A Comprehensive Indonesian-English Dictionary

The publication of this book is made possible through the generous contributions of the following companies and organizations:

American International Group
ATSGlobal Group
Empire Resources, Inc.
ExxonMobil Corporation
PT Freeport Indonesia
PT Indokor Indonesia

Citigroup
Indonesia Australia Language Foundation (IALF)
Indonesian Cultural Foundation
Robert Hornick
Rosetini, Melanita & Partners
Unocal Corporation

Centerchem Inc.
Credit Renaissance Partners, LLC
Consulate General of Indonesia (NY)
Frank and Joy Shea
Lehman Brothers Inc.
Metropolitan Life Insurance
Smith Asbury Inc.
The United States–Indonesia Society
White & Case LLP
William Milcarek/Arch Insurance Group

A Comprehensive Indonesian-English Dictionary

Alan M. Stevens

and

A. Ed. Schmidgall-Tellings

Ohio University Press
Athens

Published in association with the
American Indonesian Chamber of Commerce

Ohio University Press, Athens, Ohio 45701
© 2004 by Ohio University Press

Printed in the United States of America
All rights reserved

Ohio University Press books are printed on acid-free paper ∞

12 11 10 09 08 07 06 05 5 4 3 2

Library of Congress Catologing-in-Publication Data

Stevens, Alan M.
  A comprehensive Indonesian-English dictionary / by Alan M. Stevens and A. Ed. Schmidgall-Tellings
    p.   cm.
  Rev. ed of: Contemporary Indonesian-English dictionary. c1981
  Includes bibliographical references.
  ISBN 0-8214-1584-0 (cloth : alk. paper)
  1. Indonesian language—Dictionaries—English. I. Schmidgall-Tellings, A. Ed. II. Schmidgall-Tellings, A.
Ed. Contemporary Indonesian-English dictionary. III. Title.
  PL5076.S7 2004
  499'.221321—dc22

                        2004002570

Dedicated to the memory of Oom Ed

Contents

Preface

This dictionary is a compilation of all the roots, words, phrases, proverbs, idioms, compounds, and derivatives that the authors have found in written and spoken Indonesian. Some words that are generally used only or mostly in Malay have also been included because they appear in the Indonesian press, are known to many Indonesians, or are used in older Indonesian documents or in some regions of Indonesia. Dutch words and phrases that appear in Indonesian legal documents have also been included.

This dictionary is the result of more than twenty years of collaboration between the two authors, which ended only with the death of A. Ed. Schmidgall-Tellings in 1997. Alan Stevens has tried to honor his memory by completing the dictionary and preparing it for publication.

This dictionary would not have been possible without the help of scores of people—both Indonesians and non-Indonesians—in Indonesia, the United States, Australia, and Europe. We would particularly like to thank Oemi Schmidgall-Tellings for her many years of patient assistance to her husband, Ed; Robert Johnson and other members of Bahtera, an Internet mailing list and worldwide association of Indonesian translators and interpreters, who answered many questions about Indonesian words by e-mail; and Danielle Surkatty, who tirelessly hunted down books for me in Jakarta. Finally, the entire manuscript was read and edited by Putut Widjanarko, who made hundreds of useful suggestions for corrections and additions. I would also like to express my deepest appreciation to the editors, Gillian Berchowitz and Nancy Basmajian, and to the entire staff of Ohio University Press for all their professionalism and hard work in turning the manuscript into a published book.

For financial aid, thanks to Columbia University's East Asian Institute for providing support for a trip to Indonesia in 1989; to the U.S. Department of Education and the University of Wisconsin for support of a trip to Indonesia in 1992; and to the United States-Indonesia Society and to Queens College, CUNY for travel grants for a trip to Indonesia in 2000. And finally, I would like to state my appreciation for the financial support provided by the many companies and individuals whose contributions are acknowledged elsewhere in this book and to Wayne Forrest and Allan Harari of American Indonesian Chamber of Commerce for soliciting and organizing these contributions.

While every effort has been made to keep this dictionary free of errors or significant omissions, no work of this size and complexity can be entirely free of such errors or omissions. Users may send suggestions for improvements, additions, and corrections to alanstevens@earthlink.net.

ALAN M. STEVENS
Queens College, CUNY

Using This Dictionary

Finding the Root

Indonesian dictionaries are organized alphabetically by root, not by word. Therefore, in order to use this, or any other, Indonesian dictionary, prefixes and suffixes must be stripped off to discover the root. A list of these prefixes and suffixes follows:

Prefixes: ber- (alternate forms are bel- and be-), bersi-, di-, ke-, meN-, N-, pe-, peN-, per-, se-, ter- (alternate form te-), and reduplication.

Suffixes: -an, -i, -in, -kan.

The prefixes that cause the most problems for finding the root are *meN-* (and the nonstandard equivalent *N-*) and *peN-*. Following is a list of both the standard and nonstandard forms of the *meN-* prefix. The prefix *peN-* normally follows the rules for the standard forms of *meN-*. In the body of the dictionary we have usually given only the *meN-* form and not the corresponding *di-* form. In some cases, however, we have given the *di-* form because we were not sure whether a *meN-* form exists or we were not sure of its pronunciation or because the form in *di-* has a special meaning. Not all nonstandard forms have been entered into the dictionary because that would mean listing two or more forms for every verb that starts with *meN-* in the standard form.

The forms of the *meN-* prefix are as follows:

If the stem begins with	Standard form	Nonstandard forms
vowel	meng-	ng-
b	mem-	m- or nge-
c	men-	(me)ny- (c is lost) or nc-
d	men-	n- or nge-
f	mem-	—
g	mengg-	ng- or nge-
h	meng-	ng- (h is lost)
j	men-	nj- or nge-
k	meng- (k is lost)	ng- (k is lost)
l	me-	ng- or nge-
m	me-	nge-
n	me-	—
p	mem- (p is lost)	m- (p is lost)
r	me-	ng- or nge-
s	meny- (s is lost)	ny- (s is lost)
t	men- (t is lost)	n- (t is lost)
v	mem-	
w	me-	nge-
y	me-	nge-
z	men-	—

Monosyllabic roots may optionally prefix an <e> before the addition of the *meN-* or *peN-* prefixes, e.g., the *meN-* form of **cat** may be **mencat** or **mengecat**.

Forms other than those listed above are specifically given in the relevant entry.

The suffix *-in* occurs in Jakarta dialect for both standard *-i* and *-kan*.

To find the root from a word starting with the *meN-* prefix use the following chart, where V stands for a vowel and C for a consonant:

Standard meN-	Nonstandard meN-	Root may begin with
mengV	ngV	V, k, ng
membV	mbV	b
mendV	ndV	d
menggV	nggV	g
menyV	nyV	s, ny, c (non-standard)
memV	mV	p, m
menV	nV	t, n
menjV	njV	j
meC	nge-	r, l, w, y, b, d, g, j
	ngC	r, l

ORDER WITHIN AN ENTRY

The following order is used within each entry:

> headword (usually the root)
> expansion of an acronym, initialism, or abbreviation
> etymology and/or style. If no etymology is given, it means that the root is native or that the authors do not know the etymology. A question mark after the etymology means that the etymology is uncertain.
> pronunciation if unpredictable from the spelling
> meanings and examples. If no meaning is given for the root, the root does not occur by itself or it only occurs as the second element of compounds. The bare root may also be one of the forms of a derivative in *meN-* or a colloquial form of a derivative in *ber-*.
> idioms, phrases, and sayings (listed under the first full word of the saying)
> compounds (listed under the first element and alphabetized within each entry under the second element)
> derivatives and derivatives of derivatives.

ORDER OF DERIVATIVES

The general order of derivatives within an entry (where R stands for reduplication) is:

root (or other headword) (included within this
    are derivatives of *kurang*+headword and
    tidak+headword)

root + -nya	meN-root-i
R-root	meN-root-kan
se-root	memper-root
se-root-nya	memper-root-i
se-R-root-nya	memper-root-kan
ber-root	ter-root
bersi-root	ter-root-i
R-ber-root	ter-root-kan
ber-R-root	root-an
ber-root-an	R-root-an
ber-root-kan	ke-root-an
meN-root	ke-R-root-an
N-root	peN-root
R-meN-root	peN-root-an
meN-R-root	peN-R-root-an
N-root-in	per-root-an

Certain combinations of these affixes may also occur.

Finding Compounds

For compound words look under the first element. The compound will be entered alphabetically according to the second element. For example, *ibu jari* 'thumb' is entered under **ibu** as – *jari* and *keadaan darurat* 'emergency' is entered under **keadaan** (a derivative of **ada**) as ~ *darurat*. If the compound cannot be found under the first element, then look under the second element. Derivatives of compounds are in boldface italics and are placed immediately after the compound. For example, ***menganak-emaskan*** 'to favor' is placed right after the compound – *emas* (under **anak**) 'favorite child'.

Conventions

The following conventions are used in the dictionary:

/ is used to separate alternatives, e.g., in the book/paper should be read as 'in the book' or 'in the paper'.

[X] means the expansion of the acronym, initialism, or abbreviation used for the preceding item. See below for a discussion of acronyms and initialisms.

– means refer back to the headword (root).

~ means refer back to the nearest preceding boldface entry.

Words in boldface are headwords, derivatives of headwords, or derivatives of derivatives.

Words in italics are Indonesian examples, phrases or compounds, abbreviations, or other comments.

Words in boldface italics are derivatives of compounds and derivatives of negated words.

/ / surround a pronunciation that is not predictable from the spelling.

Roman numerals (I, II, etc.) indicate different headwords with the same spelling.

→ means a cross-reference to the word in small caps that follows the arrow.

Boldface numerals are used for different meanings of the same word.

Lowercase letters followed by closing parentheses, e.g., a) . . . b) . . . , are used for the different meanings of a compound.

Boldface italic numerals are used for different meanings of the same derivative of a compound.

Parentheses means optional.

(– X) or (~ X) means that that both – alone and – X, or ~ alone and ~ X, have the following meaning. E.g., under **canar**, (– *babi*) means that both *canar* and *canar babi* have the following meaning.

< > surround a root that is not predictable from the usual rules, usually because it is a Javanese or Sundanese root.

A dot between words means a hyphen where a hyphen could be mistaken for the – used for headwords. Under **abdi** the word –.*dalemisme* should be read as *abdi-dalemisme*.

Acronyms and Initialisms

An acronym is a word formed from the letters, initial or otherwise, of a phrase in Indonesian or another language, e.g., **ABRI** (pronounced /abri/) from *Angkatan Bersenjata Républik Indonésia* 'Indonesian Armed Forces'. In general, acronyms will not be characterized as such since they are entered in the dictionary as normal Indonesian words followed by the expansion of the acronym or a cross-reference to the expansion.

An initialism is a word formed from the names of the letters taken from an Indonesian phrase, e.g., **TNI** (pronounced /té-én-i/) from *Tentara Nasional Indonésia* 'Indonesian National Army'. In general, initialisms will be marked as such by (*init*) following the headword.

Pronunciation Notes

1. <e> is the schwa or pepet, similar to the first vowel in the English word *about*.
2. <é> is a mid-front unrounded vowel, usually closer and tenser in open syllables and more open and laxer in closed syllables. In the final syllable of Jakartanese words, however, this sound is more open.
3. Both <e> and <é> are normally written <e> in Indonesian texts.
4. <eu> in Achehnese or Sundanese words is a high central or back unrounded vowel.
5. Unless otherwise noted, <c> is similar to English <ch> in *church* though usually fronter and with less affrication.
6. Unless otherwise noted, <k> is pronounced as a glottal stop at the end of a word or before another consonant in native words or in words borrowed from Arabic. It is usually pronounced [k] before consonants in words borrowed from Dutch, English, and Sanskrit and between vowels. It may be pronounced as a glottal stop between teen vowels in the Javanese pronunciation of certain words. If final <k> is not pronounced as a glottal stop, this is indicated in the pronunciation note.
7. Within a word a glottal stop is usually pronounced between two identical vowels. This glottal stop is usually not indicated in Indonesian spelling or in this dictionary.
8. Glottal stop in a position other than those in point 6 is usually written with an apostrophe. Glottal stops not indicated by either <k> or <'> will be shown in the pronunciation note between slashes after the headword.
9. <f> is pronounced /p/ by many Indonesians.
10. <z> is pronounced /s/ by many Indonesians.
11. <v> is pronounced /f/ or /p/ by many Indonesians.
12. <sy> is similar to English <sh> in *ship* but fronter. Many Indonesians pronounce it as <s>.
13. <kh> is a voiceless velar fricative (like the German *ach* sound) but many Indonesians pronounce it as /k/ or /h/ at the beginning of a syllable and /h/ at the end of a syllable.
14. <b, d, g> are usually pronounced /p, t, k/ respectively at the end of a syllable or before a suffix.
15. <th> and <dh> in Javanese words refer to sounds made with the tip of the tongue against the alveolar ridge rather than with the tip of the tongue against the back of the upper teeth.
16. /h/ in initial position is often not pronounced in colloquial speech. /h/ in medial position between vowels is not pronounced in many words between different vowels but is pronounced between two of the same vowels. /h/ in final position is often not pronounced in some dialects.
17. Pronunciations not predictable from these rules are given in slashes after the headword or in a note at the beginning of the letter.

Abbreviations

A	Arabic		C	Chinese
abbr	abbreviation		chem	chemistry
Ac	Achehnese		cla	classical literature
acr	acronym (see note above)		col	Dutch colonial period
adj	adjective		coq	colloquial
AE	American English		cp	compare
anat	anatomical			
app	approximately		D	Dutch
			D/E	Dutch or English
Bal	Balinese		derog	derogatory
Ban	Banjarmasin			
Bat	Batak		E	English
BD	Brunei Darusalam		elec	electricity
BE	British English		e.o.	each other
BG	Bahasa Gaul (teen slang)		epist	epistolary
bio	biology		esp	especially
bot	botany			

euph	euphemism		obj	object
exclam	exclamation		O Jv	Old Javanese
			onom	onomatopoeia
fin	financial		opp	opposite
Fr	French		o.s.	oneself
G	German		Pal	Palembang
geol	geology		Pap	Papua (the former Irian Jaya)
Gr	Greek		Pers	Persian
gram	grammatical		petro	petroleum
			phys	physics
Hind	Hindi		pl	plural
			pl obj	plural object (separate single actions on more
IBT	Indonesia Bagian Timur (the eastern part of			than one object or multiple actions on a
	Indonesia)			single object)
infr	infrequent		pl subj	plural subject
init	initialism (see note above)		poet	poetic
insur	insurance		Port	Portuguese
Irja	Irian Jaya (now Papua)		Pr	Prokem (young people's disguised language)
Isl	Islam(ic)		pron	pronunciation
J	Jakarta		q.v.	which see, refer to that word
J/Jv	Jakarta or Javanese			
joc	jocular		RC	Roman Catholic
Jp	Japanese		reg	regional
Jv	Javanese		rel	religious
			rev	reverential
K	Kawi			
k.o.	kind(s) of		S	Sundanese
			sg	singular
L	Latin		Sing	Singapore
leg	legal		Skr	Sanskrit
ling	linguistics		Skr neo	Sanskrit-based neologism
lit	literally		sl	slang
			s.o.	someone
M	Minangkabau		s.o.'s	someone's
Mad	Madurese		s.t.	something
Mal	Malay		stat	statistics
math	mathematics		subj	subject
Med	Medan		Sum	Sumatra
med	medical			
mil	military		Tag	Tagalog
Min	Minahassa		Tam	Tamil
mod	modifier (used to modify a noun)			
mus	music		usu	usually
naut	nautical		voc	vocative
NTB	Nusa Tenggara Barat		vulg	vulgar
NTT	Nusa Tenggara Timur			
			zod	(sign of the) zodiac
ob	obsolete			

Etymologies

This dictionary is not meant to be an etymological dictionary of Indonesian. No attempt will be made to trace the history of a root or the many possible sources of a root. In order not to multiply possible source languages, thereby unavoidably increasing the size of the dictionary and the number of potential errors, in general the etymologies given here refer to only one rather than to the several languages or dialects which might be the source, but possibly not the only source, of the Indonesian root, with the following exceptions and notes:

In some cases two sources are given. The first is the ultimate source and the second the intermediate source. For example, (C J) means from Chinese through Jakartanese. Many of the roots marked as Jakartanese probably come from and still exist in Javanese and/or Sundanese. For the sake of simplicity the former have been marked as (J/Jv) and the latter simply as (J). Many of the roots marked as Javanese probably also exist in Sundanese. Note that the meanings given for such words in this dictionary are the meanings we have found in Indonesian contexts and do not necessarily cover all of the meanings or even perhaps the principal meaning in the source language.

The difference between the Javanese sounds /t/ and /th/ and between /d/ and /dh/ will not be marked in this dictionary unless this difference is usually marked in a certain word in Indonesian contexts.

Words from Persian probably all come through Arabic but they are listed as of Persian origin.

Recent neologisms constructed from Sanskrit roots are marked as Sanskrit neologisms. If only part of a word is such a neologism, it will usually not be marked as such.

For many Western words it is impossible to tell whether they come from Dutch, from English, or from both. In general—and in many cases this is an arbitrary decision—these have been attributed to Dutch, but sometimes (D/E) indicates that both are possible sources.

No attempt is made to determine whether words pronounced with an /e/ that are colloquial forms of the words with an /a/ in the final syllable, such as **macem** instead of **macam**, come from J, Jv, or S. They are simply cross-referenced to the form with an /a/ in the final syllable, e.g., **macem** → MACAM.

Orthography

Unless otherwise indicated, all spellings are in the post-1972 orthography, the so-called *Ejaan Yang Disempurnakan*, or EYD. The spelling of compounds and derivatives of compounds still fluctuates between spelling the compound as a single word, as two separate words, or with a hyphen. The standard form now seems to be to spell derivatives of compounds as single words, but all three possibilities appear in print for many words.

Sources

Primary Sources

The primary sources for this dictionary include newspapers, magazines and books; personal documents, government documents, ministerial decrees, business documents, and legal and court documents; tape-recorded conversations; street signs, graffiti, and restaurant menus; testimony given in Immigration Court, at civil and criminal trials and taken at depositions, all in the United States; Internet sources; and from numerous Indonesians, including the members of Bahtera (see the preface).

Secondary Sources

The following is a partial list of the hundreds of secondary sources used in the preparation of this dictionary.

Ali, A. *Al-Qur'an.* Princeton: Princeton University Press, 1988.

Anwir, B. S., et al. *Kamus Teknik Lima Bahasa.* Jakarta: Bhratara Karya Aksara, 1985.

Assegaf, I. A. *Dictionary of Accounting/Kamus Akuntansi.* Jakarta: Mario Grafika, 1991.

Badudu, J. S. *Kamus Ungkapan Bahasa Indonesia.* Bandung: Pustaka Prima, 1981.

Badudu-Zain. *Kamus Umum.* Jakarta: Pustaka Sinar Harapan, 1996.

Bakhtiar, L. *Encyclopedia of Islamic Law.* Chicago: ABC International Group, 1996.

Chaer, A. *Kamus Dialek Melayu Jakarta—Bahasa Indonesia.* Jakarta: Nusa Indah, 1976.

Cribb, R. *Historical Atlas of Indonesia.* Honolulu: University of Hawai'i Press, 2000.

Cribb, R. *Historical Dictionary of Indonesia.* Metuchen, N.J., and London: Scarecrow Press, 1992.

de Casparis, J. G. *Sanskrit Loan-Words in Indonesian.* Jakarta: Nusa, 1997.

Departemen Pendidikan dan Kebudayaan Republik Indonesia. *Daftar Istilah Warna.* Jakarta, 1984.

Departemen Pendidikan dan Kebudayaan Republik Indonesia. *Kamus Besar Bahasa Indonesia.* Jakarta, 1988.

Dewan Bahasa dan Pustaka. *Kamus Dewan (Edisi Ketiga).* Kuala Lumpur, 1998.

Djati Kerami, et al. *Glosarium Matematika.* Jakarta: Balai Pustaka, 1995.

Echols, J. and H. Shadily. *An Indonesian-English Dictionary.* 3rd ed. Ithaca, N.Y.: Cornell University Press, 1989.

Eringa, F. S. *Soendaas-Nederlands Woordenboek.* Dordrecht: Foris, 1984.

Esposito, J. L. *The Oxford Dictionary of Islam.* Oxford: Oxford University Press, 2003.

Federspiel, H. M. *A Dictionary of Indonesian Islam.* Athens: Ohio University Press, 1995.

Gonda, J. *Sanskrit in Indonesia.* New Delhi: International Academy of Indian Culture, 1998.

Grijns, C. D., et al. *European Loan-Words in Indonesian.* Leiden: KITLV, 1983.

Guritno, T. *Kamus Ekonomi Bisnis Perbankan Inggris-Indonesia.* Yogyakarta: Gadjah Mada University Press, 1992.

Hairul, A. S. *Kamus Lengkap.* Kuala Lumpur: Pustaka Zaman, 1990.

Hamid, S. R. *Buku Pintar Agama Islam.* Jakarta: Penebar Salam, 2000.

Heyne, K. *De Nuttige Planten van Indonesië.* 's-Gravenhage/Bandung: van Hoeve, 1950.

Holmes, D., and S. Nash. *The Birds of Java and Bali.* Singapore: Oxford University Press, 1990.

Horne, E. *Javanese-English Dictionary.* New Haven: Yale University Press, 1974.

Hughes, Thomas Patrick. *Dictionary of Islam.* 1885. Repr. Chicago: Kazi Publications, 1994.

Ikranagara, Kay. "Lexical Particles in Betawi." *International Journal of the Sociology of Language* (1975): 93–107.

Jones, R. *Arabic Loan-Words in Indonesian.* Paris: Cahier d'Archipel, 1978.

Karow, O., and I. Hilgers-Hesse. *Indonesisch-Deutches Wörterbuch.* Wiesbaden: Otto Harrassowitz, 1962.

Kreemer, J. *Atjèhsch Handwoordenboek (Atjèsch-Nederlandsch).* Leiden: Brill, 1931.

Labrousse, P. *Indonésien-Français Dictionnaire Général.* Paris: Association Archipel, 1984.

Lemigas. *Kamus Minyak dan Gas Bumi.* 3rd ed. Jakarta: Pusat Penelitian dan Pengembangan Teknologi Minyak dan Gas Bumi, 1995.

Leo, P. *Chinese Loanwords Spoken by the Inhabitants of the City of Jakarta.* Jakarta: LIPI, 1975.

Mackinnon, J. *Burung-burung di Jawa dan Bali.* Yogyakarta: Gadjah Mada University Press, 1991.

Martin, W. *Groot Woordenboek Nederlands-Engels.* Utrecht/Antwerp: van Dale, 1999.

Massier, A. W. H. *Beknopt Juridisch Woordenboek Indonesisch-Nederlands.* Leiden: Rijksuniversiteit Leiden, 1992.

Massier, A. *Indonesisch-Nederlands Woordenboek Privaatrecht.* Leiden: KITLV, 2000.

Monier-Williams, M. *A Sanskrit-English Dictionary.* Delhi: Motilal Banarsidass, 1990.

Moussay, G. *Dictionnaire Minangkabau-Indonésien-Français.* Paris: Association Archipel, 1995.

Muhadjir. *Bahasa Betawi.* Jakarta: Yayasan Obor Indonesia, 2000.

Pamuntjak, K. St. et al. *Peribahasa.* Jakarta: Balai Pustaka, 2000.

Pigeaud, Th. *Javaans-Nederlands Handwoordenboek.* Groningen/Batavia: J. B. Wolters, n.d.

Podo, H., and J. Sullivan. *Kamus Ungkapan Indonesia-Inggris.* Jakarta: Gramedia, 1988.

Quinn, G. *The Learner's Dictionary of Today's Indonesian.* Crows Nest, NSW, Australia: Allen and Unwin, 2001.

Rahardja, P., and H. Chambert-Loir. *Kamus Bahasa Prokem.* Jakarta: Grafitipers, 1988.

Ramali, A., and K. St. Pamoentjak. *Kamus Kedokteran.* Jakarta: Djambatan, 1994.

Robson, S., and Singgih Wibisono. *Javanese-English Dictionary.* Hong Kong: Periplus, 2002.

Salim, P., and Yenny Salim. *Kamus Bahasa Indonesia Kontemporer.* Jakarta: Modern English Press, 1991.

Salim, P. *The Contemporary Medical Dictionary English-Indonesian.* Jakarta: Modern English Press, n.d.

Saydam, G. *Kamus Istilah Telekomunikasi.* Jakarta: Djambatan, 1992.

Schmidgall-Tellings, A. Ed., and A. M. Stevens. *Contemporary Indonesian-English Dictionary.* Athens: Ohio University Press, 1981.

Soemarsono Markam. *Kamus Istilah Kedokteran.* Jakarta: Fakultas Kedokteran Universitas Indonesia, 1984.

Sudarsono, S. H. *Kamus Hukum.* Jakarta: Rineka Cipta, 1992.

Surodibroto, S. *Kitab Undang-Undang Hukum Pidana dan Kitab Undang-Undang Hukum Acara Pidana.* 4th ed. Jakarta: Rajagrafindo Persada, 1994.

Syariffudin, A. *Kamus Istilah Olah Raga Populer di Indonesia.* Jakarta: CV Baru, 1985.

Teeuw, A. *Indonesisch-Nederlands Woordenboek*, KITLV, 1990.

Tim Penyusun Kamus PS. *Kamus Pertanian Umum.* Leiden: Penebar Swadaya, Jakarta 1997.

Tim Penyusun. *Kamus Perbankan.* Jakarta: Institut Bankir Indonesia, 1999.

van den End, A. *Juridisch Lexicon Nederlands-Engels.* Zeist: Gateway, 1995.

Wandelt, I. *Kamus Dwi Fungsi.* Hürth: Bundessprachenamt, 1993.

Wasito, S. *Kamus Ensiklopedi Elektronika Inggris-Indonesia.* Jakarta: Karya Utama, n.d.

Wilkinson, R. J. *A Malay-English Dictionary (Romanised).* London: Macmillan, 1959.

Wolff, J. *Beginning Indonesian.* Ithaca, N.Y.: Cornell University Southeast Asia Program, 1980.

Woworuntu, R. *Kamus Kedokteran & Kesehatan.* Semarang: Dahara, 1993.

Zhi, K. Y. "A Study of Chinese Loanwords (From South Fujian Dialects) in the Malay and Indonesian Languages." *BKI* 143 (1987):452–67.

Zhi, K. Y. "Kata Pinjaman Bahasa Cina dalam Bahasa Melayu." *Jurnal Dewan Bahasa* (Ogos 1993): 676–702 and (September 1993): 772–95.

A

a and **A I** /a/ the first letter of the Latin alphabet used for writing Indonesian.

a II (*abbr*) are (a unit of square measure in the metric system, equal to 100 square meters or about 119.6 square yards).

a III (*abbr*) ampere.

a IV ahh (hesitation).

A V (in music) the sixth tone/note in the ascending scale of C major.

A VI car license plate for Banten.

à and **@** at. – *Rp 1.000,-* at Rp 1,000.00.

A '45 [*Angkatan '45*] the Generation of 1945.

AA car license plate for Kedu (Magelang).

aah ah. –, *itu kan proyék swasta.* Ah, that's a private project.

aala and **a'ala** dynasty; → RAJAKULA. – *Tang* Tang dynasty.

aam (*A*) general. *Rois* – General Chairman (of the *NU*); → AM.

aau ow! ouch!

ab I (*A ob*) father.

ab II (*ob*) a tin opium box/cylinder.

AB III car license plate for Yogyakarta.

aba I (*A*) father.

aba II (*Jv*) *pemegang* – *genderang* drum major(ette).
  aba-aba (*mil*) command, signal, word of command. *memberikan ~ kepada* to command, give a command to. *~ kerja* work instructions. *tanpa ~* without a word. **mengaba-abakan** to move (one's hand) in a gesture, gesture with (one's hand).
  mengabakan to drill, train (in military exercises).
  pengaba 1 *~ genderang* drum major(ette). **2** (*mil*) drill instructor.

aba III – *daba* germs, bacteria, bacilli, disease-causing microbes.

abab (*Jv*) **1** breath (from the mouth). **2** empty talk. – *besar* empty talk.
  mengababi to breathe on.

abad (*A*) **1** century. **2** era, age. **3** a long period of time. **4** eternity; *opp* AJAL. – *(al)abid* eternity. – *atom* the atomic age. – *emas* a) Golden Age. b) flourishing period. – *keduapuluh* the 20th century. – *keemasan* a) Golden Age. b) flourishing period. – *kemajuan* era of progress. – *Pencerahan* Age of Enlightenment. – *Pertengahan/Tengah* the Middle Ages.
  seabad one century, 100 years.
  berabad-abad for centuries.
  mengabad to last for centuries.

abadi (*A*) eternal, everlasting, perpetual, permanent, abiding, without end, unbreakable. *tetap* – will last for ever and ever. *tidak* – temporary, ephemeral. **ketidak-abadian** temporariness, ephemerality.
  seabadi as eternal as.
  mengabadikan and **memperabadikan 1** to immortalize, perpetuate, make s.t. last forever. *~ dengan kaméra* to take a picture of, immortalize on film. **2** to keep s.t. alive, preserve.
  terabadi(kan) immortalized, remembered forever, made permanent.
  keabadian 1 eternity. **2** durability, permanence, immortality.
  pengabadian the act of making s.t. immortal, immortalizing, perpetuating.

abadiah and **abadiat** (*A*) eternity; → KEABADIAN.

abah I direction (of compass), course, aim. *tak tentu -nya* constant change of direction.
  mengabah *~ ke* to head for, steer toward.
  mengabahkan to aim s.t. (at), steer s.t. (toward), strive (for). *Motorbotnya diabahkan ke pulau Batam.* He steered the motorboat toward Batam.

abah II → ABA I.

abah III (*Jv*) implement.
  abah-abah 1 implements, tools. **2** cords, ropes. *~ kapal* rigging. *~ kuda* harness. *~ perahu* rigging. *~ tenun* loom.

abai 1 careless, negligent, neglectful. *tidak – daripada berawas-awas* to be constantly on one's guard. **2** disregarded, neglected.
  mengabaikan 1 to neglect, ignore, disregard, pay no attention to. *Negara itu berani ~ résolusi itu.* That country had the nerve to ignore the resolution. **2** to underestimate (the enemy, etc.). *Jangan abaikan musuh yang kuat. itu.* Don't underestimate a strong enemy. **3** to break (a promise/agreement), betray (a secret) through carelessness. *~ janji* to break a promise. **4** to overlook (a fact), miss (a chance), not comply with. *Sayang sekali Anda abaikan peluang emas itu.* It's a shame you missed that golden opportunity. **5** to disappoint (s.o.'s expectations). **6** to let things drift/take their natural course, leave unfinished (of work). *~ segala sesuatu* to let things drift along/take their natural course. *tidak ~ usahanya* not slacken one's efforts.
  terabai neglected, ignored, disregarded. **keterabaian** disregard, neglect.
  terabaikan overlooked, neglected, disregarded. *Gedung itu bertahun-tahun ~.* The building was neglected for years and years. *tidak ~* nonnegligible.
  abaian (in philology) omission, textual corruption.
  pengabai 1 slovenly, sloppy, careless, nonchalant, indifferent. **2** a negligent/careless person.
  pengabaian neglecting, ignoring, disregarding, negligence, disregard, disobeying.

abaimana (*Hind cla*) the lower orifices of the body, anus and pudenda.

abaka (*D*) abaca, *Musa textilis*.

abakus (*E*) abacus.

abal-abal hardened criminal.

abandonemén (*D/E leg*) abandonment.

abandonir (*D*) **mengabandonir** to abandon.

abang I 1 older brother. – *mantu* older brother-in-law. – *saudara* older male cousin. **2** form of address for older man. "– *mau ikut?*" "Do you want to join us?" **3** form of reference by wife to husband (regardless of latter's age). *si* – (my/one's) husband. *Saya akan pergi ke mana pun si –pergi.* I'll go wherever my husband goes. **4** (*J*) term of reference for lower-class male worker. – *bécak* pedicab driver. – *Jakarta/Jakarté* Mr. Jakarta, the male counterpart of *noné Jakarta/Jakarté*. – *sabit rumput* grass mower; → PENYABIT *rumput*. – *sopir* driver. **5** more popular and respectful epithet for some prominent persons of mainly Jakarta background; in this case, the abbreviated form *bang* is usually preferred; → BANG III.
  berabang 1 to have (an) older brother(s). **2** to address (s.o.) using the term *abang*.
  berabangkan to have ... as one's older brother.

abang II (*J/Jv*) red(dish) brown. – *tua* dark red, maroon.

abang III – *pipi* Salvadori's pheasant, *Lophura inornata*.

abang-abang (*Jv*) – *lambé* a) what the listener wants to hear. b) lip service; → PENGHIAS *bibir*.

abangan I (*Jv*) Javanese who are nominally Muslim but who adhere to pre-Muslim beliefs intermixed with animist, Hindu and Buddhist beliefs. → ISLAM. *golongan* – the group of nominal Muslims.

abangan II (*J*) roof gutters.

abar I screen, shelter; wall, partition (of a room, etc.).
  berabarkan to have a wall/screen made of s.t.

abar II brake; → RÉM. – *daya* power brake. – *pintu* automatic door closer.
  mengabar 1 to brake, slow down (speed/progress/tension, etc.). **2** to lessen (the risk of war, etc.). **3** to reduce. *Obat ini dapat ~ penderitaan si sakit.* This medicine can reduce the patient's suffering. **4** to impede, hinder, delay, obstruct.

mengabarkan to reduce, lower.

terabar hindered, obstructed, impeded, etc.

abaran (*psychological*) inhibition. ~ *renjana* emotional inhibition.

pengabaran and **perabaran** screening, sheltering, braking.

Abasa (*A*) "He Frowned"; title of the 80th chapter of the Koran.

Abassiyah (*A*) Abbasid. *dinasti* – Abbasid dynasty.

abasti [*alat pembasmi tikus*] rodent exterminator.

abat → ABAD.

abaté liquid for exterminating mosquito larvae. *serbuk/obat* – larvicide powder.

pengabatéan → ABATISASI.

abatisasi exterminating mosquito larvae by using *abaté*.

abatoar (*E*) abattoir.

abau k.o. large swamp turtle, painted terrapin, *Callagur picta*.

abawi (*A*) paternal.

abaya long black coat worn by women on the pilgrimage to Mecca.

berabaya to wear such a coat.

abc and **ABC** /a-bé-cé/ alphabet, the abc's. *tidak tahu sama sekali* – not to have the slightest idea (about s.t.).

abd → ABDI.

abdas (*Pers*) (Muslim) ritual ablution before prayer.

berabdas to make one's ritual ablution before prayer.

abdi (*A*) **1** (bought) slave. **2** servant, (domestic) helper. – *dalam/dalem* (*Jv*) royal servant in the *kraton*. – *dalem jajar* (*Jv*) the lowest rank in the *kraton* administrative structure. – *dalem putih* (*Jv*) royal servant in charge of religious affairs. –*.dalemisme* serfdom. – *masyarakat* public servant. – *negara* servant of the state. – *rakyat* public servant.

berabdi to be a servant (of).

mengabdi **1** to serve, be in the service (of). *Lions Club 25 tahun* ~ *di Indonésia.* The Lions Club has served in Indonesia for 25 years. **2** to be devoted (to). **3** to live in s.o.'s house as a servant; → NGÉNGÉR.

abdi-mengabdi master-servant/patron-client relationship.

mengabdikan to make subservient to. ~ *diri di/kepada* to enter s.o.'s service/employment, devote o.s. to.

memperabdi to make subservient to. *hubungan* ~ master-servant/patron-client relationship.

pengabdi dedicated servant. ~ *masyarakat* public servant.

pengabdian 1 service. *penuh* ~ dedicated. ~ *masyarakat* public service. **2** servitude, submission, submissiveness. ~ *pekarangan/tanah* encumbrance with servitude. ~ *pekarangan jalan* right of way. **3** devotion, dedication.

abdidalemisme serfdom, servitude.

abdikasi (*D*) abdication.

abdis (*D*) abbess.

abdomén (*D/E*) abdomen.

abdominal (*D/E*) abdominal.

abdu (*A*) (from *abdi*, element used in proper names connected with one of the 99 names given to *Allah*) **1** slave. **2** servant. *Abdullah* (the Servant of God); *Abdullah bin Abdulkadir Munsyi* the name of the pioneer of modern Malay literature in the early 19th century; born in Malacca of mixed Malay-Indian parentage; Malay language teacher (= *munsyi*) and clerk of Sir Thomas Stamford Raffles (1811–1816), the first and only British Governor General of the Netherlands Indies. *Abdul Ghafur/Gafar* (the Most Forgiving Servant); *Abdul Kadir* (the Most Powerful Servant); *Abdul Rahman* (the Compassionate Servant); *Tengku Abdul Rahman* (name of a former prime minister of Malaysia); *Abdul Rauf* and *Abdurrauf* (the Loving Servant).

abécé abc (the Latin alphabet); → ABC.

abégé → ABG.

abelur → HABLUR.

abén (*Bal*) cremation ceremony.

mengabén(kan) [and **ngabén** (*coq*)] to cremate; → MEMPERABU-KAN.

pengabénan cremation.

aberasi (*D*) aberration, deviation.

abésé → ABC.

abet (*J*) **1** appearance. **2** behavior.

mengabet to behave. *bisa/tahu* ~ to know how to make a good impression (on people).

ABG (*init*) [*anak baru gedé*] adolescent, teenager.

abiad and **abiaz** (*A cla*) white. *fizah yang* – white silver.

abian (*Bal*) equal share of crop between owner and worker of the land.

abid I (*A*) pious, godly, religious, devout.

abid II (*A*) eternal, lasting, enduring.

abidin I (*A*) (plural of *abidun*) adorers of *Allah*, pious persons, the pious.

abidin II (*joc acr*) [*atas biaya dinas*] at agency expense. *haji* – s.o. who makes the pilgrimage to Mecca at government expense.

abidun (*A*) adorer of *Allah*, pious person.

Abil (*A*) (the Biblical) Abel.

abilah (*Pers*) smallpox. – *peringgi* syphilis.

abimana → ABAIMANA.

abintara (*cla*) herald; → BINTARA.

abis I (*J coq*) → HABIS. **1** well (*interjection*). – *kalo ndak di sini, ya di mana lagi saya tinggal.* Well, if not here, where do I stay then? **2** completely, totally. *édan* –. He's completely crazy.

ngabisin to use up, finish off; → MENGHABISKAN.

ngabis-ngabisin to use s.t. all up.

abis II (*D/E*) abyss.

abisal (*E geo*) abyssal.

abit (*ob naut*) bitts.

abiturién (*D*) high school graduate.

abiz (*BG*) → ABIS I.

abjad (*A*) **1** alphabet (such as *alif-ba-ta*, etc.) **2** (*ob*) the sequence of Arabic characters, each of which has a numerical value (used for counting years or for divination), i.e., *alif* = 1, *ba* = 2, *kaf* = 100, etc. *menurut* (*aturan*) – alphabetical, in alphabetical order. – *Latin/Romawi* Latin alphabet.

berabjad 1 alphabetical. **2** with an alphabet.

mengabjadkan to alphabetize.

pengabjadan alphabetization.

abjadiah (*A*) alphabetical; → MENURUT (*aturan*) *abjad*.

ablag and **ablak** (*J/Jv*) wide open; stand wide open.

seablak-ablak very wide open; very large/extended/stretched out.

mengablak [and **ngablak** (*coq*)] to be wide open (of the mouth). *Mulutnya* ~. His mouth was wide open.

mengablakkan [and **ngablakin** (*J coq*)] **1** to open s.t. wide. **2** to disclose, reveal. **3** to tell (a story).

ablasi (*D*) ablation.

mengablasi to ablate.

ablatif (*D/E*) ablative.

ablaut (*D/E*) ablaut.

ablur → HABLUR.

abnormal (*D/E*) abnormal.

keabnormalan abnormality; → ABNORMALITAS.

abnormalitas (*D*) abnormality.

abnus (*A cla*) ebony.

aboi (*C*) **1** form of address to Chinese headman. **2** Chinese village head of a *luak* (in West Kalimantan, etc.).

abolisi (*D/E*) **1** abolition. **2** pardon (for crimes committed).

mengabolisi(kan) to abolish.

abon (*Jv*) a dish of fried meat reduced to fibers.

mengabon to make this dish.

aboné (*D*) subscriber.

abonemén (*D*) **1** subscription (to a newspaper/magazine, etc.); → LANGGANAN. **2** to subscribe to, have a subscription/season ticket to; → BERLANGGANAN. *Saya* – *bis.* I have a bus commuter ticket. **3** subscription fee; → UANG *langganan*.

berabonemén to subscribe to, have a subscription to.

mengaboneménkan to subscribe for s.o.

abong-abong (*J/Jv*) just/simply because; → MENTANG-MENTANG. – *gué orang miskin, lu jangan seénaknyé menghiné, yé.* Just because I'm poor, don't insult me just because you feel like it, OK?

aborijin (*E*) aborigine. *kaum* – the aborigines (of Australia).

aborsi (*D*) abortion. *melalukan/mengadakan* – to have an abortion, abort.

mengaborsi to abort.

teraborsi aborted.

pengaborsian abortion.

abortus (*D*) abortion; → ABORSI. *mengadakan* – to abort.

mengabortus to abort.

pengabortusan aborting.

abrak (*Hind cla*) mica.

abrak-abrakan in disorder, disorderly, chaotic.

abrakadabra (*D/E*) abracadabra.

abrar (*A*) pious.

abras (*A*) leprous.

abrasi (*D*) abrasion. *termakan* – abraded.

mengabrasikan to abrade s.t.

terabrasi abraded.

abréaksi abreaction.

abreg and **abrek** (*Jv*) **seabrek** numerous, a lot. *Dara ini punya kesibukan* ~. This girl is very busy. **seabreg-abreg** in heaps.

abréviasi (*E*) abbreviation; → SINGKATAN.

ABRI /abri/ [Angkatan Bersenjata Républik Indonésia] (now replaced by TNI) 1 Armed Forces of the Republic of Indonesia. 2 a member of the Armed Forces of the Republic of Indonesia. *serombongan* – a group of ABRI members.

meng-ABRI-kan to place (a government agency, e.g.) under the control of ABRI.

ke-ABRI-an armed forces (*mod*). *dalam lingkungan* ~ in armed forces circles.

abrik → UBRAK-ABRIK.

abrikos (*D*) apricot.

abrit-abritan (*J*) to run helter-skelter.

abruk (*J*) **ngabrukin** to slam s.t. down. ~ *pantatnya di atas sofa* to slam one's behind down on the sofa.

ABS (*init*) [Asal Bapak Senang] Pleasing the Boss; → ASAL *Bapak Senang*.

meng-ABS-i and **meng-ABS-kan** to flatter.

absah (*A*) valid, legal, legitimate; → SAH. *tidak* – invalid, illegal. *Kontrak ini tidak* –. This contract is invalid. **ketidakabsahan** invalidity, illegality.

mengabsahkan 1 to legalize, legitimate, validate. 2 to endorse.

keabsahan validity, legality, legitimacy.

pengabsah validator, validation, legalizer.

pengabsahan 1 legalization, legitimacy. 2 endorsement.

absén (*D/E*) 1 absent, not present. *tidak* – not fail to appear. *tidak pernah* – *dari* never free from, never doesn't (do s.t.). *tidak pernah* – *dalam* always be present/active in, never be away from. *sudah tidak* – *lagi* to be no longer in (our) service. 2 to sign in.

mengabsén to call the roll, check attendance. ~ *diri sendiri* to answer the roll call.

absénan *daftar* ~ attendance list, roster.

pengabsénan taking attendance.

absénsi (*D*) roll call. *daftar* – attendance list, roster. *jam* – time clock.

absénteisme (*D/E*) absenteeism.

abséntia *in* – (*L*) in the absence of (the accused); → *dengan tidak* DIHADIRI.

absés (*D/E*) abscess.

absis (*D*) abscissa.

absolusi (*D*) absolution.

absolut (*D/E*) absolute; → MUTLAK.

mengabsolutkan to make s.t. absolute.

pengabsolutan making s.o. absolute.

absolutisasi (*E*) absolutization.

mengabsolutisasikan to make s.t. absolute.

absolutisme (*D/E*) absolutism.

absorbén (*D/E*) absorbent.

absorbir (*D*) **mengabsorbir** to absorb.

absorbsi and **absorpsi** (*D/E*) absorption.

mengabsorpsi to absorb.

terabsorpsi absorbed.

pengabsorpsi absorber, absorption.

absorptif (*E*) absorptive.

abstain (*E*) to abstain (from voting).

keabstainan abstention.

absté(i)n → ABSTAIN.

absténsi (*E*) abstention.

abstrak (*D/E*) 1 abstract, immaterial. 2 abstract, résumé, précis.

mengabstrakkan to abstract, make s.t. immaterial.

abstrak-abstrakan all kinds of abstractions.

pengabstakan abstracting.

abstraksi (*D*) abstraction.

berabstraksi to make abstractions, draw abstract conclusions.

mengabstraksikan to abstract.

abstraksionis (*E*) abstractionist.

abstraksionisme (*D/E*) abstractionism (style in art).

absurd (*D/E*) absurd, preposterous.

keabsurdan absurdity.

absurditas (*D*) absurdity.

ABT (*init*) [Anggaran Belanja Tambahan] Supplementary Budget.

abtar (*A*) 1 maimed (without a finger/toe/limb, etc.), crippled. 2 stumped.

abu I 1 ash(es). *tempat* – ashtray; → ASBAK. *Rumahnya menjadi* –. His house went up in flames. 2 dust. (*seperti*) – *di atas tunggul* (*M*) to occupy an insecure position. *berdiang di* – *dingin* (*M*) to obtain nothing (from brothers/family heads, etc.). *jadi* – *arang* (that is) ancient history. *terpegang di* – *hangat* to stir up a hornet's nest. – *bara* cinder. – *batu bara* coal ash. – *blarak* (*Jv*) dried coconut leaf powder (used as a cleanser). – *dasar* bottom ash/slag. – *gosok* scouring sand. – *kayu* wood ash. – *limbah* fly ash. – *soda* sodium carbonate. – *terbang* fly ash. – *vulkanik/vulkanis* volcanic ash.

abu-abu ash-gray, ashy. *udara* ~ an overcast sky. ~ *muda* light gray.

berabu dusty.

mengabu to become ashes.

mengabui 1 to spray/scatter ashes on s.t. (in planting). 2 (= **mengelabui**) to fool, trick. ~ *mata* to pull the wool over s.o.'s eyes, to deceive s.o.

mengabukan and **memperabukan** to cremate.

keabu-abuan grayish. *Rambutnya tipis* ~. His hair is thin and graying.

pengabuan cremation. ~ *mata* a) misleading, deceptive. b) camouflage, deceit.

perabuan 1 storage place for ashes. 2 container for cremation ashes. *tempat* ~ *mayat* crematorium.

abu II (*A*) father of, in proper names, such as *Abu Bakar*, etc.

abu III defeated, to lose (in certain games).

abu-abu northern bluefin tuna, long-tailed tuna, *Neothunnus rarus*.

abuan 1 part of a rice paddy yield made available to *sawah* workers; ration, share. 2 a nest egg (money saved for an emergency).

Abubakar I (*A*) one of the first companions of the Prophet Muhammad.

abubakar II (*joc acr*) [atas budi baik Golkar] by Golkar's goodwill.

abudemén (*J*) → ABONEMÉN.

abuh I (*Jv*) 1 swelling, inflammation. 2 swollen. *sakit* – a) dropsy. b) dropsical. c) edema.

abuhan to suffer from dropsy.

abuh-abuhan 1 swelling, inflammation. 2 swollen. *sakit* ~ a) dropsy. b) dropsical.

abuh II noisy; busy.

abui → ABOI.

abuk I dust. – *bunga* pollen. – *gergaji* sawdust.

abuk II (*M*) hair.

abuk III (*Jv*) **mengabuk** to take s.o. else's property by claiming that it belongs to you.

abuk-abuk *kué* ~ k.o. cake made from sugar-palm flour.

abulhayat (*A*) the father of life, i.e., rain.

abun-abun (*ob*) thoughts, ideas, ideals; → ANGAN-ANGAN. *gila di* – to hope for s.t. impossible.

abunemén → ABONEMÉN. *karcis* – (bus) commuter ticket.

abung 1 (*Mal*) pomelo. 2 the part of the coconut embryo that grows in the shell.

abur (*cla*) wasteful, extravagant, prodigal.

mengabur(kan) to waste, squander (money).

pengabur spendthrift.

abus I 1 (*col*) **1** coins of the lowest denomination. **2** very little, a bit, trifle. **3** (*geol*) shard.

abus II (*vulg*) to die, drop dead; → MAMPUS. *-lah kamu sekalian.* Drop dead all of you.

abuter [*abu terbang*] → ABU *terbang.*

abuya → BUYA.

abyad (*A*) white, clear, translucent.

ac and **AC** (*E*) /asé/ air-condition(ed). *kamar* – an air-conditioned room.
  ber-ac to be air-conditioned. *ruangan kerja* ~ an air-conditioned office.

acah I beracah-acah to pretend, feint (at an opponent).
  mengacah to act as if, pretend (in order to fool opponents), bluff.
  acahan feint, bluff, feigned attack.

acah II mengacah to violate (the law).

acak I (*J*) erratic, random, irregular, by chance. *secara* – at random, randomly.
  mengacak 1 to ransack. **2** to randomize, scramble. **3** to encrypt.
  mengacak-acak [and **ngacak-ngacak** (*coq*)] to ransack, rummage through, upset, mix up, mess up, screw up, jumble together, turn upside down. *Dépdagri diacak-acak pencuri.* The Department of the Interior was ransacked by the thieves.
  mengacakkan 1 to randomize. **2** to mess up, disarrange.
  teracak 1 scrambled. **2** encrypted.
  acak-acakan disorderly, untidy, disarranged. *dalam keadaan* ~ in a disorderly state; to be a mess. *memilih secara* ~ to choose at random.
  keacak-acakan chaos, disorder.
  pengacak randomizer, scrambler, s.t. that scrambles.
  pengacakan 1 randomizing, scrambling. **2** encryption.
  pengacak-acakan messing up, making disorderly, etc.

acak II (*coq*) – *kali* and **acak-acak** (*M*) quickly, hurriedly, in a hurry, rashly.

acan I (*ob*) **mengacan** to intend, have in mind, expect; to long for.

acan II mengacan (*cla*) to feint, mislead, trick (an opponent), bluff; → ACAH I.

acan III (*J*) *tak* – a) not yet (at all). *Saya mah kagak nyebut-nyebut nama Sur* –. I haven't mentioned Sur's name yet. b) not a single one.

acan IV (from the name Hasan; *Maluku*) (word used to refer to) Muslims; *cp* OBÉD.

acancut *taliwanda/taliwondo* (*Jv*) → CANCUT *taliwanda.*

acang I (*naut*) **1** small rod to indicate water conditions in a kettle. **2** gadget.

acang II (*Jv*) **mengacang** [and **ngacang** (*coq*)] to have an erection; → NGACENG.

acang III → ACAN IV.

acang-acang I (*M*) **1** s.o. who does errands, gofer. **2** confidant. – *alat* master of ceremonies. – *(dalam) negeri* smart people in a village.

acang-acang II *ikan* – k.o. fish, Bombay duck, *Harpodon nehereus.*

acap I 1 often, repeatedly, again and again, time and again. – *kali* often. **2** quickly, immediately, soon.
  acap-acap 1 often, repeatedly, again and again. **2** very quickly/soon.
  mengacapkan 1 to make more frequent. **2** to hasten, accelerate, speed up.

acap II 1 to be stuck deep in s.t., be buried to the top/hilt. **2** inundated, flooded (by water).
  mengacapi 1 to overflow, flood, inundate, irrigate. *diacapi air* to be flooded, inundated. **2** to soak.

acar (*Pers*) **1** pickles. **2** fresh garden salad. – *bening* uncooked pickles. – *campur aduk* mixed pickles. – *kubis* sauerkraut. – *kuning* pickled vegetables. – *matang* cooked pickles. – *mentimun* cucumber pickles. – *rampai* mixed pickles.
  mengacar to pickle, make into pickles.
  acar-acaran pickles.
  pengacaran pickling.

acara I (*Skr*) **1** item (on an agenda), agenda, schedule. *tata* – agenda. *tertib* – rules of order. **2** subject, topic, theme, program, show. *pengarah* – Master of Ceremonies, emcee. *dalam* – *rapat* on the agenda. **3** lawsuit, court case. **4** judicial procedure. *berita* – official report, deposition. *gedung* – (*ob*) court (of justice), law courts. *hari* – (*ob*) court session. *hukum* – law of procedure. **5** heading (of an article). **6** (*ob*) method, way, manner; → CARA. – *banding(an)* appeal. – *bébas* an unscheduled activity. – *berperkara* legal proceedings, litigation. – *cepat* accelerated proceedings. – *gong* closing part (of a ceremony). – *hukum* procedural (regulations). – *kebaktian* religious service. – *kesegaran* physical fitness program. – *padat* a tight schedule. – *pasang atap* topping-off ceremony. – *pembukaan* opening ceremony. – *pembuktian* listening to the evidence (at a hearing). – *pemeriksaan* investigation. – *penghiburan* reception (k.o. party). – *penglepasan/pelepasan* leave-taking, farewell. – *penuh* a full schedule. – *perdana/pokok* main item on an agenda. – *perdata* civil proceedings. – *perjalanan kapal* ship's manifest. – *pidana* criminal proceedings. – *singkat* summary proceedings. – *sipil* civil proceedings. – *surat* main contents of a letter. – *tugas* list of duties, work schedule.
  beracara 1 to have on the agenda. **2** to be involved in a lawsuit, litigate. **3** to be in session, sit (of a court).
  beracarakan to have … on the agenda/program.
  mengacara 1 to administer justice. **2** to hand down (a sentence).
  mengacarakan 1 to program; → MEM(P)ROGRAMKAN. **2** to bring to trial. **3** to place on the agenda.
  pengacara 1 counsel for the defense. **2** attorney, lawyer. ~ *Agung* (*Mal*) Solicitor General. ~ *keluarga* family lawyer. ~ *perusahaan* corporation lawyer. **3** master of ceremonies. **kepengacaraan 1** advocacy. **2** lawyers' (*mod*).
  pengacaraan programming.

acara II (*Jv ob*) **mengacarakan 1** to offer s.t. to a guest (refreshments/a chair, etc.). **2** to welcome guests on s.o.'s behalf.

acaram (*Tam? ob*) **1** wedding ring. **2** betrothal/engagement ring. **3** proof (that a bargain has been made). *uang* – earnest money.

acarawan (*Skr neo*) programmer; → PROGRAMER.

acarya 1 (*Bal*) a guru, teacher. **2** once offered as a university degree equivalent to the B.A.

acat (*J*) **acatan** remnant (of fabric), cutting.

acau mengacau 1 to be delirious, have nightmares, rave. **2** to be out of whack, to be off (of a timepiece); → ACO, KACAU.

acawi (*ob*) carpenter.

acc I (*D*) /asésé/ approved, agreed. *memberikan* –*nya* to give one's approval.
  meng-acc(kan) to approve (of), agree to. *Proyék besar harus di-acc présidén.* Big projects have to be approved by the president.

accu II (*D*) /aki/ → AKI II. – *zuur* battery acid; → AIR *aki.*

ACD → ANTI *celana dalam.*

AC-DC /asédésé/ (*E*) **1** bisexual. **2** to be between the devil and the deep blue sea, be between a rock and a hard place.

Acéh the province of Indonesia located at the northern end of Sumatra.

aceng (*Jv*) **mengaceng** [and **ngaceng** (*coq*)] **1** (*vulg*) to have an erection/a hard-on. ~ *berat* to have a big hard-on. **2** to be erect (of the penis); → ACANG II.
  acengan horny, sexually excited.

acerang 1 (*Jv*) k.o. plant, *Coleus amboinensis.* **2** (*S*) blackfellows, New Zealand cowage, k.o. medicinal herb for the liver, *Bidens pilosus.*

aceuk (*S*) older sister.

aci I 1 valid, legal. **2** okay! agreed! done (of bets)! *nggak/tidak* – a) not valid, invalid; illegal. b) canceled, could not proceed; it's off! that won't do! c) not fair. *mengambil* – to take seriously.
  mengacikan 1 to consider valid/correct/legal. **2** to validate, certify.

aci II 1 (*C*) elder sister; → ACIK. **2** (*M ob*) aunt, older woman.

aci III (*J*) **1** quintessence, essence, gist. **2** starch. **3** flour. – *jagung* cornstarch. – *ubi kayu* tapioca flour.
  acian ~ *nat* grout. – *semén* slush grout.

aci IV 1 (*Mal*) axle, shaft. **2** (*naut*) reefing-gear for rolling up sails.
  aci-aci (*naut*) reefing-gear for rolling up sails.

aci-aci 1 supposition. **2** example, model. –*nya* suppose/supposing that, take as an example, assuming that; so to speak; by chance, perhaps.
  mengaci-acikan 1 to suppose, assume, take as an example. **2** to imagine, fancy.

aci-acian belief, supposition.

acik I 1 elder sister. **2** (*M*) aunt. **3** (*ob*) older brother.

acik II → ASYIK.

acir (*J*) **mengacir** [and **ngacir** (*coq*)] **1** to dash off, run (away), walk quickly looking straight ahead. ~ *terbirit-birit* to run away as quickly as possible. **2** stiff and straight, without a bend or curve (as of a tree).

acir-aciran to run without a fixed direction (from fear, etc.).

acitra nonfigurative.

aco (*Jv*) **mengaco** [and **ngaco** (*coq*)] **1** to talk in one's sleep, be delirious; → ACAU. **2** to talk incoherently/in a confused way, talk nonsense, rave; → ACAU. **3** inaccurate; to be out of order, be off (of a watch/traffic sign, etc.). ~ *bélo* to talk through one's hat.

aco-acoan (*J*) reckless. *secara* ~ wrongly.

acu I ready, prepared.

mengacu 1 to threaten, menace (by holding up a weapon, etc.). **2** to aim, direct, point. **3** to devise, contrive, plan. *belum diacu téwas dulu* doomed before it starts. ~ *ke(pada)* a) to refer to; → MERUJUK *ke(pada)*. *dengan* ~ *ke surat ...* with reference to the letter of ... b) to be guided (by); to apply (a certain policy).

mengacu-acu to devise, contrive, plan.

mengacukan 1 to threaten with (a rifle butt, etc.), shake (one's fist) in a threatening way, point (a weapon) at. **2** to suggest, propose. **3** to consider, weigh, think over, contemplate. **4** to apply to, relate to, refer to. **5** to tune (a musical instrument).

acuan 1 reference (point), norm. *karangan* ~ reference article; → RUJUKAN. **2** application, applying. **beracuan** with a reference.

pengacu s.t. that refers.

pengacuan referential.

acu II cast, mold.

seacu to be cast from the same mold, to resemble closely.

mengacu to cast, mold (cake, etc.). ~ *ke* to be formed/molded by.

teracu molded, cast.

acuan 1 (casting-)mold, cast, model, matrix, die, form, casing. ~ *cétak* mold. ~ *kué* cake pan. ~ *sepatu* shoe last. **2** pattern. ~ *kalimat* (*gram*) sentence pattern. **3** rule. **seacuan** *bagaikan* ~ it's a perfect fit.

acuh (*M*) **1** heed, close attention, care(ful notice). **2** to care (about), pay attention (to). **3** attentive. **4** (the opposite meaning is frequent nowadays) indifferent, uncaring. ~ *tak* – indifferent, unconcerned, without interest, apathetic; → LU *lu*, *gua gua*. *bersikap tak* – to be indifferent, inattentive, heedless, negligent. *tidak/tak* – indifferent, uncaring. **menak-acuhkan** to be indifferent to. **ketak-acuhan** and **keacuh-takacuhan** indifference, lack of concern/interest, apathy.

mengacuhkan to heed, care about, be concerned about, be attentive to, mind, pay attention to, note. *tidak* ~ to ignore, disregard.

acuhan 1 s.o. that is heeded or attracts attention. *Baginya tidak menjadi* ~. He doesn't care. **2** (*J*) to care (about).

pengacuhan heeding, paying attention to.

acum incite.

mengacum to incite, instigate, stir up, stoke; to challenge (s.o. to a fight).

acuman incitement (to quarrel).

pengacum inciter, provocateur.

pengacuman instigating, provoking, incitement.

acung I point (with the finger or fingers).

mengacung to point/move upward.

mengacungi to point out, draw attention to. ~ *jempol* to applaud, acclaim, praise. *Meréka patut diacungi jempol.* They should be praised.

mengacungkan [and **ngacungin** (*J coq*)] **1** to put up (one's hand to greet or pray). **2** to raise, lift, hold up (*esp* one's hand), point s.t. ~ *ibu jarinya* to give the thumbs-up sign, indicate that s.t. is good/well done. ~ *jari berbentuk huruf V* and ~ *dua jari membentuk huruf V* to give a V for victory sign. ~ *jari satu* to give the thumbs-up sign. ~ *jari dua* to give the V for victory sign. ~ *jari tiga* to make a fuck-you sign (by making a fist and placing the thumb between the index and middle fingers). ~ *jarinya* to raise one's hand (in classroom). ~ *jempol* to give the

thumbs-up sign. *Itu patut diacungkan jempol.* We should take our hats off to that. ~ *senjata* to point a gun. ~ *tangan* to raise one's hand. ~ *telunjuk* to raise one's hand (in Indonesia, one's index finger) to ask a question. ~ *tinju* to shake one's fist.

mengacung-acungkan to keep on brandishing s.t.

teracung pointed at/toward. *dengan meriam* ~ with guns at the ready.

acungan 1 lifted (hand). *dengan/secara* ~ by show of hands. *di bawah* ~ *senjata* at gunpoint. *mendapat(kan)* ~ *jempol* to get the thumbs-up sign, be congratulated. ~ *duit kontan dari tengkulak* instant cash handed over by the middleman. *pedagang* ~ door-to-door salesman, peddler. **2** s.t. that is pointed (at).

pengacungan pointing (the finger, etc.).

acung II (*M*) **mengacung** to kick; → MENYÉPAK.

acung III amaranth (color).

ad I (*L*) – *hoc* ad hoc.

ad II introduces each item in a list.

ad III (in acronyms) → ANGKATAN *Darat*.

a.d. IV (*abbr*) [atas dasar] at, on the basis of.

AD V (*init*) → ANGKATAN *Darat*.

AD VI (*init*) → ANGGARAN *Dasar*.

AD VII car license plate for Surakarta.

ada 1 there is, there are. – *buku di atas méja.* There is/are a book/books on the table. –, *tapi tidak banyak.* There are some, but not many. *Hampir tidak* –. There are hardly any. – *apa?* What's up? What's the matter? What's going on? – *maksud* there's s.t. he wants. – *masanya* sometimes. – *orang* (this seat's) occupied, taken. – *sedia* available. – *sambungannya* (at end of a story) to be continued. – *yang* (there are) some (that are...). – *yang mérah*, – *yang biru.* Some of them are red and some are blue. *Sudah* – *pukul tujuh?* Is it seven o'clock already? – *pula* (there are) others (who). – *pula yang berpendapat* others believe that ... – *setengah jam saya tertahan.* I was held up for about half an hour. – *saja yang ...* a) there's always s.o. who or s.t. that. b) there are always. – *saja yang lolos dari perhatian.* There always are some things that escape attention. – *saja alasan.* There are always excuses. *jika* – if any, if there are any. *yang* – existing, current, remaining. *peraturan yang* – existing regulations. **2** to be (present) at/in, on (a place), be found, exist. – *di dalam rumah* to be in(side) the house. *ADA* the person is "in" his office. *tidak ADA* the person is not in (or, is "out"). *mati* – *perang* to die in war. *sesuai dengan kondisi-kondisi yang* – *dalam pasal ini* in agreement with the conditions laid down in this article. – *tidaknya* the presence or absence of, the existence or non-existence of. *belum* – not in existence, doesn't exist yet, is unheard of. **3** to stay, live (in a place). **4** to have, own, possess. *pulau yang tidak* – *orangnya* an uninhabited island. *Saudaranya* – *empat.* He has four brothers and sisters. *Berdasarkan data yang* – *pada kami.* Based on data in our possession. **5** to (really) exist. *Tuhan* –. God exists. *Orangnya sudah tidak* –. The person has passed away. **6** (to strengthen the verb) do, does, did; surely, truly, really, definitely. *Ia* – *menerima surat itu.* He *did* receive the letter; *opp* TIADA *menerima.* **7** to be, equals. *Dua dan tiga* – *lima.* Two plus three is/equals five. **8** to happen to. – *saudara melihat adik saya?* Did you happen to see my brother? – *asap* – *api* where there's smoke, there's fire. – *gula* – *semut* a) if s.o. is rich, he has many friends. b) if profit can be expected from someplace, people will go there. c) men will go to where there is a beautiful girl. – *hari* – *nasi* and *ana dina ana upa* (*Jv*) another day another meal, i.e., God will provide, so why worry? – *nyawa* – *rezeki* the future will look after itself, with time comes counsel. *tidak* – lacking, nonexistent. **ketidakadaan** lack, nonexistence. – *baiknya* it would be a good idea for (s.o. to do s.t.). – *baiknya semua pihak bersatu padu.* It would be a good idea for all parties to join together. – *main* to be unfaithful, cheat (on one's spouse).

adanya 1 the existence (of). ~ *hanya itu.* That's all there is. *sebab/karena* ~ *perang* because of the war. *tidak* ~ the absence of. *seperti apa* ~ as is. **2** so it is, amen. *Demikianlah agar Tuan maklum* ~. (*epist*) Such is the situation. **3** (*J*) the person in question/under consideration, he, she. *Belum diketahui siapa* ~. It is not yet known who the person is.

seadanya and **seada-adanya 1** whatever you have, whatever there is, whatever is available. *makan ~* to eat what is put before one, take potluck. *Makannya ~.* They ate whatever was available. *pakaian ~* any old clothes, whatever clothes come to hand. **2** not very much. *Perabotnya ~.* They don't have much furniture. *Seada-adanya silakan!* It's not much, but it comes from the heart!

ada-ada *~ saja* (exclamation suggesting that words fail one) Never at a loss for words! There's always s.t. (new)/going on! That tops it all! That takes the cake! *~ saja zaman sekarang ini!* Really, the times we live in! *Orang ini ~ saja.* a) This guy is just too much! b) This guy is always up to s.t. *~ saja! Kalau mau pulang, pulanglah!* Baloney! If you want to go home, just go! **berada-ada** to have s.t. going on behind what is said or done, have a hidden motive. *kalau tidak ~* if there isn't a good reason. **mengada-ada** and **mengada-ngada 1** to invent (an excuse), fabricate, make up (stories, etc.), talk nonsense, concoct. *bersikap mengada-ada* tendentious. **2** to give o.s. airs, boast, be pretentious, brag, act in an affected manner. *Sejak pulang dari mancanegara dia sudah ~.* After returning home from abroad, he's been putting on airs. **3** to exaggerate, overdo it. **4** to be farfetched. **mengada-adakan** to invent, fabricate, make up s.t. *~ perkara/sebab-musabab* to make a false representation, misrepresent, invent excuses. **ada-adanya(kah)** how is it possible? It's unbelievable. *~ orang mati hidup kembali!* How is it possible for a dead man to come back to life?

berada 1 to be, live, stay (somewhere). *ketika dia ~ di Jakarta ...,* when he was/lived in Jakarta ... *~ pada jalan yang tepat* to be on the right track. *... ~ di hadapan saya, notaris* (in notarial language) ... in my presence, notary public. **2** to be well off, well to do, rich. *kurang ~* lacking, deficient, scant. **kekurangberadaan** lack, deficiency, scantiness, shortage. **keberadaan 1** presence, where s.o. is, whereabouts, existence; creation (of s.t.). **2** wealth.

ada-berada there is s.t. hidden (such as a reason/intention, etc.). *tentu ada-beradanya* there must be some reason behind it.

mengadakan [and **ngadain** (*J coq*)] **1** to organize, arrange, give, have, hold, make, deliver, issue. *~ améndemén* to make/introduce an amendment. *~ dengar-pendapat* to hold a hearing. *~ diskusi/pembahasan* to hold discussions. *~ drop(p)ing beras* to make rice allocations. *~ instruksi* to give instructions. *~ konsér(t)* to give a concert. *~ konperénsi* to hold a conference. *~ pembelian* to make purchases. *~ pertemuan* to hold a meeting. *~ pidato* to make a speech, deliver an address. *~ pinjaman* to arrange for (or, take out) a loan. **2** to cause, bring about, create, establish, form, set up, launch, carry out, enter into, open up, place (an order). *~ aksi militér* to launch a military action. *~ dapur umum* to open up a soup kitchen. *~ fusi* to bring about a merger, merge. *~ hubungan* to establish relations. *~ kecepatan maksimum* to establish/set a speed limit. *~ keributan* to cause a commotion. *~ kejahatan* to commit a crime. *~ kompromi* to bring about a compromise, compromise. *~ kunjungan* to pay a visit, visit. *~ kunjungan anjang-sana* to make door-to-door calls. *~ larangan* to issue a ban/prohibition. *~ maskapai pertambangan* to set up a mining company. *~ milisi* to set up a militia. *~ partai politik* to form a political party. *~ kampanye* to launch a campaign. *~ kampanye réklame* to launch an advertising campaign. *~ latihan* to carry out exercises. *~ operasi militér* to carry out military operations. *~ perhubungan* to enter into relations. *~ perjanjian* to enter into an agreement/contract. *~ perundingan* to enter into negotiations. *~ pesanan* to place an order. *~ révolusi* to bring about a revolution. *~ salat* to say one's (obligatory) prayers. *~ sénsasi* to cause a sensation. **3** to operate, run, maintain. *~ daftar umum* to maintain public records. *~ jaringan agén-agén* to run a spy ring. **4** to get, procure, obtain.

terada (*sifat*) *~ (saja)* for want of s.t. better.

keadaan 1 situation, state, nature. *kata ~* (*gram*) adjective. *dapat menguasai ~* to be able to keep the situation under control. **2** conditions, circumstances. *dalam ~ demikian* under such circumstances. *dalam ~nya sekarang* the way things are now, as is. *~ badan* physical condition. *~ bahaya* emergency.

~ berhati-hati deliberation. *~ berkabung* in mourning. *~ cuaca* the weather, weather conditions. *~ darurat* emergency. *~ darurat militér* martial law. *~ darurat perang* martial law. *~ darurat sipil* civil emergency. *dalam ~ demikian* under such circumstances. *~ dapat masuk* accessibility. *~ diri* personal circumstances. *~ gelap* blackout. *~ gersang* arid conditions. *~ hawa* the weather, weather conditions. *dalam ~ jalan* in running condition. *~ kahar* unavoidable circumstances. *~ kas* cash situation (of a corporation; in notarial instruments). *~ kemerataan sosial* egalitarianism. *~ keras* solid state. *~ kimia* chemical nature. *~ kodrati* natural state. *~ lembab* humid conditions. *~ luarbiasa* abnormality. *~ malang* adversity. *~ memaksa* a) (state of) emergency. b) (*leg*) force majeure. *~ nyata tidak mampu* indigence. *~ pénsiun* retirement. *~ paksa* (state of) emergency. *~ perang* state of war. *dalam ~ sadar* being of sound mind. *~ sekeliling* environs. *~ sengsara* (*leg*) helpless state. *dalam ~ sulit* in a tight spot, in trouble. *~ terpaksa* emergency situation. *~ tidak bisa tidur* insomnia. *~ tidak hadir* absence. *~ tidak menentu* uncertainty. *dalam ~ utuh* intact, unscathed, in one piece. *~ yang memberatkan* aggravating circumstances. *~ yang meringankan* mitigating circumstances. *~ yang nyata/sebenarnya* reality. **berkeadaan** in the state/situation, etc. of. *putih kapas boléh dilihat, putih hati ~* (*M*) s.o.'s sincerity can best be judged from his behavior.

pengada provider.

pengadaan 1 supplies. **2** stockpiling. **3** acquisition, procurement, purchase. *~ guru bahasa Jawa* acquiring Javanese language teachers. *~ perumahan* the acquisition of housing.

adab (*A*) **1** civilization; culture, refinement. **2** good/proper behavior/manners, courtesy; erudition. *balik ~* (*cla*) unmannerly, indecent, improper (of persons); uncivilized (nation). *ilmu ~* the knowledge of good and bad for human behavior/conduct, i.e., correct forms of social intercourse. *kurang ~* ill-bred, uncultured, unmannerly; uncivilized.

beradab 1 to have/show good manners, correct forms of social intercourse; respectful (due to awe/courtesy). *Kelakuannya seperti orang tidak ~.* He behaves like an ill-bred person. **2** cultured, refined in speech/behavior, civilized. *bangsa-bangsa yang ~* civilized nations/peoples. *belum ~* not yet civilized. **kebelum-beradaban** lack of refinement. **keberadaban** politeness, civility.

mengadabi to respect, honor, treat with courtesy.

memperadabkan to refine, educate, civilize. *~ bangsa-bangsa yang terkebelakang* to civilize underdeveloped nations.

keadaban 1 refinement, culture, good breeding/manners, polish. *melanggar ~ manusia* to disregard conventionalities. **2** civilization.

pengadab civilizer, educator.

peradaban 1 culture, civilization. *perkembangan ~ bangsa Barat* the development of Western civilization. **2** etiquette, courtesy. *~ sopan* good manners.

adabiah (*A*) cultural.

adad (*A*) number. *~ catu* quantum number.

adadi (*A*) numerical.

adagio (*D*) adagio (in music).

adagium (*D*) adage.

adai-badai (*cla*) an embroidered dish-cover.

adakah whether; → APAKAH.

adakala(nya) at times, once in a while, sometimes.

adal-adal (*Jv*) croton, *Croton tiglium*.

adalah I 1 (the copulative verb) to be (usually used to emphasize the predicate noun in equational sentences, also can be followed by *merupakan* for greater emphasis). *Indonésia ~ negara hukum.* Indonesia is a constitutional state. *John ~ orang Amérika.* John is an American. **2** (an introductory emphasizer) It is ... *~ suatu usaha yang sukar sekali untuk ...* It is a very difficult undertaking to ... **3** (introducing a narrative; probably obsolete now). Once upon a time there was ... *~ seorang raja.* Once upon a time there was a king ...

adalah II and **adalat** (*A*) righteousness, justice.

adam I (*A cla*) **1** earth, land. **2** ground, soil.

Adam II (*A*) **1** Adam, the first man created by God. *anak/bani ~*

the descendants of Adam, mankind. **2** man. *kaum – dan kaum Hawa* men and women. *kulit –* new skin growing under the nail. *Nabi –* Adam.

adan I → AZAN.

Adan II (*A*) Eden.

Adan III (*A*) Aden.

adang I → HADANG. **adang-adang** screen, blinds made of thin bamboo slats (to protect against the sun/rain, etc.).

  mengadang 1 to intercept (with outstretched arms), stand in the way of, bar, block (the way), flag down (a passing vehicle); to ambush, waylay. *Orang bersenjata di sepéda motor ~ mobil yang membawa empat guru beragama Suni.* Armed men on a motorbike ambushed a car carrying four Sunni teachers. **2** (*M*) to head for.

  mengadangi and **mengadang-adangi** to intercept (with outstretched arms), bar (the way); to ambush, waylay.

  mengadangkan to stop (with one's arms/hands). *~ diri* to hold o.s. up (as).

  teradang hindered, obstructed, stopped, prevented from doing s.t. *Namun, meréka tidak berhasil mendekati kediaman Cendana karena ~ oléh aparat.* However, they did not manage to approach the Cendana residence because they were prevented from doing so by the police.

  adangan hindrance, impediment.

  adang-adangan k.o. children's game; → GALAH-GALAH *asin.*

  pengadang 1 s.o. who intercepts, highwayman, brigand, ambusher. **2** barrier, obstacle, barricade.

  pengadangan 1 place where there is an obstruction. **2** ambush, surprise attack.

adang II (*Jv*) **ngadang** *~ sego* to steam rice.

adang III aunt (mother's older sister).

adang-adang (*coq*) sometimes, now and then, occasionally; → KADANG-KADANG.

adanya → ADA.

adap I → HADAP. **ngadapin** → MENGHADAPI.

adap II (*nasi*) **adap-adapan** k.o. ceremonial rice dish.

adaptasi (*D*) adaptation.

  beradaptasi *~ ke/dengan* to adapt o.s. to.

  mengadaptasi(kan) to adapt s.t.

  teradaptasi adapted.

  pengadaptasian adapting, adaptation.

adaptif (*D/E*) adaptive, adapted to. *téknologi –* adaptive technology.

adaptor (*D/E*) adaptor.

adapun (*ob*) (introducing a sentence) well ..., as for, concerning. *– begini agaknya.* Well, it's something like this. *– raja itu berputra empat orang laki-laki.* As for that king, he had four sons.

adar I (*ob*) **mengadar** to spend the night at s.o. else's house; to go for a visit.

adar II very old.

adas (*Pers*) **1** fennel, *Foeniculum vulgare.* **2** dill, *Anethum graveolens. – cina* Japanese star anise, *Illicium religiosum. – manis* dill, *Anethum graveolens. – pedas* fennel, *Phoeniculum vulgare. – pulosari* (or, *biji – manis*) k.o. anise used in medicines. *– sowa* dill, *Anethum graveolens.* **3** (*sl*) marijuana.

adat I (*A*) **1** customary law, practices which have become unwritten local law, such as *– Minangkabau,* etc. **2** tradition, custom, habit, practice, convention. *sesuai dengan –* traditional(ly). **3** (*cla*) customs duties, tolls, taxes (in harbors, etc.). *pada –nya* usually. *hukum –* customary/unwritten law. *kata/pepatah –* words based on *adat. kurang –* a) ill-mannered, rude. b) damn! *membawa –* to menstruate. *mengisi –* to fulfill one's *adat* obligations. *pemangku –* head/chief of *adat. tahu –* to be well-mannered, polite, decent. *Itu – dunia!* That's the way of the world! *– lama pusaka usang* (*M*) custom is unchanging. *– gajah terdorong* a ruler usually misuses his power. *– diisi, lembaga dituang* (*M*) habit/custom becomes second nature. *– bersendi syarak, syarak bersendi –/kitabullah* (*M*) no deed/action should be in conflict with *adat* and religion. *– sepanjang jalan, cupak sepanjang betung* so many countries, so many customs. *– periuk berkerak, – lesung berdekak* no gain without pain. *– berkabung* funerary customs. *– bersendi syara'* custom based on Islamic law. *– cara* folklore. *– gelanggang* regulations for cockfighting.

– (dan) istiadat customs and traditions. *– yang kawi* the *adat* handed down from the past. *– kebiasaan* habits, customs. *– kemanakan* (*M*) customs concerning inheritance through the female line. *– lembaga* customs and traditions. *– pemaduan* a penalty paid by a man when taking a second wife. *– pemali* penalty paid for having violated *adat. – pembuang* penalty paid in a divorce. *– pertunangan* betrothal customs. *– resam* customs and practices; official practices. *– sopan santun* etiquette.

  beradat 1 having good manners, well-mannered. **2** to act according to *adat.* **3** customary.

  mengadatkan 1 to make into a custom/habit. **2** to ratify by *adat.*

  teradat has become a custom/habit.

  teradatkan based/formed on custom.

  peradatan customary, traditional.

adat II (*J*) **ngadat 1** obstinate, stubborn, moody, to have a temper tantrum, make a big fuss. *Istrinya suka ~.* His wife is apt to be moody. **2** to stop, stall, not run (as of a car, etc.).

adati traditional.

adawah and **adawat** (*A*) enmity.

à décharge (*Fr D*) /a désyars/ *saksi –* witness for the defense.

Adéém (*D col*) (initialism for the first three letters of *Administratur*) estate manager (of a plantation).

adegan (*Jv*) scene, act (in a movie/play/performance). *– bugil* a nude scene. *– buka-bukaan/panas* hot/sexy scene (in a movie). *– érotik* erotic scene. *– goro-goro* → GORO-GORO. *– perang* war scene. *– ranjang* a sex scene (in a film). *– séks* sex scene. *– tiwikrama* transformation scene.

  beradegan with a ... scene in it.

  pengadeganan staging. *pola ~* blocking (theatrical term).

adéh (*Jv*) **beradéh** to gallop (of horses).

adék → ADIK.

adekan → ADEGAN.

adekuat and **adekwat** (*D*) adequate.

  keadekuatan adequacy.

adem (*J/Jv*) **1** cold, cool. **2** tasteless, insipid, flat (of food). **3** quiet, tranquil, peaceful, untroubled. *– ati* k.o. medicinal plant, Indian laurel, *Litsea glutinosa. – ayem* quiet and calm. **beradem ayam** phlegmatic, imperturbable. **keademayeman** imperturbability. *uang – arem-arem* consolation money.

  mengadem to go up into the mountains (for coolness and relaxation); → NAAR *boven.*

  mengademkan [and **ngademin** (*J coq*)] **1** to refresh s.t., make s.t. cooler. **2** to put off, shelve, postpone.

  adem-ademan (*J*) **1** grown cooler. **2** calm, unconcerned. *Meréka ~ saja, meskipun Lebaran tinggal dua hari.* They were calm even though Lebaran was only two days away.

  keademan 1 peacefulness, tranquility. **2** (*Jv*) very cold/cool.

  pengadem s.t. used to cool off (such as a newspaper used to fan o.s.).

adémokratis (*D*) ademocratic.

adempauze (*D*) /adempause/ a breather, a breathing space.

adénda (*D*) addendum.

adep → HADAP.

adhan → AZAN.

adhési (*D*) adhesion.

adhésif (*D/E*) adhesive.

adhi- → ADI.

Adhi Makayasa and **Adhimakayasa** *Bintang –* the star-like decoration awarded to Armed Forces and Police Academy cadets for excellence.

Adhibhuti Antariksha motto of the First Air Operational Command: The goal must always be excellence in the air.

ad hoc (*L*) ad hoc. *panitia –* ad hoc committee.

adhyaksa (*Skr*) magistrate. *– Dharma Kartini* the women's association of the office of the public prosecutor.

adi I (*Skr*) **1** splendid, glorious, excellent. *batu setengah –* semiprecious stone. *logam –* precious metal. **2** used as a prefix meaning beautiful, excellent, superior, super-. *– bangkit* (*mil*) reveille.

  ngadi *~ sariro* to beautify one's body by putting on cosmetics, etc.

  mengadikan to improve, make superior.

adi II (*Jv*) **1** younger brother/sister. **2** spouse; → DIMAS, DIAJENG.

Adi III part of Javanese personal names, such as *Adi Sumarta*.

adiabatis (*D*) adiabatic.

adiatérmik (*D/E*) adiathermic.

adib (*A cla*) courteous, polite, respectful.

adibintang superstar.

adibunyi supersonic.

adibusana (*Skr neo*) haute couture, high fashion.

adicita ideology.

adidaya (*Skr neo*) superpower; → ADIKUASA. *negara* – superpower.

adidéwa great god.

adigang (*Skr?*) to show off one's power. –, *adigung, adiguna* to rely on one's power, authority and knowledge.

adiguna (*Skr*) superior knowledge.

adigung (*Skr*) superior authority.

adihablur (*phys*) superlattice.

adihantar superconductive.

    teradihantar superconductive. **keteradihantaran** superconductivity.

adiindividual a superhuman person.

adiinsani superhuman.

adik 1 younger sibling. *bulan* – *Maulud* (*Mal*) = *Rabiulakhir*. 2 form of address to younger sibling, wife, girlfriend, younger people in general, usually in the contracted form *dik*. 3 (*sl*) *si* – one's penis. – *bungsu* youngest sibling. – *ipar* a) husband/wife of younger sibling. b) younger sibling-in-law. – *kakak* siblings (both younger and older). – *kandung* younger sibling with the same father and mother as one. – *laki-laki* younger brother. – *perempuan* younger sister. – *sanak ayah* younger paternal nephew/niece. – *sanak ibu* younger maternal nephew/niece. – *seayah* younger sibling of another mother. – *seibu* younger sibling of another father. – *seibu sebapak* younger sibling with the same father and mother as one. – *sepupu* younger nephew/niece.

    beradik 1 to have (a) younger sibling(s). 2 to act/behave like a younger sibling. ~ *kakak* and ~ *berkakak* a) to be siblings. b) intimate, familiar.

    adik-beradik 1 brotherly, sisterly. 2 like siblings. *lima* ~ to be five siblings. *Meréka hidup* ~. They live like siblings. 3 intimate, familiar. 4 familial, within the family.

    memperadik [and **ngadik** (*Jv*)] 1 to call/consider s.o. one's own younger sibling. 2 to treat s.o. kindly.

adika (*Skr*) 1 bigger, stronger, better. 2 title for dignitaries: *Datuk Seri* – *Raja*.

adikanda → ADINDA.

adikara (*Skr*) 1 authority, power. 2 authoritative. 3 dictator, fascist.

    keadikaraan authority.

adikarya (*Skr neo*) masterpiece, masterwork.

adikodrati supernatural.

adikong (*E Mal*) aide-de-camp.

adiksi (*D*) addiction; → KECANDUAN.

adiktif (*D/E*) addictive.

adikuasa superpower. *negara* – superpower; → ADIDAYA.

adil (*A*) just, righteous, fair, impartial, unbiased, without bias/prejudice, equitable. *peraturan yang* – fair regulations. *kalau mau* – in all fairness. 2 legitimate, legal, not arbitrary. 3 honest. *operasi* – *Matoa* operation to combat the separatist movement in Irian Jaya/Papua. *tidak* – unjust, unfair, partial, not right. **ketidakadilan** injustice, unfairness.

    seadil as fair/just as.

    seadil-adilnya as fairly/justly as possible.

    mengadili [and **ngadilin** (*J coq*)] 1 to pronounce/pass judgment on, judge. *dengan tidak diadili* without trial. *bersifat* ~ judgmental. 2 to hand down (a ruling) (of a court). 3 to hear (a civil case), try (a criminal case), preside over (a court case). *Kasusnya akan diadili minggu ini*. His case goes to trial this week. 4 to try s.o., put s.o. on trial.

    mengadilkan 1 to make s.t. just. 2 (*mostly Mal*) to judge.

    teradil the most just.

    teradili can be tried.

    keadilan 1 justice, righteousness, fairness, equity. *keinsafan* ~ legal consciousness, sense of justice. *untuk* ~ pro justice. ~ *sosial* social justice. *mohon* ~ *ulangan* to introduce a demurrer. 2 honesty, candor. 3 correctness, accuracy. **berkeadilan** just, fair.

pengadil (*ob*) 1 (~ *perkara*) judge, magistrate; s.o. who administers justice. 2 referee.

pengadilan 1 (law) court, court of justice. *menghadapkan ke depan* ~ to summon before the court. *baik di dalam maupun di luar* ~ in and out of court. *mewakili perséroan di dalam/muka dan di luar* ~ (in notarial instruments) to represent the corporation in and out of court. *sidang* ~ court session. ~ *Adat* Adat Court. ~ *Agama* [PA] Religious Court. ~ *Banding* court of appeals. ~ *cepat* summary proceeding. ~ *Ékonomi* Court of Economic Delicts. ~ *Kasasi* highest appellate court, Supreme Court. ~ *kilat* summary proceeding. ~ *Landreform* Court of Land Reform Delicts. ~ *Militér* Court Martial. ~ *Negeri* [PN] District Court, court of first instance. ~ *singkat* summary proceeding. ~ *Tatausaha Negara* [PTUN] State Administrative Court. ~ *Tentara* court martial. ~ *Tinggi* appellate court, court of appeals, high court. 2 jurisdiction, (administration of) justice. 3 trial, session.

peradilan 1 (administration of) justice, judicial administration, administration of the law/the laws. ~ *bébas* a fair trial. ~ *militér* military justice. ~ *perdamaian* out-of-court settlement justice. ~ *singkat* summary justice. ~ *tata usaha negara* [Peratun] administrative justice. ~ *ulangan* court of the second instance. ~ *wasit* arbitration. 2 adjudication. 3 jurisdiction. ~ *agama* religious jurisdiction. ~ *Umum* Court of General Jurisdiction. 4 jurisprudence, case law. 5 judicial. *bantuan* ~ judicial assistance. 6 judgment. ~ *terakhir* (*religious*) the last judgment.

adilaksana (*infr mod*) professional.

adilat (*A*) justice.

Adiloka (in the *Bina Graha*, Jakarta) VIP room.

adiluhung (*Jv*) supreme, superb. *kebudayaan* – high culture.

    keadiluhungan supremacy.

adimarga (*Skr neo*) superhighway.

adinda 1 younger sibling; a courteous variant of *adik*. 2 epistolary and court use for younger sibling.

ading (*coq*) → ADIK.

adiningrat (*Jv*) 1 highest title of nobility. 2 (often spelled *Hadiningrat*) an honorific title used after the city names of Yogyakarta and Surakarta, the sites of royal courts; → NINGRAT.

ad interim (*L*) ad interim, pro tem, temporary.

    mengadinterimkan to give on a pro tem basis. *Jabatan itu akan diadinterimkan kepada menteri lain*. The position will be given to another minister on a pro tem basis.

    keadinteriman pro tem, interim.

adipasar self-service market.

adipati (*Skr*) 1 ruler, sovereign. 2 title of merit conferred by the Netherlands Indies government on a *bupati* (higher than *tumenggung*); → KADIPATÉN. – *Ario* a Javanese title used in front of Mangkunagoro, meaning "commander in chief."

adipenghantar superconductor.

adipositas (*D*) obesity.

adipura (*Skr neo*) beautiful city. *penghargaan* – an award given to cities for cleanliness.

adiraja (*Skr*) 1 emperor. 2 (*Mal Br*) (shortened to *diraja*) royal. *Angkatan Udara Diraja* Royal Air Force.

adirasa (*Skr neo*) very tasty, delicious.

adiratna (*Skr cla*) ~ *pekaca* pure-lotus jewel (symbol of a very beautiful girl).

adisional (*E*) additional.

adisiswa (*Skr neo*) model student.

adiswara (*Skr neo*) superb voice.

aditif (*D*) additive.

aditokoh 1 prominent figure. 2 mascot.

adiwangsa (*cla*) superrace.

adiwarna (*cla*) resplendent.

adiwidia (*Skr neo*) superior knowledge.

Adiyat (*A*) *al*– "Swift Horses"; name of the 100th chapter of the Koran.

adiyuswa (*Skr neo*) very old, aged.

adizalir superfluid.

    keadizaliran superfluidity.

adjéktif, adjéktip, and **adjéktiva** (*D*) adjective.

adjudikasi adjudication.

administrasi (*D*) administration. *Lembaga – Negara* [LAN] Institute for Public Administration (in Jakarta). *penyempurnaan –* administrative reform. *perubahan perilaku –* change in administrative behavior. *pranata –* administrative institutions. *– negara* state administration. *– niaga* business administration.

   mengadministrasikan to administer.

   teradministrasi administered.

   pengadministrasian administration, administering.

administratif and **administratip** (*D/E*) administrative.

administrator and **administratur** (*D/E*) 1 administrator. 2 (on a plantation) estate manager.

admiral (*D/E*) admiral.

admisi (*D*) admission (to college, etc.)

adn (*A*) paradise, Garden of Eden.

adolésén (*D/E*) adolescent.

adolésénsi (*D*) adolescence.

adon beradon to be blended (into).

   mengadon to knead, blend, mix, stir.

   mengadoni to knead.

   adonan 1 dough, batter, paste. *~ asam* leaven. *~ cair* batter. *~ kayu* ligneous stucco. 2 mixture, blend. 3 alloy.

   keadonan doughy.

   pengadonan kneading.

adopsi (*D*) adoption.

   mengadopsi to adopt. *~ anak* to adopt a child.

   teradopsi adopted.

   pengadopsi one who adopts s.t.

   peradopsian adoption (*mod*). *bisnis ~* the adoption business.

adoptif (*D/E*) adoptive.

adoptir (*D*) to adopt.

Adpél [Administrasi pelabuhan] Port Authority.

adperténsi → ADVÉRTÉNSI, IKLAN.

adpis (*D*) → ADVIS.

adpisir (*D*) advisor.

adpokat → ADVOKAT.

ad rém (*L*) ad rem, to the point.

adrénal (*D/E*) adrenal (gland).

adrénalin (*D/E*) adrenalin.

adreng (*Jv*) eager.

   keadrengan eagerness.

adrés (*D*) address. *buku –* directory. *mesin –* addressograph. *– untuk pos* mailing address.

   beradrés addressed, with the address ...

   mengadréskan to address.

adrét → ATRÉT.

ADRI [Angkatan Darat Républik Indonésia] Indonesian Army.

Adriatik (*D*) Adriatic. *Lautan –* Adriatic (Sea).

adsorbén (*D/E*) adsorbent.

adsorpsi (*D*) adsorption.

adu I pitting, matching in a contest. *– ayam* cockfight. *– ayu* beauty contest. *– bagong* boarfighting. *– bogem* to punch e.o. *– buku tangan* fisticuffs. **beradu buku tangan** to have a fistfight. **mengadu buku tangan** to have a fistfight. *– cepat* race. *– domba* ram fight. **mengadudomba(kan)** and **memperadudombakan** 1 to have rams/cocks/people fight against e.o. 2 to play off s.o. against s.o. else. **teradudomba** played off against e.o. *– fisik* tug-of-war. *– gelut(an)* a) wrestling match. b) confrontation(al). *– gembul* eating contest. *– hidung* rubbing noses. *– hukum* legal battle. *– jangkrik* cricket fight. *– jotos* fisticuffs. *– kata* war of words. *– kekuatan* power struggle. *– kening* face to face. *– kepala* head to head. **beradu kepala** to go/compete, etc. head to head. *perang – ketahanan* war of attrition. *– laga* struggle, competition. *– lari* sprint. *– layangan* kite fighting. *– lidah* verbal argument, altercation. *– manis* (*Jv*) appropriate, suitable. *– mata* exchange of glances *– muka* head-on (collision). *– mulut* dispute, war of words. *– nasib* to try one's luck. *– otot* battle of wills. *– panco* arm-wrestling. *– pandang* exchange of glances. *– peruntungan* trying one's luck. *– tenaga* test of strength. *– untung* to try one's luck. *– urat léhér* battle of wills.

   beradu 1 to collide, crash. *Ada mobil ~.* Cars have collided. 2 to fight, clash, be in conflict. *~ dengan* to contend with. 3 to have ... fight e.o. *~ ayam* to hold a cockfight. 4 to compete in. *~ lari* to run a race with. *~ kuat* to test one's strength (against). 5 to have contact with, touch. *Terdengar bunyi gelas ~.* The clinking of glasses could be heard. *giginya ~* to grind/gnash one's teeth. 6 to knock against, strike, bang. *Kepalanya ~ dengan témbok.* He banged his head against the wall. *~ bibir* (*joc*) to kiss. *~ gelas* to clink glasses, have a toast. *~ gelut* wrestling match. *~ hidung* (to have) a head-on collision. *tepuk-tinepuk bagai gelombang ~ hulu* slapping e.o. (in a friendly way) like waves dashing against e.o. *~ kening* (to meet) face to face. *~ lengan* to compete in strength. *~ lidah* to quarrel, squabble, wrangle, engage in a heated argument. *~ mata* to exchange glances (man and woman). *~ muka* to have a head-on collision. *~ nasib* to try one's luck. *~ pandang* → BERADU mata. *~ untung* → BERADU nasib. *boléh diadu* to be able to hold one's own.

   mengadu [and **ngadu** (*coq*)] 1 to bring two things together (in order to compare them), consider, weigh. *kedua benda itu bila diadu* when those two objects are compared. 2 to strike, knock, bang, dash, bump (s.t. against); to clink (glasses), toast. *Kepalanya diadunya dengan témbok.* He banged his head against the wall. 3 to have (animals) fight e.o. *~ ayam* to hold a cockfight. 4 to incite, have s.o. fight s.o. else, pit, play s.o. off against another. *Maksudnya hendak ~ kita sama kita.* His purpose was to incite us against e.o. 5 to compete in, race. *~ kekuatan* to compete in strength. 6 to test one's ... against s.o. else, play against (another team). 7 to sue, bring legal action against, lodge a complaint against. 8 to complain, file a complaint. *Saya ~ pada pimpinan mengenai pelayanan.* I complained to the management about the service. 9 to confront, have a showdown with. *Kenapa tidak kita ~ saja meréka mengenai hal itu?* Why don't we just confront them on this? *~ bibir* to kiss. *~ hidung* to rub noses. *~ kepandaian* a) to match wits. b) to test one's ability. *~ lidah* to quarrel. *~ nasib* to try one's luck, seek one's fortune. *~ pinggul* to dance. *~ tuah/untung* to try one's luck.

   mengadukan [and **ngaduin** (*J coq*)] 1 to sue, bring legal action against, take (to court). *Dia ~ paman ke pengadilan perkara.* He took his uncle to court. *~ perkara* to bring a case to court. 2 to make a complaint about, report, blow the whistle on. *Saya tidak menduga dia akan ~ saya.* I didn't think he'd report me.

   teradu the accused.

   aduan 1 competition, contest, race, fight. *~ sapi* bullfight. *~ sepuluh* (*ob*) decathlon; → DASALOMBA. 2 s.t. that is made to fight. *ayam ~* fighting cock. 3 → PENGADUAN. *tindak pidana ~* offense which is prosecuted only when a complaint is lodged.

   adu-aduan 1 contests, competitions. 2 to compete with e.o.

   pengadu 1 tattletale, tale-teller, informer. 2 plaintiff, complainant. *~ ayam* cockfight fan.

   pengaduan complaint, charge, appeal. *~ fitnah* accusation of defamation.

   peraduan 1 combat, competition, contest. 2 clinking, banging, knocking, hitting.

adu II beradu (*honorific*) to sleep. *mangkat ~* to die.

   peraduan (royal) bedchamber.

aduh 1 (exclamation of pain) ouch! ow! ooo! *–, sakitnya gigi saya ini.* Ooo, my tooth hurts. 2 Gosh! Wow! (exclamation of amazement). *– bagusnya gedung tinggi ini.* Wow, isn't that tall building beautiful! 3 (exclamation of pleasure) Oh, wow, gee!

   mengaduh(-aduh) to moan, groan.

   teraduh to utter a sudden cry of pain.

   pengaduh s.o. who complains a lot, complainer.

aduhai 1 (interjection of sadness/sorrow) oh dear. *–! Malangnya nasibku!* Oh dear! How unfortunate I am! 2 (*coq*) staggering (of prices), fantastic, great. *dengan tarif yang –* at fantastic prices. *– cakap* very good-looking. *bau yang –* a terrible smell.

aduk (*Jv M?*) mix.

   beraduk to mix, be mixed.

   mengaduk 1 to mix/put together s.t., stir. *~ semén* to mix cement. 2 to rummage through. *~ pakaian di lemari* to rummage through one's clothes in the wardrobe. 3 to disturb, rake up. *~ perkara lama* to bring/rake up the past. 4 to scramble (a signal). 5 to meddle in.

mengaduk-aduk [and **ngaduk-ngaduk** (*coq*)] 1 to mess around in, rummage through. 2 to stir up (s.o.'s emotions).

mengadukkan to knead for s.o. else. *Dengan kedua tangannya dia ~ roti bagi anak-anak yatim piatu.* With his two hands he kneaded bread for the orphans.

teraduk mixed up; disturbed, disarranged, in disarray.

adukan 1 mixture. 2 confusion, disorder. 3 mixer. ~ *telor* egg beater. 4 mortar. ~ *coran* grout.

aduk-adukan miscellaneous, mixture, variety.

pengaduk 1 mixer (the person/device), stirrer. ~ *beton* concrete mixer. 2 scrambler.

pengadukan 1 mixing, stirring. 2 agitation, roiling, stirring up.

adun I → ADON.

adun II (*cla*) beautiful, lovely (as of dress), elegant. ~ *temadun* multicolored, very lovely.

beradun to dress up, get dressed up.

mengadun(kan) to dress s.o. up.

adunan adornment, finery; cosmetics.

pengadun clotheshorse, s.o. who likes to get dressed up.

Advént (*D/E*) Advent.

Advéntisme (*D/E*) Adventism.

advérb(i)a (*D/E*) adverb.

advérbial (*D/E*) adverbial.

adverténsi (*D*) advertisement; → IKLAN.

advis (*D/E*) advice. ~ *krédit* credit advice.

mengadviskan to advise.

advokasi (*D*) advocacy.

advokat I (*D*) lawyer, attorney, solicitor.

keadvokatan attorney's, legal (*mod*). *étik* ~ legal ethics.

advokat II (*D*) *buah* ~ avocado.

adzab → AZAB.

adzan → AZAN.

adzim → AZIM.

adzmat → AZMAT.

AE car license plate for Madiun.

aék (in Tapanuli) river; → SUNGAI.

AÉKI [Asosiasi Éksportir Kopi Indonésia] Indonesian Coffee Exporters Association.

aéng (*Jv*) out of the ordinary, strange, unusual, uncommon, unfamiliar.

aér → AIR.

aérasi (*D*) aeration.

aérob (*D/E*) aerobe.

aérobatik (*D/E*) aerobatics.

beraérobatik to perform aerobatics.

aérobik(a) (*D/E*) aerobic.

aérodinamika (*D/E*) aerodynamics.

aérodinamis (*D*) aerodynamic.

Aéroflot the name of the U.S.S.R.'s national airline.

aérogram (*D/E*) aerogram, air letter.

aérologi (*D/E*) aerology.

aérométer (*D/E*) aerometer.

aéromodeling (*D/E*) aeromodeling.

aéromovél the Brazilian-made monorail bought by Indonesia.

aéronaut (*D/E*) aeronaut.

aéronautik (*D/E*) aeronautic.

aéronautika (*D/E*) aeronautics.

aéronom (*D/E*) aeronomist.

aéronomi (*D*)/*E* aeronomy.

aéronotik → AÉRONAUTIK.

aéroskop (*D/E*) aeroscope.

aérosol (*D/E*) aerosol.

aérosport (*D/E*) aerosport. *Féderasi ~ Indonésia* [FASI] Indonesian Aerosport Federation.

aérostatika (*D/E*) aerostatics.

aéstétika (*D/E*) aesthetics.

aéstétikus (*D*) aesthete.

aéstétis (*D/E*) aesthetical.

af I (*D*) free of charges. *harga ~ pabrik* price ex factory, i.e., free of charges to the purchaser until the time of removal from the factory.

af II (in acronyms) → AFRIKA.

afal I → HAFAL, APAL. **ngafalin** → MENGHAFALKAN.

afal II (*A*) /af'al/ (good) conduct/behavior (of men/animals), works (of God). ~ *dan akwal* words and deeds.

afal III (*D*) 1 offal. 2 factory rejects.

afasi(a) (*D*) aphasia.

afdal → AFDOL.

afdéling (*D*) 1 section, division, department. 2 (*col*) regency.

afdlal → AFDOL.

afdol (*A*) 1 distinguished, prominent, eminent, excellent. 2 to go well, be good, be right.

mengafdolkan to celebrate.

afdruk (*D*) (of photo) print (made from a negative).

mengafdruk to make a print (from a negative).

mengafdrukkan to have a print made (from a negative).

afdzal → AFDOL.

afék (*D/E*) affect.

aféksi (*D*) affection.

aféktif (*D/E*) affective.

Afg(h)anistan Afghanistan.

afiat (*A*) 1 health, well-being. 2 in good health. *séhat wal-* and *séhat dan -* hale and hearty, in excellent spirits, safe and sound.

mengafiatkan to restore to good health, make healthy.

keafiatan fitness, healthiness.

afiks (*D/E ling*) affix.

pengafiksan affixation.

afiksasi (*D ling*) → PENGAFIKSAN.

afiliasi (*D*) affiliation.

berafiliasi to be affiliated. ~ *dengan* a) affiliated with. b) to affiliate with.

afinitas (*D*) affinity.

afirmasi (*D*) affirmation.

mengafirmasikan to affirm.

afirmatif (*D/E*) affirmative.

afiun → APIUN.

afkir (*D*) rejected; → APKIR.

mengafkir(kan) to declare unfit for service.

afkiran rejected for use. *détonator* ~ rejected detonator.

pengafkiran rejecting, culling.

aflatoksin (*D/E*) aflatoxin.

Afrika Afrika. ~ *Barat* West Africa. ~ *Hitam* Black Africa. ~ *Selatan* [Afsél] South Africa. ~ *Timur Laut* Northeast Africa.

afrikat (*D/E ling*) affricate.

afrit I (*A*) a malicious giant spirit, evil spirit.

afrit II (*D*) ramp.

afrodisiak (*D/E*) aphrodisiac; → OBAT *kuat*.

afschuifsysteem (*D*) /afskheufsistém/ pass-the-buck system.

Afsél [Afrika Selatan] South Africa.

afsun (*A Pers/Hind cla*) sorcery, witchcraft, occult force, incantation.

aftab (*Pers ob*) sun.

afuah and **afwah** (*A*) supernatural magic power.

afyun → APIUN.

ag I (in acronyms) → AGAMA.

AG II car license plate for Kediri.

Aga I (in Turkey and India) an honorific title; *cp* BAPAK.

aga II (*ob*) → RAGA IV, PERAGA.

aga III *orang Bali* ~ the original inhabitants of Bali.

agah beragah and **beragah(-agah)an** to look/stare at e.o. provocatively/defiantly.

mengagah 1 to look at s.o. in a challenging way, stare at. 2 to tease. 3 to bring (two fighting cocks) close together to tease them into fighting.

agahari (*ob*) → UGAHARI.

agak I 1 to guess, suppose, think, believe. ~ *saya, ibu Anda sudah pulang ke Surabaya.* I thought your mother had gone back to Surabaya. 2 approximately, about. *kerbau ~ tiga* about three water buffaloes. ~ *sepuluh hari lamanya* for about ten days. 3 somewhat, rather, kind of. ~ *mahal juga buku ini.* This book is rather expensive. ~ *gerangan* supposing that.

agaknya 1 I would guess that, it seems that. 2a) I wonder. *Ke mana dia pergi ~?* I wonder where he has gone. b) (also in questions) actually, really, to be sure. *Apa ~ maksud Bapak?* What is your real intention? *Orang manakah anda ~?* Where are you actually from? **3** (used to reduce certainty and in polite conversation) apparently, it seems that; → KIRANYA. *Ia masih sakit ~.* He still seems to be sick. **4** probably, likely. *Yang ~ terlupa dalam diskusi ...* What was probably forgotten during the discussions was ...

agak-agak 1 guess, conjecture; (vague) idea, imagination. **2 to** think carefully about s.t. **3** → AGAKNYA.

seagak with the same intention.

beragak(-agak) 1 to intend, desire, wish, mean, want. *Ia sudah beberapa kali ~ hendak berkenalan dengan tetangganya yang baru itu.* More than once he has intended to get acquainted with his new neighbor. **2** (*usu* with negative) to think/consider carefully. *Ia mengatakan sesuatu dengan tidak ~ sedikit juga.* He said s.t. without thinking carefully about it.

mengagak(-agak) 1 to suppose, guess. *seperti yang diagak* as was guessed (in advance). *lain yang diagak, lain yang kena* it turned out different from what was expected. **2** to consider, think carefully about. *Ia ~ dua tiga kali sebelum mengatakannya.* He said it after careful consideration. *Kamu jangan ~ yang bukan-bukan.* Don't think about the impossible. **3** to imagine, believe.

mengagakkan to guess, think, decide, determine (carefully). *Meréka bersama-sama ~ biaya negeri.* Together they carefully determined state expenditures. *~ sénténg* (*M*) to stint, skimp, set limits on, cut corners.

mengagak-agakkan to imagine, guess, figure out.

teragak 1 (*M*) to long for, desire, crave. *Ia ~ benar ke kampungnya.* He really feels homesick. **2** guessed, thought about, anticipated. *tidak ~* unguessable. *Tidak ~ perginya.* His departure was not anticipated. **3** to pass through one's mind, think of s.t. *saya ~ untuk ...* I thought about ..., it occurred to me to ...

teragak-agak 1 (*M*) to long for, desire, crave. **2** (*usu* with a negative) to hesitate (to do s.t.).

agak-agakan guesses.

pengagak 1 estimate, guess. **2** belief, conjecture.

agak II mengagak-agakkan *~ pantatnya kepada* to stick one's buttocks out at (as an insult).

agak-agih mengagak-agihkan 1 to state clearly. **2** to find fault with, like to criticize.

agal I → AGEL 2.

agal II the leatherback sea turtle, *Dermochelys coriacea.*

agam I (*cla*) **1** virile, manly. **2** stout, sturdy, hefty.

agam II further than intended, endless, interminable. *berkepanjangan bagai ~* protracted endlessly.

beragam endless, without end.

mengagam to shelve, postpone/delay indefinitely.

agama (*Skr*) religion, religious. *memeluk ~ Islam* to embrace Islam. *menjalankan ~* to perform one's religious duties, worship. *kaum ~* the pious. *pengadilan ~* religious court. *~ animis* animism. *~ Bahai* Bahaiism. *~ belebegu* heathenism. *~ Buddha* Buddhism. *~ bumi* non-revealed religion. *~ Hindu* Hinduism. *~ Hindu Bali* Balinese Hinduism; → HINDU *dharma. ~ Islam* Islam. *~ Jawa* "religion of Java," i.e., a syncretic blend of religious beliefs. *~ Kristen* Christianity. *~ Kristen Katolik* Catholicism. *~ Kristen Protéstan* Protestantism. *~ Nasrani* Christianity. *~ samawi* the three revealed religions: Islam, Christianity, and Judaism. *~ Yahudi* Judaism.

seagama of the same religion. *orang ~* coreligionist.

beragama 1 to have a religion, be of the ... religion. *Kamu ~ apa?* What is your religion? *~ Buddha* to be a Buddhist. **2** religious, devout, pious. *kebébasan ~* freedom of religion. *kesetiaan ~* religious loyalty. *um(m)at ~* religious people. **3** to worship. *~ kepada uang* to serve Mammon. **keberagamaan 1** religiousness, religiosity. **2** (*mod*) religious. *soal-soal ~* religious matters.

mengagamakan to make s.o. religious, instill religion into s.o.

agama-agamaan false religion.

keagamaan 1 religion. **2** religious, ritual.

pengagamaan making s.t. religious.

agamani religious.

agamasasi the act of making religious.

agamawan religious person.

mengagamawankan to win s.o. over to a religion.

agamawi religious, pertaining to religion.

agami followers of a religion. *~ Islam* followers of Islam who do not practice it seriously. *~ Islam Santri* devout followers of Islam.

agamis religious, pertaining to religion.

agan I beragan (*M*) intentional. *mati ~* a) sudden death (from no visible cause, but from, e.g., a broken heart). b) suicide.

beragan-agan and **mengagan(i)** to bother, annoy, pester, tease.

agan II (*S*) short for *juragan.*

agar I (*Pers*) and *– supaya* **1** so that, in order to, for the purpose of. *– menjadi perhatian* for your attention. **2** introduces a wish, should.

agar II and **agar-agar 1** an edible seaweed, *Gracilaria lichenoides, Eucheuma spinosum.* **2** a gelatin made from it, k.o. pudding. **3** a k.o. drink; → CINCAU.

agas I various species of sand fly and gnat, *Ceratopogon spp., Phlebotomus spp.*

mengagas to swarm.

agas II → TALI *agas.*

agat (*E*) agate.

agatis *kayu ~* white dammar pine, *Agathis alba.*

agel (*J/Jv*) **1** rope made from *ijuk* or the black sugar-palm fibers. **2** fibers of the *ibul* or *gebang* palm, a tall palm with huge leaves, *Corypha utan.*

agem (*Jv*) bundle (unit of measurement for harvested rice) **1** (of plants) the number one can hold between thumb and forefinger. **2** (of raw grains) an amount weighing about 375 *kati* (231 kilograms = 509 pounds).

agén (*D*) **1** representative (of a bank/concern, etc.). **2** agent. **3** neighborhood newspaper dealer, agency. *– asuransi* insurance agent. *– beli* purchasing agent. *– dagang* commercial/manufacturer's agent. *– duane* custom's agent. *– ganda* double agent. *– jénderal* general agent. *– jual* sales agent. *– kepala* head agent. *– kuasa* agent holding a power of attorney. *– muda* subagent. *– pelaksana* executing agency. *– pembaru* trend setter. *– pembayar(an)* paying agent. *– pembelian* purchasing agent. *– penagihan* collection agent. *– penidur* sleeper agent. *– penjual* placement agent. *– penjualan* selling agent. *– perjalanan* travel agent. *– perkapalan* shipping agent. *– polisi* policeman. *– rahasia* secret agent. *– rangkap* double agent. *– samaran* undercover agent. *– surat kabar* local newspaper distributor. *– teri* minor agent. *– tunggal* sole agent/representative. **mengagén-tunggali** to be the sole agent for. **keagén-tunggalan** and **keagénan tunggal** sole agency/representation. *– umum* general agent.

mengagéni to be an agent for, represent.

keagénan and **peragénan** agency, representation.

pengagénan using agents for (products).

agénda (*E*) **1** (pocket) diary. **2** agenda. **3** agenda item.

mengagéndakan to put s.t. on the agenda (in a meeting, etc.).

pengagéndaan putting s.t. on the agenda.

ageng (*Jv*) big (of human body); *cp* AGUNG.

pengageng big shot, VIP.

agénsi (*E*) agency.

agénsia (*D*) (chemical) agent.

agih (*M*) a share agreed upon, the share to be allotted to s.o., portion. *–.– pukang* to give everything away so that one has nothing left for o.s.

beragih to make a distribution (of property).

mengagih to provide s.o. with a share, give.

mengagih(-agih)kan to distribute, share out.

teragih distributed.

agihan distribution, share, portion.

pengagih distributor.

pengagihan distributing, distribution.

peragih gift, distribution.

agio (*D*) agio, premium. *– modal* paid-in surplus. *– saham* premium on capital stock in excess of par value.

agitasi (*D*) agitation.

beragitasi to be agitated.

agitator (*D/E*) agitator.

aglaf (*A*) uncircumcised.

aglutinasi (*D*) agglutination.

agnostik (*D/E*) agnostic.
agnostisisme (*D/E*) agnosticism.
a-go-go and ago-go I (*D*) a go-go, go-go.
   bera-go-go to go-go dance.
ago-go II [aksi gobak gonjong] (to eat) dried *sago* instead of rice, since the Malay community in the Riau Archipelago could no longer afford to buy rice in 1979.
agranulositosis (*D*) anemia aplasia.
agraria (*D*) agrarian affairs.
   keagrariaan (*mod*) agrarian. *kondisi* ~ agrarian conditions.
agraris (*D*) agrarian.
agrégasi (*D*) aggregation.
agrégat I (*D/E*) electric generator set.
agrégat II (*D/E*) aggregate. *pengeluaran* – *riil* real aggregate expenditure.
agrési (*D*) aggression.
   mengégresi to launch an aggression against.
   keagrésian aggressiveness.
agrésif and agrésip (*D/E*) aggressive.
   mengagrésifkan to make aggressive.
   keagrésifan aggressiveness.
agrésivitas (*D*) aggressiveness.
agrésor (*D/E*) aggressor.
agribisnis (*D/E*) agribusiness.
   beragribisnis to be in agribusiness.
agrikultura (*D/E*) agriculture.
agro-ékologi (*D/E*) agroecology.
agroindustri (*D/E*) agroindustry.
agroindustrial (*D/E*) agroindustrial.
agronomi (*D/E*) agronomy.
agropangan agrofood.
aguk pendant, locket worn by children and brides.
agul I (*J*) proud, arrogant, boastful, overly proud of one's own achievements.
   mengagulkan to brag about, pride o.s. on, be stuck up about.
   mengagul-agulkan to glorify.
agul II (*J*) agul-agulan → UGAL-UGALAN.
agun (*M ob*) security, pledge.
   beragun backed, with collateral of. *éfék* ~ *asét* [EBA] asset-backed securities.
   mengagunkan to give/offer s.t. as collateral, encumber. *Dia* ~ *saham yang dimilikinya.* He gave the stock that he owned as collateral.
   agunan I security, collateral. ~ *pokok* principal collateral. 2 guaranteed.
   pengagunan encumbering.
agung I (*Jv*) 1 grand(iose), noble, majestic, exalted, lofty, sublime, august, illustrious. 2 great, large, main, supreme. *Gunung* – a mountain in Bali. *jaksa* – → JAKSA agung. *layar* – the mainsail. *menteri* – (*Mal*) cabinet minister. *pemerintah* – supreme government. *perasaan memandang* – pride, haughtiness. *tamu* – VIP, high-ranking visitor. *tiang* – a) the mainmast. b) the main pillar, column. *Yang Di-Pertuan* – (*Mal*) the King.
   mengagungi to boast of.
   mengagungkan and memperagungkan I to glorify, magnify. 2 to praise, commend, extol. ~ *diri(nya)* to pride o.s. (on), glory (in).
   mengagung(-agung)kan ~ *diri* to boast, brag, talk big.
   teragung most noble.
   keagungan I grandeur, magnitude, loftiness, sublimity. *menunjukkan* ~ to lord it over (others). 2 highness, majesty. 3 prestige. 4 mastery.
   pengagung zealous defender of, apostle for.
   pengagungan veneration, glorification.
   pengagung-agungan idolization.
agung II (*ob*) gong.
agung III teragung → RAGUNG.
agus I I title in Banten conferred on descendants of *radéns* married to women of lower nobility (short for *bagus*). 2 title given by parents to their young sons. *mas* – title lower than *tubagus* (short for *ratu bagus*), the highest title in Banten, carried by the male descendants in the female line of the former Sultans. 3 fair, handsome.
Agus II (*ob*) (*bulan*) – (the month of) August.
Agustus (*D*) (*bulan*) – (the month of) August.
Agustusan the celebration of Indonesian Independence Day (August 17). ber-Agustusan to celebrate August 17.
agut I agut-agut → BUTBUT.
agut II (*M*) mengagut-agut to open and close one's mouth gasping for breath.
ah I exclamation of mild protest; the speaker feels strongly or uncomfortable about s.t. or ; hey! (as a protest against s.o.'s teasing, etc.). *sudah* –! stop it! *tidak mau pergi* –! I don't *want* to go! –, *tidak apa-apa kok!* Hey, it was nothing! *Saya pulang* –! I'm going home! – ...*ih* ... *uh* sounds of pleasure.
ah II (*ob*) bisa empat – (the wife's role in Javanese society) a) *bisa omah-omah.* b) *bisa isah-isah.* c) *bisa tebah-tebah.* d) *bisa umbah-umbah*, i.e., a) keep the household. b) wash the dishes. c) make the bed. d) wash the clothing.
ah III (in acronyms) → AHLI.
A.H. IV [Anno Hejirae] follows a date in the Islamic calendar.
aha aha!
ahad (*A*) 1 one. 2 first. 3 (*hari* –) Sunday. *malam* – Saturday night. – *Palem* Palm Sunday. 4 week. *ahli-al.*– people of the covenant, i.e., Christians and Jews. 5 transmitted by only one transmitter (of a *hadis*).
   mengahadkan to unite (in marriage).
ahadiat (*A ob*) oneness (of God).
ahala → AALA.
ahang (*Pers?*) drum.
ahbar (*A ob*) news(paper); → AKHBAR.
ahdiat → AHADIAT.
ahérat → AKHIRAT.
ah-ih-éh a sound indicating indecision.
ahimsa (*Skt*) nonviolence.
ahir → AKHIR.
ahirat → AKHIRAT.
ahkam (*A ob*) laws (prescribed by religion).
ahkamul khamsaha (*A*) the fivefold division of human actions: obligatory, recommended, neutral, reprehensible, forbidden.
ahl al-bait → AHLULBAIT.
ahlak → AKHLAK.
ahlan (wa sahlan) (*A ob*) welcome!
ahlaqul (*A*) – *karimah* to be of good character.
ahli (*A*) 1 (an) authority (on), expert, specialist. 2 skilled, good at, competent. 3 member (of a family), relative(s), people; → AHLU(L). 4 (*Mal*) member (of a council/club). *bukan* – layman. *tenaga* – expert staff. *yang* – professional. – *agronomi* agronomist. – *analisa intél(l)ijén* intelligence analyst. – *anatomi* anatomist. – *andrologi* andrologist (expert on diseases of men). – *anéstési* anesthesiologist. – *antropologi* anthropologist. – *Arab* Arabist. – *arkéologi* archeologist. – *arsip* archivist. – *astronomi* astronomer. – *atom* atomic scientist. – *bahasa* linguist; → LINGUIS. – *baktéri* bacteriologist. – *bangsa-bangsa* ethnologist. – *bangunan* architect; → ARSITÉK. – *bangunan kota* city/town planner. – *barang-barang kuno* antiquarian. – *batu* petrographer. – *bedah* surgeon. – *bedah plastik* plastic surgeon. – *bedah saraf* neurosurgeon. – *bedah tulang* orthopedist. – *bidah* groups in Islam declared unacceptable. – *bina wicara* speech therapist. – *binatang* zoologist. – *bintang* astronomer. – *biokimia* biochemist. – *biologi* biologist. – *bius* anesthetist. – *bor* drilling superintendent (of an oil company). – *botani* botanist. – *bumi* geologist; → GÉOLOGIAWAN. – *cangkok jantung* heart transplant specialist. – *catur* chess master. – *ceritera* storyteller. – *cuaca* weatherman. – *darah* hematologist. – *démografi* demographer. – *dengan dadu* crapshooter. – *dérmatologi* dermatologist. – *diabétés* diabetician. – *didik* educationalist. – *disain* designer. – *dokuméntasi* documentalist. – *ékofértilitas* environmental fertility expert. – *ékologi* ecologist. – *ékonomi* economist. – *éléktronika* electronics expert. – *épigrafi* epigrapher. – *fakih* expert in canon law. – *falak* astronomers, *esp* those who calculate the beginning and end of the month of Ramadan. – *farmasi* pharmacist; → FARMASIWAN. – *fauna* zoologist. – *fikih*

scholars learned in Muslim law. – *filsafat* philosopher. – *firasat* physiognomist. – *fisika* physicist; → FISIKAWAN. – *génétika* geneticist. – *géofisika* geophysicist; → GÉOFISIKAWAN. – *géologi* geologist; → GÉOLOGIAWAN. – *gigi* dentist; → DOKTER *gigi*. – *gunung berapi* vulcanologist. – *hadis* scholars learned in the Traditions. – *hama* entomologist. – *héwan* veterinarian. – *hikmat* wizard. – *hisab dan ruyat* an expert who determines for Indonesia, Malaysia and Singapore which days certain Muslim holidays will fall on based on sightings of the moon. – *di bidang hormon* endocrinologist. – *hortikultura* horticulturist. – *hukum* legal expert, jurist. – *ibadah/ibadat* s.o. who fulfills his religious obligations. – *ikan* ichthyologist. – *ilmu alam* physicist. – *ilmu bangsa-bangsa* ethnologist. – *ilmu biografi orang yang suci* hagiologist. – *ilmu didik* educationalist. – *ilmu falak* occultist. – *ilmu jamur* mycologist. – *ilmu jiwa* psychologist. – *ilmu keturunan* geneticist. – *ilmu manusia* anthropologist. – *ilmu pelikan* mineralogist. – *ilmu pengetahuan* scientist. – *ilmu perbintangan* astronomer. – *ilmu racun* toxicologist. – *ilmu tenaga dalam* expert working with things outside the realm of the senses. – *ilmu urai* anatomist. – *imunologi* immunologist. – *jamur* mycologist. – *jantung* cardiologist. – *jasad renik* microbiologist. – *jiwa* a) psychologist. b) psychiatrist. – *kamus* lexicographer. – *kandungan* gynecologist. – *kecantikan* beautician. – *kependudukan* demographer. – *k(e)riting rambut* hair dresser (for women). – *ketimuran* orientalist. – *kimia* chemist. – *Kitab* "People of the Book" (Christians and Jews). – *konstruksi* structural engineer. – *kriminologi* criminologist. – *kriya kraton* expert in traditional ways. – *kubur* the deceased. – *listrik* electrician. – *logam* metallurgist. – *madya* [Amd] academic title received after completing a D-3 program. – *makan énak* gourmet. – *makmal* laboratory worker. – *masak* chef. – *masalah-masalah Cina* Sinologist. – *masalah-masalah Indonésia* Indonesianist. – *mékanik* mechanical engineer. – *mencopét* professional pickpocket. – *mendidik* educator. – *mengenai Mesir* Egyptologist. – *mesin* a) mechanical engineer. b) expert mechanic. – *métalurgi* metallurgist. – *métrologi* metrologist, inspector of weights and measures. – *mikologi* mycologist. – *negara* a) political scientist. b) politician. **keahli-negaraan** statesmanship. – *negeri* population of a country. – *nikah* in-laws. – *nujum* astrologist. – *nuklir* nuclear scientist. – *obat* pharmacist; → FARMASIWAN. – *ornitologi* ornithologist. – *pahat* sculptor. – *patologi* pathologist. – *patologi forénsik* forensic pathologist. – *patung/pemahat* sculptor. – *pemasangan pipa* pipe fitter. – *pembangun kota* city/town planner. – *pembikinan kapal* shipbuilder. – *pembuka tulisan-tulisan rahasia* cryptologist. – *pembukuan* certified public accountant. – *penata warna* color consultant. – *pencegah dan pengobatan penyakit tua* gerontologist. – *pendidik* educator. – *penduduk* demographer. – *peneliti* researcher. – *pengamat telapak tangan* palmist. – *pengendali pemboran (petro)* toolpusher. – *pengetahuan* scholar, scientist. – *penggunaan tanah* soil scientist. – *pengobatan kaki* pedicurist. – *pengukuran kapal* admeasurer (of ships). – *penilai/penaksir* appraiser. – *penjinak bom* demolition/bomb disposal expert. – *penjualan* sales manager. – *penyakit dalam* internist. – *penyakit kulit* dermatologist. – *penyakit telinga, hidung dan tenggorokan* ear, nose and throat specialist, otolaryngologist. – *penyakit tumbuh-tumbuhan* phytopathologist, plant pathologist. – *perancang mode* dress/fashion designer; → PERANCANG *busana/mode*. – *perawatan kulit muka* aesthetician. – *perbendaharaan* treasury accountant. – *perhotélan/peréstoranan* hotel/restaurant manager. – *perpustakaan* librarian; → PUSTAKAWAN, PUSTAKAWATI. – *peserta* shareholder (in corporation); → PEMEGANG *saham*. – *peta* surveyor. – *petilasan* archaeologist. – *pidato* orator, speaker. – *pikir* philosopher. – *pisah* analyst. – *politik* politicus; → POLITIKUS. – *praja* administrative officer. – *psikologi sosial* social psychologist. – *purbakala* archaeologist. – *racun* toxicologist. – *radio* radioman. – *radiologi* radiologist. – *ragam* (musical) composer. – *rajah* palm reader. – *rékayasa* engineer. – *rencana* planner. – *résénsi* book reviewer, critic. – *rias* makeup artist. – *risét* researcher. – *röntgén* radiologist. – *ruang angkasa* space scientist. – *rumah* the family, housemates. – *sanggul* hairstylist. – *sastra* man of letters. – *sejarah* historian; → SEJARA(H)WAN. – *seni pidato* elocutionist.

– *serangga* entomologist. – *sihir* a) hypnotist. b) sorcerer. – *sinologi* Sinologist. – *sosiologi* sociologist. – *statistik* statistician. – *stratégi* strategist. – *sufah* pilgrims in Mecca who live off the generosity of Muslims. – *sulap* magician. – *suluk* mystic, expert in *tarékat*. – *sunah/sunat* observer of traditional law. – *sunah wal jamaah* Sunni Muslims. – *syaraf* neurologist. – *tafsir* annotator, commentator. – *tanah* agronomist. – *tarikh* a) genealogist. b) historian, chronicler. – *tas(s)awuf* mystic. – *téhnik* technician. – *téknologi (makanan)* (food) technologist. – *tenung* fortune-teller. – *téori* theoretician. – *térapi* therapist. – *tulisan kode* code expert, cryptographer. – *tulisan tangan* graphologist. – *ukur (tanah)* surveyor. – *urologi* urologist. – *urusan karyawan* personnel manager. – *urut* masseur. – *ushuluddin* scholars learned in Islamic law. – *varuna* hydrographer. – *vénérologi* venereologist. – *waris* heirs (to an estate). **pengahliwarisan** appointment of an heir.

mengahlikan to specialize. ~ *diri* to specialize (in s.t.).

keahlian 1 (professional) skill, expertise, expert knowledge. *tak mempunyai/punya* ~ unskilled. **2** a trade. **berkeahlian** skilled; to have skills in a certain area. *tak* ~ unskilled.

ahlulbait (A) **1** the whole family, housemates. **2** the Prophet Muhammad's family. – *Rasul* Muslims.

ahlul hilli wal aqdi (A) authoritative elders.

ahlulkitab (A) **1** "People of the Book" monotheists other than Muslims. **2** scribe.

ahlulkubur (A) the deceased.

ahlulnikah (A) those related by marriage, in-laws, affines.

ahlulsuluk (A) mystics.

ahlunnujum (A) astrologer.

ahlusunnah (A) traditional. – *wal-jamaah* term used by Sunni Muslims to describe themselves, usually in distinction to the Syi'ah.

ahmad (A) **1** praiseworthy. **2** admired.

ahmak (A) silly, simple, stupid, dull.

ahmar (A) red.

aho an exclamation of surprise.

ahooii (E) ahoy.

Ahqaf (A) *al-* "The Dunes"; name of the 46th chapter of the Koran.

ahwal → HAL I.

Ahzab (A) *al-* "The Confederates"; name of the 33rd chapter of the Koran.

ai I an exclamation of surprise, etc.

ai II (the English personal pronoun) I.

a.i. (*abbr*) → AD INTERIM.

aib (A) **1** flaw, defect, fault. **2** a bad name/reputation. **3** scandal, disgrace, shame, ignominy. *suatu – yang tiada terhapuskan lagi* an indelible shame. *memberi –* to shame, disgrace. *menaruh –* to feel ashamed.

beraib to be/feel ashamed. *tidak* ~ shameless.

mengaibkan 1 to insult, slander, defame, criticize, condemn. ~ *nama* to bring disgrace/shame/dishonor on s.o., discredit, drag s.o.'s name through the mud. **2** to disgrace, shame.

keaiban dishonor, shame, disgrace, discredit, humiliation.

pengaiban dishonoring, shaming, disgracing.

aica aibon → LÉM *aica aibon.*

ai-con (*Mal coq*) /é-kon/ air-conditioning; → ÉKON.

aidilfitri (*cla*) → IDULFITRI.

aih → AI I.

aikyu (E) IQ.

a'immah (A) leadership.

ain (A) **1** eye. **2** essence. **3** the 18th letter of the Arabic alphabet. *nur al-* light of the eye.

ain-al-banat and **ainulbanat** (A) k.o. fabric.

ainul yakin (A) completely convinced.

air 1 water. **2** juice. *banyak –nya* juicy. – *jeruk* orange juice and other citrus drinks. **3** (*batang –*) river. *ke –* to go to the river (to relieve o.s., etc.). *anak –* tributary. **4** a drink. – *kopi* coffee (the drink). **5** liquid (in many compounds and verbs). *berhabis –* to have talked about s.t. for too long. *berkering – liur* to give advice that is ignored, waste one's breath. *buang – besar/kecil* to defecate/urinate. *gigi –* water's edge. *telah jadi –* (his money is) all gone. *kebesaran –* bewildered. *tidak lalu –* watertight. *mata –* spring; source (of river). *salah/sesat –* badly educated; → SALAH asuhan. itu hanya – mentah that doesn't amount to much. – matanya dilepasnya sepuas-puasnya. He cried his heart out. seperti – soda short-lived enthusiasm; → PANAS-PANAS tahi ayam. – kali tidak selamanya banjir life is not all beer and skittles. – laut siapa yang garamin (J) self-praise is no recommendation. – susu dibalas dengan – tuba to return good for evil. – beriak tanda tak dalam the empty vessel makes the greatest sound. – besar batu bersibak relationships fall apart after conflict. – cucuran atap jatuhnya ke pelimbahan juga and – di tulang bumbungan turunnya ke cucuran atap like father, like son. – dicincang tiada putus and – dicincang tak akan pernah putus said of relatives who make up again after a short estrangement. – dalam berenang/berkumbah, – dengkat bercébok to live within one's means. – tenang menghanyutkan still waters run deep. bagai – di daun keladi/talas inconstant, unstable, fluctuating, variable. bagai – titik ke batu a) constant dripping will wear away a stone. b) unteachable. bagai membandarkan – ke bukit to perform a Sisyphean labor. bermain – basah, bermain api letur every effort has its consequences. menepuk – di dulang it is an ill bird that fouls its own nest. – diminum rasa duri, nasi dimakan rasa sekam said of s.o. having difficulties so that everything becomes tasteless. tak – hujan ditampung, tak – peluh diurut and tak – talang dipancung the end justifies the means. pandai berminyak – a) toady. b) to flatter, cajole, wheedle. bagai mencencang – to carry coals to Newcastle. tambah – tambah sagu increased work means increased income. sekali – besar, sekali tepian beranjak/beralih (so) many heads/men, (so) many minds. ada – ada ikan one can find the means of subsistence in every country. bagai – jatuh ke pasir it is like pouring water into a sieve. sambil menyelam minum – to kill two birds with one stone. sauk – mandikan diri to stand on one's own two feet. seperti – basuh obtainable in abundance. seperti – di atas bulu bébék like water off a duck's back. – abu lye. – aki battery acid. – alas brackish water. – altar holy water. – alur wake (of ship). – ampuh flood water. – anggur a) wine. b) grape juice. – api any spirit that flares up, hydrochloric acid, vitriol, etc. – aqua distilled water; → AIR suling(an). – arwah water connected with ceremonial purification. – asam brackish water. – asin brine, saline solution. – atar rose water. – bah flood, inundation. – bakat whirlpool. – baku undistilled/unfiltered water. – balik receding tide. – baling-baling wake (of a ship). – banjir flood water. – baptisan baptismal water. – basuh tangan easy to get, plentiful. – batu/beku ice. – belanda (ob) soda water. – bena tidal water. – bendungan backwater. – beras starch. – berbalik backwater. – berolak eddy, whirlpool. – besar a) flood. b) feces, night soil. – bocor oozing water. – buah fruit juice. – buangan waste water, effluent. – bunga blessed drinking water with roses, jasmine, and ylang-ylang flowers. – busi water in a (car) battery. – combéran sewage. – cuci washing water. – cuci tangan finger-bowl water. – dadih whey. – daging meat broth. – dasar bottom water. – dingin cold water. – dukun → AIR putih. – empedu bile. – és ice water. – galian groundwater. – garam brine, salt water. – godogan (Jv) boiled drinking water. – gula molasses. – hidung nasal mucus. – hidup running water. – hujan rainwater. daérah/kawasan penangkap dan penyerap/penyimpan – hujan catchment area. – jatuh precipitation. – jeruk lemonade. – jeruk campur kécap orange juice mixed with soy sauce (used as a cough medicine). – kahwa coffee (the drink). – kaku hard water. – kaldu bouillon. – kandang liquid manure. – kapur limewater. – karbol carbolic acid, phenol. – kata-kata alcoholic drink. – kelantang bleaching water. – kelapa coconut milk. – keling high tide. – kelonyo eau de cologne. – kemih/kencing urine. – keran running/tap water. – keras hydrochloric and sulfuric acid. – ketuban amniotic fluid. – kirawa water from a flash flood. – kisi interstitial water. – koloh-koloh water in which fabric has been dipped. – kumbahan rinse water. – kumur/kusur mouthwash. – langit "water from heaven," i.e., rain. – larian runoff. – lata a small waterfall. – laut seawater. – lebah honey. – lédéng/léding running/piped-in water. – lendir phlegm. – limbah wastewater. – limun lemonade. – lisol k.o. disinfectant. – liur/ludah spit, saliva. – liur menitik saliva dripping from the mouth, drool. – lunak soft water. – madu honey. – (me)mancur

a) fountain. b) small waterfall. c) a decorative plant, Jacobinia cornea. – mandi a) bath water. b) s.t. that is normal or usual. – mani sperm, seed. – mas fluid for gilding. – masin salt water. – mata tears. – mata duyung water over which a spell has been cast. – mata pengantén mountain rose, coral vine, Antigonon leptopus. – matang boiled drinking water. – mati a) bay, inlet. b) creek. – ma'ulhayat water which has the power to raise the dead. – mawar rose water. – mejam a) unboiled water. b) latex. – mela a) waterfall. b) mountain stream. – merta jiwa rain. – minum drinking water. – muka a) facial expression. b) surface. – mukabumi surface water. – murni pure water. – najis water into which some pollution has fallen. – nanas pineapple juice. – pasang high tide. – payau brackish water. – pembersih lotion. – pendingin coolant. – pengadem "cooled water," believed to make s.o. invulnerable. – pengairan irrigation water. – peluh sweat, perspiration. – penggelontor water used for flushing. – pérak silver zinc. – peras juice, sap. – perbani neap tide. – pujaan ceremonial water. – putih (boiled) drinking water. – purwa (geol) connate water. – rabu very high tide. – raja aqua regia. – ra(k)sa mercury, quicksilver. – rebusan water left over after boiling s.t. – rendah low tide. – ruang bilge water. – ruban scum on coconut oil. – sabun soap suds. – sadah hard water. – saluran sewage. – saput (geol) pellicular water. – saringan filtered water. – seasal connate water. – sebak beginning of a flood. – seléra saliva. – sembahyang water for ritual ablutions. – sembilan (Mal) water for bathing a dead body. – sembir (geol) fringe water. – seni urine. – senyawa (geol) connate water. – serani water for baptismal purposes. – setaman (Jv) a preparation of water and three varieties of flowers used in wedding ceremonies. – siau urine. – sisa waste water. – soda soda water. – suci (Catholic) holy water. – suling(an) distilled water. – sumber spring water. – sumur well water. – suri semifermented arrack. – surut low/ebb tide. – susu mother's milk. – susu jolong colostrum. – tadahan captured rain water. – talkin water sprinkled on a grave. – tambang mine water. – tanah ground water. – tanih water near enough to the surface to be available to plant roots, ground water. – tapai arrack. – tapisan filtrate. – tawar a) fresh (not salt) water. b) unboiled water. – téh tea (the drink). – tenang slack water. – tepung tawar magic potion; → TEPUNG tawar. – terjun waterfall. – terolah treated water. – tersedia available water. – tersekap (geol) connate water. – tersenyawa water mixed with minerals. – tétés molasses. – timah tin coating. – timpas low water. – tinggi high water. – tomat tomato juice. – tolak bala water to keep diseases, etc. at a distance. – tomat tomato juice. – tua lye, lixivium. – tuban amniotic fluid. – ukup perfumed holy water. – wangi perfume, scent. – (w)udu water for ritual ablutions. – yang dipindahkan displaced water (by ship, etc.). – zamzam water from the well at Mecca.

berair 1 to have water in it; to be aqueous, not dry. **2** juicy.

mengair 1 to become/turn into water. **2** (petro) gone to water.

mengairi 1 to irrigate, water, supply with water. **2** to water down.

terairi to be irrigated.

keairan 1 flooded, inundated. **2** leaky.

pengairan irrigation, irrigating.

perairan 1 territorial waters, waterways. ~ kepulauan archipelagic waters. ~ pedalaman a) inland waters. b) internal waters. ~ téritorial/wilayah territorial waters. **2** waterworks.

airbus (D) (pesawat jét) – 320 the A-320 (jet aircraft).

Airlangga 1 Erlangga, Prince of Daha. **2** name of a university in Surabaya.

airloji (D) (ob coq) a watch; → ARLOJI.

ais (S) cloth for carrying a child on one's back or side.
  mengais to carry a child in such a cloth.
  aisan cloth for carrying a child on one's back or side.

Aisyiah and **Aisyiyah** the women's branch of the modernist, orthodox but reformist Muslim cultural organization Muhammadiyah.

Aitarak militia in the former East Timor that favored integration into Indonesia.

aiwan (Pers) hall, large sitting room.

aj (in acronyms) → AJUDAN.

aja I (*J*) → SAJA.
aja II (*Jv*) /ojo/ don't! – *dumèh* don't get on your high horse just because you ...
aja III epithet for a girl belonging to the nobility in Deli.
ajab I (*A ob*) surprised, astonished, amazed.
ajab II → AZAB.
ajag → AJAK III.
ajaib (*A*) **1** strange, abnormal. **2** astonishing, miraculous, wonderful, magic. – *di atas* – it was a miracle of miracles that.
　seajaib as amazing/astonishing/miraculous as.
　mengajaibkan miraculous, amazing.
　terajaib the most miraculous/amazing.
　keajaiban 1 miracle, wonder. **2** remarkableness, curiosity.
ajaibkhanah (*Pers cla*) museum.
ajak I invite, ask.
　mengajak [and **ngajak** (*coq*) and **ngajakin** (*J coq*)] **1** to invite, request, ask (to come along/join in doing s.t.), take s.o. out (for a meal, etc.). *Saya diajaknya tinggal di gubuk itu.* He invited me to stay in that cottage. *Dia tidak diajak berunding.* He was left out of the discussions. *Terlalu sulit diajak bicara.* It was hard to get him to talk. *yang ~ bicara* the interviewer. *yang diajak bicara* the interviewee. *~ keliling* to show/take s.o. around. **2** to persuade, induce, urge, coax, talk s.o. into. *~ ngomong-(ng)omong* to persuade/get s.o. to talk. *Dia tidak bisa diajak bergurau.* He can't take a joke. **3** to challenge (to a fight). *~ lawan berkelahi* to challenge one's opponent to a fight. **4** to propose, offer (marriage). *Ada seorang duda yang ~nya menikah.* A widower proposed to her. *~ berunding* to consult. *~ keliling* to show/take s.o. around. *~ keluar* to ask s.o. out (on a date). *~ serta* to invite along. *Tak seorang pun diajak serta.* Not one was persuaded to come along. ***mengajak-sertakan*** to invite s.o. to come along.
　mengajakkan to incite, provoke.
　terajak 1 invited along. **2** persuaded, urged, induced, coaxed.
　ajakan 1 invitation, appeal, offer, call (to do s.t.), solicitation. *~ jaman* call of the times. **2** persuasion, arrangement (for s.t. to be done). **3** stimulus.
　pengajak 1 inducement. **2** s.o. who induces.
　pengajakan inducement, inducing.
ajak II (*M ob*) **1** similar to. **2** like. **3** as.
　mengajakkan 1 to consider as. **2** to demonstrate (how s.t. is done), show by example.
ajak III (*Jv*) (*anjing* –) wild forest dog. *Cuon alpinus.*
ajal (*A*) **1** destiny. **2** term/allotted span of life, death. *menemui/sampai –nya* to die. *Sudah sampai –nya.* His time has come. *menghadapi –nya* to be dying, on the point of death. *sebelum – berpantang mati* nobody dies before his time. *– samar* a sudden or unexplained death.
　seajal *mati ~* to die a natural death (due to sickness/old age).
ajalullah (*A*) *mati* – to die a natural death.
Ajam I (*A*) Persia.
ajam II (*A*) non-Arab.
Ajami (*A*) Persian.
ajan I (*M*) → REJAN.
ajan II → AZAN.
ajang I (*Jv*) **1** object from which food is eaten, such as a plate, etc. **2** site, place, venue, arena. *– pembantaian* killing ground. *– peperangan/perjuangan/pertarungan* battlefield, battleground; → MÉDAN *laga*. *– témbakan rudal* missile launching site.
ajang II (*S*) **1** (earmarked) for. **2** property, possession. *– orang* s.o.'s property.
ajar teaching, instruction, tuition, education. *kepalang –* poorly taught. *masak –* courteous, polite, correct in behavior. *kurang –* a) ill-bred, rude, impolite, impudent, impertinent, insolent, unmannerly, having no manners, uncultured. b) (exclamation of annoyance). For heaven's sake! ***kekurang-ajaran*** impoliteness, rudeness.
　belajar 1 to study. *Ia ~ pelajarannya.* He is studying his lesson. *~ dengan bantuan komputer* [BDBK] computer-aided instruction, CAI. *~ keluar negeri* to study abroad. *~ kepada* to go to ... to study, be apprenticed to, learn from. *Viétnam ~ kepada Indonésia.* Vietnam learned from Indonesia. *~ sendiri* self-

taught. **2** to learn, to learn how to. *sesudah tamat ~* on graduation. *~ baca-tulis* to learn how to read and write. *Ia ~ bahasa Indonésia.* He is learning Indonesian. *~ berbahasa Indonésia* to learn (how) to speak Indonesian. *~ dari* to take lessons from. *~ kenal* to get acquainted with s.o., get to know s.o., make s.o.'s acquaintance. *Saya ingin ~ kenal dengan Anda.* I'd like to introduce myself. *~ lagi* to brush up on. *~ nyopir* (*coq*) to learn how to drive. **membelajarkan** to teach. *Meréka dibelajarkan menari.* They were taught how to dance. **pembelajaran** study, learning. *~ bahasa* language learning.
　mengajar [and **ngajar** (*coq*) and **ngajarin** (*J coq*)] **1** to teach s.o., drill, coach, train. *~ meréka baca-tulis* to teach them (how) to read and write. *belajar ~* to learn how to teach, learn teaching. *Jangan ajar orang tua makan kerak.* Don't try to teach people s.t. they already know. **2** to give s.o. a good lesson, give s.o. a lesson he won't forget; → MENGHAJAR.
　mengajari 1 to train, teach, instruct. *Dia diajari bahasa Belanda.* He was taught Dutch. **2** to reproach s.o.
　mengajarkan 1 to teach s.t., pass on (knowledge). *Dia ~ bahasa Indonésia.* She has been teaching Indonesian. **2** to make s.t. be a lesson (for).
　ajaran 1 teaching. *Dia tak makan ~.* He never learns. **2** warning. **3** theory, doctrine, dogma. *~ hidup* biology. *~ kejadian alam/dunia* cosmogony. *~ kesatuan/serba tunggal* monism. *~ tujuan* teleology. *~ Marx* Marxism. **4** punishment, correction; reprimand. **pemelajaran** study. *~ atas* study of. *Départemén ~ tentang Indonésia* Department of Indonesian Studies.
　pelajar 1 secondary/high school student. **2** schoolboy; schoolgirl. **3** pupil. **4** (*infr*) learned person, scholar; → SARJANA. **mempelajari 1** to study, make a close study of, learn in greater detail about, apply/devote o.s. to, concentrate on, make a point of studying ..., acquire a knowledge of. *~ dengan tekun* to study s.t. hard, pore over. *~ dunia gelandangan* to study the homeless. **2** to consider, examine closely, look into. *Rencana itu sedang dipelajari.* The plan is under consideration/is being considered. **mempelajarkan** to teach, instruct, give instruction. **terpelajar 1** *kaum ~* the intellectuals. **2** trained, practiced, schooled, learned, (highly) educated. *orang ~* an educated/learned person. *tidak ~* uneducated, ignorant. ***ketidak-terpelajaran*** ignorance. **keterpelajaran** intellectualism.
　pelajaran 1 lesson, course, subject, education, schooling, training. *~ agama* religious lesson(s). *~ manasuka* optional subject (of instruction). *~ membaca* reading lesson. *~ menengah* secondary education. *~ peraga* object lesson. *~ ulangan* brush-up course. **2** treatise, essay. *risalah ~* learned treatise. **berpelajaran** to have obtained training in school, educated. *Istrinya seorang yang ~.* His wife is an educated woman.
　pengajar 1 teacher, instructor, tutor. **2** (*infr*) teachings.
　pengajaran 1 education, teaching, instruction. *~ bahasa Indonésia* the teaching of Indonesian. *~ bersama* classroom learning. **2** experience, lesson. *Itu menjadi ~ bagi kita sekalian.* That was a lesson for all of us.
ajar II ajar-ajar (*Skr cla*) hermit, recluse.
ajat → HAJAT.
ajé gilé (*J*) what a crazy idea, what a crazy thing!
ajeg and **ajek** (*Jv*) **1** invariable, constant, steady, stable. **2** regular. *dengan –* regularly.
　keajekan regularity.
ajeng (*Jv*) younger sister; → JENG.
ajengan (*J*) **1** *bangsa –* the elite. **2** Muslim religious leader, *esp* teacher of Islam. **3** religious teacher who has no *pesantrén*.
ajér (*Jv*) to melt, dissolve; → AJUR-AJÉR.
ajeran → ACERANG.
aji I (*Jv*) **1** incantation. **2** secret formula, charm. *– antiapi* antifire charm. *– belut putih* magic power of s.o. who is successful. *– candrabirawa* incantation to conjure up a monster. *– gineng* knowledge of sexual techniques. *– halimun* a charm to make one invisible. *– kekebalan* charm which makes one invulnerable. *– kesaktian* magic formula. *– mumpung* and (*ng*) – *pumpung* (*Jv*) to be opportunistic, take advantage of an opportunity, enjoy o.s., give free rein to one's passions. *–ning saliro soko busono* (*Jv*) the fine coat makes the fine gentleman. *– pancasona* charm to

make one invulnerable to death. *- sirep* charm to put to sleep the residents of a house to be robbed.

aji-aji *~ sirep/penyirep* the art of learning how to put s.o. or an animal to sleep through sorcery. *~ roworonték* talisman to protect s.o. from death.

ajian charm; → JAMPI.

aji II mengaji [and **ngaji** (*coq*)] to read/study the Koran; → KAJI I.

ajian what one has learned.

aji III (*Jv cla*) (*sang -*) the king.

aji IV → HAJI.

Aji Suryanatakusuma the military resort command (*Korém* 091) in Balikpapan.

aji-aji k.o. marine fish, amberjack, black-banded trevally, *Seriola dumerili, Seriolina nigrofasciata*.

ajidan → AJUDAN.

ajikarma (*mil*) education of a soldier and the strength of a soldier produced by education.

ajimat (*A*) amulet, charm, talisman. *- pengasih* charm to make s.o. fall in love.

berajimat to have an amulet, etc.

Aji-no-Moto (*Jp*) MSG, Vetsin.

ajir I (*A*) laborer, hireling.

ajir II (*Jv*) k.o. bamboo used as a pole, stake (used as a marker or stake); → PATOK.

Ajisaka King Saka, an ancient monarch alleged to have invented the Javanese calendar and alphabet.

ajnabi (*A*) a man who can marry a woman because he is not a close relative (no fear of incest).

ajnas (*A*) miscellanies, sorts, kinds, variety. *tuhfatul -* (*epist*) the letter and the gifts which (theoretically) accompany it.

ajojing modern western dances.

berajojing to perform modern western dances, dance western-style.

ajol (*J*) **ajol-ajolan** to keep on lurching.

ajrih (*S*) shy, timid; respectful fear for those in high places, awe, fear.

aju put/move forward; → MAJU.

mengaju to teach, advance (an argument).

mengajukan [and **ngajuin** (*J coq*)] **1** to advance (an argument), bring (an argument) up, raise (an argument), raise/lodge an objection. *~ keberatan/éksépsi* to raise/bring up an objection. **2** to lodge (an appeal/objection), give notice of (an appeal), file (a brief/application/for asylum, etc.). *~ klaim* to submit/lodge a claim. **3** to bring the matter/case into/before the court, appeal to the court; to summon (before the court), institute (a suit/legal proceedings/an action) against, sue. **4** to produce, submit (documents as evidence). *~ sebagai barang bukti* to produce/bring in evidence. **5** to produce, bring forward (a witness). **6** to move (the time) forward, advance (a watch); → MEMAJUKAN. *~ tanggal* to postdate. **7** to put in/into action (fresh troops), throw in (fresh troops). **8** to introduce, propose (a proposal). *~ ke pengadilan negeri* to summon/bring/take s.o. before the district court.

ajuan (*ob*) proposal, suggestion, s.t. put forward or brought up.

pengaju *~ petisi* petitioner.

pengajuan submission, putting forward, filing, lodging. *~ klaim* filing a claim.

ajubila → AUDZUBILLAH.

ajudan (*D*) **1** (*mil*) adjutant. **2** chief petty officer. *- jénderal* adjutant general.

mengajudani to flank (with adjutants).

ajudikasi (*D*) adjudication.

ajujah and **ajujat** → JUJAH.

ajuk I to sound out.

mengajuk 1 to take soundings (to measure the depth of the sea, etc.). **2** to sound out s.o. to find out his/her opinion/views/feelings, seek information, probe, gauge, assess. *tak dapat ~ menimbang rasa* cannot understand s.o.'s real character or frame of mind (due to lack of acquaintance with him/her). *di laut boléh diajuk, di hati siapa tahu* who can plumb the depths of the human heart?

terajuk sounded out, tested.

ajukan sounding, guess, assumption.

keajukan can be guessed. *dangkal telah keseberangan, dalam telah ~* s.o.'s character is already well known; what is going on inside s.o. is known.

ajuk II mengajuk to mimic, imitate (in order to make fun of), mock.

ajukan and **ajuk-ajukan** mimicry, mocking, teasing, making fun of.

ajuk III → AJU.

ajun I to deviate from one's goal/target.

terajun dropped/fallen back, delayed, postponed.

ajun II (*M*) intention, purpose.

mengajun to intend, plan; to begin, start. *diajun* to be started (as of discussions, etc.). *belum diajun sudah tertarung* (*M*) there was a problem as soon as it began.

ajun III → AJUNG II.

ajung I → JUNG.

ajung II (*D*) adjunct, assistant, deputy, lieutenant; → ASISTÉN, DÉPUTI. *- komisaris (polisi)* (*coq*) deputy (police) commissioner.

ajur (*Jv*) pulverized, crushed. *mundur kita -, mandeg kita ambleg* retreat is defeat. *- ajér* completely crushed. *- kumur-kumur* crumbled to dust.

ak (in acronyms) → AKADÉMI.

akab (*A*) eagle.

AKABRI [Akadémi Angkatan Bersenjata Républik Indonésia] Republic of Indonesia Armed Forces Academy (located on Gunung Tidar, Magelang, Central Java).

akad I (*A*) contract, agreement. *putus -* void (of contract). *- jual beli* contract of sale. *- krédit* credit arrangement. *- nikah* marriage contract.

berakad to enter into an agreement/contract.

mengakadkan to enter into an agreement about, decide on.

Akad II *Hari -* (*coq*) Sunday; → AHAD.

akad III (in acronyms) → AKADÉMI.

akadémi (*D*) institute of higher education after completion of senior high school, college; usually has a three-year program leading to a B.A. *- Angkatan Laut* [AAL] Navy Academy. *- Angkatan Udara* [AAU] Air Force Academy.

akadémik (*D*) academic. *kebébasan -* academic freedom. *tenaga -* person with university training; → AKADÉMIKUS.

akadémikus (*D*) a college graduate.

akadémis (*D*) academic.

akadémisi (*D*) alumni.

akaid (*A*) dogma, correct belief. *ilmu -* dogmatism.

akak → KAKAK.

akal (*A*) **1** logic, reason(ing), presence of mind, wisdom. *banyak - yang buruk* crafty. *banyaknya -* inventiveness. *bertukar/berubah -* to go crazy, not be in one's right mind. *dalam keadaan - yang séhat* in full possession of one's faculties, sane, of sound mind. *dalam waktu tak masuk -* the incredible amount of time of. *habis/hilang/kehilangan/putus -* at one's wit's end, at a loss for what to do; to go crazy, lose one's head. *dengan sehabis -* with all one's strength and mental abilities. *lurus -* straightforward. *masak -* to have attained the age of discretion/reason. *masuk -* reasonable, logical, makes sense, advisable. *panjang -* crafty, tricky. *sempit/singkat -* narrow-minded. *tajam -* quick-witted, sharp-witted. *terang -* clever, smart. *tidak masuk (di) -* illogical, hard to believe, difficult to imagine, incredible, unreasonable, unacceptable, inconceivable, doesn't make sense. **2** a/the way to, the means of, idea. *Saya ada -.* I have an idea. *Dicarinya - supaya dapat membayar utangnya.* He looked for a way to pay his debts. *minta - (kepada)* to ask (s.o.) for a way to do s.t. **3** deception, deceit, trickery, ruse, stratagem, artifice, shrewdness. *- akar berpulas tak patah* a clever person is not easily defeated in a debate. *- tak sekali tiba* nothing comes off smoothly/without a hitch; Rome was not built in a day. *- budi* sound/common sense. *- bulus/kancil/keling/labah* a crafty trick. *- busuk* a mean/low/shabby/dirty trick. *- cerdik* deception clever idea. *- curang* fraudulent means. *- dua jengkal* to think o.s. equal to s.o. else. *- geladak* a vile trick. *- laba-laba* cunning trick. *- licik* deception. *- melintas* a sudden idea, brainwave. *- palsu* frame-up. – *panjang* crafty. – *péndék* narrow-minded. – *pikiran* reasoning. – *yang ... rahasiakan* another trick up ...'s sleeve. – *séhat* common sense. – *sejengkal* to think o.s. better than s.o. else. – *tiga jengkal* to think o.s. inferior to s.o. else. – *ubi* trick. – *waras* sound/common sense.

akal-akal pretend, feign.

seakal-akal, seakal *budi, sebudi* **seakal, seakal** *upaya* with all one's strength and mental abilities.

berakal 1 to have ideas/plans/ways; with ideas/plans/ways. **2** clever, intelligent, smart. *belum* ~ immature.

mengakal 1 to find a way to do s.t. **2** to trick, cheat, dupe, take advantage of.

mengakali [and **ngakalin** (*J coq*)] **1** to look for a way to do s.t. **2** to trick, deceive, cheat, double-cross, defraud, take advantage of, play tricks on; → MENGELABUI. **3** to get s.t. by trickery.

mengakalkan to think up a plan, work s.t. out in one's mind.

akalan 1 invention, s.t. made up. **2** trick.

akal-akalan 1 invention, fabrication. **2** tricks, deception. **3** to fabricate, invent.

pengakalan tricking.

akali (*A*) intelligent.

akaliah (*A*) cerebral.

akaliyah (*A*) rational, showing reason; → AKALIAH.

akan 1 coming, next. *minggu/bulan/tahun yang – datang* next week/month/year. **2** for (the purpose of), (in order) to. *Uang ini – pembayar utang.* This money is for paying debts. – *ganti* in lieu of. **3** about to, going to, will, shall. *Présidén – tiba pada pukul 11.00 pagi.* The president will arrive at 11:00 a.m. *(Hari) – hujan.* It's going to rain. *tidak –* and *takkan* it isn't likely to be. **4** (connective between some verbs and adjectives and their objects; can sometimes be shortened to -kan). *kenal – orang itu* to know that person. *tidak sadar – dirinya* and *tidak sadarkan dirinya* to be unconscious. **5** as to, with reference to, concerning, relating to, in regard to, about. – *halnya sédan mérah ...* As for the red sedan ... **6** (preceding the word *tetapi* it serves as an emphasizer) but, however.

akan-akan closely resembling, almost similar.

seakan-akan 1 identical, similar, almost alike. **2** (it's) as though/if.

berakan-akan (*cla*) → SEAKAN-AKAN.

mengakan (*ob*) to strive, aim for; to intend.

mengakankan (*ob*) to suppose, give an example of.

akanan 1 s.t. to be finished. **2** (*fin*) accrual.

keakanan time to come, the future.

AKAN → ANTARNEGARA.

akang 1 (older) brother. **2** wife's term of address for husband; *cp* KANGMAS, → KAKANG.

akar I 1 root, that part of a plant that is normally in the soil. *pada tingkat – padi* at the grassroots level. **2** source/origin/cause of an action/quality/condition, etc. – *segala kejahatan* the root of all evil. **3** the name of various creeping plants and lianas, such as – *bahar* bead-coral, *Plexaura antipathes* worn as a bracelet to prevent rheumatism. – *wangi* k.o. grass with fragrant root, vetiver, *Andropogon zizanioides*. **4** (*gram*) root (of a word). – *kata* (*gram*) root, stem, base. **5** (*math*) root. – *kuadrat/pangkat dua* square root. – *pangkat tiga* cube root. *menarik* – to extract the (square, etc.) root of. *bergantung pada – lapuk* to center/put all one's hopes on a powerless person. *tiada rotan – pun berguna* half a loaf is better than none. FOR OTHER PLANT NAMES BEGINNING WITH AKAR SEE THE SPECIFIC NAME. – *angin* aerial root. – *apung* floating root. – *bahar* k.o. marine plant, bead coral, used as medicine and for making into bracelets, *Plexaura sp.* – *banir* buttress root. – *batu* a fungus rhizomorph used as a bracelet against evil spirits. – *batu kelir kambing* k.o. climber, *Sarcolobus globosus*. – *belit* twining root, tendril. – *beluru* k.o. plant, St. Thomas's bean, matchbox bean, *Entada phaseoloides*. – *benang* filiform root. – *besar* blue sky flower/vine, blue trumpet vine, *Thunbergia grandiflora*. – *biji* k.o. plant, *Roucheria griffithiana*. – *binasa* scarlet leadwort, *Plumbago indica*. – *bulu* hair root. – *(ber)gantung* aerial root. – *bukit* various species of plants, *Anonaceae*. – *bumi* k.o. plant, *Rennellia paniculata*. – *cina* k.o. liana, *Limacia oblonga*. – *ca-*

bang lateral root. – *dagun* k.o. plant, *Gnetum tenuifolium*. – *egrang* tap root. – *gamat* k.o. plant, *Pericampylus glaucus*. – *gambir* a climber, jungle weed, *Combretum sundaicum*. – *gantung* aerial root. – *gigi* root of a tooth. – *isap* sucker, haustorium. – *jangkar* anchor root. – *jitah* k.o. liana. – *kambing-kambing* a climber, *Sarcolobus globosus*. – *kemenyan* k.o. climber, Chinese yam, *Dioscorea oppositifolia*. – *kuayah* → KUAYAH. – *kubik* cube root. – *kucing* k.o. climber, *Toddalia aculeata*. – *kuning/kunyit* k.o. climber used for medicinal purposes, *Fibraurea chloroleuca*. – *kupur* k.o. plant, Ceylon blackberry, *Rubus moluccanus*. – *kwadrat* square root. – *larat* → LARAT III. – *layak* k.o. plant, *Uvaria purpurea*. – *lekat* k.o. liana, betel pepper, *Piper betle*. – *lembaga* radicle, root that comes out of a seed. – *liar* adventitious root. – *lundang* k.o. nettle whose juice is used as medicine, *Pouzolzia viminea*. – *lupang* a climber, *Micaria sp.* – *lupuk* a liana, *Adenia acuminata*. – *lutut* part of root which grows up and then down toward the ground. – *mati* (*ob*) aerial root. – *melata* a) creeping root. b) to go from bad to worse, get deeper and deeper in debt. – *melibat* clinging root. – *melilit* root which wraps around. – *minyak* various species of climber, *Limacia velutina, Hypserpa cuspidata*. – *napas* pneumatophore. – *pahit* a plant used against asthma, *Cyclea laxiflora*. – *pakis* scrambling fern, climbing swamp fern, *Stenochlaena palustris*. – *pangkat dua/tiga* square/cube root. – *parsi* asparagus. – *pusat* crown root. (*penyakit*) – *putih* white root rot, a disease of rubber plants, *Rigidoporus microporus*. – *rambut* hair follicle. – *rempelas* a bush, stone leaf, *Tetracera scandens*. – *rimpang* trailing root (of turmeric/ginger). – *rumput* grass roots. – *samping* adventitious root. – *serabut* fibrous root. – *serapat* → SERAPAT. – *seruntun* → BRATAWALI. – *som* → SOM IV. – *susu* rhizome. – *tawan hutan* k.o. climbing plant, *Fissistigma melodorum*. – *tambahan* adventitious root. – *teki* k.o. plant with edible roots, *Cyperus tuberosus*. – *telanjang* bare root. – *teriba* a plant used to treat skin diseases, *Rhinacanthus nasuta*. – *tikus* a shrub with medicinal value, Indian snakeroot, *Rauwolfia serpentina*. – *tinggal* rhizome, rootstock. – *tuba* k.o. plant, derris root, *Derris elliptica, Milletia sericea*. – *tunggang* tap root. – *tunjang* prop root. – *udara* aerial root. – *ulam* k.o. decorative plant, black-eyed Susan vine, clock vine, *Thunbergia alata*. – *umbi* tuber. – *urat* k.o. herb, *Fissistigma manubriatum*. – *utama* primary root.

berakar 1 to have roots, be rooted, take root. **2** to take deep/firm root (in), be deeply rooted, take hold. *Sangat dalam* ~ *keyakinan itu.* That conviction was firmly rooted (in s.o.). *Itu sudah* ~ *dalam diri saya.* That's ingrained in me. That runs in my blood. **3** *berurat* ~ ingrained, firmly fixed/rooted. **4** to be settled and have descendants/offspring (in).

mengakar to be(come) firmly/deeply rooted, take root, become entrenched. *Organisasi itu belum lagi* ~ *ke dalam masyarakat.* That organization has not yet become firmly rooted in society.

mengakari to be rooted in.

mengakarkan to take the square root of.

akar-akaran various kinds of roots.

akar II reference to a snake (in superstitious awe and veneration).

akara k.o. fish, blue acara, *Aquidens pulcher*.

akarat (*A*) estate; land holding.

akas I agile, adroit, dexterous, nimble.

keakasan agility, adroitness, nimbleness, dexterity.

akas II (*Skr*) atmosphere; → A(NG)KASA.

akas III (*A*) **1** upside down, reversed. **2** opposite. *-nya* on the contrary.

akas IV (*Bal*) – *kaya* (*leg*) joint property (in a marriage).

akasa → ANGKASA.

akasia (*D*) acacia, *Acasia mangium* and other species.

akat → AKAD.

akaun (*E Mal*) account; → AKUN.

akaunting → PERAKUNAN.

akbar (*A*) **1** great, almighty. *Allahu –* God is great. *tahun Haji –* Great Pilgrimage Year (i.e., a year in which the first day of the Hajj ceremony, the 9th Zulhijjah, falls on a Friday). **2** mass (meeting). *rapat –* mass meeting. **3** big and important. *pertandingan –* the big (boxing) match.

Akcaya motto on the coat of arms of West Kalimantan, meaning "Never Destroyed" in the Dayak language.

akékah (*A*) ritual shaving of the head of an infant and ritual sacrifice seven days after a birth.
  berakékah to undergo this shaving.
  mengakékahkan to have (a child) undergo a ritual head shaving.

akéw (*C J*) **1** Chinese lad. **2** form of address to Chinese boys; *cp* AMOI.

akh just, in a word, in short, briefly; → AH I. *Tubuhnya semampai. Giginya putih bersih. –, menarik sekali.* She's slender; her teeth are white; in a word, she's very attractive.

akhbar (*A*) **1** news; → KABAR. **2** newspaper, daily.

akhdar (*A*) green.

akhérat → AKHIRAT.

akhiar (*A*) better; best.

akhir (*A*) **1** end, termination, close, conclusion. *malam – tahun* New Year's Eve. *pada – bulan ini* at the end of this month. *pada – pidato* in conclusion. *pada – ini* lately, of late. *perbani* – last quarter (of the moon). *tujuan* – final destination, ultimate goal. **3** final. *dengar pendapat* – final hearing. *– minggu/pekan* weekend. **berakhir minggu/pekan** to spend the weekend. *– pendidihan inti* departure from nucleate boiling [DNB]. *pada – pidato* in conclusion. *– sanad* the last person on the line of transmission of the Prophet Muhammad's words, etc. and therefore the most reliable. *– zaman* the last day. **4** (*fin*) closing.
  akhir-akhir ~ (*ini*) of late, lately, recently. *hingga* ~ *ini* till/up to now, so far. ~ *kelaknya* sooner or later.
  akhir(-akhir)nya 1 in the end, finally, sooner or later, eventually, at (long) last, in the long run. ~ *berada* to end up (in the hands of). ~ *masuk* to end up in (the hospital, etc.). ~ *menjadi* to end up as. ~ *muncul* to end/turn/wind up (in a certain place). **2** in the course of time, in due course, eventually.
  berakhir 1 to finish, end, terminate, expire, come to an end. ~ *dengan suatu kegembiraan* to have a happy ending. **2** to work/turn out in the end, end up. ~ *baik* to turn out well, work out. ~ *dengan* to wind up with, end in, conclude with. **3** to expire (of a contract, etc.). **keberakhiran** finality.
  berakhirkan to end up in/with. ~ *pembunuhan yang kejam* to end up in a cruel murder.
  mengakhiri to bring to an end, put an end to, finish, conclude, wind up, terminate. *Rapat itu diakhiri dengan lagu kebangsaan.* The meeting concluded with the national anthem. ~ *jiwa* to kill s.o. ~ *masa bujangnya/lajangnya* to get married, tie the knot. ~ *riwayat* to finish off.
  mengakhirkan to put at the back, put in the rear of, place last. ~ *jam* to set the clock back.
  terakhir 1 the latest, last, most recent, final, last time. *untuk* ~ *kalinya* for the last time. *selama beberapa tahun* ~ *ini* for the last few years. **2** lately, recently. **3** ultimate.
  akhiran 1 (*gram*) suffix, ending. **2** end. **berakhiran** to have the suffix ..., be suffixed with ... ~ *kan* to have the suffix *kan*.
  pengakhir (*mostly Mal*) last, final. *sebagai* ~ *kata* finally.
  pengakhiran 1 concluding, ending, terminating, termination. ~ *éksisténsi* phasing out. **2** conclusion, finish.

akhirat (*A*) **1** the hereafter, the next life, the afterlife. **2** eternity. **3** the Last/Judgment Day, Day of Judgment. *dunia* – our world and the next.
  keakhiratan everything related to the Last Day.

akhirulkalam (*A*) **1** end, finis (of a book/speech). **2** in conclusion, finally.

akhlak (*A*) (moral) character, morals, ethics, behavior. *krisis* – moral crisis. *pe(ng)rusak* – offender against morality. *– bejat* bad/immoral conduct/behavior.
  berakhlak to have a ... character. ~ *tinggi* to be of good character.
  keakhlakan morality. **2** moral (*mod*).

akhlakul (*A*) *– karimah/kharimah* of good character.

akhlaqiyah (*A*) moral.

akhlas (*ob*) → IKHLAS.

akhli → AHLI. *– penuh* postgraduate.

akhlul (*ob*) → AHLUL (in various words).

akhtaj (*A cla*) vassal, subject (person).

akhwan (*A cla*) brothers; → IKHWAN.

akhwat (*A*) the feminine of **ikhwan.**

akhzar (*A*) green.

aki I (*ob*) grandfather; → KAKÉK.
  aki-aki old person, senior citizen.

aki II (*D coq*) (car) (storage) battery.

akibat (*A*) **1** outcome, result, effect, aftermath, consequence. *dengan segala –nya menurut hukum* (*leg*) with all legal consequences attached to it. *– dari* arising from, as a result of. *sebab dan* – cause and effect. *sebagai* – in consequence of, as a result of, due to. *– kanker/malaria* (to die) from cancer/malaria. **2** as a result/consequence of, due to. *– hukum* legal consequences. *– jauh* far-reaching consequences. **berakibat jauh** to have far-reaching consequences. *– langsung* direct consequence. *– mutlak* necessary consequence. *– pengaruh* impact; → DAMPAK. *– sampingan* side effect.
  akibatnya finally, as a result/consequence, in the end. *pada* ~ *hanyalah satu* it amounts to the same thing, it works out the same way.
  akibat-akibat ~ *besar* far-reaching consequences.
  berakibat 1 to end in, result in. ~ *baik* to turn out well, do s.o. good. ~ *buruk terhadap* to hurt, damage. ~ *fatal* to have fatal results, cause s.o.'s death. **2** to have consequences.
  berakibatkan to result in.
  mengakibatkan to result/end in, be the cause of, have a certain effect.
  pengakibatan resulting in, causing.

akidah (*A*) **1** belief, faith. **2** confidence.

akifér (*D*) aquifer.

akik (*A*) **1** (*batu –*) agate. **2** (*siput –*) agate shell, *Helix richmondia.* *– disangka batu* humiliated by s.o. due to a misunderstanding. *– lumut* moss agate.

akikah (*A*) → AKÉKAH.

akil (*A*) intelligent, clever.

akilbalig(h) (*A*) adult (from about the age of 15).

akir → AKHIR.

akirat → AKHIRAT.

akisir battery acid.

akiték → ARSITÉK.

aklamasi (*D*) acclamation. *menerima dengan/secara* – to carry unanimously/by acclamation.

akliah (*A*) rational, logical.

aklimatisasi acclimatization.
  beraklimatisasi acclimatized.

akmal (*A*) perfect (of God).

Akmil [Akadémi Militér] Military Academy.

akné (*D*) acne; → JERAWAT.

akomodasi (*D*) accommodation.
  mengakomodasi(kan) to accommodate.
  pengakomodasian accommodating.

akomodatif (*D/E*) accommodative.

akomodir (*D*) **mengakomdir** to accommodate.

akonting (*E*) accounting; → PERAKUNAN.

akor I (*D*) → AKUR.

akor II [anti korupsi] anticorruption.

akor III (*D*) (musical) chord.

akordéon and **akordion** (*D/E*) accordion.

Akpol [Akadémi Polisi] Police Academy.

akrab I (*A*) intimate, friendly, close(ly related). *– lingkungan* environment friendly. *kurang* – not very close. **kekurangakraban** lack of closeness.
  seakrab as close/friendly/intimate as.
  berakrab-akraban to be on intimate terms with e.o.
  mengakrab to become intimate/close.
  mengakrabi to interconnect; to get close(r) to, get to know, be well acquainted with. *Jakarta mungkin dapat* ~ *warganya.* Perhaps Jakarta can get closer to its citizens. *Daérah belum terasa benar diakrabi.* They feel they don't know the province well.
  mengakrabkan to foster a closer relationship/friendship, make more intimate.
  terakrab closest, most intimate.
  keakraban 1 intimacy. **2** familiarity. **3** friendliness. **4** close relationship, solidarity, interconnection.

pengakraban fostering a close relationship.

Akrab II (*A*) Scorpio (of the Zodiac).

akram → IKRAM.

akrédit (*D/E*) **berakrédit** to be accredited. ~ *di* to be accredited to.
  mengakréditkan to accredit.

akréditasi (*D*) accreditation.
  berakréditasi accredited.
  mengakréditasi(kan) ~ *kepada* to accredit to.
  terakréditasi accredited.
  pengakréditasian accrediting.

akrési (*D*) accretion.

akriditas (*D*) → AKRÉDITASI.

akrilik (*D/E*) acrylic.

akrilonitril (*D/E*) acrylonitrile.

akrobat (*E*) acrobat. *main* – a) to perform acrobatics. b) to engage in strenuous sex.
  berakrobat to do acrobatic tricks.

akrobatik (*D/E*) acrobatics.
  berakrobatik acrobatic (*mod*).

akroléin (*D/E*) acrolein.

akromat (*D/E*) achromate.

akronim (*D/E*) acronym.
  mengakronimkan to turn into an acronym, acronymize.

akrual (*E*) accrual.

aksa (*A*) far off, remote. *masjid al* – the mosque in Jerusalem (far off from Mecca).

aksara (*Skr*) **1** letter, character. *buta* – illiterate. *tidak buta* – literate. **2** script. *tata* – writing system. **3** (alphabetical) symbol. – *Arab* the Arabic alphabet. – *baur* monogram. – *Cina/Tionghoa* Chinese characters. – *Déwanagari* the Sanskrit alphabet. – *hiéroglif* hieroglyphic script. – *Jawi* the Arabic alphabet used to write Malay. – *Kawi* letters used on Indonesian inscriptions. – *Kiril* the Cyrillic alphabet. – *Latin* the Latin alphabet. – *murda* large letter in (*Jv*) script. – *para tunanétra* Braille. – *pégon* a) Arabic script used for Javanese and Sundanese. b) Arabic writing without vowel marks. – *réncong* script used for the Kerinci language. – *rérékan* letter used to indicate foreign sounds in Javanese script.
  beraksara with letters. **keberaksaraan** literacy. *angka* ~ literacy rate.
  pengaksaraan reducing a language to writing, devising a writing system for a language.

aksarawan (*Skr neo*) literate (man).

aksarawati (*Skr neo*) literate (woman).

akséf [aksi sefihak] unilateral action.

aksélerasi (*D*) acceleration.
  beraksélerasi to accelerate.
  mengaksélerasi(kan) to accelerate s.t.
  teraksélerasi accelerated.
  pengakélerasian accelerating.

akséleratif (*D/E*) accelerative. *secara* – acceleratively.

akséleratri (*D/E*) accelerator.

aksén (*D/E*) **1** accent, stress; → TEKANAN *suara*. **2** (foreign) accent.
  beraksén to have an accent. ~ *Batak medok* to have a strong Batak accent.

akséntuasi (*D*) **1** accentuation. **2** accent. **3** stress.
  mengakséntuasi(kan) to accentuate.
  terakséntuasi accented.
  pengakéntuasian accentuating.

aksép (*D*) acceptance, written acknowledgment of a debt, promissory note, I.O.U.
  mengaksép to accept.

akséptabel (*E*) acceptable.

akséptan (*D*) acceptor (of *aksép*).

akséptasi (*D*) acceptance.
  mengakséptasi to accept.

akséptir (*D*) **mengakséptir** to accept.
  pengakséptiran acceptance.

akséptor (*E*) acceptor, i.e., a person who has expressed the willingness to use birth control measures.

aksés (*E*) access. – *di pasaran Jepang* access to the Japanese market. *jalan* – access road.

mengaksés to gain access to.

aksési (*D*) accession.

aksésibilitas (*D*) accessibility.

aksésor (*D leg*) accessory, contingent.

aksi (*D*) **1** (political, etc.) action. **2** military action. – *militér Belanda* the Dutch military action. **3** behavior (pretended or not), manners, conduct. *-nya sebagai orang kaya*. He behaves like a rich man. **4** anything undertaken to win a demand. *seperti* – excessively, immoderately. *melakukan -nya* to swing into action. – *sefihak/sepihak* unilateral action. *melakukan* – *semut* (Pramuka term) to pick up garbage to carry it to a collection center. *membuat* – to act in a play, appear on stage. **5** chic, stylish. **6** pretense, airs, showing off, put-on. *banyak* – to brag, act in a showy/flashy way. *buang/pasang* – to show off, make a show, pose. *-nya saja!* show-off! – *ambaléla* passive resistance. – *bakar-bakar* arson. – *bubar* closing down (a newspaper). – *duduk* sit-down strike (by employees). – *hambatan* delaying action. – *huru-hara* commotion. – *kéong* work slowdown. – *lamban* slowdown action. – *lambat* delayed-action. – *lambat kerja* work slowdown. – *lepas* independent action. – *mogok makan* hunger strike. – *pelambatan* delaying action. – *pemogokan* strike. – *penerbangan/udara* flight activity. – *penghambatan* delaying action. – *puasa* hunger strike. – *sepihak* unilateral action. – *tersendiri* independent action. – *turun ke jalan* street demonstration. – *unjuk rasa* (protest) demonstration.
  beraksi 1 to make a move to do s.t., swing into action. **2** to hold a demonstration. **3** to take steps/measures. **4** to behave in an affected way, show off. **5** to pretend.
  aksi-aksian to show off (to get attention). *Pistol itu dibawa cuma untuk* ~. He carries that pistol just to show off.

aksial (*D/E*) axial.

aksidéntal (*E*) and **aksidéntil** (*D*) accidental.

aksidéntalia (*D leg*) adventitious matters.

aksioma (*D*) axiom.
  mengaksiomakan to make s.t. an axiom.

aksiomatis (*D*) axiomatic.

aksis (*E*) axis, pivot.

Akt. (*abbr*) [aktuntan] accountant.

akta I (*D*) **1** official document, instrument, deed. **2** diploma, certificate, license; → AKTE. – *bébas hak* quit-claim deed. – *buru* hunting license. – *catatan sipil* certificate of civil status (for birth/death/marriage). – *di bawah tangan* private deed/instrument (not done before a notary). – *guru* teaching certificate. – *hibah* deed of donation. – *izin untuk kawin* marriage-consent license. – *jual beli* sales agreement. – *kelahiran/lahir* birth certificate; *cp* SURAT *kenal lahir*. – *kematian* death certificate. – *kenal* identification certificate. – *lepas hak* act of abdication/relinquishment (of a right). – *nikah* marriage certificate. – *notaris* notarial instrument. – *pejabat* administrative deed. – *pelepasan* → AKTA *lepas hak*. – *pembaptisan* baptismal certificate. – *pemisahan* deed of partition. – *pendirian* (of corporation) memorandum of association, articles of incorporation. – *pengalamatan* deed of superscription. – *penyimpanan* instrument of deposit. – *perceraian* certificate of divorce. – *perjanjian* contract. – *perjanjian perwali-amanatan* trust deed. – *perkawinan/pernikahan* marriage license. – *persetujuan* contract. – *perubahan* articles of amendment. – *sumpah* affidavit. – *superskripsi* deed of superscription. – *tanah* deed.

akta II (*E Mal*) act, law, regulation.

akte (*D*) deed, instrument; → AKTA. – *balik nama* deed of transfer. – *didirikannya ...* instrument setting up ... (an organization). – *jual-beli* bill of sale. – *kelahiran* birth certificate. – *notaris* notarial instrument. **mengakte-notariskan** to set up by notarial instrument. *Hotél itu sudah diakte-notariskan atas namanya*. The hotel was set up in his name by notarial instrument.

aktentas (*D*) **1** briefcase. **2** fake, bogus, phony. *kontraktor yang* – bogus contractor. *pengusaha* – fake businessman. *perusahaan* – brass-plate company. *perusahaan pelayaran* – a shipyard that has a license to operate but does not have the necessary equipment.

aktif (*D/E*) **1** active, energetic. **2** to be active (in). – *lagi* to be reinstated. **3** functioning. **4** (*gram*) active (voice). **5** active, producing profits. *neraca pembayaran* – an active balance of payments. *tak/tidak* – inactive. **ketidak-aktifan** inactivity.

mengaktifkan to activate. ~ *lagi* to revive, reinstate.

keaktifan activity.

pengaktif activator, causer, producer. *zat* ~ catalyst.

pengaktifan activation.

aktifis → AKTIVIS.

aktifitas (*D*) activity.

akting (*E*) temporarily taking over the duties of s.o. else, acting. – *ketua* acting chairman.

berakting to act, perform on the stage.

aktiva (*D*) assets; *cp* PASIVA. – *beku* frozen assets. – *berakumulasi* accrued assets. – *bergerak* movable assets. – *berisiko* risk assets. – *berwujud* tangible assets. – *dijaminkan* pledged assets. – *(yang) ditangguhkan* deferred assets. – *jaminan* pledged assets. – *lancar* current/liquid assets. – *menghasilkan* earning assets. – *modal* capital assets. – *nyata* tangible assets. – *rupa-rupa* miscellaneous assets. – *tak berwujud* intangible assets. – *tetap* fixed assets.

aktivis (*D/E*) (student) activist (*esp* after 1998), NGO activist.

aktor (*D/E*) actor. – *inteléktual* moving spirit behind s.t., instigator. – *inteléktualis ala masa* vigilante. – *pembantu* extra (in the movies), walk-on (on the stage). – *pendukung* supporting actor.

keaktoran being an actor.

aktris (*E*) actress.

aktual (*D*) 1 topical, current. 2 (of an article) timely.

mengaktualkan to actualize s.t.

keaktualan 1 topical/current interest, topicality. 2 timeliness.

aktualisasi (*D*) actualization. – *diri* self-actualization.

mengaktualisasikan to actualize, make actual.

pengaktualisasian actualizing.

aktualisir (*D*) **mengaktualisir** to actualize.

aktuaria (*D*) actuary. *ahli* – actuary.

aktuarial (*D/E*) actuarial.

aktuaris (*D*) actuary.

aktuil → AKTUAL.

aku I I, me. Usually used in prayers, among intimates, in certain types of literature, movie subtitles, etc. *Sang* - Ego. *-nya* he admitted/acknowledged.

beraku to use the word *aku*. ~ *berengkau* to use the words *aku* and *engkau* to e.o., be on a first-name basis.

beraku-aku to live/be individualistic.

beraku-akuan 1 to use the word *aku* to e.o. 2 to pledge mutual loyalty.

mengaku [and **ngaku** (*coq*)] 1 to claim (to be), identify o.s. as, consider o.s., say (about o.s.). *Dia* ~ *masih bujangan*. He said that he was still a bachelor. ~ *berjasa* to take credit (for). ~ *bernama* S. to pass o.s. off as S. 2 to confess to (an accusation/ one's sins, etc.), plead (guilty/not guilty). ~ *bersalah* to plead guilty. ~ *tidak bersalah* to plead not guilty. 3 to admit, accept and state (that one is wrong, etc.). ~ *kalah* to admit defeat. 4 to be responsible for, affirm one's readiness to, accept one's responsibility for. 5 to consider as (one's child/father, etc.). 6 (*coq*) to always talk about o.s., feel proud of o.s. ~ *telah menerima* to affirm, corroborate, confirm.

ngakunyé (*J coq*) as he claims, he says.

mengaku-aku to keep on passing o.s. off as.

memperaku 1 (*Mal*) to certify. 2 ~ *diri* to introduce o.s. *Dia* ~ *dirinya dan menyebut namanya sendiri*. He introduced himself by saying his name.

mengakui [and **ngakuin** (*J coq*)] 1 to admit, confess, concede, acknowledge. *Dia* ~ *pernah memiliki dua kg héroin*. He admitted that he had once had 2 kg of heroin. 2 to state the validity of, accept as valid, validate. 3 (*leg*) to stipulate. 4 to recognize, acknowledge. 5 to have the right to. *diakui* a) established (practice). b) certified (in a profession). c) established (of a fact). d) accredited (of a school). *diakui secara penuh* (*fin*) (based) on the full accrual method.

mengakukan ~ *diri* to admit that one is.

terakui recognized.

akuan 1 admission, confession, avowal. *surat* ~ acknowledgment. 2 ego, self. ~ *yang kedua* alter ego.

keakuan selfish attitude, egotism.

pengaku confessor, one who believes in (a certain religion).

pengakuan 1 recognition, declaration, admission, acknowledgment, avowal, testimony, evidence. 2 confession (of faith and before a priest). ~ *dosa* (*RC*) confession (in church), penance. ~ *iman* (Protestant) creed. ~ *lunas/penerimaan* evidence of payment, signed receipt. *menurut keterangan dan* ~ *pelapor* positive assurance. *surat* ~ *utang* IOU.

perakuan (*Mal*) 1 certification. 2 recommendation.

aku II mengakui to possess (said of an evil spirit).

akuan a spirit who enters s.o.'s body. *harimau* ~ were-tiger.

aku III akuan field in northern part of Java used by s.o. with *hak pertuanan* for not more than one year.

aku IV → AKI II.

akuadés aqua distillata, distilled water.

akuaduk (*D/E*) aqueduct.

akuakultur (*D/E*) aquaculture.

akuarél (*D/E*) aquarelle.

akuarium (*D/E*) aquarium. – *tanaman* terrarium.

Akuarius (*D/E*) Aquarius.

akuatin (*D/E*) aquatint.

akuifér (*D/E*) aquifer. – *bébas* unconfined aquifer. – *bocor* leaky aquifer. – *lapisan ganda* multilayered aquifer. – *ténggék* perched aquifer. – *tertekan* confined aquifer.

akuisisi (*D*) acquisition.

akuisme cult of the personality.

akuk (*M*) a chicken disease.

terakuk bent over, bowed down.

akulturasi (*D*) acculturation.

akumulasi (*D*) accumulation, accumulated. – *penyusutan* accumulated depreciation.

terakumulasi accumulated.

akumulatif (*D/E*) accumulative.

akumulator (*D/E*) accumulator. – *kalor* heat accumulator.

akun (*D*) account; → AKAUN. – *(ber)jaminan* secured account. – *gabungan* consolidated accounts. – *laba rugi* profit and loss account; → PERHITUNGAN *laba-rugi*. – *lawan* contra account. – *peruntukan* appropriation account. – *pindahan* continuing account. – *sementara* suspense account. – *tak-aktif* dormant account.

perakunan accounting. ~ *bébas* public accounting.

akuntabilitas accountability.

akuntan (*D/E*) accountant. – *bertanggung jawab/penanggung jawab* accountant in charge. – *publik* public accountant. – *Publik Berijazah/Terdaftar* Certified Public Accountant, CPA. – *swasta* private accountant (not working for the government).

perakuntanan accountancy.

akuntansi (*D*) accounting, accountancy, bookkeeping. – *berpasangan* double-entry accounting. – *biaya* cost accounting. – *dorong-turun* push-down accounting. – *keuangan* financial accounting. – *manajemén* management accounting. – *penyusutan* depreciation accounting.

akunting (*E*) → PERAKUNAN. – *manajemén* managerial accounting.

akupungtur and **akupunktur** (*D*) acupuncture.

akupungturis and **akupunkturis** (*D*) acupuncturist.

akur (*D*) 1 to accord, agree, tally, jibe, square; → K(E)LOP. *tidak* – a) (the clock) does not keep perfect time. b) do not agree, cannot get along with e.o. 2 to agree with e.o. 3 unanimous, in harmony, harmonious, congenial. 4 to harmonize, agree with. *tidak* – to disagree. **ketidak-akuran** disagreement.

(ber)akuran to make an agreement with e.o.

mengakuri to agree with, be in agreement with, approve of. 2 to agree, answer in the affirmative.

mengakurkan [and **ngakurin** (*J coq*)] 1 to check, verify. 2 to make agree, set (one's watch by s.t.). ~ *arloji* to set a watch. 3 to reconcile (disputants). 4 to harmonize, arrange in a harmonious way. ~ *warna-warna* to harmonize colors.

keakuran 1 agreement, accord(ance). *mendapat* ~ to reach/ come to an understanding/agreement, come to terms. 2 uniformity, conformity. 3 approval. 4 harmony.

pengakuran 1 harmonizing. 2 check, checking. ~ *intérn* internal check.

akurasi (*D*) accuracy; → KEAKURATAN.

akurat (*D/E*) accurate. *kurang* – less than accurate. **kekurang-akuratan** inaccuracy. *tidak* – inaccurate. **ketidak-akuratan** inaccuracy.

seakurat as accurate as.

seakurat-akuratnya as accurate(ly) as possible.

mengakuratkan to make s.t. precise/more accurate. *Data météorologi maritim yang diperlukan untuk ~ prakiraan sulit didapatkan.* The maritime meteorological data needed to make predictions more accurate are hard to come by.

terakurat the most accurate.

keakuratan accuracy.

pengakuratan making accurate.

akusatif (*D/E*) accusative.

akustik (*D/E*) acoustics. *ahli* – acoustician.

berakustik with ... good acoustics.

akustika (*D*) acoustics.

akustis (*D*) acoustic.

akut (*D/E*) acute, critical. *penderita rémétik* – a patient with acute rheumatism.

keakutan acuteness, seriousness.

akwal (*A*) words; *opp* **AFAL II.**

al I (*A*) the definite article, the, in many words of Arabic origin, such as *alhasil, alkisah, almarhum,* etc.

al II (in acronyms) → **ALAT.**

AL III [Angkatan Laut] Navy.

ala I (*A*) **1** to. **2** in, on, upon. **3** according to. – *bisa* whatever is possible. – *kadarnya* a) according to ability, to the extent of one's ability. b) what is available. c) modest, sufficient, adequate, good enough (and no more than necessary). d) bribe. *acara hiburan – kadarnya* a modest program of entertainment. *dibayar – kadarnya* to be paid modestly/moderately. *dan lain-lain – kadarnya* and other things as are fitting. – *sebentar* for a moment/short time.

ala II (*A*) **1** high. **2** "The Most High"; name of the 87th chapter of the Koran; → **A'LA.**

terala highest of the all, very high, supreme; → **TAALA.**

ala III (*D*) in the manner/style of. – *Barat* in eastern style.

ala IV disused field (but still owned).

A'la (*A*) *al–* "The Most High"; name of the 87th chapter of the Koran.

alabangka (*ob*) crowbar.

alabio *itik* – the alabio duck (originally from Amuntai, South Kalimantan).

aladdawam (*A*) for ever.

Aladin (*D*) Aladdin. *lampu* – Aladdin's lamp.

alaf (*A ob*) one thousand; → **ALF.**

alah I conquered, succumbed, defeated, beaten; → **KALAH.** – *kepada* to be susceptible to (a disease). – *oléh* defeated by. *tidak – dengan* to be no less than, be the equal of. – *bisa karena/oléh biasa* a) theory is worsted by practice. b) experience is the best teacher. – *limau oléh benalu* old employees are pushed aside by new ones; a new broom sweeps clean. – *(mem)beli menang memakai* cheap goods are the most expensive in the long run; cheap is cheap. – *sabung menang sorak* said of s.o. who never says die/who never gives up.

beralah (*M*) to give up easily, be a defeatist.

beralahan neither of the two has won, to end in a draw.

mengalah [and **ngalah** (*coq*)] **1** to admit defeat, give up, not want to defend (one's rights/standpoint, etc.), surrender, yield (the right of way). **2** to give in, make concessions. **3** permissive.

mengalahi 1 to admit defeat. **2** (*ob*) to defeat, subject.

alah-mengalahi to make concessions/give in to e.o.

mengalahkan 1 to defeat, subject, subdue, overwhelm. **2** to declare s.o. defeated, declare s.o. the loser. **3** to surpass, exceed, outdo; to oust, supersede (another language). *dialahkan* to be overgrown with (weeds/*benalu*).

teralahkan defeatable, can be beaten. *tidak ~* invincible.

alahan 1 the loser. **2** always losing. **3** loss (in gambling).

kealahan defeat.

pengalahan 1 victory. **2** concession, admission, giving in.

peralahan 1 victory, conquest, (violent) appropriation. **2** loot, plunder.

alah II (*Jv*) oh, come on now! –, *sekali seminggu, kok capék!* Come on, (you do it) once a week, and you're tired!

alah III mengalah to dam up, dike in, drain (a river to catch the fish in it).

alahan 1 old river bed. **2** (*M*) weir (across a river).

alahu → **ALLAHU.**

alai a leguminous plant, African locust bean, *Parkia biglobosa/roxburghii/javanica, Peltophorum dasyrachis.*

alai-belai (*ob*) flattery, toadyism.

alaihi (*A*) upon/to him. – *(as)salam* on him be peace! (said after the name of a prophet other than Muhammad or other revered figure mentioned in the Koran).

alaihim (*J*) very. *tinggi* – very tall.

alaika (*A*) upon/to you.

alaikum (*A*) upon/to you (plural). – *(as)salam* and *assalamu* – peace be upon you!

alak (*M ob*) **sealak-alak** just enough.

alalbahalal and **alalbihalal** → **HALAL-BIHALAL.**

alam I (*A*) **1** (– *dunia*) world, earth; kingdom, realm. *di seluruh* – all over the world. *Syah* – Lord of the Earth (a title). **2** universe.. – *terdiri dari segala* ... the universe consists of all ... **3** region, area, zone, territory. – *Minangkabau* the Minangkabau region. – *tidak beraja* a territory without a *raja*. **4** kingdom, any of the three great divisions into which all natural objects have been classified. **5** nature (as an object of study), nature/natural (*mod*), scenery. *bencana* – natural disaster. *hukum* – laws of nature, natural law. *ilmu* – a) natural science. b) physics. *pengetahuan* – natural science. **6** natural, produced or existing in nature, not artificial, not man-made. *bakat* – natural aptitude/talent/faculty. *gas* – natural gas. *karét* – natural rubber, latex. *sutera* – natural silk. *di – bébas* in the country. *di – lepas/terbuka* in the open (air), outdoors. – *akhirat* the next world, the afterlife. – *arwah* the world of the spirits. – *awang-awung* (*Jv*) the center of the universe. – *baka* the next world, the afterworld, eternity. – *barzah/barzakh* a) the period between death and judgment, purgatory, limbo. b) between truth and illusion. – *bébas* → **ALAM** terbuka. – *cita* idealism. – *dongéng* the realm of fairytales. – *fana* the perishable world. – *gaib* world of spirits. – *hayawan/haiwan(ah)/héwan* the animal kingdom, fauna. – *hidup* milieu, environment, surroundings. – *Islamiyah* the Muslim world. – *jamadah/jamadat* vegetable world. – *kabir* the wide world. – *kebinatangan* the animal kingdom, fauna. – *kekal* the next world, the place one goes after death. – *kelanggengan* → **ALAM** baka. – *khayal* fantasy world. – *klenik* world of mysticism. – *lepas* → **ALAM** terbuka. – *ma'adin* the mineral kingdom. – *madya/madyo* (*Jv*) the present world. – *mahluk halus* the world of the spirits. – *malakut* the world of spirits. – *misal* parallel world where other creatures live. – *nabat(ah)/nabtun* the vegetable kingdom, flora. – *nasut* mankind. – *nasyrah* "Expanding World"; name of the 94th chapter of the Koran. – *nyata* real life, the real world. – *pikiran* the world of ideas. – *raya* cosmos. – *sadarnya* his awareness. – *sagir* small world; humans. – *samar* the invisible world, the interval between death and the resurrection. – *sekeliling/sekitar* milieu, environment, surroundings. – *semesta* the universe. – *terbuka* nature; open-air, outdoor. *réstoran* – terbuka open-air restaurant. – *tumbuh-tumbuhan* the plant/vegetable kingdom, flora. – *wasana/wasono* (*Jv*) the hereafter.

sealam of the same nature. *daérah ~* region with a similar nature.

beralam with a ... nature. *~ lapang* easygoing, not touchy.

kealaman nature, character.

alam II (*A*) to know. *wallahu* – God only knows.

mengalami [and **ngalamin** (*J coq*)] **1** to experience, meet with (difficulties), suffer, undergo, have (s.t. bad happen to one), sustain, incur. *~ banjir besar* to have bad flooding. *~ frustrasi* to be frustrated. *~ gangguan* to have a problem (or problems). *~ jalan buntu* to reach a deadlock/an impasse, hit a dead end. *~ kecelakaan* to have an accident. *~ kerusakan* to sustain damage, get damaged. *~ krisis* to pass through a crisis. *~ luka* to receive injuries, get hurt. *~ penderitaan* to suffer. *~ perubahan* to (undergo) change. *~ rugi besar* to sustain big losses. *~ tekanan* to be under pressure/stress. **2** to become aware of, perceive. **3** to go through (experiences/adventures).

kealaman nature, character, disposition. *Pengaruh manusia terhadap ~ daérah itu besar.* Human influence on the character of that region has been great. **2** natural.

pengalaman experience. *belajar dari ~* to learn from experience. *kaya ~* and *~ segudang* to be rich in experience. *~ pahit* a bitter/hard experience. **berpengalaman** to be experienced, have had experience, with experience, (a) veteran (at s.t.). *tidak ~* a) inexperienced, green, immature. b) wet behind the ears, born yesterday. *~ perang* to be battle-hardened.

alam III (*cla*) banner, standard.

alam IV an official of religious affairs in Banten and Madura.

alam(a)ak (*sl*) great, fantastic!

alaman → HALAMAN.

alamanda allamanda, *Allamanda cathartica.*

alamar (*ob*) *penguasa* – government power holder; → AMAR.

alamas (*ob*) diamond.

alamat (*A*) **1** address. *Bagaimana -nya?* What's your address? *Jika tidak sampai kepada -nya, minta dikembalikan kepada …* In case of nondelivery, please return to … *buku* – directory. *dengan* – in care of, c/o. *si* – the addressee. **2** sign, mark, indication, signal. *tahu menilik* – to have the signs of the times in mind. **3** target. **4** beacon. **5** title (of book); → JUDUL. *– darurat* address in case of emergency. *– kawat* cable address. *– penagihan* billing address. *– pengirim* return address. *– pengiriman* shipping address. *– samaran* cover address. *– surat* a) the address on an envelope. b) inscription. *– tagih* billing address. *– tunduk* sign of surrender (such as a white flag).

sealamat *~ dengan* at the same address as.

beralamat 1 to have an address; addressed (to). **2** to indicate, be a sign of. **3** to be titled.

beralamatkan *~ di* to have … as one's address, be (located) at.

ngalamat (*coq*) omen, augury.

mengalamati to write down an address on (an envelope).

mengalamatkan 1 to address, direct (to). **2** to indicate, foretell.

teralamatkan can be addressed, (blame) can be laid at the feet of.

pengalamatan addressing.

peralamatan addressing. *sistém penamaan dan ~ komputer* computer naming and addressing system.

alamatulhayat (*A*) signs of life.

Alambhana Wana Wai the military resort command (*Korém* 121) in Pontianak.

alami (*A*) natural. *musuh* – natural enemy (of a pest). *tak/tidak* – unnatural, artificial, man-made. *secara* – in a natural way.

alamiah (*A*) **1** born, by nature. *pecandu* – a born addict. **2** natural. *secara (lebih)* – in a (more) natural way. *bentuk -nya* its natural form.

alamin (*A*) **1** confidant. **2** the universe; → ALAM *semesta.*

alan-alan (*cla*) clown. *– istana* court jester.

alang I → HALANG. **1** diagonal, transverse, across. **2** crossbeam, bar going across. **3** room divider.

beralang having a bar/wall divider.

mengalang to bar, block. *~ batang* (*ob*) to thwart s.o.

mengalang(-alang)i to thwart, hinder, impede, prevent; to obstruct.

alang-mengalangi to block/thwart e.o.

mengalangkan to lay s.t. athwart, put s.t. crosswise/across/athwart. *~ batang léhér, minta dialang-sembelih* to look for trouble/problems.

teralang 1 blocked, barred, prevented from. **2** stagnant.

alangan 1 roadblock; sandbank (in estuaries). **2** obstruction, obstacle, impediment. *~ rumah* wooden partition. **beralangan 1** blocked, obstructed. **2** to be prevented (from doing one's duty, etc).

pengalang obstacle, obstructer, impeder, thwarter. *batu ~* stumbling block.

pengalangan obstructing, impeding, thwarting.

alang II 1 middling, moderate, mediocre; only half; insignificant, unimportant. *saudaranya yang* – his in-between sibling (neither the oldest nor the youngest). *pak* – the uncle intermediate in age between the youngest and the oldest. **2** (among the Malays of North Sumatra) the third child in a family. *keris* – a kris of medium length. *– hari* (*M*) an ordinary day (not a market day).

-kah (*baiknya/besarnya*, etc.) how (good/big, etc.)!, what a …! *-kah cantik rumahmu!* What a nice house you have! *tidak* – not a little bit, a lot, very much. *– kepalang* of no importance, insignificant. *bukan – kepalang* extremely, very, too, exceedingly. *-.- berdawat, baik hitam* don't do things by halves (or, halfheartedly).

alang-alang(an) 1 (to do s.t.) halfheartedly/reluctantly. *bukan ~* a lot.

alang III (*M*) present, gift, donation. *– berjawab, tepuk berbalas* render good for good, evil for evil.

alang-alang (*Jv*) jungle/cogon grass, *Imperata cylindrica*; → LALANG.

alap I (*cla*) unhurried, sedate; well-mannered, polite. *berjalan* – *santun* to walk in a stately manner.

alap II (*J*) **mengalap** [and **ngalap** (*coq*)] to pick fruit, poke at fruit (with a stick, to make it fall off the tree). *ngalap berkah* a) to request prayers and blessings for success. b) to seek one's fortune. *ngalap mantu* to take s.o. as one's son-in-law.

pengalap *~ berkah/rezeki* fortune hunter, adventurer.

alap-alap (*Jv*) **1** common/Eurasian kestrel, *Falco tinnunculus.* **2** various species of kites/vultures/(sparrow) hawks/falcons/kestrels. *– belang* barred honey buzzard, *Pernis celebensis. – capung* black-thighed falconet, *Microhierax fringillarius. – kawah* peregrine falcon, *Falco peregrinus. – kecil* hobby, *Falco longipennus. – kukuk* cuckoo falcon hawk, crested/Pacific baza, *Aviceda subcristata. – layang* Australian kestrel, *Falco cenchroides. – macan* oriental hobby, *Falco severus. – malam* black kite, *Milvus migrans. – menara* Moluccan/spotted kestrel, *Falco moluccensis. – putih* black-shouldered/winged kite, *Elanus caeruleus/hypoleucus. – sapi* Moluccan/spotted kestrel, *Falco moluccensis. – sawah/tualang* peregrine falcon, *Falco peregrinus.* **3** (*coq*) thief. *– samber nyawa/nyowo* (*Jv*) master killer; → *jagoan* CABUT NYAWA/NYOWO. *– sepéda* bicycle thief. **4** s.o. who chases after (girls).

Alaq (*A*) *al-* "Congealed Blood"; name of the 96th chapter of the Koran.

alar I (*cla*) ruler's debt slave.

alar II rude, unmannerly.

alaram, alarem and **alarm** (*E*) alarm.

beralarm *jam ~* an alarm clock.

alas I 1 stand, foundation, base, doily, coaster. *dari – ke atas* from bottom to top. **2** mat, inner layer, lining. *kertas* – paper used as a base. *– baju* coat lining. *– beton* concrete foundation. *– bunga* torus, receptacle. *jadi – cakap* prize awarded for services. *– cangkir* saucer. *– cap* (*ob*) money paid to newly appointed official. *– cawan* saucer. *– dada* bib. (*untuk*) – *duduk* a) s.t. to sit on. b) a base. *– gurun* rocks or pebbles left in desert after erosion. *– hak* a) legal basis, legal standing. b) (basis of) title (to land, etc.). *– jerami* (straw) bedding (for cattle). *– kaki* a) footrest, footstool. b) footwear, shoes. *tanpa – kaki* barefoot. *– kasur* (bed)sheet. *– kasur bantal* bedding. *– kata* prelude, introduction (to a talk). *– kepala* head restraint (in a car). *– kubur* s.o. who takes the blame for s.o. else's mistakes/losses, etc., scapegoat. *– lantai* groundsheet. *– léhér* neck opening in coat. *– méja* table cloth. *– muatan* ballast. *– pelana* saddle cloth. *– pengetahuan* basic knowledge. *– perahu* spar under a boat. *– perut* breakfast. *– peti* lid. *– ranjang* bedsheet. *– rumah* foundation of a house. *– samar* false bottom. *– talkin* alms given to the reader of the *talkin. – tangan* hand covering (used by a woman when shaking hands with a man). *– tempat tidur* bed sheet. *– tilam* (bed)sheet. *– torak* piston head.

beralas 1 to serve/be used as an underlayer, etc. *cawan yang tidak ~* a teacup without a saucer. **2** lined. **3** to have … as a foundation/basis, be based on. *tempat tidur ~ kain hijau* a bed with a green sheet. *Kakinya ~ sepasang sandal jepit.* She was wearing thongs on her feet.

beralaskan 1 to have as a foundation/basis, be based on. **2** with a foundation/covering, etc. of. *Meréka harus tidur di lantai ~ tikar tua.* They had to sleep on the floor with an old mat under them.

mengalas(i) 1 to provide with a basis, etc., put (paper, etc.) under, lay a base/foundation. **2** to cover a floor with (mats/cloths/

paper, etc.). *Keranjang itu dialasi dengan daun pisang.* A banana leaf was put on the bottom of the basket. *dialas bagai memengat* look before you leap. *jalan dialas dengan batu* a paved road.

mengalasi (*J*) to remind/advise by stating the reasons.

mengalaskan 1 to found, ground, base. **2** to base (an opinion/accusation, etc.) on.

alasan 1 basis, foundation, ground. ~ *hukum* legal grounds. ~ *pemaaf (kesalahan)* (*leg*) ground for exculpation. ~ *pengecualian/penghapus (kesalahan)* (*leg*) ground for exclusion. ~ *pembenar* (*leg*) ground for justification. **2** motive, cause, reason. *dengan tiada* ~ without reason. *Itu bukan –!* That's no excuse! *memberi* ~ to motivate. ~ *yang dapat diterima* valid reasons. **3** pretext, evasion, subterfuge, stratagem, artifice; excuse, alibi. ~ *kancil* a (mere) pretext, cover-up, excuse, alibi; → KANCIL. **beralasan** well-founded, just; sound (reasons). *dianggap tidak* ~ to be considered unfounded/groundless.

alas II (*Jv*) forest, jungle; → HUTAN. *ayam* – wild chicken.

alas-alasan 1 forest. **2** name of a batik pattern.

alas III pengalasan k.o. courtier.

al'aswad (*A*) the black; → ASWAD.

alat I (*A*) **1** equipment, machinery, instrument, tool, device, appliance, apparatus, implement, utensil. **2** puppet, lackey, stooge; → ANTÉK, KAKITANGAN. **3** organ, means, agency, media, medium (of information), materials. – *antisadap* antibugging device. – *apung* life raft. – *bagian* part (of a machine); *cp* SUKU *cadang.* – *bakar* caustic. – *bantu* a) aid. b) accessories. c) auxiliary apparatus. d) jig. – *bantu dengar lihat* audiovisual aids. – *bayar* means of payment, currency, tender. – *bayar sah* legal tender. – *berlayar* vessel. –.– *berat* heavy machinery. –.– *berikut* accessories. – *bernafas* respiratory organs. –.– *besar* heavy equipment. – *bicara* organ of speech. – *bidik* a) sight (on a gun). b) homing device. – *bukti* evidence. – *bunyi-bunyian* musical instrument. – *cacah* counter. –.– *cerna* digestive organs. – *cukur* shaver. – *dalam* viscera. – *dapur* kitchen utensils. – *détéksi* a) detector. b) "sniffer" (at airport). – *éléktronik* electronic device. – *gali* excavator. – *gempa* seismograph. – *gések* a) string instrument. b) device for taking an imprint of credit cards. – *getar* vibrator. – *hias* toilet article. – *hias tutup dinding* wainscoting. – *hisap* drug paraphernalia for smoking narcotics. –.– *hubungan semesta* mass communications media. – *hukum* legal remedy. – *indria* sense organ. – *kandungan* womb. –.– *kantor* office equipment/supplies. – *keamanan* security organ. – *keamanan untuk memeriksa penumpang* metal detector (in airports). – *kebesaran* insignia of State. –.– *kecantikan* cosmetics. –.– *kedokteran* medical equipment. – *kekuasaan* machinery of power. – *kelamin* sex organ. –.– *kelengkapan* a) State organs, organs of State. b) paraphernalia. – *kemudi* steering gear. –.– *keperluan* necessities. – *kerajaan* insignia of royalty, regalia. – *keruk* dredger. – *keselamatan* rescue device (on board a ship). – *kontrasépsi dalam rahim* [AKDR] intrauterine (contraceptive) device, IU(C)D. –.– *kontra spionase* counterespionage devices. – *kontrol* (means of) check(ing). – *krédit* credit instrument. – *larutan* solvent. – *likwid(e) yang tidak segera diperlukan* not immediately needed liquid assets. – *masak* kitchen utensils. – *masak tekanan* pressure cooker. –.– *mesin* mechanized equipment. – *mesin tenun* power loom. – *mobil* car tools. – *musik gések/petik* string instruments. – *musik tiup* wind instrument. – *napas* respiratory organ. –.– *Negara* a) State apparatus. b) (in the U.S.A.) G-man, an agent of the FBI. – *negara penegak hukum* law-enforcement agency. –.– *olahraga* sporting goods. – *pacu jantung* pacemaker. – *pandang dengar* audiovisual aids. – *pelacak* locator. – *pelampung* lifeboat. – *peledak* explosive device. – *pelicin* a) flatiron. b) hair oil. – *pelumas* lubricator. – *peluncur rokét* rocket launcher. – *peluncur torpédo* torpedo tube. – *pemacu jantung* pacemaker. – *pemadam (busa)* (foam type) fire extinguisher. – *pemadam kebakaran* fire extinguisher. – *pemanas (air)* (water) heater. – *pemantas* cosmetics. – *pembagi suara* crossover (hi-fi equipment). – *pembakar* incinerator. – *pembantu* aid. – *pembantu instruksi* training aid. – *pembantu mendengar* hearing aid. –.– *pembayaran* a) means of payment, money, instrument. b) financial resources. – *pembayaran luar negeri* foreign exchange. – *pembayaran (yang)*

sah legal tender. – *pembersih pita vidéo* videotape cleaner. – *pembolong karcis* ticket punch. – *pembungkus* packing material. – *pembesar* a) microscope. b) enlarger. – *pemecah atom* atom smasher. – *pemecah kulit gabah* huller. – *pemercik* nozzle. – *pemerintah* government apparatus. – *pemersatu* unifying instrument. – *pemetik* mechanized picker. – *pemisah* separator. – *pemodalan* means of financing. –.– *pemotong* cutlery. – *pemotrét* camera. –.– *pemuas séks* sexual/marital aids. –.– *pemuat* cargo handling gear. – *pemukul* strike force. – *pemutar kasét* cassette player. – *pemutar lampu* light switch. – *penakut* deterrent. – *penanak nasi* rice cooker. – *penanda* marker. – *penangkap debu* electrostatic precipitator. – *penerang* lighting fixture. – *pencakar tanah* steam shovel. – *pencari* detector. – *pencari arah* direction finder. – *pencari ikan (éléktronik)* (electronic) fish finder. – *pencatat arus lumpur* mudflow sensing unit. – *pencatat curah hujan* recording rain gauge. – *pencatat gempa (bumi)* seismograph. – *pencatat kebohongan* lie detector. – *pencatat kendaraan* traffic counter. – *pencatat ketinggian permukaan air* water level recording gauge. – *pencatat radiasi* Geiger counter. – *pencatat waktu* stopwatch. – *pencegah api* fire retardant. – *pencernaan* digestive organs. – *pencium* nose. – *pencuci baju otomatik* (automatic) washing machine. – *pendarat (yang dapat dimasukkan)* (retractable) landing gear (of an aircraft). – *pendengar* listening device, earphones. –.– *pendengaran* auditory organs. – *pendérék* crane. – *pendingin* freezer. – *pendingin ruangan* air conditioner. – *penduga* water gauge. – *penetas* incubator. – *pengaman* safety device, guard. – *pengampelas* scouring pad. – *pengangkat* lifting equipment. – *pengangkutan* means of transportation. – *pengatur hawa* air conditioner. – *pengatur/pengendali lalulintas* traffic control device. – *pengatur waktu kontak* time switch and contactor. – *pengecambah* germinator. – *pengecap* organ of taste. – *pengempelas* a) scrub rag. b) abrasive. – *pengendali* control. – *pengeras suara* loudspeaker. – *pengering (rice)* dryer, desiccator. – *pengering baju automatik* automatic (clothes) dryer. – *penggalak ledak* detonator. – *penggali* excavator. – *pengganjal* prop, wedge. – *pengganjal roda pesawat* wheel chock. – *penggempur atom* cyclotron. – *penggetar* vibrator. – *penggiling padi* rice milling unit. – *penggolong* grader, sorter. – *penghembus hawa* air vent. – *penghidu* olfactory organ. – *penghilang bau* deodorizer. – *penghindar* deterrent. – *penghisap(an)* pumper. – *penghisap asap* stove/cooker hood. – *penghubung dalam* intercom. – *pengikat* binder, fastener. – *pengisap debu* vacuum cleaner. – *pengisi batu baterai* battery charger. – *penglihatan* organ of sight. – *pengocok (cocktail)* shaker. – *pengolah data* data processor. – *pengontrol (means of)* check(ing). – *penguap* evaporator, humidifier. – *penguat* a) amplifier. b) brace. – *pengukur* measuring instrument, gauge. – *pengukur tekanan napas* spirometer. – *penjumlah pengunjung* hand-held device for counting visitors, add-o-check. – *penolak* electrical insulator. – *penukar* medium of exchange. – *penukar panas* heat exchanger. – *penulis* writing materials. – *penyadap (pembicaraan)* bugging device. – *penyedot debu* vacuum cleaner. – *penyejuk* air conditioner. – *penyembur api* flamethrower. – *penyembur gemuk* grease gun. – *penyemprot gas mata* tear gas dispensing gun. – *penyemprot tangan* hand sprayer. – *penyorot* projector. – *penyosoh* polisher, whitener. – *penyulingan* distiller. – *penyuntik* syringe. – *peraba* tentacle. – *peraga* teaching tool. – *peraga anatomi* anatomical model. – *peraga(an) visual* visual aid. – *perakit* jig. – *peralatan* equipment. – *perang* military equipment, war matériel. – *perasa* one of the five senses. – *percepatan* accelerator. – *peredam goncangan* shock absorber. – *perekam* recorder. – *perekam jantung* electrocardiogram. – *perekam penerbangan* black box (in aircraft); flight recorder. – *perekam pesan* answering machine. – *perekam (suara)* tape recorder. – *perekam ténténgan* portable tape recorder. – *perintis jalan* road tracer. – *perjuangan* weapon. – *perkakas* instruments, apparatus. – *perlengkapan* instrument, apparatus. – *pernapasan* respiratory tract. – *perontok gabah* thresher (for rice). – *persisi* precision instrument. –.– *pertambangan* mining equipment. – *pertukaran* medium of exchange. – *pertukaran panas* heat exchanger. – *perumahan* furniture, household furnishings. – *perum gema* echo sounder. – *petukar* medium of exchange. – *pijat listrik* electric massager and vibrator. – *pireng*

pirsa audiovisual aids. – *potrét* camera. –.– *produksi* means of production, productive resources. – *proyéksi* projector. – *rekat* adhesive. – *révolusi* a tool of the revolution. – *rias* makeup equipment. – *Röntgén* X-ray equipment. – *runcing pénsil* pencil sharpener. – *saring* filter. – *semir* lubricating apparatus. – *senjata* armament. – *serap* absorbing agent, absorption apparatus. – *sinar tembus* fluoroscope. –.– *spionase* espionage devices. – *suling* distillation apparatus. – *suntik* (injection) syringe. – *tambahan* attachment. – *témpél* adhesives. – *tenun* loom. – *tertanam* fixtures. – *tertib* means of discipline. – *tiup* blowing engine, blower. – *tolok* gauge. – *tolong* aids. – *tubuh* organ of the body. – *tukar* medium of exchange. – *tulis* stationery. – *uji* tester. – *ukur* gauge, meter, -meter, measuring device. – *ukur hujan* rain gauge. – *ungkit* tipping device. – *vital* genitals.
  beralat to have equipment.
  beralatkan to have ... as a tool/implement.
  memperalat to use s.o. as a means to an end (or, as a tool).
  memperalati and **mengalati** to equip, fit out with.
  mengalatkan 1 to equip with, provide with, supply with, furnish with. **2** to use/treat s.o. as a tool/means/instrument.
  peralatan 1 equipment, utensils, tools, appliances, requisites, accessories. ~ *dapur* kitchen utensils. **2** instrumentation. ~ *kantor* office supplies. ~ *kesatriaan* military equipment. ~ *olahraga* sporting goods. ~ *pelengkap* accessory equipment. ~ *rias* make-up articles.
  alat-peralatan a) supplies. b) (*mil*) post equipment. ~ *dapur* kitchen utensils. ~ *éléktronik* electronic gear. ~ *mata-mata* spy gadgetry.
alat II (*M*) **1** guest (at *adat* feast). **2** feast.
  beralat 1 to call on. **2** to celebrate an *adat* feast.
  memperalatkan 1 to marry off. **2** to give a celebration for s.o.
  peralatan 1 feast, celebration. **2** *adat* (ceremonial) feast. – *lauk* feast held eight days after a wedding to introduce bride and groom to relatives.
alau I (*coq*) → KALAU.
alau II → HALAU.
alau III k.o. tree, *Dacrydium spp.*
alau IV (*burung* –) k.o. hornbill.
alawi (*A*) *kaum* – the descendants of Ali, the husband of Fatimah, the Prophet Muhammad's daughter.
albakora (*D*) albacore.
Albania Albania.
albarni (*A*) k.o. sweet.
albas (*D*) alabaster.
albino (*D*) albino.
  kealbinoan albinism.
Albion (*D*) Albion, England.
al-birr (*A*) → KEBAJIKAN.
album (*D/E*) album. – *sisipan* stock book (for stamps).
  mengalbumkan to record in an album.
  teralbum recorded in an album.
albumén and **albumina** (*D*) albumen.
aldubul (*A*) – *Akbar* Great Bear. – *Asgar* a) Lesser Bear. b) cynosure.
al-dzawq (*A*) intuition.
alé (*Ambon*) you (respectful). – *rasa béta rasa* live and let live.
alégori (*D*) allegory.
alégoris (*D*) allegorical.
aléja → LÉJA.
alék (*M*) reception, party.
  beralék to hold a reception.
aléksander (*D*) topaz.
alem (*J/Jv*) **mengalem** [and **ngalem** (*coq*)] **1** to spoil, baby s.o. **2** (*Jv*) to praise, extol.
  aleman spoiled, pampered (of a child, etc.).
alérgén (*D/E*) allergen.
alérgi (*D/E*) allergy. – *dengan/pada* to be allergic to. *penyebab* – allergen.
  beralérgi to be allergic to. ~ *debu* to be allergic to dust.
alérgik (*E*) and **alérgis** (*D*) allergic. – *terhadap* allergic to.
alesan → ALASAN.
alesduk (*D*) neckerchief, scarf.

alf(a) (*A ob*) one thousand. (*Cerita*) – *lailah wa lailah* The 1001 Nights.
alfa alpha, the first letter of the Greek alphabet.
alfabét (*D*) alphabet.
alfabétis (*D*) alphabetical.
Alfatékah and **alfatikah** (*A*) the name of the first verse of the Koran.
alfu (*A*) thousand.
alfur a term used in IBT for pagans.
Al-Furqan and **al-Furqon** (*A*) the differentiator between the right and the wrong (another name for the Koran).
alga (*D*) algae. – *perang* kelp, brown algae, *Phaeophyta, spp.*
algoja (*ob*) → ALGOJO.
algojo (*Port*) **1** hangman, executioner. **2** bully.
algojowati female executioner.
algoju (*ob*) → ALGOJO.
algoritma and **algoritme** (*D*) algorithm.
al-hajju 'arafatun (*A*) a *haji* who has made a stop at Arafat.
alhamdu first word of the *alfatékah*.
alhamdulil(l)ah(i) (*A*) **1** (when s.o. sneezes) God bless you! Gesundheit! **2** Thank God! Praise be to God!
alhasil (*A*) **1** eventually, in the end. – *ia pergi juga*. In the end he went away. **2** consequently, the result was, so. ~ *kami tidak jadi pergi*. So, we didn't go after all.
Al-Huda (*A*) the Guider (another name for the Koran).
ali I (*A*) (*ob*) high. *al* – The Exalted One (God).
  mengali to show off in order to draw attention to o.s.
ali II (*ob*) *gula* – sugar candy; → GULALI.
Ali III Muhammad's cousin and son-in-law, the fourth Caliph; → HUSAIN.
Ali IV (*A*) – *Imran* "Family of Imran"; name of the third chapter of the Koran.
ali-ali sling.
  mengali-ali and **membuang** – to sling/hurl s.t.
  pengali-ali 1 slingshot. **2** catapult, sling.
alia ginger, *Zingiber officinale*; → JAHÉ.
aliah (*A*) Muslim religious middle school.
aliansi (*D*) alliance. – *Kuning* the Yellow Alliance (between Japan and the PRC).
  beraliansi allied.
alias I (*D*) **1** alias. **2** same as, equals, meaning, i.e., *menggantungkan hélm di kendaraannya – tidak dipakai* hangs his helmet on his vehicle, i.e., doesn't use it. **3** otherwise called/named, nicknamed, also known as, aka.
Alias II (*A*) (the Biblical) Elias, Elijah.
aliat (*A*) exalted position.
Alibaba and **Ali-Baba 1** Ali Baba. **2** name for an Indonesian who is a front man for a (usually Chinese) foreign-run company; *cp* ALISAN.
alibi (*D/E*) alibi.
aliénasi (*D*) alienation.
  mengaliénasikan to alienate.
alif I the first letter of the Arabic alphabet. *tahun* – the first year in an eight-year cycle or *windu. tidak tahu di* – illiterate. *tegak (berdiri) sebagai* – bolt upright. *belum kenal* – *lémpéng* still very ignorant. *berbilang dari esa, mengaji dari* – to start from scratch/the beginning. *mengaji* –.– starting to study the Arabic writing system. *mulai dari* – *bata* from scratch/the beginning. – *benar* the alif that represents the sound /a/, *usu* only written at the beginning of a syllable. – *kecil/gantung* the symbol that replaces the *tasjdid*. – *saksi* the symbol representing long /a/. – *waslah* symbol for an elided /a/.
  alif-alif the Arabic alphabet.
  alif-alifan the letters *alif* to *ya*.
alif II (*A*) friend.
alifbata, **alif-ba-ta** and **alif ba' ta' 1** the Arabic alphabet. **2** basic principles. **3** ins and outs.
alifuru → ALFUR.
alih to change, shift, move. – *aksara* transcript. **mengalih-aksarakan** to transcribe. **pengalih-aksara** transcriber. **pengalih-aksaraan** transcript, transcription. – *ba(ha)sa* a) translation. b) translator. c) interpreter. **mengalih-ba(ha)sakan 1** to translate. **2** to interpret. **pengalih-ba(ha)saan 1** translation. **2** in-

terpretation. – *cakap* to change the subject. – *éja* transcript. **mengalih-éjakan** to transcribe. – *percakapan* to change the subject, switch to another topic. *pusat* – *muatan kapal* transshipment center. *mengambil* – *(kekuasaan)* to take over (the authority). – *générasi* change from one generation to the next. – *huruf* transliteration. **mengalih-hurufkan** to transliterate, change the spelling of. ~ *x menjadi ks* to change the spelling x into the spelling ks. – *ilmu pengetahuan* transfer of knowledge. – *janin* embryo transfer. – *kapal* transshipment. **mengalih-kapalkan** to transship. **pengalih-kapalan** transshipment. – *kécék* to change the subject. – *kedudukan* to change one's sitting position. – *krédit* credit transfer. – *milik* repossession. – *ragam* transformation. **beralih-ragam** to transform, become transformed. **mengalih-ragamkan** to transform s.t. **pengalih-ragam** transformer. **pengalih-ragaman** transformation. – *suara* dubbing. **pengalih-suaraan** dubbing. – *tanam* transplant. **mengalih-tanam** to transplant. **pengalih-tanaman** transplanting. – *téknologi* technology transfer. – *tempat* transfer from one area to another. – *tugas* transfer from one post to another. **mengalih-tugaskan 1** to send s.o. on a tour of duty. **2** to transfer s.o. (from military to civilian duties). **pengalihan-tugas** transfer to another position.

alih-alih 1 and now it turns out (contrary to expectations), but in fact, instead. *Disangkanya sudah pergi, – masih tidur.* He thought that she had left, but it turns out that she is still asleep. **2** instead of.

beralih 1 to move, shift (over), change, turn (to), move on (to). ~ *agama* to convert. ~ *ke agama Islam* to become a Muslim. ~ *kepada acara yang baru* to take up another item on the agenda. ~ *rumah* to move from one house to another. **2** to alter, change. *angin* ~ the wind has shifted. *jaman* ~, *musim bertukar* the times are changed, and we are changed with them. ~ *akal* to change one's mind. ~ *cakap* to change subjects. ~ *dari … menjadi …* to switch from … to … ~ *haluan* a) (of ship) to alter course. b) to change tack/course. ~ *hari* somewhat later in the day; afternoon. ~ *laku* to change one's behavior. ~ *pekerjaan/profési* to change jobs/professions. **3** to shoot (of stars). *bintang* ~ shooting star. **4** (*leg*) to pass, devolve.

beralihkan (*infr*) to switch over (to). *Kurangilah minum susu murni atau krim dan* ~ *ke susu skim (rendah lemak).* Drink less whole milk or cream and switch over to skim milk.

mengalih (*ob*) to change, replace. ~ *belakang* to turn around. ~ *bentuk* to change form/shape, transform. ~ *langkah* to change jobs. ~ *loka* to translocate. ~ *nama* to change names. ~ *sila* to change one's sitting position, switch crossed legs. *Dialihnya menggali.* He dug in another place.

mengalihkan [and **ngalihin** (*J coq*)] **1** to shift, move to another place, switch, divert. *Keréta api itu dialihkan dari Cirebon ke Purwokerto.* The train was diverted from Cirebon to Purwokerto. **2** to replace, change, alter. **3** to transfer, assign. ~ *… jadi* to change … into. ~ *negara dari koloni yang miskin jadi …* to change a poor colony into … ~ *pembicaraan* to change the subject. ~ *perhatian dari* to divert one's attention from.

memperalihkan to transfer.

teralih 1 to turn back (to the past). *Pikirannya* ~ *kembali ke masa lampau.* His thoughts turned back to the past. **2** to shift inadvertently.

alihan (*phys*) transition.

pengalih converter. ~ *sumbing* (*elec*) split transducer.

pengalihan 1 transfer, assignment. ~ *hak* endorsement. ~ *kekuasaan* transfer of authority. ~ *krédit* loan sale. ~ *téknologi* technology transfer. ~ *tugas* transfer to another position. **2** detour, diversion (of traffic). **3** conversion. ~ *utang* debt swap.

peralihan 1 change, alteration. ~ *agama* conversion. **2** transition(al). *aturan* ~ transitional provision(s). ~ *générasi* change from one generation to the next. *jaman/masa* ~ transition period. **3** interim. *pemerintah* ~ interim government. **4** transfer, shift, assignment, devolution. ~ *jaman* change of the times. ~ *pemerintahan* transfer of rule. ~ *milik* transfer of ownership.

alik → ULANG-ALIK.

alim I (*A* the singular of *ulama*) **1** learned. **2** pious, religious, devout. *orang* – a) a savant, theologian. b) a devoted spouse, s.o. who

doesn't cheat on his/her spouse. **3** (Muslim) cleric. – *ulama* religious dignitaries/scholars.
  sealim as pious/devout as.
  kealiman 1 learning, scholarship. **2** piety. ~ *anak* filial piety.
alim II watercress, *Lepidium sativum.*
alimat (*A*) feminine of **alim.**
alimbubu (*M*) cyclone, whirlwind.
aliméntasi (*D*) alimentation, alimony.
alimiah (*A*) and **alimiat** Age of Enlightenment; *opp* JAHILIAH.
al-Imran → ALI IV.
alin (*ob*) **mengalin** to massage the human body or part of the body so as to extract a toxic foreign substance.
  pengalin (*tepung* ~) and **alinan** substance used for massages.
alinéa (*D*) paragraph.
aling I aling-aling (*tedéng*) ~ (*Jv*) cover, concealment, protection, shield; → TÉDÉNG. *main tedéng* ~ to play hide-and-(go)-seek.
  beraling-aling to hide (behind), be in the shelter (of).
  ngaling (*J*) to hide (behind s.t.).
  mengalingi to protect/screen from sight, cover, shelter.
  mengalingkan to hide s.t.
  teraling hidden, protected.
  alingan (*J*) → ALING-ALING.
  aling-alingan 1 cover, shelter. **2** hide-and-go-seek.
  kealingan (*J*) obstructed so as to be invisible.
aling II mechanical bearing.
alip I (on the east coast of Sumatra) *main* **alip-alipan 1** to play hide-and-(go)-seek. **2** to play tag.
alip II → ALIF.
alir I flow, run. – *balik* a) reflux. b) venous return. – *golak-galik* turbulent flow. – *naik* updraft.
  beralir (*infr*) and **mengalir** [and **ngalir** (*coq*)] **1** to flow (of a river or liquid), run, stream, flow in (of profits). ~ *keluar* to stream out. ~ *masuk* to flow into. **2** to trickle/stream (down), drip. **3** to wander/travel from one place to another, migrate; → MEMBOYONG.
  mengaliri 1 to overflow s.t. **2** to flow/stream through/down. *Pagar itu dialiri tenaga listrik.* Electric current will flow through the fence. *kawat yang dialiri arus listrik* live wire.
  mengalirkan [and **ngalirin** (*J coq*)] **1** to guide, lead, drain (off) (water), channel, make s.t. flow, run (water). **2** to siphon. *Dia* ~ *cuka dari botol.* She siphoned vinegar from a bottle. **3** to shed (tears). **4** to aim, point.
  teraliri flowed through, connected (to the electricity grid/irrigation system).
  aliran 1 flow, current, stream, draft, course. ~ *air* stream. *daérah* ~ *sungai* [DAS] watershed. ~ *air tanah* groundwater flow. ~ *bada* after-flow. ~ *bawah* a) underflow. b) lower course (of a river). ~ *darah* blood circulation. ~ *gésér* shear flow. ~ *laut* ocean current. ~ *listrik* electric current. ~ *masuk* inflow. ~ *tak jenuh* unsaturated flow. ~ *tak tunak* unsteady flow. ~ *tunak* steady flow. ~ *uang kontan* cash flow. ~ *udara* airflow. **2** ideology, (spiritual, etc.) trend. ~ *kebatinan* contemporary mystical sects. ~ *kiri* the political left, the left wing. ~ *masyarakat* tendency in society. **3** rivulet, brook. **4** school (of thought). **5** pipeline; conduit, wiring. **beraliran** to follow a trend/ideology/course, be …-oriented. ~ *kanan* to be right wing. ~ *komunis* to be communist-oriented; → BERHALUAN. ~ *tengah* middle of the road.
  pengalir flow, flux.
  pengaliran 1 draining off. *daérah* ~ *sungai* catchment area. ~ *air* water drain. ~ *balik* refluxing. **2** flow, flowing. **3** drift, trend.
alir II *umpan* – floating live bait (to catch crocodiles). *tali* – line for this bait. *menahan* – to fasten the line for this bait.
  mengalir to catch (crocodiles) using this bait.
alir III (*M*) smooth (of surface).
alis (*Jv*) eyebrow.
Ali Sadikin 1 name of a former popular governor of Jakarta. **2** a batik pattern named after him.
Ali-San an Indonesian front man for a Japanese-run company.
alit I mascara.
  mengalit to apply mascara.

alit II s.t. used to strengthen sides of a basket/mat, etc.
  mengalit 1 to tie up tightly. **2** to squeeze, put pressure on. ~ *bisul* to squeeze a blister till it bursts. ~ *gasing* to wrap the cord up inside a top. ~ *perut* to eat very little because of a shortage of food.
  alit(an) *tali* ~ cord used to spin a top.
alit III (*Jv*) small, little; fragile, fine.
aliterasi (*D*) alliteration.
Aliyah (*A*) → SEKOLAH *aliyah*.
aljabar (*A*) algebra.
Aljalil (*A*) the Most Exalted (God).
Aljazair Algeria.
aljibra → ALJABAR.
Aljir Algiers.
Al-Jumhuriyah Al-Arabiyah as-Suriyah (*A*) Arab Republic of Syria.
Alkabir (*A*) the Most Great (God).
Alkadir (*A*) the Almighty (God).
alkah I (*A ob*) **1** coagulated blood (forming an embryo). **2** inmost heart, conscience.
alkah II uncultivated land.
alkali (*A*) **1** alkali, lye. **2** alkaline.
alkaloid(a) (*E*) alkaloid(s).
alkamar (*A ob*) moon; → KAMAR II.
alkari (*Port ob*) sealing wax.
alkasyaf (*A ob*) the Discoverer (God).
alkatipa (*Port ob*) carpet.
alkausar (*A*) **1** heavenly lake or river. **2** a lot. **3** "Pre-eminence"; name of the 108th chapter of the Koran.
alkéna (*D*) alkaline.
alkimi(a) (*D*) alchemy.
alketip → ALKATIPA.
alki(s)sah (*A*) **1** story, tale. **2** once upon a time, the story goes that; → KISAH.
Alkitab (*A*) **1** the Bible; → BIBEL, BIBLIA and KITAB *injil*. **2** the Koran.
alkitabiyah (*A*) biblical.
alkohol (*D*) alcohol.
  beralkohol alcoholic, containing alcohol.
  kealkoholan alcoholism.
alkoholisme (*D*) alcoholism.
alkojor (*J*) → KUJUR II.
alkonya (*A ob*) surname.
Alkoran → QUR'AN.
alku (*cla*) go-between, pimp, procurer, madam (in a brothel).
Alkuran → QUR'AN.
Alkus Sagittarius.
alkutubul (*A*) - *mu'tabarah* authentic book.
Allah (*A*) God. *dibuat karena* - *menjadi murka* - done with good intentions, but considered bad by society. *demi* - (I swear) by God. *Gusti* - God (in direct address). *hamba* - human being; mankind. *insya* - if Heaven permits, God willing. *karena* - a) for God's sake. b) gratis, free. - *azza wajallah* God Almighty. - *Maha Agung* God the Supreme Being. - *Maha Esa* the one and only God. - *Maha Rahmat* God the All-Merciful. - *Pengetahui* God the All-Knowing. - *subhanahu wa taala* [SWT] God the Most Holy (and Most High). - *Taala* God Most High. - *ya rahim* the late ...
  ber-Allah *tidak* ~ godless.
  ke-Allahan 1 Godhead. **2** divinity, deity, godlike.
Allahu (*A*) (in certain phrases) God. -*Akbar* God is Great. -*Alam* God knows best. -*mma* Oh God! -*rabi* My God!
allamah (*A*) a learned person, expert.
Allayarham (*A*) "May God have mercy on him" (the deceased).
all in (*E*) /ol-in/ everything included.
allogénik (*D*) allogenic.
all round (*E*) /olron/ versatile.
alm. (*abbr*) → ALMARHUM.
almahdi (*A*) the Messiah.
al-majmu' (*A*) compendium.
Almaktub (*A*) the Holy Book.
almalun (*A cla*) /almal'un/ the damned.
almamatér (*L*) alma mater.
almanak (*D*) **1** almanac. **2** calendar. - *dinding* wall calendar. **3** diary.

almarhum (*A*) **1** (of men) the deceased; the late. - *Dr. Lumanauw* the late Dr. Lumanauw. **2** to be deceased; to die. *Asmawi yang sudah* - Asmawi, who is deceased. *ketiganya sudah* - all three are deceased.
  mengalmarhumkan 1 to lay to rest. **2** to put out of business. **3** to kill.
almarhumah (*A*) (of women) the deceased, the late. - *Drg. Ny. Yétti R. Noor* the late Mrs. Yetti R. Noor, D.D.S.
almari (*Port*) wardrobe, cupboard; → LEMARI. - *arsip* filing cabinet. - *besi* safe.
almas (*Pers*) diamond.
almashalihul mursalah (*A*) public interest.
Almasih (*A*) *Isa* - (Jesus) Christ; → NABI *isa*.
almenak → ALMANAK.
almuazam (*A*) who is gloried; the honorable (in the address of a letter).
almukarrom (*A*) the reverend (a title). - *Bapak K.H. Abdullah* the Reverend K.H. Abdullah.
almukhallis (*A ob*) the Savior.
almukharam (*A*) Muslim scholars and elders.
almukhlis (*A*) yours truly (at the end of a letter before the signature).
Al-Nabi (*A*) the Prophet Muhammad.
Alnas (*A*) Great Bear.
alo (*S*) nephew or niece (child of an older sibling).
alofon (*D ling*) allophone.
alok (*Jv*) s.o. or a phrase (one to three syllables long) that breaks into the main playing or singing.
  mengalokkan [and **ngalokin** (*J coq*)] to yell at.
alokasi (*D*) allocation. - *upah* payroll distribution.
  mengalokasikan to allocate.
  teralokasi(kan) allocated.
  pengalokasian allocation.
alokir (*D*) **mengalokir** to allocate.
alomorf (*D/E ling*) allomorph.
alon-alon I (*Jv*) slow. - *asal/waton kelakon* slow but sure, easy does it. - *tapi mantap* slow but steady.
alon-alon II → ALUN-ALUN.
alot (*J*) **1** tough (of meat/negotiations), hard to break or tear. **2** difficult.
alpa (*Skr*) **1** careless, negligent, neglectful, forgetful, inattentive; in default. - *daripada* to neglect (one's duties). *tak* - (*daripada*) (to think about s.t.) continually, not ignore s.t. **2** unexcused (absence, on school records).
  mengalpakan 1 to neglect, forget, take no heed of, disregard. **2** to be on one's guard (against).
  teralpa(kan) neglected, disregarded, forgotten.
  kealpaan 1 carelessness, neglect, negligence, inattention, forgetfulness. **2** oversight, omission, error. ~ *manusia* human error. **3** shortcomings, deficiencies. **4** infraction. ~ *besar* major infraction. ~ *ringan* minor infraction.
alpabét → ALFABÉT.
alpaka (*D*) alpaca.
alpayaté (*Port IBT ob*) tailor.
alpérés I 1 (*Port cla*) name of the rank below lieutenant. **2** deputy administrator (during the *VOC*).
alpérés II - *batu/jawa* k.o. sea fish.
alpukah (*A*) initiative.
alpukat → ADVOKAT.
Alquran, al Qur'an, and **Al-Qur'an** (*A*) the Koran.
ALRI /alri/ [Angkatan Laut République Indonésia] the Indonesian Navy.
Al Sarq al-Awsat (*A*) The Middle East.
al-shalihun (*A*) pious people.
alsintan [Alat dan Mesin Pertanian] Agricultural Tools and Machines.
alsus [alat khusus] special tools.
Al-Syifa' (*A*) the consoler (another name for the Koran).
altar (*D*) altar.
alternasi (*D*) alternation.
altérnatif (*D/E*) alternative.
alternator (*D/E*) alternator.

altiméter (*D/E*) altimeter.

alto (*D/E*) alto (voice).

altruis (*D/E*) altruist.

altruisme (*D/E*) altruism.

altruistis (*D/E*) altruistic.

Altur Taurus.

alu I 1 rice pounder. **2** pestle. *(bagai) guna-guna –, sesudah menumbuk dicampakkan* the world's wages are ingratitude. *(bagai) dientak – luncung* defeated by a weak/stupid person. *(seperti) – pencungkil duri* an endless/hopeless task.

  beralu-alu to hit e.o. with rice pounders.

alu II → ELU.

alu-alu (pickle-handle) barracuda, *Sphyraena jello*.

alua → HALWA.

aluan (*ob*) → HALUAN.

alufoil (*D*) aluminum foil.

alum (*Jv*) drooping, withered, wilted, limp.

  mengalum to droop, begin to wither.

aluminium (*D*) aluminum.

aluminosilikat (*D/E*) aluminosilicate.

alumni (*D/E*) alumni, graduates.

alumnus (*D/E*) alumnus, graduates.

alun wave, billow.

  beralun 1 to heave, roll, pitch, billow. **2** to oscillate. **3** to keep moving.

  beralun-alun 1 to keep on rolling (of the waves). **2** to heave, pitch, roll. **3** billowing.

  mengalun 1 to heave, roll, pitch, billow. **2** to oscillate. **3** to move rhythmically.

  mengalunkan to move s.t. rhythmically/steadily. *~ azan* to recite the call to prayer.

  teralun heaved, pitched, rocked.

  alunan 1 billowing. **2** wave in hair. **3** oscillation. **4** strains (of music), rhythm. *dalam ~ impian* in the rhythm of a dream.

  pengalun oscillator.

  pengalunan oscillation, modulation.

alun-alun esplanade, square grassy area in front of the houses of regents and district heads, used for parades, sports, etc.

alung (*ob*) k.o. game of marbles.

alup (*Jv*) **mengalup** to predict bad luck from the sound of a howling dog.

  mengalupi to lament over.

alur I 1 furrow, trench, groove, gully, long deep cut in the ground/ woods, etc., fairway (of a river); slot, groove, flute, small ditch. *– dangkal* shallow fairway. **2** prong. *– dua* two-pronged. **3** plot (of a story, etc.); → ALUR *cerita*. **4** segment (of time). *– ari* channel. *– audit* audit trail. *– bajak* furrow. *– bajang* dove-tailed groove. *– balik* a change to the reverse of what one expected. *– bawahan* secondary plot. *– bibir* groove in upper lip, philtrum. *– cerita* plot (of a story, etc.). *– féli* rim gutter. *– hidung* → ALUR *bibir*. *– kerongkongan* esophagus. *– kunci/dudukan* (*petro*) key seat. *– lambat* slow lane. *– léhér* cervical groove. *– nasib dan peruntungan* one's fate and fortune. *– pelayaran* sea lane, ship channel. *– penerbangan* air route. *– pikiran* way of thinking. *– rambut* hairdo. *– ruaya* migratory pathway. *– rusuk* lateral groove. *– sesungut* antennal groove. *– sungai* river bed. *– tenggala* plowed furrow; track (through the jungle). *– tengkuk* hollow in nape of neck. *– toréhan* tapping groove.

  sealur in the same line (as), in line with.

  beralur rifled (of barrel), grooved. *laras senapan yang ~* a rifled barrel.

  mengalur-alur 1 grooved. **2** one's ribs can be counted/stick out. *Tulang rusuknya tersusun ~ dadanya*. He's as thin as a rail.

  mengalurkan to channel s.t. *Insulin segera ~ gula tersebut ke dalam sél-sél tubuh*. Insulin immediately channels the sugar into the cells of the body.

  aluran 1 (= *alur-aluran*) channel, ship-channel, navigable/navigation channel, small ditch. **2** (*Jv*) family relations. *Dia ~ keponakan saya*. He is my nephew. **beraluran** (*bio*) sulcate.

  pengaluran (*phys*) streaming.

alur II (*M*) the correct way, customs, etc. *bersua –nya* well-

fitting. *– bertempuh, jalan berturut* performed according to traditional customs.

  beralur to discuss (to arrive at the truth). *habis ~ maka beralualu* if no agreement can be reached through talk, force has to be used.

  aluran *~ adat* established custom.

alur-alur k.o. coastal tree, sea-blite, *Suaeda maritima*.

alus → HALUS. **alusan** subtlety, refinement.

alut [*alat utama*] primary tools. *– sista* [*alut utama sistém pertahanan*] defense system primary tools.

aluvial (*D/E*) alluvial.

aluvium (*D/E*) alluvium.

aluwung (*Jv*) preferable.

alvéoli plural of *alveolus*.

alvéolus (*D/E*) alveolus.

alwah and **alwat** (*A*) aloe extract. *kayu –* aloe wood, *Aquilaria malaccensis*.

alwasi(a) (*A*) the Omnipresent (of God).

al-wa'yul wathany (*A*) nationalistic viewpoint.

am (*A*) common, general, ordinary, universal. *... –nya ... khasnya ...* in general ... in particular. *orang –* the common people.

  mengamkan to make common/general/universal.

ama I 1 small insects, the natural enemies of a crop. **2** plague. **3** plant disease. **4** (*– penyakit*) germ (of a disease); → HAMA. *– kelapa* squirrel. *– mentek* rot in the roots of the rice plant. *– sékava* disease of the coconut tree. *– sundep* rice pest. *– tanaman* plant pest. *– tikus* scourge of mice (which destroy field crops).

  berama attacked by a plant disease.

ama II (*J*) → SAMA.

amabakdu (*A*) → AMMABAKDU.

amah I (*Port?*) Chinese maid/nurse.

amah II the common folk.

amai (in Bukittinggi) **1** a married woman. **2** a woman who does business independent of her husband. *–.– penggaléh* retailers.

amal (*A*) **1** good or meritorious work, mostly said of giving alms or rendering assistance, making donations or contributions to charity; charity (*mod*). *atas dasar –* charitable, philanthropic. *pertunjukan –* charity performance. **2** regular practice, action (in general). *sedikit bicara banyak –* little talk but lots of work. *– baik* good deeds/works. *– bajikan* philanthropy. *– bhakti* charity, charitable. **mengamal-baktikan** to put s.t. to charitable use. *– bidah* innovative (and so wrong) actions. *– ibadah* pious deeds. *– jari(y)ah* good/charitable deeds. *– mustahabah* actions viewed as right. *– pahala* actions that gain merit. *– saléh* pious deed.

  beramal 1 to do good deeds/works, give charity. **2** to practice austerity. *~ untuk* do a good deed by ...ing. *~ ibadah* to worship.

  mengamali to put into practice.

  mengamalkan [and **ngamalin** (*J coq*)] **1** to put into practice, apply (knowledge), implement; to practice (i.e., do s.t. on a regular basis). **2** to do, execute, cause (a drug/charm) to work. **3** to observe/comply with/live up to (God's commands). **4** to carry out (an intention, etc.). **5** to contribute.

  teramal practiced, put into practice.

  amalan 1 good works/deed. *~ bertawassul* action to petition God for help. **2** practice (i.e., s.t. done on a regular basis).

  pengamal 1 implementer/applier of an idea/doctrine/philosophy. **2** performer of good deeds, donor.

  pengamalan 1 implementation, execution, application. **2** performance (of a task). **3** contributing (ideas), making donations.

amalgam (*D*) amalgam.

amalgamasi (*D*) amalgamation.

amali applied. *ilmu –* applied science.

amali(y)ah charity (*mod*).

amamat → IMAMAT.

aman (*A*) **1** safe, not feel afraid/worried/restless/impatient. *merasa – tinggal di sini* to feel safe living here. *menjaga segala kemungkinan supaya –* to be on the safe side. **2** free from. *– pencemaran* free from pollution. *dengan –* securely, without any doubts. **3** tranquil, quiet, peaceful, secure, at peace. *negeri yang – dan makmur* a peaceful and prosperous country. *– dari(pada)* protected, (safe)guarded, secured from/against. *– sejahtera/sentosa* peaceful and tranquil. **4** (in certain terms often used with the connotation of) for the greater security of s.t., security (*mod*). *pasak* – security pin (of firearm). 5 (*cla*) message.

seaman as safe/secure as.

seaman-amannya as safe/secure as possible.

mengamankan [and **ngamanin** (*J coq*)] 1 to make peaceful, pacify (a country). ~ *hati* to quiet s.o. down. 2 to keep safe, safeguard, preserve. *diamankan dari* to be freed from. ~ *negara* to keep the country safe. 3 to defuse/dismantle (a mine/grenade, etc.); → MENJINAKKAN. 4 to restore (peace and order). 5 (*euph*) to imprison, put in prison/jail, hold (in custody); to apprehend, arrest, take into custody. 6 to quell (a revolt/uprising). 7 to regulate, control, make orderly. ~ *bus-bus antarkota* to regulate intercity buses. 8 to watch out for the safety of. ~ *diri sendiri maupun harta benda* to watch out for one's own safety and that of one's possessions. 9 to secure, put (somewhere) for safekeeping. ~ *harga* to force down the price, roll back the price. ~ *senjata (api)* to put on the safety catch.

memperaman to make safer, secure.

teraman most secure, safest.

keamanan 1 security, safety. *Déwan* ~ Security Council (of the U.N.). *Pihak* ~ The Police. ~ *bersama* mutual security. ~ *dan ketertiban* [kamtib] security and (public) order. ~ *negara* national security. ~ *swakarsa* social self control. 2 peacefulness, tranquility. *memulangkan* ~ to restore peace and order.

pengaman 1 pacifier. 2 guard, safeguard, protector; safety (*mod*), security (*mod*). 3 device to avoid accidents, fuse. *alat* ~ *kepala* and *topi* ~ protective helmet (for motorcyclists); → HEL(E)M. *alat* ~ *rumah* home security system. ~ *kilat* lightning rod. ~ *lebur* fuse. ~ *mata* safety goggles. ~ *tegangan listrik* ground.

pengamanan 1 pacification. 2 protection for, security provisions for. 3 imprisonment. 4 securing, making s.t. secure, safeguarding. *tindakan* ~ security measures. 5 relieving (pressure).

amanah and **amanat** (*A*) 1 s.t. given to s.o. to be taken care of, deposit. *barang* – goods consigned/sent out on consignment. 2 instruction, order, speech conveying a message to the people, message, mandate. – *Negara* State-of-the-Union Message. 3 (government) statement; (*mil*) order of the day. 4 security, peace. 5 reliable, trusty, trustworthy; trust (territory). *orang* – reliable person, confidant. *wilayah* – trust territory. *pecah* – to commit a breach of trust. – *anggaran* budget message. – *ganda* switch order. – *harga mati* fill or kill (order). – *Penderitaan Rakyat* Message of the People's Suffering (slogan of the Soekarno era). – *penyerahan* delivery order.

beramanat to instruct, enjoin; to issue an order (that).

mengamanati to advise, give advice to; order.

mengamanatkan 1 to (en)trust, confide, leave on trust. *Pelukis yang terkenal itu telah* ~ *segala hasil ciptaannya kepada muséum itu.* The famous painter has left all his work to the museum. 2 to order, instruct, mandate, stipulate. 3 to donate, set aside (for s.o.'s use).

pengamanat principal, mandator; → PEMBERI *kuasa.*

amandel I (*D*) almond.

amandel II (*D*) tonsil.

amandemén → AMÉNDEMÉN.

amandir (*D*) **mengamandir** to amend.

amang I mengamang(-amang), **mengamangi**, **mengamang-amangi** and **mengamangkan** (*cla*) to menace/threaten (with a weapon), challenge by gesture (as a fencer).

amang II tungsten and other impurities in tin ore.

amang III (*Bat*) – *boru* father's sibling's wife.

Aman Malindo name for the joint maneuvers between the Malaysian Royal Police and Indonesian National Police.

amansari k.o. cake made of *kacang hijau* and coconut.

amantu bil(l)ahi (*A*) I believe in God.

amar (*A*) 1 command, order, injunction. 2 (*leg*) dictum, disposition, ruling (of a court in a case). – *dan nahi* commands and prohibitions (of God). *melakukan* – *ma'ruf nahi mungkar* to do good deeds and abandon bad ones. *dengan* – *raja* by royal decree. – *putusan* (*leg*) judicial verdict, disposition, ruling.

beramar ~ *ma'ruf nahi mungkar* to instruct in doing good and in avoiding doing wrong.

mengamari to order s.o.

mengamar(kan) to command, order, instruct to do s.t.

amaran 1 order; warning, lesson. 2 disposition (in a judicial order).

amarah I → MARAH.

amarah II (*Pers*) authority.

amariyah (*A*) scenario.

amat I 1 (preceding a word) very (much); → SANGAT. – *mahal* very expensive. 2 (following a word) exceedingly, extremely. *tinggi* – extremely high.

memperamat(-amat)(kan) to make more intense, intensify, increase.

teramat(-amat) extremely, exceedingly. ~ *mahal* extremely expensive. ~ *sangat* exceedingly, extremely.

amat II observe, inspect.

mengamat(-amat)i and **memperamat-amati** 1 to pay close attention to, monitor. 2 to inspect closely/carefully. 3 to guard, watch, keep an eye on, place under surveillance. *mengamati terus-menerus* to put under continuous surveillance. *diamati* under observation/surveillance.

teramati observed, under surveillance.

amatan observation.

pengamat 1 inspector, supervisor, observer. *panitia* ~ *dan pencatat pasar* market monitoring committee. ~ *Cina* China watcher. 2 (*ob*) caretaker.

pengamatan 1 inspection, supervision. 2 observation, survey, surveying, spotting. ~ *pembaca* readership survey. 3 tracking, monitoring, surveillance. ~ *penyakit menular* epidemiological surveillance.

peramatan observation, monitoring.

amatir (*D/E*) amateur. *pemain* – nonprofessional player. *radio* – ham, amateur radio operator.

amatiran amateurish. *secara* ~ amateurishly.

amatir-amatiran amateurish; not real.

keamatiran amateur standing.

amatirisme (*D/E*) amateurism.

am-atman (*Skr*) a man who has no self.

amatur → AMATIR.

ambacang → EMBACANG.

ambah (*D ob*) vocational, trade. *sekolah* – (lower) technical school.

ambah-ambah (*J/Jv*) plague, pestilence.

ambai I purse net fixed in estuaries, scoop net.

mengambai to fish by means of such a net.

ambaian 1 the fish caught by this method. 2 place where one uses this method.

ambai II berambai-ambai 1 to flow, stream, gush. *dengan air mata* ~ with tears flowing down. 2 to spatter, sprinkle.

mengambai-ambaikan to splash (with water).

ambai-ambai 1 k.o. beach crab. 2 k.o. tree parasite which kills its host, *Rafflesia hasseltii.*

ambak (*M*) **mengambak** (*ob*) to bank/pile/heap up with earth, etc. *subur karena dipupuk, besar karena diambak* and *besar diambak, tinggi dianjung* to hold high office due to the support of underlings or followers.

ambal I (*A?*) carpet, mat, prayer rug.

ambal II berambal-ambalan to move in procession.

ambalan 1 flow (of people), group (of persons). 2 procession. 3 unit in the *Pramuka* Boy Scout Movement.

ambal-ambalan troupe, crowd.

ambal III (*M*) **mengambal** to pile up soil.

ambal IV mengambal to peep at, glance out of the corner of one's eye at, ogle.

ambalan wall-panel support.

ambaléla (*Jv*) *aksi* – passive resistance; → BALÉLA.

amban → EMBAN I.

ambang I 1 threshold, doorstep; level, margin, verge. *berdiri di* – *pintu* to stand at the threshold. *di* – *pintu* at hand. *berada di* – ... to be about to ..., be on the point/verge of ...ing. – *ékonomis* economic threshhold. *berada di* – *kebangkrutan* to be on the verge of bankruptcy. – *pintu* doorframe. – *sungai* bar, shoal, bank. 2 window sill, sill. – *atas* cap piece, lintel. – *kosén* header, lintel. 3 sleeper (of railroad tracks). 4 range (of an organism). 5 (*geol*) bar, shoal. – *batas* acceptable threshold. – *batas bahaya* safety margin – *letup* (*med*) firing level (of nerve). – *palkah* cargo hatch. – *sungai* bar, shoal.

mengambang to restrain, obstruct.

ambang II – *bébas* free float. **mengambang-bébaskan** to allow (currency) to free float. **pengambang-bébasan** free floating.

mengambang 1 to float, floating. *Mayat ~ di Kali Bekasi.* A corpse was floating in the Bekasi River. *bunga ~* floating (bank) rate. *~ terkendali* managed floating. **2** vague, imprecise, uncertain. *Rencana mutasi di Pémda Bangli ~.* Plans for transfers in the Bangli Provincial Government are vague.

mengambang-ambang to float around.

mengambangkan to float s.t. (*esp* currency).

terambang(-ambang) to float, drift about (as of shipwrecked men/timber in the sea).

pengambangan floating (of currency).

ambar I → HAMBAR.

ambar II (*A*) ambergris. *batu* – amber. – *bunga* styrax. – *darah* red spot like rubber floating in the water. – *kuning* amber.

ambar-ambar k.o. ambergris mixed with *kesturi.*

ambaradul all mixed up, confused.

ambarau (*ob*) → EMBARAU.

ambaru camp shed(ding), sheet piling.

ambasade (*D*) embassy; → KEDUTAAN *besar.*

ambasadir → AMBASADOR.

ambasador (*D*) ambassador; → DUTA *besar.*

ambasadur → AMBASADOR.

ambat → HAMBAT.

ambata-rubuh (*Jv*) in a body/group. *bersorak-sorai* – to applaud in a body.

ambau I (*ob*) bamboo floats fixed to the sides of a boat; outriggers.

ambau II (*M*) **mengambau 1** to jump off/down. **2** to surrender.

terambau fallen face down.

ambeg I → AMBEK II.

ambeg II pengambeg moneylender.

ambéien (*D*) hemorrhoids.

ambek I (*J*) stomach.

ngambek 1 to complain and whine (as of children). **2** to get angry, lose control of one's temper.

ambekan 1 quick-tempered, irascible; sulky. **2** energetic.

pengambek person who likes to complain and whine, whiner.

pengambekan whining and complaining.

ambek II (*Jv*) to breathe; breathing, respiration.

ambekan 1 breath. **2** to take a breath.

ambek III → PENGAMBEK.

ambek-parama-arta and **ambek-paramarta** (*Jv*) the ability to put important/first things first.

mengambek-parama-artakan to give (top) priority to s.t.

pengambek-parama-artaan sense of priorities.

ambelar (*J*) a string used as a mark in certain games.

ambelas and **ambeles** (*Jv*) → AMBLAS.

amben (*Jv*) **1** sash worn with wrap-around garment. **2** abdominal belt, belly-belt (of horse).

ambén (*Jv*) (bamboo) couch.

ambeng (in Ujungpandang) special place for the helmsman on board a traditional boat.

ambengan 1 (*Jv*) sacrificial meal. **2** (*S*) the place where food is laid out.

amber I (*D*) amber.

amber II (*Papua*) reference to people not from Irian Jaya.

amberal (*ob*) → ADMIRAL, LAKSAMANA.

amberi Papuan term for non-Papuans.

amberol → AMBROL.

amberuk → AMBRUK.

ambet (*J*) diaper, swaddling clothes, baby linen; → LAMPIN.

ambia → ANBIA.

ambigu (*D*) ambiguous.

ambiguitas (*D*) ambiguity.

ambik (*coq*) → AMBIL.

ambil take (*coq* for MENGAMBIL). *tidak* – *perhatian dengan* pay no attention to. *tidak* – *pusing* to not care about, not mind. *tidak (mau)* – *tahu/peduli akan* to not care a bit about; take no notice of, pay no heed to. *buruk* – misunderstanding, misconcep-

tion, misapprehension; to consider bad. *salah* – taken by accident.

seambilan (*ob*) intermarriage (between two families, etc.).

(ber)ambil-ambilan 1 give and take. **2** intermarriage (between two families/*margas,* etc.).

mengambil [and **ngambil** (*coq*)] **1** to (go) get, fetch, bring. **2** to take, withdraw. **3** to subtract. *lima diambil dua* two (subtracted) from five, five minus two. **4** to pick up (passengers, etc.). **5** take as an example. *Ambil negeri Turki.* Take Turkey, for example. *~ aci* take seriously, accept. *~ alih* to expropriate, take s.t. over; to assume (the payments on); to take charge of. *pengambil-alihan* and *pengambilan alih* expropriation, takeover, taking s.t. over. *pengambil-alihan kontrak* takeover of a contract. *~ anak* a) to adopt a child. b) (in Sumatra) marriage regulation that the wife need not leave the parents' home. *~ ancang-ancang* to get ready to do s.t. *~ angin* to get some fresh air. *~ bagian* to participate (in), take part (in), get involved (in). *~ baku piara* (*M*) to marry and live in the wife's house but the man keeps his name and inheritance rights. *~ balas* to have/take one's revenge, retaliate. *~ bandingan ke* referring/reverting to. *~ béna* to heed, care, mind, pay attention (to). *~ berat* to take s.t. seriously, take pains over. *~ buruk* to take offense. *~ campur* to meddle (in), interfere (with). *~ contoh* a) to imitate, copy. b) to copy (from). c) to take as an example. *~ di/ke/kepada hati* to take into serious consideration, take to heart. *~ foto/gambar* to take a photo/picture. *~ gampang* to take s.t. lightly. *~ gusar* to resent. *~ hak* to deprive of one's rights. *~ haluan* to determine the direction, aim, direct, go toward. *~ … halaman* to occupy/take up … pages. *~ hati* a) taking, winning, prepossessing, engaging, attractive, endearing (ways), captivating. b) to win over, curry favor with. *~ hawa sejuk* to get some fresh air. *~ ibarat;* → MENGAMBIL *contoh.* *~ ijazah* to obtain a diploma. *~ ingatan* to stamp on the mind. *~ inisiatif* to take the initiative. *~ jalan* a) to take (a certain) road, take a course. b) (to go) by way of, via; → MELALUI. *~ jalan (ke sebelah) kiri/kanan* to keep to the left/right. *~ jalan di tengah* to walk/drive in the middle of the road. *~ jalan salah* to walk/drive on the wrong side of the road. *~ kembali* to take back. *~ keputusan* to take/make a decision, decide (on). *~ kesempatan/peluang* to take advantage of the opportunity/occasion, seize/take/avail o.s. of the opportunity (to). *~ kesimpulan* to come to a conclusion. *~ keuntungan dari* to profit/benefit from, derive profit from, capitalize on. *~ kias* to draw an analogy, draw a moral. *~ langkah* a) to take a preliminary run for a jump. b) to start taking measures. *~ langkah-langkah mundur* to retreat. *~ layar* to strike sails. *~ marah* (*coq*) to get angry. *Jangan ambil marah.* Don't get angry, don't blame me. *~ menantu* to take s.o. as one's son-in-law. *~ muatan* to load, take on cargo. *~ mudah* to take s.t. lightly. *~ muka* to flatter, butter s.o. up. *~ nama dari* to take/get/derive one's name from. *~ nyawa* to kill. *~ oper* (*coq*) to take s.t. over. *~ pada* to look after, attend to (self-interest). *~ paédah dari* to profit/benefit from, take advantage of. *~ paksa* to take s.t. by force, snatch away. *~ panjang* a) to take the matter up (in court). b) to forgive/pardon mistakes. *~ pedoman* a) to use as a guideline. b) to head for. *~ peduli* (*coq*) to pay attention (to). *~ pelajaran* to learn a lesson. *~ perbandingan dari* to learn a lesson from. *~ posisi* to make/take) a stand (against). *~ prakarsa* to take the initiative. *~ pusing* to worry (over). *~ putusan* to make/take a decision, decide. *~ rantang* to order one's meals out from a restaurant or private individual; → (NG)RANTANG. *~ résiko* → MENGAMBIL *risiko. ~ ringkas/simpan/singkat* to put it briefly, shorten, condense, summarize. *~ risiko* to take the risk. *~ sempena* to benefit from. *~ sendiri* to help o.s. to (s.t. to eat or drink). *~ sikap* to adopt a position. *~ simpan/singkat* → MENGAMBIL *ringkas. ~ sumpah* to administer an oath. *~ tahu* to find out (from). *~ tanah* a) to seize land. b) (*ob*) ceremony during *Hasan Husain* feast. *~ teladan* → MENGAMBIL *contoh. ~ tempat di méja* to take a seat at the table. *~ tindakan* to take action. *~ tokoh* to recruit leading figures. *~ ujian* to take/sit for an examination. *~ untung* to benefit (from), make a profit. *~ upah* a) to work for wages. b) to accept a bribe. *~ waktu* to take time, take time off; → (ME)MAKAN *waktu.* ~ *waktu berbulan-bulan* to take months and months. *diambilnya contoh ...* he mentioned as an example ... ~ *sah saja* to consider s.t. valid. ~ *salah* to take s.t. amiss. ~ *waktu* to take the time to.

ambil-mengambil → BERAMBIL-AMBILAN.

mengambili (*pl obj*) **1** to keep taking s.t., take. **2** to nab, snatch, steal.

mengambilkan [and **ngambilin** (*J coq*)] **1** to take s.t. for s.o. ~ *adiknya kué* to take cake for his younger sibling. **2** to pass (s.t. at the table). *Tolong ambilkan gula itu.* Please pass the sugar. **3** to take (away) from. *Biaya ini diambilkan dari uang cadangan.* These charges have been taken from reserve funds.

terambil taken. *Sayang foto ini ~ kurang ke depan sedikit.* Unfortunately, this photo wasn't taken far enough forward.

ambilan 1 that which is taken. *salah ~* misunderstanding. **2** the take, receipts. **3** (*biochemical*) uptake.

pengambil taker, recruiter, maker. ~ *arus* (*elec*) contact brush. ~ *bagian* participant, partaker, participator. ~ *contoh* sampler. ~ *inisiatif* (*ob*) initiator, promoter. ~ *keputusan* decision maker. ~ *prakarsa* initiator, promoter.

pengambilan 1 intake, recruitment. **2** taking, seizure, withdrawal, retrieval, drawing. ~ *contoh* sampling. ~ *foto/gambar* a) picture taking. b) film shooting. ~ *informasi* data retrieval. ~ *jarak* establishing the proper distance. ~ *keputusan* decision making. ~ *oper* taking over. ~.~ *Pemerintah* (banking term) Government drawings. ~ *suara* a) voice recording. b) voting. ~ *sumpah* a) administering an oath. b) taking an oath. ~ *tanah* occupation of land. **3** opinion, understanding. *sepanjang ~ saya* in my opinion.

ambin I cloth used for carrying s.t. over the shoulder; strap, sling, rope, cord; string.

berambin ~ *lutut* to sit with the hands clasped in front of the knees.

mengambin to carry (a child or load) in a *sarung* slung over a shoulder.

ambinan 1 a load carried on the back. **2** knapsack, pack, satchel.

pengambin (in West Kalimantan) s.o. who carries things on the back in a *tangkin.*

ambin II sleeping platform, couch; → AMBÉN.

ambing I 1 udder. **2** mammary glands.

ambing II → OMBANG-AMBING.

ambisi (*D*) ambition.

berambisi to be ambitious, have ambitions.

ambisius (*D/E*) ambitious.

ambivalén (*D/E*) ambivalent.

ambivalénsi (*D*) ambivalence.

ambiya (*A*) (plural of *nabi*) prophets.

amblas (*J/Jv*) **1** to sink in mud, mire. **2** to disappear. **3** lost, gone, vanished. **3** totally ruined.

mengamblaskan to destroy totally.

ambleg and **amblek** (*Jv*) to give way, collapse.

ambles → AMBLAS. **amblesan** (*geol*) subsidence.

amboi 1 (exclamation of astonishment) oh! **2** terrific, fantastic. *Tubuhnya -.* She has a terrific body.

ambok ngambok arrogant, haughty.

Ambon 1 island in the central Moluccas. **2** a seaport on this island. *pisang -* the Chiquita banana.

ambong-ambong k.o. annual herb, *Bidens biternata/chinensis.*

ambrek I (*J*) **ngambrek** in a heap and unpleasant to look at.

ambrek II (*Jv*) → AMBRUK.

ambreng (*J*) **ngambreng** and **ambreng-ambrengan** (*J*) strong-smelling, can be smelled all over the place.

ambril → AMRIL.

ambrin I exhausted, all gone; → HABIS.

ambrin II (*coq*) sweetheart.

ambring-ambringan (*J*) **1** unimaginable, beyond belief, unheard of. **2** chaos, disorder, a mess.

ambrol (*Jv*) **1** to break in two, break up, collapse, burst (of dike), fall (of embankment). **2** to decline, be destroyed.

mengambrolkan to snap s.t. in two, make s.t. collapse.

ambruk (*J/Jv*) **1** to collapse, cave in. **2** to fall ill. *- lagi* to have a relapse. **3** bankrupt.

mengambrukkan to demolish, pull down.

keambrukan collapse, (down)fall.

pengambrukan demolishing, pulling down.

ambu-ambu I various species of saltwater fish resembling tuna, little tunny, *Euthynnus affinis/alletteratus, Germo sibi.*

ambu-ambu II finely ground coconut used in certain dishes.

ambuh → EMBUH.

ambul I mengambul 1 to be elastic/springy, resilient; spring. **2** to bounce (back/off), rebound, ricochet. **3** to disappear and then reappear.

mengambulkan to bounce s.t.

ambul-ambulan to bob up and down.

ambul II (*J*) **ngambul** angry and annoyed.

ambulan(s) (*E*) ambulance. *- (pengangkut) jenazah* hearse.

ambung I mengambung 1 to float up (in the air). **2** to toss up and down (of a boat).

mengambungkan 1 to toss, throw up (a ball, etc.). **2** to flatter, praise. **3** to plop/dash/bang down (with a flop). ~ *diri* to be arrogant, self-assertive.

mengambung-ambung(kan) to flatter, praise.

terambung(-ambung) 1 to float, drift about. **2** to fluctuate.

ambung II a back basket.

mengambung to carry in such a basket.

ambung III (*Jv ob*) an Indonesian-style kiss (place one's nose on s.o.'s cheek and inhale).

mengambung to kiss (in that way).

ambung-ambung a seashore shrub, beach berry, *Scaevola frutescens.*

ambur (*M*) → HAMBUR. **mengambur** to jump (into the water).

amburadul (*S*) a mess, disorganized, confused; terrible, really bad.

ambus → EMBUS.

ambyar (*Jv*) to fall apart.

ambyuk (*Jv*) **1** to swarm, flock. **2** to fall down (of a tree).

ambyur (*Jv*) to plunge into water.

AMD (*init*) [ABRI Masuk Désa] policy of having the military help in village development projects.

amdal [analisis mengenai dampak lingkungan] environmental impact analysis.

amé (*J*) → SAMA.

améba (*D*) amoeba.

amébiasis (*D*) amebiasis.

améliorasi (*D*) amelioration.

amemetri (*O Jv*) to protect the continuity of. *Ikatan - Kebudayaan Tradisional Indonésia* Union for the Protection of the Continuity of Indonesian Traditional Culture (established June 1, 1977).

amén (*A*) word uttered by beggars; → AMPUN.

ngamén 1 to beg while playing musical instruments and singing. **2** to persist like a beggar.

pengamén a singing beggar.

pengaménan singing (like a beggar).

améndemén (*D*) amendment. *mengadakan -* to amend.

améndir (*D*) **mengaméndir** to amend.

aménitas (*D*) amenity.

Amérasia (*D/E*) *anak -* Amerasian child.

Amérika (*D/E*) America. *ahli mengenai -* Americanist. *orang -* American. *- Latin* a) Latin America. b) Hispanic. *- Selatan* South America. *- Séntral* Central America. *- Serikat* [AS] the United States of America. *- Tengah* Central America. *- Utara* North America.

keamérikaan 1 Americanness. **2** Americanized.

keamérika-amérikaan Americanism.

Amérikanisasi (*D*) Americanization.

mengamérikanisasikan to Americanize.

Amérikanisme (*D*) Americanism.

amerta (*Skr*) immortal; → ANUMERTA.

ametis (*D/E*) amethyst.

amfétamin (*D/E*) amphetamine.

amfibi (*D*) **1** amphibian. **2** amphibious. *pesawat -* amphibious plane.

amfitéater (*D/E*) amphitheater.

amful → AMPUL.

ami I (*A*) 1 plentiful. 2 colloquial, not standard. *bahasa Arab yang* – nonstandard Arabic.

ami II → UMI.

amiang I (*J*) insipid, tasteless.

amiang II (*J*) to sober up, recover consciousness.

amid (*A*) dean.

amida (*D*) amide.

amien → AMIN.

amikal (*E*) amicable, friendly; → RAMAH-TAMAH.

amik-amikan (*Bal*) snacks; → NYAMIKAN.

amil I (*A*) a Muslim employee of a ward or village, a village head who records births, deaths, collects tithes, leads prayers at family parties, runs a *langgar*, etc. – *zakat* tithe collector.

amil II – *laut* a mollusk, *Fusus longissimus*.

amil III → HAMIL. ngamilin → MENGHAMILI.

amin (*A*) 1 amen! 2 so be it! *bertadah* – a) to say amen in a solemn way. b) (*ob*) to beg/ask for alms. – *yaa rabbal'alamin* (conventional end to a speech).

  beramin and mengamin to say amen, concur.

  mengamini and mengaminkan 1 to say amen (after a prayer). 2 to say yes and amen to s.t., approve of s.t.

amina (*D*) amine.

amin-amin k.o tree, *Sebastiana chamaelea*.

Aminah (Muhammad's mother) symbol of a reliable woman.

amino (*D/E*) amino.

aminoglikosida (*D*) amino glycoside.

amiotropik (*D*) amyotrophic.

amir (*A*) 1 amir, emir. 2 a title given to the Prophet Muhammad's descendants through his daughter Fatimah. 3 head of a group (of pilgrims, etc.). 4 prince. – *musafir* temporary head/leader.

amiril leader of. – *mukminin* (*A*) → AMIRULMUKMININ. – *bisy syaukah* Commander of the Faithful Muslims.

amirulbahar and amirulbahri (*A*) admiral; → LAKSAMANA.

amirulhaj and amirul haji (*A*) head/leader of a group of pilgrims bound for Saudi Arabia, etc.

amirulmukminin (*A*) Commander of the Faithful (title of the caliphs).

amis nasty smell, stinking, reeking, fetid, fishy smell.

amit I (*Pal*) pengamitan bridegroom's gift to his parents-in-law on leaving their house.

amit II (*Jv*) permission to go; → PAMIT.

amit-amit (*Jv*) 1 knock on wood, let's hope it doesn't happen, God forbid!, no way! – *jangan sampai itu terjadi pada kami.* Let's hope that doesn't happen to us. 2 I beg your pardon, excuse me (said to avoid an accusation).

amko (*ob*) k.o. *opelét*.

aml (*abbr*) [atas muka laut] above sea level.

amlas (*A*) soft.

amléng (*J?*) three-branched tool used by shoemakers.

amma (*A*) clipped form of *amma-bakdu*.

ammabakdahu and ammabakdu (*A*) and furthermore, after that, and then (in correspondence).

ammatowa (in the southern Celebes) community leader.

ammi → AMI I.

AMN [Akadémi Militér Nasional] National Military Academy.

amnésia (*D/E*) amnesia.

amnésti (*D*) amnesty. – *Internasional* Amnesty International.

amoh (*Jv*) in rags, ragged, worn out.

amoi 1 Chinese girl. 2 form of address to Chinese girls. 3 young Chinese prostitute (in Singkawang).

amok → AMUK.

amoksisilin (*D*) amoxicillin.

among (*Jv*) 1 take care of, handle, protect. – *beksa* an organization that maintains and promotes Javanese classical dancing. 2 to engage in, handle. – *tani* farmer; country person. – *usuh* education by guidance.

amonia(k) (*D/E*) ammonia.

amonium (*D*) – *sulfat* sulfate of ammonia.

Amor (*L*) Cupid.

amoral (*D/E*) amoral.

amorf (*D*) amorphous.

amortisasi (*D*) amortization.

mengamortisasikan to amortize.

amoy I (*C*) → AMOI.

Amoy II (*C*) a seaport on an island in Taiwan Strait or the island itself. *cék* – a bad check, a bounced check; → CÉK *kosong*. *si* – (reference to) garlic.

amp (*Pr*) envelope (a measure for marijuana); → AMPELOP.

ampai I (*jari* -) (rattan) scourge, lash; rod. *juran/tongkat* – divining rod (used in search of oil, etc.); → TONGKAT *peramal*.

  berampai (*M*) to hit e.o. ~ *bertinju* to hit e.o., come to blows.

  mengampai (*M*) to scourge, lash, flagellate, whip (with rattan, etc.). ~ *dengan lidi* and *memberi jari* ~ to thrash, hit.

ampai II mengampai 1 to hang on/over. 2 to hang out (to dry, of tobacco, etc.). 3 to lean (on/against). ~ *pada témbok* to lean against the wall.

  mengampaikan 1 to dry/hang out s.t. on a line in the sun. 2 to hang s.t. on a *sampiran*/coat-stand. 3 to prop (a bicycle, etc.) (against s.t.).

  terampai hung out to air, suspended. ~ *jemur* (*M*) about 8:00 a.m.

  ampaian 1 clothesline, rack. 2 suspension.

ampai III slim, slender. (*badan* -) tall and slender; → SEMAMPAI.

ampai(-ampai) jellyfish, *Scyphozoa spp*.

ampang I → GAMPANG.

ampang II (*M*) a dam, dike; → EMPANG. – *sampai ke seberang, dinding sampai ke langit* a) an irreparable break/rupture between friends. b) a job of no little importance.

ampang III (*Bat*) a large basket.

ampar I peddler; → HAMPAR. *pedagang* – peddler who spreads his wares out on a mat.

  mengampar to peddle.

ampar II (*Jv*) 1 floor. 2 (*geol*) slab.

  berampar to sit (on). ~ *di sehelai kertas koran* to sit on a newspaper.

ampas 1 waste, dregs, slag, tailing. 2 molasses. 3 feces. *memisahkan* – *dari kelapa* to separate the chaff from the wheat. *habis pati* – *dibuang* to take advantage of s.o. and then toss him away; → HABIS *manis sepah dibuang*. – *buangan* waste product. – *gabar* (*Jv*) dregs that have lost their smell. – *gandum* pollard. – *kopi* coffee grounds. – *minyak* oil waste. – *tambang* tailing. – *tebu* cane pulp, bagasse.

ampat (*coq*) → EMPAT. *si* – a rice variety, such as PB 5, PB 8, etc.

ampau → ANGPAU.

ampé (*J*) → SAMPAI.

ampéan I (*Jv*) secondary wife, concubine, common-law wife; → GUNDIK, SELIR.

ampéan II (*Jv*) hamlet, part of a *désa*.

ampek (*J*) asthma; asthmatic.

ampél (*Jv*) k.o. bamboo.

ampela (*J*) gizzard; → REMPELA.

ampelam → MEMPELAM.

ampelas → AMPLAS. mengampelas(i) to rub with sandpaper.

  pengampelas sander (the person/tool).

  pengampelasan sanding.

ampelop → AMPLOP.

Ampera I [amanat penderitaan rakyat] Message of the People's Sufferings (under President Soekarno).

ampera II and ampéra inexpensive, cheap.

ampér(e) (*D elec*) ampere.

amp(h)ibi → AMFIBI.

ampiang (*J*) tasteless, insipid.

ampik (*J*) ngampikin 1 to sweep clean. 2 to eat everything up.

ampir I (*J*) → HAMPIR.

ampir II (*Jv*) → HAMPIR. ampiran stopping off. *tempat* ~ stopping-off place, stopover.

ampitéater → AMFITÉATER.

amplas 1 1 k.o. rough-leaved fig tree, *Ficus ampelas*. 2 (leaves from this and other plants such as *Tetracera indica* used for) sandpaper.

  mengamplas(i) to (rub with) sandpaper, sand, polish.

  pengamplas 1 polisher (the person). 2 (*alat* ~) device for sand(paper)ing.

  pengamplasan ~ *kulit* dermabrasion.

amplas II (*J*) 1 dregs; → AMPAS. 2 feces; → TINJA.

amplasemén (*D*) (goods)yard. – *keréta api* railroad yard. – *langsir* shunting yard.

ampli amplifier.

amplifikasi (*D*) amplification.

amplitudo (*D*) amplitude.

amplok (*J*) seed of fruit, such as mango.

amplop (*D*) 1 envelope. 2 (*euph*) bribe (money put in an envelope); → UANG *sogok*. 3 an envelope containing about 5 grams of marijuana. *penyakit* – bribery. – *pungli* envelope containing illegal retribution.

    seamplop an envelope.

    beramplop in an envelope.

    mengamplopi, mengamplopkan [and **ngamplopin** (*J coq*)] to put s.t. in an envelope.

    amplop-amplopan to accept bribes.

    pengamplopan putting s.t. in an envelope.

ampo (*Jv*) (edible) red clay.

ampok-ampok (*J/Jv*) wall that covers the attic space under the roof.

amprah I (*J*) **ngamprah** to order or request in advance.

amprah II (*J*) **ngamprah** scattered on the ground.

amprok (*J*) – *dengan/sama* to run into s.o. unexpectedly, meet (by accident); to conflict with.

    mengamprokkan [and **ngamprokin** (*J coq*)] 1 to confront, bring face to face (such as a buyer and a seller). 2 to betroth; to marry s.o. off.

    amprokan to run into s.o., meet by accident.

amprung-amprungan (*J*) 1 always not serious. 2 always indifferent. 3 irresponsible.

ampu I 1 support, base. 2 (*mil*) cannon base.

    mengampu 1 (*cla*) to hold up by supporting the bottom with the palms of the hands, support. 2 to rule, reign over, administer (a state/kingdom, etc.).

    mengampungkan to rule over, administer.

    pengampu 1 support, prop, pillar. ~ *susu* bra; → BÉHA. 2 curator, guardian, trustee. ~ *pengawas* (*leg*) co-curator, subrogate curator. ~ *swasta* (bank) receiver.

    pengampuan guardianship, trusteeship. *ditaruh di bawah* ~ to be placed under guardianship/trusteeship.

ampu II (*M*) finger; toe; → EMPU. – *kaki* big toe. – *tangan* thumb.

ampuh I (*M*) *air* – flood.

    mengampuh(kan) to flood.

    keampuhan flooded by.

ampuh II (*Jv*) 1 efficacious, effective. 2 with supernatural power. 3 influential.

    seampuh as effective/efficacious as.

    mengampuhkan to make s.t. effective.

    keampuhan 1 effectiveness, efficiency. 2 supernatural power. 3 enormous power, potency.

ampuh III (*layar*) **pengampuh** topsail.

ampuk (*burung* –) various species of hawk owls, coppersmith barbets, puff birds, *Megalaima haemacephala indica.*

ampul I (*D*) 1 ampoule. 2 ampulla, container used in Roman Catholic church for holy oil, consecrated wine, etc. during the Mass.

ampul II (**meng)ampul** to swell out, expand (like peanuts soaked in water).

ampun 1 apology, forgiveness, pardon, excuse. 2 grace, clemency. –! Good gracious! *minta* – a) to ask forgiveness. b) (beggar's cry) have mercy! c) terrible, unbearable. *Baunya minta* –. The smell was terrible. *tanpa/tak* – mercilessly. *tidak ada* – *lagi* that was the last straw.

    berampun forgiven. *dosa tidak* ~ unmitigated evil.

    mengampuni 1 to forgive s.o. 2 to commute (a sentence).

    mengampunkan to forgive s.t.; to condone.

    terampuni pardonable. *tak* ~ unpardonable.

    terampunkan forgivable. *tak* ~ unforgivable.

    ampunan forgiveness, apology, pardon. ~ *umum* general pardon.

    keampunan 1 amnesty, pardon, forgiveness, apology. ~ *dosa* absolution. 2 reprieve.

    pengampun 1 forgiving person. 2 forgiving, pardoning.

    pengampunan 1 pardon, forgiveness, amnesty, remission, clemency. ~ *pajak* tax remission. 2 grace, absolution.

ampung → APUNG.

amput (*Jv vulg*) **mengamput** to fuck, screw. *diamput!* screw you! **amputan** 1 (*vulg*) cunt, pussy. 2 concubine.

amputasi (*D*) amputation.

    mengamputasi to amputate.

    teramputasi amputated.

    pengamputasian amputating.

amputir (*D*) **mengamputir** (*D*) → MENGAMPUTASI.

ampyang I (*J*) without its natural or customary covering. *jalan* – an unpaved road.

ampyang II (*Jv*) a delicacy containing brown sugar and ground nuts. *supermarket* – a supermarket which seems to be native-run but which belongs to nonnatives (usually Chinese); *cp* ALIBABA and BABA-ALI.

amra (*Skr*) hog-plum, *Spondias mangifera*. *mangga* – *disangka kedondong* to think that s.t. good is bad.

Amrik (*sl*) America, American.

amri → AMAR.

amril (*D*) sandpaper; → AMPLAS. *batu* – hearthstone.

    mengamril to sand, file.

amris (*A?*) gullet.

AMS (*init col*) [Algeméne Middelbare School] Upper Secondary School.

amsal (*A ob*) 1 simile(s), proverb(s), figurative language; → MISAL, UMPAMA. 2 Proverbs (in the Bible).

    beramsal having a simile. *dengan* ~ with similes.

amsiong → AMSYONG.

Amsterdam Amsterdam.

amsyong (*C J*) 1 unfortunate; bad luck. 2 broken into pieces, destroyed. 3 internal injury.

amtenar (*D col*) civil servant.

amtenarisme bureaucratic mentality.

amuba (*D*) amoeba.

amubawi amoebic.

amuh (*M*) to wish; to be willing, would like.

amuk amok, berserk.

    beramuk 1 to run amok, go berserk. 2 (*M*) to have a fight; to stab.

    mengamuk [and **ngamuk** (*coq*)] 1 to go berserk. 2 to rage; to grow worse. 3 to sweep over, knock down. ~ *hidung* to be mouthwatering (of food). *diamuk asmara* to be head over heels in love. *diamuk lindu* to be swept over by an earthquake.

    mengamukkan to incite s.o. to violence.

    amukan rage, fury; attack, spree. ~ *angin topan* raging storm. ~ *massa* fury of the mob.

    amuk-amukan knock-down, drag-out (fight).

    pengamuk person who runs amok (or, goes berserk).

    pengamukan running amok, fury, rage.

    peramukan fury, conflict.

amulét (*D*) amulet, talisman, charm.

amun → HAMUN.

amung (*Jv*) only.

    teramung only; sole; → SATU-SATUNYA, TUNGGAL.

    keamungan uniqueness.

amunisi (*D*) ammunition. – *kosong* blank cartridges. – *palsu/ tiruan* dummy ammunition.

an- I (*Gr*) prefix meaning: in-, not, without.

an II (in acronyms) → ANALISA, ANTAR, ATASAN.

ana I (*A J*) I, me. – *Muslim Sunni Syafii*. I am a Sunni Muslim of the Syafii denomination.

ana II (*Jv*) /ono/ there is; → ADA. – *dina* – *upa* (*Jv*) /ono dino ono upo/ we should not worry about tomorrow; God will provide.

anabolik (*D/E*) anabolic.

anabolisme (*D/E*) anabolism.

anaémi → ANÉMI.

anaérob (*D/E*) anaerobe.

anaérobik (*D/E*) anaerobic.

anafilaksis (*D/E*) anaphylaxis.

anafilaktik (*D/E*) anaphylactic.

anafora (*D/E*) anaphora.

anafrodisiak (*D/E*) anaphrodisiac.

anai-anai white ant; subterranean termite, *Coptotermes curvignathus*. *seperti* – *bubus* to swarm.

anak I 1 child (young human being including fetus/newborn/baby, etc.). *Seorang ibu yang sedang mengandung perlu menjaga keséhatannya supaya -nya yang di dalam kandungan juga séhat.* A pregnant woman must take care of her health so that the child still in her womb is also healthy. *- kecil yang baru dua bulan* a two-month-old baby. *-.- itu pada bermain di taman.* The children were all playing in the park. **2** s.o.'s child, offspring (including son and daughter). *- meréka kesemuanya perempuan.* All of their children are girls. **3** young of an animal; young of a plant, sapling. *- ayam* chick. *- pisang* young banana plant. **4** native (of a place). *- Jakarta* a native-born Jakartan. **5** member (of a group/certain job). *- kapal* crew member. **6** (in many compounds) smaller section of a principal object or a component part of a whole; *cp* **IBU.** *- kunci* key (of a lock). **7** (in many compounds) a small version of s.t. similar that is larger; *cp* **IBU.** *- bukit* hillock. *- baik menantu molék* to get a lot of profit. *- dipangku dilepaskan, beruk di rimba disusui/disusukan* always worrying about others rather than o.s. *- orang, - orang juga* a stranger is always a stranger. *- polah, bapak kepradah* if a child misbehaves, it's his parent's fault. *- sendiri disayangi, - tiri dibéngkéng* charity begins at home. *- seorang penaka tidak* if you have only one child, you will worry about it more. *bak - tak berbapak* like a fatherless child. *ibarat/bagai(kan) - ayam kehilangan induk* at a loss for what to do. *- Adam* a) human being. b) male person. *- adopsi* adopted/foster child. *- air* rivulet, mountain stream. *- ajaib* prodigy. *- akuan* adopted child. *alamiah (euph)* illegitimate child. *- alang* the third child (in a family). *- ali-ali* the stone thrown by a catapult/sling. *- ampang* illegitimate child. *- andaman (M)* a marriageable girl confined at home or secluded for some time before being married off. *- angin* soft breeze. *- angkat* adopted/foster child. *- angon (Jv)* boy who tends livestock, cowherd. *- angon kerbau* boy who tends water buffalo. *- angsa* gosling. *- anjing* a) puppy; → **KIRIK.** b) calf (of leg). *- asak* puppet; statue. *- asuh(an)* a) foster child. b) trainee. *- ayam* a) baby chick, poult. b) k.o. musical instrument (used in *makyung*). *- ayam umur sehari* day-old chick. *- babi* piglet, shoat, young pig. *- badung* rascal, scamp. *baduta* [bawah dua tahun] child under two years of age. *- baju* undershirt. *- balam* a couple (a man and a woman). *- balita* [bawah lima tahun] child under five years of age. *- bangsawan* a) member of the nobility. b) actor in a folk play. *- batita* [bawah tiga tahun] child under three years of age. *- batu (giling)* pestle (used in the kitchen for grinding seasonings); → **ULEKAN.** *- batu tulis* slate pencil. *- bawang* a) an insignificant person. b) a young child whom the older children take into the game but ignore; a second-class citizen. c) figurehead. *- bayi* infant in arms, nursling. *- bedil* bullet. *- belasan tahun* teenager, adolescent. *- bendungan* cofferdam. *- bengal* rascal, scoundrel. *- benua* subcontinent. *- berbakat* gifted child. *- berkundang* pampered/spoiled child. *- bermasalah* problem child. *- bersagar (M)* sickly child or one whose siblings have died. *- Betawi* a native-born Jakartan. *- bilik* small room attached to another larger room. *- bini* a) wife and child(ren). b) the entire family. *seanak-bini* with his wife and child. *- bontot (J)* the youngest child (in a family). *- brandal* rascal, scoundrel. *- buah* a) crew (member) (of a ship/airplane, etc.). b) member (of an army unit, etc.). c) group under the command of an officer, subordinates. d) employees under a superior; subordinate. e) personnel, staff. f) loyal follower, faithful adherent. *menganak-buahi* to man, staff (a ship, etc.). *- buah kapal* [ABK] (member of the) crew. *- buah pelir* epididymus. *- buangan* foundling. *- bukit* hill(ock). *- bulan* a fickle/flighty person. *- buncit* a) the youngest child (in a family). b) the last child (in a family). *- bungsu* the youngest child (in a family). *- busur* arrow. *- buyung* a) (*joc*) a pregnant woman. b) procuress, pimp. *- cabang* sub-branch. *- cacat méntal* mentally retarded child; → **TUNAGRA(H)ITA.** *- cangkokan (J)* adopted/foster child. *- catur* chess piece. *- cicit* children and grandchildren. *- corot* a child born to elderly parents. *- cucu* a) children and grandchildren. b) descendants. *- cucu Adam* descendants of Adam, mankind. *- dabus* dabus player (of Banten, West Java). *- dacin(g)* piece of metal of a specific weight used on a scale/balance. *- dagang* a)

s.o. who seeks a living abroad, foreigner. b) wanderer. *- Dalam* the *Kubus*, a primitive tribe living in the interior of South Sumatra. *- dalam perwalian* ward. *- dapat* foundling. *- dara* a) virgin, unmarried girl. b) (*coq*) bride; → **PENGANTIN** *perempuan. - dara sunti* a girl approaching puberty. *- dara tua* old maid, spinster. *- daro (M)* bride. *- daun (bio)* leaflet. *- dayung* oarsman. → **PENDAYUNG.** *- didik* a) pupil, student. b) foster child. c) juvenile offender. *menganak-didiki dirinya sendiri* to consider o.s. a pupil/student. *- domba* lamb. *- domba kecil* lambkin. *- duit* interest (on money). *- durhaka* a rebellious child. *- (e)mas* a) child bought as a slave and adopted by the master. b) a favorite child. c) favorite, a favored person. d) teacher's pet. e) Indonesian child adopted by a foreigner. *menganak-emaskan* to favor s.o., treat s.o. as a favorite. *penganakemasan* favoring s.o., treating s.o. as a favorite. *- gadis* a) virgin. b) unmarried girl. c) adolescent girl. *- gahara* a princeling (of royal parentage on both sides). *- galuh (Jv)* girl. *- gampang* illegitimate child. *- gawang* children between the ages of 9 and 15 who have been trained, *esp* in soccer to replace more senior players. *- gedanagedini (Jv)* child who has brothers and sisters (not an only child). *- gedongan* wealthy child. *- geladak/gelap* child with unknown father, illegitimate child. *- gendak* child born to one's mistress. *- genta* bell clapper. *- ginjal* adrenal gland. *- gobék* betel nut pounder. *- gondok* parathyroid. *- gugur* premature baby; stillborn child. *- gundik* child of a secondary wife. *- gunung* a) a lout; clumsy/stupid fellow; boor. b) knoll, hillock, mound. *- halal* legitimate child. *- haram (jadah)* illegitimate child. *- hasil zinah* illegitimate child. *- hilang* prodigal child. *- hitam* the eighth child (in a family). *- Indonésia* an Indonesian. *- ingusan* snotty kid, whippersnapper. *- istri* a) wife and child(ren). b) the entire family. *- jadah* illegitimate child. *- Jakarta* a (native) Jakartan, s.o. born and raised in Jakarta. *-.- jalan* street kids, urchins; → **PROKÉM 2.** *-.- jalanan* street kids. *- jari* a) finger. b) little finger, pinky. *- jawi* catamite; → **GEMBLAK.** *- jembatan* footbridge. *- jenis* subspecies. *- jenjang* ladder step. *- jentera* (wheel) spoke. *- judul* subtitle, subheading. *- kalimat (gram)* subordinate/dependent clause. *- kambing* kid. *- kandung (sendiri)* one's own flesh and blood. *- kapal* a) sailor. b) crew member. *-.- kebal* invulnerables. *- kemarin* born yesterday, inexperienced. *Dia bukan - kemarin.* He wasn't born yesterday. *- kemarin dulu/soré* born yesterday, inexperienced. *- kembar* twin. *- kembar empat* quadruplet. *- kembar lima* quintuplet. *- kembar Siam* Siamese twin. *- kembar tiga* triplet. *- kemenakan* nephew, niece. *- kencing* illegitimate child. *- keparat* accursed fellow. *- keti* small wooden ball used in certain games. *- kolak (M)* catamite. *- kolong* a) (*coq*) Army brat, soldier's child (who lives in the barracks). b) (*J*) bum living under bridges. *- komidi* member of a cast, actor. *- kompeni (coq)* a) soldier. b) term used for themselves by former Ambonese KNIL soldiers. *- kos(t)* boarder; → **INDEKSOS(T).** *- kota* a) urban child. b) satellite town. *- Krakatau* "Child of Krakatau" (in the U.S.A. called Krakatoa), i.e., the volcano that emerged from the sea in 1928 after the eruption of Krakatau in 1883. *- kualon (J)* stepchild. *- kuar* illegitimate child. *- kucing* kitten. *- kuda* a) foal. b) filly. c) colt. *- kukut* adopted/foster child. *- kunci* key (to a lock). *- kursi* rung of a chair. *- kuwalon (Jv)* stepchild. *- laki-laki* a) son. b) boy. *- latih* trainee. *- laut* arm of the sea. *- lelaki* a) son. b) boy. *- lembu* calf (the animal). *- lidah* uvula. *- limpa* a) gall bladder. b) (in some areas) bile duct. c) pancreas. *- liplap* derogatory term for Eurasian. *- lombong* mine worker. *- loncéng* bell clapper. *- luar kawin/nikah* illegitimate child. *- lumpang* pestle. *- mana?* where are you from? *- manis* spoiled child. *- manja* spoiled child. *- manusia* a) human child. b) son of man (Jesus). *- mas* → **ANAK** *emas. - masih dalam géndongan orangtuanya* infant in arms, nursling. *- mata* pupil of the eye. *- méja* table/desk drawer; → **LACI.** *- menengah* the second of three children. *- mentimun* child who is adopted and then married. *- mérah* newborn baby. *- meriam* bullet. *- muda* a) young adult/man. b) the sixth child (in a family). *- murid* pupil; school(boy/girl). *- nakal* juvenile offender. *- negara* (criminal) ward of the state. *- negeri* subject of a state, native of a country. *- neraca* weights of a scale. *- obat* a) a patient. b) sickly child raised largely on medicine. – *ontang-anting* (*Jv*) only child (without siblings). – *orang* s.o. else's child. – *orok* a baby. – *osis* senior high school student. – *pacuan* jockey; → JOKI. – *pandangan* (*Jv*) five sisters. – *panah* arrow. – *panas* child who brings bad luck. – *pancingan* → ANAK *pupuan*. – *pandak* the fifth child (in a family). – *pandawa* (*Jv*) the sons of Pandu; the five brothers who are the heroes of the Mahabharata; Yudhistira (or Puntadewa), Bima (or Bratasena, Werkudara), Arjuna (or Janaka), and the twins Nakula and Sahadewa; → PANDAWA. – *panggung* (stage) actor, player. – *panjang* the fourth child (in a family). – *panji* banner, pennant, streamer. – *partai* affiliate (of a political party). – *pasal* (budget) item. – *patung* doll. – *peliharaan* a) foster child. b) s.o. who gets special attention/treatment from a superior, favorite. – *pélor* (*ob*) bullet. – *pénak* → ANAK *pinak*. – *perahu* a) sailor. b) crew member (of a prau). – *perawan* virgin, unmarried girl. – *perempuan* a) daughter. b) girl. – *perusahaan* subsidiary (company), affiliated firm. – *pesawat terbang* air crew. – *piara* foster child. – *piatu* orphan; (in some areas) a motherless child. – *pidak pedarakan* (*Jv*) a downtrodden person; s.o. of the lowest social stratum. – *pidana* juvenile delinquent. – *pinak* descendants. **beranak-pinak 1** to have descendants. **2** to mount up (to). *Harga ini tiba-tiba ~ menjadi Rp 2.000,–.* All of a sudden the price was jacked up to Rp 2,000. c) to expand, branch out (of a company). **menganakpinakkan** to populate (a certain area) with descendants. *Médan itu bukan kota tempat suku Batak. Médan itu sudah dianakpinakkan berbagai suku, termasuk Cina dan Keling.* Medan is not a Batak town. Medan has been populated by the descendants of various ethnic groups, including Chinese and Tamils. – *pisang* a) a young banana plant (growing at the root of the mother plant). b) (*M*) name of the children in their father's *suku*, i.e., descendants in the male line of a Minangkabau family. – *prasekolah* preschooler. – *pri(y)a* a son. – *pukat* a small boat that casts sein nets. – *pungut* foster/adopted child. – *pupuan* child adopted by a childless couple. – *putih* the seventh child (in a family). – *(yang) putus sekolah* a school dropout. – *ragil* (*Jv*) the youngest child (in a family). – *raja* prince. – *rakyat* child of the common people. – *rambut* ringlet. – *remaja* adolescent, teenager. – *roda* (wheel) spoke. – *rumahan* homebody (s.o. who likes to stay at home). – *saku* a small pocket. – *sampan* (*Mal*) fisherman. – *sa(m)pi* calf (the animal). – *sanak* nephew, niece. – *sandiwara* (stage) actor, player. – *sasian* (*M*) schoolchild. – *saudara* a) nephew. b) niece. – *sekolah* schoolchild. – *semang* a) boarder. b) employee, subordinate; personnel. c) debtor. **menganak-semang** to be(come) a boarder/employee/debtor. – *semata wayang* an only child. – *sétan* a) dammit! b) you s.o.b.! – *séwa* a sublease. **menganak-séwakan** to sublet. – *singiang* imp, little devil. – *singkong* (*J*) a disadvantaged child from the inner city. – *sipil* (civil) ward of the state. – *subang* (*bot*) cormel. – *sulung* the first/oldest child (in a family). – *sulur* offshoot, sucker. – *sumbang* illegitimate child. – *sundal* a) illegitimate child. b) a strong curse: you bastard! – *sungai* tributary, affluent. *pembongkaran bangunan liar di bantaran – sungai Cisadané di wilayah Kecamatan Batucépér* the demolition of illegal buildings in the flood plain of a tributary of the Cisadane river in the Batuceper District. **menganaksungai 1** to be(come) a subsidiary. **2** to stream down (like tears/sweat/blood). – *sungsang* breech baby. – *susuan* unweaned child. – *susulan* child born to elderly parents. – *tangan* a) finger. b) apprentice. – *tangga* step of a ladder. – *tanggung* adolescent, teenager. – *tanggungan yang berwali* ward. – *tangsi* soldier's child (who lives in the barracks). – *tari* dancer. – *taruhan* favorite child. – *tekak* uvula, velum. – *telinga* a) eardrum, tympanum (of the ear). b) gristly part of the ear. – *teruna* youth. – *terlantar* neglected child. – *timangan* favorite child. – *timbangan* piece of metal of a specific weight used on a scale/balance. – *tiri* stepchild. **menganak-tirikan** and **memperanak-tirikan 1** to treat s.o. like a stepchild; to neglect. **2** to play favorites. *Jabar bagian Selatan dianaktirikan dalam pembangunan* the southern part of West Java has been neglected in the area of development. **penganak-tirian** treating s.o. like a stepchild. – *tolakan* rejected child. – *tonil* member of a cast, actor. – *torak* bobbin,

shuttle. – *tunangan* a favorite child. – *tunasosial* juvenile delinquent. – *tunggal* only child (in a family). – *turun tangga* siblings who are closely spaced in age. – *uang* interest (on money). **menganakkan** *uang* to lend money (at interest). – *ular* (young of a) snake. **menganak** *ular* to slip into line, jump the line. *Beberapa pénsiunan jatuh pingsan setelah antré berdesak-desak ~ akibat pelayanan petugas pembayaran kurang sigap.* Several retirees fainted after jostling e.o. and jumping the line because of the poor service offered by payment officials. – *umbi* (*bot*) cormel. – *usia sekolah* school-age child. – *wanita* daughter. – *wayang* member of a *wayang* performance. – *yang berangkat besar* teenager. – *yang disahkan* legitimized child. – *yang lahir dari perkawinan yang sah* legitimate child. – *yang lahir di luar nikah/kawin* child born out of wedlock. – *yang lahir di luar perkawinan yang sah* illegitimate child. – *yang terbelakang kecerdasannya* (mentally) retarded child. – *yatim* orphan; (in some areas) fatherless child. – *yatim piatu* orphan (both of whose parents are dead). – *zadah/zina* illegitimate child.

anak-anak 1 children. **2** little/small child. *mainan ~* a child's toy. **3** to still be a child. *saksinya yang masih ~* the witness who is still a child. **keanak-anakan 1** childish; to act like a child. *tabiat yang ~* a childish way of acting. **2** childlike.

beranak 1 to have a child; with a child. *~ tiga orang* to have three children. *seorang bapak ~ satu* father with one child. *keluarga ~ satu* one-child family. *~ sedikit* to have few children. **2** to give birth. *Bininya mau ~.* His wife is going to give birth. *~ tidak berbidan* to do s.t. crazy. *dukun ~* midwife. *pantang ~* birth taboos. *sakit ~* labor pains. *belum ~ sudah ditimang* to count one's chickens before they are hatched. *~ berbiak* to multiply, cause to increase in number/amount/extent/degree. *~ bercucu* a) to have children and grandchildren. b) from generation to generation. **3** together with … children. *Pak Amir ~ tiga* Amir and his three children. **4** (of money) to increase through interest. **memberanakkan** to generate money through interest.

anak-beranak husband, wife, and child(ren); accompanied by a child or by children. *kedua (orang) ~ and (orang) dua ~* one person with one child. *dia tiga ~, orang tiga ~ and ketiga ~* husband, wife and child. *empat ~* the parents and two children. *meréka ~* they and their children.

beranakkan with … children. *seorang duda yang ~ dua orang remaja putri* a widower with two marriageable daughters.

menganakkan *~ uang* to lend money at interest.

memperanakkan 1 to bear, give birth to, beget. *Siapakah yang ~ engkau ini?* Who gave birth to you? **2** to treat as one's own child. **3** to invest (money), lend money at … rate of interest. **memperanak-anakkan** to treat like a little child.

anakan 1 interest (on money). **2** doll. **3** (*Jv*) young of an animal. *~ Doberman* a Doberman pup. **4** bud on the root of some plants, tiller, seedling. *~ tumbuhan* plantlet.

anak-anakan doll, puppet. *~ mentimun* an adopted child who becomes one's wife.

peranakan 1 half-breed, half-caste. **2** Indo, i.e., a person of mixed European and Indonesian ancestry (the father must be European or an Indo himself and the mother must be an Indo or a native-born Indonesian). **3** a native of. *Jawi ~* a Tamil born in Malacca; → KELING. **4** uterus, womb. *liang ~* vagina; → P(E)RANAKAN (*Jv*).

penganak (*cla*) k.o. musical instrument.

peranak childbearing, parturition. *mendapatkan istri ~ bukan yang kosong* to get a wife who can bear children, not one who is barren.

anak II first part of some plant and animal names. – *pénak* k.o. climbing plant, *Ventilago oblongifolia*.

Anak III – *Agung* (in Bali) a caste title placed before male personal names to indicate that the person belongs to the Kshatriya caste.

anak(an)da 1 child (formal speech). **2** familiar form of address to young people.

anak(h)oda (*cla*) → NAK(H)ODA.

anakronis (*D*) → ANAKRONISTIS.

anakronisme (*D/E*) anachronism.

anakronistik (*E*) and **anakronistis** (*D*) anachronistic.

anal (*D/E*) anal.
analékta (*D*) analects.
analgésik (*D/E*) *obat* – analgesic (the remedy).
analgétika (*D*) analgesics.
analis (*D/E*) analyst. *ahli – keséhatan* medical analyst.
analisa → ANALISIS. *– dan Évaluasi* [Anév] (police terminology) analysis and evaluation. *– biaya-manfaat* cost-benefit analysis.
　menganalisa to analyze.
　teranalisa analyzed.
　penganalisa analyst. *~ politik* political analyst.
　penganalisaan analyzing.
analisir (*D*) **menganalisir** to analyze; → MENGANALISA.
analisis (*D/E*) analysis. *– ayak* screen analysis. *– luas cakup* coverage analysis. *– untaian* string analysis. *– wacana* discourse analysis.
　menganalisis to analyze.
　penganalisis analyst.
　penganalisisan analyzing.
analitik (*E*) and **analitis** (*D*) analytic.
analog (*D/E*) **menganalogkan** *... seperti ...* to draw an analogy between ... and ...
analogi (*D/E*) analogy; → RÉKABARU. *dengan mengambil – dengan, menurut –* and
　beranalogi on the analogy of, by analogy with, analogous to.
　menganalogikan *... dengan ...* to draw an analogy between ... and ...
analogis (*D*) analogic.
analuh → ANALOGI. **menganaluhkan** to make analogous.
anam I → ENAM.
anam II (*A*) mankind.
An'am (*A*) *al*– "Cattle"; name of the sixth chapter of the Koran.
anamnésa (*D*) anamnesis, patient's history taken by the doctor.
ananda → ANAK(AN)DA.
anang (*coq*) my child!
Anaprin name of a medicine for reducing fever.
anarki (*D/E*) anarchy.
anarkis (*D/E*) anarchist.
anarkisme (*D/E*) anarchism.
anarkistis (*D*) anarchistic.
anarsi → ANARKI.
anarsis → ANARKIS.
anasional (*D*) anational, not national.
anasionalis (*D*) anationalistic.
anasir (*A*) **1** element (water, fire, earth, air). **2** element (in society, etc.); → UNSUR.
anastési → ANÉSTÉSI.
anatomi (*D*) anatomy.
anatomis (*D*) anatomical.
anb. (*abbr*) [atas nama beliau] in his name, on his behalf, for.
anbar → AMBAR II.
anbia and **anbiya** (*A*) (plural of *nabi*) *al* – the prophets. *al*– "The Prophets"; name of the 21st chapter of the Koran.
anbialmursalim the 25 prophets sent by God to mankind.
anblok (*D*) en bloc, as a whole.
anca I (*M*) **1** obstacle. **2** loss, harm (resulting from a mistake, etc.). **3** handicap, disadvantage.
anca II → ANCANG.
ancah mengancahkan to destroy, annihilate.
ancai I (*M ob*) damaged, broken, destroyed.
　mengancaikan to damage, destroy, crush to bits.
ancai II neglect, disregard.
　mengancai(-ancai)kan to neglect, ignore, disregard, pay no attention to.
ancak I 1 offerings of food for evil spirits (placed in a basket). **2** k.o. rack, shelf. **3** (*M*) charm, spell. *membuang –* to provide food, etc. to evil spirits.
ancak II shelf, rack.
ancak-ancak (*M*) **1** careless, casual, indifferent to the consequences. **2** not serious, just for fun.
　mengancak-ancak 1 to fool around, do s.t. just for fun. **2** to do a futile job.
ancala (*Skr cla*) mountain.
ancam said with a threat. *–nya* he threatened.

mengancam [and **ngancam** (*coq*)] **1** to threaten, intimidate. *diancam dengan* threatened with. *diancam dengan todongan pistol* threatened with a pistol. **2** ominous, threatening. **3** (*leg*) to make liable for, make subject to, accuse of violating. *diancam dengan pasal X* subject to (violating) section X (of the criminal code).
　ancam-mengancam 1 to threaten e.o. **2** threats, threatening, blackmail.
　mengancami (*pl obj*) to threaten.
　mengancamkan to menace with, threaten with, make liable/subject to (a punishment). *hukuman yang diancamkan terhadap suatu kejahatan* the punishment for which a crime is liable.
　terancam threatened, in danger. **keterancaman** threat.
　ancaman 1 threat, menace, intimidation. *di bawah ~* under duress. *~ bahaya* threat of danger. *~ dari Utara* the threat from the North (reference to China). *dengan ~ témbakan pistol* at gunpoint. **2** punishment, penalty (for a crime). *~ hukum* penalization. *~ pidana* criminal penalty.
　ancam-ancaman threats, threatening.
　pengancam s.o. or s.t. which threatens, threat.
　pengancaman 1 threat, menace. **2** threatening, blackmail. **3** making liable for (a crime), making subject to (a provision of the penal code).
ancan (*Jv*) soil washed up from the sea; alluvial lands.
ancang (*Jv*) the distance one runs before taking a leap. *waktu –* lead time.
　ancang-ancang 1 a run (for a jump). **2** first steps, introduction. **3** preparations. **3** onset (of a syllable). (*mengambil*) *~* to make preparations.
　berancang-ancang to get ready to, make preparations for.
　mengancang-ancang 1 to take a run (for a jump). **2** to make preparations for.
　ancangan 1 approach (to a problem); → PENDEKATAN. **2** estimate; → PERKIRAAN. **3** preparation (for doing s.t.).
ancar-ancar → ANCER-ANCER.
ancelok-ancelok (*J*) jumping around; disorganized.
ancem → ANCAM.
ancémoi (*J*) snack made from coconut and cassava.
ancer-ancer (*Jv*) target, fixing (of the time/date, etc.). *– waktu kunjungan* the time set aside for a visit. *harga –* pilot price. *tanggal –* and *– tanggal* target date.
　mengancer-ancer to target, fix, set. *Pemerintah ~ daérah itu sebagai daérah transmigrasi baru.* The government is targeting that province as a new transmigration area. *diancer-ancer saja* (just) put it (down to/at), (just) mark it as about. *Diancer-ancer saja antara tahun 1830–1860.* Just put it between 1830 and 1860. *pertumbuhan yang diancer-ancer* estimated growth.
　mengancer-ancerkan *~ pada* to target for. *diancer-ancerkan selesai* targeted for completion.
ancik (*Jv*) **mengancik 1** to appear before the footlights. **2** to be on the threshhold of, be on the point of (entering/starting). *pemuda-pemuda yang akan ~ masyarakat orang déwasa* young people about to enter into adult society.
ancik-ancik (*Jv*) footstool.
ancing → HANCING.
anclep (*J*) **nganclep 1** to not return home right away. **2** to stop off somewhere.
anco (*Jv*) a large cross net.
ancoa (*C J coq*) **1** how; how are things? **2** a Chinese person.
ancol cape, peninsula.
ancuk (*Jv M vulg*) **mengancuk** [and **ngancuk** (*coq*)] to fuck, screw. *diancuk!* fuck you/it! To hell with you!
ancung → ACUNG.
ancur → HANCUR. **ngancurin** → MENGHANCURKAN.
anda I (*Skr*) *– musang* the musk gland of the civet cat.
anda II 1 you. **2** your. *–.– sekalian* all of you.
andahan transition.
andai I 1 supposition. **2** in case, if. *–kan, –pun* supposing that, let us assume. *– kata* assumption. ***perandai-kataan*** assumption.
　andai-andai supposition.
　seandainya (*jika ~*) and **andainya** suppose/supposing that, just supposing.

berandai-andai 1 to speculate, consider, weigh, think about. 2 to discuss (the possibility). 3 to seek the opinion of. 4 to take for granted.

mengandai(kan) to suppose, speculate about.

andaian assumption.

pengandaian 1 (*gram*) conditional. 2 assumption, hypothesis.

perandaian assumption.

andai II → HANDAI.

andai-andai I (*naut*) hook cleats for the stays or sheets of a boat.

andai-andai II k.o. plant, *Grewia oblongifolia*.

andak (*ob*) shortened form of *pandak*, brief, short.

mengandak(kan) 1 (~ *layar*) to reef down, take in sails. 2 (~ *belanja*) to cut down on, decrease, reduce, limit (expenses, etc.).

andakan reduction.

pengandak ropes, etc. for shortening (a sail); reef tackle.

andaka (*Skr cla*) gaur, k.o. wild buffalo, *Bos frontalis*.

andak-andak from time to time; → KADANG-KADANG.

andal I reliable, dependable; → HANDAL.

seandal as reliable as.

mengandali to have confidence in, trust.

mengandalkan [and ngandalin (*J coq*)] to rely on. *tidak bisa diandalkan* not reliable, unreliable.

terandal dependable, reliable. keterandalan dependability, reliability.

terandalkan to be relied on, can be relied on, reliable. *dukungan ~ dari* a reliable source of support from.

andalan 1 s.t. which can be depended on, mainstay. ~ *yang kokoh* firm mainstay. 2 security, guarantee, bail. *barang ~* collateral. 3 strong with magic power (of a horse, etc.). 4 reliable, dependable. *kuda ~* a horse which always wins. *orang ~* confidant. *pompa air ~* a reliable pump. keandalan reliability. ~ *diri* self-reliance.

pengandalan relying (on), reliance (on), depending (on). *mengurangi ketergantungan dan ~ pada pemerintah* reducing dependency and reliance on the government.

andal II capable, able.

keandalan capability, ability.

andal III andalan a commissioner (in the *Pramuka* Boy Scout Movement).

andal IV [analisis dampak lingkungan] environmental impact analysis.

andalas 1 name of a tree, k.o. mulberry. *Morus macroura* providing timber for poles in Sumatran houses. 2 nickname for Sumatra. *Pulau ~* Sumatra. *anak ~* a Sumatran. 3 name of a university in Padang, West Sumatra.

Andalusia (*D*) Andalusia.

andam I (*Pers*) – *surai* a) dressing of hair above the forehead. b) the hair fringe of a bride.

berandam to trim one's hair, wear hair in a fringe (of a bride).

mengandam(kan) to trim (one's hair). ~ *rambut* to trim one's hair neatly.

pengandam hairdresser.

andam II (*M*) berandam to hide.

mengandam 1 to hide, secrete. 2 to isolate, confine, lock up, seclude, segregate.

andaman isolated, secluded, kept in seclusion. *anak ~* marriageable girl (kept in seclusion); → PINGITAN.

andam III (*M*) grave. – *karam* irretrievably lost or destroyed, without hope.

andamusang musk gland of civet cat.

andan I albino.

andan II (*M*) the husband's family through a woman, or the wife's family through a man, in other words, family not through ties of blood; *opp* PESEMENDAN.

andang I rough palm-frond torch.

andang II → BELANAK *andang*.

andang-andang I (*naut*) spar, boom, yard (of a ship).

andang-andang II (*J*) mole, birthmark; → TAHI *lalat*.

andap-asor (*Jv*) humble (and courteous), self-effacing; keeping a low profile, not making o.s. stand out.

andap-gizi undernourished.

andapita (*J*) snack made from rice flour.

andapsadar subconscious (*mod*).

andar I (*Jv*) mengandarkan to tell about/explain in detail.

andaran description, circumstantial account.

andar II → BALIK *andar*, KAWIN *andar*, MATI *andar*.

andara pick up and speak, hotline delayed (a telephone service).

andarah anemia.

andarbéni (*Jv*) → HAK *andarbéni*.

andas (*M*) anvil, chopping block.

mengandaskan to use s.t. as an anvil/chopping block.

pengandas → ANDAS.

andé → ANDAI, HANDAI.

andel → ANDAL. ngandelin → MENGHANDALKAN.

andél → ANDIL.

andeng-andeng (*J*) → ANDANG-ANDANG I, II.

andépi → ANDÉWI.

anderak and anderik pitfall (to catch elephants).

anderok (*D*) slip, petticoat.

andésit (*D*) andesite.

andéwi (*D*) endive, chicory, *Cichorium endivia*.

andi I (*cla*) your/his highness (form of address to a ruler and his consort, if royal).

andi II Buginese title of nobility.

andika (*Jv*) you (to a person of rank).

mengandika (*cla*) (a person of rank) speaks.

andikara (*cla*) → ADIKARA.

andiko (*M*) penghulu – adat chief.

andil (*D*) 1 share, stock. 2 share (the part contributed by s.o.) *memberikan –nya* to make a contribution. *mempunyai/memiliki – dalam* to have a share in. *pemegang –* shareholder, stockholder. *– pendirian* founder's share.

berandil to take part, share (in).

andilau (*M*) k.o. tree, brown kurrajong, *Commersonia bartramia/echinata. tercincang/tersinggung puar, tergerak –* when s.o. is insulted, his family is also offended.

anding → BELANAK *anding*.

andir (*M*) dull, stupid; → PANDIR.

andok (*Jv*) to hang out, frequent, spend a lot of time at. *Hampir tiga hari sekali meréka – di réstoran itu.* They hang out in that restaurant about every three days. *Kalau malam Minggu, langganannya banyak yang –.* A lot of customers hang out there on Saturday night.

andon → ANDUN.

andong I (*Jv*) four-wheeled, horse-drawn carriage used as a taxi in Yogyakarta and Surakarta.

mengandong to ride in an *andong*.

andong II (*Jv*) (Hawaiian) ti plant, *Cordyline fruticosa*; → LENJUANG.

andong-andong (*Jv*) name of a *gamelan* melody.

andosan, andoseman and andosir → ÉNDOSEMÉN.

andrahi (in West Java) food a *santri* gets from home.

andrawina → ANDROWINO.

androgén (*D*) androgen.

andrologi (*D*) andrology. *dokter ahli –* andrologist.

androwino (*Jv*) 1 (official, festive) dinner, banquet; to dine. 2 recreation space. *ruang –* banquet hall.

anduh support in a sling.

menganduh(kan) to support by means of a sling. ~ *tangan* to tie a (dislocated) arm with a sling.

anduhan 1 support, prop. 2 sling, strap.

penganduh ~ *kayu* splint.

anduk (*D*) towel. – *mandi* bath towel.

menganduk to dry with a towel.

andun (*cla*) to go to.

mengandun ~ *perang* to go to war.

andung I → ANDONG II.

andung II (*M*) grandmother.

andung III (in Toba Batak) elegy, dirge.

andur buffalo cart.

ané (*J*) I, me; → ANA I.

anéh strange, odd, queer, peculiar, curious, remarkable, noteworthy. *– dibalik –* and *– bin ajaib* most remarkable, extremely strange, wonder of wonders; → BIN II. *– tak –, héran tak héran* it seems to be ambiguous. *tidak ada yang* – nothing in particular. *memandang* – to be curious about s.t.

anéhnya what is strange about s.t. *tidak ada* ~ nothing in particular. ~ *ialah* ... the strange part of it is ...

seanéh as odd/strange as.

beranéh-anéh to act strangely.

nganéh-anéhi (*Jv*) exceptional, unprecedented.

menganéhkan to be peculiar, strange, odd. *sungguh* ~ it's really strange.

anéh-anéhan an oddity.

keanéhan oddity, peculiarity, curiosity, s.t. remarkable.

anéka (*Skr* from *an* 'not' and *éka* 'one') **1** un(a)like, not the same, nonidentical, different, dissimilar; diverse, diversified; various, all kinds (of), miscellaneous, heterogeneous, assorted, variegated. **2** multi-. – *arah* multidirectional. – *arti* (*gram*) diverse meanings, polysemy. – *bahasa* multilingual. – *guna* multipurpose. – *jenis* different/various k.o., types, sorts, etc. *menganéka-jeniskan* → MENGANÉKARAGAMKAN. – *macam* various kinds/sorts/types. – *makna* ambiguous. – *muka* multifaceted. – *ragam* various, several kinds, all sorts/kinds/types. *beranéka ragam* to be varied, varying, diverse, diversified, miscellaneous. *menganéka-ragamkan* to diversify, variegate. *keanéka-ragaman* diversity. *penganéka-ragaman* diversification, varying. – *ria* various k.o. entertainment. – *ukuran* various sizes. *beranéka ukuran* of various sizes. – *usaha tani* mixed farming. – *warna* multicolor, various colors. *beranéka-warna* **1** to have various/several colors, multicolored. **2** to be varied, varying, diverse, miscellaneous. *keanéka-warnaan* a) multicoloring. b) diversity. – *warta* various news items.

beranéka various, diversified, varying, miscellaneous.

menganékakan to vary, diversify.

keanékaan diversity, heterogeneity. ~ *hayati* biodiversity.

penganékaan diversifying, diversification.

anékdote (*D*) anecdote.

anékdotik (*D*) (*secara*) – anecdotal.

anéksasi (*D*) annexation.

menganeksasi(kan) to annex.

anem → ENAM.

anémer (*D*) building contractor.

anémi (*D*) anemia.

anémon (*D/E*) anemone.

anéstési(a) (*D/E*) anesthesia, anesthesia. *ahli* – anesthetist.

anéstésiolog (*D*) anesthesiologist.

anéstésiologi (*D/E*) anesthesiology.

anfal (*D*) to have a heart attack.

Anfal II (*A*) *al-* "Spoils of War"; name of the eighth chapter of the Koran.

anfas (*A*) valuable. *tuhfatu'l-* a very valuable article (as a gift).

ang I (*M*) you (familiar).

ang II (in acronyms) → ANGKUTAN.

angabaya → ANGGABAYA.

angah (*M*) → ENGAH. *terangah* **1** tired. **2** amazed, flabbergasted (cannot say a word).

angan I **1** thought, idea, opinion, reflection, meditation, pondering, musing, contemplation, aspiration. *tidak masuk/lalu* – that's illogical. **2** (*M*) intention, purpose, aim, hope. – *lalu, paham tertumbuk* easier said than done.

angan-angan **1** thought, idea. *jalan* ~ train of thought/ideas. *sakit* ~ not quite right in the head. **2** imagination. **3** aspirations, ideals. ~*nya menjadi dokter.* He aspired to be a physician. **4** illusion, fantasy. *dalam* ~ *saja* fictitious, illusory. **5** (*M*) intention, purpose, aim, desire. *menjadi* ~ *saja* it remained an unfulfilled desire. ~ *mengikat tubuh* to look for trouble because one thinks about things too much. ~ *menerawang langit* and *menerawang di angkasa* ~ to build castles in the air. ~ *hati* heart's desire. *dimabuk* ~ crying for the moon. *panjang* ~ (*M*) (too) full of illusions. **berangan-angan 1** to meditate, ponder, muse, contemplate, daydream; → MELAMUN. **2** to dream of. *Ia tidak pernah* ~ *hidup di kota besar.* He could never have dreamed of living in a large city. **2** [= **mengangan(-angan)**] to be absorbed/lost/wrapped/buried in thought. **3** (*M*) to desire, intend, hope, wish, aim. **mengangan(-angan)kan** to picture (in one's mind), visual-

ize, envision, daydream about, dream of, aspire to, toy with the idea of, imagine, have thoughts of. **terangan-angan 1** imagined, envisioned, conceived. **2** intended, designed.

anganan 1 idea, notion. **2** reveries, daydreaming.

peranganan imagination.

angan II (*M*) **mengangan** to peer at with the head pushed forward.

angat → HANGAT.

angayemi (*Jv*) to make the household happy, i.e., the role of the husband in Javanese society.

angayomi (*Jv*) to make the household safe and stable, i.e., the role of the husband in Javanese society.

ang ciu (*C*) k.o. red Chinese liquor.

angé → HANGAT.

angék (*M*) → HANGAT. **angék-angék** ~ *tahi ayam* short-lived enthusiasm.

angél (*Jv*) difficult, hard; strange. *gampang-gampang* – *kok* seems easy but it's actually hard.

Angelsaksis (*D*) Anglo-Saxon

anget → ANGAT, HANGAT. **anget-anget** ~ *tahi ayam* short-lived enthusiasm.

ngangetin → MENGHANGATKAN.

angga antler; → BERANGGA.

berangga antlered, tined.

anggabaya (*Jv cla*) *ratu* – name of a power holder.

anggaduh (*Jv*) → HAK *anggaduh.*

anggai (*cla*) signal, sign; hint.

anggak (*Jv*) arrogant, conceited, boastful.

anggal (*Jv*) **1** slight (of illness), not serious. *Sakitnya telah* –. His sickness is no longer serious. **2** not fully occupied, free (referring to time), leisure. *masa yang* – spare time. **3** lightly laden (of boat). *perahu yang* – a lightly laden prau.

mengganggal, mengganggali and **mengganggalkan** to lighten, make s.t. light(er). ~ *muatan perahu* to lighten the boat's cargo.

anggan I (*Pal cla*) levirate (marriage).

anggan II (*M*) → ENGGAN.

anggap I think, believe, consider.

beranggap to think, believe. *Jangan* ~ *e-mail pribadi tidak dapat dibaca orang lain.* Don't think private e-mail can't be read by other people.

menganggap to consider, regard, view, suppose, believe, think, deem, take s.o. for. *Meréka* ~ *dia orang yang tidak dapat dipercaya.* They think he is an unreliable person. ~ *diri selayaknya* ... to condemn o.s. to ... ~ *énténg* to take lightly, underestimate. *Jangan* ~ *énténg lawan.* Don't underestimate your adversary. *Kalau nggak punya mobil, nggak dianggap.* Without a car you don't count for much. *apabila dianggap perlu* when (deemed) necessary, when the need arises, as (may be) required, according to requirements. ~ *rendah* to demean, downgrade. ~ *réméh* to underestimate. ~ *selayaknya* to take s.t. for granted. ~ *sepi* a) to not care about. b) to disregard, ignore, snub. ~ *wajar* to take s.t. for granted.

mengganggapi to consider, believe.

teranggap considered, believed to be.

anggapan opinion, impression, suspicion, hunch, belief, assumption. *dalam* ~ in one's imagination. *pada* ~*nya* in his opinion, to his way of thinking. ~ *dasar* basic assumption. ~ *umum* public opinion. **seanggapan** of the same opinion. **beranggapan** to be of a certain opinion.

penganggapan belief, thinking.

anggap II (*cla*) **beranggap(an)** (to dance, etc.) alternately/by turns.

beranggap-anggapan 1 to nod to e.o. **2** to bow to s.o. (to ask for a dance). ~ *minum* to drink to e.o.

menganggap to invite, ask (for a dance/to dinner).

mengganggapkan to raise/lift one's glass to.

anggapan invitation (to have a drink/to dance, etc.).

anggap III (*J*) **nganggap** to trick; to take s.t. without paying for it.

anggar I (*Pers*) – *belanja* budget. *penganggar-belanjaan* budgeting.

menganggar to calculate, estimate. ~ *belanja pésta perkawinan* to estimate the cost of the wedding.

mengganggarkan to budget. *Pemerintah* ~ *kebutuhan biaya.* The

government budgets expense needs. *uang tersebut dianggar-kan untuk* ... the money was budgeted/allocated for ...
teranggar(kan) budgeted.
anggaran 1 estimate, calculation, budget. *salah* ~ misestimated, miscalculated. ~ *belanja* budget. ~ *berimbang* balanced budget. ~ *biaya* expense budget. ~ *induk* master budget. ~ *modal* capital budget. ~ *pendapatan* revenue estimates. ~ *pendapatan dan belanja negara* state budget. ~ *perusahaan* corporate budgeting. ~ *tambahan* supplementary budget. *mata* ~ *yang menghabiskan uang* an item of loss (in a budget). *melampaui* ~ *pangkat* to live beyond one's means. **2** arrangement. ~ *dasar* [AD] a) articles of association. b) bylaws, statutes. ~ *pembangunan* project budget. ~ *pertahanan* defense budget. ~ *rumah tangga* [ART] by-laws, housekeeping rules. **3** budgeted/committed/earmarked funds, appropriation.
penganggaran budgeting.
peranggaran budgeting.
anggar II (*D*) /anggár/ main - to fence; fencing, i.e., the sport of fighting with a foil or other sword.
beranggar to fence. ~ *lidah* to argue, dispute, debate. ~ *péna* to engage in writing polemics (in newspapers), be engaged in a paper war. ~ *pikiran* to discuss, consider and argue the pros and cons.
menganggar to fence (using a weapon).
menganggarkan to fence with (a weapon).
anggar III (*D*) 1 hangar (for aircraft); → HANG(G)AR. **2** quay, wharf. **3** storage warehouse in a harbor area.
anggar IV anggar(an) perch, horizontal rod, pole, etc. in a birdcage on which birds can rest and sleep.
anggar V (*ob*) **teranggar-anggar** bumped up against everything.
anggar VI (*Jv*) belt with buckle to carry a saber, kris, or sword at one's side.
Anggara I (*Jv*) the old name for *Selasa*/Tuesday; the Sanskrit name for the planet Mars. - *kasih* a) (*S*) a Tuesday with a full moon, i.e., a lucky day. b) (*Jv*) any Tuesday *Kliwon*.
anggara II (*Skr ob*) undomesticated (of animals), wild. *satwa* - wildlife.
anggauta → ANGGOTA.
anggelan (*Jv*) terrace.
anggep → ANGGAP I.
angger fixed (of prices).
anggerék and **anggerik** → ANGGRÉK.
anggerka (*ob*) baju - long, buttoned Indian undercoat; *cp* JUBAH.
anggerung → ANGGRUNG.
anggit I fasten.
menganggit 1 to fasten (*alang-alang* grass/thatch grass, etc.) with rattan, rope, etc. **2** to stretch a piece of leather over a *gendang*, *rebana*, etc. tied up with rattan.
anggitan s.t. that has been fastened/stretched in that manner.
penganggit person who fastens/ties.
anggit II (*Jv*) design.
menganggit 1 to compose, write (poetry/a book, etc.). **2** to fabricate, invent (a story).
anggitan 1 composition, writing, essay. **2** fiction (as opposed to nonfiction); → CERITA *rékaan. bukan* ~ nonfiction. **3** concept, idea.
penganggit composer, writer.
penganggitan designing (a stage set).
angglap (*J*) → ANGLAP.
anggléng (*Jv*) boiled manioc rolled in sugar.
angglo (*J*) → ANGLO.
anggoh k.o. net for catching fish.
Anggoro the *Jv pron* of **Anggara I**.
anggota (*Skr*) 1 member (of a party/group, etc.). *calon* - aspirant member. *negara* - member nation. **2** limb, body part, member. **3** component (part). *Kata majemuk setiakawan dua* -*nya*. The compound *setiakawan* consists of two component parts. - *aktif* active member. - *biasa* rank-and-file member. - *Déwan Harian Kotapraja* alderman. - *expédite* expeditor. - *érpékad* commando; → RPKAD. - *gelap* non-card-carrying member. - *gerak* hands and feet. - *gerombolan* gangster. - *honorér* honorary member. - *kehormatan* honorary member. - *keluarga* member(s) of the fam-

ily, relative(s); → FAMILI. - *Kongrés* (U.S.) congressman. - *luar biasa* extraordinary member. - *parlemén* Member of Parliament, M.P. - *parlemén biasa* backbencher. - *pencinta* supporting-member (of the outlawed *PKI*). - *penderma* donor. - *pengganti* alternate. - *pengurus* board member, member of the committee/board. - *penuh* full member. - *perserikatan dagang* partner (in a trading corporation). - *peserta* a) associate member. b) partner (in a trading corporation); → MITRA. - *pramuka* a member of the *Pramuka* Boy Scouts. **menganggota-pramukakan** to make s.o. a member of the *Pramuka* Boy Scout Movement. - *résérse kepolisian* police plainclothesman. - *sekutu* allied member (of an association, etc.). - *Sénat* (U.S.) senator. - *serikat buruh* (trade) unionist, member of a trade union. - *tentara* soldier, military man. - *tersiar* casual member (of a political party, etc.), placed directly under the executive board). - *tetap* permanent member. - *tidak penuh* associate member.
seanggota fellow member.
beranggota 1 to have members (a party, etc.). **2** to have limbs.
beranggotakan to consist of ... members, be made up of. *komisi yang* ~ *40 orang* a 40-member commission. *anak buahnya* ~ *5 orang* with a 5-man crew.
menganggotai to become a member of (a club/association, etc.). *yang dianggotai oléh* of which ... is a member.
keanggotaan membership. *Berapa* ~*nya?* What is the membership? ~ *badan Pemerintah* government agency membership. ~ *negara* state membership.
anggrék orchid. - *bambu* kintaweed, *Arundina, spp.* - *bulan* k.o. orchid, *Phalaenopsis spp.* - *bulan raksasa* a large variety of orchid native to Kalimantan, *Phalaenopsis gigantea*. - *cakar* species of adder's mouth orchid, *Malaxis latifolia*. - *hitam* black orchid, *Coelogyne pandurata*. - *kasut* slipper plant (many species). - *kuning* yellow orchid, *Spathoglottis aurea*. - *larat* k.o. orchid with white blossoms, *Dendrobium phalaenopsis*. - *lemba* ground orchid, *Spathoglottis plicata*. - *lilin* k.o. epiphyte with white flowers, *Aerides odorata*. - *merpati* pigeon orchid, *Dendrobium crumentatum*.
penganggrékan orchid cultivation/raising.
peranggrékan orchid (*mod*).
anggrékwan orchid grower.
anggrik → ANGGRÉK.
anggrung (- *besar*) k.o. medicinal plant, charcoal tree, gunpowder tree, *Trema orientalis*.
anggu a set of s.t.; → SEPERANGKAT. - *ungkapan* (*gram*) a set of expressions.
angguk I 1 going/bobbing up and down (boats, etc.). *menurut* - *kuda* to post (on a horse). **2** a nod (with the head, indicating agreement/sleepiness). *pak/si* - a yes man, servile sycophant. - *iya* to nod in agreement. **mengangguk-mengiyakan** to nod in agreement with. - *bukan, géléng ia* to say one thing but think another. **3** pitching (of a boat).
berangguk 1 to nod in assent/approval/approvingly, bow the head, let the head fall forward. **2** to bob up and down, pitch (of a boat, etc.).
berangguk-angguk and **mengangguk-angguk** 1 to keep nodding (the head). **2** to go up and down continuously.
mengangguk and **ngangguk** → BERANGGUK.
mengangguki 1 to nod to. **2** to agree/assent to.
menganggukkan 1 to nod s.t. ~ *kepala* to nod one's head. **2** to agree to.
terangguk-angguk 1 nodding (of the head). **2** bobbing up and down (of a boat, etc.).
anggukan 1 nod (of the head). **2** nodding. **3** pitching, bobbing.
pengangguk s.o. who nods.
penganggukan nodding (the head).
angguk II (*naut*) *tali* - bobstay.
anggul beranggul and **menganggul** 1 to raise one's head. **2** (*naut*) to pitch (of a ship).
teranggul-anggul 1 to keep on raising one's head. **2** to keep on pitching, bobbing up and down.
anggun I 1 graceful, fine, elegant, sharp. **2** affected, pretentious. **3** haughty. - *halus* refined. **keanggun-halusan** refinement, elegance.

seanggun as elegant/stylish as.

memperanggun to make s.t. elegant/stylish, stylize.

keanggunan 1 grace, gracefulness, elegance, stylishness. **2** affectation, pretentiousness. **3** haughtiness.

anggun II → ANGHUN.

anggung I (*cla*) **menganggung(kan)** to lift, raise (the wings/head, etc.).

anggung II – *gaya* (*M*) confused; uncertain (what to do or which one to choose).

anggung-anggip [and **anggup-anggip** (*Mal*)] **1** up and down (motion). **2** nodding. **3** pitching (of a boat). – *bagai rumput tengah jalan* to live through hard times.

anggur I jobless, without work, unemployed.

menganggur [and **nganggur** (*coq*)] **1** to be idle/inactive/unoccupied; to be at loose ends. **2** to be unemployed, be out of work. **3** to lie idle.

menganggurkan to put out of work, make s.o. unemployed.

penganggur 1 unemployed person. ~ *terpelajar* an educated unemployed person. **2** idler, loafer.

pengangguran 1 unemployment. **2** unemployed person. *seorang* ~ *Sanusi* Sanusi, who is unemployed. ~ *terdidik* skilled unemployment. ~ *tersamar/tak kentara/terselubung/tersembunyi* disguised unemployment.

anggur II cutting, slip, scion.

menganggur 1 to take a slip from (a plant) for planting/grafting. **2** to plant (cassava, etc.) by cutting. **3** (*M*) to transplant.

anggur III (*Pers*) **1** (*pohon* –) grapevine. **2** (*buah* –) grape. **3** wine. – *apel* cider. – *beranak/bersalin* k.o. wine drunk by women who have just given birth. – *hitam* Tokay grapes. – *hijau* green grapes. – *keras* dry wine. (*buah*) – *kering* raisin. – *obat* grapefruit juice mixed with medicinal herbs.

anggur IV → ANGUR.

angguran (*J*) it would be better. – *lu ngelamun, lu bacé Qur'an.* Rather than daydream, it would be better for you to read the Koran.

anggut (*J*) → ANGGUK.

anghun (*C*) red tobacco.

angin 1 wind, breeze. **2** air. *ban* – pneumatic tire. *pintu* – porthole, vent; → PINTU *angin*. **3** flatus, breaking wind, fart. *membuang/ mengeluarkan* – to pass gas, fart. **4** rumors; unfounded news; indications, signs (of an upcoming storm/an accident, etc.). *Belum juga aku mendengar –.–nya.* I haven't heard a thing about it yet. **5** empty. *cakap* – empty talk; talk nonsense. **6** chance, opportunity, possibility. *menantikan* – *baik* to wait for a favorable opportunity. *dapat* – to get the opportunity. *tak dapat* – a) to get no chance (to). b) to get the worst of it. *berada di atas* – to prosper, thrive, flourish, be prosperous, be doing very well. *bunga* – beginning of a storm/gale; lightning or a soft breeze heralding a storm. *kabar* – rumors. *kematian* – the wind has died down. *kepala* – a) empty-headed, airhead. b) unstable, fickle (now nice, then cross). *kereta* – bicycle. *makan* – a) (*naut*) to fill with wind (of sails). b) to get some fresh air. *masuk* – → MASUK. *mata* – point of the compass. *negeri atas* – → ATAS. *negeri bawah* – Burma, Indonesia, Malaysia; *opp negeri atas* –. *perasa* – touchy, easily offended. *pistol* – air pistol. *pompa* – pneumatic tire. *rém* – air brakes. *senapan* – air rifle, BB gun. *memberikan* – to give ... the opportunity (to do s.t.). *menangkap* – to work hard with no results, be unsuccessful, fail, miss. *menggergaji* – to tack. *menjalar ke seluruh penjuru* – to spread in all directions. *menjaring* – to do s.t. useless. *menunggu* – *lalu* to wait in vain. *percaya* – *lalu* to wait for s.t. in vain. – *berputar, ombak bersabung* most difficult (of a case). *tahu di* – *berkisar* to know the capricious humor of people. *tahu di* – *turun naik* to see it coming. *kagak/nggak hujan kagak/nggak* – and *tanpa* – *tanpa hujan* and *nggak ada* – *nggak ada hujan* out of the clear blue sky. *ke mana* – *yang deras, ke situ condongnya* he will turn with every wind that blows. – *atas* wind in the stratosphere. – *badai* storm, gale, hurricane. – *baik* luck, good fortune. – *barat* west wind, westerlies. – *beliung* whirlwind, cyclone. – *beralih* shifting wind. – *berbalik* backing wind. – *bidai* steady wind from a certain direction. – *bohorok* (in the area of Deli, North Sumatra) foehn. – *brubu* (in the area of South Sulawesi) foehn.

– *buritan* tail/following wind. – *buruk* flatulence/gas that causes a stomachache. – *busuk* fart. – *darat* land breeze, offshore wind/breeze. – *desir* breeze. – *dingin semilir* soft, cool breeze. – *duduk* (*Jv coq*) a) to drop dead. b) to have a heart attack. c) a persistent cold. – *ékor duyung* wind coming from several directions. – *gending* (in the areas of Pasuruan and Probolinggo, East Java) foehn. – *gila* wind from all directions. – *gunung* landward breeze. – *gunung-gunungan* a big storm. – *haluan* head wind. – *hantu* a stroke, i.e., a sudden attack of a disease or illness, *esp* of apoplexy or paralysis. – *hembusan* breeze. – *indera bayu* typhoon. – *jahat* evil wind (that causes colds, etc.). – *jujut* draft. – *kelambu menunggal* north wind that brings rain. – *kelambu sebelah* north wind that doesn't bring rain. – *kencang* strong wind, stiff breeze . – *kepala* north-northeast wind. – *kisar* whirlwind, cyclone. – *kuat tiba-tiba* a gust. – *kumbang* (in the areas of Cirebon and Tegal) foehn. – *lalu* a) a draft. b) passing, temporary. c) rumors. – *lambung* beam wind. – *langkisau* whirlwind. – *laut* sea breeze, on-shore wind/breeze. – *lesus* (*Jv*) whirlwind, cyclone. – *limbubu* whirlwind; → HALIMBUBU. – *mati* calm, dead wind, doldrums. – *membakat* tailwind with high waves. – *mengiri* backing wind. – *menumbuk kurung* → ANGIN *membakat.* – *mumbul* updraft. – *musim* seasonable wind. – *paksa* favorable wind for sailing. – *pancaroba* shifting, changeable wind (characteristic of the transition between seasons). – *pasat* trade wind. – *pengarak pagi* morning wind. – *perkisaran* changing wind. – *puyuh/puting beliung* whirlwind, cyclone, tornado. – *ribut* storm, typhoon. – *sakal* head wind. – *salah* ill wind. – *samirana* a soft breeze. – *sapu-sapu* soft breeze. – *selatan* south wind. – *selembubu* whirlwind; → HALIMBUBU. – *semilir* soft breeze. – *sendalu* moderate wind. – *sepoi-sepoi* (*basah*) soft breeze. – *sérong buritan* tailwind. – *silang* crosswind. – *silir/siliran* soft breeze. – *sorong buritan* tail/following wind. – *sulit* hard times. – *taifan* and – *taufun* → ANGIN *topan.* – *tegang kelat* a strong wind. – *tembérang buritan/ haluan* following wind. – *tenggara mandi* swift southeast wind accompanied by waves and fog. – *tikus* wind at the beginning of the southeast wind. – *timba ruang* wind abeam, strong sidewind. – *timur* east wind, easterlies. – *timuran* easterly. – *topan* typhoon. – *tumbuk kuning* → ANGIN *membakat.* – *turun naik* intermittent wind. – *turutan* tail/following wind. – *umum* prevailing wind. – *utara* north wind. – *wambrau* (in Irian Jaya and on the island of Biak) foehn. – *yahun* → ANGIN *membakat.*

seangin a (little) bit.

berangin 1 airy, breezy, windy. *Hari ini tak* ~. It's not windy today. **2** there are indications, something turns up. *Akhirnya perkara pembunuhan* ~. Finally, something turned up on the murder case.

berangin-angin to get some fresh air. *Para penghuni rumah tahanan itu makan dan* ~ *sekitar pukul 15.00.* The prisoners eat and get some fresh air about three in the afternoon.

mengangin 1 to vanish into thin air. **2** to blow (of wind). ~ *padi* (*M*) to winnow rice.

menganginti to air, let air pass through; to fan; to spread (rumors, etc.).

mengangin(-angin)kan 1 to put out to dry in a windy place, expose to the air. **2** to send out feelers, allude to, hint at, make reference to s.t. *Dia* ~ *uang sogok.* He sent out feelers about a bribe.

memperanginkan to air, give an airing to, put out in the wind.

terangin 1 exposed to air. **2** it was to be foreseen, it was in the cards.

terangin-angin it is rumored. ~ *kabar, bahwa ...* rumors are/ have it that ... ~ *ke telinga* has/have come to one's attention.

angin-anginan 1 quick-tempered, easily angered. **2** whimsical, fickle, unpredictable, capricious. *bekerja* ~ to work in spurts.

keanginan 1 to be exposed to (or, affected by) the wind; windblown. **2** rumored about (news). **3** to become sick (of a child).

penganginan aeration, airing.

peranginan 1 (*anjung* ~) an airy room. **2** (*rumah* ~) (*ob*) bungalow, vacation cottage. **3** ventilation. ~ *silang* cross-ventilation. **4** balcony.

angina (*D*) angina.

Anging Mammiri an old name for Ujungpandang/Makassar.

angit smell of burnt rice. *memberi –* (*M*) to shame s.o.

angka I (*Skr*) **1** digit, (numerical) figure, number, numeral. *dengan – numerical*, in numbers. **2** mark, grade. *–nya matématika* his math grades. **3** grade level, class. *sekolah – loro →* SEKOLAH *ongko loro*. **4** rate, ratio. **5** dial. **6** points. *menang dengan –* to win on points. *mengalahkan dengan –* to win on points. *déprésiasi 3 –* a depreciation of three points. **7** line (in a tax form, etc.). **8** tails (of a flipped coin); *cp* GAMBAR. *– Arab* Arabic numerals (1, 2, etc.). *– beban ketergantungan* dependency ratio. *– bersusun* compound number. *– bias* refraction index. *– biasa* Arabic numerals. *– bulat* round number. *– dua* superscript 2, i.e., the symbol 2 used before the introduction of EYD to indicate reduplication of the preceding element, e.g. *orang^2 = orang-orang, ber-cakar^2 an = bercakar-cakaran*. *– ganjil/gasal* odd/uneven number. *– genap* even number. *– gugur* (school) drop-out rate. *– halaman* page number. *– huruf* alphanumerical. *– indéks* index number/figure. *– inflasi* inflation rate. *– jatuh* failing grade. *– keberaksaraan* literacy rate. *– keberuntungan* lucky number. *– kecerdasan* IQ. *– kegagalan* failure rate (of college students). *– kejahatan* crime rate. *– kelahiran* a) birth rate. b) number of births. *– kematian* a) death rate. b) number of deaths. *– kematian bayi* infant mortality rate. *– keniraksaraan* illiteracy rate. *– kepadatan* (population) density rate. *– krédit* credit points (in university). *– kriminalitas* crime rate. *– lémpéng total* total plate count, TPC. *– mati* failing grade (in schools). *– oktana* octane number. *– pandai* school grades. *– pecahan* fraction. *– pelengkap* complement. *– pengenal ékspor* export identification number [APE]. *– penghunian* occupancy rate (in a hotel). *– penuh* whole number (not a fraction), integer. *– penunjuk* index number. *– penyabunan* saponification number. *– permautan* death rate. *– putus sekolah* dropout rate. *– Romawi/Rumawi* Roman numerals. *– selamat* survival rate. *– setana* cetane number. *– sial* unlucky number. *– tanggungan* dependency ratio. *– tebal* boldface. *– tengah* median. *– tipis* narrow margin. *– tunjuk* index number. *– urut* serial number. *– utuh* whole number.

angka-angka 1 figures. *berhitung ~* to cipher. *kemampuan ~* numeracy. *~ bersusun* complex numbers. **2** → PERANGKAAN.

berangka to have a number, be numbered/indexed. *~ tahun* dated ... (with the year) ...

mengangkakan 1 to mark, number, provide s.t. with numbers, make s.t. systematic. *~ buku* to number books (in a library). *~ jumlah itu* to express these totals in numbers. **2** to rate, give a rating to. **3** to grade (exams, etc.).

memperangkakan to treat as numbers.

pengangkaan (the act of) numbering, enumerating, marking, rating, etc.

perangkaan statistics. *~ statistik* statistical figures.

angka II berangka-angka(an) and **mengangka** to think, suppose, believe, consider, deem; → SANGKA.

angkak red food coloring made by fermenting rice with monascus red, *Monascus purpureus*.

angkal-angkal black-shouldered kite, swallow-tailed kite, *Elamus caeruleus*.

angkang rickshaw.

angkar → ANGKER.

angkara (*Skr*) **1** greedy, covetous, selfish. *si –* the glutton. **2** cruel, furious, savage. **3** (*cla*) insolent, violent (*esp* towards a woman). **4** egotistical, self-centered. *hina –* very low and rude, uneducated, impertinent, conceited. **5** wild (of an animal). *– murka* greedy, voracious, covetous. **berangkara-murka** to be voracious, covetous, greedy, cruel. **keangkara-murkaan 1** greed, avarice, covetousness, selfishness. **2** cruelty, wildness, fury, savagery. **3** insolence, violence, impertinence.

keangkaraan 1 cruelty, brutality. **2** rudeness. **3** greediness, selfishness.

angkasa (*Skr*) **1** space. **2** atmosphere. **3** air. **4** sky, firmament, heavens. **5** region of the air that surrounds the earth. **6** celestial. *benda –* celestial object. *– luar* outer space. *– terbuka* open skies.

mengangkasa 1 to fly up in the air. **2** to take off (of aircraft); → LEPAS *landas*. **3** to come to the fore. *~ luar* to go into outer space.

mengangkasakan to develop s.t. to the fullest.

keangkasaan *~ luar* outer space.

angkasawan (*Skr neo*) **1** (male) astronaut. **2** (male) radio announcer.

angkasawati (*Skr neo*) **1** (female) astronaut. **2** (female) radio announcer.

angkat I take, pick up and take away. *– saja* just take it. *– barang, Tuan?* Take your bag, sir? *– méja* to clear the table.

seangkatan to lift s.t. one time.

mengangkat [and **ngangkat** (*coq*)] **1** to lift (up), raise (up), hold up. *pria dengan tangannya diangkat* the man with upraised arms. *~ alis/kening* to frown (as a sign of astonishment/amazement/surprise. *~ bahu* to shrug one's shoulders (expressing ignorance of s.t.). *~ beban* to lift weights. *~ besi* weight lifting. *~ bis* to collect letters (from the mailbox). *~ citra* to elevate one's image. *~ diri* to be arrogant. *~ ékor* to flee, run away. *~ gagang télepon* to answer the phone. *~ gelas* to toast. *~ hidangan* a) to serve food. b) to clear the table. *~ jangkar* to raise anchor. *~ jari* to raise one's thumb, make the thumbs-up sign. *~ kaki* a) to go away, depart, leave. b) to disappear. *~ kening* to knit one's brows. *~ koper* a) to pick up a suitcase. b) to clear out, leave. *~ langkah seribu* to run away as fast as possible. *~ makanan* a) to serve food. b) to clear the table. *~ mata* a) to raise one's eyes. b) to wink, blink. *~ nama* to make s.o. well-known. *~ pamor* to add luster to. *~ pantat* to clear out fast. *~ pundak* to shrug one's shoulders. *~ rumput* to weed. *~ sembah* to raise one's folded hands in homage. *~ senjata* a) to present arms. b) to take up arms. *~ sumpah* to take an oath, swear. *~ tabik* a) to greet by raising one's hands. b) to surrender. *~ tangan* a) to hold up both hands as a sign of surrender. b) to hold up one's hand to show that one is present or to answer a teacher's question. c) to defer (to), kowtow (to). d) to hold up one's hands as a sign that one is unable to do s.t. *~ tepuk* to applaud. *~ topi* a) to take off one's hat. b) to pay one's respects to, take one's hat off (to). **2** to take away, remove. *~ payudara* to remove a breast. **3** (*leg*) to lift, remove. *~ penangguhan* to lift a stay. to take/carry away. *Barang-barangnya sudah diangkat ke stasiun*. His things have been taken to the station. **5** to clear away. *~ makanan* to clear the table.

ngangkat (*coq*) → MENGANGKAT. *tukang ~* a thief.

mengangkat-angkat 1 to praise (to the skies), extol. **2** to coax, wheedle, flatter.

mengangkati (*pl obj*) to lift, carry.

mengangkatkan [and **ngangkatin** (*J coq*)] **1** to hold/lift up for. *Tolong angkatkan sepéda itu*. Pick up that bike (for me), please. **2** (*ob*) → MENGANGKAT. **3** to roll up (one's sleeves). *~ topinya akan memberi hormat* to take one's hat off (to).

terangkat 1 lifted, raised. *~nya* (*geol*) uplift. **2** can be lifted/raised. *~ kening* about 7:30–8:00 a.m. *belum ~ kening* before 7:00 a.m. **3** (*cla*) stretcher or hearse. **4** come up (for discussion), arise. *Barangkali soal potrét keluarga takkan pernah ~*. Maybe the question of a family portrait wouldn't ever come up.

angkatan 1 weight that can be lifted, burden. **2** (*coq*) s.o. who likes to be praised. *~ jempol* thumbs up (as a sign of approval).

angkat-angkatan to play at lifting.

pengangkat 1 device for lifting/carrying s.t., elevator (in some compounds). *~ pipa* casing elevator. **2** carrier, lifter. *~ sampah* garbage collector. **3** support. **4** (*coq*) flatterer, s.o. who likes to flatter.

pengangkatan 1 removal, picking up and taking away. *~ bis* letter pickup (by mailman). *~ kerangka kapal* and *~ kapal-kapal yang tenggelam* salvage. **2** (*geol*) (*~ daratan*) uplift. **3** adoption (of a child). **4** taking (an oath).

angkat II (*infr*) generation.

seangkat of the same generation. *~ siapa?* In whose generation?

angkatan 1 a group of people constituting a movement, generation, cohort. *~ muda* youth, the younger generation. *~ tua* the older generation. *~ '08* the generation of 1908 during which Budi Utomo was founded. *~ '29* the generation of 1929 during which the *sumpah pemuda* was created. *~ '45* a) the freedom generation, i.e., those who spearheaded the proclamation of

Indonesian independence on August 17, 1945. b) the group of authors and artists who emerged around 1945. ~ '66 the generation of '66, i.e., the students and youth who participated in or sympathized with the struggles that took place between 1965 and 1967; all those who were involved in these struggles. 2 expeditionary force. ~ *kelima* PKI idea of establishing a new armed force of peasants and workers. ~ *ke Timur Tengah* the expeditionary force to the Middle East. 3 class, i.e., a group of students graduating together. ~ *1988* the class of 1988. 4 any organized group of people, armed as well as unarmed, i.e., the armed forces, police force, work force, etc. 5 armed forces. ~ *Bersenjata Républik Indonésia* [ABRI and Abri] Armed Forces of the Republic of Indonesia. ~ *Angkawasan* (*poet*) Air Force. ~ *Bahari* (*poet*) Navy. ~ *Bhumiyam* (*poet*) Army. ~ *Darat* [AD] Army. ~ *Darulharab* (in Aceh) the generation preceding the ~ *Darussalam* born during the violent and turbulent political period. ~ *Darussalam* (in Aceh) the generation born at the same time that the Achehnese reconciled with the government of the Republic of Indonesia and became the *Daérah Istiméwa Acéh* [DISTA] or Aceh Special Region on May 26, 1959. ~ *kelima* a) fifth column, i.e., any group of people who aid the enemy from within their own country. b) (*PKI* jargon) fifth force, i.e., the armed workers and peasants to counterbalance the official armed forces. ~ *gabungan* unified command. ~ *Kepolisian* (*ob*) Police Force. ~ *kerja* work force. ~ *Laut* [AL] Navy. **ke-Angkat-lautan** naval (*mod*). ~ *pendidikan* class (in a military academy). ~ *pendobrak* → ANGKATAN '45. ~ *penegas* "the resolute generation," i.e., those who participated in the Second Youth Congress of 1928 and who created the *Sumpah Pemuda* ("Youth Pledge"). ~ *penerus* the force that is to replace the preceding one. ~ *Perang* Armed/Fighting Forces. ~ *perintis* "the pioneering generation," i.e., those who joined or sympathized with the ideas and aspirations of Budi Utomo in 1908. ~ *Udara* [AU] Air Force. **seangkatan 1** of the same generation. 2 of the same (air, naval, etc.) force.

perangkatan (*ob*) generation.

angkat III adopted, adoptive, foster. *anak* – adopted child. *bapak/ibu* – adoptive/foster father/mother. *orangtua* – a) adoptive/foster parents. b) host parents.

mengangkat 1 to appoint, nominate; to promote. *Ia diangkat (men)jadi walikota.* He was appointed mayor. *Léktor Madya itu diangkat (men)jadi Léktor Kepala.* The middle-level lecturer was promoted to senior lecturer. 2 to adopt. ~ *anak* to adopt a child. *Ia sudah diangkat saudara.* He was acknowledged as (s.o.'s) brother.

angkatan nomination. *surat* ~ → SURAT *pengangkatan.* ~ *negara* state appointees.

keangkatan appointment to a position.

pengangkatan appointment, nomination (to a position). ~ *beliau sebagai duta besar* his appointment as ambassador. *surat* ~ letter of appointment.

angkat IV to begin, start, commence, set about. – *bicara* a) to begin to speak, take the floor. b) to address Parliament. – *suara* to begin to speak.

berangkat 1 to begin to walk/go/leave/depart/travel, etc., start to. *Pukul berapa Anda* ~ *dari sini?* What time are you leaving here? ~ *dari kenyataan itu* starting from reality/those facts. *sebuah términal untuk yang* ~ a check-in terminal (for passengers, at an airport). *telah* ~ *déwasa* ~ *berperang* to go to war. 2 to begin to become (large/grown up, etc.). *telah* ~ *déwasa* to grow up, be a (wo)man. *sudah* ~ *remaja* to enter one's teens, come of age. ~ *tidur* to go to bed. ~ *kerja* to go to/leave for work. **memberangkatkan 1** to dispatch, move, send (off), transport (troops, etc.) to. 2 to give the departure signal (to a train). **keberangkatan** departure. **pemberangkatan** sending off, dispatch(ing). *pelabuhan* ~ port of departure.

mengangkat (to begin) to do/state, etc. s.t. ~ *nyanyiannya masing-masing* to start their respective songs.

angkat-angkatan preparation for war (in Balinese *wayang*).

keangkatan departure. *mempersiapkan* ~ *Pak Sastro* to make preparations for Pak Sastro's departure.

angkat V angkatan dress, clothes, clothing, apparel *esp* as suitable for certain occasions. *pakaian* ~ a) state robes, gala dress. b) Sunday best. c) pilgrim's attire.

perangkat 1 means, measures. 2 device, instrument. 3 set (of instruments). ~ *para pegawai negeri* ~ *kelurahan* all the government employees of the *kelurahan*. ~ *keras/lunak* hard/software. ~ *peledak* explosive device. ~ *radio* radio set. ~ *roda* bogie. **seperangkat 1** suite (of furniture), set, suit (of clothes). ~ *alat makan* a dinner set. ~ *alat minum* tea set. ~ *kursi rotan* five-piece living-room set consisting of a table and four rattan chairs. ~ *peranti baru* a new set of equipment. ~ *peraturan* a set of regulations. ~ *radio pemancar dua arah* transceiver, two-way radio. ~ *surat dividén* coupon sheet (attached to a bond; each coupon is presented for payment at the proper time). ~ *undang-undang* a set of laws. 2 (*ob*) a group, a (*gamelan*, etc.) orchestra. 3 ensemble. 4 a lot of, many. **perangkatan 1** equipment, outfit, paraphernalia. ~ *adat* the paraphernalia relevant to the performance of *adat* observances. 2 retinue (of high dignitaries).

angkau → ENGKAU.

angkél (*D coq*) money given to a new recruit/soldier. 2 to renew a contract.

angkelung → ANGKLUNG.

angker I (*S*) fiery, quick, intrepid.

angker II (*Jv*) 1 sacred, holy; haunted, bewitched; ghost (*mod*). *tempat yang* – a haunted place. 2 forbidding, unapproachable, cannot be entered/touched by anybody, such as a tree, etc. which has some magic power; inhabited by demons. 3 dangerous (because enchanted); sinister. 4 quiet, dignified, held in awe and respect. 5 (*J*) strong. 6 terrible, awful, frightening.

seangker as holy/awesome as.

keangkeran 1 holiness, sacredness. 2 awfulness, eeriness. 3 awesomeness. 4 unapproachableness.

angker III (*D*) 1 anchor; → JANGKAR. 2 rotor, armature.

angkét (*D*) inquiry, questionnaire. *hak* – right to (institute an) inquiry.

mengangkét to make an inquiry into.

angkil → ANGKÉL.

angkin (*C J*) sash made of cloth with a money pocket, worn by women market sellers.

angkit mengangkit 1 to lift a light object. 2 to lift hot pans or coals from the fire.

angklung I (*Jv*) a musical instrument consisting of a large frame on which are arrayed a number of double bamboo tubes of varying lengths and diameters which are shaken to make the music.

angklung II *burung* – chestnut-backed scimitar babbler, *Pomatorhinus montanus*.

Angkola-Mandailing a subgroup of the Batak ethnic group.

angkong I (*C ob*) k.o. two-wheeled rickshaw.

angkong II (*C J*) k.o. gambling game played with three cards.

angkong-angkong (*J*) to sit around idly and not work.

angkop (*J*) → TELUNGKUP.

angkot [*angkutan kota*] urban transportation.

Angkota → ANGKUTA.

angkrang → SEMUT *rangrang*.

angkrék → ANGGRÉK.

angkring (*Jv*) **angkring(an)** a long pole with baskets at either end carried horizontally on one shoulder; → PIKUL(AN).

angku 1 (in the Minangkabau area) form of address to maternal uncle. 2 grandfather. 3 epithet for respected persons; → ENGKU. – *palo* (in the Minangkabau area) village head.

angkudés [*angkutan pedésaan*] village public transportation.

angkuh I arrogant, conceited, haughty, proud.

seangkuh as arrogant as.

keangkuhan arrogance, conceit, haughtiness, pride.

angkuh II (*M*) appearance, look, form. *salah* – improper, unseemly, indecent. – *terbawa, tampan tinggal* all is not gold that glitters.

angkuk (*ob*) figurehead on native boat.

angkul-angkul (*Jv*) yoke for oxen.

angkup I (*sepit* -) tweezers, pincers.

angkup-angkup 1 valve. 2 (~ *besi*) tweezers, pincers.

mengangkup to hold with tweezers/pincers, pinch.

mengangkupkan ~ *jari* to make one's fingers into pincers for holding s.t.

terangkup-angkup opening and closing repeatedly (like the beak of a dying bird or the mouth of old people).

angkup II (*Jv*) sheath of an unopened leaf or flower bud of the jackfruit.

angkup-angkup k.o. tree, *Commersonia platyphylla*.

angkur (*J/Jv*) 1 forked implement or large spike for strengthening house construction. 2 armature.

angkus(a) (*Skr*) k.o. elephant goad.

angkut transport, transportation, shipping. *satu kali* – one haul.

mengangkut [and ngangkut (*coq*)] 1 to lift (heavy objects) one by one/piece by piece and carry them away. 2 to transport, convey, carry away. *Burung* ~ *sarang.* The bird carries (sprigs or grass to build) a nest. 3 to collect, gather. ~ *sampah* to collect the garbage/trash. ~ *nanah* to come to a head (of boils), suppurate. *Bengkak* ~ *darah.* The swelling contains blood.

mengangkuti [and ngangkutin (*J coq*)] (*pl obj*) to pick up, collect (garbage, etc.), lift.

mengangkutkan → MENGANGKUT.

terangkut can be transported (by).

angkutan 1 transport(ation), haulage; → PENGANGKUTAN. ~ *kelas I* trains. ~ *kelas II* buses. ~ *kelas III* taxis. ~ *kelas IV* hélicaks, *bémos, minicars* and *bajajs.* ~ *air* waterborne transport. ~ *bandar* port/harbor transport. ~ *jalan raya* highway transport. ~ *keréta api* rail transport. ~ *kota* [angkot] city/urban transportation. ~ *laut* sea transport. ~ *lintas udara* airlift. ~ *pedésaan* [angkudés] village transportation. ~ *penyeberangan* ferryboat transport. ~ *sungai* river transport. ~ *udara* air transport. ~ *udara besar-besaran* airlift. ~ *umum* public transport(ation). ~ *umum formal* buses. ~ *umum informal* transportation by *hondas, bémos,* etc. 2 freight, carriage, load. ~ *pos* mail pickup.

pengangkut 1 porter, carrier, transporter. ~ *barang* longshoreman. 2 means of conveyance, truck, van, wagon, etc. *kapal* ~ *(barang)* freighter.

pengangkutan transportation, shipping. ~ *antarpulau* interisland shipping/transportation. ~ *barang* transportation of goods. ~ *léwat/lintas udara* airlift. ~ *terus* transit.

perangkutan transport(ation).

Angkuta [Angkutan Kota] small vehicle transportation system in small urban centers.

angkut-angkut mason bee, eumenid wasp, *Eumenidae.*

anglap (*J*) menganglap [and nganglap (*coq*)] 1 to embezzle, steal (money/items, etc.). 2 not to want to pay one's debts, default on one's debts.

penganglapan embezzling.

angler I (*S*) 1 to finish. 2 finished.

angler II (*Jv*) pleasant, smooth; quiet, tranquil (of a kite in the air).

angler-anglernya *Lagi* ~ *tidur.* He is sound asleep.

angler-angleran calm, content.

Anglikan (*D*) Anglican. *kaum* – Anglicans.

angling-anglingan various species of small bushes, carnations, the *Caryophyllaceae* family of plants.

Anglir Mendung (*Jv*) name of a dance performed by four girls.

Anglisisme (*D*) Anglicism.

anglo (*C*) charcoal brazier. – *listrik* a) electric stove. b) hot plate. – *pedupaan* covered incense burner.

anglong I (*J*) nganglong to talk confusedly.

anglong II and anglung (*C ob*) pavilion, summer house.

angmor [angkutan bermotor] motorized transport.

angob (*Jv*) → ANGOP.

Angola Angola.

angomahi (*Jv*) to make a proper household for the family and provide social status, i.e., one of the roles of the Javanese husband.

angon (*Jv*) shepherd, herdsman. *bocah* – *kerbau* boy who tends the water buffalo. *bocah/tukang* – shepherd, herdsman.

mengangon(kan) to herd, tend (livestock); to graze.

angonan 1 cattle, livestock. 2 s.t. herded/tended.

pengangon boy who tends livestock, shepherd.

pengangonan 1 shepherding. 2 place where animals are taken for grazing and bathing.

angop (*J/Jv*) 1 a yawn. 2 to yawn.

angot (*J*) 1 recurring (of a disease). 2 to recur. 3 to skyrocket. 4 to talk nonsense, act somewhat crazy.

angot-angotan 1 recurrent. 2 to talk nonsense.

angpau (*C*) Chinese red paper (in which money is wrapped for children during *Imlék* celebration), alms, present.

angsa I *Skr*) goose, *Anser ferus.* – *batu* booby, *Sula spp.* – *laut* brown booby, *Sula leucogaster.* – *undan* swan, *Cygnus spp.*

angsa II [angkutan désa] village transportation.

angsana (*Skr*) (– *kembang*) k.o. tree with yellow flowers and good timber, Burmese rosewood, *Pterocarpus indicus.* – *keling* → SONOKELING.

angsang (*J/Jv*) gills.

mengangsangi 1 to clean the gills. 2 to beat.

angseg and angsek (*J/Jv*) mengangseg [and ngangseg (*coq*)] to press, urge, insist.

angséna → ANGSANA.

angsiau and angsio (*C*) red-braised cooking.

angso (*C?*) k.o. tree sap.

angsoka (*Skr*) the sacred flowering tree, *Pavetta indica,* in India, under which Buddha was born.

angsong (*J*) ngangsongin to hand s.o. s.t., thrust s.t. on s.o.; → ASONG.

angsu (*Jv*) – *kawruh* to seek out learning.

mengangsu [and ngangsu (*coq*)] 1 to gain knowledge. 2 to draw water. 3 to draw upon s.t., absorb.

angsung → ANGSONG.

angsur – *lesap* fade-out. – *timbul* fade-in.

berangsur 1 gradually (grew more or less); slowly (decreased or increased); (to pay off) little by little, a little at a time, bit by bit, in installments. ~ *baik* to improve slowly. ~ *sembuh* to be getting better gradually. 2 to move on, get up (from). *Ia* ~ *dari duduknya.* He got up from his seat. *tidak* ~ *lagi dari tempatnya* did not move (a muscle). ~ *ke depan* to move forward.

berangsur-angsur gradually, little by little, in installments.

mengangsur [and ngangsur (*coq*)] 1 to do s.t. gradually; to pay for s.t. in installments; → MENCICIL. 2 to move forward gradually. 3 to push, move s.t. forward. ~ *langkah ke negeri orang* to move to another place.

mengangsuri 1 to pay for s.t. in installments. 2 to proceed slowly with s.t.

mengangsurkan 1 to push (a chair/plate, etc.) closer (and closer) (to s.o.), extend (one's hand). 2 to deliver/sell s.t. on the installment plan. 3 to move s.t. or s.o. forward, order s.o. to move forward. ~ *para hadirin ke muka* to move the audience farther forward.

terangsur paid out in installments.

angsuran (installment) payment. ~ *kembung* balloon payment. ~ *pertama* down payment. ~ *tetap* fixed payment.

pengangsuran 1 doing s.t. in stages/bit by bit. 2 paying in installments. 3 shifting forward gradually.

perangsuran shifting forward.

angur (*Jv*) it would be better (if ...; to ...).

angus → HANGUS. – *hati* a) angry. b) yearning.

angus-angus ~ *hati hendak* ... to be eager to ...

menganguskan to scorch, singe.

keangusan scorched.

angut drowsy, sleepy.

berangut and mengangut 1 to doze off. 2 to be sleepy, drowsy. 3 to daydream.

pengangut lazy person.

anhang (*D mil*) transfer loader.

anhu (*A*) upon him. *rida allah* – may God bless him!

ani I warp (for weaving).

mengani to warp, arrange pattern on a weaver's loom.

anian warp.

pengani rack for spools.

ani II (*BD*) this; → INI.

ani-ani (*Jv*) a handheld blade used in rice harvesting.

aniaya (*Skr*) oppression, injustice, tyranny, ill treatment, mistreatment. *berbuat* – to play dishonest tricks.

menganiaya(i) to abuse, mistreat, maltreat, oppress, tyrannize, persecute, torment, harass, manhandle.

teraniaya oppressed, maltreated, mistreated, molested. *mati* ~ murdered in a violent way. *pihak yang* ~ the injured party.

penganiaya tyrant, oppressor, cruel/unjust person.

penganiayaan 1 violence, mistreatment. **2** oppression, persecution. **3** torture, torturing. ~ *atas/terhadap anggota polisi* torturing a policeman.

ani(e)m [(from *D*): <u>ANIEM</u>: Algemééne Néderlandsch-Indische Électricitéits Maatschappij or "General Netherlands-Indies Electricity Company"] **1** electric company. **2** electricity.

anih (*Jv*) ineffective (of a medicine).

anikterik (*D/E*) anicteric.

anilin (*D/E*) aniline.

animasi (*D*) animation. *melakukan* – to animate.

animis (*D/E*) animist.

animisma and **animisme** (*D*) animism.

animistis (*D*) animistic.

animo (*D*) **1** gusto, zest, spirit. **2** interest. – *masyarakat* public interest.

aning-aning a large wasp or hornet, *Apis dorsata*.

anion (*D*) negatively charged ion.

anis I (*D*) anise, anisette.

anis II various species of thrushes. – *cacing* chestnut-capped thrush, *Zoothera interpres*. – *gunung* island thrush, *Turdus poliocephalus*. – *mérah* orange-headed thrush, *Zoothera citrina*.

anja I (*M*) **beranja(-anja)** and **teranja-anja** spoiled (of a person), pampered; → MANJA.

anja II (*naut*) ship's halyard. – *bendéra* flagpole.

anjak *bidang* – (*geol*) thrust plane. – *piutang* (*fin*) factoring. **penganjak piutang** factor.

beranjak 1 to move/shift one's position slightly. ~ *dari duduknya/kursinya* to rise/get up from one's seat/chair. **2** to move toward, get close to, approach, toward. *hari yang* ~ *petang* approaching the afternoon/evening. ~ *malam* toward evening/nightfall. *belum* ~ *pergi* to show no sign of leaving (of a guest). ~ *dari sejarah* historically, based on history. ~ *déwasa* moving into adolescence. ~ *gedé* growing up. ~ *maju* to move ahead. ~ *pulang* to get ready to/start to go home. ~ *surut* to start to recede (as the tide). ~ *tua* to get/grow old. **3** to transfer, shift (to another job).

menganjak 1 to move/shift s.t. **2** to transplant.

menganjakkan ~ *langkah* to take steps.

teranjak moved, shifted.

anjakan move, shift.

penganjak (*fin*) ~ *piutang* factor.

penganjakan moving, shifting.

peranjakan transfer, removal.

anjal I elastic.

menganjal 1 to bounce, rebound. **2** to be elastic, resilient, springy.

keanjalan elasticity.

anjal II [anak jalanan] street kid.

anjambu (*Jv*) the active partner in a homosexual relationship.

anjang I (*S*) visit. – *karya* field trip.

(ng)anjang to (pay a) visit.

anjang II → PANJANG.

anjang-anjang I (*daun* –) k.o. plant, *Elaeocarpus spp.*

anjang-anjang II (*Jv*) bamboo latticework used as a support for climbing vines and providing shade for people to sit under, arbor.

anjang-anjang III 1 various species of breams: whiptails, threadfin bream, butterfly bream/whiptail, Arabian monocle bream, *Pentapodus setosus, Scolopsis ghanam*. **2** sea crab.

anjangasih visit, interview.

beranjangasih to have an interview with, interview.

anjangkarya (*S*) visit to a place to perform a task, usually undertaken by a government official; field trip.

beranjangkarya to visit a place in the framework of implementing a task; to make a field trip.

anjangsana (*Skr*) **1** a nostalgic visit. **2** friendly visit (to a neighbor/sibling, etc.). **3** house-to-house campaign.

beranjangsana 1 to visit for nostalgic reasons. **2** to visit to strengthen the ties of friendship.

anjar (*Pers*) anchor.

anjiluang (*M*) → LENJUANG.

anjiman (*E?*) *kapal* – East Indiaman (VOC ship).

anjing 1 dog, *Canis familiaris*. **2** despicable person, running-dog. *gila* – and *penyakit* – *gila* hydrophobia, rabies. *saudara* – half brother/sister (from the same mother but different father). **3** first part of the name of some animals. **4** a mild curse, damn it, shit! – *ditepuk menjungkit ékor* set a beggar on horseback and he'll ride to the devil. *bagai* – *beranak enam* said of a woman who is all skin and bones (after having had many children). *(seperti)* – *bercawat ékor* to go off with one's tail between one's legs. *bagai* – *menyalak di ékor/pantat gajah* a weak/humble person who wants to oppose a powerful person. *bagai/seperti disalak* – *bertuah* can no longer be postponed, must be granted. *melepaskan* – *terjepit* to help an ungrateful person. *sebagai/seperti* – *terpanggang ékor* get into trouble so that one doesn't know what to do (or, how to behave). *(hidup) seperti* – *dengan kucing* to be at e.o.'s throats, bicker all the time. – *yang menyalak tiada bergigit* his bark is worse than his bite. – *air* a) otter, *Lutra spp.* b) uninvited guest. – *ajak/ajag* (*Jv*) jackal; → SERIGALA. – *arau/belang* a brown-and-black-striped dog. – *betina* bitch. – *biri-biri* sheep dog. – *Cina* (an insult) Chink. – *galak* a ferocious dog. – *geladak* a stray dog, mongrel. – *gembala* a) a shepherd. b) a powerless supervisor. – *gembala Jerman* German shepherd. – *gila* mad dog. – *hérder* German shepherd. – *hutan* a) wild dog (living in the forest), *Cuon alpinus/javanicus* → (*anjing*) AJAK. b) jackal. – *jaga* watchdog. *si* – *jaga* the watchdog. – *kampung* stray dog, mongrel. – *kilat* greyhound. – *koréng* a dog with black and yellow stripes. – *kurir* messenger dog. – *laut* gray seal, *Halichoerus grypus*. – *militér* war dog. – *nibung* a dog with yellowish brown fur. – *Nica* a running dog of the *Nica*. – *pandu* scout dog. – *pelacak* tracker dog. – *pembiak* dog for breeding purposes. – *pembimbing tunanétra* seeing-eye dog. – *pemburu* hunting dog. – *pengawal* guard dog. – *penjaga* watchdog. – *perempuan* (*coq*) bitch. – *ras* pedigree dog. – *sabun* white dog. – *tanah* k.o. mole cricket, *Gryllotalpa africana/vulgaris*. – *trah* pedigree dog. – *turunan* pedigreed dog. – *tutul* Dalmatian.

memperanjing to insult s.o. by calling him a dog.

anjing-anjingan (child's) toy dog.

peranjingan dog (*mod*), canine.

anjing-anjing I (muscles of the) calf.

anjing-anjing II a fruit tree, namnam, *Cynometra cauliflora*; → NAMNAM.

anjing-anjing III (*naut*) – *perahu* loop for boat's reefing lever.

anjing-anjing IV *burung* – (white-)collared kingfisher, *Halcyon chloris*.

anjir I (*Pers*) wild fig, *Ficus carica*.

anjir II (in Kalimantan) primary canal in irrigation system.

anjir III (*vulg exclamation from anjing*) damn it, shit!

anjlog and **anjlok** (*Jv*) /anjlok/ **1** to go down, fall, drop (of prices). **2** to go downhill, get worse. **3** to jump down. – *ke titik bawah* to jump down to the lowest point. **4** (– *dari rél*) to derail.

menganjlokkan to drive down (prices).

anjlokan derailment.

keanjlokan a drop/reduction (in prices, etc.).

anjrit I (*Jv*) to scream, cry out.

anjrit II and **anjrut** → ANJIR III.

anju (*M*) **1** attempt to (jump/run), running start. **2** aim, purpose.

menganju to try/begin (to walk/stride, etc.).

menganjukan ~ *kaki* to set out, march forward.

anjuang (*M*) raised area in a traditional house.

anjung enclosed room over a porch, bay window; mezzanine. – *pengantar* visitor's gallery (at an airport). – *peranginan* airy porch.

anjung-anjung → ANJUNGAN 1.

beranjung to have such a structure.

menganjung 1 (= **menganjungkan**) to hold s.t. up high, raise s.t. up; to fly (a kite). ~ *diri* to boast, brag. **2** [= **menganjung-anjung(kan)**] to praise, flatter. **3** to jut out, protrude.

anjungan 1 outboard, raised platform at stern of Malay boat, gallery, bowsprit. **2** ship's bridge. **3** platform, rig. ~ *minyak* oil rig. ~ *minyak terapung* floating oil rig. ~ *pemboran minyak lepas pantai* offshore oil rig. ~ *pemboran* drilling platform. ~ (*ruang*) *pengantar* waving gallery (at airports). ~ *produksi* platform (in oil drilling). ~ *tunai mandiri* ATM, automatic teller machine.

anjung-anjungan 1 fulsome praise. **2** raised platform at ship's stern. **3** pavilion (at a fair).

penganjungan praising.

anjur I stuck out, protruding.

beranjur to begin to stride/step, etc.

menganjur 1 to stick/jut out, project. **2** to begin to stride, move forward. **3** (*geol*) to prograde.

menganjuri 1 to lead, head, be at the head of. ~ *rombongan unjuk perasaan/rasa* to lead the demonstrators. **2** to pioneer.

menganjurkan 1 to extend, protrude, stretch, push (one's head forward), lean (one's body out the window). *Jangan dianjurkan badan keluar jendéla.* Don't lean out the window. **2** to incite, urge, encourage. **3** to propose, recommend, advocate, move, suggest, put forward. **4** to advise s.o. ~ ... *supaya jangan* to advise ... against. **5** to hand s.t. over (by sticking it forward).

teranjur (*ob*); → TE(R)LANJUR.

anjuran 1 suggestion, proposal. **2** propaganda, agitation. ~ *yang muluk-muluk* high-sounding propaganda. **3** (at/on the) initiative (of); originates with. **4** encouragement; recommendation; invitation; impetus. **5** offer.

penganjur 1 advocate, champion, supporter; propagandist; (party) organizer. ~ *mula* initiator, pioneer. **2** (political) leader; guide. **3** promoter, mover (at a meeting); initiator. **4** instigator, provoker, provocateur. ~ *perang* warmonger. ~ *pandu* rover (in the Boy Scout movement).

penganjuran recommending, recommendation, putting forward.

anjur II → GANJUR I. **beranjur 1** to withdraw. ~ (*langkah*) *surut* a) to retreat, withdraw, pull back. b) to return/come back/revert/ refer again to (a matter/refusal).

menganjur to drag, pull. ~ *diri ke belakang* to retreat, withdraw. b) to return to (a matter, etc.). ~ *langkah* to get down to work ~ *langkah ke* to go to. *Dianjurnya ke belakang hendak melompat.* He took a running jump. *baru dianjur sudah tertarung* no sooner begun than there's a problem.

Ankabut (*A*) *al*– "The Spider"; name of the 29th chapter of the Koran.

Ankara Ankara.

ankél → ANGKÉL.

Anm. (*abbr*) [Anumerta] posthumous.

annémer → ANÉMER.

ano (*J*) hesitation word when you can't think what to say, er; → ANU. *Siapa yang – memukulnya?* Who, er, hit him? *Pak* – Mr. What's-his-name.

anonya 1 it's er (speaker can't think of the right noun to use). **2** (*euph*) (speaker doesn't want to use the right noun) his penis or her vagina.

menganokan to er (the speaker can't think of the right verb to use).

anoa(ng) the dwarf buffalo, *Bubalus depresicornis* of the Southern Celebes.

anoda (*D*) anode.

anodisasi (*D*) anodize.

penganodisasian anodizing.

anoksia (*D*) anoxia.

anom (*Jv*) **1** young. **2** vice-. *bupati* – vice-regent. *parabu/raja* – viceroy.

anomali (*D*) anomaly.

Anoman (*Skr*) the white monkey-god of the *Ramayana* epic.

anomi (*D/E*) anomie.

anona custard apple; → NONA II.

anonim (*D*) anonymous. *surat* – anonymous letter.

keanoniman anonymity.

anonimitas and **anonimitét** (*D*) anonymity.

anonser (*D/E*) announcer.

anoréksia – *nérvosa* (*D*) anorexia nervosa.

anorganik (*D/E*) inorganic.

anotasi (*D*) annotation.

beranotasi annotating.

anpal → ANFAL. **nganpal** (*J*) to hit as hard as one can.

anprah (*D*) demand, inquiry (for goods).

ansa → ANGSA.

ansambel and **ansamble** (*D*) ensemble.

ansar (*A*) **1** helpers (the people of Medina who welcomed the Prophet Muhammad when he left Mecca). **2** name of a Muslim youth organization.

ansari (*A*) *kaum* – → ANSAR.

anshorin (*E?*) local population.

ansor → ANSAR.

anstéker (*D*) cigarette lighter.

ansur (*Mal*) → ANGSUR. *tolak* – give and take.

ansyar → ANSOR.

ansyovis (*D*) (*ikan*) – anchovy.

anta I (*Skr*) **1** as far as the end/frontier; limit, border. **2** existence, nature. **3** (*math*) finite.

beranta finite.

anta-beranta the empyrean; fabled, imaginary. *negeri* ~ Utopia; → ANTAH II.

anta II (*A*) you, thou.

Antaboga (*Skr*) great sea serpent.

antagonis (*D/E*) antagonist.

antagonisme (*D/E*) antagonism.

antagonistik (*D/E*) antagonistic.

antagonistis (*D*) antagonistic.

antah I 1 rice grains left unhusked after pounding. **2** (– *kemukut*) good-for-nothing/ useless/worthless person (in society). **3** inferior item. *disisih sebagai* – segregated (due to low social status/ poverty, etc.). *tiada tahu* – *terkunyah* to be quite innocent. – *berkumpul sama* –, *beras sama beras* birds of a feather flock together. *dipilih* – *satu-satu* on close examination.

antah II → ENTAH. **antah-berantah** *negeri* ~ never-never land, fairyland.

antak → ENTAK, BERANTAKAN.

antakaranasarira (in Bali) the soul which is released during a cremation.

antakesuma and **antakusuma** (*Skr*) flowery. *baju* – a) a (magic) vest made of a flowered fabric. b) (*Jv*) in the *wayang* play, the vest worn by Gatutkaca (in order to fly).

Antakiah (*A*) Antioch.

antalas → ANTELAS.

antali marble.

antam → HANTAM.

antamir (*D*) **mengantamir** to take (the matter) up; to undertake, tackle.

antan pestle, (rice) pounder; → ALU. – *patah, lesung hilang* it never rains but it pours; misfortunes never come alone. *seperti* – *pencukil duri* a Sisyphean task.

antap I solid, compact, massive, heavy for its size (of a child, etc.).

antap II (*M*) quiet, silent, calm.

mengantapkan to quiet(en), calm (down), silence, soothe.

antar I deliver, accompany. *tukang* – *surat* mailman. – *jemput* a) door-to-door delivery. b) (in classified ads) car pool. *Dicari:* – *jemput Désa Kopi ke Harmoni.* Wanted: car pool from Desa Kopi to Harmoni and back. **mengantar-jemput** to take to and from somewhere. – *negara* between countries. **mengantar-negarakan** to ship between countries. – *pulau* between islands. **mengantar-pulaukan** to ship between islands. – *tangan* (*Mal*) to hand-deliver (a letter, etc.).

berantar accompanied, escorted. *datang tak berjemput, pulang tak* ~ to not meet or accompany, etc. properly/as one should.

mengantar [and **ngantar** (*coq*)] **1** to accompany, go with, take s.o. to somewhere. *Dia diantar naik mobil.* He was taken by car. **2** to see s.o. off. ~ *kepergian Égorov* to see Egorov off. ~ *nyawa manusia ke akhirat* to send s.o. to the next world, launch s.o. into eternity. **3** to bring s.o. home. ~ *pulang* to accompany s.o. home. **4** to introduce (a speaker, etc.). **5** to deliver (newspapers/mail, etc.). *tukang* ~ *surat* mailman.

antar-mengantar 1 to send e.o. (presents, etc.). **2** to deliver (letters). **3** intermittent. *napas yang* ~ *lepas dari dada* short of breath.

mengantari to send s.o. s.t. *Ia diantari orang kampung makanan.* The village people sent him food.

mengantarkan [and **ngantarin** (*J coq*)] **1** to accompany s.o. to a destination. **2** to see s.o. off. **3** to introduce. ~ *tamu ke pintu* to show a guest to the door. ~ *pelajaran dengan bahasa Indonésia* to use Indonesian as the medium of instruction. ~ *période transisi* to be in office for a transitional period.

terantar to be delivered/brought.

antaran 1 s.t. that is forwarded/sent/delivered. *surat* ~ letters to be delivered. ~ *pos* mail delivery. **2** (*uang* ~ and ~ *kawin*) dowry. **3** (*elec*) conductor. **4** line. ~ *balik* return line.

keantaran (*elec*) conductibility.

pengantar 1 sender, deliverer. ~ *istana* supplier/purveyor to the Royal Household. ~ *koran/suratkabar* newspaper boy. ~ *pos/ surat* mailman. **2** courier, messenger; porter, bellboy. **3** escort, convoy, usher. *kapal* ~ convoy (ship). **4** introducer; introductory. *bahasa* ~ medium of instruction. *kata* ~ preface, foreword. *surat* ~ cover letter. ~ *ékonomi* introductory economics. ~ *ilmu hukum* introductory jurisprudence. ~ *kalam/kata* preface, forward. ~ *khayal* prologue. **5** conductor (of electricity/ light/heat, etc.), lead, line.

pengantaran 1 the act/way, etc. of seeing s.o. off, etc. **2** conduction.

perantaran → PERANTARAAN.

antar II inter- (used in compounds; for examples see below).

antara I (*Skr*) **1** space between, distance between. *jarak* – *X dan Y* the distance between X and Y. – *ada dengan tiada* hardly, barely. – *lain* among others, including, inter alia. *di* – between, among. **2** in about (of time). – *lima hari* in about five days. *tak lama* – *itu* not long after that/thereafter. *pada* – *itu* at that very moment. **3** not far from. **4** in the meantime. **5** interim (decision/position), intermediate. – *kepala staf* interim chief of staff.

antaranya 1 among them. *di* ~ among others. **2** later. *tiga hari* ~ three days later. **3** distance between. ~ *dari ... ke ...* the distance between ... and Y.

seantara all around, entirely.

berantara and **berantara-antara 1** at intervals. **2** to be at a distance. **3** to have an intermediary. **berantarakan** to be separated from e.o. by.

memerantarai (from the stem *perantara*) and **memperantarai** to act as mediator for, mediate.

mengantara → MENGANTARAI 2.

mengantarai 1 to partition off, divide, separate. *Laut mana yang* ~ *pulau Jawa dengan Kalimantan?* Which sea separates Java from Kalimantan? **2** to mediate, arbitrate, be an arbitrator in. ~ *perselisihan* to be the arbitrator in a conflict.

pengantara and **perantara 1** arbitrator, mediator. **2** intermediary, middleman, agent, broker. ~ *asuransi* insurance agent/broker. ~ *bursa* stockbroker. ~ *pedagang éfék* securities broker. ~ *pertanggungan* insurance agency. **berperantara** *perundingan* ~ proximity talks.

pengantaraan intercession, mediation.

perantaraan 1 intervention, mediation, intercession. **2** liaison (office), mediator, go-between, intermediary. *tidak dengan* ~ directly (from seller to buyer). *memberi* ~ *untuk* to act as an intermediary for. *badan* ~ *pekerjaan* employment agency/ bureau. **3** *dengan* ~ by means of, via, through. *dengan* ~ *suratmenyurat* a) by correspondence. b) through the mail. *pengumuman dengan* ~ *radio* radio announcement. **4** (*ob*) relationship, social intercourse. **pemerantaraan** mediation.

Antara II the state-run news agency in Jakarta (established December 13, 1937).

antarabangsa → ANTARBANGSA.

antaragama interfaith, between religions.

antarahli (*ékonomi*, etc.) between (economics, etc.) experts.

antaraksi interaction.

berantaraksi ~ *dengan* to interact with.

Antar-Amérika Inter-American.

antaranggota between members. – *rumahtangga* between members of the family.

antarangkatan between/among forces.

antar-antar 1 (wooden) pounder to ram down (earth). **2** rotor. **3** piston rod. – *gobék* pestle of arecanut pounder. – *senapan* ramrod.

antar-ASÉAN inter-ASEAN; → INTRA-ASÉAN.

antarawak between/among members of the crew.

antarbadan between bodies. – *hukum* between law agencies.

antarbagian interdivisional.

antarbangsa 1 international. **2** interracial.

antarbank interbank.

antarbenua intercontinental.

antarbintang intergalactic, interstellar.

antarbudaya intercultural.

antarbutir *rongga* – *batuan* the space between particles of soil.

antarcabang interbranch.

antarcukong – *suap* between wheeler-dealers.

antardaérah interregional, interprovincial. *Antar kerja* – [AKAD] Interregional Job Media.

antardépartemént(al) interdepartmental.

antardésa intervillage.

antardiréksi between directors.

antardiri interpersonal.

antardisiplin (*ilmu*) between (scientific) disciplines, interdisciplinary.

antardua between two. – *étnis* between two ethnic groups.

antaréja (*Jv*) **1** a character in the *wayang* play who lives underground. **2** a thief who enters a house by tunneling under the wall.

antaréksportir between exporters.

antarélemén interelement.

antarés interglacial.

antarétnis interethnic.

antarfaksi among factions.

antarfaktor among factors. – *produksi* among production factors.

antarfakultas between schools (of a university).

antarfraksi between factions (in Parliament).

antargalaksi intergalactic.

antargali between criminal gangs; → GALI II.

antargénerasi intergenerational, between generations.

antargéng between gangs (of criminals); → GANG II. *perang* – gang war.

antargerakan between ... movements.

antargerbong between railroad cars.

antargeréjawi interdenominational.

antargigi interdental.

antargolongan intergroup, between/among/involving different groups, *esp* ethnic or racial groups in a society.

antargunung intermontane, between/among mountains.

antarhalte between (bus) stops.

antarhomoséksual between homosexuals.

antarhotél interhotel; between/among hotels.

antarhubungan interrelations, interrelationship.

antarhuta intervillage (in the Batak area).

antari (*Hind*) *baju* – inner vest under pilgrim's gown.

antar(-)iga intercostal, between the ribs.

antariksa (*Skr*) **1** sky, firmament. **2** space. *pesawat* – spaceship. *pusat* – space center. **3** atmosphere.

mengantariksa to go/be put into orbit.

mengantariskakan to send into orbit.

keantariksaan (aero)space (*mod*).

pengantariska booster.

pengantariksaan putting into orbit.

antariksawan male astronaut.

antariksawati female astronaut.

antarilmu – *pengetahuan* interdisciplinary.

antarilmuwan between scientists.

antariman between faiths.

antarindividu between individuals.

antarindustri interindustrial.

antarinsani interpersonal.

antarinstalasi between installations.

antarinstansi interagency.

antarjalin interwoven.

antarjasa interservice.

antarjawatan interoffice.

antarjemaat between congregations.

antar-jemput – *sekolah* to take to and pick up from school.

mengantarjemput to take to and pick up.

antarjuara between champions.

antarkabupatén inter-regency.

antarkader intercadre.
antarkaitan interconnection.
antarkampus between campuses.
antarkantor interoffice.
antarkaryawan between employees.
antarkaum (*Mal*) racial, communal (*mod*). *masalah* – racial problems.
antarkawasan between areas.
antarkebudayaan intercultural.
antarkecamatan interdistrict/between districts.
antarkedua between two. – *negara* between two nations.
antarkekuasaan between (sociopolitical) forces.
antarkelamin intersexual.
antarkelas intergrade.
antarkelompok intergroup.
antarkeluarga interfamily.
antarkelurahan intervillage.
antarkenalan between friends.
antarkerabat among relatives/members of the family. *perkawinan* – inbreeding.
antarkeréta between (railroad) cars.
antarkesebelasan between soccer teams.
antarklab and antarklub interclub, between clubs. – *boling* interclub bowling.
antarkomponén between components.
antarkoperasi between cooperatives.
antarkota intercity.
antarkotamadya between municipalities.
antarkubu between cliques/factions.
antarlembaga between institutions.
antarlintas intersection.
antarlogam intermetallic.
antarlokasi between locations.
antarmajalah between magazines.
antarmanajér – *tim* between team managers.
antarmanusia interhuman, between human beings.
antarmasjid between mosques.
antarmaster intermaster (in sports).
antarmasyarakat intercommunity.
antarmata – *uang* intercurrency.
antarmazhab interdenominational.
antarmédia between media. – *massa* between mass media.
antarmenteri between ministers, ministerial.
antarmérek interbrand.
antarmeréka (~ *sendiri*) between them(selves).
antarmilisi between militias.
antarmoda intermodal.
antarmolekul intermolecular.
antarmuka interface.
antarmurid between students.
antarmuséum intermuseum.
antarnapi among inmates/convicts.
antarnasabah 1 correlation. 2 among customers/clients/depositors.
antarnegara international, between/among nations; → INTERNASIONAL. *antar Kerja* – [AKAN] International Job Media.
  mengantarnegarakan to ship between countries (*esp* Indonesia, Malaysia and Singapore).
antarnegarabagian interstate, between/among states of a federal government.
antarorang interpersonal.
antarorganisasi interorganizational. – *agama* between religious organizations.
antarotot intramuscular.
antarpabrik between factories.
antarpantai intercoastal.
antarparasut *kerjasama* – (in Air Force) relative canopy.
antarparlemén interparliamentary. *Badan Kerjasama Antar Parlemén* [BKSAP] Interparliamentary Cooperation Board.
antarparpol between political parties.
antarpasangan intercouple.
antarpejabat between officials.
antarpelabuhan between ports.

antarpelajar interstudent.
antarpelaku interagent, between agents.
antarpelatda between provincial teams.
antarpemain between/among players.
antarpembalap between racers.
antarpémda between provincial governments.
antarpemerintah between governments, G-to-G.
antarpenegak – *hukum* between law agencies.
antarpenerbang between fliers.
antarpenerbit(an) between publishers.
antarpengda between regional executive boards.
antarpengusaha between/among entrepreneurs.
antarpenilai interappraisers, between appraisers.
antarpenumpang between passengers.
antarperadaban between civilizations.
antarperguruan tinggi interuniversity.
antarperkumpulan between associations.
antarperpustakaan interlibrary.
antarpérsonal interpersonal.
antarperusahaan among enterprises.
antarpeserta between participants.
antarpetani between/among farmers.
antarplanit interplanetary, between planets.
antar-Pondok Pesantrén between Islamic seminaries with attached boarding facilities.
antarpribadi interpersonal.
antarproduk between products, interproduct.
antarprofési interprofessional.
antarprogram interprogram.
antarpropinsi and antarprovinsi interprovincial; → INTRAPROVINSI.
antarpuak intergroup.
antarpulau interisland, interinsular.
  mengantarpulaukan to transport from one island to another.
  pengantarpulauan interisland transportation.
antarpusdiklat between *PUSDIKLATs*.
antarras interracial.
antarrégional interregional, between/among regions.
antarrekan between colleagues.
antarremaja interadolescent.
antarronde between rounds (in boxing).
antarruang outer space.
antarrumahsakit interhospital.
antarsaudara fraternal, between brothers.
antarsekolah interschool. *baku hantam* – fights between schools.
antarséks intersex.
antarsékte intersect.
antarséktoral intersectoral.
antarsél intercellular, located between/among cells.
antarseniman interartist.
antarsénsus intercensus. *survéi penduduk* – [Supas] intercensus population survey.
antarsesama between (community organizations) working toward the same goal. – *kita* between us all.
antarsimpatisan between supporters (of different parties).
antarsistém between systems.
antarstasiun between (railroad) stations.
antarstudio between studios.
antarsuami – *istri* between husband and wife.
antarsuku interethnic, mixed (marriage, etc.).
antartamu between guests.
antarteman between friends.
antartetangga between neighbors.
antartika (*D*) antarctic.
antartoko interstore.
antarulama between Muslim scholars.
antarumat – *beragama* between/among religious communities.
antarunit interunit.
antaruniversitas interuniversity.
antarunsur between different elements.
antarvariétas between varieties.
antarvértebra intervertebral.
antarvokal intervocalic.

antarwaktu interim, temporary.
antarwanita between women.
antarwarganegara intercitizen.
antarwartawan between reporters.
antarwilayah between regions.
Antasari name of the military resort command (*Korém* 101) in Banjarmasin.
antasid(a) (*D*) antacid.
antawacana (*Jv*) and **antawecana** dialogue, the *dalang*'s voice in the *wayang* performance which changes according to the character being played.
anté (*J*) tasteless.
anteb → ANTEP.
antédatéring (*E*) antedating.
antédatir (*D*) **mengantedatir** to antedate.
anteg (*J*) **ngantegin** to leave alone, ignore.
anték (*Jv coq*) stooge, henchman, accomplice, running dog.
  nganték to be a running dog.
antéken (*D*) **1** registered (letter). **2** to register (a letter).
antelas (*A*) (*kain* –) satin.
antelop (*D*) antelope.
antem (*Jv*) a blow with the fist; → HANTAM.
  berantem to have a fistfight; → BERHANTAM.
  berantem-anteman to come to blows with e.o.
  ngantem → MENGHANTAM.
antén (*ob*) **menganténkan** to marry off; → PENGANTÉN, PENGANTIN.
  mengenténkan to marry off, give in marriage.
anténa and **anténe** (*D*) antenna, aerial. – *dwi-arah* bidirectional antenna. – *mangkuk* dish antenna. – *menjadi satu dengan kaca depan* windshield antenna. – *parabola/parabolik* parabolic antenna. – *penguat* booster antenna. – *piring* dish antenna. – *TV* TV antenna.
anteng I (*J/Jv*) **1** quiet, calm, steady, tranquil. – *ayem* calm and peaceful. **2** not crying (of infants). **3** happy to stay at home and not go out much.
  keantengan imperturbability, calm.
anteng II (*J*) to continue to, keep on, stick to. *Dia – bekerja dari pagi sampai soré.* He kept on working from morning till night.
antep I (*J*) heavy, weighty, considerable; → ANTAP I.
antep II (*J*) **mengantep** to trust, believe in.
  mengantepi 1 to let, permit. **2** loyal to, faithful to, remain steadfast in.
anter (*coq*) → ANTAR I. **nganterin** (*J coq*) → MENGANTARKAN.
antér (*J*) **1** quiet, serene. **2** calm, composed, tranquil, self-possessed.
  antér-antér very calm/quiet.
anteré (*D*) and **anteri** → ANTRÉ.
antéro (*Port*) the whole. – *Jakarta* the whole of Jakarta.
  seantéro whole, all, entire.
  seantéronya entirely; everything.
anterpo (*D*) entrepot.
antéséden (*D gram*) antecedent.
anti- I (*D*) **1** non-; → BUKAN, TIDAK. **2** to be against. – *pada* against, opposed to. – *celana dalam* [ACD] antipanties (militant female high school and college students in Bandung circa 1968). **3** anti-, resistant. -resistant. – *berisik* soundproof. – *peluru* bulletproof. – *silau* nonglare. – *slip* nonskid.
anti II (*J*) → ÉNTÉ.
antiaborsi (*D*) antiabortion.
antiadegan – *retrain* against a retraining program.
antiair waterproof.
antialérgi (*D*) antiallergy. *obat* – antiallergic medicine.
antialkohol antialcohol.
antiaparthéid (*D*) antiapartheid.
antiapi fire-resistant, fireproof. *penyemprot* – fire extinguisher.
antiasing xenophobia.
antiasma antiasthmatic.
antibajak antipirating.
anti-Barat anti-Western.
antibatuk cough suppressant (medicine).
antibeku antifreeze.
anti-Belanda anti-Dutch.

antiberderai antishatter.
antberkarat antirust.
antibiosis (*D*) antibiosis.
antibiotik (*D*) antibiotic.
antibising noiseless.
antibocor leakproof, spillproof.
antibodi (*D/E*) antibody.
antibudaya counter-culture.
antibutir antiparticle.
anticemaran antipollution.
anticendawan *obat* – fungicide.
antidadah antinarcotic.
antidebu dust-resistant. *kacamata* – goggles.
antidemam – *berdarah* against dengue fever.
antidémokrasi and **antidémokratis** (*D*) antidemocratic.
antidengkur antisnoring.
antidéprésan antidepressant.
antidéprési (*D*) *obat* – an antidepressant drug.
antidiabétés antidiabetes.
antidioksida (*D*) antidioxide.
antidiséntri antidysentery.
antidisiplin antidisciplinary.
antidotum (*D*) antidote.
antiénzim (*D*) antienzyme.
antiflu antiinfluenza.
antifotokopi antiphotocopy, no-copy.
antigén (*D/E*) antigen.
antigendut non-fattening.
antigeréja anti-church.
antigorésan scratch-resistant.
Antigua Antigua.
antigulma antiweed.
antihama – *serangga* insecticide.
antihamil *pil* – contraceptive pill.
antihelm against (the requirement to wear) helmets.
antih mengantih to spin.
  pengantihan 1 the act of spinning. **2** spinning machine/wheel.
antihiperténsi (*D*) antihypertension.
antihistamin (*D/E*) antihistamine.
antihukuman – *mati* against the death penalty.
antihuruhara antiriot, riot (*mod*). *polisi* – riot police.
antiimigran anti-immigrant.
antiimpérialis (*D*) anti-imperialist.
anti-Indonésia anti-Indonesian.
antiinféksi anti-infection.
antiinflasi (*D*) anti-inflation.
antiinovasi against innovation.
antijamur (*D*) antifungal.
antijasad antibody.
antijudi antigambling.
antik (*D*) **1** antique, old, old-fashioned. **2** ornate, highly embellished. **3** eccentric. **4** lively, cute (of children). **5** (*sl*) code word for pornographic film.
  mengantikkan to antique.
  keantikan antiqueness.
antikabut antifog.
antikafir against unbelievers.
antikanan against the right (politically).
antikanker (*D*) anticancer.
antikapal antiship. *rudal* – antiship (guided) missile.
antikarat rustproof.
  mengantikaratkan to rustproof.
antikebakaran antifire.
antikebotakan antibaldness.
antikejahatan antievil.
antikejang antispasmodic.
antikekerasan nonviolence, nonviolent.
antikeriput antiwrinkle.
antikerudung against wearing the Muslim head covering.
antikerusuhan antiriot.
antikesuburan antifertility.
antiketuk antiknock.

antikita against us.
antiklérikalisme (D) aniclericalism.
antiklimaks (D) anticlimax.
antiklin (D) anticline.
antikoagulan (D) anticoagulant.
antikomunis anticommunist.
antikorupsi anticorruption.
antikristus (D) antichrist; → DAJAL.
antikuman antimicrobial, antiseptic. obat – disinfectant.
antikuning obat – medicine against hyperbilirubinemia.
antikup against a coup (d'état).
antikwariat (D) antiquarian.
antil → UNTAL.
antilaser /-lé-/ antilaser.
Antilés Antilles.
antiliberalisasi – borjuis anti-bourgeois liberalism.
Antil(l)a Belanda Dutch Antilles.
antilop (D/E) antelope.
antimaling theft proof.
antimandul anti-infertility.
antimapan antiestablishment.
antimasuk angin against colds.
antimerokok antismoking.
antimikrobia (D) antimicrobial agents.
antimon(ium) (D) antimony.
antimonopoli antimonopoly.
antimun (ob) → MENTIMUN.
antimuntah antiemetic.
antinarkotik(a) antinarcotic.
anting 1 weight. batu – plummet, counterweight. – neraca rides, i.e., the sliding weight on the beam of a balance/scale. 2 (in canoe racing) man hanging over the side to balance the canoe. 3 earlobe. – némpél close-set ears.
  anting-anting 1 dangling earrings for unpierced ears. 2 pendulum of antique clock.
  beranting relaying, in a relay.
  menganting 1 to hang down and swing freely, dangle. 2 pendulous.
anting-anting I (burung –) large racket-tailed drongo, Dicrurus paradiseus.
anting-anting II k.o. tree, Elaeocarpus grandiflorus.
antinomik (D) antinomic(al).
antinuklir (D) antinuclear.
antinyamuk antimosquito.
antinyeri for/against pain.
antipajak antitax.
antipangkalan – AS against U.S. bases.
antipantulan antiglare, glare proof.
anti-pasar counter-trade.
antipati (D/E) antipathy.
antipeluru bulletproof.
antipemacetan antijamming, jam proof.
antipembajakan antipirating.
antipembaruan antireform.
antipembeku – darah anticoagulant.
antipembubaran against dissolving.
antipemerintah antigovernment.
antipenawar antidote.
antipenggunaan – péstisida against the use of pesticides.
antipenjajah anticolonial.
antipenjajahan anticolonial(ism).
antipenyelundupan antismuggling.
antipenyiksaan antitorture.
antiperampok antitheft.
antiperang – bintang antistarwars.
antiperbudakan antislavery.
antiperdarahan antibleeding, astyptic.
antiperkosaan antirape.
antipesawat terbang antiaircraft. rudal – antiaircraft missile.
antipirétik (D) antipyretic.
antipirétika (D) antipyretic agents.
antipode (D) 1 antipode. 2 opposite.

antipoligami antipolygamy.
antiprotéksionis (D) antiprotectionist.
antiprotéksionisme antiprotectionism.
antiradar antiradar.
antiradiasi antiradiation.
antirampok antitheft.
antirasa – sakit against feeling sick.
antiréjim (D/E) antiregime, against the regime of.
antirématik antirheumatic.
antirésési recessionproof.
antirévolusi (D) antirevolutionary.
antirokok antismoking, nonsmoking.
antirontok obat – shampoo to arrest baldness.
antirudal balistik antiballistic missile.
antisadap antibugging (device).
antisanjungan antiflattery.
antisatelit (D) antisatellite.
antiselip antiskid.
antisémit (D) anti-Semite.
antisépsis (D) antisepsis.
antiséptik (D) antiseptic.
antiséra (D) the plural of antisérum.
antiserangga anti-insect.
antisérum (D) antiserum.
antisilau nonglare.
antisipasi (D) anticipation.
  berantisipasi to anticipate.
  mengantisipasi(kan) 1 to anticipate s.t. 2 to be prepared in advance for s.t.
  pengantisipasian anticipating.
antisipatif (E) anticipatory.
antisipatoris (E) anticipatory.
antisipir (D) mengantisipir to anticipate.
antisosial antisocial.
antistrés (D/E) antistress.
antisuap antibribe.
antisubvérsi antisubversion.
antisuper against (the use of) super-grade gasoline.
antitabrakan anticollision.
antitank (D) antitank.
antitélér antidrunkenness.
anti-terguling antirollover.
antitérorisme (D) antiterrorism.
antitésis (D) antithesis.
antitétanus (D) antitetanus.
antitikus antirat, ratproof.
antitinju antiboxing.
antitoksin (D/E) antitoxin.
antitrus (D/E) antitrust.
anti-Tuhan atheist.
antitumor antitumor.
anti-Viétnam anti-Vietnam.
antivirus antivirus.
antiwajib against obligatory … – hélm against the obligation to wear a helmet.
antiwalang sangit anti-green-rice-bug.
antiwirawan antihero.
anti-WTS antiprostitute.
antoi → ANTUI.
antologi (E) anthology.
antolojis (D) anthologist.
antonim (D/E) antonym.
antonimi (D/E) antonymy.
antop (Jv) belching; → ATOP.
antrak(s) (D) anthrax.
antrasit (D/E) anthracite.
antré (D/Fr) 1 line; → ANTRI. 2 [= mengantré and ngantré (coq)] a) to stand in line, queue up (for). ~ lift to stand in line to get in the elevator. ~ karcis to stand in line to buy tickets. b) to wait a long time.
  antréan a) a line (that one is waiting in). ~ panjang a long line. b) waiting in line. ~nya berhari-hari. One has to wait in line for days.

antré-antréan lining up.

pengantréan lining up (to buy s.t.), rush (on goods).

antreprenur (*D infr*) entrepreneur.

antri 1 to stand in line, queue up; → ANTRÉ. *tukang – karcis* s.o. who stands in line to buy movie tickets and then resells them at a higher price, scalper. **2** line, queue.

berantri 1 to line up. **2** to stand in line, queue up.

mengantri to wait in line (for a long time).

mengantrikan [and **ngantriin** (*J coq*)] to wait in line for s.t.

antrian line, queue.

antropogénik (*D/E*) anthropogenic.

antropolog (*D*) anthropologist.

antropologi (*D/E*) anthropology; → WIDYAJANMA. *– budaya* cultural anthropology. *– ragawi* physical anthropology.

antropologis (*D*) anthropological.

antropomorf (*D*) anthropomorphical.

antropomorfik (*D/E*) anthropomorphic.

antropomorfisme (*D/E*) anthropomorphism.

antroposéntris (*D*) anthropocentric.

antui *– putih/kuning/tembaga* various species of trees, *Cyathocalyx spp. – hitam* k.o. tree, *Drepananthus spp.*

antuk I collide, knock.

berantuk 1 to collide, knock against, hit (one's head against s.t.). **2** to chatter (of teeth). *gigi ~* chattering teeth.

berantukan to collide with e.o.

berantuk-antukan to keep knocking against e.o., keep colliding again and again. **bersiantukan 1** to knock against e.o. **2** to chatter (of teeth).

mengantuk to collide, knock, ram (a ship), strike against.

antuk-mengantuk to collide with e.o.

mengantukkan and **memperantukkan** to bump/strike/knock s.t. against.

terantuk collided, knocked against, bumped, in collision. *sudah ~ baru menengadah/tengadah* to lock the barn door after the horse is stolen. *~ hati* grieved, hurt.

antukan bump, collision.

antuk II mengantuk [and **ngantuk** (*coq*)] to be/feel sleepy; → KANTUK.

terantuk-antuk nodding (of one's head from sleepiness).

pengantuk sleepyhead.

antuk-antukan sleepy.

antuk III (*J*) sting (of insect); → ANTUP.

antul berantul and **mengantul** to bounce, rebound (of a ball), elastic, springy; *cp* MEMANTUL.

antun (*cla*) dandified, dressy. *orang –* a dandy.

berantun to be a clotheshorse, care about one's dress.

antung-antung hanging holder (for a kris/kitchen utensils); *cp* GANTUNG.

antup (*J*) sting (of an insect); → SENGAT.

mengantup to sting.

antusias (*D*) enthusiastic; passionate.

antusiasme (*D*) enthusiasm.

Antwérpen (*D*) Antwerp.

anu 1 (a word used to represent a pause in order to think for a moment) er, um, uh; → ANO. **2** (a word indicating a thing or s.o. which has slipped one's memory) what-you-may-call-it, what do you call it. *si –* Mr. So-and-So, Mr. What's his name. John Doe. **3** such-and-such. *di kampung –* in such-and-such kampung. **4** expressing vagueness rather than definiteness. *Tiap – dia mesti telat.* She's like always late. **5** (*math*) unknown. *persamaan dengan* 2 – an equation with two unknowns. **6** (*euph*) (when one doesn't want to say the right word) the genitals, sex organs; defecation. *–nya* his/her genitals.

menganu, menganui, and **menganukan** (*euph*) to you know what to (*euph* for to have sex with). *wanita yang dianukan pria* the woman who had you know what done to her by a man.

anuang → ANOA.

anugerah (*Skr*) **1** a gift from God, grace, mercy. **2** favor, endowment, gift (from a superior to a subordinate).

menganugerah to present (with a gift).

menganugerahi to bestow a gift (up)on, confer a favor/right/title on, grant, give a present to. *Kasman dianugerahi usia panjang.*

Kasman was granted a long life (by God). *belum dianugerahi anak* (a stereotype term in adoption procedures, etc.) they were childless.

menganugerahkan to give/confer/bestow/grant s.t.

penganugerah bestower.

penganugerahan bestowal, presentation (of a gift).

anuitas and **anuitét** (*D*) annuity.

anulér (*D*) annular. *gerhana –* annular eclipse.

anulir (*D*) **menganulir** to annul.

anum → ANOM.

anunasika → ANUSWARA.

anumert(h)a (*Skr*) posthumous(ly). *menggantikan Brigjén TNI – Mokhtar Harahap* replacing posthumously Army Brig. Gen. Mokhtar Harahap.

anus (*D/E*) anus.

anuswara (*ling*) nasal (sound).

anut meek, compliant. *– grubyug/grubyuk* to follow others blindly.

menganut(i) 1 to follow, adhere to (beliefs or religious doctrine/ political principles, etc.). **2** to practice (a certain religion/policy).

anutan 1 conviction, adherence (to a belief). **2** confidence in beliefs or religious doctrine.

penganut 1 follower, disciple, adherent. *~ cinta bébas* believer in free love. *~ garis keras* hardliner, hawk. *~ gaya hidup kelas tinggi* follower of a high lifestyle. *~ kelestarian lingkungan* environmentalist. *~ politik bébas* neutralist. **2** convert (to a religion). **3** follower (s.o. who goes along and doesn't have his own ideas).

penganutan 1 adherence. **2** (*Jv*) leader, guide. **3** a child adopted in the belief that one will then have children of one's own. **4** professing, converting to.

anyal (*Jv*) → ANYEL.

anyam plait, braid.

beranyam plaited with. *kursi yang ~ plastik* a chair plaited with plastic.

beranyamkan to be braided with.

menganyam to weave, plait, braid. *bambu yang dianyam* woven bamboo. *~ rambut* a) to braid one's hair. b) to wear one's hair in dreadlocks. *~ sasak* to make wickerwork for walls or fences. *~ tiga selang tiga* to plait by passing the weaving strip over two warp-strips. *~ tikar* to make a woven mat.

anyam-menganyam weaving, plaiting, braiding.

teranyam plaited, woven, braided.

anyaman 1 woven products, etc. *~ rambut* pigtail. *rotan ~* rattan webbing. **2** matmaking, wickerwork. **3** braid, plait, tress. **beranyaman** to be plaited with. *kursi yang ~ plastik* plastic-plaited chair.

anyam-anyaman plaited materials, webbing, wickerwork.

penganyam one who does any of the above activities.

penganyaman weaving, braiding, plaiting.

anyang I name of k.o. food (raw cockles, i.e., a type of edible shellfish, etc.) with seasonings and salt, or raw/unripe fruit with pepper and salt. *– kacang* a dish made of nuts and grated coconut.

menganyang to prepare the above food.

anyang II menganyang *~ hati* to hurt/offend, wound s.o.

anyang III (*Jv*) **menganyang** to haggle, bargain (about/over) the price.

anyang IV (*Jv*) *sakit* **anyang-anyangan/anyang-anyangen** (to have) dysuria.

anyang-anyang k.o. plant, *Elaeocarpus grandiflorus.*

anyar (*Jv*) new.

anyel (*Jv*) irritated, annoyed, peevish, petulant.

anyelir (*D*) carnation, *Dianthus caryophyllus.*

anyep (*Jv*) **1** cold, cool(er than normal); clammy, damp. **2** to be flat, insipid (of food flavor or aroma).

anyes (*Jv*) **1** cool and damp. **2** cold (of water, in a *kendi*).

anyih → ONYAH-ANYIH.

anyik → ONYAK-ANYIK.

anyir (*Jv*) **1** rancid, tasting/smelling of train oil, stinking (of uncooked fish/meat). **2** young and inexperienced.

anyut → HANYUT.

aom (*S*) servants' term of address for their master's son, young master.

aorta (*D*) aorta.

aot → AWUT.

a.p. (*abbr*) [atas perintah] on the orders of, by order of.

ap (in acronyms) → APARATUR.

apa 1 what?, what (k.o.) thing? to do what? *Hari - (sekarang)?* What day (is it today)? *Ini -?* What's this? *- namanya (itu)?* What's it called? What-do-you-call-it? *Anda lagi -?* What are you doing? *Anda sakit -?* What's wrong with you? *Perlunya -?* a) What do you want/need)? b) What's it for? *Mau -?* a) What are you going to do? b) What do you want? c) (kids, while fighting) Come on. I dare/challenge you. *Monyét itu sudah bisa -?* What k.o. things can monkeys do? *- (bahasa) Indonésianya ...?* What's the Indonesian word for ...? How do you say ... in Indonesian? **2** or (interrogative in alternative question). *Kecil - besar?* Is it small or large? *Nakal - tidak?* Was he naughty (or not)? *Iya - tidak?* Is it true (or not)? *Sudah beristri - belum?* Are you married (or not)? **3** is it the case that ...? *- iya/ya?* Is it true? Is that so? *Tamunya - banyak?* Were there many guests? **4** what, that which. *Saya tidak tahu - itu namanya.* I don't know what it's called. **5** (= apakah) whether. *Saya tidak tahu - dia sudah berangkat.* I don't know whether he's left. **6** (asks for family relationship) *Anak itu -mu?* What relation are you to that child? **7** (= apakah) (*coq*) precedes an interrogative sentence. *- dia tidak tahu?* Didn't he know it? **8** whatever, anything. *- saja* anything (at all), whatever there is. *Mau minum - ? - saja, téh boléh, kopi juga boléh.* What would you like to drink? Anything; tea or coffee will do. *Kami dapat memesan - saja yang kauperlukan.* We can order whatever you need. *organisasi - saja* any organization, no matter which. **9** (other idiomatic usages) *bukan karena - melainkan ...* simply and solely for ... *Wah, kok membeli buku Inggris -!* You've gone through all the trouble to buy an English book! *Kenapa ndak bisa tidur? Minum kopi itu -!* Why couldn't you sleep? Because I drank coffee. *- yang dikatakan/dinamakan ...* the so-called ... *-kah ... maupun ... whether ... or ... -kah berjalan kaki maupun berkendaraan, saya tidak perduli.* I don't care whether I walk or ride. *-nya yang ...?* What part/aspect of it is ...? *Satu hari dipakai saja dekilnya sudah seperti -.* After wearing it (the uniform) for one day, it's as filthy as I don't know what. *- akal?* what'll we do? *- boléh buat?* what can we do about it? what else can you do? *- daya?* what can be done? *- hendak dikata?* what more is there to say? *- kabar?* a) how are you? b) how you do? c) how is ...? *- lacur?* what can one do? *- lagi* a) what else? b) furthermore; especially; much less. *Merokok di hadapan Cik Yusuf meréka tak berani. - lagi minum dan makan.* They don't dare to smoke in front of Mr. Yusuf, much less to drink and eat. c) and on top of that. *- lagi saya ini orang melarat.* And on top of it all I'm poor. *- nian* whatever. *- pula* what else? *- pun* whatever. *- pun dia berkata, jangan menganggapnya sérius.* Whatever he says, don't take it seriously. *- pun juga* regardless, irrespective of, whether. *- pun juga keturunannya* regardless of descent. *- pun terjadi* come what may, whatever happens. *- siapa* the what and the who. ***mengapa-siapakan*** to write up, feature (in a magazine, etc.).

apanya what part of it?

apa-apa 1 something; anything, everything. *ada ~nya* there's s.t. behind that (incident). **2** (after negative) nothing. *tidak ada ~* there is nothing (going on). *tidak ~* a) there's nothing wrong, nothing at all, perfectly all right. b) it doesn't matter (at all), never mind, it's all right, no big deal. *Anjing itu tidak ~.* That dog isn't doing any harm. *mesti ada ~ dengan ...* there must be s.t. wrong with ... *tidak bisa ~* unable to do anything. **3** related to (usually in negative). *Dia bukan ~ saya.* He's not related to me. *Dia tidak ada ~nya dengan saya.* He's not related to me. **mengapa-apakan** [and **ngapa-ngapain** (*J coq*)] to do s.t. (harmful/bad) to/with. *tidak diapa-apakan lagi* (they were) not bothered any further. *Orang tua tidak akan diapa-apakan.* Nothing will be done with the elderly.

berapa (word that asks for a number as an answer) how much? how many? what amount? how? *~ kali sehari?* How many times a day? *Jam/pukul ~?* What time is it (by the clock)? *~ lama* how long? *sudah ~ lama* how long (has it been)? *~ lama*

pun no matter how long. *Tanggal ~?* What is the date? *~ saja* any amount. *~ umurnya?* How old is he (or, are you)? **seberapa** what amount, how, to what ... *~ dekat* how close. *~ jauh* to what extent, how far. *tidak ~* not so much. **beberapa** some; several, a few. *Mau ~ juga saya terima.* I'll accept whatever they want to do to me. **keberapa 1** (*yang*) ~ how many (from a certain point)? *stasiun yang ~?* How many stations (from a certain point)? **2** the umpteenth.

mengapa 1 why?, for what reason? *~ anda tidak datang kemarin?* Why didn't you come yesterday? **2** what's the matter with ..., what's with ...? *~ dia?* What's the matter with him? **3** to do what? *Sedang ~ kamu?* What are you doing? *tidak ~* it doesn't matter. **dimengapakan** to be treated in what way? *Mesti ~ barang ini?* What should we do with this?

ngapain (*J*) **1** what are you doing?, what are you going to do? **2** why, what's the point of? *~ berdébat?* What's the point of debating? **3** to do what to s.t.

mengapa(-apa)i to do s.t. to. *Diapa-apai maka ia menangis?* What did they do to him that he is crying?

mengapakan to do s.t. to, do what to. *Tidak ada yang berani ~nya.* Nobody has the nerve to do anything to him. *Barang-barang ini diapakan?* What should we do to these things?

mempengapakan → MENGAPAKAN.

apaan what kind of? *lelaki ~ lu?* (*coq*) what k.o. a guy are you? *tolong ~ dulu?* (*coq*) what should I help you with first?

apa-apaan *~ ni?* (*coq*) What's this all about? What's going on? *~ kamu ini?* What do you think you're doing?

apabila 1 when? *- ia datang?* When is he coming? **2** when. *Pasang lampu ini - sudah gelap.* Turn on the lamp when it's dark.

apai → GAPAI.

apak having a sweaty smell, musty, fusty, stuffy, frowsy (of food). **keapakan** mustiness.

apakala when, at the time that. *Dan akupun tersipu - bu Dikkha datang menyalamiku.* And even I was embarrassed when Mrs. Dikkha came and greeted me.

apal (*A*) to know by heart, memorize; → HAFAL. *Ayat ini saya sudah -.* I know this paragraph by heart.

mengapal(kan) to learn by heart, commit to memory.

ngapalin → MENGHAFALKAN.

apalan 1 material to be studied/learned/memorized. **2** s.t. to learn by heart.

apalagi 1 especially, above all, more than anything else, moreover, in addition, in particular. **2** furthermore, and on top of that. *- saya ini orang melarat.* And on top of that I'm poor. **3** to a much greater degree; (see also under APA). **4** let alone, even less.

apalah *sudi - kiranya* would you be kind enough to, please. *tak -* it doesn't matter. *- namanya* whatever-it's-called.

apam (*Tam*) cakes of steamed rice flour. *- cungkit* steamed cakes made with fermented cassava.

mengapam to cook such cakes. *- balik* (*M*) and in parts of Malaysia; → MARTABAK. *pipi seperti -* full and firm cheeks.

apar (*M*) blacksmith's workshop, smithy.

aparat (*D*) **1** apparatus, appliance, instrument, device. **2** (government) institution, officials, agency. **3** (- keamanan) law enforcement officials. *- bantu* auxiliary apparatus. *- bawah* the lower echelons of the civil service. *- intél(ijén)* a) intelligence agency. b) intelligence agent. *- penegak hukum* law enforcement (agency). *- penyaluran* distribution system.

beraparat equipped, outfitted.

aparatur (*D*) **1** apparatus, equipment. **2** machinery of the state, organ. *- bawahannya* its subordinated apparatus. *- negara* state apparatus.

aparatus (*E*) apparatus.

aparél (*D*) apparel.

apartemén (*D/E*) apartment, flat.

aparthéid (*D/E*) apartheid.

apas I neat (and nice); striking (in appearance), elegant.

apas II 1 tough luck, unlucky; → APES. **2 to** be unlucky, jinxed.

apatah → APAKAH (usually used in rhetorical questions). *- gunanya mengumpulkan uang banyak-banyak?* What's the use of collecting a lot of money?

apati (*D*) apathy.
apatis (*D*) apathetic, indifferent.
  keapatisan apathy.
apatisme apathy.
apatogén (*D*) apathogenic.
APBD (*init*) [Anggaran Pendapatan dan Belanja Daérah] Regional Revenues and Expenditures Budget.
APBN (*init*) [Anggaran Pendapatan dan Belanja Negara] National Revenues and Expenditures Budget. – *T/P* [... *Tambahan dan Perubahan*] Supplementary and Amended National Budget.
apdéling (*D*) → AFDÉLING.
APDN (*init*) [Akadémi Pemerintahan Dalam Negeri] Academy of Public Administration.
apdol → AFDOL.
apdrék and **apdruk** → AFDRUK.
apé (*J*) → APA.
apé and **apé-apé** (*J*) *kué* – a pancake made of wheat flour, sugar, and eggs.
apek → APAK.
apekir → APKIR.
apel (*D*) apple, *Malus communis*. – *hijau* Granny Smith apple. – *mérah* Red Delicious apple.
apél I (*D*) **1** roll call, muster. **2** appeal. *naik* – to file an appeal. **3** rally, assembly. – *besar* assembly, grand roll call. – *bendéra* flag roll call. – *karyawan* (government) employees' roll call. – *nama* roll call. – *kesiapan* call for preparedness. – *pagi* morning parade. – *siaga* call for readiness. – *siang* afternoon parade.
  berapél ~ *siaga* to be put on ready alert (of troops/police).
  mengapél 1 to (enter an) appeal. **2** to take roll call.
  mengapélkan to rally, assemble.
apél II (*coq*) **mengapéli** [and **ngapélin** (*J coq*)] to (pay a) visit (to) (the house of one's boy/girlfriend or fiancée). *Mély diapéli Banu.* Banu visited his girlfriend Mely.
apélatif (*D*) appellative.
apelmus (*D*) applesauce.
apem I → APAM.
apem II (*Pr*) vagina.
apéndiks (*D*) appendix.
apéndisitis (*D*) appendicitis.
apeng → APUNG.
apermut (*D*) rolled oats; → HAPERMOT.
apérsépsi (*D*) apperception.
apes (*J/Jv*) unfortunate, unlucky, to have bad luck, too bad; → APAS. *paling* – at worst.
  seapes as unlucky as.
api 1 fire (heat and light emanating from s.t. on fire), light, flame. *(kalau) ada asap (tentu) ada* – where there's smoke, there's fire. *dimakan* – to be consumed/eaten up by fire. **2** fire, conflagration; → KEBAKARAN. –! –! fire! fire! *bahaya* – danger/risk of fire, fire hazard. *bara* – embers. *batu* – a) flint. b) firebrand, instigator. *bendalu* – k.o. parasite which kills the trees to which it clings, *Loranthus sp. bunga* – a) spark. b) fireworks; → KEMBANG *api. cetus* – a) flint for making fire. b) cigarette lighter. *gorés* – matches. *gunung (ber)* – volcano. *kapal* – steamship. *kayap* – a) k.o. cancer. b) k.o. small abscess on hands or feet. *kayu* – firewood. *keréta* – train, railroad. *korék* – matches. *lidah* – tongue of flame. *loncatan* – sparks. *pedang* – flaming sword. *periuk* – bomb, hand grenade. *pucuk* – → LIDAH *api. puntung* – wood remnant still ablaze. *semut* – fire ant, *Solenopsis geminata. senjata* – firearm. *tali* –(.-) fuse. **3** spirit. – *Islam* the spirit of Islam. *bak/seperti – dalam sekam* there is a snake in the grass; → ada UDANG *di balik batu. – padam puntung berasap* things will not end there. *seperti – makan (dalam) sekam/dedak* and *ibarat – dalam jerami* a) to spread unnoticed. b) to bear malice. – *padam puntung hanyut* to be finished with that. *bersuluh minta/menjemput* – to ask again about s.t. which you already know. *meletakkan – di bubungan* to expose o.s. to unnecessary danger, incur unnecessary risks. *seperti – dengan asap* inseparable. – *kecil baik padam* to nip danger in the bud. – *lancip* a) (gasoline) blowpipe flame. b) oxygen flame. c) pilot light. – *luka* erysipelas. – *masak* fire for cooking. – *mengangah* coal fire. – *mercon/mercun* sparks from fireworks. – *neraka* the fires of

hell. – *pencucian/penyucian* purgatory, purgatorial fire. – *unggun* campfire, bonfire.
api-api 1 (= *anak* – and *batang* –) matches. **2** firefly, *Lampyris spp.* **3** fuse.
berapi 1 to have a fire. **2** to be on fire, flaming, glowing, burning. **3** volcanic. *gunung* ~ volcano. **4** to be fervent, fiery.
berapi-api 1 to see stars (in front of one's eyes), have dancing lights before one's eyes. **2** enthusiastic, spirited. **3** furious, raging; fiery, fervent.
mengapi 1 to resemble fire; firelike. **2** to fan a fire. **3** to arouse s.o.'s passions, get s.o. enthusiastic about s.t. **4** to incite, stir up.
mengapikan to light a fire to cook s.t.
mengapi-apikan to rouse, agitate, stir up, excite to action.
memperapikan to toast, roast, grill, broil.
api-apian immolation.
pengapi ignition.
pengapian igniting, ignition.
perapian 1 brazier, oven, stove, furnace. **2** ignition.
api-api 1 *pohon* – various species of mangrove, *Avicennia spp.* **2** k.o. plant, *Viscum orientale.*
apiat → AFIAT.
apik I 1 (*Jv*) smart, neat, nice, attractive, chic, tidy, orderly. *pakaian/busana* – chic clothes. **2** (*J*) very good (regarding maintenance). *dengan* – with care, very well.
  mengapikkan 1 to straighten up. **2** (*ob*) to care about; to pay attention to.
  keapikan neatness, tidiness.
  apik-apikan nicely.
apik II (*BG*) [agak pikun] pretty senile.
apikal (*D ling*) apical.
apikultur (*D*) apiculture.
apilan (*cla*) parapet, gun shield, rampart, bulwark, wooden breastwork for guns at mast of Malay pirate ship.
  berapilan with this rampart, etc.
apion (*ob*) spinning top.
apit 1 to be wedged/hemmed in between two surfaces, be between two things/persons, etc. *bulan* – the eleventh Muslim month of Zulkaedah (wedged between Ramadan and Zulhijjah). **2** → BERAPIT. – *lempang* (*naut*) the strakes on either side of a keel. **3** s.t. used as a wedge, clip, clamp.
apit-apit k.o. trap.
berapit 1 near, close to e.o. *bintang* – two stars close to e.o. **2** to be wedged between two things. *duduk* ~ to sit between two persons. *gunung* ~ a mountain between two other mountains.
mengapit 1 to squeeze (as in a press), pinch, clamp; to hold by pressing. *Ilalang itu diapit dengan buluh.* That grass was squeezed out by bamboo. *diapit tidak bersanggit, ditambat tidak berapit tali* a wife who is neglected by her husband but who is also not divorced. **2** to press, crush, etc. (with a heavy object). ~ *tebu supaya keluar airnya* to press sugarcane to extract the juice. **3** to place/put s.t. between two objects/persons, etc., flank. *Dia diapit oléh gubernur dan walikota.* He was flanked by the governor and the mayor. **4** to staple. **5** to enclose, surround.
mengapitkan to put s.t. close to s.t. ~ *pistol di pinggang* to strap a pistol to one's side.
memperapitkan to press tight, place close together, move two things closer to e.o. so that they press against e.o.
terapit 1 hemmed/wedged in, surrounded. **2** intercalated.
apitan 1 press, extractor, an instrument or machine by/in which s.t. is crushed/squeezed by pressure. ~ *minyak* oil press. ~ *tebu* cane mill. **2** electric terminal. **3** interpolation, intercalation.
pengapit 1 s.t. used as a wedge, paper clip, clamp. **2** (*cla*) a) uprights of door/window. b) adjutant. c) (*Mal*) best man at a wedding. **3** (= **apitan**) equipment used to wedge/press; a clip, clamp.
pengapitan the act of squeezing, pinching, pressing.
apit-apit I *burung* – Richard's pipit, *Anthus novaeseelandiae malayensis.*
apit-apit II k.o. wasp.
apiun (*A*) raw opium. *kembang* – poppy.
apiwan (*infr*) firefighter.
apkir (*D*) **1** rejected (for military service, etc.). **2** declared unfit, no longer usable; rejects, scrap.

mengapkir 1 to declare unfit for use/service. 2 to reject. 3 to condemn (a building). 4 to prohibit, ban.

apkiran rejected (because declared unfit for use). *barang* ~ reject(s).

pengapkiran 1 declaring unfit for service. 2 condemnation (of a building).

aplastik (*D/E*) aplastic (disease).

aplaus (*D/E*) applause.

aplikasi (*D*) application.

mengaplikasikan to apply (for a job/asylum, etc.).

teraplikasi applied.

pengaplikasian application, applying.

aplikatif (*D/E*) applicative; practical; applicatory.

aplos (*D*) → APLUS I. *pada waktu* – during the changing of the guard.

aplus I (*D*) 1 to relieve, take over. 2 relieved, changed (of the guard). 3 to redeem.

mengaplus to relieve (the guard).

aplusan turn, shift, swing. *kerja* ~ to take turns at a job. *bergantian* ~ to take turns relieving the guard.

aplus II (*D*) applause.

Apodéti [Associaçao Popular Démocratica Timorénse] Popular Democratic Association of East Timor, i.e., the original pro-Indonesian party of the former Portuguese Timor.

apokat (*D*) *buah* – → ADVOKAT II.

apolitik (*D*) apolitical.

apollo kronco rides in an amusement park.

apologétik and **apologétis** (*D*) apologetic.

apologi (*D/E*) apology.

berapologi to apologize.

apologia (*D/E*) apologia.

apologis (*D/E*) *kaum* – the apologists.

apopléksi (*D*) apoplexy.

aposisi (*D gram*) apposition.

apositif (*D/E gram*) appositive.

a posteriori and **aposteriori** (*L*) retrospectively, in retrospect.

apostolik (*D/E*) apostolic.

apostrof (*D/E*) apostrophe.

apoték (*D*) pharmacy, drug store.

perapotékan 1 pharmaceutical (*mod*). 2 pharmacy business. *suatu usaha menata kembali* ~ *di Indonésia* an effort to reorganize the pharmacy business in Indonesia.

apotéker (*D*) 1 pharmacist. 2 (*sl*) drug trafficker.

apotéma (*D*) apothem.

apotik → APOTÉK. – *hidup* a yard planted with vegetables for daily consumption.

apotiker → APOTÉKER.

appel → APEL.

appél → APÉL.

applaud 10 WP k.o. insecticide.

Apr. (*abbr*) [April] April.

aprésiasi (*D*) appreciation.

beraprésiasi to appreciate, be appreciative.

mengaprésiasi(kan) to appreciate s.t.

aprésiatif (*D/E*) appreciative.

aprésiator (*D/E*) appreciator.

April (*D*) (*bulan*) – April. – *Mop* April Fool's joke.

apriori and **a priori** (*L*) 1 a priori, before examination or analysis. 2 to make up one's mind in advance. *Saya tidak* –. I haven't made up my mind in advance.

aprit I → AFRIT.

aprit II (*J*) **aprit-apritan** to run helter-skelter/at breakneck speed, take to one's heels; → ABRIT-ABRITAN.

aprok → AMPROK.

apron (*D/E*) apron (for aircraft).

apropriasi (*D*) appropriation.

mengapropriasi to appropriate.

apsari (*Skr*) female angel, nymph.

apsir (*ob*) (army) officer; → OPSIR, PERWIRA.

apuah → AFWAH.

apu-apu k.o. floating plant, water lettuce, *Pistia strationes*; → KAPU-KAPU.

apuh wrung dry, squeezed out.

apukat → ADVOKAT I, II.

apung 1 drifting, floating. *batu* – pumice stone. 2 float, flotsam, life buoy/jacket/vest. *laksana – di tengah laut, dipukul ombak jatuh ke tepi* a creature of circumstances. – *buih* to rise and sink, go up and down.

apung-apung drift. ~ *buih* appearing and reappearing, ups and downs. ~ *kail* float. ~ *pelabuhan* buoy. ~ *pukat* float for a net.

berapungan (*pl subj*) to float around.

mengapung [and **ngapung** (*coq*)] 1 to come/rise/float to the surface, float, emerge from the water. *massa* ~ floating mass. 2 (*ob*) to fly away, soar up.

mengapungi to hover over, float around in.

mengapung(-apung)kan to set s.t. afloat. ~ *diri* to keep o.s. floating/afloat.

terapung(-apung) drifting/floating around. ~ *tak hanyut, terendam tak basah* the results/outcome are/is still uncertain. ~ *sama hanyut, terendam sama basah* in life and in death.

apungan 1 (*geol naut*) drift. 2 (*fin*) float.

pengapung floater, float. *alat* ~ float. *ban* ~ buoy. *kayu* ~ float (of a canoe).

pengapungan 1 floating. 2 floatation.

apuran (*J*) wastepipe, drain(pipe).

apus I *buluh* – yellow bamboo, *Gigantochloa apus*.

apus II (*Jv*) **ngapusi** to cheat, defraud, deceive, make a fool of.

apus-apusan deceit, cheating.

apus III → HAPUS. – *vagina* pap smear.

Aqasa Wiratangka name of the survival exercises for crew members of *Penerbad* (Army Aviation Service).

aqidah → AKIDAH. – *Islamiyah* the Islamic faith.

beraqidah ~ *Islamiyah* to have Islam as one's faith.

aqil → AKIL.

aql → AKAL.

'Aqrab and **'Aqrob** (*A*) Scorpio (in the Zodiac).

aquapolis (*D*) a community built over the water.

ar (in acronyms) → ARMADA, ARSIP.

ara I a generic name for trees of the fig type, *Ficus spp.*, and for some non-fig trees. *utang/pinjam kayu* – a debt that will be repaid when the fig tree does not produce sap, i.e., a debt that will probably never be repaid. *menanti(kan) – tidak bergetah lit.* "waiting for the sap of the *ara* tree which has none," i.e., waiting till doomsday, an endless wait. *menanti(kan) – hanyut* "waiting for the fig tree to wash away (which never happens in the desert)," i.e., tomorrow will never come, at some future time which will never arrive. – *akar* k.o. plant, *Ficus binnendykii*. – *batu* k.o. plant, billy-goat weed, *Ageratum conyzoides*. – *bertih* stinging fig, *Ficus fulva/gibbosa*. – *bukit* k.o. tree, *Pimeleodendron griffithianum*. – *buluh* k.o. fig, *Ficus villosa*. – *bungkus* k.o. fig, *Ficus annulata*. – *gajah* k.o. fig, *Ficus dubia*. – *kapuk* k.o. fig, *Ficus lepidocarpa*. – *katak* k.o. fig, *Ficus sp.* – *kelebuk* k.o. fig, *Ficus roxburghii*. – *keluak* k.o. fig, *Ficus glandulifera*. – *lumut* k.o. plant, *Croton caudatum*. – *mas* k.o. parasite. – *padi* k.o. fig, *Ficus chartacea*. – *pérak* k.o. fig, *Ficus alba*. – *songsang* k.o. plant, prickly chaff flower, *Achyranthus aspera*.

ara II → HARA I.

Arab (*A*) 1 Arab. 2 Arabic, Arabian. *bahasa* – Arabic. *Persatuan Émirat* – United Arab Emirates. *negara* – Arabia. *orang* – Arab. *tanah* – Arabia. – *Saudi* Saudi Arabia.

kearaban Arab (*mod*), of Arab background.

kearab-araban a bit Arab.

Arabica /arabika/ a coffee species.

Arabisasi (*D*) Arabization.

Arabusta [arabica + robusta] a cross between Arabica and Robusta coffee.

A'raf (*A*) al– "The Wall between Heaven and Hell"; name of the seventh chapter of the Koran.

Arafah and **Arafat** (*A*) name of a mountain and adjacent plain east of Mecca, where pilgrims spend the ninth day of Zulhijjah; → WUKUF.

Arafura *Laut* – Arafura Sea, between North Australia and South West Irian Jaya.

arah I 1 direction, course, heading, path one is taking. *dari – berlawanan* from the opposite direction. *dua –* two-way. *– ke (timur)* and *ke – (timur)* to(ward) (the east). *ke – datangnya suara itu* in the direction the voice is coming from. *–nya ke situ.* That's the way it's heading. *memberi – balik* to reverse (the direction of movement of s.t.). *tidak tahu –* to be disoriented. **2** (in the direction) of. *– barat* west of. **3** intention, aim, purpose, goal. *berkata tak tentu –nya* to speak aimlessly. *– angin* wind direction. *– gejala* trend. *– jarum jam* clockwise. *– kecenderungan* trend. *– melarikan diri* escape route. *– melintang* athwart. *– penglihatan* line of vision. *– perkembangan (ling)* drift. *– pokok* baseline. *– samping* traverse. *– serat* grain (in wood). *pada – serat* with the grain. *– terbang* trajectory. *– tindakan* policy.

searah in/of the same direction/course, going in the same direction (as). *aliran ~* direct current. *kawan ~* a like-minded person. *berjalan ~* to go in the same direction. *~ bertukar jalan* the end justifies the means. **menyearahkan 1** to direct s.t. toward. **2** (*elec*) to rectify. **tersearah** (*elec*) rectified. **penyearah** (*~ arus*) (*elec*) rectifier. **penyearahan** (*elec*) rectification.

berarah 1 to have a course/direction, to be directed. *~ kepada* to be directed toward. **2** with an aim/intention. *tak ~* aimlessly.

mengarah 1 to direct one's course, go in the direction of, head for. *~ ... pergi* to follow (with one's eyes) s.o. who is going/leaving. *~ ke lampu kuning* to be heading in a dangerous direction. **2** to point (to), aim (at), direct (at). **3** to supervise, manage, lead (a corporation/department, etc.). **4** to intend (for), aim (at). *yang diarah* the target. *diarah jiwanya* he became the target. **5** to aspire to.

mengarah-arah 1 to note and identify. **2** to direct, orientate.

mengarahi to give directions to.

mengarah-arahi to give many directions to s.o.

mengarahkan [and **ngarahin** (*J coq*)] **1** to direct, aim, point, face. *~ larasnya ke* to aim a gun at. *Arahkan TV itu kemari.* Face the TV this way. **2** to divert to(ward), steer. *Kapal diarahkan ke Belawan.* The ship was diverted to Belawan. **3** to direct (a movie, etc.). *diarahkan oléh sutradara itu.* directed by that (movie) director. **4** to target. *diarahkan ke sasaran di Éropa Barat* Western Europe is targeted (by the missiles). **5** to focus (attention) on.

mengarah-arahkan 1 to keep directing. **2** to intend, mean.

terarah 1 guided, directed, conducted, led; aimed, intended, meant. *~ kepada* directed/aimed at, targeted. **2** directional. *anténa ~* directional antenna. **keterarahan 1** directedness, directivity. **2** being guided. **3** guiding principles.

arahan 1 direction, guidance. **2** directive. *~ pentas* stage directions. **3** under the direction of, directed by. *~ Nugroho* under the direction of Nugroho. **4** (*ob*) casual additional/temporary worker, helper, assistant.

pengarah 1 director (of a corporation). *panitia ~* steering committee. **2** theater manager. *~ acara* director (TV, etc.), master of ceremonies, MC. *~ berita* news director. *~ gaya* stylist. *~ kata* narrator. *~ laku* theatrical director. **3** s.o. who or s.t. which sets the direction. **4** guide (*mod*). *rél ~* guide rails. **5** sighting equipment.

pengarahan 1 briefing; → SANTIAJI. *memberikan ~ kepada* to give a briefing to, brief. *mendapat ~* to get a briefing, be briefed. **2** directives, directions, guidelines. **3** the act of directing, steering. *pidato ~* speech which sets guidelines. *rapat ~* a) briefing. b) meeting of the steering committee. **4** alignment.

arah II (*M*) **arah-arah** about the same, almost like, alike; to resemble. *Namanya ~ nama orang Sunda.* His name is like a Sundanese name. **mengarah-arah** to resemble, look like, favor.

mengarahi (= **mengarah-arahi**) to resemble s.o./s.t. **2** to take a close look at.

arah III → ARA.

arai I (*M*) palm blossom, spadix.

arai II (*ob*) a measure for rice: two *cupak*.

arak I (*A*) rice wine, arrack. *kaki –* (*Mal*) drunkard.

pengarakan an arrack distillery. *– cap tikus* alcoholic drink made from distilled palm sap.

perarakan fermentation, making arrack. *– obat* tonic.

arak II berarak(-arak)(an) 1 to walk/march in a procession. **2** to float, drift, move slowly or easily in the air (as of clouds). *berarak ke tebing* to feel nervous all the time. *berarak tidak berlari* a collective act causing happiness need not be sped up. *angkasa ~ marak* the sky has a reddish/rosy glow (a bad omen).

mengarak [and **ngarak** (*coq*)] **1** to carry/escort in procession. **2** (*cla*) to anticipate, precede. *bintang timur ~ siang* Venus/the morning star heralds the day. **3** (*ob*) to drive a (soccer) ball (into the goal). **4** to march s.o. (in a certain direction). *~ daka(h)* to be on the point of death.

arakan and **arak-arakan** escort, procession. *~ mobil* motorcade. *~ obor* torchlight procession.

pengarak 1 participant in a procession. **2** vanguard, forerunner. *awan ~ angin* clouds are the vanguard of winds. *angin ~ hujan* wind is the forerunner of rain.

pengarakan procession.

perarakan 1 procession. **2** vehicle, etc. in a procession.

arak III berarakan (*J*) scattered, in disorder.

arakian (*cla*) then; furthermore, again; → ARKIAN.

aral (*A*) obstacle, hindrance. *– gendala/melintang/menggalang* unexpected obstacle, unforeseen event, accident. *(apa)bila/kalau tidak ada – melintang* as long as things run smoothly, if nothing intervenes, if all goes well. *berasa –* to feel discontented, unhappy about s.t.

mengarali to put an obstacle in the way of, prevent.

aram I aram-aram and **pengaram** scaffolding, temporary structure.

aram II *– temaram* a) clouded over (of the moon). b) twilight.

arang I 1 charcoal. **2** black dust which remains when s.t. has been scorched/charred, carbon. **3** shame, smear. **4** soot. *– di muka/dahi/kening* and *– yang tercoréng* an indignity one is made to suffer, insult, affront. *asam –* carbon dioxide. *batu –* pit coal. *benang –* thread stained with a mixture of soot and oil; used by a carpenter to draw a guideline on a timber. *kayu –* (*ob*) ebony; → KAYU hitam. *patah/putus –* an irreparable conflict. *pil –* activated-charcoal tablets; → NORIT. *– habis, besi binasa* an unsuccessful enterprise/undertaking. *– habis besi tak kimpal* a lot of expenses and still no profit. *membasuhkan – yang tercoréng di muka* to wipe out an indignity. *– sudah terbakar jadi bara* what is done cannot be undone, there's no use crying over spilt milk; → NASI sudah menjadi bubur. *– batok* charcoal made from coconut shells. *– batu* and *batu –* coal. *– besi* a) coke, slag. b) cinders. *– kayu* charcoal (made from wood). *– kokas* coke. *– padu* soft charcoal. *– pagu/para/para-para* soot. *– periuk* soot on pots. *– tulang* bone black.

berarang having charcoal, carbonized.

mengarang to become charcoal, carbonize.

mengarangkan to make charcoal.

pengarangan 1 carbonization. **2** place where charcoal is made. **3** charcoal brazier.

perarangan 1 place where charcoal is made. **2** charcoal (*mod*).

arang II (*M*) mouth. *mencabik –* to keep shouting.

arang-arang (*Jv*) *ikan –* black shark, *Labeo chrysophekadion*.

arang-arangan (*J*) k.o. song in *topéng Betawi*.

aran(g)semén (*D*) (musical) arrangement.

aran(g)sé and **aran(g)sir** (*D*) **mengaran(g)sir** to make a musical arrangement, arrange. **pengaran(g)sir** composer (of music), arranger. *~ musik* (music) arranger.

arap → HARAP. **ngarapin** → MENGHARAPKAN.

ararut (*D*) arrowroot, *Maranta arundinacea*.

aras I (*A*) → ARASH.

aras II (*cla*) checked, in danger (of the king in chess).

mengaras to checkmate.

aras III 1 level; border, limit. *yang –nya tinggi* high-level. **2** (*cla*) rising to a level with (the sea); surfacing. **3** (*mil*) air-target altitude. *– air* water table. *– lutut* knee-high.

mengaras to reach a limit/level. *~ awan* to the clouds. *Air ~ lutut.* The water rose knee-high.

mengarasi to delimit, define the limits of. *– air* water table.

aras IV *– kerdan* k.o. muffin, spiced puff.

aras V (*Jv*) **aras-arasan** don't feel like, feel too lazy to.

aras VI, arash and **arasy** (*A*) the throne of God.

arau I (*ob*) → KARAU.

arau II spotted (of bulls/dogs, etc.). – *batu* white dots on a dark background. – *hujan panas* red dots on a white background.

Arba(a) (*A*) (*hari* –) → RABU.

arbab (*A*) → REBAB.

arbain (*A*) forty.

    berarbain to perform forty prayers at the Nabawi Mosque in Madinah during the hajj.

arbéi (*D*) strawberry, *Fragaria spp*.

arbiter and **arbitor** (*D*) arbiter, arbitrator.

arbitrase (*D*) arbitration.

    berarbitrase to go to arbitration.

arbitrér (*D*) arbitrary.

arca (*Skr*) statue, image, bas-relief.

    mengarcakan to cast in stone.

    kearcaan sculptural.

    pengarcaan sculpting, casting into stone.

arde (*D elec*) earth, ground.

Ardhya Garini the Air Force Wives' Association.

ardi (*A cla*) mountain, the earth.

are (*D*) 100 square meters.

aréa (*E ob*) area, zone, province.

aréal (*D*) area, acreage. – *parkir* parking lot. – *temuan* situs.

arék (*Jv*) 1 child. 2 a native of. – *Surabaya/Suroboyo* a native of Surabaya.

arem (*Jv*) **arem-arem** rice prepared with coconut cream and minced meat and wrapped in a banana leaf.

    pengarem-ngarem and *tanah* **pengarem-arem** rice paddies turned over to a retired village official as a pension.

arén (*J*) areca palm tree, *Arenga sacchariferа/pinnata*; the flower stalk yields a liquid which can be made into a brown sugar or *gula –*, palm wine, etc.

aréna (*D*) arena, circle, coterie. – *parkir* parking lot.

areng → ARANG. **areng-areng** *kambang* (*J*) k.o. snack like *dodol* made from sticky rice.

arénisasi encouraging the planting of *arén* trees.

arep → HARAP. **ngarepin** → MENGHARAPKAN.

arerut → ARARUT.

ares a Balinese food made from young banana stalks and chicken.

arés I (*D*) 1 confinement, incarceration. 2 arrest, seizure, capture.

    mengarés 1 to confine, incarcerate, punish by confinement. 2 to arrest, seize, capture.

arés II (*Jv*) pith of the banana plant.

aréstasi (*D*) arrest, seizure, capture.

areuy (*S*) 1 climbing plant, climber, liana. 2 tendril of a liana.

argari → GARI.

Argéntina Argentina.

argo 1 clipped form of **argométer**. – *kuda* an overly fast taximeter. 2 – *Bromo* name of a train running between Jakarta and Surabaya. – *Dwipangga* name of a train running between Jakarta and Solo. – *Gedé* the name of a train running between Jakarta and Bandung. – *Lawu* name of a train running between Jakarta and Solo. – *Muria* name of a train running between Jakarta and Semarang.

argocycle (*D*) exercise bicycle.

argométer (*D*) taximeter.

    berargométer to be metered (of a taxi).

argon (*D*) argon.

argumén (*D*) argument.

    berargumén to argue.

arguméntasi (*D*) argumentation.

    berarguméntasi to argue, engage in an argument.

    mengarguméntasikan to argue about s.t.

arguméntatif (*D*) argumentative.

argus (*D*) guinea pig, *Cavia porcellus*.

arham (*A*) most merciful.

ari I 1 *kulit* – epidermis, scarfskin. 2 lamina.

    berari laminated.

    arian lamination.

    perarian lamination.

ari II *ular* – k.o. poisonous snake, *Doliophis spp*.

ari III ari-ari 1 abdomen. *tali ~* umbilical cord, navel string. 2 loin. 3 placenta, afterbirth. *~ biji* (*bot*) funiculus. 4 pubes.

ari IV (*Jv cla*) younger sibling.

ari V (*coq*) → HARI.

ari VI (*M*) horse corral, stall.

    mengari to corral.

aria I (*D*) operatic aria.

Aria II (*D*) Aryan.

Aria III (*Jv*) /ario/ honorific title of *bupati*.

aria IV (*ob naut*) lower away!

ari-ari umbilical cord.- *biji* funiculus.

arias *beras* – a type of high-quality rice.

arif (*A*) 1 to know, understand. 2 learned, wise, energetic, skillful. *yang* – (*Mal*) judge. 3 intelligent person. 4 capable. – *dalam segala hal itu* to understand all about that matter. *hendaklah – bahwa ...* (the reader) should pay note that ... – *bijaksana* wise. *tidak* – unable. **ketidak-arifan** lack of ability.

    mengarifi and **mengarifkan** 1 to understand, comprehend, apprehend. 2 to realize.

    terarif wisest.

    kearifan 1 learning, wisdom. 2 ability.

    pengarifan making s.o. wise.

arifin (*A*) wise men, the wise (plural of *arif*).

arih I mengarih(-arih)(kan) to put out (one's hand), put up (one's hand), hold out (one's hands to embrace s.o. or s.t. offered); *cp* MERAIH.

arih II (*M*) **mengarih** to tie, tether.

arik I mengarik 1 to grasp, hold. 2 to pull (an oar).

arik II (*A*) 1 awake, vigilant. 2 sleepless, insomniac; insomnia.

aring I k.o. trap/snare.

aring II stinking, smelly; smelling of urine.

aring III fretwork under the guard of a kris blade.

aring-aring k.o. tree, eclipta, false daisy, *Eclipta alba*; → URANG-ARING.

ariningsun (*Jv*) my younger sibling; → ADINDA.

Ario → ARIA III.

arip I (*Jv*) sleepy.

    pengarip sleepyhead.

arip II → ARIF.

aris I hem, turned-back edge (of sail).

    beraris hemmed.

    berariskan with a hem/edge made of.

aris II (*ob*) clotted/coagulated sap of a tree.

aris III (*A*) farmer.

arisan k.o. tontine; a regular social gathering for women at which every participant contributes a certain amount of money. At each meeting there is a lottery and the winner gets all the money. At the next meeting the previous winner is not allowed to participate in the lottery. Most *arisans* are held once a month and are held at the households of the participants in turn. – *call* an *arisan* in which the winner is determined by auction. – *drop* system in which members can buy s.t. one at a time in turn with each member putting in a set amount at stated intervals. – *jalan* bribe given by drivers to road officials (police, etc.). – *jedulan* club *arisan*. – *pembauran* (in Banjarmasin) an *arisan* under the aegis of the *Badan Komunikasi Penghayatan Kesatuan Bangsa*. – *piao/piau* k.o. *arisan* in which a member can get a turn first by agreeing to put in more than the others.

    berarisan to hold an *arisan*.

aris-aris (*naut*) a bolt rope, shrouds.

aristokrasi (*D*) aristocracy.

aristokrat (*D*) aristocrat.

aristokratis (*D*) aristocratic.

Aristotelés Aristotle.

arit I (*Jv*) 1 grass knife, sickle. 2 rubber-tapping knife. *kuli* – rubber tapper. *palu* – hammer and sickle. *tukang* – grass-cutter.

    mengarit 1 to cut grass. 2 to look for grass to sell as fodder.

    ngarit (*coq*) to seek spare-time employment (particularly during office hours).

    aritan s.t. cut, mowed.

    pengarit 1 mower. 2 s.o. who finds grass to sell as fodder.

arit II k.o. fish spear; → PIARIT.

aritmétika (*D*) arithmetic.
aritmia – *jantung* arrhythmia, any disturbance in the rhythm of the heartbeat.
arivé → ARRIVÉ.
ariyah (*A*) lending, loan.
arja (in Bali) a drama involving singing and dancing.
Arjuna I (*Skr*) **1** a heroic *wayang* character who has many wives and mistresses; he is the ideal man for older Javanese. **2** (*BG with lowercase a*) boyfriend, steady. **3** handsome man. – *idaman* idol; → IDOLA. – *Wiwaha* "Arjuna's wedding" to Supraba, an episode in the *Mahabharata* and subject of an old Javanese poem.
Arjuna II a corn/maize variety.
arka (*A*) weak.
arkais (*D*) archaic.
arkaisme (*D*) archaism.
arkan (*A*) (plural of *rukun*) articles of Islamic faith. *–ul iman* the major beliefs of Islam. *–ul Islam* the five pillars of Islam.
arkati (*A*) pilot, s.o. licensed to direct or steer ships into and out of a harbor or through difficult waters.
arkéolog (*D*) archeologist.
arkéologi (*D*) archeology; → WIDYAPURBA.
arkéologis (*D*) archeological.
arkhais → ARKAIS.
arkian further, moreover, besides, and then, furthermore, again.
arktik (*D/E*) arctic, North Pole; → KUTUB *utara*.
arku (*Port ob*) bow (of a kite).
arkus (in Manado) triumphal arches.
arloji (*D*) clock; watch; → AIRLOJI.
  berarloji to wear a watch, have a watch on. – *kantong/saku* pocket watch. – *tangan* wristwatch.
arma (in acronyms) → ARMADA.
armada (*D*) **1** fleet of warships, armada. *pangkalan* – naval base. **2** a country's merchant vessels. **3** fleet of cars. – *angkutan jalan raya* fleet of public transportation. – *niaga* mercantile marine, merchant fleet. – *semut* fleet of motor-driven praus; → (*perahu*) KETINTING. – *tempur* battle fleet. – *udara* the fleet of planes (owned by airlines in Indonesia).
armatur (*D/E*) armature.
Arménia (*D/E*) Armenia.
arnab (*A mostly Mal*) rabbit, hare, *Oryctolagus spp. tahun* – the year of the rabbit.
arnal and **arnél** (*D*) hairpin.
Arnas → ARSIP *Nasional*.
aro k.o. fig tree, *Ficus spp.*
arogan (*D/E*) arrogant.
arogansi (*D*) arrogance.
aroma (*D/E*) fragrance.
  beraroma aromatic.
aromatik (*E*) and **aromatis** (*D*) aromatic.
arombai Ambonese prau; → ARUMBAÉ.
aron (*J/Jv*) parboiled.
  mengaron to parboil rice for later steaming.
  aronan parboiled rice.
aronskélk (*D*) arum.
arowana (*ikan*) – arowana, dragon fish, *Scleropages formosus*.
Arpah (*A*) Mount Arafat, northeast of Mecca.
arpus 1 resin (for stringed instruments). **2** wood glue.
Arqom (*A*) one of the Prophet Muhammad's companions. *darul* – one of the places in which the Prophet Muhammad gathered with his companions for discussions.
'arrad (*A*) horoscopist, person who casts s.o.'s horoscope.
arrahman (*A*) the Merciful. – *arrohim* the Merciful and the Benevolent.
arrivé (*D/Fr*) well off, arrived (economically).
arrohim (*A*) the Benevolent.
arsén (*D*) arsenic.
arsenal (*D*) arsenal.
arsénikum (*D*) arsenic.
arsik (*M*) fish in tomato and spices; → PINDANG.
arsin stressed (syllable in meter).
arsip (*D*) archives, records, file(s). *dalam* – on file. – *aktif* active

files. – *biasa* unclassified files. – *dinamis* dynamic files. – *inaktif* inactive files. – *nasional* national archives. – *rahasia* classified files. – *statis* static files.
  berarsip archival.
  mengarsip archival.
  mengarsipkan to archive.
  kearsipan archival matters.
  pengarsip archivist.
  pengarsipan filing, archiving.
arsiparis 1 archivist. **2** file clerk.
arsipélago (*D*) archipelago.
arsipis (*D*) archivist, filing superintendent.
arsir (*D*) **mengarsir** to hatch (in drawing).
  arsiran hatching (in drawing).
arsis (*D*) arsis.
arsiték (*D*) architect. – *dalam rumah* interior designer. – *landskap* landscape architect.
  mengarsitéki to design, engineer.
arsitéktonis (*D*) architectonic.
arsitéktur (*D*) architecture.
  berarsitéktur with a ... architecture.
  berarsitékturkan ... with ... as its architecture.
arsitéktural and **arsitékturil** (*D*) architectural.
arso (*Jv*) **ngarso** in front of an exalted person.
arsu [*artileri sasaran udara*] (*mil*) radar signature seeking (missile).
arsy → ARASH.
art (in acronyms) → ARTILERI.
arta (*Skr*) money, wealth; → ARTHA, HARTA. – *Yasa* the Mint.
artal → HARTAL.
artawan → HARTAWAN.
artefak (*D/E*) artifact.
artefaktual (*D/E*) artefactual.
arteri and **artéria** (*D/E*) artery. *jalan* – arterial road.
artériografi (*D/E*) arteriography.
artériosklérosis (*D/E*) arteriosclerosis.
artésis (*D*) (*sumur*) – artesian (well).
artha (*Skr*) money. – *Kencana* and (later) *-karini* name of the women's association of the Department of Finance.
arti (*Skr*) **1** meaning, sense, idea conveyed; → ERTI, (ME)NGERTI. *pendidikan dalam* – *sempit* education in the narrow sense of the word. *mempunyai dua* – ambiguous. **2** significance, importance. *tak ada* –*nya* it is of no use/significance. – *dua* ambiguity. – *ganda* double meaning. – *harfiah* literal meaning. – *kiasan* figurative/nonliteral meaning. – *penting* significance. (*punya*) – *tersendiri* (to have) a meaning of its own. – (*yang*) *mendatang* a derived meaning. – *yang semula/asli* original meaning.
artinya I mean (*lit* "the meaning of it is"), that is, i.e., *Apa* ~? What does it mean?
  searti of similar/the same meaning, synonymous. *Carilah kata-kata yang* ~. Please look for synonyms. ~ *dengan* synonymous with.
  berarti 1 to mean, have a meaning, signify. **2** significant, meaningful, of value, important, useful. *tidak* ~ insignificant, negligible, meaningless. *cidera tak* ~ a superficial injury. **3** to be synonymous with, mean/be the same as. *Mengambil milik orang tanpa permisi* ~ *mencuri*. Taking s.o.'s property without permission is the same as stealing. *tiada/tidak* ~ meaningless, senseless, pointless. **ketidak-berartian** meaninglessness.
  keberartian significance.
  mengarti (the less frequent form; → MENGERTI the more frequent form).
  ngarti (*J*) to understand, comprehend. *sudah* ~ tamed, domesticated (of a bird, etc.).
  mengartikan [and **ngartiin** (*J coq*)] **1** to interpret, set forth the meaning of, explain, elucidate. **2** to lead one to understand, help to understand.
  terartikan (*infr*) can be interpreted.
  artian meaning, sense, interpretation. *jabatan rangkap dalam* ~ *kedinasan* holding two jobs at the same time, in the sense of service. *dalam* ~ *luas* in a broad sense.
  arti-artian various k.o. meanings.

pengartian understanding, comprehension, grasp, apprehension, perception.

artifak (*D*) artifact.

artifisial (*D*) artificial.

  keartifisialan artificiality.

artifisialitas (*D*) artificiality.

artik(a) (*D*) arctic (ocean).

artikel (*D/E*) 1 article (in newspaper). 2 clause. 3 (*gram*) article. – *karét* (*leg*) a clause subject to various interpretations. – *tentu* (*gram*) definite article. – *tak tentu* (*gram*) indefinite article.

  mengartikelkan 1 to draw up legal statutes. 2 to write an article about s.t. for a magazine/newspaper.

  pengartikelan writing up s.t. as an article.

artikulasi (*D*) articulation.

  berartikulasi to articulate (sounds).

  mengartikulasikan to articulate s.t., express (feelings, etc.).

  pengartikulasian articulating.

artikulatif (*D*) articulatory.

artikulator (*E ling*) articulator.

artileri (*D/E*) artillery.

  keartilerian artillery (*mod*).

artis (*D/E*) artist, actor. – *film* film actor. – *penata grafis* graphic art designer.

  keartisan art (*mod*).

  perartisan art (*mod*).

artisan (*D/E*) artisan.

artistik (*D/E*) artistic.

  keartistikan artistic.

artisyok (*D*) artichoke.

artona (*hama* –) pest which attacks coconut leaves.

artritis (*D*) arthritis.

arts (*D ob*) physician, general practitioner; → DOKTER.

Aru Buginese title of nobility.

aruan (*ikan* –) a) edible freshwater murrel, snakehead fish, *Ophiocephalus striatus*. b) Bombay duck, lizard fish, *Harpodon nehereus*.

aru-aru *hantu* – a malicious forest spirit.

arud (*A*) poetic meter.

aruda (*Port*) rue, *Ruta angustifolia/graveolens*.

aruh I (*Jv?*) effect; → PENGARUH.

  ngaruh to have an effect, be efficacious. *tidak* ~ it has no effect, it doesn't matter, it's not important.

  aruhan (*bio*) induction.

aruh II – *ganal* (in Central Kalimantan) a big *selamatan*.

aruk I mengaruk (*ob*) to perform a Buginese dance with a kris in the hand, pretending to attack an enemy as a token of loyalty to the *raja*.

aruk II mengaruk to disturb, bother.

  pengaruk s.o. who disturbs.

arum → HARUM. – *dalu* night-blooming jasmine, *Cestrum nocturnum*. – *manis* cotton candy.

  arum-aruman fragrances.

arumbaé Ambonese fishing boat.

arummanis → HARUM *manis*.

arun I (*M*) → HARUM.

arun II mengarun to mix, stir (rice, etc.), beat, whip.

  arunan s.o. mixed/stirred.

  pengarun s.o. or s.t. that mixes/stirs.

arung – *jeram* white-water rafting. **mengarungi jeram** to go white-water rafting. ~ *jeram di Sungai Alas* whitewater rafting down the Alas River (in Aceh).

  mengarung 1 to wade (across), walk through (shallow water/mud/a river/tall grass, etc.). ~ *rimba* to walk through the jungle. 2 to cruise. ~ *samudera luas* to cruise the wide ocean. 3 to make one's way (through difficulties, etc.).

  mengarungi 1 to cross (a river, etc.). 2 to sail across. 3 to go through/experience difficulties. 4 to plod through. 5 to traverse, go across.

  mengarungkan to sail s.t. around/across.

  (arung-)arungan 1 shallows in a river, ford. 2 riptides at sea. 3 shipping corridor.

  pengarung s.o. who wades across, s.o. who runs (the rapids).

pengarungan the act of wading/crossing, running (a river). – *jeram* running the rapids.

arus I 1 flow (of water/air/electricity, etc.), stream, current. – *masyarakat yang mudik* the stream of city-dwellers going back to their native villages, particularly to celebrate Lebaran. *dibawa* – to be swept/carried away by the stream (current). *melawan/menyongsong* – to go/run against the current, run counter to. *sumber* – source of current. 2 tide. – *antar* conduction current. – *atas* the government. – *balik* countercurrent, backwater; feedback. – *balik belakang* undertow, underflow. – *barang* flow of goods. – *bawah* undertow, undercurrent. – *bayar tunai* cash flow. – *bolak-balik* alternating current. – *dana* cash flow. – *deras* torrent. – *Gelombang Panas* Gulf Stream. – *golak-galik* convection current. – *hayati* vital fluid. – *kas* cash flow. – *khatulistiwa* equatorial current. – *kuat* high-tension current. – *kutub* polarization current. – *lalulintas/lalulalin* traffic flow. – *laut* marine/ocean current. – *lawan* countercurrent. – *lemah* low-tension current. – *listrik* electric current. – *listrik searah bertegangan tinggi* high-voltage direct current. – *modal* capital flows. – *modal masuk* net capital inflow. – *olak(an)* a) (*elec*) eddy current. b) rollers, waves. – *panas* heat wave. – *pasang surut* tidal current. – *pecah* rip current. – *pemikiran* flow of ideas. – *péndék/pintas* short circuit. – *penukar* alternating current. – *pesisir* coastal current. – *pokok* mainstream, thrust. – *pusar* (*elec* and *naut*) eddy current. – *putaran* rotary current. – *rangga* alternating current. – *searah* direct current. – *sejarah* the course of history. – *semilih* alternating current. – *séntakan* shock, surge (*elec*). – *sesat* stray current. – *Teluk* Gulf Stream. – *tukar* alternating current. – *tunai* cash flow. – *udara* air current. – *urbanisasi* the flow of people into the cities. – *utama* mainstream. **pengarusutamaan** mainstreaming.

  searus following the same trend.

  berarus and **mengarus** to flow.

  mengaruskan to make s.t. flow.

arus II → HARUS.

arus III (*A*) bridegroom.

arwah (*A*) 1 the vital element in a man. 2 the soul, spirits of the dead. 3 the late, former; ghost (of deceased person). *bulan* – the eighth month of the Arabic calendar. *doa* – prayers for a deceased person, *esp* at his grave. *hilang/terbang* – lose consciousness, faint. *kenduri* – *selamatan* in commemoration of the dead. *membaca* – and

  mengarwahkan to hold a memorial service for (the dead with recitation and a banquet).

arwana *ikan* – → SILUK II, IKAN *kayangan*. a freshwater decorative fish, *Scleropagus formosus, Osteoglossum bicirrhosum arwana*.

arya → ARIA.

Aryaduta (*Skr*) Ambassador; the name of a hotel in Jakarta (Hyatt Aryaduta Hotel).

arz (*A*) → ARDI II.

arzak (*A*) k.o. jewel.

as I (*D*) 1 axle. *negeri-negeri* – the Axis (powers). – *belakang* rear axle. – *gardan* propeller shaft. 2 axis.

as II (*D*) ace (in card deck). – *sekopong* ace of spades.

as III (*A*) myrtle.

as IV (*D*) axe.

as V (in acronyms) → ASURANSI , ASISTÉN.

AS VI [Amérika Serikat] /a-és/ the United States of America.

as VII [alaihis salam] Peace be with him (after names of prophets other than the Prophet Muhammad).

asa I (*Skr*) hope. *hilang/putus* – a) to be in despair, be desperate, be at one's wits'/wit's end, be at a loss for what to do. b) to lose hope. *memutuskan* – to make s.o. despair. – *sia-sia* idle/vain hope.

  mengasakan 1 to hope for. 2 hoping.

  asa-asaan forever/always hoping nervously, expectant.

  pengasaan (*ob*) expectation.

asa II (*M*) 1 opinion, suspicion, surmise. 2 intentional, deliberate, on purpose.

  mengasa 1 to think, suspect, surmise. 2 to do s.t. intentionally/on purpose.

asa III (*Skr*) → ESA.

asa IV (*A*) mint.

asabah and **asabat I** (*A*) **1** heirs directly related to the deceased. **2** heirs related to the deceased on the father's side. **3** heirs who get what is left over (after the estate has been distributed to other heirs).

asabat II (*A*) **1** nerve. *perang* – war of nerves. *sakit* – nervous disorder/breakdown. **2** sinew, muscle(s).

asabiah and **asabiya** (*A*) (bond of social) solidarity.

asabot → ASABAH, ASABIAH.

asad (*A*) **1** lion. **2** Leo (*zod*).

Asada Buddhist holiday celebrating Siddharta's first sermon after being enlightened.

asah I filing (of teeth/diamonds, etc.). *calak-calak ganti* – s.t. used for the time being (pending the acquisition of a better one). – *bulat* and – *papan* tooth-filing styles. – *terampil* to sharpen one's wits.

    berasah sharpened, whetted, planed, polished.

    mengasah(kan) [and **ngasah** (*coq*)] **1** to sharpen, whet, plane, grind, whet, hone. – *budi/pikiran* to sharpen one's wits, make o.s. more alert mentally. ~ *hati* to excite, irritate, make angry, vex. ~ *otak* to wrack one's brain. **2** to file down (teeth). **3** to split/cut/polish diamonds, etc.

    terasah (to get) sharpened.

    asahan 1 s.t. that has been sharpened/whetted. *intan* ~ polished diamond. **2** shavings, filings. ~ *kayu* wood shavings. **3** dust. *batu* ~ hone, grindstone, s.t. used for sharpening/whetting.

    pengasah 1 hone, grindstone. **2** sharpener, person who sharpens/whets. ~ *otak* brainteaser.

    pengasahan sharpening, whetting, grinding.

asah II → SAH.

asahan k.o. shrub, *Tetracera assa*.

asah-asih-asuh (*Jv*) to love, help and cause harmony between e.o.

asai 1 weevil. **2** rotten (of wood), moldy, mildewed.

    berasai moldy.

    mengasai to molder, be worm-eaten.

asainéring (*D*) **1** sanitation. **2** sewer. *tukang* – sewage worker.

asak crammed, packed, stuffed.

    berasak 1 (= **berasak-asak**) to be crammed, crowded, packed. **2** (*M*) to shift, move. *Ia tidak* ~ *dari tempatnya.* He stayed in place/didn't move.

    berasak-asakan to crowd, crush (of people in crowds), jostle e.o., be jammed together.

    mengasak(i) 1 to cram, gorge; to ram down. **2** to push ahead with one's body. **3** (*M*) to move, shift. *diasak layur, dicabut mati invariable*, unalterable. *sebagai ayam diasak malam* completely helpless. ~ *kaji* to switch/change to another subject. **4** to insist, urge, press. **5** to replace, supplant. **6** (*geol*) to subdue.

    mengasakkan to cram/stick s.t. (into s.t.).

    terasak 1 crammed, packed. **2** pushed aside, moved, shifted. **3** urged, pressed, compelled. *Dia merasa* ~ *untuk menjual rumahnya.* He felt compelled to sell his house. **4** (*geol*) subdued.

    asakan crowd, press (of the crowd).

    pengasak stuffing tool.

asal I (*A*) **1** origin, beginning, root, source. **2** to come from, be originally from. *Pemain-pemain* – *Indonésia.* The players come from Indonesia. **3** the original situation/place/shape/form, etc. *dikembalikan ke* –*nya* returned to their place of origin. *Catnya masih* –. It still has its original paint. *pulang* – and *kembali pada* – to return to one's original place or to the original state. *surat keterangan* – *barang* certificate of origin (i.e., a commercial document). – *ada* a) to shirk/get out of. b) it's doing OK; it will do for lack of s.t. better. – *SIM* (after an accident) this driver's license goes back to … *damai* – *damai* and – *damai saja* peace at any cost/price. *menang* – *menang* victory at any price. *kota* – *ku* my hometown. – *ayam pulang ke lumbung,* – *itik pulang ke pelimbahan* a leopard cannot change its spots. *usul menunjukkan* – the tree is known by its fruit. – *dalam* endogenous. – *jasad* organic. – *kata* (*gram*) the root of a word. – *keturunan* ancestry. – *luar* exogenous. – *muasal* causes, origins. – *mula* the cause (of s.t.). – *mulaning/usuling dumadi* (*Jv*) the origin of mankind. – *usul* a) origin, descent, stock, parentage, pedigree, antecedents, details. b) primary causes. – *usul keturunan* lineage, roots.

    asalnya originally; to derive (from). ~ *dari mana?* Where is he/are you from originally? *Kata ini* ~ *dari* … This word is derived from … ~ *sama* to be cognate.

    seasal (*dengan*) cognate, related. ~ *sepangkal* of the same family background and origins.

    berasal 1 to come from originally. *Dia* ~ *dari Boyolali.* She comes from Boyolali. **2** to emanate/stem from, be based on. *Berita itu* ~ *dari pihak resmi.* The news stems from official sources. **3** to date (back to). **4** made (in) (the place where s.t. was originally manufactured, place where s.o. was originally educated, trained, etc.; place of birth, etc.). *barang-barang yang* ~ *dari Jepang* goods made in Japan. *para guru* ~ *dari IKIP* teachers trained at IKIP. **5** to be a descendant of, come from. *Dia* ~ *dari orang baik-baik.* He comes from a good family. **6** to be a descendant of. **7** to be of high and noble social status.

    mengasalkan 1 to return/go back to the source/origin. **2** to trace the origin of. **3** (*math*) to reduce. ~ (*ke*)*pada* a) to lead everything back to. b) to derive from. *diasalkan* (*oléh*) to be caused by.

    asalan *rotan* ~ raw rattan.

asal II (*A*) **1** (– *saja* and **asalkan**) provided that, providing, as long as, on the understanding that. *Anda boléh pulang* – *pekerjaannya sudah selesai.* You can go home provided that the work is finished. – *Bapak Senang* [ABS] provided that the *Bapak* is pleased, i.e., the most important thing is to please the person in charge. – *Béta Selamat* as long as I'm OK, to look out for number one first. **2** if, subject to. – *belum terjual* subject to prior sale. **3** every. – *orang masuk diladéni* (in store) everyone who walks in is served. **4** to do in any old way, do s.t. for no good reason other than to do it. – *jadi* slapdash, to do s.t. just so that it gets done (regardless of the quality). – *jadi saja* in a slapdash manner, carelessly. *Jangan* – *jadi saja!* Don't do it carelessly. *Jangan* – *berkata saja.* Don't just speak in any old way/impulsively. – *menyetujui* to rubber-stamp s.t. *baju* – *témpél* any old piece of clothing/rag.

    seasalnya perfunctorily.

    asal-asalan 1 at will, as one wishes, according to one's whim; a perfunctory/haphazard/slipshod performance of a task or answer to a question. *bersifat* – kitch; → HANTAM *kromo. menjawab dengan* ~ to answer any old way/for the sake of saying s.t. *kuliah dengan* ~ to take courses without any goal. **2** just for show, merely symbolic.

asali (*A*) **1** original. **2** genuine, authentic. **3** to be from a good family, of noble birth; → ASLI.

asaliah → ASALI.

asam 1 sour, having a sharp taste like that of vinegar; → MASAM. **2** tamarind, sour fruit of a type of tropical tree. **3** sour (of face). **4** (chemical compound) acid. *zat* – oxygen. *Bagaimana* – *garamnya?* How do you like its taste? *sudah banyak makan* – *garam* and *tahu* – *garamnya* a) to know the ins and outs of, have a profound knowledge of. b) to have a lot of experience (in one's life). *kenyang* – *garam kehidupan* to have had a lot of experiences in one's life. *bagai melihat* – to hanker after, crave; one's mouth is watering. *kurang* – (euph for *kurang ajar*) rude, impolite. – *di darat ikan di laut* (– *garam di laut,* – *di gunung*) *bertemu dalam belanga juga* they are predestined for e.o., their marriage was made in heaven. – *amino* amino acids. – *arang* a) carbonic acid. b) carbon dioxide. – *aromatik* aromatic acid. – *arsenat* arsenic. – *askorbat* ascorbic acid. – *belérang* sulfuric acid. – *bénzoat* benzoic acid. – *bongkrék* acid produced by bacteria in coconut waste (can be fatal if eaten). – *borat* boric acid. – *butirat* butyric acid. – *caluk* k.o. tamarind with small leaves. – *cuka* acetic acid. – *empedu* bile acid. – *éncér* diluted acid. – *folat* folic acid. – *fosfat* phosphoric acid. – *fosfor* phosphoric acid. – *galat* gallic acid. – *garam* a) hydrochloric acid. b) acidic flavoring. c) life experience, joys and sorrows of life, ups and downs. *banyak makan* – *garam hidup ini* to have experienced the ups and downs of life. – *gelugur* k.o. plant with sour fruit, *Garcinia atroviridis*. – *glukomat* glucomic acid. – *Jawa* tamarind, *Tamarindus indica*. – *jeruk* citric acid. – *kandis* pieces of dried black tamarind, *Garcinia globulosa*. – *karbol* carbolic acid. – *kersik* salicic acid. – *khlorida* chloride acid. – *klorat* chloric acid. – *kolat* bile acid. – *kranji* k.o. tamarind tree, *Dialium indum*. – *kuning* → ASAM *Jawa*. – *laktat* lactic acid. – *lambung* gastric acid/juices. – *landi* k.o. tree, *Pithecelobium dulce*. – *lemak* fatty acid. – *lilin* stearic acid. – *limau* citric acid. – *minyak* oleic acid. – *nitrat* nitric acid. – *nitrit* nitrous acid. – *Padang* → ASAM *kandis*. – *pekat* concentrated acid. – *pelelah* lactic acid. – *pikrat* picric acid. – *puya* an herbaceous plant, *Oxalis corymbosa*. – *salisilat* salicylic acid. – *samak* tannic acid. – *sendawa* nitric acid. – *sianida* cyanide acid. – *sidrat* cidrate acid. – *sitrat* citric acid. – *stéarat* stearic acid. – *sulfat/sulfur* sulfuric acid. *susu* lactic acid. – *tanat* tannic acid. – *urat* uric acid.

seasam as sour as. *sudah* ~ *segaramnya* it is already perfect (of a work/actions, etc.). *kelihatan* ~ *kelatnya* to show o.s. at one's worst.

mengasam 1 to clean/wash/treat (a kris, copper or brass objects) with tamarind/acid. 2 turn s.t. to acid.

mengasami to add acid (to food), make more vinegary. ~ *hati* to hurt s.o.'s feelings.

mengasamkan 1 to marinate. 2 to pickle, preserve with vinegar/tamarind.

asaman 1 (in chemistry) acids. 2 pickled (fruits, etc.).

asam-asaman pickles, preserved (fruits, etc.).

keasaman acidity.

keasam-asaman sourish, acidic.

pengasam acidulant.

pengasaman acidification, adding acid (to food).

asan I (*M*) hope; → ASA I. – *tak* – forever/always hoping; anxious, disturbed, concerned.

asan II *ikan* – k.o. fish, sergeant major, *Abudefduf saxatilis*.

asan III → ACAN III.

asap 1 smoke, steam, vapor, fumes. *menggantang* – to build castles in the air. *menghilang* – to disappear like smoke in the sun. *mengepulkan* – *rokok* to exhale cigarette smoke. *belum dipanjat* – *kemenyan* not yet married. *tidak ada* – *tidak ada api* there is no smoke without fire. *corong/cerobong* – a) chimney. b) funnel (of a steamer). *daging* – smoked beef. *embun* – fine dewlike haze in the evening. 2 smoked. *ikan* – smoked fish. *kapal* – steamer, steamship. *perang* – mock battle. *tabir* – smoke screen. – *air* vapor. – *api* smoke. – *belérang* sulfur fumes. – *buangan* (from a bus, car, etc.) exhaust gas/fumes. – *dapur* household expenses; savings in a bank. *mempertahankan* – *dapur* to make ends meet. *ngepulnya* – *dapur* keeping the home fires burning. *turut meramaikan* – *dapur* to provide part of the household expenses. – *kemenyan* fumes of incense. **mengasap-kemenyani** to praise. – *mesiu* gun smoke. – *pelindung* smoke screen. – *perang* chemical smoke. – *racun* toxic fumes. – *ratus* smoke from the burning of a mixture of incense and other fragrant substances. – *solar* carbon monoxide. – *tangis* tear gas.

berasap 1 to smoke. *bintang* ~ comet. *membuat dapur* ~ to keep the home fires burning. *dapur tidak* ~ very poor. 2 smoky, dim, misty, steaming.

berasap-asap steaming/piping hot (cup of coffee, etc.).

mengasap 1 to become smoke, vanish into smoke. 2 vaporized. 3 (= **mengasapi**) to smoke/cure (foods). 4 to fumigate. 5 to scent, perfume.

mengasapi 1 to smoke out, fumigate. 2 to smoke (foods). 3 to scent, perfume. ~ *daging* to smoke beef. ~ *dapur* to make ends meet, provide one's livelihood. ~ *nyamuk* to drive away mosquitoes by using smoke. ~ *pakaian* to make clothes smell fragrant by burning a mixture of incense and other fragrant substances.

mengasapkan to smoke (foods).

pengasap smoker (the implement).

pengasapan 1 fumigation, smoking. 2 fogging.

perasapan equipment or incense burner for smoking clothes, censer.

asar I (*A*) 1 third daily Muslim prayer. 2 the period between 3 and 5 p.m. when this prayer takes place. – *rendah* 4–5 p.m. – *tinggi* 3–5 p.m.

asar II (in Ambon) to roast, barbecue.

asar III trace (of a memory). *tiada –nya lagi* no longer remembered at all.

asas (*A*) 1 foundation, base. 2 principle, basis. – *hukum* legal principle. –.– *hukum pidana* the principles of criminal law. – *persamaan* (*leg*) principle of equality. 3 goal, purpose, platform, set of principles. *membicarakan* – *dan tujuan partai* to discuss the platform of the party. – *pencemar pembayar* polluter-pays principle. – *persamaan* principle of equality. – *praduga tak bersalah* principle of presumed innocence. – *sumber* principle of source (of income for taxation purposes). – *tertutup* closed system of legal principles. – *tunai* cash basis. – *tunggal* the one and only principle (supposed to be Pancasila).

asasnya *pada* ~ fundamentally, basically, on principle. – *légalitas* legality principle. – *rumah* the foundation of a house.

seasas with the same foundation. *organisasi* ~ subsidiary (of a political party). *ormas yang* ~ mass organization with the same goals.

berasas ~ *kepada* and **berasaskan** to be based/founded on.

mengasaskan to base (on), found, establish.

pengasas founder.

asasi (*A*) basic, fundamental. *hak* – fundamental rights. *hak-hak* – *manusia* [HAM] human rights.

asbak (*D*) ashtray.

asbat (*A*) descendants.

asbés(tos)(*D/E*) asbestos.

asbétosis (*D/E*) asbestosis.

asbun [asal bunyi] 1 filibustering. 2 to talk for the sake of talking, love to hear the sound of one's own voice. 3 empty barrels make more noise.

asbut [asap kabut] smog.

asda [asistén daérah] regional assistant.

asdos [asistén dosén] teaching assistant.

asé I (*D*) *daging* – hashed meat, i.e., a mixture of meat and spices.

asé II → AC.

ASÉAN [Association of Southeast Asian Nations] a regional socioeconomic and cultural association formed in Bangkok, August 8, 1967; members: Indonesia, the Philippines, Singapore, Malaysia, and Thailand.

ASÉANÉKA [ASÉAN+(N)ÉKA] television arts programs of the five ASEAN nations.

aseli → ASLI.

asem → ASAM. –*!* Damn!

asem-asem ~ *buncis* sour green-bean soup.

asémbler (*D*) (automobile) assembler; → PE(NG)RAKIT.

asémbling (*D*) assembling; → PERAKITAN.

mengasembling to assemble; → MERAKIT.

pengasémblingan assembly.

asémblir (*D*) **mengasemblir** to assemble.

asep → ASAP. *bandeng* – smoked milkfish.

asép → AKSÉP.

asépsis (*D*) asepsis.

aséptik → ASÉPTIS.

aséptis (*D*) aseptic; → SUCI *hama*.

aseran (*J*) 1 hothead. 2 hot-tempered. 3 rough (language).

asesanti (*Jv*) 1 prayers. 2 to utter a slogan.

asésé (*D*) agreed! It's a deal! → ACC.

mengasésékan to approve.

asésor (*D*) accessory, additional.

asésori (*D*) accessories; → PERALATAN.

mengasésori to accessorize.

asét (*D*) asset(s). – *tidur* dead asset.

berasét with ... assets.

asetat (*D*) acetate.

asetifikasi (*D*) acetification.

asétilén(a) → ASITILÉN.

aseton (*D*) acetone.

asfal I (*A*) low (of person), despised.

asfal II → ASPAL.

asfar (*A*) cream-colored, saffron.

asfiksia (*D*) asphyxia.

asg(h)ar → ASHGHAR.

ashab (*A*) disciples, companions.

ashabah → ASABAH.
ashadu → ASYHADU.
ashar → ASAR.
ashghar (A) minor. *haji* – a *haji* who has made the minor *hajj* by skipping a stop at Arafat.
Ashr (A) al– "Afternoon"; name of the 103rd chapter of the Koran.
asi I (A) rebellious, treacherous, mutinous, insurgent, disobedient.
asi II (A) attentive. *tidak masuk* – not taken into consideration. *mengambil* – to take into account/consideration.
   mengasi to pay attention to, care, heed.
asi III (M) legal, valid. *tidak* – illegal; → ACI II.
asi IV (J) *tidak* mengasi not becoming/flattering.
   asian 1 bringing luck, lucky. 2 efficacious, effective (of medicine). *tidak* ~ not to feel pleasant; be sorry for it; → RASI.
ASI V [Air Susu Ibu] breast milk.
Asia (D) 1 Asia. 2 Asian, Asiatic. *demam/flu* – Asian flu. – *Kecil* Asia Minor. – *Tenggara* [Asteng] Southeast Asia. – *Timur Raya* Greater East Asia (Co-prosperity Sphere, under Japan during WW II).
   meng-Asia-kan to asianize.
   ke-Asiaan Asian. *suasana* ~ Asian atmosphere.
Asiad the Asian equivalent of the Olympiad.
asidosis (D/E) acidosis.
asih → KASIH. asihan love.
asik → ASYIK.
asil I → HASIL. ngasilin → MENGHASILKAN.
asil II (D) asylum.
asimétri (D) asymmetry.
asimétris (D) asymmetrical.
asimilasi (D) assimilation (in all meanings).
   berasimilasi to assimilate, become assimilated.
   mengasimilasi(kan) to assimilate s.t.
   terasimilasi assimilated.
   pengasimilasian assimilating, assimilation.
asimtot (D/E) asymptote.
asimut (D/E) azimuth.
asin 1 salty; → MASIN. 2 salted, briny. *ikan* – salted fish. *sayur* – a salt-pickled and fermented vegetable dish similar to sauerkraut. *telur* – salted duck egg. – *garam kehidupan* the vicissitudes of life.
   seasin as salty as.
   mengasin, mengasini and mengasinkan 1 to salt s.t. 2 to pickle; → MENGACAR.
   asinan ~ *sayur* a mixture of cucumber, cabbage, and bean sprouts (sometimes plus fruit) seasoned with a sauce of vinegar, salt, chili, and shrimp paste; fried peanuts and cracker crumbs are sprinkled on top.
   asin-asinan 1 all k.o. salt-pickled dishes. 2 pickle. ~ *garam* unpleasantness, trouble, worries, problems.
   keasinan salinity. ~ *air* salinity of water. *alat pengukur* ~ *air* salinometer.
   pengasin *bahan* ~ substance used for pickling s.t.
   pengasinan pickling, salting.
asin-asin a shrub with edible leaves eaten like spinach, sweet leaf bush, *Sauropus androgynus/albicans*.
asing 1 strange, foreign (country/person/religion, etc.), alien. *orang* – a foreigner. *pérs* – the foreign press. *warganegara* – a foreign national. – *tak* – semi-foreign. 2 foreigners, foreign parties. 3 separated, isolated. 4 unusual, odd, queer. *tidak* – to be usual, common. 5 (M) to be different. *tak/tidak* – *lagi* familiar, not unknown. *sudah tak/tidak* – *lagi* already familiar. *tak* – *sebagai* just/exactly as. – *maksud*, – *sampai* things take a different turn than expected. – *lubuk*, – *ikannya* so many countries, so many customs.
   berasing 1 separated, isolated, by itself, apart. *sebuah rumah yang* ~ an isolated house. 2 to change, become different.
   berasing-asingan to be different from e.o., not mix with e.o.
   mengasing *hidupnya* ~ to live isolated from others.
   mengasingkan 1 to separate, segregate. ~ *diri* to keep o.s. apart/away from others, to go into seclusion. 2 to exile. 3 to intern, jail. 4 to alienate. 5 to dispose of (by sale or other means).

memperasingkan to isolate, set apart.
   terasing isolated, separated, out of the way, far away. ~ *dari* separated/apart from. ~ *daripada* free from, without. *suatu masyarakat yang* ~ *daripada perbédaan golongan* a society free from ethnic discrimination. keterasingan 1 isolation. 2 exclusion, alienation.
   terasingkan isolated.
   keasingan 1 loneliness. 2 difference, deviation, apartness.
   pengasingan 1 exile. *di* ~ in exile. 2 internment (camp). 3 segregation, isolation. 4 isolating, exiling. 5 alienation, disposal (by sale). ~ *tanah* disposal of land.
   perasingan 1 isolated life. 2 segregation, exile, isolation. 3 internment (camp).
asingisasi foreignization.
asinkronis (D) asynchronous.
asinyasi (D) 1 order for payment. 2 draft (in banking).
asiri volatile.
asistén (D/E) 1 assistant, s.o. who assists or serves in a subordinate position. 2 (in university), assistant to a professor (B.A. holder). – *ahli* assistant professor (M.A. holder). – *apotéker* pharmacist's assistant. – *dokter* assistant to a medical doctor. – *dosén* [asdos] assistant to a university teacher/lecturer/reader, teaching assistant. – *wedana* (coq) assistant to a *wedana* (now approximately a *camat*).
   mengasist,éni to assist.
   asisténan subdistrict (under an *asistén wedana*).
   keasisténan assistantship.
asisténsi (D/E) assistance.
asitilén (D/E) acetylene.
askal (A) load.
Askaméx name of a deworming medicine, anthelmintic.
askar I (A ob) 1 soldier. 2 army, troops; → LASKAR.
askar II (Pr) cigarette.
Askés [asuransi keséhatan] health insurance.
askétis (D) ascetic (mod).
askétisme (D/E) asceticism.
askorbat (D/E) ascorbate.
askriptif (D/E) ascriptive.
Asku [Asistén Keuangan] Assistant for Finance.
asli (A) 1 original (not a copy or translation). *ijazah* – an original certificate/diploma; *opp* IJAZAH *aspal*. – *akte* original certificate. 2 genuine, authentic, real (not fake or assumed). *karangan* – a) an authentic work. b) one's own work. *nama* – one's real name (not a pseudonym). *Sumitro* – the real Sumitro (as opposed to an impersonation). *kilo* – standard kilogram. 3 indigenous, autochthonous, aboriginal, native-born. *penduduk* – indigenous people. *warganegara* – native-born citizen; *opp* WARGANEGARA *asing/bukan asli*. 4 primitive. 5 congenital, innate, inborn. *sifat* – innate quality. 6 to be of noble descent; to be from a good family. *tidak* – not authentic. **ketidak-aslian** inauthenticity.
   aslinya one's origin, where one is originally from. ~ *dari mana?* Where are you from originally? *sesuai dengan* ~ true copy.
   seasli as natural/original as.
   seasli-aslinya as natural/original as possible.
   keaslian originality, authenticity, genuineness.
Aslog [Asistén Logistik] Assistant for Logistics.
asma I (A) name. *dengan* – *Tuhan* in the name of God.
asma II (D) asthma. *serangan* – asthma attack. – *bronk(h)ial* bronchial asthma. *penderita* – an asthmatic.
asmani (Pers) heavenly.
asmara (Skr) (sexual) love, adoration, passion; → ASMORO. *bermain* – to play with fire. *jaya* – lady-killer.
   berasmara to be in love.
   mengasmarai to love.
   kasmaran love, in love, passion. – *berahi* erotic. – *ketlusuban iblis* diabolic love.
asmaradanta (Skr) snow-white.
asmaragama 1 the art of sexual relations. 2 sexual pleasure.
asmaraloka world of love/passion.
asmarawan lover.
asmatis (D) (an) asthmatic.

asmaul husna (A) the 99 names of God's greatness.

Asmén [Asistén menteri] assistant minister.

asmoro [the (Jv) pron of asmara] 1 (in port areas near Jakarta) offering a woman or girl as a k.o. pungli. 2 casual laborer.

asmu [asal muat] (newspapers) will print anything.

asnad (A) credentials, authorities for a statement.

asnaf (A) categories (of those who have the right to the zakat).

Asnawi (Pr) [asli cina betawi] a Jakarta-born Chinese.

asnowo [Asli Cino Jowo] (derog) Javanese-Chinese.

aso (J/Jv) mengaso [and ngaso (coq)] to take a break, rest; → BERISTIRAHAT.
  mengasokan to give s.t. a break/rest.
  pengasoan 1 the act/way of resting. 2 rest area; rest house.

asoi [asyik + indehoi] 1 posh. 2 passionate, hot. 3 great, super, wonderful. 4 to be absorbed in (doing s.t.); → ASSO(O)I, ASYO(I)I. masakan yang – a gourmet dish. – masoi super, great!

asonansi (D) assonance.

ason-ason (J) k.o. night bird.

asong (S) mengasong(kan) to hand s.t. to s.o., press s.t. into s.o.'s hands, hold out s.t. (a drink/food/souvenirs, etc.), thrust (one's hand) in through (the window of a train coach) to show s.t. to a passenger.
  asongan s.t. offered for sale in this way. (pedagang ~) a vendor who sells things through the windows of a train coach or bus or by going onto a train or bus when it stops at a station.

asongan → ANGSONG.

Asops [Asistén Operasi] Assistant for Operations.

asor (Jv) 1 low, inferior; opp UNGGUL. 2 humble; → ANDAP-ASOR. 3 to lose (in competition).
  asoran underdog.
  keasoran 1 humiliation. 2 defeat.

asoséris (D) accessories (to clothes/automobiles).

asosial (D/E) asocial.

asosiasi (D) association, partnership. negara – associate country.
  berasosiasi 1 to associate. 2 associated.
  mengasosiasikan to associate s.t.
  terasosiasi associated.
  pengasosisian associating.

asosiatif (D) associative.

asoy → ASYO(O)I.

asoymasoi → ASOI.

aspal I (D) 1 asphalt. 2 paved part of a road. – alam native asphalt. – cair cut-back asphalt. – panas hot mix; → HOTMIK(S). – tiup(an) oxidized asphalt.
  beraspal asphalted.
  mengaspal to asphalt (a road, etc.).
  teraspal asphalted.
  aspalan pavement.
  pengaspal asphalter.
  pengaspalan 1 asphalt pavement. 2 asphalting.

aspal II [asli tapi palsu] original but counterfeited. ijazah – an original diploma but the education is fake.

aspalisasi putting an asphalt surface on roads.

asparaga k.o. vine used in floral arrangements, leather leaf, Asparagus plumosus.

asparagus (D) asparagus.

aspék I D) aspect.

Aspék II [Asosiasi Serikat Pekerja] Association of Labor Unions.

aspéktual secara – aspectually.

aspél → ARNAL.

aspérjis and aspérsi → ASPARAGUS.

aspiran (D) aspirant, candidate.

aspirasi (D) aspiration, (political and social) desires.
  beraspirasi to have aspirations.

aspirat (D/E ling) aspirate.

aspiratif 1 aspiring (mod). 2 fulfilling aspirations.

aspirator (D/E) aspirator.

aspirin (D/E) aspirin. makan – to take an aspirin.

asprak (D) appointment, engagement.

Aspri [Asistén pribadi] personal assistant.

aspro (D) aspro, a brand name of aspirin.

Asrafil (A) the archangel Israfel.

asrafin (A) seraphim, angels.

asrakal ceremonial meal.

asrama (Skr) 1 dormitory, sleeping quarters. 2 barracks. 3 boardinghouse; → TEMPAT kos(t)/ indekos(t). 4 hostel. – biarawan abbey. – campuran coed dorm. – gundik-gundik whorehouse. – mahasiswa student dormitory. – pendidikan reformatory. – pengemis beggar's home. – prodéo (euph) prison. – tentara army barracks. – tuna tertib stockades, military prison. – wanita girls' dormitory, sorority. – wanita P house of prostitution.
  seasrama in the same dormitory. teman ~ dorm-mate.
  berasrama to live in a dormitory.
  mengasramakan 1 to put up in a dormitory. 2 to station (troops) in barracks, quarter (troops). 3 to provide accommodations for, house.
  pengasramaan the stationing (of troops) in barracks, quartering.
  perasramaan billeting.

asrar (A) secret.

asrena [asistén perencanaan] assistant for planning.

asri (Jv) beautiful, fine, pleasing to the eye; chic.
  keasrian beauty.

Asropol chlorine-like bleach.

assalamualaikum (A) peace be with/unto you; the usual Muslim greeting; the answer is: wa alaikum salam. – warahmatullahi wabarakatuh peace be with/unto you and may God bestow on you His Mercy and Blessings (a greeting).

assésoar → ASÉSOR.

assét (E) → ASÉT. berassét to have assets of.

asso(o)i → ASYO(O)I.

assoy → ASOI. assoy-assoyan having a good time/fun.

asta I → HASTA.

asta II (Skr) in compounds) eight; cp ASTAKONA. – Gatra the Eight Aspects of State and National Life; → KETAHANAN nasional.

astabrata (Skr) the eightfold teachings of Rama to Bharata.

astaga(firullah) (A) 1 God forgive me! Heaven forbid! O, my God! 2 exclamation of surprise, etc. No!
  berastaga(firullah) to say astaga.

astaganaga (BG) Gee whiz!

astagaperlah and astagapirullah → ASTAGA(FIRULLAH).

astagina (Skr) handicraft, manual training (in school).

astaka balai – (cla) hall without walls in a place where ceremonies are held.

astakona (Skr) 1 octagon. 2 polygon.
  berastakona octagonal.

astana → ISTANA.

astasatah octahedron.

astasudut octagon.

asték [asuransi sosial tenaga kerja] workers' social insurance.

Asteng [Asia Tenggara] Southeast Asia.

asténia (D) asthenia.

Astér [Asistén Téritorial] Assistant for Territorial Affairs.

asteroid (D) asteroid.

astergliserol (D) asterglycerol.

astohpirulah → ASTAGAFIRULLAH.

astra (Bal) insulting term for child born out of wedlock.

astrada [asistén sutradara] assistant movie/play director.

astral (D/E) astral.

astraléla → ASTAGA.

astringén (D/E) astringent.

astrofisik(a) (D) astrophysics. ahli – astrophysicist.

astrolog (D) astrologer.

astrologi (D/E) astrology.

astronaut (D/E) astronaut.

astronautik (D) astronautical.

astronom (D) astronomer.

astronomi (D/E) astronomy.

astronomikal (D) astronomical.

astronot → ASTRONAUT. – pendukung backup astronaut.

astronotik(a) → ASTRONAUTIK.

astul [asal tulis] just to write s.t. (of newspaper reporters); cp ASBUN.

asu I (Jv) dog. gigi – canine/eye tooth.

ASU II the Ali Surahman (cabinet); cp ASU I.

asuh rear, raise, bring up.

mengasuh 1 to bring up, rear, educate. **2** to take care of, attend to, look after, provide for. **3** to nurse, tend (a patient). **4** to organize, run (a school/radio program for small children).

asuhan 1 upbringing, rearing, fostering, nurturing. *salah* ~ poor upbringing. **2** care, provision. ~ *Rumah* Home Care. **3** guidance, leadership. *di bawah* ~ under the auspices of, sponsored by. **4** education. **5** educated (child, etc.). **6** sponsorship.

pengasuh 1 fosterer (of a child), attendant. ~ *anak/bayi* babysitter; → PRAMUSIWI. **2** guardian, caretaker. **3** host (of a show), emcee.

pengasuhan the act of nursing/taking care of, etc.

asuh-asuh and *ikan* **asuhan** k.o. marine fish, sea bream, *Lethrinus nebulosus/miniatus*.

asuk → MASUK.

asumsi (*D*) assumption.
  berasumsi to assume.
  mengasumsi to assume s.t.

asumtif (*D*) assumptive.

asung (*M*) **mengasung** to instigate, incite, stir up.
  asungan instigation, incitement.
  pengasung agitator, provocateur.
  pengasungan instigation, provocation.

asup → MASUK.

Asura and **Asuro** → ASYURA.

asurador (*Port*) insurer.

asuransi (*D*) **1** (life/fire, etc.) insurance. **2** insurance premium. *membayar* – to pay the insurance premium. **3** insurance benefit. *masuk* – a) to buy (an) insurance (policy). b) covered by insurance. – *anuitas* annuity insurance. – *bendasraya* property insurance. – *berlebih* overinsurance. – *bersama* mutual insurance. – *ganda* double insurance. – *gangguan usaha* business interruption insurance. – *ganti kerugian* property and casualty insurance. – *jiwa(sraya)* life insurance. – *jiwa kumpulan* group life insurance. – *kebakaran* fire insurance. – *kecelakaan (diri)* (personal) accident insurance. – *kelompok* group insurance. – *kematian* life insurance. – *kendaraan bermotor* motor vehicle/automobile insurance. – *kerugian* indemnity insurance. – *kesehatan* health insurance. – *kredit jiwa* credit life insurance. – *kurang* underinsurance. – *laut* marine insurance. – *mobil* car insurance. – *pemasangan instalasi bangunan* construction all-risks insurance. – *pembangunan gedung* contractor's all-risks insurance. – *pencurian* theft insurance. – *pengangkutan* cargo insurance. – *pengangkutan uang* cash-in-transit insurance. – *perjalanan* travel insurance. – *pihak ketiga* liability insurance. – *rangka kapal laut/udara* hull/aviation insurance. – *sakit* medical insurance. – *selamat be(r)layar* insurance against total loss only (for ships). – *semua resiko* against all risks. – *tabungan haji* hajj-savings insurance. – *tanggung gugat* liability insurance. – *untuk pihak ketiga* third-party insurance.
  berasuransi to have insurance, be insured. *kesadaran* ~ insurance-mindedness.
  mengasuransi(kan) to insure. *yang diasuransikan* the insured. *jumlah yang diasuransikan* the sum insured.
  pengasuransi insurer.
  pengasuransian insuring. ~ *kembali* reinsuring.
  perasuransian insurance system, insurance (*mod*).

asusila amoral, immoral. *berbuat/bertindak* – to engage in immoral practices, behave immorally. *perkara* – an amoral case.

asut → HASUT.

aswa (*Skr*) horse.

aswad (*A*) black. *hajarul* – the black stone in the Kaabah (in Mecca).

aswaja → AHLUS *Sunnah wal Jama'ah.*

aswasada (*Skr*) **1** equestrian. **2** cavalry.

aswo [asli Jowo] (*Jv*) authentic.

asyar → ASAR.

asyhadu (*A*) I testify. – *ilaha illallah* I affirm there is no god but Allah. – *Waasyhadu anna Muhammad arrasulullah* and Muhammad is His prophet.

asyik (*A*) **1** absorbed/engrossed in, wrapped up in (work), passionately addicted/devoted to. – *bermain judi* to gamble feverishly. **2** pleasant, nice, good, comfortable, snug. *nggak* – unpleasant,

not so nice. **3** to be infatuated, in love. – *berahi* infatuated. *kedua asyik-masyuk* the two lovers/lovebirds. *sepasang* – *masyuk* and *pasangan* – *asyoi* a pair of lovers. – *(dan) masyuk* a) (deeply) in love with e.o. b) a young couple. **4** animatedly. – *(ber)bicara* to talk animatedly. **5** (to study/work, etc.) diligently, industriously, zealously, assiduously, fervently. **6** (to cry) continuously, nonstop. **7** (to listen) attentively. **8** to have an eye for nothing else, do nothing but.

asyik-asyik exciting.

asyik-asyiknya madly, passionately.

seasyik as exciting as.

(ber)asyik ~ *masyuk* to fall/be in love.

berasyik-asyikan to make love.

mengasyiki 1 to excite, entertain. **2** to devour, spend all one's time on s.t.

mengasyikkan 1 to cause/make one (to be) busy/occupied with. **2** to cause/make (s.o. to be) infatuated with, make s.o. love (s.t. or s.o.). **3** absorbing, fascinating, exciting.

asyik-asyikan to do s.t. obsessively.

keasyikan 1 absorption (in s.t.), preoccupation, obsession. **2** to be obsessed by. *Dia* ~ *menghitung duitnya.* He's obsessed with counting his money.

keasyik-asyikan very infatuated/enthusiastic/zealous/absorbed.

Asymawil (*A*) Samuel.

asyobah (*A*) the person who inherits the remainder of an estate after the other heirs inherit fixed amounts.

asyo(o)i (*Pr*) swell, great.
  berasyo(o)i to shout *asyo(o)i*; → ASOI.

Asyura (*A*) **1** the 10th of Muharram (commemorating the death of Hasan and Husain). **2** the first 10 days of that month. **3** the porridge mixture eaten on that day.

at (in acronyms) → ATASÉ.

ata-été (*J*) additional needs.

atak I (*M ob*) layout, sketch. – *anju* thumbnail sketch. – *kasar* rough layout. – *kerja* shop rough.
  mengatak to arrange, put in order.

atak II (*ob*) three-wheeled car (like a *bémo*).

atal I → HARTAL.

Atal II [Atasé Laut] Naval Attaché.

atang (*Jv*) to lie on one's back.
  ngatang *terguling* ~ flipped over.

atap 1 roof, top covering of a building. *jip* – *keras* a hardtop jeep. **2** material for making roofs, roofing (such as *sirap*/sago palm leaves, etc.). – *rumbia perabung upih* good and bad articles mixed together, the good and the bad (in s.o. or s.t.). – *genting* tiled roof. – *gergaji* lean-to roof. – *gording* purlin roof. – *jerami* thatched roof. – *joglo* roof of a pyramid-shaped house used by nobility in a village. – *kaca* skylight. – *keras* hardtop. – *kubah* dome. – *langit* open-air. – *limasan* roof of a pyramid-shaped house used by those who consider themselves descendants of the original inhabitants of a village. – *mutlak* layers on top of charcoal. – *oning* awning. – *rungkup* roof that reaches almost to the ground. – *séng* corrugated-iron roof. – *serotong* roof type used by commoners. – *teritis* overhang. – *utama* main roof.

seatap under the same roof (as), in the same house.

beratap to have/use a roof; roofed. *rumah* ~ *genting* a tile-roofed house. – *langit* in the open air. *sudah* – *séng* gray-haired; → UBANAN. – *ijuk* still young. ~ *terlalu besar selagi bertiang kurang* to have a champagne taste on a beer-drinker's pocketbook.

beratapkan ... to have ... as a roof, covered with ...

mengatap to roof, put a roof on. ~ *sirih* (*M*) to make a betel quid.

mengatapi to put a roof on.

mengatapkan to use s.t. as roofing.

pengatapan roofing, covering with a roof.

ataqwa (*A*) maternal love.

atar (*A*) (*minyak* –) perfume.
  mengatari and **mengatarkan** to scent, perfume.

atas 1 up, upper, on top of, above; *opp* BAWAH. *bagian* – the upper part. *golongan* – the upper classes. *sebelah* – a) on the upper side. b) superficial. *di* – a) above, at the top. *orang di* – superiors, higher-ups. *yang tersebut di* – the above/aforementioned.

di – segala-galanya above all. *di – tanah* above ground. *di tingkat –* above the first floor. *di – sendiri* right at the top. *berada di – angin* to be far out/out in left field, to have one's head in the clouds. b) upstairs. c) exceeding, over, beyond, after (a certain hour of the day). *jumlah di – Rp 300* an amount in excess of Rp 300. *di – jam 22* After 10 at night. *yang di –* God. d) on. *di – kertas* on paper. *ke –* a) to the top, upward. b) and up. *seribu ke –* one thousand and up. *dari/hingga/sejak ini ke –, dari sekarang sampai ke –* from now on, in future, henceforth. **mengeataskan 1** to raise (a matter). **2** to hike up. *– bawah and dari – ke bawah* top-down. **2** for, on, of, with, in, by, at, into. *bertindak – usahanya sendiri* to act of one's own accord. *terima kasih – ...* thanks for ... *(dibuat) – beberapa pertimbangan* based on various considerations. *terdiri –* to consist of. *– bantuan* with the help of. *– biaya* at ...'s expense. *– dasar on grounds. – desakan* at the insistence of. *– jasa* a) on the basis of merit. b) thanks to. *– keamanan nasional* in the name of national security. *– kemauan sendiri* of one's own accord, of one's own free will, by choice. *– kesadaran sendiri* realizing what had happened. *– nama Tuhan* in the name of God. *– nama perusahaannya* on behalf of his company. *– permintaan anda* at your request. *– panggilan* on call. *– pantai* onshore. *– perintah* at the command of. *– permintaan* at the request of. *– prakarsa* at the initiative of. *– undangan* by invitation, at the invitation of. *– usul* at the suggestion of. *di bagi – dua golongan* divided into two groups. **3** superiors, above. *perintah dari –* an order from above/one's superiors. **4** due to, on account of, thanks to. *–mu* you ought to, you should. *– pertolongan gurunya* due to his teacher's help. *– usaha teman-teman saya* thanks to my friends. *negeri – angin* the countries considered as the source of winds. *orang – angin* people from those countries. *orang/pihak –(an)* superiors, higher-ups. *lapisan –(an)* upper layer, superstratum. *– nama* [a.n.] a) in the name of, on behalf of. b) registered (security, etc.). **mengatas-namakan, memperatas-namakan,** and **mengatas-namai** to act on behalf of, authorized by, do s.t. in the name of. **pengatas-namaan** putting s.t. in the name of. *– nilai* ad valorem. *– perintah* by order of, on the orders of. *– permintaan* a) on demand. b) at the request of. *– perintah* warrant. *– prakarsa* at the initiative of. *– sungai* headwaters, the upper part of a river, upstream. *– tekanan* under pressure of. *– tunjuk* bearer (security, etc.). *– undangan* at the invitation of. *– usaha* a) sponsored by; → DISPONSORI, DITAJA. b) at the instigation of. c) under the aegis/auspices of. *– usul* at the suggestion of.
beratas-atasan to compete; → ATAS-MENGATASI.
mengatas 1 to move upward, rise. **2** to aspire, rise. **3** to lodge an appeal, appeal (to a higher court). **4** always wanting to be on top. *~ alam* supernatural.
atas-mengatas 1 to go up and up. **2** to compete with e.o.
mengatasi [and **ngatasin** (*J coq*)] **1** to surpass, exceed. *~ suara* to deafen, drown out. **2** to defeat, beat. **3** to handle, overcome, surmount (difficulties, etc.), address (a problem), deal/cope with (and overcome a problem), resolve (a problem), remedy (an error). *(tidak) dapat diatasi* could (not) be overcome, (in)surmountable. **4** to have precedence over.
atas-mengatasi to compete with e.o., fight/contend for supremacy, contend for mastery.
mengataskan 1 to value higher; to favor s.o. **2** to raise, hike, lift up. *~ diri* to raise o.s. above.
memperatas *yang diperatas* God.
teratas the uppermost, highest.
teratasi can be overcome. *tidak dapat ~* insurmountable.
atasan 1 higher (things); things that are more dignified. **2** superior, manager, supervisor, higher-up. *orang ~* a superior, superiors, higher-ups; the upper class. *sekolah ~* secondary school. *~ langsung* immediate superior. **3** top (garment worn on the upper part of the body).
pengatasan overcoming.
atasé (*D*) attaché. *– angkatan laut* [atal] naval attaché. *– pendidikan dan kebudayaan* [atdikbud] educational and cultural attaché. *– kebudayaan* cultural attaché. *– militér* [atmil] military attaché. *– pendidikan* education attaché. *– perdagangan* commercial attaché. *– perhubungan* communications attaché. *– per-*

industrian industrial attaché. *– pérs* press attaché. *– pertahanan* [athan] defense attaché. *– udara* [atud] air attaché.
atau (*Skr*) **1** (introducing a synonym) or. *bébék – itik*. **2** (introducing the second of two possibilities) or. *bir – anggur* beer or wine. **3** (introducing any of the possibilities in a series) or. **4** (introducing the second of two possibilities where *baik* introduces the first) and. *baik dari tuan rumah – dari organisasi ...* both from the host and from the organization ...
ataukah 1 or. **2** whether. *~ kau mau hidup ~ ingin mati terserah kau sendiri*. Whether you want to live or die is up to you.
atavisme (*D/E*) atavism.
atawa (*coq*) or. *– ... –* either ... or ... .
atébrin (*D*) atebrine, i.e., an antimalaria medicine.
atéis (*D*) atheist.
 keatéisan atheism.
atéisme (*D/E*) atheism.
atéistis (*D*) atheistic.
atelas → ATLAS.
aténsi (*D*) attention.
atep I *buah –* peeled *enau* fruit.
atep II → ATAP.
aterét (*D*) to back up, go in reverse.
atérogénik (*D*) atherogenic.
atérosklérosis (*D/E*) atherosclerosis.
atés (*E*) attest.
Athan → ATASÉ *pertahanan*.
athar (*A*) usages set up by the Prophet's Companions.
athéis → ATÉIS.
athkal (*A*) a load (of sin).
ati (*coq*) → HATI. *diwénéhi – ngrogoh rempelo* (*Jv*) give him an inch and he'll take a mile. *– bumbu Bali* Balinese calves' liver (a dish).
ati-ati I k.o. medicinal plant, *Coleus atropurpureus/blumei*.
ati-ati II → HATI-HATI.
Atib (*A*) the angel who records all of mankind's good deeds.
atlas I (*D/E*) atlas, a book of maps. *– sejarah* historical atlas.
atlas II (*A*) satin; → ANTELAS.
atlas III (*D/E*) atlas, i.e., the upper vertebra of the neck.
atlét (*D*) athlete.
atlétik (*E*) and **atlétis** (*D*) **1** athletic. *tubuh –* an athlete's body. **2** track and field (sports).
atlétis (*D*) athletic.
atlit → ATLÉT. *– angkat besi* weight lifter. *– binaraga* → BINARAGAWAN.
ATM (*init*) ATM.
atma(n) (*Skr*) **1** soul. **2** breath.
Atmani Wedhana freshmen of the Akadémi Kepolisian [Akpol]; meaning: "with the attitude of a fighting patriot, ready to sacrifice himself in serving unselfishly."
Atmawan a male student of Atma Jaya University.
Atmawati a female student of Atma Jaya University.
Atmil [Atasé Militér] Military Attaché.
atmométer (*D/E*) atmometer.
atmosfir (*D/E*) atmosphere.
atob → ATOP.
atok *– moyang* ancestors; → DATUK.
atol (*D*) atoll.
atoli (in northern Ceram) headhunter.
atom (*D/E*) **1** atom. *bom –* atom(ic) bomb. *tenaga –* atomic energy/power. *zaman –* atomic age. **2** (*ob*) s.t. extraordinary, strange, ultramodern. *pulpén –* ballpoint pen. *selop –* plastic slippers. *tas – plastic handbag.
atomisasi (*D*) atomization.
atomistik (*D*) atomistic.
atomistis (*D*) atomistic.
Atomita a type of rice resistant to certain rice weevils and plant diseases.
Atoni an ethnic group living in Indonesian Timor.
Atonik name of a plant growth stimulant.
atop (*Jv*) belch; to belch.
atopik (*D*) atopical. *dérmatitis –* atopical dermatitis.
atos (*Jv*) hard, tough.
atraksi (*D*) attraction.

atraktif (*D/E*) attractive.

atraz (*A*) **1** objection. **2** complaint.

atrét → ATERÉT. **mengatrétkan** to back up (a car, etc.).

atribusi (*D*) attribution.

  atribusian attributed.

atribut (*D/E*) **1** attribute. **2** insignia, paraphernalia (of a political party, etc.), costume (worn by a character). **3** symbol, sign.

  beratributkan to wear the paraphernalia (of a political party, etc.).

atributif (*D/E*) and **atributip** attributive.

atrofi (*D/E*) atrophy.

atsir ether.

atsiri essential, volatile. *minyak* – essential oil; → MINYAK *kenanga*.

atu (*J*) → SATU.

Atu(d) [*Atasé udara*] air attaché.

atuh (*J*) (emphatic exclamation) *pergilah* –! go away! –, *baik!* oh, that's good! –, *syukur!* well, I'm glad to hear it. *Kasihan saya*, *anya*, –! Have pity on me!

atuk → DATUK.

atung → KATUNG. **mengatung** and **teratung-atung 1** to drift about. **2** to float, bob (up and down). **3** to flutter, hover.

atur I to arrange, place in order, regulate. – *tepat* to adjust. **mengatur-tepatkan** to adjust. **pengatur-tepatan** adjustment.

  aturnya 1 as a rule, usually, according to the regulations. **2** in fact, as a matter of fact.

  beratur arranged/placed in proper order, orderly, neatly arranged. ~ *baik-baik* well-arranged. *tidak* ~ disorderly, messy. **ketidak-beraturan** disorder, mess, untidiness.

  mengatur [and **ngatur** (*coq*) and **ngaturin** (*J coq*)] **1** to arrange, put in order. *cara* ~ *pakaian* the way one dresses. ~ *kembali jadwal* rescheduling. **2** to regulate (s.t. legally), govern (of a regulation/clause in a contract). *Peraturan di bidang lingkungan itu* ~ *ketentuan bahwa limbah tidak boléh dibuang ke laut.* The regulations in the environmental field govern the provisions that waste may not be disposed of in the sea. **3** to stipulate (provisions of the law). **4** to arrange (for), take care of s.t., settle. **5** to look after, take care of s.t. **6** to do (one's hair). **7** to string, thread. *bisa diatur* it can be arranged (through bribes, etc.). *susah diatur* hard to manage. *(di) dalam segala hal yang tidak diatur atau tidak cukup diatur dalam anggaran dasar ini, maka* in all cases not or insufficiently provided for by these articles of association.

  mengaturkan to arrange for, put in order for.

  teratur 1 orderly, properly arranged, in order, neat; → BERATUR. **2** regular, periodic, arranged in advance. *secara* ~ systematic, periodic, regular. *tidak* ~ disorganized, messy, irregular (of s.t. that usually is regular). **ketidak-teraturan** irregularity, disorderliness. **keteraturan** regularity, order. ~ *sosial* social order.

  aturan 1 arrangement, setup. ~ *rumah* the setup of a house, the way a house is organized. **2** regulation, provision, code (of rules). ~ *hukuman* penal provision. ~ *lalulintas* traffic regulations. ~ *main* the rules of the game, rules and regulations. ~ *obat* directions for using a medicine. ~ *pakai* directions for use. ~ *penutup* final provisions. ~ *peralihan* transitional provisions. ~ *permainan* ground rules. ~ *pidana* penal provisions. ~ *tambahan* supplementary provisions. ~ *umum* general provisions. **3** proper/best way to do s.t. ~ *memberantas penyakit malaria* the best way to wipe out malaria. **4** behavior, manners. *tidak tahu* ~ not know how to behave, have no manners. ~ *pranata* social customs. ~ *tertib* rules of proper conduct. **5** in fact, as a matter of fact, actually. ~*(nya) dia harus datang sendiri.* In fact, he had to come by himself. **beraturan 1** arranged properly, arranged in good order; regular. **2** to be mannerly, courteous.

  pengatur 1 controller, technician, person who arranges s.t. ~ *angkutan udara* air freight controller. ~ *farmasi* assistant pharmacist. ~ *kamar* room boy. ~ *lalulintas* traffic policeman. ~ *lalulintas udara* air traffic controller. ~ *perjalanan* tour operator. ~ *rawat gigi* dental technician. ~ *sinar* searchlight handler. ~ *téknik radio penerbangan* radio flight mechanic. **2** device/instrument used for controlling/arranging s.t., regulator, governor. *(alat)* ~ *hawa* and ~ *suhu* air-conditioner. ~ *peledak* detonator. ~ *redup terang lampu listrik* dimmer. ~ *tarik* turn-

buckle. ~ *waktu* timer (for a time bomb). **3** arranger (of music). **4** s.t. which determines s.t., factor. **5** a civil-service rank. ~ *muda* a civil-service rank. ~ *tingkat 1* a civil-service rank.

  pengaturan 1 controlling, control, arranging, arrangement(s), scheduling, handling, governing, timing. *mengadakan* ~ *dengan* to make an arrangement/settlement with. *lembaga* ~ *jemaah haji* organization which makes arrangements for pilgrims. ~ *huruf* typesetting. ~ *kembali* rescheduling. ~ *kembali pemilikan tanah* land reform. ~ *pelengkap* subsidiary arrangements. ~ *penundaan* rescheduling (of payments). **2** coordination. ~ *langkah* coordination of measures/steps. **3** adjustment, adjusting. ~ *hawa* adjusting the air-conditioning. **4** regulatory, regulating.

  peraturan 1 regulation, order, rule, ordinance. ~ *dasar* articles of association. ~ *dinas* regulations. ~ *gaji* salary scale. ~ *haid* menstrual regulation. ~ *keselamatan kerja* occupational safety regulations. ~ *majikan* company regulations. ~ *Menteri* [Permén] Ministerial Regulation. ~ *pelaksanaan* administrative/implementing regulation. ~ *Pelanggaran Pelayaran* Rules of the Road. ~ *pembangunan* building code. ~ *pemerintah* [PP and Perpém] government regulation. ~ *pemerintah pengganti* [Prp] substitute government regulation. ~ *penguasa perang* war administration regulation. ~ *peralihan* transitional regulations. ~ *permainan* rules of the game. ~ *perundang-undangan* statutes, legal provisions, laws and regulations. ~ *perusahaan* company regulations. ~ *présidén* presidential regulations. ~ *rumahtangga* housekeeping rules. ~ *tatakerja* company regulations. ~ *tatatertib* standing orders. ~ *tertib* rules of proper conduct. ~ *tingkah-laku* rule(s) of conduct. **2** system of organization, scale. ~ *gaji* salary scale. ~ *dua kamar* bicameral system. **3** *(cla)* ~ *(saudara kepada)* (to be in a) relationship (of brother with). *Bunda raja Ahmad itu* ~ *saudara dua pupu kepada ayahanda.* The mother of Raja Ahmad is second cousin to the father.

atur II (*M*) **mengaturkan:** ~ *merjan* to string red corals. ~ *hidung kerbau* to put a (nose) rope through the nose of a buffalo.

atur III (*Jv*); → HATUR. **mengaturi 1** to give. **2** to invite, ask.

  mengaturkan (and often **menghaturkan**) to offer s.t. ~ *selamat* to congratulate. ~ *selamat tahun baru* to wish s.o. a happy new year.

  matur ~ *nuwun* (to say) thank you.

atur-atur (*Jv*) **1** name of a *gamelan* melody. **2** → HATUR I.

atus leached out, all the water has leaked out.

  mengatus to leach out.

  mengatuskan to leach s.t. out.

  atusan leach(ing) solution.

  pengatusan 1 leaching out. **2** enriching ore content by leaching with a thin liquid solution.

AU (*init*) [*Angkatan Udara*] Air Force.

aubade (*D*) aubade, evening flag ceremony.

audién(si) (*E*) audience.

  beraudiénsi to have an audience. *diterima* ~ *oléh* to be received in audience by.

audio (*D/E*) audio.

audiograf (*D/E*) audiograph.

audiogram (*D/E*) audiogram.

audiologi (*D/E*) audiology.

audiométer (*D/E*) audiometer.

audiométri (*D*) audiometry.

audiovidéofil (*E*) audio-videophile.

audiovisual (*E*) and **audiovisuil** (*D*) audiovisual.

audisi (*E*) audition.

audit (*E*) audit. *juru* – (*Mal*) auditor. *laporan* – audit report. – *ketaatan* compliance audit. – *(toko) pengécér* retail audit.

  mengaudit to audit.

  pengaudit auditor.

  pengauditan auditing.

auditorium (*E*) auditorium.

audzubillah, a'udzubillah and **aud(z)ubillahi** (*A*) **1** I take refuge with God! (said in surprise, *esp* when shocked by immoral or blasphemous behavior or words). **2** damned. – *sulitnya!* damned difficult!

auk sound of barking dog, etc.

  mengauk-auk [and **ngauk** (*coq*)] to howl (of jackals).

auksi (*E?*) auction.
aula (*D*) auditorium, lecturehall.
aulia (*A*) saints, holy men.
aum (*onom*) roaring, bellowing.
   mengaum to roar, growl (of tigers), buzz (of insects), murmur (of crowds).
   mengaum-(ng)aumkan to boast of s.t.
   auman roaring. ~ *harimau* the roaring of tigers.
aung (*onom*) sound of roaring/moaning.
   mengaung to roar.
   aungan roaring, wailing.
   aungan roofbeam.
aur I generic name for many large bamboos; → AWI, BAMBU, BULUH. *bagai/sebagai – dengan tebing* very attached, devoted; to love e.o. (husband and wife). *(seperti) – ditanam, betung tumbuh* to get a windfall. *(seperti) – ditarik sungsang* very difficult. *sebagai – dengan rebung* very intimate (of friendship). – *cina* thin bamboo used for making fences, *Bambusa nana*. – *duri* thorny bamboo, *Bambusa blumeana*. – *gading* yellow/common bamboo, *Bambusa vulgaris*. – *hitam* black bamboo, *Bambusa nigra*. – *kuning* yellow bamboo, *Bambusa aspera*. – *licin* thornless bamboo. – *temiang* thin bamboo, *Bambusa wrayi*.
aur II → AWUR I. **mengaur** to act without plan or aim, do s.t. randomly/haphazardly.
   mengaur-aurkan to scatter, throw about.
   aur-auran scattered in a disorderly way.
aur III (*J?*) *tukang* – peddler.
   mengaur to peddle.
   pengaur peddler.
aur IV (*A*) one-eyed.
aur-aur spreading dayflower, *Commelina diffusa/nudiflora*.
aura (*D*) aura.
aurat (*A*) **1** parts of the body which should not be exposed (under Islamic religious law). **2** nakedness. **3** sexual organs.
AURI [Angkatan Udara Républik Indonésia] Indonesian Air Force.
aus I **1** worn-out, threadbare, shabby. **2** worn out and unusable. – *tanah* erosion; → ÉROSI, (*tanah*) LONGSOR.
   mengaus to wear out, weather.
   mengausi **1** to wear s.t. out. **2** to wear s.t. away, erode.
   mengauskan to wear s.t. out.
   keausan wear, weathering, wear and tear, attrition.
   pengausan wearing out, wear and tear.
aus II → HAUS.
ausat (*A*) middle.
Aus(s)i (*D*) Aussie, Australian.
Austin (*D*) **1** a British automobile make. **2** (any) urban bus.
Australia Australia, Australian.
Austria Austria, Austrian.
aut I (*D/E*) out of play (of the ball in a game).
aut II (*D/E*) to get out (of a club, etc.).
autarki (*D/E*) autarchy; → OTARKI.
autarkis (*D*) autarchic.
auténtik (*D/E*) **1** authentic. **2** trustworthy, reliable. **3** real, genuine; → OTÉNTIK.
auténtitas (*D*) authenticity.
auteur (*F*) author.
auto (*D*) auto(mobile), car; → MOBIL, MO(N)TOR, OTO.
autobiogafi (*D*) autobiography; → OTOBIOGRAFI.
autobis (*D*) (auto)bus.
autodidak (*D*) autodidact.
autodidaktik (*D*) autodidactic.
autofon (*D/E*) autophone.
autogén (*D/E*) autogenous.
autograf (*D/E*) autograph.
autografi (*D/E*) autography.
autografis (*D*) autographic.
autoimunitas (*D*) autoimmunity.
autokrasi (*D*) autocracy.
autokrat (*D/E*) autocrat.
autologi (*D/E*) autology.
automobil (*D/E*) automobile, (motor)car.

automotif (*D/E*) automotive.
autonomi (*D/E*) autonomy; → OTONOMI.
autopsi (*D*) autopsy; → OTOPSI.
   mengautopsi and *melakukan* – to conduct/carry out an autopsy/post-mortem.
autoskop (*D/E*) autoscope.
autropik (*D/E*) autropic.
auzubillah → AUDZUBILLAH.
avaang a tree producing oil/*minyak tengkawang*, butter tree, *Shorea spp.*, mainly found in Kalimantan; → TENGKAWANG.
aval (*D*) guarantee (of a bill).
   mengaval(kan) to guarantee (a bill).
avalis (*D*) guarantor, backer, accommodation party.
avarai, avarij and **avary** (*D leg*) marine damage.
avérsi (*D*) aversion.
avés (*ob naut*) to heave up.
avgas [aviation gasoline] (*D*) gasoline for aircraft.
AVI [Aangifte van Inlading] Shipment Declaration (in customs).
aviasi (*D*) aviation.
aviator (*D*) aviator.
Avigas → AVGAS.
avionik (*D*) avionic.
avionika (*D*) avionics.
avokat (*D*) avocado, *Persea spp.*
avontir and **avontur** (*D*) adventure.
   beravontir to go in search of adventures.
avonturir (*D*) adventurer.
Avtur [aviation turbine (fuel)] aviation turbine fuel.
awa I (*pinang* –) an areca nut with the ends cut off, split in four and dried in the sun).
awa- II (*Skr*) a privative prefix with meanings similar to English *de-* and *dis-*.
awaair free of water.
   mengawaairkan to dehydrate.
   pengawaairan dehydration.
awaarang decarbonized (*mod*).
   mengawaarangkan to decarbonize.
   pengawaarangan decarbonization.
awaasam pengawaasaman deacidification.
awaaspal awaaspalan deasphalted.
   pengawaaspalan deasphalting.
awabau free of odors, deodorized.
   mengawabaukan to deodorize.
   pengawabau deodorant.
awabenah mengawabenah to disinfect.
awabulu free of hair, depilated.
   mengawabulukan to depilate.
   pengawabuluan depilation.
awabusa to defoam.
   pengawabusa defoaming. *zat* ~ defoaming agent.
AWAC (*PT Keréta Api*) a first-class passenger car (in a train formation)
awacemar free from contamination.
   mengawacemarkan to decontaminate.
awadara deflowering (of a virgin).
awagas degasified.
   mengawagaskan to degasify.
   pengawagasan degasification.
awah vast, extensive (of a view), clear (of view).
awahama free of (pathogenic) germs, disinfected.
   mengawahamakan to disinfect, sterilize.
   pengawahama disinfectant.
   pengawahamaan sterilization.
awahidrat dehydrated.
   pengawahidratan dehydration.
awahubung disconnected.
   mengawahubungkan to disconnect.
awahutan free of forests, deforested.
   mengawahutankan to deforest.
   pengawahutanan deforestation.
awai I mengawai to wave (the hand); → MELAMBAI.
awai II (*M ob*) → AWAT II. **mengawai** to touch, feel.

terawai touched, glanced.

awai III (*M*) **berawai** (to come away) disappointed; empty-handed.

awainvéstasi disinvestment.

awak 1 body; → BADAN, TUBUH. **2** person. **3** crew member (of an aircraft/ship, etc.). **4** a) –*ku* I. –*mu* you. –*nya* he/she/they. – *tidak tahu* I don't know. b) own (language, etc.). *orang* – our people, i.e., the Minangkabau people; → URANG *awak; cp* BANGSA *déwék.* c) – *sama* – (we) among ourselves, between you and me; among friends, reciprocal. – *darat* ground crew. – *kabin* cabin crew (in aircraft). – *kapal* (ship's) crew. – *kokpit* cockpit crew (pilot and copilot). – *pesawat (terbang)* (air) crew. – *truk* truck crew (driver and assistant). – *TV* television crew.

berawak manned (spacecraft, etc.). *pesawat terbang pengintai tidak* ~ a drone (plane).

berawakkan with a crew of. ~ *empat orang* with a four-man crew.

mengawaki to man (a ship, etc.).

memperawak 1 to make use of s.o. as a crew member. **2** to call a crew (member).

pengawakan and **perawakan 1** form, shape, figure. **2** personality, posture. **3** physique. *rendah pengawakan* small of stature. **4** manning. **berperawakan** with a ... build. *lelaki* ~ *gemuk/kurus/jangkung* a man with a fat/skinny/tall body.

awakaca mengawakaca to devitrify.

awakepala decapitated, beheaded.

mengawakepalakan to behead.

awal I (*A*) **1** beginning, start, commencement. – *bermula* to start with, first of all, in the first place. – *mula* at the beginning, at first. *di* – *bulan Novémber* at the beginning of November, early in November. *dari* – *lagi* from scratch/the beginning again. *dari* – *sampai akhir* from A to Z, from start to finish, (of a book) from cover to cover. *lebih* – early (payment), at an earlier (date). *pada masa* – at an early stage. *pada* –.–*nya* when (he) first started to. *paling* – (to leave, etc.) the earliest, first. **2** early. *tahap sangat* – a very early stage. *agak* – rather early. **3** first (chairman, etc.). – *akhir* beginning and end. – *fajar* first light. – *sanad* the first name in the line of transmission of the Prophet Muhammad's words, etc., the last person to relate it orally. **4** (*fin*) opening.

awalnya (*pada*) ~ at the beginning, at first, at the outset.

awal-awalnya *pada* ~ at first, at a very early stage.

seawal as early as.

seawal-awalnya as early as possible.

berawal to begin, start, lead off. ~ *berakhir* to have a beginning and an end.

mengawal(i) 1 to begin, open, initiate. *diawali* to begin (with), be started (with). *Musibah diawali dengan terdamparnya seékor ikan besar.* The disaster started with the washing ashore of a large fish. *Upacara itu diawali dengan iring-iringan.* The ceremony began with a procession. **2** to head, be first in. **3** to precede. *Gempa itu diawali ledakan keras.* The earthquake was preceded by a loud explosion.

mengawalkan to initialize.

awalan (*gram*) prefix. **berawalan** ... to have the prefix ... *yang* ~ *meN-* (verbs) with the prefix *meN-*.

pengawal the first, initial.

awal II → KAWAL.

awalaras (*ling*) dissimilated.

pengawalarasan dissimilation.

awalemak skimmed (milk).

mengawalemakkan to skim (cream from milk).

awalengas dehumidified.

mengawalengaskan to dehumidify.

pengawalengasan dehumidification.

awam (*A*) **1** general, public. **2** lay, nonexpert. *orang* – a) the masses. b) civilian. c) nonexpert, layman. *mata* – the public's viewpoint. *si* – the man in the street. **3** common. **4** (*S*) to have no knowledge of, know nothing about. *Petugas Polrés* – *soal kartu krédit.* The Polres officials know nothing about credit cards. – *badarai* the general public.

mengawamkan 1 to announce (to the public), notify. **2** to propose, suggest, put forward.

keawaman 1 ignorance, amateurism. **2** being general, commonness.

pengawam 1 advocate, promoter. **2** profane.

awamiah (*A*) public.

awan I 1 cloud. **2** various names of cloudlike patterns, paintings, etc., such as – *biji timun* a pattern depicting cucumbers. – *bunga cengkéh* a pattern depicting cloves. **3** a very high place, the clouds. *Anganku melayang jauh tinggi di* –. My thoughts flew up into the clouds. *serasa di balik* – to be overjoyed/in seventh heaven. – *bakat kuning/mérah* yellowish/reddish-colored clouds (an unfavorable omen). – *berarak* drifting clouds. – *berawan* cloud bank. – *gelombang* clouds over mountains. – *hitam* rain clouds. – *gemawan* clouds. – *golak-galik* turbulence cloud. – *guntur* cumulonimbus clouds. – *jejak* condensation cloud. – *kelabu* sadness. – *kemawan* cumulus clouds. – *kerawang* bas-relief. – *luncur* up-glide clouds. – *mengandung hujan* rain clouds. – *panji* banner clouds, water or ice droplets on the back side of mountains in clear weather. – *pengarak hujan* clouds spearheading a storm. – *pérak* noctilucent cloud. – *pita* ribbon clouds, thin flat clouds. – *puncak* clouds hanging over peaks of mountains. – *putih*. – *rotor* clouds in the form of rolls. – *tudung* cap cloud.

berawan cloudy (sky), clouded (over), overcast, covered by clouds.

mengawan 1 to rise up into the clouds, ascend into the clouds, climb (up) into the sky, tower above everything. **2** to become cloudy/cloudy; to resemble, be like clouds or similar to them in appearance or nature. *putih* ~ *di udara* look like white clouds in the air.

keawanan cloudiness.

awan II long-armed and tailless black gibbon that lives in trees, *Hylobates, spp*; → UNGKA, WAKWAK, WAUWAU, WAWA.

awan III (*A*) helpers.

awanama (*Skr neo*) anonymous.

awang I awang-awang(an) and **awang-gemawang 1** (*cla*) space between earth and sky, atmosphere, heaven. **2** in the air, far-off, uncertain. *hidup di* –.– a) to live in the clouds (like wealthy people). b) to be very happy. *masih di* –.– in the air, in abeyance. *serasa di atas* –.– a) very high. b) very pleased; most excited; *cp* SERASA *di balik awan.*

mengawang 1 to ascend to the sky, take to the air; to the clouds. *angan/cita-cita* ~ to indulge in fantasies. *lenyap* ~ vanished into thin air. *pikirannya* ~ he aims too high. **2** at random, in the void.

mengawang-awangkan to brandish, wave s.t.

awangan without recourse to written notation, in one's head; impromptu, extemporaneous. *menghitung* ~ to do calculations in one's head. *main* ~ *saja* to play (music) impromptu/at sight, sightread. *menggambar* ~ to draw freehand.

perawangan heaven, the sky. ~ *cita-cita* castles in Spain/the air.

awang II 1 a young fellow (of a good class of society); (my) boy! **2** page (the person). – *dan dayang* male and female servants.

perawangan (*cla*) class of royal pages.

awang III berawang to be a friend, be familiar with e.o., be well-acquainted with e.o.

awang IV (in the Malay community in North Sumatra) name for the second child in a family.

awang V → MERANTI *mérah.*

awang-awangen (*Jv*) to dread having to do s.t.

awapéka desensitized.

pengawapékaan desensitization.

awapusat decentralized.

mengawapusatkan to decentralize.

awar average, damage to a ship or its cargo. – *khusus/umum* (in marine insurance) particular/general average.

awaracun detoxified.

mengawaracunkan to detoxify.

pengawaracunan detoxification.

awar-awar (*Jv*) a small tree, *Ficus septica*, whose roots are chewed as antidote to poisonous fish or crabs.

awarésin pengawarésinan deresining.

awas 1 good, sharp (of one's eyesight). *Matanya masih* –. He still has good eyesight. *kurang* – negligent. *mata kurang* – to have weak eyes. **2** to have the power to foretell the future or the unknown by occult means, be clairvoyant. **3** (word of caution) beware (of); watch out for, be on one's guard against. *– ada mobil!* Watch out for the car! *– Anjing!* (on signboards) Beware of the dog! *– copét!* Watch out for pickpockets. *–!* a) Take care! b) (strong suggestion) Be sure (to shut the door, etc.)! c) (threatening) You just wait (tomorrow I'll get you)! **4** (sports) get set! *– terhadap* to be attentive/observant, be on the alert/lookout, be watchful and ready, keep one's eyes open. *kurang* – imprudent, reckless, careless. **kekurang-awasan** imprudence, recklessness, carelessness.

berawas(-awas) **1** to be watchful, cautious, careful. **2** to check, control.

mengawasi [and **ngawasin** (*J coq*)] **1** to keep an eye on, keep watch over, watch, take care of. **2** to oversee, watch over and manage; to supervise; to superintend. *diawasi dengan ketat* to be closely supervised/watched.

mengawaskan **1** to observe carefully, pay careful attention to. *~ orang yang keluar masuk* to observe the people going in and out. **2** to supervise. **3** to survey.

pengawas **1** overseer, supervisor, control, superintendent, guardian, warden, caretaker, care. *di bawah ~ dokter* under a doctor's care. *déwan ~* supervisory board. *panitia ~* watchdog committee. *~ lalulintas udara* air traffic controller. *~ langsiran* yardmaster (in a railroad yard). *~ penjualan* sales supervisor. *~ rél keréta api* trackwalker. **2** (in races) marshal.

pengawasan care, supervision, guardianship, control, check, oversight, surveillance. *dalam ~ dokter* under a doctor's care. *~ anggaran* budgetary control. *~ berlapis* (*fin*) dual control. *~ dan pengimbangan* checks and balances. *~ keséhatan dan keselamatan* occupational health and safety supervision. *~ ketenagakerjaan* health and safety regulations. *~ kualitas* quality control. *~ langsung* on-site supervision. *~ législatif* [waslag]. legislative control. *~ masyarakat* [wasmas] social control. *~ melekat* [waskat] built-in control. *~ mutu* quality control. *~ pembangunan* [wasbang] development control. *~ persenjataan* arms control. *~ perusahaan* health and safety regulations. *~ pralaksana* preaudit. *~ purnalaksana* postaudit. *~ senjata* arms control. *~ sosial* social control. *~ tak-langsung* off-site supervision. *~ waspada* on the alert, careful. **kepengawasan** monitoring, overseeing.

awasama (*Skr neo*) dissimilated.
mengawasamakan to dissimilate.
pengawasamaan dissimilation.
awasandi (*Skr neo*) decoding.
mengawasandikan to decode.
awasayap dealation (removal of wings).
awasendi (*Skr neo*) **mengawasendikan** to dislocate.
pengawasendian dislocation.
awasenjata mengawasenjatakan to disarm.
awaserap pengawaserapan desorption.
awasuara (*Skr neo*) devoiced.
awasumbat unclogged.
pengawasumbatan unclogging.
awat I (*ob*) (= *apa buat?*) why?
awat II mengawat to hold, grasp.
awat III unplowed ground.
awatara (*Skr*) incarnation, avatar.
awatata (*Skr neo*) disorder.
awat-awat (*M*) almost not. *– sampai* almost not reaching its destination (as of a voice).
awatular decontaminated.
mengawatularkan to decontaminate.
pengawatularan decontamination.
awau gibbon; → UNGKA.
awawarna (*Skr neo*) decolorized.
mengawawarnakan to decolorize.
pengawawarnaan decolorization.
awda (*Br*) **1** you. **2** your; → ANDA.
awé (*Jv*) to call by waving.
awét (*Jv*) **1** durable, (long-)lasting, unchanging over a period of time, wears well (of clothing). **2** to stay young. *– muda* to stay young, look younger than one's age.

seawét lasts as long as, as durable as.
mengawét to can, put up (in cans), preserve (fruits/vegetables, etc.).
mengawétkan **1** to preserve/stuff (an animal's body). **2** to make s.t. last a long time.
terawét can be preserved. **keterawétan** durability, preservability.
awétan **1** preserves. **2** s.t. preserved, stuffed.
keawétan **1** life, durability (of car, etc.). **2** preservation.
pengawét **1** preservative. *~ kayu* wood preservative. **2** preserver.
pengawétan **1** conservation. *~ susu* pasteurization. **2** preservation. *~ tanah* soil conservation.
awéwé (*S*) **1** woman. **2** wife.
awi (*S*) various species of bamboo; → AUR, BAMBU, BULUH. *– andong* k.o. cream-striped bamboo, *Gigantochloa verticillata/pseudoarundinacea*. *– buluh* yellow-grove bamboo, *Schizostachyum brachycladum*. *– bunar* k.o. bamboo, *Schizostachyum blumei*. *– gereng* spiny bamboo, *Bambusa spinosa*. *– gombong* k.o. bamboo cultivated for building materials, *Gigantochloa pseudoarundinacea*. *– krisik* hedge bamboo, *Bambusa multiplex*. *– lengka* blackhair giant grass, *Gigantochloa nigrociliata*. *– tali* k.o. bamboo, *Gigantochloa apus*.
awig-awig (*Bal*) *adat* regulations.
awignam astu (namas sidem) (*Skr*) may it come true! may there be no obstacle to it!
awin → PENGAWINAN.
awing (*Pr*) thief.
awit I (*ob*) → AWÉT.
awit II (*J/Jv*) **awitan** onset (of a disease).
awloh (*J*) Allah, God.
awu (*Jv*) family relationship depending on the relative ages of the preceding generation; → KALAH *awu*.
awul-awul cotton waste.
awung-awung k.o. snack made from sticky-rice flour.
awur (*Jv*) **mengawur** [and **ngawur** (*coq*)] **1** to scatter, sow. **2** at random, aimlessly, thoughtlessly, do s.t. carelessly.
mengawuri to scatter, sow s.t.
mengawurkan **1** to sow. **2** to scatter, spread.
awur-awuran to act thoughtlessly/at random; → AWUT-AWUTAN II.
kengawuran and **pengawuran** recklessness.
awut I (*J*) tousled, tangled.
awut-awutan all tangled up, wild, disheveled, messy (of hair/thread, etc.). *pakaian ~* rumpled clothing.
awut II (*Jv*) **ngawut** to do s.t. carelessly.
awut-awutan at random, blindly, haphazardly.
AX *mobil –* a car for which the payment of import duties has been postponed temporarily.
ay. (*abbr*) [ayat] **1** verse (of the Koran, etc.). **2** article, subsection (of a law).
ayah I (more refined than *bapak*) father. *– angkat* adoptive father. *– bunda* parents. *– ibu* parents. *seayah-seibu* having the same parents. *– kandung* biological father. *– mertua* father-in-law. *– pe(r)mandian* godfather. *– pungut* a) adoptive father. b) ritual father (for certain ceremonies). *– rumah tangga* househusband. *– tiri* stepfather.
berayah **1** to have a father. **2** *~ kepada* to call/consider s.o. one's father.
berayahkan ... to have ... as one's father.
mengayahi to father.
keayahan fatherhood, paternity.
perayahan paternal.
ayah II → AYAT.
ayah III (*Hind*) Indian nurse; *cp* AMAH.
ayahan (*Jv*) task, assignment, duty, responsibility. *– Umum* Public Works (in Yogyakarta); → PEKERJAAN *umum*.
ayahanda (more refined than *ayah*; usually used in correspondence and older literature) father.
ayak I a sieve.
mengayak(i) to sift, screen.
ayakan **1** the result/output of sifting/screening. **2** sieve, screen. *~ getar* vibrating sieve. *~ kawat* wire screen.
pengayak **1** the person who sifts. **2** sieve, screen. **3** methods/ways of sifting/screening.

pengayakan 1 sifting, screening. 2 sieve.

ayak II mengayak to walk with a wobble/waddle (like a duck).

mengayakkan to wriggle, wobble.

ayak-ayak daddy longlegs, *Phalangium opilio.*

ayak-ayakan (*Jv*) k.o. Javanese musical form.

ayal (*J*) 1 be slow, delay, linger. 2 hesitate, be doubtful. *tak – lagi* a) immediately, directly, without (further) delay, forthwith. b) without any doubt, certainly.

berayal *tidak ~* promptly.

berayal-ayalan to linger, tarry; to delay; to be reluctant.

ngayal to take one's time.

mengayal-ayalin (*J*) to delay doing s.t. on purpose.

ayal-ayalan to do a job very slowly, take a long time to do s.t.; not be in a hurry.

ayam I 1 fowls (such as hen/cock/chicken). *ikan –* chicken (meat); *cp* IKAN *sa(m)pi. mati – saja* killed without much ado. *merdéka –* free as a bird, independent. *tidur-tidur –* to sleep with one eye open. *bagai – bertelur di padi* as happy as the day is long, as happy as a clam. *– ditambat disambar elang* good luck is expected, but bad luck happens. *– hitam terbang malam* difficult to figure out/detect. *– itik raja pada tempatnya* to be master in one's own house. *seperti – pulang ke pautan* in complete harmony. *– putih terbang siang* easy to detect. *– termakan rambut* very nervous. 2 (*sl*) girl, chick (*esp* a young prostitute). *– aduan* fighting cock. *– alas* wood cock/hen, jungle fowl, *Gallus gallus. – asing* (*euph*) pork. *– babon* laying hen. *– bakaran* fast-growing breed of chicken. *– balik* chicken with inverted feathers. *– bangkas* cock with white spots on its back. *– bekisar* (*Jv*) crossbreed between a Bantam (fowl) and a jungle cock. *– beku* frozen chicken. *– belanda* turkey, *Meleagris gallopavo;* → KALKUN. *– belorong* white cock. *– beroga* red jungle fowl, *Gallus gallus. – bersiang* skinned chicken. *– bertelur* layer (chicken). *– berumbun* spotted chicken. *– betina* a) hen. b) prostitute. *– biang* clucking hen, layer. *– bibit* fledgling. *– bibit induk* parent stock. *– bibit nénék* grandparent stock. *– biring* cock with yellow legs. *– borék* chicken with spotted feathers. *– broiler* broiler. *– bugil* featherless chicken. *– bulu balik* a variety of chicken with feathers "inside out," i.e., sticking out at an angle rather than lying smooth. *– bumbu acar* chicken cooked in spicy yellow sauce. *– buras* [bukan ras] a nonpedigreed chicken, not a true-bred chicken; → AYAM *kampung. – cabut tulang* galantine. *– cemani* black-boned fowl (white feathers and yellow legs). *– cenangkas* gamecock with white feathers and yellow legs. *– daging* broiler. *– dara* pullet. *– denak* a) → AYAM *alas.* b) short-legged Bantam chicken. *– galur* crossbred breed of chicken. *– goréng* fried chicken. *– goréngan* fryer. *– goréng mbok b(e)rék* chicken in a basket (simmered in spiced coconut milk) (k.o. fast food chicken). *– gulai* stewed chicken. *– Hainan* a way of preparing chicken. *– hutan* → AYAM *alas. – hutan hijau* green jungle fowl, *Gallus varius. – induk* parent stock. *– isi* dressed and stuffed chicken. *– itik* poultry. *– jago/jantan* rooster. *– jalak* speckled cock. *– jantan muda* cockerel. *– kalasan* a chicken dish prepared à la Kalasan (a place in Central Java); *cp* AYAM *mbok b(e)rék. – kalkun* turkey. *– kampung* a nonpedigreed chicken, *Gallus gallus domesticus; opp* AYAM *negeri. – kapon/kasi* capon. *– kasim* capon. *– katé/katik* short-legged Bantam chicken. *– ke(m)biri* capon. *– kécap* chicken stewed in soy sauce. *– kinantan* white cock. *– koci* large chicken with feathers on legs. *– kodok* dressed and stuffed chicken. *– kukus* steamed chicken. *– kutuk* chick. *– laga* fighting cock. *– laut* starry triggerfish, *Abalistes stellaris. – lokal* a) local chicken. b) local prostitute. *– mandul* nonlaying hen. *– masak Bali* chicken stewed in coconut milk. *– Mbok Berék* chicken cooked with coconut milk and spices. *– mék* rail. *– mutiara* helmeted guinea fowl, *Numida meleagris. – nakar* day of sacrifice (on the pilgrimage). *– negeri* pedigreed chicken; *opp* AYAM *kampung. – O* chicken cooked with taoco, ginger, and other ingredients. *– panggang* barbecued chicken. *– papak* tailless rooster. *– pedaging* a) broiler (chicken). b) (in Surabaya) pimp. *– pegar* fireback pheasant, *Lophura ignita/ rufa. – pelaga* fighting cock. *– pelesung* young man who visits a house in which there is a young girl. *– pelung* rooster with good singing voice (found in West Java). *– pemacak mancanegara*

foreign-raised chicken used for crossbreeding with domestic chickens. *– penelur/petelur* layer (chicken). *– peranggang* fryer (chicken). *– piaraan impérialis* running dog of the imperialists. *– pilas* cock with black neck and legs. *– pop* k.o. fried chicken dish. *– potong(an)* fryer (chicken). *– potong beku* frozen broiler (chicken). *– pungguk* tailless chicken. *– pupuh* fighting cock which does not use a spur. *– rambaian* chicken with long tail feathers. *– ras* pedigreed chicken. *– réd* Rhode Island Red (chicken). *– sabung(an)* fighting cock. *– sayur* potpourri. *– sebandung* twin fowl (from one egg). *– selasih* black-boned fowl. *– sembelihan* fryer (chicken). *– sétan* (*J*) → AYAM *bulu balik. – singgang* roast chicken. *– suluh* featherless chicken. *– tambatan* (*cla*) an old slave. *– tedung* red-feathered fighting cock with black eyes and legs. *– telur* layer (chicken). *– ternak* poultry. *– teruna* cockerel. *– tukung* a) featherless chicken. b) tailless chicken. *– tulak* a) chicken with upright-standing feathers like a porcupine. b) spotted chicken.

ayam-ayam watercock, wild hen, snipe, *Gallicrex cinerea.*

ayam-ayaman 1 weathercock. 2 watercock, snipe, *Gallierex cinerea.* 3 toy chicken.

ayam II mengayam to support.

ayam III (*A*) days.

ayan I (*E*) 1 zinc, corrugated iron. 2 tinplate, white iron.

ayan II epilepsy. *– menahun* chronic epilepsy.

ayanan 1 epileptic. *orang ~* epileptic (person). 2 to have/get epilepsy.

ayan III fingerbowl.

ayan IV (*A*) essences.

ayanda → AYAHANDA.

ayang (*J*) → SAYANG.

ayang-ayang k.o. plant used for medicinal purposes, *Lasianthus longifolius.*

a'yanu'l-thabita (*A*) the essence of things, fixed prototypes.

ayap feed. *– balik* feedback; → UMPAN *balik.*

seayapan eating from the same plate or bowl.

mengayap to eat or drink (by a social inferior).

ayapan food (gift or leftovers of the sovereign).

keayapan food/drinks given by the sovereign.

ayar I (*coq*) → AIR.

ayar II (*ob*) pickpocket.

ayaran *tukang ~* pickpocket.

ayat I (*A*) 1 Koranic verse. 2 paragraph, section, clause (of a law). 3 item (in bookkeeping), entry. *– kursi* verses in the Koran that explain the powers of God and that are often recited in times of danger. *– penutup* closing entry. *– penyesuaian* adjusting entry. *–.– peralihan* items running into the following year. 4 (*mostly Mal*) sentence. *– tanya* (*gram*) interrogative sentence.

seayat a verse. *~ demi ~* verse by verse.

ayat II (*A*) life; → HAYAT. *sampai akhir –nya* until the end of his life.

Ayatollah and **Ayatullah** (*A*) "Sign/Miracle of God"; a respected religious teacher (most common among Shi'ite Muslims).

ayé (*J*) → SAYA.

ayem I (*J/Jv*) 1 patient, calm, quiet, contented, satisfied, pleased. *dengan –* in peace. *– tentrem* contented, quiet. 2 (*Jv*) untroubled, comfortable.

ayeng-ayengan (*J/Jv*) 1 to go back and forth. 2 to roam around, go round and round in circles.

ayér (*coq*) → AIR.

ayid (*Jv*) 1 sticky, mucous, slimy. 2 slippery (of an eel).

ayim legal term for a woman with no husband (unmarried or widow).

ayir (*ob*) tuna fish; → TONGKOL.

ayn (*A*) name of the 18th letter of the Arabic alphabet.

ayo(h) and **ayok** come on! let's ...! *Sudah –!* OK, let's go! *-lah duluan* go ahead first.

mengayo-ayo to keep on saying "Come on!" to s.o.

ayom (*Jv*) shaded, protected, guarded, sheltered.

mengayomi to protect, shelter, shade, take care of. *diayomi oléh* under the aegis of.

terayomi protected, sheltered.

ayoman shelter.

pengayom 1 protector. **2** patron. **berpengayom** under the auspices/aegis of, sponsored by.

pengayoman 1 aegis, protection. **2** protecting, sheltering.

ayu I (*Jv*) pretty, lovely, beautiful (of a girl or woman).

keayuan beauty.

ayu II (*Jv*) *(em)bok* – and *(m)bakyu* **1** title of young ladies of lower standing. **2** form of address to an older woman.

Ayub (*A*) (the biblical) Job.

ayubagya and **ayubagyo mengayubagya** to inaugurate, install.

ayuh → AYO(H).

ayuhai hey you!

ayuk mengayuk (*vulg*) to fuck, screw.

ayum (*ob*) **mengayum** to abet, furnish with money (for bad purposes).

ayuman collusion.

pengayuman abetting, colluding.

ayun 1 oscillation, swinging back and forth. **2** sway. *dengan – dengkul* on foot. **3** swing (in boxing). *– ambung* swaying. ***mengayun-ambungkan*** to swing, rock s.t. *– temayun* a) to hang down and swing. b) to set, sink, go down. *matahari – temayun* the sun is setting, it's getting dark. ***berayun temayun 1*** to go down, set. **2** to balance o.s. *air ~ waterfall*.

seayun *~ dengan* in agreement with. *~ seperti berbuai* to be in agreement. *~ sebuaian* unanimous, in harmony.

berayun(-ayun) 1 to rock, swing, sway, go up and down. **2** to fluctuate, oscillate. *~ kaki* a) to let one's legs dangle. b) pleasant idleness, sweet doing nothing. c) to dance, shake a leg. **3** to have sex. **4** to balance o.s. *~ tambang* (*mil*) to cross by swinging on a rope.

mengayun(-ayun) 1 to rock, sway. **2** to swing, rock (a cradle). **3** (of the sun) to set, sink, go down. **4** to swing, brandish, wave (a dagger), wield. *mengayun kaki* a) to swing one's legs. b) to start off, go/move away. *mengayun kata* to weigh one's words. *~ cangkul pertama* to break ground. *~ kepal* to shake one's fist. *~ langkah* a) to start (out/off/on one's way), set out, go off, make a start. b) to take (preliminary) measures/steps, prepare to. *~ lénggang* to swing one's arms (while walking).

mengayunkan 1 to swing, move, brandish, wield. *~ cangkul pertama* to break ground (for a building, etc.). *~ palu* to swing the gavel. **2** to swing s.t. (at); to hurl by swinging s.t. *~ kaki* a) to swing one's legs. b) to start off. *~ kepal/tinju ke arah kepalaku* to swing one's fist in the direction of my head. *~ langkah* a) to take steps. b) to set off, get started. *~ tangan* one's fingers are itching (to hit him).

terayun-ayun to sway, stagger, reel, pitch, rock. *Dahan-dahan itu ~ karena tiupan angin.* The branches were swaying in the breeze.

ayunan 1 rocking, swaying, oscillation. *~ tangan* motion/movement of the hand, gesture. **2** (children's) swing (playground apparatus), hammock. **3** (rocking) cradle. **4** sling (for throwing stones). **5** fluctuation. *~ (rém, etc.)* handle (of a brake/pump). **6** oscillator, pendulum. *~ cangkul pertama* breaking ground. *~ pegas* shackle. **7** sexual intercourse. *bermain ~* to have sex.

pengayun pendulum.

pengayunan swinging, swirling, swaying. *~ cangkul pertama* ground breaking.

ayunda older sister; dear girl! (term of address).

ayut (*vulg*) **mengayut** to screw, fuck.

(ayut-)ayutan mistress, concubine.

aza → AZZA.

azab (*A*) **1** torment, torture, pain. **2** punishment. *– kubur/neraka* the torments of hell. *– sengsara* torment and misery.

mengazab(kan) to torture.

azaban torment.

keazaban torture.

azad (*Pers*) without fault.

azahar (*A?*) hazard. *– pekerjaan* occupational hazard.

azal I (*A*) without beginning, past without beginning.

azal II → AJAL.

azali (*A*) **1** of old, from time immemorial, ancient. *masa/zaman –* time immemorial, ancient times. **2** punishment after death.

azam I (*A*) greatly respected. *isim al.–* a greatly respected name (the name of God).

azam II (*A*) intention, purpose, resolution.

berazam 1 with intentions. **2** resolute, determined.

mengazamkan 1 to intend. **2** to resolve, make up one's mind.

keazaman intention.

azamat (*ob*) → AZMAT.

azan (*A*) summons/calls by the muezzin for ritual prayers.

mengazami to call s.o. to prayer.

mengazani to recite the call to prayer. *~ bayi* to recite the call to prayer over a newborn child. *~ mayat* to recite the call to prayer over the deceased at funeral rites.

mengazankan to summon/call for the ritual prayer.

azas → ASAS. **seazas:** *organisasi ~* subsidiary (of political party). *ormas yang ~* mass organization working in the same direction.

azasi → ASASI.

azemat → AZMAT.

azerbaijan (*D*) Azerbaijan.

azha (*sl*) → AJA.

azhar (*A*) shining.

azim (*A*) august, exalted.

azimat I (*A*) amulet, talisman, charm, mascot. *Lima – Révolusi Indonésia* (under the Soekarno regime around 1965) The Five Talismans of the Revolution: NASAKOM Jiwaku, Pancasila, MANIPOL/USDEK, Trisakti TAVIP and Berdikari.

azimat II → AZMAT.

azimut (*D*) azimuth. *– bintang* astronomical azimuth. *– kontra* counter-azimuth.

azis and **aziz** (*A*) **1** respected (person), honored. **2** awe-inspiring. **3** beloved, darling. **4** dear, expensive.

azl (*A*) coitus interruptus.

azmat (*A*) awe-inspiring, mighty, enormous, awful, majestic, imposing.

Azmu (*A*) Pegasus.

Azrail (*A*) Azrael, name of an archangel, the angel of death.

Aztéc (*D*) /asték/ Aztec.

azza (*A*) glorious, honored. *–.wa-jalla* may He be honored and glorified (of God).

B

b and **B I** /bé/ the second letter of the Latin alphabet used for writing Indonesian.

b II [Bin] *bin*, term used in Arabic names and some Indonesian names meaning son of. *Ibrahim – Ahmad* Ibrahim, son of Ahmad; → BIN I, IBNI.

B III (in music) the seventh tone/note in the ascending scale of C major.

B IV car license plate for Jakarta.

B2 [bahan berbahaya] hazardous materials.

B3 [bahan berbahaya dan beracun] toxic materials.

ba I the name of the second letter of the Arabic alphabet.

ba II (D) boo! *tanpa –.bi.bu* and *tanpa bilang – dan/atau bu* without saying/uttering a word.

ba III (in acronyms) → BADAN, BAHAN, BAJA, BINTARA.

ba' → BAK.

BA car license for Sumatera Barat.

baada (A) after; → BADA II. *-hu* after that; afterward.

ba'adiyah (A) to say (a prayer) in parts.

baai (D) baize.

baal (S) insensitive to pain.

Baath (A) Baath, a political party in Iraq, Syria, etc.

Baathisme Baathism.

ba'ats (A) the day the dead arise from the grave, judgment day.

bab (A) **1** gate, door. *- al Mandéb* the Gate of Tears, i.e., the name of the strait joining the Red Sea and the Gulf of Aden. **2** chapter (in a book). **3** point of discussion, topic of conversation. **4** concerning, about, on (the subject of), re. *- pemberantasan buta huruf* concerning/re: the fight against illiteracy.

baba I → BABAH. *- Ali* sarcastic reference to Chinese businessman (= *Baba*) who runs a business using a license sold to him by an Indonesian (= *Ali*) to whom the license was issued; *cp* ALI *baba*.

baba II (J) father; → ABA I, BABÉ.

baba III (*naut infr*) mouse, i.e., a knot made on a rope to keep a running eye/loop from slipping.

bababotan k.o. plant, billy-goat weed, *Ageratum conyzoides*.

babad I (*Jv*) chronicles, annals, historical accounts. *- Tanah Jawa* Chronicle of Java.

babad II → BABAT IV.

babah 1 Indonesian-born male Chinese, Indo-Chinese male. **2** form of address for an Indonesian-born Chinese male.

babahu (S) → BAU III.

babak I 1 act, scene, episode (of a play), piece (in a concert); → ADEGAN. *sandiwara dua –* drama in two acts. **2** phase, stage, series. **3** round (in boxing); set (in tennis), heat (in certain sports). *- penyisihan* elimination round. *- penyusunan peringkat* consolation round. *- pungkasan/wasana* finale, final round. *- yang terakhir* final stages.

babakan 1 phase, stage, stadium. **2** round (in boxing), set (in tennis); period. *di ~ kedua* in the second reading (in Parliament). *~ waktu* periodization.

pembabakan division into phases. *~ waktu* periodization.

babak II bruised. *- belur/bundas* (*J/Jv*) (to beat s.o.) black and blue. *dipukuli – belur* to be beaten black and blue. *membayar – belur* to pay through the nose (for s.t.).

babak III membabak to stanch/stop/check the flow of blood, etc. (from a wound).

babakan I (*J/Jv*) bark, rind (of a tree). *- kelapa* bark of the coconut palm.

babakan II (*Jv*) a new settlement on a previously uninhabited site; hamlet.

babal (*J/Jv*) pistil/bud of a very young jack fruit that is eaten as a vegetable; → KEBABAL.

babancong (S) an elevated dome-shaped structure.

babang terbabang agape; gaping (wide) (of a wound/mouth from a yawn or amazement).

baban membaban to train, educate, instruct, teach.

babar I spread, unfurl, unfold.

membabar to spread; to develop.

membabarkan 1 to spread, stretch, unfurl, unfold, hang out (washing). *~ layar* to unfurl the sails. *~ sayap* to spread one's wings. **2** to lay out, explain, set forth (an opinion, etc.). *Ia telah ~ pendapatnya kepada rakyat.* He set forth his opinions to the public. **3** to extend, spread (one's power over, etc.). *~ kekuasaannya ke negara-negara yang bertetangga* to extend its powers to neighboring countries.

terbabar 1 spread (out), unfolded, unfurled. *Layarnya ~.* The sails were unfurled. **2** developed, spread. *Cahaya perada itu ~ ke segenap penjuru.* The radiance of the gold leaf spread in every direction. **3** explained, laid out, elucidated.

pembabaran 1 spreading, stretching. **2** laying out, explaining.

babar II (*Jv*) a reddish-brown dye obtained from the bark of the indigo tree; → SOGA.

membabar to dye with *babar*, etc. (in making *batik*).

pembabaran 1 dying with *soga*. **2** making *batik* with *soga*.

babar III (*Jv*) **1** to proliferate, multiply. **2** to procreate.

babaran giving birth, confinement; to give birth.

babar IV kebabaran caught in the act (of theft/committing adultery, etc.).

babar V (*cla*) to fly about everywhere; → BEBAR.

Babaranjang *KA* – [Keréta api batubara rangkaian panjang] coal-transport train consisting of 32 vans and one administration car pulled by two locomotives, which runs from Tanjungenim to Tarahan in Lampung (South Sumatera).

babarblas and **babarpisan** (*Jv*) altogether, quite, completely.

babas carried away, drift.

membabaskan to carry away, cause to drift away, drive off course.

terbabas 1 swept away/off, carried away, driven off course, driven past one's goal in life/away from one's principles; drifted off in another direction. **2** missed, went wild/off target. **3** (*geol*) deranged.

babat I clear, cut away.

membabat 1 to clear (land by cutting growth), cut away, cut through. *~ hutan* to clear forest land. *~ rumput* to cut/mow grass/the lawn. **2** to clear away (difficulties, etc.). **3** to ban (pedicabs from certain streets/areas, etc.). **4** to root out (rebellions, etc.). *~ habis* to root s.t. out completely, clean up/out (rebellious forces, etc.). *Sarwo Édhie suksés ~ habis kekuatan pemberontakan berdarah G30S/PKI.* Sarwo Edhie was successful in rooting out the bloody rebellious forces of the G30S/PKI. **5** (in sports) to defeat, beat (one's opponents in a match).

membabati 1 (*pl obj*) to clear (a site), clear away (plants/bushes, etc.). *~ alang-alang* to clear away the elephant-grass. **2** (in sports) to defeat, beat (many opponents one by one).

membabatkan to strike a blow with (a cleaver/chopper, etc.).

babatan blow, swipe.

pembabat 1 cutter, mower. **2** mowing machine.

pembabatan chopping away, cutting down/off, felling, clearing away; → PENEBANGAN. *~ pohon-pohon mahoni di sepanjang jalan* cutting down mahogany trees along the road. *~ hutan* land-clearing.

babat II 1 group, category. **2** team (of oxen/horses). **3** pair, set. *mencari sama –* to look for an equivalent. *bukan –nya* it is not its equivalent/equal.

sebabat 1 of the same kind, homogeneous, similar. **2** congener.

babat III (M) **membabat** to bandage, wrap (a bandage) around, dress (a wound); → BEBAT.

babat IV (*J/Jv*) reticulum (of cud-chewing animals), tripe; → BABAD II. *sop –* tripe soup.

babatan original heirloom.

babawangan Chinese water chestnut, *Eleocharis dulcis*.

babé (*J*) 1 father. 2 Big Daddy (i.e., a sobriquet for President Soekarno and President Soeharto). 3 form of address to an older man or s.o. in a higher position (teacher, employer, etc.); → AYAH, BAPAK.

Babel [Bangka dan Belitung] Bangka and Belitung.

baber (*Jv*) rhubarb; → RABARBER.

babi I 1 pig, hog, swine. – *mendengkur*. Pigs grunt. *anak* – piglet. *bintang* – Venus, morning star. *daging* – pork. *gila/pitam/sawan* – epilepsy. *ular* – the black cobra. 2 term of abuse. – *lu!* you pig! 3 name of one of the *ceki* playing cards. *bagai* – *merasa gulai* behave like a bigshot/a wealthy person, etc. *kalau sorak lebih dahulu daripada tohok, tidak mati* – to count one's chickens before they hatch. – *alang-alang* Eurasian wild pig, feral hog, *Sus scrofa*. – *alu* tapir; → TENUK. – *asap* a) bacon; → SPÉK. b) ham; → HAM. – *balar* albino pig. – *baran* wild boar, *Sus vittatus*. – *batang* hog badger, *Arctonyx collaris*. – *betina* sow. – *buta* "wild hog." *membabi buta* 1 to rage, run amok, rush about in a frenzy. 2 raging. 3 demonic. 4 to act rashly/blindly. – *dara* an adult sow which has not yet brought forth young, gilt. – *duri moncong péndék* spiny anteater, short beaked echidna, *Tachyglossus aculeatus*. – *duyung* sea cow, manatee. – *gajah* tapir. – *giring* nursing sow. – *guling* (*Bal*) roast suckling pig. – *hutan* wild boar, Javan warty pig, *Sus barbatus/scrofa/verrucosus*. – *jalang* a) wild boar; → BABI *hutan*. b) slut, loose woman. *membabi jalang* 1 to commit adultery, fornicate. 2 to run wild. – *janggur* small variety of bearded wild boar. – *jantan* boar. – *jinak* domesticated pig. – *kasim* barrow, castrated pig. – *katé* miniature pig. – *kawan* → BABI *baran*. – *kécap* pork cooked in sweet soy sauce. – *lalang* sea urchin, *Diadema setosum*. – *murai* tapir. – *nangui* big bearded pig of the East Coast of Malaysia. – *ngépét* (*J*) a) s.o. who can transform himself into a boar in order to steal. b) s.o. who gets rich without hard work. – *panggang* barbecued pork. – *pejantan* boar. – *penjerit* s.o. who screams too much. – *puter* roast suckling pig. – *putih* wild boar. – *rantai* bearded wild pig. – *rusa* hog deer of Sulawesi with a pair of hornlike tusks which curve up backward from each jaw, *Babirusa alfurus/babirus(s)a*. – *suap* s.o. who bribes (soccer players, etc.). – *tanah* ant bear, aardvark. – *tunggal* solitary boar.

babi II *kayu* – → KAYU *babi*. *rumput* – weeds used as fodder for hogs, club wort, Indian heliotrope, *Adenostemma lavenia*, *Heliotropium indicum*. *rumput tahi* – k.o. herb used for medication, wild heliotrope, *Vernonia cineraria*.

babi III *burung* – a small variety of the marabou stork, *Leptoptilus javanicus*.

babi IV – *kurus* name of a tree with very hard wood, believed to be an aphrodisiac, *Eurycoma longifolia*.

babil I (*ob*) stubborn, obstinate, difficult to persuade/deal with; argumentative. – *sangat budak ini*. This servant is hard to deal with.

berbabil to bicker, wrangle, squabble.

babilan quarrel, bickering.

perbabilan squabble, quarrel.

Babil II (the Biblical) Babel. *menara* – the tower of Babel.

babinsa [bintara pembina désa] Noncommissioned Officer for Village Control.

babit membabitkan to involve/implicate s.o. in a case, cause to be caught up in s.t.

terbabit involved/implicated.

bablas (*Jv*) 1 out of sight. 2 gone, vanished, lost; passed away, dead. 3 straight ahead without a detour, direct. 4 advanced/made headway quickly, gone way ahead/too far. 5 accomplished/attained/reached one's goal.

kebablasan 1 to go far. 2 to go too far.

babon (*Jv*) 1 *ayam* – mother hen. 2 layer, laying hen. 3 mother/basic/family ...; → INDUK. 4 original text. 5 reference. *buku* – reference book.

babtis → BAPTIS.

babu I (*Jv*) female domestic servant/help, (maid-)servant; → PEMBANTU *rumah tangga*, PRT. – *anak* female servant who cares for the small children in the house. – *cuci* laundress. – *dalam* female servant who manages the household. – *jahit* seamstress. – *masak* female cook. – *nyai* (*col*) maid-servant and concubine for the European or Chinese master of the house. – *susu/téték* (*J*) wet-nurse.

membabukan to hire s.o. as a maid.

memperbabu 1 to engage/hire s.o. as a maid. 2 to treat s.t. the way one treats a maid/servant.

babu II (*A*) door, gate; → BAB

babul-jannah Gate to Heaven.

babun (*E*) baboon (mainly genus *Papio*).

babur (*cla*) *besi/keris* – iron (kris) that is supposed to expand when it enters a enemy's body.

babut (*Jv*) rug, carpet; → PERMADANI.

membabuti to carpet (a room).

baca (*Skr*) 1 (in compounds) reading. *budaya* – reading culture. *kacamata* – reading glasses. *lampu* – reading-lamp. *ruang* – reading-room. *tanda* – punctuation mark. 2 read. *Tujuh nyawa (baca: tujuh nyawa) telah dia habisi*. He killed seven people (read: seven people). – *aksara yang fungsional* functional literacy.

membaca 1 to read (a book, etc.), read s.t. out loud. ~ *batin* to read to o.s. ~ *bibir* to lip-read. ~ *dalam hati* to read to o.s. 2 to recite, chant, say (a prayer). ~ *doa* to say a prayer, recite prayers. ~ *satu per satu* to call off one by one.

membaca-baca to browse through.

membacai 1 (*pl obj*) to read thoroughly and repeatedly; to study. 2 to allude to, hint at.

mbacain and **ngebacain** (*J coq*) to reveal (s.o.'s secrets).

membacakan 1 to read s.t. out loud, read out/off. 2 to read aloud to. *Ia* ~ *anaknya cerita dongéng sebelum tidur*. She reads her child fairy tales before he goes to sleep. 3 to pronounce, say (a prayer), recite prayers.

terbaca [and **kebaca** (*coq*)] legible. *tidak* ~ illegible. **keterbacaan** legibility.

bacaan 1 reading (matter), literature. *bahan* ~ reading matter. *buku* ~ reader. ~ *untuk pemahaman* reading for comprehension. ~ *porno* pornography. 2 reading (the act of one who reads). ~*nya kurang lancar*. He is not a fluent reader. 3 recitation, incantation.

pembaca reader. ~ *éditor* (on the radio and TV) anchor(man). ~ *iseng* occasional reader. ~ *khotbah* person who gives the sermon. ~ *Menulis* Letters to the Editor (column in a newspaper).

pembacaan 1 reading, reading out (loud). *Perayaan itu didahului dengan* ~ *al-Qur'an*. The celebration was preceded by a Koran reading. 2 speech, lecture, sermon, discourse. *Acara yang kedua ialah* ~ *oléh S*. The second item on the program was a talk by S.

bacah membacah(-bacah) to cut/chop up, mince.

bacak I (*J/Jv*) wet, slushy. – *tinta* inkblot.

bacak II (*M*) (white) spots or speckles (on the skin).

berbacak-bacak speckled. *ayam* ~ a speckled chicken.

bacam → BACEM.

bacang I → EMBACANG.

bacang II (*C*) Chinese delicacy of rolls made from rice or glutinous rice filled with pork and steamed.

bacar garrulous, talks too much. – *mulut* talkative, garrulous (in a bad sense).

bacarongi (*J*) k.o. herb, water parsley/celery, *Oenanthe javanica*.

bacek → BACAK I.

bacem (*J/Jv*) soaked, pickled, marinated. *tempé* – boiled tempeh with spices, dried and then baked.

membacem to soak, marinate.

baceman soaked, marinated.

bacik ship's captain.

baciluk peek-a-boo; → CILUK...BAH.

bacin (*Jv*) stinking (as the smell of saliva/tainted fish).

backing (*E*) /béking/ backing, support; → BÉKING.

membackingi to support s.o.

backing-backingan illegal collusion.

backingisme influence-peddling.

bacok (*J/Jv*) a slash, cut, hack, stab. *kena* – to get slashed/cut/hacked/stabbed. *Sekali* –, *jatuhlah ia*. He collapsed after he was stabbed.

membacok to hack, chop, slash, cut; to stab, pierce, spear.

membacokkan to cut/hack/chop/slash with s.t.

terbacok [and **kebacok** (*coq*)] stabbed, slashed, gashed.

bacokan cut, stab; results of a stabbing, stab wound, gash, cut.

pembacok stabber, hacker.

pembacokan hacking, chopping, slashing, cutting; stabbing, piercing, spearing.

bacot (*J/Jv coq*) mouth; beak, bill (of a bird), snout, mouth (of a horse, etc.). *gedé –nya* he's got a big mouth, i.e., he talks big/a lot. *Tutup –mu!* Shut your trap!

berbacot and **membacot** to open one's mouth/trap.

bacotan talkative (but not liking to work); fussy, like to complain/grumble.

bacul timid (of a fighting cock), spiritless, lacking the spirit (to fight, etc.); cowardly. *ayam –* a cock that will not fight.

kebaculan spiritlessness; cowardice.

bacut (*Jv*) **kebacut** (now that it's) too late; (now that it has) gone too far; rash.

bad (*Pers ob*) wind. *bala –* windward. *zir –* leeward.

bada I (*M*) (*tidak*) **terbada(-bada)** 1 (in)describable. 2 (ir)repressible, can (not) be kept in/held back. *Amarahnya tidak terbada.* He could not hold his anger back.

bada II and **ba'da** (*A*) after; → BAKDA. *– kupat/Pasa* name of the feast at the end of the fasting month *Ramadan*.

bada III (*Tam*) *– pisang* a delicacy made from a banana cut into slices and baked.

bada IV *– seluang* k.o. carp, rasbora, harlequin, *Rasbora heteromorpha*.

badahu (*A*) *wa –* (and) afterward.

badai I sudden gale, hurricane, storm, typhoon. *– debu* dust storm. *– és* ice storm. *– guntur* thunder storm. *– kilat kering* dry thunderstorm. *– pasir* sandstorm. *– salju* snowstorm, blizzard. *– surya* solar storm.

berbadai to be accompanied by a hurricane. *Hujan lebat ~ melanda daérah itu.* A heavy rainstorm with gales struck that area.

membadai 1 to rage (of a storm). 2 to turn into a hurricane. 3 (*sl*) to get high (on drugs).

badai II terbadai 1 to lie on one's back; → TERSADAI. 2 to be moored (of a boat).

badak I 1 rhinoceros. 2 unable to feel/hear easily. *Dia berkulit –.* He has a thick skin, he is thick-skinned. *pekak –* hard of hearing. *– makan anak* said of a man who spoils his own child. *anak – dihambat-hambat* purposely looking for trouble. *– Afrika* (African) black rhinoceros, *Diceros bicornis*. *– air* hippopotamus, *Hippopotamus amphibius*. *– api* fierce legendary rhinoceros. *– babi* tapir. *– bengkak* small two-horned rhinoceros. *– bercula dua* two-horned (Sumatran) rhinoceros, *Rhinoceros Sumatrensis*. *– bercula satu* one-horned rhinoceros, Javan rhinoceros, *Rhinoceros sondaicus* (found in the Ujung Kulon Peninsula, Southwest Banten). *– berendam* two-horned (Sumatran) rhinoceros, *Rhinoceros Sumatrensis*. *– gajah* large one-horned rhinoceros, *Rhinoceros sondaicus*. *– hempit* smaller two-horned rhinoceros, *Rhinoceros sondaicus*. *– hitam* black rhinoceros. *– Jawa* Javan rhinoceros, *Rhinoceros sondaicus*. *– kerbau* smaller two-horned (Sumatran) rhinoceros, *Dicerorhinus/Rhinoceros Sumatrensis*. *– purba* large one-horned rhinoceros, *Rhinoceros sondaicus*. *– raya* large one-horned rhinoceros, *Rhinoceros sondaicus*. *– Sumatra* Sumatran rhinoceros, *Rhinoceros Sumatrensis*. *– sumbu* large one-horned rhinoceros, *Rhinoceros sondaicus*. *– sungai* hippopotamus. *– tampung* tapir, *Tapirus indicus*.

badak II *burung –* rhinoceros horn-bill, *Buceros rhinoceros*.

badak III *bayam –* a large amaranth/spinach variety, *Amaranthus sp.*

badakong nice, pretty.

badal I (*A*) 1 substitute, deputy (in pilgrimages to Mecca). 2 agent (in business/the mosque).

badal II (*A*) compensation. *– sakan* housing compensation.

badam I (*Pers*) 1 *buah –* almond, *Prunus spp.*, *Amygdalus communis*. *minyak –* almond oil. 2 tonsils.

badam II *bunga –* pink markings on the skin (taken as signs of leprosy).

badan (*A*) 1 body (the whole physical structure and substance of a man/animal/plant). *– saya kurang énak.* I don't feel good. I'm not feeling well. *membagi –* (*M*) (cannot do) two things at the same time. *kecil –* of small build/stature. *séhat –* fit. 2 body, the trunk or torso of a man or animal; → BODI, TUBUH. *sikap –* posture. 3 body, the main part of a structure. *– mobil* (car) body. *– pesawat* fuselage (of an airplane). 4 in person, o.s. *tuan –* the gentleman himself/in person. 5 agency, body, board, bureau, committee, commission, corps, service, group of people regarded as or functioning as a body/unit. *– pekerja* working committee. *– penasihat* advisory board. 6 corporate. *PPh –* corporate income tax. *– Adam* the human body. *– air* body of water. *– Administrasi Kepegawaian Negara* [BAKN] State Personnel Administration Board. *– amal* charitable institution. *– bertimbun tanah* (*euph*) to die. *– bijih* ore body. *– halus* ghost, invisible spirit. *– hukum* legal entity, corporate body. **berbadan hukum** which has a ... legal entity. *– intél(ijén)* intelligence agency. *– Intélijén Pertahanan* (U.S.) Defense Intelligence Agency, D.I.A. *– Intélijén Pusat* (U.S.) Central Intelligence Agency, C.I.A. *– jalan* pavement, road surface. *– kapal* casco. *– keagamaan* religious institution. *– kearsipan* archiving service. *– kehakiman* judicial body/authority. *– kelengkapan* constituent body. *– Kerjasama Ékonomi untuk Asia dan Timur Jauh* Economic Commission for Asia and the Far East, ECAFE. *– kontak* liaison. *– Koordinasi (Bantuan Pemantapan) Stabilitas Nasional* [Bakorstanas] Coordinating Board for the Consolidation of National Stability. *– Koordinasi Intélijén Negara* [BAKIN] State Intelligence Coordinating Agency. *– Koordinasi Masalah Kenakalan Remaja Penyalahgunaan Narkotika* [BAKORLANTIK] Coordinating Board for Combating Juvenile Delinquency and Drug Abuse. *– Koordinasi Penanaman Modal* [BKPM] Capital Investment Coordinating Board. *– Koordinasi Survéi dan Pemetaan Nasional* [Bakosurtanal] National Coordinating Agency for Surveys and Mapping. *– Musyawarah Désa* [Bamudés and BMD] Village Consultative Body, i.e., a legislative institution of a village administration. *– paku* the stem of a nail. *– pekerja* working committee. *– pelaksana* a) executive board. b) executing agency. *– pembentuk undang-undang* legislative assembly. *– Pembinaan Pendidikan Pelaksanaan Pedoman Penghayatan dan Pengamalan Pancasila* [BP7] Board for Developing Education and the Implementation of Guidelines for Instilling and Applying Pancasila. *– pemeriksa* investigating committee. *– Pemeriksa Keuangan* [BPK] State Audit Bureau. *– Pemerintah Harian* [BPH] Municipal Executive Board. *– penasihat* advisory board. *– penegak hukum* law enforcement agency. *– pengaduan* grievance board. *– pengaturan* regulatory body/board. *– pengawas(an)* supervisory board; trustees. *– Pengawas Pasar Modal* [BAPÉPAM] Capital Market Supervisory Agency. *– pengelola* executive board. *– Pengkajian dan Penerapan Téknologi* [BPPT] Agency for the Assessment and Application of Technology. *– pengurus* managing board. *– Penyéhatan Perbankan Nasional* [BPPN] Indonesian Bank Restructuring Agency, IBRA. *– Penyelidik untuk Persiapan Kemerdékaan Indonésia* [BPUPKI] Indonesian Independence Preparations Investigative Assembly. *– peradilan* court. *– perahu* hull of a boat. *– perantaraan* liaison board. *– Perencanaan Pembangunan Daérah* [Bappéda] Regional Development Planning Agency. *– Perencanaan Pembangunan Nasional* [Bappenas] National Development Planning Agency. *– Permusyawaratan Kewarganegaraan Indonésia* [Bapérki] Consultative Body for Indonesian Citizens (mostly of Chinese extraction). *– Pertanahan* Land Board. *– pertimbangan* advisory board. *– perwakilan* parliament, house of representatives. *– pesawat* fuselage. *– pimpinan* executive board. *– Pimpinan Pusat* [BPP] Central Executive Board. *– pusat* central committee. *– rahim* uterus. *– sinoman* association of youngsters to render aid to villagers. *– sosial* charity, relief agency. *– staf* staff division. *– Tenaga Atom Nasional* [Batan] National Atomic Institute. *– terkocak* (*M*) emaciated. *– usaha* business concern/entity, undertaking.

sebadan sexual intercourse; → SETUBUH. **bersebadan** to have sexual intercourse. *Meréka pun ~.* And then they had sex. *alat ~* (*euph*) sex organ. *~ dengan siapa saja* to be promiscuous.

menyebadani to have sexual intercourse with. **persebadanan** sexual intercourse. *~ itu sudah empat kali meréka lakukan.*

They had sex four times. ~ *léwat dubur* anal intercourse, sodomy; → SODOMI.

berbadan to have a body/figure. ~ *dua* to be pregnant. ~ *montok* to be shapely (of a woman). ~ *tampan* well-built.

perbadanan (*Mal*) board, body, committee, institution.

badang pear-shaped tray woven from rattan, etc. used for winnowing paddy, etc.

membadangkan to winnow.

badani(ah) (*A*) physical, bodily, corporeal, carnal. *keséhatan – dan rohani(ah)* physical and mental health. *melakukan hubungan –* to engage in sexual intercourse.

kebadani(ah)an physical (*mod*).

badar I a small fish species, *ikan teri* or anchovy, Makassar red fish, *Stolephorus spp.*; → BADAU, BADARI. *beroléh – tertimbakan* to get an unexpected windfall. *kalau pandai menggulai, – jadi tenggiri* if you're good at doing s.t., even bad raw material will turn out good. *melonjak –, melonjak gerundang* to imitate the rich/prominent/famous. *– kering/mersik* dried *badar*.

badar II cake of fried bananas.

badar III (*A*) full (moon) (used to depict beauty). *mukanya seperti bulan – waktu malam* she is very beautiful.

badar IV *– sila* and *raja – (cla)* a fine, white textile.

badar V (*A*) **1** *batu –* k.o. crystal used as a precious stone in rings. **2** Field of Badar, the site near Mecca where the Prophet Muhammad and his followers won their first victory in 624; seen as a victory over polytheism and a sign of divine guidance. *Selawat –* the Badar prayer, i.e., *NU*'s special prayer.

badar VI (*Jv*) **1** disclosure, revelation. **2** disclosed, revealed.

kebadaran to be disclosed/revealed.

badari and **badau** (*ob*) a fish that eats its young. *bapak – (coq)* a leader, etc. who lives at the expense of his followers.

Badawi (*A*) Bedouin.

badé I (*Bal*) a structure in the form of a mountain (= *méru*) with 11 levels and about 15 meters high (used for cremations).

badé(k) II (*J*) **membadé(k)** to guess.

badé(k)an and **badé(k)-badé(k)an 1** enigma, riddle; → TEKA-TEKI. **2** (answer to a) puzzle. *~ saya ternyata betul.* My guess turned out to be right. *seperti ~* enigmatic, puzzling, mysterious.

badé-badé (*Jv*) decorated bridal chair.

badeg (*J*) **mbadeg** and **ngebadeg** quite a lot. *Utangnya ~ di mana-mana.* He's up to his ears in debt.

badég (*Jv*) liquor made from fermented cassava or coconut-palm juice.

badek → BADEG.

bader I → BANDEL.

bader II → BADAR I.

badi (*Pers?*) **1** (*ob*) s.t. bad, such as a sickness that is caused by approaching a dead animal or a person who has been killed. **2** disease-transmitting matter, virus.

berbadi to behave like (a certain animal, etc.).

membadi to cast a spell (in order to destroy s.o.).

badik I a small, straight dagger used as a weapon.

membadik to stab with a *badik*.

badik II membadik (in soccer) to snatch the ball away and kick it from behind the opponent's lines.

badik III *– jagung* corn bud.

badis-badis k.o. decorative fish, chameleon fish, *Badis-badis burmanicus*.

badkip and **badkuip** (*D*) /batkép/ bathtub.

badminton (*D*) /bét-/ badminton.

berbadminton to play badminton.

badog (*J rude*) **mbadog** and **ngebadog** to gorge/stuff o.s., cram o.s. full of food, eat voraciously.

badogan food, grub.

badoi (*J*) obstinate, stubborn.

badong (*J*) **1** silver or gold cover for the breasts or pubic area. **2** metal chest protector. **3** winglike part of a *wayang* costume.

Badr → BADAR V.

badu and **ba'du** → BAKDU.

badug (*J*) horns (of an animal).

Badui I name of an ethnic group living in the mountains of South Banten, West Java. *orang –* Baduis; → KANÉKÉS.

Badui II Bedouin.

baduk I (*S*) **1** (of animals) to butt sideways with the head or horns. **2** to nudge s.o. with the arm or elbow. **3** to bump up against s.t.

baduk II (*Mal*) shapeless, ungainly (of a person).

badung I (*J*) naughty, mischievous; incorrigible.

kebadungan naughtiness, mischievousness; wantonness.

badung II → BADONG.

badung III → BEDUNG.

badung IV k.o. sea fish.

Badung V the Balinese name for the town of Denpasar.

badur (*J/Jv*) k.o. taro which is itchy to the touch, *Amorphophallus variabilis.*

badut (*J/Jv*) clown, comedian, buffoon.

membadut to clown/fool/play around, act silly, tell jokes.

badutan 1 joke, jest, farce. **2** target, victim.

badut-badutan to clown around, be a wise ass.

kebadutan 1 joking/clowning around. **2** ridiculousness.

pembadutan clowning around.

baduta [(di) bawah (umur) dua tahun] under the age of two, less than two years old. *anak –* toddler; *cp* BALITA.

baduyut (*S*) plant of the banyan family with rich foliage, snake gourd, *Trichosanthes villosa.*

baé I (*J/Jv*) only, solely, merely; → HANYA, SAJA, WAÉ.

baé(k) II (*J*) healthy, in good health, sound, fit, in shape; good, not defective; → BAIK.

baén-baén (*Jv*) extraordinarily (large/beautiful, etc.).

baforo (*Min*) **1** to sit on eggs, hatch, brood (of birds). **2** (*BG*) to hang around/out.

bafta(h) (*Pers cla*) (old trade name of) fine calico from Broach.

bag. (*abbr*) [bagian] part, section, department (also in acronyms).

baga lobe.

bagadang → BERGADANG.

bagai I (*Tam?*) **1** kind, sort, type, variety, species. *Beberapa – hasil lukisannya dipamérkan.* Various types of his paintings were exhibited. *banyak –nya* manifold, multifarious. **2** equal, s.t. similar, comparison, peer. *tak ada –nya* does not have an equal, unique. **3** like, as, resembling, similar to; → SEPERTI. *– kucing dengan anjing* like cat and dog. *– minyak dengan air* like oil and water.

sebagai 1 like, as (though). *Memberi fatwa ini ~ menjawab pertanyaan.* Issuing this edict is like answering a question. *~ berikut* as follows. *~ imbalan* in return, in exchange. *~ semestinya* as it should be, duly, properly. **2** to be(come), as. *mengangkat ~ ketua* to appoint/promote s.o. to the position of chairman. **3** to act as, in the capacity of, to have the position of. *~ menteri beliau tidak boléh demikian.* As minister he was not allowed to act in such a way. **4** in. *~ usaha* in an effort (to). *~ lagi/pula* likewise; the more so. *dan ~nya* [dsb] etcetera, and so forth/on.

berbagai 1 various, diverse, a number of, all kinds of, a wide range of. *~ daya upaya* various efforts. **2** to have (many) similarities (to), have (close) resemblances (to); in the ratio (of); matching. *tiada ~nya* unmatched, unequaled, without equal, peerless, incomparable.

berbagai-bagai and **bagai-bagai** all sorts of, various, several (different), divergent. *Ia berbuat ~ ikhtiar supaya terpelihara dari musuhnya.* He took various measures to protect himself against his enemies.

membagaikan (*M*) to ridicule, make fun of, mock; to humiliate, insult.

memperbagai-bagaikan to treat s.o. just as one pleases.

perbagai-bagai (*infr*) and **pelbagai** various, several (different), diverse.

bagai II (*Min*) worm-eaten. *Badannya membusuk dan –.* His body was rotting and worm-eaten.

bagaikan 1 as. **2** as if/though. *– runtuh* as if it was about to collapse. *– kera mendapat bunga* to cast pearls before swine.

bagaimana 1 how (about)? *Kalau Anda –?* How about you? *– kalau ...?* how about it if ...? what do you think of ... ? what about ... ? Suppose ...? *What do you say to ...? Tapi – kalau hal ini mémang benar adanya?* But suppose this turns out to be true? *– kalau minum és kopyor?* What do you think of having a glass of *kopyor* ice? *– kabarmu?* How are you doing? *– kabarnya?* How are things? What's new? – *nanti*? Let's think about it later. Let's see how things are a little closer to the time (used when the speaker does not want to commit himself at the present time). **2** How shall I put it? **3** how can it be! *Kamu ini –!* Oh you! How can you be like that! **4** What's with ...? **5** how do you like it? **6** what (did you just say)? excuse/pardon me. I beg your pardon (please repeat what you just said). **7** (noun +) *yang –?* what k.o. (noun)? *Kalau punya pacar ingin yang –?* What kind of a girlfriend would you like to have? *Pemecahan yang –?* What k.o. solution? **8** what do you mean by ... *Betul, Pak! Betul –?* Right, sir! What do you mean by "right?" – *lagi?* What can I do about it? How can I help it? What else (could I do)? *"Saya bukan tidak tahu peraturan itu, tapi mau – lagi, tempat ini sangat cocok buat kami," ujarnya.* "It isn't that I don't know about that regulation, but what else could I do, this place is just right for us," he said. – *pun* a) anyhow, anyway, no matter how/what. b) come what may. c) after all, all in all, in any case, by and large. d) somehow, in some way. *Saya – pun akan ke sana.* I'll get there somehow. – *pun juga* no matter how ... – *pun juga ditawar…* No matter how hard he bargained ... – *pun tidak (akan)* in no way.

bagaimana-bagaimana the details. *Bilang dong ~nya.* Come on, tell me the details. *tidak* ~ customary, usual, habitual.

sebagaimana as, like. – *mestinya* a) as it should (be done), properly. b) as such, accordingly. *Kau harus memperlakukannya ~ mestinya.* You should treat him accordingly.

membagaimanakan to do what to. *Daging ini dibagaimanakan?* What's to be done with this meat? → DIPENGAPAKAN.

bagak proud. **2** (*M*) brave, bold, tough. *Di sana banyak berkeliaran orang-orang –.* A lot of tough guys were wandering around there.

membagakkan ~ *diri* to embolden o.s.

kebagakan 1 pride. **2** bravery, boldness.

bagal I (*ob*) too big/strong, overdeveloped.

bagal II flower-stalk, peduncle (of coconut).

bagal III (*A*) mule.

bagal IV (*Jv*) ear of corn.

bagan I 1 sketch, plan, outline, scheme, design, blueprint, chart; → SEKÉT. *peta* – outline map. – *pengajaran bahasa* language-teaching scheme. **2** scaffolding, framework. **3** open platform (for drying fish, etc.). **4** quay, wharf. **5** fishing village. – *alir* flow-chart. – *aras* level scheme. – *arus* a) chart of currents. b) flow chart. – *balok* bar graph. – *bulat* pie chart/graph. – *jalur* band chart. – *kawat-mengawat* wiring scheme. – *lingkaran* circular diagram, pie chart. – *lukisan* sketch (of a picture). – *melingkar* circular graph. – *organisasi* organizational chart. – *perawakan* manning chart. – *pohon* tree chart. – *saluran* wiring diagram.

membagankan to sketch, outline.

bagan II trap net, lift net, fishing platform. – *gerak* movable lift net. – *tancap* immovable/fixed lift net.

bagang various species of marine fishes: butterfly fish, *Chelmon rostratus*; banner fish, *Heniochus acuminatus*; ocellated/six-spined butterfly fish, *Parachaetodon ocellatus*.

bagar (*M*) *gulai* – a meat-broth without coconut milk. – *kambing* a mutton dish.

membagar to roast; to cook.

bagas I 1 (of wind) strong, swift. **2** (*Jv*) (of the body) sturdy, robust.

bagas II (*E*) bagasse, sugarcane waste from sugar factory.

bagasi (*D*) **1** baggage, luggage. **2** baggage car, luggage-van (of a train), trunk (of a car). **3** carrier (of bicycle). **4** baggage/luggage rack (in train). – *cangkingan* hand baggage, hand luggage.

bagat I *ikan* – a horse-mackerel, giant trevally, big-eye trevally, *Caranx ignobilis/sexfasciatus*.

bagat II sugar palm, *Arenga pinnata*.

bagat III (= *berbagat*) spotted, with black spots on the body.

bagau various species of yellow-eyed grass. *akar* – yellow-eyed grass, *Xyris lucida*. *rumput* – yellow-eyed grass, sedge, *Xyris indica*.

bagawan → BEGAWAN.

Bagawatgita (*Skr*) the Bhagawat Gita, one of the holy books of Hinduism.

bagéa (*Min*) dish made from sago flour mixed with Java almonds and baked in sago palm leaves.

baggie (*E*) baggy (style) (trousers/shirt, etc.).

baghal → BAGAL III.

baghdla (*A*) hatred, hate, abhorrence.

bagi I (*Skr?*) **1** for, on behalf of, in favor of. *sistém kendali – dinamika politik* a control system for political dynamics. **2** (in order) to. *Ia datang kemari – menyerahkan harta bendanya.* He came here to surrender his possessions. **3** as far as … is concerned, as for, regarding, concerning. – *perkara itu* as for that matter. – *saya* as for me, as far as I am concerned.

bagi II (*Skr?*) part, share, portion. *hasil* – quotient; cp BAGI *hasil. tanda* – colon (:). – *dua* bisection. – *hasil* a) (in agriculture/mining) production sharing. b) (in banking/manufacturing) profit sharing. *berbagi hasil* to share in the profits. – *rata* equally shared/divided up. *membagi rata* to divide equally. *Harta pusaka dibagi rata kepada anak-anaknya.* His estate was divided equally among his children. *membagiratakan* to share/ divide up equally. – *rezeki* bribe. – *waktu* time share.

berbagi to share. ~ *duka* to share grief, commiserate. ~ *keuntungan* to share in the revenues. *menyatukan pemasaran minyak dan* ~ *keuntungan* pooling the oil marketing and sharing in the revenues. ~ *pengalaman* to share experiences. ~ *rasa* to share s.o.'s joys and sorrows. *Sebab itu untuk menghibur hati ibu kami ingin mencarikan teman* ~ *rasa.* Therefore, to cheer mother up we would like to look for a companion for her to share her joys and sorrows. ~ *tempat duduk* to share a seat (on a train, etc.).

membagi 1 to divide (into) ... (parts). *Tanah Jawa dibagi atas lima provinsi.* Java is divided into five provinces. ~ *dua* to halve, divide into two equal parts, bisect. **2** (*math*) to divide by (*dengan*). ~ *dua/tiga/empat* to divide by two/three/four. ~ *100 dengan 20* to divide 100 by 20. **3** to distribute, divide (among), divide up (into parts), split. ~ *kartu* to deal cards. ~ *tugas* to delegate a task. **4** to classify, group, divide up (into groups).

mbagi and **ngebagi** (*J*) to give s.o. (a share of s.t.). *Dia mendapat uang, tapi saya tidak dibagi.* He got some money, but I was not given any.

membagi-bagi to share, divide up. ~ *beban* burden-sharing.

membagikan [and **mbagiin/ngebagiin** (*J coq*)] to divide up, allocate, allot.

membagi-bagikan 1 to share. ~ *uangnya kepada orang-orang miskin* to share one's money with the poor. **2** to distribute, allocate, allot, measure out. *dibagi-bagikan* to be subdivided.

terbagi [and **kebagi** (*coq*)] **1** divided, assigned, allotted. ~ *dalam berbagai kelompok étnis* divided into various ethnic groups. ~ *sama rata* uniformly divided. *sistém komputer* ~ distributed computer system. **2** divisible. (*tidak*) *habis* ~ (in)divisible.

keterbagian (*math*) divisibility.

terbagi-bagi divided up, separated into groups.

bagian 1 share, part, portion, allowance. *di* ~ *lain dari buku ini* in another part of this book. *mengambil* ~ (*dalam*) to take part (in), participate (in). **2** part, section, piece (of s.t. larger). ~ *alas* base. ~ *atas* upper part, top. ~ *bahan* component. ~ *bawah* lower part, underside, bottom. ~ *bébas* free portion of an estate. ~ *belakang* rear (part), back(side). ~ *bersama* common area. ~ *dalam* interior, inside. ~ *ékor* tail section (of an aircraft). ~ *hidung* nose section (of an aircraft). ~ *hukum* legal department. ~ *Hukum dan Tata Laksana* Department of Laws and Operating Procedures. ~ *légitim* → BAGIAN *mutlak.* ~ *luar* exterior, outside, outer portion. ~ *mulut* mouth piece. ~ *mutlak* statutory portion of an estate. ~ *pasar* market share. ~ *pertama* first installment. ~ *rahasia wanita* a woman's private parts. ~ *sayap* wing section (of an aircraft). ~ *tambahan* appendices. ~ *teras* core sector. ~ *terlarang* private parts (of the body). ~ *terpenting* most important part, high-light. **3** constituent part. ~ *yang dapat berputar* revolving part. **4** piece, cut (off from s.t. larger). *Dia mendapat* ~ *kuénya.* He got his piece of the cake. **5** period (of time). ~ *waktu* period of time. **6** section, division, department, service. *kepala* ~ section/division head. ~ *Kendaraan* Motor Pool. ~ *Pembelian* Procurement Department. ~ *Perlengkapan* Logistics Department. ~ *tata hidangan* food and beverage department (of a hotel). ~ *Tata Usaha dan rumah Tangga* Dept. of Administrative and Domestic Affairs. **7** fate, destiny; → NASIB. *Sudah menjadi ~nya untuk hidup* *melarat*. It's his fate to live in misery. **8** part, fragment. *Cerita ~ kedua sudah tamat*. The second part of the story is over. **9** area, edge. **sebagian 1** a part/portion of, some of; partly, in part. *~ orang-orang warganegara keturunan asing* a portion of the citizens of foreign descent. *~ karena* partly because. *~ besar* for the most part, the biggest portion of which, most of, predominantly. *negara yang ~ besar penduduknya terdiri dari golongan Cina* a country the greater part of whose population is Chinese. *~ kecil* a small part/portion of. *~ kecil dari meréka kurang mampu membaca kepustakaan berbahasa Arab* a small portion of them are unable to read literature in Arabic. *~ terbesar* the greatest part of, most of. *~ terbesar penduduknya beragama Islam* most of the population is Muslim. **2** partly, partially, in some ways. **sebagian-sebagian** bit by bit, little by little.

kebagian (*J*) to obtain/get/receive a/one's share/portion of s.t., get its share, be a party to. *Saya tidak ~.* I didn't get my share. *Kampung kami belum ~ listrik.* Our *kampung* does not have electricity yet. *tidak ~ tempat* (in a movie/hotel, etc.) cannot be accommodated, there is not enough room for. *Banyak tamu tidak ~ tempat.* Many visitors could not get a seat.

pembagi 1 (*math*) divisor, denominator. *~ persekutuan terbesar* [PPT] greatest common denominator. **2** divider; distributor. *titik ~* distribution point. *~ arus* current distributor, timer. *~ arus tegangan tinggi* high-voltage current distributor. *~ suara* crossover (hi-fi equipment). *~ tegangan tinggi* high-tension distributor.

pembagian 1 distribution. *~ beras* rice distribution. *~ dalam* bribes. *~ kembali* redistribution. **2** (*math*) division. *~ berkoték* long division. **3** allotment, allocation, share, sharing. *peraturan tentang ~ keuntungan* profit-sharing regulations. *~ beban* burden sharing. *~ hak* allocation of rights. *~ laba bersih* (in corporations) the allocation of net profits. *~ rezeki* sharing of the spoils. **4** division, allotment. *~ kerja* division of labor. *~ pekerjaan* division of labor. *~ tanah* division of land into parcels. *~ tugas* allocation/distribution of duties/work. *~ warisan* allocation of an estate. **5** delegation, assignment. *~ wewenang* delegation of authority.

bagia → BAHAGIA.

bagimana (*coq*) → BAGAIMANA.

baginda (*Skr*) 'the fortunate,' i.e., His/Her Majesty (title in certain areas of Sumatra's West Coast); a title for rulers and for Ali, the Prophet Muhammad's son-in-law. *Sri –* His/Her Majesty (title for foreign rulers).

bago k.o. boat.

bagol (*J/Jv*) **mbagol** to trick, deceive.

bagong I (*ob*) big and heavy, clumsy, cumbersome; pot-bellied. *parang – a*) a big, heavy wooden knife. b) (*Mal*) my clumsy old wooden knife, i.e., my husband. *perahu –* a cumbersome prau.

bagong II (*S*) wild boar; → BABI *hutan*, CÉLÉNG.

bagongan (*Jv*) → BAHASA *bagongan*.

bagonjong → RUMAH *bagonjong*.

bagor (*J/Jv*) coarse fabric made of palm leaves.

baguk I marine catfish, *Arius spp.*, *Galeichthys spp.*

baguk II a tree whose bark is used for twine and seeds for *emping mlinjo*, *Gnetum gnemon*.

baguk III fruit section.

bagul (*ob*) **membagul** to carry on the back or the waist; to carry in a fold of a *sarong*/waist-belt.

bagup → BAKUP.

bagur heavy (gait), unwieldy, cumbersome, too big (for one's age, etc.), overgrown, grown beyond normal size, hulking.

bagus I good, fine, beautiful, nice, excellent, (of work/things), splendid, looks good (externally); → BAIK. *–!* Great! *– dilihat* nice to see, good to look at. *– dipakai* suited to the purpose, suitable for the purpose. *– kalau dipotrét* photogenic.

bagusnya the good thing to do, should. *"Liani ~nya jadi apa, mas?"* (a wife asks her husband) "What should Liani become, dad?"

sebagus as good as.

sebagus-bagusnya 1 the best possible. **2** no matter how good.

membagusi repair, touch up. *~ diri* to dress up.

membaguskan [and **ngebagusin** (*J coq*)] to improve, make better.

memperbagus to make s.t. look nicer, improve (the appearance of), decorate.

terbagus the best.

bagusan (*coq*) better, nicer, etc.

kebagusan goodness, beauty.

pembagusan enhancing, improving.

bagus II 1 (in Banten and Palembang) a title of nobility: *Radén –*. **2** (in Bandung) *Mas –* (*usu* shortened to *Masagus*). *Tu-* (from *Ratu –*) the highest title of nobility in Banten, borne by the male descendants in the female line of the former Sultanate families of Banten. **3** (*Jv*) term of address for a boy from a respectable family (shortened to *Gus*), used by servants to address the master's male children; → SINYO.

bagus III bagusan contagious skin disease, such as chicken pox.

bah I an exclamation of scorn, disgust, contempt.

bah II flood, inundation. *air –* flood water. *musim –* period of floods, the flood season. *pasang –* flood-causing high tides. *– betina* later/second flood. *– jantan* early/first flood.

bah III clipped form of **babah** and **debah**.

bahadi → BADI.

bahadur (*Pers cla*) **1** knight, warrior, hero. **2** bold, brave, courageous.

bahaduri (*Pers cla*) **1** knightly, heroic, chivalrous. **2** bold.

bahagi → BAGI.

bahagia (*Skr*) (peaceful and) happy; happiness; luck(y), good fortune; welfare. *Ia merasa –.* He is happy. *taman –* (*mil*) cemetery.

sebahagia as happy as.

berbahagia 1 to feel happy/fortunate, prosperous. *selamat ~* congratulations! **2** joyful, pleasant.

membahagiakan 1 to make s.o. happy. **2** to benefit. **3** to please, pleasing.

kebahagiaan happiness, prosperity and contentment.

bahagiawan (*Skr neo*) s.o. who is blessed.

bahak I (*M*) burst of laughter.

terbahak-bahak *ketawa ~* to guffaw, roar with laughter.

bahak II (*Jv*) white-bellied sea eagle, osprey, *Haliaetus leucogaster*.

bahala (*A*) disaster, affliction, trouble, accident, calamity; → BALA II. *bahaya dan –* dangers and calamities

bahalan (*ob*) abscess at the perineum.

baham (*J*) molar.

membaham to eat/chew with the mouth closed.

bahan I chip, flake (of wood). *besar kayu besar –nya, kecil kayu kecil –nya* they that have plenty of butter can lay it on thick.

membahan to chip, flake/peel/scale off.

bahan II 1 (raw) materials, materials still in their natural state or before processing/manufacturing; ingredients, stuff, matter, stock. *– dari luar negeri* raw materials from abroad. *– untuk membikin kué* ingredients for making cake. **2** agent, s.t. used for a certain process. *– antilucut* (*petro*) antistripping agent. **3** subject matter, theme, material, basis (of a book/for an essay). *patut dijadikan – cerita* ought to be made into a story (or, written up). *tidak menjadi – untuk disiarkan* off the record. **4** (*med*) specimen. *– aktif détérjén* surfactant. *– anti-beku* antifreeze. *– atap* roofing materials. *– bacaan* reading matter. *– baju* fabrics. *– bakar* fuel. *– bakar Élpiji* L(iquid) P(etroleum) G(as). *– bakar gas* [BBG] compressed natural gas. **mem-BBG-kan** to outfit with compressed natural gas (engines). *– bakar minyak* [BBM] fuel oil, oil-based fuel (OBF). *– bakar padat* solid fuel. *– bakar solar* high-speed diesel fuel. *– bakar pesawat terbang*; → AVTUR. *– bakar padat* solid fuel. *– bakar rokét* propellant. *– baku* a) raw material. b) base material. c) ingredient, component part, constituent. d) chemical element. e) agricultural raw produce. f) prefabricated material. g) (feed)stock. *– baku kertas* pulp. *– baku penolong* auxiliary goods. *– baku pipa plastik* PVC resin. *– baku plastik* polymer. *– baku untuk gelas* frit, the material from which glass is made. *– bangunan* building material. *– bantahan* point at issue. *– bantu* supplies. *– bekas* preused/second-hand item. *– berbahaya* [B2] hazardous materials. *– berbahaya dan beracun* [B3] toxic materials. *– berita* material for a news item. *– buangan* waste matter. *– buatan* synthetic material. – *cacah* scrap. – *cat* coloring matter. – *celup* dye-stuff. – *dalam pengerjaan* material in process. – *dalam perjalanan* goods in transit. – *dapat belah* fissionable materials. – *dasar* base. – *ékspor* export products. – *film* film stock. – *galian* ore, mineral. – *galian kalsit* calcium carbonate. – *gosok* abrasive. – *habis pakai* consumables. –.– *(keperluan) hidup* provisions, necessities of life. – *imbuhan* flux. – *induk* (in agriculture) parent material. – *inti* core stock. – *isolasi* insulation. – *jadi* manufactured articles/goods. – *keterangan* a) data. b) info(rmation). – *keterangan pokok* basic data. –.– *kimia* chemicals. – *lantai* flooring. – *lapak* non-organic waste. – *ledak* [handak] explosives. *ledakan/letupan/letusan* explosives. – *lekat* adhesive. – *lelucon* the butt of jokes, laughing stock. – *madu* nectar. – *makanan* foodstuffs. – *makanan ternak* fodder. – *masukan* input. – *mentah* raw materials. – *minyak silinder* (*petro*) cylinder stock. – *obat* remedy. – *omongan* s.t. to talk about, subject of conversation. – *organik* (*E*) and – *organis* (*D*) organic matter. – *pakaian* clothing material. – *pangan* a) foodstuffs. b) forage. – *pangan rohani* food for thought. – *pelacak* audit trail. – *pelajaran* teaching materials. – *pelanting* rolling stock (of State Railways). – *pelapis* a) coat, coating. b) lining. c) upholstery. – *pelarut* solvent. – *pelatihan* training materials. – *peledak/peletus* explosives. – *peledak pendorong* explosive charge. – *pelicin* a) lubricant. b) smear money. – *peluntur* bleach. – *pemanis* artificial sweetener. – *pembantu* auxiliaries, auxiliary materials, aids and appliances, supplies. – *pembantu makanan* food additives. – *pembersih* cleaning materials. – *pembicaraan* a) subject under discussion. b) talk of the town. – *pembungkus* packaging. – *pembunuh serangga* insecticide. – *pemeriksaan* matter under investigation. – *pemikiran* food for thought. – *pemurni* refining agent. – *penambah* additional/extra material. – *pencegat* prophylactic. – *pencelup* dye stuffs. – *pencemar* pollutant. – *penendang* propellant. – *pengajaran* teaching materials. – *pengawét* preservative. – *pengepak* packaging. – *pengering* desiccant. – *pengikat* binder. – *pengisi* filler, grouting. – *penguat badan* tonic. – *penolong* supplementary/auxiliary material. – *penutup* covering material. – *penyaring* filtering materials. – *penyedap (rasa)* seasoning, flavoring, herbs and spices (like MSG, etc.); → BUMBU *masak*. – *penyerap* absorbent material. – *penyidikan* matter under investigation by the police. – *peramu* ingredient. – *perang* agent. – *perang kimia* chemical-war agents. – *perbandingan* comparative materials. – *perbantahan* denial. – *perekat* agglutinant. – *perontok rambut* depilatory. – *pertikaian* point at issue. – *pertimbangan* food for thought. – *perusak (lapisan) ozon* ozone depleting substances. – *pewarna* coloring matter; → ZAT *pewarna*. –.– *pokok* basic commodities; → SEMBAKO. – *ramuan* ingredients. – *renungan* food for thought. – *rombakan* detritus. – *rumah* building materials. – *semburan* (*geol*) ejecta. – *sengkéta* subject of an argument. – *serahan* hand-out (at a conference, etc.). – *serap* absorbent. – *setengah jadi/olah* semifinished/manufactured goods. – *tambahan* additive. – *tambahan makanan* food additives. – *tambang* mining products, minerals. – *tertawaan* laughing-stock. – *timbunan* fill. – *uang emas* gold bullion. – *ujian* examination paper(s). – *ulang* recycle stock. –.– *yang mudah terbakar* flammables. – *warna* coloring matter.

berbahan to use a certain material/ingredient, etc. ~ *bakar* which uses ... as fuel. *jip* ~ *bakar solar* a diesel-powered jeep. *rokét pendorong* ~ *bakar padat* a solid-fuel rocket booster.

bahana I (*Skr*) 1 loud noise/sound. 2 echo, reverberation. 3 noisy, confused murmur of many sounds, cacophony.

berbahana 1 to sound loud; to speak, utter a sound. 2 to echo, reverberate.

membahana to echo, reverberate. *Masih ada orang yang* ~ *naluri kepedulian dan réla berkorban untuk orang lain tanpa pamrih.* There still are people who echo with the instinct of caring and who are willing to sacrifice themselves to others without rewards.

terbahana echoed, can be heard.

bahana II (*Skr*) clearly (visible). *tiada* – *kelihatan* not clearly visible.

bahana III (*Skr ob*) because of, due to.

bahang (*mostly Mal*) heat. – *latén* latent heat.

berbahang to be(come) hot.

membahang to heat, burn, be(come) flushed due to the heat.

pembahangan heating (up).

bahar I (*A*) sea, a large body of water such as a lake or a river. *akar* – → AKAR *bahar*.

bahar II (*ob*) linear measure (from the toes to the upward-stretched fingers).

bahar III (*J*) k.o. marine plant from which armbands, etc. are made.

bahara (*Skr*) 1 a weight which varies according to the item weighed. *agar-agar satu* – = 12 *pikul*; *kayu cendana satu* – = 6 *pikul*; *teripang satu* – = 3 *pikul*; *emas satu* – = 10 *pikul*. 2 cargo. *tolak* – ballast. – *kapal* shipload, cargo.

bahari I (*Pers? Skr*) ancient, antique. *adat yang* – old customs. *keris* – a long narrow kris. *jaman* – time immemorial.

bahari II (*Pers cla*) pretty, charming.

bahari III (*A*) marine, nautical. *bangsa* – seafaring nation. *negara* – maritime state.

kebaharian maritime, nautical. *rékayasa* ~ nautical engineering. *sejarah* ~ nautical history.

bahari(a)wan seaman, sailor.

kebahari(a)wanan 1 seamanship. 2 nautical, marine, maritime.

bahari(a)wati female sailor.

baharu → BARU. **membaharu** to modernize, modernizing.

memperbaharui to update, bring up to date, renew.

terperbaharui renewable. *tidak* ~ nonrenewable.

terbaharukan renewable. *tidak* ~ nonrenewable.

pembahahuan renewal, restoration, updating.

baharu-baharu a marine fish, spotted sickle fish, *Drepane punctata*.

bahas I (*A*) 1 debate, discussion. *ilmu* – dialectics. 2 study. 3 criticism. 4 investigation; examination.

berbahas(-bahasan) to discuss, hold a discussion, (have a) debate, argue.

membahas 1 to discuss, debate, talk over. 2 to study, deal with, address (an issue). *Pertemuan puncak itu* ~ *bahan bakar sedunia.* The summit talks dealt with world energy. 3 to criticize. 4 to review, investigate, examine, analyze, look into. *Buku ini dibagi dua. Bagian pertama* ~ *séks.* This book is divided into two parts. The first part examines sex.

membahasi (*pl obj*) to discuss.

terbahas discussed, debated, studied.

bahasan 1 criticism. 2 debate, discussion. 3 analysis, commentary.

perbahasan and **pembahasan** discussion, debate, method/results of a discussion/debate.

pembahas debater, discusser, discussant, investigator.

pembahasan 1 discussion. 2 criticism, debate. 3 investigating, looking into.

perbahasan discussion, debate, method/results of a discussion/debate.

bahas II (*ob*) backing, protection.

bahas III (*ob*) **membahas** to join pieces of wood by a wedge.

bahasa I (*Skr*) 1 language, human speech. *pengetahuan* – knowledge of languages. 2 language system common to a nation, tribe or other speech community. – *Indonésia* (the) Indonesian (language). 3 system of signs or symbols used for conveying information. – *Tarsan* (*coq*) sign language. 4 programming language. – *komputer* computer language. 5 jargon, the language of a person, group or profession. – *Prokém* Jakarta teenage slang. *bersatu* – to be in complete agreement/accord. *tidak ada kesamaan* – to be in complete disagreement. *Apa* – *Indonésianya?* How do you say it in Indonesian? What's the Indonesian word for that? *diam-diam dalam seribu* – to be conspicuously silent, as silent as the grave. – *menunjukkan bangsa* a tree is known by its fruit. – *aglutinatif* agglutinating language. – *alami* natural language. – *asal* source language. **sebahasa asal** related languages, languages having the same origin. – *asing* a) (any) foreign language. b) (the) Dutch (language) (used in some reference books in the 1950s), more recently usually refers to English. –.– *Austronésia* Austronesian languages. – *bagongan* royal-court Javanese. – *baku* standard language. – *bangsawan* Malay used by noblemen in palaces. – *basahan* (*Mal*) colloquial language. – *berfléksi* inflected language. – *bermajas* figurative language. – *berton* tone language. – *buatan* artificial language. – *buku* bookish language. – *campuran* mixed language. – *Cina Mandarin* Mandarin Chinese, Putonghua, Guoyu. – *daérah* regional/local language. – *dagang* business/commercial language. – *dalam* court language which uses a special vocabulary and is spoken in the *kratons*. – *diplomatik* (*E*) and – *diplomatis* (*D*) language of diplomacy. – *dunia* a) an international language such as English. b) an artificial language such as Esperanto. – *étnik lokal* local language, vernacular. – *fléksi* inflectional language. – *gado-gado* a mixed language. – *gaul* young people's funky language. – *gelap* jargon, cant, argot. – *gerak* sign language. – *Gerika* Ancient Greek. – *golongan* jargon, cant, argot. – *gunung* rural language. – *Guoyu* Mandarin Chinese. – *halus* a) a refined language. b) the (*Jv*) high language. – *hantu* the language spoken by *pawangs*. –.– *hidup* modern, spoken languages. – *hipotétis* hypothetical language. – *hukum* legal language, language of the law. – *ibu* mother tongue, native language. – *ibunda* (*Mal*) mother tongue, native language. – *ilmiah* scientific language. – *Indonésia* [BI] (the) Indonesian (language). – *Indonésia Jawatimuran* the type of Indonesian spoken in East Java. **membahasa-indonésiakan** to translate/ put into Indonesian. **pembahasa-indonésiaan** Indonesianization. – *induk* parent language, proto-language. – *Inggris pasaran/pijin* pidgin English (as spoken in Papua New Guinea). – *isyarat* sign language. – *Jamee* the spoken language of Tapak Tuan and southern Aceh, k.o. Minangkabau. – *Jawa dengan tulisan pégon* Javanese written with the Arabic alphabet. – *Jawa Surabayan* the Surabaya dialect of Javanese. – *Jawi* the old name for *bahasa Melayu, esp* when written in the Arabic script. – *kacauan* mixed language. – *kacok-(kacok)an* and – *kacukan* bazaar Malay, pidjinized Malay. – *kadaton* (*Jv*) court language. – *kaku* formal style. – *kalangan* jargon, cant, argot. – *kanak-kanak* the language of infants. – *kasar* vulgar language, vulgarism. – *kaum gay* /gé/ homosexual jargon. – *kawat* telegraphese. – *Kawi* Old Javanese. – *kebangsaan* a) (in general) national language. b) – *Kebangsaan* the Malay spoken in Singapore. – *kebudayaan* cultural language. – *kedua* second language, L2. – *kerabat* related language. – *kerja* working language. – *kesat* vulgar language. – *kesusastraan* literary language. – *kiasan* figurative language. – *kita* our language, i.e., Indonesian. **membahasakitakan** to translate into Indonesian. – *klasik* classical language (Greek and Latin). – *kolokial* colloquial speech. – *kolonial* Dutch. – *kolot* archaism. – *kotor* vulgar language. – *krésten* Dutch. – *kuno* a) archaic language. b) archaism. – *lagu* tone language. – *lapuk* archaism. – *laut* nautical language. – *lisan* spoken language. – *Malaysia* Malaysian. – *manusia* natural language. – *mati* dead language. –.– *Mélanésia* Melanesian languages. – *Melayu* a) (in the narrow sense) (the) Malay (language) as spoken in the Riau archipelago and part of mainland Sumatra with Pekanbaru as its capitol. **membahasa-Melayukan** to translate into Malay. b) the national language of Brunei Darussalam. c) (in the widest sense) any and all dialects of Malay/Indonesian. – *Melayu Menado* Manadonese. – *mesin* machine language. –.– *Mikronésia* Micronesian languages. – *moyang* (*ling*) proto-language. – *nada* tone language. – *nasional* national language. – *negara* state language. – *ngoko* (*Jv*) Javanese low-level language; *cp* KROMO. – *Nusantara* a) the regional/provincial languages of Indonesia. b) all the various official varieties of Malay/Indonesian. – *pantang* taboo language. – *pasar* a) bazaar Malay, pidginized Malay. b) any mixed language. – *pasarnya* in every-day language, what is usually called. *SIM atau* – *pasarnya rébewés* the SIM or what is usually called the driver's license. – *pantang* taboo language. – *pengantar* medium of instruction. – *perantaraan* language used to overcome the language barrier, *lingua franca*. – *percakapan/ pergaulan* colloquial/spoken language. – *persatuan* unifying/national language. – *pertama* first language, L1. – *pinggiran* peripheral language, a language spoken away from the center of the city. –.– *Polinésia* Polynesian languages. – *prokém* Jakarta teenage disguised language. – *purba* proto-language. – *rahasia* code. – *rakyat* colloquial language. – *remaja* teenage slang. – *resmi* official language. – *sanépa* (*Jv*) a figure of speech using a contradictory comparison implying the opposite, e.g., *pahit madu* as

bitter as honey = sweet. – *santai* informal style. – *sasaran* target language. – *sastra* literary language. – *sehari-hari* colloquial/ spoken language. – *sininya* the way we say it here (in Indonesia or in this area). – *sononya* the way they say it in their country (English/French, etc.). – *standar* standard language. – *suku* regional/provincial language. – *sulung* the first words produced by a child learning to speak. – *sumber* source language. – *susastra* belles-lettres, literary language. – *Tarzan* (*coq*) sign language eked out with gestures. – *tubuh* body language. – *tujuan* target language. – *tulis* the written language. – *turunan* daughter language. – *umum* common/popular language.
sebahasa of one language, having the same language.
berbahasa 1 to have/use/speak a language. ~ *Inggris* to speak English. ~ *Khmér* to speak Cambodian/Khmer. *Dia* ~ *dua*. He is bilingual. **2** linguistic. *kemampuan* ~ linguistic ability. *kehilangan kemampuan* ~ aphasia.
membahasakan 1 to give o.s. the title of, describe o.s. as. ~ *diri(nya)* to style o.s., give o.s. the title of. *Dr. Padmosantjojo* ~ *diri sebagai Pakdé*. Dr. Padmosantjojo calls himself *Pakdé*. **2** to address s.o. as, use the term ... to address s.o. ~ *saudara* to address s.o. as *saudara*. **3** to express, voice. *Seorang sutradara adalah seorang pencipta. Ia harus mampu membahasakan idé-idé dan alam sekitarnya dengan visualisasi.* A director is a creator. He must be able to express the ideas and nature around him in visual terms.
memperbahasakan to speak (a language). *Bahasa Melayu bukan saja diperbahasakan di ...* Malay is not only spoken in ...
kebahasaan 1 (*mod*) language. *politik* ~ language policy. **2** linguistic. *soal-soal* ~ linguistic problems.
pembahasaan language (in the abstract sense).
perbahasaan 1 proverb, idiomatic saying, figurative expression; → PERIBAHASA. **2** speech.
bahasa II (*Skr*) **1** etiquette, courtesy, good manners. *melanggar* – to commit a breach of etiquette. *tak tahu* – and *kurang* – impolite, lacking good manners. – *chastity.
berbahasa 1 to have good manners. **2** courteous, polite, cultured, refined, well-mannered. *Orang yang* ~ *tetap dihormati orang banyak*. A well-bred person is always respected by the public.
berbahasa-bahasa to speak in a very polite style, to be very polite; to stand on ceremony. *Jangan* ~, *makan kenyang tuan-tuan hendaknya*. Don't stand on ceremony; please eat as much as you like.
memperbahasakan to respect, treat s.o. with respect; to ask s.o. respectfully to.
perbahasa(an) good manners, politeness.
bahasa III a bit, slightly. *angin sepoi-sepoi* – a light breeze. *gila-gila* – slightly mad/crazy. *juling* – slightly cross-eyed. *Matanya balut-balut* –. His eyes are slightly bloodshot. *Rambutnya kusut-kusut* –. His hair is slightly tangled.
bahasa IV → BAHWA I.
bahasawan (*Skr neo*) **1** native speaker. **2** linguist.
bahasi → BAGASI.
bahawa(sa) → BAHWA I.
bahaya (*Skr*) **1** danger, hazard, jeopardy, peril, distress, risk, crisis, emergency. **2** precarious. *alat pemberi tanda* – alarm. *dalam* – in distress/danger/jeopardy. *dapat* – to be in danger. *mara* – all k.o. dangers/disasters. *mendatangkan* – *kepada* to threaten s.o. *tanda* – danger signal. – *banjir* flood danger. – *kebakaran* danger of fire, fire-risk. – *kelaparan* famine. – *khusus* named perils (an insurance term). – *kuning* the yellow peril. – *maut* mortal danger. – *pekerjaan* occupational hazard. – *ranjau* danger of (land)mines. – *rugi* risk. – *udara* air-raid warning.
sebahaya as dangerous as.
berbahaya dangerous, hazardous, perilous, precarious, critical, risky. **seberbahaya** as dangerous as.
membahayai to be dangerous for.
membahayakan to endanger, imperil, jeopardize, risk, put at risk. *tidak* ~ *jiwa* harmless, not dangerous, not life threatening.
terbahaya the most dangerous.
bahela → BAHEULA.
bahénol (*J*) sexy, sexually attractive.
baheula (*S*) in olden times, long ago. *zaman* – the old(en) days.

tahun – very old. – *bihari* in former/olden times, past and present.

bahimiah (*A*) bestial, brutish, brutal, animal-like.

bahkan 1 and even more than that, what is more, moreover, in fact. *berpuluh-puluh, – beratus-ratus tahun* for decades, in fact for centuries. **2** on the contrary, in fact. *Dia tidak miskin, – dia yang terkaya di kota ini.* He isn't poor, in fact he's the richest man in town.

bahlul (*A*) inane, buffoonish.

bahna I (*ob*) → BAHANA I.

bahna II and **bahné** (*J*) because of, due to; → BAHANA III. *Bis BOM – kerasnya kebentur pohon ...* because the BOM hit the tree so hard ...

bahri and **bahr(u)** (*A*) marine, of the sea, maritime, nautical.

bahrulhayat (*A*) sea of life.

bahtera (*Skr poet*) ark, bark, ship. – *(Nabi) Nuh* Noah's ark. – *negara* the ship of State. – *rumah tangga* the/one's journey through life.

bahu I (*Skr*) shoulder. *mengangkat* – to shrug one's shoulders (as a sign of not knowing s.t.). *tangan mencencang/memetik/menetak* – *memikul* we create our own burdens. *memikul di* – *menjunjung di kepala* one has to work according to plan in order to be safe. – *jalan* shoulder (of the road). – *landasan* shoulder of landing strip. *Roda pesawat amblas pada bagian – landasan.* The aircraft's wheels bogged down at the shoulder of the landing strip.

    sebahu down to the shoulders, shoulder-length. *berambut péndék* ~ with short shoulder-length hair.

    membahu 1 to carry on the shoulder. **2** to shoulder, support, shore up.

    bahu-membahu to do things together, help e.o.; shoulder to shoulder. *Meréka ~ memberikan bantuan.* Shoulder to shoulder they helped.

    pebahu – *layar* (*naut*) gaff.

bahu II (*Jv*) → BAU. -*désa* → BAUDÉSA.

bahu III (*D*) a unit of surface measure = 7096 square meters.

bahu IV (*Skr*) multi-.

bahu V (*C*) dried crushed meat.

bahuarti (*Skr neo*) ambiguous.

bahubahasa (*Skr neo*) multilingual.

bahubangsa (*Skr neo*) multinational.

bahuguna (*Skr neo*) multipurpose.

bahuku retribution/payment that has to be made for taking the yield of s.o.'s land.

bahulipat multiplex.

bahupada multiped.

bahureksa (*Jv*) guardian spirit.

    membahureksa to guard/protect (from ghosts or spirits which might inhabit the region).

bahusuku polysyllabic.

bahwa I (*Skr*) **1** that (introducing a subordinate clause). **2** (*leg*) whereas (introducing a point in a legal document).

bahwa II (*Skr cla*) nature, character, disposition.

bahwasanya 1 → BAHWA I. **2** (= *bahwa sesungguhnya*) truly, indeed.

bai I → BAYI.

baiat (*A*) /bai'at/ allegiance, homage paid to Muslim religious leaders.
    membaiat to take an oath of allegiance.
    pembaiatan taking an oath of allegiance.

Bai'bithama ajil (*A*) k.o. investment credit.

baid (*A*) /ba'it/ distant (of kin). *karib (dan)* – a) near and far. b) relatives and friends.

baiduri (*Skr*) opal, cat's eye.– *api* fire opal. – *bulan* moonstone. – *pandan* a green precious stone. – *sepah* k.o. precious stone in the form of a leaf or root. – *Yaman* yellow opal.

baik I 1 good, well, of good quality, worth; *cp* BAGUS. – *buruknya* the good and the bad points, the pros and cons. *dengan* – (to do s.t.) well. *berbicara bahasa Indonésia dengan* – to speak Indonesian well. *Saudara ada* –? Are you well? How are you? *jika cuaca* – weather permitting. – *dengan* on good terms with. *dengan* – duly, well. *diterima dengan* – duly received. – *dicoba* worth a try. – *lagi* a) to make up (with s.o. after a quarrel). b) to be

working again (after being broken). c) to have recovered (from an illness). **2** effective, efficacious (of medicine), of some use. *ada –nya* it has its uses, there is s.t. to be said for it. *tak berapa* – not very effective. **3** cured, become well, recovered, healed, doing well. *Lukanya sudah* –. His injuries have healed. *Keadaan ékonomi sudah* –. The economic situation has improved. *Bagaimana ayahmu? –, tuan.* How's your father? He's doing well, sir. **4** (in agreement with a command) OK, all right, yes. *Ambillah buku itu! –, mak.* Take that book. OK, mom. **5** suitable, appropriate. – *dipakai* suitable for, appropriate for. – *hati* good-natured, nice, kind, kind-hearted; honest and respectable. – *lagi* a) to make up (after a quarrel). b) to be OK/working again (of s.t. that was broken). c) to recover (from an illness). -*lah* OK, all right! -*lah, saya tidak berkeberatan kalau saudara berusaha menghubunginya dulu.* OK, I have no objection if you try to contact him first. *lebih – terlambat daripada tidak* better late than never.

baiknya it's a good idea (for s.o. to do s.t.). ~ *kita* let's. *ada ~ (bila/kalau)* (I think) it would be a good idea to. I suggest that. *Ada ~ tuan naik kelas satu saja.* It would be a good idea for you to go first class.

baik-baik 1 prudently, carefully, cautiously. *Kendarailah ~ karena jalan itu berliku-liku.* Drive carefully because the road is winding. **2** fine, good. *Apa kabar? Oh, ~ saja.* How are you? Fine. *orang ~* respectable folks, people from a good family.

sebaik 1 as good/well as. *Pénsilmu tidak ~ pénsil saya.* Your pencil isn't as good as mine. **2** (and **sebaik-baik**) as soon as, just as, the minute, while. *Pencuri itu ditangkap ~ ia memasuki rumah orang.* The thief was arrested as soon as he entered s.o.'s house. **3** no matter how good.

sebaiknya ought to, better, best, preferable; it would be best to, the best thing to do is, to be on the safe side. ~ *diam* it is best to keep quiet. ~ *daripada* it's better than.

sebaik-baiknya 1 as good/well as possible, the best one can, to the best of one's ability. *Kesempatan mencari keuntungan ini diambil ~ oléh orang asing.* Foreigners took the opportunity to seek profits as best they could. **2** the best course of action is, the best that can happen is.

berbaik to be on good terms (with), be on friendly terms (with), live in peace (with). *Ia ~ dengan orang yang sejahat itu.* He is on good terms with such a criminal. ~ *kembali* to become reconciled (*dengan*); to make up (*dengan*). *Dengan perantaraan S meréka ~ kembali.* They became reconciled through the intermediary of S.

berbaik(-baik)an to be on good terms with e.o., live in peace with e.o.

membaik to improve, become/get better, clear up (of the weather). *Cuaca ~.* The weather's cleared up. *Keadaan sudah ~.* The situation has improved. *Pusing kepalanya ~.* His headache is better.

membaiki 1 to improve s.t.; to rectify, correct; to revise; to repair, mend. ~ *duduknya* to improve one's position. ~ *jalan-jalan yang rusak* to repair the damaged roads. **2** to better (a record). ~ *rékor nasional* to better the national record.

membaikkan 1 to improve s.t., make better. **2** to repair, mend, fix. **3** to correct. **4** to further (a cause); to advance, promote. **5** to consider s.t. good.

memperbaiki 1 to improve, upgrade, remodel. **2** to rectify, correct. **3** to revise. **4** to repair, mend, fix, patch up. ~ *diri* to make o.s. comfortable (in the way one is sitting). *sedang diperbaiki* under repair. *tidak bisa diperbaiki* irreparable, beyond repair.

terbaik the best. *dokter ~ di kota ini* the best doctor in town.

terbaiki reparable, remediable, recoverable. *tidak ~* irreparable, irremediable, unrecoverable.

terperbaiki corrected (of a mistake). *Sampai tulisan ini dibuat kekeliruan tulis tersebut di atas belum juga ~.* As of this writing the writing errors have still not been corrected.

baikan (*coq*) (becoming) better, improving. *Keséhatannya hari ini ~.* His health is better today. *Ini ~ dari itu.* This is better than that; → MENDINGAN.

kebaikan 1 goodness, kindness, good nature. *Terimakasih atas ~ Anda.* Thanks for your kindness. **2** soundness. **3** use, advantage.

4 virtue. **5** benefit, good. *untuk* ~ for the good of. *Ini untuk* ~ *pagelaran itu.* This is for the good of the show. *untuk* ~ *sendiri* for my own benefit.

pembaikan 1 rectifying. **2** conditioning.

perbaikan 1 repairs. ~ *besar* overhaul. ~ *jalan* road repairs. **2** reparation, remedial. *tindakan* ~ remedial action. **3** revision. **4** reconciliation. **5** improvement, betterment; correction. ~ *nasib* improvement of one's lot (in life).

baik II – ... – ... and – ... *atau* ... both ... and ... – *saya* – *dia suka berdansa* both he and I like to dance. – ... *maupun/ataupun* ... a) both ... and ... b) neither/not ... either ... nor/or... – *ini maupun itu dia tidak suka* he liked neither this nor that, he didn't like either this or that. – ... *demikian pula* ... a) both .. and ... b) neither ... nor ...

baikot → BOIKOT.

bailéo and **bailéu** (*IBT*) village/country house.

bain (*A*) **1** clear. **2** irrevocable. – *kubro* irrevocable repudiation. – *sughro* repudiation.

bainah (*A ob*) explanation; proof, evidence.

bainai to bathe a bride in the West Sumatran way.

bainat → BAINAH.

Baipass (*coq*) the Jakarta Bypass.

Bairam (*A*) either of two Muslim festivals following the Ramadan feast.

Bais [Badan Intelijén Stratégis] Strategic Intelligence Agency.

baisikal → BASIKAL.

bait I (*A*) couplet, distich, verse.

berbait(-bait) with couplets.

pembaitan dividing into couplets.

bait II (*A*) house (usually in names of Mosques or in other religious contexts). – *Indonésia* the Republic of Indonesia's office in Mecca.

Baitulharam (*A*) the *Ka'abah* in Mecca.

Baitullah (*A*) Allah's house, i.e., the Mosque in Mecca.

Baitul Makdis (*A*) Jerusalem.

Baitulmakmur (*A*) the place passed by the Prophet Muhammad on the night of Isra and Mikraj, i.e., the meeting place of the angels.

baitulmal (*A*) (state) treasury.

Baitul Mukadas, **Baitulmukadas** and **Baitulmukaddis** (*A*) Jerusalem.

Baitul Rakhim and **Baiturrakhim** (*A*) "House of the Merciful," i.e., the name of the mosque in the *Istana Merdéka* compound in Jakarta.

Baitut Tamwil and **Baitul Maal Wattamwil** (*A*) [BMT] financing house, k.o. Islamic bank.

bai'us salam (*A*) trade margin.

baja I 1 steel. *baju* – armor. *besi* – steel. *mobil* – armored car. **2** strong, powerful, forceful. *kemauan* – an iron will. *berhati* – determined, resolute. – *batangan* steel ingot. – *beton* steel for reinforced concrete. – *cair* molten steel. – *canai dingin* cold-rolled steel [CRMI]. – *canai panas* hot-rolled steel in coils. – *cawan* crucible steel. – *cor* cast steel. – *halus* refined steel. – *kasar* crude steel. – *kil* killed steel. – *lapis séng* galvanized steel. – *lembaran* steel sheets. – *lembaran dingin* cold-rolled coil. – *lembaran panas* hot-rolled coil. – *lunak* mild steel. – *martin* open-hearth steel. – *mulia* refined steel. – *nirkarat/tahan karat/tanpa karat* stainless steel. – *paduan* alloy steel. – *paduan rendah* low alloy steel. – *pelat* sheet steel. – *pelat hitam* hot-rolled steel. – *pita* hoop steel. – *rim* rimmed steel. – *sekerup* chaser, chasing tool. – *tahan karat* stainless steel. – *tempa* hammered steel. – *tuang* cast steel. – *tulangan beton* concrete reinforcement steel sheets. – *ulet* ductile steel.

berbaja 1 of steel, tempered. *jika pisau tiada* ~, *makin dikikir bertambah tumpul* the more a stupid child is taught the stupider it gets. **2** armored.

membaja 1 as hard as steel. **2** to become as hard as steel.

membajai to harden with steel.

membajakan to steel, harden.

kebajaan hardness, toughness.

pembajaan 1 hardening. **2** hardness, obstinacy.

baja II fertilizer, manure, plant food. – *buatan* artificial fertilizer.

– *hijau* green manure. – *kandang* stable dung/manure. – *tahi kelawar* bat guano. – *tahi kuda* horse dung. – *tahi lembu* cow dung. – *uréa* a chemical manure.

membaja to fertilize, manure, enrich soil with manure.

baja III 1 coconut shell burned and mixed with oil, used for blackening teeth. **2** k.o. dentifrice.

berbaja blackened (teeth).

membaja(i) to blacken (the teeth).

Baja IV [Batak Jawa] a child of mixed Batak and Javanese parentage.

bajag → BAJAK III.

bajaj /bajay, bajéi/ a three-wheeled Indian-made passenger car which uses a 1962 150-cc Italian Vespa scooter motor.

bajak I plow. *mata* – plowshare; coulter. *dahulu* – *daripada jawi* to put the cart before the horse. – *selalu di tanah yang lembut* (– *lalu, tanah yang lembut*) the weak always have to suffer. – *sudah terdorong ke bencah* it's too late to do anything about it, there's no use crying over spilt milk. – *patah banting terambau* (*M*) misfortunes never come one at a time. – *piringan/putar* disk plow. – *singkat* moldboard plow.

membajak to plow, furrow.

terbajak plowed, furrowed.

pembajak plowman.

bajak II (*Jv*) hijack, piracy. (– *laut*) pirate; → PEROMPAK. – *udara* hijacker, skyjacker.

membajak [and **ngebajak** (*J*)] **1** to pirate (cassettes, etc.) **2** to hijack, skyjack, take over by force. **3** to steal (s.o. else's girl-/boyfriend). *Bekas pacarnya dibajak Banu.* Banu stole his former girlfriend. **4** to headhunt, recruit (executives). *Umumnya manajér yang dibajak adalah dari perusahaan-perusahaan asing.* In general the managers who have been recruited are from foreign companies.

bajak-membajak 1 pirating, hijacking. *Soal* ~ *ternyata merémbét pula ke bisnis koyo.* It turns out that pirating has also spread to the *koyo* business. **2** headhunting, recruiting.

bajakan 1 pirated. *kasét* ~ pirated cassettes. **2** hijacked, skyjacked.

pembajak 1 pirate. **2** hijacker, skyjacker. ~ *mengancam membunuh pilot.* The highjacker threatened to kill the pilot. **3** headhunter, corporate recruiter.

pembajakan 1 pirating. ~ *kasét* pirating of cassettes. **2** hijacking, skyjacking. **3** headhunting.

bajak III *sambal* – a hot condiment made from chilies, sliced onion, garlic, shrimp paste, salt, sugar, dissolved tamarind, butter and *salam* leaf.

bajan (*Pers Hind*) **1** dish, vessel. **2** fry(ing) pan; → WAJAN.

bajang I 1 spirit malignant to pregnant women and to infants. **2** *lidah* – dovetail. *baju* – (*ob*) coat with wide flags. *gelang* – (*ob*) bracelet of black thread (to ward off *bajang*s). **3** (*bio*) Lilliputian.

bajang II tenon, dovetail; → GANJAL, TANGGAM.

bajang-bajang love grass, *Andropogon/Chrysopogon aciculatus*.

bajau I **membajau** to strike, hit.

Bajau II *orang* – ethnic group which lives along the coast of East Kalimantan, Sabah, and West Sulawesi, former sea nomads and pirates.

baji 1 wedge, V-shaped piece of wood/metal used to split wood. **2** wedge/shim used to tighten up s.t. that is loose, spacer. *bersua dengan matan* (= *tahan* – *oléh kelidai*) an eye for an eye, a tooth for a tooth. – *dahan membelah dahan* the wedge from the bough splits the bough, i.e., paid back in his own coin, hoist by his own petard. – *kuku* the quick of the nail. – *pengarah* (*petro*) whipstock.

baji-baji ~ *kuku* the quick of the nail.

membaji 1 to split with a wedge. **2** to tighten up with a wedge/shim. **3** (*bio*) cuneate.

baji-baji *ikan* – (bar-tail) flathead, *Platycephalus indicus*.

bajigur (*S*) coffee with sugar and coconut milk (mixed together and then recooked; served hot; *esp* used by people who work outside at night, such as night watchmen).

bajik virtuous, beneficial, salutary, wholesome.

kebajikan 1 good deeds; goodness (of heart), kindness, generosity; benevolence; virtue, excellence. *guna* ~ (in) the interest (of), (for) the advantage (of), (for) the benefit (of). **2** benefit, benefaction, mercy; (thanks to s.o.'s) kindheartedness, good nature. *nama* ~ (to leave) a good name/reputation.

bajing I (*Jv*) squirrel, *Sciurus notatus*; → TUPAI. – *lompat/loncat/ luncat* a) thief who jumps on trucks and steals goods from them. b) opportunist. *taktik* – *loncat* hit-and-run tactics. *bicara seperti – melompat-lompat* to jump from one subject to another. – *terbang* flying squirrel, *Petinomys spp.*

bajingan 1 rascal, rogue, scoundrel, villain, sneak thief. ~ *tengik* a thorough-going rascal, an unmitigated scoundrel. **2** pickpocket. **3** gangster.

kebajingan gangsterism.

bajing II (*ob*) warm o.s. by the fire; → DIANG.

baju (*Pers*) any garment worn by men or women which slips on over the shoulders, jacket, blouse, shirt. *anak* – undershirt. *buah* – button. *tidak mengenakan* – undressed. *memelihara penyengat dalam* – to nourish a viper on one's bosom. *mencabik-cabik* – *di dada* to show off one's own disgrace. *mengukur* – *di badan sendiri* to judge others by one's own standards. – *aci* (*IBT*) jacket with a stiff high collar and no lapels, worn without a necktie. – *alang(-alang)* a short-sleeved *baju kurung*. – *anggerka* (*Hind*) a long buttoned Indian undercoat. – *antakusuma* (in the *wayang*) vest worn by Gatutkaca which enables him to fly. – *antari* long inner vest worn by pilgrims to Mecca. – *atas bawah* two-piece dress. – *ayat* jacket with verses from the Koran printed on it. – *bajang* swallow-tail jacket. – *basterop* sleeveless colorless jacket. – *bébé* woman's western-style dress. – *belah (dada)* and – *yang berbelah* jacket with open front end, closed by three buttons. – *berenang* swim-suit. – *bersayap* → BAJU *bajang*. – *besi* armor, cuirass. – *béskét* vest. – *bintan* jacket with split sleeves and gold buttons. – *biru* convict, inmate. – *blus* blouse. – *bodo* Bugis-Macassarese woman's *adat* dress. – *cina* k.o. pajamas. *si* – *coklat* Brown Shirt. – *dabal* double-breasted jacket. – *dalam* a) undershirt. b) underwear. – *dingin* a) overcoat. b) winter clothes. – *dua potongan* two-piece dress. – *ganti* change of clothes. – *guntung* short-sleeved shirt. – *halkah* chain-mail armor. – *hangat* warm clothing. – *hijau/ijo* (derogatory term for) the Indonesian soldier or army in general. *berbaju hijau* to be an army man, wear a uniform. – *hujan* raincoat. – *ihram* → *pakaian* IHRAM. – *jadi* ready-made jacket. – *jas* Western-style coat/jacket. – *jubah* gown. – *kalkah* armor, cuirass. – *kamprét* k.o. pajamas. – *kaos/kaus* undershirt. – *kebaya* woman's knee-length gown, *usu* worn with a sarong. – *kelépak* coat open at the neck. – *kemantén/kemantin* wedding dress. – *keméja* a shirt dress (for women). – *kepok* high-collared jacket. – *kodék* → BAJU *basterop*. – *kodian* ready-made clothes. – *koko* → KOKO I. – *komprang* Madurese long-sleeved collarless shirt. – *koran* American fancy shirt with pictures of newspaper articles on it. – *kotak-kotak* checked jacket. – *kotong* sleeveless jacket. – *kurung* long shirt for Sumatran women without a front opening (pulled over the head like a jumper). – *kutang* bodice. – *lama* closed jacket. – *lasak* everyday dress. – *layang* k.o. vest which enables one to fly. – *loréng* camouflage uniform. – *malam* evening jacket. – *mandi* bathing/swim suit. – *mantel* → MANTEL. – *maskat* a waistcoat (crossed in front). – *monyét* a) coveralls. b) one-piece child's play suit. – *monyét terusan* coveralls (worn by Jakarta bus drivers and conductors). – *panas* winter overcoat. – *pelampung* life-vest. – *pelindung* protective clothing. – *penangkal udara dingin* overcoat. – *pendapun* jacket decorated with gold. – *perang* battle dress. – *piyama* pajamas top. – *pokok* k.o. sleeveless jacket. – *rantai* chain-mail armor. – *renang* bathing/swim suit. – *rok* woman's western-style dress. – *safari* short-sleeved dress jacket for men (part of a suit), like a Nehru-jacket. – *sederiah* k.o. Arab waistcoat. – *seroja* k.o. Sumatran jacket decorated with gold thread. – *sika* a long sleeveless vest. – *sikap* long-sleeved *Jv* jacket. – *sirap* coat of mail. – *songsong barat* k.o. vest which enables one to fly. – *surjan* k.o. *Jv* jacket with buttons on the side. – *tanggung* open-front buttonless jacket. – *tekua* narrow jacket with broad sleeves. – *Teluk Belanga* traditional Malay dress for men, k.o. short *baju kurung*. – *teratai* → BAJU *seroja*. – *terus* gown, dress. – *tidur* nightgown. – *toro* antiquated attire of a four-wheeled horse-drawn cab coachman (made of *kain kurasi*). – *zirah* armor, coat of mail.

berbaju to have clothes on, be clothed; to wear. ~ *putih* to be a civilian, wear civvies.

berbajukan dressed as/in. *singa* ~ *domba* a wolf in sheep's clothing.

membajui to put clothes on s.o. or s.t., dress

bajul (*J*) **1** crocodile. **2** criminal; thief; pickpocket. – *buntung* (*coq*) Don Juan, playboy.

membajul 1 to be(come) a playboy/Don Juan, chase after women. **2** to steal, pickpocket.

bajupuik (in West Sumatra) system of going door to door to demonstrate, collect taxes, debts, etc.

bak I (*coq*) like, resembling. – *penari kejang* like break dancers. – *pinang dibela dua* a perfect match (of lovers).

bak II (*D*) basin, tub (for rubbish/water), vessel, box, locker. – *air* cistern. – *angkat* lift, hoist. – *bocoran* drip cup. – *cuci* sink, laundry tub. – *makanan* trough. – *mandi* bath tank (holds bath water, which is then poured on one's body for washing). – *mesin* crankcase. – *minyak* oil reservoir. – *pasir* sandbox. – *penahan* (*petro*) cather. – *penampung* reservoir. – *persnéling* gearbox. – *oli* sump. – *potrét* photo developing basin. – *rantai* (*naut*) chain locker. – *sampah* garbage can. – *serbuk bor* (*petro*) slush pit. – *siram* flushing tank. – *surat* file tray. – *tampung* sump. – *terbuka* open-back (truck), pickup truck. – *tinja* septic tank. – *transmisi* gearbox.

bak III (*C*) *tinta* – Chinese ink.

bak IV (*onom*) smacking sound.

bak V a strip of cultivated ground in sugarcane fields or a strip divided from a longer portion of land by ditches.

baka I (*A*) eternal, perpetual, lasting, constant, durable. *alam/ negeri yang* – the hereafter, the (great) beyond; eternity. *berpindah dari negeri yang fana yang negeri yang* – to pass away, die. *persahabatan yang* – everlasting friendship.

berbaka ~ *mati* all living creatures must die.

membakakan to immortalize.

kebakaan eternity.

baka II (*M*) **1** family (which has descendants). **2** hereditary traits. *saka (= pusaka)* – ancestors on both father's and mother's side; inherited estate. *membuang* – to betray one's race, renounce one's rank, bring dishonor upon one's parents' memory. *tidak membuang* – to be a chip off the old block, like father like son.

baka III *sakit* – mumps.

bakak (*ob*) *kain* – red or blue checked cloth.

bakal 1 for, destined/intended for; (of money, etc.) set aside for, appropriated/earmarked for, allocated to. *Saya ambil obat – si Dul.* I'll pick up the medicine for Dul. *Uang ini – beli apa?* What do you want to buy with that money? – *siapa?* for whom? *Hutan-hutan dirambah itu – persawahan.* Those cleared forests are set aside for irrigated rice fields. **2** prospective, future, aspirant, primordium (*bio*). – *biji* ovule, ovary (of a plant). – *buah* (*bio*) flower primordium. – *calon* future candidate. **3** elect, designate. – *guru* student teacher. – *haji* aspirant haji. – *isteri* bride-to-be, fiancée. – *menantu* future daughter-/son-in-law. – *présidén* president-elect. – *raja* crown prince. – *suami* husband-to-be, future husband. **4** (+ verb) will, is going to. *Tindakan apa yang – diambil oléh PWI?* What steps will be taken by the Indonesian Journalists Association? **5** (raw) material(s). – *baju* material for making clothing. – *janin* embryo. – *pelanting* rolling stock (of railways). – *rumah* building materials.

membakal(kan) to plan, design, contrive.

bakalan 1 will (stronger than **bakal** 4). *Tidak* ~ *ada perang.* There will be no war. *Saya tidak* ~ *mau berbuat begitu.* I wouldn't even dream of doing such a thing. **2** raw material (for making s.t.).

pembakalan the act(ion) of planning/designing.

bakalauréat, bakaloréat and **bakaloriat** (*E*) baccalaureate (degree).

bakam k.o. ruby.

bakap k.o. dark murrel, snakehead, *Ophiocephalus spp.*

bakar burn, set on fire; roasted, burned; used for burning. *bahan* – fuel. *cat* – spray paint. *ikan* – roasted fish. *jagung* – roast corn (-on-the-cob). *kayu* – firewood. *luka* – a burn. *minyak* – fuel oil. *siar* – → SIAR *bakar*. – *arang* not completely burned. – *hati* wrath, anger. – *tak berapi* not really in love. – *tak berbau* a concealed criminal intention.

membakar [and **mbakar/ngebakar** (*coq*)] **1** to roast (*saté*/banana, etc.) over coals, grill, barbecue, toast. **2** to burn s.t., set s.t. on fire, set fire to s.t., burn down. *dibakar tak hangus, direndam tak basah* a) very stingy. b) very strong/powerful. ~ *diri* to immolate o.s. ~ *halus* to refine. ~ *hati/perasaan* a) to hurt, offend. b) to provoke, fire up, instigate, incite, set off. c) to make inflammatory remarks. ~ *kayu* to burn wood. ~ *mayat* to cremate (a corpse). ~ *rumah* to set a house on fire. ~ *semangat* to fire up, instigate. ~ *téwas* to burn s.o. to death. **3** to set off (firecrackers, etc.). **4** to make s.t. by roasting. ~ *arang/bata/roti* to make charcoal/bricks/bread. **5** to be scorching (of the heat of the sun, etc.). *Matahari* ~ *dengan panasnya.* The sun was blazing hot.

membakari [and **ngebakarin** (*J coq*)] (*pl obj*) to set fire to s.t., burn s.t. up, burn s.t. down.

membakarkan to burn/roast/grill, etc. s.t. for (s.o.). *Ia* ~ *anaknya ikan asin.* He grilled salted fish for his child.

terbakar [and **kebakar** (*coq*)] **1** on fire, to catch fire. **2** burned down. *Supermarkét "Braga"* ~ *habis.* The Braga Supermarket burned to the ground. **3** set ablaze. ~ *diri* immolated (o.s.). **4** got burned, caught fire. *mudah* ~ flammable. **5** offended, hurt. ~ *hati* angry, furious.

bakaran 1 grill. **2** (*Jv*) grilled, toasted, roasted. ~ *roti* toast.

kebakaran 1 fire, conflagration. ~ *hutan* forest fire. **2** danger from fire, fire-risk, fire (*mod*). *asuransi* ~ fire insurance. **3** hit by fire; suffer from a fire; get burned by accident. ~ *jénggot* to become furious, lose one's head. **4** (BG) failing grade (marked in red on the report card). *Rapor kité kagak adé nyang* ~. We didn't get any failing grades.

pembakar 1 burner, broiler, stove. **2** arsonist; incendiary. *bom* ~ incendiary/fire bomb. *zat* ~ oxygen.

pembakaran 1 burning, cremating, incinerating. *tempat* ~ *mayat* crematorium. *tempat* ~ *sampah* incinerator. ~ *diri* self-immolation. ~ *hutan* slash and burn. **2** roasting. **3** arson. *Bagaimana dengan Sarinah serta sejumlah* ~ *mistérius lainnya belakangan ini: kebakaran atau* ~. What about Sarinah and a number of other mysterious fires: fires or arson? **4** ignition, combustion. *sistém* ~ combustion system. ~ *acar* knocking (in car engine). ~ *susulan* afterburning. **5** (pottery/brick) works, kiln. ~ *batu* brick kiln. ~ *kapur* lime kiln. **6** (kitchen) stove.

bakarah (*A*) **1** cow. **2** *al*– "The Cow"; name of the second chapter of the Koran.

bakarat I (*ob*) **1** (unmarried) girl; maiden; virgin. **2** vagina.

bakarat II (*D*) baccarat.

bakat I 1 traces, scar, vestige, track, mark, remains. **2** pockmark. **3** (foot)print. **4** sign, indication, omen, presage, portent, forerunner. – *hujan* forerunner of rain/a storm (dark clouds/wind, etc.). – *ombak* crest of a wave. – *penyakit* prodrome, i.e., warning symptoms which indicate the onset of a disease.

berbakat scarred, marked.

membakat 1 to show, signify, indicate, denote. **2** to leave traces/ marks/signs ,etc.

bakat II talent, aptitude, (natural) disposition. –*nya menurun dari orangtuanya.* He inherited his talent from his parents. – *alam* natural talent. – *bahasa* language aptitude. – *skolastik* scholastic aptitude. – *terpendam* hidden talent. *memupuk* –.– *terpendam* to encourage s.o.'s hidden talents.

berbakat talented, gifted, born (to be). ~ *démokrat* a born democrat. ~ *kriminal* with a natural criminal disposition, a born criminal. ~ *lahir* naturally talented. – *seni* artistic. ~ *untuk celaka* accident-prone. **keberbakatan** talent (*mod*). *kritéria* ~ criteria for talent.

pembakat talent(ed person). ~.~ *baru* new talents.

bakau various species of mangrove, *Bruguiera, spp., Rhizophorae spp.* and other species. *hutan* – mangrove swamp. – *akik/ minyak* oriental mangrove, *Rhizophora apiculata/conjugata.* – *bukit* k.o. tree that grows in the mountains, *Illicium cambodianum.* – *hitam/jangkar/kurap* k.o. mangrove, *Rhizophora mucronata.* – *putih* k.o. tree, *Bruguiera cylindrica.*

bak-bak-kur (*onom*) → MAIN *bak-bak-kur.*

bakcang → BACANG II.

bakda I (*A*) after (a certain event). – *Besar* name of the feast held on Besar 10. – *Haji* after *bulan Haji* or *Zulhijah.* – *isya* after the evening prayers (about 7:30 p.m.); → ISYA. – *kecil/kupat* name of the feast held on Sawal 8. – *magrib* after *magrib*. – *Mulud* a) name of the feast held on *Mulud* 12. b) the fourth Javanese month (= *Rabiulakhir*). – *Sawal* name of the feast held on *Sawal* 8.

bakda II → BADA III, IV.

bakdaddukhul and **ba'daddukhul** (*A leg*) after consummation (of a marriage).

bakdahu (*A*) after him/that. *wa* – and furthermore/then.

bakdo (*Jv*) → BAKDA.

bakdu (*A*) after that, then, further; → AMABAKDU.

bakdul (*Hind ob*) halter (for horses).

bakelit (*D*) bakelite.

bakéro (*Jp*) stupid, idiot (a term of abuse). *Ia pernah kena maki* –. He was once called an idiot.

membakéro to call s.o. an idiot. *Saya takut sama Nipong nanti saya dibakéro.* I'm afraid that the Japanese will call me an idiot.

bakét [bahan keterangan] information.

bakhil (*A cla*) miserly, mean, stingy, avaricious.

kebakhilan avarice, stinginess.

bakhsis, bakhsyis and **bakhsyisy** → BAKS(Y)IS.

baki I (*D*) small tray.

berbaki-baki by the tray-full.

baki II (*A*) → BAKA I.

baki III (*A*) **1** balance (of money), remainder, residue. **2** fund, foreign exchange. **3** relict. – *débét* debit balance. – *piutang* credit balance. – *tunai* cash balance. – *utang* debt balance.

berbaki to have a balance.

membakikan to set aside, reserve (s.t. left over).

pembakian setting aside, reserving.

baki IV beyond child-bearing age.

bakia → KIA I.

bakiah (*A*) residual.

bakiak (*C*) wooden sandals with a rubber toe strap.

bakik I pepper vine, *Piper Betle* whose leaves are chewed with betel nut and other ingredients.

bakik II → BERKIK.

bakikuk and **bakiluk** peek-a-boo.

Bakin → BADAN *Koordinasi Intélijén Negara.*

bakir sour, turned bad (of milk or coconut milk).

Bakka (*A*) the original name of Mecca.

bakmi (*C*) a vermicelli-like dish with vegetables, shrimp, shredded meat, etc., lo mein. – *kuah* boiled noodles. – *tékték* k.o. noodle dish sold by itinerant vendors.

BAKN (*init*) → BADAN *Administrasi Kepegawaian Negara.*

bako I (*M*) *induk* – relatives, kins(wo)men on the paternal side; father's family; *cp* BAKA II. *mencari* – to look for a son-in-law (so as to have descendants).

berbako ~ *kepada* to be related to s.o. through one's father's side.

bako II (*Jv*) tobacco; → TEMBAKAU. – *susur* chewing tobacco.

Bakorstanas → BADAN *Koordinasi (Bantuan Pemantapan) Stabilitas Nasional.*

Bakosurtanal → BADAN *Koordinasi Survéi dan Pemetaan Nasional.*

bakpao and **bakpaw** (*C*) **1** k.o. Chinese pastry resembling a bun, filled with pork or soybean mixture. **2** small-time. *dagang* – small business. **3** (*vulg*) sex, pussy, cunt.

bakpia (*C*) k.o. cake made from flour.

bakpuder (*D*) baking powder.

baksi (*Hind naut*) *layar* – mizzen(-sail).

membaksi to unfold the mizzen, braze the headyards aback.

baksis → BAKS(Y)IS.

bakso I (*C*) dish consisting of meat-balls and noodles in soup. *tukang* – *bakso* vendor. – *gépéng* flattened out *bakso*. – *Malang* k.o. meatball soup.

membakso [and **ngebakso** (*J*)] to eat *bakso*.

Bakso II [Batak Solo] a person who has a Batak father and a Solonese mother.

baks(y)is (*A*) **1** tip, gratuity. **2** alms. **3** douceur.

membaks(y)is to bribe.
baktau (*C*) madam, i.e., a woman in charge of a brothel.
baktéri (*D*) bacterium. – *bundar* coccus.
baktériolog bacteriologist.
baktériologi (*D/E*) bacteriology.
baktériologis (*D*) bacteriologic(al).
bakti (*Skr*) 1 homage. – *kepada Tuhan* homage to God. 2 service(s) rendered. *kerja* – volunteer work. 3 devotion, dedication, fidelity, loyalty. – *meréka kepada nusa dan bangsa* their loyalty/devotion to country and nation. 4 to be devoted.
berbakti 1 to be loyal/faithful/devoted (to). *Istri itu ~ kepada suaminya.* The wife is loyal to her husband. 2 (= membakti) to pay homage (to). *~ kepada Tuhan Yang Maha Esa* to pay homage to the One and Only God.
membaktikan 1 to dedicate/devote s.t. (to). 2 to place s.t. at s.o.'s disposal. *demi perjuangan bangsanya ~ harta bendanya* to put one's belongings at the disposal of the national struggle. *~ diri* (*kepada*) to devote o.s. (to); to be subservient (to).
kebaktian 1 faith, devotion, loyalty. 2 piety. 3 religion. 4 church/divine service, mass.
pembaktian 1 devotion, service. *~ kepada tanah air* devotion to one's country. 2 dedication, dedicating. 3 placing s.t. at s.o.'s disposal.
perbaktian devotion.
baku I (*Jv*) 1 main, essential, basic. *pangan yang* – basic food. *-nya … the main ingredient is … air* – untreated water. 2 genuine, acknowledged, full-fledged, native (of a place). *guru* – a full-fledged teacher. 3 standard. *bahasa* – standard language. *harga* – standard price. *karya* – standard work (of art). *tatabahasa* – standard grammar. *Bisa diduga, kalimat itu (saya baru saja dari luar negeri) akan* – *digunakan.* It can be expected that this sentence (I've just returned from abroad) will be used as a standing expression. *– emas* gold standard. *mutu* standard of quality. ***membakumutukan*** to standardize the quality of, exercise quality control over. *membuang limbah pada ékosistém lingkungan yang telah dibakumutukan* to dispose of waste in an environmental ecosystem the quality of which has been standardized. *– pembanding* standard of comparison. *– pincang* limping standard.
membakukan to standardize. *~ istilah* to standardize terminology (in the sciences).
bakuan 1 standard. 2 standardized. *bahasa Malaysia ~* standardized Malaysian.
pembakuan standardization. *~ bahasa Malaysia* the standardization of the Malaysian language. *~ éjaan* standardization of the orthography. *~ ganda* double standard. *~ majemuk* multiple standard.
baku II (*M*) reciprocal, mutual, e.o.; → SALING. – *baé* movement for peace and reconciliation (in the Moluccas). – *caci maki* to call e.o. names, insult e.o. – *débat* to debate e.o., argue with e.o. – *hadap* facing (e.o.). – *hantam* and *saling* – *hantam* to come to blows. ***berbaku hantam*** to come to blows. – *jotos* to fight. – *maki* to insult e.o.; a shouting match (people yelling at e.o.). – *piara* (*Min*) to live with e.o. without being married; → KUMPUL *kebo*. – *pukul* to hit e.o.; fisticuffs, fistfight. – *témbak* a) to fire/shoot at e.o. b) fire fight, shoot-out. – *tolak* to push e.o. – *tubruk* to crash into e.o. – *tuduh* to accuse e.o.
bakul I bamboo basket for rice, fruit, etc. – *beramin* openwork storage basket hung on the wall. – *berombong* cylindrical basket with a lid. – *bilah* finely woven basket. – *kerau* k.o. bamboo basket.
sebakul a basketfull. *ngomong ~ ditakar kagak ada sepiring* (*J*) much ado about nothing.
bakul II (*Jv*) 1 (*usu* a female) vendor, peddler; → MBAK *ayu bakul jamu*. 2 (in some regions) broker, middleman. – *ikan* fish monger, fish vendor. – *kecil* retailer, retail dealer. – *obrokan* a) (in Lamongan, East Java) a small rice broker. b) (in other parts of the Javanese-speaking area) retailer. – *wedang* coffee vendor.
bakulan *kaum ~* vendors.
bakul III (*ob*) the part of the table closest to the banker in a gambling game.
bakung a lily with large white flowers, *Crinum asiaticum/defixum.* – *air* a small aroid, fireweed, *Chamerion angustifolium.* – *suasa*

k.o. plant, *Susum anthelminticum.*
bakup 1 red and swollen (of cheeks from weeping or a blow). *muka* – a swollen face. 2 (*sl*) ugly.
bakut k.o. fish, marble goby, *Oxyeleotris marmorata.*
bakwan (*C*) food made from pulverized young corn mixed with soybean cakes or shrimp and kneaded together with wheat flour and then deep-fried.
bakyu → MBAKYU.
bal I (*D*) ball. – *békel* ball for playing jacks.
bal-balan (*coq*) soccer game.
bal II (*D*) bale.
berbal-bal by the bale. *~ kapas diékspor ke Jepang.* Cotton is exported by the bale to Japan.
mengebal to pack in bales.
bala I (*Skr*) troops, army; soldier. – *bantuan* reinforcements, auxiliary troops. – *Keselamatan* Salvation Army. – *tentara* fighting force, troops.
bala II (*A*) disaster, calamity, catastrophe; misery, adversity. (*doa/mandi/kenduri) tolak* – (a prayer/bath/religious meal) to avert calamity (epidemic/war/drought, etc.). *jimat penolak* – a talisman worn to avert bad luck. – *lalu dibawa singgah* purposely asking/looking for trouble. – *bencana* calamity, disaster; adversity, bad luck. – *dosa* just deserts (for having done s.t. bad). – *seribu* (*Jv cla*) magic spell which gives s.o. supernatural powers.
berbala-bala to oppose e.o.
bala III (*Jv*) – *kiwa* the left-hand group of *wayang* puppets. – *tengen* the right-hand group of *wayang* puppets.
bala IV [bala laut]. *perang* – jungle-and-sea war.
bala V → BAD.
balabad (*Pers cla*) 1 windward, west. 2 land breeze/wind.
bala-bala (*S*) a snack made of sliced vegetables, usually carrots and cauliflower, mixed with *tauge*, made into a dough by adding flour and eggs and a bit of shrimp and then deep-fried spoonful by spoonful, served with hot pepper on the side.
balad I (*A*) 1 country. 2 town, city. 3 district; province. *al–* "The City"; name of the 90th chapter of the Koran.
balad II → BALA I.
balada (*D*) ballad.
baladhika (*Skr*) 1 troop, force. 2 superior in strength, surpassing in power. – *Jaya* the military resort command (*Korém* 083) in Malang. – *Karya* private security task force.
balado I (*S*) fake, counterfeit.
balado II a way of cooking eggplant, chicken, fish, etc., fried and includes hot pepper and *belacan.*
baladupakan (*Jv*) supernumerary (actor), actor who plays a small/bit role.
balaghah (*A*) 1 eloquent. 2 rhetorical.
balah berbalah to debate, quarrel, dispute, argue.
membalah to oppose, argue against, dispute.
pembalahan arguing, disputing.
perbalahan argument, dispute, quarrel, debate. *masalah/pokok ~* crux, crucial/critical point in an argument.
balai I 1 hall, building; (research) station, center; gallery. 2 (*cla*) hall (in royal palace); pavilion. 3 (*cla*) building inside the palace grounds. 4 (*M*) market. *adat* ceremonial hall. – *agung* a) municipal/city hall. b) (*cla*) audience hall/building. – *angin* (*cla*) (vacation) cottage, bungalow. – *apit (tengah)* (*cla*) royal welcoming hall (between the royal residence and the audience). – *astaka* (*cla*) hall inside the royal palace (not walled in; place for ceremonies, etc.). – *bayu* (*cla*) (vacation) cottage; bungalow. – *bendul* reception hall for royal guests. – *benih* greenhouse. – *benih ikan/udang galah* fish/lobster hatchery. – *besar* audience hall. – *Budaya* Art Gallery, cultural center. – *budel* (*D ob*) probate court. – *dagang* chamber of commerce. – *derma* a) charitable institution. b) (*cla*) building outside the royal palace where the sovereign gave out alms. – *désa* village administration building. – *éték* village guardhouse. – *gading* (*cla*) people on both sides of the gate to the palace. – *gendang* (*cla*) building where the mosque drum was kept. – *Harta Peninggalan* Probate Court. – *istirahat* rest house. – *kambang* an artificial island with a pavilion in the center of a round pool surrounded by gardens. – *kembang (sari)* (*cla*) small house in flower park (near the royal palace).

– *keséhatan* (medical) clinic. – *kesenian* art gallery. – *kota* municipal building, city hall. – *larangan (cla)* princesses' abode in royal palace compound; → KEPUTRÉN. – *lélang* auction hall. – *madat (cla)* sentry box. – *Masyarakat* Community Center. – *mentera (cla)* reception hall for royal guests. – *pembacaan* reading room. – *pembibitan udang* shrimp hatchery. – *penelitian tanaman rempah dan obat* [Balittro] Research Station for Spices and Medicinal Plants. – *penghadapan* reception hall. – *pengobatan* (medial) clinic. – *Penyuluhan Pertanian* Rural Extension Center. – *peranginan (cla)* (vacation) cottage, bungalow. – *percobaan* experimental/research station. – *perguruan tinggi* university building. – *perpustakaan* library; → PERPUSTAKAAN. – *pertemuan* public meeting hall/room. – *Pertemuan Umum* Convention Hall. – *Prajurit* Soldiers' Home, Servicemen's Club. – *Pustaka* Government Institute of Belles-Lettres (Jakarta). – *Rendah* House of Commons, Lower House. – *ruang* → BALAIRUNG. – *sari (cla)* small house in a flower garden near the royal palace. – *seni(rupa)* art gallery. – *Sidang* Convention Hall. – *tengah (cla)* royal welcoming hall (between the royal residence and the audience). – *Tinggi* House of Lords, Upper House. – *Wartawan* Press Room/club. – *Yasa* State Railways Repair Shops. – *Yudha* War Room (in the *Istana Merdéka*).
  sebalai → SERUMPUN *Sebalai.*
balai II *burung* – tiger shrike, *Lanius tigrinus.*
balai III in disorder; → KACAU *balau.*
balai-balai bamboo cot, sitting or sleeping platform. – *mota* canvas cot.
balairung 1 *(cla)* royal reception hall. **2** (= *balérong*) *(M)* booth (in marketplace). **3** city hall.
balak I → BALOK I.
balak II → BELAK.
balakung k.o. plant that grows on water, *Hangguana malayana.*
balalaika *(D/E)* balalaika, a Russian stringed instrument.
balam I *(burung)* – turtledove, *Geopelia striata*; → MANUT; connotes loyalty, since it nods its head when s.o. snaps his fingers. *(bagai)* – *dengan ketitiran* said about two people who are always fighting with e.o., each trying to outdo the other.
balam II dimly visible, hazy (as of distant hills).
  balam-balam, berbalam-(balam) and **membalam** vaguely visible; dim.
balam III various species of sap-providing trees. – *beringin* k.o. plant, *Payena Leerii.* – *mérah* k.o. plant, *Palaquium gutta.*
balan I rock/snag, etc. hampering the flow of water in a river.
balan II *(J)* mark (on the skin from a blow, etc.).
balang I long-necked bottle or jar.
balang II *perahu/sampan* – *(cla)* two-masted sailboat.
balang III → DUBALANG, HULUBALANG.
balang IV *(J)* locust, grasshopper; → BELALANG.
balang V *(M)* → BELANG.
balang VI *(Jv) pohon* – k.o. shade tree *Pterospermum acerifolium.*
balans *(D)* **1** balance, (pair of) scales. **2** balance sheet. **3** balance, equilibrium.
balansir *(D)* **membalansir** to balance.
balap *(Jv)* race, racing. *kuda* – racehorse. *mobil/sepéda* – racing car/bicycle. – *karung* sack race. – *sepéda jalan raya* open-road bicycle race.
  berbalap to race, speed along.
  berbalapan to race e.o.
  membalap to race, speed along.
  membalapkan 1 to make (a vehicle, etc.) go fast, race (an animal). **2** to run (horses).
  balapan race, competition. ~ *kuda/mobil/motor/sepéda* horse/car/motorcycle/bicycle race.
  pembalap racer, runner. ~ *mobil* racing driver.
balapan to show (of a garment, such as a slip).
bala-pecah *(Jv)* /bolo-/ crockery, chinaware.
balar 1 albino (of buffaloes, elephants, persons); → BULÉ. **2** white-spotted (of cattle). **3** light-colored (of eyes).
balas I 1 answer, reply, response. **2** reward, recompense, remuneration. *menuntut* – to take revenge. *ada ubi ada talas, ada budi ada* – and *ada hujan ada panas, ada hari boléh* – an eye for an eye, a tooth for a tooth. – *bidan* → *balas* BIDAN. – *jasa* consid-

eration, s.t. in exchange, remuneration, compensation. – *pantun* reciting pantuns back and forth. – *petik* to kill in revenge.
  berbalas 1 to reply, answer, respond. *Maka ~lah suara dari dalam rumah.* Then a voice responded from inside the house. ~ *pantun* to sing alternating *pantun.* **2** answered, replied, responded to. *cinta yang tidak* ~ unrequited love. **3** to counterbalance. *alang berjawab, tepuk* ~ *(M)* return good for good and evil for evil.
  balas-berbalas tit for tat; to pay e.o. back.
  berbalas-balasan mutually, reciprocally. ~ *surat* to correspond.
  membalas 1 to answer. ~ *surat* to answer a letter. **2** to reply/respond to. ~ *surat Tuan tertanggal ...* in reply to your letter of. **3** to repay, pay back. ~ *kebaikan* to repay a kindness. **4** to make good, compensate. ~ *bidan (cla)* to hold a religious meal 40 days after childbirth with the intention of thanking the midwife. **5** to take revenge, retaliate, pay back in kind. ~ *budi* to return a favor/service. ~ *dendam* to take revenge. ~ *guna/jasa* to return a favor/service. ~ *kata* to respond. ~ *sakit hati* to revenge/avenge s.o. to pay s.o. back. ~ *salam* to return a greeting. ~ *serangan* to counterattack.
  balas-membalas to pay s.o. back; to get even with s.o. *atas dasar* ~ on a quid-pro-quo basis.
  membalasi to respond to, answer.
  membalaskan to avenge.
  terbalas reciprocated, requited, responded to. *cinta yang tampaknya tidak* ~ a love that apparently was not reciprocated.
  terbalaskan reciprocated, paid back.
  balasan 1 answer, reply, response. **2** reward, remuneration.
  pembalas 1 reward, recompense. ~ *jasa* compensation in services (instead of in money). **2** rewarder. ~ *dendam* avenger.
  pembalasan revenge, retaliation, vengeance, compensation; answering (back), replying, etc. *serangan* ~ counterattack.
balas II *(D)* ballast.
balasak black shark, *Morulius chrysophekadion.*
balasan *(ob)* → BALSEM.
balatentara army, armed forces; → ANGKATAN *bersenjata.* – *haluan* advance troops.
balatkom [bahaya latén komunis] latent danger of communists.
balau I various species of hard-wood commercial timber, *Shorea spp., Aglaia odoratissima.* – *betina* k.o. tree, *Swintonia floribunda.* – *betul* k.o. tree, *Shorea materialis Ridl.* – *bukit* k.o. tree, *Shorea collina Ridl.* – *bunga* k.o. tree, *Dysoxylum acutangulum.* – *laut* k.o. tree, *Shorea glauca.* – *mérah* k.o. tree, *Shorea kunstleri.* – *penyau* k.o. tree, *Upunan borneensis.*
balau II berbalau confused, chaotic.
  kebalauan confusion, chaos; → KACAU-BALAU.
balau III membalau to pare the thorns off a coconut or *durian.*
balau IV → EMBALAU.
bal-bal *main* – *(Med)* to lash out with the hand; → MAIN *pukul.*
  membal-bal to beat. *Ia dibal-bal oléh oknum LLAJR.* He was beaten by thugs of the LLAJR.
baldatun *(A)* – *thayyibatun wa rabbun ghafur* a prosperous country blessed by God.
baldi *(Port? Hind? mostly Mal)* bucket, pail, basin; → ÉMBÉR.
  sebaldi a bucketful.
baldu *(ob)* → BELEDU.
balé *(Bal)* pavilion, house, shelter, meeting place; → BALAI. – *banjar* communal meeting place of the village *banjar.* – *gedé* the reception room or guest house of a wealthy Balinese house. – *kambang* → BALAI *kambang.* – *kulkul* where the *kulkul* is placed.
baléan *(Bal) dukun*; → BALIAN.
balé-balé *(J)* → BALAI-BALAI.
balég [badan législasi] legislative body.
baléla I *(Jv)* **1** to rebel, revolt against *(terhadap).* **2** rebellion. *sikap* – resistance.
  pembaléla rebel.
baléla II *(S) ki* – lizard plant, *Tetra stigma.*
balérina *(D/E)* ballerina.
balérong → BALAIRUNG.
bales → BALAS I. **ngebalesin** → MEMBALASI.
balét *(D)* ballet. *penari* – ballet dancer.

membalétkan to choreograph.

pebalét ballet dancer. ~ *putra* male ballet dancer. ~ *putri* ballerina.

balg(h)am (*A*) mucus, phlegm.

Bali I (*pulau* –) (the island of) Bali.

bali II (*M*) *darah* – coward.

balian (*Bal* and the interior of South Kalimantan) shaman, *dukun*.

balida clown knife-fish, *Notopterus spp*.

baligh (*A*) adult, grown-up. *akil* – having reached the age of reason/discretion.

 kebalighan adulthood, manhood, womanhood.

baliho a large film poster made of hardboard.

balik I 1 upside down, topsy-turvy, reversed, inside out; the opposite side. *bulu* – ruffled (of a fowl's feathers); → AYAM *sétan/bulu balik. pada -nya* on the contrary/other hand. *Dua bis jungkir* –. Two buses turned upside down. *tunggang* – upside down, topsy-turvy; → BOLAK-BALIK. **2** behind, the other side, back/reverse side. *Ia berteriak dari - lokét.* He shouted from behind the ticket window. *di* – on the back/other side of, at the back of, behind. *di - awan* like walking on air. *di - itu* a) behind that. b) besides that. c) more than that. *di - pembelakangan/belakang(an)* behind one's back. *Di - pembelakangan/belakang(an) awak dibicarakan orang.* They/people talked about you behind your back. *datang dari - gordén* to come from behind the curtain. *pergi ke - rumah* to go to the back of the house. **3** X *di - X* a very high degree of X. *anéh di - anéh* very strange/odd; → ANÉH *bin ajaib*. *menurut cerita di - cerita* according to what people have said. *senang di - senang* very happy. **4** (to say/ask, etc.) in return, back, re-. *"Bagaimana dengan démonstran?" – Buana bertanya.* "How are things with the demonstrans?" asked Buana in return. *Ketika dia sadar ia telah dimarahi sopir, dia - mencaci.* When he realized the driver had gotten mad at him, he called him names in return. **5** to return, come/go/turn back. *Adiknya belum lagi - dari sekolah.* His brother still hasn't come back from school. *titik* – turning point. *– hari* to return the same day. *– kucing* to turn away like a coward. **6** back, again, once more. *dapat* – reversible. *garis (pem)* – tropic. *pulang* – to and fro; round trip/return ticket. *pulang - ke kantor* to go/come back to the office. *putar* – beating about the bush, evading the question/point. *timbal* – a) to and fro. b) on/from both sides. c) mutual. *- adab* ill-bred/mannered, rude, discourteous. *- andar* to go home empty handed. *- angin* k.o. antacid. *- belah* inverted, (turned) upside down. *- bokong* upside down. *- daun* the change in the tide. *- gagang* to side with the enemy, defect. *- jalan* to return without having accomplished one's purpose (or, reached one's goal). *- jungkir* to keep on turning somersaults, somersault. *- kerak* to remarry one's former spouse; → RUJUK I. *- kuang* to hang upside down. *- mata* to conspire, plot, collude (with); to allow s.o. to do wrong (or, commit a crime) (by pretending not to notice it). *- (men)jadi* to change back into. *- nama* to transfer (title). *membaliknamakan* to transfer title to. *pembalik nama* transfer agent. *- putar* play-back. *- sadar* to regain consciousness. *- sakit* to have a relapse. *- sifat poyang* atavism. *- urutan* commutation.

sebalik 1 behind, on the back side of. **2** the opposite (of). ~ *dari* instead of; → ALIH-ALIH.

sebaliknya 1 on/to the contrary. **2** on the other hand. **3** the other way (a)round, just the reverse, conversely. *(tapi)* ~ *dari/dengan* a) (but) as opposed to, as distinct from, in contrast to, contrary to. b) instead of; → ALIH-ALIH.

berbalik 1 to turn over/upside down. **2** to take another course. *Perkataannya* ~. He changed topics. **3** to reflect, reverberate, reecho, resound. *suara yang* ~ a responding sound. **4** to turn (around) (in order to or to go back). *Ia* ~ *melihat istrinya.* He turned (around) to look at his wife. **5** to change, reverse. ~ *haluan* to change direction. ~ *hati* to change one's point of view. ~ *kembali* to return, go back. ~ *muda kembali* to be(come) young again, rejuvenate. ~ *muka* a) to change one's mind. b) to desert to the enemy, defect. ~ *pikiran* to change one's ideas. ~ *pulang* to return, go/come back. ~ *tanya* to ask in (re)turn. *Ia ~ tanya dengan suara makin tinggi.* He asked in turn with an increasingly high-pitched voice. **6** to backfire,

boomerang, come home to roost, backlash. *Stratégi ini bisa* ~. This strategy can backfire.

berbalik-balik 1 to toss/to and fro/and turn (in one's sleep). **2** to keep coming back.

berbalikan to be in contradiction with/to; to be the opposite. *Ucapannya* ~ *dengan perbuatannya.* His words conflict with his deeds.

membalik 1 to ricochet, rebound, bound back, strike back. *peluru yang* ~ a ricocheted bullet. **2** to change position, turn. *Pada ke-tika tidur itu sebentar ia* ~ *ke kiri sebentar ia* ~ *ke kanan.* In his sleep, at one moment he turns to the left, the next to the right. *Orok itu sudah pandai* ~. The infant can already turn its body. ~ *tanah dengan linggis* to turn the soil with a crowbar. **3** to turn in the opposite direction, alter/change direction. *Ia* ~ *menghadap ke barat.* He turned around to face west. *tidak dapat dibalik lagi* irreversible. ~ *belakang* to desert to the enemy, defect. ~ *putaran* to invert. **4** to contradict o.s. **5** to turn s.t. over. *tak semudah* ~ *tangan* it's not as easy as turning your hand, it's not so easy.

membalik-balik 1 to turn the pages of, leaf/glance through. *Lama ia* ~ *buku catatannya.* He looked through his notebook for a long time. **2** to keep on turning/stirring s.t. ~ *kerupuk yang sedang digoréng* to keep on turning the frying *kerupuk*. **3** to turn (plans) over and over in one's mind. ~ *kaji* (*M*) to rake up old stories. ~ *mayat dikubur* not to allow the dead to rest in peace, talk about s.o. who has died.

membaliki 1 to return/go back to. *Ia* ~ *istrinya yang lama.* He returned to his former wife. **2** to turn one's back on, ignore, disregard. *Sudah cukup alasan untuk* ~ *perjanjian itu.* There are plenty of reasons for defaulting on the agreement.

membalikkan [and **ngebalikin** (*J coq*)] **1** to turn (a card/fried egg/one's face, etc.). ~ *kepala ke kiri* to turn one's head to the left. ~ *muka* to look behind one ~ *perkataannya* to distort/twist s.o.'s words; to misquote. ~ *punggungnya* to turn one's back. **2** to return s.t.; to repay, pay back, refund. ~ *uang itu kepada A* to repay the money to A. **3** to change the direction/course of (a boat, etc.); to bring/take back.

ngebalikin (*J*) to answer/talk back. ~ *omongan orangtua* to talk back to one's parents.

terbalik [and **kebalik** (*coq*)] **1** overturned, turned over, tipped (to one side), somersaulted, inside out; upside down. *Bajunya* ~. His coat is inside out. *Dunia sudah* ~. The world is topsy-turvy. ~ *akal* mad, crazy, insane. ~ *halang* contradicted. ~ *kalang* against the grain; contrary ~ *lidah* changed the subject. ~ *mata* (*coq*) waited/seen too long. ~ *pikiran* mad, crazy, insane. **2** inverted, inverse. *berbanding* ~ *dengan* inversely proportional to.

balikan 1 back. **2** feedback; → UMPAN *balik*. **3** inverse.

kebalikan 1 the reverse, inverse, the opposite; the other side (of the coin/picture). **2** reversal. **berkebalikan** ~ *dari* to be the reverse of, the complete opposite of.

pembalik 1 (*elec*) inverter, commutator. **2** retro-.

pembalikan returning, turning over/upside down, reversing, reversal, inversion, inverting. ~ *beban pembuktian* reversal of the burden of proof. ~ *kutub* polarity reversal. ~ *nama* transfer of title. ~ *putaran* inversion.

perbalikan reversal.

balik II - *adap* k.o. shrub, *Mussaenda frondosa*.

baling baling-baling 1 weathercock, weather vane. **2** screw (of a ship), propeller (of an aircraft). **3** fan, ventilator. *hati bagai* ~ *di atas bukit* vacillating. ~ *angin* fan. ~ *bertabung* ducted propeller. ~ *ékor* (of an aircraft) tail rotor blade. ~ *kemudi* rudder propeller. ~ *tunggal* single-screw propeller. **berbaling-baling** ... with ... propellers, ...-engined. *pesawat terbang* ~ *empat* a four-engined plane.

berbaling to turn, rotate (of fans/propellers/windmills).

balingan turn (of a propeller/screw, etc.).

balir → BALIGH.

balistik (*D/E*) ballistic. *proyéktil - antarbenua* intercontinental ballistic missile.

balit → BELIT.

balita [[(di) Bawah Lima Tahun]] under the age of five (of human beings); has been in business for less than five years (of companies). *anak* – preschooler; *cp* BADUTA, BATITA.

Balkan (*D/E*) the Balkans.

balkanisasi balkanization.

Balkis (*A*) *Putri* – the Queen of Sheba.

balkon (*D*) **1** balustrade, banister. **2** balcony (attached to a house). **3** gallery, balcony (in a theater). **4** railway platform.

ballada and **ballade** → BALADA.

ballok (in Ujungpandang) k.o. alcoholic drink (*tuak*) made from fermented *lontar*.

Balméra [Belawan, Médan, (Sumatra) Utara] the Belawan-Medan area in North Sumatra.

balok I (*D*) **1** beam (of wood), block. *huruf (tulisan)* – block letters. – *ambang* lintel. – *besar* (*naut*) king beam. – *cincin* ring balk. – *dukung* girder. – *gelegar* beam. – *induk* main beam. – *kasar* cant (in logging). – *kotak* box beam. – *miring* (*naut*) cant beam. – *not* (musical) staff. – *penyambung* tie beam. – *pokok* gun carriage. – *silang* a) crossbeam. b) (*mil*) cross carriage. – *rél* railroad tie. – *tarik* tie beam. – *titian* balance beam (*sports*). – *tuangan* ingot. **2** block, a counter for things which come in large blocks. *és batu empat* – four blocks of ice.

  sebalok a block of.

  balokan 1 by the bar/block. **2** ingot.

balok II insignia of *mil* rank attached to the epaulettes of a (*mil*) uniform.

balok III (Yogyakarta university *sl*) fried cassava.

balok IV → BALUK.

balon I (*D*) balloon. *ban* – large (automobile) tires. – *kabel* captive balloon. – *lampu (listrik)* light bulb. – *sabun* soap bubble. – *terbang* balloon.

  balon-balonan 1 small, inflatable bag used as a toy. *telah jadi ~ to* be a plaything/toy. **2** tentative suggestion, trial balloon. *melepaskan ~ to* throw out a feeler (to gauge opinions). **3** *~ (sabun)* soap bubble. *main ~ to* blow soap bubbles.

balon II light bulb, round neon light. – *lampu listrik* light bulb.

balon III (in East Java) whore.

balon IV [bakal calon] candidate.

balong (*Jv*) **1** puddle, mud hole. **2** (fish)pond, pool.

balot (*D/E*) ballot.

balsa (*D/E*) balsa, *Ochroma pyramidale*.

balsam → BALSEM.

balsem (*D*) bal(sa)m.

  membalsem(kan) to embalm.

  pembalseman embalming.

Baltik Baltic.

balu I (*Mal*) widow(er).

balu II dark green.

baluarti → BALUWARTI.

baluh(an) 1 wooden frame (for drumhead). **2** wooden cover of howdah.

balui (= baluian) (*ob*) a draw, quits, even (in a game).

baluk (*naut*) felucca.

balun I membalun (*cla*) to thrash with a cane/bamboo stick, beat with a stick, cane.

balun II (*M*) **berbalun-balun** in rolls, many rolls; rolling (end over end).

  membalun to roll/coil up.

balun III to recover consciousness after being in a trance.

balung I (*Jv*) bone. *sampai ke* – *sumsum* to one's very marrow.

  membalung *~ sumsum* to be/become deeply rooted, enrooted.

  balungan the basic melodic content of Javanese *gamelan* music.

balung II (*S*) **1** cock's comb. **2** (= *hantu bidari*) a mat-like waterspirit that enfolds its victim.

balung III (*cla*) – *bidai* k.o. large sea serpent that glides over water.

balur I k.o. rock-crystal; → HABLUR.

  membalur to crystallize.

balur II 1 untanned hide of an animal; → BELULANG. **2** hides and skins. **3** jerked meat (preserved by slicing into strips and drying in the sun); → DÉNDÉNG.

  membalur to dry (fish or meat).

balur III scars as a result of lashing.

balur IV (*S*) **membalur** to grease, oil.

  membaluri to smear onto s.t.

  membalurkan to smear s.t. (on s.t.).

pembaluran smearing.

balustrade (*D/E*) balustrade.

balut I bandage, dressing, wrapping. *ilmu* – wound dressing. – *kerikil* (*geol*) gravel pack. – *ketupat* wrapper made of young coconut leaves for *ketupat*.. – *luka* bandage. – *rokok* cigarette wrapper/paper.

  berbalut wrapped, bandaged.

  membalut to wrap, bandage, dress.

  balut-membalut dressings, bandaging.

  membaluti to wrap, envelop. *Stasiun keréta-api dibaluti dengan kabut.* The railroad station was wrapped in fog.

  membalutkan 1 to apply (a bandage), wrap s.t. around. *Angin ~ rok ke pahanya.* The wind wrapped the skirt around her thighs. **2** to wrap s.t. for s.o.

  balutan 1 bundle, package, parcel. **2** packing, wrapping. **3** bandage, dressing.

  pembalut 1 wrapper, wrapping. **2** bandaging, dressing. *~ kasa* sterilized gauze. *~ wanita* sanitary napkin.

  pembalutan 1 bandaging, wrapping, bundling. **2** upholstering.

balut II red and swollen (of one's eyelids from weeping).

baluwarti (*Port*) circular brick wall surrounding the *kraton*, esp the one in Surakarta.

bam I (*naut*) crosspiece (of rudder). *patah kemudi dengan –nya* all hopes were shattered.

bam II (*onom*) boom(ing noise) (of a large drum).

bamban I (*Jv*) back to the starting point, back to square one.

bamban II k.o. shrub, *Donax canniformis*.

bambang I 1 in full view. **2** flat and wide/broad; → PAMPANG. **3** (*geol*) sheet.

  bersebambang stretching out before one's eyes (fields/a poster/a tapestry).

  terbambang stretching out, displayed.

bambang II (*Pal ob*) – *kabayan* girl whom one elopes with.

  sebambang (*ob*) to run away together (to get married).

  membambang to elope, abduct a girl (to marry her).

bambangan I red snapper, *Lutjanus sanguineus*.

bambangan II bittern, *Ixobrychus spp.* – *coklat* Schrenk's bittern, *Ixobrychus eurhythmus*. – *hitam* black bittern, *Ixobrychus flavicollis*. – *kuning* yellow bittern, *Ixobrychus sinensis*.

bambu 1 bamboo. **2** (*Ac*) a measure of capacity equivalent to 2 liters. *pokrol* – a) shyster lawyer. b) (*ob*) an able debater. *rumput* – a grass species, blue-eyed grass, *Panicum montanum*. *sebilah* – a strip of bamboo used as a knife to cut the umbilical cord and for circumcisions. *seperti pohon – ditiup angin* said of a person who is friendly but firm in his opinions. – *ampel* common bamboo, *Bambusa vulgaris*. – *andong* whorled bamboo, *Gigantochloa pseudoarundinacea/verticillata*. – *apus* k.o. yellow bamboo, *Bambusa aspera*. – *ater* k.o. green bamboo, *Gigantochloa atter*. – *batu* stony bamboo, *Dendrocalamus strictus*. – *betung* large bamboo used for building houses, *Dendrocalamus asper*. – *blenduk* wamin bamboo, Buddha's belly bamboo, punting-pole bamboo, *Bambusa tuldoides/wamin*. – *cina* hedge bamboo, Chinese bamboo, *Bambusa multiplex*. – *duri* spiny/thorny bamboo, *Bambusa bambos/arundinacea/ spinosa/blumeana*. – *duri kecil* Chinese spiny bamboo, *Bambusa sinospinosa*. – *embong* k.o. bamboo, *Bambusa horsfieldii*. – *gading/kuning* yellow/golden bamboo, *Bambusa vulgaris*. – *(h)itam* black bamboo, *Gigantochloa atter/atroviolacea/ nigrociliata*. – *jalur* k.o. bamboo, *Schizostachyum longispiculatum*. – *nitu* thin-walled bamboo, *Bambusa amahussana*. – *pagar* golden goddess bamboo, silver stripe, *Bambusa multiplex*. – *runcing* bamboo spear (used as a weapon in the 1945 struggle for freedom; symbol of poorly armed but resolute freedom-fighters. ***membambu-runcingkan*** to stick a sharpened bamboo into. – *sembilang* giant bamboo, *Dendrocalamus giganteus*. – *senang* (in Sulsel) variety of bamboo that keeps clear water between its joints. – *siam* monastery bamboo, *Thyrsostachys siamensis*. – *talang* k.o. bamboo that holds a lot of water, *Schizostachyum brachycladum*. – *tali* bamboo used to make cord, *Gigantochloa, spp.* – *toi* k.o. bamboo, *Schizostachyum lima*. – *tutul* spotted bamboo, *Bambusa vulgaris*. – *ulet* string bamboo, *Gigantochloa kurzii*. – *umit* k.o. bamboo,

Schizostachyum latifolium. – *wulu* (*Jv*) k.o. bamboo, *Melocanna humilis.*

bambung (*Jv*) not conforming to proper behavior.
  bambungan vagabond, bum. *bocah* ~ juvenile delinquent.

bami → BAKMI.

bamper → BUMPER.

Bamudés → BADAN *Musyawarah Désa.*

Bamus → BADAN *Musyawarah.*

ban I (*D*) **1** (inner) tube. **2** (auto/truck, etc.) tire. *telapak* – tread (of a tire). – *angin* inflated/pneumatic tire. – *balon* balloon tire. – *buta* solid tire. – *cubles* (*E*) tubeless tire. – *dalam* (inner) tube. – *dengan pelapis kawat baja* steel-belted radial (tire). – *gembos* flat tire. – *hidup* inflated/pneumatic tire. – *kempés* flat tire. – *luar* (outer) casing (for inner tube). – *mati* solid tire. – *mobil* automobile tire. – *mobil bekas (yang divulkanisir)* (vulcanized) retread. – *padat* solid tire. – *pecah* flat tire. – *pejal* solid tire. – *pengapung* buoy. – *pinggiran putih* whitewall tire. – *pompa* inflated/pneumatic tire. – *radial* radial tire. – *sepéda* bicycle tire. – *sérap/sérep* a) spare tire. b) (pitying reference to) the Vice-President of the Republic of Indonesia. – *tanpa* – *dalam* tubeless tire. – *udara* pneumatic tire. – *vulkanisiran* retread.
  berban with/to have a ... tire. *sepéda* ~ *mati* a bicycle with a solid tire.

ban II (*D*) **1** – *KA* railroad track. **2** race track. **3** airstrip, runway; → LANDASAN (*pesawat*) *terbang.* **4** tennis court.

ban III (*D*) **1** band (worn on arm/hat, etc.), ribbon. – *arloji* watchstrap/-band. **2** belt, sash. – *angkut/berjalan* conveyor belt. – *hitam* black belt (in karate). – *kipas* fan belt. – *pengaman* safety belt. – *pinggang* belt.
  berban ... to wear a ... belt. *seorang gadis* ~ *plastik mérah* a girl wearing a red plastic belt.

ban IV (in acronyms) → BANTUAN, PEMBANTU.

banal (*D*) trite, banal.

banang (*ob*) large (in some compounds). *duku* – a large *duku, Lansium domesticum. siput* – a large snail.

banar I k.o. climbing plant, *Smilax helferi.* – *babi* k.o. plant, *Smilax sp.*

banar II *sinar* – radiant, radiating (of the rays of the sun).

banarawa → BONOROWO.

banaspati (*Jv*) an evil ghost which is invoked to frighten children.

banat I → AIN-AL-BANAT.

banat II (*ob*) **membanat(kan)** to beat, smash, thrash.

banat III *rimba yang* – virgin forest.

bancah (*M*) → BENCAH.

bancakan (*Jv*) **1** joint religious meal or *selamatan* for special occasions: child's birthday, wedding, etc. **2** dishes of food made available at such a feast. – *pitulasan selamatan* such a feast held on the 17th of August; → AGUSTUSAN.

bancang membancang to stop (by a stretched rope/rattan), tether.

bancar (*Jv*) copious and free-flowing (of mother's milk or urine, etc.).
  membancarkan to let s.t. flow freely.

bancau → BANCUH.

bancét (*J/Jv*) a rice-paddy frog.

banci I 1 transvestite. **2** hermaphrodite. **3** homosexual, homosexual prostitute. **4** an effeminate man. **5** (*infr*) impotent.
  membancikan to render powerless.
  kebanci-bancian effeminate.

banci II (*Mal*) census; → CACAH *jiwa.*

banci III adze.

bancuh (*mostly Mal*) mixed, blended, mingled.
  membancuh 1 to mix (together), stir (together) (cement and sand, etc.). **2** to shuffle (cards). **3** to knead (flour and water).
  membancuhi to mix s.t. with.
  membancuhkan to mix, blend.
  bancuhan s.t. that has been mixed, mixture, blend.
  pembancuhan mixing.

bancut I (*ob*) **terbancut** protruding, popping (of eyes, etc.); → PANCUT.

bancut II (*J*)→ BANTUT.

band I (*E*) /bén/ (a musical group) band.

band II (*E*) /ban/ (radio) band; → BAN IV. *radio transistor dari 1* – *a* one-band transistor radio.

banda (*Jv*) → BENDA.

Banda Acéh (also called Kutaraja) the capitol of the Aceh Special Region; → DAÉRAH *Istiméwa Acéh* [Dista].

bandah (*J*) causing problems for others.

bandal → BANDEL.

bandala (*ob*) bandoleer, cross belt.

bandan I (*ob*) a k.o. dance.

bandan II (*J*) a k.o. bird with a crest, like a wood hen.

bandan III k.o. fish, sea bream, *Sparus hasta.*

bandang I k.o. milk fish, *Chanos chanos.*

bandang II → BANJIR *bandang.* **bandangan** avalanche.

bandang III *penyakit* – k.o. cattle disease, rinderpest.

bandar I watercourse, ditch, waterworks, canal. *upah lalu – tak masuk* does not produce the slightest result. – *air* watercourse, canal. – *sampah* drainage canal/ditch for the removal of trash.
  berbandar to use (or, having) a *bandar. sawah* ~ *langit* rice field dependent on rain.
  membandarkan to lead/channel (water, etc.). ~ *air ke sawah* to lead/channel water to the irrigated rice fields. ~ *air ke bukit* to perform an impossible task.
  terbandar channeled.
  bandaran channel, drain, conduit (in rice fields).

bandar II (*Pers*) **1** port, seaport town; commercial/trading town/center. **2** (*Mal*) town. *datuk* – (*Mal*) mayor. *luar* – (*Mal*) rural. *to'* – (*ob*) harbormaster. – *pedalaman* dry port. – *udara* [bandara] airport.
  bandaran (*Mal*) municipal, of the town, town (*mod*).
  kebandaran (*mod*) port.
  perbandaran 1 (*ob*) Custom house; harbormaster's office. **2** (*mod*) port.

bandar III 1 croupier, banker (in some gambling games). – *dengkul* a banker without much capital. **2** wirepuller, s.o. who controls things from behind the scenes.
  membandar (*ob*) **1** to be the banker (in gambling). **2** to trade, go into business.
  membandari to be the banker (in gambling) of. *Perjudian dengan peralatan serba canggih ini dibandari oléh seorang wanita tua.* The gambling, which has completely up-to-date equipment, was bankered by an old woman.

bandar IV trader, dealer [BD] (in illegal drugs). – *kuda* horse trader. – *sayur* vegetable dealer. – *ternak* cattle dealer.

bandara I → BANDAR *udara.*

bandara II (*ob*) harlot.

bandaraya (*Mal*) municipality, city; → KOTAMADIA/-DYA.

Bandarlampung combination of the two towns of Telukbetung and Tanjungkarang, now the capital of Lampung province.

bandarsah (*ob*) small Muslim chapel; → LANGGAR, MADRASAH, SURAU.

bandéa (*Port ob*) tray.

bandel (*J/Jv*) obstinate, stubborn, difficult (in behavior).
  sebandel as stubborn/difficult as.
  membandel to act obstinate/stubborn/difficult.
  terbandel the most stubborn/difficult.
  kebandelan obstinacy, being difficult.
  pembandel a stubborn/difficult person.
  pembandelan acting stubbornly, behaving like a difficult person.

bandela (*cla*) bale, bundle, pack.

bandeng I (*Jv*) milkfish (raised in ponds along the coast), *Chanos chanos.* – *cerucut* sea banana, bonefish, *Albula vulpes.* – *isi* stuffed milkfish. – *lelaki* giant herring, *Elops hawaiensis.*

bandeng II (in tout's jargon) a piece of good luck, windfall.

banderék (*J*) → BANDRÉK.

bandering (*J*) slingshot.
  membandering to throw at with a slingshot (in order to retrieve a kite stuck in a tree, etc.).

banderol (*D*) **1** an excise band on a cigar(ette) or on its packaging. *harga* (*pas*) – the (exact) price shown on the excise stamp. **2** price tag.
  berbanderol with an excise band/price tag on it.

membanderol to put a price tag on s.t., price s.t. *kendaraan dibanderol Rp 105 juta* a vehicle priced at Rp 105 million.

bandijzer (*D*) /banéser/ band/hoop iron.

banding I 1 equal, match, peer, parallel, partner. **2** to, in a ratio of … to … *satu – satu* (ratio of) one to one. *tiada/tak ada –nya* and *tiada/tak ada tolok –nya* unexcelled, peerless, matchless, unique, incomparable, unequalled. *– berganda* constantly. *– nilai* rate of exchange.

  sebanding *(dengan)* in balance (with), comparable (to), proportionate (with), in accordance (with), equivalent (to), up to. *pengeluaran ~ pendapatan* the outlays balanced the income. *tidak ~ dengan kecakapannya* not up to his skills.

  berbanding 1 balanced, proportionate (with), in accordance (with), commensurate (with), up to, in proportion to. *Tuntutan kenaikan gaji harus ~ dengan préstasi kerja.* A demand for a pay raise should be commensurate with work performance. *tidak ~* unexcelled. *~ balik dengan* inversely proportional to. *~ sebagai* in the ratio of. *~ sebagai satu dua* in the ratio of one to two. **2** similar, parallel, equal, equivalent. **3** to be in the following proportions. *Sahamnya ~ 35 persén untuk invéstor dan 65 persén dikuasai pemilik lama.* The shares are 35 percent for the investors and 65 percent for the old owners.

  berbandingan *(dengan)* **1** in proportion (to), proportional (to). **2** in conformity/accordance (with), parallel (to). *Pengeluaran hendaknya ~ dengan pendapatan.* Spending should be in accordance with income.

  membanding to compare (two things with e.o.). *dibanding dengan* in comparison with, in relation to, compared with. *Pernahkah kau ingin tahu bagaimana nasibmu dibanding nasib kebanyakan orang?* Did you ever want to know how your fate compares with that of others?

  banding-membanding to compare with e.o.

  membandingi 1 to equal, (be a) match (for). *Mana boléh orang miskin hendak ~ orang kaya?* How could a poor man be a match for a rich man? **2** to counterbalance. *membeli senjata untuk ~ kekuatan musuh* to buy arms to counterbalance the enemy's strength.

  mem(per)bandingkan to compare (two things to e.o.), put (two things) on the same level, make (two things) comparable; to judge/measure s.t. by; to collate; to check; in comparison (with), than (in a comparison). *dibanding(kan) (dengan) bulan Désémber* compared to December.

  terbandingkan comparable. *tiada ~* incomparable.

  bandingan equal, match, parallel. *Kepandaian orang itu tiada ~nya.* That person's knowledge has no equal.

  pembanding standard (of comparison), standard against which to judge others of the same type.

  pembandingan comparison, comparing.

  perbandingan 1 comparison, proportion, ratio, rate; comparative. *keuntungan ~* comparative advantage. *~ antara modal sendiri dan utang* debt-equity ratio. *~ berat* specific gravity. *~ beratnya* relative severity. *~ garis limbah* (*geol*) waste strip ratio. *~ sistématis* systematic comparison. *~ nilai* rate of exchange. **2** relation. **3** example, parallel. **4** resemblance, similarity.

banding II (*leg*) appeal, reconsideration; appellate. *Komisi Naik –* Appeals Committee. *minta/naik –* to appeal (to a higher court). *minta – ke pengadilan tinggi* to appeal to a higher court.

  membanding 1 to appeal (a legal decision), to give notice of appeal, lodge/enter an appeal, appeal against. **2** (*M*) to suggest s.t. for consideration.

  terbanding (*leg*) appellee (in an appeal).

  bandingan appeal.

  pembanding 1 appeal. **2** (*leg*) appellant (in an appeal).

bandit (*D*) bandit. *– bertangan satu* slot machine, one-armed bandit.

  membandit (*coq*) to act like a bandit; to pinch, pilfer, steal in a sneaky way.

  kebanditan banditry.

banditisme (*D*) banditism, exploitative mentality.

bando (*D*) bandeau, hair ribbon.

bandol (*Jv*) middleman, intermediary.

bandongan (*Jv*) system of teaching in a *pesantrén*, in which the students recite the Koran all at the same time; → SOROGAN.

bandos I (*J*) → BEBANDOS.

bandos II *karang –* pumice.

bandot (*J/Jv*) **1** billy/male/he-goat, ram. **2** womanizer, lascivious old man. *– tua* dirty old man. *– yang doyan lalap rumput muda* a dirty old man who likes young girls.

bandotan chickweed, *Ageratum conyzoides.*

bandrék I (*J*) a warming drink made from heated/boiled water, sugar, ginger, and other spices.

bandrék II (*J/Jv*) master/skeleton key, pick.

  membandrék to open (a door, etc.) with such a key or pick, pick a lock.

  bandrékan s.t. that has been gotten/stolen by using such a key.

bandrék III (*Jv*) adultery.

bandrol → BANDEROL.

bandu (*Skr*) friend; comrade; relatives.

bandul pendulum (of a clock).

  membandul 1 to hang down, swing (like a pendulum). **2** to bend backward or aside to avoid an attack, etc.

  membanduli to put a counterweight on, counterbalance.

  bandulan 1 pendulum, swing. **2** counterweight, counterbalance. **3** (*vulg*) testicles, balls.

bandung I (in West Kalimantan) a motorized barge covered by a house-like roof, houseboat.

bandung II (= **sebandung**) pair, set of two. *ayam (se)–* twin-chickens (from one egg). *balai –* two halls connected by a passage(way). *rumah (se)–* semidetached house. *telur (dua) ~* two yolks in one egg, double-yolked egg.

bandusa covered wooden/bamboo bier.

bandut = **pembandut** strap/supporting belt around s.t.

  membandut to put a strap/supporting belt around s.t.

bang I (*Pers*) muezzin's call/summons to prayer. *ratib –* frequent calls to prayer.

  membangkan to call out (the summons to prayer).

bang II clipped form of **abang II**. *batik –* a sarong pattern in which red predominates. *lampu – ijo* traffic light.

bang III clipped form of **abang I**. *– Ali* popular designation for Ali Sadikin. *– Haji* popular designation for Vice-President Hamzah Haz. *– Nolly* popular designation for H. Tjokropranolo.

bang IV → BANK.

bang V (in acronyms) → PEMBANGUNAN.

bang VI (*onom*) sound of an object hitting the floor or sound of a drum, "bang!"

bangai → BENGKALAI. **membangai** to abandon.

  terbangai 1 neglected, abandoned. **2** given up, abandoned; deserted, dropped (of one's lover/ mistress).

bangang I stupid, dull-witted.

bangang II k.o. tree, *Litsea polyantha.*

bangar I putrid, decayed, bad (tasting), rotten (smelling). *busuk –* extremely rotten (smelling).

bangar II → INGAR *bangar.*

bangas k.o. tree. *– mérah* k.o. tree, *Osmelia maingayi, Memecylon garcinioides. – putih* k.o. tree, *Angelesia splendens.*

bangat I 1 fast; quick, speed(y). **2** as soon as possible. *lambat –* gradually, in the long run.

  sebangat(-bangat)nya as quick(ly)/soon as possible.

  membangatkan to quicken, speed up, accelerate, hasten.

bangat II → BANGET.

bangau stork, heron, egret. *setinggi-tinggi terbang –, surutnya ke kubang juga* east or west, home is best; there's no place like home. *– air* blue heron. *– hitam* wooly-necked stork, *Ciconia episcopus. – kambing* intermediate egret, *Egretta ibis intermedia. – kecil* little egret, *Egretta garzetta. – kerbau* cattle egret, *Bulbulcus ibis. – langka* milky stork, *Ibis cinereus. – putih* large egret, *Egretta alba modesta. – putih susu* milk-white stork, *Nucteria cinerea. – sulah/tongtong/tontong* lesser adjutant stork, *Leptoptilos javanicus.*

bangbang salmon(-colored), salmon-pink.

bangbung coconut rhinoceros beetle, *Oryctes Rhinoceros;* → KUANGWUNG.

Bangdés → PEMBANGUNAN *désa.*

bangela and **bangelo** → BUNGALOW.

bangelas → BANGLAS.

banger → BANGAR I.

banget (*J/Jv*) **1** very (much). *keliru* – very much mistaken. *tinggi* – very tall; → SANGAT. **2** serious, intense. *sakit* – seriously ill.
   kebangetan excessively, overly; → KETERLALUAN. *Dan ini isu sih ~!* This is too much!

bangga I 1 proud. *- akan/atas/dengan/karena/kepada/pada* proud of. *- pada apa?* proud of what? *- menjadi orang Amérika* proud to be an American. **2** exult, jubilate.
   berbangga and **membangga** to be/feel proud (of); to feel conceited (about).
   membanggakan 1 to give rise to pride, create pride, makes one (feel) proud. **2** to feel proud of. *yang boléh dibanggakan* s.t. one can be proud of.
   kebanggaan 1 ~ *(akan/atas)* pride (in). **2** s.t. to be proud of. ~ *kesatuan* esprit de corps, group spirit.
   pembanggaan being proud of.

bangga II (*Jv*) **1** to oppose, object, protest, obstruct. **2** to resist (authority). **3** recalcitrant, rebellious. **4** difficult, hard (of work).

Banggali → BENGGALI.

banggi (*Jv*) perverse, degenerate, disobedient.

banggréng k.o. snack made from cassava.

bangir (*J/Jv*) fine and aquiline, not flat (of the nose). *Hidungnya -.* Her nose is fine and aquiline.

bangka (*J/Jv*) stiff, hard. *tua* – old and stiff, very old. *si tua* – the old man.

bangkah 1 caste mark (on the forehead). **2** blaze on horse's forehead. **3** a notorious criminal.

Bangkahulu → BENGKULU.

bangkai I 1 carcass, corpse, dead body. *bau* – foul-smelling. *becermin –* to make a fool of o.s.; in disgrace, disgraced. *besar* – tall and spanking. *burung pemakan* – vulture. *sawan* – apoplexy. **2** cast-off snake skin. **3** the ravages of time. *ada -, ada héring* where there are prostitutes, there are customers for their services. *menjemur – ke atas bukit* to expose one's own shortcomings. *- bangunan* ruin, the remains of a ruined building. *-.- bangunan* ruins. *- kapal* shipwreck. *- mobil* jalopy, old wrecked car. *- pesawat héli* wrecked fuselage of a helicopter.
   membangkai to rot away, become a carcass.

bangkai II *bunga* – k.o. flower, *Amorphophallus titanum. kembang* – k.o. flower with edible tuber, *Amorphophallus variabilis. - raksasa* k.o. flower, *Amorphophallus titanum.*

bangkal k.o. tree, *Albizzia procera, Ctenolophon parvifolius. - kuning,* k.o. tree, *Nauclea subdita.*

bangkang I oppose, dispute, disobey.
   membangkang [and **ngebangkang** (*J*)] **1** to oppose, object to, protest, contradict, dispute with, argue with. **2** to disobey, be disobedient. **3** do not pay attention to, ignore. **4** recalcitrant, disobedient, insubordinate, stubbornly defiant.
   membangkangi to rebel against.
   pembangkang 1 dissident, dissenter. *kaum* ~ a) dissidents. b) the opposition (in Parliament). **2**a) opponent; person/group who/which opposes. b) reactionary.
   pembangkangan dissension, insubordination, disobedience, rebelliousness. ~ *sipil* civil disobedience.

bangkang II spread wide apart (of the distance between horns).

bangkang III terbangkang (*ob*) unfinished, abandoned (of work/houses, etc.).

bangkar I 1 stiff and hard (of mats). **2** rigor mortis.
   membangkar to become stiff, hard and rough to the touch.
   kebangkaran stiffness, hardness.

bangkar II snag, branches (in a stream).

bangkas 1 *ayam* – (a fighting cock) with yellow-brown and white speckles. **2** mottled.

bangkéh (*M*) **1** white blaze on horse's forehead. **2** → BANGKAS.

bangkerap (*ob*) and **bangkerut** → BANGKRUT.

bangkes (*J*) **bebangkes** to sneeze.

bangkét (*D*) **1** banquet; → ANDROWINA. **2** (fancy) cakes, pastry.

bangking I urn-shaped lacquered or brass box for clothes.

bangking II → BUNGKANG-BANGKING.

bangking III *- kembang* k.o. cookie.

bangkir → BANKIR, BONGKAR.

bangkirai k.o. tree, *Shorea balangeran/laevis.*

bangkis sneeze.
   berbangkis to sneeze; → BERSIN.

bangkit 1 to wake up, awake, rouse o.s. from sleep. rise. *Dia – dari waktu tidur.* He roused himself from sleep. **2** to rise/get up (from a chair/sleep, etc.). *Dia – dari kursinya itu.* She rose from her chair. **3** to be resurrected, rise from the dead, come back to life again. *Nabi Isa telah – dari kuburNya.* Jesus rose from the grave. **4** to arise, rise up (of feelings). *– amarah* anger rose (in him). *– hati* enthusiastic. *– hatinya setelah tahu banyak orang yang mendukungnya.* He became enthusiastic when he found out that many people were supporting him. *Rasa kasihan telah – dalam hatinya.* Feelings of compassion rose in her heart. **5** to return, come back (of a disease) *Penyakitnya yang lama –.* His old complaint came back again. **6** to rise into the air. *Debu pun – ke udara.* The dust rose into the air. **7** to rise, expand (of dough, etc.) *Lekas – adonan itu.* The dough rose quickly. **8** to rise up (in rebellion). *– menentang néo-kolonialisme* to rise up against neo-colonialism. **9** to rise (of the sun). *Sang surya – dari peraduannya.* The sun rose from his bed. *– kembali* resurgence.
   berbangkit → BANGKIT.
   membangkit 1 to excite, stimulate, inspire, incite, provoke, arouse. *~ marah* to arouse one's anger, arouse s.o. to fury. *~ nafsu makan* to tempt one's appetite, make one hungry. *~ penyakit* to look for trouble. **2** (*M*) to collect, harvest, dig up. *~ kentang* to dig up potatoes. **3** (*M*) to lift up, take away, remove. *~ batang terendam* to save from oblivion. *~ cérék* to take the kettle off the fire. *~ jemuran* to bring/take in the wash. *~ padi* to remove the dried paddy.
   membangkit-bangkit to rake up (old stories), dig up (the past). *~ (si) tambo lama* to re-open/open up old sores, rake up old stories, dig up the past.
   membangkitkan 1 to bring back to life, resuscitate, revive, revitalize. *~ dari kubur* to raise from the dead. *(yang) ~ hormat* commanding respect. *~ orang mati* to bring a dead person back to life. **2** to raise, lift up. *~ pedang ke udara* to raise his sword. **3** to bring/take in for s.o. *~ ibunya jemuran* to bring in the laundry for mother. **4** (similar in meaning to **membangkit**) to arouse, create, excite, stir up (interest/suspicion, etc.), inspire. *~ minat terhadap* to arouse interest in. *~ perangsang* to stimulate, induce (s.o. to do s.t.). *~ semangat* to motivate, inspire. *~ tawa* to provoke laughter. **5** to generate (electricity).
   terbangkit 1 awakened suddenly. **2** can be raised, etc.
   bangkitan 1 (= **bangkit-bangkitan**) reawakening of past issues. **2** (*M*) harvest.
   kebangkitan 1 resurrection. *Hari ~ Almasih* Ascension Day. **2** rise, resurgence. *penganut aliran ~* revivalist. **3** (political) uprising, insurrection, insurgence, revolt. *Hari ~ Nasional* [Harkitnas] National Resurgence Day. **4** awakening, revival, new awareness. *~ Indonésia* the new awareness of Indonesia. *~ kembali* reawakening, renaissance, revival. *~ kembali kesadaran beragama* revival of religious awareness. *~ nasional* new awakening (of the Indonesian people in opposition to the Dutch).
   pembangkit 1 generator, power plant. *~ listrik tenaga air* [PLTA] hydroelectric power plant. *~ listrik tenaga diesel* [PLTD] diesel-powered electric generator. *~ listrik tenaga gas* [PLTG] (natural) gas-powered electric generator. *~ listrik tenaga gas dan uap* [PLTGU] gas and steam powered electric generator. *~ listrik tenaga nuklir* [PLTN] nuclear powered electric generator. *~ listrik tenaga panas bumi* [PLTPB] geothermal powered electric generator. *~ listrik tenaga uap* [PLTU] steam-powered electric generator. *~ tenaga listrik* electric power generator, power station. *~ tenaga nuklir* nuclear power plant. **2** instigator, motivator, motivating force behind s.t., initiator. *~ penyakit* disease-causing agent. *~ pikiran* stimulant. *~ seléra/nafsu makan* aperitif, appetizer. **3** producer.
   pembangkitan generation (of power or energy), production (of electricity), excitation.

bangko I *ikan* – muraena, conger eel, *Ophichthus apicalis.*

bangko II k.o. tree, *Ganua motleyana;* → KETIAU.

bangkoh *kayu* – mangrove tree, *Rhizophora;* → BAKAU.

bangkok *ikan* – anchovy, *Thryssa setirostris*.

bangkong (*J/Jv*) a large variety of frog.

bangkot (*J*) 1 very old. 2 die-hard.

bangkotan very old, senile.

bangkrut (*D*) 1 bankrupt, insolvent. 2 to go bankrupt. *perusahaan-perusahaan besar yang nyaris* – moribund industries.

membangkrutkan to bankrupt.

kebangkrutan bankruptcy.

pembangkrutan bankrupting; insolvency.

bangku (*Port*) bench, stool, seat with legs. *tidak makan* – *sekolahan* uneducated. – *bubut* lathe. – *geréja* pew. – *kaki* footstool. – *kerja* workbench. – *komuni* communion rail. – *kuliah* school bench. *Di* – *kuliah ia dikenal sebagai aktivis tangguh.* During his college years he was known as a staunch activist. – *lapor penumpang* check-in counter (at airport). – *sekolah* (school) bench. *duduk di* – *sekolah* at school. – *taman* park bench.

sebangku of the same (school) bench as. *kawan* ~ classmate (seated on the same bench).

bangkut dwarfish, pygmyish, stunted.

bangku(w)ang jicama (the Spanish name, popular in the U.S.A.), *Pachyrhizus angulatus Rich.*

banglai purple ginger, *Zingiber cassumunar/purpureum* used as an antipyretic and as a liniment for lumbago.

banglas roomy, spacious. *Kamar-kamar hotél yang baru itu lebih* – : *tarif suite US$ 260.–.* The rooms of that new hotel are more spacious: the rate for a suite is US$260.00.

banglé (*J*) → BANGLAI.

banglio site for manufacturing salted fish and fish paste (in Bagansiapi-api, Riau).

banglo I k.o. fish basket.

banglo II (*E*) bungalow.

bango (*J*) → BANGAU.

bangor (*J*) 1 naughty, mischievous. 2 brutal, insolent.

bangpak (*C J*) unreliable, inferior (quality).

bangsa (*Skr*) 1 nation, people. – *Indonésia* the Indonesian nation. – *dan negara* nation and state. 2 race; clan. *kebanggaan* – racial pride. 3 (*bio*) order, family, a category in the classification of plants or animals. – *harimau* the family of tigers. 4 sort, kind, class. *pesawat terbang* – *pemburu* an aircraft of the fighter class. 5 (*ob*) sex. *Lajur yang pertama diisi dengan nama, yang kedua* –, *yang ketiga umur, yang keempat tempat tinggal.* The first column is filled out with the name, the second with the sex, the third with the age, and the fourth with the residence. 6 of noble birth, highborn. *rusak* – *oléh laku* even though of noble birth, if one behaves badly, highborn descent will not be respected. – *ajengan* the elite. – *Anglo-Sakson* Anglo-Saxon race. – *bahar(i)* seafarers. – *Barat* Westerners. – *berwarna* colored people, people of color. – *déwék* compatriots, Javanese people (term used for themselves). – *dipertuan* (in Nazi Germany) Herrenvolk, master race. – *halus* supernatural beings. – *jajahan* colonized people. – *manusia* human race. – *murni* purebred nation. – *pengembara* nomads, nomadic people. – *témpé* an insignificant and weak nation. – *ter(ke)belakang* a) backward people. b) underdeveloped nation. – *yang disenangi* favored nation. – *yang sedang berkembang/membangun* developing nation. – *yang tertindas* oppressed nation.

sebangsa fellow/of the same nation/race/kind/family/stock. *Kita* ~. We are compatriots. ~ *padi* a paddy species. *dan* ~*nya* and the like. *séminar atau* ~*nya* seminars or similar group discussions. *saudara-saudara* ~ *dan setanah air* fellow countrymen.

berbangsa 1 to belong to a particular nation by birth or naturalization. *seorang pemegang buku yang* ~ *Indonésia* a bookkeeper of Indonesian nationality. 2 (*M*) to belong to a family, be related to. ~ *kepada ibu* to be on the mother's side, be related to one's mother. 3 to belong to the nobility; of noble birth, of high and noble social status. *Ia anak orang.* ~ he's of noble birth; → BANGSAWAN. 4 national. *kehidupan* ~ national life.

membangsa to become part of a nation. *prosés* ~ *kepada pemerintah Indonésia* the process of becoming part of the Indonesian nation.

membangsakan to consider related; to connect with.

kebangsaan 1 nationality. *Apakah* ~*nya?* What's his nationality? *orang yang tak punya* ~ a stateless person. 2 national. *bahasa/*

lagu/pakaian ~ national language/anthem/costume. 3 nationalism. *semangat* ~ spirit of nationalism. 4 nobility, peerage.

berkebangsaan 1 to have the ... nationality, be of ... nationality. ~ *Indonésia* of Indonesian nationality. 2 to possess the national characteristics of.

bangsai 1 rotten, moldy (of wood). 2 to be only skin and bones, be as thin as a rail. 3 unpromising (young rice plant).

bangsal 1 shed. 2 booth, stall with a roof. 3 temporary structure (for barracks, etc.). 4 (*Jv*) hall (in palace). 5 large structure (for physical exercise/performance/public meetings, etc.). 6 ward (in a hospital).

bangsat I rascal, scoundrel, rogue, bastard, damned (also a term of abuse).

kebangsatan rowdiness, ruffianism, being a scoundrel.

bangsat II (*M*) poor, miserable (of people).

bangsat III (*J*) bedbug, *Cimex lectularius*.

bangsawan I (*Skr*) noble, aristocratic; s.o. of good family or noble ancestry. *anak* – child of a nobleman/aristocrat.

kebangsawanan nobility, aristocracy.

bangsawan II = *komidi* – Malay opera/theater; → SANDIWARA. *anak* – actor in Malay opera.

bangsawati (*infr*) noblewoman.

bangsé I → BANGSA.

bangsé II (*J*) 1 person with certain characteristics. *Babényé* – *tukang ngomél.* His father is a grumbler by nature. 2 class/group of people in the same category. –*nya orang kampung itu, nggé adé nyang mao dateng kalo diundang.* They belong to the class of villagers nobody wants to show up when invited.

bangsé III (*J*) approximately, about, around.

bangsi 1 flute. 2 k.o. flute made from the stalk of the rice plant.

berbangsi to play (on) the *bangsi*.

bangték [*pengembangan téknik*] technical development.

bangun I 1 to get up, wake up, rise (from a chair/sleep, etc.). – *kesiangan* to sleep/wake up late. – *pagi* to get up in the morning. – *tidur* to get up after sleeping. *dengan jatuh* – through failures and successes, by trial and error. *Pagi-pagi saya* –. I woke/got up early in the morning. 2 to be up, not asleep. *Ketika ia pulang itu saya masih* –. When he came home I was still up. 3 to regain consciousness. *Ia jatuh pingsan dan lama tidak* –. He fainted and did not regain consciousness for a long time. 4 to realize, be aware/conscious of. 5 to rise (of dough). 6 to liquefy (of solidified oil). *Hangatkan minyak kelapa itu, supaya lekas* –. Heat up the coconut oil so that it quickly liquefies. 7 (of the penis) to get hard, be erect; to have an erection, get it up.

sebangun arising from the same source.

berbangun (*infr*) to rise, get/stand up, get out of bed.

berbangunan (*pl subj*) to rise in a group.

membangun to lift, clear (off), rise (of fog/smoke/clouds).

membanguni (*ob*) to wake s.o. up.

membangunkan [and **mbangunin/ngebangunin** (*J coq*)] 1 to wake s.o. up. *Ibunya* ~ *anaknya pada pukul 6.* His mother wakes her child up at 6 o'clock. *Dentuman yang kuat itu* ~*nya dari tidur.* The powerful booming (of the guns) woke him from sleep. 2 to create, arouse, provoke. ~ *hasrat untuk mandiri* to create the desire to be independent. ~ *minat* to arouse/awaken interest. ~ *tresno* to awaken love.

terbangun [and **kebangun** (*coq*)] awakened suddenly. *Pada suatu malam, entah bagaimana, saya* ~ *karena mendengar suara orang bercakap di beranda.* One night, I don't know why, I woke up because I heard the sound of people talking on the veranda. ~ *dari impiannya* awakened from a dream. *tersadar dan* ~ to wake up and come to one's senses.

kebangunan 1 awakening. ~ *bangsa-bangsa Asia* the awakening of the Asian people. 2 revival, resurgence.

bangun II 1 form, (round/square, etc.) shape; → BENTUK. *méja yang bundar* –*nya* a round table. *Bulat telur* –*nya.* It is oval. 2 look, appearance; figure, posture, build. –*nya bagus.* She has a beautiful figure. 3 composition, structure. *mempelajari* – *permukaan bumi* to study the composition of the earth's surface. *perubahan* – *masyarakat* change in social structure. – *dalam* internal structure.

bangun-bangun look, appearance.

sebangun of the same form, similar. *sama dan* ~ congruent.
membangun 1 constructive. *kecaman/kritik* ~ constructive criticism. **2** to build, construct. ~ *kota baru* to construct a new town. ~ *kembali* to rebuild. *sedang dibangun* under construction. **3** to develop; → BERKEMBANG. *negara-negara yang sedang* ~ developing countries.
membangunkan 1 to build, erect, construct. *bersatu padu untuk* ~ *negara kita* to be united in building our country. **2** to develop. ~ *bangsa* to develop a nation. **3** to comply with. ~ *pusaka* to comply with the requirements of adat.
terbangun constructed, built, developed.
bangunan building, structure, erection, construction, installation. ~ *liar* illegal construction, i.e., a construction without the necessary building permit or on land not one's own, squatter's housing. ~ *militér* military installation. ~ *pabrik siap pakai* standard factory building. ~ *pemecah ombak* breakwater. ~ *pérmanén* permanent building. ~ *sémipérmanén* semipermanent building. ~ *tambahan* addition, annex. **berbangunan** with a ... structure.
bangun-bangunan buildings, structures, fortifications, scaffolding. ~ *irigasi* irrigation works.
pembangun ~ (*perumahan*) builder, constructor, developer.
pembangunan building, construction, development. ~ *berkelanjutan* sustainable development. ~ *dari atas* top-down construction. ~ *désa* [Bangdés] rural development. ~ *Jangka Panjang Kesatu/Kedua* [PJP I/II] First/Second Long-Range Development (25 years each). ~ *kepercayaan* confidence building. ~ *Lima Tahun* [Pelita] Five-Year Development (plan). ~ *masyarakat* community development. ~ *sosial* social reconstruction. ~ *yang didorong oléh negara* State-led development; → PEMBANGUNANISME.
bangun III (*cla*) blood money; wergeld.
membangun 1 (*cla*) to pay blood money. **2** (*M*) to replace a person (of another tribe) killed by a person of one's own tribe or pay a fine instead.
membangunkan (*cla*) to pay blood money.
bangun IV and **bangun-bangun** k.o. herb, k.o. Indian borage or oregano, *Coleus amboinicus.*
Bangunkarta name of a train running between Jakarta and Jombang.
bangus (*J*) (pig's) snout.
bani (*A*) children/sons/people of. – *Adam* the human race, mankind, people. – *Israél/Israil* a) Jews, Hebrews. b) "The Children of Israel"; name of the 17th chapter of the Koran.
banian I (*ob*) → BENIAN.
banian II and **baniang 1** k.o. jacket, banian. **2** traditional dress of the Central Moluccan area.
baning tortoise species, *Testudo emys/elongata* and *Geochelone emys*; gongs are made from the hard skin of this tortoise.
membaning to beat on a gong (made of such a skin).
banio k.o. tree, *Shorea leptocladus.*
banir buttress, buttress-like projection at the base of the trunk of some trees. *bertiraikan* – to have tree-buttresses for one's bed curtains," i.e., to have no house, be homeless.
berbanir with/to have a buttress-like projection etc.
banitan various species of trees, *Xylopia spp.*
banjang (*Jv ob*) k.o. fence/palisade in the sea for catching fish (used as a bow-net).
banjar I row, series, range (of mountains), battery, sequence; → DÉRÉT, LÉRÉT. – *tangki* (*petro*) tank battery.
sebanjar 1 in a row. **2** equal in value, equivalent. **3** of the same age; → SEPANTARAN.
berbanjar(-banjar) and **berbanjaran** in rows/lines/series/sequence.
membanjarkan to arrange in lines/rows, etc.
banjaran series, range. ~ *gunung Titiwangsa membagikan Semenanjung Malaysia dalam dua kawasan.* The Titiwangsa mountain range bisects the Malaysian Peninsula into two regions.
banjar II (*Bal*) the local area of the village in which community activities are organized, hamlet association. *balé* – the communal meeting place of the village *banjar*, k.o. social association where all local communal activities are organized.
banjar III mackerel.

banji (*C*) decorative wooden or porcelain trellis mounted on balcony, window, etc.
banjir (*Jv*) **1** high water; flood; inundation, *esp* water streaming down with force and en masse from areas located at a higher level causing the water in rivers to rise considerably all of a sudden. *sungai* – the river has overflowed its banks; → MELUAP. **2** to flood, overflow (of rivers). **3** a great flow or outflow; glut. *Menjelang Lebaran di pasar-pasar – tékstil.* There is a glut of textiles in markets prior to *Lebaran*. *–nya minyak* an oil glut. *–nya keinginan masuk perguruan tinggi* the rush to enroll in higher education. *– bandang* tremendous flood. *– kiriman* flood caused by rainfall, i.e., by rain that falls or fell not on the spot. *– tiba-tiba* flash flood.
membanjir to flood (of water/money); like a flood; flooded. *Uang* ~ *masuk ke dalam peti besinya.* The money flooded into his safe. *~nya minyak* oil glut.
membanjiri 1 to flood, inundate. *Air sungai* ~ *daérah itu.* The river water inundated the area. **2** to flood into, come in flocks/great numbers to. *Rapat umum itu dibanjiri orang.* People came in throngs to the general meeting. **3** to shower with (gifts, etc.). *Saya dibanjiri hadiah.* I was showered with gifts.
kebanjiran caught in a flood; flooded, overflowed, inundated, overrun. *Jalan itu* ~. The road is flooded.
pembanjiran flooding.
banjo → BANYO.
banjur membanjur to water, pour water on.
membanjuri to sprinkle, pour on to s.t.
membanjurkan to sprinkle s.t. (on to s.t.).
bank (*D*) /bang/ bank. – 46 (= BNI 1946 [*Bank Negara Indonésia 1946*]) 1946 State Bank of Indonesia. – *asal* originating bank. – *asing patungan* foreign joint venture bank. – *Bakulan* [Babak] Retailers Rank, issuing weekly and monthly loans to small farmers at weekly rates. – *Beku Kegiatan Usaha* [BBKU] Frozen Business Operations Bank. – *Beku Operasi* [BBO] suspended bank. – *berlayar* floating bank. – *beroda* mobile bank, bank on wheels. – *céwék* (*coq*) ladies bank. – *dagang* commercial bank. – *Dagang Negara* [BDN] Commercial State Bank. – *Dalam Likuidasi* [BDL] Bank in Liquidation. – *darah* blood bank. – *Désa* [BD] Rural Rank, consisting of two types of banks: *Bank Bakulan* and *Bank Tani*. – *dévisa/dévisen* foreign exchange bank. – *Donor Darah* Blood Bank. – *Dunia* World Bank, also known as International Bank for Reconstruction and Development. – *gelap* illegal bank. – *hipoték/hipotik* mortgage bank. – *Indonésia* [BI] Bank of Indonesia (the central bank). – *induk* parent bank. – *Internasional Indonésia* [BII] Indonesian International Bank. – *jaringan* tissue bank. – *keliling* bank on wheels. – *kendara lalu* drive-in banking. – *kliring* clearing bank. – *klon* clone bank. – *koréspondén* correspondent bank. – *luar negeri* offshore commercial bank. – *Mata* Eye Bank. – *milik negara* state-owned bank. – *mobil* drive-in bank. – *Muamalat Indonésia* [BMI] Indonesian Muamalat Bank (a bank operating on Islamic principles). – *pasar* market bank. – *pelaksana* handling bank. – *pembeli* lender bank. – *pembuka L/C* issuing bank. – *pemrakarsa* originating bank. – *penagih* collecting bank. – *penerbit* issuing bank. – *penerima* beneficiary bank. – *penerima transaksi* originating/receiving bank. – *penerus L/C* advising bank. – *penyalur* channeling bank. – *persépsi* collecting bank (a bank which accepts income tax payments). – *peséro* state bank. – *plecit* a company which lends out small amounts of money. – *respondén* respondent bank. – *séntral* central bank. **kebank-séntralan** (*mod*) central bank. – *Séntral Amérika* The U.S. Central Bank, the Fed. – *sirkulasi* bank of issue, central bank. – *spérma* sperm bank. – *syariah* Islamic bank. – *tabungan* savings bank. – *Tabungan Bersama* Mutual Savings Bank. – *Tabungan Pos* Post Office Savings Bank. – *Tani* [Bati] Peasants Bank, issuing loans to small farmers for one season (six months) which must be repaid in total within one month after harvest. – *Take Over* [BTO] Taken-Over Bank. – *tunggal* unit bank. – *tuyul* an ephemeral bank; → TUYUL. – *umum* commercial bank.
perbankan /perbangkan/ banking, banking sector. ~ *di negara itu sudah maju.* Banking in that country is already advanced. *lembaga-lembaga* ~ banking institutions. ~ *syariah* Islamic banking.

bankir (*D*) **1** banker, money broker. **2** financier, moneylender; → CUKONG, PEMBIAYA.

Banpol → PEMBANTU *polisi.*

Banpolantas → PEMBANTU *polisi lalulintas.*

Banprés → BANTUAN *présidén.*

bansai I → BANGSAI.

bansai II → BANZAI.

Banser [Barisan Ansor Serbaguna] Multipurpose *Ansor* Troops, i.e., the name for the black-shirt paramilitary wing of Ansor, the *Nahdlatul Ulama* youth group.

bantah dispute, squabble, quarrel, altercation. – *béntoh* all k.o. quarrels/squabbles, etc.

berbantah to wrangle, squabble, dispute, argue, quarrel, get into an argument. ~ *péna* to be polemical in print.

bantah-berbantah denials.

berbantah-bantah(an) to quarrel/fight with e.o.

membantah 1 to contradict, assert the opposite of (what s.o. else has said), deny s.o.'s statement, argue. ~ *kata-kata ibunya* to contradict what his mother says. **2** to dispute (a fact, etc.), contest (a point), challenge (a statement); to oppose (a proposal), go against. **3** to refute. **4** to deny (God's existence). ~ *janji* to break a promise. ~ ... *kepada* to protest s.t. to s.o.

bantah-membantah to contradict e.o.

membantahi to disobey (an order/a law), disagree with, dispute (a statement), object to, contest.

mem(per)bantahkan to argue over s.t. (as in a debate).

terbantahkan refutable, deniable. *tidak* ~ undeniable.

bantahan 1 refutation, denial; contradiction. **2** (a written) defense, rebuttal, challenge. **3** quarrelsome, cantankerous, contentious, disputatious; opinionated.

pembantah 1 opponent, **2** debater. **3** s.o. who likes to argue/take the opposite side.

pembantahan disputing, arguing, opposing.

perbantahan quarrel, dispute.

bantai meat (of a slaughtered animal). *tukang* – butcher, slaughterer.

membantai 1 to slaughter, butcher. *bagai kucing tidur dibantai* (*M*) like taking candy from a baby. **2** to massacre, kill off, slaughter. *Para gerilyawan* ~ *semua orang laki-laki di désa itu.* The guerrilla fighters massacred all the men in that village. ~ *habis* to wipe out, annihilate. **3** to destroy, ruin, wipe out, exterminate. *Banjir telah* ~ *habis padi yang sedang menguning di sawah.* The flood wiped out the ripening paddy in the field. ~ *dengan tangan* (*cla*) to beat up, take a swipe at s.o.

terbantai slaughtered, butchered.

bantaian 1 meat block (in a butcher shop). **2** for slaughter, to be slaughtered. *sapi* ~ slaughter cattle.

pembantai 1 butcher, slaughterer. **2** murderer.

pembantaian 1 abattoir, slaughterhouse. **2** butchering, slaughter, murder. ~ *massal* holocaust.

bantal pillow; cushion. *menyimpan uang di bawah* – to save money under the pillow, i.e., to save money at home and not deposit it in a bank. *salah* – to have a stiff neck (after sleeping). *sampul/sarung* – pillowcase. *tikar* – sleeping mat and pillow, i.e., bedding. *lepas* – *berganti tikar* to marry one's deceased wife's sister or relative. *mata* – *berjaga* a spouse who is unfaithful when her husband neglects her. *orang mengantuk disorongkan* – to obtain s.t. needed unexpectedly. – *angin* air cushion. – *duduk* seat cushion. – *galang* a) pillow (for sleeping on). b) bolster, Dutch wife (i.e., a long, cylindrical pillow embraced for coolness in the tropics). – *golék/guling* bolster, Dutch wife. – *iswari* → BANTAL *suari.* – *jangkar* (*naut*) hawse bolster. – *kembung* round pillow. – *kepala* pillow (for sleeping on). – *listrik* (*chem*) heated stand for a beaker. – *peluk* bolster, Dutch wife. – *pipih* flat pillow. – *sandar* pillow used to lean on, cushion. – *seraga* a round embroidered pillow used during wedding ceremonies. – *suari* (*cla*) k.o. square bolster with decorated ends. – *téko* tea cozy. – *tikar* all one's belongings. – *udara* airbag (in car).

bantal-bantal s.t. resembling a pillow, such as a railroad tie or sleeper, pincushion, etc.

sebantal 1 one pillow. **2** to sleep together; in bed with each other. *bagai* ~ *selapik* as one pillow and one mat, i.e., hand in glove;

very intimately associated. *Begitu dekatnya hubungan itu bagai* ~ *selapik, yang seakan-akan tak bisa dipisahkan.* They are so close that they are like hand and glove, which as it were cannot be separated.

berbantal(kan) with a pillow; to use a pillow. ~*(kan) lengan* a) to use the arm(s) as a pillow; to sleep with the head on the arms. b) to sleep pillowed in e.o.'s arms (of lovers); sleeping together, sharing the same bed. c) to sleep any place at all (because one has no permanent residence).

membantali to provide with a cushion/pillow.

memperbantal and **membantalkan** to use ... as a pillow.

bantalan 1 s.t. resembling a pillow: railroad tie or sleeper, pincushion, bearing. ~ *angin* air cushion. ~ *cap* stamp pad. ~ *gulung* roller bearing. ~ *lutut* knee pad. ~ *peluru* ball bearing. ~ *pengisi* padding. ~ *peniti* pin cushion. ~ *poros* main/shaft bearing. ~ *sandar* fender. ~ *sekoci* boat chock. ~ *stémpl* stamp pad. ~ *udara* air cushion. **2** gauge (of railroad). ~ *sempit* narrow-gauge. ~ *udara* air cushion.

bantal-bantalan s.t. resembling a pillow, such as a railroad tie or sleeper, pincushion, etc.

bantam (*D*) **1** a dwarf fowl. **2** bantam, i.e., s.t. small of its class. *kelas* – boxer of the bantamweight class.

bantar I **membantar** (*ob*) to arrest, check, restrain, resist, ward off (a disease, by magic).

bantaran (*Jv*) **1** rapid (in river), shallow, shoal (in river). **2** bottom land, i.e., low-lying grassland along a watercourse; alluvial deposit, silt (in river). **3** canal. ~ *irigasi* irrigation canal. ~ *sungai* river bottom/bed.

pembantar s.t. that wards off a disease, etc.; s.t. worn in the belief that it will protect the wearer from becoming sick, etc. ~ *demam* febrifugal. ~ *tikus* a cat raised to kill mice.

pembantaran restraining, etc.

bantar II → BANTER.

bantat I (*ob*) → PANTAT.

bantat II (*J/Jv*) not risen, doughy (of badly baked bread), not want to expand (of cake, etc.), incomplete.

bantau tennis-like net for catching birds.

banténg 1 a wild ox, Bos banteng (*Javanica*). *sebagai* – *ketaton* (*Jv*) "like a wounded banteng," i.e., to be on a rampage, rage. **2** the election symbol of the PDI. *menusuk Kabah dan* – to vote for the Muslim-backed PPP and the PDI. *terajar pada* – *pincang* it's no use trying to teach a stubborn person.

banter I (*J/Jv*) **1** quick, fast, rapidly dart/shoot ahead/forward (of a horse's gallop/stream of river, etc.). **2** pushing, energetic, with fervor/ardor, assiduously. **3** fierce (of heat, etc.), acute. **4** to rise, advance, go up (higher), move up, (of prices/the market). **5** fiery, passionate, quick-tempered. **6** (*esp J*) (too) loud (of sound). *Radio itu bunyinya* – *banget.* The radio's too loud.

membanter ~ *biola* to tune a violin.

banter II *paling* – not more than, at most/best; → PALING-PALING. *paling* – *Rp 300* not more than Rp 300.00. *Paling* – *cuma dimarahi.* At best he'll only be reprimanded.

banteras → BERANTRAS.

bantet → BANTAT II.

bantilang (in the Bulukumba regency, South Sulawesi) people's shipyard.

banting I *mercon/petasan* – firecrackers that explode when smashed on the ground. – *harga* dumping. *melakukan prakték* – *harga* to dump (goods on the market). – *stir* turning the steering wheel suddenly. **membanting stir** a) to turn the steering wheel suddenly. b) to change one's course radically. c) to reverse one's policy, i.e., to replace old methods by new ones. **pembanting-stiran** turning the wheel suddenly, reversing one's policy, etc.

berbantingan to smash against s.t.

membanting 1 to bump about. **2** to dash (as waves against cliffs/rocks, etc.). **3** to beat (laundry against rocks), slam (a door). *Ombak* ~ *pada karang.* The waves dashed against the rocks. **4** to throw down, smash, fling. ~ *diri* to throw o.s. ~ *granat ke atas méja* to dump a (hand)grenade under one's (very) nose. ~ *harga* to mark down prices. ~ *kaki* a) to stamp one's feet. b) to march in goose step. ~ *kemudi* to shift the helm, put the helm over. ~ *otak* to rack one's brains. ~ *pintu* to slam the door. ~ *tulang* to work one's fingers to the bone, work hard.

membanting-banting 1 to shake, swing. **2** to beat, knead (in making dough), stir. **3** to keep tossing up and down, moving from side to side (of a ship on the sea, a car on the road, etc.).

membantingi to smash s.t. onto s.o.

membantingkan → MEMBANTING.

terbanting [and **kebanting** (*coq*)] **1** thrown down, smashed, etc. **2** clashing. *kebanting sama pakaiannya* clashing with his clothing.

bantingan 1 smashing, throwing, shaking. **2** smashed, thrown, slashed (of prices). *harga ~* slashed prices. **3** s.t. thrown down/ smashed.

pembantingan hurling, beating, shaking, throwing down. ~ *harga* drastic price reductions.

banting II an Acehnese two-masted ship.

banting III → BANTÉNG.

bantras → BERANTAS.

bantu 1 help, assistance, aid, support, relief. *Ada yang bisa saya ~?* (in hotels/stores, asked by hotel employees/salespersons, etc.) Can I help you? **2** helper, assistant, branch, auxiliary. *guru ~* assistant/substitute teacher. *juru tulis ~* assistant clerk. *kantor pos ~* branch post office. *kata kerja ~* (*gram*) auxiliary verb. *~ laku* complicit. **pembantu laku** accomplice, accessory. **kepembantu-lakuan** complicity. *~ tulis* coauthorship. **membantu tulis** to coauthor. *dibantu tulis oléh* to be coauthored by.

berbantuan to help e.o.

membantu [and **mbantuin/ngebantuin** (*J coq*)] **1** to help, support, aid, assist. *Ia bekerja sendiri tidak ada yang ~.* He worked independently, nobody helped him. **2** to contribute, write and give or sell articles, etc. to a newspaper, magazine, etc. *Ia diminta supaya suka ~ surat kabar ini.* He was asked whether he would like to contribute to this newspaper. **3** helpful. *Staf Garuda di Halim sangat ~.* The Garuda Staff at Halim was most helpful.

bantu-membantu and **bantu-membantui** to help e.o.

mem(per)bantukan to detail, assign s.o. to assist, station s.o. (in a post). *~ (se)seorang kepada A* to assign s.o. to A. *pegawai tinggi diperbantukan* the senior official in charge.

terbantu [and **kebantu** (*coq*)] supported, helped, assisted, aided. *Ia banyak ~ dengan adanya cara belajar bersama itu.* He was very much helped by the existence of a joint study method.

bantuan 1 aid, help, assistance, support. *bala ~* auxiliary troops, reinforcements. *dengan ~* assisted by. *uang ~* support money. *~ batin* moral support. *~ cuma-cuma* grant. *~ hibah* grant (in-aid). *~ hukum* legal aid. *~ krédit* credit grant. *~ luar negeri* foreign aid. *~ moral* moral support. *~ penyelamatan* bailout. *~ Présidén* [Banprés] Presidential Aid, i.e., special funds earmarked by the President. *~ téknik* technical assistance. *~ témbakan* fire support. *~ uang* financial support. **2** cooperation, support. **berbantuan** subsidized, aided by, with the assistance of. *sekolah ~* subsidized school. *dua proyék ~ ADB* two projects aided by the ADB.

pembantu 1 helper, assistant, coworker; domestic helper, servant. *~ all-in* (in the "Krakatau Steel" complex at Cilegon, West Java) a housemaid who takes care of the house of a "bachelor," and also take care of her boss in the broadest sense of the word. *~ bupati* the present title for the former *wedana*. *wilayah ~ bupati* the former *kewedanaan*. *~ gubernur* the present title for the former *résidén*. *~ jaksa* assistant public prosecutor. *~ kejahatan/tindak pidana* accomplice, accessory to a crime. *~ lepas* free-lance assistant. *~ létnan dua* [Példa] second sublieutenant. *~ létnan satu* [Péltu] first sublieutenant. *~ létnan satu polisi* [Péltu Pol] Police first sublieutenant. *~ ordonatur* assistant to the aide-de-camp. *~ polisi* [Banpol] auxiliary police. *~ polisi lalulintas* [Banpolantas] auxiliary traffic police. *~ pribadi* personal assistant. *~ réktor* deputy president of a university. *~ rumah tangga* [PRT] domestic help; → BEDI(E)NDE. *~ tetap* permanent assistant. *~ umum* jack-of-all-trades. *~ wilayah gubernur* the former *keresidénan*. *~ yang setia* faithful servant. *~ tenaga* assistant. *~ yang segera dapat dicairkan* fast disbursement assistance. **2** correspondent. *~ lepas* stringer. *~ surat kabar* correspondent. **3** support(ing),

auxiliary, subsidiary. *sistém ~ éléktronik* electronic support system. **4** accomplice (to a crime).

pembantuan 1 assistance, support, aid, complicity (in a crime). **2** cooperation.

perbantuan 1 (*mil*) the process of attaching a military man to a civilian position on a short-term basis to perform a particular task. **2** help, assistance.

bantun I membantun(kan) 1 to pull out (hair), extract (teeth). **2** to weed (a lawn/yard).

membantuni (*pl obj*) to weed, pull s.t. out one by one.

terbantun pulled out, weeded, extracted.

bantun II sebantun k.o. tree, *Vitex coriacea*.

bantut not full-grown, whose development is arrested, aborted (of plants). *anak ~* dwarf.

membantut to hamper, hinder, impede, block. *Perjuangan nasionalis itu dibantut oléh barisan asing.* The national struggle was hampered by foreign troops.

membantuti to clog s.t. up.

terbantut 1 hampered, hindered, etc. **2** stunted, thwarted in its growth (of plants/human beings), arrested (of development).

pembantutan hindering, hampering.

banu (*A ob*) → BANI.

banyak I 1 much, many, a lot of. *~ orang* many people, a number of persons. *orang ~* the public, crowd, populace. *~nya* quantity/number of, amount. *~nya beras itu* the amount of that rice. *masih ~* there's still a lot (left over). **2** very much, a lot, quite a bit. *terima kasih ~ (atas)* thank you kindly/very much (for). *Ia ~ makan.* He's eating a lot (on one occasion). **3** (+ verb + object) often, much, habitually, to a great extent, a lot of. *Dia ~ minum bir.* He drinks a lot of beer. *OKB itu menanamkan ~ uang.* The nouveau-riche invested quite a bit of money. *~ bicara* talkative, loquacious, talks too much. *~ kali* often, frequently; → KERAP *kali*. *~ laku* whimsical, capricious, fickle. *~ makan garam* experienced, seasoned, well-versed. *~ mulut/omong* a) talkative, loquacious, a chatterbox. b) fussy, finicky, hard to please, fault-finding; → BAWÉL I, CERÉWÉT. *~ sedikitnya* and *sedikit ~nya* a) quantity, number, amount. *~ sedikitnya pelajar tergantung pada pembayaran uang sekolah.* The number of students depends on the tuition. b) more or less; a few things, a thing or two. *~ sedikitnya saya harus menggunakan wibawa pribadi saja.* I only had to use my personal authority more or less. *~ mulut* talkative. *~ terjadi* happens often, is widespread.

sebanyak as much/many as, amounting to. *Utangnya ~ bulu.* He's up to his ears in debt. *~ ini* this much.

sebanyak-banyaknya 1 as much/many as possible. **2** at (the) most, at best/the utmost. *~ dapat diberi hanya seratus ribu.* At most only one hundred thousand can be given.

berbanyak with many. *~ hati* ambivalent.

berbanyak-banyak in great/large numbers/quantities. *Meréka itu datang ~.* They came in large numbers.

membanyak to multiply, grow, increase in number. *Penonton mulai ~ setelah polisi sampai di TKP.* The spectators began to increase in number after the police arrived on the scene.

mem(per)banyaki to increase, expand, swell, add to. *~ anggota agar partai menjadi kuat* to increase membership in order to strengthen the party.

membanyakkan to increase, augment. *~ keuntungan* to increase profits.

memperbanyak(kan) 1 to increase, augment. *memperbanyak kecerdasan umum* to increase public intelligence. **2** to multiply. *lima diperbanyakkan dengan empat* five multiplied by four. **3** to reproduce, make copies of. **4** to make a lot of. *Kami mengucapkan diperbanyak terima kasih atas bantuan Anda.* We express our great appreciation for your help.

terbanyak the greatest part, the majority, most (people). *orang ~* the majority. *suara ~* majority vote.

banyakan 1 (*J*) perhaps, possibly. **2** in general, for the most part.

kebanyakan 1 quantity, amount. *Bukan ~ tetapi nilainya yang penting.* It's not the quantity but the value which is important. **2** majority, the greatest part, most, much of. *~ meréka adalah wanita.* Most of them were women. *~ orang* a) the majority of the people. b) most people. *~ daérah ini* most/much of this region. **3** ordinary, common. *orang* ~ commoner, the man in the street. **4** generally, usually. ~ *asal membayar boléh masuk.* Generally, as long as you pay, you may enter. **5** (*J*) (walked/ eaten, etc.) too much, get too much of s.t. ~ *mulut* [a direct translation of *keakéhan cangkem* (*Jv*)] to talk too much and do too little.

pembanyakan multiplying, increasing (the number of).

perbanyakan 1 (*math*) multiplication. *melakukan* ~ to multiply. **2** augmentation. **3** propagation. **4** reproduction.

banyak II (*Jv*) goose.

banyo (*D*) banjo.

banyol (*J/Jv*) **1** funny, amusing, humorous; → LUCU. **2** clown, buffoon, comedian; → BADUT.

membanyol 1 to clown around, play the fool. **2** to joke around.

ngebanyol (*J*) to joke, jest, banter. *tukang* ~ clown, etc.

banyolan 1 joke, jest. **2** clown, comedian, etc. ~ *April(an)* April Fool's Day joke. ~ *murahan* slapstick. ~ *Satu April* April Fool's Day joke.

pembanyol clown, buffoon, jester, joker.

banyu (*Jv*) water. - *bening* clear water, i.e., a mystical term peculiar to Javanese philosophical mysticism. It refers to peace in one's household, success in one's work or enterprise, cure for sickness, etc. It may also be in the form of a *slametan*, following an ascetic (religious) regimen etc. - *gégé* water warmed by the morning sun. *memandikan bayi dengan - gégé* to bathe an infant in such water.

banyu(n) k.o. lye, i.e., coconut milk with charcoal or soot, black coloring for the teeth.

banzai (*Jp*) long live!

bap (*onom*) plop!

BAP → BERITA *Acara Pemeriksaan.*

bapa (*Mal*) - *Bangsa* Father of the Nation, i.e., the sobriquet for the former Malaysian Prime Minister Tunku Abdul Rahman.

bapak 1 father; → AYAH. **2** older man; uncle; → O(O)M. **3** sir, Mr. (also a form of address). - *Présidén* Mr. President. **4** (to men) you; your; → ANDA. **5** founder, founding father; → PELETAK *dasar Républik Indonésia.* **6** big shot. -.- (*coq*) big shots (derogatory). - *angkat* a) foster father. b) a large company which helps a fledgling enterprise operating in the same field get on its own feet. - *ayam* (*coq*) a) a father who neglects his children. b) pimp. - *badari* (*coq*) a leader who uses his followers for personal profit. - *bangsa* father of the nation. - *besar* a) a higher-up, important person. b) grandfather. - *bungsu/cilik* uncle (younger brother of father or mother); → PAKLIK. - *gedé* a) a higher-up, important person. b) grandfather. c) (among the Badui) the *bupati* and *résidén*. - *indekosan* landlord. - *Kami* Our (Heavenly) Father. - *kandung* biological father. - *kecil* uncle (younger brother of father or mother). - *kualon* stepfather. - *Marhaénisme* Father of *Marhaenisme*, i.e., President Soekarno. - *mentua/mertua* father-in-law. - *muda* uncle (younger brother of father or mother). - *Negara* Father of the Nation, i.e., the President. - *pemandian* Godfather. - *Pembentuk Negara* The Founding Fathers (in the U.S.A.). - *Pembangunan* Father of Development, i.e., the first title conferred upon President Soeharto in March 1983. - *Pemerintah* reference to an official from any government agency who comes to villages located in the Cilacap Regency to bring aid in the form of rice, medicines, etc. - *pengakuan* father confessor. - *permandian* godfather. - *Rakyat* Father of the People. - *rumah yang baik* (with) due/proper care. - *saudara* uncle. - *Suci Paus* His Holiness the Pope. - *tani* the peasant, farmer. - *tiri* stepfather. - *tua* uncle (older brother of father or mother).

sebapak with the same father (but a different mother).

berbapak 1 to have a father. **2** to consider/treat as a father. ~ *kepada* to be the son of, call s.o. father.

berbapakkan to have … as one's father. ~ *seorang Belanda* to have a Dutch father. ~ *seorang tentara* to have an army man as one's father.

membapak *sifat* ~ paternalism; → BAPAKISME.

memperbapakkan to treat/consider s.o. a *bapak*.

kebapakan 1 fatherly, paternal. *sikap* ~ paternal attitude. **2** paternalistic. *Ia féodal, terlalu* ~. He's feudalistic, too paternalistic.

perbapakan fatherhood.

bapakisme /bapa'isme/ paternalism, i.e., the concept of putting emphasis on father-son type relations in the Indonesian bureaucracy, the unquestioning loyalty and obedience of underling to superior.

bapanda father (polite form of address, *esp* in correspondence).

bapang I daddy!

bapang II decorated belt buckle.

bapao → BAKPAO.

bapas [balai pemasyarakatan] rehabilitation center.

bapél k.o. *kué basah* made with *santan* and vanilla.

Bapépam → BADAN *Pengawas Pasar Modal.*

Bapérki → BADAN *Permusyawaratan Kewarganegaraan Indonésia.*

bapét (*J*) **1** broke, penniless. **2** worthless, trashy, ugly.

baplang (*J*) thick and coarse (of a moustache). - *melingker* protruding (moustache).

Bappeda → BADAN *Perencanaan Pembangunan Daérah.*

Bappenas → BADAN *Perencanaan Pembangunan Nasional.*

baptis (*D coq*) baptism, christening.

membaptis(kan) 1 to baptize, christen (a child, etc.); → MEMPERMANDIKAN. **2** to name.

baptisan baptismal. *tanda* - baptismal certificate.

pembaptis baptizer.

pembaptisan 1 baptism, christening; → PERMANDIAN. **2** introduction, (new) designation.

bapuk empty (of *padi* ear); → PUSO.

baqarah → BAKARAH.

bar I (*D/E*) bar (in a hotel/restaurant, etc.). *gadis* - bargirl.

bar II → DEBAR.

bar III (in acronyms) → BARAT.

bara I embers, cinder. *batu* - coal. *batu - muda* lignite. *jejak(-jejak)* - almost within reach. *lipan* - a red-colored centipede. *panas* - touchy, quick to take offense. *terpijak - hangat* to keep s.o. on pins and needles. - *api* live coals.

membara 1 to blaze, flash, flare up. *mérah* ~ fiery red, as red as fire. **2** to burn, be burning, fiery. *Hatinya sudah panas* ~. His heart was burning with anger.

membarakan to burn, set fire to.

pembaraan and **perbaraan** brazier, furnace.

bara II (*ob*) → BAHARA.

bara III (*ob*) → CAKAR *bara,* SARA II.

baraat (*A*) pass. *malam* - (Muslim) night of the 14th of the month of *Syaban*, when it is determined who will die in the following year. - *surat kebébasan* (letter of) safe-conduct.

baragajul → BERGAJUL.

barah abscess, boil, tumor, pustule. - *batang* elongated bubo. - *batu* a hard chronic boil. - *bir* (*A*) piles (in the anus). - *bisa* carbuncle. - *cika* intestinal ulcer. - *darah* leukemia. - *gajah* an internal tumor. - *raja* carbuncle. - *sisip* hepatic ulcer.

membarah to ulcerate, fester, abscess, suppurate.

barai *siput* - an edible saltwater shellfish, *Lingular spp.*

barak (*D*) **1** hut; → BÉDÉNG. **2** barracks. **3** quarantine.

membarak to quarantine.

barakah and **barakat** → BERKAT.

barakatuh (*A*) *wa* - and (God's) blessing.

barakuda (*E*) great barracuda, *Sphyraena barracuda.*

baran I low swampy undergrowth, bog. *babi* - wild pig living in such undergrowth.

baran II hot-/quick-tempered. *panas* - extremely hot-tempered.

baran III acorn.

barang I 1 thing, object, article; luggage, baggage; goods, property, commodities, -ware. **2** (*euph*) thing, anything unmentionable, such as drugs, genitals, etc. - *akar* (*Med*) immovables. - *anyaman* wickerwork. - *baik akar atau terlepas* movables as well as immovables. - *angkutan* freight goods. - *antaran* parcels. - *antik* antiquities. - *asal* property brought by husband and wife to a marriage. - *asal impor* imported goods. - *awét* durables. - *bacaan* reading material. - *bahan/baku* raw material. - *baru* s.t. new, a novelty, a new feature. *Film tentang pasangan lelaki-perempuan yang melarikan diri karena dikejar penjahat, atau polisi, bukanlah - baru.* A film about a couple running away pursued by criminals or the police is nothing new. - *bawaan* hand luggage. – *bawaan milik pribadi* personal effects. – *bébas* things that are freely available. – *bekas* secondhand goods. – *bergerak* movables, movable property, chattel. – *berharga* valuable articles. – *berkat* honestly obtained objects. – *besi* hardware. – *buatan ...* goods made in ... – *buatan Jepang* Japanese-made goods. – *bukti* exhibit (evidence in a Court), (documentary) evidence (in a lawsuit). – *bulk* bulk cargo. – *cair* liquids. – *campuran* general cargo. – *cangkingan* hand luggage. – *cepat* express goods. – *cétakan* printed matter. – *curah* bulk goods. – *curian* stolen goods. – *dagangan* merchandise. –.– *dalam pelayaran* goods in transit. – *ékspor* export article. – *ékstraktif* extractives. – *gadai* security, guarantee, pledge. – *galian* minerals. – *ganti* substitutes. – *gasakan* stolen goods. – *gawan* (*Jv*) property brought by husband and wife to a marriage. – *gelap* illegal/contraband goods. – *gerak* movable goods. – *gerobakan* wagon-/truck-/car-load. – *gono-gini/guna-kaya* (*Jv*) property jointly acquired during marriage. – *hantaran* parcels. – *haram* controlled substance, i.e., narcotics. – *hasil industri* industrial product. – *hutan* forest produce/products. – *ikutan* minor point. – *impor* import articles/goods, imports. – *jadi* finished goods/products, ready-made goods. – *jaminan* gage, security, collateral. – *kawasan* bonded goods. – *kebutuhan sehari-hari* daily needs. – *kelebihan* surplus goods. – *kelontong* soft goods, small wares. – *kemas-kemas* knickknacks. –.– *keperluan dapur* kitchen utensils. – *keperluan perang* war material. – *keperluan rumahtangga* household effects/utensils. –.– *keperluan selama/dalam perjalanan* a) wearing apparel. b) traveling requisites. – *kerajinan* handicrafts. – *kesenian* art object. – *kiriman* parcel, freight. – *kodian* cheap goods. – *komisi* goods on a commission basis. – *konsumsi* articles of consumption, consumer goods. – *kumanga/kumango* sundries, small wares. – *kuno* antiquities. – *larangan* contraband. – *lepas* bulk goods. – *loakan* junk, wares. –.– *logam* metal wares. – *luks* luxury items. – *makanan* foodstuffs. – *mati* inanimate object. –.– *meledak* explosives. – *mentah* raw material. – *méwah* luxury items. – *mindringan* goods sold on an installment plan. – *modal* capital goods. – *muatan* cargo, freight. – *nadirat* curio, bric-a-brac. – *niaga* commodities. – *obral* distress merchandize. – *olahan* manufactured goods. –.– *pakai habis* expendable supplies. – *palén* small wares/goods. – *pecah-belah/pecahan* earthenware, crockery, pottery. – *pengganti* substitute. –.– *penumpang* passengers goods. – *perbekalan* provisions. – *perdagangan* merchandise. – *perhiasan* jewelry items. – *perniagaan* merchandise. – *persediaan* inventory. – *pindahan* personal effects. – *potongan* (general) cargo. – *pribadi* personal effects. – *primér* primary goods. – *purbakala* antiquities. – *pusaka* heirloom. – *rampokan* loot, booty. – *rombéngan/romal* (*D infr*) rummage, rags, junk. – *ruah* bulk goods. – *sekali pakai* expendables. – *selundupan* contraband/smuggled goods. – *seni* art object. – *sepélé* trivia, bagatelles. – *serbuan* spoils of war. – *setengah jadi* semi-finished product. – *sitaan* confiscated articles/goods. – *sudah* manufactured articles, finished products. – *tahan lama* durable goods. – *tahanan* captured goods. – *tidak/tak bergerak* immovables, immovable property, fixtures. – *tak bertuan* (*usu* in ports/warehouses) unowned property, property having no owner, unclaimed goods. – *tambang* minerals. – *tanah* earthenware, pottery. – *tangkapan* confiscated goods. –.– *temuan* lost property. – *ténténgan* hand luggage. – *tenun* textiles. – *terlarang* contraband goods. – *ternama* specialty goods. – *tetap* real estate, immovable goods. –.– *timpah(an)* (*coq*) pilfered/stolen goods. – *tiruan* imitation, counterfeit article. – *umum* general cargo. – *yang akan segera habis dimakan/dipakai* expendables. – *yang dikenakan béa* dutiable goods. –.– *yang diperdagangkan* tradables. –.– *yang memabukkan* intoxicants. –.– *yang tahan lama* durable goods. –.– *yang tak dapat dipakai lagi* obsolete goods. – *yang tak tahan lama pemakaiannya* perishable goods, perishables. – *yang tidak bertuan* unowned goods. – *yang tidak dikuasai* unclaimed goods.

barang II 1 (+ interrogative and certain other words) any, ever. – *apa* no matter what. – *bagaimana* no matter how. – *bila* no matter when. – *di/ke mana* no matter where. – *kala* whenever. – *orang* whoever. – *sebentar* for a short time, no matter how long. *Biasanya Opa Simon selalu mampir – sebentar untuk menikmati segelas air jeruk segar dan sepiring kecil kué apel buatan kak Léni.* Usually grandpa Simon dropped in for a short while to enjoy a glass of fresh lemonade and a small plate of apple tart made by sister Leni. – *sesuatu* anything. – *siapa* no matter who, who(so)ever. – *siapa tidak menurutinya akan dihukum.* Whoever does not obey it will be punished. **2** (+ number) about. – *empat hari* about four days. *beras – seliter dua liter* about one or two liters of rice. – *se ... pun* (not) even a little bit. *tidak mempunyai pengalaman – sedikit pun* not to have the slightest experience. – *sejenak* just a moment. – *sementara saja* brief, short-lived. *Kasih sayang ibunya hanyalah – sementara saja.* Mother's pity was brief. – *sekali* once. – *tentu* of course, undoubtedly, without doubt, certainly, surely. – *tentu dia tahu.* Of course he knows. *Sudah – tentu ada sorga.* There's a paradise, that's for sure.

barang-barang ordinary, any old. *bukan ~ orang* no ordinary man.

se(m)barang(an) arbitrary, at one's own discretion, as one pleases, at random, for whatever reason. *Pejalan kaki yang menyeberang sembarangan dikenakan sanksi.* Pedestrians who cross at will are subject to sanctions. *Buang ludah sembarangan di Singapura kena denda 400 dolar Singapura.* Spitting for whatever reason in Singapore is fined S\$ 400.

barangan → WARANGAN.

barangkali perhaps, maybe, probably; → MUNGKIN, BOLÉH *jadi*. *Pén saya tidak ada di sini, – adik saya telah mengambilnya tadi.* My pen isn't here; maybe my kid brother took it.

barap (*ob*) **pembarap** (*Pal*) district head (under the *pesirah*).

baras (*A*) leprosy.

barase (*D*) **1** barrage. **2** jamming.

barat I 1 west. *Jawa –* [Ja-bar, Jabar] West Java. **3** – the three big western powers: The United States of America, England, and France. **2** western, Occidental; the West, the Occident. *orang –* Westerner. – *barat daya* west-southwest, WSW. – *barat laut* west-northwest, WNW. – *daya* southwest, SW. – *laut* northwest, NW. – *Tengah* the Midwest (in the U.S.A.). – *tepat* due west. – *utara laut* north-north-west, NNW.

membarat to go west(ward), westing.

membaratkan to westernize, make (an Oriental person or country) more Western in ideas and institutions, etc.

terbaratkan westernized. *Para pemimpinnya rélatif telah ~.* Their leaders are relatively westernized.

kebarat-baratan westernized, exaggeratedly western; to follow/copy western customs, behave like Westerners.

pembarat a westernized person.

pembaratan westernization.

barat II *sesat –* gone astray, confused.

barat-barat *ikan –* various species of leather-jacket, *Monacanthus chinensis, Chaetodermis penicilligerus*; filefish, *Alutera spp.*

baratisasi westernization.

barau-barau I *burung –* straw-headed bulbul, *Pycnonotus zeylanicus.*

barau-barau II *ikan –* a) barb, *Hampala macrolepidota*. b) leatherjacket, *Monacanthus spp.*

barau *pembarauan* erosion dam/dike.

baraya (*Jv*) family.

barbar (*D*) barbarian.

barbarisme (*D/E*) barbarism.

barbél (*E*) barbell.

barbir I (*D*) barber.

barbir II rosy barb, *Puntius conchonius.*

barbiturat (*D*) barbiturate.

barbur 1 to splash, plunge (in water). **2** to spend (money) recklessly. *orang –* a reckless spender.

bardi (*A*) papyrus (plant).

baréh (*M*) → BERAS.

barel (*E*) barrel [a container for petroleum containing 42 U.S. gallons (159 liters)]. – *minyak per hari* [BMPH] barrels of oil per day, BOPD.

Barélang the three Islands of Batam, Rempang and Galang.

bareng (*Jv*) together, with, along. *Mana ada orang yang mau nonton TV – sapi.* Where in the world are there people who want to watch TV with a cow. *Meréka kuliah –*. They went to school together.

bareng-bareng together, jointly. *acara mandi* ~ the ceremony of taking a bath together.

sebarengan ~ *dengan* coinciding with.

berbarengan together, at the same time, side by side, simultaneous. *Agama Hindu dan agama Budha berkembang* ~ *di Jawa*. Hinduism and Buddhism flourished side by side in Java. ~ *waktunya dengan* coinciding with, at the same time as.

membarengi 1 to accompany. *Dia tidak senang dibarengi*. He doesn't like to be accompanied. *Nyanyian bersama yang dibarengi dengan musik*. A choir accompanied by music. 2 to meet intentionally. *Saya akan* ~ *Siti di pasar*. I'm going to meet Siti at the marketplace.

membarengkan to synchronize.

pembarengan simultaneousness, synchronization.

perbarengan concurrence, conjunction, more than one at the same time. ~ *peraturan/tunggal* (*leg*) two or more offenses arising from the same action. ~ *perbuatan/jamak* (*leg*) various offenses for which one sentence is pronounced. ~ *tindak pidana* (*leg*) conjunction of punishable acts.

barep → BARAP.

barét I (*J*) scratch, abrasion, laceration.

terbarét scratched.

barét II (*D*) beret. *– hijau* a) (American) Green Berets. b) (Indonesian) beret worn by *Kostrad*. *– hitam* beret worn by the Army Cavalry and the Police Force Mobile Brigade. *– jingga* beret worn by the Air-Force Special Troops. *– kuning* beret worn by the Greater Jakarta College Students Regiment Corps. *– mérah* beret worn by *Kopassus*. *– oranye* beret worn by the Air Commandos. *– ungu* beret worn by the Marines.

berbarét to wear a beret.

pembarétan giving a beret (as a sign of membership in a special military force or having passed a certain military course).

bargas (*ob*) → BARKAS I.

bari I *papan –* movable hatch (on a ship's deck, leading to the hold).

bari II (*ob*) → BAHARI I, II.

bari III (*J/Jv*) while; → SEMBARI.

bari IV (*Pal*) *rumah –* an old house.

bari V (*IBT*) → GOTONG *royong*.

bari-bari fruit fly.

barid (*A*) messenger.

barikade (*D*) barricade.

membarikade to barricade, block.

barik-barik 1 spots or dots as on eggshells, lines or veins as in wood, marble, etc. 2 (*geol*) veinlet.

berbarik-barik veined, lined, banded, spotted.

baring I lie down.

berbaring to lie down *Dia masuk ke kamar lalu* ~ *di atas tempat tidur karena terlalu lelah*. He entered the room and then lay down on the bed because he was very tired.

membaringi to lie down on. *Dingin ambin beton yang dibaringinya*. The cement cot he lay down on was cold.

membaringkan to lay/put s.t. down. *Jenazahnya dibaringkan di ...* His (mortal) were laid to rest at ... *Mariani* ~ *bayinya*. Mariani laid her child down. ~ *diri* to stretch out.

terbaring 1 stretched out, sprawled. *Sesudah dilanggar mobil ia jatuh* ~ *di jalan*. After he was hit by a car he fell sprawling into the street. 2 to lie in state. *Jenazah masih* ~ *di kamar mayat*. The corpse was still lying in state in the morgue.

kebaringan (*infr*) bed.

pembaringan and **perbaringan** place on which to recline/lie down. ~ *raja* royal couch.

baring II (*E*) bearing.

membaring to take a bearing on. *Kita* ~ *matahari*. We are taking a bearing on the sun.

baringan 1 bearings. *mengambil* ~ to take one's bearings. 2 sextant.

baris I → GARIS. 1 row (of men/plants/books), chain (of hills). 2 line, stroke. *– baru* a new line, alinea. *– kembar* dash, hyphen. 3 rank, file. 4 vowel-point (in Arabic writing) which represents a short vowel and is followed by a vowel symbol to make them long. 5 (*mil*) drill. *sudah –nya begitu* that's his/her fate. *– di atas* sign for

the vowel a. *– di bawah* sign for the vowels e or i. *– di hadapan* sign for the vowels o or u. *– bujur* front-to-back line. *– kembar* hyphen, dash. *– kepala* running title. *– lintang* left-to-right (right-to-left) line. *– mati* symbol meaning that the consonant is not followed by a vowel. *– pejal* tight line (in printing). *– sesak* full line (in printing).

sebaris ~ *dengan* abreast of.

berbaris 1 in rows, in formation (of troops). 2 (= **berbaris-baris**) to drill, march, line up. 3 with a line/stroke; to provide with a line/stroke.

baris-berbaris marches and parades.

berbaris-baris lined up, in a line.

membaris 1 to drill. 2 to form a row/line.

membariskan 1 to put in a row, line up, draw up (soldiers). 2 to drill/march (soldiers, etc.).

barisan 1 row, line. 2 formation, rank, file, troops, forces, column. 3 front. ~ *baju biru* (Jakarta) firefighters. ~ *belakang* a) (in sports) the backs. b) rearguard. c) home front. ~ *berkuda* cavalry. ~ *depan* a) advance guard, vanguard. b) forefront. ~ *Drumband* Drum and Bugle Corps. ~ *kehormatan* honor guard. ~ *mérah* Communist troops. ~ *meriam* artillery. ~ *meriam yang bermesin* mechanized artillery. ~ *musik* marching band. ~ *Nasional* National Front. ~ *pemadam kebakaran* firemen, firefighters. ~ *pengawal* guards, escort. ~ *Sakit Hati* (*joc*) the "Sick-at-Heart Brigade," name given at various times to a number of dissident movements, including the nationalist units which refused to go along with the terms of the independence agreement with the Dutch. ~ *semut* column of ants. ~ *tiang* colonnade.

baris II (*Bal*) k.o. male war dance.

barit I (*A ob*) → BARID.

barit II (*E*) barite.

bariton (*D/E*) bariton.

barium (*D/E*) barium.

barkas I (*D*) launch, longboat.

barkas II → BERKAS.

barkat → BERKAT.

barli (*E*) barley, *Hordeum vulgare*.

barok (*D/E*) baroque.

barokah → BERKAT.

barométer (*D/E*) barometer.

baron (*D/E*) baron.

barong I (*Tag*) *– Tagalog* an embroidered Philippine shirt for men.

barong II *udang –* spiny-lobster tails.

barong III 1 a Balinese dance. 2 a mythological animal in this dance.

barongan a marine animal.

barongsai 1 male lion. 2 lion-shaped puppet carried by s.o. inside it during Chinese New Year celebrations.

baros (*Jv*) k.o. magnolia, *Magnolia blumei, Garcinia spp.*

barso (*Med*) honey, darling.

barter (*E*) barter.

membarter(kan) ~ *dengan* to barter/exchange for.

baru I → BAHARU. 1 fresh, new, newly laid (eggs), green (vegetables). *telor –* newly laid eggs. *lada yang –* fresh pepper. 2 recent, fresh, late, new. *mobil yang –* a new(-model) car. *tahun –* new year. *mendapat angin –* a) to sail before the wind. b) to be in luck. *dengan tenaga –* with fresh personnel, with a fresh staff. *pengantén –* newlyweds. *orang –* a) newcomer. b) apprentice, new recruit, novice, greenhorn. 3 modern, contemporary, new, recent. *kesusasteraan – Indonésia* modern Indonesian literature. *Orde –* the New Order (after September 1965). 4 just, just now, a moment ago. *Teman saya – datang*. My friend just arrived. *negara yang – merdéka* a recently independent country. *– ... belum ...* just ... so far, we haven't gotten to ... yet. *Ini – nasinya saja, belum lauk-pauknya*. This is just the rice, we haven't gotten to the other dishes yet. *– saja* to have just (done s.t.), no sooner. *"Kita – saja berkenalan, hati sudah bersua*. We just met e.o. and our hearts met. 5 only/not until, not till, not before, as recent as. *dan – dalam tahun tujuh puluhan ...* and not until the seventies *...Jam dua – dia datang*. He didn't arrive until two o'clock. It was two o'clock before he arrived. 6 only, just (as of now, the number is expected to increase); *cp* CUMA,

HANYA. *Anaknya sudah berapa orang? – satu.* How many children does he have now? *Only/Just one (so far). Sudah berapa lama Anda di sini? – dua minggu.* How long have you been here? Only/Just two weeks (so far).

baru-baru ~ *ini* the other day, lately, recently.

sebaru as new as.

membaru to appear/make one's appearance/come out again. *perubahan politik yang bersifat* ~ modernizing political change.

mem(per)barui 1 to renovate, renew, repair, refurbish, modernize. *bisa/dapat diperbarui* renewable. *sumber alam yang bisa diperbarui* renewable natural resources. *tidak dapat diperbarui* nonrenewable. **2** to roll over (debts). **3** to reform.

membarukan to renovate, modernize.

terbaru newest, most recent.

terbarui renewable. *tidak* ~ nonrenewable.

terbarukan renewable. *sumber énérgi yang* ~ renewable energy resources. *tidak* ~ nonrenewable.

kebaruan 1 novelty, innovation. **2** newness, being new.

pembaru reformer, renewer, renovator. *kaum* ~ reformers, renewers.

pembaruan renewal, renovation, reform, modernization, updating. ~ *data tiap dua sampai tiga tahun* updating the data every two to three years. ~ *kebijaksanaan dan struktur* policy and structural reform. ~ *keterampilan dan téknis* skill and technical reform. ~ *syarat obligasi* (*fin*) lock-up.

perbaruan extension, renewal.

baru II k.o. hibiscus tree, *Hibiscus tiliaceus. – cina* wormwood, mugwort, *Artemisia vulgaris. – laut* rosewood, *Thespesia populnea.*

barua (*Hind Mal*) pimp, madam.

barubi (*Old Jv*) plant.

baruga → BALAI *pertemuan.*

baruh 1 (*di –*) under, beneath. **2** (*M*) low-lying land, lowlands.

Baruna (*Skr*) Neptune.

barunawati (*Skr neo*) **1** (Indonesian) seaman's wife. **2** name of the Association of the Wives of Employees under the jurisdiction of the Directorate General for Sea Communications.

barung the smallest unit in the Pramuka Boy Scout Movement consisting of *siaga*s; maximum number of members = 10.

barung-barung 1 shelter, shack, platform. **2** booth, stall; → WARUNG.

Barus a place in Tapanuli, on Sumatra's west coast. *kapur –* camphor (from Barus), mothball.

barusan (*J*) – a short time ago, not long ago, just. *– berapa hari* a few days ago. *Saya – dari Bali.* I just got back from Bali.

barut I 1 bandage, dressing. **2** diaper. *tali – (Mal)* a) bandage. b) belly belt, girdle. **3** accomplice, stooge. *– gantung/keréta* navel bandage. *– keréta* swaddling clothes. *– panjang* k.o. girdle (used by women who have just given birth).

berbarut with a bandage, etc.

membarut 1 to dress, bandage. **2** to diaper.

membarutkan to wrap s.t. (around).

pembarut bandage, dressing.

pembarutan bandaging, dressing.

barut II membarut 1 to grease, smear, oil. **2** to polish, clean. **3** to caress, fondle.

membarut-barut to caress, fondle.

terbarut oiled, greased.

barut III (*Jv*) and **barutan** scratch, graze.

terbarut [and **kebarut-barut** (*coq*)] scratched, grazed.

barzakh (*A*) *alam –* a) period between death and judgment. b) Hell, Hades, realm of the dead.

barzanji (*A*) k.o. litany, hymn of praise (on the birthday of the Prophet Muhammad). *membaca –* to read from the life of the Prophet.

bas I (*D*) master, boss, foreman, head (of a company).

bas II (*D*) **1** (the instrument) contrabass, double bass. **2** (singer) bass. *– betot* bass fiddle.

bas III (*Mal*) (motor)bus; → BIS, BUS.

bas IV (in acronyms) → BASIS.

basa I (*D*) (chemical) base, i.e., a substance (e.g., an alkali) capable of combining with an acid to form a salt. *berubah dari – ke asam* to change from a base into an acid.

kebasaan alkalinity.

basa II (*Skr*) **1** language. **2** good manners; → BAHASA II. *– basi* a) etiquette, manners, conventional behavior. b) to chit-chat, exchange pleasantries. **berbasa-basi** to observe the conventional pleasantries. *Setelah dipersilahkan masuk dan ~ mohon maaf mengganggu tuan rumah, tamu yang tidak diundang itu menjelaskan maksud kedatangannya.* After being invited in and excusing himself for disturbing his host, the uninvited guest explained the purpose of his visit.

membasai and **memperbasakan** to entertain, treat in friendly way.

perbasaan pleasantries, compliments, conventionalities.

basah 1 wet, soaked. *habis –* soaking/sopping wet. **2** moist, damp, soggy. *Hawanya –.* The weather is damp. *kué –* soft sweetmeat/cake (*usu* steamed or boiled); *opp* KUÉ *kering.* **3** fresh (not dried). *daging/ikan –* fresh meat/fish. **4** profitable, lucrative, remunerative, moneymaking. *dokter –* a highly paid physician. *fakultas –* well-paid school/department. *Fakultas ékonomi dan téknik fakultas –.* The economics and engineering schools are well-paid schools. *jabatan –* a moneymaking office. *pekerjaan –* a lucrative job; *opp* PEKERJAAN *kering. tempat –* a lucrative position. *tertangkap –* caught red-handed/in the act. *– diri* in a sweat when a fever breaks. *– kerongkongan* to have lots of luck, live well. *– kuyup* soaking wet. **membasahkuyup** and **membasahkuyupkan** to soak, make s.t. soaking wet. *Air hujan ~ sepatu dan kaki celana hingga ke lutut.* The rainwater soaked his shoes and pants legs up to the knees. *– lecap* soaking wet. *– léléh* deliquescent. **kebasah-léléhan** deliquescence. *– léncong/lencun(g)* soaking wet.

sebasah as wet as.

berbasah(-basah) 1 very wet, drenched, soaking wet. **2** to get soaked (in the rain, etc.).

membasah to be(come) wet/damp.

membasahi 1 to wet, moisten, dampen. *Air matanya keluar ~ pipinya.* His tears dampened his cheeks. *~ diri* to be wringing wet. **2** to refresh, make fresh again, freshen up.

membasahkan to wet, moisten, dampen. *Hujan yang turun ~ jemuran itu.* The falling rain wet the clothes drying on the line.

terbasah the most lucrative, the wettest.

basahan 1 *bahasa ~* (*Mal*) colloquial language. *kain ~* a) s.t. that is used daily, everyday/work clothes. b) s.t. that is used while bathing, bathing suit, bath towel (wrapped around the body while bathing). **2** k.o. *Jv* traditional long wedding dress.

kebasahan 1 to get soaked. *Bajunya ~ embun malam.* His shirt got soaked from the evening dew. **2** dampness, moistness.

pembasah wetter.

pembasahan wetting, dampening, moistening.

basal I dropsy, "wet" beriberi, edema. *– api* erysipelas.

basal II (*D*) basalt.

basamo → PULANG *basamo.*

basantara (*infr*) lingua franca.

basapraja (*infr*) dialect.

basar (*D*) bazaar.

basau (*ob*) hard (of cooked potatoes or fruit, etc.).

basekat → BASKAT.

basi I 1 spoiled, stale, rotten. *Makanan ini sudah –.* This food is stale. *Telor rebus itu –.* That boiled egg is rotten. **2** out-of-date, not up-to-date. *Mode ini –.* This fashion is out-of-date. *Analisis cerita ini baik tetapi –.* This news analysis is good but not up-to-date. **3** ineffective (of medicine/a charm, etc.). **4** smelly.

membasikan to allow to turn bad/stale.

basi II 1 extra money, overtime. **2** reserves. **3** commission, percentage. **4** discount (for a large purchase).

membasi(kan) to provide such a discount or additional money.

basi III (*Port*) dish, soup tureen.

basi IV → BASA-BASI.

basikal (*E Mal*) bicycle; → KERÉTA *angin,* SEPÉDA, PIT.

berbasikal to ride a bike, go by bike.

basil (*D*) bacillus, germ.

basilér (*E*) bacillary; → DISÉNTERI *basilér.*

basilika (*E*) basilica.

basir (*A*) *Al.–* The All-Seeing (Allah).

basis (*D*) **1** basis, principle; → ASAS, DASAR. **2** base. *sistém – data* database system.

berbasis based. *perusahaan yang ~ di Hong Kong* a company based in Hong Kong. *téknologi ~ luas* a broad-based technology.

berbasiskan to have ... as a base, be based on. *dengan ~ kultural* culturally based.

basit (*A*) 1 *Al.* – The All-Embracing (Allah); → *yang* MAHAMURAH. 2 irreducible, indivisible.

Bask (*D*) Basque. *orang-orang* – the Basques.

baskara (*Skr lit*) the sun.

baskat (*E*) double-breasted coat.

baskét (*D/E*) basket. *bola* – basketball. *main bola* – to play basketball.

baskom (*D*) washbasin. *pedagang/penjual kué* – female street vendor who has a dual function, during the day she sells sweets and during the evening she sells her body.

basmallah → BISMILLAH.

basmi destroy.

membasmi 1 to exterminate, eliminate, destroy. *~ gerombolan bersenjata* to eliminate armed gangs. 2 to eradicate, wipe out, abolish, fight against. *Pemerintah berusaha keras ~ buta huruf.* The government is doing everything possible to wipe out illiteracy. *~ malaria* to eradicate malaria. *~ kejahatan* to wipe out crime. 3 to curb, quell, check, suppress.

terbasmi 1 eliminated, exterminated, destroyed. 2 eradicated, wiped out.

pembasmi eradicator, -cide, etc. *~ hama* pesticides. *~ kuman* germicides. *~ serangga* a) insecticide. b) exterminator.

pembasmian 1 annihilation, extermination. *~ serangga itu harus dilakukan secara bertahap.* The extermination of insects has to be done gradually. 2 liquidation, eradication, elimination, wiping out. *~ ketidakadilan sosial* the eradication of social injustice. *~ korupsi* the elimination of corruption.

baso → BAKSO.

basoka → BAZOKA.

basta (*D*) No more! enough!

bastar (*D*) bastard, hybrid.

membastar to interbreed.

bastaran crossbred, of mixed descent.

pembastaran 1 bastardization. 2 cross-breeding.

basuh washing, wash, scrub. *seperti air – tangan* lots of it is available. *- kapur* lime scrub. **pembasuhkapuran** lime treatment. *- lantai* ceremony at 40th day after birth.

membasuh to wash, clean with water.

membasuhi to wash away (one's sins),

basuhan s.t. that is washed.

pembasuh 1 washer, washing; laundress, washer-woman. *mesin ~ pakaian* washing machine. 2 detergent. *~ balai* legal costs. *~ dusun* (*Pal ob*) slaughter of a buffalo (to cleanse a village). *~ méja* legal costs. *~ mulut* dessert or sweets served to guests. *~ tangan* k.o. tip given to s.o. who does a job. 3 (*petro*) scrubber.

pembasuhan 1 washing, cleaning. 2 (*petro*) scrubbing.

basuk k.o. tree with yellowish timber.

basuki (*Jv*) prosperous. *kelompok masyarakat yang* – a prosperous community group.

basung I a cork-like root (e.g., from *Alstonia pneumatophora*). *bual - empty talk, rot. kayu* – touchwood.

basung II (*ob*) sebasung two dozen.

basung III cylindrical leaf wrapper (into which sago, etc. is placed).

basung IV membasung to kick (a ball) high.

basungan a kick upward (of a ball).

basut spout (of water).

berbasut and **membasut** to spout, gush (of water).

Basyah and **Basyaw** (*Pers*) Pasha.

basyir (*A cla*) herald.

bat (in acronyms) → BATALYON.

bata 1 *batu* – brick, tile. 2 turf, sod (of grass), briquette. *- genting* cinder block.

bataan s.t. that has the shape of a brick. *garam ~* salt in briquettes.

bata-bata (ter)bata-bata and **kebata-bataan** hesitating, wavering, vacillating; in doubt, ambivalent.

batagak gala (*M*) ceremony to uphold adat title.

batagor [bakso tahu goréng] meatballs and fried tofu in noodle soup.

batai various species of trees: black seed, *Albizzia falcata, Paraserianthes spp., Cassia timorensis, Derris dalbergioides*. *- laut* k.o. tree with yellow flowers, yellow flame, *Peltophorum ferrugineum*.

Batak I Batak. *orang* – a Batak (person).

ke-Batakan Batak ethnic background, Batakness.

batak II (*cla*) nomad, vagabond.

membatak 1 to rob, extort. 2 to lead a nomadic life; to live from hand to mouth, have no settled job.

pembatak robber, extortionist.

batako k.o. mass-produced brick.

batal (*A*) 1 doesn't take place, fail, be fruitless, be unsuccessful. *Misi kesenian Bali – ke India.* The Balinese art mission failed to go to India. 2 (null and) void, not valid, invalid. *Puasa seseorang itu – jika ia menghisap rokok semasa berpuasa.* Fasting is not valid if a person smokes while fasting. *- demi hukum* legally null and void. *dinyatakan* – declared null and void. *- mutlak* null and void.

membatalkan [and **ngebatalin** (*J coq*)] 1 to cancel, abolish, call off. 2 to abort. *~ tinggal landas* (of an aircraft) to abort a take off. 3 (*leg*) to vacate, set aside, declare null and void, abrogate, annul. *Hukum yang tidak adil itu dibatalkan.* The unjust law was abrogated.

kebatalan cancellation, nullification.

pembatalan 1 abrogation, cancellation, revocation. *~ persetujuan* abrogation of an agreement. 2 abolition. 3 (*leg*) setting aside, vacating, annulment. *~ pembayaran* stop payment (on a check issued by a bank). *~ terhadap pengangkatan meréka sebagai guru dan tenaga administrasi* cancellation of their appointments as teachers and administrative employees. *~ tinggal landas* aborted take off.

batalion and **batalyon** (*D*) battalion. *- zéni konstruksi/tempur* engineer construction/combat battalion.

Batan → BADAN Tenaga Atom Nasional.

batang 1 tree(trunk), stick. *- pohon asam* a tamarind tree. *- pisang* banana trunk. 2 bar, shaft, handle, rod, spindle. *cokelat* – chocolate in bars. *- joran* fishing rod. *- sabun* bar of soap. 3 stem, stalk. *- padi* a) rice stalk. b) straw. 4 a long, cylindrical part of the body. *- léhér* the nape of the neck. 5 counter for long objects (such as cigarettes/pencils/sticks, etc.). *rokok dua* – two cigarettes. *se- pohon* a/one tree. 6 counter for rivers. *se- sungai* a/one river. 7 frame of a bicycle, etc. *Sepéda ini –nya masih kuat.* The frame of this bike is still strong. *memegang –* (*J*) to be(come) a bécak-driver. 8 (*ob*) corpse, carcass, carrion. 9 (*sl*) penis. *telah menjadi* – has died. *ada – cendawan tumbuh* if you try hard, you will succeed. *angkat –, keluar cacing gelang-gelang* to perform a useless job, because it has already been done by s.o. else. *di mana – terguling di situ cendawan tumbuh* a case is settled where it occurs. *kena – hidung* to be teased/insulted. *terkena pada ikan bersorak, terkena pada – masam* hoping to come across s.o. who brings luck. *membangkitkan – terendam* (*M*) to raise a sunken log, i.e., to revive, bring s.t. back from disaster. *- air* river. *- anakan* sapling. *- angkat* boom. *- api-api* matchstick. *- atas* scion (in grafting). *- ayun* boss rod. *- bahang bakar* fuel cell. *- bawah* rootstock (in grafting). *- berkelok* k.o. decorative plant, *Pedilanthus tithymaloides variegata*. *- bor* auger stem. *- bunga* (*bio*) scape. *- canai* lace beam. *- cerita* story line, plot. *- dacing* the arm of a portable balance/scale. *- dayung* oar handle. *- dermaga* derrick boom. *- desak* strut. *- éngkol* tie rod. *- hari* a) noon. b) river. *- hidung* the bridge of the nose. *tampak – hidungnya* to show up, appear. *Tak seorang pun bintang film tampak – hidungnya.* Not a single movie star showed up. *- isap* (*petro*) sucker rods. *- jangkar* anchor shank. *- jarak* ruler. *- kalam* pen. *- kawat* wire rod. *- kayu* tree trunk. *- kemudi* steering shaft. *- kendali* control rod. *- lengan* upper arm. *- muat(an)* cargo boom. *- nadi* aorta. *- otak* brain stem. *- palang* crossbeam. *- pegangan* handrail. *- pemuat* loading boom. *- pemuntir* connecting rod. *- pendesak* strut. *- pengaduk* stirring rod. *- pengatur* regulating rod. *- pengayuh* the handle of a paddle. *- penggerak* lever. *- pengungkit* crowbar. *- rambut* hair shaft. *- sepéda* bicycle frame. *- tarik* tie iron/rod. *- tawas* styptic pencil. *- tenggorok(an)* trachea. *- torak* tie rod. *- tubuh* a) the trunk of the body, torso. b) core, principal (part). *- tubuh Undang-*

Undang Dasar 1945 the principal part of the 1945 Constitution (excluding the preamble and amendments). – *uji* test piece. – *upaman* (*petro*) polished rod. – *zakar* shaft of the penis.

batang-batang (*vulg*) to be/go in a group of all males, go stag.

sebatang a, one (counter). ~ *pénsil* one pencil. *membeli rokok* ~.~ to buy cigarettes by the piece; → KÉTÉNGAN. ~ *kara/ karang/kacang* a) without any relatives. *Pada umumnya kaum lelaki yang merantau ke Malaysia tidak membawa keluarganya. Meréka pergi dulu* ~ *kara.* Men who travel to Malaysia generally don't take along their families. They go there first without their families. b) all alone in the world. ~ *tebu* s.t. used and thrown away.

berbatang to have a trunk/stem, etc.

berbatang-batang by the bar.

membatang 1 to resemble a tree trunk (of s.t. tall and narrow). **2** to be stiff, erect.

batangan 1 bar or boom across a river. **2** bar (of soap/chocolate, etc.). *sabun cuci* ~ laundry soap in bars. ~ *baja* hot-rolled steel coils. ~ *besi* billet, i.e., an unfinished bar of iron. **3** trunk. **4** bicycle frame. **5** ingot. *Tiga* ~ *emas bernilai Rp 37,5 juta lenyap.* Three gold ingots valued at 37.5 million rupiahs have disappeared. **6** (*BG*) boyfriend. **7** (*J*) the system of leasing a *bécak* for one whole day, from 6 a.m. to 9 p.m. **8** (*mod*) log. **9** by the piece (of cigarettes, etc.). **10** (*sl*) penis.

batara (*Skr*) **1** god, male deity. **2** title for Hindu gods and the rulers of Majapahit. – *Guru* the Upper God (mythology). – *Kala* in the Javanese belief system, a spirit who takes away s.o.'s soul so that he dies. – *Tunggal* (*S*) (among the Badui people of Banten) God; → ALLAH TA'ALA, MAHAESA, SUNDA WIWITAN.

batari (*Skr*) **1** goddess, female deity. **2** title for goddesses and grand duchesses.

batas 1 limit, boundary, line or point that cannot be passed, ceiling. *garis* – a) demarcation/dividing line. b) frontier, border. c) boundary. *garis* – *landas kontinén* seabed boundary. *Pertukaran informasi dan pandangan antara kedua délégasi telah meningkatkan pemahaman timbal-balik atas persoalan yang dihadapi masing-masing dalam penentuan garis* – *landas kontinén.* The exchange of information and opinions between the two delegations has increased mutual understanding of the problems faced by each of them in determining seabed boundaries. *sudut* – border corner. *tapa* – border, frontier. **2** limit, extent. *kekuasaannya tanpa* – his power/authority is unlimited. *Kesabaran seseorang mempunyai* –*nya.* A person's patience has its limits. – .– *berlakunya* extent (of legal provisions). **3** bund, bank separating *padi* plots; → PEMATANG. *Amat berdiri di atas* – *sambil melihat ayahnya menanam padi.* Amat stood on the dike watching his father planting paddy. – *air pasang tertinggi* high water mark. – *akhir* deadline. – *bawah* floor. – *gas minyak* [BGM] (*petro*) gas oil contact, GOC. – *jangka waktu* time limit. – *kata* word boundary. – *kebudayaan* cultural boundary. – *kecepatan* speed limit. – *kesalahan* margin of error. – *kota* city limits. – *krédit* credit ceiling, line of credit. – *luar* outer limit. – *luluh* yield point. – *Maksimum Pemberian Krédit* [BMPK] Legal Lending Limit. – *negara* state border. – *pangkal* bottom dead center. – *perairan* territorial waters. – *pikiran* limits of comprehension. – *pinjaman* lending limit. – *Tanggal Internasional* International Date Line. – *teratas* ceiling. – *terbit* deadline (for publication). – *tetap* fixed line. – *tinggi* ceiling (for aircraft). – *toleransi* limit of tolerance. *di luar* – *toleransi* beyond acceptable limits. – *ujung* top dead center. – *umur* age limit. – *utang* debt limit. – *waktu* time limit, deadline. – *waktu akhir* deadline; → TÉNGGANG *waktu.* – *waktu penuntutan* statute of limitations. – *waktu yang ditentukan* the established deadline.

sebatas 1 limited/restricted to. *tak* ~ *itu* not limited to that. *Kami nggak ada hubungan apa-apa. Hanya* ~ *sababat.* We have no relationship whatsoever. It's just limited to friendship. ~ *kulit* (only) skin deep. **2** within the limits of, to the point of, border on. ~ *gunjingan* in borders on malicious gossip. ~ *tugasnya* within the limits of his duties.

berbatas to have a boundary/limit, limited. *tak* ~ boundless, limitless. *Meréka tinggal bersebelahan hanya* ~ *témbok.* They are neighbors only separated by a wall.

berbataskan to have ... as a boundary/limit/border. *Républik Indonésia* ~ *berbagai laut.* The Republic of Indonesia is bounded by various seas.

membatas to divide, separate, keep apart.

membatasi [and **ngebatasin** (*J coq*)] **1** to limit, restrict. *Dokter* ~ *makanan saya.* The physician has restricted my diet. *asap yang* ~ *jarak pandang* smoke which restricted one's vision. **2** to limit, place a limit on. *Kami terpaksa* ~ *besarnya kelas itu.* We had to place a limit on the size of the class. ~ *diri* to control o.s.

mem(per)bataskan to limit, restrict.

terbatas limited, restricted, classified. *Kesohor namanya tidak* ~ *pagar kampung kelahirannya.* His fame was not limited to his place of birth. *Daya lihat mata manusia mémang* ~. Human vision is limited. *tidak* ~ unlimited. **keterbatasan** limitation, being limited. ~ *lahan* land limitations. *Negara pulau ini berhadapan dengan momok pertumbuhan penduduk dan* ~ *lahan.* This island nation is facing the bogy-man of population growth and limitations on land.

batasan 1 border, boundary. **2** definition, demarcation. *membuat* ~ to define. *Bagaimanakah membuat* ~ *"suksés"*? How to define "success"? ~ *disain* design limitation. **berbatasan** ~ *dengan* to border on, be adjacent to, adjoining. *Indonésia* ~ *dengan Malaysia dan Brunéi Darussalam di Kalimantan.* Indonesia borders on Malaysia and Brunei Darussalam in Kalimantan.

pembatas 1 s.o. or s.t. that limits or restricts, constraint, restrictive. **2** divider. ~ *jalan* road divider. ~ *tengah* median.

pembatasan limitation, restriction. ~ *diri* self-control. ~ *kawasan* area restriction. ~ *kelahiran* birth control. ~ *penggalian tanah* restrictions on digging down. ~ *senjata* arms limitation.

perbatasan border. *daérah* ~ border region.

batau → BAKTAU.

batél (*naut ob*) two-masted ship; → BATIL III.

baterai I (*D*) **1** (– *kering*) flashlight/dry-cell battery. *radio transistor yang lemah* –*nya* a transistor radio with weak batteries. **2** working by batteries. *lampu* – flashlight. – *yang bisa dicas/diisi ulang* a rechargeable battery.

baterai II (*D*) artillery battery.

bateré → BATERAI.

bathang → BATANG 8.

bathil → BATIL II.

bathin → BATIN I.

Bathlalhuriah Al Awal (*A*) The First Hero of Independence, i.e., one of the many titles conferred upon President Soekarno.

bati (*elec*) gain. – *daya* power gain.

sebati 1 united (by common interest or love). **2** built-in.

batig slot (*D col*) budget surplus, monies transferred from Indonesia to the Netherlands during the 19th Century.

batih (*Jv*) **1** one's household. **2** nuclear family. *Di negeri Sakura ini juga dikenal prinsip keluarga* – (*yang terdiri atas ayah-ibu-anak*). In Japan the principle of a family consisting of father, mother and child(ren) is also known.

batik I (*Jv*) batik, painted and patterned fabric/cloth. – *cap* hand-blocked batik made by using a *cap*/copper stamp, *usu* of low quality. – *kombinasi* combination of – *cap* and – *tulis*. – *printing* hand-blocked batik made by using a *cap*/copper stamp, *usu* of low quality. – *tulis/tradisional* hand-drawn batik made by using a *canting* (a copper vessel with a spouted nib), more expensive than – *cap*.

membatik to do batik work.

membatiki to batik, put a batik pattern onto.

membatikkan to turn s.t. into batik.

batikan batik work.

pembatik one who works on batik, batik producer.

pembatikan 1 batik work, ways and methods of making batik. **2** place where batik is made.

batik II (*M*) papaya; → BETIK II, KATÉS, PAPAYA, PEPAYA.

batil I (*Tam*) k.o. container/bowl made from a coconut shell/silver/ brass/copper, etc. – *azimat* bowl inscribed inside with Koranic verses (used as a medicine bowl). – *belanja* bowl for dowry and kitchen money. – *lauk* food container.

batil II (*A*) → BATAL. **kebatilan** iniquity.

batil III (= batél and batéla) (*naut ob*) two-masted ship (originally from Malabar or Zanzibar).

batin I (*A*) 1 inward (feelings); one's inner-self. *bantuan* – moral support. *membaca* – to read to o.s. *dalam* – inwardly, in one's heart. *Dalam* – *meréka ketawa*. Inwardly, they laughed. *menceritakan apa yang terasa dalam* – to speak (one's mind) freely. 2 the inner/spiritual self; the secret place where man and "God" meet (its instrument is the *rasa*). *kekuatan* – spiritual/inner strength. *pertalian* – invisible ties. 3 hidden, secret, real (meaning); (the) deeper (sense of what one is reading). *Kalau tak dapat dengan lahir dengan* –. If it does not go well openly, well then (do it) in secret. *mohon maaf lahir dan* – to apologize in every way. *rupanya/pada lahirnya ... tetapi -nya ...* apparently/seemingly ... but in reality/fact ... *mengaku bersaudara lahir dan* – to want to be close friends (through thick and thin). *Sukar mengetahui/mengukur* – *seseorang*. It is difficult to figure out s.o. else's innermost feelings. 4 mental; moral. 5 mystical (power). 6 esoteric, mysterious, arcane. 7 psychic, medium. *ilmu* – mysticism. *kawin* – married in secret (not in front of the *penghulu kawin*).

   berbatin and **membatin** [and **ngebatin** (*coq*)] to talk/read silently to o.s.

   membatinkan to hide, conceal.

   kebatinan 1 the practice of contemporary Javanese mysticism as it appears in the *aliran kebatinan*; parallel to the five recognized religions: Islam, Roman Catholicism, Protestantism, Hinduism and Buddhism; → **PANCA** *agama*. 2 supernatural/inner powers, mysticism. 3 the essence of the inner man, spirituality. *ilmu ~* (theosophical) philosophy. 4 Javanese science. 5 the essence of Javaneseness.

   pembatinan internalization.

batin II 1 = *penghulu adat*, adat chief. 2 village head (in Jambi, Lampung, Palembang, the Riau Archipelago, etc.). 3 head of a *kuria*/district in Tapanuli. 4 head of a proto-Malay tribe in Malacca (Western Malaysia).

batiniah (*A*) 1 spiritual. *kekuatan* – spiritual strength. 2 inner, internal. *kepuasan* – inner satisfaction.

batiniyah → BATINIAH.

batir-batir gold sheath/loop through which a silver wire passes to fasten a kris scabbard to one's belt.

batis (*D*) batiste, a fine, sheer fabric made from any of various fibers.

batita [(*di*) bawah tiga tahun] under the age of three years; → *cp* BALITA.

batkép → BADKUIP.

batok (*J/Jv*) 1 coconut shell. 2 measurement for rice = 4 *gantangs*. *arang* – coal from coconut shells. – *kepala* skull; → TENGKORAK.

Batola [(Kabupatén) Barito Kuala] Barito Kuala Regency.

batu I 1 (natural) stone; *cp* BATA; rock, boulder; → BEBATUAN. 2 jewels (of timepiece). 3 flint (for striking a light on a cigarette lighter). 4 flashlight battery. *lampu séntér dua* – a flashlight with two batteries. 5 (chess/drafts) piece, man, any of the pieces used in playing those games. 6 classifier for teeth. *se-* *gigi* one tooth. *gigi dua* – two teeth. 7 hard attitude, like a stone. *kepala* – stubborn, obstinate, headstrong. 8 renal/urinary calculus, kidney stone. *alat pemecah* – *ginjal* nephrolithotripter. *alat pemecah* – *ginjal* ultrasonic *léwat kulit* percutaneous ultrasonic lithotripter. 9 (*sl*) kilogram of marijuana, key. *air* – ice. *anak* – (short for *anak* – *tulis*) slate pencil. *arang* – coal. *damar* – hard resin. *gula* – rock candy. *hujan* – hail. *rumah* – brick house. *tukang* – bricklayer. *kena/ketemu -nya* (*J*) a) found one's match. b) serves (s.o.) right. *Itu baru kena -nya!* That hits the nail right on the head! – *bulat tak bersanding* a brave man fears nobody. *bak* – *masuk lubang* to disappear. *hujan* – *emas di negeri orang hujan* – *di negeri sendiri, baik juga di negeri sendiri* east, west, home's best; be it ever so humble there's no place like home. – *hitam tak bersanding* to be deceptive in appearance. *seperti* – *jatuh ke lubuk* vanished into thin air; spirited away. *lémpar(kan)* – *sembunyi(kan) tangan* and *melémpar* – *sembunyi tangan* not willing to admit that one has committed an act (or, a crime). *mencampakkan* – *keluar* all lay goods on a willing horse. *mengungkit* – *di bencah* to carry out a Sisyphean task.

patah – *hatinya* his desire to finish the job, etc. that he has undertaken has completely disappeared. *seperti* – *jatuh ke lubuk* refers to s.o. who has left his *kampung* and never comes back again. – *air* river stone, river boulder. – *ajuk* stone/lead on fishing line. – *akik* agate. – *akik lumut* mossy agate. – *alam* natural stone. – *ali* stone for a sling. – *alkali* alkali rock. – *ambar* amber. – *anggur* tartar. – *anting* a) pendulum (of a clock). b) plummet. c) man hanging over the side to balance a racing canoe. – *api* a) firestone (formerly, flint or iron pyrites used for striking fire), b) flint (in cigarette lighter). c) firebrand, instigator, mischief-maker. – *apung* pumice. – *arang* coal; → BATUBARA. – *asah(an)* whetstone, grindstone. – *asas* foundation stone. *meletakkan* – *asas* to lay a foundation stone. – *badar* → BADAR v. – *baji* apex stone. – *bandul* plumb bob. – *bara* → BATUBARA. – *basurék* (*M*) inscribed stone. – *bata* → BATA. – *batan* various types of rocks and stones. – *baterai* small battery (for a flashlight/cell phone, etc.). – *beku* igneous rock. – *belanda* a) crystal. b) imitation diamond. – *berani* magnet. – *bersurat/bertulis* inscribed stone, stone tablet; → PRASASTI. – *besi* granite, ironstone. – *bintang* meteoric rock. – *bongkah* boulder. – *bongpai* (*C J*) Chinese gravestone/tombstone. – *buangan* refuse stone, gangue. – *bulan* moonstone. – *bulat* cobblestone. – *cadas* rocks. – *canai* whetstone, grindstone. – *catur* chessman. – *cermin* mica. – *cétak beton* conblock. – *cincin* semiprecious jewel. – *dacing* weights (of a *dacing*). – *dapur* hearthstone. – *darah* hematite. – *dasar* a) foundation stone. b) bedrock. – *delima* ruby, garnet. – *dolomit* dolomite. – *duga* sounding lead. – *empedu* gallstone. – *endapan* sedimentary rock. – *firus* turquoise. – *fosfat* phosphate rock. – *gamping* limestone. – *geliga* → GULIGA. – *genténg* roof tiles. – *gérétan* flint. – *gerinda* whetstone, grindstone, abrasive. – *giling* slab for grinding spices, millstone. – *ginjal* kidney stone. – *giok* jade. – *gosok* rubbing stone. – *gragal* (*Jv*) gravel [larger than *k(e)rikil*)]. – *guliga* → GELIGA. – *gurinda* whetstone, grindstone. – *hampar* flagstone. – *hias* facing stone. – *hidup* a) stones that are said to move (on sacred graves). b) k.o. curative/healing stones. c) megalith. – *hijau* serpentine. – *hijau daun* tourmaline. – *hijau laut* aquamarine. – *inti* core. – *jala* rocks for weighing down a net. – *jam* jewels (of a timepiece). – *jamhar* inferior diamonds. – *jemala* skull, cranium. – *kaca* obsidian. – *kail* sinker/lead on fishing line. – *kali* river stone. *membatu kali* to remain silent. – *kambang* pumice. – *kampak* nephrite. – *kantong/kandung kemih/kencing* kidney stone, renal/urinary calculus. – *kapur* limestone. – *karang* coral. – *karang bulan* moonstone. – *karang lingkaran* atoll. – *kawi* a) bituminous coal. b) lignite, brown coal. c) brown coal, manganese. – *kecubung* semiprecious stone, amethyst. – *kelikir* gravel. – *kendan* obsidian. – *kepala* skull, cranium; → BATOK *kepala*. – *kerikil* gravel. – *kétél* boiler scale. – *ketipé* (roof)tile fragments. – *kilang* millstone. – *kilir* grindstone. – *kisaran* millstone. – *kolar* (*J*) a) coral rock. b) pebbles, gravel. – *krakal* (*Jv*) gravel [larger than – *k(e)rikil*]. – *kubur(an)* gravestone, tombstone. – *kulansing* granite. – *kumala* jade. – *lada* gravel. – *ladung* lead, plummet/sinker on a fishing rod. – *laga* green snail, *Turbo marmoratus*. – *lanau* siltstone. – *las* emery. – *léi* (*D*) slate. – *lémpéngan* flagstone. – *lempung* clay stone. – *lengan* biceps muscle. – *loncatan* a) stepping-stone (used to step on, as in crossing a stream/soft turf, etc.). b) springboard, stepping-stone, s.t. used to better one's position or situation/attack the enemy, etc. – *lumut* jade green. – *marmar* marble. – *melintang* stumbling block, obstacle. – *mérah* brick, laterite. – *mésan/misan* tombstone, gravestone. – *minyak* tombstone. – *mulia* precious stone. – *nikmat* magic stone. – *nilam* sapphire. – *padas* rocky soil. – *pal* milepost. – *pamali* dolmen. – *panas* slag, cinders. – *pasir* sandstone. – *pecah* road metal. – *pejal* magnet. – *pelapis* facing brick. – *pelinggam* k.o. marble, alabaster. – *penarik* yellow amber. – *penarung* a) stumbling block. b) obstacle. – *pengasah* grindstone, whetstone. – *penghalang* obstacle. – *penjuru* cornerstone. – *penutup* coping. – *peringatan* stone memorial. – *permata* precious/gem stone. – *pertama* cornerstone. – *perum* sounding lead. – *pijak(an)* stepping-stone. – *pinabéténgan* (*Min*) a historic stone located at the foot of Mount Tonderukan in Central Minahasa. – *polés* polishing stone. –

pualam marble. – *puncak* a) header. b) apex stone. – *sabak* slate. – *sandungan* stumbling block, obstruction, obstacle. – *sauh* stone weighing down a Malay anchor. – *semén* conblock. – *semberani* magnet. – *sempadan* boundary marker. – *sendi* a) cornerstone. b) foundation. – *séntér* flashlight battery. – *serawak* antimony. – *siam muda* carbuncle (stone). – *slép* (D) whetstone. – *sontokan* stumbling block. – *sudut* cornerstone. – *tahan api* fire/refractory brick(s). – *tahu* gypsum. – *tanduk* hornfels. – *taker* (coq) flint. – *tapakan* stepping-stone placed at bottom of a ladder. – *tapal* boundary marker. – *tara* boundary marker. – *tegak* menhir. – *telérang* quartz. – *telinga* otolith. – *témbok* brick. – *témplék* broken stones/bricks, rubble. – *tepi* curbstones. – *tétés* dripstone. – *timbang(an)* weights (on a *dacing*). – *timbul* pumice. – *tulis* a) slate. b) inscribed stone, stone tablet; → PRASASTI. – *tumpuan* base of operations. – *ubin* floor tile. – *ujian* a) touchstone. b) criterion. c) test case. – *ukuran* landmark, guide/setting reference mark. – *ular* snakestone, bezoar. – *urat* veinstone. – *usus* intestinal calculus.

berbatu with stones, stony, contain stones.

berbatu-batu to have stones/rocks, be covered with stones/rocks.

membatu 1 to fossilize, petrify, be(come) as hard as a rock; fossilized, petrified. 2 to keep silent, refuse to talk. *diam* ~ to keep quiet. *Dia* ~ *saja bila ditanyai.* He kept quiet when he was questioned. 3 to stone, throw stones at. *Rumahnya dibatu oléh anak-anak itu.* His house was stoned by those children. ~ *runtuh/rubuh* extremely noisy, booming.

membatui 1 to pave/harden (a road), put stones on. 2 to stone, throw stones at.

batuan 1 rock, boulder. 2 lithographic, rock (mod). ~ *asal* country rock. ~ *asam* acid rock. ~ *basa* basic rock. ~ *beku* igneous rock. ~ *dasar* bedrock. ~ *endapan* sedimentary rock. ~ *induk* source rock. ~ *landas* bedrock. ~ *majir* barren rock. ~ *penudung* cap rock. ~ *penutup* overburden. ~ *samping* wall rock, country rock. ~ *séng* pitch blend. ~ *singkapan* outcropping. ~ *tegar* competent rock. ~ *terlepas* loose rock. ~ *tetap* bedrock. ~ *tudung* cap rock.

batu-batuan stones, rocks, pieces of gravel, pebbles, boulders, etc.

pembatuan 1 fossilization. 2 petrifaction.

pe(r)batuan rocky place.

batu II 1 milestone. 2 mile. *Rumahnya kira-kira lima – dari sini.* His house is about 5 miles from here.

berbatu-batu for miles and miles.

batu III in plant and animal names. *kayu* – various species of trees including *Maranthes corymbosa.* – *laga* green snail, *Turbo marmoratus.*

batubara coal. – *baki* caking coal. – *bongkah* lump coal. – *kasar* lump coal. – *kokas(an)* coking coal. – *lunak* soft coal. – *mentah* raw/rough coal. – *muda* brown coal, lignite. – *sémi antrasit* semianthracite coal. – *talam* caking coal. – *uap* steam coal, anthracite. – *wantah* raw coal.

Batujajar military training center, located 22 kilometers from Bandung (West Java), where soldiers are trained in parachute jumping.

batuk I 1 cough. 2 (the act or sound of) coughing. 3 "anybody home?" (greeting on entering a home and seeing nobody); → KULONUWUN. 4 (= berbatuk) to cough. – *bertahun-tahun* chronic cough. – *darah* to cough up blood. – *kecil* cough to clear one's throat. – *kering* phthisis, pulmonary tuberculosis. – *klimis*; → TUKMIS. – *lelah* a) whooping cough (in adults). b) (spasmodic) asthma. – *pilek* flu-like symptoms. – *rejan/100 hari* whooping cough, pertussis. – *sesak* bronchial asthma. – *teruk* tuberculosis cough.

batuk-batuk 1 coughing incessantly. 2 sputtering (of an engine); erupting (of a volcano). *Mesin mulai* ~ *dan akhirnya mogok.* The machine began to sputter and finally stalled. *oplét yang sudah pada* ~ broken-down jeepneys with "coughing" motors. *Gunung Merapi* ~. Mount Merapi is erupting. ~ *kambing* to cough to clear the throat or to attract attention, nervous cough.

berbatuk to cough. ~ *darah* spitting up of blood.

membatukkan to cough up s.t.. ~ *darah* to spit up blood while coughing.

terbatuk-batuk 1 coughed (uncontrollably and incessantly).

Matanya berair, dan sesekali dia ~, *karena asap yang pekat.* His eyes watered and he kept on coughing uncontrollably due to the thick smoke. 2 sputtering (of an engine).

batuk II (Jv) forehead; → DAHI. *setiap saat kita ketemu* – each time we have a face-to-face meeting.

batuk III (Ban) a *rambutan* variety so called because it evokes coughing when eaten in large quantities due to its very sweet taste.

batung(-batung) k.o. mollusk.

batur I (Jv) 1 servant; → BEDI(E)NDE, PEMBANTU *rumah tangga.* 2 blue-collar worker.

batur II building foundation.

bau I 1 smell, odor, fragrance, flavor, aroma, perfume, scent. –*nya setahun pelayaran.* It stinks to high heaven; you can smell it a mile away. *sudah tercium –nya* have wind/an inkling of, got wind of, found out. – *yang sangat menusuk hidung* a very penetrating odor. 2 stench, stink, unpleasant odor. 3 → BERBAU. – *busuk tidak berbangkai* groundless/unfounded criticism/slander/libel, etc. *ayam terlepas, tangan* – *tahi* s.o. who wants to defile a girl but didn't succeed in doing so only gets shame. *jauh* – *bunga, dekat tahi* love is more lasting from afar than from nearby. *sudah* – *tanah* to have one foot in the grave. – *asing* strange odor. **berbau asing** having a strange flavor/taste. **keberbau-asingan** a strange flavor/taste. – *badan* body odor. – *busuk* foul-smelling. – *harum* fragrance, pleasant odor, sweet-smelling. – *kencur* a) is only just out of the shell, is still new to the world, still in its infancy (of a business or custom). b) still very young and inexperienced, wet behind the ears. c) immature, green, untrained. *Budaya télévisi di Indonésia ini masih* – *kencur.* The custom of watching television in Indonesia is still in its infancy. – *pesing* smelling of urine.

bau-bau *ada* ~ *bacang* distantly related (of kinsfolk). ~ *sungut saja* useless, in vain.

sebau 1 having the same smell/odor. 2 similar, same, of the same type. *seragam* ~ having the same tastes. *tiada* ~ incompatible.

berbau 1 to be fragrant, smell, have an odor/scent. *Bagi kita yang bermukim di lingkungan perkotaan, seringkali menemukan kualitas air mandi atau air minum yang dikonsumsi* ~ *seperti karat dan agak keruh.* Those of us who live in urban areas often find that the bath or drinking water we consume smells like rust and is muddy. *Oléh saya* ~ *busuk.* I smelled an offensive smell. – *setahun pelayaran* to smell to high heaven. ~ *malaikat berlalu* to smell very sweet. 2 to smell of ... *Baju ini telah* – *keringat.* This jacket smells of sweat. *gadis yang* ~ *bénsin* (coq) girls interested in cars (and other luxury items). 3 to stink, have a bad/unpleasant smell. ~ *tidak énak* to have a nasty smell. 4 to show a trace (of), have some of the qualities (of), with overtones/implications of, with a ... nuance. ~ *mistik* to have a mystical connotation/implication. *tindakan kriminal* ~ *politik* criminal acts with political overtones. *getaran-getaran politik yang* ~ *militér* political tremors with military overtones. 5 to have come to (reached) one's ear, come to one's consciousness. *Telah* ~ *oléh polisi komplotan penjahat itu.* The police have become aware of that gang of bandits. *bakar tak* ~ stating disbelief in s.o. *tidak/belum* ~ *telunjukku* that cannot possibly be true. *telah* ~ *basah embacang* (the matter) became clear.

membau to smell s.t., detect an odor of s.t. (usually s.t. bad).

membaui 1 to smell, sniff at, ferret out. 2 to perceive, notice, discover, detect, observe, discern, become aware/conscious of. 3 to trace, find out about, track down.

terbau 1 smelled, sniffed, detected. 2 known.

bau-bauan perfume, scents, all k.o. smells/odors.

pembau 1 sense of smell. 2 s.o. who smells.

pembauan smelling, olfactory.

bau II (D) a square land measure; 1 *bau* = 500 *tombak persegi* = 7,096.5 square meters or about 1.75 acres.

bau III a member of the village municipal government, *esp* a hamlet headman. – *désa* (Jv reg) village headman.

bauk 1 beard, whiskers. 2 feathers/down under jaw/beak.

berbauk with whiskers, a beard, feathers/down.

bauksit (D) bauxite.

baulu (Port ob) spongecake; → KUÉ *bolu.*

baun (M) → BAU I.

baung I various species of catfish. *ikan* – a freshwater catfish, *Macrones spp.*, *Mystus Nemurus. seperti* – *dipukul* to scream bloody murder. – *akar* giant catfish, *Mystus planiceps.* – *baru/batu* k.o. catfish, *Amblyceps mangois.* – *gantang* k.o. round catfish. – *kunyit* yellowish catfish. – *pisang* k.o. catfish, *Mystus nigriceps.*

baung II (*ob*) bear; → BERUANG.

baur I 1 completely mixed, mingled together. **2** (*geol*) diffusion.

  sebaur menyebaurkan to mix/blend/combine with.

  berbaur 1 mixed (with s.t. else). *Warna air minum seringkali mirip air téh, karena* ~ *dengan sisa tanah yang belum terpisah sempurna.* The color of the drinking water often looks like tea because of the remains of the soil which have not been completely separated out. ~ *menyatu dengan* to become one with. **2** to associate/group together (with). *hidup* ~ to live together as husband and wife; to be married.

  membaur 1 to assimilate. *Cina WNA atau WNI yang tak mau* ~ *bisa pilih Béijing atau Taiwan.* Chinese of foreign or Indonesian nationality who do not want to assimilate may choose between Peking or Taiwan. **2** to diffuse, spread.

  membauri to mix into s.t., blend into, mingle with, assimilate into.

  membaurkan 1 to mix s.t. (with). **2** to put s.o. among. **3** (= **memperbaurkan**) to allow to mingle/mix. *Pemuda dan pemudi diperbaurkan supaya dapat kenal-mengenal.* The youngsters (boys and girls) were allowed to mingle to get to know e.o. **4** to integrate. **5** (= **memperbaurkan**) to marry off.

  terbaur mixed up, diffused. **keterbauran** (*phys*) diffusivity.

  bauran 1 mix, mixture (of food, etc.). ~ *pemasaran* marketing mix. **2** dissolve (in film making). **3** (*phys*) diffusion.

  kebauran fusion, mix, mixture.

  pembaur (*phys*) diffuser.

  pembauran 1 (the act of) mixing/blending, assimilation, integration. **2** mixture, blend. ~ *bangsa* assimilation. *Konsépsi* ~ *bangsa mémang paling tepat dan usaha-usaha konkrét harus ditingkatkan untuk mengadakan* ~ *di segala bidang kehidupan.* The concept of mixing races is the correct one and concrete efforts must be increased to bring it about at all levels of life. **3** (*phys*) diffusion.

  perbauran 1 (social) intercourse, association (with other people). **2** marriage.

baur II (*Skr*) **1** a fishing rod. **2** sword of office.

baureksa (*Jv*) guardian spirit/ghost.

  membaureksa to protect/guard (of a spirit, etc.).

bausastra (*Jv*) dictionary; → KAMUS.

bausuku (*Jv ob*) statute/compulsory laborer in the rice field given to the village head.

baut (*D*) **1** bolt, pin, stud, screw. **2** (*coq*) strong-arm man. – *jangkar* anchor bolt. – *kembang* expansion bolt. – *pasak* cotter pin. – *pengikat* set stud. – *penyétél udara* idle mixture adjustment screw. – *siku* hook pin.

  membaut to bolt.

  pembautan bolting.

ba-véto (*Min*) to contribute one's bit, put in a word; to interrupt. *Yah, mémang wanita Minahasa suka* – *kepada pria atau suaminya, sebab meréka tidak mau dirémèhkan begitu saja.* Yeah, Minahasan women like to contribute their bit to the men because they don't want to be considered unimportant just like that.

bawa carry, bring. *mau* – *cara sendiri* self-important, conceited.

  membawa [and **mbawa/ngebawa** (*coq*)] **1** to bring, carry, take (along). *Anak-anak* ~ *buku bacaan.* The children were carrying books to read. **2** to transport, bring (along), carry with one, deliver. *Hari ini ia tidak* ~ *uang sepésér pun.* Today he doesn't have a penny in his pocket. **3** to escort, accompany. ~ *anak ke sekolah* to escort/accompany a child to school. **4** to bring about, give rise to, cause, result in. *kecelakaan yang* ~ *maut* a fatal accident. **5** to involve/implicate s.o. *Jangan sampai* ~ *nama baik keluargamu.* Don't go so far as to drag your family's good reputation through the mud. **6** to bring up (an issue for discussion). ~ *acara* to direct the entertainment at a (musical) show, party or the like. ~ *adat* to menstruate. ~ *agama* to embrace/adhere

to a religion. ~ *alamat* to give one's address. ~ *aturan sendiri* at one's own discretion. ~ *bekas* to result/end in, conclude with. ~ *berahasia* to admit to the secret. ~ *berat* to be pregnant. ~ *berkeliling* to show/take s.o. around a place. ~ *berunding* to invite s.o. to participate in a discussion. ~ *bulan* to menstruate. ~ *diri* a) to go/move to ...; to flee. b) to adjust/adapt (to a situation). ~ *diri seorang saja* to have nothing to do with s.o., have no dealings with s.o. *pandai* ~ *diri* to know how to behave/conduct o.s.; easy going. ~ *duduk* to invite s.o. to have a seat. ~ *gelak* to make s.o. laugh. ~ *gigi saja* to come empty handed (without bringing a gift). ~ *halnya* to go seek a living. ~ *hasil* to pay off, be successful. ~ *hati* a) to pour out one's heart, unbosom o.s., tell/reveal one's feelings/secrets, etc. b) to discourage, frighten. ~ *hidup* to go to seek a living. ~ *iman* to embrace (Islam, etc.), convert to (Islam, etc.). ~ *jalan* to show the way. ~ *kabur* to run off/away with. ~ *kacau* to create confusion. ~ *kakinya* to go from place to place without any particular purpose/destination. ~ *ke* to take s.t. out on s.o. else. ~ *ke air* to circumcise. ~ *keliling kota* to take s.o. around the city. ~ *kembali* a) to bring back, return s.t. b) ~ *kembali ... kepada* to carry back (to). ~ *ke tengah* to put forward. ~ *lagu* to sing a song. ~ *laku* a) to go/move to ... ; to run away to ... ; to flee/escape/take to one's heels/run away. b) to adjust/adapt (to a situation). ~ *lari* to escape with, abduct. ~ *makna* to contain a meaning/sense. ~ *masuk* to bring s.t. in, let s.t. come in. ~ *masuk hati* to discourage, frighten. ~ *mati/maut* a) to take s.t. to the grave. b) to be fatal, mortal. ~ *mobil* to drive a car. *Dia* ~ *kendaraan sendiri.* He drove his own car. ~ *mulut* a) to eat and run. b) (*Mal*) to tell s.t. about s.o. to s.o. else. ~ *nama* to implicate s.o. ~ *nama beberapa kedutaan besar asing* to implicate some foreign embassies. *gerakan-gerakan* ~ *nama agama* movements under cover of religion, movements which use religion as a cover. ~ *nasib* to go seek a living. ~ *nyawa* to seek safety in flight. ~ *pergi* a) to walk off with, take s.t. away. *Pengunjung itu* ~ *pergi kunci rumah.* The guest walked off with the house key. b) to abduct, run away with. ~ *perut* to come empty-handed asking for food. ~ *pulang* a) to take home. b) to bring back. ~ *rezeki* to bring luck. ~ *salah* to misunderstand. ~ *senjata api* to carry a firearm. ~ *serta* to take along with one. ~ *sial* to bring bad luck. ~ *singgah* to invite s.o. to stop by/in/at, drop by. ~ *soal* to put forward a problem. ~ *suara* to deliver a speech. ~ *tari* to give a dance performance. *dibawa arus* to be carried along by water, waves, etc., drifting. *dibawa berkenalan* taken to making s.o.'s acquaintance. *dibawa cakap* taken to have a talk/chat (with). *dibawa juga makan-makan angin* taken for a breath of fresh air anyway. *dibawa kemuka pengadilan* to be summoned before the court. *Sakit, lebih-lebih dibawa menelan itu.* It especially hurts when he tries to swallow. *Dan beberapa kali malam hari Lisa telah dibawanya makan ke réstoran.* And several times at night Lisa agreed to go eat with him in a restaurant. *dibawa kabur* to be carried off, be spirited away (by thieves). *dibawa karena* because/on account of, owing/due to; as a result of, as a consequence of. *dibawa lahir* innate, inborn, congenital. *boléh dibawa ke tengah* to be able to hold one's own. *untuk dibawa bepergian* for your travels (a medicine), to be taken on a trip.

  membawa-bawa 1 to take (s.o.) away/out, transport, convey. *dibawa-bawa* portable. *mesin tulis yang dapat dibawa-bawa* a portable typewriter. **2** to implicate, involve, mention. *Jangan* ~ *saya dalam urusan itu.* Don't involve me in that matter.

  membawakan [and **mbawain/ngebawain** (*J coq*)] **1** to take/fetch/carry for, bring (s.t. for s.o.). *Istriku* ~ *saya oléh-oléh.* My wife brought me back a present (from her trip). *Anak-anak berebut mau* ~ *koper saya.* The kids were fighting with e.o. wanting to carry the trunks for me. *seperti kucing dibawakan lidi* shy, timid, bashful. **2** to cause, result/bring in, produce. *Usaha yang* ~ *keuntungan.* A profit-making venture. **3** to read for/to, recite. *Bésok ia akan* ~ *puisi ini di atas pentas.* Tomorrow he is going to recite this poem on the stage. **4** to sing (a song, etc.). **5** to be the master of ceremonies of. *Karena dia masih ada kesibukan, acara ini saya yang bawakan.* Because he's still busy, I'll be the master of ceremonies of the program. ~ *diri* to know how to behave in public. ~ *politik* ... to conduct a ... policy. ~ *tabiat* to know how to behave in public. ~ *tari* to give a dance performance.

terbawa 1 [= **terbawakan** (and **kebawa** (*coq*)] taken/carried away, carried off. ~ *arus* carried along (without any will of one's own). ~ *oléh suasana tegang* carried away by the tense atmosphere. ~ *perasaan* to get carried away. *Saya ikut, sudah kebawa suasana.* I joined in, carried away by the atmosphere. **2** taken/brought unintentionally. *Wah, buku saya ~ Wirono.* Goodness, my book was (unintentionally) taken by Wirono. **3** ~ *oléh* caused by, due to. ~ *oléh keadaan masyarakat* due to the social situation. **4** able to carry. *tidak ~* unable to carry. *Saya perlu bantuan anda karena saya tidak ~ barang-barang yang banyak itu.* I need your help because I can't carry so much baggage. ~ *masuk* involved, implicated.

terbawa-bawa [and **kebawa-bawa** (*coq*)] **1** involved, implicated. *Kepala kampung itu pun ~ juga dalam urusan itu.* Even the village head was implicated in that matter. *kecil teranja-anja, besar ~* as the twig is bent the tree is inclined. **2** to persist, not go away for a long time. **3** carried away.

bawaan 1 load, cargo, burden, belongings, effects; s.t. carried (by). *Tamu meletakkan ~nya di lantai.* The guest put his belongings on the floor. *sebuah tas jinjing ~ T* a handbag carried by T. **2** property, goods, estate (*esp* brought to a marriage), dowry. *Apabila bercerai, ~ perempuan tetap menjadi hak si perempuan.* When there is a divorce, the wife's property remains hers. **3** presents, gifts. *Bila nénék datang, tentu banyak ~ untuk cucu-cucunya.* When grandmother comes, undoubtedly she is going to bring a lot of gifts for her grandchildren. **4** congenital (defect), inborn. *faktor ~* predisposing factors. **5** result, outcome, effect, consequence. *Kekacauan ini adalah ~ perang yang baru lalu.* This chaos is the result of the war that was just over. ~ *hidup* way of life. *menjadi ~ hidup si atlit* to become the athlete's way of life. **6** s.t. driven/ridden in. *Ésok harinya, ketika Rachmat akan menjemput pemakai mobil itu, ternyata mobil ~nya itu telah tidak ada di tempatnya lagi.* The next morning, when Rachmat wanted to pick up the person who uses the car, it turned out that the car he drove was not where it had been (because it was stolen). **berbawaan** (*M*) to correspond, match, go along with; → SEPADAN. *Lénggangnya ~ dengan pinggangnya yang ramping.* The swaying of her arms while walking matches her slender waist.

bawa-bawaan goods, wares, commodities, baggage.

pembawa 1 carrier, bearer, conveyor. **2** deliverer. **3** leader, s.o. who runs s.t. **4** feeder, device that feeds. ~ *acara* M.C., emcee, master of ceremonies. ~ *bendéra* flag carrier, standard-bearer. ~ *berita/kabar* courier; informant, reporter, agent, anchorman. ~ *jalan* guide. ~ *mobil* driver, chauffeur. ~ *modérnisasi* agent of modernization. ~ *penyakit* carrier. ~ *pesan* messenger. ~ *pos* mailman. → JURU *bicara*, PENYAMBUNG *lidah*. **sepembawa** ~ *kaki* wherever one's feet take one, no matter where; as far as one's feet can take one.

pembawaan 1 (= **bawaan**) congenital (defect); (natural) disposition, aptitude, talent; inclination, tendency, bent, propensity, one's nature. *Jangan anda marah, mémang sudah ~ adik saya itu.* Don't be angry, my younger brother is just like that. *Meskipun ada ~ berdagang, harus ada modal juga.* Even though you have a talent for trade, you also have to have capital. **2** delivery. ~ *barang-harang itu dilakukan pada malam hari.* Those goods are delivered in the evening. **3** feeding (material into a machine). **4** gift, present. **berpembawaan 1** with a ... disposition/demeanor, by nature. ~ *kalem* with a calm disposition. **2** talented, competent.

bawab (*A*) doorkeeper.

bawah 1 under, sub-, lower. *bibir ~* lower lip. *dunia ~* underworld, dregs (of society). *~ angin* leeward. *negeri ~ angin* the Malay archipelago. *~ atas* bottom-up, from the bottom up. *pembangunan ~ atas* bottom-up development. *~ baku* substandard. *~ kulit* subcutaneous. *~ laut* underwater, submarine. *~ permukaan* a) under the surface, subsurface. b) (*petro*) down hole. *~ sadar* subconscious. *~ tanah* a) underground, subterranean. b) clandestine, covert. *~ tangan* a) underhanded, under-the-table. b) private,

not drawn up before a notary. *~ umur* underage. **2** (with the prepositions *di*, *ke*, and *dari*) under, beneath, below. *di ~* below, beneath, under. *orang di ~* subordinate, underling. *di ~ bendéra* under the wing of. *di ~ ini* hereunder, mentioned below. *sebagai di ~ ini* as follows. *di ~ garis kemiskinan* below the poverty level. *di ~ harga* below the original price. *di ~ kendali* under the control of. *di ~ ketiak* under the influence of (one's parents, etc.). *di ~ ketiak istrinya* to be henpecked by one's wife. *di ~ (kolong) langit (ini)* here below, in this world. *memproduksi di ~ lisénsi* to produce under a license. ~ *komando* under the command of. **membawah-komandokan** to put under the command of. *(di) ~ perintah* to be under the orders of, subordinated to. **membawahperintahkan** to put under the orders of, subordinate. *di ~ payung* under the aegis of. *di ~ permukaan* subsurface. *di ~ pimpinan* under the leadership of, led by. *di ~ duli baginda* (*ob*) to prince/king ruler. *~ sadar* subconscious. *~ tanah* underground, subterranean. *di ~ tangan* a) done privately, not before a notary. b) underhanded, not above board. *~ tekanan* in contact (with the enemy). *ke ~* downward, and under, and less. *umur dua puluh satu tahun ke ~* 21 (years old) and under. **mengebawahkan** to lower, take down. **terkebawah** lowermost, bottommost. *dari ~* from below/the bottom. *Ia mulai karirnya dari ~.* He began his career from the bottom. *~ Komando Operasi* [BKO] (*mil*) Under Operational Command.

sebawah(an) *orang ~* subordinate, inferior, underling.

membawah (*ob*) to work under s.o., place o.s. under s.o.'s command.

membawahi to subordinate, be in charge of, have under one. *Kelompok profési tersebut harus mampu tampil sebagai kelompok yang tidak dibawahi oléh instansi lainnya.* The professional groups must be able to appear to be groups which are not subordinate to other agencies.

membawahkan to have as a subordinate/underling; to govern/rule manage (an area, etc.).

terbawah 1 lowest. **2** ~ *oléh* headed by.

bawahan 1 (*orang*) ~ subordinate, underling. *opp* ATASAN. *Sebagai ~ saya harus mematuhi keputusan atasan saya.* As a subordinate, I must obey my superiors' decisions. *hubungan ~* (*gram*) subordination. **2** bottom (a garment worn on the lower part of the body).

pembawah (*math*) denominator.

bawak (*ob*) → BAWA.

bawal (*ikan*) ~ *cermin* silver pomfret, *Parastromateus cinereus, Pampus argenteus.* (*ikan*) ~ *hitam* black pomfret, *Parastromateus/Formio niger.* ~ *(ke)tambak* Chinese silver pomfret, *Pampus chinensis.* ~ *putih* silver pomfret, *Pampus argenteus.* ~ *selatan* white pomfret,

bawang a generic name for onions/leeks, etc. *makan ~* to be angry. *pemakan ~* quick-tempered, hothead. *(kelakuan) anak ~* (behavior of) nothing, s.o. who counts for nothing. *menjadi anak/pupuk ~* to keep one's mouth shut, keep mum. *kuéh ~* sticks formed of wheat flour, coconut milk, eggs, onions and then deep fried. *rusak ~ ditimpa jambak* a person is ruined by his own splendor. ~ *acar* pickled onion. ~ *Benggala/Bombai/Bombay* large onions imported from India, *Allium fistulosum.* ~ *cina* white onion, *Allium fistulosum.* ~ *daun/hijau* leek, *Allium ampeloprasum.* ~ *hutan* → KULIM. ~ *kucai* Chinese chives, *Allium odorum.* ~ *mérah* red onion, shallot, *Allium cepa*; → BRAMBANG, EMAS *mérah.* ~ *préi* leek, *Allium ampeloprasum.* ~ *putih* garlic, *Allium sativum.* ~ *sayuran/sop* leek, *Allium ampeloprasum.* ~ *semprong* → BAWANG *daun.* ~ *tembaga* → BAKUNG.

berbawang with onions (in it), containing onions.

membawang to become angry, fly into a rage, lose one's temper.

membawangi to add onions to.

pembawang hothead, s.o. who gets angry easily.

bawasir (*A*) hemorrhoids, piles.

bawat I *payung ~* long-handled umbrella of state.

bawat II and **terbawat** drooping, hanging down (of ropes). *mata ~* sleepy/drowsy eyes.

bawél (*Jv*) **1** nagging, complaining. **2** chatterbox, tattler; → CERÉWÉT.

terbawél the most nagging/complaining.

kebawélan being a chatterbox/complainer.

bawon (*Jv*) sharecropping (with harvester); the share of *padi* for each female cutter in the harvest, i.e., ¼, ⅕, or ⅙ of the crop reaped.

    membawoni to give s.o. his earned portion of the harvest. *Di kabupatén Ngawi cara memanén ada yang dengan ani-ani, kemudian langsung pulang dan dibawoni di rumah.* In the Ngawi regency harvesting is done with a small knife and then it's taken home and shared out at home.

    bawonan 4, 5, or 6 parts for the owner of the *padi*, and one part for the harvester.

baya I (*Skr*) age; → PANTARAN, UMUR, USIA. *sudah/telah* – mature, no longer young. *separuh/setengah* – middle-aged. *ibu separuh – ini* this middle-aged woman. *lelaki setengah* – a middle-aged man.

    sebaya of the same age. *kawan/teman* ~ peer, contemporary.

    berbaya *sudah* ~ old, aged.

baya II → BAHAYA.

bayabaduri a spiny plant, amaranth, *Amarantus spinosus*.

bayak short and fat, paunchy, obese; big-bellied (of a pregnant woman).

    membayak to be squat/paunchy.

    terbayak squashed down flat.

    kebayakan corpulence, stoutness, obesity.

bayam amaranth (similar to spinach), *Amaranthus spp.* – *badak* a large spinach variety, *Amanthus sp.* – *berduri* → BAYAM duri. – *besar* k.o. shrub, *Deeringia amaranthoides.* – *duri* spiny/thorny amaranth, a spiny spinach variety, *usu* used as a remedy against swellings, *Amaranthus spinosus.* – *ékor kucing* love-lies-bleeding, *Amaranthus caudatus.* – *gelatik/kakap* Chinese spinach, Joseph's coat, *Amaranthus tricolor.* – *itik/monyét* amaranth, *Amaranthus blitum.* – *mérah* a spinach variety whose stem and leaves are red colored, used as an antidysentery remedy, red cockscomb, love-lies-bleeding, *Aerva sanguinolenta.* – *putih* vegetable used in preparing *sayur, Amaranthus lividus.* – *selasih* Chinese spinach, red spinach, loves-lies-bleeding, *Amaranthus caudatus.*

bayan I *burung* – long-tailed parakeet, *Palaeornis longicauda.*

bayan II (*A*) clear, explained. *talak* – third and final divorce of Muslims. *ilmu* – exegesis (of the Koran).

    membayankan to clarify, explain, elucidate.

bayan III (*ob*) → KEBAYAN.

bayan-bayan various species of fishes, wrass, tuskfish, *Bodianus spp., Choerodon spp., Cheilinus spp., Thallosoma spp.*

bayang I 1 shadow. 2 image. 3 imagination. *di* – *kata* behind the words, one's true intent. – *kias* indirection, implication. **membayang-kiaskan** to imply, say by implication, state indirectly.

    bayang-bayang 1 shadow, shade. *Mukanya tidak kelihatan nyata karena ia berdiri pada* ~ *pintu.* His face was not clearly visible because he stood in the shadow of the doorway. 2 reflection, image (reflected in a mirror or in water). *melihat ~nya di air* to observe his reflection in the water. ~ *kaca* mirror image. 3 vague outline, silhouette. *tertampak* ~ *orang di dalam kebun pada waktu malam* the vague outline of a person was visible in the yard during the evening. 4 imagination, fantasy. *Semuanya hanya* ~ *belaka.* Everything was mere fantasy. 5 s.o. unimportant. *buntar* ~ the middle of the day (when the sun is at the zenith). *dimabuk* ~ wanting the impossible. *ibarat* ~ *badan* inseparable, said of persons who are frequently seen in e.o.'s company. *kain* ~ loosely woven cloth. *tidak kelihatan ~nya* he was nowhere to be seen. *menangkap* ~ pointless, fruitless. *serasa* ~ unconscious. *singkat* ~ signs of a short life. *Sudah tampak ~nya akan berhasil.* The signs indicate that it will be successful. *takut akan* ~ afraid of his shadow, of s.t. nonexistent. *takut akan ~nya sendiri* afraid of one's own shadow. ~ *disangka tubuh* to expect s.t. that is not yet sure. ~ *sepanjang badan/tubuh* to live within one's means. *mengukur* ~ *sepanjang badan* to cut one's coat according to one's cloth. ~ *tidak sepanjang badan* have a champagne taste on a beer drinker's pocketbook.

    berbayang(-bayang) 1 to be like a shadow/reflection, shaded. *Liuk-lambai ranting-ranting kayu yang berbayang-bayang di air.* The reflection in the water of the branches of the tree was

swaying from left to right. *tanda air berbayang* shaded watermark. *tanda air berbayang yang merupakan bagian intégral kertas* a shaded watermark that forms an integral part of paper. 2 imagined, to be present in the mind (of an image); to have s.t. in one's mind. *Melimpahnya makanan di Hari Raya nanti tidak berbayang.* The abundance of food on the forthcoming holiday cannot be imagined.

    membayang to appear/become visible vaguely, flash (across). *Pada wajahnya* ~ *rasa cemas.* A feeling of worry flashed across his face.

    membayang(-bayang)i 1 to shade, overshadow, darken. *Kondominium yang tinggi itu membayang-bayangi rumah-rumah di sekelilingnya.* The high condominium overshadowed the surrounding houses. 2 to shadow, trail, follow s.o., keep a close eye on. *Agén intélijen itu membayangi aktivis kampus tersebut.* The intelligence agent shadowed those campus activists. 3 to obsess, hang over, cast a shadow over. *Penggunaan narkotika selalu membayangi kaum remaja.* The use of drugs always hangs over young people.

    membayang(-bayang)kan 1 to picture to o.s., imagine, fancy, conceive (of). ~ *berbagai jalan yang dapat ditempuh* to picture to o.s. the various ways which could be taken. 2 to hint at, allude to. ~ *isi hatinya dalam surat kepada kekasihnya* to allude to what was in his heart in a letter to his sweetheart. 3 to hold out to s.o. the prospect that ... ~ *hadiah* to hold out the promise of a gift. 4 to call to mind, call up before the mind. 5 to sketch, outline.

    terbayang [and **kebayang** (*coq*)] brought to light, revealed; imagined. *hujan yang terbayang* threatening to rain. *invasi terbayang* an imaginary invasion. *dari ... terbayang ...* from ... we can conclude that ... *kebayang oléh saya* I can imagine. *Kebayang oléh saya problém-problém wajah ini.* I could imagine the problems of this face. *Kebayang 'kan berapa besar pengeluaran saya.* Now you can imagine, can't you, how large my expenses are.

    terbayang(-bayang) sketched out, appear vaguely. *terbayang-bayang di mukanya/hadapannya* sketched out ahead of him. *terbayang-bayang dalam ingatannya* sketched out in his mind.

    terbayangkan *tidak* ~ unimaginable, inconceivable. *Tidak* ~ *oléh penduduk bahwa dalam waktu hanya 14 hari, wajah désa telah berubah.* The population couldn't imagine that in only 14 days the face of the village could change. *Téknologi modérn telah memberi manusia kemampuan yang belum pernah* ~ *sebelumnya.* Modern technology has given mankind capabilities that could never have been imagined before.

    bayangan 1 reflection, shadow, silhouette, image. *berlatih tinju* ~ shadow boxing. ~ *hujan* rain shadow. ~ *ikutan* afterimage. 2 stand-in, reserve, understudy. *pemain* ~ a reserve player. 3 vague idea, image, illusion; s.t. seen in one's mind's eye, s.t. imagined, what one imagines. ~ *ibunya* an image of his mother seen in his mind's eye. ~ *ikutan* afterimage. ~ *kejadian* illusion. ~ *khayal* phantasmagoria, weird spectacle. *di dalam* ~ *saja* only in one's imagination, false. *belum ada ~nya* not the faintest trace of it was to be found. *kelihatan ~nya* there is evidence of. *Kapan menikah? Wah, masih belum ada* ~, *nih.* When do you plan to get married? Gee, I still don't have the faintest idea. 4 disguised. *kartél* ~ a disguised cartel. 5 shadow, unofficial. *pemerintah* ~ a shadow government, government in exile. *términal* ~ an unofficial bus terminal. 6 shading (on a map).

    bayang-bayangan image; s.t. imagined.

    pembayang ~ *mata* eye shadow.

    pembayangan 1 idea, notion, image. 2 imagination, suggestion. 3 reflection. ~ *udara* mirage, fata morgana. 4 shadowing, following closely.

    perbayangan imagination.

bayang II *kayu* – ironwood tree; → KAYU *ulin.*

Bayangkara → BHAYANGKARA.

Bayangkari → BHAYANGKARI.

bayar pay. – *untuk sekali nonton* pay per view. – *atas perintah* pay to order. – *atas unjuk* pay to bearer. – *pramuat* freight prepaid.

    berbayar (*M*) paid.

    membayar 1 to pay. ~ *berangsur-angsur* to pay in installments. ~ *atas nama* to make out (a check) to. ~ *créng* (*coq*) to pay cash.

~ di belakang to pay later. *tanpa dibayar* for free, without payment. *Harap dibayar harganya.* Please pay the price. *~ hajat* to fulfill a vow (by holding a *selamatan*). *~ hutang* to pay debts. *~ di muka* to pay in advance. *~ kaul* to redeem a pledge. *~ kembali* to pay back, refund, reimburse. *~ lebih dahulu* to pay in advance. *~ lunas* to pay off/in full. *~ mahal* to pay dearly. *Keselamatan dan kesehatan kerja harus dibayar mahal dengan nyawa.* Employment safety and health have to be paid for dearly with one's life. *Kuwait harus ~ mahal atas sikapnya.* Kuwait has to pay dearly for its position. *dibayar di muka* prepaid. *~ murah* to pay little. *dibayar murah* grossly underpaid. *masih harus dibayar* accrued. *~ niat* to redeem a pledge. *~ puasa* to fast to make up for days not fasted. *~ tinggi* to pay a lot. *~ tunai* to pay cash. **2** to pay for. *~ kejahatan* to pay for a crime.

membayari [and **ngebayarin** (*J coq*)] **1** to pay for s.t. *"Sekali-kali ngebayarin céwék cakap kan tidak jadi soal," seloroh Adi.* "Once in a while, paying for a cute chick isn't a problem, is it?" said Adi jokingly. **2** to pay s.o.

membayarkan 1 to pay (a price). *tanggal dividén dapat dibayarkan* the date the dividend has be paid. **2** to pay with (in the form of). *~ nyawa* to pay with one's life. **3** to spend (money) on.

terbayar(kan) paid. *tak ~* unpayable. *utang tak ~* unpaid debts.

bayaran 1 money paid, sum. **2** pay(ment), salary, wages. *~mu berapa?* What's your salary? **3** paid, s.o. who is paid or s.t. that is paid for. *pemain ~* a paid player, a professional. *serdadu ~* mercenary.

pembayar payer, (used) to pay for. *Uang yang meréka peroléh, sebagian digunakan ~ sekolah dan keperluan lainnya.* Part of the money they earn is used to pay for school and other necessities. *alat ~* means of payment, money. *~ pajak* taxpayer. *~ utang* a) scapegoat. b) debt payer.

pembayaran payment. *untuk ~ (fin)* in reimbursement. *alat ~* means of payment, money. *alat ~ sah* legal tender/currency. *~ angsuran* on account. *~ bersyarat* payment under reserve. *~ cicilan pokok* amortization. *~ dengan jangka waktu* deferred payment. *~ di muka* advance payment, prepayment. *~ ditunda* deferred payment. *~ kembali* repayment, refund, reimbursement. *~ penyelesaian* payment for honor. *~ pertama* flag fall (in taxicab, etc.). *~ rutin* recurring payment. *~ tertunda* deferred payment.

bayas a small wild palm, *Oncosperma horridus. - betina*, k.o. palm, *Pinanga scortechinii.*

bayat I (*A*) allegiance, homage (to a religious Muslim leader); → BAIAT.

membayat to honor, respect.

bayat II freshman (in college).

membayat to initiate, haze.

pembayatan initiation, hazing.

bayata male freshman.

bayati female freshman.

bayem → BAYAM.

bayén (*Jv*) to give birth.

bayi (*J/Jv*) *anak/jabang* - baby, infant. *masih* - still young and inexperienced. *- ikan* fry, spawn. *- ikan mas* goldfish fry. *- mérah* newborn baby. *- tabung* test-tube baby. *- terlantar* foundling.

berbayi with/to have a baby.

kebayi-bayian babyish.

Bayinah (*A*) *al-* "Evidence"; name of the 98th chapter of the Koran.

bayonét (*D/E*) bayonet. *dengan - terhunus* with fixed bayonet. *dengan ujung -* at bayonet point.

berbayonét with/to have a bayonet.

membayonét to bayonet, stick with a bayonet.

bayu I (*Skr poet*) breeze, wind. *Betara -* Vayu, the Hindu god of the winds.

bayu II (*ob*) slave, servant.

bayu III stale; → BASI I.

bayuan left-over food from the previous day.

kebayuan staleness (of food/drink).

bayu IV → MBAKYU.

bayuh (*cla*) each wife's turn for a polygamous husband's visit; a wife's conjugal rights.

bayung I a small chopper.

bayung II (*J*) k.o. climbing plant, *Triomma malaccensis. sulur -* (*ob*) k.o. decorative motif; → LEMBAYUNG.

bayung III bayung-bayung scarecrow.

bayur I various species of trees with useful timber, some with bark for tanning, *Pterospermum spp. - betina* k.o. tree, *Sterculia jackiana. - jantan,* k.o. tree, *Pterospermum javanicum. - laut* k.o. large buttressed tree, looking-glass mangrove, *Heritiera littoralis.*

bayur II → KUTU *bayur.*

baz (*Pers cla*) falcon.

bazar (*Pers*) bazaar; → PASAR.

bazari (*Ac*) *kaum -* retailers.

bazoka (*D*) bazooka.

BB I [Bau-Badan] body odor, BO.

BB II [Bibliothéca-Bogoriénsis] Bogor Library.

BB III (*init*) [Binnenlands(ch)-Bestuur] (Netherlands Indies) Civil Service; → PAMONG *Praja.*

BB IV car license for Tapanuli.

b/b (*abbr*) [berat/berat] by weight.

BBG [Bahan-Bakar-Gas] Gas Fuel.

mem-BBG-kan to gas up.

BBKK [Béa Balik Nama Kendaraan Bermotor] Transfer-of-Title-To-Motorized-Vehicle-Fee.

BBM [Bahan Bakar Minyak] Fuel Oil, Oil-Based Fuel (OBF).

BBN [Béa Balik Nama] Transfer-of-Title Fee, i.e., fee on transfer of property.

BBNKB [Béa Balik-Nama-Kendaraan Bermotor] Transfer of Motor Vehicle Title fee.

BC [Béa (dan) Cukai] Customs and Excise (office).

BCA [Bank Central Asia] Asian Central Bank.

Bc.Ac.P. [Baccalauréat Akadémi Pos] Bachelor of the Postal Academy.

Bc.A.K. [Baccalauréat Administrasi Kepegawaian] Bachelor in Personnel Management.

Bc.Hk. [Baccalauréat Hukum] Bachelor of Laws.

Bc.I. [Baccalauréat Imigrasi] Bachelor of Immigration.

Bc.KWN. [Baccalauréat Keuangan Negara] Bachelor in State Finances

Bc.T.T. [Baccalauréat Télepon dan Télegrap] Bachelor in Telephone and Telegraph.

BD and **B.D. I** drug dealer; → BANDAR IV.

BD II [barat daya] southwest.

BD III car license for Bengkulu.

BDB [Bébas Dari Béa] **1** duty-free. **2** tax-free (used as a franking mark).

BE car license for Lampung.

bé clipped form of **babé.**

béa (*Skr*) **1** duty, tax, levy, excise. **2** charge, fee, dues, toll. **3** expense, cost. *- angkut(an)* cost of transport, carriage, fare. *- balik nama* transfer-of-title fee. *- cukai* [BC] customs and excises. **kebéa-cukaian** the customs and excises field. *satu kerjasama bidang ~ antarnegara ASÉAN* an ASEAN Interstate cooperation in the customs and excises field. *- ékspor* export duty. *- impor* import duty. *- keluar* export duty. *- kepil* mooring fee. *- labuh* anchorage fee. *- légalisasi* legalization fee (for official documents). *- lélang* public auction dues. *- masuk* import duty. *- masuk tambahan* countervailing duties. *- masuk yang tinggi* tariff barrier. *- meterai* tax stamps, stamp duty. *- pabéan* customs duties. *- pelabuhan* port charges, harbor dues. *- pemindahan hak* transfer-of-title fee. *- perambuan* beaconage. *- pindah nama* transfer-of-title fee. *- pos* postage. *- tetap* fixed duty/tax. *- warisan* inheritance tax.

membéa to tax, impose a tax on.

pebéan (*infr*) [and **pabéan** (*Jv*)] customs office. **kepabéanan** customs (*mod*).

pembéaan taxing, imposition of customs duties.

béa-cukaiwan customs officer.

béasiswa (*Skr neo*) scholarship, fellowship. **membéasiswai** to grant a scholarship to s.o. **kebéasiswaan** pertaining to scholarships

béaya (*ob*) → BIAYA.

bebal 1 stupid, dull, foolish, mentally deficient. **2** hard to understand. *salah* – mistake, error.

kebebalan stupidity, foolishness.

bebalisme anti-intellectualism.

beban 1 burden, load, (shoulder-)load (as yoke). – *orang kulit putih* the white man's burden. *kuda* – packhorse. *percobaan* – a) load test. b) severe test. **2** responsibility, burden, charge, obligation, onus, care, liability. *menerima* – *untuk* to assume the obligation to. **3** stress, strength. *dengan latihan* – stress training. **4** *(elec)* charge, load. **5** charges, expense. *tiada* – *mencari* and *tak bahu galas* to ask for trouble, let o.s. in for unnecessary trouble. – *berat senggulung batu* a great responsibility. *ibarat* – *sudah ke tepi* it's now the right time to do s.t. – *bank* bank charges. – *belum dibayar* accrued charges. – *ditangguhkan* deferred charges. – *guna* payload (of a missile). – *hanyut* wash load. – *jasa* service charges. – *ikatan* encumbrance. – *kerja* workload. – *kesalahan* fault. – *keuangan* financing cost. – *maksimum* *(elec)* maximum capacity, peak load. – *méntal* mental stress. – *pembuktian* burden of proof. – *penyetimbang* ballast. – *pokok penjualan* cost of goods sold. – *puncak (elec)* peak load. – *tambahan* assessment. – *tetap* a) fixed expenses. b) dead load. – *usaha* operating expenses. – *yang ditangguhkan/ditunda* deferred liabilities. – *yang masih harus dibayar* accrued charges/ expenses. – *yang melekat* carrying charges.

membeban burdensome.

membebani 1 to load on s.t. **2** to burden, be a burden on s.o., be an onus on. *Sementara Kasparov sangat dibebani méntal untuk menang.* Meanwhile there was a great mental onus on Kasparov to win. **3** to charge s.o. (a certain amount of money), charge s.o. with the responsibility for s.t. *dibebani untuk membayar* charged with paying. *tidak akan ~ keuangan negara* at one's own expense, without cost/charge to the state. **4** to encumber.

membebankan 1 to put/lay s.t. on s.o.'s shoulders, place (a burden) on. *~ tanggung jawab kepada* to put the responsibility on. **2** to impose s.t. on s.o., charge. *~ biaya perkara kepada terdakwa* to make the defendant pay court costs.

terbebani burdened. *~ oléh jumlah kematian yang terus meningkat akibat naiknya angka bunuh diri dan tindak kejahatan* burdened by the ever-increasing number of deaths due to the raise in the suicide rate and criminal acts.

pembeban freighter.

pembebanan 1 (act of) putting a burden on, loading, packing, burden. *~ lebih* overloading. *~ pembuktian (leg)* onus probandi, the burden of proof. *~ rugi ke belakang (in accounting)* carry back. **2** encumbrance. **3** debiting (an account).

bebandos *(J)* k.o. delicacy (made of cassava).

bebangkis *(J)* → BANGKIS.

bebang terbebang and **kebebangan 1** stopped, halted. **2** constipated. **3** asphyxiated. *mati ~* stillborn, dead when delivered during childbirth.

bebar and **membebar** to scatter, disperse, fly off in all directions; → SEBAR I.

berbebaran *(pl subj)* to scatter/disperse in all directions.

terbebar scattered, dispersed.

bebaran scattering, dispersal.

bebarik *(geol)* veinlet, stringer.

bébas 1 free, unhampered, unimpeded, at liberty, not imprisoned. *démokrasi yang* – *baku hantam* a free-for-all democracy. *dibeli* – bought over the counter. *Sebagian obat yang dibeli* – *atau yang dirésépkan, belakangan diketahui berisi tepung.* Some of the medicines bought over the counter or by prescription later on were found out to contain flour. *laut* – the open sea. *penjualan* – free sale. *terjun* – free fall, the part of a parachute jump that precedes the opening of the parachute. *dengan* – freely, at will. – *dari* free/exempt/immune from (taxes/military service/ criticism, etc.), unhampered by. – *dari hukuman* to be unpunished, get away with s.t. –*nya gedung itu dari alat sadap suara* the debugging of that building. **2** released/discharged/absolved/freed from (responsibilities/obligations, etc.); *(leg)* acquitted, declared/pronounced not guilty, dismissed of the summons. – *dari segala tuduhan dan tuntutan* discharged from further prosecution. **3** free of. – *bécak* free of *bécak*. **4** indepen-

dent, free. *politik* – a free/independent policy. *politik* – *aktif* Indonesia's active and free foreign policy which is not bound by any ideology, doesn't belong to any bloc and actively participates in taking the initiative to develop international friendship and cooperation. *tidak* – dependent, not independent. **ketidakbébasan** dependency. – *air* anhydrous. – *bayar pajak* tax holiday. – *béa* a) duty free. b) toll-free (of telephone call). *toko* – *béa* duty-free shop. – *bécak* pedicab-free (zone). – *bidan a selamatan* given on the fortieth day after childbirth. – *bocor* leakproof. – *bunga* grace period. – *buta huruf* free of illiteracy. **membébasbutahurufkan** to teach s.o. to become literate, teach s.o. how to read and write. – *cacat* free from defects, zero defects. – *cacing* worm-free. – *calo* free of (ticket, etc.) scalpers. – *gula* sugarfree. *jalan* – *hambatan* toll road free from obstacles (that can cause traffic jams). – *hutang* debt free. – *militér* demilitarized. **membébasmilitérkan** to demilitarize. **pembébasmilitéran** demilitarization. *Rencana ~ Béirut Timur.* The demilitarization of East Beirut. – *murni* acquitted/exonerated from further prosecution. **membébas-murnikan** to acquit/exonerate from further prosecution. *Majelis hakim yang diketuai S tak disangka, ~ "orang kuat" di kota itu, GBH alias A, 26 tahun, dari tuntutan penyelundupan.* The panel of judges headed by S unexpectedly acquitted the "strong man" in that city, GBH, alias A, 26, from charges of smuggling. – *ongkos* cost-free. – *ongkos kirim* no postage required. – *pajak* tax free. – *pemeliharaan/perawatan* maintenance-free. – *pilih* free choice. – *pulsa* toll-free (of telephone call). – *rokok* free of (cigarette) smoke, smoke free, smokeless. – *senjata* weapon-free (zone). – *setelah dimuat* free on board, FOB. – *tugas* exempted from duty, relieved of duty, on inactive duty. **membébas-tugaskan** to exempt from duty, relieve s.o. of his/her duties. **pembébas-tugasan** exemption/ release from duty. – *tuntutan (leg)* harmless, blameless.

sebébas as free as.

sebébas-bébasnya as free(ly) as possible.

membébaskan [and **ngebébasin** *(J coq)*] **1** to allow, permit. *Ibu tidak akan ~ kami keluar bermain sebelum pukul 4.00 soré.* Mother won't allow us to be outdoors to play before 4:00 p.m. **2** *(leg)* to dismiss (a summons), acquit, declare/pronounce not guilty, set free, liberate, absolve, exonerate. *dibébaskan dari segala tuduhan dan tuntutan* to be dismissed of the summons/ action, be discharged from further prosecution. **3** to give/grant independence/freedom. *Dalam negara démokrasi yang sesungguhnya, pérs dibébaskan untuk memberi penerangan kepada khalayak ramai.* In a real democratic state, the press has been granted the freedom to inform the public. **4** to free, relieve, exempt (from taxes, etc.), grant (a tax holiday) to. *Meréka dibébaskan dari pungutan bunga.* They got a grace period. *dibébaskan dari tugasnya* (s.o. has been) relieved of his duties. *dibébaskan dengan perjanjian* to be paroled. **5** to acquire (land) compulsorily (for development), expropriate (land). *~ diri* to get rid of. *hak ~ diri dari kesaksian* right to claim exemption from giving testimony.

terbébas free (of), released. *Industri tékstil tak ~ dari hambatan.* The textile industry is not free of obstacles.

terbébaskan to be relieved of (one's thirst, etc.).

bébas-bébasan 1 permissive. **2** licentious.

kebébasan 1 liberty, freedom. *~, persamaan dan persaudaraan* liberty, equality, fraternity/brotherhood: rallying cry of the French Revolution. *~ akadémi* academic freedom. *~ beragama* freedom of worship, religious freedom. *~ berbicara* freedom of speech. *~ berbuat* freedom of action. *~ beréksprési* freedom of expression/speech. *~ berfikir* freedom of thought. *~ bergerak* freedom of movement. *~ berkontrak* freedom to enter into contracts. *~ berorganisasi* freedom of organization. *~ berpendapat* freedom of expression. *~ berperasaan* freedom of ideas. *~ bepergian* freedom of movement. *~ bersaing* freedom of competition. *~ berserikat dan bersuara* freedom/right to organize and vote. *~ berusaha* free enterprise. *~ dalam hidup* permissiveness. *~ dari kepapan* freedom from poverty. *~ dari ketakutan* freedom from fear. *~ di laut* freedom of the seas. *~ intéléktual* intellectual freedom. *~ kekuasaan* freedom of authority. *~ kekuasaan kehakiman lemah penyebab muncul-*

nya korupsi keadilan. A weak judicial freedom of authority is the cause of the emergence of judicatory corruption. ~ *kréatif* creative freedom. ~ *memilih* freedom of choice. ~ *mimbar* academic freedom. ~ *pendapatan* freedom of opinion. ~ *pérs* freedom of the press. ~ *politik* political freedom. ~ *pribadi* privacy. ~ *tanpa batas* unlimited freedom. ~ *untuk berbuat* laissez faire, laissez aller. 2 independence.

pembébas 1 liberator, emancipator, deliverer. 2 security, guarantee.

pembébasan 1 liberation, release, deliverance, emancipation. *gerakan* ~ liberation movement. 2 acquittal, discharge. *memberi* ~ *kepada diréksi* to discharge the management of (responsibility for their actions). 3 exemption. ~ *béa masuk* exemption from import duties. ~ *diri* recusal. ~ *pajak* tax exemption/holiday. 4 freeing up, acquiring, acquisition (of land for development). ~ *tanah* land acquisition, expropriation. 5 remission (of debts).

bebat bandage, dressing, wrapping; → BALUT, PERBAN.

membebat(i) to bandage, dress, wrap. *Perawat itu* ~ *kaki saya yang luka dengan perban.* The nurse wrapped my injured foot with a bandage. ~ *muka* to cover one's face from shame.

membebatkan to bandage with s.t.

bebatan bandage, dressing.

pembebat dresser, s.o. who bandages/dresses/wrapped.

pembebatan bandaging, dressing, wrapping. *gunting* ~ bandage scissors.

bebatuan stones. *lapisan* – (in the ground) stratum of stones.

bebauan perfumes; → BAU.

bébé I dress, gown; → GAUN.

berbébé to wear a dress/gown.

bébé II (*D*) [B(innenlands) B(estuur)] civil service.

bébi (*ob*) baby; → BAYI.

bébék I (*J/Jv*) duck; → ITIK. *seperti* – *dengar geluduk* "like a duck hearing the thunder," i.e., to stare like a stuck pig. – *betutu* a Balinese duck dish. – *Manila* Manila duck; → MENTOG.

membébék 1 to quack, utter the cry of a duck or a sound resembling it. 2 to imitate, echo/repeat s.o.'s words. 3 to follow s.o. (without thinking).

pembébék a mindless follower.

pembébékan mindless following.

bébék II (*M*) bleating (of a goat).

membébék 1 to bleat. 2 to bawl, howl.

bébékan bleat.

bébék III → MOTOR *bébék.*

bébékisme following the leader without thinking (like ducks in a row).

bebeksan (*Jv ob*) → BEKSAN.

bebel (*coq*) → BEBAL

bebenah (*J*) to tidy up, put in order, arrange neatly; to clean and arrange/put in order, make (a bed, etc.); → BENAH.

bebencé long-tailed nightjar.

bebenyut → BELIBIS.

bébér (*Jv*) spread out, opened up; → WAYANG *bébér.* – *bentang* fully spread out, revealed in detail. *membébérbentangkan* to explain in detail, lay out.

membébér 1 to unfold, unfurl, open up (a rolled umbrella/sail, etc.). *Layarnya mulai dibébér.* They began to unfold the sail. 2 to reveal, disclose, unveil, give away (a secret, etc.).

membébérkan 1 to unroll, unfold, etc. 2 to explain, describe, lay out, set forth. *Tolong bébérkan persekongkolan itu.* Please explain the plot in detail. 3 to reveal, unveil, divulge. *Rahasia negara itu dibébérkan di hadapan publik.* The state secrets were revealed in public.

bébéran 1 s.t. unfolded/displayed. 2 explanation, analysis.

pembébér unfolder.

pembébéran 1 unfurling (a flag), unrolling (a carpet). 2 explanation, description, analysis, laying out, setting forth. 3 disclosure (of a secret), divulgence.

beberapa several, some, quantity of indefinite number; → BERAPA.

bebercak spotted, speckled. *sebuah ikat kepala* – a spotted/mottled/speckled head kerchief; → BERCAK.

beberék → BERÉK-BERÉK.

bebesaran (*J*) mulberry, *Morus alba.*

bebet (*Jv*) k.o. wraparound worn by men.

bébét (*Jv*) ancestry, lineage.

bébi (*E*) baby.

bebidung to pester.

bebika (*Ambon*) a cake consisting of yeast, sugar, coconut milk, rice flour, sago, vanilla, salt, and eggs, mixed up, kneaded, and baked.

béblat → BIJBLAD.

bebodoran (*S*) clown, comedian, buffoon; → BODOR. *untuk* – jokingly.

bebogohan (*J*) 1 to mate. *sepasang cicak lagi* – a pair of mating house lizards. 2 amusement (park).

bebola – *bulu* hairball.

bébong (*Pr*) servant; → BABU.

bebonténgan k.o. weed, Chinese/red sprangletop, *Leptochloa chinensis.*

beboréh → BORÉH.

bebotoh (*J*) 1 rascal, rogue, scamp. 2 referee. 3 gambler.

bebotok *ikan* – fish cooked in banana leaves au bain marie.

bebrayan (*Jv*) 1 to gather, assemble. 2 community.

bébrék (*Jv*) **membébrék** to expand (of a crack/wound/fire/farmland/trade).

bebuahan fruits; → BUAH.

bebuka (*Jv*) introduction, preface, foreword; → BUKA.

bebukitan hills; → BUKIT.

bebuyutan (*Jv*) ancestral, from generation to generation. *musuh* – sworn/traditional/hereditary enemy, archenemy; → BUYUT.

becak fleck, spot, stain, dot; pimple.

berbecak-becak 1 spotted, stained, dotted, with specks/dots. 2 dingy, muddy, grimy, dirty. *Celananya* ~. His pants are grimy.

bécak (*C*) 1 a form of pedaled three-wheeled rear-driven pedicab that carries the passengers in front of the driver, a bicycle-propelled rickshaw. *abang/penarik/sopir/tukang* – becak/pedicab driver. 2 (*ob*) rickshaw (a two-wheeled vehicle) pulled by a person. 3 (*coq*) DC-3 aircraft. – *air* pedal-boat. – *dayung* man-driven pedicab. – *komplit* (*J*) pedicab complete with prostitute passenger. – *motor* [*bémo*] any k.o. motor-driven pedicab.

sebécak (to ride) in the same pedicab. *Joni* ~ *dengan Yusuf.* Joni and Yusuf were riding in the same pedicab.

berbécak to ride in a pedicab.

berbécak-bécak(an) to ride around in a pedicab.

membécak [and **mbécak** (*coq*) and **ngebécak** (*J*)] 1 to drive a pedicab, → NARIK *bécak. Membécak hanya menuntut tenaga fisik dan keuletan.* Driving a pedicab only demands physical strength and stamina. *"Kalau kita bisa hidup di désa, Pak, buat apa kita harus susah-susah ngebécak di Jakarta ini?"* "If we could live in our village, sir, why would we work our asses off driving a pedicab in Jakarta?" 2 to ride in a pedicab. *"Mbécak dén?"* "Do you want to ride in a pedicab, sir?"

perbécakan pedicab (*mod*). *Tak ada dualisme dalam kebijaksanaan* ~. There is no double standard in pedicab policy.

bécakwan pedicab driver.

becanda → BERCANDA.

bécék (*J/Jv*) 1 muddy, marshy, swampy, soggy. 2 soft and wet.

berbécék muddy.

bécéng (*sl*) pistol, revolver. *Bila sudah diberi peringatan tidak mau menyerah, bahkan melakukan perlawanan, si – bisa ikut bicara.* When they refused to surrender after being warned, and, in fact, resisted, the pistol spoke out.

becik (*Jv*) – *ketitik ala ketara* (*Jv*) the good will make itself known, along with the bad.

bécok noisy, loud.

becokok → BICOKOK.

becuk *ikan* – parrot-wrasse, chiseltooth wrasse, *Pseudodax moluccanus.*

bécuk (*Mal*) noisy, loud (of talking).

becus (*J/Jv*) (mostly with negative *tidak* -) *tidak* – incapable, incompetent. **ketidak-becusan** inability, incompetence.

béd (*D*) bed. - *susun* bunk bed.

béda (*Skr*) 1 difference. *tak jauh* – *dengan* didn't differ much. - *harganya tidak seberapa.* The difference in price isn't so great. *tak jauh* – *dengan* didn't differ much from. 2 balance, remainder. 3 inequality.

bédanya the difference. *Itu kan tak ~ dengan animisme.* It's not much different from animism.

berbéda 1 to be different/unequal/divergent. *agak ~ dari peringatan Proklamasi* rather different from the Proclamation commemoration. *~ pendapat* to disagree, have a different opinion. *~ dengan* unlike. 2 to vary, be diverse/various. 3 to be different from e.o. by, a difference of. **keberbédaan** difference.

berbéda-béda to vary, varying, differing.

berbédaan (*coq*) to be different from e.o.

mem(per)bédakan and **membéda(-béda)kan** 1 to discriminate, tell apart, tell one from the other. *membédakan mana yang benar, mana yang salah* to tell right from wrong. *tanpa ~* regardless of. 2 to treat differently. 3 to be picky/choosy.

terbédakan distinguishable. *tak ~* undifferentiated. **ketakterbédaan** indistinguishability.

pembéda distinguishing, distinctive, differential. *harga ~* differential price.

pembédaan 1 distinction, differentiation, differential. *~ upah* wage differential. 2 discrimination, favoritism, unfair treatment. *politik ~ warna kulit* apartheid (in South Africa). *~ bendéra* flag discrimination. 3 classification (by differences).

pembéda-bédaan favoritism, discrimination, unfair treatment.

perbédaan 1 difference, distinction. *~ graduil/tingkat* difference in degree. *~ kurs* conversion rate. *~ tingkat suku bunga* interest differential. 2 disparity. 3 discrimination. *~ umur* age discrimination, ageism.

bedah 1 operation, surgery. *ahli ~* surgeon. *ilmu ~* surgery. *ruang ~* operating room. 2 (*Jv*) torn, broken/forced open. *- Caesar* Caesarian section. *lahir léwat -* Caesar born by Caesarean section. *- jantung koronér* cardiopulmonary bypass. *- jantung terbuka* open-heart surgery. *- kosmétis* cosmetic surgery. *- mayat* autopsy. *- mulut* oral surgery. *- perut* laparotomy. *- pintas jantung* bypass heart surgery. *- plastik* plastic surgery. *- rongga dada* thoracic surgery. *- tulang* orthopedics.

membedah 1 to operate on, cut open. 2 to split s.t. open.

bedahan 1 surgery. *~ plastik* plastic surgery. 2 scar, cicatrice. 3 analysis. 4 dissection. 5 incision.

pembedah 1 surgeon. 2 s.t. used to perform surgery (a knife, etc.).

pembedahan operation, surgery. *~ jantung terbuka* open-heart surgery. *~ pintas jantung* coronary artery bypass grafting. *~ plastik* plastic surgery.

perbedahan operation, surgery. *~ kosmétis* cosmetic surgery. *~ plastik* plastic surgery. *~ terbuka* open surgery.

bedak 1 face/talcum powder. *dasar -* foundation, i.e., a cosmetic cream, liquid, etc. over which other makeup is applied. *- dasar* base (for makeup). *- dingin* k.o. facial powder put on before going to sleep. *- kasar* powder made from rice. *- talk* talcum powder. *- toko* store-bought powder. 2 (*sl*) heroin.

berbedak 1 to put powder on o.s., put on one's makeup. 2 powdered.

membedaki 1 to powder s.t. 2 to patch up. *~ jalan-jalan bopéng* to patch up potholed streets.

membedakkan to apply (a powder).

bedal I membedal to hit, whip, beat, strike.

bedal II (*J coq*) to run off, gallop away (of a horse, etc.). **membedal** 1 to run wild. 2 to run away from home.

bedama (*Jv ob*) cleaver, chopper; → PARANG.

bedan-bedan heat spots, nettle-rash wheals.

bedangkik stingy.

bedar viceroy; → WIZURAI. *kapal -* viceroy's ship.

bédar → BIDAR.

bedara → BIDARA.

bedaru → DARU-DARU.

bedawang → PADMASANA.

Bedawi (*A*) Bedouin.

bedaya (*Jv*) 1 female court dancers. 2 a classical female dance, *usu* performed by nine dancers at a time, representing the nymphs of *Nyai Loro Kidul.* *- ketawang* a sacred, magic and religious dance symbolizing the sensual love between *Nyai Loro Kidul* and *Sultan Agung.* This dance may only be staged in the main front veranda of the palace, during a *jumenengan* and *wiyosan* ceremony of the prince.

bédé → BANDAR III 3.

bedebah (*Pers*) 1 misery, distress. 2 accursed. 3 wretch. *si -* stinker. *Kedua jung itu berisi orang-orang Marxist para – politik yang lagi diuber-uber oléh polisi dan agén rahasia Kuomintang.* The two junks were loaded with Marxists, political wretches who were being pursued by Nationalist Chinese police and secret agents. *lima perampok* – five wretched robbers. 4 jerk! (a mild insult).

bedegap strong, sturdy, well built.

bedegong (*S*) 1 ill-mannered/-bred. 2 stubborn, opinionated.

bedék → BIDIK.

bedél (*Jv*) operation, surgery; → BEDAH. **membedél** 1 to operate on. 2 to lance. **bedélan** 1 incision. 2 scar. **pembedélan** operation.

bedéng I (= **bédéngan**) (*Jv*) 1 loose soil which has been raised as a dike (sometimes planted with vegetables) in a rice field. 2 embankment, dike. 3 raised seedbed for tobacco seeds.

bédéng II shed, barracks.

bedés (*Jv*) monkey.

bedhol → BEDOL.

bedikar → BADIK I.

bedil (*Tam*) gun, rifle. *obat -* gunpowder. *menghadapkan – pulang* to harm one's own family. *menjual - kepada lawan* to foul one's own nest. *- angin* air rifle. *- bambu* empty threat. *- bedal* various firearms. *- buluh* (*coq*) empty threat. *- locok* (*ob*) musket, blunderbuss.

berbedil with/to have a rifle, armed.

berbedil-bedilan (*coq*) to shoot at e.o.

membedil to shoot (at) s.t. with a rifle.

membedili to shoot at.

bedilan shoot-up.

bedil-bedilan *~ sumbat* popgun.

sepembedil within gunshot, as far as a rifle shot.

bedinde (*D ob*) domestic help; → PEMBANTU *rumah tangga.*

bedog (*Jv*) 1 cleaver, chopper; → PARANG. 2 short-handled axe.

bedol (*Jv*) 1 pulled out, torn out, uprooted; → CABUT. 2 relocated. *- désa* an uprooted village. ***membedol-désa(kan)*** to move an entire village. *- modal* divested capital. *- santri* a relocated Islamic seminarian.

membedol [and **mbedol** (*coq*)] 1 to (re)move, relocate, transfer one's office/business. *Gedung Kantor Kabupatén Semarang yang sangat bersejarah itu dibedol, dipindahkan ke Bukit Kalipancung.* The historic Semarang Regency Office Building was moved, relocated to Balai Kalipancung. *Sebelas désa di Gresik akan dibedol.* Eleven villages in Gresik will be uprooted. 2 to break up (in order to move a household/establishment/family, relocate families, *esp* away from Java); → MENTRANSMIGRASIKAN. *~ brankas* to break open a safe.

terbedol uprooted.

bedolan 1 the result of moving/pulling out s.o., drop-out. *anak ~* a school dropout. *ongkos ~* transportation costs. 2 calling in (or, sending for) a *penghulu* to solemnize the wedding of the bride and groom at home; i.e., outside the office of the *penghulu.*

pembedolan relocation.

bedoyo → BEDAYA.

bedudak (*J*) → BELUDAK.

beduk /beduk/ and **bedug** (*Jv*) a large drum suspended horizontally in a mosque to summon to prayer.

bedukang *ikan -* k.o. freshwater catfish, *Arius leptocephalus.*

bedung diaper, swaddling cloth. **membedung** to diaper, swaddle (an infant). **bedungan** swaddling.

beduri → BAIDURI.

Beduwi Bedouin.

bé-éng (*J*) very, extremely. *gedé -* very big.

béga I berbéga and **membéga** 1 to move, stir. 2 to circle around (of predatory birds). **berbéga-béga** to circle around frequently. *Setiap tengah hari elang terbang ~ mengitari Gunung Tigo.* Every noon hawks fly in circles around Mount Tigo. **membégai** to circle around.

béga II membéga 1 to aim (a weapon). **2** to direct, aim, point. **3** to aim at.

begadang (*J*) to stay up till late at night.

begaduh → BERGADUH.

begadring → BEGANDRING.

begah (after eating) too full, stuffed.

bégak smartly dressed, a clotheshorse.

bégal (*Jv*) (street)robber.
  membégal to rob, hijack.
  bégal-bégalan robbery, hijacking.
  pembégal robber, hijacker.
  pembégalan 1 (street) robbery. **2** misappropriation.

begana (*J*) rice with spices.

begana-begini (*J*) to make pretexts. *tanpa* – straight, point blank, without further ado.

begand(e)ring (*D coq*) meeting.

begané (*J*) k.o. spiced mutton dish.

begap and **bégap** sturdy, compact, dense, robust; *cp* TEGAP.

begar 1 (still) hard (of food that will not cook). **2** can no longer be changed (as to character/bad behavior), confirmed (bachelor, etc.). **3** rough (as to the make of an article).
  membegar to be stubborn.
  kebegaran perseverance, stubbornness.

bégar → BÉGA I. **berbégar** to circle/pivot around.
  membégar to turn, pivot.
  membégari to circle around, encircle.
  pembégaran and **perbégaran** carrousel, merry-go-round.

begasi → BAGASI.

begasing → GASING.

begawan (*Skr*) **1** originally one of the names of Vishnu, Shiva, Krishna, and Rama. **2** title of honor for religious leaders, scientists. – *ékonomi* economist (title for several famous Indonesian economists, including Sumitro Djojohadikusumo). – *(yang) waskito* wise sovereign/leader of noble descent. *Pak Harto sebagai* – *yang waskito*. Pak Harto as a wise sovereign.
  kebegawanan *fungsi* ~ in front.

begéng (*J*) gaunt, skinny.

begénggék (*Jv*) whore.

begidik → BERGIDIK.

begini 1 like this. –, *bukan begitu*. It's like this and not like that. *Ceritanya* –. This is how the story goes. *Dengan pendapatan* –, *apa meréka masih tergoda untuk melakukan jalan béngkok?* With such an income, would they still be tempted to do s.t. immoral? – *perkataannya: "Aku tak suka mendengar katamu lagi."* This is what he said: "I don't want to hear what you're saying any more." **2** well! now! (to enter into the conversation). – *Marti, soalnya.* Well, Marti, the problem is this. – *hari* at this hour of the day/evening. *Mengapa kau makan* – *hari?* Why are you eating so early? – *ini* (emphatic) like this. – *pun* nevertheless, for all that. – *salah, begitu salah* damned if you do and damned if you don't.

beginilah (intensive) then, therefore, so. ~ *kita akan pergi saja.* So, we'll just go.

begini-begini as things are now, still just this way. *Kalau setelah 34 tahun kita merdéka perékonomian kita masih* ~ *saja, akibat negara masih berada terus dalam tahap mencari-cari.* If after 34 years of economic freedom we are still like this, the result is still at the seeking stage.

sebegini as much (as this), of such a size/an amount (accompanied by gestures of the hand). *Pesawat-pesawat* ~ *biasanya sanggup menempuh jarak maksimum 5 jam terbang.* Planes of such a size can usually cover a maximum distance of 5 flight hours. *hanya* ~ only as much/little as this.

membeginikan to do like this. *sebuah komédi yang longgar dalam struktur yang bisa dibeginikan-dibegitukan* a comedy that's loose in structure that can be molded in any direction.

beginian (*coq*) like/such as this; to do s.t. like this. *Udah sering* ~ *ya kamu?* Do you do this often?

begitu 1 like that, in that way, therefore, so, thus. *Bukan* –? Isn't it like that? Isn't that so? *Kalau* –, *mengapa?* If it's like that, why is that so? *bukan* –! no way! *bukan begini, tetapi* – *seperti yang berada di pojok sana itu.* It isn't like this, but like that, like the one in the corner over there. – *dong!* That's more like it! – *juga* likewise, similarly, and further, and also, as well as. –*lah* a) that's the way it is with …, that's the way thing are with … *Tina* –*lah.* That's the way it is with Tina. b) yes, that's about the way it is. –*lah lebih kurang.* That's more or less the way it is. c) and so on, and so forth. – *pula* likewise, similarly. – *pun* as well, and also. *Kamu diundang* – *pun adikmu.* You were invited and so was your younger brother. *(dengan)* – *saja* simply, offhand, without much ado, without making a fuss over it. *Kegemukan itu tidak datang* – *saja.* Obesity doesn't appear out of the blue. **2** very, too. *Ia* – *baik kepadaku.* He's very good to me. **3** (*coq*) immediately after, as soon as, when. – *dibayar, boléh dibawa.* As soon as it's paid for, you can take it with you. – *kapal merapat, penumpang pada turun.* As soon as the ship docked, the passengers disembarked.

begitu-begitu so-so, nothing to brag about. *Karena pertandingannya* ~ *saja, hanya beberapa pertandingan penting saja yang saya saksikan di Stadion.* Because the matches were so-so I only watched some important matches in the Stadium. *masih* ~ *juga* still so-so, not too great.

sebegitu as … as that. ~ *banyaknya* as many as that. ~ *jauh* to the extent that, to that extent.

membegitukan [and **mbegituin** (*J coq*)] **1** to treat s.t. like that. *Tak seorang pria yang akan mau dibegitukan.* No man wants to be treated like that. **2** (*euph*) to have sexual intercourse with. *Anak itu bercerita pada ibunya bahwa ia habis dibegituin oléh seorang laki-laki.* That child told her mother that she had sexual intercourse with a man (against her will).

begituan (*euph*) s.t. unmentionable, you know what (such as feces). *Jika téknologi WC keréta api berubah, maka petugas kontrol rél akan merasa lebih senang, sebab meréka tak perlu takut menginjak* ~. If the technology of the restrooms in railway trains changes, the track inspectors will feel more comfortable, because they need not be afraid of stepping on you know what. *perempuan* ~ prostitute.

bégo (*J*) idiot, cretin, imbecile, slow-witted. *berlagak* – to play the fool, pretend to be ignorant.
  kebégoan stupidity, imbecility, idiocy.

bégonia (*D/E*) begonia, Begoniaceae.

begroting (*D ob*) budget, estimate.

begu forest demon. – *ganjang* (*Bat*) a ghost that can be instructed to kill s.o.

beguk goiter. *kelenjar* – thyroid gland; → GONDOK, GONDONG.

begundal (*Jv*) **1** accomplice, henchman, stooge, crony; → KAKITANGAN. **2** (*J*) rascal, scoundrel.

begundalisme cronyism.

béha (acronym from Dutch *bustehouder*) bra, brassiere; → BH.

behagi (*ob*) → BAHAGI.

behandel (*D ob*) and **membehandel 1** to take care of, treat (a patient). **2** to handle (kindly/roughly, etc.).

behari (*ob*) → BAHARI.

behaya (*ob*) → BAHAYA.

behéna worth paying attention to; → BÉNA.

beheula → BAHEULA.

BEJ ~ BURSA *Éfék Jakarta.*

béj (*E*) beige.

bejad → BEJAT.

bejana (*Skr*) **1** vessel, vat, chamber, still, pot, cask. **2** vase. **3** bushing. – *berhubungan* communicating vessels. – *kakus* toilet tank. – *pasir* sandbox. – *pelerai* (*petro*) knockout drum. ~ *pemasak* still. ~ *pengokas* coking still. – *sorong* bedpan. – *(ber)tekan(an)* pressure vessel.

bejat I (*Jv*) damaged (of earthenware/wood, etc.).
  membejati and **membejatkan** to damage, spoil.
  pembejatan damaging.

bejat II depraved, perverted, wanton, corrupt, rotten, immoral.
  membejatkan to corrupt, spoil, deprave.
  bejatan depravity, perversity, corruption.
  kebejatan depravity, corruption, wantonness, immorality.

béjé fishpond dug in a lake, filled in the rainy season but dry in the dry season.

bejibun (*J*) → BERJIBUN. *Duitnya* –. He's rolling in money.

bejo (*Jv*) lucky.

bejuwit striated grassbird/warbler, *Megalurus palustris*.

bék I (*D J*) 1 head of a neighborhood. 2 district, neighborhood.

bék II (*E*) (in soccer) fullback. – *kanan/kiri* right/left fullback.
membék to play as fullback.

bék III (in acronyms) → PERBEKALAN.

béka I berbéka(-béka) to chat.
membéka to talk pleasantly to, chat up.

béka II (*M*) presently, by and by.

bekah cracked, slit.

bekakah the offering of a sacrifice in the month of *Sapar* (the second month of the Muslim year) to ward off epidemic diseases at the village of Gamping (Yogyakarta).

bekakak (*J/Jv*) grilled. – *ayam* grilled, whole chicken, on the spit (not cut in pieces, usually for a ceremonial meal).

bekakas → PERKAKAS.

bekal I 1 victuals (food or money for a journey). *Kami membeli nasi rames untuk – di jalan*. We bought cooked rice with side dishes to eat on the trip. 2 s.t. useful in the future, equipment needed for success. *ilmu pengetahuan adalah – untuk hari tua* knowledge is capital for old age. – *hidup* a) victuals. b) s.t. needed for success in life. – *kantor* office supplies. – *makanan* packed rations. – *pakai* used supplies. – *pokok* basic allowance.

berbekal 1 with/to have supplies/provisions. 2 to be supplied/armed with. *Tanpa harapan muluk dan hanya ~ ongkos sejalan, Rukmana berangkat ke Bandung*. Without high hopes and only supplied with a one-way fare, Rukmana left for Bandung. *~ undang-undang baru itu* armed with the new law.

berbekalkan to be provided/supplied/furnished with. *hanya ~ apa yang sangat dibutuhkan* only provided with what is absolutely necessary.

mem(per)bekali to supply/provide s.o. (with s.t.), furnish s.o. (with s.t.).

membekalkan to supply/furnish s.t.

(bekal-)bekalan all k.o. supplies.

pembekalan supplying, provisioning. *~ perhubungan* communications.

perbekalan 1 provisions, victuals, stock, equipment, outfit. 2 provisioning, supply of food, equipment. *alat ~* travel outfit. 3 orientation course, briefings, period of pre-job training for prospective members of the Indonesian Parliament.

bekal II pembekal (in the Hulu Sungai Tengah Regency, Kalimantan) village head.

bekam I cupping-glass; → KOP.
membekam to cup (by heated glass, incision or pinching).
pembekam s.t. or s.o. that cups.

bekam II (*J*) membekam 1 to clench, hold (prey) tight (in one's grip). 2 to hold in (one's feelings, etc.).

bekam III (and bekaman) bruise, swelling (from being pinched).
terbekam swollen (from being pinched).

békang → BIKANG.

bekantan a large monkey species of Kalimantan with a long nose and reddish-brown hair-colored skin, proboscis monkey, *Nasalis larvatus*; → *si* HIDUNG *mancung*.

bekap membekap to close, gag (the mouth/nose/eyes); to seize, capture. *~ mulut seseorang* to gag s.o. *~ mulut* to silence, hush.
membekapkan to hold s.t. (against). *Salah seorang pelaku mengeluarkan sapu tangan dan ~nya ke hidung dan mulut korban*. A sailor took out a handkerchief and held it against the victim's nose and mouth.
terbekap covered up.

bekas I 1 mark, trace, print, spot. – *darah* blood traces, bloodstain. – *jari* fingerprint. – *kaki* footprint. – *luka* scar, cicatrix. – *réman* skid mark. – *sidik jari* fingerprints. – *tangan* a) signature. b) handwriting. c) product of one's pen, one's writings. d) handiwork. e) blow, hit, strike. 2 traces, remainder, remnant, remains, vestige, ruin, debris. *runtuhan – gedung-gedung besar* the ruins/rubble of large buildings. 3 (before a noun) former, late, retired, ex-, previous; → MANTAN. – *Ibu kota Negara Républik Indonesia Yogyakarta*. the former capital of the Republic of Indonesia, Yogyakarta. – *istri* ex-wife. – *pacarnya* his former girlfriend. – *présidén* former president. 4 (following a noun)

secondhand, used, preowned. – *pakai* used, secondhand. *alat pacu jantung* – *pakai* a used pacemaker. *barang-barang* – secondhand goods. *mobil sédan* – *pakai* a (pre)used sedan car. *pakaian* – hand-me-downs. *perangko* – a used/cancelled stamp.

berbekas and membekas 1 to leave an imprint/a trace, mark with traces, leave a trace. *bilang lenyap tak berbekas* disappeared without a trace. *Yang membekas tentang peristiwa ini hanyalah penderitaan yang dirasakan penumpang*. What left an impression of this event was only the anguish the passengers went through. 2 to have/leave an impression (on). *Orang itu tidak berbekas sama sekali pada saya*. That person didn't impress me at all. *tidak membekas ke luar* invisible, not seen. *berbekas dalam hatinya* to make a deep impression.

membekasi to leave a trace on.

membekaskan 1 to leave (an impression). *Kata-katanya ~ kesan pada saya*. What he said made an impression on me. 2 to leave s.t. behind.

bekasan secondhand.

bekas-bekasan leftover, residue, remainder.

bekas II (*mostly Mal*) depository, repository, receptacle, container. – *sirih* betel nut holder. – *tinta* inkwell.

bekasam → PEKASAM.

bekat *penuh* – (*cla*) chock-full, crammed full.

bekatul (*J/Jv*) bran.

bekel I (*Jv*) hamlet head. – *bhayangkara* commander of the troop of royal officials at the time of Majapahit.
perbekel (*col*) village head.

bekel II → BEKAL.

békel (*D*) game of jacks.

békén (*D*) well-known, famous; → TERKENAL, TERNAMA. *yang* –.– celebrities.
sebekén as famous/well-known as.
membekénkan to make s.o. be well-known.
membekén-bekénkan to make s.o. become more known. *banyak penyanyi békén, yang sesungguhnya tak perlu dibekén-bekénkan lagi léwat penampangan wajah* many well-known singers, who don't actually need to be made better known through their appearances.
terbekén [and kebekén (*coq*)] most famous, best known. *Abdul Malik Karim Amarullah lebih kebekén dengan panggilan (Buya) Hamka*. Haji Abdul Malik Karim Amarullah is better known by the name of (Buya) Hamka.
kebekénan fame.

béker I (*D*) alarm clock.

béker II (*D*) 1 trophy. 2 cup, beaker.

bekicot (*Jv*) a large species of land snail, *Achatina fulica*. – *darat* escargot, *Achatina variegata*.

bekikuk crossbreed between a Bantam (fowl) and a *bekisar*.

bekil *ikan* – red snapper, *Lutianus spp*.

béking (*E*) 1 backing, clout. *Pemilik pabrik itu punya* –. The factory owner has a powerful friend (or, has protection from s.o. with power). 2 patron.
membéking to back, support. *Judi gelap itu dibéking "orang kuat."* The illegal gambling was backed by a "strong man."
béking-membékingi backing, clout. *Kalau ~ itu sudah bukan rahasia lagi*. Backing is no longer a secret.
béking-békingan patronage.

békingisme practice of seeking and relying on support from influential figures in (often) questionable projects.

bekisar (*Jv*) crossbreed between a Bantam (fowl) and a jungle cock.

bekisting (*D*) framework, mold.

bekléding (*D*) upholstery of a car interior.

béklés (*E*) backlash.

beklid (*D*) upholstery. *ahli* – upholsterer, *esp* of car interiors.
membeklid to upholster of car interiors.

béko (*J*) *sabun* – bar of soap, soap in bars.

bekoar (*J*) to speak loudly.

bekos (*Jv*) mbekos to snort with rage (of buffaloes).

békot → BOIKOT.

beksan (*Jv*) Javanese dance; → JOGÉT.

beku 1 coagulated, congealed. *darah* – congealed blood. *darah – di dalam hati* one's heart stands still, one's blood runs cold. **2** frozen (of water/a bank account, etc.). *Simpanan di bank itu masih –.* The deposits in that bank were still frozen. *air –* ice. **3** stiff, hard, inflexible, rigid. *Pikirannya/Otaknya –.* He is rigid in his thinking. *– kepolitikan* politically inflexible.

sebeku as frozen as.

membeku 1 to freeze, congeal, solidify. **2** to clot. **3** to stiffen. *~nya jaringan darah* frostbite. *laksana embun ~* like frozen dew.

membekukan 1 to freeze/congeal s.t. *Adakah cairan yang tidak dapat dibekukan?* Are there liquids which cannot be frozen? *Uang simpanan dalam bank dibekukan.* Deposits in the bank were frozen. *Hubungan antara kedua negara itu dibekukan.* Relations between those two countries were frozen. **2** to suspend, make inoperative. *Karena pergolakan politik, DPR negara itu dibekukan oléh présidénnya.* Due to the political upheaval, Parliament in that country was suspended by its president. **3** to shelve (a proposal, etc.).

terbeku frozen.

bekuan 1 s.t. coagulated, clot. *~ darah* blood clot. **2** s.t. frozen.

kebekuan 1 coagulation. **2** freezing, frigidity. *~ hati istriku mencair lagi.* My wife warmed up to me again. *pencairan ~ daging* the thawing of meat. **3** rigidity.

pembeku coagulant. *kotak ~* freezer (in a refrigerator); → RUANG *pembekuan.*

pembekuan 1 coagulation, congealing, consolidation. **2** freezing (of bank accounts, etc.). *~ 90% dari semua uang simpanan di bank-bank* the freezing of 90% of all deposits in the banks. *~ pada anggota badan* frostbite. *~ pembangunan* zero growth. **3** stiffening.

bekuk (*Jv*) **membekuk 1** to bend/fold s.t. hard in two; → MELIPAT. *~ tongkat besi* to bend an iron rod in two. **2** to defeat (the enemy). **3** to seize, arrest, apprehend, take into custody, capture. *Polisi berhasil ~ penjahat ulung itu.* The police managed to apprehend the professional criminal. *~ batang léhér* to arrest, apprehend. **4** (*coq*) to trick, swindle.

terbekuk 1 seized, arrested. **2** bent in two. **3** swindled.

pembekuk s.o. who captures/arrests.

pembekukan 1 arrest, capture, etc. **2** (*coq*) tricking, swindling.

bekuku(ng) *ikan* – sea bream, *Sparus hasta.*

bél I (*D*) (metal bicycle, etc.) bell. *– bahaya* alarm buzzer. *– bubaran* dismissal bell (in school).

membél and **mengebél 1** to ring a bell. **2** to call (on the telephone).

pengebélan ringing.

bél II (in acronyms) → BELA I.

bela I defend, take care of (frequently confused with **béla**). *– diri* self-defense. *Dia menémbak perampok bersenjata itu sebagai tindakan – diri.* He shot the armed robber in self-defense. *pasukan – diri Jepang* Japan self-defense force. *– paksa* (*leg*) self-defense (necessary violence in defense of one's own or s.o. else's body/virtue/property).

membela 1 to take care of, nurse, look after (a child/plant/boat/the sick), rear, raise. *~ orang sakit* to look after (or, care for) the sick. *Orang itu ada ~ beberapa burung.* That man did raise some birds. **2** to save, rescue, retrieve. *Ia dapat ~ jiwa seorang anak yang malang itu.* He managed to rescue that unfortunate child. **3** to protect, defend, maintain. *Ia tidak hanya ~ negara, tetapi juga kebenaran dan keadilan.* He didn't only defend the state, but also truth and justice. *~ diri* to get defensive.

bela-belain (*J*) to make every effort to, try one's hardest to.

terbela can be defended, defendable.

belaan protection.

pembela 1 provider, nurse. *~ orang sakit* nurse. **2** defender, counsel, apologist. *~ Tanah Air* [Peta] Defender of the Fatherland (during the Japanese occupation).

pembelaan 1 care, nursing. *~ orang sakit* patient care. **2** (*leg*) defense, plea. *~ perkara itu diserahkan kepada seorang penasihat hukum.* The defense of that case was handed over to a legal counselor. *pidato ~* plea. **3** defense. *~ darurat/terpaksa* self-defense.

bela II → BALA.

bela III *– beli* to go shopping.

béla (frequently confused with **bela I**) **1** (*cla*) sacrifice or live for s.o. else (by suicide/stabbing o.s./jumping in a fire, etc.). **2** avenger, s.o. who takes revenge, etc. (for the killing of one's boss, friend, etc.). *mencari –* to seek revenge. *menuntut –* to demand revenge, avenge s.t. *– sungkawa* → BÉLASUNGKAWA.

membéla to avenge. *Aku hendak pergi ~ kematian rajaku.* I want to avenge my king's death. *Jika benar ia mati terbunuh, kita sekalian akan -nya.* If it is true that he was killed, all of us will avenge him.

membélai to follow s.o. in death, sacrifice o.s. for.

terbéla avenged.

pembéla avenger.

pembélaan revenge, vengeance.

belabas (*cla*) silk interwoven with gold thread.

belabat → BELEBAT I.

belacak mud-skipper, goby, *Periophthalmus spp.*

belacan I a paste of prawns and fish fry (used as a relish); → T(E)RASI.

belacan II (*Jv*) k.o. wild cat.

belacan III various species of song birds; → (*burung*) KELICAP.

belacu unbleached calico/cotton.

beladau a tiny curved dagger.

beladu (*J*) bobbin, spool, reel.

belaga (*J*) = *berlaga* → LAGA.

belagu → BERLAGU.

belah I 1 crack, slit, (*geol*) cleavage. *Tanah – karena kemarau.* The soil cracked because of the dry season. **2** broken into two or more parts. *Pinggan itu retak saja dan tidak –.* The plate was only cracked and not broken into pieces. **3** divided (in two, three, etc.). *– tiga/empat* divided in three/four. **4** side, part (refers to parts of the body which occur in pairs). *kedua – mata/pipi/tangan* both eyes/cheeks/hands. **5** side, party (refers to opposing groups/parties, etc.). *Kedua – pihak ini akan bertemu untuk menyelesaikan segala kontrovérsi.* The two parties will meet to resolve all controversies. *pecah –* a) earthenware, ceramics. *barang pecah –* crockery, plates and dishes. b) to create friction. *politik pecah –* politics creating friction. *retak menanti –* "the crack awaits the split," i.e., the situation is precarious and ominous. *seperti pinang – dua* exactly identical, like two peas in a pod. *politik – bambu* policy of divide and conquer. *– betung* a long rip. *– buluh* wide stripes (on a garment). *(baju) – dada* (shirt, blouse) open in front. *– perlapisan* (*geol*) bedding cleavage. *– rekahan* (*geol*) fracture cleavage. *– hancur* split and crushed, pulverized. **membelah-hancurkan** to pulverize, devastate, etc. *– hati* heart lobe. *– ketupat* rhombic, lozenge-shaped. *– mulut* ceremony to name an infant. *– paru* lobe of lung. *– rambut* part (in one's hair).

sebelah 1 one half; one of a pair; → BELAH. *mata ~* one eye. **2** toward, on the side of, in the direction of, next door. *~ barat* toward the west. *~ sini* on this side, over here. *~ sana/situ* in that direction, over there. *~ kanan/kiri* to the right/left, on the right/left side. *anak gadis ~ rumah* the girl next door. *~ dia* on his side, in his direction. *berat ~* a) biased, one-sided. b) heavy on one side. *kamar ~* the next room. *lihat ~(nya)* please turn over, P.T.O. *orang ~* neighbor. *rumah ~* next door. **3** direction. *datang dari ~ selatan* to come from the south. *di ~* next to, at the side of, next door. *di ~ kanan* on the right side, over to the right. *pergi ke ~ kiri* to go to the left. **bersebelahan** adjacent, contiguous. *persis ~* right next to. **sebelah-menyebelah 1** side by side; opposite e.o. **2** on both sides of, on either side of. *Daniél dan Sondang duduk ~nya.* Daniel and Sondang sat on either side of her. *orang ~* neighbors. **menyebelah** *kepada* and **menyebelahi** to take s.o.'s side, side with s.o. *Di antaranya ada yang menyebelah kepada musuh.* Among them are some who sided with the enemy. *Pendiriannya tak tetap selalu ~ siapa yang menang.* He trims his sails to every wind. **menyebelahkan 1** to put/set aside. *Perasaan curiga harus disebelahkan.* Suspicious feelings have to be set aside. **2** to be/sit, etc. next to. *Ia duduk ~ istrinya.* He sat next to his wife. **3** to separate, sever, divide. *~ pelajar-pelajar yang berkelahi* to separate the students who were fighting.

berbelah 1 to divide, break/split up. **2** divided, not united. *Perdana*

Menteri menasihatkan rakyat bersatu dan jangan ~ supaya negara akan maju. The prime minister advised the people to unite and not be divided so that the country will advance.

berbelah-belah uncertain, vacillating.

membelah 1 to cut, divide, separate. *serambut dibelah tujuh* a tiny bit. *seperti pisang dibelah dua* like a banana cut in two, i.e., identical. **2** to cut open, cleave through, rip apart. *Kapal ~ ombak.* The ship cleaved through the waves. *Kalau tidak percaya belahlah dadaku.* If you don't believe me, well, cut open my heart. *~ angkasa/bumi* deafening, earsplitting, ripping apart. *panasnya ~ benak* suffocatingly hot, stifling. *~ laut/samudra* to cleave through the sea/ocean. **3** to cut across, take a shortcut.

terbelah [and **kebelah** (*coq*)] split, broken up, cut, bisected. *Sampan nelayan itu ~ dua karena terlanggar batu karang.* The fishing boat broke in two because it struck a coral reef. *pribadi yang ~* and *~nya kepribadian* split personality. *Frankfurt, kota yang ~ dua oléh sungai Main di Éropa* Frankfurt, a city bisected by the Main river in Europe. **keterbelahan** being split (in intention), irresoluteness.

terbelahkan fissionable. *Di antara isotop-isotop uranium yang ~ adalah U-235 dan U-233.* Among the fissionable isotopes of uranium are U-235 and U-233.

belahan 1 a split, crack. *~ pada pasu bunga itu masih belum ditampal.* The crack in the flower pot has not been patched yet. **2** portion, part, half, section. *~ papaya itu disimpan dalam peti pendingin sebelum dihidang.* The section of papaya was stored in the freezer before being served. *dalam ~ kedua abad ke-20 ini* in the second half of the 20th century. *pekan lalu penduduk di ~ lain kota di Jawa Timur itu* last week residents at the other end of the town in East Java. *~ bumi/dunia* hemisphere. *~ dada* the part of the body between the breasts, cleavage. *~ diri/hati/jiwa/nyawa* a) one's better half (= wife). b) sweetheart. *~ sisiran* part (in one's hair). **3** (*geol*) fissure. **4** fragment, shard. *~ gelas* shard of glass. **berbelahan** with a split/crack.

pembelah splitter, cutter. *~ inti* atom splitter. *~ kayu* woodcutter.

pembelahan 1 division, splitting, separation. *~ inti/nuklir* nuclear fission. **2** fission, parting, scission.

belah II (*M*) **belahan** distantly related. **berbelahan** of common descent.

belah III (*bot*) gill.

belahak membelahak to clear one's throat, hawk.

belai I stroke, caress.

membelai 1 to stroke, caress, fondle. *Ia terus menggéndong dan ~ Natalia yang tampak belum segar.* She kept on carrying and caressing Natalia who didn't appear to be healthy yet. **2** to flatter, coax, cajole, wheedle.

membelai-belai to keep on caressing/stroking/fondling. *Ibu itu ~ anaknya dengan penuh kesayangan.* The mother repeatedly/kept on caressing her child lovingly.

membelaikan to stroke/caress with. *Tangannya dibelaikannya pada punggung anjingnya.* He stroked the back of his dog with his hand.

belaian 1 stroking, caress, fondling. **2** flattery.

belai II → BELU *belai*.

belajar → AJAR I.

belak white spots (on one's skin, etc.), veins (in wood/stone); → BALAR.

berbelak with/to have spots/veins.

belaka (*Skr*) **1** only, solely, merely. *bohong –* just lies. **2** wholly, entirely, completely, altogether. *dibuat daripada emas –* made of pure gold. *wanita –* all of them women, only women. *habis –* utterly finished. **3** very.

belakang 1 back (behind the chest). *berasa pegal pada –nya* to have a pain in one's back, have a stiff feeling in one's back. *sumsum –* spinal cord. *tulang –* spine, backbone. **2** part of an object that can be considered as the back of it. *– layar* hidden, not known to the public. *– tangan* the back of the hand (as opposed to the palm of the hand). *– parang* the back of a chopping knife. **3** back(side) [as opposed to the front(side)], behind, rear. *lampu –* rear/tail light. *latar –* background. *pemain –* (in soccer, etc.) back. *pintu –* backdoor. *roda –* rear wheel. *– kapal* stern,

aft. **4** (in a document) on the back, on (the) back of this. **5** following, ensuing, next, coming after, later. **6** tails (of a flipped coin). *paling –* most recently. *– hari* later, in the future. *untuk – hari* for the future. *tahun –* next year. *itu perkara –* that's a matter for later concern, that's not important right now. *berpaling – to look backward. membalik –* to desert to the enemy, be a turncoat. *membayar –* to pay on credit. *dari –* a) in the back. *Dia menusuk saya dari –.* He stabbed me in the back. b) from the back. *Dari – céwék itu kelihatan hébat, séksi.* From the back, that girl looked gorgeous, sexy. c) from back. *Saya dapat melihatnya jauh dari – sini.* I can see her from way back here. *di –* a) behind, at the back. *Ia duduk di –.* He sat at the back. *bersembunyi di – lemari* to hide behind the wardrobe. *di – layar* behind the scenes, not out in the open. *berdiri di – pemerintah* to stand behind the Government. *berbicara di – s.o.* to talk/gossip about s.o., talk behind s.o.'s back. *Kalau sudah memberi sedekah jangan memaki-maki di –.* If you have given alms (to s.o.) don't use abusive language about him behind his back. b) (who comes, etc.) afterward, later (on). *orang –* the servants. *orang-orang yang datang di –* those who came later. *orang-orang yang di –* those who will be born in the future. *Tak boléh tidak di – akan dihukum juga.* It cannot be otherwise, those at the back will also be sentenced. *di – ini* who'll be mentioned later. c) later. *Di – kabar ini akan diberi pula keterangan yang lebih lanjut.* After this news, further information will also be given. d) abaft. *di – buritan* astern. e) to keep a low profile. *Dia orang penting tetapi senang di –.* He's an important person but he likes to keep a low profile. *di – mata* out of sight. *ke –* a) backward, back. *menoléh ke –* to look back. *undur ke –* to back up. b) and before. *pada tahun 1960-an ke –* in the 1960s and earlier. c) (polite and refined) to go to the bathroom. *Maaflah, saya hendak ke – sebentar.* Excuse me. I would like to go to the bathroom for a moment. d) to the rear/back. **mengebelakangkan 1** to move/turn s.t. back. *Dengan sengaja arlojinya itu dikebelakangkannya.* He turned his watch back intentionally. **2** to turn one's back on s.t., ignore, neglect. *Kepentingan sendiri hendaklah dikebelakangkan.* Self-interest should be placed last. **terkebelakang 1** fallen behind, be left behind, pushed into the background; backward, neglected. *Dia jauh ~ dari teman-temannya.* He has fallen behind his friends. *dana bantuan untuk daérah-daérah yang ~* assistance funds for backward areas. *Dunia komunis Blok Éropah Timur di bawah Uni Soviét berada 10 sampai 15 tahun ~.* The East Europe communist bloc countries under the Soviet Union are 10 to 15 years behind. *~ dari jadwal* behind schedule. **2** latest, most recent. *Menurut kabar yang ~, perundingan di Austria sudah berakhir dengan kegagalan.* According to the latest news, the discussions in Austria ended in failure. **keterbelakangan 1** backwardness. *~ méntal* mental retardation, Down syndrome. **2** arrears. **3** underdevelopment. *~ di bidang ilmu pengetahuan* underdevelopment in the scientific sector.

berbelakang-belakangan and **berbelakangan** back to back, with the reverse side to e.o. *duduk ~* to sit back to back. *Dua baris polisi bersenjata berdiri ~.* Two rows of armed police stood back to back.

membelakang 1 facing backwards. *muka menghadap, hati ~* to be a sly and tricky person. **2** to turn one's back. *~ saja melihat aku.* He turned his back when he saw me. *~ bulat kepada* to turn against s.o. **3** to remain/stay behind. *Mengapa kamu ~ saja, ayoh lekas!* Why do you stay behind, come on hurry up!

membelakangi [and **ngebelakangin** (*J coq*)] **1** to turn one's back on, have one's (its) back to. *Ia selalu ~ saya, tak mau berhadapan muka.* He always turns his back on me and doesn't want to look me in the eye. *~ lénsa* (in the caption of a picture) back to camera. *saling ~* back to back. **2** to turn away from, disregard. *Anak muda yang sedang mabuk berahi itu dibelakanginya.* She ignored the young man who was drunk with sexual desire. **3** to mislead, deceive.

belakang-membelakangi to turn their backs on e.o., back to back.

membelakangkan 1 [= **memperbelakangkan** (*ob*)] to postpone, put off, delay. *Jangan dibelakangkan!* Don't put it off! **2** to disregard, ignore. *Dia tidak mau dibelakangkan dalam pimpinan* *perusahaan itu.* He doesn't want to be ignored in the leadership of the enterprise. **3** to pass over (for promotion).

terbelakang 1 the last. **2** left back/behind, underdeveloped, backward. **3** the most recent, latest. **4** behind. ~ *jadwal* behind schedule. **keterbelakangan** backwardness, underdevelopment.

belakangan 1 recently, of late, not long ago, a short time ago. ~ *ini* recently. ~ *ini banyak orang yang mendirikan konglomerat.* Recently many persons have established conglomerates. **2** finally, at last, in the end. ~ *ini mengaku juga.* Finally he did confess. **3** (*J*) to come too late, be late. *Orang datang* ~ *tidak boléh masuk.* Late-comers are not admitted. **4** the back/reverse side of s.t. **5** stop press. ~ *dikirim* (of letters) forwarded.

pembelakangan 1 turning one's back to/on, placing s.t. at the back or behind. **2** ignoring, disregarding. **3** (*M*) back, reverse side. *Di balik* ~ *awak dicibirkan orang.* Behind your back people look down on you. *PT Usindo* ~ *berubah nama menjadi PT Jaya Bhakti, lalu berubah lagi menjadi PN Tjipta Niaga.* Usindo, Inc. changed its name to PT Jaya Bhakti and then changed it again to PN Tjipta Niaga.

belakin → BELANGKIN.

belalah (*ob*) → LALAH I.

belalai 1 trunk (of an elephant/tapir), proboscis. **2** (*– penyedot*) an elongated mouth-part in certain insects, proboscis. **3** tentacle. *– besi* the steel (swinging) arm of a (hoisting/elevating/lifting) crane. *– gajah* (at airports) telescopic gangway/aerobridge, airbridge (ramp between the terminal and the plane); → GARBARATA.

belalak I membelalak wide-open and staring (of eyes); → MEMBELIAK, TERBELIAK. *Matanya* ~ *memandang lawannya.* His eyes were wide-open staring at his opponent.

membelalaki to gaze/look at with large eyes, stare down.

membelalakkan 1 to open the eyes wide. *Dia tidak menjawab pertanyaanku, melainkan* ~ *matanya.* He didn't answer my question, but (on the contrary) stared at me with eyes wide open. **2** to stare at s.o.

terbelalak wide open, staring.

belalakan stare.

belalak II *– mata* k.o. marine fish, *Pellona kampeni/ditchela.*

belalang I a generic name for grasshoppers, stick-insects, leaf-insects, mantises, etc. *buta* – blind stare. *mata* – prominent eyes. *Pak* – a figure in folklore who is always lucky. *nujum Pak* – a forecast whose success depends on luck. *seperti paha* – said of thighs which are broad at the base and get more slender going downward, in older literature a reference to a beautiful woman. *(bagai) mencari* – *atas* to carry out a job that cannot succeed. *mata* – *belum pecah, sudah hendak membuta* to go to bed with the chickens. *– dapat menjual* s.t. easy to get, therefore valueless, for instance, a prostitute. *– telah menjadi belang* a stupid and contemptible person has become smart and noble. *lain ladang lain* – when in Rome, do as the Romans do. *– centadu* → BELALANG *sentadu.* *– kacung* a brown-colored locust which attacks coconut trees. *– kembara* migratory locust, *Locusta migratoria.* *– kerit-kerit* mole cricket. *– padi* locust. *– ranting* stick-insect. *– sembah/sentadu* praying mantis. *– sengit* → WALANG *sengit.*

belalang II (*M*) staring (of eyes); → MEMBELALAK.

membelalang to stare.

membelalangkan to open (one's eyes) wide.

belalang III k.o. fish, spotwing flying gurnard, *Dactyloptena macracantha.*

belalit (*geol*) stock work.

belam I *– api* a glowing piece of wood kept burning for some purpose. **membelam** to burn.

belam II membelam to get dark.

terbelam 1 vaguely visible, indistinct. **2** to disappear (into the darkness).

belam III (*ob*) **membelam** to stuff in.

belambang flooring of split *nibung* palm trunks.

sebelambang a bundle of black sugar palm fibers.

belambangan large log.

belampah (in Palangkaraya) to dig for diamonds.

belan I crossbar, bolt.

membelan to bar (a door/fence, etc.) with a crossbar.

belan II (in the southeast Moluccas) a traditional racing prau.

belanak *ikan* – gray mullet, *Mugil spp.* *– andang/anding* greenback mullet, *Liza subviridis.* *– jumpul* k.o. mullet, *Mugil planiceps.* *– kedera/putih* blue-tail/longarm mullet, *Valamugil cunnesius/ seheli.* *– rapang/tamuk* diamond scale/squaretail mullet, *Liza vaigiensis.*

Belanda I (*D*) **1** Dutch, Netherlands. *negeri* – the Netherlands. *orang* – Netherlander, Dutchman. *bahasa* – Dutch (the language). *masuk* – (*ob*) to put on the same level as a European. *seperti* – *kesiangan* (*col*) to behave like a Dutchman. *Tenang!* – *masih jauh.* Relax. We're safe for now, i.e., the danger/problem isn't immediate. *air* – (*ob*) soda water. *ayam* – turkey. *batu* – imitation diamond. *beras* – wheat. *durian* – a) jackfruit. b) soursop. *halwa* – chocolate. *jam* – on time; *opp* JAM *karét.* *kapur* – chalk (for writing). *kucing* – rabbit. *nangka* – custard apple, *Anona Squamosa.* *sagu* – starch; → ACI II. *terung* – eggplant. *timun* – a nonsweet watermelon species. *bagai/seperti* – *minta tanah* and *dulu permata intan, sekarang batu* – give him an inch and he will take an ell. *– berkulit sawo matang* Eurasian, Dutch-Indonesian. *– didong* a full-blooded Dutchman; → *orang* DIDONG. *– hitam* a) negro. b) (*col*) collaborating Indonesian. c) Surinamese. *– hitam serdadu* the black Dutch soldier i.e., a) the Ambonese soldier. b) the black Surinam negro with Dutch citizenship who during the Dutch colonial period served in the Netherlands Indies army or police. c) the South African negro who mainly served in the army of the Dutch East India Company. *– indo* Eurasian of Dutch extraction, Dutch Indonesian. *– kertas* Indonesian who has become a Netherlander on the basis of certain regulations. *– tempé* a derogatory reference to a Dutch Eurasian. *– tiga suku* an Indonesia who took Dutch citizenship at the time of the Indonesian Revolution. *– totok* a full-blooded Dutchman. **2** any westerner/European. *orang* – any European or Westerner. *– Inggris* Englishman, Britisher. *– Rusia* Russian.

membelandakan 1 to translate into Dutch. **2** to put on the same level as a Dutchman (regarding one's rights), treat s.o. as Dutch.

kebelanda-belandaan Dutchified, westernized, too western.

belanda II *– mabuk* Indian cuckoo, *Cuculus micropterus.*

belandang I (*Jv*) **membelandang** head over heels; helter-skelter.

membelandangkan to carry s.t. away.

belandang II (*Jv*) (in Jember, East Java) middleman (in the tobacco trade).

Belandanisasi Dutchification, Hollandization.

belandar (*Jv*) roof frame.

Belandawi Dutch (*mod*).

belandis (*col*) native Indonesian with pro-Dutch leanings.

belandong (*Jv*) woodcutter, lumberjack.

belandongan cut wood.

belandung too large, oversize.

belang 1 variegated; spotted, blemished. *anjing* – a spotted dog. *hidung* – s.o. who always runs after women, womanizer. *kucing* – a multicolored cat. **2** striped. *harimau* – *Sumatera* the striped royal tiger. *kuda* – a) zebra. b) piebald pony. *ular* – a spotted, poisonous snake. *si* – the tiger. *Karena habitatnya terganggu si* – *berkeliaran di jalan raya dan bahkan sampai masuk ke kampung-kampung.* The tiger is hanging around on the highway and even manages to enter kampongs, because his habitat has been disturbed. **3** stain, blot, spot, blemish. **4** true colors (bad character of s.o.). *Ia digelédah dan ketahuan* –*nya.* He was frisked (by Customs officers) and what he was up to was discovered. *(harimau) menunjukkan* –*nya* to show one's true colors. *orang mati meninggalkan nama, harimau mati meninggalkan* –*nya* the evil that men do lives after them. *– bonténg* (*J*) streaked all over. *bahasa Indonésia* – *bonténg campuraduk dengan bahasa daérahnya* the Indonesian language is all mixed up with its regional languages. *– cecak* spot, mark.

berbelang(-belang) striped, spotted.

berbelang (*bio*) variegated.

membelangi to spot, stain, make stains on.

belanga earthenware cooking pot. *kurang setris se–* one more slice and the pot would be full, i.e., just short of success. *memancing dalam* – to look for favors among one's relatives/friends. – *sekat* cooking pot with compartments.

belangah and **terbelangah** (*ob*) to be wide open.

belangir(an) *pohon* – k.o. tree, *Shorea balangeran*.

belangkas I female king-crab, *Limulus moluccanus. bagai* – like king-crabs, i.e., inseparable (because a pair of king-crabs walk about clinging to e.o.).

belangkas II chopper, small knife.

belangkin (*E*) 1 asphalt. 2 black shoe polish. 3 pitch.

belangko → BLANGKO.

belangsak (*J*) **kebelangsak** *hidup yang* ~ a hard life.

belanja 1 expenditures, expenses, housekeeping money, (money for) purchases. 2 wages, pay, salary. 3 to make purchases, buy things; to go/be shopping. *anggaran* – budget. *uang* – housekeeping money. *harus diberikan* – *terus* should be continuously provided with funds. *pandai* – knowing how to make ends meet. *tukang* – shopper. – *angus* money paid by bridegroom's family toward wedding expenses. – *belanji* to go shopping. – *dapur* daily kitchen expenses. – *hangus/hantaran* contribution of the groom to marriage expenses. – *jarak jauh* teleshopping. – *menyusu/menéték* money paid to the bride's mother. – *negeri* government expense. – *pasar* money for the market. – *pegawai* personnel expenditures. – *rokok* cigarette allowance. – *tumpangan* board, money paid to stay in lodgings.

berbelanja to shop, go shopping.

membelanjai to finance, subsidize, pay the expenses of, support financially. *Pemerintah* ~ *perjalanannya*. The government paid for his trip.

membelanjakan to spend (money), lay out (money). ~ *banyak uang* to spend a lot of money.

terbelanjakan spent.

belanjaan (*J*) 1 items bought, shopping. *daftar* ~ shopping list. 2 to go shopping.

pembelanja and **pebelanja** shopper, customer.

pembelanjaan 1 spending. ~ *défisit* deficit spending. 2 financing.

perbelanjaan 1 expenses, budget. 2 shopping. *pusat* ~ shopping center.

belanjawan (*Mal*) budget, estimate of future income and expenditures; → ANGGARAN *belanja*.

belantan cudgel, club, truncheon, nightstick; *cp* ANTAN.

membelantan to club, hit with a truncheon.

belantara (*Skr*) 1 *hutan/rimba* – the jungle, wilderness, primeval/virgin forest, the bush. *padang* – a) desert. 2 fields and forests. – *beton* (facetious reference for Jakarta given by Ali Moertopo) concrete jungle.

belantik I a spring-gun or spring-bow (used in hunting).

belantik II *bintang* – (the three middle stars of) the constellation Orion.

belantik III (*Jv*) broker, middleman in the livestock (such as, cows/buffaloes/goats) trade.

belantuk k.o. fish, marble goby, *Oxyeleotris marmoratus*.

belar (*ob*) **membelar** 1 to roam/wander about, drift from one place to another. 2 to swarm, teem, run around everywhere (as ants/mob/children).

belarak dried coconut leaf; → ABU *blarak*.

belas I – *hati* compassion. – *kasihan* compassion, pity, mercy, sympathy. *timbul* – *kasihan melihat anak itu*. Seeing that child, he felt pity. **berbelas-kasihan** compassionate, have a heart. *Aku tidak mau kau* ~ *kepadaku*. I didn't want you to pity me. **membelas-kasihani** to pity, be sorry for, commiserate with. *Para cacat sama sekali tidak minta dibelas-kasihani dan tidak minta pelayanan khusus*. The handicapped didn't at all ask for sympathy and special services.

berbelas-belasan to have a compassionate relationship with e.o.

memelas 1 pitiful. 2 miserable.

membelaskan ~ *hati* to arouse s.o.'s pity.

pembelas compassionate, sympathizing.

belas II formative for the numerals between 11 and 19. *dua* – 12. *tiga* – 13. etc. *yang kelima* – the 15th.

sebelas eleven (11). **kesebelasan** 1 (number of) eleven. 2 (in sports) eleven, team. ~ *sépakbola* soccer team.

belasan 1 between 10 and 20; dozens. *Pemerintah India memberlakukan jam malam pada* ~ *kota India untuk menghentikan aksi kekerasan berdarah*. The Indian government put a curfew into effect in dozens of Indian towns to halt the bloody violent actions. 2 about 10. *Ia berpisah sudah* ~ *tahun dengan suaminya*. She has been separated from her husband for about 10 years. *anak* ~ *tahun* teenager, adolescent. *Meréka berusia* ~ *tahun*. They are teenagers.

belasah membelasah to club, cane, switch, lash, whip.

belaster → BLASTER.

belasting (*D*) tax; → PAJAK.

bélasungkawa (*Skr*) condolences. *menyampaikan* – *pada keluarga* to express one's condolences to the family.

berbélasungkawa to express one's condolences.

belasut grumbling, growling, snarling.

membelasut to grumble, growl, snarl.

membelasuti to growl/snarl at.

belat I a type of large bamboo screen used for trapping fish. It has three cordate chambers, an outer (*sayap*), inner (*bunuh-paril*) and inmost (*bunuh-mati*); → KÉLONG I. – *angkit-angkit* awning.

membelat to catch fish with this k.o. trap.

belat II (*M*) splint.

membelat to put a splint on.

membelatkan to use s.t. as a splint.

belat III – *belit* crooked, devious, artful, cunning; insincere; → BELIT.

belat IV k.o. tree, *Ixora grandifolia*.

belata k.o. fish, *Selar spp*.

belati (*Hind cla*) foreign, from or of another country. *pisau* – a broad-blade knife. *tali* – hemp rope.

belatik (*Jv ob*) → GELATIK.

belatuk *burung* – a generic name for woodpeckers, *Picus spp*.

belatung (*J*) maggot (in corpses, etc.), botfly, *Cuterebra, spp*.

belau I (*D*) 1 blu(e)ing (used in wash water). 2 blue.

kebelau(-belau)an bluish.

belau II *ikan* – a herring species, *Dorosoma sp*.

belau III (ber)**belau-belau** to flicker, blink, shimmer (before one's eyes).

belawan k.o. tree, *Terminalia citrina*.

belayar → LAYAR I.

beldu → BELEDU.

belebas (*Tam*) 1 vertical and horizontal laths for affixing palmleaf walls or thatch. 2 transverse lath for warp in loom. 3 ruler, measure, measuring-rod.

belebat I k.o. cake made of mashed banana with yams wrapped in banana leaves and steamed.

belebat II initial steps in *pencak*.

belebegu → AGAMA *belebegu*.

beleda gruel of *kacang ijo, Phaseolus aureus*, eaten with syrup.

belédang *ikan* – k.o. sea eel (white with a thin flat body), *Dorosoma chacunda*. – *kering* said of a tall thin person.

belederu → BELEDU.

beledi → BALDI.

beledu (*Port*) velvet.

membeledu velvety.

belegar (*onom*) sound made by an explosion.

beleguk (*onom*) bubbling sound.

belegur (*onom*) bang! (sound of the roar of guns).

beléh (*Jv*) **membeléh** to slaughter.

beléhan butcher's meat.

beléid (*D ob*) policy; → KEBIJAKSANAAN. *Indonésia tak akan mengubah* – *penanaman modalnya*. Indonesia will not change its capital investment policy. – *pemerintah* government policy.

belék I → BLÉK.

belék II (*Jv*) (minor) operation (on a part of the body).

membelék to operate on.

belékan incision.

bélék I (*J/Jv*) 1 inflamed (of eyes). 2 conjunctivitis, pink-eye. **bélékan** to suffer from conjunctivitis/pink-eye.

bélék II membélék to scrutinize closely, pore over; → BIDIK.

belekék k.o. snipe, swamp bird.

belekok (*Jv*) *burung* – (*sawah*) Javan pond heron, *Ardeola speciosa*.

belél bell-bottom (of trousers).

belél to fade away (of color), stone-washed. *Ia mengenakan celana jin – biru luntur dengan sobékan kecil di sana-sini.* He put on his faded blue jeans with small tears here and there.

belélang terbelélang wide open (of eyes).

belélék wide open (of eyes).

   membelélékkan to open wide.

belélétan to stick (to). *Kuah gado-gado – di baju itu.* Some gado-gado sauce was stuck to the shirt.

belembang (*M ob*) bundle. *liuk se–* a bundle of black sugar palm fibers.

beléncong (*Jv*) hanging lamp used at *wayang* performances.

belendung (*Jv*) **membelendung** to swell, dilate, expand (like leather coming into contact with hot water).

béléng (*M*) **berbéléng** and **membéléng** to turn around.

   membéléng(-béléng) to turn s.t. around. *membéléng badan* to shift (in one's sleep).

belenggu (*Tam*) **1** handcuffs, fetters, shackles (of wood or iron). **2** s.t. that is thought to curb (one's freedom, etc.).

   membelenggu 1 to handcuff s.o., shackle, put s.o. in chains/irons. *Polisi ~ penjahat itu.* The police shackled the criminal. **2** to curb s.o.'s freedom.

   membelenggukan to shackle/fetter, etc. with.

   terbelenggu 1 handcuffed, tied, chained, shackled. **2** captivated (of one's heart). *Hatinya ~ oléh kecantikan gadis itu.* He was captivated by that girl's beauty.

   belengguan s.t. used to fetter/shackle.

   pembelengguan handcuffing, shackling, fettering.

beléngkét (*J*) **membeléngkét** to stick, adhere, cling. *Anak itu terus ~ pada ibunya.* That child keeps on clinging to his mother.

   membeléngkétkan to affix, attach, stick on, glue. *~ pengumuman pada témbok univérsitas* to attach the announcement to the wall of the university.

beléngkok (*J*) **1** to curve, bend (of a river, etc.); curved, bent; → BÉNGKOK. **2** insincere, dishonest.

   membeléngkok 1 to curve, bend. **2** to be insincere/dishonest.

   membeléngkokkan 1 to bend s.t. **2** to turn s.t., change (the topic).

   beléngkokan a turn/bend in a road.

beléngkong → BELÉNGKOK.

beléngsét ectropion, with the lower eyelid turned inside out; → LÉNGSÉT.

belenting swollen. *Perut orang sakit itu –.* The patient's stomach was swollen.

   membelenting to be swollen.

   membelentingkan to make s.t. swell.

belentung a large tree frog which on rainy days goes: tung, tung, tung, black-spined toad, *Bufo asper/melanostictus*.

belépotan (*J*) messy, greasy, muddy, dirty, filthy, soiled, smeared. *Hidungnya – sambal.* Your nose is smeared with *sambal. Akibat hujan abu itu, kendaraan-kendaraan bermotor angkutan umum jurusan Yogyakarta-Semarang dan Solo-Semarang, Jumat pagi – dengan abu kendati tipis.* Due to the ash rain the public transport motor vehicles on the Yogyakarta-Semarang and Solo-Semarang run were covered Friday morning with an ash layer, though it was very thin. *Pokoknya, dengan uang lima ratus saja bisa ngibing sampai – keringat.* The main thing is, for only five hundred (*rupiahs*) you can dance with a *dogér* till you are soaked with sweat.

bélér (*sl*) drunk.

belér (*J/Jv*) **mbeléri** to cut with a sharp object.

   kebelér to get cut by a sharp object.

beléra weaver's sword.

belérang sulfur. *asam –* arsenic. *– bang* k.o. rat poison.

   membelérang 1 to sulfur. **2** to become sulfurous.

belérong (*M*) → BALAIRUNG.

belésék (*J*) stuck (in the ground/mud).

   membelésék [and **mbelésék** (*coq*)] to get stuck.

   membelésékkan to stick s.t. (in the ground/mud).

   kebelésékan stuck.

belet (*Jv*) **kebelet** to have to go to the bathroom immediately (you can't wait any longer).

belét (*D*) appointment. *(me)minta – X* to ask whether Mr. X can be seen. *Rumah itu dapat dilihat setelah diminta –.* The house may be viewed by appointment.

beletak-beletok and **beletar-beletur** (*J onom*) the sound of crackling objects like wood, etc. burning.

belétér to babble, chatter, talk incessantly; → LÉTÉR.

beletok and **beletuk** (*J*) cracking sound (such as cracking one's knuckles).

   membeletokkan to crack (one's knuckles).

Bélgia Belgium.

beli buying, purchase, purchasing. *daya –* buying/purchasing power. *harga –* purchase price. *"Mau – apa Pak?"* (asked by salesperson in stores) "May/Can I help you?." *– belah* (*Sg Mal*) shopping. *pusat kawasan – belah* shopping center. **membeli-belah** to shop, go shopping. *Menjelang Tahun Baru Cina, ramai orang sibuk ~.* Just before Chinese New Year the public is busily engaged in shopping. *– putus* (system of) purchasing directly by check and not by a letter of credit. *– utang* leveraged buyout.

   berbeli (*Mal*) bought, paid, payable. *Ambil sajalah, tak usah ~.* Just take it, it doesn't have to be paid for.

   berbeli-beli(an) 1 buy for e.o. **2** to shop, go shopping. *Singapura murah dalam segala hal buat berbeli-beli.* Singapore is cheap in all respects for shopping.

   membeli 1 to buy, purchase. *mahal dibeli sukar dicari* s.t. hard to get (very rare/scarce). *(k)alah ~ menang memakai* cheap is cheap, cheap goods are dearest in the long run. *sistém ~ kembali* buy back system. *~ akad* to buy on contract. *~ berutang* to buy on credit. *~ bini* marriage by purchase in Tapanuli; the spouse is given a bride price in order to be completely free from her family and become the full right of her husband's family. *~ haji* to pay s.o. else to carry out the *hajj* for s.o. who is sick, unfit or feeble. *~ laki* to give money to a wife or co-wife so that she is willing to separate from her husband so that he can be gotten by the buyer. *~ ramék-ramék* (*M*) to buy retail. *opp* MEMBORONG. *~ séwa* to hire-purchase, buy on credit. *~ tunai* to buy for cash. **2** to buy off (by bribery, etc.). *dibeli* can be bought, for sale. *Tiap orang dibeli.* Everyone can be bought. Everyone has his price. **3** to obtain s.t. through great sacrifice.

   membelikan [and **mbeliin/ngebeliin** (*J coq*)] **1** to buy s.t. for s.o. *Ia ~ anaknya mainan.* He bought a toy for his child. **2** to buy with/using. *~ ke/kepada/pada* to spend money on. *Uang itu dibelikannya kepada beras.* He spent the money on rice.

   terbeli [and **kebeli** (*coq*)] **1** bought. *~ kerbau bertuntun* to buy a pig in a poke. **2** affordable. **3** taken a bribe, corrupted. **4** buyable. *masih ~ kantung saya* I can afford it.

   belian 1 s.t. bought/purchased, merchandise. *budak ~* bond slave. **2** (= **beli-belian**) (*coq*) buying things, shopping. **3** what one buys. *~nya* what he bought.

   pembeli 1 buyer, purchaser *~ adalah raja* the customer is king. *~ harus berhati-hati* caveat emptor. *~ kembali* repurchaser. *~ siaga* ready buyer. *~ tunai* a buyer who pays cash. *~ tunggal* single buyer. **2** s.t. used to buy. *Aku sempat menjual bajuku untuk ~ bola.* I managed to sell my coat to buy a (soccer) ball.

   pembelian purchase, acquisition, buying. *~ atau penjualan ke depan* hedging; → LINDUNG *nilai. ~ mobil tanpa dikenai béa masuk* duty-free purchase of cars. *~ oléh pemerintah* government procurement. *~ suara* buying votes.

belia (*Skr*) **1** young, youthful. *muda –* young and fresh, in the bloom of youth. *usia –* a young age. **2** youth; → PEMUDA. *Menteri – dan Sukan* (*Mal*) Minister of Youth and Sports.

beliak membeliak and **terbeliak** wide open and staring (of eyes), expose the whites of the eyes; bulging.

   membeliakkan *~ mata* to glare, open the eyes wide.

belian I (*cla*) shaman, witch doctor. *hantu –* the tiger spirit in incantations.

   berbelian to call a shaman to cure an illness.

belian II *pohon –* the Borneo/Kalimantan iron-wood tree, *Eusideroxylon zwageri*.

beliau 1 (respectful) he, she, they. **2** person. *kedua – itu* both of them.

   beliau-beliau (*itu*) those gentlemen (derisively).

beliawanti (*BD*) and **beliawati** (*Mal*) (*Skr neo*) female youth, young woman, girl; → PEMUDI.

belibas k.o. marine fish, rabbit fish, *Siganus oramin*.
belibat double-bladed (of an oar).
belibis *burung* – lesser tree duck, whistling teal, *Dendrocygna javanica*. – *kecil* lesser tree duck, *Dendrocygna javanica*. – *kembang* whistling tree duck, *Dendrocygna arcuata/javanica*. – *totol/tutul* spotted whistling duck, *Dendrocygna guttata*.
belida *ikan* – large river featherback, *Notopterus chitala/notopterus*.
beligat weaver's tie.
beligo and **beligu** wax gourd, *Benincasa cerifera/hispida*.
belik (*Jv*) a small spring, well.
belikas spool of thread.
belikat the space between the shoulder blades. *tulang* – the shoulder blades.
beliku bent (like an elbow), winding, meandering (of road/river); → LIKU.
belimbing I ridged longitudinally.
  membelimbing ridged longitudinally, corrugated.
belimbing II *pohon* – (*manis/besi*) carambola, *Averrhoa carambola*. *halwa* – syrup mixed with *belimbing*. – *asam/batu/buluh/sayur/wuluh* star fruit, *Averrhoa bilimbi*.
  belimbingan shaped like a carambola.
  belimbing-belimbingan k.o. weed, *Oxalis spp*.
belimbing III leather-back sea turtle, *Dermochelys coriacea*; → KATUNG I.
belimbing IV a tart-yellow color. *kuda betina berwarna* – a tart-yellow colored mare.
belincong and **belincung** → BELIUNG.
beling I 1 fragment, splinter (of glass/shell), potsherd (of a pot). 2 porcelain. *pak/pencari* – (in Jakarta) rag-picker/gatherer (of scrap iron/cables/worn-out articles/junk/secondhand goods (old radios, etc.).
beling II *pecah* – (*J*) k.o. plant, *Strobilanthus crispus*; → DAUN *keji beling*.
beling III (*Jv*) (*usu* **mbeling**) disobedient, rebellious. *puisi mbeling* poetry against established conventions. *seniman beling* anti-establishment artist.
belingkang terbelingkang sprawled; → GELIMPANG.
belingsat (*J*) **belingsatan** in disarray, a mess; chaotic, disorganized, in total confusion. *lari* – to run helter-skelter.
belingut and **terbelingut** (*ob*) sprained.
belinjan (*Ban*) tomato; → TOMAT.
belinjo 1 *pohon* – tree with edible seeds, *Gnetum gnemon*; → MELINJO. 2 (*coq*) bullet (of a pistol/rifle).
belintang *kayu* – crossbars (of fences); → LINTANG.
  berbelintang(an) athwart, (to lie) across (as of a beam/tollgate, etc.). *Pokok kayu itu ~ di tengah jalan.* The tree trunk lay across the middle of the road.
  membelintang 1 to lie athwart. 2 to cut across.
  membelintangi to lay s.t. across. ~ *jalan* to lay (a rope) across the road (to prevent passage).
  membelintangkan to place across/athwart. *Di jembatan itu dibelintangkan orang batang-batang kayu.* People lay trees across the bridge.
  terbelintang lying across, athwart.
belirang → BELÉRANG.
belis (*A J*) 1 Satan, demon, devil, bad/evil spirit; → SÉTAN. *Istilah popnya bagi sétan itu yakni* –. The popular term for demon is "belis." 2 troublemaker.
  kebelisan 1 possessed by the devil; → KEMASUKAN/KESURUPAN *sétan*. 2 to act in a strange way.
belisah → GELISAH.
belit (*J*) 1 turn, twist. 2 curve, bend. – *pusing* squirm, wriggle; crooked, cunning, deceitful, dishonest, underhanded. *Hati-hati dengan orang itu, banyak – pusingnya.* Watch out for that guy, he's very tricky.
  berbelit(-belit) 1 to wind, twist around. *Seékor ular ~ di dahan itu.* A snake twisted around the branch. 2 winding, twisting, sinuous (road). 3 tangled, complicated, intricate, involved. *Masalah itu sangat ~.* That problem is very complicated. 4 related, connected, more interconnected. *Perkara itu ~ dengan perkara korupsi di Jakarta.* That case was related to a corruption case in Jakarta. 5 rambling, to beat around the bush.

membelit 1 = berbelit. 2 to involve/implicate. *Untuk meringankan hukumannya ia mencoba ~ seorang pegawai tinggi.* To lighten his sentence he implicated a high-ranking official.
  belit-membelit intertwined, interlaced.
  membelit-belit to wind/twist around.
  membeliti to go around s.t., encircle. *Jalan itu ~ kawasan baru itu.* The road encircles the new area.
  membelitkan 1 to wind/wrap/twist s.t. around. *Anak gajah itu ~ belalainya pada ékor ibunya.* The baby elephant wound its trunk around its mother's tail. 2 to complicate, make complicated/intricate. *Dia sengaja ~ perkara itu.* He purposely made the case complicated.
  terbelit 1 involved/entangled in. 2 twisted. ~ *utang* up to one's neck in debt.
  belitan 1 intricacies, complications. ~ *birokrasi* bureaucratic intricacies. ~ *utang* mountains of debt. 2 kink, twist. 3 connection, relationship.
  pembelitan entanglement, complication.
belitung I *siput* – mangrove creeper snail, blunt creeper, *Cerithidea obtusa*.
belitung II common dolphin fish, *Coryphaena hippurus*.
Belitung III Billiton.
beliung 1 carpenter's adze. 2 a small axe; → KAPAK I. 3 pick. *puting* – whirlwind; → PUTING. *bagai – dengan asahah* inseparable.
beliut and **terbeliut** bent, twisted; → LIUT.
Belméra [Belawan-Médan-Tanjungmorawa] the Belawan-Médan-Tanjungmorawa toll road.
belo *ikan* – a) shad, *Dorosoma chacunda*. b) (*esp*) herring, *Clupea kanagurta*.
bélo (*J*) *ngaco* – to talk nonsense.
bélo-bélo (*Min*) *sogili* liver.
belobor → BLOBOR.
belodok I prominent, protruding (of eyes).
belodok II → GELODOK III.
béloh (*ob*) stupid, dumb.
belok I (*J*) muddy.
belok II (*D*) 1 block. 2 pulley. 3 prisoner's stocks.
  membelok to place in the stocks.
  pembelokan (*ob*) jail, prison, incarceration.
belok III (*J*) wide-eyed.
bélok bend, curve, turn.
  bélok-bélok (*naut*) tack.
  berbélok to turn, curve. ~ *ke* to turn to (the right/left), turn off to. ~ *kucing main daun* to do s.t. skillfully.
  berbélok-bélok 1 with/to have curves; to wind, twist; winding, twisting; tortuous, sinuous. *jalan yang ~* a winding road. *Jalannya ~.* The road is curvy. 2 frequently turning. *Ia berlari ~.* He kept turning as he ran.
  membélok ~ *ke* to turn/veer/bear to (the right/left).
  membéloki to (make a) turn.
  membélokkan 1 to turn s.t., change the direction of. *Mobil kubélokkan masuk ke garasi.* I turned the car into the garage. 2 to divert, detour (traffic), distract. ~ *hati* to persuade. ~ *percakapan* to change subject, turn the conversation in another direction. ~ *perhatian* to divert s.o.'s attention.
  terbélok(kan) turned, veered.
  bélokan curve, bend, turn; deflection. ~ *dalam* convex bank. ~ *luar* concave bank.
  pembélok deflector, deflecting.
  pembélokan turning, shift (in policy, etc.). ~ *politik luar negeri ke arah perdamaian dan persahabatan* a foreign policy shift toward peace and friendship.
  perbélokan 1 turn, shift. 2 curve.
belokok thorny catfish, *Megalodoras uranoscopus(?)*.
belolang small boat with outriggers.
belolok → BELULUK.
belom and **belon** (*coq*) → BELUM.
belonggok k.o. tree, *Alseodaphne peduncularis*.
belongkang river barge/cargo boat.
belongkéng k.o. edible univalve mollusk, *Ellobium sp*.
belongsong I (*Jv*) material (paper/bamboo, etc.) for wrapping fruits while still on the tree to hasten ripening.

berbelongsong wrapped in such material.

membelongsongi to wrap s.t. in such material.

belongsong II (*Bal*) a fabric of mixed cotton and silk.

belontang an East Kalimantan statue of the departed spirits.

belontok *ikan* – marble goby, *Oxyeleotris marmoratus*.

belo'on → BLO'ON.

beloon (*S*) /belo'on/ a net *esp* for catching shrimps.

belorok → BLOROK.

bélot 1 accomplice (of the other party). **2** turncoat, deserter, defector. **3** apostate. **4** betrayer, traitor. – *kerja* stoppage, cessation (of work).

berbélot and **membélot 1** to defect (to the enemy). *Seorang mata-mata terkenal Rusia telah ~ ke Inggris untuk mengungkapkan rahasia-rahasia nuklir yang vital.* A well-known Russian spy defected to England to reveal vital nuclear secrets. **2** treacherous, traitorous.

pembélot deserter, turncoat, defector. *Tabloid itu menyebutkan ~ itu sebagai Kolonél F. D.* The tabloid said that the defector was Colonel F. D.

pembélotan 1 treason, treachery, betrayal. **2** defection, desertion. *~ itu berlangsung ketika pesawat yang ditumpanginya singgah di Bandara Heathrow, London, dalam penerbangan dari Jenéwa menuju Chicago.* The defection took place when the plane he was flying in stopped at Heathrow Airport, London, in its flight from Geneva to Chicago.

belu – *belai* chatter, gossip.

beluam (*cla*) Buddhist monk's collecting bag.

beluas k.o. fish.

belubu earthen jar.

belubur square rice bin.

beludak I *ular* – a) hooded snake, *Naia tripudians*. b) pit viper, *Agkistrodon rhodostoma*.

beludak II → BLUDAK.

beludar → BLUDER.

belud(e)ru → BELEDU.

beluhan → BALUHAN.

beluk I (*Jv*) plague in rice (the stalk borer).

beluk II → SELUK *beluk*.

beluk III – *watu* Asian barred owlet, *Glaucidium cuculoides*.

belukang (*ob*) → BEDUKANG.

belukap k.o. mangrove, *Rhizophora mucronata*.

belukar brushwood, thicket, undergrowth, secondary forest, scrub. – *sudah menjadi rimba* an irreparable mistake. *dari semak ke* – out of the frying-pan into the fire. – *muda* land that has been left for some time not attended to until it has become a small forest again. – *teduhan* undergrowth. – *tua* land that has become forest again.

membelukar to go to weed, become scrub.

membelukari to cover with brush or s.t. similar.

beluku (*Jv*) plow; → LUKU. *bintang* – Orion.

belukut → MELUKUT.

belulang 1 rawhide. **2** corn, callus. **3** untanned leather. *tulang* – bones. *(tinggal) tulang* – nothing but skin and bones. – *kering* s.o. who is all skin and bones.

berbelulang and **membelulang** callous, horny (hands); → KAPALAN.

beluluk 1 fruit of the sugar palm. **2** (*Jv*) very young coconut.

belum 1 not (yet). *Saya* – *mendengar dari dia.* I haven't heard from him yet. – *waktunya* It's not time for it yet. *Saya* – *berkenalan dengannya.* I haven't met him yet. *orang yang umurnya/usianya* – *delapan belas* a person under the age of 18. **2** no (answering a question containing *sudah* or *belum*). *Apa sudah makan?* –. Have you eaten (yet)? No, I haven't. *Sudah kawin?* –. Are you married? No. **3** not including, exclusive of, not counting, before (counting), still left out. *Ongkosnya Rp 5.000,* – *pajaknya.* It costs Rp 5,000.00, not including taxes. – *dipersoalkan* still left out of consideration. **4** not quite, almost. – *500 penduduk* almost/not quite 500 inhabitants. *kalau* – if not (yet); until. *Saya tidak akan berangkat kalau* – *menerima kabar dari X.* I'm not leaving till I hear from X. – *ada* doesn't/didn't exist, unknown. *Waktu itu organisasi demikian* – *ada.* At that time, such an organization didn't exist. *Bosnya* – *ada.* a)

The boss isn't in/here yet. – *ada duanya* unequalled, matchless, unparalleled. *Hal seperti ini* – *ada duanya.* This is s.t. new/unheard of. **kebelum-adaan** unavailability as of yet. – *apa-apa ... sudah ...* nothing's happened yet, but ... is already. – *apa-apa anggota DPR kok sudah membéla Pak K.* Nothing's happened yet, but the members of the DPR are already defending Mr. K. – *disuruh sudah pergi,* – *dipanggil, sudah datang* a word to the wise is sufficient. – *duduk berlunjur dahulu* and – *duduk sudah berlunjur* to work too hastily; preparations are not yet that completed, work has just started. – *beranak sudah ditimang* don't count your chickens before they are hatched. – *ajal,* – *mati* one doesn't die before one's time. – *déwasa/akil balig* underage. – *juga* still not (though expected to by now). *Lama dia menunggu,* – *juga penjaga télepon menjawab.* He waited for a long time, but the switchboard operator still didn't respond. *belum ... juga* still doesn't/hasn't. *Jika sampai tanggal 25 Maret dia* – *menjawab juga ...* If he still hasn't responded by March 25th. – *juga ... sudah ...* no sooner ... then. – *juga naik panggung, meréka sudah teriak-teriak.* No sooner did they get on stage, then they (the audience) screamed and screamed. – *lagi* a) not yet, not to mention, without even talking about. *Itu sudah cukup mahal* – *lagi ongkos pengangkutan yang ékstra.* That's already expensive enough, not to mention the extra transportation costs. b) still haven't (even though expected to). *Sudah jam tiga dan suaminya* – *lagi pulang dari kantor.* It's already three o'clock and her husband still hasn't come home from the office yet. c) even before (doing s.t.). – *lagi meléwati pintu* even before passing through the door. – *lama (ini)* just recently, not so/very long ago. *Saya melihatnya* – *lama ini.* I saw him not so long ago. – *pai* (*cla*) and – *pernah* never has/have up to now. *Ayah* – *pernah ke Amérika.* Father has never been to America. – *... pisan* (*J*) generally/on the whole not yet. – *bisa nulis pisan* on the whole, he cannot write yet. – *pula* exclusive of, not including/counting. *Ia banyak memiliki lahan yasan* – *pula yang di mancanegara.* He owned a lot of real estate not including his property abroad. – *tentu* (it's) not necessarily (the case), it's not certain that.

belum-belum nothing has happened yet, (subject) hasn't done anything yet. *~ kok sudah menyemprot saya.* I haven't done anything yet and you're already scolding me. *~ sudah* still hasn't/haven't yet. *Buku Sulawesi Selatan ~ sudah mendapat banyak saingan atau merebut pembeli, di samping belum jelas juga ségmén pasar yang akan membelinya.* South Sulawesi books still haven't had a lot of competition to get buyers and besides that it's not clear what market segment will buy them.

sebelum before, prior to; *opp* SETELAH. *Meréka menghadiri résépsi ~ pertemuan itu.* They attended a reception before the meeting. *Berpikirlah ~ berbicara.* Think before you speak, look before you leap. *~ hari ini berakhir* before the day is over.

sebelumnya 1 beforehand, in advance, previously. *Anda harus memesan tempat ~.* You should reserve seats in advance. *Dia* – *dipekerjakan di Pertamina.* He was previously employed by Pertamina. *tahu ~* to have prior knowledge. *~ dan sesudahnya* (in correspondence) in advance. *terima kasih ~* thanks in advance. – *dan sesudahya saya mengucapkan banyak terima kasih atas kesediaan saudara untuk menjawab pertanyaan-pertanyaan.* In advance, I thank you very much for your willingness to answer these questions of mine. **2** previous. *édisi ~* previous edition.

belumpai → BELUM *pai*.

belun (*J*) → BELUM.

belungkang (*Jv*) **1** butt end of palm leaf stalk. **2** a young coconut split in two.

belungkur *ikan* – greater lizard fish, *Saurida tumbil*.

belungsing membelungsing to snarl at.

belunjur to stretch one's legs; → UNJUR. *belum duduk,* – *dahulu* "stretch one's legs before being seated," i.e., a) count one's chickens before they are hatched. b) be familiar too soon, be overly familiar.

beluntas marsh fleabane, a swamp gardenia favored for hedges; the leaves are edible and used for medicines, *Pluchea indica*.

belur I → HABLUR I.

belur II lesion, welt. *babak –* black and blue.
   berbelur-belur covered with welts.
beluru *akar –* St. Thomas's bean, a big climber with enormous pods, *Entada phaseoloides.*
belus I slipping off easily, loose (of rings/in a socket); → CELUS.
belus II (*D*) blouse; shirt.
belusetun Korean angelfish, *Pomacanthus semicirculatus.*
belustru an edible plant, k.o. luffa, *Luffa cylindrica.*
belut the *sawah* eel, Asian swamp eel, *Monopterus albus. sebagai – diketil/diketir ékor* "like an eel whose tall has been cut," i.e., to dash off. *sebagai – jatuh/pulang ke lumpur* to be in seventh heaven. *licin sebagai –* as slippery as an eel. *bagai menyukat – hidup* carry coals to Newcastle. *– kena ranjau/getah* it's a good horse that never stumbles.
   berbelut to catch eels, fish for eels. *kena kecipak orang ~* implicated in s.o. else's case.
belutisasi pisciculture of *belut,* the breeding and rearing of eels.
beluwek (*J*) crumpled, rumpled; worn out; discolored, faded.
bembam membemban to roast s.t. (in hot ashes).
bemban I k.o. shrub (used for roofing/baskets, etc.), *Donax arundastrum.*
bemban II a conical wicker trap with a spring catch that lifts fish and trap out of the water.
bemban III *ikan –* k.o. freshwater fish, two-spotted glass catfish, butter catfish, *Ompok bimaculatus.*
bémbar → MIMBAR.
bembarap (*ob*) k.o. litter, sedan chair.
bembeng (*Jv*) cylindrical, thick around.
bémbét → BIMBIT.
bémo [bécak bermotor] a three-wheeled taxicab.
   membémo to go by *bemo.*
   membémokan to use s.t. as a *bemo.*
bémper → BUMPER.
bén (dance) band.
bena I flood(-tide), flux. *air –* tidal wave.
bena II (*J*) **membenai** and **membenakan** to put in order, make (a bed); → BENAH.
béna (*Skr*) 1 interesting, worth paying attention to (because it is important or extraordinary). *cantik manis terlalu –* extremely beautiful (woman). *Apa –nya kepadaku barang itu?* Of what interest is that to me? 2 (after a negative) (not) so/very. *tiada berapa –* not so extraordinary. *– tak –* indifferent, unconcerned, nonchalant.
   membénakan (*usu* after a negative) (not) heed, pay (no) attention to; to consider (un)important. *Ia tidak ~ bahaya yang mengancamnya.* He paid no attention to the danger threatening him.
   pembénaan and **perbénaan** attention.
benah I (*J/Jv*) clear away, straighten up, fix up.
   be(r)benah(-benah) to clear things away, put things (back) in order, tidy up. *~ diri* to get ready/prepared.
   membenahi 1 to clean up, make (the bed). 2 to beautify (a city). 3 to arrange, straighten out, tidy up, fix up. *~ diri* to get ready. *Dia sudah dapat ~ dirinya, tidak lagi bergantung kepada orangtuanya.* He can get himself ready, he no longer has to depend on his parents. 4 to rehabilitate, reform.
   membenahkan to put in order, set s.t. out in an orderly way.
   terbenahi fixed/straightened up.
   benahan s.t. that has been fixed/straightened up.
   pembenahan arrangement, revision, tidying up (a room), rehabilitation, reform. *~ kota* city beautification.
benah II an insect rice-pest, *Nephotettix bipunctata.*
benak I 1 (*– tulang*) marrow (of bones); → SUMSUM. *mengisap/ mencarak/mencucup –* to extort money from s.o. *Pertanyaan yang masih menggayut di – saya adalah siapakah orang-orang yang kami temui tadi.* The question that still haunts me is who are the people we met a while ago. *tidak bisa melupakan kejadian itu dari –nya.* Cannot put that event out of his mind. *– kepala* brains. *– kuku* quick (of the nail). 2 (*– otak*) brains, mind.
   berbenak to have brains. *tidak ~* very dull/stupid. *tiada ~* to do s.t. rashly.
benak II (*ob*) 1 having a false ring to it. 2 obtuse, dull, unresponsive.

benalu 1 tree parasite, epiphyte, *Loranthaceae;* → PARASIT, PASILAN. *– api* various epiphytes that kill the plant on which they grow, *Solenopsis geminata.* 2 sponger, parasite, freeloader.
   membenalu to be a sponger, be a freeloader.
   membenalui to sponge off, be a parasite on.
   pembenaluan sponging off, being a parasite on.
benam set, sunk. *– matahari* sunset, sundown. *– timbul* countersunk (of screws).
   berbenam and **membenam** 1 disappear, out of sight, not seen for a long time, bury o.s. *Entah karena malu entah karena apa ia selama itu ~.* Whether due to embarrassment or due to s.t. or other, he has not been seen all this time. 2 to be/sink beneath (the water/mud, etc.), sunk (in sadness), not floating to the surface. *Coba lihat baik-baik, apa yang ~ dalam kolam itu.* Please look carefully at what has sunk in the pool.
   membenamkan 1 to immerse s.t. (in water/mud, etc.), cause s.t. to sink, drown. *… kataku sambil ~ puntung rokok ke asbak …* I said while putting out my cigarette in the ashtray. *~ diri* to sink, down, set. *~ diri di kursi* to sink down into a chair. *Sejam matahari ~ diri.* The sun set an hour ago. 2 to invest (money). *~ uang* to invest money. 3 to drive s.t. (into). *~ paku pada témbok* to drive a nail into a wall. 4 to keep quiet about s.t. (a case/ scandal, etc.), shelve, try to hide. 5 to sink/scuttle (a ship). 6 to put s.t. on ice/the back burner. *Rupanya perkara ketidakjujuran dalam départemén itu dibenamkan.* It seems that the case of fraud in that ministry was shelved. 7 to incarcerate, jail. *Dia dibenamkan dalam penjara karena curanmor.* He was imprisoned for car theft. 8 to suppress (feelings, etc.). *~ ambisi beberapa tokoh yang melirik pada kursi Waprés* to suppress the ambitions of some leading figures who glanced at the Vice President's seat stealthily.
   terbenam 1 driven deeply (into the wall/mud, etc. so that it's no longer visible), sunken/caved (in). *Mobil itu mogok karena rodanya ~ dalam lumpur.* The car got stuck because the wheels were sunk in the mud. 2 drowned. *Orang itu mati ~.* That person drowned. 3 flooded, inundated. *Karena banjir yang meluap sawah-sawah ~ sehingga padinya rusak.* Because of the flood the rice fields were inundated and the rice was ruined. 4 disappeared (from one's field of vision), set (of the sun). *Matahari ~.* The sun has set. 5 hidden between s.t. *Kampung itu seolah-olah ~ di antara bukit-bukit.* It's as if the village is hidden between the hills. 6 buried (in/under). *Ia ~ dalam utang.* He's up to his ears in debt. *~ dalam pelukan* locked in an embrace. 7 locked up (in a room/at home), not coming out. *Sudah seminggu ini dia ~ saja di kamarnya setelah mengalami musibah itu.* He locked himself up in his room for a week after he went through that disaster. 8 put on ice/on the back burner, shelved.
   benaman 1 s.t. submerged. 2 the liquid left over after s.t. has been immersed in it.
   pembenaman 1 subsidence. 2 embedding.
benang thread, yarn. *buku/geléndong –* a spool/bobbin of yarn. *salah –* a) wrongly woven. b) indisposed, unwell. *setukal –* a bundle of yarn; a hank; → TUKAL. *Dia tarik – berniaga.* He did an honest trade. *– jangan putus tapi tepung jangan tersérak* if there is a dispute, try to end up with both sides satisfied. *berolah raga tanpa ditutupi selembar – pun* to engage in physical exercise stark naked. *putus – boléh dihubung, patah arang sudah sekali* "broken thread can be joined, charcoal broken is done for," i.e., some quarrels can be patched up, others never. *bagai – dilanda ayam* all in a tangle, disheveled. *menegakkan/mendirikan – basah* to (try to) make wet cotton stand on end, i.e., a hopeless task, a waste of time. *melanggar – hitam* to break various k.o. taboos and restrictions. *sehari selembar –, lama-lama jadi sehelai kain* many a little makes a mickle. *terpijak – arang hitam tampak* one has to have the courage to be responsible for the consequences of one's actions. *tidak makan – (M)* illogical. *seperti mencabut – dari gumpalan tepung* it's like looking for a needle in a haystack. *– arang* a) a charcoal line drawn by carpenters to guide them in their cutting or carving. b) a boundary line beyond which one should not go. *ikut – arang* to stick close to the rules. *memijak – arang orang* to encroach on the rights or privacy of others, "tread on people's toes." *– basah* a really

wrong case. – *bol* rather thick yarn (for sewing mattresses). – *bola* thread rolled like a ball (without spool), the middle part of the ball is empty in order to be stuck within a rotating axle. – *bulu* wool yarn. – *e(mas)* gold-colored very thin wire (used for embroidering or weaving). – *gelasan* thread coated with ground glass for kite fighting. – *gigi* dental floss. – *ikat* twine. – *karap* threads in the warp heddles. – *karat* rubber thread. – *kusut* tangled thread. *menelusuri – kusut ihwal pembangunan dua gedung tambahan* to straighten out the tangled knot about the construction of two annexes. – *lungsin* warp. – *makao* gold or silver thread. – *mas* gold thread. – *mentah* yarn which has not yet been twined. – *mérah* the leading thread, the way that s.t. runs. **membenang mérah** to run through (as the leading thread). – *nenas* yarn made of pineapple fibers. – *nilon* nylon thread. – *pakan* woof. – *pancarona* varicolored thread. – *pembersih gigi* dental floss. – *pengaman* security thread, i.e., a colored thread running through the paper of a piece of paper money to deter counterfeiting. – *putih* still pure, like a very young child. – *raja* a) rainbow. b) → BENDÉRA *benang raja*. – *salib* cross hairs. – *sari/serbuk* stamen (of a plant). – *sek(e)rup* screw thread. – *sela* thread with several strands. – *sutera* silk thread. – *tali kincir* thread in the process of being woven.

sebenang a tiny bit.

berbenang 1 with/to have threads, with a … thread. **2** thready, stringy.

berbenang-benang fibrous.

membenang 1 thready, like a thread, filiform. **2** uninterrupted, at a stretch. *Kita bekerja haruslah seperti ~.* We have to work systematically. **3** fibrous.

benar 1 accurate, precise, right, correct, true. *Jawabannya – semua.* All his answers were correct. *Éjaan kata itu –.* The spelling of that word is right. *–lah seperti kata anda.* What you say is true. *ada –nya* to be right. **2** unbiased, just, fair. *Keputusan hakim hendaknya –.* The judge's decision should be fair. **3** honest, sincere, truthful. *Orang itu amat –.* That person is very honest. **4** reliable, trustworthy; valid, legal, authentic. *Kalau itu berita RRT –.* If that was a news item from the Republic of Indonesia Radio, it must be reliable. *surat keterangan yang –* a valid/authentic statement. *berkata – to speak frankly/one's mind.* **5** very, extremely, really. *Mahal – buku ini.* This book is extremely expensive. *Pagi – ia sudah berangkat.* He left very early in the morning. *– sendiri* and *bersikap mau – sendiri* self-righteous.

benar-benar 1 closely, accurately. *Nasihat gurunya ~ dipegangnya.* He followed his teacher's advice closely. *Pandanglah ~ wajahnya.* Look closely at her face. **2** really, very, extremely.

sebenar (*Mal*) true, real.

sebenarnya 1 actually, in truth; in fact, as a matter of fact. *sesuai dengan keadaan yang ~* in accordance with the actual situation. **2** it is really true that. *~lah dia tidak mau datang, karena takut kalau-kalau kaumarahi.* It is really true that he didn't want to come, because he was afraid that you might reprimand him. **3** properly, rightly. *diperlakukan dengan tiada ~* to be treated improperly. *dengan ~* properly (drawn up, in official reports). **4** true. *utara ~* true north.

berbenar (*M*) → BERBENAR-BENAR.

berbenar-benar (*M*) to talk candidly/straightforwardly, tell the truth.

membenar (*M*) → BERBENAR-BENAR, MEMBENAR-BENAR.

membenar-benar 1 (*M*) I to speak/say candidly. *Ia minta belas kasihan dan ~ serta mengakui kesalahannya.* He asked for compassion and spoke candidly as well as admitted his mistake. **2** to ask, request. *Meskipun telah berkali-kali ia ~ tidak dikabulkan juga.* Although he had asked frequently, his request still wasn't granted.

membenari (*M*) to advise s.o. *Ibu tidak bosan-bosan ~ anaknya yang nakal itu.* Mother never got tired of giving advice to her naughty child.

membenar-benari to do/take s.t. seriously.

membenarkan 1 (and **memperbenar**) to correct, set s.t. right/straight. *Ia mencoba ~ kata-katanya yang telah terlanjur –.* He tried to set straight the words he had spoken hastily. *Guru menyuruh murid ~ kesalahannya.* The teacher ordered the pupil to correct his mistake. **2** to confirm. *Ia tidak menyangkal dan tidak pula ~ desas-desus itu.* He neither denied nor confirmed those rumors. **3** to approve. *Pemerintah tidak pernah ~ tindakan yang menyalahi undang-undang negara.* The Government never approves of measures violating state laws. **4** to permit, allow, yield to, sustain (an objection), justify (an action). *Pihak majikan tidak ~ tuntutan kaum buruh.* Employers don't yield to the demands of workers. *tidak dapat dibenarkan* unjustified. **5** to exonerate. **6** to acknowledge.

terbenar the truest.

benaran 1 genuine. **2** (*coq*) to do s.t. right. *~ aja dong!* Hey, do it right!

kebenaran 1 correctness, accuracy, rightness. *Ia masih menyangsikan ~ berita itu.* He still questions the accuracy of that news. **2** sincerity, honesty, truth. *~ yang diajarkan oléh agama* the truth taught by religion. *~ yang menyeluruh* the whole truth. **3** reliability, trustworthiness, fidelity. *Tidak seorang pun menyangsikan ~ hatinya.* Nobody doubted his trustworthiness. **4** approval. *Dengan ~ yang dipertuan, kami masuk istana.* With the approval of the sovereign, we entered the palace. **5** reality, fact. **6** confirmation, proof, evidence. **7** (*J*) by chance/accident, coincidentally; → KEBETULAN. *Nah, ~ dia datang sekarang, kita dapat bertanya langsung kepadanya.* Take a look, he might be coming now, we can ask him directly.

pembenar s.t. that justifies, justification, justificatory, justifying.

pembenaran 1 justification, approval, legitimization. **2** confirmation.

benara I (*Tam cla*) laundryman.

membenara to wash clothes.

benara II (*A ob*) → MENARA.

benatu laundryman; → PENATU.

bencah bog, marsh, swamp. *sawah –* (*ob*) irrigated rice field.

berbencah(-bencah) marshy, swampy, soggy, muddy, oozing.

membencah 1 to become soggy, wet, marshy, swampy, etc. **2** to splash, make s.t. wet or soggy. *Ia dibencah air got yang berlumpur.* He got splashed with water from the muddy gutter.

membencahkan to splash with s.t.

bencahan splash.

bencana (*Skr*) affliction, calamity, catastrophe, disaster, cataclysm. *bala –* (case of) emergency. *berbuat – atas* to damage/harm. *dalam –* (to be) in danger. *hari –* a disastrous day. *– alam* natural disaster, "act of God." *– kematian* danger of life, deadly danger. *Ia meloloskan diri dari – kematian* he escaped death.

membencanai 1 to bring bad luck (to). **2** to disturb, inconvenience. **3** to deceive, mislead, cheat.

membencanakan 1 to endanger, jeopardize. **2** to disturb, inconvenience.

béncang-béncul full of pimples (of the face).

bencar dazzled (by glare).

bencat → GENCAT.

bencés (*gay sl*) effeminate, gay.

bencét membencét 1 to push, press. **2** to single out (for criticism), pick on.

benci I hate, aversion, dislike. *– aku!* How awful! Oh, no! *– akan/kepada/terhadap* to hate, loathe, despise. *– dan marah dan dengki* hate, anger, spite.

berbenci(an) to hate e.o.

membenci to hate, dislike, have an aversion to, despise. *Ia ~ ketidakadilan.* He hates injustice. *yang dibenci* odious, hateful. *saling ~* to hate e.o.

benci-membenci to hate e.o.

membencikan 1 to inspire/cause hatred, fill with hate, hateful, odious. *yang dibencikan kepada* what one has against s.o. **2** → MEMBENCI.

kebencian 1 hatred, hate, object of hatred, aversion. *menabur benih ~ di antara penduduk* to sow the seeds of hatred among the population. *~ pada orang asing* xenophobia. *~ pada perempuan* misogyny. **2** (= **kebenci-bencian**) inspired by hatred, vindictive.

pembenci 1 hater. **2** s.t. that makes s.o. hate. *obat –* a talisman/charm to make s.o. hate s.o., e.g., to make a girl hate a rival suitor.

benci II [ben(ar-benar) ci(nta)] (*BG*) to really love e.o.

bencirit (*J*) to have an involuntary bowel movement.

béncong (*Pr*) 1 homosexual, gay. 2 female impersonator; → BANCI.

benda (*Skr*) 1 thing, object. 2 matter. 3 collateral. *tanah dan – yang ada di atasnya* (in documents) the land and the buildings/ structures erected thereon (or, with the buildings and structures thereon; and anything upon it; and its appendages). *harta –* wealth, riches, property. *kata/nama –* (*gram*) noun, substantive. *mata –* valuables. *– angkasa* celestial body/object, space object. *– asing* foreign body/matter. *– bergerak* movable property. *– berharga* valuables. *– (yang) bertubuh* physical object. *– buang(an)* excrement, manure. *– buatan* artifact. *– cair* liquid. *– duniawi* worldly matters. *– hidup* animate object. *– ikutan* minor matter. *– keras* a blunt instrument. *– koléksi* collectable (item). *– langit* celestial body. *– langit tak dikenal* unidentified flying object, UFO. *– letupan* explosive material. *– luapan* explosive matter. *– mati* inanimate object, immovables. *– padat* solid matter, solids. *– pakai* consumer goods. *– penangkis* antibody. *– perniagaan* merchandise. *– pos* stamps, postcards, etc. *– pos bercétakan prangko* prestamped postal items. *– rampasan* confiscated goods. *– sitaan* attached/seized goods. *– tanah* land (as property). *– terbang anéh* unidentified flying object, UFO. *– tetap* real estate; → LAHAN *yasan. – tidak bergerak* real estate. *– (yang) tidak bertubuh* intangible object. *– tuang* casting from mold. *– yang tak dikenal* unidentified flying object, UFO. *– yang terikut* foreign matters.

berbenda to be well-to-do, be well off.

membendakan 1 to make s.t. materialize, reify. 2 to make a noun of, nominalize. *Fungsi "nya" pada "tingginya" untuk ~ kata sifat "tinggi."* The function of *"nya"* in *"tingginya"* is to make a noun of the adjective *"tinggi."*

kebendaan 1 collateral. 2 material. *kekuatan ~ dan kerohanian* material and spiritual strength. 3 materialism. 4 object, item. *~ bergerak* movable property. *~ tak bergerak* real estate. *~ tetap* real estate. 5 worldly goods.

pembendaan 1 materialization. 2 nominalization.

perbendaan material, stock, provisions.

bendahara (*Skr*) 1 treasurer (of an organization/foundation/club, etc.); → BENDAHARI. 2 bishop (in chess). 3 (*cla*) the title of a very exalted Malay State official, *usu* ranking next to the heir-apparent in old time Malay, in effect, the Prime Minister. *– (M)* a title used, for instance, in *Datuk/Sutan (Datuk) – di Sungai Tarap* name of a dignitary in the Minangkabau area, domiciled at Sungai Tarap.

perbendabaraan 1 treasury. *~ kata* vocabulary. *~ negara* State Treasury. 2 riches, wealth. 3 list of valuables.

bendaharawan treasurer, bursar.

bendahari (*Hind*) 1 (*cla*) *penghulu –* in medieval Malaka, the ruler's chamberlain, secretary and treasurer. 2 treasurer.

bendahariwati female treasurer.

bendal membendal(kan) 1 to arouse. 2 to reflect.

bendalu → BENALU.

bendang (*Mal*) wet rice field.

bendaniah material.

bendar → BANDAR.

bendari I → BENDAHARI.

bendari II ship's cook.

bendawi material. *kebutuhan –* material needs.

bendé (*Jv*) small copper or brass gong; → CANANG.

béndel (*D*) bundle. *se– surat* a bundle of documents, a file.

membéndel(kan) 1 to bundle. file. 2 to bind (books).

pembéndelan binding.

bendela → BANDELA.

bénder (*D*) (book)binder.

bendéra I (*Port*) flag, colors. *apél – 17-an* and *upacara – 17-an* flag ceremony on the 17th of each month in commemoration of Indonesia's Independence Day (August 17). *hidup di bawah – negara lain* to live under the flag of another country. *– Benang Raja* the four-color flag of the separatist Republik Maluku Selatan. *– bintang kejora* the flag used by those trying to achieve a free Papua. *– biru* the blue flag flown in coastal towns on the Island of Java to indicate that it is too dangerous for ships to moor

there. *– kebangsaan* national flag. *– kemudahan* flag of convenience. *– kuning* yellow jack, a yellow flag, flown on a ship as a sign of quarantine or elsewhere as a sign that a death has occurred. *Di Jakarta, jika ada – kuning berkibar di ujung jalan, itu tanda ada orang meninggal dunia.* In Jakarta if a yellow flag is flying at the end of a street, it is a sign that s.o. has died. *– mérah* a) a flag *usu* flown in case of fire. b) (*naut*) a red burgee, designating in the International Code of Signals the letter "B" flown by itself to show that a vessel is carrying, loading, or discharging explosives or highly inflammable material. *– mérah putih* the Indonesian flag. *– negara* state flag. *– penungkul* flag of truce. *– Pusaka* the Indonesian Red-and-White Flag flown when President Soekarno and Vice-President Hatta proclaimed Indonesia's Independence on August 17, 1945, now stored and protected by the Indonesian Government. *– putih* the white flag flown when asking for surrender or peace. *– salah* (in sports) penalty flag. *– setengah tiang* flag flown at half mast. *– ular-ular* long narrow banner. *– yang memudahkan* flag of convenience.

berbendéra to fly the ... flag. *kapal ~ Panama* a ship flying the flag of Panama.

membendérai to dress with flags.

bendéra II k.o. decorative fish, Moorish idol, toby, *Zanclus cornutus/canescens*.

benderang I (*cla*) *tombak –* State lance/spear with tuft of horsehair.

benderang II *bulan –* full moon. *terang –* brilliantly lit.

membenderang(i) to light up, illuminate, spread light on.

benderung (*cla*) 1 passage between two (palace) buildings. 2 passage in a prince's audience rooms.

bendésa (*Bal*) village head.

béndi I (*Hind*) a two-wheeled horse-drawn carriage.

berbéndi and **membéndi** to ride in such a carriage.

béndi II (*Hind*) *kacang/sayur –* okra, *Hibiscus esculentus*.

béndi III (*Pr*) police.

bendir (*Jv ob*) small gong.

béndiwan a *béndi* driver.

bendo I (*Jv*) chopper, wooden knife.

bendo II (*S*) k.o. headdress.

bendoro (*Jv*) title of nobility.

bendosa (*Jv*) catafalque.

benduan (*Hind*) convict.

bendul I crossbeam. *pak/si –* duffer, dullard. *– jendéla* window frame. *– pintu* threshold beam.

bendul II swollen (of eyes); → BENGUL.

bendul III (*cla*) room where the king holds private meetings.

bendung (*J/Jv*) 1 fishpond (in a river, at sea). 2 irrigation overseer. 3 weir, dam. *– balas* counterdam. *– penangkap air* check-dam. *– penumpang air* reservoir dam.

membendung 1 to dam up. *Sungai yang besar itu dapat dibendung.* That large river can be dammed. 2 to stop, check, arrest, stem, curb. *Aturan itu dimaksudkan untuk ~ pemasukan barang-barang méwah.* That regulation is meant to curb the importation of luxury items.

membendungi to dam up, embank.

terbendung dammed up, stopped, checked, etc. *tidak ~* uncontrollable, irresistible.

bendungan dam, dyke, weir, barrage, embankment. *anak ~ cofferdam. anak ~ awal/utama* primary cofferdam. *~ élak* coffer dam. *~ gelombang* breakwater. *~ pelimpah* spillway. *~ penangkap air* and *– pengélak (peti)* cofferdam.

pembendung 1 dam, weir, dyke. 2 (s.t.) that stops/checks/dams up/halts/puts an end to, etc.

pembendungan damming up, embanking, embankment; controlling, containment. *politik ~* containment policy.

bénefaktif (*E*) benefactive.

bener → BENAR. *yang – aja* be serious, don't kid around.

ngebenerin (*J coq*) to repair, renovate. *duit buat ~ atap yang rusak* money to repair a damaged roof.

beneran real(ly). *Kamu gila ~ atau gila-gilaan?* Are you really crazy or are you just acting crazy? *senapan ~* a real rifle/gun; *opp* SENAPAN *mainan.*

pembeneran justification, justifying; repairing, renovating.

benerang → BENDERANG.

béng (in acronyms) → BÉNGKÉL.

bengah (*ob*) **1** arrogant, conceited; → PONGAH. **2** pedantic.
  kebengahan 1 arrogance, conceit. **2** pedantry.

bengak-bengok to talk a lot, talk loudly. *Kami tidak suka –.* We don't like to talk a lot.

bengal 1 (temporarily) deaf, numb. **2** stubborn, obstinate. **3** (*J*) naughty, mischievous, incorrigible. **4** impudent, forward.
  kebengalan 1 recalcitrance, rebelliousness, stubbornness. **2** impudence, impertinence, forwardness.

bengang I and **terbengang 1** wide open (of a hole/mouth/wound, etc.). *seperti kena si –* struck dumb. **2** amazed, flabbergasted.
  membengang to open wide (of a hole/mouth, etc.).
  terbengang wide open.

bengang II buzzing/ringing (in one's ears).
  berbengang to have a ringing in the ears.

bengang III (*J*) gonorrhea.
  bengangan to suffer from gonorrhea.

bengang IV (*Jv*) k.o. tree, *Neesia altissima*.

béngang-béngut all twisted up.

bengap I 1 (temporarily) deaf; → PEKAK. **2** dull, not clear (of the ring of forged coins).

bengap II 1 to hesitate, stammer; hesitating, stammering. **2** speech impediment.

bengap III (*J*) swollen (of the face).

bengawan (*Jv*) **1** large river. – *Solo* the Solo River. **2** marsh, swamp; lake. **3** name of a train running between Jakarta and Solo.

béng-béng k.o. chocolate snack.

bengeb (*Jv*) → BENGAP.

bengék I *sakit* – a) asthma. b) asthmatic wheezing.

bengék II *téték* – trifling matters, trivialities. → TÉTÉK II.

bengén (*Jv*) of old, in former times, in times gone by. *jaman –* in olden times. *wong jaman –* an old timer.

bengep → BENGAP.

benggal benggal-benggil (*ob*) → BENGKAK *bengkil*.

Benggala (*D?*) Bengal. *bawang –* Bengal/large onion. *kambing –* k.o. large goat (with long hair). *rumput –* guinea-grass *Panicum maximum*.

Benggali *orang –* Bengali, a native of Bangladesh.

benggandering (*D ob*) meeting, assembly.

benggil and **berbenggil** bumpy (of one's forehead from a knock).

bénggol I swollen, (to form) a lump.

bénggol II (*col*) a two-and-a-half-cent coin.
  bénggolan a two-and-a-half-cent piece.

bénggol III = **bénggolan 1** gang leader. **2** leader, crack (swimmer, etc.), (party) boss. *seorang bénggolan dalam kasus pencurian mobil* an expert car thief.

bengik → BENGÉK I.

bengis I 1 cruel, harsh. **2** strict, severe. *Seorang raja yang sangat – terhadap rakyatnya.* A prince who was very cruel towards his people. *– bertimpal –, kejam berbalas kejam* an eye for an eye and a tooth for a tooth.
  sebengis as cruel/harsh as.
  membengis to become cruel, harsh, etc.
  membengisi to deal harshly/cruelly with. *Jika tidak dibengisi, tak akan takut orang-orang itu.* If you don't deal harshly with them, those people will not be afraid.
  terbengis the cruelest.
  kebengisan cruelty, harshness, ferocity, authority, rigor.
  pembengis a harsh person.

bengis II (*M*) angry, furious, irate.
  membengis to become angry, etc.
  membengisi to reprimand, scold.
  membengiskan to make s.o. angry.

bengkah split, cleft, cracked.
  bengkahan crack, flaw.

bengkak 1 swelling, abscess, growth, tumor. – *pada kakinya sudah dibedah.* The swelling on his leg was operated on. **2** bloated, swollen, puffed up. *Kakinya – karena sakit béri-béri.* His legs were swollen from beriberi. **3** cancer. *lain –, lain bernanah* to suffer for the mistake of others, get the blame for s.o. else's mistakes. – *bengkil* covered with lumps/bumps. – *lapar* malnutrition, edema.

membengkak 1 to swell, puff up. **2** to increase, expand. *Ternyata jumlah bécak malahan semakin ~.* On the contrary, it turns out that the number of pedicabs has been increasing more and more.
  membengkakkan to increase, expand. *~ biaya légalisasi surat-surat* to raise the legalization fees for documents.
  bengkakan swelling, lump, bump.
  kebengkakan swelling.
  pembengkakan 1 swelling (of one's face/brain, etc.). *~ prostat* enlarged prostate. **2** increase, rise, advance.

bengkal I kebengkalan to choke (on s.t.), swallow s.t. the wrong way; → KESELAK.

bengkal II k.o. tree, *Nauclea spp.* – *puri* Leinhardt tree, *Nauclea orientalis*.

bengkalai and **terbengkalai** unfinished, half-done/finished, got stuck in the middle, incomplete. *Proyék yang – itu telah dapat diselesaikan.* The unfinished project was completed. *Duduk –* to sit around and do nothing. **menterbengkalaikan** to leave s.t. unfinished/half-done, neglect. *~ tugasnya* to neglect one's duties.
  keterbengkalaian neglect, disregard for.
  membengkalaikan 1 to leave unfinished, etc. **2** to neglect, not take care of, ignore, disregard. *Beberapa invéstor tidak aktif dan ~ izin prinsip.* Some investors were inactive and neglected their principle licenses.

bengkang → BENGKIL I.

béngkang (*J*) – *béngkok/béngkong/béngkung* winding, twisting, not straight; broken (of language). *dengan bahasa Indonésia yang – béngkok* in broken Indonesian.

béngkap (*D*) boots, leggings.

bengkar membengkar to open up, expand (of bud/fruit); → ME(NG)KAR.
  pembengkar opener.

bengkarak skeleton, bare bones.

bengkaras k.o. plant, *Norrisia malaccensis*.

bengkarung skink, *Lygosoma spp.*; → KADAL. – *ular* k.o. lizard, *Tachydromus spp.*

bengkatak k.o. monitor lizard, komodo dragon, *Varanus komodoensis*.

bengkawan 1 roof-lath (to which *nipah* leaves are attached for roofing). **2** (*Mal*) a counter word for *atap*. *25 – atap* 25 pieces of *atap*.

bengkawang stag horn fern, *Gleichenia linearis*.

bengkayang (*ob*) gorged, glutted, stuffed (from overeating).

béngkél (*D*) **1** (work)shop. – *asah* grindery. – *bubut* turning shop. – *canai* rolling mill. – *cor* foundry. – *frais* milling shop. – *ketok (magic)* body shop. – *las* welding shop. – *lukis* painter's studio. – *mobil* auto repair shop. – *roti* bakery. – *téater* theater workshop. – *tempa* smithy. – *tuang* foundry.
  membéngkél to operate a workshop.
  membéngkélkan to take (a car) into an auto repair shop for repairs.
  perbéngkélan repair shop (*mod*).

bengkelai I → (BER)KELAHI.

bengkelai II → BENGKALAI.

béngkéng 1 annoyed, irritated, touchy. **2** excitable, impetuous. **3** stubborn.
  membéngkéngi 1 to be angry/irritated with. **2** to tease, nag, pester.

béngkér (*D*) bunker, casemate.

bengkil I (*ob*) and **bengkang-bengkil** puffed up, swollen.

bengkil II → BENGKAK *bengkil*.

bengkoang → BENGKUANG.

bengkok (*Jv*) **1** form of land tenure (i.e., land given in usufruct to members of the village administration as a k.o. salary). **2** land taken care of by a village head to finance the village organization. *kepala désa yang mendapat gaji – tanah sawah* the village head who get a *bengkok* salary of rice field land.

béngkok 1 bent, crooked (of lines/conduct), garbled (of a news-item). *pikiran –* dishonest. *berpikir yang –* twisted way of thinking. *Kesemrawutan dan keterbelakangan pendidikan kita sekarang ini sebagian disebabkan oléh cara berpikir kita yang –.* The confusion and backwardness of our education nowadays is partly caused by our twisted way of thinking. *Tongkat ini agak –.* This cane is somewhat bent. **2** cunning, crafty, astute. *– hati* unreliable, undependable, dishonest. **3** unscrupulous.

membéngkok 1 to bend, become bent. *Banyak tiang télepon ~ karena terserang tornado.* Many telephone poles became bent due to the tornado. **2** to turn, make a turn. *Di depan kantor pos ia ~ ke kiri.* In front of the post office he turned to the left.

membéngkokkan 1 to bend s.t. *Jangan kaubéngkokkan apa yang sudah lurus.* Don't bend what is already straight. **2** to turn s.t. *Gadis itu ~ skuternya di depan rumahnya.* The girl turned her scooter in front of her house. **3** to clinch (a nail).

béngkokan camber.

pembéngkokan 1 bending, curvature. **2** distortion, twist, perversion (of the facts).

béngkol (*J*) bend, curve.

béngkolan bend, curve; → PÉNGKOL.

béngkong I (*Jv*) crooked, curved.

béngkong II (*J*) *tukang* – circumciser.

bengkos membengkos to gasp.

bengku *pohon* – a tree producing *damar*/resin and its fruits provide oil for lamps, *Ganua motleyana.*

bengkuang I screw pine, the leaves of which are used for plaiting fine baskets and mats, *Pandanus atrocarpus..*

bengkuang II jicama, yam bean, a brown-colored root resembling a turnip; crisp, white flesh with a mild flavor, similar to a water chestnut, *Pachyrhizus angulatus/bulbosus/erosus* used in making *rujak.*

bengkudu → MENGKUDU.

Bengkulu Bencoolen (town and province in Southwest Sumatra).

bengkunang (larger) dwarf mouse-deer of Java, *Tragulus napu/ napo.*

bengkung I bent, crooked.

membengkung bent, crooked.

membengkungkan to bend s.t.

bengkung II (*Jv*) long cotton band worn around the midsection by women after childbirth to hold the muscles firm.

benglé (*Jv*) (medicinal) ginger-like herb (an ingredient of a *jamu* mixture), *Zingiber cassumunar.*

bengoh (*ob*) to work hard.

bengok I (*J*) *sakit* – goiter, mumps; → BEGUK, GONDOK.

bengok II (*M*) → BENGUK I.

bengok III water hyacinth, *Eichornia crassipes.*

bengok IV (*Jv*) **membengok** to shout, yell.

bengong (*J/Jv*) **1** stunned, bewildered, taken aback. *granat* – stun grenade. **2** to be deep in thought.

membengong stunned. stupefied. *~ kagum* stupefied with astonishment.

membengongkan [and **ngebengongin** (*J coq*)] to confuse, stupefy.

terbengong-bengong 1 discomfited, put out. **2** stared blankly, looked stupefied/with mouth hanging open.

béngot twisted, awry, slanting; → SÉRONG.

béngsrat (*S*) (only as part of a compound) *janda* – a woman who remained a virgin though married.

bengu (*J*) stinking (of a corpse), stale-smelling (of tobacco).

benguk I dejected, low(-spirited), depressed, despondent, discouraged, sulky.

membenguk to become despondent, sulk.

benguk II (*Jv*) *kara* – plant with large pods, Florida velvet bean, *Mucuna pruriens/utilis.*

bengul (*J*) red and swollen (of the eyes) (after crying).

bengung (*J*) **mbengung** to mumble.

beniaga → BERNIAGA.

benian box (for valuables).

benih 1 seed; breeding animals, breeding fish; sperm, semen; → BIBIT. *Pekebun itu menyemai bermacam-macam – bunga di kebunnya.* The gardener sowed the seeds of various flowers in his garden. *– lelaki* sperm. **2** seedlings. *– padi* rice seedlings. *– padi itu akan dipindah ke sawah bila sudah berumur 40 hari.* The rice seedlings will be transplanted to the rice fields when they are 40 days old. **3** germ. *– penyakit cacar* smallpox germ. *Untuk menjauhkan diri daripada penyakit cacar, – cacar hendaklah disuntikkan ke tubuh kita.* To avoid smallpox, smallpox germs

should be inoculated into our bodies. **4** cause, origin, source, seed (of s.t.). *– dendam bersemi pada awal 1988.* The seeds of revenge sprouted in early 1988. *Ketidakadilannya merupakan – pemberontakan di kalangan pengikutnya.* His injustice is the cause of the rebellion among his followers. **5** descendant. *Dia itu adalah – orang bangsawan.* He is a descendant of nobility. **6** fry. *– ikan bandeng* milkfish fry. *ahli/ilmuwan* – breeder. *– bersértifikat* certified seed. *– dasar* foundation seed. *– perselisihan* the seeds of dissension/discord. *– penjenis* breeder seed. *– pokok* stock seed. *– ras* seed true to type. *– sebar* extension seed.

berbenih to germinate; to bear seeds.

membenih deep-seated, at the base of s.t.

membenihi to impregnate s.o.

membenihkan to germinate s.t.

pembenih breeder.

pembenihan 1 nursery, seedbed. **2** hatchery (for fish). *~ benur/ udang* shrimp hatchery. **3** breeding. *~ buatan* artificial breeding.

perbenihan nursery (*mod*). *Ia ahli di bidang ~.* He's an expert in the nursery sector.

benik (*sl Solo*) illegal drug.

bening clear, transparent, limpid; → JERNIH. *getah* – lymph. *kelenjar* – lymph gland. *selaput* – cornea.

sebening as clear as.

membeningkan 1 to make s.t. clear, clarify. **2** to purify, cleanse.

beningan overhead transparency.

kebeningan 1 transparency, clarity (of water, etc.). **2** clearness, purity.

pembening purificatory, purifying.

pembeningan purification, cleansing.

benitan various species of trees whose wood is used for making ships' masts, *Goniothalamus ridleyi, Xylopia caudata, Arytera littoralis.*

bénjal *– bénjol* bumpy, lumpy.

bénjol lump, bump, swelling [on (fore)head]. *– akar* root nodules. **(ber)bénjol-bénjol 1** black and blue. **2** covered with lumps, bumpy, knotty, knobby.

bénjolan swelling. *~ di payudara* fibrocystic disease.

benjut (*J/Jv*) lump (on the head), bump (resulting from a blow or bump); → BÉNJOL. *Kepalanya –.* He has a bump on his head.

bénkap (*D*) → BÉNGKAP.

bénsin (*D*) gasoline. *céwék/gadis bau* – a girl who is always after boys who have a lot of money and who own a motorcycle/car. *– alam* natural gasoline. *– bébas timbal* unleaded gasoline. *– bertimbal* leaded gasoline. *– campuran* mixed gasoline. *– murni* pure gasoline. *– prémium* premium-grade gasoline. *– sumur* casing-head gasoline. *– supér* super-grade gasoline. *– yang tak mengandung timbal* unleaded gasoline.

berbénsin with ...gasoline. *~ timbal* with leaded gas.

bénsol high-octane gasoline for planes.

benta I sore, boil (on upper lip).

benta II *rumput* – a ricegrass, cut grass, used for fodder, *Leersia hexandra.*

bentak (*J*) say in a harsh way, snap. *–nya* he snapped.

membentak 1 to snap at, snarl at, scold. **2** to bark out, snarl (orders).

membentaki to snarl at.

bentakan snarl, snapping, growl, bark, scolding.

bentala (*Skr*) the earth.

bentan relapse, the return of a sickness.

bentang → RENTANG I. **1** lay/spread out. **2** span (of a bridge). *– alam* landscape. *– bébér* laid out. **membentang-bébérkan** to unfold, explain. *– budaya* cultural landscape.

membentang 1 to spread out, open up by unfolding/unrolling/unfurling. *Dia duduk bersila di atas permadani yang telah dibentang dalam kamar itu.* She sat cross-legged on a carpet that had been spread out in the room. **2** to spread, extend, stretch, lead (to). *Jalan ini ~ sampai bandara.* This road leads to the airport.

membentangi 1 to spread s.t. out on, unroll s.t. over. *~ seluruh lantai dengan permadani* to spread a carpet out over the entire floor. **2** to spread out over s.t.

membentangkan 1 to spread s.t. out, unfold. *Ibu ~ taplak itu sebelum menghidangkan makanan kepada tetamu.* Mother unfolded the tablecloth before serving food to the guests. **2** to pitch (a tent). **3** to explain, lay out, set forth, present. *Dia ~ penda-patnya di hadapan kami.* He laid out his opinion in front of us.

terbentang unrolled, (to lie) spread out, unfolded, opened up. *Saya tidak gentar apa yang ~ di depan saya.* I'm not afraid of what lies ahead of me.

bentangan 1 s.t. that's unrolled/unfolded/spread out. *kain ~* banner. *~ alam* landscape. *~ langit* firmament, heavens, sky. **2** span (of bridge). *~ tengah* main span. *~ sungai* span over a river. **3** landform. **4** array.

pembentangan 1 unfurling (of a flag), unrolling (of a carpet). **2** laying out, presenting, presentation, explanation, exposition. *~ tahunan* annual report. **3** straining, stretching.

perbentangan extension.

bentangur k.o. trees yielding good timber for masts and scaffolding, *Calophyllum spp. - ara* k.o. tree, *Calophyllum kunstleri. - batu* k.o. tree, *C. pulcherrimum. - belulang* k.o. tree, *C. lanigerum. - besar* k.o. tree, *C. pulcherrimum. - bunga* k.o. tree, *C. inophyllum/lanigerum. - mumut/pasir → **BENTANGUR** ara.*

bentar I sebentar 1 a moment/instant, a short while. *~!* Just a moment/minute *~ ya.* Just a moment, please. *ala ~* for a moment/ short time. *tiap ~* every moment, all the time, at any moment. *Seperempat abad adalah waktu yang tidak ~.* A quarter of a century is not a moment of time. *tidur barang ~* to take a quick nap. *~ antaranya* soon, before long. *~ lagi* a little longer, soon. *~ lagi dia datang.* He'll come in a few moments/minutes. *Lebaran tinggal ~ lagi.* Lebaran is just around the corner. **2** later (in the day). *~ soré* this afternoon. *~ malam* this evening, tonight; → **NANTI** *malam. ~ ini* this very instant/minute. *~ tadi* earlier. *~ ... kemudian* now ... now/then ... one moment ... the next ...

sebentar-sebentar and **sebentar-bentar 1** (at) any time/moment, all the time, keep on ...ing. *~ dia melihat ke arah jalan.* He kept looking in the direction of the street. **2** from time to time, now and again, again and again. **3** for a short time only.

sesebentar frequently, often, again and again. *Dengan tongkatnya pengemis itu melangkah tertatih-tatih seorang diri. ~ berhenti dan menadahkan tangan.* With his cane the beggar stepped gropingly along alone. From time to time he stopped and held out his hand. **sebentaran** just a minute, a short while.

bentaran ephemeral.

bentar II (*Bal*) *candi -* split gate without a top, often at the entrance to the outer courtyard of a temple.

béntar (*M*) *jalan -* bypass.

berbéntar(-béntar) to go/run around. *mengambil jalan -* to make a detour.

membéntar to run around s.t. *Kuda itu lari ~ lapangan.* The horse ran around the field.

membéntari to circle, run around, circumnavigate.

mem(per)béntarkan to run (a horse around the field).

perbéntaran arena for horses to run around in.

bentara (*Skr*) herald, s.o. who makes public announcements and carries messages for the ruler.

bentaus and **bentawas** → **MENTAUS**.

béntéh a game consisting of knocking one's tibia against that of one's opponent.

berbéntéh and **membéntéh** to play that game.

bénténg 1 fortification, wall built around a town to defend it from enemy attacks. **2** fortress, bastion, town/place surrounded by a defensive wall; → **BALUARTI**. *suatu - kejahatan, kebiadaban dan kekejian moral* a bastion of criminality, debauchery and moral shame. **3** rook, castle (in chess); → **TIR I.**

berbénténg fortified.

membénténg to form a rampart around, defend.

membénténgi to fortify, strengthen with a fort/walls, etc., embank, dam in/up.

bénténgan 1 dyke, bank, dam. **2** battlement.

perbénténgan fortification.

bénter → **BÉNTAR**.

benterok → **BENTROK**.

béntés → **BÉNTÉH**.

bentét (*J/Jv*) **1** cracked, burst open. **2** to burst open.

béntét *- biasa* long-tailed shrike, *Lanius schach. - cokelat* brown shrike, *Lanius cristatus. - loréng* tiger shrike, *Lanius tigrinus.*

bentik ocean layer inhabited by organisms.

bentil *- susu* nipple, teat, tit; → **PENTIL**.

berbentilan (*bio*) muricate.

béntoh → **BANTAH**.

bentok (*J*) **membentok** to bump into.

kebentok bumped into, run into.

béntol small swelling.

bentong stain, spot, speck, spatter, splotch.

berbentong-bentong and **berbentongan** to be completely covered with stains.

membentongi to stain, spot.

bentos flora and fauna that live permanently on the floor of the sea.

bentrok (*J/Jv*) **1** to bicker, squabble, disagree, quarrel. *Kamu sering - sama ortumu?* Do you often squabble with your parents? **2** to conflict (with). *Keteranganmu itu - dengan bukti yang diperoléh.* Your statement conflicts with the evidence (we have) obtained. **3** to collide (with). *Kapal penumpang itu - dengan kapal barang.* The passenger ship collided with a freighter. **4** clash, conflict, quarrel. *- fisik* physical clash. *seratus lebih mahasiswa Bandung terlihat - fisik dengan aparat keamanan* more than 100 university students in Bandung were involved in a physical clash with law enforcement.

berbentrok 1 to quarrel, squabble, bicker. **2** to collide, clash.

berbentrokan 1 to collide with e.o. *Rupanya ada mobil ~.* Apparently there were cars which collided with e.o. **2** to have a difference of opinion, clash.

membentrokkan 1 to crash s.t. into. **2** to set (people) (against e.o.), cause (people) to fight, bring about conflict between. *Ia ~ kedua partai itu.* He made the two parties fight with e.o.

bentrokan 1 to quarrel, clash, come into conflict. **2** clash, conflict. *Istilah triad markét antara Jepang, Amérika dan Éropah Barat ternyata menuju arah persatuan yang bersifat kerja sama (collusion) daripada ~ (collision).* The term triad market among Japan, America and Western Europe has turned out to be heading in the direction of a unit which is characterized by collusion rather than by collision. *~ pendapat* clash of opinions. *~ senjata* armed clash.

pembentrokan 1 clash, conflict, dispute. **2** collision, clash.

perbentrokan 1 clash. **2** crash, collision.

bentuk I 1 form, shape, type, -form. **2** pattern and arrangement of a written article. *salah -* misshapen, deformed, disfigured. *- antara* (*geol*) sequential form. *- badan hukum* legal status. *- benang* filiform. *- coba* by trial and error. *- ilmu - kata* (*gram*) morphology. *- kembar* (*ling*) doublet. *- koli* coliform. *- médan* terrain feature. *dalam - natura dan kenikmatan* in kind and in benefit. *- peralihan* (*geol*) passage form. *- ragam* (*ob*) form and type. *- seasal* (*ling*) cognate. *- tasrif* (*ling*) conjugated form. *- Usaha Tetap* [BUT] permanent establishment (of a business for tax purposes).

sebentuk similar in form.

berbentuk 1 in the shape/form of; to take the form of, have the shape of, shaped. *~ busur* arched. *~ kubus* cubical. *~ memanjang* oblong. *~ sél* cellular. *~ tabél* tabular. **2** to take shape/ form.

membentuk 1 to establish, set up, form (an association/party, etc.), create. *~ organisasi baru* to establish a new organization. *~ ulang* to reform, reconstitute. **2** to form, compose, make up (a Cabinet). **3** to mold.

membentukkan 1 to form, shape. **2** to create, establish, set up.

terbentuk 1 formed, established, set up. *Kini telah ~ suatu badan.* Now a committee has been established. *tidak ~* a) not formed, formless. b) cannot be formed. **2** composed (of).

bentukan 1 s.t. formed/shaped/made/set up. *tim ~ Présidén ...* the team set up by President ... *kata ~* (*gram*) derivative. **2** style. *PKI ~ baru.* The new-styled Communist Party of Indonesia. **3** learning. *~ dasar* basic training.

pembentuk 1 maker, creator. *~ kabinét* Prime Minister, Premier. *~ opini* opinion maker. *badan ~ undang-undang* legislature. **2** what is used to form s.t. *Awalan, akhiran dan sisipan ialah morfém ~ kata.* Prefixes, suffixes and infixes are morphemes used to form words.

pembentukan formation, establishment, building; shaping, forming, training. ~ *bangsa* nation building. ~ *harga* price formation. ~ *kabinét* cabinet formation. ~ *kata-kata baru* formation of new words, neologism. ~ *kebiasaan* habit forming. ~ *modal* capital formation. ~ *pemerintah baru* the formation of a new government. ~ *pendapat* opinion building. ~ *pegunungan* orogeny. ~ *persediaan* stockpiling.

bentuk II 1 bend, curve. **2** numeral coefficient for curved objects, like rings, hooks, watches, etc. *Kini tubuhnya gemuk, di léhérnya ada lilitan kalung dan di pergelangan tangannya ada se- arloji.* His body is fat now, a necklace is wound around his neck and there is a watch on his wrist. *se- cincin* a ring. *se- kail* a fish hook.

berbentuk to be bent/curved.

membentuk to curve, arch, bend, have curves. *Alisnya ~ seperti taji.* His eyebrows are curved like a cock's spur.

membentukkan to curve/bend s.t.

bentul (*Jv*) blue taro, *Xanthosoma violaceum*.

bentulu k.o. fish, sucker barb, *Barbichthys laevis*.

bentur I (*J/Jv*) collide, bang, knock, conflict.

berbenturan to collide (with e.o.); to be in conflict (with), come into conflict (with), conflict (with); to quarrel. *Kedua mobil yang ~ itu mengalami kerusakan hébat.* The two cars which collided were severely damaged. *Pendapat meréka selalu ~.* Their views were always in conflict.

membentur to come into contact with, collide with, bump into, knock against, hit. *Mobilnya ~ pohon.* His car banged against a tree. *Bola ~ tiang gawang, sehingga tidak menghasilkan gol.* The ball hit the goal post, so that it didn't score a goal.

membenturkan to crash/ram/bang s.t. *Kepalanya dibenturkan témbok.* His head was banged against the wall.

terbentur [and **kebentur** (*coq*)] **1** collided (with), bumped (against). *Kepalanya ~ pada tiang télepon.* His head bumped against a telephone pole. **2** confronted with, run into, encounter s.t. which obstructs/gets in the way. *Usahanya gagal karena ~ biaya produksi yang tinggi.* His business failed because it ran into high production costs. **3** to meet with (difficulties).

benturan 1 clash, conflict. ~ *antarperadaban* clash of civilizations. ~ *kepentingan* conflict of interest. **2** impact, collision.

kebenturan to collide with.

pembenturan clash, conflict.

perbenturan clash, collision, impact, shock. ~ *budaya* culture shock. ~ *kepentingan* conflict of interests.

bentur II membentur to bend down (of branches full with fruits), be flexible (as a cane).

membenturkan to flex s.t.

benturung weasel, Malayan civet, bear-civet, *Arctictis binturong, Viverra tangalunga.*

bentus (*Jv ob*) **terbentus** collided; → BENTUR I.

benua 1 continent, one of the main land masses (Europe, Asia, Africa, etc.). **2** a large country, empire, kingdom, realm. – *hitam* Africa. – *kangguru* Australia. – *kecil* subcontinent.

kebenuaan continental.

benuang I (*ob*) large, having a large spread of horns or antlers. *kerbau – a* huge buffalo. *rusa – a* large sambur-deer, *Cervus equinus.*

benuang II *pohon –* **a**) a tree with soft light wood, *Octomeles sumatrana.* **b**) Buddha coconut, *Sterculia alata.* *– laki* k.o. tree, *Duabanga mollucana.*

benuas k.o. tree, *Shorea laevis/kunstleri.*

benum (*D ob*) appointed (to a post).

membenum to appoint.

benuman 1 appointment. **2** appointed.

pembenuman appointing, appointment.

benur shrimp fry. *pembibitan –* shrimp hatchery.

benyai 1 soupy, too watery (of cooked food, *esp* rice), soggy. **2** spiritless.

benyawak (in Sumatra); → BIAWAK.

benyék 1 soft, tender, weak. **2** overripe, bruised (of fruit). **3** (*Jv*) (of wounds) watery and infected.

benyoh to work hard.

bényot askew, awry, skewed.

bénzéna (*D*) benzene.

béo I the *tiung* or mynah bird. – *Nias* Sumatran hill myna, *Gracula religiosa robusta.*

membéo(i) to parrot, imitate.

pembéo s.o. who likes to parrot (imitate), copy-cat.

pembéoan parroting, imitating.

béo II (*sl*) pedicab.

béol (*J*) /bé'ol/ **1** to (take a) shit. **2** to lie. *tukang –* liar, bullshit artist.

béongan (*gay sl*) a gay person, homosexual. *Doi hémong –.* He's a male prostitute.

Béos the downtown railroad station in Jakarta.

Bepékét [Belawan-Penang-Phuket] the ferry connection between Belawan, Penang, and Phuket in Thailand.

Béppan (during the Japanese occupation) the Japanese Special Task Unit within the 16th Army Headquarters which was responsible for counterintelligence and special operations.

ber- also see entries beginning with **br-**.

bera I 1 red and swollen (of cheeks from a toothache). **2** dark red (of blushing cheeks/worn roof tiles).

membera to blush, flush, (turn) color.

bera II (*K*) lord; → BHRA.

bera III (*Jv*) fallow; → BERO. *sawah –* a rice field lying fallow.

memberakan to allow (agricultural land) to lie fallow temporarily. *Aréal persawahan luas telah diberakan.* The rice-field area was allowed to lie fallow.

berabé (*J*) **1** difficult, hard, bothersome, annoying. **2** complicated. *membuat –* to make things difficult. *Kalau dua-duanya diam bisa –.* If both are quiet then there will be the devil to pay. **3** (*coq*) a mild exclamation of annoyance or exasperation.

memberabékan to make things hard, make for trouble.

beragan (*ob*) *mati –* to die without visible cause, die from natural causes; → AGAN.

berahi (*Skr*) **1** passionate love, passion, sexual desire, lust. **2** estrus, the period of heat/rut. *api –* the heat of passion. – *kelamin* to be in heat.

memberahikan 1 to titillate. **2** to charm, enchant. **3** to be mad about, love. *Pria itu sangat ~ wanita yang muda itu.* The man is very much in love with the young woman.

keberahian lust, passion. *Gambar porno bisa membangkitkan ~.* Pornographic pictures can give rise to lust.

Berahman(a) (*Skr*) a Brahmin.

Berahmani a female Brahmin.

berai and **berberaian** dispersed, scattered, in disorder; → CERAI.

memberai-beraikan 1 to throw into disarray. *Meréka berhasil ~ pasukan musuh.* They succeeded in throwing the enemy's troops into disarray. **2** to spread, scatter. *Dialah yang ~ kabar bohong itu.* He's the one who spread that false news.

terberai scattered, disordered.

beraian scattering, divergence. ~ *téktonik* tectonic divergence. *Di daérah sekitar Florés-Sumba terjadi kegiatan ~ téktonik.* There is tectonic divergence activity in the region around Flores and Sumba.

pemberaian scattering, dispersion.

beraja (*J*) *bintang –* falling star.

berak sunk (into water or mud).

memberakkan to put s.t. under water.

terberak sunk (into water or mud).

bérak 1 human excrement, night soil, feces; → TAHI, TINJA. *muntah – [muntabér]* k.o. cholera. **2** (= **membérak**) to defecate, have a bowel movement. – *air* diarrhea. – *darah* a) dysentery. b) melena. – *kapur* pulorum disease.

bérak-bérak diarrhea.

membéraki 1 to defecate in(to)/on. *Machrum ~ sumur tetangganya, Darso.* Machrum defecated into his neighbor Darso's well. **2** to disgrace, dishonor, humiliate. ~ *nama keluarganya karena perbuatan yang tercela* to dishonor one's family's name by a shameful act.

membérakkan to defecate/eliminate s.t.

terbérak-bérak to accidentally defecate in one's pants (from fright, etc.). *Karena dihardik, anak kecil yang ketakutan itu ~ di celananya.* Because he was scolded, the small child who was afraid accidentally soiled his pants. *Maling itu digebuki sampai ~.* The thief had the shit beaten out of him.

berakah proud, arrogant.

berak-berok (*Jv*) to cry, shout, bawl.

beraksa I (*Skr*) *kuda* – a legendary Pegasus.

beraksa II (*Skr*) *pohon* – k.o. banyan tree with beautiful flowers, *Cassia fistula*.

beram I (*J*) rice spirits, a liquor made of fermented rice; → BREM.

beram II cardinal red (color).

berambang (*Jv*) red onion, shallot, *Allium ascalonicum/cepa*.

beramin k.o. basket that is hung up.

beranang (*Jv*) *mérah* – fiery red, red as fire.

beranda (*Port*) 1 veranda, porch; → SERAMBI. – *muka* front veranda. 2 (*naut*) ship's cabin. – *stasiun* platform.

berandal (*J*) 1 rogue, rascal, scoundrel. 2 bandit, gangster.
  memberandal 1 to behave like a rogue/rascal. 2 to engage in banditry.
  berandalan roguish, rascally.
  keberandalan roguery, rascality, knavishness.

berandang 1 conspicuous, striking, clearly visible, obvious. 2 striking, noticeable.

berandi (*D*) brandy, cognac.

bérang 1 furious, infuriated, enraged, raging, very angry. 2 fury, rage, anger. *naik* – and
  membérang to rage, be violently angry (in actions or speech), be forceful/violent/uncontrolled, fulminate, seethe, run amok/wild, go berserk.
  membérangi to be angry at, inveigh/fulminate against, jump down (s.o.'s) throat.
  kebérangan fury, anger.
  pembérang hothead, impetuous/angry person.

berangai *mati* – a) asphyxia. b) apparently dead, in a state of suspended animation; → MATI *suri*. *perahu* – pirates' prau.

berangan I chestnut, *Castanea javanica*. – *babi* k.o. tree, *Lithocarpus rassa*. – *bukit* → BERANGAN *duri*. – *dangkal* k.o. chestnut tree, *Castanopsis argentea*. – *duri/haji* chestnut, *Castanopsis javanica/megacarpa*. – *gundul* chestnut, *Castanopsis sumatrana*. – *landak* k.o. tree, *Quercus spicata*. – *padi* k.o. tree, braided chestnut, *Castanopsis inermis/sumatrana*.

berangan II arsenic; → WARANGAN.

berangan III → BERANG-BERANG.

berangas barnacle.

berangasan (*Jv*) irascible, hot-tempered.

berang-berang otter. – *berkumis* "mustached" otter, *Lutra sumatrana*. – *bulu licin* "smooth-haired" otter, *Lutrogale perspicillata*. – *cakar kecil* "small-clawed" otter, *Aonyx cinerea*. – *utara* northern otter, *Lutra lutra*.

berangkal (*Jv*) rubble, cobble.

berangkat 1 to leave; → BERTOLAK. *Pukul berapa* – *dari sini*? What time are you leaving here? *Meréka* – *ke Bandung*. They left for Bandung. 2 to have just become, begin to become (big/grown up, etc.). *telah* – *déwasa* to grow up, be a (wo)man. *wanita yang* – *hamil* a woman who has just become pregnant. *sudah* – *remaja* to come of age. – *dari* to start from/with. – *dari pemikiran bahwa ...* starting with the idea that ... – *dari kenyataan itu* starting from those facts. *sebuah términal untuk yang* – departure terminal (at an airport). – *bekerja* to go/leave to/for work. – *berperang* to go to war. – *tidur* to go to bed.
  memberangkatkan to dispatch, move, send (off), transport (troops, etc.) to. *Meréka diberangkatkan sebagai transmigran khusus.* They were transported as special transmigrants.
  keberangkatan departure, going away, starting out. *mempersiapkan* ~ *Pak Sastro* to make (the necessary) preparations for Pak Sastro's departure.
  pemberangkatan departure, sending, dispatch, forwarding, embarkation. *pelabuhan* ~ port of embarkation. ~ *dengan kapal* shipment. ~ *jenazah* the funeral will leave at ...

berangsang berangsangan to be angry, furious.
  memberangsang to become angry, become furious.
  memberangsangkan 1 to make s.o. angry. 2 to encourage, cheer up. 3 to instigate, incite.
  berangsangan 1 easily angered. 2 instigation.
  pemberangsang hothead; quick/hot short-tempered.

berangsong → BERONGSONG.

berangta (*Jv ob*) desire (of love), desiring; languishing (of love).

berangti (*Jv*) → BERANGTA.

berangus 1 muzzle. 2 bridle.
  memberangus 1 to muzzle (a dog). 2 to control, bridle, muzzle (the press).
  pemberangus 1 s.o. who muzzles/silences s.o. else. 2 muzzle.
  pemberangusan control over, muzzling. ~ *pérs* muzzling the press. ~ *pihak oposisi* muzzling the opposition.

berani I 1 audacious, courageous, have the courage to; plucky, valiant. – *mati* a) to look death in the face, have no fear of death. *barisan* – *mati* suicide command. b) (expression often used to add force to an oath) strike me dead, so help me God. – *mati kalau saya bohong*. God strike me dead if I lie. – *betul!* what a nerve! 2 bold, daring, brave. *melancarkan serangan* – to launch a daring strike. *Biasanya masakan Muangthai lebih* – *dalam rempah-rempah, sehingga rasanya agak menyengat*. Thai food is usually more strongly seasoned (than Chinese food), so that it tastes rather sharp. 3 impudent, insolent, shameless, brazen, vulgar. *adegan yang* – *sekali* an indecent/indecorous scene. – *sama* to dare to be disrespectful to. 4 (*coq*) to be able (to pay a certain amount). – *hilang tak hilang*, – *mati tak mati* fortune favors the bold. – *malu, takut mati* have the guts to perform a forbidden job, but regret after having noticed it. – *menjual*, – *membeli* a) look before you leap. b) not only having the courage to order s.t., but also to carry it out. – *buka*, – *bayar* not afraid to suffer a financial loss. *anjing galak, babi* – both parties are equally strong. *malu* –, *mati takut* discretion is the better part of valor. *tidak* – afraid. **ketidak-beranian** fear, cowardice. *Itu disebabkan* ~ *PDI menampilkan calon alternatif*. That was caused by the PDI's fear of putting up an alternative candidate. – *candang* (*Mal*) dauntless, reckless. – *lalat* to pretend to be brave, but when facing the foe to run away. – *(ber)sumpah* a) to have the courage/nerve to take an oath, dare swear (that s.t. is really the case). b) to guarantee, warrant s.t. *Saya* – *sumpah bahwa emas ini tulén*. I guarantee that this gold is pure. – *udang* to be/act like a coward.
  berani-berani unmotivated/groundless courage, courage uncalled-for, have the nerve to. *Ia* ~*nya mencantum S.H. di belakang namanya, padahal belum lulus*. He had the nerve to put S.H. after his name even though he had not graduated yet. ~ *takut* ambivalent.
  seberani as brave as.
  seberani-beraninya no matter how courageous.
  berberani-berani to try/attempt to act courageously. *Jangan* ~ *diri menentang penguasa*. Don't be so bold as to oppose the authorities.
  memberani *semakin* ~ increasingly daring.
  memberanikan to encourage, incite, stimulate, rouse. *Ia pun pandai pula* ~ *hati anak buahnya*. He also knew how to encourage his team. ~ *diri* to pluck up one's courage, take heart, be so bold (as to).
  terberani the bravest.
  berani-beranian (*J*) to dare, presume, have the courage/nerve to do s.t. improper/out of the ordinary. *Belum punya uang sudah* ~ *melamar anak saya*. You have no money and you have the nerve to ask for my daughter's hand in marriage.
  keberanian 1 courage, valor, fearlessness. 2 bravery, boldness. *dengan* ~ *sendiri* on one's own initiative, of one's own accord.
  pemberani 1 a courageous/brave/bold person. *Pasukan* ~ *Penjaga Gunung Api Indonésia* Indonesia's Brave Band of Volcano Watchers. 2 daredevil. 3 hero.

berani II *batu* – lodestone, k.o. iron that is magnetic. *besi* – a) magnetic iron. b) magnet.

beranta I (*ob*) a Malay river boat.

beranta II (*Jv*) → BERANGTA.

berantak memberantakkan to break, crush, throw into disorder.
  berantakan (*J*) 1 broken (down), in pieces, dilapidated. 2 in total disorder, a mess, scattered all over. 3 collapsed (of a defense).
  keberantakan disorder, confusion, chaos.

berantam to fight; → BERHANTAM.

Berantas I the *Brantas* river, the largest river in East Java, known for its devastating floods.

berantas II memberantas 1 (originally) to combat, fight against (floods, etc.). ~ *buta huruf* to combat/fight against illiteracy. ~ *kejahatan* to combat crime. **2** to abolish, eradicate, exterminate (insects, etc.), wipe out, eliminate, destroy. ~ *coro* to exterminate roaches.
  memberantasi (*pl obj*) to wipe out, eliminate.
  terberantas eliminated, destroyed, wiped out.
  pemberantas 1 destroyer, vandal. **2** exterminator. (*obat*) ~ *hama* pesticide.
  pemberantasan extermination, destruction, control, stamping/wiping out. ~ *hama* pest control. ~ *hama tikus* extermination of rodents.
berapa → BERAPA (under *apa*).
beras 1 uncooked rice with the husk removed. *Diambilnya – dan ditanaknya.* She took some uncooked rice and she cooked it. **2** grain, seed; cereals. *induk* – (M) wife, spouse. *kerbau* – a small type of water buffalo. *ada –, taruh dalam padi* "if you have husked rice, keep it in with the unhusked rice," i.e., a secret should be well-kept. *– secupak ikan sejerak, madar* to work one's fingers to the bone and just make enough to live on. *tak – antah dikikis* the end justifies the means. *– Amérika panjang* long-grain rice. *– basah* s.t. worthless. *– Belanda* pearl-barley. *– bergizi* enriched rice. *– bersih* clean rice (not containing foreign matter). *– bertih* a) rice fried without oil. b) parched rice (used by magicians). *– campur* rice consisting of two or more paddy varieties. *– cerah* rice without the pericarp, white rice (cleaned). *– Cianjur* rice consisting of medium grains. *– dagang* imported rice (from abroad). *– droping* allocated rice. *– fitrah* rice earmarked as an obligatory gift at the end of the fasting month. *– gandum* bulgur. *– giling* milled rice, mechanically ground rice. *– Irvin* rice made from corn which after undergoing certain chemical processes no longer has the outer skin of its corn kernels. *– jagung* rice mixed with corn. *– jatah* allocated rice. *– Jepang* rice consisting of small, nearly round grains resembling barley. *– jernih* ground rice whose grains do not calcify. *– kencur* a mixture of powdered raw rice and medicinal roots for massaging, saffron-colored rice. *– kepala* prime quality rice. *– ketan* glutinous rice. *– ketas* various k.o. rice. *– kumbah* s.t. worthless. *– kuning/kunyit* saffron rice. *– lembab* s.t. worthless. *– méja* white, good-quality rice. *– menir* very small broken grains of rice. *– menurun* low-quality rice that ripens in a short time. *– mérah* reddish-brown rice. *– patah* broken grains of rice. *– pecah kulit* [PK] rice with inner bran layer. *– pera* granular, dry rice. *– perélék* rice grains which have dropped from sacks during transportation. *– petas* various k.o. rice. *– pulut* glutinous rice. *– putih* white top-quality rice. *– recak(-recak)* pieces of rice which have broken off during pounding. *– rendang* soaked rice used as medicine for stomach ailments. *– Saigon* medium-grain rice. *– Saigon Bandung* slender, medium-grain rice. *– Siam* lower-grade rice. *– sosoh* rice without pericarp. *– tékad* the popular name of "artificial rice" made from *ketéla, jagung,* and *kacang. – tipar* rice from dry-rice field. *– tua usia simpan* raw husked rice in a state of decay. *– tumbuk/tuton* (*Jv*) hand-pounded rice. *– utuh* whole (not broken) rice. *– wutah* (*Jv*) spilled rice (from sacks, etc.).
  berberas with/having rice.
  berasan imitation *beras.* ~ *gaplék* dried sweet potatoes which are then pounded.
  perberasan rice (*mod*).
beras-beras I *ikan* – k.o. fish, drummer fish, k.o. chub, *Kyphosus cinerascens.*
beras-beras II *pohon* – a tall tree with useful timber, *Trigonochlamys griffithii.*
berat 1 heavy, hard to lift/move, weighty. *alat-alat* – heavy-duty equipment (such as, tractors/tow-trucks/cranes, etc.). *industri* – the heavy industries. **2** heavy (of high specific gravity; of concentrated weight for the size). *Peti yang – itu tidak dapat diangkat oléh tenaga manusia.* That heavy crate cannot be lifted by human power. *-nya* weight. **3** severe (of illness), serious (of injuries). *menderita luka-luka* – to suffer serious injuries. *-nya* severity. **4** difficult/hard to bear, severe (of troubles/punishment). *Kematian ibunya merupakan cobaan – untuk gadis itu.*

Her mother's death was a severe blow for the girl. *Titiek Wardiono – meninggalkan keluarga.* It was hard for Titiek Wardiono to leave his family. **5** heavy, difficult to move (of limbs, etc.). *mata terasa* – to be sleepy. **6** to favor, lean toward, take a particular side. *– (ke)pada* to take s.o.'s side, side with s.o. *Kau lebih – padaku?* Do you lean more toward me? Are you on my side? **7** (*dalam* –) pregnant, expecting (a baby). *Istrinya sedang dalam –.* His wife is expecting. **8** (*coq*) unpleasant, problematic, difficult. *Kalau sudah ketahuan, – kita.* If it is discovered, we're in trouble. **9** strong (of suspicion/drink). *– dugaanku bahwa dia akan setuju.* I have a strong suspicion that he'll agree. *dengan –* reluctant(ly), unwilling(ly), disinclined (to). *Dengan – ia mengeluarkan Rp 16.000.* Reluctantly he took 16,000 rupiahs (out of his pocket). **10** to have more (votes), have command over the votes (during an election). *Wartawan menanyakan apakah Golkar masih akan – di DKI Jakarta.* The reporter asked whether Golkar will still have command over sufficient votes in the Jakarta Special Region. **11** weight. *– badan* body weight. *angkat* – weight lifting. *kelas* – a) heavyweight (boxing). b) dangerous. *tapol-tapol kelas* – dangerous political detainees. *kelebihan* – overweight. *titik* – a) center of gravity. b) the main point, gist of the matter. *– pada mata orang lain* respected by others. *pengangkat* – weight lifter. **12** oppressive (of weather). *– sama dipikul, ringan sama dijinjing* share one's joys and sorrows; share the sweet and bitter of life. *berapa – mata memandang, – juga bahu memikul* however heavy it may look, it is still heavier on the carrier's shoulder. *– atas* top heavy. *– atom* atomic weight. *– berpesan* to give explicit instruction. *– bersih* net weight. *– bibir* taciturn, always silent, not liking to talk, uncommunicative; → PENDIAM. *– dibongkarkan* weight delivered. *– dimuatkan* weight shipped. *– ékor* lazy, idle, indolent, slow. *– énténgnya hukum* sentence, punishment. *– hati* a) unwillingly, reluctant. *Saya mengembalikan penghargaan dengan – hati.* I returned the award reluctantly. b) do not want/wish. c) to have the inclination/tendency to. d) to have strong suspicions. **berberat hati** to be unwilling. *– hidup* body weight of cattle before slaughtering, live weight. *– imbangan* counterweight. *– jenis* specific gravity. *– kaki* lazy. *– ke atas/puncak* top-heavy. *– kendala* slow on the uptake, slow to understand. *– kepala* stupid, slow-witted. *– kotor* gross weight. *– lidah* a) taciturn. b) cannot talk well. *– mata* sleepy. *– mati* dead weight. *– menolak* doesn't turn people down easily. *– mulut* taciturn. *– otak* a) stupid, slow-witted. b) anxious, restless. *– pinggul* a) lazy. b) lazy bones, sluggard, idler. *– puncak* top heavy. *– ringannya biaya perawatan* the amount of maintenance costs. *– sapih* body weight of cattle when weaned. *– sebelah* one-sided, biased, partial. *tidak – sebelah* unbiased. **keberatsebelahan** one-sidedness, partiality. *– siku/tangan* lazy. *– telinga* hard of hearing; → PEKAK. *– timbangan* s.t. petty that seems important. *– tulang* lazy, indolent.
seberat 1 as heavy as. **2** weighing, with a weight of. *satelit* ~ *3 ton* a three-ton satellite.
berberat to have a certain weight; with a weight of, weighing. *Nanas Sarawak* ~ *sampai 12 kilogram.* Sarawak pineapples weigh up to 12 kilograms.
memberat 1 to become heavy/heavier. *merasa sesuatu yang* ~ *di dalam dadanya* to feel s.t. heavy in his chest. **2** to appear (to be) heavy. *Susu kambing itu tergayut-gayut dan* ~. The goat's udders were hanging down and appeared to be heavy.
memberati 1 to add weight to, weigh down. ~ *kailnya dengan sedikit timah* to add weight to his fishhook with a little bit of lead. **2** to burden, weigh on, worry, trouble. *Soal-soal rumahtangga sering* ~ *pikirannya.* Household problems often weigh on his mind.
memberatkan 1 to increase the burden/weight/load (so that s.t. sinks, etc.). *Jangan* ~ *beban ibu dengan kehendak yang bukan-bukan itu.* Don't increase mother's burdens with nonsensical desires. **2** to aggravate. *hal-hal yang* ~ aggravating circumstances. *saksi yang* ~ witness for the prosecution. **3a)** to prefer (to). **b)** to stress, lay stress on, emphasize, accentuate. *Soal golongan lebih diberatkan daripada kepentingan negara.* Group interests are more emphasized than national interests. **c)** to attach importance/value to, set/put value on, care for. **4a)**

(~ *kepada*) to assign, delegate, ascribe, attribute. *Jangan ~ tugas itu hanya kepada seorang saja.* Don't assign that task to only one person. b) to put/lay the blame on. *pandai ~ diri* to know how to behave with aplomb (in order to be honored), assert o.s. (by keeping one's distance). 5 be a burden to, be burdensome. ~ *hati* to grieve, hurt, offend. 6 (*leg*) for valuable consideration, onerous. *persetujuan ~* an agreement for valuable consideration. 7 (*leg*) incriminating.

memberat-beratkan ~ *diri* to strike a strong/forceful attitude, take heart, steel one's nerves, pull o.s. together.

memperberat 1 to weigh down, load. 2 to make more serious.

terberat 1 the heaviest. 2 the most serious/severe, etc.

keberatan 1 weight, heaviness. *surat ~* declaration of complaint. 2 unwilling, reluctant. *Dia seakan-akan ~ hendak menolong kami.* It seems as if he is reluctant to help us. 3 (*J*) too heavy, overloaded. *Tak terangkat oléhnya karena ~.* He couldn't lift it because it was too heavy. 4 difficulty. 5 objection, legal objection, petition for relief. 6 burden (of taxation). 7 draw-back.

berkeberatan (*atas*) 1 to have objections (to), raise objections (to), object (to), take exception (to). 2 to raise difficulties, have scruples (about ... -ing).

pemberat 1 weight. 2 ballast.

pemberatan 1 ballasting. 2 aggravation, making heavier, etc.

berau (*in South Sulawesi*) **memberaukan** to allow land to lie fallow. *Di Sulawesi Selatan tanaman kedelai bahkan kini dimanfaatkan pada lahan yang biasa diberaukan setelah panén padi.* In fact, in South Sulawesi the planting of soybeans is nowadays being utilized on land which is *usu* allowed to remain fallow after the rice harvest.

berba [*berlapis baja*] armored (car, etc.).

Bérber (*D*) *orang –* Berber.

bercak (*Jv*) 1 pocked, pockmarked. *– bawaan* birthmark. *– benih/cokelat/daun/hitam* various k.o. plant diseases, purple/brown/leaf/black spot. *– daging* brownish-red spot in an egg. *– darah* blood spot in an egg. *– mérah-mérah* red marks on face. 2 small holes.

berbercak-bercak spotted, dotted.

berbecakan covered with spots.

terbercak spotted.

Bérce (*D*) diminutive of the male proper name, Bert.

bercik → PERCIK.

bercokok (*J*) a small crocodile species, *Crocodilus sp.*; → BICOKOK.

berdikari [*berdiri di atas kaki sendiri*] to be self-reliant.

memberdikarikan to make self-reliant/sufficient. *Tahun 1967 PN Postél diberdirikarikan.* In 1967 the Postal and Telecommunications State Corporation will be made self-reliant.

keberdikarian standing on one's own two feet, independence, self-reliance.

berdus → PEREDUS.

berédel → BRÉIDEL.

beregong → BERIPAT.

berekah → BERKAH.

bérék-bérék *burung –* bay-headed/chestnut-headed bee-eater, *Merops sumatranus.*

beréken (*D ob*) to figure (out).

berem → BREM.

bérem (*D*) **béreman** (graded) verge, shoulder (of the road).

beremban crossbar (for a dam/door). *– peti* cofferdam.

berembang *pohon –* a seaside tree, *Sonneratia spp. buah –* (*cla*) the knob-like fruit of this tree, which gives its name to the knob at the apex of the mast of a boat.

berén (*E*) Bren(gun).

beréncét various species of babblers, *Napothera spp.*

beréndéng (*J*) in a row, consecutively; close (to*)*, next (to), side by side. *pengantin duduk –* the bride and groom sat side by side. → RÉNDÉNG I.

beréndi (*D*) cognac, brandy.

berenga → BERNGA.

berengau k.o. trumpet.

beréng-beréng flat knobless Chinese gong, cymbals.

berenggil protruding, sticking out (of crab eyes/the pit of the cashew-nut/kris out of belt/head above water/snake from a hole, etc.).

beréngkés (*Pal*) k.o. way of grilling.

beréngsék (*coq*) 1 rude, ill-bred, malicious, wicked, mean, nasty. 2 arbitrary, high-handed, indescribable, outrageous, shocking. *–!* what a nerve! 3 useless, lousy. *mobil –* a useless car.

keberéngsékan 1 lousiness (of traffic conditions), rottenness. 2 outrageousness.

beréngséng (*onom*) snoring noise.

berengut memberengut to scowl, be surly/sour/sullen.

berénjolan (*J*) uneven, rough, rugged, potholed (of a road).

beréntang memberéntang to pull away from (an embrace, etc.).

memberéntangkan 1 to pull/tug/jerk (s.t.) away (from). 2 to exert o.s., try hard, do one's utmost; to devote s.t. to; to concentrate on.

terberéntang (to rise) sharply (of a road).

berenti → BERHENTI.

beréo (*J*) full beard; → BERÉWOK.

berérot (*J*) to walk one after the other, walk in single file.

berés (*M ob*) very cold, ice-cold.

bérés (*J/Jv*) 1 in order, neat. *Rumah tangganya –.* Her household is neat. 2 settled (of a quarrel/problem, etc.). *Persoalannya sudah –.* The problem has been settled. 3 paid off (of debts). *Utang saya sudah –.* My debts have been paid off. 4 (*coq*) (all) taken care of, all done. *Jangan khawatir, pokoknya –.* Don't worry, the main thing is that it's all taken care of. *sudah –!* it's all taken care of! no sweat! *Kurang – ingatannya.* He's not right in the head. *tanggung –* leave it to me! I'll take care of it. It'll be all right! *kurang –* a) not quite right in the head. b) not in good order, in disorder, a mess (of work). **kekurang-bérésan** disorderliness, messiness. *tidak –* disorderly, in disorder. **ketidak-bérésan** 1 disorder, disorderliness. *Dia mencium ~ itu.* He noticed the disorder. 2 irregularities.

berbérés(-bérés) to take steps, get ready (to do s.t.).

memberési and **memberéskan** [and **mbérésin/ngebérésin** (*J coq*)] 1 to put in order, neaten up, tidy up (a room), arrange, take care of. ~ *tempat tidur* to make a bed. 2 to settle, conclude. 3 to pay off (debts), liquidate. 4 (*coq*) to kill, take care of. *"Komandan pemberontakan dibéréskan."* The rebel commander was taken care of.

terbérés most in order, neatest.

kebérésan order(liness), tidiness, neatness.

pembérés liquidator.

pembérésan 1 cleaning away/up, arrangement. 2 paying, paying off (a debt), settlement, liquidating. 3 discharging (from responsibility).

berésok and **berésuk** tomorrow. *–nya* the next morning.

berét (*J/Jv*) scratched.

bérét I (*ob*) *cérét –* a) bit by bit, little by little. b) coming out a little at a time (of diarrhea).

bérét II (*J*) difficult, exacting, demanding, making lots of objections.

beréwok (*Jv*) with (side-)whisker(s).

beréwokan bewhiskered.

bergajul (*J*) 1 rogue, knave, rascal, scoundrel, villain. 2 vandal, hooligan.

bergajulan to act like a scoundrel, etc.

kebergajulan 1 roguery, villainy, knavery. 2 vandalism, hooliganism.

bergas I (*Jv*) neat, smart.

bergas II (*D J*) ferry boat. *pulau Seribu yang dicapai dengan naik – kapal férry penuh sesak* Pulau Seribu reached by boarding a chock-full ferry.

bergedél (*D*) → PERGEDÉL.

berguk (*A*) and *– melayah* a long veil (with eyeholes only) for women pilgrims.

berhala (*Skr*) (animistic) idol, image. *sembah –* a) idolatry. b) to worship idols. *penyembah –* idolater. *penyembahan –* idolatry.

memberhalakan to idolize, worship idols/images. ~ *ilmu pengetahuan* to worship science.

keberhalaan idolatry.

pemberhalaan idolatry, idolization. ~ *matéri* idolization of material wealth or riches, serving Mammon. *Rasa solidaritas masyarakat semakin menipis, ~ matéri makin menonjol.* Feelings of social solidarity are lessening and idolatry of material goods is appearing.

berhana → SEBERHANA.

beri give, grant, provide. - *tahu* → MEMBERITAHU.

memberi 1 to give, grant, provide. *Ia ~ uang kepada pengemis itu.* He gave that beggar money. *~ pertolongan* to help, give assistance. *diberi ber-* ... to be provided with, be given. *diberi beratap* (the house) was provided with a roof, roofed. *diberi berawalan* to be provided with a prefix, prefixed. *diberi bergambar* provided with illustrations, illustrated. *diberi berjangkar* provided with an anchor, anchored. *diberi berkaki* mounted on a stand. *Kaléng ini diberinya berlubang.* He made a hole in this can. *diberi bernama* to be called/given a name. *diberi berpintu* to be provided with a door. *diberi bertali* tied with a rope. *diberi bertanda* to be indicated. *diberi bertitian* to be bridged. *tidak diberi* denied, refused, rejected. **2** (*coq*) to allow, permit. *Ibu tidak ~ anak-anaknya bermain-main dengan anak yang berandal itu.* Mother didn't allow her children to play with that bad kid. *tidak diberi masuk* not allowed to enter, off limits. **3** to add s.t. to s.t. else, apply s.t. to s.t. *~ gula pada air téh itu* to add sugar to the tea. *~ betas hendak paha* give him an inch and he will take a mile. *~ aib* to shame, disgrace. *~ alamat* to give a signal/cue. *~ angin* to favor, encourage, promote, facilitate. *~ angit* (*M*) to embarrass. *~ celaan* to criticize, find fault with. *~ ciri* to mark, characterize. *~ dahsyat* to frighten, scare. *~ gelar* to award a degree, bestow a title. *~ gemuk* arming (a sounding device to take samples of the ocean floor). *~ hati* a) to encourage, embolden. b) to spoil, pamper, indulge. c) to give in (to s.o.). *~ hormat* to extend regards, salute. *~ ingat* → *memberi* INGAT. *~ isi* to conjure up spirits so that they enter a kris. *~ isyarat* a) to give a signal/cue. b) to give s.o. a hint. *~ izin* to permit, allow. *~ jalan* to yield (the right of way), let s.o. pass, let s.o. get by. *~ kesaksian* to testify. *~ kesempatan* to provide an opportunity. *~ keterangan* to provide information, inform (the authorities, etc.), testify. *~ keterangan lebih jauh* to provide further information, go into details. *~ krédit* to grant credit, provide a loan. *~ kuasa* to authorize, empower. *yang ~ kuasa* (*leg*) principal. *~ leta* to show contempt toward. *~ makan* to feed (an animal). *Ayah sedang ~ makan sapinya.* Father fed his cows. *~ malu* a) to discredit. b) to make s.o. look like a fool. c) to embarrass. *Perbuatanmu yang tidak baik telah ~ malu keluarga kita.* Your bad behavior has embarrassed our family. d) to affront. *~ muka* to be lenient to, give in to. *~ nomor* to number. *~ peluang* to provide an opportunity. *~ perlawanan* to resist, put up resistance. *~ pinjaman* to lend. *~ rezeki* to bring luck. *~ salam/selamat* to extend/convey greetings, say hello. *~ semangat* to inspire, stimulate. *~ suara* a) to approve or disapprove. b) to vote (for = *kepada*). *~ tahu* to tell, let know, inform; → MEMBERITAHU. *~ tanda* a) to make a sign (with the hands). b) to mark. *~ telinga* to lend an ear, listen. *~ tempat* to make room. *~ waktu* to allow time (for s.t. to happen or s.o. to do s.t.).

beri-memberi to give e.o., give and take.

memberikan 1 to give, hand over, provide. *~ angin* to give ... the opportunity (to do s.t.). *~ ganti rugi* to reimburse. *~ hasil* to give a result. *~ inspirasi dan imajinasi bagi* to give s.o. inspiration and imagination. *~ izin* to give permission, permit. *~ pandangan* to express an opinion. *~ perlawanan* to resist, put up resistance. *~ suara* to (cast one's) vote. **2** to administer (medicine).

berian 1 gift, present, award; → PEMBERIAN. **2** dowry given to brides, bride price.

pemberi 1 giver, bestower, donor, provider. *~ amanat* a) adviser. b) principal (in a business deal). *~ aval* (*fin*) guarantor, benefactor, accommodation party. *~ gadai* pledgor. *~ hadiah* rewarder. *~ hipoték* mortgagor. *~ krédit* lender. *~ kuasa* (*leg*) principal. *~ pekerjaan* employer. *~ pemudahan* (*leg*) accessory after the fact. *~ pinjaman* lender, obligee. *~ pinjaman terakhir* lender of last resort. *~ titipan* depositor. *~ tugas* principal. *~ waralaba* franchisor. **2** generous, open-handed, liberal.

pemberian 1 gift, grant, award, present, bestowal, assignment. *~ amanat* mandate, commission. *~ amnésti* granting amnesty. *~ grasi* pardon, grant of pardon. *~ hak* assignment of title. *~ kerja*

providing employment, employing, hiring. *~ kuasa/tugas* (*leg*) delegation of authority, authorization, power of attorney, mandate. *~ naséhat-naséhat perkawinan* marriage counseling. *~ nyata* informal gift. **2** delivery, provision, supply, giving, extending (credit). *~ izin* licensing, issuing. *~ krédit* extending credit. *~ makanan* feeding. *~ nomor* numbering. **3** administering (a medicine). *~ tunggal* single administration.

beriang (*M*) water monitor lizard, *Varanus salvator*; → BIAWAK.

beriani (*Pers*) rice that is cooked with ghee or fat obtained from cow's milk.

béri-béri I (*D/E*) beri-beri. - *kering* marasmus.

béri-béri II *kambing* - sheep; → BIRI-BIRI.

berida (*Skr*) **1** aged, old. **2** senior. **3** experienced. *bangsawan* - the old/true nobility.

berik (*D naut*) brig, a two-masted vessel.

berinda (*Sg*) **seberinda 1** a group (family, etc.). **2** all, the whole. *~ tubuh* over the whole body; → SEKUJUR *tubuh*.

beringas and **beringasan** wild, raging, furious. *dengan mata* - with angry eyes.

keberingasan rage, fury, wildness, ferocity.

bering-bering → BERÉNG-BERÉNG.

beringin 1 banyan tree, *Ficus benjamina*. **2** the election symbol used in general elections by Golkar. - *kembar* two banyan trees at the north *alun-alun* of the Surakarta Palace. - *putih* the white banyan tree, creeping fig, *Ficus radicans variegata*, symbol of old age. - *sungsang* "an upside down banyan tree on the face of the moon," man in the moon.

beringis beringinsa to grimace, smirk, make a wry face.

beringsang (*J*) stifling hot, sultry, oppressive; → GERAH. *Dia tak bisa tidur juga karena - kekenyangan.* He also couldn't sleep because it was stifling hot.

beripat (*Belitung*) k.o. game involving fighting with rattan sticks.

berisik (*J*) loud, noisy, tumultuous, uproarious. *dengan suara* - in a loud voice. *Suaranya -.* He has a loud voice. *Telinganya -.* His ears were ringing.

berita (*Skr*) **1** news, news item. **2** communication, announcement. **3** notification, tidings, report, message. **4** proclamation. *tokoh yang membuat* - news maker. *warta* - news items. - *acara* a) minutes. b) notification. c) official report, deposition. **memberita-acarakan** to issue (an official report, etc.). - *acara pemeriksaan* [BAP] official report, deposition. - *acara persidangan* court record, transcript. - *acara rapat* agenda. - *acara serah terima* record of transfer (of property, etc.). - *angin* rumors. - *balasan* response. - *bulanan* monthly report. - *burung* rumors. - *cuaca* weather report. - *dalam negeri* home news. - *dengkul* rumors. - *duka* death notice, obituary. - *hasutan* seditious news. - *intérlokal* news transferred through a long-distance call. - *kapal* shipping intelligence/news. - *kawat* cablegram. - *keluarga* births, marriages and deaths (notices). - *kematian* death notice, obituary. - *kilat* bulletin. - *lutut* secondhand news. - *Negara* State Gazette (for private and commercial laws); → LEMBARAN *Negara*. - *murahan* juicy bit/piece of news. *Koran-koran Amérika yang membuat - murahan itu hanya beberapa saja.* Only a few American papers carried that juicy bit of news. - *panggilan ganda* multiple call messages. - *panél* banner headline (in newspaper). - *pasar* market report. - *peringatan* warning. - *radio dengkul* rumors. - *segera* urgent message. - *sepekan* weekly news. - *sesaat* feature. - *téndénsius* slanted news. - *terkini* latest news. - *terlambat* a belated report/news item.

berberita to report, inform, make known. *pergi tempat bertanya, pulang tempat ~* (*berkenaan dengan orang cerdik pandai*) when you leave, ask (for his advice), when you return, make a report (said about a wise man).

memberitakan to report, tell, relate. *tidak diberitakan* off the record.

terberita reported, heard (as news). *belum ~* (it) has not yet been reported.

pemberita reporter, news correspondent. *~ injil* evangelist.

pemberitaan 1 communication, information, announcement. **2** notification. **3** news report/story, report(ing). **4** (*PC*) preaching (of the Gospel).

beritahu memberitahu to tell, inform. *Dia diberitahu bahwa dia* *telah lulus pemeriksaan.* He was told that he had passed the examination.

memberitahui to inform s.o.

memberitahukan 1 to tell about, report (on), recount, notify (s.o.) of. *Pak Guru akan ~ hasil ujian kepada murid-muridnya.* The teacher will report (on) the results of the test to his pupils. **2** to announce. *Surat-surat kabar ~ kejadian itu.* The newspapers announced the event.

terberitahu reported.

pemberitahuan announcement, communication, notice, notification. *~ barang masuk untuk dipakai* entry for home use (a Customs document). *~ gugatan* summons, subpoena. *~ pajak* tax notice. *~ penarikan* notice of withdrawal. *~ penghentian* notice of dismissal. *~ resmi* a legal/official notice.

beritawan (*Skr neo*) reporter, news correspondent.

berjuis (*ob*) → BORJUIS.

berkah → BERKAT.

berkas I 1 a bundle (of papers, etc.) fastened together, a bunch (of grapes, etc.), a sheaf (of paddy, etc.). *- isoglos* (*ling*) isogloss bundle. **2** a file, folder (for letters, etc.), dossier. *- perkara* file/ dossier of a lawsuit. *Sejumlah petugas PMT masuk ke dalam gedung itu untuk mengambil -.- kantor meréka.* A number of Indonesian Red Cross personnel entered the building to remove their office files. **3** (lawyer's) brief. *- pemeriksaan terhadap NU belum dapat dilimpahkan ke Kejaksaan, karena menunggu pengakuan dari salah seorang tersangka pelaku penculikan dan pembunuhan terhadap I. B. alias R yang belum tertangkap.* The NU investigative brief could not be presented to the Office of the Attorney General yet, because a confession could not be obtained from the alleged kidnapper and murderer of I. B., aka R, who is still at large. **4** beam, shaft, ray (of light). *- cahaya/ sinar* beam/shaft of light.

memberkas 1 to put into a file, make a file on. *Penyidik di Polsék ini memberkas perkaranya termasuk berita acara penyitaan barang-barang bukti tersebut.* The Police precinct investigators made a file of the case, including the report on the seizure of those goods. **2** to bundle up, tie into a bundle. *~ rumput kering* to tie hay into a sheaf. *bagai tanduk diberkas* very hard to bring together (because not of the same mind). *bagai tanduk diberkas* very hard to unite. **3** to arrest, capture, detain. *kelima tersangka yang diberkas* the five arrested suspects. **4** to beam (of light).

memberkasi to bind, fasten, tie into a bundle/bunch/sheaf.

memberkaskan to put s.t. together in a dossier/file (in order to submit it to the court).

terberkas bundled, tied, bound together.

berkasan bunch/sheaf, bundle.

pemberkas bundler.

pemberkasan 1 bundling, binding, making into a file/dossier, filing system. *~ abjad* alphabetical filing system. **2** arresting.

berkas II (*D cla*) launch, longboat.

berkat (*A*) **1** blessing (divine favor bestowed directly or through the intercession of s.o.). *Tuhan sumber segala -.* God is the source of all blessings. *memberi -* to give one's benediction/ blessing. *- Paus* papal blessing. *memohon -* to ask for s.o.'s blessings. **2** blessed, fortunate. *Marilah kita berdoa bersama-sama kepada Allah dalam bulan puasa yang - ini.* Let us pray together to Allah in this blessed fasting month. *Tidaklah - bagi kita menipu orang yang membeli barang daripada kita.* It isn't a blessing for us to deceive people who buy goods from us. **3** as a result of, thanks to. *- penggulawéntahnya apik, anak-anaknya pada jadi orang semuanya.* Thanks to their fine upbringing, his children have all become good adults. **4** (*coq*) to produce s.t. good; useful, profitable, doing well. *Uangnya banyak, tetapi tidak -.* He has a lot of money but nothing that is good. **5** (*Jv*) gift (and reward) in the form of blessed food (and money), from a *slametan* taken home by the participants after they have eaten a portion of it, *esp* to those who had prayed. *- bersyarat* conditional blessing. *- terselubung* blessing in disguise.

memberkati 1 to bless, give one's blessing/benediction to. *Walaupun miskin, meréka tetap berdoa semoga Tuhan ~ kehidupan meréka sekeluarga.* Even though they are poor, they still pray

that God will bless their lives and that of their family. **2** to ask for blessings for. *Penghulu itu ~ kedua pengantin.* The penghulu asked for blessings for the newlyweds. **3** to bring good/blessings. *barang curian tidak akan ~* ill-gotten gains seldom prosper.

te(r)berkati blessed.

berkatan (*Jv*) food taken home from a *slametan*.

keberkatan blessing.

pemberkat God.

pemberkatan blessing, consecration.

Berkeley Mafia (and **Mafia Berkeley**) term used for American-educated economists brought in by President Soeharto in 1966 to form a new economic policy for the government.

berkicot → BEKICOT.

berkik *burung* – pintail snipe, *Capella stenura.*

berkil *ikan* – sea-perch, red snapper, *Lutjanus erythropterus.*

bérko (*D? brand name ob*) electric bicycle light.

berkok and **berkuk** *burung* – the larger thick-billed green pigeon, *Treron capellei magnirostris;* → PUNAI.

berkung a small *sampan.*

berlau blue; → BELAU.

berlian (*D*) a brilliant, polished diamond.

berlukar (*ob*) → BELUKAR.

berma (*cla*) red, scarlet.

bermat a one-masted ship.

bermi a climber that grows in water, thyme leaved gratiola, *Herpestis monniera.*

bermis [beton ringan (dari batu) pamis] lightweight concrete made from pumice stone.

Bernama [Berita Nasional Malaysia] *Kantor Berita* – Malaysian National News Agency.

bernang → BERENANG.

bernas 1 full, well-filled (of grain/seed/breasts/boil, etc.). **2** plump (of infants). **3** spirited, lively, animated (speech). **4** reliable. *Janjinya selalu -.* His promises can always be trusted.

bernga larvae of insects, maggots.

berniaga → NIAGA.

bero → BERA. **memberokan** to let (land) lie fallow.

berobot I (*J*) to come out quickly.

berobot-berobot (constant) rattling, crackling (of rifle fire or farts), (repeated) explosions (of firecrackers).

memberobot to crackle, rattle (of a rifle).

berobotan constantly/repeatedly crackling, rattling, exploding (of many rounds/firecrackers).

berobot-berobotan crackling; rat-a-tat-tat. *Khalayak dikagétkan pula dengan ~ berasal dari senjata api.* The public was also frightened by the crackling of firearms.

memberobotin (*J*) to make s.t. crackle.

berobot II (*J*) **berobot-berobot** to eat noisily. *Makannya ~ sebentar saja sudah habis dua piring.* He ate noisily, in no time at all he had finished two helpings.

beroci (*Hind*) fine silk of Bharoch (in Gujerat).

berocot (*J*) to come into the world, be born.

diberocotin (*vulg*) to be born.

bérod I skinned, peeled off. *Tangannya pada - jatuh dari motor.* His hands were skinned because he fell off his motorcycle.

bérod II (*J*) *ikan* – lesser spiny eel, *Macrognathus aculeatus.*

beroerte (*D ob*) /berurte/ stroke (of apoplexy).

beroga *ayam* – red jungle-fowl, *Gallus ferrugineus.*

berogol → BORGOL.

berok (*J*) abdomen. *turun –* hernia; → BURUT.

bérok a small *sampan.*

berokar (*E*) broker; → MAKELAR.

berokat (*D*) brocade.

beroklak corrupted pronunciation of the name of the laxative "Brooklax."

beronang *ikan* – a poisonous coral fish, the streaked spine foot, *Siganus vermiculatus/virgatus.*

berondong fusillade. *kena –* to get shot.

memberondong 1 to fire (off) a volley. **2** to bombard, shell, pepper. *~ dengan pertanyaan* to bombard/pepper s.o. with questions. **3** to fire a burst at. *Suami-istri téwas diberondong peluru penjahat.* The couple was killed by a burst of bullets from the criminals.

memberondongkan to shower, fire off (a volley). ~ *peluru senapan mesin ke arah pengemudi mobil* to fire off a volley of machine-gun bullets in the direction of the drivers.

berondongan 1 barrage, salvo, volley. **2** popped. *jagung* ~ popcorn.

pemberondongan bombardment.

bérong (*ob*) → SÉRONG.

berongkos a vegetable side dish seasoned with *kluwak*.

berongsang (*M*) **memberongsang** to flare up (of anger), be in a foul mood.

berongsong (*Jv*) **1** material (paper/bamboo, etc.) for wrapping fruits while still on the tree, to hasten ripening or to protect against birds, squirrels, bats, etc. **2** muzzle (for dogs), curbing (of a newspaper).

memberongsong 1 to wrap (fruits on the tree to protect them). **2** to muzzle (dogs), curb (a newspaper); → MEMBRÉIDEL.

beronjong 1 a large basket. **2** gabion (for reinforcing a dam).

beronok name given to several k.o. edible sea slugs; → TERIPANG. - *landak*, k.o. sea slug. - *pisang*, k.o. sea cucumber/slug, *Colochirus sp.*

beronsang → BERONGSANG.

berontak 1 insurrection, rebellion, revolt. **2** to revolt; → MEMBERONTAK. **3** to struggle.

memberontak to revolt, mutiny, rebel, show resistance.

memberontaki 1 to rebel against. **2** to resist, struggle against.

memberontakkan to make s.o. revolt.

pemberontak rebel, mutineer, rioter, revolutionary, insurrectionist. ~ *bersenjata* armed rebel/insurgent.

pemberontakan mutiny, rebellion, insurgence, insurrection, riot. *Sampai satu ketika ia terlibat dalam* ~ *yang dipimpin Kahar Muzakar.* So that at one point he got involved in the rebellion headed by Kahar Muzakar. ~ *yang didukung RRC* an insurrection supported by Communist China. ~ *gerilya* guerrilla rebellion.

berosot (*J*) **memberosot** [and **ngeberosot** (*J*)] to slip/slide off.

beroti a horizontal lath, rung.

bersagi (*ob*) → PERSEGI.

bersat → BERSESAT.

bersih 1 clean, free from dirt. *Dia mandi dan mengenakan pakaian yang* -. She bathed and put on clean clothes. **2** free from pollution, unadulterated, pure. *air* - clean water. *udara* - clean air. **3** clear, cloudless. *langit* - *bertabur bintang* a clear and starry sky. **4** honest, sincere. *menolong orang yang susah itu dengan hati* - to offer help sincerely to s.o. in trouble. **5** morally pure, innocent. *gadis yang* - an innocent girl. **6** not involved in unlawful actions. **7** clean (not corrupt). *pemerintah* - a clean government. **8** neat, orderly, clean (copy). *laporan yang diketik dengan* - a neatly typewritten report. **9** net, after deducting all expenses or extras. *Setelah pembungkusnya dibuang, berat* - *barang itu hanya 50 Kg.* After the wrapping was discarded, the net weight of the goods was only 50 kilograms. *keuntungan* - net profit. *pendapatan* - net income. **10** (*coq*) all gone (of money/food served, etc.). *Hidangan di méja itu sudah* -. The food served on the table is all gone. *tidak* - dirty. **ketidak-bersihan 1** dirtiness. **2** involvement in corruption. - *désa* (*Jv*) annual purification of the village from evil spirits. - *dari stok* out of stock. - *diri* indication that s.o. was not involved in the G30S/PKI coup. *transmigran yang tidak* - *diri* a transmigrant who was involved in the G30S/PKI attempted coup. - *lingkungan* politically clean, an indication that s.o.'s close family was not involved in the G3OS/PKI coup. - *nagari* (*Jv*) (in Tulungagung) cleansing the town of all disturbance. - *suci* pure, innocent. **membersih-sucikan** to purify.

bersih-bersih everything is clean, all clean. *Pakaian anak-anak* ~. The children's clothing is all clean.

sebersih as clean as.

berbersih-bersih to clean everything up. *Kerja ibu pagi-pagi* ~ *di rumah sebelum ke pasar.* Mother's job at home in the morning is to clean up before going to the market.

membersihkan [and **mbersihin** (*J coq*)] **1** to clean. **2** to purify. **3** to purge (politically). **4** to clear/mop up. ~ *sisa-sisa gerombolan* to mop up the remnants of the gangs. **5** to restore (s.o.'s good name). ~ *nama itu dari tuduhan palsu* to restore the good

name of s.o. falsely accused. ~ *diri* to clear one's name (of an accusation).

terbersih and **tebersih** the cleanest.

bersihan (*med*) clearance, volume of blood cleansed of a substance per unit of time.

kebersihan 1 cleanliness, tidiness, neatness, hygiene. ~ *mulut* oral hygiene. ~ *pribadi* personal cleanliness. **2** purity. ~ *hati* purity of heart.

pembersih 1 cleaner, cleanser, detergent, purifier; purist (in language). ~ *air* water purifier. ~ *gigi palsu* denture cleanser. ~ *kaca* glass cleaner. ~ *klosét* toilet bowl cleaner. ~ *lantai* a) floor polisher. b) floor cleanser. ~ *udara* air purifier. **2** cleanup man, custodian. ~ *petugas ruangan* janitor. ~ *wajah* facial cleanser.

pembersihan 1 cleaning, cleansing. ~ *étnis* ethnic cleansing, genocide. ~ *gigi palsu* cleaning one's dentures. **2** purification (of water, etc.). **3** purge, purging. **4** mopping up, clearing away. *gerakan* ~ mopping-up operation. ~ *tanah* land clearing. **5** raid, round up. **6** catharsis.

bersil membersil to protrude, bulge, appear partially, emerge (as a snake from a hole or a ship from behind a cloud or island).

bersin to sneeze; → BEBANGKIS.

bersit sebersit (a small quantity). ~ *cahaya* a ray of light. ~ *harapan* a flicker of hope. ~ *rasa haru* a bit of emotion. ~ *senyum* a flicker of a smile. ~ *sinar* a ray of light.

membersit 1 to appear, make one's appearance, become visible, emerge. **2** to bead, form into beads, stand out in drops. *Keringat* ~ *di dahinya.* Sweat stood in drops on his forehead. **3** to surge, rise, spring up. *kenangan itu yang kini* ~ *di benaknya* memories that now came to mind.

membersitkan to bring out, produce, show, protrude, exude (an odor).

terbersit emerge, appear, come over one, well up. *Dalam benakku* ~ *dendam.* A feeling of hatred came over me. *Akhirnya,* ~ *idé untuk membuat média khusus yang harganya mudah dijangkau.* Finally, he hit upon the idea of making a special media which everyone could afford.

bersitan radiation, emanation, spouting/squirting out; expansion.

bersut membersut 1 to spit (of cats). **2** to snarl (of dogs). **3** to look gruff/surly, act sour, surly. **4** to glare/glower at.

pembersut a sour person.

bertam I *pohon* - bertram palm (split for wattled house panels), *Eugeissona tristis.*

bertam II *burung* - Malayan black wood-partridge, *Melanoperdix nigra.*

bertih to roast rice in the husk. *beras* - toasted rice, used *esp* in magic ceremonies. *seperti* - *direndang* incessant rattling of rifle fire.

beruang I the Malayan bear, *Ursus malayanus.* - *cokelat* Ursus arctor, the brown bear. - *damar* → BERUANG *madu.* - *és/kutub* polar bear, *Ursus/Thalarctos maritimus.* - *madu* honey bear, *Ursus malayanus.* - *matahari* sun bear, *Helarctos malayanus.* - *mainan* toy/teddy bear. *si* - *Mérah* the U.S.S.R. - *polar* polar bear, *Ursus maritimus.*

beruang-beruangan toy bear, teddy bear.

beruang II → EMPEDU *beruang.*

beruas *pohon* - a wild mangosteen, *Garcinia celebica/hombroniana.*

beruaya → RUAYA.

berudu tadpole; → CÉBONG, GERUNDANG.

beruga (in NTB) k.o. shelter.

berui sawfish, *Pristis cuspidatus*; → YU *parang.*

berujul (*Jv*) a small plowshare.

beruk pigtailed monkey, *Macacus nemestrinus*, that can be trained to pick coconuts and durians. *serah* - and - *hantar hasil* the mumps; → BEGUK. *digila* - *berayun* only manipulated/victimized by beautiful women. *mabuk/dimabuk/dilengah karena* - *berayun* busily paying attention to s.t. useless by throwing away time (or other resources). *berhakim kepada* - to ask for justice from a greedy person; both litigants will lose financially. *bertukar* - *dengan cigak* one should not throw away old shoes before one has got new ones. *anak di pangku dilepaskan,* - *di rimba disusukan* sell not the skin before you have caught the

bear; don't count your chickens before they are hatched. *bagai – kena ipuh* to wriggle and writhe in pain, etc.
berumbun (*M*) **terberumbun** in bold relief (as a mountain/rock/house/carving).
berumbung I 1 cylinder; cylindrical. **2** (*elec*) bus.
berumbung II *pohon* – k.o. tree with hard timber, *Adina rubescens*.
berunai *pohon* – a tree, *Antidesma neurocarpum/alatum*.
berunang k.o. long basket (carried on the back).
berungut memberungut 1 to grumble. **2** surly, sour; → RUNGUT.
memberunguti to be surly toward, grumble about.
pemberungut a sour person.
beruntun (*J*) consecutively; → RUNTUN.
beruntus (*J*) pimples, rash.
beruntusan covered with rash/prickly heat.
berurte (*D ob*) (to have) a stroke/seizure.
berus I (*D/E*) brush.
memberus to brush, groom.
berus II k.o. mangrove tree, *Bruguiera cylindrica*, → BAKAU *putih*.
beruwas → BERUAS.
berwari (*M*) then, further, next.
berzanji → BARZANJI.
bes (in acronyms) → BESAR.
besagi (*ob*) → PERSEGI.
be'sai (*C J*) **1** ugly. **2** damaged. **3** out of order, unusable.
besalén (*Jv*) **1** blacksmith's shop, smithy, forge. **2** kris-making site.
bésan people whose children are married to e.o. *memulangi* – to marry one's cousin (i.e., the *anak mamak kandung*). – *sebantal* if husband and wife each have a child by a former marriage and they intermarry, the parents become – *sebantal*.
berbésan and **bésanan** to be related to e.o. through the relationship of *bésan*. *belum beranak sudah* ~ don't count your chickens before they are hatched.
perbésanan the relationship between *bésans*.
besar I 1 large, big; *opp* KECIL. *bangunan yang* – a large building. *bertubuh* – to be a big person. **2** grand, prominent, notable. *orang* – a notable, dignitary, bigwig. *perlombaan senjata yang* – a big arms race. **3** adult, grownup. *orang* – an adult, grownup; → ORANG *déwasa*, DÉWASAWAN. **4** important, great, considerable (amount, etc.). *bahaya* – a great danger. *belanja yang* – considerable expense. **5** highest, supreme. *guru* – professor. *markas* – [Mabés] headquarters. **6** measurement, size. *-nya size* – *badannya* his bodily measurements. **7** difficult to surmount. *masalah* – a problem difficult to surmount. **8** to grow up, be raised. *Anak Blitar yang – di Kediri*. A native of Blitar who grew up in Kediri. *Embah kita ini kelahiran Klatén, Jawa Tengah – di Suriname*. Our grandmother was born in Klaten, Central Java, and grew up in Suriname. **9** very, enormously, considerably. *Bu Lurah menjadi marah* –. The spouse of the Village Head became very furious. *air* – flood, inundation; → BANJIR. *buang air* – to defecate. *bencana* – catastrophe, calamity. *buku* – ledger (in bookkeeping). *dosa* – a grave sin. *duta* – [Dubés] ambassador. *empat* – → EMPAT *besar*. *hari* – a) holiday. b) feast day. *hutan* – primary forest. *jalan* – highway, main road; → JALAN *raya*. *makan* – feast, big dinner. *negara* – a powerful/influential country. *pengurus* – executive board. *perang* – great war. *perkara* – an important matter. *perut* – pregnant, expecting. *rapat* – congress, meeting. *sungai* – large stream. *untung* – an enormous profit. – *kayu* – *bahannya*, – *periuk* – *keraknya* they that have plenty of butter can lay it on thick. – *pasak daripada tiang* to live beyond one's means. *tidak* – not big. *ketidak-besaran* unimportance. – *akal* (*cla*) smart. – *bangkai* tall, robust, sturdy. – *cakap* a) talkative. b) arrogant, conceited. – *empat* the four high-ranking officials in the Minangkabau. – *gabuk* a) large but empty rice kernel. b) a heavy body but still stupid (of a child). – *hati* a) proud, haughty, arrogant. b) cheerful, in high spirits, joyful, elated. **berbesar hati** to be happy, proud, cheer up. **membesarkan hati** to cheer s.o. up, be encouraging. – *hidung* proud, haughty, arrogant. – *jiwa* magnanimous, unselfish. **kebesaran jiwa** magnanimity, unselfishness. – *kalang* cowardly. – *kécék* a) talkative. b) arrogant, conceited. – *kecilnya* a) size. – *kecilnya telur tidak terlalu tergantung pada keturunan ayam*. The size of

the eggs does not depend too much on the pedigree of the chicken. b) amount. *Perhitungan – kecilnya séwa biasanya tergantung pada* … The calculation of the amount of the rental usually depends on … c) extent. – *kecilnya suatu kerusakan akan ditentukan bersama oléh kedua belah pihak* the extent of the damage shall be determined jointly by the two parties. – *kepala* a) stubborn, obstinate. b) conceited, stuck-up. *Suksés telah membuat – kepalanya*. Success has gone to his head. – *lambung* a big eater, gluttonous, voracious. – *lengan* to be powerful/mighty/influential. – *mulut* a) talkative. b) arrogant, conceited. c) shameless, brazenfaced, impudent, impertinent. – *péndék* a) chubby. b) plump. c) short and stout. – *perut* a) gluttonous, voracious. b) pregnant; *cp perut* BESAR. – *rabu* slow-witted. – *risiko* risky, a big risk.
sebesar 1 as big as. *Dia tidak* ~ *saya*. He isn't as big as I (am). **2** to the amount of, amounting to. *utang* ~ *satu juta* a debt amounting to one million rupiah. ~ *nyata* as big/large as life, life-sized.
sebesar-besarnya as large/big, etc. as possible. *Kami mohon maaf* ~. We deeply apologize.
berbesar-besar to increase, worsen (of an illness, etc.). *Demamnya* ~ *setelah kena hujan*. His fever worsened after he got caught in the rain.
membesar 1 to become/grow big/tall. *Bengkak itu* ~. The swelling became bigger. **2** to augment, increase. **3** to pretend to be a big shot, be arrogant/self-assertive, boast.
membesarkan [and **ngebesarin** (*J coq*)] **1** (= **memperbesar**) to enlarge, increase. ~ *invéstasinya* to increase his investment. **2** to bring up, rear, raise. (usually passive). *Saya dibesarkan di Jakarta*. I was brought up in Jakarta. **3** to expand, broaden, widen. ~ *tanah jajahan* to expand the subjugated territory. ~ *jurang perbédaan antara miskin dan kaya* to widen the gap between the poor and the rich. **4** to increase (the number of). ~ *pasukan pemeliharaan perdamaian* to increase the number of peace-keeping forces. **5** to honor, hold in high esteem. ~ *nabi Muhammad s.a.w.* to hold the Prophet Muhammad in high esteem; → S.A.W. **6** to turn up (the volume). ~ *api* to feed the fire. ~ *belanja* to increase expenses. ~ *diri* to pride o.s., boast, brag. ~ *hati* a) to encourage. *Ada orang yang perlu dibesarkan hatinya untuk maju dalam hidup*. Some people need to be encouraged in order to move ahead in life. b) encouraging. *Pembangunan ékonomi Indonésia tahun-tahun terakhir ini sangat* ~ *hati*. Economic developments in Indonesia have been very encouraging these last few years. c) to cheer up. *Dia sedih. Seseorang harus* ~ *hatinya*. She's depressed. S.o. should cheer her up. ~ *kerak nasi* to add unneeded expenses. ~ *lampu* to turn up the lamp. ~ *mata* to open one's eyes wide. ~ *modal* to increase the capital. ~ *nafsu* to give free rein to. ~ *semangat* to encourage. ~ *suara* to raise one's voice.
membesar-besarkan to exaggerate, blow up, blow out of (all) proportion, make a big deal out of, overemphasize. *Dia senang* ~ *segala sesuatu*. He likes to exaggerate everything. *Jangan* ~ *apa saja*. Don't make a big deal out of everything. *Dia cenderung* ~ *segala sesuatu yang bersifat négatif*. She tends to blow negative things out of proportion. *Dia* ~ *peranannya di bidang politik*. He overemphasized his role in politics. *Ia* ~ *kekayaannya*. He exaggerated his wealth.
terbesar 1 biggest, largest. **2** oldest, first-born. *anak* ~ *dari keluarga Ny. Encum* the oldest child of Mrs. Encum family; → ANAK *sulung*.
besaran 1 extent, size, magnitude, amount, quantity. ~ *tarif bis kota* the size of the city-bus rate. **2** (*coq*) bigger.
besar-besaran 1 large-scale (of military operations, etc.). *secara* ~ on a grand/large scale. *memperingati ultahnya secara* ~ to celebrate his birthday on a grand scale. *penangkapan secara* ~ large-scale arrests. **2** pompous, sumptuous, magnificent. *Pésta pernikahan itu dirayakan secara* ~. The wedding party was celebrated in a pompous fashion. **3** massive. *balasan* ~ massive retaliation.
kebesaran 1 greatness, grandeur, magnitude. ~ *kerajaan Hindu-Jawa Majapahit* the grandeur of the Majapahit Hindu-Javanese empire. **2** honor, state, pomp. *Pemakaman berlangsung dengan* ~ *militér*. The funeral took place with military

honors. *pakaian* ~ full dress. **3** (*J*) too big. *Bajunya* ~ *sedikit.* His coat is a bit too big. ~ *air* bewildered.

pembesar l big shot, dignitary, important person, bigwig. ~ *kapal* the ship's officers. **2** magnifying.

pembesaran l enlargement, blow-up (of a photo). ~ *léver* enlargement of the liver, hepatomegaly. ~ *limpa* enlargement of the spleen, splenomegaly. **2** increase, expansion.

perbesaran magnification.

Besar II the 12th (lunar) month of the Muslim calendar.

Besaran *Lembu* ~ the cow given by the Sultan of Yogyakarta to the poor and needy in his administrative area on the 10th of the Javanese lunar month of Besar on the occasion of *Idul Korban.*

besar III and **besaran** → BEBESARAN.

bések (*Jv*) k.o. closed basket.

besel (*Jv*) bribe.

beselah → BESLAH.

beselit → BESLIT.

besengék (*Jv*) curried chicken, meat, etc.

besér bed-wetting, incontinence. – *mani* spermatorrhoea, wet-dream.

besét I (*J/Jv*) skinned, flayed, fleeced.

  membesét to skin, flay, fleece.

besét II (*D ob*) taken (of a seat), occupied (of a town).

  membesét to take (seats), occupy (a town).

besi l iron. *angkat* – weight lifting. *baju* – armor, coat of mail. *batu* – granite. *bijih* – iron ore, hematite. *gubal* – pig iron. *kayu* – various species of iron wood providing hard timber, *Eusideroxylon zwageri. kikir* – iron file. *pagar* – iron fence. *pandai* – blacksmith. *pukul* – hammer. *serbuk* – filings. *tabir* – a) iron curtain. b) safety curtain. *tahi* – rust. *Wanita* – Iron Woman, i.e., the British Prime Minister Margaret Thatcher. **2** tool made of iron. *menempa* – *di waktu panas* and *tempalah* – *waktu masih panas* strike when the iron is hot. *memegang* – *panas* to do s.t. but be worried/frightened. *baik di* – *bajai/diringgiti* (*M*) to improve s.t. that is already good. – *aji* a revered kris. – *baja* steel. – *batang* iron bar. – *bekas* scrap iron. – *belérang* ferrous sulfide. – *berani* magnet. – *berbaja* tempered steel. – *berombak* corrugated iron. – *beton* iron rods for reinforced concrete. – *bulat* iron bar. – *buruk* scrap iron. – *cabang* a metal truncheon with two tine-like projections that emerge from the junction of the shaft and handle. – *cor* cast iron. – *cor kasar* pig iron. – *dadur timah* tin-plated iron. – *debus* a sharp iron device used in *debus* performances. – *duga* sounding line. – *galbani* galvanized iron. – *gubal* pig iron. – *hiasan* ornamental ironwork. – *Karsani* iron from Khorassan, a good-quality iron. – *kasar* pig iron. – *kawi* manganese, sacred iron. – *kejen* pig iron. – *keropos* sponge iron. – *kuda* horseshoe. – *kuning* magic iron. – *lancér* scrap iron. – *lantai* sheet iron. – *lantak(an)* iron bar. – *lémpéng(an)* sheet iron. – *lunak* nonmagnetic iron. – *mérah* red-hot iron. – *pamor* k.o. white steel forged on a kris, etc. – *papan* iron plate. – *pelat* sheet iron. – *putih* tin (plate), white iron. – *sadur séng* zinc-plated iron. – *sadur timah* tin-plated iron. – *sekrap* scrap iron. – *sembrani* magnet. – *siku* angle iron. – *spons* sponge iron. – *tanah* less good iron. – *tempa(an)/tempawan* wrought iron. – *tua* a) scrap metal. b) worthless. ***membesi tua* 1** to become scrap. **2** to become worthless. ***membesi-tuakan*** to (turn s.t. into) scrap. ***pembesituaan*** scrapping (of sunken ships, anything that is no longer useful). – *tuang(an)* cast iron, magic iron from tusks of a fabulous boar.

  berbesi with/containing iron, ferruginous, ferrous.

  membesi (to become) as hard as iron, iron-hard, (to be) like iron.

  besian iron (*mod*).

  pembesian ironwork.

besing → DESING.

besit I (*D*) property.

besit II → BETIK. **terbesit** became known. *Pernah* ~ *berita, Sungailiat akan segera jadi kota madia yang kedua di Pulau Bangka.* Once rumors had it that Sungailiat would soon become the second municipality in Bangka.

besit III membesit to whip.

besit IV → BERSIT.

béskal (*Jv*) → FISKAL.

beskap (*Jv*) and **beskat** *baju* – a tight-fitting short jacket (with high-closed collar, long sleeves, with two wide flaps folded over the breast and buttoned-up at the shoulders).

besk(u)it (*D*) biscuit, cracker; → BISKUIT.

beskup (*Jv*) **membeskup** to seize, confiscate; → BESLAH.

beslah (*D*) seizure, confiscation.

  membeslah to seize, confiscate.

  beslahan seized.

  pembeslahan seizure, confiscation.

beslit (*D*) **1** letter of appointment. **2** decree, ordinance.

bésok 1 tomorrow, the day after today; → ÉSOK. – *atau lusa* one of these days. – *saja!* wait till the time comes. **2a)** (*Jv*) soon, afterwards, later, in the future, at some future time. b) next ... the coming ... *bulan Séptémber* – next September. *minggu/tahun* next week/year. – *ésok* (*Jv*) tomorrow morning. – *lusa* a) tomorrow or the day after. b) in the future. – *malamnya* the next/following evening. – *pagi* tomorrow morning. – *paginya* the next/following day in the early morning hours; → KEÉSOKAN *paginya.*

  bésoknya the next/following morning.

  bésok-bésok later on, in the future. *Ah, saat ini belum terpikirkan. Entah* ~. Well, at the moment I'm not thinking about it yet (i.e., marrying). But, who knows about the future.

  bésok-bésoknya 1 the day after tomorrow. **2** later. ~ *saya tak bisa mengira-ngira apakah ini suatu jebakan.* Later I could not figure out whether this was a trap.

besot (*J*) badly scratched, lacerated. – *kulitnya* his skin was chafed.

  kebesot scratched; → BARÉT.

bestari (*Skr cla*) expert, skilled; well-educated, wellborn and well-bred. *muda* – young and bright.

bestÉk I → BISTIK.

bestÉk II (*D*) (in building construction) (tender) specification.

bestél (*D*) **1** to order (goods from). **2** ordered. **3** shipment of goods (at a railway station, etc.).

  membestél to (place an) order (for).

  bestélan 1 order; (goods) ordered. **2** parcel. **3** (*J*) (soccer, etc.) player borrowed from another club.

  pembestélan delivery. – *éksprés* special delivery. – *surat* mail delivery.

bestéler (*D*) mailman, delivery man.

bestik → BISTIK.

bestir (*D coq*) executive board (of an organization, etc.); → PENGURUS *besar. priayi* – civil service.

bestral (*D*) **pembestralan** X-ray treatment.

besuk (*D*) /besuk/ **1** visit to a sick person. **2** to pay a visit, make a call.

  membesuk to visit (s.o. in a hospital), see, etc.

  pembesuk visitor, caller.

bésuk → BÉSOK.

besus (*Jv*) to like to get dressed up.

besusu an edible tuber, *Pachyrrhizus erosus*; → BENGKUANG.

besut I membesut 1 to refine metals. **2** to repair, mend. **3** to improve, make better.

  besutan refined.

besut II membesut to spurt, gush, spout, squirt (of water/blood, etc.).

  membesutkan to cause (water/blood, etc.) to spout.

  besutan made by. *film* ~ *sutradara N. A.* a movie made by director N. A.

  besut-besutan outpourings.

besuta (*cla*) a fine silk fabric.

besutan (*Jv*) k.o. folk performance.

bet (*J*) zip! – *(h)ilang* to disappear with lightning speed.

bét (*E*) bat (of table tennis, etc.).

BETA [Benda-Terbang-Anéh] UFO.

béta 1 (*Hind cla*) servant; slave. **2a)** (*cla*) I (used by persons holding an important position, in correspondence, etc.). b) (in literature) I. *saudara* – my brother. c) (in Ambon) I.

  berbéta and **membéta** to use *béta* (when speaking to s.o.).

Betacipok [Bekasi-Tangerang-Cibinong-Depok] the Bekasi-Tangerang-Cibinong-Depok area around the Greater Jakarta Special Capital Region.

betah (*Pers*) **1** (*Jv*) to feel comfortable/at home, get used to (staying at a new place, etc.). *Turis asing harus dibikin –*. Foreign tourists should be made to feel at home. **2** to keep doing s.t. for a long time. *– bicara* to be in a talkative mood. *Astiti yang paling – kalau télepon.* Astiti talks your ear off when she talks on the telephone. **3** (to feel) well, to recover, be getting better (after an illness), convalescent.

membetahi to feel at home in/at.

membetahkan to make s.o. feel at home. *~ diri* to make o.s. feel at home.

kebetahan comfortable feeling, feeling of being at home.

betahak *(J)* to belch; → BESERDAWA.

betak-betak I tattered, dilapidated; torn, in rags.

betak-betak II a skin disease, miliaria, prickly heat; → BETIK-BETIK.

betangur *(– laut)* k.o. tree which produces *tamanu* oil, *Calophyllum inophyllum.*

betapa 1 (followed by an adjective + *-nya*) how …! (exclamatory); → ALANGKAH. *– girangnya hati ibunya kalau mendengar kabar itu!* How elated his mother will be when she hears the news! **2** no matter how much, however much. *– dicarinya, tak bertemu.* No matter how much he looked for it, he didn't find it. **3** (not followed by an adjective + *-nya*) how. *– banyak orang Indonésia …* how many Indonesians … **4** as, like. *diperlakukan – adat orang dahulu kala* to be treated as was the custom in the old days. *– lagi/pula* a) not to mention, to say nothing of, let alone, and even more so. b) so much the more. *–pun* in any case, be that as it may. *– tidak?* How could that not be the case?

betara *(cla)* → BATARA.

betari *(cla)* → BATARI.

betas opened (of a seam), split (of cloth), cracked (of eggshell).

membetas to tear open, split, crack (open).

betatas sweet potato, *Ipomoena batatas.*

Betawi the Indonesian version of the Dutch name Batavia, former name of Jakarta. *bahasa/omong –* Jakartanese. *orang –* a native of Jakarta. *– orak (ob)* people of *Jv* origin who lived in the Batavia region.

kebetawian Jakartanese *(mod).*

pembetawian Jakartanization.

perbetawian Jakartan.

betay → KARTU

bété 1 *(BG from E BT = bad trip)* in a bad mood. **2** [from BT birahi tinggi] very horny.

kebétéan feeling in a bad mood, moodiness.

bétel *(D ob)* chisel.

betemak *burung –* Malayan hawk-owl, *Ninox scutulata.*

betet I *(J)* deformed (of the leg from beriberi).

betet II *– wuk-wuk.* Wuuussh *(onom)* sound made by gasoline set on fire. *Tiba-tiba, – terdengar suara bénsin disulut.* All of a sudden, the sound was heard of gasoline set on fire.

bétét red-breasted/mustached parakeet, *Psittacula alexandri.*

beti I *(Skr M) tanda –* documentary evidence, *corpus delicti.*

berbeti to have proof/evidence, be proved, be proven.

terbeti proved.

beti II and **beti-beti** a small tree, white berry bush, *Flueggia virosa.*

béti-béti *(Hind cla)* palace slave girls.

betik I *(A)* papaya, *Carica papaya;* → KATÉS, PAPAYA. *– belulang* papaya with red flesh. *– bubur* papaya with yellow flesh.

betik II *(M)* news.

terbetik it has become known, it leaked out. *ada kabar ~* there is a report abroad. *~ berita* rumor has it (that). *~ dalam/di hati* it flashes into one's mind. *tidak ~ ke luar* did not show it, did not betray one's feelings.

betik-betik 1 German measles. **2** spot, rash (on skin).

berbetik-betik spotty.

betina 1 female, woman (in South Sumatra); → PEREMPUAN, WANITA. **2** female (of animals). *anjing –* bitch. *kuda –* mare. **3** applied figuratively to inanimate objects, from some sexual connotation, such as, *embun –* light dew; *opp embun jantan* (heavy morning dew). *kasau –* common rafters. *ketam –* grooving plane. *kokot –* eye of clasp. *papan –* board with grooved edge. *stéker –* *(elec)* jack.

membetina to be (like) a female. *pria yang ~* effeminate.

beting reef, sandbank, shoal, ridge; → GOSONG I. *seperti – dipalu ombak* like a reef, pounded by waves, i.e., helpless. *– berkunjur* reef with sharp drop-off. *– buta* shoal. *– gisik* beach ridge. *– karang* coral reef. *–.– pasir* shallows, sandbar.

berbeting with/to have sandbanks.

membeting to form a sandbank; like a sandbank.

terbeting stranded, run aground.

betis I I *(buah/jantung/perut) –* calf (of the leg). *– shinbone*, fibula. *– bagai bunting padi* a calf like a swelling rice grain, i.e., a mark of beauty. **2** lower part of the leg. *diberi – hendak paha* (if you) give him an inch he will take an ell/mile.

sebetis to the calf, calf-length.

betis II k.o. tree, *Palaquium spp., Payena utilis.*

betok I *ikan –* climbing perch, walking fish, *Anabas scandens/testudinus;* → PUYU II.

betok II burnt by acid, etched.

beton *(D)* concrete. *– baja* reinforced concrete. *– berbesi/bertulang* reinforced concrete. *– bis* concrete tube. *– mol(l)en* concrete mixer. *– pratekan* prestressed concrete. *– tulang* reinforced concrete.

membeton 1 (to become) hard as concrete. **2** to reinforce with concrete.

betonisasi the introduction of concrete. *– bantalan rél kereta api* the introduction of concrete for railroad sleepers/ties.

bétor [*bécak motor*] motorized pedicab.

betot *(J/Jv) – urat* → TARIK *urat.*

membetot 1 to pull out, extract. **2** to snatch. *~ jam tangannya* to snatch his wristwatch. **3** to affect (of a disease). **4** to strum (a guitar).

terbetot [and **kebetot** *(coq)*] snatched; pulled out. *merasa hatinya ~* to be overjoyed or saddened, very touchy.

betotan strumming, playing (a string instrument).

pembetot player (of a string instrument).

betuah → TUAH.

betuk → BETOK I.

betul 1 (up)right, honest. *– hati* honest, straightforward. **2** right, exactly, precisely. *Rumahnya berhadapan – dengan rumahku.* His house is right across from my house. *sebelah selatan –* due south. **3** truly, really (not a lie). *– saya datang tadi.* Really, I came a while ago. **4** correct, right, accurate. *jalan yang –* the right way. *Arti kata ini tidak –.* The meaning of this word is incorrect. **5** true, real, genuine (not artificial). *orang Surabaya –* a real Surabayan. *Ini bukan emas –.* This is not genuine gold. **6** upright. *berdiri –* to stand upright. **7** very, extremely. *Mahal – kamus ini.* This dictionary is extremely expensive. **8** for sure. *Dia tahu – persediaan kopi di dapur sudah tidak ada sama sekali.* He knows for sure that the coffee supply in the kitchen is all gone. *– tidaknya* either right or not; the truth (of the matter). *Pertanyaan tentang – tidaknya desas-desus itu.* A question regarding the truth of the rumors. *Yang – (s)aja!* Be serious! *bungkuk baru – (buta baru celik)* to run hog-wild.

betul-betul really, truly, indeed. *Opelét ~ berakar bagi masyarakat Indonésia.* The opelet has really taken root in Indonesian society.

sebetulnya in fact, actually, indeed. *~ tempat pemakaman di sana sudah penuh.* In fact, the burial site over there is already full.

berbetul *(ob)* to arrange, order, marshal (facts/data, etc.), straighten (one's clothing).

berbetulan in accordance with *(dengan),* to coincide (with). *Usulnya ~ dengan usul ketua.* His proposal is in accordance with that of the chairperson. *Hutnya ~ dengan hari Natal.* His birthday coincided with Christmas.

membetul 1 straight. *berjalan ~* to walk/go straight. **2** to straighten out.

membetuli 1 to repair (damage), correct. *~ rumahnya yang bocor* to repair his leaking house. **2** to put in order, straighten up. *Wanita itu ~ letak seléndangnya.* The woman adjusted her shawl. **3** to agree with, come up to. *~ permintaannya* to agree with his request. **4** to aim directly at. *Nakhoda berusaha ~ pulau itu.* The ship's captain tried to aim directly at the island.

membetulkan [and **mbetulin** *(J coq)*] **1** to repair, fix, adjust. *Dia ~ letak kacamatanya.* She fixed/adjusted her glasses. **2** to straighten. ~ *letak topinya* to straighten one's hat. ~ *letak duduknya* to twist and turn (in one's seat). **3** to affirm, confirm. *Ia selalu ~ apa yang dikatakan orang itu.* He always confirms what is said by that person. **4** to correct, rectify. *Murid itu telah ~ kesalahannya.* The pupil has corrected his mistake. **5** to send (out) for repair. *Saya sudah beberapa kali ~ tas itu ke Laba-Laba.* I've sent this bag several times to Laba-Laba for repair.

betulan l vicinity. *di ~* a) close by, off (the west coast of Kalimantan). **2** (*coq*) real, genuine. *Ia dokter gigi ~.* He is a real dentist (not a would-be one). **3** (*coq*) precisely, exactly, actually, really.

betul-betulan for real, really.

kebetulan l coincidentally, unexpectedly. *bukti yang ~ ada* unexpectedly present evidence. *Penjahat yang telah lama dicari itu tertangkap dengan cara ~ saja.* The criminal long looked for was apprehended by chance. *karena sesuatu ~* due to a coincidence. *~ yang bertali-tali* a coincidence. **2** unintentionally. *Témbakannya ~ mengenai dadanya.* The shot unintentionally hit his chest. **3** fortunately. *~ anda datang awal, jadi anda tidak ketinggalan keréta api.* Fortunately, you came early, so that you didn't miss the train. **berkebetulan** to be simultaneous (by chance), coincide, coincidentally. *Sebenarnya hanya ~ saja kami datang bersama-sama.* In fact, only coincidentally did we come together.

pembetulan l repair, fixing. **2** correction, fixing up. *~ kesalahan itu bisa dibuat nanti.* That mistake can be corrected later. **3** amendment, revision.

betung I large (in certain compounds), e.g., *bambu/buluh* – a large bamboo species, *Dendrocalamus asper.* *katak* – a large species of frog that makes loud sounds, *Pufo sp.* *rumput* – a large grass/rattan species, *Equisetum debile, Daemonorops didymophylla.* *tebu* – a large sugarcane. *– ditanam, aur tumbuh* disappointed in one's expectations. *berteduh di bawah* – to obtain unsatisfying assistance. *bagai/seperti membelah* – and *memijakkan – sebelah* unfair, unjust, biased.

betung II pipe through which water or sewage flows.
  membetung to form a pipe through which water, etc. can flow.
  pembetung s.o. or an implement that conveys water, sewer, etc.

betur – *belulang* k.o. tree found in Bangka and Belitung, *Calophyllum lanigerum*; → **BINTANGUR** *belulang*.

betutu I a freshwater carp, sucker barb, *Barbichthys laevis.*

betutu II k.o. shrub related to the camellia, *Eurya japonica.*

betutu III (*Bal*) chicken fillet. *– bébék* a duckling broiled in banana leaf.

bewés → **RÉBEWÉS**.

béwok (*Jv*) (side-)whisker(s).

béybéh → **CUWÉK** *béybéh*.

béza (*Mal*) → **BÉDA**.

bezét (*D*) occupied (of seat, etc.).
  membezét to occupy.

bezuk (*D*) (hospital) visit. *waktu* – visiting hours (in hospital).
  membezuk to visit (in hospital).

BF [Blue Film] pornographic movie.

BG car license for Sumatera Selatan.

bgm (*abbr*) → **BAGAIMANA**.

bgt (*abbr*) → **BANGET**.

bh I (*init*) /béha/ (the Dutch *abbr* for buste houder) bra, brassiere.

bh II (*abbr*) [buah] counter word.

bh- III also see entries beginning with **b-**.

BH car license for Jambi.

bhakti (*Skr*) → **BAKTI**. *– Wanita* the women's organization which has under its wing the State Secretary (= *Sékrétariat Negara*) and 18 nondepartmental institutions. *– Wisatastri* the women's organization under the jurisdiction of the Directorate General of Tourism.

bhara (in acronyms) → **BHAYANGKARA**.

Bharada [Bhayangkara dua] Private Second Class (in the national police force).

Bharaka [Bhayangkara Kepala] Head Private (in the national police force).

Bharatayud(h)a → **BRATAYUD(H)A**.

Bharatu [Bhayangkara satu] Private First Class (in the national police force).

Bharawisata [Bhayangkara wisata] Tourist Police, part of the Yogyakarta Police force consisting of members who are relatively fluent in speaking a foreign language.

Bharma (*Skr*) fire. *Yudha – Jaya* (motto of the Jakarta Fire Department) Greater Jakarta Fire Fighters.

Bhaskara Jaya the military resort command (*Korém* 084) in Surabaya.

Bhayangkara **1** The Police Force of the Republic of Indonesia. **2** Private (lowest set of ranks in the Police Force). **3** (*cla*) the Police Force of the *Majapahit* Empire

Bhayangkari the Policemen's Wives' Association.

bhiku, bhikku, bhikkbu and **bhikkshu** Buddhist monk, lama; → **BIKU**.

bhi(n)néka (*Skr*) not one, many, of various types. *- Tunggal Ika* motto of the Republic of Indonesia State Coat of Arms, meaning: Unity in Diversity. **kebhinnéka-tunggal-ikaan** "unity-in-diversityness."
  kebhinnékaan diversity. *Indonésia yang dikenal ~nya itu sebenarnya sudah memiliki pola-pola yang satu sama lain mendukung.* Indonesia, which is known for its diversity, actually already has a pattern of mutual support. *~ bahasa* multilingualism. *~ manusia* human diversity *~ Karya Abdi Negara* motto of *Korpri*, meaning: Work Diversity of Public Servants.

Bhirawa Anoraga motto of the *Brawijaya* Army Division, meaning: Courageous but Humble.

Bhra name of the Majapahit dynasty.

Bhrawijaya name of the army division stationed in East Java.

Bhuana Sakti sword of honor conferred upon high-ranking Air Force retirees.

Bhuda Buddha, Bhuddist.

Bhumibhakti Adiguna the motto of the National Land Affairs Board, meaning: excellent service to the earth.

Bhumi Pura Yaksha Purna Wibawa the guiding principle of the Directorate General of Immigration, meaning: Guardian of the Gate to a Sovereign State.

bhuwana agung microcosm.

bi I (*A*) in, at, on (place and time); with (indicating connection/association/attention); through, by means of (designating instrumentality or agency); for (= at the price of); by (= in the amount of); by (introducing an oath). *-hi* on/with him. *-smillah* In Allah's/God's name.

bi II clipped form of **bibi**.

BI III [Bahasa-Indonésia] the Indonesian language.

BI IV [Bank Indonésia] Bank of Indonesia, the Indonesian central bank.

bi- a combining form meaning "two," used in the formation of compound words, such as, *bifokal, bilatéral*, etc.

bia I → **BÉA**.

bia II (in acronyms) → **BIAYA**.

bia-bia (*J*) various species of swamp plants, swamp potato, pickerel weed, *Monochoria vaginalis/hastata, Sagittaria sagittifolia.*

biadab (*Pers*) **1** impolite, rude, disrespectful, discourteous, ill-mannered, unmannerly (of person). **2** uncivilized, primitive, wild.
  terbiadab the most uncivilized.
  kebiadaban **1** rudeness, disrespect, disrespectful behavior. **2** primitiveness, backwardness (of a race).

biadat (*A*) unsociable.

biadi (*M*) pinworm, *Oxyuris/Enterobius vermicularis.*

biah (*A ob*) synagogue, temple, church.

biak I **1** prolific, fertile, productive, fruitful (of plants, etc.). *(ber)kembang* – and **berbiak kembang** to proliferate. *memamah* – to ruminate, chew the cud. *pemamah* – ruminants. **2** proliferation. *- bikér/dara* parthenogenesis.
  berbiak and **membiak** **1** to multiply, flourish, increase. *Ayam ternakan jenis ini ~ dengan cepat.* This type of breeding chicken multiplies fast. **2** to proliferate.
  membiakkan **1** to breed (of animals/plants), raise, rear, cultivate. *Ayah bermaksud hendak ~ ayam lalu menjualnya untuk meninggikan pendapatannya.* Father wants to raise chickens and sell them to increase his income. **2** to make s.t. proliferate. **3** to seed (clouds).
  biakan **1** s.t. that is bred/reared/cultivated. *ikan ~* cultivated

fish. **2** culture (in an artificial medium). ~ *jaringan* tissue culture. ~ *murni* (*bio*) pure culture. ~ *pemula* starter culture. ~ *sediaan* stock culture.

pembiak s.t. that breeds, product of breeding/rearing.

pembiakan 1 breeding, raising, rearing, cultivation, cultivating, multiplication. ~ *awan* cloud seeding. ~ *ternak itu berhasil*. The cattle breeding was a success. **2** proliferation.

biak II (*M*) wet, damp.
  membiaki to wet, dampen.
biak III k.o. tree, kratom plant, *Mitragyna speciosa*.
biak IV cud.
  membiak to chew one's cud.

biang I 1 mother, dam (of animals). b) parent (of plants). *ayam –* hen, the female of the domestic chicken; → BIANG *ayam*. *kucing –* pussycat. **2** largest one, master. *– jambrét* the ringleader of a gang of pickpockets. *– jari* thumb. *– kasét* master cassette. *– keladi* a) k.o. taro, the tuber of the *keladi* (a tuberous plant, *Colocasia antiquorum/esculenta*). b) instigator, troublemaker. b) and *– kerok* (*coq*) a member of a group who is regarded as its intellectual leader or planner (*esp* in unlawful acts), ringleader, mastermind. **membiang-keladikan** to mastermind s.t. *– tangan* thumb. **3** (basic/primary) cause. *Tentu, isi dari télepon itu membuat ribut-ribut dan jadi – khéki!* Naturally, what was said over the telephone caused a fuss and became the primary source of frustration. *– macet di sini adalah kendaraan umum*. The basic cause of the traffic jam here is public vehicles. *– penyebab* main cause. *– rampok* mastermind of a robbery. **4** (*J*) wife, spouse; mother. *Pak Dugel bercucu delapan dan beranak empat dari dua –*. Dugel has eight grandchildren and four children from two wives. **5** big, large. *ondél-ondél – a large ondél-ondél*. **6** (*J*) purebred, thoroughbred, pedigreed (not mixed with other races). **7** essence. *– menanti tembuk* relationship that is almost severed. *– ayam* pure line chicken. *– arak* pure arrack (a strong alcoholic drink made from rice). *– besi* iron ore. *– cuka* mother of vinegar (used as a starter to make vinegar). *Hendaknya susu segar dibawa dengan diberi – és pada bagian tepinya*. Fresh milk should be transported with dry ice on the sides. *– kambing* pedigreed goat. *– keringat* prickly heat. *– kopi* essence of coffee. *– lebah* queen bee. *– minyak wangi* k.o. fragrant essence. *– roti* (*J*) yeast. *– selisih* source of a disagreement. **membiang-selisihkan** to make s.t. into the source of a disagreement.

biang II (*M*) nearly perforated (of fabrics); critical (of affairs). *– menanti tembuk* a case almost settled (such as, divorce, etc.), a critical moment.

biang-biang ~ *kain* (no longer) know for sure (but yet vaguely remembering).

biang III very small openings (as slits in a wall or roof which is leaking).

biang-biang (*ikan –*) wingfin anchovy (always salted), *Setipinna breviceps/taty*.

biang-biut (*seperti ular kena palu*) (*ob*) writhing and twisting (like a beaten snake), crooked (of lines), zigzag, askew.

bianglala (*J*) rainbow.

biaperi (*Hind cla*) merchant, trader (Hindu, Persian and Arab).

biar 1 let, allow, permit. *– dia pergi, sebentar lagi juga kembali*. Let him go; he'll be back anyway in a few minutes. **2** so that, in order to. *Berilah aku uang, – aku beli baju itu*. Give me some money, so that I can buy the coat. *Panggillah – datang*. Tell him to come. **3** better, rather, prefer. *– putih hilang jangan putih mata* and *– mati daripada menanggung malu* better death than enduring disgrace. *– lapar daripada mengemis* prefer hunger to begging. **4** whether. *– mahal, – murah, tak akan saya beli*. Whether it's cheap or expensive, I won't buy it. *– bagaimana* (*pun*) be that as it may, come what may. *– begitu* nevertheless, nonetheless. *– d(ah)ulu* not now. *– nanti* so that (it) would be. *dengan maksud – nanti dipenatukan oléh pelayan* with the intention that the (clothes) would be taken to the laundryman by the bellboy. *– seketika pun* not even a minute. *–pun begitu/ demikian* nevertheless. *-pun siapa* and *– siapa pun* whosoever. *– … maupun … maupun … –pun …* and *baik pun … –pun …* a) both … and … b) *– (pun) … atau …* (or, *– … – …*) either … or … *– lambat asal selamat* better late than never, slow but sure.

membiarkan, memperbiar (*ob*) [and **ngebiarin** (*J coq*)] **1** to let, allow, keep, permit, tolerate, let s.o. have his way, give permission or leave to. *Krisis ékonomi global déwasa ini terlalu berbahaya dibiarkan ditangani oléh ahli-ahli keuangan*. The current global economic crisis is too grave to be left to financial experts. ~ *berlalu* to let s.t. pass by, pass up. ~ *hidup* to leave s.t. running. ~ *terbuka* to keep s.t. open. **2** to abandon, neglect, ignore, disregard, let s.t. pass by unnoticed, leave s.t. unfinished. *biarin* (*coq*) forget about it!

biar-membiarkan to be tolerant, live and let live.

terbiar let, allowed. ~ *begitu saja* abandoned (without further ado).

pembiaran permission, letting, permitting.

biara (*Skr*) **1** monastery (for men). **2** convent (for women). **3** nunnery. **4** ancient Hindu monastery ruins in Sumatra.

membiara to live in a monastery. *Setelah hidup – 47 tahun suster Mary kagét naik pesawat terbang*. After having experienced a 47-year monastic life, sister Mary was startled to board a plane.

pembiaraan retreating to a monastery.

biarawan monk. *calon –* novice.

biarawati nun.

biar-biar k.o. small intestinal worm, *Filaria loa. – naik ke mata* to keep on neglecting s.t. that causes danger to o.s.

biarinisme go-to-hell-ism.

bias I 1 deviation, deflection, refraction. *– cayaha* refraction. **2** ray (of light).

berbias with a refraction, refracted.

membias 1 to be deflected from one's course (of ships), slant (of slanting rain). *Air hujan ~ masuk ke dalam rumah akibat angin yang kencang*. Rainwater was deflected into the house due to a strong wind. **2** to change course, drift off, be driven off course.

membiaskan 1 to deflect, change course. *Angin ribut yang turun itu telah ~ perahu meréka ke timur laut*. The typhoon that was coming down deflected their prau in a northwestern direction. **2** to refract.

terbias 1 drifted off, driven off course, diverted from the original direction; deflected. **2** refracted.

biasan 1 diversion, deviation, deflection. **2** refraction; refracted.

pembiasan 1 deflection, deviation, refraction. ~ *sinar* diopter. **2** reflection.

bias II (*E*) bias, prejudice.

berbias biased.

biasa (*Skr*) **1** common (people/cold/stock); ordinary (people), commonplace; as always. *luar –* beyond the ordinary, extraordinary. *rumah –* an ordinary house. *seperti –* as usual, as always. **2** to be accustomed/used to. **3** customary, usual, habitual. *alah bisa oléh –* practice makes perfect; experience is the best teacher.

biasanya usually. *Kursus itu ~ berlangsung selama 6 bulan*. The course usually lasts for six months.

biasa-biasa so-so, not bad. *"Bagaimana, Lidya?" tanya Suara Karya. ~ aja*. "How are you, Lidya?" asked Suara Karya. "So-so."

sebiasa as ordinary, etc. as.

membiasakan to accustom, familiarize, habituate (s.o. to s.t.). ~ *diri* to get o.s. used to s.t. to make it a habit/practice to, make a habit/practice of, accustom o.s. to.

membiasa-biasakan to make s.t. seem normal/customary.

terbiasa to be/get used/accustomed to s.t., acquire a taste for s.t. *Orang Indonésia sudah ~ dengan kenaikan harga, apa pun alasan yang melatarbelakanginya*. Indonesians are used to rising prices whatever the reasons behind it are.

kebiasaan habit, custom, usage, practice. ~ *membaca* reading habit. ~ *makan* eating habits. **kebiasaannya** as a rule, normally, usually, mostly, generally, ordinarily. *sebagaimana ~* as is one's habit.

pembiasaan habituating, familiarizing, accustoming.

biau berbiau embroidered.

biawak 1 iguana and other large lizards, *Varanus salvator*. **2** a little flirt. *– kudung masuk kampung* a thief known by the public. *bila pula – duduk* an impossibility. *mendukung – hidup* bring a hornets' nest down about one's ears. *– air* water monitor, *Varanus salvator. – bersirip* finned monitor lizard, found on Togean

Island, Poso Regency, Central Sulawesi. - *komodo*; → KOMODO. - *kudung* Dumeril's monitor, *Varanus dumerili*. - *puru* lizard with ridged hide, clouded monitor, *Varanus nebulosus*. - *riang-riang* a large species of iguana or monitor lizard, *Varanus salvator*. - *serunai* k.o. iguana with long stretched out head, black rough-neck monitor, *Varanus rudicollis*.

membiawak to creep (like an iguana) on all fours.

biawan k.o. freshwater fish.

biawas guava, *Psidium guajava*; → JAMBU *klutuk*.

biaya (*Skr*) expenditure, expense, expenses, cost, outlay, charge, fee. *atas* - at the expense of. *atas* - *saya* at my expense. *didasarkan pada* - *dan manfaatnya* based on cost and benefit. *ékonomi* - *tinggi* high-cost economy. - *acara* cost of litigation. - *administrasi* administrative expenses, maintenance fee. - *aktiva tetap* capital expenditure. - *angkutan* transportation costs. - *bank* bank charges. - *batas* (*infr*) marginal costs. - *bunga* interest expenses. - *dana* cost of funds. - *dasar* first cost. - *daur ulang* recycling charge. - *(dibayar) di muka* prepaid expenses. - *dinas* work expenses. - *fiskal* departure tax. - *hidup* cost of living. - *ikatan* commitment fee. - *inklaring* (D) (Customs) clearance charges. - *kawat* cable charges. - *keluaran* output cost. - *labuh léna* demurrage. - *lain-lain* miscellaneous expenses. - *langsung* direct costs. - *makan* subsistence expenses. - *makelar* brokerage fee. - *marginal* marginal costs. - *masuk* admission/entrance fee. - *militér* military expenditures. - *modal* cost of capital. - *muat(an)* shipping charges, freight(age). - *operasi* operating cost. - *pekerja* labor costs. - *pelabuhan* dock charges, wharfage. - *pelayanan* service costs. - *pelengkap* supplementary cost. - *pembangunan* sunk cost. - *pembelian* acquisition cost. - *pembuatan* manufacturing/production costs, cost of manufacturing/production. - *pemeliharaan* maintenance costs. - *penagihan* cost of recovery, collection costs. - *pencatatan* recording fee. - *pendaftaran* filing fee. - *pengelolaan* operating expenses. - *pengganti* replacement cost. - *penggiatan* operating costs. - *penggudangan* carrying cost. - *penghidupan* cost of living. - *penginapan* hotel expenses. - *penjualan* sales expenses. - *penundaan* towage. - *penyimpanan* (safe-)custody fee. - *penyusutan* depreciation expense. - *perang* war expenditure. - *perawatan* nursing expenses; hospital fees. - *perizinan* licence fee. - *perjalanan* travel expenses. - *perkara* costs of litigation. - *peroléhan* original cost, acquisition cost, carrying cost. - *pinjaman* borrowing costs/fee. - *pokok* basic cost. - *produksi barang* cost of goods manufactured. - *rambu* beaconage. - *sampan* lighterage. - *seluruh* all-in cost. - *sempadan* marginal cost. - *siluman* bribes. (*dengan*) - *swadaya* (at) their own expense. - *tak langsung* indirect costs. - *tak terduga* unforeseen expenses. - *tambahan* surcharge, additional charges; → TUSLAH. - *tambangan* freight. - *tenaga (kerja)* labor costs. - *terikat* committed cost. - *terkait* imputed cost. - *terpakai* expired cost. - *tetap* fixed/overhead costs. - *tidak langsung* overhead. - *tombok* out-of-pocket costs. - *tongkang* lighterage. - *tunggu* standby cost. - *uang/untuk menarik dana* cost of money. - *udara* airfreight. - *umum* overhead. - *usaha* operating expenses, the cost of doing business. - *utama* prime cost. - *variabel* variable cost. - *yang masih harus dibayar* accrued expense.

berbiaya to have expenses, etc. *pelayanan keséhatan* ~ *murah* low-cost health service.

membiayai [and **ngebiyaiin** (*J coq*)] to finance, pay for, pay the expenses of, defray/bear the cost of; to pay s.o.'s way.

membiayakan to spend (money), lay out (money).

pembiaya financier.

pembiayaan 1 financing. ~ *awal* prefinancing. ~ *bersama* co-financing. ~ *bertahap* take-out loan. ~ *kembali* refinancing. ~ *konsumén* consumer finance. ~ *pascapengapalan* post-shipment financing. ~ *perdagangan internasional* international trade finance. 2 upkeep.

Bibel (D) Bible; → BIBLIA.

bibi(k) (*Pers?*) 1 younger sister of father or mother; also the spouse of a *paman*, thus an aunt. 2 (*J*) term of address for a female domestic help, *usu* shortened to **bi**. 3 reference for any female worker. 4 term of address for a middle-aged woman of lower social status. 5 (*cla*) a married woman, lady; → NYONYA.

bibinda → BIBI(K).

bibir 1 lip. - *atas/bawah* upper/lower lip. - *arat delima* "lips like a ripe (open) pomegranate (the color of red lips)"; in Old Malay literature often used as a metaphor for "beautiful lips of a woman." 2 (anything like a lip in structure or shape) edge, rim, brink, verge, border. - *belanga* the rim of a large earthenware cooking pot. - *cawan* the edge of a (tea)cup. - *jurang* edge of the precipice. - *mangkok* lip of a cup. - *sumur* the rim of a well. 3 mouth or tongue (in the sense of words, etc.). - *berat* - taciturn, uncommunicative, closemouthed. *panjang* - a) backbiting, slanderous. b) like to tell/repeat things heard. *tebal* - taciturn, uncommunicative, closemouthed. *tepi* - lip edge. *di* - *saja* in words only. 4 genital labia. *bergetah* -*nya* very clever in persuading/flattering. *di* - *mata* right in front one's eyes (very near). *di* - *saja* only lip service, all talk and no action. *Selama ini pemerintah dinilai bahwa memberantas korupsi secara di* - *saja dan tidak dengan tindakan*. Up to now the government has been judged to only combat corruption through mere lip service and not through actions. *Belum kering ludah di* - *membicarakan penemuan*. One has hardly finished talking about the discovery. *Katanya dengan suara di* -. He said mumbling. *menjadi buah* - to be the talk of the town. *menjilat* - a) to lick one's lips. b) get s.t. serious consideration. *mudah menggerakkan* - easily said. *tinggal menghapus* - to get nothing, be disappointed, unsuccessful. *tipis* -*nya* a) like to chatter/talk. b) quarrelsome, talkative. *Tutup* -*mu!* Shut your mouth! → TUTUP *mulutmu*. -*nya bukan diretak panas* his words/remarks were not uttered in vain. - *Asia Tengah* the border of Central Asia. *Teluk Oman di* - *Asia Tengah*. The Gulf of Oman at the border of Central Asia. - *bak mandi* the edge of a bath tub. - *hutan* the edge/fringe of a wood, the verge of a forest. - *jalan* the side of a road, roadside. - *jendéla* window sill. *melongok dari* - *jendéla* to stare out from the window sill. - *mata* eyelid. - *méja* table edge. - *nét* the edge of a (tennis) net. - *panggung* apron of a stage. - *pantai* the edge of a beach. - *Seméru* the lip of the crater of Mount Semeru. - *sumbing* harelip. - *Sungai Batanghari* the bank of the Batanghari River. - *tabir* the end of a screen. - *taman nasional* the edge of the national park. - *tangan* the side of the hand. - *telaga* the edge of a lake/pond.

berbibir with/to have a lip. *aktris* ~ *sénsual* an actress with sensual lips.

membibiri to provide s.t. with a lip/edge.

bibis (*Jv*) water beetle.

bibit I 1 seedling, seed. *Kacang itu sempat membiak* - *dalam jangka beberapa bulan saja*. Beans manage to sprout in just a couple of months. - *tembakau Virginia* Virginia tobacco seeds. 2 germ (for proliferation/cultivation, etc.). *kebun* - nursery (for young trees), seedbed. *kuda* - studhorse, stallion, brood mare. 3 source, origin, cause or beginning of anything. -.- *pemberontakan* the seeds of revolt. 4 germ, bacteria. - *penyakit* disease/pathogenic germ(s). - *penyakit cacar* smallpox bacteria. 5 the younger Generation, future students, cadre, etc. *Murid-murid SMA dididik sebagai* - *untuk perguruan tinggi sénior*. High School students are educated as cadres for colleges. *mencari* - talent scouting. 6 fledgling, neophyte, novice. -, *bébét dan bobot* (or, any other sequence of these three words). a) Javanese saying referring to the three elements taken into consideration for a harmonious marriage: (equal) origin, descent and position. b) birds of a feather flock together. - *ayam* day-old chicken, DOC. - *badai* storm cell. - *banting* milkfish fry; → NÉNÉR. - *énten* graft. - *ikan* fry (i.e., small fish). - *induk* parent stock (*esp* of chickens). - *kentang* seed potato. - *minyak wangi* perfumed compounds. - *nénék* grandparent stock (*esp* of chickens). - *opium* poppy seed. - *perselisihan* reasons for a conflict. - *sapi* breeding stock. - *sebar* final stock (*esp* of chickens). - *udang windu* tiger prawn for breeding purposes; → BENUR. - *unggul* top-quality seeds.

sebibit of the same origin. *dulur asal* ~ (*Jv*) descendants of the same father and mother.

berbibit 1 to have germs. 2 to have ... seeds. 3 to have a certain origin, be descended (from). ~ *kepada* to be descended (in the father's line) from.

membibit to become germs, grow, shoot, spring up, germinate

membibitkan 1 to sow. **2** to produce, give rise to.

pembibitan 1 seed/nursery bed. **2** growth, cultivation of seedlings. **3** talent scouting. **4** breeding. ~ *ternak* livestock breeding.

bibit II membibit to carry s.t. with the finger tips; → MEMBIMBIT.

Biblia (*L*) Bible; → BIBEL.

biblikal (*D*) biblical.

bibilograf (*D*) bibliographer.

bibliografi (*D/E*) bibliography.

bibliografis (*D*) bibliographic.

biblioték and **bibliotik** (*L*) library; → PERPUSTAKAAN, TAMAN *pustaka*.

bibliotékaris (*D*) librarian; → PUSTAKAWAN/-WATI.

bicana → BIJANA.

bicara (*Skr*) **1** to speak; to talk, telling. *Siapa yang pandai – Indonésia? Who can speak Indonesian? Dia tidak banyak –*. He doesn't talk much. *sedikit – banyak bekerja* saying little but doing a lot. *angka-angka lain yang –* other telling figures. *tanpa/dengan tak banyak –* without much ado, without making a great fuss. **2** meeting, discussion. *Rasanya tak perlu diadakan – lagi.* It seems that it is unnecessary to hold discussions again. **3** trial or case (in court). *–nya belum diputuskan* no discussion has as yet been taken regarding this case. *habis –!* that's final! that's the end of it!; → HABIS *perkara*. **4** (*cla*) advice. *Apa –?* What should we do? **5** (*ob*) idea, opinion. *pada – patik* in my opinion/judgment. *budi –* common sense, intelligence; → AKAL *budi. tidak/tak – sepatah pun* not say a word. *memasang – ini-itu* to talk about this and that. *Nama ini mungkin tidak banyak (ber)– bagi pembaca.* This name probably does not mean much to the reader. *Tidak satu pun yang berani buka –.* There wasn't one who had the nerve to open his mouth (and tell the truth). *Clurit pun ikut –.* The *clurit* also spoke up. **6**a) conversation (in general). *saling tukar – tentang …*to enter into a conversation about … b) call (a telephone conversation). **7** busy, engaged (of a telephone line). *lagi/sedang –* line/number is busy. **8** (*J coq*) *– bérés!* leave it to me! everything will be taken care of! *– énak!* definitely/absolutely delicious! *alat –* a) mouthpiece of telephone. b) organ of speech (the tongue, vocal chords, etc.). *angkat –* (to begin) to deliver a speech, speak. *corong –* microphone, loudspeaker. *film –* talking film. *gedung –* a) meeting hall. b) (= *rumah –*) (*ob*) courthouse. *jam –* office hours. *juru –* [*jubir*] spokesman. *mesin/peti –* phonograph. *tukang –* speaker.

berbicara 1 to talk, chat. *lawan ~* person with whom one is conversing, interlocutor. *si ~* the speaker. *~ dengan/pada* to talk with, speak to. *~ di muka mikropon* to go on the air. *fakta-fakta yang ~* bold facts. *fakta yang telah ~ sendiri* the facts speak for themselves. *Meréka belum ~ satu bahasa.* They're not on the same wavelength yet. **2** to discuss, deliberate, debate. **3** to give/state/express one's opinion/view(s) on/of. **4** meaningful.

membicarakan [and **memperbicara** (*ob*)] to discuss, debate, argue, talk about, deliberate. *~ tempat* to reserve seats (in a restaurant, etc.); → MEMESAN *tempat*.

pembicara 1 speaker, spokesman, discussant. *~ tamu* guest speaker. *~ utama* keynote speaker. **2** (*ob*) counsel, adviser, attorney.

pembicaraan 1 talk, discussion, conversation. *melangsungkan ~ empat mata dengan* to hold a private conversation with. *~ jarak dekat* proximity talks. *~ pembuka jalan* preliminary talks. *~ Pengurangan Senjata Stratégis* Strategic Arms Reduction Talks, START. *~ politik* political talks. *~ (secara) blak-blakan* open talks. *Kisah itu menjadi ~ ramai.* The story was the talk of the town. **2** (telephone) call. *~ interlokal* long-distance call.

perbicaraan (*Mal*) trial, court case.

bicokok (*J*) **1** k.o. small crocodile. **2** accomplice, henchman; accessory; → KAKI *tangan*. **3** petty swindler/thief/criminal; a greedy person.

bicu(-bicu) jack (machine for raising a heavy weight off the ground); → DONGKRAK.

membicu to jack up.

bid (in acronyms) → BIDANG.

bida I (*cla*) clipped form of **bidadari**.

bida II (in northern Jakarta) collector of sand (for building purposes).

bidadara sprite.

bidadari I (*Skr*) **1** fairy, nymph, angel. **2** houri, one of the beautiful virgins provided in paradise for all faithful Muslims. **3** a beautiful woman.

bidadari II *ikan* – angel fish, Pomacentridae.

bidah, bidaah and **bid'ah** (*A*) **1** innovation/modernization of Islamic teachings not guided by the Koran and Hadis. **2** teachings deviating from the true religion. **3** deceitful, lying; lie; liar. *– hasanah* beneficial innovation. *– madzmumah* blameworthy innovation. *– yang makruh* neutral innovation. *– sesat* erroneous innovation. *– yang sunat* beneficial innovation. *– tercela* blameworthy innovation.

membidahkan to innovate (in religion).

kebida(a)han innovation, modernization.

pembidah innovator, innovating (in religion).

bidai I 1 thin strips of rattan or bamboo tied parallel (for screens/window blinds/mats, etc.). **2** splint (for a broken limb). *memasang –* to splint. **3** Venetian blind.

berbidai-bidai 1 in long, thin parallel lines. **2** black and blue.

membidai 1 to hang blinds, etc. **2** to put (an arm/leg) in a splint.

bidai II goal, home, line in games (such as *kasti*, etc.).

bidak (*A*) pawn (in chess). *– dilantik* (in chess) a pawn which reaches the opponent's back row and is exchanged for a more valuable piece, promoting a pawn.

bidal I and **bidalan** saying, maxim, proverb.

bidal II thimble.

bidan (*Skr*) *dukun* midwife, obstetrician; → DUKUN *bayi. balas/bébas/berlimau* – a *selamatan* held 40 days after childbirth. *– désa* [*bidés*] village midwife. *– perawat berijazah* registered nurse, R.N. *– tarik/terjun* midwife who has been called for suddenly without earlier notice (she has to be paid extra). *– tempah* midwife who has been called for in advance.

berbidan to use the services of a midwife/obstetrician. *beranak tiada –* in trouble through one's own fault.

membidan to be a midwife.

membidani 1 to help a woman in childbirth. **2** to bring s.t. into being, bring about. *Soenarto termasuk salah seorang otak yang ikut ~ lahirnya Sumpah Pemuda yang bersejarah itu.* Soenarto is one of the brains who helped bring about the historic Youth Pledge.

kebidanan midwifery, obstetric. *départemén ~* maternity/obstetrics department (in a hospital). *ilmu ~* obstetrics.

bidang 1 numerical coefficient for wide and flat objects, like sails, land, mats, etc. *se- tanah* a piece/plot of land. *kajang dua –* two palm-leaf mats (for covering goods/ boats, etc.). **2** unit of length, approximately 5 *hasta*. *Seléndang itu empat – panjangnya*. The shawl is about 70 *hasta* long. **3** broad (of chest/shoulders/cloth/sail/mat, etc.), capacious, spacious. *Dadanya –.* He has a broad chest. **4** field/department of study or activity, area, sphere. *di – politik* in the field of politics, the subject of politics. *masing-masing untuk –nya* everyone with his own area/field of responsibility. *– kerja* field of operations. *– peminatan* concentration (in higher education). **5** sector. **6** (*math*) plane (surface with fixed limits), surface, -hedron. *ilmu ukur –* plane geometry. **7** area, scope. **8** aspect, viewpoint. **9** face (in a mine). *– alas* base. *– batas* plane (for leveling). *– empat* tetrahedron. *– enam* hexahedron. *– jalan* roadway. *– kerja* working face. *– lingkup* scope. *– miring* inclined plane. *– pakaian* fabric. *– rata* (*math*) even level. *– tanah* plot of land. *– temu* interface. *– usaha* line of business.

sebidang on the same plane, planar.

membidang to be active in the field/sphere/domain of, be active in the … field.

membidangi to cover, deal with (certain sectors in Parliament, etc. by certain committees into which Parliament has been divided), subordinate … sectors.

membidangkan 1 to spread/stretch s.t. on a frame. **2** to expand. *~ bahu* to square one's shoulders. *~ dada* to brag, boast. **3** to group/classify according to subject/field.

bidangan (*ob*) piece, patch/plot of land.

pembidangan 1 frame for stretching (hides/embroidery), stretcher, tenter (frame). **2** grouping/classifying according to subject/field. *~ tugas* division of labor.

bidar 1 *sampan –* (*cla*) large, rowed war boat. **2** (*Jv*) dugout canoe. **3** rowboat used for racing (in Palembang, South Sumatra).

bidara (*Skr*) various species of coastal trees, *Zizyphus rotundifolia.* *– cina* Chinese date, *Zizyphus jujuba. – laut* k.o. small tree reputed to be an aphrodisiac, *Eurycoma longifolia;* → TONGKAT *ali. – putih* strychnine tree, *Strychnos lucida. – upas* k.o. tree, *Merremia mammosa.*

bidari I (*ob*) (in sports) goal, base(-line) or stopping place in *kasti*, a game similar to baseball or softball.

bidari II → BIDADARI.

bidas – *anak panah* to draw a bow.

  membidas 1 to spring/swing back (of traps); to draw (a bow). **2** to rebound. **3** to react (of persons), counter (verbally), retaliate (with an offensive). **4** to push through, penetrate, enter.

  membidaskan to release s.t. so that it springs forward.

  bidasan 1 penetrating movement. **2** reaction. **3** attack.

  pembidas 1 lance. **2** shock (*mod*). *pasukan ~* shock troops.

  pembidasan releasing, release.

bidat → BIDAH.

bidik aim.

  membidik 1 to aim/shoot at. **2** to peer at, lie in wait for. **3** to take aim.

  membidikkan to aim/point s.t. *~ kaméranya* to aim one's camera.

  bidikan 1 a shot, aim. *~ tepat* well-aimed shot. **2** s.t. aimed at, target, s.t. carefully chosen.

  pembidik 1 sight (of a gun, etc.). **2** s.o. who aims.

  pembidikan aiming, targeting. *ladang ~* practice range, rifle range.

bido (*Jv*) k.o. bird, crested serpent eagle, *Spilornis cheela.*

biduan (*Skr*) (male) singer, vocalist.

biduanda (*cla*) title for valets.

biduanita female singer.

biduk k.o. boat used for fishing or carrying cargo on rivers. *anak-anak –* those on board a *biduk. bintang –* the Great Bear. *cerana –* pedestal salver for betel requisites resembling a *biduk. bersatu – dengan* to cooperate, act/work together. *lain –, lain digalang* the wrong boat is put on the stocks (for repair), i.e., barking up the wrong tree, giving an irrelevant answer. *– keluarga* married life. *– lalu kiambang bertaut* said of relatives who make up again after a short separation. *– tiris menanti karam* can no longer be helped. *ada – serempu pulau* unfulfilled desires; to have beautiful wife but now want an inferior mistress.

  sebiduk in the same *biduk. ~ dan setujuan* to work toward the same goal. *~ seperasaan* to be a couple.

  berbiduk 1 to go boating; to embark on a *biduk;* to use a *biduk.* **2** to live in marriage (with).

  berbiduk-biduk to go boating for pleasure.

bidur slab of tin, ingot; a weight = 2 *kati.*

biduran [and **biduren** (*Jv*)] **1** (to have) nettle rash, hives, urticaria. **2** wheal.

biduri I (*Skr*) **1** opal, cat's eye; → BAIDURI. **2** quartz (semiprecious stone). *– bulan* a very black opal.

biduri II k.o. tree, madar plant, *Calotropis gigantea.*

biduwati → BIDUANITA.

biénale (*D*) biennial.

bier (*D*) → BIR.

bif (*E*) beef. *kornét (–)* canned corned beef; → DAGING *kornét/susur.*

bifokal (*E*) bifocal.

bifstik (*E*) beefsteak.

bigair (*A*) except, with the exception of, excluding; → KECUALI.

bigami (*D/E*) bigamy.

bigamis (*D*) bigamist.

bigas (*Ban*) healed, cured, restored to its original condition, back to normal.

bigu (*ob*) Buddhist monk/priest; → BHIKU.

bihalal → HALAL-BIHALAL.

bihara → BIARA.

biharawan → BIARAWAN.

bihari (*S*) formerly, in former times.

bihausy (*ob*) → BIUS.

bihun (*C*) rice sticks made from shaped boiled rice, dried.

bihus → BIUS.

Bija I (*Skr*) part of an honorific (= *vijaya* conqueror), eggs *Seri – Diraja.*

bija II (*M*) seed, pip, stone of fruit; → BIJI.

bijak (*Skr*) **1** clever, intelligent, bright, smart, wise. *Iskandar kembali ke kota Susa dan mengumpulkan semua orang – yang ada.* Alexander returned to the town of Susa and gathered all the wise men there were. *– amat* too clever by half. **2** (*M*) fluent, able to speak smoothly and readily, clever at talking.

  sebijak as prudent/cautious/intelligent as. *Saya akan mempertimbangkannya ~ mungkin.* I'll take it into consideration as prudently as possible.

  terbijak the wisest.

  kebijakan 1 cleverness, intelligence, skill, prudence, discernment, smartness. **2** policy, measure (taken); → KEBIJAKSANAAN. *pembuat ~* policy maker. *– angkasa terbuka* open-sky policy. *– bertetangga baik* good-neighbor policy. *– harga* pricing policy. *– kawasan* district/regional policy, *– luar negeri Indonésia* Indonesian foreign policy. *– perlindungan sosial* social defense policy. *– uang ketat* tight money policy, TMP. *– Australia putih* white-Australia policy. *– makro ékonomi Indonésia* Indonesia's macroeconomic policy.

bijaksana (*Skr*) **1** astute, shrewd, sagacious, discerning, wise. **2** discreet, prudent, tactful, clever, judicious, political.

  sebijaksana as wise(ly) as.

  berbijaksana to be wise.

  terbijaksana the wisest.

  kebijaksanaan 1 wisdom, sagacity. **2** tactics, policy. *atas ~ sendiri* by one's own action. *~ Australia putih* white Australian policy. *~ keamanan nasional* national security policy. *~ kompétisi* competition policies. *~ menyeluruh* overall policy. *~ pandang ke Timur* look-East policy. *~ pemerintah* government policy. *~ pengetatan uang* tight money policy. *~ penyesuaian* policy of adjustment. *~ senyum* smiling policy. **3** according to (or, as required by) circumstances, according to the exigencies of the case; to use one's own discretion/judgment, act as one thinks fit, discretionary, voluntary. *Itu terserah kepada ~ Tuan.* I leave it to your discretion. **4** irregularities, bribing, violation of regulations.

bijaksanawan (*Skr neo*) wise man.

bijan sesame (seed), *Sesamum orientale. minyak –* sesame oil. *menabur – ke tasik* "sowing sesame on water (where it will not grow)," i.e., a wasted effort.

bijana (*ob*) *jana/tanah –* fatherland.

Bijblad (*D*) /béblat/ Supplement to the Statute Book.

biji I (*Skr*) **1** seed, pip, stone of a fruit which is hard and can be planted. *akar –* name of a plant species, *Roucheria griffithiana. jambu –* common variety of guava. *pisang –* a seed-filled banana species whose leaf provides wrappers. *– ketimun* cucumber seed. **2** small legume, such as, *– kacang* peanut. *– kedelai* soy bean. **3** numerical coefficient for eggs/eyes/baskets, etc. in lieu of *buah, butir,* etc. *dua – durian* two durians. *beberara – telur ayam* a few chicken eggs. **4** (*J*) sometimes also used as a numerical coefficient for human beings and animals. *orang tiga –* three persons. *menabur/menanam – atas batu* to cast pearls before swine. *kena –nya!* grabbed by the balls. *– inti* kernels. *– jakar* testicles. *– jambu médé/monyét* cashew nut. *– kacang* k.o. plant, asthma weed, *Euphorbia hirta. – kemaluan* testicles. *– kenari* Javanese almond, *Canarium commune. – longkong* chance(s), possibilities. *– mata* a) eyeball. b) darling, sweetheart. *– padi* unhusked rice. *– pelir/pelér* (*J*) testicles. *– penangkar* breeder seed. *– perabot* (*euph*) testicles. *– polongan* bean seed. *– pala* nutmeg. *– ratap/sabak* tear(s). *– salak* (*euph*) clitoris. *– sawit* palm kernels. *– tepus* light-colored alluvial tin. *– zakar* testicles. **5** (*J*) grade, mark (the symbol used in the rating of conduct/proficiency, etc. of students), point (in sports).

  berbiji with/to have pips/seeds. *~ sabak* to weep, cry.

  membiji 1 to become/produce seed. **2** (*coq*) to grade, mark.

  bijian grain, granular (form).

  biji-bijian cereals, grains (*padi, jagung, kacang,* etc.).

  pembijian 1 seeding. **2** grading, marking.

biji II *ikan – nangka* spotted golden goatfish, *Upeneus, spp., Parupeneus, spp.*

bijih ore; rocks, earth or sand which contain metal. – *beku* igneous ore. – *besi/timbal* iron/tin ore. – *degil* refractory ore. – *pejal* massive ore. – *rapung* float ore. – *teréka* inferred ore. – *terkira* indicated ore. – *terperoléh* recoverable ore.

bik contracted term of address of *bibi(k)*; → BIBI(K) 1.

bika – *ambon* cake containing yeast, sugar, coconut milk, rice flour, sago, vanilla, salt, eggs mixed together, kneaded, and then baked on a hot plate.

bikang I a pastry of rice flour that has been diluted, provided with sugar, vanilla, and coconut milk, and then baked in a pan. – *ambon* → BIKA *ambon*.
  pembikangan baking pan.

bikang II (*J*) woman, female; spouse, wife.

bikarbonat (*E*) bicarbonate.

bikin make, do.
  membikin [and **ngebikin** (*J*)] 1 to do, make, manufacture, build, construct, produce. *Itu kita – sendiri.* We made it ourselves. *dibikin menurut ukuran* made to measure, custom-made. 2 (plus adjective) (*coq*) to make, cause s.t. to become. ~ *besar* to enlarge. ~ *betul* to repair. ~ *capék* to tire, fatigue. ~ *sakit* to hurt s.o. ~ *salah* to do wrong. ~ *takut* to frighten, scare. ~ *tinggi* to raise. 3 to cast a spell on. *Ayahnya sudah tidak ada. Dibikin lurahnya.* His father is already dead. The village head cast a spell on him.
  membikin-bikin to fabricate, make up. *dibikin-bikin* artificial, contrived, devised, unnatural, disfigured (writing); far-fetched, strained.
  membikinkan [and **ngebikinin** (*J coq*)] to make for. *Dibikinkannya adiknya mainan.* He made a toy for his younger brother.
  terbikin done, made, manufactured.
  bikinan make, product of. *senyum* ~ a simper. *komponén* ~ *manusia* man-made element. *mobil* ~ *Jepang* Japanese-made car.
  bikin-bikinan fake, counterfeit.
  pembikin maker, manufacturer. ~ *uang palsu* counterfeiter (of money).
  pembikinan manufacture, production. ~ *pabrik* fabrication. ~ *uang* coinage.

bikini (*D/E*) bikini.
  berbikini to wear a bikini. *Wanita-wanita asing* ~ *muncul di Pasir Putih Situbondo.* Foreign women wearing bikinis showed up at Pasir Putih in Situbondo.

bikir (*A*) 1 virgin. 2 virginity.

bikonkaf (*D*) biconcave.

bikonvéks (*D*) biconvex.

biksu (*Prakrit*) /biksu/ Buddhist monk or ascetic.
  kebiksuan Buddhistship. *melepaskan* ~*nya* to renounce one's Buddhistship.

biksuni /biksuni/ female Buddhist monk.

biku I → BHIKSU.

biku II 1 narrow lace edging in a zigzag pattern, serrated, scalloped (pattern), frills. 2 (*geol*) dissection.
  berbiku-biku toothed, serrated (edges), zigzagged.
  membiku (*geol*) to dissect.
  terbiku (*geol*) dissected.

bikulturalisme (*D*) biculturalism.

bikuni → BIKSUNI.

bila I (*Skr?*) 1 when, at what time; → KAPAN. – *Anda berangkat?* When did you leave? 2 (*coq*) if, when, whenever. *Ia baru menjawab – ditanya.* He answered when asked. – *mungkin* if possible. – *perlu* if necessary. – *saja* and *barang* – it doesn't matter when, at any time, whenever.
  bila-bila whenever, anytime; → KAPAN-KAPAN.

bila II → BÉLA II.

bilabial (*D*) bilabial.

bilad (*A ob*) country.

bilah 1 piece/strip of bamboo/wood/rattan, etc., lath. *pagar dari – buluh* a fence of strips of bamboo (or, of bamboo laths). 2 s.t. resembling a lath (*esp* a kris, knife, sword, etc.). 3 gill (of a mushroom). 4 classifier for all k.o. weapons of sharpened metal: knives, chisels, daggers, hatchets, needles, spears, etc. *Dengan se– golok meréka coba mencongkél pintu kamar tidur.* They tried to open the door of the bedroom with a crowbar-like prying

tool. *Tiga orang Indonésia dipergoki menyelundupkan 68 – keris ke Malaysia.* Three Indonesians were caught smuggling 68 krises into Malaysia.
  bilahan strip, piece, lath. ~ *piano* piano key.

bilai I (*M*) hem, border, edge, fringe, s.t. added to s.t.
  membilai 1 to add s.t. to an edge, border, etc. to make it longer/wider; to lengthen (a *kain*). ~ *lengan baju* to lengthen a sleeve. 2 to insert. 3 to fill/crown a tooth. ~ *gigi dengan platinum* to fill/crown a tooth with platinum. 4 to supplement (insufficient) income, with savings or from other sources.

bilai II (*ob*) weal, welt; → BILUR.

bilakmata Bengal quince-tree, *Aegle marmelos*; → KAWISTA, MAJA I.

bilal (*A*) muezzin, one whose task it is to announce the five daily prayer times. – *maséhi* chaplain.

bilamana when(ever); → BILA. –.– *juga* anytime.

bilamasa (*ob*) when(ever).

bilang I 1 (*coq*) number (1, 2, 3, etc.), figure; enumeration; → BILANGAN. *dengan modal yang tidak lagi – juta, tetapi sudah milyaran* with a capital no longer running into the millions, but already in the billions. 2 = SEBILANG.
  sebilang each, every. ~ *hari* each/every day. ~ *kali* each/every time. ~ *waktu* each/every time, always, at all times.
  sebilangan a number/total part of; as much as, amounting to, to the amount of. ~ *besar dari penduduk kampung saya berpendidikan tinggi.* Most of the inhabitants of my kampung have had a higher education.
  berbilang 1 some, several, a few. *uang* ~ a) a certain amount of money. b) a lot of money. ~ *aulia dan budiman* many saints and sages. ~ *bulan/hari* for months/days. ~ *jam* a few hours. ~ *kali* again and again, repeatedly. ~ *kata* (though not yet put on paper) in so many words. ~ *langkah* to jump a few steps. ~ *liter* a number of liters. ~ *puluhan* tens of (rupiahs). ~ *ratus/ribu* by the hundreds/thousands. ~ *untung* to estimate. *hanya* ~ *waktu saja* (within) a short time. 2 to count, reckon. *hidup di désa – gobang, hidup di kota ~ rupiah* (*col*) in the villages people reckon by 2 1/2-cent coins, in the cities by rupiahs. ~ *dari esa, mengaji dari alif* to start from scratch.
  membilang 1 to count (1, 2, 3, etc.), reckon, count out, enumerate. ~ *dari satu sampai seratus* to count from one to hundred. *tidak ~ tempo* not to be particular about a few hours, to have a lot of time for s.t. *tidak ~ lawan* to shrink from nobody. 2 to remember, mind, pay attention to, consider, take into account. *Rupanya banyak orang kaya saja yang dibilang.* It seems that only rich people are considered. *tidak ~ rasa orang* not to take people's feelings into consideration. 3 to include in counting/groups, etc. *Saya dibilang pekerja harian.* I was counted in the group of daily workers. 4 to predict. *Dicarinya seorang dukun yang pandai~ nasibnya.* He looked for a dukun who could predict his future.
  membilangkan to remember, mind, pay attention to, take into account. *tidak ~ kaya dan miskin* irrespective of rich and poor.
  terbilang [and **kebilang** (*coq*)] 1 calculable, countable. *tidak ~ banyaknya* an incalculable/innumerable number. 2 reckoned/counted/included among; inclusive of, including. *harga Rp 10.000 ~ ongkos kirim* (a price of) 10,000 rupiahs including cost of shipment. *Suatu kali saya bertandang ke rumah seorang kawan lama yang ~ berada.* Only once did I pay a visit to the home of an old friend reckoned among those well-off. 3 to be famous, renowned, illustrious, celebrated.
  kebilang (*J*) reckoned/counted/included among. *Pada tahun 1980 keduanya tamat dari sebuah SMA yang ~ ngetop di Solo.* In 1980 both (children) graduated from a Senior High School reckoned among the best in Solo. *banyaknya tidak ~* an innumerable number.
  bilangan 1 number, figure. *kata* ~ numeral. ~ *satu sampai tiga puluh* the numbers 1 to 30. ~ *anu* unknown quantity. ~ *asli* whole numbers. ~ *berpangkat* (*math*) power. ~ *bulat* a round number. ~ *cacah* integer. ~ *catu* quantum number. ~ *dasar* cardinal number. ~ *ganjil/gasal* odd number. ~ *genap* even number. ~ *pecahan* (decimal/complex, etc.) fraction. ~ *perpecahan* decimals. ~ *persepuluhan* decimal. ~ *pokok* cardinal

number. ~ *prima* prime number. ~ *urut(an)* ordinal number. ~ *utuh* a round number. ~ *variabel* a variable. ~ *yang dibagi* (*math*) dividend. 2 total (amount), sum total, quantity, amount. *Tidak diketahui benar ~nya.* The quantity/total amount is not exactly known. 3 (*Mal Sg*) (serial) number (of a newspaper/journal). 4 group, section, class. *Meréka termasuk ~ orang-orang alim di kampung ini.* They belong to the group of pious people in this kampong. *tidak masuk ~* be of no/little account. 5 calculation. *Menurut ~ baru itu kurang baik untuk menikahkan anak.* Based on calculations that day is not so favorable for marrying off a child. 6 fate. *sudah sampai ~nya akan mati* his days are numbered. 7 *Kitab ~* Numbers.

kebilangan to be famous, renowned, illustrious, celebrated.

pembilang 1 (*math*) numerator. 2 (the person) counter, teller.

pembilangan 1 enumeration, counting. 2 calculation to find out whether one has bad or good luck, whether it is a bad or good day to embark upon s.t.

bilang II (*coq*) to say, tell, relate. *Siapa – saya tidak suka makan durian?* Who says that I don't like to eat durian? *sonder – item-putih* (*coq*) and *sonder –.–* (*coq*) without saying a word, without opening one's mouth.

bilang-bilang *jangan ~, ya* don't say anything, don't tell.

membilang (not used in the active form, only the forms **bilang** and **dibilang** are used) *boléh dibilang* people say, you could say, practically speaking. *boléh dibilang mahal* people say that it's expensive.

membilangi [and **ngebilangin** (*J coq*)] to inform, report; to advise. *Sudah dibilangi, tidak menurut.* We've already advised them but they didn't obey.

mbilangin (*J*) (not used in the active form, only the form **dibilangin** is used) *udah dibilangin* I told you (so) (but you didn't listen to me).

membilangkan to say, tell, relate, disclose, narrate.

bilangan (*J*) 1 area, region. *Tinggalnya di ~ Ciputat.* He lives in the Ciputat area. 2 near, not far from, in the neighborhood/vicinity of. *Saya mau berhenti di ~ Hotél Indonésia.* I would like to stop near Hotel Indonesia. 3 near relatives, family. *Dia masih ada – sama Bupati Bekasi.* He's related to the Regent of Bekasi.

bilang-bilang (*M*) k.o. purslane, *Portulaca oleracea. rendah – disuruki/diseluduki, tinggi kayu ara dilangkahi* "a low purslane is crawled for, a high fig tree is stepped over," i.e., in doing s.t. or confronting s.o. one should act properly.

bilas I (*J*) rinse. – *logam* grid blasting.

berbilas to bathe o.s. for the second time in clean water (i.e., in fresh water after having taken a swim in the sea or a swimming pool).

membilasi to rinse s.t. off.

membilas(kan) to rinse (with clean water after washing), cleanse, wash off. *Dia ~ pakaian yang telah dibasuh itu sebelum menjemurkannya.* She rinsed the clothes that had been washed before drying them in the sun.

bilasan 1 rinsate. 2 rinsed.

pembilasan 1 rinsing, cleaning. 2 (*petro*) stripping, scavenging.

bilas II *mata –* with poor vision (owing to disease).

bilateral (*D*) bilateral. *perjanjian –* bilateral agreement.

bilau *kacau –* in confusion; → KACAU *balau.*

bilhak (*A*) in truth, truly; in fact.

biliar (*D*) billiards.

bilik I 1 room (in a house/office, etc.); → KAMAR I. 2 chamber, specifically either of the two lower chambers on each side of the heart. – *air* (*Mal*) lavatory. – *bacaan* reading room. – *bersekat* cubicle. – *bersolék* makeup room. – *di bawah tanah* cellar. – *gelap* darkroom (for developing films). – *gerakan* (*Mal*) operation room. – *gerbong* railway compartment. – *jantung* ventricle. – *kerja* office. – *kuliah* (*Mal*) lecture room. – *loténg* attic. – *makan* dining room. – *mandi* bathroom. – *markonis* telegraph operator's cabin. – *mata* chamber of the eye. – *pencoblosan* voting booth. – *réhat* (*Mal*) recreation room. – *sekat* a room divided up by partitions. – *suara* voting booth. – *télepon umum* public telephone booth. – *tidur* bedroom. 3 (*Mal*) apartment.

sebilik of/in the same room. *berdua ~* roommates.

berbilik-bilik with/to have rooms/compartments, compartmentalized.

bilik II (*Jv*) wickerwork of bamboo slats as (house) wall; → GEDÉK, TEPAS.

bilingual (*E*) bilingual.

bilingualisasi bilingualization. – *syarat mutlak memasuki éra globalisasi.* Bilingualization is an absolute condition for entering the era of globalization.

bilingualisme (*D*) bilingualism.

bilion (*E*) 1 billion (in the U.S.A. and France). 2 thousand million (in England and Germany).

bilis I bleary (-eyed), inflamed.

bilis II (*Mal*) *ikan –* anchovies, *Anchoviella indica, Stolephorus spp.*; → TERI.

bilis III → ANGIN *sepoi-sepoi.*

bi(l)lahi (*A*) by God.

biliun (*D/E*) billion; → MILYAR.

biloh k.o. monkey.

bilon (in West Kalimantan) helicopter. *bapak –* helicopter pilot.

biludak *ular –* black cobra.

biluk crooked, bent, turn, curve.

bilur lash, welt (from caning).

bilyar (*D*) billiards.

bilyét (*D*) 1 form. 2 card, ticket. – *giro* transfer form. – *perbendaharaan* treasury bill.

bilyétris conductress (on *Bima, Mutiara,* and *Parahyangan* trains).

bilyun (*D*) trillion.

Bima I *Raden –* second of the five *Pandawa* brothers of the Mahabharata, distinguished by his might and intrepidness. *kuku – →* KUKU *Bima.*

Bima II [Biru-malam] the blue-colored night express between Jakarta and Surabaya.

Bimas 1 [Bimbingan massal (Swa Sembada Bahan Makanan)] Mass Guidance, a program introduced in 1965 which includes the promotion of the use of pesticides, high-yielding seeds, and other means of increasing crop yield, as well as money known as *krédit –* agricultural credits. *padi –* rice varieties provided or recommended by the government. – *Nasional* and – *Gotong Royong.* 2 [Bimbingan Masyarakat] Community Guidance.

membimaskan to organize s.t. as a Bimas.

pembimasan Bimasization.

Bimasakti (*Skr*) 1 Milky Way, Galaxy. 2 code name given by the *Gestapu/PKI* to the *Lubang Buaya* volunteers in their abortive coup staged on September 30, 1965. 3 G30S troops with the assignment of occupying the Jakarta Radio Station and Telephone Exchange.

bimbang I 1 worried, anxious. *Orangtua anak itu – karena demamnya makin bertambah naik.* The parents of that child were worried because his fever was increasingly on the rise. 2 uncertain, doubtful, hesitant. *Saya tidak menyerahkan uang itu kepadanya karena saya masih – tentang kejujurannya.* I didn't turn the money over to him because I was still in doubt about his integrity. – *hati* doubtful.

membimbangkan 1 to be(come) anxious about s.t., worry about. *Hubungannya dengan pemuda itu ~ kami.* His relationship with that young man worries us. ~ *kepercayaan* to betray a trust/confidence. 2 alarming, disquieting, disturbing. *kabar-kabar yang ~* alarming news.

terbimbang(-bimbang) anxious, preoccupied.

kebimbangan anxiety, distress, uneasiness (of mind), restlessness.

pembimbang worrywart.

bimbang II k.o. *adat* ceremony/feast.

bimbang III to take turns, by turns.

Bimbél → BIMBINGAN *belajar.*

bimbinan (*J*) the crop (of a bird).

bimbing *berbimbing* guided/led by the hand. *Yang buta datang ~.* The blind man arrived led by the hand. ~ *tangan* and **berbimbing-bimbing(an)** *tangan* a) hand in hand, holding hands. b) to cooperate, support/help e.o.

membimbing 1 to guide/lead by the hand. *Ibu ~ anaknya (se)waktu menyeberangi jalan raya.* Mother led her child when crossing the highway. 2 guide, instruct, direct, conduct, run (a

meeting). *Kita harus ~ rakyat yang masih sukar mengerti.* We have to guide the people who still don't understand. *Jika tidak dibimbing, tak mungkin memahami isi buku ini.* Without guidance, it's impossible to understand the contents of this book.
terbimbing guided, supervised.

bimbingan 1 guidance, leadership, counseling, instruction. *~ Kemasyarakatan dan Pengentasan Anak.* Social Guidance and Child Care. *~ lapangan* field guidance. *memberikan ~ kepada bawahannya* to give instructions to his subordinates. *~ belajar* [*Bimbél*] preparation/remedial course for university students. **2** introduction, preface.

pembimbing 1 guide, leader. **2** preface, introduction (to a science), introductory (level course). *kata ~* opening/prefatory remarks. **3** counselor (in a college/university, etc.). *guru ~* teacher counselor.

pembimbingan 1 accompaniment, supervision. **2** guidance, directing.

perbimbingan direction, orientation, guidance.

bimbit membimbit 1 to carry a light object dangling in the hand (such as keys/a handbag/duster, etc.); → MENJINJING. **2** to lead/ guide s.o. by the hand; → MEMBIMBING. *Anaknya ~nya menuruni tangga.* His child led him by the hand down the stairs.

bimbitan 1 carried by hand. **2** guidance, leadership. **3** parcel. **4** preface.

bimbuluh [*bimbingan dan penyuluhan*] guidance and counseling.

bin I (*A*) **1** term used as indicator of filial relationship: son of, e.g., *Ali – Abdullah* Ali, son of Abdullah; → IBNI (for offspring of royalty) and IBNU; *cp* BINTI. **2** father's name. *Sudah sahlah dia, namanya, -nya dan tempat tinggalnya serupa.* It must be him, his name, his father's name and his domicile are similar.

bin II (*A*) *qualitative + – + qualitative* forms an affective expression indicating a high degree: *ajaib – ganjil, anéh – ajaib, ganjil – ajaib,* and *héran – ajaib* very strange/odd. *kalut – kacau* extremely confused. *sah – resmi* very official. *serakah – tamak* extremely greedy.

bin III (in acronyms) → BINA, PEMBINAAN.

BIN IV [*Badan Intélijén Negara*] National Intelligence Board (replaced Bakin).

bina I (*A*) building, construction, erection, structure, edifice, establishment, development. *- bicara* speech therapy. *- Graha* Executive Building. *Diréktorat Jénderal - Karya* Directorate General of the Unemployed. *Pendidikan - Kelas* Ground School Training. *Diréktorat Jénderal - Marga* Directorate General in charge of highways, road development and maintenance. *- negara* statecraft. *- raga* bodybuilding. *- téknik* [*binték*] technical development. *- tumbuh* establish and grow. **membinatumbuhkan** to establish and make s.o. grow. *pentingnya dibinatumbuhkan iklim keterbukaan antar-OPP* the importance of the realization of an open climate between participating organizations in the general elections. *Diréktorat Jénderal - Tunawarga.* Directorate General in charge of Correctional Institutions. *- Usaha Nasional (Bahana)* National Business Management, i.e., a state-owned enterprise established to supply investment capital for smaller firms. *- Waluya* Health Care. *- watak* character building. *- Wisata* Tourism Management. *- Wismabumi* (*infr*) real estate; → LAYAN *yasan.*

membina 1 to build, erect, construct, create, establish, form, found. *~ hubungan langsung dengan* to build direct connections with. *~ negara baru yang adil dan makmur* to build a new, just and prosperous state. *~ rasa kepercayaan* confidence building. **2** to encourage, arouse, promote, stimulate, foster. *~ minat suka membaca* to stimulate/arouse interest in the pleasure of reading. *~ bahasa Indonésia* promote the (use of the) Indonesian language. **3** to cultivate, develop, improve, build up, upgrade, advance. *~ para petani* to upgrade farmers.

terbina 1 built, erected, constructed. **2** fostered, promoted. *mengutamakan ~nya manusia-manusia kréatif* to prioritize the fostering of creative men.

binaan 1 building, construction, structure, erection. *lingkungan ~* building environment. **2** fostered, cultivated.

pembina 1 builder, constructor, establisher, former. *~ bangsa* nation builder. **2** worker, performer, operative. *~ kerja* welfare

worker. **3** manager, supervisor, administrator, officer-in-charge. *~ perusahaan* manager; → MANAJÉR. *~ pramuka* (in the Pramuka Boy Scout Movement) scout master (from 26 years up). *~ pramuka putri* (in the *Pramuka* Boy Scout Movement) den mother (for cub scouts). *~ pramuka tunaraga* handicapped scout master. *~ satpam* security guard supervisor. **4** patron. **5** (training) coach. **6** *~ utama* and *~ utama madya/muda* various civil service ranks. **7** (an army term from the early 1960s) trainer, supervisor, shaper, molder, control (in the intelligence sense).

pembinaan 1 building, construction, establishment, creation, formation. *~ bangsa* nation building. *~ kader* cadre formation. *~ krédit* (*fin*) nursing of credit. *~ rasa nasionalisme* nation building. **2** cultivation, development, improvement, advancement, fostering, promoting, promotion. *Pusat ~ dan Pengembangan Bahasa Départemén Pendidikan dan Kebudayaan.* Language Advancement and Development Center of the Department of Education and Culture (in Jakarta). *Disiplin pegawai memerlukan prosés ~ keuletan dan kesabaran.* The improvement of employees' discipline needs a process of perseverance and patience. *~ masyarakat* community development. *~ olahraga* sports development. *~ perumahan* housing development. *~ sosial* social development. **3** codification, arrangement. *~ hukum nasional* codification of national law. **4** supervision, management, guidance, control, administration. *~ kepegawaian* personnel management. **5** indoctrination.

bina II (*ob*) → BÉNA.

Bina Graha → BINA *Graha.*

binal (*J*) **1** obstinate, stubborn. **2** disobedient (of children), refusing to obey, insubordinate. **3** naughty (eyes); wild, undomesticated, untamed (of horses and other animals). *kuda -* a skittish horse (unmanageable by the driver of the cart). *perempuan -* a wanton woman.

kebinalan 1 disobedience, insubordination. **2** wildness, savageness.

binan (*gay sl*) gay, homosexual; → BANCI.

binantu (*M*) son-/daughter-in-law.

binar 1 bright. **2** (*ob*) ray, beam, gleam, radiance.

berbinar-binar 1 to shine, beam, radiate, gleam. **2** to see stars, have dancing lights before the eyes. **3** radiant/luminous (of eyes/light).

membinar to sparkle, flash.

binara (*ob*) → MENARA.

binaraga bodybuilding. *alat-alat -* sport equipment.

binaragawan (male) bodybuilder.

binaragawati female bodybuilder.

binasa (*Skr*) **1** destroyed, ruined, wrecked. **2** to be killed/slain, perish, fall in battle (of enemies).

membinasakan to destroy, annihilate, ruin, eradicate, exterminate, wreck. *nafsu ~ diri* self-destructive desire.

terbinasa destroyed.

kebinasaan damage, destruction, extermination, eradication.

pembinasa destroyer, eradicator.

pembinasaan complete destruction, extermination, annihilation, eradication.

binatang 1 animal, beast; vermin. **2** s.o. who is brutal/ferocious/gross/vile/a brute. **3** animal (as a pejorative term). *-, lu!* You're an animal! *- berdarah dingin/panas* cold-blooded/warm-blooded animal. *- berkantung* (*perut*) marsupial. *- berkuku ganjil* perissodactyl (such as, the Sumatran tapir, *Tapirus indicus*). *- beruncang* marsupial. *- buas* beast of prey, predator. *- buruan* game. *- dwikatup* bivalve. *- ékonomi* economic animal. *- jinak* domesticated animal. *- kerat* rodent. *- kerikit* rodent. *- kulit-duri* porcupine. *- lata* reptile. *- liar* wild animal. *- lunak* mollusk. *- melata* reptile. *- memamah biak* ruminant. *- mengerat* rodent. *- menyusui* mammal. *- merusak* vermin. *- pengerat* rodent. *- penggangsir* burrowing animal. *- perusak* vermin, pest. *- piaraan* pet, domesticated animal. *- politik* political animal. *- rumah* pet. *- ternak* livestock (horses, cows, buffalos). *- timangan* pet. *- yang bertulang belakang/punggung* vertebrates.

membinatangi *~ diri* to act like an animal.

membinatangkan to treat like an animal.

kebinatangan beastly, bestial (instincts), brutal, brutish (lusts); animal characteristics, inhuman behavior, ferocious, savage, brute.

pembinatangan bestialization.

binatara (*Jv*) an important person.

binatu (*Tam*) laundryman; → DOBI, MENATU, PENATU. – *kimia* dry cleaner.

binawah (*M*) a brute (of a man).

binawan (*infr*) developer.

bincacak and **bincacau** (*M ob*) cursed (son).

bincana (*ob*) → BENCANA.

bincang I berbincang(-bincang) to debate, discuss, deliberate.

mem(per)bincangkan to discuss, talk about.

perbincangan 1 discussion, talk, deliberation. 2 meeting, conference.

bincang II (*ob*) → PINCANG.

bincang-bincut full of small pimples (on the forehead),

bincu (*ob*) lipstick; → GINCU.

bincul and **bincut** swelling, lump, bump, hump; → PUNUK. *Di Jawa, lukisan banténg sering digambar memiliki –*. In Java a picture of the *banténg* is frequently depicted with a hump.

membincul gibbous.

bindam 1 (*ob*) bruised, swollen (due to beating/kicking, etc.). 2 (*med*) hematoma.

bindeng (*J/Jv*) nasal (sound), nasalized.

binder (*E*) 1 bookbinder. 2 binder, i.e., a detachable cover of clasps or the like for holding magazines or sheets of paper together.

membinder to bind.

bindu lathe; → BUBUT IV.

membindu to (shape on a) lathe.

binéka → BHINNÉKA.

binen (*D coq*) to be successful, have arrived.

binér (*D*) binary.

bing → DEBING.

bingal (*ob*) → BENGAL.

bingar → (B)INGAR-BINGAR.

bingas quick-tempered; wild, fierce (of animal); → BERINGAS.

membingas to become quick-tempered/wild/fierce.

bingit 1 unpleasant; uncomfortable. 2 (*M*) jealous, envious.

pembingit envious person.

bingka → BIKANG I.

bingkah 1 classifier for earth/chalk/rice, etc. which is *usu* kneaded in the fist into a solid ball. 2 (*geol*) block.

sebingkah ~ *tanah* a clod/chunk/lump/fistful of earth.

berbingkah-bingkah in lumps/chunks/clods of earth.

membingkah(i) to hoe (earth) to make it into lumps.

bingkahan lump, clod, chunk.

bingkai rim (of wood/rattan, etc.); molding; edging (of a basket/ winnowing tray, etc.); felloe (of wheels), frame (of eyeglasses/ door/picture, etc.); edge (of eye socket), brim. – *hiasan* trim. – *pintu* door frame.

berbingkai with/to have a rim, edge, frame or border.

berbingkaikan framed/rimmed, etc. with.

membingkai(kan) to frame, put an edging around.

bingkaian frame.

bingkang (*ob*) → BIKANG.

bingkap (*D*) leggings, puttee.

bingkas 1 elastic, springy, resilient, rebounding, recoiling. 2 went off, sprung (of a trap). – *bangun* to bounce/jump up quickly. – *kenyal* elastic rebound.

berbingkas and **membingkas** 1 to spring back, rebound, bounce. 2 to spring up, move/get up all of a sudden; to awaken, revive quickly. 3 resilient, elastic.

bingkatak (*M*) a small crocodile species, estuarine/swamp crocodile, mugger, *Crocodilus palustris*; → BUAYA *katak*.

bingké – *siram* k.o. potato cake.

bingkil (*Jv*) → BÉNGKÉL.

bingkis parcel, package, complimentary gift; → BUNGKUS.

membingkis(kan) to send a gift/present/souvenir (accompanied by a letter).

bingkisan 1 gift, present, (*euph*) bribe. 2 souvenir. 3 parcel, package.

bingo I (*D/E*) bingo.

bingo II a three-wheeled motorized vehicle in Banjarmasin.

bingung 1 upset, confused, bewildered, perplexed, amazed, panicky, mixed up (in one's mind). 2 to lose one's bearings. 3 (*M*) stupid, foolish, dull, muddle-headed.

membingungkan 1 to confuse, fluster, bewilder, daze, puzzle, perplex. 2 mystifying, confusing. 3 to be uneasy at.

kebingungan 1 confusion, bewilderment, panic, perplexity. 2 to be confused, panic, lose one's head/bearings.

perbingungan confusion, panic.

bini wife; → ISTRI. *anak* – family; → ISI *rumah*. *laki* – husband and wife. – *aji* (*cla*) concubine of a *raja*. – *gahara* (*cla*) legal wife. – *gelap* illegal wife. – *muda* a) second and *usu* younger wife. b) concubine, mistress. – *lari* wife married by elopement. – *piaraan* paramour, mistress. – *simpanan* mistress. – *tua* first and *usu* older wife.

berbini (of a man) to be married to.

berbinikan (of a man) to be married to. *Tidak patut engkau ~ perempuan nakal itu*. It is improper for you to be married to that wanton woman.

memperbinikan 1 to take ... as a wife, get married to. 2 to marry off.

bini-binian 1 polygamous, likes to get married. 2 mistress, illegitimate concubine. *orang ~ beranak tak boléh disuruh* an impermanent job always brings losses. **berbini-binian** marrying again and again.

binjai *pohon* – a fruit-tree, cashew apple, *Mangifera caesia*, whose oval-shaped fruit, containing a large, hard seed, grows in clusters; *cp* LANGSAT.

binjat (*M ob*) **membinjat** to lift.

binnen (*D*) → BINEN.

Binnenlandsch Bestuur [BB] (*D col*) the Indies administrative apparatus.

binojakrama festival.

binokular (*D/E*) binoculars. *Komét Halley tampak di –*. Halley's comet is visible with binoculars.

binomium (*E*) binomial.

bint → BINTI.

bintak *perahu* – k.o. boat.

bintal I → BINTIL.

bintal II [pembinaan méntal] mental/psychological development.

bintalak (*M*) boundaries of farm land.

bintan *pohon* – k.o. tree, *Cerbera manghas*, which grows along river edges and whose roots mixed with areca nuts are frequently used as a purgative.

bintang 1 star. *batu* – a) meteorite. b) crystalline rock. *cirit* – a) shooting/falling star, meteor. b) meteorite. *ilmu* – astronomy. *Perang* – Star Wars, *aka* Strategic Defense Initiative; → PRAKARSA *Pertahanan Stratégis*. *ramalan* – horoscope. *tahi* – → CIRIT *bintang*. *sebanyak – di langit* as many as there are stars in the sky. 2 any diagram or figure that resembles a star. *bendéra bulan* – a flag depicting the crescent and star symbol of Islamic nations. *Bendéra Malaysia mempunyai bulan sabit dan – pecah empat belas pada satu sudut*. The Malaysian flag has the crescent and a star with 14 rays in one corner. 3 the symbol of the PPP (party). 4 planet or heavenly body regarded as influencing a person's future. *Ia dilahirkan dalam naungan – Léo*. She was born under the sign of Leo. 5 fate, destiny, luck, fortune. *–nya gelap* and *gelap –nya*. He had a run of bad luck. *–nya naik* his star is rising. He is fortunate/prosperous/doing well. *Mulai terbuka –nya*. His star is in the ascendant. 6 constellation (showing the picture of an object or animal). – *biduk* Great Bear. – *pari* Southern Cross. 7 medal, decoration or the like, often used as an award for meritorious work. – *Mahaputra Ad(h)iprana* medal presented to a foreigner as a token of appreciation for his outstanding service to promote closer relations between Indonesia and his country. – *jasa* decoration. 8 asterisk (*), star (among other things used as indicator for the quality ranking of hotels in advertising). 9 star-shaped military insignia symbol of rank. *jendéral – tiga/empat* a three/four-star general (more frequently used is the form *berbintang*, see hereunder). 10 (= bintang-bintang) covered with spots, spotted, speckled. *harimau* – the common leopard. 11 star (person famous as a singer/actor/actress/sports figure, etc.). – *film* movie star. – *sandiwara* stage star. – *lapangan hijau* and – *sépak bola* a brilliant soccer player. **12** the best in one's domain. – *kelas* the best of the class. – *di langit boléh dibilang, tetapi arang di mukanya tak sedar* see the mote in one's brother's eye and not the beam in one's own. – *Asad* Leo. – *babi/barat* Venus, morning star. – *belantik/beluku* Orion. – *beraja* shooting/falling star, meteor. – *beralih* comet. – *berapit* double star. – *berasap* comet. – *berédar* planet. – *berékor/berkoték/berbuntut/bersapu* comet. – *bertualang* comet. – *biduk* Great Bear. – *biri-biri* the Ram. – *curat* falling star. – *Delu* Aquarius. – *Dharma* medal of honor presented by the government to prominent officials in appreciation for services beyond the call of duty. – *dua belas* the Zodiac. – *gelap* bad luck. – *gemintang* stars. – *gugur* shooting/falling star, meteor. – *Hamal* Aries. – *Hut* Pisces. – *Jadi* Capricorn. – *jasa* order of merit. – *jatuh* meteor. – *Jauza* Gemini. – *Jung* Great Bear. – *Johar* Venus. – *jung* Great Bear. – *Kala* Scorpio. – *Kambing Batu* Capricorn. – *kartika* Pleiades. – *Kaus* Sagittarius. – *keberanian* medal of valor. – *kehormatan* medal of honor. – *Kejora* a) Venus, morning star. b) symbol used by those trying to achieve a free Papua. – *Kembar* Gemini. – *kemintang* all k.o. stars. – *kemuka* comet. – *kutub* Polar Star. – *laut* starfish. – *Marikh* Mars. – *Mahaputra* civilian order of merit. – *Mayang* Virgo. – *meluku* Orion. – *Mengkara* Cancer. – *mintang* stars. – *Mizan* Libra. – *Musytari* Jupiter. – *Naga* Milky Way. – *Néptun* Neptune. – *Neraca* Libra. – *pagi* morning star. – *pari* Southern Cross. – *Pemanah* Sagittarius. – *pengarahan* lodestar. – *Pluto* Pluto. – *puyuh* Pleiades. – *Sakti* military order of merit. – *Sapi* Taurus. – *sapu* comet. – *Sartan* Cancer. – *Selatan* a) Southern Cross. b) Southern Cross, i.e., the code name for the Joint Indonesian-Australian naval exercises held in Australian waters. – *siarah/syarat* planet. – *Sidik Sakti* Medal for Supernatural Investigation, i.e., an award for appreciation presented by the Chief of Police to a detective who has distinguished himself. – *Singa* Leo. – *Sunbulat* Virgo. – *tamu* guest star. – *tanjung* military decoration. – *télévisi* TV star. – *terang* good luck. – *Thaur* Taurus. – *tiga beradik* Orion. – *timur* Venus, morning star. – *tohok* Southern Cross. – *tujuh* Pleiades. – *Uranus* Uranus. – *utara* North Star. – *utarid* Mercury. – *Waluku* Orion. – *Waruna* Neptune. – *zohrah* Venus. – *Zuhal* Saturn.

sebintang to harmonize, agree, be well matched. ~ *dengan* compatible/suitable/matching with. *Ketiga-tiganya tidak ~ dengan dia*. None of the three agreed with him.

berbintang 1 to have stars/a star; with stars. *langit tiada ~* a starless sky. ~ *gelap* to have a run of bad luck, be down on one's luck. ~ *mujur* to be fortunate/lucky. **2** indication of the rank of a military man. *Jénderal ~ lima Douglas MacArthur*. Five-star general Douglas MacArthur. **3** quality rating for hotels (in advertising material indicated by printed stars). *Hotél ~ lima itu punya pembangkit listrik sendiri*. The five-star hotel has its own generator set. *Di Bali saat ini tersedia sekitar 11.000 kamar, terdiri dari 6.000 kamar hotél ~ dan 11.000 kamar hotél non-bintang*. In Bali, at the moment, there are about 11,000 rooms, consisting of 6,000 rooms of quality-rated hotels and 5,000 rooms of non-rated hotels. **4** to be born under the sign of. *gadis Amérika yang ~ Pisces ini* this American girl born under the sign of Pisces.

berbintang-bintang 1 with a lot of stars, starry; star-spangled. **2** to see stars (from hunger, after a blow, from a fever/strong light, etc.). **3** open to the sky (of a roof with holes).

membintang 1 to be expressed in stars. *Industrialisasi berarti produksi dengan angka-angka ~*. Industrialization means production in figures expressed in stars. **2** star-shaped.

membintangi to star/act in (a movie/play, etc.).

bintangan 1 star(s), constellation, figure or design like a star. **2** with white spots (in the center of one's eyes).

bintang-bintangan 1 to see stars (from hunger, after a blow, from fever, strong light, etc.). **2** open to the sky (of a roof with holes).

perbintangan 1 astronomy. **2** astrology. **3** horoscope. **4** starhood.

bintangur → BETANGUR. – *belulang* → BETUR *belulang*.

bintara (*Skr?*) noncommissioned officer, N.C.O., noncom; in

ABRI the ranks between corporal (*kopral*) and lieutenant (*létnan*): sergeant (*sérsan*), sergeant major (*sérsan mayor*) and warrant officer (*pembantu létnan*). – *dan tamtama* enlisted men. – *pelatih* drill sergeant. – *tinggi* senior NCO.

bintat → BINTIT.

bintayung frigate bird, *Fregata andrewsi*.

binték → BINA *téknik*.

binteng (*Jv*) – *jahé* snack made of sticky-rice flour and ginger.

binti (*A*) term used as indicator of filial relationship: daughter of, e.g., *Siti Aishah – Mat Ali* Siti Aishah, daughter of Mat Ali.

binti-binti *burung* – deep-blue/blue-eared kingfisher, *Alcedo meninting*.

bintih → BÉNTÉH.

bintik I (white) spots or speckles (on the skin or on a plant); → BERCAK. – *hitam* blackhead. – *layu* spotted wilt. – *putih* white spot (a plant disease).

berbintik-bintik covered with (white) spots or speckled (on the skin), speckled, mottled.

berbintikan dotted.

membintik to form a spot/speckle.

bintik II drop (of liquid). – *air* drop of water. – *tinta* ink spot.

berbintik-bintik with drops, to pearl, form in beads, stand out in drops (of perspiration).

membintik to form a drop.

bintikan drop. ~ *keringat* drop of perspiration/sweat.

bintil 1 small swelling such as caused by a mosquito bite. **2** a sty in the eye. **3** nodule. – *akar* root nodule.

berbintil to have such swellings, etc.

berbintilan warty.

bintit → BINTIL.

bintrok sexy.

bintul → BINTIL 1.

bintul-bahar mermaid.

bintur lift net (for catching shrimps/crabs).

binturong and **binturung** bearcat, a variety of civet cat with tufted ears and a long, hairy tail that can be used to hang onto trees, etc., *Arctis binturong*.

binuang → BENUANG II.

binun (*Pr*) → BINGUNG.

bio (*C*) Chinese temple; → KLÉNTÉNG.

bioaktif (*E*) bioactive.

bioaktivitas (*E*) bioactivity.

bioaktivator (*E*) bioactivator.

bioantropologi (*D/E*) bioanthropology.

biodata (*D/E*) biodata.

biodégradasi (*D*) biodegradation.

    kebiodegradasian biodegradation.

biodivérsitas (*E*) biodiversity.

bioétika (*E*) bioethics.

biofarmaseutik biopharmaceutical

biofértilisasi (*E*) biofertilization.

biofiltrasi (*E*) biofiltration.

biofisik (*E*) biophysic(al).

biofisika (*D*) biophysics.

biogas (*D/E*) biogas.

biogénik (*E*) biogenic.

biogéograf (*E*) biogeography.

biograf (*D*) biographer.

biografi (*D*) biography.

    membiografikan to write a biography of. *Bukunya ~ 111 wartawan "tiga zaman."* His book gives the biography of 111 reporters who experienced the three periods (of Indonesian history). *tokoh yang dibiografikan* person about whom a biography has been written.

biografis (*D*) biographic(al.)

bioindikator (*E*) bioindicator.

bioindustri (*D/E*) bioindustry.

biokatalis (*E*) and **biokatalisator** (*D*) biocatalyst.

biokimia biochemistry.

biokimiawan biochemist.

biokimiawi biochemical.

bioklimat (*E*) bioclimatic.

biokong (C) temple attendant.
biokonvérsi (D) bioconversion.
biola (*Port*) violin.
    berbiola 1 to have a violin. 2 to play the violin; → (BER)MAIN *biola*.
    pembiola violinist.
biolistrik bioelectricity.
biolog (D) biologist.
biologi (D/E) biology. *ahli – molécular* molecular biologist. – *molékular* molecular biology.
biologik (E) and **biologis** (D) biologic(al). *memenuhi kebutuhan – nya* to meet the biological needs (of inmates).
biologiwan biologist.
biomagnétisme (D/E) biomagnetism.
biomassa (D) biomass.
    membiomassa to biomass.
biomédis (D) biomedical.
biomékanik (E) biomechanical. *laboratorium –* biomechanical laboratory.
biomékanika (D) biomechanics.
biométrik (E) biometric(al).
biomolékular (E) biomolecular.
biomorfik (E) biomorphic.
biong land speculator.
bioprosés (D/E) bioprocess.
biopsi (D/E) biopsy.
biopsikologi (D/E) biopsychology.
bioremédiasi (E) bioremediation.
bioritme (D/E) biorhythm.
biorotor (D/E) biorotor.
biosfér (D/E) biosphere.
biosida (D) biocide.
biosintésis (D/E) biosynthesis.
bioskop (D) cinema, movie theater. – *misbar/openkap* drive-in (theater); → MISBAR. – *papan tengah* second-run theater. – *sinéplék* cineplex. – *utama* first-run theater.
    perbioskopan 1 movie (*mod*). *kehidupan ~* movie life. *organisasi ~* movie organization. *tokoh ~* movie magnate. 2 the (world of) movies.
biota (D/E) biota. – *laut* marine biota.
bioték(nologi) (D/E) biotechnology. *ahli –* biotechnologist.
biotipe (D/E) biotype.
biotis (D) biotic.
biotop (D) biotope.
biotrop [biologi tropikal] tropical biology.
bipak → BIWAK.
bipang (C?) *kué –* k.o. snack made from sticky rice.
bipédal (E) biped.
bipolar (E) bipolar.
bipolarisasi E bipolarization.
bir (D) beer. – *hitam* stout. – *kaléngan* canned beer, beer in cans. – *pletok* (*J*) k.o. non-alcoholic drink. – *tong(an)* draft beer.
    ngebir (*coq*) to drink beer. *Rini kebagian peran gadis nakal, suka – dan perokok berat.* Rini was allotted the role of a wanton girl, fond of drinking beer and a chain smoker.
birah I a large taro variety, *Alocasia indica/macrorrhiza*, that causes itching; the root is tasty after boiling. *seperti – tidak berurat* very lazy (every moment lying down). *seperti – tumbuh di tepi lesung* like a child growing fast. – *air*, k.o. plant, *Aglaonema marantifolium*. – *hitam*, k.o. jungle aroid, *Alocasia denudata*.
birah II 1 itchy. 2 horny, sexually excited.
    kebirahan 1 itch, itchiness. 2 sexual excitement, horniness, lust.
birahi (*Skr*) 1 *asyik/cinta gila* – love, deep/strong affection. *memancing –* to rouse/stir up sexual desires. *menyaksikan dua insan itu melampiaskan – séksnya* to witness the two human beings indulging in sexual pleasures. 2 love to (babble/joke, etc.), fond of (music). 3 estrus, being in heat. *rasa –* a) love, affection, sexual passion, amorousness. – *tenang* (of cattle) silent heat.
    membirahikan 1 to love, be in love with. 2 to charm, fascinate. 3 to arouse lust.
    kebirahian 1 love, affection, sexual passion, amorousness. 2 estrus.
birai 1 low wall, balustrade, parapet. 2 banister. 3 fringe at edge/end. 4 edge of a blank page. 5 picture frame.

    berbirai with/to have a balustrade. *balkon ~* balcony with a balustrade.
biram I (*cla*) elephant.
biram II (*cla*) a snake with two heads on either end of the body (in fables).
biram III (dark) red.
birama (*Jv*) tempo, meter (in music).
biras I (*cla*) relationship between two men who have married sisters or two women who have married brothers.
    berbiras to be brother/sister-in-law (of).
biras II – *sementung* k.o. shrub, *Alsodeia lanceolata*.
birat 1 a scar on the mouth or lips. 2 welts from a caning.
    berbirat having such a scar or marks.
biri → KEBIRI.
biri-biri I (*Hind?*) (*kambing –*) sheep, *Ovina spp*.
biri-biri II (*E?*) *penyakit –* beriberi. – *basah* beriberi with dropsy. – *kering* beriberi with atrophy.
birih → BIRAI.
biring I k.o. skin disease. – *peluh* German measles.
biring II yellowish red (of a fighting cock/skin from chafing), brownish orange.
birit (*J*) the buttocks, ass.
    terbirit-birit to have an accidental discharge of feces. *lari ~* to run helter-skelter, take to one's heels, run like hell.
Birma Burma.
birmang (*IBT D*) neighbor.
biro (D) bureau, department, office, agency. – *ahli* firm of surveyors. – *arsiték* architectural bureau. – *bangunan* builder's office. – *Dunia Pandu Putra* Boy Scouts World Bureau. – *Hubungan Masyarakat* Public Relations Office. – *iklan* advertising agency. – *konsultasi* consultation center. – *Pengapalan Indonésia* Indonesian Cargo Control Agency. – *Penyelidikan Fédéral* (U.S.) Federal Bureau of Investigation, FBI. – *Perancang Nasional* [Bapenas] National Planning Bureau. – *perjalanan* travel bureau, tourist office. – *perkawinan* matrimonial agency. – *Pusat Statistik* [BPS] Central Bureau of Statistics. – *wisata* tourist office.
birokrasi (D/E) bureaucracy.
birokrat (D/E) bureaucrat.
birokratik (E) and **birokratis** (D) bureaucratic.
birokratisasi (D) bureaucratization, i.e., the system whereby leaders have become bureaucrats only responsible to their office, department, superiors, and subordinates, so that they do not have relations with society at large.
    membirokratisasi to bureaucratize.
birsam pleurisy.
biru I 1 blue, bluish green. *meninju mata orang sampai –* to give s.o. a black eye. – *Bén Hur* cyan blue. – *Bérlin* Prussian blue. – *ceraka* flax blue. – *cuci* bluing. – *giok* jade green. – *jelak* vivid blue. – *keabu-abuan* grayish blue. – *kehijauan* turquoise blue. – *kelasi* navy blue. – *keunguan* purple blue. – *kobalt* cobalt blue. – *langit cerulean/sky* blue. – *laut* marine blue. – *lebam/legam* black and blue. – *logam* metallic blue. – *muda* light blue, azure. – *panci* fog blue. – *pelangi* spectrum blue. – *pirus* turquoise. – *pucat* pale blue. – *putih* tranquilizer. – *telang* reddish blue. – *tua* dark blue. 2 bruised. – *sembam* swollen (of a bruise). 3 (*coq*) better than average (of grades).
    sebiru as blue as.
    membiru to turn blue.
    membirukan to make/paint s.t. blue.
    kebiruan 1 excessively blue. *badan –* cyanosis. 2 (of batik) too deeply dyed.
    kebiru-biruan bluish.
biru II → HARU *biru*.
biru III – *laut* various species of godwits, *Limosa spp*.
biruang (*ob*) → BERUANG.
biru-biru folds at the edge of a dress; plaited (at the edges of material, etc.).
    berbiru-biru pleated.
    membiru-biru (*cla*) to fold, pleat.
bis I (D) (mail)box. – *surat* mailbox.
    membiskan to mail (a letter).

bis II (D) bus (public conveyance; → BUS. – *air* water bus. – *antarkota* intercity bus. – *bertingkat* double-decker bus. – *cepat* express bus. – *Jumbo* the double-decker Volvo bus of the Jakarta Transport Company (PPD). – *kilat* express bus. – *kota* city/local bus. *perbis-kotaan* city bus (mod). – *kota jangkung* the double-decker Leyland bus. – *luar kota* intercity bus. – *malam* "night bus," i.e., a long-distance overnight bus. – *tiga tingkat* three-level bus," i.e., a passenger bus consisting of three types of passengers: a) those squatting on top of the roof; b) those with a seat; c) strap-hangers. – *tompok* (in Surabaya) the double-decker Volvo bus.

bis III (D) (metal) tube.

bis IV (D) piping (in trimming a dress, etc.), trimming. *Pada pinggiran jas diberi – beludru.* A velvet piping was put on the seam of the coat. – *bantalan* bushing.

bis V (D) 1 –.– bis, bis ... ! Encore, encore... ! (a demand by the audience, shown by continued applause, for the repetition of a piece of music, etc.). 2 (leg) bis, the second section under the same article number.

bisa I (Skr) 1 venom, the poison secreted by some snakes, spiders, insects, etc., introduced into the body of the victim by bite or sting; *cp* RACUN. *ular* – a venomous snake. – *ular* snake venom. 2 venomous, poisonous. *ada ular yang –, ada yang tidak* some snakes are venomous, some are not. 3 poison, s.t. considered harmful/destructive to society. *Péndéknya, ajaranmu itu – bagi kita sekalian.* In short, your teachings are a poison for all of us. *alah – oléh biasa* theory is worsted by practice. *pisau senjata tiada –, – lagi mulut manusia* words are sharper than a weapon. – *kawi* (cla) a mysterious power (such as a calamity brought on by a curse, etc.) that falls on s.o. due to breaking *adat*, etc. – *penyengat* wasp's venom.

   bisa-bisa venomous, poisonous.

   berbisa venomous, poisonous.

   kebisaan 1 (to be) poisoned. 2 toxicity, virulence.

bisa II (Skr J/Jv) 1 can, be able to, be capable of, know how to. *Apa –?* Is that possible? *Mana –!* How is it possible! *paling –* at (the) most. *Ia umur lima sudah – baca.* He could read when he was five. – *aja kau ini* you've always got s.t., there's always s.t. up with you. *tidak – tidak* undoubtedly, absolutely, just must *Orang Indonésia tidak – tidak harus menerima naséhat ahli-ahli asing.* Indonesians absolutely must accept the advice of foreign specialists. – *jadi ia tidak datang.* It's quite sure he won't come. *tidak – jadi* impossible, incredible. – *juga* and *juga –* a) will also be possible. b) will be all right, too. – *saja* a) (they) can of course, certainly it can be done. – *saja meréka datang ke Jakarta.* Of course they can come to Jakarta. b) It's all right, of course. – *sekali* very able/clever. – *tidur?* Did you sleep well? 2 to manage to (do), succeed in (do)ing. *Ia – menahan marahnya.* He managed to control his anger. 3 to (do) in accordance with one's nature. *Macan – mengaum.* Tigers roar.

   bisanya what one is capable of. *atas ~* on one's own, independently. *~ bisa, tapi dia hanya malas.* He can do it, he's just lazy.

   bisa-bisa it's quite possible that, there is a possibility that/of ...-ing. *~ uang itu untuk membeli TV.* It's quite possible that the money will be used to buy a television set. *Itu ~ kamu sajalah.* It's up to you.

   sebisa *~ mungkin* as much as possible. *~ saya* as far as I'm able to.

   sebisa-bisa if possible. *~ harus menang.* If possible I have to win.

   sebisa(-bisa)nya 1 to try one's best; to the best of one's ability, according to one's capability, to the fullest extent. *Aku mesti mampir, ndak tahu kapan; sebisaku.* I'll drop by, I don't know when; whenever I can. 2 if at all possible; as much as possible. *Kerjain ~ ajé.* Just do it, if at all possible.

   membisa(-bisa)kan (Jv) to make s.o. able to do s.t., make it possible for s.o. to do s.t.; to do one's best. *Ujiannya mémang susah, tapi dibisa-bisakan lho!* The test is hard, but do your best! *Aku tahu bésok sibuk, tapi cobalah dibisakan.* I know you're busy tomorrow, but do try to work it in.

   kebisaan ability, capability.

bisaé (C coq) ugly, bad, horrible looking.

bisai (cla) fine, pretty, nice, handsome; a dandy *seperti – makan sepinggang* really reasonable/fair/just.

bisan → BÉSAN.

bisawab → BISSAWAB.

bisban (D) seam binding (in clothing).

bisbol (E) baseball. *pemain –* baseball player. *penggemar –* baseball fan.

bisbul (S) velvet apple, *Diospyros blancoi.*

biséksual (D/E) bisexual.

biséksualitas (D) bisexuality.

biséktris (D) bisector.

biséps (D/E) biceps.

bisik whispering, say in a whisper.

   bisik-bisik secretly, quietly.

   berbisik(-bisik) 1 to whisper. 2 whisperingly, in a whisper.

   berbisikan to whisper to e.o.

   membisiki to whisper/speak softly to, whisper in (s.o.'s ear).

   mem(per)bisikkan 1 to whisper s.t. (in s.o.'s ear); to inform of secretly. 2 to prompt, suggest, inspire, instigate.

   terbisik whispered.

   bisikan 1 whisper, whispering. 2 suggestion, prompting, inspiration, instigation. *~ ghaib* inspiration. *~ hati* conscience; → KATA/SUARA hati. *menurut ~ hati/kalbu* conscience, the dictates of one's heart.

   pembisik 1 whisperer. 2 inspirer, s.o. who has s.o.'s ear. 3 (theater) prompter.

bisilabik (E) disyllabic. *kata –* disyllabic word.

bising 1 noise (of chatter/traffic), rustle; rustling, buzzing. 2 with ringing ears. 3 din, uproar,

   sebising as noisy as.

   berbising to make noise, be noisy.

   membisingi to deafen.

   membisingkan 1 to make one's ears ring. 2 ear-splitting, deafening.

   terbising the noisiest.

   bisingan noise.

   kebisingan 1 noise, noisiness, uproar, tumult, clamor. 2 to have a ringing in one's ears.

bisinosis (D) brown lung, byssinosis.

biskal → FISKAL.

biskit → BISKUIT.

biskop I (D RC) bishop; → USKUP.

   kebiskopan bishopric, diocese.

biskop II (coq) → BIOSKOP.

biskuit (D/E) biscuit, rusk. – *mari* k.o. biscuit. – *nasib* fortune cookie.

bislah → BESLAH.

bislit → BESLIT.

bismi (A) in the name of. *-Ilah(i)* in the name of God. *-Ilahirrahmanirrahim, -llahirrokhmanirrokhim* and *-lahirahmanirrahim* in the name of God the Merciful, the Compassionate.

bismut (D) bismuth.

bisnis (E) business. *untuk keperluan –* for business purposes. *melakukan –* to do business. *dunia –* business world. *orang –* businessman. *tokoh –* tycoon. *– éceran* retail business. *– utama* core business. *– waralaba* franchise business.

   sebisnis in the same business.

   berbisnis to do business.

   membisniskan to deal in (a product).

   pebisnis business person.

bisnisman (E) businessman.

bisnismén (E) businessmen.

bisniswan → BISNISMAN.

bisniswati businesswoman.

bison (D/E) bison, *Bison americanus.*

bispak (BG) [bisa dipakai] easily approachable for sex, a slut.

bissawab (A) *wallahualam* – and only God knoweth the truth.

bissu (Bugis) transvestite priest.

bisték → BISTIK.

bistél → BESTÉL.

bistik (D) beefsteak. – *komplit* steak dinner. – *lidah sapi* ox tongue steak.

bisturi (Pers) (surgeon's) lance.

bisu 1 dumb, mute, unable to speak, silent; → GAGU, KELU. *film –* silent movie. – *seribu bahasa* not to say a word. – *batu* totally mute. **kebisu-batuan** total muteness. – *tuli* deaf and dumb. **2** silent(ly), noiseless(ly).

bersibisu to keep silent, behave as if one knows nothing.

berbisuan not to speak to e.o.

membisu to keep silent, not say anything.

membisukan to silence.

kebisuan 1 muteness, dumbness. **2** silence.

bisul boil, sore, ulcer, pustule, tumor, abscess. – *hampir memecah* a difficulty almost surmounted. – *jerawat* blister. – *lada* a painful boil. – *perut* gastric ulcer. – *sabut* carbuncle. – *selinap* a boil that doesn't break but gradually disappears.

berbisul ulcerated.

membisul to turn into a boil, etc.

bisulan to have boils, suffer from boils.

bit I (*D*) beet. – *gula* sugar beet.

bit II (*D*) bit (for horses).

bit III (*E*) byte.

bitbit k.o. bird, plaintive cuckoo, *Cacomantis merulinus (threnodes)*.

Bitel (*E*) The Beatles.

berbitel-bitelan to act like the Beatles, imitate the Beatles.

biti (*Skr*) *tanda* – a piece of evidence, proof; → BETI I.

biti-biti (*Skr cla*) – *perwara* court ladies, (lady's) maids.

bitila (*E ob*) betteela (coarse flannel).

biting (*J/Jv*) a bamboo splinter used for pinning leaf-wrapped food.

membiting to fasten with a *biting*.

bitingan such a splinter.

bitis k.o. tree, *Madhuca utilis, Palaquium Ridleyi*.

bitu (*S*) to burst (of tires).

bitumén (*D/E*) bitumen; bituminous.

berbitumén bituminous.

biuku water tortoise, flat-shelled turtle, *Notochelys platynota*. *mata* – lackluster/dull eyes.

biul Javan ferret-badger, *Melogale orientalis*.

bius (*Pers*) **1** unconscious, unaware, in a swoon. **2** stunned, intoxicated, drugged, stupefied. **3** anesthesia. – *lokal. kena* – to be anesthetized. *obat* – a) anesthetic. b) narcotics, drugs. c) opiate, soporific (used by thieves). – *total* general anesthetic.

membius(i) and **membiuskan 1** to anesthetize, put to sleep, make unconscious. **2** to drug, dope, knock s.o. out. **3** to soothe, tranquilize.

terbius stunned, knocked unconscious, put to sleep. **keterbiusan** unconsciousness.

kebiusan 1 to become unconsciousness. **2** unconsciousness.

pembius 1 anesthesia, anesthetic. **2** anesthetist.

pembiusan anesthetization, doping, drugging; → ANÉSTÉSI.

biut I (*ob*) chronic (of illness that takes a long time to recover from), stubborn (of disease).

biut II *biang* – writhing and twisting.

biwak (*D*) bivouac.

berbiwak to bivouac.

biwada (*Jv*) honor, esteem, veneration.

biyaya → BIAYA.

biyayakan (*Jv*) to keep moving around restlessly (in such a way as to disturb others).

biyuh-biyuh (*Jv*) exclamation of astonishment.

biyung (*Jv*) mother.

biyung-biyung 1 calling out for one's mother. **2** screaming in pain.

biza (*ob*) → BÉDA.

bizurai (*cla*) viceroy.

BK car license for Sumatera Utara.

BKPM → BADAN *Koordinasi Penanaman Modal*.

BL car license for Aceh.

bl- also see entries beginning with **bel-**.

BL [Barat Laut] Northwest.

B/L Bill of Lading.

blaar (*onom*) sound of an explosion.

blabar (*Jv*) overflow, overstatement.

bla-bla-bla (*E*) blab-blab-blab.

berbla-bla-bla to talk. *meluangkan waktu untuk ~ sedikit bercerita tentang Indonésia* to have the opportunity to say a few words and tell about Indonesia.

blacan → BELACAN.

blaco → BELACU.

blader (*Cilacap*) sludge, i.e., any heavy, slimy deposit, sediment, or mass as the waste resulting from oil refining, etc..

bladerdéég (*D*) puff-paste.

blado (*Jv*) broke, penniless.

blagu (*sl* from *berlagu?*) cocky.

blak (*onom*) → DEBLAK I.

blaka (*Jv*) to have the courage to speak one's mind.

blakasuta (*Jv*) frankly, openly, without mincing matters.

blak-blakan (*Jv*) straightforward, frank, concealing nothing. *Meréka mengadakan tukar-pikiran secara –*. They had a straightforward exchange of views.

blam (*onom*) boom (sound of an explosion).

blandang (*Jv*) broker. *Petani lebih suka melégo tembakaunya kepada –*. Farmers prefer to sell their tobacco to brokers.

Blandis native Indonesian with pro-Dutch leanings.

blandong (*Jv*) lumberjack working on a contract basis.

blandrék mblandrék → BANDRÉK II.

blang-bleng (*Jv onom*) sound of bomb explosions.

blanggur (in East Java) a large fireworks bomb that explodes in the air. – *boléh dibunyikan sebagai tanda berbuka puasa oléh mesjid-mesjid*. Fireworks may be exploded as a sign of breaking the fast by mosques.

blangko (*D*) **1** blank, empty (of an empty form to be filled in). **2** to abstain (in voting). **3** form to be filled in.

blangkon (*Jv*) *ikat*-style headgear permanently sewn in shape.

blangkréh (*Jv*) in disorder/the wrong place.

blangsak (*J*) **keblangsak** troubled. – *wajah Partono, bengap ditampar Yayuk*. Partono's face was troubled, swollen and beaten by Yayuk.

blangwér → BRANDWÉER.

blanko → BLANGKO.

blantik (*Jv*) **1** trader in horses/buffaloes/chickens/ducks/weapons. **2** purchaser of items which after having been repaired, are sold again. **3** middleman, broker.

blantika 1 firmament. **2** world. – *musik* the world of music.

blarak → BELARAK.

blas (*Jv*) (not) at all. *nggak ngerti* – I don't understand at all.

blasak (*Jv*) **keblasak** to get lost.

blaster (*Jv*) **1** bastard, hybrid, crossbreed. **2** k.o. bird, a crossbreed between a *puter* and a *perkutut*.

blasteran of mixed blood. *anak ~* child of mixed blood. *bank ~* an Indonesian bank in joint enterprise with a foreign bank. *seorang wanita ~ Jawa-Belanda* a woman of mixed Javanese and Dutch blood.

blasur (*Jv*) mixed. *Sulit berbicara dalam bahasa Jawa genap, umumnya sudah pating – bercampur dengan bahasa Indonésia.* It's difficult to talk in pure Javanese, usually it's mixed with Indonesian.

blater (*J*) popular, friendly, outgoing.

blau → BELAU.

blazer (*E*) blazer.

bledék (*Jv*) thunder with lightning.

bledug I (*Jv*) elephant's cub.

bledug II (*Jv*) mud.

blégo (*Jv?*) tallow or wax gourd, *Benincasa hispida*.

blegudrék → BLUDRÉK.

bléh (*J*) man, bud (as a vocative).

bléjét (*Jv*) **membléjéti** to rob, strip (of possessions/power, etc.). **pemblejétan** stripping (of power, etc.). *~ KGP akhir-akhir ini banyak dilakukan oléh orang dalam sendiri*. The recent stripping naked of the KGP was carried out by its own insiders.

blék (*D*) tin, can.

blékan in cans. *Korma itu dibelinya ~*. He bought the dates in cans.

blekék (*Jv*) little green heron. – *Asia* Asian dowitcher, *Limnodromus semipalmatus*. – *kembang* greater painted snipe, *Rostratula benghalensis*.

bleketépé (*Jv*) roughly woven coconut leaves (for walls/roofs/temporary sheds, etc.). *rumah yang beratapkan –* a house roofed with this material.

blekok (*Jv*) → BELEKOK.

blembem (*Jv*) k.o. grass, ratana grass, *Ischaemum spp.*

bléncong (*Jv*) hanging oil lamp for lighting the *wayang.*

blénder (*E*) (food) blender.
  memblénder to blend in a blender. *cairan yang diperoléh dengan ~ kulit nenas* the liquid obtained by crushing pineapple husks in a blender.

blendhak-blendhuk (*Jv*) bulging (of cheeks/belly, etc.). *yang perutnya –* whose belly is bulging.

blendok (*Jv*) resin.

blendong foreign (non-Indonesian) homosexual.

bleng I (*onom*) sound of an explosion (of a bomb). *– lagi!* another bomb explosion!

bleng II (*Jv*) saltwater spring.

bléngah-bléngah (*Jv*) **1** pretty, yellowish-brown complexion. **2** pleasing in appearance/facial features.

blentang-blentong (*Jv*) spotted, covered with blemishes.

blépot (*J/Jv*) full of (dirt/mud/soil, etc.).
  blépotan covered with (dirt, mud, etc.). *Bajunya ~ lumpur.* His coat is all covered with mud.

bles (*onom*) whoosh (sound of s.t. moving fast).

blesek (*J/Jv*) crammed, stuffed.
  membleseki to stuff, cram (with food, etc.).
  memblesekkan to cram/stuff/shove s.t. (into).
  keblesek stuffed into some place.

bletak (*J onom*) bang!

bletok (*Jv*) mud.

bléwah (*Jv*) **1** melon, *Cucumis melo.* **2** cantaloupe.

blijvers (*D col*) Dutch who stayed on in Indonesia after retirement; *cp* TRÉKKERS.

blik (*D*) → BLÉK.

blinger (*Jv*) **keblinger** misled, deceived, cheated, taken in.

blingsatan (*J*) uncomfortable, worried, uneasy, restless, nervous. *Negeri-negeri Barat – melihat pembangunan militér RRC.* The western countries are uneasy at seeing the military buildup of the PRC.

Blitar town in East Java.
  Blitaran of this town. *bahasa Inggris ~* broken English.

blits (*D*) flash. *memotrét memakai –* to take pictures with a flash.

bliyér (*Jv*) **mbliyér 1** to dissemble, sham, pretend, feign. **2** to behave/answer foolishly.

bln (*abbr*) [*bulan*] month.

blobor (*Jv*) blotch.
  mblobor to run/flow out (of a liquid/paint. etc.), bleed through (of one page onto the next).

blog weblog, an Internet publishing tool.
  ngeblog to communicate using this tool.

blok I (*D*) **1** block, bloc (a group of nations acting together in support of e.o.). **2** (a group of buildings regarded as a unit) block. *Rumah saya tiga – lagi dari sini.* I live three blocks away. **3** roll (of material). **4** (piece of wood, etc.) block. *– Barat/kapitalis* the capitalist bloc. *– komunis* the communist bloc. *– Sovyét* the Soviet bloc. *– Timur/komunis* the communist bloc.
  ngeblok (*coq*) to side with a certain bloc. *sudah ~ ke Barat* It has already sided with the western bloc.

blok II (*D*) **memblok** to block, obstruct.

blokade (*D*) blockade. *melakukan –* to blockade. *– air* (*petro*) water block.
  memblokade to blockade, block, close. *~ jalan* to block, seal off (a street).

blokir (*D*) **memblokir 1** to freeze (a bank account). *~ cék* to stop payment on a check. **2** to suspend (a license). **3** to blockade, seal off.
  blokiran blockage.
  pemblokiran 1 blockading, blocking. **2** suspension, suspending.

bloknot(es) (*D*) notebook, note pad.

blokosuto → BLAKASUTA.

blon → BELUM.

blonda (*D*) blond. *rambut –* blond hair. *Seorang perempuan bermata biru dan berambut –.* A woman with blue eyes and blond hair.

blondotan (*Jv*) tomato; → TOMAT.

blong (*Jv*) to fail (of brakes). *Mobil itu mengalami kecelakaan karena rémnya –.* The car had an accident because the brakes failed.

blongkotan (*J*) full-fledged. *anak Betawi –* a full-fledged Jakartan.

blo'on and **bloon** (*J*) foolish, stupid. *Wartawan sekarang pintar-pintar, sedangkan wartawan dulu –.* The reporters of today are very smart, whereas reporters used to be stupid.
  memblo'oni to make a fool of s.o., trick.
  keblo'onan stupidity.

blorok (*Jv*) speckled, spotted (of an animal). *ayam –* a speckled hen. *Si – adalah ayam betina yang molék, gemuk dan selalu sibuk bekerja.* Spotty is a pretty, fat, and always very busy hen. *si –* and *Banténg –* the 40-mm AA-gun used by the Indonesian freedom fighters around 1945.

blorong (*Jv*) black and white striped.

blotong (*Jv*) **1** dregs, lees, sediment, sludge, deposit (of oil/sugarcane factory). **2** (in Kutoarjo) the dregs of tea.

blubut out-and-out. *Sorge mémang seorang gombunis yang –.* Sorge was really an out-and-out commie.

bludag (*Jv*) and **bludak membludak** [and **mbludak** (*coq*)] **1** to erupt. **2** full-breasted (woman).

bludas-bludus (*J*) to go in and out without permission. *Armada Sovyét – di Samudera Indonésia.* Soviet fleets are secretly slipping in and out of the Indonesian Ocean.

bluder (*D*) *roti –* Dutch-style vanilla cake with raisins.

bludrék (*D*) **1** (high) blood pressure, hypertension. **2** to have hypertension/high blood pressure. *Suami saya itu –.* My husband has high blood pressure.
  bludrékan hot-tempered.

Blue mushroom (*E*) mushroom growing on cattle dung mixed with eggs and fried, used by drug addicts.

blug (*J onom*) a thud. *Dengan rasa enggan aku menuju kamar dan –, aku jatuhkan diri berbaring di atas ranjang.* Reluctantly I went to the room and threw myself down on the bed with a thump.

blujin(s) (*E*) blue jeans. *Pemakai – merosot.* Wearers of blue jeans are on the decline.
  berblujin(s) to wear blue jeans.

bluk (*Jv onom*) bang! (the noise made by falling heavy objects); → BLUG.
  bluk-bluk with a bang.

blumkol (*D*) cauliflower.

blunder (*D*) blunder.

blur (*onom*) splash! (the noise made by jumping into water).

blus (*D*) blouse.

blustru → BELUSTRU.

bluwak (*Jv*) sweet melon, *Cucumis melo.*

bluwek → BELUWEK.

bluwok (*Jv?*) milky stork, *Mycteria cinerea. – hitam* wooly necked stork, *Ciconia episcopus. – sayap mérah* painted stork, *Ibis leucocepha. – tongtong* lesser adjutant stork, *Leptopilus javanicus.*

BM car license for Riau.

bmt (*abbr*) [*bawah muka tanah*] below the surface of the earth.

BMT → BAITUL *Maal Wattamwil.*

BMW *Kota* – [Bersih, Manusiawi dan Berwibawa] Clean, Human and Authoritative (of Jakarta). *menjadikan Jakarta sebagai kota –* to make Jakarta a clean, humane, and authoritative city.

BN car license for Bangka/Belitung.

bo and **bo'** (*BG voc*) man, buddy.

boat I (*E*) boat. *– pancung* a long prau with outboard motor.

boat II and **bo'at** (*Pr*) /bo'at/ drug, narcotic (such as valium/mogadon, etc.).
  ngeboat to use such a drug.

bob I (*E*) bouffant, a woman's or girl's short haircut.
  ngebob to have that k.o. hairdo.

bob II → MANYALA *bob.*

boba (*ob*) scabies, ulcer, abscess.

bobin (*D*) bobbin, spool.

bobok I (child's language) to sleep. *nina –!* (a lullaby) rest, my baby, rest! hushaby baby. *–.– siang* [BBS] (illicit) sex in the afternoon.
  membobokkan to rock (a child) asleep.

bobok II (*J*) **membobok** to bore a hole in s.t. (a wall, for example, to make a door).
  memboboki to bore a hole in s.t.

bobokan l opening, bole. **2** passage, corridor.

bobok III (*Jv*) traditional herbal remedies used as a painkiller applied to the human body.

boboko (*S*) a coarsely plaited basket, round of shape, about one foot high and one foot in diameter, provided with a footing, *usu* used as a rice bowl.

bobol (*J/Jv*) l break, burst, fall apart, collapse. *Tanggulnya –*. The dike collapsed. **2** broken through (of the defense), (in sports) scored. *Gawangnya –*. The goal was penetrated, i.e., a goal was scored (by the other team).

membobol(i) to force entry, break into, burgle. *Apoték Angkasa dibobol maling*. The Angkasa pharmacy was broken into by thieves.

membobolkan l to break/force open, force entry into, break through. *~ gawang* (in soccer) to break through the defenses and score a goal. **2** to defraud. *~ beberapa buah bank* to defraud several banks.

kebobolan l to be broken into/through. *Dan banyak orangtua yang merasa ~ kocéknya untuk membiayai hobi baru anak-anaknya itu*. And the financing of their kids' new hobby hit the parents in their pocket. **2** penetration, breaking into/through. *~ gawang* to score a goal. **3** loophole. **4** to be burglarized/defrauded of. *Perusahaan negara ~ pajak puluhan milyar*. State companies were defrauded of tens of billions. **5** to be scored off (in a game). *tidak ~ satu gol pun dalam tiga pertandingan terakhir* not to have a single goal scored off them in their last three games.

pembobol l s.o. who breaks into. **2** defrauder. *~ bank* bank defrauder.

pembobolan l breaking into. **2** scoring (a goal). **3** defrauding. **3** theft. *~ 485.000 kartu krédit* the theft of 485,000 credit cards.

bobos l torn/ripped open, pierced through. **2** a large leak.

membobos *ramai* ~ to come/go en bloc/as a group/all together. *suara ~* the noise of many voices sounding through (a window). *~ masuk* to enter in throngs (into a defeated town). *bagai anai-anai* ~ "like a disturbed ants' nest," i.e., a) crowded (in the street). b) (go to meet the enemy) in great numbers.

terbobos torn open, ripped apart.

bobot (*Jv*) l weight; a weight. *–, bébét, bibit* (*Jv*) a) heredity, worldly wealth, and moral character (the criteria for evaluating a prospective son-in-law) (or, in another sequence: *bibit, bobot, bébét*). b) birds of a feather flock together. *susut – badan* a) to slim down. *– atom* atomic weight. *– isi* density. *– jenis* specific gravity; → **BERAT** *jenis*. *– lawan* counterweight. *– mati* dead-weight. **berbobot mati** to have a dead weight of. *– muat* tonnage. *– punggah* shipping weight. *– spésifik* specific gravity; → **BERAT** *jenis*. **2** seriousness, high quality.

sebobot as heavy/high-quality/serious as.

berbobot l to weigh. **2** serious, of high quality, substantial, substantive, influential. *seniman-seniman ~* artists of consequence. **3** weighted. *rerata ~* weighted average.

berbobotkan to be weighted toward.

terbobot the heaviest, the most serious, highest-quality.

memboboti to add seriousness to. *~ diri* to burden o.s.

membobotkan to weigh.

bobotok (*M*) dish accompanying rice of steamed shredded; coconut, salted fish, and chili wrapped in banana leaf; → (**BE**)**BOTOK**.

bobrok (*J/Jv*) l dilapidated, rickety, in bad condition, ruined, broken down (of a building). *rumah –* a ramshackle house. **2** depraved, immoral, degenerate, rotten. *Pendidikan agama harus dapat menolong memperbaiki masyarakat yang –*. Religious education must be able to help reform an immoral society.

sebobrok as depraved/degenerate as.

membobrokkan l to ruin. **2** to deprave, degenerate.

kebobrokan l dilapidation, collapse. **2** corruption, decay, degeneration, depravity. *~ moral* moral depravity.

bocah (*Jv*) child, kid. *saben – nggawa/nggowo rejeki déwé* (*Jv*) every child brings his own luck. *masa –* childhood. *– angon* shepherd. *– bajang* a child (1-7 years old) whose hair has not been cut yet, *esp* in rural areas, considered a way to avert illness; → **ANAK** *bajang*. *– belasan tahun* teenager. *– cilik* a) a small/little child, *–.– cilik* small fry. *– ingusan* snotty kid. *– prasiswa* preschooler.

kebocah(-bocah)an childish, childlike.

bocél (*Jv*) chipped, nicked.

membocélkan to chip, nick.

bocélan chip, nick.

bocok (*ob*) mosquito-net awning (for a cradle).

bocong (*J*) (big-bellied) pitcher.

bocor l a leak, hole. *membunuh –* to stop a leak. **2** to leak, be leaky, leaking. *Émbér ini –*. The bucket is leaking. **3** to be punctured, flat (of a tire). *Ban belakang – rupanya*. It looks like the rear tire is flat. **4** to take on water (of a ship). *bermulut –* to talk too much, reveal secrets. *Jangan percayakan rahasiamu kepada orang yang bermulut –*. Don't entrust your secrets to a person who talks too much. **5** to leak (of a secret), become known. *Rahasia itu –*. The secret got out. **6** to trickle/ooze out, filter through, transpire. **7** to escape (of gas, etc.). **8** to leak through (of a liquid). *Hujan – di situ*. The rain is coming in there. **9** to bleed. *Karena dia jatuh dari atap kepalanya –*. Because he fell off the roof his head was bleeding. **10** a) to have frequent bowel movements, suffer from diarrhea. *Karena suami saya makan terlalu banyak cabai, maka sekarang dia –*. Because my husband ate too many chilies, he's suffering from diarrhea now. b) to urinate frequently. *Kalau makan banyak ketimun kadang-kadang –*. If you eat a lot of cucumbers sometimes you have to urinate frequently. *– bacir* leaking everywhere (as an old boat). *– mulut* to let one's tongue run away with one, blab (a secret).

membocori to put a hole in, penetrate (the opposing team's goal).

membocorkan [and **ngebocorin** (*J coq*)] l to puncture s.t. **2** to leak (secrets). *~ rahasia* to divulge/reveal a secret, give away a secret (to the enemy). *~ uang negara* (*euph*) to embezzle State funds.

terbocor leaked (out).

bocoran l leak, hole, crack. *~ léding* leak in the water pipe. **2** liquid/gas etc. that gets out or in. **3** leaked. *~ ujian* leaked exam.

kebocoran l leakage. **2** leaking (of a secret). **3** puncture, flat.

pembocor s.o. who leaks examination papers. *Tujuh ~ dipériksa*. Seven persons who leaked (examination papers) were investigated.

pembocoran leaking, causing a leak. *~ rahasia médis tentang itu oléh tim dokter RRT yang merawat Bung Karno, telah menjadi pangkal sebab lahirnya Gerakan 30 Séptémber di tahun 1965 yang fatal itu*. Leaking the medical secret by PCR's medical team who took care of Bung Karno was the basis for the birth of the September 30 Movement in the fatal year of 1965.

bodi (*E*) l (human) body (*esp* as a sex object). **2** body (of an aircraft/car, etc.).

bodo I (*J*) → **BODOH**.

bodo II (*Jv*) (in Pati, Central Java) celebration at *Lebaran*; → **BAKDA**. *– kupat* name of the feast celebrated on *Sawal* 8.

bodo III → **BAJU** *bodo*.

bodoh [and **bodo** (*J*)] l stupid, silly, idiotic, foolish; ignorant. **2** (pronounced in a somewhat long-drawn out tone) what do I care! *bikin – sama* (*coq*) to fool, make a fool of. *membuat diri –* a) to play dumb. b) to behave like a fool. c) indifferent. *masa – a*) do as you like/please; I leave it up to you. b) indifferent, careless, laissez-faire. *sikap belaga –* (*coq*) indifference, uncaring. *– politik* apolitical (having no interest or involvement in politics).

sebodo I don't care. *~ téing* (*J*) I don't give a damn.

sebodoh as stupid as.

sebodoh-bodohnya no matter how stupid.

berbodoh(-bodoh) *~ diri* to pretend ignorance.

membodoh to play dumb, pretend to be innocent.

membodohi [and **mbodohin** (*J coq*)] to take in, cheat, trick. *Meréka dibodohi mentah-mentah oléhnya*. They were taken in completely by him.

membodohkan and **memperbodoh(kan)** l to consider/regard as stupid, insult one's intelligence. **2** *~ diri* to pretend ignorance. **3** to fool, dupe, deceive, cheat, defraud.

terbodoh the stupidest.

bodoh-bodohan to play dumb.

kebodohan l stupidity, ignorance. **2** (*J*) to be wrong, be mistaken.

pembodohan deceit, cheating, fraud, deception.

bodok (*Jv*) leprosy in its initial stage.
bodol I (*J/Jv*) **1** pulled out (of feathers/hair, etc.). **2** full of holes.
bodol II (*D J*) estate, inherited property.
bodol III loose woman.
bodong I (*Jv*) protruding (of navel), umbilical hernia. *jeruk –* sour lime, *Citrus aurantifolia;* → JERUK *nipis*, LIMAU *asam.*
   membodong bossed, herniated.
bodong II (*ob*) a squall (of wind).
bodong III counterfeit, fake; → GIRIK *bodong.*
bodor (*J*) *tukang –* clown, comedian, buffoon; → BEBODORAN.
bodrék → BODRÉX. *wartawan –* hack reporter.
Bodréx k.o. anti-flu medicine.
Boer (*D*) /bur/ a South Afrikaner whose ancestors were Dutch colonizers.
boés (*J*) sore on lips (from *seriawan,* etc.).
boga (*Skr*) food; → JASABOGA.
   berboga to eat.
bogam tinsel spangles on an aigrette, etc.
bogang (*ob*) *telanjang –* stark naked.
bogél (*J*) naked, nude, insufficiently covered; → BUGIL. *ayam –* a chicken without feathers. *telanjang –* stark naked.
   berbogél naked, nude.
   berbogél-bogél to prance around in the nude.
   membogéli to strip, denude.
bogem (*J/Jv*) *– mentah* blow with the fist, punch.
bogénfil (*D*) bougainvillea.
bogi (*E*) (*keréta –*) buggy (a light carriage with two wheels and a single seat, *usu* drawn by a horse).
bogoh (*J*) (*– pada*) to like, be fond of; → BEBOGOHAN.
bogol (*ob*) → BORGOL.
bogor I (*Jv*) tree from which *mlinjo* chips are made, *Gnetum gnemon.*
Bogor II the name of the town that was formerly called Buitenzorg (West Java).
bogot (*ob*) extremely rotten. *hitam –* hideously black.
bohay (*BG*) sexy.
Bohémian (*E*) Bohemian.
bohlam (*D ob*) **1** arc lamp. **2** electric light bulb.
bohok → BUHUK.
bohong l a lie, falsehood, s.t. untrue. **2** to lie. *–!* You're lying! *– pada orang* to lie to s.o. *berbuat –* to (tell a) lie, deceive. *kabar –* canard. *orang –* liar. *– besar* a big lie.
   berbohong and **membohong** to (tell a) lie, deceive. *berbohong untuk menjaga perasaan* to tell white lies. *Ah, membobong kamu!* Ah, you're lying!
   membohongi [and **ngebohongin** (*J coq*)] to lie to, deceive. *Jangan bohongi saya.* Don't lie to me. *~ diri sendiri* to deceive/delude o.s..
   membohongkan l to deny s.t. *Segala tuduhan saksi dibohongkannya.* He denied all the accusations of the witness. **2** to consider s.t. untrue. **3** to lie about s.t.
   memperbohongkan to falsify, lie about.
   bohongan fake, bogus. *perusahaan ~* a bogus company.
   bohong-bohongan false, fake. *loteré ~* a fake lottery.
   kebohongan lie, falsehood. *~ yang lekas diketahui orang* a lie that spread like wild fire.
   pembohong liar.
   pembohongan lying.
bohorok foehn (on Sumatra's east coast; from May through September).
boi (*E*) [in Medan, now (*ob*)] boy, a male domestic worker or servant: a patronizing term applied by Caucasians to nonwhites; → JONGOS.
boikot (*E*) boycott. *– luas* secondary boycott. *– terbatas* primary boycott.
   memboikot to boycott.
   terboikot boycotted.
   boikotan s.t. boycotted.
   pemboikot boycotter.
   pemboikotan boycotting.
boil (*Pr*) /bo'il/ automobile, car; → MOBIL.
bo'ing (*sl*) illegal drugs.

bojo (*Jv*) spouse.
bojod and **bojot** (*J/Jv*) damaged; rotten.
bok I (*J*) **1** mother; → EMBOK. **2** grownup woman of lower and middle class. **3** (*reg*) *– ayu* older sister; → AYU.
bok II → BOKS.
bok III (*E*) box.
bokal beaker.
bokap (*Pr*) father; → BAPAK.
bokar I (*ob*) jug.
bokar II [*bahan olah karét*] raw material for rubber slabs.
bokbrok → BOBROK.
bokca (*Pers cla*) wallet of Buddhist monk.
boké(k) (*C J*) **1** broke, poor, penniless. *Menjelang akhir bulan kantong lagi –.* Near the end of the month I'm broke. **2** to have a hard time (with). *siswa yang merasa – dengan bahasa asing* a college student who has a hard time with foreign languages.
bokép (*Pr from bépé,* the initials of English *blue film*) porno film.
   ngebokép to watch dirty movies.
bokér (*Pr*) shit; → BÉRAK.
   bokér-bokér to have diarrhea.
bokét → BUKAT.
bokin (*Pr*) wife; girlfriend; → BINI.
bokji (*C?*) thin ear-shaped tree-bark fungus used for soups; → JAMUR *kuping.*
bokoh (*cla*) weak (in body); soft.
bokong I 1 *balik –* inside out (as coats). **2** buttocks; hip, rump. **3** (*J*) back (part).
   membokong [and **mbokong** (*coq*)] **1** (*J*) to attack from behind/the rear. **2** to read in reverse (from the end to the front). **3** to carry out s.t. in secret (without announcing it beforehand).
   membokongi to stick one's behind out at s.o.
   bokong-bokongan → MAIN *backing.*
   pembokongan surprise attack (from behind), stab in the back.
bokong II (*M ob*) **l** swollen. **2** red and swollen (of eyes). **3** puffed up. **4** bumpy.
bokop swollen (of one's cheeks from weeping/eyes etc.). *mata –* a black eye.
bokor 1 open (brass) bowl. **2** cup (given as a prize, *usu* made of metal). *– Kencana Astagina* Octagonal Gold Cup, symbol of excellence in shadow-play performance.
bokot membokot to cover up (for protection).
boks I (*D*) **1** playpen. **2** booth. *– télepon* (*umum*) (public) telephone booth.
boks II (*E*) box, short newspaper article or ad enclosed in borders.
boksen (*D*) **1** to box. **2** (the sport of) boxing.
bokser (*D*) boxer.
boksit (*D*) bauxite.
   berboksit bauxite-bearing.
boksu (*C*) Christian Chinese minister/priest.
boktor k.o. stem borer, *Xystrocera festiva.*
bol I (*J/Jv*) rectum, anus.
bol II *jambu –* a guava variety, rose apple, *Eugenia malaccensis.*
bol III (*D*) Bols (trademark of a certain liquor), Dutch gin.
bol IV (*D*) bowl.
bol V feather (on a hat, etc.).
bola I (*Port*) ball, sphere, globe (a round glass cover for a lamp, etc.), billiard ball. *bermain –* to play soccer. *kamar –* (*col*) (social) clubhouse. *lapangan –* soccer field. *méja –* billiard table. *rumah – (col)* (social) clubhouse. *sépak –* soccer. *– itu bundar* that's the way things are, that's the way the cookie crumbles. *menjadi – ping-pong* to send s.o. from pillar to post. *– adil* k.o. game in which the players bet on which slot a ball will go into. *– air* water polo. *– bekél* small ball used in games. *– baskét* basketball. *pebola baskét* basketball player. *– bopéng* golf ball. *– bulutangkis* shuttlecock. *– bumi (dunia)* globe. *– cocok* matched ball (in a game). *– cogok* (in soccer) a ball put into play again. *– gada* baseball. *– gelinding* bowling ball; bowling. *bermain – gelinding* to bowl. *– golf* golf ball. *– huruf IBM* IBM letter ball. *– kaki* soccer. *– kasti* → KASTI. *– keranjang* basketball. *– kristal* crystal ball. *– lampu* a) a round glass cover, globe. b) (electric) light bulb. *– langit* celestial sphere. *– mata* eyeball. *belakang – mata* fundus. *gerakan mata – cepat* rapid eye movement, REM.

gerakan – *mata tenang* nonrapid eye movement, NREM. – *per-mainan* plaything. – *ping-pong* ping-pong ball. – *salju* snowball. – *sépak* soccer ball. – *sétan* small ball in a gambling game. – *sodok* billiards. – *tampar* volley ball. – *tampel* tennis ball. – *tangan* handball. – *tangkas* pinball machine. – *tangkis* badminton; → BADMINTON. – *ténis* tennis ball. – *ténis méja* Ping-Pong ball. – *tojok* billiards. – *tongkat* field hockey. – *voli* volleyball.

membola like) a ball, spherical; (to become) ball-shaped.

ngebola (*sl*) to pick s.o.'s pocket.

bola II delivery boy.

bolak round (of eyes). – *balik* a) (to walk) up and down, to and fro; toss/turn (in one's sleep). b) back and forth. *Bis itu pergi ke Bandung – balik.* That bus goes back and forth to Bandung. *diplomasi – balik Henry Kissinger* Henry Kissinger's shuttle diplomacy. *karcis – balik ke Surabaya* a round-trip ticket to Surabaya. *pesawat ruang angkasa – balik* and *pesawat – balik antariksa* space shuttle. *harus berpikir – balik* should consider thoroughly. *Pikirannya – balik.* a) He weighs the pros and cons. b) He is wavering/vacillating/unstable (also of politics: an opportunist). c) restlessly wandering/roaming thoughts (of an insomniac). *cakap – balik* prevaricate. *kata – balik* cannot rely/depend on s.o.'s words. d) (to hear) time and again (certain reports). *Dan Namalui (Ménlu PNG) – balik minta maaf.* And Namalui (Papua New Guinea's Foreign Minister) again and again asked for forgiveness. e) *diputar – balik* (the coin) was turned and turned around. f) alternating. *arus – balik* alternating current. – *balik melintasi* to pass frequently (a group of people). g) multiple entry. *visa khusus yang bersifat – balik* a special multiple entry visa. h) backward and forward. ***membolak-balik*** to turn over and over, toss; to turn s.t. over, leaf through. *dibolak-balik bagaimana juga* no matter how the matter is twisted/turned around. ***membolak-balik(kan)*** *1* to turn over (the leaves of a book/the soil, etc.). *Petani-petani sedang ~ tanah sawahnya yang pecah berbongkah-bongkah untuk ditanami padi gora.* The farmers were turning over the soil of their rice paddies which was broken in chunks in order to plant it with *gora* rice. *2* to examine carefully. *Kerja ~ potongan kéramik yang jumlahnya ribuan bagi Naniek bukan hal aneh.* The job of closely examining the thousands of ceramic pieces is nothing new to Naniek. ***pembolak-balikan*** *1* tossing, spinning around and around. *2* to twist, distort (words/facts, etc.).

bolang-baling I *1* weather/wind vane. *2* propeller (of an aircraft); screw (of a vessel). *3* pointer showing the direction of the wind; → BALING-BALING.

berbolang-baling with a weather vane/propeller/screw.

bolang-baling II k.o. cake.

boléh I *1* can, could, to be able to. *Dengan uang sebanyak itu meréka – hidup senang.* With that much money they can live comfortably. – *dikatakan* it can be said (that). *Di Indonésia Geraldine Page – dikatakan tidak dikenal, padahal beberapa filmnya sudah masuk.* It can be said that Geraldine Page is unknown in Indonesia, although some of her films have come in (to the country). – *dikatakan kosong* practically empty. *Apa – buat?* What can be done about it? What is to be done? What else could we do? *2* may, be allowed, permitted. – *tanya, ya* (*coq*) excuse me, may I ask a question? *Anak-anak – menonton.* Children are allowed to see the movie. *3* all right, go ahead. – *déh/dah* (*coq*) all right, go ahead. *4* yes, OK. "*Mau pisang.* "*–*" "Would you like a banana?" "Yes." *–lah* a) OK. b) it's OK. – *jadi* perhaps, possibly; probably. *akan tetapi sangat – jadi bahwa ...* but it might well be that ... *tak – jadi* impossible; → MUSTAHIL. **keboléh-jadian** probability. – *juga* a) maybe, not unlikely/impossible, quite possible. b) (*coq*) fair, not too bad, it'll do; → LUMAYAN, MENDINGAN. *tak – tidak* a) have to, be obliged, can't avoid, can't be otherwise, must; → *tak* DAPAT *tidak*. b) certainly, no doubt. *seberapa –* → SEDAPAT-DAPATNYA. *Mana/Masa –!* What a ridiculous idea! What are you talking about! – *diadu* and – *dibawa ke tengah* to be able to hold one's own.

boléhnya (*ob*) *1* (*J*) one's own gain, what one has gotten. *Ini ~ beli, bukan mencuri.* He bought this with his own money and didn't steal it. *2* (*J*) how is it possible. *3* (on the analogy of Javanese *oléh*) an auxiliary word to form a predicate regarded as im-

portant. *Dengan dada terbusung ~ Tambera pergi ke rumah.* Completely full of himself Tambera went home.

boléh-boléh *~ saja* it's quite allowed.

seboléh-boléhnya *1* in so far as this is possible. *2* with all one's might and main. *3* to the best of one's ability/power.

mem(per)boléhkan [and **ngeboléhin** (*J coq*)] to permit, allow. *masyarakat yang bercorak sékular dan serba memboléhkan* a secular and permissive society.

boléhan passable, O.K., not bad. *Di antara meréka ada saja yang ~.* There are always some among them who are not bad to look at. *Ia berasal dari SMA yang –.* He graduated from an OK Senior High School.

keboléhan ability, skill, capability. *~ banding* comparability.

berkeboléhan to have the ability to.

pemboléhan permission. *~ pulang* permission to return home.

boléh II (*cla*) to get, receive, obtain; → OLÉH.

boléro (*D*) bolero.

berboléro to wear a bolero.

boling (*E*) bowling.

peboling bowler, a participant in a bowling game; → PEBOLER. *PBI menentukan ~ untuk kejuaraan dunia Oktober mendatang.* The Indonesian Bowling Association determines the bowlers for the world championship next October.

boljug [boléh juga] pretty good/nice.

Bolmong [Bolaang-Mongondow] a regency in North Sulawesi.

bolong I (*Jv*) *1* perforated, pierced. *2* with a hole (opening) in it. *Kantongnya –.* a) There was a hole in his pocket. b) He is broke; → TONGPÉS. *sundal –* female devil with a hole in her back; → KUNTIANAK, KUNTILANAK, LANGSUIR, PONTIANAK. *uang –* coin with a hole in its center, such as, the *kelip*. – *melompong* (*coq*) completely empty. *3* (*J*) no longer a virgin.

berbolong-bolong perforated, pierced.

membolongi *1* to put a hole through. *2* to deflower.

mbolongin (*J*) to deflower (a girl).

bolongan *1* hole, perforation. *2* place where the handle of a shadow puppet is stuck.

kebolongan hole, perforation.

bolong II (*J*) broad (daylight), *usu* combined with *siang (hari)* to become *siang (hari) –*. *Penodong yang beraksi di siang – merampas uang Rp 5 juta.* The holdup man who carried out his action in broad daylight stole five million rupiahs. *tengah hari –* broad daylight.

bolong III k.o. tube for carrying water, etc.

bolos I (*J/Jv*) *1* to skip, cut (class). – *makan dari kantin* to skip eating in the clubhouse. *2* to be out, absent (from work, etc.). *3* (*J*) to gain entrance to (a film showing/soccer match, etc.) without paying. *4* with a hole in it.

membolos *1* to sneak away from one's obligations, desert, go AWOL. *2* to play hooky, skip work, cut class. *3* to escape, flee.

mbolos (*coq*) *tukang ~* a habitual truant, s.o. who dodges work.

pembolos truant, deserter, s.o. who cuts classes, one who dodges his responsibilities.

pembolosan truancy, absenteeism.

bolos II → BULUS I.

bolot I (*ob*) **membolot** to wrap, bundle up.

pembolotan the act of wrapping/bundling up.

bolot II (*Jv*) grime, dirt on one's body (from not having a bath for a long time); → DAKI.

bolotu (*naut*) sailboat (from Central Sulawesi).

bolpén (*D*) and **bolpoin** (*E*) ballpoint pen.

bols (*D*) gin.

bolsak (*D*) mattress; → KASUR.

Bolsyevik (*D*) Bolshevik.

Bolsyevis (*D*) Bolshevik.

bolu I (*Port*) – (*kukus*) (steamed) sweet, white cake made of wheat flour; resembles a pile of mashed potatoes on top of a cupcake. – *suji* k.o. cake made with *suji*.

bolu II (in Ujungpandang) k.o. milkfish; → BANDENG II.

bolui (*C*) penniless, broke.

bom I (*D*) *1* bomb, charge, mine. *pelémpar –* (*mil*) bomb thrower, bomber. *pesawat pelémpar –* bomber (the airplane). *2* (*sl*) fart, shit. – *api* incendiary bomb. – *asap* smoke bomb. – *atom* atom bomb. **pembom-atoman** the dropping of an atom bomb. – *bakar* incendiary bomb. – *bénsin* Molotov cocktail. – *bersampul* letter bomb. – *brisan* brisant/high-explosive bomb. – *cahaya* flash bomb. – *fosfor* phosphorus bomb. – *H/Hidrogén* hydrogen bomb. – *kambang* sea mine. – *laut* depth charge – *mobil* car bomb. – *Molotov* Molotov cocktail. – *napalm* napalm bomb. – *nuklir* nuclear bomb. – *peledak* high-explosive bomb. – *pembakar* incendiary bomb. – *pembunuh api* fire-extinguishing bomb. – *pintar* smart bomb. – *rakitan* homemade bomb. – *sebar* cluster bomb. – *surat* letter bomb. – *tarik* a bomb which has to be detonated by pulling a pin. – *waktu* time bomb. – *zar(r)ah* atomic bomb. – *zat air* H-bomb.

membom and **mengebom** [and **ngebom** (*coq*)] **1** to bomb. *Tentara Sekutu ~ kubu pertahanan Jepang.* The allied forces bombed Japanese bunkers. **2** (*sl*) to steal.

ngebom (*sl*) to fart, take a shit.

membomi and **mengebomi** to bomb, drop a bomb on.

pembom and **pengebom** **1** bomber. *pesawat ~* bomber (the aircraft). *~ berat* heavy bomber. *~ jarak-jauh* long-range bomber, *~ raksasa B-25* the B-25 giant bomber. **2** bomber, bomb hurler/thrower.

pemboman and **pengeboman** (the act of) bombing. *~ tukik* dive bombing.

bom II (*D ob*) pole, shaft of a carriage.

bom III (*D ob*) boom, i.e., a barrier of chains or poles over a river to obstruct navigation, toll-bar, Customs. *pegawai –* Customs officer.

bomba (*Port*) **1** (*ob*) pump, squirt, syringe, hose (of a fire-engine); → POMPA. **2** (*Mal*) *ahli –* fireman. *balai –* fire station. *pasukan – fire brigade;* → PEMADAM *kebakaran.*

bombardemén (*D*) bombardment, strafing.

bombardir (*D*) **membombardir 1** to bombard; to bomb, shell (*esp* with aircraft using grenades). **2** to bombard, shower (with questions). *Dia dibombardir dengan berbagai pertanyaan.* He was bombarded with various questions. **3** to appoint s.o. to a position who doesn't have the qualifications.

terbombardir bombarded. *~ oléh zarah lain* bombarded with other particles.

pembombardiran shelling, bombarding.

bombas (*D*) high-flown (words).

bombasme (*D*) pomposity, bombast. *gaya –* bombastic style.

bombastis (*D*) bombastic, pompous.

bomber I (*E*) bomber (an airplane.).

bomber II fat, obese.

bombon → BONBON.

bombong (*Jv*) optimistic, confident.

  membombong 1 to stimulate, inspire, encourage. **2** to protect.

bomoh (*Mal*) medicine man, shaman; → DUKUN.

bon I (*D*) (in a restaurant/hotel, etc.) check, bill. *Minta –nya!* The check, please! **2** (*ob*) receipt/voucher for payment.

  berbon and **mengebon** [and **ngebon** (*coq*)] **1** to buy s.t. on credit. **2** to buy s.t. on a charge account or with a credit card. *ngebon potong gaji* (when buying items from a government office cooperative) to settle one's account by means of automatic salary deductions.

bon II mengebon 1 to borrow a player from another club. **2** (police term) to torture, maltreat (a suspect). **3** to take a suspect or suspect out of a prison ostensibly to interrogate him or to put him to work.

bon III (*D*) union, alliance, bond. *– Bécak* Pedicab Drivers union.

  mengebon to unionize.

bonafid(e) (*D*) and **bonafit** (*infr*) **1** bona fide. **2** in good faith, without deception.

  kebonafidan bona fides, reliability.

bonafiditas bona fides, reliability.

bonang I (*Jv*) a musical instrument consisting of 10–14 upside-down bronze kettles placed in 2 rows next to one another on a low rack (beaten with two sticks).

bonang II *ikan –* k.o. fish, longfin batfish, *Platax teira*.

bonanza (*E*) bonanza, windfall, godsend.

bonbon (*D*) bonbon, candy. *– karét* chewing gum; → KARÉT, PERMÉN.

boncél I (*J*) small. *si –* Tom Thumb.

boncél II carved, notched.

boncélan (*S*) k.o. fish, *Ophiocephalus, spp.*

boncéng (*J/Jv*) to share in, take part in. *Pada suatu malam Rusman bertamu untuk – menonton TV.* One evening Rusman paid a visit to watch television with them. *tukang –* sponger, cadger, parasite, freeloader.

  berboncéngan to ride tandem. *Dua orang yang ~ sepéda motor, téwas seketika akibat tabrakan dengan sebuah bis.* Two persons riding tandem on a motorcycle were killed instantly due to a collision with a bus.

  memboncéng 1 to ride on the back of a bicycle, motorcycle, etc.; → MENGOJÉK. *Ia bersepéda dan adiknya disuruhnya ~.* He rode on his bike and told his younger brother to ride on the back of the bicycle. **2** to get a lift on. *Ada dua orang hendak ~ mobil saya, tetapi saya tolak.* There were two people who wanted to get a lift in my car, but I refused. **3** to give s.o. a lift. *Orang tua itu diboncéngnya dengan sepéda-motor.* He gave that old man a lift on his motorcycle. *(orang) yang dibonceng* s.o. who bums a ride. **4** to ride without paying. *Banyak orang yang ~ keréta api disuruh turun lalu digiring ke kantor polisi.* Many people who rode the train without paying were instructed to get out and were then carried off to the police station. **5** to freeload, sponge (off s.o.), use s.o. else's influence etc. for one's own advantage, use s.o. else's property. *A selalu ~ kepada temannya.* A is always sponging off his friend. *Kalau boléh saya hendak ~ suratkabar anda.* If I may, I would like to also read your newspaper.

  memboncéngi 1 to get a ride from. *Saya diboncéngi Machmud.* I gave Machmud a lift on my bike. **2** to follow, accompany.

  memboncéngkan [and **mboncéngin** (*J coq*)] to give s.o. a ride on the carrier of one's bicycle, etc. *Seorang ayah ~ anaknya di belakang Véspanya dan menyelip di antara keramaian lalu-lintas dalam mengantar anaknya ke sekolah.* A father gave his child a ride on the back of his Vespa scooter and cut in to the hustle-bustle of the traffic in bringing him to school. *Dadang mengemudikan sepéda motor Binter ~ iparnya, Amung.* Dadang drove a Binter motorcycle with Amung, his brother-in-law, riding on the back of the motorcycle.

  terboncéng 1 given a ride. **2** sponged, cadged.

  boncéngan 1 to ride with s.o. on the back of a bicycle, etc. **2** carrier on back of bicycle, etc. *barang ~* goods clandestinely slipped through (i.e., not recorded in Customs documents) by being sent along with other goods.

  pemboncéng 1 s.o. who rides on the back of a bicycle, etc. **2** hitchhiker. **3** fellow traveler. *Sedang Walikota Surabaya disebutkannya sebagai ~ PKI.* Whereas the Mayor of Surabaya was mentioned as a fellow traveler of the Communist Party of Indonesia. **4** sponger, freeloader.

  pemboncéngan 1 obtaining a ride. **2** sponging, cadging.

boncis → BUNCIS.

boncol (*J*) swollen, bumpy, protruding (*esp* of one's forehead).

boncong (*ob*) round bottomed (earthenware) water jar.

boncos (of) low quality.

bond (*D*) → BON III.

bonda (*ob*) → BUNDA.

bondan (*Jv*) a classical dance showing a woman caring for her child.

bondang *– kampung* village constabulary.

bondo (*Jv*) capital (investment). *– déso* (also in Jambi) village property, i.e., land about two hectares placed at the disposal of members of the village administration as k.o. salary.

bondol (*J/Jv*) various species of sparrows and munias. *burung –* Java sparrow/munia/mannikin k.o. paddy bird, *Lonchura leucogastroides*. *– haji* white-headed munia/mannikin, *Lonchura maja*. *– hijau* pin-tailed parrot finch, *Erythrura prasina*. *– tuli* black-faced munia, *Lonchura molucca*.

bondon I [boncéngan Don Juan] and [Bonéka Donto] easy lay, slut; → PERÉK.

bondon II bung.

bondong (*M*) crowd, in throngs. *– air, – ikan* where one sheep goes follows another.

  sebondong-bondong in groups.

  berbondong-bondong and **berbondongan** in crowds/droves.

  bondongan crowd, stream (of people).

bondot (*J*) bundle (of firewood/rattan, etc.).

membondot to tie/bundle together.

bonék [*bondo nékat*] young soccer hooligans (used for supporters of Persebaya).

bonéka (*Port*) **1** doll, puppet. *pemerintah* – puppet government. **2** figurehead, s.o. whose actions, ideas, etc. are controlled by another. – *pajangan* mannequin. – *salju* snowman. – *tali* marionette.

membonékakan and **memperbonéka(kan)** to treat/use as a puppet. *membonékakan diri* to play the role of a puppet.

bonéka-bonékaan puppet, stooge.

bonékawan puppeteer.

bonét (*E*) bonnet, k.o. hat (worn by judges/university professors, etc.).

bong I (*ob onom*) a resounding sound, that produced by a falling crate, etc.

bong II (= **bongpai**) (*C*) **1** Chinese grave. **2** Chinese graveyard.

bong III (*Jv*) (– *supit*) circumciser.

bong IV (in South Sumatra) a floating, primitive bamboo toilet in a river.

bong V (*C?*) bong, k.o. of pipe for smoking narcotics.

bongak I 1 (*ob*) arrogant, haughty, proud; → PONGAH. **2** (*ob*) to lie, deceive. **3** (*M*) stupid.

membongak to boast, brag.

bongak II (*ob*) lie.

bonggol I 1 hump (of a camel, etc.); → PUNUK. **2** gnarl (on a tree); knot (on a mace). **3** (*euph*) penis. **4** (*bot*) capitulum. – *lengan* head of humerus. – *siku* olecranon.

bonggol II (*J*) **membonggol** to beat.

membonggoli(n) to beat up.

bongin a commercial plant, dika tree, *Irvingia malayana*; → PAUH *kijang*.

bongkah 1 lump, hunk, chunk, nugget, block, clod. – *emas* a gold nugget. – *és* pack ice. **2** counter for things that come in chunks, etc.

berbongkah-bongkah in chunks/fragments.

membongkahi to hoe s.t. into clods.

bongkahan 1 lump, chunk, bulk. ~ *kapur* a lump/chunk of limestone. **2** lumped (together).

bongkak arrogant, haughty, proud (of an adult); insubordinate (of children).

bongkal → BUNGKAL.

bongkang → BUNGKANG.

bongkar I – *bangkir* (turned) upside down, topsy-turvy, scattered all around. *membongkar-bangkir* to turn over, put in disorder. *Polisi ~ rumah karena mencari tanda bukti.* The police turned the house upside down in search of evidence. ~ *seseorang dengan sengaja untuk menghinanya* to keep on insulting s.o. intentionally to humiliate him. – *muat* loading and unloading (from a boat/ship, etc.). – *muat kayu* loading and unloading logs. – *muat lepas dermaga* → RÉDE transport. – *muat sendiri* self-loading and unloading (system). – *muat tanpa sandar*; → RÉDE transport. – *pasang* taken apart and put back together, overhauled. *membongkar-pasang* to take apart and put together again, overhaul.

membongkar 1 to unload, discharge, remove cargo/freight, unship. *Buruh pelabuhan itu sedang ~ (muatan) kapal.* Dock laborers were unloading that ship. *Kapal itu akan ~ muatannya di pelabuhan berikutnya.* The ship is going to discharge its cargo at the next port. **2** to force/break open (a door/lock, etc.), open up, break into. *Dia terpaksa ~ jendéla kamar itu.* He had to force the window of that room open. *Kami harus ~ konténer besar dari kayu itu.* We had to open up the large wooden container. *Rumahnya dibongkar orang.* His house was broken into. **3** to do (a room). *Kamar tamu itu dibongkar ibu lalu divakumnya karena tamunya mau datang.* Mother did the guest room then vacuumed it because her guest was arriving. **4** to demolish, pull/tear down (a house, etc.). *Bangunan tua ini harus dibongkar.* This old building must be demolished. **5** to dig up (old memories), expose, bring to light, reveal, disclose. ~ *kisah-kisah lama* to rake up old stories. *Surat ini ~ suatu rahasia.* This letter reveals a secret. *Dia ~ persekongkolan itu di depan polisi.* He revealed the plot to the police. ~ *jaringan mata-mata Soviét*

to expose the Soviet spy-ring. ~ *prakték-prakték penggelapan* to disclose malpractice/illegal practices. ~ *rahasia* to disclose/reveal/divulge a secret. ~ *kebenaran* to reveal the truth. ~ *kejahatan* to expose evils. **6** to take/pull apart, overhaul (an engine/bicycle, etc.), dismount, dismantle. *Mesin mobil itu harus dibongkar seluruhnya.* The entire engine of the car has to be taken apart. **7** to unpack, remove the contents of. *Tolong saya ~ koper ini.* Help me unpack this trunk. ~ *paksa* to force open. ~ *sauh* to weigh anchor. ~ *susunan* to reshuffle; → RISAFEL.

membongkari (*pl obj*) to take apart, demolish, etc.

terbongkar 1 turned over, demolished, pulled down, overhauled. **2** [and **kebongkar** (*coq*)] disclosed, unveiled. *Jaringan mata-mata di Prancis ~.* The espionage network in France was unveiled. ~*nya kawat sandi* the deciphering of coded cables.

bongkaran 1 what has been turned upside down. **2** (unloaded) cargo. *Barang-barang ~ dikeluarkan dari gudang.* The (unloaded) goods were cleared from the warehouse.

kebongkaran (*coq*) robbed, broken into a house. *Si A ~.* A's house has been broken into.

pembongkar unloader, housebreaker, demolisher, s.o. who reveals/exposes.

pembongkaran 1 demolition, pulling down (of a house, etc.). **2** unloading, discharge. **3** forcing open, breaking into, burglary. **4** unmasking, revealing, exposure, exposing. ~ *jaringan mata-mata* exposing a spy ring.

bongkar II name of a *ceki* card.

bongkas → BUNGKAS.

bongko (*Jv*) k.o. cake made with peanuts. – *kopyor* k.o. steamed cake made with rice flour and coconut milk. – *menir* cooked rice with coconut milk. – *pisang* k.o. cake made with rice and bananas.

bongkok *si* – a) hunchback. b) pistol, revolver. c) shrimp. d) the tow truck of the Mobile Brigade Search and Rescue Team. e) a diesel locomotive provided with a crane for lifting derailed train coaches or overturned railway carriages; → BUNGKUK.

membongkok to bend over.

membongkoki (*pl obj*) to bend/twist s.t.

membongkokkan to bend s.t.

bongkol → BONGGOL. **1** lump, hump. **2** outgrowth. **3** knot (in a tree). **4** head (of lettuce).

bongkong (*M*) **1** misshapen, deformed, be out of proportion. **2** stupid, retarded, mentally deficient. *mati* – to die in vain.

bongkor k.o. basket (of bark, for collecting honeycombs).

bongkoran (*Jv*) lying fallow.

bongkot (*J/Jv*) **1** stem, stalk, stump (of a tree). **2** cabbage stalk. **3** (*bio*) caudex.

bongkotan with a stump, etc.

bongkrék (*Jv*) peanut residue, remains of peanuts after the oil has been extracted; → BUNGKIL. *témpé* – fermented bean cake made with peanut residue.

bonglai cassumar ginger, *Zingiber cassumunar*, used as a febrifuge and in embrocations for lumbago.

bonglak (*J*) broken off (of round things, such as, marbles, etc.).

bongméh (*C J*) **membongméh 1** to take one's pulse. **2** to feel s.o. out, sound s.o.

bongok I short and stumpy; squat.

bongok II (*M*) stupid.

bongor → BUNGUR.

bongpai (*C*) gravestone.

bongsang (*J*) fruit basket.

bongso (*IBT*) youngest, last (of children); → BUNGSU. *saudara* – youngest brother.

bongsor (*J/Jv*) **1** tall and oversized (of body), growing fast. **2** to thrive. *anak/bayi* – a child/baby who is thriving.

bonjol and **bonjolan** (*ob*) **1** bump, bump, protuberance. **2** projecting outward. **3** to protrude.

berbonjol humped.

mbonjolin (*J*) to defeat, beat (in sports).

bonjor (*M ob*) fortification.

bonorowo (*Jv*) low-lying arable land (in the rainy season inundated), generally located at estuaries of river basins; excellent land for planting kenaf.

bonsai (*Jp*) bonsai.

membonsaikan to dwarf by bonsai. *Jambu dibonsaikan.* A guava tree has been dwarfed.

pembonsai bonsai grower.

bontak (*M*) chubby, bulging (of cheeks).

bonto(h) (*J*) no longer fresh (of fish), rotten.

bontos I cross cuts at both ends of a log.

bontos II pitch, the thick residue obtained after straining tar.

bontot I (*J*) youngest.

bontot II (*Jv*) **membontot** to wrap food in leaves for a trip.

bontotan food supply wrapped in leaves from the teak tree.

bonus (*D/E*) bonus.

bonyok I (*J*) (beaten) black and blue. *Muka ini rasanya sudah –.- kena gebuk.* It looks as if his face has been beaten black and blue.

bonyok II and **bonyor** (*Jv*) overripe (of fruits), soft and rotten (of fish/meat, etc.).

bonyok III (*Pr*) [bokap + nyokap] parents.

bonyor → BONYOK I.

booking (*E*) /buking/ to book (a seat, etc.). *Saya – tikét Malaysian Airlines systém untuk pulang-pergi Médan-Pénang-Médan.* I booked a seat with MAS for a roundtrip Medan-Penang-Medan.

bo'ol (*J*) anus, rectum; → ANUS, DUBUR, PELEPASAN 4.

membo'ol and **ngebo'ol** to sodomize.

bo'ol-bo'olan sodomy.

boom (*D ob*) /bom/ Customs Office; → BOM III.

boomklérk (*D ob*) /bomklérek/ Customs clerk.

boomzaken (*D ob*) /bomsaken/ Customs business.

bo'ong (*J*) → BOHONG.

boorwater (*D*) /borwater/ boric acid.

bopelo (*J D*) the popular name for a (public) square in Jakarta, near the place where formerly the van Heutz monument was located.

bopéng (*C?*) **1** pock(mark), a scar on the skin left by a pustule caused by smallpox or some other disease. **2** pockmarked. **3** damaged by syphilis. **4** potholed (of streets due to heavy rainfall).

membopéngkan to make s.o. pockmarked, pothole.

bopéngan pockmarked, potholed.

boper (*E*) buffer. – *angin/udara* air buffer.

bopét → BUFÉT.

bopo(k) (*C*) **1** damaged, worn out, in bad shape. **2** (physically) weak.

bopong (*J/Jv*) **membopong** to carry in the arms, *esp* against the chest.

bopongan 1 carried in the arms. **2** sling for carrying in one's arms.

pembopong supporter.

Bopunjur [Bogor-Puncak-Cianjur] the Bogor-Puncak-Cianjur region.

bor I (*D*) drill, auger, bit. – *batu* rock drill. – *bit* auger. – *cekrék* ratchet drill. – *kecil* gimlet. – *kotrék* brace (the tool). – *linggis* pick hammer. – *listrik* electric drill. – *pahat* chisel auger. – *paku* gimlet. – *pembenam* countersink. – *pilin* screw auger. – *putar* rotary drill. – *séndok* auger bit. – *sentak* small compressed-air drill. – *tanah* earth auger. – *tangan* hand drill. – *tekan* drill press. – *tutukan* percussion drill. – *udara* air drill. – *ulir* twist drill.

membor and **mengebor** [and **ngebor** (*coq*)] to drill, bore.

pembor and **pengebor 1** (foreman) driller. **2** drilling (instrument).

pemboran and **pengeboran 1** (*petro*) drilling. ~ *darat* onshore drilling. ~ *keluar* drilling out. ~ *lepas pantai* offshore drilling. ~ *minyak di darat* onshore oil drilling. *téhnik ~ lumpur* drilling-mud technology. ~ *sisipan* infill drilling. ~ *tembus* drilling in. ~ *terarah* directional drilling. **2** (oil-well) drilling site.

bor II (*D*) **1** nameplate (on building). **2** blackboard.

borak I (*A*) the Prophet Muhammad's horse, a winged steed with human head which carried him to heaven, k.o. Pegasus; → BOURAQ.

borak II (*D*) borax.

borak III insipid (of tobacco).

boraks → BORAK II.

borang I (*Mal*) (application or official) form. – *langganan* subscription form.

borang II (*J*) booby trap of sharpened bamboo points stuck in the ground.

borang III (*S*) various species of trees, *Trevesia spp.*

borat (*D*) borate.

Borbon (*D*) Bourbon.

borboran (*J*) bloody; blood-stained; covered with blood.

borci (*Tam ob*) k.o. gold paper used in decoration.

bordél (*D coq*) gold paper used in embroidery; → BORDIR.

borderi spangles.

bordés (*D*) balustrade.

bordil (*D*) brothel.

bordir (*D*) embroidery.

berbordir embroidered. *Tuti yang ketika itu belum dandan, mengenakan kaos mérah ~ bunga dan celana hot pants biru.* Tuti, who at that time was not yet dressed up, put flower-embroidered red socks on and wore blue hot pants. *gaun ~* an embroidered gown.

membordir(kan) to embroider s.t. (on to s.t.).

bordiran embroidery.

bordir-bordiran embroidery.

bordu (*Port naut ob*) gunwale, railing.

boreh (*D*) **1** security, guaranty, an asset used to secure a loan. **2** guarantor. *menjadi –* and

memborehi to become surety (for), put up security for.

memborehkan to put s.t. up as security/collateral.

borehan *uang ~* security, guaranty.

boréh (*Jv*) cream ointment, yellow cosmetic.

memboréhi to apply such a cosmetic on.

borék *bapak –, anak berinték* "if the father is spotted, the offspring will be speckled," i.e., like father, like son.

borg → BOREH.

borgol (*J*) handcuffs, manacles; → BELENGGU.

memborgol to (hand)cuff, put cuffs on. *Dengan tangan diborgol, Ny. LKL diserahkan ke Kejaksaan Tinggi.* Handcuffed, Mrs. LKL was transferred to the High Prosecutor's Office.

borgolan handcuffs.

pemborgolan handcuffing, cuffing.

borhan (*A*) proof, evidence; → BURHAN.

borju bourgeois.

borjuasi (*D*) bourgeoisie.

borjuis (*D*) bourgeois.

borkol (*D*) kale.

bornal (*naut*) scupper.

Bornéo an island politically divided among the Republic of Indonesia (Kalimantan), Malaysia (called Sarawak) and Brunei Darussalam. *orang –* Borneans.

Bornean tallow (*E*) or Tilipe nuts, the export name for the *tengkawang* nuts.

boro (*Jv*) **1** to go to another place (away from home) to stay and work there as a casual worker, etc. *rumah –* (in Surabaya) dwelling for seasonal workers, for out-of-town workers who will stay there for a short time. **2** (*esp* in Semarang) vagabond, wanderer; → PENGEMBARA.

boro-boro (*J*) **1** let alone, much less. – *seratus pérak, sepérak saja saya tidak punya.* I don't even have one rupiah, let alone one hundred. **2** instead of; → ALIH-ALIH. – *pergi libur, kami merancang mengisi liburan untuk Karang Taruna.* Instead of going on vacation, we planned to spend the vacation at *Karang Taruna.* **3** to say nothing of, not to mention. *Tapi bila nasib sial, – untung, seharian penuh tak mendapat uang.* But when luck is not with you, to say nothing of profit, you won't make any money the entire day.

boroh → BOREH.

borok → BURUK. **1** ulcer, boil; scabies; abscess; suppurating skin disease. **2** (*coq*) to have an ulcer/scabies, etc. **3** potholes (in a street). **4** rottenness, decay, deterioration. *melenyapkan – perkumpulan itu* to eliminate the deterioration of the club.

berborok to have ulcers, ulcerated.

memborok to ulcerate, suppurate, fester.

borokan to suffer from ulcers, etc., ulcerated.

borong wholesale. *Toko itu tidak menjual secara écéran tapi secara – saja.* That store doesn't sell retail but only wholesale. *pasar –* wholesale market. *pedagang –* wholesaler.

memborong 1 to buy up (an entire lot/a large quantity), buy s.t.

wholesale. *Kain putih itu diborong pedagang-pedagang dari pedalaman.* The white fabric was bought wholesale by merchants from the interior. 2 to walk away with. *Dia berhasil ~ 2 buah piala.* He succeeded in walking away with 2 trophies. 3 to rent, hire. *Mobil itu diborong satu minggu.* The car was rented for a week. 4 to do (a job) on a contract basis. *Pekerjaan itu diborong tukang cat.* The job was contracted for by a painter. 5 to hold a number of (jobs). *Ketiga jabatan tinggi itu diborongnya semua.* He himself took in hand all three top positions.

memborongi (*pl obj*) to buy up.

memborongkan 1 to sell wholesale. *Ayah saya telah ~ hasil tanamannya kepada seorang pedagang Cina.* My father sold the yield of his crops wholesale to a Chinese merchant. 2 to make a contract with, contract out. *Pemerintah telah ~ pembangunan rumah-rumah murah itu.* The government has contracted out the building of inexpensive houses.

borongan 1 job/piece work, contracted. *pekerjaan ~* work contracted for. *penerbangan ~* charter flight. 2 wholesale. *Jeruk ini dijual ~.* These oranges are sold wholesale.

pemborong 1 wholesaler. 2 contractor.

pemborongan contracting, tendering, act of buying or selling wholesale. *~ pekerjaan* contracting for work.

boros 1 spendthrift, extravagant, wasteful, lavish. *orang – a spendthrift. Uang simpanannya sedikit saja karena dia bersikap –.* He has only a few savings because he's a spendthrift. 2 loose, unwound. *Tali gasingnya –.* The string of his top got loose.

memboros 1 to let out, ease off (a rope). 2 to spend freely/lavishly, squander, waste, expend uselessly.

memborosi (*pl obj*) to squander, waste.

memboroskan to spend freely, squander, waste. *Harta peninggalan orangtuanya habis diboroskannya.* He squandered his parents' estate down to the last penny.

keborosan extravagance, wastefulness, prodigality. *Oléh karena ~nya, gajinya yang besar itu tidak cukup untuk menanggung keluarganya.* Owing to his extravagance, his large salary was insufficient to support his family.

pemboros spendthrift, squanderer, wastrel.

pemborosan wasting, waste of money, squandering, extravagance. *~ uang dan tenaga* a waste of money and energy.

borstel (*D*) brush.

bortel → WORTEL.

boru (*Bat*) daughter of the ... clan. *– Nasution* daughter of the Nasution clan.

borwater (*D*) boracic lotion.

bos I (*D*) bundle (of grass, etc.), bunch (*of rambutan*, etc.), small carton (of cigarettes).

bos II (*E*) boss, head (of a company or organization).

bosah-basih (*Jv*) in confusion, confused, in a mess.

bosan (*Jv*) tired/sick (of), bored (with), fed up (with). *Saya sudah – makan ikan.* I'm sick of eating fish. *– dengan/pada* sick/tired of, fed up with. *– hidup* world weary.

bosan-bosannya *tidak ~* untiring, unwearyingly, unflagging.

membosankan [and **ngebosanin** (*J coq*)] 1 to bore, satiate, make s.o. tired of. *Acara-acara resmi di Washington ~ para pengusaha yang ikut misi.* The official agendas in Washington were boring the businessmen who joined the (trade)mission. 2 boring, tedious, monotonous. *pekerjaan yang ~* a monotonous job.

kebosanan 1 boredom, tiresomeness, tedium, weariness, ennui. *~ ini mendadak berubah menjadi kegembiraan.* This boredom suddenly changed into enthusiasm. 2 disgust, aversion, dislike. 3 (*J*) repletion, satiation, saturation.

pembosan s.o. who becomes bored/gets fed up very easily/quickly.

pembosanan boring, wearying.

bosanova bossa nova.

berbosanova to dance the bossa nova.

bosé → JAGUNG *bosé.*

bosen → BOSAN. **mbosenin** and **ngebosenin** (*J coq*) → MEMBOSANKAN.

boséta (*Port ob*) a small basket or box.

bosman (*D*) boatswain.

bosor 1 pierced, with a hole in it; broken through; → BOCOR. 2 *– makan* gluttonous, voracious.

bostan (*cla*) → BUSTAN.

bot I (*E*) *sepatu –* boots.

bot II (*D*) boat (which uses an engine or motor). *– polis marin* PD marine police boat.

bot III (*D J*) 1 bread. 2 word shouted by the bread man in selling his merchandise along the street.

bota → BUTA II.

botak I bald(headed).

membotak to become bald. *Kepalanya mulai ~.* He's getting bald.

membotaki 1 to shave s.o. bald. 2 to strip completely bare.

membotakkan to make bald. *Penyakit itu telah ~ kepalanya.* The illness has made him bald.

kebotak(-botak)an baldness.

botak II *burung –* lesser adjutant stork, *Leptoptilos javanicus;* → BURUNG *babi.*

botana various species of decorative fishes, surgeons. *– biru* powder blue surgeonfish/tang, *Acanthurus leucosternum. – kacamata* red-tailed surgeonfish, Achilles tang, *Acanthurus achilles. – kasur* clown surgeon/tang, striped surgeonfish, *Acanthurus lineatus*

botang → BUTANG.

botani (*D*) botany.

botanikus (*D*) botanist.

botanist (*D/E*) botanist(s).

botaniwan botanist.

botapora (*Port ob*) pin-money.

bot, bot (*onom*) beep, beep (sound of a horn).

botékan (*Jv*) chest to store herbal preparations in traditional houses on Java, *usu* located in the center-room of the house.

botelir (*D*) steward (on a ship).

boti → BO'AT II.

boti-boti a sailing prau of the Buton islanders (South Sulawesi).

botik → BUTIK.

boto (*J*) and **botoh I** (*S*) (to look) pretty, charming, attractive.

botoh II (*Jv*) 1 gambler. *– kartu* s.o. who plays cards for money. 2 arbiter, referee.

berbotoh to bet.

botohan bet.

botok (*Jv*) dish of steamed shredded coconut, salt fish, and chili, wrapped in banana leaf; → BEBOTOK.

botol (*E*) 1 bottle. *membawa – (minuman) sendiri* bring your own bottle, BYOB. *tukang –* junkman (who mainly deals in used bottles). 2 bottled (in set expressions). *téh –* bottled tea, tea in bottles. *susu –* bottled milk. *– air* canteen, i.e., a metal flask, *usu* encased in canvas, for carrying drinking water. *– dot* baby bottle. *– hampa udara* thermos bottle. *– semprot* siphon. *– takaran* flask with graduated markings. *– udara* compressed air bottle. *– vakum*

berbotol-botol several/some/a few bottles, many bottles. *Minuman keras diténggaknya ~.* He downed a few bottles of alcoholic drinks.

membotoli to bottle, put s.t. in a bottle.

membotolkan to bottle s.t.

pembotolan bottling.

botor (*J/Jv*) *kacang –* winged bean, *Psophocarpus tetragonolobus.*

botram (*D*) lunch box.

bot-répot (*Jv*) troubles. *ikut membantu –nya di rumah tangga mertua* to lend a hand in the troubles of the in-laws' household.

botulisme (*D/E*) botulism. *– bayi* infant botulism. *– luka* wound botulism. *peracunan pangan* food-poisoning botulism.

bou → BO.

bouraq (*A*) a winged bird with the body of a horse and the face of a fairy wearing a crown on her head ridden by the Prophet Muhammad.

Bouraq Indonesian Airlines name of a privately owned airline; → *kuda* BERAKSA.

bouwhéér (*D ob*) /bohér/ building contractor.

boven (*D ob*) /bofen/ *naar –* /nar bofen/ (to go) to the mountains (for relaxation or sexual fun).

bow → BO.

bowés (*D*) *nomor –* license number registration card; → NOMOR *bewés.*

bowling (*E*) → BOLING.

bowong a person (= *wong* in Javanese) who pulls a plow to replace a water buffalo (= *kebo* in Javanese).

boy → SELONONG *boy*.

boya I (*E*) (*naut*) buoy.

boya II to fall to pieces.

   memboya to let fall to pieces.

boyak I 1 insipid (due to dryness/rottenness, etc.); monotonous, tedious (of work). **2** dissatisfied; bored.

   memboyakkan to bore.

   keboyakan dissatisfaction; boredom.

boyak II squat, short and fat.

Boyan (*Mal*) (*Pulau* –) the Isle of Bawean, between Java and Kalimantan. *orang* – a "Boyanese," i.e., a person from Bawean.

boyas (*ob*) big- (pot-)bellied, having a big belly from pregnancy.

Boyo clipped form of Suroboyo (= Surabaya).

boyo-boyo (*naut*) hatch-beam.

boyok (*Jv*) waist, the small of the back. *penyakit* – kidney ailment.

boyong (*Jv*) to move with one's family/all one's belongings elsewhere; *cp* BORO. – *pulang* to go back home.

   berboyong to migrate, immigrate, emigrate, transmigrate, move, resettle, relocate. *Banyak petani* ~ *ke Lampung.* Many peasants are relocating to Lampung.

   memboyong 1 to (re)move/transfer/shift elsewhere. **2** to capture, carry off. *Tim Jakarta* ~ *piala "Proton Fulét Électronic Industrial.* The Jakarta team carried off the "Proton Fulet Electronic Industrial" cup.

   boyongan 1 s.o. who relocates to another place. **2** movement, removal, migration, immigration, emigration. **3** to move, go (somewhere else).

   pemboyong migrant, immigrant, emigrant.

   pemboyongan migration, immigration, emigration, migration, movement, removal.

boyot (*S*) to emerge slowly.

bozah (*Pers*) fermented spirits.

BPKB (*init*) [Buku Pemilik Kendaraan Bermotor] Motor Vehicle Owner's Book.

BPPN (*init*) [Badan Penyéhatan Perbankan Indonésia] Indonesian Bank Restructuring Agency, IBRA.

BPPT → BADAN *Pengkajian dan Penerapan Téknologi.*

BPS [Badan Pusat Statistik] Central Bureau of Statistics.

br- I also see entries beginning with **ber-**.

br II (*abbr*) → BORU.

B.R. III [barang] illegal drugs.

braak (*onom*) sound of slamming, breaking, colliding.

Brahman (and **Brahmin**) (*cla*) member of the highest, or priestly, class among the Hindus; *cp* KESATRIA, SUDRA, WAISYA.

Brahmana member of the first Hindu caste of priests (in Bali).

Brahmani (*cla*) a woman of the Brahman class.

brai → CUT *brai*.

B.R.Aj. [Bendara Radén Ajeng] title for an unmarried princess.

brak, brak (*onom*) cracking sound of breaking tiles.

brambang (*Jv*) shallot, red onion, *Alium cepa*; → BAWANG *mérah*.

   brambangan French grass?, *Aneilema malabaricum*.

brandal → BERANDAL. **brandalan** troublemaker, juvenile delinquent.

brander (*D ob*) burner.

brandgang (*D ob*) fire lane.

brandwéér (*D ob*) fire department; → BRANWIR, DINAS *kebakaran*, PEMADAM *kebakaran.*

brangasan 1 (*Jv*) hot, spicy. **2** (*J*) pugnacious, competitive, bellicose, irascible.

brang-bring-bréng (*onom*) sound of hammering/construction.

branggah (*Jv*) *tanduk* – widespread antlers.

brangkar → BRANKAR.

brangus → BERANGUS.

branjang (*Jv*) small square fishing net.

   branjangan (*Jv*) Australasian bush lark, *Mirafra javanica.*

brankar (*D ob*) stretcher.

brankas (*D ob*) strongbox, safe.

brantam → BERHANTAM.

Brantas name of a train running between Jakarta and Kediri; → BERANTAS.

Branti name of the airport in Banjarlampung.

branwir → BRANDWÉÉR.

braok loud, shrill (of voices).

Brasil(ia) Brazil(a).

braso Brasso, a brand name of a brass, copper; chromium, etc. cleanser and polisher.

   membraso to apply this cleanser to s.t.

brata penyepian (*Bal*) vow (of abstention).

bratawali (*Jv*) /broto-/ a plant whose bitter-tasting leaves are used in folk medicine, *Tinospora tuberculata.*

Bratayud(h)a (*Jv*) a Javanese version of the heroic struggle between the five Pandawa and their cousins, the Kurawa, as described in the Indian epic poem, the *Mahab(h)arata.*

bratu (*Jv*) **1** advance money [to gamble (further) with; advance (on loan)]. **2** bonus.

Bravo Hotél CB-er's term, used jokingly to refer to BH 'bra'; → BH.

Brawijaya → BHRAWIJAYA.

bray → CUTBRAI.

brayat (*Jv*) nuclear family, parents and their children.

BRD I [Bank Rakyat Désa] Village Bank.

BRD II [Barat-Daya] Southwest, S.W.

brebet-brebet (*onom*) to defecate by fits and starts combined with farting; *opp* PLUNG.

brédel (*D*) → BRÉIDEL.

breg (*onom*) sound of s.t. heavy falling, crash.

bregedél (*D*) minced meat ball; → PERKEDÉL. – *jagung* corn-patties.

bregogo (*Jv*) military company of the Yogyakarta *kraton.*

bréidel (*D*) **1** bridle, ban, prohibition. **2** closing down (a newspaper, etc.).

   membréidel 1 to bridle, curb. **2** to ban, revoke a (newspaper's) license, close down.

   pembréidelan 1 bridling, curbing. **2** ban, prohibition, closing down.

bréien (*D ob*) to knit.

bréksi (*geol E*) breccia.

brem (*Jv/Bal*) **1** rice brandy, a sweet sherry made from fermented black rice. **2** k.o. cookies made of fermented rice.

brén (*D*) clipped from of **bréngun**.

   membrén to shoot with a bren-gun.

bréndi (*E*) brandy.

brengbrengan (*Jv*) strong smelling.

brengos (*Jv*) **1** mustache. **2** block chief (in a prison).

   brengosan mustachioed.

bréngsék (*J*) **1** bad, evil, wicked, mean, rude, **2** lousy, rotten. *cuaca yang* – lousy weather. *mobil* – jalopy. **3** arbitrary, high-handed. **4** unfit for use, unserviceable. **5** (*sl*) damn it! –*! Mau tau urusan orang!* Damn it! You're always sticking your nose into s.o. else's business!

   sebréngsék as lousy/rotten as.

   terbréngsék the worst/lousiest.

   kebréngsékan garbage, junk, anything worthless; lousiness (of traffic conditions, etc.).

brenjol and **brenjul** (*Jv*) uneven, rough, bumpy.

   membrenjol-brenjolkan to turn over (soil). *Sekarang dengan adanya gardening, tanah malah dibrenjol-brenjolkan.* Now that there is some gardening, the soil is being turned up.

brenti → BERHENTI.

bret 1 (exclamation used to express sudden and swift action), zap. *Tangan panjang main* – *aja.* It was a great day for pickpockets. **2** sound made by a rapidly spreading fire. –*. Api menjilat sekujur tubuh Djunaidi.* Whoosh. The fire licked at Djunaidi's body. **3** sound of a knife slashing through s.t.

brétél (*D*) suspenders.

brevét (*D*) **1** brevet, badge. **2** k.o. license.

brevir (*D*) breviary.

bréwok (*Jv*) long sideburns.

   bréwokan with sideburns.

bridge (*E*) /brits/ **1** bridge (the card game). *main* – to play bridge. **2** bridge (of a ship).

bri(e)fing (*E*) briefing; → SANTIAJI.

brig (in acronyms) → BRIGADE, BRIGADIR.

brigade (*D*) brigade. – *Anjing* K-9 Brigade. – *Mobil* [Brimob] Mobile Brigade. – *Satwa* K-9 Brigade. – *Tempur* Combat Brigade.

brigadir (D) brigadier. - *jénderal* [brigjén] brigadier general. - *polisi* police brigadier.

brigjén [brigadir jénderal] brigadier general.

brik (E) (CB-term) a call.

ngebrik to call.

brikdéns (E) break-dance.

brikét (D/E) briquette.

pembrikétan molding into briquettes.

bril (D ob) eye-glasses; → KACAMATA I.

brilian and brilyan (D) brilliance.

kebrilyanan brilliance, brilliancy.

Brilkrim (E) brand name of a hair cream, Brillcream.

Brimob [Brigade-mobil] Mobile Brigade.

bringas → BERINGAS.

brinji (Jv?) Javan streaked bulbul, golden bulbul, *Ixus virescens/ affinis*.

brintik (Jv) curly (haired), kinky.

brintil (Jv) curly, kinky. *rambut* – curly/kinky hair.

bripét → BREVÉT.

Bripda [Brigadir Polisi Dua] Second Police Brigadier.

Bripka [Brigadir Polisi Kepala] Chief Police Brigadier.

Briptu [Brigadir Polisi Satu] First Police Brigadier.

brisan (D) *bom* – highly explosive/brisant bomb.

brisik (J/Jv) 1 noisy, tumultuous, boisterous. 2 uproar, noise. *dengan suara* – in a loud voice. *Telinganya* –. His ears are ringing.

brital → BRUTAL.

Britania Raya Great Britain.

Britis (E) British.

B.R.M. [Bendara Radén Mas) title for a young unmarried prince.

brobos (Jv) to crawl through an opening, creep under. *upacara* – to "honor" a corpse, request a favor by respectfully bending the back and crawling under the bier that is ready to be carried on the shoulders to the cemetery, one after the other.

brobot → BEROBOT.

brocél (Jv) uneven, not smooth.

brodkas (E infr) broadcast.

brodol (Jv) timeworn.

brojol (Jv) m(em)brojol 1 to come out (of a hole). 2 to come out (unexpectedly).

brok (Jv) ngebroki to occupy (a house).

brokat (D) brocade.

broker (E) broker.

brokohan (Jv) a religious ritual for a child at birth when the umbilical cord drops off.

brokoli (E) (*sayur* –) broccoli.

brom (E) broom.

bromocorah (Jv) 1 riffraff, rabble, scum, underworld. 2 Robin Hood. 3 habitual criminal, recidivist, ex-convict.

bromocurah → BROMOCORAH.

bromokroso (D) flower parade.

brompit (D) motorbike.

broncés → ONCÉS.

brondol (Jv) 1 to molt, shed one's feathers. 2 to fall off.

brondong I → BERONDONG. - *jagung* a) popcorn. b) an infectious sexual disease, *Kondiloma akuminata*; → JÉNGGÉR *ayam*.

brondongan (Jv) salvo, (volley of) gunfire.

brondong II (sl) gigolo (for older women).

brongkol (Jv) lump under the skin.

brongkos (Jv) a vegetable side dish seasoned with *kluwak*.

bronjong (Jv) 1 (cylinder-shaped) large bamboo basket (for packing sugar/pigs, etc.). 2 gabion, a wire basket filled with stones, etc. used to prevent floods/landslides, etc.

bronk(h)itis (D) bronchitis. - *kronis* chronic bronchitis.

bronkhus (E) bronchus, windpipe.

bronki (D) bronchi

bros I (D) crisps, brittle.

bros II (E) brush cut.

bros III (D) brooch.

brosot (Jv) membrosot to sneak out (without saying good-bye).

brosur (D) brochure.

membrosurkan to put out in the form of a brochure.

broti → BEROTI.

brotowali → BRATAWALI.

B.R.T. (abbr) [Bendara Radén Tumenggeng] title for a courtier.

bruder (D) Roman Catholic clergyman/friar.

bruderan Catholic seminary.

kebruderan Christian brothers' school.

brujul (Jv) a small plow without a moldboard.

membrujul to plow.

brujulan plowing.

bruk (onom) crash! sound of s.t. falling down.

brunai → BERUNAI.

Brunei Darussalam the State of Brunei the Abode of Peace.

brunét (D) brunette.

brus (E) brush.

Brussel Brussels.

brutal (D/E) 1 brutal.

kebrutalan brutality.

brutalisme (D/E) brutalism.

bruto (D) gross (weight, profit, etc.).

brutu (Jv) coccyx (of chickens where the tail-feathers grow).

bruwet (Jv) indistinct, obscure. *Tampangnya* –. His features were not clearly visible.

bt (abbr) [Binti] daughter of (in Muslim names).

BT (init) → BÉTÉ.

btj (abbr) [bagian tiap juta] parts per million.

BTL [Batak Témbak Langsung] straight-shooter Batak, a reference to the supposed blunt and straightforward style of Bataks.

bu 1 (the clipped form of *ibu* mother. 2 (term of address) mother; wife; order and/or higher-status woman. 3 [vocative short form for female domestic servant *babu*] *bu!* - *dé* (Jv) short for *ibu gedé* aunt (parent's older sister). - *guru* (in addressing a female teacher) teacher! - *lik* (Jv) short for *ibu cilik* aunt (parent's younger sister). - *Tjitro* Mrs. Tjitro, a name closely linked to the best Yogyakarta *gudeg* sold in restaurants in Jakarta and other cities.

buagus very good; → BAGUS.

buah 1 fruit (growing on tree). *Pohon ini tak berapa banyak –nya*. This tree does not bear a lot of fruit. 2 classifier for either large objects without any definite shape or kind, such as, *dua – kampung*, or for abstracts, such as, *beberapa – aliran kebatinan* several mystical trends. 3 seed that is quite big and hard. - *kemiri/ keras/kéréh* (in West Sumatra) candlenut, *Aleurites moluccana*. 4 part of s.t. that resembles a fruit. - *guli* marble. 5 result, outcome. *Inilah – daripada jerih payah orangtuamu*. This is the result of the efforts of your parents. 6 origin, subject, topic, theme. - *percakapan* a) the subject/topic of discussion. 7 the outcome/result of the discussion. - *masak tercantung tinggi, akan dijolok penggalah singkat, akan ditingkat batangnya licin* a) unable to achieve one's aspirations. b) (M) wants to study to get a high position, but doesn't have the money to do so. *sebab – dikenal pohonnya* a tree is known by its fruit. - *yang manis berulat di dalamnya* when the fox preaches, guard your geese. FOR NAMES OF FRUITS NOT FOUND HERE UNDER BUAH SEE THE SPECIFIC NAME. - *apokat/adpokat/ alpokat/alpukat* avocado. - *anggur* grape. - *apel* apple. - *ara* fig, *Ficus spp*. - *atep* (J) sugar-palm fruit eaten for dessert; → KOLANG-KALING I. - *baju* button. - *badam* almond, *Prunus spp*. - *baju* button. - *bengang* fruit which bursts open when ripe. - *beraksa* bullock's heart (formerly used as weights for scales). - *berangan* chestnut. - *berembang* a) the knob-like fruit of the *berembang* tree, *Sonneratia caseolaris*. b) the knob at the apex of a boat's mast. - *betis* calf (of the leg). - *bibir* subject/topic of conversation, much talked of, the talk of the town. **membuah-bibirkan** to discuss, converse, make s.t. the subject of conversation. *Bandar udara Soekarno-Hatta hendaknya menjadi - bibir. Bahkan agar dibuah-bibirkan ke seantéro dunia*. The Soekarno-Hatta airport should become the talk of the town. In fact, it should be the subject of conversation throughout the world. - *cakap* subject/topic of conversation, to be much talked of. - *catur* chess piece (any of the pieces used in the game of chess). - *céri* cherry. - *cinta* child. *Suami-istri Hérry dan Ninung, pasangan remaja yang bahagia, saat ini, menanti kepastian hadirnya - cinta meréka*. At this moment the happy, teenage married couple Herry and Ninung are waiting for the certainty of the appearance of their new arrival. – *congklak* seeds, shells of the *lokan*, etc. used in playing *congklak*. – *dacing* (scale) weights. – *dada* (woman's) breast, bosom; → PAYU-DARA. – *dadu* die. – *dam* checker piece. – *enau* sugar-palm fruit eaten for dessert; → KOLANG-KALING. – *ganda* (*bio*) aggregate fruit. – *geli-geli* kidneys. – *geluk* nut. – *ginjal* kidneys. – *gundi* k.o. fruit. – *harapan* hope. – *hasil* work, opus. – *hati* a) sweetheart, darling. b) favorite, any person whom one cherishes. – *hidup* fresh fruit. – *jingah* k.o. sweet-potato fritters. – *kacapuri* a *durian* fruit that has grown inside another. – *kalam* product of a pen, writings. – *kaléngan* canned fruit. – *kandungan* baby. – *karangan* work of literature. – *karangan ulung* masterpiece. – *karya* one's works. – *kata* subject/topic of conversation. – *kendaga* schizocarp. – *kering* dried fruit. – *keringat* the fruits of one's labor. – *kesenian* work of art. – *ginjal* kidneys. – *khuldi* the apple (in the garden of Eden). – *léci* litchis. – *lengan* biceps; → BISÉPS. – *lidah* subject/topic of conversation. – *mahoni* a fruit used as medicine against hypertension. – Makassar k.o. medicinal plant, Makassar kernels, *Brucea javanica*. – *mata* a) eye ball. b) apple of the eye, any person whom one loves. – *melaka* k.o. cake. – *mentéga* an edible fruit of a tree (ebony) with very hard wood, velvet apple, *Diospyros discolor*. – *mentah* unripe fruit. – *meriam* cannon ball. – *mimpi* s.t. seen in a dream. – *mulut* subject/topic of conversation, talk of the town. – *naga* dragon fruit, pitahaya, *Hylocereus undatus*. – *nona* custard apple, *Annona reticulata*. – *pala* nutmeg. – *pantat* the buttocks. – *pelaga* cardamom, *Amomum cardamomum*. – *pelajaran* subject of study. – *pelir* testicles. – *pembicaraan* subject/topic of conversation. – *péna* product of the pen, writing. – *perdébatan* subject of debate. – *perkakas* (*euph*) testicles. – *perkawinan* child, offspring. – *perundingan* subject of the discussions. – *pidato* subject of a speech. – *pikiran* reflection, contemplation, thought, idea, opinion, brainchild. – *pinggang* kidneys. – *polongan* a leguminous plant. – *punggang* kidneys. – *ranum* overripe fruit. – *rengas* k.o. cake. – *sabun* fruit from a tree, *Sapindus rarak*, which is used as soap. – *segar* fresh fruit. – *séri* cherry. – *semu* accessory fruit. – *sesentul* fruit that has pips. – *sulung* the first fruit, – *susu* Jamaican honeysuckle, passion fruit, *Passiflora laurifolia*. – *tahun* s.t. rare and unusual. – *tangan* a) a gift brought back from a trip; → OLÉH-OLÉH. b) literary work, creation. – *tasbih* a) rosary, string of beads for keeping count of prayers. b) type of plant, canna, *Canna orientalis*. – *tempurung* avocado, *Persea gratissima*. – *terlarang* forbidden fruit. – *tikus* wild water lemon, love-in-a-mist, *Passiflora foetida*. – *timbangan* (scale) weights. – *tunggal* simple fruit. – *tutur* subject/topic of conversation. – *undi* die. – *usaha* fruits of one's labor. – *zakar* testicles.

buah-buah scrotum.

sebuah (a counter) a, one – ~ *rumah* a house. ~ *cita-cita mulia* a noble aspiration. **menyebuahkan** (*infr*) to unite, make into one

berbuah 1 to bear fruit. *Rambutan itu sudah* ~. The *rambutan* tree has borne fruit. **2** to be successful. *Bisnisnya* ~. His business was successful.

berbuahkan to produce, yield. *Padi itu* ~ *emas*. The rice has produced gold.

membuah 1 to ripen. **2** to turn to fruit.

membuahi to impregnate, inseminate, fertilize.

membuahkan 1 to produce, yield, cause, bring forth. *Gerakan yang mendadak itu ternyata* ~ *hasil*. The surprise move turned out to be successful. ~ *kemungkinan-kemungkinan baru* to open up new possibilities. ~ *uang* to produce income. **2** to give birth to. ~ *seorang bayi yang lahir muda* to give birth to a premature baby. ~ *anak* fertile, able to bear children. *Suzzanna sudah memeriksakan diri ke dokter ahli kandungan, konon masih bisa* ~ *anak*. Suzzanna was examined by a gynecologist and she is still able to bear children. *tidak* ~ *turunan* to be childless. *Istrinya yang pertama tidak* ~ *turunan*. His first wife was childless.

terbuahi fertilized (of a flower, etc.).

buah-buahan 1 various fruits **2** artificial fruits. ~ *campur* mixed fruit, fruit cocktail.

pembuahan 1 impregnation, insemination. **2** fertilization, conception (conceiving in the womb), ovulation. ~ *alamiah* natural/in vivo insemination. ~ *buatan* artificial insemination. ~ *sendiri lengkap* autogamy.

perbuahan (*bio*) infructescence.

buai 1 swing, rock (as a cradle), sway. **2** (*phys*) pitch.
   berbuai(-buai) to swing, sway.
   membuai(kan) 1 to swing/rock s.t., make s.t. fluctuate. **2** to stroke.
   terbuai 1 swung. **2** lulled.
   terbuai-buai swinging, swaying, rocking, vibrating.
   buaian 1 cradle, gun cradle, swinging cot, hammock. **2** pendulum. ~ *diguncang, anak dicubit* to have a few tricks up one's sleeve.

buak I membuak to bubble up; → MEMBUAL.

buak II (*M ob*) to act strangely, improperly, in an unstable, fickle way.
   buak-buakan *orang* ~ k.o. Jekyll and Hyde personality, s.o. who can be nice but then can turn around and be vicious.

bual 1 bubbling (up), spouting, gushing out. **2** brag(ging), boast(ing). – *basung* hot air. ***membual basung*** to talk nonsense.
   berbual(-bual) and **membual 1** to boil over, bubble up. **2** to talk big, brag, chatter away.
   membualkan 1 to gossip about. **2** to brag about. **3** to expel s.t., spout. **4** conceited, proud.
   bualan 1 bubbling (up). **2** gossiping.
   pembual braggart, loudmouth.
   perbualan chatter.

buana (*Skr*) universe, world. – *agung* macrocosm. – *alit* microcosm.

Buanawan reporter for the daily "Berita Buana."

buang throw away, discard [appears in many compounds and other connections where also **membuang** and (to a lesser degree) **membuang-buang** could have been used, for instance: *hukuman* – exile, expulsion.] – *adat* to be ill-mannered. –.– *air* to suffer from diarrhea. – *air besar* to defecate. – *air darah* to suffer from dysentery. – *air kecil* to urinate. – *aksi* to have an attitude. – *ancak* to put a tray of offerings of food out for the spirits. – *angin* to break wind, fart. – *arang (di muka)* to eliminate shame. – *badan* (*sl*) to refuse to take responsibility for, wash one's hands of, completely ignore; → CUCI *tangan*. – *baka* to drag the good name of one's ancestors/family through the mud, dishonor the family name. – *belakang* a) to flee, escape, run away. b) to not want to know a thing about s.t. – *bicara* to acquit, dismiss a case (in court). – *bini* to divorce one's wife. – *bom* (*coq vulg*) to take a crap. – *dadu* to shoot dice. – *diri* a) to commit suicide. b) to withdraw, retreat. c) to go into seclusion, isolate o.s. – *hajat* to relieve o.s. *Sehabis* – *hajat memakai celananya kembali*. After relieving himself he put on his pants again. – *hamil* to abort. – *hidup* to expel, exile. – *ingus* to blow one's nose. – *jangkar* to cast anchor. – *keringat* to work hard. – *lambai* to wave the hands (in dancing). – *langkah* a) to flee, escape, run away. b) to execute certain steps (in *silat*, etc.). – *lelah/letih* to take a break/rest. – *lendir* (*vulg*) to get sexual satisfaction, get one's rocks off. – *malu* a) to take revenge. b) to circumcise. c) to get rid of one's shame. – *masa* to waste time. – *mata ke* to look at, glance at. – *muka* a) to turn one's eyes away, look the other way, turn one's back on. – *muka kepada orang-tua* to disregard one's parents. b) to be contemptuous/disdainful. – *mulut* to say s.t. vaguely/not straightforwardly. – *nahas* to get rid of ill-luck. – *nama* to disgrace/bring shame upon one's name. – *nyawa* a) to die; to sacrifice o.s. b) to risk one's life. – *obat* to fire a shot at random. – *ongkos* to spend money; to be fortunate. – *pandang* to look at, glance at. – *peluru* to put the shot. – *penat* to take a break/rest. – *sauh* to cast/drop anchor. – *senyum* to smile. – *sepanjang adat* to expel from customs and traditions. – *setir* to turn the steering wheel sharply. – *sial* to get rid of bad luck. – *sikap* a) to walk, etc. in an affected manner. b) to get rid of an attitude. – *sipat* (*Pal*) to do s.o. bodily harm. – *tabiat* to act differently than usual. – *tangan* to swing one's hand to hit/beat, etc. – *témbakan* to fire a shot at random. – *témpo* to waste time. – *tenaga* to work hard. – *tingkah* a) to walk, etc. in an affected manner. b) to get rid of an attitude. – *tubuh ke laut* to plunge into the sea. – *undi* a) to shoot dice. b) to draw lots. – *waktu* a) to waste time. b) to devote time to.

membuang 1 to throw, hurl, fling. **2** to throw away, discard, get rid of. *habis manis sepah dibuang* to take advantage of s.o./s.t. and then toss him/it away; to be ungrateful to s.o. ~ *kerja* to fire, dismiss from a job. ~ *lalu* to slow down. **3** to divert (from a course, etc.), deflect. *lalu lintas yang dibuang ke Pecenongan* the traffic which was diverted to Pecenongan. **4** to remove, delete, get ride of, strike out. *Koma di kalimat ini baik dibuang saja.* It would be better to omit the comma in this sentence. **5** to waste, squander (money). **6** to exile, banish. *Dahulu banyak orang Indonésia dibuang ke Boven Digul.* Formerly many Indonesians were exiled to Boven Digul. **7** to eliminate from the body. ~ *air besar* to defecate. ~ *air darah* dysentery. ~ *air kecil* to urinate. ~ *anak* to refuse to acknowledge one's child. ~ *angin* to pass gas, break wind, fart; → **KENTUT.** ~ *aksi* to strike an attitude. ~ *anak* to no longer recognize a child. ~ *ancak* to offer food to spirits. ~ *angkar* to cast anchor. ~ *arang di muka* to get rid of shame. ~ *asmara* to make love. ~ *baka* to sully the name of one's ancestors. ~ *bala* to avoid conflicts or illnesses. ~ *belakang* a) to run away, flee, retreat. b) to turn one's back on a problem. ~ *belakang* to retreat. ~ *belanja* to throw away money on useless items. ~ *bini* to divorce one's wife. ~ *dadu* to play dice. ~ *diri* a) to commit suicide. b) to withdraw into solitude. c) to leave one's home area for faraway places. ~ *garam ke laut* to do s.t. useless. ~ *hajat* to defecate. ~ *hamil* to have an abortion. ~ *hidup* to exile. ~ *ingus* to blow one's nose. ~ *lambai* to wave one's hands (in a dance). ~ *langkah* a) to flee, escape, run away. b) to take a step backward (in *pencak*). ~ *lelah/letih* to take a break, rest. ~ *ludah* to spit. ~ *malu* a) to get rid of shame. b) to take revenge to wipe out shame. ~ *mata* a) to avoid looking at s.t. (for instance, s.o. disliked), turn away/aside. b) to glance at. ~ *muka* a) to avert one's eyes, be unwilling to look at. b) to dislike. c) to not pay attention to. ~ *muka kepada orang-tua* to disregard one's parents. ~ *mulut* to say s.t. insincerely. ~ *nama* to disgrace s.o.'s name. ~ *napas panjang* to exhale. ~ *nyawa* a) to die. b) to sacrifice one's life. c) to face mortal danger intentionally. ~ *pal* (*naut*) to tack, sail in a crisscross way against the wind. ~ *pandang* to glance (at), look around (at). ~ *penat* to take a break, rest. ~ *peran* (*naut*) to turn (a ship/kite, etc.) to the left and to the right. ~ *perum* to take a sounding to find out the depth. ~ *sampah* to throw away the garbage. ~ *sauh* to drop anchor. ~ *senyum* to smile. ~ *sepanjang adat* to expel s.o. from the *adat* community on account of his opposing the *adat*. ~ *setir* to turn the steering wheel, make a sharp turn. ~ *sial* to try to get rid of bad luck by holding a *selamatan*. ~ *sipat* (*Pal*) to do s.o. bodily harm. ~ *sirih* to expel s.o. from a group. ~ *tangan* a) to sway with the hands when walking. b) to move the hands to deliver a blow (in *silat*, etc.). ~ *témbakan* to fire a shot in a ceremony honoring s.o. ~ *témpo* to waste time. ~ *tenaga* to work hard. ~ *tingkah* to have an attitude. ~ *tolak bala* to get rid of the ballast of a ship to make it lighter. ~ *tubuh ke laut* to plunge into the sea. ~ *tuduhan* to deny an accusation. ~ *undi* to draw lots to determine the winner. ~ *utang* to shift a debt to a relative of s.o. who has not paid the debt. ~ *waktu* to waste time.

membuang-buang to throw away s.t. repeatedly, fritter away. ~ *langkah* to pay a visit (to). ~ *mata ke* to keep an eye on s.t. ~ *pandang* to look around. ~ *penat* to stretch one's legs. ~ *tingkah* to strike a pose. ~ *uang* to waste/squander/fritter away money.

membuangi (*pl obj*) to throw away, etc.

membuangkan to throw away, discard, cast off. *Siapakah yang ~ bermacam jenis sampah di pinggir jalan?* Who discarded all k.o. trash by the roadside?

terbuang [and **kebuang** (*coq*)] thrown away, discarded, expelled, abandoned. *Anak ~ itu ingin kembali kepada orangtu-anya yang membuangnya.* The abandoned child wanted to return to his parents who abandoned him. *Meréka adalah anak-anak ~.* They were abandoned kids.

terbuang-buang wasted, not put to proper use. *Sayang 'kan, waktumu ~ untuk berfoya-foya saja selama ini.* It's a pity, isn't it, that so far your time has been wasted in just throwing money around.

buangan 1 s.t. that is thrown away/discarded/abandoned, trash. *anak ~* abandoned child, foundling. *manusia ~* human trash. *orang ~* exile. **2** waste, tailing, trash. **3** sewage.

pembuang 1 thrower, hurler. ~ *bom* bomb thrower. **2** disposer, disposal. **3** exhaust.

pembuangan 1 dump, place for dumping garbage, outlet. ~ *air* drainage. ~ *waktu* waste of time. **2** isolation. **3** disposal, exhaust. **4** exile, banishment.

buang II (*M*) k.o. beetle.

buanget (*sl*) very much; → **BANGET.**

buani universal.

buanyak a lot, many; → **BANYAK.**

buar extravagant, wasteful; spendthrift, s.o. who likes to squander money.

pembuar spendthrift, wastrel.

buari (*ob*) jerked meat; → **DÉNDÉNG.**

buas 1 savage, wild, fierce (of animals). **2** vicious, fierce, ferocious, violent, cruel.

membuas to fly into a rage, rage, be(come) violent.

membuaskan to drive s.o. wild.

kebuasan fierceness, ferocity, savageness, cruelty.

pembuasan driving s.o. wild.

buat I do, make. *Apa boléh ~?* What can you do about it? Nothing can be done about it.

berbuat 1 to do, behave, act (in a certain way). *Aparat keamanan agar ~ adil.* The forces of security should act in a just way. ~ *aniaya* to play dishonest tricks. *tidak bisa ~ apa-apa* cannot do a thing. *Hanya Pak Marto yang tak ~ apa-apa.* It was only Marto who didn't do a thing. *Belum mampu ~ banyak.* Not yet able to do a lot. *Agar ~ lebih banyak untuk perdamaian dan kemakmuran.* To do more for peace and prosperity. ~ *begitu* to act like that, act in that way. ~ *bodoh* to play the fool. ~ *cabul* to do s.t. immoral (such as live together without being married). ~ *céndol* to do s.t. immoral. ~ *curang* to commit fraud. ~ *demikian* to act in that way. ~ *dosa* to sin. ~ *hal-hal yang lucu* to play jokes. ~ *iseng* to be unfaithful to one's spouse. ~ *itu* (*coq*) to have sexual intercourse. ~ *jahat* to do s.t. bad, make trouble. ~ *jasa* to render a service. ~ *kebajikan* to confer a benefit. ~ *korupsi* to act in a corrupt way. *tidak dapat ~ lain se-lain* cannot do other than. ~ *leluasa* to act freely. *tempat ~ maksiat* place where sins are committed. ~ *mesum* to act immorally. ~ *nakal* to act dishonestly, cheat. ~ *nékad* to act in despair. ~ *néko-néko* to do as one pleases. ~ *olah* to be tricky. ~ *onar* to raise a fuss, make a big fuss. ~ *perkara* to take legal action. ~ *salah* to make a mistake. ~ *sama* to do the same. ~ *seke-hendak hatinya* to act as one pleases, do s.t. to one's heart's content. ~ *semaunya* to act as one pleases. ~ *sérong* to cheat (on one's spouse, etc.). ~ *tidak patut* to do s.t. improper. ~ *tidak terpuji* to do s.t. unethical. ~ *sekehendak hatinya* to do s.t. to one's heart's content. ~ *semaunya* to do as one likes. *Meréka ~ seperti itu karena lapar.* They acted like that because they were hungry. ~ *sesuatu yang berguna* to do s.t. useful. ~ *sesuka hati kita* to do as we wish/like. *Ia bisa ~ sesuka hatinya.* He could do as he wished/liked. ~ *tak terpuji* to act in an unethical way. **2** to do it, make love. *Meréka sering ~ di rumah jika tidak ada orang.* They often made love at home, when nobody was there.

membuat 1 to make, build, manufacture, produce, turn out, set up. ~ *rumah* to make/build a house. ~ *sabun* to manufacture soap. **2** to treat/act/behave toward. *Saya tak tahan melihat dia dibuat begitu.* I can't stand to see him treated like that. **3** to do. *Apa yang hendak dibuat, nasi telah menjadi bubur.* What can we do, what is done cannot be undone. ~ *céndol* to do. s.t. immoral. **4** to cause, make, bring about, turn s.t. (into s.t.), induce. ~ *bagus* to beautify. ~ *bodoh* a) to consider/regard as stupid; deceive, cheat, defraud. b) to act/pretend to be stupid. ~ *marah* to anger, make s.o. angry. ~ *palsu* to forge (a document). ~ *takut* to frighten, make s.o. afraid, scare. **5** to use for, make into. *Janganlah kain itu dibuat baju.* Don't make that material into a dress. **6** to commit. ~ *gawé* to commit adultery. ~ *laku bukan-bukan* to pass the time. ~ *naskah pidato* speechwriting. ~ *perhitungan* to take revenge. ~ *ulang* to reproduce. *Film itu tidak bisa dibuat ulang lagi.* The film cannot be reproduced. **7** (= **membuat-buat** *muka*) to pretend, feign. **8** to cajole, wheedle, fawn on s.o. ~ *susah* to get (o.s.) into trouble. **9** to enter into, conclude (an agreement/contract, etc.). **10** to draw up, draft (a deed/notarial instrument). ~ *surat* to draft/draw up a letter. *dibuatnya* a) (= *dibuat oléhnya*) he made. b) as a result, in consequence of this, owing to this. *Di daérah itu timbul penyakit pést sehingga tak sedikit orang yang mati dibuatnya.* The plague has broken out in that area, so that many died as a result of this. *dibuat menurut ukuran* to be custom-made.

membuat-buat to do s.t. in a fake k.o. way, make up, invent, pretend to do s.t. *dibuat-buat* faked, made up, invented. *Dengan langkah yang kubuat-buat saya masuk ke dalam réstoran itu.* I pranced into the restaurant.

membuatkan [and **mbuatin/ngebuatin** (*J coq*)] to make/do/ prepare s.t. for s.o. else. *Saya ~ anggarannya.* I drew up a budget for him. *~ surat kematian* to draw up a death certificate for s.o. *~ istana raja* to make/build a palace for one's ruler.

memperbuat 1 to make/do s.t. for (with some effort). *~ laporan mengenai kejadian itu* to draw up a report on the event. **2** (*coq*) to make fun of, play tricks on, tease.

terbuat made, manufactured.

buatan 1 artificial, mannered, affected, unnatural, disguised (handwriting), false. *senyuman yang ~* a false smile. *gigi ~* false tooth. **2** invented, devised, contrived, fabricated. *Kerugian sebanyak itu hanya ~ saja.* Such a large loss was just invented. **3** product of, made in. *~ Jepang* made in Japan.

buat-buatan imaginary, simulated, invented, false.

pembuat 1 doer, perpetrator, culprit. **2** maker, producer. *~ gaduh/resah* trouble maker. *~ kebijaksanaan* policy maker. *~ keputusan* decision maker. *~ kunci* locksmith. *~ naskah pidato* speechwriter. *~ undang-undang* lawmaker, legislator. **3** s.o. who drafts/draws up documents. **4** maker, device that makes s.t. *~ éskrim* ice cream maker. *déwan ~ undang-undang* legislative assembly. *perusahaan ~ kapal* shipyard.

pembuatan production, manufacture, construction. *dalam ~* under construction. *~ hujan kimiawi* cloud-seeding. *~ jalan* road construction. *~ kapal* shipbuilding. *~ pabrik* manufacture, fabrication.

perbuatan 1 act, deed, action. *~ berlanjut* (*leg*) continued act. *~ cabul* lewdness, indecent/obscene act, sexual abuse. *~ curang* fraud. *~ halal* legal action. *~ hukum* legal act(ion). *~ kejahatan/pidana* criminal act, crime. *~ lanjutan* (*leg*) continued act. *~ melawan/melanggar hukum* illegal action. *~ pelaksanaan* overt acts (toward the commission of a crime). *~ penguasa melawan hukum* unlawful government act. *~ persiapan* preparatory act. *~ pidana* criminal action. *~ Rasul-Rasul* (*Bible*) Acts of the Apostles. **2** behavior. **3** performance.

buat II 1 for. *~ apa?* What for? Why? *~ sementara* for the time being, temporarily. **2** (in order) to.

buaya 1 crocodile, alligator, *Crocodilus spp.* **2** (*coq*) bad guy, scoundrel, low-life, philanderer. *~ stasiun* riff-raff who hang around the railroad station. *~ uang* money lender (at exorbitant rates). **3** fan, enthusiast. *~ bioskop* movie fan. *adakah ~ menolak bangkai* what is bred in the bone will come out in the flesh. *tak akan terlawan ~ menyelam* a powerful person cannot be opposed. *~ darat* womanizer. *~ jolong-jolong* false gharial, *Tomistoma schlegeli*. *~ katak → BUAYA tembaga. *~ muara* estuary crocodile, *Crocodilus porosus*. *~ pandan* a green crocodile. *~ pasar* pickpocket. *~ senjolong* false gharial, *Tomistoma schlegeli*. *~ tangsi* bullying Army brat. *~ tembaga* estuary crocodile, *Crocodilus porosus*.

membuaya 1 to be/act like a crocodile, e.g., to crawl, creep. **2** (*coq*) to cheat, deceive, trick.

membuayai 1 to cheat, trick, deceive. **2** to bully.

buaya-buaya I (*naut*) step for a mast.

buaya-buaya II *burung ~* brown-winged king-fisher, *Pelargopsis amauroptera*; → RAJA *udang.*

bubar (*Jv*) **1** to disperse, scatter. **2** (*mil*) dismissed!

membubarkan [and **ngebubarin** (*J coq*)] **1** to disperse, break up, dissolve (a contract), close down (a business). **2** to dismiss.

terbubar dispersed, broken up, dissolved.

bubaran dissolution, dispersal, dismissal.

pembubaran 1 dispersion, dissolution, liquidation. *~ perkawinan* dissolution of a marriage. *~ perséroan* liquidation of a company. **2** abrogation (of a contract).

bubaran (*Jv*) k.o. Javanese musical form.

bubéng 1 nameless. **2** rascal.

bubrah (*Jv*) **1** destroyed, torn to pieces. **2** scattered, dispersed (of a crowd). **3** out of order, not working.

bubras (*Jv*) scraped off (of skin).

bubu river fish trap (made of wire netting and bamboo).

membubu 1 shaped like or resembling such a fish trap. **2** to catch fish using that method.

bubuh membubuh to affix, place on, attach, add. *~ harga* to set a price. *~ tandatangan* to affix one's signature.

membubuhi 1 to add (s.t.) to. **2** to affix, attach. **3** to embellish (a story).

membubuhkan 1 to add s.t. **2** to affix, place s.t., add s.t.

terbubuhi added to, affixed to.

bubuhan 1 s.t. affixed, stuck on, addition. **2** mark-up.

pembubuhan affixing, placing on, adding.

bubuk I various species of wood-maggots, weevils (in rice), moths (in clothes). *dimakan ~* worm-eaten. *~ beras* rice weevil, *Calandra oryzae*. *~ buku* bookworm, *Anobium panicum*. *~ kayu* wood maggot, powder-post beetle, *Lyctus brunneus*. *~ tembakau* tobacco weevil, *Lasioderma serricorne*.

bubuk II 1 powder, powdered substance. *~ bakar (kué)* baking powder. *~ beras* rice powder. *~ besi* iron dust. *~ kadal* lizard powder, *Pulv. Maboyae multifasciatae*, a traditional medicine used against eczema. *~ kayu* sawdust. *~ kopi* ground coffee. *~ mesiu* gunpowder. *~ pemutih* bleaching powder. *~ pengembang roti* baking powder. *~ roti* bread crumbs. *~ sabun* soap powder. *~ tulang* bone meal. **2** powdered. *kopi ~* powdered coffee.

membubuk 1 to crush to a powder, pulverize. **2** to turn to dust.

bubukan s.t. that has been ground up or turned into powder.

pembubukan pulverizing.

bubuk III (*ob*) **membubuk** to boil in water.

bubul I 1 sore on palm of hand or sole of foot. **2** corn on hoof of animal.

bubulan to have such a sore.

bubul II membubul to repair (fishing nets, etc.).

bubul III membubul to soar, rise.

membubulkan to make s.t. soar/rise.

bubun-bubun (*M*) → UBUN-UBUN.

bubung 1 crest, top, ridge. **2** (*phys*) lift.

membubung to crest, peak. *~ tinggi* to skyrocket.

membubungkan and **memperbubungkan** to make s.t. rise.

bubungan 1 ridge, pitch. **2** cam, tappet. *~ antar* guide cam. *~ atap* ridge. *~ minyak* oil drip. *~ rol* roller tappet.

bubur 1 porridge. **2** pulp. *nasi sudah menjadi ~* what's done cannot be undone. *~ kayu* wood pulp. *~ kertas* paper pulp. *~ ketan* sticky-rice porridge. *~ mérah* k.o. rice porridge with palm sugar. *~ nasi/pulut* rice porridge. *~ semén* cement slurry. *~ sumsum/ sungsum* a dish made with rice flour, *santan*, pandanus leaves, and a sweet sauce.

membubur 1 to make s.t. into porridge. **2** to become mushy.

bubus I (*M*) **membubus** to swarm out (like ants out of a nest).

bubusan culvert.

bubus II bald/hairless (from an illness).

bubut I badger, *Mydaus meliceps*.

bubut II (*J/Jv*) **membubut** to pluck/pull (out), extract.

membubuti to pluck (hair, fur, a chicken).

bubut III (*naut*) stay, brace. *~ belakang* backstay. *~ muka* jib stay.

bubutan stay, guy. *tali ~* halyard.

bubut IV (*J/Jv*) lathe.

membubut to operate a lathe.

bubutan lathe. *~ prisma* gantry lathe.

pembubut 1 lathe operator, turner. **2** lathe.

pembubutan lathe work.

bubut V various species of birds: coucals, malkohas, crow-pheasants, *Centropus spp.*; → BUTBUT. *~ alang-alang/kecil* lesser coucal, *Centropus bengalensis javanensis*. *~ besar* greater coucal, *Centropus sinensis*. *~ hitam* Sunda coucal, *Centropus nigrorufus*. *~ jambul* chestnut-winged cuckoo, *Clamator coromandus*. *~ kembang* red-billed malkoha, *Phaenicophaeus javanicus*.

bucu corner, edge.

berbucu with ... corners/edges.

membucu to stick out.
bud (in acronyms) → KEBUDAYAAN.
Buda → BUDHA.
budak 1 slave. 2 servant. 3 (*ob*) young person. – *belian* bondsman. – *dalam* servant in the palace. – *gembala* shepherd. – *jarahan* slave captured in battle. – *suruhan* servant, errand boy. – *lampau tua tidak* between youth and manhood.
membudak to be(come) a slave.
membudakkan and **memperbudak** 1 to enslave. 2 to treat s.o. like a slave.
kebudak-budakan childish.
pembudak slave holder.
pembudakan 1 enslaving. 2 treating as a slave.
perbudakan slavery, servitude, bondage.
budal-budél and **budal-badil** (S) to run in all directions, scatter.
budanco (*Jp*) rank in Japanese defense units during occupation.
Budapés Budapest.
budaya (*Skr*) 1 civilization, culture; → ADAB, KULTUR. 2 practice, s.t. generally done or accepted. – *télepon* k.o. self-censorship by newspaper editors.
sebudaya with/of the same culture.
berbudaya to have a ... culture.
membudaya to become generally adopted, find/receive/obtain acceptance, be accepted, take root, be entrenched (in a society). *Secara diam katebélece itu sudah ~ di masyarakat, termasuk dalam belantika dunia bisnis, pemerintahan, perbankan dan lainnya.* Quietly the short note from a prominent person to s.o. asking a favor for the bearer has been accepted in society, including in the business world, government, banking, etc.
membudayakan to cultivate/instill/impart, achieve acceptance of. *~ tata krama bertélepon* adapting to telephone etiquette.
terbudaya enculturated.
kebudayaan culture, cultural. *catatan ~* cultural notes. *Départemen Pendidikan dan* [Dépdikbud] Department/Ministry of Education and Culture. *~ étika/nilai* cultural ethics/values. *perjanjian ~* cultural accord/agreement. *~ amplop* the custom/way of life of giving and accepting cash-stuffed envelopes by certain journalists; → AMPLOP. *~ baur* mixed. **berkebudayaan** to have a culture, be civilized. *Cara-cara tadi masih terlalu kasar. Ya berarti kurang ~.* The methods just mentioned are still too rude which means (they are still) less civilized.
pembudayaan cultivation, cultivating.
perbudayaan culture. *~ hati/otak/tangan* culture of the heart/head/hands.
budayawan (*Skr neo*) cultured man, culture-bearer, cultural elite.
budayawi (*infr*) cultured.
budé (*Jv*) aunt.
budeg and **budek** (*Jv*) 1 deaf. 2 anonymous, only in the compound *surat –* anonymous letter.
membudekkan to deafen.
budel (*D ob*) (personal) estate, property, goods and chattels, movables.
budeng (*Jv*) → LUTUNG.
Budha 1 Buddha, Gautama Buddha. – *stick* k.o. marijuana. 2 Buddhist.
Budhin (*D*) Buddhist.
Budhisme (*D*) Buddhism.
budi (*Skr*) 1 sense, mind, reason, intellect, intelligence. *akal –* common/sound/good sense. 2 character, nature, disposition. *orang yang baik –* a kind hearted person. 3 kindness, goodness, good deed. 4 way, effort, endeavor. *Tidak didapatnya – untuk membusukkan nama saingannya itu.* No ways were found of slandering his competitor. 5 trick, artifice. *baik –* kind-hearted. *bermain –* to deceive, double-cross. *bertanam –* to do good. *hina – of low character. kedapatan/ketabuan –* one's bad intentions are already known. *Dia banyak lepas –.* He has put many persons under an obligation. *membalas –* to return a benefit. *menanam –* to do good. *rendah –* of low character. *tinggi –nya* he is high-minded/of high character. *utang –* debt of gratitude, moral obligation. **berutang budi** to feel morally obliged, have moral obligations. *ada ubi ada tales, ada – ada bales* nothing for nothing. *– bahasa* good manners/breeding, amiable, politeness,

civility. **berbudi bahasa** polite. *– bicara* common sense. *– Nurani Manusia* Social Conscience of Man. *– pekerti* character, nature, disposition. *– Utomo* "High Endeavor," i.e., the 1908-grouping of Javanese medical students in Batavia (Jakarta) with the purpose of promoting Javanese cultural ideals.
sebudi *~ akal* with might and main, with all one's moral force.
berbudi 1 to have intellect/sense, etc. 2 intelligent, smart, sensible, wise, level-headed. 3 to have a good character; to be honest. *tidak ~* bad, evil. 4 to be generous.
memperbudikan to trick, cheat.
perbudian (*M*) to deceive, fool, cheat.
budidarma (*Jv*) philanthropy.
budidaya I (*Jv*) culture (of plants and animals), cultivation. *kebun –* plantation, a large farm or estate. *– ayam petelur* breeding of layers. *– hutan* silviculture, agroforestry. *– laut* sea farming, mariculture. *– lorong* alley cropping. *– perlebahan* apiculture. *– tembakau* tobacco cultivation.
membudidayakan to cultivate, grow, breed, raise.
kebudidayaan plantation (*mod*).
pembudidaya cultivator.
pembudidayaan cultivation.
budidaya II (*ob*) to strive after, aim at, effort to achieve one's goal.
budiman (*Skr*) clever, intelligent, learned, wise, sensible. *pembaca yang –* respected/valued reader.
budirahayu (*Jv*) virtue, virtuousness.
budu a type of food made of pickled anchovy.
budug and **buduk** 1 (*Jv*) leprosy in its initial stage; → BODOK. 2 mangy (of dogs).
budur (*M ob*) **membudurkan** *~ mata* to open one's eyes wide, stare.
terbudur protruding (of eyes).
bueesar (*coq*) very big.
buén (*Jv*) jail, prison; → BUI I. *Dulu narapidana disebut orang – atau pesakitan.* Formerly a convict was called a prisoner or *pesakitan*.
bufét (*D*) 1 (furniture) buffet, sideboard. 2 (in a station, etc.) buffet, refreshment bar. 3 smorgasbord.
bug(h)a (*A*) opposing a lawful ruler.
bugang → KEMBANG *bugang*.
bugar → PUGAR I. *segar/séhat –* safe and sound, hale and hearty, in perfect good health, fit.
kebugaran health, fitness. *~ jasmani* physical fitness. *pusat ~ jasmani* physical fitness center. *pusat ~* fitness center.
bugbelah, **bugduwo** and **bugtelu** names of *ceki* cards.
bugenfil and **bugenvil** (*D*) bougainvillea, *Bougainvillea glabra*.
buger → BUGAR.
bugi-bugi (*E*) boogie-woogie (dance).
bugil uncovered (in general), bare, stripped, naked; → BOGÉL. *ayam – a)* a featherless chicken. b) a plucked chicken. *kaki –* barefoot; → KAKI *telanjang/terbuka. mata –* naked eye; → MATA *telanjang. telanjang –* stark naked. *– ria* porno. **berbugil-ria** pornographic.
berbugil to act in the nude, be naked (in public).
membugili to undress s.o.
membugilkan to undress s.o. *~ diri* to strip o.s. naked.
bugilan and **kebugilan** nakedness.
bugilisme (*infr*) nudism.
Bugis I Buginese. *orang –* a Buginese (of the southern part of Sulawesi).
bugis II *kayu –* k.o. tree used for its timber, *Koordersiodendron pinnatum*; → RANGGU.
buh (*onom*) puffing sound (of blowing out candles).
buhu leaves of the *Padbruggea/Millettia dasyphylla* used to treat infections.
buhuk (*M*) goiter, struma.
buhul (*M*) knot (of rope/string); → SIMPUL I. *– cinta* ties of love. *– mati* hard knot. *– sentak* slip knot.
membuhul(kan) 1 to tie in a knot, tie (in a knot/a necktie). 2 to strengthen, make the ties closer. *membuhulkan hubungan darah* to strengthen blood ties. 3 to establish, make. *membuhulkan tali persaudaraan* to make friends, establish friendly relations. 4 to enter into, conclude (an engagement). *membuhul jandi* to conclude/enter into an engagement. *mengebat erat-erat, membuhul mati-mati* when entering into a contract it should be arranged as well as possible.

buhul-membuhul to make knots.

terbuhul knotted, fastened.

buhulan knot.

buhur → BUHUL.

bui I (*D coq*) jail, prison.

membui to jail, imprison, incarcerate.

pembuian jailing, imprisonment, incarceration.

bui II (*D*) buoy.

buih foam, froth, bubbles. *siapa pandai meniti –, akan selamat ke seberang* it's dogged does it. *– sabun* soapsuds.

berbuih(-buih) and **membuih(-buih)** foamy, frothy, bubbly. *~ mulut* to incessantly talk about (others/an event, etc.).

membuihkan to make foam/froth/lather.

pembuihan frothing, lathering.

Buitenzorg (*D*) /boitensorekh/ the colonial name for Bogor.

bujal 1 protruding, sticking out, jutting out. **2** umbilical hernia. **3** navel.

membujal to protrude, stick out.

bujam (*ob*) receptacle (for betel/tobacco) made from plaited screw-pine leaves.

bujang I 1 bachelor, young man; unmarried, not (yet) married; spinster. **2** adults of marriageable age. **3** widow or widower, divorcee. **4** (*Mal*) all by itself. *kopi – just coffee (without cakes, etc.).* **5** (*vulg*) penis. **6** domestic help; → PEMBANTU *rumah tangga. sebagai – baru berkeris* (*M*) arrogant, conceited. *– (ber)cerai* divorce(e). *– jalang* prostitute. *– juandang* k.o. spirit that can bring good or bad luck to a gambler. *– lapuk* confirmed bachelor. *– mati lakinya* widow. *– serabutan* handyman, jack-of-all-trades. *– talang* childless widow. *– tua* confirmed bachelor.

membujang 1 to live a bachelor's life; single, celibate. **2** to be(come) domestic help.

bujangan bachelor, young man.

pembujang bachelor.

pembujangan celibacy.

bujang II perbujangan and **pebujangan** (*cla*) royal attributes (such as, a ship/sword/audience hall).

bujangga → PUJANGGA.

bujét (*E*) budget.

bujétér (*E*) budgetary.

bujubusét gracious me! (a mild expletive).

bujuk I persuasive talk, coaxing, cajoling, flattery. *kena – to be misled, get talked into s.t. – cumbu* flattery and caresses. *– rayu* flattery. **membujuk rayu** to flatter.

membujuk to talk s.o. into s.t., mislead s.o. by words, incite, instigate

membujuki (*pl obj*) to coax, cajole.

membujukkan to coax/cajole for s.o. else.

terbujuk persuaded, cajoled, talked into (doing s.t.), charmed.

bujukan persuasion, flattery, cajolery.

pembujuk persuader, inciter. *~ hati* s.t. used to cajole, etc.

pembujukan persuasion, flattery, wooing.

bujuk II k.o. snakehead fish, *Channa/Opiocephalus lucius*.

bujung (*J/Jv*) → BURU. **bujungan** fugitive, person run after; → BURONAN.

bujur 1 oblong. **2** longitude, meridian. **3** longitudinal, lengthwise. **4** length. **5** counter or numerical coefficient for long objects. *– angkasa* celestial longitude. *– panjang* oblong. *– sangkar* square; quadrangular. *– sirih* oval. *– sungsang/telur* ellipse, elliptical.

membujur 1 to stretch, run, extend. **2** to be stretched out, stretching out (on), lying alongside. **3** longitudinal.

membujuri to stretch out/extend along, travel the length of.

membujurkan to stretch/lay s.t. out lengthwise/longitudinally.

terbujur stretched out. *Mayat kedua kakak beradik yang sewaktu ditemukan ~ terkapar berdampingan di lantai.* When they were found, the corpses of the two brothers were stretched out on the floor stiff and lying next to e.o.

bujuran length.

bujut 1 tangled, complicated. **2** tousled.

buk I (*Jv*) **1** arch, arched vault (of a bridge). **2** a small bridge over a stream.

buk II (*onom*) thud, bang.

buk III (*D infr*) book.

membuk to book, reserve.

buka 1 (*coq*) to open. *tidak berani – mulut* afraid to open one's mouth. *Toko itu – pukul 8 pagi.* That store opens at 8 a.m. *– kata ... tutup kata* quote ... unquote. **2** opening, wide. *jalan raya – lima depa* the main road which is five fathoms wide. *– pintu* upon entering, flag-drop (initial charge in a taxicab). *– puasa* breaking the fast, eating after the fast.

buka-buka to leaf through (a book/magazine, etc.).

berbuka 1 to take off (a garment). **2** *~ puasa* to break the fast. *Meréka akan diajak untuk bersama-sama ~ puasa di rumahnya.* They will be invited to break the fast together at his house.

membuka 1 to open. *~ bungkusan/lemari/mata/pintu* to open a package/cupboard/one's eyes/a door. *~ paksa* to force s.t. open. *~ si tambo lama* to open up old sores, rake up the past. **2** to take off (one's clothes). *~ baju/pakaian/topi* to take off one's coat/one's clothes/one's hat. **3** to loosen, untie, unbind, undo. *~ simpul* to untie/undo a knot. *~ tali* to loosen a cord. **4** to spread s.t. out, extend. *~ paha* to spread one's legs (for sex). *~ tangan* to extend the hand. **5** (*coq*) to turn on. *~ lampu* to turn on a lamp. **6** to reclaim, open up for use. *~ hutan* to reclaim a forest. *~ jalan* a) to clear/break a way. b) to yield. c) to do pioneering work, be at the forefront. *~ kebun* to clear the ground/forest for a garden. *~ tanah* to clear land. **7** to give/afford s.o. an opportunity; → PELUANG. **8** to embark upon, begin, open, etc. *~ bicara/kata* to begin to speak, take the floor. *~ faal* to view one's horoscope. *~ percakapan* to begin/open a conversation. *~ nujum* to consult one's horoscope. *~ serangan* to launch an attack. **9** to found, establish, open up. *~ perusahaan/sekolah/warung* to establish an enterprise/school/roadside stall. *~ hati/pikiran* to broaden one's mind, inspire. *~ rahasia* to disclose/reveal a secret. **10** to arouse s.t. (such as hunger, etc.). *~ nafsu/seléra* to arouse one's appetite (*esp* sexual desires) (one's taste). *~ langkah* to pluck up one's courage. **11** to inaugurate, make official. *~ bangunan baru* to inaugurate a new building. **12** to leave uncovered (part of the body in *silat*). **13** to show. *~ kedok* to unmask. *~ warna* to reveal s.o.'s true colors.

membuka-buka to leaf through s.t.

membukai 1 to open for. *Dia ~ pintu untuk ibu.* He opened the door for mother. **2** (*pl obj*) to open. *Pekerjaannya tak lain dan tak bukan ~ pintu dan jendéla.* His job was none other than opening doors and windows over and over again.

membukakan [and **ngebukain** (*J coq*)] **1** = **membuka**. **2** to open for. *~ adiknya jendéla* to open the window for his younger sibling. **3** to reveal, open up.

terbuka [and **kebuka** (*coq*)] **1** open, ajar. *Pintunya ~.* The door is open/ajar. *secara ~* openly. *bercakap secara ~* to speak openly (not on camera). **2** public. *rapat ~* an open/public meeting. *tempat ~* a public place. *~ kepada orang ramai* open to the public. **3** open-minded, open. *kami ~ akan* we are open-minded toward. **4** sincere, straightforward, honest, fair. *hati ~* frank, outspoken, openhearted; cheerful, in high spirits. **5** disclosed, overt, not hidden, open. *pengangguran ~* overt unemployment. *surat ~* an open letter. *tangan ~* openhanded, generous. **6** available, open. *tidak ~* closed. **ketidak-terbukaan** closeness, non-openness, secretiveness, nondisclosure. **7** [Tbk] publicly traded. **keterbukaan 1** openness, candor, frankness, outspokenness, openheartedness. **2** (*fin*) disclosure. *~ bank* bank disclosure.

bukaan 1 opening, aperture, gap. *~ gas* throttle. *~ rana* aperture. **2** (*elec*) break. **3** opener.

buka-bukaan to have nude scenes (in a movie). *tanpa ~* without any nude scenes.

pembuka 1 device to open s.t., opener. **2** s.o. or s.t. that opens s.t. *makanan ~* hors-d'oeuvre. *~ akal* s.t. that broadens the mind. *~ botol* corkscrew; → KOTRÉK. *~ jalan* a) trailblazer, pioneer. b) advance motorcycle escort, outriders. *~ kaléng* can opener. *~ kata* preface, introduction. *~ pintu mobil* doorman. *~ seléra* aperitif.

pembukaan 1 opening. *~ itu tinggal menunggu gong saja.* The opening (of the office) is only waiting for the beating on the gong. **2** clearing (of land), reclaiming. *~ lahan/tanah* land clearing. **3** beginning, opening, commencement. *~ upacara* opening ceremony. *~ penawaran* tender. **4** preamble. *~ UUD 45* Preamble to the 1945 Constitution.

perbukaan 1 ending of the fast. **2** (= **pebukaan**) food taken in breaking the fast. *~ sudah tersaji di méja tinggal menyantannya lagi.* The food served at breaking the fast has already been laid out on the table waiting to be consumed.

bukan 1 a negative used to contradict an impression that is, or may be, in s.o.'s mind, *usu* used before noun phrases. *– itu* not that (but rather s.t. else). *Orang Minang – harus kawin dengan orang Minang, orang Madura tidak mesti hidup bersama orang Madura, tidak!* A Minangkabauer doesn't have to marry a Minang wife, a Madurese doesn't have to live together with a Madurese spouse, no way! **2** tag question at the end of a sentence: isn't he, aren't you, don't you, won't they, can't she, shouldn't he, etc. *– buatan* real, not fake. *– hanya (saja) – orangnya ...* not the kind of person to ... *tetapi ... not only ... but also ... –kepalang* not a little, a lot. *– main* considerable, a great deal, serious. *– tidak* it's not in-/un-. *– tidak mungkin* it's not impossible. *– tidak tahu* it's not unknown.

bukannya it's not (but in fact the opposite). *~ apa* it's not nothing. *Itu ~ berkurang.* It didn't decrease (but in fact increased).

bukan-bukan nonsense, bizarre. **berbukan-bukan** to talk nonsense.

sebukan seia *~* in complete agreement.

membukankan to deny.

bukat dirty; black; muddy, turbid. *– likat* very muddy.

membukat to become turbid (of water).

bukau valley.

bukét (D) bouquet.

buking (E) booking, reservation.

membuking to reserve, book.

membukingkan to reserve for s.o.

terbuking booked, reserved.

bukingan booked up, reserved.

pembukingan booking, reserving.

bukit hill; mountain. *anak –* hillock. *– adi paya* a rich/noble man becomes poor/humble. *– Barisan* a) a mountain range that stretches from north to south Sumatra. b) name of Military Region Command I North Sumatra. *– berapit* hills connected by a low col. *– bukau* a) hills and valleys. b) land not yet worked on, virgin land, wilderness. *– kembar* female breasts. *– pasir* (sand)dune. *– perabung* hogback. *– Tur Sina* Mount Sinai. *– serinding* tor.

berbukit with hills. *kawasan ~* a hilly area. *di balik pendakian ~* one difficulty after another.

berbukit-bukit hilly.

membukit 1 to resemble a hill. **2** to form a hill, pile up, accumulate.

perbukitan 1 range of hills, lower chain of mountains. **2** (mod) hill. *Orang-orang suku ~* hill tribes.

buklét (E) booklet.

bukrah (A) **1** tomorrow. **2** mañana, at some indefinite time in the future; → BÉSOK.

bukti (Skr) **1** proof, evidence. *– yang nyata/terang* conclusive (documentary) evidence. *– yang sah* admissible evidence. *barang/ tanda –* evidence, exhibit. *surat –* document (in a case). **2** certificate, (leg) title deed. *– asal-usul* certificate of origin. *– diri* identity/ID card. **membukti-dirikan** to prove one's identity. *– garansi* guaranty, warrantee. *– hak* title deed. *– kas* cashier's receipt. *– keuntungan* stock certificate. *– lawan* evidence to the contrary, rebuttal. *– mendukung* supporting evidence. *– unyatadiri* identity/ID card. *– pelanggaran (tilang)* traffic ticket. *– pelunasan* quittance. *– pembukuan* voucher. *– pengujian* (automobile) test certificate. *– penimbunan* warrant, warehouse receipt. *– penjualan* proof of purchase. *– perlawanan →* BUKTI lawan. *– saksi* a) evidence. b) testimony. *– sangkalan →* BUKTI lawan. *– serah* delivery bill. *– setor(an)* statement that a certain amount of money has been deposited, deposit receipt. *– terima* receipt. *– tertulis/tulisan* written evidence. *– utang* debt instrument.

berbukti to have proof/evidence.

membuktikan [and **mbuktiin/ngebuktiin** (J coq)] **1** to prove, confirm, demonstrate, show, be demonstrative of. **2** to (really/actually) give evidence of. **3** to ascertain, see for o.s.

terbukti 1 proven (correct), confirmed (by the evidence). *Keempat orang itu ~ melakukan kegiatan spionase.* It has been proven that the four persons carried out espionage activities. *~ secara sederhana* proven summarily. *~ sah* legally proven. **2** turned out to be justified. **3** fulfilled, kept (of a promise).

pembukti 1 witness. **2** proof.

pembuktian 1 proving, verification. **2** proof, evidence. *~ sebab* verification of cause. *~ secara sederhana* summary proof. *~ terbalik* reversal of the burden of proof.

buku 1 (D) book. *memegang –* bookkeeping, accounting. *pembatas –* bookend. *pemegang –* bookkeeper, accountant. *pindah –* transfer from one account to another. *tahun –* fiscal year. *tata –* bookkeeping, accounting. *toko –* bookstore. *tutup –* closing of the books (to draw up the profit and loss account). *tidak masuk –* to be of no account, receive no consideration; → tidak masuk HITUNGAN. *– acara* program book. *– acuan* reference book. *– agénda* agenda book, diary. *– ajar* textbook. *– alamat* address book. *– amanat* (fin) book. *– babon* reference book. *– bacaan* reading book, reader. *– bacaan komik* comic book. *– bajakan* pirated book. *– bekas* used/secondhand book. *– berkabung* book of condolence, mourning book. *– besar* (general) ledger. *– besar pembantu* subsidiary ledger. *– biru* blue book. *– catatan* (computer) notebook. *– catatan kas* cashbook. *– catatan terjinjingkan* portable notebook. *– cék* checkbook. *– ceritera* story book. *– daftar peserta* register of shareholders. *– dagang* trade directory. *– daras* textbook. *– ékspédisi* delivery book. *– geréja* church/prayer book. *– harian* diary, day book. *– harian pos* mail log. *– hijau* health certificate for haji's. *– hitam* blacklist. **membuku-hitamkan** to put on the blacklist; cp DAFTAR hitam. *– hukum* penal code. *– ilmiah populér* popular science book. *– ilmu pengetahuan* science book. *– induk* registry. *– jiplakan* plagiarized book. *– kas* cashbook (to register all incoming and outgoing moneys). *– kenang-kenangan* souvenir book. *– kerja* work book, log. *– kir* motor vehicle inspection book. *– komik* comic book. *– kuning* the yellow-colored booklet containing: (I) International Certificate of Vaccination and (II) Personal Health History. *– Lintas Batas* Border Crossing Book. *– log* logbook. *– manéuver* (naut) bell book. *– nikah* marriage book/registry. *– nilai* grade book. *– notasi kantor Polisi* police blotter. *– nilai* (teacher's) grade book. *– notés* (ob) notebook. *– novél* novel. *– nyanyian* songbook. *– olah gerak* (naut) bell book. *– panduan/pedoman* manual. *– pedoman pemilik* owner's manual. *– pelajaran* textbook. *– pelaut* seaman's book. *– pelengkap* subsidiary ledger. *– pemilik Kendaraan Bermotor* Motor Vehicle Owner's Book (owner gives car title, tax statements, etc. to police in exchange for this record book). *– pemutaran* scenario. *– pendaftaran* register. *– pengumpulan* compilation. *– penuntun* manual. *– peta* atlas. *– petunjuk* directory. *– petunjuk télepon* telephone book/directory. *– petunjuk terbitan Déplu* diplomatic list. *– picisan* dime novel. *– pintar* vademecum. *– putih* a) white book, an official report annually issued by the government. b) criticisms of the New Order government by ITB students (1978). *– rapor* (teacher's) grade book. *– référéns(i)* reference book. *– résépsi* reception/guest book. *– rujukan* reference book. *– saku* pocket book. *– sebaran* brochure, pamphlet. *– sekolah* textbook. *– séri* serial. *– setoran* deposit book. *– sijil* muster roll. *– silsilah* a) (of persons) book of genealogy, register. b) (of dogs/horses, etc.) stud-book. c) (of cattle) herd-book. *– simpanan/tabungan* savings/pass book. *– tagihan* collection book. *– tahapan* savings/pass book. *– tambahan* subsidiary ledger. *– tamu* guest book. *– téks* textbook. *– télepon* telephone book/directory. *– tulis* exercise book.

berbuku(-buku) in books, by the book.

membukukan 1 to publish as a book. *Banyak cerita kuno belum dibukukan.* Many ancient stories haven't been published in book form. **2** to note down, record/enter (in the account books), register. *Pada tiap-tiap hari akuntan itu ~ segala penjualan dan pembelian yang dilakukan.* Every day the accountant records all sales and purchases made. *~ kemenangan* to record a victory.

terbukukan booked, recorded, chronicled. *Dan kini Hotél Ibis Cikarang sudah ~ sebagai satu dari 4 Hotél Ibis yang ada di*

Jabotabék. And now the Ibis Cikarang Hotel has been put down as one of the 4 Ibis hotels in the Jabotabek region.

bukuan entry (in bookkeeping).

kebuku-bukuan bookish.

pembukuan recording, entry, bookkeeping, record keeping, registration, booking, posting (an item in a ledger), accounting/ bookkeeping records. ~ *berdampingan* side-by-side posting. ~ *beruntun* multiple posting. ~ *ganda* double-entry bookkeeping. ~ *kembali* reversing/compensating entry. ~ *muatan* cargo booking.

perbukuan book matters, book (*mod*). *Dunia ~ dan anak-anak*. The world of books and children.

buku II 1 joint (of the bones), knot (in wood), knuckle, vertebra. **2** counter or numeral coefficient for objects that come in lumps/ grains/pellets/cakes, etc.; lump, pinch. *garam tiga* – three lumps of salt. *se– sabun* a bar of soap. **3** a roll, wad. *tembakau lima* – five wads of tobacco. *mengadu* – (*M*) to quarrel, fight. *mengadu* – *lidah* to dispute, squabble, wrangle. *bertemu ruas dengan* – and *bertemu* – *dan ruas* to be well-matched. *pilih-pilih ruas, terpilih pada* – (or, *terkena* – *buluh*) choosing the interspace (of a bamboo) and running up against the node, i.e., however carefully you plan you may run up against difficulties. – *buluh* bamboo node. – *jari* knuckle. – *kaki/lali* ankle bone. – *léhér* cervical vertebra. – *lima* fist. – *tebu* knot in sugarcane.

berbuku 1 with/to have a joint; jointed, etc.; vertebrate, knotty, lumpy. *buluh* ~ knotty bamboo. **2** in clods/lumps, etc.; clotted. *Gula itu* ~ *karena kena air*. Sugar becomes lumpy when it comes into contact with water.

membuku 1 to become lumpy. *Aduklah terus adonan supaya jangan* ~. Stir the dough constantly so that it doesn't become lumpy. **2** to be pent up (of emotions). *Segala yang* ~ *dalam dadanya dikeluarkannya belaka*. He got everything off his chest that was pent up in him.

terbuku 1 pent up. **2** lumpy.

perbukuan joints, articulations.

bukung (*Jv*) **1** tailless; → BUNTUNG. **2** short-haired (of woman).

bukur I (*Jv*) → BUTIR.

bukur II (*M*) shaved. **membukur** to shave.

bukut (*M*) **membukut 1** to cover, wrap. **2** to keep quiet about s.t. **pembukut** covering, cover, wrapping.

bulai → BULÉ.

bulakan (from *S ci-bulakan*) fountainhead.

bulak-balik → BOLAK *balik*.

bulalai (*M*) → BELALAI.

bulan I month. *hari* – date (of the month). *sehari* – the first of the month (of January, February, etc.). *dua hari* – the second of the month (of January, February, etc.). *awal* – the beginning of the month. *cukup –(nya)* she has reached the end of her pregnancy. *datang* – a) to menstruate. b) menstruation; → HAID, MÉNS(TRUASI). *genap/sampai –(nya)* to reach term (of a pregnancy). *habis* – a) the end of the month. b) payday. *pengujung* – the last two days of the month. *sayup/tanggung/ujung* – toward the end of the month (from the 27th through the 30th or 31st; when salary has almost been used up for daily expenses). – *apit* the month wedged between Islam's two great feasts (*Idul Adha* and *Idul Fitri*), the eleventh month of the Muslim calendar (*Zulkaédah*). – *bakti* community service month. – *ber* months ending in *ber* (September, October, November, December), the rainy months. – *lemang* the month of Sya'ban. – *neda* the first half of the month when one still has some money. – *ruah* the month before Ramadhan, i.e., *Syahban*. – *sabit* waning moon. – *s(e)tor* month of payment. – *Suci* → RAMADAN. – *sura/asyura* the first Muslim month (*Muharram*). – *tabut* 1–10 *Muharram*, the month of the *Hassan-Husain* commemoration (in west Sumatra and Bengkulu). – *timbul* waxing moon. – *tua* toward the end of the month (from the 27th through the 30th or 31st).

sebulan-bulannya the whole month.

berbulan 1 for a month. ~ *madu* to honeymoon. **2** to last/stay a month.

berbulan-bulan month after month, for months on end, month in and month out. ~ *dia tidak mengirimi istrinya nafkah*. For months on end he hasn't sent money to his wife for household expenses.

bulanan monthly. *gaji* ~ monthly salary. *majalah* ~ monthly magazine. *majalah tengah* ~ biweekly magazine. *séwa* ~ monthly rent.

bulan II moon; → REMBULAN. *anak* – beginning of the crescent. *anggrék* – name of an orchid species, *Phalaenopsis amabilis*. *baiduri* – opal. *cerah* – moonlight. *gelap* – moonless night, new moon. *kandang* – halo around the moon. *(seperti) kejatuhan* – to get a windfall, hit the jackpot. *kelapa (dimakan)* – coconut with soft and spongy meat; → KELAPA *kelapa/puan*. *mata* – phase of the moon. *pendaratan di* – moon landing. *terang* – a) full moon. b) moonlight. *bagai/seperti* – *dengan matahari* unanimous, at one, in harmony; *siang bagai hari, terang bagai* – very obvious (of a mistake, etc.). *bak* – *kesiangan* pale. – *baru* new/waxing moon. – *bintang* crescent-and-star symbol of Islamic nations. – *gelap* a) moonless night, new moon. b) everything one does brings bad luck. – *gerhana/kapangan* part of the moon or the entire moon being covered by the earth's shadow, eclipse of the moon. – *kesiangan* pallid moon visible during daylight. – *madu* honeymoon. **berbulan madu** to go on one's honeymoon. – *mati* dark of the moon. – *muda* a) waxing moon. b) first part of the month when one's salary hasn't been spent yet. – *naik* very first part of the waxing moon. – *penuh/purnama* full moon. – *sabit* crescent. – *Sabit Emas* The Golden Crescent (in the Middle East): Iran, Afghanistan, and Pakistan; *cp* SEGI *tiga emas*. – *susut/surut* waning moon. – *tilem* new moon. – *timbul* waxing moon. – *tirus* waning moon. – *tua* waning moon, the end of the month when one's salary has been spent.

berbulan with/to have a moon. *malam* ~ moonlit night.

membulan 1 to become/be visible like a moon. ~ *penuh* like a full moon (of a woman's face). **2** to go to the moon.

membulankan to send (a spaceship) to the moon.

bulan-bulanan target, goal, purpose, object. *Penumpang bus kota menjadi* ~ *tukang copét*. City bus passengers have become the target of pickpockets. *menjadi* ~ to be talked about.

bulan III *ikan* – and *ikan* **bulan-bulan** giant herring, Indo-Pacific tarpon, *Megalops cyprinoides*.

bulan IV *kayu* – various species of trees including *Fagraea crenulata* and *Endosperma spp*.

bulang I 1 headdress, headgear, turban. **2** means by which artificial spurs are attached to the legs of a fighting cock. – *dagang* the spur attached to the cock's natural spur on the right leg. – *hulu* a) headdress. b) (*cla*) darling, sweetheart. – *kanan/kiri* the spur attached to the right/left leg.

bulang-bulang s.t. that has been wound/twisted around the head (a *kain*/string of flowers, etc.).

berbulang 1 with a headdress. **2** tied-up spurs (fighting cock).

membulang 1 to wind/twist round (the head). **2** to tie on spurs (to a cock).

terbulang tied on spurs. ~ *ayam betina* a coward.

pembulang s.o. who provides a fighting cock with spurs.

bulang II bougainvillea, a type of climbing plant with flowers. – *akar* a climbing plant, *Smythea pacifica*. – *gajah/hitam/kecil/tikus* various species of shrubs, *Canthium sp*.

bulangan k.o. tree shrub, small cashmere tree, *Gmelina asiatica*.

bulang-baling propeller, windmill; → BALING-BALING.

bular I whitish discoloration of the eye, *esp* due to cataracts.

bular II – *mata* (*M*) tired weary eyes.

bulat 1 round (as a ball), spherical. *Dapatkah kau buktikan bahwa bumi* –? Can you prove that the earth is round? **2** round, circular. *kayu* – round logs stripped of branches. *pusat* – the center of a circle. *rumah* – (*M*) k.o. house. *Roda sepéda berbentuk* –. Bicycle wheels are circular. **3** whole, complete. *angka* – a whole number. **4** unanimous, complete(ly). *dengan suara* – unanimously. *telanjang* – stark naked. *Meréka telah* – *menyetujui usul itu*. They unanimously agreed to that proposal. – *air oléh pembuluh*, – *kata oléh mufakat* and – *air di pembuluh*, – *kata di mupakat* agreement can be achieved through deliberations. – *boléh digulingkan, pipih/pecak boléh dilayangkan* deliberations are finished and a conclusion has been reached. – *berisi* fat. – *bujur* oval. – *buluh* cylindrical. – *bumi* (terrestrial) globe. –

cekung concave. – *cembung* convex. – *gépéng* round and flat. – *hati* a) honest, sincere. b) determined, resolute. – *kata/mufakat* total consent, agreement. – *lipir* round and flat. – *lonjong* oval. – *mata* eyeball. – *mufakat* in total agreement. – *niat* determination. – *nyempluk* round and firm. – *panjang* elliptical. – *penuh* fat. – *pikiran* determined, resolute. – *pipih* flat and round (as a coin). – *silinder* cylindrical. – *sungsang* obovoid. – *tékad* determined, resolute. – *telor/telur* oval-shaped (of an egg), ovoid. **membulat telur** ovoid. – *tongkol* shapelessly round, chubby. – *torak* cylindrical.

bulat-bulat 1 round. *Apakah gunanya benda yang ~ ini?* What is the use of this round object? 2 wholly, completely, totally. *Pendapat orang itu diterimanya ~.* He accepted that person's opinion in its entirety. *menelan ~* a) to swallow s.t. whole. b) to accept in its entirety.

sebulat 1 unanimously. *dengan ~ hati* with all one's heart. 2 totally, entirely, completely.

membulat 1 to appear to be round, become round. *Karena gemuknya tubuhnya ~.* Since he was fat, his body appeared to be round. 2 to be unanimous.

membulati 1 to take over, grab. *untuk mencegah suara yang didapat oléh suatu partai terbesar ~ segala kursi dalam DPR* to prevent the votes gotten by a majority party from taking over all the seats in the DPR. 2 to draw a circle around s.t.

membulatkan 1 to round off. *~ ke atas/bawah* to round up/down. 2 to make (a decision), concentrate, make perfect. *~ hati* to take a firm decision to, resolve to. *~ ingatan* to concentrate, devote one's attention to, devote o.s. fully to. *~ kemauan* to make a firm decision. *~ mufakat* to reach agreement. *~ niat* to make up one's mind to, resolve to. *~ pikiran* to concentrate, devote one's attention to, devote o.s. fully to. *~ suara* to come to an agreement. *~ tékad* to make a firm decision. *~ tinju* to clench one's fist.

memperbulat to make rounder.

bulatan 1 ring, circle. *~ lonjong* oval. *~ mérah* red circle. 2 roundness, rotundity. 3 sphere. 4 hemisphere. *setengah ~ selatan/utara* southern/northern hemisphere. 5 (*geol*) lobe. **berbulatan** concentric.

kebulatan 1 roundness, sphericity, circle. 2 rounding off, completeness, fullness. *~ bumi dapat dibuktikan dengan mudah.* The earth's roundness can easily be proved. 3 determination, resolution, firmness, agreement, concurrence, unanimity. *dengan ~ suara* unanimously. *~ tékad* a) self-confidence, determination. b) unanimity.

pembulat s.t. which rounds out or off.

pembulatan 1 rounding, rounding off. *~ ke atas* rounding up. *~ ke bawah* rounding down. 2 concentrating. 3 making (a decision). *~ pikiran* decision. *~ tenaga* power concentration.

bulbul (*Pers*) nightingale.

buldan (*A*) cities, towns.

buldog (*D*) /buldok/ bulldog.

buldoser (*D*) bulldozer.

membuldoser to bulldoze, demolish by bulldozer(s).

pembuldoseran bulldozing, demolition by bulldozer(s).

bulé(k) (*Jv*) 1 (*orang* -) white person, Caucasian, western(er). *bahasa* – a western language. *Inggris* – a native-born Britisher. – *kampung(an)* a Caucasian who lives an Indonesian life-style. 2 albino. 3 slur term for a light-skinned person.

buléng (*J*) k.o. Betawi performance.

bulet → BULAT.

buletin (*D*) bulletin.

bulevar (*D*) boulevard; → ADIMARGA.

Bulgaria (*negeri*) – Bulgaria. *orang* – Bulgar(ian).

bulgogi (Korean) BBQ meat.

bulgur precooked, cracked wheat (imported from the U.S.), eaten as rice, rather rough.

bulian ironwood tree, *Eusideroxylon zwageri*.

buli-buli 1 small flask/bottle. 2 small glass bulb forming part of s.t. – *di ujung térmométer itu diisi dengan raksa* the small glass bulb at the end of the thermometer is full of mercury.

bulir 1 ear of corn. 2 bunch, sheaf, cluster (of paddy, etc,). 3 (*bot*) spike.

berbulir(-bulir) 1 with/to have ears. 2 in bunches/clusters. 3 in drops/beads (of sweat). *"Wah, lumayan," ~ ucapnya seraya menghapus keringet yang di léhérnya.* "Well, it's reasonable," he said wiping drops of sweat off his neck.

membulir *~ kain* to roll up fabric.

buliran spikelet.

Bulog [Badan Urusan Logistik] Logistics Management Board, i.e., a State agency with monopolistic powers in the production, purchase, and distribution of basic staples, of which the most important is rice.

mem-Bulog-kan to place under the control of *Bulog*. *Kopra dan minyak goréng perlu di-Bulog-kan.* Copra and cooking oil need to be placed under the control of *Bulog*.

Buloggate name of a scandal linked with Bulog.

bulpar → BULEVAR.

bulsak → BOLSAK.

bultok lineated barbet, *Megalaima lineata*.

bulu 1 (body) hair. 2 feather, wool, down, fluff. 3 small plant hairs; → MIANG. 4 appearance, true self. *berganti/bertukar* – a) to molt. b) to change shape. c) to change one's attitude/point of view. *kelas* – featherweight class (in boxing). *menunjukkan/memperlihatkan* – to show one's true colors/character. *memilih/memandang* – to show partiality, discriminate. *tidak/tanpa memilih/memandang* – without respect of persons, not discriminating against, regardless of who it is. – *akar* root hair. – *ayam* a) chicken feather. b) feather duster. c) k.o. tiny sea fish, *Thryssa sp.* d) k.o. lug (sail). – *babi* a) hog's bristles. b) k.o. sea-urchin (an animal with quills), *Echinus esculentus.* – *balik* ruffled fowl feathers. – *bumbu* fine hairs. – *cambuk* flagellum. – *domba* wool. – *getar* cilium. – *hidung* hair in nostrils. – *jarum* pin feather. – *jubah* cape feather. – *kaca* glass mineral wool. – *kalong* a) down. b) anal hair. – *kapas* down. – *kempa* felt (the fabric). – *kening* eyebrow. – *kuduk/kodok* hair of the nape; mane (of horse). – *kumis* bristle. – *landak* quill (of a porcupine). – *lawi* the very long tail feathers (of a chicken, etc,). – *léhér* hackle feather. – *mata* eyelash. – *mink* mink (fur). – *pahat* smooth feathers. – *rambai* the very long tail feathers (of a chicken, etc.). – *remang* bristles. – *roma* fine hairs on the body. *membangunkan/mendirikan* – *roma* to make one's hair stand on end. – *sua(k)* hackles on neck (of a rooster). – *tangkis* badminton. *pemain* – *tangkis* badminton player. **pebulu-tangkis** badminton player. **perbulu-tangkisan** badminton (*mod*). *dunia ~ Indonésia* Indonesian badminton world. – *tengkuk* hair of the nape; mane (of horse). *Membikin berdiri – tengkuk kita.* It gave us the creeps. It made our flesh crawl.

sebulu of the same (political, etc.) orientation, on a par (with). *tak ~* disagree, be contrary to. *Bukan rahasia lagi bahwa kedua tokoh itu tidak ~ dalam isyu amandemén konstitusi.* It no secret that the two leading figures don't see eye to eye in the constitution amendment issue.

berbulu hairy, having feathers/hair/fur, etc.; frayed (of rope). *kepala sama ~, pendapat berlain-lainan* (so) many men, (so) many minds. *~ hati* angry. *~ kapas* fluffy. *~ kasap* coarse-haired. *~ mata melihat* to feel disgusted at seeing s.t.

membului to pluck (a chicken, etc.). *Ayam yang telah disembelih itu dibuluinya bersih-bersih.* He plucked the slaughtered chicken clean.

bulu-bulu 1 feather duster. 2 various plant names. *daun* – k.o. climbing plant, *Tragia hirsuta. pohon* – a tree with red-colored hard and heavy timber which can reach a height of 25 meters with a diameter of 60 centimeters; used for wedges, crossbars, etc., *Pellacalyx axillaris.* **membulu-bulu** to dust, wipe off.

bulug (*A*) adulthood, maturity; → KEDÉWASAAN.

buluh 1 a generic name for many species of bamboo, *Bambusa spp.*; → AUR, BAMBU, PERING II, PRING. 2 large pipe. 3 (*bio*) culm. *harimau* – wild cat, *Felis planiceps. menebas – serumpun/seperdu* the name of the entire family dragged through the mud. – *akar* bamboo with a large and strong stem *usu* used for house poles in villages, *Dendrocalamus pendulus.* – *apoa* yellow bamboo, *Gigantochloa apus.* – *bangi* reed pipe. – *betung* bamboo with a large and strong stem *usu* used for house poles in villages, *Dendrocalamus asper.* – *bungkok* k.o. bamboo, *Dendrocalamus/*

Schyzostachyum caudatum. – *cina* k.o. bamboo, *Bambusa multiplex/nana*. – *gading* ivory bamboo, *Bambusa vulgaris*. – *karah* → KARAH II. – *kasap*, k.o. bamboo, *Ochlandra ridleyi*. – *kuning* yellow bamboo. – *luléba* k.o. bamboo, *Bambusa atra*. – *néhé* k.o. bamboo, *Schizostachyum brachycladum*. – *perindu* a) k.o. Jew's harp. b) k.o. bamboo, *Bambusa magica*. – *tambiang* k.o. bamboo, *Schizostachyum blumei*.

pembuluh tube, piping, artery. ~ *balik* vein. ~ *darah* blood vessel. *dalam* ~ *darah* intravenous. ~ *karét* rubber hose. ~ *kencing* urethra. ~ *kerongkongan* larynx, esophagus. ~ *makanan* alimentary canal. ~ *mekar* varicose veins. ~ *nadi* artery. ~ *napas* windpipe, trachea, respiratory tract. ~ *rambut* small artery. **berpembuluh** to have an artery, etc.

Buluh Tombang the name of the airport in Tanjungpandan, Belitung.

buluk (*J*) mold, must, mildew.

bulukan musty, moldy, mildewed (of cigarettes, etc.).

bulung bole (of a tree).

bulur (= **buluran**) (*cla*) starvation, hunger; famished, starving, ravenous; (to have) a ravenous appetite; starved; very hungry. **kebuluran** to starve to death. *mati* ~ to starve to death.

bulus I 1 penetrated, entered, pierced; → BOLOS II. **2** to be struck by a blow (in a fight/*pencak*, etc.).

bulus II (*Jv*) large freshwater turtle, *Tryonix sp. akal* – a crafty trick. **bulus-bulusan** *main* ~ to play hide-and-go-seek.

bulus III 1 bald, bare, stripped of (hair/blisters/ornaments, etc.). **2** childless, sterile. **3** poor.

bulus IV and **bulus-bulus** *ikan* – Australian/silver whiting, *Sillago maculatus/sihama*.

bulyon I (*D*) bouillon.

bulyon II (*D*) bullion.

bum I (*D ob*) a barrier of chains or poles formerly used to obstruct navigation, tollgate; → BOM II. *pegawai* – customs officer.

bum II (*E*) boom, a rapid increase in price, development, etc. – *dalam konstruksi perumahan* a boom in housing construction.

bum III (*onom*) a deep, prolonged, resonant sound

bum IV (*A*) owl.

bumantara (*Skr cla*) **1** firmament. **2** (air)space, outer space, atmosphere.

bumban (*cla*) wreath, garland (for beautifying/decorating the head).

bumbu (*Jv*) **1** (– *masak*) a general term for spices, flavorings, seasoning and herbs (used in cooking). **2** (non-literal sense of) spice, flavor. *yang banyak* –*nya* spicy. *dengan* – flavored by, with some (in it). *Aksi dengan* – *bentrokan*. Demonstrations with some clashes. – *masak* flood seasoning. – *penyedap (makanan/masakan)* condiment, flavoring (spices added to a food to give it a certain taste).

berbumbu spiced.

berbumbukan spiced/flavored with ...

membumbui 1 to season, spice. **2** to make s.t. (a speech/conversation, etc.) more attractive, spice up. *Rupanya kabar itu telah dibumbui banyak-banyak*. It seems that the news has been spiced up quite a bit.

terbumbui spiced (up) (with s.t.).

bumbu-bumbuan spices, flavorings.

bumbun I 1 shade, shelter (under leaves). **2** hunter's tree hut for watching game birds/tigers, etc.

bumbun II (*M*) heap, pile (of paddy/earth/sand, etc.).

membumbun 1 to pile/heap up (paddy). **2** to dam up, embank. **3** to accrue. **4** to loosen and pile up soil.

terbumbun piled up.

bumbunan accretion.

pembumbunan 1 accretion. **2** filling, loosening and piling up soil (around a plant).

bumbunan → UBUN-UBUN.

bumbung I 1 bamboo cylinder (for water), large section of bamboo used as a water-vessel. **2** tube, pipe, sheath. – *pengebun* tubing for condensation. – *sangkar* (elevator) shaft. **3** (*bio*) follicle.

bumbung II (= **bumbungan**) ridge; → BUBUNG.

bumel (*D*) *keréta api* – slow train; → SEPUR *ejes-ejes/klutuk/trutuk*.

bumerang (*E*) boomerang.

membumerang to hit as a boomerang.

bumi (*Skr*) **1** soil, earth, ground, land. *gas* – natural gas. *gempa* – earthquake. *hasil* – agricultural produce. *ilmu* – geography. *intan* – a gem/jewel/precious stone with a dark luster. *di (muka)* – *(ini)* (here) on earth. *orang* – native: → BUMIPUTRA, PRIBUMI. *pajak* – land tax. *sedekah* – a sacrificial feast for the well-being of the village. **2** world; → DUNIA, JAGAT. *ke* – into the ground. **mengebumikan 1** to bury, inter. **2** to ground, find grounds for (an argument). **pengebumian** burial. *antara* – *dan langit* between the devil and the deep blue sea. *(se)bagai/kaya/seperti* – *dan langit* as different as night and day. – *berputar, zaman berédar* a) other days, other ways; other times, other manners; the times are changed, and we are changed with them. b) time goes on. – *mana yang tidak kena hujan* it is a good horse that never stumbles. *di mana* – *dipijak di sana langit dijinjing* a) when in Rome do as the Romans do. b) to conform to all wishes, obey all commands (i.e., the motto of *Kodam* III/17 Agustus). *sebesar-besar* – *ditampar tak kena* more difficult than it looks at the first glance. *terban* – *tempat berpijak* vanished/dissipated hope. *adi* – *langit* (*M*) s.o. in whom hope has been centered (from whom always hope could be expected, etc.). – *angkat* pillage, brigandage. – *B(h)rawijaya* the poetic name for East Java. – *hangus* scorched earth (in war). **membumihanguskan** to subject to scorched-earth policy. **pembumihangusan** scorching the earth, razing. – *Indonésia* Indonesia. – *Lambung Mangkurat* Banjarmasin. – *Moro* Morokrembangan, Surabaya, i.e., the navy training center. – *rata* level with the ground. **membumi-ratakan** to raze to the ground. – *Perkémahan* Camping Ground (of the *Pramuka* Boy Scout Movement). – *putera* → BUMIPUTERA. – *Réncong* Aceh. – *Siliwangi* the IKIP-building grounds in Bandung, the former Villa Isola. – *Sriwijaya* the poetic name for the South Sumatra area around Palembang.

sebumi on the (same) earth.

membumi 1 to land (of aircraft); → MENDARAT. **2** to (be)come part of the local culture/scene, become part of one's nature. **3** to stand with both one's feet on the ground. **4** realistic, down-to-earth. **5** (*ob*) to settle/remain to stay in a certain place, maintain a permanent residence.

membumikan (*elec*) to ground. *sirkit dibumikan* grounded circuit.

kebumian (*mod*) earth, geo-.

pembumi (*elec*) s.t. that grounds, grounding.

pembumian 1 burial. **2** (*elec*) grounding.

bumiah and **bumiawi** earthly, terrestrial, worldly.

bumiput(e)ra (*Skr neo*) **1** indigenous, native, aborigine; → PRIBUMI. **2** (*Mal*) Malays.

kebumiputraan nativeness, indigenousness.

bumiputraisme nativism.

bumper (*E*) bumper. – *belakang* rear bumper. – *muka* front bumper.

bumpet (*Jv*) clogged (of a ditch/one's nose, etc.)

bun I (*ob*) a small brass box (for betel/tobacco, etc.).

bun II (*Jv*) dew; → EMBUN.

buna k.o. fish.

bunar → AWI *bunar*.

bunbun → BUMBUN. **bunbunan** → BUMBUNAN.

buncah (*M*) **1** in confusion, confused, tangled. **2** in a commotion. *perut* – nauseous, nauseated.

membuncah to be upset.

membuncahkan 1 to confuse. **2** to alarm, upset, disturb.

terbuncah disturbed, upset.

kebuncahan (*Med*) corruption.

buncang unstable, unsteady, wobbly.

berbuncang-buncang swaying from side to side.

terbuncang 1 swung. **2** blown away.

buncéng → BONCÉNG.

bunci I (*C coq*) a set of cards having the value of 13.

bunci II (*Jv*) transvestite.

buncis (*D*) string bean. *kacang* – and – *mérah* kidney bean, *Phaseolus vulgaris*.

buncit I 1 distended (of the belly), bloated. **2** (*vulg*) pregnant, knocked up.

membuncit to appear inflated/swollen. *penyakit perut* ~ schistosomiasis.

membuncitkan 1 to inflate, swell, puff out. 2 to cram.

buncit II (*J/Jv*) and **buncitan** 1 the latest, last, final. 2 youngest (of a child). *nomor* – final digit (of a number). *paling* – last of all.

buncul → BONCOL, BONJOL.

bunda the polite form for "mother;" → (I)BUNDA. – *alam* mother nature. – *(Suci) Maria* (The Virgin) Mary.

bundak (*M ob*) in confusion; tumult, uproar; disturbance.

membundak to create confusion.

bundan (*Jp*) military squad (during the Japanese occupation).

bundar I round, globular, rounded; → BULAT. *si* – (*col*) the silver guilder. – *gemuk* plump. – *panjang/telur* cylindrical, oval. – *telur* ovate. **membundar telur** ovate. – *telur sungsang* obovate.

membundar 1 to form a circle, be rounded. 2 to circle (of airplane above a town, etc.).

membundarkan to make round, round.

bundaran 1 circle. ~ *lalu lintas* traffic circle. ~ *panjang/telur* a) cylindrical. b) oval (table). ~ *semanggi* (highway) cloverleaf. 2 rotunda. 3 s.t. round, such as a hoop, disk, etc.

kebundaran roundness.

pembudaran rounding.

bundar II (*D*) (scrub-)brush; → GUNDAR, SIKAT I.

bundas (*Jv*) abraded (of the skin).

bundel I (*D*) 1 bundle, sheaf. 2 collection, set. 3 bound volume.

sebundel a bundle/stack, etc. ~ *surat kaléng* a stack of anonymous letters.

membundelkan to bundle s.t., put into bundles. 2 to collect, put into a set.

bundelan bundle.

pembundelan bundling.

bundel II knot.

membundel to knot, become knotted.

membundeli to knot/tie a knot onto s.t.

bundelan knot.

bunder → BUNDAR I.

bundet (*Jv*) 1 entangled (of thread/rope, etc.). 2 complicated. *Masalah ini masih* –. This issue is still complicated.

Bundo Kandung (in West Sumatra a popular term for a respected) woman; *lit* "mother of one's own flesh and blood."

bunduk (*A*) 1 bastard. 2 hybrid; → ANAK *haram*, HARAM *zadah*.

bundung liver fluke (a cattle disease).

bung I 1 (elder) brother. 2 buddy (when addressing waiters/peddlers/pedicab drivers, etc.). 3 in addressing high-ranking, generally respected person, such as – *Karno* (President Soekarno), – *Hatta* (Vice-President Moh. Hatta), – *Kecil* (Sjahrir, the leader of the now defunct *Partai Sosialis Indonésia* or Indonesian Socialist Party), – *Tomo* (Soetomo, the leader of the freedom struggle in East Java).

bung II (*onom*) sound produced by beating a *gendang*.

bung III clipped form of **rebung**.

bunga I 1 flower; → KEMBANG. *Mariam sedang memetik – di halamannya.* Mariam was picking flowers in her garden. 2 blossom. 3 indicator for the species of various flowers, such as – *mawar* rose, – *melati* jasmine. 4 flowery pattern/design on cloth, etc. – *pada kain itu* the flowery patterns on that cloth. 5 belle. – *dipersunting* a married girl. – *yang layu balik kembang* a) to take back one's words. b) an ape's an ape, a varlet's a varlet, though they be clad in silk and scarlet. *lémpar – dibalas lémpar tahi* repay good with evil; return evil for good. *jauh bau –, dekat bau tahi* familiarity breeds contempt. *membuang – ke jirat* to cast pearls before swine. – *dipetik perdu ditendang* and –*nya dipersunting, pangkal – dibéraki* aiming at making profits, being out for profit making, wanting to live in clover. – *gugur petik pun gugur* nobody dies before his time. FOR NAMES OF FLOWERS NOT FOUND HERE UNDER BUNGA SEE THE SPECIFIC NAME. – *air mawar* damask rose, *Rosa damascena*. – *angin* a soft breeze as the foreboding of a storm. – *api* a) fore-whorls. b) spark. – *apiun* poppy. – *badam* maculae in leprosy. – *bahasa* proverbs. – *bakung* lily, *Crinium asiaticum*. – *ban* tread (of tire). – *bangkai* snake plant, devil's tongue, leopard palm, *Amorphophallus titanum Becc.* – *bangsa* the hope of the nation, i.e., the nation's youth, the flower of the nation. – *barah* maculae in leprosy. – *berita* subject of the news. – *berpu-*

tik pistillate flower. – *bersari* staminate flower. – *bibir* a) flattery, sweet words; → ABANG-ABANG *lambé*. b) *menjadi* – *bibir* to become the subject of conversation. – *bundai/bondé* (*coq*) flower in a hair bun. – *cagak hidup* annuity. – *campak* initial symptoms of measles. – *daun hanjuang* dracaena. – *désa* village belle. – *és* frost-flowers. – *hati* sweetheart. – *kacapiring* gardenia. – *kain* flowered decorations on fabric. – *kancing* calendula, *Calendulla offisinalis*. – *kantil* champaka, *Michelia alba*; → CEMPAKA. – *karang* coral sponge. – *kehidupan* luxury in life. – *keras* artificial flower. – *kertas* a) artificial flowers. b) bougainvillea. – *kesturi* scorpion orchid, *Arachnis flos-aeris/moschifera*. – *kol* cauliflower. – *kubur* flowers put around a grave, *usu kemboja*. – *kuku* lunula, the half-moon at the base of nails. – *kundai/kondé* flowers in a hair-do. – *kupu-kupu* butterfly tree, *Bauhinia purpurea*. – *kusta* maculae in leprosy. – *landak* a bush with spiky bracts, *Barleria prionitis*. – *latar* (*coq*) prostitute; → WTS. – *lau* k.o. orchid, *Phalaenopsis amabilis*. – *lawang* a) nutmeg skin, *Cinnamomum cassia*. b) clove-tree, *Eugenia aromatica*. – *lotus* lotus. – *mas* (*Mal*) artificial trees made of gold, formerly paid as tribute to Siam's kings. – *matahari* sunflower, *Helianthus annuus*. – *mawar* rose. – *melati/melur* jasmine, *Jasminum sambac*. – *méntéga* k.o. oleander, *Nerium indicum*. – *opium* poppy. – *merak* → KEMBANG *merak*. – *pagoda* pagoda plant, *Clerodendron buchanani*. – *pala* mace. – *palawija* shortlived blossoming nonperennials. – *pamor* figures on kris, damascene. – *pasir* fine sand. – *pekan* jasmine, *Jasminum grandiflorum*. – *pukul empat* k.o. flower, four-o'clock, *Mirabilis jalapa*. – *puru* secondary stage yaws. – *rampai* a) bunch of flowers, small bouquet. b) anthology. c) medley. **membunga-rampaikan** to anthologize. – *raya* a) hibiscus, *Hibiscus rosasinensis*. b) prostitute; → WTS. – *sanggul* flower in a hair bun. – *sedap malam* tuberose, *Polianthes tuberosa*, long golden-brown dried stems for soup and *jamu*, various Indonesian herbal medicines. – *sepatu* hibiscus, *Hibiscus rosasinensis*. – *serunai* bell-mouthed chrysanthemum, *Wedelia biflora*. – *sisir* flower in a hair bun. – *tabu* impatiens. – *tahi* dirty words. – *tahi ayam* shrub verbena, *Lantana camara*. – *taluki* pink carnation. – *tanah* topsoil, humus. – *tepung* refined flour. – *teratai* lotus. – *tiruan* artificial flowers. – *tulip* tulip. – *warung* food stall with charming waitresses to attract truck drivers, etc.; → WARUNG *berbunga/sénggol*.

berbunga 1 to flower, (be) in bloom, blossom. ~ *semangatnya* to be pleased as Punch. *tidak* – *és pada ruang pembekuan* no frost in the freezer. – *kembali* to revive, return to life, live again (of s.o.'s hope). 2 successful, fruitful, productive, yielding. *Pekerjaannya sudah* ~. His work has already borne fruit.

berbunga-bunga 1 flowered. 2 flowery. *Dia senang kain cita yang* ~ . She likes flowered chintz. 3 elated, frantic with joy, wild. *Hati Jasiran* ~. *Secara tak terduga, Darni, 21, gadis yang ditaksirnya, nyamperin dan mengajaknya jalan-jalan.* Jasiran was elated. Unexpectedly, Darni (21), the girl he is after, called on him and invited him to go for a walk.

membunga like a flower. ~ *bakung* resembling the lily with large white flowers, *Crinum asiaticum*.

membungai to decorate with flowers, embellish.

membunga-bungai to decorate, dress up, beautify with flowers.

bunga-bungaan 1 all k.o. flowers. 2 artificial flowers. 3 floral decoration.

perbungaan inflorescence.

bunga II (banking term) interest (on money). *suku* – interest rate. – *abadi* perpetual interest. – *alé* compound interest. – *andaian* imputed interest. – *antarbank* interbank call money. – *berbunga/berganda* compound interest. – *belum dibayar* accrued interest. – *berjalan* accrued interest. – *biasa* simple interest. – *cagak hidup* annuity. – *déposito* interest on deposits. – *ditambahkan* add-on rate/interest. – *kekal* → BUNGA *abadi*. – *kotor* gross interest. – *krédit* interest on a loan. – *majemuk* compound interest. – *mengambang* floating rate. – *modal* interest on capital. – *moratoir* statutory interest. – *nol* zero interest. – *pinjaman* interest to be paid on a loan. – *pinjaman jangka péndék* short-term loan interest rate. – *pukul rata* flat rate. – *resmi* legal interest rate. – *selama hidupnya* annuity. – *tanah* land rent. – *tetap* perpetual interest. – *tridasa* Boston interest. – *tunggakan* interest in arrears. – *tunggal* simple interest. – *uang* interest. – *untuk selama hidup seorang* annuity. – *yang masih harus dibayar* accrued interest.

berbunga 1 to bear/carry interest; interest bearing. **2** with interest (of money).

bunga-berbunga *dengan* ~ at compound interest.

membungai to earn interest.

mem(per)bungakan to loan at interest.

pembungaan interest.

pebunga ~ *uang* a) (*ob*) rentier, man of (independent) means. b) moneylender, loan shark.

perbungaan investment.

bungalan buff (colored).

bungalo (*E*) bungalow.

bungaran first, introductory, preliminary. *nomor* – premier issue (of a newly published magazine); → NOMOR *perdana*.

bungkah → BONGKAH.

bungkal 1 lump, chunk, piece. **2** weight, sinker (for fishing net, etc.). **3** (*cla*) measure of weight for gold (= 1/16 *kati*). – *yang betul* (*M*) a just/righteous administration of justice. *mengambil – kurang* was offended at/by it.

berbungkal-bungkal and **berbungkalan** in chunks/hunks/lumps.

membungkal to turn into chunks.

terbungkal lumped.

bungkalan lump, chunk, piece.

bungkam 1 silent, quiet, speechless, mute. **2** abstain (politically); to remain/keep silent. **3** to misfire, fail to go off or discharge (of firearm) (due to magic/sorcery).

berbungkam to remain silent.

membungkam 1 to remain silent. **2** to silence, squelch (a radio signal).

membungkamkan to silence/gag s.o., impose silence on. *Mulut istrinya segera dibungkamnya sehingga tak dapat berteriak-teriak.* He gagged his wife so that she could not keep screaming. *Diambilnya bermacam-macam tindakan untuk* ~ *pemimpin kita.* He took a number of steps to silence our leaders.

terbungkam silent, silenced.

kebungkaman silence, quiet.

pembungkam 1 s.t. that makes s.o. keep quiet. **2** silencer, muzzle, gag.

pembungkaman silencing, squelching.

bungkang lying stretched out (like a corpse). – *bangking* sprawled all over.

bungkar → BONGKAR.

bungkas uprooted.

bungkem → BUNGKAM.

bungker (*E*) bunker, pillbox. – *atas tanah* hardened site. – *bawah tanah* underground shelter. – *pertahanan* defensive bunker.

bungkil (*Jv*) residue after extracting oil from copra, etc., cake. – *kedelai* soybean meal. – *kopra* copra cake.

bungking lying on its back.

bungkuk 1 bent over. **2** crooked, hunch-backed. *si* – shrimp. *si tua* – an old person. **3** hooked (of the nose). – *hati* dishonest. – *sejengkal tidak terkedang* stubborn. – *sabut* bent over from age. – *udang* bent over (with age, etc.).

bungkuk-bungkuk cringing.

berbungkuk to be bent over.

berbungkukan (*pl subj*) to bend over.

membungkuk 1 to stoop over, duck down. **2** to take a bow.

membungkuk-bungkuk 1 to bow down. *berjalan* ~ to walk bent over. **2** to stoop so low (as to). *Tak sudi aku* ~ *minta pertolongan kepadanya.* I'm not prepared to stoop so low as to ask for his help.

membungkuki to bend toward/in the direction of.

membungkukkan to bend (one's back) down.

terbungkuk stooped over, bent down.

terbungkuk-bungkuk all bent over (due to the weight of s.t. on the back or old age, etc.).

bungkuk-bungkukan to keep on bending/bowing.

pembungkukan bending, stooping over, bowing down.

bungkul I → BONGKOL.

bungkul II cauliflower; → KOL *kembang*.

bungkus 1 s.t. wrapped up (in paper/leaves/cloth, etc.), wrapped

---

pack, package, packet. *satu – candu* a packet of opium. *nasi –* rice wrapped in banana leaf. *rokok dua –* two packs of cigarettes. **2** wrapping material. *kertas – kacang goréng* paper used to wrap fried peanuts. *hantu –* ghost that looks like a dead body with a sheet around it. *ketumbuhan –* undeveloped smallpox. *telur –* an egg in which there is a dead chicken embryo. **3** counter for wrapped objects, pack, package, parcel. *se- rokok* a pack of cigarettes. – *bingkis* all k.o. wrappings.

berbungkus wrapped (up).

membungkus 1 to wrap s.t. (up). **2** to conceal, keep secret.

membungkusi 1 to wrap around, envelop. **2** (*pl obj*) to wrap, etc.

membungkuskan to wrap s.o. for s.o.

terbungkus wrapped (up), packaged.

bungkusan package, parcel.

pembungkus 1 wrapping (paper). ~ *mayat* shroud. **2** s.o. who wraps/packages.

pembungkusan wrapping, packing, packaging.

bunglai cassumar ginger, *Zingiber cassumunar*.

bungli k.o. tree, Indian trumpet flower, *Oroxylum indicum*.

bunglon (*Jv*) **1** various species of chameleon. **2** s.o. who vacillates. **3** opportunist.

membunglon to change sides depending on the circumstances, vacillate.

bungsang → BONGSANG.

bungsil (*J*?) very young coconut; → MUMBANG.

bungsu 1 youngest/last (child) in a family. **2** the last (rain during the rainy season, etc.).

bungur k.o. tree producing timber, (Queen) crape myrtle, rose of India, *Lagerstroemia speciosa*.

buni I 1 k.o. tree, Chinese laurel, *Antidesma bunius*. **2** berry.

buni II → BUNYI.

buni III → SEMBUNYI.

bunian invisible forest elves.

bunjai (*M*) → GUNJAI, JUMBAI.

bunker (*E*) /bungker/ bunker; → BUNGKER.

buntak 1 stumpy, squat, short and fat, beamy (of a boat). – *bayang-bayang* high noon. **2** (*M*) round.

kebuntakan stumpiness, squatness.

buntal I → BUNTEL II.

buntal II 1 bloated, swollen, inflated (of one's stomach). *bagai – kembung* arrogant but stupid. **2** various species of puffers. – *batu* k.o. puffer, *Lactoria spp*. – *duri/landak* barbed puffer, porcupine fish, *Diodon hystrix*. – *pisang* various species of boxfish, *Ostracion spp*. and other species.

berbuntal to inflate, blow up.

buntalan bubble. ~ *udara* air bubble.

buntang I 1 staring, with eyes fixed. **2** stiff (of a dead body), tense.

berbuntang 1 staring, with eyes fixed. **2** to be stretched out stiff (of a dead body).

membuntang to stare, wide open (of eyes).

membuntangkan to stretch s.t. out.

terbuntang 1 wide open, staring. **2** stiff (of a dead body).

buntang II berbuntang to rise/float to the surface, emerge from the water.

membuntang to rise/float to the surface, emerge from the water.

membuntangkan to bring s.t. to the surface, make s.t. rise to the surface, raise.

terbuntang to rise/float to the surface, emerge from the water.

buntang III part of a spinning jenny.

buntar → BUNDAR. – *bayang-bayang* high noon.

buntat I gallstone. – *hendak jadi gemala* to have ridiculous pretensions.

buntat II → BUNTET I.

buntek → BUNTAK.

buntel I 1 bundle. **2** knapsack; → BUNTIL II.

membuntel to bundle s.t. up.

buntelan 1 bundle. **2** knapsack.

pembuntelan packaging, bundling.

buntel II (*Jv*) wrapping.

membuntel to wrap s.t. up.

buntelan s.t. wrapped up.

pembuntelan (dental) crown, crowning.

buntel III → BUNTAL II.
buntet I (*Jv*) 1 clogged (up), blocked. 2 unexpressed (of thoughts)
buntet II → BUNTAT I.
buntil I (*Jv*) dish made of grated coconut, spices, and fish wrapped in taro leaves.
buntil II and buntilan knapsack, cloth bag.
bunting 1 pregnant (*usu* said only of animals), knocked up (of humans). 2 swollen, full (with fruit). 3 loaded (of firearms). – *bantang/besar* heavily pregnant. – *gelap* pregnant with an unknown or secret father. – *harimau* irritable during pregnancy. – *jolong* pregnant for the first time. – *kecil* in early pregnancy. – *kerbau* pregnant for more than nine months. – *muda* in the first trimester of pregnancy. – *padi* calves like swelling rice grains. – *sarat/tua* swollen with pregnancy.
membunting 1 to become pregnant, conceive. 2 to have the shape of a fully formed rice grain.
membuntingi 1 to make s.o. pregnant. 2 to carry (a child in one's womb).
membuntingkan 1 to impregnate, make pregnant. 2 to carry (a child/foal).
buntingan pregnancy, gestation.
kebuntingan 1 pregnancy. 2 womb.
pembuntingan impregnation.
buntu 1 blocked, clogged, come to a dead end. *Pikiran saya* –. I didn't know what to do. – *akal* to be at a loss, at one's wits' end. 2 deadlocked. *perdébatan* – a deadlocked debate.
membuntu to be blocked, obstructed.
membuntukan 1 to block, obstruct, impede. 2 to deadlock, cause a deadlock.
terbuntu clogged.
kebuntuan 1 deadlock, dead end, impasse. ~ *pikiran* out of ideas. 2 obstruction, hindrance, stoppage.
buntul trunk-fish, cow-fish, *Ostracion quadricornis*.
buntung (*J/Jv*) 1 maimed, amputated, lopped off. 2 bad luck; unlucky, unfortunate, suffering a loss. *untung atau* – profitable or losing, profit or loss. *mencari untung sementara yang lain biarkan* – one's man's meat is another man's poison.
membuntungi and membuntungkan to cut off, amputate, lop off.
kebuntungan amputation.
buntut I 1 tail, posterior, end, hind part, rear, behind, bottom, buttocks. *pada* – *bulan/tahun ini* the end of this month/year. 2 consequences, aftermath. *Itu merupakan* – *dari meledaknya sebuah bom.* This is the aftermath of a bomb explosion. *belum tentu untung –nya* it is not clear how it will turn out. 3 track. 4 trace. *Tidak kelihatan –nya.* He hasn't shown up. 5 the last one in a series. – *belangkas* braided girl's hair. – *kapal* ship's stern. – *kuda* a) ponytail (hairdo). b) horse's tail. *membuntut* – *kuda* to tie in a ponytail. – *Nalo* betting on the 'tail' (the last two digits of a lottery). – *perarakan* the rear of a procession. – *perkara* the consequences of a case.
buntutnya 1 after it, etc. 2 s.o. left behind.
buntut-buntutnya aftermath.
berbuntut 1 to lead to, result in. *Insidén itu* ~ *ketegangan yang cukup lama.* The incident led to a long period of tension. ~ *panjang* to have serious consequences. 2 with a tail. *bintang* ~ comet.
berbuntut-buntut in a line, in rows, one after the other, in single file, in succession. *berjalan* ~ to walk one after the other.
membuntut to follow, trail after, pursue.
membuntuti [and mbuntutin (*J coq*)] to track down, trace, follow, tail, tailgate. *Dia dibuntuti polisi.* The police were tailing him.
buntutan (*nomor* ~) the last digits of a number that is bet on.
pembuntut s.t. or s.o. that tracks/follows.
pembuntutan tracking.
buntut II various species of shrubs and trees. – *bajing* k.o. plant, *Uraria crinita.* – *bajung* foxtail palm, *Wodytia spp.* – *baung/paya* k.o. shrub. – *kucing* hornworth, *Ceratophyllum demersum, Uraria spp.*
buntut III *ikan* – *kerbau* lizard fish, *Saurida tumbil.*
buntut IV (*M*) female genitals, vagina.

bunuh kill, murder. *hukum* – to sentence to death. – *mati* inmost chamber of a fish trap. – *paril* inner chamber of a fish trap; → BELAT I.
(ber)bunuh-(bunuh)an, bunuh-membunuh and bersibunuh to kill e.o.
membunuh 1 to kill, murder. ~ *diri* to commit suicide. ~ *nafsu* to kill one's desire, turn one off. ~ *waktu* to kill time. 2 to get rid of (s.t. unwanted), eliminate, erase, cross out. 3 to put out, extinguish (a fire/a light). 4 to plug (a hole, etc.), stop (a leak).
membunuhi [and mbunuhin (*J coq*)] (*pl obj*) to kill, murder.
terbunuh killed, murdered.
bunuhan 1 killing, murder. 2 s.o. used for killing. 3 murder victim, s.o. who is to be killed. 4 back part of a fish trap.
pembunuh 1 killer, murderer, assassin. ~ *bayaran* paid assassin/murderer, hit man. 2 s.t. that kills, -cide. ~ *jamur* fungicide. ~ *kutu busuk* bedbug exterminator. ~ *putih* narcotics. ~ *serangga* insecticide. ~ *waktu* time killer. 3 lethal. *zat* ~ lethal substance.
pembunuhan murder, homicide, killing, assassination. ~ *berencana/dengan rencana/terencana* premeditated murder. ~ *besar-besaran* wholesale killings, genocide. ~ *diri* suicide. ~ *karakter* character assassination.
bunut I k.o. small tree, *Pternandra coerulescens.*
bunut II small spots/streaks.
bunyi I 1 sound, noise. – *ledakan* explosion. 2 cry (of an animal). 3 what s.t. sounds like, how s.t. reads, the content of s.t. *Surat ini –nya begini.* The letter reads as follows. – *alir* (*ling*) liquid. – *cina karam* an infernal racket. – *desis* (*ling*) sibilant. – *geletar/getar* (*ling*) trill. – *gésér* (*ling*) fricative. – *hidup* (*ling*) vowel. – *kembar* (*ling*) diphthong. – *letupan* (*ling*) stop.– *lanjut* (*ling*) continuant. – *luncuran/pelancar* (*ling*) glide. – *menggelegar* sonic boom. – *murai* at dawn, at daybreak. – *pepet* (*ling*) schwa. – *sampingan* (*ling*) lateral. – *sengau* (*ling*) nasal. – *sentuhan* (*ling*) flap, tap. – *serangkap* (*ling*) diphthong. – *surat* contents of a letter. – *tekak* (*ling*) glottal stop.
sebunyi 1 like-sounding. 2 in agreement.
berbunyi 1 to make a noise. 2 (it) reads. *Surat keputusan itu* ~ *sebagai berikut.* The decision reads as follows. 3 to ring (of the telephone). 4 to be heard (of a sound). *Tapi sejak tahun itu krédit sepéda tak* ~ *lagi.* But since that year nothing more has been heard of bicycle credits.
membunyikan 1 to sound s.t., play (an instrument). ~ *mercon* to set off fireworks. 2 to turn on (a radio, etc.).
memperbunyikan to let s.t. be heard.
bunyi-bunyian all k.o. noises and sounds.
pembunyian 1 making noise. 2 (*ling*) phonation.
bunyi II → SEMBUNYI.
bupati (*Skr*) 1 regent, government official in charge of a regency (the next level below province). 2 high officials at the royal courts in Yogyakarta and Surakarta.
bupét → BUFÉT.
bur (*onom*) splashing sound.
bura spit(tle), s.t. spit from the mouth.
membura 1 to blow strongly. 2 broken into pieces. *Pada saat itu hatiku sangat* ~. At that time my heart was broken. 3 to fire (s.o. from a job). ~ *api* to fan a fire (with bellows). ~ *musuh* to spray the enemy (with bullets).
memburakan to spit out. spew forth, spout, spray.
burai berburai 1 gushing out. 2 projecting, sticking out, protruding. 3 to spill, flow out; → BERJURAI-JURAI. *Rambutnya* ~ *diembus angin.* Her hair was disheveled blown by the wind. 4 leaked (of a secret).
memburai to flow out, pour forth. *Keluh-kesah* ~ *dari mulutnya.* Complaints poured out of her mouth.
memburaikan to pour s.t. out, radiate. *Wajahnya* ~ *ketenangan.* Her face radiated calm.
terburai gushed forth, poured out. *Ususnya* ~. Her guts poured out.
burak → BORAK I.
burakah → BERAKAH.
buraksa → BERAKSA.
buram I 1 blueprint. 2 sketch, draft.

memburam(kan) to sketch, draft, make a blueprint of, design, plan.

buram II 1 obscure, dim, dark, vague. **2** gloomy. **3** dull, translucent; → CURAM, MURAM, SURAM.

   seburam as dark/gloomy as.

   memburam to darken, become obscure.

   memburamkan to discourage, depress.

   terburam the darkest/gloomiest.

   keburaman dullness, gloominess, translucency.

bura(n)sang angry.

buraq → BORAK I.

buras I (*coq*) **1** wiped out, all gone, entirely out of. *Hartanya – di méja judi.* He lost everything at the gambling table. **2** loss, damage. **3** compensation (for damages).

   memburas to delete, wipe out, erase.

buras II small talk, chit-chat

   memburas 1 to chatter away. **2** to coax, persuade, flatter (into doing s.t.).

   buras-memburas to chatter, talk.

   memburaskan to talk about, chatter away about.

   pemburas chatter-box.

buras III k.o. rice cake made with coconut milk and wrapped in banana leaves.

buras IV memburas to have diarrhea.

burat I [*bubur serat*] pulp.

   pemburatan pulping.

burat II (*Jv*) → BORÉH.

burayak fish or shrimp larva. *– kebul* small fish larva. *– putihan* large fish larva.

burdah (*A*) **1** poems in praise of the Prophet Muhammad. **2** sheepskin coat.

burem → BURAM.

bureng (*Jv*) dull, lackluster, dim, hazy.

   pemburengan making s.t. unclear, obfuscation.

bures → BURAS I.

burét (*D*) burette.

burhan (*A*) evidence, proof.

buri (*Jv*) **1** backside, buttocks. **2** back.

burik (*J/Jv*) **1** speckled (of feathers). **2** pockmarked.

   memburik speckled, punctate.

burit 1 anus, rear end. **2** back part of s.t. *main –* and

   seburit → SEMBURIT.

   memburit to have anal intercourse.

buritan poop deck, stern (of a ship). *berhaluan/bergilir ke ~ to* be henpecked. *di ~* astern.

burj (*A*) fort.

Burjamhal (*A*) Aries.

burjasmani (*A*) ecliptic.

burjo [*bubur (kacang) ijo*] mung-bean porridge.

burjuis (*D*) bourgeois.

burjuldalu (*A*) → DALWU.

burjulmizan → MIZAN.

burjussunbulat → SUNBULAT.

burjusyamsi (*A*) orbit of the sun.

burkak (*A*) veil worn by female Muslim pilgrims; → CADAR.

burnus (*A*) cloak.

buro → BIRO.

burokrasi (*D*) bureaucracy.

buron (*J/Jv*) pursued (*usu* by the law), on the run, at large; → BURU.

   memburon to pursue, hunt down.

   buronan fugitive, wanted (by the law).

   pemburon(an) hunting down (fugitives).

bursa (*D*) **1** stock exchange, market. **2** mart, office. *berita –* stock exchange report. *kurs –* stock quotation. *– berjangka* futures market. *– buku* book fair. *– éfék(-éfék)* stock/securities exchange. *– Éfék Jakarta* [BEJ] Jakarta Stock Exchange. *– kesempatan kerja* employment agency. *– komoditi* commodities exchange. *– pariwisata* travel mart. *– saham* stock exchange. *– tenaga kerja* employment office. *– uang* check cashing office. *– wisata* tourist office.

   membursakan to put on the stock exchange.

bursuasi → BORJUASI.

buru I hunt, chase after/down. *– sergap* [buser] pursuit and attack. **memburu-sergap** to track down and stop (crime). **keburusergapan** (crime) fighting.

   berburu to go hunting (after game). *Malam ini kami akan ~ rusa.* This evening we're going deer hunting.

   berburu-buru (*pl subj*) to chase, hunt down. *Penduduk kampung itu ~ pencuri ayam.* The villagers hunted down the chicken thieves.

   memburu 1 to chase, hunt, pursue. *diburu anjing* chased by a dog. **2** to hunt for (a job, etc.), pursue (wealth). *diburu waktu* with a time value. *koran yang diburu waktu* newspaper that has a time value.

   memburui (*pl obj*) to hunt s.t.

   buruan 1 prey, game. **2** (*orang*) ~ fugitive, hunted person.

   pemburu 1 hunter. *~ berita* newshound. *~ foto* paparazzi. **2** fighter. *~ jét* jet fighter. *~ kejahatan* crime fighter. *~ laba* profiteer. *~ mata-mata* spy-catcher. *~ sergap* fighter interceptor (plane). **3** hunting (*mod*). *anjing ~* hunting dog. *hantu ~* (*cla*) a spirit resembling a dog, the specter huntsman, Shiva. *kapal ~* destroyer (a highly maneuverable warship to chase enemy ships). *Pesawat (terbang) ~* fighter (plane) (a highly maneuverable airplane to pursue enemy aircraft).

   pemburuan hunting. *~ liar* poaching.

   perburuan 1 hunting. *~ liar* poaching. **2** hunting equipment. **3** hunting ground.

buru II buru-buru hurriedly, hastily, in a hurry. *Jangan ~ pulang.* Don't go home so fast!

   berburu-buru in a hurry, quickly. *Ayah ~ berangkat ke kantor.* Father left for the office in a hurry.

   memburu-buru and **memburu(-buru)kan** to hasten, hurry/speed s.t. up, rush. *Jangan kauburu-buru.* Don't try to hurry him up.

   terburu [and **keburu** (*coq*)] **1** timely, just in time, on time, not late. *masih ~* still able to catch (the train, etc.). *Saya tidak ~.* I wasn't late. *Meréka ~ tertangkap.* They were arrested just in time. *Sudah gini hari mana ~?* How could you be on time so early in the morning? **2** too early/soon, premature, hasty, ahead of time. *~ cemas* anxious ahead of time. *~ nafsu* impetuous(ly), reckless(ly), in a hurry, prematurely, excited. **keterburuan** haste, hurry.

   terburu-buru hasty; hastily, hurriedly, quickly. *Jangan ~!* Don't be in such a hurry! *Ini keputusan yang ~.* This was a hasty decision.

   buruan (*coq*) hurry, in a hurry, hurry up (and). *~ gabung.* Hurry up and join!

   keburuan hurriedly, in a hurry.

buruai tadpole; → (KE)CÉBONG.

buruh laborer; → PEKERJA. *Hari – Nasional* Labor Day. *banyak memerlunakan/memakai –* labor intensive; → PADAT *karya. hari –* labor day. *kaum –* laborers. *partai –* labor party. *serikat –* labor union. *– bangunan* construction worker. *– borongan* pieceworker. *– cuci* washerwoman. *– darat* shore staff (of shipping company). *– halus* white-collar worker; → *pekerja* KERAH *putih.* *– harian* day laborer. *– kasar* manual laborer, unskilled worker. *– keréta api* railroad worker. *– kontrakan* contract worker, laborer working on a contract basis. *– lepas* casual laborer. *– minyak* oil worker. *– musiman* seasonal worker. *– pelabuhan* dock-worker, longshoreman. *– percétakan* printing-office worker. *– rendahan* low-income worker. *– semusim* seasonal worker. *– tambang* mineworker. *– tani* farmhand, agricultural laborer. *– terlatih* skilled worker. *– upah-batas* marginal worker.

   memburuh to work as a laborer. *Ia sehari-hari ~ tani di kebun itu.* In his daily life he works as a farmhand on that plantation.

   buruhan daily wage(s), daily pay.

   perburuhan (*mod*) labor, work; matters concerning workers. *départemén ~* department/ministry of labor. *hukum ~* labor law. *undang-undang ~* labor act.

buruhwati (*infr*) female worker.

buruj (*A*) **1** fort(ress); sign of the Zodiac. **2** *al-* "Celestial Signs"; name of the 85th chapter of the Koran.

buruk 1 ugly, hideous, horrible, unpleasant to look at. *Lukisannya itu – dan tiada seorang pun yang hendak membelinya.* His painting is hideous and no one wanted to buy it. **2** old and no good any more, worn out, dilapidated, decayed. *Tiang-tiang rumahnya telah* –. The poles of his house are already decayed. **3** bad, evil, wicked. *Kelakuannya sangat* –. His behavior is very bad. *berbuat* – to act badly. *mendapat nama* – to get a bad name. *mengambil* – a) to think mistakenly. b) to be mistaken. *angin* – (*coq*) a wind causing an upset stomach. *hari* – an unlucky day. *kabar* – bad news. *nasib* – to be unlucky, have bad luck, misadventure. *Apa –nya?* What is wrong with it? *tak ada –nya* it can do no harm, there's nothing wrong with it. *baik –nya* and – *baiknya* a) ups and downs (of fortune). b) the pros and cons (of a matter). *Meréka berbahas tentang* – *baiknya orang beristri lebih dari satu.* They discussed the pros and cons of having more than one wife. *tidak ada –nya* it won't hurt, there's nothing wrong with. – *perahu,* – *pangkalan* it's no use crying over spilt milk; what is done cannot be undone. – *muka cermin dibelah* it is an ill bird that fouls its own nest. – *ambil* a) unjust. b) to consider s.t. bad. c) to misunderstand; misunderstanding, misconception, misapprehension. – *gizi* malnourished. – *hati* evil at heart. – *laku* ill-behaved, badly behaved. – *makan* greedy, gluttonous. – *mulut* course/unrefined in speech. – *perut* a) to eat a lot. b) susceptible to diseases. – *pinta* to have bad luck. – *sangka* misinterpreted, suspected wrongly; viewing others with suspicion. **berburuk sangka** to view others with suspicion, have preconceived notions. – *siku* to take back what one has given to another person.

seburuk as bad as.

seburuk-buruknya no matter how bad it is.

berburuk(-buruk) to be on bad terms with e.o.

memburuk to rot, decay, become bad/useless, go bad, deteriorate; deteriorating.

memburuk-buruknya 1 the worst. *Inilah pengalaman saya* ~. That was the worst experience for me. **2** however bad ... may be. ~ *hasilnya tidak akan membuat engkau dipecat dari pekerjaan itu.* However bad the outcome may be it will not affect your being fired from that job.

memburukkan 1 to spoil, make worse. **2** to disgrace, defame, abuse, say bad things about. *Ia dituntut karena* ~ *nama Menteri Keuangan.* He was prosecuted because he dragged the Finance Minister's name through the mud.

memburuk-burukkan to defame, vilify.

memperburuk to make worse, worsen.

terburuk the worst.

keburukan 1 ugliness. **2** bad point, weakness.

pemburukan 1 rotting, deterioration. **2** defamation, slandering.

burun 1 desert; → GURUN. **2** → KAMBING *burun.*

burung I 1 bird. **2** (often) prefixed to names of birds (also see the specific bird name). **3** (*coq*) an infant's penis. *cerita* – rumors. *daun* – a shrub, *Rhincanthus nasuta. Perhimpunan* – Indonesia, Ornithological Society of Indonesia. – *terbang dipipis lada* don't count your chickens before they are hatched. *satu sangkar dua* – two women both having the same man as their lover. *kuat* – *karena sayap* every man has his strong points. FOR OTHER NAMES OF BIRDS BEGINNING WITH BURUNG SEE THE FOLLOWING WORD. – *angin ribut* albatross. – *angklung* chestnut-backed scimitar babbler, *Pomatorhinus montanus.* – *anis mérah* orange-headed thrush, *Zoothera citrina.* – *babi* adjutant stork, *Leptoptilus javanicus.* – *badak* hornbill, *Buceros rhinoceros, Dichoceros bicornis.* – *balai* thick-billed shrike, *Lanius tigrinus.* – *bangau* various species of herons. – *berkik* snipe, *Gallinago spp.* – *besi* Asian fairy-bluebird, *Irena puella.* – *buaya* k.o. kingfisher, *Pelargopsis malaccensis.* – *bunga api* orange-bellied flower pecker, *Dicaeum trigonostigma.* – *cabé* scarlet-headed flowerpecker, *Dicaeum trochileum.* – *cenderawasih* bird of paradise, *Cicinnurus regius.* – *dara* pigeon, dove. – *déwata* bird of paradise; → CENDERAWASIH. – *elang* various species of hawk. – *gagak* crow, *Corvus macrorhyncus.* – *gelatik* Java temple/rice bird. – *gelatik Indo* a Java temple bird but with white feathers. – *geréja* sparrow, *Passer montanus.* – *gosong* various species of brush-turkey, *Aepypodius spp.* and *Megapodius spp.* – *hantu* scops owl, *Otus scops.* – *hiburan* bird kept for one's pleasure, pet bird. – *hong* phoenix. – *jalak* star-

ling. – *janggut* grey-cheeked bulbul, *Alophoixus bres.* – *jantung* little spider hunter, *Arachnothera longirostra.* – *jenjang* crane. – *jinak* tame bird. – *kacamata* oriental white-eye, *Zosterops palpebrosus.* – *kaléng* starling. – *kékék* mangrove kingfisher, *Halcyon chloris.* – *kenari* canary. – *kendali* Asian palm swift, *Cypsiurus balasiensis.* – *kepudang* golden oriole. – *kesturi* parroquet. – *kopi-kopi* chestnut-backed scimitar babbler, *Pomatorhinus montanus.* – *kuda-kuda* red-fronted laughing thrush, *Garrulax rufifrons.* – *kuntul* white heron. – *kuntul kepala mérah* (in Irian Jaya) eastern sarus crane, *Grus antigone sharpii.* – *kunyit* k.o. oriole, *Micropus melanocephalus.* – *lang* hawk. – *layang-layang* swallow. – *lembu* dusky-gray heron, *Ardea sumatrana.* – *lipat* Blyth's hornbill, *Rhyticeros plicatus.* – *luntur* blue-tailed trogon, *Harpactes reinwardtii.* – *madu* brown-throated sunbird, *Anthreptes malacensis.* – *madu gunung* Kuhl's sunbird, white-flanked sunbird, *Aethopyga eximia.* – *malas* long tailed nightjar, *Caprimulgus macrurus bimaculatus.* – *maléo* a fowl species found in the Gorontalo area (North Celebes). – *manyar* weaverbird, *Ploceus spp.* – *mas* Nicobar pigeon, *Caloenas nicobarica.* – *merak* peacock. – *merpati* pigeon. – *merpati kebutan* racing pigeon. – *merpati klépékan* decoy pigeon. – *murai* magpie. – *namdur* various species of bowerbird, *Chlamydera spp.* – *nasar* vulture. – *nilam* golden oriole. – *nuri raja* (in Irian Jaya) Pesquet's parrot, *Nestor pesquet.* – *océhan* talking bird. – *ongklét* crested jay, *Platylophus galericulatus.* – *paok* banded pitta, *Pitta guajana.* – *pegar* pheasant. – *pelituk* woodpecker. – *pemangsa* bird of prey. – *perantau* migratory bird, bird of passage. – *pingai* white crow (a symbol of the miraculous). – *putar* turtle dove, *Turtur spp.* – *pipit* sparrow. – *puyuh* quail; → PUYUH I. – *remetuk* fly-eater, golden-bellied gerygone, *Gerygone sulphurea.* – *segan* long tailed nightjar, *Caprimulgus macrurus bimaculatus.* – *sepah gunung* Sunda minivet, *Pericrocotus miniatus.* – *sepah kecil* small minivet, *Pericrocotus cinnamomeus.* – *serak* owl. – *serambi* Vogelkop bowerbird, *Amblyornis inornatus.* – *sétan* (in some areas of Central Java) pelican. – *sriwang* Asian paradise flycatcher, *Terpsiphone paradisi.* – *sorga* bird of paradise. – *suangi* k.o. owl. – *tahun* wrinkled hornbill, *Aceros corrugatus.* – *tebang mentua* helmeted hornbill, *Rhinoplax vigil.* – *tikus* Javan tesia, *Tesia superciliaris.* – *udang* small blue kingfisher, *Alcedo coerulescens.* – *undan* pelican, *Pelicanus conspiculatus.* – *unta* ostrich, *Struthio camelus.* – *upik* milky stork, *Ibis cinereus.* – *wilis* k.o. emerald-colored bird.

burung-burungan bird-like, toy bird.

burung II → DAUN *burung.*

burus (*A*) leprosy.

burut (*med*) hernia, rupture, prolapse; → KONDOR. – *pusar* umbilical hernia. – *rahim* prolapsed uterus.

pemburutan prolapse.

bus I (*D*) (city) bus; → BIS II. – *air* river bus. – *bertingkat* double-decker bus. – *gandéng* articulated city bus. – *laut* k.o. ferry (boat) plying between Jakarta and *Pulau Seribu.* – *ompréngan* bus used illicitly to earn extra money. – *surat* mailbox. – *témpélan* (the term used by *Perum PPD*) to refer to the articulated city bus. – *tingkat* double-decker bus.

bus II (*onom*) hissing sound of air escaping.

busa I 1 froth, scum, foam, lather. *Sabun yang baik mutunya banyak –nya.* A good-quality soap has quite a lot of suds. *Kocok putih telur sampai –!* Beat the egg white until it is stiff. **2** foam at the mouth (from talking a lot), froth (on liquids/beer etc.), foam (of liquid in fermentation). – *pérak* silver sweepings. – *sabun* soapsuds.

berbusa 1 to foam, froth, lather (of soap); frothy, lathery **2** to foam at the mouth.

membusa 1 to foam (of water/the mouth, etc.); foamy. *laut* – foamy sea. **2** to froth (of beer); frothy. **3** to sparkle (of wine).

membusakan to make scum/foam.

busa II (*M*) *tukang* – bellows puller.

berbusa and **membusa 1** to blow/breathe out forcefully. **2** to pant, gasp (for breath).

membusa-busa to pant, gasp for breath.

membusakan 1 to blow up (a balloon). **2** to blow s.t. out; to spray s.t.

pembusa 1 bellows puller. **2** (glass) blower.

busah → BUSA I.

busai spread, scatter.

  membusai to spread, be scattered/propagated.

  membusaikan to spread, scatter s.t.

  terbusai spread, scattered.

  busaian ~ *rambut* a head of hair.

busana (*Skr*) clothing, wearing apparel, attire, garment, dress. *dalam keadaan tanpa* – in the nude. *Operasi* – Operation Clothes, i.e., the operation launched in 1964 to clothe the people of Irian Jaya. *peragaan* – fashion show. – *berbunga-bunga* a flowery dress. – *jadi* ready-to-wear garment. – *kerja* work clothes. – *Muslim* Islamic clothing. – *sedia* simple dress. – *gala* evening dress. – *pantai* beach wear. – *pernikahan* wedding dress. – *prima* haute-couture. – *renang* swimwear. – *santai* leisure wear. – *siap pakai* ready-to-wear. – *siap pakai gaya kantor* office-style ready-to-wear clothing.

  berbusana dressed, to dress. ~ *terbaik* best-dressed.

  membusanai to put clothing on s.o., clothe.

  membusanakan to clothe.

  pebusana dresser. ~ *terbaik* best-dressed.

busar → BUSUR. *seperti* – *Arjuna* a simile for a beautiful arm.

buser [buru sergap] pursuit and attack.

busét I (*J*) Oh Lord! Good gracious/grief!

busét II (*ob*) *sakit* – dysentery.

bushido (*Jp*) bushido.

busi I (*D*) sparkplug.

busi II (*Hind? cla*) rice bran.

busi III (*Jv*) dry and flaking (of skin).

busih landfill.

busik white spots on hands and feet.

bustan (*Pers*) garden.

bustanulathfal (*A*) kindergarten.

buster booster (for automobiles).

busuk 1 rotten (literally and as an insult). **2** rot, blight (in names of plant and animal diseases). – *bangar* very bad. – *basah* wet rot. – *batang* stem rot. – *bonggol* rhizome rot. – *budi* of bad character. – *hati* a) envious. b) heart rot (a disease of plants). – *kayu* butt rot. – *kering* dry rot. – *kuku* foot rot. – *lahak* very bad. – *pangkal* butt rot. – *tangan* light-fingered.

  sebusuk as rotten as.

  membusuk to rot, decay, putrefy, become rotten. *dalam keadaan* ~ in a state of putrefaction. *cepat* ~ highly perishable.

  membusuki to denigrate.

  membusukkan 1 to defame, denigrate. **2** to let s.t. rot.

  busuk-membusukkan to denigrate e.o.

  terbusuk the rottenest.

  kebusukan 1 rot. **2** evil.

  pembusuk rot, rotting.

  pembusukan rot, rotting, rottenness, putrefaction.

busung (*J/Jv*) swollen, bloated, distended, bulging. – *air* dropsy. – *dada* conceited. – *darah* swelling prior to menstruation. – *kelaparan* edema. – *kencing* swelling of bladder due to holding in urine. – *kulit* water-filled swellings under the skin. – *lapar* edema. – *perut* bloat in the stomach.

  membusung to inflate, blow up, distend, bulge, swell. ~ *dada* to brag, boast.

  membusungkan to blow s.t. up, distend s.t., make s.t. distend. ~ *dada* to swell with pride.

  terbusung swollen, bloated.

busur 1 bow (used with arrows). **2** arc, arch, quadrant. **3** cotton-gin. **4** blow-link (s.t. made of – *api* fire arc. bamboo that gives a humming sound to a kite). – *cahaya* electric arc. – *derajat* protractor. – *kompas* compass graduation. – *panah* bow and arrow.

  membusur 1 to shoot with a bow and arrow. **2** to curve, be shaped like an arc, bow-shaped. **3** to clean (cotton) with a cotton-gin.

busut 1 mound, hillock, hummock. **2** anthill, termite nest. – *juga yang ditimbun anai-anai* a) the rich get richer. b) once guilty, always assumed to be guilty. – *betina* large round anthill. – *jantan* small pointed anthill.

  membusut mound shaped, mounded. *kerak nasi* ~ *jantan* there are a lot of left-overs (after a feast).

busyét (*J*) Oh, my God! Gosh!

but I (*Pers*) idol.

but II (in acronyms) → KEBUTUHAN.

BUT III → BENTUK *Usaha Tetap*.

buta I 1 blind, unable to see; → TUNANÉTRA. *Matanya* –. He is blind (usually in one eye), blind in one eye; *cp* TOJI. *Kedua-belah matanya* –. He is blind in both eyes. *menjadi* – to go blind. *orang* – blind (wo)man. *kaum* – the blind. *si* – the blind-person. *perigi* – a) a dried-up well. b) a well without a cover. *uang* – → GAJI *buta*. **2** dark. *gelap* – pitch black. *malam* – pitch-black night. **3** ignorant, not know anything about s.t. – *hukum* ignorant of the law. – *huruf* illiterate. **kebuta-hurufan** illiteracy. **4** furious. *si* – *membilang bintang di langit* to carry coals to Newcastle. *seperti orang* – *kehilangan tongkat* be in a tight spot. – *akan* blind to. – *baru celik/melék/melihat* to go/run hog wild. *si* – *baru melék* – s.o. who runs hogwild. *tidak sepésér* – broke, penniless. – *hukum* ignorant of the law. – *rabun* myopic (when objects look like smoky shadows). – *warna* colorblind. *Sudah malam dan saya masih* – *sama sekali keadaan Jakarta*. It was night and I was still completely unused to the Jakarta scene. **5** ignorance. **6** blank, not written on, not marked. *gaji* – a salary without having to work for it. *makan gaji* – to have a sinecure/soft job. *surat* – an anonymous letter (not marked with the sender's name). **7** to act blindly/recklessly. *malam* – a pitch-black night. *perigi* – a dried-up well. – *akal* obtuse. – *ayam* a) near-sighted. b) twilight blindness. – *belalang* blind stare. – *bular* blind from cataracts. – *celik/céméh/cémér* a) blind in one eye. b) blind with the eyes open. – *hati* a) cold, unfeeling, heartless. b) cruel, harsh. – *kayu* completely illiterate. – *kemajuan* backward. – *kesip* blind from a lost eyeball. – *larang(an)* myopic; myopia. – *malam* night blindness. – *mereloh* totally blind. – *pendengaran* a) deaf. b) to refuse to listen. – *perasaan* insensitive, unfeeling. – *perut* a) unfeeling. b) unable to tell one taste from another, not fussy about eating. c) to eat forbidden food (such as pork) by pretending not to know what it is. – *picak* blind in one eye. – *senja* twilight blindness. – *siang* day blind. – *tuli* a) deaf and blind. b) ignorant. **membuta tuli** to act recklessly. **membuta-tulikan** to pull the wool over s.o.'s eyes. – *warna* colorblind. – *warta* ignorant of current events.

  sebuta as blind as.

  membuta 1 to pretend to be blind. **2** (*vulg*) to sleep, doze off. **3** (to act, etc.) blindly/recklessly.

  membutakan 1 to blind s.o. **2** to dazzle. **3** to keep s.o. in ignorance. ~ *mata terhadap kenyataan* to blind o.s. to reality.

  buta-butaan recklessly, wildly.

  kebutaan blindness.

buta II a well which has no (wooden) cover over it.

buta III (*Skr*) demon, giant, ogre. – *cakil* (*Jv*) (mythological demon with protruding lower jaw and raised eyeteeth.

buta-buta k.o. tree, *Excoecaria agallocha*. – *badak* k.o. tree, *Cerbera manghas*.

butak I → BOTAK.

butak II → BUTEK.

butala (*Skr*) earth, soil.

butana I and **butane** (*D*) butane (gas).

butana II *ikan* – various species of surgeon fish, *Acanthurus triostegus*; unicorn fish, *Naso brevirostris*.

butang (*Port*) button (on clothing); → KANCING I.

butarepan (*Jv*) **1** competition, rivalry. **2** jealousy (between spouses).

butas [buton aspalt] Buton asphalt.

butbut the crow-pheasant, short-toed coucal, *Centropus rectunguis* and other species.

butek (*J/Jv*) **1** turbid, thick, muddy (of water). **2** confused, in confusion, stressed out. *pikiran yang* – a troubled mind.

butik (*D/E*) boutique.

butir 1 particle, corpuscle; grains, small seeds. *Ibu tua itu mengumpulkan* –.– *beras yang tercécér di lantai truk*. The old lady collected rice kernels scattered on the floor of the truck. **2** tiny bit. *tidak ada satu* – *pun* there isn't a scintilla of. **3** data, (minute) facts, details, point (in a contract), item. –.– *kesepakatan* points in an agreement. **4** round (of ammunition). **5** counter/classifier for small round objects, such as, eggs/coconuts/grains/gems/

bullets, etc. *tiga – telur* three eggs. *dua – peluru* two rounds. *– darah* blood corpuscle. *–.– darah mérah* red blood corpuscles. *–.– pokok* essentials.

sebutir l (*counter*) one, a. **2** a particle, small amount. *~ harapan* a flicker/ray of hope.

berbutir granulated.

berbutir-butir in/many ... (whatever is being counted). *~ telur* many eggs.

membutir l to granulate, be grainy. **2** to be detailed, in detail.

membutirkan to relate in detail, give details about.

butiran l grain, s.t. granular. *~ keras* (*geol*) rigid grain. *~ lunak* (*geol*) ductile grain. **2** bullet (in typography). **3** point, item.

berbutiran granulate.

butir-butiran grains.

kebutiran granularity.

pembutiran granulation.

buto jockey (at bull races).

buto ijo (*Jv*) a green ogre.

butongpai (C) a system of self-defense (a blend of *kungfu* and *karaté*)

butsarman [kebutuhan dasar manusia] basic human needs.

butuh I (*Jv*) *– akan/dengan/(ke)pada* need for, necessity of. *Anak itu masih – bimbingan.* That child still needs guidance.

membutuhi (*ob*) and **membutuhkan** to need, want, require. *membutuhi kebutuhan hidup* to require the necessities of life. *Negara Indonésia masih membutuhkan invéstasi modal asing.* Indonesia still is in need of foreign capital investments.

kebutuhan need, necessity, want, requirement. *menurut ~* as and when required, according to requirements, as (may be) required, as the need arises, as circumstances require. *~ akan tanah* greed for land. *~ biologis* biological needs. *~ berpréstasi* need for achievement. *~ dan pengadaan* supply and demand. *~ fisik* physical need. *~ hidup* necessities of life. *~ hidup yang layak* proper necessities of life. *~ jasmani* material needs. *~ lain* other needs, extras. *~ kantor* office supplies. *~ pokok* basic necessities. *~ pokok sehari-hari* basic necessities of life.

butuh II (outside Java) penis.

butul (*Jv*) **butulan** side (*mod*). *jalan ~* side street. *pintu ~* side door, side entrance.

butun(g) *pohon –* k.o. tree, *Barringtonia asiatica*; → PUTAT *laut*.

butut (*J*) worn out, threadbare, unfit for use. *Dia gemar mengenakan celana jin –.* He likes to wear prewashed worn-out jeans.

terbutut totally worn out.

bututut brown-throated barbet, *Megalaima corvina*.

buuanyak (*coq*) a whole lot, a great deal of. *Anak buahnya – sekali.* He has a lot of underlings.

BUUD [Badan Usaha Unit Désa] cooperative village organization.

buwana (*ob*) → BUANA.

buwés (*D*) driver's license; → RÉBEWÉS.

buya (in Sumatra) religious pundit; → AJENGAN (in West Java), KIAI (in Central and East Java).

buyar (*J/Jv*) **1** scattered (of birds when startled), blown away, dispersed (in all directions). *awan –* scattered clouds. **2** to run (of ink on blotting paper), spread. *kertas –* blotting/tissue paper. **3** vanished (into thin air). **4** to break down (of a pesticide). **5** to break down, fall through (of talks). *Harapan-harapan itu –.* Those expectations vanished into thin air. *Gencatan senjata – lagi.* The ceasefire fell through again.

membuyarkan to disperse, scatter s.t. around. *~ asumsi itu* to destroy that assumption. *~ rencana Pemerintah Indonésia* to make a mess of the Indonesian government plans.

buyung I (*Port?*) **1** big-bellied pitcher, round-bottomed (earthenware or metal) water-jar, urn. *mak – (joc)* a) a pregnant woman. b) procuress, matchmaker. *pecah –, tempayan ada* there is no shortage of women (to take as a wife). **2** (*bio*) utricle.

buyung II (*M*) vocative for boy (in calling); → AWANG II.

buyung III k.o. decorative plant, *Hibiscus mutabilis*.

buyung-buyung k.o. plant, *Vernonia cinerea*.

buyur (*J*) **membuyur** to water, pour water on; → MENGGUYUR.

buyut **1** great-great-grandparent(s). **2** a sacred place of worship/veneration. **3** great-grandchild.

kebuyutan **1** hereditary, heritable. *musuh ~* hereditary enemy. *permusuhan ~* hereditary enmity. **2** trembling, shaking (due to old age). **3** holy site.

BVA [Bursa Valuta Asing] Foreign Exchange Market.

BW I first-class passenger car (in train formation).

BW II (*D leg*) [Burgelijk Wetboek] Civil Code.

byar (*Jv onom*) come on (of lights), sudden brightness/light; *cp* PET. *Mak – lampunya bernyala lagi.* Suddenly the lights came on again, the lights all of a sudden lit up again. **2.172** *désa di Jatim sudah –.* 2,172 villages in East Java have already been hooked up on the electric light system. *~ pet* to go on and off. *Néonnya – pet.* The neon lights went on and off. *Pacaran dengan céwék yang manis sudah – pet.* His romance with that sweet girl was on-again off-again.

byar-byar the light suddenly dawned.

membyarkan to switch off (lights, etc.).

byur (*Jv onom*) **1** *mak –* plop! (sound of s.o. jumping or s.t. falling into the water). **2** whish (sound of s.t. whizzing by fast).

C

c and **C I** /cé/ the third letter of the Latin alphabet used for writing Indonesian. Note – When this letter should be pronounced as *sé*, as in *AC*, this will be indicated immediately following the lemma, thus /asé/. When this letter should be pronounced as *k*, as in Coca Cola, it will be indicated so immediately after the lemma, as in /Koka Kola/.

c II symbol for centi-; → SÉNTI-.

C III Roman numeral for 100.

C IV Celsius or centigrade.

ca I the sixth letter in the Arabic alphabetical order used to spell, for example, *cari*.

ca II (C) Chinese tea.

ca III (C *J*) to eat (rice, etc.).

ca IV (in acronyms) → CALON.

ca V (C) **1** cooked in sauce. **2** a dish made from a combination of meat/shrimps and vegetables (mushrooms, leek, broccoli, bamboo shoots, cauliflower), broth, and corn starch.
   mengeca to stir fry.

cab (in acronyms) → CABANG.

caba I → CALON *bintara*.

caba II reckless, frivolous.

cabai I (*Skr*) chili, red pepper; → LOMBOK.. *Ia menumbuk – untuk membuat sambal.* She's pounding chili to make a spicy paste. *kecil-kecil – rawit* small but feisty. *mendapat – rawit* to get a scolding. *siapa makan – ialah kepedasan/berasa pedas* and *siapa yang makan – mesti dia sendiri yang kepedasan* (or, *dialah yang kepedasan*) as you sow, so shall you reap. *– alas* → CABAI *jawa*. *– besar* Spanish (red) pepper, *Capsicum annuum*. *– jawa* long pepper, a creeping plant resembling *sirih* or *merica* growing in coastal areas; the seeds are blackish-brown colored and are *usu* used as a traditional *jamu* ingredient, *Piper retrofractus*. *– keriting* a small, curly, red chili, somewhat larger than the *cabai rawit*. *– mérah* Spanish (red) pepper, *Capsium annuum*. *– panjang* → CABAI *jawa*. *– rawit/sétan* a) small, very sharp (green or red) pepper, *Capsicum frutescens*. b) a small but very active person.
   kecabaian 1 too spiced, have a burnt taste from eating red peppers. **2** (of a person) restless, fidgety. *seperti orang ~* to fidget.

cabai II bird species – tree creeper, *Dicaeum spp.*; → CABÉ-CABÉAN.

cabak I (*Jv*) various species of nightjar and related birds. *– gunung* Salvadori's nightjar, *– India* grey nightjar, *Caprimulgus indicus*. *– maling* large-tailed nightjar, goatsucker, *Caprimulgus macrurus*. *– maling kota* savanna nightjar, *Caprimulgus affinis*. *– wono* Javan frogmouth, *Batrachostomus javensis*; → SEGAN *jawa*.

cabak II torn wide open.

cabang 1 branch, bough, spur, ramification, prong. *Pohon ini banyak –nya.* This tree has many branches. **2** branch establishment/office; division or part (of a body of learning); subdivision (of a family of languages). *Bank Indonésia mempunyai banyak –nya di seluruh Indonésia.* Bank Indonesia has many branch offices throughout Indonesia. *Botani ialah – biologi.* Botany is a branch of biology. *Bahasa Indonésia ialah – rumpun bahasa Melayu-Polinésia.* The Indonesian language is a branch of the Malayo-Polynesian language family. **3** fork, the point where a river/road, etc. divides into two or more branches. *Sungai itu banyak –nya.* That river has many branches/arms. **4** chapter, affiliation (of an organization/club, etc.). *–.– Golkar terdapat di mana-mana.* Chapters of Golkar are found everywhere. *– arus* shunt. *– atas* a) top-level, first-class (player), top-seeded. b) the higher echelons, the elite. *– dua* bifurcation. *– jalan* side road, bystreet, byway. *– pegunungan* mountain spur. *– pembantu* sub-branch. *– tempur* combat arm.
   bercabang 1 to have branches (of trees/enterprises, etc.). *Pohon kelapa mémang tidak ~.* In fact coconut trees have no branches. **2** to branch off, divide into branches, fork, split, bifurcate. *Jalan itu ~ tiga.* That road splits into three branches. **3** to be of two (minds, etc.). *lidah ~* deceitful, double-tongued, untrustworthy. *~ hati/pikiran* ambivalent. *~ dua* two-fold, two-pronged. *pikirannya ~ (dua)* he is in doubt. *~ hati/pikiran* ambivalent.
   cabang-bercabang and **bercabang-cabang** to have many branches, branch off, split, fork (in numbers), fork in many different directions. *Tanduk rusa ~.* Deer antlers have many branches.
   mencabang to branch, ramify.
   mencabangkan 1 to graft, transplant. **2** to set up a branch/affiliate.
   mempercabangkan to cause to branch off (or, to have ramifications).
   kecabangan branch.
   pencabangan 1 branching. **2** grafting, transplanting.
   percabangan 1 branching, forking. *~ jalan/sungai* branching of road/river. **2** ramification.

cabar I 1 timid, faint-hearted, cowardly, fearful. **2** discouraged, disheartened, downhearted. *– hati* cowardly. **3** without effect, ineffective, powerless (of charms/spells/magic), pusillanimous.
   mencabarkan *~ hati* a) to discourage, dishearten. b) to frighten.
   kecabaran insipidity, cowardice, discouragement.

cabar II (*M*) **1** careless, rash, nonchalant. **2** careless about spending money.

cabar III (*Mal*) **mencabar** to challenge (to a fight).
   cabaran challenge.
   pencabar challenger.
   pencabaran challenge.

cabau (*M*) claw, paw.
   mencabau to claw, scratch.

cabé I (*J*) → CABAI I. *– lempuyang* a folk medicine brewed from the wild ginger plant, *Zingiber spp.*, and chilies; it is used as a cough suppressant and decongestant.
   cabé-cabéan various k.o. chilies.

cabé II → BURUNG *cabé*.

cabik 1 torn, snagged, tattered. *Baju pengemis itu – dan kotor.* The beggar's clothes were torn and dirty. **2** lacerated, mangled (of prey). **3** classifier for pieces/strips of paper/cloth/read, etc. *se-kertas* a piece of paper. *kain dua –* two strips of cloth. *beberapa – roti* some slices of bread.
   cabik-cabik 1 torn to shreds/ribbons, tattered, ragged; → COBAK-CABIK. *Bajunya ~.* His coat was all tattered and torn. *~ arang* frail, fragile (of almost broken relationships). **2** shreds, torn-up pieces. *~ kertas* shreds of paper. *~ bulu ayam* reconcilable controversy.
   mencabik 1 to tear into strips/tatters, rip up, cut up into strips. *~ arang/mulut* (*M*) to cry out, scream. *~ baju di dadanya* to wash one's dirty linen in public. **2** to lacerate, mangle.
   cabik-mencabik to lacerate e.o., rip e.o. up.
   mencabik-cabik to tear/rip/shred frequently/again and again.
   mencabikkan → MENCABIK.
   tercabik torn/tattered, got ripped. *Lengan bajunya ~.* The sleeve of his coat was torn.
   tercabik-cabik 1 torn to pieces, shredded. *Rasa harga dirinya ~.* Her pride was torn to shreds. **2** lacerated, hurt (of feelings).
   cabikan 1 tear, rent, rip, split. **2** piece, shred. *~ kertas bungkus* shreds of wrapping paper.
   pencabik *~ bas* bass player. *~ karcis* ticket taker (in movie theaters); → PENYOBÉK *karcis*.
   pencabikan tearing, ripping, laceration.

cabin roasted sugar-palm stalks.

cabir torn to pieces, torn into long strips; → CABIK, COBAR-CABIR.
   bercabiran (*pl subj*) in rags, torn up.
   cabiran rag, tatter.

cabis (*Jv*) traditional visit by the parents of *santriwans* to a *pondok* to submit gifts in the form of rice or money to the *Kiai*.

cabit → CABIK.

cablak (*J*) to have a big mouth. – *blaka* (*Jv*) candid and open. *Antara lain sifat-sifat masyarakatnya yang –.* The characteristic features of the society are, among other things, candor and openness.

cabo (*C J*) loose woman, prostitute, whore. – *embun* prostitute who operates in the open air.

   nyabo to engage in promiscuous sex, be a slut.

cabol → CÉBOL.

cabuh (*M*) in a commotion, in an uproar, in confusion.

   kecabuhan commotion, uproar, confusion, tumult, upheaval.

cabuk I a syphilitic ulcer (*esp* on the lower leg). *penyakit – putih* mildew (in apple trees).

cabuk II *ikan –* wolf herring, *Chirocentrus dorab*.

cabuk III → CAMBUK.

cabul I 1 immoral, licentious, indecent, outrageous (behavior). *perempuan –* a loose woman, prostitute, whore. **2** obscene, dirty, pornographic, lascivious. *Lima remaja usia sekolah menengah dihukum karena berbuat –.* Five high-school-aged students were punished because they had engaged in obscene behavior. *bacaan/gambar –* pornographic reading matter/photos. **3** rape, sodomy.

   bercabul 1 to behave in an outrageous manner, act immorally; → BERBUAT *cabul*. **2** to rage (of an epidemic/war), rampage, operate unchecked, go on the rampage. **3** rampant. *Kejahatan jenis ini mémang makin ~.* This type of crime is, in fact, increasingly rampant.

   bercabul-cabulan to do dirty things to e.o.

   mencabuli 1 to stain, besmirch (s.o.'s name). **2** to rape, molest (a woman), violate (rights/sovereignty, etc.). *~ hak-hak asasi manusia* to violate fundamental human rights.

   mencabulkan *~ diri* to prostitute o.s.

   tercabuli got violated/raped.

   kecabulan pornography, obscenity, immorality, profligacy.

   pencabul pornographer, immoral person.

   pencabulan 1 rape (of a woman). **2** violation (of the law).

   percabulan 1 obscenity, licentiousness, profligacy. **2** sex (*mod*). *Ketika berkunjung ke salah satu kota terbesar di AS, lelaki ini menghabiskan waktu masuk-keluar toko ~.* When visiting one of the largest cities in the U.S., this gentleman wasted his time going in and out of sex shops.

cabul II → CÉBOL.

cabup [calon bupati] candidate for regent.

cabur I kecaburan uproar, disturbance, chaos.

cabur II (*M*) → CEBUR.

cabut I pull/yank out. – *bulu* hair tweezers. – *gigi* extraction. – *malu* to save face. – *masuk* (*petro*) round trip (pull out and reinsert an oil drill).

   bercabut drawn (of a weapon), pulled out, extracted. *main ~ to* play blackjack; → SELIKURAN.

   bercabut-cabutan to tear away at e.o.

   mencabut [and **nyabut** (*coq*)] **1** to pull/take out, pull off, extract, take off, remove, draw (out), pull up, strip. *~ cincin* to take off a ring. *~ gigi* to extract a tooth. *~ kartu* to draw a card. *~ nyawa* to take s.o.'s life. *~ paku* to pull out a nail. *~ rambut* to pull out hair. *~ rumput* to pull up grass. **2** to win (a prize), draw (a winning number). *~ loteré* a) to win a prize in a lottery. b) to draw a lottery. *~ malu* to save face. *~ undian* a) to win a prize in a lottery. b) to draw a lottery. **3** to draw, pull out. *~ keris/pistol/répolpér* to pull out a kris/pistol/revolver. **4** to cancel (an order/expired passport, etc.), nullify, annul, rescind, reverse (a decision, etc.). **5** to withdraw (a draft bill/coins from circulation, etc.), recall (a promise/order, etc.), revoke/repeal (a decree), abolish (subsidies/rights), countermand (an order), retract (a statement), lift (an embargo), kill (a news story). *~ blokade* to lift a blockade. *Émbargo minyak telah dicabut.* The oil embargo has been lifted. *~ gugatan* to withdraw a suit. *~ hak* to abolish rights. *~ kata* to take back one's words. *~ kepercayaan* to withdraw one's confidence from s.o. *~ perkara* to withdraw a suit. *~ SIM-nya* to suspend (temporarily) one's driver's license. *Filipina ~ tuntutannya atas wilayah Sabah.* The Philippines has withdrawn its claim to Sabah. **6** to quote, copy (from a book, etc.).

mencabuti [and **nyabutin** (*J coq*)] (*pl obj*) to pull/pluck/draw out again and again/repeatedly, pull up (weeds). *~ rambut janggutnya* to pull out the hairs of one's beard.

mencabutkan 1 = mencabut. **2** to take out, draw, extract for s.o. else. **3** to reverse, revoke, lift (an embargo) for s.o. else. **4** to annul, nullify for s.o. else. **5** to quote for s.o. else.

tercabut drawn, (can be) pulled. *tidak ~* irrevocable (resolution). *~ di kartu mati* or *~ pada kertas mati* unlucky.

cabutan 1 extraction; the draw (as in a race, etc.). *~ alis* eyebrow tweezers. *~ selubung* (in mining) casing spear. **2** (in forestry) wilding, wrenching.

pencabut 1 withdrawer, drawer, puller, extractor. *~ nyawa* s.o. who takes s.o.'s life. **2** rescinder. **3** stripper. *~ selubung* (in mining) casing spear.

pencabutan 1 cancellation, repeal, retraction, withdrawal, revocation, rescission, lifting (an embargo), abolition. **2** expropriation (of title to land), deprivation (of rights, etc.). *~ hak-milik* expropriation. *~ instansi* withdrawal from (legal) proceedings. *~ izin operasi* the revocation of operating licenses. *~ jam malam* lifting of curfew. *~ kebudayaan* cultural deprivation. *~ pengakuan* derecognition.

percabutan withdrawing, revoking.

cabut II (*sl*) **1** to take off, go (home). *–!* city bus conductor's command to driver to start off on the last leg. *– lari* to run away, beat it. *–, yo/yuk!* come on, let's go! **2** to leave, depart. *Ia pernah – dari Balikpapan.* He once left Balikpapan. *Ketua Déwan Kesenian Jakarta yang akrab dengan panggilan Gus Dur ini langsung – ke Banten.* The Chairman of the Jakarta Arts Council who is intimately known by the name of Gus Dur immediately left for Banten.

mencabut to leave, abandon, give up, desert. *Meréka sepakat pula untuk ~ rumah dan memindah ke lokasi lain.* They have also agreed to abandon their houses and to move to another location.

caca I (*cla*) k.o. salad.

caca II cha-cha, a ballroom dance of Latin-American origin.

cacad → CACAT.

cacadan (*Jv*) whiffletree of a plow.

cacah I tattoo. *mesin –* perforating machine. *– lubang* perforation.

   bercacah 1 tattooed. **2** vaccinated.

   mencacah 1 to perforate. **2** to tattoo. **3** to give an injection to, inoculate. *Dokter ~ pasiénnya.* The physician inoculated his patient.

   mencacahkan to tattoo s.t.

   mencacah-cacah to repeatedly prick (the skin with a needle).

   cacahan 1 the thing tattooed. **2** tattooing. *~nya bagus sekali.* The tattooing is very nice.

   pencacah 1 tattooer, tattooist. **2** device for putting tattoos on the skin or for punching holes in paper, etc. *~ lubang* punch (the tool).

   pencacahan 1 tattooing. *~ kulit* tattooing the skin. **2** marking, branding. **3** specifications.

cacah II (*Jv*) minced, chopped up. *daging –* minced meat.

   mencacah to chop up into small pieces, mince (meat). *~ daging* to mince meat.

   cacahan chip. *~ kayu* wood chip.

   pencacah chopping knife, cleaver.

cacah III (*Jv*) number, amount. *– jiwa* a) (the size of the) population. *-nya tidak kurang dari sejuta.* The population is at least a million. b) census; → SÉNSUS. *mendaftar ~* to keep census records. **bercacah jiwa** with a population of; to have a population of. **mencacah-jiwa** to take a census, – enumerate. **pencacah jiwa** census taker. **pencacahjiwaan** census (of population).

   tercacah counted. **ketercacahan** countability.

   cacahan 1 digital. *komputer ~* digital computer. **2** count.

   pencacahan 1 census taking. *~ Cénsus Lengkap* [PCL] Complete Census Calculation. **2** enumeration, counting.

cacah IV (*Jv*) a farm worker who stays and becomes a member of the village.

cacah V (*M*) → CECAH.

cacak I perpendicular (of s.t. long that has been driven into the ground). *– lari* to run quickly. *ranjau – caltrop of bamboo/*

iron (set up in path or pit to trap enemies/game/pests). *- tong-gak* standing up straight as an arrow.

mencacak 1 to stand upright, vertical. *~ tonggak* to stand up straight as an arrow and motionless. *~ seperti tiang bendéra* to stand proudly/haughtily. *~ belat* to set a trap. **2** to stick s.t. vertically into the ground. *~ tiang bendéra* to stick a flagpole vertically into the ground. *~ lari* to run quickly.

mencacakkan 1 to stick s.t. vertically into the ground, plant s.t. upright. **2** to erect. *~ patung* to erect a statue.

tercacak implanted vertically; erected, stood upright/erect (of a stake/mast/tail/penis, etc.). *Bendéra Sang Mérah Putih berkibar-kibar pada tiang yang ~ di hadapan déwan itu.* The Red-and-White flag fluttered on the pole which was erected in front of the council.

cacak II (*M*) **mencacak 1** to pinch. **2** to pickpocket, steal.
pencacak pickpocket, thief.

cacak III (*Jv*) **1** elder brother. **2** term of address for older man. **3** → CAK II.

cacang (*M*) sappan tree, *Caesalpina sappan*; → SEPANG.

cacap I hair wash (to stimulate hair growth).
mencacap 1 to shampoo. **2** to wet one's head.
mencacapi 1 (*ob*) to inundate, flood; → MEMBANJIRI, MENGGENANGI. **2** to soak.

cacap II (*M*) **mencacap** to caress, stroke.

cacar I 1 pock mark. **2** smallpox. *benih/obat* – vaccine (lymph). *mantri* – vaccinator. *tanam* – to vaccinate against smallpox. *- air* chickenpox, varicella. *- ayam* fowl pox. *- benih* vaccine. *- betul* → CACAR *nanah*. *- cair* chickenpox. *- daun* a clove-plant disease, phylosticta. *- jaluntung/monyét* chickenpox. *- nanah* pus that produces pus blisters. *- pohon* blight. *- sapi* cowpox. *- téh* blister blight (a tea plant disease). *- ulang* revaccination, booster shot. *- unggas* fowl pox.

bercacar 1 to get a vaccination shot. **2** vaccinated. *Murid-murid di kelas ini semua sudah ~.* The pupils of this class have all been vaccinated.

mencacar to vaccinate (against smallpox).
cacaran pock-marked.
pencacar 1 vaccinator. **2** the instrument used in vaccinations.
pencacaran vaccination (against smallpox). *~ di kampung itu dilakukan oléh mantri –.* The vaccination against smallpox in that village was done by a vaccinator.

cacar II restless, capricious, fickle.
bercacar to be restless, keep on moving around.
mencacar to keep on moving s.t.

cacar III (*Jv*) **mencacar** to cut away (shrubs/bushes, etc.).

cacat 1 blemish, flaw, stain, physical disability, defect (in body/work/product/writing/behavior, etc.); defect, disfigurement, shortcoming. *Apa -nya kalau kita menjemput dia.* What harm is there in meeting him? *Barang ini - sedikit.* This article is somewhat damaged. *Hanya satu -nya.* It has only one disadvantage. *orang/penderita/penyandang –* an invalid, a handicapped/disabled person. *tiada - sedikit juga* a) stainless, spotless, perfect. b) unhurt. **2** blot, shame. *tanpa -* zero-defect. **3** disabled; disability. **4** distortion. *-.- cempedak, -.- nak hendak* sour grapes. *- badan* physical defect. *- bawaan* innate/congenital defect. *- bentuk* malformation. *- cedera/cela* various defects and flaws. *- daksa* physical deficiency. *- fungsi otak minimal* minimal brain dysfunction. *- grahita* mental deficiency. *- hukum* legally defective. *- ingatan* psychological defect. *- jantung bawaan* congenital cardiac defect. *- jasmani* physical handicap; physically handicapped. *- kehendak* vitiated consent. *- lihat* poor vision. *- logat* speech impediment. *- méntal* imbecile, mental deficiency. *- nétra* eye defect. *- penglihatan* poor vision, such as far- or near-sightedness, astigmatism, cataracts, etc. *- rungu* hearing loss. *- sejak lahir* congenital defect. *- sosial* socially handicapped. *- tersembunyi* hidden defect. *- tubuh* physically handicapped (person); → TUNADAKSA. *- tungkai* paraplegic. *- véteran* disabled veteran. *- yuridis* judicial error.

bercacat 1 infirm, invalid, disabled, handicapped. *Anak-anak nakal itu selalu mengéjék orang tua yang ~ itu.* Those naughty children always make fun of that disabled old man. **2** with/to have a defect, defective, faulty. **3** in discredit (of s.o.'s name).

mencacat to criticize, censure, disparage, find fault with, point out s.o.'s faults.

mencacati 1 to mutilate, injure, harm, hurt, damage. **2** to outrage, molest, violate.

mencacatkan to damage, hurt.

tercacat 1 damaged, defective. **2** criticized.

cacatan criticism.

kecacatan 1 disability, physical defect, handicap. **2** criticism.

pencacat s.o. who likes to point out others' faults, fault-finder.

pencacatan 1 defect. **2** disabling.

cacau 1 inconstant, fickle, changeable. **2** nervous. **3** chattering away.

mencacau 1 to be inconstant, fickle, restless, changeable, always on the move; (of a man) always remarrying. **2** to rave, be delirious, talk incoherently; → MENGIGAU.

pencacau 1 s.o. who is full of hot air, gas-bag. **2** (*cla*) saying/aphorism to throw an opponent off.

cacengklok knee hollow.

caci I abuse, mockery, scorn, ridicule, contempt, sarcasm, (critical) remark, criticism. *- maki* abuse, scorn, ridicule, name-calling. *mencaci-maki(kan)* to jeer at, mock, abuse, scorn, blame, chide. *caci-makian* insulting language.

bercaci-cacian to criticize/insult/scold e.o., exchange abuses, jeer at e.o.

mencaci 1 to insult, humiliate, offend, criticize. **2** = *mencaci maki*.

cacian ridicule, scorn, term of abuse, mockery, abuse, derision, vituperation.

pencaci person who scorns/abuses.

pencacian ridiculing, humiliating, offending, criticizing.

caci II (*cla*) reefing-gear.

cacibar great-eared/Malaysian nightjar, *Eurostopodus temminckii*; → TAPTIBAU.

cacil (*ob*) much too small for its purpose, such as one animal mating with another.

cacing I 1 worm. **2** intestinal worms. *- hendak menjadi ular naga* the humble man acts as if he were noble. *seperti - kepanasan* to be restless (due to difficulties/illness/shyness). *sebagai - gila* to run around and not stay home (of a woman). *- batang tenggorokan* gapeworm, *Syngamus trachea*. *- belut* nematode. *- benang* threadworm, *Strongyloides stercoralis*. *- cambuk* whipworm, *Trichuris trichiura*. *- darah* cesspit worm, k.o. blowfly, *Chrysomyia megacephala*. *- daun* various species of leaf-worm. *- gelang(-gelang)* round/galley worm, *Ascaris lumbricoides*. *- gelembung* k.o. tapeworm in domesticated animals. *- gerumit* nematode. *- gila* (*M*) a) a worm that turns when touched. b) a woman who likes to roam around. *- gilik* k.o. long worm. *- gulung* earthworm. *- hati* liver fluke. *- jangkar* anchor worm, *Lernae cyprinacea*. *- jantung* heartworm. *- kalung* → CACING *gelang*. *- kayu* timber worm. *- kerawit* threadworm, *Oxyurus vermicularis*. *- ker(e)mi* thread/pin worm, *Enterobius vermicularis*. *- keruit* pinworm, *Oxyuris* spp. *- kompos* → CACING *tanah*. *- laor* (IBT) → NYALÉ. *- laut* serpula. *- paru-paru* lungworm. *- perut/pipih/pita* tapeworm, *Taenia saginata*. *- rambu* maggots in sores, whipworm. *- rambut kuda* horse-hair worm. *- ségmén* annelid. *- susu* k.o. intestinal worm. *- tambang* hookworm, *Ancylostoma duodenale, Necator americanus*. *- tanah* earthworm, *Lumbricus rubellus*. *- tiang* sea-worm. *- usus* intestinal worm.

bercacing 1 to have worms in it, be wormy. **2** worm-shaped. *seperti diberi minuman air ~* as if forced/coerced (into doing s.t.).

cacingan to have worms, be wormy. *jamu/obat ~* worm medicine, anthelmintic.

cacing II (*burung -*) hill blue flycatcher, *Cyornis banyumas*.

cad (in acronyms) → CADANGAN.

cadai I (*ob*) **mencadai** to joke; to mock/scoff at, make fun of.

cadai II (*ob*) piece of cloth worn when bathing for purposes of modesty.

bercadai to wear such a piece of cloth.

cadang *suku –* spare parts.

bercadang to be ready/prepared.

mencadangkan 1 to reserve, earmark (money for emergencies/

payment of debts), budget. **2** to set aside, lay aside, place in reserve, accrue. ~ *uang untuk hari tua* to put money aside for one's old age. *Biaya pengembangan dicadangkan pada tanggal kontrak.* Development costs are accrued at the contract date. **3** to designate, nominate. **4** to propose, suggest, put forward. **5** to plan, arrange beforehand, intend.

cadangan 1 reserve, reserves, funds put aside for emergencies, spare, accrual. *pasukan* ~ reserve troops. *perwira* ~ reserve officer. *sebagai* ~ in reserve. *uang* ~ reserve funds, money set aside. ~ *bersyarat/darurat* contingency reserves. ~ *diam* secret/hidden reserves. ~ *emas* gold reserves. ~ *keamanan pangan* food reserves. ~ *lebih* excess reserves. ~ *modal* capital/statutory reserves. ~ *pasti* proved reserves. ~ *pengurasan* reserves for depletion. ~ *penyangga* buffer stock, i.e., a stock of commodities retained to offset price fluctuations. ~ *rahasia* secret/hidden reserves. ~ *tak terduga* contingency reserves. ~ *tegakan* standing stock (in the lumber business). ~ *terbukti* proved reserves. ~ *terduga* possible reserves. ~ *teréka* inferred reserves. ~ *terkira* indicated reserves. ~ *teruji* proved reserves. ~ *terukur* measured reserves. ~ *terunjuk* demonstrated reserves. ~ *tujuan* appropriated reserves. ~ *umum* general reserves. ~ *utang* liability reserve. ~ *wajib* legal reserves. **2** proposal, scheme, motion. *balasan* ~ counterproposal ~ *perdamaian* peace proposal. ~ *tak percaya* motion of no confidence; → MOSI *tak percaya*. **3** plan, project. ~ *lima tahun* five-year plan; → RENCANA *lima tahun*. **4** prospective replacement, substitute, reserve.
pencadang proposer, s.o. who moves adoption of a motion.
pencadangan 1 reserve, reserving. **2** reservation, setting aside, allowance. **3** nomination.
percadangan reserves.
cadar (*Pers*) **1** (a woman's) veil. **2** *kain* – (bed)sheet. **3** (*elec*) shield. **4** (*anat*) velum.
bercadar 1 with/to have a veil; veiled, masked. *Dua orang laki-laki* ~ *hitam merampas kalung emas bernilai Rp 100.000,–.* Two men wearing black masks stole a gold necklace worth Rp 100,000.00. **2** shielded.
mencadari to veil, put a veil on.
cadas (*S*) **1** sandstone. **2** (in a broader sense) stone, rock(y ground). **3** rock (music).
cadek (*J*) thickset, squat, short and thick.
cadék → CALON *Dharma Éka Karma.*
cadél (*J*) **1** to substitute 'l' for 'r' when speaking. **2** to speak with a lisp. **3** to speak imperfectly, have a speech defect, speak with slurred speech. *Terima kasih Bapak Présidén ujar seorang bocah agak –, setelah présidén selesai memberi amanat.* "Thank you, Mr. President," said a lisping boy after the president had delivered his speech.
cadik I outrigger (of boat). – *pengisbang*
bercadik with outriggers. *biduk* ~ boat with outriggers.
cadik II (*M*) → CERDIK.
cadir → CADAR.
cadok (*Jv*) nearsighted, myopic.
cadong (*Jv*) one's share/portion.
menyadong [and **nyadong** (*coq*)] to ask for s.t. ~ *dawuh* to ask for orders/instructions from a superior, i.e., to ask s.o. what to do, wait for instructions. *orang* ~ *dawuh* s.o. who waits for instructions, s.o. who is not a self-starter.
pencadong s.o. who gets a share.
Caduad [Cadangan Umum Angkatan Darat] Army General Reserve.
caduk (*geol*) upheaval. – *kucing* a cat with a curly tail.
mencaduk to raise (the head, as of a snake about to strike, a swan's neck, an elephant's trunk).
mencadukkan to lift s.t., raise up s.t.
tercaduk lifted up in a curve (as a snake about to strike, etc.).
cadung bercadung to sprout, germinate.
mencadung to stand up straight, lift one's head.
caem (*sl*) cute.
caéng (*S*) a measure for *padi* = 200 *ikat*.
Cafétaria /kafé-/ → KAFÉTARIA.
cagak (*J/Jv*) **1** (wooden forked) pole, fork, post (used for support). **2** crossing. **3** support, mainstay. – *bendéra* flagpole. – *hidup* life annuity. – *jalan* crossroads. *jalan* – *tiga* three-forked road. – *listrik* utility pole. – *potrét* tripod for a camera. – *télepon* telephone pole.
bercagak 1 forked. *jalan* ~ road which forks. *hati* ~ insincere, disingenuous. *pikiran* ~ thoughts which run wildly in every direction. **2** supported/rested on. *tulang* ~ cheekbone, zygomatic bone.
mencagak 1 to prop up with a pole. **2** to support (financially). **3** standing upright. **4** (pickpocket jargon in Jakarta city buses). to take s.t. with two fingers. *Pada saat penumpang bergoyang-goyang akibat injakan rém korbannya dicagak kantongnya.* When the passengers were swaying because the brakes had been stepped on the victim's purse was snatched with two fingers.
mencagakkan 1 to mount on a stand. **2** to prop, support, sustain. **3** to drive (into the ground); → MEMANCANGKAN.
tercagak 1 supported, on a stand. **2** standing upright, clearly visible (because it's sticking out). **3** (= **mencagak**) driven in, set up.
cagar I 1 pledge, guarantee, security. **2** advance money/payment, down payment.
mencagarkan to mortgage, pawn, give s.o. s.t. as security/collateral for payment of a debt or loan, provide advance money.
cagaran security, guarantee, collateral.
pencagaran pledging as a security.
cagar II reserve, preserve. – *alam* nature preserve. ***pencagaralaman*** conservation of natural beauty. – *alam laut* marine reserve. – *budaya* culturally protected area. – *ikan* fish reserve.
pencagaran setting aside a reserve.
cagil mencagil to disturb, bother.
cagu I → CALON *guru.*
cagu II k.o. leprosy that causes the extremities to rot away, whitlow.
cagub → CALON *gubernur.*
caguh → CAGU II.
caguma → CALON *guru agama.*
cagun (*M*) **mencagun** to appear above the surface, rise to the surface (of water).
cagut (*ob*) **mencagut** to bite (of a snake), peck (of fowls/birds with long beak); → MEMATUK.
cah I (interjection to express dissatisfaction/humiliation, etc.) oh! hey! eh!
cah II (*Jv*) clipped form of **bocah**. – *ayu* girl! – *bagus* a) boy! b) a boy used in pederasty; → GEMBLAK I.
cahang tasteless, insipid, destitute (of taste); → CAMPAH I.
cahar loose (of a bowel movement). *sakit* – diarrhea; → DIARÉ.
mencahar to purge, open/relax the bowels.
pencahar (*obat* ~) aperient, laxative.
cahara → CARA.
cahari → CARI.
cahaya (*Skr*) **1** sparkle, gleam, shine (of metal/gems/stars). **2** light (of the sun/moon/lamp), ray, beam. **3** brilliance, glow. **4** facial expression. *-nya pucat* she looks pale. – *alam* natural light. – *baur* diffused light. – *bintang* starlight. – *bulan* moonlight. – *hati* generosity, openhandedness. – *hidup* zest for life. – *iman* devotion. – *kilat* flash of lightning. – *laser* laser beam. – *majemuk* light consisting of component parts (in physics). – *mata* a) look, glance. b) facial expression. c) sweetheart, beloved. – *matahari* sunshine, sunlight. – *muka* a) complexion. b) facial expression. – *pantul* reflected light. – *silau* glare. – *sorot* search light. – *udara* aurora borealis.
bercahaya(-cahaya) to gleam, beam, shine, radiate, glisten, be luminous. *Matanya tidak* ~. His eyes are not sparkling. *Mukanya* ~. Her face was beaming.
bercahayakan to be lit by s.t.
mencahayai 1 to illuminate, light up. **2** to shed light on. **3** to expose (a film).
mencahayakan 1 to cause to shine/radiate. **2** to radiate, send out (beams).
tercahaya exposed. *tidak* ~ underexposed. *Foto tidak* ~ *sebagian.* Part of the picture was underexposed.
kecahayaan luminosity.
pencahayaan 1 illumination, lighting. **2** exposure (of film). *kurang* ~ underexposure.
percahayaan illumination, lighting.
cailah (*coq*) O my God!

caing I caing-caing in tatters/rags, torn into small pieces (of cloth, meat); → CUANG-CAING.

bercaing-caing and mencaing-caing in tatters; to tear to pieces.

caing II (S) measurement for paddy (1 *caing* = 200 ikat).

cair 1 liquid, fluid. *barang/benda* – a liquid. *dalam bentuk* – in liquid form. *cacar* – chicken pox. 2 watery, liquid, weak, aqueous. *téh* – weak tea. 3 to be watered down. *Mencapai persetujuan sekarang, bésoknya – lagi.* Today an agreement is reached and tomorrow it is watered down again. *menjadi – kembali/lagi* a) (diplomatic relations) have been reestablished. b) (of funds) liquid. c) (of funds) have been released, made available. *Honor guru sekolah menengah pertama belum juga –.* The honorariums of junior high school teachers are still not forthcoming. 4 leakage, exposure (of secrets/information/news, etc.), trickled out, filtered through (of rumors). 5 available, disbursed, at s.o.'s disposal. *Krédit itu belum –.* The credit is not yet available (or, has not yet been disbursed).

mencair 1 to become liquid/fluid, liquefy, melt. *Logam yang dipanaskan lama-lama ~.* Heated metals gradually melt. 2 to become normal, be normalized, be repaired again (of relationships). *Hubungan diplomatik yang membeku selama seperempat abad baru saja ~.* The frozen diplomatic relations (with the Peoples Republic of China) for 25 years have recently been normalized. 3 to dissolve, disappear (into s.t. larger).

mencairkan 1 to liquefy, melt, dissolve, dilute, water down. *Cepat atau lambat hubungan diplomasi RI-RRC akan dicairkan.* Sooner or later diplomatic relations between the Republic of Indonesia and the Peoples Republic of China will thaw. *Kebijakan dérégulasi akan dicairkan kekentalannya untuk mengakomodasikan kepentingan kekuatan kelompok kepentingan.* The deregulation policy will be watered down to accommodate the importance of the strength of the interest groups. 2 to cash. *~ cék (perjalanan)* to cash a (traveler's) check, convert a (traveler's) check into cash. *Pembagian dividén ini akan segera kami lakukan dengan mengirimkan cék langsung kepada pemegang saham yang dapat dicairkan di seluruh cabang-cabang Bank Bumi Daya tanpa dibebankan biaya oléh bank.* We will immediately put into effect these dividend distributions by forwarding a check directly to the shareholders which can be cashed at any branch office of Bank Bumi Daya without being debited with charges by the bank. 3 to disburse, make available (funds). 4 to thaw. 5 to release. *~ uang* to release assets (previously frozen). 6 to mollify, soothe the temper of, appease; to make less intense/severe/violent. *~ kekerasan hati para téroris* (psychiatrists tried) to mollify the terrorists (in their demands). 7 to lift (a suspension).

mempercairkan to turn s.t. into a liquid.

tercair 1 disbursed. 2 liquefied.

tercairkan disbursed, available (of funds). *belum ~* undisbursed. *utang luar negeri yang belum ~* undisbursed off-shore/foreign loans.

cairan fluid, liquid, solution. *kehilangan ~ tubuh* dehydration. *~ bubut* cutting fluid. *~ gas bumi* liquefied natural gas [LNG]. *~ ketuban* amniotic fluid. *~ pembersih* cleanser, cleaning fluid. *~ pembersih rambut* shampoo; → SAMPO. *~ pendingin* refrigerant. *~ penghapus* correction fluid, white-out. *~ telur beku* frozen egg.

kecairan liquidity.

pencair 1 flux, liquefier, liquefacient, diluent, (of paint) thinner, solvent. 2 defroster.

pencairan 1 liquefaction, solution (of a solid). 2 disbursement, making available (of funds). *~ pinjaman luar negeri* the disbursement of off-shore (foreign) loans. 3 normalization (of relationships). *~ hubungan diplomatik dengan RRC.* The normalization of diplomatic relations with the PRC. 4 thawing. *~ dan pembekuan yang berulang kali akan merusak mutu daging.* Frequent thawing and freezing will destroy the quality of meat. 5 lifting (a suspension).

cais rein(s), bridle.

caisim and cai siem (C) mustard greens, *Brassica juncea.*

cajar → CALON pelajar.

cak I (*onom*) smack, sound made by smacking lips, chewing sound made when eating/walking through muddy soil.

bercak-cak to smack one's lips repeatedly.

cak II form of address used in calling pedicab drivers. –! Cab! (in summoning a passing pedicab).

cak III (*Jv*) 1 (in Surabaya and other parts of East Java) brother, buddy. – *dan ning* (in a contest, title for) the best young man and young girl (of Surabaya). 2 a title. – *kopi* coffee seller. – *Nur* nickname for Nurcholish Madjid.

cak IV various species of birds. – *padang* k.o. finch, Richard's pipit, *Anthus novaseelandiae malayensis.* – *padi* chestnut munia, *Munia maya.* – *raja* tree sparrow, *Passer montanus.* – *raya* Baya weaverbird, *Ploceus philippinus;* → (*burung*) MANYAR.

cak V measurement of size as much as can be enclosed between the two hands by putting together the two thumbs and the two forefingers.

cakadés → CALON kepala désa.

cakah 1 wide apart (of an angle/feet astride, etc.), obtuse angle. 2 widely curved (of buffalo's horns, etc.), straight to the left and right (not curving or bending).

mencakah widened (of an angle/fork/branch, etc.). *berjalan ~* to walk with legs wide apart.

cakak (M) quarrel, fight.

bercakak to quarrel, fight, be at loggerheads; → CEKAK II, GONTOK-GONTOKAN.

pe(n)cakak fighter, tough, brawler, quarrelsome fellow.

cakakah sacred kingfisher.

cakalang I ikan – skipjack tuna, *Katsuwonus pelamis.*

cakalang II → CIKALANG.

cakal-bakal (*Jv*) 1 founder of a village/settlement. 2 founding fathers; → CIKAL bakal.

cakalélé war dance (of the Moluccas and Minahasa).

cakap I 1 talk. *banyak –* too much talk. *Jangan dengar –nya yang bukan-bukan itu.* Don't listen to his nonsense. *memutuskan –* to interrupt s.o. 2 words. *tinggi –* high-sounding words. 3 speech. *juru –* spokesman; → JURU bicara, JUBIR. 4 language. – *Inggris* a) English (language) b) (*coq*) to speak English. – *angin* a) meaningless/empty talk, nonsense. b) boasting. – *besar* boasting. – *ke langit* boasting. – *kosong* nonsense. – *olah-alih/pancaroba* chatter, small talk. – *tinggi* boasting.

bercakap 1 to talk, (have a) chat. *~ angin* to (have a) chat. *~ perut* to ventriloquize. 2 to (be able to) speak (a language), express o.s. in a language. *~ Inggris* to (be able to) speak English.

bercakap-cakap to converse, speak/talk to e.o., have a talk.

mencakapi (*ob*) to bring s.o. into the conversation; to address/accost s.o. (in the street).

mencakapkan and mempercakapkan 1 to discuss, deliberate over, talk about. *Meréka sedang ~ pésta semalam.* They were talking about last night's party. 2 to use/speak a language. *Semua rakyat Indonésia harus berusaha ~ bahasa Indonésia, karena inilah bahasa kebangsaannya.* The entire population of Indonesia must try to speak Indonesian, because this is their national language.

cakapan dialogue. *~ tunggal* monologue.

percakapan 1 talk, conversation. *bahasa ~* spoken language. *~ ilmiah* scientific conversation, colloquium. 2 (telephone) call.

cakap II 1 able, capable. 2 intelligent, bright, perceptive, clever, skillful. 3 to have the ability/competence, to be able/competent, qualified. – *berbuat hukum* full legal capacity. – *bertindak (hukum)* of full legal capacity. 4 nice, good-looking, beautiful, pretty, handsome, choice, exquisite. – *perawakannya* she has a beautiful figure. – *benar rupanya, rupa yang –* and *roman mukanya –* handsome, comely, good-looking. 5 (M) dexterous, adept, adroit; quick, shift. *tidak –* unable. **ketidak-cakapan** inability, incapability.

bercakap (*cla*) to be (cap)able; to undertake to do s.t.; to have the courage (to perform s.t.), venture. *Inilah perjurit yang ~ mencuri keris laksamana itu.* This is the soldier who dared to steal *laksamana's* kris.

mempercakap(kan) to make able/competent, enable.

kecakapan 1 ability, capability. 2 intelligence, skill, competence, cleverness, attainments. *~ bahari* seamanship. *~ berpidato* rhetorical skill. *~ bertindak* full legal capacity. *~ poténsial* potential ability.

cakar I 1 claw (of animals/birds/hammer); (animal's) paw; (bird's) foot. **2** scratch (with a claw/rake/pen). **3** rake, harrow, scraper, scratcher. – *ayam* a) a scrawl, illegible handwriting. b) rings under the eyes, crow's feet. c) k.o. plant, *Selaginella doederleinii*. – *balar/baler/bara* badly scratched, scratched all over. – *bébék* illegible writing. *Tim – Beruang* Steamed Bear Paws, i.e., an expensive delicacy made from the front paws of a bear. – *besi* k.o. iron pincers (for pinching burning iron, etc.). – *kucing* k.o. plant, *Ucaria tomentosa*.

bercakar 1 to have claws, clawed. **2** scratched **3** to scratch e.o.

bersicakar, ber(si)cakar-cakaran and **cakar-mencakar** to scratch e.o.

mencakar(i) 1 to scratch, scrape (with a scratcher). **2** (*ob*) to scratch, scrape (for food, of chickens, etc.); → MENGAIS.

mencakarkan to scratch with.

tercakar scratched, scraped.

cakaran a scratch made by claws.

cakar-cakaran at odds, at each other's throats, at loggerheads. *Meréka sedang ~ satu sama lain.* They are at each other's throats.

pencakar 1 scraper, scratcher, harrow. *~ langit* skyscraper. **2** s.o. who scratches.

pencakaran scratching.

cakar II (in Central Sulawesi) cheap second-hand clothing brought in by small motorboat from Tawao and Sandakan, Malaysia.

cakar-uwa (in Karangbolong) a stick or hook to which end a pocket has been attached and used to detach the nests of swallows from the wall of a cave.

cakatan → CEKATAN.

cakau → CEKAU.

cakawari (*ob*) ancestors, forefathers, progenitors (of the fifth generation back).

cakcakan (*Bal*) (in cock fighting) the defeated cock may be taken by the organizer of the fight and used for offerings.

cak-cék 1 active. **2** to make swift motions.

cakela (*Hind*) *rumah –* brothel.

cakep → CAKAP II.

cakepan (*Jv*) a debt to a broker/middleman.

cakera → CAKRA.

cakeram → CAKRAM.

cakerawala → CAKRAWALA.

cakerawati → CAKRAWATI.

cakiak → BAKIAK.

cakil I (*Jv*) a bamboo peg used to hold bamboo wall sections in place.

cakil II (*Jv*) a puppet figure acting as ritual antagonist to the hero in certain combat scenes of a *wayang* performance.

nyakil with a protruding lower jaw.

cakim [calon-hakim] aspirant judge.

caking (*ob*) **cakingan** → CANGKINGAN.

cakmar I → COKMAR.

cakmar II → CAMAR I.

cakmau → CAMAU.

cako (*D*) shako.

cakot (*J/Jv*) **1** the way a horse bites, to bite (of horses); → COKOT. **2** (s.o. with) protruding upper teeth.

nyakot bite (like a horse).

cakra (*Skr*) **1** wheel. **2** quoit (used as a weapon or for a game). **3** disk, discus. **4** weapon used by the god Vishnu; → CAKRAM. **5** name of a *ceki* card. – *ajna* the third eye (of mysticism). – *bubungan* cam. – *pilih* dial. – *potong* cutting disc. – *sakang* shim.

Cakrabirawa President Soekarno's palace guard.

cakra-cikri k.o. plant, chinaberry, *Melia azedarach*.

cakrak (*Jv*) handsome, good-looking.

cakram (*Skr*) **1** disk. **2** discus. *lémpar –* discus-throwing. **3** discoid. – *angka* telephone dial. – *keras* hard drive. – *magnétik* magnetic disk. – *nomor* telephone dial. – *padat* compact disk, CD. – *putar* telephone dial.

cakrawala (*Skr*) **1** atmosphere, sky. **2** the revolving vault of heaven, the heavenly bodies in space (the moon/sun, etc.), firmament, heavens. *selagi ada perédaran –, yaitu bulan dan matahari as* long as the heavens, namely the moon and sun, revolve. **3** horizon. *Kami berusaha memperluas – kerjasama kami di masa*

mendatang. We'll try to broaden our horizon of cooperation in the future. – *Baru* New Horizon, i.e., the code name for the joint Indonesian-Australian naval maneuvers held in Indonesian waters; *cp* BINTANG *Selatan*.

bercakrawala *~ luas* to have a broad horizon.

cakrawati (*Skr*) **1** (*cla*) absolute sovereign ruler, Supreme Ruler, one who rules the world. **2** government (of a country), administration.

cakruk (*Jv*) guardhouse (for *jaga malam*)

cakti (*Skr?*) the sacred devolution of power to a moral and righteous force – i.e., to President and General Soeharto, the guarantor of the TNI-AD.

caku (*Pers ob*) knife.

cakué (*C*) fried flour cake.

cakuk → CANGKOK III.

cakul [catatan kuliah] course notes.

Cakung the bonded warehouses at Cakung (Bekasi).

men-Cakung-kan to store imported goods in the Cakung bonded warehouses.

pen-Cakung-an the storing of imported goods in the Cakung bonded warehouses.

Cakungisasi the removal of imported goods from a ship moored at Tanjungpriok (Jakarta), directly into the *Cakung* bonded warehouses.

cakup I mencakup 1 to seize (suddenly), snap, snatch (with both hands/in the mouth, etc.). **2** to catch (with/in the mouth). *Anjing itu ~ tulang yang dilémparkan kepadanya.* The dog caught the bone thrown to him. **3** to keep on opening one's mouth as though breathing in air, open one's mouth wide so as to take in air.

mencakup-cakup to keep on opening one's mouth.

mencakupi to scoop up.

mencakupkan to scoop up (and pour into one's mouth).

tercakup 1 caught. **2** caught up in s.t., embroiled.

pencakup a trap (for rats/pigs, etc.).

cakup II (*Jv*) scoop, ladle. – *lindung* (*fin*) coverage.

secakup a ladleful.

mencakup 1 to scoop (up); to ladle up (with vessel or hands). **2** (= **mencakupi**) to cover (various subjects, in a speech/discussion, etc.), comprise, consist of, encompass, include, entail, address; → MELIPUTI. *Daérah lain yang diperlukan untuk penunjang pembangunan bendungan ~ 621,06 ha.* Another area needed to support the construction of the dam covers 621.06 hectares.

cakup-mencakup to overlap.

mencakupi to cover, include.

tercakup included (under the scope of), came under, contained, covered.

cakupan 1 scope, coverage, range. *wilayah ~* catchment area. **2** handful, as much as can be carried in both hands. *Pemerintahan Daérah yang mengembang ~ kerja yang cukup besar dalam kegiatan pemerintahan, kemasyarakatan dan pembangunan* a regional government that carries quite a large workload in administrative, social, and development activities. **3** to hire a prostitute for the night.

pencakupan coverage, covering, scope.

cakur (*M*) → CEKUR.

cakus (*M*) **mencakus** to take (food) a little at a time.

cakwé (*C*) fritter of twisted fried dough.

cal I (*coq*) shawl, muffler.

cal II in acronyms → CALON.

cala → COLA-CALA.

calabikang (*ob*) a pastry of rice flour, sugar, and coconut milk.

caladi (*S*) various species of woodpecker. – *batu* pygmy woodpecker, *Dendrocopos kizuki*. – *kelabu* gray-capped woodpecker. – *kundang hutan* orange-backed woodpecker, *Reinwardtipicus validus*. – *tikus* rufous piculet, *Sasia abnormis*. – *titik* Sunda woodpecker, *Dendrocopos moluccensis*. – *ulam* fulvous-breasted woodpecker, *Dendrocopos macei*.

calak I (*M*) talkative, chatty, loquacious, insincere (in speech); nagging, to poke one's nose into s.o. else's business. – *mata* all-seeing eye.

calak II 1 good, beautiful, nice. *mengendarai mobil yang –* to drive a beautiful car.

calak III (*M*) cosmetic; mascara; → CELAK.
calak IV calak-calak (*M*) grindstone, whetstone. *~ ganti asah, menanti tukang belum datang* to use s.t. temporarily until s.t. better comes along.
  mencalak to hone, sharpen (of knives); to polish (diamonds, etc.).
calak V (*Jv*) circumcizer; → BONG III.
calang I → PENCALANG.
calang II 1 bare, leafless (of trees). **2** undecorated, unadorned, bare.
calang III (*Jv*) **mencalang** to be on the look-out for, spy on, observe.
  pecalang k.o. security guard.
  pencalang spy ship, reconnaissance craft.
calar scratch on the skin (caused by a thorn, etc.), laceration. *– balar* full of scratches, all scratched up.
  bercalar to be scratched, scraped.
  mencalarkan to scratch (all) over, scratch with.
  tercalar scratched, scraped.
  calaran scratch, scrape.
Calcusol name of a medicine in capsule form used against renal calculus prepared from the leaves of *Sonchus arvensis*.
calég → CALON *anggota législatif*.
calhaj → CALON *haji*.
cali (*infr*) female *calo*.
calincing → CALINGCING.
caling I → COLAK-CALING.
caling II (*J*) **1** tusk, canine-tooth; → TARING. **2** name of a *ceki* card.
calingcing (*S*) k.o. medicinal weed, Indian/lavender sorrel, yellow oxalis, *Oxalis barrelieri*.
calit smear, spot, stain (with ink/dirt, etc.); → PALIT I.
  bercalit to be smeared/stained/dirty.
  mencalit to smear s.t.
  mencalitkan to smear s.t. (on). *Jangan ~ tinta pada bajumu.* Don't smear ink on your shirt.
  tercalit smeared, stained, dirtied.
calo (*C? J*) **1** middleman, broker, agent. **2** hustler, tout, scalper. **3** canvasser. **4** shill. *– bis* s.o. who looks for bus passengers at a bus terminal (he gets a tip from the bus conductors for his services). *– gituan* pimp. *– karcis* ticket scalper. *– kewarganegaraan* citizenship broker (mostly used by people trying to obtain Indonesian citizenship). *– paspor* passport broker (contacted by persons who want to speed up business). *– pencari pekerjaan* job-seeking mediator. *– tanah* real estate broker. *Kedua – tanah pemalsu stémpel itu kini dalam pemeriksaan Polsék Cengkaréng.* The two real estate brokers, counterfeiters of the seal, are now under investigation by the Cengkareng Precinct Police. *– télepon* middleman to speed up telephone installation. *– tenaga kerja* manpower/work force recruiter. *– tikét* ticket scalper. *– WTS* pimp; → WTS.
  nyaloin (*J*) to sell s.t. on the black market. *"Sedang ngapain, Dé?" "Sedang ~ tikét keréta," jawabku seénaknya.* "What are you doing, De?" "I'm selling railway tickets on the black market," I answered pleasantly.
  mempercalokan to sell through the intermediary of a broker. *WTS-WTS kita juga dipercalokan ke Tawao.* Our prostitutes are also sold to Tawao through the intermediary of pimps.
  caloan s.t. obtained through a scalper, scalped. *harga karcis ~* the price of tickets obtained through a scalper.
  pencalo scalper.
  pencaloan scalping (tickets), selling on the black market.
  percaloan broker (*mod*), scalping (tickets, etc.). *Prakték ~ semakin menjadi-jadi di kantor BPN (Badan Pertanian Nasional) di lima wilayah DKI Jakarta.* The practice of brokering is happening more and more in BPN offices in the five regions of DKI Jakarta.
caloisme the mentality of making money by being a middleman/scalper.
calok I → CALO.
calok II (*Mad*) coconut cleaver.
calon (*Jv*) **1** candidate (for the function of), aspirant, s.o. trained for a post/task, fledgling, prospective, aspiring. **2** nominee. **3** applicant. **4** fiancée. *– akar* radicle. *– anggota* a) aspiring member (of a club, etc.). b) associate (of a professional association).

– anggota législatif [calég] candidate legislative member. *– baptisan* catechumen. *– bayi* fetus. *– biarawan/biarawati* novitiate. *– bintara* [caba] aspiring noncommissioned officer; → BINTARA. *– dropingan* a candidate submitted by the authorities/government in case they cannot agree on a candidate put forward by a lower-level agency. *– gubernur* [cagub] candidate governor (of a province). *– guru* [cagu] prospective teacher, teacher-in-training. *– haji* [calhaj] aspiring pilgrim to Mecca. *– hakim* [cakim] candidate judge. *– harapan* favorite son (in elections). *– ibu* mother-to-be. *– janin* morula. *– jururawat* student nurse. *– kepala désa* [cakadés] village head candidate. *– mahasiswa* [cama] male freshman. *– mahasiswi* female freshman. *– menantu* prospective son/daughter-in-law. *– mertua* [camér] prospective parents-in-law, parents-in-law to be. *– notaris* [CN] candidate notary. *– orangtua pemelihara* (*leg*) potential adoptive/foster parent. *– opsir* cadet. *– orok* fetus. *Tapi N merahasiakan siapa ayah – oroknya.* But N kept secret who the father of the fetus is. *– pegawai* [capég] candidate employee. *– Pegawai Negeri Sipil* [CPNS] Candidate Civilian Government Employee. *– pelajar* prospective student. *– pembeli* potential buyer. *– pemimpin* future leader(s). *– pendéta* vicar. *– penerbang* pilot-in-training. *– penulis* aspiring writer. *– perwira* [capa] officer candidate. *– présidén* a) candidate for president. b) president elect (in the U.S.). **kecalon-présidénan** candidacy for president. *– siswa* [casis] aspiring student. *– spésialis* resident. *– tamtama* [catam] aspiring lower-ranking enlisted man (between private and corporal). *– taruna* [catar] aspiring cadet. *– transmigran* prospective transmigrant. *– véteran* [cavét] prospective veteran. *– wakil gubernur* [cawagub] candidate deputy governor (of a province). *– wakil présidén* [cawaprés] candidate vice president (of the Republic of Indonesia). **mencalon-wakil-présidénkan** [mencawapréskan] to nominate for vice president.
  mencalonkan to nominate/name as a candidate (for a post, etc.). *~ diri* to run for office.
  tercalonkan nominated, put up as a candidate. *Nama-nama di atas mungkin ~.* The above names might be put into candidacy.
  calon-calonan nominating not seriously.
  pencalon nominator.
  pencalonan 1 nomination, designation. **2** candidacy.
calonisasi nominating.
calui (*C J*) to take bribes; to be bribable.
caluk I (*Bal*) a seasoning paste made from ground shrimp or fish, used as an ingredient for sambal.
caluk II *pisau –* chopping-knife, cleaver.
caluk III widower; → DUDA.
calung I 1 (*M*) bamboo water vessel. **2** bamboo dipper (for water or oil). **3** tin cup for collecting latex.
calung II (*Jv*) a musical instrument, k.o. *gambang*, consisting of pieces of bamboo which are hung and which are beaten at by two pieces of wood. *Untunglah ia juga lainnya, mempunyai kerja sambilan: sebagai pembuat alat kesenian, seperti –.* He is lucky, as are the others, that they have side jobs: like makers of objects of art, such as, *calung. tukang – calung* player.
calung III name of a welcoming dance to honor tourists disembarking at Cilacap.
calus → CELUS.
cam I (only with a negative) interested, taken by. *tak berapa –* not very interested. *kurang –* uninterested.
  mencam to bear s.t. in mind.
  mencamkan 1 to pay close attention to, note, observe carefully. *Ia ~ dengan baik apa yang sedang dilihatnya.* He observed carefully what he was seeing. **2** to inculcate, instill, implant, imbue. *Camkanlah nasihat itu dalam hatimu!* Take that advice to heart. **3** to convince. *Kita harus ~ pikiran rakyat bahwa kemerdékaan tidak berarti boléh berbuat sekehendak hati.* We have to convince the people that independence doesn't mean that we can do whatever we like. *Karena kurang ~, dia kecopétan di depan bioskop itu.* Due to his inattention, he was pick-pocketed in front of the cinema.
cam II → KECAM.
cam III (in acronyms) → KECAMATAN.

cama → CALON *mahasiswa.* –.*cami itu berpakaian putih dan berdasi hitam.* The freshmen (male and female) were dressed in white with black neckties.

camar I *burung* – sea mew, common tern, *Sterna hirundo.* – *besar* great/large crested tern, *Thalasseus bergii cristatus.* – *hitam* brown noddy, *Anous stolidus pileatus.* – *jambu* roseate tern, *Sterna dougallii bangsi.* – *kecil* Chinese little tern, *Sterna albifrons sinensis.*

camar II (M) greedy, gluttonous. – *uang* money-grubbing.
  kecamaran greed, gluttony.

camat (*J/Jv*) subdistrict head, i.e., the head of a third-level autonomous region or *kecamatan.*
  kecamatan 1 subdistrict under *camat's* jurisdiction, i.e., a subdivision of a *kabupatén* or *kotamadya.* 2 subdistrict head's office/residence. sekecamatan of the same district. *Haji Mansyur, 56, yang* ~ *dengan Unem, lebih berhasil.* Haji Mansyur, 56, of the same subdistrict as Unem, was more successful.

camau *pohon* – a tree whose roots have medicinal properties against gonorrhea, *Dracaena angustifolia.*

cambah shoot, bud, seed-bud (in coconut), bean sprouts; → KECAMBAH.
  bercambah to spring up, germinate, bud.

cambang sideburns, side whiskers; → JAMBANG II. – *bauk* whiskers and beard.
  bercambang to have/wear sideburns/side whiskers. *Rambutnya gondrong,* ~ *pula.* He has long bushy hair and also wears sideburns. ~ *lebat* to wear thick/bushy sideburns, with thick/bushy sideburns.
  cambangan whiskered.

Cambodge (*Fr*) Cambodia; → CAMPA II, KAMBODIA, KAMBOJA II, KAMPUCHÉA.

cambuk (*Pers*) 1 whip (to frighten animals), sjambok. 2 driving force, incentive, impulse, impetus, stimulus. – *petir* thunderclap.
  mencambuk 1 to (strike with a) whip, lash, beat. ~ *kuda itu supaya ia berlari* to whip that horse so that he runs. 2 to whip up.
  mencambuki to lash, scourge, flagellate, whip.
  mencambukkan to whip with s.t.
  cambukan lash (of the whip).
  pencambuk whipper.
  pencambukan whipping, lashing.

cambul → CEMBUL.

cambung (M) a large bowl (for rice/fruits, etc.).

cambut (M) → CAMBUK.

camca (C) a small long-bowled spoon (for tea/soup).

camcau → CINCAU.

cami → CALON *mahasiswi.*

camik (*Jv onom*) the sound made by moving the lips when chewing on s.t.
  mencamik to have a snack, nibble.
  camikan /cami'an/ snacks, refreshments.

camil (*Jv*) → CAMIK. mencamil [and nyamil (*coq*)] to have a snack, nibble at. *Kami berjalan santai kembali ke hotél sambil* ~ *jeruk, kacang Arab dan jajanan yang semuanya sangat murah!* We walked back leisurely to the hotel nibbling at an orange, okras, and various cheap snacks.
  camilan snacks, refreshments.

campa I *harimau* – (M) golden cat, *Felis temminckii.*

Campa II former kingdom in Indo-China, Cambodge. *beras* – a short-grained rice. *padi* – the plant that produces this rice.

campah I flavorless (of food), insipid, tasteless. – *cahang/hambar* totally tasteless.

campah II leachate.

campak I throw, cast. – *buang* wooden javelin. – *bunga dibalas dengan – tahi* to pay back good with evil, be rewarded with ingratitude.
  mencampak to throw, cast. ~ *jala* to cast a net. ~ *uang* to throw away money.
  mencampakkan 1 to throw, cast. *Jutaan gadis dunia ketiga dicampakkan ke dunia pelacuran.* Millions of girls from the third world have been thrown into the world of prostitution. ~ *diri* to throw o.s. down. ~ *dirinya ke atas kursi* to throw o.s. down in a chair. ~ *jala* to cast/throw out a net. ~ *kopiahnya ke tanah*

to throw his fez down on the ground. 2 to discard, throw away, cast aside, delete (from the agenda, etc.), get rid of. *Singapura minta agar masalah Timtim dicampakkan dari agénda PBB.* Singapore asked to delete the East Timor issue from the United Nations agenda. ~ *istri yang pencemburu* to cast aside a jealous spouse.

tercampak 1 thrown out, discarded, cast aside. *Sekitar 20 km dari pelabuhan Belawan sampan bermotor meréka terserang badai ombak setinggi 10 méter yang berhasil menggulung sampan meréka. Dan meréka pun* ~ *keluar sampan.* Approximately 20 kilometers from the port of Belawan their motorized sampan was hit by a hurricane and 10-meter-high waves that overturned their sampan. And they were flung out of their sampan. 2 knocked down. *Anak itu jatuh dan* ~ *ke atas batu.* The child fell down and was smashed onto the rocks. 3 run aground, cast ashore. *Meréka* ~ *ke sebuah pulau yang kosong.* They were cast ashore onto a deserted island. 4 crashed, smashed. *Pesawat itu* ~ *di léreng Gunung Kalora.* The plane smashed into the slope of Mount Kalora.

pencampakan casting aside, discarding, getting rid of, throwing out.

campak II *penyakit/sakit* – measles, morbilli. – *Jerman* German measles, rubella.

campal (*J*) mencampal and nyampalin (*J*) to step on s.o.'s heels or shoes.

campalan notches cut in a coconut tree so that it can be climbed.

campang I paddle.
  bercampang and mencampang to paddle from the bows (of a boat).

campang II → COMPANG *camping.*

campin I 1 deft, adroit, skillful, competent. 2 able, capable, clever. *pedagang yang* – *menjalankan modal* a trader adept at managing capital.
  secampin as clever/smart as. *Tidak banyak orang kita yang* ~ *Encik dalam menjalankan modal.* Not many of us are as adept as Encik at managing capital.

campin II (*E*) champion.

camping I → COMPANG-CAMPING.

camping II (*E*) /kam-/ 1 camping. 2 to go camping. *Meréka mau* – *di Pantai Trikora.* They would like to go camping at Trikora Beach.
  bercamping to camp (out). *Kawasan Carita yang berujud teluk kecil ini juga menyediakan aréal untuk* ~. The Carita district which is in the form of a small bay also provides an area for camping.

camplungan cesspool.

campuh (*Jv*) *perang* – free-for-all battle.
  bercampuh to fight with e.o., have a fight (*usu* using sharp weapons).

campung I broken/lopped/chopped off.
  mencampung to break/lop/chop off (the end of s.t.).
  tercampung 1 broken/lopped/chopped off. 2 (*petrol*) topped. *minyak bumi* ~ topped/reduced crude.
  campungan and pencampungan topping (in mining).

campung II (M) → CEMPLUNG.

campur 1 mixed, mingled, blended, different things put together. *logam* – alloy of two or more metals. *pérak* – impure silver. – *dalam* to interfere/meddle in. 2 associated with s.o.; lived together. *ikut/turut* – to be/get involved, take part. 3 to get involved. 4 to have sexual intercourse. – *aduk/baur* mixed together, intermixed, hodgepodge, mishmash. *masyarakat yang* ~ a mixed community. **bercampur-aduk/-baur** mixed up, confused. **mencampur-adukkan/mencampur-baurkan** to mix, mingle (substances), blend (of tea/coffee), alloy (metals). *Film Indonésia itu kerap dicampur-adukkan dengan pelbagai rupa kebudayaan.* Indonesian films are frequently mixed up with various kinds of cultural forms. **pencampur-adukan/-bauran** and **percampur-adukan/percampur-bauran** mixing, mixture, blending, alloying. – *air* mixed with water. *Susu – air tampak lebih cair daripada susu murni.* It seems that milk mixed with water is more liquid than pure milk. – *bicara* to break/enter into conversation. (*ber*)*campur gaul* to associate/

mix (with), keep company (with), rub elbows (with). – *kaya* joint property acquired at marriage. – *kebo* a) a gathering of water buffaloes. b) living together without being married; → KUMPUL *kebo*. – *kode* (*gram*) a) interference. b) code switching. – *mulut* to break/enter into conversation. – *sari* mixed, assorted, miscellaneous, pell-mell, in confusion. – *tangan* and **bercampur tangan** to meddle (in), associate (with), have dealings (with).

bercampur 1 to mix different things together. ~ *dengan* to mix with. *sisa-sisa makanan ~ dengan minyak* leftovers mixed with oil. *benci ~ sayang* hate-love relationship. *putih ~ kuning* yellowish white. ~ *darah dengan bangsa Belanda* of mixed Dutch blood, with some/a touch of Dutch blood. **2** to mingle, blend in. *Dia bisa ~ dengan penduduk setempat.* He can blend in with the local population. **3** to meddle/interfere (in). *Meréka tidak ~ dengan urusan itu.* They have nothing to do with that matter. ~ *mulut* to interrupt, stick one's two cents in (to a matter). **4** (~ *gaul*) to get along (with), associate (with), have social relations (with). *Kita harus tahu bagaimana ~ dengan sesama teman.* We have to know how to get along with our friends. **5** (*coq*) to have sex(ual intercourse). *Belum menikah, tetapi keduanya sudah ~.* They're not yet married, but they have already had sex.

bercampurkan to be mixed in with.

mencampur to mix (together), blend. *Dia ~ pasir itu dengan kapur dan semén.* He mixed the sand with lime and cement.

nyampur-nyampur (*coq*) all mixed up.

mencampuri [and **nyampurin** (*J coq*)] **1** to mix s.t. with s.t. else, introduce s.t. into s.t. else, add s.t. to s.t. else. *Jangan kaucampuri apa-apa obat ini!* Don't mix anything into this medicine. **2** to meddle/interfere with, get involved in. *Ia mémang suka ~ perkara orang.* He really likes to poke his nose into other people's business. **3** to associate, have to do with, have social relations with. *Jangan sekali-kali ~ orang jahat!* Don't have anything to do with criminals! **4** to have sex(ual intercourse) with. *Seorang pemuda diciduk karena disangka ~ istri orang.* A man was arrested because he was thought to have had sex with s.o. else's wife.

mencampurkan and **mempercampurkan 1** to mix, mingle (substances), blend (tea/coffee), alloy (metals). ~ *gula pada obat itu* to mix sugar into the medicine. **2** to throw/jumble together. *Jangan ~ masalah ini dengan perkaramu itu.* Don't throw that problem in with your problem. **3** to involve/implicate s.o. in. ~ *diri* to involve o.s. in.

tercampur [and **kecampur** (*coq*)] mixed, blended.

campuran 1 mixture, medley, blend, composite. ~ *sarat* rich mixture. **2** hodgepodge, jumble. **3** interference, meddling, intervention. **4** (social) intercourse. **5** mixed (blood/farming, etc.). *kawin ~* a mixed marriage (different religions/nationalities/races, etc.). **6** hybrid. *téknologi ~* hybrid technology.

kecampuran (*Jv*) to get s.t. mixed into it, be mixed with s.t. *batuknya yang acap ~ darah mérah* his cough, which was often mixed with red blood.

pencampur mixing, mixer. *unsur ~* additive. *mesin ~ aspal* asphalt mixer.

pencampuran (the act of) mixing/blending. ~ *berbagai aspék itu menunjukkan bagaimana bisa jadi rumitnya sebuah tuntutan pemalsuan obat.* Blending those aspects indicates how complicated a charge of counterfeiting medicine can be. ~ *tambahan* admixture.

percampuran 1 mixture, blend(ing), mixing, alloy, medley, jumble. ~ *antara suku-suku Proto-Malay dan Mélanosoid melahirkan penduduk di pulau-pulau Indonésia Timur seperti di Maluku dan Timor yang kulitnya coklat tua dan rambutnya keriting.* A mixture of Proto-Malays and Melanosoid groups gave rise to the inhabitants of the Eastern Indonesian islands such as the Moluccas and Timor whose skin color is dark brown and hair is curly. ~ *harta* confusion of property. **2** ~ *tangan* interference (in), meddling (with), intervention. **3** (social) intercourse, association.

campursari catchcrop, i.e., a fast-growing crop at a time when the ground would ordinarily lie fallow; rotation of crops, crop rotation; → TUMPANG *sari*.

camuk I (*M*) a stab, strike.
  mencamuk to stab, strike, run amok; to whip/spur up; → KECAMUK.
camuk II whore.
camuk III → CARI *muka*.
camur scattered.
  mencamurkan to scatter (money/flowers, etc.); → MENGHAMBURKAN.
can (*E*) chance, opportunity. *Banyak – yang dibuangnya.* He threw away lots of chances.
canai 1 grinding, sharpening. *batu –* whetstone, grindstone. *tukang – (scissors)* grinder. **2** board, drum. *papan –* pastry-board. *– rém* brake drum. **3** roll(er). *– giling* grinding roller.
  mencanai 1 to smooth, polish. ~ *diri* to spruce o.s. up. **2** to grind (gems), sharpen (knives) on a grindstone, roll (pastry). **3** to pull s.o.'s leg, fool, double-cross. **4** to smooth (the way).
  canaian 1 the object ground/sharpened, etc.; method of polishing, etc. **2** Spartan training.
  pencanai 1 grinder, polisher. **2** grinding tool.
  pencanaian grinding shop.
canak mencanak to stick up, stand straight, be erect/vertical.
canang I 1 small (bossless) gong (used for making announcements/proclamations). *menjadi –* much-discussed, well-known. **2** alarm, signal.
  bercanang to use a gong (for announcements).
  mencanangkan 1 to announce/proclaim by beating a gong. **2** to propagandize for, spread.
  tercanang(kan) announced, proclaimed.
  pencanang proclaimer, announcer.
  pencanangan proclaiming, proclamation, announcing
canar (*Pers*) (*– babi*) various species of plane trees, *Smilax helferi* and others.
cancang I post, pile.
  mencancang 1 to erect, put up. **2** to lift, stick s.t. up in the air.
  tercancang erected, stuck up, rising to a point (of ears/headdress/tail of animals); → PANCANG.
cancang II (*M*) → CENCANG II.
cancang III (*Jv*) **mencancang** to tether, tie up; → CANGCANG I.
  mencancangkan to tie/tether to s.t.
  tercancang tied, tethered.
cancut (*Jv*) **1** loincloth; → CAWAT. **2** to tuck the end of one's *kain* into the front of the waist band.
  (ber)cancut ~ *taliwanda/taliwondo* a) to wear a loincloth; (only) dressed with a loincloth (for heavy work). b) with united strength, with a united effort, with combined/concerted effort; to put one's shoulder to the grindstone, roll up one's sleeves (to fight, etc.). *Mari ~ taliwanda berusaha bersama mengatasi soal pangan.* Come on, let's roll up our sleeves and with concerted efforts overcome the food problem.
  mencancut(kan) to roll up (one's sleeves/*kain*, etc.).
canda I (*Skr*) (*J*) joke, fun. *Jangan suka –!* Don't joke around! **2** whim, caprice, behavior. **3** (*M*) likeness.
  bercanda 1 (*J*) to joke around, fool around. **2** to be capricious.
  canda-bercanda joking/fooling around.
  mencandakan and **mempercandakan** to make a fool of s.o., make fun of s.o., pull s.o.'s leg.
  candaan humor, joke, joking.
  percandaan joking.
canda II (*– kemudi*) the strip of wood at the stern of a boat to which a rudder is attached. *– peti* a secretaire, a box divided into compartments, cabinet (for keeping jewelry/money, etc.).
canda III (*cla*) a short spear, lance, javelin.
canda IV *tak –* (*I*) don't mind.
candai (*M*) → CINDAI I.
candak (*J*) *– cekel* to seize (illegally) the goods of a debtor who is unable to settle his debts. *– kulak* purchasing goods with limited capital for immediate resale at a profit.
  mencandak to catch, seize.
  tercandak [and **kecandak** (*coq*)] caught, seized.
candala → CENDALA.
candan → KECANDAN.
candang *berani –* (*cla*) dauntless, fearless, courageous.

candat grapnel anchor, multiple hooks on a float sticking out in different directions (used to catch cuttlefish, or fish up sunken objects); → CANDIT.

candatan (psychological) inhibition.

candera → CANDRA I, II.

candi (*Skr*) a Buddhist or Hindu temple, shrine, mausoleum. - *bentar* (*Bal*) split gate without a top, frequently at the entrance to the outer courtyard of a temple. - *Borobudur* the Buddhist temple near Yogyakarta (Central Java). - *induk* a large temple surrounded by a number of small temples. - *Lorojonggrang* 'Slender Virgin' temple of the Prambanan complex near Yogyakarta (Central Java). - *perwara* a minor temple which surrounds the *candi induk*.

mencandikan and mempercandikan to turn s.t. into a *candi*, enshrine.

pe(r)candian temple complex. *Kompléks ~ Dieng diperkirakan dibangun akhir abad ke-VIII.* It is estimated that the Dieng Hindu temple complex was constructed at the end of the eighth century.

candik (*cla*) concubine, mistress. *gundik* - various concubines.

candil k.o. snack made from sticky-rice flour.

candit s.t. with a wide and curving end, fluke (of an anchor).

candra I (*Skr*) moon; → BULAN II. - *sengkala* (*Jv*) chronogram used to express dates.

candra II (*Skr*) demigod.

candra III (*Jv*) hidden intention/purpose, allusion, insinuation, symbol.

bercandra to have a hidden intention.

mencandra 1 to predict, prognosticate. 2 to allude (to), hint (at). 3 to describe, characterize.

pencandraan 1 allusion, hint, insinuation. 2 description, characterization.

Candra Bhakti Panca Windu 'Forty-Year Devotional Superiority,' i.e., the name given to the 40th anniversary of the PNI (1927-67).

candrabirawa → AJI *candrabirawa*.

Candradimuka (*Skr*) 1 *Kawah* - a cauldron shaped like a cow into which according to Buddhist teaching a man was thrown to be 'boiled' in scalding water for supernatural powers and strength. 2 Spartan training (for military officers). 3 Armed Forces Academy in Magelang (Central Java).

candramawa (*Jv*) a cat with a particular coat and eye coloring, said to have the magical power to kill a mouse just by staring at it.

candrasa (*Jv cla*) a legendary sword (in the *Ramayana* epic).

candrasengkala (*Skr*) lunar chronogram.

candu 1 prepared opium, opium ready for use, a type of substance prepared from poppy seeds. *biji* - poppy seed. *menteri* - (*ob*) manager of the State monopoly of opium production and distribution. *pajak* - (*ob*) public opium den, opium farm. *pakter* - opium leaseholder. 2 addiction, craving. -*nya orang Rusia pada teka-teki silang* the Russian addiction to crossword puzzles. - *gelap* black-market opium. - *kasar* raw opium.

mencandu 1 [and menyandu (*infr*)] (of smoking tobacco) to be covered in tar. *Pipanya tak pernah dibersihkan hingga ~.* His pipe is never cleaned, so that it is covered in tar. 2 [and nyandu (*coq*)] to be or have become addicted to. *Ia sudah ~ minum kopi setiap pagi.* He has become addicted to drinking coffee every morning.

mencandui to be addicted to, very fond of, infatuated with, mad about. *Ia ~ permainan judi itu.* He's addicted to gambling.

mencandukan to addict, cause s.o. to become addicted.

kecanduan 1 addiction, drug dependence. 2 addicted. *~ héroin* addicted to heroin. *penderita ~ narkotik* narcotics addict.

pe(n)candu [and penyandu (*infr*)] 1 opium smoker. 2 fan, devotee, zealot, fanatic; addict, avid. *~ alkohol* alcoholic (the person). *~ bioskop* movie fan. *~ bola* soccer fan. *~ buku* bookworm (the person). *~ bulutangkis* badminton fan. *masyarakat ~ bulutangkis* a public crazy about badminton. *~ burung* bird lover. *~ cerita silat* martial arts stories fan. *~ film* film fan. *~ ganja* pothead, pot smoker. *~ ikan* fish lover. *~ joging* jogger. *~ judi* gambler. *~ kerja* workaholic. *~ klab malam* nightclub habitué. *~ komputer* computer hacker. *~ minuman* drinker,

boozer. *~ morfin* morphine addict. *~ narkotika* narcotic addict. *~ pertaruhan uang* inveterate gambler. *~ rokok* chain smoker. *~ (sépak) bola* soccer fan.

percanduan 1 opium trade. 2 drug problem.

candung a small curved wood-knife with blade and handle fashioned from one piece of metal.

cang I (*onom*) clanging (loud ringing sound of a train, etc.).

cang II (*C*) *kué(h)* - a type of rice dumpling wrapped in bamboo leaves (similar to *ketupat*).

cang III a square lift-net (for catching fish).

cangah (*M*) mencangah to gape, be open wide (of mouth).

tercangah gaping, opened widely.

cangak I → CONGAK I. mencangak to raise head and chin, crane forward and look up, rubberneck.

tercangak-cangak to look around uncertainly.

cangak II (*Jv*) *bangau* - heron, *Ardea cinerea rectirostris*. - *abu* gray heron, *Ardea cinerea*. - *laut* great-billed heron, *Ardea sumatrana*. - *mérah* purple heron, *Ardea purpurea*.

cangal-congol (*J*) to keep protruding/sticking out.

cangam (*M*) → CENGAM. mencangam to catch in the mouth, snag/snatch with the mouth.

cangantu (*C J*) uncle's spouse or aunt's husband (who is older than mother or father in a family relationship).

cangap I 1 having a triangular notch/groove/nick (at the edge of a pole). 2 k.o. forked punt-pole, two-pronged pitchfork (spear, etc.).

bercangap split, cleft.

mencangap force open (the mouth of animals).

cangap II greedy, gluttonous.

cangbok (*C J*) uncle's spouse (who is older than father or mother in a family relationship).

cangcang I (*J/Jv*) mencangcang to fasten to a rope, tether, tie up.

cangcang II (*M*) → CENCANG.

cangcaratan (*S*) k.o. tree, *Nauclea lanceolata*.

cang-cing-cong (*onom*) derogatory imitation of a person speaking Chinese.

cangcorang (*J*) a large, green grasshopper variety, praying mantis.

cangga (congenital) deformation.

mencangga to deform.

kecanggaan (congenital) deformation.

canggah I 1 a forked branch (of a tree). 2 forked punt pole.

bercanggah 1 to use a forked punt-pole. 2 forked.

canggah II grandchild of a grandchild, great-great-grandchild. *Rudy Ismanto, - dari nénék itu.* Rudy Ismanto is the great-great-grandson of that old woman.

canggai I 1 nail (of the little finger) left long for adornment. 2 gold or silver sheath for long fingernails (used for adornment).

canggai II Shanghai fried (peanuts).

canggat 1 nail (of the little finger) left long (for adornment). 2 gold or silver sheath for long fingernails, also for adornment (used by dancers and brides).

canggih I 1 sophisticated, up-to-date. *peralatan* - sophisticated equipment. 2 great, fantastic. *Gila, bodi céwék itu - sekali!* Wow, that girl's body is fantastic! 3 experienced.

secanggih as fantastic as. *taksi ~ itu* such a fantastic cab.

mencanggihkan and mempercanggih to make more sophisticated, bring up to date. *~ peralatan* to bring equipment up to date.

tercanggih most up-to-date/sophisticated. *Pabrik yang di Indonésia ini disebut ~ mengamankan lingkungannya dibanding pabrik Ciba-Geigy lain.* This most up-to-date Indonesian factory is preserving the environment more than other Ciba-Geigy factories.

kecanggihan 1 artificiality, mannerism, refinement. 2 experience. 3 sophistication. *~ inteléktual tampil sebagai faktor penentu jaman pembangunan.* Intellectual sophistication appears as a determining factor in the era of development.

pencanggihan sophistication. *Kita tidak boléh terbawa oléh perubahan dan ~ dari produk.* We can't be carried away by changes and sophistication of products.

canggih II (*Jv*) 1 fussy, fastidious. 2 boisterous, rowdy. 3 artificial, unnatural.

canggu (*M*) → CAGU(H), KELURUT.

canggung I 1 awkward, clumsy, stiff, maladroit, unused to. *Si bulé itu masih – makan dengan tangan.* The westerner was unused to eating with his hand. *Susunan kata-kata dalam kalimatnya –.* The word order in the sentence is awkward. *Tidaklah – baginya.* It will not be difficult for him. 2 uneasy, gauche, (feel) out of place, uncomfortable, ill at ease. *Saya selalu – bila bercampur dengan meréka yang kaya itu.* I always feel ill at ease when mingling with the rich. *Orang désa itu – ketika pertama kali datang di kota.* Those country people were uncomfortable when they came to town for the first time. 3 inadequate, insufficient (of knowledge/money, etc.). *Kepandaianmu serba –.* Your skills are in every way insufficient (for that job). 4 k.o. Malay dance (in the northern part of West Malaysia).
   secanggung as awkward as.
   mencanggungkan embarrassing, causing s.o. to feel ill at ease.
   kecanggungan 1 clumsiness, awkwardness. 2 unease, feelings of discomfort.
canggung II (*M*) = tercanggung 1 feeling lonely/deserted. 2 dissatisfied, disappointed.
   mencanggungkan 1 to make s.o. feel lonely. 2 to dissatisfy, cause dissatisfaction.
canggung III dead branch of tree trunk that floats half out of the water.
cangik (*Jv*) 1 the name of a clown, the maidservant to a princess in the *wayang.* 2 underbite.
cangip → CUNGAP *cangip.*
cangkang I (*Jv*) snail-shell; shell.
cangkang II crude, extremely rude, ill-mannered.
cangkat 1 a low hill, hillock, rise. 2 (of water) shallow, not deep.
cangkau → CENGKAU I, II.
cangkél (*J*) stuck fast, attached firmly.
   mencangkél 1 to stick (fast), get stuck. 2 = mencangkélkan.
   mencangkélkan 1 to hang, hook on to s.t.; to link, join, connect. 2 to carry (a child) on one's waist.
cangkelong I (*J*) 1 – *candu* opium pipe (of bamboo). 2 *pipa –* tobacco pipe. 3 any modern foreign-made pipe.
cangkelong II (*Jv*) *tas –* double bag worn over the shoulder, shoulder basket.
   mencangkelong [and nyangkelong (*J*)] to carry s.t. (on a shoulder strap) by one's side under the arm.
cangkem (*Jv*) mouth.
cangkerang → CANGKRANG.
cangkih(-mangkih) → CONGKAH *cangkih.*
cangking I mencangking [and nyangking (*J/Jv*)] 1 to carry a light article dangling in one's hand (while walking), hand-carry (letters, etc.). 2 to pick up, lift s.t. with both hands. ~ *anak* to pick up a child.
   cangkingan hand-, portable; → JINJINGAN. *barang-barang ~* hand-baggage, portable articles. *générator ~* portable generator. *pedagang ~* huckster carrying portable merchandise (to evade duties imposed by customs officers on imported goods); → JÉNGÉK II.
cangking II (*naut*) halyard.
cangkir I cup (for tea/coffee). – *piring* a) china. b) cups and saucers.
cangkir II spur, hind-claw (of birds/chickens, etc.).
cangklék (*Jv*) mencangklék to carry on the waist or hip. *Seorang gadis – tas keluar.* A girl carrying a (school)bag on her hip left the house.
cangklékan 1 (*J*) split bamboo used for storing fodder for goats. 2 (*Jv*) a wooden sickle holder tied to the hip.
cangklong I → CANGKELONG I. (*J*) pipe. *Ia tertawa ngakak sambil mengisap –nya.* He roared with laughter while smoking a pipe. *mengisap – éks luar negeri* to smoke an imported pipe.
cangklong II → CANGKELONG II. (*Jv*) mencangklong [and nyangklong (*J*)] to carry s.t. by hanging it over (the shoulder or arm/ a bicycle handlebar, etc.). *Rok mini hitam ketat, rambut tergerai dan ~ tas kecil hitam. Pas benar Euis berlaku sebagai gadis binal menanti pacar.* A tight black miniskirt, loose hair, and a small black bag. Euis was behaving exactly like a disobedient girl waiting for her boyfriend.
   tercangklong to dangle, hang down. *Tas kecil ~ di pundaknya.* A small bag was dangling at her back.

cangkok I 1 cutting, shoot, graft. 2 not genuine, false, imitation. 3 transfer.
   mencangkok 1 to take a cutting from a living plant for starting a new plant. 2 to tie up/attach (broken limbs, etc.). 3 to transplant. 4 to transfer (a university student to another institution, for further study).
   nyangkok (*J*) to adopt (a child).
   mencangkokkan to transplant (a human organ), graft. ~ *jantung* to transplant a heart.
   cangkokan 1 grown from a cutting, transplant, graft. *Pohon mangga ~* a mango tree raised from a cutting from another tree. 2 false, imitation. 3 (*geol*) hybridized.
   kecangkokan transplantation.
   pencangkokan 1 propagation by cuttings. 2 affixation, attachment. 3 transplant(ing) (human organs). ~ *ginjal* kidney transplant. ~ *janin* fetus transplant. ~ *jantung* heart transplant.
cangkok II (*Jv*) landowner (as contrasted with sharecropper or *indung*).
cangkok III 1 hook. 2 hooking small proas to a sailing ferry boat using a *tukang cangkok* or *pencangkok* who uses a grappling iron. – *pangkal* butt hook. – *tanjul* choker hook.
   mencangkok to hook a small prau (to another boat).
   pencangkokan hooking s.t. on etc.; → *pedagang* CANGKINGAN, JÉNGÉK II.
cangkol I (*J/Jv*) *kancing –* hook-and-eye fastener.
   mencangkolkan to hang up (clothing). ~ *baju* to hang up a shirt.
   tercangkol hung up.
   cangkolan hook, hanger. ~ *baju* shirt/dress hanger.
   pencangkolan hooking up.
cangkol II cangkolan k.o. card game.
cangkoréh (*Jv?*) k.o. bamboo, *Dinochloa scandens.*
cangkrang I 1 a dry branch (of a tree). 2 cover (of a battery lamp), hard outer shell. 3 a wreck.
cangkrang II chicken pox.
cangkrang III spading fork.
cangkriman (*Jv*) riddle, enigma, conundrum. *Teman Karim ada yang hanya main keléréng, bermain –.* Some of Karim's friends only played marbles and some played riddles.
cangkring (*Jv*) k.o. herbal plant, naked tree, coral bean, *Erythrina fusca*, the roots of which are used to cure *béri-béri.*
cangku (*C*) → CENGKAU.
cangkuk I → CANGKOK I.
cangkuk II 1 hook, curved or bent piece of metal. – *pangkal* butt hook. – *tanjul* choker hook. 2 iron elephant goad; →CANGKOK III.
   bercangkuk to have/use a hook.
   mencangkuk to hook.
   mencangkukkan to attach a hook to.
   tercangkuk hooked, snagged.
cangkuk III k.o. medicine (dried flowers of *Schima noronhae*, imported from Java); → PUSPA.
cangkuk IV (*M*) fish pickled in brine along with bamboo shoots.
cangkul hoe, mattock.
   mencangkul to hoe.
   mencangkuli (*pl obj*) to hoe away at (a field, etc.).
   pencangkul s.o. who hoes.
   pencangkulan hoeing, digging, ground-breaking.
cangkum mencangkum to embrace, hug.
cangkung *besar* – squatting with the knees far apart; conceited, stuck-up.
   bercangkung and mencangkung to squat on one's haunches; → JONGKOK I, TINGGUNG. *Dia duduk mencangkung.* He is squatting.
cangkup mencangkup to eat with one's palm and fingers.
cangkurileung (*S*) → KEPUDANG.
canguk mencanguk to sit/stand with head lowered.
cangut to protrude, stick out (of kris hilt from waist-belt).
cantas (*Jv*) 1 handsome. 2 intelligent, dynamic.
   kecantasan 1 handsomeness. 2 intelligence, dynamism.
cantél I (*Jv*) hook. *jarum/peniti –* safety pin.
   mencantél to hook on.
   nyantél (*coq*) 1 to hook on. 2 to get stuck, cannot be released. *Sumbangan korban banjir masih banyak yang ~.* A lot of the

contributions for the flood victims got stuck (i.e., didn't get distributed).

mencantéli to put a hook on (to s.t.).

mencantélkan to hook s.t., put s.t. on a hook. ~ *baju pada kapstok* to put a jacket on a hook.

kecantél (*coq*) to get caught/stuck/hooked/snagged. *Celana saya* ~ *paku*. My pants got caught on a nail. *Dia* ~ *wanita asing*. He got led to the altar by a foreign woman.

tercantéli to have stuck to one, have (clothing) on one.

cantélan hook, clasp, clip, hanger. *Sehelai celanaku tergantung di* ~. A pair of my pants hung on a hanger.

pencantélan hooking up, connecting.

cantél II (*Jv*) sorghum, *Andropogon sorghum*. - *berjambul* millet.

cantengan (*J/Jv*) to get/have a whitlow.

canterik → CANTRIK.

cantik I 1 (originally in Indonesia only referring to women) pretty, charming, sweet, attractive, beautiful, cute, lovely. *si* – the beauty. - *rupanya* she has a pretty face. **2** (nowadays also can refer to inanimate objects) pretty, good. *Jakét yang menurut Emma* - *(istilah Médan tentu) dipakainya terus*. She keeps wearing the jacket which according to Emma is beautiful (certainly a Medan term). *Bis-bis kota yang* -.- *itu*. The attractive city buses. - *jelita/molék* very pretty/charming, etc. - *manis* k.o. *kué manis*.

secantik as beautiful as.

bercantik-cantik dressed up, stylishly dressed; beautified; to dress in style, groom o.s.

mencantikkan to make pretty, beautify, fix up.

mempercantik to make s.t. look nicer, decorate, fix up. ~ *pembukuan* window dressing (in bookkeeping).

tercantik most beautiful. *Gadis di tengah itu yang* ~ *di antara kelima gadis itu*. The girl in the middle is the most beautiful of the five girls.

kecantikan 1 beauty. **2** sweetness, charm. *ahli* ~ beautician, beauty specialist. *salon* ~ beauty parlor. ~ *abadi* eternal beauty.

cantik II (*M*) flirtatious, lascivious, lustful.

canting 1 oil dipper (coconut (made of bamboo). **2** (*Jv*) a small nib for applying melted wax film etc.). - *témbokan* nib used to cover up parts of *batik* so that they do not absorb any color. **3** a small copper vessel with a spouted nib for applying melted wax to fabric being batiked.

cantol (*J/Jv*) a hook, bail; → CANTÉL I.

mencantol 1 to hook on (to), attach/stick (to). **2** to be attached (to). **3** to hook (illegally) up to (a telephone or power line).

nyantol (*coq*) to get held back, stuck, be affected. *Tak hanya dépositonya yang tak dapat diambil uang tabungannya pun* ~. It's not only his checking account that he couldn't draw on but his savings were affected as well.

mencantoli to stick/attach to s.t. *Gelar tersebut sudah sekian lama* ~ *Ménwa*. This title has stuck to Menwa for such a long time.

mencantolkan to hook on to, hang up. *Ia* ~ *topinya pada kapstok*. He hung his hat on a clothes tree.

tercantol [and **kecantol** (*coq*)] **1** hooked on, hung up. **2** hooked, snagged, got led to the altar. *Putri Caroline* ~ *peténis Argéntina Guillérmo Vilas*. Princess Caroline got led to the altar by the Argentine tennis player Guillermo Vilas. **3** to be held back (in school).

cantolan (influential) connection.

pencantolan connection (usually an illegal connection to a telephone or power line).

cantrik (*Jv*) **1** pupil who lives in the home of a Hindu/Buddhist *guru* and does service for him as well as learns from him. **2** assistant to a clergyman/priest. **3** helper (of a *dukun*). **4** follower (*esp* mystical).

cantum grafting. - *hijau* green budding. - *jemala* crown grafting. - *sanding* approach grafting.

bercantum 1 to close up, heal (of a wound); to join together (of feathers/papers, etc.). **2** to touch. *carik-carik bulu ayam, lama-lama* ~ *juga/pula* a dispute between relatives will end peacefully because they love e.o.

mencantum 1 to lie touching e.o., make contact with. **2** to pin, affix/attach (with a pin).

mencantumi to add to, affix.

mencantumkan 1 to pin up, stick up, stitch up. **2** to carry (an article in a newspaper/magazine, etc.). **3** to interpolate. **4** to attach, stick. **5** to mention, make mention of, cite, state, put down (s.t. on a form). **6** to specify, take up, include. *Panggilan itu* ~ *agénda, tanggal, waktu dan tempat rapat*. (in notarial instruments) The convocation specifies the agenda, date, time, and place of the meeting.

tercantum 1 included, inserted. ~ *dalam hati* cherished (in one's heart). **2** specified (in a law or contract), stated, taken up.

cantuman 1 s.t. attached, stuck/pinned on. **2** s.t. included, mentioned.

pencantuman inclusion, insertion, incorporation.

cantun (*ob*) → CANTUM.

cao I (*C coq*) to go. *Gua mau* – *dulu, ada appointment*. I have to go now, I have an appointment.

cao II → CINCAU.

caos (*Jv*) **1** to perform guard duty for s.o. of high status. **2** to visit respectfully (a higher-up). **3** to prepare and/or serve food and refreshments (for a high-ranking person). - *bekti* to kneel and bow (as in prayer) as a token of loyalty (before a *raja*). - *dahar* a) to lay out food for persons of high rank, also referring to a ritual carried out in the month of Sura which takes the form of scattering flowers in the sea, e.g., at Popoh beach in the Tulungagung regency. b) offering to avert evil.

cap I (*Hind*) **1** (inked/rubber) stamp. **2** seal. *cincin* – signet/seal ring. **3** stamp, imprint, impress. *Surat keterangan yang tidak ada* – *lurah, tidak laku*. A certificate without the village head's stamp is invalid. **4** print. - *huruf* letter; *opp* HURUF *tulis*. *tukang* – print printer. *canting* – a small copper vessel with a spouted nib for applying melted wax to fabric being batiked. **5** (trade)mark (which contains a design, picture or photograph), label. *bir* – *Jangkar* "Anchor" beer; the bottle shows the picture of an anchor. - *Macan* Tiger Balm; the little pot in which the balm is sold has a label depicting a tiger. **6** label, character, nature, disposition. *kelihatan* -*nya* his true character came out. *sudah mendapat* – *kurang baik* labeled as less good. - *air* watermark. - *batu* lithography. - *dagang* trademark. - *empu jari* thumbprint. - *jadi* s.t. done without much effort. - *jari* fingerprint. - *jempol* thumbprint. **mencap jempol** to provide with a thumbprint. - *kempa* (*ob*) seal of the Sriwijaya empire. - *lak* wax seal. - *mohor* a) government seal. b) a die for coins, etc. - *mutu* hallmark. - *panas* brand (for cattle). **mencap-panas** to brand. - *parap* signature stamp. - *pos* postmark. - *Sulaiman* five-pointed star.

mencap and **mengecap 1** to put one's stamp on, stamp. **2** to print (books/*kain*, etc.). **3** to brand, provide with a mark. *Ia* ~ *semua sapinya dengan besi panas*. He branded all his cattle (to show ownership). **4** to label, consider, regard (as). *Pahlawan nasional dicap oléh pihak sana sebagai pemberontak*. The national hero was labeled a rebel by the opposition.

mencapi 1 to stamp, label, affix a stamp to. **2** to label s.o. (as s.t.).

mencapkan and **mengecapkan 1** to stamp, place a stamp/mark on. **2** to print s.t. for s.o. else. **3** to label/brand) s.o.

cap-capan 1 all k.o. labels. **2** with a false seal and therefore not genuine.

pengecapan and **pencapan 1** (the act of) stamping. **2** printing house.

cap II (*cla*) *secap* as much as can be held between the two thumbs and forefingers joined.

cap III (*onom*) sound of noisy eating or chewing.

cap IV (*C J*) ten. *sa*– ten. - *go* fifteen. – *tiau* 10,000,000.

cap V (*J*) to do s.t. without cause/warning. - *paké* to use s.t. without warning. - *témbak* to shoot without prior warning.

cap VI (*onom*) sound made when a knife penetrates s.o.'s body. *Dan di saat itu*, -, -, *tusukan belasan pisau bersarang ke sekujur tubuh Asep*. And at that moment, wham, wham, scores of knife-thrusts hit Asep's body.

capa I wild camphor plant, *Blumea balsamifera*, the roots and leaves of which are used as medicine.

capa II k.o. gambling game of heads or tails.

capa III → CALON *perwira.*
capah I (*M*) → CAKAH.
capah II wide platter (similar to a tray, made of wood); *cp* CAPAR I.
capai I reach. *- témbak* range (of guns). *- terbang* cruising radius (of aircraft).
   mencapai 1 to reach out for s.t. *ibarat si cébol hendak ~ bulan* wanting s.t. impossible, being over-ambitious. 2 to reach. *Umurnya sudah ~ 80 tahun.* He has reached the age of 80. *mudah dapat dicapai* a) within easy reach. b) easy to achieve. *~ suatu kesepakatan* to reach an agreement. 3 to amount to (a certain amount). *Daftar tunggu pemohon télepon di Jakarta ~ hampir 140 ribu.* The waiting list of applicants for a telephone in Jakarta almost reaches the 140 thousand mark. 4 to get, obtain (s.t. by hard work), arrive at, gain, attain, achieve, accomplish (one's purpose), reach (a target/goal). *~ cita-cita* to realize one's dream. *~ kemenangan yang gilang-gemilang* to achieve a glorious victory. *~ hasil yang memuaskan* to show satisfactory results. *berhasil ~ gelar doktor* to succeed in getting one's Ph.D. *siapa yang hendak dicapai* (advertising term) target audience. *~ puncak* to reach a climax, come to a head, culminate.
   tercapai [and kecapai (*coq*)] achieved, reached, accomplished, carried out; affordable (of price). *yang belum pernah ~* all-time (high). *tidak ~* unobtainable, inaccessible; affordable. *tapi kesepakatan tidak ~* but agreement could not be reached. ketercapaian accessibility.
   capaian 1 result, s.t. obtained/achieved. 2 access.
   pencapai aim. sepencapai arm's length, as far as one can reach.
   pencapaian achievement, accomplishment. *~ tujuannya* achievement of one's goals. *~ targét Pajak Bumi dan Bangunan* achieving Ground and Buildings Tax targets.
capai II tired, exhausted; → CAPÉ(K). *- hati* bored, irritated.
capai-capainya *tidak ~* without stopping, ceaseless.
   secapai as tired as.
   secapai-capainya no matter how tired.
   kecapaian 1 weariness, fatigue. 2 fatigued, worn out. *Terlalu ~ karena bekerja berat atau kurang istirahat juga faktor timbulnya serangan asma.* Overexertion from hard work or lack of rest is also a factor in having an asthma attack.
capak I (*cla*) ignored, neglected.
   mencapak and mempercapak 1 to underestimate, underrate, take lightly, be indifferent to. *Karena terlalu mencapak lawannya, dia kalah dalam pertandingan itu.* Because he underestimated his opponent, he lost the contest. 2 to ignore, disregard. *biar sejengkal lautan, jangan dicapak* don't underestimate the number of your opponents.
   tercapak ignored, neglected.
capak II tercapak sit with legs spread apart (as if riding on a motorcycle); → CELAPAK.
capak III (*M*) smacking (of the lips while eating).
   mencapak(-capak) to smack the lips (while eating).
capal (*Hind*) sandals (with leather soles).
capang wide spread (of ears/nostrils, etc.), wide and curving (of horns/moustache, etc.), long and broad (of ears).
capar I k.o. vase or pot made of wood; → CAPAH II.
capar II (*Jv*) bean sprouts.
capcai (*C*) 1 chop suey. 2 medley.
capcap → CAPAK III.
capég → CALON *pegawai.*
capék → CAPAI II.
capelin (*J*) → CAPIL, CAPING II.
capelok → CAPLOK.
capém → CABANG *pembantu.*
capéo → CAPIO.
capgomé(h) and Cap Go Méh (*C*) the 15th day of the first month of the Chinese calendar, i.e., after *Imlék*, Chinese New Year.
capgotun (*C J*) fifteen *rupiahs.*
capiau → CEPIAU.
capik I lame, paralyzed, limping.
capik II → CAPAI II.
capil (*Jv*) a tapering sun-hat made of plaited bamboo; → CAPING II.
caping I piece of metal (*usu* copper in the shape of a betel leaf) used as cover for a girl's pubic area; scutcheon (over keyhole); ankle-

guard (of soccer players). *memecah -* (*Med*) (formerly) to marry a girl; (nowadays) to brag, boast.
caping II (*Jv*) a broad woven bamboo hat worn as a sunshade or umbrella by villagers, farmers, etc.; → CAPIL, CAPELIN. *- gunung* a large hat of this type. *- kerosok* a finely woven hat of this type.
   bercaping to wear such a hat.
capio k.o. hat.
capit (*Jv*) tweezers; → SEPIT I.
   mencapit to snap at, pinch with pincers.
capita sélécta (*L*) /kapita sélékta/ selected chapters.
Capjigwéé (*C J*) December.
capjiki and cap jie kie (*C*) gambling game which uses 12 cards or dice.
capjitunpoa (*C J*) twelve and a half *rupiahs.*
caplak (*J/Jv*) various species of ticks and flies, such as dog tick, horsefly, cattle tick, *Rhipicephalus sp., Haemaphysalis renschi,Boophilus microplus.*
caplang (*Jv*) prominent, sticking out (of ears).
caplok (*J/Jv*) mencaplok 1 to snatch, snap, seize in the mouth (of crocodiles), make a sudden bite, swallow whole. 2 (*coq*) to pinch, steal. 3 (*coq*) to annex, incorporate the territory of a State into another State.
   mencaploki (*pl obj*) to snatch, etc.
   tercaplok grabbed, snatched, annexed.
   caplokan spoils, s.t. seized.
   pencaplokan annexation.
Capra Beetle /kapra/ name of a species of beetle found in the rice imported from Pakistan.
caprés [calon présidén] presidential candidate.
   mencapréskan to nominate for president.
cap-sah-taipo (*C*) a Chinese gambling game which uses 13 cards.
capsai (*C*) *judi* - k.o. gin rummy.
captain (*E*) /kaptén/ (in sports/some airlines/some shipping companies) captain; → KAPTÉN.
captun (*C J*) 10 *rupiahs.*
capuk pockmarked, freckled.
capung (*J*) dragonfly. *pesawat -* Piper Cub (a lightweight aircraft).
car (in acronyms) → CARAJA, CARAKA I.
cara (*Skr*) 1 way, manner, method, technique. *Bagaimana - menulis huruf Arab ini?* How do you write this Arabic letter? *Begitulah - orang membuat tapai.* That's the way people make fermented cassava. *- berpikir* way of thinking. *- hidup* life style. 2 style, fashion. *- Barat/Timur* Western/Eastern or Asian style/way of doing things. *- menulis* writing style. 3 custom, tradition, habit. *Perkawinan - Barat tidak sama dengan - kita.* A Western wedding is not the same as our kind of wedding. 4 according to; like, resembling; as a ..., by the ..., -ly. *- adat lama* according to old customs. 5 (in a) in the language/dialect of ... *- Jakarta disebut "tampek," - Jawa "gabak" dan - Malaysia "campak"* In the Jakarta dialect (measles) is called "tampek," in the Javanese language "gabak" and in the Malaysian language "campak". *- artikulasi* (*ling*) manner of articulation. *- bekerja* working method, procedure, modus operandi, manner of working/operating. *- bergaul* manners. *- beristirahat* at ease, parade rest. *- berpikir* way of thinking, world view, general attitude. *- bersiap* at attention. *dengan - yang cepat* on an expedited basis. *- Chicago* a la Chicago, i.e., violent. *- hidup* lifestyle. *- hidup menyendiri* exclusivism. *- kerja* a) procedure. b) how s.t. works. *- kuno* archaism. *- laksana* MO, modus operandi. *- lepas* free-range (way of raising poultry). *- memasak* cuisine. *- mengajar* teaching method. *- pembayaran* method of payment. *- pemeristiwaan* case method. *- pendekatan* approach. *- pengerjaan* operations. *- pengisian* directions for completing (a form). *- penyajian* method of presentation. *- perjuangan* mode/method of warfare, fighting method. *- terakhir* last resort. *- transportasi* transportation modal. *- ucap* articulation. *- uji untuk kerja* performance test method.
   cara-cara 1 many k.o. ways/methods/styles, etc., customs and traditions. *~ konvénsional* conventional methods. 2 ceremony. 3 indications; model, specimen.
   secara 1 in a ... manner, in the manner/method/way. *Perselisihan itu diselesaikan ~ damai.* The conflict was settled in a peaceful

manner. 2 according to, in accordance with (*adat*, etc.). *Perkawinan akan dilangsungkan ~ adat keraton.* The wedding will be performed in accordance with *keraton* traditions. 3 as if, like, resembling, as; as a function of. *bertindak ~ laki-laki* to act like a man. *disambut ~ tamu* to be received/welcomed as a guest. 4 in a ... way/manner/fashion, by the ... ; ...-ly, ... -wise. *~ adat* according to custom. *~ anumerta* posthumously. *~ besar-besaran* on a large scale. *~ damai* peacefully. *~ bersudut* angular. *~ bertahap* in stages, phases. *~ blak-blakan* openly, frankly. *~ buatan* artificially. *~ damai* peacefully. *~ diam-diam* covertly. *~ dua-duaan* privately. *pembicaraan ~ dua-duaan* a private talk. *~ gelap* clandestinely, illegally. *~ G to G* Government to Government. *~ hina* in an offensive way. *~ kebetulan* by chance/accident. *~ kecil-kecilan* on a small scale. *~ kekerasan* rigorously. *~ k(e)satria* sportsman-like. *~ langsung* directly. *~ lisan* orally, by word of mouth. *~ luas* broad, extensive. *~ mandiri* independently. *~ mencolok* strikingly. *~ musyawarah* by mutual agreement. *~ naluri* instinctively. *~ oglangan* by turns. *Suratkabar-suratkabar harian yang terbit di Yogyakarta sejak hari Senin yang lalu telah terbit ~ oglangan.* Since last Monday the daily papers published in Yogyakarta have been published by turns. *~ padatnya* in short, to be concise. *~ panjang lébar* in depth, extensively. *~ perseorangan* in person, personally. *~ resmi* officially, formally. *~ rukun* harmoniously. *~ sahabat* amicably. *~ sepihak* unilateral. *~ singkat* concisely, briefly. *~ tambal-sulam* in a makeshift way. *~ teka-teki* enigmatically, mysteriously. *~ tersurat dan tersirat* verbatim et literatim, literally and figuratively. *~ tidak langsung* indirectly. *~ tidak merata* unevenly, inequitably. *~ tidak resmi* informally, unofficially. *~ timbal balik* conversely.

kecaraan (*gram*) modality.

carabikang and **cara bikang** → CORO *bika*.

carah (*M*) **bercarah** retail, in small quantities.

    mencarah 1 to (distribute) in small quantities. **2** to (cut s.t.) into small pieces. **3** to be in the retail business.

    mencarahkan to sell s.t. retail.

    carahan s.t. sold in small quantities.

caraja (*Skr mil*) escort.

carak I mencarak *~ air* to drink by pouring water into the mouth from the spout of a kettle, etc. *telur* to swallow the contents of an egg by opening the shell and pouring the egg into one's mouth. *~ benak* to extort money from s.o., take usurious interest.

carak II (*ob*) **mencarak 1** to become visible, appear (the sun etc.). **2** to open (the cards in a game).

carak III log, records.

    mencarak to log.

carak-carik in tatters; → CORAK-CARIK.

caraka I (*Skr*) **1** courier, messenger. **2** mailman. **3** envoy. *Média –* "Media of the Envoys," i.e., the name of the Indonesian-language monthly magazine published by the Indonesian Embassy in Washington, D.C. *– Loka* the building managed by the women's association of the Department of Foreign Affairs (Jakarta). *- negara* foreign service officer. *- yudha* (*infr*) military attaché.

caraka II the Javanese alphabet; → HANACARAKA.

caram → ACARAM.

caran (*M*) **bercaran** to squabble, wrangle.

carang small boughs and branches of a tree, leaf-bearing twigs (of creeping or climbing plants), tendril. *sirih –* young betel leaves. *- berdapa* k.o. *kué basah* made with bananas.

    bercarang 1 to have branches. **2** to branch out.

    mencarang 1 to look like the curving leaf-bearing twigs. **2** to pluck young betel leaves.

    carangan (*Jv*) a play that departs from the events depicted in epics or in mythology.

carap transform.

    pencarapan transformation.

carat (*ob*) → CARAK I.

carder (*E*) /karder/ s.o. who commits credit card fraud over the internet.

carding (*E*) /karding/ credit card fraud over the Internet, cyberfraud.

carép [calon réporter] cub (reporter).

cari (*Skr?*) **1** (*coq*) look for, seek (= **mencari**). *tukang – adperténsi* advertising salesman. **2** possession, property; joint earnings of a husband and wife. *- angin* to take a break. *– duit sendiri* to earn one's own money. *Lebaran serta hari-hari raya lain, sejenak membuka kesempatan – duit.* Lebaran and other holidays for a short time affords people the opportunity to get money or make a living. *- gampang* easygoing. *– iseng* to loiter (as a prostitute looking for business). *- kabar* to make inquiries. *- kerja* to find/look for work. *Di Jakarta ini orang sulit – kerja.* In Jakarta it's hard for people to find work. *- muka* try to make up with s.o., cajole s.o. *tim – dan selamatan* an SAR-team. *- teman* looking for company (usually for sexual purposes).

secarian joint property (of husband and wife).

bercari (*M*) to be looked for, be sought after. *kata dahulu berte-pati, kata kemudian kata ~* a promise must be fulfilled, it may only be changed after negotiating.

bercari-cari 1 to look for (s.t., evidence, etc.). **2** far-fetched, recherché, artificial, invented, fabricated, made-up, trumped-up, concocted. *alasan yang ~* a trumped-up argument.

bercari-carian 1 to look for e.o. **2** = *bermain cari-carian* to play hide-and-go seek.

mencari [and **nyari** (*coq*)] **1** to look for, seek, hunt for, look up (a word, in a dictionary, etc.); to find. *Bapak ~ apa?* (in stores) What can I do for you? *tugas ~ dan menyelamatkan* search and rescue task. *dicari* (in want ads) wanted (a salesgirl, etc.). **2** to strive/endeavor to obtain income/livelihood/subsistence, etc. *seperti ~ jejak dalam air* like looking for a needle in a haystack. *enau ~ sigai* a woman looks for a man. *~ umbut dalam batu* to be in a hopeless situation. *~ akal* to look for a way (out), think of a way (to do s.t.), take pains, endeavor, exert o.s. *~ amannya* to take no risks. *~ angin* to go get a breath of fresh air. *~ bakti* to divide property/possessions between husband and wife (when separating). *~ bako* (*M*) to select a son-in-law. *~ bala* to look for trouble. *~ balas* to seek revenge. *~ béla* to kill s.o. so that his spirit joins s.o. else after their death. *~ berita* a) to try to obtain news. b) to gather and look for data to write a news item. *~ daya upaya* to take pains, endeavor, exert o.s. *~ duit* to make a living. *~ énaknya saja* to be selfish, egoistical, look for the easy way out. *~ fasal* to look for a motive (to quarrel). *~ gampang* easygoing. *~ gara(-gara)* to look for trouble, create problems. *~ helah* to look for an excuse (to do s.t.). *~ hindu* to trace family ties. *~ hitungan* to solve an arithmetical problem. *~ ikan* to go fishing. *~ ikhtiar* to take pains, make an effort, endeavor. *~ ilmu* to seek knowledge. *~ info* to find out. *~ jalan* to search for a means/course of action. *~ jalan gampang* to take the line of least resistance. *~ jalan keluar dari kemelut* to find a way out of a crisis. *~ jejak* to trace, track. *~ jejak di air* to do s.t. useless. *~ kelebihan* to better o.s. *~ keringat* practice, exercise. *~ kerja* to look for employment/a job. *Saya hijrah ke Jakarta ~ kerja.* I moved to Jakarta to look for a job. *~ kesalahan* a) to look for mistakes. b) to nitpick. *~ keterangan* a) to inquire. b) to investigate. *~ kutu* a) to go through s.o.'s hair to pick out lice or nits. b) to disgrace. *~ kutu dalam ijuk* to do s.t. very difficult. *~ langkah* to look for a suitable moment to quit. *~ lantai terjungkat* to find fault with others. *~ lantaran* to look for a reason (to quarrel). *~ lawan* to look for a quarrel. *~ makan* to try to make a living, earn one's bread. *~ muka (kepada)* a) to cajole, wheedle, try to make up with s.o. b) to seek praise, fish for compliments. *~ nafkah* to make/earn one's livelihood. *~ nama* to seek fame. *~ nasi* to make a living. *~ pasal* to look for an excuse (to quarrel). *~ pekerjaan* to look for employment/a job. *~ pemancar gelap/tersembunyi* to seek hidden, clandestine CB-sets, i.e., fox hunting. *~ pengalaman* to go looking for different experiences. *~ penyakit* to look for trouble. *~ perkara* to look for a reason (to quarrel), look for trouble. *~ pikiran* to take pains, endeavor, make an effort. *~ rezeki* to look for a way to make a living. *~ risik* to make secret inquiries. *~ sebab* to look for a reason (to quarrel). *~ selamat* to keep on the safe side, play for safety. *~ selisih* to provoke a fight, look for trouble. *~ senangnya saja* to only look after one's own self-interest. *~ sesuap nasi* to earn one's keep. *~ seteru* to provoke a fight, etc. ~ *silang* to look for a fight. ~ *tahu* to find out, discover. ~ *uang* to make a living.

mencari-cari 1 to hunt for, look all over for, grope for. **2** to ask/look for (trouble). **3** to create, fabricate, trump up. *alasan yang dicari-cari* trumped-up/invented arguments. ~ *kesalahan* to nitpick; nit-picking, finicky, fussy; to find fault with (s.o.).

mencarikan [and **nyariin** (*J coq*)] **1** to look for s.t. for s.o. *Ketika itu, Mirin, tetangga kita yang baik itu, bersedia menolongku ~ kerja di kota.* By that time, Mirin, our kindhearted neighbor, was willing to help me find a job in town. **2** to seek. ~ *penyelesaian* to seek a solution. ~ *perut (yang tak berisi)* to earn one's bread/livelihood.

carian s.t. that is looked for.

pencari searcher, finder, detector. ~ *arah* direction finder. ~ *bakat* talent scout. *misi* ~ *fakta* fact-finding mission. ~ *jejak* stalker, tracker. ~ *keadilan* litigant. ~.~ *kemungkinan perdamaian* peace feelers. ~ *kerja* s.o. looking for work. ~ *mangsa* a) hooker, prostitute. b) predator. ~ *nafkah* breadwinner. ~ *untung* fortune seeker, adventurer.

pencarian 1 search, quest; seeking, searching. *dalam* ~ wanted (by the police). ~ *dana* seeking funding. *Pusat* ~ *dan Penyelamatan* SAR/Search and Rescue Center. **2** (often **pencaharian**) occupation, profession. *mata* ~ means of livelihood. **3** prospecting. **sepencarian** joint property (of husband and wife).

carik I 1 a torn/ripped piece (of paper/cloth). – *kenangan* (philatelic) souvenir sheet. **2** classifier for letters, paper, etc.
secarik a piece, sheet, coupon, counterfoil. ~ *diploma* a diploma. ~ *kertas* a piece/sheet of paper. ~ *surat* a letter.
bercarik-carik in tatters, torn to shreds.
mencarik to tear bits off, rip.
mencarik-carik(kan) to tear to shreds.
tercarik(-carik) torn, pulled apart.
carikan a torn off piece, scrap.

carik II (*Jv*) secretary, writer, clerk (to a *lurah*).

carik III – *hantu/kapan* spotted wood owl, *Strix seloputo*.

carima [pemancar-penerima] transceiver.

caring I (*ob*) **mencaring** to violate (rights).

caring II (*Jv*) to dry o.s. off in the sun.

carmuk → CARI *muka*.

carok (*Mad*) killing s.o. because one feels one's honor has been insulted.

carper [cari pergaulan] to look for social intercourse.

carpon (*S*) [carita pondok] → CERPÉN.

carter (*E*) charter. *pesawat* – chartered plane. – *masa* time charter. – *partai* charter party. – *sejalan* voyage charter. – *waktu* time charter.
mencarter to charter (a plane, ship). ~ *kapal berbendéra asing asal seluruh awaknya berkebangsaan Indonésia* to charter a foreign-flag vessel as long as the entire crew is Indonesian.
carter-mencarter chartering.
mencarterkan to charter out.
carteran chartered. *pesawat* ~ chartered plane.
pencarter charterer, shipper.
pencarteran chartering.

caruh → CERUH.

caruk I mencaruk 1 (*cla*) to peel the bark (of a tree). **2** to make a runnel in bark; to tap a tree (for its latex).

caruk II (*ob*) gluttonous, greedy.
mencaruk to eat greedily/a lot.

caruk III → CERUK.

carut obscene (language), vulgar, indecent, filthy (speech). – *capai/marut* dirty talk, obscene language.
bercarut(-carut) and **mencarat(-carut) 1** to talk dirty, use bad/foul language, revile. **2** to use obscene/vulgar words to s.o. *bercarut bungkang* (*M*) to use obscene language. *Pernah meréka bercarut bungkang menjawab si penélepon ketika ada kebakaran di kawasan Hélvétia (Médan).* They had used obscene language in answering the caller when there was a fire in the Helvetia area (Medan).
mempercaruti to use foul/obscene language to s.o.
kecarutan obscenity.
pencarut foul-mouthed fellow.

pencarutan obscenity.

carut II scratches, marks from scratches. – *marut* all scratched up.

cas I (*E*) **1** charge (of storage battery). – *aki* battery charger. **2** (*sl*) to eat.
mencas to charge. ~ *aki* to charge a (car) battery.
mencaskan to charge an accumulator/storage battery with electric power.
pengecasan charging.

cas II *main* – game in which one tries to trip s.o. up.
mencas and **mengecas** to kick s.o. to trip him up.
mencaskan and **mengecaskan** to knock s.o. down by kicking.

cas-cis-cus 1 to talk big, boast. **2** to speak a language fluently (like a native). *Istrinya berbicara* – *dalam bahasa Jepang dengan Jonathan.* His wife spoke fluent Japanese with Jonathan.
bercas-cis-cus to speak a language fluently (like a native speaker).
cas-cus(an) 1 to talk big, boast. **2** to use many foreign words.

casis I (*E*) chassis.

casis II → CALON *siswa*.

casmah → TESMAK.

cassette (*D/E*) /kasét/ **1** cassette. **2** cassette tape recorder; → KASÉT. *membunyikan* – to play the cassette tape recorder.

cat (*C?*) **1** paint. *minyak* – linseed oil. **2** tint, coloring. – *air* watercolor. – *alis* eyebrow pencil. – *antara* undercoat. – *bakar* spray paint. – *batik* coloring matter used to color batik cloth. – *besi panas* hot stamping. – *bibir* lipstick; → GINCU, LIPSTIK, PEMÉRAH *bibir*. – *dasar* first coat of paint, primer. **mencat dasar** to prime. – *duko* spray paint. – *kéramik* glaze. – *kuku* nail polish. – *luar* outer coating. – *marka jalan* road marking. – *minyak* oil paint. – *pelapis* coatings. – *penahan api* fireproof paint. – *pewarna rambut* hair-coloring. – *rambut* hair coloring. – *semprot* spray paint.
bercat painted, colored. *Rumah itu* ~ *putih.* That house has been painted white.
mencat and **mengecat** to paint, color. *Dengan* ~ *mobil, sehari rata-rata meréka berpenghasilan antara Rp 3.000,- sampai Rp 4.000,-.* By painting cars, they could make about Rp 3,000.00 to Rp 4,000.00 a day. ~ *rambut* to dye one's hair.
pengecat painter.
pencatan and **pengecatan** painting, paint job. ~ *gedung baru itu memakan waktu kira-kira sebulan.* It will take about a month to paint that new building.

catak (*Jv*) horsefly (family *Tabanidae*); → PIKAT I.

catam → CALON *tamtama*.

catat note, record(s). – *kumpul* register and collect. **mencatat-kumpulkan** to take stock. – *pinggir* marginal note. **mencatat-pinggiri** to comment on.
mencatat [and **nyatat** (*coq*)] **1** to make a note of, note/write down, keep a record of. **2** to register, list (stock on an exchange). **3** to have/achieve (success); to make, win, score, chalk up. *Dalam tahun ini perséroan kita* ~ *keuntungan yang lumayan.* This year our company has made a substantial profit.
mencatati (*pl obj*) to note, etc.
mencatatkan [and **nyatatin** (*J coq*)] to enter/write down (in a notebook), record, mark. ~ *diri/nama* to enter/put down one's name (in), register (one's name) (with), sign up, enroll, apply (for) (membership). *Dia sudah* ~ *diri untuk kursus itu.* He has signed up for the course. *Kapan saudara akan* ~ *diri di univérsitas ini?* When are you going to enroll at this university?
tercatat [**kecatat** (*coq*)] **1** noted/written down, recorded, (the record) stands at, on record. ~ *dalam sejarah* made history. *Préstasinya* ~ *dalam sejarah.* His achievement made history. *Dia orang terpéndék yang* ~ *dalam sejarah.* He's the shortest man on record. **2** registered. *dengan surat* ~ by registered letter/post, under registered cover. **3** to stand at/be. *Harga beras impor itu* ~ *320 dolar per ton.* The price of imported rice is 320 dollars per ton. *Korban jiwa* ~ *100 orang.* The number of victims stands at 100. **mentercatatkan** to have (a letter) registered. *Tolong, tercatatkan surat ini.* Please, have this letter registered.
catatan 1 note, memorandum. **2** (business/medical, etc.) records. *buku* ~ notebook. ~ *bawah* footnote. ~ *harga* price

quotation. ~ *harian* diary. ~ *harta benda* inventory. ~ *huku-man* rap sheet. ~ *jiwa* census (of population). ~ *kaki* footnote. ~ *kesimpulan* concluding notes. ~ *kriminil* criminal record. ~ *pelaksanaan* performance records. ~ *penangkapan* arrest record, rap sheet. ~ *pinggir* a) marginal notes. b) commentary. ~ *rapat* minutes/notes (of a meeting). ~ *samping* marginal notes. *Kantor ~ Sipil* Registry of Births, Deaths, and Marriages, Vital Statistics Bureau, Civil Register. ~ *tambahan* additional notes, postscript. ~ *upah* payroll records. **3** annotation, comments, endorsement. *dengan* ~ with the annotation/endorsement. **bercatatan** with/to have an annotation, annotated.
pencatat 1 registrar. ~ *rapat* minutes clerk. ~ *waktu* a) timekeeper. b) stopwatch, time recorder. **2** device that records, detector, counter, -graph. *alat* ~ *gempa (bumi)* seismograph. *alat* ~ *kebohongan* lie detector. *alat* ~ *kendaraan* traffic counter. *alat* ~ *radiasi* Geiger counter.
pencatatan 1 registration, enrollment, recording, listing, notation. ~ *beban atas hak* registration of an encumbrance. ~ *data pasién berbasis komputer* computer-based patient record. ~ *diri* registration. ~ *jiwa* census (of the population). ~ *kembali* relisting. ~ *sipil* civil registry. **2** quotation (of a price). **3** listing (of stock on an exchange).
caték (*J/Jv*) **mencaték** to bite (of a snake or dog).
catet → CATAT. **nyatetin** (*J coq*) → MENCATATKAN.
catok vise, clamp.
catol (*J*) **mencatol** to peck (of a chicken when eating).
cator [béca-(ber)motor] motorized pedicab.
catu (*Jv*) portion, ration, allocation, share, supply. *mendapat – beras 2 kg sehari* to get a daily rice allocation of 2 kilograms. *– daya* power supply.
mencatu 1 to ration, limit amount (of gasoline per day, etc.). ~ *bénsin pada saat bénsin kurang* to ration gasoline when gasoline is in short supply. **2** to allot (a certain quantity), supply, dole out. **3** to distribute. **4** to charge (a battery).
mencatukan to distribute, ration/dole out, allot s.t.
catuan portion, ration, allocation, share, supply. ~ *daya* power supply.
pencatu ~ *daya* power line.
pencatuan 1 rationing. **2** allotment, allocation. **3** distribution.
catuk I mencatuk 1 to peck (of a bird), bite (of a snake). *Ayam ini suka benar ~ telurnya.* This chicken really likes to peck at her eggs. **2** to injure with the point of a weapon; to chop (up). *Ia ~ kepala orang itu dengan bayonét.* He injured that person's head with a bayonet. ~ *kelapa* to chop up a coconut.
catuk II 1 large hammer. **2** pickax, mattock.
mencatuk to hew, back, chop, cut, knock, hit.
catuk III 1 a tablespoon. **2** a coconut-shellful. **3** measure of capacity for rice (= 1/8 *cupak*).
catuk IV tercatuk *duduk* ~ to sit with the head slightly bowed. *Orang itu duduk ~ sambil merenung dengan muka yang muram.* That man sat with his head slightly bent while staring with a depressed face.
catur I (*Skr*) chess. *buah* – chessman. *papan* – chessboard. *tapak* – the squares on a chessboard.
bercatur 1 to play chess. **2** checkered (material).
caturan check(er)ed design.
pecatur chess player.
percaturan 1 chess game. **2** chessboard. **3** game of politics, policy. ~ *internasional* international policy. ~ *politik* political life. ~ *uang* financial policy.
catur II (*Skr*) (in compounds) four. – *Brata* the four guiding principles for carrying out the duties of Army Finance Office employees. – *Dharma Éka Karma* [cadék] the four duties of the Armed Forces. – *jalma* the four Hindu castes. – *kembar* quadruplets. – *Krida* the four activities. – *lipat* fourfold. – *Prasetya* the four pledges of the national police force. – *Tertib* the Four Orders (relating to land registration). – *Tunggal* The Four-in-One Unit (consisting of the Army Police, Civil Service, and the People). – *Upaya* the Four Efforts (a political slogan). – *Wangsa* a) the four castes in Bali. b) (*leg*) the police, public prosecutor, judge, and attorneys. *keluarga – Warga* (in the framework of birth control) an ideal family consisting of father, mother, and

two children. – *windu* 32 years. – *wulan* quarter (of the school year).
catur III (*Jv*) talk, chatter.
bercatur to talk, speak, discuss.
caturan subject of discussion.
percaturan discussion, talk, conversation.
caturangga (*Skr*) chessboard; → PAPAN *catur*.
caturangkap [catur+rangkap] quadruple.
caturisme the game of politics.
caturwulan quarter (of a year), four months; trimester (in schools).
catus → CETUS.
catut I (*J*) **1** tweezers (to extract facial hair, etc.). **2** pincers, nippers (to extract nails).
mencatut to extract, pull out.
catut II *harga* – an illegal (higher than the official) price, a high price. *tukang* – a) an extortionate dealer in the black market. b) ticket scalper; → CALO *tikét.* c) black marketer, swindler. – *pantat* "scalping of buttocks," i.e., keeping seats in train compartments warm until s.o. shows up who is willing to pay a certain amount of money to the *tukang – pantat* who has illegally occupied the seat, with the only purpose of "chasing him away" from "his seat" which, in fact, is yours because you have paid for it!
bercatut to work as a scalper.
mencatut [and **nyatut** (*coq*)] **1** to carry out illegal trade; to become a black marketer. **2** to deal in s.t. and make an extremely high profit, sell on the black market. **3** to deceive, trick, double-cross s.o. **4** to use (or misuse) (power, s.o.'s name/a function, etc.).
mencatutkan → MENCATUT 2.
catutan 1 income from carrying out illegal trade, etc. **2** illegal transactions, black-market dealing.
pencatut 1 black marketer. **2** scalper; → TUKANG *catut.*
pencatutan carrying out illegal trade, etc, misuse of. ~ *nama* the misuse of the name of.
percatutan illegal trading, scalping, black-marketeering.
catutisme the "art" of black-marketing.
cauhué (*C*) poor quality goods.
cauk → CAUNG.
caul (*Pers?*) *kain* – a) fine embroidered fabric from the Indian port of Chaul. b) shawl.
caung sunken, hollow (of cheeks, due to age, toothlessness).
causa (*D*) /kausa/ reason, provision (in a contract).
cawagub [calon wakil gubernur] candidate for vice governor.
cawai *burung* – k.o. magpie.
cawak I dimple, dent. – *pipi(t)* dimple on cheeks.
bercawak with/to have dimples; dimpled. *Senyumnya ~.* When she laughs she has dimples in her cheek.
cawak II neck strap, k.o. leash (for dogs).
cawan (*C*) **1** mug, cup without a handle/ear. **2** k.o. rice bowl. **3** crucible. **4** cupful. – *lebur* crucible. – *Pétri* Petri dish. – *pinggan* chinaware, porcelain ware. – *sarapan* breakfast cup.
mencawan concave.
cawang I → CABANG.
cawang II (*S*) check mark, marginal note.
mencawangi to mark, put a mark on.
tercawang marked.
cawaprés → CALON *wakil présidén.* **mencawapréskan** to nominate for vice president.
cawat 1 (bather's) loincloth. **2** suspensory bandage.
bercawat to wear a loincloth. ~ *ékor* with one's tail between one's legs (of dogs); tail down. *sepuluh jung datang, anjing ~ ékor juga* junks may arrive (laden with cloth) but a dog's only cloth is his tail.
mencawatkan to wear s.t. as a loincloth.
cawé-cawé (*Jv*) to join in (s.o. else's affairs). *Meréka adalah sumber pengetahuan, panutan, pengawas yang tak perlu harus selalu bertentangan dengan pemerintah. Peranan meréka tak perlu – ikut memerintah.* They are the source of knowledge, leaders, and overseers who should not always be in conflict with the administration. It isn't necessary for them to join in in governing (the country).
cawet → CAWAT.

cawi-cawi *burung* – drongo, king-crow, *Dicrurus sp.*

cawis (*Jv*) ready, all set.

    mencawiskan to prepare s.t.

    cawisan s.t. prepared in advance, stock.

Cawu → CATUR *wulan.*

cawuh (*Jv*) mixed, blended; not sharply distinct. *Berasnya – dengan gabah.* The husked rice grains were mixed in with the unhusked ones.

caya → CAHAYA.

CBSA (*init*) [Cara Belajar Siswa Aktif] Active Pupil Teaching Method.

cc /cécé/ cubic centimeters.

CC-PKI /sé-sé-pé-ka-i/ [Céntral Comité Partai Komunis Indonésia] Central Committee of the Communist Party of Indonesia, outlawed in 1966.

cd I [celana dalam] underpants, panties.

cd II → KERTAS *cd.*

CD III CD, compact disk.

cé I the name of the letter c.

cé and cé' II clipped form of CÉWÉK.

cebak (mineral) deposit. *– emas* gold deposit.

    mencebak to dig (out), excavate, mine.

    cebakan 1 digging, excavation. **2** ore, mineral. **3** (mineral) deposit. *~ berlapis* bedded deposit. *~ bijih* ore deposit. *~ laut* marine deposit. *~ yang disimpulkan* inferred reserves. *~ tersebar* disseminated deposit.

    pencebak miner, digger.

    pencebakan excavation, digging.

    percebakan mine.

ceban (*C J*) ten thousand (rupiahs).

cebar (*Mal*) **cebaran** challenge.

cebar-cebur splashing (of bathers); → CEBUR.

    bercebar-cebur to splash around.

cebelus → JEBLOS. **mencebeluskan** to put in a hole.

cébi (*J*) in vain, for nothing.

cebik sulk, pout.

    mencebik to pout, sulk, be sulky, make a face at (i.e., purse one's lips in a derisive fashion, in mimicry). *Kasdan ~ karena bencinya kepada saya.* Kasdan pouted at me because he hated me.

    mencebikkan 1 *~ bibir* to make a face (at s.o.). **2** to insult s.o.

    cebikan sulky expression.

cebil → CEBIK.

cebir 1 chipped, torn at the edge. **2** shred, fragment, scrap, chip.

    secebir a shred/scrap (of cloth/paper).

    mencebir to chip.

cebis → CEBIR.

ceblang-ceblung (*Jv*) awkward (in speaking).

céblék I (*J*) k.o. basket.

céblék II (*J*) thin and flat.

céblék III hollow (cheeks).

ceblok I (*J*) **nyeblok** to walk through a slushy and muddy place.

    ceblok-ceblokan forced to walk through such a place.

ceblok II (*Jv*) **nyeblok** to work under a mutual agreement in which A agrees with B that, if he plants rice for A free of charge, he will be entitled to cut the rice during harvest time for a certain wage, *usu* in the proportion 10:1 or 12:1 of the harvest.

ceblok III (*Jv*) to crash (of aircraft).

cébok 1 a scoop, water dipper, ladle (half coconut shell with handle). **2** to clean one's anus with water after defecation (nowadays using bottles filled with water); to clean one's genitals after urinating.

    bercébok → CÉBOK 2.

    mencébok 1 to ladle/dip up (water with a vessel or hands). **2** to clean the body/anus and genitals after defecation or urinating.

    mencéboki [and **nyébokin** (*J coq*)] → MENCÉBOK 2.

    cébokan small trough for water for washing o.s.

cébol (*Jv*) **1** (*orang –*) dwarf, midget. **2** badly proportioned, out of proportion, abnormally short. (*si*) *– hendak mencapai bintang/bulan* and *– nggayuh lintang* (*Jv*) one who attempts things beyond his ability, one who wants to reach for the moon, one who wants to seek the impossible; to cherish an unrealized desire.

    pencébolan stunting.

cébong (*J/Jv*) tadpole.

cébrés (*BG*) [céwék bréngsék] bitch (dysphemism for a woman).

cebur (*onom*) sound of s.t. being plunged or thrown into water; plop!

    bercebur to plunge (into water).

    mencebur [and **nyebur** (*coq*)] **1** to jump/plunge into water. **2** to plunge (into some line of work, etc.). **3** make a splashing sound.

    menceburi to plunge into, get involved in, mix in s.t.

    menceburkan [and **nyeburin** (*J coq*)] to plunge/throw s.t. into water. *~ diri ke (dalam)* to throw o.s. into (business, etc.); to plunge into (misery); to meddle with, interfere in; to join in.

    tercebur [and **kecebur** (*coq*)] **1** fallen/plunged (into water). *Truk angkut beras tercebur ke laut.* A rice truck plunged into the sea. *tercebur dalam lumpur* sunken in the mud. *Seorang gadis téwas kecebur sumur ketika ia sedang menimba air.* A girl fell in a well while drawing water and was drowned. *Tenaga asing téwas kecebur kétél uap.* A foreign worker died when he fell into a steam kettle. **2** engaged/involved in.

    penceburan slashing down.

cecadu various species of fruit bat.

cecah trace (amount). *tiap –* each moment.

    sececah 1 a moment, an instant, a twinkling of an eye, awhile. *~ mata* at a glance, in a wink. **2** a little bit, a touch of, trace (amounts of). *~ garam* a pinch of salt (a quantity held between forefinger and thumb).

    bercecah in small amounts, bit by bit.

    mencecah 1 to touch s.t. lightly. *Bajunya ~ tanah.* Her dress touched the ground. *~ bahu* (hair) down to the shoulders. **2** to step on, touch with the feet. *~ bumi* to step on the ground. *sejak ~ bumi* from one's childhood. **3** to pick up s.t. with the tips of the fingers. *~ garam* to take some salt between forefinger and thumb.

    mencecahkan 1 to dip, put the tip of s.t. (into). *~ ikan dalam kécap* to dip fish into soy sauce. **2** to touch with. *~ kaki ke tanah* to touch the ground with the feet, plant the feet on the ground. *~ péna ke tinta* to dip a pen into ink. *~ tandatangan* (*ob*) to place one's signature on, sign. **3** to affix.

    tercecah 1 *~ (ke)pada* barely dipped into. **2** touched lightly.

cecak I → CICAK.

cecak II (*M*) **mencecak 1** to pinch. **2** to steal, pickpocket. *~ tonggak* to start carving a house post/pole (ceremonially).

    pencecak pickpocket.

cecak III freckled, tabby (of cats, etc.), speckled, spotted.

cecap I mencecap 1 to taste (with the tip of the tongue or touch with the finger and then put on the lip). **2** to enjoy. *Dari kecil saya belum pernah ~ kesenangan dalam hidup ini.* I've never had any pleasure in my life since I was little.

    tercecap *~ air* just touching (the water as a bridge in a flood).

cecap II *burung* – a sunbird, *Leptocoma hasselti?*

cecar (*J*) **mencecar** to keep on (doing s.t. to s.o.), press, bombard with questions, interrogate. *Dicercanya Dinem untuk berterus terang.* He pressed Dinem to speak the truth.

    mencecarkan to keep on (asking questions or doing s.t.).

    cecaran bombarding. *~ pertanyaan* interrogation.

    pencecaran *~ pertanyaan* interrogation.

cecat → CACAT.

cecawi → CAWI-CAWI.

cécé I (*J*) great-great grandchild; → CICIT I.

cécé II (*J*) young jackfruit; → GORI.

cécé III [cc] cubic centimeters.

cécéh (*coq*) a boy's penis.

cecek (*Jv*) point, dot (over an i), ornamental dots (on a *batik* pattern).

cecéng (*C J*) one thousand (rupiahs).

cecengklok → CACENGKLOK.

cecer → CECAR.

cécér dripping/dribbling away.

    bercécéran (*pl subj*) to dribble away (as flour from a torn bag/money from a pocket), spill all over, be scattered all around.

    mencécérkan 1 to pour s.t. out. **2** to scatter s.t. around.

    tercécér [and **kecécéran** (*coq*)] **1** fallen out (on the way). **2** spilled, poured out (little by little), scattered. **3** left back/behind. *~ di belakang* and *~ dari* backward, left behind (in study/progress, etc.). **ketercécéran** scattering.

cecéran left behind, abandoned. *beras* ~ rice sweepings, i.e., rice kernels swept up from the route between a port area and the warehouse in which the bales of rice are stored

cecéré (*J*) 1 small. *ikan* – a small river fish, *Rasbora argyrotaenia* (*Blkr.*). *masih* – still young, not yet experienced. 2 small fry, commoner, worthless/good-for-nothing fellow. 3 cockroach.

cecincin annular.

cécok → CÉKCOK.

cecongok → CECUNGUK.

cecongor (*J*) face, mug.

cecoro (*Jv*) cockroach; → CORO I.

cecuit (*onom*) hissing sound.

cecuitan hissing.

cecunguk (*S*) 1 cockroach. 2 plainclothesman, spy. 3 petty criminal. 4 a nonentity, a nothing, a loser.

cecuping auriculate.

cecurut shrew.

cédal (*Jv*) (*berlidah* –) to have a k.o. speech defect or childish pronunciation, inability to pronounce a trilled *r*.

cédéér (*D*) /sédér/ **mencédéér** to cede.

cédént (*D*) /sé-/ assignor, transferor.

cedera I (*Skr*) dispute, quarrel, disagreement, discord, conflict.

bercedera to (have a) quarrel, disagree. *Tak lama kemudian ia ~ dengan pimpinan rédaksi.* Not long afterward, he had a quarrel with the head of editing.

mempercederakan to set people against e.o., make people quarrel.

kecederaan and **percederaan** dispute, quarrel, disagreement, discord, dissension.

cedera II (*Skr*) 1 flawed, defective. *Dia tidak mau menerima barang-barang yang – itu.* He didn't want to accept the defective goods. 2 injury, wound; injured, wounded. *Seorang ahli asing téwas dan empat orang téknisi – berat akibat meledaknya stabilisator pompa lumpur perusahaan minyak "Mobil Oil."* A foreign expert was killed and four technicians were seriously wounded as a result of an explosion of a dredger at "Mobil Oil." 3 loss, harm, damage. *kena –* a) attacked/investigated/searched/raided suddenly/unexpectedly. b) to be ruined. c) to suffer (from hard times). *tanpa –* unscathed. *– janji* default. *– tekanan berulang-ulang* repetitive strain injury.

bercedera flawed, defective.

mencederai (*M*) to hurt, injure, (inflict) damage on, wound (feelings). *Dua ribu pasukan Irak berhasil ditéwaskan dan dicederai dalam serangan baru Iran.* Two thousand Iraqi troops were killed and wounded in fresh Iranian attacks.

mencederakan to injure, hurt.

tercedera 1 injured, hurt, wounded (of feelings). 2 (*M*) ailing, suffering.

pencedera s.o. who injures/violates.

pencederaan injuring, hurting.

cedera III 1 treachery, disloyalty, faithlessness. 2 breach of contract. 3 attack/killing in a treacherous/sneaky way. *– janji* no fulfillment, nonperformance, default.

bercedera to be treacherous/disloyal.

mencedera(kan) 1 to betray. 2 to attack in a treacherous/ sneaky way, assassinate.

mencederai to betray, be treasonous to.

kecederaan 1 betrayal, treachery. 2 disloyalty, unfaithfulness.

pencederaan 1 the act of betraying, being disloyal. 2 the act of attacking, etc. in a treacherous/sneaky way.

cedera IV → CENDERA II.

ceding 1 small, little, scrubby, diminutive, thin and out of condition (of plants/children, etc.), measly. 2 backward.

cédok dipper, scoop; → CIDUK.

mencédok 1 to scoop up (of liquids), ladle up (with hands or dipper). 2 (*coq*) to arrest.

mencédokkan to use s.t. to scoop/ladle up.

pencédok scoop, dipper, ladle.

pencédokan scooping, ladling.

cédong → CÉDOK.

cedra → CEDERA.

ceduk I shrunken (of cheeks), sunken (of eyes due to lack of sleep or illness).

ceduk II (*M*) **terceduk** ~ *seléra* appetite-stimulating.

cedut (*Jv*) **mencedut** to jerk, pull.

cedut-cedut to throb (of a wound).

cegah (*Jv*) say by way of prohibition. *daftar – Tangkal* a list of prohibitions and preventions, i.e., an immigration document consisting of the names of persons who are not allowed to enter or leave the country, comparable to a blacklist. *Ktihn dimasukkan dalam daftar – Tangkal.* Ktihn's name has been inserted in the list of "Unwanted Arrivals." *– resiko* hedging; → PELINDUNG *nilai.*

mencegah 1 to forbid, prohibit, prevent, not allow, restrain, hold back. *Ia tidak sanggup ~ hawa nafsunya.* He was unable to hold back his lust. *~ kehamilan* to prevent conception. *~ kelaparan* to free from hunger. *~ perluasan* to prevent the spread of, nonproliferate. 2 to guard against, combat. *Segera diambil tindakan untuk ~ penyakit cacar.* Immediate steps were taken to combat smallpox. 3 to keep s.o. away (from). *~ anak-anak itu dari bahaya* to keep the children away from danger.

tercegah forbidden, prohibited, under control. *tak ~* uncontrollable, indomitable, not prevented/precluded.

cegahan inhibition, inhibiting.

pencegah 1 preventer, preventative, deterrent. *~ semburan liar* (*petro*) blow-out preventer. *~ tubrukan dari sisi* side-impact bars (of a car). 2 anti-. *alat ~ pencuri* antiburglar contrivance. *~ penghamilan* contraceptive. *obat ~ penyakit* prophylactic medicine. *pil ~ beranak* birth control pill.

pencegahan 1 prevention, deterrence, preventive. *secara ~* preventive. *~ banjir* flood prevention. *~ kejahatan-kejahatan menurut prosédur hukum* procedural crime prevention. *~ kejahatan situasional* situational crime prevention. *~ kejahatan yang beroriéntasi pada pelaku kejahatan* offender-oriented crime prevention. *~ kejahatan yang bersifat sosial édukatif* socio-educative crime prevention. *~ kejahatan yang mengikutsertakan masyarakat* community crime prevention. *~ pencemaran* pollution prevention. *~ penyakit* preventive medicine. *~ perkawinan* interruption of a marriage. *~ perlawanan countermeasure. *~ yang beroriéntasi pada korban* victim-oriented prevention. 2 not being allowed to leave Indonesia.

cegak upright, erect; → TEGAK.

cégak 1 strong and active, robust. 2 strong and swift. 3 (*M*) recovered and healthy again.

cegar I shallow rapids.

cegar II (*M*) healthy again after an illness; → SEGAR.

cegar III *burung* – white-crowned forktail, *Enicurus leschenaulti*.

cegas → CERGAS.

cegat (*J/Jv*) **mencegat** [and **nyegat** (*coq*)] 1 to block, impede, thwart, prevent. *~ kesalahan cétak pada suratkabar* to prevent typos/typographical errors in newspapers. 2 to ambush, lie in wait for. *Tentara meréka dicegat musuh.* Their army was ambushed by the enemy. 3 to wait for (s.t. to come along), flag down (a vehicle). *~ taksi* to flag down a cab.

mencegati (*pl obj*) to stop, block, etc.

tercegat stopped short, choked up (of the throat/voice).

cegatan 1 ambush. 2 interception, stopping. 3 checkpoint.

pencegat s.o. or s.t. that blocks/stops/impedes/ambushes, etc.

pencegatan interception, ambushing, on-the-spot check.

cegluk (*onom*) gulping sound.

berceglukan to make such a sound.

ceguk I a swallow, gulp; → TEGUK I.

seceguk a gulp (of water, etc.).

ceguk II (*Jv*) hiccup, sob.

terceguk-ceguk to sob.

cegukan 1 to hiccup. 2 hiccup.

cék I (*D*) a check. *dibayar dengan –* to be paid by check. *menarik –* to draw/write a check. *mengeluarkan –* to issue a check. *penarik – s.o.* who writes a check. *penarikan –* the drawing of a check. *– atas unjuk* bearer check. *– berjaminan* certified check. *– fiat* certified check. *– gantung* a) (*Med*) a postdated check. b) outstanding check. *– kedaluwarsa* stale check. *– kosong* a bad/ bounced check. *– lunas* canceled check. *– luwes* rubber check. *– mundur* postdated check. *– pelancong* traveler's check. *– pelanggan* customer's check. *– pembawa* bearer check. *– pembayar* *upah* payroll check. – *perjalanan* traveler's check. – *perseo-rangan* personal check. – *pos* postal check. – *perjalanan BRI* [Cékpébri] BRI traveler's check. – *pribadi* personal check. – *putih* check that looks like a bank check and used as 'legal' tender, but issued by a large crumb rubber plant to replace cash money in the Sambas regency in West Kalimantan (early 1981). – *terjamin* bank/certified check. – *tertolak* bad check. – *tunai* bank check. – *undur* post-dated check. – *wisata* traveler's check. – *(yang diberi tanggal) mundur* and – *yang diberi tanggal lebih kemudian daripada tanggal penarikannya* a postdated check. – *yang tidak cukup dananya* a check with insufficient funds, bad/bounced check.

cék II (E) check, control, verification. – *dan cék lagi* check and recheck. *sistim – dan recék/pengecékan kembali* check-and-recheck system. – *in* check in. – *out* check out.

men(ge)cék [and **ngecék** (*coq*)] to check, control, verify. *Polisi mengecék laporan kematian.* The police verified the report on the death. *mencék dan mencék lagi/ulang* to check and recheck. *dicék kebenarannya* its authenticity was checked. *"Saya ngecék apa Agnes sudah pulang dan tidur bersama Mbak Rus," ujar Ivan.* "I checked to see whether Agnes had come home and was sleeping with Mbak Rus," said Ivan.

pencékan and **pengecékan** check(ing), control, verification. *tempat-tempat pencékan* checkpoints. *pengecékan beberapa kali* check and recheck. *melakukan dua langkah pencékan* to double-check. *melakukan pengecékan silang* to cross-check.

cék III clipped form of *encék*, title used in addressing Chinese born in China.

Cék IV Czech.

Cék V – *gu* (*Mal Med*) teacher.

cekah bercekah 1 to tear/burst/split open (of fruits). **2** torn, burst, split.

mencekah 1 → BERCEKAH. **2** to break open (a mangosteen, etc.) by squeezing (it) between the hands.

mencekahkan to break s.t. open.

cekak I the space between the index or middle fingers and the thumbs of both hands held together. *baju – musang* a jacket with a high collar.

secekak a quantity that can be held between thumb and index or middle finger, a pinch (of).

bercekak – *pinggang* with hands on hips (a provocative gesture).

mencekak 1 to grasp between the forefinger and thumb. **2** to grab hold of and squeeze.

mencekakkan to place (one's fingers) on s.t.

cekakan 1 s.t. held between those fingers. **2** strangle-hold.

cekak II (M) quarrel.

bercekak to quarrel, fight. ~ *henti, silat terkenang* an idea that comes too late is useless.

mempercekakkan to fight/contend for. *Kedua pria itu berkelahi ~ wanita cantik itu.* The two men fought over the beautiful woman.

cekak III (*J/Jv*) **1** short, brief. *cerita ~* [cerkak] short story. **2** insufficient (of money). *Uangnya –.* He doesn't have enough money. *bangsa kantong –* (*J*) those who are (always) short of money. *Réstoran itu boléh dikunjungi tamu berkantung –.* Customers who don't have a lot of money can go to that restaurant. **3** curt, short. – *aos/aus* clear and succinct, curt.

cekak IV and **cekakan** the smallest package in which morphine is sold.

cekakak I (*J/Jv*) – *cekikik* and **(ber)cekakakan** to laugh out loud, convulse with laughter; → NGAKAK.

cekakak II (white-collared) kingfisher, *Halcyon chloris*. – *cina* black-capped kingfisher, *Halcyon pileata*. – *gunung/Jawa* Javan kingfisher, *Halcyon cyanoventris*. – *hutan* banded kingfisher, *Lacedo pulchella*. – *mérah* ruddy kingfisher, *Halcyon coromanda*. – *sungai* collared kingfisher, *Halcyon chloris*.

cekal I – *hati* strong, sturdy, bold, determined, unwavering, resolute, firm, staunch, steadfast, intrepid.

mencekal to bear, stand, suffer, endure, tolerate.

mencekalkan ~ *hati* to take heart, pull o.s. together.

cekal II mencekal 1 to seize with the hand, grab, snatch, grasp, catch. **2** to arrest, apprehend. **3** (*Jv*) to pawn; → GADAI *cekelan*.

mencekali to grasp, grab hold of.

cekalan 1 grip. **2** seized.

cekal III [cegah tangkal] not allowed to leave or enter Indonesia.

tercekal not allowed to leave or enter Indonesia.

pencekalan not allowing s.o. to leave or enter Indonesia.

cekalang → CAKALANG.

cekam I → CENGKAM I. grasp, grip.

mencekam 1 to grasp, grip, seize tightly in the hands. *dicekam ketakutan* to be seized by fear, fear-stricken. **2** gripping, engrossing. **3** tense. *semencekam* as tense as.

mencekami to grip.

mencekamkan 1 gripping, engrossing. **2** to put (one's claws into).

tercekam stricken, in the grip of, oppressed. *Abdul Latief, Dirut PT Sarinah Jaya sedang ~ memandangi bangunan yang terbakar.* Abdul Latief, managing director of PT Sarinah Jaya was stricken when he saw the burning building. *ketercekaman* oppression. ~ *sivitas kedua akadémi ini berawal dari diperoléh-nya penjelasan resmi.* The oppression of the community of these two academies started when he got an official explanation.

cekaman grip, hold, oppression.

pencekam gripper.

cekam II dibble-stick for planting rice or corn. *tilam –* mattress stuffed and sewn, quilted mattress.

mencekam to plant with a dibble-stick.

cekam III quilted mattress.

mencekam to make a quilted mattress.

cekang 1 taut (of muscles, etc.), tight. **2** narrow.

cekap I → CEKAK I.

cekap II (*Mal*) → CAKAP II. **kecekapan** efficiency.

cekar turn ship's wheel hard.

cekarau (M) → CIKARAU. – *besar* to boast, brag, talk big.

cekat I nimble, adroit. – *dua tangan* ambidextrous. *tidak –* not skillful, awkward. **ketidak-cekatan** awkwardness.

bercekat to act smart, be skillful/adroit.

cekatan 1 skillful, adroit, nimble. **2** quick-witted, smart.

kecekatan 1 skill, adroitness, dexterity. ~ *tangan* sleight of hand. **2** slyness, cleverness, intelligence.

cekat II → CEGAT.

cekau mencekau to grab, snatch, seize with the hand/claw, beak, etc.

cekauan grip. *dalam ~* in the grip/power of.

cékcok (*J/Jv*) quarrel, squabble, disagreement, discord, bickering, wrangling. – *mulut* squabbling. *Tetapi yang ditegur tersinggung sampai terjadi ~ mulut.* But the one addressed was so offended that a squabble occurred.

bercékcok to squabble, bicker, quarrel, etc.

bercékcokan to squabble with e.o.

mempercékcokkan to bicker/dispute about s.t.

percékcokan quarrel, squabble, etc.

cékdam (E) check dam.

cek-del (*coq*) frank, outspoken, open.

cekék → CEKIK I. – *léhér* cutthroat. *tarip – léhér* cutthroat rates.

cekel → CEKAL II.

cékél I miserly, stingy, niggardly. – *berhabis, lapuk berteduh* though all too stingy, all wealth will be gone.

cékél II (*Jv cla*) a pupil of a Hindu ascetic.

cékél III k.o. short spear/javelin.

céker (*E Med*) teller (in a bank).

céker I (*J/Jv*) **1** claw. **2** foot (*esp* of fowl). **3** k.o. dish made of chicken.

mencéker to scratch around (of chickens); *cp* CAKAR I.

cékér I stingy, miserly; → CÉKÉL I.

mencéker to scratch around (of chickens).

cekeram partial payment in advance, down payment; → CENG-KERAM I.

cekerau → CEKARAU.

ceketing k.o. bird, red wattled lapwing, *Lobivanellus indicus atronuchalis*.

ceki (C) **1** (*main –*) **1** name of a Chinese card game using small playing cards (for gambling). **2** *daun/kartu –* small Chinese playing cards (120 in total).

cekibar and **cekiber** (*J*) flying lizard, *Draco volans*.

cekih mencekih to open s.t. a bit.

tercekih slightly open and showing the insides (of mussels/a door, etc.).

cekik I 1 choking. – kedadak choking and vomiting. 2 k.o. curse.
mencekik 1 to throttle, strangle, choke s.o. 2 to eat up, gobble up, swallow up, kill. *Industri-industri kecil hendaklah dilindungi, supaya jangan dicekik pengusaha besar.* Small industries should be protected so that they are not gobbled up by big entrepreneurs. ~ *léhér* very expensive. 3 killing, murderous.
mencekiki (*pl obj*) to strangle, etc.
mencekikkan to strangle with s.t.
tercekik [and kecekik (*coq*)] 1 strangled, choked (to death). ~ *utang* be up to one's ears in debt. *Inalum (Indonésia Asahan Aluminium) ~ utang.* The Indonesia Asahan Smelting Co. is up to its ears in debt. 2 cut short, nipped in the bud.
cekikan strangulation, strangling.
pencekik 1 strangler. 2 killer.
pencekikan strangling, throttling.
cekik II bercekik (*M*) to quarrel, wrangle, fight. – *merih* quarrel.
bercekik-merih to quarrel.
mempercekikkan to squabble/argue over.
cekikik (*J*) → CEKAKAK cekikik.
nyekikik to giggle, chuckle.
cekikikan ketawa/tertawa ~ to giggle, chuckle.
ceking (*J/Jv*) – *t(e)répés* thin, slender, scrawny, skinny, as lean as a rake.
kecekingan 1 thinness. 2 to be too thin.
céking (*E*) checking, control, verifying. *belum melakukan – atas duduk persoalan yang sebenarnya* still hasn't checked out the actual situation.
mencéking to check, control, verify.
pencékingan control, verification.
cekit I mencekit 1 to nibble/peck at. *Burung ~ makanannya.* The bird pecked at the food. 2 to take s.t. between the index finger and thumb. ~ *makanan lalu dibawa ke mulut untuk dikecap* to pick up the food and then put it in one's mouth to taste it. 3 to distribute bit by bit.
cekit-cekit prickling.
cekit II bercekit-cekitan to quarrel, squabble. *Anak-anak itu ~, tak ada yang mau mengalah.* The kids were squabbling, nobody wanted to give in.
ceklak → CEKLÉK. – *ceklék* to keep on clicking. – *ceklék menekan tombol kaméranya* to keep on clicking the shutter of his camera (to take more than one picture). *"Begini caranya, Nyonya," katanya sambil menekan kombinasi nomor alat pengaman ini. – ceklék, pintu pun terbuka.* "It's like this, ma'am," he said, pressing on the combination lock. Click, and the door opened.
ceklék (*J onom*) click (of a camera shutter/lock, etc.).
menceklék to click, take (pictures), turn on (a switch).
cékli (*Jv*) small but attractive, nice.
ceklik → CEKLÉK.
ceklop (*onom*) the sound of sucking.
cekluk (*Jv*) tercekluk slipped and fell.
céko I (*Jv*) misshapen, deformed, disfigured. *Tangannya –.* His hand was deformed.
Céko II Czech.
cekoh (*C J*) two and a half (rupiahs); → RINGGIT I.
cekok I 1 traditional medicine forced into the mouth of an unwilling child. 2 force-feeding.
mencekok 1 to forcefully administer (a liquid medicine) to an unwilling child. 2 to indoctrinate.
mencekoki to feed (a child) forcefully, force down (a child's throat).
mencekokkan 1 to force s.t. down a child's throat. 2 to force s.o. to swallow s.t., force-feed, force to take in (students), hammer/pound s.t. into s.o.'s head.
cekokan 1 medicine administered in that way. 2 indoctrination.
pencekokan administering medicine in that way.
cekok II – *manis* a vegetable, *Sauropus albicans* (eaten as spinach).
cekop – *manis* k.o. shrub used by women during lactation, sweet leaf bush, *Sauropus androgynus*.
cekor → CEKUR.

Cékoslowakia Czechoslovakia.
cekot (*Jv*) cekot-cekot throbbing pain (in one's head, etc.)
cékpoin (*E*) checkpoint.
cekrék (*Jv*) to click (of a spring). *bor* – ratchet (hand)drill.
cekrékan k.o. musical instrument made with bottle tops nailed to a board.
cekrém advance money, down payment.
cekrés (*onom*) *suara* – clipping sound (of scissors).
mencekréskan to use s.t. to clip with. ~ *gunting* to cut with scissors.
ceku I menceku to stick s.t. (with a pointed object). *Dia ~ tangan saya dengan kukunya.* He stuck his nail into my hand.
mencekukan to stick (a pointed object) into s.t. ~ *jarum suntik ke lengan* to stick a needle into s.o.'s arm.
ceku II nausea.
menceku to feel like vomiting, nauseated.
cekuh I mencekuh to reach for s.t., (in one's pocket), pick s.t. (out of one's pocket).
cekuh II → CEKUR.
cekuk I → CEKOK II.
cekuk II → CEKUNG, LEKUK.
cekung 1 sunken, hollow (of one's cheeks/eyes). 2 concave (of mirrors/lenses). – *batu bara* coal basin. – *kepala* hollow at the lower back of the head.
mencekung 1 to be sunken, hollow, concave. 2 to sink in(ward).
mencekungkan to form a hollow in, form a concave depression in.
cekungan 1 shale. *Indonésia déwasa ini sudah menemukan lagi sebanyak 50 ~ minyak yang mengandung k.l. 200 milyar barrel.* Indonesia has now again found fifty oil shales which contain approximately 200 billion barrels. 2 cavity. 3 (sedimentary) basin, shelf. ~ *Banda* Banda Basin. ~ *benua* continental shelf. ~ *Pasifik* Pacific Basin. ~ *resapan* infiltration basin. 4 (*coq*) hollow, sunken (in).
kecekungan concavity.
pencekungan hollowing out.
cekup I mencekup to cover s.t. with the palm of the hand, catch (a fly, etc.) under the hand.
cekup II → CEKUT.
cekur k.o. herbal weed, galanga, *Kaempferia galanga*, used in medicines. – *jerangau, ada lagi di ubun-ubun* to be still green/inexperienced, still wet behind one's ears; → KENCUR. – *manis* a shrub, the leaves of which are eaten as vegetables, sweet shoot, *Sauropus albicans/androgynus.*
cekut mencekut to hold/pick up between the tips of the thumb and three fingers (of food).
cela (*Skr*) 1 defect, flaw, imperfection, shortcoming; → CACAT. 2 shame, disgrace. 3 criticism.
bercela damaged, disgraceful, shameful, with shortcomings/defects. *tidak/tanpa ~* flawless, perfect.
mencela(kan) 1 to condemn, denounce, disapprove of. *patut dicela* condemnable, improper. 2 to blame, find fault with. 3 to criticize, slander, defame, pick on. 4 to refute (a theory).
tercela 1 condemned, disapproved of, objectionable, disgraceful. 2 culpable, improper. ketercelaan culpability. *Dalam kasus ecstasy kita juga harus melihat sejauh mana ~nya.* In the case of ecstasy, we also have to see how far the culpability extends.
celaan 1 criticism, disapproval. 2 blame, condemnation.
kecelaan 1 fault, defect, shortcoming. 2 disgrace, shame, ignominy. berkecelaan 1 to have defects/shortcomings, 2 ignominious, humiliating.
pencela critic.
pencelaan 1 criticism. 2 disapproval. 3 blame.
céla (*M*) k.o. cotton fabric with checkered design.
celadi various species of woodpecker, crimson-winged woodpecker, *Picus puniceus.*
celaga I tiller (of boat), helm. – *tangan* hand tiller.
celaga II soot; → JELAGA.
celah 1 gap, empty space, slit, fissure, crack, crevice, cleft. 2 (*leg*) loophole. – *batu* fissure in rock. – *bibir* harelip. – *bukit* pass between hills, col. – *dada* space between the breasts, cleavage. – *gigi* space between the teeth. – *gunung* mountain pass. – *hukum* loophole in the law. – *insang* gill cleft. – *jari* space between the fingers. – *kangkang/kelengkang* crotch, perineum.– *kening*

space between the eyebrows. – *kisi-kisi* spaces between trellises. – *lantai* crevices between floorboards. – *paha* groin. – *pegunungan* mountain pass. – *pintu* slit, slightly ajar, not properly closed (of door). – *suara* glottis. – *Timor* Timor Gap.

bercelah to have space between, gapped.

bercelah-celah ~ *putihnya* (painted) unevenly white.

mencelahi to pass through a gap in.

mencelahkan to make (a path) into.

celak 1 – *mata* a) mascara, eye shadow. b) a derogatory term for Islam/Muslims. **2** to apply/wear eye shadow, wear mascara.

bercelak to apply/wear eye shadow.

mencelak(i) to use an eyebrow pencil on.

célak (*M*) **bercélak** and **mencélak** to sparkle, gleam, shine, flash, glitter.

tercélak sparkled, gleamed, etc. *Tak dapat dia melihat dahi yang ~, lantas pusing.* He cannot see a beautiful girl or he falls in love with her immediately.

celaka (*Skr*) **1** misfortune, bad luck, calamity, disaster, catastrophe; unfortunate, unlucky, to be down on one's luck, have a run of bad luck. *Wah, sekarang ini – aku!* Oh-oh, I'm out of luck now! *mendapat –* a) to meet with an accident. b) to have a run of bad luck. *Apa –!* What can I do! → LACUR I. *nasib –* an accursed fate. – *dan sengsara* affliction. **2** (exclamation showing anger/cursing/frustration, etc.) (what a) bad luck! damn it. *kita kehabisan bénsin!* Damn it, we're out of gas! – *duabelas/tigabelas!* what (a piece of) bad luck! – *orang itu! Berani dia menipu saya!* The hell with him! He has the nerve to cheat me! *Ah –, kunci kontak saya hilang!* Damn it, I've lost my ignition key!

celakanya 1 unfortunately, it's too bad, it's a pity that. ~ *ia baru membayar untuk barang itu!* It's too bad that he had just paid for those goods! **2** as (bad) luck would have it.

mencelakai to do damage to, hurt. *Awas kalau berani* ~ *diriku!* Watch out if you dare hurt me!

mencelakakan 1 to bring disaster/misfortune/ruin down on s.o., cause trouble for s.o. ~ *dirinya sendiri* to bring ruin upon o.s. **2** to embarrass, humiliate.

kecelakaan 1 accident, mishap, bad luck. *undang-undang* ~ workmen's compensation act. ~ *kerja* occupational accident. ~ *lalin/lalu-lintas* traffic accident. ~ *penerbangan* air crash. **2** misfortune.

pencelakaan causing misfortune.

celalét (*J*) trunk (of an elephant) .

celam-celum tramping in and out of a house without ceremony, running in and out of s.o.'s house without regard for anyone.

celamitan (*J*) greedy, selfish, covetous.

celampak mencelampak(kan) to throw away, toss down, hurl.

tercelampak thrown away; → CAMPAK I.

celana (*Skr Hind?*) trousers, pants. – *banjir* high-water/roll-up pants. – *belél* stonewashed/prewashed faded pants. – *berenang* swimming trunks. – *buntung* short trousers. – *cutbrai* bell-bottom trousers. – *dalam* underpants, panties. – *gombyor* baggy pants. – *jéngki* blue jeans. – *jin(s) (warna biru)* (blue) jeans. – *kaos* swim trunks. – *katok* short pants, shorts. – *kodok* children's playsuit. – *kolor* men's drawstring briefs. – *kombor* Madurese traditional calf-length loose-fitting pants. – *komprang* broad, long pants. – *kuda* (riding) breeches. – *lévis* Levi's. – *merangsang* hotpants. – *monyét* children's playsuit. – *Napoléon* blue jeans. – *pangsi* black pants (used in *silat*). – *panjang* (long) trousers. – *pembalap sepéda* bike pants. – *péndék* short trousers. – *pof* plus fours. – *puntung* shorts. – *renang* bathing suit/trunks. – *sepan* tight-fitting trousers. – *setengah tiang* high-water pants. – *sport péndék putih* white sports shorts.

bercelana 1 to wear trousers. *Meréka* ~ *abu-abu.* They wore gray pants. ~ *jin(s)* to wear jeans. **2** to put one's trousers on, get dressed.

mencelanai to put trousers on, make … wear trousers.

celang mencelang to look at with wide-open eyes, look fixedly at, stare at without seeing.

celangak wide open (of a door); → CELANGAP.

mencelangakkan to open widely (of a door).

celangak-celinguk (*J*) to look left and right (in bewilderment, etc.).

celangap (*J*) agape (of mouth). *dengan –* a) open-mouthed. b) yawning.

mencelengapkan to open (the mouth) wide.

celang-cepun (*J*) unsystematic, uneven, disorderly.

celapak mencelapaki to straddle s.t.

tercelapak astride, straddling.

celar(i) *kain –* silk with gold thread embroidery at the edges.

celaru disorder.

celas-celus passing or going in and out (of a house) without ceremony.

celat (*J*) **mencelat 1** to jump/dart far or high, fly off. **2** to soar, skyrocket (of prices). **3** to pop out, protrude.

celatuk (*ob*) **bercelatuk** to joke, jest, banter.

célé (*J*) k.o. cotton fabric with checkered design.

Celébes (*D*) the former name for Sulawesi; → SULAWESI.

celebuk (*onom*) sound made by stones/pebbles, etc. falling into water, flop! plop!

bercelebuk to make this noise.

celédang-celédong and **celédang-celédok/celéduk** to sway one's hips while walking.

celeguk (*J*) **celegukan** gulp.

celeguri → SELEGURI.

célék (*M*) blind in one eye.

celékéh smeared with sticky dirt, smudged, stained, dirty; → SELÉKÉH.

celemék 1 apron. **2** bib.

celémot (*Jv*) **celémotan** dirty (mouth not wiped off after eating).

celémpong a small gong; → TELÉMPONG.

celempung I → CEMPLUNG.

celempung II (*Jv*) a zither-like *gamelan* instrument with 13 double strings, played by plucking.

céléng I (*Jv*) **1** (in Central and East Java) wild boar; → BABI *hutan*, BAGONG II. *sakit –* epilepsy. – *kondé/kundai* reference to a loose woman **2** (*derog*) a mild insult.

céléng II mencéléng to save up money.

mencélengi [and **nyélengi** (*coq*)] to save up (money).

mencélengkan to save (money) for s.o.

célengan 1 savings. **2** money box, piggybank.

celengap tercelengap uncovered, without a cover.

celéngkak-celéngkok zigzagging, winding, twisting (of road, etc.).

celéngkang-celéngkok (-celéngkong) winding, tortuous, sinuous; → CELÉNGKAK-CELÉNGKOK.

celentang (*J*) to lie on one's back; → TELENTANG.

celep (*J/Jv*) dye; → CELUP.

mencelep to dye.

celepan dyed goods.

celepa → SELEPA.

celepak → CELAPAK.

celepik I (*onom*) sound made by a small object falling (such as, a lizard falling to the floor from the ceiling).

celepik II folded-over end of a piece of fabric or paper.

celepok and **celepuk I** (*onom*) sound of a splash/a heavy mass falling into s.t. soft.

celepuk II *burung –* (*J*) Indian scops owl, collared/lesser scops owl, Otus bakkamoena. – *gunung* Javan scops owl, Otus angelinae. – *kalung* collared scops owl, Otus bakkamoena. – *Maluku* Moluccan scops-owl, Otis magicus. – *mérah* reddish scops-owl, Otus rufescens.

celetuk (*J*) interrupt.

menceletuk [and **nyeletuk** (*coq*)] to interrupt.

terceletuk interrupted.

celetukan interruption, intervention.

celi 1 (*J*) **1** accurate, precise. **2** (*J*) keen, sharp-eyed.

celici stingy, tight-fisted.

celih lazy, sluggish; reluctant to work.

pencelih s.o. who hates to work.

celik 1 open (of the eyes). *Saya tidak dapat tidur semalam, mata saya – sepanjang malam.* I couldn't sleep last night, my eyes were open all night. **2** (can) see, sighted. *buta –* blind with the eyes open. **3** aware/conscious of. *buta baru –* to become arrogant/proud because one has obtained wealth or a high position, etc.; → BUTA *baru melék.* – *huruf* literate. ***kecelik-hurufan*** literacy.

mencelik 1 can/able to see. **2** with open eyes; to open.

mencelikkan ~ *mata* a) to open one's eyes. b) to open one's eyes to the fact that. *Pengalaman yang buruk ~ matanya bahwa kawan pun tidak selalu jujur.* The bad experience opened his eyes to the fact that even friends are not always honest.

pencelikan ~ *mata* glance.

celingak-celinguk (*Jv*) looking around. *Setiap saya keluar dari kamar saya, saya selalu ~ mencari wartawan, tetapi tidak seorang pun yang saya lihat.* Every time I leave my office, I always look around for newspaper reporters, but I couldn't see anybody; → CELINGUK. **2** sightseeing.

celinguk (*Jv*) **celingukan** to look left and right apparently confused/perplexed/bewildered/puzzled.

celingus (*Jv*) embarrassed, shy, unsociable.

celis mencelis to chop up into small pieces, mince.

celit (*J*) **mencelit** to stick out, protrude.

celok (*ob*) → MÉNCLOK.

celomés (*ob*) **1** sickly, weak, full of suffering. **2** fussy, hard to please, fault-finding.

celomok bercelomok and **tercelomok** full of streaks and scratches, pockmarked (of one's face).

celong sunken (of an eyeball, etc).

celongok (*J*) to stick out, protrude.

celopar fussy, hard to please, never satisfied, always nagging.

celoréng (*Jv*) k.o. musical instrument consisting of a metal bar or plate which is struck with a stick.

celorot (*Jv*) flash.

mencelorot to flash.

celos I → CELUS.

celos II (*J*) **mencelos** ~ *hatinya* to be frightened.

celot mencelot to stick out, protrude, bulge out.

celotéh chatter, idle talk, blather.

bercéloteh and **menceloteh** to talk idly, babble, chatter away.

mencelotéhkan to babble about s.t.

celotéhan babbling.

Célsius (*D*) /sél-/ centigrade, Celsius.

celuk ... bah peek-a-boo; → CILUK BAH.

celuk menceluk to grope (in a hole/pocket) for s.t., put the hand into s.t./water etc. in order to get an object.

celulut (*burung* -) k.o. plover.

celum-celam → CELAM-CELUM.

celung I (*J*) hollow, sunken (of cheeks).

celung II (*onom*) ~ *celang* jingling/tinkling sound.

celung III stall for an elephant or buffalo.

mencelung(kan) to drive an animal into such a stall.

celup *téh* – flow-thru tea bag. *tukang* – dyer. – *dingin* quenching. – *minyak* oil bath.

bercelup coated.

mencelup 1 to soak o.s. **2** to dye s.t. **3** to dip, soak.

mencelupkan [and **nyelupin** (*J coq*)] to dip/soak/immerse s.t. (in a liquid). *Meréka duduk di tepi kolam sambil ~ kaki ke dalam air.* They were sitting at the edge of the pool and dipping their feet in the water.

tercelup [and **kecelup** (*coq*)] to get dipped/soaked inadvertently.

celupan 1 dyeing. **2** dyed article. **3** immersion. ~ *minyak* oil quenching.

pencelup 1 dyer. **2** dye. ~ *listrik* immersion heater.

pencelupan 1 immersion, dip. **2** dyeing. *pengawas bidang industri* ~ dyeing supervisor. **3** dye works.

celupak (*Jv*) earthenware oil lamp (in the shape of a small bowl, coconut oil is used as fuel).

celupar garrulous; → CELOPAR.

celur *sumpah* – oath taken by dipping one's hand into boiling water/oil or molten tin.

bercelur ~ *minyak/tangan* to swear/take an oath by immersing one's hand in boiling oil or water.

mencelur(kan) to dip in boiling water (of eggs/vegetables/a fowl to remove its feathers, etc.).

penceluran dipping s.t. in boiling water.

celuring (*Jv*) a xylophone-like *gamelan* instrument.

celurit → CLURIT.

celurut (*J*) various species of shrew, k.o. mouse with a strong disagreeable odor, *Crocidura spp*. – *air* Sumatran water shrew, *Chimarrogale sumatrana*. – *rumah* house shrew, *Suncus murinus*.

celus slipping on and off readily (of a ring), easily passed through (as through a gap).

celus-celus passing in and out freely, as s.o. on intimate terms with a household.

mencelus and **tercelus** to slip away, slip into (for example, a muddy pool of water).

celut (*M*) **mencelut** to steal.

pencelut thief.

celutak (*J*) **1** greedy-guts, willing to eat anything. **2** taking s.t. that he shouldn't take.

celutuk *burung* – snipe (a bird species).

céma (*M*) accusation, charge, indictment, impeachment. *tanda* – exhibit, evidence.

mencéma to lay an accusation, accuse, make a charge against.

tercéma accused, charged, blamed.

cémaan 1 accusation, etc. **2** allegation.

cemak-cemék (*J*) to keep handling s.t.

cémang-cémong dirty, filthy.

cemani (*Jv*) totally black, black throughout. *ayam* – (*Jv*) black-boned chicken. *hitam* – jet black, pitch dark.

cemantél (*Jv*) hooked (on to), hanging (from); → CANTÉL I. *Keméjanya* – *di pintu.* His shirt is hanging on the door.

cemar 1 dirty, foul, soiled, unclean. *kain* – and *membawa* – to menstruate. **2** tarnished, besmirched, blemished. *Sudah* – *namanya.* His reputation has been tarnished. **3** obscene, filthy, indecent. *perkataan yang* – obscene words, filthy language. **4** polluted (environment). – *noda* disgrace. **mencemar-nodai** to disgrace, cast aspersions on.

bercemar 1 soiled, filthy. **2** to dirty, tarnish, dishonor (one's own reputation). ~ *kain* menstruating. ~ *duli* a) (originally) to deign to proceed (honorific, of a Ruler's progress). b) willing to go somewhere in response to an invitation. ~ *duli* to go on foot.

mencemari 1 to soil, defile. **2** to stain s.o.'s reputation, disgrace. **3** to pollute.

mencemarkan 1 to make s.t. dirty. ~ *kaki* to visit my humble abode. ~ *tangan* useless, pointless. **2** to disgrace, bring disgrace to. *Pedagang mobil itu telah memfitnah dan ~ nama baik si B.* The car salesman libeled and disgraced the good name of B. **3** to pollute, contaminate. ~ *udara* to pollute the air.

tercemar 1 tarnished, dirtied, stained, soiled. ~ *kain* menstruating. ~ *kening/muka* to be shamed. **2** polluted. *Sungai yang bermuara di Teluk Jakarta telah ~.* The river which runs into Jakarta Bay has been polluted.

cemaran impurity, pollutant, contamination. ~ *mikroba* bacterial contamination.

kecemaran 1 dirt, filth. **2** dirtiness. **3** obscenity. **4** defilement.

pencemar 1 defiler. **2** polluter. *prinsip* ~ *membayar* polluter-pays principle. *bahan* ~ pollutant.

pencemaran 1 pollution, contamination. ~ *lingkungan* environmental pollution. ~ *udara* air pollution. **2** slander. ~ *tertulis* libel, libelous article.

cemara I (*Skr*) **1** tuft/pendant of horse-hair (under the blade of a spear). **2** wig, chignon. **3** yak tail, fly-brush. **4** hair-bun stuffed with fake hair.

cemara II (*Skr*) *pohon* – (*laut*) casuarina tree, k.o. evergreen tree, *Casuarina equisetifolia*. *ayam* – a chicken with needle-leaved feathers. – *gunung* k.o. mountain casuarina, *Casuarina junghuhniana*. – *Pasifik* Pacific yew tree.

cemarut obscenity; → CARUT I. – *perfilman* obscenities in a film.

cemas 1 – *hati* worried, apprehensive, concerned, upset, uneasy, disturbed, anxious, nervous. *dengan* – on tenterhooks, anxiously. *Ia menyatakan rasa -nya yang mendalam atas ...* He expressed his profound concern over ... . **2** afraid, frightened. **3** discouraged, pessimistic.

cemas-cemas nearly (happened), almost, narrowly escaping. ~ *mati* barely escaping death.

secemas as anxious/nervous as.

bercemas anxious, nervous, uncomfortable, on edge, uneasy.

mencemas to become anxious.

mencemasi to worry about, be concerned about.

mencemaskan 1 to alarm, disturb, perturb, upset; alarming, disturbing. 2 to scare, frighten; scary, frightening. 3 to worry about, be concerned about, be what is of concern. *tidak pernah ~ bahaya* never worried about danger. *yang dicemaskan* what one worries about. 4 alarming, critical.

tercemas worried, anxious.

kecemasan 1 anxiety, worry. 2 alarmed, uneasy, in danger. *Ali dalam ~*. Ali is in danger. 3 concern, apprehension. *~ sérius* serious concern. 4 fear. 5 (*Mal Sg*) emergency, crisis.

pencemas 1 pessimist, worrier. 2 worried, brooding. 3 coward.

cemat *sauh* – kedge (anchor). *tali* (**pen**)**cemat** warp.

mencemat to warp, shift, tow (a ship).

cematan various species of evergreen trees, *Dacrydium spp.*

cembala (*D*?) harpsichord

cémbéng → CINGBING.

cemberut (*J*) sour (of look), sullen. *– asam seperti cuka-biang* as sour as a lemon.

cemberutan to have a sour face, pout.

cembul 1 tobacco/gambier, etc. box made of metal (put on a *cerana*, (round or oval-shaped) bowl or tray for keeping articles used in betel chewing, or *puan*, a gold or silver plate (for betel, *usu* used by the queen or bride). *– dengan tutupnya* to go together (or, get along) very well. *– dapat tutupnya* found its mate. 2 a small head on s.t. larger. *– pedang* the head of sword hilt.

cembung (*J/Jv*) 1 chubby (of cheeks), round and plump (face). 2 convex.

mencembung to curve, be convex.

mencembungkan to curve s.t.

kecembungan convexity, curvature.

cembur → CEBUR.

cemburu 1 jealous, envious. *– buta* madly jealous. 2 suspicious, mistrustful.

secemburu as jealous/envious as.

bercemburu → CEMBURU.

mencemburui to be envious of, feel jealous of. *"Héran, saya kan sudah péot dan tak cantik, apa yang mau dicemburui," kata istrinya.* "I'm surprised; I'm old and not pretty, what are you jealous of?" said his wife.

mencemburukan 1 to make s.o. jealous/envious. 2 to be jealous/envious of.

cemburuan 1 envious (jealous of) e.o. 2 jealous (by nature). 3 envy, jealousy. **bercemburuan** jealous of e.o.

kecemburuan 1 jealousy, envy. 2 resentment, grudge, suspicion.

pencemburu 1 suspicious person. 2 jealous person.

cemceman (*coq*) a female secretary who is also the boss's mistress; → GULA-GULA.

cémé → CÉMÉH I, CÉMÉK I.

cemééh → CEMOOH.

céméh I (C?) 1 optic atrophy, extremely near-sighted, nearly blind but with eyes open. 2 blind in one eye.

céméh II (*J*) Chinese game played with small cards.

céméh III → CÉMÉK II.

cémék I (C?) 1 blind in one eye. *si –* the one-eyed man. 2 blind with eyes wide open. *di negara orang-orang buta, si – menjadi raja* in the kingdom of the blind the one-eyed man is king.

cémék II → RÉMÉH *cémék*.

cemeki (*Hind*) spangles, sequins, beads sewn to the edges of a veil/shawl; → JEMEKI.

cémén 1 cartoonishly unsophisticated; nerd, loser. *tukang –* circus monkey. 2 cheap.

ceme(ng)kian *pohon* – purging croton, *Croton tiglium.*

cémér blind but eyes are open.

cemerlang 1 sparkling, shining, brilliant, bright, gleaming, dazzling. *Pépsodént memberi Indonésia senyum yang semakin –*. Pepsodent gives Indonesia a more sparkling smile. *Ia itu orang –*. He's a bright person. 2 to glitter, sparkle, shine (brightly). 3 outstanding, excellent.

secemerlang as brilliant as.

mencemerlangi to add luster to.

mencemerlangkan 1 dazzling. 2 to brighten up s.t.

tercemerlang the most sparkling/brillant.

kecemerlangan 1 radiance, glow, luster, glitter. 2 glory, splendor, brilliance.

pencemerlang s.t. which brightens, brightening (agent).

cemerut → CEMBERUT.

cemeti (*Tam*) 1 whip (for a horse, etc.). *– déwa/malaikat* and *sinar – malaékat* thunder and lightning ("caused by the cracking of the whips of the angels who during a thunderstorm fire and strike the demons"). 2 stimulant, encouragement.

mencemeti to whip.

cemetuk present, offering (given according to customs and rituals).

bercemetuk to present s.t. with ceremony.

cémi marijuana cigarette, joint.

cemil (*Jv*) *makanan* – tidbit.

secemil a little bit.

nyemil (*coq*) to take a little bite. *Seperti tak mau berhenti ~*. You can't take just one bite.

nyemilan (*coq*) take small bites.

cemilan snacks.

cemlorot (*Jv*) shining.

cemol (*Jv*) **mencemol-cemol** to grab with the whole hand.

cemomot unclean, dirty (of face).

cémong (*J*) dirty (of face), soiled.

cemooh (*M*) mockery, ridicule, taunt, insult, gibe, teasing, making fun of.

bercemooh to jeer.

mencemooh to mock, scoff, taunt, insult, make fun of, jeer at.

mencemoohkan to make fun of, poke fun at, scorn, ridicule, tease, sneer at, put down.

cemoohan insult, teasing, sneering.

pencemooh taunter, jeerer, insulter.

pencemoohan insult, taunt.

cempa (*Jv*) *padi* – paddy plant that produces short-grained rice.

cempaka (*Skr*) 1 various species of gardenia, magnolia, and frangipani. *– Ambon* banana shrub, *Michelia figo*. *– biru* frangipani, *Plumiera acutifolia*. *– gading/putih* champaca, white jade orchid tree, *Michelia alba*. *– gunung* k.o. frangipani, *Talauma rumphii*. *– hutan* k.o. gardenia, *Gardenia griffithii*. *– kemboja/ kubur/mulia* west Indian jasmine, *Plumiera acuminata*. *– kuning* alamander, ironwood tree, *Michelia champaca*. 2 a gemstone with the color of the *Michelia champaca*, like topaz.

cempala I quick, lively, mobile (of doing s.t. indecent or thoughtless). *– mulut* thoughtless, rash (likes to hurt people's feelings, etc.). *– tangan* use (physical) violence/one's fists, quick with the hands (likes to beat/slap, etc.).

cempala II (*Jv*) one of a pair of wooden mallets used by the *dalang* for producing sound effects and musical signals, by hitting a wooden puppet chest, during shadow-play performances.

cempana I → JEMPANA.

cempana II k.o. plant which causes itching, *Teysmanniodendron pteropodium.*

cempé and **cemplé** (*Jv*) lamb; kid (young of the *wedus*).

cempedak *pohon* – k.o. breadfruit tree, *Artocarpus spp.*, the fruit resembles a jackfruit; → NANGKA. *seorang makan –, semua kena getahnya* one rotten apple will decay a bushel. *daripada – baik nangka* better s.t. than nothing at all.

cempék (*M*) chipped/torn/broken at the edge.

cempelik pitch and toss (k.o. game in which two coins are used), game of heads-or-tails.

cempelung I → CEMPLUNG.

cempelung II k.o. row boat.

cémpéng → CÉMPÉK.

cempera bercempera scattered, strewn about.

cemperai *pohon* – k.o. shrub (with edible leaves), *Champereia griffithii* (and other species).

cemperling *burung* – glossy tree-starling, *Aplonis strigatus*. *mata –* red eyes.

cempiang (C) robber, roughneck, hoodlum.

cémpin (*E*) champagne; → SAMPANYE.

cemping a piece of cloth, rag, small fragments/remnants; → CAMPING I, COMPANG-CAMPING.

cemplak mencemplak [and **nyemplak** (*coq*)] to kick start, kick or hit s.t. (a horse/starter of a vehicle) to make it start or go.

cémplak (*J/Jv*) **nyémplak 1** to hug/clasp s.t. (a Dutch wife, i.e., a bolster or long round pillow) between the two thighs during sleep. **2** to jump on and sit on the carrier of a bike, attached on top of the rear wheel fender.

cemplang (*J/Jv*) **1** tasteless, without taste, bland. **2** in bad/poor taste, dissonant. **3** insipid (remarks/anecdotes), boring.

cempléngan (*J*) doubtful, dubious; confused, upset, bewildered.

cemplongan (*Jv*) the deep ditches or holes in which sugarcane is planted, minimum tillage.

cemplung (*Jv onom*) **1** plop! the sound of s.t. thrown or falling into water; → PLUNG, PLUNG-LAP. **2** pit toilet.

mencemplung [and **nyemplung** (*coq*)] **1** to plunge, plop. **2** to jump into the water.

mencemplungi 1 to plunge s.t. (into water or other liquid). *Anak itu ~ batu ke dalam kolam.* The boy threw stones in the pond. **2** to immerse s.t. in a liquid. *Téhnya dicelupi gula.* He put sugar in his tea. **3** (*M*) to interfere/intervene in the private matters of others.

mencemplungkan to plunge s.t. (into). *~ diri* to throw/plunge o.s. into (the field of politics/work/study, etc.). *Dia perlu waktu bertahun-tahun untuk secara langsung ~ diri dalam kehidupan orang Jawa.* He needed years and years to directly throw himself into the life of the Javanese.

tercemplung [and **kecemplung** (*coq*)] **1** fallen in s.t. accidentally. **2** implicated.

cemplungan cesspool.

cempo (*Jv*) → CEMPA.

cempoa (*C*) abacus (for calculating purposes); → SWIPOA.

cempolong plastic piping.

cempor (*Jv*) *lampu –* oil lamp (without a lamp chimney).

cempréng (*J/Jv*) shrill, strident (noise, voice).

cempuk (*Jv*) → CIPLUK.

cempuling → TEMPULING.

cempung → CEMPLUNG.

cempurit (*Jv*) the main stick made of buffalo horn for manipulating a leather puppet plus the puppet's arm to which it is attached in the shadow play. *memegang –* a) to pull the strings. b) to have supreme power.

cemuas streaked all over, daubed (with soot/dirt/chalk), dirty (as a child's face or hands) from food; → JEMUAS.

cemuh → CEMOOH.

cemuk I mencemuk to hit, strike (with a stick, etc.); → CAMUK I.

cemuk II pod (of beans, etc.).

cemuk III shaft. *– cerobong* chimney shaft. *– tambang* mine shaft.

céna (*Skr*) **1** mark, scar (on fighting cock, evidence of his prowess), back to normal health (of a fighting cock after a fight). **2** proof, evidence.

kecénaan marked, scarred.

cenak *tulang –* collarbone, clavicle.

cenaku → CINDAKU.

cenal-cenil (*Jv*) **1** elastically. **2** rhythmically. *seorang wanita dengan lénggang-lénggoknya yang –* a woman with her rhythmically swaying hips.

cenangau a smelly flying rice-bug very destructive to paddy, gundhi bug, *Leptocorisa varicornis*; → WALANG *sangit*.

cenangga (*Skr*) congenital deformation. *– tangan* a deformed hand.

cenangkas (*cla*) a heavy cutlass.

cenayang a medium in spiritualism, psychic.

cencadu → SENTADU I.

cencala I *burung –* fantail flycatcher, pied fantail, *Rhipidura javanica*.

cencala II (*Skr*) prone to say improper things, say whatever comes to mind without thinking of the consequences; → LANCANG *mulut*.

cencaluk relish made of small prawns, flavor (of prawn pickle).

cencang I slash, cut (with a cutlass/cleaver). *sekali –* in one stroke. *– air* unbreakable (of family ties, etc.). *– dua segeragai* to kill two birds with one stone.

   bercencang slashed, cut, chopped. *Ibu membeli daging ~.* Mother bought chopped meat. *~ air* (connected) unbreakably.

   mencencang 1 to chop/cut up fine/in bits, mince. *~ berlandasan, melompat bersitumpu* to always act in a proper way. **2** (*ob*) to kill brutally (by slashing with a chopper/cleaver, etc.).

   tercencang chopped, slashed.

   cencangan chopped up (meat).

cencang II (*M*) *– latih* rice paddy cleared by o.s. (to become one's property). *mencencang(-melatih)* to break up ground to make it into a rice paddy.

cencaru *ikan –* horse-mackerel, hardtail scad, *Megalaspis cordyla*. *– makan pedang* slow but profitable work.

cencawan kneecap, patella.

cencawi *burung –* king-crow, *Dicrurus longicaudatus intermedius*.

céncéng mencéncéng to run away with one's tail between one's legs (like a dog).

céncong → CINCONG.

cencurut → CELURUT.

cendaku → CINDAKU.

cendala (*Skr*) **1** pariah (in caste system). **2** mean, dishonorable, low (of conduct).

   kecendalaan dishonor, lowness.

cendana I (*Skr*) *pohon –* sandalwood tree used for incense and perfumes, *Santalum album*. *Pulau –* Sumba. *sudah gaharu – pula, sudah tahu bertanya pula* to ask about s.t. that one already knows the answer to. *– janggi/Zanggi* red sandalwood, *Pterocarpus santalinus*, used by Hindus for caste-marks. *– kering* a) dried sandalwood. b) a has-been.

Cendana II reference to former President Soeharto's residence on Jalan Cendana in Jakarta and by extension a reference to him and his family.

céndang (*M*) squinting, cross-eyed, cockeyed; → JULING.

cendawan 1 fungi. **2** mushroom, toadstool. **3** mildew, mold (on cheese, damp clothes). *mabuk –* lovesick (of a woman). *tumbuh sebagai – habis/di musim hujan* and *tumbuh mencendawan* to spring up like mushrooms. *sebagai – dibasuh/disesah* very pale. *– batang* fungus growing on dead logs, *Lentinus exilis*. *– bintang/kelemayar* incandescent fungus. *– (muka) (ha)rimau* k.o. fungus, *Rafflesia hasseltii*. *– karat* rust (a disease of plants). *– mérah* k.o. fungus, *Polystictus sanguineus*. *– telinga* tree ear, black fungus, *Auricularia polytricha*.

   bercendawan moldy.

   mencendawan to spring up like mushrooms.

cendayam (*cla*) fair, beautiful, pretty.

cendekia (*Skr*) **1** intelligent, clever, smart, learned, educated, skillful. **2** cunning, shrewd. **3** intellectual. *kaum cerdik –* intellectuals, intelligentsia.

   kecendekiaan 1 learnedness. *pusat ~* center of excellence. **2** shrewdness.

   pencendekiaan intellectualization. *~ Bahasa Indonésia* the intellectualization of the Indonesian language.

cendekiawan (*Skr neo*) **1** male intellectual. **2** the educated class. *kaum –* the intellectuals.

   kecendekiawanan intellectualism.

cendekiawati (*Skr neo*) female intellectual.

cendéla → JENDÉLA.

cendera I (*Skr*) → CANDRA.

cendera II (*Skr*) *– mata* a) souvenir, memento, keepsake. b) beloved, darling.

cendera III (*Skr cla*) deep (of sleep), fast (asleep).

cenderadimuka → CANDRADIMUKA.

cenderai *pohon –* and *– hutan* small trees (with leaves used medicinally), tili, *Grewia paniculata*.

cenderasa (*Skr cla*) magic sword, the sword of Rawana.

cenderawasih (*Skr*) **1** *burung –* bird of paradise, *Paradisa apoda/tomentosa*. **2** (*P*) name of the Army division stationed in Irian Jaya.

cenderung 1 slanting, tilted, sloping, leaning; → CONDONG. *Tiang itu sedikit karena ditiup angin kencang.* The pole was tilted a little bit because it was blown by a high wind. **2** interested (in), inclined to(ward), like, prefer. *Adik saya lebih – kepada masak-memasak.* My younger sister is more interested in cooking. **3** tend to, be prone to, apt to, given to. *Dia – bohong.* He's prone to lying. *– untuk celaka* accident prone. **4** to side (with), be biased (toward). *– hati kepada* to (be on the same) side, take part. *Selaku wasit, jangan sekali-kali – kepada salah satu pihak.* As an arbiter, don't ever side with one of the parties. *– ketat* tight bias (in economic policy).

   mencenderungi to have an inclination toward, tend toward.

   mencenderungkan to tend/incline/lean toward. *~ diri* to bend over, duck (to avoid s.t.).

kecenderungan 1 interest, inclination, preference. *Kaidah mengajar ini harus disesuaikan dengan ~ para pelajar.* This teaching method has to be adapted to the students' interest. 2 tendency, prone(ness). *~ penyesuaian* tendency of adaptation. 3 trend. *~ besar* megatrend. *~ ke arah keduniawian* secular trend. *~ antiékspor* antiexport bias. 4 bias. *~ global* global trend. **berkecenderungan** to have the tendency to.

céndok → SÉNDOK.

céndol a layered cooling drink of dark brown palm sugar syrup topped with snowy coconut milk and ice; it also contains gelatinous green shreds made from mung bean flour.

cendra → CENDERA I, II.

cendrong (M) → CENDERUNG.

cenduai (cla) magic spell to charm and entice women. *minyak –* love-philter.

bercenduai to flirt (with a girl), chat up.

cendur → CINDURMATA.

cenéla (Port) slipper.

céng I (C J) thousand.
   secéng one thousand (rupiahs); → CECÉNG. *Ayo dong sini, nanti saya pijitin. Murah kok, ~.* Come over here, I'll give you a massage. It's cheap. One thousand (rups). *~ ni yé* (rude epithet for policeman) one thousand rupiahs, right?

céng II (C) molasses, syrup.

cengak – *cenguk sendirian* to sit somewhere doing nothing; → CENGOK.

cengal *pohon* – various species of large trees with hard commercial timber, *Balanocarpus spp., Hopea sangal.*

cengam mencengam to seize in the mouth (as a dog/crocodile, etc.), snap, clutch, grasp (in the same way).

cengang amazed, astonished. *– bengang* totally astonished.
   bercengang(an) and bersicengang amazed, dumbfounded, flabbergasted, bewildered, stunned, astonished.
   mencengangi to be amazed at.
   mencengangkan and mempercengang(kan) 1 to amaze, astonish, confound, perplex, nonplus, astound, perplex. *Tapi jawaban yang diterimanya tambah mencengangkan.* But the answer he got astonished him even more. 2 amazing, astonishing.
   tercengang(-cengang) astonished, amazed, flabbergasted. mentercengangkan to astonish, amaze. ketercengangan astonishment, amazement.
   cengangan amazement, astonishment.
   kecengangan 1 amazement. 2 out of amazement.

cengap I mencengap to snap at and catch with the mouth.

cengap II mencengap to pant, gasp (for breath).

cengar-cengir 1 (S) to boast, brag. 2 (Jv) to cry (of babies). 3 (J) to smile foolishly/sheepishly or from shyness; to grin, grimace.

céngbéng (C) → CINGBING.

céngcong → CINCONG.

céngéh and céngék (J) a very small, spicy hot red pepper variety, *Capsicum annuum;* → CABAI *rawit.*

céngéng 1 whine, be a crybaby, snivel. *Jangan –!* Don't be a crybaby! 2 tearful, sentimental, overly emotional.
   kecéngéngan 1 whining, sniveling. 2 sentimentality. 3 to be overemotional.

cengéngés (Jv) mencengéngés to sneer/jeer at.
   cengéngésan to keep jeering/sneering.
   kecengéngésan grin, sneer.

cengér (Jv) the cry of a newborn baby; → CENGAR-CENGIR.

céngét shrill (of sounds).

céngggék → TÉNGGÉK.

cénggér → JÉNGGÉR.

cenggéréng (Jv) grated and fried condiments used in cooking.

cenggérét (J) → TONGGÉRÉT.

cénggo (C J) one thousand five hundred (rupiahs).

cengi cruel.

cengir sheepish smile, grin.
   nyengir (J) to grimace, have a sheepish smile (or, a foolish grin) on one's face.
   menyengirkan to put on (a sheepish smile).

cengis I smelling nasty, nauseating, loathsome, stinking (of a strong scent/rotten fruit or food), repugnant.

cengis II embarrassed. *– tidak tahu apa yang hendak dikatakannya* embarrassed and not knowing what he wanted to say.
   mencengis-cengis to act shy, unsure of how to behave.

cengkah (Jv) to oppose, resist, set o.s. against.

cengkal I (Jv) linear measure of about 12 feet. *mantri –* surveyor.

cengkal II a protective covering of curved wood or pressed coconut fibers for preventing a newly circumcised penis from rubbing against the sarong.

cengkaling white camphor → KOLANG *kaling.*

cengkam I 1 grip, squeeze, grasp (with the fingernails or claws). 2 control, power, authority, domination. *kuku –* ingrown toenail. *– kera* cannot escape.
   mencengkam 1 to grasp, grip, claw. 2 to dominate, control. 3 to squeeze, seize firmly. 4 gripping, engrossing. 5 to be ingrown (of a toenail).
   mencengkamkan 1 to claw at, press one's nail into one's prey. 2 gripping.
   tercengkam gripped, grasped, seized.
   cengkaman grip, grasp, hold, squeeze.
   pencengkam clamp.

cengkam II and cengkaman – *harimau* k.o. small tree, *Trevesia cheirantha.*

cengkang → CEKAK II.

cengkar (Jv) arid, infertile (land).

cengkaruk a cake of fried glutinous rice and coconut.

cengkat (J) to stand on one's heels.

cengkau I (C) 1 agent, dealer, broker (in valuables/marriage). 2 pimp.

cengkau II → CENGKAM I.

cengké → CENGKÉH.

cengkedi ghostly or malignant powers and influences.

cengkéh I 1 *buah –* clove (the spice). 2 *pohon –* the clove-tree, *Eugenia aromatica.* 3 *bunga –* a clovehead pattern (in silverware), from petals with a tiny central boss.
   bercengkéh spiced (up) with cloves.
   percengkéhan cloves (mod).

cengkéh II (C) 1 a card game. 2 (Jv) clubs (in card deck).

céngkék tight at the waist, narrow-waisted (of a person, etc.), thinner at the center.

cengkeling → SENGKELING.

cengkelong (Jv) markdown.
   mencengkelong to withdraw money in installments.

cengkeram I grip, hold, seize; → CENGKAM I. *daya – ban* tread gripping power (of tires).
   mencengkeram 1 to grip, seize, grasp. *Ban radial Goodyear itu ~ dengan pasti pada waktu pengeréman mendadak.* The Goodyear radial tires have a secure grip at moments of slamming on the brakes. *Tangan saya ~ keras lengan kursi yang saya duduki.* I held tight the arm of the chair I sat in. 2 to keep tight control over s.t., dominate.
   mencengkeramkan to seize/hold firmly (with the fingernails or claws), press down with the nails or claws.
   tercengkeram gripped, grasped.
   cengkeraman grip. grasp, hold. *~ Uni Soviét di Afghanistan makin kokoh.* The Soviet Union's grip on Afghanistan is becoming increasingly firm.
   pencengkeraman seizing.

cengkeram II 1 part payment in advance, down payment. 2 guarantee, mortgage, pledge, security. *memulangkan ~* to cancel a contract.
   mencengkeramkan to deposit, entrust.
   cengkeraman grip. *~ maut* grip of death.

cengkerama (Skr) 1 (cla) journey, travel, tour (just to enjoy o.s.). 2 sociable chat/talk just to amuse o.s.
   bercengkerama 1 (cla) to go sight-seeing for fun. 2 to have a chat (as an amusement/way of entertaining o.s.), amuse o.s.

cengkerawak (S?) *burung –* yellow-crowned bulbul, *Pycnonotus zeylanicus;* → CUCAK *rawa.*

cengkerik → JANGKRIK I.

cengkering I a tree species, *Erythrina ovalifolia.*

cengkering II (Mal) chicken pox.

cengkerma → CENGKERAMA.

cengkerung (ob) hollow, sunken (of one's eyes, etc.).

céngki (C J) lucky (in gambling).

cengkih → CENGKÉH.

cengking (onom) yelping, yapping, squealing (of a dog).
bercengking to yelp, yap, squeal.

cengkir (Jv) very young coconut.

cengklak (J) mencéngklak to carry a child on the hip.

céngkok I twisted; bent at the end, like a hockey stick. – belédok zigzag, twisting and turning.

céngkok II leaf-monkey, Semnopithecus pruinosus.

céngkok III style of singing. Dengan – yang khas, mirip Dolly Parton, biduanita asal Ujungpandang membawa penonton marak. In her trademark affected style of singing, resembling that of Dolly Parton, the Ujungpandang-born singer, regaled the spectators.

céngkol bent, twisted (of a leg, from birth or accident).

cengkolong (ob) → CENGKELONG.

céngkong deformed (of an arm).

cengkudu → MENGKUDU.

cengkung I sunken, hollow (of one's cheeks/eyes). – mengkung very hollow (of cheeks, etc.).

cengkung II (onom) a loud noise (such as, that of a yelping dog). – cengking all k.o. noises, such as the yelping of dogs, people bickering, etc.

cengkung III bercengkung to squat, bend over; → CANGKUNG.
mencengkungkan to bend (one's body) over.

cengkurai kain sutra – (cla) a mottled silk fabric.

cengkuyung → TENGKUYUNG.

céngli (C) reasonable, stands to reason, plausible, normal, fair.

cengo(k) confused, look blank, dumbfounded, at a loss for what to do.

cengung tercengung gazed in astonishment, astonished, dumbfounded.

cengut (M) tukang – loafer.
mencengut and tercengut amazed, gazing in open-mouthed astonishment, disappointed.

cenil – tepung k.o. dessert made from cassava.

cénok various species of birds, malkoha, Rhinortha spp., Rhopodytes spp.

centadu → SENTADU.

centang (M) – peren(t)ang in disorder/a mess, totally chaotic. Maafkan saya karena ruangan saya yang – perenang ini. Sorry, my office is a mess. kecéntang-peren(t)angan chaos.

céntang I (Jv) check mark, (correction) mark (like an inverted letter v).
mencéntang to tick/check off (items on a list), place a checkmark next to.

céntang II (J) mencéntang to hit, strike.

cénté k.o. plant, Lantana camara. – manis k.o. coffee cake.

centéng and cénténg (C J) 1 guard, watchman (of a building/factory, etc.). 2 supervisor, overseer in a plantation (which belongs to private ownership). 3 opium sales inspector. 4 bouncer, hired thug.

centerik → CANTRIK.

centét I (J/Jv) small, stunted, shrunk.
kecentét stunted (in growth).

centét II economical, saves money.

centil I → SENTIL I.

centil II coquettish, flirtatious.
kecentilan coquetry, coquettish manners.

céntong (J/Jv) spoon. – nasi rice spoon, ladle (with a handle).
secéntong a spoonful (of).
mencéntong(kan) to scoop out, ladle out, serve s.t. with a ladle.

Central Committee Partai Komunis Indonesia /Séntral Komité …/ [CC-PKI] Central Committee of the Communist Party of Indonesia.

centung tuft, crest (of a bird); lock of hair (that is tied up).

cenung tercenung 1 contemplative, pensive, musing. 2 flabbergasted, dumbfounded, looking without seeing. Mendengar keterangan dari Pak Samekto tadi, anak-anak jadi ~. After having heard Mr. Samekto's explanation just now, the children became flabbergasted.

cenut-cenut → SENUT-SENUT.

céos mencéos to hiss (sound produced when striking a match). Gérétan –. The match hissed.

cep (Jv) all of a sudden quiet. – klakep suddenly (they became) quiet. mencep-klakepkan to silence s.o. menanti dicep-klakepkan waiting to be silenced.

cepak I (onom) smacking sound (of s.o. eating); sound of lapping (a liquid); → CAPAK III.
mencepak-cepak and mencepak-cepok to smack one's lips (over food), make a smacking sound (while eating or drinking).
kecepak bunyi – ombak the sound of waves beating against the shore.
cepakan smacking sound.

cepak II (J) crew cut (haircut). cukuran – crew-cut haircut.

cepak III a spade (for digging)

cépak (J) 1 to walk with legs wide apart. 2 to limp.

cepaka (ob) → CEMPAKA.

cepal – cepol to hit e.o.; → CEPOL.

cepat 1 quick, fast, speedy, rapid, swift; express; → DERAS I, KENCANG I, LAJU I. bis – express bus. keréta api – fast train. lari – to run fast. surat – express letter. tulisan – shorthand, stenography. 2 in a hurry, hurry up. 3 soon. lebih – lebih baik the sooner the better. 4 speed, pace, velocity. Sekarang –nya 55 mil sejam. Nowadays the speed is 55 miles an hour. 5 early. 6 first, foremost. yang – dapat first come first served. siapa – dia dapat the early bird catches the worm. terlalu – bisa tersesat haste makes waste. – akhir final/ultimate velocity. – atau lambat sooner or later. – awal initial velocity. – baik quickly on good terms again. – darah short/quick-tempered, irascible. – habis to sell like hotcakes, goes fast (like money). – hati easily insulted/offended/hurt, thin-skinned. – jalan speed (of a car). – kaki fleet, speedy, swift of foot. – kaki (ringan tangan) dexterous, deft, adroit. – kiri left-handed. – lambat(nya) sooner or later, – lidah/mulut/muncung rash, hasty, garrulous, talks too much. – membusuk highly perishable. – panén quick-yielding. – paruh rash, hasty, etc. – pikir mentally agile. – réaksi velocity of reaction. – rusak perishable. (makanan) – saji fast (food). – tangan light-fingered, thievish. – tepat a) fast and accurate. b) quiz contest.

cepat-cepat in a hurry, do s.t. in a rush. ~ pulang to rush home.

secepat as fast as. ~ kilat quick as lightning, with lightning speed.

secepatnya very soon, in the near future.

secepat-cepatnya as fast as possible.

bercepat-cepat, bersecepat and bersicepat 1 to race e.o. 2 to hurry up, speed up. 3 in haste, hastily.

mencepat 1 to accelerate, speed up, become faster. 2 to speed s.t. up.

mencepatkan and mempercepat(kan) 1 to quicken, speed up, hasten, accelerate, race (an engine). mempercepat pembangunan to speed up developments. 2 to set s.t. for an earlier time/hour, advance, move forward, do s.t. earlier. Pertunjukan akan dipercepat sejam dari yang sudah ditentukan. The show will be moved forward one hour from the appointed time.

tercepat the fastest/swiftest.

cepatan (J) 1 faster, quicker. 2 hurry up. – dong! hurry up!

kecepatan 1 (rate of) speed, velocity, swiftness. Ia mengendarai mobilnya dengan ~ 55 mil sejam. He drove his car at a speed of 55 miles per hour. Dengan ~ tinggi, truk itu berlari membawa muatan cabé. The truck left at a high speed carrying a load of red peppers. batas ~ speed limit. pada ~ at a rate/speed/velocity of. ~ awal initial velocity. ~ imbas downwash. ~ jelajah cruising speed. ~ nisbi relative velocity. ~ suara speed of sound. ~ tangan (in conjuring tricks) sleight of hand. ~ terbesar/tertinggi top speed. ~ tinggi high velocity. 2 (J) to be fast, gain (time). Jam tangan saya ~ lima menit. My wristwatch is five minutes fast. 3 too fast, too soon, early. berkecepatan to have a speed of. Kedua kendaraan itu ~ cukup tinggi. The two cars moved at a rapid rate.

pemercepat 1 precipitating, accelerating. faktor ~ precipitating factor. 2 accelerator. ~ bak gear box.

pencepat accelerator, s.o. who accelerates/increases the speed of s.t.

pencepatan acceleration, speeding s.t. up. alat ~ accelerator.

percepatan 1 acceleration. 2 velocity.

cepatu → SEPATU.

cepebri → CÉK perjalanan BRI.

cepék (C J) one hundred (rupiahs/cubic centimeters, etc.).
cepékan one hundred (rupiah) bill.
cepékcéng (C J) one hundred thousand (rupiahs).
cepéng (J) a halfcent.
cepéngan low-class. *tempat pelacuran kelas ~* low-class brothel.
cépér 1 shallow (of dish for serving or holding food). *Piring – atau piring dalam?* Is it a shallow or a deep dish? *dapat piring –* to be unlucky, unfortunate. 2 k.o. metal serving tray.
cepet → CEPAT. cepetan faster.
cepiau (*Port*) hat, soldier's cap.
bercepiau to wear such a cap.
cepis chip.
cepit device to hold/press things together; → JEPIT, SEPIT I.
mencepit to pinch (as a crab, etc.), squeeze between two things.
tercepit [and kecepit (*coq*)] squeezed/trapped between two things.
cepitan a clip. *~ kertas* paper clip.
ceplas-ceplos 1 (*Jv*) speaking one's mind, speaking out frankly. *bicara –* to tell s.t. in no uncertain terms. 2 (J) to walk to and fro; → CEPLOS.
ceplek (*onom*) clicking sound.
céples (*Jv*) to look exactly like, resemble.
ceplok I (J) stamp, seal, mark.
nyeplokin to stamp, seal, mark.
ceplok II (J) 1 round. *telor –* fried egg sunny side up. 2 (colored) rosette-shaped ornaments (on a pillow/cushion). *– piring* a round white plate-shaped flower, cape jasmine, *Gardenia augusta.*
ceplok-ceplok covered with round figures.
mencepok [and nyeplok (*coq*)] to fry an egg.
ceplos (J/Jv) 1 (*onom*) sound produced by s.t. bursting or exploding, such as a balloon, etc. 2 to state precisely. *ceplas.–* to say outright/in plain terms, without mincing words. *bicara ceplas.–* to blurt out, tell s.t. in plain terms or in down-to-earth language. *Kalau bicara, suaranya selalu lantang, dan dalam forum-forum seperti panél diskusi atau séminar ia selalu bicara ceplas.–.* When he speaks, he always has a piercing voice, and in forums, like panel discussions or seminars, he always speaks in down-to-earth language.
menceploskan 1 to say s.t. in down-to-earth language, blurt s.t. out. 2 to make a direct hit on s.t., make s.t. burst. *~ bola ke dalam gawang* to smash the ball into the goal.
ceplosan s.t. blurted out, uninhibited comment.
keceplosan *~ omong* to say whatever comes to mind, blurt s.t out. *Saya kira meréka ~.* I guess they just said whatever came to mind.
céplukan (*Jv*) /céplu'an/ k.o. wild shrub; also, its edible grape-like fruit, *Physalis angulata/minima.*
ceplus menceplus to press, put (in).
cepo I fragile, brittle, breakable.
cepo II (C J) broke, without any money.
cepok → CEPAK I.
cepokak devil's fig, turkey berry, *Solanum torvum.*
cepol I (*Jv*) 1 to come loose, break/tear off, detached, drawn/pulled out, extracted. 2 jerked/torn open (of corn cob). 3 damaged, spoiled.
mencepol [and nyepol (*coq*)] to pull/tear loose, tear s.t. out.
cepol II (J) mencepol [and nyepol (*coq*)] to beat, strike, knock, hit. *Cepol kepalanya!* Hit him on the head!
nyepolin (J) to thrash/trounce s.o.
cepolan a blow, punch.
cepol III bun (of the hair).
cepon (*Jv*) k.o. bamboo basket.
ceprat-ceprot (*onom*) pounding sounds.
ceprét (*onom*) sound of clicking (of a camera shutter, etc.); → JEPRÉT.
menceprét 1 to snap (a photograph). 2 to squash s.t.
céprét → PERCIK. mencepréti to squeeze (s.t.) onto s.t.
mencéprétkan to water, sprinkle, spray, spatter.
kecéprétan 1 sprinkled, spattered. 2 to get one's share of the pie (from what s.o. else acquired by luck).
cepu → CEPUK I.

cepua → SWIPOA.
cepu-cepu k.o. small white bird.
cepuh mencepuh(kan) to dip s.t. in a liquid; → CELUP.
cepuk I (J) 1 round wooden/silver china box with a convex lid for betel perquisites; k.o. box (made of *mengkuang* leaves) for food and clothes, etc. *– bunga* anther. 2 (*naut*) pivot bearing. *bagai – dengan tudungnya* to match perfectly, a perfect match. 3 tube (for toothpaste, etc.).
cepuk II (*onom*) sound of s.t. hitting water (such as, when washing clothes/a stone is falling in water, etc.). *– cepak* noisy.
mencepuk(-cepuk) to splash, hit the surface of the water.
cepuri (*Jv*) masonry wall around a house or garden.
cer (in acronyms) → CERITA.
cerabah 1 grubby, untidy, slovenly, dirty. 2 not neatly done, careless. 3 rude, ill-mannered.
cerabih (*ob*) bercerabih and mencerabih to chatter, babble, prattle, chitchat, talk rubbish.
cerabut tercerabut torn up by its roots, uprooted. ketercabutan 1 uprooting. 2 rootlessness. *Yang sudah dan sedang terjadi adalah ~ akar budaya.* What has been and is happening is the uprooting of their cultural roots.
ceracah (*onom*) sound of running water or of rain drumming on s.t.
menceracah to babble (of a brook), drum (of rain)
ceracak → CERANCANG.
ceracam haphazard, at random.
menceracam to do things haphazardly.
ceracap 1 bamboo castanets. 2 cymbals.
ceracapan (J) eaves.
ceracas-cerocos to chatter away.
ceracau menceracau 1 to be delirious. 2 to chatter away.
penceracau chatterbox.
cerah I 1 clear (of weather/daylight/complexion/light). *saat-saat –* happy moments. *hari –* a) it's nice weather. b) (in) broad daylight. 2 radiant (face), brilliant, glorious, bright (prospects, future), sharp (of a photograph). *mempunyai masa depan –* to have a bright future. 3 auspicious. 4 brightness. *– anggun* facelift. mencerah-anggun to give s.t. a face-lift. *Mesjid Attaubah di séntral Anyer yang semula kusam dicerah-anggunkan dengan cat dan pagar baru.* The Attaubah Mosque in Central Anyer (Banten) which at first was lackluster has been given a facelift with paint and a new fence. *– budi* enlightened. *– ceria* bright and shiny, brightened/cleared up. *– cuaca* clear weather. *– ria* luminous.
secerah as bright/clear as.
mencerah 1 to become clear, clear/brighten up. 2 to become/get better, improve (of the situation/perspectives, etc.).
mencerahi to illuminate.
mencerahkan 1 to brighten, light up, lighten, illuminate. *Cahaya lilin itu ~ ruang yang kecil itu.* The light of the candle lit up the small room. 2 to make s.t. radiant/beam/shine, make s.o. happy/cheerful, cheer s.o. up.
kecerahan 1 clear-sightedness. 2 brightness, splendor, glory, brilliancy, glamour, bright spot. 3 sharpness, clarity.
pencerah brightener, brightening, s.t. that makes s.t. shine/gleam.
pencerahan brightening, lighting, illumination. *Abad/Masa/Zaman ~* the Enlightenment.
cerah II (S) crack, fissure, crevice, slit.
cerai 1 separated (from), loose. *padi –* quick-ripening small-grained paddy. *tanda –* hyphen; → TANDA *sémpang.* 2 (of persons) divorced. *surat –* divorce certificate. *minta –* to file for divorce. *Dia tidak boléh berbuat apa-apa melainkan meminta – dari suaminya.* She was not allowed to do anything but file for divorce from her husband. *– anjing* (*coq*) a divorce without any (Muslim religious) procedure (because of the expense). *– berai* dispersed, scattered (of crowds/armies), in disorder. bercerai berai to be scattered, become dispersed. menceraiberaikan to make fall apart/to pieces, scatter, disperse, leave behind. tercerai berai separated, dispersed, scattered. *Massa ~ oléh témbakan.* The masses scattered because of the shooting. perceraiberaian dissension, discord, disunity, dispersal. *– dahar*

guling judicial/legal separation, separation from bed and board. – *gantung* divorce without legal sanction. – *gugat* divorce on grounds of a legal action. – *hidup* separation of husband and wife in which both are still alive, separated. – *mati* separation of husband and wife due to the death of one of them, widowed. – *méja dan ranjang/tempat tidur* separation from bed and board. – *susu* weaning. – *tembilang* separation of husband and wife due to the death of one of them.

bercerai 1 to be divorced, separated (of a married couple). *Karena tidak ada kecocokan, akhirnya suami-istri itu ~ juga.* Because they couldn't get along, finally the couple divorced. ~ *kain* irreparable break. **2** to part, separate, split off. *Di sini jalan kami ~.* Our ways part here. *Lengannya ~ dari tubuhnya ditetak oléh musuhnya.* His arm parted from his body when it was slashed by the enemy. ~ *kasih* to stop loving e.o.

bercerai-cerai and **berceraian** broken up into fragments/pieces.

mencerai 1 to part. ~ *rambutnya* to part one's hair. **2** to isolate o.s., keep to o.s. **3** to divorce.

menceraikan 1 to separate, divide. ~ *sebuah kata atas sukunya* to divide a word into syllables. **2** to separate, pull apart (people fighting). **3** to divorce, repudiate (one's wife); → TALAK. *Karena sebab yang kecil itu maka ia diceraikan suaminya.* For such a petty reason she was divorced by her husband. **4** to wean (a child). ~ *menyusu* to wean (a child).

memperceraikan to separate (people fighting).

tercerai 1 separated, apart, scattered, isolated. **2** divorced.

cerai-ceraian frequently divorcing.

penceraian 1 separation, divorce. **2** division, partition, splitting. ~ *suku kata* (*gram*) syllabification of a word.

perceraian divorce, separation. ~ … *dengan* divorce … from. ~ *lanréporem/landréform* a formal divorce based on the Agrarian Basic Law (under President Soekarno).

ceraka I a stand on which clothes are laid out for fumigating with incense.

ceraka II k.o. herbal plant, Ceylon/white leadwort, *Plumbago zeylanica*.

cerakin I (*Pers*) portable chest/box with partitions for medicinal herbs; → PEDADAH.

cerakin II *pohon –* k.o. tree, purging croton, physic nut, *Croton tiglium*.

ceramah I lecture, talk, speech. – *tamu* guest lecture.

berceramah to give/deliver a lecture/talk.

menceramahi to lecture to.

menceramahkan to lecture on s.t., give a talk/speech on s.t.

penceramah lecturer. ~ *tamu* a) guest lecturer. b) guest speaker.

penceramahan lecturing.

ceramah II 1 talkative, garrulous, chatty; → RAMAH. **2** fussy, quarrelsome, hard to please, fault finding.

cerana (*Skr*) a (copper/silver, etc.) pedestal salver on which are placed the various vessels used for holding the requisites for betel-chewing. *menerima –* to receive a tray, i.e., to receive a marriage proposal; → PINANG. – *biduk* such a salver in the form of a riverboat.

cerancang bercerancang(an) bristling (of thorns), spiky (of caltrops), prickly.

cerang (*cla*) an abandoned and partly overgrown clearing in the jungle. *pelanduk di dalam –* and *pelanduk di – rimba* a) to lose one's head, be desperate. b) very nervous, restless, worried. – *rimba* a clearing in the forest.

ceranggah (*pl* of *canggah*) many-tined, forked (of antlers), branched; → CANGGAH I.

berceranggah 1 to have forked antlers. *rusa ~* a deer with many tines. **2** prickly, thorny, pointy, spiky.

berceranggah-ceranggih bristling unevenly (as of teeth).

cerangka (*cla*) garbage disposal.

cerap attentive, observant. *kurang –* inattentive. *Anak itu kurang – saja tampaknya.* The child seems inattentive. *tak –* I don't know (in courtly language).

mencerap 1 to pay attention to, take note of. **2** to perceive.

mencerapkan to take note of, respond to.

tercerap perceptible.

cerapan 1 perception, observation. **2** image. **3** response.

pencerapan perception, observation.

cerat spout, nozzle (of a kettle), spigot, tap, cock; (*petro*) bleeder.

bercerat with a spout/nozzle.

mencerat 1 to pour s.t. out through a nozzle/faucet/spout. **2** to drink from a spout. **3** (*petro*) to bleed down/off. **4** to squirt (out).

ceratan a small spout/tap.

penceratan throttling.

ceratai (*M*) lively conversation.

mencerataikan to discuss s.t. in a lively way.

ceratak-cerotok (*J*) reckless, inconsiderate.

ceratuk berceratukan and **menceratuk** to sit or squat in a row (as of pupils or of birds on an electric wire) with heads bowed down.

cerau (*onom*) the sound of pouring (water/grain/rain).

cerawat (*Skr cla*) arrow of fire, rocket. – *bahaya* distress flare. – *payung* rocket flare.

cerbak (*Jv*) gluttonous, ravenous, voracious, omnivorous.

cerbér → CERITA *bersambung*.

cerbergam → CERITA *bergambar*.

cerbersam and **cerbung** → CERITA *bersambung*.

cerca (*Skr*) **1** derision, mockery, ridicule, slander, abuse, insult. **2** criticism, reprimand. – *maki* taunt, scorn, ridicule.

mencerca(i) to reprimand, vilify, defame, abuse, insult, slander, revile, censure.

mencercakan to criticize and vilify.

cercaan verbal attack, reprimand, disdain.

pencerca 1 critic. **2** a scold, faultfinder.

pencercaan criticism, vilification.

cercah secercah a scintilla, an iota. ~ *cahaya* a shaft of light. ~ *mata* in passing, at a glance. ~ *harapan* silver lining. ~ *rasa* a slight feeling (of).

cercak I slightly pockmarked (on the skin); → BERCAK.

cercak II → CERACAP.

cercap (*ob*) **mencercap** to flop about (of a fish, out of water).

cerdas 1 intelligent, smart, educated, clever, shrewd, skillful. **2** alert (of the body), agile, fit, healthy, well developed. – *cermat* contest of wits. – *tangkas* a) intelligent. b) quiz contest.

secerdas as intelligent as.

mencerdaskan to sharpen/improve (one's way of thinking/reasoning/mind).

tercerdas the most intelligent, smartest.

kecerdasan intelligence, astuteness, development, advancement. ~ *buatan* artificial intelligence. ~ *émosional* emotional development. ~ *jamak* multiple intelligences. ~ *spiritual* spiritual development.

pencerdas s.t. that sharpens (s.o.'s mind).

pencerdasan sharpening (one's mind, etc.).

cerdét [cerita détéktif] detective story.

cerdik 1 intelligent, smart, clever, bright. *kaum – cendekia/pandai* and *kaum – cendekiawan* the intellectuals, the educated class. **2** cunning, shrewd, sly, artful, crafty. – *buruk/busuk* deceptive, likes to trick people.

secerdik as intelligent/cunning as.

tercerdik the most clever/intelligent.

kecerdikan 1 cunningness, shrewdness, craftiness. **2** intelligence, cleverness.

ceré (*Jv*) *padi –* quick-ripening small-grained rice.

cerecak → CERCAK I.

cerecat (*onom*) chirping.

bercerecat-cerecat to chirp.

cerecéh (*onom*) screeching/chirping sounds.

bercerecéh and **mencerecéh** to screech, chirp, talk nonsense.

cerecék *ikan –* a freshwater carp, skin-head barb, *Cyclocheilichthys apogon*.

cerecis (*onom*) sizzling.

bercerecis-cerecis to sizzle.

cérék I 1 kettle. **2** kettle-shaped water vessel. **3** watering can. – *daun* pitcher.

secérék a potful.

cérék II and **secérék** (*daun*) – k.o. plant, *Clausena excavata*; → SICÉRÉK.

cérék III various species of plover. – *besar* a) greater sand plover,

Charadrius leschenaultii. b) black-bellied plover, *Pluvialis squatarola*. – *kalung hitam* little ringed plover, *Charadrius dubius*. – *kernyut* Pacific golden plover, *Pluvialis fulva*.

ceremai and **cereme** → CERMAI.

ceremongan (*J*) dirty, soiled, stained (of one's face/hands/clothes); → CEMONG.

cerempung k.o. boat-shaped, four-string plucked zither.

cerenah → CERNA.

cerengkan sloppy (about work).

ceret → CIRIT. – *beret* bad diarrhea.
  menceret to have diarrhea.

ceret I various species of bush warbler. – *coklat* chestnut-backed bush warbler, *Bradypterus castaneus*.

ceret II → CEREK I.

cerewet 1 quarrelsome, cranky, nagging, like to complain, fussy, contrary (in personality). **2** critical, faultfinding, hard to please, difficult to manage. **3** to have a sharp tongue. **4** to talk too much, make a fuss about s.t. **5** freakish, whimsical, capricious, wayward.
  secerewet as nagging/faultfinding, etc. as.
  tercerewet the most nagging/faultfinding, etc.
  mencereweti [and **nyerewetin** (*J coq*)] always scolding about s.o., finding fault with, constantly critical of.
  kecerewetan faultfinding, censoriousness, nitpicking. ~ *logika* the nitpicking of logic.

cergam → CERITA *bergambar*.

cergamis(t) cartoonist, writer of comic strip; → CERGAM.

cergas energetic, active, enterprising, agile, nimble, dynamic.
  secergas as energetic/agile/nimble as.
  mencergaskan to activate, enliven.
  kecergasan 1 activity, activeness. **2** agility, verve.

ceri (*ob*) → CERIA II.

ceri (*E*) Japanese cherry, strawberry tree, *Muntingia calabura*.

ceria I (*cla*) **1** pure, clean, clear. **2** cheerful, bright (of the countenance). **3** cloudless (of the sky).
  seceria as cheerful, etc. as.
  menceriakan to purify, cleanse. ~ *diri* to clean o.s.
  keceriaan 1 purity. **2** cheerfulness.
  penceriaan purification.

ceria II (*Skr*) stereotyped words (like a mantra) read at the moment of the installation of a ruler. *membacakan* – to read out an address/special words of loyalty to a ruler on his accession (like a loyalty oath); → CIRI I.

cericap *burung* – → KELICAP.

cericau (*onom*) cackling.
  bercericau to talk nonsense, yap, cackle.

cericip (*onom*) chirping, chatter (of birds).

cericit I (*onom*) sound made by brakes squealing, squeaking.
  mencericit to make that noise.

cericit II (*onom*) twitter, warble, chatter. – *burung* the chirping of birds.

ceridau (*onom*) sound of many people bustling about, e.g., of children leaving school, etc.

ceriga I (*Skr*) dagger.

ceriga II → CURIGA.

cerih dregs, residue.

ceringis a big grin.

ceriping → CRIPING.

cerita (*Skr*) **1** story, narrative, account, report, tale, plot. *bukan – baru* it's an old story, it's nothing new. *–nya begini…* the story goes like this … the facts of the case are as follows …; → BEGINI. **2** gossip, idle talk, prattle. *banyak* – to talk big, boast. *dengan tidak banyak* – stripped of all unnecessary verbiage, in a nutshell. **3** (it's just an) invention. **4** twitter (*esp* of the *murai* or magpie robin). *– secuil jadi segunung* to make a mountain out of a molehill. *tak panjang* – a) without further ado. b) straight away. *– anak* [cernak] children's story. *– (ber)bingkai* frame story. *– bergambar* [cerbergam] cartoon. *– bersambung* [cerbung] serial(ized story). *– binatang* fable. *– bohong* a hoax. *– burung* rumor, gossip. *–.– burung mengatakan bahwa …* rumors have it that … *– busah* an invented story. *– cekak* [cercak] short story. *– keberhasilan* success story. *– kedewasaan* myth. *– keper-*

wiraan epic. *– kriminal* [cerkrim] detective story, murder mystery. *– lama* saga. *– lucu* funny story. *– miring* biased story. *– panjang* [cerpan] long story. *– picisan* novelette. *– pendek* [cerpen] short story. *– perjalanan* travel story, account of a journey/voyage, itinerary. *– rakyat* folklore. *– rekaan* [cerkan] fiction. *– sejarah* historical fiction. *– Seribu Satu Malam* The Arabian Nights. *– silat* [cersil] martial arts stories. *– usang* an old story.

bercerita 1 to tell a story, relate, narrate. *Mereka asyik ~ tentang hal-hal yang saya tidak mengerti.* They talked animatedly about matters I didn't understand. **2** storytelling, chitchatting. **3** to twitter (*esp* of the magpie robin).

menceritai to tell a story to, relate to. *Anak-anak diceritai ibu.* Mother told the children a story.

menceritakan [and **nyeritain** (*J coq*)] **1** to relate/tell s.t. to s.o. **2** to talk about, tell, relate, recount, disclose. *Jangan ~ hal ini kepada siapa-siapa.* Don't talk about this to anybody. *Jangan ceritakan pada siapa pun juga.* Don't tell anybody. **3** to hand down.

ceritaan (*J*) narration, report, story. *jadi ~ orang* much-discussed, much talked-of.

pencerita narrator, storyteller.

penceritaan the telling of a story.

ceritera → CERITA.

ceriwis (*J*) nagging, fussy, finicky, hard to please.

ceriwit red-wattled lapwing, *Lobivanellus indicus*.

cerkam (*ob*) → CENGKAM.

cerkan → CERITA *rekaan*.

cerkas → CERGAS.

cerkau → CEKAU. **mencerkau** to scratch, keep grabbing at, seize, abrade (skin).

cerkrim → CERITA *kriminal*.

cerlang 1 bright, brilliant (of colors), shining, gleaming, glittering, resplendent, glorious; → CEMERLANG. **2** to open and roll the eyes. *– budaya* local genius. *– cemerlang* brilliance and splendor.
  mencerlang to glitter, sparkle, shimmer, shine, gleam.
  mencerlangi to light up, illuminate.
  kecerlangan 1 brightness, luster, gleam, glimmer. **2** splendor, magnificence, glory, fame.

cerlih *tupai* – a small species of squirrel, *Callosciurus spp.*

cerling → JELING, KERLING II. **mencerling 1** to look at from the corner of the eye. **2** to ogle.

cermai *pohon* – a tree with small, yellowish, sour fruits with a hard seed, preserved and eaten as a side dish, Malay/Otaheite/star gooseberry, *Phyllanthus acidus*. *– belanda* k.o. tree, Surinam cherry, *Eugenia michelii*.

cermat 1 conscientious, careful, cautious, punctual, accurate, meticulous. **2** thrifty, economical, careful about spending money. *kurang* – inaccurate. **kekurang-cermatan** inaccuracy. *tidak* – inaccurate. **ketidak-cermatan** inaccuracy.
  secermat as conscientious, etc. as.
  mencermat to pay careful attention to.
  mencermati 1 to observe, examine. **2** to economize on.
  mencermatkan to be accurate in/with, do s.t. with care. ~ *belanja* to be careful about (expenditures), be economical of, economize in, retrench (expenses).
  kecermatan 1 care, thoughtfulness, caution, heed, accuracy, precision. **2** thriftiness, economical. *permainan ~* k.o. bingo.
  pencermat s.o. who pays attention to s.t.
  pencermatan 1 attention, care. **2** economizing.

cerme → CERMAI.

cermin 1 mirror. *gambar* – image. *Ketika pertama kali menerima pakaian seragam, tak henti-hentinya ia berdiri di depan – memeriksa dirinya dalam pakaian Hansip.* When he got his uniform for the first time, he couldn't stop standing in front of the mirror admiring himself in his Civil Defense Corps uniform. *Dia tentang – toiletnya.* (She stood) in front of her dressing table. **2** (shining) example. *Apa yang dialami ayahnya itu jadi – bagimu.* What was experienced by his father becomes a shining example for you. **3** reflection. *Surat kabar ialah – isi hati rakyat.* A newspaper is the reflection of the people's feelings. *buruk muka – dibelah* to lay the blame on s.o. else for one's mistakes. *– balik* distorting mirror. *– bantal* small mirror on a pillow. *– batu* k.o. herbal plant, *Pentasacme caudatum*. *– cekung* concave mirror. – *cembung* convex mirror. – *dinding* wall mirror. – *hidup* exemplary example. – *mata* (M) glasses, spectacles. – *muka* mirror (to look at one's own face. – *pembesar* magnifying glass. – *perbandingan* instruction, lesson. – *spion* outside rearview mirror (of car). – *tegak* full-length mirror. – *telinga* otoscope. – *terus/tilik* (*cla*) crystal ball. – *wasiat* a magic mirror with supernatural powers.

be(r)cermin 1 to look (at o.s.) in a mirror. ~ *bangkai* to live in shame. *daripada hidup ~ bangkai lebih baik mati berkalang tanah* better dead than to live in shame. **2** with/to have a mirror. *Ada tas yang ~, ada yang tidak.* There are handbags that have mirrors and those that don't. **3** to take an example (from). ~ *di air keruh* to follow a bad example. ~ *dalam hati sendiri* to examine/look at) o.s. carefully. *Jika tiap-tiap orang mau ~ dalam hati sendiri, niscaya diketahuinya bahwa dirinya pun tidak bersih dari cacat dan cela.* If s.o. wants to examine himself carefully, he will undoubtedly find out that he himself is not free from any faults or flaws. ~ *diri* to see one's own faults.

mencermini 1 to hold a mirror up to s.o. **2** to look at s.t. or s.o. in a mirror. *Cerminilah bangkai dahulu.* You ought to be ashamed of yourself first.

mencerminkan to reflect, mirror, portray, picture, depict.

mempe(r)cermin 1 to use s.t. as a mirror. **2** to always see/watch.

te(r)cermin reflected, mirrored, portrayed, pictured, depicted.

ketercerminan reflection.

cerminan reflection.

pencerminan reflection. ~ *kelemahan intérnal* a reflection of an internal weakness.

cerna (*Skr*) **1** digested (of food). *salah* – indigestion, dyspepsia. **2** disintegrated, dissolved.

mencerna 1 to be crushed and dissolved. **2** to think s.t. over, sleep on s.t. **3** to digest.

mencernakan 1 to dissolve, digest. **2** to assimilate, absorb and incorporate (into one's thinking), think over, register, take in.

tercerna digested, dissolved; assimilated. **ketercernaan** digestibility.

kecernaan digestion.

pencerna digester.

pencernaan 1 digestion. ~ *makanan* digestion. **2** digestive. *alat ~* digestive organ. *saluran ~* alimentary canal. **3** assimilation. **4** dissolving, rotting.

cernak → CERITA *anak.*

ceroboh I 1 indecent, improper, immoral, disrespectful. **2** rough, rude, unmannerly, bad-mannered, insolent, impudent, boorish. **3** unscrupulous, low, vile, bad, heartless.

menceroboh to act indecently/improperly, etc.; to violate, dishonor.

mencerobohi to commit an indecent/improper act toward s.o.

kecerobohan indecent/improper, etc. behavior, indecency, rudeness, insolence, impudence.

ceroboh II (*J*) careless, negligent, inattentive, irresponsible, imprudent, reckless, rash.

seceroboh as careless, rash, etc. as.

kecerobohan recklessness, irresponsibility. *Kecelakaan lalulintas yang nyaris membawa korban jiwa itu terjadi karena ~ pengemudi kendaraan itu yang ngebut dengan kecepatan tinggi.* Traffic accidents which almost caused deaths occur due to the recklessness of the drivers who drive their vehicles recklessly at great speed.

ceroboh III (*Jv*) slovenly, sloppy, untidy, disorderly.

kecerobohan untidiness, sloppiness.

cerobong 1 chimney(-shaft), flue. **2** funnel (on a ship). **3** (– *kapal*) smokestack.

bercorobong with a flue, etc.

cerocok I 1 palisade, lattice, trellis. **2** jetty; mooring; landing-stage, pier, quay, wharf. **3** fisherman's rattle. **4** breakwater.

cerocok II (M) (cylindrical) funnel, spout, nozzle.

bercerocok to flow (through a funnel, etc.).

cerocos [and **nyerocos** (*Jv*)] **1** to pour/stream/flow out; → CROCOS. **2** (*onom*) the sound produced by red-hot iron when plunged into water.

mencerocos to rattle on, words come pouring out of one's mouth.

cerocosan to pour, drip (profusely). *Keringat ~ dari pori-pori badannya.* The sweat poured out of his pores.

cerompong muzzle (of a gun/cannon).

ceronggah → CERANGGAH.

ceropong → CEROMPONG.

cerorot k.o. snack made from rice flour, palm sugar, and coconut milk steamed in a cone-shaped leaf.

cerotéh → CELOTÉH.

cerotok arranged in a (sitting or squatting row); → CERATUK.

cerowok mencerowok to scratch (with the nails). *Kuku gadis itu ~ muka pria yang menggodanya.* The girl's nails scratched the face of the man who was bothering her.

cerpan → CERITA *panjang.*

cerpelai (*Skr/Tam*) mongoose, *Herpestes spp.;* → GARANGAN II.

cerpén → CERITA *péndék.* **mencerpénkan** to write a short story about.

cerpénis short story writer. *Siapa – yang paling jempolan di "Kompas Minggu?" Jawabnya Yanusa Nugroho!* Who is the best writer in the "Sunday Edition of Kompas"? The answer is Yanusa Nugroho.

cerpu (*Tam*) sandal (similar to a *terompah*).

cersil → CERITA *silat.*

cerucuh (*cla*) k.o. ship.

cerucuk pile (driven into the ground).

cerucup I pointed, tapering, ending in a sharp point. – *atas* gable.

bercerucup and **mencerucup** to end in a point, taper (to a point), come to a point.

cerucup II love grass, *Chrysopogon aciculatus.*

cerucut → KERUCUT.

ceruh (entirely) cleaned (of rice after milling or pounding), twice-milled (of rice (to make it white).

menceruh to pound rice a second time (so as to whiten it).

ceruk 1 corner (in a room); hole, hollow (in the wall, ground, etc.), nook, recess, cranny, niche, alcove, small compartment. *Jangan menyorok di -.-!* Don't hide in corners! **2** blind alley, lane. **3** inlet, a small bay. **4** shaft. **5** mountain cave. **6** (*anat*) alveolus. **7** (*geol*) cockpit. – *bénténg* passage connecting parts of a fortress. – *gunung* valley. – *kubur* hole in the ground for a grave. – *meruk* all k.o. holes; nooks and crannies. – *rantai* chain locker. – *rantau* from all nooks and corners. – *pasar* niche market. – *pasut* tidal inlet. – *tétés* drip channel.

berceruk-ceruk full of nooks and crannies.

menceruk 1 to dig a hole/crevice. **2** to go into a hole, hollow, cranny, etc.

ceruk-menceruk to look/search in every nook and cranny.

cerukan (*fin*) overdraft. *pinjaman ~* overdraft loan.

cerukcuk → TERUCUK.

cerun sloping (of a hill/roof).

cerup (*onom*) the audible sound of lapping/sipping up (water, etc.). **mencerup** to lap/sip/suck up.

ceruput → CERUP.

cerurut → CELURUT.

cerut I constriction.

mencerut to wind s.t. around tightly, tighten, rope off, squeeze tight, constrict, compress on all sides (as a python/belt/hangman's noose).

mencerutkan to tighten (one's belt).

pencerut 1 (*naut*) guy wire. **2** constrictor.

pencerutan constricting.

cerut II → CERUTU.

cerutu (*Tam*) cigar, cheroot; → LISONG, SERUTU, SIGAR II.

bercerutu to smoke a cigar.

cerwatélis [*pencuri kawat télepon dan listrik*] s.o. who steals electric and telephone cables.

cés (*J*) **men(ge)cés** to charge (a battery).

cespleng (*Jv*) **1** efficient, effective, to have the desired result, hits the spot, cure instantly, provide instant relief; → MANJUR, MUJARAB. *obat yang murah, aman, tapi sangat* – an inexpensive, safe but effective medicine. **2** to hit home/the mark. *karikatur-karikatur yang* – cartoons which hit home. **3** straightforwardly. *Biasanya kalau dikritik para pejabat lalu tidak bicara* – (*terus terang*) *di antara sesamanya.* When criticized, the officials usually do not talk straightforwardly to their peers.

céss (*D*) /sés/ **1** a tax, an assessment. **2** (in Indonesia) a surcharge on export products from plantations levied by the local regional government.

céssie (*D fin*) /sési/ assignment.

cét → CAT.

cetai (**ber**)**cetai-cetai** (to be) in tatters/rags, to pieces.
　mencetai-cetai to tear to pieces.

cétak 1 print (used in making books, etc.). *barang/benda* – printed matter. *besi* – cast iron. *huruf* – (printing) type. *jumlah* – circulation (of a newspaper, magazine); → OPLAH, TIRAS. *kantor* – printing office, print shop. *média* – print media. *mengulang* – to reprint. *mesin* – printing press. *ongkos* – printing expenses. *salah* – misprint. *seni* – typography. *tinta* – printer's/printing ink. *tukang* – printer. **2** fold, matrix. **3** impression. *bagaimana* – *begitu kuéhnya* like father, like son. – *awal* preprint. – *balik* reverse printing. – *batu* lithography. – *biru* blueprint. – *cahaya* light printing. – *coba* (galley) proof. *Belum semua penerbit bisa menyerahkan contoh – coba untuk buku-buku.* Not all publishers can submit (galley) proofs for books. – *dalam* rotogravure. – *datar* offset. – *jempol* thumbprint. – *kasa* screen printing. – *keluar* bleeding. – *kembali* reprint. **mencétak kembali** to reprint. – *lepas* offprint. – *miring* italics. **mencétak miring** to italicize. – *ofsét* offset printing. – *rekam kasét* videocassette reproduction. – *rompak* (*Mal*) piracy (of cassettes/books). – *sablon/saring* screen printing, serigraphy; → SÉRIGRAFI. – *semprot* spray print. **mencétak semprot** to spray print. – *talam* galley proof. – *tambahan* reprint. – *timbul* relief printing, intaglio. – *tinggi* letterpress. – *tunggal* monoprint. – *ulang(an)* reprint.

bercétak printed. *Kertas itu ~ timbal balik.* The paper has been printed on both sides.

bercétakkan imprinted with. *kartu nama ~ tinta* emas business/calling cards imprinted with gold.

mencétak [and **nyétak** (*coq*)] **1** to print (books/banknotes, etc.). *~ buku/surat kabar* to print a book/newspaper. *sedang dicétak* in press. **2** to stamp/print (a motif/repeated figure in a design) on a piece of cloth. *~ kain sarung* to print a sarong fabric with a certain motif; → BATIK *cap*. **3** to cast (iron, etc.). *~ roda* to cast a wheel. **4** to achieve, produce. *~ kemenangan yang gilanggemilang* to achieve a glorious victory. **5** to mint, strike. *~ uang* to mint/strike money. **6** to make, score, reap. *~ gol* (in soccer) to score a goal. *~ suksés besar* to reap a great success. **7** to turn out (doctors, etc.; by a university or other establishment). *Kami tidak akan ~ calon-calon birokrat yang hanya berambisi menjadi pegawai negeri.* We don't turn out aspiring bureaucrats who only have ambitions to become government employees. *~ sarjana* to turn out candidates for a doctor's degree. **8** to make, earn, gain, book. *~ uang* to earn money. *Tahun lalu cuma bisa ~ keuntungan Rp 10 juta.* Last year a profit of only 10 million rupiahs was earned. **9** to lay out, arrange according to a plan. *kemampuan ~ sawah* the ability to lay out rice paddies.

cétak-mencétak printing.

mencétakkan 1 to have s.t. printed up, ask to print s.t. up. *~ kartu undangan* to have invitation cards printed up. **2** to print for. **3** to publish (a book, etc.).

tercétak 1 printed. **2** cast.

cétakan 1 print(ing), printout. *barang ~* printed matter. *~ biru* blueprint. *~ dalam* rotogravure. *~ percobaan* proofs. *~ percontohan* rush print. *~ ulangan* reprint. **2** publication. *~ awal* advance copy, initial publication. **3** edition, printing, issue. *~ pertama* first edition. **4** mold, mould, matrix, pan. *alat ~ bodi mobil* mold for casting car bodies. **5** graduate; → LULUSAN, TAMATAN, WISUDAWAN.

pencétak 1 printer. **2** printing press. **3** s.o. who scores (a goal). *~ gol* (in soccer) goal-getter/scorer. *~ gol terbanyak* (in soccer) top scorer. *~ laser* laser printer. *~ uang kertas* banknote printer.

pencétakan 1 printing, pressing. **2** laying out (of rice paddies). *Réalisasi ~ sawah sampai Oktober 1984 baru mencapai 193.583 héktar.* Actual laying out of rice paddies as of October 1984 has only amounted to 193,583 hectares. **3** molding.

percétakan printing office, print shop, press. *~ Negara* Government Printing Office. *~ ofsét* offset printing office. *~ Uang* The Mint.

cetar-cetér 1 (*onom*) cracking sounds (of a horsewhip/gunfire/fireworks). **2** to keep cracking (of whips); → CETÉR.

cetat-cetét (*onom*) clicking sounds.

ceték I and **céték** (*Jv*) **1** shallow (of water, river); → DANGKAL I. *Kalinya – atau dalam?* Is the river shallow or deep? **2** superficial, inexperienced, having limited/little knowledge. *pengetahuan yang –* superficial knowledge.
　seceték as shallow/inexperienced as.

ceték II (*onom*) clicking sound.
　mencetékkan to click on s.t.

céténg → JINJING I, TÉNTÉNG I. **mencéténg** to carry in one's hand (or, lift with one hand).

cetér (*onom*) cracking sound (made by a horsewhip); → CETAR-CETÉR.

cetera I (*Skr cla*) canopy, state umbrella (with a hanging fringe). – *jantung* diaphragm.

cetera II → CERITA.

ceteri (*Hind*) small tent on a boat for protection from the elements.

Ceteria (*Skr cla*) the second, or warrior, Hindu caste; → CATUR *wangsa*.

cetét (*Jv*) **mencetét-cetét** *~ tangannya* to snap one's fingers while simultaneously making a soft sound to a turtledove, encouraging it to coo.

céthok (*Jv*) antique. *montor –* an antique car

céti I (*Malayalam?*) **1** merchant from Malabar or Coromandel (in India). **2** moneylender who usually loans money at a very high interest rate, usurer.

céti II go-between, matchmaker, pimp.
　mencéti to act as a matchmaker.

cetiao and **cetiau** (*C*) one million (rupiahs).

ceting (*Jv*) small container for serving rice; → BOKOR.

céting (*E*) to chat (on the Internet).

cetok (*J*) headgear (used by Chinese farmers). – *topi* pith helmet.

cétok (*Jv*) trowel.

ceto-wélo-wélo (*Jv*) crystal-clear.

cetrak → CETRÉK. (*J*) – *cetrék* to keep on striking a match but it doesn't light.

cetrék mencetrékkan to turn on or off a switch.
　nyetrékin (*J*) to strike (a match).
　cetrékan 1 switch. **2** flick of a switch.

cetrong racket-tailed treepie, *Crypsirina temia*.

cetus (*onom*) **1** sound produced by scraping iron over a stone, etc. – *api* (*M*) a) flint for making fire. b) spark. **2** outburst, irrelevant remark.

mencetus 1 strike. *~ api* to strike fire. **2** to strike a flint/match/lighter; to flash. **3** to flare up, flash (of a flame). **4** to burst from one's lips. **5** (*M*) a) to launch an attack; to bite/hurt s.o. silently/stealthily. b) to find fault.

mencetuskan 1 to light, ignite, set on fire, strike (a match). **2** to create, come up with, start, launch, spark, provoke, kindle, incite. *~ diskusi* to provoke a discussion. *~ gagasan* to come up with an idea. *~ kerusuhan* to incite a riot. *~ perang* to start a war. *~ révolusi* to spark a revolution. **3** to spit out (words).

tercetus 1 kindled, enkindled, sparked. **2** come up with. *Gagasan itu ~ daripadanya.* He came up with that idea. **3** said unexpectedly, came out of one's mouth.

cetusan 1 *~ api* spark, flash. **2** outburst, utterance. *~ hati* heartfelt cry.

pencetus 1 spark, impetus. **2** s.o. who ignites. *~ idé* sponsor, idea man, initiator.

pencetusan igniting; ignition, sparking, launching.

cetya (Buddhist) altar.

ceuk → ACEUK.

céwang (*M*) changeable (in ideas), fickle.

céwé (*Mal*) a taboo word as a substitute for names of animals, snakes, etc., whose real name it is taboo to mention due to superstitious awe and veneration, for instance, in encountering them in the jungle, such as – *angin* deer, – (*meng*)*aum* tiger, – *céblék* k.o. snake, – *duri* porcupine, – *épék* rhinoceros, – *untut* elephant.

céwék (*J*) **1** girl, woman, female. – *bulé* Caucasian girl. – *komérsil/pasaran* whore. – *orderan* call girl. – *matré* gold digger; → MATA *duitan*. **2** girlfriend.

bercéwék-céwék to go looking for girls.
CFW reference to a dining railway coach.
CGI Consulative Group on Indonesia.
chiak → CIAK III.
chi(e) /ci/ → CI II.
chiménk (*BG*) marijuana; → CIMÉNG.
chro(o)m (*D*) /krom/ → KROM.
chudancho (*Jp*) /cudanco/ company commander of the *Peta* during
    the Japanese occupation.
Chuo Sangi-in (*Jp*) /cuo sangi-in/ Central Advisory House (in
    Jakarta) during the Japanese occupation.
chusétsu (*Jp*) /cusétsu/ submission to the fatherland.
ci- I (contraction of Sundanese *cai* 'water, river') first element in
    many place and river names in West Java, such as Cimahi (a
    town), Citarum (a river), etc.
ci II (C) a weight, 1/10 of a *tahil*, used in illegal drug traffic.
ci III → ENCIK.
ciak I (*onom*) twitter, chirping (of birds, etc.). - *ciap/miak* a) all
    k.o. chirping sounds. b) to cry, whimper (of children).
    berciak(-ciak) and menciak(-ciak) to twitter, chirp.
    ciakan peep, cheep.
ciak II *burung* - name for a variety of finches, sparrows, munia, etc.
    - *gajah* weaver-finch, *Ploceus spp.* - *padi* rice bird, sharp-tailed
    munia, *Munia oryzivora*. - *raja* sparrow, *Passer montanus*. -
    raya weaver-finch, *Ploceus spp.* - *rumah* (house-)sparrow,
    Passer montanus.
ciak III (C) to eat. - *kopi* bribable.
ciaka (C) barefoot.
cialat (C) damn it, uh-oh! (said on running into a problem); →
    CELAKA.
ciam (C) needle.
ciami(k) (C) 1 good-looking. 2 of good quality. 3 will sell well com-
    mercially (of a film, etc.).
    keciamikan good looks, beauty.
ciamsi and ciam sie (C) to predict the future by casting sticks.
ciap (*onom*) twittering, chirping (of birds, chickens). - *miap* all k.o.
    chirping sounds.
    seciap ~ *bak ayam, sedencing bak besi* unanimous.
    menciap(-ciap) to twitter, chirp, titter. *Menciapnya anak ayam
    hutan sudah jarang terdengar.* The chirping of wood-hen
    chicks is seldom heard; → CIAK I.
    ciapan twitter, chirp.
ciar (*onom*) sound of screaming/bawling.
    berciaran (*pl subj*) to scream/bawl.
    menciar-ciar to bawl (of infants), cry without stopping (of chil-
    dren).
    terciar-ciar to bawl.
ciat sound made when attacking in martial arts. En garde! - *ciut*
    creaking, squeaking.
ciau I (*ob*) → CIU I.
ciau II menciau (*Mal*) to row (a boat) standing (by using a long
    oar).
cibai (*J*) little girl's vagina.
ci-bie (*E*) /si-bi/ citizen band.
cibir (*M*) curling one's lip (in ridicule), sneering. *tak ada -, tak ada
    cemooh* there's no turning up of noses at and scoffing at e.o.
    mencibir to curl up one's lip (in contempt). *dengan ~* sarcasti-
    cally. *sambil ~* sneering(ly).
    mencibiri to sneer at, look down on, ridicule.
    mencibirkan 1 ~ *bibir/mulut* to turn up one's nose. *Telah lampau
    masa ketika kita ~ bibir mencemoohkan pengobatan dengan ra-
    muan-ramuan tradisional.* The time is at an end when we
    turned up our noses and scorned treatments with traditional
    herbs. 2 to mock, scoff at, jeer at, sneer at, ridicule.
    tercibir curled up (of one's lip in contempt).
    cibiran mocking, derision, contempt, disdain, scorn.
    pencibiran mocking, disdaining, scorning.
cibit → CUBIT.
ciblék [cilik betah melék] (*Jv*) young prostitute. - *céwék* female
    prostitute. - *lanang* male prostitute.
ciblon (*Jv*) k.o. drum.
cibuk (*M*) → CÉBOK.

cibung large earthen pitcher for keeping a supply of water or rice
    handy.
cica bulbul. - *rante* orange-spotted bulbul, *Pycnonotus bimaculatus*.
cicah → CECAH.
cicak house lizard, *Hemidactylus frenatus. jadi - kering* to become
    as thin as a rail. - *kubin/terbang* flying lizard, *Draco volans*; →
    CEKIBAR.
cici I → CICIT I.
cici II various species of cisticola bird, *Cisticola spp.* - *mérah*
    golden-headed cisticola, *Cisticola exilis*.
cicih little boy's penis; → CÉCÉH.
cicik I (*onom*) sound of boiling water.
    mencicik 1 to hiss, fizzle (of boiling water). 2 to pour (with per-
    spiration), stream.
cicik II → JIJIK.
cicik III form of address and reference for one's elder sister.
cicil I (*Jv*) *secara* - in installments.
    mencicil [and nyicil (*coq*)] to pay in installments, pay off little by
    little.
    cicilan installment, tranche. *dengan ~ yang ringan* with afford-
    able installments, on easy terms. *masa ~* installment period.
    pencicilan and penyicilan paying s.t. off in installments.
cicil II (*J*) mencicil to watch with wide-open eyes.
cicinda (*formal*) great-grandchild.
cicip I *tukang* - taster (of tea, etc.).
    mencicip to taste (food during its preparation to check the sea-
    sonings).
    mencicipi [and nyicipin (*J coq*)] 1 to taste (food/drinks, etc.),
    sample, nibble on. *Sayur itu dicicipinya.* She tasted the vege-
    table soup (while she was cooking it). 2 to get acquainted with,
    experience, enjoy. *~ pendidikan* to enjoy/receive an education.
    pencicip taster.
    pencicipan tasting.
cicip II (*onom*) cheep, twitter.
    mencicip to cheep, twitter, chirp (of birds, etc.).
cicir → CÉCÉR.
cicit I great-grandchild.
cicit II (*onom*) squeak, twitter, creak.
    mencicit to squeak (of mice), twitter (of birds), creak (of hinges).
cicit III crested green wood-partridge, *Rollulus roulroul*.
cicunguk → CECUNGUK.
cidera → CEDERA. - *janji* breach of contract, default; non-
    fulfilment, nonperformance.
Cidés Center for Information and Development Studies.
cidomo (*in Lombok*) a vehicle which is a combination of an ox-
    drawn cart (*cikar*) and a two-wheeled horse-drawn cab (*dokar*)
    using motorcar (*motor*) wheels and tires, but pulled by a horse.
cidra → CEDERA.
ciduk (*Jv*) → CÉDOK. menciduk [and nyiduk (*coq*)] 1 to ladle,
    scoop (a liquid). 2 to arrest, apprehend (for criminal or politi-
    cal causes).
    terciduk arrested, apprehended.
    cidukan grip, clutches. *Orang-orang itu berusaha melarikan
    diri dari ~ ABRI.* Those people attempted to escape from the
    grip of the Armed Forces of the Republic of Indonesia.
    penciduk scoop, dipper.
    pencidukan arrest, apprehension.
ciék (in Sawahlunto, West Sumatra) *ijazah - baduo* marriage li-
    cense.
cigak (*M*) k.o. leaf monkey, *Semnopithecus pruinosus*. *bertukar
    beruk dengan -* it is six of one and half a dozen of the other.
cigau a fierce animal, the crossbreed of a lion and a tiger.
cigok mencigok ~ *keto* stick one's head into.
cih shame on you!, exclamation of disgust, disapproval.
cihuuuiiii and cihuy (*sl*) great! *Céwéknya -, a!* The girls were
    knockouts!
cik I clipped form of *encik*.
cik II 1 clipped form of *kecik II. mak -* aunt (youngest sister of
    father or mother). *pak -* uncle (youngest brother of father or
    mother). 2 clipped form of *encik*.
cik III (*M*) dung.
cik IV skat! shoo! (to dogs).

cik V (*D*) chic.

cik VI (*C*) → CHI(E).

cika severe pain in the stomach and bowels with diarrhea, colic. – *kedadak* diarrhea with vomiting, cholera.

cikal I (*Jv*) **1** first-born, oldest child. **2** first (of s.t.). *proyék* – pilot project; → PROYÉK *perintis/pola*. – *bakal* first tillers of the land, founder of a village, ancestor, pioneer, forerunner. *secikal-bakal* of the same ancestor. *sanak saudara* ~ family of the same ancestor. *bercikal-bakal* to originate (from).

cikal II (*Jv*) young coconut.

cikalan (*J*) scrap, refuse, cuttings. *kaléng* – tin scrap/refuse, tinplate scrap/cuttings.

cikalang → CAKALANG. *burung* – frigate bird, *Fregata spp.* – *bintayung* Christmas-island frigate bird, *Fregata andrewsi*.

Cikapur [Cikampék-Karawang-Purwakarta] the development of these three towns.

cikar I (*Jv*) bullock/horse-drawn cart.

cikar II to put the steering wheel hard over, hard a-port or hard a-starboard (of the steering wheel). – *kanan* starboard hard – *kiri* port hard.

pencikaran ~ *kemudi* (on sea) = BANTING *s(e)tir* (on land).

cikarau (*M*) an edible plant that grows in swamps/marshland.

mencikarau to meddle/interfere with.

cikarwan cart driver.

cikat → CEKAT.

cikeruhan (*S*) (in Sumedang) → KETUK *tilu*.

cikok (*C*) spoon, ladle.

cikrak I (*Jv*) → JINGKRAK. **cikrak-cikrak** to jump with joy.

cikrak II (*J/Jv*) wastebasket, dustpan.

cikrak III various species of leaf-warbler, *Phylloscopus spp.*

ciku *buah* – sapodilla. *pohon* – sapodilla tree, *Achras zapota*; → SAWO I.

cikukua various species of friarbird or leatherhead, *Philemon spp.* – *Seram* gray-necked friarbird, *Philemon subcorniculatus*. – *Timor* helmeted friarbird, *Philemon buceroides*.

cikun (*M*) **bercikun-cikun 1** to hide, conceal o.s. **2** (to do s.t.) secretly/surreptitiously.

cikut cikutan (*J*) to hiccup.

cilaka → CELAKA.

cilap I tercilap-cilap to flicker, flutter, wave.

cilap II → CILOK I.

cilat trick, dodge.

mencilat to deceive.

cilawagi (*ob*) forefathers/ancestors of the fifth generation back.

Cilé Chile

cili (*E*) chili, red pepper, *Capsicum annuum*. *lada* – bird pepper, cayenne, *Capsicum frutescens*. – *besar* large pepper. – *padi* a small, very hot k.o. chili → CABAI *rawit*.

cilik (*Jv*) little, small. *pahlawan* – a minor hero. *wong* – the man in the street.

cilim → CULIM.

ciling (*M*) wild boar; → CÉLÉNG. – *menurun* name for a certain way to wear a turban.

cilok I (*M*) **mencilok** to steal.

pencilok thief.

cilok II a sweet or salty delicacy made from seasoned tapioca flour.

ciloték → CELOTÉH.

ciluk ... bah and **cilu(uu)p ... ba** peek-a-boo, i.e., a children's game in which s.o. hides his/her face behind a newspaper, etc. and says "*ciluuup*," and then suddenly reveals it, calling out "*ba!*".

cim (*C*) clipped form of **encim**.

ciméng (*C? BG*) marijuana, pot.

nyiméng and **ngeciméng** to smoke marijuana/pot.

cimi-cimi (*J*) reluctant, unenthusiastic.

cimplong (*C*) *dadu* – k.o. dice game.

cimplung food prepared by boiling in sap or sweet juice, candied food.

mencimplung to candy food.

cimplungan candied food.

cimpring k.o. *krupuk*.

cimpung (*ob*) → KECIMPUNG I.

Cina 1 China, Chinese (formerly derogatory but less so now).

negeri/tanah – China; → TIONGKOK. *bangsa/orang* – a Chinese; → TIONGHOA. *bahasa* – Chinese (the language). **2** name of a *ceki* card. *bunga* – gardenia. *dawat* – India ink. *lada* – capsicum, *Piper caba*. *sebagai* – *karam* and – *kebakaran jénggot* very noisy, a pandemonium. – *Bénténg* Tangerang-born Chinese. *kelebon* – *gundulan* (*Jv*) to be cheated. – *kolong* Chinese mineworker. – *ku(n)cir* former male Chinese who wears a pigtail. – *mindering* itinerant Chinese vendor who sells his wares to customers on easy terms. – *peranakan* Indonesian-born Chinese of mixed Chinese-Indonesian parentage. – *perantauan* overseas Chinese. – *téko* Chinese farmer. – *totok* newly arrived Chinese in Indonesia.

mencina to become Chinese.

mencina-cinakan to consider a Chinese. "*Saya tetap dicina-cinakan*," keluh nyonya itu dengan getir kepada Tempo. "I keep on being considered Chinese," the woman complained bitterly to Tempo.

kecinaan Chinese (*mod*). *idéntitas* ~ Chinese identity.

percinaan Chinese (*mod*).

pecinan Chinatown.

cinabuta (*Skr*) divider, i.e., the man who marries a woman who has been divorced three times (based on Muslim law); → TALAK *tiga*, in order, thereafter, to divorce her again so as to enable her to remarry the first husband who repudiated her three times; → MUHALLIL.

cinafikasi sinicization.

cinangga → CENANGGA.

cincai (*CJ*) **1** *-lah* a) it's OK, agreed. b) never mind, it's all right, no big deal, it doesn't matter at all. *uang* – bribe. *Dalam hal ini penggunaan falsafah – yang mengandung makna négatif dalam kehidupan perékonomian harus dilenyapkan dalam prakték bisnis di negara kita.* In this case the application of the philosophy of "no big deal" which implies a negative sense has to be eliminated in business practices in our country. **2** worthless, of low quality.

cincai-cincai not really (careful/faultless), arbitrarily.

cincang *tukang* – (*coq*) film editor; → CENCANG I.

mencincang(kan) 1 to mince, chop. **2** to slaughter, kill cruelly/ in a barbaric manner.

cincangan s.t. minced, chopped (up). ~ *daging* chopped meat.

pencincangan chopping up.

cincaru → CENCARU.

cincau (*C*) **1** k.o. gelatin used to make a k.o. drink and this drink. **2** *daun* – k.o. climbing plant, *Cyclea spp.*, the leaves of which can be squeezed out to become a viscous, gelatinous mass to form the main substance of the drink of that name; some molasses syrup is added to taste. – *hijau* k.o. plant, *Cyclea barbata*. – *hitam* k.o. plant, *Mesona palustris*. – *minyak* k.o. plant, *Stephania hermandifolia*. – *perdu* k.o. plant, pink heart, *Melastoma polyanthum*.

cincay → CINCAI.

cincin I 1 (finger)ring. – *sebentuk* a/one ring. **2** round ferrule; round link; washer for bolts, faucets, etc. – *antara* washer (the device). – *baji* (*petro*) doughnut (oil term). – *belah rotan* a plain wedding ring, from the inside flat and outside round. – *belakang* breech ring (of a cannon). – *berapit* ring with one big stone in the middle and two smaller stones at the sides. – *bindu* machine-made ring. – *cap* signet ring. – *dalam rantai* chain link. – *emas* a) a gold ring. b) species of snake. – *garam sebuku* ring with a single stone. – *hidung* nose ring (for animals). – *hitam* black ring (a disease of cabbages). – *ikat Éropa* ring with claw-setting. – *kawin* wedding ring. – *lenja* gimbals. – *peluncur* drive band (for ammunition). – *pembuka* (*bio*) annulus. – *perapat* O-ring. – *s(e)témpel* signet ring. – *tanam* ring with a stone inset. – *tanda* (*pertunangan*) engagement ring. – *tanya* ring given to the parents of a girl when asking for her hand in marriage. – *torak* piston ring. – *tunang* engagement ring.

pencincinan ringing, putting a ring around.

cincin II k.o. cake made with bananas and rice flour.

cincing (*Jv*) **mencincing** to rise up (of skirt, etc.).

mencincingkan ~ *kain* to hold up a sarong on one side when walking.

cincoan → CINGCOAN.

cincong (C?) fuss, big deal, uproar. *banyak –nya* to be difficult/ exacting hard to please. *tidak banyak –* a) easygoing, not finicky. b) without much ado/fuss.

cincu (C) 1 owner's agent on a (Chinese) ship. 2 ship's captain. 3 (in Aceh) bus conductor.

cinda clipped form of **cicinda**.

cindai I (*Hind*) 1 printed silk fabric. *ular –* name of a snake the skin color of which resembles the color of this fabric. *– kara* k.o. fabric. 2 waist-sashes (of the same fabric). *mati berkapan –* to die with a good name. *– hari* k.o. flowered *cindai*.

cindai II *si –* (*M*) k.o. female ghost (who *esp* targets pregnant women and babies); → KUNTILANAK.

cindaku (*M*) were-tiger; → CINDEKU.

cindan clipped form of **kucindan**.

cindé (*Jv*) → CINDAI.

cindeku → CINDAKU.

cinderamata (*Skr*) souvenir. *tempat penjualan –* souvenir shop

cinderawasih → CENDERAWASIH.

cindil (*J/Jv*) baby mouse.

cindo (*Pal*) good-looking.

cindramata → CINDERAMATA.

cindurbuta (*M*) → CINABUTA.

cindurmata 1 souvenir, gift. 2 darling, sweetheart.

cinénén various species of tailorbird, *Orthotomus spp. – abu/kelabu* a) ashy tailorbird, *Orthotomus ruficeps*. b) olive-backed tailorbird, *Orthotomus sepium. – gunung* mountain tailorbird, *Orthotomus cuculatus*.

cing I (*onom*) clink, i.e., a sharp clinking sound, as of coins clinking together, etc.; → DENCING.

cing II (*C J*) 1 clipped form of *encing*, used in calling or as a term of address for uncle or aunt (younger than father or mother). 2 general term of address, man. *Gila –!* It was crazy, man!

cingah → CINGANGAH.

cingak (*Jv*) to open one's eyes in surprise; → CLINGAK-CLINGUK.

cingak-cinguk (*Jv*) → C(E)LINGAK-C(E)LINGUK. *Bobby – seperti mencari: "Ibu tadi mana ya mas?"* Bobby was astonished as though looking for s.o.: "Where was mother earlier, Buddy?"

cingam (*Tam?*) k.o. small coastal mangrove tree, *Scyphiphora hydrophyllacea*, the wood of which is used for making ladles, etc.

cingangah (*M*) **tercingangah** wide open (of mouth), agape.

cingantu (*C J*) uncle's wife or aunt's husband (father's or mother's younger sibling).

Cingbing (C) special day of cemetery-cleaning and praying held by the Chinese in early April; → CÉNGBÉNG.

cingbok (*C J*) uncle's wife (father's or mother's younger sibling).

cingcai → CINCAI.

cingcau → CINCAU.

cingcay → CINCAI.

cingcoan *– alis putih* white-browed short wing, *Brachypterix sp.*

cingcong → CINCONG.

cinggé (C) pageant, parade featuring floats.

cingkat young coconut; → CENGKIR.

cingkau → CENGKAU I.

cingkéh (*ob*) → CENGKÉH.

cingkong (C) *– kepiting* a dish made of crab claws.

cingkrang (*Jv*) to be short (of money/trousers).

    kecingkrangan to live in poverty. *Hidup wredatama golongan kecil ~ dan pas-pasan*. The minor government retirees are living in poverty and on a shoestring.

cingkuk (in Jambi) a black monkey species.

cinguk (*Jv*) **cingak-cinguk** astonished, amazed, dumbfounded; → CINGAK.

cingur the cartilage and meat of a bull's snout and ears which is used as a salad ingredient.

cining k.o. dessert made from cassava.

cino (*Jv*) → CINA.

cinsé (*J*) (a derogatory term for) a Chinese, Chink.

cinta (*Skr*) 1 *– akan/dengan/(ke)pada* to (be in) love with, have strong/deep tender feelings for. *sangat – pada diri sendiri* narcissistic; → NARSISISTIK. *Ia – dengan gadis itu.* and *Ia – gadis itu.* He loves that girl. 2 (*– kasih*) love, affection, strong liking (for one's country/close ones/parents/freedom, etc.). *berseminya –*

love in bloom. *hubungan – benci* a love-hate relationship. *jatuh – to* fall in love. *– kepada kampung meréka* their homesickness/ nostalgia. 3 desire, yearning/longing for. 4 (*cla*) sorrow, regret, pain, distress, grief. *Tiada terperikan lagi –nya ditinggalkan ayahnya itu.* His sorrow was indescribable when left by his father. *– itu buta* love is blind. *– bébas* free love. *– berlarat-larat* deep love which lasts a long time. *– birahi* passionate longing, love's desire. *perasaan – diri* narcissism; → NARSISISME. *– kasih* love, affection. *bercinta-kasih* to love, feel affection. *– kasih-persaudaraan* brotherly love. *– kepada tanah air* chauvinism, patriotism. *– laut* sea mindedness. *– menyala-nyala* ardent love. *– monyét* puppy love, infatuation. *– pada pandangan pertama* love at first sight. *– platonik* platonic love. *– pura-pura* hypocritical affection. *– rasa* affection. *– segi-tiga* love triangle. *– sepihak* one-sided love. *– tak berbalas* unrequited love. *– tanah air* love for one's country, patriotism. *– udara* air mindedness. *– yang mendalam* profound love.

bercinta 1 to be in love (with). *meréka yang sedang ~* the lovers. 2 to be sad, grieve.

bercinta(-cinta)an 1 to be in love with e.o., be continually in love. 2 to talk sweet nothings (of lovers).

bercintakan 1 to be in love with. 2 to long for. 3 to mourn for, grieve over, pine for.

mencinta 1 (*cla*) to grieve/mourn for, feel/express sorrow for. 2 (= **mencintakan**) to lust after (a woman). 3 to be in love with.

mencintai 1 to long for, desire (a woman). 2 to love. *Aku mencintaimu teramat sangat.* I love you very, very much.

cinta-mencintai to be in love with e.o.

mencintakan to long for, desire.

tercinta dear, beloved, much loved. *kekasihku ~* my beloved sweetheart.

kecintaan 1 (*cla*) concern, worry, sadness. 2 (*cla*) to mourn for, pine for, bemoan. 3 longing, yearning, desire. 4 love (and affection). *~ pada diri sendiri* narcissism. *~ terhadap laut* love of the sea. 5 s.o. or s.t. which one loves, one's favorite. *Ibu terdengar menyanyi di kamar. Lagu ~nya.* We could hear mother singing in her room. Her favorite song.

pencinta and **pecinta** lover, (ardent) fan, devotee. *pencinta alam* nature lover. **kepencintaalaman** love of nature. *– damai* pacifist, peacenik. *– lingkungan* environmentalist. *~ seni/kesenian* art lover/buff. *– sépakbola* soccer fan, devotee of soccer. *– tanah air* patriots.

pencintaan loving.

percintaan 1 love. 2 love affair, romance. 3 mourning, sorrow. 4 longing. **bepercintaan** to be involved in a love affair.

cintamani (*Skr*) 1 legendary wish-gem, philosopher's stone (helps to make one's wishes and dreams come true). 2 brilliantly golden-yellow legendary snake, the finding of which betokens good fortune in love.

cintawan (*Skr neo*) lover. *– agung* great lover.

cinténg → CÉNTÉNG.

cintrong (*Pr*) love; → CINTA. *jatuh – to* fall in love. *mabuk – kepada* madly/head over heels in love with.

cintrong-mencintrong to be in love with e.o.

cintuh (*ob*) → SENTUH.

cintungan Javanese bishipwood, *Bischofia javanica*.

ciocing (C) salty soy sauce; → KÉCAP *asin*.

ciok (*ob*) → CIAK I, CIAP. **menciok-ciok** to peep, chirp, squeak (of birds, etc.).

ciongsam (C) cheongsam.

cip I (*onom*) cheep, cheep. **mencip(-cip)** to cheep.

cip II (*E*) chip (in golf). **mencip** to chip. **cipan** a chip.

cipai k.o. leaf monkey, *Semnopithecus melalophos*; → SIMPAI II.

cipan I (*cla*) battle axe.

cipan II tapir, *Tapirus indicus*.

cipit → SIPIT.

ciplak I → JIPLAK.

ciplak II (*J*) chewing food in a noisy way, smacking. **menciplak** [and **nyiplak** (*coq*)] to chew food in a noisy way, smack.

ciplakan 1 to smack (one's lips). 2 to chew on s.t. in a noisy way.

cipluk (*Jv*) thick and fat, plump.

ciplukan → CÉPLUKAN.

cipoa I (*C*) abacus; → SWIPOA.

cipoa II (*C*?) 1 crooked, not straightforward, dishonest, swindling. 2 bullshit!, lies.

mencipoa to cheat s.o. *Lu dicipoa orang tua mau ajé, sialan lu!* (*J*) How is it possible that you were cheated by an old man, you're so unlucky!

cipoh common iora, *Aegithina tiphia*.

cipok (*coq*) kiss (with the lips).

bercipok to kiss e.o.

mencipok [and **nyipok** (*coq*)] to kiss. *Darni telah dicipok kakék-kakék di keréta api.* Darni was kissed by the old men in the train.

cipok-mencipok to kiss e.o.

mencipoki (*pl obj*) to kiss.

cipok(-cipok)an kissing e.o. *Sudah lazim anak-anak sekarang ~.* It's s.t. quite common for children nowadays to kiss e.o.

ciprat (*J/Jv*) – *ciprét* to spatter/splatter all over. *Airnya – ciprét.* The water splashed all over.

bercipratan to splash e.o.

menciprat [and **nyiprat** (*J*)] to splatter. *Air hujan nyiprat-nyiprat, aku kecipratan basah.* The rain water splattered and I got all wet.

menciprati [and **nyiprati** (*coq*)] to splash/spatter onto. *Kalau malamnya panas ~ mori, batikannya tidak baik.* If the hot wax spatters onto the cloth, the batik won't turn out well.

mencipratkan [and **nyipratkan** (*coq*)] to splash/spatter, sprinkle s.t. (onto). *Pastor ~ air suci pada anak yang dibaptis.* The priest sprinkled holy water on the child he was baptizing.

terciprat [and **kecipratan** (*coq*)] 1 to get spattered. 2 to be showered with. *~ bagian* to get one's share. 3 (*coq*) to get hooked into (a system). *belum ~ terang-benderang listrik PLN* (the village) has not yet been hooked up to the electric lighting system of the State Electricity Company.

cipratan splash, spatter, sprinkle.

pencipratan sprinkling.

cipta (*Skr*) 1 create, creative. *daya* – creative force/power imagination. *hak* – copyright. (*Diréktorat Jénderal*) – *Karya* (Directorate General of) Housing, Building, Planning, and Urban Development. 2 (concentration of) thought, idea, aspiration. *mengheningkan* – to meditate, purify one's thoughts, observe a moment's silence.

mencipta(kan) [and **nyiptain** (*J coq*)] 1 to conceive, create (by supernatural power). *Tuhan ~, langit dan bumi.* God created the heavens and the earth. 2 to make, produce. *~ lukisan yang bagus* to make a nice painting. 3 to devise, contrive, invent. 4 to compose, put together in literature/musical, etc. form. *Lagu kebangsaan Indonésia Raya diciptakan oléh Wagé Rudolf Supratman.* The national anthem "Indonesia Raya" was composed by Wage Rudolf Supratman. 5 to achieve, win. *Dia menciptakan rékor dunia.* He won the world record.

tercipta created, composed, etc.

ciptaan 1 creation, composition, make, invention. *~ péna* product of one's pen. *~ sastra* literary work. 2 composed, invented, created. *lagu klasik ~ komponis terkenal Beethoven* a classical melody composed by the famous composer Beethoven.

pencipta 1 creator, designer, maker. 2 composer, inventor. *Brahma ialah déwa ~.* Brahma was the god of creation. *~ mode* fashion designer. *~ lagu* composer. *~ pasar* market maker.

penciptaan creation, composition.

Cipuja name of a train running between Jakarta and Kroya.

Cipularang [Cikampék-Purwakarta-Padalarang] the toll road Cikampek-Purwakarta-Padalarang.

ciput I (*J*) small and round. *kondé* – a small and round hair bun.

ciput II 1 → SIPUT. 2 (*M*) penis.

ciput III k.o. head covering placed under a *jilbab*.

ciput IV → KECIPUT.

CIQ [Customs, Immigration and Quarantine]. *Di Halim prosés pemeriksaan – dilaksanakan penuh.* At Halim (Perdanakusuma International Airport, Jakarta) the CIQ-investigation procedures are fully implemented.

cir shame on you!

cirat (*Jv*) – *cirit* emerging little by little.

circir small bell.

circuit (*E*) /sir-/ → SIRKUIT.

Cirebon (frequently pronounced Cerbon) a port town in West Java; → CI, REBON I.

Cirebonan of Cirebon. *gaya* – style of Cirebon, Cirebon style.

ciri I (*Skr Jv*) 1 distinguishing/identification mark, hallmark. 2 characteristic, feature. *– wanci (lelai ginawa mati)* (*Jv*) defects and bad manners last forever, an incurable defect of character. *– khas* distinctive trait/characteristic feature, hallmark. *– gaya* style. *Monumén Nasional (Monas) merupakan – khas Jakarta.* The National Monument is the hallmark of Jakarta. **bercirikhaskan** with/to have distinctive features. *~ Islam itu* with distinctive Islamic features. **kecirikhasan** distinctiveness. *~ pengaman* security feature. *– pemusatan* centricity.

berciri to have the characteristic of.

bercirikan to be characterized by. *Dia Indonésia asli, namanya saja ~ kedaérahan.* She's a native Indonesian, only her name shows regional characteristics.

mencirikan and **mempercirikan** to characterize, mark, characteristic. *bau yang sangat ~* a very characteristic smell.

kecirian identifying characteristic.

penciri earmark.

pencirian characterizing, marking, differentiation.

ciri II (*Skr Mal*) the coronation formula used in certain Malaysian states.

cirit 1 excrement, feces, droppings. 2 sediment, dregs, grounds, waste. *– kopi* coffee grounds. 3 discharge (from any bodily orifice/nose/eye/ear). 4 diarrhea. *termakan (di) – berendang* (to be under the spell of black magic so that) one is fully dominated by s.o. else. *– bintang* meteorite, shooting star; → TAHI *bintang.* *– birit* bad diarrhea. *– kopi/madat/minyak* coffee/opium/oil dregs. *– mirit* a bad case of diarrhea.

mencirit to have/suffer from diarrhea.

menciritkan to discharge s.t., defecate s.t. *~ tunjang* (*M*) to give birth.

tercirit [and **kecirit** (*coq*)] discharged feces inadvertently; to have diarrhea.

cis I (exclamation showing feeling of hate/anger/dislike, etc.) (for) shame on you! *~ !, tak tahu malu!* Shame upon you; you're impudent/shameless! 2 (*Jv*) bah!

cis II *pistol/senjata* – (*coq*) a revolver/rifle using small pellets.

Cisemar name of a train running between Cirebon and Semarang.

cit I squeak (of mice), twitter (of birds).

cit II chintz.

cit III (*C*) to wipe, clean off.

cita I (*Skr*) 1 feeling(s) (mainly in compounds). *besar –* in ecstasy. *duka –* a) sorrow, grief, distress, sadness. b) condolence. *datang menyatakan duka – kepada* to condole with. *suka –* joy, gladness, pleasure. 2 (*cla*) concentration of thought; → CIPTA. 3 longing/yearning for; → CINTA. *– rasa* (good) taste. *bercita rasa tinggi* to be high class, have good taste.

cita-cita 1 ideal(s), aspirations. *Dunia mahasiswa adalah dunia yang penuh ~ dan harapan.* The world of college students is a world full of ideals and expectations. 2 wish, desire, ambition. **bercita-cita** 1 to desire, hope, expect, long. *bangsa yang ~ luhur* a nation with high hopes. 2 to have aspirations/ambitions, be ambitious. **bercita-citakan** *~ menjadi* to have ambitions to. *DKÉ, yang ~ menjadi Ibu Guru* DKE, who had ambitions to become a teacher. **mencita-citakan** 1 to hold as an ideal. 2 to long/yearn for. *yang (telah lama) dicita-citakan* what has been desired (for a long time). 3 to dream of s.t.

mencitakan to long for, want to.

cita (*Port from Hind*) II chintz, k.o. fabric. *– sayur* poor quality fabric.

citak (*ob*) → CÉTAK.

Citgwéé (*C*) (the month of) July.

citpé(k) (*C J*) seven hundred (rupiahs).

citra (*Skr*) likeness, portrait, image. *merusak – para petugas keséhatan* to damage the image of the health officials. *pembangunan –* image building. *– Allah* Imago Dei. *– bisnis* business image. *–*

dengaran auditory image. – *diri* self-image. – *kekuasaan* image of power. – *mérek* brand image. – *Panca Yudha Jaya* the military resort command (*Korém* 082) in Mojokerto. – *produk* product image. – *tubuh* body image. – *usaha* corporate image.

secitra in the image (of).

mencitrakan to project an image of s.o.

citraan imagery.

pencitra imager, imaging. *Radar ~ Surya* Solar Imaging Radar.

pencitraan 1 description. 2 image, imaging.

Citrajaya name of a train running between Jakarta and Kroya.

ciu I (*cla*) ceremonial sitting-mat of three layers with gold and silver decorations.

ciu II (C) an alcoholic beverage made of fermented rice; → BREM. – *bekonang* a traditional liquor. – *bumbon* a spiced alcoholic beverage.

ciu III – *besar* white-browed shrike-babbler, *Pteruthius flaviscapis*. – *kecil* chestnut-fronted shrike-babbler, *Pteruthius aenobarbus*.

cium 1 kiss (Javanese/Muslim style: placing nose on cheek and inhaling). 2 (nowadays also) a kiss with the lips. *daya* – (sense of) smell, olfactory organ, power of smell/scent. *Banténg sangat tajam daya –nya.* The wild buffalo has a very sharp power of smell. *kehilangan daya* – anosmia. *peluk – dari* (in correspondence) hugs and kisses from. – *maut* the kiss of death.

bercium(-cium)an to kiss e.o.

mencium [and **nyium** (*coq*)] 1 to kiss (as described above). *Orang Prancis, prianya mempunyai kebiasaan untuk ~ tangan wanita.* The French people, the men (among them), have the custom of kissing a woman's hand. 2 to smell, sniff. *~ bunga mawar* to smell a rose. 3 to get wind of s.t., sniff out s.t., sense, learn (of news/information, etc.). *~ adanya organisasi di bawah tanah* to sniff out a subversive organization. *~ perbuatan ini* to get wind (or, become aware) of this action. 4 to collide with, hit, bump against. *dicium mobil* to be hit/knocked down by a car. *~ jejak* to trace. *~ kabar* to get to hear. *~ tanah* to bite the dust, be killed (*esp* in a battle). *~ telapak kaki* to surrender. *Orang setua itu sudah ~ bau tanah.* Such an old man has one foot in the grave.

cium-mencium 1 kissing. 2 to kiss e.o.

menciumi [and **nyiumin** (*J coq*)] 1 (*pl obj*) to kiss. 2 to gather information about, find out about, make inquiries into; to investigate, detect.

menciumkan to have s.o. sniff s.t. *~ obat bius kepada si sakit itu* to have the patient sniff an anesthetic.

tercium 1 kissed inadvertently. 2 gotten wind of s.t., found out, learned about. *Rencana démo ini telah ~ petugas intélijén.* Intelligence agents got wind of these demonstration plans. **keterciuman** sense of smell.

ciuman 1 kiss, kissing. *Ada hikayat Injil Perjanjian Baru yang berkisah tentang ~ Yudas Iskariot.* In the New Testament there is a Biblical story that tells about Judas Iscariot's kiss. *~ pergaulan* social kissing. *~ Prancis* French/tongue kissing. 2 sniffing. 3 collision. *~ maut* kiss of death.

pencium (sense of) smell, olfactory organ.

penciuman 1 sense of smell. *Tajam ~nya.* He has a good nose for. 2 (the act of) smelling/kissing, sniffing out.

ciung – *air* gray-cheeked tit babbler, *Macronous flavicollis*.

Ciung Wanara (S) by the Sundanese considered the founding father (= *cikal bakal*) of their former kings.

ciup → CIUT II.

ciut I (*J*) 1 narrow. 2 shrunk, shortened, contracted. 3 (*hati* –) frightened. *Melihat delapan mobil pemadam api kebakaran dan dua ambulans "siap tempur" di seputar landasan terbang, hati ini rasanya – juga.* Upon seeing eight fire trucks and two ambulance cars "combat ready" around the runway, I became rather frightened. – *hati* discouraged.

berciut and **menciut** 1 to become narrow, tighten; to decrease, become less and less, shrink (of cloth, etc.). *Dana yang tersedia semakin ~.* Available funds are increasingly decreasing. *Hatinya ~ mendengar bentakan itu.* His heart shrank when he heard the crash. 2 to become despondent/dejected.

menciutkan to limit s.t., narrow down s.t., make s.t. smaller. *~ matanya* to squeeze one's eyes closed. *~ nyali lawan* to make an opponent pull back.

keciutan 1 narrowness. 2 contraction.

penciutan 1 shrinkage, becoming smaller/fewer/less, reduction. *~ krédit* credit contraction *~ luas* shrinkage of an area. 2 austerity. 3 damping.

ciut II (*onom*) squeak, creak (noise when opening a door, rubbing two things together, etc.).

berciut-ciut and **menciut-ciut** to squeak, creak.

ciutan squeak(ing), creak(ing).

civic mission (E) /sivik misyen/ civic mission.

mencivicmissionkan to use for civic mission purposes.

civitas (L) /si-/ → SIVITAS. – *académia* community of scholars.

ck(k), ck(k), ck(k) sound of clucking tongue *usu* showing disapproval, tsk, tsk, tsk!

claim (E) /klém/ claim.

menclaim to make a claim.

clamit(an) (*Jv*) greedy, grasping.

clash (E) /klés/ – I/II the first/second police action; → KLÉS II. *Waktu – II saya berada di Kediri.* During the Second Police Action I was in Kediri.

cleguk (*Jv onom*) gulp(ing). *clegak.* – to down s.t. in a series of gulps.

clemang → CLEMONG. – *clemong* to keep on blurting s.t. out. *Keduanya mengaku – clemong saja ketika diperiksa polisi karena tak tahan menanggung siksaan.* Both of them admitted that they blurted things out when they were questioned by the police because they couldn't stand the torture.

clemong (*Jv*) to blurt s.t. out.

nylemong to blurt s.t. out.

clemongan s.t. blurted out.

clérét (*Jv*) – *gombé1* flying lizard; → CICAK *terbang*. – *tahun* whirlwind, tornado, cyclone; → ANGIN *puyuh*. *Lebih kurang 48 rumah rusak berat dan ringan serta ratusan pohon tumbang akibat – tahun.* About 48 houses were heavily and slightly damaged and also hundreds of trees were toppled as a result of a hurricane.

clila-clili (*Jv*) to look about shyly.

climén (*Jv*) on a small scale, with little fanfare, simple (not elaborate, of a feast). *Perkawinan Anne cuma – saja.* Anne's wedding was very simple.

clingak-clinguk (*Jv*) 1 astonished, amazed, dumbfounded, bewildered, puzzled. 2 to look around everywhere (searching for s.t. or s.o., as though one has lost s.t.). *Malam itu juga penduduk berduyun membantu polisi mencari Suyanti, dan Suparno ikut –.* That night the residents helped the police look for Suyanti, and Suparno also looked around.

clingkrak-clingkrik (*Jv*) 1 again and again kicking upstairs. 2 up and down.

clingus (*Jv*) bashful (about being seen), shy, timid; → PEMALU.

clola-clolo (*Jv*) distraught.

clonéh (*Jv*) *pating* – parti-colored, varicolored, of various colors.

clométan (*Jv*) to make a lot of noise but no sense.

clorot → CEROROT.

clurit (*Mad*) a small Madurese sickle-shaped knife. *bersenjata* – and **berclurit** to be armed with a *clurit*.

clutak (*Jv*) always getting at the food, always sticking one's nose into other people's business.

co and **co' I** clipped form of COWOK.

CO II [céwék orderan] call girl.

coaching (E *coq*) /kocing/ directions given by a superior to an inferior on how to behave or how to improve performance, etc.

mencoaching to give such directions.

coak (*J*) **mencoaki** to tear up, shred.

coakan s.t. torn, shred. *~ piston* a cut made in the top of a racing-cycle piston to make it lighter.

coan (C) profit, gain, advantage.

coang I (*M*) **bercoang(an)** and **mencoang** to stick/point up all over (as of spears), protrude, stick out, stick up, rise up. *Dari jauh tampak mercu suar – ke langit.* From afar the lighthouse could be seen rising up to the sky.

mencoangkan to extend/stick/point s.t. up, offer s.t., hold s.t. up.

tercoang extended/sticking/pointing up.

coang II (*M*) **mencoang-coang** to walk up and down without any definite destination or specific intention.

Coast Guard (*E*) rescuers of drowning persons in the Taman *Impian Jaya Ancol* in Jakarta.

cob (in acronyms) → PERCOBAAN.

coba 1 (to get s.o.'s attention) hey, say. *– apakah ini baik?* Hey, is this O.K.? *E, – rasanya.* Here, take a taste. **2** to (do s.t.) and see what happens, let (me). *– saya tanyakan dia dulu ya.* Let me ask him first (and see what he says). **3** please; → HARAPLAH, HENDAKLAH, SILAKAN. *– ambilkan buku itu.* Get that book (for me), please. *– kalau* assuming/supposing that ... *– kalau abangnya ada di situ* supposing that his brother was there *– dan salah* trial and error. *– ribut* make a fuss. **mencobaributkan** to make a fuss about s.t. *Budayawan Y.B.M. mengatakan bahwa soal séks adalah soal yang alamiah, masalah sehari-hari yang biasa. Tapi selalu saja ingin dicobaributkan.* Culture-bearer Y.B.M. said that sex is s.t. natural, a common everyday matter. But people always like to make a fuss about it. *– trobos* attempted smuggling. **mencoba-troboskan** to try to smuggle s.t. into the country. **4** (*sl*) believe it or not, can you believe it.

coba-coba experimental, pilot, on a trial basis; to give s.t. a try. *produksi ~* experimental/pilot production, production on a trial basis. *Ia hanya ~ memperbaiki tapi sebenarnya tidak bisa.* He's doing what he can to repair it, but actually he doesn't know how. *Jangan ~, ya.* Don't even think about it.

mencoba [and **nyoba** (*coq*)] **1** to try (out), test. *Setelah terjadi transaksi jual beli, maka lelaki itu kemudian minta untuk ~ mobil di jalan umum.* After the sales transaction was concluded, the gentleman made a test-drive over public roads. **2** to taste, take a taste of (food/drinks, etc.). *Sop buntut itu dicobanya.* She tasted the oxtail soup. **3** to try on. *~ jas baru* to try on the new coat. **4** to try to do/carry out s.t. *Tahanan itu ~ melarikan diri.* The detainee tried to escape. *~ dan salah* and *~ dan mencoba lagi* trial and error.

mencoba-coba to make an attempt to.

mencobai 1 to (put to the) test, try (out). **2** (*pl obj*) to try repeatedly.

mencobakan [and **nyobain** (*J coq*)] **1** to try s.o. out, test on s.o. *Ia ~ ketrampilannya.* He tried out his skill. **2** to try s.t. on s.o. *Soal-soal ini bisa kita cobakan kepada anak-anak yang hendak menempuh ujian.* We can try them on kids who are going to take the exam.

tercoba tried, tested.

cobaan 1 test, examination. **2** experiment, (clinical) trial. **3** trial, difficult time that must be passed through, ordeal. *Kita mengalami banyak ujian dan ~.* We are undergoing many tests and trials.

pencoba 1 examiner. **2** experimenter.

pencobaan (the act of) trying (out), testing. *~ mesin baru* testing of a new engine.

percobaan 1 test. *anjing ~* test dog. *kelinci ~* guinea pig. *~ asam* acid test. *~ beban* a) load test. b) severe test. **2** trial, experiment. *balai ~* experimental/research station. *kebun ~* experimental garden. *pelayaran ~* and (less frequent) *~ berlayar* trial run (of a frigate/ship, etc.). **3** specimen. *nomor ~* specimen copy (of a magazine). **4** attempt. *~ membunuh* and *~ pembunuhan* attempted murder. **5** proof. *~ cétak halaman* page proof.

cobak (*coq*) → COBA.

cobak-cabik torn into shreds/ribbons in tatters.

coban a needle of horn/bamboo used in embroidery, sail making, making or mending fishing nets, etc.

cobar-cabir in rags, tattered and torn, torn everywhere; → CABIR.

cobék I (*Jv*) earthenware bowl (in the shape of a saucer) used for grinding/crushing spices; → CUIK I.

cobék II torn; to tear, shatter, tatter; → SOBÉK.

cobék-cobék torn, shattered, tattered.

mencobék to tear.

coblong (*J*) with a hole in it, perforated.

bercoblong with holes in it.

mencoblongi to make a hole in s.t.

coblongan hole made in s.t.

coblos (*J/Jv*) **mencoblos** [and **nyoblos** (*coq*)] **1** perforate. **2** to vote for s.o. (by perforating an election symbol).

tercoblos perforated. *~ peluru* riddled with bullets.

coblosan general elections (by perforating an election symbol); → PEMILIHAN *umum*, PEMILU.

pencoblos [and **penyoblos** (*coq*] such a voter.

pencoblosan [and **penyoblosan** (*coq*)] voting (in the above way). *~ tanda-gambar* voting by perforating an election symbol.

Coca Cola /koka kola/ Coca Cola.

cocak(rawa) (*Jv*) → CUCAK *rawa*.

cocang (*C? J*) braid (of hair).

cocok I 1 a sharp object used to pierce, pin, prick (such as a needle/skewer, etc.); → CUCUK I. **2** classifier for things strung/fastened together by means of a pin/skewer, etc. *saté empat –* four skewers of satay; → SUJÉN I, TUSUK. *– hidung/keluan* (*M*) nose-band, ring put through the nose of a cow/buffalo. *– kondai/sanggul* hairpin. *– tanam* farming. **mencocok tanam** to farm, be a farmer.

bercocok to wear a hairpin.

mencocok [and **menyocok** (*coq*)] **1** to pierce, thread (needle), stab, prick, make a hole, etc. with a sharp object, puncture. *~ mata* to put out s.o.'s eyes. **2** to put a ring through the nose of a cow/buffalo. **3** to join/string together by piercing. *~ kajang* to make a mat. **4** to poke (with a sharp object).

mencocok-cocok perut *~* stinging pain in the stomach.

mencocoki (*pl obj*) to put holes in.

mencocokkan and **menyocokkan** to pierce, prick, stab, thread, pin s.t.

tercocok pierced, stabbed, pricked, stuck, threaded. *~ hidung/mata* (*M*) cheated (e.g., to buy s.t. worn out at a high price).

cocokan implant.

pencocok 1 skewer. **2** electric light plug.

cocok II (*Jv*) /cocok/ **1** similar, identical, in accord; to agree, tally, jibe. *Keterangan Pemerintah – dengan keadaan yang sebenarnya.* The government's Statement (of Policy) is in accord with the real situation. *Pendapat saudara – dengan pendapat saya.* Your opinion is similar to mine. **2** correct, right, precise, exact, fitting. *Arloji saya tidak –.* My watch doesn't keep good time. **3** to appeal strongly to, to be to one's taste, suit. *Kalau –, boléh anda beli.* If you like it, you can buy it. **4** to be effective, have an effect, produce the desired results (as of medicine, etc.). *Obat ini sudah diminumnya, tetapi tidak –.* He has already taken this medicine, but it has had no effect. **5** to agree, have an understanding between/among. *Kita semua – untuk mengemukakan keberatan kepada yang berwajib.* There is an understanding among all of us to propose the objections to the proper authorities. **6** to fit, be suited, suitable, serve/fulfill the purpose, lend itself to the purpose, go well (with s.t.). *Perkataannya – dengan perbuatannya.* His words fit his deeds. *Kunci ini – dengan lemariku.* This key fits my cupboard. *Tanah itu – tidak untuk tanaman tembakau.* The soil is not suitable for growing tobacco. *Rumah ini – sekali untuk rumah makan.* This house lends itself very much to a restaurant. **7** in proportion (with). *Hadiah sebanyak itu sudah – dengan jasanya.* Such a large gift is in proportion with his services. *– dengan ukuran cita* to come up to. **8** to come true. *Ramalannya –.* His prediction came true. **9** to get along well (of people). *tidak –* not fitting, unsuitable, disparate, incompatible. **ketidak-kecocokan** mismatch, lack of fit, unsuitability, disparity, incompatibility.

secocok (*Mal*) fitting, appropriate.

mencocoki to agree to.

mencocokkan [and **nyocokin** (*J coq*)] **1** to set right, correct. **2** to compare, check (out), match up, check (against), verify. **3** to set, adjust (a watch). *~ diri* to adjust o.s. (to s.t.). **4** to harmonize. **5** to stick s.t. (into s.t.).

tercocok adapted, in accord.

kecocokan 1 agreement, consensus, concord, like-mindedness, harmony. **2** suitability, fit, conformity.

pencocokan verification, proof. *~ jangka panjang* long-run proof. *~ kurva* (*math*) curve matching. *~ silang* cross-reference.

cocol I (*J*) **mencocol** to dip (a pen in ink/finger in water, etc.), **mencocolkan** to dip.

cocol II **mencocol** to stick (out), protrude, project.

coco méo and **cocomeo 1** the downtrodden. **2** mild, friendly teasing insult.

cocor I mencocor ~ *bola* to lift up a ball with the tip of the toe/shoe.

cocor II (*Jv*) 1 bill, beak. 2 (of aircraft) nose. *Baling-baling tunggal ukuran 2,08 méter di – pesawat berwarna biru kelabu, memutar seperti mengebor udara.* The 2.08-meter single propeller at the nose of the blue-and-gray-colored aircraft rotated as if it were drilling the sky. *(si) – mérah* the Mustang P-51 Dutch fighter plane used in combating Indonesian freedom fighters around 1947. *– mérah* prostitute.

   mencocor 1 to peck (with the beak). 2 to kick (a ball) with the tip of the foot.

cocor III *– bébék* k.o. decorative plant, *Kalanchoe spp.*

cocot (*J/Jv*) 1 beak, bill. 2 (*vulg*) mouth.

codak mencodak to pick up one's head (of a snake/swimmer, etc.), lift up s.t.

   mencodakkan to hold s.t. up (head, etc.), hold the head aloft.

   tercodak lifted up.

codang → CODAK.

codét (*J*) marks (of cuts/bruises) on the face, forehead, etc.

codot (*J/Jv*) 1 various species of fruit bat, *Cynopterus spp. – punggung gundul* naked-backed fruit bat, *Aethalops alecto.* 2 various species of dawn bat, *Eonycteris spp.* and other species. 3 scoundrel, villain.

coék → COBÉK I, CUIK I.

coél (*J*) → CUIL I. mencoél [and nyoél (*coq*)] 1 to touch slightly with the tip of a finger. 2 to warn, reprimand.

   kecoél (*coq*) 1 touched slightly with the tip of a finger. 2 reprimanded.

cogah (*M*) 1 strong, robust, vigorous, muscular. 2 chic, smart (of dress). 3 rich.

cogan (*Pers*) (State) emblem (flag, spear), symbol, sign. *– alam* (*cla*) trowel-shaped royal spear with gold trimmings at the edges. *– kata* slogan, motto.

cogok I tercogok be upright, erect; → CONGGOK.

cogok II mencogok 1 to be born, see the light of day, come into the world. 2 to crop up, arise, show up, loom into sight. *Dia ~ lagi di pasar itu dan langsung dicokok polisi.* He showed up again in the market and was immediately arrested by the police. *Mempelai pria yang ditunggu-tunggu tidak ~.* The groom whom they were waiting for didn't show up.

coin (*E*) /koin/ coin.

cok I (in acronyms) → PENCOCOKAN.

cok II (*E*) chock.

cokar game played on a boat-shaped board with ten small holes and two large holes at the end; sometimes cowry shells are used in this game; → CONGKAK II.

cokék (*C? J*) a traditional dance of the Tangerang area, accompanied by *gambang keromong.*

cokél (*Jv*) → CONGKÉL. mencokél 1 to dig or gouge (out). 2 to pick.

cokelat → COKLAT.

cokér I (*Jv*) mencokér to peck around for food.

cokér II [cowok kerén/Kristen] name of a gang in Ambon.

cokét mencokét to take a little of s.t., take/break off a small piece of s.t.

cokin (*Pr*) (a slur for) Indonesian-born Chinese; → CINA.

coklat (*D*) 1 *pohon –* cacao tree, *Theobroma cacao,* whose seeds are made into a powder. 2 chocolate, a drink made by adding sugar and milk/hot water to the above powder. 3 chocolate, sweet substance made with cocoa powder, sugar, etc. 4 chocolate, a reddish-yellow brown color. *Gadis itu mengenakan seragam – dengan pét putih.* The girl was wearing a reddish-yellow uniform with white cap. *– betas* sugared caraway seeds (to be sprinkled on bread). *– sampang* rosewood (in color). *– susu* milk chocolate. *– tembakau* snuff brown.

   secoklat as brown as.

   mencoklat to become brown.

   mencoklati and mencoklatkan to make s.t. brown, darken.

   kecoklatan cacao (*mod*). *Tingkat ~nya sempurna dan aromanya pun bagus.* The cacao level is perfect and the aroma is also good.

   kecoklat-coklatan brownish.

cokmar (*Pers cla*) war-club, mace (that was hurled).

coko (*Jv*) k.o. children's game; PANJAT *pinang.*

cokok I (*M*) mencokok to seize, apprehend, take into custody, arrest, capture, catch, etc. *Dua hari setelah kejadian, delapan tersangka pelaku dapat dicokok.* Two days after the incident, eight suspects were taken into custody.

cokok II cries/shrieks of a hysterical person when excited; → LATAH.

cokol (*J*) bercokol 1 to sit/squat together in a group. 2 to live (in), infest (a place of criminals, etc.). 3 implanted, ensconced, lodged. *kepentingan ~* vested interest.

   mencokol to occupy a place.

   mencokoli (*pl obj*) to occupy a place.

   mencokolkan to put s.t. down (somewhere).

cokola (*ob*) chocolate.

cokor (*J/Jv*) paw, claw.

   nyokor 1 to go barefoot. 2 to eat with the fingers.

Cokorda and Cokordé (*Bal*) a caste-marking title placed before personal names to indicate that the person who bears this title belongs to the Kshatriyas, e.g., *Ida – Gdé Mayun.*

cokot (*Jv*) → CAKOT. mencokot [and nyokot (*coq*)] 1 to bite. 2 to drag s.o. in, involve.

   cokotan a bite of s.t.

cokrém [cowok krémpéng] a skinny guy. *Idola remaja Jakarta: – ternyata bukan pria yang tinggi dan segar jasmani.* The ideal of the Jakarta teens: a skinny guy and not a physically fit and tall man.

cokri (*Pr*) woman, girl; → CÉWÉK.

cokromanggilingan (*Jv*) (the world goes) as a mill wheel does (it has its ups and downs).

col (*Jv*) not proportionally divided.

cola-cala and cola-colo (*ob*) to talk nonsense, engage in small talk.

colak *pohon –* k.o. tree which produces an acid toxic to fish, *Callicarpa maingayi.*

colak-calik (*Jv*) 1 to make frequent one-day excursions. 2 shuttle service.

colak-caling (*ob*) in disorder, confused, entangled.

colak-colék (*J*) to touch repeatedly with the fingertips. *main –* to paw a girl/woman by touching her with the fingertips.

colang-caling → COLAK-CALING.

colék I a lick.

   secolék a small piece taken of s.t., an amount that is touched or taken (with the finger tips).

   mencolék 1 to pick out s.t. with a pin or the tip of a finger (such as pomade with a fingertip/lime for a betel squid), touch slightly. *dituduh ~ pantat seorang wanita* to be accused of slightly touching a woman's behind. 2 to pick at. *~ tahi telinga dengan korék telinga* to pick at one's earwax with an ear pick. 3 to scratch, strike. *~ gérétan* to strike a match. 4 to tap s.o. on the shoulder to attract his/her attention.

   mencolékkan to touch, etc. with s.t., press s.t. (into s.t.), put s.t. (onto s.t.).

   tercolék [and kecolék (*coq*)] touched, affected. *Rata-rata udara Lawang yang sejuk dan bersih cocok untuk orang berumur, apalagi yang kondisi jasmaninya sering ~ penyakit.* On the average the air of Lawang is cool and clean, correct for the aged, above all for those whose physical conditions are frequently affected by complaints/illnesses.

   colékan touch (with the tip of the finger).

   pencolék 1 s.t. used for picking up. 2 s.o. who touch.

   pencolékan picking out, touching.

colék II (*M*) mencolék to instigate, provoke, incite.

colén a small lamp.

coléng (*J*) mencoléng to steal.

   pencoléng thief. *~ mobil diringkus polisi.* The police apprehended the car thief.

   pencoléngan theft, stealing.

colét → COLÉK I.

coli I (*Hind ob*) k.o. breast covering or bra; → BÉHA.

coli II (*sl vulg*) to masturbate, jerk off.

   mencoli(kan) [and nyoliin (*J coq*)] to masturbate s.o., rub (a part of the body) in a sexual way.

colok I 1 *lampu –* torch, made of a piece of twisted cloth dipped in oil (used as a light). 2 a palm-leaf rib provided with resin/damar or sulfur to function as a light or to replace a match, etc. **3** white stripes on the tail of a black dog.

menyolok [and **menyolok/nyolok** (*coq*)] to light up, illuminate.

mencoloki to illuminate with a torch, etc.

colok II (*M*) → CELUP. *jatuh/turun –nya* in reduced circumstances, went downhill, come down in the world.

mencolok 1 to dip s.t. (into a liquid), immerse (in a liquid). **2** to dye, color *usu* by dipping in a liquid.

colok III (*J*) → COBLOS. – *mata* cynosure, center of attention.

mencolok [and **nyolok** (*coq*)] **1** eye-catching, striking, conspicuous, obvious. *dengan tidak ~ (mata)* unobtrusively. **2** offensive, shocking, annoying, irritating, provoking. **3** to stick s.t. into. ~ *mata* to stick s.t. into s.o.'s eye. **4** to vote for. ~ *tanda gambar* to vote for s.o. by perforating an election symbol; → MENCOBLOS.

kecolok 1 gotten stuck in the eye. *Matanya ~.* He got poked in the eye. **2** s.t. caught one's eye. *Matanya ~ tape recorder.* The tape recorder caught her eye.

tercolok perforated.

kecolokan conspicuousness.

colok IV (*Jv*) **mencolokkan** to plug in, connect, hook up. ~ *kabel adaptor ke stopkontak* to plug the adapter cable into the socket.

colokan (electric) plug. *kabel-kabel listrik yang lengkap dengan ~nya* electric cables complete with their plugs.

colong (*J/Jv*) steal; → CURI. *tinggal gelanggang – playu* (*Jv*) to leave the arena irresponsibly and go on the run.

colong-colong stealthily, clandestinely.

mencolong [and **nyolong** (*coq*)] to steal. *nyolong peték* (*Jv*) to belie/disprove the prediction, turn out differently from what was expected, have a deceptive appearance. *Canada bersedia tetap dalam ICCS sampai tanggal 31 Méi. Eh, ~ peték alias di luar dugaan.* Canada is prepared to remain in the ICCS until May 31. Eh, this is contrary to expectations. *nyolong waktu* to get away (in a hurry).

colong-menyolong theft. ~ *sepéda sudah merupakan hal yang normal.* Bicycle thefts have already become s.t. usual.

nyolongin (*J coq pl obj*) to steal.

colongan stolen. *sepéda motor ~* a stolen motorcycle.

colong-colongan to steal things right and left. *orang main ~ ceritera* people commit plagiarism left and right.

kecolongan robbed, stolen. *Oriéntasi Program Studi dan Pengenalan Kampus ini disusun ketat, sehingga kemungkinan ~ dari unsur négatif dapat terhindar.* This Orientation Program on Study and Getting Acquainted with the Campus has been drafted rigidly, so that the possibility that it was stolen from negative elements could be avoided.

pencolongan theft, stealing.

colot (*J/Jv*) **mencolot** to leap, jump up (like frogs).

nyolot (*sl*) angry, upset.

Colt /kol/ a small Japanese-made Mitsubishi suburban bus.

berkolt to use a Colt.

coma /ko-/ → KOMA.

comat-comot to jostle/elbow e.o.

combér (*Jv*) **kecombéran 1** open sewage ditch. **2** basin for household waste water.

(pe)combéran 1 (drainage) ditch, drain, sewer. **2** cesspool; septic tank.

combi (*G*) /kombi/ station wagon. *sebuah mobil – VW* a Volkswagen station wagon.

comblang (*C J*) **1** *mak* – go-between, matchmaker (for matching marriage partners). **2** pimp, procurer, pander; → JOMBLANG, MUNCIKARI. **3** go-between, intermediary, middleman. *Negara itu, yang ékonominya dan keberadaannya sangat bergantung pada Amérika Serikat, tak bisa menolak tekanan Mak –.* That country, whose economy and existence is most dependent on the United States of America, cannot refuse the pressure of its Go-Between.

mencomblang to act as a go-between/procurer.

mencomblangi [and **nyomblangin** (*J coq*)] **1** to act as a middleman/procurer for, fix s.o. up with s.o. (on a date, etc.). *kakak dan teman yang dulu ~ kami* an older brother and friend who formerly acted as our procurer. **2** to act as a middleman for/in. *Boléh dikatakan bahwa Amérika Serikat yang ~ pertemuan ini sebagai*

bagian dari stratégi menyusun "tata dunia barunya". It can be said that it was the U.S.A. that acted as a middleman in this meeting as part of its strategy to arrange a "new world order."

percomblangan matchmaker (*mod*).

combol (*ob*) doorknob; → TOMBOL.

combong (*J*) a small kris (with a perforation in the blade as an amulet).

combor (*Jv*) horse feed: grass, rice bran, and rice husks mixed with water.

combro(k) (*J*) k.o. food made of cassava filled with *oncom. tukang* – person who produces or sells this food.

comék I (*J*) hairs that grow between the chin and lower lip (an imperial beard).

comék II a small cuttlefish, squid, *Loligo spp.*

comél I dainty, pretty, attractive. – *cantik* extremely beautiful.

comél II (*J*) **1** grumbling, nagging, grousing. **2** grumbler, grouser.

mencomél to grumble, nag, grouse. *Anak itu masuk ke kamarnya sambil ~ tak keruan.* The child went into his room grumbling terribly.

mencoméli to grumble at, scold, reprimand. *Sang suami dicoméli istrinya terus-menerus.* The husband was scolded by his wife without stop.

comélan scolding, reprimand.

kecomélan to be reprimanded.

pencomél grumbler, grouser.

pencomélan grumbling, nagging.

Commanders Call (*E*) /ko-/ the meeting of commanders of *Kodam, Kodak,* etc.; → RAPAT *Komandan.*

Comanditaire Vennootschap (*D*) /komanditére fenotskap/ a firm including one or several partners whose liabilities go only as far as the amount of capital they have put into the company, while the managing partner(s) remain(s) fully responsible for the firm's liabilities; → CV.

comor → COMOT I.

Comoro air base in Dili (in the former Timor Timur).

comot I – (*momot*) stained, soiled, smeared, grimy, dirty (of one's face/body, etc.).

bercomot to be dirty, grimy, smeared.

comot II (*J*) **secomot** a little bit. ~ *senyum* a trace of a smile.

mencomot 1 to take s.t. between the fingertips (said of s.t. granular, such as, rice kernels/sand, etc.). **2** to take into custody, nab, arrest, catch (a criminal). *Penjahat itu dicomot oléh polisi.* The criminal was arrested by the police. **3** to pick up, grab, snatch. *Pemerintah Afganistan mulai memaksa pelajar sekolah menengah atas untuk menjadi tentara. Bahkan terkadang ~ saja para pemuda itu dari jalan-jalan.* The Afghani government has begun to force senior high school students to become soldiers. In fact, once in a while the students are just grabbed off the streets.

nyomot (*coq*) to shoplift; → MENGUTIL. ~ *tas di toko "Dickens & Jones, Ltd."* to shoplift a handbag at "Dickens & Jones, Ltd."

mencomoti (*pl obj*) to grab, steal, etc.

mencomotkan (*sl*) to steal s.t.

comotan 1 theft. **2** stolen. *hasil ~* loot.

pencomotan picking (up), grabbing.

compang-camping/-compéng torn, in rags/tatters (of a garment), frayed (at the edges).

compéng frayed at the edges.

compés chipped, jagged (at the edge) (of a plate/knife, etc.).

compo /kompo/ → KOMPONÉN.

compoh (*C*) cook (on a ship).

compréng compréngan (*Jv*) (in Indramayu, Cirebon) a small fishing boat with sail, about 10 meters long and 2 meters wide. *Sejak berumur 10 tahun ia mengikuti jejak orangtuanya melaut dengan ~.* Since the age of 10 he has been following in his parents' footsteps going to sea in a *compréng.*

comro (in West Java) k.o. cake made of cassava.

concong (*ob*) **menconcong** to walk straight ahead without looking to the left or right.

conderong → CENDERUNG.

Condét area in the Greater Jakarta Special Capital Region; almost all the residents are native-born *orang* Betawi; it's a large salak-producing area and cultural preserve.

condong 1 sloping, slanting, tilted; → CENDERUNG. *Tiangnya – sedikit.* The pole is somewhat slanting. **2** slightly crazy. *pikiran – crazy. – ingatan* slightly crazy. *– mondong* all aslant (of pillars, trees). **3** to set, sink, go down (of the sun). *Matahari – ke barat.* The sun sets in the west. *hatinya – (ke)pada* to be inclined to one party, in favor of, take s.o.'s side. **4** (M) to trim one's sails to every wind. **5** tendency.
  mencondongkan 1 to bend, lean. *~ badan ke depan* to bend/lean forward, stoop. **2** to incline, tend. *~ kepada* to favor, **3** to show affection for.
  tercondong inclined. *~ balik* reclined.
  kecondongan 1 tendency, penchant. **2** inclination, leaning. **3** bias.
condrong → CENDERUNG.
Conéfo /ko-/ [Conference of the New Emerging Forces] /ko-/ President Soekarno's concept of a rival organization to the UN.
conét menconét pointed and upturning (as a mustache).
cong (Madura and East Java) vocative for a child.
congak I bercongakan (*pl subj*) to stick up.
  mencongak 1 to raise head and chin (as buffaloes do when they sense danger), look upward (of a startled animal/swimmer). **2** to stick out, protrude. *Tonggak ~ sedikit di atas air.* The pole stuck out a little above the water.
  mencongakkan to lift up, raise. *~ kepala* to lift/raise one's head, tilt up s.o.'s head.
congak II (*J*) **mencongak** to do mental arithmetic.
congcong I telescope snail, *Telescopium telescopium.*
congcong II (*J*) **mencongcong** to pierce, penetrate.
  kecongcong pierced, penetrated.
congcorang (*J*) k.o. grasshopper, "flying leaf."
congéh open, gaping (of wound).
  mencongéh and **tercongéh** open, gaping.
congék (*J*) **1** pus running from the ear; → KOPOK II. **2** (*rude*) deaf. *penyakit –* middle-ear infection, *Otitis media.*
conggah → CONGKAH.
conggét tergonggét-conggét bobbing/moving up and down (as a wagging tail).
conggok erect, upright (of one's head); → CONGOK.
  mencongok to stand or sit upright.
  mencongokkan to put upright.
  tercongok pointing upward, erected.
congkah to stick out (aslant). *– cangkih* to stick out in all directions, project spikily (as branches of trees), jagged. *– mangkih* not properly piled up or arranged.
congkak I proud, conceited, arrogant. *– bongkak* very arrogant. *– dan ria* arrogant and haughty.
  mencongkak to stick one's nose up in the air arrogantly.
  mencongkakkan to stick s.t. up (arrogantly).
  kecongkakan pride, arrogance, conceit. *~ kekuasaan* arrogance of power.
congkak II 1 cowry-shells used in playing the game mentioned below. **2** a game for girls called by this name in Sumatra and *dakon* in Java, popular throughout Indonesia. It consists of a *papan –,* i.e., a boat-like wooden board with a large hole at each end (= *rumah*). On both sides of this board are five, seven, or nine smaller holes. Each hole is filled with seven beans, pebbles, or cowry-shells, the so-called *buah –.*
congkang → JONGKANG.
congkar-cangkir projecting spikily.
congkék (*Jv*) *– GAYA II. memperkenalkan – (gaya) sindén Widuwati Nyi Tjondrolukito* to introduce the style of the singer Widuwati Nyi Tjondrolukito.
congkél mencongkél to pick (a lock), open with a lock pick. *Mobil yang parkir di halaman Hotél Angkasa dicongkél pintunya.* The door of the car parked in the lot of the Hotel Angkasa was forced open.
  congkél-mencongkél to remove, take off. *~ dop mobil* removing hubcaps with an extractor (i.e., to steal them).
  mencongkéli (*pl obj*) to remove.
  pencongkél s.o. who removes s.t.
  pencongkélan removing, taking off.
congkelang → CONGKLANG.
congki I (*C*) a game similar to chess.
congki II (*Pr*) key.

congklak → CONGKAK II.
congklang (*J onom*) sound of galloping.
  mencongklang to gallop, canter swiftly/fast.
  mencongklangkan to make s.t. gallop, gallop.
congkok I (*J*) cover, lid.
congkok II (*J*) to squat; → JONGKOK I.
congkok III *macan –* golden cat.
congkong I (*M*) **mencongkong** to squat.
congkong II (*M*) sentry box.
congkong III wood chip.
congkrah (*Jv*) to quarrel.
congo(k) (*J*) pickpocket, petty thief.
congok mencongok (to sit or stand) erect, upright; → CONGGOK.
  mencongokkan to erect, pull s.t. up.
congol (*J*) **mencongol** to protrude, stick out.
congor (*J/Jv*) **1** snout, muzzle. **2** cowcatcher (of a locomotive). *Tampaknya – lokomotif yang ditabrak, sehingga loko tergésér arahnya dan keluar rél.* It seems that the locomotive's cowcatcher was hit, so that the locomotive was pushed to the side and derailed.
congsam (*C*) cheongsam, a type of slim-fitting dress with a high collar and side slits worn by Chinese women.
congti, Cong Tifu and **Cong Tipu** (in the Tanjungpriok port area, Jakarta) **1** thieves and small-fry Mafia-type thugs. **2** request for or collection of money under duress.
conték cheat on exams.
  contékan crib sheet (for cheating on exams).
conténg scrawl, scribble, doodle; smear, stain, blemish. *– moréng* all smeared.
  berconténg-conténg scrawled, scribbled; smeared, smudged, smirched, soiled.
  menconténg(-conténg) to soil, dirty, smear, daub, scrawl, scribble.
  menconténgkan to streak/scrape s.t. (on).
  terconténg smudged, blotted, soiled; scrawled, defamed, besmirched, disgraced. *~ arang* disgraced s.o.
  conténgan scrawl, scribble.
conto → CONTOH.
contoh 1 sample, specimen. *tidak cocok dengan –nya* not corresponding to the sample. **2** model. *Guru membuat – di papan tulis.* The teacher made a model on the blackboard. **3** pattern. *Dalam majalah wanita selalu dimuat –.* – *menggunting baju.* Women's magazines always carry dress-making patterns. **4** mock-up, model. **5** example, instance. *mengambil – dari* to imitate, follow the example of. *sebagai –* for example/instance. *menanam –* to set/show give a good example. *– acak* random sample. *– buang air stool* specimen. *– cacat* defective sample. *– inti* core sample. *– sembarangan* random sample. *– tanah* soil sample.
contohnya for example/instance.
mencontoh [and **nyontoh** (*coq*)] **1** to copy, imitate, follow. **2** to be modeled/patterned after. *dicontoh dari* on the model of. **3** to exemplify.
mencontohi to follow the example of, do s.t. by following an example.
mencontohkan 1 to copy, imitate, exemplify. **2** to give as an example, show by example, exemplify, illustrate. *Coba contohkan bagaimana dia jatuh.* Show me how he fell.
mempercontohkan to give as an example, show by example, exemplify, illustrate.
percontoh sample. *~ acak* random sample. *~ setangan* hand specimen.
percontohan and **percontoh** (*infr*) **1** specimen, sample. *nomor ~* specimen/sample copy, specimen (of a newspaper/magazine, etc.); advance copy (of a magazine, etc. still to be published). **2** model. *désa ~* model village (superseded by *désa teladan*). *proyék ~* pilot project.
pemercontoh 1 (*petro*) corer. **2** (*geol*) sampler.
pemercontohan sampling, (*petro*) coring. *~ inti* core sampling. *~ samping* side-wall coring. *~ teras* coring.
contok (*J*) **mencontok** to sock, hit with the fist.
contong (*Jv*) cone-shaped paper/leaf wrapper or container (for peanuts/sweets, etc.).
conyang (*C?*) k.o. alcoholic drink.
cop I foul, expression said when a player makes/says a false start

in a game; if the opponent is late in shouting this, move or foul stands and counts (against him).

cop II → CUP I, II.

cop III /kop/ → KOP I.

copak-capik 1 to walk with a limp due to lameness or paralysis. **2** to move (the mouth) constantly.

copar → CUPAR I, II.

copét (*J/Jv*) *tukang* – a pickpocket. – *séks* molester.

  mencopét to pickpocket, pilfer.

  nyopét (*coq*) to be a pickpocket.

  mencopéti (*pl obj*) to pickpocket.

  tercopét pickpocketed. *Penjaga toko* ~. A store watchman was pickpocketed.

  kecopétan to be the victim of a pickpocket. *Aku* ~ *dompétku*. My wallet was lifted. *Pak, mau melapor. Saya* ~, *uang dan surat-surat keterangan, semuanya hilang.* Sir, I would like to report s.t. My money and documents have been pickpocketed, I lost them all. *Mengapa* ~? How could you have been pickpocketed?

  pencopét pickpocket.

  pencopétan pickpocketing, pilfering. *Saya terkena* ~. I was pickpocketed.

copi and **copy** (*D/E*) /kopi/ → KOPI II.

coplok (*J/Jv*) to break off, come loose (of a button/tooth/nail, etc.); → COPOT.

  mencoplok 1 to get loose. **2** (*sl*) to fire s.o.

  mencoplokkan 1 to loosen. **2** to break off s.t., detach.

coplot → COPLOK.

copol → CUPUL.

copot (*J/Jv*) **1** to come loose/off/out, gotten loose (of a bike chain/teeth/buttons/pages in a book, etc.), fall out. *Giginya* –. His tooth fell out. *Jantung saya mau* –. My heart skipped a beat. *Sekrupnya* –. The screw came loose. *Rodanya* – *satu dari as-nya.* One of the wheels came off the axle. *Tapal kuda itu* –. The horseshoe came off. **2** removed, taken off (clothes). **3** a mild exclamation, goodness gracious.

  mencopot [and **nyopot** (*coq*)] **1** to dismiss, discharge, fire, unseat, relieve (of one's post). *Banyak pegawai yang dicopot.* Many employees were fired. ~ *seseorang dari kedudukannya* to unseat s.o. **2** to take s.t. off, remove s.t., pull out s.t. ~ *kacamata* to take one's glasses off. *"Sepatunya dicopot dulu, dik," tegur wanita ber-baju biru kotak-kotak itu dengan ramah.* "Take off your shoes first, young man," the woman dressed in a blue checkered blouse said in a friendly way. *Ia* ~ *cangklong dari mulutnya.* He pulled the pipe out of his mouth. **3** to dismantle, take apart, untie.

  nyopot (*coq*) ~ *dari* to desert, leave (one's political party). ~ *sebelum tamat* to drop out (of students).

  mencopoti [and **nyopotin** (*J coq*)] **1** (*pl obj*) → MENCOPOT. **2** to snatch. ~ *arloji tangan* to snatch a wristwatch.

  mencopotkan 1 to set loose (a dog), take s.t. off, remove s.t., undo (clothes). ~ *cincin* to take off a ring. **2** to dismantle, take s.t. apart. **3** to pull out (nails). **4** to snatch. ~ *hati* quite taken aback (with fright). **5** to take s.t. off, etc. for s.o. else.

  pencopotan 1 dismantling. **2** discharge (from office).

coprak-coprak (*J onom*) sound of galloping.

copul → CUPUL.

cor (*Jv*) *besi* – cast iron. *beton* – reinforced concrete. *tukang* – (metal)founder. – *baja* steel casting.

  men(ge)cor to cast (metal).

  coran cast-iron. *pipa* – cast-iron pipe.

  pengecor s.t. that casts (metal).

  pengecoran 1 casting. *upacara* ~ *tiang pancang oléh Duta Besar H. Achmad Tirtosudiro* the cornerstone laying ceremony by Ambassador H. Achmad Tirtosudiro. **2** foundry. ~ *beton* concrete mixer. ~ *cétak* die casting. ~ *terakhir* topping up (of a building under construction).

corak 1 (fabric) design, motif, pattern. **2** stripe (on a flag). **3** color. – *politiknya tidak tegas.* His political color is unclear. **4** type, form, structure, feature, characteristic. – *pikiran* attitude. – *ragam* sorts, kinds, types. **bercorak ragam** manifold, multifarious.

  bercorak 1 with/to have a pattern, patterned. **2** with stripes, striped. **3** with a color, tinged, characterized. *informasi* ~ *kebudayaan yang mempunyai tugas mendidik* cultural-educative information.

  mencoraki to model.

corak-carik tattered, in tatters/rags.

  mencorak-carikkan to tear s.t. to bits.

corang → CURANG.

corat-corét 1 scratches, scribbles. **2** graffiti; → CORÉT I.

  pencorat-corét graffiti-artist/writer. *Polsék Tébét menertibkan remaja* ~ The Tebet police station has taken care of the graffiti-writing young people.

corék I 1 stripe, line. **2** scratch, graze.

  mencorék 1 to scratch out. **2** to nullify, annul, cancel, abolish, revoke.

corék II → CURIK.

corék III (*J*) hard of hearing.

coréng 1 (thick) stripes, streaks, scratches. **2** smear. – *moréng* full of streaks and scratches, streaked all over, daubed (with soot/dirt/chalk), completely smeared and streaked. **bercoréng-moréng** to be streaked, smeared, scribbled on. *Kertas putih itu* ~ *sehingga tidak dapat lagi ditulisi.* The white paper was scribbled all over so that it couldn't be written on any more. **mencoréng-moréng 1** cross out, daub, streak. **2** to tattoo. **tercoréng-moréng** to be smeared (of one's reputation). **kecoréng-moréngan** smears, crossings out.

  bercoréng(-coréng), **bercoréngan** and **bercoréng-coréngan 1** daubed, streaked, scrawled over, striped. **2** tattooed. *macan bercoréng* striped tiger.

  mencoréng 1 to smear. ~ *arang ke kening* to smear (the reputation of). ~ *muka* to give s.o. a bad name. *Hambat-menghambat ini tentu* ~ *muka tuan rumah, sebagai penyelenggara paméran.* All these kinds of obstacles have certainly given the host, the organizer of the show, a bad name. **2** to scribble on. **3** to tattoo.

  mencoréngi (*pl obj*) to smear, etc.

  mencoréngkan to smear, scrape s.t. on.

  tercoréng scratched, scrawled, streaked.

  coréngan 1 scratch, streak. **2** scribbling, graffiti.

  pencoréng s.t. that scribbles over/crosses off.

  pencoréngan smearing, sullying.

corét I 1 scratch, stripe; → CORÉNG. *gambar* – sketch, draft, (sketchy) outline, pen drawing. – *dinding* graffiti.

  corét-corét 1 scratches, doodling, scratching. **2** graffiti. *gambar* ~ sketch; caricature. *tulisan* ~ worthless scribbling (an article/book, etc.). **mencorét-corét 1** to scribble (down), jot (down). **2** to scrawl graffiti. **3** to sketch s.t.

  bercorét with scratches, scratched, striped.

  mencorét 1 to cross/strike out, delete, wipe/blot out, cancel. **2** to nullify, annul, abolish.

  mencoréti 1 (*pl obj*) to streak s.t. **2** to scribble on.

  mencorétkan to cross/wipe blot out s.t.

  tercorét 1 streaked, scribbled on. **2** struck off (a list of candidates/participants).

  corétan 1 stripe, stroke, scratch. **2** sketch, pen drawing. **3** note, annotation. **4** erasure, crossing off, correction, deletion.

  pencorétan erasure, deletion, removal, cancellation, scratching out. ~ *pembukuan* deletion of a record.

corét II (*M*) **mencorét** to gush/spout out.

coro I (*Jv*) **1** (a large species of) cockroach. **2** a lowly person. **3** (in Indonesian nationalist circles during the Dutch colonial period) spy, traitor; stooge, lackey; → CECUNGUK, LIPAS.

coro II – *bika* round pancake-shaped snack made from rice flour and coconut milk.

coroh (*S*) k.o. skin disease, white spots (on hands).

corok-corok cream-vented bulbul, *Pycnonotus simplex*.

corong I (*Jv*) **1** tube, pipe, shaft, funnel, chute. **2** loudspeaker, receiver (telephone). **3** mouthpiece, s.o. who speaks for s.o. else. **4** mine shaft. *lampu* – spotlight. – *asap* chimney. – *bicara* megaphone. – *cukong* mouthpiece. – *dengar* ear trumpet. – *halo-halo* bullhorn. – *hawa* ventilation duct. – *isi* hopper, funnel. – *klakson* hooter. – *kuping* headphone. – *lampu* lamp chimney. – *pembesar suara* loudspeaker. – *pencurahan* hopper funnel. – *penerima* receiver. – *pengeras suara* megaphone. – *radio* microphone. – *suara* megaphone. – *télepon* telephone set. – *tuang* running head, runner, hopper (car).

  bercorong with a tube (etc.); to use a loudspeaker, etc.

mencorongkan 1 to broadcast. **2** to shape s.t. into a funnel.

corongan chute.

pencorongan broadcasting.

corong II mencorong 1 to shine, glare. **2** to radiate. **3** to light up, illuminate (with a searchlight/spotlight). **kemencorongan** grandeur, pomp, splendor.

mencorongkan to make s.t. shine.

corot I spout, mouth (of a kettle, etc.), nozzle. – *minyak* syringe. – *pelita* wick-holder.

bercorot with a spout/mouth.

mencorotkan to spout/spit forth.

corot II (arrived) last.

mencorot to become the last; (to come) lastly.

pencorot s.o. who arrives late, straggler, laggard, afterthought.

corps (*D*) /koreps/ corps; → KORPS. – *Diplomatik* Diplomatic Corps, Corps Diplomatique. – *inténdans Angkatan Darat* Army Quartermaster Corps. – *Polisi Militér* Military Police.

cosblong (*J*) in high spirits, cheerful; *cp* PLONG I.

cotét → CONÉT.

coto (*in Makassar/Ujungpandang*) k.o. beef *soto*.

cotok bill, beak. *salah – melantingkan* to have the courage to correct a mistake. *mékanisme harga – pelatuk* trigger-price mechanism.

mencotok to peck at, tap at.

mencotoki to peck away at, tap away at.

cover (*E*) /kover/ → KOVER.

cowék and **cowét** (*J*) → COBÉK I.

cowok (*J*) **1** guy, boy, male. **2** boyfriend.

cowokan boy-crazy.

cowong (*J*) to talk at the top of one's lungs.

CPNS (*init*) → CALON *pegawai negeri sipil.*

c.q. (*abbr*) [casu-quo] (*L*) /céki/ or ... as the case may be, in this instance, attention. *Pelaksanaan semua Undang-Undang – Peraturan Pemerintah RI.* The implementation of all Laws or Government Regulations of the Republic of Indonesia as the case may be.

craas ... craas ... (*onom*) slashing sounds.

crat (*onom*) sound of s.t. squirting out. – *crét/crit* (*Jv*) repeated squirts of water or feces. *Airnya ~.* The (tap)water is dripping.

creambath (*E*) /krimbat/ **1** a steamed-in shampoo plus a neck and shoulder massage. **2** to get such a shampoo.

creb ... creb ... (*onom*) slashing sounds.

créngkéngan (*Jv*) spear

crét 1 sound of emission of bird droppings. **2** sound of feces during diarrhea. – *crat* a) repeated acts as above. b) to keep on going to the bathroom.

crét-crét (*onom*) squirt, sound of squirting/spraying. *Tiba-tiba, "Crét, crét!" Seseorang menyemprotkan sesuatu ke arah mata Sapto.* Suddenly, squirt, squirt. Somebody sprayed something toward Sapto's eyes.

ngecrét 1 to squirt. **2** to ejaculate, come.

crigis (*Jv*) to nag, bother. *gadis yang* – a nagging girl.

cring (*onom*) jingling sound.

criping and **crimping** (*Jv*) fried chips (made from cassava, etc.). – *kentang* potato chips. – *ketéla* cassava chips. – *pisang* fried banana chips.

crit → CRÉT.

crocos (*Jv*) *pating* ~ (plural) flowing in profusion; → CEROCOS.

nyrocos (*coq*) to flow/pour out. *~lah info dari mulut perjaka itu.* Information poured out of the young man's mouth.

crongos (*Jv*) buck-toothed.

nyrongos to stick out, protrude.

croot (*onom*) spurting/squirting sound, for example when s.o. is blowing his nose the Indonesian way, i.e., by shutting off one nostril, or the sound of ejaculating; → CROT.

crootin (*J vulg*) to come, ejaculate.

crop-crop (*onom*) sound of clanging metal.

cross-boy /krosboy/ male juvenile delinquent.

cross-girl /krosgirel/ female juvenile delinquent.

cross-mama /krosmama/ irresponsible adult female.

cross-papa /krospapa/ irresponsible adult male.

crot ngecrot → NGECRÉT, CROOT.

cruat-cruit (*onom*) sound of a lot of people talking all at once.

c.s. (*abbr*) [cum-suis] (*L*) /sé-és/ and associates. *–nya* one's friends/buddies. *Penerima-penerima krédit itu adalah si – diréktur utama.* The buddies of the chief director got credits.

CSIS (*init*) Center for Strategic and International Studies.

cu I (*ob*) → CIU.

cu II clipped form of **bungsu.**

cua (*ob*) disappointed, regretful.

cuaantik (*sl*) gorgeous. *Cowoknya ganteng, céwéknya –!* The guys were dashing and the gals were gorgeous.

cuaca (*Skr*) **1** weather. *terang* – clear, bright weather. – *menjadi gelap* it's getting dark. **2** clear, bright (of weather). – *dingin* a cold snap. *ilmu* – meteorology. *peramal* – weatherman. *ramalan* – weather forecast. – *baik* nice weather, not overcast and not raining. – *buruk* foul weather. – *kabut* dense fog.

bercuaca with ... weather, with a ... climate.

cuah (*exclam*) nonsense!

cuai 1 insignificant, unimportant, inferior. **2** heedless, negligent, careless, thoughtless, indifferent.

mencuaikan 1 to underestimate, underrate, look down on, despise. **2** to neglect, treat as s.t. unimportant.

kecuaian 1 insignificance, unimportance, inferiority. **2** negligence, carelessness, indifference.

pencuaian 1 disregard, disdain. ~ *mahkamah* contempt of court. **2** negligence, carelessness.

cuak I (*ob*) decoy (such as a buffalo/elephant, etc.).

cuak II nervous, scared (as a player before a match).

cuak III (*C*) (police, etc.) informer.

cual (*cla*) silk (fabric, cloth) in the first stage of its manufacture.

cuali → KECUALI.

cuan (*C*) (to make a) profit.

cuana → CERANA.

cuang → COANG I.

cuang-caing torn to shreds.

bercuang-caing (to be) in tatters/rags.

cuantik (*sl*) very beautiful; → CANTIK.

cuap(-cuap) (*Pr*) (CB-er term) to chat, talk (using a *CB-radio*). *tukang* – radio broadcaster. *tukang – pacu-jalur musik* disc jockey.

mencuapkan to announce. *meréalisasikan program muluk yang pernah dicuapkan semasa kampanye* to put on a high-sounding program that was announced during the campaign.

cuar mencuar and **tercuar** to stick up high (of a mast), stick out (of knees, etc.).

mencuarkan to stick s.t. up high.

tercuar stuck up high.

pencuaran (*geo*) upcoming.

cuat bercuatan (*pl subj*) to protrude/stick out.

mencuat 1 to protrude, stick out erect (of small objects, such as a cigarette from one's lips). ~ *ke langit lepas* to rocket skyward. *batang besi beton ~ keluar* reinforced concrete bars are sticking out. ~ *ke permukaan* to surface, come to the fore. **2** to move with a rapid motion, such as to fly to the side, or to spring back. **3** (*geol*) to obduct.

mencuat-cuat to keep on moving with a rapid motion, vibrate.

tercuat shot up, stuck up and erect.

tercuat-cuat sticking up.

cuatan 1 s.t. that protrudes, obduction, peg. **2** reflection (of feelings). **3** rapid movement, spring.

pencuatan protruding, obduction.

cuat-cuit → CRUAT-CRUIT.

cuba (*mostly Mal*) → COBA.

cuban → COBAN.

cubang rainwater catcher.

cubit pinch; → GETIL.

secubit 1 pinch, nip, tweak. **2** just a little bit (of salt/snuff).

bercubitan to pinch e.o.

mencubit [and **nyubit** (*coq*)] **1** to pinch, nip (between the thumb and finger). **2** (*coq*) to pinch, steal.

cubit-mencubit to pinch e.o.

mencubiti (*pl obj*) to keep pinching, pinch.

cubitan pinch.

cubit-cubitan to pinch e.o.

pencubitan pinching.

cublik (*Jv*) oil lamp.
cubluk (*Jv*) **1** a pit for trapping animals. **2** leaching pit (used as a toilet).
cubung → KECUBUNG.
cubung-cubung 1 swarm of flies (over a carcass of dead animals, etc.). **2** maggot, larva (of flies).
cuca I → CERCA.
cuca II (*cla*) magic formula, spell to silence or confuse an enemy or cure wounds or illness.
  mencuca to pronounce the magic formula so as to cure wounds or cast a spell on enemies.
cucak (*burung*) – *rawa* yellow-crowned bulbul, *Trachycomus zeylanicus*; → BARAU-BARAU I.
cucau and **cucaw** (*sl*) needle (for injecting illegal drugs).
cuci I wash. *babu* – female house servant in charge of the laundry, wash(er)woman. *mesin* – (*pakaian*) washer, washing machine. *mesin* – *piring* dishwasher (the equipment). *papan* – scrub board. *sabun* – laundry soap. *tahan* – washable, fast (color). *tukang* – a) launderer, laundryman; → PENATU. b) dishwasher (the person). – *asam* pickling, curing. – *balik* backwash. – *cétak film warna* (in ads) developing and printing of color film. – *darah* hemodialysis. – *film* developing a film. – *gudang* warehouse sale/clearance. – *lambung* gastric lavage. – *mata* a) to use an eyewash. b) to feast one's eyes, look around, sightsee, watch the girls go by. *Di sinilah orang dapat ngopi sambil* – *mata*. Here one can drink coffee and watch the girls go by. – *muka* to wash one's face. (*makanan*) – *mulut* dessert. – *nama* to clear one's name. – *otak* brainwash. **mencuci otak** to brainwash; brainwashing. *Kita hanya mengharapkan agar para sejarahwan Indonésia jangan mau dicuci-otaknya.* We only hope that Indonesian historians will not be brainwashed. – *perut* to take a purgative/laxative. – *pucat* stonewash. **mencuci pucat** to stonewash; stonewashing. *Celana jin(s) yang terbuat dari bahan dénim masih popular, apalagi yang dicuci pucat.* Denim jeans are still popular, above all the stonewashed ones. – *rambut* to shampoo one's hair. – *tangan* a) to wash one's hands (with water). b) do not want to accept responsibility for s.o.'s faults; do not want to meddle.
bercuci (*Mal*) to be circumcised.
mencuci [and **nyuci** (*coq*)] **1** to wash, cleanse. ~ *kendaraan* to wash a car. ~ *léhér* to eat well, have a good meal. ~ *mata* to look around, sightsee. ~ *tangan* a) to wash one's hands (with water). b) to attempt to show that one is guiltless. *dapat dicuci dengan tangan* hand-washable. *dicuci kering* dry-cleaned. *Dan bila ada waktu baru dibawa ke binatu yang profésional untuk dicuci kering* and if there's time it's taken to the laundry to be dry-cleaned. **2** to develop (film). *dan* ~ *dan mencétak film warna* to develop and print color film. **3** to wash, launder, do the laundry. ~ *pakaian* to wash the clothes. ~ *uang* to launder money. **4** to purge (the stomach), purify (the soul).
mencucikan [and **nyuciin** (*J coq*)] **1** to wash s.t. for s.o. **2** to have s.t. washed, send to the laundry. *Salman masih sendirian. Masih makan diwarung-warung dan masih* ~ *pakaiannya kepada bik Inah, tetangganya.* Salman is still single. He still eats out in roadside stalls and sends his clothes to Inah, his neighbor, to be laundered. **3** (*Mal*) to have s.o. circumcised.
tercuci washed.
cucian laundry (to be washed), wash. *pelayan untuk* ~ washwoman. *tempat* ~ laundry tub.
pencuci 1 equipment, s.t. used to wash/clean. **2** way/method of washing. **3** launderer, laundryman, laundress. (*alat*) ~ *baju* (*otomatis*) (automatic) washer/washing machine. ~ *darah* hemodialysis. ~ *kaca* (*mobil*) (car) windshield wiper. *mesin* ~ *darah* hemodialysis machine. ~ *muka* washbasin; → BASKOM. ~ *mulut* dessert. *Pembeli lalu memilih minuman dan* ~ *mulut.* The buyers (in a fast-food restaurant) then choose a drink and dessert. ~ *perut* purgative, laxative. ~ *piring* a) dishwasher (the person). b) *alat* ~ *piring* dishwasher (the equipment). ~ *rambut* shampoo. ~ *tangan* finger bowl. *tempat* ~ *tangan* washstand. ~ *uang* money launderer.
pencucian 1 cleansing, washing. ~ *film* film developing. ~ *otak* brainwashing. ~ *vagina* vaginal douche. **2** laundering. ~ *uang*

money laundering. *Pelarangan bank untuk menerima prakték uang harus dirumuskan secara berhati-hati dalam UU Perbankan mendatang.* Prohibiting banks from accepting laundered money must be carefully formulated in the next banking bill. **3** laundromat. **4** place where film is developed. **5** catharsis.
cuci II – *maki* abuse, revile, scorn, taunt. **mencuci maki** to abuse s.o., call s.o. names, taunt, ridicule.
cucu grandchild. *anak* – descendant. *beranak* – with all one's children (i.e., children + grandchildren). – *Adam* human beings; mankind. – *cicit* grandchildren and great-grandchildren. – *sepupu* sibling's grandchildren.
  bercucu 1 to have grandchildren. **2** to address s.o. as *cucu*. *Saya* ~ *kepadanya*. I call him grandson.
cucuh mencucuh and **menyucuh** to kindle a fire, set fire to, fire (a weapon). ~ *meriam* to fire a gun/cannon.
  pencucuh 1 kindling. **2** instigator.
cucuk I (*Jv*) **1** decorative hairpin; → COCOK I. **2** beak, bill. **3** thorn. **4** (*mil*) front line (of troops). **5** spearhead. **6** row; cord.
bercucukan to peck e.o.
mencucuk to peck with the beak; to prick, stick.
mencucuki (*pl obj*) to prick, stick, peck.
mencucukkan to stick up (someplace), stick (s.t. somewhere), install, locate, place. *Parabola tadi lalu dicucukkan di wuwungan rumah Siregar.* The dish was installed on the top of Siregar's roof.
  tercucuk to be stuck (in).
cucuk II (*ob*) **kecucukan** inquisitiveness, curiosity.
cucuk III → COCOK II.
cucuk IV – *rawa* (*Jv*) yellow-crowned/straw-headed bulbul, *Pycnonotus zeylanicus*.
cucukan (*Jv*) /cucu'an/ (in Solo and Yogyakarta) ~ *tumbak* to gossip; → RUMPI.
cucul (*Jv*) to take off (one's clothing), get undressed.
cucunda (*cla*) (polite form of address) grandchild; → CUCU.
cucung (*ob*) (word used to call a grandchild) my grandchild.
cucup → KECUP. **mencucup 1** to sip, suck. **2** to kiss (audibly). ~ *benak* to be a blood sucker.
cucur I flow, trickle (in small quantities). – *darah* bleeding, hemorrhage.
bercucuran (*pl subj*) to gush forth, flow (of blood), stream, run (of sweat). *Peluhnya* ~ *karena ia bekerja keras.* He was sweating because he was working hard.
mencucur to flow, trickle.
mencucuri to let water, etc. fall or drip on s.t., drip, pour, anoint.
mencucurkan to sprinkle (a liquid). ~ *air mata* to have tears in one's eyes. ~ *darah* to shed blood. ~ *keringat/peluh* to sweat, toil (and moil), drudge away.
tercucur dripping, falling in drops. *kuah* ~ *ke nasi, nasi akan dimakan juga* (*M*) a perfect match.
cucuran 1 outpouring, flood. **2** place where water pours/floods out. ~ *air* eaves, gutter. ~ *air mata* flood of tears. ~ *atap* eaves, gutter. *air* ~ *atap jatuhnya ke pelimbahan juga* as the tree so the fruit; like father, like son. ~ *darah* bleeding, hemorrhage. ~ *keringat/peluh* sweat, perspiration.
pencucuran flowing, outpouring.
cucur II (*naut*) bowsprit. *layar* – jib.
cucur III (*kué* –) a fried sweet made of rice flour and brown sugar.
cucur IV *burung* – a) large frogmouth, *Batrachostomus auritis*. b) goatsucker, *Caprimulgus sp*.
cucurut → CELURUT.
cucut I (*J/Jv*) *ikan* – shark, *Pleurotremata spp.*; → HIU, YU. – *biru besar* blue shark, *Prionace glauca*. – *botol* bottle shark, spiny dog fish, *Centrophorus atromarginatus/Squalus mitsukurii*. – *buta* (tawny) nurse shark, *Nebrius concolor*. – *gergaji* sawfish, *Pristis cuspidatus*. – *lanyam* sandbar shark, *Carcharinus limbatus*. – *macan* tiger shark, *Galeocerdo cuvieri*. – *mako* mako shark, *Isurus glaucus*. – *mandrong* k.o. shark, guitar fish, *Rhinobatus thouin*. – *martil* hammerhead shark, *Sphyma zygaena*. – *pedang* (*Jv*) → CUCUT *gergaji*. – *poto* leopard/tiger shark, *Stegostoma tigrinum*. – *putih besar* great white shark, *Carcharodon carchias*. – *rongcéng* hammerhead shark, *Sphyma zygaena*. – *tekéh* sand shark.

cucut II mencucut to suck, lap, lick up. ~ *benak* to extort money from s.o.

cudanco → CHUDANCO.

cuék (*J*) → CUWÉK, CUAI. **nyuékin** → NYUWÉKIN.

cugat mencugat raised (of one's head).

  mencugatkan to raise (one's head).

cuh 1 on! (cry to hunting dogs, to encourage them). **2** skat! (to chase away a dog); → CIH.

cui I (*M*) penis.

cui II (*Min*) *lémon* – a type of small citrus fruit.

cuik I → COBÉK I.

cuik II (*J*) *ikan* – steamed and salted fish.

  mencuik to steam and salt fish.

cuil I mencuil to touch slightly, nudge (with the tip of a finger in order to say s.t.). *"Ayo kita buru-buru berangkat, supaya jangan tergoda dengan pelayan," ajak sopir ~ bahu kernétnya, setelah mengisi perut.* "Come on, let's leave right away, so that we're not seduced by the waitresses," persuaded the driver while lightly touching his assistant's shoulder, after having filled their stomachs.

cuil II (*J*) a torn/chipped-off fragment, chunk.

  secuil 1 spark, trace, touch, bit, glimmer, scintilla. *tak ada ~ pun niat untuk membunuh* there wasn't even a spark of intention to kill. *mori ~* a fragment of white calico. *terasi ~* a bit of shrimp paste. *~ demi ~ dikunyahnya dan ditelannya kué itu.* Bit by bit he chewed and swallowed the cake. *~ catatan dunia pendidikan Indonésia.* Cursory notes on the Indonesian educational world. *~ senyum* a trace of a smile. **2** very few, some. *Orang Betawi asli sudah tinggal ~.* There remain only a mere handful of native Jakartanese. *andil ~* small parts. **3** slightest. *tak punya keterampilan ~ pun* don't have the slightest skill. *Ia tidak memberikan penjelasan ~ pun tentang maksudnya melepaskan témbakan.* He didn't give the slightest explanation as to the purpose of his shooting.

cuilah → DUIL(L)AH.

cuit I – *gamit* nervous movements of the fingers. **mencuit-gamit** to move (one's fingers) nervously.

  bercuit-cuit to move the fingers nervously.

  mencuit to touch s.t. with the tip of the finger, nudge s.o. to get his attention, poke, tap

  cuitan nudge, poke.

cuit II (*onom*) **1** peeping, chirping. **2** screeching.

  bercuit and **mencuit 1** to peep, chirp, squeak (of birds). **2** to screech.

cuk I (*E*) choke (of a car).

cuk II (*J*) mosquito larvae; → UGET-UGET.

cuk III *burung* – *padang* k.o. minivet, *Pericrocotus cinereus/roseus*.

cuk IV (*C*) (in gambling) house cut, rake, money given to person who holds card games or cockfights.

cuka (*Skr*) vinegar. *makan* – to get a taste of vinegar (of a wife neglected for a mistress). *minum* – *pagi hari* to get out of bed on the wrong side. *– belanda* wine vinegar. *– getah* (*Mal*) formic acid. *– jawa* vinegar prepared from the juice of the sugar palm, *Arenga pinnata. – kayu* resinate. *– méja* table vinegar. *– minyak* (*in Ambon*) (mild exclamation) gosh.

cukai 1 tax, customs duty, excise tax, tariff; → BÉA, PAJAK. **2** [= *cuké* (*Jv*)] part of the earnings of a harvest on privately owned land levied by the landholder. *– bir* excise tax on beer. *– gula* excise tax on sugar. *– korék api* excise tax on matches. *– minuman keras* excise tax on spirits. *– minyak tanah* excise tax on kerosene. *– tembakau* excise tax on tobacco.

  bercukai taxed.

  mencukai to tax, levy taxes/customs/duties, etc. on, impose/lay/place a duty/excise on, levy a duty/excise on. *Gula mérah dicukai.* An excise tax has been imposed on brown sugar.

  pencukaian tax (*mod*), taxing.

cukam marks due to pressure.

  mencukam(kan) to put pressure on s.t.

  tercukam marked up (due to pressure).

cuké I (*C*) client, customer.

cuké II → CUKAI.

cuki I (*C*) a game like checkers. *kasur* – a stitched-through mattress. *papan* – the board used to play the above game.

bercuki to play such a game.

cuki II (*J vulg*) cunt; → CIPUT II, MÉMÉK II, PUKI I. *– mai* "your mother's cunt," kiss my ass! fuck you!

  mencuki (*vulg*) to fuck.

cukil (*J?*) → CUNGKIL. *-.– gigi* to pick one's teeth.

  mencukil 1 to gouge out, pick one's teeth. **2** to engrave.

  cukilan 1 extract (from book, document etc.). **2** engraving.

cukin (*C*) **1** bib, small napkin used to cover the chest when eating. **2** loin-cloth (used when bathing). *seléndang* – k.o. cloth used in the *cokék* dance.

  penyukin the woman who distributes *seléndangs* to the male dancers (in the *cokék* dance).

cukir → CUNGKIL.

cukit 1 fork (used for eating together with a spoon). **2** (*Jv*) chopsticks. **3** (*Jv*) bamboo sticks used (in pairs) for mixing tobacco and opium for smoking. *– gigi* toothpick.

cukong I (*C*) wheeler-dealer (a term for the vastly wealthy Chinese financiers of key Indonesian political figures).

  bercukong with/to have a financier.

  mencukongi to back, finance, pay for (has bad connotation).

  cukong-cukongan to act like a *cukong* (but not having sufficient capital).

  percukongan and **pencukongan** wheeling and dealing.

cukong II [*pucuk singkong*] the tip of the young cassava leaf.

cukongisme wheeler-dealerism, wheeling-dealing.

cuku (*Tam*) dried *gambir* root.

cukup 1 enough, sufficient, adequate. *Berasnya – untuk dua hari.* There's enough rice for two days. *Uang saya tidak –* I haven't got enough money. *–! Good enough! – sekian sajalah!* That's enough! *Kamar ini – untuk dua orang.* This room is sufficient for two persons. *Itu –!* That will do! **2** precisely, exactly (... years old). *Tahun ini umurnya – tujuh puluh tahun.* This year he'll be exactly seventy (years old). *– sembilan bulan* a) precisely nine months (pregnant). b) the end of the month (i.e., payday in Indonesia). *Penduduknya tidak – dua juta.* It has less than 2 million residents. **3** complete, full. *– dengan* complete/full with. *Ada sebuah mesjid besar – dengan tabuh dan menaranya.* There's a large mosque complete with a large drum and minaret. **4** quite, very, enough. *– banyak yang berpendapat Singapura hanya menarik untuk beberapa hari; meréka tidak mempunyai kesenian, tidak ada kebudayaan yang mantap.* Quite a few are of the opinion that Singapore is only interesting/attractive for a couple of days; it has no art objects, it has no established culture. *telah – menjalankan hukumannya* to have served one's sentence. *– punya nama* quite well-known. *sebuah perguruan tinggi yang – punya nama di Yogyakarta* a very well-known university in Yogyakarta. *– berani* brave enough (to do s.t.). **5** passing (grade in school). **6** (*coq*) all you have to do is. *– jawab beberapa pertanyaan.* All you have to do is answer a few questions. *tidak –* insufficient. **ketidak-cukupan** insufficiency. *– bulannya* ready to give birth. *– hitungannya* dead. *– jelas* self-explanatory, sufficiently clear. *– mutu* qualified. *– persenjataannya* armed to the teeth. *– ramai* rather busy. *– umur* a) adult, mature. b) obsolete. *belum – umur* minor, underage. *– umur terbatas* (*leg*) limited legal capacity.

  secukupnya (to an) adequate (amount/degree) for the purpose. *garam ~* a) the right amount of salt. b) salt to taste. *dengan ~* sufficiently.

  secukup-cukupnya well-calculated.

  mencukupi [and **nyukupin** (*J coq*)] **1** (to be) sufficient/adequate. *tak ~* insufficient, inadequate. **2** to fulfill, comply with, meet, come up to. *~ kebutuhan penduduk* to meet the needs of the populace. **3** to make up, complete, supplement. *untuk ~ kekurangan tenaga dokter* to make up the shortage of medical doctors. **4** (in correspondence) in reply to. *~ surat Anda tanggal 6 April* in reply to your letter of April 6.

  mencukupkan to make sufficient/suffice/adequate, supplement, complete. *Ia berusaha ~ gaji yang diperoléhnya setiap bulan.* He tried to make the salary that he received monthly sufficient.

  mencukup-cukupkan to make s.t. be sufficient/suffice, have enough (money) to live on.

  tercukupi sufficed, made sufficient. *setelah pangan ~* after there is sufficient food.

cukupan 1 just enough, adequate, will do. *Baju itu ~ untuk adik saya.* The shirt will do for my little brother. 2 mediocre, fair. *Ujiannya angkanya ~.* His exam grades were fair. *si ~* the adequates (between the haves and the have-nots).

kecukupan 1 sufficiency, adequacy; be enough. *Orang datang begitu banyak sehingga méja dalam réstoran itu tidak ~.* So many people came that there weren't enough seats in the restaurant. 2 well off, to have (more than) enough. *Hidupnya sekarang bisa ~ sebab usahanya maju.* He lives well now, because his business has improved. **berkecukupan** to have a good life, to have no shortage of money.

pencukupan (efforts to achieve) sufficiency.

percukupan complement.

cukur shave (*coq*) → BERCUKUR. *pisau –* razor. *tukang –* barber. *– batok* (to have) the hair cut at the sides and bottom, leaving the hair on the crown in a coconut-shell shape. *– gundul* (to have) the hair cut completely off. *– komplit* "complete shave," this includes not only a haircut, but also trimming of sideburns and mustache. *– krukat* (to have) a crew cut. *– poni* (for girls; to have) bangs cut at the forehead. *– suci* tonsure. *– tentara* (to have) a crew cut.

bercukur 1 to shave o.s. *~ dengan pisau silét lebih mudah dan senang* to shave with a safety razor is easier and pleasanter. 2 to be shaven. *Janggutnya tidak ~.* His beard was not shaven. 3 to get a haircut.

mencukur [and **nyukur** (*coq*)] 1 to shave s.o., cut s.o.'s hair. 2 to defeat badly, overwhelm. *dicukur gundul* (in sports) to be beaten badly.

mencukuri (*pl obj*) to shave.

mencukurkan to shave with s.t.

tercukur 1 shaved. 2 can be shaved.

cukuran a *selamatan* at which the hair of a 40-day-old baby is cut.

pencukur 1 barber. 2 a shaver (the instrument). 3 shaving. *krim ~* shaving cream.

pencukuran shaving.

cula (*Skr*) 1 horn of the rhinoceros and of the hornbill. *si – dua* the Sumatran rhino. 2 *– tupai* a) the penis of a squirrel (believed to be a powerful aphrodisiac). b) an aphrodisiac talisman in the shape of a squirrel's penis.

bercula horned.

culak I → COLAK.

culak II menculak to stick up high (as a mast).

culan (*C?*) a plant whose flowers are used to scent tea and clothes, Chinese perfume plant, *Aglaia odorata*, → PACAR *cina*.

culas I lazy, work-shy (stronger than *malas*). *Mahasiswa sekarang berhati ~.* Nowadays, university students are work-shy.

culas II (*M*) insincere, unfaithful, crafty, dishonest.

keculasan dishonesty.

cules → CULAS I.

culi → COLI I.

culiah (*ob*) Muslim Indian merchants from Malabar.

culik I (*Jv*) (= **culik-culik**) female nocturnal cuckoo, *Eudynamis orientalis*, whose cry, according to folk belief, announces the approach of thieves; → KULIK-KULIK, TUHU.

culik II (*J*) 1 (*cla*) a spirit who kidnaps children. 2 bogeyman who pries people's eyes out to gratify the troll under the bridge or to offer them as a sacrifice on starting a building. 3 s.o. who steals or abducts children. 4 kidnapper, abductor.

menculik [and **nyulik** (*coq*)] 1 to abduct, kidnap. 2 to elope with. 3 to pilfer, pinch. 4 to decapitate (or, abduct a child) in order to put the head under a building.

menculiki (*pl obj*) to kidnap.

terculik *si ~* the kidnap victim.

penculik kidnapper, abductor.

penculikan kidnapping, abducting.

culik III → COLÉK I.

culika (*Jv*) 1 deceiver, impostor, cheat, fraud. 2 thief.

culim (*Hind?*) k.o. tobacco or opium pipe.

seculim one pipe-full (of opium or tobacco).

Cultuurstélsel (*D*) /kul-/ the force-crop "Cultivation System" introduced by the Dutch colonial government (1830–70).

culun (*M? BG*) 1 naïve and inexperienced. 2 strange, weird, odd, unstylish.

cuma only, just, merely (no expectation that it will increase; *cp* BARU). *Uangnya – seratus rupiah.* He has only one hundred rupiahs. *Ia tidak belajar, – bermain-main saja.* He was not studying, he was just playing around. *– secéng* [cuci mata sembari ngécéng] (*BG*) just hanging around watching the girls.

cuma-cuma *secara ~* free, for the asking (with no money changing hands).

bercuma in vain, to no purpose. *mati ~* died in vain.

mempercumakan 1 to waste (time/energy, etc.). 2 to give s.t. free of charge.

percuma useless, vain, fruitless, a waste of time. *dengan ~* free (of charge), gratis. *Obat-obatan diberikan dengan ~.* Medicines were provided free of charge. *perjanjian dengan ~* agreement for no consideration (where no money changes hands).

cumadong dawuh (*Jv*) to wait for instructions (in a humble way).

cuman (*J*) 1 only; → CUMA. *Saya – makan ubi sepotong.* I have only eaten a slice of yam. 2 however, but (don't). *Adik boléh main di sini, – jangan berisik.* You may play here, but don't make a lot of noise. *Kemarin duit saya ada seribu, sekarang – seratus pérak.* I had a thousand rupiahs yesterday, now I have only have a hundred.

cumbang (*Jv*) (to have) sexual intercourse. *Pengungkapan ajaran-ajaran moral diselang-selingi dengan adegan – sanggama yang riuh dan tuntas.* The expression of moral teachings has been alternated with tumultuous and conclusive scenes of sexual intercourse.

cumbu 1 flattery, endearment. 2 joke, banter. *– dan belai* sweet words and caresses. *– rayu* compliments, sweet words. **bercumbu rayu** to seduce, tempt, lure. **mencumbu rayu** to sweet-talk, soft-soap, persuade with promises.

bercumbu(-cumbu)(an) 1 to joke, banter back and forth. 2 to make love. *Kupu-kupu malam itu merayu laki-laki yang léwat untuk bercumbu ke rumah liliput atau semak di tepi kali.* The prostitutes are courting men passing by to make love in huts or in the shrubs along the river bank.

mencumbu(i) 1 to fondle, caress. 2 flatter, coax. 3 to make love (to). *Sekali témpo dia coba-coba mencumbu sang Nona Manis.* One day he tried hard to make love to the sweet girl.

cumbuan 1 endearments, flattery, compliments. *bujuk ~* coaxing, wheedling, cajoling. 2 jokes.

cumbu-cumbuan making love/out.

pe(n)cumbu s.o. who is good at bantering/flirting/making love.

percumbuan lovemaking.

cumbul → CEMBUL.

cumengkling (*Jv*) a very shrill and high-pitched sound, but sweet and pleasant to listen to.

cumepak (*Jv*) in stock, on hand, available, ready.

cumi-cumi (*C?*) 1 (*ikan –*) cuttlefish, squid, *Loligo indica*. 2 riff-raff, rabble, scum; → BROMOCORAH. 3 police spy, stool pigeon.

cumil → COMÉL.

cuming (*J*) only, merely; → CUMA. *– gelar* a mere title. *Anaknya – satu.* He has only one child.

cum laude (*L*) /kum/ cum laude, with honor. *meraih gelar doktor dalam ilmu sastra dari Univérsitas Indonésia dengan prédikat – to get a doctorate in literature from UI with honors.

cum suis (*L*) /kum/ 1 with his friends/companions/associates. 2 with affiliates; → C.S.

cun I (*C*) Chinese inch, 1/10 foot.

cun II (*E*) tune in.

mengecun to tune in.

pengecunan tuning in.

cunam tweezers, tongs, forceps.

mencunam to tweeze.

cunda → CUCUNDA.

cundang I (*M*) → KECUNDANG. instigation, provocation. *kena –* to be provoked.

mencundang to instigate, provoke, incite, spur/egg on.

kecundang provocation, instigation. *Kau menjadi korban karena termakan ~ orang.* You became a victim because you were eaten up by s.o.'s provocative actions. *~ jangan diperbanyak.* Don't provoke people. *~ lebih bagai kebaji* provocation is more wicked/evil than magic.

cundang II (*J*) **becundang, mencundang** and **nyundang** to sleep with the feet elevated.

cundrik (*Jv*) poniard.

cunduk (*Jv*) hair ornament.

bercunduk to wear such an ornament.

cung I (*Pal*) egg plant.

cung II clipped form of **kacung**.

cungak → CUNGAP.

cungap – *cangip* and – *cungip* panting, gasping for breath.

mencungap to open one's mouth wide.

tercungap open wide, gaping.

cunggar (to have an) erection; → NGACENG.

Cungit Ngacung (*Min*) a Moluccan species of banana; the fruit appears to look upward; *cp* NGACENG.

cungkil (= **pencungkil**) object (like a toothpick, etc.) used to pick or gouge s.t. out of a hole; → CUKIL. – *ban* tire remover. – *ajai* toothpick.

bercungkil 1 gouged/dug out. **2** vaccinated, inoculated.

mencungkil 1 to lift, dig out. ~ *kuman dengan alu* to do s.t. useless. ~ *ban* to remove a tire. **2** to gouge out. ~ *kelapa* to gouge out a coconut. ~ *mata* to gouge out the eyes. **3** to pick at. ~ *gigi* to pick one's teeth. ~ *telinga* to remove earwax. **4** to vaccinate, inoculate.

mencungkili (*pl obj*) to pick, pry, etc.

mencungkilkan to pick, pry, etc. for s.o. else.

cungkilan 1 vaccination, inoculation. **2** gouge. *kelapa/nyiur* ~ a coconut hard enough to be gouged (for its milk).

pencungkil object (like a toothpick, etc.) used to pick or gouge s.t. out of a hole. ~ *és* ice pick. ~ *gigi* toothpick.

pencungkilan gouging out.

cungking (C?) trawler.

cungkok (*C sl*) Chinese (from China); → TIONGKOK.

cungkup (*Jv*) (memorial) tomb in the shape of a house.

cungo *tukang* – pickpocket; → CONGO.

cunguk → CECUNGUK.

cungul mencungul to appear/emerge at the surface.

mencungulkan to stick s.t. out.

cungur (*J/Jv*) snout; → JUNGUR.

cunia and **cunya** (C) barge, flat-bottomed ship.

cuntel → CUTEL.

cunting → CONTÉNG.

Cuo Sangiin (*Jp*) Indonesian advisory body during the Japanese occupation.

cup I (*onom*) sound of s.t. immersed in water.

cup II 1 (*onom*) hush! (parent to crying child), halt! stop! silence! **2** → COP II. **3** mine! (word which children use to lay claim to s.t.).

mencupkan to take a break in playing (a game).

cup III (*onom*) sound of a kiss on s.o.'s cheek.

cup-cupan smooching.

cupai (*M*) neglectful, careless.

mencupaikan to neglect, procrastinate, delay, postpone, be careless, be inattentive.

tercupai neglected, disregarded.

cupak I 1 cubic measure for rice, etc. of uncertain capacity, *usu secupak* = ¼ *gantang* or half a coconut shellful, ca. 0.780 kilograms.

secupak ¼ of a *gantang*. *(yang)* ~ *takkan jadi segantang* who was born as a donkey will never die as a horse, a leopard doesn't change its spots.

mencupak to measure by the *cupak*.

cupak II (*M*) – *asli* traditional customs. *membawakan – ke negeri orang* to keep one's (own) customs and traditions (in a foreign country).

cupak III (*Jv*) bowl of opium pipe.

cupak IV *pohon* – k.o. tree (with fruit like the *duku*), carambola, *Baccaurea dulcis*; → KETUPA I.

cupak V small carrying bag for betel requirements made from woven bamboo with a black and red painted Dayak mask motif on it.

cupak VI *penyakit* – vitiligo

cupang I love-bite, hickey.

nyupangin (*J*) to give s.o. a love-bite.

cupang II (*Jv*) black magic.

nyupang to possess black magic.

cupang(-cupang) *ikan* – croaking gurami, Betta fighting fish, *Ctenops vittatus, Betta splendens*. – *bintik* dwarf gurami, *Ctenops pumilus*. – *hias* k.o. decorative fish.

cupar I dirty mouthed, like to say dirty words.

mencupar 1 to talk dirty. **2** to talk nonsense.

cupar II sneering.

mencupar to twist things around, confuse matters.

cupar III (*J/Jv*) (said of a man) stingy, miserly, and likes to meddle in what are usually female household chores.

cupat → CUPET.

cupeng (*Jv*) cover for grown-up girl's private parts (in the *Keratons*, made of gold).

cupet (*J*) **1** too tight, not large enough, skimpy, inadequate, too short. *Soalnya uang belanja dapur terasa menjadi – (sempit) setelah ada pengumuman Pemerintah bahwa gaji pegawai negeri naik lima belas persén.* The case is that the household money is felt to become barely sufficient after a government announcement that the salaries of the government employees will increase 15 percent. **2** narrow(-minded), short-sighted. **3** petty, narrow, bigoted. *seorang yang – pikiran* a narrow-minded person; → PICIK. *pengetahuan yang –* a narrow knowledge.

kecupetan 1 narrowness, narrow-mindedness. **2** to be pinched for room, cramped for space.

cuping 1 lobe (of the ear or nostril). **2** handle, ear-like projection. – *hidung* nostrils. *tidak memperlihatkan – hidungnya* didn't appear/show up. – *cangkir* handle of a cup. – *telinga* ear lobe. – *sayap* flaps (on aircraft).

bercuping with a handle, lobed.

cupit Chinese chopsticks; → SUPIT I.

cuplak → CELUPAK.

cuplik (*Jv*) **mencuplik 1** to pick out part of s.t., quote, cite, extract. **2** to sample.

mencupliki to cite, quote.

cuplikan 1 quotation, citation, extract. **2** sample; sampling. *mengambil* ~ to take a sample.

pencuplik (*elec*) sampler.

pencuplikan 1 quoting, citing. **2** sampling.

cupluk (*J*) family toilet.

cupu(-cupu) 1 jewelry box. **2** hole for boat's mast, mast hole. **3** threshold, doorsill; → CEPUK I.

cupul 1 too short (of cord, etc.), too loose (of string on parcels, etc.), untidy (of strings, etc.). **2** too little (of amounts).

cur (*onom*) **1** rushing sound (of water). **2** sizzling sound (of food being fried).

cura I joke, jest. *berbuat* – and **bercura** to joke, jest, banter, play the fool. *tidak* ~ serious, earnest.

cura II (*M*) **cura-cura** harsh, abusive words. **bercura-cura** and **bercura-bura** to abuse s.o., call (s.o.) names, utter indecent words.

curadi (*geol*) phenoclast.

curah large quantity, bulk, in large amounts. *barang* – bulk goods. – *hujan* rainfall, precipitation. – *hujan Désémber di Jakarta di atas perkiraan*. The December rainfall in Jakarta was above expectations. – *jantung* cardiac output. – *pendapat* brainstorming.

mencurah to pour down (of rain), precipitate.

mencurahi 1 to pour down on, flood. *Hujan lebat* ~ *sawah*. Torrential rains poured down on the irrigated rice fields. **2** to bestow upon, shower. *Ia dicurahi kepercayaan kami.* He was given our full confidence. *seperti* ~ *garam ke laut* like carrying coals to Newcastle. ~ *isi hatinya* to pour out one's heart. ~ *perhatian terhadap* to pay attention to. ~ *perhatiannya untuk menulis buku-buku pelajaran bahasa Indonésia* to turn one's attention to writing Indonesian textbooks. **3** to pour (water) on.

mencurahkan 1 to pour s.t. (on). *curiga dicurahkan kepada* the suspicion fell on. *hujan sebagai dicurahkan* a downpour, heavy shower. **2** to dedicate, devote. ~ *tenaganya kepada* to devote one's energy to. **3** to expend (energy), express (one's feelings), pay (attention). ~ *(isi) hati* to pour out one's heart, share one's problems (with s.o. else). ~ *waktu* to devote/spend one's time.

tercurah(kan) ~ *ke(pada)* dedicated/devoted (to), focused (on). *Seluruh perhatianku* ~ *padamu*. All my attention was focused on you.

curahan 1 outpouring, outflow, bestowal, expression, pouring out. ~ *hati* [curhat] (*BG*) pouring out one's heart, sharing one's feelings. ~ *kasih sayang* outflow of love and affection. ~ *waktu orangtua bagi anak meréka* the devotion of time of parents to their children. **2** precipitation. **3** bulk. *kapal* ~ bulk carrier. **4** outfall (in mining).

pencurah s.t. that pours, pourer.

pencurahan 1 precipitation. **2** outpouring, effusion, devotion, expression. ~ *rasa* outpouring of feelings. ~ *tenaga* devotion of energy. **3** bestowal.

curai (*M*) **1** loose, detached, separate. **2** clear, evident. **3** resolution (of an image).

mencuraikan 1 to loosen, untie, disentangle, unravel. **2** to separate, isolate, resolve (images). **3** to explain, clarify.

curaian 1 separation. **2** explanation. **3** resolution.

pencuraian 1 resolution, resolving. ~ *tinggi* high resolution. **2** loosening, disentangling, separating. **3** explaining, clarifying.

curam steep, sheer, precipitous, abrupt (of a cliff/abyss, etc.).

mencuram to become steep; sloping, on an incline, inclined.

kecuraman steepness, precipitousness, abruptness.

curang (*J/Jv*) **1** dishonest, deceitful, fraudulent, insincere, unethical, unfair. **2** cheating (of a spouse). *perbuatan* – fraud, swindle. *persaingan* – unfair competition. *tidak* – candid, frank.

mencurangi to deceive, mislead, cheat, defraud, swindle, foul (in sports).

tercurang the most dishonest, etc.

curangan deceit, fraud.

kecurangan 1 deceit, deception, fraud, unfairness, dirty trick. ~ *pajak* tax fraud. **2** foul (in sports).

curanmor → PENCURIAN *kendaraan bermotor*.

curapi (*geol*) pyroclast.

curas → PENCURIAN (*dengan*) *kekerasan*.

curat I spout (of kettle, etc.), nozzle; → CERAT.

mencurat to gush forth/out, pour out.

mencuratkan to have poured down.

pencuratan spouting forth.

curat II → PENCURIAN (*dengan*) *pemberatan*.

curdiri (*geol*) autoclast.

cureng (*J/Jv*) **mencureng** and **nyureng** to squint at s.t./s.o. with half-closed eyes (due to the glare).

tercureng-cureng squinted at.

curhat → CURAHAN *hati*.

curi (*Hind?*) theft, steal, rob. – *bongkar* break-in, burglary. – *gait* shoplifting.

mencuri [and **nyuri** (*coq*)] **1** to steal s.t.; to rob s.o. ~ *hati* to steal s.o.'s heart. ~ *mata* to do s.t. while others aren't watching. ~ *pandang* to sneak a look. ~ *tulang* to loaf about, (be) idle, pretend to work hard. **2** → CURI-CURI.

mencuri-curi [and **curi-curi** (*coq*)] to do s. t. surreptitiously/on the sly, secretly/stealthily/in a clandestine way. *secara mencuri-curi* secretly, clandestinely. ~ *kesempatan* to take advantage of an opportunity. ~ *rute* (of city bus) to deviate from the prescribed route (to earn more money). *Saya suka ~ nyetir mobil milik orangtua.* I like to drive my parents' car without their knowledge.

nyuri-nyuri (*coq*) to steal repeatedly.

tercuri stolen, plagiarized.

curian stolen. *barang* ~ stolen items, loot.

kecurian 1 to get robbed, lose s.t. through theft. *Sabtu malam lalu dia ~ mobil sédan Toyota Corolla warna putih.* Last Saturday night his white Toyota Corolla sedan was stolen. **2** theft.

pencuri thief; → MALING. *Diduga ~ mobil itu menggunakan kunci palsu.* It is assumed that the car thief used a master key.

pencurian 1 theft, robbery. ~ (*dengan*) *kekerasan* [curas] theft with violence, armed robbery. ~ (*dengan*) *pemberatan* [curcat] aggravated theft. ~ *kawat télepon* theft of telephone wires. ~ *kendaraan bermotor* [curanmor] car theft. ~ *paksa* armed robbery. **2** defalcation.

curiah (*M*) **1** talkative, garrulous, chatty. **2** friendly, amicable.

curiga I (*Skr*) suspicious, distrustful, have doubts, doubtful, hesitant. *Walaupun saya bersedia menolongnya, dia masih – tentang kejujuran saya.* Although I'm willing to help him, he still has doubts about my sincerity.

bercuriga to suspect, be suspicious.

mencurigai to suspect/distrust s.o. *Kita boléh ~ dia, tetapi jangan langsung menuduh.* We might distrust him, but let's not accuse him directly.

curiga-mencurigai mutual suspicion.

mencurigakan to arouse suspicion, be suspicious. *Tindakannya itu ~ karena itu kita harus berhati-hati terhadapnya.* His actions are suspicious and that's why we must be careful about him.

tercuriga the suspect. *para ~* the suspects.

kecurigaan doubts, suspicion, distrust, mistrust. *Gerak-geriknya telah menimbulkan ~ di hati saya.* His movements made me suspicious.

curiga II (*Jv*) kris.

curik (*ob*) k.o. short dagger, poniard.

curing (*geol*) karst.

curjasad (*geol*) bioclast.

curna (*cla*) dissolved, destroyed; → CERNA.

curu (*M*) **mencuru** to have diarrhea.

curubah epiclast.

curudut anguclast.

curug and **curuk** (*Jv*) waterfall.

curulat spheroclast.

curut Japanese scad, *Decapterus maruadsi*.

cus I 1 (*onom*) (imitation of the sound produced by pouring water over burning coals, etc.) sst!

cus II shh, be quiet!

cut (*onom*) squeaking.

cutak (*S*) district. *kepala* – district head.

cutam (*Tam? Mal*) black and gilt niello from Siamese Malay.

cutbirahi pun on *cutbrai*; → BIRAHI.

cutbrai and **cutbray** *celana* – bell-bottom trousers.

cutel (*Jv*) the end (of a story, film, etc.). *tanpa/tidak ada* – endless, interminable.

cuti (*Hind*) **1** vacation, holiday. **2** leave, furlough. *mengambil – tahunan* to take annual leave. – *bersalin* maternity leave. – *besar* long leave. **mencuti-besarkan** (*euph*) to grant long leave (with the underlying idea of dismissing s.o.). – *bersalin* maternity leave. – *dengan tetap mendapatkan upah* paid holiday. – *di luar tanggungan* unpaid leave (for government employees). – *dibayar* paid leave. – *dinas* official leave. – *haid(h)* leave due to menstruation. – *hamil* pregnancy leave. – *luarbiasa* extraordinary leave. – *melahirkan* maternity leave. – *panjang* long leave. – *sakit* sick leave. – *studi selama setahun* a one-year sabbatical (leave) (for lecturers/professors). – *tahunan* annual leave.

bercuti 1 to go on vacation. **2** to be on leave.

mencutikan to give/grant leave, furlough.

pencutian being sent on leave.

cuwap → CUAP.

cuwawakan (*Jv*) (to laugh) at the top of one's voice (improperly) with the mouth wide open. *dengan gaya* – with an open mouth.

cuwék indifferent; → CUAI, CUÉK. – *bébék/béybéh/bléh* couldn't care less, completely indifferent.

nyuwékin to ignore, pay no attention to, be indifferent to.

cuwil I secuwil a (little) bit.

mencuwil to touch slightly, nudge.

cuwil II (*Jv*) damaged (earthenware, etc.), with a piece broken off; → CUIL II.

mencuwil to take a little bit of s.t.

cuwilan a little bit.

CVS [Commanditaire Vennootschap] (*D*) Limited Partnership.

CW I a passenger car (in train formation).

cw II abbreviated form of *céwék*.

cylinderkop pakking (*D ob*) gasket.

D

d and **D I** /dé/ the fourth letter of the Latin alphabet used for writing Indonesian.

D II car license plate for Bandung.

3D [Duit, Dulur dan Dalit] (*Jv*) Money, Relatives, and Close Unity (in village development).

4D [Duit, Dukun, Dukungan dan Déking] Money, *Dukun*, Support, and Backing.

5D [Datang, Duduk, Dengar, Diam dan Duit] Attend, Sit Down, Listen, Be Quiet, and Get Money (of members of the *DPR*).

6D [Datang Daftar/Absén, Duduk, Diam dan Duit serta Dengkur] Come, Attend/Sign In, Sit Down, Be Quiet, Get Money, and Snore (of members of the DPR).

D-1 [Diploma Satu] one-year diploma program.

D-2 [Diploma Dua] two-year diploma program.

D-3 [Diploma Tiga] three-year diploma program.

da I (*M*) clipped form of **uda** "older brother".

da II (in acronyms) → DAÉRAH, DAYA, DUA, MUDA.

da III -nda and **-anda** used as polite suffixes for certain words indicating family relationships; → ANAKDA, ANAKANDA, ANANDA, IBUNDA.

da IV → ADA.

DA V car license for South Kalimantan.

d/a (*abbr*) [dengan alamat] in care of, c/o.

daayah and **da'ayah** (*A*) Muslim propaganda or proselytizing.

dab (*E*) **mendab** and **mengedab** to dub (a film).
  pendaban dubbing; → SULIH *suara*.

daba (*hawa*) – 1 foul air, strong smell. 2 breath of suspicion. 3 passion, lust.

dabah → DABAT, DEBAH.

dabak (*M*) **mendabak** (to show up) unexpectedly, all of a sudden, suddenly; → MENDADAK.

dabal I (*A ob*) bag/pouch attached to one's waist-cloth or belt.

dabal II (*E*) double. *baju* – double-breasted jacket. – *setengah tiang* dress coat.

dabaran (*A*) (the star) Aldebaran.

dabat (*A ob*) animal for slaughter.

dabih (*M*) **mendabih** to slaughter. ~ *menampung darah* very greedy/selfish.
  pendabihan 1 slaughter. 2 abattoir, slaughterhouse.

dabik (*M*) **mendabik** to beat (one's chest) (as a sign of daring or pride).

dabing (*E*) dubbing; → DAB, SULIH *suara*.
  mendabing to dub, make another sound track on a movie film, *esp* in a different language.

dabir (*Pers ob*) clerk, scribe.

dablek, dableg (*Jv*) and **ndableg** 1 stubborn, obstinate. 2 indifferent.
  kedablegan 1 stubbornness, obstinacy. 2 indifference.

dabok (*M*) → DEBAR.

dabu-dabu – *manis* k.o. sweet and hot sauce.

dabung berdabung to file, cut level (of teeth).
  mendabung to cut level (of teeth, prior to filing).

dabus (*A*) (in Serang, Banten, West Java) performance in which the players stab themselves with sharp objects, eat shards of glass, cut their tongues, roll over barbed wire, etc. *anak* – participant in this performance. *besi/mata* – awl used in this self-stabbing scene. *main* – and
  berdabus put on, give such a performance.

dabyah ngedabyah to hold one's ground, last for a long time.

dacin(g) (*C*) steelyard, scale, type of instrument for weighing consisting of a graduated rod, a pan or scale, and a weight. *anak/buah/batu* – piece of metal of a specific standard heaviness used on the scale in weighing. *lidah* – marking on this rod to indicate the exact weight of s.t.
  mendacin(g) to weigh with a *dacin(g)*.

dad (*A*) name of the 15th letter of the Arabic alphabet.

dada chest. *Ini –ku, mana –mu?* This is my chest, where's yours?" i.e., a challenge to fight. If you want to fight, come on. *buah* – female breast, bosom; → PAYUDARA. *rongga* – chest cavity (containing the heart and lungs). *membusung* – to brag, boast. *mengusap/mengurut* – to control/have control over one's feelings. *sakit* – tuberculosis. *sempit* – very touchy, irritable, prickly, quick/short-tempered. *tiba di – dibusungkan, tiba di perut dikempiskan* to act unfairly in reaching a decision. – *ayam* chicken-breasted. – *bidang* broad-breasted. – *burung* pigeon-breasted. – *kempis* concave chest. – *lapang* patient, calmly tolerating delay, phlegmatic. – *lega* relieved. – *manuk* pigeon breasted.

berdada-dadaan and **dada-mendada** to fight at close quarters, hand-to-hand fighting.

mendada to stick out one's chest (in defiance), strut, face up to an attack.

dadah I 1 medicines, medicinal herbs. 2 (*Mal*) narcotics. *pembawa* – drug trafficker.
  berdadah doped, drugged.
  mendadahi to dope/drug s.o.
  terdadah doped.
  pedadah container for herbs.
  pendadah 1 drug addict. 2 place for storing medicines.
  perdadahan and **pendadahan** doping.

dadah II (*Jv*) to massage by pressing softly on (a baby).

dadah III mendadah to expose; → DEDAH.
  mendadahkan to expose
  pendadahan exposure.

dadah IV (*D coq*) to say good-bye/hello, bye-bye.

dadaisme (*D/E*) dadaism.

dadak I (*J/Jv*) instant. *kopi/mi* – instant coffee/mie.
  mendadak 1 suddenly, all of a sudden, unexpectedly, overnight. *Meréka pasti bakal kaya* ~. They will certainly become rich overnight. ~ *sontak* quite suddenly. ~ *sontak saluran listrik padam* ~. Quite suddenly there was a power failure. **2** unannounced, surprise. *inspéksi* ~ [sidak] an unannounced inspection. **kemendadakan** suddenness, spontaneity.
  terdadak unexpectedly, surprised. "*Jangan sampai kita merasa* ~ *ada ini, ada itu,*" *ucapnya.* "By all means, let's not be surprised, with all k.o. excuses," he said.
  dadakan overnight, instant, sudden, unannounced. *ékspér(t)* ~ an instant expert. *orang kaya* ~ s.o. who becomes rich overnight. *secara* ~ instantly, instantaneously. *serangan udara* ~ a preemptive air strike.
  pendadak s.t. sudden. *pertemuan* ~ emergency meeting.
  pendadakan surprise, surprise attack.

dadak II → KEDADAK.

dadal I (*Jv*) swept away (of bridge, etc. by the current).
  mendadal to break down.
  dadalan breakdown, disruption.

dadal II revocation of rights to land when the user moves or passes away.

dadali I (*Jv*) *manuk* – k.o. swallow.

dadali II Moluccan kestrel, *Falco moluccensis*.

dadap I various species of trees, *Erythrina spp.* – *ayam/laut* Indian coral tree, *Erythrina orientalis*. – *duri/serep* December tree, *Erythrina subumbrans*. – *hias* coral tree (used as shade tree in coffee plantations), *Erythrina variegata*.

dadap II (*Jv*) *si – dan si Waru* A and B (two hypothetical persons); *cp* POLAN.

dadap III (*cla*) metal shield.
  mendadap to shield.
  dadapan shielding.

dadar I 1 *telur* – and – *telur* a) omelet. b) scrambled eggs. – *gulung* wheat flour crepe, *usu* green in color; rolled around a mixture of coconut and brown sugar.

mendadar to make an omelet of.

dadar II (*Jv*) **1** test, trial. **2** training.

pendadaran 1 testing. **2** touchstone. **3** (*mil*) training (center); → KAWAH *Candradimuka.*

dadék (*M ob*) **terdadék** lost, gone astray.

dadén (*Jv*) to build a fire by sprinkling it with a little bit of petroleum to facilitate burning. *Sekarang ini minyak tanah hanya digunakan untuk –.* Nowadays petroleum is only used for lighting firewood.

dadi I (*ob*) → DADIH.

dadi II (*Jv*) → JADI I.

dadia (*Bal*) extended family.

dadié (*Bal*) community worshipping place.

dadih (*Skr*) **1** coagulated milk (from goats/cows/water buffaloes), curd, curdled milk. *air –* whey. **2** (*M*) frozen buffalo milk, eaten with *emping pulut*, brown sugar, and coconut. *– darah* coagulated blood. *– jalang* diluted milk. *– kering* butter. *– pekat* curds, curdled milk.

berdadih curdled.

mendadih to curdle, form or cause to form curds.

mendadihkan to condense.

pendadih coagulating agent.

pendadihan coagulating, condensing.

dading (*D leg*) out of court settlement.

dadu I (*Port*) **1** *buah –* die, dice. *main/membuang –* to shoot dice. **2** cube. *– guncang* (in Jambi) k.o. gambling game consisting of a die, dice shaker, and an illustrated board depicting animals, such as, snakes. *– pusing/putar/sintir* roulette.

berdadu to shoot dice.

dadu II pink, roseate. *méga –* the roseate clouds.

mendadu to become pink in color.

kedadu-daduan pinkish. *serbuk ~* pinkish powder.

Dadu III Aquarius.

daduh (*ob*) **mendaduh 1** to sing. **2** (= **mendaduhkan**) to put (a child) to sleep by singing lullabies.

daduk (*ob*) **mendaduk** to beg for alms, panhandle.

pendaduk beggar, panhandler.

dadun mendadun to air-dry tobacco leaves.

dadung I (*ob*) **berdadung** to sing a lullaby.

mendadung(kan) to put (a child) to sleep by singing lullabies.

dadung II (*Jv*) thick rope (*esp* for leading cattle), halter, hawser. *– kepil* mooring hawser.

mendadung to tether using such a rope.

dadya (*Bal*) clan.

daéng Buginese/Makassarese title of nobleman (not a prince), somewhat lower than *keraéng; cp* ANDI. **2** older brother (vocative). **3** term of address for an older man. *Silakan duduk, –.* Please, be seated, sir.

daérah (*A*) **1** region, territory; regional, local. *bahasa –* regional language (such as, Sundanese, Javanese). **2** environs, vicinity, surroundings, neighborhood. **3** province. *Kepala –* [KDH] (Provincial) Head or Governor. **4** outlying district. **5** area with a similar climate/population, etc.; zone, belt. **6** position. *– aliran sungai* [DAS] Watershed. *– angkutan* (*mil*) drop area. *– antar* interregional. *– asuhan* nursery (for fish). *– bahagian* component state. *– banjir* flood plain. *– bantai* killing ground. *– batubara* coal belt. *– Bébas Bécak* [DBB] Pedicab-Free Zone. *– Bébas Militér* Demilitarized Zone, DMZ. *– bébas témbakan* free fire zone. *– belakang* hinterland. *– berbahaya* danger zone. *– berbukit* hilly country/land. *– bina* development zone. *– buta* blind zone. *– dataran tinggi tengah* the Central Highlands (in Vietnam). *– démilitarisasi* demilitarized zone. *– désa* rural area. *– distribusi* distribution point. *– gawang* goal zone. *– Haram* Forbidden Zone (area around Mecca and Medina). *– hawa dingin* frigid zone. *– hawa panas* tropics. *– hawa sedang* temperate zone. *– hijau* (PKI-term) an area in which the army is strongly represented. *– hitam* a) red-light district. b) crime-ridden area. *– hukum* (*leg*) jurisdiction. *– hulu* headwaters. *– hulu sungai* catchment area. *– hutan* forest area. *– iklim* climatic region. *– Istimewa Acéh* [Dista] Aceh Special Region (in northern Sumatra). *– Istiméwa Yogyakarta* [DIY] Yogyakarta Special Region (in Central Java). *– jabatan* district. *– jajahan* colony. *–*

jalur hijau greenbelt. *– jantung* heartland. *– jelajah* range (of an animal). *– kandung beras* rice bowl, i.e., a region in which rice is grown. *– kantong* enclave. *– katulistiwa* equatorial zone. *– kediaman* residential area. *– kepolisian* [Dak] Police District. *– kericuan* trouble spot. *– kering* arid region. *– khatulistiwa* tropical/equatorial area. *– Khusus Ibukota Jakarta Raya* [DKI Jaya] Greater Jakarta Special Capital Region (with provincial status). *– kosong* thinly populated area. *– kota* urban area. *– kumuh* slum. *– kutub* polar region. *– lampu mérah* red-light district. *– larang témbakan* no-fire zone. *– luah* discharge area. *– luar* external zone. *– majir* barren zone. *– mata air* headwaters. *– mati* dead space. *– mencari makan* feeding ground (for fish). *– mérah* (PKI term) an area in which the Communist Party of Indonesia is strongly represented. *– meriam* gun position. *– milik jalan* right of way. *– militér* military area. *– minus* an area that does not grow or raise enough food to support itself; *opp* DAÉRAH *surplus. Maluku masih tergolong – minus héwan ternak.* The Moluccas is still a low cattle-producing area. *– negara* national territory. *– Nyiur Melambai* reference to Northern Sulawesi. *– operasi militér* [DOM] zone of military operations. *– Otonomi Khusus Nanggroe Acéh Darussalam* Darussalam Aceh Nanggroe Special Autonomous District. *– oséanik* oceanic territory. *– pabéan* Custom Zone. *– padi* rice belt. *– panas* tropics. *– pandangan* field of vision. *– pantai* waterfront area. *– pasang surut* intertidal zone. *– pedalaman* hinterland, inland. *– pedésaan* rural area. *– pegunungan* mountainous regions. *– pemberangkatan* pick-up zone. *– pemilihan pemungutan (suara)* electoral district. *– pemindahan* transfer point. *– penampungan air* drainage area. *– penangkapan ikan* fishing grounds. *– pendaratan* landing zone. *– pendudukan* occupied zone. *– penerjunan* drop-zone. *– pengaruh* sphere of influence; → LINGKUNGAN *pengaruh. – penghasil karét* rubber-producing area. *– pengiriman pos* postal zone/code. *– pengungsian* refugee area. *– penunjang* hinterland. *– penerjunan* drop zone. *– penyangga* buffer zone. *– penyekat* buffer-zone. *– peralihan* watershed. *– perkémahan* camp ground. *– perlindungan* prohibited area. *– perbatasan* frontier/border zone (with provincial status). *– perkotaan* urban area. *– pertokoan* shopping center. *– Perwalian* trust territory. *– pesisir* a) coastal area. b) (in Java) the regions along Java's north coast. c) (also, in Java) the regions outside the principalities (of Yogyakarta and Surakarta). *– pinggiran* a) outskirts (of a city), periphery, perimeter. b) borders. c) (in Jakarta, the neighborhoods of) Pal Merah, Kebayoran Lama, Tanggerang, Kramat Pulo, Klender, and Pasar Rebo. *– putih* (PKI term) an area in which the Communist Party of Indonesia is weak. *– rahasia* genital area. *– rawan pangan* an area that does not grow enough food to support itself. *– remang-remang* dark and dangerous neighborhood. *– sabuk hijau* green belt. *– sebaran* distribution, range (of a plant or animal). *– seberang lautan* (*ob*) overseas territories (viewed from the Dutch standpoint). *– sedang* temperate zone. *– senja* twilight zone. *– serba kekurangan* an area that does not grow enough to support itself. *– singgahan* staging area. *– sungai* catchment basin/area. *– surplus* an area with enough food to feed itself plus some left over; *cp* DAÉRAH *minus. – swapraja* autonomous region. *– swasembada* area which can supply its own needs. *– Swatantra Tingkat I* First Level Autonomous Region. *– Swatantra Tingkat II* Second Level Autonomous Region. *– tadah(an)* catchment area. *– tak bertuan* no-man's land. *– takluk* dependency. *– tangkapan air* catchment area. *– tapak* site zone. *– tatapraja* administrative unit. *– terbatas* restricted area. *– terbelakang* underdeveloped regions. *– terjepit* enclave, pocket. *– terlarang* prohibited/restricted area. *– tetangga* neighborhood. *– tidak bertuan* no man's land. *– Tingkat I* [(Dati I/Dati Satu] First Level Region, i.e., the former *Provinsi* or Province. *– Tingkat II* [Dati II/Dati Dua]: a) *kabupatén* governed by a *bupati* and b) *kotamadaya* governed by a *walikotamadya* (= mayor of a municipality). *– tropika* tropics. *– udik* uplands. *– upah* payroll. *– waktu* time zone. *– yang banyak gangguannya* trouble spot. *– yang bergolak* hot spot. *– yang dikosongkan dari militér* demilitarized zone. *– yang mengenal empat musim* the West, western countries. *– yang tidak dikenal* terra incognita.

sedaérah 1 of the same area/region/province. 2 regional, local. *teman* ~ person from the same region.

sesedaérah → SEDAÉRAH-SEDAÉRAH

sedaérah-sedaérah on a regional basis, regionally.

berdaérah with/to have regions.

memperdaérah to turn into a region/province, treat like a region.

kedaérahan 1 provincialism, regionalism. 2 local, regional, provincial.

pendaérahan regionalization.

perdaérahan local, regional.

daérahisme regionalism, provincialism.

daérahnisasi regionalization.

daf (in acronyms) → DAFTAR.

dafnah (*A*) *pohon* – laurel, *Lauris nobilis*.

daftar (*Pers*) list, register, roster, catalog, table, roll, slate. – *abjad* alphabetical list. – *absénsi* attendance list, roster. – *acara* program. – *anak buah kapal* muster. – *angka* report card (in school). – *bahari* muster. – *barang* packing list. – *budel* inventory of an estate. – *buku* booklist, catalog. – *catatan sipil* civil register. – *cegah tangkal* and – *cekal* [cegah dan tangkal] list containing the names of certain individuals who are not allowed to leave or enter the country (an immigration document). – *darab* multiplication table. – "*F*" PKI Communist Party of Indonesia's list containing the names of hardcore members. – G list of prescription drugs. – *gaji* payroll. – *giliran sidang* docket. – *hadir* attendance list, roll, roster. – *harga* price list. – *hitam* blacklist. *sudah masuk* ~ *polisi* already black listed by the police. **mendaftar-hitamkan** to blacklist. – *induk* master list. – *isi (buku)* table of contents (of a book). – *isian* form (to fill out), questionnaire. – *isian pertanyaan* questionnaire. – *isian proyék* [DIP] list of project contents. – *istilah* glossary of terminology. – *kali-kalian* multiplication table. – *kartu* card index. – *kata* wordlist, glossary. – *kelahiran* registry of births. – *kematian* mortality table. – *kepustakaan* bibliography. – *lampiran gaji* pay slip. – *logaritma* logarithmic table. – *makanan* menu. – *muatan* waybill, manifest. – *nama* a) list of names, roll. b) nomenclature. – *nilai* (in schools) a) examination results. b) (school) transcript. – *nilai ébtanas murni* [daném] Ebtanas Murni test results. – *nomor yang keluar* list of drawings. – *orang rusak* [DOR] and – *orang tercela* [DOT] list of people not allowed to engage in banking activities. – *orang yang akan dibunuh* hit list. – *pasang surut* tide table. – *pelaku* cast of characters, dramatis personae. – *pelayaran* log. – *pembagian* distribution list. – *pembayaran* payroll. – *pemilih* voters registration, electoral register. – *pengawasan* watch list. – *pengecékan* checklist. – *penunjuk* index, register (in book). – *periksa* checklist. – *perjalanan* schedule, timetable, itinerary. – *permintaan* a) application form. b) questionnaire. – *persidangan* docket. – *pertanyaan* questionnaire. – *pokok* principal register. – *présénsi* attendance list. roster. – *pustaka* bibliography. – *riwayat pekerjaan* record of service. – *sérep* waiting list. – *susunan berkala* periodic table. – *tak-hadir* attendance record. – *tunggu* waiting list. – *umum* public record. – *umur piutang* aging schedule (of receivables). – *upah* payroll. – *usaha* program, schedule. – *usulan projék* [DUP] list of project proposals.

berdaftar (*mostly Mal*) registered.

mendaftar 1 to enter (into records), book, register, record, enroll. 2 to sign up, register, enroll o.s., place o.s. on a list, check in. *Tahun lalu, murid yang ~ di sekolah itu cuma 45 siswa.* Last year only 45 students enrolled in the school. 3 to draw up a list/inventory.

mendaftari (*pl obj*) to register, record, etc.

mendaftarkan [and ndaftarin/ngedaftarin (*J coq*)] 1 to record. 2 to register, enroll/enlist s.o., sign up. ~ *diri* to enter one's name, enroll o.s. *Saya sudah ~ diri di univérsitas itu.* I've registered at that university.

terdaftar [and kedaftar (*coq*)] 1 registered (mail), enrolled, listed, etc. 2 chartered (analyst, etc.).

daftaran list.

pendaftar 1 enroller, recorder, registrar. 2 registrant.

pendaftaran enrollment, registration, listing. *uang* ~ registration fee. ~ *Jiwa* → CATATAN Sipil. *kantor* ~ *tanah* real estate registry;

→ KADASTER. ~ *ulang* reregistration. ~ *Warga* → CATATAN Sipil. ~ *keberangkatan* (at airport) check-in. ~ *tanah* land survey.

dafti (*Pers*) rosary.

dag (in acronyms) → PERDAGANGAN.

daga I (*Skr*) insubordination, resistance, willful disobedience; → DAGI, DAHAGA II. – *dagi* all k.o. resistance. *Anggota-anggota partai terlarang itu mengadakan – dagi dalam negeri.* The members of that party put up all k.o. domestic resistance.

mendaga to rebel against authority, be insubordinate. *Pemimpin orang-orang yang ~ itu ditangkap oléh alat-alat negara.* The leaders of the rebels were arrested by the state apparatus. ~ *arus* to go against the current, run against the tide.

daga II → DAHAGA I.

daga III (*M*) terdaga accidentally bump into. *Kepalanya ~ dengan keras ke dinding itu.* His head bumped hard into the wall.

dagang I trade, commerce, business. *bahasa* – business/commercial language. *hitung* – commercial arithmetic. *kantor* – business office. *kaum* – traders. *orang* – merchant, trader. *sekolah* – business/commercial school. – *bersambut* a) buying merchandise on credit. b) consignment. – *gelap* contraband/smuggling trade. – *sapi* horse-trading, trafficking in votes, political bargaining.

berdagang to trade, deal, do business, be in business; to trade/deal in. ~ *kayu* to deal/trade in timber. ~ *kecil-kecilan* to carry on a small-scale business.

mendagangkan and memperdagangkan to trade, buy and sell. *tak boléh diperdagangkan* nonnegotiable.

dagangan merchandise, commodities, wares. *Dari tadi belum ada ~nya yang laku.* His wares have not been selling well. ~ *bersambut* goods bought with a loan.

pedagang merchant, trader. ~ *acung* peddler who offers his wares (cigarettes/drinks/snacks, etc.) to prospective buyers (in cars) at road intersections. ~ *antara* middleman, distributor. ~ *asongan* peddler who offers his wares (cigarettes/drinks/snacks, etc.) to prospective buyers (in cars) at road intersections. ~ *barang rombéngan/bekas* junkman. ~ *batang* small fishmonger. ~ *(ber)keliling* traveling salesman. ~ *besar* wholesaler. ~ *bumbon* (*Jv*) peddler of kitchen necessities, *esp* spices. ~ *écéran* retailer. ~ *girlan* (in Bogor) street vendor; → GIRLAN. ~ *grabakan* (*Jv*) vendor of raw and dry materials. ~ *kadal* retail fishmonger. ~ *kaki-lima* sidewalk vendor. ~ *kecil* retailer. ~ *kecil léséhan* (*Jv*) street vendor who sells his wares spread out on the ground. ~ *keliling* traveling salesman. ~ *kéténgan* retailer. ~ *menengah* middle class trader. ~ *minuman keliling* traveling street vendor of drinks. ~ *misbar* sidewalk vendor. ~ *obligasi tanpa jaminan pemerintah* junk bond trader. ~ *oprokan* (*Jv*) vendor who sells his wares in a disorderly heap. ~ *partai besar* wholesaler. ~ *pengécér* retailer. ~ *perantara* middleman, commission agent. ~ *pertengahan* a) middle class trader. b) tradesman, shopkeeper. ~ *pikulan* vendor who uses a shoulder pole to carry his wares. ~ *sayur gelaran* produce vendor who displays his wares on a mat. ~ *sunggén* (*Jv*) vendor who moves from one place to another.

pendagangan trading, dealing in.

perdagangan trade, commerce, business. *imbangan* ~ trade balance. *pusat* ~ trade center. *utusan* ~ trade envoy. ~ *antardaérah* inter-regional trade. ~ *antarpulau* interisland commerce. ~ *banyak pihak* multilateral trade. ~ *bébas* free trade. ~ *berjangka* futures trading. ~ *besar* wholesale trade. ~ *budak* slave trade. ~ *daging mentah* (*coq*) "raw flesh" trade, i.e., prostitution. ~ *dalam negeri* [dagri] domestic trade. ~ *écéran* retail trade. ~ *gelap* illegal/contraband/smuggling trade. ~ *kecil* retail trade. ~ *komoditi penyerahan kemudian* commodities futures trading. ~ *luar negeri* [daglu] foreign trade. ~ *mengumpul* collective trade. ~ *multilateral* multilateral trade. ~ *orang dalam* insider trading. ~ *penyaluran* distribution trade. ~ *penyerahan kemudian* futures trading. ~ *perbatasan* border trade. ~ *pulau* insular trade. ~ *Républik Indonésia* [Dagri] Republic of Indonesia commerce. ~ *sapi* a) horse trading. b) trafficking in votes. ~ *seberang laut* overseas trade. ~ *silang* cross trade. ~ *tanpa warkat* scripless trading. ~ *tetap* regular trade. ~ *timbal balik* countertrade, CT. ~ *transito* transit trade. ~ *tukar-menukar* barter trade, countertrade. ~ *wésel* bill trading. ~ *yang diatur* managed trade.

dagang II foreign, in or from some other place, abroad. *anak/orang* – alien, wanderer, tramp; → PERANTAU. *perahu* – ship from elsewhere, trading ship. *laki pulang kelaparan, – lalu ditanakkan* to help strangers but neglect one's own family. – *piatu* all alone in the world. – *santri* Muslim seminarian from abroad (not a resident).

berdagang (*ob*) to go abroad, travel in a foreign land, live in a foreign country.

dagang III (*M*) **mendagang** to carry s.t. on a carrying pole over the shoulder; → MEMIKUL. ~ *barang* to carry goods on such a pole.

dagangan commodities which are carried on a carrying pole.

pe(n)dagang carrying pole; → PIKULAN.

dag-dig-dug (*onom*) sound/feeling of palpitating heart (from fear). *Hatinya* –. He was scared. *menunggu dengan hati* – to wait with one's heart beating.

dagé (*Jv*) fermented product (of grated coconut, etc.). – *gembus* k.o. *témpé bongkrék.*

dagel I (*J*) **bedagel** to be dirty from a lot of body dirt or dried sweat.

ndagel to become dirty because of a thick layer of body dirt.

dagel II (*J*) *tukang* – clown, comedian.

mendagel [and **ndagel** (*coq*)] to clown around, speak and act comically, do s.t. that is amusing; → MELAWAK.

dagelan 1 jest, joke. **2** clownishness, farce, humorous show.

dagi → DAGA I, DAHAGA II. **mendagi** to offer resistance.

pendagi resister, rebel, insurgent.

daging 1 meat. **2** flesh. **3** pulp (of fruit). *darah* – and – *darah* one's own flesh and blood; → DARAH. *Sudah menjadi darah* – *pada dia.* It has become second nature to him. *nama* – surname, family/last name (not a *gelar* or endearment). *saudara* – distant relatives. *bagai duri dalam* – a thorn in the flesh. – *anak sapi* veal. – *asap* smoked meat. – *asé* hash. – *asin* salted/pickled meat. – *awét* preserved meat. – *babi* pork. – *basah* fresh meat. – *beku* frozen meat. – *buah* mesocarpium. – *cacah/cincang* (raw) ground beef. – *darah* one's own flesh and blood. **sedaging sedarah** and **sedarah sedaging** one's own flesh and blood, blood relatives. – *domba* lamb. – *gandik* eye steak. – *gigi* gums; → GUSI. – *giling* meat cut into small pieces. – *gulung* roulade. – *has* sirloin. – *kain* unprocessed material (to be woven into textiles, etc.). – *kaléng* canned beef. – *kancing* muscle, gristle. – *kering* dried meat. – *kornét* corned beef. – *lebih* a) tonsils. b) penis. – *lembu* beef. – *liat* tough meat. – *manis* beauty spot. – *mati* meat from animal not ritually slaughtered. – *menémpél* calloused wart. – *mentah* a) raw meat. b) a piece of ass, i.e., a woman considered as sex object. – *mérah* red meat *esp* beef. – *numbu* (*coq*) a) tumor. b) polyp. – *pacak* roast beef. – *rapuh* tender meat. – *sapi* beef. – *sapi haas* fillet. – *segar* fresh meat. – *susur* corned beef. – *tétélan* meat scraps. – *tumbuh* a) tumor. b) polyp. c) wart.

berdaging 1 to be fleshy, thick, big, stout. *tidak* ~ *lagi* a) grown thin. b) become poor. **2** well-to-do.

mendaging 1 to be(come) fleshy (arms, etc.); to be firm (of the flesh of a *durian*). **2** to close up, heal (of wounds or cuts). **3** to put on weight.

mendagingi to be flesh of/for, form part of.

terdaging 1 to cut into the flesh. **2** to be hurt (of s.o.'s feelings), cut to the quick.

kedagingan carnal (of lust, etc.). *nafsu* ~ sexual desires.

pedaging *ayam* ~ broiler.

pendaging meat eater, s.o. very fond of meat.

pendagingan materialization, actualization. ~ *dari nafsu-nafsu dan keinginan* materialization of passions and desires.

daglu → PERDAGANGAN *luar negeri.*

dagri → PERDAGANGAN *dalam negeri.*

dagu 1 chin. **2** corner under the guard of a keris blade. *seperti janggut pulang ke* – in the right place. – *keris* handle end of a keris. – *lentik* chin which curves outward.

berdagu with a chin. ~ *dua* with a double chin.

dah I (*cla*) service, duty.

dah II (*J coq*) **1** particle giving or requesting permission, agreement; → DÉH. *biar* – go ahead, then, O.K. **2** emphasizer. *Lihat – ke sané, adé apé tuh?* Look over there, what's up there?

dah III the clipped form of *sudah.*

dah IV (*D coq*) a greeting comparable to "bye." *dah-dah* bye-bye!

dah V (*J*) comparable to Indonesian *ya. Saya lupa apé – namanya?* I've forgotten, what's his name again? (I can't think of it now).

dahaga I (*Skr*) **1** thirst. *mati* – to die of thirst. *melepaskan/menghapuskan* – to quench one's thirst. **2** to be/get thirsty. **3** desire; desirous. *orang* – *diberi air* to help/teach s.o. who really wants help/learning.

berdahaga thirsty.

mendahagakan to thirst/long for s.t., wish, want. ~ *pendidikan* to long for an education.

kedahagaan thirst, thirstiness.

dahaga II (*Skr*) resistance, opposition, rebellion, insubordination. – *dahagi* various k.o. resistance; → DAGA I, DAHAGI.

mendahaga to be insubordinate.

dahagi resistance, opposition, mutinous(ness), insubordination; → DAGI.

menda(ha)gi to put up resistance, rebel, be insubordinate.

dahak phlegm, mucus (from the mouth); → RIAK III.

berdahak and **mendahak** to clear the throat noisily, hawk.

mendahakkan to hawk s.t. up.

pendahak s.o. who hawks up a lot.

daham (*onom*) hem; → DEHEM.

berdaham and **mendaham 1** to cough, clear one's throat. **2** to clear one's throat to attract attention or express surprise.

dahan I bough, branch. *harimau* – a large tiger-cat or small leopard, *Leopardus sp. besar kayu besar -nya* they that have plenty of butter can lay it on thick. – *pembaji batang* to use one's master's wealth as one's own.

berdahan with branches, ramified.

mendahan to grow branches, branch out.

(dahan-)dahanan branches.

dahan II (*ob*) → PENDAHAN.

dahanam (*onom*) boom, rumble.

berdahanam to boom, rumble.

dahar (*Jv*) to eat. *caos* – to offer food to the spirits. – *kembul* (*Jv*) to eat together. *Tak jarang tamu yang datang diminta untuk* – *kembul bersama dengan keluarganya.* Guests who come to see (us) are often invited to stay to dinner with the family. – *klimah* Javanese Islamic wedding meal.

dahasyat → DAHSYAT.

dahél (*D J*) **1** daily work. **2** day laborer.

dahi 1 forehead, brow. **2** front. – *layar* top part of a sail. – *sehari bulan* a beautiful forehead.

dahiat (*A*) calamity.

dahina during the day, by day.

dahlia (*D/E*) dahlia, *Dahlia pinnata.*

Dahr (*A*) *ad*– "Time"; name of the 76th chapter of the Koran.

dahri(ah) (*A*) *kaum* – atheists, infidels.

dahsyat (*A*) **1** terrifying, dreadful, horrible. **2** imposing, awesome.

sedahsyat as dreadful/horrible as.

mendahsyat to become terrifying/horrible, get worse.

mendahsyatkan and **memperdahsyat(kan)** to terrify, horrify, frighten.

kedahsyatan 1 terror, dread, horror. **2** awesomeness. **3** severity.

dahu (*S*) k.o. tree, New Guinea walnut, *Dracontomelum mangiferum.*

dahuk greedy, covetous; → LOBAK, TAMAK.

dahulu → DULU. – *bajak daripada sapi* to put a younger person in charge instead of an older one, do s.t. that goes against the usual order of things.

dahulu(-dahulu)nya formerly.

berdahulu-dahuluan and **dahulu-mendahului** to try to get ahead of e.o., try to be first.

bersidahulu to try to get ahead of.

mendahului 1 to be/go ahead of, be in advance of s.o. else, precede. *dengan* ~ *pengesahan* in anticipation of the ratification of. ~ *jamannya* to be ahead of one's time. ~ *waktu* to do s.t. ahead of time. **2** to do s.t. first/before s.o. else does it, preemptive (strike).

mendahulukan 1 to put s.t. first/before, give priority/precedence to, prioritize. *Dahulukan pangan!* Food comes first! *Keluarga saya harus didahulukan.* My family must come first. **2** to allow s.o. to go first.

terdahulu 1 the earliest. ~ *dari itu* before that. ~ *daripada waktunya* premature. **2** preliminary.

terdahului to be preceded (by), gotten ahead of. ~ *daripada waktunya* premature.

kedahuluan 1 before s.t. ~ *sang surya* before the sun rose. **2** to be preceded (by). ~ *oléhnya.* He went first.

pendahulu predecessor, first person to do s.t.

pendahuluan 1 preface, forward, preamble. **2** preliminary, preparatory.

dahyang (*Jv*) guardian spirit.

dai and **da'i I** (*A*) s.o. who proselytizes, spreads Islam, tries to improve thought and behavior in line with Islamic beliefs.

dai II (*E*) die (the tool).

daidan (*Jp*) battalion.

daidanco (*Jp*) battalion commander.

daif (*A*) /da'if/ **1** weak, feeble. **2** incompetent, incapable.

mendaifkan 1 to humiliate, insult, regard as insignificant. **2** to weaken.

kedaifan 1 weakness. **2** contempt, scorn, considering weak. **3** inferiority.

daim (*A*) /da'im/ durable, long-lasting, enduring, permanent, perpetual.

dain (*A*) /da'in/ debt.

daing dried fish. *minta darah pada* – to try to get blood out of a stone.

mendaing to dry (fish).

mendaing-daing to slice (fish) for drying.

Dairi a subgroup of the Batak ethnic group.

daitia (*Skr*) giant.

dajal (*A*) **1** a supernatural being which tempts humans in the days before Judgment Day. **2** s.o. who tempts people to be against religion or behave sinfully. **3** liar. **4** devil (in general). *al masih al* – false Christ.

dak I → NDAK.

dak II (*D*) roof.

dak III (*onom*) boom.

dak IV (in acronyms) → MENDADAK, DAÉRAH KEPOLISIAN.

DAK V → DANA *alokasi khusus.*

daka(h) (*A*) (burial pegs holding) the planks covering the niche for the body in an Islamic grave.

dakak-dakak k.o. snack made of cassava.

dakap → DEKAP I.

dakar I 1 stubborn, obstinate. **2** bold, determined.

berdakar to do as one pleases.

kedakaran obstinacy.

dakar II → ZAKAR.

dakep → DEKAP I.

dakhil (*A*) **1** internal, inner. **2** intimate, close.

daki I 1 grime, dirt, filth. **2** s.t. bad that is hidden, skeletons in the closet. *Dia tahu di mana tersembunyi* – *dan kerak tiap orang di kotanya.* He knows where everyone in his town's skeletons are hidden. – *dunia* filthy lucre.

berdaki grimy, filthy.

daki II mendaki 1 to climb (a mountain, etc.). **2** to rise, slope upwards. *jalan* ~ a sloping road. **3** towards. ~ *tengah hari* towards noon.

mendakikan 1 to raise, lift, move upward. ~ *perkara* to appeal a case (to a higher court). **2** to make s.t. climb/go up.

terdaki climbable.

dakian slope, incline, rise.

pendaki climber.

pendakian 1 ascent, climbing. **2** pass (in mountains). **3** slope, incline, rise.

perdakian climb.

dakik I (*Jv*) bombastic, pompous.

dakik II (*A*) indivisible.

dakik-dakik (*Jv*) **ndakik-dakik** elaborate, sophisticated, detailed.

dakocan(g) (*Jp*) **1** inflatable doll. **2** insulting name for Malaysia during the *Konfrontasi.*

dakon (*Jv*) k.o. game using cowry shells on a board with depressions; → CONGKAK II.

dakron (*E*) Dacron.

daksa (*Skr*) **1** skilled, capable. **2** proper.

daksina (*Skr*) south. *dari* – *ke paksina* from south to north.

daktilo- (*D*) having to do with the fingers.

daktilografi (*D*) fingerprinting.

daktur → RÉDAKTUR.

daku I → AKU I.

daku II mendaku → MENGAKU.

dakwa (*A*) charge, accusation, indictment. –.*dakwi* mutual recriminations.

berdakwa to litigate, sue.

mendakwa 1 to accuse, charge with a crime, indict. **2** to sue, take to court.

mendakwai to claim, demand.

mendakwakan and **memperdakwakan 1** to sue over, bring (a case) to court. **2** to charge with. *Tindak pidana itu didakwakan kepadanya.* He was charged with that crime.

terdakwa the accused, defendant; → TERGUGAT.

dakwaan accusation, charge, indictment.

pendakwa plaintiff, accuser; → PENGGUGAT.

pendakwaan indictment, indicting, charging, complaint.

dakwah (*A*) (Islamic) proselytism, mission, attempt to improve behavior in line with Islamic thinking.

berdakwah to do this activity. *semangat* ~ missionary spirit.

mendakwahkan to missionize, spread the faith, proselytize.

pendakwah (Islamic) missionary.

pendakwahan deliver a sermon on.

dal I (*Jv*) the fifth in a cycle of eight years.

dal II (*Hind*) k.o. pulse, dal, pigeon pea, *Cajanus indicus.*

dal III (*A*) name of the eighth letter of the Arabic alphabet.

dal IV (in acronyms) → PENGENDALIAN.

dalal (*A*) intermediary, broker, go-between.

dalalah I (*A*) female go-between, marriage broker.

dalalah II (*A*) exegesis (of the Koran); → DALIL

dalalat (*A*) deviation (from the truth).

dalam I 1 deep, far below the surface. *Sungai ini* – *sekali.* This river is very deep. **2** deep, not superficial, profound. *pengetahuan yang* – profound knowledge. **3** deep, not shallow. *piring* – soup bowl. **4** deep-seated. *ketidakpercayaan yang* – deep-seated distrust. **5** inner, internal, under, not visible from the outside. *baju* – underwear. *ban* – inner tube. *orang* – insider. *penyakit* – internal disease. – *laut dapat diduga,* – *hati siapa tahu* who can plumb the depths of the heart?

dalamnya depth.

dalam-dalam deeply. *menyedot pipanya* ~ to inhale one's pipe deeply.

sedalam 1 as deep as. **2** to a depth of.

sedalam-dalamnya 1 sincerely, deeply, seriously. *menyatakan turut berdukacita* ~ to express one's deepest sympathies. *Nasihat ibunya diresapinya* ~. He absorbed his mother's advice seriously. **2** as deep(ly) as possible.

berdalam-dalam to intensify, worsen. *Perdébatan sudah* ~. The debate intensified.

mendalam 1 in-depth, in detail, thorough, profound, deep. *berpikir lebih* ~ to think more in depth. *secara* ~ in depth. **2** to grow worse, intensify. *Penyakit itu telah* ~. The illness has grown worse. **3** to become ingrown, deep-rooted, deep-seated. **4** to deepen.

mendalami [and **ngedalamin** (*J coq*)] to go/delve deeply into, steep o.s. in, have a deep understanding of. *Tujuannya untuk* ~ *ajaran Wéda kitab suci Hindu.* His goal is to delve into the Vedic learning of the Hindu holy books.

mendalamkan to deepen s.t.

memperdalam to make deeper, increase (knowledge, etc.), broaden (one's knowledge of), specialize in.

memperdalami 1 to deepen. **2** to go more deeply into s.t.

terdalam the deepest.

dalaman guts, bowels, entrails, intestines, viscera.

kedalaman 1 depth. **2** profundity, deepness, shallowness. **3** draft (the depth that a ship displaces). **4** (*J*) too deep. *Jangan* ~ *dua méter sudah cukup.* Don't go too deep, two meters is enough. **berkedalaman** with a depth of.

pedalaman 1 the interior, hinterlands. **2** the area not in the hands of the Dutch during the Indonesian Revolution. **3** deepening.

pendalaman 1 deepening, making deeper. ~ *selokan* deepening drains. **2** going deeply into.

dalam II 1 in, inside, within, on. *di – rumah* inside the house. *– hati* to o.s. *katanya – hati* he said to himself. *akan mulai dipasarkan – waktu satu tahun lagi* will be marketed within one year. *– hal* in case, if. *– hal ini* in this case. *– pada itu* meanwhile, in the meantime. *– perjalanan politiknya* on her political journey. **2** when (doing s.t.). *– arsip* on file. *– berat/dua* pregnant. *– dua tengah tiga* a) unable to decide what to do. b) dishonest, unethical. *– janji* engaged. *– kekeringan* in trouble. *– negeri* domestic. *– telangkai* a girl whose hand has been asked in marriage.
  terdalam inmost, innermost.

dalam III (*Jv*) palace.

dalang 1 narrator and puppeteer at a *wayang* performance. **2** mastermind, behind-the-scenes power.
  berdalang and **mendalang** to perform the *wayang*.
  mendalangi to be (the mastermind) behind, mastermind, manipulate. *Dia dituduh ~ penculikan mantan présidén.* He was accused of masterminding the kidnapping of the former president.
  mendalangkan 1 to manipulate the puppets in a *wayang* performance. **2** to mastermind, be the mastermind behind.
  pedalangan having to do with the *dalang*. ~ *wayang* puppetry.
  pendalangan 1 manipulating puppets. **2** masterminding.
  perdalangan (*mod*) having to do with the *dalang*.

daldaru k.o. climbing plant, *Psychotria sarmentosa*.

dalem → DALAM. **ngedalemin** → MENDALAMI.

dalfin → LUMBA-LUMBA.

dalia → DAHLIA.

dali-dali k.o. tree used for light construction, *Strombosia javanica*; → DEDALI.

dalih 1 excuse, pretext, argument, subterfuge. *dengan – tertentu* under certain conditions. **2** to argue (as an excuse). *"Kita tidak bisa apa-apa," -nya.* "We couldn't do anything," he said as an excuse.
  berdalih 1 to look for an excuse/pretext, use s.t. as an excuse. **2** to quibble.
  berdalih-dalih(an) to blame e.o.
  berdalihkan to use s.t. as an excuse/pretext.
  mendalih to use as an excuse.
  mendalihkan to blame s.t., use s.t. as an excuse.
  pendalih s.o. who likes to argue.
  pendalihan using s.t. as an excuse/pretext.

dalik → DOLAK-DALIK.

dalil (*A*) **1** argumentation. **2** theorem, thesis. **3** argument, grounds (for a law suit). *untuk –* in support of (an argument). *– akali* rational argument. *– alhayat* vital signs. *– gugatan* (*leg*) allegations (in the statement of claim). *– naqli* arguing by referring to the Koran. *– lancung* false syllogism. *– qadi* decisive proof.
  berdalil valid, founded on arguments.
  mendalili to make an argument (that).
  mendalilkan 1 to postulate, set forth (an opinion, etc.). **2** to argue for (an opinion, etc.). *Bank N tetap ~ bahwa perséroan tidak berkewajiban untuk membayar fee.* Bank N has continued to argue that the company is not obligated to pay the fee.
  pendalil arguer, s.o. who argues for a certain position.
  pendalilan argumentation (based on evidence).
  perdalilan evidence, proof.

dalkhana (*Pers*) veranda.

dalmas [pengendalian massa] crowd control.

Dalu I → DALWU.

dalu II (*J/Jv*) fully ripe.
  kedaluan overripe.

daluang paper made from wood.

dalu(w)arsa → KEDALUWARSA. **berdaluwarsa** expired.

dalung 1 large copper tray. **2** lamp used at *wayang* performances.

daluwarsa (*Jv*) overdue, expired; to lapse. *tanggal/waktu –* expiration date.
  mendaluwarsa to postpone, delay, defer, put off.
  kedaluwarsa 1 expired, out-of-date. **2** superannuated.

Dalwu (*A*) Aquarius.

dam I (*D*) **1** checkers. **2** checked (pattern). *buah –* piece (in checkers). *main –* to play checkers. *papan –* checkerboard.

dam II (*onom*) thumping, slamming noise; → GERDAM.

dam III (*D*) dam, weir. *– penahan érosi* retaining wall; → TURAP I. *– pengendali* check dam. *– penggelontor* splash dam.
  pendaman damming up.

dam IV (*A*) a religious penalty. *kena –* to be fined for a religious offense.

dam V (*C*) greedy, gluttonous. *– ciak* gluttonous.

dam VI (*Pers*) whiff, breath.

dam VII (in acronyms) → DAÉRAH *militér*.

damah (*A*) a diacritic above an Arabic letter indicating the vowel /u/.

damai 1 peace. *secara –* peaceful(ly) **2** peaceful.
  sedamai as peaceful as.
  sedamai-damainya as peacefully as possible.
  berdamai 1 to be peaceful, be reconciled, come to an agreement, come to terms, (*leg*) settle out of court. **3** to be negotiable (about the price, etc.). *harga boléh –* the price is negotiable. *pembayaran bisa ~* terms negotiable.
  mendamaikan 1 to come to an agreement about, settle. *perbédaan yang tak bisa didamaikan* irreconcilable differences. **2** to bring peace between (different parties), reconcile.
  memperdamaikan to reconcile (different opinions).
  terdamaikan can be reconciled. *tidak ~* irreconcilable.
  kedamaian state of peace, tranquility. ~ *hati/rohani* peace of mind.
  pendamai peacekeeper. *menjadi ~* to mediate.
  pendamaian (*theology*) atonement, reconciliation.
  perdamaian 1 peace. **2** reconciliation. **3** settlement.

damak 1 (blowpipe) dart. **2** (*geol*) spicule.
  mendamak to shoot a dart from a blowpipe.

damal slow (of boats).

daman (*Pers naut*) sheet (of a sail).

damar I 1 dammar, *Agathis damara*. **2** resin. **3** torch that uses resin as fuel, oil lamp. *– alam* natural resin. *– batu* hard resin. *– daging* soft red resin, *Agathis beccarii*. *– hablur* crystal resin. *– hitam* the black heart of the *Shorea multiflora*. *– léléh* soft resin. *– lilin* → MERSAWA. *– mata kucing* cat's eye resin, *Hopea globosa*. *– pilau* East Indian kauri, *Agathis spp*. *– putih* white damar from the *Vateria indica* tree. *– urat* substance similar to resin derived from the *Agathis beccarii* tree.
  berdamar 1 using resin. **2** to collect resin. **3** resinous.
  mendamar to collect resin.
  mendamari 1 to light up, illuminate. **2** to apply resin to.
  pendamar resin collector.
  pendamaran 1 place where resin is collected. **2** torch that uses resin as fuel.

damar II k.o. tree, *Canarium secundum* and other species.
  berdamar to play a game with the nuts of this tree.

damas I (*D*) damask.

damas II out of money (spent on useless things).

damat (*ob*) noisy; → AZMAT.

damawi (*A*) blood (*mod*).

damba I long for, yearn for.
  mendamba(kan) to long for, crave, covet. *R ~ anak tahun ini.* R longs for a child this year.
  dambaan 1 (s.t.) longed for, yearned for. *Rumah yang séhat adalah ~ setiap insan yang tahu dan mengerti akan kebutuhan keséhatan.* A healthy home is what every human being who knows about and understands health needs longs for. **2** longing.
  kedambaan longing, yearning, desire for.
  pendamba s.o. who longs after or yearns for s.t.
  pendambaan and **perdambaan** longing, yearning, desire for.

damba II mendamba to embrace.
  mendambakan ~ *diri* to throw o.s. down.

damba III sulky, sullen.

damban → LAMBAN.

dambin I (*M? onom*) thud, thump. *–.dambun* series of thuds/thumps.
  berdambin to thud, thump.

dambin II very fat.

dambir → GELAMBIR.

dambun (*onom*) boom.
  berdambun(-dambun) to boom.
  mendambunkan to make s.t. boom/resonate.

dané → DAMAI.

damén (*Jv*) → JERAMI.

dames (*D*) (*mod*) lady's, for women.

dami → DAMAI.

damiah (*A*) a wound.

damik (*M*) mendamik ~ *dada* to beat one's chest in anger.

damir I (*A*) symbol used in Arabic script to indicate a closed syllable.

damir II (*A*) conscience.

dampa (*Jv*) shingles, herpes; → SINAGA.

dampak 1 impact, effect. 2 collision. – *ganda* multiplier effect. – *ikutan* side effect. – *lingkungan* environmental impact. – *sampingan* side effect.

   berdampak 1 to have an impact/effect. *ion négatif yang ~ positif* negative ions with a positive effect. 2 to collide (with), bump (into).

   mendampak 1 to hit, collide with. 2 to have an effect (on).

dampal 1 sole (of the foot). 2 palm (of the hand)

dampar I beach, wash ashore.

   berdampar to become beached.

   mendampar 1 to become beached. 2 to cast ashore. 3 (*geol*) to aggradate.

   mendamparkan 1 to cast ashore, wash ashore. 2 to beach (a boat).

   terdampar 1 stranded, beached, run aground, washed ashore. 2 end up (in), fall (into s.o.'s hands). keterdamparan being stranded.

   damparan 1 s.t. beached/cast ashore. 2 (*geol*) aggradation. 3 (*forestry*) waif.

   kedamparan → PERDAMPARAN 1.

   pendamparan 1 running aground. 2 (*geol*) aggradation.

   perdamparan 1 (*leg*) increase by alluvial deposition. 2 stranding, grounding.

dampar II (*Jv*) 1 throne. 2 low table.

dampil berdampil touching, close to.

   mendampil(kan) to put (one's body) close to s.o. else, juxtapose. *Dia ~ tubuhnya kepada kekasihnya.* She put her body close to her lover's.

   terdampil juxtaposed.

   dampilan juxtaposition.

damping I close/near by, adjacent.

   sedamping-dampingnya as close as possible.

   berdamping next (to).

   berdampingan next to e.o., side by side, adjacent, contiguous, coexisting. *hidup ~ secara berdamai* peaceful coexistence.

   mendampingi [and ngedampingin (*J coq*)] 1 to accompany, go alongside of, stand next to, flank. 2 to work closely with. 3 to provide support for.

   mendampingkan to move s.o. close to s.o. else. ~ *tubuh ke tubuh orang lain* to move one's body close to another person's body.

   terdamping ~ (*di*) *dalam hati* close to one's heart.

   kedampingan 1 closeness, proximity. 2 (*math*) adjacency.

   pendamping 1 s.o. who goes along with one, colleague, associate, right-hand man, companion. ~ *hidup* one's spouse. 2 runningmate (of the president). 3 co-. ~ *pengemudi* co-driver. 4 supplementary (funds), side (dish). 5 s.o. who provides support for. ~ *anak* teacher's aide.

   pendampingan 1 going alongside of, standing next to, flanking, working closely with s.o., assistance. 2 providing support for.

   perdamingan working closely with.

damping II (*M*) berdamping to engage in antiphonal singing.

damping III (*E*) dumping (of products on the market).

dampit (*Jv*) boy-girl twins.

damprat (*J*) scolding, verbal abuse. *kena* – to get scolded.

   mendamprat to scold.

   mendamprati (*pl obj*) to scold.

   mendampratkan to pour out (one's abuse).

   dampratan scolding, verbal abuse.

   pendampratan scolding.

dampu (*J*) k.o. children's street game like hopscotch.

dampul (*Jv*) mendampul [and ndampul (*coq*)] to live together as man and wife without being married; → KUMPUL *kebo*.

   dampulan living together as man and wife.

   pendampul s.o. to live with.

dampung (*onom*) beating sound.

   berdampung-dampung to beat, throb.

Damsyik (*A*) Damascus.

dan I 1 and. (*buah*) *apel* – (*buah*) *Persik* apples and peaches. *baju mérah* – (*baju*) *putih* a red and white jacket. *Dia memohon-meminjam.* He begged and borrowed. 2 in contrast, but. *Minyak nabati tercernakan* – *minyak mineral tidak.* Vegetable oil is digestible and/but mineral oil is not. –/*atau* and/or. – *juga* and also. – *lagi* and moreover. – *lain-lain/sebagainya/selanjutnya/seterusnya*, etc.

dan II → KAN III.

dan III (*Jp*) degree of expertise in karate and other martial arts, *usu* indicated by wearing a cloth belt of a particular color.

dan IV (in acronyms) → KOMANDAN.

dana (*Skr*) 1 funds, (financial) means, money. *peminjam* – obligor, lender. *penyandang/penyuntik* – financier. *seluruh* – *dan daya* all funds and forces. 2 (*cla*) gift, alms; liberal, generous. – *abadi* endowment fund. – *Alokasi Khusus* [DAK] Special Grant. – *Alokasi Umum* [DAU] Block Grant. – *anggaran* budgetary funds. – *antarbank* call money. – *bantuan* financial aid. – *berédar/berputar* revolving fund. – *bersama* mutual fund. – *cadangan* reserve fund, sinking fund. – *darurat* contingency fund. – *dipusatkan* funds channeled from the ministry of finance to the department of defense and security. – *disalurkan* funds channeled from the department of defense and security to military units. – *hibah* endowment fund. – *hutang* amortization fund. – *imbalan* countervalue funds. – *Internasional untuk Pembangunan Pertanian* International Fund for Agricultural Development. – *jaminan* a) guarantee fund. b) collateral. – *mengendap* (*fin*) core deposits. – *Monétér Internasional* International Monetary Fund, IMF. – *nganggur* idle money. – *Pelestarian Alam Sedunia* World Life Preservation Funds. – *pelunasan obligasi/sekaligus/utang* sinking fund. – *pendamping* auxiliary funds. – *penebusan* redemption fund. – *pengukuran* grading fee (for logs). – *pénsiun* retirement fund. – *pénsiun dan tunjangan* retirement and relief fund. – *penumpu* leverage. – *penyangga harga* price support funds. – *penyusutan* depreciation fund. – *piatu perang* war orphan fund. – *pinjaman* loan proceeds. – *Satwa Dunia* World Wildlife Fund. – *segar* fresh money. – *semalam* overnight money. – *siaga* standby loan. – *siswa* scholarship. – *sosial* charitable donation (either government or private). – *talangan* bail-out funds. – *tarik* refunding, refinancing. – *terpakét* block grant. – *terpusat* funds distributed directly by the Finance Department to the military. – *utang* amortization fund. – *yang dipakai menjamin* guarantee fund. – *yang disimpan di bawah bantal* money not deposited with a bank, but kept at home ("under the pillow"). – *yang siap dioperasikan* loanable funds. – *wasiat* escrow funds.

   mendana (*ob*) to beg for alms.

   mendanai [and ngedanain (*J coq*)] to finance, fund. *Proyék Data Akuisisi itu didanai dari Pinjaman lunak Pemerintah Australia.* The Data Acquisition Project was funded by soft loans from the Australian government.

   mendanakan to fund, provide funds for.

   memperdanakan to grant (funds as a subvention).

   kedanaan (*mod*).

   pendanaan funding, financing, paying for. ~ *kembali* refinancing. ~ *mikro* microfinancing. ~ *modal véntura* venture capital financing. ~ *proyék* project financing.

danaréksa mutual fund.

danasiswa (*Skr neo*) scholarship.

danau I lake. – *kawah* crater lake. – *musiman* ephemeral lake. – *terlingkung* land-locked lake.

   berdanau with/to have a lake.

danau II mendanau to perform an immoral act.

danawa (*Skr cla*) giant, demon.

dancuk (*vulg*) → DIANCUK.

danda (*Skr*) club, stick.

dandan I (*J*) clothes, dress, attire, outfit.

   berdandan 1 adorned, ornamented, decorated. 2 dressed. ~ *rapi* well-dressed.

   mendandan(i) [and ngedandanin (*J coq*)] 1 to dress s.o., adorn, decorate. ~ *pengantin* to dress the bride. 2 to equip. *Meréka ~*

kapal untuk berlayar. They equipped the ship for sailing. **3** to repair, fix. *Jalan-jalan rusak karena tidak didandani bertahun-tahun.* The streets were damaged because they hadn't been fixed for years.

dandanan 1 attire, trimmings, outfit, dress, toilet, grooming. *~ muka* makeup. *~ rambut* hairdo, hair-style. **2** layout (of a newspaper).

pendandanan 1 dressing up. **2** laying out.

dandan II (*naut*) projecting platform or gallery over the deck of a ship. *- haluan* the prow platform.

mendandani to equip with such a platform.

dandan III ship's cable.

dandang I 1 (copper) vessel for steaming rice. **2** boiler, vessel for boiling liquid.

dandang II a large dugout; → DENDANG II.

dandang III *burung* – great cormorant, *Phalacrocorax carbo sinensis*; → DENDANG I.

dandanggula (*Jv*) Javanese meter (in music).

dandi I (*Hind cla*) **1** a lute. **2** small Tamil kettledrum (a musical instrument often mentioned in literature).

berdandi to play the lute.

dandi II spotted, mottled. *rusa* – a deer with spotted markings.

dandi III → DÉNDI.

dandim [komandan distrik militér] military district commander.

daném → DAFTAR *nilai ébtanas murni.*

dang I (*cla*) an honorific given in old romances to ladies of a court; *cp* DAYANG.

dang II (*Jv*) **ngedang** to steam (rice, etc.).

dangai k.o. cake made of flour, sugar, and coconut cream.

dangak → DONGAK.

dangar (*ob*) → DANGAU.

dangau a temporary hut erected to camp out in and watch the paddy fields.

dangdang → DANDANG I.

dangdangan (*S*) k.o. ditch.

dangdut → DANGDUT.

dangdut popular music with strong beat reminiscent of Hindi or Arabic music. *film* – a film with *dangdut* music accompaniment.

berdangdut 1 to make *dangdut* music. **2** to dance to such music.

ndang-ndut to make that k.o. music. *lagu-lagu berirama ~* melodies in the *dangdut* rhythm.

mendangdutkan to turn s.t. into *dangdut* music.

pedangdut a *dangdut* musician.

dangdutwan male pop musician.

dangdutwati female pop musician.

danghyang (*Jv*) guardian spirit(s); → DANYANG.

dangir (*J*) **mendangir** to hoe.

mendangiri (*pl obj*) to hoe.

pendangir 1 person who hoes. **2** hoeing equipment.

pendangiran hoeing.

dangka I → SANGKA I.

dangka II (*ob*) **terdangka-dangka** to land, approach land.

dangkal I 1 shallow. *laut* – a shallow sea. **2** trivial, superficial. *intérprétasi* – a superficial interpretation.

sedangkal as shallow as.

mendangkalkan 1 to make shallower. **2** to consider trivial/unimportant.

memperdangkal to make shallower.

dangkalan 1 shoals, shallows. **2** shelf (in ocean).

kedangkalan 1 shallowness. **2** superficiality, triviality. *~ pikiran* narrow-mindedness.

pendangkalan 1 becoming shallow (of a river, etc. due to sedimentation), silting up. **2** making shallower, lowering (the water level). **3** trivialization, making/considering s.t. unimportant.

dangkal II 1 infertile (of land), barren. **2** (*J*) hard and dry (of fruit). **3** half-hearted, unfinished, incomplete. *- dangkalan* completely unlucky.

dangkal III (*J*) spots (on clothing).

dangkap berdangkap to grapple (two people grasping hands in fighting, etc.).

dangkar I → DANGKAL.

dangkar II very brave.

dangkar III mendangkar to roll up (a mat, etc.).

Dankolaops → KOMANDAN *Komando Pelaksana Operasi.*

dangku k.o. fruit with edible fruits, *Pimeleodendron macrocarpum.*

dangkung I k.o. leprosy.

dangkung II (*M*) **mendangkung** to punch.

dangsa → DANSA.

danguk berdanguk, mendanguk and **terdanguk** to sit with one's hands on one's chin.

dani → UDANI.

danramil → KOMANDAN *Koramil.*

danrém → KOMANDAN *Korém.*

danrés [komandan résimén] Regiment Commander.

danru [komandan regu] Team Commander.

dansa (*D*) (western-style) dance, dancing. *lantai* – dance floor. *malam/pésta* – dance party, dance. *- dansi* dancing. **berdansa dansi** to dance and dance.

berdansa to dance.

mendansikan to dance s.t.

pedansa dancer.

dansanak (*M*) blood relations on one's mother's side; → SANAK. *- anjing* sibling with a different father. *- bapa/ibu* cousin. *- kandung* full sibling. *- sebapak* sibling with same father.

berdansanak to have such relatives.

dansék [komandan séksi] section commander.

danta (*Skr*) tooth. *- asmara* beautiful white teeth.

danton [komandan peleton] platoon commander.

Danu(h) 1 archer. **2** (*zod*) Sagittarius.

danur putrefaction, putrefying corpse.

danwil [komandan wilayah] regional commander.

danyang supernatural guardian of a tree, house, etc. *- désa* guardian spirit of a village.

danyon → KOMANDAN *Batalion.*

daon (*Pr*) marijuana.

dap (*A*) small drum.

dapa (*ob*) slave sent as gift to one's future in-laws.

dapar buffer.

dapat 1 can, be able to, capable of, -able/-ible, may. *tidak* – *tidak* cannot fail to, must. **2** to get, etc.; → MENDAPAT. **3** be gotten/obtained, be found/located. *Sudah –?* Have you gotten it yet? *masih tidak – juga* still couldn't be found/located. *– pun ... takkan* even though ... will not. **4** adopted. *anak* – an adopted child. *– durian runtuh* to get a piece of good luck without having to work hard for it. *– atur* adjustable. *– balik* reversible. *– berubah* subject to change. *– dibatalkan* revokable, voidable. *tidak – dibatalkan* non-revocable. *– diganti* interchangeable. *– dikatakan* one might say. *– dikerjakan* feasible. *– dimakan* edible. *– ditagih* payable (of a debt), collectable. *– ditukar* convertible. *– gerak* movable. *– gésér* sliding. *– hati* to get the courage to. *– jalan* transportable. *– kain kotor* to menstruate. *– larut* soluble. *– lengkung* flexible. *– lipat* hinged. *– masanya* a) to take place. b) to see one's chance (to do s.t.). *– muai* expandable. *– muka* to become famous. *– nyala* inflammable. *– pecah* fragile. *– pindah* movable. *– putar* revolving. *– tembus* permeable. *– tukar* interchangeable.

sedapat upon receiving/getting. *~ mungkin* as much as possible.

sedapat-dapatnya as much as one can, to the fullest extent (possible), whatever one can.

berdapat 1 decent, reasonable (of a price). **2** to meet up (with).

berdapat-dapat to be a lot. *Utangnya ~.* He has a lot of debts.

berdapatan to meet up with e.o.

mendapat 1 to get, obtain, receive; to come up with (an idea). *~ angin* a) to get a good wind (of a ship). b) to get lucky. *~ halangan* to menstruate. *~ hati* a) to take courage. b) to like s.t. *~ kain kotor* to have one's period, menstruate. *~ kopi pahit* get yelled at, scolded. *~ malu* to be embarrassed. *~ nama* to become famous. *~ pisang berkubak* to get s.t. good without having to work hard for it. **2** to find, meet with, (go to) see s.o.

mendapati 1 to find, discover, notice. *Saya ~ dia mabuk.* I found him drunk. **2** to meet up with, come across, experience.

mendapatkan [and **ndapatin/ngedapatin** (*J coq*)] **1** to get, obtain, procure, come up with, find. *cara ~ bayi laki-laki atau perempuan* how to get a boy or a girl. *~ diri* to realize that one has done s.t. wrong. **2** to go to see s.o., visit. **3** just before, prior to. *~ Hari Natal* just before Christmas.

memperdapat to get, obtain. *~ persetujuan* to reach agreement.

terdapat 1 found, discovered. *tidak juga ~* could not be found/ arrived at. **2** can be found, to exist. **keterdapatan** occurrence, existence (of s.t. somewhere).

dapatan income, s.t. obtained.

kedapatan found, discovered. *Seorang intél ~ menyusup di antara meréka.* An intelligence agent was discovered infiltrated among them. *~ budinya* his evil actions were discovered.

pendapat 1 opinion, idea, thinking (about s.t.). *pada ~ saya* in my opinion. *~ akuntan* auditor's certificate, accountant's opinion. *~ hukum* legal opinion. *~ menyangkal/tidak setuju* adverse opinion. **2** conclusion. **sependapat** of the same opinion, in agreement. **berpendapat** to have an opinion, be of the opinion (that).

pendapatan 1 income, earnings, revenue, return. *~ asli daérah* [PAD] provincially generated revenue. *~ bersih* net income. *~ Kena Pajak* [PKP] taxable income. *~ kotor* gross income. *~ lain-lain* miscellaneous income. *~ tertunda* deferred income. *~ Tidak Kena Pajak* [PTKP] nontaxable income. *~ tidak tetap* nonfixed income. *~ usaha* operating income. *~ yang masih harus dibayar* accrued income. **2** yield, output. *~ sawah* wet-rice field yield. **3** (*math*) product, result, solution. **berpendapatan** with an income/yield (of).

dapet → DAPAT. **ndapetin/ngedapetin** → NDAPATIN.

dapra fender (a cushion of rope hung over the side of a ship to protect it when mooring).

daptar → DAFTAR.

dapuk (*Jv*) **mendapuk** to assign s.o. the role (of).

dapur I 1 kitchen. **2** cuisine. **3** stove, oven, furnace, hearth, fireplace. *untuk membuat – berasap* to make ends meet. *– saya bisa ngebul.* I can make ends meet. **4** kiln. *– api* hearth, fireplace. *– arak* distillery. *– batu* brick kiln. *– bedil* (*cla*) pan (of a flint-lock). *– berita* editorial room (of a newspaper, etc.). *– cawan* crucible kiln. *– kapur* lime kiln. *– koran* (*coq*) newsroom (of a newspaper). *– lapangan* field kitchen. *– leburan* blast furnace. *– matahari* solar oven. *– mobil* mobile field kitchen. *– pengering* drying over. *– semén* cement kiln. *– tinggi* blast furnace. *– tukang besi* smithy, forge. *– tungkik* blast furnace. *– umum* soup kitchen, canteen.

sedapur in the same kitchen.

kedapuran kitchen (*mod*), culinary.

pendapuran furnace.

perdapuran kitchen (*mod*), culinary.

dapur II dapur-dapur the external part of an object. *~ bahu* the part of the body under the shoulder, thorax. *~ susu* the part of the body under the breasts.

dar I (*A*) (in compounds) **1** house surrounding a yard; dwelling, residence. **2** yard. *– al-aitam* and *– ul-aitam* orphanage. *– ul-akhirat* the hereafter. *– ul-Arqam* the house of Arqam, named after a friend of the Prophet who donated his house for Islamic missionary activities. *– ul-asyikin* the world of passions. *– ul-atsar* museum. *– ul-baka* the hereafter. *– fana* the transitory world. *– ul-harb* the non-Muslim world. *– ul-ilmu* university. *– ul-iqab* hell. *– ul-Islam* a) the Muslim faith. b) [DI] a rebel movement in southern Celebes in the 1950s. *– ul-jalal* heaven. *– us-salam* a) Baghdad. b) Aceh. c) Brunei. d) seventh heaven. *– ul-sawab* heaven.

dar II → DOR. **dar-dér-dor** and **dar-dor 1** (sound of) shooting. **2** (sound of) explosions.

dara I (*Skr*) **1** virgin, maiden, young girl. *hilang –nya* lost her virginity. **2** nubile, able to bear young. **3** virginity.

kedaraan virginity.

perdaraan virginity.

dara II *burung –* pigeon, *Columba domestica. – batu* bridled tern, *Sterna anaethetus. – kipas* fantail pigeon. *– laut* tern, *Sterna hirundo. – laut hitam* noddy, *Anous spp. – laut jambu* roseate tern, *Sterna dougallii. – laut putih* white tern, *Gygis alba. – mahkota* crowned pigeon, *Goura cristata. – putih* pied imperial pigeon. *– tiram* gull-billed tern, *Gelochelidon nilotica.*

darab I (*A mostly Mal*) multiple, multiplication, product.

mendarab to multiply.

pendarab multiplier.

daraban multiplication.

darab II blow, smack.

mendarab to hit, smack.

darah blood. *– beku* coagulated blood, gore. *– belut* k.o. climbing plant. *– biru* blue blood. *– dalem* blue blood. **berdarah dalem** to have an aristocratic ancestry. *– daging* a) flesh and blood. b) internalized. **mendarah-dagingkan** to internalize, inculcate. inculcation. **pendarah-dagingan** internalizing, inculcating. *– dingin* cold blooded, phlegmatic. *– hidup* fresh blood, gore. *– jernih* of noble blood. *– kotor* menstrual blood. *– lintah* thick and sticky. *– mati* coagulated/dried/congealed blood. *– mérah* arterial blood. *– muda* impatient, quick to anger. *– nifas* a) afterbirth. b) postnatal hemorrhage. *– pahit* magic power. **berdarah pahit** to have magic power. *– panas* hot-headed. *– putih* a) vaginal discharge. b) aristocratic. **berdarah putih** to be of aristocratic blood. *– rendah* low blood pressure. *– tinggi* a) high blood pressure. b) to get angry.

sedarah 1 of the same blood, closely related. **2** incest, incestuous. *perkawinan ~* incestuous marriage.

berdarah 1 to bleed. **2** bloody. **3** to have ... blood, be a member of the ... ethnic group. *~ campuran* of mixed blood. *~ bali* cowardly. *~ hangat* warm blooded. *~ jernih* aristocratic. *~ muda* to act without thinking. *~ ningrat* to be of noble descent. **4** to be talented in. *~ seni* to be artistic.

berdarahan covered in blood, all bloody.

mendarah 1 to become dark red in color like blood. **2** to hemorrhage.

mendarahi to bleed on, smear with blood.

pendarah a weapon, etc. that has claimed victims.

pendarahan bleeding, hemorrhaging. *~ otak* cerebral hemorrhage, stroke.

perdarahan bleeding, hemorrhage.

daraj (*A*) parchment.

darajat → DERAJAT.

daras (*A*) Koran recital.

mendaras to recite the Koran.

pendarasan recitation of the Koran.

darat 1 land (as opposed to ocean or sky). **2** the interior. **3** mountainous. **4** (*petro*) on-shore. **5** (*mining*) overland. *– darau* plateau. *– pokok* mainland.

mendarat 1 to land, touch down. *sudah ~ melaut* to have traveled everywhere. **2** to go into the interior.

mendarati to land on, disembark at.

mendaratkan 1 to land (a plane, etc.). **2** to put (a boat) ashore. **3** to disembark, offload (passengers/freight). **4** to ground (airplanes). **5** to land (a blow on s.o.).

daratan 1 mainland, dry land. **2** landing place. **3** solid ground, bottom.

pendarat 1 landing (*mod*). *~ ayun* swing landing (for parachute training). **2** rope which ties a ship to the dock, landing gear.

pendaratan 1 landing, putting ashore, disembarking. **2** dock, pier.

darau → DARAT.

dardar (*A*) elm tree.

dargah (*Pers*) palace.

dari 1 from. *Dia berangkat – Semarang.* He left from Semarang. **2** starting from, beginning at. *~ ... sampai* from ... till ... *Rapat berlangsung – pukul 19.00 sampai 22.00.* The meeting lasted from 7 p.m. to 10 p.m. **3** coming from. *Saya – Australia.* I'm from Australia. **4** since, from some point in time. *– dulu/tadi* for some time. **5** because, for, due to. *maka – itu* thus, therefore, that's why. *Hal itu dilakukannya – kemauannya.* He did that of his own free will. *– sebab itu* for that reason. **6** than. *Harganya lebih mahal – emas.* It's more expensive than gold. **7** made of, out of. *méja – jati* a table made of teak. *dibuat – emas* made of gold. **8** of *sepotong – kué ini* a piece of this cake. *Ini rumah – Menteri.* This is the Minister's house. **9** regarding, concerning. *– utang-piutang diperlukan bukti tertulis* written proof is required regarding/of debts.

sedari since (the time that).

dari-dari → LABI-LABI I.

darih (A) mausoleum.

daripada 1 (rather) than, instead of. 2 it would be better/preferable to.

darjah → DERAJAT.

darji (Pers) tailor.

darma (Skr) 1 duty, obligation. 2 contribution to social and humane institutions.

darmabakti (Skr neo) 1 services rendered, devotion (to duty). 2 volunteer work, contribution to social or humane ends or institutions.

   berdarmabakti 1 to devote o.s. to, perform/carry out one's duty. 2 to do/perform one's volunteer work.

   mendarmabaktikan to dedicate, devote. ~ kemampuan keinsinyurannya bagi pembangunan dan kejayaan bangsa dan negara to devote one's engineering skills to the development and glory of the people and nation ~ dirinya kepada masyarakat to devote o.s. to community service.

darmaga → DERMAGA.

darmasarjana scholarship, grant.

darmasiswa student scholarship stipend; → BÉASISWA.

darmawisata 1 picnic, excursion. 2 school trip. – kota city tour.

   berdarmawisata 1 to go on a picnic/excursion. 2 to take a school trip.

darmawisatawan s.o. who goes on an excursion.

darsana → JAMBU.

dart (E) dart; → PASER II. olahraga lémpar – darts.

daru(-daru) pohon – a tree with commercial timber, Urandra/Cantleya corniculata.

daruju (Jv) sea holly, holly-leaved mangrove, Acanthus ilicifolius.

darulakhirat (A) the highest heaven.

darulaman (A) abode of peace/security.

darulbaka (A) the hereafter, the next world.

darulfana (A) the present or sublunary world.

darulhar(a)b (A) non-Muslim countries, war zone.

darulislam (A) 1 areas under Muslim authority. 2 Darulislam [D.I.] Muslim rebel movement which operated in the eastern part of West Java and the southern Sulawesi in the 1950's.

daruljalal (A) lowest level of heaven.

darullulum (A) university.

darun (M) sedarun together, in unison.

darunu mark of ownership, brand.

darurat (A) 1 emergency. 2 necessity. mendarat – to crash-land (of aircraft). melakukan pendaratan – di laut (of aircraft) ditching, crash landing. bekalan – emergency rations. jembatan – emergency/temporary bridge. keadaan – an emergency (situation). rém – emergency brake. undang-undang – emergency regulations. – sipil civil emergency.

   kedaruratan state of emergency. ~ diam silent emergency.

   mendaruratkan 1 to compel, force. 2 to declare an emergency about.

darus → DARAS.

darus(s)alam (A) 1 abode of peace (Aceh and Brunei). 2 Jerusalem.

darussawab (A) Garden of Eden.

darwis I (Pers) dervish, mendicant friar.

darwis II → SADAR wisata.

darwis III (Jv) [modar ya wis] dead in the water.

darzi → DARJI.

das I (onom) 1 boom (of gun). 2 rifle shot, gunshot.

das II (in acronyms) → DASAR.

dasa (Skr) -teen, 10 digit. – tahun decade.

dasadarma (Skr neo) the 10 Boy Scout obligations.

dasalomba decathlon.

dasamuka ten-headed (monster; in the wayang = Rawana, the mortal enemy of Rama).

dasar I 1 bottom, floor (of the sea/ocean, etc.), bed, ground, benthic. – bukti grounds (for an argument). – laut bottom of the sea, seabed. – samudra ocean floor. 2 the lowest part, bottom (of a wok/bottle, etc.). – botol bottom of a bottle. 3 floor (of a house, etc.). rumah papan, -nya ubin a wooden house with a tile floor. 4 background. gambar bulan sabit putih pada – warna hijau the picture of a white crescent moon on a green

colored background (the symbol of Islam). 5 paint that functions as a ground-color. 6 basic material. rupa-rupa – buat gaun various sorts of material for a gown. 7 foundation. Gotong-royong itulah – masyarakat Indonésia. Mutual cooperation is the foundation of Indonesian society. 8 basis, principle, grounds. atas – pesanan on request. atas – a) on grounds of. b) at (a certain price). pada -nya basically, fundamentally, at heart. 9 basic, bases of. – kimia basic chemistry. – bunga (bot) torus, receptacle. – ganda double bottom (of a vessel). – hukum legal ground. – kebenaran (leg) justification. – kering dry base (mining). – masyarakat foundations of society. – mudasir that's the way it is. – negara national principle – pajak tax basis. – pemaaf (leg) justification, ground for exculpation. – pemberatan pidana (leg) ground for an increase in penalty. – pembuktian legal grounds. – pemikiran basic/underlying idea. – pengenaan pajak [DPP] tax basis. – penilaian basis for judgment. – pénsiun final pay (used for determining pension). – peradilan (leg) trial basis. – persahabatan basis of friendship. – samudera ocean floor. – sungai riverbed. – timbal-balik principle of reciprocity. – tuduhan (leg) basis of the charge. – pembicaraan the subject under discussion. – tukar terms of trade.

   sedasar based on, on the basis of. Dukungan sosial harus meliputi tingkat intervénsi berbéda ~ tempat tinggal, makanan dan transportasi. Social support must cover varying levels of intervention based on residence, food, and transportation.

   berdasar 1 founded, well-grounded. tidak ~ samasekali completely unfounded. 2 to be based (on). 3 to have a base of.

   berdasarkan 1 to be based/founded on, rest on, on the basis of, emanating from. ~ pilih kasih on the basis of favoritism. 2 under (the terms of a contract, etc.), pursuant to (the law). ~ kontrak under contract.

   mendasar 1 fundamental, basic. perbédaan yang ~ a fundamental difference. 2 to set out on display.

   mendasari to form the basis/foundation/principle of. ~ gugatannya it forms the basis of his lawsuit.

   mendasarkan to base s.t. (on). Pendapat itu didasarkan pada dugaan belaka. That opinion was based on a mere hunch.

   dasaran 1 solid ground, bottom. 2 (coq) since, because.

   pendasar founder, (founding) father.

   pendasaran foundation.

dasar II (J) 1 (congenital) nature, character. – kepandaian menggambar natural drawing skill. 2 inherent, unalterable, by nature. – gatel horny bastard! – maling, di mana saja dia nyolong. He's a thief by birth, that's the way he is. – manusia, sudah ngantuk, tidurlah meréka. It's inherent in the nature of men that when they are sleepy, they go to sleep. – mudasir through and through by nature. – mudasir anak bengal. He was born naughty, and that's the way he will always be! 3 damn it!

dasariah fundamental, basic.

dasarian a 10-day period. curah hujan selama satu – a 10-day period's rainfall.

dasasila (skr neo) 10 principles. – Bandung the 10 principles (of the Asia-Africa Conference in Bandung, 1955).

dasatitah the Ten Commandments.

dasawarsa (skr neo) decade, decennium.

dasbor (E) dashboard. – berwajah menawan an attractive dashboard panel.

dasi (D) tie, necktie. – jepitan clip-on tie. – jerat garrote. – kupu-kupu bow tie. – panjang necktie. – péndék short necktie.

   berdasi with a necktie; to wear a necktie.

dastar and daster I → DESTAR.

daster II (E) duster, housecoat, lab coat.

   berdaster to wear a duster/lab coat.

dastur (naut) layar – studding-sail.

dasun (M) garlic, k.o. Allium. – tunggal a single/solitary garlic (not a dual or triple one). hidung bak/seperti – tunggal a well-shaped nose: round at the end and sharp at the back. hidung mendasun tunggal to have such a nose.

Daswati [Daérah Swatantra Tingkat I] First Level Autonomous District.

dat → ZAT.

data (E) data, information. sistém basis – database. kedap – data proof. – *dasar/pokok* basic data, database. – *keluar* output. – *masuk* input. – *pribadi* personal information. – *statistik* statistical data. – *téhnik* technical data.

mendata(kan) to collect data on, record, document.

terdata documented, recorded. *rumah kos yang belum* ~ boarding houses which have not yet been recorded.

pendataan data collection, documentation, recording.

datang 1 to come, arrive. *Pukul berapa bapak* –? What time did you arrive? *Jam berapa dia* –? When did he come? When do you expect him? *Suatu ketika, barangkali anda pernah* – *periksa ke dokter umum.* At one time, maybe you had to go to a general practitioner for a checkup. *–nya* his/her/its/their arrival. *air tidak* – the water doesn't run (from the pipe). *perai* – a) (to go) to and fro, (to go) backward and forward. b) to call on a person, drop in a person's house/office, etc. again and again. – *(ter)lambat* to arrive (too) late. – *menyerang* to attack, come at. **2** to come (from) (refers to one's hometown/birthplace, etc.), be (from, *dari*). *Ia* – *dari Surabaya.* He's from Surabaya. **3** *(yang) akan* – a) [in (the)] future, later, afterward. *perkembangan-perkembangan yang akan* – future developments. b) approaching, forthcoming, next (week/month, etc.), next (copy of a newspaper, etc.). *(hari) Jumat yang akan* – next Friday. *minggu yang akan* – next week. **4** to, till. *dari permulaan* – *kepada kesudahannya* from beginning to end, from start to finish; (of a book) from cover to cover. *sudah* – *pada saatnya* the moment has arrived. **5** to fall (of night). *bila malam* – when night falls. – *kepada* to call on. *Dia* – *kepadanya meminta pekerjaan.* He called on him for a job. – *nampak/tampak muka, perai/pulang nampak/tampak belakang/punggung* one should always be correct in one's behavior (when visiting or leaving s.o.'s house). – *seperti ribut, pergi seperti semut* a sickness comes very quickly, but disappears slowly. – *tak berjemput, pulang tak berhantar* a gate-crasher. *dari mana –nya cinta, dari mata turun ke hati* where does love come from, from the eyes down to the heart. – *akal* to have an inspiration. – *bulan/haid* to have one's period, menstruate. – *hati* to have the heart to. – *silih-berganti* to come and go. *pemerintahan* – *silih-berganti, tapi…* administrations come and go, but …

datang-datang 1 on arrival, as soon as one arrived. ~ *saya sudah disuruhnya membelikan rokok.* As soon as I arrived, he asked me to buy him cigarettes. **2** to come often/again and again, keep (on) coming. ~ *lain ke rumah bila senang.* Come as often as you like. **3** suddenly, all of a sudden; → TIBA-TIBA. ~ *saya disembur.* Suddenly I was abused.

sedatang (up)on the arrival of.

berdatang ~ *sembah (cla)* to approach s.o. respectfully, say s.t. respectfully, use courteous language.

berdatangan *(pl subj)* to come, arrive. *Ratusan détéktip dan mobil antipeluru* ~. Hundreds of detectives and bulletproof cars arrived.

mendatang 1 to come all of a sudden; (an idea) all of a sudden struck (s.o.). **2** accidentally, by chance. *jika ada aral* – in case an unforeseen event occurs; → ARAL *melintang*. **3** derived (word). *kata-kata* ~ derived/affixed words. **4** (forth)coming, upcoming, next. *tanggal 21 Maret* ~ next March 21. *di waktu* ~ and *pada masa* ~ in the future. *masih 15 bulan* ~ still 15 months to go. **5** *orang* ~ foreigner, nonnative.

mendatangi [and **ngedatangin** *(J coq)*] **1** to enter, get into, go into, get to, access. *mudah didatangi* easy to get to, convenient. *sukar didatangi* hard to get to, inconvenient. *Tempat-tempat itu sukar didatangi.* Those places are hard to get to. **2** to visit, pay a call on *(usu* with an unfavorable connotation). *Toko itu didatangi polisi.* That store was visited by the police. **3** to attack, invade. **4** to provide with a prefix and/or suffix. *Kata "kerja" bila didatangi awalan "ber" menjadi "bekerja" bukan "berkerja."* The word "kerja" when prefixed with the prefix "ber" becomes "bekerja" and not "berkerja."

datang-mendatangi to visit e.o.

mendatangkan [and **ngedatangin** *(J coq)*] **1** to import. *Tidak perlu lagi* ~ *pakan ternak dari luar negeri.* It is no longer necessary to import animal feed from abroad. **2** to bring, bring in, bring about, cause. *yang* ~ *bahaya maut* dangerous, perilous, involving danger to life. ~ *hasil* to pay off, work out well. ~ *laba* profitable. ~ *uang* to bring in money. **3** to summon.

datangan arrival.

kedatangan 1 arrival. ~ *délégasi Indonésia disambut dengan hangat.* The arrival of the Indonesian delegation received a warm welcome. **2** to receive, have s.o. come to one; to be attacked; to be afflicted. ~ *tamu* to have visitors. *Rumahnya* ~ *gerombolan.* His house was invaded by a gang. ~ *penyakit mata* to have eye problems.

pendatang 1 visitor. **2** s.o. who arrives, stranger (a person/foreigner/nonnative). ~ *baru* a newcomer. ~ *kebelakangan* latecomer. *orang* ~ foreigner, stranger, newcomer. **3** presentiment.

pendatangan importation (of commodities).

datar 1 flat, level, smooth. **2** monotonous. *suara* – monotonous. *Tak banyak jalan* – *dalam kehidupan ini.* The road of life is bumpy. **3** superficial. **4** horizontal.

sedatar equally smooth/flat/level.

mendatar 1 to be level, level off. *Jalan itu* ~. The road is level. **2** horizontal, cross. *balok* ~ a crossbeam.

mendatarkan to level, flatten, (make) smooth.

dataran plain, level land. ~ *banjir* flood plain. ~ *luas* broadland. ~ *pantai* coastal plain. ~ *rendah* lowland. ~ *Tempayan* Plain of Jars (in Vietnam). ~ *tinggi* upland, plateau, high plains.

kedataran 1 flatness. **2** superficiality, shallowness. **3** monotony.

pendataran leveling (off).

pedataran plateau; plain.

datatamak penalty paid for having sexual relations with an underage girl.

dateng → DATANG. **ngedatengin** → NGEDATANGIN.

dati I family-owned land which cannot be subdivided.

DATI II [Daérah Tingkat] administrative level. – *I* Province. – *II* Regency.

datia *(Skr)* → DAITIA.

datif *(D gram)* dative.

datin *(Mal)* **1** title given to the wives of *datuk*. **2** honorary title for female (equivalent to *datuk*).

dating *(E)* **1** date. **2** dating.

Dato' → DATUK.

datu I 1 *(ob)* sovereign, monarch, king; → DATUK, RATU. **2** *(M)* medicine man, shaman; → BOMOH, DUKUN. **3** *(J)* a holy person, saint; a deceased person.

kedatuan *(ob)* **1** kingdom. ~ *Sriwijaya* the Sriwijaya Kingdom (of Sumatra).

datu II kedatuan *(M)* k.o. dance.

datuk 1 head, elder. **2** grandfather. **3** *(M)* an honorific title, i.e., a *gelar* for people of high status or older people within the group. **4** idol (in Chinese temple); → TOAPÉKONG. **5** (taboo term for) tiger. *si* – reference to the Sumatran elephant. – *bandar (Mal)* mayor; → WALIKOTA(MADYA). – *bendahara (cla)* royal treasurer. – *nénék* ancestors. – *petinggi* adat chief. – *saudara* great-uncle.

datuk-datuk ancestors.

berdatuk to address s.o. with *datuk*.

memperdatuk and **mendatukkan** to call s.o. *datuk*, consider s.o. as one's master.

datum *(D)* date (on the calendar).

berdatum dated.

datung *(ob)* my grandfather!

DAU → DANA *alokasi umum*.

Daud *(A)* David, author of the Psalms/*kitab Zabur*.

daudan preserved eggs wrapped in rice.

dauk I *(Jv)* gray (of horses). *kuda* – roan. – *ruyung* k.o. gray (horse).

mendauk to become grayish.

dauk II *(A)* voluptuous.

daulah *(A)* empire, state; → DAULAT. – *Islamiyah* Islamic State. – *Usmaniyah* Ottoman Empire.

daulat *(A)* **1** sovereignty. **2** *(cla)* blessing, prosperity. – *rakyat* sovereignty of the people. **3** *(cla)* (magical) welfare/good (of monarch). **4** *(cla ob)* ominous influence, curse. – *tuanku (cla)* your majesty!

berdaulat 1 sovereign. *hak* ~ sovereign rights. *merdéka dan* ~ free/independent and sovereign. **2** to dominate, be(come) dominant. **3** *(ob)* blessed.

mendaulat 1 to take control of. 2 to give s.o. the job of. 3 to force (s.o. to do s.t.), fire s.o.

mendaulati to take control of, dominate.

mendaulatkan 1 to take control/possession of s.t. 2 to proclaim. 3 to force, compel, coerce. 4 to take/snatch (away) (s.o.'s rights/position from s.o.), appropriate.

daulat-daulatan (*coq*) passing the buck.

kedaulatan sovereignty. ~ *hukum* legal sovereignty. ~ *negara* sovereignty of the state. ~ *raja* royal sovereignty. ~ *rakyat* sovereignty of the people. **berkedaulatan** to have sovereignty.

pendaulat 1 s.o. who reins/rules. 2 s.o. who engages in violent actions.

pendaulatan 1 appropriation, (unlawful) possession (of). 2 dismissal, ousting, firing; depriving, deprivation

daun 1 leaf. *tulang* – veins of a leaf. 2 the first element in the names of many plants. 3 lobe, leaf-like/-shaped objects. 3 blade (of an oar). 4 blade, plate (in some compounds). FOR OTHER PLANT NAMES BEGINNING WITH DAUN SEE THE FOLLOWING WORD. – *asem (kecil)* yellow wood sorrel. – *ati-ati* k.o. decorative plant used as medicine for hemorrhoids, *Coleus atropurpureus.* – *baling-baling* propeller/screw blade. – *bawang* spring onion. – *beludu* a decorative plant, purple passion plant, *Gynura aurantica.* – *birarut* k.o. herb, *Halopegia blumei.* – *buah* (*bio*) carpel. – *bulu ayam* k.o. bushy perennial plant, *Desmodium gangeticum.* – *bunga* petal. – *bungkus* wrapper. – *burung* k.o. medicinal tree, *Rhinacanthus nasutus.* – *ceki* small Chinese playing cards. – *dayung* blade (of an oar). – *deres* Pouzolz's bush, *Pouzolzia zeylanica.* – *déwa* k.o. croton, *Gynura procumbens/pseudo-china.* – *duduk* three-flowered desmodium, *Desmodium triquetrum.* – *ékor belangkas* k.o. plant, *Gnetum brunonianum.* – *emas* marijuana. – *éncok* Ceylon leadwort, *Plumbago zeylanica.* – *gagang* (*bio*) bract. – *gamet* beach morning glory, railroad vine, *Ipomea pes-caprae.* – *ganja kering* dried ganja leaves. – *gantilan* (*bio*) bracteole. – *gésér* leaf (of a table). – *getang* k.o. medicinal herb, alphabet plant, paracress, toothache plant, *Spilanthes acmella.* – *hidup* (*ob*) touch-menot, *Biophytum sensitivum.* – *iler* k.o. decorative plant used as medicine for hemorrhoids, *Coleus atropurpureus.* – *inggu* a medicinal plant, asafetida, *Ruta angustifolia.* – *jarum* conifer. – *jendéla* window shutter. – *jeruk purut* citrus leaf. – *jingga* orang leaf. – *jinten* k.o. plant similar to oregano, *Coleus amboinicus.* – *kaki kuda* a medicinal plant, Indian pennywort, *Centella asiatica.* – *katuk* sweet-leaf bush, *Sauropus androgynus.* – *keji beling* Persian shield, *Strobilanthes spp.* – *kelopak* (*bio*) sepal. – *kemudi* rudder. – *kentut* skunk vine, *Paederia scandens.* – *kepialu* k.o. medicinal plant, *Vitis trifolia.* – *kemarogan* k.o. plant, *Gymnopetalum leucostictum.* – *kemudi* (*naut*) afterpiece of rudder. – *kentut* Chinese fever vine, skunk vine, *Paederia foetida.* – *ketumbar* Chinese parsley, coriander; → **KETUMBAR.** – *kipas kapal* ship's screw. – *kumis kucing* k.o. bush, cat's whisker, *Orthosiphon grandiflorus.* – *kuning* yellow leaf. – *kuping gajah* begonia. – *kupu-kupu* a shrub, white dwarf orchid tree, *Bauhinia acuminata.* – *lada* k.o. plant, *Spilanthes acemella.* – *lalu* k.o. climbing plant. – *landep/landak* k.o. jasmine, *Barleria prionitis.* – *lindung* bract. – *lumut* an herb, prayer plant, *Maranta leuconeura.* – *lurik* a decorative plant, seersucker plant, *Geogenanthus undatus.* – *madu* Philippine violet, *Barleria cristata.* – *mahkota* petal. – *mangkok* k.o. shrub, *Nothopanax scutellarium.* – *méja* table-leaf. – *muda* a young girl. – *nasi* row of bushes indicating the boundary of land ownership. – *neraca* (pair of) scales. – *padi* k.o. small knife. – *panah* a decorative plant, stardust plant, *Syngonium albolineatum.* – *panahan* k.o. plant, *Eupatorium triplinerve.* – *pangkur* the wooden piece into which the blade of a hoe fits. – *panjang* k.o. herb, Indian lettuce, *Lactuca indica.* – *patola* jewel orchid, *Macodes petola.* – *payung* umbrella palm, joey palm, *Johannesteijsmannia altifrons.* – *pelindung* bract. – *penumpu* stipule. – *penutup* calyx. – *pérak* a) k.o. plant used for cattle fodder, silver leaf, Spanish clover, *Desmodium uncinatum.* b) k.o. decorative plant, aluminum plant, *Pilea cadierei.* – *pintu* leaf of a door. – *penumpu* stipule. – *poko* k.o. wild mint, *Mentha arvensis/javanica.* – *prasmanan* k.o. plant, *Eupatorium triplinerve.* – *préi* leek. – *putri* k.o. plant,

Mussaenda spp. – *rahat* part of spinning wheel for winding thread. – *rebah bangun* mimosa, *Mimosa pudica.* – *rokok* cigarette paper. – *rusa* k.o. plant, scarlet hygro, sessile joyweed, *Alternanthera sessilis.* – *salam* (*Jv*) bay leaf. – *sambung nyawa* k.o. tree, *Gynura procumbens.* – *sang* joey palm, *Johannesteijsmannia altifrons.* – *sangkétan* prickly chaff flower, devil's horsewhip, *Achyranthes aspera.* – *saputangan* a decorative plant, *Maniltoa grandiflora/schefferi.* – *séndok* k.o. plantain, *Plantago major.* – *simbukan* k.o. shrub, *Saprosma ternatum.* – *sudamala* mugwort, *Artemisia vulgaris.* – *tampar hantu* k.o. plant. – *telinga* auricle, outer edge of the ear. – *tempuyung* sow thistle, *Sonchus arvensis.* – *tembaga* flame violet, *Episcia cupreata.* – *ténda* (*bio*) tepal. – *terup* European playing-cards. – *tunjang* stipule. – *tuntang* stipule. – *urat* plantain, *Plantago major.* – *wungu* caricature plant, *Graptophyllum pictum.* – *zébra* wandering Jew, *Zebrina pendula.*

daun-daun foliage, leaves.

sedaun *makan* ~ a) to eat from one dish. b) to be friends. *dunia tak* ~ *kélor* there are plenty of fish in the sea, i.e., there are lots of possible lovers available.

berdaun 1 to have leaves. 2 leafy.

berdaunkan to have ... as leaves/a leaf.

mendaun to be like a leaf, leaf-like, foliate. ~ *kayu/kunyit* a lot.

daunan, daun-daunan and **dedaunan** leaves, greenery, foliage.

perdaunan foliation.

daur (*A*) 1 rotation. 2 circle, cycle. 3 turn. 4 vicissitude. 5 age, period, epoch. 6 roundabout way. – *besar* cycle of 120 years. – *haid* menstrual cycle. – *hidrologi* hydrological cycle. – *hidup* life cycle. – *hidup produk* product life cycle. – *hidup rata-rata* average life. – *iklim* climatic cycle. – *kecil* cycle of 8 years; → **WINDU** I. – *ulang* recycling. *kertas* – *ulang* recycled paper. *mendaur-ulang(kan)* to recycle. *dapat didaur-ulang* recyclable. **pendaur-ulang** recycling (machine/plant). **pendaur-ulangan** [and **pendauran-ulang** (*infr*)] recycling.

mendaurkan to (re)cycle.

terdaurkan (re)cycled. *sampah* ~ recycled garbage/trash/waste.

dauriah (*A*) cyclical.

da'wa → **DAKWA.**

da'wah → **DAKWAH.**

dawai 1 string, cord. 2 metallic wire; → **KAWAT** I. – *duri* barbed wire. – *gelang* (telegraph, etc.) cable. – *piano* piano string. **berdawai** with strings. *instrumén* ~ stringed instrument.

dawai-dawai k.o. plant, *Smilax calophylla.*

dawam → **ALADDAWAM.**

dawas exhausted (of soil).

dawat (*Pers*) ink. *bagai* – *dengan kertas* inseparable. – *cina* India ink. **berdawat** with ink. *Alang-alang* ~ *biarlah hitam.* If you do s.t., don't do it half-heartedly.

dawet (*Jv*) cold drink consisting of a mixture of coconut milk with Javanese sugar, rice flour, and *céndol.*

dawuh (*Jv*) order, instruction.

dawukbang (*Jv*) dappled, blackish-brown mixed with white spots.

dawul-dawul (*Jv*) untidy, messy.

daya I 1 power, might, force, strength, energy, vigor, capacity, impetus. – *dan dana* energies and funds. *Apa –?* What can we do? 2 influence, effect. 3 expedient, remedy, way out, way of escaping, makeshift, resource. – *absorpsi* absorptive capacity. – *air* hydraulic power. *sumber* – *air* hydraulic power source. – *alami* force of nature. – *ampuh* life span. – *angan* inspiration. – *angkat* a) lifting power. b) bearing capacity. – *angkut* carrying capacity. – *antar* conductivity. – *apung* buoyancy. – *atom* atomic energy. – *awét* keeping qualities (of food), shelf-life. *Ikan segar –.-nya rendah.* The shelf life of fresh fish is low. – *baca* reading capacity. – *banding* comparability. – *batin* inner strength. – *baut* inner strength. – *bekerja* working power, energy. – *beli* purchasing power. **berdaya beli** to have ... purchasing power. *Désa-désa* ~ *rendah membutuhkan beras murah.* Villagers with low purchasing power need inexpensive rice. – *bertahan* stamina. – *bertelur* laying ability (of fowls). – *berubah* changeability. – *biak* propagative capacity. – *bukti* probatory force, evidentiary value. – *cahaya* illuminating power. – *capai* access, accessibility. – *cengkeram* holding ability (of a tire). – *cerap* power of observation.

– *cerna* digestibility. – *cipta* creativity. **berdaya-cipta** to be creative. – *citra* (power of the) imagination. – *cium* sense of smell, ability to sniff things out. – *cium berita* nose for the news. – *cuci* washing capacity. – *dengar* auditive force. – *dipindah-tangankan* transferability. – *dorong* thrust. – *dukung* portative power, carrying/bearing capacity, support capacity. **berdayadukung** to have a carrying capacity of. – *éféktif* effective power (of an engine). – *gabung* affinity. – *gaib* supernatural power. – *gerak* a) mobility, motility, kinetic energy. b) drive. – *gerak empat roda* four-wheel drive. **berdaya-gerak** to have mobility, be mobile. *tak* ~ immobile, incapacitated. – *gesit* maneuverability. – *guna* efficiency, productivity. **berdaya-guna** efficient, productive. **keberdaya-gunaan** efficiency. **mendaya-gunakan** to use efficiently, exploit. **kedaya-gunaan** efficiency, productivity. **pendaya-gunaan** efficient/productive use of. – *guna catu* quantum efficiency. – *guna perusahaan* productivity. – *hangus* flammability. – *hantar* conductance, conductivity, conduction capacity. – *hantar panas* thermal conductivity. – *hasil* productivity. – *hembus* wind power. – *hidup* a) vital power, vitality. b) life, length of time s.t. is active. – *hisap* a) suction power. b) absorptive capacity. – *ikat* binding force. – *ikhtiar* initiative, drive. – *ingat* memory, retentiveness, ability to recall. – *isi* loading capacity. – *jangkau* range (of a TV station, etc.). – *jelajah* cruising range (of an aircraft). – *juang* fighting spirit. – *kandung air* water-holding capacity. – *karya* work capacity. – *kata* catchword, motto. – *kebal* immunity, resistance. – *kembali* ability to spring back, resilience. – *kecambah* germinative power. – *kejut* shock action. – *kenyal* resilience, resiliency, spring. – *kerja* a) work capacity. b) energy. c) ability to work. – *kerja cepat* fast acting. – *khayal* power of imagination. – *kikis* erosivity. – *kuda* [DK] horse power. – *kupas* hulling rate. – *laksana* creativity. – *laku* validity. – *laku surut* retroactive effect. – *lampu* wattage. – *larut* solubility. – *lawan* resistance. – *ledak* explosive power. – *lekat* adhesion. – *lenting* resilience, flexibility. – *lentur* pliancy. – *lihat* visual acuity. – *listrik* electric power. – *lulus* permeability. – *magnit* a) magnetic power. b) power of attraction. – *mampu* carrying capacity. – *memproduksi* productivity. – *mengikat* (*chem*) combining power. – *muai* expansion capacity. – *muat* carrying capacity. – *pakai* wearability, life span. – *paksa* (*leg*) force majeure. – *pancar* radiating capacity, emissivity. – *pecah* crushing strength. – *pegas* elasticity. – *péka* sensitivity. – *pembéda* distinguishability. – *pemikat* attraction. – *penalaran* reasoning power. – *penarik* attractiveness, drawing power. – *pendorong* motivating force. – *penerimaan* receptivity. – *pengangkut* carrying capacity. – *pengantar* conductivity. – *pengertian* comprehension. – *penggak* deterrence. – *penggerak* a) driving force, kinetic energy. b) motivation. – *penghancur* destructive force. – *pengikat* demand. – *pengisap* absorptive capacity. – *pengisian* charge capacity. – *penjiwa* power of inspiration. – *penyatu* power to unify. – *penyinaran* ability to illuminate. – *peramal* predictability. – *perang* fighting ability. – *perékaan* inventiveness. – *perusak* destructive force. – *pesona* personal magnetism, charisma. – *pijar* burn quality. – *pikat* charm, appeal. – *pikir* intelligence. – *pikul* carrying capacity. – *pisah* resolution, resolving power. – *pukau* appeal. – *pukul* striking power. – *racun* toxicity. – *rambat* reproductive power. – *pompa* pump output. – *prabawa* ability to influence people. – *racun* toxicity. – *regang* tensile strength. – *rekat* adhesive power. – *rentang* tensile strength. – *resap* absorptive power. – *rohani* spiritual force. – *saing* competitiveness. – *samar* apparent capacity. – *sekat* insulating power. – *serap* absorptive power, absorbency, permeability. **berdaya serap** absorbent. **kedayaserapan** absorptivity. – *serap jenis* absorptivity. – *serbu* striking power. – *simak* comprehension. – *suai* adaptability, adjustability. – *surut* retroactive effect. – *tahan* durability, endurance, strength, resistance, stamina. **kedaya-tahanan** endurance, stamina. – *tahan lama* stamina. – *tahan panas* heat resistance. – *tak sungguh* apparent power. – *talar* reasoning power. – *tampung* occupancy rate, capacity. – *tanggap(an)* responsiveness. – *tangkal* deterrence. – *tangkap* a) apprehension. – *tangkis* ability to resist, resistance. – *tarik* a) attractive output/power, attractiveness, appeal. b) traction, tensile force. – *tarik séks*

sexiness, sex appeal. **berdaya tarik** to be attractive. – *tekan* compressive strength. – *témbak* fire power. – *tembus* transparency. – *tempuh* stamina. – *terbang* cruising range. – *tersambung* (*elec*) service (of ... volts). **berdaya tersambung** with electrical service (of ... volts). – *tersedia* available power. – *tetas* hatchability. – *timbang* judgment. – *tolak (balik)* recoil. – *tuas* leverage. – *tumbuh* viability. – *ujud* enforcement. – *ungkapan* expressiveness. – *upaya* efforts. **sedaya-upaya** to the best of one's ability, utmost. **berdaya-upaya** to work hard at, try hard to. **mendaya-upayakan** to do one's best to, make every effort to. – *usaha* initiative.

sedaya ~ *mungkin* as much as possible.

berdaya 1 powerful. **2** to be able to, be capable of ... -ing. ~ *rendah* low-income. *tidak* ~ a) powerless, helpless; to succumb. *tidak* ~ *terhadap* to be powerless against. b) impotent. **ketidak-berdayaan 1** powerlessness, helplessness. **2** impotence. **keberdayaan** strength, power.

memberdayakan to empower. **pemberdayaan** empowerment.

mendayai 1 to strengthen. **2** to influence.

terdaya able, capable.

kedayaan ability, capability, force.

pendayaan influence.

daya II (*tipu* –) a) ruse; cunning, craft, artifice; trickery. b) seduction (of the devil), temptation. *Apa* –? What on earth is to be done?

mendaya, mendayai and **memperdayai** to deceive, trick, cheat.

memperdaya(kan) and **mendaya(kan)** to trick, fool, cheat, deceive.

te(r)pedaya tricked, cheated, fooled, deceived. *tidak* **teperdayakan** cannot be deceived, uncheatable.

pemerdaya con-man.

pemerdayaan fraud.

pendayaan deceit, fraud, deception.

perdayaan deceit, trickery.

daya III → BARAT *daya*.

dayah I (*Pers*) **1** wet nurse. **2** governess.

dayah II (*Ach*) Islamic boarding school; → PESANTRÉN.

Daya(k) Dayak.

dayak (*BG*) unwelcome guest, gate-crasher.

dayan (*A*) *ad* – a name of God, the Reciprocator.

dayang (*cla*) **1** girl. **2** lady-in-waiting. **3** (modern meaning) chaperone.

dayang-dayang (*cla*) lady-in-waiting, handmaid.

mendayangi to serve (s.o. in court).

pendayang 1 (*cla*) young lady. **2** prostitute.

pendayangan female attendants in the palace.

perdayangan seraglio, female court servants.

dayu I 1 (*onom*) moaning, groaning, rumble. **2** sighing, plaint.

mendayu 1 to moan, groan. **2** to rumble (of distant thunder). **3** to lull (to sleep).

mendayu-dayu to lull to sleep.

mendayukan to sing a lullaby to, lull to sleep.

dayu II → IDA (AYU).

dayuh (*M*) **terdayuh** ~ *hati* and **terdayuh-dayuh** moved, touched; sad, depressed.

dayuk (*M*) **terdayuk** *pinggang* swaying the hips.

dayung 1 oar, paddle. **2** pedal (of a bicycle, etc.). **3** fin (of fish); → SIRIP. *sekali merengkuh – dua, tiga pulau terlampaui* to kill two birds with one stone. – *batang* oar with a long handle. – *gébéng* oar with the blade nailed to the handle. – *golék* European oar. – *kebas/kibas* oar with a long handle. – *mayung* all k.o. oars, etc. – *peminggang* oar in the middle of a boat. – *sepéda* bicycle pedal. – *tudung belanga* round oar.

sedayung ~ *sampan* in tune/line (with).

berdayung 1 to row, paddle. **2** to pedal.

mendayung 1 to row/paddle s.t. ~ *kano* to row a canoe. **2** to steer (a ship). ~ *(di) antara dua karang* between the devil and the deep blue sea. **3** to pedal.

dayung-mendayung rowing.

mendayungkan 1 to move s.t. ahead by rowing/paddling. **2** to row s.o. across.

pendayung 1 oar, paddle. **2** oarsman, rower.

pendayungan 1 rowing, paddling. 2 pedaling.
dayus (*A*) 1 despicable, hateful. 2 pimp.
  mendayus to despise.
DB car license for Minahasa/Manado.
dbp (*abbr*) [di bawah pimpinan] directed by.
DD car license for South Sulawesi.
DE car license for South Maluku.
dé I name of the letter d.
dé II → ADIK.
dé III (in acronyms) → DÉPUTI.
debah (*A*) **mendebah** to slaughter.
debak (*onom*) thud. – *debuk* thudding.
  berdebak to thud.
debam (*onom*) crash (of s.t. heavy falling).
  berdebam to fall with a crash.
deban → DEBAM.
debap (*onom*) light noise of s.t. falling, slap.
  berdebap and **mendebap** to make a slapping sound.
debar (*onom*) pulsating, beating, throbbing. – *jantung* heartbeat, pulse.
  berdebar to pulse, palpitate, beat (of the heart), throb, pound.
  berdebar-debar(an) to pound, keep on throbbing.
  mendebarkan to make s.t. pound/throb. ~ *jantung* exciting, thrilling, suspenseful, heart-pounding.
  debaran flutter, throb, pulsation, palpitation.
  pendebar s.t. that makes s.t. pound/beat.
  perdebaran pounding, throbbing, beating.
débarkasi (*D*) debarkation.
debas (*onom*) breathy sound.
débat (*D/E*) debate.
  berdébat to debate.
  berdébat-débatan to debate with e.o.
  mendébat to argue, argue about s.t., debate s.t.
  memperdébatkan to debate about s.t., make s.t. the subject of discussions.
  pendébat debater.
  perdébatan 1 debate, debating, deliberations. 2 the subject of debate.
débét → DÉBIT I.
debik I (*onom*) bleat.
  berdebik and **mendebik** to bleat.
debik II (*onom*) slapping sound.
  mendebik to make a slapping sound. ~ *mata parang* to resist authority.
debil (*D*) mentally retarded.
debing (*onom*) hollow sound (of a small drum).
  berdebing to make a hollow sound, boom.
débirokratisasi debureaucratization.
débit I (*D/E*) debit.
  mendébitkan to debit.
  pendébitan debiting.
débit II (*D*) flow velocity, rate of flow. – *air* discharge. – *keluar* outflow. – *masuk* inflow.
  mendébitkan to discharge.
débitor and **débitur** (*D*) debtor. – *utama* primary debtor.
deblak I (*onom*) slapping sound.
  mendeblak to slap.
deblak II (*J*) **ndeblak** to collapse, fall down.
déboasasi deforestation.
debog (*Jv*) banana-tree log used as puppet rack.
debos (*coq*) **ngedebos** to boast.
debu 1 dust. 2 silt. – *batu* rock dust. – *(h)embus* blowing dust. – *kikir* filings. – *layang* drifting dust. – *lembab* inert dust. – *mérah* red haze. – *radioaktif* radioactive fallout.
  berdebu dusty.
  mendebu to become like dust; powdery.
  debuan dust.
  pendebuan dusting.
debuk (*onom*) pound, smash, thud. – *debak* thumping. **berdebuk-debak** to keep on thumping.
  berdebuk to thud.
  mendebuk to hit s.t. hard.

debum (*onom*) the muffled sound of blows. – *debam* muffled sounds.
  berdebum to make a muffled sound.
debun → DEBAP.
debung (*onom*) boom, thud, resonant sound.
debup (*onom*) crashing sound of light object falling.
  berdebup to make a crashing noise, with a crash. *jatuh* ~ to crash down.
debur (*onom*) noise of waves smashing or heart pounding.
  berdebur and **mendebur** to pound (on the shore of waves).
  mendeburkan to make s.t. pound.
  deburan pounding.
debus I (*onom*) whistle, rustle, flap.
  berdebus to whistle, rustle, flap.
debus II → DABUS.
debus III empty (of a fishing net).
debut (*onom*) hiss, sizzle, farting noise.
  berdebut to hiss, sizzle, make a farting noise.
début (*D*) debut, first appearance.
decah I (*onom*) chewing noise.
  mendecah to chew.
decah II (*Jv*) puddle.
decak (*onom*) clicking sound. – *sungai* outflow, rate of flow.
  berdecak to make a clicking sound. ~ *nikmat* to click one's tongue with pleasure.
  berdecak-decak ~ *kagum* to click one's tongue in amazement.
  mendecak to make a clicking noise.
  mendecakkan to make s.t. click, click (one's tongue, etc.).
  decakan clicking noises (made by the tongue).
decap I (*onom*) sound of smacking lips, clicking. – *decup* clicking. **berdecap-berdecup** clickety-clack.
  berdecap-decap to smack one's lips.
  mendecap-decap to smack one's lips.
decap II flashing.
  mendecap-decap to flash, flicker.
decéh and **decih** (*onom*) clicking sound.
  berdecih and **mendecih** to make a clicking sound.
  mendecihkan to click.
déch → DÉH.
decing (*onom*) clinking, jingling, ringing, clattering.
  mendecing to clink, clatter, jingle.
decit (*onom*) twitter, squeal, chirp.
  berdecit and **mendecit** to twitter, squeal, chirp.
  decitan twittering.
decup (*onom*) plop, small object falling into water.
  berdecup to make that noise.
decur (*onom*) spurt, sound of water gushing out.
  mendecur to (make a) spurting (sound).
decus (*onom*) → DESUS.
decut (*onom*) sucking noise.
  berdecut to make a sucking noise.
dedah uncovered, exposed; → DADAH III.
  mendedahkan 1 to uncover, open up, expose. 2 to remove (one's clothing).
  terdedah wide open, uncovered, exposed, revealed.
  pendedahan uncovering, exposure.
dedai berdedai-dedai in large groups, in long strings.
dedak I bran. *makan* – very poor. *minta* – *kepada orang mengubik* to seek help from s.o. who is very poor. – *halus* chaff. – *kasar* husks.
  berdedak still has some husk on it (of rice).
dedak II grievance.
  mendedak to feel aggrieved.
dedak III crowded.
  berdedak-dedak closely packed.
dédal (*Port*) thimble.
dedali → DALI-DALI.
dedalu (- *api*) mistletoe; → BENALU.
dedangkot → DEDENGKOT.
dedap k.o. tree used as props for betel-vines, *Erythrina*, *spp. laksana bunga* –, *mérah ada berbau tidak* beautiful but stupid. – *batik* coral tree, *Erythrina variegata*. – *hantu* k.o. small tree, *Erythrina fulgens*. – *laut* hibiscus, *Hibiscus tiliaceus*.
dedar feeling ill, slightly feverish.

dedara → DARA I.

dedaré (*J*) chick.

dedas I (*onom*) crackling sound.
  mendedas to crackle.

dedas II feeling of not having completely emptied one's bladder.

dedau (*onom*) shriek, screaming.
  mendedau to shriek, scream.

dedaunan 1 foliage. 2 leafy vegetables.

dédé (*vulg*) genitals.

dedek → DEDAK I.

dédél ripped, torn.
  mendédél(i) to rip, tear.

dedemenan (*J*) sweetheart.

dedemit evil spirit, ghost; → DEMIT.

dedengkot (*S coq*) big shot, magnate, well-known.

deder (*J*) mendeder to sow seeds; to cultivate.
  dederan seedling; seedbed.
  pendederan 1 sowing; cultivating. 2 seedbed.

dederuk mourning dove.

dedes (*J*) mendedes to question, interrogate.

dédés I (*S?*) 1 musk. 2 civet cat.

dédés II slice.
  mendédés to cut into thin slices.

dédét (*Jv*) *jual* – to sell s.t. to an employee and take payment out of his/her salary.

dédikasi (*D*) dedication.
  berdédikasi to be dedicated.
  mendédikasikan to dedicate.

dédolarisasi stopping the use of the dollar as a standard for the valuation of currency.

déduksi (*D*) deduction.
  mendéduksikan to deduct.

déduktif (*D/E*) deductive.

dedulang pink shower tree, *Cassia javanica*; → DULANG-DULANG.

dééskalasi (*E*) de-escalation.

défaitis (*D?*) defeatist.

défaitisme (*D?*) defeatism.

dé fakto (*D*) de facto.

défénsif (*D/E*) defensive.
  berdéfénsif to be on the defense.

défilé (*D mil*) review, parade.
  berdéfilé to pass/march in review.

définisi (*D*) definition.
  mendéfinisikan to define.
  terdéfinisikan defined.
  pendéfinisi definer.
  pendéfinisian defining.

définitif (*D/E*) definitive.

défisiénsi (*D*) deficiency.

défisit (*D/E*) deficit.

déflasi (*D*) deflation.

déforéstasi (*D/E*) deforestation.

déformasi (*D*) deformation.
  mendéformasi(kan) to deform.
  terdéformasi deformed.
  pendéformasian deformation.

degam (*onom*) booming, thundering.
  berdegam and mendegam to boom, thunder.

degan (*Jv*) – *ijo* young green coconut.

degap I (*onom*) rapping/tapping noises (of heels/horseshoes). – *degup* tapping, hammering.
  degap-degap rapping/pounding noises.
  berdegap-degap to rap, tap; to pound.
  degapan rapping, tapping.
  degap-degapan pounding.

degap II (*M*) sturdy, robust, strong.

degar (*onom*) 1 rolling/reverberating noise (of thunder/cannons). 2 sound of smashing s.t. down.
  degar-degar noise of rolling thunder. ~ *merpati* trouble between husband and wife. ~ *perapatan* trouble in the family which leads to greater harmony. berdegar-degar to make the noise of rolling thunder.

degaran reverberating noise.

degdeg (*Jv*) throb, pulsation.
  degdegan to throb, beat, pulsate.

dégen (*D*) foil (k.o. sword).

dégénérasi (*D*) degeneration.

deger → DEGAR.

degil obstinate, naughty, troublesome (child), insubordinate, rebellious, intractable.
  sedegil as obstinate/stubborn as.
  berdegil to be insubordinate/obstinate.
  mendegilkan to make s.o. insubordinate.
  kedegilan naughtiness, being troublesome, insubordination, obstinacy.

deging berdeging to persevere.

dégléng (*Jv*) 1 eccentric. 2 not straight, at an angle.

dégradasi (*D*) degradation.
  mendégradasikan to degrade.

degub berdegub throbbing, exciting.
  deguban throb.

deguk (*onom*) gulping/gurgling noise.
  berdeguk to gulp, gurgle, make a gulping/gurgling noise.

degum (*onom*) noise of cannon shots. – *degam* explosive noises.
  berdegum and mendegum to make the noise of cannon shots.

degung (*onom*) 1 noise of a gong. 2 Sundanese *gamelan*.

degup (*onom*) 1 thud, crash. 2 gulping. – *hati* heart beat.
  berdegup(-degup) 1 to make crashing noises. 2 to gulp.
  berdegupan to beat, palpitate.
  mendegupkan to make s.t. beat/palpitate; exciting. ~ *hati* to make one's heart pound; exciting.
  degupan beat. ~ *jantung* heart beat.

degur (*onom*) sound of waves crashing.
  berdegur to smash (of waves).

déh (*J*) 1 particle urging s.o. to do s.t. *Makan* –. Come on and eat. 2 particle showing agreement. *Baik* –. Oh, all right. 3 particle emphasizing that s.t. is true. *Puas* –! I assure you, you'll be satisfied.

deham berdeham(-deham) and mendeham(-deham) to clear one's throat.

dehem → DEHAM. mendehem(i) 1 to clear the throat (at) (a falling star to make a wish). 2 to signal by clearing the throat.

déhidrasi (*D*) dehydration.

dehim (*onom*) sound of a suppressed cough.

dehoi → INDEHOI.

dehok (*onom*) groaning.
  berdehok-dehok to moan and groan.

déhutanisasi deforestation.

dék I (*E*) deck. – *muka* forward deck.

dék II (*D*) cover, blanket.
  dék-dékan to cover o.s., cover one's ass.

dékade (*D*) decade.

dékadén (*D/E*) decadent.

dékadénsi (*D*) decadence.

dekah (*onom*) laughing.
  berdekah-dekah to guffaw, roar with laughter.

dekak I → DEKAH.

dekak II (*onom*) clicking.
  berdekak-dekak to click (of one's heels on the pavement, etc.).

dekak-dekak abacus.

dekam berdekam 1 to crouch, sit in crouched position. 2 to be cooped up (in a place). 3 to be in jail. 4 to stick (in one's mind), obsess.
  berdekam-dekam to coop o.s. up.
  mendekam 1 to crouch. 2 to be cooped up. 3 to be in jail.

dekan bamboo rat, *Rhizomys sumatrensis*.

dékan (*D*) dean. – *ahli* dean of academic affairs.
  mendékani to be dean of.
  kedékanan deanship.

dekap I with folded arms.
  sedekap folded (of one's arms).
  berdekap ~ *tangan* with folded arms.
  berdekap(-dekap) to embrace, hug.
  berdekap(-dekap)an and bersidekap to embrace/hug e.o.
  bersedekap with arms folded.

mendekap to embrace, hug, take in one's arms, cuddle. ~ *tangan/tubuh* to sit around and not do any work.

mendekapi to embrace, hug.

mendekapkan to squeeze to o.s. in an embrace, hug.

dekapan embrace, hug, arms (in the sense of an embrace).

pendekap bracket, brace. **sependekap** as much as can be embraced, armful.

dekap II (*onom*) palpitation, beating.

berdekap(-dekap) to palpitate, beat.

dekap III → DEKAT.

dékar mendékar to fight with a sword; → PENDÉKAR.

dekat 1 near, close by, next to; vicinity. *sudah* – to be near, approaching. **2** almost, nearly. – *seminggu* almost a week. – *rezekinya* make a profit easily.

dekat-dekat ~ *jauh* so near and yet so far. *Jangan* ~*!* Stay away!

sedekat as close(ly) as.

sedekat-dekatnya as close(ly) as possible.

berdekat to be near(by).

berdekat-dekat 1 to get close to e.o., associate. **2** to be next to e.o.

berdekatan and **berdekat-dekatan** near, next/close to e.o., adjacent, contiguous. *Rumah kami* ~. Our houses are next to e.o.

mendekat 1 to approach, get close, draw near. **2** to reconcile.

mendekati [and **ngedekatin** (*J coq*)] **1** to approach, get close (up) to, get near, close with (the enemy). *tidak bisa didekati* unapproachable. *kalau pada suatu saat Anda didekati oléh seseorang yang belum dikenal* if some time you are approached by a stranger. **2** to be close to, almost. *Umurnya* ~ *40 tahun.* He's almost 40.

dekat-mendekati to approach e.o.

mendekatkan to put s.t. close (to s.t. else), bring s.t. closer. *stratégi* ~ *pasién dengan dokter melalui Internét* strategies for bringing the patient closer to the doctor via the Internet. ~ *perbédaan* to reconcile differences.

memperdekat(kan) to make s.t. move closer, reconcile.

terdekat closest. *keluarga* ~*nya* her closest relatives.

terdekati approachable. *tidak* ~ inaccessible.

dekatan 1 (*coq*) (come) closer. **2** proximate.

kedekatan nearness, closeness, proximity, propinquity.

pendekatan 1 approach. **2** rapprochement. **3** approximation.

perdekatan approach.

dékblad (*D*) wrapper (of a cigar).

dekep → DEKAP I.

deket → DEKAT. **ngedeketin** → NGEDEKATIN.

dekih (*onom*) chuckle, snigger, snicker.

mendekih and **terdekih(-dekih)** to chuckle, snigger, snicker.

dekik (– *pipi*) dimple, indentation.

dekil (*J*) very dirty, filthy.

déking (*D*) **1** (protective) cover(ing). **2** collateral. **3** protection by an important person. – *emas* gold reserves.

mendéking to cover, protect.

mendékingi to protect.

dekit (*onom*) snigger.

déklamasi (*D*) declamation.

berdéklamasi to declaim.

mendéklamasikan to declaim s.t.

pendéklamasian declaiming.

déklamator (*D*) declaimer, reciter.

déklarasi (*D*) declaration.

mendéklarasikan to declare.

déklérer (*E?*) declarer (in a card game).

déklinasi (*D*) **1** declination. **2** (*gram*) declension.

dékolonisasi (*D*) decolonization.

dékomposisi (*D*) decomposition.

Dékon [Déklarasi ékonomi] Economic Declaration (pronounced by Sukarno in 1963).

dékonstruksi (*D*) deconstruction.

dékor (*D/E*) decor.

dékorasi (*D*) decoration.

dékoratif (*D/E*) decorative.

dekrét and **dékrit** (*D*) decree.

mendekrétkan to decree.

deksa well-built.

déksel (*D*) small cover.

deku (*Jv*) **berdeku** to be in a kneeling position.

mendeku to kneel.

dekuk curved, bent over.

mendekuk(-dekuk)kan to bend, fold.

dekunci k.o. tree, *Gastrochilus pandurata*.

dekung (*onom*) → DEGUNG.

dekur (*onom*) → DEKUT.

dekus (*onom*) snarl, hiss, spit, snort.

berdekus and **mendekus** to hiss, spit, snort.

dekut (*onom*) cooing noise.

berdekut and **mendekut** to coo.

dekutan cooing.

delah k.o. sea bream, yellow tail fusilier, *Caesio erythrogaster*.

delamak (*M*) embroidered fabric used in marriage ceremonies. *seperti kudung dengan* – inseparable.

delan ripple.

berdelan to ripple.

delap I gun smoke.

delap II ill-mannered, shameless, brazen.

delapan eight. – *belas* 18. – *enam* 86. **mendelapan-enamkan** to settle s.t. privately (outside the legal system). – *puluh* 80.

berdelapan to be (in a group of) eight.

kedelapan 1 eighth. **2** all eight.

perdelapan eighth.

delas land which has been cultivated and then allowed to lie fallow so that it returns to secondary growth.

delat berdelat-delat glittering, twinkling.

délégasi (*D*) **1** delegation. **2** delegate.

mendélégasikan to delegate.

délégasian delegated.

pendélégasian delegation (of s.t.). ~ *wewenang* delegation of power.

délégir (*D*) **mendélégir** to delegate.

delemak → DELAMAK.

déleman → DÉLMAN.

déléngék (*J*) **ndéléngék** and **ngedéléngék** to get a look at s.t. without paying.

delep (*Jv*) **mendelep 1** to sink. **2** to hide (behind s.t.).

mendelepkan to hide s.t.

delepak lamp consisting of a wick placed in a plate of fuel.

delér (*D col*) title for members of the Raad van Indie.

deles (*Jv*) pure-bred, pure-blooded, of unmixed blood.

déligir (*D*) **mendéligir** to delegate.

deli → DELIK I.

delik I k.o. tree, *Memecylon caloneuron*.

delik II (*Jv*) wide-open (of the eyes).

mendelik 1 to stare, glare (at). **2** to hide.

mendeliki to stare/glare at.

mendelikkan to open (one's eyes) wide.

delikan /delikan/ and **deli'an** / **1** peek-a-boo. **2** to play hide-and-go-seek.

délik (*D*) delict, offense, misdemeanor, punishable act, wrongdoing. *kena* – found/proven guilty of an offense. – *aduan* complaint (offense). – *biasa* ordinary offense. – *harta benda* property offense. – *kesusilaan* indecent assault. – *kulpa* culpable offense. – *omisi* offense of omission. – *pérs* press offense. – *susila* crime against morality. – *tunggal* sole offense.

délikat (*D/E*) delicate, ticklish, requiring careful handling.

delikatés (*D*) delicacy.

delima I (*Skr*) *pohon* – pomegranate, *Punica granatum. warna* – *merekah* a split pomegranate (showing its red content), a simile for ruby lips. – *batik* k.o. small pomegranate. – *burung* k.o. bush, *Memecylon dichotomum.* – *gading* small pomegranate used as a medicine. – *hutan* k.o. shrub, *Gardenia tubifera*.

delima-delimaan plant family, *Punicaceae*.

delima II *batu* – ruby, a red precious gem(stone).

delimukan emerald dove, *Chalcophaps indica*.

délinéasi (*D/E*) delineation.

delinggam 1 annatto tree, *Bixa orellana*. **2** red-lead; → SEDELINGGAM.

délinkuén (*D*) delinquent.

délinkuénsi (*E*) delinquency. – *remaja* juvenile delinquency.

delir → DELÉR.

délist (*E*) delist.

　mendélist to delist.

délisting (*E*) the removal (of a security) from the group listed with a particular stock exchange.

délko (*D*) car battery.

délman (*D*) a 2-wheeled horse-drawn carriage with the passenger seats right across the axle-tree and a small door at the back; the cabman sits on a bench placed parallel with the axle-tree in front of the passenger seats.

delong (*ob*) sunken (of eyes).

　mendelong 1 sunken (eyes). **2** to be taken aback.

delongop (*Jv*) **mendelongop** yawning, wide-open (of the mouth).

délta (*D/E*) delta.

delu I mendelu fed up. ~ *dalam hati* to be fed up.

delu II → DALU I.

deluang → JELUANG.

delujur → JELUJUR III.

délusi (*E*) delusion.

délusif (*E*) delusive, delusory.

delut → JELUT.

dem (*E*) car dump.

déma [déwan mahasiswa] university student council.

démagog (*D/E*) demagogue.

démagogi (*D/E*) demagoguery.

démagogik (*D/E*) demagogic.

demah anything heat(ed) (such as stones/ashes/leaves/hot-water bottles, etc.) to cure sore parts of the body, warm compress.

　mendemah to apply such a compress to a sore part of the body.

　pendemahan compress.

demam 1 fever, condition of the body with temperature higher than normal. **2** to have/run a temperature, be feverish. *orang* – fever patient. **3** fad. – *berdarah* dengue, hemorrhagic fever, DHF, breakbone fever. – *berganti hari/berselang/(ber)selang-seling* intermittent fever. – *bintik* spotted fever. – *cupak* slight fever. – *dangdut* pop-music fever. – *dingin* fever with the shakes. – *emas* gold fever/rush. – *gigil* fever with the shakes. – *kaméra* nervous before the camera, camera shy. – *kéong* schistosomiasis. – *kepialu* prolonged fever, typhoid. – *ketulangan* rheumatic fever. – *kuning* yellow fever. – *kura(-kura)* malaria with enlarged spleen. – *mengambuh* relapsing fever. – *meroyan* puerperal fever. – *panas* high fever. – *panggung* stage fright. – *parit* trench fever. – *politik* political excitement/agitation. – *puyuh* slight fever. –.– *puyuh* to pretend to be ill. – *rabu kembang* fever in lung disease. – *rématik* rheumatism. – *sejuk* fever with the shakes. – *selesma* influenza, flu. – *sépakbola* soccer fever. – *siput* schistosomiasis. – *susu* puerperal fever. – *ternak* tick fever (of cattle).

　demam-demam feverish.

　berdemam 1 feverish. **2** to have a fever.

　mendemami to infect (with a fever), make feverish. *Suasana Lebaran masih ~ kota Jakarta.* A *Lebaran* atmosphere has infected Jakarta.

demama (*A*) kettle drum.

deman → DEMEN.

demand (*E*) (economic) demand; → PERMINTAAN.

demang (*J/Jv*) **1** district head (first in Java and later in South and Central Sumatra). **2** (*cla*) title for district head, like – *Lébar Daun.* – *tani* (in Central Java) an agricultural district officer. **3** (*col*) honorific title bestowed by the Netherlands Indies government on prominent Indonesian chiefs (in the *Priangan* region).

demap (*ob*) glutton; voracious, gluttonous.

　mendemap to be gluttonous.

　pendemap a glutton.

démarkasi (*D*) demarcation.

dembai *berjalan* **berdembai-dembai** to walk along chatting and joking.

dembam (*onom*) thud.

　berdembam to fall with a thud.

dembum → DEBUM.

dembun (*onom*) sound made by beating a mattress, thump.

berdembun(-dembun) to thump.

demdem → DUMDUM.

demek (*J*) moist, damp, humid.

demen (*J/Jv*) to like, be fond of; → SUKA.

　kedemenan like, love.

démés (*J*) large and flat (nose).

demi 1 for (the sake of). – *kepentingan* in the interest of, for the benefit/sake of. – *keséhatan* for the sake of one's health. **2** X after X. *satu – satu* one after the other. *seorang – seorang* one (person) after the other. **3** as soon as, when. *Pintu rumah ditutup – tersiar kabar musuh mulai masuk ke kota.* The doors of the houses closed as soon as the news spread that the enemy had started to enter the city. **4** in the name of, on, by (in oaths). – *Allah* by God. **5** (*cla*) as, like. *Suaranya merdu – buluh perindu.* Her voice was as sweet as the Aeolian harp.

demik (*M*) **mendemik** to slap, smack (with the palm).

demikian 1 thus, such, so. *karena dengan* – because in this way. *dengan* – therefore, to this end, in this way. *dalam hal yang* – in such case. *kalau mémang* – if that is the case, if so. *sehingga dengan* – so that in this way. *tidak – mahal* not so expensive. **2** according to, so said. – *Antara* according to Antara. – *suratkabar X memberikan .../memberitahukan* the newspaper X reported that ... **3** in closing to letters and official documents. – *agar maklum* and – *supaya saudara maklum* and – *supaya saudara maklum adanya* the above has herewith been brought to your attention. –*lah* in witness thereof. –*lah naskah ini dibuat di Jakarta.* In witness thereof this document was drawn up in Jakarta. – *juga/pula* likewise, the same goes/is true for. –*lah halnya* that's the way it is, that is the situation. *dalam – itu* at that time.

　sedemikian such. ~ *lama* for such a long time. ~ *rupa sehingga* in such a way that.

démilitarisasi (*E*) demilitarization.

　mendémilitarisasikan to demilitarize.

démisionér (*D*) lame duck, outgoing. *kabinét* – outgoing Cabinet. *Kabinét itu adalah* –. The Cabinet has tendered its resignation.

　mendémisionérkan ~ *kabinét* to dissolve a Cabinet.

　pendémisionéran ~ *kabinét* dissolution of a Cabinet.

démistifikasi (*E*) demystification.

　mendémistifikasikan to demystify.

demit → DEDEMIT.

démitologisasi (*D*) demythologization.

démo I [délman bermotor] a 3-wheeled motorized vehicle powered by a German-made D.K.W. engine; the front wheel is steered by means of an elongated tubular handlebar on which controls for transmission and throttle are mounted. Brake and clutch are on the floor of the vehicle and are foot-operated.

démo II clipped form of **démonstrasi**.

　berdémo to demonstrate (against).

　mendémo(kan) 1 to demonstrate. *enam résép bufét yang didémokan* the six buffet recipes which were demonstrated. **2** to demonstrate against. ~ *majikan buron* to demonstrate against the fugitive boss.

　pendémo demonstrator.

démobilisan (*D*) demobilized soldier.

démobilisasi (*D*) demobilization.

　mendémobilisasikan to demobilize.

démograf (*D*) demographer.

démografi (*D/E*) demography. *ahli* – demographer.

démografis (*D*) demographic.

démokrasi (*D/E*) democracy. – *langsung* direct democracy. – *liberal* (western) liberal democracy. – *Pancasila* Indonesian-style democracy (based on the *Pancasila*). – *Parleméntér* parliamentary democracy. – *Pelibatan* participatory democracy. – *penindasan* pressure democracy. – *Perwakilan* representative democracy. – *terkendali* controlled democracy (of Singapore); *cp* DÉMOKRASI *terpimpin.* – *terpimpin* guided democracy (under President Soekarno).

　berdémokrasi democratic.

　mendémokrasikan to democratize.

　pendémokrasian democratization.

démokrat (*D/E*) democrat. *Partai* – Democratic Party.

démokratik (*E*) and **démokratis** (*D*) democratic.
 mendémokratiskan to democratize.
démokratisasi democratization.
démokratisator (*E*) democratizer. *ABRI sebagai* –. The Republic of Indonesia Armed Forces as the democratizer.
démokratisir (*D*) **mendémokratisir** to democratize.
démolisi (*D*) demolition. – *bawah air* minesweeping.
démon (*D/E*) demon.
démonis and **démoniak** (*D*) demoniac(al).
démonstran (*D*) demonstrator; → PENGUNJUK *rasa. kaum/para* – demonstrators. – *antiperang* antiwar demonstrator.
démonstrasi (*D*) demonstration, display, exhibition; → UNJUK *rasa.*
 berdémonstrasi 1 to demonstrate. **2** to protest.
 mendémonstrasi to demonstrate against.
 mendémonstrasikan 1 to demonstrate, display s.t. **2** to demonstrate against s.t.; → MELAKUKAN/MELANCARKAN *unjuk rasa.*
 pendémonstrasi demonstrator.
 pendémonstrasian demonstrating.
démonstratif (*D/E*) demonstrative.
démonstrator (*E*) demonstrator.
démoralisasi (*D*) demoralization.
 mendémoralisasikan to demoralize.
démoralisir (*D*) **mendémoralisir** to demoralize.
démosi (*E*) demotion.
dempak 1 broad and flat (of a hat/roof of a house, etc.). **2** short and stout (of people), stocky.
dempal (*Jv*) strong.
dempam → DEMBAM.
dempang I (*onom*) clang of hollow things (empty tins, etc.).
 berdempang-dempang clanging of empty tins, etc. *cakap ~* to boast, chatter away.
dempang II → DAMPING I.
démpél (*Jv*) near.
 berdémpélan nearby, close.
 mendémpél to stick/stay together, be close to e.o., crowd together.
démpét I and **dempét** (*J/Jv*) growing as one (said of two separate things) (such as Siamese twins/bananas grown together), stuck together. *pisang* – two bananas growing in one skin. *rumah* – a duplex (house).
 berdémpét packed/pressed/stuck close together.
 berdémpét-démpét and **berdémpét(-démpét)an** to be packed close together, stick close together, jammed, close to e.o.
 mendémpét 1 to get stuck (to s.t.). **2** to connect, link up, jam, squeeze.
 mendémpéti to get close to.
 mendémpétkan to press things together (until they join or stick together).
 terdémpét [and **kedémpét** (*coq*)] jammed, wedged in.
démpét II name of a *ceki* card.
dempir (*onom*) shrill/strident/piercing (sound).
 berdempir to make a shrill sound, to ring a bell/cymbal.
dempit → DEMPÉT.
démplon (*Jv*) chubby, plump.
démplot [demonstration-plot] (*E*) experimental plot.
dempok (*onom*) sound of collision, bumping.
 berdempok to collide (with), bump (against).
 terdempok 1 accidentally bang/bump into, bump against. **2** collided, bumped.
 mendempokkan to cause to collide, knock s.t. into s.t.
dempol → DEMPUL I.
dempuk → DEMPOK.
dempul I (glazier's) putty, caulk, gypsum. – *kayu* wood putty.
 berdempul caulked, puttied.
 mendempul to caulk, putty.
 dempulan s.t. caulked, puttied.
 pendempulan calking, puttying.
dempul II (*Jv*) various species of trees, black currant tree, *Antidesma ghaesembilla* and *Glochidion spp.*
dempung (*onom*) plopping sound of stones or fruit into water; splash, sound of s.t. falling into water.
 berdempung(-dempung) to splash.

demung I (*ob*) → DEMANG.
demung II (*Jv*) musical instrument (with *gamelan*, k.o. xylophone of metal plates).
dén I (*Jv*) **1** clipped form of *radén.* – *ajeng* title for an aristocratic girl. – *ayu* title for a married female aristocrat. – *bagus* a) title for high-status men and boys. b) form of address used to a rat (in imploring it not to damage things in the house). **2** form of address from wife to husband; *cp* MAS.
dén II (*M*) I, me (of superiors familiarly to inferiors).
dén III (in acronyms) → DÉTASEMÉN.
déna → DINA I.
dénah I 1 ground plan, sketch, outline. **2** plan, design, blueprint.
 mendénah make such a plan.
dénah II *hantu* – an evil spirit which causes diseases of the feet. *penyakit* – a disease of the feet (ascribed to this evil spirit).
denai trail, spoor, track of a wild animal in the forest or jungle.
 mengikut – to track, follow an animal track. *bagai anjing melintang* – very happy/arrogant. *bagai* – *gajah lalu* trail of ruin.
denak and **dénak** decoy (used in hunting). *seperti* – *mencari lawan* very brave.
Dénas [Déwan Nasional] National Council.
dénasakomisasi dissolution of the *Nasakom* ideology of President Soekarno by the New Order.
dénasionalisasi denationalization.
dénaturasi (*D*) denaturing.
denawa I (*Jv*) demon, giant.
denawa II (*Jv*) village police official, village messenger.
dencang (*onom*) rattling/clanging sound. – *dencing* jingling.
 berdencang to rattle/clang.
dencing (*onom*) jingling sound of coins; → DECING, DENTING.
 sedencing *~ uang* a small coin.
 dencingan jingling.
déncis (*D*) sardines; → SARDÉN.
dencit (*onom*) squeaking.
 mendencit to squeak.
denda (*Skr*) fine, penalty, demurrage. *kena* – fined, incurred a fine. – *bunga* penalty. – *cerukan* overdraft penalty. – *damai* (out of court) settlement. – *darah* blood money. – *kubra* (*Jv*) communal fine if a murderer isn't caught or is unknown. – *pati* penalty imposed on a murderer.
 mendenda(i) to fine/penalize.
 dendaan 1 fine, penalty. **2** fining, penalizing.
 pendendaan fining, penalizing.
dendam 1 – *hati* hate, spite, grudge, grievance, resentment, hard feelings. **2** revenge, vengeance. *–nya selesai sudah* he took revenge. *melepaskan/membalas* – to take revenge, pay s.o. back. *menaruh* – to have a grudge/spite against s.o., bear s.o. a grudge. *dan tidak menaruh* – *kepada siapa pun, dengan kasih kepada sesama manusia* with malice toward none, with charity for all. *menaruh* – *tak sudah* (*M*) to keep (on) sulking endlessly. *rindu* – hankering, yearning, longing, desire. – *benci* deep resentment. – *berahi* passionate love. – *darah* blood feud. – *kasemat/kasumat/kesumat* enmity, rancor.
 berdendam to resent, bear a grudge, sulk. *dengan* ~ to hate, dislike. ~ *hati* to bear malice.
 berdendam-dendaman to have hard feelings toward e.o., bear a grudge toward e.o., be resentful toward e.o.
 dendam-mendendam to hate/resent e.o.
 mendendam(i) to have/bear a grudge against, hurt s.o. out of spite, resent.
 mendendamkan to resent s.t., be sore about s.t., be vexed with.
 kedendaman revenge, resentment, grudge, malice, spite.
 pendendam 1 resentful person, avenger. **2** resentful, vengeful, vindictive.
 pendendaman revenge.
dendang I *burung* – large-billed crow, *Corvus macrorhynchus*; → GAGAK. – *air* cormorant, *Phalacrocorax carbo.* – *laut* brown booby/gannet, *Sula leucogaster plotus.*
dendang II (*cla*) a large dugout.
déndang song (while working). *dengan* – a) singing. b) easily.
 berdéndang to sing (while working). *sambil* ~ *biduk hilir* to kill two birds with one stone. *perut* ~ a growling stomach.

mendéndang to sing, croon, chant.

mendéndangkan 1 to sing s.t. **2** to sing for.

pendéndangan singing.

dendem → DENDAM.

déndéng (C?) dried jerked meat. – *belado* (M) jerked fried meat. – *ragi* dried jerked meat with seasoned grated coconut.

mendéndéng to make *déndéng*.

denderang (*onom*) **1** drumming sound. **2** pounding sound of footsteps.

denderangan 1 drumbeat. **2** pounding of footsteps.

déndi (E) dandy.

berdéndi to play the dandy.

déndritik (D) dendritical.

déndrologi (D/E) dendrology.

dengak (*ob*) **mendengakkan** to bend s.t. forward.

terdengak (to sit) bent forward.

dengan 1 with, along with, in the company of *Ia datang – istrinya.* He came with his wife. *Makan minum di réstoran – teman-temannya.* Eat and drink in a restaurant (together) with his friends. **2** in accordance/agreement/conformity with. *Dia sepaham – saya.* He shared my views. *sesuai – permintaan* in accordance with one's request. **3** of, with. *penuh – manusia* full of people. **4** by means of, with (the help of). *menulis – bolpén* to write with a ballpoint. *dipukul – tongkat* beaten with a stick. – *alamat* [d/a] in care of, c/o. – *jalan* by means of. **5** in (in imprecations). – *nama Tuhan* in the name of God. – *nama Nabi Allah* in the name of the Prophet. *sampai* – up to and including, through. *sampai – 5 Novémber* up to and including November 5, through November 5. *dari tanggal 6 Novémber 1996 sampai – tanggal 1 Januari 1997* from November 6, 1996 to January 1, 1997 inclusive. – *tiada/tidak* and *tiada* – without; → TANPA, TIDAK PAKAI. – *tidak malu-malu* shamelessly, impudently, brazenly. **6** at (a cost of). – *harga $69,95* at $69.95. **7** as. *sama* – the same as. **8** in the way of. – *begitu* in that way, thus. **9** (introduces adverbial expressions) – *lisan* verbally, orally. – *hormat* (in letters) dear. – *ini* hereby. – *sekaligus* all at once, simultaneously, all together. – *sendirinya* automatically. – *sepatutnya* fittingly, properly. – *sewajarnya* naturally. – *tidak* without. – *tidak malu-malu* without reservation. – *tiada* without. – *tulisan* in writing, written.

dengap I pounding (of the blood).

berdengap to pound (of the blood).

dengap II (*onom*) panting.

berdengap and **mendengap** to pant.

terdengap to pant.

dengar 1 to hear. **2** to hear about, learn about. **3** to listen to. – *pendapat* (public) hearing.

dengar-dengar (I've) heard that. ~ *bisa bikin séhat* I've heard that it can make you healthy.

berdengar (M) to be heard/listened to.

mendengar 1 to hear. *saksi yang didengar keterangannya* the witness whose testimony was heard. **2** (*leg*) noted (in decrees, etc.).

mendengari to listen to, pay close attention to.

mendengarkan 1 to listen to. *Siaran radio atau suara dapat didengarkan nyaris bersamaan.* Radio broadcasts and voices can be listened to almost in real time. **2** to obey, comply with.

memperdengarkan 1 to make/allow s.o. to hear s.t. **2** to present, perform, play (a musical selection, etc.). *Radio BBC yang ~ bacaan ayat-ayat al-Qur'an* BBC radio which presents readings of sections of the Koran.

terdengar 1 heard, audible, can be heard. *tidak ~* inaudible.

keterdengaran 1 (sense of) hearing. **2** audibility.

terdengarkan audible.

dengar-dengaran 1 to like to listen. **2** as if one hears s.t., to hear s.t. vaguely, think one hears s.t. **3** to listen to e.o. **4** to listen (to), obey. ~ *akan firman Tuhan* to obey God's commands.

kedengaran 1 audible, can be heard. *Bunyinya tidak ~ oléh orang lain.* The sound was not audible to other people. **2** (it) sounds. ~ *janggal.* It sounds odd.

pendengar s.o. or s.t. who/which hears, hearer, listener. ~ *dada* stethoscope. ~ *tengah* middle ear.

pendengaran 1 (sense of) hearing. ~ *saya kurang tajam.* My hearing isn't very sharp. **2** what has been heard. **sependengaran** according to what s.o. has heard.

déngdét (J) not straight, slanted.

denger → DENGAR. **ngedengerin** (J *coq*) → MENDENGARKAN.

dengih (*onom*) groan, moan, gasp.

terdengih-dengih groaning, moaning, gasping.

dengik (*onom*) light slapping sound.

terdengik to make that sound.

denging (*onom*) whistling/ringing/buzzing sound.

berdenging and **mendenging** to make a whistling, ringing, buzzing sound.

dengingan whistling, ringing, buzzing.

dengkang (*onom*) croaking.

berdengkang to croak.

berdengkang-dengkang to croak.

déngkang-déngkol bent over, twisted.

déngkék name of a *ceki* card.

déngkél I dry, without sap.

déngkél II swollen ankles.

dengkéng (J) **ndengkéng** and **ngedengkéng** to lean forward.

dengki 1 spite, envy, hatred. **2** spiteful, envious.

berdengki (~ *hati*) spiteful, full of spite/hatred.

berdengki-dengkian to hate e.o.

mendengki to envy.

kedengkian spite, hatred; envy, jealousy.

pendengki spiteful/envious person.

pendengian spite.

dengkik weak (from hunger).

dengking (*onom*) yelp.

berdengking and **mendengking** to yelp.

mendengking to yelp at s.t.

dengkingan yelp.

dengkir (*onom*) noise made by grasshoppers.

mendengkir to make that noise.

dengklang lame, limping.

mendengklangkan to lame, cripple, hobble.

déngkol twisted/bent downward.

dengkul I (J/Jv) **1** knee. **2** (in compounds) based on hard work or talk, etc. but not real. *modal* – sweat equity. *seénak – sendiri* to do as one pleases. – *kopong* to get too much sex.

sedengkul knee-high, reaching to the knee.

mendengkul 1 to knee s.o. **2** to kneel down. **3** (*coq*) to take s.t. through corruption.

dengkul II hornless.

dengkung (*onom*) **1** roar, rumble. **2** yelp, grunt, yowl. **3** clang.

berdengkung and **mendengkung 1** to roar, rumble. **2** to yowl.

dengkur (*onom*) **1** snoring noise. **2** grunting noise.

berdengkur and **mendengkur** to snore, grunt.

dengkuran snoring, grunting.

pendengkur snorer, grunter.

dengkus (*onom*) snort, sniffle, whinny.

berdengkus and **mendengkus** to snort, sniffle, whinny.

dengkut → DEKUT.

dengu I → DUNGU.

dengu II berdengu and **mendengu** to breathe noisily.

denguk I (*onom*) sobbing.

mendenguk to sob.

denguk II mendenguk to lower the head.

terdenguk with the head lowered.

dengung (*onom*) humming/buzzing/droning/wailing/roaring sound.

berdengung and **mendengung 1** to hum, buzz, drone, roar. **2** to resound, reverberate.

mendengungkan 1 to make s.t. hum/buzz/roar. **2** to preach (s.t. to s.o.).

dengungan 1 hum, buzz, drone, roar. **2** propaganda.

pendengung s.t. that buzzes, etc., buzzer.

dengus (*onom*) snort, sniff, chugging noise.

berdengus and **mendengus** to snort, sniff, chug.

mendengus-dengus to keep on snorting, sniffing, chugging.

mendenguskan to make s.t. snort/sniff/chug.

dengusan snort, sniff, chug.

dengut (*onom*) resounding/reverberating sound.

berdengut and **mendengut** to resound, reverberate.
berdengut-dengut to keep on reverberating.
terdengut resounded, reverberated.
dénim (*E*) denim.
denok (*Jv*) term of address for young girl; → NOK.
dénok I (*Jv*) chubby, plump, buxom.
kedénokan chubbiness, plumpness.
dénok II (*J*) poinsettia, *Euphorbia pulcherrima.*
dénotasi (*D*) denotation.
dénotatif (*D/E*) denotative.
dénpom [détasemén polisi militér] military police.
densanak → DANSANAK.
dénsitas density; → KEPADATAN.
dentam (*onom*) crackling (sound of gunfire), pounding of metal on metal. – *dentum* explosions.
berdentam to crackle (of gunfire), pound (of metal on metal).
berdentaman crackling (of gunfire), pounding.
mendentamkan 1 to make s.t. crackle, crackling. **2** to pound s.t. on s.t. else.
dentaman crackle, pounding.
dentang (*onom*) clang, rattle, ringing. – *denting* jingle-jangle. **berdentang-denting** jingling, rattling.
berdentangan to jingle, rattle, clang.
mendentangkan 1 to make s.t. jingle/ring. **2** to ring out.
dentangan clang, ringing.
dentar (*onom*) slamming, clanging.
berdentar to slam, clang.
denting (*onom*) clink, tinkle, clatter.
berdenting and **mendenting** to clink, tinkle, clatter.
berdenting-denting and **berdentingan** to keep on clinking, etc.
mendentingkan to make s.t. clink, etc.
dentingan clink, tinkle, clatter.
dentum (*onom*) bang, booming noise, knocking.
berdentum to boom.
berdentuman to keep on booming.
mendentum to knock (of an engine).
mendentumkan to make s.t. boom.
dentuman bang, boom.
dentung (*onom*) bang, boom.
berdentung to bang, boom.
dentur (*onom*) bang, pop.
mendentur to bang, pop.
denyar flash, flashing. – *kilat* flash of lightning.
mendenyar to flash, flicker.
denyaran flash, flicker.
denyit (*onom*) squeak, squeal, shriek.
berdenyit to squeak, squeal, shriek.
denyitan squeak, squeal, shriek, squeaking, squealing, shrieking.
denyut (*onom*) pulse, heartbeat, throb, beat, impulse. – *hati* heartbeat. – *jantung* heartbeat. – *nadi* pulse.
berdenyut and **mendenyut** to beat (of the pulse, etc.).
mendenyutkan to make s.t. throb, heart-pounding.
denyutan 1 pulse, heartbeat. **2** impulse.
déodoran (*D/E*) deodorant.
dép I (*D*) **mendép** and **mengedép** to shelve, put off indefinitely.
dép-dépan *main* ~ to withhold complaints/information, don't take seriously.
pen(ge)dépan shelving, putting off.
Dép II (in acronyms) → DÉPARTEMÉN.
depa a fathom, the span from finger-tip to finger-tip of the outstretched arms, roughly six feet. *beroléh sehasta hendak se*– give him an inch and he wants an ell. – *agung* about three meters.
mendepa(i) to measure in fathoms.
mendepakan ~ *tangan* to spread one's arms.
Dépag [Départemén Agama] Department/Ministry of Religious Affairs.
dépag → DÉPAK, SÉPAK.
depak (*onom*) clatter, the sound made by the clatter of a horse's hooves or a book falling to the floor.
berdepak and **mendepak** the clatter of a horse's hooves.
mendepakkan to make that sound with. ~ *lidah* to smack one's lips.

dépak and **depak mendépak 1** to kick (a ball, etc.), kick away. **2** to discharge, dismiss, fire, oust, throw out.
terdépak discharged, dismissed, fired, ousted.
pendépakan 1 kicking. **2** dismissal, ousting, firing.
depan 1 before. **2** front (of a house, etc.), at (the gate), off (the coast). **3** next, (forth)coming. *bulan/minggu/tahun* – next month/week/year. *di* – a) in front of. b) ahead. c) in the presence of, before. *di* – *umum* in public, publicly. *ke* – a) to the front. b) ahead, into the future, looking forward. *mengedepan* to come to the fore/front; → MENGEMUKA. *Masalah Hak Asasi Manusia (HAM) tetap merupakan isu global yang* ~. The problem of Human Rights continues to be a global issue which is coming to the fore. *mengedepankan* to put forward, advance (a claim, etc.), propose, make (a motion); → MENGEMUKAKAN. ~ *otot* to flex one's muscles (as a show of strength). *buat ke* – henceforward, henceforth, in future, from this time on. *hari/masa* – future. *kaca* – windshield.
berdepan 1 openly, not in secret, right to s.o.'s face. **2** (*mostly Mal*) to come face to face (with).
berdepan(-depan)an to face e.o., face to face.
mendepan to advance, move forward.
mendepankan to put forward, propose.
terdepan 1 foremost, front (seat, etc.); → HADAP. **2** first, in the lead (in contest, etc.).
depang berdepang to stretch one's arms out sideways. ~ *tangan* to stretch one's arms out sideways.
mendepang 1 to stretch one's arms out sideways. **2** to bar/block the way with both arms.
mendepangkan to stretch (one's arms out).
depap (*onom*) sound produced by slapping the palm of the hand on a hard surface, etc.
dépar [Départemén] (in acronyms) department.
Déparlu [Départemén Luar Negeri] Department/Ministry of Foreign Affairs
déparpolisasi decrease in the number of political parties.
Déparpostél [Départemén Pariwisata Pos dan Télékomikasi] Department/Ministry of Tourism, Postal Service, and Telecommunications.
départaisasi (*E*) departyization.
départemén (*D/E*) **1** department, ministry. **2** (*E*) department, one of the sections of a university dealing with a particular field of knowledge. – *Agama* [Dépag] Department of Religion. – *Dalam Negeri* [Dépdagri] Interior Department. – *Dalam Negeri dan Otonomi Daérah* Department of the Interior and Regional Autonomy. – *Hukum dan Perundang-Undangan* Justice Department. – *Kebudayaan dan Pariwisata* Department of Culture and Tourism. – *Kehutanan* [Déphut] Forestry Department. – *Kehakiman* [Dépkéh] Justice Department. – *Kehakiman dan HAM* [Dépkéhham] Department of Justice and Human Rights. – *Kelautan dan Perikanan* Department of the Oceans and Fisheries. – *Keséhatan* [Dépkés] Department of Health. – *Keuangan* [Dépkéu] Department of Finance. – *Koperasi, Pengusaha Kecil & Menengah* Department of Cooperatives, Small & Medium Enterprises. – *Luar Negeri* [Déplu] Foreign Department. – *Pemukiman dan Prasarana Wilayah* [Dépkimpraswil] Department of Settlement and Regional Infrastructure. – *Pendidikan dan Kebudayaan* [Dépdikbud] Department of Education and Culture. – *Pendidikan Nasional* [Dépdiknas] National Education Department. – *Penerangan* [Déppen] Department of Information. – *perdagangan* [Déperdag] Department of Commerce. – *Perhubungan* [Dépérhub] Department of Communications/Transportation. – *Perindustrian* [Déperin] Department of Industry. – *Perindustrian dan Perdagangan* [Déperindag] Department of Industry and Commerce. – *Permukiman dan Prasarana Wilayah* [Kimpraswil] Department of Settlement and Regional Infrastructure. – *Pertahanan* Department of Defense. – *Pertahanan dan Keamanan* [Déphankam] Department of Defense and Security. – *Pertahanan AS* The Pentagon. – *Pertambangan* [Déptan] Department of Mining. – *Pertambangan dan Énergi* [Déptambén] Department of Mining and Energy. – *Pertanian* [Déptan] Agriculture Department. – *Sosial* [Dépsos] Department of Social

Services. – *Tenaga Kerja* [Dépnaker] Department of Manpower. – *Tenaga Kerja, Transmigrasi dan Koperasi* [Dépnaker-transkop] Department of Manpower, Transmigration and Cooperatives. – *Transmigrasi* [Déptrans] Department of Transmigration.

sedépartemén in the same department.

départeméntal (*D/E*) departmental.

depati (*ob*) → (**A**)DIPATI.

Dépdagri → DÉPARTEMÉN *Dalam Negeri.*

Dépdikbud → DÉPARTEMÉN *Pendidikan dan Kebudayaan.*

Dépdiknas → DÉPARTEMÉN *Pendidikan Nasional.*

dépéndén (*E*) dependent.

dépéndénsi (*E*) 1 dependency, dependence. 2 (colonial) possession.

Déperdag → DÉPARTEMÉN *Perdagangan.*

Déperhub → DÉPARTEMÉN *Perhubungan.*

Déperin → DÉPARTEMÉN *Perindustrian.*

Déperindag → DÉPARTEMÉN *Perindustrian dan Perdagangan.*

dépersonalisasi (*D*) depersonalization.

dépersonalisir (*D*) **mendépersonalisir** to depersonalize.

Dépertan → DÉPARTEMÉN *Pertambangan.*

Déphub → DÉPARTEMÉN *Perhubungan.*

Déphut → DÉPARTEMÉN *Kehutanan.*

depik k.o. fish, *Rasbora tawarensis.*

dépinisi → DÉFINISI.

dépisen → DÉVISA.

Dépkéh → DÉPARTEMÉN *Kehakiman.*

Dépkéhham → DÉPARTEMÉN *Kehakiman dan HAM/Hak Asasi Manusia.*

Dépkés → DÉPARTEMÉN *Keséhatan.*

Dépkéu → DÉPARTEMÉN *Keuangan.*

Dépkimpraswil → DÉPARTEMÉN *Pemukiman dan Prasarana Wilayah.*

déplak (*J*) **mendéplak** to fall into a sitting position or with the legs up.

deplék (*J*) **mendeplék** to hide.

déplési (*D*) depletion.

deplok mendéplok to fall into a sitting position.

Déplu → DÉPARTEMÉN *Luar Negeri.*

Dépnaker → DÉPARTEMÉN *Tenaga Kerja.*

Dépnakertranskop → DÉPARTEMÉN *Tenaga Kerja, Transmigrasi dan Koperasi.*

dépo → DÉPOT.

dépok (*Jv*) holy man's shrine; → PADÉPOKAN.

  mendépok to reside, live.

  pendépokan camp, dormitory.

déponir (*D*) **mendéponir** to push out of sight, sweep under the rug.

  pendéponiran pushing s.t. out of sight, sweeping under the rug.

déportan (*D*) deportee.

  pendéportasian deportation.

déposan (*D*) depositor.

déposito (*D*) deposit. – *berjangka* time deposit, certificate of deposit, CD. – *dengan pemberitahuan* deposit on call.

  mendépositokan to deposit (money in a bank).

  pendépositoan depositing.

dépot (*D*) 1 depot, warehouse, site. 2 stand, store.

Déppén → DÉPARTEMÉN *penerangan.*

déprési (*E*) depression.

déprésiasi (*E*) depreciation; → PENYUSUTAN.

  terdéprésiasi depreciated.

déprok (*J/Jv*) **mendéprok** 1 to sit down with the legs to the side. 2 to horn in on s.t.

Dépsos → DÉPARTEMÉN *Sosial.*

Déptambén → DÉPARTEMÉN *Pertambangan dan Énérgi.*

depun hem, edge.

  mendepun to hem, edge.

  pendepun *baju* ~ a blouse decorated with gold thread.

depus (*onom*) sound made by the wind, movement of air, sighing.

députasi (*D*) deputation.

députi (*D/E*) deputy.

dera 1 whipping. 2 castigation.

  mendera 1 to whip, flog. 2 to be painful. 3 to castigate. 3 to punish.

  deraan 1 whipping, flogging. 2 castigation. 3 punishment.

derai I scattered.

  berderai(an) to be scattered all over.

  menderai(-derai)kan to scatter. *menderaikan air mata* to shed tears.

  deraian scattering.

derai II granule, grain, drop.

  berderai 1 granulated, loose (of soil). 2 in small drops. **keberderaian** granularity.

  menderai(-derai)kan 1 to granulate. 2 to make s.t. into small drops, etc.

  penderaian 1 granulation. 2 making into small drops.

derai III (*onom*) sound made by drops of water falling on a surface, pattering, tinkling laughter.

  berderai and **menderai** to make that sound. *titik hujan* ~. Drops of rain splattered down.

  berderai-derai to keep on making that sound.

  derai-menderai to keep on making that sound.

  menderai(-derai)kan 1 to make s.t. make that sound. 2 to shed (tears).

  deraian 1 patter(ing sound). 2 flowing (of tears).

derai IV berderai-derai 1 in large quantities, in droves. 2 without stopping.

derajah → DERAJAT.

derajang k.o. plant, *Lepisanthes kunstleri.*

derajat (*A*) 1 degree (of angle/temperature/family relationship, received at graduation, etc.). 2 level, rank, position (in society). 3 standard. – *berita* degree of urgency of messages. – *biasa* normal degree. – *bujur* degree of longitude. – *busur* degree, arc (of a circle). – *garis lintang* degree of latitude. – *keasinan* salinity. – *kecairan* fluidity. – *kejenuhan* degree of saturation. – *kelembapan* humidity. – *kepercayaan* reliability. – *kilat* highest degree of urgency. – *penghidupan* standard of living. – *segera* immediate, urgent (of messages). – *tolok* standard meridian. – *utama* prime meridian. – *waspada* state of alert.

  sederajat of the same degree, at the same level; equal, equivalent. **menyederajatkan** to place on the same level. *tidak* ~ unequal. **ketidak-sederajatan** inequality.

  berderajat to have a grade/degree, etc. of ...

  menderajatkan to make the same degree, rank the same, put at the same level.

  penderajatan grading, ranking.

derak (*onom*) crack (as of a branch breaking), creak, squeak. – *derik* constant creaking. **berderak-derik** to keep on creaking. – *deruk* constant creaking.

  berderak(-derak) and **menderak-derak** to make a cracking noise, creaking, squeaking.

  menderak-derakkan to gnash (one's teeth).

  derakan creak, crack, squeak.

deram (*onom*) thunder, rumble, roar.

  berderam and **menderam** to rumble, thunder.

deram-deram k.o. pastry made from flour and palm sugar.

derana (*ob*) patient, doesn't lose hope easily.

derang I (*onom*) ting, clatter, clank.

  berderang and **menderang** to clatter, resonate.

derang II (*M*) **berderang** to break (of daylight).

derap (*onom*) trotting, tramping, pattering, clopping. – *irama* rhythmic movement. – *langkah* a) sound of tramping feet. b) speed of movement. – *sepatu* sound of footsteps. – *révolusi* the progressive march of the revolution.

  sederap in agreement, in unison, coherent. **kesederapan** coherence.

  berderap and **menderap** 1 to make a tramping/clopping sound, patter. 2 to trot (along).

  menderapkan to make (a horse, etc.) trot.

  derapan trotting, tramping, pattering.

deras I 1 swift (of a current/movement). 2 fast (of s.o. or s.t. running). 3 heavy (of rainfall).

  deras-deras swiftly.

  berderas to run swiftly.

  menderas 1 fast-flowing, swift. 2 full of energy, energetic.

  menderaskan to speed up, accelerate, make s.t. flow or run faster.

  derasan torrent.

kederasan 1 force, intensity. **2** speed.
penderas s.t. that speeds s.t. up or makes it louder, accelerant. ~ *suara* microphone.
penderasan rapids, cataract.
deras II → DARAS.
deras III (*onom*) crunching sound.
derau (*onom*) **1** sound of rushing water or of rain falling. **2** noise (in general).
  berderau and **menderau** to make noise, be noisy.
  berderau-derau and **menderau-derau** to make a lot of noise.
  derauan rushing/roaring sound.
dérégulasi deregulation.
dérék I (*E*) crane, derrick, boom. – *induk* quarry crane. – *jalan* (traveling) crab. – *kambang* floating crane. – *mesin* crane. – *pemboran* drilling derrick. – *petikémas* container crane.
  mendérék to tow (a vehicle).
  pendérék tower.
  pendérékan towing.
dérék II → DÉRÉT.
derél I → DRIL I.
derél II (*D*) volley (of gunshots), salvo.
  menderél to shoot a volley at.
  penderélan volleying, salvo.
derep (*Jv*) services at the rice harvest.
  menderep [and **nderep** (*coq*)] to harvest rice (for a share of the crop).
  penderep s.o. who harvests rice (for a share of the crop).
deres → DERAS.
dérés I (*Jv*) **mendérés** to tap a palm for toddy; → SADAP I.
  pendérés tapper.
dérés II → DARAS.
derési (*D*) drainage.
derési (*D*) passenger carriage (of train).
dérét 1 row, column. **2** (*math*) series, progression. **3** serial. *secara* – serial(ly). – *acak* random series. – *berhingga* finite series. – *hitung* arithmetic progression. – *ukur* geometric progression.
  sedérét 1 abreast (of), in (the same) line (as). **2** a line/sequence of.
  berdérét 1 in rows, in a line; to form a line, line up. **2** serial.
  berdérét-dérét to line up, lined up, in a row. *Di samping piring kiri kanan,* ~ *séndok atau garpu.* Next to the plates on the right and left, the spoons and forks were lined up.
  berdérétan to be lined up, in rows.
  mendérét to be lined up, in rows.
  mendéréti to line s.t. up (with s.t.).
  mendérétkan and **memperdérétkan** to line s.t. up in a row/series/sequence.
  dérétan column, row, line; series, progression, array.
  pendérétan sequencing.
deretak (*onom*) clickety-clack.
  berderetak to make that noise, click and clack.
dergama (*Jv*) libel.
derhaka → DURHAKA.
derham → DIRHAM.
deriji → JERUJI.
derik (*onom*) grate, creak.
  berderik to creak.
  berderik-derik to keep on creaking, make grating noises.
  derikan grating noise.
deril → DRIL I.
dering I (*onom*) **1** burring/whirring/ringing sound, ring, clink, chirp. **2** tinkling sound.
  berdering and **mendering** to ring, tinkle, chirp, clink, burr, whir. *masuk dalam kawanan gajah berdering* when in Rome do as the Romans.
  berderingan (*pl subj*) to tinkle, etc.
  mendering to tinkle, ring, clink, whir.
  deringan ring, tinkle, chirp, clink, burr, whir.
dering II k.o. tree, *Cryptocarya griffithiana.*
deringo sweet flag, *Acorus calamus.*
derip punch (the tool).
deris (*onom*) rustling sound, sound made when cutting cloth.
  berderis and **menderis** to make such a sound.

derit (*onom*) creaking/squeaking sound.
  berderit and **menderit** to make such a sound.
  deritan creaking.
derita (*Skr*) suffering.
  menderita 1 to suffer. *Perempuan paling* ~ *akibat HIV/AIDS.* Women suffer the most from HIV/AIDS. **2** to have (a particular disease). *Dia* ~ *flu.* He has the flu.
  menderitai to suffer from s.t.
  terderita bearable. *tidak* ~ unbearable.
  terderitakan bearable. *siksa yang tak* ~ *lagi* unbearable torture.
  deritaan suffering.
  penderita 1 person who suffers from (an illness, handicap). ~ *cacat* handicapped. ~ *cacat nétra* a blind person. **2** victim. ~ *kecelakaan* accident victim. **3** (*gram*) grammatical object.
  penderitaan 1 suffering, agony, anguish. **2** hardship. **sependeritaan** suffering the same fate. *kawan* ~ fellow-sufferer.
dérivasi (*D*) derivation, formation (of a word). – *balik* (*gram*) back formation.
  berdérivasi derived.
dérivatif (*D/E*) derivative.
derjat → DERAJAT.
derji (*cla*) tailor.
derkuku – *sopa* ruddy cuckoo dove, *Macropygia emiliana.*
derma (*Skr*) alms, charity. gifts/donations to the poor, contribution; funds, money (for such a purpose); → DARMA. *mengumpulkan* – to take up a collection.
  be(r)derma to give alms/a contribution, make donations, donate.
  mendermakan to give/grant/donate s.t.
  penderma 1 generous, charitable. **2** donor, contributor, supporter. *anggota* ~ a) donor. b) contributor, supporter. ~ *darah* blood donor.
  pendermaan donation, contribution. ~ *darah* blood donation.
dermacipta (*Skr neo*) grant.
dermadara (*ob*) legal wife.
dermaga (*J/Jv*) quay, pier, wharf. – *terapung* floating quay.
derman (*Jv*) having many children (of a woman).
dermaputra (*ob*) son.
dérmatolog (*D*) dermatologist.
dérmatologi (*D/E*) dermatology.
dermawan philanthropist.
  kedermawanan philanthropy.
dermawati female philanthropist.
dermayu a shortened form for the place name Indramayu in West Java in *mangga* – one of the finest mango varieties.
dermimil (*Jv*) **ndermimil** to mutter, mumble (*esp* in saying prayers).
dermolen (*D*) merry-go-round, carousel.
derobos (*J*) **menderobos 1** to enter by force. **2** to break down.
dersana (*Jv*) a variety of rose-apple or *jambu bol.*
dersik (*onom*) sound of sighing or rustling (of s.t. in the wind).
deru (*onom*) roar, howl, rumble (of very strong wind, thunder).
  berderu and **menderu(-deru)** to roar, howl, rumble (of very strong wind/thunder).
deruji → JERUJI.
deruk (*onom*) crack, crash.
  berderuk and **menderuk** to crack, crash.
derum I a word of command to make an elephant kneel.
  menderum to kneel (of an elephant/buffalo, etc.). *Kerbau* ~ *di bawah pohon yang rindang.* A water buffalo kneeled under a shady tree.
  menderumkan to make (an elephant/buffalo, etc.) kneel.
derum II (*onom*) rumbling sound, the sound of falling tree, thunder, engine, etc. – *kendaraan* roar of a (car) engine.
  sederum (to sound) together, in chorus.
  berderum and **menderum** to rumble, roar, drone.
  menderumkan to cause to rumble/roar/drone.
  deruman rumble.
  penderuman rumbling.
derun and **derung** → DERUM II.
derup → DERAP. – *derap* (*onom*) sound of footsteps.
derus (*onom*) rubbing/scraping sound, rustling noise.
  berderus and **menderus** to make such a sound.
derut (*onom*) a dull scraping sound.

menderut to make such a sound.

dérwis(y) (*Pers*) a dervish, mendicant friar.

dés (in acronyms) → DÉSA.

désa (*Skr*) 1 village, rural settlement, country(side). *orang* – villager. 2 place. *bertandang* – to wander from place to place. *anak* – a) villager, countryman. b) hamlet. *Pulau Buru terdiri atas 27 – dan 31 anak –.* Buru consists of 27 villages and 31 hamlets. – *abdi* area that the sultan's servants live in. – *kaputihan/keputihan* area near a mosque in which devout Muslims live and which is free from taxation. – *mijén* area given by the king to certain families who live there without paying taxes. – *pakuncén* (*Jv*) village charged with watching over graves. – *peristiwa* village created for transmigrants. – *perdikan* (*ob*) village exempted from paying taxes. – *Praja* village government. – *swadaya* traditional village. – *swakarya* transitional village. – *swasembada* advanced village. – *tertinggal* backward village.

sedésa from the same village. *wanita ~nya* his fellow-villager.

kedésaan rural, village (*mod*).

pedésaan 1 rural. *pembangunan ~* rural development. 2 rural area.

perdésaan rural.

desah (*onom*) 1 rustling, murmuring. 2 puffing, wheezing. 3 (*elec*) noise (on a line).

berdesah and mendesah 1 to rustle, murmur. 2 to puff, wheeze. 3 (*elec*) noisy.

berdesahan rustling, puffing, wheezing.

mendesahkan to make s.t. rustle/murmur/puff/wheeze.

desahan 1 rustle, murmur. 2 puff, wheeze.

désain (*E*) design. – *grafis* graphic design.

mendésain to design.

pendésain designer.

désainer (*E*) designer.

desak I push, press, urge. – *turun* urge downward. mendesak-turunkan to urge s.o. to decrease s.t. *Meréka didesak-turunkan tingkat produksi.* They were urged to decrease production.

berdesak to crowd (together), jostle e.o.

berdesakan and berdesak-desak(an) to crowd e.o., jostle e.o. *~ masuk* to push one's way into.

mendesak 1 to push (with one's body). *~ mundur* to push back. 2 to urge, insist, press, put pressure on. *Sejumlah tokoh partai ~ Bank Dunia menunda pertemuan CGI.* A number of party leaders urged the World Bank to postpone the meeting of the CGI. 3 urgent, pressing. *masalah yang ~* pressing problems. *Waktu ~.* Time is running out. 4 to instigate, incite, provoke.

kemendesakan pressure, urgency.

mendesak-desak to press in on.

mendesaki to push/press its (one's) way into, crowd through.

mendesakkan 1 to urge, insist on. *Meréka ~ penyelidikan pemerintah atas pelanggaran hak asasi.* They insisted on a government investigation into violations of human rights. 2 to push for (s.t. to happen). 3 to press/push s.t. (into s.t.).

terdesak 1 squeezed, pressed. *~ uang* short of money, hard up. 2 suppressed, exploited. 3 to be forced to, have to. *~ buang hajat* to have a strong urge to go to the bathroom. 4 urged, pressed, pestered (to do s.t.). 5 backed into a corner, trapped.

desakan 1 push, shove. 2 pressure, urging, insistence, urgent request. *atas ~* at the insistence of. *~ masa* the pressure of the times. 3 tension, strain. 4 strong claim. 5 instigation. *~ hati* dictates of the heart.

desak-desakan 1 to push e.o. 2 pushing and shoving

pedesak pressure (*mod*).

pendesakan 1 pushing, pressing, urging. 2 displacement.

desak II (*onom*) crinkling/crumpling sound (of paper).

berdesak and mendesak to make a crumpling noise.

désakralisasi desacralization.

désalinasi desalination.

désapraja → DÉSA *praja*.

desar (*onom*) hiss, swish.

berdesar and mendesar to hiss, swish.

desas-desus 1 rumors. 2 sound of whispering; → SAS-SUS.

mendesas-desuskan to spread rumors about.

desau (*onom*) 1 sound of waves breaking. 2 humming/rustling sound.

berdesau and mendesau 1 to smash (of waves on the shore). 2 to make a humming/rustling sound.

desauan 1 smashing, breaking (of waves). 2 hum, rustle.

Désawarnyana an alternate name for the Nagarakertagama, *q.v.*

déségregasi (*D*) desegregation.

desek → DESAK I.

désélerasi (*D*) deceleration.

Désémber (*D*) December.

déséntralisasi (*D*) decentralization.

mendéséntralisasikan to decentralize.

terdéséntralisasi(kan) decentralized.

désérsi (*D/E*) desertion.

désértir (*D*) deserter, defector.

mendésértir to desert, defect.

dési (*D*) tenth.

désibél (*D*) decibel.

desih (*onom*) whispering, sound of breathing.

berdesih to make that sound.

desik (*onom*) rustling (of leaves/paper).

berdesik and mendesik to rustle.

berdesik-desik to keep on rustling.

désikan (*E*) desiccant.

désiliter (*D*) deciliter.

désimal (*D*) decimal.

désiméter (*D*) decimeter.

désinféksi (*D*) disinfectant.

désinféktan (*E*) disinfectant.

desing (*onom*) whistling/whizzing sound (of bullets passing overhead).

berdesing and mendesing to whiz.

berdesingan (*pl subj*) to whiz.

desingan whiz.

désintegrasi (*D*) disintegration.

desir (*onom*) rustling (sound of leaves blowing in wind), swish, hissing, fizzing, splutter.

berdesir and mendesir to rustle, fizz, hiss, splutter.

mendesirkan to make s.t. rustle, etc.

desiran rustle, hiss, fizz, splutter.

desis (*onom*) hiss, wheeze, whistle.

berdesis and mendesis to hiss, etc.

berdesis-desis to keep on hissing, etc.

berdesisan (*pl subj*) to hiss, etc.

mendesiskan to make s.t. hiss, etc.

desisan hissing.

desit → DESIR.

déskripsi (*D*) description.

mendéskripsikan to describe.

pendéskripsian describing, description.

déskriptif (*E*) descriptive.

déso (*Jv*) → DÉSA. ndéso to go to the village.

déspot (*D/E*) despot.

déspotisme (*D/E*) despotism.

destar (*Pers*) head-cloth. – *habis kopiah luluh* (*M*) to suffer great misfortunes.

berdestar to wear a head-cloth.

déstinasi (*D*) destination.

déstruksi (*D*) destruction.

déstruktif (*D/E*) destructive.

desuk (*onom*) crinkling, crumpling (paper).

berdesuk and mendesuk to make a crinkling/crumpling noise.

desup (*onom*) sound of s.t. falling into mud, etc.

desur (*onom*) scraping sound (as of brushwood being dragged along).

berdesur to scrape.

desus (*onom*) whispering.

berdesus and mendesus to make a whispering noise.

berdesus-desus and mendesus-desus to keep on making a whispering noise.

mendesuskan to rumor, spread rumors about.

pendesus whisperer, gossip.

desut (*onom*) sound of the wind, strong breath, murmur.

mendesut to make that sound.

détail (*E*) detail.

mendétail in detail. *secara ~* in detail.
détailman (*E*) medical sales representative.
detak (*onom*) ticking, tapping, beating, throbbing, thumping, clicking, clippety-clop. *- detik* tick-tock, clickity-clack. **berdetak-detik** to make clicking noises. *- hati* impulse. *- jam* ticking of the clock. *- jantung* beating of the heart.
berdetak and **mendetak** to beat, tick, throb, thump.
berdetakan (*pl subj*) to click.
mendetak to click s.t.
mendetakkan to click (the tongue), make s.t. make ticking, etc. sound.
detakan tick, tap, click, beat, throb.
detap (*onom*) dripping sound of the rain.
mendetap-detap to drip (of the rain).
detar (*onom*) shivering, vibrating, noise of rolling wheels, sizzle.
berdetar and **mendetar** to make those sounds.
detas (*onom*) cracking, breaking (egg shell, thread).
berdetas and **mendetas** to make a cracking sound.
berdetasan (*pl subj*) to make cracking sounds.
détasemén (*D*) detachment. *- 81* counterterrorist unit. *- polisi militér* [dénpom] military police.
détaséring (*D*) temporary detachment of personnel.
détasir (*D*) **mendétasir** to detach, dispatch, detail.
détdot (*onom*) sound of car horn, toot, honk.
berdétdot to toot, honk.
détéksi (*D*) detection.
mendétéksi to detect,
terdétéksi detected.
pendétéksi detector. *~ asap* smoke detector. *~ uang* money detector.
pendétéksian detection.
détéktif (*D/E*) detective. *- swasta* private investigator.
détéktor (*D/E*) detector. *- logam* metal detector. *- ranjau* mine detector.
détél → DÉTAIL.
déténsi (*D*) detention.
déténte (*D*) detente.
détérgén and **détérjén** (*E*) detergent. *- bubuk* powdered detergent. *- krim* cream detergent.
détériorasi (*E*) deterioration.
détérjén (*E*) detergent.
détérminan (*D*) determinant.
détérminasi (*D*) determination.
détérminatif (*D/E*) determinative.
détérminis (*D*) determinist.
détérminisme (*D/E*) determinism.
détérministik (*E*) and **détérministis** (*D*) deterministic.
détia and **détya** (*Skr*) demon; → DAITIA.
detik (*onom*) **1** tick, sound made by ticking clock. *pada - terakhir* at the last minute. *- hati/jantung* palpitation (of the heart), heartbeat. **2** second (unit of time), moment, instant.
sedetik 1 a moment, momentary. **2** a second.
berdetik to tick (of a clock).
berdetik-detik *~ lamanya* for seconds on end.
mendetik to tick, vibrate.
terdetik to make a ticking sound.
detikan pulsation; vibration.
détil → DÉTAIL.
deting → DENTING.
détoksifikasi (*E*) detoxification.
détonator (*D/E*) detonator.
detuk (*onom*) dull noise.
detup (*onom*) sound of light popping (of corn fried without oil/a firecracker).
berdetup to pop, explode lightly.
detus (*onom*) **1** popping sound. **2** light beating (of heart).
berdetus and **mendetus 1** to pop. **2** to beat (lightly).
detusan popping, beating.
deuheus (*S*) near, close to (of an inferior with respect to a superior); → DEKAT.
ngadeuheus to have an audience with the kyai.
dévaluasi (*D*) devaluation.

mendévaluasikan to devaluate.
pendévaluasian devaluation.
dévaluir (*D*) **mendévaluir** to devaluate.
devéloper (*E*) developer; → PENGEMBANG.
déviasi (*D*) deviation.
dévisa and **dévisén** (*D*) reserves, foreign exchange.
dévosi (*D*) devotion; → PEMUJAAN.
déwa (*Skr*) **1** god; godhead. **2** idol, false god. **3** Savior. *- déwi* gods and goddesses. *- pelindung/penolong/penyelamat* guardian angel. *- pencipta* God the Creator. (*si*) *- Perang* (the ancient Roman) God of War.
berdéwa(kan) to have as god.
mendéwa(-déwa)kan and **memperdéwa(kan) 1** to deify, worship as a god. **2** to idolize; to be crazy about. *~ uang* to worship money.
kedéwaan divine(ness), godliness.
pendéwa 1 idolater. **2** devotee, admirer.
pendéwa(-déwa)an and **perdéwaan 1** deification. **2** idolization.
déwadaru a tree with commercial timber, *Urandra corniculata*; → DARU-DARU.
déwal(a) (*Pers*) stone wall built around a castle or city.
déwaloka abode of the (Hindu) Gods; → KAYANGAN I.
déwan (*Pers*) **1** council, committee. **2** board, agency. **3** (*cla*) court (of justice). *- angkutan* board of transportation. *- banding* board of appeal. *- diréksi* Managing Board, Board of Directors. *- Ékumini* Ecumenical Council. *- Geréja* Synod. *- Geréja-Geréja Sedunia* [DOD] World Council of Churches, WCC. *- Guru pada perguruan Tinggi Kedokteran* Faculty of Medicine. *- haminte* (*col*) municipal council. *- Harian* Executive (Committee). *- Internasional Kesejahteraan Sosial (Kawasan Asia dan Pasifik Barat)* Regional International Council on Social Welfare (of Asia and the Western Pacific). *- Jawatan dan Kepangkatan* Selection Board. *- juri* judges (in a competition). *- Keamanan* Security Council. *- Kehormatan* Review Board, Honor Council. *- Komisaris* (of an Inc. or Ltd.) Board of Commissioners. *- Kota* City Council. *- kurator* Board of Regents. *- lalu lintas* traffic board. *- Mahasiswa* [Déma] Student (Representative) Council. *- Menteri* Cabinet Council. *- Monétér* Monetary Board. *- Nasional* National Council (1957–59). *- Negara* (*Mal*) Senate. *- Niaga* Board of Trade. *- Pangan Dunia* World Food Council. *- Parampara* Advisory Council. *- pastoral* pastoral council. *- Pembina* Board of Patrons. *- pemisah* arbitration panel. *- penaséhat* Board of Advisors. *- Pengawas* Supervisory Board. *- Pengawas Keuangan* Fiscal Auditing Office. *- Penguji* Board of Examiners. *- Pengurus* Managing Board. *- Penyantun* Board of Regents. *- Perancang Nasional* National Planning Board. *- Pertahanan Keamanan* National Security and Defense Council. *- Pertimbangan Agung* [DPA] Supreme Advisory Council, an organ provided for in the 1945 Constitution. *- Perusahaan* Enterprise Council (under President Soekarno). *- Perwakilan Rakyat* [DPR] People's Representative Council, House of Representatives, Parliament. *- Perwakilan Rakyat Daérah* Provincial Parliament. *- Pimpinan* a) Board of Directors. b) (of political party) Executive Committee. *- Rakyat* (*col*) People's Council. *- Rédaksi* Editorial Board. *- Réklaséring Pusat* Central Probation Board. *- Sesepuh* Council of Elders.
déwana (*cla*) madly in love.
déwanagari (Asian) Indian alphabet.
déwangga (*Skr*) **1** tapestry or figured fabric named after India's reputed inventor of weaving. **2** orange-red, yellowish-red.
déwani (*infr*) council member.
déwasa I (*Skr*) **1** grown-up, adult. *belum -* juvenile, minor. **2** mature, fully grown. *- kelamin* sexually mature. *belum/tidak -* underage. **kebelum-déwasaan** and **ketidak-déwasaan** being a minor, minority.
sedéwasa as adult/grown up as.
mendéwasa to grow up, become an adult.
mendéwasakan to mature s.t., make more mature. *~ pandangan moral seseorang* to make s.o.'s moral views more mature.
kedéwasaan adulthood, growth, maturity.
pendéwasaan 1 bringing to adulthood. **2** development (to adulthood/maturity). **3** (*leg*) (declaring) of age.

déwasa II (*Skr*) time, moment, date (*esp* in compounds). – *dulu* formerly. – *ini* now, nowadays, at this moment/date, currently. – *itu* at that time.

déwasawan (*Skr neo*) adult, grown-up, mature person.

déwata I (*Skr*) godhead, divinity. *burung/unggas/manuk/paksi* – the bird of paradise. – *mulia raya* (*cla*) the heavenly gods.

  mendéwatakan to idolize, deify.

  kedéwataan 1 realm of the supernatural beings. 2 divine(ness), godlike.

  pendéwataan idolizing, deifying.

déwata II → CENDERAWASIH.

déwé(k) (*Jv*) 1 one's own, self. 2 the most, -est. *sing gedé* – the biggest.

  déwékan /déwé'an/ alone.

déwi 1 (*Skr cla*) goddess. 2 fairy. – *Fajar* Aurora. – *Fortuna* Goddess of Fortune. – *Pertiwi* the Earth Goddess, *aka Ibu Pertiwi*. – *Sri* a) wife of Vishnu, Goddess of the Rice Crop. b) rice plant. c) beautiful (woman); beloved, darling.

déwi-déwi (*naut*) davit.

de yure (*L*) de jure.

dg and dgn (*abbr*) [dengan] with.

DG car license for North Maluku.

DH car license for Timor and surrounding islands.

dhaif → DAIF.

dhal (*A*) name of the ninth letter of the Arabic alphabet.

dhalim → LALIM.

dhar (*A*) *ad* – a name of God, the Punisher.

dharma → DARMA. – *Karya Kencana* Development Award. – *Pertiwi* association of wives of the Indonesian armed forces. – *Pusaka 45* instilling the principles of the 1945 Constitution into the Armed Forces. – *Puspha* principles of the army women's corps. – *Wanita* organization of civil servants' wives.

dharmais [(Yayasan) Dharma Bhakti Sosial] Social Service Foundation.

dhat → ZAT.

d.h.i. [dalam hal ini] in this instance/case.

Dhirot Saha Jaya the military resort command (*Korém* 081) in Madiun.

dholim → LALIM. kedholiman tyranny, oppression.

dhuafa → DUAFA.

dhudhur → LOHOR.

dhuha (*A*) *adh* – "The Morning Hours"; name of the 93rd chapter of the Koran.

dhuhur → LOHOR.

dhuja (*Skr? mil*) badge at regiment and battalion level.

di I 1 a locative preposition: at, in, on. *ada* – *rumah* to be at home. *tinggal* – *Jakarta* to live in Jakarta. – *méja* on the table. 2 now also used as time-indicating prepositions: in, on. – *bulan Juli* in July. – *saat itu* at that moment/time. – *Senin* on Monday. 3a) of. *takut* – *kuat orang* afraid of human strength. *Sebenarnya dulu Lusi senang* – *musik pop dan jazz*. In fact, formerly Lusi was fond of pop and jazz music. b) from. *Aku datang* – *air.* I came from the river (after having relieved myself). c) about. *tak tahu* – *alif* illiterate. 4 to. *tidak jelas* – *saya* it's not clear to me. 5 through, by. *Orang Belanda mati* – *pangkat, orang Cina mati* – *kaya dan orang Melayu mati* – *angan-angan.* A Dutchman dies by his position, a Chinese by his wealth, and a Malay by his ideals. – *kita ini* this/our country. *jauh* – *mata, jauh* – *hati* far away from the eye(s) far away from the heart, i.e., out of sight out of mind. *jauh* – *mata dekat* – *hati* absence makes the heart grow fonder.

di II noble, the clipped form of *adi* (in certain titles), i.e., *dipati* for *adipati* (regent/ruler/sovereign). *diraja* for *adiraja* (*Mal*) royal.

DI III [Darul Islam] a movement that fought for an Islamic state.

dia he, she, it (though less frequent for non-humans); → IA I. – *orang* (*coq*) they. –.– *juga* always the same person. *Itu* –! a) That is it/him/her! b) Precisely! Exactly! That's right! *si* – a) boyfriend, girlfriend. b) (*joc*) one's penis.

  dianya that one, him/her. *Antara ~ dan wartawan tidak ada masalah.* There are no problems between him and the journalists.

berdia and ~ *beraku* to be on familiar terms with s.o., use the more intimate forms.

  mendiakan 1 to address s.o. with *dia.* 2 to treat s.o. (such as a family member) disrespectfully by referring to him/her by *dia.*

  diaan *gaya* ~ he-man style (in novels).

diabétés (*D/E*) diabetes.

diafragma (*D*) 1 diaphragm. 2 midriff.

diagnosa and diagnose (*D*) and diagnosis (*E*) diagnosis.

  mendiagnosa and mendiagnosis to diagnose.

  pendiagnosaan diagnosing.

diagnostik (*D/E*) diagnostic.

diagonal (*D/E*) diagonal.

diagraf (*E*) diagraph.

diagram (*D/E*) diagram. – *balok* block diagram. – *bélok* three-dimensional diagram. – *kué/serabi* pie graph.

diah → DIAT I.

diajeng (*Jv*) (little) sister (term of address, also for one's spouse).

diaken and diakon (*E*) deacon.

diakonat (*D*) deaconate.

diakonés (*D*) deaconess.

diakoni corporate body to carry out charity services.

diakritik (*E*) and diakritis (*D*) diacritic(al).

diakronik (*E*) and diakronis (*D*) diachronical.

dialék (*D/E gram*) dialect. – *sosial* social dialect.

  berdialék with a ... dialect.

dialéktik(a) (*D*) dialectic(s).

  mendialéktikkan to use dialectics about s.t.

dialéktis (*D*) dialectical (materialism).

dialéktologi (*D/E*) dialectology.

dialisis (*D/E*) dialysis.

dialog (*D/E*) dialogue. – *antariman* interfaith dialog. – *Utara-Selatan* The North-South Dialogue [between the eight major non-communist industrial (northern) countries and the southern Third World countries]. – *wisata* travel dialogue.

  berdialog to hold a dialogue.

  mendialogkan to hold a dialogue on.

dialogis (*D*) dialogic(al), (a discussion) between two people.

diam I 1 quiet, silent (not talking), taciturn. 2 to keep silent, say nothing. *Anak itu* – *saja ketika ia bersembunyi di belakang pintu.* That child just kept silent when he hid behind the door. – *dalam seribu bahasa* to be as silent as the grave. 3 to remain motionless/tranquil/still/at ease. *Rumah adalah benda yang* –. A house is real property. 4 (to remain sitting) idly, inactively. – *itu emas* silence is golden.

  diam-diam quietly, secretly, silently. ~ *makan dalam* unreliable. ~ *ubi (berisi)* ~ *penggali berkarat* still waters run deep. *dengan/secara* ~ in secret, secretly, covertly. *secara* ~ *dan terang-terangan* covertly/implicitly and overtly/explicitly.

  berdiam(-diam) ~ *diri* a) to keep silent, say nothing. b) to do nothing.

  berdiam-diaman to refuse to speak to e.o.

  mendiam silently, in silence. ~ *diri* to remain silent.

  mendiami [and mengediami (*infr*)] to refuse to talk/say anything to.

  mendiamkan and memperdiamkan 1 to ignore, pay no attention to. 2 to silence s.o. 3 to keep quiet about s.t., do nothing about s.t. 4 to keep s.t. from moving.

  terdiam 1 quietest. 2 to become speechless/silent, keep silent. 3 to become motionless.

  kediam(-diam)an stillness, silence.

  pendiam a taciturn/reserved person who prefers to be by himself, introvert. kependiaman taciturnity, silence. *Sulit juga menggambarkan* ~ *almarhum.* It is rather difficult to picture the silence of the deceased.

  pendiaman silence. ~ *radio* radio silence.

diam II and berdiam 1 to reside, live, dwell. 2 stay, abide. 3 residing, living.

  mendiami [and mengediami (*cla*)] to live/dwell/reside in, occupy, inhabit.

  terdiam resided, dwelled.

  kediaman *tempat* ~ residence, dwelling-place, home, domicile, abode.

diaméter (*D/E*) diameter.

berdiaméter with a diameter of ...

dian I 1 candle. 2 kerosene/oil lamp. 3 burning. *minyak* – burning oil. – *Ékawati* the women's association of the Department of Information.

  berdian to use a candle, etc. for illumination.

  mendiani to illuminate s.t. with a candle, etc.

  pendianan candling.

dian II *burung kaki* – red-shank, *Tringa totanus eurhinus*.

diang I **berdiang** to warm o.s. next to the fire. *sambil ~ nasi masak* to kill two birds with one stone.

  mendiang 1 to warm s.t. on the fire. *bagai pucuk pisang didiang* weak as a kitten. 2 to put s.o. near the fire (of a drum so that the head stretches).

  mendiangkan to warm up, heat (by putting near a fire).

  pendiang stove.

  pendiangan and **perdiangan** 1 hearth, fireplace. 2 special hearth used to warm a woman after childbirth. 3 stove.

diang II → MENDIANG.

diapositif (*D/E*) diapositive.

diar (*M*) → BIAR.

diaré (*D*) diarrhea.

dias clipped form of **diapositif**.

diat I (*A*) compensation for bodily harm, murder or manslaughter, blood money.

  mendiatkan to pay such compensation.

diat II **pendiat** (*cla*) elephant's skin.

diatonik (*E*) and **diatonis** (*D*) diatonic.

diayah (*Mal*) proclamation, propagation (of an ideology/doctrine/opinion, etc.).

dibacah (*Pers*) preface.

dibaj (*Pers*) silk fabric.

didaktik (*E*) and **didaktis** (*D*) didactics.

didéh (*Jv*) black pudding of coagulated chicken or beef blood.

didih boil, boiling. *titik* – boiling point.

  berdidih to boil.

  mendidih 1 to boil s.t. 2 to seethe with rage. *Darahnya ~.* He is furious/enraged.

  mendidihkan to boil s.t., make s.t. boil, bring s.t. to a boil. *~ darah* to make one's blood boil, enrage, enraging.

  pendidih boiler.

  pendidihan boiling.

didik education. *anak* – pupil.

  mendidik 1 to bring up, rear, educate. 2 educational, instructive, pedagogic.

  mendidikkan to impart/instill (knowledge) into s.o.'s mind, teach (a subject or pupils), educate.

  terdidik educated. **keterdidikan** state of being educated.

  didikan 1 pupil, disciple; graduate. *Dia ~ Univérsitas Indonésia.* He is a graduate of the University of Indonesia. 2 education, upbringing. 3 educated. *anak ~* pupil.

  pendidik educator, instructor.

  pendidikan 1 education. 2 (in compounds) a school subject. 3 training. 4 pedagogy. *~ agama* religion (a school subject). *~ (ber)kelanjutan* continuing education. *~ dan kebudayaan* education and culture. *~ dan latihan* [diklat] education and training. *~ dasar* a) basic training. b) basic education. *~ dasar dan menengah* [dikdasmén] basic and secondary education. *~ formal* formal education. *~ jasmani* physical education. *~ kawiryan* military training, ROTC. *~ keagamaan* religious education. *~ kejuruan* vocational training. *~ kekaryawanan* occupational education. *~ kelompok* group education. *~ keniagaan* business education. *~ keséhatan* health education. *~ ketrampilan* skills, vocational training (a school subject). *~ kewarganegaraan* civics (a school subject). *~ lanjutan* advanced education. *~ latihan kerja* on-the-job training. *~ latihan pertempuran* combat training. *~ moral Pancasila* Pancasila moral education (a school subject). *~ non-formal* informal education. *~ paksa* compulsory education. *~ para* airborne training. *~ pembentukan* basic training. *~ permulaan* preliminary training. *~ pertama* basic training. *~ rakyat* public education. *~ sejarah* history (a school subject). *~ séks* sex education. *~ seni* art (a school subject). *~ seumur hidup* lifelong education. *~ terpadu* integrated training. *~ tinggi* [dikti] higher education. *~ umum* general education. *~ untuk orang déwasa* adult education.

  sependidikan with the same education, educated at the same institution. **berpendidikan** to be educated/trained.

didis I **sedidis** a thin slice (of meat, etc.).

  mendidis to cut into slices.

didis II (*J/Jv*) **mendidis** 1 to delouse, look for vermin, such as nits and lice (in one's hair/clothes or between the feathers). 2 to examine; → SELIDIK.

  ndidis (*sl*) to steal s.t. from s.o. who is asleep.

didong I 1 *orang* – Frenchman. 2 European, foreign(er). *Belanda* – Frenchman.

didong II opinionated, stubborn.

didong III 1 (*ob*) *komidi* – k.o. puppet show. 2 dance and musical performance. 3 (*Ac*) traditional art of the Gayo area presented by singing *Pantuns* while dancing.

  berdidong to perform a dance and musical show.

diem I (*L*) *per* – per day, daily.

diem II → DIAM. **ngediemin** (*J coq*)] → MENDIAMKAN.

dienul Islam Islamic religion; → DIN.

diés (*L*) day. *– natalis* dies natalis, anniversary (of a university, etc.).

diesel (*D*) /disel/ → DISEL. *mesin* – diesel engine. *minyak* – diesel oil.

  mendieselkan to convert to diesel engines.

dieselisasi /diselisasi/ the introduction of locomotive, diesel-powered.

diét I (*D*) diet.

  berdiét to diet.

  pediét dieter.

Diét II name of the Japanese Parliament.

diétis (*D*) dietician.

diferénsial (*D/E*) differential. *hitungan* – differential calculus.

diferénsiasi (*D*) differentiation.

  berdiferénsiasi to be differentiated.

  mendiferénsiasikan to differentiate.

  terdiferénsiasi(kan) differentiated.

difinisi → DÉFINISI.

difinitif → DÉFINITIF.

difraksi (*D*) diffraction.

diftéri (*D*) diphtheria.

diftong (*D/E gram*) diphthong.

difusi (*D*) diffusion.

  berdifusi to diffuse.

digdaya (*Jv*) supernatural; unconquerable, invulnerable, impervious to weapons.

  kedigdayaan invulnerability, supernatural power.

digit (*E*) /dijit/ digit.

digital (*E*) /dijital/ digital. *komputer* – digital computer. *télepon* – digital telephone.

  mendigitalkan to digitize.

digjaya → DIGDAYA.

digraf (*gram*) digraph, i.e., a combination of two letters to express a single sound (such as ng, ny).

digrési (*D*) digression.

Digul short for Boven Digul, a place in Irian Jaya (in the Dutch colonial period used as a place of exile).

  mendigulkan to exile to Boven Digul.

  pendigulan exiling to Boven Digul.

digulis *bekas seorang* – a person exiled by the Dutch to Boven Digul.

digung (*Jv*) *kaum* – the upper class, elite.

diit → DIÉT I. diet. *ahli* – dietician.

  berdiit to diet.

dijit (*E*) digit.

dik I → ADIK, form of address to younger sibling and to younger people, including waiters in restaurants, etc. "–, 20 tusuk saté ayam, satu lontong, sepiring nasi, air jeruk satu dan bir kecil sebotol lagi," katanya. "Waiter, 20 sticks of chicken satay, one lontong, one serving of white rice, one orange juice, and another small bottle of beer," he said.

dik II (in acronyms) → PENDIDIKAN.

dikara → ADIKARA.

dikau form of **engkau** after words ending in n. *dengan* – with you.

dikbud [pendidikan dan kebudayaan] education and culture.

dikdasmén → PENDIDIKAN *dasar dan menengah.*

dikir → ZIKIR.

dikit (in proverbs) a little bit. *– hujan banyak yang basah* a minor problem which has serious consequences.

dikitnya at least; → SEDIKITNYA.

sedikit a little bit. *~ demi ~* little by little, step by step. *tidak ~pun* not the least bit, not at all. *~.~* a little bit. **sesedikit-sedikitnya 1** as little as possible. **2** at least.

sedikit-dikitnya at (the very) least.

berdikit-dikit 1 little by little. **2** (to set money aside) bit by bit.

dikitan a little bit.

dikjur [pendidikan kejuruan] vocational training.

diklat [pendidikan dan latihan] educational and training (center). *– intérn* in-house training.

diko (D) spray paint (for cars, etc.).

mendiko to apply spray paint to s.t.

dikotomi (D/E) dichotomy.

mendik(h)tomi to draw a dichotomy between.

dik(h)otomis dichotomous.

dikrit (D) decree.

diksa (Skr) initiation.

berdiksa to be initiated (into the Buddhist monkshood).

diksi (D) diction.

diktat (D) **1** mimeographed lecture notes. *mahasiswa –* a college student who mainly studies from mimeographed lecture notes, without paying any attention to the books prescribed by his professors; → MAHASISWA *fotokopi.* **2** news item read out on the radio.

diktator (D/E) dictator.

mendiktatori 1 to exercise dictatorship over. **2** to be dictatorial to.

diktator-diktatoran to be overbearing, dominating.

kediktatoran 1 dictatorship. **2** dictatorial. *pemerintah ~* dictatorial government.

diktatorial (D) and **diktatoris** (D) dictatorial.

diktatur (D) dictatorship.

dikté (D) dictation; → IMLAH.

mendikté 1 to dictate (to). **2** to give orders (to), order s.o. around.

mendiktékan to dictate.

pendiktéan dictating.

dikti [pendidikan tinggi] higher education.

diktir (D) **mendiktir** to dictate.

diktum (D) dictum, verdict, judicial ruling.

dil *buah –* k.o. hockey. *(ber)main –* k.o. hockey game.

dila(h) 1 k.o. torch of the fruit of the castor oil plant. **2** oil lamp.

dilak (S) **mendilak** to look at s.o. in annoyance, role one's eyes in annoyance.

dilalah (Jv) corruption of Arabic *takdir Allah* God predestination.

ndilalah and fate would have it that ..., it so happened that ..., chance would have it that ... *~ masuk bersamaan dan pengaruh hippies, ganja, free sex dan sebagainya.* It so happened that (this type of music) entered (the Third World) at the same time as the influence of hippies, marijuana, free sex, and the like.

dilam patchouli, *Pogostemon patchouli;* → NILAM I.

dilasi (D) dilation.

dilem → DILAM.

diléma (D/E) dilemma.

dilématik (E) and **dilématis** (D) problematic. *Rokok bagi kita adalah masalah –.* Cigarettes are a problem for us. *situasi –* dilemma.

diler (E) dealer.

diletan (D) dilettante.

diletantisme (D/E) dilettantism.

diling (E) (commercial) dealings. *– dengan turis* dealings with tourists.

Diljapol [pengadilan-kejaksaan-kepolisian] Court of Justice-Public Prosecutor's Office-Police.

dilman → DÉLMAN.

dim I (D) **1** inch. **2** decimeter.

dim II (E) dim. *lampu –* parking lights.

men(ge)dim to dim (the lights).

dim III (in acronyms) → DISTRIK *militér.*

dimas (Jv) term of address to younger brother.

diménsi dimension; → MATRA.

berdiménsi with/to have a dimension (of). *masalah ékonomi ~ politik* economic problems with a political dimension.

dimensional (D/E) dimensional.

dimi (A) a non-Muslim who believes in a religion which was founded by a prophet with a revelation from God, such as a Christian or Jew.

dimik-dimik (Jv) imperfect (of pronunciation).

berdimik-dimik to have an imperfect accent.

diminutif (E gram) diminutive.

dimma (A) non-Muslim subjects or minorities living in Muslim countries who, in return for paying a capital tax, enjoy protection and safety.

dimmi → DIMI.

dimpit → DÉMPÉT I.

dimstok (D) carpenter's rule.

din and **dien** (A) (Muslim) religion, faith (common in men's names). *hari – and Yaumuddin* Day of Judgment. *– al-hubb* religion of love. *-ul Islam* Islam.

dina I (Skr) → HINA *dina..*

dina II (Jv) day (opp MALAM I). *ana – ana upa* (Jv) /ono dino ono upo/ don't worry about tomorrow; God will provide.

dinamik(a) (D) **1** dynamics. **2** dynamic.

dinamis (D) dynamic.

mendinamiskan to dynamize.

kedinamisan dynamism.

pendinamis dynamist.

pendinamisan dynamization.

dinamisasi dynamization.

mendinamisikan to dynamize.

dinamisator (D) dynamist.

dinamisir (D) **mendinamisir** to dynamize.

pendinamisir s.o. who dynamizes.

dinamisme (D/E) dynamism.

dinamit (D/E) dynamite.

mendinamit to dynamite.

pendinamitan dynamiting, blowing up (with dynamite).

dinamo (D/E) dynamo.

dinamulya activity. *– kelautan* sea-mindedness.

dinar (A) **1** former gold coins issued by Islamic governments (now mostly used as jewelry). **2** monetary unit of Algiers, Bahrain, Iraq, Jordan, Kuwait, Tunis, South Yemen and Yugoslavia.

dinas (D) **1** service, agency (of the government). **2** term of office. **3** to perform the duties of one's office; to be on duty. **4** official. *paspor –* service passport. *surat –* official letter. **5** length of service. **6** official. *mobil –* official car. *pakaian –* uniform. *paspor –* official/service passport. *untuk –* for official use. *– Aéronautika dan Angkasa Luar* NASA. *– ajikarma* service for military mental education. *– aktif* active service. *– baru* the new schedule (for trains).- *Giro dan Cepos* Postal Check and Clearing/Transfer Service. *– Invéstigasi Fédéral* FBI. *– jaga malam* night duty. *– keamanan* security service. *– kebakaran* [DK] Fire Department. *– kebersihan* sanitary service. *– kehutanan* forestry service. *– kepanduan* pilot service. *– ketentaraan* military service. *– luar* duty outside the office. *– malam* (to work on) the night shift. *– pemeriksaan* inspectorate. *– pendahulu* service for transmigrants. *– Pendidikan Masyarakat* (U.S.) Board of Education. *– penyelidik* intelligence service. *– Purbakala* Archaeological Service. *– Rahasia* Secret Service. *– Sékuriti* Security Service. *– tentara* military service. *– traksi* haulage.

sedinas (working for) the same agency or department. *Bharatu NP mengakui ~ bersama tiga temannya.* Private First Class NP admitted that he worked with three of his colleagues (in the same department).

berdinas to serve, be on duty.

mendinaskan to put s.t. into service.

dinasan schedule (for trains), service. *~ baru* new service.

kedinasan 1 service (mod). **2** services. *~ umum* public services.

dinasti (D/E) dynasty; → RAJAKULA.

dinda → ADINDA.

dindang (ob) → DÉNDANG I.

dinding I wall (a vertical, solid structure of stone/brick/wood/ *gedék*, etc., forming one of the sides of a building or room). *lampu* – wall lamp/light/fixture. – *sampai ke langit, empang sampai ke seberang* do s.t. completely, don't do things halfway. – *teretas, tangga terpasang* proof of intention. – *antara* partition. – *atas* hanging wall. – *batas* partition. – *bawah* foot wall. – *bertulang* reinforced wall. – *dalam* a) soffit. b) inner wall. – *hias* paneling. – *kabi* lining at the underside of a wall (of wood/plastic, etc.). – *jantung* myocardium. – *lingkar* enclosure. – *lintang* septum. – *mati* blind wall. – *pemisah* partition. – *penahan* retaining wall. – *penupang* supporting wall. – *pisah* partition. – *Ratapan* Wailing/Western Wall. – *sekat* bulkhead. – *sél* cell wall. – *sendi* pilaster. – *Tangis* the Wailing/Western Wall (in Jerusalem). – *témbok* mortar wall. – *tepas* a wall made from the main ribs of the *kumbar* leaves. – *tiang* piling. – *tupang* supporting wall. – *yang sudah jadi* dry wall.
  berdinding to use/have a wall, walled.
  berdindingkan to have a wall (made) of. *Warung-warung yang bermunculan* ~ *bilik.* The road-side stalls which sprang up have walls of plaited screen. *Sebuah rumah petak* ~ *gedék.* A house with several rented cubicles which uses plaited bamboo walls.
  mendinding 1 to form a wall. 2 to wall (in).
  mendindingi 1 to wall s.t. in, put a wall around. 2 to block, keep s.t. from entering.
  mendindingkan to make s.o. into/use s.o. as a wall. ~ *tangan* use one's hands to shade one's eyes or cup one's ears.
  terdinding walled in, screened/partitioned off.
  pendinding s.t. used as a wall, screen, partition, etc.
  pendindingan 1 walls, masonry, brickwork. 2 walling in, bricking up.
dinding II **mendinding** form of marriage in which the husband has to work for the wife's parents to pay the bride price.
diné (*D*) dinner (party).
dines → DINAS.
ding (*Jv*) particle that contradicts and corrects what (the speaker) has just said. *Saya baru berumur 9 tahun, eh 10 tahun* –! I'm only 9 years old, eh 10 years old!
dingding → DINDING I.
ding-dong 1 (*onom*) clinking sound of coins/slot machine. 2 parlor games, such as video games, pin-ball machines.
dingin 1 cold, cool, frigid. 2 not close (of friendship, etc.). *nasi tak* –, *pinggan tak retak* to do s.t. thoroughly. – *hati* not happy; to feel indifferent. – *kepala* doesn't get angry easily, cool-headed. – *tangan* a) (about a doctor or midwife) whose patients get well. b) (about a farmer) whose crops grow well, has a green thumb. – *tertulang* chilled to the bone.
  sedingin as cold as.
  sedingin-dinginnya the coldest, no matter how cold (s.t. is).
  berdingin-dingin (to walk around, etc.) in the cold.
  mendingin to become cold, cool off/down. *tak menghangat* ~ doesn't care, indifferent.
  mendingini to cool s.t. off/down.
  mendinginkan 1 to chill, make s.t. cold. 2 to cool off/down.
  kedinginan 1 cool, cold, chill, chilliness. 2 to feel cold. 3 (*Jv*) too cold/cool.
  pendingin 1 coolant, refrigerant, cooling (*mod*). *gudang* ~ cold storage. ~ *mata* joy, pleasure. ~ *ruangan* room air conditioner. ~ *udara* air conditioner. **berpendingin** *udara* air-conditioned. 2 cooler.
  pendinginan cooling, cooling down/off.
dingkelik → DINGKLIK.
dingkik (*Jv*) **dingkik-mendingkik** to check (up) on e.o.
  mendingkik(-dingkik) to follow s.o. secretly/surreptitiously, steal upon s.o. (*esp* from behind)
dingkis *ikan* – a small edible fish, rabbit fish, *Siganus spp.*
dingkit (*M*) **berdingkit-dingkit** to jostle e.o., crowd; in throngs.
dingklang (*Jv*) lame, crippled.
  mendingklangkan 1 to lame, cripple. 2 to sabotage.
dingklik (*Jv*) footstool, k.o. tabouret.
dingkrak → JINGKRAK.
dingkring (*J*) hop (walk on one foot).

dini 1 early. *diagnosa* – early diagnosis. *Sistim peringatan* – early warning system. *secara* – early on, at an early stage. 2 premature. *lahir* – born prematurely; → PRADINI. *Ibu dan ayah dijemput terlalu* –. Father and mother were picked up too early (at the train station). 3 young. *Usia meréka masih begitu* –. They are still so young. 4 real time. – *hari* → DINIHARI.
  sedini ~ *mungkin* and **sedini-dininya** as early as possible.
  kedinian very early in the morning; → DINIHARI. *Ketahuilah bakat anak anda secara* –. Know your child's talents at an early stage.
dinihari 1 daybreak, dawn, very early in the morning, from about 3 till 5 o'clock in the morning, aurora. *hulu* – about 4 o'clock in the morning. 2 (in news media, etc., also) the period between 24:00 and 04:00 hours. *Kapal itu berangkat Senin* – *jam 01.00 menuju Belawan, Médan.* The ship left Monday at 1 a.m. for Belawan, Medan.
diniyah (*A*) religious. *masalah* – problems related to religious law. 2 a *madrasah* for religion.
dinosaurus (*D*) dinosaur.
dinul-Islam (*A*) Islam.
diode (*D/E*) diode.
dioksid(a) (*D*) dioxide. – *arang/karbon* carbon dioxide.
dioksin (*D/E*) dioxin.
diorama (*D/E*) diorama.
diosis (*E*) diocese.
dip I [Displaced Indonesian Person] *orang* – a displaced Indonesian person, i.e., s.o. who was taken out of Indonesia by the Japanese during World War II.
DIP II [Daftar Isian Proyék] detailed list for a project.
dipan (*D*) divan, sofa.
dipati *adat* chief of the *Anak Dalam*; → ADIPATI.
dipidén → DIVIDÉN.
dipisi → DIVISI.
diploma (*D/E*) diploma; → IJAZAH.
diplomasi (*D*) diplomacy.
  berdiplomasi diplomatic.
  mendiplomasikan to negotiate about.
diplomat (*D/E*) diplomat.
  kediplomatan diplomatic.
diplomatik (*E*) and **diplomatis** (*D*) diplomatic.
  kediplomatikan diplomatic.
dipo → DÉPO.
Diponegoro the Army division stationed in Central Java.
dir (in acronyms) → DIRÉKTUR.
dirah /dir'ah/ → ZIRAH.
diraja (*Skr mostly Mal*) → ADIRAJA.
dirayat (*A*) knowledge.
diréksi (*D*) (managing) directors, board of (managing) directors.
diréktif (*D*) directive.
diréktor (*D*) managing director. – *utama* [dirut] head managing director (similar to CEO).
diréktorat (*D*) directorate. – *intédans* quartermaster corps. – *jénderal* [ditjén] directorate general.
diréktris (*D*) 1 directress, headmistress. 2 mother superior.
diréktur (*D*) managing director, member of the board of management. – *geladi* (*mil*) director of training. – *inténdans* quartermaster director. – *jénderal* director general. – *kepatuhan* compliance officer. – *muda* assistant director. – *pelaksana* managing director. – *pembinaan lembaga* director for administration. – *umum* [dirum] general director. – *utama* [dirut] general/chief director, director-in-chief, president director.
  mendirékturi to direct.
dirga and **dirgahayu** (*Skr*) long live..., good luck to.
dirgantara (*Skr*) 1 aero-. *olahraga* – aerosports. 2 air, atmosphere. 3 airspace.
  kedirgantaraan aerial, avionics.
dirham (*A ob*) various gold and silver coins with Arabic lettering on them.
diri I 1 self, person. *di dalam* – to o.s., mentally. *nama* – proper name. – *présidén* the person of the president. *seorang* –*(nya)* alone, all by o.s. 2 o.s., himself, herself, themselves (in reflexive verbs, such as) *melarikan/membawa* – to run away. *Begitu*

melihat korbannya terkapar, pelaku segera melarikan –. As soon as he saw the victim sprawling, the perpetrator immediately ran away. *membuang –* to commit suicide. *minta/mohon –* to beg leave to depart. *membunuh –* to commit suicide. *menahan –* to contain/restrain o.s. *mengkhususkan –* to specialize. *mengundurkan –* to withdraw (o.s.). *Ia kehilangan –.* He became bewildered. *antara – kita sendiri* just between us/ ourselves. *pada – sendiri* as such, in itself/themselves; *cp* SENDIRI. *–ku (sendiri)* I myself. *–mu* yourself. *–nya* a) himself, herself, itself, themselves. b) he, she (*emphatic*). *waktu –nya di Semarang* when he was in Semarang. 3 (*gram*) person. *– yang ketiga* the third person (also sometimes used in lieu of the first and second persons in letter writing). 4 (*ob*) one's. *tak tahu –* doesn't know one's place, to have insufficient knowledge of one's own actions, etc. *– orang* individuals. *– sendiri* he/she him/herself. **berdiri sendiri** separate, individual. **kediri-sendirian** individuation.

dirinya he, she.
mendiri (*gram*) reflexive (verb).
kediri egotistical.
diri II berdiri 1 to stand. *Karena tidak ada tempat duduk yang kosong, saya terpaksa ~.* Because there was no vacant seat, I was forced to stand. *~ tegak* to stand at attention. 2 to get up. *Sekalian hadirin bersama-sama ~ menyanyikan lagu Indonésia Raya.* All the attendees got up (from their seat) at the same time to sing the Indonesia Raya anthem. 3 to be established, be in existence. *Républik Indonésia ~ sejak tanggal 17 Agustus 1945.* The Republic of Indonesia has been in existence since August 17, 1945. *~ sendiri* a) to be on one's own. b) to be independent/self-sustaining. *sudah ~ di ambang liang kubur* to have one foot in the grave. *~ di belakang layar* to stay in the background. *~ di atas kaki sendiri* [berdikari] a) to stand on one's own two feet. b) to be self-reliant. *~ di atas tanduk kesulitan* having to choose between two difficulties, be on the horns of a dilemma. *~ di luar pagar* to be an outsider, not be in on s.t. *~ lutut* to sit with the knees raised. *~ saja* to stand by helplessly. *~ sama tengah* to be neutral. *~ tegak* to stand up straight, stand at attention. *~ urut* to stand in line. **memberdirikan** to put/set s.t. up, erect. *Meréka ~ papan réklame yang besar.* They put up a large billboard.
berdiri-diri to stand around.
sendiri *q.v.*
mendiri → MANDIRI.
mendirikan [and **memperdirikan** (*infr*) and **ndiriin/ngediriin** (*J coq*)] 1 to set up, erect, establish. 2 to make s.t. stand up. *~ bulu roma* to make the hairs on one's head stand up. 3 to build, construct. 4 to develop (self-confidence). *mendirikan benang basah* to do s.t. that's a waste of time, do s.t. impossible.
terdiri 1 to consist (of), be composed (of), be made up (of). 2 to come (in sizes). *~ dari empat ukuran* it comes in four sizes. 3 to stand up suddenly. *~ seorang orang tua* an old man stood up.
kedirian 1 existence. 2 nature, character, individuality.
pendiri founder. **sependiri** as tall as s.o. standing up, the height of s.o. standing up, standing height.
pendirian 1 establishment, founding. 2 erecting. 3 opinion, attitude, position. **berpendirian** to have ... as a position, be of the opinion ...
dirigén and **dirijén** (*D*) musical conductor.
diris mendiris 1 to water (plants). 2 to irrigate (rice fields). *~ hati* to calm s.o. down.
pendiris sprinkler (the device). *~ hati* (*ob*) refresher.
Dirjén → DIRÉKTUR *Jénderal.*
Dirum → DIRÉKTUR *Umum.*
dirus mendirus to water, wet; to flush with water; → JIRUS I.
mendiruskan 1 to pour out. 2 to water, irrigate.
pendirus watering can.
pendirusan 1 irrigation. 2 fountain (watering place, spa). 3 bathroom.
Dirut → DIRÉKTUR *Utama.*
dis (in acronyms) → DINAS.
disagio (*D fin*) difference in exchange rate which can lead to a financial loss.

disain (*E*) design, style, pattern. *– baku* standard design.
berdisain with/to have a certain design. *~ artistik* with an artistic design.
mendisain to design.
pendisain designer.
pendisainan designing.
disainer (*E*) designer; → PENDISAIN. *~ mode/pakaian* fashion designer.
disel → DIESEL.
diselisasi → DIESELISASI.
disémbarkasi (*D*) disembarkation.
disént(e)ri (*D/E*) dysentery. *– amuba(wi)* amoeba dysentery. *– basilér* bacillary dysentery.
disérsi → DÉSÉRSI.
disértasi (*D*) dissertation.
disfungsi (*E*) dysfunction.
disharmoni (*D/E*) disharmony, discord.
disidén (*D/E*) dissident.
disimilasi (*D*) dissimilation.
disinféksi (*E*) disinfection.
mendisinféksi to disinfect. *~ lénsa kontak* to disinfect a contact lens.
disinféktan (*E*) disinfectant.
disinséntif (*E*) disincentive.
disintégrasi (*D*) disintegration.
berdisintégrasi to disintegrate; disintegrated.
disipasi (*D*) dissipation.
disipel (*D*) disciple.
disiplin (*D/E*) discipline. *ketiadaan –* lack of discipline. *Di kalangan pegawai negeri ketiadaan –.* Among government employees there is no discipline. *– bangkai/mati* rigid discipline. *– diri/ pribadi* self discipline. *kurang –* less disciplined. **kekurangdisiplinan** lack of discipline. *tidak –* undisciplined. **ketidakdisiplinan** lack of discipline.
berdisiplin disciplined.
mendisiplin(kan) to discipline, regiment.
terdisiplin disciplined.
kedisiplinan discipline, training, coaching.
pendisiplinan disciplining. *langkah-langkah ~* disciplinary measures.
displinér (*D*) disciplinary.
disjoki (*E*) disk jockey.
diskaun (*E*) discount.
diskét (*E*) diskette, floppy disk.
mendiskétkan to store on a diskette.
disko (*D/E*) disco(theque). *joki –* disc jockey. *musik –* disco-music.
berdisko to dance to disco music.
mendiskokan to put a certain type of music to a disco-rhythm. *~ jaipongan* to put jaipongan music to a disco rhythm.
disko-diskoan to like to go to discos.
pedisko disco dancer.
diskon → DISKAUN.
diskontir (*D*) **mendiskontir** to discount.
diskonto (*D*) (rate of) discount, (bank) rate. *– wésel* bill discount.
mendiskontokan to discount.
pendiskontoan discounting. *~ wésel ékspor* discounting an export draft.
diskoték and **diskotik** (*D/E*) discotheque.
diskowan (*infr*) male disco lover.
diskowati (*infr*) female disco lover.
diskrédit (*D/E*) discredit.
mendiskréditkan to discredit. *~ pemerintah* to discredit the government.
terdiskréditan discredited.
pendiskréditan discrediting.
diskrépansi (*D*) discrepancy; → KETIDAK-SESUAIAN.
diskriminasi (*D*) discrimination. *– rasial* racial discrimination.
mendiskriminasi(kan) to discriminate against. *~ orang asing* to discriminate against foreigners.
terdisrikrinasi discriminated.
pendiskriminasian act of discriminating, discrimination.
diskriminatif (*E*) discriminatory.

diskriminir (*D*) **mendiskriminir** to discriminate.

diskus (*D*) discus.

diskusi (*D*) discussion. *panél* – and – *panél* panel discussion. – *tak resmi* informal discussion.

  berdiskusi to hold discussions, discuss.

  mendiskusikan to discuss, talk over.

  pendiskusi discussant.

  pendiskusian discussing.

diskusiwan discussant.

diskwalifikasi (*D*) disqualification.

  mendiskwalifikasi(kan) to disqualify.

diskwalifisir (*D*) **mendiskwalifisir** to disqualify.

dislokasi (*D*) **1** dislocation. **2** (*mil*) deployment

disonan (*D/E*) dissonant, discord.

disonansi (*E*) dissonance.

disorganisasi (*E*) disorganization.

disoriéntasi (*E*) disorientation.

disosiasi (*E*) dissociation.

disparitas (*D*) disparity.

dispénsasi (*D*) **1** dispensation. **2** exemption (from some provision of the law). *memberikan* – *kepada* to grant dispensation to.

  mendispénsasikan to grant dispensation to.

dispérsi (*D/E*) dispersion.

  mendispérsikan to disperse.

disposisi (*D*) disposition.

disproporsi (*E*) disproportion, lack of balance.

disproporsional (*E*) disproportional, unbalanced.

disrupsi (*D*) disruption.

Dista → DAÉRAH *Istiméwa Acéh.*

distansi (*D*) distance.

distilasi (*D*) distillation.

  mendistilasi to distill.

distilat (*D*) distillate.

distilir (*D*) **mendistilir** to distill; → MENYULING.

distingsi (*D*) distinction.

distingtif (*D*) distinctive.

distorsi (*D*) distortion.

  mendistorsikan to distort.

  terdistorsi distorted.

  pendistorsian distorting.

distribusi (*D*) distribution.

  mendistribusikan to distribute.

  terdistribusi distributed.

  pendistribusi distributor.

  pendistribusian distributing.

distributif (*D/E*) distributive.

distributor (*E*) distributor; → PENDISTRIBUSI.

distrik (*D col*) **1** (administrative) district (the former *kawedanan*). **2** section designated for a certain purpose (elections, etc.). **3** (*Bat*) (in *HKBP* terminology) provincial level.

  sedistrik of all the districts of.

  kedistrikan district (*mod*).

disyuntif (*D*) disjunctive.

dit (in acronyms) → DIRÉKTORAT.

diték (*E*) detect.

  menditék to detect. *Wartawan 'Pelita' mencoba mengunjungi beberapa pasar untuk ~ apakah kecemasan itu beralasan atau tidak.* A reporter of "Pelita" made an attempt to visit several markets to find out whether that concern was motivated or not.

ditéksi (*E*) detection.

ditéktif → DÉTÉKTIF.

ditel (*D*) detail.

  menditel to detail.

ditérgén (*E*) → DÉTÉRGÉN.

ditibani (*Jv*) → TIBA II.

Ditjén → DIRÉKTORAT *Jénderal.*

dito (*D*) ditto.

div (in acronyms) → DIVISI.

divan (*D*) divan, sofa.

divérgén (*D*) divergent.

divérgénsi (*D*) divergence.

divérsifikasi (*D*) diversification.

mendivérsifikasikan to diversify.

dividén (*D*) dividend. – *agio* agio dividend. – *akhir* final dividend. – *berakumulasi* accrued dividend. – *diléwatkan* passed dividend. – *disahkan* declared dividend. – *ditahan* stock dividend. – *ditunda* deferred dividend. – *ékstra* extra dividend. – *khusus* special dividend. – *manasuka* optional dividend. – *nalatif* cumulative dividend. – *obligasi* bond dividend. – *pilihan* optional dividend. – *primér* primary dividend. – *saham* stock dividend. – *sementara* interim dividend. – *stok* stock dividend. – *super* super dividend. – *terléwat* past dividend. – *tunai* cash dividend. – *utang* liability dividend.

divisi (*D*) **1** division (of military or corporation). **2** phylum. – *baja/(ber)lapis baja* armored division.

  berdivisi-divisi in divisions/large numbers.

diwal(a) → DÉWAL(A).

diwan → DÉWAN.

DIY (*init*) → DAÉRAH *Istiméwa Yogyakarta.* **se-DIY** the entire Special Region of Yogyakarta. *Para bupati ~* (all) the regents of the entire Special Region of Yogyakarta.

DK I (*init*) [Daya Kuda] Horsepower.

DK II (*init*) [Dinas Kebakaran] Fire Department.

DK III (*init*) [Déwan Keamanan] Security Council (of UN).

DK IV car license for Bali.

DKI Jaya (*init acr*) → DAÉRAH *Khusus Ibukota Jakarta Raya.*

dkk (*abbr*) [dan kawan-kawan] et al., and others

DL car license for Sangihe/Talaud.

dlaif → DAIF.

dlamir (*A*) conscience, inner feelings; → HATI *nurani.*

dléwéran (*Jv*) to flow, ooze. *keringat yang* – sweat that is dripping down.

dll (*abbr*) [dan lain-lain] etc.

dlm (*abbr*) [dalam] in.

dls(b) (*abbr*) [dan lain sebagainya] and so forth.

dluha (*A*) after dawn (prayer).

DM car license for Bolaang Mongondow/Gorontalo.

DN car license for Central Sulawesi.

dng (*abbr*) [dengan] with.

do I (*D*) do, the first note in the musical scale.

do II (*E*) drop-out (from school/university).

  mendo(kan) to expel (a student) from school/university. *Tahun lalu UGM terpaksa ~ salah satu dari meréka.* Last year Gadjah Mada University was forced to expel one of them.

doa (*A*) **1** prayer, communication with God, a request to God. – *nya didengarkan Tuhan.* God listened to his prayers. *membaca/minta* – to pray, say a prayer; to devoutly hope. **2** incantation, magic formula. – *arwah* prayers for the dead. – *berkat* a blessing. – *hajat* special prayer (to request s.t. from God). – *istighfar* to pray for forgiveness. – *halimun* mantra for making o.s. invisible. – *iftihah* opening prayer. – *kualat* prayer not to be punished by a higher authority. – *kunut* a) special prayers on the 16th night of the month of *Ramadan.* b) a prayer said in time of danger. – *maulid* prayer on the Prophet's birthday. – *pematah lidah* magic formula to silence an enemy; → PEMBUNGKAM. – *pendinding* prayer for protection. – *pengasih* magic formula to cause s.o. to fall in love. – *restu* blessing. – *sanjung* eulogy. – *selamat* benediction. – *syafaat* Catholic creed. – *tawasul* a prayer concerning some personal matter.

  berdoa and **mendoa** to pray, say a prayer, devoutly hope. *Berdoa dan bekerjalah.* Pray and work. *Berdoalah kepada Tuhan.* Pray to God. *Saya berdoa mudah-mudahan Diréktur yang baru dapat meningkatkan soal pembinaan dan pengembangan bahasa.* I pray that the new Director can step up the guidance and development of the (Indonesian) language.

  mendoai to say a prayer on behalf of s.o.

  mendoakan [and **ngedoain** (*J coq*)] to pray for. *Doakanlah saya.* Pray for me.

  pendoaan praying.

doane → DUANE.

doang(an) (*J/S*) only, merely. *minum bir* – to drink only beer.

doank → DOANG.

doba (*A*) gourd.

dobel (*D*) **1** double; → GANDA I. – *gardan* four-wheel drive. **2**

doubles (in sports). – *campuran* mixed doubles. – *pria/putri* men's/women's doubles.

mendobel to double (in card games).

mendobelkan to double, duplicate.

dobelan s.o.'s double/counterpart.

pendobelan doubling, duplicating.

dobellup and **dobelop** (*D infr*) double-barreled. *bedil* – a double-barreled gun.

Doberai *Jazirah* – the former Vogelkop or Kepala Burung in Irian Jaya.

doberak → DOBRAK.

dobi (*Hind*) laundryman, dhobi; → BENARA I, PENATU.

   berdobi and **mendobi** to have the wash/laundry done.

   mendobikan to have s.o. do the laundry, send the laundry out to be done.

dobis (*Jv*) percussion cap (of percussion rifle).

doblé I (*D*) → DUBLÉ.

doblé II (*J*) with protruding lower lip.

dobol I (*Jv*) with holes in it, perforated. *karung* – a sack with many holes in it.

   mendobolkan to pierce, perforate. ~ *kartu pemilihan* to vote.

dobol II (*J*) **mendobol** to spread rumors, gossip.

dobol III (*Jv*) sagging (of intestines/uterus), bulging.

dobol IV (*Jv vulg*) and **ngedobol** to take a shit.

   ngedobolin 1 to shit on. **2** to cheat, trick.

dobol V → DOBEL.

dobolo k.o. card game.

dobrak (*D*) smashed, broken open (of door/gate, etc.).

   mendobrak to force, batter/break down, break through (a door/locks/defenses).

   dobrakan breaking down, break-through.

   pendobrak 1 s.o. who forces s.t. open. ~ *almari besi* safecracker. **2** wrecker, demolisher. **3** an instrument that breaks through.

   pendobrakan 1 breaking down/open. ~ *rumah* housebreaking, burglarizing. **2** break through. **3** burglary.

dodél (*Jv*) **mendodél** to cut into.

dodét (*J/Jv*) torn/cut open.

   mendodét to tear/cut open (so that the contents comes out).

   pendodétan tearing off.

dodok I (*Jv*) informer, stool pigeon.

dodok II (*Jv*) **1** to (go) sit. **2** to squat, kneel sitting on one's hams.

dodok III hammering flat, body work.

   mendodok to hammer s.t. flat.

dodol I a confection made of pounded glutinous rice with coconut milk and palm sugar; sometimes fruits are added.

dodol II cartridge. – *peledak* blasting cartridge.

dodol III → DOGOL II.

dodong I (*ob*) a curved dagger; → BELADAU.

dodong II (*M*) **terdodong** premature, rash, too hasty; (went) too far; → TELANJUR. ~ *melakukan sesuatu* to do s.t. hastily.

dodor (*J*) **kedodoran 1** fitting badly, too large or too long (of a garment). **2** to be unable to keep up with, be no match for, be unequal to; to give up, lose (the battle).

dodos mendodos 1 to plane s.t. smooth. **2** to enlarge a hole.

   mendodosi 1 to dig up. **2** to pilfer.

dodot I → DEBUS I.

dodot II (*Jv*) (batiked) court dress (folded around lower part of the body and legs, about 4 x 2.20 meters). *mengenakan* – to put on such a wraparound garment.

doelmatighéid (*D*) /dulmatikhhéit/ appropriateness.

doeloe (in the old spelling) formerly; → DULU. *témpo* – the past, the good old days.

doér → DOWÉR.

dogdog 1 (*J*) a small drum. **2** (*onom*) sound made by such a drum.

dogél tailless, featherless (fowl).

dogéng tailless; → DOGÉL.

dogér (*J/Jv*) **1** *tari* – k.o. street dance performed by women. **2** a female dancer.

   mendogér [and **ndogér** (*coq*)] **1** to engage a female dancer in this dance. **2** to dance the *dogér* together.

dogma (*D/E*) dogma.

dogmatik(a) dogmatics.

dogmatis (*D*) dogmatic.

   kedogmatisan dogmatism.

dogmatisme (*D/E*) dogmatism.

dogol I 1 hornless (of cattle). **2** combless (of roosters). *udang* – → UDANG *dogol*.

   berdogol with a swelling (on the head).

dogol II (*J*) stupid, dull.

   kedogolan stupidity.

dogol III (*Jv*) Danish seine net.

doha (*A*) → LOHA. *sembahyang* – (voluntary) forenoon prayer.

dohok (*M*) **terdohok** pushed forward.

doi (*Pr*) /do'i/ boy/girl friend. *si* – that certain s.o. (often a lover); → *si* DIA.

doif → DAIF.

dojo (*Jp*) dojo, i.e., a school/practice hall where karate, judo, or other martial arts are taught.

dok I (*D/E*) /dok/ dock. – *angkat* lift deck. – *apung* floating deck. – *darat* dry dock. – *gali* dugout dry dock on the beach. – *tarik* slipway.

   mendok(kan) and **mengedok(kan)** to dock.

   pengedokan docking.

dok II /dok/ clipped form of **dokter**.

dok III (in acronyms) → DOKTRIN, DOKUMÉN.

dokar (*E*) dokar, a two-wheeled, horse-driven cab.

   berdokar to ride on such a vehicle.

dokarwan dokar driver.

dokat (*Pr*) money, dough.

dokim [*dokumén imigrasi*] immigration document.

doking (*E*) dock(ing).

doklonyo → KELONYO.

dokoh I pendant for a necklace. – *sehari bulan* pendant worn by a bride.

   berdokoh to wear such a pendant.

   memperdokoh to use s.t. as a pendant.

dokoh II → DUKUH I.

dokok-dokok k.o. cake made of rice flour, sugar, bananas, and coconut, wrapped in a banana leaf and steamed.

dokter (*D*) doctor, physician. – *ahli* specialist. – *ahli kulit* dermatologist. – *ahli mata* ophthalmologist. – *ahli penyakit dalam* internist. – *ahli tulang* orthopedic surgeon. – *anak* pediatrician. – *basah* highly paid doctor. – *bedah* surgeon. – *bedah syaraf* neurosurgeon. – *gigi* dentist. – *gula* production manager (on sugar plantation). – *héwan* veterinarian. – *jaga* doctor on call, attending physician. – *jantung* cardiologist. – *Jawa* (*col*) doctor who trained at a medical school specifically for Indonesians during colonial times. – *jiwa* psychiatrist. – *kacamata* optician. – *kandungan* obstetrician. – *kedokteran* medical doctor. – *kering* low-paid doctor. – *kulit* dermatologist. – *kuping* ear doctor. – *langganan* family doctor. – *lokal* practicing doctor who has not passed the state licensing exams yet. – *mata* eye doctor. – *pemeriksa* medical examiner. – *penerbang* flight surgeon. – *pengirim* referring doctor. – *prakték* medical practitioner. – *umum* GP, general practitioner.

   berdokter 1 to go to the doctor for treatment. **2** to have a doctor.

   mendokteri to doctor, treat, patch up.

   mendokterkan to take s.o. to the doctor.

   kedokteran medical, having to do with medicine. *fakultas* ~ medical school. ~ *gigi* dentistry. ~ *kehakiman* forensic medicine.

doktor (*D*) doctor, Ph.D. – *honoris causa* and – *kehormatan* honorary Ph.D./doctor.

doktoral (*D*) doctoral.

doktoranda (*D*) **1** female candidate for a Ph.D. **2** title for a woman who has a BA in the humanities.

doktorandus (*D*) **1** male candidate for a Ph.D. **2** title for a man who has a BA in the humanities.

doktrin (*D/E*) doctrine.

   berdoktrin to have a doctrine.

   mendoktrin(kan) to indoctrinate.

doktrinér (*D/E*) doctrinaire.

doktrinir (*D*) **mendoktrinir** to indoctrinate.

doku (*Pr*) money, dough; → DUIT.

dokudrama documentary (stage-)play.

dokumén (D/E) document. – akséptasi documents against acceptance [D/A]. – bayar documents against payment [DP]. – bukti pembayar payment certificate. – bukti penerima receipt. – lengkap full set of documents. – pemuatan udara airways bill. – pengapalan shipping documents. – rahasia classified document. – sumber source document. – terbuka unclassified document. – tertutup classified document.
  pendokuménan documentation.
dokuméntalis (D) documentalist.
dokuméntasi (D) documentation.
  berdokuméntasi documented.
  mendokuméntasikan to document.
  pendokuméntasian documentation.
dokuméntator (D) documentator.
dokuméntér (D/E) documentary.
dokuméntir (D) mendokuméntir to document.
dokun k.o. decorative fish, spanner barb, Puntius lateristriga.
Dokuritsu Jumbi Chosakai (Jp) Independence Preparations Investigation Committee; → PANITIA Penyelidik Persiapan Kemerdékaan.
dol I (Hind) k.o. drum (the musical instrument).
dol II ship's mast.
dol III (Jv) 1 damaged due to overuse, such as threads of a screw that is stripped. 2 (coq) crazy, mad, frantic, wild.
dol IV empty (of the stomach).
dolak-dalik changeable, unstable, vacillating.
dolan (Jv) 1 to enjoy/amuse o.s. 2 to make an excursion, make/take a trip.
  dolanan 1 to play (a game). 2 toys, playthings.
dolar I (E) dollar (esp the U.S. dollar). – A.S. U.S. dollar. – Malaysia the Malaysian ringgit. – minyak petrodollar.
  sedolar a dollar.
  mendolarkan to convert to dollars.
  pendolaran conversion to dollars.
dolar II pohon – the Ti plant.
dolarsén cent of U.S. dollar.
dolat → DAULAT.
dolbon [modol di kebon] to dispose of human waste in an open field/yard.
dolfin (E) dolphin.
dolim (ob) → LALIM.
dollar → DOLAR.
dolle Mina (D) women's libber.
Dolly name of a red-light district in Surabaya.
dolmén (D/E) dolmen.
Dolog [Dépot logistik] depot for staple foods (rice, etc.).
dolok I (unsawn) (tree-)trunk.
dolok II (ob) mountain.
dolomit (D) dolomite.
dom I → PEDOMAN.
dom II (D) cathedral (church).
dom III (Bal) k.o. card game.
DOM IV → DAÉRAH Operasi Militér.
domah pendomah gift presented by a ruler's envoy.
doman (ob) → PEDOMAN.
domba (Pers) 1 sheep. mengadu – to play one off against the other. 2 (Christian) congregation. para – the congregation. 3 old goat (older man who likes young girls). – Allah lamb of God. – betina ewe. – ékor gemuk fat-tailed sheep. – garut sheep with large curved horns. – hitam black sheep. – merino merino sheep. – pejantan stud sheep.
domblong (Jv) mendomblong to stare openmouthed.
dombrong → GOMBOR, GOMBRONG.
doméin (D) domain; → RANAH. – negara state property. – publik public domain.
doméstik (E) domestic.
domina (D) female Protestant minister.
dominan (D/E) dominant.
dominasi (D) domination.
  berdominasi to be dominant.
  mendominasi(kan) to dominate.
  pendominasi s.o. or s.t. that dominates, dominating.

pendominasian domination.
dominé (D) pastor, minister.
dominir (D) mendominir to dominate.
domino (D/E) domino.
domisili (D) domicile. – hukum yang tetap permanent legal domicile.
  berdomisili domiciled.
  mendomisilikan to domicile.
domot stupid.
dompak I berdompak and mendompak to rear, prance, buck (of horses, etc.).
dompak II and berdompak packed too tight, too close (to e.o.).
dompét 1 wallet, purse. 2 (eyeglass) case. 3 pouch (for carrying tobacco). 4 relief funds. – banjir relief fund for flood victims. – gantungan kunci key case. – kemanusiaan relief funds. – kempés/tipis broke, without any money.
domplang (J) leaning forward or backward, sloping.
  domplangan 1 seesaw. 2 crossing gate.
dompléng (Jv) coincidental. Sifatnya hanya –. It's just a coincidence.
  mendompléng [and ngedompléng (coq)] to get s.t. for free from s.o., sponge (off), live (somewhere for free). Meréka ~ di rumah famili atau kenalan. They live for free in a relative's or a friend's house. ~ kendaraan to get a hitch.
  mendompléngi to get the free use of, join with s.o. in using s.t., exploit.
  mendompléngkan to use s.t. belonging to s.o. else for free.
  dompléngan getting s.t. for free, hitching a ride.
  pendompléng non-paying passenger.
  pendompléngan getting s.t. for nothing, hitching a ride.
dompo → DAMPA.
dompol (Jv) bunch, cluster.
  sedompol a bunch. ~ rambutan a bunch of rambutan.
  dompolan bunch.
Donal Bébék Donald Duck.
donasi (D) donation.
donat (E) donut.
donatir, donator and donatur (D) donor.
Donau Danube.
doncang (M) mendoncang to jump, pounce.
dondang I 1 rocking, swaying. 2 cradle.
  berdondang to rock back and forth.
  mendondang(kan) to rock s.t.
  dondangan 1 rocking, swaying. 2 cradle, swing.
  pedondang back stay.
dondang II → DÉNDANG I, II.
donder (D) anger, bawling out, scolding. Ia kena – pacarnya. His girl friend bawled him out.
  mendonder to bawl out, get angry at, scold.
  donderan scolding, bawling out.
dondon I the same color and pattern.
  sedondon of the same color and pattern.
dondon II mendondon to pawn.
dong I (J) 1 what I'm saying is true even though your words or actions seem to deny it. Kalau mémang punya hutang, harus dibayar –! If you have debts, they have to be paid! 2 indicates a strong command. Minta ke Sékjén –! Ask the secretary general!
dong II → DORANG I, II.
donga incantation.
dongak elevation; → KETINGGIAN.
  mendongak to look upward.
  mendongakkan to point (one's head) upward (to look up). Kepalanya didongakkan ke jendéla kokpit. He pointed his head up to the cockpit window.
  terdongak lifted up.
dongan (Bat) clan-mate, person in the same marga.
dongbrét (in Indramayu) female street dancer.
dongdot prostitute, call girl, whore.
dongéng (Jv) 1 fairy-tale, traditional story. 2 made-up story. – rakyat folktale. – sasakala legend.
  mendongéng 1 to tell fairy-tales. 2 to talk nonsense.
  mendongéngi to tell stories/fairy-tales to. Dia ~ kita tentang fakta sejarah. He told us fairy-tales about history.

mendongéngkan to tell tales about.
dongéngan 1 made-up stories. 2 myth, legend.
pendongéng 1 story teller, narrator. 2 s.o. who likes to fabricate stories.
dongkak (*M*) **mendongkak** to prance, rear up.
dongkék (*J*) **ndongkék** to force s.t. open.
dongkél (*Jv*) jack, lever.
   mendongkél 1 to lift/pry up/jimmy open/up. 2 to remove s.o. from his position, oust. ~ *habis* to get rid of s.t. completely. 3 to reveal (a secret).
   terdongkél pried/jimmied open.
   dongkélan jack, lever.
   pendongkél 1 jack, lever. 2 s.o. that ousts s.o. from his position.
   pendongkélan 1 jacking, levering. 2 ousting, removal.
dongker (*D*) dark; → TUA. *warna biru* – dark blue.
dongkol I (*J*) **mendongkol** [and **ndongkol** (*coq*)] annoyed, irritated, upset, mildly angry. **kemendongkolan** irritation, annoyance.
   mendongkolkan [and **ngedongkolin** (*J coq*)] to irritate, annoy; irksome, irritating.
   kedongkolan irritation, annoyance, mild anger.
   pendongkol a malcontent.
dongkol II (*Jv*) former, ex-; → MANTAN.
   dongkolan retired person.
dongkol III 1 hornless; → DUNGKUL I. 2 powerless, impotent.
dongkrak (*D*) (automobile) jack.
   mendongkrak 1 to jack up. ~ *produksi* to jack up production. 2 to puff s.o. up by flattery. 3 to support.
   terdongkrak [and **kedongkrak** (*coq*)] jacked up.
   dongkrakan raising, hoisting, hiking. ~ *atas nilai* raising the grade (in school).
   pendongkrakan hoisting, jacking up.
dongkrok (*Jv*) **ndongkrok** 1 to slump. 2 to be inactive.
dongo and **dongok** 1 heavy, clumsy, hulking. 2 stupid, idiotic.
dongong (*Jv*) **mendongong** and **ndongong** to stare openmouthed.
donk → DONG I.
donor (*E*) donor. *negeri* – donor nation. – *darah* blood donor.
   mendonorkan to donate s.t. *Kedua matanya sudah didonorkannya di bank mata.* He has donated his eyes to an eye bank.
   pendonor donor. ~ *darah* blood donor.
   pendonoran donation, donating.
donto (*S*) nicely shaped, sexy, voluptuous; → BAHÉNOL.
doos → DOS.
dop I (*D*) cap. – *mobil/roda* hubcap.
dop II (*D*) baptism.
   mendop and **mengedop** to baptize.
dopércis (*D*) green peas.
doping (*D/E*) doping. – *darah* blood doping (in sports).
dopis caps (for toy guns, etc.).
dor I (*onom*) 1 bang! boom! (imitating the sound of a gun). 2 shot. *sekali* – with one shot. *Résidivis B berlumuran darah kena* – *setelah melakukan penodongan.* The repeat offender B, smeared with blood, was shot after a holdup.
   mendor and **mengedor** 1 to fire at, shoot. *Seorang anggauta polisi didor.* A member of the police was shot. ~ *mati* to shoot dead. *Penyelundup obat-obatan kepada pihak komunis akan didor mati.* Smugglers of medicines to the communists will be executed. 2 to shoot down.
   mendorkan to have s.o. fire a gun.
   doran gunfire.
   dor-doran shooting, gunfire. ~ *lagi di Siprus.* Again shooting in Cyprus.
dor II → DAUR.
dorak (*A*) jar.
doraka → DURHAKA.
dorang I (*IBT*) they, their, them. *Paling-paling* – *cuma periksa kitorang punya pas.* At the most they only inspect our passes.
dorang II *ikan* – (*J*) pomfret, *Stromateus niger*; → BAWAL.
doréng (*Jv*) 1 streaked, spotted, marbled. 2 camouflaged (clothing); → LORÉNG. *baju* – (*mil*) a camouflage jacket.
dorgok → SENJATA *dorgok*.
dormansi (*E*) dormancy; → MASA *tidur*.

dorna (*J*) → DURNO.
dorodon (*E?*) drawdown, a lowering of water surface level.
dorong push. *keréta* – push cart. – *turun* (accounting term) pushdown.
   mendorong 1 to push/shove/drive forward. *Meréka beramai-ramai* ~ *mobil yang mogok.* They pushed the stalled car. *didorong oléh sekadar rasa ingin tahu* driven by curiosity. 2 to move (forward) forcefully. *Seorang di antaranya tampil* ~ *ke depan.* One of them appeared to move forward. 3 to urge (s.o. to do s.t.). *Teman-temannya yang* ~ *dia agar menerima tantangan lawannya itu.* It was his friends who urged him to accept his enemy's challenge. 4 to stimulate, motivate, provide the impetus for; stimulative. *meningkatkan bantuan yang bersifat* ~ to increase stimulative aid. 5 (*leg*) to incite, instigate.
   dorong-mendorong to push e.o., jostle.
   mendorongi (*pl obj*) to push.
   mendorongkan to push, move s.t. forward.
   terdorong 1 driven, stimulated. ~ *oléh keinginan* driven by desire, motivated. 2 premature, rash, (over-)hasty, going too far, too late (of s.t. already past and irreversible). *kata/mulut* – let one's tongue run away with one. *kaki* ~ *badan merasa, lidah* ~ *emas padahannya* one has to keep one's promises. ~ *waktu* pressed for time. 3 [= **kedorong** (*coq*)] pushed, shoved.
   dorongan 1 motivation, stimulus, incentive, impetus, urge. *memberi* ~ to encourage. 2 drive, thrust, propulsion. ~ *batin* motive. ~ *hati* impulse. *mudah terpengaruh oléh* ~ *hatinya* impulsive. ~ *kehendak* will-power. ~ *permintaan* demand pull. ~ *séks* libido, sex drive. ~ *téknologi* technology push.
   pendorong 1 incentive, motive, impetus, stimulus, motivation. 2 stimulator, propelling force, booster. 3 s.t. which promotes, promoter, organizer. 4 plunger (of syringe), driver.
   pendorongan 1 pushing forward, propulsion. 2 instigation, stimulus, motivation.
dorsal (*D/E*) dorsal.
dorslah and **dorslag** (*D*) carbon copy, c.c. *kertas* – carbon copy paper.
dorsum (*E*) dorsum.
dortrap (*D*) bicycle with pedal brake.
dos (*D*) 1 cardboard box, carton. 2 cardboard. – *pancuran* shower stall.
   berdos-dos in boxes.
dosa (*Skr*) 1 sin, guilt. 2 crime, offense. – *asal* original sin. – *syirik* the sin of disbelief.
   berdosa to be sinful, commit a sin. *tidak* ~ innocent, not guilty. **ketidak-berdosaan** innocence.
   mendosai to sin against s.t.
   kedosaan sinfulness, guilt.
   pendosa sinner.
   pendosaan sinfulness, guilt.
dosén (*D/E*) university-level instructor, lecturer. – *luar biasa* adjunct instructor. – *negeri* instructor appointed by the state. – *pembimbing* teacher's aide. – *tamu* visiting lecturer. – *terbang* visiting instructor who flies to the university where he is lecturing. – *tetap* permanent instructor.
   kedosénan (*mod*) instructor, lecturer.
doser clipped form of **buldoser**.
dosin dozen; → LOSIN, LUSIN.
dosir I (*ob*) **mendosir** to teach at a university.
dosir II (*D*) dossier, files.
dosis (*D*) dose, dosage. – *berlebih(an)* overdose. – *maut* lethal dosage. – *penunjang/rumatan* maintenance dose. – *penyembuh* curative dose. – *yang tepat* the correct dose.
   mendosiskan to determine (the proper) dose.
doski (*Pr*) he, she; → DOI.
dot I (*D*) nipple (of nursing battle), pacifier.
   men(ge)dot to give a nipple/pacifier to, pacify.
dot II (*onom*) beep.
doti magic incantations.
douane (*D*) → BÉA *dan cukai*, DUANE.
Double Tén (*E*) the anniversary of the People's Republic of China (October 10).
dowél *kayu* – round timber, logs.

251

dowér (*J/Jv*) pouting, protruding (of one's lower lip).

doyak octopus; → SOTONG.

doyan (*J/Jv*) to like, be fond of, care for (*esp* of food/money/sex, etc.) *Seorang mahasiswa sénior yang – gonta-ganti pacar.* A senior male college student who likes to keep changing girlfriends. – *ngobrol* talkative.

   mendoyani to like s.t., have a taste for s.t.

   kedoyanan favorite (food).

doyong (*J*) (dangerously) inclined, leaning, slanting, sloping. *menara* – leaning tower.

   mendoyong sloping, inclined.

   doyongan slope, inclination.

dozer bulldozer; → BULDOSER. *diterjang* – bulldozed.

DPA [Déwan Pertimbangan Agung] Supreme Advisory Council.

dpk (*abbr*) [yang dipekerjakan] *q.v.*

DPP I [Déwan Pimpinan Pusat] Central Leadership Council (at the national level).

DPP II [Dada, Pinggang dan Paha] Chest, Waist and Thigh (the vital measurements).

DPR [Déwan Perwakilan Rakyat] Parliament.

DR car license for Lombok.

dra (*abbr*) [doktoranda] → DOKTORANDA.

draf I (*D/E*) (rough) draft, design.

draf II (*E*) (bank) draft. – *bank* bank draft.

draf III (*D*) bolt.

drag (*E BG*) **ngedrag** 1 to drag race. 2 to burn *putauw* on tin foil and inhale it.

dragon (*E*) 1 trademark of a Japanese water pump. 2 water pump (in general).

draimolen (*D*) merry-go-round, carousel.

drainase and **drainasi** (*D*) drainage.

Drakula Dracula.

dram (*E*) drum (musical instrument).

drama (*D/E*) 1 drama, tragedy. 2 dramatic event. – *gang* (*Bal*) popular folk theater.

   berdrama to perform a drama.

   mendramakan to dramatize.

   kedramaan dramaturgy.

   pendramaan and **perdramaan** dramatization.

dramatari drama with dance; ballet; → SENDRATARI.

dramatik (*E*) and **dramatis** (*D*) dramatic.

   sedramatis as dramatic as. *tidaklah ~ laporan pengacara* not as dramatic as the lawyer's report.

   mendramatiskan to dramatize.

dramatisasi (*E*) dramatization.

   berdramatisasi dramatized.

   mendramatisasi(kan) to dramatize.

dramatisir (*D*) **mendramatisir** to dramatize.

dramator dramatist.

dramaturg (*D/E*) dramatist.

dramaturgi and **dramaturji** (*D*) dramaturgy.

dramawan male dramatist.

dramawati female dramatist.

drambén (*D/E*) marching band.

drap → DERAP.

drastis (*D*) drastic.

drat (*D*) (screw) thread.

   mendrat to thread (a screw).

drég (*E sl*) **ngedrég** inhaling heroin smoke through the nose, chase the dragon.

dréi (*Jv*) screwdriver; → OBÉNG I.

drél fusillade, salvo.

   men(ge)drél 1 to fire a volley. 2 (*J*) to shoot.

   pendrélan firing a volley.

drésoar (*D*) sideboard, buffet.

drh (*abbr*) → DOKTER *héwan*.

dria sense; → INDERA II.

dribel (*E*) **mendribel** to dribble (in sports).

dril I (*D*) drill, twilled linen.

dril II (*E*) drill, training.

   men(ge)dril to drill.

   pendrilan drilling.

drim (*E*) (oil) drum; → DRUM.

dringo → DERINGO.

drip I (*J ob*) act (of theater).

drip II (*D?*) punch (the tool).

drok (*E naut*) drogue.

dron (*E mil*) drone.

drop I (*E*) (air)drop.

drop II (*D/E*) drop (such as cough drop/lozenge).

drop III (*E*) **mendrop** and **mengedrop** 1 to drop off (persons from a car, etc.). 2 to distribute/provide/deliver supplies, etc. 3 to disembark. 4 to unload. 5 to make available, furnish, release (money/funds). 6 to abandon, waive, relinquish, drop (demands).

   drop-dropan supply distributions.

   pendropen and **pengedropan** dropping (of supplies, etc.).

droping (*E*) allocation, provision/delivery of supplies, etc.

dropout (*E*) dropout (from school/university); → JEBOLAN, MOGOL.

drs (*abbr*) → DOKTORANDUS.

drum (*D/E*) 1 drum (musical instrument). 2 oil drum. – *sampah* trash can.

drumband and **drumbénd** (*D/E*) marching band.

drumer (*D/E*) drummer.

Ds (*abbr*) [Dominus] Protestant clergyman.

DS car license for Irian Jaya/Papua.

dsb (*abbr*) [dan sebagainya] etc.

dsl (*abbr*) [dan selanjutnya] and so forth.

DSPP [Daftar Susunan Personil dan Peralatan] Personnel and Equipment List.

dst (*abbr*) [dan seterusya] and so on.

dto (*abbr*) [ditandatangani oléh] signed by.

du (in acronyms) → DUTA, TERPADU.

dua two. *pangkat* – square, quadrate. *titik* – a) colon (punctuation mark). b) division sign. *dalam* – (*ob*) and *berbadan* – to be pregnant. *dalam – satu* one out of two. *tiada – bodohnya* extremely stupid/dull. *telah – kepalanya* to be drunk/intoxicated. *dalam – tengah tiga* unfair, dishonest, deceitful. *sudah lima belas dan tengah – puluh* it's six of one and half a dozen of the other. – *angka* double digit. – *arah* a) duplex. b) ambivalent. – *badan senyawa* (they are) hand in/and glove. – *belas* twelve. *celaka – belas* a) bad luck. b) unlucky person. – *bulanan* bimonthly. – *hati* hesitant. **menduahati** to be undecided. **menduahatikan** to raise doubts in, make s.o. hesitant. – *jurusan* two-way (ticket). – *kali* twice, two times. **mendua kali** to do s.t. twice. **mendua-kalikan** to multiply by two, double s.t. – *kali lipat* twofold. **menduakakali-lipatkan** to duplicate. – *mingguan* biweekly. – *nilai* ambivalent. – *poros* biaxial. – *puluh* twenty. *main – puluh satu* to play blackjack. – *likur* twenty-two. – *mingguan* biweekly. – *sama* two all (score in sports). – *sejoli* a married couple. – *spasi* double space. – *tak* two-stroke.

duanya *tak ada ~* second to none, unequalled, unrivalled, unparalleled. *Kehidupan malam Bangkok tak ada ~ di Asia Tenggara.* Night life in Bangkok is unparalleled in Southeast Asia.

dua-dua 1 two by two, each time two. *Masuklah ~.* Please enter two by two. 2 both. *dalam ~ hal* in both cases. **dua-duanya** both (of them). *~ bodoh.* Both of them are stupid.

sedua share cropping. **menyeduai** to farm land or raise cattle for s.o. else and share in the profits. **menyeduakan** to have s.o. do this.

berdua 1 a group of two, two of. *Meréka duduk ~.* The two of them sat together. *antara kita ~* just between the two of us. 2 in private.

berdua-dua 1 just the two (of us, etc.). 2 in twos, two by two, in groups of two.

berduaan [and **duaan** (*coq*)] in private, tête-à-tête.

berdua-duaan in a pair, just with one other.

mendua 1 to be ambiguous, ambivalent. 2 to be in doubt, hesitate, be of two minds. 3 to trot (of horses). 4 to (break) in two. **kemenduaan** 1 ambiguity. 2 duality. 3 indecisiveness.

menduai [and **ngeduain** (*J coq*)] 1 to add one to make it two. *~ istri* to marry so that one has two wives. *~ laki* to commit bigamy (of women). 2 to steal s.o.'s boy-/girlfriend.

menduakan to double, duplicate. *~ Allah* to be a polytheist. *~ istri* to take a second wife. *~ suami* to commit bigamy (of a woman).

memperdua 1 to divide in half, halve. 2 to till another person's land or raise another person's cattle and divide the crop or profit in half.

memperduakan 1 to double. 2 to have s.o. raise another person's crops or cattle and divide the profit in half.

duaan to be a pair, consist of two, be a couple. ~ *waé* (*Jv*) tête-à-tête, private.

kedua 1 the (set of) two, both. ~ *anak itu* both/the two children. ~ *belah kakinya/matanya/tangannya/telinganya* both his legs/eyes/hands/ears. 2 (*yang*) – the second. *anak* (*yang*) ~ the second child. 3 another. *Viétnam* ~ another Vietnam. (*untuk*) – *kalinya* for the second time. 4 secondary. *kerugian* ~ secondary damages. *peroléhan* ~ (*petro*) secondary recovery.

kedua-dua, keduanya and **kedua-duanya** both. *Ali dan Amin* ~ *bermain ténis dengan baik.* Both Ali and Amin play tennis well.

pendua 1 (s.t. used as a) reserve, duplicate. 2 copier.

penduaan raising other people's cattle or crops and dividing the profits in half.

perdua half, halves. **seperdua** one half of. ~ *dari kekayaannya* half of his assets. ~ *umur* to be middle aged.

perduaan 1 → PENDUAAN. 2 half; → PERDUA.

duafa (*A*) the unfortunate; → DAIF.

duai *ipar* – brother-in-law, sister-in-law.

duaja banner, standard.

duakutub bipolar.

dualis (*D gram*) dual.

dualisme (*D/E*) dualism, double standard.

dualistis (*D*) dualistic.

duane (*D*) customs.

duangsom → DWANGSOM.

dub I (*D col mil*) sergeant major.

dub II (*E*) dub, put a sound track on a film.

mendub and **mengedub** to dub.

penduban dubbing.

dubalang (*M*) village policeman; → HULUBALANG.

dubang (*Jv*) red spittle from chewing betel.

dubés [*duta besar*] ambassador.

berdubés to have an ambassador.

mendubéskan to appoint s.o. as ambassador. 2 to send s.o. into limbo.

dubilah → DUILAH.

dublé (*D*) goldplated.

dubuk (*ob*) hyena, *Hyaena crocutus/striata*.

dubur (*A*) anus.

duda (*J/Jv*) widower, divorcé. – *cerai* separated (from one's spouse). – *kembang* a young and childless widower.

menduda *hidup* ~ to live a widower's life.

peduda widower.

dudu mendudu 1 to follow from behind, trail after. 2 to race ahead. 3 forced to follow from behind.

duduk I 1 to sit (down). –*lah* sit down, have a seat. 2 to settle (of liquids). *Jangan kauminum kopi itu, biar* – *dulu.* Don't drink the coffee, it has to settle first. 3 the situation, the facts of the case. *menceritakan* – *soalnya* to tell all the facts of the case. – *nya* the way it fits (together) *Motor ini belum baik* –*nya.* This engine is not put together well. *tentang* –*nya perkara* regarding the facts of the case. *Saya tahu* –*nya perkara.* I know the ins and outs of the matter. 4 (*petro*) bottom-supported (as opposed to floating) (of drilling platforms). 5 (mainly *Mal*) to stay, live, reside. – *berkisar, tegak berpaling* do not want to keep one's promise, break one's promise. – *sama rendah, berdiri/tegak sama tinggi* what's sauce for the goose is sauce for the gander. *belum* – *belunjur dulu* (or, *telah belunjur/sudah mengunjur/hendak belunjur*) to count one's chickens before they are hatched. – *meraut ranjau, tegak meninjau jarak* to be a workaholic. – *belunjur* to sit with the legs stretched out in front of one. – *bercengkerama* to sit around and chat. – *berhadapan* to sit facing e.o. – *berjuntai* to sit with legs dangling. – *berkokol* to sit hunched up, crouched down. – *bersanding* to sit around and do nothing. – *bersanding* to sit side by side, sit close together (figuratively of bride and groom). – *bersila* to sit cross-legged/with one leg placed over the other. – *bersimpuh* to

sit with the legs folded back (of women). – *bertimpuh(an)* to sit with the legs turned to the right and bent back toward the body, while the left arm rests on the ground. – *bertinggung* to squat; → BERJONGKOK. – *bertolak punggung* to sit back to back. – *bertongkat lutut* to sit with one leg pulled up and put on the seat. – *bertopang dagu* to sit with chin in hands. – *lurus* to sit upright/straight. – *manis* to sit around. – *mencangkung* to squat. – *perkara* (*leg*) the facts of the case. – *perut* to be pregnant. – *seméja dengan* to sit at the same table as. – *tegak* to sit upright/straight. – *terbengkalai* to do nothing. – *termenung* to be lost in thought.

duduk-duduk to sit around/back and relax, hang out. *Mari kita* ~ *di beranda.* Let's sit and relax on the porch.

berduduk to have a seat, be seated.

menduduki [and **mengeduduki** (*infr*) and **ngedudukin** (*J coq*)] 1 to occupy (a region/country, etc.), fill, hold (a position). ~ *posisi yang menonjol* to occupy a prominent position. ~ *tempat kedua* to be in second place, the runner-up. ~ *tempat kedua setelah ...* and ~ *urutan kedua sesudah ...* to rank second to ... ~ *tempat teratas* to rank first.... 2 to sit on/in. ~ *kursi itu* to sit on that chair. ~ *tikar* to sit on a mat. 3 (*infr*) to stay at, live in, reside at.

mendudukkan 1 to make/have s.o. sit down, seat s.o. 2 to place, put. *Kita harus* ~ *persoalan itu pada proporsi yang sebenarnya.* We have to put this problem in its proper perspective. 3 to let s.t. settle. *Dudukkan kopi itu.* Let the coffee settle.

terduduk 1 to flop down, fall into a sitting position. *Dia tergelincir dan jatuh* ~ *di atas lantai yang basah itu.* He slipped and fell to a sitting position on the wet floor. 2 settled (as of coffee/tea, etc.), sedimented.

dudukan 1 pedestal. *Tinggi patung setengah badan ini bersama* ~*nya adalah 2,55m.* The height of this bust together with its pedestal is 2.55 meters. 2 seat (in a car and a piece of machinery), bed/socket (in some compounds). ~ *empuk yang dapat distél mundur-maju* soft seats which can be adjusted forward and backward. ~ *peluru* ball socket. 3 bearing.

kedudukan 1 home, residence, domicile, location. ~ *hukum* legal domicile. 2 station, assigned post. 3 position. ~ *bawahan* subordination. ~ *komando* commanding position. ~ *kunci/pengunci* key position. 4 standing, status, rank. ~ *dalam hukum* legal status. ~ *perkawinan* marital status. 5 the real situation (of a case, etc.). 6 behind, derriere. 7 seat, where one sits. **sekedudukan** 1 of the same status/standing/position. 2 having sexual intercourse. **bersekedudukan** (*ob*) to live together as husband and wife without being legally married. **berkedudukan** 1 to hold/take/occupy a position. 2 to be established, be set up. 3 to be located/based/domiciled (at/in).

penduduk 1 inhabitant, resident, person who lives somewhere. 2 occupier (of a country, etc.). *daérah yang padat/rapat* ~*nya* a densely populated area. *daérah yang tipis* ~*nya* a sparsely populated area. ~*nya sesak/padat* overpopulated. ~ *asing* resident alien. ~ *asli* the first/earliest known inhabitants of a region/country, natives. ~ *pesisir* coastal dwellers, *esp* the Malay ethnic population of northeastern Sumatra; → MAYA-MAYA II, SUKU Déli. ~ *pribumi* native population. **berpenduduk** to have a population; be populated. **kependudukan** 1 residence, residential affairs, population (*mod*). *Bagian* ~ Section for Residential Affairs. 2 population (*mod*). *masalah* ~ population problems.

pedudukan bottom, buttocks, posterior.

pendudukan 1 occupation. *tentara* ~ army of occupation. *zaman* ~ occupation period (regarding Indonesia, refers to the Japanese occupation). 2 area/country, etc. occupied by a foreign power.

duduk II and **berduduk** *dengan* a) to be married to. b) to be engaged to.

mendudukkan 1 to marry off s.o., give away s.o. in marriage. 2 to arrange a marriage between a couple, promise (a daughter/son) in marriage, betroth, affiance.

duduk III fishtail palm, *Caryota mitis*. – *kijang* a climbing plant, *Strophanthus dichotomus*.

dudus (*Jv*) ceremony at which bride's hair is washed.

mendudus to perform that ceremony on.
dudut I (*J/Jv*) **mendudut** to pull out, jerk. ~ *jantung* heartrending.
dudut II (child's language) penis.
duél (*D/E*) **1** duel. – *artileri* artillery duel. **2** (*joc*) collision.
  berduél 1 to fight a duel. **2** to collide.
  duél-duélan to pretend to fight.
duét (*D/E*) duet.
  berduét to sing a duet.
Dufan [Dunia fantasi] Fantasy Land, the Indonesian counterpart of Disneyland.
duga I guess, estimate, sounding. *batu* – sounding lead. *salah* – miscalculation. *tali* – sounding line.
  duga-duganya apparently, it would seem.
  menduga 1 to guess, surmise, assume, suppose, expect, predict. **2** to suspect, presume, allege. *hal-hal yang tidak dapat diduga terlebih dulu* unforeseen circumstances. **3** to fathom (the depth of the sea/mind, etc.), take soundings. **4** to sound out.
  menduga-duga to presume in advance, expect. *secara* ~ presumably. *tanpa diduga-duga* quite unexpectedly.
  mendugakan to take a guess at.
  terduga(-duga) 1 expected, predicted. **2** alleged. *tidak* ~ unexpected, unpredictable, unforeseen. *biaya tidak terduga* unforeseen expenses.
  dugaan 1 guess, assumption, expectation. **2** presumption, suspicion, allegation. *di luar* ~ contrary to expectations, unexpectedly, much to one's surprise. *hal-hal di luar* ~ contingencies. *mempunyai* ~ *keras* to have a strong suspicion. ~ *waktu awal* estimated time of departure, ETD. ~ *waktu datang* estimated time of arrival, ETA.
  penduga gauge, depth finder, s.t. that sounds, guesses, etc., sounder. *gelas* ~ gauge glass. ~ *gema* echo sounder.
  pendugaan 1 fathoming, assuming, guessing, assuming, estimation. ~ *kompas* compass bearing. **2** alleging, allegation.
duga II (*M*) **menduga 1** to oppose, fight back. **2** to overcome, surmount.
  ber(si)duga to compete with e.o. (to do s.t.).
  berduga-duga to race with e.o.
dugal I 1 nausea. **2** nauseated. **3** squeamish.
  mendugal to be nauseated.
  mendugalkan to nauseate, make nauseous, sicken.
dugal II (*Jv*) **ndugal** rowdy, rude.
dugang supporting rope.
  mendugang to hold up with a rope. ~ *perintah* to disobey an order.
dugas mendugas to walk fast.
dugdéng (*Jv*) magically invulnerable.
dugdér (*Jv*) week of festivities leading up to Ramadan.
dugem [dunia gemerlap malam] nightlife, club going.
dugong → DUYUNG.
duh → ADUH.
Duha (*A*) *ad*– "Early Hours of the Morning"; name of the 93rd chapter of the Koran.
duhai → ADUHAI.
duhu (*ob*) village which is the administrative center.
dui(l)lah (*A coq*) exclamation of surprise, O my God.
duit (*D? C? sl*) money, dough. – *ayam* (*col*) k.o. money used during colonial times. – *garis* (*col*) small coin of the colonial period. – *kecil* small change. – *mérah* (*col*) 1/20 of a rupiah. – *panas* illegally gotten money. – *récéh* small change. – *rokok* a tip. – *selawat* money paid to s.o. who reads prayers at a *selamatan*.
  seduit (*col*) five-sixths of a cent.
  berduit rich, well-off.
  menduitkan to turn into cash, cash in.
  duitan *mata* ~ money hungry.
duit-duit red-wattled lapwing, *Lobivanellus indicus atronuchalis*.
duk I clipped form of **dupak** "kick". *main* – to kick.
duk II clipped form of **handuk** "towel".
duk III (in acronyms) → DUKUNGAN.
duka (*Skr*) sadness, grief, sorrow, misery. – *derita* misery. – *lara* misery. – *nestapa* misery, sorrow.
  berduka (~ *hati*) to be sad/miserable.
  mendukakan 1 to make s.o. miserable, distress. **2** distressing.
  kedukaan sadness, misery, sorrow.

keduka-dukaan to be in mourning.
dukacarita and **dukacerita** (*Skr neo*) sad story, tragedy.
dukacita (*Skr*) grief, sadness, sorrow, misery.
  berdukacita to grieve, be grief stricken, mourn, go into mourning. *Saya turut* ~. My condolences.
  mendukacitakan 1 to mourn, grieve for. **2** to make s.o. miserable.
  kedukacitaan sadness, mourning, grief.
dukan (*A*) shop, booth.
dukana lustful, lascivious, sensual, voluptuous.
dukanestapa sadness, grief.
dukat (*D*) ducat.
dukhan (*A*) *ad*– "Smoke"; name of the 44th chapter of the Koran.
duko (brand name of a) rustproofing paint.
  menduko to apply that paint to.
duku I k.o. tree and its fruit, lanson, *Lansium domesticum*.
duku II (*M*) not smooth or even.
  berduku-duku wavy, not smooth or flat.
dukuh I (*J/Jv*) hamlet, a few houses in a cluster.
  sedukuh the entire hamlet.
  pe(r)dukuhan 1 hamlet, the administrative unit below the *kelurahan*. **2** (*mod*) hamlet.
dukuh II butcher; → JAGAL II.
dukun (*Jv*) **1** traditional healer, medicine man. **2** spiritual counselor. – *bayi* midwife. – *beranak* midwife. – *buaya* specialist in dealing with crocodiles. – *buntut* s.o. who claims to be able to predict the winning lottery number. – *calak* circumciser. – *jampi* one who uses traditional medicine. – *japa* expert in spells and incantations. – *klenik* sorcerer. – *paraji* (*S*) midwife. – *patah* s.o. who knows how to set broken bones. – *pengantén* specialist in wedding decorations and make-up. – *peraji* midwife. – *peréwangan* medium. – *petungan* expert in numerology. – *pijet/pijit* masseur. – *rias* s.o. who applies makeup to a dancer, etc. – *santét* sorcerer, user of black magic. – *sihir* sorcerer, user of black magic. – *siwér* specialist in preventing natural disasters such as keeping away the rain when one is holding a feast. – *susuk* specialist in putting metals or materials into the body for strength, etc. – *tenung* sorcerer, user of black magic. – *tiban* s.o. who is granted the power to become a *dukun* overnight. – *urut* abortionist. – *wiwit* specialist in harvest rituals and ceremonies.
  berdukun 1 to seek the help of a *dukun*. **2** to work as a *dukun*.
  mendukuni 1 to treat illness by means of a *dukun*. **2** to put under a *dukun*'s spell.
  mendukunkan 1 to cause s.o. to become ill by sorcery. **2** to take to a *dukun* for treatment.
  pe(r)dukunan 1 sorcery. **2** involved in *dukun* activities. *tokoh* ~ a *dukun* figure. **3** charlatanism.
dukung support. *sebagai* – *terhadap* in support of.
  berdukung 1 to sit on s.o.'s shoulders, be carried on the back or shoulders. **2** to overlap, one on top of the other.
  mendukung 1 to support, endorse, espouse. *AS Kembali* ~ *Pinjaman Bagi Indonésia*. America Again Supports Loans for Indonesia. **2** to carry on the back or hips. ~ *belakang* to carry on the back. ~ *kélék* to carry on the hip.
  mendukungi (*pl obj*) to support.
  terdukung supported, endorsed, espoused.
  dukungan 1 support, endorsement, backing. **2** carried on the back. *anak* ~ *ibu* a child carried on his mother's back.
  pendukung 1 supporter, exponent, proponent, advocate. **2** s.o. who carries s.o. or s.t. on the back or hips. **3** support, bearer, pedestal, bracket.
  pendukungan support, supporting, endorsing.
Dul contracted form of names containing -**dul**, e.g., *Abdullah*.
dulag the drum beaten on *Lebaran* and at the end of *Ramadan*.
dulang I 1 k.o. round tray from South Sumatra. **2** printer's galley. **3** (*geol*) pan. *bagai* – *dengan tudung* right for e.o. *lain* – *lain kaki, lain orang lain hati* to each his own, de gustibus non disputandum est. – *alas* a) tray for carrying food. b) coaster. – *pelanda* gold-mining pan. – *putar* lazy Susan (a rotating tray). – *rendah* low tray for serving food. – *tinggi* tray with legs for serving food.
dulang-dulang small tray used for washing heirlooms.
  mendulang to pan for gold.
  pendulang prospector (for gold, etc.).

pendulangan 1 prospecting (for gold, etc.). 2 printing a galley.

dulang II (*Jv*) **mendulang** to feed a child premasticated food.

dulang III mendulang to rise up in puffs of smoke.

dulang IV pink shower tree, *Cassia fistula*.

dulang-dulang I part of a boat's mast.

dulang-dulang II → DULANG IV.

duli (*Skr cla*) 1 dust (on the bottoms of the feet). 2 foot. 3 part of some royal titles. – *baginda* Your Majesty. – *syah alam* your majesty.

  berduli 1 to be dusty. 2 to walk (of royalty).

dulillah → DUILAH.

dulu (short for *dahulu*) 1 formerly, previously, in the past, used to. *dari – mula* from the very beginning. *lebih* – earlier, prior. *témpo* – (often spelled **doeloe**) the (good) old days, the past (*esp* under Dutch rule). – *daripada* prior to. – *kala* formerly, used to. 2 (in negative commands) (not) just yet, (not) before doing anything else. *Jangan mandi –!* Don't bathe just yet! 3 (in statements and positive commands) now (rather than later, used as a softener). *nanti* – one moment please. *Saya pergi –.* I'm leaving now. 4 before, prior to. *siapa – siapa dapat* first come, first served (in advertisements).

  dulunya formerly, previously.

  dulu-dulu formerly, used to. *seperti yang selalu kita lakukan ~* as we always used to do. *~ sekarang sekarang* what's past is past.

  berdulu-duluan and **dulu-mendului** to try to get ahead of e.o.

  mendului [and **ngeduluin** (*J coq*)] to precede, go before.

  mendulukan to give priority to.

  duluan before (s.o. else), sooner (than s.o. else). *Aku ~.* I'll go first. *Siapa ~ dialah yang punya.* First come, first served.

  keduluan preceded (by s.o.). *Dia ~.* S.o. else got there before him. *Kita tidak ~ oléh Australia.* Australia didn't get there before us.

dulur (*Jv*) sibling.

dum I (*onom*) plop! (the sound); → REDUM I.

dum II mengedum to dump (goods on the market).

dumal → DUMEL.

dumdum (*D*) dumdum (bullet).

duméh (*Jv*) just because. *Aja –.* Don't imagine too much (because ...).

dumel (*J/Jv*) **mendumel** and **ngedumel** to grumble, grouch.

dumolit a tablet manufactured by the Dume pharmaceutical industries which is frequently used as a substitute for narcotics.

dumping (*E*) dumping (goods on the market).

dumung (*Jv*) a poisonous snake.

dunah (*Pers?*) decoy(-bird).

dunak (*Jv*) a large basket (for rice).

dung I (*onom*) sound made by a drum.

Dung II short for **Badung V.**

dungak → DONGAK.

dungas snort; → DENGUS

  berdungas and **mendungas** to snort.

dungkul I 1 hornless or with downward curving horns (of a bullock). 2 powerless.

dungkul II k.o. evil spirit.

dungu stupid, mentally retarded.

  sedungu as stupid as.

  mendungukan to cheat s.o., make s.o. appear stupid/foolish.

  kedunguan stupidity.

dungun *pohon* – k.o. coastal tree, looking-glass mangrove, *Heritiera littoralis*. – *darat* k.o. mahogany tree, *Tarrieta javanica*.

dunia (*A*) the (physical) world. *harta* – the riches of this world. *perédaran* – the chances and changes of mortal life. – *merubah dan kita ikut berubah* the times are changed, and we are changed with them. – *ini tidak selébar daun kélor* and – *ini tidak selébar telapak tangan* with time comes counsel. – *akhirat* the next world, the hereafter. *dari – lalu ke akhirat* (faithful) unto death. – *anak-anak* child world. – *(yang) baka* the afterworld. – *Barat* the West. – *binatang* fauna. – *(yang) fana* the temporal world. – *ghaib* the mysterious world. – *héwan* fauna. – *hitam* the underworld. – *kehéwanan* fauna. – *ketiga* the Third World. – *kiamat* Armageddon. – *leta* corrupt world. – *luar* the outside world. – *luaran* (*infr*) the outside world. – *maya* the virtual world (of the Internet). – *merdéka* the free world. – *olah-*

raga the world of sports. – *pedagang* commercial world. – *perdagangan* the world of commerce. – *persurat-kabaran* the press world. – *perusahaan* commerce and industry, industrial life. – *ramai* general society. – *saudagar* the world of commerce/business. – *selebihnya* the outside world. – *timur* the East, the Orient. – *tumbuh-tumbuhan* flora. – *usaha* the business world.

  sedunia 1 worldwide, the whole wide world, international. *kongrés pemuda ~* international youth congress.

  berdunia 1 to be in the world, live. 2 to strive for wealth, pleasure, etc.

  mendunia 1 to come into existence/being/the world, see the light of day. 2 secular.

  menduniakan 1 to broadcast. 2 to secularize. 3 to create a world market for.

  keduniaan 1 worldly, secular, earthly. *kesenangan ~* earthly pleasures. 2 mundane.

  penduniaan secularization.

duniawi (*A*) worldly, secular. *kekayaan* – earthly riches.

  menduniawikan to secularize.

  keduniawian 1 worldly, secular. 2 secularism. 3 materialism; materialistic.

  penduniawian secularization.

duniawi(y)ah (*A*) → DUNIAWI.

  keduniawian worldliness.

dunsanak → DANSANAK.

dup (*D*) baptism.

  men(ge)dup to baptize.

dupa (*Skr*) incense. *membakar* – to burn incense. – *bakar* burning incense. – *pakai* incense put into clothing to make it smell better.

  mendupai 1 to burn incense for. 2 to hold s.t. over burning incense. 3 to put incense into clothing to make it smell better.

  pedupaan 1 censer. 2 burning of incense.

  pendupaan 1 burning of incense. 2 putting incense into clothing.

  perdupaan burning of incense.

dupak (*J/Jv*) **mendupak** [and **ndupak** (*coq*)] to kick with the side of the foot.

dupléks (*E*) duplex, folded twice.

dupli(e)k (*D leg*) rejoinder.

duplikasi (*E*) duplication.

duplikat (*D*) duplicate, carbon copy.

duplikator (*D*) duplicator, copier.

duplisir (*D*) **menduplisir** to double.

duplo (*D*) in duplicate. *Surat itu diketik –.* The letter was typewritten in duplicate.

dur I (*A*) pearl; → MUTIARA I.

dur II (*Skr*) (usu as part of a name or as the first part of a word) bad, evil, wicked.

dura I (*Skr*) anxious, worried, troubled, disturbed. *Ibu berhati – karena adik perempuanku sudah senja belum juga pulang.* Mother is worried because her daughter hasn't come home and it's getting dark.

dura II (*Skr*) 1 distant, far away. *langit yang* – the distant sky. 2 distal.

duraka → DURHAKA.

durasi (*D/E*) duration.

  berdurasi with/to have a duration, last. *sebuah film untuk télévisi yang terdiri dari enam épisode ~ 48 menit* a TV film consisting of six episodes which lasts for 48 minutes.

durat (*A*) pearl; → DUR I.

duratif (*D/E*) durative.

durbasa (*Skr*) a coarse/rough language.

durén (*J*) → DURIAN.

Durga (*Skr*) consort of Shiva; goddess of death and destruction.

durhaka (*Skr*) 1 insurgent (against God/authority/one's parents). 2 rebel, mutineer. 3 rebellion, mutiny; mutinous; disloyal, rebellious. 4 godless, wicked, unholy.

  berdurhaka 1 to rebel, revolt (against). 2 to be insubordinate. 3 to sin (against).

  mendurhaka 1 to offer resistance. 2 to mutiny, rebel. 3 to be unfaithful. *~ sumpah sendiri* to break one's oath.

  mendurhakai 1 to revolt/rebel against s.t. 2 to betray.

kedurhakaan 1 rebelliousness, mutiny. 2 wickedness.

pendurhaka 1 rebel, insurgent, mutineer. 2 traitor.

pendurhakaan 1 rebellion, revolt, insurrection, mutiny. 2 treachery.

duri I 1 thorn, burr. 2 (fish-)bone. 3 spine, quill (of porcupine). 4 difficulty. *menempuh hidup baru, yang banyak –* to start on a new life with its many difficulties. *bagai – dalam daging* like a thorn in one's side. *– cangkang* k.o. thorny plant, *Opuntia schumanii. – dalam daging* a thorn in the flesh. *– lengkung insang* gill rakers. *– paku* spike. *– témpél* prickle.

berduri 1 thorny, prickly. 2 barbed. *kawat ~* barbed wire. *sepatu ~* spike shoe.

berduri-duri 1 to have many thorns. 2 to have a lot of difficulties.

menduri 1 like a thorn, thornlike. 2 sharp, hard, biting, hurts one's feelings. *~ hati* painful. *mengeluarkan ucapan-ucapan yang ~* to say things which hurt s.o.'s feelings.

duri II → DURIAN.

duri III *ikan –* various species of catfish, *Arius spp.* and *Macrones nemurus.*

duri IV *akar –* name of a thorny plant. *buluh –* name of a thorny bamboo. *– landak* agave, *Agave americana.*

durian the durian fruit, *Durio zibethinus. lempok –* (in Bengkulu) delicacy made of glutinous rice, coconut milk, durian, and palm sugar; → DODOL I. *– jarang jatuh di siang hari* the durian fruit seldom falls during (broad) daylight. *kepala –* the first durians to fall. *– jatuh sarung naik* the durians fall and the sarungs come up (because durian are believed to be an aphrodisiac). *(men)dapat – runtuh* and *beruntung memperoléh – runtuh* to hit the jackpot. *(seperti) mentimun dengan –* next to a dangerous neighbor, uneasy bedfellows. *– Belanda/Betawi* (*infr*) soursoup, *Anona muricata;* → SIRSAK. *– burung* k.o. durian, *Durio carinatus. – daun* k.o. durian, *Durio oxleyanus. – hutan* k.o. durian, *Durio malaccensis. – kucing titun* (in Medan) the most expensive, choice durian. *– kuning* k.o. durian, *Durio graveolens. – monthong* a superior variety of durian. *– nyekak/pulu* k.o. durian, *Durio kutejensis;* → LAI II. *– tembaga* a durian variety whose flesh is yellow-colored like copper, considered the best.

durias (*Hind*) muslin (thin, fine material).

duriat → ZARIAH, ZURIAT.

durit (*D*) durain, dull coal.

durja (*Skr*) countenance, face, look, appearance. *jamjam –* expression. *tinggi –* an arrogant expression. *– berseri* a bright countenance. *– muram* a gloomy/depressed expression.

durjana (*Skr*) evil, wicked. *laki-laki –* a criminal; → PENJAHAT. *perempuan –* prostitute.

kedurjanaan evil, crime.

durjasa (*Skr neo*) discredit, disservice.

durkarsa (*Skr*) 1 malicious, malevolent. 2 maliciousness, malevolence.

durkarya misdeed.

durma (*Jv*) a classical verse form.

durna → DURNO.

durno (*Jv*) 1 a *wayang* character. 2 intriguer, schemer, plotter, double-tongued opportunist. 3 (during the G30S) reference to Dr. Soebandrio.

durno-mendurno to accuse e.o. of intrigues; the pot calls the kettle black.

mendurnoi to incite s.o. to do s.t. bad.

durnois 1 intriguer, schemer, etc. 2 (during the G30S) a follower of Dr. Soebandrio.

durnoisme scheming, intrigue, Machiavellianism.

dursila (*Skr*) 1 immoral, wicked, sinful, unethical. 2 evil spirit. 3 giant of the forest.

kedursilaan immorality, sinfulness.

duru (*M*) **berduru(-duru)** in throngs/droves.

dus I (*D*) consequently, so, therefore. *–, dia benar.* So, he was right.

dus II (*D*) cardboard box; → DOS.

dus III (*D*) shower (bath).

dus IV (*Jv*) **mendus** to plate (a metal object). *didus emas* gold-plated.

dusanak → DANSANAK.

dusel (*Jv*) **mendusel** to snuggle up.

dusi mendusi (*M*) to be half awake, feel drowsy.

dusin I → LUSIN.

dusin II (*J*) **mendusin** 1 to wake up. *Saya ~ pukul tiga malam.* I woke up at three o'clock at night. 2 to realize, be aware of; to become conscious. *Baru kemudian saya ~ bahwa saya sudah tertipu oléhnya.* It was only later that I realized that he had tricked me.

dusta (*Skr*) 1 lie, falsehood; → BOHONG. 2 lying. *berbuat –* to (tell a) lie.

berdusta and **mendusta** to (tell a) lie. *Anak itu selalu suka ~.* That child always likes to tell lies.

mendustai to lie to s.o., deceive s.o.

mendustakan 1 to deny, say s.t. is untrue. *~ adanya Tuhan* to deny the existence of God. 2 to lie about s.t.

kedustaan lying, falsehood. *bagaimanapun ~ disembunyikan akhirnya akan ketahuan juga* the truth will out.

pendusta liar.

pendustaan 1 lying, deceit, deception, fraud. 2 denial.

dustur (*A ob*) laws; regulations, rules.

dusun I hamlet; → DUKUH I. *orang –* a) hamlet resident. b) country bumpkin.

pedusunan a group of hamlets.

dusun II (*Mal*) orchard.

duta (*Skr*) envoy, ambassador. *– besar* [dubés] ambassador. **menduta-besarkan** a) to appoint s.o. as ambassador. b) to send s.o. to limbo. *– besar berkuasa penuh* ambassador plenipotentiary. *– besar luar biasa dan berkuasa penuh* ambassador extraordinary and plenipotentiary. *– besar Vatikan* papal Nuncio. *– istiméwa* special envoy. *– keliling* roving ambassador, ambassador-at-large. *– luar biasa dan berkuasa penuh* envoy extraordinary and minister plenipotentiary. *– pengembara* roving ambassador, ambassador-at-large. *– perdamaian* goodwill ambassador. *– perubahan* agent of change. *– pribadi* personal envoy (of the president).

kedutaan legation, embassy. *~ besar* [kedubés] embassy.

peduta and **penduta** envoy, emissary.

perdutaan mission, legation, delegation.

dutawati ambassadress, Mrs. Ambassador.

dutawisata → PRAMUWISATA.

duwegan → DEGAN.

duwet (*Jv*) k.o. tree, *Eugenia, spp.;* → JAMBLANG.

duwit → DUIT.

duyun berduyun-duyun in throngs/droves.

duyunan a stream (of people).

duyung dugong, sea cow, manatee, *Halicora dugong/Dugongus marinus/Trichochus dugong. air mata –* dugong's tears, *akar minyak tangis –* dugong's cry oil, a love potion; when smeared over a woman, she will immediately fall in love.

dwangsom (*D leg*) penalty.

dwarapala (*Jv*) gatekeeper statue.

dwi- (*Skr*) (prefix used to form neologisms) two-, bi-, di-, dual, duo-.

dwiabad bicentennial.

dwiarah bidirectional, two-way.

dwiarti (*Skr neo*) ambiguous; → TAKSA.

kedwiartian ambiguity; → KETAKSAAN.

dwibahasa (*Skr neo*) bilingual.

berdwibahasa to be bilingual.

kedwibahasaan bilingualism.

dwibahasawan and **dwibasawan** bilingual (person).

dwibelah double-sided.

dwibudaya (*Skr neo*) bicultural (like British and French culture in Canada).

dwibulanan bimonthly (magazine).

dwicabang two-pronged.

dwicakap (*Skr neo*) dialogue.

dwicekung biconcave.

dwicembung biconvex.

dwidarma (*Skr neo*) double duty.

dwidasa (*Skr neo*) twenty.

dwidasawarsa (*Skr neo*) 1 twenty years. 2 twentieth anniversary.

dwidaun bifoliate.

dwidéwan bicameral (legislature).

dwidharma (*Skr neo*) two principles taught to 7–10 year olds (obey your parents and be brave and do not give up hope).

dwifokus bifocal.

dwifungsi 1 (in general any) dual function/job/occupation. **2** the dual function concept which states that the military's role is not simply to protect the nation in wartime, but also to undertake the task of building the nation.

    berdwifungsi to hold two functions concurrently, wear two hats. *Sekalipun ~, tentara Indonésia tetap masih juga berfungsi sebagai tentara konvénsional.* Although the Indonesian army has a dual function, it also still functions as a conventional army.

    mendwifungsikan to give s.t. a dual function.

    pendwifungsian making s.t. have a dual function.

dwiganda double, twofold, in duplicate.

    mendwigandakan to double.

dwiguna (*Skr neo*) dual-purpose.

dwihuruf 1 digraph. **2** diphthong.

dwi-istri bigamy.

dwikelamin bisexual.

dwikembar doublet.

dwike(warga)negaraan dual citizenship.

Dwikora [Dwi komando rakyat] People's Twofold/Dual Command [under President Soekarno] comprising: **1** Strengthening the defense of the Revolution. **2** Supporting the struggle for independence of the peoples of Malaya, Singapore, and Borneo.

dwikutub bipole, bipolar.

dwilambang → DWIHURUF.

dwilingga (*Skr neo*) **1** full reduplication, for instance, *méja-méja, mlaku-mlaku,* etc. **2** reduplication of the initial syllable, for instance, *lalaki, papacangan,* etc.

dwilipat double, twofold, in duplicate.

dwilogam bimetallic.

dwilomba biathlon.

dwimakna ambiguous.

    kedwimaknaan ambiguity.

dwimarga (*Skr neo*) two-way (traffic).

dwimata binocular.

dwimatra (*Skr neo*) two-dimensional.

dwimingguan biweekly.

dwimuka ambivalent.

    kedwimukaan ambivalence.

dwimusim bimonsoonal.

dwinikah bigamy.

dwipa (*Skr*) **1** island. *Jawa* – the island of Java. **2** continent.

dwipaksa (*ling*) *katakerja* – a verb which is both passive and active, for instance, *Dadanya tembus oléh tombak.* His chest was pierced through by a lance and *Tombak itu tembus ke dadanya.* The lance pierced through his chest; *masuk sekolah* to go into a school building, i.e., a person is entering the building and *masuk angin* to catch a cold, i.e., the cold has entered a person's body.

Dwipangga name of a train running between Jakarta and Solo.

dwipartai two-party. *sistém* – two-party system.

dwipecahan two-pronged.

dwipekan two weeks.

    dwipekanan biweekly.

dwiperan dual role.

dwipihak bilateral, bipartite.

dwipurwa (*Skr neo*) initial syllable reduplication with the vowel replaced by the schwa, such as, *beberapa, sesama, tetapi, tetangga,* etc.

dwirangkap double, twofold, in duplicate.

dwireti → DWIARTI.

dwirunjung biconical.

dwirupa (*Skr neo*) dimorphic.

    kedwirupaan dimorphism.

dwisatya (*Skr neo*) two promises made by 7-10-year-olds (to carry out one's duties and to do good every day).

dwisegi two-sided, with two aspects.

dwisisi two-sided, bilateral.

dwisuku (*ling*) disyllabic.

dwisyarat biconditional.

dwitahap two-stage.

dwitahun(an) biennial, biannual.

dwitarung duel.

dwitransitif (*ling*) *katakerja* – ditransitive verb, i.e., a verb that takes both an indirect and a direct object.

dwitunggal 1 twosome, duumvirate. **2** President Soekarno and Vice-President Hatta.

    kedwitunggalan duumviracy.

dwiwarna (*Skr neo*) **1** two-tone, bicolor, with two colors. **2** the Indonesian red and white flag. *Sang* – the Indonesian Red-and-White Flag. – *purwa cendekia wusana* [Motto of *Hankamnas* (National Defense and Security) training courses] emphasizing patriotism and fighting spirit above profession.

dwiwasana (*Skr neo*) imperfect reduplication of the last part of a word, i.e., *cengenges.*

dwiwindu 16 years.

dwiwulanan bimonthly.

dz- also see entries beginning with **d-, l-** or **z-**.

dzariyat (*A*) 'Scattering Winds"; name of the 51st chapter of the Koran.

dzat → ZAT.

dzawul faraidh (*A*) the heirs who have the right to receive part of an estate according to the Koran in the percentages specified there.

dzikir → ZIKIR.

dzimmi → DIMMI.

dzuntiqam (*A*) a name of God, the Retaliator.

E

é and É I the fifth letter of the Latin alphabet used for writing Indonesian.

é II 1 (exclamation used to attract attention, express surprise, etc.) hey, hi, say. -, *lihat rumah terbakar di sana!* Hey, look there's a house on fire over there! -, *mari!* Hey (you), come here! 2 (particle of hesitation, pause in speech, self correction) eerh, eh, um, I mean. *Di situ kan dangkal lautnya. Tidak begitu dangkal, -, dalam.* The sea is shallow over there, isn't it. Not so shallow, eh (I mean), deep.

E III car license plate for Cirebon.

EA car license plate for Sumbawa.

éak (*onom*) cry, wail (of an infant).
mengéak-éak to cry, wail. *Kenapa orok itu terus-menerus ~, apakah ia sakit?* Why does the baby keep on crying, is he sick?

EB car license plate for Flores.

ebam (*naut*) cross-piece of rudder; → BAM I.

ébam (*ob*) k.o. oval-shaped lidded porcelain pot for water.

éban → HÉBAN I. mengéban to throw, hurl, fling. *sudah diéban, dihéla pula* to retract what one has just said, undo what one has just done.

ebang call/summons to prayer; → BANG I.
mengebangkan to call/summon to prayer.

ébég (*Jv*) *jaran* - a village folk dance using a bamboo-plaited hobby horse.
(ébég-)ébégan a hobby horse used for this dance; → KUDA *képang*.

ébék tent-flap, awning (for ship or over window); → KERAI.

ébéng → IBING I.

ébi (*C*) dried and salted shrimps.

éblég and éblék (*Jv*) a circular green board with a white rim and a handle used at train stations as a signal for departing trains.

éboh (*M*) noisy, clamorous; → HÉBOH.

ebom → BOM I, II, III.

ebon → BON I, II, III.

éboni (*E*) ebony, *Diospyros spp.*; → KAYU *hitam*.

ébonit (*D*) ebonite, vulcanite, i.e., a hard black vulcanized rubber.

ebor → BOR.

ébro [Éérste Bataviaanse Rijtuig Ondernéming (*D*) [First Batavian Carriage Enterprise] name of a four-wheeled carriage chartered vehicle.

Ébta [Évaluasi Belajar Tahap Akhir] Final Stage of Study Evaluation.
meng-Ébta-kan to take one's *EBTA*.

Ébtanas [Évaluasi Belajar Tahap Akhir Nasional] National Final Stage of Study Evaluation.
berébtanas to take the Ebtanas test.
mengébtanaskan to test in that test. *mata pelajaran yang diébtanaskan* the subjects tested.

écé (*Jv*) mengécé to make faces at, poke fun at, make fun of, ridicule.
écéan kidding/fooling around.

ecék → CÉK I, II, III.

écék (*coq*) écéknya apparently, it seems that. *~ ada tabrakan mobil.* There seems to have been an automobile accident.
écék-écék 1 not serious, appears to be s.t. but really isn't. *perang ~* phony war, mock battle. 2 small, of little value. *proyék ~* a small project. 3 suppose that. *~ saya ini menjadi raja.* Suppose that I were king. berécék-écék to pretend. *Ia ~ saja bekerja.* He pretended to work.

écék-écék I maraca(s).

écék-écék II (*Jv*) to challenge/threaten verbally.

écéng (*J*) an aquatic plant found in rice paddies, yellow sawah lettuce, *Limnocharis flava* and duck lettuce, *Monochoria hastata* eaten as a raw side dish. - *gondok* water hyacinth, *Eichornia crassipes*, with swollen petioles that float on water and lavender flowers, an obstacle to water traffic. - *padi* an aquatic plant, pickerel weed, *Monochoria vaginalis*.

écér (*Jv*) mengécér(kan) to sell retail.
ngécér (*J*) to buy or sell in small quantities.
écéran 1 retail. 2 by the single copy (of a newspaper/magazine, etc.); by the one (of eggs/ cigarettes, etc.).
pengécér retailer. *warung ~* (roadside) retail store. *~ koran* newspaper street vendor.
pengécéran retailing.

éco (*Jv*) tasty, delicious.

eco-ecoan (*J*) arbitrary, high-handed, indiscriminate(ly), at random, on the off chance.

ED car license plate for Sumba.

édah → IDAH II.

édamatik electronic advertising.

édan (*Jv*) 1 insane. 2 mad, crazy, wild, frantic. - *kasmaran/kesemaran* madly/head over heels in love.
édan-édanan to go crazy/nuts.
keédanan 1 head over heels in love. 2 craziness, foolishness.
keédan-édanan to act crazy.

edap → DAP.

édap → IDAP.

édar beréder [and mengédar (*inf*)] 1 to revolve, move around a central point or axle, move in a circle, orbit around a point, rotate. *bintang ~* a planet. 2 to circulate, be in circulation (of circulars/money) from one hand to another. *Daftar ini sudah ~ di kampung saya.* The list has been circulating in my area. *Uang kertas baru mulai ~.* The new bank notes will go into circulation. 3 to shift, move on to another place. *~ dari méja makan ke kamar rékréasi* to move from the dining room to the rec room. *zaman ~ musim berubah* time moves on; other times, other manners. 4 to circle (of a flying plane). 5 to be in effect (of the value of money). 6 to be available (on the market).
mengédari 1 to revolve/rotate/circle around s.t. *Bulan ~ bumi.* The moon revolves around the earth. 2 to travel over, traverse, roam, explore. *~ dunia* to travel around the world. 3 to circle around, encircle. *jalan yang ~ Jakarta* the roads which encircle Jakarta.
mengédarkan and memperédarkan [and ngédarin (*J coq*)] 1 to hand/pass/send around. *Seorang gadis ~ talam berisi kué.* A girl passed around a tray with cookies. 2 to cast (one's eyes/glance) at. *Kuédarkan pandanganku ke segenap penjuru ruangan.* I cast my eyes around all corners of the room. 3 to circulate (money/circulars/letters, etc.). 4 to distribute (products).
édaran 1 s.t. circulated; memo, pamphlet, leaflet. *surat ~* a circular. *~ pérs* press release. 2 orbit, cycle.
pengédar 1 distributor (of newspapers/magazines, etc.). *~ film* film distributor. 2 dealer, pusher. *~ narkotika/obat bius* drug dealer.
pengédaran circulating, dealing in, etc.
perédaran 1 circulation. *~ darah* blood circulation. *~ uang* the circulation of money. *~ udara* air circulation, ventilation. *~ usaha* turnover, sales; receipts; → OMSÉT. *kegiatan ~ uang* cash flow. *menarik dari ~* to withdraw s.t. from circulation. 2 rotation, revolving. *~ bumi dan bulan* the revolution of the earth and the moon. 3 orbit (of stars). 4 revolution (of a wheel). *~ dunia* a) the course of the earth. b) the vicissitudes/ups and downs of life. *datanglah ~ zaman* the tide turned, the state of affairs was completely reversed. 5 distribution. berperédaran with ... circulation.

édé (*J*) → IDAH II.

édelwéis the Indonesian variety of this flower, *Anaphalis javanica*.

édi (*joc*) → ÉJAKULASI *dini*.

édisi (*D*) 1 edition, the total number of copies of a book, etc. printed from the same plates, type, etc. and published at about the same time. 2 any of various regular issues of a newspaper. - *Minggu* the Sunday edition. - *pendahuluan* bulldog edition. - *percobaan* trial edition.

mengédisikan to publish, issue.

édit (*E*) **mengédit** to edit. ~ *kembali* to re-edit.

éditan edited.

pengédit editor.

pengéditan editing.

éditing (*E*) editing; → PENGÉDITAN.

éditor (*E*) editor; → PENGÉDIT. – *bahasa* copy editor. – *fiksi* fiction editor (in a publishing house). – *naskah* copy editor. – *pengelola* managing editor. – *sains* science editor.

éditorial (*E*) editorial; → TAJUK *rencana*.

éditorialisasi (*D*) editorialization.

mengéditorialisasi to editorialize.

éditur → ÉDITOR.

édokolonye (*D*) eau-de-Cologne.

édukasi (*D*) education; → PENDIDIKAN.

édukatif and **édukatip** (*D/E*) educative, instructive.

édukator (*E*) educator; → PENDIDIK, AHLI *mendidik*.

é-é I (children's language) doo-doo, faeces.

é-é II (exclamation of warning) watch out, be careful. –, *kalau benar, benar mati sih, lu tangis*. Watch out what you say; if she really dies, you'll cry.

ééé (interjection of amazement) (Oh) my God! –, *anaknya mati ... anaknya mati ... Ayo, lari*. My God, the kids died ... the kids died ... Come on, let's run away.

eem-eem (children's language) delicious, yummy!

éf the name of the letter F.

éfék I (*D/E*) effect, consequence, result. – *biologis* biological effect. – *berantai* chain reaction. – *darab* multiplier effect. – *ékstérnal* externalities. – *fisika* physical effect. – *keracunan* poisonous effect. – *menétés ke bawah* trickle-down effect. – *penenang* calming/tranquillizing effect. – *pengeluaran* spreading effect. – *racun* → ÉFÉK *keracunan*. *menétralisir* – *racun* to detoxify. – *rumah kaca* greenhouse effect. – *régrés(s)i* regressive effect. – *samping(an)* side effect(s). **beréfék sampingan** with/to have side effects. – *tertekan* suppressed effect. – *tétésan ke bawah* trickle-down effect.

éfék II (*D*) securities, stocks, and shares. *Bursa* – Stock Exchange. *Bursa* – *Jakarta* [BEJ] Jakarta Stock Exchange. *Bursa* – *Surabaya* [BES] Surabaya Stock Exchange. – *bersifat tertutup* closed-end fund.

éfékten → ÉFÉK II.

éféktif and **éféktip** (*D/E*) effective.

mengéféktifkan to make s.t. (become) effective.

keéféktifan effectivity, effectiveness.

pengéféktifan (causing) effectiveness, making s.t. effective. ~ *pemantauan* the effectiveness of the monitoring.

éféktifitas, éféktivitas, and **éféktifitét** (*D*) effectivity.

keéféktifitasan effectiveness.

éféminasi (*E*) effeminization.

éféndi (*A*) master (title of address for aristocrats).

éfékten → ÉFÉK II.

éfisién (*E*) efficient; → BERDAYAGUNA. *tidak* – inefficient. ***ketidak-éfisiénan*** inefficiency; → INÉFISIÉNSI.

mengéfisiénkan to make efficient.

keéfisiénan efficiency.

pengéfisiénan making efficient.

éfisiénsi (*E*) efficiency; → KEÉFISIÉNAN, KEBERDAYAGUNAAN.

pengéfisiénsian making effective.

ef-kos (*E J*) of course; → MÉMANG, TENTU *saja*.

éfoni → ÉFONI.

egah glorious; glory, fame; → GAH I, MEGAH.

mengegahkan ~ *diri* to glorify o.s., boast.

égah mengégah to walk with long jerky steps, walk with long steps and to thrust the shoulders forward with each step, wobble (of cyclists).

terégah-égah wobbling (as a stake in a stream).

égal (*D*) smooth, level, even, equal.

égalisasi (*D*) equalization.

égalisator (*D*) equalizer.

égalitas (*D*) smoothness, evenness.

égalitér (*E*) *bersifat* – egalitarian.

egat (*ob*) **mengegatkan** to cut off, carve (meat).

Égéa Aegean. *Laut* – Aegean Sea.

égendom → ÉHENDOM.

égerang → ÉGRANG.

égés-égés (*sl*) rubbing up against e.o.

Égiptologi (*D/E*) Egyptology.

égla (*Jv*) clearly visible (from afar), apparent, noticeable.

mengégla to become visible/clear.

égo (*D/E*) ego.

égois (*D/E*) egoist.

égoisme (*D/E*) egoism.

égoistik (*E*) and **égoistis** (*D*) egoistic.

egol → GOL I.

égol I (*J*) **mengégol** [and **ngégol** (*coq*)] to move/lift with a lever, lever/jack up, raise.

mengégoli (*pl obj*) to pry up, move s.t. with a jerk.

terégol-égol with jerks, jerkily.

égol II (*Jv*) **mengégol** to sway one's hips.

mengégoli to turn one's backside on s.o. and shake it (as an insult).

égol-égolan (*J*) to move one's backside and hips back and forth.

égos (*J/Jv*) **mengégos** to get out of the way, avoid, shun, evade. *Dia tidak bisa* ~. He couldn't get out of the way.

mengégosi to dodge, avoid, evade.

mengégoskan 1 to avoid (a collision with s.t./a subject of conversation), evade. **2** to move s.o. aside. **3** to swing s.t. to and fro. ~ *pantatnya ke kiri dan ke kanan* to swing one's backside from left to right (when walking); → MENGÉGOT.

égosan sidestep, feint, evasion.

égoséntris (*D*) egocentric.

égot (*J*) **mengégot** [and **ngégot** (*coq*)] to walk wobbling one's buttocks (like a duck).

égotisme (*D*) egotism.

EGP [Émangnya Gua Pikirin] (*sl*) What do I care? Who cares?

égrang (*Jv*) stilts; → JANGKUNGAN. *main/naik/berjalan dengan* – to walk on stilts. *permainan* – walking on stilts.

egung → GUNG I, II.

eh and **éh 1** (exclamation of disgust/rejection) ugh. –, *jangan dekat-dekat saya!* Ugh, don't come near me! **2** (exclamation of annoyance at doing s.t. wrong). damn it! –, *salah lagi!* Damn it, another mistake. **3** (particle of self-correction) *Setelah bertengkar ...* –, *bermusyawarah.* After quarreling, uh (I mean) coming to an agreement. **4** (exclamation of amazement/awe) wow!

ehem and **éhem** (*interj*) **1** hem, hum; a cough or clearing the throat made to get s.o.'s attention, etc. **2** cough. *Permén VICKS Pengusir Si* –. VICKS Sucking Candy, the Expeller of the Cough.

éhendom (*D*) fully owned land, property.

ehm 1 whatsis, what-do-you-call-it. *Rupanya, dia sudah punya ...* –. It seems that she already has a ... you know what I mean (a boyfriend). **2** (introduces an aside) eerh, ahem. *Kak Léri yang kécé selangit* (–, *muji biar dimuat nih*) ... Beautiful Lei [eerh, this should be put in (the newspaper)] ... **3** uh-huh, yes; → HE'E. *Mau pergi ke Pekan Raya?* –. Are you going to the Fair? Uh-huh.

éi (exclamation of surprise). –, *itu namanya bikin bodoh kita itu*. Well, that just makes you stupid.

éigen (*D*) /éhen/ *dengan* – *gemakken* with every comfort/convenience.

éigendom /éhendom/ (*D*) → ÉHENDOM.

éit (exclamation used when trying to avoid physical or verbal attack) wait a minute! hold on!

éja (*A*) **mengéja** to spell (a word).

mengéjakan to spell out (to s.o.).

éjaan spelling, orthography. ~ *Républik/Suwandi* the orthography used for Indonesian from 1947 to 1972. ~ *van Ophuysen* the orthography used for Indonesian from 1901 to 1947. ~ *Yang Disempurnakan* [EYD] the Reformed Spelling (introduced on August 16, 1972).

pengéja speller.

pengéjaan spelling out.

éjakulasi (*D*) ejaculation. – *dini* premature ejaculation. – *terputus* coitus interruptus.

beréjakulasi to ejaculate.

ejan → REJAN. **mengejan** [and **ngejan** (*coq*)] to force, strain, press down (of woman in labor, during a bowel movement, etc.).

diejan-ejan (M) far-fetched (idea/solution/comparison); imposed/enforced/forced on, forced (joy).
mengejankan to squeeze s.t. tight.
pengejanan straining (during a bowel movement).
éjawantah (*Jv*) visible, manifest.
    mengéjawantah to realize the form of, take form, become visible (*esp* of deities).
    ngéjawantah *déwa* ~ the creator.
    mengéjawantahi to realize, accomplish.
    mengéjawantahkan to manifest, materialize.
    teréjawantah to be manifested.
    pengéjawantahan 1 manifestation. 2 personification.
éjék mocking, ridiculing, making fun of.
    mengéjék [and **ngéjék** (*coq*)] to mock, ridicule, make fun of, taunt.
    éjék-mengéjék to ridicule e.o.
    mengéjéki [and **ngéjékin** (*J coq*)] to ridicule, make fun of.
    mengéjékkan 1 to mock, make fun of. 2 scornful, mocking.
    éjékan 1 mockery, ridicule, derision. 2 laughing-stock. *gambar* ~ caricature, cartoon. *nama* ~ nickname, sobriquet.
    éjék-éjékan *menjatuhkan* ~ *kepada* to boo, heckle.
    pengéjék mocker, taunter.
    pengéjékan ridiculing, taunt, making fun of.
ejing k.o. game of nine pins/skittles.
ejung → JUNG.
ék I (*D*) **mengék** to calibrate.
ék II (*D*) oak.
ék III (in acronyms) → ÉKONOMI.
éka I (*Skr*) mono-, one.
    keékaan oneness, unity; → KESATUAN. ~ *dan keanékaan* unity and diversity.
éka II [*ékstrém kanan*] extreme right.
ékaba(ha)sa (*Skr neo*) monolingual. *Kamus* – *Bahasa Indonésia* Indonesian Monolingual Dictionary.
ékaba(ha)sawan (*Skr neo*) monolingual person.
Éka Dasa Rudra (*Bal*) the most important ritual of purification and sacrifice, held once every Balinese century. Dedicated to the 11 (= *éka dasa*) sacred directions of the world, it is supposed to restore the harmony between the forces of nature and man.
Éka Dharma Sakti (*Skr neo*) name of the women's organization under the jurisdiction of the Department of Manpower, Resettlement and Cooperatives.
Ékadyasa (*Skr neo*) name of the women's organization under the jurisdiction of the Department of Air Communications.
ékahablur single crystal.
ékalapis monolayer, simplex.
ékamarga (*Skr neo*) one way (traffic). *lalu-lintas* – one-way traffic.
ékamatra (*Skr neo*) one-dimensional.
ékanada (*Skr neo*) monotonous.
Ékaprasetia/Ékaprasetya Pancakarsa (*Skr neo*) The Sole Determination to Implement the Five Desires, i.e., *Pancasila*, Guidelines for Experiencing and Implementing *Pancasila* (Suharto speech in 1978).
ékaristi (*D*) (Roman Catholic) Eucharist.
ékasabda monologue.
ékasama (*Skr neo*) identical.
ékasila (*Skr neo*) monoprinciple, i.e., making *Pancasila* into one principle (1960s).
ékasuku (*Skr neo ling*) monosyllabic.
ékawarna (*Skr neo*) monochromatic.
ékawarsa (*Skr neo*) one year. *polis* – term insurance.
ékbang → ÉKONOMI *dan pembangunan*.
ékbis [ékonomi dan bisnis] economy and business.
éke → IKKE.
ékéh-ékéh (*M*) **terékéh-ékéh** panting.
ékék – *geling* short-tailed magpie, *Cissa thalassina*.
ékér-ékéran (*Jv*) to come to blows; → CAKAR-CAKARAN.
ékho (*D*) echo; → GEMA.
éki [ékstrém kiri] extreme left.
ekik → KIK III.
ékivalén → ÉKUIVALÉN.
ékivalénsi → ÉKUIVALÉNSI.
ékléktik (*E*) eclectic.

ékléktikus (*D*) eclecticist.
ékléktis (*D*) → ÉKLÉKTIK.
ékléktisisme (*D/E*) eclecticism.
éklips (*D/E*) eclipse; → GERHANA.
ékliptika (*D*) pertaining to the ecliptic.
ékliptis (*D*) ecliptic.
éko → ÉKHO.
ékodémografi (*D/E*) ecodemography.
ékolog (*D*) ecologist; → AHLI *ékologi*.
ékologi (*D/E*) ecology.
ékon (*Mal*) → AI-CON. *berékon* air-conditioned.
ékonom (*D*) economist.
ékonométri (*D/E*) econometrics. *ahli* – econometrician, econometrist.
ékonomi (*D/E*) 1 economy. *fakultas* – school of economics. 2 economics. – *berancangan/berencana* planned economy. – *biaya tinggi* high-cost economy. – *campuran* mixed economy. – *kedai* traditional economy of small shops, small profit margins, bargaining, etc. – *kota* urban economics. – *lemah* small-capital economy. – *makro/mikro* macro/micro-economics. – *pasar* market economy. – *pedésaan* rural economy. – *pemerintahan* political economy. – *perusahaan* business economics, industrial economy. – *produktif* productive economy. – *rumah* household finances. – *sihir* voodoo economics. – *terpimpin* guided economy (under President Soekarno). – *terpusat* centralized economy. – *yang tergantung kepada ékspor* export-driven economy.
    berékonomi 1 to make use of one's economic knowledge when doing s.t. 2 to economize, make economies.
    mengékonomikan to economize on s.t.
    keékonomian economic (*mod*).
    pengékonomian economizing. *dengan tujuan* ~ *pemakaian bahasa* with the purpose of economizing on the use of language.
    perékonomian 1 economy. 2 economic affairs.
ékonomis (*D*) economic(al), thrifty, frugal.
    berékonomis to economize, reduce one's expenses.
    mengékonomiskan to make s.t. economical.
    keékonomisan economy, frugality, thrift(iness).
ékonomisasi mengékonomisasi to economize.
ékor I 1 tail (of animals, insects, etc.); → BUNTUT I. *dengan* – *di antara kaki belakang* with one's tail between one's legs. 2 queue, a line/file of persons, etc. waiting to be served; rear, the part of an army, procession, motorcade, etc. farthest away from the front. – *iring-iringan* the rear part of the procession, motorcade, etc. – *kodi* the bottom-most piece of clothing in a pile, i.e., the worst. – *mata* (outer) corner of the eye. *melihat dengan* – *mata* to look sideways (at). – *pipit* spit curl between temple and ear. – *pulau* downstream part of an island. 3 classifier for birds, cattle, and other animals. *se* – *burung* a bird. *belalang dua* – two grasshoppers. *lima puluh* – *ternak* fifty head of cattle. *lima* – *marmot* five guinea pigs. 4a) classifier for children. *anak empat* – *itu* those four kids. b) by extension can be used for s.o. not fully an adult. *Aku satu di antara 11* – *mahasiswa* I was one of these 11 students. 5 part of s.t. that resembles a tail. – *belangkas* a) the king-crab's tail. b) a style of coiffure, a bayonet or hairpin that resembles the king-crab's tail. – *cicak* hair that grows between the ear and cheeks, sideburns. – *kuda* a) pony tail, a style of hairdo; → BUNTUT *kuda*. b) ravels. – *layang-layang* the tail of a kite. – *lipas* (*Mal*) → ÉKOR *cicak*. – *pipi* lower part of the cheek. – *tikus* a) a small round file. b) a rat's tail. 6 result, consequence, aftermath (of the war, etc.) (usually bad); → BUNTUT. *Kejadian itu masih ada –nya*. This event had an aftermath. 7 the last digits in a lottery number; → LOTERÉ *buntut; cp* KEPALA 7, 8.
ékor-ékor aftermath.
berékor 1 with/to have a tail; tailed. *bintang* ~ comet. *lada* ~ cubebs, *Piper cubeba*. *membagi* ~ (*math*) long division. 2 with consequences. ~ *panjang* with/to have a lot of consequences, to result in a great number of problems.
berékor-ékor one after/behind the other, single file; to form a long line, queue up.
mengékor [and **ngékor** (*coq*)] 1 to follow, imitate, copy. 2 to follow closely (from behind), shadow, track, trail, tag along; → MEMBUNTUTI. 3 to be/hang down like a tail.
mengékor-ékor to follow along mindlessly.

mengékori → MENGÉKOR 2.

pengékor follower, pupil; disciple, imitator.

pengékoran 1 following, shadowing, tracking, etc. 2 imitation.

ékor II the first part of many plant and animal names. – angin k.o. herbal plant, k.o. plantain, *Plantago major*. – anjing k.o. bush, *Uraria lagopoides*. – cenderawasih decorative plant, *Phyllanthus alternifolia*. – hangus k.o. herring, *Clupea atricauda*. – keledai a decorative plant, *Sedum morgalianum*. – kucing an herb, chenille plant, *Dysophylla auricularia*. – kuning a) yellow tail, *Caesio erythrogaster*. b) k.o. herbaceous plant, *Utricularia flexuosa*. (ikan) – mérah caesio, *Caesio xanthonotus*. – musang a decorative plant, keeled tassel fern, *Lycopodium carinatum*. – serigala fox tail (a disease of plants). – tikus watermelon plant, *Peperomia sandersii*. – tupai k.o. palm, *Justicia betonica*.

ékor III murai/merbah – gading Asian paradise flycatcher, *Terpsiphone paradisi*.

ékor IV kurang –! (*euph* for) kurang ajar! damn it!

ékornia water hyacinth, *Eichornia crassipes*.

ékosistém (D/E) ecosystem.

ékoték [*ékonomi dan téknis*] economic and technical.

ékrak (*Jv*) trash basket.

ékral (*coq*) → IKRAR.

éks I the name of the letter x.

éks II (D) 1 ex-, former, previous(ly); → BEKAS 3, MANTAN. – *Létkol Untung* ex-Lieutenant Colonel Untung. – *présidén* former president. 2 a has-been. *Dia kan sudah –*. She's a has-been, isn't she? 3 (exported or imported) from. – *impor* imported. *udang – Taiwan* shrimps (exported) from Taiwan. 4 shipped on, coming out of, ex. *30.000 ton beras – K.M. Neptune* ex M. V. Neptune. 5 from, derived/coming out of, resulting from. *30.000 ton beras – pinjaman kepada berbagai negara* 30,000 tons of rice derived from a loan made to various countries. 6 (*leg*) in/by virtue of, under. – *Pasal 5* by virtue of Article 5, under Article 5.

éks. III (*abbr*) [*éksémplar*] copy (of a book/magazine, etc.).

éksais (*Mal*) excise (tax).

éksak (D/E) exact.

éksakta (D) exact sciences, such as physics, biology, and chemistry.

éksaltasi (D) exaltation.

éksamen (D/E) examination; → UJIAN.

mengéksamen to examine, test.

éksaminandus (D) examinee.

éksaminasi (E) examination.

mengéksaminasi to examine, look into.

éksaminator (D) examiner.

ékségésis (D/E) exegesis.

 éksékusi (D) 1 execution (putting to death). 2 enforcement, execution (of a decision/contract).

mengéksékusi to execute.

mengéksékusikan to execute (a decision).

teréksékusi (to be) executed. ~ *mati* to be executed, put to death.

pengéksékusian executing.

éksékutif (D/E) executive (*mod*). *kelas* – executive class (in airplanes). *penumpang kelas* – executive-class passenger. – *muda* junior executive.

ékselénsi (D) his Excellency.

éksém → ÉKSIM.

éksémplar (D) copy (of a book/magazine, etc.).

éksémplifikasi (E) exemplification.

ékséntrik (D/E) eccentric.

keékséntrikan eccentricity.

keékséntrik-ékséntrikan rather eccentric.

éksépsi (*D leg*) objection, exception, demurrer.

éksépsional (E) and éksépsionil (D) exceptional.

éksérsisi (*D mil*) drill.

éksés (D/E) excess.

beréksés to go too far.

éksésif (D/E) excessive.

éksibisi (E) exhibition; → PAMÉRAN.

beréksibisi to exhibit, show.

éksim (E) eczema.

éksindustri the former ... industry. – *kayu gergajian* the former sawn-timber industry.

éksipién (E) exipient.

éksis (E) to exist.

éksisténsi (D) existence.

éksisténsialis (D) existentialist.

éksisténsialisme (D/E) existentialism.

éksisténsiil (D) existential.

éksit (E) 1 exit. 2 to leave/drop out of school.

mengéksitkan to expel, dismiss.

ékskavasi (E) excavation.

éksklamasi (D) exclamation.

éksklusi (D) exclusion.

éksklusif (D/E) exclusive.

seéksklusif as exclusive as.

mengéksklusif to exclude o.s.

mengéksklusifkan to make exclusive.

keéksklusifan exclusiveness, exclusivity.

pengéksklusifan exclusion.

éksklusivisme (D/E) exclusivism.

éksklusivitas (D) exclusivity.

ékskomunikasi (D) excommunication.

mengékskomunikasikan to excommunicate.

ékskrési (D) excretion.

ékskul extracurricular.

ékskursi (D) 1 excursion, outing, trip; → DARMAWISATA. 2 (= berékskursi) to make an excursion.

éksodus (D/E) exodus. *melakukan* – and beréksodus to go on an exodus.

éksogami (D/E) exogamy.

éksogén (D/E) exogenous.

éksotérmis (D) exothermic.

éksotik (E) and éksotis (D) exotic.

éksotisitas (E) exoticism.

éksotisme (D/E) exoticism.

ékspansi (D) expansion. *politik* – policy of expansion, expansionism. – *usaha* business expansion.

berékspansi to expand, carry out an expansion (of territory).

ékspansif (D/E) expansive.

ékspansionis (D/E) expansionist. *politik* – expansionalism.

ékspansionisme (D/E) expansionism.

ékspedisi I (D) 1 forwarding, dispatch; shipping, shipment. 2 forwarding/shipping agency.

mengékspedisikan to forward, dispatch; to ship.

pengékspedisian forwarding, shipping.

ékspedisi II (E) (military/scientific) expedition. – *Kutub Selatan* Antarctic Expedition.

ékspedisi III (*D leg*) copy, duplicate of sentence.

ékspéditor and ékspéditur (D) forwarding/shipping agent.

ékspéktoran (E) expectorant.

ékspénsif (D/E) expensive.

ékspér (D/E) expert; → AHLI, PAKAR.

ékspérimén (D/E) experiment.

berékspérimén (*dengan*) to experiment (on/with).

mengékspériménkan to experience/try out s.t.

ékspériméntal (E) experimental.

ékspériméntasi (E) experimentation.

ékspérimentil (D) experimental.

ékspért → ÉKSPÉR.

ékspértis (E) expertise; → KEPAKARAN.

ékspirasi (D) expiration.

ésplan (E) explant.

éksplisit (D/E) explicit.

mengéksplisitkan to make explicit.

éksploat (*D leg*) writ (of a process server).

éksploatasi → ÉKSPLO(I)TASI. mengéksploatasi(kan) to exploit.

éksploatir → ÉKSPLOITIR.

éksploitasi (D) 1 exploitation, working, running, operating, developing. *biaya/ongkos* – working expenses, operating costs. 2 exploitation, taking unfair advantage of.

mengéksploitasi(kan) 1 to exploit, make the most of, put to good use, develop, exploit for profit, bring into production. 2 to exploit, take advantage of.

pengéksploitasi exploiter.

pengéksploitasian exploiting (for profit), working, using.
éksploitir (D) mengéksploitir to exploit, gain an advantage from.
éksplor (D/E) mengéksplor to explore.
éksplorasi (D) exploration.
    mengéksplorasi to explore.
    pengéksplorasian exploring.
éksplosi (D) explosion.
éksplosif (D/E) explosive.
éksplotasi (D) exploitation.
ékspo (D/E) expo.
éksponén (D/E) 1 representative, s.o. who is an example or sym-
    bol (of s.t.). – Angkatan 66 member of the generation of 66.
    ~ daérah regional notables. 2 (math) exponent.
ékspor (D/E) export. barang-barang – export commodities.
    mengékspor to export.
    mengéksporkan to export (goods).
    pengékspor exporter, exporting (mod). negara-negara ~ min-
    yak oil-exporting nations.
    pengéksporan exportation.
éksportasi (D) exportation.
éksportir (D) exporter.
ékspos (E) expose; → DEDAH.
    mengékspos to expose, reveal.
    pengéksposan exposing, revealing.
éksposé (D/E) exposé; airing.
éksposisi (D) 1 exposition; → PAMÉRAN. 2 exposition, explanation,
    statement; → KETERANGAN.
éksprés (D/E) 1 express; → ÉSPRÉS. keréta api – express/fast train.
    2 special delivery. surat – special-delivery letter.
éksprési (D) expression. muka/wajah – facial expression.
    beréksprési to express o.s. kebébasan ~ freedom of expression.
    mengéksprésikan to express, show.
    teréksprési (to be) expressed.
    pengéksprésian expression (of s.t.), expressing.
éksprésif (D/E) expressive.
    keéksprésifan expressiveness.
éksprésionis (D/E) expressionist.
éksprésionisme (D/E) expressionism.
éksprésionistik (E) and éksprésionistis (D) expressionistic.
ékstase (D) ecstacy, rapture.
ékstasi (E) ecstacy (an illegal drug).
éksténsi (D) extension.
éksténsif (D/E) extensive.
éksténsifikasi (E) extensification.
ékstérior (E) exterior.
ékstérn (E?) 1 external. 2 s.o. connected with, but not living in, an
    institution, extern.
ékstérnalitas (E) externality.
ékstorsi (E) extortion.
ékstra- (D/E) 1 extra-, very. -hémat extra-economical. -sérius ex-
    tremely serious. 2 extra-, beyond, besides, outside. – komptable
    non-budgetary, non-balance sheet. – utarin extrauterine. 3 ex-
    tra, supplementary, additional. gaji – additional salary. pelakon
    – supernumerary (actor). 4 previews, trailer, fragments of
    forthcoming film(s) shown during the main film performance.
ékstraberat extremely difficult.
ékstradisi (D) extradition. perjanjian – extradition agreement.
    mengékstradisi(kan) to extradite. bisa/dapat diékstradisikan
    extraditable.
    pengékstradisian extradition.
ékstra(ber)hati-hati extra-careful, extra-cautious.
ékstrahémat very economical.
ékstrainténsif extra-intensive.
ékstrak I (D/E) extract, essence. kopi – concentrated coffee. –
    ganja hashish. – hati liver extract.
    mengékstrak to extract.
    pengékstrakan extracting.
ékstrak II (D/E) excerpt, quotation.
ékstrakeras very intensive. bekerja – to work very hard. risét – in-
    tensive research.
ékstraketat extremely tight (security).
ékstraksi (D) extraction.

mengékstraksi to extract.
    pengékstrasian extraction.
ékstraktif (E) extractive.
ékstrakurikulér (E) extracurricular.
ékstramarital (E) extramarital.
ékstraméwah very luxurious.
ékstranéi (D) external candidate (who participates in senior high
    school final exams, etc.).
ékstraordinér (D/E) extraordinary.
ékstraparleméntér (D/E) extraparliamentary, nonparty (cabinet).
ékstrapolasi (D) extrapolation.
    mengékstrapolisikan to extrapolate.
ékstrasérius very serious.
ékstrasibuk very busy.
ékstratéritorial (D) extraterritorial. tanah-tanah dengan hak –
    extraterritorial lands.
ékstrauniversitér (E) college-student group organized on the
    basis of a political, religious, or other nonacademic affiliation.
ékstrawaspada extremely on the alert.
ékstrém (D/E) extreme. dalam bentuk –nya in the extreme. –
    kanan [éka] extreme right. – kiri [éki] extreme left. – lainnya
    [éla] other extremes.
    mengékstrémkan to make extreme.
    keékstréman extremism.
ékstrémis (D/E) extremist.
ékstrémisme (D/E) extremism.
ékstrémitas (E) extremity.
ékstrim → ÉKSTRÉM.
ékstrimis → ÉXTREMIS.
ékstrinsik (D/E) extrinsic.
ékstrovér(t) (D/E) extrovert.
ékstrusi (D) extrusion.
éktohormon (D/E) ectohormone.
éktoparasit (D/E) ectoparasite.
éktotérmik (D/E) ectothermic.
ékuator (D/E) equator.
Ékubang(kesra) [Ékonomi, keuangan, pembangunan (dan kesejah-
    teraan rakyat)] Economic, Financial, Development (and Social
    Welfare) (affairs).
ékuilibrium (D) equilibrium.
Ékuin [Ékonomi, keuangan dan industri] Economic, Financial, and
    Industrial (affairs). Ménko – Coordinating Minister for the Eco-
    nomic, Financial, and Industrial Sector.
ékuiti (E) (financial) equity.
ékuivalén (D/E) equivalent.
ékuivalénsi (D) equivalency.
ékuméne (D) ecumenism.
ékuménis (D) ecumenical.
ékwator → ÉKUATOR.
él the name of the letter L.
éla I → ÉLO.
éla II [ékstrém lainnya] other extremes.
élaborasi (D) elaboration.
    mengélaborasi(kan) to elaborate.
elah mengelah to sigh.
    elahan a sigh.
élah(an) (A) tactics, devices; excuse, subterfuge, evasion; → HÉLAT,
    TRIK.
élak say evasively. Entah ya, –nya. Not that I know of, he said eva-
    sively.
    mengélak 1 to dodge, duck, move quickly aside in order to
    avoid/escape s.t. 2 to avoid, escape, keep/get away from doing
    s.t. Dia suka ~ daripada membuat kerja yang susah sedikit.
    He likes to avoid doing difficult jobs.
    mengélak-élak evasive (reply).
    mengélaki (pl obj) to avoid, evade, dodge; → MENGÉLAKKAN 1.
    mengélakkan 1 to shun, avoid, evade, shirk, dodge. tidak dapat
    diélakkan (lagi) inevitable, unavoidable; → tak TERÉLAKKAN. 2
    to shunt to the side. ~ tangannya moving her hand to the side.
    terélakkan avoidable, can be avoided. tak ~ unavoidable, inevi-
    table.
    élakan avoidance.

pengélak dodger. ~ *pajak* tax dodger. ~ *wajib militér* draft dodger.

pengélakan act of shunning, avoidance, disclaiming, shirking.

élan (*D*) élan, vigor, impetuosity.

elang I various species of predatory birds, such as buzzards, eagles, hawks, kestrels, kites, falcons, ospreys, goshawks. – *alap* Meyer's goshawk, *Accipiter meyerianus*. – *belalang* black-thighed falconet, *Microhierax fringillarius*. – *berjambul* crested serpent eagle, *Spilornis cheela*. – *bondol* brahminy kite, *Haliastur indus*. – *cina* pied harrier, *Circus melanoleucus*. – *garis dagu* besra sparrow hawk, *Accipiter virgatus*. – *hindék/kepala putih/ rimba* mountain hawk-eagle, *Spizaëtus cirrhatus*. – *hitam* Indian black eagle, *Ictinaëtus malayensis*. – *jambul (malam)* crested serpent eagle, *Spilornus cheela*. – *jawa* Java eagle, *Spizaëtus bartelsi*. – *kangok* gray-headed fishing eagle, *Ichtyopaga ichtyaëtus*. – *kelabu* gray-faced buzzard eagle, *Butastur indicus*. – *kelabu besar* buzzard, *Buteo buteo*. – *kuik* secretary, crested serpent-eater, *Spilornis cheeta*. – *laut burik* osprey, *Pandion haliaëtus*. – *laut/putih/siput* white-bellied sea eagle, *Haliaeëtus leucogaster*. – *lebah* resident honey buzzard, *Pernis apivorus*. – *malam* bat hawk, *Machaerhamphus alcinus*. – *mérah* brahminy kite, *Haliastur indus intermedius*. – *perut karat* rufous/chestnut-bellied eagle, *Hieraaetus kienerii*. – *rajawali* gray goshawk, *Accipiter soloensis*. – *rinték* gray-faced buzzard, *Butastur indicus*. – *tikus* black-winged/-shouldered kite, *Elanus caeruleus*. – *tiram* osprey, *Pandion haliaetus*. – *tutul* spotted harrier, *Circus assimilis*. – *ular* crested serpent eagle, *Spilornis cheela*.

elang II reference to the joint air maneuvers conducted between Indonesia and another Southeast Asian country. – *Indopura* between Indonesia and Singapore. – *Malindo* between Malaysia and Indonesia. – *Thainésia* between Thailand and Indonesia. – *Seberang* between Indonesia and New Zealand.

élastik (*D/E*) 1 elastic. 2 rubber. 3 a rubber band.

élastis (*D*) elastic, resilient.

   keélastisan elasticity, resilience.

élastisitas and **élastisitét** (*D*) elasticity.

élastomér (*D*) elastomer.

elat → LAT II.

élco /élko/ [eligible couple] eligible couple (for birth control).

élefantiasis (*D/E*) elephantiasis; → UNTUT.

élégan (*D/E*) elegant, stylish; → ANGGUN I.

   seélégan as elegant as.

   mengélégankan to make elegant.

   keéléganan elegance.

élégansi (*D*) elegance.

élégi (*D/E*) elegy.

elek (*J*) reluctant, unwilling, averse.

   elek-elekan reluctantly. *Cepetan sedikit, jangan pakai ~ nanti dimarahi ayah.* Hurry up a little bit, don't hold back or father will scold you.

élék (*Jv*) ugly, bad.

éléktone (*E*) Electone, brand-name for the Yamaha piano or organ.

éléktrifikasi (*D*) electrification.

   mengéléktrifikasi(kan) to electrify.

éléktris (*D*) electric(al); → LISTRIK.

   mengéléktriskan to electrify; → MENGÉLÉKTRIFIKASIKAN.

éléktrisir (*D*) **mengéléktrisir** to electrify; → MENGÉLÉKTRIFIKASIKAN.

éléktro (*D*) electro-, electrical. *insinyur* – electrical engineer. *téknik* – electrical engineering.

éléktroda and **éléktrode** (*D/E*) electrode. – *pentanahan* grounding rod.

   beréléktroda with electrodes.

éléktrodinamika (*D/E*) electrodynamics.

éléktrofisiologis (*D*) electrophysiological.

éléktroforésa (*D*) electrophoresis.

éléktrokardiografi (*D/E*) electrocardiography.

éléktrokardiogram (*D/E*) electrocardiogram.

éléktrokimia (*D*) electrochemistry.

éléktrokusi (*D*) electrocution.

éléktrolisa and **éléktrolisis** (*D*) electrolysis.

éléktrolit (*D/E*) electrolyte.

éléktrolitis (*D*) electrolytic.

éléktromagnét and **éléktromaknét** (*D/E*) electromagnet.

éléktromagnétis and **éléktromaknétis** (*D*) electromagnetic.

éléktromagnétisme and **éléktromaknétisme** (*D/E*) electromagnetism.

éléktrométalurgi (*D/E*) electrometallurgy.

éléktrométer (*D/E*) electrometer.

éléktron (*D/E*) electron.

éléktronik (*E*) electronic.

   mengéléktronikkan to electronify (a musical instrument).

éléktronika electronics. – *daya* power electronics. – *udara* avionics.

éléktroskop (*D/E*) electroscope.

éléktrotéknik (*D/E*) electrotechnics, electrical engineering.

élemén (*D/E*) 1 element; → ANASIR, UNSUR. 2 a device or wire coil that becomes glowing hot (in an electric oven), cell.

éleméntér (*D/E*) elementary.

éléng slanting to one side, rocking (of boat, etc.).

él-én-ji [LNG (Liquefied Natural Gas)] natural gas frozen and compressed into a liquid for shipment in pressurized containers.

élévasi (*D*) elevation.

   berélévasi ... to have an elevation of ...

élévator (*D/E*) elevator; → LIFT. – *timba* bucket elevator.

éliksir (*D/E*) elixir.

éliminasi (*D*) elimination.

   mengéliminasi(kan) to eliminate.

   pengéliminasian eliminating, elimination.

éliminir (*D*) **mengéliminir** to eliminate. ~ *kedwiartian* to disambiguate.

éling (*J/Jv*) 1 to come around/to, regain consciousness, become aware again. 2 to recollect, remember; to think over, reflect, meditate (on), mull (over). – *lan waspodo* (*Jv*) alert and cautious.

élips (*D/E*) ellipse.

élipsis (*D/E*) ellipsis.

élipsoide (*D/E*) ellipsoid.

éliptis (*D*) elliptic(al).

élit (*D/E*) elite. *kawasan* – the fashionable section of town. *pasukan* – elite troops.

   keélitan elitism.

   keélit-élitan elitism; → ÉLITISME.

élite (*E*) → ÉLIT. – *pemimpin* the ruling elite.

élitis (*E*) elitist. *pola hidup* – elitist lifestyle. *sikap* – elitist attitude.

élitisme (*D/E*) elitism.

élmaut (*A*) death; → MAUT.

élmu (*Jv*) → ILMU. – *kanoman* knowledge for use. – *kanuragan* physical knowledge.

elo → LU I.

élo ell, linear measure about 0.688 meters = ca. 45 inches.

   éloan by the ell.

élok 1 good; fine. *cerita yang* – a good story. 2 beautiful, handsome, pretty. *anak yang – parasnya* a good-looking child. – *basa* polite, courteous, correct in behavior. – *budi* of good character. – *buruknya* ... the good and bad aspects of .... – *laku* well-behaved. – *rupa* good-looking.

   éloknya fortunately, luckily, by chance.

   seélok as beautiful/fine/good as.

   seélok-élok as soon as, the minute (s.t. happens) (it is followed by s.t. else). ~ *saja kami keluar, hujan pun turun dengan lebatnya.* The minute we left the house, it began to rain heavily.

   seélok-éloknya the best thing/way, most appropriate thing/way. ~ *uang simpanan anda diinvéstasikan dalam saham.* The best thing would be to invest your savings in stocks.

   mengélokkan and **memperélokkan** to improve (the condition of), make better, beautify.

   keélokan 1 beauty, loveliness, splendor. 2 goodness.

   pengélokan enhancement.

elon I (*J/Jv*) and **kelon** (*Jv*) **mengelon(i)** 1 to lie down with a child to put it to sleep. 2 to rear/bring up/take care of children.

elon II (*J*) → BELUM.

élon (*Jv*) **mengéloni** to favor, foster, promote, encourage, side with, treat with partiality; → KÉLON.

élpiji (the English pronunciation of LPG) liquefied petroleum gas, generally a mixture of propane and butane; → LPG. – *berte-kanan* pressurized LPG. – *campuran* mixed LPG.

ELS [Europése Lagere School] European Elementary School, i.e., during colonial times an elementary school which covered the first seven grades; it was open to both Dutch and native children; the medium of instruction was Dutch.

éltor El Tor (cholera).

elu I mengelu(-elu)kan 1 to crane (one's neck). **2** to welcome/ meet s.o. (at the airport/station, etc.).
  elu-eluan a warm/hearty welcome.
  pengelu(-elu)an act of welcoming, welcome.

elu II mengelu-elu to come in waves, reverberate.

elu III (*J*) → LU I.

eluk → LUK.

elung arc, curve; → LUNG I.

elus (*Jv*) **mengelus(-elus)** [and **ngelus-ngelus** (*J*)] **1** to caress, stroke. **2** to coax, persuade by soothing words. ~ *dada* to hold in one's feelings of anger, etc.
  mengelusi to stroke, make stroking motions on.
  elusan 1 caress. **2** coaxing, flattery.
  pengelusan caressing.

elut mengelut to permit.
  elutan permission.

éluviasi (*E*) eluviation.

éluvium (*E*) eluvium.

em exclamation expressing hesitation. –, *takut aku.* I'm (too) scared (to go, etc.).

ém 1 the name of the letter *m*. **2** (*coq*) menstruation (from the pronunciation of the name of the first letter of *ménstruasi*).

e-mail (*E*) /imél/ e-mail.

émail (*D*) **1** enamel, porcelain glaze. **2** enamel of the teeth.
  mengémail to enamel.

emak mother, mom; → MAK I.

emam (children's language) to eat.

éman (*Jv*) feeling of compassion/pity/regret; it's a pity. *Apakah tidak – melepas jabatan DPRD?* Isn't it too bad to have to give up your position in the DPRD?
  éman-éman regrettable, too bad, it's a pity. *Ah ~ benar, roknya sobék.* Oh, it's too bad her skirt is torn.

émanasi (*D*) emanation.

emang (*S*) uncle (parent's younger brother).

émang (*J coq*) of course, indeed, it is true, no doubt, in (point of) fact, as a matter of fact, certainly, be sure; → MÉMANG. – *benar* it's certainly true.
  émangnya 1 actually, really. **2** do you (really) think that ...? → MÉMANGNYA. ~ *aku ini buta?* Do you think I'm blind?! ~ *gua pikirin* [EGP] What do I care? Who cares?

émansipasi (*D*) **1** emancipation, i.e., the freeing of slaves. **2** similar legal rights (for women as for men).
  berémansipasi to be emancipated. *wanita ~* emancipated women.

émansipatoris (*E*) emancipative.

emas I (*Skr*) **1** gold; → MAS I. *abad* – Golden Age. *arloji/cincin/piala* – a gold watch/ring/cup. *hati* – a heart of gold. *hujan* – laburnum. *kesempatan/peluang* – a golden opportunity. *berkesempatan/berpeluang* – to have a golden opportunity. *tambang* – a) gold mine, i.e., a mine yielding gold. b) goldmine, i.e., a source of wealth or profit. *zaman* – → ABAD *emas*. **2** gold-colored. *pisang* – a sweet, gold-colored, finger-size banana variety. **3** s.t. regarded as having the value of gold. – *cokelat* clove (the spice). – *hijau* vanilla (the fruit). (*si*) – *hitam* petroleum, oil. **4** bribe, payola, kickback; filthy lucre. *kena* – bribed, bought off. **5** (*ob*) a gold coin: 1/10 *tahil. utang – dapat dibayar, utang budi dibawa mati* debts in gold can be paid off, but moral obligations are carried to the grave. *tak – bungkal diasah, tak rotan akar pun jadi* half a loaf is better than none. – *berpeti, kerbau berkandang* possessions have to be kept in their respective places. *menilai mana yang – mana yang loyang* to sift/separate the chaff from the wheat/grain. – *batang(an)* gold ingot. – *bébas* free milling gold. – *belanda* 18-carat gold. – *bersih* pure gold. – *cokelat* cloves. – *galian* gold mixed with stones and liquid. – *hijau* a) cloves. b) vanilla. c) marijuana. – *hitam* petroleum, oil. – *intan/inten* a) jewelry. b) treasure. – *juita* (*poet*) sweetheart, beloved. – *kawin* dowry

(from the groom's side to the bride). – *ker(a)jang/kerancang* a) tinsel. b) tinfoil. – *kertas* gold leaf/foil. – *kimpal* gold nugget. – *kodok* platinum. – *lanar* fine gold like sand found in mud banks. – *lancung* imitation gold. – *lantak(an)* → EMAS *batang*. – *lembaran* gold leaf. – *liplap* → EMAS *lancung*. – *mentah* raw gold. – *mérah* a) gold boiled in sulfur so that it turns light red. b) red onion, *Allium cepa*. – *muda* yellow gold (less than 18 carats). – *murni* pure/24-carat gold. – *padu* a) gold which has been cleaned and formed into nuggets. b) alloyed gold. – *pasir* gold dust/nuggets. – *perada* → EMAS *kertas*. – *pérak* wealth, riches. – *pukal* → EMAS *kimpal*. – *putih* → EMAS *kodok*. – *sepuluh mutu* → EMAS *murni*. – *tambang* gold dug up from a mine. – *tempaan* a) → EMAS *kimpal*. b) words of praise directed toward a beautiful woman. c) → EMAS *juita*. – *tempawan* a) native gold. b) golden girl. – *terupan* scrubbed gold. – *tongkat* low-quality gold. – *tongkol* gold nugget. – *tua* solid gold, high-alloy gold. – *tulén* 24-carat gold. – *urai* → EMAS *pasir*. – *utama* pure/24-carat gold.
  beremas 1 to wear gold ornaments; to have valuable objects, expensive articles, jewelry. **2** wealthy, well-to-do, rich.
  mengemas golden; gold-like, resembling gold; to become/turn golden. *Padi kuning ~.* The rice became golden yellow.
  mengemasi 1 to gild. *jambangan pérak yang diemasi* a silver-gilt vase. **2** to bribe, buy/pay off.
  emas-emasan (*J*) **1** imitation gold. **2** gold-colored louse or insect, parasite of vegetables in the squash family.
  keemasan 1 gilded, gold-plated. *lancang ~* a gold(-plated) boat-shaped receptacle for betel articles. **2** golden. *abad ~* → ABAD *emas*. *masa ~* economic boom. *zaman ~* → ZAMAN *emas*.
  kemasan → KEMASAN (under k).
  peremasan 1 objects made of gold or with a layer of gold, jewelry. **2** gilding.

emas II various forms of address; → MAS II.

emas III *ikan* – carp; → MAS IV.

emas IV *burung* – fiery minivet, *Pericrotus sp.*

emat I (*D*) measurements (of a shirt/coat/pants, etc.). *mengambil* – to measure s.o. (for a shirt, etc.).

emat II (*Pers*) checkmate! (in game of chess).
  mengemat(i) to checkmate.

embacang horse-mango, *Mangifera foetida*. *busuk-busuk* – and – *buruk kulit* from the outside it/he looks bad/stupid but actually it/he is excellent/smart. *menyimpan – busuk* wanting to keep a secret which the public has known for a long time.

embah (*Jv*) **1** grandparent: grandfather or grandmother. **2** (taboo word) reference to the elephant (in Lampung, South Sumatra). – *Jawér* the invisible spirit in charge of the Jatiluhur water reservoir.

embak → MBAK.

embak-embak (*J*) **1** to move up and down (like the wings of a flying bird). **2** to wave, beckon.

embal I (*ob*) damp, humid (not totally dried yet).

embal II (*J*) **ngembal** to rebound (as s.t. elastic); → MEMBAL.

émbalase (*D*) packing.

embalau stick-lac (imported formerly as dye), shellac; resin for fixing hafts.

emban I waistband; breast band; belly band (for horses). – *ékor* band under horse's tail. – *perut kuda* horse's belly band.
  mengemban 1 to carry a child in a shoulder strap or *seléndang* on one's chest. **2** to carry on the back. **3** to carry out (a task/order, etc.) ~ *amanat rakyat* to carry out the people's mandate. ~ *dawuh* to carry out an order. ~ *kewajiban* to devote o.s. selflessly to a task. ~ *tanggung-jawab* to bear/assume the responsibility. ~ *tugas* to devote o.s. selflessly to a task.
  mengembani to assign s.o. the task of carrying out s.t. *Ia diembani tugas itu.* He was assigned that task.
  mengembankan 1 to carry out, execute (for s.o.). **2** to assign, to give s.t. as a task. *Tugas itu diembankan kepadanya.* The task was assigned to him.
  teremban carried.
  pengemban 1 repository. ~ *tunggal* sole repository. **2** guardian, caretaker (of culture). ~ *Ampera* guardian of the Message of the People's Suffering. **3** carrier (of a hereditary disease).
  pengembanan carrying out, execution (of a task).

emban II (*Jv ob*) nurse (for children). *(e)mbok* – female nursemaid.

émbar (*S*) **mengémbarkan** to proclaim, make known, announce.
  émbaran information, data.

embara → KEMBARA. **mengembara** to wander about, roam around, go from place go place.
  mengembarai to roam over/through, rove, wander/travel over. *Ia ~ Indonésia.* He roamed around Indonesia.
  mengembarakan to let s.t. (one's imagination, etc.) wander.
  pengembara wanderer, traveler, explorer, rover. *duta ~* roving ambassador.
  pengembaraan 1 act of traveling, travel, act of roving, etc. **2** place where one wanders/roams, etc. **3** adventure.

embaran(g) and **embarau 1** wooden/stone embankment at the edge of the sea or along a riverbank. **2** piling (of a pier).

émbargo (*D/E*) embargo.
  mengémbargo to embargo.

émbarkasi (*D*) embarkation.

embaru a fibrous shrub, cottonwood, *Hibiscus tiliaceus;* → BARU II.

embat mengembat 1 to lash/whip/thrash with a strip of bamboo, a piece of rope, etc.; → SEBAT I. **2** (*J*) to take, steal. **3** to speed up (a car, etc.). **4** to swallow.
  mengembatkan to use s.t. ... to hit, hit with s.t.
  pengembat s.o. or s.t. that hits.
  pengembatan (*J*) stealing.

embek (*J*) physical condition due to lack of vitamins or food.

embék 1 goat (and other animals belonging to the same family). **2** bleat (*onom*), sound produced by a goat, sheep, etc.
  mengembék to bleat (like a goat, etc.).
  embékan bleating.

émbék → ÉBÉK.

embel I (*J*) to be elastic, be springy. – *embul* to be continuously elastic (as if having springs).

embel II (*J/Jv*) marsh/swamp/morass covered with reed varieties.

embél (*J*) pulled downward (of a tree branch, etc.).
  mengembélkan [and **ngembélin** (*J*)] to pull s.t. downward (of a tree branch).

émbél I mengémbéli to cause to fray or unravel.

émbél II (*J/Jv*) **émbél-émbél** addition, things added, supplement, (unimportant) added details, appendage, unimportant side issue. *tanpa –* unembellished, informal. *upacara singkat tanpa ~* a brief informal ceremony. **mengémbél-émbél** to add a detail. **mengémbél-émbéli** to add an unnecessary detail to. *tidak usah diémbél-émbéli "haji"* unnecessary to add (the title of) "haji." **mengémbéli** to supplement, add a detail to.
  émbél-émbélan 1 small and unimportant details. **2** all needless appurtenances.

émbér I (*D*) pail, bucket.
  seémbér a pailful of.
  berémbér-émbér by the bucketful, bucketsful.

émbér II (*BG*) → ÉMANG.

embes → REMBES.

émbét (*J/Jv*) **keémbét** implicated, involved.

embi (*J*) aunt (wife of an uncle); → EMBIK II.

embih I (*ob*) term used for a female child.

embih II outward appearance.
  seembih outwardly similar.

embik I (*onom*) bleating of a goat; → EMBÉK.
  mengembik to bleat.
  embikan bleating.

embik II → EMBI.

émblém (*D*) emblem.

embok (*Jv*) **1** mother, mom. **2** (*– ayu*) older sister and older (full) niece. **3** polite appellation for a somewhat older respectable woman.

embol mengembol hidden.

émbol (*J*) swelling; lump, bump, bruise (on one's forehead from a knock).
  mengémboli to swell s.t. up, puff out, blow up; to stick s.t. out, protrude.
  terémbol sticking out, protruding.

émboli (*D med*) embolism.

émbosur (*D*) embouchure.

émbrat (*J/Jv*) a large can for watering a garden.

embrek (*J*) **ngembrek 1** unpleasant to look at. **2** to be, stay.

émbrio (*D/E*) embryo.

émbriogénésis (*D/E*) embryogenesis.

émbriologi (*D/E*) embryology.

émbrionik (*E*) and **émbrionis** (*D*) embryonic.

embuai (*cla*) court damsels.

embuh I (*cla*) wish, want, like, yearn for. *hidup segan, mati tak –* reluctant to (work to) live, reluctant to die, i.e., a lazy person.
  mengembuhi to accept, agree to.
  embuh-embuhan although, even though.

embuh II → MBUH.

embuk → HAMA *tebu.*

embun 1 dew; → BUN II. **2** haze, thin mist. **3** condensed vapor. *cabo – (J)* a prostitute who operates in the open air. *kering –* after the dew has evaporated, early morning. *kertas –* blotting paper. *tadah –* the topmost banana in a bunch. *lenyap seperti – kena panas* to disappear like snow in the sun. *seperti – di atas daun* changing all the time (of wishes/intentions). *seperti – di ujung rumput* quickly evaporating (as of love, etc.). *– asap* fine dew like haze in the evening (due to cool temperature). *– beku* frost. *– betina* small drop of dew. *– jantan* large drop of dew. *– kering* about 7 a.m. *– pagi* morning mist/fog. *– rintik* → EMBUN *betina.* *– salju* frost.
  berembun 1 dewy, bedewed, covered with dew, in the dew. **2** to spend the night out in the open. *Ia terpaksa ~ dan beratapkan langit hitam.* He was forced to spend the night out under the dark sky.
  mengembun to condense, turn into dew; dewlike. *Udara yang cukup sejuk akan ~.* Sufficiently cool air will condense.
  mengembuni to wet s.t. drop by drop.
  mengembunkan and **memperembunkan 1** to expose to the dew, bedew. **2** to make s.o. stay out overnight.
  embunan moisture, condensate, condensation.
  keembunan bedewed, covered with dew.
  pengembun condenser.
  pengembunan 1 condensation. *~ bertahap* (*petro*) fractional condensation. **2** fogging. *mencegah ~* to prevent fogging (in cars), defog.

embun-embunan (*Jv*) fontanel.

embung I a small, traditional reservoir for catching rainwater.

embung II (*J*) reluctant, unwilling.

embung III (in Nusa Tenggara Barat) k.o. dam, dike.

embung IV oldest son.

embus I (*ling*) aspirated. *p –* aspirated p; → HEMBUS.
  berembus 1 to blow (of the wind, etc.). *Angin pagi ~.* The morning wind began to blow. **2** to breathe. *Napasnya sudah tak ~ lagi.* He has died.
  mengembus 1 to blow (of the wind). **2** to exhale, breathe. **3** to blow out. *Tolong embus lilin itu.* Please blow out the candle.
  mengembusi to blow/breathe on.
  mengembuskan 1 to breathe, blow out (a candle), puff out (smoke). **2** to exhale. *~ napas (yang) terakhir/penghabisan* to breathe one's last, die.
  embusan 1 bellows. **2** blower. **3** puff. *~ napas* a sigh. **4** (*ling*) aspiration. **5** suggestion.
  pengembus bellows.
  pengembusan exhaling, puffing out.

embus II (*coq*) go away, beat it!
  mengembus (*coq*) to run away, flee.

embut I mengembut-embut and **terembut-embut** to go/rise up and down (like an infant's fontanel, etc.), throb (of the pulse), rise and fall (of the chest of a sleeping person), pulsate.
  embut-embutan to palpitate (of the heart).

embut II edible pith.
  embut-embutan 1 *rambutan* fruit of which the hairy part of the skin has been removed so that only the cuticle or epidermis skin remains. **2** the words uttered when removing such a skin so that (based on superstition) the epidermis skin doesn't break.

emeg and **emek** (*J*) distended (of the stomach) due to having eaten one's fill.

émfiséma (*E*) emphysema.

émigran (*D/E*) emigrant.

émigrasi (*D*) emigration.

　berémigrasi to emigrate.

　mengémigrasikan to cause to emigrate.

　pengémigrasian emigration.

emik (children's language) to drink.

éminén (*D/E*) eminent, well-known; → TERKENAL.

éminénsi (*D*) eminence.

émir (*D from A*) emir.

émirat (*D*) emirate. *Persatuan Arab* – United Arab Emirates, UAE.

emis (*Jv*) → KEMIS. **mengemis** to beg (*esp* on the street), panhandle.

　mengemisi to beg for.

　pengemis beggar (*esp* on the street), panhandler.

　pengemisan begging.

émisi (*D*) 1 (*fin*) emission, issuance (of stocks/shares/paper money, etc.). *penjamin* – underwriter. *– baru* new issue. *– laris* oversubscription. *– lebih* overissue. *– terbatas* private offering. 2 emission (of a gas/semen, etc.).

émitén (*bank D*) banker, issuer.

émiter (*D*) one who issues a stock, issuer.

emoh (*Jv*) unwilling (to do s.t.), not want (to do s.t.); → MOH. *Dia – ikut.* He didn't want to go along.

　mengemohi to refuse/reject s.t., not want s.t. *Pil itu diemohi.* Those pills have been rejected.

émok (*S*) the gracious way for a woman to sit; on the floor with the upper part of the body resting on the arm, the legs somewhat bent and then stretched sideward; → SIMPUH I.

emol mengemol 1 to annoy s.o. 2 to behave in an improper way.

émolumén (*D*) emolument, perquisite.

emong (*Jv*) **mengemong** to take care of/bring up (children); → AMONG, MOMONG, MONG, PAMONG (PRAJA).

　emongan s.t. taken care of.

émosi (*D/E*) 1 emotion. 2 emotional, full of emotion, upset.

　berémosi 1 emotional. 2 to have strong feelings.

émosional (*E*) and **émosionil** (*D*) emotional.

émosionalisme (*E*) emotionalism.

empak (*J*) broken off (of a branch).

empal (*J/Jv*) meat sliced about one-half inch thick, seasoned and then fried in oil. *– gentong* Cirebon specialty made from beef parts. *– gepuk* beef fried in this way.

　perempalan pruning.

empan I (*Jv*) *– papan* a) (to act) with discretion (considering to whom and where one is speaking). b) the appropriate circumstances, the right time and place.

empan II (*J*) to eat.

　mengempani [and **ngempanin** (*J*)] to feed.

　empanan food.

empan III (*J*) → UMPAN.

empang 1 dam/dike/dune/sand hill to contain water. 2 (saltwater, embanked) fishpond near the shore where certain sea fish, such as *bandeng*, are cultivated, aquaculture pond. 3 a dike or dam for regulating the flow of water. 4 ornamental garden pond. *– sampai ke seberang, dinding sampai ke langit* can no longer be settled (of a conflict); permanently not want to reconcile; cannot be softened (of a regulation). *– KA* railroad crossing barrier.

　mengempang 1 to block the flow of (water), dam up. 2 to stretch right across, put across; to thwart, impede, intersect, obstruct. 3 to stop, check, block.

　terempang stopped, barred, blocked. *tiada ~ peluru oléh lalang* the desires of a man in power cannot be contained by the weak.

　empangan 1 fish-pond. 2 dam. 3 barrier.

　pengempang dam. *~ air* sluice. *~ minyak* (*petro*) containment boom.

　pengempangan damming, obstructing, blocking, barring.

émpang (*Jv*) (man-made) fishpond.

empap (*M*) 1 to dash down; throw away; fling. 2 to gamble by throwing up a coin, flip a coin. *pergi –, pulang emban* to make no profit, come out even, be a wash.

　berempap to flip a coin.

　mengempap 1 to put s.t. on top, press/weigh down on, crush. *Ular itu tidak akan lekas mati, kalau tidak diempap dengan batu.* The snake won't die quickly if it isn't crushed with a stone.

2 to strike/hit/beat, etc. with a wide, thin, and flat object. *~ ikan dengan daun dayung* to hit a fish with the flat side of an oar.

　mengempapkan 1 to dump/slam down (s.t. heavy), throw, dash, fling. *Dia mengangkat peti itu kemudian ~nya ke tanah.* He lifted the case and slammed it down on the ground. *~ badan ke kasur* to throw o.s. down on the bed. 2 to strike, etc. with s.t. wide and flat. *~ telapak tangan* to strike with the palm of the hand.

　terempap fallen face down.

　pengempapan curing (of vanilla beans).

émpar centrifugal.

　mengémpar to be off course, drift from its course (of a ship); to be derailed. *berjalan ~* to walk in a splay-footed way.

　terémpar 1 (of a ship) drifted (off), make leeway. 2 leaning to the outside.

　pengémpar centrifuge.

empas I → HEMPAS. **mengempas** 1 to throw/fling/dash down. 2 to slam (the door/window, etc.). *Wiratno ~ pintu kamarnya.* Wiratno slammed the door to her room. 3 to wreak (one's fury) on, vent (one's rage) on. 4 (of waves against rocks) to pound, beat on. *Ombak ~ pantai dengan keras.* Waves pounded wildly on the shore.

　mengempaskan 1 to toss (s.t. against s.t.). 2 to slam (the door). *~ diri* a) to throw o.s. down (with grief/joy, etc.). b) to toss (around).

　terempas 1 thrown, flung, hurled (as waves or boat against cliffs). 2 thrown down.

　empasan 1 breakers, surf. *tempat ~ ombak* breakwater. 2 the rolling (of waves). *~ balik* backwash. *~ gelombang* breakers.

empas II refuse (of coconut/tapioca), dregs; → AMPAS.

empas-empis I (*J*) to breathe slowly and with great difficulty (of a dying person); to breathe one's last, be at one's last gasp. *perusahaan yang ~* a dying business.

empas-empis II empty; emptied.

empat four. *jam –* four o'clock. *– jam* four hours. *rencana – tahun* four-year plan. *segi –* quadrangle. *silang –* intersection. *simpang –* where four roads cross. *tengah –* three and a half. *– belas* fourteen. *– beranak* parents and two children. *– bersaudara* o.s. and three siblings. *– besar* the four powerful nations (U.S., USSR, China, Japan); the four important persons; the four big water reservoirs (in the Bengawan Solo project). *– dasawarsa* 40th anniversary. *-likur* (*Jv ob*) twenty-four. *– lima hari* four or five days. *– macan kecil Asia* Hong Kong, Taiwan, South Korea, and Singapore. *– mata* face to face, privately. *– penjuru alam* the four points of the compass. *– (per)segi* square. *– persegi panjang* rectangle. *– pihak* a) a quadrilateral temporary administration. b) quadripartite, quadrilateral, four-part. *– puluh* forty. **mengempat puluh** *hari* to honor the deceased with a ceremony held on the 40th day after the death. *– satu* card game similar to black jack. *– sekawan/serangkai* group of four, quadrumvirate. *– suara* in four-part harmony. *– tak* four cycle. *– tepas dunia* the four corners of the world.

　empat-empat by/in fours. *Murid itu berjéjér ~.* The pupils sat in rows of fours. *~nya* all four of them. **berempat-empat** by/in fours, (to line up) in rows of four.

　berempat to be four, make four in all. *kita/meréka ~* the four of us/them.

　memperempat to divide into four equal parts.

　keempat 1 the set of four. *~ buku ini* these four books. *~ meréka itu* the four of them. 2 fourth. *yang ~* the fourth (in a series). *untuk ~ kalinya* for the fourth time.

　keempat-empat all four. *~nya* all four (of a group of four), all four of them. *Anaknya ~nya jadi dokter.* All four of his children are doctors.

　perempat quarter, fourth. **seperempat** a quarter. *~ jam* a quarter of an hour. *jam/pukul lima kurang ~* a quarter to five.

　perempatan 1 intersection, crossroads. 2 a fourth.

émpati (*D/E*) empathy.

empé ngempé to attract attention.

émpé → PÉMPÉK.

empedal gizzard → REMPELA.

empedu gall, bile. *batu –* gallstone. *kandung/pundi-pundi –*

gallbladder. *bagai – lekat di hati* most intimate, inseparable (of friends/lovers). *susu dibalas* – to bite the hand that feeds you. *– ayam* chicken gall (a folk cure for malaria). *– beruang* k.o. tree, *Brucea amarissima*.

empé-empé → EMPÉK-EMPÉK I.

empék (*C J*) father; → BAPAK.

empék-(empék) I (*C J*) 1 old Chinese man. 2 appellation for old Chinese man.

empék-empék II a Palembang, South Sumatra delicacy, k.o. fishcake.

empela → EMPEDAL.

empelai (*ob*) → MEMPELAI.

empelas 1 k.o. trees, *Ficus ampelas/Tetracera indica* whose leaves are used for scouring or polishing. *– putih* stone leaf, *Tetracera scandens*; → MEMPELAS. 2 (*kertas –*) sandpaper; → AMPLAS I.

berempelas scoured, already smoothed.

mengempelas(i) to scour/scrub with sandpaper.

pengempelas abrasive, scourer.

émpelop → AMPLOP.

empelur pulp. *– gigi* inside of tooth containing nerves.

empénak (*ob*) *bujuk* – persuasion and sweet-talk.

mengempénak to spoil, pamper, pet.

empéng (*Jv*) pacifier, teething ring.

mengempéng [and **ngempéng** (*coq*)] to nurse, suckle.

ngempéngan (*J*) 1 to chew on a pacifier. 2 to suck on the nipple of a woman's breast which is no longer producing milk. 3 to suckle another woman's child. 4 to still be dependent on one's parents.

empéngan *anak ~* suckling.

émpér (*Jv*) 1 verandah, porch, piazza; → SERAMBI. 2 covered verandah to house or *pendapa/pendopo* (a roof extension of the main or center roof), k.o. penthouse.

ngémpér (*J*) 1 to make an *émpér*. 2 to live in s.o.'s *émpér*.

émpéran 1 → ÉMPÉR. 2 doorway (of a store/movie house, etc.).

empet I (*J*) to feel annoyed; → DONGKOL I, JÉNGKÉL, KESAL.

ngempet to feel annoyed.

empet II → EMPÉT II.

empét I (*S*) the fixed mouthpiece of a flute or trumpet.

empét-empét paper trumpet, balloon with a whistle.

empét-empétan (*J*) a trumpet made of paper.

empét II **empét-empétan** (*J/Jv*) crowded, jammed; jostling e.o.

empeyak (*J*) outbuilding, outhouse, annex (attached to the main building).

ngempeyakin to construct such a house.

empéyék cracker made with dried fish, etc. and fried with rice flour.

empik (*ob*) **mengempik** to have a strong desire for s.t.

emping I a crisp chip resembling a potato chip, made from young rice plants, pounded flat, dried and fried or (= *– mlinjo*) made from the meat of the seed of old *mlinjo, Gnetum gnemon. sudah biasa makan* – has had lots of experiences. *– balado* dish of hot and spicy *emping. – berantah* said of s.o. who is invulnerable to sharp objects. *– tersérak hari hujan* said about s.o. who is unlucky in business.

memperemping and **mengemping** to make s.t. into *emping*.

emping II *– teki* → RUMPUT *teki*.

émpirik (*E*) and **émpiris** (*D*) empirical.

émpirisme (*E*) empiricism.

empis → EMPAS-EMPIS.

émplasemén (*D mil*) 1 emplacement (of gun). 2 railway yard. *– langsir* marshalling/shunting yard, siding.

emplek (*J*) **ngemplekin** to dump/slam down.

emplék I (*S*) classifier for pieces, parts, fragments, sheets.

emplék II (*Jv*) sheet, layer.

émplék (*Jv*) *– wedang kopi* canvas-roofed roadside stall which sells hot coffee.

émplék(-émplék) (*Jv*) a sloping roof extending out from a wall or building. *– dari bambu* such a roof made of bamboo.

emplep (*J*) **ngemplepin** to prevent exposure to the sun or to air.

keemplep not exposed to the sun or to the air, closed up.

emplok (*J*) a mango or *embacang* seed (usually after the pulp has been eaten).

émplop → AMPLOP.

empo (*C?*) **mengempo** to carry on the waist/hip.

émpoh overflow (of a river, etc.), flood → BAH II, BANJIR.

mengémpoh(i) to flood, inundate.

keémpohan flooded, inundated.

pengémpohan flooding, submersion, inundation.

empok (*J*) 1 older sister. 2 title for lower-class women from Jakarta.

empok-empok lower-class women from Jakarta; *cp* ABANG-ABANG.

empol (*J*) tree trunk; → BATANG.

empon-empon (*Jv*) (medicinal) tubers or roots, such as *kunyit, jahé*, etc.

émpong cluster (of fruit).

émporium (*E*) emporium.

empos I **mengempos** [and **ngempos** (*coq*)] 1 to ripen fruit artificially; fruit are put into a barrel provided with a small opening and then the mass of fruit is covered with leaves and carbide smoke is introduced into the opening. 2 (*J*) to exterminate rodents by smoking them out of their holes.

mengemposi 1 to breathe on. 2 to suggest. 3 to infuse ... into. 4 to instigate.

emposan 1 the way fruit are ripened. 2 artificially ripened fruit. *mangga ~* artificially ripened mangos. 3 the opening in the barrel described above. *~ tikus* smoking rodents out of their holes.

pengempos s.t. used to smoke (rodents out of their holes).

pengemposan smoking (rodents out of their holes).

empos II (*J*) **mengempos** [and **ngempos** (*coq*)] 1 to deflate, let out (air/gas, etc.) (from a container, etc.). 2 to leak. 3 to fart.

empot I k.o. marine plant (that is believed capable of making a woman regain her youth).

empot II *– ayam* squeezing tight, contractions.

empot-empotan (*J*) 1 to be out of breath, breathless, winded. 2 to palpitate, beat, throb (of the heart); → BERDEBAR-DEBAR. *Hatinya ~ menunggukan istrinya yang sedang mau melahirkan*. His heart was throbbing waiting for his wife to give birth. 3 to tire o.s., overwork o.s.; → MEMBANTING *tulang*. 4 contracting, squeezing tight (of the vagina/anal passage). 5 impatient, restless.

émprak (*Jv*) k.o. Arabian music accompanied by dancing.

empu I (*Old Jv*) 1 appellation for: master, chief, ruler, poet, man of letters, philologist, linguist, craftsman; → MPU. 2 armorer. O, *– ngku!* O, my lord! *– Sindok* King Sindok, i.e., the first ruler of East Java. *– Panuluh, – Prapanca*, and *– Sedah* all well-known men of letters of previous centuries. *– Gandring* craftsman or maker of krises under Ken Arok. *kelas –* master, world-class. *sang – berambut putih* the gray eminence, i.e., a name for the author Prof. Dr. Sutan Takdir Alisjahbana. *– pembuat topéng* master mask maker.

mengempu 1 to honor, respect, revere. *~ orang-orang tua itu* to honor the elders. 2 to bring up, raise; to act as a guide to (an apprentice). *Ia ~ kami supaya menjadi orang bermanfaat*. He brought us up to be useful persons.

mengempukan to consider/acknowledge s.o. as a master craftsman. *Empu itu mungkin seniman, mungkin juga diempukan karena kesenimannya*. That craftsman is possibly an artist; it's also possible that he is considered a master craftsman because of his artistic ability.

keempuan 1 mastership, craftsmanship. 2 being a master craftsman.

empu II the main tuber or bulb or a tuberous or bulbous plant. *– kunyit* the main tuber of the turmeric, *Curcuma domestica. – jari* thumb. *– kaki* big toe. *– tangan* thumb.

empuan (*cla*) lady (= *perempuan*) in titles. *(t)engku* – appellation for a queen/*raja*'s spouse; → PEREMPUAN. *datuk* – appellation for a *datuk*'s spouse.

empuh overflowing, flooded.

Empu Jaya name of a train running between Jakarta and Lempuyang.

empuk 1 soft, not hard. *duduk di kursi yang –* to sit in a soft chair. *pendaratan –* a soft landing (of aircraft). 2 not tough (of meat), tender. 3 fine, delicate (in texture), not hard, not shriveled up. 4 soft from repeated use, well-worn. *Kain itu sudah –.* That cloth is soft. 5 soft and pleasant (of one's voice). 6 simple, easy. *cara paling – untuk* ... the easiest way to ... 7 easy to defeat or trick. *sasaran –* an easy target (for criminals).

seempuk as soft/tender as.

mengempukkan to soften, tenderize (meat).

terempuk the softest.

keempukan softness.

pengempuk 1 softener, tenderizer. ~ *daging* meat tenderizer. **2** padding, stuffing.

pengempukan softening, tenderizing.

empul (*ob*) **mengempul** to drift about due to strong winds or currents (of boats).

empulur pith or soft core of palm trees; → EMPELUR.

mengempulur to discard the pith.

empung-empung (*J*) to take/make use of the opportunity; → MUMPUNG.

empunya 1 (*cla*) the/its owner; → EMPU I, PUNYA. **2** to have, possess, own. *si – kemalangan* the unlucky person. *yang –* a) the owner. b) the haves. *yang – cerit(er)a* the narrator. *Dia yang – rumah.* He is the owner of the house. *yang tak –* the have-nots. *si – the* owner. *si – cerita* the storyteller.

mengempunyai → MEMPUNYAI.

empus → EMBUS I, EMPOS I.

empyak → EMPEYAK.

émrat (*J*) → ÉMBRAT.

ému (*D/E*) emu.

émulasi (*D*) emulation.

émulsi (*D*) emulsion.

mengémulsi(kan) to emulsify.

pengémulsian emulsifying.

émulsifikasi (*D*) emulsification.

emut (*Jv*) putting s.t. in the mouth so as to suck on it (for instance, by toothless persons/babies, etc.).

mengemut [and **ngemut** (*coq*)] to put s.t. in the mouth so as to suck on it; → MUT-MUTAN.

én I (*D*) and. *potlot, pulpén, bolpoin, – karét penghapus* pencils, pens, ballpoints, and erasers. *– toh* and yet. *beruang – toh tidak berbahagia* rich and yet (in spite of it) not happy.

én II the name of the letter *n*.

énak (*Jv*) **1** delicious, tasty, appetizing, savory. *Makanan ini – rasanya.* This food is delicious. **2** good, enjoyable, desirable, pleasant, happy. *kehidupan yang –* the good life. *cuma/hanya tahu – sendiri saja* from selfish motives, selfishly. *– ya* a) it feels good (e.g., stretching the muscles). b) (sarcastic, to s.o. who didn't show up for work) taking it easy, huh? *nggak – dilihat orang* it won't be good/nice for others to see. **3** pleasing to the senses *esp* smell. *bau yang tidak –* an unpleasant odor. **4** healthy, well, in good health. *tidak – badan* not in good shape (physically), not feeling well. *Badannya kurang –.* He doesn't feel too good. **5** refreshed. *Badan terasa –.* One feels refreshed (after a shower). **6** deep, profound, sound (of sleep). *tidur – to* sleep soundly. **7** pleasing, comfortable, at ease, relaxed. *tempat duduk kurang –* an uncomfortable chair. *– dibaca* easy reading. *tidak – hatinya* a) uncomfortable, not relaxed. b) worried, anxious, restless. **8** spicy, peppery, piquant; → GURIH. *– hati* (*usu* with a negative) *tidak – hati* unhappy, displeased. *– kepénak* (*Jv*) comfortable, pleasing, pleasant, gratifying, easygoing. *sikap – kepénak* an easygoing attitude. *tidak – unpleasant.*

ketidak-énakan discomfort, displeasure, irritation.

énaknya 1 it is advisable, better, the easy/best way to do s.t. is to. *Tidak ada bis di sini, ~ berjalan saja.* There's no bus here; we'd better walk. **2** the good thing about it is. *~ meréka membayar dengan dolar Amérika.* The good thing was that they paid in U.S. dollars. **3** the pleasure/convenience of. *~ memiliki lemari és LG* the convenience of owning an LG refrigerator.

énak-énak (*coq*) **1** comfortably, undisturbed, relaxed, at one's ease. *pada waktu saya ~ rebah-rebah* when I was lying down comfortably. **2** sound (asleep). *~ tidur* to sleep soundly. **3** to enjoy o.s., take it easy. *Meréka ~ saja, sedangkan teman-teman sibuk bekerja.* They were just taking it easy while their friends were busy working. *– pahit* to have its ups and downs.

seénak as nice as, equally pleasant/tasty, etc. *~ perut* whatever (you) feel like (without considering others). *dengan ~ udel(nya)* (*Jv*) in whatever way I find pleasant; to my heart's content.

seénak(-énak)nya (with positive connotations) when it's conve-

nient, make o.s. comfortable; (with negative connotations) as one pleases, just the way one feels like, at will, to take one's time (about doing s.t.), do s.t. carelessly, act inconsiderately. *~ lho orang Yogya jalannya.* Yogya people walk just as they like. *Datanglah ~.* Come whenever it's convenient. *duduk ~* to make o.s. at home.

berénak-énak to do s.t. with pleasure, enjoy doing s.t., have the leisure to do s.t., do s.t. to one's heart's content. *Jangan ~ tidur.* Don't sleep to your heart's content.

mengénakkan [and **ngénakin** (*J coq*)] **1** to make s.t. agreeable/pleasant/comfortable. *Énakkan dudukmu.* Make yourself comfortable in the chair. **2** to inspire, encourage, reassure; reassuring. *Pernyataan itu tidak ~.* That statement is not reassuring. **3** agreeable, pleasant.

mengénak-énakkan mouthwatering.

memperénak to make s.t. more agreeable/pleasant. *Ia ~ letak duduknya.* He made himself more comfortable in his chair.

terénak most delicious, tastiest, etc.

énakan 1 recuperating, recovering, feeling/getting better (after an illness). *Saya merasa ~.* I'm feeling better. **2** preferably, better, a good idea. *~ tinggal di rumah sakit saja.* It would be better just to stay in the hospital. **3** (*coq*) to feel at ease/comfortable. *Aku pemalu, enggak ~ sama orang.* I'm shy and don't feel comfortable around people.

énak-énakan (*coq*) **1** to relax, take it easy. **2** spicy. **3** delicacies.

keénakan 1 ease, comfort, happiness, pleasure, delight, satisfaction. **2** (*J*) with pleasure. *Saya merintih ~.* I moaned with pleasure. **3** to get pleasure/satisfaction from, be pleased/happy to, it feels good to; to be engrossed in doing s.t. *~ ya, dibébaskan dari tugasmu.* You must be pleased to be relieved of your duties. *Kita ~ ngobrol jadi lupa waktu.* We were so engrossed in our conversation that we forgot the time. **4** to do as one pleases, do whatever one likes.

enal → NAL I.

enam six. *jam –* six o'clock. *– jam* six hours. *-belas* sixteen. *– likur* (*Jv*) twenty-six. *– puluh* sixty.

enam-enam by sixes, in groups of six. **berenam-enam** by/in sixes, (to line up) in rows of sixes.

berenam to make six, six in all. *kita ~ the/all six of us.

keenam 1 the set of six. *~ majalah ini* these six magazines. **2** sixth. *yang ~ the* sixth (in a series). *untuk ~ kalinya* for the sixth time. **sekeenam** one sixth.

keenam(-enam)nya all six (of a set of six).

perenam sixth part. **seperenam** one sixth.

enap I → ENDAP I. *tanah –* firm alluvial deposit.

mengenap to settle (of soil).

enapan sediment, deposit.

enap II (*M*) silent, quiet; → DIAM I.

mengenap-enap(kan) to think over thoroughly, consider carefully, examine in great detail.

enau sugar palm, *Arenga pinnata/saccharifera*; → ARÉN, KABUNG III. the flower stalk of the palm yields a liquid which can be made into brown sugar, palm wine, etc. *– mencari/memanjat sigai* refers to a woman looking for a man. *mati – tinggal di rimba* when an unimportant person dies, nobody talks about him again. *Bukan sigai yang menampar –, tetapi – yang menampar sigai.* It is not the man who seduces the woman but the woman who seduces the man. *– sebatang dua sigainya* refers to a woman with two husbands.

encang I mengencang to step on s.t. unintentionally. *Ia ~ beling sehingga kakinya berdarah.* He stepped on broken glass so that his foot bled.

encang II mengencang to strike s.t. hard with a hammer, smash.

encang III (*J*) older sibling of father or mother; older first cousin of father or mother.

encéh (*Jv*) glazed Chinese jar (for soy sauce, etc.).

encék (*J*) **1** an adult Chinese man. **2** term of address for such a man. **3** a full-blooded Chinese; → SINGKÉH. **4** father's younger brother.

encék-encék full-blooded Chinese.

encék (*Jv*) winnow of bamboo wickerwork (covered with a piece of white cloth, for offerings).

encél beréncél-éncél by turns, in turn, alternately; → BERSELANG-SELANG.

énceng → ÉCÉNG.

éncér (*J/Jv*) **1** weak, diluted, thin. *kopi/téh* – weak coffee/tea. *susu* – thin (diluted) milk. **2** watery (of porridge, etc.), not viscous enough. **3** liquefied, dissolved. **4** (*coq*) quick, prompt to understand/learn, bright, perceptive, smart. – *pikirannya/otaknya* he is smart. **5** (*coq*) trivial, unimportant. *Ia mengganggap* – *penentangnya*. He did not take his opponents seriously. – *suai* diluted. *pengéncér-suaian* (*petro*) cut-back.

mengéncérkan to liquefy, dilute, weaken, thin.

memperéncér to make s.t. thinner/more dilute.

éncéran 1 diluting, thinning down (of a color). **2** liquid that results from a dilution.

keéncéran 1 too weak/thin/watery, etc. **2** diluteness, thinness. ~ *otak* intelligence.

pengéncér 1 thinner. *bahan* ~ (paint) thinner. **2** (*petro*) flux.

pengéncéran dilution, diluting, thinning.

encik 1 form of address to respectable or unknown people; title before a name, if the title is not *Datuk* or *Tengku*. – *Ali dengan istrinya* – *Maimunah* Mr. Ali and his wife Mrs. Maimunah. **2** – *laki-laki* host. – *perempuan* hostess. **3** (in West Sumatra) title for female schoolteachers; *cp* ENGKU. **4** (*J*) → ENCÉK.

berencik to use *encik* when talking to s.o. *Hamid bila berbicara dengan saya selalu* ~. Hamid always uses *encik* when talking to me.

memperencik to call s.o. *encik*.

encim (*C J*) **1** a married Chinese woman. **2** term of address for such a woman. **3** term of address for a Chinese store owner's wife. **4** term of address for father's younger brother's wife.

encing (*C J*) father's or mother's younger sibling; father's or mother's younger first cousin.

encit I (*C*) cotton print, chintz.

encit II (*J*) **mengencit(kan)** and **ngencit(in)** to wipe s.t. with a cloth.

encling → KUDA *képang*.

éncok (*Jv*) arthritis, inflammation/stiffening of a joint, gout, rheumatism, lumbago, rheumatic pain in the lumbar region. *kena* – to suffer from rheumatism.

éncot (*J*) lame, crippled.

encrit I (*J/Jv*) **seencrit** a little (bit), a bit, some; → SEDIKIT.

seencrit-encritné only that much. *Duit tinggal* ~. Only that much money was left.

encrit II (*J*) **ngencrit** to make/defecate in one's pants; → KECEPIRIT.

enda (*J*) **ngendain** to pay attention to, care about, be concerned with; to listen to. *Anaknya tidak* ~ *saya sama sekali*. His child didn't pay any attention to me. *Anda harus* ~ *petuah ortu*. You have to listen to your parents' advice.

éndah (*ob*) → INDAH I.

endak I (the clipped form of **hendak**) to desire, wish, want.

endak II (*Jv*) no, not; → NDAK I.

endak III → GENDAK.

endal mengendal 1 to cram, stuff; → MENJEJAL. **2** elastic, resilient, springy; → MENGANJAL.

endam → HENDAM, ANDAM II.

éndang (*cla*) **1** (*Hind*) nun. **2** wife or daughter of a Hindu ascetic.

endap I – *tuang* pour out after settling. *mengendap-tuangkan* to pour out the excess liquid after the solid has settled at the bottom of the container.

endap-endap sediment, dregs. ~ *darah* blood precipitate.

mengendap 1 to settle, precipitate. **2** to remain/stay (where they are and not be used); to be present in s.t. ~ *di gudang* (the goods) remained in the warehouse. *kemanisan yang* ~ *pada air tapé* the sweetness that is present in fermented cassava water. ~ *di rékening* to stay (of funds) in an account (and not be withdrawn).

mengendapi to settle at/in.

mengendapkan to allow s.t. to precipitate/settle.

terendap 1 settled, precipitated. **2** deposited.

endapan 1 sediment. **2** fall-out. **3** (mineral) deposit. ~ *cebakan* mineral deposit.

endap-endapan (also → ENDAPAN) sedimentation, precipitation; fallout. ~ *darah* blood precipitation. ~ *kopi* coffee grounds. ~ *lumpur* mud deposit. ~ *radioaktif* radioactive fallout; → JATUHAN *radioaktif*.

pengendap 1 clarifier. *instalasi* ~ clarification plant. **2** sump (*mod*).

pengendapan sedimentation, settling. *bak* ~ sedimentation vessel.

endap II endap-endap main ~ to play hide-and-go-seek.

berendap(-endap) and **mengendap(-endap) 1** to bend, stoop. **2** to creep, crawl. **3** to approach in a crouching position, spy on, lie in ambush for. *secara berendap-endap* secretly, in secret.

mengendap-endap *berjalan/menyelinap* ~ to stalk, steal up on s.o., bend over to watch.

mengendapkan 1 to bend s.t. down. ~ *badan* to avoid being noticed by lowering o.s. to a crouching position. **2** to embezzle, steal (money). **3** to conceal, not notify the authorities about, etc.

terendap put away in a secret place, hidden.

terendap-endap → MENGENDAP-ENDAP.

endas I (*Jv*) head (of the human body).

endas II mengendas to put s.t. on the chopping block.

endasan chopping-block; → LANDASAN.

endasemenda (*M ob*) several family relations by marriage (to a matrilineal tribe); → SEMENDA.

éndémi (*D*) endemic (the noun).

éndémis (*D*) endemic. *daérah* – *malaria* an area in which malaria is endemic.

éndér (*S*) fennel, *Foeniculum vulgare*; → ADAS.

énderia sense organs; → INDERIA.

endilau k.o. tree that is useful for reforestation, brown kurrajong, *Commersonia bartramia*.

endog → ENDOK.

éndogami (*D/E*) endogamy.

éndogén (*D*) endogenous.

endok (*Jv*) egg.

éndokardinologi (*D/E*) endocardinology.

éndokarditis (*D/E*) endocarditis.

éndokrin (*D/E*) endocrine. *ahli* – endocrinologist.

éndokrinologi (*D/E*) endocrinology.

endon (*J/Jv*) **ngendon 1** to go to another place and stay there for some time. **2** to play soccer, etc. away from home.

(e)ndonan *orang* ~ a) a visitor from another region; s.o. who is not a local. b) s.o. who sleeps at s.o. else's house.

pengendonan visiting.

éndong I (*Jv*) **mengéndong** to pay a visit to s.o.

éndong II (*ob*) → INDUNG I, II.

éndong III *pohon* – k.o. frangipani.

éndoprak (*J*) **1** to fall flat on one's face. **2** severely ill and unable to get up.

éndors (*D/E*) **mengéndors** to endorse (a draft/check, etc.).

éndosan (*D*) endorser.

éndosemén (*D*) endorsement (of a draft/check, etc.). – *atas tunjuk* endorsement to bearer. – *(dalam) blangko* blank endorsement. – *pinjam nama* accommodation endorsement. – *tanpa nama* blank endorsement.

mengéndoseménkan to endorse.

éndosir (*D*) **mengéndorsir** → MENGÉNDORS.

éndrin (*E*) Endrin, brand name of a rat poison.

mengéndrin to poison with Endrin.

enduk (*Jv*) term of address for little girl; → GENDUK.

endul (*Skr ob*) swinging cradle, sling.

endung → INDUNG.

éndung (*J*) **mengéndung** to sleep away from home; → MENGINAP.

endus (*J*) **mengendus** [and **ngendus** (*coq*)] **1** to sniff, smell. **2** to get wind of, suspect, find out, detect, perceive, begin to know/understand.

ngendusin (*J coq*) **1** to have s.o. smell/sniff s.t. **2** to be awake; → MENDUSIN.

terendus came to be known, discovered, found out. *tidak* ~ *oléh bininya* (his fooling around with other women) was not sniffed out by his wife.

endusan 1 a whiff. *mendapat* ~ to get a whiff of, find out about. **2** a keen nose for. ~ *politik* a keen nose for politics.

pengendus sniffer.

pengendusan sniffing out s.t.

endut (*J*) drooping, flabby, potbellied (big and wrinkled); → GEMBROT, GENDUT.

endut-endutan (*J*) throbbing, palpitating, pounding (of a headache), beating (of the heart from emotion).

enek (*J/Jv*) disgusting, nauseating, sickening; unsavory, repulsive.

enem → ENAM.

enéng (*J*) pet name for little girls.

énérgétik (*E*) energetic.

énérgi (*D/E*) energy. *krisis* – energy crisis. – *matahari* solar energy. – *nuklir* nuclear energy. – *panas bumi* geothermal energy. – *séksual* libido. – *surya* solar energy.

énérjétik (*E*) → ÉNÉRGÉTIK.

énérji (*E*) and **énérsi** (*D*) → ÉNÉRGI.

enes (*Jv*) sad, melancholy, sorrowful, grieved.

  mengenes [and **ngenes** (*coq*)] to languish from grief/heartbreak, be sad/grieved, distressed. *mati ngenes* to die of a broken heart.

  mengeneskan [and **ngenesin** (*J coq*)] to bring sorrow to, give/cause pain to, distress, grieve, afflict; distressing.

engah I (*J*) to see, realize (the danger/one's error, etc.), be aware, be conscious; → NGEH. *Ia baru – bahwa pulpénnya dicopét.* He just realized that his pen had been pickpocketed.

  ngengain to remind.

engah II mengengah-engah and **terengah-engah** gasping for breath, out of breath, panting.

  engahan panting, gasping, suffocating.

engah III terperengah seized with fright and confused.

engak 1 dazed, lost in thought, confused, bewildered. **2** drowsy, sleepy.

engap (*J*) **1** stifling, sultry, oppressive. **2** tight in the chest, unable to breathe.

  mengengap-engap, terengap-engap, and **engap-engap(an) 1** to gasp for breath. **2** with a lot of trouble, with difficulty.

engas (*J*) **1** bad smell, stench, stink. **2** body odor after working/playing, etc. too long in a hot place.

engeh → ENGAH.

enggak (*J*) → TIDAK. *Saya – tahu.* I don't know. *Kamu kenal pada dia? – .* Do you know him? No.

  enggak-enggak *yang ~* absurd, ridiculous.

énggal (*J*) free of child care responsibilities.

enggan I unwilling, reluctant, not wanting to, disinclined to, not feeling like; → EMOH, OGAH. *tak* – to be willing to, have the guts to. – *jikalau* (*cla*) only if; except; unless and until. – *seribu daya, mau sepatah kata* if one does not want to do s.t., there are always many excuses. *Jangan – bertanya.* Feel free to ask questions.

  enggan-enggan hesitatingly, hesitantly; unable to make up one's mind to.

  berenggan-enggan to keep saying one is unwilling, keep on refusing.

  mengenggani 1 to dislike. **2** to reject.

  mengenggankan to disapprove of, dislike, refuse.

  enggananan reluctance.

  keengganan unwillingness, reluctance, dislike, refusal, aversion.

enggan II → PERENGGAN I.

enggang hornbill, *Aceros spp. yang – sama – juga, yang pipit sama pipit juga* birds of a feather flock together. *selama – mengeram* quite a long time. *pipit meminang anak –* a poor person wants to marry the daughter of a wealthy man, i.e., an impossibility. *makanan – hendak dimakan oléh pipit* to want to be the equal of rich/noble people; to want to do s.t. beyond one's abilities. *mendengarkan cakap –* listen to the coaxing of the enemy. – *badak* rhinoceros hornbill, *Buceros rhinoceros.* – *buluh* bushy-crested hornbill, *Anorrhinus galeritus.* – *gading* white-beaked/helmeted hornbill, *Rhinoplax/Buceros vigil.* – *gunung* bar-pouched wreathed hornbill, *Aceros undulatus.* – *hitam* black hornbill, *Anthracoceros malayanus.* – *jambul putih* white-crowned hornbill, *Berenicornis comatus.* – *kondé* bushy-crested hornbill, wreathed hornbill, *Anorrhinus galeritus/Aceros undulatus.* – *lilin* pied hornbill, *Anthrococeros spp.* – *musim* wreathed hornbill, *Rhyticeros undulatus.* – *papan* great hornbill, *Buceros bicornis.* – *raja* rhinoceros hornbill, *Buceros rhinoceros.* – *Sumatera* plain-pouched hornbill, *Rhinoplax subruficolis.* – *tirangga* → ENGGANG *gading.*

enggen (*J*) → ENGGAN I.

énggét (*J*) → SÉNGGÉT I. **mengénggét** to knock/bring down s.t.

(usually fruits) by using a pole; (sometimes a knife, with the blade pointed downward, is attached to the end of the pole).

enggil (*ob*) **berenggil(an)** serrated, toothed.

énggok (*Jv*) **mengénggok** to detour, turn (to the side).

  mengénggokkan to turn/detour s.t.

  énggokan curve, bend, turn (in a road/river, etc.).

eng(g)ro (from French: en gros) wholesale.

engkah I (*C*) glue, paste.

engkah II (*J*) a large crack (in wall, etc.).

engkah-engkah(an) half-ripe (of fruit); → MENGKAL.

engkak I (*Jv*) crow, *Corvus enca.*

engkak II k.o. tart.

engkalé and **engkali** (*J*) → BARANGKALI.

engkang (*S*) term of address for elder brother; → KAKAK I, KANG I.

éngkang (*M ob*) **mengéngkang** to walk with the legs apart; → MENGANGKANG.

éngkar → INGKAR.

engkas-engkis (*J*) **1** constricted, bronchial, asthmatic. **2** to be at the point of death due to old age.

engkau you (used by people of the same status or to juniors or inferiors).

  berengkau to use *engkau* in one's conversation with s.o., be on familiar terms with s.o.

  memperengkau to call s.o. *engkau.*

engkék mengengkék to lever up; → UNGKIT.

éngkel (*D*) simple, single; → SINGGEL. *kacamata* – nonbifocal glasses. *kain* – single-width cloth.

éngkél (*Jv*) **ngéngkél** to keep on arguing.

  éngkél-éngkélan to argue.

engket-engket k.o. mango tree.

engkét-engkét (*J/Jv*) **1** to walk on tiptoe. **2** (*onom*) creaking sound made by a pole carried on the shoulders.

éngkét-éngkét pest of the mango tree, trunk borer, *Batocera rufomaculata.*

engkim (*C*) wife of mother's younger brother.

engkis-engkis (*J*) → ENGKAS-ENGKIS.

éngklé a children's game similar to hopscotch; → PÉTAK *gunung.*

éngklék (*J*) **ngengklék** to have a numb arm from carrying a heavy load.

engko (*C coq*) older brother.

éngko (*D*) partner. *beli* – to buy s.t. collectively.

  beréngko to be allied (with), be in partnership (with).

  éngkoan 1 partnership; trading company. **2** to be partners.

éngkol 1 crank (of car) *lubang* – crank slot. *poros* – crankshaft. **2** wrench. *memutar poros – mesin* to crank (a car).

  mengéngkol 1 to crank (a car). **2** to tighten or loosen nut and bolt with a wrench. **3** handle.

  éngkolan ~ *motor* crank handle. ~ *pintu* door handle.

engkong (*C*) grandfather; → KAKÉK.

engku 1 (*cla*) title for s.o. of royal descent. **2** form of address to respectable persons (such as – *guru*). **3** (*M*) a) form of address to maternal uncle. b) appellation for grandfather (*datuk*); → ANGKU. **4** (*C*) form of address for mother's younger brother. – *muda* a) form of address to newlywed son-in-law. b) young gentleman.

  berengku to be called *engku.*

engkuk I (*Jv*) and **engkuk-engkuk** (*J*) a barbet-like bird which makes the sound "kuk-kuk."

engkuk II plant pest.

engkuk-engkuk (*Jv*) **mengengkuk-engkuk** to bend/push down, grab and shake.

éng-ong (*J*) striped; → LURIK.

engos (*J*) **engos-engosan** out of breath.

éngsel and **éngsél** (*D*) **1** hinge, joint. **2** switch, points (in a railroad system). – *buku* hinge. – *cabut* French-hinge. – *kupu-kupu* (*J*) a flat hinge on a box lid which makes it impossible to remove the lid without damaging the hinge. – *lonjat* cocked hinge. – *patrom* (*J*) a hinge which enables a door leaf to be lifted without damaging the hinge. – *peluru* ball-in-socket joint.

  beréngsél hinged, with hinges.

engso (*C*) term of address for older brother's wife or woman of that generation.

éngsot → INGSUT. **beréngsot(-éngsot)** and **mengéngsot** to shift, move slightly/slowly.

mengéngsotkan to move s.t. slightly, shift.

enjak → INJAK. **mengenjak** to step/tread/trample on (a pedal/person being massaged, etc.).

mengenjak-enjak to stamp one's feet.

enjal I **mengenjal** to drop/fall down with a thud.

enjal II → ANJAL I. **mengenjal** to ricochet, rebound, recoil, spring out, bounce back; to be resilient/elastic.

enjal III **mengenjal** to stuff, cram.

enjam → HUNJAM.

enjelai a cereal, Job's tears, *Coix lachryma Jobi*; → JELAI I.

enjid and **enjit** (*J*) grandfather; → KAKÉK.

énjima → ÉNZIM.

énjin (*E*) engine.

énjiniring (*E*) engineering.

enjot (*J/Jv*) → ENJUT, GENJOT. 1 to move up and down. 2 to use the pedals (of a bike, etc.), pedal, treadle.

mengenjot [and **ngenjot** (*coq*)] ~ *sepéda* to cycle, (ride a) bicycle.

enjot-enjotan to jump, bounce up.

pengenjot ~ *(pédal) bécak* a *becak* driver.

pengenjotan pedaling.

enjut **mengenjut** to move s.t. up and down slowly; to pull up and down (as a fishing line); to pull o.s. up and down (on a branch).

énklave (*D/E*) enclave.

eno (*J*) /ono/ there; → (*Jv*) ANA II. – *dia*. There he is!

énokulasi (*D*) inoculation.

enol → NOL.

enom (*Jv*) young; → ANOM.

énsi clipped form of **énsiklopédi**.

énsiklik (*D*) encyclical (letter).

énsiklopédi (*D*) encyclopedia.

énsim → ÉNZIM.

énsopor (*E*) and so forth, etc.

entah 1 (= **entahkan**) (an expression of doubt) don't know, who knows, I wish I knew. *-lah* and ~, *ya* I don't know. 2 it is unknown (or, known but not important in the context). *Namanya Dave – apa nama belakangnya*. His name is Dave – who knows what his last name is. *– ... – ... and – ... atau ...* either ... or ... (unknown which). *Kursi itu dibeli – oléh ayahnya – oléh kakéknya*. The chair was bought either by his father or by his grandfather. *– Garuda, Merpati atau apa saja* either Garuda, Merpati, or whatever it is. *– bagaimana* somehow, for some reason. *– benar – tidak* whether it is true or not. *dan – apa lagi* and so on, etc. *– mengapa* I don't know why. *– dari/ke mana* I don't know where.

entah-entah 1 not know. 2 maybe, possibly (but one hopes not). ~ *dia datang*. Let's hope he doesn't come, but who knows. ~ *dia sudah tidak ada lagi di situ*. There is a chance he is no longer there. 3 → BERENTAH. 4 (*ob*) descendants in the fifth or sixth generation. 5 (*ob*) calculation of the smallest monetary value.

berentah to say *entah* (while speaking or answering a question).

entah-berentah (*M*) a thing (or things) the exact word for which is not known or not recalled or is avoided at the moment of speaking; s.t. inexpressible; → ANU. *negeri* ~ (*cla*) never-never land, fairyland.

entak → HENTAK. **mengentak** 1 to trample/step on, stamp/press/push/pound hard. ~ *kakinya* to stamp (with) one's feet. 2 to stab (with a spear/dagger, etc.). *Anjingnya luka dientak orang*. S.o. stabbed his dog and wounded it. 3 to sting, smart (of a wound). 4 (= **mengentak-entak**) to beat/throb/palpitate (of the heart/fontanel/ear, etc.). *Hatinya* ~. His heart palpitated; → BERDEBAR-DEBAR. 5 to batter.

mengentak-entak(i) 1 to throb, thud, pound. 2 to keep bumping (with one's buttocks) against (the wall, etc.).

mengentakkan 1 ~ *diri* to flop/flop down, drop with a thud, sit down with a thump, sink down (on a chair, etc.). 2 to swat with s.t.; to dash/crash (of trees) to the ground. ~ *kaki* to stamp the feet (in anger). ~ *kedua belah kakinya* (*mil*) to click one's heels.

terentak thrown down, lie sprawled.

entakan 1 stamping (of the feet). 2 stroke (in typing). ~ *se-menit* [ent/men] strokes per minute.

pengentak pestle, (rice) pounder.

entang *tak* – a) doesn't care about. b) isn't interested in. c) doesn't want to.

entar and **'ntar** [the clipped forms of **(se)bentar**] (*J*) 1 a moment/second. –, *tunggu di sini!* A moment, just wait here! 2 soon, in (less than) no time. – *malam* tonight. 3 or else in no time at all; → NANTI II. *Jangan main di jalan – ketubruk mobil*. Don't play in the street (or else) in less than a minute you'll be hit by a car.

entaran for a moment. *Pinjam dong sepédanya* ~. Lend me your bike for a minute.

entar-entaran not carry out s.t. immediately, put off (indefinitely), postpone; linger, dawdle. *Jangan pakai* ~. Don't goof off. ~ *malam* tonight; → NANTI *malam*, SEMALAM *ini*.

entas (*Jv*) **mengentas** 1 to take s.t. in. ~ *jemuran* to take in the laundry. 2 to remove, take out. ~ *sayuran yang sedang direbus dari kualinya* to remove the boiled vegetables from the pan. 3 to extricate s.o., pull out. ~ *meréka yang terjerumus ke dalam lembah kesengsaraan* to extricate those who have fallen into the cesspool of misery.

mengentaskan ~ *anak* to raise a child till he becomes self-sufficient.

pengentasan ~ *anak* child care.

énté (*A J*) you.

enték-entékan (*Jv*) to the bitter end. *Saya hayati – tokoh itu*. I'll support that prominent figure to the bitter end.

énten (*D*) graft.

mengénten to graft (s.t. onto).

énténg (*Jv*) 1 light (in weight). 2 of little or no importance, not serious, trivial, light. *hukuman* – a light sentence. *makanan yang* – a snack. *Sakitnya sudah* –. His illness has improved. *Janji-janji – atau berat?* Are those idle or serious promises? 3 easy, natural. *bacaan yang* – easy/light reading. 4 mild, not sharp or strong (in taste, etc.). 5 easily gotten. – *jodoh* said of s.o. who finds his/her mate easily. – *rejeki* said of s.o. who gets money easily.

seénténg as light as.

mengénténgi to alleviate.

mengénténgkan and **memperénténg** [and **ngénténgin** (*J coq*)] 1 to lighten, relieve. ~ *tubuh dengan membuang air kecil* to relieve o.s. 2 to decrease, reduce (expenses), economize. 3 to alleviate (a punishment), mitigate. 4 to consider unimportant, take for granted.

terénténg the lightest.

énténgan 1 (*Jv*) to enjoy helping others. 2 (*coq*) lighter, easier.

énténg-énténgan unimportant, petty, slight. *Ia dapat bekerja* ~. He can do some light work.

keénténgan 1 lightness. 2 easiness, ease.

pengénténg s.t. which relieves, relief. *tuas* ~ relief lever.

pengénténgan lightening, making easier.

énternit → ÉTÉRNIT.

Éntero Vioform Enterovioform, an antidiarrhea remedy.

enti I → HENTI.

enti II (*J*) → NANTI.

entimun → MENTIMUN.

enting-enting (*Jv*) (– *kacang*) peanut stick dipped in palm sugar. – *gepuk* triangular shaped peanut and sugar snack. – *wijén* k.o. sesame brittle.

entit (*Jv*) **ngentit** to steal, pilfer (small things).

éntitas (*D*) entity.

ent/men → ENTAKAN *semenit*.

entod (*J*) **ngentod-entodin** make s.t. run in fits and starts.

entod-entodan by fits and starts.

éntog (*Jv*) and **éntok** Manila duck; → MENTOG.

éntomolog (*D*) entomologist.

éntomologi (*D/E*) entomology.

éntomologis (*D*) entomological.

entong (*J*) 1 a boy, lad, youth. 2 form of address to a boy.

éntot (*J vulg*) **mengéntot** [and **ngéntot** (*coq*)] to fuck.

mengéntotkan [and **ngéntotin** (*J coq*)] to fuck s.o.

éntot-mengéntot fucking.

mengéntoti (*pl obj*) to fuck.

éntotan fucking, fuck.

pengéntotan fucking.

éntré (*D*) admission(fee).

éntri (*E*) (dictionary) entry. – *pokok* main entry.
  mengéntrikan to enter (words in a dictionary).
entrog (*Jv*) **mengentrog(-entrog)** to shake up.
éntropot (*D*) entrepot. – *umum* general entrepot.
entuk (*J*) **1** to reach, go up to/as far as. **2** to hit, contact. *Kepalanya – ke dinding*. His head hit the wall.
entut – *kerbau* k.o. bird, yellow wagtail, *Motacilla flava*.
enyah (*coq*) to go away. – *dari sini!* Beat it! Get away from here!
  mengenyahkan 1 to kick out, expel, oust, eject, remove. **2** (*coq*) to kill, murder, assassinate, wipe out.
  pengenyahan 1 fleeing. **2** elimination, assassination. **3** expulsion (of undesirables). **4** abolition.
enyak I mengenyak to press/thrust/push/tread down (the earth around the roots, etc.). *duduk ~* to flop down, drop with a thud, sit down with a thump, sink down (into a chair, etc.).
  mengenyakkan *~ diri* to drop back (into a chair, etc.), throw o.s. down.
  terenyak and **te(r)perenyak** flopped down suddenly, fallen with a flop.
enyak II (*Jv*) **1** mother. **2** form of address to older woman or one in higher position, teacher, employer, etc.; → IBU.
enyék (*Jv*) answer in a mocking way.
  mengenyék [and **ngenyék** (*coq*)] to mock, belittle, put down.
enyot (*J*) → NYUT. **ngenyot** to suck (the teat).
énzim (*D*) enzyme. – *amilase* amylaceous enzyme. – *protéase* protease enzyme.
énzimatik (*D*) enzymatic.
epak → PAK I, III.
épakuasi → ÉVAKUASI.
épakué (*D ob*) evacuee.
épék (*Jv*) (narrow outer) belt, sash (of velvet/leather, etc.) with a buckle used to hold the wider abdominal belt under it.
éphorus (*Bat*) leader of the Council of the Protestant Batak Christian Church.
épidémi (*D*) epidemic; → WABAH.
épidémik (*E*) → ÉPIDÉMIS.
épidémiologi (*D/E*) epidemiology.
épidémiologis (*D*) epidemiological.
épidémis (*D*) epidemic (*mod*). *penyakit –* an epidemic disease.
épifit (*D/E*) epiphyte.
épigon (*D/E*) epigony, epigones.
épigoni (*D/E*) epigony, epigones.
épigraf (*D/E*) epigraph.
épigrafi (*D/E*) epigraphy; → WIDYALÉKA. *ahli –* epigraphist, epigrapher.
épigram (*D/E*) epigram.
épik (*D/E*) epic.
épilépsi (*D*) epilepsy.
épilog (*D/E*) epilog.
épis (*D*) epic (*mod*).
épiséntrum (*D*) epicenter.
épiskop (*D/E*) episcope.
épisode (*D/E*) episode.
épistémologi (*D/E*) epistemology.
ÉPO [Exit Permit Only] /éksit pérmit onli/ Exit Permit Only.
  meng-ÉPO-kan to expel (from a country).
épok I (*D*) epoch.
épok II a lidded, envelope-shaped bag for holding betel nut chewing ingredients.
époksi (*E*) epoxy. *perekat –* epoxy resin.
épolét (*D*) epaulet. *menyemat –* to fasten an epaulet. *penyematan –* fastening an epaulet.
épos (*D*) epic; → WIRACARITA.
épot (*J*) very busy; → RÉPOT.
Épsom (*E*) *garam –* Epsom salts.
epyur (*Jv*) **mengepyuri** to lavish s.o. with s.t. *diepyuri air* sprinkled with water.
ér I name of the letter *r*.
ér II (*J*) → AIR.
éra I (*S*) to be/feel ashamed.
éra II (*D/E*) era.
éradikasi (*E*) eradication.

erak I → RAK II.
erak II (*ob*) tired, weary, fatigued, exhausted. *melepaskan –* to rest, take a break.
erak III → UANG *erakan*.
erak IV (*onom*) screeching sound.
  mengerak to make a screeching sound.
érak I berérak and **mengérak 1** to uncoil, unwind (as of a snake/coil of rattan). **2** to fall apart, separate, get free, edge away (from e.o. like boxers).
  mengérak(kan) to loosen, separate, uncoil.
érak II (*Jv*) **1** hoarse (of voice). **2** sore (of throat).
eram I mengeram 1 to sit on eggs, hatch, brood. **2** to sit crouching (of a tiger ready to jump at its prey). *gajah ~* the crouching elephant, i.e., the shape of a Minangkabau house. **3** (*coq*) to sit at home brooding (of people).
  mengerami to brood, sit on (eggs) to hatch them. *Ayam ~ telur itik*. A chicken sat on duck eggs to hatch them. *~ telur orang* a) (*M*) to marry/have intercourse with a pregnant woman (s.o. else's wife). b) to take care of s.o. else's affairs without getting the benefits.
  mengeramkan to have eggs hatched by another hen, duck, etc.
  pengeram layer. *alat ~* incubator.
  pengeraman the act of hatching, brooding, incubating.
eram II (*M*) sagging, sunken, curved downward (of the floor/ground/road, etc.).
erang groaning, moaning (from pain); → RINTIH.
  mengerang(-erang) to groan, moan (in pain).
  erangan groaning, groans, moan(ing). *suara ~* groaning.
érang I (*cla*) dark blue, dark black (of complexion).
  keérang-érangan dark bluish.
érang II oblique, twisted. – *érot* zigzag, askew, awry.
  mengérang to twist.
Érasmus Huis /hés/ and *Gedung –* the Dutch Cultural Center in Jakarta.
erat 1 firm, tight; (to hold) firmly, tightly. *Ikatan itu harus –*. The fastening must be tight. **2** close (of friendship/relationships); → KENTAL. *Persahabatan meréka masih –*. They are still close friends. **3** firm (of a promise).
  erat-erat tight(ly), firmly.
  seerat-eratnya as firm(ly)/tight(ly) as possible.
  mengeratkan and **mempererat(kan) 1** to tighten (bonds), draw (bonds/ties) closer, knit (ties) more closely. **2** to strengthen/consolidate (unity/one's grip on s.t.), tighten. *Eratkan ikat pinggang!* Tighten your belts!
  tererat the tightest/closest.
  keeratan relationship, kinship, intimacy, close friendship, closeness.
  pengeratan tightening up, closing up, making closer.
érbis passion fruit, *Passiflora quadrangularis*; → MARKISA.
ércis (*D*) peas, *Pisum sativum*.
eréh (*Jv ob*) **mengeréh** to be placed under the rule of, be under the authority of.
érék-érék (in Samarinda, Ujungpandang, etc.) k.o. upright roulette.
éréksi (*D*) erection. *mengalami – malam hari* to have a nocturnal erection.
éréktil (*D/E*) erectile.
eréng I (*burung –*) king vulture, *Torgos calvus*; long-billed vulture, *Gyps indicus nudiceps*; brown white-backed vulture, *Pseudogyps bengalensis*.
eréng II (*S*) cross-lath (of wood or bamboo) put over the roof rafter.
éréng (*M*) slanting, tilted, sloping, askew, lopsided; → MIRING. *– géndéng* things that contradict *adat*, improper behavior, etc.
  éréng-éréng a slope.
  mengéréng to lean to one side; slanting, oblique.
  teréréng inclined, awry.
ér-ér-i (*pron* of RRI: *Radio Républik Indonésia*) Republic of Indonesia Radio.
eret → ERAT.
érét I (*J/Jv*) **mengérét** to drag (forcibly) along the ground; → MENYÉRÉT.
  érétan 1 sledge, sleigh. **2** (*J*) *~ sungai* ferryboat controlled by a bamboo pole about 4 meters long which is used to push the boat. **3** slide, (moving) table, carriage. *~ gergaji* saw carriage.

pengérét puller, dragger.

pengérétan 1 dragging. 2 sledge, sleigh. 3 baggage cart.

érét II (*J*) **mengérét-érét** [and **ngérét-érét** (*coq*)] 1 to persuade, talk into, win over. *Kepindahan penduduk dari daérah genangan jangan dipaksa atau diérét-érét*. Don't force or try to talk people from moving away from the flooded area. 2 to ask s.o. for s.t. (by flattery/deceit, etc.); to extort money from s.o., wheedle s.t. out of s.o.

pengérét (*J*) s.o. good at getting s.o. to do s.t. for one's personal gain.

pengérétan persuading. *perempuan* ~ (*J*) a) a woman who is after one's money, a gold-digger. b) s.o. clever at winning another person's favor for personal gain.

érgonomi (*D*) ergonomics.

érgonomis (*D*) ergonomical.

erik mengerik 1 to scream, shout, screech. 2 to trumpet (of elephants). 3 to neigh (of horses). 4 to chirp (of crickets).

éring → ÉRÉNG.

Éritréa Eritrea.

érloji and **érluji** (*J*) → ARLOJI.

érmil (*E coq*) airmail.

érobik(a) → AÉROBIKA.

érok-érok (*Jv*) a perforated scoop or slotted spoon, a kitchen utensil of wicker-work, tin(plate), or white iron, used for removing frying foods from the pan and draining them.

érong I 1 (*naut*) *lubang* – and **érong-érong** scupper hole. 2 (*geol*) weephole.

érong II (*C cla*) k.o. small Chinese teacup.

Éropa(h) (*Port*) 1 Europe. – *Timur* Eastern Europe. 2 European.

se-Éropa(h) all-Europe.

mengéropahkan to Europeanize.

keéropahan European (*mod*). *status ~nya* its European status.

Éropanisasi (*D*) Europeanization.

Éropés and **Éropis** (*D*) European, i.e., refined, delicate. *seperangkat tata cara yang sungguh* – really European formalities.

Éroséntrisme (*D/E*) Eurocentrism.

érosi (*D*) erosion. – *ceburan* splash erosion. – *genangan* puddle erosion.

mengérosikan to erode.

terérosi eroded.

érot I wry (of one's neck/face), askew, deformed, distorted; → MÉNCONG, PÉOK. *érang* – and – *bényot/bérot* crisscross, zigzag.

mengérotkan 1 to distort (*esp* the mouth), deform, twist, turn awry. 2 to skew.

érotan deformation, distortion.

keérotan distortion.

érot II (*J*) → LÉROT, RÉROT.

berérot(an) 1 to go in single file in a large crowd. 2 in a row, following e.o.

érotik (*E*) and **érotis** (*D*) erotic; → CABUL I, PORNO.

érotisme (*D*) eroticism.

érpah (*D*) long lease (75 years) of land out of the free domain.

érpak the right to make full use of real estate belonging to s.o. else by paying yearly rent; → HAK *guna pakai*.

érpékad /ér-pé-kat/ Army Para Commandos Regiment; → RPKAD.

érpot (*E*) airport; → BANDARA I.

érrata (*D/E*) errata.

ér-té (*pron* of RT: Rukun Tetangga) neighborhood association. *pak* – the RT head.

erti → ARTI, MENGERTI. **ngerti** (*Jv*) to understand, know. *Saya tidak* ~ *namanya*. I don't know his name. *Rupanya ia tidak* ~ *maksud perkataan itu*. It seems he didn't understand the meaning of what was said.

mengerti to understand (and **ngertiin** (*J coq*)]; → MENGERTI.

dimengerti to be understood.

mengertikan 1 to explain, make clear. 2 to make s.o. understand. *Mémang sukar* ~ *orang setolol dia*. You're right, it's hard to make s.o. as stupid as he is understand.

pengertian 1 understanding, comprehension, knowledge. *dalam* ~ *bahwa* on the understanding that. *kurang* ~ lacking in comprehension. *menanamkan* ~ to make s.o. understand s.t. ~ *umum* generalization. 2 understanding, agreement. *belum ber-*

temu titik ~ they have not yet come to terms. **3** interpretation, explanation. *kekurang-pengertian* misunderstanding, lack of understanding.

eru (*pohon* –) casuarina, *Casuarina equisetifolia*; → CEMARA II, RU I. *seperti pucuk* – to set one's sails to every wind.

érupsi (*D*) eruption.

ér-wé I (*pron* of RW: RUKUN WARGA) Citizens Association; i.e., an administrative organization comprising several RTs; → RW II.

ér-wé II (*pron* of RW: Rintik Wu'uk) dog meat (which is used in the preparation of a well-known Manadonese dish).

és I the name of the letter *s*.

és II (*D*) ice. *hujan* – hail. *lemari* – ice-box, refrigerator; → ÉSKAS, FRISIDÉR, PETI *és. Harap disimpan di lemari* –. Keep refrigerated. *zaman* – ice age. – *Apollo* popsicle. – *balok(an)* ice in blocks. – *batang(an)* ice in blocks. – *batu* ice cube. – *blok* cube-shaped flavored ice. – *buah* tutti-frutti. – *campur* ice mixed with fruits and syrup. – *cipok* popsicle. – *curai* ice plate. – *daratan* glacier. – *gandul/gantung* shaved ice on a dried rice straw suffused with a sweet syrup. – *Ganéfo* flavored ice in a plastic bag. – *gepukan* crushed ice. – *gosok* shaved ice. – *jus* blended fruit juice and crushed ice. – *kantong plastik* popsicle. – *kas* ice-box. – *kering* dry ice. – *kombor serut* ice shavings with sweeteners and milk or coconut milk. – *konsumsi* ices. – *kopi* iced coffee. – *kopyor* a beverage, consisting of the soft meat of a special variety of coconut, served with syrup and crushed ice cubes; → KELAPA *kopyor*. – *krim* ice cream. – *lalang* drift ice. – *lembaran* pack ice. – *lilin* popsicle. – *loli* lollipop. – *longsor* avalanche. – *mambo* popsicle. – *paparan* shelf ice. – *perongkol* ice cube. – *Petojo* block ice (originally made in the ice factory in the Petojo area of Jakarta). – *plastik* popsicle. – *prongkol* ice in large chunks. – *puter* (Indonesian style) ice cream. – *roli* popsicle. – *roti* ice-cream bread. – *serut* a) shaved ice. b) food containing ice. – *setrup* cold beverage made with fruit syrup. – *Shanghai/Syanghai* a fruit cocktail mixed with sugared jelly covered with shaved ice. – *soklat* iced chocolate drink. – *tébak* shaved ice made by a spinning shaving machine. – *téh* iced tea. – *téler* a fruit cocktail with topping of condensed milk suffused with shaved ice. – *tepian* marginal ice.

berés to be frozen.

mengés [and **ngésin** (*J*)] to freeze, put on ice, cool with ice.

pengésan 1 icing. 2 glaciation.

esa and **ésa** variant form of *sa* or *se* meaning "one," used in certain expressions. *Tuhan yang* – the One God. – *hilang, dua terbilang* (motto of the Siliwangi Army Division stationed in West Java) "For each man fallen, two will spring up to replace him." *membilang dari* –, *mengaji dari alif* to start from scratch. *kurang* – *tiga puluh* thirty minus one *si* – (*Min*) one's better half, life partner.

(ber)esa-esaan 1 alone. 2 lonely; loneliness.

mengesakan ~ *Tuhan* to acknowledge the oneness of God.

keesaan unity. ~ *Tuhan* the Oneness of God.

ésabahasa monolingual; → ÉKABAHASA.

keésabahasaan monolingualism.

esah (*A*) legal, legitimate; to validate, confirm; → SAH I.

mengesahkan to legalize, validate, confirm.

pengesahan legalization, legitimating, validation, confirmation.

ésai I (*E*) essay.

ésai II (*J*) it's unimportant, forget about it.

esak I *sakit* – a) asthma. b) shortness of breath; → ASMA II, SESAK.

esak II mengesak and **teresak(-esak)** sobbing.

esang mengesang to blow one's nose; → KESANG I.

és-dé (*pron* of SD: Sekolah Dasar) Elementary School.

ései (*D*) essay. *penulis* – essayist.

éséis (*D*) essayist.

esék (*E*) esék-esék sex.

esék *demam* – dermatosis accompanying tuberculosis.

éselon (*D*) echelon, level, rank. – *atas* top echelons. – *I* Directors General and Secretaries General. – *II* Directors. – *III* Subdirectorate Heads. – *IV* Division Heads.

éselonéring (*D*) dividing up into echelons, ranking.

és-ém-a (*pron* of SMA: Sekolah Menengah Atas) Senior High School.

és-ém-pé (*pron* of SMP: Sekolah Menengah Pertama) Junior High School.

ésens (*D/E*) essence; → BIANG 7.

ésénsi (*D*) quintessence, gist, substance.

ésénsial (*E*) and éséniil (*D*) essential. *tidak* – nonessential.

ésénsialia (*D*) essential problems.

ésénsialitas essentiality.

éser (*D*) iron.

és-ér (*pron* of SR: Sekolah Rakyat) Elementary School (now superseded by *És-dé*).

ését (*pron* of EZ: Économische Zaken) i.e., the now-defunct (Netherlands Indies Department of) Economic Affairs. *harga* – the official price (stipulated by that department).

és-ha (*pron* of S.H.: Sarjana Hukum) Master of Laws, LL.M.

éskadron (*D*) squadron.

és-ka-ka-a (*pron* of SKKA: Sekolah Kesejahteraan Keluarga Atas) Senior High School for Domestic Sciences.

éskalasi (*D*) escalation.
    mengéskalasi to escalate.

éskalator (*E*) escalator.

éskas (*D ob*) icebox, refrigerator.

éskatologi (*D/E*) eschatology.

éskatologis (*D*) eschatological.

Éskimo Eskimo.

éskrim (*E*) ice cream.

éskul (*E BG*) school.

Éslandia Iceland.

ésok 1 the early morning, forenoon, the early/first part of the day, from midnight to noon (poetic or literary version of *bésok*). – *hari* tomorrow. *hari* – a) tomorrow. b) the future. – *lusa* a) tomorrow. b) the day after tomorrow. c) one day (in the future); → BÉSOK. – *pagi* and *pagi* – tomorrow morning. *petang* – tomorrow afternoon/evening. 2 at a later time, later, some time from now. *kalau sudah mendapat ijazah* – when you get your degree later.

ésoknya 1 the next/following morning. 2 the next/following day. *petang –nya* the next afternoon/evening.

bérésok (*Mal*) tomorrow; → BÉSOK. ~ *harinya* the next/following day.

mengésokkan ~ *(hari)* to postpone until the following day.

keésokan ~ *harinya/paginya* the following day/morning.

(ke)ésokannya the following morning.

ésot berésot(-ésot) to keep on moving around.
    mengésot to move/push forward, shove; → INGSUT.

ésotérik (*D/E*) esoteric.

ésotérisme (*D/E*) esotericism.

ésprés (*D*) 1 fast. *Kalau* – *bayar dobel*. If you want it fast (i.e., special delivery), you have to pay double. 2 express/fast train; → ÉKSPRÉS.

ésrar (*RC*) *tanda* – the Holy Sacraments.

éstafét and éstapét (*D*) relay race. *tongkat* – baton.
    mengéstafétkan to relay, pass s.t. to s.o. else (as in a relay race).

éster (*D/E*) ester.

éstétik (*E*) and éstétis (*D*) aesthetic.

éstétika (*D*) esthetics.

éstétikus (*D*) esthetician.

éstéwé [[*pron* of stw: *sudah tuw(w)a*] already old; → MÉNOR.

éstimasi (*E*) estimation.

éstrus (*D/E*) estrous, in heat.

ÉT (*init*) [éks tapol] former political prisoner.

étalase (*D*) show window.

étan (*D/E*) ethane.

étanol (*D/E*) ethanol.

étape (*D*) stage (in route), stretch, route, run. – *terakhir* the final stretch.

étatisme (*D*) étatism, statism, state control.

étatis (*D*) statism, étatism.

éték I (*Jv*) ngéték-étékkan to show (a part of the body, etc.).

éték II (*M*) → MAK *éték*.

éték III ngéték to crave.

étép → PUTAUW.

éter (*D*) ether (all meanings).

étérni(e)t (*D*) asbestos cement board, cement-asbestos board.

ét(h)anol (*D*) ethanol.

étik (*D*) ethics. *kode* – code of ethics. *Kode – Jurnalistik* Journalists' Code of Ethics. *Kode – Lingkungan Insinyur* Green Code for Engineers.

étika (*D*) ethics.

étikét I (*D*) label, tag.
    berétikét with/to have a label/tag; labeled, tagged. – *harga* price tag.

étikét II (*D*) etiquette; → TATAKRAMA. – *berbahasa* linguistic etiquette.

étil (*D*) ethyl.

étilmétansulfonat (*E*) ethyl methane sulfonate.

étimologi (*D/E*) etymology.
    mengétimologi to etymologize.

étimologis (*D*) etymologic.

étiologi (*D/E*) etiology.

Étiopia Ethiopia.

étis (*D*) ethical.

étnik (*E*) and étnis (*D*) 1 ethnic. *masalah* – ethnic problems. 2 ethnic group.
    keétnisan ethnic (*mod*).

étnisitas (*E*) ethnicity.

étnograf (*D*) ethnographer.

étnografi (*D/E*) ethnography.

étnografis (*D*) ethnographic.

étnolinguistik (*D/E*) ethnolinguistics.

étnolog (*D*) ethnologist.

étnologi (*D/E*) ethnology.

étnologis (*D*) ethnologic(al).

étnomusikolog (*D*) ethnomusicologist.

étnomusikologi (*D/E*) ethnomusicology.

étnoséntrisme (*D*) ethnocentrism.

étologi (*D/E*) ethology.

étos (*D*) ethos. – *kerja* work ethic.

étsa (*D*) etching, engraving. – *ulang* back etching.
    mengétsa to etch, engrave.
    pengétsaan etching, engraving.

éufemisme (*D/E*) euphemism; → PENGHALUSAN *bahasa*.

éufemistik (*E*) and éufemistis (*D*) euphemistic.

éufoni (*D/E*) euphony.

éuforia (*D/E*) euphoria.

éuforis (*D*) euphoric.

euis (*S*) *si* – the beautiful (woman).

Éurasia (*E*) Eurasian.

Éurodolar (*D*) Eurodollar.

Éurokomunis (*D*) Eurocommunist.

Éurokomunisme (*D*) Eurocommunism.

Éuromisil (*E*) Euromissile.

Éuroséntris (*D*) Eurocentric.

éustasi (*E*) eustacy.

éustatik (*E*) eustatic.

éut(h)anasia (*D*) euthanasia.

éutrofikasi (*D*) eutrophication.

Éva 1 Eve. 2 woman personified.

évakuasi (*D*) evacuation.
    mengévakuasi(kan) to evacuate.
    terévakuasi evacuated.
    pengévakuasian evacuation.

évaluasi (*D*) evaluation; → NILAI. – *Belajar Tahap Akhir* → ÉBTA.
    mengévaluasi to evaluate.
    pengévaluasi evaluator.
    pengévaluasian evaluation.

évaluatif (*E*) evaluative.

évaluir (*D*) mengévaluir to evaluate.

évangéli (*D*) gospel, evangel.

évangélis (*D*) evangelist.

évangélisasi (*D*) evangelization.

évapotranspirasi (*D*) evapotranspiration.

évokasi (*D*) evocation.

évokatif (*D/E*) evocative.

évolusi (*D*) evolution.
    berévolusi to evolve.

évolusionér (*D*) evolutionary.

éwa (*Jv*) **1** antipathy, aversion, dislike (of/for). **2** to have a dislike of/for, feel an aversion (to).

 mengéwakan to treat with disdain.

éwan → AIWAN.

éwé (*J vulg*) fucking, sex.

 ngéwé to have sex, fuck.

 ngéwéin to fuck s.o.

 éwéan fucking, sex.

éwét (*Pr*) girl; → CÉWÉK.

éwuh (*Jv*) and – *pakéwuh* uneasiness, awkwardness; uncomfortable, ill at ease. – *oyo ing pambudi* in a dilemma. *rasa – pakéwuh* to feel uncomfortable/ill at ease. *tidak – pakéwuh* without feelings of dislike/discomfort, at ease, relaxed.

 mengéwuhkan to embarrass.

éx- see entries with ÉKS-.

éyang (*Jv*) **1** grandfather. **2** grandmother. – *kakung* grandfather. – *putri* grandmother.

ÉYD [Éjaan Yang Disempurnakan] the Reformed Spelling (introduced on August 16, 1972). **meng-kan** to spell according to the new orthography.

éyél (*Jv*) **mengéyél** [and **ngéyél** (*coq*)] unwilling to yield, not wanting to give in, obstinate/stubborn.

 kengéyélan stubbornness.

 éyél-éyélan sticking to one's guns, be firm.

éyong (*Jv*) **mengéyong(-éyong)** to rock.

ÉZ → ÉSÉT.

F

/f/ is usually pronounced /p/ by most Indonesians. If a word beginning with the letter f cannot be found below, look for it under p.

---

f and **F I** the sixth letter of the Latin alphabet used for writing Indonesian.

F II car license plate for Bogor.

fa I name of the 20th letter of the Arabic alphabet.

fa II the fourth note in the musical scale.

fa III and **Fa** (*abbr*) [firma] firm, company.

faahisyah (*A mod*) homosexual.

faal I (*A*) **1** deed, act, good works. **2** function, performance (as of organs of the body). *ilmu – alat tubuh* physiology. *– jantung* cardiac functions. *– paru* lung function. *– véntrikel kanan/kiri* right/left ventricle function.

faal II (*A*) sign, omen; prophecy; → FIRASAT. *membuka –* to make a prophesy.

   memfaalkan to predict, prophesy, foretell (based on cabalism).

faali (*A*) **1** automatic or natural working or movement of parts of the body, physiological; → FAAL I. *prosés penurunan fungsi – tubuh* decline in the physiological functions of the body. **2** automatically or naturally.

fabel (*D*) fable.

FABIONI → FAKULTAS *Biologi* (*Univérsitas*) *Nasional*.

F-ABRI → FRAKSI *Angkatan Bersenjata Républik Indonésia*.

fabrik → PABRIK.

fabrikan (*D*) → PABRIKAN.

fabrikasi (*D*) → PABRIKASI. **memfabrikasi** to manufacture. *Komponén éléktronik mikrocip yang dirancangnya harus difabrikasi di sebuah pabrik di Inggris*. The microchip electronic components which he is designing must be manufactured in a factory in England.

factor (*D*) /faktor/ a type of financing firm, common in the garment industry, which furnishes cash to cover seasonal fluctuations in revenue in exchange for the company's accounts receivable.

Factorij (*D col*) /faktorai/ the Batavia-based office of the Nederlandsche Handel Maatschappij (Netherlands Trading Company), directing its affairs in the whole of the Netherlands Indies.

factoring (*D*) /faktoring/ the act of doing business as, or with, a factor, *q.v.*; → ANJAK *piutang*.

fadiga (*Port ob*) blennorrhoea.

fadihat (*A*) shame, disgrace, infamy.

   memfadihatkan to humiliate, disgrace.

fadil (*A*) eminent, excellent, prominent, famous.

fadilat and **fadzilat** (*A*) excellence, prominence, virtue.

faduli (*A*) → PEDULI. *si –* (*Mal*) busybody.

fadzilat → FADILAT.

faédah (*A*) **1** use, usefulness, utility. *Apa –nya?* What good is it? **2** (*ob* and *Mal*) profit, advantage, benefit. *– perubatan percuma* free medical benefits. *bagi –* in the interest of.

   berfaédah 1 useful, helpful, beneficial. **2** (*Mal*) profitable, advantageous.

   memfaédahkan to put s.t. to use, take advantage of, make use of. *Rumah itu sekarang difaédahkan untuk asrama*. The house is now being used as a dormitory.

   kefaédahan utility, usefulness.

fagéti (*Port esp Ambon*) fireworks.

fagot (*D*) bassoon.

faguam (*ob*) → PEGUAM.

faham → PAHAM. **sefaham** of one mind, like-minded.

fahisyah → FAAHISYAH.

fahombé stone-jumping sport of the Nias Islanders (on Nias off Sumatra's west coast); an activity once used to train young men for battle and to prove a young man's fitness for marriage, now a tourist spectacle.

fahrasat (*A*) list; index, catalog.

Fahrenhéit (*D/E*) Fahrenheit, F.

Fahutan → FAKULTAS *Kehutanan*.

faidah → FAÉDAH.

fail (*E*) file, holder for keeping papers, etc. together for reference purposes.

failasuf (*A*) → FILSUF.

failit (*D*) bankrupt; → PAILIT.

fair I (*D/E*) /fér/ fair, honest.

fair II (*D/E*) /fér/ fair, festival; → PÉR III.

Faissements-Verordening (*D col*) the 1905 bankruptcy law.

fait accompli (*E/Fr*) /fétakompli/ fait accompli, an accomplished fact, s.t. already done.

   memfait accompli to present with a fait accompli. *Ia mengemukakan mengapa ia merasa difait accompli*. He presented the reason that he felt that he had been presented with a fait accompli.

fajar (*A*) dawn, daybreak, aurora; red glow in the sky indicating sunrise. *harian –* morning paper. *– buta* still pitch dark. *– kemerdékaan* the dawn of independence. *– kizib* reddish colors in sky before dawn. *– menyingsing/merekah* daybreak; red of dawn. *– senja* twilight. *– sid(d)ik* true dawn, daybreak. *– Utama* name of a train running between Jakarta and Semarang or between Jakarta and Yogyakarta.

   fajar-fajar at dawn.

   berfajar to dawn.

Fajr (*A*) *al–* "Dawn"; name of the 89th chapter of the Koran.

fakar (*A*) *dul–* famous sword (belonging to Muhammad).

FAKÉD → FAKULTAS *Kedokteran*.

fakhar (*A*) glory.

fakih (*A*) expert in *fikh*/Muslim law.

fakir (*A*) **1** poor, destitute, needy; religious mendicant. **2** (sometimes used to mean) I (the personal pronoun for the first person singular, by writers in a poem, etc.). *– miskin* poor and miserable; the poor.

   kefakiran poverty.

faks (*E*) fax. *mesin –* fax machine.

faksi (*D*) faction.

faksimili (*D/E*) facsimile.

   memfaksimil to fax. *Pernyataannya difaksimili ke kantor berita Reuters di Nikosia*. His statement was faxed to the Reuters office in Nicosia.

faksionalisme (*D/E*) factionalism.

fakta (*D*) fact. *– berbicara sendiri* the facts speak for themselves. *– nyata* hard fact.

   faktanya the fact is (that).

   berfakta factual.

   memfaktakan 1 to make factual. **2** to prove with facts.

faktir → FAKTUR.

faktor (*D/E*) factor. *– kunci* key factor. *– pemersatu* unifying factor. *– pendorong dan penarik* push and pull factor. *– penentu* determining factor. *– penghambat* retarding factor. *– perancu* confounding factor. *– waktu* time factor.

faktorial (*E*) factorial.

faktual (*E*) and **faktuil** (*D*) factual; → BERFAKTA.

faktur (*D*) invoice. *– asli* original invoice. *– fiktif* a fake/fictitious invoice.

fakultas (*D*) one of the major disciplines of an Indonesian university, department/school of a university, faculty. *– Arsitéktur dan Lan(d)skap Univérsitas Trisakti* [FAL-Usakti] Department of Architecture and Landscaping, Trisakti University (Jakarta). *– Biologi* (*Univérsitas*) *Nasional* [FABIONA] Faculty of Biology, National University (Jakarta). *– Ékonomi Univérsitas Indonésia* [FE-UI] School of Economics, University of Indonesia (Depok). *– Hukum Univérsitas Indonésia* [FH-UI] Faculty/School of Law, Law School, University of Indonesia (Depok). *– Hukum dan Ilmu Pengetahuan Kemasyarakatan* [FHIPK] or [FH dan IPK] School of Law and Social Sciences. *– Ilmu-Ilmu Sosial Budaya Univérsitas Hasanudin*

[FIISBUD-, Unhas] School of Sociocultural Sciences, Hasanudin University (Ujungpandang). – *Ilmu Komunikasi Univérsitas Padjadjaran* [FIKOM-Unpad] School of Communications Science, University of Padjadjaran (Bandung). – *Ilmu Pasti dan Pengetahuan Alam* [FIPPA] School of Mathematics and Physics. – *Ilmu Pendidikan Univérsitas Cenderawasih* [FIP-Uncén] Faculty of Pedagogy, Cenderawasih University (Jayapura). – *Ilmu Sosial dan Ilmu Politik Univérsitas Gadjah Mada* [FISIPOL, UGM] School of Social Sciences and Politics, University of Gadjah Mada (Yogyakarta). – *Kedokteran Univérsitas Indonésia* [FK-UI] Medical School, University of Indonesia (Depok). – *Kedokteran Univérsitas Sumatera Utara* [FAKED-USU] School of Medicine, University of North Sumatra (Medan). – *Kedokteran Gigi Univérsitas Indonésia* [FKG-UI] School of Dentistry, University of Indonesia (Jakarta). – *Kedokteran Héwan* [FKH] School of Veterinary Medicine. – *Keguruan dan Ilmu Pendidikan* [FKIP] School of Teacher Training and Pedagogy. – *Kehutanan Institut Pertanian Bogor* [Fahutan-IPB] School of Forestry, Bogor Institute of Agriculture. – *Keséhatan Masyarakat* [FKM] School of Public Health. – *Ketatanegaraan dan Ketataniagaan Univérsitas Tujuhbelas Agustus* [FKK-Untag] School of Political Science and Business Administration, University of August Seventeen (Jakarta). – *Matématika dan Ilmu Pengetahuan Alam Univérsitas Airlangga* [FMIPA-Unair] School of Mathematics and Physics, Airlangga University (Surabaya). – *Kelompok Nonéksakta* Faculty of Humanities and Social Sciences. – *Pasca Sarjana Institut Pertanian Bogor* [FPS-IPB] (Post)graduate School, Bogor Institute of Agriculture. – *Pendidikan Bahasa dan Seni* [FPPS] School of Language and Arts Education. – *Pendidikan Ilmu Pengetahuan Sosial* [FPIPS] School of Social Sciences Education *IKIP Negeri*, Medan. – *Pendidikan Olahraga dan Keséhatan* [FPOK] School of Sports and Health Education. – *Pendidikan Téknologi dan Kejuruan* [FPTK] School of Technical and Vocational Education. – *Perikanan Univérsitas Riau* [Faperi-Unri] School of Fishery, University of Riau (Pekan Baru). – *Perikanan Institut Pertanian Bogor* [Faperikan-IPB] School of Fishery, Bogor Institute of Agriculture. – *Pertanian Univérsitas Tadulako* [Faperta-Untad] School of Agriculture, University of Tadulako (Palu). – *Peternakan Institut Pertanian Bogor* [FAPÉT-IPB] School of Animal Husbandry, Bogor Institute of Agriculture. – *Psikologi Univérsitas Indonésia* [F.Psi-UI] School of Psychology, University of Indonesia (Depok). – *Sastra Univérsitas Indonésia* [FS-UI] School of Literature, University of Indonesia (Depok). – *Seni Rupa dan Désain Institut Téknologi Bandung* [FSRD-ITB] School of Fine Arts and Design, Bandung Institute of Technology. – *Téknik Sipil dan Perencanaan Institut Téknologi Bandung* [FTSP-ITB] School of Civil Engineering and Planning, Bandung Institute of Technology. – *Téknologi dan Mékanisasi Pertanian Institut Pertanian Bogor* [Fatéméta-IPB] Department of Technology and Agricultural Mechanization, Bogor Institute of Agriculture. – *Téknologi Mineral Institut Téknologi Bandung* [FTM-ITB] Faculty of Mineral Technology, Bandung Institute of Technology. – *Téknologi Pertanian Institut Pertanian Bogor* [FTP-IPB] Faculty of Agricultural Technology, Bogor Institute of Agriculture. – *Théologia* [FTh] School of Theology.
  sefakultas of the same faculty, in the same school. *teman ~* fellow faculty member.
fakultatif and **fakultatip** (*D*) optional.
fakultét (*D ob*) → FAKULTAS.
fakulti (*Mal*) → FAKULTAS.
fal I (*A*) omen.
FAL II → FAKULTAS *Arsitéktur dan Lan(d)skap*.
falah (*A*) victory.
falak (*A*) vault of heaven, celestial sphere. *ilmu –* astronomy.
falakiah (*A*) **1** astronomical. **2** astrology, astronomy.
Falaq (*A*) "Daybreak"; name of the 113th chapter of the Koran.
Falasha Ethiopians who practice a form of Judaism.
Falastin (*A*) Palestine.
Falastini (*A*) a Palestinian.
Falastiniyyin (*A*) Palestinians.

Falintil (*Forças Armadas do Libertaca° Nacional do Timor-Ésté*) Armed Forces of National Liberation of East Timor: Fretilin's armed forces.
falka → PALKA.
fals (*D*) false (of musical tone), off-key.
falsafah and **falsafat** (*A*) philosophy. – *amalan* situational ethics. – *burung onta/unta* an ostrich-like policy, denial, i.e., to pretend that a problem does not exist. – *hidup* philosophy of life. – *Melayu Islam Beraja* [MIB] Royal Islamic Malay Philosophy (comparable to Indonesia's *Pancasila*). – *padi* with wisdom comes modesty.
  berfalsafah to philosophize, be philosophical.
  berfalsafahkan based on the philosophy of. *negara yang ~ Pancasila* a nation based on *Pancasila*.
falsafi (*A*) philosophical. *problém –* a philosophical problem.
falsifikasi (*D*) falsification.
fam (*Min*) family name.
famili (*D*) **1** family. **2** relative. *dengan dalih dipanggil seorang –nya* under the pretext of having been called by a relative. – *pak anu* (*coq*) the system in which s.o. is quickly hired for a job when he happens to be a relative of a certain big shot. **3** related. *ada hubungan – dengan* to be related to. *tidak ada sangkut paut – dengan* unrelated to.
  sefamili of the same family. *~ dengan ketimun* belonging to the same family as the cucumber.
  berfamili to have a family. *~ dengan* to be related to.
  berfamilikan to have ... in one's family. *~ janda yang kaya* to have a rich widow in one's family.
  kefamilian family-like.
  perfamilian family relations/affairs, family (*mod*).
familia (sporadically) family (a subdivision in the classification of plants).
familiar (*D/E*) **1** familiar, informal. **2** accustomed to, used to.
familiarisasi (*D*) familiarization.
familiér (*D*) → FAMILIAR. friendly. *Malam silaturrahmi itu berlangsung dalam suasana –*. The amicable soirée took place in a friendly atmosphere.
FAN → FRAKSI *Amanat Nasional*.
fana (*A*) brief, perishable, transitory, transient, fleeting; *opp* ABADI. *dari negeri yang – ke negeri yang baka* from the perishable to the imperishable world, from earth to heaven.
  kefanaan transitoriness, fleetingness. *segala perselisihan ~* all temporal disputes.
fanatik (*D/E*) fanatic.
  kefanatikan fanaticism.
fanatikus (*D*) a fanatic.
fanatisme (*D*) → KEFANATIKAN. – *buta* blind fanaticism.
fani (*ob*) → FANA.
fans (*E*) fan(s), supporter(s). *Anggap saja dia itu –mu.* Just think of her as one of your fans.
  ngefans to be a fan (of). *Ia mémang ~ berat pada Tyson.* He's really a devoted fan of Tyson.
fantasi (*D*) fantasy, imagination. *saputangan –* fancy handkerchief. *tenaga –* power of imagination.
  berfantasi to fantasize, indulge in fantasies.
  memfantasikan to fantasize about.
fantastik (*E*) and **fantastis** (*D*) fantastic.
  sefantastis as fantastic as. *tidak – skandal krédit Bapindo* not as fantastic as the Bapindo credit scandal.
FAO [Food and Agricultural Organization].
Faperi → FAKULTAS *Perikanan*.
Faperikan → FAKULTAS *Perikanan*.
Faperta → FAKULTAS *Pertanian*.
Fapét → FAKULTAS *Peternakan*.
faraaidl, **faraid** and **fara'idz** (*A*) religious obligations; → FARDHU. *hukum –* Muslim law of inheritance.
farad khana (*Pers*) guesthouse.
faraj (*A ob*) vagina, vulva, pudendum.
farak (*A*) **1** irregularity. **2** difference, distinction, (*fin*) spread.
  faraknya it concerns. *empat ~* it concerns four problems, four problems are involved. *jauh ~* there's a big difference.
faraku (*Port*) to faint.

Faransa (*A*) France.

Faransawi (*A*) French.

fard(h)u I (*A*) obligatory (by religious law), duty; → PERLU. *salat* – obligatory prayer. *-(l-)ain* religious obligation incumbent on all Muslims individually. *-(l-)kifayah* collective religious obligation (not incumbent on all Muslims).

memfard(h)ukan to oblige, require.

fardu II (*ob*) package, parcel.

farik (*A*) different, discrete, distinctive, separating.

faring (*D*) pharynx.

faringal (*D*) pharyngeal.

faringitis (*D/E*) pharyngitis; → RADANG *tenggorokan*.

farinya (*Port ob*) meal, flour.

Faris (*A*) Persia; Iran.

Farisi I (*A*) Persian.

farisi II Pharisee, hypocrite.

farji (*A ob*) → FARAJ.

fark (*A*) separation, severance, division, partition.

farmakodinamik (*D/E*) pharmacodynamic.

farmakognosi (*D*) pharmacognosy.

farmakokinétik (*E*) pharmacokinetics.

farmakoklinik (*D/E*) pharmacoclinic.

farmakologi (*D/E*) pharmacology. *ahli/pakar* – pharmacologist.

farmakopé (*D*) pharmacopoeia.

farman → FIRMAN.

farmasi (*D*) pharmacy.

kefarmasian pharmaceutical. *perkembangan dunia ~ di Indonésia* the development of the pharmaceutical world in Indonesia.

farmasis (*E*) pharmacist; → APOTÉKER.

farmasiwan → FARMASIS.

farming (*D/E*) farming; → USAHA *tani. Akadémi – Gajahmungkur* Gajahmungkur Farming Academy (Wonogiri). *Sekolah – Menengah Atas* [*SFMA*] Senior High School for Farming (at Sekawul, Ungaran, Central Java).

farsakh (*A cla*) linear measure of about 6–7 km or about 3 miles, parasang.

Farsi (*A?*) Persian; Iranian.

fas (in acronyms) → FASILITAS.

fasa (*D*) phase.

fasad (*A*) damage, flaw. *–fil ardhi* and *–fi alardi* discord in this world.

fasaha(h) (*A*) purity of the language; fluency, eloquence; → FASIH.

fasakh (*A*) divorce by judicial decree (due to physical or mental disability of the husband, etc.); → PASAH I.

memfasakh to divorce by such decree. *Tapi masalah keperawanan tak bisa sebagai alasan untuk ~ istri.* But the question of virginity cannot be a reason for divorcing one's wife.

fasal (*A*) **1** paragraph, section, chapter. **2** concerning, as to, regarding; → PASAL.

fase (*D*) → FASA. *– percobaan* pilot phase.

fasét (*D*) facet.

FASI → FÉDÉRASI *Aéro Sport Indonésia*.

fasial (*D*) facial.

fasid (*A*) → FASAKH. **memfasidkan** to dissolve, annul (a marriage).

fasih (*A*) fluent (in speaking a language), glib, voluble. *– lidah* (and *berlidah –*) eloquent.

sefasih as fluent as.

fasih-memfasih *~ langkah* to keep up the martial art of *silat*.

memfasihkan to make fluent.

memperfasihkan to make s.t. fluent. *~ lidah bahasa Belanda* to keep up one's Dutch.

kefasihan eloquence, fluency.

fasihat (*A*) eloquence.

fasik (*A*) godless, sinful, dissolute, iniquitous, nefarious; trespasser, sinner; fornicator; s.o. not meeting the legal requirements of righteousness (Muslim law).

kefasikan godlessness, sin.

fasilitas (*D*) facility, facilities. *Memiliki – bola gelinding.* It has a bowling alley. *– keimigrasian* [faskim] immigration facilities. *– kesejahteraan* welfare facilities. *– krédit* credit (facilities). *– lapangan ténis di dalam dan luar ruangan* indoor and outdoor tennis court facilities. *– rawat-nginap/perawatan-menginap* in-patient facilities. *– sosial* [fasos] social facilities. *– télékomuni-* *kasi* [fastél] telecommunications facilities. *– umum* [fasum] public facilities.

fasilitasi (*D*) facilitation.

memfasilitasi to facilitate s.t., provide facilities (for). *Pemerintah tidak cukup hanya ~ bagi perusahaan yang mengkhususkan diri dalam pengolahan limbah.* It is not enough for the government to provide facilities for companies that distinguish themselves in processing waste.

pemfasilitasian facilitating.

fasilitator (*E*) facilitator.

fasilitét (*D*) → FASILITAS.

Fasilkom [Fakultas Ilmu Komputer] School of Computer Science.

fasis (*D*) fascist.

fasis-fasisan fascistic.

kefasisan fascism.

fasisme (*D*) fascism; → KEFASISAN.

fasistis (*D*) fascist (*mod*).

faskim → FASILITAS *keimigrasian*.

fasos → FASILITAS *sosial*.

fastabikhulkhairat (*A*) and **fastabiqul khairat** competing in doing good deeds.

berfastabikhulkhairat to compete in this way. *Dimintanya dapat ~ dalam mempersatukan bangsa dan negara manapun.* He asked them to compete in doing good deeds in unifying any nation and country.

fastél → FASILITAS *télékomunikasi*.

fastiu (*A IBT*) bored; boredom.

fasum [fasilitas umum] public facilities.

fatah I (*A*) opener (the person), unlocker. *al –* a) God (the unlocker of mercy). b) the main wing of the PLO. *ya – al kulub* O unlocker of hearts! (a traditional heading for a letter of enquiry).

fatah II (*A*) a vowel point above the line representing short *a* or, if followed by alif, long *a*.

fatahah → FATAH II.

fatal (*D/E*) fatal. *– bagi* fatal to.

kefatalan fatality.

fatalis (*D*) fatalist.

fatalisme (*D/E*) fatalism.

fatalistik (*E*) and **fatalistis** (*D*) fatalistic.

fatamorgana (*D*) fata morgana.

fatan (*A*) intelligent, clever.

Fatayat NU Young Women's Organization of the Nahdlatul Ulama party.

Fatéméta → FAKULTAS *Téknologi dan Mékanisasi Pertanian*.

fath (*A*) "Victory"; name of the 48th chapter of the Koran.

fathah → FATAH II.

fathiyah (*A*) openness; → KETERBUKAAN.

fatihah (*A*) **1** the confession of faith. **2** the first *surah*/chapter of the Koran.

fatik (*E*) fatigue; → KELELAHAN.

fatir I (*A ob*) unleavened.

fatir II (*A*) "The Originator, The Angels"; name of the 35th chapter of the Koran.

fatsal → FASAL, PASAL.

fatsoen and **fatsun** (*D*) decorum, good manners.

fatur (*A*) **1** meal breaking a fast (in the evening); → SAUR I, SAHUR. **2** breakfast; → SARAPAN.

fatwa (*A*) **1** legal decision, edict, i.e., the findings of a competent *mufti* or Muslim jurist. **2** good advice, counsel. **3** admonition, warning; → PETUA(H). *surat – waris* document stating that property has been willed to s.o.

berfatwa to advise, give advice (generally on religious matters).

memfatwai to advise s.o.

memfatwakan to give ... as advice, advise.

fauna (*D*) fauna, the animals of a specified region.

fauteuil (*Fr D*) armchair.

fauvisme (*Fr D*) fauvism.

favorit (*D/E*) favorite; → PRIMADONA.

memfavoritkan to favor.

kefavoritan favoritism.

pemfavoritan favoritism, favoring.

favoritisme (*D/E*) favoritism; → PEMFAVORITAN.

fayit → FAILIT.
FBSI → FÉDERASI *Buruh Seluruh Indonésia*.
FDKB → FRAKSI *Démokrasi Kasih Bangsa*.
FE → FAKULTAS *Ékonomi*.
Feb. (*abbr*) [Fébruari] February.
Fébruari (*D*) February.
fédayeen (*A*) /fédayin/ Palestinian fighter.
féderal (*D/E*) federal.
féderalis (*D/E*) federalist.
féderalisme (*D/E*) federalism.
féderalistis (*D*) federalistic.
féderasi (*D/E*) federation. – *Républik Jerman* Republic of Germany. – *Aéro Sport Indonésia* [FASI] Aero Sport Federation of Indonesia. – *Buruh Seluruh Indonésia* [FBSI] All-Indonesia Labor Federation. – *Perhimpunan Bank Perkréditan Rakyat Indonésia* [Férbapri] Federation of Indonesian People's Credit Bank Associations.
fediah → PEDIAH.
feduli (*A ob*) → PEDULI.
fékih → FIKIH.
fékunditas (*E*) fecundity.
félbét (*D*) camp bed.
féli → VÉLI.
féllah (*A ob*) agriculturalist, farmer; → PETANI.
félspar (*D*) fel(d)spar.
fémifobia (*E*) femiphobia.
Fémina name of a biweekly magazine for women.
féminin (*D/E*) feminine.
  kefémininan femininity.
féminisme (*D/E*) feminism.
féminis(t) (*D/E*) feminist.
féminitas (*E*) femininity.
fenér → FINÉÉR.
féng shui (*C*) geomancy.
fénilbutason and **fénilbutazon** (*E*) phenyl butazone.
fénilétilamin (*E*) phenyl ethylamine.
fénol (*D/E*) phenol.
fénolik (*E*) phenolic. *senyawa* – phenolic compound.
fénologi (*D/E*) phenology.
fénomén(a) (*D*) phenomena.
fénoménal (*D/E*) phenomenal.
fénoménologi (*D/E*) phenomenology.
fénoménologik (*E*) and **fénoménologis** (*D*) phenomenological.
fénomin (*D/E*) phenomenon (the person).
fénotip(e) (*D/E*) phenotype. *pemeriksaan* – phenotype examination.
féntilasi → VÉNTILASI.
féodal (*D*) feudal.
  keféodalan feudalism.
féodalis (*D*) feudalist.
féodalisme (*D*) → KEFÉODALAN.
féodalistik (*E*) and **féodalistis** (*D*) feudalistic.
Férbabri → FÉDERASI *Perhimpunan Bank Perkréditan Rakyat Indonésia*.
féri (*D*) ferry; → KAPAL *penyeberangan*.
  perférian ferry system, ferry (*mod*).
Feringgi (*A Pers?* through *Port*) Portuguese, Westerner.
férmén (*D/E*) ferment.
férméntasi (*D*) fermentation; → PERAGIAN.
  memférméntasikan to ferment. ~ *biji-biji kakao* to ferment cacao seeds.
  terférméntasi(kan) fermented.
féromon (*D/E*) pheromone.
féronikel (*D/E*) ferronickel.
férosemén (*D/E*) ferrocement.
férosilikon (*E*) ferrosilicon.
fértil (*D/E*) fertile.
fértilisasi (*D*) fertilization. – *in-vitro* in-vitro fertilization, IVF.
fértilitas (*D*) fertility. *ahli* – fertilizer (the person). *tingkat* – total total fertility rate, TFR.
féstival (*D/E*) festival. – *film* film festival. – *masakan Indonésia* Indonesian food festival.

memféstivalkan to hold a festival on ...
fétakompli (*Fr D*) fait accompli.
  memfétakomplikan to confront with a fait accompli.
fétisisme (*D/E*) fetishism.
fétor (*Port*) (in Nusa Tenggara) **1** village chief. **2** chief of an ethnic group.
  kefétoran 1 viceroyalty. **2** village.
fétsin → VÉTSIN.
FHIPK → FAKULTAS *Hukum dan Ilmu Pengetahuan Kemasyarakatan*.
FH-UI → FAKULTAS *Hukum Univérsitas Indonésia*.
fi (*A*) in, at, (up)on, regarding. *–l alam* on earth, in the world. *–l hal* now, immediately. *–l sabilillah* in Allah's cause.
fiah (*A*) (clandestine) cell.
fiasko (*D/E*) fiasco.
fiat (*D/E*) fiat. – *éksékusi* order for execution.
  memfiat to issue a fiat.
fiber (*D/E*) fiber; → SERAT. – *optik* optical fiber.
fibrasi (*D*) vibration.
fibril (*D/E*) fibril.
fibrilasi (*D*) fibrillation. – *véntrikular* ventricular fibrillation.
fibrin (*D/E*) fibrin.
fibrinogén (*D/E*) fibrinogen.
fidah (*A ob*) silver.
fides (*L*) faith.
fidiah → PEDIAH.
fidusia (*D*) fiduciary.
fidyah (*A*) compensation/substitution/alternative (*usu* in the form of food, such as rice, etc.) that has to be paid by a person who has to leave the *salat* or skip *puasa* due to illness or old age.
fifty-fifty (*E*) fifty-fifty. *kans Indonésia* – Indonesia has a fifty-fifty chance.
figh → FIKH.
figur (*D/E*) **1** shape, appearance. **2** person, (leading public) figure.
figuran(t) (*D*) an extra (actor), s.o. who has a walk-on role, supernumerary.
figuratif (*D*) pictorial.
fihak (*A*) → PIHAK. **kesefihakan** bias, one-sidedness.
fiil I (*A*) (good) action, work. *kata* – (*gram*) verb.
Fiil II → FIL.
FIISRUD → FAKULTAS *Ilmu-Ilmu Sosial Budaya*.
fikh (*A*) and **fikih** the system of jurisprudence; the legal foundation of Islamic religious, political and civil life.
fikir (*A*) → PIKIR. **berfikir** to think. ~ *yang berulang* to rethink.
fikrah (*A*) ideology, way of thinking. – *Islamiyah Indunisiyah* Indonesian Islamic viewpoint.
fiksasi (*D*) fixation.
fiksi (*D*) fiction. – *ilmiah/sains* science fiction. – *hiper* hyperfiction.
fiksyen (*E*) fiction; → FIKSI.
fiktif (*D*) fictitious, imaginary.
  kefiktifan fictitiousness.
Fil (*A*) "The Elephant"; name of the 105th chapter of the Koran.
filamén (*D/E*) *benang* – filament polyester.
filantrop (*D*) philanthropist.
filantropi (*D/E*) philanthropy.
filantropis (*D*) philanthropic.
filantropisme (*D/E*) philanthropism.
filariasis (*D/E*) elephantiasis.
filateli (*D/E*) philately.
  perfilatelian philatelic, philatelic matters.
filatelis (*D/E*) philatelist.
filem → FILM.
filharmoni (*D*) philharmonic.
filial (*D*) branch (office).
filigram (*D*) watermark, filigrain.
filing I (*E coq*) **1** lottery prediction, hunch. **2** feeling.
filing II (*E*) filing. – *kabinét* filing cabinet.
Filipina Philippines.
film (*D*) /filem/ **1** film, movie. *bintang* – movie star. *kru* – film crew. *industri* – film industry. *main* – to act in a film. *mencuci* – to develop film. *Pekan* – *Indonésia* Indonesian Film Week. *pemain* – film actor. *pemutaran perdana* – *ini* this movie's premiere/first

showing. *pengunjung* – moviegoer. *pertunjukan perdana/pertama* – film premiere. *seni* – art of the film. *tampil dalam* – to appear in a film. *-nya laris* full house. – *3D* three-dimensional film. – *aksi* action film. – *anak-anak* children's movie. – *animasi* animated film. – *bak-buk-bak-buk* (*coq*) action film. – *ber-ASA rendah/tinggi* film with a low/high ASA index (indicating sensitivity to light). – *berbiaya murah* low-cost film. – *berbugil-ria* pornographic film. – *berwarna* color film. – *bertéma(kan)* ... a film with a ... theme. – *(ber)warna* color film, film in color. – *bicara* talking picture. – *biru* blue/pornographic film. – *bisu* silent film. – *cabul* blue/pornographic film. – *cerita* nondocumentary film. – *dagelan* comedy. – *dalam negeri* domestic film. – *dibintangi* S a film starring S. – *dokuméntér* a documentary motion picture. – *dor-doran* action film. – *érotik* (*E*) and – *érotis* (*D*) erotic/pornographic film. – *érotis lunak* softcore porn film. – *fiksi ilmiah/ilmu* science-fiction film. – *flora dan fauna* nature film. – *gituan* pornographic film. – *hiburan* feature film. – *hitam putih* a movie in black and white. – *horor* horror film. – *hot* hardcore porn film. – *humaniora* film about the humanities. – *iklan* advertising film. – *jorok* hardcore porno film. – *kacangan* second-rate film. – *kartun* movie cartoon. – *keluarga* family film. – *keras* action film. – *koboi* cowboy movie, western. – *kodian* serial (of an inferior quality). – *komédi* a comedy. – *kultural-édukatif* educational-cultural film. – *laga* action film. – *layar kaca* small-screen film. – *layar lébar* wide-screen film. – *layar-tancap* film shown on a moveable screen pegged into the ground. – *mandarin* a Chinese film. – *misbar* a film shown in the open air; → MISBAR. – *mistik* a mystery (film). – *musik* musical (film). – *noncerita* a documentary (film). – *olahraga* sports film. – *panas* hardcore porn film. – *perang* war movie. – *perdana* film shown for a premiere. – *porno/pornografi(s)* a pornographic film. – *promosi* a promotional film. – *sandiwara* screenplay. **memfilmsandiwarakan** to make into a screenplay. – *sejarah* historical drama. – *séks* porno film. – *seram* horror movie. – *séri* serial. – *séri mini* miniseries. – *silat* kung-fu film. – *téatris* theatrical film. – *télévisi* TV film. **memfilmtélévisikan** to make into a TV film. *Élvis difilmtélévisikan* a TV film has been made about Elvis. – *ukuran 35 mm* a 35-mm film. – *unyil* porno film. – *vidéo* video film (for a VCR). – *wéstern* a western (film). – *yang menegangkan* a thriller. – *yang sudah siap édar* a film which has passed the board of censors and is ready for distribution. **2** film, i.e., a fine, thin skin, surface, layer or coating. – *tipis yang terbuat dari polimér* a thin film made of polymer.
    memfilmkan to film.
    perfilman 1 filming. **2** film production.
filmiah film (*mod*), filmic.
filmis (*D*) **1** cinematographic. **2** sensational.
filmisasi (*E*) filmization.
filmologi filmology.
filmologis (*D*) filmologic.
filolog (*D*) philologist.
filologi (*D/E*) philology.
filologis (*D*) philological.
Filopur a trade name for a water purifier.
filosof (*D*) philosopher. – *fénoménologi* phenomenological philosopher.
filosofi (*D/E*) → FILSAFAT.
    berfilosofi to philosophize.
filosofik (*E*) and **filosofis** (*D*) philosophic(al).
filsafah and **filsafat** (*A*) philosophy. – *akhlak* ethics. – *ilmu pengetahuan* epistemology.
    berfilsafah to philosophize, speculate, theorize, moralize.
    memfilsafahkan to philosophize about.
    kefilsafahan philosophy, philosophical.
    kefilsafah-filsafahan pseudo-philosophical.
filsafati (*A*) → FILOSOFIS, KEFILSAFAHAN.
filsafi (*A*) philosophic. *kaum* – philosophers.
filsuf (*A*) philosopher.
filter (*D/E*) filter (also in cigarette). – *air* water filter. – *minyak* oil filter.
    berfilter with a filter. *rokok* ~ filter tip cigarette.
filum (*D*) phylum.

fin (*E*) fin, an underwater swimmer's rubber flipper; → SEPATU katak. – *swimming* skin diving.
final (*D/E*) **1** final. **2** (in sports) finale.
    memfinalkan to finalize.
finalis (*D/E*) finalist (in contests).
finalisasi (*E*) finalization.
finansial (*E*) and **finansiil** (*D*) financial.
finansir (*D*) financier; → CUKONG I, PENYANDANG *dana*.
    memfinansir to finance.
finéc and **finék** [finansial-ékonomi] financial-economic (matters).
finéér and **finir** (*D*) veneer.
finis (*D/E*) finish (in sports).
finisying and **finishing** (*E*) finish, finishing.
Finlandia Finland.
FIPIA → FAKULTAS *Ilmu Pasti dan Alam*. Mathematics and Natural Science Faculty.
fiqh and **fiqih** (*A*) → FIKIH. *kaidah-kaidah* – legal maxims. *usul* – legal theory. – *munakahat* marriage law. – *siasah* political jurisprudence.
firajullah → FIRJATULLAH.
firak (*A*) group.
firaon → FIRAUN.
firasah and **firasat** (*A*) **1** countenance, face, facial expression, appearance, aspect, looks, air. *ilmu –* a) physiognomy. *ahli* – physiognomist. b) characterology, ethology. **2** sign(s) on s.o.'s face from which his future can be seen forty days in advance. **3** presentiment, hunch, omen, feeling (that s.t. is going to happen). *ilmu –* art of prediction or prognostication. *mendapat* – to have a hunch, have the feeling that something is going to happen. – *jelék* a bad omen.
    berfirasat to have a hunch.
    memfirasatkan to have a hunch about/that.
Firaun (*A*) Pharaoh.
firdaus (*A*) **1** (Christian) paradise. **2** second heaven (in Islamic theology).
firdausi (*A*) paradisiacal, heavenly.
firjatullah (*A*) Allah's joy.
firkah (*A*) sect.
firma (*D*) business firm, i.e., a company in which the owners are fully responsible for the company's liabilities.
firman (*Pers*) **1** order, command, decree, commandment (*esp* of God or the king). **2** the word of God, apocalypse. *seperti – Allah* in accordance with God's word.
    be(r)firman to order, command.
    memfirmankan to order/command s.t.
firqah (*A*) group, troop, detachment, party, company, band.
firus I (*A*) *batu* – a turquoise; → PIRUS.
firus II (*D*) → VIRUS.
FIS → FAKULTAS *Ilmu Sosial*.
fisi (*E*) fission. – *inti* nuclear fission.
fisibel (*E*) feasible. *Proyéknya sudah distudi dan sangat –*. The project has been studied and is very feasible.
fisibilitas (*E*) feasibility.
fisik (*D*) physical. *ahli térapi* – physiotherapist. *kekuatan* – physical strength. *térapi* – physical therapy.
fisika (*D*) *ilmu* – physics. *ahli* – *atmosfér* atmospheric physicist. *ahli* – *inti* nuclear physicist. *ilmu* – physics. – *atomistik* atomic physics. – *bahan* materials physics. – *batuan* lithogic physics. – *inti* nuclear physics. – *lanjut* advanced physics. – *lingkungan* environmental physics. – *murni* pure physics. – *nuklir ékspériméntal* experimental nuclear physics. – *perbintangan* astrophysics. – *rokét* rocket physics. – *terapan* applied physics.
fisikal (*E*) physical.
fisikalistis (*E*) physical. *pembangunan yang sangat* – a very physical development.
fisikawan physicist. – *zarah keunsuran* elementary particle physicist.
fisikawi (*D*) physical (*mod*). *perlakuan* – physical treatment.
fisiognomi (*D/E*) physiognomy, facial features and expressions. *ahli* – physiognomist.
fisiograf (*D*) physiographist.
fisiografi (*D/E*)) physiography.
fisiografis (*D*) physiographic.

fisiokrat (*D/E*) physiocrat.
fisiolog (*D*) physiologist.
fisiologi (*D/E*) physiology. *ahli* – physiologist.
fisiologik (*E*) and **fisiologis** (*D*) physiologic.
fisiopatologis (*D*) physiopathologic.
fisiotérapi (*D/E*) physiotherapy.
fisiotérapis (*D/E*) physiotherapist.
FISIP(OL) → FAKULTAS *Ilmu Sosial dan Politik*.
fisis (*D*) → FISIK.
fiskal 1 (*D*) fiscal, having to do with the public treasury or revenues, tax; → PAJAK. *surat* – document showing that the exit tax was paid. *tahun* – fiscal year. **2** civil service employee in charge of the interests of the State, public prosecutor.
fiskus (*D*) fiscal; treasury, Internal Revenue Service, taxman.
fistan (*Pers*) shirt.
fistél (*D*) fistula.
fit (*D/E*) fit, in good physical condition.
fiting (*D/E*) light socket, fixture, fitting (of a bulb).
fitnah (*A*) false accusation, slander, libel, calumny, backbiting. *kena* – to be slandered. – *secara tertulis* libel. – *itu lebih kejam dari pembunuhan*. Slander is crueler than murder.
  memfitnah(kan) to accuse falsely, slander, libel, defame.
  terfitnah slandered, libeled, defamed.
  pemfitnah slanderer, backbiter.
  (pem)fitnahan 1 slander, libel, defamation. **2** slanderous, libelous.
fitofarmaka phytopharmacies.
fitogéografi (*D/E*) phytogeography.
fitohormon (*D/E*) phytohormone.
fitométer (*D/E*) phytometer.
fitopatologi (*D/E*) phytopathology.
fitoplankton (*D/E*) phytoplankton.
fitotérapi (*D/E*) phytotherapy.
fitotoksin (*D/E*) phytotoxin.
fitotoksoid (*D/E*) phytotoxoid.
fitr → FITRI II.
fitrah I (*A*) obligatory tithe, alms in the form of a *kulak* of rice, etc. given by each Muslim at the end of the fasting month; → ZAKAT.
  berfitrah to give a tithe or alms.
  memfitrahkan to observe/carry out the giving of a tithe or alms on behalf of s.o.
fitrah and **fitrat II** (*A*) **1** natural tendency/characteristics. **2** religious beliefs/inclinations. – *insaniyah* human nature. – *politik* political tendency.
  kefitrahan religiosity.
fitri I (*A*) natural, pure; → FITRAH II.
fitri II (*A*) end of the fast, breaking the fast; → BERBUKA *puasa*, FUTUR I.
fitri(y)ah (*A*) natural; → FITRI II.
fitrin (*D*) vitrine.
fitur (*E*) feature (special characteristic of a product).
fityah (*A*) slave (*esp* one who is emancipated).
FK → FAKULTAS *Kedokteran*.
FKG → FAKULTAS *Kedokteran Gigi*.
FKH → FAKULTAS *Kedokteran Héwan*.
FKIP /éf-kip/ → FAKULTAS *Keguruan dan Ilmu Pendidikan*.
FKM [Front Kedaulatan Maluku] Front for the Sovereignty of the Moluccas.
FKMUI → FAKULTAS *Keséhatan Masyarakat Univérsitas Indonésia*.
F-KP → FRAKSI *Karya Pembangunan*.
fla → VLA.
flaai (*E sl*) /flai/ high on drugs.
flakon (*D*) bottle, flask.
Flam (*D*) *orang* – a Flemish person.
flamboyan I (*D*) flamboyant tree, *Poinciana regia*.
flamboyan II (*D*) showy, flamboyant.
flaménco (*D/E*) /flaméngko/ flamenco dancing. *penari* – flamenco dancer.
flamingo (*D/E*) *burung* – flamingo, *Phoenicopterus ruber*.
flanél (*D/E*) flannel.
flat (*D/E*) apartment, flat. – *jejaka* bachelor flat.
flavoprotéin (*D/E*) flavoprotein.
flégmatis (*D*) phlegmatic.

flék → VLÉK.
fléksi (*D*) flexion, bending; inflection, inflectional. *bahasa* – inflectional language.
fléksibel (*D/E*) flexible. *jam kerja* – flex time.
  sefléksibel as flexible as.
  kefléksibelan flexibility.
  memfléksibelkan to make s.t. flexible. *Ménpora menganggap BKK itu perlu difléksibelkan*. The Minister of State for Youth and Sports thinks that it is necessary to make the BKK more flexible.
fléksibilitas → KEFLÉKSIBELAN.
flénsa I → INFLUÉNSA.
flénsa II (*D/E*) flange.
flés (*D*) flask; → PELÉS.
flésko (*Port Manado*) square bottle.
flin-flan denigrating form of *plin-plan*.
flis (*D*) fleece (from sheep).
Flit (*D*) trademark of an insecticide spray.
  memflit to spray with Flit.
Flobamora [Florés, Sumba, Timor dan Alor] the islands of Flores, Sumba, Timor and Alor.
floém (*D*) phlegm.
flokulasi (*E*) flocalation.
floor (*E*) /flor/ audience; → HADIRIN.
flop I (*D/E*) flop, failure.
flop II *gaya* – technique at high jumping.
flora (*D/E*) flora, plants of a region.
floral (*E*) floral. *bermotif* – with a floral motif.
florét (*D*) foil (fencing sword).
Florida Pantai Suralaya at Merak, Banten, West Java.
florikultura (*E*) floriculture.
flotasi (*D*) flotation.
flotila (*D/E*) flotilla.
Flotim [Florés Timur] East Flores (Regency).
flu (*D/E*) flu, influenza. – *céléng* swine flu. – *Hongkong* Hongkong flu. – *sanum* meningitis.
flugel (*G D*) grand piano.
fluks (*D/E*) flux.
fluktuasi (*D*) fluctuation. – *harga* price fluctuation.
  berfluktuasi to fluctuate.
fluktuatif fluctuating. *Harga komoditi itu sangat* –. The prices of those commodities fluctuate a lot.
fluor (*D*) fluorine.
fluorésénsi (*D*) fluorescence.
fluorida (*D*) fluoride.
fluoridasi (*E*) fluoridation.
fluorosis (*E*) fluorosis.
fly → FLAAI.
fly-over (*E*) /flai ofer/ and **flypass** /flaipas/ overpass.
FMIPA → FAKULTAS *Matématika dan Ilmu Pengetahuan Alam*.
fobi (*D*) phobia; to have a phobia. *Saya* – *dengan ular*. I have a phobia about snakes.
fobia → FOBI.
fobik (*E*) phobic (the person).
fohte (*D ob*) foxtrot.
fokstrot (*E*) foxtrot.
fokus (*D/E*) focus. *menjadi* – *perhatian* to be the center of interest, be in the limelight.
  berfokus ~ *pada* to be focused on.
  berfokuskan to be focused on.
  memfokuskan to focus. ~ *perhatiannya kepada* to focus one's attention on. *Peningkatan program KB di Jabar difokuskan ke désa*. Boosting family planning in West Java is focusing on villages.
  terfokus ~ *pada* focused on. ~ *kepada pelanggaran* offense-centered.
  pemfokuskan focusing. ~ *kepada pasar-pasar negara-negara dinamis* focusing on the markets of dynamic countries.
folan → POLAN.
folat (*E*) folate. *asam* – folic acid.
folder (*D/E*) folder.
foli (*D*) foil.
folikel (*D/E*) follicle.

folio (*D/E*) foolscap-size (paper) (about 33 x 21.5 cm).
folklor(e) (*D/E*) folklore. *ahli ilmu* – folklorist. – *bukan lisan* non-verbal folklore. – *lisan* verbal folklore. – *sebagian lisan* partly verbal folklore.
folklorik (*E*) folkloric.
folkloris (*D*) folklorist.
fon (*E*) phone.
fondamén (*D*) foundation (of a building, etc.).
fondasi (*D*) foundation; → FONDAMÉN.
   berfondasi(kan) to be founded on.
   memfondasikan to found, lay the foundations of.
fonds (*D*) /fon(s)/ fund(s).
   fonds-fonds securities (banking).
foném (*D/E ling*) phoneme.
fonémik (*E*) and **fonémis** (*D*) (*ling*) phonemic.
fonétik (*D/E ling*) phonetics.
fonétis (*D ling*) phonetic.
fonim → FONÉM.
fonis (*D ling*) phonic.
fonograf (*D/E*) phonograph.
fonografi (*D/E*) phonography.
fonogram (*D/E*) phonogram.
fonologi (*D/E ling*) phonology.
fonologis (*D ling*) phonological.
fons → FONDS.
fontén (*D*) fountain.
fora (*D pl*) forums. – *internasional* international forums. – *multilateral* multilateral forums.
forénsik (*D/E*) forensic. *ahli* – forensic expert. *kimia* – forensic chemistry.
forés (*Min*) inner gallery.
fork (*E*) /forek/ bicycle fork.
forklift(t) (*E*) forklift. *operator* – forklift operator.
form I (*D/E*) form.
form II (*E*) form (to be filled in); → FORMULIR.
formal (*D/E*) formal.
   memformalkan to formalize.
   keformalan formality.
   pemformalan formalization. ~ *itu seharusnya berjalan bertahap.* Formalization should go in stages.
   formal-formalan in a formal way, to be formal.
formaldehid (*E*) formaldehyde.
formalin (*D/E*) formalin.
   berformalin containing formalin.
formalisasi (*E*) formalization. – *kehidupan dengan atribut-atribut Islam* formalization of life with Islamic attributes.
formalisir (*D*) **memformalisir** to formalize.
formalisme (*D/E*) formalism. – *yang mematikan* deadening formalism.
formalistik (*E*) and **formalistis** (*D*) formalistic.
formalitas (*E*) formality.
formasi (*D/E*) 1 formation. – *kemampuan dasar* formation of basic skills. 2 appointment to a position in the government.
format (*D/E*) format, form, size. – *baku* standard size. – *bersinambung* continuous form. – *lembaran* individual form.
   berformat in ... format. ~ *besar* in large format.
formatir (*D*) 1 prime-minister-designate, i.e., a person appointed by the head of state to form a cabinet of ministers. 2 leader designate (of an organization).
formatur → FORMATIR.
formiat (*D*) formic. *asam* – formic acid.
formika (*D*) formica.
formil → FORMAL. **keformilan** formality.
formol (*E*) formol.
formula (*D/E*) formula; → RUMUS.
formulaik (*E*) formulaic.
formulasi (*D*) formulation; → PERUMUSAN.
   memformulasikan to formulate.
formulir (*D*) → FORM II. 1 declaration, official form. – *bentuk K-2* the popular reference to the *SBPOA/Surat Bukti Pelaporan Orang Asing* Foreigners Registration Certificate. – *daftar barang bawaan penumpang* and – *pabéan* customs declaration.

– *lamaran* application form. – *pendaftaran* registration form. – *pertanyaan* questionnaire. 2 table. – *angkatan udara* air movement table.
   memformulir to formulate.
forna and **forno** (*Port*) (in Ambon) oven.
fors (*D/E*) force, violence.
forsa (*IBT*) robust, sturdy, strongly built; strong-minded.
forsir (*D*) **memforsir** to force (s.o., a door/lock, etc.), burst open (a door), strain (one's voice).
fortifikasi (*D*) fortification.
   memfortifikasi to fortify. *difortifikasikan vitamin A* fortified with vitamin A.
Fortuna *Déwi* – the goddess of fortune.
forum (*D/E*) forum. – *dialog* brief seminar.
forwarder (*E*) forwarder. *Gabungan – dan Ékspédisi Indonésia* [Gaféksi] Indonesian Forwarders and Forwarding Agents Association.
fosfat (*D/E*) phosphate. – *batu* rock phosphate.
fosfatida (*E*) phosphatide.
fosfolipid (*E*) phospholipid.
fosfor (*D*) phosphorus.
fosforilasi (*E*) phosphorylation.
fosil (*D/E*) fossil.
   memfosil to fossilize.
fosilisasi (*D*) fossilization.
Fosko [Forum Studi dan Komunikasi] Study and Communication Forum.
foto (*D*) photo, snapshot. *mencétak* – to print (photos from a negative); → MENGAFDRUK. *tukang* – (*coq*) photographer; → FOTOGRAFER, MAK/MAT *kodak.* – *berita* news photo. – *berwarna* color photo. – *bugil* nude photograph. – *hitam putih* black-and-white picture. – *holografi* holographic photo. – *langsung jadi* Polaroid picture. – *ronsen/rontgen* X-ray (photograph). – *ronsen dada* chest X-ray. – *udara* aerial photograph. – *warna* color photo.
   berfoto 1 to be photographed. ~ *bersama* to take a group photograph. 2 to take pictures. *mengambil kesempatan* ~ to take the opportunity to take pictures.
   memfoto(kan) to photograph, take a photograph/picture of.
   pemfotoan photographing, picture-taking.
fotodinamik (*D/E*) photodynamic(s).
fotoéléktrik (*D/E*) photoelectric.
fotogénik (*D*) photogenic.
fotograf (*D*) and **fotografer** (*E*) photographer; → MAK/MAT *kodak.* – *mode* fashion photographer.
fotografi (*D/E*) photography. – *désain grafis* graphics-design photography. – *jarak-dekat* close-up. – *jurnalistik* photojournalism. – *periklanan* advertising photography.
fotografis (*D*) photographic.
fotogramétri (*D/E*) photogrammetry.
fotogramétris (*D*) photogrammatic. *pemetaan* – photogrammatic mapping.
fotojurnalistik (*D*) photojournalism.
fotokaméra (*D*) camera.
fotokatalisis (*E*) photocatalysis.
fotokimia (*D*) photochemistry.
fotokopi (*D/E*) photocopy. *mesin* – photocopier.
   memfotokopi(kan) to photocopy, make a copy of.
   terfotokopi photocopied.
   fotokopian photocopy. *lima* ~ *ijazah* five photocopies of a diploma.
   pemfotokopian photocopying (*mod*). *téknik* ~ photocopying techniques. *usaha* ~ photocopying business.
fotolisis (*E*) photolysis.
fotométer (*D/E*) photometer.
fotomodél model, s.o. who poses for a photographer. – *kalénder* pin-up girl.
foton (*D/E*) photon.
fotorésis (*D/E*) photoresist.
fotosénsitif (*E*) photosensitive.
fotosfér (*D/E*) photosphere.
fotosintésa and **fotosintésis** (*D*) photosynthesis.

fotostudio (*D*) photographic studio.
fototustél (*D*) camera; → FOTOKAMÉRA, KAMÉRA, TUSTÉL.
fotovoltaik (*E*) photovoltaic.
fotowan (*infr*) photographer; → *mak/mat* KODAK.
foya (*D? Port?*) **foya-foya** escapades. *urusan* ~ philandering.
  (ber)foya-foya 1 to enjoy o.s., relax, have fun, take it easy. **2** to throw money around, be extravagant.
  memfoyakan to enjoy s.t.
  memfoya-foyakan to spend (money) wildly. *Uang hasil curian itu difoya-foyakannya bersama teman.* He and his buddies spent wildly the money they had stolen.
F-PDI → FRAKSI *Partai Démokrasi Indonésia.*
FPMIPS → FAKULTAS *Pendidikan Ilmu Pengetahuan Sosial.*
FPOK → FAKULTAS *Pendidikan Olahraga dan Keséhatan.*
F-PP → FRAKSI *Persatuan Pembangunan.*
FPS → FAKULTAS *Pasca-Sarjana.*
FPsi → FAKULTAS *Psikologi.*
FPTK → FAKULTAS *Pendidikan Téknologi dan Kejuruan.*
fragmén (*D/E*) fragment.
  memfragmén(t)kan to fragment.
fragméntaris (*D*) fragmentary. *secara* – scrappily, in a fragmentary way.
fragméntasi (*D*) fragmentation.
  terfragméntasi fragmented. *~nya lahan pertanian* the fragmentation of agricultural lands.
frais (*D*) (milling) cutter, mill, reamer.
fraksi (*D*) **1** fraction. **2** faction, group which acts together in Parliament or in local councils (a *fraksi* may be a party, a group of parties or individuals, or a splinter group). **3** (*petro*) cut. – *Amanat Nasional* [FAN] National Mandate Faction. – *Angkatan Bersenjata Républik Indonésia* [F-ABRI] Republic of Indonesia Armed Forced Faction. – *Démokrasi Kasih Bangsa* [FDKB] National Love Democratic Party. – *inti* (*petro*) heat cut. – *Karya Pembangunan* [F-KP] Functional (Group) Development Faction. – *Partai Démokrasi Indonésia* [F-PDI] Indonesian Democracy Party Faction. – *Partai Golkar* [FPG] Golkar Party Faction. – *Persatuan Pembangunan* [F-PP] United Development (Party) Faction. – *ringan* (*petro*) light ends. – *Utusan Daérah* [F-UD] Provincial Representatives' Faction.
fraksionasi (*E*) fractionation.
fraktur (*D/E*) fracture.
frambos (*D*) raspberry.
frambosen (*D*) raspberry (*mod*). *setrup* – raspberry-flavored syrup.
frambusia (*D*) yaws.
franc franc (the unit of currency).
franchise (*E*) franchise; → WARALABA.
fran(g)ko → PRANGKO.
Fransiskan (*D*) Franciscan. *pater* – Franciscan father. – *Asisi* Francis of Assisi.
Frans Kaisiéo the name of the airport in Biak.
frasa and **frase** (*D*) phrase.
fraséologi (*D/E*) phraseology.
frater (*D*) friar.
  frateran friary.
fratérnal (*E*) fraternal (twins).
fratérnalistis (*D*) fraternalistic.
fratérnitas → FRATERAN.
fraude (*D*) fraud.
fregat (*D*) frigate. – *berpeluru kendali antiudara* a frigate armed with antiaircraft missiles.
frékuén (*D/E*) frequent.
frékuénsi (*D*) frequency. – *ultratinggi* ultra high frequency.
  berfrékuénsi with a frequency. ~ *tunggal* with a single frequency.
frékuéntatif (*D/E*) frequentative.
frékwénsi → FRÉKUÉNSI. – *nada/terdengar* audio-frequency.
frénologi (*D*) phrenology.
fréon (*D/E*) Freon.
frésko (*D/E*) fresco.
Frétilin [Frénte Révolucionária do Timor-Ésté Indépéndénté] Revolutionary Front for the Liberation of East Timor, in Portuguese Timor; → PRÉTÉLIN.
frigidair → FRISIDÉR.

frigiditas (*D*) frigidity.
frikatif (*D/E ling*) fricative.
friksi (*D*) friction.
friser (*E*) (*infr*) freezer (in refrigerator); → RUANG *pembekuan.*
frisidér (*D/E*) refrigerator.
frit (*D*) frit, i.e., the basic material used in glass-making.
frobel (*D col*) kindergarten.
front (*D/E*) front. *organisasi* – front organization. – *belakang* home front. – *Pembébasan Nasional Moro* Moro National Liberation Front, MNLF. – *pertempuran* battle front.
frontal (*D/E*) frontal. *serangan* – a frontal attack. *tabrakan* – head-on collision.
frontir (*E*) frontier.
fronton jai alai.
fruktose (*D/E*) fructose; → GULA *singkong. sirup* – *kadar tinggi* high-fructose syrup.
frustrasi (*D*) **1** frustration; → KEGAGALAN. *membuat* – to cause frustration. **2** to be frustrated.
  berfrustrasi to be frustrated.
  kefrustrasian frustration.
FSRD → FAKULTAS *Seni Rupa dan Désain* (ITB).
FTM → FAKULTAS *Téknologi Minéral* (ITB).
FTSP → FAKULTAS *Téknik Sipil dan Perencanaan* (ITB).
fuad (*A*) heart; emotions; inner feelings. – *al-zakiah* sincere/pure heart.
F-UD → FRAKSI *Utusan Daérah.*
fufu (*Min*) method of smoking fish.
fugur (*A?*) an immoral act.
fukaha (*A*) plural of *fakih.*
fukara (*A*) plural of *fakir.*
ful (*E*) full. – *angin* air-conditioned.
  memfulkan to turn up to high, turn on full blast. *meski AC sudah ia fulkan* even though he had turned the AC up to high.
fulan (*A ob*) *si* – so and so; → POLAN.
fuli (*D*) mace (of nutmeg).
fulminan(t) (*E*) fulminant.
fulpén (*D*) → VULPÉN.
fulus (*A*) **1** money, lucre (often in an unfavorable sense). **2** covetous.
fumarol (*D/E*) fumarole.
fumigasi (*D*) fumigation.
  memfumigasi to fumigate.
fumigator (*E*) fumigant.
fundamén (*D*) foundation, basis.
fundaméntal (*E*) fundamental.
fundaméntalis (*D/E*) fundamentalist.
fundaméntalisme (*D/E*) fundamentalism. – *Islam* Islamic fundamentalism.
fundaméntil (*D*) → FUNDAMÉNTAL.
fungi (*E*) fungi, *pl* of *fungus.*
fungisida (*D*) fungicide.
fungistatik (*D*) fungistatic.
fungsi (*D*) **1** function. **2** occupation, employment. – *mengatur* regulatory function. – *pembangunan* developmental function.
  berfungsi to function, work. ~ *ganda* to have a dual function. *tidak* ~ *secara sempurna* malfunctioning. *tidak* ~ out of order, not functioning. **ketidakberfungsian** being out of order, malfunction(ing).
  memfungsikan have s.t. function (as), to put into use. *Bangunan itu belum difungsikan.* The building is not in use yet. *tidak difungsikan lagi* decommissioned, disused.
  pemfungsian (the act of) having s.t. function, putting s.t. into use.
fungsional (*E*) functional.
  pemfungsional putting into use. ~ *bajaj di jalan-jalan* putting bajajs into use on the streets.
fungsionalis (*D*) functionalist.
fungsionalisasi (*D*) functionalization.
  memfungsionalisasi to functionalize.
fungsionalisme (*D*) functionalism.
fungsionaris (*E*) functionary, official.
fungsionil (*D*) → FUNGSIONAL.
fungus (*D/E*) fungus.

Funisia Phoenicia.
fuqoro wal masakin (*A*) the poor.
furadan an insecticide available in Indonesia.
furak (*A ob*) dissimilarity, difference; → FARAK.
Furat Euphrates.
furdah (*A*) harbor, port.
furing → VURING.
furkan (*A*) **1** Scriptures which reveal the true and the false in life, i.e., the Old and New Testaments and the Koran. **2** "The Distinction"; name of the 25th chapter of the Koran.
Furnifair [Furniture fair].
furud (*A*) lawful share.
furu'i(y)ah (*A*) branch (*mod*), subsidiary matters.
furu' and **furu(k)** (*A*) deductions, conclusions derived from Islamic principles.
fusa (*E*) explosive fuse.
fusi (*D*) **1** merger, amalgamation, coalition. **2** (*phys*) fusion. – *dingin* cold fusion.
    berfusi to merge, amalgamate.
    memfusikan to merge/amalgamate s.t.
    terfusi fused.

perfusian merger, amalgamation, fusion.
fusta (*D cla*) a (Portuguese) ship.
Fusyilat (*A*) "Explanation"; name of the 41st chapter of the Koran.
futbal (*D/E*) **1** soccer ball. **2** soccer.
futuat (*A*) generosity.
futur I (*A*) break the fast; → FATUR.
futur II (*E gram*) future (tense).
futuris (*D/E*) futurist.
futurisme (*D/E*) futurism.
futuristik (*E*) and **futuristis** (*D*) futuristic.
futurolog (*D*) futurologist.
futurologi (*D/E*) futurology. *penganut aliran* – futurologist.
futurologis (*D*) futurological.
futurologiwan (*D*) futurologist.
fuya → FOYA.
fu yong hay (*C*) egg foo young.
Fv (*D leg*) [Faillissements-verordening] Bankruptcy Law.
FVI [Friesche Vlag Indonésia] the name of a Dutch dairy operating in Indonesia.
fyord (*D*) fjord.

G

g and **G I** /gé/ the seventh letter of the Latin alphabet used for writing Indonesian.

G II (*abbr*) [Gunung] Mountain, Mt. *G. Slamet* Mt. Slamet.

G III car license plate for Pekalongan.

G IV clipped form for **gay**.

G30S, G 30 S and **G-30-S** [Gerakan-30-September] the 30 September (1965) Movement.

ga I the 26th letter of the Arabic alphabet.

ga II (in acronyms) → GABUNGAN.

ga III and **ga'** → ENGGAK.

gaang (*S*) /ga'ang/ mole cricket; → ORONG-ORONG II.

gab (in acronyms) → GABUNGAN.

gabag (*Jv*) measles; → GABAK II.

   gabagen to have the measles.

gaba-gaba 1 coconut palm fronds used as a decoration; → JANUR. **2** gates decorated in that way, a triumphal arch made of those fronds. *Warga kota Médan agar memeriahkan HUT-38 Proklamsi Kemerdékaan 7 Agustus 1983 mendatang. Setiap kelurahan agar memasang – selambat-lambatnya harus selesai 15 Agustus.* The residents of Medan should celebrate the 38th anniversary of the Proclamation of Independence next August 17 (1983) in a grand way. Each village should put up ceremonial decorations which must be completed not later than August 15. **3** a thatched roof made of that material.

   bergaba-gaba with a decoration made of coconut leaves. *Segala pihak gubuk itu diberi ~ daun kelapa muda.* All sides of the hut are decorated with young coconut leaves.

   menggaba-gabai to decorate s.t. with such leaves.

gabah I rice in the husk (after threshing). *mesin pengering* – dryer. *- kering giling* [GKG] ground dry rice grains. *- kering panén* [GKP] harvested dry rice grains. *- kering simpan* [GKS] stored dry rice grains.

   menggabahkan to leave ... as unhusked rice.

   penggabah huller.

gabah II (*A*) dome, vaulting; → KUBAH.

gabah III (*J/Jv*) reckless, daring, rash; → GEGABAH.

gabai (*M*) **menggabai** to reach for s.t. (by stretching out one's arms); → GAPAI.

   tergabai to hang at an angle.

gabai-gabai (*M*) hair bun decoration made of thin gold.

gabak I (*M*) cloudy, overcast, dull (of weather). *hari* – a cloudy day. *nampak – di hulu* bad weather is heading this way.

   bergabak overcast.

   menggabak 1 gloomy, dark, overcast, dull. **2** to pour forth (of tears).

gabak II (*Jv*) measles.

   gabaken (*coq*) to have the measles.

gabar volatile.

gabardin (*E*) gabardine.

gabas done in a hasty, careless manner/style, rough; hurriedly, hastily, quickly.

   menggabas to hurry up, accelerate, quicken, speed up s.t.

   tergabas hurriedly, hastily, quickly, in a hurry.

gabes (*J/Jv*) tasteless, bland.

gabir (*M ob*) awkward, clumsy, stiff.

gableg and **gablek** (*Jv*) *tidak* – to have/own nothing.

gablog and **gablok** (*J/Jv*) **menggablog** and **nggablog** to slam shut.

   menggablokkan and **nggablokkan** to slam s.t. hard (a door, etc.).

Gabon Gabon.

gabruk (*J/Jv onom*) sound made by a heavy object falling down.

   menggabrukkan [and **nggabrukin** (*J coq*)] **1** to let s.t. fall (producing the sound "bruk"). *sembari gabrukin pantatnya di jok taksi* while flopping his rear end down on the taxi seat. **2** to put s.t. on s.t. else carelessly. **3** to dump down, slam down.

gabuk I (*J/Jv*) **1** empty (of rice-husk). **2** childless, infertile, barren. *besar -* (*coq*) big but weak.

gabuk II (*M ob*) → GABAK I. **menggabuk** overcast.

gabung bundle, sheaf, cluster, string. *bunga anggrék dua* – two bunches of orchids. *kacang panjang tiga* – three bunches of long beans.

   segabung one bundle/sheaf/bunch *~ kunci* a bunch of keys.

   bergabung 1 to join (up), link up, join forces, be with, merge. *Ia akhirnya ~ pada laskar BPRI.* Finally, he joined the Indonesian People's Revolutionary Front. *Saya akan ~ dengan kamu sebentar lagi.* I'll be with you in a minute. **2** to get together. **3** joined, combined.

   menggabung 1 to merge, join, unite, combine. *Gonta-ganti nama seolah sudah menjadi "hobi" Départemén Perdagangan. Juga sudah berkali-kali digabung dengan départemén lain, dan sekian kali pula berdiri sendiri kembali.* It's as if changing names again and again has become a "hobby" of the Department of Trade. It was also, again and again, merged with another department, and, for the n'th time, it also stood on its own two feet again. **2** to put together into sheaves.

   menggabungi to merge into, become merged with.

   menggabungkan [and **nggabungin/ngegabungin** (*J coq*)] **1** to bundle together, bale, bring together, collect, tie up together. **2** to unite, join, combine, link up, merge, fuse, annex. *~ dua perkumpulan* to merge two parties. *~ diri pada* to associate/align o.s. with, enter into partnership with. *~ diri* to join.

   tergabung 1 affiliated, joined, united, fused, merged. *negara-negara yang ~ dalam G-7* the countries which have joined the G-7/Group of Seven. **2** connected (with), related (to).

   gabungan 1 combined, joint, consolidated, collective, composite. *neraca ~* consolidated balance sheet. *sidang ~* joint session. *indéks harga saham ~* composite stock price index. *~ biaya* combined costs. **2** alliance, union, federation, consolidation, merger, fusion, community. *~ béa* customs union. *~ otak* brain trust. *~ tentara* joint force. *Partai Persatuan Pembangunan (PPP) adalah ~ beberapa partai Islam.* The United Democratic Party (PPP) is a merger of several Islamic parties. *~ keuntungan dan kerugian* community of profit and loss. **3** (*elec*) gang(ed).

   penggabung combiner, combination.

   penggabungan 1 combining, uniting, merging, merger, consolidating, joining, joinder. *~ gugatan* consolidation of claims. *~ perkara* consolidation of cases. *~ usaha* merger. **2** (*elec*) ganging.

   pergabungan association, union, federation, fusion.

gabus I *ikan* – a freshwater fish, murrel, *Ophicephalus striatus*. *Ikan -lah yang suka memakan anaknya.* The murrel likes to eat its young.

gabus II cork, round piece of cork used as a bottle stopper. *kayu* – spongy wood (from the *pohon -*, *Alstonia scholaris/Sonneratia acida*) (used to whet knives, etc.). *sutera* – crêpe. *topi* – pith helmet, topee; → TOPI *prop. - botol* cork in a bottle. *- kaki* (*Mal*) doormat.

   menggabus 1 to cork, close with a cork. **2** to whet (one's knife, etc.) on this.

   gabusan k.o. plant used as fodder, silky sesban, *Sesbania sericea*.

   penggabus 1 whetstone. **2** polisher, abrasive.

   penggabusan spongification.

gacoan (*J/Jv*) /gaco'an/ **1** boyfriend, girlfriend. **2** partner, companion.

gacok I and **gacuk** marble used in children's game which the player thinks will make him defeat the other players.

   gacokan such a marble.

gacok II (in *Sumut*) s.o. who is paid to take an examination for another person, ringer; → JOKI II.

   menggacok to help s.o. answer examination questions for money.

gacong I (*S*) to harvest paddy in s.o.'s rice field for a wage of 1/10 of the yield.

gacong II → GANCO.

gada (*Skr*) club, bludgeon. – *getah* (rubber) truncheon.

menggada to club, bludgeon.

penggada 1 s.o. who hits with a club/bludgeon. **2** club, bludgeon.

penggadaan clubbing.

gada-gada a row of small pennons, vane. – *angin* wind vane.

gadai pledge, security, collateral, pawn. *jual* – k.o. conditional sale. *rumah/pajak* (*M*) – pawnshop. *surat* – mortgage bond. *cekelan* (*Jv*) pawning. – *terdorong kepada Cina* s.t. lost is gone forever.

bergadai to borrow money (by pawning s.t. as collateral).

menggadai to mortgage, borrow money on s.t. using it as collateral. *tanah yang digadainya* the land he mortgaged.

gadai-menggadai pawning.

menggadaikan 1 to pawn, pledge s.t. as a security. ~ *emas* mortgaging gold. **2** to mortgage s.t. ~ *nyawa* (*Mal*) to risk one's life. ~ *rohnya pada iblis* to sell one's soul to the devil.

tergadai(kan) pawned, mortgaged. *orang* ~ pawnee. *tergadai kepala* very embarrassed.

gadaian item that is pawned/mortgaged. *menebus* ~ to redeem s.t. that has been pawned.

penggadai pawner, pledgee.

pegadaian pawnshop.

penggadaian 1 pawning, mortgaging. **2** pawnshop.

gadamala Java galingale, k.o. rhizome, *Languas galanga*.

gadang I (*M*) big, large, great; → GEDANG. *Datuk* – the Sumatran elephant.

menggadang 1 to bring up, rear. **2** to boast, brag.

gadang II large round tray for winnowing; → BADANG, TAMPAH.

menggadangkan to winnow.

gadang III be(r)gadang to stay awake until late at night or early in the morning on certain social occasions, such as parties, *selamatans*, playing cards, etc.

menggadangi to hold a wake over, (keep) watch over.

gadang IV (*Jv*) **menggadang(kan)** to hope for, expect, look forward to.

gadar (*J*) → KADAR I.

gadén → SURAT *gadai/gadén*.

gading I 1 elephant tusk. **2** ivory. **3** ivory-colored. *tak ada – yang tak retak* there's no ivory which is not cracked, i.e., nothing is perfect, no rose without a thorn. *bila ada (or, telah dapat) – bertuah, tanduk tidak berguna lagi* "when you've gotten some lucky ivory, the horn of a dead buffalo is thrown away," i.e., the new drives out the old. *kalau gajah harapkan –nya* (*M*) a person honors s.o. because he expects s.t. in return.

bergading 1 to have tusks. *yang* ~ (*M*) a powerful (person), pillar of society. *telah mati yang* ~ a powerful/respected person has died. **2** having/with ivory.

menggading 1 to stab with a tusk. **2** to resemble ivory, ivory-like.

gading II (in many plant and animal names, referring to its ivory color). *aur/buluh, bambu* – large, common (yellow-colored) bamboo, *Bambusa vulgaris. enggang* – white-beaked hornbill, helmeted hornbill, *Rhinoplax vigil. kelapa/nyiur* – a coco palm species with ivory-colored nuts. – *punai* – the pink-headed pigeon, jambu fruit dove, *Leucotreron jambu. seri* – srigading flower, night jasmine, *Nyctanthes arbortristis*.

gading III the pair of bride's pages who fan the bride and groom on the dais.

gading-gading 1 ribs (of a boat), frame. **2** rim (of a wheel).

gadis 1 girl, young lady, unmarried woman, maiden; → ANAK *dara*. **2** still pure (not yet married or having had relations with men), virgin. **3** virginity. *Meskipun sudah berumur tiga puluh tahun, tetapi masih* –. Even though she's already 30 years old, she's still a virgin. *Sudah hilang –nya*. She has lost her virginity. **4** an animal that has no young or hasn't laid eggs yet. *ayam* – a non-egg-laying chicken. *kerbau* – a water buffalo that has had no young. *si bujang* – (*M*) bisexual, transvestite; → BANCI, WARIA. *Tuan* – (*M*) title for a descendant of a female Minangkabau *raja. seperti* – *sudah berlaki* a lazy or slovenly girl. *bagai – jolong bersubang* full of o.s. and arrogant (from having become rich overnight/holding an important position, etc.). *Dia bukan – muda lagi*. She's no spring chicken. – *Aron* (*Bat*) female worker

in Tanah Karo. – *bar* bar girl. – *besar* girl about 18 years of age. – *kecil* a young girl of about 13–14 years of age. – *kelinci* bunny (of the Playboy Club). – *pemerah* milkmaid. – *pemijit* masseuse. – *pengiring pengantin* bridesmaid. – *rompong* a girl who is no longer a virgin. – *sampul* cover girl. – *sial* a girl who can't find a man. – *tanggung* teenage girl. – *taruhan* a girl kept secluded, *esp* at home. – *tua* old maid, spinster.

bergadis *tidak* ~ deflowered, no longer a virgin.

menggadis to remain unmarried/single.

menggadisi to deflower s.o.

kegadisan 1 maidenhood, virginity. *Dia menyerahkan ~nya*. She surrendered her virginity. **2** chastity.

kegadis-gadisan girlish (although already married).

gado I (*Jv*) **gado-gado 1** a dish made from vegetables, potatoes, tempeh, tofu, boiled eggs, etc., together with a peanut sauce. **2** hodgepodge, mishmash, mess. *bersifat* ~ heterogeneous. *lagu* ~ potpourri, medley.

menggado to nibble at the side dishes which accompany the *rijsttafel* without the rice. ~ *saja!* Just have a nibble!

kegado-gadoan mishmash, hodgepodge.

gado II (*coq*) → GADUH I.

gado III → GADUH II.

gadon (*Jv*) a dish made from a seasoned mixture of chopped meat, eggs, and coconut milk wrapped in a banana leaf.

gadri (*Jv*) rear porch.

gadu I (*Jv*) *musim* – dry season.

gadu II k.o. tree, *Trigonostemon longifolius*.

gaduh I (*Jv*) share cropping (fields tilled or cattle bred by another person in exchange for part of the yield, *usu* a half or a third of the yield).

menggaduh to till or breed in a share-cropping arrangement.

menggaduhkan to have s.t. tilled or bred by another in a share-cropping arrangement.

gaduhan s.t. lent under this arrangement. *ternak* ~ cattle given as a loan.

penggaduh share cropper.

penggaduhan having s.t. tilled or bred by another in a share-cropping arrangement.

gaduh II 1 bustle, commotion, tumult, upheaval. **2** noise, uproar, hullabaloo. *tingkat* – noise level. *berbuat* – to create a disturbance. **3** noisy, tumultuous. *Jangan* –! Don't make so much noise! – *hati* nervous, restless.

bergaduh [and **begaduh** (*coq*)] **1** to quarrel, have a fight. *Kita tidak patut* ~ *dengan anggota-anggota keluarga kita sendiri*. It's wrong to quarrel with our own family members. **2** to make noise, cause an uproar. *Jangan* ~ *di sini karena ayah sedang tidur*. Don't make noise in here, because father is sleeping. **3** mixed/mingled together. *Yang buruk dengan yang baik* ~, *susah dibédakan lagi*. The bad and the good are mixed together, it's hard to tell them apart again.

menggaduh to disturb, bother.

menggaduhkan 1 to make trouble for/in, disturb, cause disturbance in. *Ada anasir-anasir yang hendak* ~ *daérah itu*. There were elements who wanted to make trouble for that area. **2** to disturb, interrupt, bother. *Jangan* ~ *orang yang lagi bekerja*. Don't disturb s.o. who's working. **3** to make a fuss (about). *Jangan engkau* ~ *tentang makan dan minum*. Don't make a fuss about the food and drinks.

mempergaduh-gaduhkan to start a fight between.

kegaduhan 1 quarrel, riot, disturbance, uproar, revolt, rebellion, insurrection. **2** commotion, tumult, upheaval, hullabaloo. ~ *di désa itu semakin meluas*. The tumult in that village spread further. **3** noise.

penggaduhan (the act or way of) disturbing, bothering, causing trouble, etc.

pergaduhan quarrel, commotion, tumult, upheaval, disturbance. ~ *itu telah dapat diselesaikan*. The rebellion could be quelled.

gaduk (*M*) proud, conceited, uppity, arrogant, presumptuous.

bergaduk and **menggaduk** to boast, brag. *bergaduk diri, saku-saku diterbangkan angin* to brag a lot, but actually be broke.

menggaduki to be arrogant to s.o.

gadung 1 a climbing plant from whose tubers a narcotic is made, wild yam, *Dioscorea spp. mabuk* – a) intoxicated (from eating those tubers). b) madly/head over heels in love; to be sunk in thought, daydream; somewhat crazy. **2a)** (*NTT*) forest tuber. b) (in Southern Garut) forest mushroom; → JAMUR *hutan. hijau* – light green. – *cina* a climbing plant, Chinese sarsaparilla, *Smilax china.*

gadungan (*Jv*) **1** not genuine; false, fake, imitation, bogus. *pemimpin/polisi/tentara* ~ a bogus leader/policeman/military man. **2** self-styled, pretend, would be. **3** were-. *macan* ~ were-tiger (k.o. werewolf), human being in the form of a tiger.

gaé(k) (*J M*) old; past one's prime.

gaét hook; → KAIT. *kena* – hooked. *Suaminya pernah kena – penyanyi.* Her husband once got hooked by a singer. *tukang* – pickpocket.

menggaét 1 to hook, grab with a hook. ~ *buah dari pohon* to hook fruit down from a tree. **2** to steal, rob. *Tukang copét ~ dompétnya.* A pickpocket stole his purse. **3** to hook, catch, attract; to get hold of. *gadis yang pandai ~ orang berduit* a girl who knows how to hook wealthy people. ~ *hatinya* to capture his/her fancy. *tahu caranya ~ duit orang* to know how to get hold of s.o.'s money. **4** to get, snatch, snare. ~ *pelanggan baru* to snare/get new subscribers (to a newspaper, etc.). ~ *posisi itu ia telah bekerja keras.* He worked hard to snare that position.

menggaéti (*pl obj*) to hook, etc.

tergaét [and **kegaét** (*coq*)] hooked, robbed, snared, caught up. *Kabel dasar laut diduga ~ jangkar.* Underseas cable believed snared in anchor.

gaétan hook.

penggaét ~ *barang dari/di toko* shoplifter; → PENGUTIL.

penggaétan 1 hooking. **2** capturing, attracting.

gafar, gafir, and **gafur** (*A*) **1** forgiving, pardoning. *al-* the All-Merciful, Great Pardoner (Allah). **2** an alternate name for the 40th chapter of the Koran; → MUKMIN.

gaga (*Jv*) → GOGO I.

gagah 1 smart, handsome, dashing. *Naik mobil dianggap lebih – daripada naik bécak.* Going by car is considered more prestigious than going by bécak. **2** brawny, strong, mighty, forceful, robust, valiant. *Orang itu masih – meskipun usianya sudah lanjut.* That person is still robust even though he's old. **3** brave, dauntless, audacious, courageous. *Ibu itu merasa bangga melihat anak laki-lakinya yang – itu.* The mother was proud to see her dashing son. – *berani/perkasa/perwira* courageous.

segagah as dashing/strong, etc. as.

bergagah 1 to be sturdy. **2** splendid, powerful and influential. *masih* ~ still going strong, hale and hearty, in good shape.

bergagah-gagahan 1 to challenge e.o.'s strength/bravery. **2** to show off, try to impress people, brag.

menggagah 1 to do s.t. with all one's strength, act firmly. **2** to take up s.t. wholeheartedly.

menggagahi 1 to overpower, defeat. *Pemerintah telah berjaya ~ kaum komunis.* The government managed to defeat the Communists. **2** to violate (a law). **3** to molest, rape (a woman). *Dia dihukum karena ~ seorang gadis.* He was sentenced because he molested a girl. ~ *diri* to pull o.s. together. **4** to take great pride in.

menggagahkan 1 to make ... look important, do s.t. in order to appear smart/strong, etc. *Kesombongannya hanya untuk ~ diri.* His arrogance was only to make himself look important. **2** to consider s.t. or s.o. strong, etc.

tergagah the most dashing/strong, etc.

gagah-gagahan for show, showing off; to give o.s. airs, try to make o.s. look better than one really is. *Gelar MBA yang disandangnya palsu, katanya, untuk ~.* His MBA degree was fake, he said; it was just for show.

kegagahan 1 courage, spirit, bravery, firmness. **2** pretension, airs. **3** boldness, impertinence. ~ *lelaki* virility.

penggagahan 1 rape, sexually molesting. **2** violating. **3** overpowering.

gagai menggagai to clamber up (a tree) using one's hands and feet.

gagak various species of crows. *burung* – large-billed crow, *Corvus macrorhynchus. selama* – *hitam, selama air hilir* forever, always, eternal. *seperti burung – pulang ke benua* after coming home from abroad, one has not changed a bit, plus ça change. *ketika – putih, bangau hitam* in the distant past. – *gunung* blue-green magpie, *Kitta chinensis.* – *hutan* slender-billed crow, Stresemann's Bush-Crow, *Corvus enca.* – *kampung* large-billed crow, *Corvus macrorhynchos.*

gagal 1 failed, frustrated, didn't occur, abortive, misfired. *kudéta yang – di Indonésia* the abortive coup d'etat in Indonesia. *kup yang* – the coup that failed. **2** to fail, be unsuccessful, not succeed in, fizzle out, go wrong. – *ginjal* kidney failure. – *jantung* heart failure. – *komunikasi* failure of communication. – *mengisi pos tersebut* failed to fill the post. – *total* failed totally.

menggagalkan to frustrate, foil, sabotage, make s.t. fail, defeat, thwart, abort. *Dia mencoba ~ perjanjian itu.* He tried to sabotage the agreement.

kegagalan failure, fiasco, miscarriage, flop; unsuccessful (of negotiations). ~ *membayar* default. *Pihak Indonésia, Malaysia, Filipina dan Thailand tidak akan mengalami – membayar utang luar negeri, meskipun nilai yén terus menguat terhadap dolar AS.* Indonesia, Malaysia, the Philippines and Thailand will not default on paying their foreign debts even though the value of the yen continues to appreciate against the US dollar.

penggagal s.o. or s.t. that foils or causes s.t. to fail. *kelompok ~ pemilu* a group that causes the election to fail.

penggagalan foiling, making s.t. fail. *keberhasilan ~ pengédaran ganja* success in foiling marijuana trafficking.

gagang I 1 stalk (of a leaf/flower, etc.), stem (of a flower), peduncle. **2** handle, haft, hilt, knob. **3** (*M*) aerial root; stump, stub (of a creeping plant). *seperti sirih pulang ke* – to retrace one's steps, go back to where one started from. – *bunga* stem. – *kacamata* earpiece (of eyeglasses). – *kemudi* rudder. – *kipas* propeller shaft. – *pedang* hilt of a sword. – *péna* penholder. – *pintu* door handle. – *pisau* handle of a knife. – *sapu* broomstick. – *senapan* rifle butt. – *télepon* telephone handset. *mengangkat/mengambil – télepon* to pick up the phone. **4** counter for such plants.

bergagang to have/use a handle.

gagang II – *bayem* black-winged stilt, *Himantopus himantopus.*

gagap I to stammer, stutter. *orang* – stammerer, stutterer.

bergagap(-gagap) 1 stammering, stuttering. **2** nervous, agitated; hurriedly, in a hurry.

menggagap to stammer, stutter.

tergagap-gagap in fits and starts, not smooth or fluent. *Dia menjawab pertanyaan saya dengan ~.* He answered my question in a stammering way.

kegagapan 1 stammering, stuttering. **2** nervousness.

penggagap stammerer, stutterer.

penggagapan stuttering.

gagap II (*J*) **menggagap(i)** to feel/grope/fumble around for, grope (one's way); → GAGAU I.

gagap-gagap groping/fumbling around.

menggagapi to grope/feel around for s.t.

gagas menggagas to think up, dream up, devise, improvise, contrive, invent. ~ *sebuah pertemuan di Pelabuhan Ratu* to improvise a meeting in Pelabuhan Ratu.

menggagasi and **menggagaskan** to design, think/dream up, contrive, devise, have the idea of. *Ia juga menggagasi kerja sama téknis antara UI dan Victorian Institute of Forensic Sciences.* He also dreamt up the idea of technical cooperation between UI and the Victorian Institute of Forensic Sciences.

tergagas thought up, devised, dreamt up.

gagasan idea, notion, concept(ion), viewpoint, way of thinking. *Itu mémang merupakan suatu ~ yang baik.* That's really a good idea. ~ *yang bisa diinvéstasikan* an idea that can be invested in.

penggagas idea-man, designer, creator, inventor.

penggagasan figuring s.t. out, coming up with an idea.

gagau I menggagau to grope around. *Kamar itu sangat gelap dan karena itu saya ~ hendak mencari sakelar.* The room was pitch dark, and so I groped around looking for the switch. ~ *dengan belalainya* to fumble with the trunk (of an elephant).

tergagau-gagau groping with hands stretched out (of the blind).

gagau II (*M*) **bergagau-gagauan** to scream horribly from shock or fear.

tergagau scream suddenly at the top of one's voice (from shock or fear).

gagit – *noni* k.o. cookie.

gagu (*J/Jv*) dumb, mute, speechless. *Dia seperti orang* –. He stood tongue-tied.

menggagu to be dumb, unable to speak.

kegaguan muteness, speechlessness.

gaguk → GAGAP I.

gah I dignity, fame, distinction, greatness, a sense of greatness; → (M)EGAH.

gah II → OGAH I.

gaham (*M*) bluster, threat, intimidation; → ANCAMAN.

menggaham to threaten, try to intimidate.

gahar I menggahar to scour, scrub, abrade.

penggahar scrubber.

penggaharan abrasion.

gahar II (*S*) **1** tasty in a sharp way, scrumptious. **2** (*BG*) rough, vicious, heavy (of music).

gahara (*Skr*) of royal birth on both sides. *anak/raja yang* – a prince of fully royal descent.

gahari (*Skr*) moderate, middle; → UGAHARI. *kaum – dan digung* the middle class and the elite.

menggahari to moderate.

penggahari moderator. *Dalam séminar yang dipimpin ~ Dr. Boediono, juga diperlihatkan oléh Nurimansyah bahwa éfisiénsi berbagai industri terus menurun.* In the seminar led by moderator Dr. Boediono, Nurimansyah also showed that the efficiency of various industries has continued to decline.

gaharu (*Skr*) *kayu* – aloe wood, agar wood, fragrant eaglewood, *Aquilaria malaccensis*. *seperti buku* – to show one's excellence/superiority no sooner than necessary. *sudah – cendana pula (sudah tahu bertanya pula)* to ask about s.t. that one already knows the answer to. *– buaya* k.o. aloe wood, *Gonystylus bancanus*. *– candan* k.o. aloe wood, *Gonystylus miquelianus*. *– cina* joss sticks. *– hitam* k.o. aloe, *Gonystylus macrophyllus*. *– laka* k.o. aloe, *Aetoxylon sympetalum*.

gai (*E naut*) guy; → GIUK.

gaib (*A*) **1** hidden, concealed, obscured. **2** to disappear, vanish. **3** mysterious, occult, esoteric. *alam* – the invisible world. *daya* – magical power. *ilmu* – mysticism, magic, occultism, metaphysical. *kuasa* – occult power. *Ada beberapa hal yang ingin saya kemukakan tentang masalah* –. There are some things I want to present about the occult.

menggaib to disappear, become invisible; to make o.s. invisible.

menggaibkan ~ *diri* to make o.s. invisible.

gaib-gaiban mysterious happenings.

kegaiban **1** mysteriousness; mystery. **2** paranormality, the occult, metaphysics.

gaibana (*Pers*) profligate.

gaid (*E*) (tourist) guide; → PEMANDU *wisata*.

gail → GUAL *gail*.

gaing (*naut*) sheer, shallow fin-keel made of wood.

gairah (*A*) **1** passion, ardor, eagerness, spirit, enthusiasm, fervor, strong desire. **2** ambitious, desirous, ardent. *– berdikari* the spirit of self-sufficiency. *– hidup* zest for life, love of life. *– makan* ravenous hunger. *– séks* sexual desire, libido. *Parfum dapat pula meningkatkan – séks.* Perfumes can also increase sexual desire. *– syahwat* sexual desire, libido.

bergairah to have/feel passion/desire/enthusiasm, be passionate/enthusiastic/fervent, -minded, get excited/enthused. *Ia semakin ~ untuk memajukan désa* he is increasingly enthusiastic about making villages progress. *~ séks yang luar biasa* to have an extraordinary sex drive. *~ angkasa* airminded (interested in aerospace). *tidak begitu ~* not very excited, lukewarm.

menggairahi to be passionate/enthusiastic about.

menggairahkan **1** to stimulate, arouse, turn on, stir up, activate, encourage. *Peraturan itu untuk ~ ékspor.* That regulation is for encouraging exports. **2** delightful, enchanting, tempting, seductive. *Dalam cahaya remang-remang, alangkah ~ wanita cantik itu.* How enchanting that beautiful woman is in the dim light. *~ hati* a) to charm. b) charming. **3** exciting, arousing, thrilling. *satu tahapan yang ~* an exciting stage.

kegairahan passion, lust, desire, ambition, enthusiasm, -mindedness. *~ angkasa* airmindedness. *~ cinta* eroticism.

penggairahan **1** stimulation, encouragement. *gerakan ~ pedésaan* the movement to stimulate villages. **2** excitement, animation.

gairat → GAIRAH.

gaiser (*E*) → GÉYSER.

gait hook; → GAÉT, KAIT I.

menggait 1 to pull, hook, pluck, etc. s.t. with a hook attached to a pole, etc. *~ buah* to pluck fruit (from a tree). **2** to get/wheedle s.t. out of s.o. *Maksudnya tidak lain hendak ~ kantung orang.* He only intends to wheedle money out of people. **3** to steal, rob, swipe.

menggaitkan to pluck, hook, wheedle (for s.o. else).

tergait hooked.

gaitan 1 hook, snare. **2** way of snaring s.t. **3** point of application/attack.

penggait 1 hook, snare. **2** person who hooks. **3** s.t. which connects two opposing things.

gajah I (*Skr*) **1** elephant. **2** term for Police wreckers or tow trucks. **3** bishop (in chess game). **4** a descriptive epithet meaning large or huge, gigantic. *badak* – Javan rhinoceros, *Rhinoceros sondaicus*. *barah* – a carbuncle. *belalai* – a) trunk of an elephant. b) telescoping gangway (at airports); → GARBARATA. *Gedung* – (National Museum at Lapangan Merdeka, Jakarta). *ilmu/hikmat/mantra* – magic formula to tame an elephant. *nyamuk* – a large mosquito. *pawang* – s.o. who practices black magic to tame/catch/treat, etc. elephants. *penghulu* – *keraton* employee in charge of elephant care. *(gendutnya) seperti* – *bengkak* very fat. *– seékor, gembala dua* s.o. who wears two hats. *– mati karena gadingnya* to have an accident because of one's superiority/character, actions, etc. *– mati, tulang setimbun* when a wealthy person dies, he leaves behind a large estate. *– berjuang sama* –, *pelanduk/kancil mati di tengah-tengah* when the elephants fight, the ants are trampled. *seperti – masuk kampung* a powerful person can do what he pleases among the weak. *– derum tengah rumah* the arrival of a VIP. *seperti ditempuh – lalu* s.t. that cannot be covered up (or, hidden). *terdorong – karena besarnya* to do s.t. bad due to one's power. *– ditelan ular lidi* the child of an important person fell in love with a child of a lower status. *– dialahkan oléh pelanduk* a powerful person can be defeated by a clever person. *– lalu dibeli, rusa tidak terbeli* to do an important job overlooking the little things which, actually, are needed to complete the job. *– Afrika* African elephant, *Loxodonta africanus*. *– Asia* Asian elephant, *Elephas maximus*. *– bara* a black elephant. *– barat* a children's game. *sebesar/segedé – bengkak* as big/huge as an elephant. *– bertarung* a fighting elephant. *– butang* a small elephant with long and straight tusks. *– gambut* a huge elephant with large, white tusks. *– guling* two strings of jasmine flowers, a decoration for a hair bun. *– hotong* a small elephant with small reddish-colored tusks. *– India* Indian elephant, *Elephas maximus belangensis*. *– jinak/lalang* a tame elephant. *– laut* a 45-ton floating crane used at the Port of Tanjungpriok. *– liar* wild elephant. *– Mada* a) the *Mapatih* of *Majapahit*. b) name of a university in Yogyakarta [*Gama* spelled Gadjah Mada]. *– mengkona* a tuskless elephant. *– menong* pendant for a necklace with a horse figure. *– menyusu* attached shed, annex. *– meta* rutting elephant. *– mina* a) whale. b) a design of the *makara*, a sea-monster with the head of an elephant and the body of a fish. *– oling* k.o. batik pattern. *– putih* white elephant. *– Sri Lanka* Sri Lankan elephant, *Elephas maximus maximus*. *– Sumatera* Sumatran elephant, *Elephas maximus sumatranus*. *– terbang* jumbo jet, the Boeing 747. *– tunggal* solitary rogue elephant.

bergajah 1 to have/use an elephant. **2** to ride an elephant.

menggajah to look like an elephant, appear to be huge.

gajah-gajahan *main ~* to play chess. *sakit ~* elephantiasis.

gajah II *burung* – whimbrel, *Numenius phaeopus variegatus*. *burung gembala* – white-winged black jay, black magpie, *Platysmurus leucopterus*.

gajahan curlew, whimbrel, *Numenius phaeropus*. *– besar* curlew, *Numenius arquata*.

gajak 1 behavior. *– yang tidak terpuji* bad behavior. 2 measure. 3 posture, carriage.

gajaménong a seahorse (used as an aphrodisiac).

Gajayana name of a train running between Jakarta and Malang.

gaji (*D*) salary, pay, income, wages. *– dan upah* payroll. *makan –* to work for wages, be a wage-earner, get a salary, be in the pay of. *– bermula* starting salary. *– bersih* net wages, take-home pay. *– borongan* piece rate. *– bulanan* monthly pay. *– buta* pay without work, sinecure wages. *makan – buta* to have a paid sinecure, a soft job. *– cuti* vacation pay. *– dasar* base pay. *– harian* daily wage. *– kotor* gross wages. *– mingguan* weekly pay. *– percobaan* probationary salary. *– permulaan* starting salary. *– pokok* base pay. *– tunjangan* benefit. *– yang dibawa bersih ke rumah* and *– yang diterima sebenarnya* take-home pay.

bergaji to get paid a salary, be paid (a certain amount). *Pegawai negeri kecil ~ pas-pasan.* Minor civil servants just get by on their salary.

menggaji 1 to pay (salary/wages). *Kami ~ pembantu kami 50 ribu sebulan.* We paid our domestic help 50 thousand a month. 2 to employ, hire. *Dia ~ tiga orang untuk membantunya di toko.* He employed three persons to assist him in the shop.

tergaji salaried.

gajian 1 (*orang*) ~ a) (domestic) servant. b) s.o. who works for wages. (*hari*) ~ payday. 2 paid.

penggajian payment of salary/wages, etc.

gajih I (*Jv*) fat (of meat).

bergajih fatty.

gajih II (*ob*) → GAJI.

gajul I (*ob*) rascal, scoundrel; → BAJUL 2, BERGAJUL, BARAGAJUL.

be(r)gajul (*J*) rascal, scoundrel, villain; criminal.

gajulan and **bergajulan** to raise hell, act like a scoundrel.

pergajulan (*coq*) criminal.

gajul II (*Jv*) **menggajul** to kick with the tip of the foot.

gajus *pohon –* cashew-nut tree, *Anacardium occidentale*.

gak (*J*) no; not; → NGGAK.

gakang → GA'ANG, ORONG-ORONG II.

gakari task.

gakin [keluarga miskin] poor families.

gal (in acronyms) → TUNGGAL.

gala I (*Skr*) resin, pitch; → DAMAR I. *– lembut* tar.

gala-gala a mixture of pitch and resin used for caulking boats.

bergala attached, stuck. *tidak ~* boundless, unbounded. *Sukacitanya beroléh hadiah itu tiada ~.* His joy at getting the reward was boundless.

menggala-gala to stop up, close.

gala II **segala** all.

segala-galanya all of them, everything; → SEGALA.

gala III (*M*) **gala-gala** a small resin-collecting bee, *Melipona laeviceps*; → KELULUT II.

gala IV (*D*) gala. *malam –* gala evening. *– premiér* gala premiere.

menggala-premiérkan to show (a film) at a gala premiere. *– Puspa Séna* Women Soldiers Training/Indoctrination. *– Yudha* (*mil*) Field Test.

gala V → GALAH.

galaba(h) (*ob*) moved, touched, affected, sad.

galagasi (*J*) a poisonous spider.

galah 1 pole, stake, stick. 2 punting pole. 3 jumping pole. *lompat –* pole vault. *bagai – di tengah arus* a) to shiver and shake. b) constantly complaining. *bagai – dijual* all one's property is gone (gambled away, etc.). *– asin* children's team game; → GALASIN. *– canggah* punting pole with a forked end for pushing against snags/tree trunks, etc. *– pancang* mooring pole. *– sanggamara* harpoon. *– unjam* mooring pole.

galah-galah ~ *asin/panjang* a children's game (with lines resembling partitions drawn on the ground).

bergalah to have/use a punting pole, punt. *segan ~ hanyut serantau* if you're lazy, you'll just drift along. *~ hilir tertawa buaya, bersuluh di bulan terang tertawa harimau* all useless acts will be ridiculed by the wise.

menggalah(i) 1 to push with a punting pole. 2 to get s.t. (fruit, etc.) with a pole.

menggalahkan to push s.t. with a pole.

penggalah punting pole. **sepenggalah** the length of a pole. *matahari telah tinggi ~* around 7 a.m.

galai → GALI III.

galak I 1 (*esp* of animals) fierce, savage, wild, cruel, vicious. *Awas anjing –!* Beware of the dog! 2 violent, fiery, aggressive, belligerent, fanatic, combative, pugnacious. *sifat –* pugnacity. 3 bad-tempered. *Guru matématika kami – sekali.* Our math teacher is very bad-tempered. *Dia – dan kata-katanya jorok.* He's belligerent and foulmouthed. *perempuan yang –* virago, Xanthippe, fishwife. 4 stern, severe, mean.

segalak as fierce/violent/vicious, etc. as.

segalak-galaknya ~ *macan, tiada macan makan anaknya sendiri* however ill-natured a tiger may be, he'll never eat his young, i.e., however bad a father/mother may be, he/she will never destroy his/her own child.

bergalak and **menggalak** to become fierce/wild, etc., rage.

menggalakkan and **mempergalak** 1 to encourage, promote. *Pemerintah berusaha ~ penanaman modal asing dengan berbagai cara.* The government tries to promote foreign capital investments in various ways. *Undang-undang Nomor 11 itu digalakkan lagi.* Law Number 11 was promoted again. 2 to incite, instigate, stir up. *~ ayam sabung agar mau berlaga* to incite fighting cocks to fight.

tergalak the most vicious, etc.

kegalakan fierceness, aggression, violence.

penggalak 1 encourager, enthusiastic supporter. 2 stimulus, spur, impetus. 3 primer.

penggalakan incitement, encouragement, promotion. *~ objék-objék pariwisata* the promotion of tourist objects.

galak II (*ob*) **penggalak** powder in the touchhole of early firearms.

galak III (*M*) → GELAK.

penggalak s.o. who laughs easily.

galaksi (*D/E*) galaxy.

galan (*D*) gallant.

galang 1 prop, support, underlayer, girder, transverse bar, point on which s.t. rests. *– atap* roof girders. *– kepala* headrest, pillow. *– perahu* rollers for hauling up boats.

bergalang 1 propped, shored up, supported, with a support. 2 docked, put into dock, dry-docked. *perahu ~* a boat in dock. *~ tanah* (*euph*) dead, passed away.

menggalang 1 to support, prop, shore up. *Kepalanya digalang dengan bantal.* His head was supported by a pillow. *Balok-balok itu gunanya untuk ~ perahu.* Those beams are used to shore up boats. 2 to provide a basis/firm footing (for). *~ persatuan seluruh rakyat untuk menghadapi ancaman musuh* to lay the basis for the unity of the entire population to face a hostile threat. 3 to provide leadership for. 4 to promote, cultivate, encourage. 5 to collect (money). 6 to establish (an alliance/relations). 7 to consolidate, gather (one's forces).

menggalangi to stabilize, provide support for.

menggalangkan 1 to use s.t. for support. 2 to put (a boat) into dry-dock. *~ perahu yang rusak* to dry-dock a damaged boat. *~ batang léhér* to sacrifice o.s. for s.t. important, for instance to defend one's country, etc. 3 to rest s.t. (on s.t.).

tergalang propped, supported, placed in dry dock, etc. *lidah ~* struck dumb.

galangan 1 slip, dry dock. 2 shipyard. *~ kapal* dockyard, dry dock. *~ sérét* slipway. *~ terapung* floating dock. *~ utama* main slipway.

penggalang 1 supporter. 2 pillar, supporting device.

pegalangan dock.

penggalangan 1 support. *Meréka mendukung pula sepenuhnya upaya ~ dana dari masyarakat.* They fully support efforts for financial support from the community. 2 providing leadership for. 3 stabilization (measures). 4 (*mil*) conditioning (in psychological operations).

galang II **penggalang** member of the *Pramuka* Boy Scout Movement from 12 to 15 years old, scout.

galang III (galang-)**galangan** (*ob*) *~ sawah* dike, bund; → GALENGAN.

galang IV → ALANG I. **menggalang** to lie athwart, be/get in the way, block; → MELINTANG. *jika tiada aral ~* and *kalau tidak ada aral ~* if all goes well.

menggalang-galang(i) to prevent, hinder, get in the way of. *Barang kehendaknya tiada yang berani ~*. Nobody has the nerve to get in the way of what he wants.

tergalang held back, blocked.

galang V – *gulung* back and forth. **bergalang-gulung** to roll back and forth. *Bekas macan bola Iswadi Idris tak lagi ~ di lapangan dengan anak asuhannya*. The former soccer star Iswadi Idris will no longer roll back and forth over the (soccer) field with his trainees; → GULUNG.

galanggasi (*J*) → GALAGASI.

galant → GALAN.

galantin (*D/E*) galantine.

galar (*Jv*) 1 a mat made of bamboo which has been pounded flat. *Di atas gambut itu akan dipasang setebal 10 séntiméter*. A 10-centimeter-thick mat will be placed on top of the turf. 2 joist, beam.

galas 1 carrying pole. 2 load, burden; merchandise, commodities (carried on a shoulder pole). *(bagai) menyandang – tiga* an easy job but one that is hard to carry out. *– terdorong kepada Cina* s.t. that has already gone so far that it cannot be stopped. *sambil menyeruduk/menyuruk – lalu* while having a good time, one's desires are reached or not forgotten.

menggalas 1 to carry on a pole over the shoulder. 2 to hawk, peddle, vend. 3 to carry on retail trade (in). *tiada beban batu digalas* to look for trouble. *jalan dipindahkan orang ~* customary law or language is changed by foreigners/outsiders.

menggalaskan to lay (a burden on s.o.'s shoulders).

tergalas carried.

penggalas 1 hawker, peddler. 2 carrying pole.

penggalasan 1 trading center. 2 trading, hawking, peddling.

galasin → GALAH *asin*.

galasuh backhoe.

galat error; → RALAT. *– kelola* (*fin*) mismatch.

galau (*M*) in confusion/an uproar, confused. *Semakin dipikirkannya, semakin – perasaannya*. The more he thought about it, the more confused he felt. *Lili hanya bisa menangis manakala hatinya sedang –*. Lili could only cry when she felt confused.

bergalau 1 tumultuous, noisy, uproarious, confused and boisterous. *suara ~* cacophonous sound. 2 confused; upset. *Anak muda itu memandang saya sambil tersenyum, di wajahnya terbayang perasaan yang ~*. The youngster looked at me smiling; a confused expression flitted across his face. *kata banyak kata ~* (*M*) so many men, so many minds.

bergalauan (*pl subj*) confused, upset.

menggalau to become tumultuous/confused.

menggalaukan 1 to confuse. 2 to be confused about s.t.

galauan and **kegalauan** confusion, hubbub, brouhaha, upheaval, hullaballoo. *Dalam ~, lapar dan kedinginan, Dinem toh masih sempat khawatir akan keselamatan kekasihnya*. In the confusion, hunger, and cold, Dinem still managed to think about his sweetheart's safety.

penggalauan confusion, upheaval.

galawadi (*J*) k.o. children's game using short sticks of wood.

galbani (*D*) **menggalbani** to galvanize.

galbanisasi → GALVANISASI.

galéh (*M*) 1 a stick for carrying s.t. over the shoulder. 2 a shoulder-load; → GALAS.

galeng (*J/Jv*) **bergaleng** marked, with marks on it.

galengan (*Jv*) bund/dike in rice field; → GALANG III.

galeri (*D/E*) gallery. *– Nasional* National Gallery.

pergalerian gallery (*mod*).

galgal (*ob*) 1 hurried, in a hurry/rush, in haste. 2 passionate, quick-tempered, fiery.

gali I dig (up), (in mining) cut. *– dan timbun/urug* cut and fill.

menggali 1 to dig (for), quarry. *~ emas* to dig for gold. 2 to elicit, evoke. *~ keterangan* to elicit information. 3 to lift, dig (up) (potatoes, etc.), excavate. *~ ubi* to dig up tubers. 4 to dredge up (old memories/stories). *Mata pemuda ini menatap jauh ke sebuah gerbong kereta yang telah usang, seakan ~ kenangannya yang tertinggal di sana*. The young boy's eyes were fixed far off on a worn-out railroad car, as if he was dredging up old memories which had been abandoned there. 5 to burrow, dig.

~ diri to dig in. *~ lubang menutup lubang* to borrow from Peter to pay Paul. 6 to delve/go deeply (into). 7 to discover (by going deeply into s.t.).

menggali-gali to dig up dirt on people.

tergali dug up, excavated.

galian 1 excavations, diggings, s.t. dug up, minerals that have been mined. *~.~ tanah di sekitar Jakarta mengakibatkan kehilangan lahan subur*. Excavations around Jakarta have resulted in the loss of fertile land. *air ~* ground water. 2 surface-mine. 3 ditch; → PARIT.

gali-galian 1 all k.o. minerals. 2 tubers.

penggali 1 tool used for digging: spade, shovel, trowel, etc. *diam-diam ~ berkarat, diam-diam ubi berisi* rest makes rusty. 2 digger. *~ emas* gold digger. *~ kubur* grave digger. *~ sirtu* digger of sand and stone; → SIRTU.

penggalian 1 digging (up), excavating. 2 unearthing. 3 mining, quarrying. *~ pasir* quarrying for sand.

gali II [Gang Anak Liar or Gerakan Anak-anak Liar] gang of habitual criminals and thieves operating in large cities in Central Java.

pergalian *dengan cara ~* like criminal gangs. *Kita mémang tidak réla terhadap sebagian anggota masyarakat mempertahankan hidupnya dengan cara ~*. We are unwilling for some members of the community to defend their lives like gangs of criminals.

gali III (*Port*) galley.

galian *– putri* a *jamu* for tightening the vagina. *– singset* k.o. *jamu* for slimming down the body.

galias (*Port*) a large three-masted galley.

galib (*A*) 1 victorious, successful. 2 normal, ordinary, usual, common, habitual. *(pada) -nya* usually, customarily. *-nya siapa yang datang pertama membuka pintu*. Usually, whoever gets here first opens the door. *sudah -nya* has become the custom.

menggalib(kan) to accustom, habituate, familiarize.

kegaliban custom, habit. *~nya* usually, customarily, normally.

galibut (*E cla*) galliot, a large row-boat.

galigata urticaria.

galih (*Jv*) heart, core, kernel, pith (of wood). *– asam* the heart of the tamarind tree.

galing (*S*) curly (of hair).

galing-galing (*Jv*) k.o. grapevine, *Vitis trifolia*; → KAPIALUN.

galir 1 slipping off, loose, not fitted or fixed properly (of keys/curtains); elastic. 2 smart, bright, spry, sprightly. 3 fluent, well-spoken, eloquent, articulate.

galis (in *Sumbar*) shrewd, astute; → LIHAY, LIHAI.

galium (*D/E*) gallium.

galiun(g) (*E ob naut*) galleon.

galodo (in Sumatra) mudslide and flood (from a volcanic eruption).

galo-galo (*ob*) → SEGALA.

galon (*E*) gallon.

bergalon-galon by the gallon.

galu-galu (*M*) paddy almost ripe and with soft contents (suitable for making *emping*).

galuh (*Jv cla*) 1 silver. 2 gem (a term of endearment for a princess), e.g., *Radén – Cendera Kirana, putri Daha*. 3 name of a train running between Tanah Abang and Banjar.

galuk (*M*) water-dipper made of coconut shell; drinking cup.

Galungan (*Bal*) the Balinese New Year according to the Wuku calendar. It lasts 10 days and occurs every 210 days; → NYEPI.

galur I 1 furrow, groove, gully; channel; → JALUR I. *susur –* pedigree, ancestral line, lineage, parentage, family tree, descent. 2 variety, strain, line. *– murni* inbred line, pure line.

bergalur-galur grooved, furrowed. *uratnya ~* his veins look like grooves, i.e., he's muscular.

menggalur(-galur) to trace/investigate the origins of an event, etc.

menggalurkan to trace the origins of s.t.

galuran tracing back into s.t.

penggaluran parentage, descent.

galur II (in Central Kalimantan) torrent.

galvanis (*D*) galvanic.

galvanisasi (*D*) galvanization.

menggalvanisasikan to galvanize.

galvanométer (*D/E*) galvanometer.

galyas (*Port naut*) k.o. warship.

gam I (*onom*) boom; a deep, prolonged, resonant sound; → DEGAM.

GAM II [Gerakan Acéh Merdéka] Free Aceh Movement.

Gama [Gadjah Mada] University (in Yogyakarta). – 61 dry-field rice with a high average yield

gamak 1 hesitant, reluctant. *tidak* – not hesitant, unhesitating. **2** probe. – *dan galat* trial and error.

gamak-gamak at random; (play it) by ear. ~ *seperti menyambal* by trial and error.

menggamak(-gamak) 1 to take s.t. in the hand (to appraise s.t., estimate the weight of s.t., etc.). *Ia menggamak-gamak berat barang itu sebagai tiga ons.* He estimated the weight of that object (by taking it in the hand) at three ounces. **2** to guess, surmise. *Jawaban yang diberinya mungkin salah karena ia hanya menggamak-gamak saja.* The answer he gave might be wrong because it was only based on a guess. **3** to brandish (a weapon). *Ia berteriak dengan sekuat tenaga sambil menggamak pistolnya.* He shouted at the top of his lungs, brandishing his revolver.

tergamak 1 had the heart/nerve to ... *Saya tak sangka anda ~ melakukan perbuatan terkutuk itu di depan orangtua saya.* I didn't think that you had the nerve to do that damned deed in front of my parents. *tidak* ~ a) invaluable, inestimable, incalculable. **2** unflagging, undaunted.

gamal I 1 *pohon* – a plant which is used to exterminate elephant grass, *Gliricidia spp.* **2** (*acr*) [ganyang mati alang-alang] Root Out Elephant Grass.

menggamalkan to plant with *gamal* trees. *tanah dapat digamalkan kembali* the land could be replanted with *gamal.*

gamal II (*A*) camel.

gamalisasi planting of *gamal* trees to eliminate elephant grass.

gamam I (*cla*) doubtful, dubious, uncertain, unsure; worried, confused, nervous; dumbstruck, unable to act due to shock, etc. *Karena merasa bersalah, ia menjadi* – *ketika ditegur.* Since he felt guilty, he was dumbstruck when he was reprimanded; → GAMANG, GEMAN.

tergamam → GAMAM.

gamam II (*M*) **menggamam** to hold s.t. in the mouth (sweets, etc.) but not chew it; → GUMAM.

gaman (*Jv*) (heirloom) weapon (such as a kris inherited from one's grandfather, etc.); → GEGAMAN.

bergaman armed.

gamang (*M*) **1** suffer from vertigo, afraid of heights. **2** phobic. – *tinggi* acrophobia.

menggamang to be nervous.

menggamangkan dizzying, making one nervous.

tergamang feeling all alone and sad. *Ia pun* ~ *ditinggalkan orangtuanya.* He felt abandoned by his parents.

kegamangan -phobia, *esp* acrophobia, fear of heights. ~ *berada di ruangan sempit* claustrophobia.

penggamang s.o. who suffers from a phobia, *esp* acrophobia. *Orang* ~ *mati jatuh (orang pendingin mati hanyut)* if you are afraid, you will fail.

gamat I menggamat to touch (strings/harp, etc.); → GAMIT.

gamat II sea cucumber, *Stichopus badionata.* – *pisang* a coral reef sea cucumber, beche-de-mer, *Stichopus variegatus.*

gamat III bergamat to sing.

menggamat to sing s.t.

gamat IV *akar* – k.o. plant, *Pericampylus glaucus.* – *hutan* a climber, *Pterisanthes cissoides.*

Gamawan male student at Gadjah Mada University.

Gamawati female student at Gadjah Mada University.

gambang (*Jv*) xylophone-like instrument. – *keromong* k.o. *gamelan* used to accompany *Betawi* drama (*lénong* and *cokék*).

gambar 1 picture, reproduction (of a printed photo in a newspaper/magazine, etc.), illustration, drawing. **2** painting. **3** map. **4** sketch. *buku* – sketchbook. *juru* – a) draftsman. b) illustrator. *kantor* – topographical office. **5** heads (of a flipped coin); → *cp* ANGKA. *komidi* – (*infr*) movie, motion picture. *pandai* – draftsman. *tukang* – a) draftsman. b) (pickpocket jargon heard on Jakarta city buses) the person who picks out the victim to be robbed. *wayang* – (*infr*) movie, motion picture. – *angan-angan*

(thought) image, s.t. seen in one's mind's eye. – *bagan* sketch, draft. – *bagian* detailed drawing. – *bumi* (geographical) map. – *cermin* reflected image. – *cétak biru* blueprint. – *corét* pen drawing, sketch. – *dénah* ground plan. – *éjékan* caricature. – *garis* line drawing. – *hias* illustration. – *hidup* movie, motion picture. – *hijau* (*infr*) blueprint. – *iklan* show card, picture poster. – *kaca* slide (for projection on screen). – *kena* (*mil*) cone of fire. – *komik* comic, cartoon strip. – *kulit* decorated dust jacket (of a book). **menggambarkuliti** to provide (a book) with a decorated dust jacket. – *lucon* caricature. – *lukis* painting. – *mati* portrait, still life. – *muka* frontispiece. – *perkenaan* (*mil*) dispersion pattern. – *potrét* photograph. – *rékaan* composite drawing. – *rencana* preliminary drawing. – *sampul* cover photo. – *sénter* (lantern) slide. – *sindiran* caricature; political cartoon. – *situasi* site plan. – *sorot* (lantern) slide. **memutarkan** – *sorot* to show a slide. – *tanda* vignette. – *tangan* free-hand sketch. – *telanjang* pin-up picture. – *témpél* a) sticker; → STIKER. b) poster. – *timbul* bas-relief. – *transparan* slide. – *ukur* surveyor's plan.

segambar in the image of. ~ *dan serupa dengan* in the image and shape of.

bergambar 1 to have o.s. photographed, pose (for a picture), have a picture of o.s. taken. **2** with pictures, illustrated. *majalah* ~ an illustrated magazine.

menggambar 1 drawing (a school subject). ~ *mistar* geometrical drawing. ~ *mesin* mechanical drawing. **2** to draw, sketch.

menggambari to illustrate, decorate with pictures, draw pictures on.

menggambarkan [and **ngegambarin** (*J coq*)] **1** to draw (a picture), illustrate, portray, represent. **2** to reproduce, describe, depict. **3** to imagine.

tergambar 1 pictured, portrayed, represented. **2** to be expressed, be outlined, stand out (against).

tergambarkan described, depicted. *Dan baru dalam film inilah* ~ *bagaimana kehidupan sehari-hari keluarga M.* And it was only in this film that the M. family's daily life was depicted. *tidak* ~ indescribable.

gambaran 1 image, illustration, drawing, picture. ~ *grafik* graph. ~ *kepribadian* image; → CITRA. **2** idea, impression. **3** description, account (of s.t. that occurred). **4** expectations, dreams (of s.t. that might occur).

gambar-gambaran set of pictures.

penggambar 1 draftsman. **2** illustrator. ~ *peta* cartographer.

penggambaran 1 drafting. **2** description, depiction.

gambas (*Jv*) pumpkin, gourd, angled luffah, *Luffa acutangula.*

gambir I gambier, *Uncaria gambir*; its leaves produce a k.o. tannin (used in betel chewing/tanning). *bunga* – k.o. jasmine, *Jasminum grandiflorum.* – *bulu-bulu* k.o. climber, *Uncaria cordata.* – (*h*)*utan* downy jasmine, *Jasminum pubescens/Trigonopleura malayana.*

Gambir II (*Tanah Lapang*) – (*coq*) Merdeka Square (in Jakarta).

gambir-gambir studs (placed on shoes to prevent slipping).

gambit (*D/E*) gambit.

gamblang (*J/Jv*) clear, plain, distinct, obvious, explicit. *Masih* – *dalam ingatan kita.* It is still fresh in our minds.

segamblang as clear as.

segamblang-gamblangnya as clear(ly) as possible.

menggamblangkan to make clear, clarify, make explicit/understandable.

tergamblang clearest.

kegamblangan clarity, explicitness.

gamblok I (*Jv*) papaya.

gamblok II (*Jv*) **nggamblok 1** to hold on to s.t., be attached to s.t. **2** to join s.t.

gamblong (*Jv*) tapioca residue.

gambot boxy (of shape).

gambrang (*J*) and **gambreng** (*Jv*) with thick hair (of mustache, etc.).

gambréng (*J*) to talk in a loud voice.

gambuh I (*Pal*) **1** k.o. dance. **2** dancer. *bermain* – and **bergambuh** to dance that dance.

gambuh II (*Jv*) a Javanese meter.

gambuh III → GAMBUS.

gambur (*M*) → GEMBUR I.

gambus (*A*) a six-stringed Arab musical instrument resembling a lute. *orkés* – a lute ensemble. *tari* – dance accompanied by a lute orchestra.

bergambus and **menggambus** to play that instrument.

gambusan *malam* ~ an evening event with lute music.

gambut bog peat. *tanah* – peat soil, soil that is loose and soft, fen.

gambyong (*Jv*) *tari* – a classical dance performed by women.

nggambyong to perform that dance.

game (*E*) /gém/ 1 game. 2 contest, competition. 3 game!, expression signaling end of a game.

gamelan (*Jv*) a set of musical instruments making up a Javanese/ Sundanese/Balinese, etc. orchestra.

gamet (*Jv*) various species of plants, including *Polygonum perfoliatum*.

gamét (*D/E*) gamete, reproductive cell.

gamik → GAMIT.

gamis (*A*) Arab shirt, chemise, i.e., a shirt-like dress with an unfitted waistline. *Sambil menyibak – panjang, tuan Sulaiman memperhatikan tingkah dan paras Ruminten.* Pulling aside his long shirt, Mr. Sulaiman observed Ruminten's demeanor and expression.

gamit gamit-gamit *menjadi* ~ to get talked about.

bergamit 1 to nudge, touch e.o. lightly with a finger, signal e.o. with the finger. *Dua remaja itu* ~ *dan bertukar kerling*. The two young people signaled each other with their fingers and exchanged glances. 2 to wave. *Daun pokok kayu* ~. The leaves of the tree waved. 3 to pluck, touch (the strings), twang (a guitar), etc.

bergamitan to nudge e.o.

menggamit 1 to touch (with the finger), nudge. ~ *dengan mata* to wink at. *Ketika gadis itu léwat di depan kami, ia ~ku dengan mata.* When the girl passed in front of us, she winked at me. 2 to beckon with the finger. *Dia* ~ *ke arah kawannya untuk memanggilnya.* She beckoned in her friend's direction to call her. 3 to pluck, strum. ~ *kecapi, gambus, dll.* to pluck at the *kecapi*, *gambus*, etc.

gamit-menggamit to touch e.o.

menggamit-gamit(kan) 1 to tap/touch with a finger, beckon. 2 to solicit.

tergamit touched, nudged.

gamitan 1 touch. 2 keyboard.

gamit-gamitan 1 s.t. that is talked about a lot, the talk of the town. 2 touching, nudging.

gamma the third letter of the Greek alphabet.

gampang 1 easy, easily; → MUDAH. 2 (pronounced with a somewhat long-drawn-out tone on the second vowel) I'll cross that bridge when I come to it. 3 easy-going. *anak* – a child of doubtful paternity, illegitimate child. *(men)cari* – to take the line of least resistance, take the easy way out, easy-going. *supaya* – in order to facilitate. – *marah, tapi* – *baik lagi.* He's quick to anger, but also quick to recover. *uang* – *datang melayang* easy come, easy go. – *terkena* subject/susceptible/liable/prone to. *Dia* – *terkena pilek.* She's prone to catching cold.

gampangnya *untuk* ~ to make it easy, give an easy example, for convenience sake.

gampang-gampang very easy. ~ *sukar* it looks easy but it's hard, it's harder than it looks. ~ *sulit/susah/angel* (*Jv*) fickle, unpredictable, i.e., sometimes easy to please and sometimes not. *Rustam mengingatkan dalam mendapatkan kartu PWI terdapat* ~ *sulit.* Rustam reminded us that one will meet with unforeseeable circumstances in obtaining an Indonesian Journalists Association card. *Déwasa ini bisnis pupuk di negeri ini dapat dikatakan* ~ *susah.* It can be said that nowadays the fertilizer business is unpredictable.

segampang as easy as. *Menjaring pinjaman dari luar negeri tidak akan lagi* ~ *kemarin.* Obtaining offshore loans will no longer be as easy as before.

menggampangi to make s.t. easy.

menggampangkan [and **ngegampangin** (*J coq*)] 1 to make easy/ easier, facilitate. *Cara itu hanya untuk* ~ *pengerjaannya.* That

method was only to make his performance easier. 2 to underestimate, have a low opinion of, disparage. *Jangan* ~ *persoalan yang penting itu!* Don't underestimate that important problem!

mempergampang to make s.t. easy/easier, alleviate.

tergampang the easiest/simplest.

gampangan (*J*) 1 easier. ~ *berbicara daripada bekerja/mengerjakannya* easier said than done. 2 easy. *wanita* ~ loose woman. *Saya ini dikiranya* ~ *apa?* Does he think that I'm easy?

gampang-gampangan *secara* ~ *saja* avoiding the difficulties, taking the easy way out.

kegampangan (*coq*) too easy.

penggampangan simplifying, simplification.

gampar (*J*) **menggampar** to strike, beat, hit.

menggampari (*pl obj*) to strike, beat, hit.

gamparan (*J/Jv*) k.o. wooden clog/shoe, sandals.

gamping (*Jv*) limestone (unburned).

bergamping lime-bearing.

gampingan calcareous, limey.

gampong (*Ac*) village; → DÉSA.

gamuh k.o. necked bottle-shaped water jar.

gan (*S*) clipped form of **juragan**. "*Ya, –, penumpang kurang.* "Yes, sir, there are fewer passengers."

gana I (*A*) 1 rich, wealthy. 2 All-Sufficing (an attribute of God).

gana II an evil spirit.

gana III digit.

bergana digital.

gana-gini I (*Jv*) twins consisting of a boy and girl.

gana-gini II (*Jv*) husband and wife's joint property acquired during marriage and which is divided up in case of divorce, community property.

ganal-ganal almost, as good as closely resembling, almost identical. – *mati* practically dead.

ganang → GUNUNG *ganang*.

ganar dizzy, bewildered, confused.

ganas 1 ferocious, fierce, savage, cruel; ill-natured, malicious, virulent. 2 dangerous. 3 malignant (of a tumor).

seganas as fierce as.

mengganas 1 to become violent/terrorize, run wild. *Pengacau semakin* ~ *di daérah itu.* The trouble-makers are becoming even more violent in that area. 2 to rage. *Wabah koléra* ~ *di Kalkuta.* Choleras is raging in Calcutta.

mengganasi to become violent toward, attack viciously.

mengganaskan to make s.t. more violent/vicious.

terganas the most vicious, fiercest.

keganasan ferocity, violence, viciousness, barbarity.

pengganas terrorist.

pengganasan (*Mal*) terrorism.

gancang nimble, agile, lively.

menggancangkan to make ... agile.

gancaran (*Jv ob*) prose.

gancél (*J*) simple/easy (to answer).

ganco and **gancu** 1 a long crook for pulling down fruit or branches. 2 hooks used to hold open a mosquito-net. 3 pickax. 4 a pole with a hook on the end (used for looking for salable items in trash cans). 5 boathook.

menggancu to fasten with a hook.

ganda I (*Hind?*) 1 -fold (in certain expressions, such as twofold/ threefold, etc.). 2 double. *Pesawat latih HS Hawk mempunyai tempat duduk –.* The HS Hawk training plane has tandem seats. *menjalani pekerjaan* – to take up a side line. *arti* – ambiguity. *berlipat* – multifarious, manifold; → LIPAT. *dua kali* – twice (as much), twofold. *dua kali* – *lebih mahal* twice as expensive. 3 multiple. *pengaruh* – multiple effects. 4 (in tennis, etc.) doubles. – *campuran* mixed doubles. – *pria/wanita* men's/women's doubles. 5 duplicate.

berganda manifold, multifarious. *penghasilan* ~ multiple income. ~ *sisi* multifaceted, many-sided/-faced. *Abdurrahman Wahid sangat beralasan menyebut kepribadian L.B. Moerdani* ~ *sisi.* Abdurrahman Wahid has good reason to mention L. B. Moerdani's multifaceted personality.

ganda-berganda and **berganda-ganda** doubled, multiplied, increased. *Pada tahun silam perdagangan ayah saya telah* *mendapat keuntungan yang* ~. Last year my father's business had increased profits.

mengganda 1 to double, multiply/increase by two. **2** to clone.

menggandakan 1 to multiply, increase, augment. **2** to multiply (in mathematics). *~ bilangan dua dengan empat hasilnya delapan.* Multiplying the number two by four equals eight. **3** to clone.

mempergandakan 1 to multiply, increase. **2** (*math*) to multiply. **3** to double and redouble, multiply, increase the total many times over.

kegandaan 1 ambiguity, double entendre. **2** multiplicity.

penggandaan 1 doubling, multiplying. **2** cloning. **3** multiplexing (in telecommunications).

pergandaan multiplication, reduplication. *~ sepuluh* tenfold increase.

ganda II (*J*) **1** opponent of unequal strength. **2** handicap.

mengganda to dare to stand up (to s.o. stronger); to be a match for s.o., be able to cope with s.t.

ganda III (*Jv*) odor, fragrance, aroma.

gandai (*mil*) standard (on vehicles).

gandal I → GANDAR I.

gandal II obstruction, obstacle, hindrance.

gandalan and **penggandal** obstruction, obstacle, hindrance.

gandala(n) → KENDALA.

gandan *kain gebar* – silk coverlet.

gandang k.o. tree, corkwood, *Carallia brachiata.*

gandapita → ANDAPITA.

gandapura (*Skr*) a plant whose seeds smell of musk and are an article of trade, musk mallow, *Abelmoschus moschatus;* the liniment made of this plant contains as active ingredients: methyl salicyl, cayenne pepper, oil of clove, oil of peppermint, oil of turpentine, and is used for the relief of pain associated with arthritis and rheumatism.

gandar I 1 carrying pole. **2** lever for rice-pounder. **3** arm of scales. **4** (wheel) axle. *– belakang* rear axle. *– mata* axis of the eye. *– poros* axle, rod on which a wheel turns.

bergandar to have an axle. *~ dua* biaxial, with two axles.

menggandar to carry on the shoulders with a pole. *~ air dua kaléng* to carry two cans of water on the shoulders with a pole.

menggandari (*pl obj*) to carry on the shoulders with a pole.

gandaran 1 load (carried on the shoulders with a pole). **2** ballast.

penggandar and **penggandaran** carrying pole, yoke.

gandar II (*J*) **menggandar** to drive (a car); to ride (a horse, bicycle) **gandaran** vehicle, carriage, means of transportation; → KANDAR I, KENDARA. *~ kuda* horse-drawn vehicle. *~ motor* motor vehicle.

gandarasa flavor.

gandaria(h) 1 a tree with small, round, dark green, very sour, edible fruit, plum mango, *Bouea macrophylla.* **2** lavender, lavender blue.

gandarokam and **gandarukam** (*Jv*) k.o. tree that yields a gum used for soldering, *Colophonium spp.*

gandarusa (*Skr*) a fragrant plant used in magic and medicine, *Justicia gendarussa, Gendarussa vulgaris.*

gandar(u)wa (*Jv*) k.o. semi-divine being.

gandasturi (*J*) a pastry made of wheat flour mixed with coconut milk, saltwater, and small peas.

gandasuli medicinal herb with sweet-smelling flowers, white ginger, *Hedychium coronarium,* symbol of disloyalty. *Jika – dikirim kepada kekasih itu tandanya bahwa kekasih itu tidak setia atau dianggap telah merusakkan kesetiaannya.* If sent to a sweetheart it is a sign that the sweetheart is not faithful or is considered to have broken his/her loyalty.

gandék I (*Jv*) (royal) envoy.

gandék II (*Jv reg*) (in Karangbolong) guard; → PENJAGA.

gandén (*Jv*) wooden hammer, mallet.

gandéng (*J/Jv*) hooked/joined together. *kapal* – tugboat. *kena –* to fall in love. *– rénténg* and *bergandéng-rénténg* **1** linked to e.o. **2** always together (in every activity). *Kedua saudara itu selalu – rénténg yang mencerminkan adanya kerukunan.* The two brothers are always together, which shows that they are in harmony with e.o.

bergandéng 1 to join together in doing s.t., (do s.t.) together. *Pesawah-pesawah itu ~ untuk menjual padi supaya lekas selesai.*

The rice growers joined together to harvest the paddy in order to finish the job fast. **2** arm in arm, with linked arms. *Meréka berjalan* ~. They walked arm in arm. **3** coupled. *~ dengan* joined with, in tandem with, coupled with; in connection with, together with, alongside. *~ tangan* hand in hand.

bergandéngan 1 joined, coupled. **2** to cooperate, join in with. *Indonésia harus ~ dengan negara-negara Asia.* Indonesia has to cooperate with Asian countries. *truk ~* a truck with a trailer. *~ tangan* to join hands, arm in arm, hand in hand. **3** related (to).

menggandéng 1 to hold/lead by the hand. **2** to take up with, have a (romantic) relationship with. *Ketika Lina hamil tua, sang suami malah ~ wanita lain.* When Lina was in an advanced stage of pregnancy, her husband, on the contrary, took up with another woman. **3** to tow alongside. *Motorbot itu ~ dua buah perahu.* The motorboat towed two praus alongside. **4** to pull, haul, drag (railway cars, etc.). *Lokomotif itu ~ dua belas gerbong.* The locomotive hauled twelve cars.

menggandéngi to go hand in hand with.

menggandéngkan and **mempergandéngkan 1** to place alongside (of). *Tukang perahu itu ~ perahunya dengan perahu yang besar.* The boatswain placed his boat alongside a large prau. **2** to link, hook together, join, couple. *Beberapa buah wagon digandéngkan dengan kereta api yang akan berangkat ke Jakarta.* Several cars were hooked onto the Jakarta-bound train.

tergandéng joined together, coupled.

gandéngan 1 link, connection. **2** with joined hands, hand in hand. *Kedua anak muda itu berjalan ~.* The two young people were walking hand in hand. **3** trailer. *truk tidak ada ~nya* a truck without a trailer. **4** appendix (to a document). **5** (*J*) partner; wife, husband; sweetheart. *Ngomong-ngomong saudara sudah punya ~, apa belum?* By the way, are you married, or not?

penggandéngan coupling, connection.

pergandéngan parallelism.

gander(u)wo → GENDRUWO.

gandes (*Jv*) gracious, graceful, elegant, charming, attractive.

gandéwa (*Jv*) archer's bow.

gandi (*cla*) **1** archer's bow. **2** hammer.

bergandi archery. *main –* archery.

menggandi to hammer.

gandik 1 gold frontlet decorating a bride's fringe, a tiara. **2** decoration on the hilt of a kris.

gandil thorn.

gandin → GANDÉN.

ganding I (*M*) equal, match, peer; → BANDING I, TANDING I.

berganding(an) to vie, compete.

menggandingkan and **mempergandingkan 1** to compare s.t. (with s.t. else). **2** to match s.o. (with s.o. else).

terganding equaled, matched. *Kekayaannya tak ~ oléh orang lain.* His wealth is unequalled by others. **2** can be overcome/exceeded.

pengganding competitor.

ganding II berganding(an) joined; → GANDÉNG.

gandingan appendix.

gandok(an) (*Jv*) pavilion, wing (of a house).

gandol → GANDUL.

gandola (*Skr?*) Ceylon spinach, *Basella rubra.*

gandorio (*Jv*) → GANDARIA.

gandos (*J/Jv*) cookie made of rice flour, mixed with coconut and salt, then fried. *– wingka* a variety of such a cookie.

gandringan (*ob*) meeting.

gandrum → JAGUNG *cantél.*

gandrung I (*J/Jv*) **1** infatuated, enamored, in love, fond (of); to long (for). *– kuda putih alias céwék bulé* crazy about a white horse alias a white girl. *Buruh Jepang – pada pekerjaan.* Japanese workers are workaholics. *Meréka sedang – dengan pekerjaan-pekerjaan manajérial seperti keuangan.* They are in love with managerial jobs, such as finances. **2** minded. *– olahraga* sportsminded. *– révolusi* dedicated to revolution. *– udara* air-minded.

menggandrungi 1 to be very fond of, be enamored of, be infatuated with. *Ia ~ gadis berkulit kuning itu.* He's infatuated with the girl with the light brown complexion. *digandrungi publik* to be in vogue with the public. **2** to interest s.o. in, show (an) in-

terest in. *Mistik belakangan ini ternyata semakin banyak di-gandrungi masyarakat dari kalangan élite atau masyarakat menengah atas.* The elite and the middle classes have recently been showing an interest in mysticism.
menggandrungkan to long/yearn for. *Para guru ~ sarana pen-didikan yang serba lengkap.* Teachers have been longing for complete educational facilities.
kegandrungan (state of) love, being in love, attachment, devo-tion. *~ kepada* fondness for. *~ menggunakan jasa bank* loving to use the services of a bank.
penggandrung lover, enthusiast, -phile.
gandrung II k.o. millet, sorghum, *Andropogon sorghum.*
gandu *buah* the hard, black fruit (of the *merbau*-tree, ironwood, *Intsia bakeri*), used as a marble in some children's games.
ganduh I (*M*) lagniappe, extra, small addition given in order to please a customer. *tidak lalu –nya* didn't succeed.
berganduh and **mengganduh** to barter and also give extra money.
memperganduh(-ganduh)kan to treat s.t. as an object to bar-ter, give in exchange.
ganduh II berganduh mixed, blended.
gandul hanger, pendulum; → BANDUL.
bergandul [and **bergandulan** (*pl subj*)] to hang down/suspended.
menggandul 1 to hang, suspend. *Sebuah pistol ~ pada ikat ping-gangnya.* A pistol was hanging from his belt. *Banyak penumpang ~ pada pintu bus.* Many passengers were hanging on to the door of the bus. **2** pendulous.
mengganduli 1 to hang on. *diganduli ngantuk* to be overcome with sleepiness. *Anak itu meréngék sambil ~ tangan ibunya.* That child was whining while hanging on to his mother's hand. **2** to be the support for. *Dia kini sudah diganduli 2 bocah.* Now he has to support two children. **3** to provide with a pendulum/counter-weight. *Ia ~ ujung bambu pengérék timbanya dengan batu.* He attached a stone as a counter-weight on to the bamboo end of his well hoist.
menggandulkan to hang s.t. (on s.t. else), attach, suspend s.t.
gandulan 1 pendulum. **2** a decoration hanging down from a neck-lace.
gandum (*Pers*) **1** wheat, *Trificum sativum. tepung –* wheat flour. **2** corn. *– hitam* rye.
gandung I light logs attached as outriggers to a prau to give it greater steadiness.
bergandung 1 to be fitted with outriggers. **2** to be loaded on the outriggers.
menggandung to carry cargo on the outriggers.
penggandung outrigger.
gandung II → PÉLA GANDUNG.
gandungan → GADUNGAN.
gandut (*J*) → GANDUL.
Ganéfo [Games of the New Emerging Forces] Games of the New Emerging Forces (under President Soekarno).
ganésha (*Skr*) **1** elephant. *"Pak, pak, ada – masuk kampung. Buaanyak.* Dad, dad, there are elephants coming into our kam-pung. A whole lot." **2** in Hindu mythology, the fat-bellied elephant-headed son of Shiva; the Household God, or God of Prosperity. **3** the symbol of ITB.
gang I [Gg] (*D*) **1** alley. *– buntu* dead-end alley. **2** passage. **3** nar-row street. **4** hallway. **5** corridor. *– Lokomotip* a rice trading center in Jatinegara (Jakarta). *– mobil* driveway.
gang II (*E*) /géng/ **1** gang, a group of law-breakers, etc.; → GÉNG. **2** gang, buddies, group (of friends).
segang of the same gang. *Saya bersama teman-teman ~ pasti nonton.* I definitely go to the movies with friends of the same gang.
gang III *– asam* k.o. braised beef from Kalimantan.
Gangga (*Skr*) and *Betara –* the holy Ganges.
ganggam bauntuik (*M*) right to use (land).
ganggang I berganggang 1 to warm o.s. (by a fire). **2** to roast/smoke/warm over a fire.
mengganggang 1 to put s.t. over the fire to dry or cook. *~ pakaian yang basah* to dry wet clothing. **2** to toast (bread), grill (fish); *cp* PANGGANG.
terganggang toasted, grilled.

ganggangan warmth.
ganggang II (*M*) **1** a narrow opening between two objects, crack, slit. *menéngok dari – pintu* to look/peep through a slit in the door. **2** wide apart. *Persahabatan meréka semakin –.* Their friendship is getting further and further apart.
berganggang 1 with/having a space/gap between. **2** to be di-vorced (husband and wife).
mengganggang 1 to split apart (of joinery), open up. *papan ~ a* split board/plank. **2** no longer on close terms (of friends). **3** to open s.t. a crack/a little bit. *~ pintu* to open the door a crack.
mengganggangkan to open s.t. a crack.
ganggang III algae, seaweed. *– biru* blue algae, *Cyanobacteria. – laut* seaweed, sargassum.
ganggu *– gugat* sue, challenge, contest. *mengganggu gugat 1* (*leg*) to sue, institute proceedings against, take legal action against. **2** to impeach. **3** to challenge, contest, question. *~ suatu keputu-san* to contest a decision. *tidak boléh diganggu-gugat* unim-peachable, inviolable, irreversible, irrevocable. *Présidén tidak dapat diganggu-gugat.* The President cannot be sued. *terganggu-gugat* to be challenged/contested. *pengganggu-gugat* s.o. who challenges/contests (a decision). *pengganggu-gugatan* taking legal action against.
mengganggu [and **nggangguin** (*J coq*)] **1** to disturb, trouble, bother. *Jangan ~ anjing itu.* Don't disturb the dog. **2** to inter-fere with, disrupt, upset, interrupt. **3** to annoy, tease, harass. **4** to affect, impinge on, harm, hold up (the line). **5** to jam (a gun/broadcast). *~ hati* to upset s.o. *~ keamanan* to disturb the peace. *~ kepentingan* to harm s.o.'s interests. *~ keséhatan badan* to damage s.o.'s health. *~ ketenteraman rumah* to tres-pass. *~ ketertiban umum* to disturb public order. *~ pikiran* a) to bother/nag s.o., haunt s.o. b) to disturb, upset.
terganggu [and **kegangu** (*coq*)] **1** interfered with, interrupted, out (of electric power). *tidak ~* unperturbed. *Perlombaan itu ~ oléh hujan.* The race was interrupted by the rain. **2** disturbed, bothered. *Keséhatannya ~.* He didn't feel well. *~ otaknya/pikirannya.* He isn't quite right in the head. *~ pikiran* crazy. **3** jammed (of telecommunications).
gangguan 1 interference, hindrance; interruption, nuisance, bother, annoyance, disturbance, problem. **2** outage (of electric power). **3** jamming. *~ jantung* heart failure. *~ jiwa* mental ill-ness. *~ keamanan* disturbance of the peace. *~ lalu-lintas* traffic problems. *~ listrik* a) outage/interruption of electricity. b) static. *~ kepanikan/panik* panic attack. *~ perut* stomach upset. *~ séksual* sexual harassment; → PELÉCÉHAN séksual. *~ suara* flutter. *~ téknik* technical difficulties. *~ tidur* sleep disorder.
pengganggu 1 disturber, teaser. *peralatan éléktronik ~* electronic counter measures, ECM. **2** pest.
pengganguan 1 disturbance, interference. *~ ketenteraman rumah* trespass. **2** annoyance. **3** jamming.
ganggut mengganggut 1 to draw, pull. **2** to tug at, yank out.
gangrin (*D/E*) gangrene.
gangsa I (*Skr*) brass, bell-metal.
gangsa II (*Skr*) **1** goose; → ANGSA I. **2** *– batu* various species of boo-bies including Abbott's booby, *Sula abbotti.*
gangsa III menggangsa to shift, transplant.
gangsal (*ob*) → GASAL.
gangsang → GASANG I.
gangsar (*Jv*) prosperous (in business), successful.
gangsi (*ob*) perfume(s), scent.
menggangsi to perfume (clothes).
gangsing → GASING.
gangsir I (*Jv*) mole cricket, short-tailed cricket, *Brachytrypes por-tentosus;* → GASIR. *tukang – rumah* burglar.
menggangsir to tunnel under a wall (to burglarize a house).
penggangsir burrower.
penggangsiran undermining, tunneling.
gangsir II (*Jv*) **gangsiran** (reference to certain Yogyakartan deli-cacies) **1** a snack of fried *mlinjo* skin. **2** dishes which accom-pany fried seasoned beef.
gangster (*E*) gangster.
gani (*A*) **1** rich. **2** the all-rich (God).
ganih I (*ob*) female elephant tusk; → GENIH.

ganih II (*M ob*) white. *kain* – white cloth.

ganimah (*A*) spoils of war; → RAMPASAN *perang*.

ganitri (*S*) k.o. tree, rudraksha berry, *Elaeocarpus ganitrus*.

ganja I (*Hind*) (steel) cross-piece of kris blade, the guard at the top of a kris blade. – *iras/menumpu* a kris with the guard and blade in one piece. – *datang/rawan* guard that is joined to the blade.

ganja II (*Hind*) marijuana, *Cannabis sativa*.
  berganja [and **ngeganja** (*coq*)] to smoke pot/marijuana. *Dia suka ngeganja.* He likes to smoke pot.
  mengganja to drug, intoxicate.

ganjais pot smoker, pothead.

ganjak → ANJAK. **berganjak 1** to shift, move, budge (slightly). *tidak mau ~ dari duduknya* does not want to move from one's seat. **2** to shake. *Pendiriannya tiada ~*. His opinion is unshakable.
  mengganjak(-ganjak) and **mengganjak(kan)** to move, budge, shift s.t. slightly. *Karena sangat berat, tidak dapat diganjak sedikit jua.* Because it was very heavy, it could not be moved even a little bit.
  terganjak shifted, moved, budged. *Batu sebesar itu tidak dapat ~ oléhnya.* Such a large rock cannot be moved by him.
  ganjakan shift.
  pengganjakan shifting, shift.

ganjal shim, wedge, chock; a bit of wood, paper, small stone, etc., slipped under s.t. (to prevent it from wobbling or moving or to raise it). *Mobil yang mogok di tanjakan langsung diberi –*. A chock was put behind the car that stalled on the slope (to prevent it from rolling backward). – *kaki* foot-rest. – *lunas* (*naut*) keel block.
  berganjal with a prop/wedge/chock.
  mengganjal 1 to prop s.t. up (to make it stable), shim. *Dia ~ kaki kursi dengan kertas.* He propped up the leg of the chair with paper (so that it wouldn't wobble). **2** to supplement. *~ belanja hari ini* to supplement today's (kitchen) expenses. **3** to put a chock/wedge under/behind. *Ia ~ roda mobilnya dengan balok kayu.* He put a block of wood as a chock behind the back wheel of his car. **4** to take the edge off (one's hunger). *~ perut* to be filling, stick to one's ribs (of food). *~ lapar seusai sidang-sidang* to take the edge off one's hunger after the sessions have finished. **5** to stick (in one's craw), bother, stand in the way. *Ada sesuatu yang terasa ~ di hati saya.* It is as if there's s.t. that's bothering me. *Tapi ada sesuatu yang ~.* But there was s.t. that was bothering him. *Yang mungkin masih ~ adalah jumlah hotél di Batam masih kurang.* What probably still stands in the way is the inadequate number of hotels in Batam.
  ganjal-mengganjal to block e.o.'s way.
  mengganjali to prop up/open with a wedge/prop/shim/chock. *Pintu itu diganjali.* The door was propped open. *~ méja yang goyang* to prop up a wobbly table.
  mengganjalkan to use s.t. as a wedge/prop/shim/chock.
  terganjal 1 to have a problem/impediment. *Masih ~ soal harga dengan Gappri.* There is still a problem in the matter of the price with Gappri. **2** not fluent/glib. *~ lidah* unable to speak. **3** propped up, shimmed. *Kaki méja itu ~ dengan kertas sehingga tidak timpang lagi.* The leg of the table was propped up with paper so that it was no longer wobbly.
  ganjalan 1 support, prop, chock, shim. *~ perut* a bite, s.t. to put in one's stomach. **2** impediment, choke.
  pengganjal 1 s.t. to take the edge off (one's hunger). *~ perut* anything to take the edge off of one's hunger. **2** prop, wedge, chock, shim. *alat ~ roda pesawat* wheel chock. *~ pintu* door stop. *~ bahu* shoulder pad. *~ ruang kosong* (in newspaper) stopper.
  pengganjalan 1 scaffolding, supporting. **2** wedging, propping up.

ganjar mengganjar(i) 1 to repay, reward, give s.t. that s.o. deserves (thanks/repayment for services or good deeds, etc.). *Orang kaya itu telah mengganjar Sumitro, karena Sumitro telah menyelamatkan anaknya.* That wealthy person rewarded Sumitro, because he had rescued his child. **2** to punish, sentence. *Hakim mengganjar pencuri itu tiga tahun penjara.* The judge sentenced the thief to three years in jail. *diganjar hukuman 6 bulan penjara* sentenced to 6 months in prison.
  mengganjarkan 1 to reward with. **2** to sentence with.

terganjar rewarded, blessed.
  ganjaran 1 reward, present, gratuity. *sebagai ~* in return (for s.t. done). **2** punishment, conviction.
  pengganjaran rewarding, blessing.

ganjat 1 cramps, to have a cramp. **2** taut (of thread).
  terganjat cramped. *Kakinya ~.* He had a cramp in his leg.

ganjawan pot smoker, pothead; → GANJAIS.

ganjel → GANJAL. *tukang –* (in pickpocket jargon) the person who distracts the attention of the victim so that the pickpocket can pick his pocket.
  mengganjel [and **ngganjel** (*coq*)] to be thorny (of a problem). *Nampaknya masih ada beberapa perkara yang ~ hubungan Malaysia-Brunéi.* It seems there still are some thorny problems between Malaysia and Brunei. *~ mata* to be an eyesore.
  ganjelan 1 shim. **2** thorn in the flesh. *Okinawa ~ antara Jepang-AS.* Okinawa is a thorn in the flesh of Japan and the US. *Ia menceritakan ~ hatinya yang selama ini terpendam.* She spoke about what was bothering her and told him what she had kept to herself.

ganjen (*J*) lively and flirtatious (of girls), coquettish, likes to play around (of men).
  keganjenan flirtatiousness, coquettishness.

ganjil 1 odd, uneven (of numbers). *3, 5, 7 dan 9 semuanya adalah angka –*. 3, 5, 7, and 9 are all odd numbers. **2** extraordinary, exceptional, abnormal, eccentric, quaint. *– dari biasa* different from the ordinary.
  seganjil as exceptional/abnormal as.
  berganjil *bergenap* – a) to play dice and bet on odds or evens. b) strange, odd, unusual.
  mengganjil to be strange, act oddly (different from the usual).
  mengganjilkan 1 to make s.t. odd/uneven. *Pengurus yang empat orang itu harus diganjilkan.* The four-man board of directors has to be made an uneven number. **2** to be odd/strange/unusual. *Meskipun perangainya ~, orangnya baik.* Even though his behavior is odd, he's a good person. *Rupanya saja yang ~, tetapi sebenarnya tidak.* It only seems odd, but actually it isn't.
  keganjilan abnormality, strangeness, oddity, queerness. *~ kelakuannya menghérankan anak-anaknya.* The strangeness of his behavior surprised his children.

ganjur I (*M*) pulling back (a kite string). *perjalanan si – lalai, dari pergi surut yang lebih* describes the slow and graceful way girls walk in *Jv wayang* plays, not in a hurry.
  berganjur *dibawa ~* to be invited to go to a quiet place (in order to negotiate, etc.). *pergi ~* to leave (a crowded place, etc.).
  berganjur-ganjur *~ surut* vacillating.
  mengganjur to draw/pull back. *~ tali layang-layang* to pull back on a kite string. *~ diri/surut* to withdraw, retire, pull back. *Meréka hendak ~ diri dahulu supaya dapat berpikir agak tenang.* They wanted to withdraw first so that they could think in quiet. *diganjur surut bagai bertanam* always walking backward like paddy planters in a rice field. *~ hari* to postpone, put off.

ganjur II (*Jv*) a pike, lance.
  mengganjur to lance, spear, stab.
  mengganjuri (*pl obj*) to lance, spear, stab.

ganjur III (*Jv*) a rice plant pest, gall midge, *Orseolia oryzae*.

gank → GANG II 2.

ganta *– berganti* to alternate/succeed e.o.; → GANTI I. **berganta-ganti** to change frequently, keep on changing. *Sepulang kerja, saya terpaksa bersusah payah ~ angkutan untuk mencapai tempat tinggal saya.* Going home after work, I was forced to go to a lot of trouble and keep on changing transportation to reach my house.

gantal (*Jv*) during a wedding ceremony, a rolled-up betel leaf tied with yarn that the bride and groom throw to e.o. as a sign that they promise to give and take from e.o.

gantang a cubic measure for rice, etc. equal to 3.125 kg, around one quart. *penuh sudah bagai –* chock-full.
  segantang one quart. *~ beras* a quart of rice. *secupak tak jadi ~* you can't make a silk purse out of a sow's ear; things are what they are fated to be.
  menggantang to measure with a *gantang*. *~ anak ayam* to do s.t. very difficult that is useless and probably won't succeed. *~*

asap to build castles in the air, to hope for the impossible. *bagai* ~ *anak ayam* to look for a needle in a haystack.

gantar (*S*) (a long, thin, straight) bamboo pole (mainly used to dry clothes or to pick fruits, and as a carrying pole).

gantél (*J*) **menggantéli** to hang/be hanging from.
  menggantélkan to hang s.t.
  gantélan hanger.

ganteng (*Jv*) handsome, good-looking (*esp* of a man), dashing. *berpakaian* – to be dressed elegantly.
  seganteng as handsome as.
  mengganteng [and **ngganteng** (*coq*)] to act like s.o. who thinks he is good-looking.
  terganteng the best looking, the handsomest.
  kegantengan handsomeness.

ganténg (*J*) coagulated, congealed, thickened (of sugar); → **KENTAL**.
  mengganténgkan to coagulate, congeal, thicken (of a sauce).

ganti I 1 deputy, successor. **2** replacement, substitute. *sebagai – nya* a) as a substitute for. b) instead/in place of. **3** compensation, indemnification. **4** –*!* (in shortwave communications) over! **5** (often used instead of **mengganti**) to change, replace, substitute. *Kalau kau sudah capék, saya – angkat air itu.* If you're tired, I'll lift up that water in your place. – *bus empat kali* to change buses four times. *sekarang – cerita saya* and now I want to tell about s.t. else. – *keréta api* to change trains. – *kulit* to slough, cast its skin (of a snake), molt. – *nama* to change one's name. *Ia hampir 29 hari tidak – pakaian.* For almost 29 days he hasn't changed his clothes. – *pesawat* to change planes. *Dia sudah berulang kali – suami.* She has changed husbands again and again. – *bulu* to molt, shed feathers. – *ganda* double indemnity. – *kerugian* compensation, indemnity, indemnification. **menggantirugikan** to compensate, indemnify. *Tanah masyarakat digantirugikan pemerintah.* Community lands are indemnified by the government. – *lapik* to marry a deceased spouse's sister or a deceased husband's brother; → **TURUN** *ranjang.* – *rugi* compensation, indemnification, recompense (for property taken by the state, etc.); → **PAMPASAN.** – *tangan* (done) by another person. – *tikar* to marry a deceased wife's sister or a deceased husband's brother; → **TURUN** *ranjang.*

ganti-ganti by turns, in turn, alternately; → **GONTA-GANTI.** ~ *mitra séks* to keep on changing sex partners.
  seganti ~ *setungguan* (in *Sumsel*) an eye for an eye; → **NYAWA** *ganti nyawa.*

berganti 1 to turn, change, become different, turn into. ~ *bulu* a) to molt, shed feathers. b) to change one's attitude. ~ *haluan* to change course. ~ *keréta api* to change trains. *Hari* ~ *minggu, minggu* ~ *bulan, dia belum juga pulang.* Days turned into weeks, weeks turned into months, and he still hadn't come home. *hari* ~ *hari* day after day. **2** to change, replace. ~ *keméja* to change shirts. *saling/silih* ~ to replace e.o. *patah tumbuh, hilang* ~ "the broken grows, the lost is replaced," i.e., the king is dead, long live the king.

ganti-berganti → **BERGANTIAN.**
berganti-ganti → **GANTI-GANTI.**

bergantian in turn, one after another/the other, to take turns, alternate, do things in shifts. *Semua penduduk kampung itu* ~ *datang mendaftarkan nama meréka.* All the villagers came to register their names one after the other. *Keluarga terdekatnya secara* ~ *menunggu di kamarnya.* Her closest relatives waited in turn in her (sick) room.

mengganti 1 to replace (with s.t. else), change s.t. (into s.t. else). *Kartu Tanda Penduduk (KTP) yang lama akan diganti.* The old Resident Identification Cards will be replaced. ~ *persnéling* to shift gears. ~ *uang* to refund money. *Buku kau yang hilang saya – dengan yang ini.* I'll replace your lost book with this one **2** to pay back, reimburse, compensate. *Siapa yang akan* ~ *kerugian sebanyak itu?* Who will reimburse such a loss? **3** to succeed. *Bila Ketua Umum berpénsiun nanti, siapakah yang akan ~nya?* When the General Chairman retires, who will succeed him?

menggantikan [and **nggantiin/ngegantiin** (*J coq*)] to replace, substitute for, take over for, sit/fill in for, cover for, supercede. *Anak bupati* ~ *ayahnya bila berhalangan.* The son of the regent

takes over for his father when he is occupied. ~ *lapik* to marry the former spouse of one's brother.
  memperganti-gantikan to keep on changing s.t.

tergantikan replaceable. *Di Bali kentongan benar-benar merupakan alat komunikasi yang belum* ~. In Bali the *kentongan* really is a communication device that cannot yet be replaced. *tidak* ~ irreplaceable. *Kasih sayang ibu pada anak tak* ~. A mother's love for her children is irreplaceable.

gantian → **BERGANTIAN.**

pengganti 1 replacement, successor, substitute, stand-in, make-up. *atas/kepada* ~ (a bill of exchange) to bearer. *tanggal* ~ make-up date. ~ *hak* substitute holder of rights. ~ *lemak* fat substitute. ~ *pelaku* stand-in. *sebagai* ~ in lieu of. *Kartu nama ini sebagai* ~ *surat undangan* This name card is in lieu of an invitation. ~ *suku cadang* replacement parts. **2** compensation. ~ *jasa* compensation for services.

penggantian 1 replacement, change, changing, substitution. *direncanakan sebagai* ~ *armada tua yang terkena pembesituan.* planned as a replacement for the old armada which is being scrapped. ~ *biaya* compensation. ~ *kerugian* ~ *pejabat dalam pemerintahan adalah hal yang lumrah* changing officials in the government is a common thing. ~ *tenaga* replacements. ~ *warna* change of color. **2** recompense. ~ *jasa* recompense for services.

pergantian 1 change(over), replacement, transfer. **2** place or time where/when s.t. changes. ~ *abad* turn of the century. **3** (*leg*) representation, substitution (of one heir for another). ~ *alamat* change of address. ~ *lampu mérah ke ijo itu nggak seberapa lama.* The change from red to green doesn't take that long. ~ *nada suara* modulation. ~ *kekuasaan* transfer of power. *pada* ~ *tahun* at the end of the year. *merayakan* ~ *tahun* to celebrate New Year's. ~ *sekutu* shifting of alignments. ~ *siang dan malam* the change from day to night. ~ *tahun* turn of the year (when one year turns into the next).

ganti II k.o. root, Angelica root?, *Ligusticum acutilobum.*
gantih (*M*) **menggantih** to spin thread.
ganting (*J*) → **GANTÉNG.**
gantol (*Jv*) (large) hook (on a pole); sling, grappling iron.
  menggantol to hook on.
gantolé 1 (*Ujungpandang*) dragonfly. **2** hang glider.

gantung 1 hang, suspend. – *diri* to hang o.s. – *sungsang* to hang upside down. *jembatan* – suspension bridge. *lampu* – hanging lamp. *menghukum* – to sentence to death by hanging. **2** defer, adjourn, deferred (of divorce/marriage, etc.). – *bicara* to adjourn a case. *dicerai* – not divorced, but also not sent home (of a spouse). *kawin* – a legal marriage but one not yet made official by a ceremony, or the married couple is not yet living together. *pusaka* – estate awaiting distribution. **3** contingent. *kewajiban* – contingent obligation. – *kapal* award for s.o. helping a grounded ship. – *kemudi* k.o. port tax. – *layar* (*cla*) fee for sailors helping the shipwrecked.

bergantung 1 to hang, be suspended. *Anak itu* ~ *di dahan pohon itu seperti kera.* That child is hanging on the tree branch like a monkey. *Ia* ~ *pada ambang pintu bus.* He was hanging on to the doorstep of the bus. ~ *di awang-awang* uncertain. ~ *di ujung rambut* his fate hangs by a thread. *Engkaulah tempatku* ~. You're the one on whom I rely. ~ *tidak bertali* (= *sehasta tali*) a) a spouse left behind by her husband but not divorced. b) the situation of a mistress. c) up in the air, not firm. ~ *pada akar lapuk* and ~ *pada tali rapuh* to make one's life dependent on a weak or unstable person/job, etc. **2** ~ *[(ke)pada]* to depend on, be dependent on. *Meskipun sudah kawin, tetapi hidupnya masih* ~ *pada orangtuanya.* Even though he's married, he's still dependent on his parents. **3** to be at the mercy of. *Sekarang meréka* ~ *kepada musuh.* Now they are at the mercy of the enemy. **4** to count on, bank/rely on. *Jangan* ~ *padanya.* Don't count on him. **5** to delay, defer, postpone, suspend. *Kejuaraan tidak* ~. The championship wasn't suspended. **6** to be up to, for … to decide, (I) leave it to you. *Berhasil tidaknya* ~ *pada kita sendiri.* Whether it will succeed or not is up to us ourselves. *tidak* ~ independent. **ketidak-bergantungan** independence.

bergantungan (*pl subj*) to hang, be suspended.

menggantung 1 to hang s.t. up. *~ jas hujannya pada paku di dinding rumahnya* to hang his raincoat on a nail in the wall of his house. *~ seragam* to retire from the military. **2** to hang (a person). *Ia tidak ~ diri, melainkan digantung orang.* He didn't hang himself, but he was hanged. **3** to hang, be suspended. **4** adjourned, suspended. *Perkara itu masih ~, belum putus juga.* That case is still adjourned; no decision has been reached yet. *~ talak* to hold up or hamper a divorce requested by a spouse. *digantung* to be out of commission. *Ratusan truk digantung.* Hundreds of trucks were out of commission. *~ tak bertali* not given support but also not granted a divorce.

menggantungi 1 (*pl obj*) to hang. *Algojo itu sudah biasa ~ orang.* An executioner is used to hanging people. **2** to hang on/around. *Léhérnya digantungi dengan rantai emas.* A gold chain hung around her neck.

menggantungkan 1 to hang (up). *Gantungkan peta ini di témbok.* Hang this map up on the wall. *Di depan toko itu digantungkan papan nama yang besar.* In front of the store hung a large sign. **2** *~ [ke(pada)]* to have s.t. depend (on). *Anak yatim itu ~ hidupnya pada orang tua asuhnya.* That orphan makes his life dependent on his foster parents. *~ diri dari/kepada* to depend on, be dependent on, sponge off. **3** to bet on. *Jangan ~ pada rencana ini.* Don't bet on this plan. **4** to delay, defer, postpone, put off, adjourn. *~ talak* to get a conditional divorce.

mempergantungi to hold on to, rely/depend on. *Sejak ibu bapaknya meninggal, ia ~ paman dan bibinya.* Since the death of his parents, he has relied on his uncle and aunt.

tergantung 1 hanging, supported, suspended. *Di dalam kamarnya ~ beberapa buah lukisan yang indah.* In his room hang some beautiful paintings. **2** to depend (on). *~ (dari)pada* dependent (on). *~ keadaan* it depends on circumstances, wait and see; → TERSERAH *nanti*. **3** postponed, delayed, deferred, put off. *tidak ~* independent. ***ketidaktergantungan*** independence. *~ Proton dari Jepang semakin terlihat pada sédan vérsi-vérsi baru yang akan diluncurkan mulai tahun depan.* The independence of the Proton (car) on Japan can be seen more and more from the new versions of sedans which will be launched starting next year. **ketergantungan** dependence. *mengurangi ~ pada serat impor* to decrease dependence on imported fibers. *saling ~* and ***kesalingtergantungan*** interdependence, interdependency; → SALING.

gantungan 1 hook, hanger, mounting. *~ baju* clothes hanger/hook. *~ kunci* key ring. *~ pakaian* coat hanger. **2** s.t. depended on. *~ hidup* refuge, protection, s.t. or s.o. one can rely on. *Tanah itu merupakan ~ hidup rakyat di situ yang hidup sebagai petani sawah atau petani tambak ikan.* The people there depend on the land for their living as rice or fish farmers. *~ jiwa* sweetheart. *~ ke atas* an undeserved promotion. **3** pylon, post. *tiang ~* gallows. *~ senjata* weapons pylon. **4** fixture. *~ lampu* lamp fixture. **5** gallows.

penggantung s.t. to hang s.t. from. *~ mangkuk* cup hook. *~ manusia* lyncher.

penggantungan 1 hanging, suspending, suspension. **2** gallows.

pergantungan 1 hanger. **2** scaffold. *tiang ~* gallows.

ganung (*Jv*) heart of various fruits (*nanas, kapok*, etc.)

ganyah menggganyah 1 to rub, massage, scrub, scour. **2** to hit, attack. *Pendududuk Tambon Baroh, Acéh Utara, tak putus diganyah kebocoran amoniak.* The population of Tambon Baroh, North Aceh, was constantly attacked by ammonia leaks.

ganyang (*Jv*) **mengganyang 1** to crush, destroy, liquidate, eliminate. *~ Malaysia!* (slogan during the Confrontation of 1963–69) Crush Malaysia! **2** to devour, eat up (raw) (of animals). *Ular ~ mangsanya.* A snake devours its prey. **3** (*joc*) (of people) to eat up, attack (food). **4** to beat, defeat.

terganyang 1 crushed. **2** devoured. **3** defeated.

ganyangan s.t. destroyed, etc.

pengganyang destroyer, smasher.

pengganyangan crushing, destruction, annihilation, liquidation. *merasakan pahit-getirnya sebagai seniman yang jadi sasaran ~ PKI* to feel the bitterness of life as an artist who became the target of PKI annihilation.

ganyar hard (of uncooked potatoes/yams, etc.), tough.

ganyong (*J/Jv*) k.o. tuberous plant, edible canna, purple arrowroot, *Canna edulis/indica.*

ganyut (*ob*) → GANYAR.

gaok (*Jv onom*) **1** cawing sound. **2** *burung –* crow.
menggaok to caw.
gaokan cawing.

gap I (*onom*) **1** the sound of slapping on a table. **2** the sound of a heartbeat; → DEGAP I.

gap II (*E*) gap; → KESENJANGAN. *– antara yang miskin dan yang kaya* the gap between the poor and the rich.

gapa(h) I (*J*) skillful, adroit; capable, able, clever.
kegapahan capability, ability; skill, adroitness.

gapah II (*S?*) *– gopoh/gupuh* to do s.t. in haste/a hurry (due to lack of time).

gapai bergapaian to seize/catch hold of/grip e.o. *Lutung dan kera itu ~ di akar yang berjela-jela.* Long-haired black monkeys and apes seized e.o. on the dangling roots.
menggapai 1 to extend the hand out to reach s.t., reach out to touch s.t. **2** to convey, extend (one's intention/aspirations, etc.). *~ cita-citanya* to convey one's aspirations. **3** to reach. *Sebagai imbalannya, Riau Pos kini bisa ~ pembaca di Kepulauan Riau lebih pagi.* As compensation, the *Riau Post* can now reach the reader in the Riau Archipelago earlier. **4** to attain (after hard work).
menggapai-gapai to keep on reaching out (to grab s.t.), try hard to achieve s.t. *Orang yang hampir tenggelam ~.* A person who is drowning keeps on reaching out (for help).
menggapai(-gapai)kan to extend one's hand as if trying to grab hold of s.t.
tergapai-gapai kept making (involuntarily) grasping movements, keep on reaching out. *Tangannya ~ kecemasan karena hampir lemas ia dalam air itu.* His hand kept reaching out nervously because he was almost drowning in the water.
penggapaian 1 extending the hand, reaching out. **2** conveying, extending.

gapapa [*enggak apa-apa*] it doesn't matter, I don't care.

Gapasdap [Gabungan Pengusaha Angkutan Sungai, Danau dan Penyeberangan] Association of River, Lake and Ferry Entrepreneurs.

gapé (*J*) have a sure hand at, be great at. *Dia – bahasa Inggris.* Her English is great.

gapik → GOPOH *gapah/gapik/mamang.*

gapil meddlesome. *– mulut* fault-finding, fussy, finicky, hard to please. *– tangan* meddlesome.
menggapil to meddle, interfere (in s.o.'s affairs, etc.).

gapit (*Jv*) **1** pincers, clamp, tongs. **2** handle (of *wayang* puppet).
menggapit to nip.

gaplé(h) (*J*) domino (card game). *main –* to play dominoes.
pegaplé(h) domino player.

gaplék (*Jv*) peeled, sliced, and dried cassava.

gaplok (*J/Jv*) slap (in the face), box on the ear.
menggaplok to slap on the cheek.
menggaploki (*pl obj*) to hit (again and again), slap.
gaplokan slap, box on the ear.

Gapmmi [Gabungan Pengusaha Makanan Minuman Indonésia] Indonesian Association of Food and Beverage Entrepreneurs.

gapruk (*J*) **menggaprukkan** to drop s.t. with force.

gapték [gagap téknologi] computer illiterate/ignorant.

gapura (*Skr*) gateway, entrance. *– kehormatan* triumphal arch.

gar I (*onom*) sound of rattling; → DEGAR.

gar II (in acronyms) → ANGGARAN, GARNISUN.

gara I → GAHARA.

gara II (*ob*) → GARAH I.

gara-gara 1 (in the *wayang* play) scene which occurs at or shortly after midnight in which the clowns appear with their master, the hero of the play; this constitutes the turning point in the play. **2** bustle, commotion, tumult, upheaval. *Perkara itu akan dapat menimbulkan – dalam masyarakat.* That case will cause an uproar in the community. *–mu!* It's all your fault! *mencari –* to look/ask for trouble. **3** idea, instigation. *Ini –nya siapa ya?* Whose bright idea was this? Who's the wise guy? **4** (just) because, (just) due to the fact that. *Bupati pernah memarahi D. – belum pindah ke rumah dinas.* The regent once got mad at D.

just because he hadn't moved into the official residence yet. *Penduduk mulai mengungsi – Gunung Merapi akan meletus.* The residents began to run away because Mt. Merapi was about to erupt.

bergara-gara to make a big fuss.

garah I (*M*) **menggarah** to scare off, try to frighten, chase away, drive away (birds in rice fields, etc.).

penggarah rope with noisemakers attached stretched across rice field; when shaken it frightens birds away.

garah II and **garah-garah 1** jest, joke. **2** in/for fun, as a joke.

bergarah(-garah) to joke, jest.

mempergarahkan to make a fool of s.o., make fun of s.o., pull s.o.'s leg, poke fun at s.o.

garai 1 (in *Sumbar*) sorghum. **2** midrib.

garam 1 salt. **2** chemical compound obtained when an acid is combined with a metal. *Mahasiswa itu mencampurkan sejenis logam dengan asin untuk mendapatkan – yang dikehendakinya.* The student mixed a kind of metal with salt to produce the salt he wanted. **3** (*coq*) fertilizer resembling salt. *asam* – hydrochloric acid. *kurang* – insipid, boring, without any taste. *Pidatonya kurang –.* His speech was boring. *sudah banyak makan (asam) –, sudah makan – (dunia ini)* and *banyak menelan – hidup* seasoned, well-versed, having had a lot of experience. *Ia sudah 30 tahun makan – pelayaran.* He has 30 years of sailing experience. *belum banyak makan – young* and inexperienced. *– dikulumnya tak hancur* s.o. who can keep a secret. *– di laut, asam di gunung bertemu dalam belanga juga* if a man and a woman are destined for e.o., they will finally meet. *bagai – jatuh ke air* advice which is easy to accept. *membuang – ke laut* to carry coals to Newcastle, carry owls to Athens. *sebagai – dengan asam* a perfect match. *– abu* alkali. *– amonium* ammonium acetate. *– asam cuka* acetous salt. *– bata(an)/brikét* salt in briquettes. *– batu(an)* rock salt. *– bukit batu* rock salt. *– curai* salt which contains no iodine. *– dapur* kitchen salt, sodium chloride. *– darat* mineral salts. *– épsom* Epsom salt. *– galian* mineral salts. *– halus* table salt. *– hancur(an)* table salt. *– hidup* life experience. *– hirup* smelling salts. *– Inggris* Epsom salt. *– kapur* calcium. *– kasar* kosher salt. *– konsumsi* edible salt. *– krosok* coarse salt, salt prepared by salt makers in the simple, traditional manner. *– laut* sea salt. *– méja* table salt. *– mesiu* saltpeter. *– reruk* (*Jv*) salt scraped out of brine. *– sian* cyanide. *– yodium* iodized salt.

segaram *sudah seasam ~nya* it's perfect the way it is.

bergaram 1 containing salt. **2** salty. **3** to form salt crystals. *tidak ~* a) unsalted. b) insipid, boring. *hidupnya sudah ~* to have had a lot of experience.

menggaram 1 to become salty/like salt. **2** to make/produce salt. **3** (*M*) to lick at salt (of cattle).

menggarami 1 to salt, put salt on. **2** to make s.t. worse. **3** to season, spice, spice up (a conversation); → MEMBUMBUI.

menggaramkan to turn s.t. into salt.

garam-garaman various k.o. salt.

kegaraman salinity, saltiness.

pe(ng)garaman 1 salt pan. **2** salt making.

garan I (*J/Jv*) handle, *esp* of a tool; → PEGANGAN, TANGKAI. *– arit* sickle handle. *– pecut* whip handle. *– pisau* knife handle. *– wayang* puppet-handling stick.

garan II (*coq*) → GERANGAN.

garang I 1 wild, savage, ferocious, vicious, fierce. *binatang yang – a* vicious animal. **2** cruel, despotic, tyrannical. *raja yang – a* despotic king. **3** aggressive. **4** (*M*) very hard. *– bekerja* very hard working. *– makan* a hearty eater. **5** vivid (of colors).

menggarang to rage, storm, become violent, fly into a rage.

menggarangkan 1 to cause to become fierce. **2** to stir up, incite, instigate, stimulate.

kegarangan fierceness, savagery, aggression. *~nya mengesankan* their savagery left an impression.

garang II (*Jv*) **menggarang 1** to roast (food) over coals. **2** to dry s.t. near a fire. *~ tembakau* to dry tobacco.

garangan 1 dried near a fire. *tembakau ~* dried/smoked tobacco. **2** equipment for drying (clothing, etc.) or broiling (food).

penggarang grill.

penggarangan drying, roasting.

garangan I (*M*) → GERANGAN.

garangan II (*Jv*) various species of mongoose, *Herpestes spp.*

garansi (*D*) guarantee, warranty. *– bank* bank guarantee/indemnity.

bergaransi guaranteed. *pemulangan ~* guaranteed repatriation.

garantung (*Bat*) xylophone.

garap (*Jv*) **menggarap 1** to till, cultivate (the soil). *~ sawah* to till a rice field. **2** to make a fool of s.o., make fun of s.o., pull s.o.'s leg, tease. *Digarap begitu saja kok nangis.* I was only teasing, don't cry! **3** to undertake, execute, carry out, work on, tackle (a problem). **4** to rape (a woman), have sex with. *Selesai ~ Khodijah, Jono kembali mengancam.* After raping Khodjiah, Jono threatened her again. **5** to break/force open. *~ brankas* to force open a safe.

menggarapkan to till for s.o. else.

tergarap 1 tilled. *tanah ~ 3 héktar* 3 hectares of tilled soil. **2** tillable. *Yang – oléhku sendiri hanya sehéktar.* I could till only one hectare by myself. **3** executed, carried out. **4** raped.

garapan 1 tillage. **2** tilled. *~nya sendiri 5 ton padi gabah.* He himself tilled 5 tons of *padi gabah.* **3** carried out. **4** task, s.t. to do, assignment.

penggarap 1 tiller. **2** executor, s.o. who carries out s.t.

penggarapan 1 tillage, tilling, working (the soil). *Tabunganku untuk membiayai ~ sawah.* My savings went to cover the expenses of working the rice field. **2** carrying out, doing. *~ berita-selidik* doing investigative reporting.

garar → GHARAR.

garas I menggaras to gobble up, guzzle; → GARES I.

garas II → GARES II.

garasi (*D*) garage.

menggarasikan to garage, put/keep in a garage.

garau hoarse, rough (of the voice).

garba (*Jv ob*) **1** womb. **2** depository; reservoir, container. *– Ilmiah* Alma Mater.

garbarata jetway, airbridge (leading to an airplane).

garbis (*Jv*) melon; → BLÉWAH.

garda *– depan* avant garde.

gardan → KARDAN.

gardu (*Port*) **1** guardhouse, sentry post. **2** bus shelter. **3** (*mil*) depot, magazine. *– jaga* guardhouse. *– jaringan listrik* substation (for electricity distribution). *– listrik* powerhouse, generating plant. *– pembangkit* powerhouse. *– penjagaan* guard post. *– ronda* patrol. *– télepon* (*umum*) (public) telephone booth. *– transformator* transformer station.

garebeg and **garebek** (*Jv*) the three Muslim feasts of *– Maulud* on the 12th of *Rabiulawal, – Puasa/Poso* (*Jv*) on the first of *Syawal,* and *– Besar Haji* on the 20th of *Zulhijab.*

garédéng (*M*) tassels, fringe.

garem → GARAM.

garéng I (*Jv*) k.o. cicada, tree cricket.

Garéng II son of Semar and brother of Petruk (in the *wayang kulit/orang*).

gares I (*S*) **ngegares 1** (of animals) to feed. **2** (of human beings) to gobble, stuff o.s.

garesan 1 (of animals) fodder. **2** (of human beings) food, chow, grub.

gares II (*Jv*) shin.

garéséh gibberish; → KELÉSÉH-PÉSÉH.

gari (*Hind*) handcuffs, manacles.

menggari to handcuff.

tergari handcuffed. *A lari dengan tangan ~.* A. ran away handcuffed.

penggarian handcuffing.

garib (*A*) strange, peculiar, rare; rarity.

garindin → GERINDIN.

garing I 1 crisp(y) (of toast), hard, dry and easily broken (of food). **2** cooled down (of a relationship). **3** (*Jv*) dry, barren, arid. **4** (of a joke) old, stale.

menggaringkan to dry out, make s.t. crispy.

kegaringan crispiness.

garing II (*M*) *ikan –* k.o. river fish, *Labeobarbus tambra.*

garing III (*cla*) a deep shoulder basket.

garis → BARIS. **1** line, stripe, stroke, dash. **2** (*mil*) line. *– pertahanan* line of defense, defense line. **3** scratch. **4** directive, line of action. **5** front (line). **6** curve. **7** outline. **8** (*sl*) ounce of marijuana. – *air rendah* low-water mark. – *akhir* (in sports) finish (line). – *alas* base (line). – *arah* line of direction, trajectory. – *arsiran* hatching (in drawing). – *bagi sudut* bisector, bisecting line. – *balik* tropic. – *balik Sartan/selatan* tropic of Capricorn. – *balik utara* tropic of Cancer. – *balok* bar (of music). – *batas* frontier, border, boundary. – *bawah* underline, underscore. **menggaris-bawahi 1** to underline, underscore. **2** to emphasize, stress. **penggaris-bawahan 1** underlining, underscoring. **2** emphasizing, stressing. – *bayangan* hachure, hatch lines. – *belakang* a) home front. b) rear guard. – *berat* median line. – *besar* outline. –.– *Besar Haluan Negara* [GBHN] Broad Outlines of the Course of the Nation. *dalam – besarnya* in broad terms, broadly speaking. – *biku-biku* zigzag line. – *bujur/busur* meridian, degree of longitude. – *dalam* depth contour. – *dasar* base line. – *daya* line of force. – *démarkasi* demarcation/dividing line. – *depan* front line. – *édar* orbit. – *édar matahari* ecliptic. – *gelombang* wavy line. – *gencatan senjata* cease-fire line. – *grafik* curve (line on a graph). – *haluan* line of action, directive. – *hidup* a) fate, destiny. b) one's life/life story. – *hirarki yang bercabang dua* (*mil*) dual command. – *horisontal* horizontal line. – *hubung* hyphen. – *incang-incut* crisscross line. – *Jadi* tropic of Capricorn. – *kaki* base line. – *ke atas/bawah/samping* ascending/descending/collateral line (of kinship). – *keibuan* matrilineal line. – *kendali* constraint line. – *keras* (in politics) hard-line. – *ketinggian* contour line. – *keturunan* line of descent. – *keturunan lurus* direct line of descent. – *khatulistiwa* equator. – *kodrat* one's fate. – *komando* chain of command. – *lengkung* curvature. – *lintang* (degree of) latitude. – *lintasan* ballistic curve. – *lurus* straight/direct line, lineal. – *lurus ke atas* ascending direct line. – *lurus ke bawah* descending direct line. – *lurus maupun – ke samping* both in the lineal and in the collateral line. – *mata* eye liner. – *mendatar* horizontal line. – *menengah* diameter. – *menyimpang* collateral line (of descent). – *mérah tebal* stern warning. – *miring* slant line. – *nadi* pulse curve. – *pandangan* sight line. – *pantai* coastline. – *partai* party line. – *pemisah/pisah* a) partition/dividing line. b) (between regions) boundary/demarcation line, line of demarcation. – *penglihatan* line of sight. – *penyekat* slant line. – *perbatasan* border line. – *peredaran* orbit. – *perhatian* underlining. – *petunjuk* guide line. – *pilih* slant line. – *potongan* secant. – *putus-putus* dashed line. – *sama tinggi* contour line. – *samping* a) line at side of paper marking off margin. b) collateral line (of relationship). – *segi tiga* triangle. – *sejajar* parallel (line). – *sekat* slant line. – *sempadan* (*bangunan*) [GSB] building line, alignment. – *silang* intersecting line. – *silang pembidik* reticule. – *singgung* tangent. – *sipatan* building line, alignment. – *start* starting line. – *sudut-menyudut* diagonal (line). – *tanda hubung* hyphen. – *tangan* lines on the palm; → RAJAH I **2**. – *tangan tidak bisa ditentang* one's fate cannot be avoided. – *tanggal* date line. – *tarikh* date line. – *tegak* (*lurus*) perpendicular. – *tengah* diameter. **bergaris tengah** with a diameter of. – *tepi* line at side of paper marking off margin. – *tinggi* a) perpendicular (in a triangle). b) contour line (on a map). – *tinggian* high-water mark. – *titik* dotted line. – *tolak* starting line. – *unting-unting* plumb line. – *vértikal* perpendicular. – *wajah* profile. – *waktu internasional* international date line.

segaris on the same line, collinear, in line (with). ~ *dengan* in line with. ~ *dengan kemerosotan nilai sosial masyarakat sekelilingnya* in line with the decline of social values in the surrounding society.

bergaris lined (of paper); with lines.

bergaris-garis with many lines.

menggaris 1 to draw a line. **2** to scratch. **3** to outline, determine (a line of action). **4** to be in the shape of a line.

menggarisi 1 to draw lines on. *Ia sedang ~ kertas itu* he was drawing lines on that paper. **2** to underline, underscore.

menggariskan 1 to outline, determine/establish (a course of action). *peraturan yang telah digariskan* regulations which have been outlined. **2** to state, say (of a law). **3** to draw a line for s.o. else.

tergaris scratched.

garisan lines (on face), feature.

penggaris 1 ruler; → MISTAR. **2** s.o. who draws lines.

penggarisan 1 drawing lines, scratching. **2** outline. *Perlu ~ yang tegas sebelum kontrak manajemén Bapindo dilakukan.* A firm outline is needed before Bapindo's management contract is drawn up.

pergarisan lineation.

garisah (*A*) → GARIZAH, NALURI.

garit I 1 scratch. **2** (*geol*) striation.

bergarit to be scratched. *tak ~* unscratched, unscathed.

menggarit to scratch.

garit II (*M*) movement.

menggarit to move. *tidak ~* to stay put.

menggaritkan to move s.t.

garizah (*A*) instinct; → NALURI.

garizahi (*A*) instinctive.

garmén (*E*) garment.

garnis (*E*) garnish; → PENGHIAS *makanan*.

garnisun and **garnizun** (*D*) garrison.

garnitur (*D*) fittings, mounting.

garocoh-pocoh (*M*) to proceed very thoughtlessly. *Para sopir diminta jangan sembarangan setop dan – tak keruan.* The drivers were asked not to stop just anywhere and go ahead thoughtlessly.

garong (*J/Jv*) **1** robber, holdup man. **2** burglar, housebreaker. *kucing –* a) a wild cat species (larger than the domesticated cat). b) a face full of lines and scratches.

menggarong [and **nggarong/ngegarong** (*coq*)] **1** to rob, hold up. **2** to plunder, pillage, loot.

kegarongan to be robbed. *Jadi Saudara yang ~?* So, you were the one who was robbed?

penggarong 1 robber, holdup man. **2** burglar, housebreaker. **3** plunderer, pillager, looter.

penggarongan 1 robbery, holdup, banditry. **2** plundering, pillage, looting.

garot (*J/Jv*) **nggarot 1** to gnaw at/on. **2** to eat s.t. without peeling it or cutting it into small pieces.

garpu (*Port*) **1** fork. **2** tine, prong. *serangan – empat* a four-pronged attack. – *jerami* pitchfork. – *penala* tuning fork. – *sepéda* bicycle fork. – *tala* tuning fork. – *tanah* pitchfork. – *tarik* spading fork.

bergarpu to use a fork.

menggarpu to pick up with a fork.

garteng [*garis tengah*] diameter.

garu I 1 scratch, harrow, rake. – *bajang* stretch lines left after pregnancy; → BAJANG I. – *piring* disc harrow.

bergaru to scratch (the skin) continuously. *Pria itu ~ karena diserang agas.* That man kept on scratching because he was attacked by gnats.

menggaru 1 (in agriculture) to harrow, rake. **2** to scratch (with one's nails; less hard than *garuk*).

tergaru-garu to keep on scratching.

penggaru rake, harrow.

penggaruan raking, harrowing.

garu II aloeswood, fragrant eaglewood, *Aquilaria malaccensis*; → GAHARU. *Kayu jati dan – sudah hampir punah.* Teak and aloeswood are almost extinct.

garuda (*Skr*) **1** griffin. **2** the mythical bird that transported the god Vishnu through space. **3** the eagle in the state coat of arms of the Republic of Indonesia. **4** the state-run Garuda Indonesian Airways. *Maka kami semua bersepakat membatalkan perjalanan naik –.* Therefore, all of us agreed to cancel the trip on Garuda airlines. **5** (*joc*) Good And Reliable Under Dutch Administration. – *Dempo* the military resort command (*Korém* 044) in Palembang. – *Hitam* the military resort command (*Korém* 043) in Lampung. – *Mas* the military resort command (*Korém* 041) in Bengkulu. – *Putih* the military resort command (*Korém* 042) in Jambi. – *Yaksa* honorary saber (of *ABRI*).

menggarudai to put wings on s.t.

garuk I scratch. *kena – razia gelandangan* apprehended/arrested in a raid on homeless drifters. *main –* to apprehend/arrest needlessly/without provocation. *tukang – (J)* s.o. who eats and runs.

bergaruk(-garuk) [and **garuk-garuk** (*coq*)] **1** to keep on scratching (one's head/arm/skin, etc. because it itches). *Tak henti-hentinya ia ~ kepalanya.* He couldn't stop scratching his head. **2** to root up. *Anjingnya ~ di tanah.* His dog was rooting up the earth.

menggaruk 1 to scratch (one's head, etc.). **2** to curry (horses). **3** to claw, scratch (of a tiger/cat, etc.). **4** to harrow, rake. **5** (*coq*) to apprehend, round up, arrest (vagabonds, etc.). **6** to steal, embezzle, misappropriate. *Tanah jajahan diperlukan untuk ~ kekayaannya.* A colony is necessary in order to steal its riches. *hendak ~ tidak berkuku* wanting to do s.t. but lacking the means. *Tidak ada orang ~ ke luar badan.* One usually takes sides with his relatives/members of the group, etc. in case of a conflict. *kini gatal bésok digaruk* to be too late in giving help.

menggaruk-garuk to keep on scratching/raking. *~ kepala* to keep on scratching one's head. *Kasim berpikir lalu ~ kepala.* Kasim was thinking and then scratched his head.

menggaruki (*pl obj*) to scratch.

menggarukkan 1 to scratch/rake with s.t. **2** to scratch/rake for s.o. else.

tergaruk [and **kegaruk** (*coq*)] **1** got scratched, inadvertently scratched. **2** rounded up, apprehended.

kegaruk (*coq*) to get robbed. *Bank asing ~ ratusan juta.* Foreign banks have been robbed of hundreds of millions.

garukan 1 s.t. that has been scratched, way of scratching s.t. **2** arrest, apprehension, capture.

penggaruk scraper, curry-comb, harrow.

penggarukan scratching, scraping away at; arresting; arrests, arresting. *mengadakan ~* to make arrests.

garuk II hoarse, husky (of voice).

garung I (*M*) **1** loud cry/weeping, groan, moan. **2** roar (of a storm/ waves, etc.); → GERUNG.

menggarung 1 to cry, weep, groan in pain, growl. **2** to roar.

penggarung a whiner.

garung II → GARONG.

garut I menggarut to scratch away by rubbing, abrade, chafe.

garut II k.o. arrowroot, *Marantha arundinacea*.

garwa (*Jv*) and **garwo** (*Jv*) wife. *- ampéyan/ampil* any wife of a sultan other than the legal spouse; → SELIR I. *- padmi* the first wife in a polygamous royal marriage.

bergarwa *~ pada* to have ... as one's spouse.

gas I (*D*) **1** gas. **2** aerosol gas. **3** the gas (as a symbol of acceleration in a car). *kedok –* gas mask. *kokas –* gas coke. *kompor –* gas cooker. *lampu –* gas lamp. *minyak –* kerosene. *pabrik –* gas works. *pembakar –* gas burner. *pipa –* gas pipe. *saluran –* a) (main conduit) gas main (inside the house); gas pipes. *tér-mométer –* gas thermometer. *topéng –* gas mask. *menancap/ menginjak –* a) to accelerate, step on the gas. b) to expedite (one's work). *menekan –* to accelerate, step on the gas. *– air* water gas. *– air mata* tear gas. *– alam* natural gas. *– alam cair/ yang dicairkan* liquefied natural gas, LNG. *– alam yang dimampatkan* compressed natural gas. *– asam arang* carbon dioxide. *– asap* flue gas. *– bakar* combustion gas. *– basah* (*petro*) wet gas. *– bekas* exhaust gas. *– bio* biogas. *– buang(an)* exhaust gases/ fumes. *– bumi* natural gas. *– bumi cair* liquefied natural gas, LNG. *– cair* liquid gas. *– cerobong* flue gas. *– ikutan/iring* casing head gas, associated gas. *– karbit* acetylene. *– kecut* sour gas. *– kilang* refinery gas. *– korék* cigarette lighter fuel. *– lamban* inert gas. *– langka* rare gas. *– lemas* choking gas. *– lembam* inert gas. *– letus* explosive gas. *– métan* methane. *– minyak cair* liquefied petroleum gas, LPG. *– mudah terbakar* highly combustible. *– mulia* noble/inert gas. *– oksigén* oxygen gas. *– peledakan* after-gas. *– pendingin* Freon. *– penghujung* (*petro*) end gas. *– racun* poison gas. *– rawa* marsh gas, methane. *– saraf* nerve gas. *– sempurna* ideal gas. *– sisa* residual gas. *– sisa pembakaran* exhaust gases/fumes. *– sumur* well/free gas. *– tambang* fire-damp. *– tanur* flue gas. *– tertawa* laughing gas. *– yang berdiri sendiri* non-associated gas. *– yang bergabung dengan minyak* associated gas.

bergas gaseous, containing/full of gas.

menggas and **mengegas 1** to volatilize, evaporate. **2** [= meng(e)gaskan] to accelerate, speed up (a car), step on the gas. *mobilnya digas* he stepped on the gas.

menggasi and **mengegasi** to step on the gas, press down on the accelerator.

penggasan and **pengegasan** fumigation.

gas II (in acronyms) → TUGAS I.

gasa → GAZ.

gasak hit, strike.

bergasak (*Mal*) to go for e.o.

menggasak 1 to strike, hit, beat, attack. *Ia ~ lawannya dengan tinju.* He hit his opponent with his fist. *Ia ~ kaki temannya hingga jatuh terjungkal.* He struck his friend's leg so that he tumbled forward. **2** to seize, snatch (by force); to steal, misappropriate, embezzle. *~ uang kantor* to misappropriate office funds. **3** to swallow, gulp (down), eat up, devour. *Meréka ~ saté itu hingga tinggal satu dua tusuk saja.* They gulped down the satay until only one or two skewers were left. **4** to defeat, drub (in a game). **5** to smash, break down. *~ pintu* to break down a door. *~ lari* to take off like a shot. *– saja!* Do it now! Go for it (and ask questions later)!

menggasaki (*pl obj*) to hit, etc.

menggasakkan 1 to hit/smash with. *~ kail ke dalam belahan kayu* to smash the hook into a piece of wood. *~ tinjunya kepada lawan* to smash one's fist into one's opponent. **2** to thrust, stick. *Pembunuh itu ~ belati itu ke dalam perut suaminya.* The murderer stuck the *belati* in her husband's stomach.

gasakan 1 blow, hitting. **2** stolen (*mod*). *barang ~* stolen goods.

gasak-gasakan 1 to hit e.o. **2** to compete with e.o.; to defeat e.o. (in competition).

penggasakan 1 hitting, beating. **2** seizing, stealing. **3** devouring. **4** smashing, breaking down.

gasak-gusuk (*J*) → KASAK-KUSUK.

gasal uneven, odd; → GANJIL. *bilangan yang –* an uneven number.

gasang I lascivious, lewd, hot (of person), sensual, voluptuous, horny, sexually aroused.

kegasangan horniness, sensuality, voluptuousness, lust.

gasang II (*M*) in a hurry; → GESA.

menggasang to urge s.o. to do s.t. right away.

gasifikasi (*E*) gasification.

menggasifikasikan to gasify. *Sangat poténsial pula sél yang digerakkan oléh batu bara yang digasifikasikan.* Cells activated by gasified coal have a great potential.

gasing (spinning) top.

bergasing to spin a top.

gasingan a spin of a top.

gasir I (*J/Jv*) mole cricket; → GANGSIR I.

gasir II (*J*) a hole through which a thief tunnels under and into a house.

menggasir [and **nggansir/ngegasir** (*coq*)] to burglarize/break into a house by digging a hole under the foundation. *Para tersangka berhasil masuk rumah dengan jalan menggasir.* The suspects were able to enter the house by digging a hole under the foundation.

kegasiran to have one's house broken into. *S ~.* S's house was broken into by s.o. digging a hole under the foundation.

gaskét (*E*) gasket.

gasohol [gasolin+alkohol] (*E*) gasohol.

gasolin (*D/E*) gasoline.

gasométer (*D/E*) gasometer.

gasos (*BG*) [gagap sosial] socially awkward.

gastrik (*E*) gastric.

gastrin (*D/E*) gastrin, i.e., a hormone in the stomach that stimulates production of gastric juices.

gastritis (*D/E*) gastritis.

gastroéntéritis (*D/E*) gastroenteritis.

gastronom (*D/E*) gastronome.

gastronomi (*D/E*) gastronomy.

gastrula (*E*) gastrula.

gastrulasi (*E*) gastrulation.

Gasyiyah (*A*) *al–* "The Overpowering"; name of the 88th chapter of the Koran.

gatak (*J*) **nggatak** to punch.

gatal 1 itch. *Kepala saya –.* My head itches. *– kuping/telinga mendengarnya* one does not want to hear it. **2** itchy, irritating, cause an irritating sensation. *Ulat ini – benar*. This caterpillar really causes itching when touched. *daun –* stinging nettle, *Laportea decumana Wedd*. *sakit –* scabies. *semut –* black stinging ant, *Tetraponera rufonigra*, which causes itching. **3** horny, hot, lascivious, in heat. *Lelaki – itu sangat ditakuti oléh gadis-gadis kampungnya*. The village girls were very much afraid of that horny guy. **4** itching/eager to do s.t. *Kakinya sudah gatal-gatal hendak melantai*. His feet were already itching to go onto the dance floor. *kini – bésok digaruk* help that came too late. *lain – lain digaruk* there's neither rhyme nor reason to his answer. *kuping siapa –, dialah menggaruk* you reap what you sow. *– gusi* hungry, thirsty. *– kaki* restless, always on the move. *– mata* man who likes to look at or bother women. *– menémbak* trigger-happy. *– mulut* chatty, talkative. *– réla* loose, lascivious. *– tangan* to have itchy fingers (e.g., draw graffiti/interfere/look for a fight). *– telinga* unhappy about hearing s.t.

gatal-gatal itching/eager (to do s.t.). *~ tangan* looking for a fight.

menggatalkan to itch, irritate. *Getahnya kalau kena akan ~ badan*. When the latex is touched, it will irritate the body.

gatalan always horny/hot.

kegatalan 1 itching, itchiness, irritation. **2** to be horny. *Ia ~.* (said of a woman) She has hot pants. **3** lasciviousness, lechery, sexual desire, horniness. *~ tangan →* GATAL *tangan*.

gatalbirah *burung –* black hornbill, *Anthracoceros malayanus*; → KÉKÉK II.

gaték I and **gatékan** (*Jv*) bright, quick to catch on.

gaték II [gagap téknologi] computer illiterate/ignorant.

gatel → GATAL.

gatél (*Jv*) head of the penis, glans penis.

gateng I *ikan –* a fish species found in the Gua Konthe in the Gunungkidul area.

gateng II [garis tengah] diameter.

gatép and **gatét** *pohon – pahit* Tahitian/Polynesian chestnut. *Inocarpus edulis*.

gathuk → GATUK.

gatot (*Jv*) a dessert made of cassava, brown sugar, and coconut.

Gatotkaca the N-250 aircraft manufactured by Nurtanio Aircraft Industry; → GATUTKACA.

gatra I (*Skr gram*) **1** clause. **2** syntactic unit. **3** main element in sentence formation: subject, predicate, object. **4** aspect.

Gatra II (*Skr*) *– Loka →* BINA *Graha*.

gatrik (*S*) a boys' game in which a sharp piece of wood is struck with a small stick.

gatuk (*Jv*) **1** to match. *nggak –* (*coq*) I disagree. *Nggak – dengan pengurus yang dulu*. I don't agree with the former board. **2** *othak-athik –* in complete agreement/harmony, perfectly matched. *Ia meneruskan membaca sambutannya meskipun agak tidak othak-athik – dengan yang dibacakan terdahulu*. He kept on reading his welcoming speech even though it didn't quite match what he had been reading before.

menggatuk-gatukkan to match up, connect. *~ komponén itu* to match the components up with e.o.

Gatutkaca and **Gatutkoco** (*Jv*) **1** the name of one of Bima's sons in the *Mahab(h)arata*, called upon when the fighting gets rough in the *wayang* play; a warlike figure from the *wayang purwa*. **2** reference to a pilot (because Gatutkaca was able to fly). **3** the code name given by the *Gestapu/PKI* to the Air Force Base guards. **4** the code name for Omar Dani, Chief of the Air Force in 1965. **5** the *C-30S* reserve troops.

gauk I (*M*) **1** long-billed jungle crow; *Corvus macrorynchus*; → GAOK. **2** (*onom*) the cawing of a crow.

menggauk to caw.

gauk II (*coq*) siren.

gaul associate, mix. (*ber)campur –* to be good friends. *Ia bercampur – dengan anak-anak lainnya*. He is good friends with the other children.

bergaul 1 to socialize, make friends, get along with people. *Anda perlu ~.* You need to socialize. **2** to associate, run/hang around with, get involved (with). *Saya tidak ~ dengan penjahat itu*. I don't associate with that criminal. *Dia tidak akan ~ dengannya*. He's not going to run around with her. *mau ~* to get out

and meet people. *pandai ~* to be a good mixer, smooth in social relations. *~ ria* to have fun together.

menggaul to mix, blend (ingredients/food). *Saya ~ nasi saya dengan kuah dan sambal*. I mixed my rice with sauce and *sambal*.

menggauli 1 to associate with, mix with. **2** to have sexual intercourse with. *sang wanita yang sudah meréka gauli* the woman with whom they had sexual intercourse.

mempergauli to associate with, mix with. *Ia hanya mau ~ orang yang sederajat dengan dia*. He only wants to associate with persons of the same rank.

menggaulkan and **mempergaulkan 1** to mix s.t. (into), blend s.t. (into). *Ia menggaulkan beberapa butir telur pada adonan itu*. He mixed some eggs into the dough. **2** to let s.o. associate/be friendly (with). *Ayahnya mempergaulkan anaknya dengan anak-anak di kampungnya*. The father lets his child associate with the children in his village.

pergaulan 1 (close) association, social intercourse, companionship. *~ kita dengan meréka hanya merugikan kita*. Our association with them only hurts us. *luas ~nya* he has a large circle of friends. **2** sexual intercourse. *~ bébas* free sex, sexual intercourse outside of marriage, promiscuity. **3** society, community. *~ hidup/ramai* social intercourse.

gaum → GAUNG I.

gaun (*E*) gown. *– malam* evening outfit. *– mini* minidress. *– modél karung* (*coq*) sack dress. *– panjang* long dress *– pengantin* wedding dress, bridal gown. *– rumah* housecoat. *– sepan* tight gown/dress. *– tidur* nightgown.

bergaun to have/wear a gown, be dressed in a gown. *Dua pramugari ~ batik mendapat sambutan hangat*. Two airline stewardesses wearing batik gowns got a warm reception.

gaung I echo, reverberation.

bergaung and **menggaung** re-echo, reverberate.

menggaungkan to make reverberate.

gaungan echo.

gaung II (*M*) (shore) hole.

menggaung to dig a hole.

gaut (*M*) *– gapai* to scratch/scrape hard; wonder what to do next.

menggaut to pull s.t. toward one.

gauw and **gaw** (*C?*) one-gram packet of illegal drugs.

gawah forest, jungle.

gawai I (*Port naut*) topsail.

gawai II (*Jv*) **1** work, activity, services. **2** job, task; → GAWÉAN. **3** (*Bal*) lewdness, prostitution; a lewd act(ion). *– raja* (*Bal*) forced (statute) labor. **4** function. *struktur –* functional structure. **5** device.

pegawai and **pagawai** (*Jv*) employee, official; → KARYAWAN.

gawal (*M*) (social) error, gaffe, mistake. *sepandai-pandai tupai melompat, sekali – juga* it is a good horse that never stumbles.

gawan (*Jv*) what one brings (to a marriage).

gawang I 1 gate(way). **2** (in soccer) goal posts. *penjaga –* goalie, goalkeeper. **3** hurdle (in a race). *lari –* hurdle-race. *– pintu* door frame.

gawang-gawangan (in croquet) wicket(s).

penggawang goalie, goalkeeper.

gawang II **tergawang-gawang** waving the arms in the air (to drive away animals).

gawar s.t. showing quarantine or barring access, warning.

gawar-gawar ropes attached with coconut fronds and hung out to indicate that passage is blocked (due to an infectious disease, etc.).

gawat 1 critical, crucial, serious. *– darurat* emergency. **2** alarming, dangerous, terrifying, risky, explosive (situation), sensitive (topic). *masalah –* an alarming problem. **3** (*sl*) too much!

menggawat to be critical/dangerous/risky.

menggawatkan 1 to make critical, endanger. **2** critical, dangerous.

kegawatan 1 seriousness. **2** danger, risk.

gawé (*Jv*) **1** work. *nyari ~* (*coq*) to look for a job. **2** feast.

gawéan work, job.

gawi (*Ban*) → GAWÉ. *– manuntung* to do thoroughly. *– Manuntung Waja Sampai Kaputing* (Motto of *Kodam* VI Tanjungpura) = Never Surrender and work hard like steel until the end. *–*

sabumi mutual aid; → GOTONG *royong*. - *sabumi bastari* mutual aid work group.

gawir (*S*) a steep mountain slope with an abyss at the lower end, escarpment.

Gawitra the Petroleum Museum (in Jakarta).

gawuk (*Jv vulg*) cunt, pussy.

gay (*E*) /gé, gai/ gay, homosexual.

gaya I (*Skr*) → DAYA I. force, power, potential; powerful. *kalah –* to be less energetic. *– air* water power. *– alami* natural force. *– angkat* lift. *– apung* buoyancy. *– atom* atomic power. *– badan* physical force. *– basa* basicity. *– berat/bobot* gravitation, gravity, gravimetric. *– dorong* propulsion power, thrust. *– gabung* affinity. *– gerak* motoric force. *– gésér* shear force. *– hidrolik* hydraulic power. *– kuda* horsepower. *– lembam* inertia. *– lentur* flexibility. *– pancar gas* jet propulsion. *– pegas* elasticity, resilience, spring. **bergaya pegas** resilient. *– penahan* drag. *– pendorong* driving force. *– perekat* adhesive strength. *– pikul* carrying capacity. *– puntir* torque. *– pusaran* centripetal force. *– pusingan* centrifugal force. *– putaran* torque. *– rentang* tensile force. *– saran* suggestive power. **bergaya saran** suggestive. *– séks* sex appeal. *– selingkung* house style. *– semu* inertia. *– séntrifugal/séntripetal* centrifugal/centripetal force. *– tahan(an)* resistance. *– tarik* attractive force/strength. *– tegang* tension. *– tekan* compressing force. *– torsi* torsion. *– traksi* traction. *– uap* steam power. *– udara* aerodynamics.

gaya-gayanya seemingly.

bergaya to be strong/powerful/forceful/potent. *tidak ~ lagi* powerless, impotent.

menggaya to have an effect on, encourage.

penggaya a powerful person.

gaya II (*Skr*) **1** form, style, model; stroke (in swimming). *Ia tertarik dengan – rambut saya.* She was attracted by my hairstyle. **2** style, looks, appearance, manner; way(s). *– Jawa* the Javanese way. **3** smart, stylish, fashionable, elegant. *dengan –nya* proudly. *penuh –* swanky, stylish. *– aku* first-person (narrative style). *– alami* natural look. *– bahasa* linguistic style. *ilmu – bahasa* stylistics. *– baru* a) new-style, new-fangled. *ujian – baru* new-style examinations. **menggayabarukan** to bring a new style to s.t. b) name of a train running between Jakarta and Surabaya. *– bébas* freestyle (in swimming). *– berganti* relay (in swimming). *– berjalan* gait. *– Cina* (in fashion designing) Chinoiserie; → ENCIM. *– dada* breast stroke. *– hidup* life style. *– hidup méwah* luxurious lifestyle. *– hidup sederhana* simple/plain lifestyle. *– katak* breast stroke. *– kepemimpinan* leadership style. *– kupu-kupu* butterfly stroke. *– laku* behavior. *– lama* old style. *– nungging* doggy style (sex from the rear). *– punggung* back stroke. *– tulis* writing style. *– Yunani Baru* Neo-Greek style.

gaya-gayanya in an affected way.

bergaya 1 elegant, in good taste, stylish. *Ia ~ dalam film itu* He was elegant in that film. **2** in the style/manner of. *sebuah gedung ~ Spanyol* a building in the Spanish style. **3** to show off.

bergaya-gaya 1 with airs/affectation. **2** to put on airs, pose; to be affected. *jalan ~* to walk in an affected manner.

menggaya to put on airs.

menggaya-gayai to inspire, encourage.

menggayakan to give a style to.

penggayaan stylization.

gayal I 1 elastic, supple, resilient. **2** tough (of meat); → KENYAL.

gayal II → KHAYAL.

gayam I *pohon –* Tahitian/Polynesian chestnut, *Inocarpus edulis*.

gayam II k.o. bivalve mollusk, *Asaphis deflorata*.

gayang staggering, unsteady, swaying (of the body from dizziness/intoxication), dizzy, giddy.

gayang-gayang a hanging shelf (in kitchen).

gayang(-gayang) k.o. plant, the leaves of which are used against headaches, *Inocarpus edulis*.

gayat dizzy, suffering from vertigo.

gayau k.o. game of quoits.

gayem (*Jv*) **menggayem** to ruminate, chew the cud.

gayeng (*Jv*) pleasant, warm, cordial. *suasana – a* cordial atmosphere. *Sidang menjadi – ketika pembicara ...* The session became pleasant when the speaker ...

kegayengan pleasantness, warmth, cordiality.

Gayo an ethnic group in southern Aceh, Sumatra.

gayot hills, mountains, valleys on the sea floor.

gayuh I (*Jv*) **bergayuh** to dangle, hang low.

bergayuhan (*pl subj*) to dangle.

menggayuh to dangle.

gayuhan place where s.t. is hanging.

gayuh II ideal, what one is reaching for.

menggayuh to achieve, grasp, get what one is reaching for.

gayuk menggayuk to reach out for, grasp, seize, clutch.

gayun → AYUN.

gayung I water dipper, ladle (with a handle, made of a coconut shell/sheet metal/aluminum, etc.). *– bersambut, kata berjawab* a) to parry/ward off s.o.'s attack, defend o.s. b) to make a response (to s.o.'s remarks, etc.), accept a challenge. *Kerjasama dengan Trading House – bersambut.* Cooperation with Trading House has been accepted. *sebab takkan – disambut, kalau tidak ...* because one wouldn't jump at the chance, if he didn't ... *"Kamu mau jadi istriku?" – bersambut.* "Do you want to marry me?" She accepted. **menggayungsambuti** to accept. *Keterangan Dubés Amérika W di Riau yang digayungsambuti oléh Sinar Harapan dalam tajuknya tanggal 29 Méi 1986 sangat menarik perhatian kita.* The explanation of American Ambassador W in Riau, which was accepted by Sinar Harapan in its editorial of May 29, 1986, was very interesting to us.

bergayung to use a *gayung* (for bathing, etc.).

menggayung to ladle/scoop (water with a *gayung*).

gayung II 1 k.o. walking stick used as a weapon. **2a**) blow with the fist. b) saber stroke. c) strike, slash, hit (with a weapon). d) (*M*) motion, action (in stabbing with a spear, cutting with a cleaver, etc.); attack, charge (with a sword, etc.). **3** magic spell, incantation used to kill/hurt s.o. from afar. *ilmu – k.o.* spell to kill, hurt, etc. s.o. from afar. *– main –* (*ob*) art of fighting. *– tua, – memutus* words of the elderly are *usu* right.

bergayung to practice *gayung* self-defense tactics.

menggayung 1 to strike/slash/hit s.o. (with a weapon). **2** to use the feet (in *pencak*). **3** to cast a spell on s.o. from afar (in order to kill/hurt, etc.).

gayut 1 hanging, suspended. **2** relevant. *tidak – irrelevant.*

bergayut to hang (like fruit or a monkey from a branch/a person from a rope, etc.), be suspended. *askar – (Mal)* airborne troops.

bergayutan (*pl subj*) to hang down and swing.

menggayut to be suspended/hanging.

menggayuti to hang over (one's head), hover over, be present in. *Beban berat di pundak yang selama ini ~ dirinya hilang seketika.* The heavy burden on his shoulders, which up till now has been hanging over him, has all of a sudden disappeared. *Wajah sedih ibu terus ~ benakku.* Mother's sad face is always in my mind. *digayuti rasa khawatir* anxiety hovers over him. *walaupun masih digayuti beberapa persyaratan* even though it is still subject to a number of conditions.

menggayutkan to hang (up) s.t. *Dia ~ topinya yang baru pada paku di dinding.* He hung his new hat on a nail in the wall.

tergayut hanging, suspended, caught on s.t. high up.

gayutan 1 hook, hanger. **2** relationship, connection, relevance.

kegayutan relevance. *Ia bertanya, apakah ~ pembicaraan seperti ini.* He asked what the relevance is of discussions like this. *Di sini ada ~ untuk melakukan kerjasama antara Dépparpostél dengan berbagai Départemén lainnya.* There is s.t. relevant here to bringing about cooperation between the Ministry of Tourism, Post and Telecommunications, and several other ministries.

gaz (*Pers ob*) a linear measure of various lengths (about 33 inches or 83.83 centimeters), ell.

gazal (*Pers*) Persian poem, consisting of eight lines each ending in the same word, telling of one's passion.

gazébo (*E*) gazebo.

GBHN [Garis-garis Besar Haluan Negara] Broad Outlines of the Nation.

gbr (*abbr*) → GAMBAR.

gbt and **gbt-an** → GÉBÉTAN.

Gd (*abbr*) → GEDUNG.

Gdé (*Bal*) name element placed before personal names to indicate the firstborn child, such as *I Gdé Putu Wirata*.

gé name of the letter *g*.

gebah I (*S*) to intimidate, browbeat.

gebah II (*J*) **menggebah** to chase/drive away (animals/beggars, etc.); → MENGUSIR.

gebahan *pedagang* ~ street vendor who sells on sidewalks without permission and can be chased away at any time by local authorities.

gebang *pohon* – a tall palm with huge leaves, gebang palm, *Corypha spp.*

gebar I *kain* – cover (such as a blanket/sheet, etc.).
  bergebar blanketed.

gebar II **mengebar** to vibrate.
  gebaran vibration.

gébéng (*J*) *dayung* – an oar with a blade nailed to the shaft. *perahu* – a boat with a tiny cabin or palm-leaf awning.

geber I (*Jv*) screen (in *wayang* play); → LAYAR I 4.

geber II (*S*) **menggeber** 1 to accelerate, quicken. *Pada saat mengendarai, jangan langsung* ~ *gas*. While driving, don't step on the gas right away. **2** to play (a song). **3** (*BG*) to have sex with.

geber III → GEBAR II.

gébér (*J*) wattle (on birds/cattle).

gébés (*Jv*) **menggébés-gébés** to shake s.t. held in the beak.
  menggébés-gébés to shake the head as a sign of dislike, refusal, unwillingness, etc.

gébét (*BG*) **menggébét** to date s.o.
  gébétan a date, s.o. whom one approaches to be a boy-/girlfriend.
  pergébétan dating.

geblak (*Jv*) **menggeblak** to fall backward/on one's back.

geblas (*Jv*) **menggeblas** to leave in a rush, rush away.

geblek I (*J/Jv*) stupid, dumb; → GOBLOK.

geblek II (*Jv*) a snack made from grated cassava.

geblok (*J/Jv*) **1** roll/bolt (of cloth). **2** wad (of banknotes).
  segeblok a roll (of cloth), a wad (of banknotes).
  geblokan *cita* ~ cotton (in a roll).

gébok (*J*) **menggébok** to strike (a blow) at, hit with a ball or stone.

gebos I (*J*) **menggebos** to snap at, scold, reprimand; → MEMBENTAK.
  gebosan reprimand.

gebos II (*Jv*) to release a puff of smoke.

gebot **menggebot** **1** to beat the stems of fibrous plants to separate the fibers from the other parts. **2** to knock paddy kernels from the ear.

gebrak (*J/Jv*) blow. *sekali* – all at once, in one blow. *Memberantas perjudian dan prostitusi tak bisa sekali* –. Eradicating gambling and prostitution cannot be achieved all at once.
  gebrak(an) to pound away at e.o.
  menggebrak **1** to hit hard (with the hand or weapon, etc.) at, strike a blow or blows with the fist or a hard object. *Partai itu* ~ *putaran pertama kampanyenya*. The party hit hard at the first round of its campaign. **2** to attack, use force against, strike out at. **3** to instigate.
  gebrakan **1** blow (with the fist). *Hanya dengan beberapa* ~ *saja dua dari orang garong yang mendatangi rumah Nyi Encur diringkus oléh istri korban yang pandai main pencak silat*. With only a few blows two of the bandits who entered Nyi Encur's house were grabbed by the victim's wife, who is a *pencak silat* expert. **2** attack, charge, assault, raid. **3** beat (of music). **4** a hit, winner.

gebrés (*Jv*) **1** to snort (of horses). **2** to sneeze.

gebruk (*Jv*) thud.

gebrus (*J*) **nggebrus** **1** to snap at. **2** to flare up (of a fire).

gebu I **menggebu(-gebu)** **1** to flare up (of fire/revolt), rage (of fury, etc.). *Dengan semangat yang menggebu-gebu CCR menuliskan panjang lébar hipotésanya itu dalam lima penerbitan bersambung*. Most enthusiastically CCR wrote elaborately about his hypothesis in five successive publications. **2** to be high/strong (of excitement/passions, etc.). *Dulu waktu masih di désa keinginan untuk melihat megahnya kota Jakarta begitu menggebu*. When he was still in the village, he had a strong desire to see the luxury of Jakarta. **3** to break out (of strike/wars/riots/rebellion, etc.). *Dalam tahun 1945 menggebulah pemberontakan nasional*. In 1945 the national revolt broke out.

gebu II (*J*) soft, crunchy, crisp (delicious to eat, because it is not hard); neither too soft nor too hard (such as sweet potatoes, etc.).

gebu III (*Mal*) fine (of textiles), floury (of peeled potatoes), loose (of soil), soft (as a woman's hand).

gebuk (*J/Jv*) blow.
  menggebuk to hit, whack, thrash, beat.
  menggebuki [and **nggebukin/ngegebukin** (*J coq*)] (*pl obj*) to beat up, hit again and again. *Meréka terus* ~ *anjing itu sampai mati*. They beat the dog until it was dead.
  menggebukkan to beat with s.t.
  gebukan blow, stroke, hit.
  gebuk-gebukan beating, thrashing.
  penggebuk thrasher, flogger, hitter. *karena posisi* ~ *berdiri di belakang korban* since the hitter was standing behind the victim. ~ *dram* drummer.
  penggebukan hitting, thrashing, flogging, beating, whacking.

gebung (*Jv*) bunch, bundle (of grass/straw).

gebyagan (*Jv*) performance, official presentation.

gebyah-uyah (*Jv*) overgeneralization.
  menggebyah-uyah and **nggebyah-uyah** to overgeneralize. *untuk mencegah gambaran yang nggebyah uyah* to avoid an overgeneralized picture.
  menggebyah-uyahkan ~ *sesuatu* to overgeneralize s.t.

gebyar I (*Jv*) **1** glitter, sparkle, shine. **2** glance, sight, view.
  menggebyar(gebyar)kan to promote s.t. *Apalagi bila itu terjadi menjelang digebyarkannya Tahun Kunjungan Wisata 1991 oléh pemerintah*. Especially since that happened just as the government was about to promote the 1991 Year of the Tourist.

gebyar II – *gebyur* splash around; → GEBYUR.

gebyok and **gebyog** (*Jv*) wooden wall of a house. *rumah-rumah* – houses with walls made of wood.

gebyur (*J/Jv*) **menggebyur** to jump into the water with a splash.
  menggebyur-gebyur to splash around in the water.
  menggebyurkan to splash s.t. around/out.
  gebyuran splash. ~ *dengan air seémbér* a splash with a bucketful of water.

gecak (*J/Jv*) **menggecak** **1** to press/beat/smash s.t. flat. **2** to beat up, pound, thrash. *Ngomong, nanti gua gecak!* Talk or I'll smash you!

gecar (*J*) trembling, shaking; → GENTAR, G(EM)ETAR.
  menggecarkan to make s.t. quiver/tremble/shake.

gecek → GECAK.

gecer → GECAR.

gécol (*J*) **nggécol** to slip, slide.

gecul (*Jv*) **1** roguish, impish. **2** funny, comical.

gedabah triangular gold hair ornament.

gedabak (*ob*) → GEDEBAK.

gedabir loose skin in old people, dewlap of ox, gills (of a rooster); → GELAMBIR.
  bergedabir to have loose folds of skin.

gedana-gedini (*Jv*) boy-girl sibling combination.

gedang I (*M*) large, big. *rumah* – a Minangkabau family house in the form of a ship with ridges of buffalo horns.
  menggedangkan to enlarge, increase, expand.
  kegedangan size.

gedang II (*S*) papaya. **2** (*Jv*) banana.

gedé (*J/Jv*) large, big; important; much. – *rasa* [GR] Don't act like a big shot! Don't brag!
  segedé as big as.
  menggedékan [and **nggedéin/ngegedéin** (*J coq*)] to enlarge, make larger.
  tergedé the biggest.
  gedéan (*coq*) larger, bigger; more; very large.
  gedé-gedéan on a large scale.
  kegedéan too large/big. – *empyak kurang cagak* (*Jv*) to have Champagne tastes on a beer budget.
  penggedé authority, big shot, V.I.P.
  penggedéan making s.t. larger.

gedebak (*onom*) sound of s.t. heavy falling. – *gedebuk/gedebur* (*onom*) sound of several heavy objects falling, thudding (of falling fruit/tramping feet). ***bergedebak-gedebuk*** to make that noise.

bergedebak to make that noise.
bergedebakan (*pl subj*) to make that noise.
menggedebak to stamp one's foot/feet.
menggedebakkan to stamp (the feet, etc.).
gedebam (*onom*) sound made by s.o. falling on the ground.
gedebar – *gedebur* (*onom*) splashing sound.
gedebeg (*Jv*) load-cart (with wheels without spokes).
gedeblak-gedebluk (*J*) sound of people fighting.
gedebog and **gedebok I** (*Jv*) 1 stem of a banana tree (in which shadow play leather puppets can be stuck). 2 dried skin of banana trunk.
gedebok II → GEDEBUK.
gedebong → GEDEBOG.
gedebrak-gedebruk → GEDEBAK *gedebur*.
gedebuk (*onom*) thudding, stamping, pounding.
　bergedebuk(an) to thud, with a thud.
gedebum → GEDEBUK.
gedebung I a square of cloth folded to hold betel or tobacco, handkerchief for wrapping betel or tobacco.
gedebung II → GEDEBOG.
gedebur → GEDEBAK *gedebur*.
gédég (*Jv*) to shake the head. *membuat orang* – to make people shake their head.
gedek (*J*) be annoyed at, dislike.
gedék (*J/Jv*) panel of braided or woven bamboo. *pagar* – a wall built of such panels. *rumah* – a house made of bamboo panels.
gedembai evil spirit that can turn one into stone.
gedembal → GEDÉMPOL.
gedémpol hefty, obese, pudgy, corpulent, fat, stout. *gemuk* – fat and pudgy.
gédéng (*J/Jv*) 1 sheaf (of rice), bunch (of red onions, etc.). 2 counter for such objects.
　nggédéng 1 to tie into a sheaf. 2 to marry off.
gedibal dirt on the bottom of shoes; the lowest of the low, scum.
gedik I flail (used in agriculture).
　bergedik-gedik trembling, quivering.
　menggedik-gedikkan to shake (the legs).
　kegedikan shaking.
gedik II → GEDÉK.
gedobrol (*Jv*) **menggedobrol** to talk nonsense.
gedobros (*Jv*) **menggedobros** to talk nonsense.
gedog I (*Jv*) a small gong in the *gamelan* orchestra.
gedog II (*Jv reg*) decision. *membikin* – to make/come to a decision.
gedog III (*J/Jv*) blow, rap.
gedok menggedok to weave.
　gedokan 1 k.o. handloom. 2 agricultural implement for separating grain from chaff.
gedombak k.o. tambourine of which only one side is closed by bide.
gedombrongan (*J*) too large (of clothing); slovenly.
gedong → GEDUNG. **gedongan** *anak* ~ (*J*) children of well-to-do parents (living in brick or stone buildings).
gedor (*J*) **menggedor** 1 to bang/knock at (the door). 2 to plunder, pillage, loot, sack.
　menggedori (*pl obj*) to pound on.
　gedoran 1 bang, loud knocking. 2 *barang* ~ loot, items obtained by looting.
　penggedor robber, burglar, looter.
　penggedoran 1 pounding. 2 robbery, burglary.
gedruk (*Jv*) **menggedruk** to stamp with the foot on the ground.
　menggedrukkan to stamp (the feet).
　gedrukan stamping.
gedubang large *kléwang* in Aceh, *usu* used for hunting, etc.
gedubrak (*onom*) crash!
　menggedubrak to make a crashing sound.
gedu(m)brang (*onom*) cacophony. – *gedu(m)bréng* (*onom*) (noisy discordant). *musik* – *gedu(m)bréng* music that made a noisy discordant.
gedu(m)bréng (*onom*) slam-bam.
gedubuk (*J onom*) stamping sound.
　gedubukan to stamp around.
gedul (*J*) stubborn.
gedumbréng → GEDUMBRANG *gedumbréng*.

gedung 1 building of brick or stone (as *opp* to wood/bamboo, etc.), premises. *rumah* – a brick/concrete building. *Rumah –nya cukup megah untuk ukuran désa.* His brick house is rather luxurious for rural standards. 2 building that houses an organization. – *Wanita* Women's Club. 3 palace outbuilding where food is stored and prepared. – *acara* (*ob*) law courts. – *apartemén* apartment building, condominium. – *arca* name for the National Museum at Jalan Merdeka Barat, Jakarta. – *berlantai/bertingkat satu/dua* a one-/two-story building. – *bertingkat* highrise. – *bicara* (*ob*) a) meeting hall. b) courthouse. – *bioskop* movie theater. – *Bulat/Bundar* the building housing the attorney general's office. – *Conéfo* (under President Soekarno) Conefo Building. – *flat* apartment building. – *Gajah* the National Museum (Jakarta). – *induk* main building. – *instansi* a) government-owned building. b) building owned by a private firm. – *jangkung* high-rise. – *jeneng* (*Jv*) "yellow building," i.e., the Sultan's office in the Yogyakarta Kraton. – *madat* "opium building," a building in Jakarta which had this function during the Dutch colonial period; now used as the building of the central administration of the University of Indonesia on Jalan Salemba Raya. – *olahraga* sports hall. – *papak* (*S*) brick building with a flat roof. – *pemerintah* public building. – *pencakar langit* skyscraper. – *Putih* the White House (in the U.S.). – *peraih langit* skyscraper. – *perkantoran* office building. – *Pinter* "intelligent building," i.e., the building of *Bank Negara Indonésia* 46 on Jalan Jenderal Sudirman in Jakarta. – *Pola* Blueprint Hall (Jakarta, Jalan Pegangsaan Timur 96); from this site the proclamation of Indonesia's independence was made on August 17, 1949. – *Saté* "Barbecued Meat Building," i.e., the epithet given by the population of Bandung to the Office of the Head of the First Level Region (the Governor's Office). – *sekolah* school building. – *serba guna* all-purpose building. – *yang menjangkau awan* skyscraper.
gedungan 1 domesticated, house (*mod*). *anjing* ~ a dog as domestic animal. 2 rich (because they live in big houses). *orang* ~ rich people.
geduyut bergeduyut to droop, bend (from heavy branches, etc.).
gé ér, géér and **kegééran** → GEDÉ *rasa*.
gegaba → GABA-GABA.
gegabah (*J*) 1 hasty, rash, reckless, inconsiderate, thoughtless. *tindakan yang* – a hasty/reckless action. 2 at random, wildly, arbitrarily. *dengan* – to have the nerve to.
　bergegabah to act rashly.
　kegegabahan rashness, recklessness. *Inilah* – *yang keléwat batas.* This is a recklessness going beyond all bounds.
gegadan (*ob*) seemly, respectable, reputable; properly, – decently.
gegai not sturdy/firm (of construction).
gegajahan – *kecil* little curlew, *Numenius minutus*. – *sedang* whimbrel, *Numenius phaeopus*.
gegak and – *gempita* uproar; → GEGAP II.
　menggegakkan deafening, ear-splitting.
gegala caulking, pitch; → GALA I.
gegaman (*Jv*) hand weapon.
　pergegaman arsenal, armory.
gegan tergegan startled, surprised, shocked. *Ayah* ~ *dari tidurnya karena pencuri masuk rumah.* Father was startled awake because thieves entered the house.
gegana (*Skr*) 1 air. 2 sky. 3 an elite branch of the police force often used as the bomb squad. *Détasemén* – *Brigade Mobil Polda Métro Jaya* Greater Jakarta Metro Area Police Mobile Brigade Elite Detachment.
gegaokan → GAOKAN.
gegap I tergegap-gegap haltingly, haltingly (in speaking); → GAGAP I.
gegap II – *gempita* uproarious, tumultuous, noisy, clamorous, deafening. *serangan nuklir yang* – *gempita* a massive nuclear attack.
　segegap-gempita as tumultuous as. *Penjualan buku ilmiah tak* ~ *seperti rékor yang pernah dicapai buku.* The sale of scientific books is not as brisk as the record once achieved by the book.
　menggegap-gempitakan to make uproarious. ~ *seluruh rakyat* to bring the crowd to a roar. **kegagap-gempitaan** clamor, uproar, tumult.

bergegapan (*pl subj*) noisy, thunderous
menggegap-gegap to thunder.
menggegapkan deafening, ear-splitting.
gegap III tergegap-gegap stammering, halting (of speech).
gegar 1 quivering, shaking. 2 shock. – *budaya* culture shock. – *otak* (brain) concussion.
bergegar and menggegar 1 to vibrate, shake. *Bumi bergegar karena gempa*. The ground shook from an earthquake. 2 to rumble.
bergegar-gegaran to keep on rumbling.
menggegarkan to shake, convulse, jerk, make s.t. rock/sway.
tergegar vibrated, shook. *Karena dentuman bom itu kaca-kaca jendéla gedung itu ~*. Because of the bomb blast the window-panes of the building shook.
gegaran shaking, shock, blast. ~ *bom* bomb blast.
gegares (*J rude*) to stuff o.s.
gegas bergegas(-gegas) and tergegas(-gegas) 1 hasty, hurried. *Ia berjalan ~ ke sekolah takut terlambat*. He walked hurriedly to school, afraid of being too late. 2 to hasten.
bergegasan (*pl subj*) to hurry.
menggegas(kan) and mempergegas to hasten, speed up, accelerate.
gegasing → GASING.
gegat I a small insect which bores holes in clothes, books, etc., silverfish, *Tineola tripa*.
gegat II loosely (connected), not strong, weak in construction (of houses, boats).
gegat III menggegat to bite down hard on. ~ *gigi* to gnash one's teeth.
gegau tergegau startled, surprised, shocked.
gegawan (*J*) small gifts of food brought along on a visit.
gegawar → GAWAR-GAWAR.
gegayaan stylish, in style; → GAYA I.
gegayuhan (*Jv*) objective, aspiration.
gégé (*Jv*) speeding-up process.
nggégé (to try) to anticipate. ~ *mangsa/mongso* to speed up the normal pace, try to force s.t. before its time. *Aja ~ mangsa*. Don't be premature.
Gegelang one of the four kingdoms at war in the *Hikayat Panji: Jenggala* (Mojokerto), *Daha* (Kediri), *Singosari* (Malang), and *Gegelang* (Ponorogo).
gegep I (pickpocket jargon on Jakarta city buses) arrest.
menggegep to arrest, apprehend. *Kalau ada béndi, kita bisa digegep*. If there's a policeman around, we could be arrested.
gegep II → GEGAP II.
gégép (*S*) pliers, forceps, tongs.
geger → GEGAR.
gégér (*Jv*) 1 noise, uproar, bustle, commotion, tumult, panic, turbulence. 2 in chaos, panicked.
bergégéran (*pl subj*) to be in an uproar.
menggégéri [and nggégéri (*coq*)] to create a sensation, make/cause a stir.
menggégérkan 1 to cause a panic/uproar/tumult/stir. 2 controversial.
gégéran and kegégéran 1 commotion, tumult. 2 fighting, personal conflict.
gegetar tinsel flowers fixed on a wire for headdress of a bride.
gegetuk → GETUK I.
gegetun I (*J*) 1 surprised, dumbfounded. 2 regret, disappointment.
gegetun II (*J*) fed up, angry and annoyed/irritated.
gegoakan screeching; → GAOK, GOAK.
gegunungan mountains.
geguyon(an) joke; → GUYON.
géisha (*Jp*) geisha.
gejaban whimbrel.
gejah (*J*) muddy.
gejala (*Skr*) 1 symptom(s), sign (of illness, etc.). 2 indication(s), traits (of bad language/influence, etc.), tendency. 3 trend. 4 phenomenon. – *awal* early symptoms. – *bisnis* business phenomenon. –.-*flu* flu-like symptoms. – *hamil* signs of pregnancy. –.-*permulaan* early symptoms. – *putus obat* withdrawal symptom. – *takut tua* gerontophobia.

menggejala to become a trend. *Hidup bersama di luar nikah déwasa ini nampaknya mulai ~ di negeri kita*. It seems that living together outside of marriage has become a trend recently. *Penyelundupan ~ lagi*. Smuggling is on the rise again.
penggejalaan indication, sign.
gejol (*BG*) petting, making out (without intercourse).
gejolak 1 disturbance, upheaval. – *dalam* domestic/internal disturbances. – *sosial* social unrest. 2 fluctuation (in prices). 3 flame, fire, ardor, passion, desire. *Tak dapat dia menahan – hatinya karena kegembiraan yang luar biasa itu*. He was unable to restrain himself because of his extraordinary happiness.
bergejolak 1 to flare up (of fire/feelings, etc.), flame high. 2 to heave violently (of the sea in a storm). *Ombak ~ menaik-turunkan kapal*. The rough seas tossed the ship around. 3 to fluctuate. 4 volatile.
menggejolakkan to arouse (the interest of).
gejos (*J onom*) sizzling sound when water is poured over hot embers or when hot iron touches water.
bergejos and menggejos to sizzle (when glowing coals are poured over water). *Besi panas itu ~ ketika dicelupkannya ke dalam air*. The hot iron sizzled when he dipped it in the water.
menggejoskan to put s.t. into hot water and so produce a sizzling sound.
gejrot (*S*) nggejrot to spatter (of liquid).
gejrotan a spatter.
gejug → MENGGEJUK.
gejuju (*M*) menggejuju to pile/heap up (of clouds/smoke, etc.).
gejuk (*Jv*) menggejuk to kick (in fighting/martial arts, etc.).
menggejukkan to kick (one's feet).
gejukan a kick.
gék-sor (*S*) *réstoran* – fast-food restaurant.
gél (*E*) jelly.
gela leak, with open seams (of boats).
gelabak → GELÉTAK.
gelabaran sleepy.
gelabat (*Jv*) film, skin.
gelabir → GELAMBIR.
gelabur menggelabur to plunge into water.
geladah menggeladah to search, go through (s.o.'s pockets), ransack (a house), frisk; → GELÉDAH.
penggeladahan search, frisking. ~ *badan* body search. ~ *rumah* house search.
geladak I 1 (*naut*) (ship's) deck. *penumpang* – deck passenger. – *anjungan* bridge deck. – *antara* tween-decks. – *bawah* lower deck. – *belakang* afterdeck. – *kimbul* poop deck. – *muka* foredeck. – *penerbangan* flight deck. – *penumpang* passenger deck. – *utama* main deck. 2 (*Jv*) floor.
menggeladak ~ *jalan* to construct a road.
geladak II (*J*) 1 wild, untamed (of dogs and women), mongrel. 2 criminal.
geladeri (*coq*) gallery.
geladi → GLADI.
geladir (*J*) 1 mucus, phlegm. 2 slime.
gelagah → GLAGAH.
gelagak → GELEGAK.
gelagap (*J*) tergelagap and gelagapan 1 nervous, agitated. 2 confused, perplexed. 3 stammer, stutter. 4 to gasp for breath; → GLAGEPAN.
gelagar I (*onom*) boom.
bergelagaran (*pl subj*) to thunder, boom (of cannons).
gelagar II 1 reinforcement, girder, beam. 2 dam, barrage (to hold back water). – *beton* pier head. 3 purlin.
gelagat (*J/Jv*) 1 look, appearance, aspect. 2 sign, indication. – *zaman* sign of the times. 3 symptom. *melihat –nya* a) there are signs that, there is every indication that. 4 judging from the manner/way in which (s.t. behaves, etc.). 5 looks as though, to all appearances. *nampak* – everything points to the fact that. – *masa* conditions of the time(s), state of affairs.
bergelagat to behave/conduct o.s.
gelagepan → GLAGEPAN.
gelak 1 laughter. 2 to laugh. – *bersenyuman* to smirk, laugh with

one's tongue in one's cheek. – *gejolak* a raucous laugh. – *manis* sweet smile. – *nabi* suppressed laugh. – *senyum* slight smile, smirk. – *sétan* satanic laughter. – *mumbling/sumbing* titter, sly laugh, snigger. – *tawa* burst of laughter. **bergelak tawa** to burst out laughing. – *terbahak-bahak* to roar with laughter.

gelak-gelak *tertawa* ~ to roar with laughter.

bergelak-gelak to chuckle.

menggelakkan l to laugh at, ridicule, deride. 2 to make s.o. laugh.

tergelak(-gelak) laughed, roared with laughter.

gelakak to roar with laughter, chuckling laugh.

gelalar menggelalar to resist (of a dog or goat being dragged on a leash), tugging (to get free).

gelam I l *pohon* – cajuput, paper bark tree, *Melaleuca cajuputi/leucadendron*, which grows in wet soil or water and provides timber for boats, posts, and firewood, bark for caulking and torches, and pharmaceutical oil. 2 agate (color).

gelam II *burung* – chestnut/cinnamon bittern, *Ixobrychos cinnamomeus.*

gelama *ikan* – various species of croakers, jewfish, *Sciaenidae*. – *batu/hitam* k.o. fish, *Johnius spp*. – *bongkok* k.o. fish, yellow croaker, *Johnius sina*. – *cerua* k.o. fish, grayfin croaker, *Pseudosciaena aneus, Pennahia macrocephalus*. – *jarang gigi* k.o. fish, *Otolithes spp*. – *papan* k.o. fish, soldier croaker, *Nibea soldado*. – *pérak* k.o. fish, pawak croaker, *Pennahia pawak*. – *pisang* k.o. fish, big-eye croaker, *Pennahia macrophthalmus*.

gelamai pounded glutinous rice (*pulut*) with coconut milk and sugar, similar to *dodol*.

menggelamai to make this k.o. *dodol*.

gelambir l dewlap, rooster's wattles, also skin fold under the chin of older people. 2 (*anat*) lobe.

bergelambir(an) and **menggelambir** to hang in folds (of skin of old people, *esp* on the belly), hang loosely; with dewlaps.

gelana → GUNDAH *gulana*.

gelandang I **bergelandang(an)** to loaf about/around, wander about, lounge. *Akhir-akhir ini nampak bertambah banyak orang yang bergelandangan di jalan-jalan.* Recently more and more people have been wandering about the streets.

menggelandang l to loaf about. 2 to arrest for vagrancy.

gelandangan vagrant, vagabond, loafer, drifter. ~ *perempuan* prostitute, female drifter.

penggelandangan and **pergelandangan** vagrancy.

gelandang II (*Jv*) **menggelandang** to drag away by force.

gelandang III (in sports) half-back. – *kanan* right back. – *kiri* left back. – *tengah* mid-fielder (in soccer)

gelandot and **gelandut bergelandot** to hang/hold on to s.t.

menggelandot to hang. *Di punggung-punggung meréka ~ ransel lengkap.* Full knapsacks were hanging on their shoulders.

menggelandoti to hang down on.

gelang l bracelet, circular band, bangle. 2 ring, washer, girdle, race. – *antar* guide ring. – *bajang* amulet of black thread worn by babies to prevent disasters. – *bayonét* locking ring. – *besi* handcuffs. – *borstel* rocker ring. – *cekam* tie-down ring. – *emas* gold bracelet. – *getah* rubber band. – *ikat* fastening ring. – *jalan* race. – *jam* watchband. – *jarak* spacer. – *kaki* anklets. – *kana* (*Jv*) decorated armlet worn by children or newlyweds. – *kancingan* clinch ring. – *karét* rubber band. – *kepil* (*naut*) mooring ring. – *keroncong* anklets with small tinkling bells. – *kompas* gimbal. – *kunci* key ring. – *panggul* pelvic girdle. – *patah semat* bangle with a pattern of ribbed sections. – *peluru* ball race. – *penghubung* coupling ring. – *penutup* washer. – *pintu* ring into which a door bar is placed. – *puyuh* pastern (of a horse). – *raja* spindle worm. – *rantai* a) link of chain. b) chain-bracelet. – *raya* spindle worm. – *sekerup* eye screw. – *sérét* slip ring. – *silinder* piston ring. – *tanah* earthworm. – *tangan* armlet, bracelet. – *trétés* a bracelet decorated with precious gems. – *tutup* washer. – *until* bracelet with a twist in it.

gelang-gelang l ring-shaped objects. 2 ~ *raya* tapeworm. *Ascaris lumbricoldes*. ~ *tanah* round or galley worms, *Ascaris spp*.

bergelang to wear/have a bracelet.

bergelang-gelang with rings on it.

gelangan l bracelet. 2 hoop.

pergelangan s.t. circular. ~ *kaki* the narrow part of the leg just above the ankle, tarsus. ~ *tangan* wrist.

gélang I purslane, *Portulaca oleracea*. – *laut/pasir/tanah* sea purslane, *Sesuvium portulacastrum*. – *susu* (*J*) snakeweed, *Euphorbia Hirta*.

gélang II **tergélang-gélang** glittering, shining.

gelanggang l arena, open space, field, ring, forum. 2 circle around (the moon/sun/a carbuncle/ wound, etc. – *ayam* site for cock fighting. – *Balap Sepéda* Velodrome Sports Center. – *bergumul* wrestling ring. – *buku* book fair. – *bulan* halo around the moon. – *dagang* trade fair. – *dunia* world fair. – *hidup* a) society. b) life. – *Mahasiswa* College Student Center. – *mata* bluish color around the eye. – *matahari* halo around the sun. – *olahraga* sports center. – *pacuan kuda* racecourse. – *Pembinaan Bangsa dan Persahabatan Antar Bangsa* Center for Nation Building and International Understanding (in Jakarta). – *perang/perjuangan* battle arena, battlefield. – *permainan anak-anak* children's playground. – *pertempuran* battle arena, battlefield. – *pertemuan* a) society. b) life. – *politik* political arena. – *remaja* youth center. – *renang* swimming pool. – *Samudra* Oceanarium. – *susu* the dark circle around the nipple, areola. – *tinju* boxing ring. – *Wanita* Exhibit of Articles made by Women.

bergelanggang l to have an aureole, halo, nimbus. 2 to be a circular area for a public event. ~ *di mata orang banyak* obvious, conspicuous, striking.

menggelanggang to hold a (cock)fight.

gelangsar I bergelangsaran and **menggelangsar** to slide, slip, glide.

tergelangsar slid, slipped, glided, slipped down; → TERGELINCIR, TERSELIP. *Anak itu ~ karena lantai licin*. The child slipped because of the slippery floor. *Matahari mulai ~ ke barat*. The sun began to sink in the west.

gelangsar II bergelangsar to surf (with a board); → BERSELANCAR.

gelantang (*J*) **menggelantang** to bleach (laundry); → KELANTANG I.

gelanting and **gelantong** → GELANTUNG.

gelantung bergelantung to dangle, steady o.s. by holding onto s.t. above one.

bergelantungan l to dangle. *Pada pinggangnya ~ Colt besar*. A large Colt dangled from his hip. 2 (*pl subj*) to dangle. *meréka yang ~ di besi pegangan di dalam bus kota* the straphangers on the city bus.

menggelantung to dangle, swing (on the gallows), hang down. *Ketiga penjahat yang sudah ~ di bak truk hendak menurunkan sebagian muatan*. The three criminals, who were dangling off the truck, wanted to lower part of the cargo.

menggelantungi to hang/dangle over s.t.

tergelantung hanging, dangling.

gelantut (*J*) **gelantutan** to hang down, swing.

gelap l dark. *Ia mengenakan kopiah hitam, berkeméja safari warna biru, celana agak –*. He wore a black fez, blue safari shirt, and rather dark-colored pants. *habis – timbul/terbit/lah terang* after rain comes sunshine, behind the clouds the sun is shining. 2 unclear, obscure. 3 clandestine, surreptitious, secret, subversive, illicit, illegal (immigrant, etc.). *bank* – illegal bank. *barang-barang* – illegal commodities, contraband. *candu* – unlicensed opium. *dagang* – smuggling. *garam* – bootleg salt. *istri* – mistress. *malam* – dark night (because of no moon, fighting, etc.). *mata* – to run amok, go berserk. *mata-mata* – detective. *pasar* – black market. *pikiran* – mental derangement, completely confused. *senjata* – illegal weapons. *taksi* – gypsy cab. *tokoh* – sinister character/figure. *uang* – illegal money. – *bulan* dark of the moon. – *buta/gulita/katup/pekat* pitch black. – *hati* fallen into evil ways. – *mata/pikiran* a) to run amok, go berserk. b) mentally deranged. – *otak* stupid. – *pendengaran* uninformed. – *samar muka* unable to see one's hand before one's face. – *temaran* pitch-dark.

segelap as dark as.

bergelap-gelap l to sit in the dark. 2 to be dishonest.

menggelap l to become/turn dark. *Hari kian ~*. It became darker and darker. 2 to abscond. 3 to make a fool of o.s.

menggelapi to darken.

menggelapkan l to darken, obscure. *Ruang depan sudah digelapkan*. The front room has already been darkened. 2 to embezzle, misappropriate. *Dia dihukum karena ~ uang.* He was sentenced because he embezzled money. **3** to tamper with (legal documents/evidence, etc.).

tergelap the darkest.

gelapan darkness. *di ~ malam* in the darkness of the night.

gelap-gelapan clandestinely, in secret. *bacaan porno yang beredar ~* pornographic literature circulating clandestinely.

kegelapan 1 darkness, obscurity; somberness. *dalam ~* backward. **2** overtaken by darkness. *Pulanglah sekarang supaya jangan ~ di jalan.* Go home now so that you don't get caught out after dark. **3** to go crazy.

kegelap-gelapan 1 semi-darkness, twilight, dusk, gloaming. **2** half-mad.

penggelap embezzler. *~ pajak* tax dodger.

penggelapan 1 blackout. *Dalam waktu perang setiap malam diadakan ~ di seluruh tanah Jawa.* During the war there was a blackout over all of Java every night. *masa ~* the dark ages. **2** embezzlement, misappropriation. *melakukan ~* to embezzle, misappropriate. **3** fraud, defalcation. **4** tampering with (for criminal purposes). *~ asal-usul* tampering with a person's status.

gelapur → GELEPUR.

gelar I 1 (honorary) title. *memakai/memegang/menyandang ~* to bear a title. **2** degree, academic title. *lembaga pencétak ~* degree mill. **3** alias, nickname. **4** designation. **5** membership's name (given when men marry in their village, in the Minangkabau), *suku-*name. *~ dokter* physician's degree. *~ kebangsawanan* title of nobility. *~ kesarjanaan* lowest academic degree. *~ pusaka* hereditary title.

bergelar 1 to bear a title, have the title of. **2** nicknamed. **3** named, by the name of, called.

menggelari and **menggelarkan** to name, give a (nick-) name to, entitle.

gelaran 1 title. **2** k.o. *adat* chief.

gelar-gelaran phony title.

penggelaran bestowal of title/degree.

gelar II (*Jv mil*) (battle) array, deployment. *Hal ini dikatakan oléh Menteri M. Jusuf dalam ~ pasukan Brigade Marinir di bumi Marinir Karangpilang Surabaya.* This was said by Minister M. Jusuf in a battle array of troops of the Marine Brigade at the Karangpilang Marine Grounds in Surabaya.

menggelar 1 to deploy, spread out (troops) so as to form an extended front/line. *"Setiap pagi saya ~ pasukan di jalan untuk menanggulangi kemacatan lalu-lintas," kata Létkol Pol Riyanto, Kapolrés Jakarta Pusat.* "Every morning I deploy my troops in the streets to cope with traffic jams," said Police Lieutenant-Colonel Riyanto, Police Chief of the Central Jakarta Jurisdiction. **2** to hold, put on. *~ démonstrasi* to hold a demonstration. *~ konsér piano* to perform a piano concerto.

menggelarkan and **mempergelarkan** to show (a drama, etc.), perform, stage (a play). *~ senyum akrabnya* (she) flashed her friendly smile.

gelaran mat. *Kami sekeluarga semua tidur sekamar. Anak-anak di ranjang, saya dan Mas Jumin ~ di bawah.* We all slept in one room. The children in bed, Jumin and I slept on a mat on the floor.

pergelaran 1 place/venue where a performance/show is given. **2** show, recital. *~ langsung di panggung* life show.

pagelar mempagelarkan to perform, show. *~ kelompok musik kamar "Nusantara Chamber Orchestra"* to stage the chamber music group Nusantara Chamber Orchestra. **pagelaran** and **pegelaran** performance, show, display. *~ bunga* flower show. *~ jazz* jazz concert. *~ kesenian* art exhibition. *~ lukisan* exhibition of paintings. *~ musik* orchestra. *~ perdana* preview.

penggelaran (*mil*) deployment. *Den Haag menolak ~ peluru kendali jelajah dari Amérika Serikat.* The Hague rejected the deployment of U.S. cruise missiles. *~ rudal nuklir jarak jauh sedang* the deployment of medium-range nuclear missiles.

gelar III (*Jv*) **pagelaran** the front part of the *kraton* in which officials jointly pay their respects to the sultan.

gelar IV (*J/Jv*) to spread/lay (out). *~ perkara* (*leg*) presentation of a case. *~ tikar* to spread a mat (made of palm leaves; to display merchandise, etc. on sidewalks).

tergelar spread out.

gelas (*D*) **1** drinking glass, tumbler. **2** glass, glazed (*mod*). *~ baterai* battery jar. *~ bertangkai* a small stemmed glass, such as a wineglass, goblet. *~ kimia* beaker. *~ penduga* gauge-glass. *~ piala* beaker. *~ takar* calibrated beaker. *~ timpus* flute. *~ ukur* calibrated beaker.

bergelas *tali ~* string coated with glass powder.

bergelas-gelasan (*M*) kite fighting using the above string.

menggelas to coat kite string with glass powder.

gelasan 1 k.o. paste from pulverized glass, white of egg, and joiner's glue, with which the string of the fighter kite is coated. *~ mati* glass shards used to coat the kite string. **2** coated (string).

gelasak doormat.

gelasar → GELANGSAR I.

gelasir (*D*) icing, glazing.

menggelasir to ice, cover with icing.

gelatak I (*ob*) → GELÉTAK.

gelatak II talkative.

gelatak III → GELITIK.

menggelatak to tickle.

gelatang (*J*) → GELANTANG I, KELANTANG.

gelatik (*Jv*) various species of nuthatch and tit. *burung ~* Java sparrow/rice bird, *Munia/Padda oryzivora. ~ batu* great tit, *Parus major. ~ munguk* various species of nuthatch, *Sitta spp.*

gelatin (*D/E*) gelatin.

gelatinisasi gelatinization.

gelatuk (*onom*) chattering.

menggelatuk to chatter (of teeth, from cold/fear); to shiver (with cold), tremble (with fear).

gelawai k.o. tree, *Buchanania sessilifolia.*

gelayangan (*J*) **bergelayangan** to wander/roam/rove about.

gelayar gelayaran (*Jv*) to totter, stagger.

gelayut (*J*) hang, dangle.

bergelayut to hang, swing.

bergelayutan (*pl subj*) to hang, swing.

menggelayut to droop, sag, hang down; to fall, descend. *Ketika malam larut dan sepi ~.* When it was late at night and silence had fallen. *~ tubuh lawan* (in boxing) to clinch.

menggelayuti to hang/hover over s.t., haunt, trouble. *Suasana di rumah kami digelayuti duka yang amat dalam.* The atmosphere in our house was haunted by a deep sadness.

menggelayutkan to hang s.t. (around s.t.). *Dia mengiyakan dan ~ tangannya di léhérku.* She hooked her hand around my neck.

tergelayut to hang down, dangle.

gelayutan 1 s.t. which dangles. **2** to hang on.

gélé (*sl*) marijuana.

gelebak and **gelebap** (*onom*) sound of a thud (as of falling coconuts/books), crash!

bergelebak to thud, crash.

gelebar tergelebar to fall and scatter all over.

gelébar bergelébar and **menggelébar** to wave, float, fly, flutter.

tergelébar waved, floated, etc.

gelébat double-bladed paddle.

gelébér (ber)gelébéran to hang down, droop, hang in folds (of dewlap, old skin, loose coat); → GELA(M)BIR.

gelebuk (*onom*) thud (of fruit falling); → LEBUK II.

gelebur menggelebur to plunge/jump (into).

gelebyar bergelebyar to fly/flutter around.

bergelebyaran (*pl subj*) to fly/flutter around.

menggelebyar to fly, flutter.

geleca (*ob*) a light feather mattress.

gelécék menggelécék and **tergelécék** to skid, slip, slide.

gelecik → GELÉCÉK.

gelédah menggéledah to search, go through (s.o.'s pockets), ransack (a house), frisk, carry out a house search, raid.

menggelédahi (*pl obj*) to search, etc. repeatedly.

penggéledah raider.

penggelédahan 1 search, raid, sweep (by police). *~ rumah* raid on a house/premises. **2** ransacking.

geledang menggeledang to stretch out the arms at right angles to the body (to ward off a blow, etc.).

geledeg (*Jv*) case, chest, box.

gelédék (*J*) thunder, lightning. *sebagai – di siang hari bolong* like a bolt from the blue. *Sambar –!* May I be struck by lightning (if I'm lying, etc.), (I) swear to God!

    menggelédék 1 to roar, boom, thunder; thundering, thunderous (voice). **2** to bang (of a gun); a fierce shot.

    menggelédéki to thunder/roar, etc. at.

gelédékan pushcart.

geleding menggeleding to warp (of wood), sag.

geleduk (*J*) **menggeleduk** to fall head forward.

geledur menggeledur to hang down in folds (like the skin on an obese person).

gelegah → GELAGAH, GLAGAH.

gelegak bergelegak and **menggelegak 1** to boil (of water), bubble, effervesce, fizz. **2** to seethe. *Kemarahan ~ di hatinya*. He seethed with rage. *Darah panas Lastri ~*. Lastri's hot blood seethed. **3** to wheeze.

    menggelegakkan 1 to boil, bring s.t. to the boil. **2** to make s.t. or s.o. seethe.

gelegapan → GELAGAPAN, GLAGEPAN.

gelegar I beam, girder on which the floorjoints rest.

gelegar II (*onom*) rumbling. *Terdengar bunyi – peluru*. The rumbling sound of shells could be heard. *– buluh* a lot of talk and no action.

    bergelegar(an) and **bergelegar-gelegar** to keep rumbling (of thunder).

    menggelegar 1 to explode. *Granat ~ di tengah-tengah orang*. A grenade exploded in the crowd. **2** to boom, rumble.

    menggelegarkan 1 to make s.t. thunder/rumble, blast out. **2** to say s.t. in a boastful way.

gelegata k.o. eczema, nettle rash, hives, urticaria.

gélék I 1 to roll over. **2** to run/roll over, knock down. *Mati digélék mobil*. Run over and killed by a car. **3** to roll s.t. up into a cylinder.

    tergélék run over, knocked down.

gélék II (*M*) **menggélék** to dodge.

    menggélék(kan) ~ *diri* to get out of the way; to avoid, evade s.t.

gélék III (*sl*) marijuana, pot. *ngisap –* to smoke pot.

    ngegélék to smoke pot. *Biang kerok pemeras sewaktu sedang ~ diciduk Polri*. While smoking pot, the mastermind of the extortionists was apprehended by the police.

gelekak menggelekak to peel off (of paint/bark), crumble away (of the plaster on a wall); → KELUPAS.

gelékék menggelékék to giggle; → TERPINGKAL-PINGKAL.

gelema phlegm, mucus in the throat.

gelemak a heavy burden/load. *dibenam – utang Pertamina* to groan under a heavy burden of Pertamina's debts.

gelemat (*cla naut*) decking over the bow and stern of a boat, containing cabins.

gelémbéran (*J*) wattle (of roosters), dewlap (of cattle); with wattles/dewlaps; → GELAMBIR.

gelémbong wide (fencing) pants.

gelembung 1 (water) bubble. **2** balloon. **3** (*anat*) alveolus, vesicle. **4** swollen. *– air* water bubble. *– empedu* gall bladder. *– kencing* urinary vesicle. *– paru-paru* alveolus (of the lung). *– renang* swim bladder. *– sabun* soap bubble. *– udara* air bladder.

    bergelembung 1 with bubbles in it. **2** to swell up, become swollen.

    bergelembung-gelembung to bubble, fizz.

    menggelembung 1 to swell up, become swollen/inflated/bloated. **2** to grow, increase, expand.

    menggelembungkan 1 to blow up, inflate. **2** to make s.t. grow/increase/expand; to bloat, distend. *digelembungkan menjadi* to be expanded into.

    gelembung-gelembungan 1 to blow bubbles. **2** all k.o. bubbles.

    penggelembung s.t. that bubbles.

    penggelembungan expansion, bloating, swelling. ~ *wilayah industri* expansion of industrial areas.

gelembur wrinkle, groove, ripple.

    menggelembur wrinkled, lined, grooved (of the skin).

    menggelemburkan to wrinkle/line/groove s.t.

gelémpang → GELIMPANG.

gelémprang (*onom*) high-pitched sound.

bergelémprang to make a high-pitched sound.

gelenang → GENANG. **tergelenang** flooded, inundated. *Air yang ~ di jalan itu berpancaran ketika mobil léwat*. The water which inundated the road splashed whenever a car passed by.

gelénang set of three small gongs in the *gamelan* orchestra.

gelendo (*J*) residue, sediment, deposit, dregs.

geléndong bobbin, spool, reel, hoop, roll, drum. *– besi* iron hoop. *– kabel* cable drum. *– kumparan* shuttle. *– silang* turnstile.

    menggeléndong to wind (thread/a film, etc.) around a spool.

geléndot menggeléndot to lean (on). *Ny. Murni mengelus salah seorang cucunya yang ~ di pangkuannya*. Mrs. Murni stroked one of her grandchildren who was leaning on her lap.

    menggeléndoti to lean on.

géléng to shake (one's head). *– seperti (si) patung kenyang* (*M*) arrogant.

    bergéléng(-géléng) to shake the head.

    menggéléng 1 to shake (one's head). **2** to refuse, deny.

    menggéléngkan to shake (one's head).

    tergéléng-géléng shaking of the head (in surprise/amazement).

    géléngan shaking, movement. ~ *kepala* shaking the head.

gelénggang → GELINGGANG.

gelentang *– golék/guling –* rolling over and over; to tumble.

    bergelentang and **menggelentang** to roll around, wallow.

gelentar → GELETAR.

gelenting (*onom*) tinkling sound.

gelenyar tingling.

    menggelenyar to tingle.

geléong → GELIANG.

gelépak → GELÉTAK.

gelepar flap, flutter; → GELEPUR.

    bergelepar(an) and **menggelepar(-gelepar) 1** to flutter, sprawl, flounder. *menggelepar di tempat* to hover (of an aircraft). *anak elang yang menggelepar* a fluttering baby eagle. *Ibu tidak tahan melihat udang-udang yang menggelepar di tanah itu*. Mother couldn't stand seeing those shrimp floundering on the ground. **2** to have convulsions, convulse, twitch.

    menggeleparkan to flap, beat. ~ *sayap* to flap its wings (of a cock).

    geleparan fluttering.

gelépék menggelépék to hang down slack, droop (of flags/sails of a boat when there's no wind).

gelepok (*J*) **1** blow, hit. **2** (*onom*) pow!

gelépok and **gelépot** dirty, muddy.

gelepung (*onom*) sound of an object falling heavily into the water.

    bergelepung to make that sound.

gelepur attack (of a fighting cock). *tinggi –, rendah laga* much ado about nothing.

    menggelepur to attack (of a cock).

gélér → GILIR.

gelésék → GELÉSÉR.

gelésér menggelésér 1 to keep on moving. **2** to start rotating (of wheels, etc.). **3** to move, roll on (like a ball). *Kiper itu gagal menangkap bola ~ di tanah*. The keeper failed to catch the ball rolling over the ground.

    menggelésérkan to cause (a ball, etc.) to roll.

gelésoran (*Jv*) to roll over the ground. *Lantas meréka – di pinggir pantai*. And then they rolled over the sand along the beach.

gelésot menggelésot to move up (while sitting), push up.

geléta a long-necked water-jar.

geletak (*J*) *– geletik* and *– geletuk* to chatter (of teeth).

geletak bergelétakan (*pl subj*) to sprawl.

    menggelétak to sprawl, lie on the ground, lie down.

    menggelétakkan to throw/fling s.t. down.

    tergelétak lie (sprawling) (on the ground).

geletar shivering, trembling.

    bergeletar(an), **geletaran**, and **menggeletar** to shiver (with cold), tremble (with fear), quake, shake, shudder.

    menggeletari to chill, make s.o. shiver.

    menggeletarkan to make s.t. tremble.

gelétek → GELÉTAK.

geléténg ghost crab, *Ocypode ceratophthalmus*.

geletik I (*onom*) tick (of clocks).

geletik II menggeletik to wriggle, hop (as fish/prawns/grasshoppers), twitch, squirm.

geletik III menggeletik 1 *hati* ~ to palpitate, throb (of a heart). 2 to tick (of a clock).

geleting menggeleting to tinkle, jingle (like coins rubbing together).

geletis menggeletis to sprawl, flounder.

geletuk (*onom*) chattering.

  bergeletukan (*pl subj*) to chatter.

  menggeletuk to chatter (of teeth).

geléyot (*S*) menggeléyot to toss to and fro.

geli 1 ticklish; to tickle. 2 amusing, facetious. 3 pleasure, fun. 4 peevish, irritated. 5 to shiver, shudder. 6 gruesome, creepy, weird. *habis/alah – oléh gelitik, (habis bisa oléh biasa)* one gets used to everything. *– geman* to shiver (with cold, fear), shudder (with horror); irritated. *– hati* tickled, amused. *– pahit* a bitter laugh. *– sendiri* to laugh to o.s.

  menggeli to encourage (a game-cock).

  menggelikan 1 ridiculous, amusing, comical, humorous. ~ *hati* to amuse, be amusing. 2 to tickle, tickling.

  kegelian 1 to feel like laughing. 2 very amused. *Ia tertawa* ~. He laughed from amusement.

  penggeli 1 joker. 2 joking. ~ *hati* joke, jest; amusing.

geliang *– geliut* writhing and twisting from the waist up. **menggeliang-geliut(kan)** to make s.o. writhe and twist.

  menggeliang to writhe.

geliat *– geliut* to stretch.

  bergeliatan (*pl subj*) to squirm around.

  menggeliat 1 to stretch. 2 to twist. 3 to show signs of life. *tetap* ~ to stay/still be alive.

  menggeliatkan 1 to stretch s.t. ~ *badan* to stretch o.s. (after sleeping). *Dia bangun sambil mengangkat kedua belah tangannya ke atas dan* ~ *badan*. He woke up and raised both his arms and stretched. 2 to twist, distort.

  tergeliat strained, dislocated, sprained, twisted, distorted; → TERKILIR. *Dia terjatuh ke dalam lubang itu dan* ~ *kakinya*. He fell into the hole and sprained his foot.

  penggeliatan stretching.

gelibir menggelibir and **tergelibir** drooping/bent down because of its weight, pendulous.

gelicik I tergelicik skidded, slipped; → TERSELIP.

gelicik II menggelicikkan to avoid, evade. *Dia memeléngkan kepalanya ke kiri untuk* ~ *tinju lawannya itu*. He turned his head to the left to avoid a blow from the fist from his opponent.

geliga → GULIGA.

geli-geli I *buah* – kidneys.

geli-geli II k.o. aquatic aroid plant, *Lasia spinosa*.

geligi I menggeligi to shiver, chatter.

geligi II → GIGI *geligi*.

geligin a cross-rod holding the cloth against the yard beam in a weaver's loom.

geligis menggeligis to shudder (because of fever/fright, etc.), tremble, quiver, chatter (of teeth).

geligit to bite repeatedly; → GIGIT.

gelimang pool, puddle; pile (of mud/money/pleasure/luxury).

  bergelimang(an) to be covered with mud, smeared with dirt, stained, soiled. *hidup bergelimang uang* rolling in money. *Hidupnya selalu bergelimang dengan kemelaratan*. She has always lived in misery.

  menggelimang to be smeared.

  menggelimangi 1 to dirty, soil, defile, pollute, besmirch. 2 to swamp/inundate/flood with.

  tergelimang all covered with (dirt).

  gelimangan pool. *Dia duduk di dalam* ~ *cahaya*. He was sitting in a pool of light.

gelimantang menggelimantang to radiate (of light).

gelimbir sagging, pendulous (of old or fat cheeks); → GELAMBIR.

  menggelimbir to sag.

  gelimbiran sagging, pendulous.

gelimir tissue, membrane.

gelimpang bergelimpangan to sprawl, lie outstretched, sprawled out (as of dead or exhausted men). *Tiga orang pengendara sepéda motor, Sabtu siang* ~ *di aspal, menderita luka berat dalam peristiwa tabrakan*. Three motorcycle drivers, sprawled on the asphalt Saturday afternoon, received serious injuries due to a collision.

  menggelimpang to sprawl, lie with the arms and legs loosely spread out. ~ *di atas sofa karena ia terlalu lelah* to lie sprawling on the sofa because he was so tired.

  menggelimpangkan to sprawl (one's body).

  tergelimpang sprawled, lying down (from exhaustion, etc.). *Ikan paus yang mati* ~ *di atas pasir di pantai itu*. The dead whale sprawled on the sand of the beach.

  gelimpangan ~ *dalam uang* to be rolling in money.

gelimun bergelimun enveloped, wrapped (up), engaged in.

  menggelimuni to envelop, cover.

gelinang menggelinang to pour forth (of tears).

gelincir menggelincir to slip, skid, slide, almost fall when one loses one's balance. ~ *lidah* to make a slip of the tongue.

  menggelincirkan 1 to cause to skid/slip. 2 to sidetrack.

  tergelincir 1 to slide, slip, fall (into bad habits). *Ia jatuh* ~ *karena lantai sangat licin*. He slipped and fell because the floor was very slippery. 2 setting (of the sun). *Matahari sudah* ~ *menandakan senja sudah mendatang*. The sun was setting, a sign that evening was near. 3 ~ *lidah* to put one's foot in one's mouth, make a slip of the tongue. *Dia meminta maaf karena* ~ *lidahnya*. He said he was sorry for his slip of the tongue.

  penggelinciran skidding, sliding.

gelincuh tergelincuh stumbled, tripped.

gelinding wheel.

  bergelinding(an) to roll.

  menggelinding 1 to roll along/on, get moving. 2 to taxi (of an aircraft).

  menggelindingkan to roll s.t. ~ *keluar dari hangar* to roll (an airplane) out of the hangar.

  gelindingan s.t. that rolls, caster.

  penggelindingan the roll-out (of an aircraft).

gelindung → GELÉNDONG.

gelinggam I 1 red lead. 2 red dye (made of *Pixa orellana*).

gelinggam II (*M?*) gelinggaman → GELI *geman*.

gelinggang k.o. shrub with medicinal uses, *Cassia alata*.

gelingsir bergelingsir and **menggelingsir** 1 to move slowly downward or upward. 2 to set, go down (of the sun). 3 to slide/slip down.

  menggelingsirkan to cause to move down.

  tergelingsir slid/slipped down.

gelinjang bergelinjang to splatter.

  menggelinjang 1 to become turbulent, excited. *Minah sudah merasa seperti jabang bayi sedang* ~ *mencari jalan keluar*. Minah felt like an infant getting all excited trying to find a way out. 2 to prance (of horses). 3 to bounce up and down, rear (of a horse). 4 to jump up and down (with joy).

  menggelinjangkan to move s.t. up and down.

  tergelinjang to jump up and down.

gelintang mengelintang and **tergelintang** fall down and sprawl (on the ground, etc.).

gelintar menggelintar to walk about searching for s.t.

gelintin bergelintin 1 to stick, glue, paste. 2 sticky, gluey, viscous.

gelinting (*J/Jv*) menggelinting 1 to roll (a cigarette); → TINGWÉ. ~ *rokok kawung* to roll a cigarette from the dried leaves of the sugar palm tree. 2 to writhe (in pain, etc.).

  gelintingan rolled (of cigarettes, etc.).

  penggelinting roller (the person).

gelintir (*J/Jv*) 1 small round object, grain, pellet, particle. 2 a small (unimportant) group (of persons). *beberapa – manusia* small knots of people. *beberapa – anak-anak muda* some youngsters. 3 classifier for persons. *tujuh – penumpang* seven passengers. 4 (*coq*) defeated (in a match/competition). *Dalam babak sémifinal juara Malaysia telah –*. In the semifinal round Malaysia's champion was defeated.

  segelintir a very few, a minute fraction, a small number. ~ *manusia* a very small number of people, very few people. ~ *umat manusia* a handful of people.

  menggelintir to form/roll into pellets or small balls.

  menggelintiri (*pl obj*) to roll into pellets.

gelintiran grain, pellet.

gelipang → GELIMPANG.

gelipar and **tergelipar** distorted or bent (of a kris/weapon, etc.) from hitting a hard object.

gelis → GEULIS.

gelisah worried, anxious, restless, nervous. *Nafsu makannya normal, sedangkan tidurnya* –. His appetite was normal, but his sleep was restless. *– belia* restless. *– resah* very nervous.

  bergelisah to be nervous, fidget.

  menggelisah to fidget, move around restlessly.

  menggelisahi to bother, disturb.

  menggelisahkan 1 to alarm, disturb, perturb; disturbing. *Itu pengumuman yang* ~. It was a disturbing announcement. **2** to upset, cause anxiety.

  kegelisahan unrest, restlessness, anxiety, concern, uneasiness. ~ *sosial* social unrest.

  penggelisah worrywart.

gelita → GELAP, GULITA. **kegelitaan** darkness, obscurity.

gelitar menggelitar to struggle.

gelitik 1 tickle, tickling. **2** stimulus, incitement, instigation. **3** quivering, throbbing.

  menggelitik 1 to tickle. ~ *perasaan* amusing. **2** to tillate, tickle (one's nose). *Asap saté* ~ *seléra pejalan kaki*. The shish kebab smoke tickled the pedestrians' noses. **3** to stir up, rouse, prod, encourage, incite (s.o. to take a certain action). ~ *hati* to pound, thud, beat faster (of the heart out of fear, etc.). ~ *hati pembaca* it makes the reader's heart beat faster.

  menggelitiki (*pl obj*) to tickle.

  tergelitik 1 tickled. **2** stimulated.

  gelitikan 1 tickling, tickle. **2** stimulation, incitement.

  penggelitik 1 tickler. **2** stimulant.

geliting → GELITIK.

geliut → GELIANG, GELIAT.

gelo (*Jv*) disappointed. *merasa* – to feel disappointed

gélo (*J*) foolish, silly, mad, crazy.

gelobak seriously injured, damaged.

gelobok menggelobok to gurgle (of a vessel dipped into water); → GEROBOK I.

gelocak swishing around (of water).

gelodar I muddy, turbid (of water).

gelodar II menggelodar to flounder around (of a fish out of water).

gelodok I (*Jv*) case, box.

gelodok II (*Jv*) beehive made from pieces of coconut tree trunk.

gelodok III *ikan* – mudskipper, *Periophthalmodon schlosseri*.

gelogok I (*onom*) gulping noise, glug.

  menggelogok 1 to gulp/swig down (a liquid). **2** to boil, bubble (of hot water). **3** to spill or pour out a large quantity.

gelogok II (*M*) a threat. *salah* – to do s.t. hurriedly (without due consideration).

gelohok tergelohok wide open, gaping.

gelojak → GEJOLAK.

gelojo(h) (*Port?*) **1** gluttonous. **2** greedy for, keen on.

  menggelojo(h) to be gluttonous.

gelokak menggelokak to peel off (of paint, etc.); → GELOPAK.

gelomang → GELUMANG.

gelombang 1 long, rolling waves, rollers. **2** band, wavelength (radio). **3** wave, series (of strikes/suicides, etc.). **4** phase, stage, facet. *– bunga lepang* whitecap. *– bunuh diri* wave of suicides. *– bunyi* sound wave. *– cahaya* light wave. *– duabelas* (*M*) k.o. sword dance. *– éléktromagnétik* electromagnetic wave. *– getaran/kejut* shock wave. *– kepala kera* cross seas. *– ledakan* blast wave. *– mangkuk* eddy. *– melintang* transverse wave. *– memanjang* longitudinal wave. *– mikro* microwave. *– mikro digital* digital microwave. *– panas* heat wave. *– panjang* roller. *– pasang* tsunami. *– pasat* waves caused by the trade winds. *– péndék* shortwave, microwave. *– radio* radio waves. *– réaksi* a wave of reactions. *– samudera* ocean wave. *– tekan* pressure wave. *– udara* airwaves. *– ultrasonik* ultrasonic wave. *– ultraviolét* ultraviolet wave.

  bergelombang 1 to have waves, be choppy. *Lautnya agak* ~. The sea was rather choppy. **2** to have radio waves. **3** wavy, curly, bumpy, choppy. *Rambutnya* ~. Her hair is wavy. **4** in waves (as flights of aircraft), successive. *Sekitar 150 orang diterbangkan dari Jayapura ke Waména secara* ~. About 150 people were flown from Jayapura to Wamena in waves. ~ *naik* to go up and down, fluctuate. **5** corrugated.

  bergelombangan (*pl subj*) to surge, roll (of waves).

  bergelombang-gelombang in waves.

  menggelombang to wave, surge.

  menggelombangkan to make wavy.

  penggelombang ~ *rambut* hair waver (*mod*).

  penggelombangan causing s.t. to wave/surge.

gelompar menggelompar to jump/leap up quickly.

gelondangan (*J*) (feels/looks) empty.

gelondong roll, bunch.

  gelondongan → GLONDONGAN I, II.

gelonéng a small gong.

gelonggong bergelonggong with a hole made in it (as of a coconut by a squirrel), perforated.

gelongsong → KELONGSONG.

gelongsor I bergelongsor to flush.

  gelongsoran flushing, draining. *suara* ~ *air klosét* the flushing sound of a toilet bowl.

gelongsor II bergelongsor to slip, slide.

  menggelongsor 1 to slide down (a tree trunk, etc.). **2** to slip down (of a soccer player).

  tergelongsor to slip/slide down.

gelonjak bergelonjak and **menggelonjak** to jump/leap/start up; → LONJAK.

  bergelonjakan (*pl subj*) jump/leap around.

gelontor flush, drain.

  menggelontor 1 to drain, flush; to flush/wash away. **2** to flood (the market). **3** to overwhelm.

  menggelontorkan to flood (the market), pour in lots of s.t.

  gelontoran 1 flushing, draining. *suara* ~ *air klosét* the flushing sound of a toilet bowl. **2** flood, flooding (the market).

  penggelontor flush, s.t. that flushes. *tombol* ~ flush knob.

  penggelontoran draining, flushing.

gelopak menggelopak to peel off (of paint, etc.), → KELOPAK.

gelora I (*Skr?*) **1** tempestuousness, boisterousness, turbulence; turbulent, stormy. *musim* – the stormy season. **2** breakers, surf, bore; raging (of the sea). **3** excitement, enthusiasm, agitation, thrill. *– hati* strong feelings of anxiety, passion, restlessness. *– semangat* enthusiasm, strong emotion.

  bergelora 1 billowy, with great waves. *Nelayan-nelayan tidak turun ke laut dalam musim hujan karena laut* ~. Fishermen don't go down to the sea during the rainy season because of the high seas. **2** worried, disturbed. **3** flaring up, raging, seething.

  menggelora 1 to be stormy. **2** to be ardent, enthusiastic, passionate.

  menggelorakan to incite, spur on, stir up, whip up, incite. *Ucapan oléh pemimpin itu telah dapat* ~ *semangat mencintakan tanahair di kalangan muda-mudi*. What that leader said spurred the spirits of love for their nation among the young people.

  penggelora s.t. or s.o. that spurs on, incites, etc.

  penggeloraan inciting, spurring on, whipping up, stirring up.

Gelora II [Gelanggang olah raga] Athletic Stadium.

gelorat → DARURAT.

gelosang (*M*) **menggelosang** to be in a hurry.

geloso (*J*) **menggeloso** to writhe (from pain).

gelosok menggelosok to scrub vigorously (an intensive form of *gosok*).

gelosor → GELONGSOR I.

gelotak menggelotak to remove a hard husk, split a coconut husk.

gelotrak (*onom*) rattling sound.

  menggelotrak to rattle.

geluduk (*Jv*) thunder; → GELÉDÉK.

  bergeluduk and **menggeluduk** to thunder.

  geludukan thundery.

geluga (*Jv*) red dye. *kayu* – the tree (the Annato, *Pixa orellana*) from which this red dye is obtained.

gelugur I (with) grooves, striped.

gelugur II *pohon* – k.o. tree with juicy fruit, *Garcinia macrophylla*.

asam – yellow-orange fluted fruit of the *Garcinia atrovirides*, used as a seasoning for curries and for cleaning krises.

gelugut bergelugut and **menggelugut 1** to shiver, quiver (from cold/fear). **2** to chatter (of the teeth).

geluh clay, mud, loam. *tanah* – loamy soil.

geluk 1 a water vessel made of coconut shell. **2** (*bio*) nut.

gelulur menggelulur and **tergelulur 1** to slip and roll (as a soccer player). **2** to slip off (as a garment).

gelumang bergelumang smeared with (mud/blood, etc.).

menggelumang to wallow in (mud, etc.).

menggelumangi to smear s.t. (with s.t.).

gelumat (*cla*) loud, noisy, boisterous, tumultuous, uproarious; roar, uproar. – *suara orang bersorak-sorak di tanah lapang itu terdengar sampai jauh.* The tumultuous sound of people shouting on the field could be heard far away.

gelumbang → GELOMBANG.

geluncang tergeluncang hovering. ~ *antara tradisi dan modérnisasi* hovering between tradition and modernization.

geluncur → GELONGSOR II.

gelundung I (*Jv*) **1** rolling. *batu* – rolling stone. **2** roll, reel.

bergelundungan (*pl subj*) and **menggelundung** to roll (downward or along a path). *Batu itu menggelundung ke bawah.* The rock rolled downward.

menggelundungkan to make s.t. roll, roll s.t.

gelundungan reel.

gelundung II a ghost whose head rolls over the ground with a broad grin.

gelundung III → GELONDONG.

gelung I 1 coil (of rope/rattan/snake). **2** bun (of hair). **3** curve, bend, turn, winding. **4** loop.

segelung a coil.

bergelung 1 to coil (of a rope/snake); coiled. **2** to shrink, cringe. *tidur* ~ *karena dingin* to sleep curled up because of the cold. **3** to wear a bun of hair.

menggelung 1 to curve s.t. into a coil. **2** to coil (the hair into a bun, a rope).

menggelungi to coil/wrap up s.t.

menggelungkan to coil/curve s.t. into a circle.

tergelung 1 curled/coiled up. **2** knotted, in a knot. **3** looped.

gelungan 1 circle, coil (of rope, etc.). **2** curve, bend (in road).

gelung-gelungan 1 coil. **2** bun.

penggelungan rolling, coiling.

gelung II – *tekuk* a Central Javanese traditional hairdo.

gelungsur → GELONGSOR II.

geluntung I (*J*) **geluntungan** to wander around.

geluntung II (*J*) **geluntungan** big piece.

gelup menggelup to fall out (of teeth).

gelupas → KELUPAS.

gelupur menggelupur to move and flap about (of the wings of a slaughtered fowl or a fish out of water), struggle convulsively.

gelut wrestle, fight. *adu* – to wrestle. *jago* – wrestler.

bergelut 1 to wrestle, roll around, romp. *Anak-anak kecil itu suka* ~ *dan berguling-guling di padang itu.* The little children wrestled and rolled around in the field. **2** to fight, struggle. *Pencuri itu berusaha* ~ *dengan polisi itu untuk melepaskan diri.* The thief tried to struggle with the police to get free. ~ *senda* (*ob*) to jest, joke. ~ *dengan* to struggle with, have to contend with, deal with. *sehari-hari* ~ *dengan komputer* to deal with computers on a daily basis.

bergelut-gelutan to horse around, roughhouse.

menggelut to try to wrestle s.o. down. *Salah seorang dari kedua perampok itu* ~ *saya.* One of the two robbers tried to wrestle me down.

menggeluti 1 to wrestle with, deal with. *masalah yang digeluti mahasiswa-mahasiswa* problems with which college students have to wrestle. **2** to overcome, engulf. *digeluti ketakutan* to be overcome with fear. *digeluti sepi* to be engulfed in silence.

gelutan wrestler, fight.

pegelut wrestler.

penggelut aficionado.

pergelutan wrestling, fighting.

gelutuk → GELETUK.

geluyur → KELUYUR.

gém – *kembang rose* small, round, frosted flour snack.

gema echo, reverberation, repercussion. – *duga* echo-finder.

bergema to echo, reverberate. *tak* ~ anechoic.

menggema to resound, echo, reverberate.

menggemai 1 to echo back. **2** to echo in.

menggemakan to make s.t. echo/resound/reverberate.

gemah (*Jv*) (of a country, etc.) prosperous, thriving. – *ripah* prosperous and populous. *kegemah-ripahan* affluence, prosperity. – *ripah loh jinawi* prosperous, rich, and fertile.

gemak I (*Jv*) female quail; → PUYUH I.

gemak II (*M*) → GAMAK.

gemal segemal a handful (of paddy).

bergemal-gemal in handfuls/bunches/bundles.

menggemal to hold (a bunch, etc.) in the hand.

gemala (*Skr*) bezoar stone found in snakes, dragons. – *hikmat* magic bezoar.

gemalai → GEMULAI.

gemam → GUMAM.

gemampang (*Jv*) to take things easy, irresponsible, apt to take things too lightly.

geman to be afraid, frightened.

menggemani to be afraid of.

penggeman coward.

gemang I squat and thick; barrel-shaped.

gemang II (*M*) nervous, scared, afraid.

penggemang coward.

gémang *ikan* – k.o. catfish, *Plotosus anguillaris. ikan* – *darat* k.o. catfish, *Silurichthys phaiosoma.*

gemap tergemap taken aback, thunderstruck, dumbfounded.

gemar – *akan* to take pleasure in, be fond of, delight in. – *akan makanan Éropah* to like European food. – *lekas menémbak* trigger-happy.

bergemar to be happy/pleased/delighted; to enjoy/amuse o.s., rejoice, be glad.

menggemari to like very much, be very fond of.

menggemarkan to make s.o. happy, please, pleasing, delightful, satisfactory.

kegemaran 1 hobby, likes. **2** habit. ~ *membaca* reading habit. **3** pleasure, delight. **4** fashion.

penggemar lover, fan, devotee, aficionado. ~ *berat batu pirus* a lover of turquoise. ~ *kesenian* art lover. ~ *perangko* philatelist. ~ *sandiwara* theater-goer. ~ *sulap* magic fan.

pergemaran (*ob*) pleasure, diversion, amusement.

gemas (*J*) **1** annoyed, irritated. *Dia merasa* – *apabila melihat orang memukul pengemis itu.* He felt annoyed at seeing s.o. hit the beggar. **2** sick of, fed up with. **3** to get carried away (by feelings), moved emotionally to do s.t. physical; → GEMES. *Sangat* – *aku melihat bayi yang mungil itu.* I get carried away when I see that cute baby (I could eat him up).

menggemaskan [and **gemasin** (*J*)] **1** to irritate, annoy, arouse anger; frustrating, getting on one's nerves. **2** provocative.

kegemasan 1 annoyance, nuisance, irritation, aggravation, vexation. ~ *hati* anger. **2** strong feelings.

gemati (*Jv*) careful, solicitous, caring.

menggematéni to consider s.t. important/necessary.

gemaung echoing, reverberating, humming; → GAUNG I.

gemawan flying clouds. *awan putih* – fleeting white clouds.

gembak → GOMBAK.

gembala I (*Skr*) **1** herdsman. **2** tamer. **3** shepherd, pastor; pastoral (letter). – *anjing* dog-boy. – *ayam* poultry-tender. – *gajah* mahout. – *kambing* goatherd. – *kuda* groom. – *onta* camel driver. – *pintu* gatekeeper. – *rajawali* (*ob*) falconer. – *sapi* cowherd. – *singa* lion-tamer.

bergembala to have a shepherd.

menggembala to guide, lead, direct. *Dia* ~ *pikiran rakyat ke jurusan toleransi.* He led the people's thoughts in the direction of tolerance.

menggembalai and **menggembalakan 1** to herd, rear (animals). **2** to guide, tend (people). **3** to guide, tend.

kegembalaan being a herder/shepherd.

penggembala herder, s.o. who herds. ~ *bébék* boy who tends ducks. ~ *sapi* cowboy (also in the U.S.).

penggembalaan 1 (shep)herding. ~ *melénglang* nomadic herding. **2** *tanah* ~ grassland, pasture.

gembala II (in the names of birds that accompany certain animals). *burung – gajah* black magpie, *Platysmurus leucopterus. burung – kera* rail-babbler, *Eupetes macrocercus. Burung – kerbau* buffalo mynah, *Acridotheres fuscus torquatus. – pelanduk* green-breasted/hooded pitta, *Pitta sordida. – rimau* orange-breasted trogon, *Harpactes oreskios.*

gembar-gembor (to make) a big deal (of s.t.). *tanpa –* without fanfare. *-nya sala yang banyak, tetapi bukti pekerjaannya tak ada* much ado about nothing.

bergembar-gembor to cry out, brag.

menggembar-gemborkan 1 to trumpet forth, announce at the top of one's voice. **2** to crow over (one's successes). *tidak ~* to play down, not make a big deal out of.

penggembar-gemborkan trumpeting forth, announcing, crowing over.

gémbél I (*J*) wanderer, vagabond, tramp, drifter; panhandler, bum.

gémbél II (*J/Jv*) tangled (hair), with densely tangled hair.

gembeléng → GEMBLÉNG.

gembéng (*J/Jv*) to cry easily. *si –* crybaby.

gemberéng a small Chinese gong; → BERÉNG-BERÉNG.

gembil (*Jv*) fat, plump (of cheeks). *Pipinya –.* Her cheeks are plump.

gembili a) (*ubi –*) k.o. yam, *Coleus tuberosus. – belanda* potato; → KENTANG. b) (*Jv*) birch rind yam, *Dioscorea aculeata.*

gembira 1 excited, enthusiastic, exuberant, glad, happy, in a good mood, pleased. *dengan –.* *secara –* enthusiastically. *Ayah sungguh – karena ia berhasil memenangi hadiah pertama.* Dad was very pleased when he managed to win first prize. **2** cheerful, gay, festive. *malam –* festive evening/night. *naik –* to get excited. *– ria* great pleasure. **bergembira ria** to be overjoyed.

segembira as happy/overjoyed as.

bergembira to rejoice, be glad, be enthusiastic, have good time, enjoy o.s., have fun, cheer up. *Murid-murid ~ karena semuanya lulus dalam ujian.* The students rejoiced because all of them passed the exams.

menggembirai to cheer s.o. up.

menggembirakan 1 to make s.o. happy, gladden, gratify. *Pujian diberikan guru untuk ~ hati murid-muridnya.* The teacher praised the students to make them happy. **2** to satisfy, satisfying, satisfactory, gratifying, rewarding (experience), favorable. *Hasil pekerjaanmu cukup ~.* The results of your work are very satisfying. **3** to encourage, encouraging. **4** to enliven, make livelier.

mempergembira ~ *hati* to cheer (o.s.) up.

kegembiraan 1 joy, cheerfulness, high spirits. **2** happiness, pleasure.

penggembira 1 a cheerful person, cheerful. *Ia ~ dan selalu banyak tertawa.* She's a cheerful person and she always laughs very easily. **2** cheerleader. **3** person who is not an active participant (at a conference) or not a serious player (in sports).

gemblak I (*Jv*) catamite, a boy used in pederasty; → CAH *bagus.*

menggemblak to be a pederast, have homosexual relations (with other males).

gemblakan 1 homosexuality, pederasty, sodomy between males, *esp* as practiced by a man (*warok*) with a boy (*gemblak*). **2** catamite, boy who has sex with an older man; → WAROK II.

penggemblakan pederasty.

gemblak II (*Jv*) tinker, tinsmith, brass worker.

gembleng (*Jv*) **bergembleng** to unite, united; to join, joined.

tergembleng united, joined. *selama buruh belum ~ dalam suatu organisasi raksasa* as long as the workers are not united in a gigantic organization.

penggemblengan union, junction.

gembléng menggembléng 1 (*Jv*) to flatten, roll (metal). **2** to forge, weld; to train, educate, (undergo tough) training. *Para taruna itu sudah digembléng.* The cadets have been through the mill. **3** to steel, harden.

menggembléngkan to gather (all one's forces).

tergembléng hardened, forged.

gembléngan 1 hardened. **2** forging, training. **3** s.o. that has undergone training.

penggembléng trainer, forger, uniter.

penggembléngan forging, tough training.

gemblep (*Jv*) chubby-cheeked.

gemblok (*Jv*) padlock; → GEMBOK.

menggemblok to lock (with a padlock).

gémblok (*Jv*) **menggémbloki** to cling to.

gemblokan (*J*) k.o. Betawi theater.

gemblong (*J*) snack made of smashed (steamed) glutinous rice or cassava.

gemblung I (*Jv*) not in one's right mind, not quite right in one's head.

gemblung II (*S*) big-bellied, corpulent.

gembok (*Jv*) padlock. *– pasak* mortise lock.

bergembok to be provided with a padlock, padlocked. *pintu besi ~* a padlocked iron door.

menggembok to lock (with a padlock), padlock.

tergembok padlocked.

penggembok s.o. or s.t. that locks.

gémbol (*Jv*) **menggémbol** to carry with one (in a bag/pocket/clothes).

gémbolan parcel carried by s.o. in his/her sash.

gembolo (*Jv*) the larger variety of the *gembili.*

gembong I (*Jv*) *macan –* the Bengal/striped royal tiger. **2** cock of the walk, champion. **3** leader, leading/top figure, boss, big wheel. *– gerombolan* gang leader. *– politik* political big shot, politico.

menggémbongi to be the brains behind, be the ringleader of.

gembor I (*J*) large. *pisang –* a large banana.

gembor II (*Jv*) watering can.

gembor III → GEMBAR-GEMBOR. **menggemborkan** to make a lot of noise about s.t.

gembor-gemboran a big to-do, hullabaloo.

gembor IV k.o. tree, *Alseodaphne umbelliflora.*

gembos (*Jv*) **1** punctured, flat (of a tire). **2** deflated.

menggembos to go flat (of a tire).

menggemboskan 1 to deflate (a tire). **2** to reduce the number of votes gotten by a mass organization, etc. **3** to free from political pressure.

penggembos *kelompok ~* group which deflates the vote of another party.

penggembosan 1 deflation (used about the decrease in voting strength of the parties opposing *Golkar*, particularly of the PPP). **2** political decompression.

gembréng (*Jv*) **1** flat knobless Chinese gong, cymbals. **2** oil tin. *lampu –* hanging lamp (with tin screen).

menggembréng to clatter.

gembrobyos (*Jv?*) pouring out (of sweat).

gembrot (*J/Jv*) **1** bulky, ponderous. **2** slobby.

kegembrotan obesity, corpulence.

gembuk (*Jv*) black and blue (from a fight, etc.), skinned and bruised.

gembul I **1** gluttonous. *dengan –* greedily. **2** glutton.

gembul II full, plump (of figure).

kegembulan fullness, plumpness; distention (of stomach).

gembung 1 bloated (face), swollen (vein), puffed, chubby (of cheeks). *– perut* flatulence. **2** (*geol*) vesicle.

bergembung to be swollen, swell up. ~ *dada* to be proud, be puffed up with pride.

menggembung to increase, grow. *Gappri kini telah ~ menjadi "sepuluh besar".* Gappri has grown into one of the "big ten."

menggembungkan to blow up, inflate, puff up. ~ *dada* to puff out one's chest, put on airs.

tergembung set, spread (of sails).

gembungan swelling.

penggembungan inflating.

gembur I 1 loose (not tightly packed) (of soil), sandy (road), crumbly (of bread). **2** overripe, bruised (fruit); crumbling (of floury potatoes).

gembur-gembur *sakit –* dropsy; → BASAL.

menggembur to turn overripe, etc.

menggemburkan to loosen (the soil).

penggembur device to loosen.

penggemburan loosening (the soil).

gembur II (*onom*) roar(ing) (of a gun).

menggembur to roar.

gembus (*Jv*) a dish made from leftover bean cake.

gembut bergembut-gembut and menggembut to pulsate (of an infant's fontanel), go up and down (of turf under one's tread).

gemebyar (*Jv*) shiny; brightness.

gemedé (*Jv*) (also *gumedé*) prominent, wanting to shine, grandiose, haughty.

gemelai → GEMULAI.

gemelegar → GELEGAR I.

gemelentam (*onom*) banging (of guns/crackers/falling articles).

gemeletak (*onom*) chattering (of teeth).

bergemeletak to chatter.

gemeletap (*onom*) continuous tapping (of the fingers on table, etc.).

bergemeletapan to keep on tapping.

gemeletik (*onom*) pinging.

gemeletuk → GELETUK.

gemelugut shivering (with cold/ague/fear); → GELUGUT.

gementam (*onom*) banging (of guns), sound of slamming.

gementar shaking (from cold/ague/fear), trembling all over; → GENTAR. *badan – kedinginan* shivering with cold.

gemerasak (*onom*) cracking (of the ice), squeaking (of boots).

gemercak (*onom*) splash of oars or paddles.

gemerecik (*onom*) spattering.

bergemerecik to spatter.

gemerecing → GEMERENCING.

gemereget to be angry.

gemerencang (*onom*) clanging (of a sword/bell).

bergemerencang to clang.

gemerencik (*onom*) spattering, splattering, splashing.

gemerencing (*onom*) jingling (coins), tinkling (bangles).

bergemerencing to jingle, tinkle.

gemerencung (*onom*) clanging (as in a smithy).

gemerericik (*onom*) continual rustling or crackling.

gemeresak and gemeretak (*onom*) crackling of dry leaves. *- daun yang bergésékan* the crackling of leaves rubbing against e.o.

gemeresik and gemerisik (*onom*) sound of rustling or crackling.

bergemerisik to rustle.

gemeretak (*onom*) chattering sound.

menggemeretak to make s.t. chatter.

gemeretuk and gemeretup (*onom*) chattering sound.

gemerincing (*onom*) jingling sound.

bergemerincing to jingle.

gemerencingan jingling.

gemerisik → GEMERSIK.

gemerlap glittering, shimmering (eyes), sparkling (diamonds), flickering, twinkling (stars).

menggemerlapi to illuminate, decorate.

gemerlapan (*pl subj*) sparkling, shiny.

kegemerlapan glitter, shimmer, sparkle, twinkle.

gemerocok → GEMERCAK.

gemersik (*onom*) rustling (of paper, etc.).

gemersikan rustling.

gemertak (*onom*) pattering (rain), chattering (of teeth).

gemertap (*onom*) clattering, pattering (of rain).

gemertuk and gemertup → GELETUK.

gemerusuk (*onom*) rustling.

gemerutuk (*onom*) clatter; → GELETUK. *suara – rantai jangkar yang diturunkan* the clatter of the dropping of anchor chains.

gemes → GEMAS. *–nya!* You're/He's/She's so cute I could eat you/him/her up!

nggemesin 1 to annoy, irritate. 2 annoying, provocative.

gemetar and menggemetar to tremble/shake all over; → GETAR. *Badannya – karena diserang penyakit malaria.* He's shivering with malaria. *Tangannya – bila dia lapar.* His hands shake when he's hungry.

bergemetaran (*pl subj*) to tremble, shiver.

menggemetarkan to make s.t. tremble, make s.o. shiver.

gemetaran tremor.

gemi I *ikan* – k.o. remora or sucking fish, *Echineis naucrates*.

gemi II (*Jv*) –, *nastiti, lan ngati-ati* thrifty, thoughtful, and careful.

gemik (*M*) menggemik to beckon with the fingers to call s.o.

gemil (*J*) to want, be attracted to.

gemilang shining, dazzling, glittering; → GILANG *cemerlang/gemilang*.

segemilang as brilliant(ly) as.

kegemilangan glittering, radiance, luster.

penggemilangan glamorization.

gemilap lustrous; → GILAP.

géminasi (*D*) gemination.

geming (*J*) bergeming (nowadays frequently also *tak bergeming*) not move a limb/hair/eyelid, not raise/lift a finger, never move/budge, stay put. *Hatinya tak –.* He remained indifferent (when threatened).

nggeming to not move a bit.

kegemingan stubbornness.

tergeming stopped. *tak ~* unstoppable

Gémini (*D/E*) Gemini (the constellation).

gemintang star(s), constellation realm of stars.

geminte (*D col coq*) municipality.

gemirang cheerful, merry.

gemit → GAMIT.

gempa (*Skr*) (earth)quake, tremor. *Bandung digoyang –* Bandung was shaken by a tremor. *Kota Semarang digoncang –.* Semarang was hit by an earthquake. *– bumi* earthquake. *– (bumi) awal* foreshock. *– gelora* violent shaking. **menggempar-gelorakan** to shake s.t. *– kiamat* the final earthquake (that precedes the end of the world). *– pendahuluan* foreshock. *– susulan* aftershock. *– téktonik* tectonic quake. *– utama* main shock. *– vulkanik* volcanic quake.

bergempa to quake (of the earth).

menggempakan to shake, shock; to cause a quake.

kegempaan 1 quiver, vibration; seismic. 2 seismic. *daérah ~* seismic zoning.

pergempaan (*mod*) earthquake.

gempal I firm, strong, sturdy, stout, robust. *– kukuh* extremely strong, sturdy.

menggempal-gempalkan to contract (the muscles).

kegempalan sturdiness, firmness, solidity.

gempal II → GUMPAL.

gempar 1 bustle, hubbub, commotion, tumult, uproar. 2 tumultuous, uproarious, in a commotion/an uproar.

menggemparkan 1 to cause a commotion/stir, controversial. 2 sensational, shocking. 3 fantastic, terrific.

kegemparan tumult, stir, commotion, shock, uproar.

gempel (*J*) to stick/clump together, adhere.

gémpél (*Jv*) dried up and pasty.

gempét (*J*) menggempét to press down on.

gempil (*Jv*) chipped, damaged.

gempilan sliver, splinter.

gempita → GEGAP II *gempita*. menggempita to be loud/noisy/boisterous.

menggempitakan to sound loudly, make s.t. resound/thunder.

gemplok (*J*) bunch, bundle.

gempol (*S?*) k.o. tall tree, Leichhardt tree, *Nauclea cordatus/orientalis*.

gémpor (*J*) paralyzed, lame; broken. *Kakinya jadi – sehabis ketubruk.* His leg was fractured after the collision. *Skuter – énté bawain ke mari.* Bring your broken-down scooter here.

gempriang (*onom*) sound made by shattered glass.

bergempriang to make that sound. *Suara piring – karena dibanting ke lantai.* The sound a plate makes when smashed on the floor.

gempul-gempul to gasp (for breath), panting, puffing.

gempur menggempur 1 to attack, assault, assail. 2 to destroy, wreck, demolish. *~ musuh yang mendarat di pantai selatan* to attack the enemy who landed on the south coast.

gempur-menggempur to attack e.o.

tergempur attacked, assaulted.

gempuran attack, assault, charge. *~ musuh tak tertahankan* an attack which could not be resisted.

penggempur attacker, destroyer, s.o. who attacks and destroys. *pasukan –* shock troops.

penggempuran assault, attack, destruction, annihilation.

gemuk 1 fat, stout, plump, corpulent, obese. *bertambah –* to gain weight. **2** fertile, rich (of soil). *Tanaman ini subur karena tumbuh di tanah yang –.* This plant is prolific because it grows in fertile soil. **3** profitable, lucrative (of airline routes/government posts, etc.). *Garuda masih berkonséntrasi mengincar jalur-jalur –.* Garuda is still concentrating on targeting lucrative routes. *dubés pada pos yang –* an ambassador at a lucrative post. **4** suet, fat, grease. *Mesin ini membutuhkan – agar lancar berputar.* The engine needs grease so that it will run smoothly. **5** (*ob*) manure, fertilizer. *– gandar* axle grease. *– gembrok* fat slob. *– gempal* pleasingly plump, nicely rounded (of a girl). *– kimplah-kimplah* heavy set. *– lapis* slushing grease. *– lembék* flabby. *– padat* plump. *– perapat* (*petro*) dope. *– talek* tallow. *– terokmok* (*J*) chubby.

segemuk as fat as.

menggemuk 1 to grease, oil. **2** to become fat.

menggemuki to grease, lubricate, oil.

menggemukkan [and **nggemukin/ngegemukin** (*J coq*)] **1** to fatten (up), fertilize, manure. *industri ~ sapi* feedlot industry. **2** to be profitable/lucrative. **3** fattening.

mempergemuk (*~ diri*) **1** to fatten o.s. up, enrich o.s. **2** to gain weight.

tergemuk the fattest, etc.

kegemukan 1 fatness, obesity, corpulence. **2** greasiness. **3** to become fat/overweight, be too fat. *~ menyeluruh yang berlebihan* morbid obesity.

penggemuk fattening, fattening agent.

penggemukan 1 fattening up. **2** greasing, lubricating, oiling.

gemulai supple, flexible, pliant, waving, drooping, graceful (of body), swaying as of coconut fronds; → GEMALAI.

menggemulai to sway.

menggemulaikan to make s.t. sway back and forth.

gemuntai rolling, roll after roll (of breakers); → GULUNG.

bergemulung to roll (of crowds/breakers).

gemuntur thundering; → GUNTUR.

gemunung mountains; → GUNUNG.

gemuruh rolling (of thunder), rumble (of machines), roaring (of waters/a crowd); rushing (of blood from excitement); → GURUH.

bergemuruh and **menggemuruh** to roar, thunder, make a loud sound. *tepuk sorak bergemuruh* thunderous applause.

menggemuruhkan 1 to make s.t. make a thunderous noise. **2** to make s.t. rush (from excitement). *~ hati* highly exciting.

kegemuruhan uproar, tumult.

gén (*D/E*) gene. *– penekan* suppressor gene.

genah (*Jv*) proper, correct. *enggak/tidak –* not right, improper.

segenahnya properly, correctly.

menggenahkan to correct, straighten out.

genahar furnace for smelting metal, for boiling down sugar, etc. (not used for cooking).

genang – minyak oil slick.

bergenang 1 to stand (of pools of water in rice fields, etc.), be stagnant, not flowing (of water). *Nyamuk selalu bertelur dalam air yang ~.* Mosquitoes always lay eggs in stagnant water. **2** to trickle, drip, fall in drops (of tears).

menggenang 1 (*air*) *mata ~* (with) tears in one's eyes. **2** to drain water (to a lower level). **3** to flood, inundate.

menggenangi 1 to irrigate, water. **2** to inundate, flood.

menggenangkan to hold back (water) so that it doesn't flow.

tergenang 1 flooded. **2** welled up. *~ air mata* tears welled up.

tergenangi 1 *– air* flooded, inundated, deluged. *Sekitar 450 kilométer persegi wilayah Ibukota ~ air.* Around 450 square kilometers of the area of the capital were inundated. **2** covered with tears. *mata ~* eyes glistening with tears.

genangan 1 pool, puddle. *~ air* puddle of water. *~ air mata* welling up of tears. *~ darah* blood bath. **2** inundation. **3** calm.

kegenangan flooded, inundated.

penggenangan 1 irrigation. **2** deluge, flood, overflow (of water), inundation.

genap 1 exact, enough, sufficient, as much/many as is necessary. *Setelah menimbang – sekati ia pun membungkus kentang itu.* After weighing exactly a kati he wrapped up the potatoes. *– berumur 18* exactly 18 years old. *– 200 tahun* a full 200 years. *hidup dengan segala –* to have everything one needs. *telah – bulannya* a full-term baby (of nine months). *– setahun yang lalu* exactly a year ago. **2** even, not odd (of numbers). **3** completely, fully, totally. *rézim yang tumbang – sudah* a regime which has been completely overthrown. *masuk tak –, keluar tak ganjil* an insignificant person, a nobody. *dibilang – dipapar ganjil* calculated in passing it's a profit, but after checking it's a loss. *empat gasal, lima – (M)* "(with him) four is odd and five is even," i.e., you never know what he's going to say. *sudah –* everyone's here (of a group of people gathering together).

segenap 1 each and every. *~ kali* every time. **2** all, entire. *~ hadirin bertepuk tangan.* the entire audience applauded. **3** even, even in number.

menggenapi 1 to complete the number. *Baik kita genapi supaya menjadi dua puluh.* We should make it complete by making it come to 20. **2** to increase so that it's enough, complete. *untuk ~ pesanan-pesanan yang telah saya terima* to complete the orders that I received.

menggenapkan 1 to make up the numbers, complete. **2** to make s.t. even.

kegenapan completeness, fullness.

penggenap complementary, supplementary; complement.

penggenapan (mostly in religious contexts) fulfillment, consummation.

gencar 1 incessant, sustained, repeated, unbroken (in length/of volleys), nonstop (of shelling, etc.), unending. **2** violent, vehement, fierce, intensive.

menggencar 1 to become incessant. **2** to become violent.

menggencarkan 1 to keep on doing s.t. without stop. **2** to intensify.

mempergencar to intensify, do s.t. again and again.

gencaran violent movement.

kegencaran vehemence, violence, intensity.

gencar-gencarnya incessantly, keep on.

gencat 1 suspended, stopped, ceased. **2** stunted (in growth).

bergencatan to cease. *~ senjata* to lay down one's arms, declare a cease-fire. *Selagi orang sibuk dengan wereng cokelat, rupanya kutu loncat enggan ~ senjata.* While people are busy with the cocoa pest, it seems that the *kutu loncat* doesn't want to declare a cease-fire.

menggencat to suspend, stop, cease. *~ senjata* to cease firing.

tergencat suspended, stopped, ceased, halted.

gencatan cessation. *~ perang/senjata* cease-fire, truce, armistice.

penggencatan putting a stop to, halting.

géncél I 1 tassels. **2** counter for lengths of rope.

géncél II (*Jv*) rest, remainder.

gencer → GENCAR.

gencét (*J*) **menggencét 1** to squeeze (from both sides), flatten out, press flat, crush. *Pegulat itu ~ lawannya sehingga tak dapat bergerak sama sekali.* The wrestler pressed his opponent down so that he was completely unable to move. **2** to keep down, oppress, suppress. **3** to treat s.o. unfairly, discriminate against.

tergencét 1 squeezed, pressed, oppressed. *Rakyat yang ~ oléh penjajah.* The people were oppressed by the colonizers. **2** in a tight spot. **3** pinned down.

gencétan 1 squeeze, pressure. **2** oppression. **3** buckling.

gencét-gencétan to oppress.

penggencétan 1 squeezing, pressure. **2** oppression, suppression. **3** unfair treatment, discrimination.

géncét (*J*) grown together (of two fingers/bananas, etc.). *pisang –* two bananas grown together; → PISANG démpét.

gencir to slip, skid; → GELINCIR.

gendaga → KENDAGA.

gendak (*J*) lover (of either sex); mistress; → KENDAK. *melakukan –* to commit adultery.

bergendak(an) to have a lover/mistress, have an affair (with).

bergendakkan to have ... as a lover.

menggendaki to have a love affair with.

gendakan lover.

pergendakan concubinage.

gendala (*Skr*) → KENDALA.

gendam (*Jv*) a charm, magic spell. *tukang* – hypnotist. – *pengasihan* love potion, a magic spell to make s.o. fall in love.

menggendam to cast a spell (on); to cause a miracle to happen.

gendaman charm, magic spell.

gendang I kettledrum. *menitir* – to beat a drum with swift rapping motions. *bagaimana bunyi* –, *begitulah tarinya* and *bagaimana bunyi* –*nya, begitulah tepuk tarinya* to dance to s.o. else's tune. – *Batak* name given to certain instruments of the monochord and primitive zither type. – *hati* inspiration, inner voice. – *keling* drum (both sides of which are beaten by the drummer). – *kembang* two-sided drum. – *meléla* drum (one side of which is beaten with the hand and the other with a drumstick). – *nadi* beat of the pulse. – *pendengar* tympanum, eardrum, tympanic membrane. – *perang* war drum. – *raya* large drum used to summon people to mosque; → BEDUK. – *suling* drum and fife. – *serama* → GENDANG *meléla*. – *telinga* eardrum.

gendang-gendang membrane.

segendang ~ *sepenarian* of the same mind/opinion.

bergendang to (beat a) drum. ~ *lutut* to sit around idly. ~ *paha* to feel schadenfreude, malicious pleasure in s.o. else's troubles. ~ *tangan* to clap one's hands in rhythm with the music.

menggendangi to drum on.

gendangan membrane.

gendang II segendang a roll (of paper, etc.).

gendang-gendis k.o. vegetable that grows in underbrush.

gendar a Central Java delicacy made from rice; → KERAK *gendar*.

gendari (*mil*) service standard of a high-ranking official of the armed forces.

géndél (*Jv*) *penyakit* – trematode.

gendeng I (*Jv*) crazy, not in one's right mind.

gendeng II *roda* – flywheel.

géndéng (*M*) oblique, slanting, inclined. – *éréng* various tricks. *tabu di léréng dan* – wise, quick to understand s.o.'s sarcasm. – *rénténg* a credit system in which the delinquent part becomes the joint responsibility of the entire group of peasants.

bergéndéng to stand at an angle.

bergéndéng-géndéngan to stand close to e.o., not in line.

menggéndéng to stand at an angle.

menggéndéngkan to slant s.t., (cause to) incline.

tergéndéng inclined, slanting.

gendér (*Jv*) *gamelan* instrument, xylophone with bronze keys suspended over bamboo sounding tubes.

génder (*E*) gender.

genderang war-drum, state/processional drum; → GENDANG. *Golkar tidak akan menari dengan* – *orang lain*. Golkar will not dance to another party's tune.

génderisasi genderization.

gendéwa (*Jv*) bow (for shooting arrows).

gendi → KENDI I.

gending (*Jv*) melody (of *gamelan*). – *sriwijaya* a court dance (of Palembang).

gendir → GENDÉR.

gendis k.o. tree, *Aphanamixis grandifolia*.

gendit → KENDIT.

gendola Ceylon/Malabar spinach, *Basella rubra*.

gendon I k.o. maggots found in the remains of rattan, etc.

gendon II (*Jv*) edible soft inner skin of the areca palm.

géndong *kuli* – porter.

menggéndong 1 to carry (children/*jamu* bottles by female *jamu* vendors, etc.) on the back or hip. **2** (*vulg*) to fuck, screw.

menggéndongkan 1 to hang s.t. (in a sling/scarf, etc.). **2** to carry for s.o.

géndongan 1 burden, s.t. carried on the back or hip. **2** carrying cloth.

penggéndong carrier. ~ *jamu* a woman who peddles medicinal herbs.

géndong II segéndongan ¹/₁₂ of the entire estate in the form of land.

géndot name of a *ceki* card.

gendruwo (*Jv*) ghost, *esp* a garden/forest spirit that manifests itself by throwing stones and other objects on the roofs of houses, by spitting at or spattering s.o., an animal, or other objects with red sirih-juice, by knocking on doors and windows, or by shaking them.

genduk (*Jv*) little girl; unmarried adolescent girl (as a term of address *usu* shortened to *nduk*).

gendut 1 with a big belly, paunchy. **2** pregnant. **3** well-lined (purse); to have plenty of money, be well heeled.

segendut as big-bellied/paunchy as.

menggendut to swell up.

menggenduti to make s.t. swell up.

menggendutkan 1 to fatten s.t. **2** to fill s.t. up. ~ *kantong sendiri* to line one's own pockets.

kegendutan 1 paunchiness, corpulence. **2** too fat.

généalogi (*D/E*) genealogy.

généalogis (*D*) genealogical.

généng (*M*) spoiled; fine, handsome, beautiful.

généralis (*D/E*) generalist.

généralisasi (*E*) generalization.

menggénéralisasikan to generalize.

penggénéralisasian generalization, generalizing. ~ *terhadap buku-buku terjemahan bukankah sesuatu yang gegabah?* Isn't it rash to generalize about translated books?

généralisir (*D*) **menggénéralisir** to generalize.

générasi (*D*) generation; → ANGKATAN. – '45 and – *empat-lima* the generation of 1945, i.e., (a) the freedom fighters who spearheaded the revolution prior to the proclamation of independence on August 17, 1945; (b) the group of authors and artists who emerged around that time. – *muda* the younger generation, teenagers. – *penerus* a) the next generation. b) the successor generation, i.e., the second generation after the revolution. – *taruna* the younger generation. – *tua* older generation. – *wreda* the older generation.

segénérasi of the same generation. *kawan-kawan* ~*nya* her peers.

génératif (*D/E*) generative, pertaining to the production of offspring.

génerator (*D/E*) generator.

générik (*E*) generic. *nama/obat* – a generic name/medicine.

génésis (*D/E*) genesis, origin, creation, beginning.

génetif (*D/E gram*) (the) genitive (case).

génétik (*E*) and **génetis** (*D*) genetic. *cacat* – a genetic defect/deformity.

génétika (*D*) genetics. *ahli* – geneticist. *skrining* – genetic screening.

géng (*E*) gang.

genggam 1 fist. **2** jaw, clamp (in names of tools). – *kera* held onto for dear life. – *tangan* a) vice clamp. b) stingy, tight-fisted. **3** handful. **4** hand-held.

segenggam a handful. *beras/kacang* ~ a handful of rice/peanuts. ~ *kecil* a little bit. – *digunungkan, setitik dilautkan* very much appreciated.

bergenggam-genggam in handfuls, by the handful.

bergenggaman ~ *tangan* hand in hand.

menggenggam 1 to grasp, clutch, seize/hold in the fist. ~ *rahasia* to keep a secret. ~ *tangan* to clench one's fist. ~ *erat membuhul mati* to keep one's promise/word/pledge. ~ *tak tirus* a miser. *digenggam tiada tirus* very thrifty. *seperti* ~ *bara terasa hangat dilepaskan* to try a job, and, when it's not to one's liking, to leave it and look for another. *digenggam takut mati, dilepaskan takut terbang* said of s.o. who has a girlfriend who's very young, still too young to marry. ~ *tangan* tight-fisted. **2** to control, rule, govern.

menggenggami (*pl obj*) to grasp, clutch, etc.

menggenggamkan to clench (one's fingers or fist). *Anak itu* ~ *tangannya menahan kemarahan*. The child clenched his fists trying to suppress his anger. ~ *ke tangan* to put into s.o.'s hand.

tergenggam 1 grasped, clutched, gripped. *barang* ~ *terlepas* s.t. already possessed is lost again (i.e., to suffer a loss). **2** controlled, ruled, governed.

genggaman 1 fistful, handful. **2** grip, might, control, clutches. *sudah dalam* ~ *pemeras, dll.* already in the grip of blackmailers, etc.

penggenggam 1 clamp, fastener. **2** holder (of power, etc.).

penggenggaman grasping, gripping.

genggang 1 cleft, chink, crack, fissure, crevice, slit. **2** ajar, slightly open; → GANGGANG II.
  tergenggang to be ajar (of a door, etc.).
génggang (*E?*) *kain* – a striped fabric, gingham.
génggong k.o. Jew's harp made of bamboo.
géngsi (*A*) **1** prestige, honor, social status. *demi* – for effect. *turun* – to lose one's prestige. **2** descent, relations, relatives. *membanggakan ketinggian –nya* to be proud of one's descent.
  bergéngsi prestigious. *univérsitas yang ~ tinggi* a high-prestige university.
géngsot and **bergéngsot** to dance (in the western style). *main* – to play around (with prostitutes).
géngster (*E*) gangster.
génial (*D*) genius.
  kegénialan geniality.
génialitas geniality.
genih and **genis I** the teeth in a cow-elephant corresponding to the tusks in the male.
genis II (*ob*) → GENIT.
genit coquettish, flirtatious, alluring, cute.
  menggenit to act coquettishly, etc.
  menggenitkan to make (o.s.) act coquettishly, etc.
  genit-genitan *main* – to flirt, act coquettishly.
  kegenitan coquetry, coquettishness.
génital (*D/E*) genital.
génitalia (*L*) genitals. – *wanita* female genitals.
génitif (*D/E gram*) genitive.
génius (*E*) genius.
génjah (*Jv*) **penggénjah** quick-ripening (paddy).
génjang 1 awry, crooked, aslant. **2** parallelogram. – *génjot/génjut* all awry, zigzag.
genjé (*S*) **1** k.o. Indian herb; → GANJA II. **2** *pohon* – k.o. shrub, *Clerodendron indicum*.
génjér (*J*) water lettuce (*esp* on irrigated rice fields), eaten as vegetable, *Limnocharis flava*.
Génjér-Génjér the PKI anthem.
genjik (*Jv*) **1** young pig, piglet (of wild boar). **2** you pig! (term of abuse).
genjlong (*Jv onom*) pounding noise.
  menggenjlong to fall with a bang.
  menggenjlongkan to drop s.t. that makes a pounding noise.
genjot (*J*) **menggenjot 1** to pedal a bike/pedicab, etc. **2** to strike hard, attack. **3** to work (a foot-operated sewing machine, etc.). **4** to intensify (one's efforts in studying/working). **5** to trouble s.o. **6** to stimulate. **7** to wolf down, eat up.
  menggenjotkan to pedal for s.o. else.
  genjotan stroke, kick, attack.
  penggenjot ~ (*pédal*) *bécak* pedicab driver.
  penggenjotan stimulating, encouraging.
génjot *génjang-génjot* awry; → GÉNJANG.
genjréng (*Jv*) (*onom*) the sound of metal clanging, clink; → KONTAN I, TUNAI. *dibayar* – to be paid cash.
  genjréng-genjréng ~ *pegang sitar* to strum/twang a guitar.
genjrét *lari* – to take suddenly to one's heels.
genjring (*Jv*) (small) tambourine.
genjrit → GENJRÉT I.
genjur stiff (of hair, leaves); → KEJUR I.
génsét (*E*) [*génerator sét*] generator set.
génsi → GÉNGSI. *Di Indonésia kata perempuan itu –nya merosot dramatis.* In Indonesia the prestige of the word *perempuan* has declined drastically.
genta (*Skr*) **1** large (church) bell. *anak* – clapper. **2** cattle-bell. – *bahaya* alarm. – *geréja* church bell. – *tangan* handheld bell. – *suara* echoing voice.
  bergenta to ring (out).
gentak (*ob*) → ENTAK.
gentala (*Skr?*) a magic wheeled car. *naga* – a fabled dragon of monstrous size.
gentar 1 vibration, quivering, quiver. **2** shiver (with cold or fear); fear, afraid. *tak* – fearless, undaunted; → GETAR.
  bergentar and **menggentar** to vibrate, quiver, tremble.
  menggentarkan 1 (= **menggentari** and **mempergentari**) to ter-

rify, terrorize; terrifying. **2** to make s.o. tremble/shiver. *Ancamannya itu tidak dapat ~ aku.* His threats couldn't make me tremble. **3** to make s.t. vibrate.
  gentaran jitter, dither.
  kegentaran 1 vibration. **2** fright, shivers.
  penggentar 1 terrorist. **2** terrifying. **3** coward.
  penggentaran 1 terror. **2** vibration. **3** deterrence.
gentas 1 plucked off (flowers), broken off (a stalk). **2** over, ended, past. *Musim durian tahun ini sudah* –. This year's durian season has ended.
  menggentas to pluck off, break off.
gentat (*cla*) dented (as a bad lemon/plum), shrunk (at one side).
gentayangan (*J*) (= **bergentayangan**) to roam about, wander aimlessly. *Meréka itu dituduh bersekongkol dengan agén KBG hingga bébas – di semua ruang rahasia di sana.* They were accused of conspiring with agents of the KBG and so they were free to roam about in top-secret places there.
géntél pill, pellet.
  menggéntél(i) to roll (s.t. into a pill) in one's fingertips.
genténg (roof-)tile. *atap* – tiled roof. – *berombak* corrugated tile. – *kodok* k.o. thick, strong tile.
  menggenténg(i) to tile, cover with tiles.
  pergenténgan imbrication.
genténgisasi tiling of roofs.
genter → GENTAR.
gentét (*J*) **menggentét** to open up.
géntét (*J*) **segéntét** a bundle/package.
genting I 1 narrow/small in the middle; slender; neck (of a bottle). – *tanah* isthmus. **2** pass, narrow way over or through mountains/ hills. **3** critical, tense, precarious, endangered (of species). – *menanti putus, biang menanti témbak* (*M*) a case which is almost solved. – *putus, biang tembus* (*M*) a case which has been solved or definitely decided. – *senting* hair-splitting. **4** frayed, thinning.
  menggenting 1 to become small/narrow/precarious. **2** to become critical/tense.
  menggentingkan 1 to narrow down, make smaller/tighter/ more critical. **2** to make s.t. critical/tense.
  gentingan isthmus.
  kegentingan 1 crisis, critical situation, emergency. **2** to overact, exaggerate.
  pegentingan isthmus.
  penggentingan making s.t. critical/tense.
genting II → GENTÉNG.
gento (*Jv*) bandit.
gentong (*J/Jv*) earthen pitcher for keeping a supply of water, *beras*, etc. handy. – *pendaringannya mulai miring* he could no longer make ends meet.
gentur (*Jv*) persevering (in asceticism/meditation).
gentus (*J*) **1** push, shove. **2** angry, hurtful, sharp words.
  ngegentus to push, shove.
  gentusan 1 push, shove. **2** (in soccer) head-ball.
génus (*D/E*) genus.
gényéh menggényéh to rub, massage.
gényot oblique, slanting, sloping.
géoarkéologi (*D/E*) geoarcheology.
géodési (*D*) **1** geodesy. **2** geodetic. – *fisik* physical geodesy.
géo-ékologi (*D/E*) geo-ecology.
géofisik (*E*) and **géofisis** (*D*) geophysical.
géofisika geophysics.
géofisikawan geophysicist.
géograf (*D*) geographer.
géografi (*D/E*) geography. – *ékonomi dan sosial* socioeconomic geography.
géografis (*D*) geographical.
géokimia geochemistry.
géol (*S*) **bergéol** and **menggéol** to sway, swing (of women walking and twitching their hips).
géolog (*D*) geologist.
géologi (*D/E*) geology.
géologis (*D*) geological.
géologi(a)wan male geologist.

géologi(a)wati female geologist.
géomagnétik (*E*) geomagnetic.
géomansia (*E*) geomancy; → FÉNG SHUI.
géométri (*D/E*) geometry. *ahli* – geometrician. – *diferénsial* differential geometry.
géométrik (*E*) and **géométris** (*D*) geometrical.
géomorfologi (*D/E*) geomorphology.
géonomi (*D/E*) geonomy.
géopolitik (*D/E*) geopolitics. *ahli* – geopolitician.
géopolitis geopolitical.
géosains (*E*) geoscience. – *laut* marine geoscience.
géoséntris (*D*) geocentric.
géosfér (*D/E*) geosphere.
géososiologi (*D/E*) geosociology
géostasionér (*D*) geostationary.
géostratégis (*D*) geostrategical.
géotéknologi (*D/E*) geotechnology.
géotéktonik (*E*) and **géotéktonis** (*D*) geotectonic.
géotérmal (*E*) geothermal.
géotérmis (*D*) geothermic.
gepai → GAPAI.
gépak (*J*) a kick.
   menggépak to kick.
gepar → GELEPAR.
gépéng I (*J/Jv*) flat (because squeezed between two surfaces), skinny; → PIPIH.
   menggépéngkan to flatten s.t.
gépéng II [gelandangan dan pengemis] homeless drifters and panhandlers.
gepit (*Jv*) **menggepit** to squeeze. ~ *rokok* to squeeze a cigarette; → JEPIT.
geplak I (*J*) a sugar-coated snack of rice flour and grated coconut.
geplak II (*onom*) slap! flap! smack! bang!
gepok (*J*) bundle, sheaf.
   segepok a bundle, sheaf, wad. ~ *album* a bunch of albums. ~ *uang* a wad of money.
   bergepok-gepok in bundles/piles/wads, bundles and bundles (of).
geprak (*J*) **menggeprak** to hit (with a *sapu lidi*/punting pole, etc.).
geprok → GEPOK.
gepuk I (*M*) fat, plump (of children).
gepuk II (*Jv*) **menggepuk** to hit, beat.
gepuk III (*S*) and **gepuk-gepuk** k.o. *empal daging*.
gepyok (*Jv*) **nggepyok** to hit, whack, thresh.
   penggepyok thresher. – *padi* thresher of unhusked rice; → PERONTOK *padi*.
ger- also see entries beginning with **ger-**.
ger I (in acronyms) → GERAKAN.
ger II (*Jv*) ha-ha-ha (interjection indicating loud laughter). *mengundang* – *seluruh pengunjung* to make the visitors laugh.
   ger-geran to roar with laughter.
gera menggera to frighten s.o., chase away.
   penggera s.o. or s.t. that frightens/startles. ~ *burung* scarecrow.
gerabah (*Jv*) earthenware, crockery.
gerabak I (*ob*) → GERABANG.
gerabak II (*M*) **menggerabak** to flow (of tears).
   menggerabakkan to shed (tears).
gerabak III (*J onom*) clattering noise. – *gerubuk* a) clattering, clatter. b) to do s.t. rashly.
gerabang torn, tattered, with large holes in it.
geracak → GERECAK.
geradah → GELÉDAH.
geradi (*Port ob*) iron grating.
geragai hook for catching crocodiles.
   menggeragai to catch (crocodiles with this hook).
geragal (*Jv*) → KERAKAL.
geragap (*Jv*) a sudden start (*esp* from sleep).
   menggeragap and **geragapan 1** to act flustered/startled. *Saya* ~ *bangun*. I was startled from sleep. **2** (to look) bewildered, perplexed. **3** to have trouble speaking because of nervousness. **4** to grope around.

geragas I menggeragas to tear at one's hair with one's fingers or a comb in anger or excitement, run one's fingers through one's hair; to claw at, paw.
geragas II (*Jv*) **nggeragas** gluttonous, eat too much.
geragau I menggeragau to sprawl, flounder about.
geragau II *udang* – small shrimps, *Mysis sp.*, from which *trasi/belacan* or fish-paste is made.
geragau III (*Mal*) *Encik* – derisive nickname for Portuguese Eurasians.
geragih runner (of a plant).
geragot → GRAGOT.
geragu(k) (*ob*) → GERAGAU II.
gerah I (*J/Jv*) **1** feverish. **2** hot, stifling heat, sultry.
   gerahan trouble, difficulty.
   kegerahan 1 to suffer from stifling heat (due to threatening rain). **2** mugginess. **3** to get angry.
gerah II → GERUH *gerah*.
geraham molar. – *bungsu/déwasa* wisdom tooth.
gerai I (*cla*) bridal dais.
gerai II 1 (*Mal*) **1** stall, small open-fronted shop, table, etc. used for selling things, counter. **2** retail outlet.
gerai III menggerai to dig, bore, excavate.
   penggerai gimlet, drill.
gerai IV (*M*) loosened (of hair), hanging down loosely.
   bergerai to hang down loosely.
   menggerai to make s.t. wave to and fro.
   menggeraikan to let down/loosen one's hair.
   tergerai hanging-down/unloosened (of hair). *rambutnya yang* ~ *bébas* her hair, which was hanging down freely.
gerak 1 movement. *tenaga* – kinetic energy. – *batin/hati* impulse, intuition, presentiment. **2** twitch (of one's eyelid/lips/shoulder, etc. considered formerly as an omen/sign/indication). – *badan* physical exercise, gymnastics, calisthenics. – *balik* withdrawal. **bergerak balik** to withdraw. – *bangkit* upward movement. – *batin* inspiration. – *bolak-balik* alternating movements, reciprocating (engine). – *cepat* a) lightning speed. b) quick reaction. – *gempa* a) earth tremor. b) a hair ornament which shakes when the wearer moves. – *gerik* a) movements. b) gestures. c) steps. – *geriknya mencurigakan* his movements were suspicious. **menggerak-gerikkan** to move, make (movements/gestures), take (steps). – *harga* price fluctuation. – *hati* inner feeling. – *jalan* a) hike, long march. b) race walking. – *jalan beranting* relay march. – *kaki* footwork. – *lakuan* acting. – *langkah* a) gesture, motion, movement. b) conduct, behavior, comportment. *sebagai penyemangat* – *langkah bangsa dan Pemuda Pelajar Indonésia di masa perang kemerdékaan* as a stimulant for the conduct of the Indonesian nation and Student Youth during the struggle for independence. – *lembung* (*mil*) envelopment. – *lintas alam* cross-country march. – *maju* (*mil*) approach. – *mata* twitch. – *mundur* (*mil*) withdrawal, disengagement. **bergerak mundur** to withdraw. – *putar* rotary/circular motion. – *rasa* presentiment. – *surut* ebb tide. – *tangan* gesture. – *tipu* trick move (in sports). – *torak* piston stroke. – *tubuh* gesture.
gerak-gerak *sudah ada* ~*nya* there are (positive) indications/signs.
   bergerak 1 to move, change position, be in motion. *Pengemis itu* ~ *dari satu tempat ke tempat yang lain untuk meminta sedekah.* The beggar moved from place to place asking for alms. *barang* ~ personal property/estate, chattel. *Barang tidak* ~ immovable property, real estate (property). *Jangan* ~! Don't move! Freeze! ~ *maju/mundur* to advance/retreat. *bagai* ~ *bumi Allah* shocked. ~ *naik* to move up, rise. **2** to move (off/onto). *Selepas memberkas barang-barangnya maka* ~*lah dia ke bandar udara Soekarno-Hatta.* After packing up his things, he moved on to Soekarno-Hatta Airport. **3** to operate, run. *Persatuan itu hanya dapat* ~ *dengan adanya derma-derma yang dikumpulkan.* The association can only operate with the contributions that it collects. **4** to engage/be active (in a business), go into action. *Hanya ada dua perusahaan yang* ~ *dalam bisnis tersebut.* Only two companies are engaged in that business. **5** mobile. *télékomunikasi* ~ mobile telecommunications.
   bergerak-gerak *hatinya* ~ *untuk* he feels inclined to, he'd like to.

menggerakkan 1 to move, set/put in motion, drive, actuate, power. *Sampai sekarang ia belum dapat ~ kakinya.* He is still unable to move his legs. *~ hati* a) moving, touching, pathetic. b) irritating. **2** to stimulate, motivate, activate, induce (s.o. to do s.t.). *~ invéstasi di Indonésia* to stimulate investment in Indonesia.

tergerak set/put in motion, moved, affected. *~ (di) hati* got an idea/impulse. *~ hati* a) to want, desire; impulsive. b) to be touched/moved/affected/agitated/excited. *~ hatinya* impressed by, felt drawn to. *~ juga hatiku oléh kata-katanya yang halus dan sopan itu.* I also felt affected by his gentle and polite words.

tergerakkan set in motion.

gerakan 1 movement, motion, travel (of part of a tool). *~ Acéh Merdéka* [GAM] Achehnese Freedom Movement. *~ badan* physical exercise. *~ (di) bawah tanah* resistance movement, underground. *~ bibir* lip movements. *Saya dapat membaca ~ bibirnya.* I can read his lips. *~ kebangsaan* nationalist movement. *~ Kebébasan Wanita* Women's Lib. *~ Kiri Baru* New Left. *~ lonjak* heaving. *~ Mahasiswa Nasional Indonésia* [GMNI] Indonesian National College Students Movement. *~ maju* (mil) advance. *~ maju musuh* (mil) hostile advance. *~ memisah* separatism. *- oléng* roll, rolling motion. *~ operasi militér* (various) military operations of the Indonesian Army to crush internal uprisings. *~ pasukan* troop movement. *~ Pengacau Keamanan* [GPK] troublemakers (euphemism for separatist movements). *~ Rakyat Indonésia* [Gerindo] Indonesian People's Movement. *~ Séptémber 30* [Gestapu] the leftist coup of the September 30 (1969) movement. *~ Wanita Indonésia* [Gerwani] Indonesian Women's Movement. *~ Zionis* Zionist movement. **2** activity, action.

penggerak 1 motor. **2** mover, initiator, motivating force. **3** pacemaker. **4** drive (of engine), actuator. *~ mula* prime mover. *~ pembangunan* agent of development. *~ utama* prime mover. *~ empat roda* four-wheel drive. *~ roda belakang* rear-wheel drive. *~ roda depan* front-wheel drive.

penggerakan activation, activating, drive, driving. *~ kekuatan rakyat* activation of people's strength.

pergerakan movement. *~ politik* political movement. **sepergerakan** belonging to the same movement. *saudara ~* friend in the same movement.

Gerakhas Malaysia's Special Forces.

geram I (*Pers*) **1** furious, angry. **2** (*ob*) passionate.
menggeram to become furious.
menggeramkan 1 to make s.o. furious/angry, infuriate. **2** to arouse s.o.'s passions.
geraman fury, anger.
kegeraman rage, fury, anger.

geram II (*onom*) growling sound.
menggeram to growl.

geraman → GERAHAM.

geramang (*Jv*) *semut* - red ant, *Formica sanguinea*.

gerami → GURAMI.

geramsut (*A*) cloth from which Arab zouave jackets are made.

geranat → GRANAT.

gerang burnt coconut husk and oil used for blackening teeth.
menggerang to blacken the teeth with this substance.

gérang → BÉRANG.

gerangan -ever, it is possible that (mark of doubt/uncertainty/assumption/possibility in a question). *Bulan purnama - jatuh daripada langit yang ketujuh?* Can it be that the full moon has fallen from the seventh heaven? *Apakah - yang menyusahkan hatimu?* What could be the matter with you? *mengapa* - why ... at all. *Mengapa - dia pergi bekerja?* Why on earth does she go to work at all?

geranggang (*Jv*) bamboo spear.
menggeranggang to spear.

gerangsang passionate, quick-tempered, fiery.

gerangsangan (*Jv*) wanting to eat everything one sees; to eat compulsively

gerantak menggerantak to stamp (one's foot).

gerantam (*onom*) thundering (sound of cannon, explosions, etc.).

gerantang 1 loud, noisy, boisterous. **2** roaring. **3** snarling. **4** boasting, bragging. *- keling* (an empty) bluff.
menggerantang 1 to beat a can, etc. to frighten away tigers, etc. **2** to snarl at s.o.
menggerantangi 1 to snarl at s.o. **2** to intimidate.

geranyam (*M?*) **menggeranyam 1** to tingle (of the elbow or knee when struck). **2** to quiver (of heat haze).

gerapa-gerépé (*J*) to grope around (in the dark).

gerapai menggerapai to grope around, grope one's way; to cling to, clutch/grasp at.

gerapik → GRAFIK.

gerapu and **bergerapu** rough, coarse (of skin, etc.).

gerapyak → GRAPYAK.

gerasakan rough (to the touch).

gerasut → GERAMSUT.

gerat (*onom*) noise of chewing, scraping.
menggeratkan to gnash (one's teeth).

geratak (*J*) **menggeratak** to go around and around looking for s.t.
menggeratakkan to search/look for s.t. here and there.

geratih (*M*) trot (of horses).
menggeratihkan to trot (a horse).

geratil (*Jv*) **menggeratili** to touch (in an improper way), feel up.

gerau (*ob*) chef, cook.

gerawan (*M*) color-blending/-mixing (in the atmosphere).

gerawat menggerawatkan to leave s.o. in the lurch, desert s.o.

gerayah (*Jv*) to grope around. *Tangannya -.- kepada amplop itu.* His hand was groping around for the envelope.

gerayak (*Jv*) holdup man, robber.
menggerayak to rob, plunder.
penggerayak robber.
penggerayakan robbery.

gerayang (*J*) **bergerayangan** (*pl subj*) to roam/wander about, drift from one place to another. *Banyak perompak ~ di daérah itu.* Many pirates roamed about that area.
menggerayang 1 to feel, grope, fumble; to grab, grabble. **2** to approach, draw near to (with the intention of robbing/stealing, etc.). *~ rambut* to scratch one's head with one's fingertip. **3** to creep (as lice in hair).
menggerayangi 1 to touch (improperly in order to steal s.t. or to feel up a woman). *Tangannya digerayangi pencopét yang berusaha untuk membélot jam tangannya.* His hand was touched by a pickpocket who tried to snatch his wristwatch. *Pria itu ~ tubuh wanita itu sehingga dia berteriak.* The man touched the woman's body and she screamed. **2** to feel, grope (an object), run one's fingers over. *Salah seorang pemuda tersebut kemudian mendekati pengemudi dan menodongkan senjatanya sementara tangannya ~ kantong baju pengemudi tersebut.* One of the young men in question then approached the driver and threatened him with his weapon while his hand groped in the pockets of the driver's coat. **3** to frisk, probe around in. *Sejak semula nafsu wartawan memasuki ruang sidang yang ketat dijaga, tak padam juga walau berkali-kali meréka diusir dan digerayangi.* From the beginning the desire of the journalists to enter the closely guarded meeting hall could not be extinguished, although they were frequently thrown out and frisked. **4** to break into, ransack. *~ brankas yang ketika itu terbuka* to ransack an open safe. **5** to infest, roam about in. *Komplotan penodong bersenjata tajam akhir-akhir ini mulai ~ jalan tol Jagorawi.* Lately a ring of holdup men armed with sharp weapons has started to roam about the Jagorawi toll road.

gerayangan touch, grope, frisk.

penggerayang s.o. who likes to feel up women, frotteur.

penggerayangan groping, touching, frisking, patting down (to look for weapons), feeling up.

gerbak menggerbak 1 to spread, be pervasive (of scent); → S(EM)ERBAK. **2** to flow, stream, gush. *Karena sedihya ~lah air matanya.* She was so sad that the tears streamed forth. **3** to fall (of several things). **4** to make a falling sound (of heavy fruits).

gerbang I - *gersul* hanging down loose and disheveled (of hair).
menggerbang disheveled (of hair).
menggerbangkan 1 to spread s.t. out wide. **2** to undo (one's hair).
te(r)gerbang(-gerbang) spread out, loose (of hairdo).

gerbang II 1 gate, front/main gate, entrance, port; → GAPURA. 2 threshold. *memasuki - hidup baru* to embark on a new life (i.e., married life). - *masuk* entryway. - *pengaman* metal detector. - *tol* tollgate. - *utama* main gate.

gerbang III (*onom*) - *gerbik* to make loud noises (like one possessed).

Gerbangkertasusila [Gersik-Jombang-Kertosono-Surabaya-Sidoarjo-Lamongan] the greater Surabaya region.

gerbas - *gerbus* (*onom*) rustling sound.

gérbera (*D*) gerbera (a flower), *Gerbera jamesonii*.

gerbong railway coach. - *barang* freight car. - *dater* open goods van (no roof and side walls). - *ékor* the last train coach (in train formation). - *kelas bisnis* business-class car. - *kelas ékonomi* economy-class car. - *kelas éksékutif* executive-class car. - *penumpang* railroad passenger car. - *réstorasi* diner, dining car. - *tangki (minyak)* tank car.

gerbus I menggerbus to hull (coffee beans).

gerbus II → GERBAS-GERBUS.

gerda → GARUDA.

gerdak (*onom*) thudding sound.

gerdam (*onom*) slam, thud, sound of a heavy object hitting the floor.
  menggerdam to thud, slam (to the floor).

gerdan(g) (*D?*) propeller shaft.

gerdum → GERDAM

gerebeg I → GREBEG.

gerebeg II and gerebek menggerebek 1 to raid, assault, storm, swoop down on. 2 to surround, gang up on. 3 to round up (suspects), seize, search. 4 to ransack.
  gerebekan 1 (in soccer) scrimmage. 2 raid.
  penggerebekan 1 raid, raiding, rounding up. 2 ransacking.

gerecak (*onom*) bubbling/fizzing sound.
  menggerecak(-gerecak) to bubble, fizz, seethe.

gerécok (*J*) menggerécok to nag, annoy, bother.
  menggerécoki to nag.
  penggerécok nag, bother, nuisance.

geréforméérd (*D*) reformed (church).

geregetan (*Jv*) (pent up) furious, raving, raging, mad, unable to restrain one's feelings.

geréh *ikan* - a small flat round dried salted fish

gerehak hawking, expectorating.

geréja I (*Port*) church. - *Advént Hari Ketujuh* Seventh Day Adventist Church. - *Anglikan* Anglican Church. - *Ayam* a Protestant Church (in Jakarta, with a weathervane attached to the top). - *Béthél Injil Sepenuh* Bethel Full Gospel Church of God. - *Katolik Bébas* [GKB] Free Catholic Church. - *Ortodoks* Orthodox Church. - *Pantékosta* Pentecostal Church.
  segeréja going to the same church.
  bergeréja ecclesiastic(al). *kehidupan ~ di tengah masyarakat* ecclesiastic life amid the community.
  kegeréjaan ecclesiastic; church (matters). *kebaktian ~* church service.

geréja II *burung* - sparrow, *Passer montanus*.

geréjani ecclesiastic.

geréjawan churchgoer.

geréjawi ecclesiastic. *provinsi* - ecclesiastic province.

gérék - *dada* bit brace. - *kayu* auger, gimlet. - *kotrék* ratchet drill. - *pnéumatik* pneumatic hammer. - *tangan* gimlet, auger, hand-drill.
  bergérék-gérék 1 to be perforated. 2 with (to have) holes or openings in. *Papan itu ~ karena dimakan anai-anai.* That board has holes in it because it was eaten away by termites.
  menggérék 1 to drill, perforate, make a hole in or through. *~ lubang di témbok* to drill/make a hole in the wall. 2 to bore (by a rodent). *Kelapa itu digérék tupai.* The coconut was bored into by a squirrel.
  menggérékkan 1 to use s.t. (a drill/auger, etc.) to make a hole. 2 to drill or bore for s.o. 3 to hammer s.t. in. *~ tutur kata ke telinga* to keep on giving advice.
  gérékan drilled, (hole) made by a drill.
  penggérék 1 drill. *~ kecil* gimlet. *~ polong* pod auger. 2 driller (the person). 3 natural enemy of a crop. *~ batang* borer that attacks black pepper plants in Bangka and Lampung, *Lo-*

phobaris piperis. *~ batang cokelat* cocoa stalk borer, *Zeuzera coffeae*. *~ batang padi bergaris* striped rice plant borer, *Chilo suppresalis Walk.* *~ batang padi kuning* yellow rice plant borer, *Tryporyza interculas Walk.* *~ batang padi mérah jambu* pink rice plant borer, *Sesamia inferens Walk.* *~ batang padi putih* white rice plant borer, *Tryporyza innotata Walk.* *~ buah kakao* cocoa-moth, *Conopomorpha crameria*. *~ daun* leaf borer. *~ kulit* bark beetle. *~ kuncup kapas* cotton bud borer, *Heliothis armigera*. *~ lubang jarum* pinhole borer. *~ polong* pod borer, *Etiella zinckenella*. *~ pucuk tebu* sugarcane sprout borer, *Scirpophaga nivella*.
  penggérékan drilling/boring a hole.

gerelap → GELAP.

gerem → GERAM I.

geremang → GERMANG.

geremeng vibration.

geremet → GREMET.

geremut → GERMUT.

geréndel → GRÉNDEL.

gerendeng (*J/Jv*) menggerendeng to mumble, grumble, growl.

geréndéng (*M*) menggeréndéng to assume a threatening/fighting attitude (of a fighting cock or animal).

gerénék → GERENIK.

gereneng (*Jv*) menggerenengi to grumble to/about.

gereng (*J*) to howl.
  gereng-gereng to growl (of a dog/tiger).

gerengseng I a large cooking utensil made of brass or copper.

gerengseng II (*Jv*) enthusiasm, urge, desire.

gerenik (*onom*) trilling (of voice).
  menggerenik (*cla*) to vibrate, quiver (of one's voice).

gerenjal-gerenjul bumpy, rough, uneven.

gerénjéng (*Jv*) (aluminum) foil. - *mas* (*Jv*) gold-leaf.

gerentam menggerentam to stamp one's feet.

gerentang → GERENTAM.

gerenyam menggerenyam to have a tingling sensation (of the funny bone when hit).

gerenyau capering about (of little girls), impudent.

gerényéng and tergerényéng(-gerényang) to grimace, grin.

gerényét and menggerényét to twitch (of muscles), tic.

gerenying → GERÉNYÉNG.

gerényit → GERÉNYÉT.

gerényot and gerényut 1 smirking, grimacing. 2 not perfectly round, irregular.
  menggerényot to smirk.
  menggerényotkan *~ bibir* to smirk.

gerépé menggerépé to grope around.

gerépék (*cla*) menggerépék to be a dirty person (who doesn't wash after defecating).

gerepes restless.

gerépés I menggerépés to fidget with the fingers

gerépés II (*J*) bergerépés 1 uneven, not smooth. 2 = gerépésan (*Jv*) worn out.

geréséh-péséh → KARÉSÉH-PÉSÉH.

gerésék (*onom*) clatter.
  menggerésék to rustle, rattle, clatter.

gerét (*J*) menggerét 1 to scratch, scrape. 2 to squeak, squeal.
  menggerétkan to scratch with s.t. *~ gérétan* to light a match.
  gérétan 1 matches. 2 a lighter. *~ gas Ronson* a Ronson butane lighter.

gérét → SÉRÉT. menggérét to tow, drag along.
  menggérét-gérét to keep on towing/dragging along.
  gérétan pull, drag.

geretak (*onom*) grinding, grating, gnashing.
  menggeretak 1 to grind, grate, gnash one's teeth. 2 to crackle.
  menggeretakkan to gnash (one's teeth).

gerétang (*M*) menggerétang to threaten, be aggressive.

geréték (*onom*) crinkling, crackling.

geretuk (*onom*) rapping/tapping sound.
  menggeretuk to make that sound.

gergaji (*Skr*) a saw. *serbuk* - sawdust. *seperti - dua mata* to play a double game and take advantage of both sides, a double-edged knife, the knife cuts both ways. - *balik/band/balok* cross-cut saw. – *bermesin* chainsaw. – *besi* hacksaw. – *bolak-balik* cross-cut saw. – *bundar* buzz saw. – *gelung* band saw. – *gorok* hand-saw. – *halus* fret saw. – *induk* head saw. – *lingkar* circular saw. – *lintang* cross-cut saw. – *logam* hacksaw. – *mesin* chainsaw. – *pemangkas* pruning saw. – *piring* circular saw. – *pita* band saw. – *potong* cross-cut saw. – *rantai* chainsaw. – *tangan* handsaw. – *tank/tarik* cross-cut saw. – *ukir* fret saw.

menggergaji 1 to saw, cut with a saw. 2 (*naut*) to tack, seesaw. ~ *angin* a) to tack. b) to do s.t. useless.

gergajian s.t. sawed, sawn.

penggergaji sawyer.

penggergajian sawing. ~ *kayu* a) sawmill. b) sawmilling.

gergajul → BERGAJUL.

gergap k.o. monkey.

gergasi (*Skr*) giant; → BUTA III, RAKSASA.

ger-ger ger-geran (*Jv*) to roar with laughter; → GER I. *Ia disambut dengan* ~ *oléh wakil-wakil rakyat itu.* He was greeted by the laughter of the representatives of the people.

keger-geran laughter.

gerha (*Skr?*) wife, spouse.

gerham → GERAHAM.

gerhana (*Skr*) 1 eclipse (of the sun/moon/great men, etc.). – *bulan* lunar eclipse. – *matahari* solar eclipse. – *matahari total* total solar eclipse. – *menggelang* annular eclipse. – *sebagian* partial eclipse. – *mutlak* total eclipse. 2 to be beset by problems.

geri I slight movement, shrug.

geri II various species of starlings, *Aplonis spp.*

geriak – *geriuk* rumbling (of the stomach from hunger).

menggeriak to swarm, crawl around in large numbers.

geriap I (*J?*) **menggeriap** to become smaller (of sleepy eyes, fading lamplight).

geriap II (*J*) 1 startled and scared. 2 loosened (of hair).

gériatri (*D*) geriatrics.

gériatrik (*E*) and **gériatris** (*D*) geriatric.

geribik (*Jv*) woven-bamboo panel used as a screen or as a splint for a broken limb.

gericau (*onom*) twitter, chirp, screech; repeated sound that is harsh and jarring, like sounds of birds, monkeys, etc.

menggericau to twitter, chirp, chatter, screech.

geridik menggeridik ~ *bulu* to make one's flesh creep, make one's hair stand on end.

geridip I menggeridip to glitter, sparkle.

geridip II (*J*) to like to fiddle with things for lack of anything better to do.

geridit – *pidit* chock-full, packed.

gerigi serration, cog.

bergerigi serrated, jagged; cogged.

gerigik a bamboo water vessel with handle.

gerigis serrations, cogs.

bergerigis serrated, cogged.

gerigit menggerigit to gnaw (away) at.

gerih → GERIT-GERIT I.

gerik → GERAK *gerik*.

gerilya (*D*) guerrilla. – *kota/perkotaan* urban guerrilla. – *politik* political guerrilla.

bergerilya to wage guerrilla warfare.

menggerilya(i) to wage guerrilla warfare against.

gerilyawan male guerrilla fighter.

gerilyawati female guerrilla fighter.

gerim (*D?*) *kain* – a coarse flannel cloth.

gerimis 1 (*hujan* –) drizzling rain, drizzle. 2 snow (on the TV screen). *Siaran TV masih saja* –. TV broadcasts are still blocked by snow.

bergerimis and **menggerimis** 1 to drizzle. 2 to trickle.

gerincing (*onom*) sound of jingling.

bergerincing to jingle.

menggerincingkan to jingle (one's money), rattle (one's saber).

gerincingan rattling. ~ *pedang/senjata* saber-rattling.

gerinda grindstone, emery wheel, abrasive. *batu* – whetstone, a stone used for filing teeth.

menggerinda to grind, whet, sharpen.

gerindin (*M*) shivers (a horse disease).

gerinding I k.o. mouth-organ, Jew's/mouth-harp made of bamboo.

gerinding II (*J*) **bergerinding** and **menggerinding** (one's hair) stands on end.

gering sick, ill (used about kings). – *bersalin* labor pains. – *tengah* stomachache. – *ulu* headache.

kegeringan sickness, illness, ailing.

penggering magic means of making s.o. ill.

penggeringan 1 sickly, always ill. 2 magic spell for causing s.o. to become ill.

gering-gering → GIRING-GIRING I.

geringging(en) → GRINGGINGEN, KESEMUTAN.

geringsing I 1 curly. 2 various k.o. batik and weaving designs.

geringsing II distorted (of grimace/smirk).

bergeringsing to distort (the face in a smirk).

gerinjal (*ob*) → GINJAL.

gerinjam 1 whetstone (for filing teeth); → GERINDA. 2 tool for cleaning ears.

menggerinjam 1 to whet clean. 2 to pick out.

gerinting – *air* k.o. grass (cattle fodder/forage), *Chamaeraphis aspera.*

gerinyau menggerinyau to itch, feel ticklish.

gerinyut → GERÉNYOT.

gerip I (*D*) slate pencil.

gerip II various k.o. climbing plants; → GERIT-GERIT I.

geripel (*D ob*) slate pencil.

geripir (*D ob*) court clerk.

geripis → GERÉPÉS.

gerisik (*onom*) sound of rustling.

menggerisik to rustle.

gerising → GERINGSING II.

gerit (*onom*) screeching sound (of pencils/pens), creaking; → KERIT I.

bergerit and **menggerit** to screech, creak.

gerita → GURITA I.

gerit-gerit I *akar* – *putih* a generic name for a number of wild rubber vines, *Urceola brachysepala* Hook.

gerit-gerit II *ikan* – spiny eel, *Macrognathus aculeatus.*

geriting k.o. tree, *Lumnitzera littorea/coccinea*; → TERUNTUM.

geritis (*M*) **menggeritis(kan)** ~ *gigi* to gnash one's teeth.

gerlap menggerlap to glitter, flicker, twinkle; → GEMERLAP.

gerling (*ob*) → KERLING I.

gerlip menggerlip to glitter, shimmer.

germang menggermang to stand on end (of hairs) due to fear/nausea. *Melihat ular menggeliat-geliat seperti itu* ~ *bulu romaku.* Seeing the wriggling snake made his hair stand on end.

tergermang giving spasmodic starts (as from St. Vitus's dance).

germo (*Jv*) 1 pimp, procuress, matchmaker. 2 female brothel keeper, madam.

menggermoi to pimp for, act as a pimp for. *Istrinya ia jual sebagai pelacur, digermoinya sendiri.* He sold his wife into prostitution. He pimped for her himself.

kegermoan pimping (*mod*). *Dalam dunia* ~ *salah satu faktor keberhasilan bisnis terletak pada WTS yang dipekerjakan.* In the world of pimps, one of the factors for business success lies in the prostitutes hired.

penggermoan pimping.

germowan procurer, pimp, matchmaker.

germut menggermut to swarm (of ants/people).

menggermuti to surround, swarm around.

gero (*Jv*) **menggero** to roar.

geroak (*J*) with a large tear in it.

gerobak I (*J/Jv*) 1 cart. 2 wagon. 3 van. *mobil/oto* – truck. – *barang* baggage car/trolley. – *batu bara* coal car. – *dorong* pushcart, wheelbarrow. – *gandéngan* trailer (of a truck). – *héwan* cattle car. – *keréta api* wagon, truck (for cattle, open or flat). – *kuda* horse box. – *lembu* oxcart, bullock cart. – *roda* wheelbarrow. – *sampah* garbage cart. – *sapi* oxcart, bullock cart. – *sorong/tangan* handcart, pushcart. – *tambahan* trailer (of a truck). – *ungkit* car that tips to empty its load.

bergerobak in cartloads.

bergerobak-gerobak by the cartload, cartloads and cartloads.

gerobak II (*Pr*) [*gerombolan-Batak*] gang of Bataks.

gerobok I **bergerobok** and **menggerobok** to gurgle (of a vessel dipped into water), bubble up; → GELOBOK.

gerobok II (*J/Jv*) **1** (bamboo) cupboard for food. **2** large clothes chest.

gerocok (*onom*) sound of bubbling water.

bergerocok(an) to bubble over (of water, with life).

geroda (*ob*) → GARUDA.

gerodak (*onom*) rumble, clatter.

menggerodak to rumble, rattle.

menggerodaki to rummage around in (a box, etc.), break into (a place).

gerodok (*onom*) bubbling sounds.

gero-gero (*Jv*) to wail, roar.

gerogi → GROGI.

gerogoh menggerogoh(i) to make a grab for s.t.

gerogol 1 (*Pal*) house on a raft. **2** (*Jv*) palisade (on the beach), stockade.

gerogot (*J*) → GERAGOT. **menggerogoti 1** to gnaw all over. *– barang logam* corrosive. **2** to steal, embezzle (little by little). **3** to make inroads on, riddle s.t. with, undermine, nibble away at, eat into. *Jepang yang sudah ~ sebagian besar pasaran mobil Amérika dan Éropa memprogramkan produksi 250 ribu mobil listrik, tahun 1998.* Japan, which has made inroads on the greater part of the American and European car markets, has programmed a production of 250,000 electric cars in 1998. *Bisnisnya masih saja digerogoti inéfisiénsi.* The business is still riddled with inefficiencies.

tergerogoti undermined.

gerogotan 1 marks of being eaten (away). *Roti yang dijualnya, ternyata tidak bébas dari ~ tikus-tikus.* The bread he was selling was not free of marks of being eaten by rats. **2** stealing, embezzlement. **3** undermining, erosion.

penggerogot embezzler. *~ uang* corruptor.

penggerogotan 1 stealing, embezzling. *~ uang negara* embezzlement of state funds. **2** impairment (of capital).

gerohok [and **gerohong** (*J*)] **1** (to have) holes (of trees/fences/teeth), decayed. *Giginya –.* His teeth are decayed. **2** hollow (of tree).

bergerohok with holes in it.

gerojog and **gerojok** (*Jv*) water falling.

menggerojok 1 to fall, falling (of water). **2** to distribute (a lot of). **3** to flood (the market).

menggerojoki to flood (an area/the market).

gerojokan 1 waterfall, cataract. **2** a flood (of goods/water, etc.). **3** distribution (of goods, etc.).

gerombol bergerombol and **menggerombol 1** to come together, meet, assemble, flock together, stay together. **2** to meet/get together as a group. **3** to form a gang. *selalu bergerombol* to stick close to e.o., be clannish.

gerombolan 1 group, troop. **2** gang, band. *~ bersenjata* armed band. **bergerombolan** in groups.

gerombong gerombongan troop; → ROMBONG II.

gerompok → KELOMPOK.

gerong I 1 (*J*) holes, openings in the ground. **2** (*Jv*) hollow, sunken (of one's eyes).

gerong II (*M*) trumpet (of elephants), roar (of tigers), howl (of dogs), moan (from pain).

geronggang I hollow, cavity.

bergeronggang with holes, cavities, with a large hole in it.

menggeronggang to pierce, make a hole in.

menggeronggangi to go through and come out the other side, penetrate.

tergeronggang pierced, with holes in it.

penggeronggangan caving (in).

geronggang II handle of a *tuai*/small knife for cutting ears of rice.

geronggang III various species of trees which produce timber for houses, mampat, *Cratoxylon spp.*

gerong-gerong k.o. fish, golden trevally, *Gnathanodon speciosus.*

geronggong I (*J*) hollow; → GERONGGANG I.

geronggong II → GERONGGANG III.

geronjal (*Jv*) bumpy.

bergeronjal to jump up and down.

geronjalan with bumps in it.

gerontang I (*J*) **menggerontang** roaring (success); alarming, intimidate, intimidating,

gerontang II → GERANTANG. *– keling* threat with nothing to back it up.

gérontokrasi (*D*) gerontocracy.

gerontol (*Jv*) salted shredded coconut mixed with cooked maize seeds, eaten as a snack.

gérontologi (*D/E*) gerontology. *ahli –* gerontologist.

gerontong → GERANTANG I.

geronyot → KERNYUT II. **menggeronyot** to throb (of an abscess), give a twinge (of neuralgia/gout).

geropés → GERUPIS.

geropyak (*Jv*) booming, thudding

bergeropyak with a thud.

geropyok (*Jv*) **menggeropyok 1** to chase in order to catch, hold a battue. **2** to attack, assault.

penggeropyokan 1 battue, roundup (of suspects). **2** razzia, raid.

geros I (*J*) **menggeros** to snore.

geros II (*D/E*) gross, 144 of a kind.

gerosak and **gerosok** rustling; → KEROSOK I.

bergerosok and **menggerosok(-gerosok)** to rustle.

gerosokan 1 rustling. **2** roaring noise.

gerot-gerot *ikan –* the grunter, silver grunt, javelin-fish, *Pristipoma/Pomadasys hasta.*

gerotong → GERANTANG.

gerowong (*J*) a large hole (in tree).

gerowot → GEROGOT.

geroyok → KEROYOK.

gerpol [*gerilya politik*] leftish political guerrilla warfare.

menggerpol to launch a leftish political guerrilla war.

menggerpoli to launch a leftish political guerrilla attack on.

penggerpol leftish adherent of political guerrilla warfare.

gerpolis "gerpolist," i.e., an adherent of political guerrilla warfare.

gerr → GER II.

gersak (*onom*) the sound of stepped-on dry leaves. *– gersik* crackling sounds.

menggersakkan to rustle s.t.

gersang 1 dry (of hair/sand/timber), arid. **2** infertile (land), sterile, barren. **3** miserable, pitiful, empty (of one's life).

menggersang to be(come) dried up.

menggersangkan 1 to dry up. **2** to make sterile, infertile.

kegersangan 1 dryness, aridity. **2** barrenness, infertility, sterility.

gersik I (*onom*) sound of grinding/crunching.

menggersik to grind, crunch.

gersik II gravel, sand, shingle.

gertak I **menggertak** to swarm, crowd, crawl, or move in large numbers as of ants, bees, etc. *Beratus-ratus ékor semut ~ ke tempat air gula itu tertumpah.* Hundreds of ants swarmed over the place where the sugar water had spilled.

gertak II (*Jv*) snarl, threat, menace. *– gerantang/sambal/sambel* empty threat, big talk, bluff. *– gertuk* rumbling (of the stomach from hunger).

menggertak(i) 1 to snarl/snap at, bluff, intimidate. **2** to spur on, encourage.

menggertakkan 1 to spur, stimulate, excite. *Mendengar orang menjerit itu segeralah kudanya digertakkannya.* Hearing the people scream, he spurred on his horse. **2** to gnash (one's teeth). *~ gigi/geraham* to gnash one's teeth. **3** to spur on (a horse).

gertakan 1 threat, threatening. **2** snarl(ing). **3** bluff. **4** spurring on (of a horse).

penggertak 1 snarler, bluffer. **2** snarl, bluff. **3** whip used to spur on.

gertap I → GERLAP.

gertap II (*J*) **menggertap** to droop (of sleepy eyes), grow small (of a fading lamp).

gertik (*onom*) creaking.

menggertik to creak, crack.

gertuk → GERTAK *gertuk*.

geru (*onom*) roaring sound.

menggeru to roar (of tiger), trumpet (of elephant).

gerubuk I → GEROBOK II.

gerubuk II → GERABAK III.

geruduk (*Jv*) **gerudak-geruduk** to follow the crowd.

gerudukan going along as one of a group. *Jangan ~ masuk kampus.* Don't crowd onto the campus.

penggerudukan crowding (into).

gerugul → GEROGOL.

gerugut bergerugut and **menggerugut** deeply wrinkled, corrugated (of tree trunks).

geruh I misfortune, bad luck. *- gerah* all k.o. misfortunes/mishaps. *- tak mencium bau* you never know when misfortune will hit.

kegeruhan misfortune, bad luck.

geruh II (*onom*) snoring.

bergeruh and **menggeruh** to snore.

geruit menggeruit to wriggle around, squirm.

geruk I *- gerak* (*onom*) sound made by an object being dragged along.

menggeruk-geruk to make the sound of s.t. being dragged along.

geruk II k.o. wrapper put around fruit on the tree to prevent it from dropping off too soon.

gerumbul I (*Jv*) **1** underbrush. **2** (*reg*) hamlet.

gerumbul II gerumbulan → GEROMBOLAN.

gerumit menggerumit 1 to putter around, tinker (with), do handicrafts, do small jobs. **2** (*J*) to move very slowly.

gerumpung (*J/Jv*) with a misshapen nose.

gerumuk menggerumuk to huddle/hunch up, crouch down.

gerumus (*onom*) murmuring sound.

menggerumus to murmur.

gerumut (*J*) **menggerumut** to swarm; to creep on (bit by bit).

menggerumuti to swarm over s.o. (in a crowd), crowd e.o. out.

gerun I afraid, horrified with fear.

bergerun *tiada* ~ fearless.

menggerunkan 1 awe-inspiring. **2** terrifying, fearsome, scary.

gerun II (*M*) jungle. *kambing* - wild goat, serow, *Capricornis sumatrensis*.

gerundal → GERUNDEL.

gerundang (*M*) tadpole. *seperti* - *yang kekeringan* floundering about and nobody wants to help.

gerundel (*Jv*) **menggerundel** to grumble, complain.

gerundelan grumbling, complaining.

gerung moaning (from pain), roaring sound.

menggerung(-gerung) 1 to yelp, whine, squeal, moan, groan. **2** to roar.

tergerung uttered a cry of pain, burst out wailing.

gerunggang (*M*) *pohon* - a tree with purple flowers, *Cratoxylon arborescens/formosum*.

gerunyam menggerunyam to mutter, mumble.

gerup frame for the comb in a loom.

gerupis menggerupis to tinker/putter at.

gerupuk (*M*) **menggerupuk** to trip, fall down.

menggerupukkan to cause the downfall of, make s.o. stumble, trip up.

tergerupuk tripped, stumbled. *Karena jalan licin dan malam gelap, beberapa kali ia ~.* Because the road was slippery and the night dark, he stumbled several times.

gerus I *siput* - tiger cowry, a large cowry shell, *Cypraea tigris*, used for polishing cotton cloth.

menggerus to polish s.t. in that way.

gerusan polished. *kain* ~ cotton cloth used for polishing.

gerus II (*Jv*) **menggerus 1** to rub/grind down, pulverize in a pestle. **2** to scour (off), grind off. **3** to erode.

tergerus scoured/ground down.

gerusan 1 scouring, rubbing down. **2** s.t. scraped.

penggerus scraper. *mesin* ~ pulverizer.

penggerusan grinding, scouring, scraping.

gerut (*onom*) crunching/scraping noise.

gerutan scrape.

gerut-gerut → GEROT-GEROT.

gerutu I rough (of skin/bark), coarse (of texture).

gerutu II grumbling, grumble. *-nya* he grumbled.

menggerutu to grumble, complain.

menggerutui to grumble at/about.

gerutui grumbling, gripe, complaint.

penggerutu grumbler, complainer.

penggerutuan grumbling, complaining.

gerutup and **gerutus** (*onom*) the noise of artillery fire/firecrackers.

menggerutup to crackle and bang (of a fusillade).

geruyak menggeruyak to shake.

gesa hurry, haste.

(ber)gesa-gesa hastily, hurriedly.

menggesa to hasten, speed up, ask to do s.t. quickly, urge forward. *Pegawai itu ~ orang-orang bawahannya supaya menyelesaikan kerja meréka dalam témpo masa sebulan.* The officials hurried their subordinates to finish the work within one month.

menggesa(-gesa)kan and **mempergesa** to hurry up, accelerate, quicken, speed up.

tergesa in a hurry. **ketergesaan** hurry. *Dalam pelaksanaan hukuman mati tidak ada ~.* In executing a death sentence there's no hurry.

tergesa-gesa in haste, hastily. *Dia ~ pulang.* He hurried home. *Jangan ~!* Take your time! Don't be in a rush! **ketergesa-gesaan** hurry, haste. *~nya menulis kelihatan juga di akhir buku.* The hurry in which he wrote is also noticeable at the end of the book. *~nya meninggalkan rumah akhirnya malah membuatnya bertambah gelisah.* His haste to leave the house finally made him even more nervous.

penggesaan speeding up; → PERCEPATAN.

gesau → DESAU.

gésék rub, scrape; → GÉSÉL, GÉSER. *orkés* - string orchestra.

bergésék to rub, scour, scrape, rub against.

bergésékan to rub against e.o.

menggésék 1 to rub, move a thing backward and forward on the surface of another. **2** to play (a musical instrument). *~ biola* to play the violin. **3** to swipe (a card through a card reader).

menggéséki to rub against s.t.

menggésék(-gésék)kan and **mempergésék-gesekkan** to rub a thing against another. *~ geraham* to gnash one's teeth. *~ tangan* to rub one's hands.

gésékan and **gésék-gésékan** friction, rubbing. *Hindari gésék-gésékan yang mengganggu stabilitas.* Avoid frictions which can disturb stability.

penggésék 1 one who scours/rubs/plays. *~ biola.* violinist. *~ sélo* cellist. **2** bow of a violin.

pergésékan friction, rubbing.

gésél rub, brush against; → GÉSÉK, GÉSER.

bergésél to brush/rub against, touch lightly, brush together (of two persons or objects). *Anak-anak yang bermain di kamar itu sering ~ badan karena kamar itu agak sempit.* The kids playing in the room often brushed against e.o. because the space was rather narrow.

bergésélan to rub against e.o.

menggésél to touch, brush, rub. *Dia coba membuat api dengan ~ dua batang kayu.* He tried to make a fire by rubbing two sticks together.

menggésélkan to rub s.t. (against s.t.). *Ia ~ bokongnya yang gatal pada dinding.* He rubbed his itchy backside on the wall.

tergésél rubbed/brushed against s.t. *Mobilnya bercalar-calar karena ~ tiang lampu.* His car was scraped because it brushed against the lamp post.

gésélan rubbing, chafing, abrasion.

gésér → GÉSÉK, GÉSÉL. **1** (*ling*) fricative, spirant. **2** shear. *- angin* wind shear.

bergésér 1 to rub/brush against. *~ bahu* to rub shoulders. **2** to move, shift, change position. *Guru itu tidak membenarkan murid-muridnya ~ dari tempat masing-masing.* The teacher did not allow the students to move from their places. **3** to shuffle along. *~ maju* to shove ahead, push forward. **4** shear.

bergéséran to rub against e.o.

menggésér 1 to rub against. *Mobil itu rusak sélebornya, karena ~ témbok.* The fender of the car was damaged because it rubbed against the wall. **2** to move, shift, transfer. *~ duduknya* to move one's seat. **3** to move/push aside, shift out of the way, remove (from office), get rid of, kick s.o. out, purge. *Bagaimana meréka bisa ~ dia dari jabatannya sekarang?* How could they have removed him from his present office? **4** (*mil*) to deploy.

gésér-menggésér frictions. *Cerita panjang ~.* it's a long story of frictions

menggésérkan 1 to move/shift s.t. *Ketika melihat kedatanganku,* *dia lalu ~ pantatnya.* When he saw me, he moved his behind over. **2** (*coq*) to pinch, pilfer, steal.

tergésér shifted, moved, pushed aside, overthrown.

géséran 1 abrasion. **2** grazing (of s.t. briefly rubbing against s.t.).

penggésér converter. *~ ke bawah* down converter.

penggéséran moving, shifting, relocation, displacement, deployment.

pergéséran 1 rubbing, scouring, abrasion, friction. *~ dengan atmosfér* friction with the atmosphere. **2** shift, tour of duty (in the army), transfer (from one post to another to get rid of s.o.), reshuffle. *~ kabinét* cabinet reshuffle. **3** quarrel, disagreement, conflict, argument. **4** shift, displacement. *~ ke kanan/kiri* a shift to the right/left. *~ kekuasaan/kekuatan* power shift. *~ yang bersifat tidak kontinu* discrete shift.

gesit (*J*) adroit, skillful, clever, agile, active, nimble.

menggesitkan to speed up, accelerate.

tergesit the most adroit.

kegesitan nimbleness, agility, skill, adroitness, handiness.

géspér (*D*) buckle, clasp.

menggéspérkan to buckle, clasp.

gésrék (*Jv*) **menggésrék** to graze/rub against.

Gestapu [Gerakan Séptémber Tiga Puluh] the left-wing September 30 movement.

Gestapuisme "Gestapuism," i.e., the actions and practices carried out by the *Gestapu.*

gesut menggesut to wipe away, rub off.

geta (*Skr*) dais, sleeping platform, broad sofa or couch. *- kerajaan* royal divan. *- pemanjangan* bridal couple seat. *- peraduan* state bed.

getah 1 sap; latex or gum produced by trees and organs; birdlime. **2** (vegetable) gum, resin. **3** juices produced by an organ of the body. *kena/ketiban* (*Jv*) - a) spattered with latex. b) caught with birdlime. c) (to suffer) the bad consequences of s.o. else's actions. *bagai - dibawa ke semak* a more and more confusing case. *seorang makan nangka, semua kena -nya* one rotten apple in the basket disgraces all the perfect fruit. *niat hati nak - bayan, sudah tergetah burung serindit* the wife one gets is far less then the one dreamed of. *daun dapat dilayangkan, - jatuh ke perdu juga* another relative cannot be the same as one's own flesh and blood. *burung boléh lupa akan -, - takkan lupa kepada burung* a debtor may forget the creditor, but not the other way around. *berseléléran bagai - dilélang* an incoherent discussion which gets off the subject. *- terbangkit kuaran tiba* a miscalculation. *- arab* gum Arabic. *- asap* smoked rubber sheet. *- bening* lymph. *- burung* birdlime. *- damar* copal. *- hangkang* k.o. plant, *Palaquium leiocarpum. - karét* latex, rubber sap. *- lambung* gastric juices. *- lendir* mucus. *- luka* pus. *- manis* gamboge yellow. *- padu* coagulated rubber. *- pankréas* pancreatic juice. *- perca* gutta-percha. *- perut* gastric juice. *- purwa* (*petro*) existent gum. *- radang* exudate. *- rokok* tar (of a cigarette). *- sundai* k.o. plant, *Payena leerii. - susu* rubber from the *Willughbeia firma* plant. *- tubuh* secretion (from the body). *- upil* rubber from the *Willughbeia coreacea* plant.

bergetah 1 sticky, sappy, viscous, juicy. **2** to tap rubber, etc. *~ bibirnya* tempting, cajoling, alluring, seductive. *~ hatinya* insincere. *~ mulutnya* sharp and hurtful words.

menggetah 1 to become sap. **2** to tap (a tree), collect (sap from a tree). **3** to catch s.t. with birdlime. *~ bawang* to utter sharp and hurtful words. *~ hati* to win s.o. over (to one's side).

menggetahkan to make s.t. into sap.

tergetah 1 smeared with sap/resin. **2** became implicated.

getah-gatahan apocynaceae.

penggetahan secretion.

getak *- getuk* (*onom*) knocking/pounding sound.

getang I cloth, skin or paper tightly stretched to cover the open end of a *rebana*/tambourine, bottle, *gendang*/drum, etc.

menggetang to cover. *~ gendang* to make a drum head taut.

penggetang *kulit ~* eardrum, tympanum.

getang II *daun -* k.o. vegetable, toothache plant, *Spilanthes acmella.*

getap I menggetap (to break) with a crack, crunch, gnash. *~ geraham* to gnash one's teeth.

getap II (*Jv*) **getapan 1** easily frightened/startled. **2** quick to take offense, touchy. **3** hotheaded.

getap III (*J*) steadfast, resolute, uncompromising.

getar 1 trembling, shaking. **2** (*ling*) trill. *- gemetar* trembling all over.

segetar a slight tremble.

bergetar 1 to shake, tremble. **2** to vibrate, quiver, shudder (with horror). **3** horrible, ghastly, startling.

menggetar 1 to shake, tremble. **2** to shake s.t., make s.t. shake. *Ledakan itu ~ jendéla dan pintu rumah.* The explosion shook the windows and doors of the house.

menggetari (*pl obj*) to shake s.t., make s.t. tremble.

menggetarkan 1 to deter. *Senjata ketinggalan zaman tidak ~ lawan.* Obsolete weapons do not deter opponents. **2** horrifying, horrible. *Ledakan itu ~.* The explosion was horrible. *~ hati* heart-moving. **3** to shake s.t., make s.t. shake/tremble/quake.

tergetar(-getar) to tremble, vibrate.

getaran 1 shiver(s), quiver, shudder, vibration. *~ gelombang* shock wave. *~ hati/jiwa* emotion. *~ laut* seaquake. *~ sendiri* natural vibration. **2** (*ling*) trill. **3** pulsation. **4** frequency (of a sound wave).

penggetar 1 vibrator. **2** (*ob*) tyrant; (reign of) terror.

getas I (*Jv*) **1** frail, brittle, fragile. **2** irritable, touchy.

bergetas *~ hati* easily offended, irritable.

kegetasan crispiness, brittleness.

getas II (*J*) clear, obvious, plain, manifest.

getas III (*- jawa*) k.o. snack made from sticky rice.

géték I immodest, indecent, shameless (in talk/conduct, of women).

géték II (*J/Jv*) **1** (bamboo) raft; → RAKIT I. **2** ferryboat.

getem-getem (*Jv*) to express anger by gestures.

getet (*J*) **menggetet** and **nggetet 1** to snip at, cut off a bit. **2** to take a bit of.

geti-geti a sweetmeat made from peanuts and sugar.

getik (*J*) **menggetik 1** to touch (with the finger, etc.), tap lightly. **2** to flick with one's fingers.

getikan pinch (of s.t.).

getil segetil pinch (of s.t.).

menggetil to hold with two fingers, pinch, nip between thumb and forefinger; → GETIK.

getir I (*Jv*) **1** bitter, tart, harsh (in the mouth). **2** bitter (experience). *sikap -* cynicism.

menggetirkan to make bitter, embitter, exasperate.

kegetiran bitterness, embitterment, exasperation.

getir II → GETIL.

getis fragile, brittle, frail.

géto I (*D/E*) ghetto.

géto II (*BG*) → GITU.

getok (*J onom*) pounding sound. *- tular* (*Jv*) word of mouth, from mouth to mouth, hearsay. *dengan - tular mewartakan* to report by word of mouth. **menggetok-tularkan** to spread (news) by word of mouth.

menggetok 1 to hit, knock on s.t. (with a hammer/one's knuckles/a gavel, etc.). *Kepala korban digetok dengan gagang senjata api.* The victim's head was hit with the butt-end of a rifle. **2** to smooth s.t. out.

getokan s.t. used for hitting/knocking, stick, club. *~ hoki* hockey stick.

getol (*J/Jv*) **1** industrious, diligent, hard-working. **2** enthusiastic.

menggetol(i) to be keen on s.t., be persevering/persistent.

kegetolan industriousness, diligence.

getrok (*J onom*) sound of things striking against e.o.

menggetroki (*pl obj*) to strike s.t. frequently (to remove the contents of bottles/cans, etc.).

getu menggetu to nip (a flea/bug) to kill, crush (a small insect, etc.) with the fingernails, pinch between thumb and forefinger.

getuk I (*J/Jv*) snack made from yams or cassava (which have been crushed and to which sugar and coconut have been added). *- lindri* (*Jv*) the same as above with additional aromatic ingredients.

getuk II → GETAK *getuk.*

getun (*J*) → GEGETUN I.

geuchik (*Ac*) village head.

geudeu-geudeu (*Ac*) Acehnese wrestling

geulis (*S*) beautiful.

géwang I mother-of-pearl; → GIWANG I.

géwang II ear stud; → GIWANG II.

géwang III gebang palm, *Corypha elata*; → GEBANG.

gewésten (*D col*) regions, small territorial units.

géyat-géyot to dance around.

géyong I (*J*) thick-set woman with a large behind.

géyong II (*Jv*) to dangle.

géyot → GÉYAT-GÉYOT.

géyser (*D*) geyser.

gh- also see words beginning with **g-** or **r-**.

ghaib → GAIB.

ghairah → GAIRAH.

ghalat → RALAT.

gharar (*A*) (the Islamic business principle forbidding) uncertainty in a business transaction, lack of transparency.

ghayn (*A*) name of the 19th letter of the Arabic alphabet.

gi I (*Hind*) ghee (clarified butter).

gi II clipped form of PERGI.

gi III (*C?*) 0.1 gram (in the drug trade).

GIA [Garuda Indonesian Airlines] Garuda Indonesian Airlines.

gial I (*Jv*) – *giul* ticklish.
　menggial to squirm (when tickled).
　tergial(-gial) squirming (from being tickled).

gial II slow to obey an order.

giam *pohon* – k.o. hardwood tree, *Cotylelobium spp.*

giat 1 active, busy. *bekerja* – to work hard. *tidak* – inert. **2** energetic, strong, powerful, forceful, zealous, aggressive. – *malam* nocturnal. – *siang* diurnal.
　segiat as active as.
　segiat-giatnya as actively as one can.
　bergiat to be active, do one's best to. *Keluarga itu ~ memajukan réstoran yang baru saja dibuka itu.* The family did its best to make the new restaurant a success.
　menggiat to be(come) active.
　menggiatkan and **mempergiat(kan) 1** to activate. **2** to encourage. *Pemerintah setempat ~ rakyat menaikkan hasil pertanian.* The local government encouraged the people to increase agricultural production. *menggiatkan kembali* to revive, bring back to life. **3** to emphasize, add/lend force to, intensify.
　kegiatan 1 activity, action, operation. **2** (social) function. **3** measure, step taken. *mengadakan ~.~ éksplorasi dan éksploatasi atas bahan tambang ini* to explore and exploit these mining products. *~ ékstrakurikulér* extracurricular activities. *~ kegemaran* amateurism. *~ pengamanan* security measures. *~ penyelidikan* surveillance operation. *~ perédaran uang* cash flow. *~ tertutup* covert operation. **4** energy, ardor. **berkegiatan** to be active.
　penggiat and **pegiat 1** activist, activator. **2** actuator.
　penggiatan 1 activation, encouragement. **2** boosting (a battery).

gibang (*J*) **menggibang** to obstruct (the way), barricade (a street), block (a road).

gibas I → KIBAS II (*A*) *kambing* – a fat-tailed sheep.

gibas II → KIBAS I.

gicu (*BG*) → GITU.

gidig and **gidik** (*J*) **bergidik 1** to shudder, shiver (because of some gruesome or weird event or situation) **2** afraid. *~ tengkuk* one's skin crawls, one's hair stands on end. **3** to get excited.
　menggidik(-gidik) to give one the creeps, make one's flesh creep, make one squirm.
　menggidikkan to make s.o. shiver, give s.o. the creeps.

gidu (*J*) nettle rash, hives, urticaria; → WIDUREN.

gigau → IGAU. **menggigau 1** to talk in one's sleep. **2** to be delirious.

gigi 1 tooth. **2** the serrated or rippling edge of anything. *menunjukkan* – to show one's teeth. *akar* – root of a tooth. *daging* – gums. *dokter* – dentist. *pencungkil* – toothpick; → SELILIT, TUSUK *gigi*. *sakit* – toothache. *salut* – tooth enamel. *saraf* – dental nerve. *tukang* – one who makes dentures. *tulang* – dentine. **3** gear (of a transmission), cog. – *satu* first gear. *masuk* – *dua* in second gear. – *persnéling* transmission gear. **4** edge. – *hutan* edge of the forest. – *tanggal rawan murah* to get a chance when it's too late. *lunak* – *daripada lidah* very gentle/mild. – *dan lidah adakalanya bergigit juga* husbands and wives or siblings are sometimes also at odds with e.o. – *air* a) the rippled surface of water. b) the edge of the sea (on the beach), sea-line, horizon.

– *akhir* final gear. – *anjing/asu* upper canine tooth, eyetooth. – *bayi* baby teeth. – *benar* permanent teeth. – *berdukung* overlapping teeth. – *buatan* artificial tooth, denture, dental prosthesis. – *bungsu* wisdom tooth. – *déwasa* adult/permanent teeth. – *garpu* tines of a fork. – *geligi* all the teeth in one's mouth. – *geraham* molar. – *geraham bungsu* wisdom tooth. – *gergaji* teeth of a saw. – *gerigi* gears, cogs. – *hutan* the uneven fringes of the jungle, edge of the wood(s). – *jentera* sprocket. – *ka(m)pak* large front teeth. – *laut* high-water mark. – *manis* incisor. – *palsu/pasangan* false tooth. – *pengiris* incisor. – *sambut* overbite. – *sayap kumbang* blackened teeth. – *sejati* permanent teeth. – *semara danta* snow-white teeth. – *seri* four largest teeth in horses; incisor. – *sisir* teeth of a comb. – *sulung* the four front teeth. – *susu* milk teeth, baby teeth. – *taring* a) eyetooth, canine. b) fang. – *telur* part of the beak of a chick for breaking out of the egg. – *tetap* permanent tooth. – *tikus* small evenly spaced teeth. – *tiruan* false teeth, dentures.
　gigi-gigi 1 tread (of tires). **2** perforations (at edges of stamps, etc.).
　bergigi 1 with/to have teeth. *tidak ~* toothless. **2** to have authority. *tidak ~* powerless, dead as a doornail. *belum ~ hendak mengunyah* to have no power yet but already want to take action. **3** with a gear/cogwheel. *keréta api ~* cog railroad. *~ rendah* with a low gear.
　menggigi *~ air* to appear on the horizon.
　penggigian gear, toothing.
　pergigian dentition, dentistry.

gigih I (*M*) **1** (stand) firm, persevering, stubborn, obstinate, adamant. *Partai itu – mempertahankan démokrasi.* The party firmly defended democracy. **2** grim, fervent, tenacious, unyielding. *perjuangan yang lebih* – a grimmer/more intensive struggle.
　segigih as fervent(ly)/adamant(ly)/tenacious(ly) as.
　bergigih to persevere.
　kegigihan tenacity, obstinacy, perseverance, persistence, stubbornness.

gigih II (*Jv*) cooked sticky rice.

gigih III (*ob*) → GIGIL. **menggigih** to shiver (with), shudder (at).

gigil shiver, shudder. *demam* – fever with ague. – *kedinginan* cold shiver.
　menggigil to shiver, tremble (from cold/fear, etc.), chatter of teeth. *~ kedinginan* to shake with cold. *~ ketakutan* to shiver from fear.
　menggigilkan 1 to make s.o. shiver/shudder. **2** horrible, ghastly.
　gigilan shiver, shudder, jitter. *~ émosi* a shiver of emotion.

gigir I → GIGIL.

gigir II (*Jv*) – *gunung* mountain ridge.

gigis bergigis serrated.

gigit bite. – *jari* to feel disappointed/frustrated.
　segigit a bite (of s.t.).
　bergigit(an) to bite e.o. *gigi dengan lidah ada kalanya ~ juga* close family members sometimes also quarrel.
　menggigit 1 to bite. *digigit kobra* bitten by a cobra. *~ bibir saja* to restrain one's anger. *~ gigi* to hold back one's anger. *~ jari* to be disappointed because s.t. didn't work out. *~ lidah* (*M*) a) confused, perplexed, ashamed. b) not daring to speak openly. *~ pangsa* to profit (from s.t.). *~ telunjuk* to be disappointed. **2** to pinch, squeeze. *Sepatu itu terasa ~ karena sempit.* The shoe seems to be pinching because it's too tight. **3** biting (cold, etc.), scathing (criticism, etc.). *dalam hawa dingin ~* in biting cold. *anjing yang menyalak tiada ~* his bark is worse than his bite. *belum bergigi sudah ingin ~* has no power but wants to take action.
　menggigiti (*pl obj*) to bite, etc.
　tergigit [and **kegigit** (*coq*)] **1** bitten. **2** bitten unintentionally. *~ lidah* unable to take action because of a debt of gratitude to s.o. *~ oléhku lidahku ketika sedang makan tadi.* I accidentally bit my tongue when I was eating. **3** taken in by trickery.
　gigitan a bite. *mendapat ~* to get bitten.
　penggigit biter.
　penggigitan biting.

gigolo (*D/E*) gigolo.

gigrig (*Jv*) to fall, drop off. *Tidak – bulunya.* It's not shedding its feathers.

gijuhéi (during the *Jap* occupation) volunteer for military duty.

gila 1 mad, crazy, idiotic, silly, foolish. *main* – a) to joke around, jest, banter. b) to act arbitrarily. 2 – *akan* mad about, infatuated/obsessed with. – *amuk* to run amok. – *angin* mentally unbalanced. – *anjing* rabies. – *asmara* madly in love. – *asyik* madly in love. – *babi* epilepsy. – *bayang-bayang* wanting the impossible. – *berahi* to fall in love, be madly in love. – *bola* soccer-crazy. *orang* – *bola* soccer fan/fanatic. – *burung* bird lover. – *gadis* fond of girls, girl-crazy. – *harta* money-mad. – *hati* fall in love, be madly in love. – *Hongkong* Hong Kong syndrome. – *hormat* status conscious, demanding respect (or adulation) from one's subordinates. – *isim* religion-mad. – *jabatan* status conscious. – *judi* gambling-mad. – *kasmaran* fall in love, madly in love. – *kebangsaan* chauvinistic, ultranationalistic. – *kekuasaan* power-hungry. – *kerja* workaholic. *seorang – kerja* a workaholic. – *laki-laki* boy crazy. – *mambang* fashion plate, a woman who loves to dress up. – *pangkat* office seeker. – *perempuan* girl-crazy. – *renang* not quite right in one's head, a bit crazy. – *turunan* proud of one's origin/descent. – *uang* money-mad. – *wanita* woman-crazy.

gilanya the crazy thing (about it) is ...

gila-gila ~ *air/bahasa/basa* somewhat crazy.

segila as crazy as.

bergila-gila to fight back crazily (as a lunatic would); to behave like a fool, fool around.

menggila 1 to be an aficionado of. ~ *burung* bird-lover. 2 to increase in intensity, get crazier/wilder. *Démonstrasi mahasiswa di Koréa Selatan makin ~ saja.* Student demonstrations in South Korea were getting wilder. 3 to go up like crazy (of prices). *Harga makin ~ sehingga terasa nilai uang makin merosot.* Prices were going up like crazy so that it felt like the value of the money was going down. 4 to be very fond (of), be crazy (about). *digila talak tiga* to still want one's ex-wife after the third and final divorce.

menggila-gila to fight back like crazy.

menggilai to drive s.o. mad. *Demiklanlah kelakuan orang yang digilai pangkat.* That's the way a person who desperately wants a position behaves.

menggila(-gila)kan and **mempergilakan** to drive s.o. mad/wild, make s.o. crazy. *Gadis itu betul-betul telah ~ dia sehingga ia lupa akan studinya.* That girl really drove him mad so that he forgot about his studies.

tergila the craziest.

tergila-gila infatuated (with), crazy (about), obsessed (with). *Gadis itu ~ kepada pemuda ganteng itu.* The girl was crazy about that good-looking guy.

gila-gilaan 1 to act (like a) crazy (person); like crazy. *pengusaha yang berékspansi ~* businesses that expanded like crazy. 2 to act wild, do things that are wild/exciting.

kegilaan 1 madness, insanity, dementia. 2 mania, craze. 3 stupidity, folly.

kegila-gilaan 1 maniacal, possessed. 2 not quite right in the head.

penggila aficionado, s.o. who is crazy about s.t.

gilaf (*ob*) → KHILAF.

gilang – *cemerlang/gemilang* glittering, scintillating, glorious.

gilap burnished. – *gemilap* lustrous, glittering.

menggilap lustrous, glittering.

menggilapkan to make s.t. gleam, polish.

gilapan glazing.

gilas crush, grind. *mesin* – roller, cylinder.

menggilas 1 to pulverize, crush, grind; to roll, flatten. ~ *cabé di batu cobékan* to grind hot peppers in a mortar. 2 to run over (s.o./a dog, etc.), knock down, run into s.o., collide with (another car). *Kerbau itu mati digilas keréta api.* The water buffalo was run over and killed by a train. 3 to stifle, suppress, silence (opposition). *Apakah yang dapat kulakukan untuk ~ semua perasaan?* What can I do to suppress all my feelings?

menggilaskan to run down/over.

tergilas [and **kegilas** (*coq*)] run over. *Ali téwas seketika ~ truk angkutan tanah di Jalan Merdéka.* Ali was killed outright, knocked down by a truck transporting sand on Jalan Merdeka.

gilasan crushing, squashing.

kegilasan collision, crash, smash.

penggilas 1 crusher, pulverizer, grinder. 2 roller, cylinder. 3 rolling pin. ~ *és* ice crusher. ~ *jalan* road roller.

penggilasan crushing, grinding, smashing, shattering.

gilau → KILAU.

giles → GILAS.

gili I (*M*) **menggili(-gili)** 1 to tickle. 2 to incite, egg on.

gili II (*Jv*) a (reef) island (in the sea). *Lokasi itu terlindung oléh – di sekitarnya.* The site was protected by a reef around it.

gili-gili 1 earthen dike. 2 sidewalk.

gilig (*Jv*) and **gilik I** 1 round, oval. 2 chubby.

gilik II → GÉLÉK I. **menggilik** to grind (down), pulverize, crush.

gilik III → GILI I. **menggilik** to tickle.

giling grind, mill, roll. *batu* – grindstone. *anak batu* – rolling pin. *masa/musim – tebu* milling period of sugarcane factory. *beras* – milled rice; *opp* BERAS *tumbuk*.

giling-giling steam roller.

bergiling to roll, turn.

menggiling 1 to roll (cigarettes). 2 to mill (rice), grind (spices), press (sugarcane). ~ *beras menjadi tepung* to grind rice into flour. 3 to flatten (with a roller), run over (with a vehicle). 4 to knead. ~ *adonan kué* to knead dough.

menggilingkan to mill/grind for s.o. else.

tergiling 1 milled. 2 run over (by a car).

gilingan 1 ground, milled. ~*nya halus* it was ground fine. 2 mill; millstone. 3 act/way of milling.

penggiling grinder, roller, mangle. ~ *beras* rice huller. ~ *beton* cement mixer. ~ *jalan* steam roller.

penggilingan 1 (rice-)mill. 2 milling. ~ *bola* ball milling.

giliper (*coq*) → GERIPIR.

gilir (one's) turn. – *kerja* shift (at work). *singgah pada dia* – to wait one's turn. *pada –nya* in turn. *tunggu –* to wait one's turn. – *ganti* take turns. **(ber)gilir-ganti** alternately. – *kerja* shift.

bergilir 1 to change, rotate, turn (of seasons). ~ *ke buritan* to be a henpecked husband. *Musim ~ lagi, kini musim panas telah mulai.* The season has turned, the hot season is starting now. 2 by/in turns, turn (and turn) about, alternately. *Untuk pergi berbelanja ke pasar dapat dilakukan secara ~.* Going shopping in the market can be done by turns.

gilir-bergilir to take turns, alternate. *Meréka ~ mendapat arisan itu.* They took turns getting the *arisan*.

bergilir-gilir alternately, in turns. *suka dan duka ~* happiness and sorrows alternate.

bergiliran (*pl subj*) to take turns, (do things) in shifts. *Anak-anak yang bermain kasti itu ~ memukul bola.* The children playing *kasti* took turns hitting the ball.

menggilir 1 to take turns. 2 to take turns with.

menggiliri to take turns with. *Kalau meréka ~ seorang perempuan, saya juga ikut.* When they take turns with a woman, I join in.

menggilirkan to have s.o. do s.t. alternately. *Ketua RT ~ anggota-anggota RT-nya meronda.* The head of the RT had the members of the RT take turns doing the rounds.

mempergilirkan 1 to have s.o. do s.t. alternately, have s.o. take a turn. 2 to have (s.o.) take a turn with, turn s.t. over (to). *Tongkat komando dipergilirkan ke Angkatan Udara.* Command was turned over to the Air Force.

giliran 1 turn, opportunity, move. *pada ~nya* in his turn. ~ *gelap* blackout, outage. ~ *kerja* (work)shift. ~ *pemadaman (listrik mati)* blackout, power outage. 2 shift (at work).

kegiliran to get/take one's turn. ~ *kerja* work shift. *yang dibagi dalam tiga ~ kerja* it was divided into three shifts.

penggiliran rotating, rotation, making people take turns.

pergiliran rotation. ~ *tanaman* crop rotation.

gilotin (*D*) guillotine.

gim I (*D*) short for *gymnasium*.

gim II (*J*) gold thread.

gim III (*E*) → GAME.

giman [*gigi mancung*] a sharp/pointed tooth.

gimana (*coq*); → BAGAIMANA. – *sih*? What's with ...? *É, – sih, wartawan-wartawan ini kalau nulis?"* "Hey, what's with these reporters when they write?"

menggimanakan to do what to. *Meréka itu digimanakan, ditindak keras.* What's to be done to them, they should be treated firmly.

gimbal I (*Jv*) unkempt hair. *rambut –* a hair lobe.

gimbal II (*Jv*) a dish made of fried flour chips containing shrimp or fish. *– udang* shrimps baked in flour.

gimnasium (*D col*) gymnasium, grammar school.

gimnastik (*D*) gymnastics.

gimpal a large gold/silver pendant.

gin (*E*) gin.

ginang-ginang → RENGGINANG.

gincu (*C*) (*– bibir*) lipstick. *– pipi* rouge.
  bergincu to wear/put on lipstick, with lipstick on.
  menggincu to apply lipstick to, color.

Gincung Pridina (*mil*) the principle of always giving priority to the state.

gindé (in Bengkulu) village chief.

ginding (*S*) beautifully dressed up; to dress up with nice clothing.

ginékolog (*D*) gynecologist.

ginékologi (*D/E*) gynecology.

ginggang and **gingham** striped fabric; → GÉNGGANG.

gingkang (*C*) → GINKANG.

gingsi → GÉNGSI.

gingsir (*J/Jv*) **menggingsir** and **ngengingsir 1** to shift, displace. **2** to change place.

gingsul (*J/Jv*) irregular (of teeth), one or more teeth are protruding outward.

gingsut (*ob*) → INGSUT.

gini I (*coq*) → BEGINI. *kaya –* like this. *– saja!* let's just do it like this! *–.–, ya* it's like this, let me explain. *– hari* a) for this time of the day. b) nowadays.
  segini as much as this (making a gesture with the hands showing the size).

gini II → GANA-GINI I, II.

ginjal kidney. *anak –* adrenal gland. *batu –* stone in the kidney, renal calculus. *ada batu dalam –nya* he suffers from kidney stones. *kegagalan –* renal failure. *ahli –* nephrologist. *radang –* nephritis.
  mengginjal kidney-shaped.

ginjéan Chinese motherwort, bloody flower motherwort, *Leonurus sibiricus.*

ginjel → GINJAL.

ginkang (*C*) (art of) bodily/physical control/relief.

gino [gigi nongol] prominent front teeth.

ginséng 1 any of several plants of the genus *Panax, esp P. pseudog-inseng,* of eastern Asia, having an aromatic root. **2** the root of the plant shaped like a man. **3** medicine (made from the ginseng root).

ginsi → GÉNGSI.

gintil pellet, pill, tablet.
  menggintil to turn into a pellet.
  penggintil so. that makes pellets.

gintungan k.o. tree, bishop wood, *Bischofia javanica.*

gintur (*BG*) to sleep.

giok (*C*) → BATU giok.

gip(s) (*D*) **1** gypsum. **2** plaster (of Paris).
  menggip(s) to plaster, put a cast on.

gipsi (*E*) Gipsy.

gir (*E*) gear (of a car/motorcycle, etc.). *– belakang* sprocket wheel. *– depan* chain gear.

girai → GÉRAI.

giral (*D*) *uang –* deposit money; → GIRO.

giralisasi payment by money transfer.

giran person who has a demand deposit account.

girang cheerful, glad, joyful, elated. *Tante –* "Merry Aunt," i.e., a married woman from the upper classes who chases after younger men. *– gembira/gemirang* overjoyed.
  segirang as cheerful as.
  bergirang to be happy. *~ hati* to be cheerful.
  girang-menggirang joyful.
  menggirangkan 1 to gladden, cheer s.o. up, make s.o. rejoice, delight. **2** rejoicing. **3** delightful.
  kegirangan 1 gladness, joy, mirth. **2** gleefully, with joy. *menangis ~* to weep with joy.

kegirang-girangan elated, exuberant, full of joy, joyful, overjoyed.

penggirang cheerful person.

girap-girap (*Jv*) and **girap-gemirap** to be startled. *membuatnya –* startled her.

giras (*Hind*) *kain –* coarse linen.

giri (*Skr*) mountain (in place names, such as *Inderagiri*).

girik (*Jv*) **1** documentary evidence, document in support, *esp* a temporary deed of ownership where a permanent deed is not available. **2** land tax assessment paper. **3** certificate of *Ipéda* tax payment. **4** schedule of rounds by guards. *– bodong* a counterfeit *girik;* → ASPAL II.
  menggirik to assess.

girikan (*Ban*) farm implement.

girik-girik (*M*) betel-nut pounder. *~ telah mengguncang* (*M*) already very old, senile.

giring drive, herd.
  menggiring 1 (*Mal*) to drive wild animals. **2** to herd cattle, escort a criminal, etc. to a certain place. *Polisi itu ~ para penjahat ke rumah tahanan.* The police herded the criminals into the jail. **3** (in soccer) to dribble. *Ia mendapat bola dan terus ~nya ke mulut gawang lawannya.* He got the ball and dribbled it to in front of the other goalie.
  menggiringkan 1 to escort, take s.o. somewhere. **2** to herd for s.o. else.
  tergiring driven.
  giringan procession.
  penggiringan 1 driving, herding. **2** escorting (a criminal).

giring-giring I 1 bells (on anklets). **2** bicycle bell.

giring-giring II various plants with seeds that rattle in their shells and which can be used for green manure, *Crotalaria spp.* and others.

giris (*Jv*) frightening(ly). *Angin bertiup –.* The wind was blowing terrifyingly.
  menggiriskan to frighten, make s.o. shiver/chilly. *Boléh jadi tangan yang dipotong itu untuk ~ warga kota.* The cut-off hand might have been to frighten the residents of the city.

girlan [pinggir jalan] (in Bogor) sidewalk.

girli [pinggir kali] river edge.

giro (*D*) **1** demand deposit. **2** transfer, clearing. *– bilyét* (*D*) clearing forms issued by a bank in the form of a checkbook. *– pos* clearing forms issued by a post office.

giroh → GAIRAH.

giroskop (*D/E*) gyroscope.

giru *ikan –* clown fish, *Amphirion polymus.*

gisar I 1 to roll s.t. between the two hands. **2** to insert s.t. while rotating it (like a cork into a bottle). **3** to rub two things together to make a fire. **4** to rub s.t. by rotating the hands.

gisar II → KISAR.

gisi → GIZI.

gisik I → GÉSÉK. **menggisik** *~ mata* to rub one's eyes.

gisik II (*Jv*) and **gisikan** beach, shore, foreland (of a river). *– pasiran* sandy beach. *– penghalang* barrier beach. *– tenggelam* drowned beach.

gisil → GÉSÉL. **menggisil** to scour.

gisir → GÉSÉR. **menggisir** to rub.

gita (*Skr*) hymn. *– Jaya* "Song of Greater Jakarta," name of the official hymn of the Greater Jakarta Capital Region. *– Karya* name of a printing house in Jakarta (formerly O. Kolff). *– puja* hymn.

gitar (*D/E*) guitar. *– bas* bass guitar. *– klasik* classical guitar. *– listrik* electric guitar. *– pengiring* accompaniment guitar.
  bergitar to play the guitar.
  menggitar 1 to play the guitar. **2** with an hourglass figure, curvaceous (said of a woman).
  penggitar guitarist.

gitaris (*D/E*) guitarist.

gitchu (*BG*) → GITU.

gitek (*S*) to shake one's behind.

gites (*Jv*) **menggites** to kill (lice) by pressing with the thumbnails.

giti former, ex-; → LAMA. *dokter – yang selama ini sudah bekerja* the ex-doctor who is still working.

gitik (*Jv*) **menggitik 1** to beat. **2** to stimulate, excite. **3** (*vulg*) to screw, fuck.

giting (*sl from tinggi*) high (on drugs).

gitok (*Jv*) nape of the neck. *Membikin -nya mengkirig.* It made his hair stand on end.

gitu (*coq*) → BEGITU. *Jangan – dong!* a) Don't act like that! b) Don't say that! *kaya* – like that.

gitu-gitu so-so. *"Tapi réstoran yang ada kok makanannya ~ saja," tutur Amler.* "But the food in the existing restaurants is just so-so," said Amler. *~ lagi* the same thing (over and over again).

segitu as much as that (making a gesture with the hands to show how much is meant).

begituan (*vulg*) to screw, fuck.

menggitukan [and **menggituin** and **nggituin** (*J coq*)] (*vulg*) to fuck, screw; → MENGANUKAN, MENYEBADANI. *Saya lihat Tina digituin Dicky, tapi saya tak ikut-ikutan gituin Tina.* I saw Dicky screwing Tina, but I didn't join in screwing her.

gituan (*vulg*) **1** shit. **2** screwing, fucking. *Seorang tukang sapu yang disapa menjawab: "Hotél ini mémang tempat ~, pak."* A sweeper who was accosted answered: "This hotel is a whore house, sir." *film ~* pornographic film. *penyakit ~* venereal disease. **3** reefer, marijuana cigarette.

gitu-gituan in that way (implying it's bad).

giuk (*naut*) *- dalam* inboard guy. *- luar* outboard guy.

penggiuk unofficial banker in a card game.

giur menggiurkan 1 to arouse desire, tempting. **2** sexy. **3** exciting. *~ hati* charming, enchanting.

tergiur charmed, enchanted, fascinated, excited, tempted, excited.

tergiurkan gullible. *Pajangan iklan bagi konsumén kaya yang ~.* The advertising displays are for rich gullible consumers.

penggiur s.o. arousing/enticing.

giwah (*Pers*) sandals.

giwang I mother-of-pearl.

giwang II (*C?*) ear stud (with one stone).

gizi (*A*) nutrition, nutrient, nutritive element. *ahli* – nutritionist. *bahan* – nutrients. *ilmu* – science of nutrition, dietetics. *kaya* – nutritious, full of nutrients; nourishing. *kekurangan* – not nutritious. *kelebihan* – overnutritious. *nilai* – nutritional/food value. *pangan* – nutrient. *penyakit kurang* – marasmus.

bergizi nutritious, nourishing. *makanan ~* nutritious food.

pergizian related to nutrients.

gl- also see entries beginning with **gel-**.

gladi (*Jv*) drill, training, rehearsal; → LATIHAN. *– Berganda* (*mil*) Joint Training (carried out by the Armed Forces Reserve Officers School of the Department of the Interior). *– bersih* dress rehearsal. *– kotor* general rehearsal prior to the *– resik. – resik* dress/general rehearsal. **bergladi-resik** to hold a general rehearsal. *– tangguh* survival exercise.

gladiator (*D*) gladiator.

gladiol (*D*) gladiola.

glagah (*Jv*) wild sugarcane grass, thatch grass, k.o. reed grass in watery places, *Saccharum spontaneum. - p(e)rumpung* (*Jv*) Eulalia grass, *Miscanthus/Eulalia japonica.*

glagepan (*Jv*) to stammer (from stress).

glamor (*E*) and **keglamoran** glamour. *Mémang, kehidupan seorang artis sarat dengan keglamoran.* Indeed, the life of an artist is full of glamor.

glamur [golongan-lanjut-umur] senior citizens.

glangsi (*Jv*) coarsely twisted sack for sugar (in sugar manufacturing).

glasial (*D/E*) glacial. *masa* – glacial epoch.

glasiasi (*D*) glaciation; → PENGÉSAN.

glasir (*D*) glaze, icing.

mengglasir to glaze, ice.

glasnost (*Russian*) openness; → KETERBUKAAN.

glasur → GLASIR.

glaukoma (*D*) glaucoma.

glayung (*Jv Jatim*) one sheaf (two bunches of newly harvested rice bound together); about 12 *kati.*

glazur → GLASIR. **berglazur** glazed.

glebagan and **glebakan** (*Jv*) crop rotation (sugarcane and rice).

gléca-glécé (*Jv*) moody.

glécé (*Jv*) **ngglécé** to joke.

glédég (*Jv*) **glédégan** hawker's cart.

glédék → GELÉDÉK.

glegar-gleger (*Jv*) to drone/rumble/roar/boom loudly (cannon shots/grenade explosions, etc.).

glégék (*Jv*) **glégékan** to belch.

glek (*onom*) sound made by gulping down a drink: glug. *Dan, – racun itu masuk ke lambungnya.* And, glug, glug, the poison went into his stomach.

mengglek to gulp down. *Dulu, opium diglek bersama anggur.* Opium used to be gulped down with wine.

glembug (*Jv*) *– Sala Solo* sweet talk in order to tempt/deceive.

glendem (*Jv*) **ngglendem 1** to speak softly and melodiously. **2** to do s.t. sneakily.

glenggem → GLENDEM.

glenik (*Jv*) to chat (about trivial matters), make empty promises.

gletang k.o. weed, *Spilanthes labadicensis sp.*

glétser (*D*) glacier.

glidig (*Jv*) to work as a laborer, *usu* in sugar factories or sugarcane fields.

glikogén (*E*) glycogen.

glikosa → GLUKOSA.

glinding (*Jv*) (in Pekalongan) horse-drawn buggy; → DOKAR.

gliserin (*D/E*) glycerin.

gliserol (*D/E*) glycerol.

global I (*D*) roughly, in rough outline.

global II (*E*) global. *Para pemimpin dunia harus bersatu mencegah kita menuju déprési –.* World leaders have to unite to prevent us from heading for a global depression. *perundingan –* global negotiations.

globalisasi (*E*) globalization.

globe (*D*) globe.

globulin (*E*) globulin.

glogor (*Jv*) **ngglogori** to rattle on. *Suaranya mulai ~.* His voice began to rattle on.

glondongan I (*Jv*) **1** log, i.e., a portion or length of the trunk or of a large limb of a felled tree. **2** reel (of film), roll (of paper). *secara – (buy or sell) as one complete package.

glondongan II (*Jv*) a large young milkfish; → NÉNÉR.

glontor (*Jv*) **ngglontor** to flush. *Pengaliran air Jatiluhur terlebih dahulu diglontor.* The flow of Jatiluhur water was first flushed.

glos (*D ling*) gloss.

glotal (*D ling*) glottal.

glotalisasi (*D ling*) glottalization.

glotis (*D/E ling*) glottis.

glukosa (*D*) glucose.

GM (*init*) → GERMO.

GMF (*init*) Garuda Maintenance Facility.

go I (*C*) five.

go II and **GO** [Gonorrhea] gonorrhea.

goa → GUA I.

goak → GAOK.

goal (*E*) → GOL I.

goansiau (*C*) lantern festival.

goba(h) lagoon, slough.

gobah → GUBAH II 2, KUBAH.

gobak and **gobag** (*Jv*) (*– sodor*) a child's game played on a badminton court in which players try to keep s.o. from entering a square.

goban (*C J*) fifty thousand.

gobang I (*col*) a copper coin with a hole in the middle valued at two and a half cents; → BÉNGGOL II. *film kelas tiga –* low-class film.

segobang a two-and-a-half-cent coin.

gobang II (*Jv*) large, heavy (rectangular) knife (for carving tobacco).

gobar (*A*) gloomy (of sky), dejected, somber, depressed. *- hati* sad.

go bék (*E*) (to) go back.

gobék areca nut pounder. *anak/mata* – pestle.

menggobék to pound/pulverize/crush with that device.

gobét (*J*) **1** slicing knife with a serrated blade. **2** knife for chopping tobacco leaves.

menggobét to cut with such a knife.

gobi – *blirik* k.o. swamp fish, bumblebee catfish, *Brachygobius doriae*.

goblék (*J*) **1** come off, succeed. **2** as one pleases; at any price/cost. *Aing ngomong asal – (saja)*. Aing talked just for the sake of talking; → ASBUN.

goblok (*J/Jv*) stupid, idiotic, moronic.

segoblok as stupid as.

nggoblok-goblokin to make s.o. stupid.

tergoblok the stupidest.

kegoblokan stupidity, idiocy, imbecility.

gobnor (*ob*) → GUBERNUR.

gocan (*J*) restless, to toss and turn (in one's sleep, etc.).

gocap (*C*) fifty (rupiahs).

gocék (*Jv*) **menggocék** ~ *bola* (in soccer) to get hold of the ball.

gocéng (*C*) five thousand.

gocét (*J*) tricky foot movement (in sports).

gocoh bergocoh to box, spar with.

bergocoh-gocohan to box with e.o.

menggocoh to hit with the closed fist.

menggocohkan to hit with.

pergocohan fight, tussle.

goda tempt.

menggoda 1 to (attempt to) seduce, allure, tempt, try to make s.o. do s.t. immoral. *Iblis selalu ~ manusia untuk berbuat jahat*. The Devil always tempts human beings to act badly. *digoda Sétan* tempted by the Devil. **2** to tease, torment, harass, plague. *Kau terus ~nya sehingga dia menangis*. You kept on teasing him until he cried.

menggodai [and **nggodain/ngegodain** (*J coq*)] (*pl obj*) to keep on tempting/teasing, etc.

menggodakan tempting, seductive.

tergoda 1 tempted, seduced. *Kalau imanmu teguh, engkau takkan ~ oléh bujukannya*. If your faith is strong, you won't be tempted by his enticements. **2** harassed, bothered.

godaan 1 seduction, temptation. *Gadis itu terpikat kepada ~ pria yang ganteng dan tampan itu*. The girl was attracted to the dashing and handsome man's temptations. **2** plague, torment. ~ *duniawi* worldly temptations. ~ *sétan* temptations of the devil.

penggoda seducer, tempter, tormentor, tease.

penggodaan seducing, tempting.

godak (*cla*) rice mixed with all k.o. side dishes.

menggodak ~ *nasi* to cook rice together with the side dishes in one pot.

godal-gadul (*Jv*) to bounce back and forth.

godam sledgehammer.

menggodam to hit with (a sledgehammer/bludgeon/fist, etc.). *digodam tiada indah, ditémbak tiada lut* an invulnerable person.

penggodam mace, club.

godang (*Bat*) great, grand. *sinode* – grand synod.

godék I (*Jv*) side whiskers, sideburns; → CAMBANG.

bergodék with sideburns. *Pria ~ itu seorang pastor*. The man with sideburns is a pastor.

godék II (*J*) shaking, wagging.

menggodékkan to shake, wag.

tergodék-godék to wag back and forth (of a dog's tail).

godok and **godog** (*J/Jv*) boiled. *mi* – boiled noodles.

menggodok 1 to boil. **2** to hatch, plan, draw up (a set of laws or regulations). *Sidang ~ usul-usul yang masuk TR*. The session drew up suggestions for the TR. **3** (*mil*) to train. **4** to prepare, draw up, consider. *Pengganti gubernur Jawa Tengah kini sedang digodok*. A replacement for the governor of Central Java is now under consideration.

tergodok prepared, trained.

godokan 1 boiled. *air* ~ the water in which s.t. has been boiled. **2** done and soft. **3** fully considered. **4** (*mil*) trained, molded. **5** training, molding; effect.

penggodokan 1 boiling. **2** hatching, planning, drawing up. *dalam prosés* ~ in the planning stage. **3** (*mil*) training.

godot (*J*) **menggodot 1** to saw through/off. **2** to cut into (a loaf, etc.). ~ *ketupat* to cut into a *ketupat*. **3** to fleece s.o. (down to the last penny). ~ *hati* painful, sad.

goék (*onom*) sound of clearing the throat.

menggoék to clear one's throat.

gogah (*Pers*) din, noise.

gogo I (*Jv*) dry/nonirrigated rice field; → HUMA, LADANG. *padi* – rice grown on dry rice field. – *rancah* rice cultivation on nonirrigated rice field.

gogo II (*E*) go-go dance.

bergogo to dance this dance.

gogoh menggogoh to shiver (from ague), quiver (of trees).

gogok I (*Jv*) **menggogok 1** to gulp down water from an earthen water pitcher, etc. without touching the mouth. **2** to guzzle.

penggogok an alcoholic, drunkard.

gogok II k.o. necklace.

gogol (*Jv*) person who has rights to parts of common land.

gogos (*Jv*) washed away (soil); undermined.

menggogos to undermine, sap.

tergogos washed away. ~ *banjir* washed away by a flood.

gogrog (*Jv*) **1** to fall off (prematurely). **2** to lose. *SOKSI semakin – !* SOKSI is losing more and more members!

gogrogan s.t. fallen off.

goha → GUA I.

gohiong → NGOHIANG.

gohok (*J*) k.o. plant with sour purple fruit, *Eugenia polycephalata*.

gohong (*M*) hole, cave.

gojag-gajeg (*S*) hesitant, undecided.

gojék and **gojékan** to fool around, laugh and joke around.

gojlok and **gojlog** (*J*) **menggojlok 1** to shake, give s.o. a good shaking. **2** to haze (new students, etc.).

menggojloki (*pl obj*) to shake, etc.

kegojlok-gojlok shaken up, jolted.

(peng)gojlogan hazing (in a rough way in colleges).

gokar(t) (*E*) go-cart, mini racing car.

gokdor [*disogok lalu dor*] loaded and then bang; → DORGOK, SENJATA *dorgok*. *pistol* – muzzle loader.

gokil (*Pr*) crazy; → GILA.

gol I (*D*) **1** goal. **2** score, point. **3** to be successful, win. *Kalau usul yang kuajukan itu – kita akan merayakannya*. If the proposal I submitted wins, we'll celebrate. *tak bakalan –* will not succeed, fail. *mencétak –* to score a goal.

meng(e)golkan 1 to score (a goal). **2** to make a success of, be successful at. **3** to push s.t. through to acceptance/victory.

pengegolan pushing s.o. through to victory.

gol II (in acronyms) → GOLONGAN.

golak – *galik* a) to turn repeatedly/over and over; → BOLAK-BALIK. b) convection. *menggolak-galik* to turn over and over. *menggolak-galikkan badan* to turn over and over (in one's sleep). – *gejolak* flare-up.

bergolak 1 to boil (of water). **2** to seethe, churning. *laut ~* churning sea. **3** to be in commotion, turbulent, churn(ing). **4** to riot, take to the streets.

bergolak-golak to keep on boiling.

menggolak to boil, brew.

golakan turbulence, seething.

pergolakan commotion, difficulties, troubles, turbulence, violence, upheaval.

golang (*S*) **menggolangkan** to make s.t. turn; to put s.t. into circulation; to make (money) productive.

penggolangan putting s.t. into circulation.

golbi (*D*) fly (of trousers).

golék I easily swaying; easily shaken or rolled; rolling, rocking. *hantu –* a sheeted ghost believed to propel itself by rolling along the ground. *bantal –* Dutch wife, long pillow. – *gelantung* to roll over and over.

golék-golék to lounge around.

bergolék 1 roll over and over (like a ball), pitch (of boats), tumble. *Gundunya ~ masuk ke dalam lubang*. The marble rolled and went into the hole. **2** to roll over (on), lie down (on). *Anak itu ~ di atas tikar*. The child rolled over on the mat.

bergolékan (*pl subj*) roll over and over.

bergolék-golék to roll over and over.

menggolék 1 to roll s.t. **2** to lay s.t. down.

menggolékkan 1 to make s.t. roll, roll s.t. **2** to lay s.t. down (on), put s.o. to bed. ~ *badan* to lie down.

tergolék 1 sprawled, stretched out. **2** rolled over. *Bus itu ~ ke lembah karena pecah ban.* The bus rolled over into the valley because a tire burst.

tergolék-golék rocked repeatedly. *tertawa ~* rocking with laughter.

golék II (*S*) three-dimensional wooden puppet. *wayang –* (performance with) those puppets, k.o. marionettes. *– jénggél/jonggol* tumbler (an easily tipped, self-righting toy).

golékan (*Jv*) doll, puppet.

Goléklemah [Golongan-ékonomi-lemah] economically weak group.

goléng (*J*) **menggoléng** to touch, nudge.

golér (*J*) **bergolér 1** to lie around (in bed, etc.). **2** to turn, roll over.

menggolérkan 1 to lay s.t. down. **2** to roll s.t. over.

tergolér lying down, sprawled.

golf (*E*) /golef/ (to play) golf.

pegof golfer.

golfer (*E*) golfer.

golfisasi the construction of golf courses.

Golkar [Golongan Karya] Functional Work Group.

menggolkarkan to make s.o. a member of Golkar. *Saya datang bukan untuk ~ TATN.* I have not come to Golkarize the TATN. *~ diri* to join Golkar.

kegolkaran Golkar affairs. *Jutaan kader Golkar di désa-désa paham akan ~nya.* Thousands of Golkar cadres in the villages are thoroughly conversant with Golkar matters.

golkaris a member of Golkar.

Golkarisasi "Golkarization," i.e., efforts to make people become members or supporters of Golkar.

golok 1 machete. **2** (*J*) k.o. short sword. *– pencincang daging* chopper, cleaver, mincing knife.

bergolok to be armed with a *golok*. *Pemuda ~ ngamuk di lokasi WTS Rawa Bangké.* A young man armed with a *golok* ran amuck in a Rawa Bangke brothel.

menggolok to slash with such a weapon.

golong I (*Jv*) **bergolong-golong** in groups.

menggolong to group, become a group.

menggolongkan to group, classify into groups, group.

tergolong 1 grouped, classified. *Sebagian besar WNT ~ sebagai orang yang dikenai hukuman ringan.* Most of the WNT are classed as people who have been convicted of a misdemeanor. **2** to belong to, be included in (a group/class). *Beliau ~ orang bangsawan yang berdarah putih.* He belongs to the class of blue-blood aristocrats. *~ tua* to be a senior citizen.

golongan group, grouping, classification, circle, cohort, faction, class, wing (of a party). *masuk ~* to belong to. *~ A, B, C* the three different classes of persons apprehended after the uprising of 1965. *~ atasan* elite, upper class. *~ berpenghasilan rendah* those in the low-income bracket. *~ beruntung* the privileged. *~ bintara* noncommissioned officers. *~ darah* blood type. *~ desakan* pressure group. *~ ékonomi lemah* lower-income group. *~ fungsional* functional group. *~ gaji* wage scale. *~ harapan bangsa dan nusa/negara* the hope of the nation, the younger generation. *~ karya* functional group; → GOLKAR. *~ kepentingan* interest group. *~ keras* (in politics) the hawks. *~ lunak* (in politics) the doves. *~ masyarakat* social classes. *~ mayoritas/mayorität* the majority. *~ ménak* the feudal class. *~ menengah* the middle class. *~ merugi* the underprivileged. *~ minoritas/minorität* the minority. *~ ningrat* the aristocracy. *~ pertengahan* a) the middle class. b) tradespeople, trading class(es), small-sized industry and craftsmen. *~ pangkat* rank group. *~ PGPN/Peraturan Gaji Pegawai Negeri* government employees. *~ penekan* pressure group. *– Pilih Semua* [Golpis] Vote-For-All Group. *~ Putih* [Golput] White Group, nonvoting group. *~ sayap kiri* the left wing. *~ tamtama* enlisted men. *~ terbesar* the majority. *~ terkecil* the minority. *~ ultra-kanan* the ultra-right. *~ umur* age group. *~ upah* wage bracket.

penggolong (*ling*) classifier.

penggolongan grouping, classifying. *~ rakyat* ethnic groupings.

golong II → GULUNG.

golong III (*M*) **menggolong** to oppress, dominate. *Engkau bukan menolong, melainkan ~.* You're not helping, you're dominating.

golonganisme group spirit.

golpi → GOLBI.

Golpis [Golongan Pilih Semua] Vote-for-All Group, *q.v.*

Golput [Golongan Putih] Group of Abstainers from Voting, *q.v.*

menggolput to act as a member of this group.

golputwan abstainer from voting.

gom (*D*) gum. *– arabika* gum Arabic.

gomar (*J*) clown.

gombak 1 crest (of bird). **2** forelock (of a person's hair/horse's mane) **3** tuft (of grass). **4** collar. *– keméja* ruffles on a shirt.

bergombak with a forelock, etc.

menggombak to cut hair; → MEMANGKAS 2.

gombakan forelock.

gombal (*Jv*) **1** rag(ged clothing), rags. *Bagaikan – meréka bergulung di bawah jembatan.* They huddled under the bridge like a bunch of rags. **2** worthless, good-for-nothing, of poor quality. **3** bullshit! *rayuan –* false flattery, coaxing, wheedling. *bupati –* a good-for-nothing regent. *ngomong yang –.–* nonsense, rubbish. **4** to say in a flattering way.

bergombal → GOMBAL 2.

menggombal to coax, wheedle.

menggombali to make sexual advances to.

penggombal flatterer.

kegombalan 1 worthlessness. **2** pretexts, poor excuses, etc.

gombalisasi (*sl*) **menggombalisasi** → MENGGOMBALI.

gombang I (glazed earthenware) water jar.

gombang II (*M*) handsome, good-looking. *– di labut* a) proud, conceited. **2** all that glitters is not gold.

gombéng menggombéng to widen, enlarge (a hole).

gombenis, gombinis, and **gombunis** commie (insulting word for Communist).

gombés (*J*) deflated; → KEMPÉS.

gombol → GEROMBOL.

gombong → KOMBONG II.

gombor too big (clothing), loose-fitting (clothes). *Dia bercelana panjang – berwarna hitam soré ini.* That afternoon she wore black, loose-fitting pants.

gombra (*J*) **1** a woman with long hair. **2** a talkative woman.

gombrang (*Jv*) **menggombrang** to cut/lop off.

gombroh → GOMBOR.

gombrong → GOMBOR.

kegombrongan being too big/loose.

gombyok I (*Jv*) fringe, tassel.

gombyok II (*Jv*) bunch.

segombyok a bunch. *~ kunci* a bunch of keys.

gompal (*J*) and **gompel** (*Jv*) broken, cracked, chipped, damaged. *Pisau cukurnya sudah –.* His razor was damaged. *Cangkirnya –.* The cup is chipped.

gompyok (*J*) dense and thick (of fruit/hair/leaves/rain/rice grains).

gonad (*E*) gonad, sexual gland.

goncang 1 shaky, shaking. **2** shaken, concussed. *– gancing* a) to fluctuate. b) fluctuation. *– otak* concussion (of the brain). *– syaraf* nervous breakdown. **3** unstable, shaky.

bergoncang 1 to shake, rock, sway, wobble. *Seluruh pondok kecil itu ~ apabila ditiup angin.* The entire hut shook when the wind blew. **2** shaky, unsteady, unstable, fluctuating.

menggoncang(kan) to shake (up), rock, upset, shock. *Kerusuhan yang berkesinambungan itu akan ~ keamanan negara.* The continuous riots shook up the country's security. *~ iman* to shake one's faith. *~ suasana* to shake up the situation.

tergoncang shaken, troubled. *~ hati ibu mendengar cerita sedih itu.* Mother was shaken when she heard the sad story.

tergoncang-goncang to keep on shaking.

tergoncangkan shakable.

goncangan 1 shock, emotion. **2** fluctuation, wobbling. **3** rock(ing), shaking, jolt.

kegoncangan 1 shock. **2** commotion, turmoil. **3** fluctuation. *~ harga* price fluctuations. *~ imannya* tempted to act in an immoral way.

penggoncang shaker. *~ koktail* cocktail shaker.

penggoncangan shaking, churning.

pergoncangan 1 shaking, wobbling. **2** shock, commotion.

goncéng → BONCÉNG. **menggoncéng** to hitch a ride (on the carrier of a bicycle or motorbike).

gondang I (S) large mortar for rice, rice pounding block.

gondang II (Jv) k.o. fig tree, *Ficus variegata*.

gondang III 1 (*siput* –) snails, *Ampullarius spp.* and *Cyclophorus spp.* **2** marine univalve mollusks, *Tonna spp.*

gondang IV k.o. traditional Batak music.

Gondangdia a residential area in Jakarta with many *gondang* or fig trees, *Ficus variegata*.

gondas-gandes (Jv) sexy.

gondél (Jv) hung down from s.t. *gelung* – a hair bun hanging down (low on the back of the neck).

menggondéli to hang/hold on. *digondéli oléh bandulan-bandulan yang dibuatnya sendiri* to be hung from weights which he made himself.

gondok I (M) short and thick (of pouter pigeon, knife, neck, horns).

gondok II goiter. *kelenjar* – thyroid gland. *penyakit* – goiter (the disease). – *laki* (S) Adam's apple. – *nadi* (*med*) aneurism.

gondokan suffering from goiter.

gondok III (J/Jv) **1** angry, furious. **2** annoyed. *rasa* – feeling of discontent. *menimbulkan rasa* – to bring about a feeling of discontent.

menggondokkan to infuriate.

gondokan easily annoyed.

kegondokan fury, anger, grudge.

gondol (Jv) **menggondol 1** to seize and carry off s.t. in the mouth or beak (of dogs/cats/birds). **2** to run away with, steal, abscond with. *Pencuri semalam* ~ *TV dan radio.* Last night the thief ran off with a TV and a radio. **3** to walk away with (a prize/victory, etc.). ~ *gelar* to earn a degree. ~ *médali* to win a medal.

tergondol 1 seized and carried off. **2** stolen. **3** attained, gotten.

penggondol s.o. who walks away with (a prize, etc.).

gondola (E) gondola (suspended underneath a balloon).

gondong I (J) mumps; → BEGUK.

gondongan to have the mumps.

gondong II (Jv) shuttle (of a loom).

gondorokem and **gondorukem** (Jv) → GANDAROKAM.

gondoruwo → GENDRUWO.

gondrong (J/Jv) long and bushy, unkempt (of hair). *rambut* – *acak-acakan sebatas pundak* shoulder-length, long and unkempt hair. *si Empat* – the Beatles.

menggondrongkan ~ *rambutnya* to let one's hair grow long and bushy.

kegondrongan and **penggondrongan** having long and bushy hair.

gong I (D) gong. *acara* – closing/signature tune (of a program). – *pelaung* gong struck to call people or to convey messages to another ship. – *pengerah* gong struck to muster people in an emergency.

menggongi [and **ngegongi** (J)] **1** (originally) to beat the gong. **2** to say yes and amen to everything (in order to be through with it).

menggongkan to say yes to s.t.

gong II (*onom*) **gong-gong-gong!** woof-woof-woof!

gonggo (J/Jv) spider. *sarang* – cobweb.

gonggok k.o. millipede, *Chilognatha spp.*

gonggon k.o. edible mollusk, *Strombus canarium Isabella.*

gonggong I → GONDOL.

gonggong II (*onom*) bow-wow.

menggonggong to bark.

menggonggongi to bark at.

gonggongan barking.

gonggong III k.o. card game.

gongli (S) [*bagong liar*] "dizzy pig," i.e., a loose teenage girl, a slut.

pergonglian prostitution by such a teenage girl.

gongséng I (J) **menggongséng** to dry-fry; → KELAPA *gongséng.*

gongséng II (Jv) the string of bells tied around the anklets of a *topéng* dancer.

gongso (Jv) → GONGSÉNG.

goni (Hind) **1** jute. **2** gunnysack; → GUNI.

menggonikan to put s.t. into a gunnysack.

gonjak (S) *kena* – to have one's leg pulled.

menggonjakkan to make a fool of s.o., make fun of s.o., pull s.o.'s leg.

gonjang-ganjing (Jv) to shake, rock, tremble. "*Bumi* –," *kata orang Jawa.* "The world is rocking to its foundations," say the Javanese. *tanpa banyak* – without much ado.

menggonjang-ganjingkan to shake the foundation of s.t.

gonjing (Jv) to rock, roll, be in danger of capsizing, be in imminent danger of collapse.

gonjok menggonjok(kan) to ridicule.

gonjong (M) and **bergonjong** to taper (like the *rebung* or bamboo shoot), tapering. *rumah* – traditional Minangkabau house (with rising roof ends).

gono-gini → GANA-GINI II.

gonoré (D) gonorrhea.

gonta-ganti (Jv) to keep on changing. – *mitra séks* to keep on changing sex partners.

bergonta-ganti to keep on changing/alternating.

penggonta-gantian constant changing/alternating.

gontai (M) slow, sluggish, indolent. *Dengan* –*nya ia melangkah masuk hotél.* She walked into the hotel slowly.

bergontai to move slowly, shuffle along, shamble along.

bergontaian (*pl subj*) to move slowly.

menggontai to do s.t. (working/walking, etc.) slowly, slack off (at work).

menggontaikan to move s.t. slowly.

mempergontai 1 to slow down (the pace). **2** to delay, put off till later, postpone.

tergontai-gontai 1 slowed down. **2** delayed, put off, postponed.

gontok (Jv) **gontok-gontokan 1** violence. *tanpa* ~ without violence. **2** brawling. **3** to be at e.o.'s throats, come to blows. *Partai itu akhirnya akan bubar karena anggota-anggotanya* ~. The party finally was going to be disbanded because its members were at e.o.'s throats. *Jangan* ~! Don't fight with e.o.!

bergontokan to be at loggerheads, quarrel.

gontokan 1 fight, fisticuffs. **2** quarrel.

gontométri (D) gontometry.

gonyak (*ob*) **menggonyak(kan)** to ridicule.

gonyéh menggonyéh to munch (of the toothless), chew between toothless gums.

gonyél menggonyél to massage/squeeze/knead gently.

gonyoh menggonyoh to scrub hard, scour, wipe clean.

gonyohan 1 s.t. scrubbed/scoured/wiped clean. **2** scourge.

gopék, go pék, and **nggo pék** (C J) five hundred (rupiahs).

gopékan a 500-rupiah bill.

gopoh hurried, hasty; (hustle and) bustle, haste. – *gapah/gapik/mamang* hurriedly, in a hurry.

gopoh-gopoh hurriedly, in a hurry.

tergopoh-gopoh hurried, hasty.

kegopohan haste, rush.

gora [*gogo rancah*] rice cultivation on a nonirrigated rice field.

gorab and **gorap** (A) dhow, Arab ship.

gorden(g), gordén(g), and **gordin** (D) curtain. – *gulung* window shade, blinds

bergordin with/to have drapes. *Ruangannya* ~. The room had drapes.

gorék → KORÉK I. – *api* matches.

menggorék-gorék *hati* ~ one's heart is quivering, throbbing.

menggorékkan to scrape s.t.

penggorékan scratching.

gorék-gorék k.o. climbing plant, *Caesalpinia jayabo.*

goréng fried, fry. *ikan* – fried fish. *minyak* – cooking oil. *nasi* – fried rice. *pisang* – and – *pisang* fried banana fritters. *laku/laris seperti pisang* – to sell like hot cakes.

menggoréng 1 to bake, fry. **2** (in soccer) to dribble. **3** (*fin*) to manipulate (stock prices), corner (the market).

menggoréng-goréng (in soccer) to dribble.

goréng-menggoréng (*fin*) manipulating (stock prices), cornering (the market).

menggoréngkan to fry for s.o.

tergoréng fried. ~ *tanpa minyak* tricked.

goréngan 1 roast (meat); fried; baked. ~ *kambing* k.o. goat stew. **2** (in soccer) dribble. **3** manipulated, cornered (the market/stock prices).

goréng-goréngan fried foods.

penggoréng 1 fryer, s.t. used for frying. *minyak* ~ cooking oil. *panci* ~ frying pan, wok. 2 s.o. who manipulates (stock prices) or corners (the market).

penggoréngan 1 frying. 2 frying pan, wok. 3 (*fin*) manipulating, cornering.

gorés 1 scratch, graze. 2 line scratched into s.t. – *api* matches. - *péna* writings.

bergorés(-gorés) 1 to be scratched. 2 with/to have lines.

menggorés(-gorés) 1 to scratch, graze. 2 to injure, hurt. ~ *hati* to hurt s.o.'s feelings.

menggorési to put a scratch on s.t., scratch lines on s.t.

menggoréskan to scratch with. ~ *gérétan* to light a match.

tergorés [and **kegorés** (*coq*)] 1 scratched. 2 engraved. ~ *di hati* unforgettable. *yang* ~ *dalam hati* what is engraved in one's heart.

gorésan 1 scratch, scratches, lines. 2 impression.

penggorés scratcher, scraper.

penggorésan scratching.

gorét scratch; → GORÉS.

menggorétkan to scratch s.t.

gorga (*Bat*) k.o. of Batak carving.

gori (*Jv*) young jackfruit, *Artocarpus integra*, used in cooking, *esp* in preparing *gudeg*.

gorila (*D*) gorilla.

gorilya (*sl?*) thief. – *kayu* lumber thief.

goroh (*M*) **menggoroh** to slaughter; → GOROK.

gorok menggorok 1 to slaughter, cut the throat of. 2 to cheat (by charging cutthroat prices).

penggorokan slaughtering, massacre.

gorong-gorong I (*Jv*) culvert, k.o. sewer (for irrigation).

gorong-gorong II mole cricket, *Gryllotalpa africana/vulgaris*; → ANJING *tanah*.

goroso (*NTB*) sloping dry rice field.

gosip (*E*) gossip. – *murahan* cheap gossip.

bergosip to gossip.

menggosipi, [**nggosipin** (*J*)] and **menggosipkan** to gossip about. *Nina terkejut digosipi koran.* Nina was shocked to be gossiped about in the papers. *Ronny yang doyan nggosipin anak-anak sekampus* Ronny, who likes to gossip about fellow students.

pergosipan gossiping.

gosip-gosipan to gossip.

gosipol (*E*) 1 a toxic pigment derived from cottonseed oil, made nontoxic by heating. 2 basic ingredient of a male contraceptive pill used in China.

gosok rubbing, friction. *obat* – scouring powder. – *gigi* a) toothpaste. b) toothbrush.

bergosok 1 to scour, rub, scrub, brush, shine, polish. 2 scoured, rubbed, scrubbed, polished, brushed. *Sepatunya yang baru* ~ *itu kelihatan berkilat.* His polished new shoes seemed to shine. 3 to rub (against s.t. else).

bergosokan to rub against e.o.

menggosok 1 to polish, shine, brush. ~ *gigi* to brush one's teeth. ~ *sepatu* to shine one's shoes. 2 to rub. ~ *mata yang gatal dengan punggung tangan* to rub one's eyes with the back of one's hand. ~ *badan dengan minyak tawon* to give one's body a rubdown with *tawon* oil. 3 to incite, stir up. ~ *orang agar dia mau berkelahi dengan orang yang menghinanya.* To incite people so that they want to fight with people who insult them. 4 to iron. ~ *baju* to iron a shirt.

menggosok-gosok 1 to incite, instigate. 2 to polish. 3 to rub.

menggosoki (*pl obj*) to rub.

menggosokkan to use s.t. to rub with, to rub s.t. (on s.t.). *Ayah* ~ *obat itu ke badannya.* Father rubbed the medicine on his body.

menggosok-gosokkan to snuggle s.t. up against s.t. else.

mempergosokkan to rub (s.t. against s.t. else).

tergosok rubbed.

gosokan 1 s.t. that has been rubbed/ironed. *Berlian itu halus* ~*nya.* The gem has been rubbed smooth. 2 polishing. 3 inciting, incitement, instigation. 4 incentive.

gosok-gosokan incitement.

penggosok 1 *alat* ~ abrasive, scourer. *kulit* ~ chamois leather, shammy. 2 s.o. who polishes. ~ *sepatu* bootblack. 3 instigator, provocateur.

penggosokan 1 scrubbing, brushing, polishing. ~ *intan itu dilakukan oléh tenaga-tenaga ahli.* The stones are polished by experts. 2 attrition. 3 ironing. 4 instigating, provoking.

gosong I sandbank, sandbar.

gosong II (*Jv*) burned, scorched.

menggosongkan to burn, scorch.

gosong III *burung* – various species of scrub fowl and incubator bird, *Megapodius spp. - Maluku* Moluccan scrub fowl, *Eulipoa wallacei.*

got (*D*) 1 gutter, drain. *koran* – gutter press. 2 ditch.

gotan (*Jv*) drainage channel.

gotés (*cla*) **menggotés** to pluck (off), pick.

gotiau (*C*) five million.

Gotik (*E*) and **Gotta** (*D*) Gothic.

gotok menggotok to boil (balls of opium).

gotong – *royong* to share the burden, work together in mutual cooperation. **bergotongroyong** to work together, cooperate with e.o. in doing a job. *Orang-orang kampung itu* ~ *membersihkan ladang itu.* The villagers worked together to clean the field. *menggotongroyongkan* to do s.t. by mutual assistance. *Ini berarti bahwa beban biaya memelihara infrastruktur ékonomi dan sosial digotongroyongkan dengan daérah.* This means that the expense of maintaining the economic and social infrastructures are done by mutual assistance with the provinces. **kegotongroyongan** mutual assistance, cooperation.

menggotong to carry a heavy burden with others.

gotongan shared burden.

penggotong 1 s.o. who carries such a burden. 2 stretcher.

gotperdom (*D*) Damn it!

gotri I (*Jv*) 1 pellets, shot (for a shotgun). 2 slug.

gotri II (*Jv*) ball bearing.

gotrok (*Jv*) lorry (a flat wagon without sides, fitted to run on rails for the transportation of sugarcane, etc.); → LORI I.

go tu hél (*E*) to go to hell.

menggo-tu-hélkan to send to hell.

gou (*C*) low-level drug dealer.

gowok I (*Jv*) k.o. plant and its edible berry, *Eugenia polycephala.*

gowok II (*Jv*) a woman who teaches a young man about sex.

goyah unstable, unsteady, rickety (of chairs, etc.), shaky, wobbly (of teeth), labile, fluid (situation). – *hati* shaky (of one's resolution, etc.).

bergoyah to totter, stagger, shake, wobble.

menggoyahkan 1 to shake s.t., make s.t. wobble/shake. 2 to shake (s.o.'s resolution), make s.o. waver. *Bujuk rayumu tidak mampu* ~ *imanku.* Your blandishments cannot shake my faith.

tergoyah(kan) shaken, wobbly, etc. *Hatiku* ~ *oléh takhyul.* I was shaken by superstition. *tak* ~ unshakable, unwavering (decision), unswerving (resolution).

kegoyahan instability, uncertainty.

penggoyahan shake-up.

goyak (*M*) **menggoyak** to shake/rock s.t., make s.t. wobble

goyang 1 shaky, wobbly, unsteady, loose, wiggling; →GOYAH. *kursi* – rocking chair. *Paris* – k.o. shiny fabric. *tanah* – earthquake. 2 uncertain, changeable, unstable. – *gayong* to shake back and forth. (*hidup*) – *kaki* to be idle, laze about. **bergoyang kaki** to take it easy, be idle. – *kepala* head shake. **bergoyang kepala** to shake one's head. – *lidah* to have a feast; eat, drink, and be merry. 3 swaying, rocking. – *ngebor* gyrations, erotic hip movements. – *Madura* reference to the supposed erotic movements of Madurese women during sex. – *pinggul* to sway one's hips.

(ber)goyang 1 to rock, wobble, sway. *iman* ~ one's faith is shaken. ~ *iman* a) to be tempted to act in an immoral way. b) to fall in love at first sight. ~ *lutut* to not work, sit around idly. ~ *pantat* to wiggle one's behind back and forth; → MIGAL-MIGUL. 2 to fluctuate.

bergoyang-goyang to sway back and forth.

bergoyangan (*pl subj*) to sway, rock.

menggoyang 1 to shake, rock, wobble. 2 to sway, swing (of branches, etc.), wave. 3 to waver, vacillate, fluctuate. *harga karét* ~ the price of rubber fluctuated. ~ *lidah* to lick one's chops. ~ *sumur* (*petro*) stop-cocking (a well).

menggoyangkan to shake, sway, jiggle. ~ *kepala* to shake one's head. ~ *lidah* mouthwatering. *Pemberontakan itu telah ~ kedudukannya sebagai raja.* The rebellion shook his position as king.

tergoyang shaken, rocked, etc. *Keamanan negara itu ~ juga oléh perang dunia.* The nation's security was shaken by the world war.

tergoyang-goyang to keep on shaking/rocking.

goyangan and **kegoyangan** oscillation, fluctuation, precariousness.

penggoyang s.o. who shakes.

penggoyangan shaking.

goyoh (*M*) **tergoyoh(-goyoh)** staggering from side to side.

goyor (*Jv*) lightweight (of fabric).

gr- also see entries beginning with ger-

GR → GEDÉ *rasa.*

grabadan (*Jv*) to hawk, peddle.

grabah (*Jv*) earthenware, crockery.

grad (*D*) degree (of blood relationship, consanguinity)

gradag (*Jv onom*) dragging sound.

gradagan clatter.

gradah → GELADAH, GELÉDAH.

gradak-gruduk (*Jv*) to do s.t. in a hurry or too hastily.

gradasi (*D*) gradation.

gradual (*E*) and **graduil** (*D*) gradual, by degrees.

graf (*D/E*) graph.

grafik (*D*) graph, diagram, chart. *- balok/batang* bar chart. *- lingkaran* pie chart. *- pérsonil* list of personnel.

kegrafikan and **pergrafikan** graphic arts.

grafika 1 graphic. **2** graphic arts, graphics.

kegrafikaan graphic (*mod*).

grafikawan graphic artist.

grafis (*D*) graphic. *seni –* graphic arts.

pegrafis graphic artist.

grafit (*D/E*) graphite, plumbago.

grafiti (*D/E*) graffiti.

grafolog (*D*) graphologist, handwriting expert.

grafologi (*D/E*) graphology.

gragal (*Jv*) gravel, pebbles.

gragas (*Jv*) **nggragas 1** gluttonous. **2** acquisitive.

gragot (*J*) **menggragoti** to bite off, gnaw, nibble, munch, chew s.t. off.

graha (*Jv*) building, house (in recent compounds and names). *- Karana* Auditorium (in the MPR Building). *- Pemuda* or *Gedung Pusat Komunikasi Pemuda* [PKP] Youth Communications Central Building. *- Purna Yudha* Veterans Building. *- Remaja* Youth Hostel. *- Sabha Paripurna* Hall for Plenary Sessions (in the MPR Building). *- Sawala* the Department of Finance building. *- Tama* (Domed) Main Building (in the MPR compound). *- Widya Patra* the Indonesian Petroleum Museum. *- Wisata Pramuka* Pramuka Boy Scout Hostel.*- Wiyata Yudha* Army Command and General Staff College (in Bandung).

grahawan (male) housekeeper (in hotels, etc.).

grahawati (female) housekeeper (in hotels, etc.).

grahita (*Skr*) comprehension, mental grasp.

graita the ability to grasp s.o.'s meaning, comprehension; →GRAHITA.

grajén (*Jv*) sawdust, wood filings.

gram (*D/E*) gram (unit of weight).

gramatika (*D*) grammar.

gramatikal (*D/E*) grammatical.

kegramatikalan grammaticalness.

grambyang (*Jv*) **menggrambyang** to stray, wander (of thoughts). *Pikirannya ~.* He's daydreaming.

gramofon (*D/E*) phonograph.

Granada [(Gedung) Graha Purna Yudha] → GRAHA *PurnaYudha.*

Granagraha Committee Room (in the MPR Building).

granat (*D*) **1** grenade. *pelémpar –* grenade launcher. **2** shell. *- asap* smoke grenade. *- asap fosfor* white phosphorous grenade. *- bénsin* Molotov cocktail. *- brisan* high explosive shell. *- manggis* baseball grenade. *- nanas* pineapple grenade. *- pengejut* stun grenade. *- plastik* concussion grenade. *- rokét* rocket grenade. *- tangan* hand grenade. *- yang digerakkan tenaga rokét* rocket-propelled grenade, RPG.

menggranat to throw a grenade at.

penggranatan attack with grenades.

granit (*D/E*) granite.

granulasi (*D*) granulation.

granulosit (*E*) granulocyte.

grapak-grupuk (*Jv*) hasty, hurried.

grapyak (*Jv*) familiar, friendly, courteous, polite to a guest, amiable.

grasa-grusu → GRUSA-GRUSU.

grasi (*D*) pardon, clemency, mercy. *permohonan –* petition for clemency. *Permohonan – ditolak Présidén pada Oktober 1984.* A petition for clemency was denied by the President in October 1984. *- bersyarat* (*leg*) conditional pardon.

gratak (*Jv*) (little kids) cannot leave anything alone.

menggrataki to wreck.

gratifikasi (*D ob*) **1** bonus. **2** dividend.

gratis (*D*) gratis, free (of charge). *Dia mau –.* He wanted it for nothing.

menggratiskan to issue/give away for free. *Pemerintah Républik Cina (Taiwan) mulai 1 Méi 1987 ~ visa bagi pengunjung berkebangsaan Indonésia.* Starting on May 1, 1987, the Government of the Republic of China (Taiwan) will issue visas for visitors of Indonesian nationality free of charge. *digratiskan menginap di hotél prodéo* to be imprisoned.

gratisan for nothing/free. *film ~* a film shown free of charge.

penggratisan the issuance of s.t. free of charge. *Sebelum ~ ini, setiap pemohon visa Taiwan dikenakan biaya Rp 24.000.* Prior to this issuance (of visas) free of charge each applicant for a Taiwanese visa was subject to a Rp 24,000 fee.

gravifoton (*E*) graviphoton.

gravir (*D*) **menggravir** to engrave.

gravitasi (*D*) gravitation.

graviton (*E*) graviton.

G.R.Ay. (*abbr*) → GUSTI *Radén Ayu.*

grayak (*Jv*) k.o. worm, *Spodoptera Litura.*

Grebeg (*Jv*) celebration of the three annual Muslim religious festivals: *- Maulud, Bakda Pasa,* and *Besar* in the kratons. *- Syawal* celebration organized by the Yogyakarta Kraton at the end of the *Idul Fitri* prayer (*Syawal* 1) in the form of a procession of a pyramid-like structure of food taken to the *Pasar Kauman* mosque where it is distributed to members of the community.

grécok (*J*) to trouble, bother, worry, annoy.

Green Campus (*E*) reference to the Bogor Institute of Agriculture.

grégél (*Jv*) loosened grip.

menggrégéli and **nggrégéli** to lose one's grip on s.t.

greges I (*Jv*) feverish.

nggreges to be feverish.

greges II *- otot* horsetail, *Equisetum debile.*

greget (*Jv*) a strong urge, intense feeling.

menggregetkan to infuriate s.o.

gregetan 1 angry. **2** to become angry, lose one's temper.

gréhon (*E*) greyhound.

gremet (*Jv*) **nggremet** to creep along, move at a crawl's pace.

menggremeti to infiltrate.

grempel (*Jv?*) **grempelan** clod, lump, nugget (of gold), morsel.

gréndel (*D*) latch, bolt (of a door/window). *- pintu* door bolt.

menggréndel to bolt, latch. *Pintu digréndel kembali.* The door was bolted again.

penggréndelan bolting, latching.

grendeng (*Jv*) **menggrendeng** to grumble.

grengseng (*Jv*) zest, spirit, enthusiasm.

nggrengseng *~ dengan usul-usulnya* full of suggestions.

grénjéng (*Jv*) silver paper, tinfoil; → KERTAS *grénjéng.*

grépé I (*J*) **menggrépé** [and **nggrépé/ngegrépé** (*coq*)] to grope one's way, feel, feel up.

grépé-grépéan to grope e.o.

grépé II → GONGLI.

grés (*Jv*) brand-new, the latest, most up-to-date.

grésék (*Jv*) to rummage, hunt around in (trash bins/garbage cans). *jago –* collector of used articles; → PEMULUNG. *Dari hasil – mencari kaléng bekas karton dan koran bekas dia bisa membeli radio transistor.* From the proceeds of rag picking (looking for used cans, cardboard, and old newspapers) he was able to buy a transistor radio.

grétek (*Jv*) fussy, finicky, hard to please.

grha → GRAHA.

gria → GRAHA. – *kinarya* production house. – *Purna Bakti Polri* Republic of Indonesia Police Retirees Building

griesneel (*D*) /grisnél/ semolina.

grifir (*D*) clerk (of the court), recorder, registrar.

Grika Greek. *bangsa* – Greeks.

gringgingen (*Jv*) pins and needles; → KESEMUTAN.

gringsing (*Jv*) k.o. batik design, the so-called flaming cloth.

grip I (*D*) slate-pencil; → GERIP I.

grip II (*E*) grip. – *setang* handlebar gear change.

gripfrut (*E*) grapefruit.

griya I → GRAHA. – *busana* fashion-house. – *wartawan* "Journalist House," i.e., the name for the journalists' house at Cipinang Muara, Jakarta.

griya II (*Skr*) house, home. – *Karya* rest place for locomotive engineers at a number of stations. – *patungan* time share.

grodok (*onom*) crashing sound.

grogi (*E*) **1** groggy, unstable, stunned, dazed, dizzy. **2** scared, feeling awkward and embarrassed.

grojog (*Jv*) water falling.
  menggrojog to fall (of water).
  menggrojogi to pour water over, flush.
  grojogan waterfall, cataract; → AIR *terjun*.

grontol → GERONTOL.

gropyok (*Jv*) **menggropyok** to round up, raid.
  gropyokan drive, roundup. *Pembasmian hama tikus itu dengan cara ~*. The rats were eradicated in a roundup.
  penggropyokan raid, raiding.

gros (*D*) gross (= 12 dozen, 144 pieces).

grosir (*D*) wholesaler.

grosse (*D leg*) (*– akte*) process server's copy, executory copy, counterpart original, first authenticated copy.

grotésk (*D/E*) grotesque.

growak (*Jv*) with a hole in it.

grumosol (*E*) grumosol, a soil composition.

grup (*D/E*) group. – *penjajagan* advance group.

grusa-grusu (*Jv*) reckless, rash, impetuous. *mengambil keputusan –* to jump to conclusions.

gruwung (*Jv*) without a nose. *hidung –* a nose which has been eaten away by leprosy.

gu (*ob*) yoke-mate, partner; → REGU.
  segu a pair of (shoes, etc.), a group of.

gua I (*Skr*) **1** cave, cavern, grotto. *ahli –* speleologist. *ilmu –* speleology. *menelusuri –* to explore caves; caving. **2** cradle. – *garba* womb.

gua II (*C J*) I, me, my.

gual I (*M*) **menggual** to drum.
  pengggual drummer.

gual II – *gail* shaky, loose (of teeth/posts).

guam I (*Mal*) dispute, litigation. *anak –* litigant.
  beguam to quarrel, dispute.
  perguaman issue in litigation, case, suit.
  peguam attorney; lawyer.

guam II thrush, sprue; → SERIAWAN.

guano (*D/E*) guano.

guar (*S*) **mengguar 1** to take apart, knock down, dismantle (of a car/engine). **2** to unpack, unwrap (a present). **3** to look into, investigate.

Gub clipped form of **Gubernur**. *Pak –* (in Jakarta) the appellation for one of the former Governors *Ali Sadikin*.

gubah I menggubah to arrange, adapt, compose. *Penyanyi ~ lagu-lagunya*. The singer arranged his songs.
  gubahan composition, arrangement, adaptation. *~ Bach* arrangement on a theme of Bach.
  penggubah 1 composer. **2** author. **3** arranger, adapter.
  penggubahan 1 composing. **2** arranging, adapting.

gubah II (*A*) **1** burial/grave mound. **2** dome, vaulting.

gubal I 1 cambium, cellular tissue under bark, sapwood. **2** roughly cut block, lump. *teras terunjam – melayang* "a tree's core is firmly fixed in the ground but its soft-wood blows away," i.e., blood is thicker than water. – *besi* pig-iron. – *tersisip* included sapwood.

gubal II crude, unrefined.

gubal III (*mostly Mal*) **menggubal** to draw up, draft, formulate, legislate.
  penggubal legislator.
  penggubalan drawing up, drafting, legislating.

gubang I (*cla*) *perahu –* k.o. sailing boat (of the *Orang Laut*).

gubang II notch cut in tree trunk for climbers.

gubang III → GOBANG II.

gubar → GOBAR.

gubel (*Jv*) **menggubel** to keep begging, keep after s.o. (to do s.t.), nag.

gubernemén (*D coq*) government.

gubernur (*D*) I governor, head of a *Daérah Tingkat I* and governor of an institution, such as a bank. – *Akabri* Governor of the Republic of Indonesia Armed Forces Academy. – *Bank Indonésia* Governor of the Bank of Indonesia. – *Lémhanas* Governor of the National Resistance Institute. *Pembantu –* title of the former (Dutch) resident.

(ke)gubernuran 1 residence or office of a *Kepala Daérah Tingkat I*. **2** Governor General, G.G., the representative crown in the former Netherlands Indies.

gubis (*Jv*) cabbage; → KUBIS.

gubit (*M*) **menggubit** to beckon to.

gubris (*J coq*) **menggubris 1** to pay attention to. *Dia tidak ~ peringatan kami*. He paid no attention to our warning. **2** to listen to. *Pemuda itu tidak ~ siapa saja*. That young man didn't listen to anybody. **3** to care, give a damn; → PEDULI. *Dia tidak ~*. He didn't care. *Larangan polisi tidak digubris*. The police prohibition was ignored.
  tergubris paid attention to, noted.
  gubrisan attention (paid to s.t.).

gubuk and **gubug** (*J/Jv*) **1** (bamboo) hut, shack. **2** partitioned-off compartment, booth. **3** shelter in rice field (where the farmers keep watch when the crop is standing).

gucek (*J*) **menggucek** and **nggucek** (*coq*)] to rub one's eyes.

guci (*C*) earthenware jug. – *wasiat* a) secret. b) soil corrector (used in agriculture to improve soil conditions).

gudam → GODAM.

gudang 1 warehouse, storehouse, shed, silo. **2** storage room, godown, pantry. – *api* magazine, storage place for dangerous chemicals, etc. – *bawah lantai* cellar. – *dingin* cold storage. – *gandum* granary. – *industri berizin* licensed manufacturing warehouse, LMW. – *laut/éérste linte* (*D*) deep-sea godown (along the quays). – *mesiu* a) powder keg. – *mesiu Balkan* the Balkan powder keg. b) powder magazine. – *pabéan* bonded warehouse. – *pembongkaran peti kémas* container freight station. – *pendingin* (*an*) cold storage. – *penyimpanan barang-barang* warehouse. – *persediaan* stock room. – *senjata* armory, arsenal, magazine. – *umum* public warehouse.
  segudang a warehouse-/silo-, etc. full. *~ beras* a silo-full of (hulled) rice. *~ pengalaman* quite a lot of experiences. *Biasanya orang yang baru selesai tugas, entah tugas apa saja, pasti membawa ~ pengalaman*. A person who just has completed his assignment, any assignment, usually surely comes away with quite a lot of experiences.
  bergudang-gudang 1 several warehouses. **2** by the warehouse.
  menggudangkan to store, put in a warehouse, stock up on.
  kegudangan storage room (*mod*). *tata usaha ~* storage room administration.
  penggudangan storage. *fasilitas ~* storage facilities.
  pergudangan warehouse, storage (*mod*). *~ berikat/di luar pabéan* bonded warehouse.

gudangan (*Jv*) steamed mixed vegetables with grated coconut and chili peppers; → LALAP 2.

gudé (*Jv*) pigeon pea, k.o. shrub, the bean of which can be made into a bean cake, *Cajanus cajan*.

gudek and **gudeg** (*Jv*) a type of food made from young jackfruit. – *géndongan* the *gudek* sold in restaurants or permanent roadside stalls. – *jalanan* the *gudek* sold along the streets and in markets. – *léséhan* the *gudek* sold in the evening hours, when the customers sit on a *tikar* spread over the sidewalk.

gudél I (*J/Jv*) water buffalo calf.

gudél II plaque (on teeth).

gudep [gugus depan] 1 (*gram*) initial cluster (of consonants). 2 a *pramuka* formation.

guderi (*J*) k.o. fine carpet.

gudi I (*ob*) betel tray; → CERANA.

gudi II 1 shipyard. 2 dry dock.

gudik I and **gudig** (*J/Jv*) scabies, mange.

  gudigan and **gudiken** scabby, mangy, scurfy.

gudik II tergudik-gudik to wag (of a dog's tail), flop/flounder around (of a fish out of water).

gudir gelatin.

gudu-gudu hookah.

gudus rampart.

gué (*C J*) → GUA II. I, me, my. – *nggak mau* I don't want to. *semau* – at my (own) discretion, as I think fit, just as I please.

guedé (*sl*) very big; → GEDÉ.

gugah (*Jv*) arousal, excitation.

  menggugah 1 to arouse/wake up s.o. *Ibumu akan saya gugah.* I'll wake up your mother. ~ *bakat sebagai ...* to bring out one's talent as. 2 to excite (feelings, etc.), stimulate, stir up. ~ *hati/semangat* to encourage, stir up. ~ *bakat ... sebagai* to bring out (s.o.'s talent for). *Tempat indah itu benar-benar ~ bakat saya sebagai penyair.* That beautiful place really brought out the poet in me. 3 compelling.

  menggugahkan to wake s.o. up on s.o. else's behalf.

  tergugah 1 awakened, aroused. 2 encouraged. ~ *hati* to get excited about; → TERANGSANG. *Dia tidak bisa ~ hatinya karena apa pun.* He can't get excited about anything. *Setiap pengunjung paméran ~ hatinya untuk menyayangi tanaman langka.* Each visitor to the exhibition was encouraged to love scarce crops.

  gugahan excitation.

  penggugah stimulator, s.o. who arouses.

  penggugahan excitement, stimulation.

gugat I (*leg*) complaint, claim. – *asal/asli* original complaint. – *balik/kembali* counterclaim. – *konvénsi* original complaint. – *penyangkalan* attempt to disavow a child. – *rékonvénsi* counterclaim.

  menggugat 1 to accuse, indict. *Indonésia ~.* Indonesia Accuses. 2 to sue, bring legal action against. ~ *balik* to counter sue. ~ *... ke pengadilan* to take ... to court. 3 to sue for. ~ *cerai* to sue for divorce. 4 to claim, demand. *Pernah rumah itu digugat seseorang.* That house was once claimed by s.o. ~ *pusaka* to claim a heritage. 5 to protest against, contest, challenge. *Saya tidak akan menggugat-gugat keputusanmu.* I won't contest your decision.

  gugat-menggugat and **gugat-ginugat** claims and counterclaims.

  menggugatkan to make a claim/demand about/for. *apa yang digugatkan terhadap tergugat* what is demanded of the respondent.

  tergugat 1 (*leg*) defendant. *Kuasa NV. Ketaren memohon pengadilan menghukum ~ membayar Rp 300 juta.* NV. Ketaren's attorney asked the court to sentence the defendant to pay Rp 300 million. 2 (*leg*) respondent. ~ *dalam kasasi* respondent in cassation. ~ *dalam konvénsi* original respondent. ~ *dalam rékonvénsi* respondent in the counterclaim. ~ *penjamin* impleaded party, third-party defendant. 3 accused. 4 contested, challenged.

  gugatan 1 accusation. 2 complaint, suit, claim. ~ *antara* interim claim. ~ *asli* original complaint. ~ *balasan/balik* counter claim. ~ *dalam konvénsi* original complaint. ~ *dalam rékonvénsi* counterclaim. ~ *dalam sengkéta tanah* complaint in a land dispute. ~ *malpraktik* malpractice suit. ~ *perceraian* divorce action. ~ *perdata* civil complaint. ~ *perwakilan* class-action suit. ~ *pidana* criminal complaint. ~ *provisi* application for interim relief. 3 criticism, protest.

  penggugat (*leg*) plaintiff, accuser, claimant, complainant, petitioner. ~ *asal* original plaintiff. ~ *dalam konvénsi* original plaintiff. ~ *dalam rékonvénsi* plaintiff in a counterclaim. ~ *dalam/untuk kasasi* appellant in cassation. ~ *dalam penanggungan/untuk jaminan* impleading party. ~ *intervénsi* intervenor. – *konvénsi* plaintiff in the original complaint.

  penggugatan 1 accusation, indictment. 2 demand, claim.

gugat II shaking, shock.

  menggugat to shake, shock.

gugon-tuhon (*Jv*) superstition.

gugu I (*Jv*) **menggugu** to believe (in), trust. *Ali tidak dapat digugu.* Ali is not to be trusted.

  tergugu believed, trusted.

gugu II tergugu-gugu to stammer, stutter.

guguh I (*M*) **mengguguh** 1 to beat (a drum). 2 to rap, knock (at the door).

guguh II (*Jv*) very old.

guguk I hillock, knoll, dune. – *pasir* sand dune.

guguk II (*Jv*) **(se)ngguguk** restrained (laughing, crying). *nangis ngguguk* to cry in a stifled manner.

  mengguguk to sob.

  terguguk *menangis ~* to cry in a stifled manner.

  terguguk-guguk *Dia menangis ~.* She wept in a repressed way.

gugup I (*J/Jv*) nervous, jumpy, panicky, jittery. *Jangan –!* Don't be nervous! Take it easy! *Dia – karena akan bertemu dengan pacarnya lagi.* He's nervous about seeing his girlfriend again. *Penduduk ibu kota benar-benar menjadi – karena semua publisitas mengenai skandal itu.* The residents of the capital had a real case of the jitters, with all the publicity about the scandal. *masih –* not yet bold enough to say s.t. right out.

  gugup-gugupnya *tidak ~* not be afraid (to say s.t., etc.).

  segugup as nervous as.

  menggugupkan to make s.o. nervous. *Jangan ~ supir, nanti menabrak!* Don't make the driver nervous or else he'll have a collision!

  tergugup nervous, confused.

  gugupan to be upset.

  kegugupan 1 nervousness. 2 panic.

  penggugup a nervous person.

gugup II noisy.

gugur I 1 to fall off (too early, of leaves/unripe fruits, etc.). 2 to fall out (of hair/teeth, etc.). *Rambut anda –?* Is your hair falling out? 3 to be killed (in action/battle), be slain, perish, fall. 4 to cave in (of soil/a river bank, etc.). 5 to fail to pass (in school). *Anaknya yang lain sudah – di kelas I atau II.* Her other child failed to pass in either grade I or grade II. 6 to be born prematurely (of a fetus, etc.). *anak –* a prematurely born child. 7 to crash (of aircraft). 8 to be null and void (of a legal action), fail (of a motion), lapse (of a license). 9 to be eliminated (in an athletic contest). *bintang –* falling star. *musim –* fall, autumn. *Sembahyangnya –.* His prayers were not answered. – *satu tumbuh seribu* one falls and a thousand spring up. – *ajar* dropout (from school). *Lagu – Bunga* "Song of the Fallen Flowers (of the Nation)," i.e., a melody played every November 10 in honor of the fallen heroes. – *gunung* (*Jv*) a) forced, compulsory, unpaid labor during exceptional events, disasters, etc., levee en masse. b) voluntary labor service, work assignment. – *haknya* his rights have lapsed. – *hati* to fall in love. – *iman* to be led astray (away from the right course). – *kandung(an)* miscarriage. – *salju* avalanche. – *sekolah* dropout (from school). – *talak* divorced by the husband. – *tempur* killed in action.

  berguguran (*pl subj*) to fall (off). *Daun-daun itu ~ di sana-sini.* The leaves fell here and there. *Tétésan air ~ di atas kepala saya.* Drops of water fell on my head.

  menggugurkan [and **ngegugurin** (*J coq*)] 1 to cause to fall off (fruits from a tree), drop. *Dia ~ buah-buah kelapa yang sudah tua.* He dropped old coconuts. 2 to produce an abortion, abort. 3 to annul. ~ *bukit* to level/raze (to the ground) hills (for military purposes). ~ *gunung* to cause a mountain slope to come down (in order to be able to dig rocks). ~ *hak* to renounce/give up/waive a right. ~ *iman* to tempt, lead away from the right path, make s.o. renounce his religion. ~ *kandungan* to have an abortion.

  guguran 1 fallout. ~ *batuan* pyroclastic. ~ *nuklir* nuclear fallout. 2 aborted fetus. ~ *spontan* spontaneous abortion.

  keguguran 1 miscarriage, abortion. 2 to be killed (in action). 3 falling out. *mencegah ~ rambut* to prevent hair from falling out. 4 to have a miscarriage. ~ *tanah* erosion.

  pengggugur ~ *daun* defoliant.

  pengguguran 1 abortion. ~ *kandungan/kehamilan/janin* (induced) abortion. 2 loss (of leaves by deciduous trees).

gugus 1 group, force (a group of people). **2** cluster. *– depan* [gudep] initial cluster (of consonants). **b)** a *pramuka* boy scout formation. *– konsonan (ling)* consonant cluster. *– pengendali mutu* [GKM] total quality control, quality assurance. *– sekoci* boat/landing wave. *– tugas* task force. *– vokal (gram)* vowel cluster.

bergugus-gugus and **menggugus** in groups (islands, stars etc.), in batches/clusters, e.g., of *rambutan, langsat*, etc.

gugusan group, *(mil)* detachment. *~ pulau(-pulau)* archipelago. *~ bintang* constellation.

guha → GUA I.

guit mengguit to nudge with the foot, finger. *Ketika gadis itu léwat di depan meréka, ia ~ kawan di sampingnya sambil membisik-kan sesuatu.* When a girl walked by in front of them, he nudged his friend in the side and whispered s.t.

mengguit-guit to move around slightly.

terguit nudged.

gujirak(-at) → GUNJING-GUJIRAK.

gukguk mengguguk to sob, → GUGUK II.

tergukguk to break into sobs.

gul I → GOL I.

gul II *(Pers)* rose.

gula *(Skr)* sugar. *hitam-hitam – jawa* said of a woman who has dark skin but is attractive. *mati semut karena –* ants die for the sake of sugar, i.e., tempting objects may lead to danger. *penyakit –* diabetes; → DIABÉTÉS. *ada – ada semut* bees flock to honey. *seperti – dalam mulut* an easy job, as easy as pie. *semanis-manis – ada pasir dalamnya* where there's smoke there's fire. *– anggur* grape sugar, glucose, dextrose. *– arén* sugar from the areca palm, made into cakes. *– asam* lactose. *– batu* lump sugar, sugar candy. *– bit* beet sugar. *– cair* high fructose syrup. *– coklat* heroin mixed with caffeine. *– darah* blood sugar. *– enau* palm sugar. *– halus* refined sugar. *– hias* confectioner's sugar. *– hitam* caramel. *– jawa* coconut sugar from the areca palm in the form of half spheres. *– kacang* → AMPYANG II. *– kasar* raw sugar. *– kelapa* **a)** sugar made from coconut-palm sap. **b)** striped red and white (colors of flags/decorations). *– kembang* lump sugar. *– kental* dextrose, corn/grape sugar. *– kristal* crystalline sugar. *– lontar* → GULA arén. *– mangkok* bowl-shaped cane sugar. *– mérah* **a)** brown sugar. **b)** → GULA arén. *– nyiur* sugar made from coconut-palm sap. *– obat* medicated syrup. *– otot* glycogen. *– pasir* **a)** granular sugar. **b)** (in Ujungpandang) code word for gunpowder, used for fishing. *– rafinasi* refined sugar. *– rawak* sugar syrup. *– singkong* fructose. *– tanjung* coarse-grained brown sugar. *– tarik* candy floss, spin sugar. *– tebu* cane sugar, sucrose. *– tétés* molasses. *– tumbu* (in Kudus, Central Java) brown sugar (packed in a medium-sized round open basket with a square bottom). *– ubi manis* beet sugar.

gula-gula 1 bonbon, candy, sweets. **2** *(coq)* anything that gives pleasure. **3** mistress, concubine; → GUNDIK.

bergula 1 to contain sugar, sugared. **2** sugar-coated. *tablét ~ a* sugar-coated tablet.

menggula *(coq)* to bootlick, brown-nose.

menggulai to sugar, sweeten.

pergulaan sugar *(mod)*, relating to sugar.

gulai currying; curried food. *– ayam* chicken curry. *– babat* tripe with coconut milk. *– bagar* mutton curry. *– gajébo (M)* k.o. cooked brisket. *– kambing* goat/lamb curry. *– lemak* a stew with a lot of *santan. – paku* curried fiddlehead ferns.

menggulai to prepare curry.

menggulaikan to prepare curry for s.o.

gulai-gulaian all k.o. curries.

gulali *(Jv)* a syrupy confection.

gulamah silvery-white fish, croaker, *Sciaena russeli*.

gulambai *(M) (hantu) –* a spirit that can cause a house to burn down.

gulana → GUNDAH *gulana*.

gulang-gulang *(M)* shelter for rice planters from which ropes are stretched in all directions to which rags are attached to chase away birds.

gulang-guling flip-flop.

gular → GALIR. *Pendiriannya gular.–.* He trimmed his sails according to the wind.

gulat wrestling (the sport); → GELUT, GUMUL. *ahli/jago –* wrestler; fighter. *pertunjukan –* wrestling match.

bergulat 1 to fight, struggle. *Dia sedang ~ dengan lawannya.* He's fighting with his opponent. **2** to wrestle, struggle with. *Ia ~ lagi dengan buku.* He was again struggling with his books.

menggulati 1 to wrestle with, fight against. **2** to combat.

tergulat enmeshed, caught up in.

pegulat wrestler.

pergulatan 1 wrestling, scuffle. **2** fight, combat, battle (of life), struggle.

gulawantah and **gulowantah** *(Jv)* **ngulawantah** to bring up, rear.

penggulawantahan 1 care, paying attention. **2** close supervision.

gulden *(D col)* guilder.

gulé → GULAI.

gulem *(J)* **1** cloudy, overcast. **2** sad, gloomy.

gulet → GULAT.

guli *(Hind)* marble; → GUNDU, KELERÉNG. *main –* to play marbles.

guliga *(Skr cla)* bezoars found in fish, snakes, and porcupines, used as talismans.

guling roll. *babi –* (in Bali) roasted suckling pig. *bantal –* bolster, Dutch wife. *– gantang/garak/gelantang* rolling over and over (or, from side to side).

berguling 1 to roll, turn over. **2** to sleep with a bolster.

berguling-guling to keep rolling around.

bergulingan *(pl subj)* to roll around.

mengguling to roll (around).

menggulingkan 1 to roll s.t., make s.t. roll; to roll with. **2** to break up (a gang/organization), topple. **3** to overthrow, topple. *~ pemerintah yang sah* to overthrow the legal government. **4** to defeat (in sports).

terguling 1 rolled (over), overturned, turned over. **2** toppled, overthrown. *Kabinet yang baru ~.* The new cabinet was overthrown.

terguling-guling rolling over and over.

pengguling overthrower, deposer.

penggulingan toppling, overthrow. *~ présidén* the overthrow of the president.

pergulingan 1 turn. *~ tahun* turn of the year. **2** revolving, turning.

gulir roll; → GULING, GULUNG.

bergulir 1 to roll on, go, move, get going/moving. *Kasus ini lalu ~ ke pengadilan.* The case went to court. **2** to evolve, change. **3** revolving (credit, etc.).

menggulir to roll on, go, move.

menggulirkan 1 to make s.t. roll, roll. *Digulirkannya badannya ke atas kasur.* He rolled onto the mattress. **2** to put s.t. into action, launch. **3** to topple, overthrow.

tergulir rolled.

penggulir s.o. who overthrows.

pengguliran 1 launching. **2** overthrowing.

gulita → GELITA.

gulma weed. *– air* aquatic weed, *Eichornia crassiper, Azolla pinnata. – padi* rice weeds. *– tahan* noxious weed.

gulu *(Jv)* neck. *– menjing* Adam's apple. *– banyak* **a)** swan-like neck. **b)** long thin object formed like a gooseneck.

guludan *(Jv)* garden/flower bed, ridge of sugarcane field, bund.

gulung roll. *– gemulung* to roll on and on. *– tikar* to go bankrupt, go out of business. *– transformator* (on signboards) transformer winding. *se-* a roll of. *kawat se-* a roll/coil of wire. *tikar dua –* two mats.

bergulung 1 by the roll. *Dia membeli kertas ~.* He bought paper by the roll. **2** rolled up (of sleeves). *Lengan keméjanya ~ hingga ke siku.* The sleeves of his shirt were rolled up to the elbow. **3** rolling (in). *~ dengan* rolling in (debt, etc.).

bergulung-gulung in many rolls, roll after roll (of waves), rolling.

menggulung 1 to roll, roll up. *~ celana* to be ready to get down to work. *~ lengan (baju)* to roll up one's sleeves, get down to work. **2** to wind s.t. **3** to put an end/stop to s.t. *~ tikar* to go out of business. **4** (in sports) to defeat, beat. **5** (in computers) to scroll. *~ ke bawah* to scroll down.

menggulung-gulung *~ perut* it's hateful.

gulung-menggulung rolling over and over.

menggulungkan 1 to roll up. **2** to put an end/stop to s.t. **3** to furl (a sail).

tergulung 1 rolled up. **2** quelled (of a rebellion), nipped in the bud, stamped out, put out of business.

gulungan 1 roll. *Kertas dijual dalam ~.* Paper is sold in rolls. **2** scroll. *~ Laut Mati* Dead Sea Scrolls. **3** (*elec*) winding. *~ angker* armature winding. *~ poros* shaft winding. **4** turn(ing). *se~* a roll (of s.t.).

penggulung 1 reel (of fishing rod). **2** roller.

penggulungan 1 rolling up. **2** putting an end to s.t., putting s.o. out of business. *~ komplotan perampok* putting a gang of robbers out of business. **3** defeating, beating.

gulut bergulut(-gulut) and **tergulut(-gulut)** head over heels, (run) helter-skelter, in a hurry.

menggulut to hurry/speed up, accelerate.

gum (*onom*) sound of booming (cannon); → DEGUM.

gumal 1 crumpled, rumpled. **2** wrinkled, creased; → KUMAL.

bergumal to run into. *~ dengan kekurangan kertas* to run into a paper shortage.

menggumalkan to crease, rumple, crumple.

gumala → GEMALA.

gumalai → GEMULAI.

gumam mumbling.

bergumam and **menggumam** to mumble (under one's breath), speak indistinctly; to grumble. *senyum/tertawa ~* to smirk.

menggumamkan to mumble s.t.

gumaman mumble, murmur.

gumampang (*Jv*) be unreliable, irresponsible.

gumanak (*Bal*) a musical instrument in the Balinese *gamelan*.

gumantung (*Jv*) **1** to hang down, hanging. *buah* – fruit growing on trees; → GANTUNG 2. **2** suspended.

Gumarang name of a train running between Jakarta and Surabaya.

gumatok (*Jv*) fixed, invariable.

gumba protuberance on an elephant's forehead or a horse's withers.

gumbaan a farm implement, k.o. pump.

gumbang I → GOMBANG I.

gumbang II short open-necked coat.

gumbar soft pith of palms.

gumbira → GEMBIRA.

gumboro (*Jv*) *penyakit* – Infectious Pursal Disease, IPD.

gumbuk (*cla*) **menggumbuk 1** to coax. **2** to deceive.

penggumbuk 1 coaxer. **2** deceiver.

gumelar (*Jv*) spread out, unfolded, revealed; → GELAR II. *segala yang* – the earth and everything in it, i.e., all that is spread out before us.

gumelaran revelation.

gumpal 1 spherical clod/lump (of dough/tobacco). **2** ball (of thread), wad. *– darah* blood clot. *– emas* gold nugget.

segumpal a clod (of earth), lump (of sugar). *~ awan* a rain/storm cloud. *~ katun* a wad of cotton.

bergumpal to clot, mass together, concentrate.

bergumpal-gumpal and **bergumpalan** in clumps. *Awan gelap bergumpal-gumpal datang dari timur.* Billowing dark clouds came from the east.

menggumpal 1 to assemble, coagulate, congeal. *Gagasan ini ~ menjadi tékad.* The idea congealed into a determination. **2** to build up, collect, assemble. *Kekesalan ~ di jantungnya.* Disappointment built up in his heart. **3** to crumple, rumple. *Digumpalnya surat itu.* He crumpled up the letter.

menggumpalkan to mash together, crumple up, make s.t. into a wad.

tergumpal massed together, concentrated, congealed.

gumpalan mass, agglomeration, lump, clod, clot. *~ awan* a mass of clouds, cumuli. *~ lemak* fetlock (of a horse). *~ orang* a small crowd of people. *~ rambut* coiffure.

penggumpalan agglutination.

pergumpalan agglutination.

penggumpalan clotting.

gumpel → GUMPAL.

gumpil (small) clod or lump.

gumuk (*Jv*) small hill, knoll, dune.

bergumuk hilly.

gumukan hill.

gumul bergumul 1 to wrestle. **2** (*vulg*) *~* (*bersama*) to screw, fuck. **3** to struggle.

menggumul 1 to wrestle. **2** to struggle.

menggumuli 1 to wrestle with. **2** (*vulg*) to screw, fuck.

gumulan s.t. that one struggles with.

pergumulan 1 wrestling. **2** struggle.

gumun (*Jv*) astonished, astounded. *– aku!* I'm astounded.

gun (*Jv*) weaver's comb to separate the threads.

guna I (*Skr*) **1** use, advantage, benefit. *Apa –nya?* What's the point? *banyak –nya* it has a lot of uses, it's useful. *salah* – misuse. *serba* – multipurpose. *tanpa* – useless. *tidak ada –nya* a) that (sentence) makes no sense. b) it's useless. **2** function. **3** virtue, quality. *tak tahu membalas* – doesn't know how to show one's gratitude. *– bangunan* building. *– ganda* double benefit. *– usaha* long lease.

gunanya *tidak ada ~* it's useless, what's the point.

seguna *~ sekaya* community property (when divorced it has to be split equally).

berguna 1 useful, beneficial, fit for use, suitable. *pekerjaan yang ~* useful work. **2** appropriate (to the purpose), necessary.

menggunakan and **mempergunakan** [and **nggunain/ngegunain** (*J coq*)] to use, utilize, make use of, avail o.s. of, employ, apply, have at one's disposal, exercise (one's rights). *tidak dapat digunakan* unusable. *~ lagi* to reuse, put back into service. *~ waktu* to make use of one's time.

kegunaan use, purpose, utility.

pengguna user. *~ akhir* end-user. *~ jasa* employer.

penggunaan 1 use, usage. **2** employment. *cedera-cedera karena ~ yang berlebihan* injuries due to overuse. *~ bahasa* (*gram*) language use. *~ berlebihan* excessive use. *~ obat perangsang* doping. *~ tunggal* single usage.

pergunaan use, utilization, application

guna II (*Skr*) for, in order to, to. *– kepentingan* for the sake of. *menyurat – minta uang* to write in order to ask for money. *– mengejar waktu* to lose no time.

guna-guna magic spell for doing harm to another, charm, formula, black magic.

mengguna-gunai to put a curse on, use black magic on s.o.

gunawan I (*Skr*) **1** virtuous, meritorious. **2** (*ob*) useful.

gunawan II (*Mal*) skilled in magic.

guncang shake; → GONCANG.

berguncang(-guncang) to shake, rock.

berguncang-guncangan (*pl subj*) to shake, rock.

mengguncang to stagger, shake, rock, oscillate. *Lembaga Bantuan Hukum (LBH) Semarang diguncang kemelut intérn.* The Semarang Legal Aid Foundation was rocked by an internal crisis.

mengguncang-guncang *~ bahunya* shaking (with laughter).

mengguncangkan to rock, shake. *Dua ledakan ~ Kuwait.* Two blasts rocked Kuwait.

terguncang shaken, rocked. *~ rokét* shell shock.

guncangan shock, oscillation.

keguncangan strong emotion.

pengguncang shaker; oscillator.

gunci 1 curl (in hair). **2** fringe.

guncip shears.

gunda goose weed, *Sphenoclea zeylanica.*

gundah sad, despondent, depressed, unhappy, worried, anxious. *– gulana* brooding, melancholy, apathetic. **bergundah gulana** to brood. **bergundah hati** sad.

menggundahkan and **mempergundahkan** *~ hati* to sadden, depress, discourage, dishearten.

kegundahan dejection, low spirits, worry, depression.

gundal I mark/tally to show where one has stopped counting (marked by a notch/a knot in a string/a scratch, etc.).

gundalan tally.

gundal II (*cla*) **1** servant, follower, helper, associate. **2** stooge, accomplice, henchman, partner in crime.

begundal scum.

pergundalan slavery.

gundal III gundal *gandil* (*J*) to swing back and forth, dangle, hang down and sway (such as the udders of a walking cow).

gundang throat, gullet.

gundar (*M*) clothes/shoe brush; → BUNDAR II.

menggundar to brush (one's hair).

gundi (*buah* -) k.o. fruit.
gundik 1 illegal wife, concubine, mistress (housekeeper of European or Chinese). 2 common-law wife. 3 queen of white ants. – *candik* all k.o. concubines.
  bergundik to have a concubine/mistress.
  menggundiki to take … as one's mistress.
  mempergundikkan to take a woman as concubine/mistress.
  pergundikan concubinage, polygamy.
gundil I (*Jv*) hairless paddy.
gundil II Javanese in Arabic script without vocal marks; → HURUF *Arab gundul*.
gundu 1 k.o. nut, the meat of which has been taken out and replaced by lead, used as a marble. 2 marble; → GULI, KELÉRÉNG. *main* – to play marbles.
  bergundu to play marbles.
gunduk 1 small pile. 2 (*anat*) colliculus.
  bergunduk(-gunduk) piled up, in piles.
  menggunduk 1 to pile up. 2 to look like a pile.
  menggunduk(-gunduk)kan to heap/pile up, accumulate.
  gundukan 1 hillock, mound. 2 heap, pile, stack; group, cluster.
gundul 1 bald. – *pacul* completely bald, bald as a billiard ball. 2 barren. *tanah yang* – barren land. 3 leafless (of trees). *pohon* – leafless tree. 4 fleeceless, hairless (of sheep).
  bergundul bare-headed (because not wearing headgear); not covered with vegetation; leafless.
  menggundul 1 to go bald. 2 to shave s.o. bald. 3 to deforest. 4 to defeat, trounce. 5 to clean out, strip s.o. of everything he owns.
  menggunduli 1 to defeat, trounce. 2 to clean s.o. out, strip. 3 to denude.
  menggundulkan 1 to make bald. 2 to strip s.o. of his possessions.
  kegundulan baldness.
  penggundulan 1 shaving s.o. bald. 2 denuding. ~ *hutan* deforestation. ~ *luas* clear cutting. 3 stripping s.o. of his possessions.
gung I gong.
  meng(e)gungkan to beat a gung.
gung II (*onom*) sound of rumbling, booming; → DEGUNG.
gung III (*Jv*) – *liwang-liwung* dense (of jungle).
gung IV (in acronyms) → AGUNG I.
gung V (*Jv*) – *binatara* a celebrated and important person.
gunggung (*Jv*) sum, total.
  menggunggung to total up.
  gunggungan total.
gungsing (*S*) globular bell.
guni (*Hind*) jute. *karung* – jute gunnysack; → GONI.
gunjai fringe (of a scarf/curtain), tassels (on a bridal aigrette), tuft. *sampai ke* –*nya* in every detail.
gunjang-ganjing (*S*) to shake, tremble; commotion. *bumi* – the earth shook.
gunjing (*M*) slander, libel, gossip. – *gujrak/gunjrat* all k.o. slander.
  bergunjing to gossip.
  menggunjing to slander, revile, abuse (a person), grumble at, malign (behind one's back).
  menggunjingi, menggunjingkan, and **mempergunjing(kan)** to gossip maliciously about, say bad things about.
  gunjingan malicious gossip. *menjadi* – and (*men*)*jadi bahan ~ orang* to be the talk of the town.
  pergunjingan malicious gossip, gossiping.
guntai I → GONTAI.
guntai II (*S*) absentee. *tanah* – land given to a third party for tilling.
guntak (*onom*) rattling of seeds in a dry pot.
guntang I (*cla*) fisherman's float.
guntang II (*Skr ob*) protected.
guntang-guntang spool in a loom.
guntara [*pegun sementara*] (*geol*) eustatism, eustacy, eustatic.
  keguntaraan eustatic.
guntil small pouch.
gunting 1 scissors, shears. *kena* – laid off (from one's job). *mata* – the sharp edge of scissors. *tukang* – *rambut* barber. *seperti* – *makan di ujung* words that are quietly successful in reaching the target. – *bajak* shears. – *besi* iron cutter. – *inggeris* trickery. – *kaléng* tin snips. – *karcis* ticket punch. – *kabun* pruning

shears. – *kuku* nail clippers. – *mesin* hair clippers. – *pagar* hedge clippers. – *rambut* haircut. – *rumput* grass cutter. 2 the cut (of an article of clothing).
  menggunting 1 to cut (off), clip (off). ~ *karcis* to punch tickets. ~ *lidah* to interrupt. ~ *pita* to cut the ribbon. 2 to cut off, intercept. 3 to trim, cut hair. 4 to deceive, swindle. ~ *dalam lipatan* to deceive one's own relatives/friends. ~ *hati* to hurt s.o.'s feelings. 5 (drivers' jargon) to take a shortcut; → MEMOTONG.
  mengguntingi (*pl subj*) to cut with scissors/shears.
  tergunting cut, sheared. *hati* ~ hurt, one's feelings are hurt.
  guntingan 1 cut-off piece. 2 (*press*) cutting, clipping. 3 quotation. ~ *berita/pérs* press clipping. 4 cut, style (of clothing). 5 cutter. ~ *kuku* nail clippers.
  pengguntng 1 clipper. 2 scissors, shears. ~ *dalam lipatan* deceiver, cheater (of one's own family or friends). 3 various k.o. shearwaters (birds); → PENGGUNTING.
  pengguntingan 1 cutting, snipping (a ribbon, etc.). 2 devaluation (of the rupiah). 3 layoffs. ~ *dalam lipatan* deceit, deception (of one's own family or friends).
guntung blunt, cut off, short (of shorts), truncated. *baju* – short-sleeved shirt. *celana* – cut-off trousers. *pusaka* – heirloom with no heirs and thus fallen into the hands of the state.
  mengguntung to top (a tree), truncate (a cone), cut off.
guntur thunder; → GELUDUK, GURUH II. *mengharapkan* – *di langit, air di tempayan dicurahkan* to throw away old shoes before one has gotten new ones.
  berguntur and **mengguntur** 1 to thunder. 2 to boom, resound, blast.
  menggunturkan to strike, drive, inflict, give forth, etc. with loud noise or violent action.
gunung 1 mountain. *seri* – (*cla*) beautiful from a distance. *takkan lari* – *dikejar (bilang kabut tampaklah)* haste makes waste. *maksud hati memeluk* –, *apa daya tangan tak sampai* – to have high ideals, but not the means to achieve them. *niat hati nak peluk* –, *terpeluk biawak sial* good intentions lead to hell. – *jua yang dilejang panas the rich get richer. *tak ada* – *yang tak dapat didaki* where there's a will there's a way. – *api* volcano. **kegunung-apian** volcanology. – *berapi* volcano. – *berapi yang tidur* a dormant volcano. – *és* iceberg. – *ganang* various/ranges of mountains. – *gemunung* mountain chain. – *Jati* name of the Jakarta-Cirebon fast train. – *pasir* sand dune. – *Srandil* Mount Srandil in Cilacap (Central Java), considered to be the center of the Island of Java. – *sulah* bald mountain. – *Tidar* Mount Tidar, south of Magelang (Central Java), considered to be the nail that fastens the Island of Java to the earth. 2 name of a *ceki* card.
  segunung as high as a mountain. *Dongkolnya* –. His anger was sky high.
  bergunung-gunung mountainous.
  menggunung 1 to look like a mountain. 2 to mount/pile up. *sampah* ~ the trash was piling up (like a mountain).
  menggunungkan to make s.t. into a mountain.
  gunungan 1 (in the *wayang* play) a symbolic triangle figure placed in the middle of the screen. The top corner depicts the world of God (*Arupadatu*), and the other two corners depict the world of mankind (*Rupadatu*) and the spirit world (*Kamadatu*). 2 the mountain of food in the Sekaten ceremony in Central Java. 3 heap, mass (like a mountain). ~ *runtuhan* heap of ruins, mass of debris.
  gunung-gunungan 1 a small mountain, mountainous. 2 a high stack/pile/heap.
  pe(r)gunungan mountainous. *daérah* ~ mountainous region. ~ *Alpen* the Alps. ~ *Dafonsoro* the former Cyclops Mountains in Irian Jaya. ~ *Pirénéa* Pyrenees.
guoblok (*coq*) very stupid; → GOBLOK.
gup (*onom*) a thudding sound: plop! flop!
gupak (*J*) **ngegupak** 1 to roll (over the ground, in the mud, etc.). 2 to wallow in a mud hole (of buffaloes). 3 to have lots of experience; to spend a lot of time at.
gupermental (*D*) governmental.
gupérnemén (*D*) government.
gupernur → GUBERNUR.
gupuh (*Jv*) → GOPOH.

gurab (*A*) → GORAB.

gurah I (*Jv*) method of healing by rinsing. – *mata* k.o. method of healing eye disease by rinsing.
bergurah to gargle, rinse (one's mouth with water).
menggurah 1 to clean one's mouth with water. **2** to clean (a barrel, etc.) with water.

gurah II *pohon* – k.o. mangrove tree, *Sapium indicum*, whose fruits are used to stun fish.

guram I (*J*) faded, dull, dim, somber, gloomy, grim. *masa depan* – a bleak future.

guram II → GUREM.

gurami (*Jv*) *ikan* – fresh-water carp, gurami, *Osphromenus olfax.*

gurandil small-scale gold panner.

gurat 1 scratch, line; feature. – *tangan* lines on the palm. **2** pin. *intan* – diamond pin. – *belah* bolt pin. **3** pen. – *tulis* recording pen. – *batu* (*S*) unyielding, inflexible, tenacious.
bergurat scratched, lined; with lines.
bergurat-gurat 1 all scratched up. **2** covered with lines.
menggurat 1 to scratch. **2** to scratch out. **3** to make a strong impression on.
menggurati 1 to scratch, make lines. **2** to draw stripes; to leave traces. **3** to cross out. **4** to sketch, make a sketch of.
mengguratkan to mark, tick off, engrave.
tergurat scratched, incised.
guratan 1 line, stripe; groove, wrinkle. **2** underlined. **3** (*geol*) striation. **4** sketch. ~ *nasib* fate.
pengguratan scratching.

gurau joke, jest, banter; → SENDA *gurau*.
bergurau to joke around, banter.
bergurauan to joke around with e.o.
mengguraukan and **mempergauraukan** to make a fool of s.o., make fun of s.o., pull s.o.'s leg, poke fun at s.o.
gurauan joke, jest, bantering, prank.
pergurauan joking around, bantering.

gurda → GARUDA.

gurdan *ringgit* – Mexican dollar on which there is the picture of a bird; → RINGGIT *burung*.

gurdi (*Tam*) drill, auger, gimlet.
menggurdi to drill/bore with a gimlet.

gurem (*Jv*) **1** chicken flea. **2** trivial, insignificant, of little importance. *partai* – a small, ill-defined (political) party. *petani* – small farmers. – *bawang* k.o. flea, *Thrips tabaci.*

guri I short, round earthenware pot.

guri II dry dock.

guribang (*J*) hibiscus, *Hibiscus rosasinensis.*

gurih deliciously pungent/piquant (with a salty taste liked fried fish).
kegurihan 1 pungency, piquancy. **2** too pungent.

gurik (*ob*) → URIK I. **menggurik** to pick/pluck in.

gurila (*ob*) → GERILYA.

gurinda → GERINDA.

gurindam (*Skr*) couplet, poem made up of 2 rhyming lines of equal length.
bergurindam to recite such couplets.

guring I (*ob*) → GULING.

guring II (*Ban*) to sleep. *tempat* – hotel, inn.

guris → GORÉS. *senyum* **berguris-guris/mengguris/terguris** a trace of a smile.

gurit (*Jv*) k.o. verse, poem.
menggurit to write poetry.
guritan poetry.

gurita I (*Skr*) *ikan* – octopus, *Octopus vulgaris.*
menggurita to spread (like an octopus).

gurita II (*Jv*) abdominal/umbilical belt.

guru I (*Skr*) **1** teacher, instructor, mentor. **2** one's personal spiritual adviser. *Batara* – Divine Teacher = Shiva. – *kencing berdiri, murid kencing berlari* the teacher urinates standing up and his pupils urinate running, i.e., pupils are apt to carry the results of their teaching to extremes. – *agama* s.o. who teaches the Islamic religion in government or private schools. – *angkat* unlicensed teacher. – *bangsa* a national figure who leads the way for his/her people. – *bantu* assistant teacher. – *besar* professor; →

MAHAGURU, PROFÉSOR. **keguru-besaran** professorship. – *désa* village schoolteacher. – *Huria* (*Bat*) elder of the church. – *Injil* preacher, evangelist. – *jaga* substitute teacher. – *kehormatan* honorary professorship. – *kepala* principal, headmaster. – *kunjung* a teacher who teaches by going to his/her students. – *(me)ngaji* s.o. who teaches the elementary principles of Islam, such as Koranic reading, in a mosque, *musholla*, or village. – *pengawas* housemaster/mistress. – *penolong* auxiliary teacher. – *putra* male teacher. – *putri* female teacher. – *sulih* substitute instructor. – *tamu* visiting professor.
berguru 1 ~ *dengan* (*infr*) and ~ *kepada* to learn from/study under a teacher, be a student of, study with a teacher. ~ *dahulu sebelum bergurau* sweet is repose after the work is done. **2** to act as a teacher. *Ia sebenarnya bukan* ~, *tetapi pandai* ~. In fact, he is not a teacher, but he cleverly acts as such.
bergurukan to be taught by, have ... as a teacher.
mengguru to act like a teacher.
menggurui [and **ngguruin/ngeguruin** (*J coq*)] **1** to teach s.o. **2** to advise s.o. **3** to lecture, give s.o. a lecture, talk down to. *Jangan mulai* ~ *saya*. Don't start lecturing me.
memperguru to consider/treat as a teacher.
mempergurui (*M*) to take lessons in.
guru pedantic.
keguruan teacher (*mod*). *fakultas* ~ school of education. *Institut* ~ *dan Ilmu Pendidikan* [IKIP] Institute of Teacher Training and Pedagogy.
keguru-guruan pedantic.
pengguruan (*M*) *tangkap* ~ a dangerously learned grip (in *silat*). **sepengguruan** as clever as (in *silat*).
perguruan 1 school, educational institution. ~ *menengah* secondary school. ~ *rakyat* institute of mass education. ~ *rendah* elementary school. **2** education. ~ *déwasa* adult education. ~ *tinggi* a) higher education. b) graduate school. c) academy, college. ~ *tinggi* college, university, academy. ~ *Tinggi Dakwah Islam* [PTDI] College for Islamic Missionary Work. ~ *Tinggi Ilmu Kepolisian* [PTIK] Police Science Academy. ~ *Tinggi Negeri* [PTN] State-run University. ~ *Tinggi Swasta* [PTS] Private University. **seperguruan** of one/the same academy/college/university. *rekan/teman* ~ fellow student.

guru II (*Bat*) → DUKUN

guruh I (*A*) sunset, sundown.

guruh II thunder, loud noise which *usu* follows a flash of lightning. – *harapkan di langit, air tempayan ditumpahkan* to count one's chickens before they are hatched. – *gemuruh* thunderous (of applause, etc.). *darah* – *gemuruh* one's blood pounds.
berguruh and **mengguruh 1** to thunder, boom. **2** thunderous.

gurun desert, wasteland. – *Gobi* Gobi desert. – *pasir* wasteland (desert, etc.). – *Sahara* the Sahara. – *tandas* complete wasteland.
pengguruan turning s.t. into a wasteland/desert.

gurung I (*Jv*) **1** windpipe, esophagus, gullet. **2** culvert.
gurungan culvert.

gurung II a pole with a hook to pluck fruit from trees so that they don't fall to the ground.

gurur (*A*) **1** wishful thinking, false hopes, illusions. **2** vanity.

gus I → SEKALIGUS.

gus II (*Jv*) young man (friendly term of address).

gus III → BAGUS II.

gus IV (in acronyms) → GUGUSAN.

gusah (*Jv*) **menggusah** to chase away.

gusar I 1 angry, offended, annoyed. – *akan* angry with. *mengambil* – to resent. *Jangan* –! Don't be offended! – *hati* angry. **2** harassment.
menggusari to be angry at, chide.
menggusarkan to anger, make s.o. angry, provoke s.o. to anger.
kegusaran anger, fury, rage.

gusar II (*S*) **menggusar** to file one's teeth.
gusaran tooth-filing (ceremony).

gusel (*J*) **menggusel** to embrace; to kiss repeatedly, cuddle, hug.
gusel-guselan 1 to pet. **2** petting.

gusgus (*J*) **1** a skin disease of the hands and feet. **2** bad, of poor quality.

gusi I gums.

gusi II *layar* - (*naut*) mizzen sail; → LAYAR *baksi*.

gusti I (*Jv*) lord, master. - *Allah* God. - *Kan(g)jeng* your Majesty. - *naib* k.o. *penghulu*. - *pangéran ngabéhi* oldest son of a monarch but not the crown prince. - *Pangéran Haryo* [GPH] a royal title in Yogya and Solo. - *Radén Ayu* [G.R.Ay.] title for a married princess.

gusti II (*Pers*) wrestling.

  bergusti to wrestle.

Gusti III (*Pal*) – *Ngurah* caste-indicating title placed before a male personal name to indicate that the person belongs to the Vaisyas. – *Ayu* caste-indicating title placed before a female personal name to indicate that the person belongs to the Vaisyas.

gusur (*J*) *kena* - *haknya* had their rights trampled on. *terkena* - leveled, torn down (of illegally built houses).

  menggusur 1 to drag along, pull. *Sang korban digusur oléh lokomotip*. The victim was dragged along by the locomotive. **2** to demolish, raze, flatten, pull down (a house). *Pemerintah DKI ~ bangunan-bangunan liar di pinggir kali itu*. The DKI government demolished the illegal houses at the edge of the canal. **3** to evict (squatters). *force s.o. to move.*

  menggusuri (*pl obj*) to demolish, etc.

  tergusur [and **kegusur** (*coq*)] **1** swept away, razed, wiped out, demolished, evicted. *Meréka yang ~ rumahnya diberi ganti rugi yang wajar*. Those whose houses were demolished were given reasonable compensation. **2** s.o. whose land has been confiscated.

  gusuran 1 expropriated (property). **2** vacated (area). **3** razed, torn down (of a house). **4** displaced.

  penggusur expropriator.

  penggusuran and **pergusuran 1** sweeping away, razing, wiping out. **2** eviction, evicting (squatters).

gutgut I (*J*) **ng(e)gutgut** to nibble.

gutgut II large crow-pheasant, *Centropus sinensis eurycercus*; → BUBUT V.

gutik (*M?*) **menggutik 1** to pinch between thumb and finger. *Ia ~ anak itu hingga menangis*. He pinched the child until he cried. **2** to touch with the fingertip. **3** to pluck (the strings of an instrument).

gutuk (*Jv*) worthwhile.

gutural (*D ling*) guttural.

guyah → GOYAH.

guyang (*J/Jv*) to bathe, take a bath.

guyon (*Jv*) **1** object of laughter; a laughingstock, farce. *Pencopotan Vér dan Ramos, misalnya, sangat boléh jadi hanya sekadar –.* It is quite possible that the removal of Ver and Ramos, for instance, was just a farce. *bahasa Indo* – the amusing, joking language of Eurasians (a mixture of Dutch and Indonesian). *film* – a comedy. – *parikeno* ostensibly joking but actually serious. **2** to joke/kid around.

  berguyon to joke/kid around.

  guyonan jokingly.

  guyon-guyonan joking, joke.

guyot flat underwater mountain.

guyu (*Jv*) **mengguyu** and **ngguyu** to laugh; → GUYON.

guyub and **guyup** (*Jv*) **1** unanimous, of one mind, harmonious. **2** close to e.o., friendly, mutually helpful. – *rukun* close and harmonious.

  keguyuban concord, harmony, unity, communality of interests.

  guyuban community. ~ *bahasa* speech community.

  peguyuban 1 solidarity, community (of interests). **2** association, club, union, party. ~ *keluarga* family union. ~ *Widiyani/Widyani* Community of Scholars; → PAGUYUBAN.

guyur (*J/Jv*) **berguyur** dripping, bathed (in sweat, etc.).

  berguyuran (*pl subj*) to pour forth/out. *Hujan mortir ~*. A rain of mortar fire poured forth.

  mengguyur 1 to pour water, etc. in large amounts on, drench, shower (with). *Daérah-daérah Kabupatén Cianjur termasuk Puncak diguyur hujan*. The Cianjur region, including Puncak, was drenched with rain. *diguyur dengan sanjungan dan puji-pujian* showered with praise. *Sewaktu-waktu Médan bisa mendadak diguyur gelap*. At any time Medan can suddenly be covered in darkness (due to a power outage). **2** to splash, spray. ~ *seluruh badannya dengan air* to splash his entire body with water.

  mengguyurkan 1 to pour s.t. out in large amounts. ~ *air* to pour/sprinkle) a lot of water on. **2** to flush out s.t. with water.

  terguyur [and **keguyur** (*J*)] poured, sprinkled, sprayed.

  guyuran 1 splash. **2** large amounts of liquid. *di tengah-tengah ~ hujan* in a driving rain storm.

  pengguyuran pouring out.

guwé and **gwé** [and **gw** (*abbr*)] → GUÉ.

H

Words beginning with an H not found under this letter might be found under the vowel immediately following this letter, such as *(h)abis, (h)utang,* etc.

h and H I /ha/ the eighth letter of the Latin alphabet used for writing Indonesian.

H II (*abbr*) [Haji] → HAJI I.

H III (*abbr*) [Hijrah] → HIJRAH.

H IV car license plate for Semarang.

3-H Konsép – (*Bat*) the 3-Ha concept consisting of *Hamoraon* (Wealth), *Hagabéon* (Descendants/Prosperity), long life, and *Hasangapon* (Prestige).

ha I (*A*) **1** the seventh letter of the Arabic alphabet used for writing certain Arabic words with Jawi characters, represents a rough h. **2** the 31st letter of the Arabic alphabet used for writing Indonesian/Malay words and certain other Arabic words, represents a smooth h.

ha II 1 (exclamation of satisfaction or triumph) ha, hey! *–!, dapat juga saya menyelesaikan PR itu.* Hey, I was able to finish the home work. **2** (exclamation used to tease or make s.o. realize the result of s.t. prohibited, etc.). hey! *–! Rasakan, anda sekarang tahu akan gatalnya getah pohon itu.* Hey! Now you know how itchy the sap of that tree is.

ha III (*onom*) sound indicating laughter, usually repeated: **haha** or **ha-ha-ha;** → GERR.

ha IV (*abbr*) [héktar] hectare.

haah /ha'ah/ yes, yeah. *–, betul!* Yeah, that's right!

haai (*E*) high (on drugs); → HAI II.

haas (*D*) /has/ fillet of beef; → DAGING *has.*

haatzaai (*D*) – *artikelen* articles (in the press) spreading hatred.

haba I (*Mal*) heat.

haba II container for holding live fish.

habah (*A Hind ob*) barleycorn (also as a measure of weight or value = a small amount).

habaib (*A*) *pl* of HABIB 2.

habat berhabat half one's children are boys and half are girls.

habek (*J*) to eat; to stuff one's mouth with food.

habelur → HABLUR.

habib (*A*) **1** friend (of God), beloved (of God). **2** a form of address for a *Sayyid.*

habibi (*A*) my sweetheart/darling/love.

Habiburrahman (*A*) God, the Merciful, the Loving One.

Habil (*A*) (the Biblical) Abel.

habis I 1 all gone, used up, spent, depleted, nothing is left, (s.o. is) out of (s.t.), wear off (of the effects of a medicine). *Uangnya –.* His money is all gone. *Uangnya – ke baju saja.* He spends all his money on clothes. *Kesabaran saya –.* I'm out of patience. *Gula kami –.* We're out of sugar. *Apa bénsinnya –?* Are we out of gas? **2** all, wholly, totally, entirely, fully, completely, thoroughly. *mengkritik –* to criticize thoroughly. *Rumahnya – dimakan api.* His house burned down completely. *Padinya – dimakan tikus.* The rice was all eaten up by the rats. *Padinya sudah – dijual.* The rice was all sold. *– terbakar* to burn down. *Kamus itu – jual.* The dictionary was completely sold out. *– diborong oléh* completely bought up. *– dipesan* fully booked up (of hotel reservations). *Yakub percaya – kepada ibunya.* Yakub trusts his mother completely. **3** to spend, be spent in, require, consume (of time/amounts of money). *hari – dengan* the day was spent in. *Untuk belanja di pasar – tiga puluh ribu rupiah.* To shop in the market you need 30,000 rupiahs. **4** to end, be the final part of; (to be) over, finished. *tak – di situ* it didn't end there. *Cerita ini belum –.* The story isn't finished yet. *–lah riwayatnya.* His life is over. *– sudah riwayat Lébanon.* Lebanon is finished. *– bulan/tahun ...* a) at the end of ... the month/year. b) after the month/year ... was over, i.e., at the beginning of the next time period. **5** to expire, lapse, come to an end, terminate. *Visanya dinyatakan – masa waktunya.* Her visa was declared expired. *tak ada –nya* endless, without end, unending. *pertempuran yang tak ada –nya* an endless war. *tak/tidak – + verb* to

keep on (trying to) ... *tidak – mengerti* to keep on trying to understand (and failing). *tidak – pikir* to keep on worrying, can't stop thinking about. **6** (+ a verb) after ... -ing. *– makan, bagaimana kalau kita nonton bioskop?* After eating, what about going to the movies? *– dari* to have visited/been to. "*Gué dengar lu – dari Bali, Ridzal*" "I heard you've just been in Bali, Ridzal." **7** (*coq*) what (happened) then/after that/next? *Sesudah engkau ditanyai ini itu, – ...* After you were questioned about this and that, what happened next? **8** well (what do you expect?); well (that's the way it is); well (what should ...)? *– selalu kaumarahi, tentu saja tak betah.* (It can't be helped) because you're always mad at me, of course I don't feel comfortable here. *– mesti bagaimana?* Well, what do I have to do then? *– di Jakarta!* well, that's the way it is in Jakarta! **9** expendable. *bahan –* expendable materials (such as filter paper, etc.). *– berkelahi ingat silat* not to think of the best solution until after s.t. is over. *– manis sepah dibuang* to take advantage of s.o. or s.t. and then throw him/her/it away. *– akal* to be at one's wits end. *– buku* close the books. **menghabis-bukukan** to close out the books (in bookkeeping). *– dibagi* divisible (number). *– hati* a) frightened. b) to have had it (with), be finished (with). *– hati saya kepadanya* I'm finished with her. *– kalas* exhausted. *– kesabaran* out of patience. *– perkara* that's final, that's it, period! *– rantas* completely wiped out (of plants). *– tahun* end of the year. *– témpo* expired, no longer in effect. *– tenaga* exhausted. *– terkuras* all gone, used up, wiped out. *– waktu* expired, no longer in effect.

habis-habis through and through, thoroughly, in every which way. *Kita cakapkan ~ tentang hal ini.* We discussed this matter thoroughly. *tak ~* and *tak ~nya* endless(ly), continually, never ending, keep on (doing s.t.). *memakan ~, menyuruk hilang-hilang* to cover up s.t. (so that nobody can know about it).

sehabis 1 after (something is finished). *~ penat berkeliling sambil menunggu kalau-kalau ada pembeli, ia beristirahat.* After tiring himself out going around looking for buyers, he took a break. *~ itu* after that, afterward. **2** to an extreme degree of, as far as ... *menjangkau ~ tangan* to work one's fingers to the bone. *dengan ~ akal* with all one's strength and mental abilities.

sehabisnyé (*J*) after. *~ sulap* after the sleight of hand.

sehabis-habis(nya) all of it/them, the whole lot, entirely, completely. *~ busuk* completely rotten. *~ tenaga* as much as one could, to the utmost of one's power, at the top of one's. *dengan ~ kekuatan* with all one's might.

berhabis to spend, waste, squander. *~ air* to have talked about s.t. for too long. *~ tenaga* to waste one's energy. *~ uang* to spend money right and left, squander money. *~ waktu* to waste/fritter away one's time.

menghabisi 1 to end, finish (off). *Pidato itu dihabisinya dengan seruan supaya ...* He ended the speech by appealing to ... **2** to kill, destroy, do away with. *~ nyawa* to kill, murder. b) to commit suicide. *~ umur* a) to spend one's life. b) to die; → TUTUP *usia.* **3** to erase, eradicate, abolish, obliterate. **4** to spend (time). *~ malam* to spend the night.

menghabis(-habis)kan 1 to spend, devote (time/money/labor/ the day, etc.) to some purpose. *~ biaya* to spend money recklessly. *Hari-hari Minggu biasanya kami habiskan untuk jalan-jalan di Balbao Park.* We usually spend Sundays taking a walk in Balbao Park. *Setelah mengunci pintu kamarnya dicobanya duduk di méja tempat ia biasa ~ jam-jamnya untuk belajar.* After locking the door to her room, she tried sitting at the table where she usually spends hours studying. *~ liburan di* to spend one's vacation in. *~ waktu* to spend/kill time. *Meréka ~ waktu bermain kartu, ngobrol dan lain sebagainya.* They kill time playing cards, chatting and the like. **2** to complete, finish, bring to an end. *Dia pergi ~ kerjanya yang terbengkalai.* He went to complete his unfinished job. ~ *hidup* to end/live out one's days. 3 to finish (off/up), use/eat up, consume entirely, devour, swallow (up), wipe out. *Habiskan!* Finish it up! (of the remaining food). *Macan yang berkeliaran ~ tujuh ékor kambing.* Roaming tigers devoured seven goats. *Dihabiskannya mata sapi dan toastnya.* He finished up his fried eggs and toast. ~ *tenaga* to exhaust o.s. 4 to kill, murder. *Keris ini akan ~ siapa saja yang coba mengganggu adinda.* This kris will kill anyone who tries to bother you.

habis-habisan and **berhabis-habisan** 1 to the last (man/penny), till the bitter end, with all one's might, without mercy. *Tetangga saya kemalingan sampai habis-habisan.* My neighbor was robbed of every last thing he owns. 2 to an extreme degree, as much as ... *Ia dicaci-maki ~.* He was reviled to the nth degree, abuse was poured on him. *dianiaya habis-habisan* to be tortured to death. *usaha habis-habisan* all-out efforts.

kehabisan 1 (is/was) finished, *tak pernah ~* inexhaustible. 2 to be/run out of, have no ... left. ~ *akal* to be at one's wits end. *Ia tak pernah ~ akal.* He never runs out of ideas. ~ *bénsin* out of gas. ~ *darah* (s.o.) loses blood (in an accident, etc.). ~ *ikhtiar* to be at one's wits end. ~ *jawab* to be at a loss for an answer. ~ *karcis* to run out of tickets. *Karena takut ~ karcis, saya segera membeli dua lembar yang nomornya berurutan.* Because I was afraid they would run out of tickets, I immediately bought two with sequential numbers. ~ *makanan* to run out of food. ~ *nafas* out of breath. ~ *oksigén dalam darah* asphyxiated. ~ *stok* out of stock. ~ *tempat* sold out (of seats). ~ *tenaga* exhausted, out of energy. ~ *uang* broke, out of money. 3 to miss/be left out. *Lekas pesan, jangan ~!* Order right now, don't miss out!

penghabis s.o. who uses up. ~ *duit rakyat* s.o. who uses up the people's money.

penghabisan 1 (the) very last, (the) last (one to). *Dialah yang ~ keluar dari rumah.* He was the last one out of the house. 2 for the last time, final. *perpisahan ~* a final farewell. 3 last, final. *stasiun ~* terminal station, last stop; → **TÉRMINAL**. *ujian ~* final examination. **penghabisannya** finally, in the end. ~ *tiada siapa pun yang berdaya.* Finally, there was nobody left who had the strength.

habis II (*A*) inalienable (property, etc.).

habitat (*E*) habitat.

habitus (*D*) habit.

habluk (*A Hind*) white spots on a background of different color, spotted, stained. *kuda –* a piebald horse.

hablun (*A*) relationship. *- min Allah* and *–inallah* the relationship between man and God. *- min al-nas* and *–inannas* the relationship between men.

hablur (*Pers*) rock crystal.
   berhablur crystalline.
   menghablur to crystallize, form crystals.
   menghablurkan to crystallize, cause s.t. to form into crystals.
   penghabluran crystallization.

Habshah (*A*) Abyssinia, Ethiopia.

Habshi and **Habsyi** (*A*) *negeri –* Abyssinia, Ethiopia. *orang –* Abyssinian, Ethiopian; African black.

habuan (*cla*) share (of money/food), portion; → **ABUAN**.

habuk dust; → **ABUK I**.

habur (*ob*) **menghabur** ~ *uang* to spend money recklessly; → **MENGHAMBUR**.

hacih, hacing, haciu and **hacu** (*onom*) atchoo! (sound made when sneezing).

had I (*A mostly Mal*) 1 limit, boundary. *tanpa –* without limits, limitless. *- laju* speed limit. 2 until, as far as.
   berhad limited, Ltd., Incorporated, Inc. (of a corporation). *Pustaka Zaman Sdn ~* Pustaka Zaman, Pt. Ltd.
   menghadkan to limit.
   terhad limited. *Dia mempunyai pengalaman ~ dalam perkara itu.* He has limited experience in that matter.

had II (*A*) punishment for condemned behavior.

hadal abyss, sea level at more than 6,000 meters.

hadam (*A mostly Mal*) digested (of food).
   menghadamkan to digest.

terhadam digested.

penghadam s.t. that helps to digest food.

penghadaman digestion.

hadanah (*A leg*) child custody.

hadang → **ADANG I**. **menghadang** to intercept, obstruct, block (the way). *Begitu membuka pintu depan, ia langsung dihadang perampok bergolok.* As soon as he opened the front door, his way was blocked by a robber waving a machete. ~ *musuh* to intercept the enemy. ~ *pintu* to block the door(way).

penghadang holdup man, highway robber.

penghadangan ambush(ing), robbing.

hadap 1 front. 2 direction (upstream, etc.), direction faced, facing. *tidak berketentuan – belakangnya* it's not clear which is the front and which is the back. *tak tentu –* a) the aim/purpose/goal/object is uncertain/dubious/questionable. b) do not do a thing, do not take any action. *Ke mana – rumah itu?* Which direction is the house facing? *perékonomian yang hanya satu – saja* an economy which only looks in one direction. *- angin* windward. *- kanan/kiri* (*mil*) eyes right/left! *- muka* face, confront. **berhadapan muka** to meet face to face. **menghadapmukakan** to confront. *Dua orang saksi akan dihadapmukakan dengan terdakwa.* Two witnesses will be confronted with the accused.

sehadap bersehadap(an) to face/confront e.o.

berhadapan 1 ~ (*dengan*) to (meet face to) face, (to stand/sit) opposite *Rumahnya ~ dengan kantor pos*. His house faces the post office, his house is opposite the post office. 2 to be on hostile terms (with). 3 to have the courage to face (bullets), have the courage to hold one's own (with). ~ *dengan musuh* to face up to the enemy, to have the courage to face the enemy. ~ *muka* to be confronted with, face to face. ~ *manis mulutnya, di belakang lain bicaranya* sweet-mouthed in front of people, but talking evil behind their back.

berhadap-hadapan 1 opposite e.o. 2 (to say s.t.) to one's face, (to speak as) one man to another, face to face. 3 (to fight s.t. out) openly, publicly; → **BERMUKA-MUKA**. *berhadap(-hadap)an muka/mata* (to see, etc. s.o.) personally, meet face to face.

menghadap 1 (*ke* or with direct object) a) (with the front/back, etc.) to face, facing. b) (thoughts were) directed to. 2 (the house) faces (toward/in a certain direction). 3 (to go) in a certain direction. 4a) to obtain an audience with, appear before, pay one's respects (to). *dihadap oléh* to be granted/given an audience with. b) to go to speak to (an employer), report to (a superior). ~ *ke pengadilan* to be summoned to appear in Court, be summoned to Court. ~ *Tuhan* a) to pray. b) to pass away. 5 to make an appearance (in court), turn to (the police, etc.).

menghadapi 1 (to stand/sit) before, opposite, facing, (to sit) at (the table), to be present at. 2 to experience, go through (hard/bad) times, get into trouble/difficulties with. ~ *jalan buntu* to reach a deadlock, fail, fall through. ~ *masa sulit* to go through hard times. 3 to face (up to), be faced with, confront, meet, encounter, deal with. *Meréka itu duduk ~ berbagai-bagai makanan yang lezat citarasanya.* They were sitting in front of various delicious dishes. *Apa yang harus anda perbuat jika anda ~ musuh yang lebih kuat?* What should you do if you faced a stronger enemy? *banyak ~* to be plagued with, face a lot of. ~ *dengan berani* to stand up to. ~ *hidup* to face up to life's problems, keep going. ~ *secara langsung* to face head-on. ~ *surut* to face backwards. 4 to be prepared to meet (contingencies, etc.). 5 to look forward (to the future), have ... ahead/ahead of/before/in front of one, in anticipation of. ~ *panén buruk* in anticipation of a poor crop. *tugas yang dihadapi* the work at hand. 6 to be on the eve/threshold of, be within striking distance of ... -ing. ~ *ajalnya* to be/ill dying, be at the point of death, be on one's deathbed. 7 to face (the facts/danger), put one's mind to (the subject), give some thought (to the matter). 8 to adjust/adapt o.s. to s.t. else/new.

menghadapkan 1 (= **memperhadapkan**) to confront, (come face to) face, oppose, contest, contend, compete with. *dihadapkan pada satu di antara dua* to be faced with a dilemma. 2 to set s.t. in front of, put/set before/in front of s.o.; to offer. 3a) to send/direct (a boat to). b) to turn (one's look/fury, etc.)

on s.o.; → MENUJUKAN. c) to level (reproaches) at. 4 ~ *kepada hakim* and ~ *ke (muka) pengadilan* to take to court, summon before the Court. 5 to put forward, propose (terms, conditions).

terhadap 1 concerning, having to do with, in regard to, regarding, about, for, of. *Penculikan ~ seorang anak SD Taranika digagalkan Satpam.* The kidnapping of a child from the Taranika Elementary School was thwarted by *Satpam. Pengakuan ~ Singapura.* The recognition of Singapore. 2 (change/conversion of s.t.) (in)to. *penukaran uang rupiah ~ dolar Malaysia* the conversion of rupiahs into Malaysian dollars. 3 aimed at, directed to, turning toward. *Hatinya sudah ~ ke Jawa.* His heart is already turning toward Java. 4 against. *diambilnya tindakan ~ ... he took measures against ...*

hadapan 1 facing front. *pintu ~* front door. 2 in the presence of, before. 3 next. *bulan ~* next month. 4 face, façade, frontage.

hadap-hadapan *nasi-nasi ~* (*Mal*) glutinous rice which is placed in front of the bridal dais during the *bersanding* ceremony.

penghadap (in notarial and legal language) person appearing, party (to a suit).

penghadapan appearance, being party (to a suit). ~ and *balai ~* audience hall.

perhadapan (face-to-face) confrontation.

hadar (*A*) *mati -* to die unavenged.

hadas (*A*) to be impure in regard to Muslim rites. *mandi - a* to perform ritual ablution after being defiled. *- besar* a ritual impurity which requires bathing for absolution, such as menses, childbirth, emission of semen. *- kecil* a ritual impurity which requires ablutions for absolution, such as urination and defecation.

hadat I (*ob*) council, college.

hadat II → ADAT I.

hadhanah (*A*) child care.

hadi (*A*) *al-* The Guide (a name of God).

hadiah (*A*) 1 gift, present; → KADO, OLÉH-OLÉH. 2 prize, s.t. awarded to s.o. who succeeds in a competition, etc. 3 bonus, premium. 4 award, reward. 5 bribe. *- dari tangan ke tangan* (*leg*) informal gift. *- hiburan* consolation prize. *- kerja -Lebaran* a *Lebaran* bonus. *- Natal* Christmas gift. *- Nobél* Nobel Prize. *- penghibur* consolation prize. *- perpisahan* present given to s.o. leaving (a job, etc.). *- pertama* first prize. *- pintu* door prize. *- Pulitzer* Pulitzer Prize. *- sastra* literary prize. *- setia* consolation prize. *- ulang tahun* birthday present. *- undian* lottery prize.

berhadiah 1 with/carry a prize/present, etc. *loteré/undian ~* lottery with prizes. *teka-teki ~* puzzle with prizes. 2 to give presents, present gifts.

menghadiahi to give a prize/present/award, etc. to.

menghadiahkan to present, reward, award, bestow, recompense.

penghadiahan presenting, rewarding, awarding.

hadi(i)d (*A*) "Iron"; name of the 57th chapter of the Koran.

hadir (*A*) to be present, be in the place in question; to appear, present o.s. *daftar -* attendance list, roll. *tidak -* absent; → *menghukum secara* VERSTÉK. *memberikan keputusan tidak -* to condemn/sentence s.o. by default/in absentia. *Ia dihukum dengan tak -nya.* He was sentenced in absentia. **ketidakhadiran** absence, abstention.

berhadir (*cla*) to be present (with arms). *menghimpunkan orang dan disuruh ~ senjata* to assemble people and instruct them to be present with arms.

menghadir to attend.

menghadiri to attend, be present at, go to. *dengan dihadiri (oléh)* in the presence of.

menghadirkan 1 to cause to attend/be present at. 2 to summon (to appear in court). *Majelis hakim yang mengadili perkara subvérsi terhadap A.M.F. akhirnya mengabulkan permohonan pihak terdakwa untuk ~ Létjén (Purn.) Ali Sadikin sebagai saksi a décharge.* The tribunal of judges adjudicating the subversion trial of A.M.F. finally granted the request to summon Lieutenant-General (Ret.) Ali Sadikin to appear in court as a witness for the defense.

kehadiran 1 presence, attendance. *tanpa ~ tertuduh* in the absence of the accused. ~ *militér* military presence. 2 s.t. in, s.t. that exists in. *salah satu ~ Islam* s.t. that exists in Islam.

penghadir (*infr*) attendee; → HADIRIN.

penghadiran presence, attendance at.

hadirat (*A*) 1 presence (before God). *berkumpul menghadap – Allah* to assemble before God. *pulang ke – Tuhan* to pass away, die; → PULANG *ke haribaan Tuhan*. 2 (*cla*) (used as a title) His Excellency/Majesty. *dipersembahkan ke – Baginda* to be presented to His Majesty.

hadirin (*A*) *para –* the audience, those present, attendees. *Para – yang terhormat!* and *– dan Hadirat* Ladies and Gentlemen!

hadis (*A*) a collection of the traditions relating to the sayings and deeds of the Prophet Muhammad. *– ahad* a tradition recounted by only one person. *– daif* weak/unreliable traditions. *– fikli* Muhammad's behavior as guidance. *– Hasan* traditions that are probably true. *– kauli* Muhammad's sayings as guidance. *– kudsi* commands from Gabriel to the Prophet, not recorded in the Koran. *– masyhur* traditions that are recounted by three different *sanad*. *– mutawatir* traditions that are recounted by many *sanad*. *– nabi* traditions that are considered accurate. *– sahih/ syahih* reliable sayings of the Prophet, strong traditions.

hadist and **hadits** → HADIS.

hadlir → HADIR.

hadlirat → HADIRAT.

hadlirin → HADIRIN.

hadrah and **hadrat** (*A*) k.o. chant of praise to Allah accompanied by a tambourine.

Hadramaut district of southern Arabia. *putra –* an Arab.

hadyu (*A*) sacrificial (animal).

hadzir → HADIR.

hafal (*A*) *– (di luar kepala)* to know by heart, have memorized; → APAL.

menghafal(kan) and **menghafali** to memorize, learn by heart, commit to memory. *Ia tampil melawak secara spontan dan tanpa harus menghafal skénario.* He appeared and told jokes spontaneously without having memorized the script.

terhafal memorized.

terhafalkan can be memorized.

hafalan 1 memorized (lesson). 2 s.t. to memorize.

penghafal s.o. who memorizes (e.g., the Koran).

penghafalan memorizing.

hafaz → APAL, HAFAL.

hafidz, hafil, hafis and **hafidz** (*A*) 1 male reciter of the Koran from memory, male Koranic memorizer; guardian (of the Koran). 2 well-versed in the Koran, knowing it by heart.

hafidzah and **hafidzoh** female reciter of the Koran from memory.

haga k.o. tool used to measure tree heights.

hah (interjection to indicate astonishment/amazement/surprise).

haha (*onom*) ha! ha! ha! representing laughter; → GERR. *– hihi* repeated laughter. **berhaha-hihi** laughing. *Kartun bukan hanya sekedar ~.* Cartoons are not just for laughs.

hai I 1 hey! (exclamation used to attract attention) *–! Awak tidak diperkenankan masuk ruang itu!* Hey! You're not allowed to enter that room! 2 (exclamation used to show sorrow or to arouse sympathy) *–! Malangnya nasibku!* Boy, am I unlucky! 3 (exclamation to express surprise/disbelief/suspicion, etc.). *–! Sudah dia membuat kerja itu?* What! He finished the job?

hai II (*E sl*) high (on drugs).

ngehai to be(come) high (on drugs).

haibah and **haibat** (*A*) → HÉBAT.

haid (*A*) 1 menses. 2 menstruation. *mati/berhenti -* and *saatnya henti-haid* menopause. *- pertama* menarche.

haik (*A*) the white veil worn by Arab women, which also covers the face, except the part above the nose that is left uncovered.

haika (*A*) non-Muslim place of worship.

hail → HAID.

hailai jai alai, pelota.

Hainan 1 Hainan. 2 a way of cooking rice. *- polos* rice cooked in chicken broth.

hairan → HÉRAN.

haisom (*C*) sea slug/cucumber; → TERIPANG.

Haiwa (*A*) Eve.

haiwan → HÉWAN.

haiwanat (A), beasts, fauna.

haiwani (A) living, animate. *roh* – the spirit of life in animals, anima.

haiwaniah and **haiwaniat** (A) 1 fauna, beasts. 2 beastly; → HÉWANAH, HÉWANAT.

haj → HAJJ.

hajab → AZAB.

hajad → HAJAT.

hajah → HAJJAH.

hajam → HAJIM.

hajar I (A) – *al-aswad* and – *ul-aswad* the black stone in the wall of the Kaabah.

hajar II (J) **menghajar** 1 to beat up. *Pencoléngnya dihajar massa.* The thief was beaten up by the mob. 2 to beat, defeat.

hajaran beating up, thrashing.

hajar III penghajaran discipline; → PENGAJARAN.

hajat (A) 1 banquet, ceremonial meal. *Bahkan bila panén sawah, ladang atau kebun berhasil baik, meréka melaksanakan pésta perkawinan putra maupun putrinya dan –.– lainnya* In fact, when the wet-rice, dry-rice or garden harvest is good, they hold marriage celebrations for their sons or daughters and other banquets. *ada* – to organize a banquet. – *perkawinan* wedding feast/party. 2 occasion, reason for a celebration. *Apa –nya?* What's the occasion (for the celebration)? 3 wish, want, intention, desire. *Apa –(mu)?* a) what do you want? b) what do you mean? c) what are your intentions? *membayar/menunaikan* – to fulfill a vow (*esp* by holding a *selamatan*). 4 need, requirement, necessity. *doa/salat/sembahyang* – special prayer (to request s.t. from God). – *hidup* necessities of life. 5 feeling of urgent need to defecate or urinate, tenesmus; → KEBELET. *kada* – to defecate. *buang/melakukan* – to relieve o.s. – *besar* feces; → TINJA. – *kecil/seni* urine.

berhajat 1 to intend, wish. 2 (= berhajatkan) to need/require/want s.t. *berpuluh juta orang yang berhajatkan barang-barang keperluan hidup* tens of millions of people who need the necessities of life. 3 to relieve o.s. *Ia mati-matian menolak ~ besar di pispot.* He refused to the death to defecate in a pisspot.

menghajati to desire, long for. *berharap apa yang dihajatinya akan berhasil* to hope that what one desires/longs for will be realized.

menghajatkan 1 to aspire to, wish for, aim at. *~ ketenangan dan kedamaian* to wish for quiet and peace. 2 to want, need, require.

hajatan occasion, reason for a celebration. *~ besar* grand ceremonial banquet.

haji I (A) 1 *fardu* – the fifth of the five obligatory Muslim duties requiring a Muslim (who has sufficient means) to make the pilgrimage to Mecca to carry out various religious services linked to that duty or obligation. *Meréka telah pergi ke Mekah untuk menunaikan fardu* –. They went to Mecca to fulfill the *hajj* obligation. *s.o.* who is leaving for Mecca to carry out the *fardu* – or to make the *hajj*. *bakda* – festival celebrated on 10 *Zulhijjah*. *bulan* – the pilgrimage month: *Zulhijjah*, i.e., the 12th month of the Muslim year. *hari raya* – celebration taking place on 10 *Zulhijjah*. *jemaah* – a group of pilgrims/*calon haji* leaving for Mecca. *kapal* – ship used for transporting pilgrims to Mecca. *lebaran* – festival celebrated on 10 *Zulhijjah*. *naik* – to make the pilgrimage to Mecca. *penaik* – pilgrim to Mecca. *pergi* – to make the pilgrimage to Mecca. *rukun* – all the acts that must be carried out to become a full-fledged *haji*. *syéh/syéikh* – person who provides housing or camping services for Muslim pilgrims and who escorts them to observe their religious duties. 3 title for a man who has made the *hajj* [H]; *H(aji) Moh. Natsir.* cp HAJJAH. – *akbar* a full-fledged *haji*; → WUKUF. – *badal* a pilgrim who goes to Mecca to represent a sick person, etc. – *besar* a full-fledged *haji*. – *ifrad/kecil* a) a domestic helper who goes to Mecca with a pilgrim when still not an adult. b) to make the pilgrimage before being an adult. – *kecil* pilgrimage outside the pilgrimage season. – *keluaran Singapura* (viewed from the Indonesian standpoint) s.o. who in his intention to make the pilgrimage to Mecca is stranded in Singapore and does business

there. – *kiran* → HAJI *qiran*. – *laut* a pilgrim who uses a ship to make the required trip to Mecca; *cp* HAJI *udara*. – *mabrur* a *haji* whose deeds are in agreement with religious laws; *cp* HAJI *mardud*. – *mardud* a *haji* whose deeds are in opposition to religious laws; *cp* HAJI *mabrur*. – *Péking* the nickname given to Dr. Soebandrio, Prime Minister under President Soekarno during the abortive Communist coup owing to his orientation toward the People's Republic of China. – *nazar* vow to undertake the pilgrimage. – *orang lain* to undertake the pilgrimage on behalf of s.o. else (because he is too old or sick to go). – *plus* a more complete and therefore more expensive version of the pilgrimage. – *qiran* a pilgrim who does both the *hajj* and the *umrah* at the same time. – *sunat* (*coq*) a) a domestic helper who goes to Mecca with a pilgrim when still not an adult. b) to make the pilgrimage before being an adult. – *titipan* a person who makes the *haji* for s.o. else, *usu* an older person who cannot make it. – *turis* a *haji umrah*. – *udara* a pilgrim who uses a plane to make the required trip to Mecca; *cp* HAJI *laut*. – *umrah/umroh* a so-called "tourist pilgrim" who makes the *haji* to Mecca off season and *usu* visits only certain places. – *widak* a *haji* to whom a k.o. extreme unction is administered by the Prophet Muhammad before his death.

berhaji to make the pilgrimage to Mecca.

menghajikan to send to Mecca, have s.o. become a pilgrim.

pehaji pilgrim (to Mecca).

penghajian (*mod*) pilgrim.

haji II *paku* – cycas (tree), *Cycas rumphii*.

Haji Hasan Aroeboesman name of the airport in Ende.

hajib (A) concierge, door-keeper.

hajim (A) barber (*dukun* and k.o. surgeon at the same time).

hajj (A) 1 Muslim pilgrimage to Mecca. *amir al*– and *amirulhaj* leader of a pilgrimage. *pergi* – to make the pilgrimage to Mecca. 2 "The Pilgrimage"; name of the 22nd chapter of the Koran.

hajjah (A) title for a woman who has made the *hajj*; *cp* HAJI.

hajrah and **hajrat** → HIJRAH.

haju menghajukan to put forward; → AJU.

hak I (A) 1 right. 2 property, ownership, title, interest. 3 competence, competency; duty, obligation. 4 truth. *al* – the Truth, the Real, the Absolute, *i.e.*, God. *kaul al* – these words are the truth. – *alyakin* absolute truth. *Orang yang tidak berijazah guru sebenarnya tidak ada* – *mengajar di sekolah-sekolah negeri.* Those who have no teacher's certificate are, in fact, not entitled/qualified to teach in government schools. *yang menjadi* – (s.t.) to which one is entitled. – *agunan* security right. – *agunan atas kebendaan lainnya* other security right. – *améndemén* right to move an amendment. – *andarbéni* (*Jv leg*) right of possession. – *anggaduh* (*Jv leg*) the right to use the land (considered owned by the sultanates of Yogyakarta and Surakarta). – *angkét* right to make inquiries (in Parliament). – *asasi* fundamental rights. – *asasi manusia* [HAM] human (fundamental) rights. –.– *asasi manusia yang tidak boléh dilanggar* inalienable human rights. – *asimilasi* work release (from prison). – *atas air* water rights. *pemegang* – *atas nama* franchise holder (of). – *atas kekayaan intéléktual* intellectual property rights. – *atas tanah* land rights. – *bébas bersyarat* conditional release (from prison). – *beli kembali* pre-emption. – *berkumpul dan berapat* right of association and assembly. – *bertanya* the right to ask questions in Parliament. – *besit* property rights. – *bujét* budgetary right (in Parliament). – *bungkam* the right to remain silent. – *cipta* copyright. – *cuti menjelang bébas* prerelease leave (from prison). – *didahulukan* priority right, benefit, privilege. – *dipilih* the right to be elected. –.– *ékonomi* economic rights. – *érpah* (*col*) long-lease rights. – *érpah kecil* (*col*) shorter lease rights. – *gadai* (right of) lien. – *gugat* right to sue, legal standing. – *guna air* water-use rights. – *guna bangunan* [HGB] building rights. – *guna pakai* the right of use. – *guna usaha* [HGU] leasehold. – *hipoték* mortgage rights. – *hukum* legal right. – *ikut menentukan* right to have a say. –.– *individual* individual rights. – *ingkar* a) right of objection/challenge. b) right to refuse to reveal a secret, (attorney/doctor) privilege. – *intérpelasi* right of interpellation. – *istiméwa* privilege, preferred right. – *jaminan* security right/interest. – *jawab* right of reply. – *jual* right of sale. – *kebébasan berpendapat* freedom of expression. – *kebendaan* real property rights. – *kekayaan intéléktual* intellectual property rights. – *kepemilikan (fin)* abandonment. – *keperdataan* civil rights. – *kepunyaan* property rights. –.– *kewargaan* civil rights. – *kuasa* might makes right. – *kuasa bapak* patriarchate. – *kuasa ibu* matriarchate. – *kuasa pertambangan* [HKP] mining rights. – *lintas damai (naut)* right of innocent passage. – *lungguh (Jv)* right of appanage. – *maro* sharecropping rights. – *membatalkan véto* power, right of veto. – *memesan éfék terlebih dahulu* preemptive right. – *menahan* right of retention. – *memilih* voting rights, franchise. – *meminta keterangan* right/power of asking questions (or, of questioning ministers, to put questions to ministers) right of interpolation. – *menahan* right of retention. – *mendahulu(i)* preferential rights. – *mendarat* landing rights (for aircraft). – *mendasar* fundamental rights. – *mendiami* occupancy rights. – *mengadakan penyelidikan* right to make inquiries. – *mengadakan perubahan* right to move an amendment. – *mengadakan pertanyaan* right of interrogation. – *mengundurkan diri* right to decline to give evidence, privilege. – *menikmati hasil* right of use and enjoyment, usufruct. – *menjalankan régrés* and – *menuntut (ber)balik* power of recourse. – *milik* property/proprietary rights, ownership, title. – *milik adat* traditional property rights. – *milik intéléktual* intellectual property rights. – *milik jaminan* fiduciary ownership. – *milik perindustrian* industrial property rights. – *milik pribadi* private ownership. – *minoritas* minority interest. – *mogok* right to strike. – *mutlak* natural rights, absolute title. – *nikmat (hasil)* right of enjoyment. – *nikmat hasil* right of use and enjoyment. – *numpang-karang* building and planting rights. – *oktroi (ob)* patent. – *pakai* right of use. – *patén* patent rights. – *pembetulan* right of rectification. – *penayangan* performing rights. – *pendahuluan* right of priority. – *penentuan/pertuanan* right of disposition over. – *pengabdian tanah (leg)* easement. – *pengarang* copyright. – *pengusahaan hutan* [HPH] Forest Concession Rights. – *peralihan* transitional law. – *perbendaan* → HAK *kebendaan*. – *pilih* right to vote, voting rights; electoral franchise, suffrage. – *pribadi* individual rights. – *prioritas* priority right. – *pungut* gleaning rights. – *punya* property rights. – *pusaka* inheritance. – *régrés* right of recourse. – *réténsi* right of retention. – *sanggan* right to work the land. – *séwa* right to lease. – *séwa tanah* leasehold. – *suaka* right of asylum. – *suara* franchise, voting rights. – *suci* divine right. – *tanggungan* security right/interest, hypothecation. – *terdaftar* listed option. – *tolak* right of refusal. – *tunggal* exclusive/sole right. – *ulayat* communal right of disposal. – *untuk didahulukan* right of priority. – *usaha* right to use (land). – *utama* right of priority, privilege, benefit. – *waris* inheritance rights. – *yang telah diperoléh* acquired rights. – *yang tidak bisa diganggu-gugat* prerogative. – *yasan* individual right of disposal.

berhak 1 to have/reserve the right, be in a position (to). **2** (to be) authorized, qualified, entitled. *~ memilih* to be entitled to vote. *yang ~* rightful, lawful, rightful claimant. *yang tak ~* unrightful, unlawful.

menghaki to have the right to s.t.

menghakkan to confirm/give the right to.

hak II (D) /hak/ heel (of shoe). – *sepatu* shoe heel. – *tinggi* high heel.

berhak heeled. *sepatu ~ tinggi* high-heeled shoes; → SEPATU *jinjit*.

hak III (D) /hak/ hook, i.e., a small metal catch inserted in an eye to fasten clothes together.

hakaik (A) *pl* of **hakékat**.

hakam (A) arbiter, mediator, jury.

hakékat → HAKIKAT.

haken (D) to crochet.

HaKI [Hak Kekayaan Intéléktual] Intellectual Property Rights.

hakikat (A) facts, truth, *esp* Divine Truth, that which is true and cannot be denied, essence. *pada –nya* in fact/truth, actually. *satu agama yang benar-benar –nya* the True Faith. *pada –nya* by far, in many ways, to a certain extent, in essence, basically.

hakiki (A) true, real, intrinsic. *pada –nya* in fact/truth, actually.

hakim (A) **1** judge; arbitrator. **2** (*ob*) the authorities, the government. **3** (*cla*) learned/wise man, sage, scholar. *main – sendiri*

take the law into one's own hands. – *agung* Supreme Court judge. – *anggota* associate justice. – *banding* appellant court. – *garis* (in soccer) linesman. – *ketua* presiding judge, chief justice. – *komisaris* supervisory judge. – *militér* military judge. – *Negara (Mal)* Lord President. – *nonpalu/non-yustisial* nonpresiding judge, i.e., a judge who does not take on lawsuits. *Hakim itu kini dinonaktifkan, menjadi – nonpalu.* That judge is now deactivated and has become a nonpresiding judge. – *pengadilan rendah (Mal)* magistrate. – *pengawas* supervisory judge, examining magistrate. – *pengawas daérah* [hawasda] regional supervisory judge. – *perwira* judicial officer. – *pidana* judge in a criminal case. – *tinggi* high-court judge. – *wasit* arbiter, arbitrator.

berhakim *~ kepada* to ask the judgment of, consult s.o., ask s.o. to arbitrate.

menghakimi to sentence, convict, pass sentence on. *Pencuri itu dihakimi massa.* The thief was judged by the mob.

hakim-hakiman would-be judicial. *vonis ~* a would-be judicial sentence.

kehakiman 1 justice. **2** juridical, legal; judicial. *Départemén ~* Ministry of Justice. *kekuasaan ~* judicial authority. *Menteri ~* Minister of Justice. *susunan ~* judicial organization. *~ militér* military justice.

penghakiman punishment.

hakimah (A) wise (woman).

hakir (A) mean or degraded person.

hakulyakin (A) absolute truth.

hal I (A) **1** problem, matter, case; cause, reason. **2** situation, incident, affair. **3** concerning, regarding, about, in the matter of. *ada –* there's s.t. going on. *dalam –* in case (of), if, when it comes to. *dalam – ini* in this instance. *dalam – ini bertindak berdasarkan …* (in notarial instruments) acting for the purposes of these present on the basis of … *dalam – ini juga* in this case as well, here again. *dalam – itu* in that case. *dalam segala –* in every respect. *dari –* concerning, regarding, about. *dengan – yang demikian itu, maka …* accordingly/in this way/thus. *karena satu dan lain –* for one reason or another. *mengenai – itu* pertinent, to that effect. *mengenai – tersebut* (in letters) in reference to. *pada –* whereas, in fact, as it turned out; → PADAHAL, PERIHAL. – *a(k)hwal/i(k)hwal* events, occurrences, circumstances. – *ini* this. – *itu* that. – *kewiraan* an act of heroism. – *mana* which. *salah pengertian tentang perjuangan klas, – mana adalah tipikal bagi burjuasi* a misunderstanding about the class struggle, which is typical of the bourgeoisie.

halnya the case is/with. *demikian ~ dengan* this was also the case with. *sebagaimana ~ dengan* as is the case with.

berhal 1 to be concerned, have s.t. to do with the matter. *Jika ada orang yang ~ dan minta pertolongan kepadanya, selalu diterimanya dengan senang hati.* If there is s.o. concerned who asks him for help, he is always received pleasantly. **2** to be prevented (from coming) because one is otherwise occupied. *Dia ~ sebab itu dia tidak dapat datang.* He couldn't come because he was otherwise occupied.

terhal prevented (due to circumstances).

hal II galvanized sheet iron.

hal. III (*abbr*) page of a book; → HALAMAN II.

hala (*mostly Mal*) direction. *tidak tentu –* aimlessly.

sehala going in the same direction, *jalan ~* one-way street. *secara ~* unilaterally.

berhala in the direction of.

menghala to be in a certain direction. *~ ke barat* lying in a westerly direction.

menghalakan to direct, point (a weapon) at, aim.

kehalaan directivity, directionality.

halai-balai neglected.

menghalai-balaikan to neglect.

halaik (A) infidel.

halak (Bat) man; → ORANG I. – *hita* villager, country fellow; → ORANG *kampung*.

halal I (A) **1** lawful, legitimate (according to Islamic law). **2** permissible (according to divine law, e.g., of food), kosher. *dengan cara –* honestly, legally.

menghalalkan to allow, permit. *~ hutang* to forgive a debt.

~ *segala macam cara untuk mencapai tujuan(nya)* the end justifies the means.

kehalalan legitimacy.

penghalalan legitimizing.

halal II (*A*) – *bihalal* asking forgiveness on Lebaran day for mistakes and sins committed during the previous year. *pertemuan* ~ post-fasting informal get-together for the above purpose. ***berhalal bihalal*** to pay one's respects to e.o. in order to ask forgiveness for mistakes and sins committed.

halaman I 1 yard, open space near a house, garden, grounds. – *dalam* inner court. – *istana* palace grounds. – *muka* front yard. – *pabrik* factory grounds. – *rumah* yard. – *rumput* lawn. – *sekolah* schoolyard. – *tengah* inner courtyard. **2** premises. *kampung* – a) birthplace. b) native village.

halaman II page (of a book/newspaper, etc.); → KACA II, MUKA, PAGINA. – *judul* title page. – *kanan* recto. – *kiri* verso. – *muka* front page. – *putih* blank page. – *tengah* centerfold.

berhalaman with/have pages. *destar* ~ (*cla*) k.o. full turban.

berhalaman-halaman pages and pages.

halamanisme *kampung* ~ provincialism

halang I → ALANG I. **1** weir. **2** interdiction. – *rintang* steeplechase.

menghalang to obstruct, impede, hinder, prevent, block. ~ *pandanganku* to block my view.

menghalangi to hamper, hinder, impede, obstruct, stand in the way of, prevent; to resist, oppose, stand up against (tyranny, etc.). *Ia tidak dapat dihalangi*. He cannot be opposed.

menghalang-halangi to block, get in the way of, obscure (the view).

menghalangkan to put an obstruction in front of, obstruct. *Pengacau-pengacau telah* ~ *beberapa batang kayu di jalan raya itu*. The trouble-makers put some logs across the main road.

terhalang hampered, obstructed, impeded, prevented. *Pembinaan jalan* ~ *karena musim hujan*. Road construction was impeded due to the rainy season.

halangan 1 prevention, hindrance, impediment, obstacle, obstruction. *ada* ~ s.t. has come up (that prevents me from doing that). ~ *dan gangguan* let or hindrance. ~ *perkawinan* hindrance to a marriage. **2** (*elec*) impedance. **berhalangan** to be prevented (from doing s.t.), be unable (to come), be unavoidably absent. *Jika Ketua Panitia* ~ *untuk memimpin rapat, maka rapat dipimpin oléh seorang anggota.* When the Chairman of the Committee is unavoidably absent and cannot lead the meeting, the meeting shall be led by a member. ~ *hadir* to be prevented from attending.

kehalangan impeded, obstructed.

penghalang 1 s.t. that obstructs, obstructer, obstacle, bar, barrier, hindrance, stumbling block. ~ *lalu lintas* an obstacle to traffic. ~ *kemajuan* a barrier to progress. **2** (*elec*) impeder.

penghalangan obstruction, prevention.

halang II → ALANG.

halaqah and **halaqoh** (*A*) **1** the system used in *pesantrén* in which the pupils have to sit in a cross-legged position in front of the teacher; *cp* SOROGAN. **2** seminar.

halat → ALAT II.

halau drive/chase away.

menghalau(kan) 1 to drive, herd. *Petani itu menghalau kambing-kambingnya masuk ke kandang.* The farmer drove his goats into the barn. **2** to chase/drive away, repel, drive back. *Tangannya bergerak-gerak untuk menghalau lalat yang berkerumun di atas makanan.* His hand moved back and forth to chase away the flies circling over his food. ~ *mentah-mentah/tegak-tegak* to chase away brusquely. **3** to embargo. *menghalau ékspor dari produk yang bersifat péka sekali untuk dikirim ke negeri-negeri komunis* to embargo the export of most sensitive products for shipping to Communist countries. **4** to avert (danger).

terhalau driven

penghalau 1 driver, beater. **2** means of repelling/getting rid of, repellant. *obat* ~ *serangga* insect repellant.

penghalauan 1 chasing/driving away. **2** herding.

halayak → KHALAYAK.

halazuun (*A*) escargot, *Achatina variegata*; → BEKICOT.

halba(h) (*A*) Greek hay, fenugreek, *Trigonella foenum-graecum*, whose seeds are imported for medicine.

haléja (*Hind*) a fabric of mixed silk or cotton; → LÉJA.

haléluya (*D*) hallelujah.

halia ginger, *Zingiber officinale*; → JAHÉ.

halilintar 1 (flash of) lightning (in the sky). **2** thunderbolt, burst of thunder. *batu* – celt, neolith. *bagaikan* – *di hari bolong* like a bolt from the blue, like a thunderclap out of a clear blue sky.

halim I (*A*) kind, gentle, good-tempered.

Halim II the former international airport in Jakarta; short for *Halim Perdanakusuma*.

halimah (*A*) **1** a forgiving woman. **2** a woman's first name.

halimbubu (*M*) whirlwind.

halimun 1 (*S*) mist, fog. **2** (= **halimunan**) dark, invisible. *mantera/doa ilmu* – charm/spell to make o.s. invisible. *orang* – invisible elves, fairies.

halintar → HALILINTAR.

halipan centipede, *Chilipoda/Lithobius/Scutigera spp.*; → LIPAN.

halir → ALIR I.

halkah (*A*) **1** (ankle) bracelet, anklet. **2** link. – *berséngkang* (*naut*) stud link.

halkum (*A*) **1** Adam's apple, larynx. **2** throat; → LEKUM.

halma (*D*) Chinese checkers.

halo I (*D*) hello. –, *Sutomo di sini! sambutnya di pesawat télepon*. "Hello, Sutomo speaking," he said on the phone.

halo-halo (*coq*) microphone. **berhalo-halo** to talk on the phone. ~ *tanpa éngkol* to make a telephone call with a push-button or dial telephone (not one operated with a crank); → TÉLEPON *éngkol*.

menghaloi to call s.o., speak on the telephone to. *yang dihaloi* person called (over the telephone).

halo II (*D*) halo, nimbus.

haloba (*A*) covetousness, greed; → LOBA.

halogén (*D/E*) halogen.

halsduk (*D*) scarf, neckerchief.

halte (*D*) stopping place (for public transportation); → SÉLTER, TEMPAT *perhentian*. – *bis* bus stop. – *keréta api* train stop; station.

halter (*D*) dumbbell, bar bell.

halua → HALWA.

haluan I 1 (*naut*) prow, bow. *angin* – head wind. **2** s.t. that precedes. – *kata* preface. **3** direction, course, orientation. – *Negara* Official Political Course of the Nation; → GBHN. *beralih/memutar/mengubah* – to change course/direction. **4** aim, purpose, wish. – *baling-baling* (*naut*) screw post. – *dempak* (*naut*) straight course. – *hidup* aim in life. – *kata* preface, forward. – *pepat/tegak* (*naut*) straight course. – *tubruk* ram bow.

sehaluan in agreement, of the same aim, to have the same aspirations. *partai-partai politik yang* ~ like-minded political parties. ~ *sama tengah* neutral, unbiased.

berhaluan to have/follow a course/direction, oriented toward. *kaum* ~ *keras* the hardliners. *meréka yang* ~ *kanan* right wingers. ~ *ke buritan* to be a henpecked husband, be tied to one's wife's apron-strings. ~ *kiri* left wingers. ~ *maju* to be progressive. ~ *melar* to have an expansionist policy.

menghaluankan to aim at, direct to, guide.

haluan II (*A*) a present.

halu-lasung (*Ban*) farm implement.

Haluoléo the military resort command (*Korém* 143) in Kendari.

halus fine, consisting of very small or fine particles. *Tepung adalah lebih* – *daripada garam*. Flour is finer than salt. **2** fine, not rough/coarse, delicate, smooth. *Papan itu diketam sehingga* –. The board was planed until it was smooth. *Kulit mukanya* –. She has fine skin on her face. *Pesawat itu mendarat dengan* –. The plane made a soft landing. **3** polite, refined, courteous, refined. *Istrinya mempunyai budi pekerti yang sungguh* –. His spouse has a really refined character. *bahasa* – refined language. **4** sweet (of voice). *Céwék itu menyanyi dengan suara yang merdu lagi* –. The girl sings in a melodious, sweet voice. **5** indirect, subtle. *perintah* – gentle command. – *makannya* working imperceptibly. **6** invisible (of spirits/elves). *orang/makhluk* – a ghost. **7** (in some compounds) small. *usus* – small intestine.

sehalus as fine/refined as.

berhalus(-halus) to be/act in a refined way.

menghalus to become fine/soft/polite.

menghalusi 1 to treat gently. *Anak nakal itu tidak dapat dihalusi.* That naughty child cannot be treated gently. **2** to deceive, trick, cheat. ~ *musuh* to trick the enemy. **3** to investigate thoroughly, go into carefully. *Perkara itu tidak perlu dihalusi lagi.* It isn't necessary to investigate that case again.

menghaluskan to refine, make thin/fine. ~ *jalan* to grade a road. ~ *kayu* to finish wood. ~ *sawah* to level off a rice field.

memperhalus(kan) to refine, make finer.

terhalus the finest, etc.

halus-halusan refined matters.

kehalusan 1 gentleness, subtlety. **2** gentility, breeding. **3** daintiness, smoothness.

penghalus refiner, (material for) finishing.

penghalusan refining, refinement. ~ *bahasa* (*gram*) euphemism; → ÉUFEMISME.

halusinasi (*D*) hallucination.

halusinogén (*D/E*) hallucinogen.

halwa (*A*) fruits, etc. prepared in syrup. - *cabai* hot peppers prepared in syrup. - *mata* any thing that pleases the eye (such as a movie, etc.). - *telinga* musical treat.

ham I (*D*) ham (meat).

HAM II (*init*) → HAK *asasi manusia.*

hama 1 the natural enemies of a crop, plant disease, pest; → AMA I. *ilmu* - entomology. **2** plague, scourge. *penyakit* - microbes, germs (of a disease), bacteria. *kena* - infected. *suci* - aseptic, sterilized. - *bawang* a rice pest, gall midge, *Orseolia oryzae.* - *beluk* → BELUK I. - *bodas* pest which attacks vegetables, onion thrips, *Thrips tabaci.* - *busuk pangkal batang,* a pest which attacks black pepper plants, *Phytophthora capsici.* - *ganjur* midge. - *golok/kapak* pests of the *cendana* plant. - *kelapa* squirrel. - *kepik* → KEPIK II. - *kutu* k.o. plant pest, *Planococcus spp.* - *kutu sisik* scale insect pest, *Chionaspis.* - *mentek* rot in the roots of the rice plant (according to folk belief, eaten up by *sétan-sétan kerdil*). - *mérah* spider mite, *Tetranychus bimaculatus.* - *oléng-oléng* bee-hole borer, *Duomitus ceramicus.* - *pembawa/penular penyakit* germs which transmit disease, vector. - *penggérék* borer. - *putih* caseworm, *Nymphula depunctalis.* - *sexava* disease of the coconut tree. - *sundep* rice pest. - *tanaman* plant pest. - *tebu* sugarcane pest, *Lepidiota stigma;* → SEREH. - *tikus* scourge of mice (destroying field crops). - *tungro* virus carried by the - *wereng hijau.* - *uret* grub. - *wereng coklat, Nila parvata lugens,* pest which attacks *padi* plants.

menghamakan to infect, contaminate.

terhama infected (by a plant disease, etc.), contaminated.

kehamaan infection.

hamak (*A*) surly, hard to work with.

Hamal (*A*) (*Burjamal*) - Aries (*zod*).

hamar → KHAMAR.

hamasida insecticides.

hamba I 1 slave, serf, servant, vassal, person who is the property of another and bound to serve him. **2** (humbly) I, we; me, our; my, your humble servant. - *disuruh guru pergi ke kantor pos.* I was ordered by the teacher to go to the post office. *tuan* - my master (of a servant to his master; very respectful). **3** yes, sir. *Betulkah ini adikmu? -!* Is this really your younger brother? Yes, sir! - *Allah* servants of God, mankind; → MANUSIA. - *bayar* slaves given by a master to settle a debt. - *belian* slave. - *berutang* debt-slave. - *hukum* (*ob*) servants of the law, the police. - *péna* (*joc*) journalist. - *raja* a) servant of the *raja*, court servant. b) (*cla*) a *rajah*'s debt-slave. - *sahaya* (*cla*) all k.o. bought slaves. **penghambasahayaan** slavery, serfdom. - *tebusan* bought slave (i.e., bought from his original creditor). - *tuan* your servant, I (very respectful). *menjadi* - *uang* to serve Mammon, be a slave to debt. - *waris* wives and children of debt-slaves. - *wét* (*ob*) servants of the law, the police. - *yang hina* your humble servant, I.

berhamba 1 to be a slave/servant. *Keempat orang itu* ~ *kepada raja.* Those four were servants of the king. **2** to have/own slaves/servants. *Saudagar itu* ~ *tiga puluh orang.* That merchant owned thirty slaves. **3** to use *hamba* (call themselves *hamba*). *Ia selalu* ~ *bila bercakap-cakap dengan saya.* He always called himself *hamba* when talking to me.

berhambakan to have ... as a slave.

menghamba(i) to serve. *menghamba kepada nusa dan bangsa* to serve one's homeland/country and nation.

menghambakan 1 to treat/regard as a slave, enslave. **2** (= **memperhamba, memperhambai** and **memperhambakan**) to make o.s. the slave of, subordinate o.s. to. ~ *diri* to make o.s. the servant of, enslave o.s to. *yang diperhamba* your humble servant, I.

hambaan servitude.

kehambaan humility, servitude.

penghamba a slave to. ~ *obat-obat terlarang* a slave to illegal drugs.

penghambaan enslaving.

perhambaan servitude, subservience, slavery, bondage.

hamba II *burung* - *kera* large racquet-tailed drongo, *Surniculus lugrubis;* → ANTING-ANTING I.

hambal rug; → AMBAL I.

hambar I tasteless, insipid, flat; → CEMPLANG, TAWAR II **2.** *Masakannya - rasanya.* Her cooking is tasteless. **2** cold, indifferent, spiritless, vapid. *Terhadap suaminya ia mengambil sikap yang - saja.* She was cold and indifferent to her husband. *senyum yang -* a cold smile.

sehambar as tasteless as.

menghambar to become tasteless/vapid.

menghambari-hambari ~ *hati* to discourage.

menghambarkan to make s.t. tasteless/flat.

kehambaran vapidness, insipidity, insignificance.

hambat I - *glotal* (*infr*) glottal stop.

menghambat to delay, retard, slacken, slow down, hamper, impede, obstruct, stand in the way of, snarl (traffic). *Kelangkaan semén harus secepatnya diatasi karena akan* ~ *pembangunan.* The lack of cement must be overcome quickly because it will hamper construction.

terhambat obstructed, hindered, impeded.

terhambat-hambat delayed, hampered, impeded, obstructed. *Dan apakah masih ada ancaman lain yang sewaktu-waktu bisa membuat bisnis kita* ~? And are there other threats that might from time to time hamper our business? *tidak* ~ unimpedable, not to be checked, cannot be obstructed.

hambatan 1 obstruction, obstacle, constraint, restraint, resistance. ~ *ékspor secara sukaréla* voluntary export restraints. ~ *buang* back pressure. ~ *tumbuh* stunting. ~ *udara* drag. **2** bottleneck. **3** (*ling*) closure. **4** (*elec*) resistance. **keterhambatan** resistivity.

kehambatan obstruction.

penghambat 1 obstacle, barrier. ~ *masuk* entry barrier. **2** blocker, inhibitor. **3** retardation.

penghambatan 1 obstruction, obstacle, impediment, hindrance. **2** inhibiting, inhibition.

hambat II **menghambat** and **memperhambat** to pursue, chase, run after, dog (s.o.'s footsteps), grab hold of.

penghambat pursuer.

hambung → AMBUNG. **menghambungkan** to throw upward, toss up.

hambur I **berhamburan** (*pl subj*) **1** spread/scattered/strewn about (as rice from a sack). *beras* ~ *dari guni yang bocor itu.* Rice (kernels) were scattered all about from the leaking guni-sack. *lari* ~ to run helter-skelter in large numbers. **2** to trickle down, flow (of tears). *Air mata* ~ *membasahi pipinya.* Tears rolled down her cheeks.

menghambur 1 to be dispersed/diffused. *~lah bau busuk dari mulutnya.* A rotten smell escaped from his mouth. **2** to scatter s.t. about, throw about, strew (flowers). **3** to run helter-skelter, rush (in[to]). *Lalu tak dapat menahan air matanya, diam-diam menangis, dia segera* ~ *ke kamar.* Then, unable to hold back her tears and crying silently, she immediately rushed into her room.

menghamburi to sprinkle/strew/sow on. *Setelah mayat dimakamkan kubur dihamburi bunga.* After the corpse was buried, the grave was strewn with flowers.

menghamburkan 1 to throw (away), cast, fling, toss (in the air), pour, shed, spread, scatter, spit. *Gunung berapi itu* ~ *lava.* That volcano spit forth lava. *Ia* ~ *air mata.* He shed tears. ~ *jala* to cast a net. **2** to spew, spit forth (insults). ~ *angkara* *murka* to give free reign to one's greed. **3** to waste, squander, fritter away. *Kerjanya ~ uang melulu.* All he does is waste money. *~ kata-kata* to pour out a flow/torrent of words (in reprimanding s.o.).

terhambur scattered, strewn, etc.

hamburan 1 s.t. that has been scattered/strewn about, scattered, squandered. **2** scattering, dispersion.

kehamburan dispersal.

penghambur 1 (*elec*) scatterer. **2** squanderer (of money), waster (of time).

penghamburan 1 spreading, dispersing, dispersal, strewing. *~ inséktisida* spreading of insecticides. **2** waste, wasting, squandering.

hambur II berhamburan (*pl subj*) to jump down, dive. *Anak-anak itu ~ ke sungai.* The children dived into the river.

menghambur to jump. *~ bangun* to jump/leap/start up, jump to one's feet. *~ ke laut* to jump into the sea. *~ ke samping* to jump aside. *Menghamburlah dari sini!* Beat it!

menghamburi to jump/leap/spring into, pounce on. *Ia membungkukkan badannya sedikit hendak ~ kolam renang.* He bent his body somewhat to jump into the swimming pool.

menghamburkan 1 to make/let s.o. jump. *~ diri ke dalam* to throw o.s. into (education, etc.). *~ kudanya* to let his horse jump. **2** fruitless, vain, futile.

hamburger (*E*) hamburger. *kedai* – hamburger joint.

hamburgerisasi hamburgerization. *– dunia* the hamburgerization of the world.

hambus berhambus and **menghambus** to go away, leave.

hamdalah → ALHAMDULILLAH(I).

hamd(u) (*A*) praise. *alhamdulillah(i)* a) praise be to God. b) (*coq*) thank God.

Hamengku Buwana and **Hamengkubuwono** (*Jv*) name of each Sultan of Yogyakarta.

hamid (*A*) praised.

hamik (*A*) stupid, foolish, silly.

hamil (*A*) **1** pregnant (more polite than *bunting*). **2** pregnancy. *pil anti–* birth control pill. **3** impregnated. *– anggur* molar pregnancy, *mola hydatidosa ~ muda* pregnant for less than six months. *– pertama* first pregnancy. *– tua* pregnant for more than six months.

menghamili and **menghamilkan 1** to make (a woman) pregnant; to impregnate. *Noor membantah sebagai orang yang ~ Éha.* Noor denied that he was the one who had made Eha pregnant. **2** to be pregnant with, carry. *Wanita itu sangat séhat ketika ~ anak sulungnya.* That woman was very healthy when she was pregnant with her oldest child.

kehamilan pregnancy. *keracunan ~* toxemia. *~ remaja* teenage pregnancy.

penghamilan fertilization, impregnation, making s.o. pregnant, pregnancy.

haminte (*D ob*) municipality.

hamis → AMIS.

Haml (*A*) Aries (*zod*).

hampa 1 empty; → PUSO I. *Padi yang – itu dipisahkan daripada padi yang berisi.* The empty rice plants were separated from the full ones. *– beras* said about a rice plant that is empty. *– berat* rice plant which is not completely full. **2** fruitless, vain, futile. *– gulana* completely empty/without result. *– guna* useless, no good. *– hati* disappointed. *– udara* vacuum. **3** stupid, dumb.

berhampa *~ tangan* empty-handed, unsuccessful, fruitless.

menghampa to become empty.

menghampakan 1 to empty s.t. *Boléhkah saya ~ bakul ini?* May I empty this basket? **2** to frustrate; to disappoint. *Saya terpaksa ~ permintaan anda.* I was forced to disappoint you in your request.

kehampaan 1 emptiness, vacuum. *~ tinggi* high vacuum. **2** disappointment; failure, frustration. *Dia sudah mengalami banyak ~ dalam hidup.* He has experienced many disappointments in his life.

penghampaan emptying. *pompa ~* vacuum pump.

hampai (*M*) **menghampaikan** to spread; to hang up. *~ sayap* to depend on; → AMPAI II, HAMPAR.

hampal (*S*) k.o. fish, *Hampala macrolepidota*.

hampar spread out.

sehampar a spread-out area of.

berhamparan (*pl subj*) spread/laid out everywhere, stretched, extended, reached.

menghampar 1 to spread (out flat). *Sawah yang ~ luas itu ditumbuhi lalang.* The broad rice fields were overgrown with elephant grass. **2** → MENGHAMPARKAN.

menghampari to spread s.t. over s.t. else. *Lantai pelupuh itu dihampari dengan tikar pandan putih.* A white pandanus mat was spread over the pounded-bamboo floor.

menghamparkan 1 to lay out, spread out. *Meréka ~ sehelai tikar di bawah pohon beringin itu.* They spread out a mat under the banyan tree. **2** to define, explain, elucidate, make clear. *Pak guru sedang ~ soal itu kepada Marsidi.* The teacher explained the problem to Marsidi. **3** to spread (one's wings).

terhampar 1 (to lie) spread out. *Di lantai ~ permadani yang indah.* A beautiful rug was spread over the floor. **2** laid out, explained.

hamparan 1 s.t. that is spread out, such as a carpet, mat, rug, etc. **2** plain, level. **3** extent.

penghampar spreader. *peralatan ~ campuran aspal* asphalt finisher.

penghamparan spreading, extending.

hampas → AMPAS.

hampedal → EMPEDAL.

hampedu → EMPEDU.

hampir 1 near, close (to); → DEKAT. *Perhentian bus terletak – dengan rumah saya.* The bus stop is located close to my house. *– menangis* close to tears. **2** almost, nearly. *Anak-anak itu – dilanggar oléh sebuah truk.* The children were almost hit by a truck. *– selesai* close to completion. *– serupa* nearly identical. *– sial* a narrow escape. *Matahari – terbenam..* The sun has almost set.

hampir-hampir very nearly, almost (expected to but didn't). *~ dia tidak mempercayai matanya sendiri.* He almost didn't believe his own eyes. *Meréka ~ sepakat.* They were very close to an agreement. *~ tidak* almost didn't (expected not to but did). *Penduduk di sana menjadi sangat biasa, ~ tidak punya rasa takut lagi, meskipun sebenarnya hidupnya terancam.* People living there got used to it and were almost no longer afraid even though their lives were threatened.

berhampir to be near, nearby.

berhampiran *~ dengan* to be near/close to/in the vicinity of.

menghampir to draw near, approach, come up to. *Dia berlari ~.* He ran up.

menghampiri to come close/near to, approach. *Pengemis itu ~ saya.* The panhandler approached me.

menghampirkan to bring s.t. near to, bring over. *Dia ~ kursinya pada jendéla.* He brought his chair over to the window.

terhampir nearest.

terhampiri approachable.

hampiran 1 nearness, proximity, vicinity, neighborhood. **2** (*math*) approximation.

kehampiran vicinity.

penghampiran approximation, approach.

hampirata penghampirataan (*geol*) penplanation.

hampulur → EMPELUR.

hamud (*A*) acid. *kadar –* (degree of) *acidity. – amino* amino acid. *– cuka* vinegar.

hamuk → AMUK.

hamun coarse and abusive language, abuse.

berhamun-hamun to curse, use abusive language.

menghamun(i) to abuse, curse, scold. *Majikannya menghamun dan memakinya karena merusakkan mesin yang baru itu.* His boss cursed and scolded him because he had broken the new machine.

hamzah (*A*) the glottal stop and the name of a letter in the Arabic alphabet.

han (in acronyms) → PERTAHANAN.

hana (*M*) abandoned, deserted (of islands/villages etc.).

hanacaraka (*Jv*) the Javanese alphabet.

hancing stinking (of urine).

hancur 1 crushed, smashed, shattered, broken to pieces, pulverized, destroyed. *Gelas yang jatuh itu –.* The glass that fell down smashed. **2** dissolved, dissolve. *dapat – sendiri* biodegradable. **3** to be ruined, in ruins. *– berantakan/berkeping-keping/binasa* completely smashed, etc. *– hati* deeply grieved, brokenhearted. *– lebur/luluh/lumat* a) smashed, shattered. b) dissolved. **menghancurleburkan** and **menghancurluluhkan 1** to smash/shatter s.t. **2** to dissolve s.t. *– rembas* completely destroyed. *– remuk* smashed to bits.
berhancuran (*pl subj*) crushed, smashed, destroyed.
menghancur 1 to break up into pieces. **2** to perish.
menghancurkan 1 to smash, destroy, ruin, crush, shatter, break/smash to pieces, wreck, tear down, vandalize. *mudah dihancurkan* vulnerable (of submarine, etc.). **2** to dissolve. **3** to smelt (ore). **4** destructive. *prakték ~* destructive practices. *~ hati* heart-breaking.
hancur-menghancurkan to destroy e.o.
terhancurkan breakable.
hancuran 1 fragment(s), rubble, debris. **2** destruction. **3** (diluted) solution, dilution.
hancur-hancuran totally shattered.
kehancuran destruction, annihilation, ruin. *saling memastikan ~* mutually assured destruction.
penghancur 1 crusher, shredder. *~ batu* stone crusher. *~ dokumén/kertas* document/paper shredder. **2** destructor (the person).
penghancuran crushing, shattering, smashing, destruction, devastation, ravaging, vandalizing. *~ diri sendiri* self-destruction.
handai I 1 friend, comrade. **2** associate, companion. *– taulan/tolan* friends, comrades, pals.
berhandai-handai to be on friendly terms with e.o.
handai II (*M*) **berhandai-handai** to talk. → BERCAKAP-CAKAP.
perhandai talkative, loquacious.
handak [bahan peledak] explosives.
handal 1 reliable, renowned, well-known, of good repute; → ANDAL I. **2** experienced, skillful.
menghandalkan to depend on.
terhandal the most reliable.
kehandalan and **keterhandalan** reliability.
handalan reliable.
handam (*M*) *– karam* to suffer a heavy loss (in business).
menghandam to confine/shut up (a marriageable girl) at home; → MEMINGIT.
handasah (*A*) *ilmu –* mathematics *esp* geometry.
handel I (*D*) trade, commerce.
handel II (*E*) handle.
handelar (*D*) merchant, dealer, trader.
handelmaatschappij (*D*) /-matskapai/ trading company.
handeuleum (*S*) caricature plant, *Graptophyllum pictum*, which can reach a height of 1–3 meters; seven leaves of this plant mixed with turmeric and brown palm sugar and boiled are used as medicine against hemorrhoids.
handikap (*E*) handicap.
berhandikap to be handicapped, have a handicap.
handil drainage canal, outlet.
handuk (*D*) towel; → TUALA. *– mandi* bath towel. *– muka* face towel. *– tamu* guest towel.
berhanduk (provided) with a towel.
menghanduki to wipe off s.o. with a towel.
handukan (*coq*) wrapped in a towel.
hang I (*cla*) title for men in Old Malay literature (preceding their names), such as, *– Jebat*, *– Kasturi*, *– Tuah*, etc; *cp* DANG I. *– Nadim* name of the airport on Batam Island. *Univérsitas – Tuah* Hang Tuah University, Surabaya.
hang II (*M ob*) you; → ANDA II, ANG I, ENGKAU.
hangar (*D/E*) (aircraft) hangar.
menghangarkan to put s.t. in the hangar.
hangat 1 (piping) hot. *Nasinya masih –.* The rice is still (piping) hot. **2** hearty, cordial, warm. *dengan –* warmly. *salam –* warmest regards. *sambutan –* an enthusiastic reception/welcome. **3** (giving) a little bit less than the actual weight. *Toko ini – timbangannya.* This store cheats on weight. **4** fierce, urgent, acute,

of interest now, topical (event/question), timely (of an article in a newspaper), most recent, current. *sedang – diperbincangkan* is much talked about. *masih – dalam benak kita* is still fresh in our minds. *berita –* current events. *débat –* heated argument. *– hati* delighted, pleased. *– pijar* white-hot.
hangat-hangat *~ kuku* lukewarm. *~ tahi ayam* short-lived enthusiasm, flash in the pan; → ANGAT-ANGAT *tahi ayam*, PANAS-PANAS *tahi ayam*. *~nya* to be at its height. *Ketika kasus yang melibatkan Ria Irawan lagi ~nya* when the case involving Ria Irawan was still at its height/peak. *Sekarang sedang ~nya orang membicarakan soal itu.* Nowadays people are busily discussing that issue.
berhangat *~ diri* to warm o.s. (by the fire, etc.).
menghangat 1 to become hot, heat up. *tidak ~ mendingin* does not make one happy or unhappy. **2** to become critical. *Judi buntut ~ di Ampenan.* Illegal gambling on the 'tail' or the last two or three digits of the outcome is becoming a problem in Ampenan.
menghangati 1 to warm up (food, etc. that has become cold). **2** to give a warm feeling to.
menghangatkan 1 to warm up. **2** to heat up s.t. *~ suasana politik* to heat up the political atmosphere.
kehangatan 1 (*coq*) too hot; → KEPANASAN. **2** heat, warmth. *~ kasih sayang* the warmth of love and affection. **3** tenseness (of the political situation, etc.). **4** overcome by heat.
penghangat heater, warmer.
penghangatan heating, warming (up). *~ bumi* global warming.
hanggar → ANGGAR III, HANGAR. *keluar –* rolled out (of an aircraft).
hangit smell of burnt rice crust or smell of burning cloth; → ANGIT.
hangus 1 scorched, singed, burnt. *bumi –* scorched earth. *Nasinya –.* The rice was burnt. **2** confiscated, (pronounced) forfeited. *Uang régistrasi itu dianggap –.* The registration fee was considered forfeited. **3** to expire, fall/become due, mature (of bills). *Kalau dana yang disediakan itu tidak diselesaikan, otomatis akan –.* If the funds made available are not settled, they will automatically become due. **4** (*coq*) all gone/used up (of money). *belanja/uang –* bridegroom's share of wedding expenses; *opp* MAHAR, EMAS KAWIN. *uang –* (in banking) points (the individual and not the bank pockets the difference). *– tiada berapi, karam tiada berair* to have a problem. *– daun* leaf scorch, a disease attacking sugarcane. *– hati* a) furious, angry; irritated. b) yearning, longing.
hangus-hangus *~ hati* to be keen on s.t.
menghangus to scorch, singe; to smolder.
menghangusi to burn/scorch s.t. *Kulitnya dihangusi oléh matahari.* The sun burnt his skin.
menghanguskan to burn, set fire to, singe, scorch, roast until burned. *~ hati* to anger s.o., make s.o. angry.
terhanguskan scorched, singed, burned.
kehangusan 1 scorching, singeing. *~ hati* a) intense feelings of anger/irritation/grief. b) longing. **2** scorched, singed.
penghangusan heating (up).
hanif (*A*) **1** sincere in one's inclination to Islam. **2** orthodox.
hanjakal (*S*) to be sorry for s.t., regret s.t.
hanjaliwan → ULAR *hanjaliwan*.
hanjet (*J*) → HANJUT.
hanjuang (*S*) → LENJUANG.
hanjut menghanjut to beat, hit, thrash.
Hankam(nég) [pertahanan dan keamanan (Negara)] (State) Defense and Security.
Hanoman → ANOMAN.
Hanra [Pertahanan rakyat] civil defense unit.
Hansip [Pertahanan sipil] paramilitary civil defense corps, member of the paramilitary civil defense corps. *kawin –* marriage a la *hansip*, i.e., to have already had sexual intercourse before being officially married. *seragam –* a *hansip* uniform. *– lalulintas* popular reference to *Banpolantas*.
menghansipkan to give s.o. paramilitary civil defense corps training. *16 wartawan dihansipkan oléh Bupati.* Sixteen journalists were given paramilitary civil defense corps training by the regent.
kehansipan relating to the activities of the paramilitary civil defense corps. *Para wartawan itu mendapat penataran tentang*

~. All the journalists received upgrading on the activities of the paramilitary civil defense corps.

hansop (*D*) play- and sleepwear with short sleeves and legs for boys and girls.

hantam blow (with the fist). *baku* – fistfight, scuffle. – *kromo* a) to strike out blindly. b) to do as one pleases. – *kromo!* attack! *main – kromo* to take a strong line or strong action. **menghantam-kromokan 1** to act in a careless, perfunctory manner. **2** to overgeneralize. **penghantam-kromoan** acting carelessly. – *saja* to do as one pleases.

  berhantam 1 to fight, come to blows. **2** to collide (with). **3** to infringe (on).

  bersihantam and **hantam-menghantam** to come to blows with e.o.

  menghantam 1 to hit/beat/strike hard. *Orang itu ~ anak tirinya sehingga pingsan.* That man hit his stepchild until he passed out. **2** to bang on (a door/s.o.'s head). **3** to assess, impose, hit (with a tax). *Barang itu dihantam pajak.* A tax was imposed on those goods. **4** to ram into. ~ *tiang télepon* to ram into a telephone pole. **5** (*coq*) to attack (food). *Mari, kita hantam saté panas ini!* Come on, let's attack this hot satay!

  menghantami (*pl obj*) to hit, beat, attack, etc.

  menghantamkan to strike/beat with. *Anak itu ~ kakinya di lantai.* The child pounded the floor with his foot.

  terhantam [and **kehantam** (*coq*)] struck, hit.

  hantaman blow, punch, beating. ~ *ombak* beating of the waves, wash.

  penghantam (*mod*) strike. *kekuatan* ~ strike force.

  penghantaman striking, hitting hard at.

hantap (*S*) various species of trees, *Sterculia spp./Planchonia valida.*

hantar I menghantar(kan) to place, lay down, spread (out).

  berhantaran (*pl subj*) to lay scattered everywhere.

  terhantar 1 placed, laid down, spread out. **2** abandoned, neglected.

hantar II menghantar(kan) to accompany; → ANTAR I.

  hantaran conduction.

  terhantar conductible. **keterhantaran** conductivity.

  penghantar conductor. ~ *panas* heat conductor.

hantem → HANTAM.

hantir (*D*) **menghantir** to handle, wield.

hantu I 1 phantom, ghost, demon, specter, apparition, evil spirit. *Ia percaya pada* –. She believes in ghosts. *dirasuk* – to be attacked by an evil spirit. *jari* – middle finger; → JARI *malang/mati/panjang. kena* – to suffer from a disease/craziness, etc. from being attacked by evil spirits. *rumah* – Masonic Lodge. **2** (*hantu + noun*) to be a fiend for, be addicted to. – *bola* soccer fan. – *judi* professional or addicted gambler. *takutkan* – *pélokkan bangkai* and *takut di* –, *terpélok ke bangkai* from the frying pan into the fire. – *air* water spirit. – *angin* spirits of the storm. – *aru-aru* spirit of the forest. – *bangkit/bungkus/kapan* shrouded ghost that feeds on the blood of babies; → PONTIANAK. – *buni(an)* k.o. elf. – *haru-haru* (*M*) a spirit who kidnaps people. – *jembalang* soil gnome. – *kangkung ngéang-ngéang/ngiang-ngiang* spirit of a stillborn child. – *lembalang* gnomes who damage crops. – *kelaparan* specter of hunger. – *kocong* → HANTU *pocong.* – *laut* a) St. Elmo's fire. b) sobriquet for the navy amphibious tank. – *mambang* weird-shaped clouds. – *mérah* fire (personified); → JAGO *mérah.* – *pocong* ghost wrapped in a winding sheet. – *puaka* tutelary spirit. – *rimba* a) spirit of the woods, jungle spirit. b) reference to the infantry. – *siluman* k.o. elf. – *tuyul* evil spirit that can be ordered to steal money.

  berhantu haunted, possessed. *rumah* ~ haunted house.

  menghantu 1 to become a ghost. **2** to hover around.

  menghantui 1 to haunt, obsess. *dihantui ketakutan* to be obsessed by fear. **2** to scare.

  hantuan dreadful vision.

hantu II *burung* – a) scops owl, *Otus scops malayanus.* b) Ceylon fish owl, *Ketupa zeylonensis leschenault.*

Hanuman (*Skr*) the monkey god of the Ramayana.

hanura [hati-nurani-rakyat] the people's conscience.

hanya only, just; except, other than, no more than, nothing but; merely; → CUMA. *Anaknya* – *dua orang.* She has only two chil-

dren. – *Tuhan yang mengetahui.* Only God knows. *Itu – rencana.* That was no more than a plan. *Cerita itu – dua halaman.* The story occupies no more than two pages. – *... saja* only, just. *Itu – untuk main-main saja.* That was just for fun. – *saja marga Simarémaré memberi syarat untuk menyetujui penyerahan tanah ulayat itu.* Only the Simaremare clan placed conditions on agreeing to the transfer of communal reserved land. *tidak* – not only. *Saya menyadari hal itu tidak – sekarang tetapi sudah lama.* I've been aware of that case not just now but for a long time.

hanyir stinking (of uncooked fish/meat/eggs, etc.), fetid, smelly, rancid; → ANYIR.

hanyut 1 to drift, be carried away (by the current), washed away. – *dibawa untung* to go where the winds of fortune take one – *mengikuti ke mana saja alur mengalir* (a Javanese saying) to float following the stream wherever it goes. – *menjauhi* drifting away from. *balok itu – dibawa air pasang.* The beam was carried away by a high tide. **2** to go/travel, etc. far away, wander far away. *Ada baiknya saya – ke negeri lain.* It would be a good thing for me to travel to another country. – *serantau* to wander far away. **3** to skip/slide away. **4** to be carried away (by s.t.), be crazy about. *Meréka – dibuaikan lagu yang berirama lembut.* They were carried along rocked by the soft rhythm. *orang* – a) drowned person. b) vagrant, tramp, homeless person. *malu berkayuh, perahu* – if you're too proud to paddle, your boat will drift. *terapung tak – terendam tak basah* there's no decision yet.

  berhanyut to slip/slide away.

  berhanyut-hanyut 1 drifting about (of boats/flotsam/persons/conversation). *Dua hari dua malam perahu meréka ~ dibawa ombak.* For two days and two nights their boat drifted about on the waves. **2** to wander/roam about. *Biar aku ~ ke rantau orang.* Let me wander about abroad. **3** to go on and on endlessly. *Ceritanya ~.* His story went on and on.

  menghanyut to drift along.

  menghanyutkan 1 to set adrift, wash/carry away, wash out (a road). *Biduk dihanyutkan arus.* The river boat was carried away by the current. **2** to carry along (of one's thoughts, etc.).

  terhanyut(kan) carried along (by the current).

  hanyutan 1 drift, drifting. **2** outwash.

  penghanyutan 1 washing away. **2** outwash.

hao (*C*) filial piety.

hap (*onom*) sound of sucking s.t. into one's mouth.

hapa small gauze bag used for dealing with fish in fish tank.

hapak → APAK.

hapal → HAFAL. **hapalan** memorized (lesson). *Inggris* ~ memorized (phrases of) English.

hapas → APAS I.

hapé (*initials of hénpon*) cell phone, mobile.

hapermot (*D*) oatmeal.

haplologi (*D gram*) haplology.

hapsak [hari peringatan kesaktian] – *Pancasila* Anniversary of Pancasila's Supernatural Power.

hapus 1 come off, wiped off/out, erased (s.t. written on a blackboard, etc.; a spot/blame, etc.). *Corat-corét pada dinding itu tidak akan* –. The graffiti on that wall won't come off. **2** to disappear, vanish. *Jika peperangan berkecamuk sekarang, ada kemungkinan manusia akan – dari permukaan bumi ini.* If a war flairs up now, there's a possibility that mankind will vanish from the face of the earth. **3** blotted out (memory), obliterated, annulled, paid off (a debt), remitted (of a punishment, etc.). – *karena daluwarsa* (*leg*) the statute of limitations has expired. – *nya kewenangan menuntut pidana dan menjalankan pidana* (*leg*) statute of limitations. – *buku* write off, wipe off the books. **menghapusbukukan** to write off. *Krédit macet yang dihapusbukukan itu akan diambil alih suatu badan hukum yang sahamnya dimiliki bank-bank pemerintah.* The bad loans that were written off will be taken over by a corporate body whose stock is owned by government banks. – *hama* sterile. **menghapushamakan** to sterilize. **penghapus hama** sterilizer. – *kaca* windshield wiper.

  menghapus(kan) 1 to wipe off, erase, clear (the table/lips, etc.). ~ *air matanya* to wipe away one's tears. ~ *arang di muka* to blot/wipe out disgrace/shame. ~ *bibir* disappointed. ~ *dosa* a) to cleanse o.s. from sins. b) "forgive us our trespasses." **2** to close/shut down. *Lima dari sembilan Lembaga Pemasyarakatan yang ada di Pulau Nusakambangan segera dihapus, sesuai (dengan) instruksi dari Départemén Kehakiman.* Five of the nine Penitentiaries on the Island of Nusakambangan will soon be closed down in conformity with an instruction from the Ministry of Justice. **3** to annul, cancel, repeal, rescind, revoke (a law). **4** to annihilate, destroy (a city/land, etc.); to eradicate, root out (a population/race, etc,); to strike s.t. out. **5** to extinguish, blot out, obliterate, remit/write off (a debt/taxes/punishment/sentence), release. **6** to abolish, do away with, cancel, annul (a contract/agreement).

terhapus 1 disappeared, wiped out, deleted. *Iklan anda akan ~ secara otomatis.* Your ad will be automatically deleted. **2** repealed. **3** null and void.

terhapuskan can be deleted/wiped out. *kesan tak ~* an indelible impression.

penghapus 1 wiper. ~ *kaca* windshield wiper. **2** eraser, s.t. that wipes out s.t. ~ *hama* an antiseptic. ~ *papan tulis* blackboard eraser. ~ *tinta* white-out, ink eraser.

penghapusan 1 annihilation, destruction, eradication, abolition, extermination; wiping out, extinction. ~ *persediaan* disposal of inventory. **2** canceling, repeal; discharge, redemption, remission, writing off (of debts). ~ *pencatatan* (*fin*) delisting. **3** dismissal. **4** removal, elimination. ~ *gemuk* grease removal. ~ *hama* disinfecting.

Haqqah (*A*) "The Truth"; name of the 69th chapter of the Koran.
haqqul-yakin → HAKULYAKIN.
har I (*A*) warm.
har II (in acronyms) → HARI, PEMELIHARAAN.
hara I *ikan* – a freshwater fish, *Osteochilus melanopleura*.
hara II 1 food/nutritive substances/material, nutritious matter. **2** nutrient. *miskin akan* – nutrient-poor, poor in nutrients. *pengayaan zat-zat* – nutrient enrichment. *unsur* – nutrients.
hara III → HIRU-HARA.
harab (*A*) war. *darul* – abode of war, i.e., the non-Islamized regions.
harafiah (*A*) literal; → HARFIAH.
  keharafiahan literalness. *penerjemahan ~* literal translation.
harak (*cla*) **terharak-harak** torn to pieces. *Maka baju Laksamana pun ~ terkembang beterbangan.* Then the admiral's coat unfolded and flew about everywhere,
harakah I (*A*) movement. *– Islam* Islamic movement.
harakah II and **harakat** (*A*) **1** one of the vowel points in Arabic writing. **2** *huruf* – vowel. *– rangkap* diphthong.
harakiri (*Jp*) harakiri, suicide.
  berharakiri to commit harakiri/suicide.
haral → ARAL.
haram (*A*) **1** prohibited, banned, forbidden by Islam; *opp* HALAL. **2** illegal, illegitimate. *anak* – illegitimate child, bastard; → HARAMJADAH. *pendatang* – (*Mal*) term used in Malaysia to refer to Indonesians who have entered the country without valid immigration papers, illegal immigrant. **3** pure (ritually, of persons/food/beverages), sacred (of places). *tanah* – Mecca and surrounding areas. *Di tanah – terlarang berperang.* It is prohibited to wage war in Mecca. *Baitul–* the Kaaba in Mecca. *Masjidil–* the holy mosque in Mecca. **4** (*coq*) truly, really. *Saya -mengambil buku itu.* Really, I didn't take that book. **5** (*coq*) not in the least, not at all, by no means, no way. *Dia lari terus, – tidak menoléh ke belakang.* He kept on running, and did not look back at all. **6** (*coq*) not (one of), there is not one. *– seorang pun di antara meréka tahu bahwa meréka dikepung.* Not one of them knew that they were encircled. *– jadah/zadah* (*q.v.*) bastard, illegitimate child.
  mengharamkan 1 to consider unlawful. *Agama Islam ~ pernikahan antara saudara kandung.* Islam considers a marriage between brothers and sisters by the same mother to be unlawful. **2** to refuse, oppose. *Rakyat ~ pemerintahan bonéka.* The people rejected a puppet government. **3** to vow not to do s.t.
  pengharaman prohibition, ban.
  perharaman (*mod*) proscription.
Haramaian (*A*) twin-city name for Mecca and Medina.

haramay (*S*) white ramie, *Boehmeria nivea*, from whose fibers yarn and rope are made.
haramjadah (*A*) illegitimate child, bastard; → ANAK *haram*.
  mengharamjadahkan to treat like a leper. *Komité itu diharamjadahkan, bahkan orang lépra kata meréka masih lebih dihargai dari komité itu.* The committee was treated like a leper, in fact even lepers are treated with more respect than the committee was.
harang → ARANG I.
haranggasu (*S*) build-up of soot.
harap 1 and **haraplah** please, kindly. *– tunggu sebentar.* Please wait a minute! *Haraplah dikirim dengan segera.* Kindly send it immediately. **2** hopefully, we hope, it's to be hoped; → MOGA-MOGA, MUDAH-MUDAHAN. *– Tuhan akan memberkati hidup engkau.* We hope (or, it's to be hoped) that God will bless your life. **3** (you) should. *– maklum* you should know. **4** hope. *penuh –* full of hope. *hilang/putus –* to lose hope. *berbesar –* to have high hopes. **5** to have hope in, hope. *Saya – ia datang.* I hope (that) he comes. *– akan* to hope for s.t. **6** to ask politely. *Saya – anda bayar utang anda.* I'm asking you to pay your debt. **7** wish that s.t. may happen. *– hati* heart's desire, fondest wish. *– maklum* please note, N.B.
harap-harap ~ *cemas* hovering between fear and hope; restless, nervous. *Akréditasi diterima dengan ~ cemas.* The accreditation was received nervously. **berharap-harap** ~ *cemas* to be between hope and disappointment. *Kini seluruh peserta mulai ~ cemas menunggu hasil.* Now all the participants began to be between hope and disappointment waiting for the result.
  berharap to hope, expect, look forward to. *Kami ~ para majikan membaca tulisan yang penting ini.* We hope that the employers will read this important notice. *Kami ~ anda dapat melunasi utang dengan segera.* We hope (i.e., request) that you will settle your debt immediately.
  berharapkan to hope for s.t., have hopes for. *Meréka ~ perlindungan.* They hoped for protection.
  mengharapi to look forward to, in advance of.
  mengharap(kan) 1 to hope for s.t., expect s.t., look forward to; in expectation of. *Saya mengharapkan agar susuk dikembalikan kepada saya.* I hope that the change is returned to me. *seperti diharapkan* as expected. **2** to rely/depend on s.t. or s.o.; can count on (reimbursement, etc.). *Dia mengharap bantuan moril.* He is depending on moral support. **3** should, please. *Diharap para penumpang segera masuk pesawat.* The passengers should board the plane immediately. *mengharap hujan di langit, air di tempayan ditumpahkan* s.t. unexpected occurs.
  mengharap-harapi to give s.o. hope.
  memperharap(kan) to please s.o., make s.o. happy.
  terharap-harap always hoping/expecting. ~ *saja* disappointed.
  harapan 1 hope. *menyatakan/menyampaikan ~ supaya ...* to express the hope that ... *sebutir ~* a flicker of hope. *Itu memberi ~ baik.* That augurs well. *memberikan ~ besar* promising. *~ku ialah agar ia kelak menjadi dokter.* My hope is that he will become a physician. **2** expectation. *jauh dari ~* far from expectations. *memenuhi ~* to come up to expectations. *~ hidup* life expectancy. *~ yang meningkat* rising expectations. *Pulau ~* "Island of Expectations" one of the names given to Sumatra. **3** s.o. on whom one's hopes have been placed. *~ bangsa* "the hope of the nation," i.e., young people. *~ terbaik* best-guess. *wanita ~* (*euph*) prostitute. **berharapan 1** to have hope. **2** hopeful.
  harap-harapan always hoping/longing/yearning for, in expectation, expectantly.
  pengharapan 1 hope, expectation, reliance. *Tipis ~nya.* He has little hope that s.t. will happen. **2** placing hope in, hoping for. **berpengharapan** to hope that, hoping/in the hope) that.
harapiah → HARAFIAH.
harasia (*coq*) → RAHASIA.
harawan (*ob*) *tunggang* – the manubrium sterni, the uppermost of the three bony segments constituting the sternum/breastbone (in horses a sign of strength).
harbor (*E*) hardboard.
hardam (*Pers ob*) constantly.

hardik 1 stern, severe, acrimonious, sharp. 2 scolding, reprimand, rebuke; → BENTAKAN.
  menghardik(kan) to use sharp/harsh words (when angry, etc.), give a rebuke/scolding to, rebuke, scold, reprimand.
  hardikan scolding, rebuke, reprimand.
Hardiknas → HARI *Pendidikan Nasional.*
hardolin (in Kuningan, West Java) lazybones.
hardtop (*E*) hardtop. *sebuah jip* – a hardtop jeep. *kendaraan Toyota* – a Toyota hardtop car.
harem (*D*) harem, seraglio.
haréndong (*S*) various k.o. plants, *Melastoma/Clidemia spp.* and others.
harfiah (*A*) 1 literal, word for word. *terjemahan* – a literal translation. 2 verbal.
harga (*Skr*) 1 price, rate, value. *dengan – murah* at a low price. *dengan – Rp 10.000* at (the price of) Rp 10,000.00. *pasang – to set a price. –nya akan anjlok.* The price will drop. – *yang dipasang seminim mungkin* the lowest possible price set. 2 (self-)esteem, (self-)respect; worth, importance. *tahu akan – dirinya* a) (sufficient) sense of self-respect. b) to know what one is worth. – *diri* self-esteem, self-respect, pride. – *diri nasional* national self-respect. 3 use, benefit, meaning. *tahan* – a) to stick to a price. b) to maintain/keep up one's standing. *ada rupa ada* – the value of goods follows from their condition or quality. – *ancer-ancer* basic/guiding price. – *atap* ceiling price. – *bahan* price of materials. – *baku* standard price. – *banderol* price shown on the tax stamp. – *banting(an)* slashed price, bargain. – *barang* commodity price. – *bayangan* under-the-counter price (paid to get s.t. in short supply). – *bébas* free-market price. – *beli* purchase price. – *berdamai* price to be arranged/agreed upon. – *berlaku* current market price. – *bersaing* competitive price. – *borongan* a) wholesale price. b) price contracted for. – *dasar* floor price. – *dibanting* dumping price. – *di dalam negeri* domestic price. – *di luar* unofficial/black-market price. – *di luar negeri* foreign price. – *disesuaikan* (*euph*) a price increase. – *diskon* discount price. – *éceran* retail price. – *éceran tertinggi* [HET] highest retail price. – *EZ [EZ* stands for the Dutch [*Departement van Économische Zaken* = Department of Economic Affairs] (*D ob*) /ését/ the official price determined by this department. – *gelap* black-market price. – *gila* (*coq*) a crazy price, i.e., a price which is either too low or too high. – *grosir* wholesale/trade price. – *jadi* a) price agreed upon after bargaining. b) exercise price. – *jual* sale/selling price. – *jual éceran* retail sales price. – *jual minimum* minimum selling price. – *karét* (*coq*) "elastic price," i.e., not a fixed price. – *kurang* balance (after deducting a down payment). – *langganan* subscription rate. – *langit* ceiling price. – *limit* floor price, lowest price at which s.t. will be offered. – *luar(an)* free-market price. – *mati* a) fixed price. b) rock-bottom price. c) bottom line. *Inilah yang merupakan* – *mati bagi Muangthai.* This is the bottom line for Thailand. – *melawan* competitive price. – *mengangkasa* sky-high price. – *miring* (*coq*) lower than usual price. – *obral* reduced price. – *pabrik* manufacturer's price. – *pakan ternak* price of cattle fodder. – *pagu* ceiling price. – *paku* fixed price. – *pantas* reasonable price. – *partai* wholesale price. – *pas/pasti* fixed price. – *pasar(an)* market price. – *patokan* benchmark/check price. – *pembelian* purchase price. – *penawaran* price offered. – *pengangkutan* freight rate. – *penjualan* sale/selling price. – *penutupan* closing price. – *penyelesaian* (*fin*) settlement price. – *permintaan* offer price. – *peroléhan* (*fin*) cost (of acquisition). – *plafon(d)* ceiling price. – *pokok* (*produksi*) cost price, production cost. – *pokok pembelian* cost of goods purchased. – *pokok penjualan* cost of goods sold. – *primér* pegging. – *puncak* top price. – *putus* agreed-upon price. – *rata-rata* average price. – *resmi* official price. – *rincih* retail price. – *rumah* price of houses. – *sasaran* target price. – *satuan* unit price. – *sementara* provisional price. – *setengah mati* bargaining price. – *séwa* rental cost. – *sisa buku* book value. – *taksiran* assessed/appraised value. – *tanda masuk* [HTM] cost of admission. – *tawaran* bid price. – *tercatat* list price. – *terendah* floor price. – *terjangkau* affordable price. – *terpasang* posted price. – *tertinggi* ceiling price. – *tetap* fixed price. – *tunai* cash price. – *uang*

rate of exchange. – *umpan* loss leader. – *umum* common/general price. – *wajar* fair price.
  harganya selling for, with a price of.
  seharga 1 of the same price. 2 for the amount of, at, valued at, worth. *dijualnya ~ Rp 4 juta* sold for 4 million rupiahs. *~ Rp 300.-* at Rp 300.00. *bangunan ~ Rp 200 juta* a building valued at 200 million rupiahs.
  berharga 1 to cost, have a price of, be worth. *~ sedolar.* It's worth one dollar. *tidak –* worthless, useless; invalid (of votes/stock, etc.). 2 valuable, of importance/great value, priceless. 3 valid.
  seberharga as valuable as.
  menghargai 1 to price, fix the price/value of. *~ dirinya* a) to have sense of self-respect. b) to know what one is worth. 2 to assess, evaluate, appraise. 3 to appreciate, value, esteem. *~ apa yang kita lakukan* to value/appreciate what we did.
  harga-menghargai to appreciate/value e.o.
  menghargakan 1 to offer s.t. at a certain price. *~ barang dagangan dengan harga yang pantas* to offer merchandize at a reasonable price. 2 to appraise, evaluate, assess. 3 to appreciate; → MENGHARGAI.
  terhargai the most valuable/respected.
  terharga(i) and **terhargakan** 1 valued, priceless. *tiada terhargai* not respected. *tiada terharga(kan)* priceless, invaluable. 2 assessed, estimated.
  penghargaan 1 honor, respect, appreciation. *~ positif tanpa syarat* an unconditional positive appreciation. 2 value, valuation, assessment, appraisal.
harhar (*A*) burning.
Harhubnas → HARI *Perhubungan Nasional.*
hari 1 day [both the day of 24 hours (*seharmal*) and the daylight hours alone]. *Ia tidak suka keluar pada – berhujan.* He doesn't like to leave home on a rainy day. *pada suatu –* a) someday (in the future). b) one day (in the past). 2 (*siang –*) daytime, the time from sunup till sundown. 3 any part of the day. *malam –* night-time. *petang –* afternoon. *siang –* daytime. *tengah –* midday, noon. *se– bulan* the first (of the month). *dua belas – bulan Syaban* the twelfth day of the month of *Syaban.* 4 the nonreferential pronoun "it" referring to weather conditions, part of the day, etc. – *gelap/jam enam* it's dark/six o'clock. – *hujan* a) it's raining. b) a rainy day. – *sudah malam* it's night. – *sudah tinggi* it's already late in the day. – *sudah hampir magrib ketika hujan mulai turun.* It was nearing sunset when it started to rain. 5 time or period (in the past/future, etc.). *Tak lupa ia menyimpan uang untuk – tua.* He didn't forget to save money for his old age. *Di – tuanya dia memilih nyepi di désa kelahirannya di Batujamus, Jawa Tengah.* In his old age he chose to go into seclusion at his native village in Batujamus, Central Java. *begini –* at this time (of the day). *belakang –* later, afterward. *dalam satu dua – ini* one of these days, some day soon. *dini –* very early in the morning, the time between midnight and sunup. *dua – sekali* every other day. *ésok –* tomorrow; → BÉSOK. *– ini* and *ini – (coq)* today. *kemudian –* later, afterward. *malam –* night. *Mobil – Bésok* The Car of the Future. *pada – itu juga* that very day. *pagi –* morning. *petang –* evening. *saban –* every day, daily. *saban –nya* day in and day out. *sampai pada – itu* to date. *sepanjang –* all day long. *ada – ada nasi* God will provide. – *acara* (*ob*) (court) session. – *akhirat* the future. – *Asyura* the 10th of Muharram. – *baik* (to have) a good day. – *baik bulan baik* (*Mal*) feast day, holiday. – *bakat* expiration date. – *bayar* a) (*ob*) payday. b) due date. –*.–* belakangan ini these days, nowadays. – *berlakunya ...* the date of validity of ... – *bersejarah* an historic day. – *bertanggal mérah* holiday. – *besar* a day celebrated in commemoration of an important event, holiday. – *besar nasional* a national holiday. – *biasa* workday, weekday. – *bulan* (*Mal*) [hb] date (of the month). – *Buruh* Labor Day. – *buruk* unlucky day. – *cuti* a day off (from work). – *demi –* day after day. – *depan* the future. – *depan kita terletak di tangan para pemuda.* Our future lies in the hands of our young people. – *din* doomsday. – *dividén* declaration date. – *émisi* date of issuance. – *ésok* the future. – *gajian* payday. – *gugur* due date. – *hisab* judgment day. – *imbang* a day with changeable weather. – *ininya* today's. *Amérika harus menjawab persoalan – ininya.*

America has to answer today's problems. – *hujan* rainy day. – *jadi* a) (lower case) anniversary. b) (upper case) Christmas. – *jatuh (témpo)* expiration/maturity/due date. – *kejepit nasional* → HARPITNAS. – *kelahiran* birthday. – *kemudian* the future, later on. – *kerja* a) business day. b) workday, weekday. – *kiamat* resurrection day. – *krida* athletics' day (for government employees). – *libur* holiday. – *mambang* the setting sun. – *matahari* solar day. – *Minggu* Sunday. **berhari minggu** to spend one's Sunday. – *naas* unlucky day. – *nanti* the future. – *pengeposan* mailing day (of a letter, etc.), date postmarked. – *perhitungan* → HARI *hisab*. – *sial* unlucky day. – *sidang* hearing/court date. – *takwim* a) a 24-hour period from 00.00 to 24.00. b) a calendar day. – *Syak* 30th of *Sya'ban*. – *tasyrik* sacrificial days (11, 12, 13 *Zulhijah*). – *tua* old age. – *tuntut bayar* due date. – *ulang tahun* birthday. – *wafat* day of one's death. – *ABRI* Republic of Indonesia Armed Forces Day (October 5). – *Adhyaksa* Attorney General's Office Day (July 22). – *AIDS Sedunia* World AIDS Day (December 1). – *Air Sedunia* World Water Day. – *Aksara Internasional* [HAI] and – *Aksarawan Sedunia* International Literacy Day (September 25). – *Amal Bhakti (Départemén Agama)* Day for the Devotion of Good Deeds (of the Department of Religious Affairs) (January 3). – *Anak Nasional* [HAN] National Children's Day (July 23). – *Angkatan Perang* Combat Forces Day (October 5); → HARI *ABRI*. – *Arafah* the day on which a group of pilgrims gather at the plain of *Arafah* to perform the *wukuf* on the ninth of the month of *Zulhijah*. – *Arba* Wednesday. – *Armada* Fleet Day (December 5). – *Artileri* Artillery Day (December 4). – *Arwah* All Souls' (Day). – *Asadha* the celebration of the first day of the dissemination of the teachings of Buddha. – *Asyura* the tenth day of the month of *Muharam*. – *Balita* Preschoolers' Day (November 25); → BALITA. – *Bank* Bank Day (July 5). – *Béa dan Cukai* Customs and Excise Day (November 1). – *Bébas Rokok Sedunia* World Nonsmoking Day (May 31). – *Berkabung Nasional* National Mourning Day (September 30). – *Berkabung Nasional Korban 40.000 Jiwa Sulawesi Selatan* National Mourning Day for the 40,000 Victims of South Sulawesi (December 11). – *Bersyukur* (U.S.) Thanksgiving Day (third Thursday in November). – *B(h)akti Adhyaksa* Public Prosecutor's Devotion Day (July 22). – *B(h)akti AURI* Air Force Devotion Day (July 29). – *B(h)akti Pariwisata, Pos dan Télekomunikasi* [Parpostél] (Department of) Tourism, Post and Telecommunications Devotion Day (September 27). – *B(h)akti Pekerjaan Umum* [PU] Public Works Devotion Day (December 3). – *B(h)bakti Transmigrasi* Transmigration Devotion Day (December 12). – *Bhayangkara* Police Day (July 1). – *Brigade Mobil* [Brimob] Mobile Brigade Day (November 14). – *Buku* Book Day (May 21). – *Bumi* Earth Day (April 22). – *Buruh* Labor Day (May 1). – *Cinta Puspa dan Satwa Nasional* National Love of Fauna and Flora Day (November 5). – *Dharma Karyadhika* Department of Justice Duties Day (October 30). – *Dharma Samudera* Ocean Duties Day, commemorating the Arafura Sea battle on January 15, 1962. – *Diréktorat Jénderal Perguruan Tinggi* Higher Education Directorate General Day (April 14). – *Diturunkan Al-Qur'an* Day of the Descent of the Koran *(Ramadan 17)*. – *Doa Sedunia* [HDS] World Day of Prayer (the first Friday in Lent) – *Dokter Nasional* National Physicians Day (October 24). – *émisi* date of issuance. – *Film Nasional* National Film Day (March 30). – *Ganéfo* Games of the New Emerging Forces Day (November 25). – *Guru Internasional* International Teachers Day (October 5). – *Hak-Hak Asasi Manusia* Human Rights Day (December 10). – *Ibu* a) (Indonesian style) Mothers Day (December 22). b) (International style) Mothers Day (the second Sunday in May). – *Industri (National)* (National) Industrial Day (July 13). – *Infanteri* Infantry Day (December 15. – *Jadi Diréktorat Hukum TNI-AD* Armed Services-Army Law Directorate Anniversary (March 1). – *Jadi Diréktorat Keséhatan TNI-AD* Armed Services-Army Health Directorate Anniversary (October 26). – *Jadi Kabupatén Banyumas* Founding of Banyumas Day (April 6). – *Jadi Korps Marinir TNI-AL* Armed Services-Navy Marine Corps Anniversary (November 15). – *Jadi Kota*

Bogor Anniversary of the Town of Bogor (June 3). – *Jadi Kota Boné* Anniversary of the Town of Bone (April 6). – *Jadi Kota Garut* Anniversary of the Town of Garut (March 17). – *Jadi Kota Médan* Anniversary of the Town of Medan (July 1). – *Jadi Kota Samarinda* Anniversary of the Town of Samarinda (January 21). – *Jadi Kota Tasikmalaya* Anniversary of the Town of Tasikmalaya (August 21). – *Jadi POM ABRI* Republic of Indonesia Armed Forces Military Police Anniversary (May 11). – *Jadi Radio Républik Indonésia* Republic of Indonesia Radio Day (September 11). – *Jadi Wanita Angkatan Udara* (*WARA*) Air Force Women's Anniversary (August 12). – *jatuh* maturity/due date. – *Jumat Agung/Besar* Good Friday. – *Kanak-Kanak Nasional* National Children's Day (June 6). – *Kanak-Kanak Sedunia* International Children's Day (June 1). – *Kartini* Kartini Day (April 21). – *Kasada/Kasodo (Jv) Kasada* Day (December 11). – *Kasih Sayang* Valentine's Day (February 14). – *Kebaktian Sosial* Social Devotion Day (December 20). – *Kebangkitan Nasional* [Harkitnas] National Awakening Day (May 20). – *Kebébasan Pérs Sedunia* World Press Freedom Day (May 3). – *Kejadian* Christmas (December 25). – *Kejaksaan* Public Prosecutors Day (July 22). – *Keluarga Nasional* National Family Day (June 29). – *Kemenangan Buruh* Labor Victory Day (May 1); → HARI *Buruh*. – *Kenaikan Isa Almaséh* and – *Kenaikan Tuhan Yésus ke Sorga* (Christian) Ascension Day (Holy Thursday; 40 days after Easter Sunday) – *Kependudukan Sedunia* International Population Day (July 11). – *Kepolisian* Police Day (July 1). – *Keréta Api* Railway Day (September 28). – *Kesaktian Pancasila* [HAPSAK] (Commemoration of) Pancasila Sanctity Day (September 30–October 1); → HARI *Pancasila*. – *Keséhatan Jiwa Sedunia* World Mental Health Day (October 9). – *Keséhatan Nasional* [HKN] National Health Day (November 12). – *Kesetiakawanan Sosial Nasional* [HKSN] National Social Solidarity Day (December 20). – *Keuangan* Finance Day (October 30; this was the first day that Indonesian republican money was circulated in 1945). – *Kewaspadaan Nasional* National Vigilance Day (September 30). – *Koperasi* Cooperative Day (July 12). – *Krida* Day of Extracurricular Activities (in schools); officialized on *TNI-AD* Armed Services-Army anniversary (March 11). – *Krida Pertanian* Day of Extracurricular Activities of the Department of Agriculture (June 21). – *Lahir Pramuka* Pramuka Anniversary Day (August 14). – *Lahirnya Pancasila* Anniversary Day of Pancasila (October 1). – *Lebaran* Lebaran Day. – *Lingkungan Hidup Sedunia* World Environment Day (June 5). – *Listrik Nasional* [HLN] National Electricity Day (October 27). – *Mahsyar* Resurrection Day. – *Miraj Nabi Muhammad SAW* (Muslim) Ascension Day. – *Nasional Australia* Australian National Day (January 26). – *Nasional Bahari* National Seamen's Day (September 23). – *Natal* Christmas Day (December 25). *Mengucapkan selamat* – *Natal dan Tahun Baru.* Merry Christmas and a Happy New Year. *merayakan* – *Natal* to celebrate Christmas; → KRISMESAN, NATALAN. – *Nuzulul Qur'an* the day the Koran descended from Heaven. – *Olahraga Nasional* National Sports Day (September 9). – *Pahlawan* Heroes' Day (November 10). – *Pancasila* Pancasila Day (October 1). – *Pangan Sedunia* [HPS] World Food Day (October 16). – *Pantekosta/Kenaikan Isa Al Masih)* Whitsuntide/Ascension of Jesus Christ (June 18). – *Pattimura* Pattimura Day (May 15). – *Payung* Wing Day (of the Republic of Indonesia Air Force). – *Pekerja Nasional Indonésia* Indonesia National Workers Day (February 20). – *Pemasyarakatan* Penitentiary Day (April 27). – *Pembalasan* Judgment Day. – *Pembasmian Malaria* Malaria Eradication Day. – *Pemberantasan Buta Huruf Internasional* International Combating Illiteracy Day (September 6). – *Pendidikan Nasional* [Hardiknas] National Education Day (May 2). – *Penentuan* D-Day. – *Penerbangan Nasional* [Harpenas] National Aviation Day (April 9). – *Penggelaran* (Army) Commencement/Inauguration) Day. – *Perhotélan* Hotel Business Day (July 25). – *Perhubungan Nasional* [Harhubnas] National Communications Day, *aka* – *Transport dan Komunikasi Nasional* National Transport and Communications Day (September 17). – *Peringatan Kesaktian Pancasila* [HAPSAK] (Commemoration of) Pancasila Sanctity

Day (September 30–October 1); → HARI *Pancasila*. – *Peringatan Pahlawan Raja Sisingamangaraja XII* Commemoration Day of the National Hero Raja Sisingamangaraja XII (June 17). – *Perkebunan* Plantation Day (January 31). – *Pérs Nasional* [Ripenas and HPN] National Press Day (February 9). – *Perserikatan Bangsa-Bangsa* (PBB) United Nations Day (October 24). – *Pertanian-Koperasi dan Keluarga Berencana* [Pertasikencana] Peasants-Cooperation and Family Planning Day (July 12). – *Perum Penerbitan dan Percétakan BALAI PUSTAKA* Public (State) Corporation *Balai Pustaka* Day (September 22). – *Postél* Post Office and Telecommunications Day (October 8); *cp* HARI *B(h)akti Pariwisata, Pos dan Télékomunikasi*. – *Pramuka* Pramuka (August 14); → HARI *Lahir Pramuka*. – *Proklamasi/Kemerdékaan* Independence Day (August 17). – *Radio* Radio Day (September 11). – *Raya* holiday. – *Raya Haji* and – *Raya Idul Adha* the great Muslim feast of Immolation or Greater Bairam, on the tenth of *Zulhijah*, the twelfth and last month of the Muslim year, following completion of the pilgrimage to Mecca; animals are slaughtered *usu* goats or lambs. This occasion is the climax of the *hajj*. – *Raya Idul Fitri* Feast of Breaking the *Ramadan* Fast or Lesser *Bairam*, on the first day of *Syawal*, the tenth month of the Muslim year, i.e., the so-called Javanese New Year or Lebaran day. – *Raya Orang Kudus* All Saints' Day. – *Raya Santa Perawan Maria diangkat ke Surga* (August 15). Virgin Mary's Ascension Day. – *Robo* the last Wednesday in the month of *Syafar*. – *Sandang Nasional* National Clothes Day (September 16). – *Saraswati* Saraswati (the Hindu Protector of Sciences, Culture and Art) Day (August 21). – *Sarjana* Commencement/Graduation) Day (September 29). – *Sumpah Pemuda* [Harsumda] Youth Pledge Day (October 28). – *Syukuran* (U.S.) Thanksgiving Day. – *Tani* Peasants' Day (September 24). – *Tanpa Rokok Sedunia* World Non-smoking Day (May 31). – *Ulang Tahun Akadémi Angkatan Bersenjata Républik Indonésia* [Akabri] Anniversary Day of the Republic of Indonesia Armed Forces Academy (December 15). – *Ulang Tahun Angkatan Muda Pembaruan Indonésia* [AMPI] Anniversary Day of the Young Generation for Indonesia's Renovation (June 28). – *Ulang Tahun Badan Kerjasama Organisasi Wanita* [BKOW] Anniversary Day of the Women's Organizations Cooperative Body (May 20). – *Ulang Tahun Badan Pembekalan* [Babék] Anniversary Day of the Supply Board (June 29). – *Ulang Tahun Badan Pembinaan Hukum* [Babinkum] *ABRI* Anniversary Day of the Republic of Indonesia Armed Forces Law Development Board (December 3). – *Ulang Tahun Bank Dagang Negara* [BDN] Anniversary Day of the State Commercial Bank (April 11). – *Ulang Tahun Batalyon Infanteri 201/Jakarta Raya Yudha* [Yonif 201/Jaya Yudha] Anniversary Day of the 201st Infantry Battalion/Greater Jakarta Military (July 31). – *Ulang Tahun Bhayangkara* Police Anniversary Day (July 11); → HARI *Bhayangkara*. – *Ulang Tahun Brigade-Mobil* [Brimob] Mobile Brigade Anniversary Day (November 14); → HARI *Brimob*. – *Ulang Tahun Dharma Pertiwi* Anniversary Day of Dharma Pertiwi (Women's Association of the Department of the Interior). – *Ulang Tahun Diréktorat Keuangan Angkatan Darat* Anniversary Day of the Army Financial Directorate (October 27). – *Ulang Tahun Divisi Infanteri I Kostrad* Anniversary Day of the Kostrad First Infantry Division (December 22). – *Ulang Tahun Divisi Siliwangi* Siliwangi Division Anniversary Day (May 20).– *Ulang Tahun Garuda* Indonesian Airways Garuda Indonesian Airways Anniversary Day (January 26). – *Ulang Tahun Golongan Karya* [Golkar] *Golkar* Anniversary Day (October 20). – *Ulang Tahun Grand Hyatt Jakarta* Jakarta Grand Hyatt Anniversary Day (July 23). – *Ulang Tahun Himpunan Pengarang Indonésia "Aksara"* Anniversary Day of the Indonesian Writers Association "Aksara" (May 2). – *Ulang Tahun Hotél Indonésia* Anniversary Day of Hotel Indonesia (August 5). – *Ulang Tahun Indonesian Hotel & Restaurant Association* [IHRA] Anniversary Day of the Indonesian Hotel & Restaurant Association (February 9). – *Ulang Tahun Ikatan Kesejahteraan Keluarga ABRI* [IKKA] Anniversary Day of the Republic of Indonesia Armed Forces Families Welfare Union (July 14). – *Ulang*

Tahun Indonesisch-Nederlandsche School [INS] Anniversary Day of the Indonesian-Dutch School (May 31). – *Ulang Tahun Intégrasi Timtim* Anniversary Day of East Timor's Integration (July 17). – *Ulang Tahun Kabupatén Bekasi* Anniversary Day of the Bekasi Regency (August 15). – *Ulang Tahun Kelompok Usaha Sahid* Anniversary Day of the Sahid Trading Company (July 5). – *Ulang Tahun Keséhatan Jiwa Sedunia* World Mental Health Anniversary Day (October 9). – *Ulang Tahun Kodam IV/Sriwijaya* Anniversary Day of *Kodam TV/Sriwijaya* (April 25). – *Ulang Tahun Kodam VIII/Brawijaya* Anniversary Day of *Kodam VIII/Brawijaya* (December 17). – *Ulang Tahun Kodam IX/Udayana* Anniversary Day of *Kodam IX/Udayana* (May 27). – *Ulang Tahun Kodam XVII/Cenderawasih* Anniversary Day of *Kodam XVII/Cenderawasih* (May 17). – *Ulang Tahun Komando Pasukan Khusus* [Kopassus] Anniversary Day of the Special Forces Command (April 25). – *Ulang Tahun Komando Cadangan Stratégis Angkatan Darat* [Kostrad] Anniversary Day of the Army Strategic Reserve Command (March 6). – *Ulang Tahun Komando Daérah Militér Jakarta Raya* [Kodam Jaya] Anniversary Day of the Greater Jakarta Military Area Command. – *Ulang Tahun Komando Khusus* [Kopassus] Anniversary Day of the Special Forces Command (April 25). – *Ulang Tahun Komando Lintas Laut Militér* [Kolonlamil] Anniversary Day of the Military Sea Lanes Command (July 3). – *Ulang Tahun Komando Pendidikan Tentara Nasional Indonésia-Angkatan Udara* [Kodikau] Anniversary Day of the Educational Command of the Armed Services-Air Force (November 15). – *Ulang Tahun Komando Pertahanan Udara Nasional* [Kohanudnas] Anniversary Day of the National Air Defense Command (February 9). – *Ulang Tahun Komando Stratégis Angkatan Darat* Anniversary Day of the Army Strategic Command (December 20). – *Ulang Tahun Komando Stratégis Nasional* Anniversary Day of the National Strategic Command (December 20). – *Ulang Tahun Komité Olahraga Nasional Indonésia* [KONI] Anniversary Day of the Indonesian National Sports Committee. – *Ulang Tahun Korém 131/Santiago* Anniversary Day of the *Korém 131/Santiago* (January 4). – *Ulang Tahun Korps Pegawai Républik Indonésia* [Korpri] Anniversary Day of the Republic of Indonesia (Government) Employees Corps (November 30). – *Ulang Tahun Korps Wanita Angkatan Laut* [Kowal] Anniversary Day of the Navy Women's Corps (January 5). – *Ulang Tahun Kota Administratif* [Kotif]) *Cilegon* Anniversary Day of the Cilegon Administrative Town (July 20). – *Ulang Tahun Kota Cirebon* Anniversary Day of the Town of Cirebon (September 26). – *Ulang Tahun Kota Jakarta* Anniversary Day of the City of Jakarta (June 22). – *Ulang Tahun Kota Madya Manado* Anniversary Day of the Manado Municipality (July 14). – *Ulang Tahun Kota Médan* Anniversary Day of the City of Medan (July 1). – *Ulang Tahun Kota Padang* Anniversary Day of the City of Padang (August 7). – *Ulang Tahun Kota Palémbang* Anniversary Day of the City of Palembang (June 7). – *Ulang Tahun Lembaga Bantuan Hukum* Anniversary Day of the Legal Aid Institute (October 28). – *Ulang Tahun Lembaga Pertahanan Nasional* [Lémhannas] Anniversary Day of the National Defense Institute (May 24). – *Ulang Tahun Paguyuban Wehrkreise III Yogyakarta* Anniversary Day of the Yogyakarta IIIrd Defense District Association (an association of former fighters in the March 1, 1948 General Attack on Yogyakarta) (December 30). – *Ulang Tahun Palang Mérah Indonésia* [PMI] Anniversary Day of the Indonesian Red Cross (September 17). – *Ulang Tahun Partai Démokrasi Indonésia* [PDI] Anniversary Day of the Indonesian Democratic Party (January 10). – *Ulang Tahun Pasukan Pengamanan Présidén* [Paspamprés] Anniversary Day of the Presidential Security Guard. – *Ulang Tahun Pemerintah Daérah Tingkat I* [Pémda Tk I] *Bali* Anniversary Day of the First Level Provincial Government of Bali. – *Ulang Tahun Perairan dan Udara* [AIRUD] (Police) Sea and Air (Corps) Anniversary Day (December 1). – *Ulang Tahun Persatuan Insinyur Indonésia* [PII] Anniversary Day of the Indonesian Engineers Association; → INSINYUR. – *Ulang Tahun Persatuan Istri AURI* [PIA] "Ardhya Garini" Anniversary Day of the Republic of Indonesia Air Force Wives

Association "Ardhya Garini" (November 25). – *Ulang Tahun Perusahaan Pertambangan Minyak (dan Gas Bumi) Negara (Pertamina)* Anniversary Day of the State Oil (and Natural Gas Mining Company (December 10). – *Ulang Tahun Polisi Militér* [POM] Military Police Anniversary Day (June 22). – *Ulang Tahun Provinsi Lampung* Anniversary Day of Lampung Province (March 21). – *Ulang Tahun PT Bouraq Indonésia Airlines* Anniversary Day of Bouraq Indonesian Airlines Inc. (April 1). – *Ulang Tahun PT Sandoz Biochemie Farma Indonésia* Anniversary Day of Sandoz Biochemie Farma Indonesia Inc. (March 26). – *Ulang Tahun Pusat Pendidikan Hukum Diréktorat Hukum TNI-AD* [Pusdikkum Ditkumad] Anniversary Day of the Armed Services-Army Legal Directorate of the Law Educational Center (June 5). – *Ulang Tahun Pusat Pendidikan Marinir* [Pusdikmar] Anniversary Day of the Center for the Training of Marines (November 27). – *Ulang Tahun Real Estate Indonésia* [REI] Indonesian Real Estate Anniversary Day. – *Ulang Tahun Républik Maluku Selatan* [RMS] Anniversary Day of the Republic of South Moluccas (April 25). – *Ulang Tahun Rumah Sakit Persatuan Geréja-Geréja Injil* [RS-PGI] Cikini Anniversary Day of the Cikini Hospital of the Churches of the Gospel (March 11). – *Ulang Tahun Rumah Sakit Pusat Angkatan Darat* [RSPAD] Anniversary Day of the Army Central General Hospital (July 26). – *Ulang Tahun Satuan Pengamanan* [Satpam] Security Units Anniversary Day (December 30). – *Ulang Tahun Sekolah Olahraga Ragunan* Anniversary Day of the Ragunan Sports School (January 15). – *Ulang Tahun Sekolah Staf Komando Angkatan Laut* [Séskoal] Anniversary Day of the Navy Staff and Command School (November 28). – *Ulang Tahun Soekarno/Bung Karno* Soekarno Birthday (June 6, 1901). – *Ulang Tahun Suara Pembaruan* Anniversary Day of Suara Pembaruan (February 4). – *Ulang Tahun Supersemar* Supersemar Anniversary Day (March 22). – *Ulang Tahun Taman Impian Jaya Ancol* [TIJA] Anniversary Day of the Jaya Ancol Dream Park (February 28). – *Ulang Tahun Taman Ismail Marzuki* [TIM] Ismail Marzuki Cultural Center Anniversary Day (October 8). – *Ulang Tahun Taman Mini Indonésia Indah* [TMII] Anniversary Day of the Beautiful Indonesian Mini Garden (February 22). – *Ulang Tahun Tentara Rakyat Mataram* Anniversary Day of the Mataram People's Army (December 15). – *Ulang Tahun TNI-AU* Anniversary Day of the Armed Forces-Air Force (April 10). – *Ulang Tahun Trikomando Rakyat* [Trikora] Anniversary Day of the People's Threefold Command (December 19); → TRIKORA. – *Ulang Tahun Wisuda Para* Wing Day (of the Republic of Indonesia Air Force).

sehari a/one day. *Kabar dari Acéh ~ dua yang lalu mengungkapkan ...* News from Aceh a couple of days ago reveals ... *dari ~ ke ~* day after day. *~ Sesudahya* The Day After. *~ semalam* around the clock, 24 hours; → SEHARMAL. *~ suntuk/sontok* all-day, all day long, the whole day. **seharian** the whole day, all day long. *karena ~ hujan turun* because it had rained the whole day. **keseharian 1** daily. *barang-barang keperluan hidup ~* the daily necessities of life. **2** daily life. *dipraktékkan dalam ~* to be put into effect in daily life. *Dalam ~nya, di rumah, di luar rumah, dan di mana saja, kedisiplinan yang dimilikinya mémang tercermin.* In his daily life in and out of the house, and wherever he might be, the discipline he possesses shows.

sehari-hari 1 daily, every day. *tugasnya ~* his daily assignment. **2** colloquial. *bahasa ~* colloquial language.

sehari-harian all-day long, the whole day. *~ kerjanya hanya tidur.* All he does is sleep all day long.

berhari-hari(an) day after day, for days and days, day in and day out, for days on end. *Berhari-hari Hasanuddin berjalan.* Hasanuddin walked for days and days.

harian 1 daily, diurnal. *pekerja ~* daily worker. **2** duty, in charge of day-to-day activities. *pengurus ~* executive committee (in charge of day-to-day activities). *perintah ~* order of the day. **3** daily newspaper. *~ pagi/soré* morning/evening paper.

haribaan → RIBA. lap. *Anak itu meletakkan kepalanya ke – ibunya.* The child laid his head on his mother's lap. *pulang ke –Nya* (*euph*) to die, pass away.

harim (*A*) wife.

harimau I 1 tiger. **2** leopard. **3** a fierce person; → RIMAU. *– mati meninggalkan belang, gajah mati meninggalkan gading, manusia mati meninggalkan nama* when a tiger dies, it leaves its stripes; when an elephant dies, it leaves its tusks; when a man dies, he leaves his reputation. *terlepas dari mulut buaya masuk ke mulut* – out of the frying pan and into the fire. *sudah masuk ke dalam mulut* – irretrievably lost. *– ditakuti sebab giginya* authoritative persons are feared for their powerful influence. *– mengaum takkan menangkap* barking dogs seldom bite, his bark is worse than his bite. *anak – takkan jadi anak kambing* a courageous person won't become a coward. *membangunkan – tidur* to awaken sleeping dogs. *– akar* common leopard, *Felis pardus. – anjing* golden cat, *Felis temminckii. – Bali* Bali tiger, *Panthera tigris balica. – belang kasau* tiger, *Felis tigris. – belang tebuan* common leopard, *Felis pardus. – bintang* common leopard, *Felis pardus. – buluh* wild cat, *Felis planiceps. – compok* golden cat, *Felis temminckii. – dahan* clouded leopard, *Felis nebulosa. – daun pinang* name given to the tiger when the black markings are not extensive. *– gadungan/jadi-jadian* weretiger. *– kertas* paper tiger. *– kijang* golden cat, *Catopuma temminckii. – kumbang/peturun* black panther, *Felis pardus niger. – loréng Jawa* Java tiger, *Panthera tigris sondaica. – puntung perun* black panther, *Felis Pardus niger. – Sumatera* Sumatran tiger, *Panthera tigris sumatrensis. – sancang* variety of tiger found in West Java, *Felis tigris. – tarum* black panther, *Felis pardus niger. – telap* golden cat, *Felis temminckii. – terung kasau* royal tiger, *Felis tigris. – tutul* common leopard, *Felis pardus.*

mengharimaui to be violent/savage towards, scold harshly.

harimau II *– lalat* a jumping spider.

haring I (*D*) *ikan* – herring.

haring II → ARING I.

haring III → ARING II.

harini (contraction of *hari ini*) today.

haris (*A*) watchman, guard.

harisah (*A*) *bubur* – a broth eaten on 10 *Muharram.*

harkat (*A*) **1** standard, level. **2** rate (of exchange). **3** dignity, (social) status, standing, position, value. **4** (*phys*) valence.

seharkat equal in value, equivalent.

mengharkatkan to rate s.t.

pengharkatan rating. *~ krédit* credit rating. *~ préstasi* performance rating.

Harkitnas → HARI *Kebangkitan Nasional.*

harlah [hari lahir] anniversary.

berharlah to celebrate an anniversary.

harmal [hari malam] (space of) 24 hours. *tiga –* three full days.

seharmal (= *sehari semalam*) one full day.

harmoni (*D*) harmony.

keharmonian harmony.

pengharmonian harmonizing.

harmonik (*E*) and **harmonis** (*D*) harmonic. *tidak –* inharmonic. **ketidakharmonisan** disharmony. *~ sosial* social disharmony.

mengharmoniskan to harmonize.

keharmonisan harmonization. *~ sosial* social harmonization.

harmonika (*D/E*) harmonica.

harmonisasi (*D*) harmonization. *menciptakan – antara industri besar dan kecil* to create harmony between large and small industries.

mengharmonisasikan to harmonize.

terharmonisasi harmonized.

harmonium (*D/E*) harmonium.

harnal (*D*) hairpin.

harnét (*D*) hairnet.

harpa (*D*) harp.

Harpenas → HARI *Penerbangan Nasional.*

harpis (*D*) harpist.

harpitnas [hari kejepit nasional] a day taken off from work because it's sandwiched between two holidays.

harpun (*D/E*) harpoon.

harpus (*D?*) resin used by violinists.

Harsumda (*acr*) → HARI *Sumpah Pemuda.*

hart (*D*) heart(s) (in card deck).

harta (*Skr*) property, wealth, goods, possessions, assets, estate. *- asal* property brought to a marriage. *- babon* (*Jv*) capital assets. *- bawaan* dowry brought to a marriage by either side. *- benda* wealth, riches, property. *- bergerak* movable property. *- bersama* joint property/assets. *- bersih* net asset. *- bersyarat* contingent asset. *- berwujud* tangible assets. *- binatok* assets brought to a marriage by the groom. *- campur* community property. *- carian* joint property obtained during a marriage. *- dunia* worldly goods. *- gawan* (*Jv*) property brought to a marriage. *- gono-gini* (*Jv*) joint property. *- hébah/hibah* family property given away by general consent. *- karun* a) hidden treasure. *mengumpulkan - karun* treasure hunt. b) ownerless fortune/wealth/riches or of obscure origin. *- kawin* dowry given by bridegroom to bride. *- kekayaan* assets. *- kumpul* joint property. *- milik* property. *- pailit* bankruptcy estate. *- pelayaran* assets gained abroad. *- pembawaan* personal assets brought by either side to a marriage. *- pembujangan* assets brought by the groom to a marriage. *- penantian* wife's separate property. *- pencarian* earned wealth. *- (pen)dapatan* wife's separate property. *- peninggalan* estate. *- pusaka* heirloom, ancestral/inherited property. *- rampasan* booty, loot. *- (se)pencarian* joint earnings of husband and wife (shared in a divorce), community property. *- sésan* property brought by the wife to the marriage. *- silih jarih* (*M*) a Minangkabau form of land ownership. *- surut* wasting assets. *- tak-bergerak* real property. *- tak berwujud* intangible assets. *- terpendam* buried treasure. *- tetap* unmovable property. *- tua* (*M*) (inalienable) family matrilineal possessions. *- usaha* working/operating assets. *- wakaf* legacy left to charity. *- warisan* estate, inheritance. *- wujud* tangible assets (of a corporation).
   seharta ~ *semilik* joint property and assets. (*kawin dengan dasar*) ~ *semilik* to marry on the basis of community property.
   berharta 1 well-to-do, well-off. **2** propertied.
hartal (*Hind*) **1** a yellow face powder, ochre; saffron. *- nikel* nickel green. **2** a general strike.
hartati 1 sugar. **2** sweet. **3** woman's name.
hartawan (*Skr*) rich, well-to-do. *kaum -* rich people, the rich.
harti → ARTI.
haru moved, touched. (*rasa -*) emotion. *Matanya berkedip-kedip menahan -.* Her eyes blinked, controlling her emotions. *- biru* and *- hara* noise, uproar, bustle, commotion, tumult, upheaval.
   mengharu-biru(kan) to create chaos, cause/make a stir. *Masalah krédit macet yang ~ selama dua pekan terakhir ini mémang tak ada hubungannya langsung dengan asuransi déposito.* The problem of bad debts, which has caused quite a stir over the past two weeks, actually has no connection with deposit insurance. **terharubiru** created a chaos, chaotic.
   mengharu to disturb, perturb, pester, alarm, confuse.
   mengharukan 1 to move, touch, affect; moving, touching, affecting. **2** to stir, disturb, perturb, confuse, confound.
   terharu moved, affected, touched. **keterharuan** emotion, feelings.
   keharuan 1 emotion, feeling. **2** emotional.
   pengharu troublemaker.
   pengharuan confusion, perturbation, disturbance.
haruan a coarse freshwater fish, snakehead, *Channa striata*, caught for food, *esp* in rice fields.
harum 1 fragrance, odor, smell. *- menghilangkan bau* legitimizing a questionable undertaking by implying direct association with another activity, person, or institution which is above reproach. **2** fragrant, aromatic. *- namanya* to be famous/well-known. *- manis* cotton candy; → ARUMANIS.
   seharum as fragrant as.
   mengharum 1 to be(come) fragrant, be scented/perfumed. **2** to become famous/well-known.
   mengharumi to make fragrant, perfume.
   mengharumkan 1 to make s.t. smell sweet, make aromatic. **2** (~ *namanya*) to be(come) famous.
   terharum the most fragrant.
   harum-haruman perfumes.
   keharuman 1 fragrance, perfume, smell. **2** fame, reputation.
   pengharum means of making s.t. smell sweet.

Harun (*A*) (the biblical) Aaron.
harung → ARUNG.
harus I must, should, ought to, have to, be obliged to, have no choice but, need to. *Air sumur - dimasak sebelum diminum.* Well water must be boiled before drinking. *Saya - menélepon.* I have to make a phone call. *tidak -* do(es) not have to, need not; → *tidak* USAH.
   haruslah it must (we cannot get away from it); it goes without saying.
   harusnya should have (but didn't).
   seharusnya 1 should have (but didn't). **2** should, rightly, fittingly, proper(ly); → SEMESTINYA, SEPATUTNYA.
   mengharuskan to oblige, compel, force, require, demand. *Pluralitas agama ~ adanya dialog.* A plurality of religions demands that we have a dialog.
   keharusan necessity. *suatu ~* a must. *~ yang tak terélakkan* a sine qua non, an absolute necessity. **berkeharusan** to be compelled, required.
harus II → ARUS I.
harya (*Jv*) male nobility title, grand.
haryapatih grand duke.
   keharyapatihan grand duchy. *~ Luksémburg* Grand Duchy of Luxembourg.
has I (*D*) *daging -* fillet, tenderloin.
has II (*D*) gauze, fine screening.
has III → KHAS.
has IV → AS I.
hasab (*A*) → HISAB.
hasad (*A*) envy, spite.
   berhasad jealous, envious.
hasai → ASAI.
hasan I (*A*) **1** plausible (of a tradition or *Hadis*). **2** beauty.
Hasan II a male name; → HUSAIN. *- dan Hamzab* Hansel and Gretel.
hasanah and **hasanat** (*A*) good deed/act.
Hasanuddin (*ob*) name of the Army division stationed in South and Southwest Sulawesi.
hasar (*D*) game of chance.
hashis *daun -* hashish.
hasiat → KHASIAT.
hasib (*A*) **1** highly valued (attribute of God). **2** reckoner, calculator, arithmetician.
hasidah (*A*) k.o. cake eaten at *Asyura*.
hasil (*A*) **1** yield, produce, proceeds (from the sale of ...), harvest, crops, product(s), production. **2** income (of a person), earnings, gain, return, profits. **3** result, outcome, success, effect. *membuahkan -* to yield/produce/show results. *tidak membuahkan/membawa -* unsuccessful, fails to produce any results. *- air marine* product. *- alami* natural products. *- bagi* (*math*) quotient. *- bagi pemilihan* electoral quotient. *- baik* success. *- bersih* net profits. *- buatan* work of art. *- buatan tangan* handmade. *- bumi* agricultural/farm produce/products, crops. *- guna* effective, effectiveness; → SANGKIL I. **berhasil guna** to be effective. **keberhasilgunaan** effectiveness; → KESANGKILAN. *- hutan* forest product(s) (such as rattan/resins from various Indonesian trees, *esp* from *Dipterocarpus* trees, lumber, etc.). *- hutan ikutan* minor forest products. *- ikutan* by-product, derivative. *- jadi* result. *- jarah* booty, loot. *- jual* proceeds (of a sale). *- kali* (*math*) product. *- kalori* caloric effect. *- karya/kerja* performance; → KINERJA, PÉRFORMANSI, PÉRFORMENS. *- kotor* gross profits. *- lestari* sustainable yield. *- mahsul* various products (of a country). *- padi* rice harvest. *- panén* the harvest. *- pemilihan* election results. *- pendapatan karcis masuk* box-office (gate) receipts. *- penjualan* proceeds of a sale. *- perampokan* loot. *- Perdagangan Negara* State Trading Earnings. *- perkiraan* estimation results. *- perdata* civil fruit. *- révaluasi aktiva tetap* fixed asset revaluation reserves. *- samping(an)* a) by-product. b) side effect. *- sesaat* standing crop. *- tahunan* annual yield. *- tambang* mining products. *- tanah* agricultural/farm produce/products. *- tempaan* forging. *- ternak* pastoral products. *- tetap* standing crop. *- turut* by-product, derivative. *- uji* a) test results. b) assay. *- usaha* operating results. *- utama* principal product. *- yang akan diterima* (in bookkeeping) collectable profits. *- yang menurun* diminishing returns.

berhasil 1 to produce, yield, bring in, realize. *Kebunnya sudah ~.* His plantation is already producing. **2** to succeed, make it; successful; profitable, advantageous. *bekas tukang kebun yang ~* a former gardener who has made it. *dalam hal pihak penjual tidak ~ untuk menyerahkan* in case the selling party fails to deliver. **3** ~ (*+ a verb*) to manage to, be able to, succeed in. *Kini meréka ~ memperbaiki rumah-rumahnya.* Now they are able to renovate their houses. *Usaha meréka ~ digagalkan oléh Angkatan Darat Yaman.* The Yemeni Army was able to thwart their efforts. *~ melampaui* to make it through, live through. **keberhasilan** success. *kurang ~* less successful. **kekurangberhasilan** less successfulness. *tidak ~* unsuccessful. **ketidakberhasilan** failure, lack of success. *Para pemimpin PDI yang paling bertanggung jawab atas keberhasilan dan ~ KLB.* The leadership of the Indonesian Democratic Party is most responsible for the success and lack of success of the extraordinary congress.

menghasilkan 1 to produce, bring in/forth. *Daérah manakah yang ~ karét?* Which provinces produce rubber? *Séks diakui cuma punya tujuan tunggal yaitu ~ keturunan.* It has been recognized that sex has only one sole purpose, to procreate. **2** to make successful. *Ketekunanlah yang sudah ~ bisnisnya.* It's perseverance that made his business successful. **3** profitable. **4** to create, make, produce, come up with. *Ia adalah seorang pengarang yang sudah ~ lebih dari 10 cerpén.* He's a writer who has produced more than 10 short stories.

kehasilan production; income, earnings. *Upah sawah itu kadang-kadang sama dengan ~ yang diperdapat.* The payment for work in the rice fields sometimes equals the earnings obtained.

penghasil 1 producer. **2** breadwinner. *Tidak ada satu pun yang memberi stigma pada pria jika istrinya yang sebenarnya merupakan ~ utama dalam rumah tangga.* Nobody blames a man if he has a wife who is actually the main breadwinner in their household.

penghasilan 1 production. **2** yield. **3** income, earnings, emolument. *~ atas invéstasi* return on investment. *~ bunga* interest income. *~ negara* national income. *Gaji dan ~ lain para anggota Diréksi ditetapkan oléh Menteri.* The salary and other emoluments of the members of the Management shall be determined by the Minister. *orang-orang yang tinggi ~nya* those in the higher income brackets. *~ sekali banyak* mass production. *alat ~ means* of production. *pajak ~* income tax. *~ kena pajak* taxable earnings. *~ tidak kena pajak* nontaxable earnings. **berpenghasilan** to have income. *negara ~ menengah/rendah/tinggi* middle-/low-/high-income country. *Masalah perumahan bagi kebanyakan kaum yang ~ pas-pasan, merupakan probléma tersendiri.* The question of housing for the majority of people who are on a subsistence level of income constitutes a special problem. *negara Arab ~ minyak* an Arab oil-producing country.

hasis (*A*) hashish.

hasrat (*A*) longing, desire, urge, eagerness, need for, propensity for. *~ belajar* eagerness to learn. *~ hati/jiwa* motivation. *~ kuasa* need for power. *~ membunuh* blood lust. *~ séksual* lust.

berhasrat to have a wish to, desire.

menghasratkan to long/wish for, desire. *~ sebuah rumah idaman* to long for a dream house.

terhasrat longed/wished for, desired. *Ia peroléh apa yang ~.* He got what he wished for.

kehasratan wish, desire, longing.

hasta (*Skr*) cubit, i.e., the length from the elbow to the top of the middle finger = about 18 inches or 45.72 centimeters, a linear measure. *lengan ~* forearm. *tulang ~* ulna.

sehasta one cubit. *diberi sejengkal hendak ~* (or, *diberi ~ hendak sedepa*), *beroléh ~ hendak sedepa* give him an inch and he'll take a yard, i.e., to want more and more, never have enough. *mencari ~ yang sejengkal* (*M*) to look into the closeness of family relations.

menghasta to measure in cubits. *~ kain sarung* a fruitless act.

hastakarya handicrafts.

hasud I (*A*) envy, jealousy; → DENGKI, IRI *hati*.

menghasud to envy, be envious of.

penghasud envier.

hasud II → HASUT.

hasung (*M*) to incite, instigate; → ASUNG.

hasut (*A*) **menghasut(kan)** [and **menghasuti** (*pl obj*)] **1** to instigate, incite, excite. *Ia ~ masyarakat agar menentang kedatangan dokter tersebut.* He incited the community to oppose the arrival of the physician. **2** to goad, provoke.

terhasut agitated, disturbed, annoyed.

hasutan incitement, provocation.

penghasut agitator, inciter, provocateur. *~ rakyat* rabble-rouser.

penghasutan goading, agitating, provoking, incitement, excitation, provocation.

hasyarat (*A*) *binatang ~* disgusting animals, such as, rats, snakes, frogs, scorpions, ants, and insects, all of which are *haram*.

hasyiah (*A*) **1** annotation, gloss. **2** side, edge.

hasyis (*A*) hashish.

Hasyr and Hasyar (*A*) "The Assembly"; name of the 59th chapter of the Koran and the name of the day men will assemble on the field of Mahsyar to be judged by God.

hata → HATTA.

HATAH → HUKUM *antar tata hukum.*

hatam → KHATAM.

hati I liver; → LÉVER II, LIMPA. *Satu daripada fungsi ~ manusia ialah membersihkan darah.* One of the functions of the human liver is to purify the blood. *penyakit ~* hepatitis; → HÉPATITIS. *penyakit pengerasan ~* cirrhosis of the liver. *ibarat ~ ayam tercemar empedu, dimakan pahit tidak dimakan rasanya éman-éman* it's like a chicken liver polluted by bile, eaten it's bitter, not eaten it's regrettable, i.e., damned if you do, damned if you don't; → MALAKAMA. *~ ayam* chicken liver. *saté ~ ayam* chicken liver satay. *~ ikan hiu* shark liver. *ékstrak ~ ikan hiu* shark liver extract, squalese.

hati II 1 heart. *~nya berdebar-debar karena ketakutan.* Her heart pounded with fear. **2** heart, marrow, pith. *~ pohon* the heart of a tree. **3** heart (the seat of the emotions and feelings), mind, mood, disposition. *~ saya tidak ke situ.* I'm not in the mood for it. *~ sudah tak sedap lagi* a) peevishly, testily. b) uneasy. *selalu dekat di ~* keeping in touch. *tahu isi ~ seseorang* to know what's going on in s.o.'s heart. *bicara dengan ~ terbuka* to be open with s.o. *baik ~* kindhearted, good-natured/tempered. *bakar ~* to make s.o. angry, mortify. *berahi ~ (kepada)* to be passionate/aroused/mad about/infatuated. *berat ~* a) oppressed, heavy-laden; to fear, shrink from, be reluctant to. b) to incline toward, care for, be in sympathy with. *keputusan itu diambil dengan berat ~* bercabang to be of two minds, hesitate, vacillate. *berbalik ~* to become hostile. *bercagak ~* insincere. *besar ~* a) proud. b) glad, happy, pleased, elated. *bimbang ~* doubtful, hesitating, vacillating. *buah ~* sweetheart. *bulat ~* a) determined, resolute, firm. b) with all one's heart, wholeheartedly. c) obstinate, stubborn. *buruk/busuk ~* evil-minded, depraved, atrocious. *dapat ~* a) to please, give pleasure, seduce s.o. *dalam ~* to o.s., in one's own mind. *berkata dalam ~* membaca dalam ~ to read to o.s. *simpan dalam ~* to keep s.t. to o.s. *dari ~ ke ~* from one person to another, personal (talk, etc.). *datang ~* to take courage. *dengki ~* envy, spite. *geli ~* to feel like laughing; tickled, intrigued. *gerak ~* impulse, urge; intuition, presentiment. *gusar ~* angry. *hangat ~* delighted, pleased, elated. *hulu ~* pit of stomach, solar plexus. *iri ~* envious, jealous. *jantung ~* a) heart. b) favorite child, darling, apple of one's eyes. *jatuh ~ kepada* to fall in love with. *jauh ~ (ob)* to feel offended. *jauh di mata, jauh di ~* out of sight, out of mind. *jauh di mata, dekat di ~* absence makes the heart grow fonder. *kata ~* a) conscience, inner voice. b) effusion, outpouring. *kaya ~* generous, openhanded. *kecil ~* a) annoyed, irritated, offended, hurt (of feelings). b) cowardly, timid, fainthearted. *kecut ~* afraid, frightened, scared. *keras ~* firm, persevering, stubborn. *keruh ~* a) malicious. b) dirty, corrupt. *kurang ~* spiritless. *lapang ~* a) relieved. b) broadminded, tolerant. c) free from care, unconfined (of feelings). *lega ~* relieved, solaced. *lemah ~* without willpower/energy. *lembut ~* gentle, tender, considerate. *lubuk ~* the depths of one's heart; the subconscious. *lurus ~* honest, straight. *makan ~ (berulam jantung)* to eat one's heart out, brood. *melepaskan ~* to give free rein to one's feelings, allow one's feelings to flow freely. *membakar* – a) to hurt (deeply). b) to incite, instigate, stir up. *memberi* – to encourage. *membesarkan* – a) to gladden, rejoice, delight, encourage. b) to take heart, pull o.s. together. *membulatkan* – to make a decision. *memikat* – to seduce, entice, charm, lure. *menambat* – to charm, enchant, fascinate, captivate, enthrall. *menarik* – to captivate, grip, fascinate, attract (one's attention). *menaruh* – *kepada* to be in love with. *menawan* – to steal s.o.'s heart. *mencuri* – to prepossess in one's favor. *mendua* – a) to hesitate, waver. b) to simulate, feign, sham, pretend. *mengambil* – to flatter, cajole, seduce, insinuate o.s. into s.o.'s favor, impress favorably. *mengandung* – a) to harbor a grudge against, b) to take an interest in. *mengembangkan* – a) to stimulate, incite. b) to cheer s.o. up. *menghiburkan* – to entertain, amuse. *menjadikan* – to grieve, hurt, offend. *menjolok* – to sound s.o. (on/as to/about). *menusuk* – to hurt, offend. *murah* – generous, openhanded, unstinted. *panas* – ardent, excited, inflamed. *patah* – brokenhearted, desperate, discouraged. *puas* – satisfied. *rendah* – humble, modest, unpretentious. *sakit* – offended, harboring resentment. *sedap* – contented, glad, happy. *sedu* – sad, sorrowful, unhappy, depressed. *segan* – reticent, reserved, not forthcoming. *sejuk* – cheerful, happy. *sempit* – irritated, impatient. *senang* – contented, satisfied. *senang* – *memandanginya* he has a pleasant personality, he is a pleasant-looking person. *dengan segala senang* – with the greatest pleasure. *dengan setengah* – *salah* reluctantly, unwillingly, grudgingly, with an ill will. *suka* – pleased, contented. *susah* – morose, sullen, sourfaced, moody. *tawar* – dejected, depressed, cast down, disheartened. *tegar* – stubborn. *terang* – bright, intelligent, perspicacious. *tinggi* – haughty, proud, arrogant. *ada* – *pada* to have an inclination to. *tak sampai* – don't have the heart to. – *bagai baling-baling* an unstable standpoint. – *baja* firmness, a strong will. **berhati baja** firm, strong-willed. – *batu* a heart of stone. **berhati batu** to have a heart of stone, be insensitive (to feelings). – *beku* cold and unfeeling. – *bejat* pervert. – *cekal* brave, steadfast. – *dingin* unwilling(ly). – *emas* a heart of gold. – *kayu* pith. – *kecil* the deepest internal feelings. – *kecilku menyesal.* I regret it deeply. *dalam* – *kecil* in the back of my mind. – *kecut* → KECUT *hati*. – *keruh* worried, troubled. – *muda* young at heart. *orang tua yang* – *muda* an old person who is young at heart. – *mulia* generous, bighearted. – *nurani* a) conscience; super ego. b) innermost feelings. – *rapuh* brittle heart (a disease of trees). – *rotan* rattan core. – *sanubari* the (human) heart, deepest internal feelings. – *terbuka* frank, straightforward. – *terlonjak* overjoyed. – *yang susah* a feeling of depression.

hatinya one's heart, feelings. *kurang énak* ~ resentful, full of rancor. *membaiki* ~ to make (it) up again with him. *timbul dalam* ~ *akan* a) inclined, disposed to. b) to take a fancy to it. *dengan setulus-tulus* ~ with perfect single-mindedness. ~*nya berkait* two-faced, to say one thing and believe another.

hati-hatinya *sampai ke* ~ to the core, throughout, through and through, to the bottom of one's heart.

(ber)sehati unanimous, harmonious, in harmony, at one, in unison, united. **kesehatian** unanimity, agreement.

berhati 1 to have a heart. **2** kind, sympathetic. ~ *berjantung* to be sensitive, be delicate. *tidak* ~ *(berjantung)* a) insensitive, hard. b) shameless, unashamed. ~ *berlian* to be good-natured/tempered, be kindhearted. ~ *bimbang* to be worried/anxious. ~ *binatang* to be inhuman. ~ *emas* to have a heart of gold. ~ *iblis* to be a bad person. ~ *jantan* brave. ~ *keras* to have strong ideals. ~ *lapang* patient, relaxed. ~ *mutu* doleful, sad, gloomy. ~ *pilu* to be sad. ~ *putih* to have honest and straightforward intentions. ~ *rawan* melancholy. ~ *rendah* to be humble/modest. ~ *tungau* to be a coward. ~ *walang* to be worried/anxious. ~ *waja* to be persevering.

hati III attention. *dengan sepenuh* – with complete attention.

hati-hati attentive, prudent, careful, cautious; (of a cry/shout) take care, watch out, be careful/on your guard. ~ *anjing galak* beware of the dog. ~ *banyak anak-anak* watch out for children. ~ *kalau menyeberang!* Take care in crossing the street! *Kita harus bertindak* ~. We have to act cautiously/prudently. *kurang* ~ imprudent, careless. **kekurang-hati-hatian** impru-

dence, carelessness. **berhati-hati 1** to pay attention, take care. **2** attentively, carefully, prudently. **3** accurate, exact. **4** be careful, (do s.t.) carefully, (to listen to a suspect) with reservations. ~*lah bila mengemudikan mobil!* Be careful when you drive a car! **kehati-hatian 1** prudential, prudent. *prinsip* ~ prudential principles. **2** prudence. *mencerminkan* – *Indonésia dalam menyéléksi calon-calon dutabesar negara-negara besar yang ditempatkan di Jakarta* to reflect Indonesia's prudence in selecting candidate ambassadors of large countries who will be stationed in Jakarta.

memerhatikan, memperhatikan [and **merhatiin** (*J coq*)] **1** to heed, observe, pay attention to, watch, take note of, consider. *Pihak polisi telah memerhatikan segala gerak-gerik orang itu.* The police observed all the movements of those people. *Meréka tidak memperhatikan sedikit pun nasihat guru besar.* They didn't pay the slightest bit of attention to the professor's advice. *Pokoknya, siapa aja yang pimpin negara ini harus perhatiin nasib rakyat kecil.* The main thing is, anyone who leads this country must consider the fate of the man in the street. *tidak diperhatikan* unwanted, left out, ignored. **2** in light of. **3** attentive. **perhatikan(lah)** attention! **terperhatikan** paid attention to.

perhatian 1 attention, notice. –! Attention, please! **2** interest. *menaruh* – *terhadap* to show interest in. *dalam* ~ *khusus* special mention (of payments on debts).

pemerhati 1 observer. ~ *bulu tangkis* badminton observer. ~ *hukum* legal observer. ~ *masalah komputer* observer of computer problems/questions. – *masalah sosial-politik* observer of sociopolitical questions, sociopolitical observer. ~ *sosial-ékonomi pertanian dan pedésaan* village and agricultural socio-economic observer. **2** interested person.

hatif (*A*) voice. – *(al-ghaib)* voice (of an invisible person), mysterious voice.

Hatiwasda [Hakim-Tinggi-Pengawas-Daérah] High Judge Provincial Overseer.

hatsil → HASIL.

hatta (*Skr cla*) (– *maka*) then, further, next, and then.

hatur I (*Jv*) **menghatur** to offer/present (to). **menghaturkan 1** to offer/present s.t. to a high-ranking person. ~ *surat kepada Bapak Gubernur* to present a letter to the Governor (of a territory). **2** to express. ~ *selamat* to offer congratulations, congratulate.

hatur II → ATUR I.

haud (*A*) tank, cistern (*esp* in mosques).

hau-hau (*C?*) → MAIN-MAIN. in fun, joking, not serious. *Ini bukan usaha* –. This is a serious matter. *perusahaan* – dummy corporation, fictitious company.

haudah → HOWDAH.

haul I (*A*) **1** strength. **2** power, might.

haul II (*A*) **1** a full year. *Zakat untuk binatang-binatang dikenakan kalau binatang-binatang itu dimiliki tuannya selama satu tahun, yaitu cukup* –. A tithe on animals is levied when they have been in the possession of the owner for one year, that is, one full year. **2** annual commemoration of the death of a prominent person or the anniversary of s.o. in office.

haulan → HAUL II 2. *Gus Dur pada* ~ *Bung Karno.* Abdurrahman Wahid at the annual commemoration of the death of *Bung Karno*.

hauri (*A*) houri.

haus I 1 thirsty. **2** eager (for), hungry for. – *dahaga* a) very thirsty. b) craving. – *darah* bloodthirsty, bloodlust. – *informasi* hungry for information. *si* – *perang* warmonger. – *séks* hungry for sex, horny. **menghausi** to thirst for s.t.

menghauskan 1 to make one feel thirsty. *Matahari yang terik dengan cepatnya telah* ~ *pekerja-pekerja itu.* The strong sun quickly made the workers thirsty. **2** to be hungry for, have a strong desire for, thirst for. *Kanak-kanak yang tinggal di kampung-kampung terpencil* ~ *ilmu pengetahuan.* Children who live in isolated villages are hungry for knowledge.

kehausan 1 thirst. **2** eagerness, hunger for. **3** of/from thirst. *Meréka sesat di gurun dan mati* ~. They got lost in the desert and died of thirst. **4** to suffer from thirst.

haus II worn out; → AUS I. *Baju itu telah – dan tidak dapat dipakai lagi.* The dress is worn out and can't be worn again.

havermut → HAPERMOT.

hawa I (*A*) **1** air, gas. *mengambil –* to take a walk in the fresh air. **2** weather. **3** climate. *sudah serasi dengan –* to be acclimatized. *– daba* odor, smell. **berhawa-daba** to try to get, have aspirations for. *~ saja terhadap pekerjaan itu saya belum, apalagi melamarnya.* I have no aspirations for the job, much less will I apply for it. *– darat/laut/panas/sedang* continental/marine/tropical/temperate climate.

   berhawa with/to have a certain climate. *~ dingin/sejuk* air-conditioned.

   menghawa to volatilize, evaporate.

   penghawaan 1 ventilation. *~ silang* cross-ventilation. **2** evaporation.

hawa II (*A*) impulse, craving, lust. *– harta* craving for wealth. *– nafsu/napsu* passion, lust.

hawa III (*A*) *si –* the woman. *Sitti –* Eve. *kaum –* the fair/weaker sex, women.

Hawai Hawaii(an).

hawalat (*A*) (money) deposit.

hawar blight, i.e., a disease characterized by the rapid and extensive discoloration, wilting, and death of plant tissues. *– daun* leaf blight. *penyakit – daun karét Amérika Selatan* South American Leaf Blight, SATB. *– kalung* halo blight. *– kecambah* seedling blight. *– kedelai* bacterial blight. *– pelepah* sheath blight.

hawar-hawar → AUR-AUR.

hawari (*A*) Christ's disciples, apostles.

hawatir → KHAWATIR.

hawiah (*A*) the lowest level of hell.

haya oh boy!

hayal → KHAYAL.

hayali → KHAYALI.

hayam → AYAM I.

hayat I (*A*) life. *ada –* to be alive. *selama/sepanjang – dikandung badan* as long as I live. *ilmu –* biology. *tanda –* sign of life, keepsake.

   berhayat *tak ~* without life, lifeless.

   menghayati 1 to instill, familiarize with, make familiar with, educate, school, inspire. *di dalam usaha mengerti dan ~ nilai dan perilaku yang terkandung dalam Cyberspace, términologi …* in an effort to understand and instill the values and behavior in cyberspace, the terminology … **2** to make a commitment to, be committed to.

   kehayatan (*mod*) life, vital.

   penghayat instiller. *~ aliran kepercayaan* instiller of faith.

   penghayatan instilling. *~ kejahatan* school of crime.

hayat II (*cla*) *baju –* k.o. jacket.

hayati (*A*) **1** alive, vital. **2** biological, bio-. *keanékaragaman –* biodiversity.

hayo → AYO. come on! *Siapa – yang jadi suami saya dulu?* Come on. Who will be the first to marry me?

hayu → AYU I.

hayun → AYUN.

hazanah → KHAZANAH.

hazar (*Pers*) nightingale.

HB [Hindia Belanda] (*col*) Dutch East Indies.

HBS [Hogere-Burgerschool] (*col*) a five-year senior high school.

h.c. (*abbr*) → HONORIS CAUSA.

HCS [Hollands-Chinese School] (*col*) Dutch-Chinese School, i.e., an elementary school for Chinese which covered the first seven grades. Hollands (Dutch) refers to the language used as medium of instruction; *cp* ELS, HIS.

HD [Harley Davidson] trademark of an American-made motorcycle.

HD-wan Harley Davidson owner or rider.

hé I hey (there)! **2** eh? huh? hm? *Percaya atau tidak kamu, –?* Do you believe it, huh?

hébah (*A*) **1** gift; → HIBAH. **2** (*Mal*) announcement, broadcast. *juru –* radio announcer, broadcaster.

   menghébahkan 1 to announce, broadcast. *Meréka ~ berita yang baik itu.* They announced the good news. **2** to spread, *Orang*

yang mula-mula ~ ajaran Islam tidak diketahui dengan pasti. It is not known precisely who first spread Islam.

   penghébah announcer, broadcaster.

   penghébahan announcement, announcing.

héban I **menghéban** to throw/hurl s.t. heavy with both hands. *sudah dihéban dibéla pula* it never rains but it pours.

héban II (*A*) awe-inspiring.

hébat (*A*) **1** terrible, terrific, dreadful. *Sungguh – bunyi ledakan tadi.* The sound of the explosion a moment ago was really dreadful. **2** serious, severe, intense, strong. *perlawanan –* strong opposition. *saingan –* intense competition. *Sakitnya –.* He was seriously ill. **3** extraordinary, wonderful, grand, great, breathtaking. *– nampaknya.* He looks great. *Wah – lho!* Great! Good for you! *Pemandangan itu –.* The scenery was breathtaking. *Bentuk badannya –.* She has a great figure. *Memperoléh paspor bukan sesuatu yang –.* Getting a passport is no big deal. *– kelé-wat-léwat* really terrific.

   hébatnya and to top it all.

   sehébat as terrific as.

   menghébat 1 to get/grow worse, worsen, deteriorate. *Hura-hara itu –.* The rioting was getting worse. *Keadaan ~.* The situation is getting worse. **2** to run high (of feelings), flare up, rage, get out of control. *pada waktu ~nya* at the height of.

   menghébatkan and **memperhébat(kan)** to intensify, heighten, escalate, step up. *Penjagaan terhadap térorisme diperhébat.* Security against terrorism was stepped up.

   hébat-hébatan on a large scale, intensive(ly).

   terhébat the most terrific, etc.

   kehébatan 1 intensity. **2** grandeur.

   penghébatan intensification, escalation. *~ peperangan* escalation of the war.

héboh 1 noise, uproar, hullabaloo, tumult, commotion, upheaval, sensation. **2** scandal, scene, row, fuss, stir, furor.

   menghébohkan 1 to cause a tumult/commotion, create a sensation, sensational, controversial. *berita ~* sensational news. **2** to get excited about s.t. *Apa yang dihébohkan?* What's all the fuss about?

   kehébohan uproar, tumult.

hébring (*Pr*) great! terrific! magnificent! splendid!; → HÉBAT. *Memasuki kompléks yang beraspal dengan tatanan pepohonan yang terawat rapi, berdérét rumah –.* Entering a complex which was paved with rows of neatly cared for trees with lines of fantastic houses.

hédonis (*D*) hedonist.

hédonisme (*D/E*) hedonism.

hédonistik (*E*) and **hédonistis** (*D*) hedonistic.

he'e(h) and **he-e(h) 1** m-hm, uh-huh (informal yes). **2** yes, that's right.

hégémoni (*D/E*) hegemony.

hégémonik (*E*) hegemonic.

héh hey!

héhéhéhé don't make me laugh. *Meréka mau jadi kelinci percobaan –.* They would like to become guinea pigs, don't make me laugh.

hehem coughing.

héiho (*Jp*) non-Japanese conscript (during World War II).

héja → ÉJA.

héjrah → HIJRAH.

hék (*D*) **1** gate (*usu* made of iron). **2** fence; → PAGAR.

héksaklorofén (*D*) hexachlorophene (a bactericide used in soaps).

héksamétér (*D*) hexameter.

Héksmi [Himpunan Ésékutif Muda Indonésia] Indonesian Junior Executives Association, Indonesian Jaycees.

héktar (*D*) hectare.

   berhéktar-héktar hectares and hectares. *~ tanah yang dimilikinya* the hectares and hectares of land he owns.

héktogram (*D*) hectogram.

héktoliter (*D*) hectoliter.

héktométér (*D*) hectometer.

héla I pull, drag, haul.

   menghéla to drag, pull, haul (along the ground). *~ kotak yang kosong itu ke tempat sampah* to drag the empty box to the garbage heap. ~ *napas dalam-dalam/panjang-panjang* to take a deep breath, breathe deeply. ~ *napas lega* to breath a sigh of relief. ~ *surut* to withdraw, pull back. *bagai ~ rambut dalam tepung* the straw that broke the camel's back.

menghélakan 1 to drag s.t. along the ground. *Dihélakannya anaknya itu dengan perlahan-lahan menuju mobil yang sudah menanti.* She pulled her child slowly toward the waiting car. 2 *(ob)* to aim. ~ *senjata* to aim a rifle.

terhéla pulled, dragged. *tidak ~* immovable.

hélaan dragging, pulling, drawing, traction. ~ *napas* sigh, gasp.

penghéla s.o. or s.t. that pulls/drags, etc. *séktor ékonomi ~* leading economic sector.

penghélaan drawing, pulling, traction.

héla II → HÉLAT.

hélah 1 reason, excuse, pretext. 2 trick, ruse.

berhélah to look for excuses.

menghélah to trick, fool.

penghélahan tricking, fooling.

helai 1 sheet (of paper/woven material, etc.). 2 classifier (for thin objects, such as, leaves/paper, etc.). *tiga – sapu tangan* and *sapu tangan tiga* – three handkerchiefs.

sehelai one piece. ~ *napas* a sigh. ~ *papan* one board/plank. ~ *rambut* a single hair. ~ *sepinggang* the clothing on one's back.

berhelai(-helai) in sheets, with loose sheets.

helaian sheet.

hélak → ÉLAK.

helang → ELANG I.

helat 1 guest (at a celebration/party); stranger. 2 (traditional) party, banquet (at a wedding/circumcision); → ALAT II.

memperhelatkan ~ *perkawinan* to celebrate a wedding.

perhelatan celebration. (traditional) party, banquet (at a wedding/circumcision); → ALAT II.

hélat 1 trick, ruse. 2 excuse, pretext.

berhélat 1 to use a trick. 2 to use an excuse.

menghélat to cheat; → KILAH I.

hélem → HÉLM.

héli clipped form of hélikopter.

berhéli to use a helicopter. ~ *ke P. Seribu* by helicopter to Pulau Seribu.

hélicak *(acr)* → HÉLIKOPTER *bécak*.

hélikopter *(D/E)* helicopter, chopper. *Semua peserta akan diterbangkan dengan ~.* All the participants will be flown in by helicopter. *– antikapalselam* antisubmarine helicopter. *– bécak* a three-wheeled motorized becak, using a Lambretta scooter motor; the passengers, who sit in front of the driver, are in a closed dome-like compartment. *– bermeriam* helicopter gunship. *– penyapu ranjau* mine-sweeping helicopter. *– segala cuaca* all-weather helicopter. *– serang* attack helicopter. *– serbaguna* utility helicopter. *– yang diperlengkapi dengan meriam* helicopter gunship.

berhélikopter *polisi-polisi ~* police officers in helicopters, helicopter police officers.

héliograf *(D/E)* heliograph.

hélioséntrik *(E)* and hélioséntris *(D)* heliocentric.

héliotrop *(D/E)* heliotrope, *Heliotropium peruvianum.*

hélipad and hélipéd *(E)* helipad, a takeoff and landing area for helicopters.

hélium *(D/E)* helium.

hélm *(D)* /hélem/ 1 helmet (of an army man/motorcyclist, etc.). 2 pith helmet worn as a sunshade. *– bangunan* hard hat; → TOPI *proyék*. *– kuning* yellow helmet worn by *tukang ojék* in Bogor. *– penyelamat* crash helmet (used by motorcyclists). *– putih* white pith helmet. *– putih biasa dipakai oléh tuan-tuan tanah di jaman penjajahan.* The white pith helmet was usually worn by the landlords during the colonial period.

perhélman helmet *(mod)*.

hélmisasi the introduction/use of crash helmets. *Pelaksanaan – di 7 jalur kota Surabaya ternyata berjalan dengan lancar dan berhasil.* It seems that the introduction of crash helmets on 7 city roads in Surabaya is going well and is successful.

hem I (exclamation of distaste) ugh!

hem II wow. *Ya, saya punya seorang mami, Pémi namanya. Kalau*

memasak ayam, – lezat sekali rasanya. My mommy, her name is Pemi, when she cooks chicken, wow, it's really delicious.

hém *(D)* (western-style man's) shirt. *– batik* batik shirt. *– kutungan* a short-sleeved shirt. *– lengan panjang* short-sleeved shirt. *– lengan péndék* short-sleeved shirt. *– strip* striped shirt. *– yang berlengan panjang* long-sleeved shirt.

hémar *(A)* zebra.

hémat I 1 *(A)* 1a) thrifty, economical, frugal. b) thriftiness), economy. *pembakar –* economical burner. 2a) prudent, careful, cautious. b) prudence, care, caution. 3a) attentive, careful. b) attention, carefulness. c) ambition. *– (dan) cermat* careful, attentive. *Perkataan gurunya itu didengarnya dengan – dan cermat.* He listened to his teacher's words attentively. *– pangkal kaya* thrift is the foundation of wealth. *sia-sia – hutang tumbuh* penny wise and pound-foolish.

sehémat as economical as.

berhémat 1 to be economical; calculating. *Kalau hendak menyimpan uang, haruslah – membelanjakan uang.* If you want to save money, you have to spend money wisely. 2 to be cautious/careful. *ingat sebelum kena, ~ sebelum habis* look before you leap.

menghémat to economize, cut down (on expenses), save (time/money), cut corners. *Untuk mengulur-ulur anggaran, anda harus ~.* In order to stretch your budget, you've got to cut corners. ~ *tenaganya* to save one's energy. *Kanak-kanak sejak kecil perlu dilatih ~ uang.* From the time children are small, they have to be taught to spend less. ~ *waktu* to save time.

menghématkan to save (on), reduce (spending), spend less.

terhémat the most economical.

hématan calculation, computation.

kehématan economy, thriftiness.

penghémat s.t. that saves, saving. *sistém ~ bahan bakar* fuel saving system.

penghématan retrenchment, cut (in wages), curtailment, cutback, austerity. *untuk ~ tempat* for the sake of saving space. *Panitia itu tidak berpendapat bahwa ~ baik.* The committee doesn't believe in austerity.

hémat II *(A)* opinion, judgment. *menurut/pada – saya* in my opinion.

hématolog *(E)* hematologist; → AHLI *darah*.

hématologi *(D/E)* hematology.

hembalang berhembalang to roll, turn over and over, tumble. *lari ~* to run helter-skelter (or, in every direction).

menghembalangkan to sling, throw, hurl.

terhembalang rolled, turned over and over, tumbled.

hembus → EMBUS I. berhembus to blow. *Angin ~ kencang.* The wind blew strongly.

menghembuskan to breathe. *Belum sempat dokter menolong, korban sudah ~ nafasnya terakhir.* The physician was unable to help when the victim breathed his last. ~ *isu* to spread rumors.

terhembus 1 blown about (in the wind). 2 spread (of a rumor).

hembusan blowing. *waktu bagaikan ~ angin yang begitu cepat pergi* time flies.

penghembusan blowing. ~ *isu* spreading rumors. ~ *napas* expiration.

hémeralopi(a) *(E)* hemeralopia.

hémes → HÉMONG.

hémisélulosa *(E)* hemicellulose.

hémisfér *(D/E)* hemisphere.

hémodialisis *(E)* hemodialysis.

hémofilia *(E)* hemophilia. *penderita –* hemophiliac.

hémoglobin *(D/E)* hemoglobin.

hémong *(Pr)* gay, homosexual; → HOMO.

hémoragi *(D)* hemorrhage.

hémostatis *(E)* hemostatis.

hempang → EMPANG. menghempang to block. ~ *masuknya kayu curian* to block the introduction of stolen timber.

hempap → EMPAP.

hempas → EMPAS I.

hémpét → IMPIT.

hendak 1 (future marker) shall, will. 2 to intend to, plan to, be about to, on the point of ...-ing, willing, prepared; → AKAN, INGIN, MAU. *Dia – berangkat.* He is going to leave. *Mereka da-*

tang kemari – bertemu dengan Ketua DPR. They came here to see the Chairman of Parliament. *Tidak – menerima tamu itu.* Not willing/prepared to receive the visitor. **3** in order to; → UN-TUK. *ingin* – want to. *Uang – membuat belanja sesén pun tiada.* They don't even have a penny to go shopping. *– pun* even though/if. *– pun dikatakan cantik tidak juga.* Even if it is said that she's beautiful, she isn't. *– pun … tapi (tiada dapat karena …)* even though … but (it cannot be because ...). *– akan* and *– kan* to wish, want, desire (to have/own/possess/take, etc.). *Bukankah – akan mas kita.* it isn't that they want our gold. *Suaminya dalam masa beberapa bulan ini suka bercakap tentang hajatnya –kan seorang anak lelaki.* These last few months her husband has wanted to talk about his strong desire to have a son. *–lah* a) please, be so kind as. *Hendaklah diperhatikan benar nasihat itu.* Please, take the advice truly to heart. b) it is requested that ...; say, might. *Kalau mau séhat, hendaklah dimakan makanan bergizi.* If you want to be healthy, you must eat nutritious food.

hendaknya 1 it is/would be desirable, the (very) best thing you can do, the best thing/plan will be ...; should; → MUDAH-MUDA-HAN. *Aksi unjuk rasa ditangani secara bijaksana.* It's desirable that demonstrations be handled wisely. **2** (voluntative) let's. **3** it is to be hoped that, I hope that ... *jangan ~* I hope not.

meng(e)hendaki 1 to want, wish for, desire, have in view. *(yang) tidak dihendaki* undesirable. *lebih dikehendaki* preferable. **2** to require, need, demand, call for. *~ kesabaran* to require patience.

kehendak wish, want, desire, will, demand. *~ alam* nature, the natural/ordinary course of events. *atas ~ sendiri* of one's own accord/free will, on one's own initiative. *~ hati* one's desire. *sekehendak hatinya* **1** arbitrary. **2** to one's heart's content, absolute, unlimited. **berkehendak** to (entertain a) wish, intend to, hope to. *Saya ~ supaya adik saya akan mendapat keputusan yang baik dalam pemeriksaannya.* I hope that my younger sibling gets a favorable decision in his examination. **berkehendakkan** to have a desire for. *Ia menghadapi kewajiban memenuhi hati suaminya ~ anak lelaki.* She faces the obligation to fulfill her husband's desire to have a son.

hendam (M) *– karam* destroyed, wiped out.

hendap → ENDAP I, II.

héndel (D) handle. *– kunci pintu ruang tamu* door-key handle to the guest room.
menghéndel to handle.

héng (D) hand! (s.o. touched the ball with his hands in soccer).

hengah → ENGAH II.

hengit terhengit-hengit ailing for a long time.

héngkang (C) **1** to go away, withdraw, run away, flee. *–nya modal (keluar negeri)* capital flight; → PELARIAN *modal.* **2** to resign (from an association/party, etc.). *Datuk Asri lantas – dari PAS, dan bersama dengan beberapa pengikutnya, ia mendirikan Hizbul Muslimin.* Datuk Asri resigned immediately from the All-Malay Islamic Party and together with some of his followers, he set up the Hizbul Muslimin (Legion of Muslims).
sehéngkangnya *~ dari* after leaving/deserting from. *Cambridge membuka pintu lébar-lébar bagi Salam sebagai tenaga pengajar ~ dari Univérsitas Panjab.* Cambridge opened the door wide to Salam as an instructor as soon as he left Panjab University.
penghéngkang refugee. *Kapal-kapal pun diserobot oléh para ~ Albania dari bandar-bandar di negerinya.* The ships were grabbed by the refugees from Albania from the towns in their country.

hening 1 clear, clean (of water/intentions); → BENING. *Air perigi yang – itu digunakannya untuk mencuci pakaian.* He used the clean well-water to wash the clothes. **2** pure, free from impurities. **3** quiet, hushed, calm (of mind), silent, still. *di – malam* in the still of the night. *– sepi/sunyi* deathly quiet.
sehening as silent as.
berhening-hening to keep silent.
menghening to become silent.
mengheningkan 1 to clear, clean (from impurities). **2** to purify. **3** to make quiet, silence. **4** to concentrate s.t., meditate upon. *~ cipta* (Jv) a) to concentrate/purify one's thoughts, meditate. b) to stand in silence, bow one's head for a few moments

of silence; → SEMADI, TEPEKUR. **5** *diheningkan saja* (the statement) was ignored, no notice was taken of (the statement).
terhening to be silent; silenced, reduced to silence.
keheningan 1 clearness, cleanliness. **2** purity, calmness. **3** quietness, silence, stillness. **4** sincerity.
penghéningan 1 (the act of) purifying, purification, cleansing. *~ cipta* prayer (for the dead/good fortune, etc.). **2** (mystical) inner concentration.

henjot → ENJOT.

hénpon (E *hand phone*) [HP] cell phone, mobile.

hentak menghentak 1 to stamp, put (one's foot) down with force. *Kakak ~ kakinya ke lantai karena merajuk.* Older sister stamped her foot on the floor in a sulk. **2** to stomp on. *Kucing itu mati dihentak orang.* The cat died because s.o. stomped on it.
menghentak-hentak to throb, pulsate, palpitate; to tap (of the feet to music). *Hatinya ~ mendengar kabar itu.* His heart pounded hearing the news.
menghentak(-hentak)kan to smash, pound. *Anak itu menghentakkan tasnya ke atas méja.* The child smashed the purse down on the table.
terhentak stamped, smashed, stomped, etc.
hentakan stamping, pounding, stomping.
penghentak pestle, pounder.

hentam I → HANTAM.

hentam II menghentam(kan) *~ kaki* to stamp, put (one's foot) down with force.

hentar penghentar (Lutheran) pastor; → ANTAR I.

henti stopping, stop. *tiada –* without stop, continuously.
henti-hentinya *tanpa/tiada ~* ceaselessly, without stop.
berhenti 1 to stop, halt. *~!* avast! *tak ~nya* incessantly, unceasingly. *tanpa ~* incessantly, unceasingly. *tanda ~* stopping signal. *tempat ~* stopping/halting place, stop. *~ berdenyut* to skip a beat (of one's heart). **2** to end, finish, terminate, cease, be over. *Peperangan telah ~.* The war is over. **3** to (take a) rest (from work), pause, be still. *(hendak) ~ (dulu)* to take a rest. **4** to retire, withdraw, quit (a job), resign; to leave (stop being a member of a party, etc.). *minta ~* to tender one's resignation. *~ dengan hormat* to take an honorable discharge. **memberhentikan 1** to stop, bring to a standstill. **2** to dismiss, discharge, fire. **keberhentian 1** dismissal, discharge. *~ sementara* suspension. **2** withdrawal, retreat, resignation (from a job, etc.). **pemberhentian 1** dismissal, discharge, removal from office. *~ atas permintaan sendiri* dismissal at one's own request. *~ dengan mendapat hak pénsiun* dismissal with pension rights. *~ seketika* immediate dismissal. *~ sementara* suspension (of an employee). *~ tidak dengan hormat* dishonorable discharge (military). **2** walkout. *~ buruh* work stoppage. **3** suspension (of payment). **4** (infr) stop. *~ bis yang beratap* bus shelter; → SÉLTER *bis. ~ sela* shutdown.
berhenti-henti *tidak ~* repeatedly, without stopping.
berhentikan *~ lelah* to (take a) rest/break.
menghentikan and **memperhentikan 1** to (cause to/make s.t) stop, put a stop to, halt, flag down (a vehicle), turn off. *Mobil itu segera dihentikannya.* He immediately stopped the car. *Beberapa pompa bénsin di sepanjang Jalan Pramuka menghentikan kegiatannya karena listrik padam.* Several gas stations along Pramuka Road closed down due to an outage. *menghentikan penat* to (take a) rest. **2** to end, terminate, finish, conclude. *perintah ~ témbak-menémbak* a cease-fire order. *menghentikan larangan/tegah* to avoid prohibited things. *tidak bisa menghentikan tangan* a) to keep working continuously/uninterruptedly. b) cannot sit still. **3** to discharge, dismiss, fire. *diberhentikan dengan hormat* given an honorable discharge. **4** to suspend, abolish (temporarily), break off (talks). *Aturan penjagaan kampung akan dihentikan.* Village vigilance regulations will be suspended.
terhenti 1 come to a stop suddenly. **2** stopped, break down (of talks). **3** arrested (development). **keterhentian** sudden stoppage, impasse.
terhenti-henti with interruptions.
hentian (ling) stop.
penghentian 1 stopping, halting. *~ pembayaran* stop payment

(of a check). **2** suspension (of hostilities), cessation, stoppage. ~ *permusuhan* armistice. ~ *untuk sementara waktu* suspension.

perhentian 1 suspension (of hostilities), cessation, stoppage. **2** stop; → STOPAN. ~ *bis* bus stop. ~ *perjalanan sebelum mencapai tujuannya* stopover. ~ *tembak-menembak* ceasefire.

henyak → ENYAK I.

hépar (*D/E from Greek*) liver.

hépatitis (*D/E*) hepatitis.

hépéng (*Bat*) money.

hér (*D*) *héroriéntasi* (reorientation), *hérrégistrasi* (reregistration) and in *ujian* – reexamination.

héran (*A*) 1 surprised, astonished, amazed; surprise, astonishment, amazement. – *melihat/memikirkan* to be astonished over. **2** a wonder. *tidak – kalau/bila* no wonder that, it is not surprising that. **3** strange, odd, curious, bewildering, puzzling. – *bin ajaib* by a miracle, it was a miracle that, wonder of wonders, that is the limit, that beats everything.

menghéran to be amazed/surprised at.

menghérani 1 (*pl obj*) to surprise. **2** to admire.

menghérankan 1 to amaze, astound, puzzle; amazing, astounding, startling, puzzling. **2** to be puzzled about s.t.

terhéran-héran greatly amazed/astonished/surprised. *Kita menjadi ~ mengapa tamu-tamu Indonésia ini melakukan tindakan bermusuhan dengan cara melakukan kegiatan mata-mata.* We were greatly surprised at these guests of Indonesia taking hostile steps by engaging in spying.

kehéranan 1 surprise, amazement, astonishment. **2** (= **kehéran-héranan**) stupefied; strangeness, oddity.

hérba (*D*) herbs.

hérbal (*D/E*) herbal.

hérbarium (*D/E*) herbarium.

hérbisida (*D*) herbicide.

hérbivor(a) (*D*) herbivore.

hérbras (*D?*) gerbera, *Gerbera spp*.

hérder (*D*) (*anjing –*) sheepdog.

hérdines (*D*) corvée services.

hérdislokasi (*D*) redislocation (of one's shoulder, etc.).

héréditas (*E*) heredity.

héréditér (*D/E*) hereditary.

héréng menghéréngkan to slant, slope, tilt.

terhéréng slanted, sloped, tilted; → ÉRÉNG.

hériditas → HÉRÉDITAS.

hériditér → HÉRÉDITÉR.

herik mengherik to scream, shout, trumpet (of elephants); → ERIK.

hering → ÉRÉNG I.

héring (*E*) herring.

hérmafrodit (*D/E*) hermaphrodite.

hérmandad (*D ob*) the police.

hérménéutik(a) (*D*) hermeneutic(s). – *filsafati* philosophical hermeneutics.

hérmétis (*D*) hermetic.

hérnia (*D/E*) hernia, rupture; → BURUT.

héro (*E*) hero, principal figure; → PAHLAWAN.

héroik (*E*) and **hérois** (*D*) heroic.

kehéroikan heroism.

héroin (*D/E*) heroin.

héroisme (*D/E*) heroism.

hérordening (*D*) replanning.

héroriéntasi (*D*) reorientation.

hérot → ÉROT I.

hérpétologi (*D/E*) herpetology. *ahli* – herpetologist.

hérrégistrasi (*D*) re-registration.

hérscholing (*D*) /hérskoling/ refresher course, retraining.

hérut → ÉROT I.

hétero clipped form of **hétero***séksual*.

héterodoks (*D/E*) heterodox.

héterodoksi (*D*) heterodoxy.

héterofil (*D/E*) heterophile.

héterogén (*D/E*) heterogeneous.

kehéterogénan heterogeneity.

héterogénitas (*E*) and **héterogénitét** (*D*) heterogeneity.

hétero*séks* clipped form of **hétero***séksual*. *orang* – a heterosexual individual.

hétero*séksual* (*E*) and **héterosé***ksuil* (*D*) heterosexual.

hétero*séksualitas* (*D*) heterosexuality.

hévéa (*D*) a common variety of rubber tree.

héwan (*A*) animal, beast. *dokter* – veterinary surgeon. *ilmu* – zoology. *penyakit* – cattle plague. – *bantai* cattle for slaughter. – *berbelalai panjang* the elephant. – *bertulang belakang* vertebrate. – *beruas* arthropod. – *buruan* game, wild animals. – *hadyu* sacrificial animal. – *jinak* domestic animal. – *korban* sacrificial animal. – *kunyah* ruminant. – *liar* wild animal. – *mammal/menyusui* mammal. – *melata* reptiles. – *mentari* one-celled animals. – *penarik* draft animal. – *pengerat* rodent. – *piaraan* a) domestic animal. b) pet. – *potong* slaughter cattle/stock. – *tak bertulang belakang* invertebrates.

kehéwanan 1 bestiality. **2** fauna; relating to animals. *fakultas ~* school of veterinary medicine. **3** (*ob*) live-stock.

héwanah and **héwanat** (*A*) fauna, animal kingdom.

héwani (*A*) animal (*mod*). *lemak* – lard oils. *protéin* – animal protein.

héwaniat (*A*) beastlike.

hia (*C*) k.o. herbaceous plant, *Artemisia vulgaris*.

hianat → KHIANAT.

hiang → YANG I.

hiansay → KIANSAY.

hiap (*A?*) restless.

hias decorate, ornament. *ikan* – ornamental aquarium fish. *méja* – dressing table. *tukang* – decorator. *kendaraan* – *bunga* float (in a parade). – *daif* (*A*) window dressing (banking term), misrepresentation of s.t., so as to give a favorable impression. – *daun* foliage (as a design element).

berhias 1 ~ *diri* to adorn/beautify/make up (o.s.), dress up, embellish. *janda ~* a childless widow or divorcee who may dress as a virgin bride for her second wedding. ~ *mandi* ~ ceremonial bathing of the bride when she is adorned for her wedding. **2** (= **berhiaskan**) decorated/adorned/beautified with. *Pemilik rumah yang ~ sepasang gading gajah masing-masing sekitar 1,5 méter itu, di Jalan Daksa I, Kebayoran Baru, kini menjelang 60 tahun.* The owner of a house adorned with a pair of elephant tusks, each about 1.5 meters long, at Jalan Daksa I, Kebayoran Baru, is now approaching his 60th birthday.

berhiaskan to be decorated with.

menghias, menghiasi and **memperhiasi** to decorate, put ornaments on, adorn, make more beautiful by placing adornments on or in, embellish, garnish (cakes). *Dinding itu dihiasi gambar-gambar.* The wall was decorated with pictures. *Dia menghiasi rambutnya dengan bunga-bungaan.* She adorned her hair with flowers. *bintang-bintang yang menghias angkasa* stars which embellished the sky. *majalah yang di(per)hiasi gambar* an illustrated magazine.

terhias decorated, adorned, etc.

hiasan adornment, decoration, ornament, embellishment. ~ *bibir* lip service. *Ini hanya ~ bibir karena terbentur pada pengadaan lahan.* This is only lip service because it runs up against the availability of land. ~ *dinding* wall decoration. ~ *janur kuning* decoration of young coconut leaves.

penghias decorator, illustrator. ~ *bibir* lip service. ~ *étalase* window dresser. ~ *makanan* garnish (on food). ~ *sampul depan* cover girl.

penghiasan ornamentation, decorating.

perhiasan 1 decoration, ornament. **2** jewelry. ~ *kulit* tattooing. ~ *Natal* Christmas ornaments. ~ *tingkat tinggi* fancy jewelry. ~ *tingkat tinggi menurut définisinya adalah untuk suatu "peristiwa agung," atau peristiwa yang sangat luar biasa.* Fancy jewelry, by definition, is for an "impressive event," or a very uncommon event. **berperhiasan** to be decorated with. *Céwék 25 tahun itu adalah cukup tidur di vila méwahnya di sebuah bukit dekat Kota Cannes, ~ cukup kalung berlian besar.* The 25-year-old girl slept well in her luxurious villa on a hill near Cannes adorned with plenty of big diamond necklaces.

hiasinta (*D*) hyacinth.

hiat and **hiatus** (*D*) hiatus.

hiba → IBA.

hibah (A) **1** gift (during one's lifetime). **2** donation, grant. *– wasiat* legacy, bequest. **menghibahwasiatkan** to bequeath.

menghibahi to donate to.

menghibahkan to give (during one's lifetime; an Islamic practice), grant, donate.

hibahan grant, bequest.

penghibah donor.

penghibahan donation, gift.

hib(b)at (A) love, affection.

hibernasi (D) hibernation.

hibiskus (D/E) hibiscus.

hibrid(a) (D/E) hybrid. *– jagung* corn hybrid

hibridisasi (D) hybridization.

hibuk (J) busy; → SIBUK I. *– dan riuh berseling gaduh menyambutku di términal udara.* Business and crowds alternating with noise greeted me at the air terminal.

kehibukan business, activity.

hibur berhibur to amuse/entertain o.s.

menghibur 1 to amuse, entertain, divert. *~ diri* to distract/amuse o.s., relax. *untuk ~ diri* for amusement. **2** to console, comfort, relieve, cheer up, alleviate (grief/pain). *Seorang petugas Bala Keselamatan ~ para korban.* A Salvation Army official comforted the victims. *~ diri* to console o.s. *~ hati* to be a consolation (to).

menghiburi 1 to entertain/amuse s.o. **2** to divert, comfort, console, offer solace to.

menghiburkan 1 to entertain, amuse. **2** to console, comfort, cheer up. *Saya berusaha ~ hati adik saya, karena dia kelihatan sakit.* I tried to cheer up my younger brother, because he seemed to be ill.

terhibur comforted, consoled, relieved. *Setelah mendengar berita dari suaminya, ~lah sedikit hati Roosnani.* After having heard the news from her husband, Roosnani was somewhat relieved. *tidak ~* not to be comforted, disconsolate, inconsolable.

terhiburkan consolable. *kedukaan yang tidak ~* an inconsolable grief.

hiburan recreation, distraction, amusement, entertainment. *pusat/taman ~* amusement center/park, place to amuse o.s. *Tempat ~ yang satu-satunya di kota itu ialah sebuah bioskop.* The only place for amusement in that town is a movie theater.

penghibur 1 entertainer, performer. *wanita ~* hospitality girl, prostitute. **2** consoler, comforter. *untuk ~ hati* a) to console. b) for relaxation. **3** diversion.

penghiburan 1 entertaining, amusing, diverting. **2** entertainment, recreation, amusement. *ruang ~* recreation room. **3** consolation.

hidam → IDAM I.

hidang serve, offer, present.

menghidangi to serve (s.t.) to s.o.

menghidangkan 1 to serve/offer/present food/drinks, etc. *Bapak sedang menolong ibu ~ makanan untuk sarapan pagi.* Father was helping mother serve food, etc. for breakfast. **2** to present, introduce, show, exhibit. *Toko Buku Gramédia ~ kamus-kamus terbaru keluaran Malaysia.* The Gramedia Book Store exhibited the latest dictionaries published in Malaysia.

terhidang served, offered. *air téh yang ~* the tea that was served.

hidangan 1 dishes, food that is served, meal. *~ kilat* (infr) fast food. *réstoran ~ kilat* fast food restaurant. *~ laut* sea food. *~ rohani* spiritual nourishment. **2** presented, showed, exhibited. *busana ~* clothing exhibited (in a fashion show). **3** (= **penghidangan**) presentation, performance. *~ sandiwara* stage performance. **sehidangan 1** a course (in a meal), plateful. **2** the same dish. *makan ~* to eat from the same dish (together).

penghidangan presenting, serving.

hidap menghidap to suffer from a disease or an illness (for a long time); → IDAP I.

hidayah and **hidayat** (A) (God's) guidance.

hidmat → KHIDMAT.

hidran (D) (*pompa*) *–* hydrant.

hidrat (D) hydrate. *– arang/karbon* carbohydrate.

hidraulik (E) and **hidraulis** (D) hydraulic.

hidraulika (D) hydraulics.

hidrofilik (E) hydrophilic.

hidrofobik (E) hydrophobic.

hidrogén (D/E) hydrogen. *bom –* hydrogen bomb.

hidrogénasi (D) hydrogenation.

terhidrogénasi hydrogenated. *mentéga putih ~* hydrogenated shortening.

hidrogéologi (E) hydrogeology.

hidrogéologiwan hydrogeologist.

hidrografi (D/E) hydrography.

hidrografis (D) hydrographic.

hidrokarbon (E) hydrocarbon.

hidrokraker (E) hydrocracker.

hidroksid(a) (D) hydroxide.

hidrolis → HIDRAULIK.

hidrolisis (E) hydrolysis.

menghidrolisis to hydrolyze.

hidrolistrik (E) hydroelectric.

hidrologi (D/E) hydrology. *ahli –* hydrologist.

hidrologis (D) hydrological.

hidrométer (D/E) hydrometer.

hidrométéorologi (D/E) hydrometeorology.

hidroponik (E) hydroponics.

berhidroponik hydroponic.

hidrosfér (D/E) hydrosphere.

hidrostatika (D) hydrostatics.

hidu menghidu to sniff, smell, scent.

hidung nose. *–nya tertarik oléh wangi saté yang dibakar.* The smell of barbecued sate tickled his nose. *Ia tidak menampakkan batang –nya.* He didn't show up. *besar –* proud, arrogant. *di muka –* under one's (very) nose. *tajam –* a keen nose. *potong – rusak muka* it's an ill bird that fouls its own nest; don't cut off your nose to spite your face. *– dicium, pipi digigit* feigned/simulated love. *– bajak* beak (of a plowshare). *– bak/sebagai dasun tunggal* a beautifully pointed nose. *– belang* Don Juan, playboy, ladies' man, womanizer, philanderer. *para – belang yang mencari kepuasan séks* the womanizers who were looking for sexual satisfaction. *sepasang merpati – belang* a couple of lovebirds. *– beringus* a nose full of mucus. *– cérét* the spout of a kettle. *– kapur* Don Juan, playboy, womanizer. **berhidung kapur 1** to seduce women. **2** to have one love affair after another. *– ketam* handle of a plane. *– mampet* clogged nose. *– mancung* sharp, fine-shaped nose. **berhidung mancung** with a sharp, finely shaped nose. *– (mancung-)melengkung* aquiline nose. *si – mancung* k.o. monkey; → BEKANTAN. *(beroléh) – panjang* to look blank/foolish. *beroléh – panjang* to be shamed. *– papar* flat nose. *– péok* pug nose. *– pésék* flat nose. *– pésék melébar* saddle nose. *– pintu* latch, wedge plate. *– putih* Don Juan, playboy, ladies' man, womanizer, philanderer. **berhidung putih 1** to seduce women. **2** to have one love affair after another. *– yang menjungkat* turned-up/pug nose.

berhidung to have a nose, (provided) with a nose.

menghidung 1 (= **kehidung-hidungan**) speak nasally, be nasal. **2** always following/obeying, compliant.

hidup 1 live, be alive, living; *opp* MATI I. *Ibunya masih –.* Her mother is still alive. *kebahagiaan –* happy life. *matahari –* the rising sun. *seumur –* as long as I live, lifelong. **2** to live, stay, reside, dwell. *binatang-binatang yang – di air* animals that live in the water, aquatic animals. *– di kota besar tidak selamanya lebih senang daripada – di désa-désa.* Urban living is not always more comfortable than living in a village. **3** to live, pass one's life in a specific way. *Pada masa ini keluarganya – berbahagia dan méwah.* At this time his family is living in a happy and luxurious way. *Kita harus – dengan hémat.* We have to live economically. *Itulah –.* C'est la vie, that's life. *– atau mati!* sink or swim! *– terus bergulir* the show must go on. **4** to live (by), make one's living (by). *Orang-orang di kampung ini – dari/dengan bercocok tanam dan bersawah.* The villagers live by farming and working the rice fields. *Lembu, kambing dan kuda – dengan rumput.* Cows, goats, and horses feed on grass. **5** long live, (three) cheers for ...., hail to ... *– Indonésia!* Long live Indonesia! *Meréka* *menyeru,"-.–!"* They shouted out "Hail, hail!" **6** not forgotten, immortal. *Meskipun orangnya telah mati, tetapi namanya tetap –.* Though the person has passed away, his name is still alive. **7** still working/going/running, active (of volcanoes). *Walaupun jam tangan ini telah dijatuhkannya tetapi masih – lagi.* Although he dropped his wristwatch it's still working. *Di Indonésia masih masih terdapat beberapa buah gunung berapi yang –.* There are still some active volcanoes in Indonesia. **8** still burning, on fire, aflame, aglow. *Arang di dalam dapur masih – lagi.* The charcoal in the kitchen is still burning. **9** fresh (not preserved) *susu –* fresh milk. **10** in operation, running, start up (of an engine). *Pabrik gula itu masih –.* That sugar factory is still in (full) operation. **11** lively, active (market). *Menjelang hari Lebaran, perdagangan kain dan cita – kembali.* Prior to Lebaran day, trading in sarongs and chintzes is active again. **12** lifelike, looks alive. *benar-benar – lukisan ini* this drawing is really lifelike. **13** live (not recorded). *musik –* live music. *cara –* lifestyle, style of living. *darah –* fresh blood (not coagulated). *daun –* sensitive plant, *Mimosa pudica;* → PUTERI *malu.* *gambar –* movie, motion picture. *hikayat –* biography. *huruf –* vowel. *matahari –* the east. *pandangan –* view/philosophy of life, weltanschauung. *riwayat –* biography. *sikap –* attitude to life. *teman –* life-partner. *mencari –* to make attempts to save o.s. *– sama –, mati sama mati* at one, in harmony, of one mind, unanimous. *antara – dengan mati/napas satu dua* to hover between life and death. *– segan mati tak mau* shy of working for a livelihood but unwilling to die (said of the lazy). *– dikandung adat, mati dikandung tanah* as long as one lives, one has to follow the existing regulations and customs, after one's death everything is up to God. *– dua muara* to wear two hats. *– kayu berbuah, manusia biar berjasa* it's nice when one is still alive to do good for o.s. and for the community. *– sandar-menyandar umpama aur dengan tebing* a) a married couple who love e.o. b) a loyal friend who is willing to help. *– tidak karena doa, mati tidak karena sumpah* build on your strength and ideas and don't expect help from others. *daripada – bercermin bangkai, lebih baik mati berkalang tanah* it's better to die than to bear disgrace. *jauh berjalan banyak dilihat, lama – banyak dirasa* having had plenty of experience in life; → *sudah banyak makan* GARAM. *kalau bangkai galikan kuburnya, kalau – sediakan buaiannya* first wait quietly to see what's going to happen, and than make your decision. *– berkebau-kerbau* to live together without being married, shack up; → KUMPUL *kebo. – bermasyarakat* to be out on one's own (of children). *– berpisah* separated from bed and board. *– bersama* a) co-existence. b) gregariousness. *– bersama secara damai* peaceful co-existence. *– dengan segala genap* to live the good life, live in clover. *– di bawah tangan orang* to be subordinate to others, be dependent on others. *– hina* to lead a rotten life. *– kelamin* sex life. *– longgar* to live in (grand) style, live beyond one's means. *– jujur* to live an honest life. *– kebingungan* to go around in a state of confusion. *– mati* a) on-off. b) life or death (decision, etc.). *menghidupmatikan 1* to switch/turn on and off. *~ listrik* to turn the electricity on and off. *~ mesin listrik* to switch an electric engine on and off. *2* to have the power of life and death over. *Walikota berwenang ~ organisasi massa di wilayahnya.* The mayor has the power of life and death over the mass organizations in his territory. *– menderita* to live through hell. *– menetap* sedentary life. *– menyendiri* to live a solitary life. *– morat-marit* to lead a precarious existence. *– pisah* long-distance marriage, to live apart. *– rukun-damai* to live in harmony/concord. *– selamanya* to go through life. *– sendiri* to make it on one's own terms, to continue to exist, endure, subsist, survive. *– Senin-Kemis* to live from hand to mouth. *– sesat* to be led astray. *yang – terlama* the survivor, the surviving (spouse). *– terus* to continue to exist, endure, subsist, survive.

hidup-hidup (while still) alive. *ditangkap ~* to be captured alive.

sehidup *~ semati* a) in life and in death, for life, lifelong. b) (during the Japanese occupation interpreted as) one lives (i.e., the Japanese) and one dies (i.e., the Indonesians). *Ia menjanjikan ~ semati dengan seorang pemuda.* She promised a young man to live with him for life.

berhidup to live life (in a certain way). *~ méwah* to lead a luxurious life.

menghidupi 1 to allow s.o. to live, keep alive, let live. *Pembunuh yang tertangkap tidak akan dihidupi lagi.* The captured killer won't be allowed to live. **2** to maintain, support, provide sustenance for, take care of. *Siapa ~ siapa?* Who supports whom? *Pria itu harus ~ istri dan anak-anaknya.* That man has to support his wife and children.

menghidupkan 1 to resuscitate, resurrect, revive, restore/bring back to life; to put new life into, revivify. *Tuduhan ~ séktarianisme dibantahnya.* He denied the accusation that he had revived sectarianism. *Pembajaan yang teliti dapat ~ pohon itu.* A thorough fertilization can bring the tree back to life. *Seni batik dihidupkannya.* He revived the art of batik. *~ lagi* to breathe new life into. **2** to switch/turn on, activate, start up. *~ lampu/radio* to turn on the light/radio. *~ mesin* mobil to start a car. *~ kembali* to revive.

memperhidup(kan) to enliven, stimulate, strengthen, invigorate.

terhidup keterhidupan viability.

hidupan living organism. *Ikan paus adalah ~ laut yang terbesar sekali.* The whale is the largest maritime living organism. *~ liar* wildlife. *Hutan alam adalah habitat utama ~ liar.* Virgin forests are the primary habitats for wildlife. *Masyarakat Pelestari ~ Liar Indonésia* [MPHLI] Indonesian Wildlife Conservation Society.

hidup-hidupan living organisms.

kehidupan 1 life. *bidang ~* walk of life. *~ beragama* religious life. *~ berbangsa dan bernegara* life as a nation and as a state. **2** livelihood, sustenance. **3** mode of living. *~ berdampingan* coexistence. *~ berdampingan secara damai* peaceful coexistence. *~ bermasyarakat* social life. *~ duniawi* worldly life. *~ keakadémian* academic life. *~ keluarga yang berantakan* broken homes. *~ malam* night life. *~ pernikahan* married life. *~ pribadi* privacy. **berkehidupan** to live. *Meréka ~ di atas sampan.* They live on boats.

penghidup starter, s.t. that ignites s.t. else.

penghidupan 1 way of living, livelihood, sustenance. *~ dengan biaya tinggi* high cost of living. *~ malam/spiritual* night/spiritual life. **2** starting (an engine).

hiéna (D) hyena.

hiérarki (D) hierarchy.

higiéne (D/E) hygiene.

higiénis (D) hygienic.

higina (D) hygiene.

higrométer (D/E) hygrometer.

higroskop (D/E) hygroscope.

higroskopis (D) hygroscopic.

hih → IDIH, IH.

hihid (S) a flat bamboo-plaited fan (for making a kitchen fire).

hijab (A) curtain, veil.

hijah (A) single act of pilgrimage.

hijau 1 green. *baju –* a) green uniform. b) military man. *berpakaian –* to be an army man. *gaun berwarna – telur bébék* a Williamsburg-green gown. *lampu –* a) green-colored traffic light used to signal drivers, pedestrians, etc., that they may proceed. b) permission, consent; approval; authorization. *Lampu – DK PBB untuk invasi Haiti.* Authorization of the United Nations Security Council for an invasion of Haiti. *lapangan –* sports grounds. *si – (coq)* the greenback, U.S. dollar. *Bila si – jatuh.* When the dollar falls. **2** unripe. *Mangga itu masih –.* The mango is still green/unripe. **3** inexperienced. *gadis itu masih – that girl is still inexperienced. *– daun.* a) leaf-green, chlorophyll. b) *tidak mengerti – daun* be inexperienced. *Mas'ud, bocah tiga tahun yang belum mengerti – daun, Jumat pekan lalu téwas tertémbak di Modung, Pangkalan, Madura.* Mas'ud, an innocent little boy of three, was shot to death at Modung, Bangkalan, Madura, Friday of last week. *– gadung* light green. *– jelak* vivid green. *– kaki* olive brown, khaki. *– laut* aquamarine. *– lumut* moss green. *– muda* light green. *– nuri* parrot green. *– pupus* yellowish green. *– tanaman* chlorophyll. *– tembaga* verdigris. *– tentara* army green. *– tua* dark green. *– zamrud* emerald green.

hijaunya the greening of (*usu* reference to the military) *semakin*

~ *komposisi kabinét* the increasing number of army men in the cabinet.

sehijau as green as.

sehijau-hijau ~ *taman sendiri, lebih hijau taman tetangga* the grass is always greener on the other side of the fence.

menghijau 1 to be(come) or turn green. *Bocah-bocah tak berbaju menggiring sapinya ke hamparan rumput yang ~ di tepi hutan.* Naked children herded their cattle to a carpet of grass which was turning green on the edge of the forest. 2 to appear to be green, look green. *Padang rumput di hadapan kami ~.* The meadow in front of us appeared to be green.

menghijaukan 1 to (make) green. ~ *pagar* to paint the fence green. 2 to (re)forest, plant trees. ~ *daérah-daérah yang tidak ditumbuhi tanam-tanaman* to reforest areas on which trees are not growing.

hijauan greens (for cattle fodder), forage. ~ *kering* hay. ~ *potong* cut forages.

hijau-hijauan greenery.

kehijauan 1 greenness. 2 unripeness, immaturity. 3 inexperience.

kehijau-hijauan greenish.

penghijau greening, s.t. that makes s.t. green.

penghijauan 1 greening. 2 the green revolution. ~ *dunia* the greening of the world. 3 planting. 4 reforestation. 5 militarism; militarization, i.e., the appearance of large numbers of military officers as ministers, directors-general, governors, and local administrators, since the mid-1960s.

hijaunisasi "greenization," painting objects green in support of the PPP.

Hijaz (*A*) the original name of Saudi Arabia.

Hijr (*A*) "The Hejirah"; name of the 15th chapter of the Koran.

hijrah (*A*) 1 Muhammad's flight from Mecca to Medina (ca. A.D. 622). *tahun –* the year of the *hijrah*, A.H. 2 the evacuation of Indonesian army troops from pockets in Dutch-occupied West Java to Indonesian-occupied Central Java in conformity with the Renville Agreement. 3 evacuation (to save one's life). *–nya tenaga intéléktual dan profésional* brain drain of intellectuals and professionals. 4 (in politics) to switch parties.

berhijrah 1 to evacuate. 2 to emigrate.

menghijrahkan to evacuate s.o.

penghijrahan 1 evacuation. 2 emigration.

hijriah (*A*) related to the *hijrah*. *tahun –* the era which begins at Muhammad's flight from Mecca to Medina, A.H.

hik (*Jv*) snack food sold off a cart.

hikayat (*A*) 1 story, tale, annals, romance (a Malay literary genre). *– hidup* biography, curriculum vitae. *– Raja-Raja Pasai* history of the Rajas of Pasai. *– Tanah Melayu* Malay Annals. 2 history.

berhikayat to tell/relate/narrate a history.

menghikayatkan to tell/relate/narrate the history of.

hikmah and **hikmat** (*A*) 1 wisdom; (deeper) insight. *dipimpin oléh – kebijaksanaan* to be led by wise guidance. 2 divine wisdom. 3 supernatural (power), magic, witchcraft, sorcery. *ahli –* magician. *batu/gemala –* magic stone. *mengambil –* to learn from s.t. *Ahli sihir itu dihormati oléh umum karena ia dipercayai mempunyai – (kebijaksanaan)* The magician was respected by the public because they believed he possessed magic powers. *– (kebijaksanaan) musyawarah* (a phrase in notarial instruments on foundations, etc.) wisdom born of consultation.

berhikmat 1 (supernaturally) gifted/talented. 2 to have wisdom; wise, insightful. *slogan yang –* a wise slogan.

menghikmat(i) to bewitch, enchant, fascinate, cast a spell over. *Ilmu pengetahuan telah menghikmatinya.* Science has cast a spell over him.

hikwan (*C*) fish balls.

hilaf → KHILAF.

hilah → HÉLAT.

hilal (*A*) new crescent moon; → RUKYAH *hilal.*

hilalang → LALANG I.

hilang 1 lost, gone, disappeared, vanished, missing. *Anaknya –.* His child disappeared/got lost. *Uangnya –.* His money is gone. *dinyatakan – sama sekali* to be declared a total loss. *orang –* missing person. 2 sank, wrecked (of ship). 3 passed away. *Ayahnya*

– pada pertengahan bulan lalu. His father passed away the middle of last month. 4 thrown away. *Akibat kelemahan administrasi itu, –lah waktu satu tahun bagi CW, untuk mengenyam keadilan.* As a result of weakness of the administration, a period of one year was thrown away for CW to enjoy justice. 5 (+ *di-*) completely. *Surat-surat berharga – dicuri.* Valuable documents were stolen. *Suara musik dari radio kasét tidak terdengar jelas, – ditelan tawa ria anak-anak itu.* The sound of music from a cassette radio couldn't be heard clearly because it was drowned out by the cheerful laughter of the children. *esa –, dua terbilang* a) tried hard until one's goal is achieved. b) (motto of the Siliwangi Army Division stationed in West Java) For each man fallen, two will spring up to replace him. *– dicari, terapung direnangi, terbenam diselami* to investigate a matter in detail. *– satu, sepuluh gantinya* for each man fallen, two will spring up to replace him. *– tak bercari, lulus tak berselam* everything leaves one cold, don't care a bit. *– tak tentu rimbanya, mati tak tentu kuburnya* a) vanished into thin air. b) a thing the outcome of which can be predicted. *tunggang – tak* - fortune favors the bold. *– akal* to lose one's head. *– arwah* a) faint, be unconscious. b) lost one's senses. *– dara* (a deflowered girl) no longer a virgin. *– dalam tugas* missing in action, MIA. *– dari mata* disappeared/vanished (from sight). *– gaib* vanished into thin air. *– harapan* abandoned hope. *– hayat, padam jiwa* passed away. *– ingatan* a) unconscious, fainted. b) forgetful. c) crazy, insane. *– keberanian* cowardly. *– kedengaran* faintly audible. *– kelihatan* sometimes discernible, faintly visible. *– keberaniannya* lost courage. *– kesabaran* to lose one's patience. *– kikis* entirely lost/vanished/disappeared/faded away, swept away. *– lenyap/tak berbekas/ketentuan rimbanya* vanished into thin air, disappeared without (leaving) a trace. **menghilanglenyapkan** to cause to disappear. *– malu* lost one's self respect. *– muka* to lose face. *– napas* apnea, breathlessness. *– nyawa* passed away. *– pencaharian* to lose one's livelihood. *– pikiran* at a loss for words. *– redam* completely lost. *– semangat* a) to lose one's enthusiasm, get discouraged. b) to faint, fall unconscious. *– seri* evaporate, evaporated. *– suara* aphonic. *– tempur* missing in action. *– terkikis* lost, vanished, disappeared.

hilang-hilang 1 a) ~ *timbul* (*antara ada dengan tiada*) (*dalam ingatan*) to have a faint/dim recollection. b) (*dalam pikirannya*) to vacillate, waver. 2 (of the voice) barely audible. 3 to bob up and down, float (in water). 4 (of a street) almost inundated/flooded street(s). **sehilang-hilang** ~ *dari mata* until one has lost sight of s.o. or s.t.

menghilang to disappear, vanish. *Meréka ~ di tikungan jalan.* They disappeared around the corner (of the street).

menghilangkan [and **menghilangi** (*ob*)] 1 to make s.t. or s.o. disappear/go away. 2 to eliminate, wipe out, get rid of, do away with, remove. 3 to omit, delete, leave out. ~ *baunya* to deodorize. ~ *capai* to relax. ~ *diri* to disappear. ~ *haus* to quench one's thirst. ~ *kantuk* to ward off sleep. ~ *kata* to omit/leave out a word. ~ *kelelahan* to rest, take a break. ~ *kesan* to remove an impression. ~ *lapar* to satisfy one's hunger. ~ *nyawa* to kill, take s.o.'s life. ~ *payah/penat* to rest, take a break. *untuk ~ rasa sunyi* to relieve one's loneliness. ~ *sakit* to deaden the pain. ~ *salah pengertian* to clear up a misunderstanding.

kehilangan 1 disappearance, loss, deficiency. ~ *darah* loss of blood. ~ *mémori* dementia. ~ *kejantanan* impotence. ~ *kontrol* loss of control. 2 to lose; lost; suffer the loss of s.t. or s.o. due to death, negligence, accident, etc. ~ *akal* to lose one's head. ~ *cairan badan* dehydrated (of a person). ~ *idéntitasnya* lost its identity. ~ *jejak* to lose track of s.o. ~ *kejantanan* to become impotent. ~ *keseimbangan* to lose one's balance. ~ *muka* to lose face. ~ *nyawanya* to lose one's life. ~ *pandangan* blackout (of pilot due to G-force). ~ *pedoman* to be lost, not knowing what to do. ~ *pegangan* to lose one's bearings.

penghilang s.t. which removes/deletes s.t. ~ *cat/pernis kuku* nail-polish remover. ~ *karat* rust remover. *krim ~ sélulit* cellulite removing cream.

penghilangan 1 omission. 2 de-. ~ *bau* deodorizing. ~ *és* deglaciation. ~ *warna* decolorizing.

hilap → KHILAF.

hilat → HÉLAT.

hilau (*M ob*) berhilau(-hilau) to perform a death dance.

hilir 1 down river, downstream; *opp* HULU. *ke* – to go/sail downstream. *industri* – downstream/secondary industry; *opp* INDUSTRI *hulu*. 2 lower course/reaches (of a river), river mouth, estuary. – *malam mudik tak singgah, daun nipah dikatakan daun abu* to feel ashamed, reluctant, etc. because of a debt of honor. *seorang ke* – *seorang ke mudik* there's no agreement. *sudah terlalu* – *malam, apa hendak dikata lagi* a wrong act that cannot be helped. *tidak tentu* -*nya, tidak berketentuan bulunya* the aim and goal are uncertain. *tidak mengetahui bulu* -*nya* undecipherable as to the beginning and end, incoherent. – *malam* late (at night). – *mudik* (to go) to and fro, back and forth. *orang yang* – *mudik* commuter. *tak tentu* – *mudiknya* cannot make heads or tails of it, can make no sense of it. *belum tentu* – *mudiknya* it's not yet sure how things will develop/turn out. *Kita mulai omong-omong ke* – *ke mudik.* We began to chat about all sorts of things. **menghilirmudiki** to go back and forth over. **menghilirmudikkan** can make or break.

sehilir going downstream together. – *semudik* having the same aim, having the same goals. ***bersehilir-semudik*** ~ *dengan* to go through thick and thin with.

berhiliran always flowing, to flow here and there. ~ *air matanya* his tears flowed.

menghilir to sail to the mouth of a river or estuary.

menghiliri to go downstream on. ~ *sungai* to follow a river downstream, sail to the mouth of a river or estuary.

menghilirkan 1 to let (a raft, etc.) go downstream, set (a raft, etc.) adrift in the direction of the current, float s.t. downstream. 2 to divert (a conversation).

berkehiliran certain, sure of. *dengan tidak* ~ (*ob*) arbitrary.

hiliran downstream; → HILIR 1.

him (in acronyms) → PERHIMPUNAN.

himah → HÉMAT I.

himar (*A*) zebra.

himat → HÉMAT I.

himbau call, appeal. *siamang* – howling-monkey, howler.

menghimbau 1 to call. *Ibu* ~ *nama anaknya yang telah hilang itu.* Mother called out the name of her child who had disappeared. 2 to appeal to (s.o. or s.t.). *Ketua Umum PDI* ~ *anggotanya supaya membantu mengentaskan kemiskinan.* The PDI's General Chairwoman made an appeal to the membership to assist in relieving poverty.

terhimbau 1 called. 2 appealed.

himbauan 1 call. 2 appeal.

penghimbauan appeal, call (to do s.t.).

himén (*E*) hymen.

himmah and himmat → HÉMAT. *tinggi* – full of ambition/aspirations.

himne (*D*) hymn.

Himpemi [Himpunan pengusaha muatan Indonésia] Indonesian Freight Forwarders Association.

himpit pressed/very close together.

berhimpit(-himpit)(an) to push/press/squeeze e.o., jostle/ elbow e.o., crowd. *Ramai orang berhimpit-himpit menaiki bus itu.* The people crowded onto the bus. *Lapangan yang luasnya sekitar satu setengah kali lapangan bola, penuh sesak dengan massa, yang berhimpit-himpitan hingga ke jalanan di sekitar lapangan.* The stadium, which was as big as one and a half ball fields, was full of people who were crowding e.o. out into the roads surrounding the stadium.

menghimpit to crush, press/squeeze (down on). *Janganlah* ~ *kotak ini karena ia berisi bunga hidup.* Don't press on this box because it contains fresh flowers.

menghimpitkan to press down on, squeeze. *Dia* ~ *tanah liat itu dengan batu.* He pressed down on the clayey soil with a rock.

memperhimpit(-himpit)kan to squeeze things together.

terhimpit crushed, squeezed, pressed down on, wedged in between two things.

himpitan crushing, squeezing, pressure.

penghimpitan crushing, squeezing.

himpun gather, assemble.

berhimpun to gather, crowd together, assemble. *Sejumlah besar rakyat Korut* ~ *di Lapangan Kim Il Sung.* A large number of North Koreans gathered in Kim Il Sung Stadium.

menghimpun(kan) 1 to gather, assemble, bring together. *menghimpunkan anak buahnya* to assemble his followers. 2 to collect. *Pergelaran ini khusus untuk menghimpun dana.* This performance was specially given to raise funds. 3 to accumulate. *menghimpunkan kekayaan* to accumulate wealth. 4 to accrue.

terhimpun 1 gathered, assembled. 2 accrued, accumulated.

himpunan 1 assembly, gathering; association. ~ *Éksékutif Muda Indonésia* Indonesian Jaycees. ~ *Mahasiswa Islam* [HMI] Islamic Students Association. ~ *Pengusaha Muda Indonésia* [HIPMI] Indonesian Young Entrepreneurs Association. 2 compilation, collection 3 (*math*) set. 4 (*geol*) assemblage.

penghimpun 1 collecting, storage. *wadah* ~ reservoir. ~ *listrik* storage battery. 2 compiler, collector.

penghimpunan 1 assemblage, coming together, gathering. 2 collecting, putting together. 3 accumulation.

perhimpunan 1 association, club, union. ~ *memancing* fishing club. 2 meeting, assembly. ~ *agung* (*Mal*) convention. 3 meeting place.

hina (*Skr*) 1 despicable, contemptible, disgraceful. *Perbuatan itu sangat* – *dan keji.* That behavior was very disgraceful and shameful. 2 mean, humble, degraded (of persons). *gubuk* – a humble hut (in talking about one's own house, denigrating o.s. or making it appear as if one is not too well-off). 3 miserable, worthless. – *angkara* despicable. – *budi* bad behavior. – *dina/ lata/papa* very contemptible/despicable. – *mulia* a) high and low. b) – *mulianya* standing, status, reputation. *ketahuan* – *mulianya* to know the true status.

sehina ~ *semalu* to share contempt and shame, having the same destiny, be partners in distress

berhina ~ *diri* to humble/humiliate o.s.; modest, humble.

menghina(kan) 1 to humiliate, insult, despise, scorn, revile. *Dia telah* ~ *saya di hadapan teman-teman saya.* He humiliated me in front of my friends. 2 to hold in contempt, offend, be offensive to, defame. *Karangannya dalam surat kabar itu dipandang* ~ *gubernur.* His newspaper article was considered offensive to the governor.

memperhina to despise, insult.

terhina insulted, humiliated, etc. *Wanita itu merasa sungguh* ~ *apabila dituduh menjadi seorang pelacur.* The girl really felt humiliated when she was accused of having become a prostitute.

hinaan insult, taunt, affront, revilement, humiliation.

kehinaan 1 lowness. 2 baseness, meanness.

penghina s.o. who insults.

penghinaan 1 humiliation, abasement, revilement, opprobrium. 2 insult, contempt, scorn, defamation, libel. ~ *berdarah* blood libel. ~ *ringan* defamation (of character). ~ *terhadap lembaga/ wibawa peradilan* contempt of court.

hinai → INAI.

hinap menghinap-hinap to consider, weigh, think about.

Hinayana the more conservative form of Buddhism, practiced in Sri Lanka, Burma, Thailand, and Cambodia.

hincit run away, leave quickly.

hindar menghindar 1 to give way/ground, yield. 2 to evade, dodge, avoid, shun; to withdraw (from), get away (to), turn aside, make way/room. ~ *dari tanggung jawab* to avoid responsibility. ~ *diri* to get away. 3 evasive. *jawaban* ~ an evasive answer.

menghindari to avoid, evade, get around, get out of (doing s.t.), stay out of the way of. *tidak bisa dihindari* unavoidable. ~ *untuk* to refrain from (doing s.t.).

menghindarkan 1 to move s.t. out of way so that it can be avoided/evaded/gotten around, avoid, sidestep. ~ *perang nuklir* to avoid a nuclear war. *keberatan itu dapat dihindarkan dengan mudah* that objection/difficulty could have easily been gotten around. 2 ~ *daripada* to safeguard, save, protect (o.s.) against. ~ *diri dari* to refrain from, avoid. ~ *dirinya daripada celaan dan cacian* to protect o.s. from criticism and insult.

terhindar 1 avoided, evaded, escaped. *Dia* ~ *dari bahaya maut.* He cheated death. 2 safeguarded, protected. ~ *dari tekanan* protected against stress.

terhindari avoided. *tidak* ~ unavoidable.

terhindarkan avoidable. *tidak* ~ inevitable, unavoidable. *Kenaikan harga semén tak* ~. The rise in cement prices is unavoidable.

hindaran ~ *ke kiri/kanan* deviation/deflection to the left/right.

penghindar evader, dodger, avoider. ~ *pajak* tax dodger.

penghindaran setting s.t. to the side so that it can be avoided, avoidance, evasion, dodging. ~ *diri* self-avoidance. ~ *pajak* tax evasion.

Hinderordonnantie (*D col*) [HO] Nuisance Law.

Hindia (*D ob*) Indies. *Lautan/Samudera* – Indian Ocean. - *Barat* West Indies. - *Belanda* Netherlands [HB] (Dutch) East Indies. – *Molék* an art movement of the late 19th and early 20th centuries.

hindék → ELANG *hindék*.

Hindu I 1 Hindu; Indian. *agama* – Dharma (the official name of) Balinese Hinduism. **2** of or pertaining to Hindus or Hinduism.

menghindukan to Hinduize.

kehinduan (*ob*) of or pertaining to Hindus or Hinduism.

hindu II (*M ob*) **1** mother. **2** ancestors; family. *mencari* – to trace one's family; → INDU, INDUK.

hinduisasi Hinduization.

hinduistik (*E*) and **hinduistis** (*D*) of or pertaining to Hindus or Hinduism.

hingar – *bingar* noise, hubbub, tumult, uproar; → INGAR. *kehingar-bingaran* noisiness, noise, tumult, tumultuousness, boisterousness.

menghingar to make noise.

hingaran hubbub, tumult.

kehingaran noise, tumult.

hingga 1 limit, boundary; end. *tak ada –nya* endless, interminable, unlimited, unbounded. **2** up to, as far as, by (a percentage). – *betis* up to the calf. *harganya melonjak* – 80% the price rose by 80%. **3** (= *sehingga*) until, till; so that (showing the result of an action), and so. – *kini/sekarang* hitherto, till now. – *kini ke atas* from now on. – *saat ini* heretofore.

sehingga so that, and so. *Dia sakit,* ~ *dia belum dapat pergi ke kantor.* He's sick and so he can't go to the office yet.

berhingga limited, finite. *tidak* ~ boundless, unlimited, infinite. *kesenangan yang tidak* ~ infinite pleasure.

menghinggakan and **memperhinggakan** to fix a limit, define, determine.

terhingga limited, finite. *tidak* ~ unlimited, without limit. *terimakasih yang tidak* ~ lots of thanks.

perhinggaan limit, boundary; verge.

hinggap 1 to perch, alight, settle. *Kupu-kupu* – *di jendéla.* A butterfly alighted on the window. **2** to infect (of a disease). *hendak* – *tiada berkaki* wishing to do s.t. but unable to do it.

berhinggap-hinggapan (*pl subj*) to perch.

menghinggap to strike with an illness, infect with an illness. *Orang itu telah dihinggap penyakit taun.* that person was struck by cholera.

menghinggapi 1 to alight on, sit down on. **2** to affect (of an illness, etc.), attack, infect.

menghinggapkan to perch/set s.t. (somewhere), implant. ~ *rasa takut di hatinya* to implant fear in their hearts.

terhinggap infected (by a disease).

hinggut **menghinggut** and **terhinggut-hinggut** to shake, rock, sway, swing.

hingkik barred eagle owl, *Bubo sumatranus.*

hintai **menghintai 1** to spy upon, watch surreptitiously. **2** to lie in wait for; → INTAI.

hio (*C*) joss stick. *Gadis bergaun malam itu sedang sembahyang pakai* –. The girl in the evening gown was praying with joss sticks.

hio-bio (*IBT*) a Moluccan song of welcome.

hioko (*C*) *jamur* – dried mushrooms (used in cooking).

hiolo (*C*) incense burner.

hip I (*D*) -.– *hura!* hip, hip, hurray!

hip II (in acronyms) → HIMPUNAN.

Hipadwipa name given to West Kalimantan because of its richness in diamonds.

hiperaktif (*E*) hyperactive; → LASAK *berlebih.*

hiperaktivitas (*E*) hyperactivity.

hiperbarik (*E*) hyperbaric.

hiperbol(a) (*D*) hyperbola.

hiperbolik (*E*) and **hiperbolis** (*D*) hyperbolic.

hiperbolisme (*D/E*) hyperbolism.

hiperglikémia (*E*) hyperglycemia.

hiperkalésterolémi (*E*) hypercholesterolemia.

hiperkorék (*E*) hypercorrect.

hiperréalistik hyper-realistic.

hiperséks (*E*) oversexed.

hiperséksualitas (*E*) hypersexuality.

hipersénsitif (*E*) hypersensitive.

hipersonik (*E*) hypersonic.

hiperténsi (*D*) hypertension.

hipertrofi (*D*) hypertrophy.

hipervéntilasi (*D*) hyperventilation.

hipi and **hip(p)is** (*E*) hippy, hippies, hippy-like (about tourists/ clothing, etc.).

hipnose (*D*) and **hipnosis** (*E*) hypnosis.

hipnotérapi (*E*) hypnotherapy.

hipnotis (*D*) hypnotic. *ahli* – hypnotist.

menghipnotis to hypnotize.

terhipnotis hypnotized. *Sekian banyak pemujanya seakan* ~. It was as if so many of his admirers had been hypnotized.

penghipnotis hypnotist.

hipnotisir (*D*) hypnotist.

menghipnotisir to hypnotize.

hipnotisme (*D/E*) hypnotism.

hipofise (*D/E*) hypophysis.

hipoglikémia (*E*) hypoglycemia.

hipokalsémia (*E*) hypocalcemia.

hipokolésterol (*E*) hypocholesterol.

hipokondriak (*E*) hypochondriac. *penderita* – hypochondriac.

Hipokratés (*E*) Hippocrates.

hipokrisi (*D/E*) hypocrisy.

hipokrit (*D/E*) hypocrite; → MUNAFIK.

hipoksia (*E*) hypoxia.

hiponim (*gram*) hyponym.

hipopotamus (*D/E*) hippopotamus.

hipostasti (*E*) hypostasis.

hipotaksis (*E*) hypotaxis.

hipotalamus (*D/E*) hypothalamus.

hipoték (*D*) mortgage.

menghipotékkan to mortgage (a house, etc.).

hipotenusa (*D*) hypotenuse.

hipotérmia (*D/E*) hypothermia.

hipotésa and **hipotése** (*D*) hypothesis.

hipotétis (*D*) hypothetic(al).

berhipotétis hypothetical.

hippies → HIPIS.

hipuk **menghipuk** to cultivate (plants), raise (vegetables); → IPUK.

HIR (*D leg*) [Herziene Indonesisch Reglement] → RÉGLEMÉN *Indonésia yang diperbarui.*

hirap disappeared, vanished.

menghirap 1 to disappear, vanish (of wanted persons). **2** to go into hiding. *Orang-orang itu* ~ *karena dicari polisi.* Those people went into hiding because the police were looking for them.

hirarki (*D*) hierarchy.

hirarkis (*D*) hierarchical.

hirau interested. *tidak* – uninterested, do not care a bit.

menghirau(kan) to care about, trouble o.s. about, pay attention to. *tidak* ~ to ignore. *Anak itu tidak* ~ *nasihat ibunya.* The child ignored his mother's advice.

hiris → IRIS I, II.

hiru-biru → HARU *biru.*

hiru-hara commotion, tumult, upheaval.

hiruk – *pikuk/piruk* noise, din, commotion, tumult, uproar, hubbub, confusion, clamor. *kehiruk-pikukan* noise, etc.

menghiruk to cause a commotion/uproar.

menghirukkan 1 to create an uproar in, cause to be very noisy/uproarious. **2** to make a fuss over s.t.

kehirukan noise, commotion, etc.

penghiruk rioter, s.o. who causes a commotion/disorder.

hirup inhale, suck in (through the mouth/nose).

menghirup 1 to sip, gulp, lap (up), slurp. ~ *kopi* to sip coffee. **2** to draw (on one's cigarette), inhale. **3** to breathe in, inhale; → ISAP. ~ *udara* to take a walk in the fresh air.

menghirup-hirup to snivel, blubber.

terhirup sipped, inhaled, breathed; swallowed (by accident) (e.g., a mosquito, when one's mouth was open).

hirupan 1 sniff; gulp, sip, slurp. **2** (*ling*) implosive.

penghirup 1 inhalant. **2** inhaler.

penghirupan inhalation, inhaling.

his I fie! for shame!

his II labor pains.

HIS (*init*) [Hollands Inlandse School] Dutch-Native (read: Indonesian) elementary school for Indonesians which covered the first seven grades. *Hollands* (Dutch) refers to the language of instruction; *cp* ELS, HCS.

hisab (*A*) **1** computation, calculation, reckoning. *ahli* – mathematician; → MATÉMATIKAWAN. *ilmu* – mathematics; → MATÉMATIKA. **2** care, heed, pay attention to. *Apa –mu kepadanya?* What's it to you?

menghisab(kan) 1 to compute, calculate, count, sum up. **2** to heed, care for. **3** to take into account.

terhisab(kan) counted, reckoned, calculated. *tidak* ~ countless, innumerable.

penghisaban calculating, computing.

hisak → ISAK.

hisap menghisap to take a drag (on a cigarette). *Ia mengambil sebatang rokok dan dihisapnya dalam-dalam.* He took a cigarette and took a deep drag; → ISAP.

menghisapi (*pl obj*) to suck.

penghisap smoker, s.t. that sucks. ~ *asap* smoke eater. ~ *candu* dope addict.

penghisapan 1 extortion. **2** exploitation. **3** suction.

Hisbullah (*A*) "Legion of Allah," i.e., the former *Masyumi* youth given paramilitary training.

Hisbul Wathan (*A*) "Legion of the Fatherland," i.e., the name of the *Muhammadiyah* Boy Scout Movement.

hisit (*C*) shark fin (for soup).

Hispania Spain. *orang* – Spaniard.

Hispanik (*E*) Hispanic.

histéri(a) (*D*) hysteria.

histéris (*D*) hysterical.

histologi (*D/E*) histology.

histologik (*E*) histologic.

histopatologi (*E*) histopathology.

histori (*D*) history.

historik (*E*) and **historis** (*D*) historic(al).

historikus (*D*) historian.

historiografi (*D*) historiography.

historisitas (*E*) historicity.

hit (*E*) hit (pop music).

hitam 1 black, dark (in color). **2** under a cloud. *Sépakbola kita semakin* –. Our soccer games cannot bear the light of day (due to briberies). **3** code word for various k.o. drugs. *domba* – the black sheep (of the family). *dunia* – underworld. *ilmu* – black magic. *kambing* – the black sheep (of the family). *kayu* – ebony, *Cratoxylon celebicum. orang* – a black person, *esp* a Negro. – *bagai pantat belanga* as black as the ace of spades (regarding s.o.'s character). – *gula Jawa* really black but attractive/cute to look at. – *dikatakan putih, putih dikatakan* – not telling the truth. – *mata itu mana boléh bercerai dengan putihnya* to be inseparably tied to e.o. (of lovers); → MIMI *dan mintua. rapor* – a good school report. – *tahan tempa, putih tahan sesah* can stand e.o.'s test. – *arang* carbon black. – *birat* ugly person with dark skin. – *bogot* intense black. – *di atas putih* in writing, in black and white. – *gading* ivory black. – *hangus* carbon black. – *jelaga* pitch black. – *jengat* pitch black. – *kecoklat-coklatan* brownish black. – *kelam* pitch black. – *kumbang* pitch black. – *kusam* dull

black. – *lakan* glistening black. – *lampu* lampblack. – *langit* pitch black. – *legam* pure black. – *lotong* brownish black. – *manggis* purplish black. – *manis* dark brown complexion (considered attractive). – *mata iris* (of the eye). – *pekat* inky black. – *platina* platinum black. – *putih* black and white. (*sudah*) *tentu* – *putihnya* a) to know for sure where one stands or, how s.t. will end up. b) it has already been decided. **menghitam-memutihkan** and **menghitamputihkan** to do as one likes with, be in charge of, control. – *sabak* slate gray. – *tedas* pitch black. – *tulang* bone black. – *usam* swarthy.

sehitam as black as. ~ *kuku* (*pun*) (not) (even) a bit, (not) at all. *Ia tak menyesal* ~ *kuku pun.* He didn't regret it one bit.

menghitam to become black, appear to be black. *Jalan raya* ~ *karena orang banyak.* The highway was black with people.

menghitamkan 1 (= **menghitami**) to blacken, make black, darken. *obat untuk* ~ *rambut* hair-coloring (black). *Orang tua yang berambut putih itu mencoba* ~ *rambutnya.* The gray-haired old man tried to color his hair black. **2** to speak evil of, sully (s.o.'s reputation). **3** (*M*) to leave (the country, etc.) forever.

terhitam the blackest/darkest.

kehitaman 1 blackness. **2** very black.

kehitam-hitaman blackish.

penghitam blackener, s.t. that blackens. ~ *alis* eyebrow pencil.

penghitaman 1 blackening, making black. **2** blacking out (an article, etc., by censorship).

hitung calculation, computation, reckoning, counting. *ilmu* – arithmetic. *mesin* – (electronic) calculator. *salah* – miscalculation. – *dagang* commercial/business arithmetic. – *mundur/menurun* (*infr*) countdown. *melakukan* – *mundur* to countdown. – *panjang* on the average, mean, by and large; → RATA-RATA. – *potong* (to sell) by the piece, apiece. – *ratusan* by/in hundreds, by the hundred. – *ulang* recalculation.

hitung-hitung 1 all things considered, all in all. *Katanya, banyak untuk melanjutkan rintisan nénéknya,* ~ *melestarikan cita-cita nénék.* They say, a lot is only to continue the pioneering efforts of her grandmother. All things considered, to preserve her grandmother's aspirations. **2** (*coq*) just think of it as. *"Saya cuma mau cari keringat kok," ujar Widi. "Ya,* ~ *refreshing," tambah Réza.* "I just want some exercise," said Widi. "Just think of it as refreshing," added Reza.

berhitung 1 to make calculations, calculate, count. *pengajaran* ~ arithmetic instruction. ~ *angka-angka* to compute, calculate, do arithmetic/math. *tidak* ~ *benar* (money, etc.) is no object for him. ~ *di kertas* to make calculations on paper. ~ *kepala/mencongak* to do/perform mental arithmetic. **2** to confer, discuss, talk about. ~ *nasib peruntangan* to talk about the vicissitudes to s.o. or e.o. **3** (*M*) to audit profit and loss (in commerce, etc.).

menghitung 1 to add up, figure out. *bagaimana cara* ~ *pengeluaran dan pemasukan uang* how to figure out the receipts and expenditures. **2** to count. *Hitunglah berapa orang yang sudah datang.* Count how many persons have already come. *Ini bisa dihitung dengan jari.* You can count this on your fingers. *Kalau tak dapat menghitung, baik kuhitungkan.* If you can't count, let me count it. ~ *mundur* to count down. ~ *surat suara* to count the ballots. *sebagai* ~ *bulu kambing* a Sisyphean task. **3** to determine, calculate. *Harga barang-barang itu dihitung dengan dolar.* The price of these commodities is calculated in dollars. *dihitung ratusan/ribuan/puluhan* to be determined in hundreds/thousands/tens. **4** to include, belong to, consider (as). *Rupa-rupanya aku ini tidak dihitung pegawai negeri.* Apparently I'm not considered a government employee. *Daérah itu boléh dihitung daérah yang makmur.* That area may be considered one of the prosperous areas. **5** to count/rely on. *Sudah dihitung pasti, kau bakal datang.* We're counting on you to come.

menghitung-hitung to take things into consideration. *Kalau dihitung-hitung, jatuh biayanya malah lebih murah.* All things considered, in fact, it turns out to be cheaper.

menghitungi (*pl obj*) to count.

menghitungkan to count for s.o.

memperhitungkan 1 to calculate, give an estimate of, figure out. *Sebelum diperhitungkan dengan teliti, tidak dapat menentukan*

berapa ongkos pembuatan rumah ini. Before it is calculated precisely, the cost of building that house can't be determined. **2** to compensate, counterbalance, make up for, cover (debts). *Tunggakan hutangmu akan diperhitungkan dengan gajimu bulan depan.* Your arrears will be made up for by your next month's salary. **3** to consider, take into consideration, figure in, weigh, think about, contemplate. *Saya terpaksa ~ perkara ini sebelum dapat memberi kamu jawaban.* I'm compelled to take this matter into consideration before I can give you an answer. *setelah diperhitungkan* after due consideration, on second thought. *yang tidak diperhitungkan* unforeseen (expenses in a budget). **4** to add s.t. (to). *Commercial Paper Bapak sebesar Rp 2 milyar diperhitungkan dengan kewajiban Bapak kepada kami sebesar Rp 43 milyar.* We have added your Commercial Paper of Rp 2 billion to your obligations to us of Rp 43 billion.
terperhitungkan can be figured out.
terhitung 1 included (in the calculation), inclusive of (charges). *belum ~* not counting, excluding. *belum ~ ongkos kirim* shipping charges not included, excluding shipping charges. *boléh ~ kepada* can be ranked among, can be included in. *tak ~* countless, innumerable, numberless. **2** *~ mulai/sejak tanggal* commencing on, as of, taking effect on, effective, dating from, counting from, starting from. **3** considered (as being). *Dia ~ anak yang normal.* He was considered a normal child.
hitungan 1 calculation, computation, reckoning, count. **2** (point under) consideration. *~ nya begini* you figure it out like this. *Jangan banyak ~.* Don't talk too much. *masuk ~* to take into account/consideration, deserve/receive consideration. *tidak masuk ~* not to be considered, not taken into consideration. *mencari ~* to do sums. *~ angka-angka* calculation. *~ diferénsial* differential calculus. *~ mundur* countdown. *tinggal ~ hari lagi* you can count the days till then. **berhitungan** *~ dengan* to take into account/consideration.
penghitung 1 counter, checker, meter, recorder. *~ Geiger* Geiger counter. **2** bank teller.
penghitungan calculation, counting, reckoning, estimation. *~ mundur* countdown. *~ surat suara* the counting of ballots. *dalam prosés ~* being considered.
perhitungan 1 calculation, computation, clearing, settlement (of account). *~ awal* preaudit. *~ dugaan* calculus/theory of probabilities. *~ laba rugi* a) balance; → NERACA. b) profit and loss account/statement. *~ tahunan* annual financial statement. *~ yang dilakukan bersama oléh Départemén Keuangan dan Départemén Pertambangan dan Énérgi* the computations made jointly by the Department of Finance and the Department of Mining and Energy. **2** (bookkeeping) account, figures. *memberi ~* to account for (one's deeds). *minta ~* to ask for an account (of one's deeds). *~ antarbank* clearing. *~ habis* final settlement. *~ harga pokok* cost accounting. *~ kemudian* open account. *~ laba rugi* profit and loss figures. **3** consideration, opinion, judgment. **4** calculating. *Saya nggak terlalu ~ kok.* I'm not too calculating, really.
hiu shark. *ékstrak minyak hati –* shark liver extract, squalene; → YU.
hiung (S) **menghiung** to scream, howl (of wind).
hiuran → IURAN.
hiwalah (A) **1** money order. **2** transfer of a debt to a third party.
hiya oh yes.
hiyang (ob) god. *– Agni* God of Fire; → YANG I.
hiyayat (A) gift of life.
hiyu → YU I.
Hizbé Islami (A) Islamic Alliance.
Hizbullah → HISBULLAH.
hizib (A) group, party.
Hj (abbr) → HAJJAH.
HKBP (init) [Huri Kristen Batak Protéstan] Batak Christian Protestant Church.
HKN (init) → HARI Keséhatan Nasional.
HKSN (init) → HARI Kesetiakawanan Sosial Nasional.
hla → LHA.
hlm (abbr) → HALAMAN II.
HLN (init) → HARI Listrik Nasional.
hlo → LHO.
ho (exclamation of surprise) oh! *–! Saya tidak sangka kamu ber-*

jalan di belakang saya. Oh! I didn't realize you were walking behind me.
H.O. I [Hongeroedeem] (D) /hongerudim/ malnutrition.
HO II [Hinderordonnantie] (D) Nuisance Law.
Hoakiau (C) overseas Chinese.
hoana (C) native, aborigine; → PRIBUMI, WANNA.
hoayi (C) s.o. of mixed Chinese-Indonesian origin.
hobat charm, magic formula/spell, black magic. *orang –* witch, sorcerer, magician, wizard.
  menghobat(kan) to bewitch, cast a spell on, charm.
  hobatan charm, magic formula.
hobi (E) hobby, enjoyable pastime. *Rekan ini mémang punya – tidur.* This colleague of mine is really a sleepyhead.
  berhobi to have (as) a hobby. *Saya ini ~ memburu satwa.* My hobby is big game hunting.
  pe(ng)hobi hobbyist.
hobo (D/E) hobo.
hodah → HOWDAH.
hodeng (D ob) posture, comportment, attitude; → TINGKAH laku.
hoé (C) "hoey," i.e., a secret society.
hofméster (D) steward (on board a ship).
hoga-hoga to go on a spree. *Uangnya untuk –.* He spends wildly.
hoi (interjection used to get s.o.'s attention) hey! *–! Jangan petik bunga di kebun saya!* Hey! Don't pick the flowers in my yard!
hoisum → HAISOM.
hojah and **hojat** → HUJAH I, II.
hoka(h) (A) hookah, water pipe, k.o. smoking pipe in which the smoke is drawn through water; → ROKOK hoka(h).
Hokbén clipped form of Hoka Hoka Bento, a chain of popular Japanese restaurants.
hoki I (E) hockey. *– és* ice hockey.
  (ber)main – to play hockey.
  pehoki hockey player.
hoki II (C) luck. *Rupanya – belum ada pada almarhum.* It seems that the deceased had no luck; → KEBERUNTUNGAN.
  hoki-hokian trust in blind luck. *Usaha rekaman mémang kayak judi, ~.* The recording business is really like gambling, trusting in blind luck.
Hokian(g) (C) relating to Fukien province (esp the Amoy and Chang-chow divisions, not Fuchau itself).
hokie and **hokki(e)** → HOKI II.
hokok (Jp) *– kepada* to report (in the Japanese way, by bowing or saluting to a superior).
hol (A) annual, ritual feast given in commemoration of s.o.'s death. *menepati –* to hold such a feast.
Hol(l)an → HOLLANDS.
holé deception. *tukang –* swindler.
holiganisme (D) hooliganism.
holisme (D/E) holism.
holistik (E) holistic.
Hollands (D) Dutch. *– spréken* to speak Dutch. *seorang notaris kawakan yang bisa – spréken* an experienced notary public who can speak Dutch.
holomini (Pap) penis-sheath; → KOTÉKA.
holopis (Jv) to work together cooperatively; yo-heave-ho; → TU-WA-GA. *– kuntul baris* words chanted by a group of workers to keep their concerted movements in rhythm. **berholopis-kuntul-baris** to work together in a group.
Holosén (D) Holocene.
hom (Pap) taro.
hombo (in Nias) jumping. *– batu* stone jumping; → FAHOMBÉ.
hombréng (Pr) [homo bréngsék?] gay, homo.
homéopat (D) homeopath.
homéopati (D) homeopathy.
homing (E mil) homing.
homo (D) homosexual. *orang –* a homosexual.
  berhomo and **menghomo** to commit homosexual acts with. *Dia ~ S.* He committed homosexual acts with S.
  menghomoi to commit homosexual acts with. *Polisi tak dapat memastikan apakah dia benar ~ anak-anak angkatnya itu.* The police couldn't confirm whether he really had committed homosexual acts with his adopted children.

kehomoan homosexuality. *Para gay yang diwawancarai di berbagai tempat tak ada yang mencemaskan ~nya sebagai nasib buruk.* None of the gays who were interviewed in various places regretted their homosexuality as a bad fate.

homofil (*D/E*) homophile, homosexual.

homofon (*D/E*) homophone.

homofoni (*D/E*) homophony.

homogén (*D*) homogeneous.

  kehomogenan homogeneity.

homogénitas (*D*) homogeneity.

homograf (*D/E*) homograph.

homologasi (*D leg*) approval.

  menghomologasikan to approve.

homologi (*D/E*) homology.

homonim (*D/E*) homonym.

  berhomonim homonymous. *kata-kata yang* ~ homonymous words.

  kehomoniman homonymy.

homonimi (*D/E*) homonymy.

homorgan (*D*) homorganic (sound).

homoséks homosexual.

homoséksual (*E*) and **homoséksuil** (*D*) homosexual.

homoséksualitas (*D*) homosexuality.

homowan (male) homosexual. *protés kaum* – protest of the homosexuals.

homowati female homosexual, lesbian.

hompimpa a children's game for three players. They all chant *hompim-pa* and on the last syllable they each hold out a hand face up or face down. The winner is the one whose hand is different from the other two.

honai (*Pap*) round house.

honar → ONAR I.

Honda I 1 brand name of a Japanese make of motorcycle. **2** (in Nias) any brand of motorcycle. – *bako* a Honda motorcycle purchased from the receipts of a tobacco harvest. – *bébék* the 80-cc Honda motorcycle resembling a duck.

  ber-Honda to ride a Honda motorbike. *Perampok ~ menyikat TV dan radio.* Bandits on a Honda motorbike stole a television and radio set.

honda II [*honoré (pemerintah) daérah*] honorary worker/teacher who works for an honorarium.

  menghondakan to hire such a worker/teacher, etc. for a honorarium/stipend.

honda III (in Bandung) an *oplét*.

Hondanisasi the introduction of Honda outboard motors for fishing boats.

Hondawan I a Honda motorcyclist; → HONDA I.

hondawan II an honorary worker hired by a regional/local government; → HONDA II.

hondayung (*joc*) bicycle; the term is a blend of *Honda* "Honda" and *dayung* "pedal."

hondoh-pondoh (*M*) in throngs; → BERDUYUN-DUYUN. *Meréka itu – ke puskésmas.* They went in throngs to the clinic.

honé → HONAI.

hong I culvert, sewer.

hong II → BURUNG *hong.*

hong III (*Skr*) the Sanskrit and Buddhist "om," a word signifying the Hindu Trinity, used by Malay medicine men.

Hongaria Hungary.

hongerloon (*D*) /hongerlon/ starvation wages.

hongeroedeem (*D*) /hongerudim/ and **hongerudim** → H.O. I

honghiam (*C*) risk.

hongi a heavily armed fleet of praus at the time of the Dutch East India Company (1602–1800) used during a project to destroy nutmeg trees where they were growing in abundance (to keep the market price of nutmegs at a high level). *pelayaran* – an expedition with such a fleet.

honghouw (*C*) empress.

hongkoé (*C*) → HUNGKUÉ, HUNGKWÉ, HUNKWÉ.

hongsip (*C*) rheumatism.

honjé (*J*) k.o. fruit-bearing plant, *Nicolaia spp.*

honor clipped form of **honorarium.** – *secara borongan* flat payment. *Kasino dkk dari Prambors waktu itu minta – secara borongan Rp 10 juta.* Kasino and friends from Prambors at that time asked for a flat payment of Rp 10 million.

  menghonor to give s.o. a honorarium.

honorarium (*D*) **1** honorarium, remuneration, stipend. **2** payment for services.

  menghonorarium to give a honorarium.

honorér (*D*) **1** honorary. *anggota* – honorary member. **2** paid by honorarium and not by salary. *pegawai* – hired on a contract basis (not permanently and consequently receiving a honorarium and not a fixed salary).

honorifik (*E*) honorific.

honoris causa /honoris kausa/ [h.c.] (*L*) honorary. *doktor* – honorary doctor, doctor h.c.

honyok terhonyok ~ *pada* slammed against.

hoop (*D ob*) /hop/ head overseer (in sugarcane field); → HOP I.

hoopéng, hooping, hoping (*C*) close friend.

hop I (*coq D*) head, chief.

hop II stop! (said by city bus conductors to the driver).

hopagén (*D col*) police sergeant.

hopbiro (*D col*) police headquarters.

hopéng and **hoping** (*C*) close friend.

hopjaksa (*D col*) chief public prosecutor.

hopkantor (*D col*) head office.

hopyes (*D*) hard coffee-flavored caramel.

horak menghorak to unveil, unwind; → ORAK I.

horas I (*Bat*) long live!

horas II (*Port*) time, hour.

horbo (*Bat*) water buffalo; → KERBAU.

hordéng (*D*) curtains, drapery.

horé (*E*) hurray! hurrah!

horég (*Jv*) to shake as a result of a strong force. "*Rumah saya terasa –,*" *kata seorang nénék.* "I felt my house shaking to its foundations," said an old lady.

horison (*D/E*) horizon. – *alam* visible/apparent horizon. – *nyata* celestial/rational horizon.

horisontal (*D/E*) horizontal.

hormat (*A*) **1** respect, esteem, honor, high regard. *dengan* – a) with respect, respectfully. b) *Dengan* – (in correspondence) Dear Sir. *dengan segala* – with all due respect. *diberhentikan (tidak) dengan* – to be (dis)honorably discharged. *kurang* – impolite, ill-mannered, rude. *merasa* – to feel honored. **2** courteous, well-mannered, respectful. *Gadis itu cantik lagi* –. That girl is pretty and well-mannered. **3** salute. *memberi* – *pada bendéra/ panji* to salute the flag. **4** sincere, trustful. – *dan salam,* – *dan takzim/taklim* and – *saya* (in correspondence) yours faithfully/ truly, sincerely/respectfully yours. – *dan salam dari* with the compliments of. – *pada orangtua* filial piety.

  berhormat honored, respected, esteemed. *Ia seorang yang* ~ *di kampungnya.* He's a respected person in his area.

  berhormat-hormat to exchange courtesies, be courteous to e.o.

  menghormat to respect, show respect to.

  menghormati 1 to (pay) respect (to), show respect for, to pay homage/tribute to, honor. *Anak-anak wajib* ~ *orang tuanya.* Children should respect their parents. *Perjanjian Saling* ~, *Persahabatan, dan Kerjasama.* Treaty of Mutual Respect, Friendship, and Cooperation (between Indonesia and Papua New Guinea). *untuk* ~ in honor of. **2** to regard, think highly of. **3** to look up to. ~ *manula* to look up to the elderly.

  hormat-menghormati to exchange courtesies, show respect to e.o.

  terhormat 1 respected, honorable. *orang yang* ~ persona grata. *Bapak-bapak dan Ibu-ibu yang* ~! Ladies and Gentlemen! **2** high-class. *kelab malam yang* ~ a high-class nightclub. **3** refined. *wanita* ~ a refined lady.

  kehormatan 1 courtesy, honor (*mod*), honorary. *barisan* – honor guard. *nama* ~ courtesy title, epithet. *tamu* ~ visiting dignitary. *visa* ~ courtesy visa. *dikebumikan dengan penuh* ~ to be interred with full honors. ~ *prajurit* soldier's honor. **2** honor, reputation. **3** dignity. ~ *kemanusiaan* human dignity. **4** a woman's chastity/purity/honor. *Ia kehilangan ~nya.* She lost her virginity. ~ *kesusilaan* decency. **berkehormatan** to have a sense of honor/self-respect.

penghormat that which respects/honors, that which is done as a form of respect/honor. *barisan* ~ → BARISAN *kehormatan*.
penghormatan high respect/esteem, honor, homage. *memberikan* ~ *terakhir kepada pusara almarhum S.* to render the last honors to the grave of the late S.
hormon (*D/E*) hormone. - *kelaki-lakian* androgen. - *kewanitaan* estrogen. - *pertumbuhan* growth hormone.
hormonal (*D/E*) hormonal.
Hormuz (*A*) *Selat* - Strait of Hormuz.
horok-horok k.o. dessert made from rice flour.
horor (*E*) horror. *adegan/film* - horror scene/film.
horoskop (*D/E*) horoscope.
hortikultur(a) (*D*) horticulture. *petani* - horticulturist.
hortikulturis (*E*) horticulturist.
hoskut (*D*) housecoat, dressing gown.
hospital (*D*) hospital; → RUMAH *sakit*.
  menghospitalkan to hospitalize.
hospitalisasi (*E*) hospitalization.
hostél (*E*) hostel.
hostés (*E*) 1 hostess, girl in nightclub, etc. 2 prostitute.
hosti (*D*) host, consecrated wafer. - *Suci* Holy Host.
hot (*E*) 1 hot, sexy, passionate. *celana* - hot pants. *lagu-lagu* hot songs. - *pants* hot pants. *berhot pants* to wear hot pants. 2 sexually aroused, horny. *Aku rasa* -. I feel horny.
  menghotkan to jazz up.
hotdog (*E*) /hotdok/ hotdog.
hotél (*D*) hotel. *keluar* - to check out. *masuk* - to check into a hotel. *meninggalkan* - to check out of a hotel. - *berbintang* a hotel that has been given a rating of a number of stars. - *berbintang lima* a five-star hotel. - *bertaraf Internasional* a hotel of international standards. - *kelas kambing/krések* fleabag hotel. - *megah* luxury hotel. - *melati* inn, guesthouse, lodging, non-star hotel; → LOSMÉN. - *mercusuar* luxury hotel (under President Soekarno). - *prodéo* (*euph*) prison, jail. *menghotélprodéokan* to imprison, incarcerate, jail.
  sehotél in the same hotel (as).
  menghotélkan 1 to put in a hotel. 2 (*euph*) to imprison.
  perhotélan hotel (*mod*). *bisnis* ~ hotel business. *pengelolaan/manajemén* ~ hotel management. *sekolah* ~ hotel school.
hotélir (*D*) hotelkeeper.
hotib → KHATIB.
hotmiks (*E*) hot mix.
  berhotmiks hot mixed. *Jalan-jalan utama di kota Purwokerto kini sudah lébar dan* ~. The main roads in Purwokerto are now already wide and hot mixed.
hotperdom (*D*) goddamn!
houder (*D ob*) /hoder/ magazine for firearms.
houver /hower/ → HOUDER.
howdah (*A*) seat of platform for one or more persons, *usu* with a railing and canopy, placed on the back of an elephant.
howitser (*D*) howitzer.
hoyak (*Jv*) → OYAK I. **menghoyak-hoyak** to shake up. *Singgasana para déwa (konkrétnya, para menteri) seperti dihoyak-hoyak.* It was as if the throne of the gods (i.e., the ministers) had been all shaken up.
hoyong to swerve; → OYONG I. *Tiba-tiba pesawat* - *ke kiri.* All of a sudden the airplane swerved to the left.
HP I (*init*) → HÉNPON.
HP II (*init*) homepage.
HPH (*init*) → HAK *pengusahaan hutan*.
HPS (*init*) → HARI *Pangan Sedunia*.
HSU [[Kabupatén] Hulu Sungai Utara] North Hulu Sungai (Regency in South Kalimantan).
HT (*init*) Handy Talky.
HTI (*init*) → HUTAN *Tanaman Industri*.
hu (*C*) piece of paper placed over entrance door of a house as a good luck charm.
Hua (*A*) He, God (for Islamic mystics).
huana → WANNA.
huap (*S*) → SUAP. 1 a bite. 2 a mouthful. - *lingkung* an old custom in which newlyweds put a ball of rice in e.o.'s mouth.
hub (in acronyms) → HUBUNGAN, PERHUBUNGAN.

hubad [*perhubungan angkatan darat*] Army Communications.
hubah (*A*) love.
hubaya-hubaya warning! watch out! - *jangan* absolutely not. *Saya berdoa kepada Allah - jangan salah lagi.* I prayed to God not to sin again.
hubb (*A*) love. - *ahl al-bayt* love for the descendants of Muhammad. -*ul watani minal imani* and -*ul wathon minal iman* (a saying often quoted in newspapers) love of one's native land is part of faith.
hububan (*Jv*) bellows.
hubung connect, join, link.
  berhubung 1 to be connected (with s.t.), be joined/linked/coupled/attached (to s.t.). *Paviliun itu* ~ *dengan rumah induk.* The pavilion is connected to the main building. 2 to be connected/related to, in connection (with). *Kedatangannya* ~ *dengan pembukaan kantor cabang baru.* His arrival was in connection with the opening of a new branch office. 3 (*coq*) a) since, seeing that. ~ *terlibat dalam gerakan séparatis* since he was involved in a separatist movement. b) because of, due to, owing to. ~ *naiknya harga kertas* because of the increase in the price of paper. ~ *dengan* in consequence of, as a result of, in pursuance of, pursuant to, on the strength/basis of, in connection with, in reference (or, referring) to. ~ *dengan surat Tuan tertanggal 6 April* in reference to your letter of April 6. - *péndék/singkat* short circuit; → KORSLÉTING.
  berhubungan 1 = berhubung. 2 to be connected (with e.o.), be in contact/touch (with e.o.), be related (to s.t.), have s.t. to do (with). *Harap* ~ *dengan R.* Please, contact R. *Ini* ~ *dengan pekerjaan Anda.* This has to do with your job. *Anak itu selalu* ~ *dengan ibunya.* That child is in constant touch with his mother. ~ *badan* to have sexual intercourse. 3 to communicate (with), get/keep) in touch (with). *bejana* ~ communicating vessels. *tidak* ~ to have no connection (with), no bearing (on).
  menghubungi to communicate with, get in touch with, make contact with, contact (s.o.). *tidak dapat dihubungi untuk dimintai keterangan* to be unavailable for comment.
  memperhubungi to put s.t. or s.o. in contact (with).
  menghubungkan [and **memperhubungkan** (*infr*)] 1 to connect, relate, associate. 2 to put s.o. in contact/touch with s.o. else. *Hubungkan saya dengan Surabaya.* Connect me with Surabaya. *Hubungkan saya dengan manajér.* Put me through to the manager. ~ *calon pembeli mobil dengan pramuniaganya* to bring the prospective car buyers in contact with the salesman.
  terhubung connected, related, linked. *Di Indonésia hanya Pusat Ilmu Komputer Univérsitas Indonésia yang* ~ *ke Internét.* In Indonesia only the Computer Center of the University of Indonesia is connected to the Internet. **keterhubungan** connectedness, relatedness, relationship. *Pemilihan adalah éksprési dari rasa* ~ *seseorang dengan suatu masyarakat tertentu.* Elections are an expression of the relationship of a person with a certain community.
  hubungan 1 contact, connection, link(ing), association. *putus* ~ to lose contact, break up. 2 relationship, tie, connection, communication, correlation, context. *dalam* ~ *ini* in this context. *dalam* ~ *kelompok* in groups. *yang erat* ~*nya dengan* that/who/ which is closely linked to. *memulihkan* ~ to restore relations. *menggalang* ~ *erat dengan Iran* to cultivate close relations with Iran. *prosés awal pemupukan* ~ *baik* the initial process of fostering good relations. 3 cam. 4 coupling (in poetry). ~ *antaragama* interreligious relationships. ~ *antarpulau/antarkepulauan* interinsular communications. ~ *badan/intim/kelamin/tubuh* sexual relations/intercourse, carnal knowledge. *melakukan* ~ *badan* to have sexual intercourse; → BERSEBADAN. ~ *bapak-anak* patron-client relationship. ~ *bawahan* subordination. ~ *bébas* free sex. ~ *dagang* trade relations. ~ *darah* blood relationship, consanguinity. ~ *dasar* underlying relationship. ~ *dérét* (*elec*) parallel connection (in wiring). ~ *dinas* employment. ~ *diplomatik* diplomatic relations. *memutuskan/menjalin* ~ *diplomatik dengan* to sever/establish diplomatic relations with. ~ *famili* family relationship. ~ *gelap* illicit relations. ~ *insani* human relations. ~ *jabatan* employment. ~ *jajar* (*elec*) parallel connection. ~ *kalimat* (*gram*) (sentential) context. ~

kekuasaan power relations. ~ *keluarga* family relationship. ~ *kerja* engagement, employment. ~ *masyarakat* [humas] public relations; → PR XV. ~ *nyawa* sweetheart. ~ *péndék* (*elec*) short circuit; → KOR(T)SLÉTING. ~ *persaudaraan* ties of blood. *tidak ada* ~ *persaudaraan antara kita* there are no ties of blood between us, we are not related to e.o. ~ *saling melengkapi* complementary relationship. *séks di luar* ~ *perkawinan* extramarital sexual relations. ~ *semenda* relationship by marriage. **berhubungan semenda** to be related by marriage. ~ *singkat* (*elec*) short circuit; → KOR(T)SLÉTING. ~ *suami-istri* husband and wife relationship. *melakukan* ~ *suami-istri* to have sexual intercourse between husband and wife. ~ *susuan* relationship by wet nurse. **berhubungan susuan** to have had the same wet nurse. ~ *télepon* telephone connection. ~ *télepon langsung* hot line, direct connection. ~ *terbatas/tertutup* closed circuit (in electricity). ~ *timbal-balik* a) correlation, interaction. b) two-way (traffic); → LALULINTAS *dwimarga.* ~ *usaha* business relationship. **sehubungan** ~ *dengan* 1 in connection with, with regard to. ~ *dengan ini* in this connection. 2 due/owing to, because of, given. ~ *dengan naiknya harga beras* due to the increase in the price of rice. 3 pursuant to, under. ~ *dengan Keputusan Diréktur Jénderal Pajak No. ...* pursuant to Director General of Taxes' Directive Number ...

penghubung 1 link, connection, connecting part. *kata* ~ (*gram*) connecting word. ~ *télepon* telephone operator. 2 liaison, contact. *perwira* ~ liaison officer.

penghubungan connecting, relating.

perhubungan communications (highway/radio, etc.), relations. *Menteri* ~ [Ménhub] Minister of Communications. *memegang* ~ *yang baik dengan* in good terms with. ~ *keluarga semenda* affinity. ~ *langsung* point-to-point communication. ~ *majikan-buruh* labor relations. ~ *perdagangan* trade relations.

Hud (*A*) "Hud"; name of the 11th chapter of the Koran.

hudai shallow washbasin.

Hudaibi(y)a (*A*) → PERJANJIAN *Hudaibi(y)a.*

hudhud (*A*) hoopoe bird, *Upupa epops.*

hudud (*A*) (Islamic) criminal law.

huduh → ODOH.

hudur (*A*) presence.

hugin (*C*) donation, gift.

huh hey! ha! ah! oh! "~, *lagi-lagi kak Addy bolos,*" *katanya di dalam hati.* "A-ha, Addy played hooky again," he said to himself.

hui I → HWÉÉ.

hui II – *boléd* (*S*) sweet potato, *Ipomoea batatas.*

hujah I (*A*) slander, calumny, defamation, blasphemy.

menghujah to slander, calumniate, defame, blaspheme.

penghujah ~ *Allah* blasphemer.

penghujahan ~ *Allah* blasphemy.

hujah II (*A mostly Mal*) evidence, argumentation. –*ulbalig(at)* (evidence of) adulthood.

berhujah to argue.

hujan I 1 rain. *Kita akan keluar bila* – *berhenti.* We'll leave the house when the rain stops. *curah* – rainfall. *daérah penangkap* – catchment area. *musim* – rainy season. 2 to rain. – *sudah agak menipis* it has almost stopped raining. *tidak* – *tak angin* and *kagak* – *kagak angin* (*coq*) out of the clear blue sky. – *salju* (to) snow. 3 shower (of s.t.), in abundance/large quantities. – *peluru* a shower/rain of bullets. *tiba-tiba turun* – to rain cats and dogs. – *emas di negeri orang* – *batu di negeri sendiri, baiknya di negeri sendiri* there's no place like home; east or west, home is best. *sedia payung sebelum* – prevention is better than cure. – *berbalik ke langit* and *terbalik* – *ke langit* (*infr*) the world upside down. *bagai* – *jatuh ke pasir* it is like pouring water into a sieve. *ada* – *ada panas, ada hari boléh balas* there's always an opportunity to take revenge (or, to return a favor). *mengharap* – *dari langit, tapi air di tempayan dibuang* count one's chickens before they are hatched. – *abu* ash rain. – *angin* rain and wind, gust of rain. **menghujananginkan** to expose to the weather. – *asam* acid rain. – *awal* first rain of the rainy season. – *badai* rainstorm. – *batu/beku* hail. – *belérang* rain of sulfur (from volcano). – *buatan* artificial rain. – *bungsu* last rain(s) of the rainy season. – *buntut* steady drizzle. – *debu* dust storm. –

deras downpour. – *emas* laburnum. – *és* hail, sleet. – *gerimis* a) drizzle. b) (*coq*) to drizzle. – *kerikil* hail. – *lalu* passing rain. – *lebat* downpour. *Tiba-tiba turun* – *lebat sekali.* All of a sudden it poured. – *lesak* heavy rain that goes on for a long time. – *manik* fine rain. – *merata* steady rain. – *panas* rain with sunshine, sun shower. **menghujanpanaskan** to expose to all sorts of weather. – *peluru* hail of bullets. – *rambun* hail. – *renik-renik/renyai/rintik-rintik* drizzle. – *turun rintik-rintik.* It drizzled. – *salju* snowfall. – *singkat tak merata* brief scattered showers. – *sulung* first rain of the rainy season. – *tropis* tropical/ torrential rains.

sehujan having the same (amount of) rainfall.

berhujan rainy. *hari* ~ a rainy day. *di suatu siang* ~ on a rainy afternoon. *pada suatu malam* ~ on a rainy evening. ~ *berpanas* in rain or shine. *Meréka* ~ *harus mengantar surat-surat.* They have to deliver the mail in rain or shine.

berhujan-hujan to walk/play in the rain on purpose. "*Kukira tak lama lagi* – *akan reda, mas,*" *jawab* Nining. "*Aku tak dapat* – . *Badanku mudah terserang penyakit.* "I guess that the rain will slow down soon," answered Nining. "I can't play in the rain. I easily become ill."

menghujan rain down, come down in buckets like rain. *Peluru pun* ~ *datangnya.* Even bullets rained down.

menghujani 1 to rain on, pour down heavily on. 2 to bombard, attack constantly (with). *dihujani bacokan golok* to be showered with machete-cuts. *dihujani pertanyaan* to be bombarded with questions. *dihujani dengan bom* to be showered with bombs.

menghujankan 1 to expose to the rain, drench in the rain. *Dia* ~ *papan-papan itu selama beberapa hari.* He exposed the boards/planks for some days to the rain. 2 to bomb, shell. *Pasukan Viétnam telah* ~ *bom ke atas kota itu.* Vietnamese troops shelled that town.

memperhujankan to let s.t. be rained on, expose to the weather. ~ *garamnya* to ignore one's own relatives.

hujan-hujanan → BERHUJAN-HUJAN.

kehujanan caught in the rain. *hari* ~ day of rain; rainy/wet weather.

penghujan rainy. *hari* ~ a rainy day. *musim* ~ rainy season.

penghujanan bombardment, rain. ~ *bom atas populasi-populasi yang tidak mempunyai pertahanan* a rain of bombs on defenseless populations.

hujan II – *emas* k.o. plant, yellow bells, yellow trumpet flower, *Tecoma stans.*

hujan-hujan *burung* – black and red broadbill, *Cymbirhynchus macrorhyncus* and dusky broadbill, *Corydon sumatranus.*

hujat → HUJAH I.

hujjaj (*A pl of haji*) *Jamiyatul* – *Indonésia* Indonesian Hajis Association.

hujung → UJUNG I.

Hujurat (*A*) *al*– "Apartments"; name of the 49th chapter of the Koran.

huk I (*D*) (in boxing) hook. – *kiri* left hook.

huk II (*D*) corner (of room).

hukah → HOKAH.

hukama (*A*) jurists (*pl of* **hakim**).

hukéng (*C*) slices cut off a large roll of *bakso* mixture served on a *saté* stick.

huk ... huk... (*onom*) coughing sound. *Baru dihisapnya rokok itu beberapa kali, dia batuk* ~ He had just taken some puffs on the cigarette when he coughed and coughed.

hukmi (*A*) legal.

huknah (*A*) clysm.

hukum I (*A*) 1 right, law; legal, judicial. *badan* – legal entity. *bantuan* – legal aid/assistance. *batal menurut* – legally null and void. *ilmu* – jurisprudence. *demi/karena* – by law. *ketidakpastian* – legal uncertainty. *menurut* – lawful, rightful, legitimate. *mewakili di dalam dan di luar* – (in notarial instruments) to represent in legal and other proceedings (or, in and out of Court). *minta* – *kepada* to seek justice from. *negara* – constitutional state. *négosiasi keringanan* – plea bargain. *pendapat* – legal opinion. *penegak* – law enforcer. *perbuatan melawan* – illegal act. *perkosaan* – violation of the law. *dari segi* – from a legal standpoint. *secara –* judicially. *tata –* legal structure. *urusan –* legal affairs. **2** verdict, sentence, judgment. **3** commandment. *– acara* law of procedure. *– acara perdata* law of civil procedure. *– acara pidana* law of criminal procedure. *– acara sipil* law of civil procedure. *– adat* customary/adat law. *– administrasi* administrative law. *– agama* religious law. *– agraria* agrarian law. *– alam* natural law. *– Allah* divine law, God's justice/decree (*esp* of death). *– antarbangsa* law of nations, jus gentium. *– antargolongan* [HAG] intergroup law. *– antara negara* international law. *– antar tata hukum* [HATAH] conflict of laws. *– asasi* basic law. *– bangsa-bangsa* international law. *– bangunan* building law. *– benda* property law. *– besi oligarki* iron law of oligarchy. *– bukti* law of evidence. *– bunuh* death penalty. *– bunyi* (*ling*) sound law. *– dagang* commercial/mercantile law. *– darurat* emergency powers. *– disiplin* disciplinary law, code of conduct (for a profession). *– éksékusi* right to levy execution. *– fiskal* tax law. *– gantung (sampai mati)* death by hanging. *– geréja* canon law. *– geréja Katolik* Catholic canon law. *– hutan rimba* law of the jungle. *– internasional* [HI] international law. *– Islam* Islamic law. *– kanonik/kanun* canon law. *– kebendaan* law of property. *– kebiasaan* unwritten/customary law. *– kekayaan* property law. *– kekeluargaan* family law. *– kelambatan* of inertia. *– keluarga* family law. *– kerakal* hard labor (as punishment, crushing stones). *– kerja* labor law. *– ketenagakerjaan* labor law. *– keuangan* monetary law. *– kewarisan* law of inheritance. *– kisas* capital punishment (in retaliation). *– kodrat* natural law. *– kuasa ibu-bapak* parental rights. *– laut* maritime law, law of the sea. *– lingkungan* environmental law. *– madi* material law. *– maritim* maritime law. *– mati* death penalty. *– niaga* commercial/mercantile law. *– pailit* bankruptcy law. *– pajak* tax law. *– pasung* sentence to the stocks. *– pelengkap* supplementary law. *– pembuktian* law of evidence. *– pendamping* supplementary law (*adat* and *syariat* law). *– pengikatan* law of obligations. *– penjara* sentence to imprisonment. *– peralihan* transitional law. *– perang* laws of war. *– perburuhan* labor law. *– perdata* civil law. *– perdata internasional* [HPI] international civil law. *– perikatan* law of obligations, contract law. *– perkawinan* marriage/matrimonial law. *– perselisihan* law of conflict. *– perséroan* corporate law. *– perutangan* law of obligations. *– pidana* criminal law. *– positif* positive law (not *adat* or *syariat* law). *– privat* private law. *– publik* public law. *– rimba* law of the jungle. *– Romawi* Roman law. *– sipil* civil law. *– syara/syariat* (Muslim) canon law. *– taklik* suspended sentence. *– tak tertulis* unwritten/common/consuetudinary law, lex non scripta. *– tantra* administrative law; → SWATANTRA. *– tatalingkungan* environmental law. *– tatanegara* constitutional law. *– tata pemerintahan* administrative law. *– tata usaha negara* administrative law. *– tuntutan* law of procedure. *– warganegara* citizenship law. *– waris(an)* law of inheritance/succession. *– yang sepuluh* the Ten Commandments (in the Bible).

berhukum 1 to make use of the law. *pergi ~ kepada* to seek justice from. **2** (*ob*) to litigate.

menghukum 1 to sentence, condemn. *~ denda* to fine. *– gantung* to sentence to death by hanging. *Pengédar obat bius itu telah dihukum gantung.* The drug trafficker was sentenced to death by hanging. *Hampir seluruh dunia ~ dasar perbédaan warna kulit Afrika Selatan.* Almost the entire world condemns South Africa's apartheid policy. *dihukum* to be in jail. *dihukum berat* convicted of a felony. **2** to punish, penalize. *Sejumlah anggota Polri di Tanjunglinang dihukum disiplin di muka umum.* Disciplinary punishment was carried out in public against a number of police officers. **3** to order (of a court) (s.o. to do s.t.).

menghukumi to pass judgment (on).

menghukumkan to make ... into a law, enact.

terhukum 1 sentenced, condemned, punished. *Saya merasa sebagai ~ karena terpaksa menghentikan merokok.* I felt as if I was being punished because I was forced to stop smoking. **2** convict(ed person). *~ itu ditahan di Rutan Salémba.* The convict was detained in the Salemba Correctional Facility.

hukuman 1 punishment, sentence, condemnation. *kena ~* (in sports) to be disqualified. *sebagai ~* as punishment. *~ badan* corporal punishment. *~ bersyarat* suspended sentence. *~ buang* expulsion. *Dia juga dijatuhi ~ buang.* He was also expelled. *~ dalam sél* solitary confinement. *~ denda* to be fined. *~ gantung* sentence of death by hanging. *~ kawalan* sentence with restricted freedom of movement. *~ kerakal* forced labor, penal servitude. *~ kerja* punishment by hard labor. *~ kurungan* (be sentenced to) detention, imprisonment. *~ mati* death sentence. *~ pancung* sentence of death by beheading. *~ penjara* imprisonment. *~ penjara seumur hidup* imprisonment for life, life (long) imprisonment. *dapat dihukum dengan ~ penjara* to be liable to imprisonment. *diganjar/dijatuhi ~ 6 bulan penjara* to be sentenced to a six-month jail term. *~ percobaan* probation. *~ perjanjian* suspended sentence. *~ pokok* principal punishment. *~ rajam* sentence to stoning (to death). *~ sél* solitary confinement. *~ seumur hidup* life imprisonment. *~ témbak* death sentence by firing squad. *~ tutupan* imprisonment, incarceration. **2** sentenced, condemned. *orang ~* convict, prisoner.

kehukuman legal, juridical. *syarat-syarat ~* legal conditions.

penghukum s.o. who judges or sentences.

penghukuman sentence, sentencing. *kesalahan ~* wrongful conviction. *~ bersyarat* suspended sentence. *~ yang untuk pertama kali dihukum* first offender. *~ permintaan dan penawaran* the law of supply and demand.

perhukuman (*mod*) judicial, legal. *istilah ~ yang tepat* the correct legal term.

hukum II (*Min*) *– besar* district head. *– kedua* subdistrict head. *– uma* village head.

hukumiah legal (*mod*).

hula-hula I a Hawaiian native dance with waving movements of the arms and body.

hula-hula II (*Bat*) the name of a leg of the *daliban natolu*. In the hierarchical system of the Bataks, the term refers to the *marga* of the wife's side.

hulam → ULAM.

huler (*E*) (rice) huller.

hulu 1 upstream. *– sungai* reaches/upper course of a river, headwaters; → UDIK I; *opp* HILIR. *di – sungai ada air terjun* there is a waterfall at the upper course of the river. *industri –* upstream industry. **2** base, beginning. *– hati* pit of the stomach, solar plexus. *– malang* the root/beginning of all misery. *– musim* beginning of the season. **3** handle, haft, hilt. *– cangkul* handle of a hoe. *– keris/pisau* kris/knife hilt. **4** interior, hinterland, back country. **5** (*cla*) head. *sakit – (ob)* headache. *kalang –* pillow; → BANTAL. *orang –* country bumpkin. *– hilir* a) upper and lower course of a river. b) lower and upper ends, beginning and end. *Kita mulai omong-omong ke – ke hilir.* We began to chat about all sorts of things. *tidak tahu – hilirnya* you can make neither head nor tail of it. *– mujur pandai bertengkar, – baik pandai memakai* (*M*) to get along fine with others, easygoing. *ke – kena bubu, ke hilir kena tengkalah* cannot avoid danger. *jikalau di – airnya keruh, tak dapat tidak di hilirnya keruh juga* it doesn't rain but it pours. *– dinihari* just before dawn. *– hati* pit of the stomach. *– kembar* biceps. *– kepala* crown of the head. *– ledak* warhead. *berhulu(kan) ledak* fitted with a warhead. *– ledak banyak* multiple warhead. *– ledak nuklir* nuclear warhead. *– perang* warhead.

berhulu(kan) 1 with a hilt (of). *keris ~ gading* a kris with an ivory hilt. **2** to originate/begin from (*di*), have its upper reaches at (*di*). *Sungai Cisadané berhulu di Gunung Pangrango.* The Cisadane River has its upper reaches at Mount Pangrango. **3** to have a warhead.

menghulu to go/sail upstream/up river; → MUDIK.

menghulukan (*ob*) to lead, head.

hulu-huluan, pehuluan (*ob*) and **penghuluan** headwater area.

penghulu village head. **kepenghuluan** (in Riau, etc.) village.

pe(r)huluan interior, inland.

hulubalang 1 (*ob*) army commander. **2** (*Ac*) k.o. district head. **3** k.o. bodyguard. **4** k.o. village security guard; → DUBALANG.

menghulubangi to command, be commander of.

hulur → ULUR I.

huma 1 dry rice field. **2** newly cleared forest land.

berhuma 1 to have/own a dry rice field or newly cleared forest land. **2** to work in a dry rice field or on newly cleared forest land.

memperhuma to work a piece of land to turn it into a dry rice field.

perhumaan 1 act of working on newly cleared forest land or in a dry rice field. **2** land that is turned into unirrigated rice fields.

human I 1 (D) humane. **2** (E) human.

Humanika [Himpunan Masyarakat untuk Kemanusiaan dan Keadilan] Community Association for humanitarianism and Justice.

humaniora (D) the humanities, arts and humanities.

humanis (D) humanist.

humanisasi (E) humanization.

humanisma and **humanisme** (D) humanism.

humanitas 1 humanity. **2** (E) mankind.

humanitér (D) humanitarian.

Humas [Hubungan masyarakat] Public Relations. *seorang –* public relations man/officer. *Ia didampingi –nya.* He was accompanied by his public relations man.

kehumasan public relations (*mod*).

humbalang → HEMBALANG.

humban → UMBAN.

humbar menghumbar to let loose, leave unattended.

humbas berhumbas to run away, flee.

menghumbas to do s.t. quickly.

humor (D) humor, comic.

berhumor to jest, joke, tell jokes.

humoris (D) humorist.

humoristis (D) humorous, comical.

humus (D/E) humus.

Humuzah (A) al– "The Slanderer"; name of the 104th chapter of the Koran.

hun (C) a small weight for opium (1/100 *tail*).

huncué (C) (opium) pipe.

hungkué and **hungkwé** (C) **1** *tepung –* flour made from mung beans. **2** gelatinous pudding made with this flour.

huni inhabit. *layak –* inhabitable. *Luas wilayah daratan Irian Jaya yang layak – perlu diteliti secara cermat.* The inhabitable range of the Irian Jaya mainland needs careful research. *tidak layak –* uninhabitable, unfit for human habitation. *Rumah baru yang kini siap dialokasikan tidak layak –.* The new houses now ready to be allocated are unfit for (human) habitation. *– kontrak* occupied and leased. **menghuni-kontrak** to occupy and lease (a house).

berhuni 1 occupied, inhabited. *Rumah itu ~.* That house is occupied/inhabited. **2** guarded, watched over. *tempat ~ a* haunted place.

menghuni 1 to occupy, inhabit, live/dwell/reside in. *Selama ia pergi, sayalah yang ~ rumahnya.* In his absence, I lived in his house. *Rumah susun Kebon Kacang siap dihuni.* The walk-ups at Kebon Kacang are ready to be occupied. *Pulau itu belum dihuni manusia.* That island is not yet inhabited by men. *Bangunan yang dihuni penduduk dinyatakan sudah tidak memenuhi syarat untuk dihuni lagi.* The building which was occupied by residents has been declared uninhabitable. **2** to be infested with. *sungai yang dihuni buaya* a crocodile-infested river.

menghunikan 1 to settle s.o. (somewhere). *200 KK akan dihunikan di Kecamatan Cibinong.* Two hundred families will be settled in the Cibinong subdistrict. **2** to guard, (keep) watch over. *Hunikan barang-barang ini, saya hendak ke belakang.* Watch this stuff, I have to go to the bathroom.

hunian 1 residence. *daérah ~* residential area. *Kampung di Indonésia bukanlah daérah ~ saja, tetapi juga merupakan daérah ékonomi.* Kampongs in Indonesia are not only residential areas, but also constitute commercial areas. **2** occupancy. *tingkat ~* occupancy rate (of hotel, etc.).

pehuni → PENGHUNI 2.

penghuni 1 inhabitant, occupant, occupier (of a room, etc.). *~ bui* jailbird. *~ kolong jembatan* inhabitant of the space beneath a bridge. *~ rusun/rumah susun* high-rise apartment house occupant. **2** (M) guardian spirit. *Rumah itu ada ~nya.* The house is haunted. **berpenghuni** inhabited, occupied. *Di sana sekarang terdapat 227 rumah yang sudah siap dan ~.* Now,

there are 227 houses finished and occupied. *Pulau itu tidak ~ kecuali héwan-héwan.* That island is not inhabited by men but rather by animals. *tidak ~* uninhabited. **berpenghunikan** to be inhabited/occupied by. **kepenghunian** inmate. *meningkatkan ~ solidaritas* to increase inmate solidarity. *subkultur ~* inmate subculture.

penghunian occupation (of a dwelling).

perhunian occupation (of a house), habitation. *tingkat ~ kamar* occupancy rate (of a hotel).

hunjam plunge, dive.

menghunjam 1 to dive down (of a hawk/plane, etc.). *Burung elang itu ~ ke arah sekumpulan anak ayam.* The hawk dived down in the direction of a bunch of chicks. **2** to stab, thrust, plunge (a knife, etc.) into s.o. or s.t. *Pelaku langsung ~ cluritnya tepat mengenai perut bagian kiri W.* The perpetrator immediately stabbed his sickle-shaped knife right into the left side of W's stomach. **3** to have entered/penetrated (one's heart). *Rasa kasih sayang sudah ~ benar ke dalam hati sanubarinya.* His feelings of love have really penetrated his deepest innermost self.

menghunjami (*pl obj*) to stab.

menghunjamkan 1 to make s.t. dive down. *~ layangannya menuju ke tanah* to make his kite dive downward. **2** to stab, thrust, plunge (a spear, etc.) (into s.o.), rain (blows) (down on), plant (roots), embed s.t. (into). *Dihunjamkan lembingnya ke perut binatang itu.* He stabbed his spear into the stomach of the animal. *~ lutut nan dua* (M) to kneel.

terhunjam 1 embedded, stuck, planted in the ground, rooted. *Jénderal (Purn) Abdul Harris Nasution, seorang tokoh militér légéndaris yang nyaris ~ tikaman pisau di tahun 1965.* General (ret.) Abdul Harris Nasution, a legendary military figure, who was almost stabbed in 1965. **2** (regarding feelings) buried, kept locked up inside. *Kalau perasaan begini yang ~ di dalam hati sanubari, alamat dunia akan celaka.* If feelings are buried deep in the heart like that, the world will be a bad place.

hunjaman stab, thrust, plunge, sticking s.t. (into s.t.).

penghunjam → tenggal plowshare.

penghunjaman thrusting, sticking.

hunjin (C) contribution (paid for membership of a club, etc.).

hunjuk → UNJUK I.

hunkwé → HUNGKUÉ.

hunsa (A) good deeds, benevolent service; → KEBAJIKAN.

hunting (E) **1** (for telephones) hunting, queuing. **2** (in Kuta-Legian, Bali) chasing after white women who are looking for Balinese men. *Adegan baku – ini mencapai puncaknya di disko-disko léwat pukul 12.00 malam.* These acts of hunting reach their climax in the discos, after midnight.

huntsa (A) *– musykil* bisexual.

hunus menghunus(kan) to unsheathe, draw (a sword, etc.), draw out s.t. *Ia ~ bayonét.* He drew his bayonet. *~ cincin* to take a ring off one's finger.

terhunus unsheathed (a bayonet/dagger, etc.). *memegang pedang ~* to hold an unsheathed sword in one's hand. *dengan bayonét ~* with fixed bayonet. *pistol ~* an unholstered pistol.

hunyi → HUNI.

hup (command of bus passenger to driver) hold on, don't start yet!

hupmas [Hubungan Masyarakat dan Pemerintah] Public and Government Relations.

hura (D) hurrah! hurray!

(ber)hura-hura 1 to shout hurrah. *Meréka berhura-hura di hotél tempat meréka menginap.* They shouted and shouted in the hotel where they were staying. **2** to have a good time.

huria (Bat) **1** district. **2** (PC) parish.

huru *pohon –* various species of trees, Litsea spp. and others. *– tangkalak* k.o. tree, Litsea chinensis and others.

huruf (A) letter(s) of the alphabet. *buta –* a) illiterate. b) illiteracy; → BUTA I. *dengan –* spelled out in words (rather than numerical). *mata –* letter. *tahu mata –* literate. *menurut –* word by word, verbally, literally, verbatim (translation). *– Arab gundul* Arabic characters used in writing Indonesian/Malaysian but omitting the vowel points. *– awal* initial letter. *– balok* block letter. *– benar* consonant. *– besar* uppercase/capital letter.

menghuruf-besarkan to capitalize, write s.t. in uppercase letters. – *bunyi* vowel. – *cétak* printed character, print letter. – *corét* strikeout. – *emas* gold lettering.– *gésér atas* superscript. – *gésér bawah* subscript. – *harakat/hidup* vowel. – *ikat* monogram. – *Jawa* Javanese characters. – *jawi* Arabic script for writing in Indonesian/Malaysian. – *kamariah* (in Arabic) moon letters, sounds which do not cause assimilation of the last sound of the definite article. – *kapital* uppercase letter. – *kecil* lowercase letter. – *kurus* condensed type. – *Latin* Roman script. – *lepas* typed letters not connected to e.o., block letters. – *majemuk* digraph. – *mati* consonant. – *miring* italics. – *mula* initial letter. – *paku* hieroglyph, cuneiform characters. – *panggilan* call letter (of a ship). – *pégon* Arabic letters used to write Javanese. – *rangkap* digraph. – *Rumi* (Indonesian or Malaysian with) Roman characters. – *saksi* vowel mark in Arabic script. – *sambung* connected letters in script. – *syamsiah* (in Arabic) sun letters, sounds which cause assimilation of the last sound of the definite article. – *tebal* boldface type. – *timbul* raised embossed letter. – *tong* (*coq*) musical note. – *tulis* handwritten character, script.
berhuruf with ... characters. *bacaan yang ~ Latin* reading material in Roman characters.
hurufiah (*A*) → HARFIAH.
huru-hara commotion, tumult, disturbance, uproar, riot(ing).
berhuru-hara to be in an uproar.
menghuru-harakan to instigate rioting/disturbances.
hurup → HURUF.
hus hush! be quiet!
menghus(-hus)kan to hush s.o. up.
husada (*O Jv*) medicine, health.
pehusada healer, therapist.
Husain the Prophet Muhammad's grandson, the youngest son of Fatimah with Baginda Ali (the Prophet's son-in-law), Hassan's younger brother. Husain during his tenure as caliph was ambushed and killed by his enemies in Karbala. After his head was cut off, it was pierced by a bayonet and later carried around by the enemies who shouted: Husain! Husain! Husain! At that very moment, it is alleged, a mysterious flying animal, in the shape of a bird with the body of a horse with wings and a human face (the *buraq*), arrived to pounce on and seize the head to fly with it to heaven. This event is still annually commemorated on the 10th of *Muharram* by the Shi'a community, *esp* in Iran, but also in Padang and Bengkulu (West Sumatra) under the name of *keramaian Hasan-Husain*; → BOURAQ *Indonesian Airlines*.
husap → USAP.
husar (*D*) hussar. *selada* – Russian salad.
husarenslah (*D*) Russian salad.
Huséin Sastranegara air base in Bandung.
Husni Thamrin a street in Jakarta named after Mohammad Husni Thamrin, a well-known nationalist, native of Jakarta.
meng-Husni Thamrin-kan to improve shantytowns. *Memberi bantuan untuk memperkeras jalan itu sekaligus ~ lingkungannya.* To grant aid in order to harden the roads and at the same time improve the shantytowns in the surroundings; → PROYÉK MHT.
husnudh-dhon (*A*) good prejudice.
hust hush!
husuk → KHUSUK.
husus → KHUSUS.
Hut I (*A*) Pisces (*zod*).
HUT II [Hari Ulang Tahun] 1 birthday. *merayakan –nya* and *ber-*

HUT to celebrate one's birthday. 2 anniversary, commemoration.
hut III (in acronyms) → KEHUTANAN.
huta (*Bat*) a Toba-Batak settlement, i.e., a very small cluster of houses standing like an island in the midst of a rice field; many Toba-Batak names have *huta* as their initial element: *Hutabarat, Hutagalung, Hutapéa, Hutauruk*, etc.
hutan 1 forest, wood. 2 wild (animals, etc.) *anjing* – jackal. *ayam* – jungle fowl. *babi* – wild boar. – *orang* a) forest dweller. b) aborigine of East Sumatra. c) orangutan; → MAWAS I. – *alam/asli* natural/primeval/native/virgin forest, jungle. – *alam produksi* natural production forest. – *bakau* mangrove forest. – *belantara* jungle, wilderness. – *belukar* underbrush forest. – *beton* concrete jungle (describing a city). – *cadangan* reserved forest. – *cemara* coniferous woodland. – *daratan rendah* lowland forest. – *daratan tinggi* highland forest. – *hujan* rainforest. – *hujan tropis/tropika* tropical rainforest. – *jati* teak forest. – *kayu* woodlot. – *kemasyarakatan* community forest. – *kota* city park. – *larangan* forest in which it is forbidden to fell trees, forest preserve. – *lepas* big primeval forest. – *lindung* protected forest. – *milik* privately owned forest. – *muda* forest recently planted with trees. – *musim* monsoon forest. – *negara* national forest. – *pantai* coastal forest. – *payau* tidal forest. – *perawan* virgin forest. – *percobaan* experimental forest. – *pertanian* agroforest. – *produksi* production forest. – *rimba* forest primeval, jungle. *tidak diketahui – rimbanya* he was nowhere to be seen, there was no sign of him (anywhere). – *rimbun* deciduous woodland. – *suaka (alam)* [HSA] forest preserve. – *suaka margasatwa* animal preserve. – *tanaman* plantation. – *tanaman industri* [HTI] industrial forest. – *terusan* coppice forest. – *tropis/tropika* tropical forest. – *tropis/tropika basah* tropical rainforest. – *tropis/tropika dataran rendah* lowland tropical rainforest. – *tua* a forest with old trees. – *tetap* permanent forest. – *turis* tourist forest, national park. – *tutupan* forest in which it is forbidden to fell trees; forest preserve. – *wisata* forest for tourists, national park.
berhutan wooded.
menghutan to become forest, grow back (of a forest). *Ladang yang ditinggalkan itu ~ lagi.* The abandoned arable land became a forest again. *kembali ~* to turn back into forest.
menghutani to afforest, reforest.
menghutankan 1 to turn into a forest, forest. *~ kembali* to reforest. 2 to abandon to the jungle.
kehutanan 1 forestry, forest (*mod*). 2 silviculture, silvicultural.
penghutanan afforestation.
perhutanan forestry.
hutang → UTANG.
Huud → HUD.
huwayu (*Jv*) beautiful (of women). – *manyala* of rare beauty.
huwi → HUI II. various species of plants. – *blicik* a plant with contraceptive powers, *Dioscorea bulbifera*. – *sawut* k.o. tree, *Dioscorea pentaphylla*.
huyung menghuyungkan to make s.o. stagger.
terhuyung-huyung to stagger, sway, swing, oscillate, move first to the right then to the left.
HVS → KERTAS *HVS*.
Hwa hwéé (*C*) a popular Chinese gambling game based on combinations of pictures and riddles.
hwaméi (*C*) *burung* – spectacled laughing thrush, *Carrulax canorus*.
hwana → WANNA.
Hwéé (*C*) *Tionghoa Siang* – Chinese Trade Association.
hyang → YANG I.
hy- see words beginning with HI-.

I

i and I I /i/ 1 the ninth letter of the Latin alphabet used for writing Indonesian. 2 the Roman numeral for 1.

I II (E) /ai/ I (the pronoun). *I mau ke pasar.* I'm going to the market.

I III (Bal) caste title placed before male and female personal names to indicate that the person belongs to the Sudra caste, such as *I Nengah Wédja*. – *Déwa* caste title placed before male personal names to indicate that the person belongs to the Vaisya/Waisya caste. – *Desak* caste title placed before female personal names to indicate that the person belongs to the Vaisya/Waisya caste. – *Gusti Agung* and – *Gusti Ngurah* caste title placed before male personal names to indicate that the person belongs to the Kshatriya caste, such as *I Gusti Ngurah Oka*.

I IV (sl) the illegal drug Ecstasy; → INÉX.

ia I (third-person singular pronoun) he, his, she, her, it, its. *Amérika Serikat menyatakan, – tak akan membiarkan keseimbangan di Timur Tengah berubah.* The U.S. stated that it would not tolerate a change in the balance of power in the Middle East.

ia II (emphatic form of) yes. – *dong!* of course! – *ini* and – *itu* namely, id est, i.e.; → YAKNI, YAITU.

seia ~ *sekata* to be in complete agreement.

beria to say yes, assent; → YA I. ~ *berbukan* to negotiate, consult.

beria-ia 1 to discuss, negotiate, deliberate. 2 to keep on agreeing/saying yes.

mengiakan to agree to/with, assent to. *Bukan orang yang ~ saja apa yang dikatakan kepadanya.* He's not the kind of person who just agrees with everything said to him.

pengia yes man. *Pemimpin itu mengelilingi dirinya dengan ~.* That leader surrounded himself with yes men.

IAIN (init) [Institut Agama Islam Negeri] State Institute of Islamic Studies; a university-level institute administered and financed by the Department of Religion which offers Islamic subjects and a general education.

ialah 1 (copula between third-person subject and the predicate) is, are; → ADALAH I. *Orang itu – orang Indonésia.* That person is an Indonesian. *Bahasa resmi Negara Républik Indonésia – Bahasa Indonésia.* The official language of the Republic of Indonesia is Indonesian. 2 – *karena/sebab* because, due to. – *karena kurang hati-hatinya* due to carelessness.

iang (ob) god, idol; → SANG *yang*, YANG I.

ianjo (Jp) (during the Japanese occupation) bordello, brothel.

ianya (M) (emphatic) he, she. *Mendengar témbakan yang begitu gencar, Iskandar Alisyahbana terbangun; dikiranya témbakan itu membunuh anjing hérdernya. Dibiarkan begitu – kembali tidur.* Hearing such sustained shooting, Iskandar Alisyahbana suddenly woke up thinking that the shooting had killed his German shepherd. He didn't do anything about it and just went back to sleep.

iau (onom) meow, mew, cry (of a cat).

mengiau to meow, mew, cry.

iba I (A) 1 pity, sympathy, compassion, commiseration. *memasang rasa* – to try to arouse s.o.'s pity. *Di Jerman pengemis tidak memasang rasa – dengan pakaian compang-camping, tapi menampilkan keahlian beratraksi.* In Germany beggars don't try to arouse people's pity by wearing ragged clothes, but rather by showing off their interesting skills. *menaruh – pada diri sendiri* to indulge in self-pity. 2 feel pity/sorry (for), be moved/affected/touched. *Semua orang – melihat anak-anak itu menangis memanggil ibunya.* Everyone felt sorry for the children who were crying and calling out for their mother. – *hati* concerned, solicitous, compassionate. – *kasihan* compassion, sympathy, pity; → BELAS *kasihan*.

beriba-iba pitiful, moving, touching, pitiable. ~ *minta tolong* to ask for help by trying to make s.o. feel pity.

mengiba(-iba) touched, emotional.

mengibai to pity, feel pity/sorry for. *Tidak usah kau ~ meréka yang tidak mau menolong diri meréka.* You needn't feel sorry for those who don't want to help themselves.

mengibakan 1 (~ *hati*) to make s.o. feel pity, moving. *Berita kematian anaknya sungguh ~ hati.* The news of her child's death was really moving. 2 to sympathize with, feel pity for, sorry about. *Tidak usahlah anda ~ nasib pria yang tidak berguna itu.* You needn't feel sorry for what happened to that useless man.

keibaan 1 grief, sorrow, regret, remorse. 2 compassion, pity.

pengiba [and peiba (M)] person who feels pity/sorry, loving person.

iba and iba' II (A) refusal, denial.

ibadah and ibadat (A) 1 service to God, worship, religious devotion/observance. 2 god-fearing, pious. 3 religious feelings, piety. *ahli* – s.o. who fulfills his religious duties/obligations. *rumah* – house of worship. *melakukan/menjalankan* –.– *keagamaannya* to perform one's religious duties/obligations. – *haji* the pilgrimage to Mecca, the fifth pillar of Islam. – *mahdhah* religious obligations. – *puasa* the fast, the fourth pillar of Islam. – *shalat* the five daily prayers, the second pillar of Islam. – *sosial* social obligations. – *sunah* a nonobligatory action. – *wajib* an obligatory action.

beribadah 1 to perform one's religious duties/obligations. 2 religious, pious, devout.

keibadahan religious duties/obligations, worship.

peribadah pilgrim.

peribadahan 1 observance of religious duties/obligations. *Musik merupakan bagian ~ orang Kristen.* Music is part of Christian religious observance. 2 worship. *rumah/tempat ~* house of worship.

ibah → HIBAH.

ibak → IBA II.

iban I various k.o. crustaceans.

Iban II *orang* – the Iban, a tribe in Kalimantan.

ibarat (A) 1 like, similar to. *melukiskan suasana – kiamat* to depict a situation similar to the end of the world. 2 parable, moral (of a story). *Cerita-cerita – banyak terdapat dalam kesusasteraan Melayu Lama.* Many parables can be found in Old Malay literature. *Cerita ini –nya barang siapa makan cabai dia yang merasa pedas.* The moral of this story is: As you sow, so shall you reap. 3 metaphorical.

beribarat 1 to contain a lesson, have a moral, have a symbolic meaning. *Dia gemar sekali membaca cerita-cerita ~.* He loved to read stories with a moral. 2 to tell a story (or, give advice) that has a lesson/symbolic meaning. *Ketika ia sedang ~, ada seorang yang bertanya, katanya.* When he was giving advice with a moral, s.o. asked a question, he said.

mengibaratkan 1 to make a comparison (with), compare s.t. (to). *Kalau kita ibaratkan dengan pertunjukan wayang, maka itu sama dengan banyak pemain yang dibébérkan di layar tapi tidak ikut main.* If we compare it to a *wayang* performance, it's like a group of actors spread out on a screen but not taking part in the show. 2 to tell parables to. *Tiada lupa ia ~ anak-anaknya supaya jangan menempuh jalan yang sesat.* He did not forget to tell parables to his children so that they would not take the wrong path. 3 to be likened to, considered. *Diibaratkan kita orang alim.* We are considered pious people.

ibarat-mengibaratkan to tell stories with a moral. *Di samping ~ kehidupan duniawi, dia mengungkapkan bahwa suksés hidupnya itu semata-mata adalah anugerah Tuhan.* Besides telling moral tales about life in the real world, he also revealed that the secret of his success is a gift from God.

pengibaratan comparison, symbolizing.

ibar-ibar a dugout canoe.

IBB [Indonésia Bagian Barat] the Western Part of Indonesia; cp IBT.

Iben Sekedai (in Bengkulu) the Raf(f)lesia plant.

iberani → IBRANI.

ibidem (*L*) *ibidem*, in the same place.

ibing I (*Jv*) **ngibing** to dance with a *pengibing*.

   pengibing a female dancer who dances with men without touching them. ~ *ronggéng* k.o. taxi dancer, i.e., men pay to dance with her and it possibly leads to sexual intercourse; → RONGGÉNG.

ibing II (*J*) **pengibing** (teenager slang in the Tanjung Priok port area) s.o. who looks for goods which have fallen off trucks.

iblik k.o. dance peculiar to the Diëng Plateau area in Central Java.

iblis (*A*) Satan, devil, demon. *digoda* – tempted by the devil. *kemasukan* – possessed by the devil; → SÉTAN. *biar* – *asal dikenal* better the devil you know than the one you don't know.

ibni (*A*) son of (royalty) (in personal names), such as *Abdul Halim Mu'adzam Shah* – *Sultan Badlishah*.

ibnu (*A*) **1** son of (in personal names), such as *Umar* – *Khatab*; → BIN I. **2** a first name, such as – *Sutowo*.

ibra I (*A*) **1** acquittal, remission (of debts/sins), exemption (from taxes). **2** liberation.

IBRA II (*acr*) Indonesian Bank Restructuring Agency.

Ibrahim (*A*) **1** (the biblical) Abraham. **2** "Abraham"; name of the 14th chapter of the Koran.

Ibrani (*A*) Jewish; → YAHUDI. *orang* – a Jew.

ibrit (*J*) **mengibrit** and **ngibrit** to run away.

IBT [Indonésia Bagian Timur] the Eastern Part of Indonesia; *cp* IBB.

ibtida (*A epist*) beginning, exordium. *huruf al.*– introductory words of a chapter.

ibtidaiyah (*A*) elementary. *madrasah/sekolah* – elementary school; → SD.

ibu 1 mother; → BIANG I, INDUK, INDUNG I. – *dari segala pertempuran* the mother of all battles. **2** married woman. *kaum* – a) mothers. b) housewives. c) married women. **3** spouse, wife. *Ménpén H. Ali Budiardjo bersama* –. Information Minister H. Ali Budiardjo and his wife. **4** maternal. **5** form of address to older women or s.o. higher in status than the speaker. – *Agung* Supreme Mother, i.e., Fatmawati Soekarno. **6** (in many compounds) main or most important part of s.t.; *cp* ANAK. – *akar* main root, taproot. – *angkat* foster mother. – *ayam* mother hen. – *bapak* parents. ***keibubapakan*** parental. – *baptisan* godmother. – *dapur* cook. – *Dharma Pertiwi* wife of a member of the Armed Forces. – *gedé* a) grandmother. b) parent's older sister. – *guru* female teacher. –*nya guru* (*Jv*) female teacher. – *jari* thumb. *menjepit* – *jarinya di tengah telunjuk dan jari tengah* to stick the thumb between the index finger and the middle finger (= a fuck-you sign). – *kaki* big toe. – *kandung* birth mother (not by adoption or foster). – *kejahatan* source of evil. – *Korps Taruna Akmil* the Mother of the Military Academy Cadet Corps, i.e., Mrs. Tien Soeharto. – *kos* landlady. – *kota* and *ibukota* a) capital city (of any administrative district). b) (*usu* capitalized) Jakarta, the capital of Indonesia. ***beribu kota*** to have ... as its capital (city). *Républik Démokrasi Kongo yang* ~ *kota Kinshasa* the Democratic Republic of the Congo with Kinshasa as its capital. ***beribukotakan*** with ... as its capital. *Suriname* ~ *Paramaribo*. The capital of Suriname is Paramaribo. ***mengibukotakan*** to make ... the capital city. ~ *Samarinda* to make Samarinda the capital (of East Kalimantan). – *Kota Kedua RI* Bogor. – *kunci* lock. – *mata angin* cardinal points of the compass. – *mertua* mother-in-law. – *Negara* First Lady, the president's wife. – *negeri* capital city. ***beribunegerikan*** to have ... as its capital (city). ~ *Payakumbuh* to have Payakumbuh as its capital. – *panah* bow (of a bow and arrow). – *pasir* pebble; gravel. – *pejabat* a) the mother of an official. b) the wife of an official c) (*Mal*) head office; → KANTOR *pusat*. – *pejabat bank itu terletak di Kuala Lumpur*. The headquarters of the bank is located in Kuala Lumpur. – *pengganti* surrogate mother. – *Pertiwi* a) Mother Earth. b) native country. c) fatherland, motherland. – *pintu* door post. – *puru* primary stage of yaws. – *roti* yeast. – *rumah* main house. – *rumah tangga* housewife. – *sungai* main/principle river. – *suri* queen/royal mother. – *susu* wet nurse. – *tangan* thumb. – *tangga* banister(s). – *tentara* main body of an army, main force. – *tiri* stepmother. – *tunggal* single mother. – *Utama* Eminent Mother, i.e., Ibu Wongsoredjo, General Ahmad Yani's mother.

ibu-ibu 1 ladies. **2** of an age to be a mother, older woman.

   seibu with the same mother.

   beribu 1 to have a mother. **2** to call s.o. mother.

   beribukan to have ... as a mother.

   mengibui to mother.

   keibuan 1 motherhood, maternity. **2** motherly, maternal.

   keibu-ibuan motherly.

   peribuan 1 women's rights movement. **2** matriarchal.

ibuisme the ideology of motherhood.

ibuk → HIBUK, SIBUK I.

ibul *nibung* – a large thornless palm variety with poisonous fruit, *Orania macrocladus*.

ibun (*S*) dew.

ibunda mother (politer than *ibu* and usually epistolary).

ibung (*ob*) mother.

ibus gebang palm, a variety used for mat-making, *Corypha gebanga*.

i.c. (*abbr*) [in casu] (*L leg*) in this instance.

icak icak-icak (*M*) **1** to pretend, make believe, feign; → PURA-PURA, SOK I. ~ *tidak tahu* to pretend not to know, play dumb. **2** pseudo, not genuine, fake, false. *kepala désa* ~ pseudo-village head. **bericak-icak** to pretend, make believe, feign.

   mengicak to simulate.

   icakan pretended, feigned, counterfeit, sham.

   icak-icakan false, pretend.

icip (*J*) morsel, (food) sample, taste (of); → CICIP I.

   icip-icip sample, taste. *gula* ~ small amounts of sugar given out as samples, etc.

   mengicipi [and **ngicipin** (*J*)] to try/taste (food).

ICMI [Ikatan Cendekiawan Muslim se-Indonésia] All-Indonesia Muslim Scholars Association.

icrit (*Jv*) small amount.

   ngicrit-icrit (*usu* in passive) *diicrit-icrit* to do s.t. in small amounts, do s.t. little by little.

id (*A*) feast (day), festival, holiday. – *al-adha*, –*ul Adha*, –*uladha* and –*ulkorban* the Feast of the Sacrifice or Greater *Bairam*, celebrated on the tenth day of *Zulhijjah* (the last month of the Muslim year); the climax of the *hajj*, following completion of the pilgrimage to Mecca; goats, lambs, and cows are usually sacrificed. – *al-fitr/–ul Fitr/–ulfitri* the Feast of Breaking the fast of *Ramadan* or Lesser *Bairam*, celebrated on the first day of *Syawal* (the tenth month of the Muslim year), i.e., the so-called Javanese New Year; → LEBARAN. – *al-kiswa* the Festival of the *Kiswa*, celebrated in the month of *Syawal* on the occasion of carrying the *Kiswa* from Cairo to Mecca; → KISWA. – *al-milad* Christmas.

Ida (*Bal*) – *Anak Agung* a caste title placed before personal names to indicate that the person belongs to the Kshatriya caste. – *Ayu* a caste title placed before female personal names to indicate that the person belongs to the Brahman caste, such as *Ida Ayu Nyoman Rai*; → DAYU II. – *Bagus* a caste title placed before male personal names to indicate that the person belongs to the Brahman caste, such as *Ida Bagus Balik Ambara*. – *Betara* Goddess of the Southern Ocean; *cp Nyi Loro Kidul*. – *Cokorda/Cokorde* a caste title placed before male personal names to indicate that the person belongs to the Kshatriya caste. – *Sang Hiang Widhi Wasé*, – *Sang Hyang Widhi Wasa*, and – *Sangyang Widi Wassa* The One and Only God; *cp* TUHAN *yang Maha Esa*.

idafat (*A gram*) genitive.

idafi (*A*) additional; relative.

idah I (*A*) a love token given by a man to a woman at a betrothal or at the beginning of a sexual liaison. – *gelap* love token given at the beginning of a sexual liaison. – *terang* love token given at a betrothal.

   mengidah to court s.o. by giving him/her a love token.

   mengidahkan to offer s.t. as a love token.

idahan and **pengidah** a love token given at a betrothal or at the beginning of a sexual liaison.

idah II (*A*) – *bain* period (generally 100 days) during which a divorced woman is not allowed to remarry (because she might be pregnant with her former husband's child).

idam I (*Tam*) **1** longings/cravings of a pregnant woman (for certain k.o. food). **2** craving, desire, strong wish.

mengidam [and **ngidam** (*coq*)] **1** to long for (or, crave) certain k.o. food (of a pregnant woman). **2** to become pregnant, conceive.

mengidam(-idam)kan 1 to crave, want to eat. *Istrinya ~ buah-buahan yang kecut.* His wife craved sour fruit. **2** to have a strong desire for. *Ibunya ~ seorang dokter sebagai menantu.* Her mother wanted a doctor as her son-in-law.

idam(-idam)an 1 s.t. craved/longed for. **2** aspirations, hopes, ideals, dream (*mod*). *rumah idaman keluarga anda* your family's dream house.

pengidaman longing for, craving.

idam II → IDAP I.

idang → HIDANG.

idap I mengidap to suffer from a chronic disease. *~ penyakit* to suffer from, have (a disease). *~ obat bius* to be addicted to drugs. *~ perut* to be hungry.

mengidapkan 1 to suffer from, have (a disease). **2** chronic, prolonged (illness).

teridapkan *tidak ~* unbearable.

idapan 1 a chronic illness. **2** sickly, ailing, in poor health.

pengidap sufferer, s.o. who has (a disease). *~ narkotik* drug addict.

pengidapan suffering (from a disease).

idap II → IDEP.

idar → ÉDAR.

idas seidas a twist (of thread).

mengidas to twist/twine threads.

idayat → HIDAYAT.

'iddah → IDAH II.

idé (*D*) idea; → GAGASAN. *- komunisme* the idea of communism.

seidé with the same ideas.

idéal (*D/E*) ideal, perfect. *Ia adalah pria yang - untuk wanita itu.* He's the perfect man for that woman.

mengidéalkan to make ideal.

pengidéalan making ideal.

idéalis (*D/E*) idealist.

beridéalis idealistic. *Jangan terlalu ~.* Don't be too idealistic.

idéalisasi idealization.

mengidéalisasikan to idealize.

idéalisir (*D*) **mengidéalisir** to idealize.

idéalisme (*D/E*) idealism.

idéalistik (*E*) and **idéalistis** (*D*) idealistic.

idem (*D/E*) ditto. *- dito* ditto (stronger than *idem* alone).

idéntifikasi (*D*) identification.

mengidéntifikasi(kan) to identify.

teridéntifikasi(kan) identified.

pengidéntifikasian identification.

idéntifisir (*D*) **mengidéntifisir** to identify.

idéntik (*D/E*) identical.

mengidéntikkan to identify. *~ diri* to identify o.s.

keidéntikan identity, resemblance.

pengidéntikan identifying.

idéntitas (*D*) identity; → JATI *diri*.

beridéntitas to be identified (as). *~ sebagai agén KGB* to be identified as a KGB agent.

mengidéntitaskan to identify.

pengidéntitasan identity, identification.

idéograf (*D/E*) ideograph.

idéografi (*D/E*) ideography.

idéogram (*D/E*) ideogram.

idéologi (*D/E*) ideology.

beridéologi to have an ideology; ideological.

beridéologikan to have ... as one's ideology. *~ Pancasila* to have *Pancasila* as one's ideology.

mengidéologikan to ideologize.

idéologis (*D*) ideological.

idéologisasi (*D*) making (s.t.) an ideology.

idéologiwan (*D*) ideologist, ideologue.

idep (*Jv*) eyelash(es).

idep-idep (*Jv*) it would be better (to do s.t.) rather than.

ider (*Jv*) → ÉDAR, IDAR. **ider-ider** to walk around, travel about.

ngider to wander around, travel about, ride/drive around. *Ia semalaman ~ dengan mobilnya keliling Jakarta.* He drove around Jakarta all night long.

ngiderin (*J coq*) to wander around some place.

Idhata the association of female workers and wives of employees of the Department of Education and Culture.

IDI [Ikatan Dokter Indonésia] Association of Indonesian Physicians.

idih (*usu* dragged out: idiiiih) (*coq*) exclamation of disgust, yuk!

idiil (*D*) ideal, not real, imaginary.

idil → IDUL.

idilis (*D*) idyllic.

idin → IZIN.

idiolék (*D/E gram*) idiolect.

idiom (*D/E gram*) idiom.

idiomatik (*E*) and **idiomatis** (*D*) idiomatic.

idiosinkrasi (*D*) idiosyncrasy.

idiot (*D/E*) idiot.

idmar (*A gram*) ellipsis.

idola (*D*) idol.

mengidolakan to idolize.

Idris and **Idrus** (*A*) (the biblical) Enoch.

idu I (*Jv*) spittle, spit. *- abang* → DUBANG.

idu II → HIDU.

idul → following entries.

iduladha → under ID.

idulfitri → under ID. **beridulfitri** to celebrate *Idulfitri*.

idulkorban and **idulkurban** → under ID.

idung → HIDUNG.

idup → HIDUP. **ngidupin** → MENGHIDUPKAN.

idzin → IZIN.

ied → ID. *sembahyang -* mass prayer held in the open on *Idulfitri*. *-ul Adha* → ID*ul adha*. *-ul Fitri* → ID*-ul fitri*.

if (in acronyms) → INFANTERI.

if(f)ah (*A*) self-restraint, abstinence, maintaining one's purity.

ifkun (*A*) slander, calumny.

ifrit (*A*) evil spirit.

iftar (*A*) to break the fast; → BERBUKA *puasa*.

iftitah (*A*) opening (prayer/speech, etc.). *khutbah -* opening speech.

iga (*Jv*) rib. *- landung* a long rib. *- péndék* seventh rib. *- selungkang* false rib. *- wekas* (*Jv*) short rib.

igal I mengigal(-igal) 1 to spread its tail and strut around. **2** to dance around while moving the body around.

mengigalkan to dance (a dance).

igal-igalan dancing around.

igal II (*A*) band around a headdress.

igama → AGAMA.

igamah (*A*) foreign resident permit.

igau I mengigau [and **ngigau** (*coq*)] **1** to talk in one's sleep. **2** to be delirious. **3** to sleepwalk, walk in one's sleep.

mengigaukan to dream about, rave about, talk deliriously about.

terigau talked about in one's sleep.

terigau-igau dreamt. *~ kepada* dreamt about s.t.

igauan 1 delirium. **2** nonsensical talk, prattle.

igau-igauan talking in one's sleep; to be delirious, be half awake.

pengigau s.o. who talks in his sleep.

pengigauan talking in one's sleep.

igau II (*M*) noisy, chaotic, with lots of commotion.

terigau startled.

igau-igauan very noisy, boisterous.

igel → IGAL I.

igir (*Jv*) mountain ridge.

igo → IGAU I.

ih exclamation of disgust; → IDIH.

iham-iham (*J onom*) clicking of the tongue.

ihdom (*D ob*) fully owned land.

ihik-ihik-ihik (*onom*) sobbing sounds.

ihlas → IKHLAS.

ihram and **ihrom** (*A*) in a state of purity; consecration. *baju/pakaian -* clothing which pilgrims to Mecca are required to wear.

berihram to wear such clothes.

ihrom → IHRAM.

ihsan (*A*) good deeds/works, charity, benevolence.

ihsanat (*A*) good deeds/works.

IHSG → INDÉKS *Harga Saham Gabungan.*

ihtiar → IKHTIAR.

ihtifal (*A*) party, social gathering.

ihtikar (*A*) to hoard (grain, etc.) in order to sell it at a higher price; to corner, monopolize (the market in a certain food, etc.).

ihtilam (*A*) wet dream.

ihtimal (*A*) to take away, take along with.

    mengihtimalkan to give, assign (a duty) to s.o.

ihwal → HAL I.

ija → IJO.

ijab (*A*) 1 bid, offer, tender of goods. 2 answer to a prayer. – *kabul/nikah* signing the marriage contract and accepting the bride, solemnization of a marriage.

    mengijabkan 1 to offer. 2 to answer a prayer. 3 to perform a marriage ceremony, solemnize a marriage.

ijabah and **ijabat** (*A*) favorable reply; approval, granting a wish, answering a prayer.

ijajah → IJAZAH.

ijajil (*A*) devil.

ijama → IJMA.

ijarah (*A*) 1 price. 2 rent, leasing; k.o. Islamic leasing system in which goods are bought by the bank and then rented to the client.

ijas (*A*) 1 (black) prune. 2 dark purple (in color).

ijasah → IJAZAH.

ijazah (*A*) 1 permission, permit, license. 2 diploma, certificate.

    berijazah 1 to have a diploma/certificate. ~ *Sarjana Muda* to have a B.A. degree. 2 certified, licensed. *bidan* ~ certified midwife. *tak* ~ unlicensed, uncertified.

ijil (*A*) calf (young of a cow); → GUDÉL I.

ijin (*A*) → IZIN. *kartu* – *masuk* entrance card. *surat* – *mendarat* landing permit, permission to disembark. *surat* – *menetap* resident permit. – *Kerja Tenaga Asing* [IKTA] Foreign Worker's Work Permit. – *terlebih dahulu* prior consent.

    ngijinin (*J coq*) to allow, permit.

ijma', **ijmah**, and **ijmak** (*A*) 1 consensus of opinion, *esp* on a religious point. 2 common accord/agreement.

    berijmak to agree, come to an agreement/understanding. *150 ulama* ~ *bahwa pajak adalah wajib.* 150 Muslim scholars agreed that taxes are obligatory.

ijmal (*A*) summary, epitome.

    mengijmalkan to summarize, epitomize.

ijo (*J/Jv*) green; → HIJAU. – *royo-royo* fresh green, green as grass.

    mengijo to buy paddy, etc. while it is still green (or, before it is ripe); → IJON.

ijon (*Jv*) the purchase of paddy, etc. while it is still green (or, before it is ripe). *sistém* – "ijon system," i.e., the system by which a peasant mortgages the crop (for money) before it is harvested.

    mengijon and **ngijon** to buy up (paddy standing in the field). ~ *mahasiswa* to recruit college students before they have completed their studies by granting them a one-year scholarship.

    mengijonkan to sell rice before it is harvested.

    pengijon purchaser of paddy, etc. while it is still green (or, before it is ripe).

    pengijonan buying or selling rice before it is harvested.

ijtihad and **ijtihat** (*A*) 1 interpretation through reasoning and judgment of the Koranic code, conclusion formed after careful study of the evidence, conviction based on such conclusions. 2 investigation, opinion. *pada –nya* in his opinion.

    berijtihad to interpret (according to one's opinion).

ijtima and **ijtima'** (*A*) lunar conjugation (used to determine the time for religious observance).

ijtimaiyah (*A*) 1 social. 2 socialist(ic). 3 sociological. *sayuun* – social affairs.

ijuk I black sugar palm fiber (used for brooms/rope/roofing). *tali* – rope made from this fiber.

    mengijuk bristly, bristling (like a mustache).

ijuk II (*M*) **terijuk** embarrassed.

ik (*D*) I (the personal pronoun).

ika I → ÉKA.

ika II (in acronyms) → IKATAN.

ikab (*A*) punishment.

Ikadin [Ikatan Advokat Indonésia] Indonesian Attorneys Association.

ikal 1 (of hair/tendrils) curly, wavy. – *galing* ringlet. – *manis* slightly curly. – *mayang* more tightly curled, ringlets (like the curl of a palm blossom). *Tubuhnya kecil dengan rambut* – *mayang.* He is small and has curly hair. 2 loop. 3 shavings. – *baja* steel shavings. – *tembaga* copper shavings.

    berikal 1 curly, wavy. 2 looped.

    berikalkan with a curl of.

    mengikal 1 to curl, make curly, wave. 2 to become curly/wavy.

    mengikalkan to curl the hair for s.o. else.

    ikalan 1 loop. 2 (*Jv*) spool, reel, bobbin. ~ *benang* cotton-thread reel/bobbin.

    keikalan curliness, waviness, curl.

    pengikalan looping.

ikamah and **ikamat** (*A*) muezzin's second and last call to prayer.

ikan 1 fish. *nyawa* – breathing one's last. *daérah penangkapan* – fishing grounds. 2 (*Jv*) meat of any kind, any meat dish which accompanies rice. – *ayam* chicken meat. – *babi* pork. – *sapi* beef. *seperti* – *pulang ke lubuk* east, west, home is best; there's no place like home. *seperti* – *dalam belanga* like shooting fish in a barrel, within easy reach. *seperti* – *dalam air* very happy. – *biar dapat, serampang jangan pukah* don't let the work go to waste, any work performed should be useful. – *terkilat jala tiba* quickly understanding what s.o. is saying before he even finishes saying it. – *gantung, kucing tunggu* the tortures of Tantalus. *kuat* – *karena radai (kuat burung karena sayap, kuat ketam karena sepit)* everyone has his own strengths. *terkilat* – *di dalam air, sudah tahu jangan betinanya* a sharp-witted person can tell s.o.'s intentions or intelligence as soon as he starts talking. *ibarat* – *dan air* hand in glove. FOR NAMES OF FISHES OTHER THAN THOSE BELOW SEE THE NAME OF THE FISH. – *air tawar* freshwater fish. – *asap* smoked fish. – *asin* salted fish. – *babi* spiny coral fish, *Holacanthus sp.* – *baja* freshwater decorative fish, tiger barb, *Puntius tetrazona.* – *bakar* grilled/roasted fish. – *balur* k.o. jerked fish. – *bambangan* sea perch, *Lutianus sanguineus.* – *basah* fresh fish. – *batak* k.o. fish found in Lake Toba. – *baung* freshwater catfish, *Macrones spp., Mystus nemurus.* – *bawal* pomfrey. – *belida* a) a large river featherback, *Notopterus notopterus.* b) clown knifefish, *N. chitala.* – *belanak* gray mullet, *Mugil spp.* – *belut* a swamp eel, *Monopterus albus.* – *bentik* fish that live between the land and the continental shelf. – *bilih* k.o. fish, *Mystacoleucus padangensis.* – *bulu ayam* k.o. anchovy, Macassar red fish, *Coilia spp., etc.* – *buntal* puffer, globe-fish, *Crayracion immaculatus.* – *buru* k.o. decorative fish, *Chanda buruensis.* – *cakalang* skipjack tuna, *Katsuwonus pelamis.* – *cuik* (*J*) steamed and salted fish. – *cuka* fried pickled fish. – *cumi-(cumi)* a small cuttlefish, squid, *Loligo spp.* – *darat* freshwater fish. – *duri* catfish, *Arius, spp.* – *duyung* dugong, a large whale-like mammal, sea cow, manatee, *Dugong dugon.* – *ékor kuning* yellowtail (a tasteless, medium-sized fish). – *emas* goldfish, carp, *Cyprinus carpio.* – *gabus* a murrel, *Ophiocephalus sp.* – *garing* a freshwater carp, *Labeobarbus.* – *gemi* sucking fish, remora, *Echineis naucrates/ albsescens.* – *gendang-gendis* an ornamental aquarium fish. – *gerot-gerot/gerut-gerut* grunter (fish), *Pristipoma spp.* – *gépéng* flounder. – *glodok* mudskipper, *Periophtalmus spp.* – *gurami* (*Jv*) a freshwater carp, k.o. gurami, *Osphromenus olfax.* – *hias* an ornamental aquarium fish. – *hias néon tétra* neon tetra, *Paraceirodon inesi.* – *hiu* various species of shark. – *hiu paus* whale shark, *Rhincodon typus.* – *hiu tenggiri* man-eating shark, *Galeocerdo rayneri.* – *hiu todak* sawfish, *Pristis cuspidatus.* – *jelawat* maroon shark, *Leptobarbus hoeveni.* – *jolong-jolong/julung-julung* a) garfish, *Hemiramphus spp.* b) needlefish, *Xenentodon canciloides.* – *juara* a river catfish, *Pangasius sp.* – *kaca* Javanese ricefish, *Oryzias javanicus.* – *kacang-kacang* barracuda, *Sphyraena spp.* – *kakap* a) a marine fish species, often referred to as a giant perch. b) big shot, big fish (among criminals); *opp* TERI. – *kakap mérah* red snapper, *Lutianus argentimaculatus.* – *kakap putih* sea bass, *Lates calcalifer.* – *kakatua* parrot fish, *Callydon sp.* – *kaléngan* canned/tinned fish. – *kambing-kambing* blue ring angelfish, *Pomacanthus annularis.* – *kelabau* a carp, *Osteochilus melanopleura.* – *kembung* horse mackerel, *Caranx spp.* – *kembung banjar* k.o. mackerel. – *kepala timah* a freshwater cyprinid. – *kerapu* grouper. – *kering* dried fish, *usu* salted. – *ketutung* an ornamental aquarium fish. – *koan* grass carp, *Ctenopharyngodon idellus*. – *kulari* → KULARI. – *landak* k.o. porcupine fish, *Diodon hystrix*. – *layang-layang* the flying fish, *Exocoetus volitans*. – *layaran* marlin, sailfish, *Istiophorus gladius*. – *lélé* k.o. catfish, *Clerius melanoderma*. – *léma* k.o. fish, *Rastreliger kanagurta*. – *lembu* long-horned cowfish, *Ostracion cornutus*. – *lemuru* k.o. sardine, *Sardinella longiceps*. – *lidah* k.o. sole, *Synaptura panoides*. – *lidi* grooved razorfish, *Centriscus scutatus*. – *limbat* walking catfish, *Clarias nieuhofi*. – *lindung* (*Jv*) eel. – *lodan* (*Jv*) whale. – *lombalomba/lumbalumba sungai/air tawar* freshwater dolphin, *Orcaella brevirostris*; → PESUT. – *mangsi* cuttlefish, *Sepia* spp. – *mas* goldfish; carp, *Cyprinus carpio*. – *mérah* red sea-perch, *Lutianus roseus*. – *moa* → IKAN mua. – *mola* silver carp, *Hypopthalmichthys molitrix*. – *mua* Asian swamp eel, *Monopterus albus*. – *mujair* tilapia, a freshwater fish, *Tilapia mossambica*. – *Napoléon* giant wrasse, *Cheilinus undulatus*. – *nila* a parrot fish, *Pseudodax sp*. – *nilem* k.o. fish, *Osteochilus hasselti*. – *noméi* Bombay duck, *Harpodon nehereus*. – *Nun* a legendary fish which carries the earth on its back. – *oték* a) a sea fish, *Arius utik*. b) a sea fish, *Tachysurus utik*. – *padi* freshwater decorative fish, Japanese killifish/medaka, *Oryzias latipes* and other species. – *pari* various species of ray, skate, *Rhinoptera javanica*. – *paus* whale. – *paus abu-abu* gray whale, *Eschrichtius robustus*. – *paus biru* blue whale, *Balaenoptera musculus*. – *pecak* halibut. – *peda* salted fish. – *pépés* spiced fish roasted or steamed in a banana leaf. *pépés* – *mas* spiced goldfish roasted or steamed in a banana leaf, considered an aphrodisiac in West Java. – *raya* whale. – *rucah* fish not eaten but turned into fishmeal, fertilizer, etc. – *salem/salam* salmon. – *sayap* Indian hatchet fish, *Laubuca laubuca*. – *sebelah* k.o. flatfish, Indian halibut, *Pseudorhombus arsius*. – *selar* horse mackerel, *Caranx kalla*. – *semah* river carp, *Tor douronensis*. – *senangin* edible thread-fish, *Polynemus tetradactylus*. – *senjolong/senjulung* garfish, *Hemirhamphus* spp. – *sepat siam* snakeskin gourami, *Trichogaster pectoralis*. – *siram dabu-dabu* k.o. fish dish made with tomato sauce and onions. – *sotong* cuttlefish, *Sepia* spp. – *suji* various black marlin, *Makaira indica*. – *tamban* pilchard, sardine, *Clupea* spp. – *tambera* a freshwater carp, *Labeobarbus tambra*. – *tapa(h)* a giant river catfish, *Callichrous pabda/Wallago tweediei*. – *tawas/tawes* Java barb, *Puntius javanicus* and other species. – *tembakul* mudskipper, *Periophtalmus* spp. – *tempaus* whale. – *tenggiri* Spanish mackerel, *Scomberomorus* spp. – *teri* a) various k.o. very small marine fish, Makassar red fish, *aka* anchovy, *Stolephorus* spp. b) small fry, petty thief; *opp* KAKAP. – *terubuk* herring, *Clupea macrura*. – *todak* keeled nettlefish, spearfish, *Platybelone argalus platyura*; Square-tail alligator gar, *Tylosurus leiurus*. – *tombro* (*Jv*) freshwater carp, *Labeobarbus tambra*. – *tongkol* tunny fish, *Thynnus thunnina*. – *torpédo* grass carp, *Ctenopharyngodon idella*. – *ubi* lizard fish, *Synodus* spp. – *ubur-ubur* jellyfish, *Scyphozoa* spp. – *ulang-uli* an ornamental aquarium fish, clown loach, *Botia macracanthus*.

ikan-ikan ship's log, float for measuring a ship's speed.

berikan 1 abounding in fish, full of fish. 2 *pergi* ~ to go fishing.

ikanan fish.

pengikan 1 fisherman. 2 (*M*) s.o. who loves to eat fish.

perikanan fishing, fishing industry, fishery. ~ *laut dan darat/air tawar* sea and land/freshwater fishery. ~ *rakyat* artisinal fisheries. *ahli* ~ piscatologist.

Ikapi [Ikatan Penerbit Indonésia] Indonesian Publishers Association.

ikat 1 band, string, cord. 2 bunch, bundle, sheaf. 3 frame(work). 4 counter for tied bundles/bunches. *rambutan se-/dua* – one/two bunches of *rambutan*. 5 fastening/setting (of a ring). *cincin yang longgar –nya* a ring with a loose setting (for its gems). 6 (*Jv*) a plaited *batik* headcloth which is wrapped around the head; → DÉSTAR. 7 k.o. woven fabric found in parts of the Lesser Sundas. – *erat* a tight binding. **mengikateratkan** to tighten (a binding). – *janji* commitment. – *janji terdukung* back-to-back commitment. – *kepala* a) headband. b) *batik* headcloth. – *kepala mérah* red headband, symbol of Christians. – *kepala putih* white headband, symbol of Muslims. – *kolam* stone edge of a pool. – *kursi* seatbelt. – *léhér* scarf. – *perang* (*cla*) battle-array. – *pinggang* waistcloth, belt, girdle; → SABUK I. – *satu* a tied bundle. **mengikatsatukan** to tie/fasten together into a bundle. – *teguh* tie firmly. **mengikat-teguhkan** to tie s.t. up tight.

ikat-ikat *tanpa* ~ without any strings, no strings attached.

seikat a bundle, s.t. tied up. ~ *bagai lidi* in agreement.

berikat 1 bound, tied together. 2 with/having a band/belt, etc. of. *pedang* ~ *mas* a sword mounted with gold. 3 bonded. *kawasan* ~ bonded zone. 3 (*Mal*) allied, united, joint. *Bangsa* ~ United Nations; → PERSERIKATAN *Bangsa-Bangsa. Kuasa-kuasa* ~ Allied Powers, the Allies.

berikatkan to use s.t. as cord/tie/band.

mengikat 1 to tie (up), fasten, bind (together, into bundles/bunches). ~ *kayu api* to tie firewood up into bundles. ~ *mata* to fascinate, attract one's attention. 2 binding (of a contract, etc.). *tidak* ~ nonbinding. ~ *diri* to commit o.s. (to). ~ *diri dalam perkumpulan* to join a club. ~ *diri untuk membayar pada tanggal ...* to commit o.s. to paying on ... ~ *hati/perhatian* captivating, appealing, fascinating. *cerita yang* ~ *hati* a fascinating story. *perjanjian yang* ~ a binding agreement. *Imbauan présidén tentang sawah perlu diikuti peraturan* ~. The president's proposals on wet-rice fields must be followed up by binding regulations. 3 to enter into (a contract). ~ *perjanjian* to enter into a contract/agreement. ~ *dinas* to enter into a service contract (with a government agency). 4 to compose/write (verses/poetry, etc). ~ *pantun* to compose a quatrain. ~ *kalimat* to compose a sentence. 5 to set/mount (diamonds, etc.); to hem, edge, put a border around. ~ *intan dengan suasa* to mount diamonds with pinchbeck. ~ *mas* gilded. ~ *perang* to send soldiers into battle. ~ *perigi* to put a border (of wooden beams) around a well.

mengikati (*pl obj*) to tie, etc.

mengikatkan 1 to attach/fasten/tie/secure s.t. (to s.t. else). *Ikatkan tali ini pada tiang itu*. Fasten this rope to that pole. ~ *ke léhér* to wrap s.t. around s.o.'s neck. 2 to bind, commit. ~ *diri* to commit o.s. (to), promise (to). ~ *dirinya kepada orang lain* to commit o.s. to another person.

terikat 1 bound, fastened, attached, tied down (by obligations). *tak* ~ nonbinding. ~ *akar* permanently attached (to the soil). ~ *kontrak dengan* bound by a contract to. 2 committed. 3 liable. 4 captivated. 5 tangled (of wire, rope). 6 restricted. *penulis tak* ~ freelance writer. ~ *oléh* addicted to. ~ *secara hukum* legally bound. **keterikatan** tie, bond; commitment, encumbrance. ~ *historis* historic ties.

ikatan 1 club, organization, union, association, society. ~ *Dokter Indonésia* [IDI] Indonesian Medical Association. 2 bundle, bunch. ~ *hanyutan* boom (for transporting logs). ~ *kayu* bundling (for transporting timber). 3 commitment, bond; allegiance. *ada ~nya* there's a string attached, there's a catch to it. *tanpa* ~ *apa-apa* with no commitment, with no strings attached. ~ *dinas* commitment to work for the government after graduation. ~ *moral* moral commitment. ~ *kawin/nikah/perkawinan* bonds of matrimony. ~ *orangtua dan anak* parent-child bonding. ~ *panén* crop lien. 4 contract, agreement; contracted for. ~ *dinas* a) service contract. b) conscription. *dalam* ~ *kontrak* under contract. ~ *pembelian* purchase agreement. 5 (literary) composition. 6 bond, chemical bond. 7 bracing, brace. ~ *busur* arch brace. 8 setting (of a jewel). **seikatan** belonging to the same organization. **berikatan** to have a contract. ~ *dinas* to have a service contract to work for the government after graduation.

ikat-ikatan (*cla*) poetry.

keikatan commitment.

pengikat s.t. used for tying/binding/fastening. ~ *gigi* braces.

pengikatan 1 tying, binding, obligating. 2 fastening, fixing. 3 connection. 4 federating.

perikatan 1 relationship. 2 alliance, federation, merger. *Beberapa partai politik yang sehaluan sedang berunding untuk membentuk sebuah* ~. Some political parties which are moving in the same direction are discussing forming a federation. 3 (*leg*) obligation, commitment, (formal) agreement. ~ *akibat* obligation to guarantee a certain result. ~ *bébas* natural obligation. ~ *bersyarat* conditional obligation. ~ *dengan ketetapan waktu* and ~ *dengan waktu yang ditentukan* obligation with a time limit. ~ *hasil* obligation to guarantee a certain result. ~ *usaha* obligation to perform to the best of one's abilities. ~ *yang dapat dibagi-bagi* divisible obligation.

ikébana (*Jp*) the Japanese art of flower arranging.

ikel → IKAL.

iket → IKAT.

ikhbar (*A*) **1** to inform, report to. **2** to tell, narrate, relate.

ikhlas (*A*) **1** sincere, honest, truthful, straightforward. **2** ready, prepared, willing. **3** wholehearted. *dengan tulus* – a) sincerely, seriously. b) carefully. *penerimaan dengan* – wholehearted acceptance. **4** "Pure Faith"; name of the 112th chapter of the Koran. *belum* – not yet willing/ready, etc. **kebelum-ikhlasan** not being willing/ready, etc.

seikhlas as sincer as.

mengikhlaskan 1 to devote o.s. to. **2** to do s.t. wholeheartedly/ with devotion. **3** not be particular (about), accepting.

keikhlasan 1 sincerity, honesty, truthfulness. **2** devotion. **3** readiness, willingness.

pengikhlas devotee.

ikhtiar (*A*) **1** free choice/will; decision. **2** ways and means, efforts, endeavor, initiatives. *habis* – all means have been tried. *mencari suatu* – *untuk membébaskan kawannya* to look for a way to free their friend.

berikhtiar to try, make an effort to, see to it that. *Kamu semua harus* ~ *untuk menyelesaikan masalah ini.* All of you have to try to settle this problem. *tidak* ~ at a loss, unable to find a way.

mengikhtiarkan to succeed in doing s.t., choose a line of action to do s.t., find the ways and means for doing s.t., arrange for doing s.t.

pengikhtiaran making an effort to, seeing to it that.

ikhtiari (*A*) spontaneous, optional, voluntary, of one's own will/ choice.

ikhtikar (*A*) monopoly, hoarding (illegal under Islamic law).

ikhtilaf (*A*) difference (of opinion), discrepancy; diversity, variety, deviation (of compass).

ikhtilah and **ikhtilat** (*A*) free social relations of men and women who are not related.

ikhtisar (*A*) **1** summary, résumé, précis, outline, statement, minutes (of a meeting), abstract (of s.t. written). *Buku ini memuat* – *tatabahasa Indonésia.* This book contains a summary of Indonesian grammar. **2** diagram, tableau.

berikhtisar summarized.

mengikhtisarkan to summarize, condense, make a synopsis of.

pengikhtisaran summarizing, condensing.

ikhtisariah (*A*) brief, condensed.

ikhtiyath (*A*) prudence; → KEHATI-HATIAN.

ikhwal → HAL I, IHWAL.

ikhwan (*A*) **1** brothers; friends. **2** alumnus of the *Pesantrén Suryalaya* in Tasikmalaya, West Java. – *al-zaman* contemporaries.

seikhwan in a brotherhood/fraternity; of the same race, fraternal.

ikhwani (*A*) brotherly, fraternal.

Ikhwanul Muslimin (*A*) Muslim Brotherhood.

ikhwanun (*A*) *kullul-Muslimin* – all Muslims are brothers.

IKIP [Institut Keguruan dan Ilmu Pendidikan] Institute of Teacher Training and Pedagogy.

ikke (*Indonesian-Dutch*) (the pronoun) I.

iklab (*A*) correct pronunciation.

iklan (*A*) **1** advertisement. **2** announcement, notice. – *atap* sky sign. – *baris* classified ad. – *kecil* classified ad. – *layanan masyarakat* public service ad. – *luar* outdoor advertising. – *mini* classified ad. – *témbak* a "shotgun-approach" advertisement placed in a small newspaper without the consent of the business enterprise concerned. The newspaper then tries to force the business to pay for the ad.

beriklan 1 to have advertisements. **2** to advertise. *Anda ingin* ~ *di berbagai média daérah?* Do you want to advertise in various regional media? **3** to be advertised. *Sampai mendekati akhir tahun ini, hanya obat-obatan yang masih terus gencar* ~ *léwat PT Matari Advertising.* Until close to the end of the year, only medicines have kept on being advertised through the Matari Advertising Agency. *cara* ~ advertising method.

mengiklankan to advertise, promote.

keiklan-iklanan advertising.

pengiklan advertiser.

pengiklanan advertising s.t., the act of advertising.

periklanan advertising, publicity. *ahli* ~ advertising expert. *perusahaan* ~ advertising agency.

iklanisasi commercialization through advertising.

periklanisasian (*mod*) advertising.

iklas → IKHLAS.

iklim (*A*) **1** climate. **2** atmosphere. – *invéstasi* investment climate. – *politik yang baik* a favorable political climate/atmosphere. – *usaha* business climate. **3** weather. – *antara* the climate in the period between the two monsoons. – *panas* tropical climate. – *sedang/sederhana* temperate climate.

beriklim with a ... climate. ~ *dingin* to have a cold climate.

mengiklim to become the climate (of a place).

teriklim acclimatized.

keikliman climatological.

ikmal (*A*) sighting the moon so as to begin or end Ramadan.

ikon (*D/E*) icon.

ikonis (*D*) iconic.

ikonografi (*A*) iconography.

ikrab (*A*) intimate, close.

ikral → IKRAR.

ikram (*A*) veneration, worship, reverence.

ikrar (*A*) **1** oath, pledge, vow. – *bersama* collective vow. **2** avowal, affirmation; acknowledgment, attestation, declaration. – *talak* declaration of divorce. **3** charter. – *Atlantik* Atlantic Charter; → PIAGAM *Atlantik*.

berikrar to pledge, take a vow. ~ *setia* to pledge allegiance.

mengikrarkan to pledge, promise; to acknowledge. ~ *akad nikah* to take the vows of marriage. ~ *janji* to make an agreement. ~ *sumpah* to take/swear an oath. ~ *tauhid* to attest to the oneness of God, acknowledge that God is One.

iksan → IHSAN.

iksir (*A ob*) elixir.

ikterus (*D*) icterus, jaundice.

iktibar → ITIBAR.

iktidal (*A*) **1** straight; balanced. **2** (in praying) to stand upright after bowing (*rukuh*) and before prostrating o.s. (*sujud*).

beriktidal 1 believing, convinced. **2** to aim at s.t.

mengiktidalkan to be convinced of s.t.

iktikad → ITIKAD.

iktikaf → ITIKAF.

iktiologi (*D/E*) ichthyology.

iktisab (*A*) (legitimate) profit (making under Islamic law).

iktisad (*A*) economy.

ikut 1 to come/go along with, join (s.o. in doing s.t.), participate, take part. – *saya* come with me. *Pernah pula selama tujuh tahun ia* – *seorang dokter di Bandung.* He also worked with a physician in Bandung in order to gain experience. – *kami!* Follow us! – *angin* to set one's sails to every wind. – *berbicara* to join in the conversation, put one's two cents in. – *berdukacita* to convey one's condolences. – *berperang* to fight, serve (in the military). – *bersuara* to have a voice/say in the matter. *tidak* – *campur* to stay out of the picture, not get involved. – *dalam* to participate/ take part in. – *dalam acara* to be on (stage, etc.). – *dalam acara musik* to take part in a musical performance. – *duduk* to sit in (on). – *duduk di panitia* to be on a committee. – *gembira* to share in s.o.'s happiness. – *kuliah* to take a course. – *latah* to reflect, echo. *tidak* – does not participate. **ketidak-ikutan** nonparticipation. – *membayar* to chip in, pay one's share. *Saya mau* – *membayar.* I would like to chip in. – *nimbrung* (*coq*) to put one's two cents in, make one's contribution. – *numpang orang* to get a ride (in s.o. else's vehicle). – *rasa (dalam)* to give free rein to one's feelings (in). – *serta* to participate/take part, join (a game, etc.). *Adam Malik pada tahun 1937* – *serta dalam membentuk Kantor-Berita "Antara."* Adam Malik took part in the formation of the "Antara" News Agency in 1937. *Dalam rombongan présidén* – *serta ...* In the president's entourage were included ... – *serta perkelompokan* unlawful assembly. **mengikutsertakan** to make ... participate/take part, include. *Negara-*

negara yang ~ pemainnya adalah Inggris, Dénmark, Swédia, ... Countries which had their players participate were England, Denmark, Sweden, ... **keikutsertaan** participation; complicity. *~ meréka amat membantu prakarsa kami mengurangi stok dunia* ... their participation very much helped our initiatives to decrease the world's stock of ... **pengikutserta** participant. **pengikutsertaan** participation, taking part. **tidak ikut serta** does not participate/take part. **ketidakikut-sertaan** not participating/taking part, nonparticipation. *~ wakil-wakil parpol dalam Kabinét Pembangunan IV sekarang* ... the nonparticipation of the political parties' representatives in the Fourth Development Cabinet is ... *- tertawa* to join in the laughter. *- tua* to grow up. *- urun rembuk* to want to put in one's own word. *Berbicara soal musik dangdut, saya ingin - urun rembuk.* Talking about *dangdut* music, I wanted to put in a word. **2** to be/go/stay with s.o. (in their house/vehicle, etc.); to work for s.o., serve s.o.; to go along with s.o. (as a dependent). *- suami* housewife, accompanying her husband (in passports/biographies, etc.). **3** also, too, as well; → LATAH I.

ikut-ikut to copy, imitate, get involved in. *Jangan ~!* Stay out of this! Mind your own business! *Ia hanya ~ saja.* He has no principles, he's just a follower/hanger-on.

berikut 1 together/along with, including. *akan dijual sebuah rumah ~ pekarangannya* for sale: house and land. **2** following, (as) mentioned/stated below. *keterangan ~* the following information/explanation, the explanation stated below. *sebagai/seperti ~* [sbb] as follows/mentioned below. *surat yang bunyinya sebagai/seperti ~* a letter which reads as follows, a letter to the following effect. *yang ~* the following, the next one. **berikutnya** the following/next. *hari ~* the next/following day. *tahun-tahun ~* the following years. *Siapa ~?* Who's next?

berikut-ikut one following the other, one after another/the other, successive. *~ meréka keluar kamar itu.* They came out of the room one after another.

mengikut [and **ngikut** (*coq*)] **1** to go along with, accompany. *Dia akan ~ ayah ke Bogor.* He'll go with father to Bogor. *~ jejak* to follow suit. **2** to copy, imitate. *Murid selalu ~ kelakuan gurunya.* Students always imitate their teacher's behavior. **3** to follow, obey, comply with, adhere to. *Ia tidak mau ~ nasihat dokternya.* He doesn't want to follow his doctor's advice.

mengikuti [and **ngikutin** (*J coq*)] **1** to follow, shadow, tail, pick up (the track); → MEMBUNTUTI. *~ arah jalan jarum jam* clockwise. *Ia diikuti Polsus KA berseragam dengan borgol tercantél di géspérnya.* He was followed by a uniformed Special Policeman of the State Railways with handcuffs hooked to his belt buckle. *polisi ~ buronan itu* the police tracked down the fugitive. *~ jejak* a) to follow suit, follow in s.o.'s footsteps, do the same. *~ nasihat* to follow s.o.'s advice. **2** to attend, take part in, participate in, take (a course). *~ konperénsi* to take part in a conference. *~ kuliah/pendidikan* to take a course/courses. *~ upacara* to take part in a ceremony. **3** to observe, pay attention to, obey. **4** to keep up/pace with, keep abreast of. *tidak ~ perkembangan zaman* does not keep abreast of the times. *~ zaman* to keep up with the times. **5** to be like/similar. *Dia ~ ibunya.* She's like her mother.

mengikutkan 1 to have/let ... follow, continue/go on with. **2** to add. **3** to enclose, attach. **4** to have/let ... participate/take part in, include. *Dia diikutkan.* He was included (in the operation).

memperikutkan to have/let ... follow, continue/go on with.

terikut inclusive, enclosed, included. *benda-benda yang ~* foreign matter.

ikutan 1 worthy of imitation. **2** model, example, s.t. to be followed/imitated. **3** s.t. that goes along with s.t. else. *angin ~* tail wind. *hasil ~* by-product. **4** (*geol*) associated (mineral). **5** (*coq*) to go along in, ... along, do s.t. with others. *Éd mengajak penonton ~ nyanyi.* Ed asked the audience to sing along. *~ urun rembug* to put one's two cents in.

ikut-ikutan 1 to follow blindly, not have one's own opinion, be a copycat. *Jangan ~!* Don't be a copycat! Don't try to keep up with the Joneses! **2** to get in on the act.

keikutan participation.

pengikut 1 adherent, supporter, follower. *~ buta* s.o. who follows blindly. **2** participant. *~ kursus* student in a course. *~ ujian* examinee. **3** partner. **4** fellow traveler. **5** (*geol infr*) associated (mineral). **kepengikutan** following, participating.

pengikutan following (s.o. or s.t.).

ilafi (*A*) *roh -* the finest spirit that can see God.

ilah I (*A*) **1** a god; a false god, idol. **2** my God! **berilah** *tak ~* godless. **mengilahkan** to deify. **keilahan** godhead, divinity.

ilah II → ILAT I.

ilahi (*A*) divine. *menghadap -* (*euph*) to pass away, die. *ya -!* Oh my God!

keilahian divinity.

ilahi(y)ah and **ilahi(y)at** (*A*) divinity, theology.

ilai mengilai(-ilai) to whinny (of horses), whoop (of gibbons), roar with laughter.

ilak I (*M*) weaver's measure of width of cloth to be woven. *bagai - bercerai dengan benang* irreparably separated.

ilak II (*A*) annulment.

ilak III → ÉLAK.

ilalang cogon grass, *Imperata cylindrica;* → ALANG-ALANG, LALANG I. *laksana batang - terhembus angin* irresolute, wavering, hesitant.

ilam-ilam dimly visible, vague, hazy.

ilang → HILANG. **ngilang** → MENGHILANG. **ngilangin** → MENGHILANGKAN.

Ilanun the name of a tribe of pirates from Mindanao, Philippines; pirate; → LANUN.

ilapat (*Jv*) omen (in reality or in a dream).

ilar → ILER I.

ilas (*J*) **mengilas** to step/tread on, crush, squash underfoot.

ilas-ilas → ILES-ILES.

ilat I (*A*) **1** bad luck, misfortune, accident. **2** illness, malady. **3** disadvantage. *Apa -nya?* What's the drawback? What's the problem with it? **4** handicapped, crippled, disabled, invalid.

ilat II (*Jv*) tongue. *- ngigel* mouthwatering. *- ujar* speech defect.

ilat-ilatan (*Jv*) *pohon -* a tall wild tree whose sap can be used as a medicine against boils, *Ficus callosa.*

ilau → KILAU.

ilégal (*D/E*) illegal.

iler (*J*) drooling saliva, slobber. **mengiler** [and **ngiler** (*coq*)] **1** to drool, slobber. **2** to drool over s.t., crave, (subject's) mouth waters. **mengilerkan** to make s.o. drool. **ileran** to salivate, drool.

ilér (*Jv*) mayana plant, *Coleus atropurpureus/scutellarioides.*

iles → ILAS.

iles-iles (*Jv*) a tuberous forest plant, k.o. *badur,* only eaten in times of famine, *Amorphophallus variabilis, Tacca palmata.*

ilham (*A*) **1** divine inspiration, revelation. **2** inspiration. **mengilham(i)** to inspire s.o. **mengilhamkan** to inspire with s.t. **terilhami** inspired. *Pelukis kita, Srihadi Soedarsono, ~ pantai Cherating.* Our painter, Srihadi Soedarson, was inspired by Cherating Beach. **pengilham** inspiration, inspirer. **pengilhaman** inspiration.

ili (*J*) **mengili** to evacuate, flee (natural disasters, etc.).

iling (*Jv*) **mengiling** to pour s.t. out carefully. **ilingan** s.t. poured out. **pengilingan** pouring out.

ilir → HILIR.

illat (*A*) reason, cause, motive. *Kita harus melihat - diharamkannya judi itu.* We must look at the reasons for forbidding gambling.

ilmiah (*A*) scientific. *orasi/pidato -* scientific lecture. **mengilmiahkan** to treat in a scientific manner, base s.t. on science. **keilmiahan** scientific (*mod*). *kader ~* scientific cadres.

ilmia(h)wan, ilmiyawan scientist; → ILMUWAN.

ilmiyah → ILMIAH.

ilmu (*A*) **1** science, knowledge. **2** supernatural knowledge, (writing with) esoteric wisdom → NGÉLMU. *contohlah - padi, makin/kian berisi makin/kian runduk* follow the example of the wisdom of the rice plant, the fuller it is, the more humble it is, i.e., remain modest. – *adab* ethics, moral philosophy. – *administrasi negara* public administration. – *aéronautika* aeronautics. – *agama* theology, religious science. – *agronomi* agronomics. – *akhirat* eschatology. – *akhlak* characterology, ethics. – *alam* a) natural science. b) physics. – *alam inti* nuclear physics. – *alat* the study of *tauhid*. – *alik* mysticism. – *aljabar* algebra. – *angka* numerology. – *arti kata-kata* semantics; → SÉMANTIK. – *asihan* the art of arousing feelings of love in a member of the opposite sex. – *astronautika* astronautics. – *atom* atomic theory. – *badi* science of metaphors. – *bahan* the study of commodities. – *bahari* navigation. – *bahas* dialectics. – *bahasa* linguistics. – *bahasa terapan* applied linguistics. – *baka* genetics; → GÉNÉTIKA. – *balaghah* science of rhetoric. – *bangsa* ethnology. – *bangun* morphology; geometry. – *bangunan* structural/building engineering. – *barang-barang kuno* antiquarianism. – *batin* a) esoteric learning, mysticism. b) the art of hypnotizing. – *batuan* lithology. – *bayan* exegesis. – *bedah* surgery. – *bedah syaraf* neurosurgery. – *belajar bahasa* language learning. – *belanja* corporate finance (a university subject). – *bentuk* morphology. – *bentuk kata* (*ling*) morphology. – *berat* theory of gravity. – *bercocok tanam* and – *bertanam* plant breeding, plant cultivation. – *bintang* astronomy. –.– *budaya* the humanities. – *bumi* geography. – *bumi alam* physical geography. – *bumi perékonomian* economic geography. – *bumi sosial-ékonomi* socioeconomic geography. – *cendawan* mycology; → MIKOLOGI. – *cuaca* meteorology; → MÉTÉOROLOGI. – *dagang* the study of trade and commerce, commercial science. – *dakwah* the study of the Islamic faith. – *diagnostik klinis* clinical diagnostics. – *éksakta* exact sciences, the hard sciences, such as mathematics, physics, etc. – *faal* physiology. – *fakih* canon law. – *falak* a) astronomy (*usu* limited to the calculation of the first day of the lunar month, eclipses, etc.). b) astrology. – *faraid* the laws governing inheritance/succession. – *fik(i)h* canon law, jurisprudence, study of Islamic law. – *firasat* physiognomy. – *fisik* physical sciences. – *fisika* physics. – *fisika atom* atomic physics. – *gaib* mysticism, occultism. – *gaya* mechanics. – *gaya bahasa* stylistics. – *gayung* incantation used to injure or kill s.o. from a distance. – *gejala penyakit* symptomatology. – *gendam* knowledge of how to cast a spell on s.o. – *géodési* geodesy. – *gizi* dietetics, study of nutrition. –.– *hadith nabi* the study of the traditions of the Prophet. – *halimunan* spell used to make o.s. invisible. – *hama* entomology. – *handasah* geodesy, geometry. – *hayat* biology; → BIOLOGI. – *héwan* zoology. – *hisab* arithmetic. – *hitam* black magic. – *hitung* arithmetic. – *hukum* jurisprudence. – *huruf* assigning numerical values to important words and phrases for divination. – *iklim* climatology. – *inti* nuclear physics. – *istilah* terminology. – *jaringan tubuh* histology. – *Jawi* philosophical mysticism. – *jiwa* psychology. – *jiwa analitis* analytical psychology. – *jiwa perusahaan* industrial psychology. – *jiwa tingkah-laku* behaviorism. – *jiwa urai* analytical psychology. – *kalam* doctrine, scholastic theology (of a religious faith). – *kampung halaman* folklore. – *karang-mengarang* the art of writing. – *katak* (*M*) acting without thinking in advance. – *keakhiratan* eschatology. – *kebatinan* philosophical mysticism. – *kebidanan* midwifery, obstetrics. – *kedokteran* medical science. – *kedokteran hukum* forensic medicine. – *kedokteran gigi kehakiman* forensic odontology. – *kedokteran kehakiman* forensic medicine. – *kedokteran mulut* oral medicine. – *kehutanan* forestry, silviculture. – *kejahatan* criminology. –.– *kelautan* maritime sciences. – *kenegaraan* political science. – *kependudukan* demography. – *keperawatan* nursing. – *keprajuritan* military science. – *kesaktian* occultism. – *keséhatan* hygiene. – *keséhatan masyarakat/umum* public health. – *kesejahteraan keluarga* home economics. – *kesenian* esthetics. – *ketabiban* medical science. – *ketatanegaraan* public administration. – *keturunan* genetics. – *kewarganegaraan* civics. – *kewiraan* military science. – *kira-kira* arithmetic. – *klenik* occult sciences, black magic. – *komputer* computer science. – *komunikasi massa* communication science; → PUBLISTIK. – *lambang* heraldry. – *lingkungan manusia* human ecology. – *lughat* philology. – *ma'ani* rhetoric. – *mantik* logic. – *masyarakat* social sciences.

– *mesin* mechanics. – *musik daérah* ethnomusicology. – *nah(w)u* syntax; → SINTAKSIS. – *nujum* astrology, astronomy. – *obat(-obatan)* pharmacology. – *optik* optics. – *panas* black magic. – *pasti* mathematics; → MATÉMATIK(A). – *patirasa* immunology; → IMUNOLOGI. – *pemasyarakatan* penology. – *pemerintahan* science of government. – *pendidikan* pedagogy. – *pengajaran bahasa* language teaching. – *pengetahuan* science; knowledge. – *pengetahuan alam* (natural) science. –.– *pengetahuan kemasyarakatan* social sciences. – *pengetahuan khayali* science fiction. –.– *pengetahuan terpakai* applied science. – *pengobatan radang usus dan perut* gastroenterology. – *penyakit* pathology; → PATOLOGI. – *penyakit gigi dan mulut* oralogy. – *penyakit kanak-kanak* pediatrics. – *penyakit kulit* dermatology. – *penyakit tua* gerontology; → GÉRONTOLOGI. – *penyangga gigi* periodontology. – *penyirep* → SIREP. – *penyutradaraan* directing (plays/films). – *peran* acting (on stage, etc.). – *perbintangan* a) astronomy. b) astrology. – *perkamusan* lexicography. – *perkebunan* horticulture. – *perokétan* rocket science. – *pertambangan* mining engineering. – *pertanian* agriculture. – *pesawat* mechanics. – *peta* cartography; → KARTOGRAFI. – *petilasan* archaeology. – *pidato* rhetoric; → RÉTORIK. – *politik* political science, politics. – *psikiatri* psychiatry; → PSIKIATRI. – *purbakala* archaeology. – *putih* white magic; *opp* – *hitam*. – *rajah* palm reading. – *ramalan bintang* astrology; → ASTROLOGI. – *sabda* art of casting a spell on s.o. – *salik* mysticism. – *saraf* neurology. – *sejarah* history; → HISTORI. – *sél* cytology. – *serangga* entomology; → ÉNTOMOLOGI. – *sérologi* serology; → SÉROLOGI. – *sihir* a) hypnosis. b) shamanism. – *silat* art of self-defense. –.– *sosial* social sciences. – *suara* acoustics. – *sufi* Sufism. – *suluk/sunyata* mysticism. – *surahi* knowledge of the Koran. – *susila* ethics. – *syirik* polytheism; → POLITÉISME. – *tabib* (*ob*) medicine. – *tanah* pedology. – *tanah pertanian* agrogeology. – *tanaman* botany; → BOTANI. – *tarikat/tasawuf* mysticism. – *tasyrih* anatomy; → ANATOMI. – *tatabahasa* grammar. – *tatalingkungan* ecology. – *tatapérsonalia* personnel management. – *tatarias* cosmetology. – *téater* dramaturgy. – *téknik* technology; → TÉKNOLOGI. – *téknologi dirgantara* aerospace science and technology. – *teras* nuclear physics. – *terpakai* applied science. – *toksikologi* toxicology; → TOKSIKOLOGI. – *tongkat* stick fighting. – *tulisan rahasia* cryptography; cryptology. – *tumbuh-tumbuhan* botany; → BOTANI. – *ukur* geometry. – *ukur analitis/analitika* analytic geometry. – *ukur bumi* geodesy. – *ukur melukis* descriptive geometry. – *ukur ruang* stereometry; → STÉRÉO. – *ukur tanah* surveying. – *ukur sudut* goniometry. – *ukur tanah* surveying. – *urai* (*tubuh*) anatomy; → ANATOMI. – *usaha negara* public administration (term used at Gadjah Mada University). – *us(y)uluddin* knowledge of Islamic tenets. – *utama* mainstream science. – *watak* characterology. – *wiraniaga* salesmanship. – *yang dominan dipergunakan* mainstream science.

berilmu knowledgeable, erudite, scholarly, learned.

mengilmukan to make s.t. scientific.

keiluman scientific.

ilmuwan scientist; → ILMIAWAN. – *agronomi* agronomist. – *hukum angkasa* specialist in aerospace law.

ilok (*Jv*) *ora* – improper, out of place, in poor taste.

ilték [*ilmu dan téknologi*] science and technology.

ilu moving, touching, affecting, pathetic.

ilung(-ilung) water hyacinth, *Eichhornia crassipes*.

ilusi (*D*) illusion.

ilusif (*E*) illusive.

ilusionis (*D/E*) illusionist.

ilusionisme (*D/E*) illusionism.

ilustrasi (*D*) illustration.

berilustrasi illustrated.

mengilustrasikan to illustrate.

ilustratif (*D/E*) illustrative.

ilustrator (*D/E*) illustrator.

Ilyas (*A*) (the biblical) Elias.

Ilyasa (*A*) (the biblical) Elijah.

imago (*E*) image, imagery. *Dia sengaja membungkus sajaknya dalam –.– supaya rahasia tetap ada dalam sajaknya.* He purposely wraps his poems in images so that there is always a secret in his poems. – *auditif* auditory image.

imaji (*E*) image.

imajinasi (*D*) imagination. *penuh* – imaginative.

berimajinasi to be full of imagination.

mengimajinasikan to imagine, figure/picture s.t. to o.s.

pengimajinasian imagining.

imajinatif (*E*) imaginative.

imajinér (*D*) imaginary.

imak (*M*) imitation.

mengimak(-imak) 1 to imitate (a sound/action, etc.), ridicule s.o. by imitating him, mock. 2 to simulate.

imakan the result of imitating.

pengimak imitator.

pengimakan imitating.

imalat (*A*) coalescence (of sounds), e.g., *insya Allah* becomes *in-syallah*.

imam (*A*) 1 a Muslim who is competent to lead prayers. 2 leader of the congregation of a mosque in prayer. – *yang empat* the founders of the four sects (*mazhab*): *Syafii, Hanafi, Hambali,* and *Maliki*. 3 Roman Catholic priest. 4 (in a few titles) "leader." – *Bonjol.* 5 leader (in general). 6 the priest who presents the *kurban misa* or communion or who leads Roman Catholic church services. – *Mahdi* Messiah. – *tentara* army chaplain.

berimam to have/act as group-prayer leader.

mengimami to lead (prayer services).

keimaman priesthood.

pengimaman leading prayer services.

imamah and **imamat** (*A*) 1 leadership; → KEPEMIMPINAN. *Sakramén* – Ordination of a Roman Catholic priest. 2 Leviticus (in the Bible).

imamiah (*A*) imamate.

iman (*A*) faith, belief, creed. *bergoyang* – a) to (be tempted to) act in an immoral way. b) to fall in love at first sight. *kegoncangan – nya* (tempted) to act in an immoral way. *Dia mengalami kegoncangan –nya.* She acted in an immoral way. *membawa* – to convert (to Islam). *menggoyangkan* – to tempt, make s.o. act in an immoral way. *meruntuhkan* – tempting, seductive. *teguhkan – mu!* be firm, keep the faith! *–lah engkau!* cheer up! keep smiling!

seiman of the same faith/religion. *keluarga-keluarga yang ~* families who have the same faith.

beriman 1 to believe, have faith, have a creed/religion. *~ kepada takdir* to believe in destiny. 2 faithful. *seorang yang ~ a* believer. *yang ~* the faithful. *~lah!* cheer up! 3 to be morally and spiritually sound.

berimankan to believe in.

mengimani 1 to trust (in God). 2 to believe in, profess (Islam, etc.).

mengimankan 1 to trust (in God). 2 to believe in, profess (Islam, etc.).

keimanan belief, conviction, steadfastness (against temptation).

pengiman believer.

im(m)anén (*D/E*) immanent.

imang mengimang-imang to coddle, pamper; → TIMANG I.

imani (*A*) faithful.

imarah and **imarat** (*A*) position of an *amir*, rulership.

im(m)ateriil (*D*) non-material, non-physical, emotional (damages).

IMB → IZIN *mendirikan bangunan.*

imba (*Jv*) nim tree, *Azadirachta indica.*

imbak mengimbak-imbak to wander about; to flutter/hover around.

imbal I counter, compensating, matching. – *beli* counter purchase. – *produksi* counter production. ***mengimbal-produksikan*** to offset. – *swadaya* matching grant.

mengimbali to pay back, repay (good for good, etc.).

imbalan 1 compensation, indemnification, reward, recompense; retribution. *dengan ~* compensated. *sebagai ~* in return/exchange (for). *Apa yang saya peroléh sebagai ~?* What will I get in return? *tanpa ~* uncompensated, unpaid. *~ ikatan* retainer. *~ jasa* (professional) fee, honorarium. *untuk ~nya* in compensation. *~ uang* indemnity. *~ yang terukur* measured consideration. 2 counter-value. *dana ~* counter-value funds.

pengimbalan compensating, indemnifying, reward(ing).

perimbalan compensation.

imbal II 1 one-sided, unsteady. 2 unequal, unbalanced. 3 slanting, sloping, askew, lopsided.

mengimbal slanting, leaning to the side.

imbal III (*Jv*) to remove/transfer (a heavy load) (onto a truck, etc.).

imbang I 1 in equilibrium, evenly balanced. 2 balance. 3 one's match, one's equal (opponent). 4 draw, having an equal score (in a game).

seimbang in balance, balanced, equal(ly balanced), in proportion; to suite. *Hukuman itu adalah ~ dengan kesalahannya.* The punishment suits the crime. *secara ~* in a balanced way. *dengan hal tersebut* similarly. *tidak ~* unbalanced, out of proportion (to). *perékonomian yang sangat tidak ~* a highly unbalanced economy. *perjanjian yang tidak ~* an unequal/lopsided treaty. ***ketidakseimbangan*** imbalance, disequilibrium. **menyeimbangkan** and **memperseimbangkan** to balance, bring into equilibrium, equalize, make s.t. proportionate/equal. *Indonésia mendesak AS ~ neraca perdagangan.* Indonesia urged the US to balance the trade budget. *~ neraca perdagangan RI-Koréa* to balance the Republic of Indonesia-Korea balance of trade. **keseimbangan** balance, stability (of a ship), equilibrium, harmony, proportionality. *~ kekuatan* balance of power. *~ kepentingan* balance of interest. *~ pembayaran* balance of payments (between countries). *(berada) dalam ~* to be in balance, in a state of equilibrium. *hilang/kehilangan ~* to lose one's balance. *téori ~ umum* general equilibrium theory. **berkeseimbangan** to be well-balanced. **perseimbangan** balance, equilibrium, harmony. **penyeimbang** balancer, balancing, matching. *kekuatan ~* matching force. *mesin ~* balancing machine. **penyeimbangan** stabilizer. *~ yang sudah dipasang* built-in stabilizer.

berimbang 1 (to be) in balance, balance/even out, be equal, measure up to, match, matched, comparable. *Kekuatan kedua negara itu ~.* The two nations are of equal strength. *Tindakannya tidak ~ dengan kata-katanya.* Her deeds don't measure up to her words. 2 to be proportional (to), (be) in proportion (to). *Hadiah yang diberikan ~ dengan jasa yang diperbuatnya.* The reward granted was proportional to the service rendered. *tidak ~* out of balance, out of proportion.

mengimbangi [and **ngimbangin** (*J coq*)] to equal, match, repay/return (an equal amount of s.t.). *Kebaikan saya tidak diimbangi dengan kebaikan, melainkan dengan kejahatan.* My kindness was not repaid with kindness, but with evil. *~ angka* (in sports) to equal the score.

mengimbangkan to (keep in) balance, make equal, equalize. *Untuk ~ pemasukan dan pengeluaran uang, akan diadakan penghématan.* To keep income and expenses in balance, cuts will be made.

memperimbang(kan) to (keep in) balance.

imbangan balance, match, counterweight. *Aku ~mu.* I'm your equal! You'll have to deal with me! *menurut ~* proportional.

berimbangan to be proportional (to), (be) in proportion (to).

imbang-imbangan almost similar/equal.

pengimbang s.t. that balances/equalizes, match.

pengimbangan balance, equalization.

perimbangan balance, proportion, parity. *~ bisa mencegah perang* an equal balance can prevent war. *Waktu itu ~ kasar antara Amérika dan Soviét belum tercapai.* At that time a rough parity between America and the Soviets had not yet been achieved. *~ kekuatan* balance of forces. *fasilitas ~ neraca pembayaran* facilities for balancing the budget.

imbang II uncertain, unsure; worried, anxious.

imbang-imbangan *hati ~* unsure, in doubt; worried, anxious.

imbas 1 air current (caused by s.t. passing by, a swinging object, etc.). *sekali –* a glimpse. 2 electric current. 3 effect, impact. 4 induction, enduksi. *– timbal-balik* mutual induction.

seimbas at first glance. *~ lalu* at first glance.

mengimbasi 1 to spread (to), affect, have an effect on. *Kami sangat berharap bahwa suasana kerja sama akan ~ juga ke Asia.* We hope that the spirit of cooperation will also spread to Asia. 2 to induce (air or electric flow). 3 to blow on (of a breeze). 4 to pass a current through.

terimbas 1 affected. 2 induced.

imbasan 1 air current. ~ *hantu* (*cla*) a ghost passing by (which causes an illness). 2 induced. 3 induction.

keimbasan inductivity.

pengimbas inductor, inducer.

pengimbasan induction.

imbau (*M*) call, summon, appeal.

mengimbau 1 to call, summon, mention (s.o.'s name). *Azan magrib ~ dari masjid.* The evening call to prayer called out from the mosque. 2 to appeal to, call upon, urge. *diimbau berbunyi, dilihat bersua* (*M*) whatever he says must be true.

mengimbaukan to call for, appeal for (s.t. to be done).

terimbau called, summoned.

imbauan call, summons, appeal, urging. ~ *moral* moral suasion. ~ *yang menyatukan/mengikat* rallying call.

imbésil (*D*) imbecile, idiot.

imbésilitas (*D*) imbecility.

imbit (*ob*) **mengimbit** to move, migrate.

imbo built-in.

imbuh 1 extra, supplement, a small addition given to a customer, lagniappe. 2 (*geol*) recharge, flux.

mengimbuh(kan) to give s.t. extra, add a little bit (to the price paid/ingredients, etc.).

mengimbuhi 1 to give s.o. a supplement. 2 to accompany s.o. or s.t. with.

imbuhan 1 (*gram*) affix. 2 money paid as a consolation. 3 redundant.

pengimbuhan (*gram*) affixation.

iméj (*E*) image.

imél (*E*) e-mail.

ngimélin (*J coq*) to send s.t. by e-mail.

imet → HÉMAT I.

imigran (*D/E*) immigrant. – *gelap* [IG] illegal immigrant.

imigrasi (*D*) immigration.

berimigrasi to immigrate.

mengimigrasikan to bring s.t. to immigration.

keimigrasian immigration. *bidang ~* the field/area of immigration. *tugas ~* immigration duty.

imigrasiwan immigration officer.

imigrésen (*E Mal*) immigration. *jabatan* – immigration office.

imil (*E*) e-mail.

iming (*Jv*) **iming-iming** lure, enticement, bait. **mengiming-iming** to allure, entice, tempt. *Hadiah yang ditawarkan cukup ~ publik.* The prize offered is really enticing for the public. **mengiming-imingi** to allure/entice/tempt. *Tidak sedikit wartawan yang hijrah, karena diiming-imingi gaji yang lebih besar.* Many reporters went over (to another magazine) because they were enticed by a higher salary.

mengimingkan to use s.t. to tempt. s.o.

(iming-)imingan enticement, temptation, lure, bait.

pengiming-iming temptation, s.t. or s.o. who tempts.

imitasi (*D*) imitation.

imitator (*D*) imitator.

IMKA [Ikatan Maséhi Kepemudaan Am] YMCA.

imkan (*A*) power, strength.

mengimkankan 1 to enable. 2 to strengthen, reinforce.

imkanur (*A*) – *rukyat* possibility of seeing the moon.

imlah and **imla(k)** (*A*) dictation.

mengimlahkan and **mengimlakkan** to dictate.

Imlék (*C*) calendar. *tahun baru* – Chinese New Year.

ber-Imlék to celebrate Chinese New Year.

immatériil → IMATÉRIIL.

imobilisasi (*D*) immobilization.

imoral (*E*) and **imoril** (*D*) immoral.

imoralitas (*D*) immorality.

impak (*E*) impact; → DAMPAK.

impang → ÉMPANG.

impas I (*J*) 1 paid off, no balance of debt on either side. *titik* – break-even point. 2 balanced, even.

mengimpas(kan) to pay off (a debt).

impas(e) II (*D*) impasse, deadlock.

impék → IMPAK.

impén (*Jv*) a dream.

impératif (*D/E*) 1 imperative, obligatory, binding. 2 (*gram*) imperative (mood).

impérfék (*D/E*) imperfect.

impérféksi (*D*) imperfection.

impérialis (*D/E*) imperialist.

impérialisme (*D/E*) imperialism. – *budaya* cultural imperialism.

impérialistis (*D*) imperialistic.

impérium (*D*) empire.

impérméabel (*D*) impermeable.

impérsonal (*E*) impersonal; → TANDIRI.

keimpérsionalan impersonality.

impérsonalitas (*E*) impersonality.

impes → IMPAS I.

impi dream, imagining; → MIMPI.

mengimpi [and **ngimpi** (*coq*)] to dream, imagine.

mengimpikan [and **ngimpiin** (*J coq*)] to dream of, see in a dream; to long for.

mengimpi-impikan to dream of; to long for. *bangsa Filipina yang masih ~ révolusi akan datang* Filipinos, who are still dreaming that the revolution will come.

terimpi-impi dreamt of, imagined. *tak ~* undreamt, not dreamt of, unimagined.

impian dream, s.t. in one's imagination, (in) fancy; dream world, utopia. ~ *dan kenyataan* dream and reality. ~ *jebol* a dream that was dashed. ~ *keinginan* wishful thinking.

pengimpi dreamer.

pengimpian dreaming.

impit very close together, close to e.o.

berimpit(-impit)(an) to squeeze together, push/shove e.o. *Ramai orang kelihatan berimpit-impit menaiki bus.* People could be seen crowding and shoving to get on the bus. *Meréka harus tidur berimpit.* They have to sleep crowded together.

mengimpit to squeeze, press/pin down on/on all sides. *Setumpuk kertas itu diimpit dengan stépler.* The stack of paper was held down by a stapler. *sudah jatuh diimpit tangga* one bad thing after another.

mengimpitkan to crush/squeeze (close) together.

memperimpit(-impit)(kan) to squeeze/crush together.

terimpit 1 squeezed, crushed, wedged, pressed. *Supir truk itu ~ sampai mati.* The bus driver was crushed to death. 2 in a tight spot.

impitan 1 pressure, crushing, squeezing. *tidak dapat lepas dari ~ orang banyak* cannot escape from public pressure. 2 overlap.

pengimpitan crushing, squeezing.

implantasi (*D*) implantation.

implemén (*E*) implement.

impléméntasi (*E*) implementation.

mengimpléméntasikan to implement.

pengimplémentasian implementation.

implikasi (*D*) implication. *Apa –nya?* What are the implications?

berimplikasi to have implications. *masalah kemiskinan yang ~ politis* the issue of poverty which has political implications.

mengimplikasikan 1 to implicate. 2 to imply.

terimplikasi(kan) implicated; implied.

implisit (*D/E*) implicit.

mengimplisitkan to make implicit.

impor(t) (*D*) import. *barang-barang* – imported goods.

mengimpor to import.

pengimpor importer.

pengimporan importing, importation.

importasi (*E*) importation.

importir (*D*) importer. – *aktentas* "briefcase importer," i.e., an Indonesian whose sole office is his briefcase and whose sole function is to obtain licenses and foreign-exchange permits while his Chinese silent partner continues to manage the business; *cp* ALIBABA, ALI-SAN, BABA *Ali.* –.– *Bénténg* "Bulwark Importers," i.e., a group of smaller local importers who were encouraged by the Indonesian government to form a "bulwark" against foreign competition and to whom the government gave the right to deal in special categories of goods.

mengimportir to import.

impotén (*D/E*) impotent.

impoténsi (*D*) impotence.

imprégnasi (*D*) impregnation.

imprésariat (*D*) office of an impresario.

imprésario (*E*) and imprésaris (*D*) impresario.

imprési (*D/E*) impression.

imprésif (*D/E*) impressive.

imprésionis (*D*) impressionist.

imprésionisme (*D/E*) impressionism.

imprésionistik (*E*), imprésionistis (*D*) impressionistic.

improvisasi (*D*) improvisation.

   berimprovisasi to improvise. *menciptakan peluang* ~ to create an opportunity to improvise.

   mengimprovisasikan to improvise s.t.

improvisator (*D*) improviser.

improvisir (*D*) mengimprovisir to improvise.

impuls (*D/E*) impulse.

impulsif (*D/E*) impulsive.

impun → HIMPUN.

Imran (*A*) al-" "The Family of Imran"; name of the third chapter of the Koran.

imsak (*A*) 1 abstinence (from food, etc.). 2 (time in) the later part of the night (when fasting begins).

imsaki(y)ah (*A*) 1 examination, test. 2 (ceremony at) promotion (in Islamic schools). 3 fasting calendar.

imtihan (*A*) examination.

imun (*D/E*) immune; → KEBAL. - *terhadap* to be immune to. *Siapa saja tidak - terhadap bahaya itu.* Nobody is immune to that danger.

   mengimunkan to immunize.

   keimunan immunity.

imunisasi (*E*) immunization.

imunitas (*D*) immunity; → KEKEBALAN. - *diplomatik* diplomatic immunity.

imunofarmakologi (*E*) immunopharmacology.

imunologi (*D/E*) immunology.

imunologik (*E*) immunologic. *défisiénsi* - immunological deficiency.

imunotérapi (*E*) immunotherapy.

imut I and imut-imut I (*S*) to smile. *Mukanya* ~. He's smiling.

imut II and imut-imut II (*Pr*) lovely, good-looking, cute.

in I (*E*) to be in/popular/fashionable. *Budaya tari kejang sedang - di antara remaja.* Breakdance culture is in among teenagers. *lagu yang lagi* - a popular song.

in II (*A*) if; (in the phrase) *-sya Allah* God willing.

in III (in acronyms) → INDUK, INSTRUKSI.

ina (*ob*) mother.

inabah (*A*) drug addict.

in absentia (*L*) /in apséntia/ in one's absence. *mengadili* - to try in absentia.

inai (*A*) 1 henna, a dye used for coloring fingernails and toenails. 2 henna tree, *Lawsonia inermis*, anatto, safflower; → PACAR I. *malam* - night when a bride's nails and toenails are stained with henna (for her wedding). *malam - curi* when this ceremony is performed privately. *malam - besar* when this ceremony is performed publicly. *meletakkan* - to put henna on one's nails. *tari* - dance performed at the ceremony described above. *kaki tertarung - padahannya (mulut terdorong emas padahannya)* as you have made your bed so must you lie in it. - *tertepung, kuku tanggal* the straw that breaks the camel's back. - *ayam* balsam, *Impatiens balsamina*.

   berinai to color one's nails with henna.

   menginai to color s.o.'s nails with henna.

inaktivasi (*E*) inactivation.

   menginaktivasi to inactivate.

inang I 1 nursemaid. 2 wet nurse. 3 host (to a parasite, etc.). - *akhir* end host (of a parasite). - *antara* intermediate host. - *pengasuh* governess. - *penularan* disease vector.

   menginang to be a nursemaid/wet nurse to.

inang II (*Bat*) mother; → IBU.

   inang-inang woman who takes the boat that runs between Belawan, the port of Medan, and Singapore or Tanjung Priok to bring in goods illegally.

inangda princely/court foster mother.

inap stay overnight, spend the night.

   menginap [and nginap (*coq*)] 1 to stay over, spend the night somewhere (other than one's house). ~ *di rumah prodéo* and ~ *di LP* to spend time in prison. ~ *semalam* to spend the night, stay overnight. 2 in(patient); → RAWAT *nginap*.

   menginapi to stay in/at/with.

   menginapkan 1 to provide s.o. with a place to spend the night, put s.o. up for the night. *Ia diinapkan tiga hari di rumah saya.* I put him up for three nights. 2 to put/keep s.t. somewhere for the night, leave s.t. overnight. *Seluruh pusaka itu nanti akan diinapkan semalam di pendapa kabupatén.* All the heirlooms will be kept in the *pendapa* of the regent's house for the night. *Sayur bayam tidak boléh diinapkan.* You can't leave spinach soup overnight.

   inapan stay (in a hotel).

   penginap s.o. who puts s.o. up for the night, host.

   penginapan *hotél* ~ place to stay for the night, inn, hotel, lodgings. *rumah* ~ *kecil* bed and breakfast. *rumah* ~ *tamu* guest house.

inas *pekung* - a carbuncle on the nape of the neck.

inaugurasi (*D*) inauguration; → PELANTIKAN.

inayah and inayat (*A*) help (from God), assistance, aid.

inca-inca and inca-binca (*ob*) in pieces, in confusion.

incak (*Jv*) ngincak to tread/step on; → INJAK.

incang → INCENG.

incang-incut not straight, crooked, zigzag, askew.

incar I drill, bore.

   mengincar to drill, bore (a hole).

incar II (*J*) mengincar [and ngincar (*coq*)] 1 to aim (a gun/slingshot, etc.) (at), look at s.t. with one eye closed (e.g., while aiming), zero in on. 2 to peer at, spy on, watch, have one's eyes on.

   mengincari to target, have one's eyes on.

   incaran 1 focus of attention. *Indonésia merupakan daérah* ~ U.S. Indonesia is the region on which the Soviet Union is focusing its attention. 2 watchful eye. 3 target. *gadis* ~*nya* the girl he has in mind.

   pengincar having one's eye on; targeting.

   pengincaran targeting.

in casu (*L*) /in kasu/ in this case, *in casu. Biaya dibebankan kepada Pemerintah Daérah, - kepada DKI Jakarta.* Expenses are charged to the provincial government, in this case to the Jakarta Special Capital Province.

inced (*J*) somewhat crippled/lamed. *jalannya -, kakinya kena duri.* He walked with a limp (because) he had stepped on a thorn.

incek (*Jv*) ngincek to step on.

incék → ENCIK.

inceng (*Jv*) nginceng to take a look/peek (at), peer out (at). ~ *dari belakang témbok* to peer out from behind the wall.

   ngincengkan 1 to take a look at, peer out at. 2 to aim, direct. ~ *bedil* to aim a gun; → INCAR II.

incer → INCAR II.

inci (*E*) inch.

incim → ENCIM.

incit leave! go away!; → ENYAH, USIR.

   mengincitkan to kick out, send away.

   terincit kicked out, sent away.

incling (*Jv*) → KUDA *képang*.

incognito (*D*) /inkokhnito/ incognito.

income (*E*) /inkam/ income.

in concreto (*L*) /in kon(g)kréto/ in concreto, concretely.

incrit (*J/Jv*) seincrit a little bit; → SEDIKIT.

   mengincrit-incrit to give out s.t. in small amounts, dole out bit by bit. *Membayar kembali pinjamannya diincrit-incrit, saya jadi gondok.* He repaid the loan bit by bit, (and) I got annoyed.

incu (*S*) grandchild.

incut I 1 lame, limping, crippled; → PINCANG I, TIMPANG. 2 deformed, distorted.

   terincut-incut limping, crippled.

incut II → INCANG-INCUT.

inda → INDAK.

indah I 1 beautiful, pretty, charming, picturesque; → BAGUS I, CANTIK I, ÉLOK. **2** beautiful, exquisite, esthetically pleasing. *bunga/musik/puisisi yang* – exquisite flowers/music/poetry.
  seindah as beautiful as.
  memperindah(kan) to beautify, adorn, embellish. *Gedung bertingkat itu baru-baru ini diperindah dan diperbarui.* The high-rise building was recently beautified and renovated.
  terindah the most beautiful.
  keindahan beauty. *perasaan* ~ esthetic feeling. ~ *alam* beauty of nature. ~ *tunggang serasi* dressage.
  pengindahan beautifying, beautification, embellishment.
indah II pay attention (to), care (about), show interest (in). *Tiada ia – akan diriku lagi.* She doesn't care about me any more. *tak – akan* to be indifferent to.
  mengindahkan 1 to pay attention to. *tidak* ~ to ignore. *Céwék yang cantik itu tidak ~nya.* That attractive girl ignores him. **2** to consider s.t. seriously. *Larangan itu tidak pernah diindahkannya.* He never pays any attention to that prohibition.
  pengindahan (paying) attention (to), (taking) consideration (of).
  perindahan attention, consideration, interest in. *kurang mendapat* ~ doesn't receive enough attention.
indak → ENDAK II, TIDAK.
Indamardi [Industri, Dagang, Maritim, dan Pendidikan] Industry, Commerce, Maritime (Affairs), and Education. *Kota* – Surabaya.
indang I mengindang to winnow rice by moving a sieve from right to left and away from o.s. with upward jerks. *diindang ditampi beras, dipilih antah satu-satu* (M) be very careful in choosing a son-in-law or a daughter-in-law; → BIBIT, BOBOT, BEBET.
  terindang *tidak* ~ *dedak, berbiak lagi* (M) to be powerless/impotent/helpless.
indang II female ascetic/hermit/recluse, nun.
indang III ancestral spirits.
indap → ENDAP I.
indar → HINDAR.
indarus (M) defeated (of a fighting cock) and forfeited to the winner.
indayang (M) frond of a coconut palm.
indehoj, in de hooi, in de hooy, in de hoy, and **indehoy** (D) to make out, have illicit sexual relations.
  berindehoy to make out, have illicit sex.
  keindehoyan making out, having sex. *tanda-tanda* ~ signs of having made out.
indekos (D) **1** to take s.o. in as a boarder/paying guest; to be a boarder/paying guest; → KOS(T). **2** to house (an office) in (another, larger office). *bayaran – hanya Rp 50.000* room and board are only Rp 50,000. *Kamar – yang saya tempati keadaannya amat menyedihkan.* The condition of the room I boarded in was pathetic. *Kota* – Yogyakarta.
  berindekos to board (with). *Pemuda itu* ~ *di tetangga.* The young man is boarding with a neighbor.
  mengindekosi to board at, be a boarder at. *Rumahku diindekosi anak dua.* Two children are boarding in my house.
  mengindekoskan to put s.o. out to board, board s.o. somewhere. *Meréka harus* ~ *anaknya.* They had to put their children out to board.
  indekosan boarder. *Dia menerima* ~ *anak-anak muda.* She takes in youngsters. *mahasiswa* ~ university student who is a boarder.
indéks (D/E) **1** index, a list of names, titles, etc., *esp* an alphabetical list indicating where a book, etc. can be found. **2** index, a figure indicating the relative level of prices compared to that of an earlier date; → DAFTAR. *– harga konsumén* [IHK] consumer price index. *– harga saham gabungan* [IHSG] composite stock price index. *– fisik kualitas hidup nasional* national physical quality of life index. *– préstasi* [IP] grade-point average. *terusan* running index.
  pengindéks indexer.
  pengindéksan indexing.
indéksasi (E?) indexation.
inden (Jv) spindle, pivot, axis.

indén (D) order for goods accompanied by partial payment (or, a deposit) for those goods.
  mengindén to order goods and pay a deposit/indent.
  pengindén person who orders goods in this way.
indéntor person who orders goods and pays a deposit/indent.
indépéndén (D/E) independent. *mahasiswa* – nonaffiliated college student.
indera I (Skr cla) **1** divinity, gods. *(raja/batara)* – Indra; → INDRA. **2** divine; all-powerful, might.
  mengindera divine.
  keinderaan abode of the gods (or, of Indra).
indera II (Skr) sense organ, one of the five senses. *– keenam* sixth sense, intuition. *– mata* sense of sight. *– pencium* nose. *– pendengar* ears. *– penglihat* eyes. *– peraba* skin. *– perasa* tongue. *– warta* a nose for news.
  mengindera to sense. *Negara-negara bertéknologi tinggi memiliki kemampuan* ~. High-tech nations have sensing abilities.
  pengindera sensor.
  penginderaan sensing, reconnaissance (by machines). ~ *jauh (dengan satelit)* remote sensing (by satellite). ~ *jarak jauh* long-range reconnaissance.
inderaja → PENGINDERAAN *jauh.*
inderalaksana k.o. tree which produces gum, *Acacia farnesiana.*
Inderaloka (Skr) the abode of Indra.
inderawasih (ob) → CENDERAWASIH.
inderawi → INDRAWI.
inderia → INDRIA I.
inderiawi → INDRIAWI.
India India. *kelas* – low-class.
Indian (E) American Indian, native American.
  meng-Indiankan to indianize, i.e., to provide Indonesians (*esp* Jakartans) with housing (now in the Condét area of Jakarta).
  indian-indianan *main* ~ to play cowboys and Indians.
indiferén (E) indifferent.
indigo (D/E) indigo, a blue dye for *batik.*
indik (J) *mindik-mindik* (Jv) to sneak toward s.t. in order to grab it.
  mengindik [and **ngindik** (coq)] to sneak up on, inch toward, approach in a crouching position, stalk. *Macannya* ~ *biri-biri itu.* The tiger was stalking the sheep.
  ngingik-ngindik (J) **1** to sneak toward s.t. in order to grab it. **2** to eye, ogle. *Pria itu lagi* ~ *anak prawannya si Amir.* That guy still has his eye on Amir's daughter.
indikasi (D) indication, sign. *ada* – (coq) was involved in the G30S movement. *Ada – korupsi.* There are signs of corruption.
  berindikasi 1 to show indications/signs of. **2** suspicious.
  mengindikasikan to indicate, point out.
  terindikasi there are indications that.
  pengindikasian indicating, pointing out.
indikatif (D/E) indicative, showing signs.
indikator (D/E) indicator. *– Dini Ékonomi* Leading Economic Indicators.
inding menginding 1 to watch expectantly. **2** to listen to attentively.
indisiplinér (D) undisciplined, bad. *kelakuan/tindakan* – bad behavior.
individu (D/E) individual, person.
  keindividuan individuality.
individual (E) individual (mod).
individualis (D/E) individualist.
individualisasi (E) individualization.
individualisir (D) **mengindividualisir** to individualize.
individualisme (D/E) individualism.
individualistis (D) individualistic.
individualitas (D) individuality.
individuil (D) individual (mod).
Indo I 1 Eurasian, i.e., a person of mixed European and Indonesian ancestry (the father must be European or an Indo himself and the mother must be an Indo or a native-born Indonesian); → PERANAKAN **2** any person of mixed Indonesian ancestry. *– Arab* s.o. of Arab and Indonesian ancestry. *– Belanda* s.o. of Dutch and Indonesian ancestry. *– Cina/Tionghoa* s.o. of Chinese and Indonesian ancestry.

keindo-indoan being Eurasian, condition or state of being a Eurasian. *Si cantik yang ~ ini cuwék saja.* The beautiful Eurasian woman was indifferent.

Indo II clipped form of **Indonésia**.

indoktrinasi (*D*) indoctrination; *cp* SANTIAJI.

  mengindoktrinasi to indoctrinate.

  terindoktrinasi indoctrinated.

  pengindoktrinasian indoctrination.

indoktrinator (*E*) indoctrinator.

indoktrinir (*D*) **mengindoktrinir** to indoctrinate.

indolén (*D/E*) indolent. *bangsa yang* – an indolent people.

indolénsi (*D*) indolence.

Indologi (*D*) Indonesian studies.

Indonésia 1 Indonesia. 2 Indonesian (*mod*). *ahli* – Indonesianist. *bahasa* – [BI] Indonesian, the Indonesian language. *berbahasa* – a) to speak Indonesian. b) Indonesian-language, in Indonesian. *surat kabar berbahasa* – an Indonesian-language newspaper. ***membahasaindonésiakan*** MENGINDONÉSIAKAN. *lebih* – *daripada orang* – to carry an imitation too far, more royalist than the king. – *I* license-plate number of the presidential limousine. – *II* license-plate number of the vice-presidential limousine. – *Raya* a) Greater Indonesia. b) name of the Indonesian national anthem.

  Indonésianya the Indonesian for it. *Apa ~?* How do you say it in Indonesian? *~ (adalah/ialah)* ... in Indonesian it is ...

  se-Indonésia all-Indonesia. *para remaja ~* all-Indonesia youth.

  ber-Indonésia 1 to be Indonesian. *ada upaya lebih ~* there are efforts to be(come) more Indonesian. 2 to speak Indonesian. *Ia ~, antara lain katanya,* ... Speaking Indonesian, he said, among other things, ...

  mengindonésia to be(come) Indonesian. *Tampak sekali hasrat kuat Anton Moeliono mengajak penutur BI tertib, cermat, dan ~.* Anton Moeliono's strong desire to urge Indonesian speakers to be courteous, accurate, and Indonesian is very clear.

  mengindonésiakan 1 to Indonesianize, make s.o. into/become an Indonesian. *upaya ~ warganegara keturunan Cina melalui pergantian nama* efforts to Indonesianize citizens of Chinese descent through name changes. 2 to translate s.t. into its Indonesian equivalent, express in Indonesian. *Ratusan kata-kata asing belum diindonésiakan oléh TÉMPO.* Hundreds of foreign words have not yet been translated into their Indonesian equivalents by TEMPO.

  keindonésiaan 1 Indonesian (*mod*). *prinsip ~* Indonesian principles. 2 Indonesianness, state or condition of being Indonesian.

  pengindonésiaan Indonesianizing, Indonesianization. *~ Bahasa Indonésia* the Indonesianization of Indonesian, i.e., the replacement of foreign words by Indonesian equivalents.

indonésiani Indonesian.

Indonésianis (*E*) Indonesianist.

Indonésianisasi (*D*) Indonesianization.

Indonésianisme (*D/E*) Indonesianism.

Indonésianistik (*E*) Indonesian (*mod*). *dalam suatu bidang* – in a field of Indonesian studies.

Indonésia-séntris Indonesia-centric.

Indonésiawan (*infr*) a male Indonesian.

Indonésiawi Indonesian (*mod*). *Saudara Achmad Ali menganggap SK Gubernur itu sudah cukup fair atau sangat* –. Achmad Ali considered the Governor's Directive very fair or very Indonesian.

Indopura [*Indonésia-Singapura*] Indonesia-Singapore. *Elang* – reference to the Joint Indonesian-Singaporean Air Operations Maneuvers.

indra I → INDERA I, II.

Indra II Indonesian Debt Restructuring Agency.

indralaksana → INDERALAKSANA.

indraméga k.o. snack made from sticky-rice flour.

indranila (dark) bluish green.

indrawi sensory. *pengalaman* – sensory experience.

indria I → INDERA II. **berindria** to have a sense. *~ keenam* to have a sixth sense.

  pengindria sensor, detector. *~ asap* smoke detector.

  pengindriaan sensing. *~ jauh* remote sensing.

indria II *taman* – a) playground. b) *Taman* – Kindergarten (of the *Taman Siswa*).

indriawi sensory.

indu (*M*) 1 mother; → IBU, INDUK. 2 ancestors.

  seperinduan *~ kambing* a litter of goats.

induk 1 mother (mostly of animals), dam; → BIANG I, IBU, INDU. *kapal* – a) mother ship. b) aircraft carrier. *negara* – homeland, motherland. 2 main, master, principal (mostly in compounds), center (for an activity). *kamar tidur* – master bedroom. *kunci* – master key. *pita suara* – master tape; → KASÉT biang. *rencana* – master plan. *rumah* – main building. 3 essence, quintessence, central/main part, nucleus, origin, core, source. *seperti anak ayam kehilangan* – at a loss for what to do. – *administrasi* administrative center. – *ayam* mother hen; → BABON. – *babi* sow. – *bako* (*M*) all the relatives on one's father's side. – *bala* (*ob*) ringleader. – *bangsa* stock, race. – *beras* (*M*) wife, spouse. – *berlian* a large diamond. – *cuka* essence of vinegar; → BIANG cuka. – *jari* thumb; → IBU jari, JEMPOL. – *jenis* genus. – *kaki* big toe; → IBU kaki. – *kalimat* (*gram*) main clause. – *karangan* editorial; → TAJUK rencana, ÉDITORIAL. – *karbol* concentrated carbolic acid. – *keluarga* superfamily (in taxonomy). – *kerbau* female buffalo. – *keréta api* locomotive; → LOKOMOTIF. – *madu* honeycomb. – *nasi* (*M*) spouse, wife. – *padi* the first rice stalks harvested. – *pasukan* main body (of troops). – *pembasuh* swivel. – *penyalur* chief distributor. – *perusahaan* holding company, parent company. – *pisang* the first banana tree planted, later surrounded by shoots; *cp* ANAK pisang. – *roti* leaven, yeast for making bread; → BIANG roti. – *rumah* main building. – *semang* a) adoptive mother. b) female employer. c) landlady. – *semang WTS* madam, woman in charge of a bordello; → MU(N)CIKARI. – *sutera* cocoon of a silkworm. – *taman ternak* cattle breeding center. – *tangan* thumb; → IBU tangan. – *tangga* banister; → IBU tangga. – *tentara* (*mil*) main body of an army. – *utang* principal (of a debt).

induk-induk (*Med*) women.

  seinduk having the same mother but different fathers.

  berinduk 1 to have a mother. *seperti anak ayam tidak ~* at a loss for what to do. 2 to be descended (in the female line) from. 3 to be based, be derived. *Pendidikan politik générasi muda harus ~ pada pendidikan politik nasional.* Political education for the younger generation must be based on national political education. 4 to be under (a parent organization).

  menginduk *~ ke* to be under (a parent organization).

  mengindukkan to be a subsidiary. *Serikat Buruh Kereta Api (SBKA) ~ ke Séntral Organisasi Buruh Seluruh Indonésia (SOBSI).* The Railway Workers Union is a subsidiary of the All-Indonesia Federation of Workers Organization.

  perindukan 1 (from the same) family, (having the same) mother. 2 a unit in the *Pramuka* Boy Scouts Movement. **seperindukan** a brood, litter, etc. all from the same mother.

induksi (*D*) induction; → IMBAS.

  menginduksikan to induct.

  terinduksi inducible.

  penginduksi inductor.

induktif (*D/E*) inductive.

indung I 1 mother; → INDUK. 2 origin of s.t. – *madu* honeycomb. – *mutiara* mother-of-pearl, pearl oyster. – *telur* ovary.

indung II (*Jv*) people who reside in a village but lack the rights of ownership because they are not members of the communal group according to customary law.

  ngindung to occupy (a house) erected on s.o.'s property

  mengindungkan to let s.o. occupy a house on one's property after he has paid a deposit.

  pengindung s.o. who lives in another person's house or on another person's property.

indusemén (*E*) inducement.

industri (*D/E*) industry. *gudang* – *berizin* licensed manufacturing warehouse, LMW. – *bayi* infant industry. – *berat* heavy industry. – *besar* large-scale industry. – *hilir* downstream industry. – *hilir kimia* chemical downstream industry. – *hulu* upstream industry. – *kecil* small-scale industry. – *kerajinan* home/handicrafts industry. – *kimia* industrial industry. – *kimia yang berdasarkan* *hasil pertanian* agro-based chemical industry. – *madya* mid-level industry. – *manufaktur* manufacturing industry. – *métal* meta(lurgical) industry. – *pariwisata* tourist industry. – *pedésaan* rural industry. – *pembantaian kapal tua* ship-breaking industry. – *pembikinan barang-barang jadi* manufacturing industry. – *perbukuan* book industry. – *perkebunan kayu* timber industry. – *primér* primary industry. – *prosésing* processing industry. – *rékayasa* engineering industry. – *ringan* light industry. – *rumah (tangga)* cottage industry. – *sékundér* downstream industry. – *yang masih bayi* infant industry. – *yang beroriéntasi (pada) ékspor* export-oriented industry. – *yang menua* mature industry. – *yang menyenja* sunset industry. – *yang sudah tak layak lagi di negaranya* sunset industry. – *yang tidak berbasiskan bahan mentah* non-resource-based industry.

mengindustri to industrialize.

mengindustrikan to industrialize s.t.

pengindustrian industrializing, industrialization.

perindustrian industrial.

industrial (*E*) industrial.

industrialis (*D/E*) industrialist; → INDUSTRI(A)WAN. *kaum – besar* captains of industry.

industrialisasi (*D*) industrialization. *menuju –* industrializing. – *yang sangat tergantung kepada impor* import-dependent industrialization.

mengindustrialisasi to industrialize.

industrialisir (*D*) **mengindustrialisir** to industrialize.

industriawan industrialist. – *minyak* oil tycoon.

industriil (*D*) industrial.

industriwan → INDUSTRIAWAN.

inefisiénsi (*D*) inefficiency.

inéks and **inéx** (the illegal drug) Ecstasy.

inélastis (*E*) inelastic.

inep → INAP.

inérsi (*E*) inertia.

inf- → also see entries beginning with **inp-**, **inv-**.

infak (*A*) (– *amal*) gift of money, charity. *gerakan –* movement to have Muslims contribute to development.

infanteri (*D/E*) infantry.

infantil (*D/E*) infantile; → KEKANAK-KANAKAN.

infantilisme (*D/E*) infantilism.

infaq (*A*) → INFAK. **menginfaqkan** to contribute (money).

infark (*D*) infarction, heart attack. – *miokardial* myocardial infarction.

inféksi (*D*) infection; spreading an infection. *gigitan nyamuk yang –* a mosquito bite which spreads an infection.

menginféksi to infect.

terinféksi infected.

penginféksian infecting.

inférior (*D/E*) inferior.

inférioritas (*D*) inferiority.

inférno (*D/E*) inferno.

infértil (*D/E*) infertile.

infértilitas (*D*) infertility.

infiks (*D/E gram*) infix; → IMBUHAN.

infiltran (*D*) infiltrator.

infiltrasi (*D*) infiltration.

berinfiltrasi to infiltrate.

menginfiltrasikan to infiltrate.

infiltrir (*D*) **menginfiltrir** to infiltrate.

infinitif (*D/E gram*) infinitive.

infitah (*A*) opening; open door.

inflamasi (*D*) inflammation.

inflasi (*D*) inflation. *laju –* rate of inflation. – *inti* core inflation.

keinflasian to suffer from inflation.

inflatoar and **inflotoir** (*D*) inflationary.

infléksi (*D*) inflection.

influénsa (*D*) and **influénza** (*E*) influenza; → FLU.

influks (*E*) influx.

info clipped form of **informasi**. *mendapatkan – dari tangan pertama* to get first-hand information. *akibat salah –* as a result of misinformation.

menginfokan 1 to inquire after. 2 to inform, advise.

infogirl female police informant.

informal (*E*) informal.

informan (*D/E*) 1 informant, source of information. 2 informant, native speaker who acts as an assistant.

informasi (*D*) information, tip. *mendapat – bahwa* got a tip that. *pemberi –* informant. *saling memberikan –* to exchange information. – *péka* sensitive information.

berinformasi 1 to have information. 2 to ask for information.

menginformasikan 1 to inform. *Para karyawan ~, bahwa meréka menggunakan perumahan Krakatau Steel tidak cuma-cuma.* The employees informed (us) that they were not using Krakatau Steel housing for nothing. *perlu diinformasikan* it is worth noting (that). 2 to report on, provide information about. *Calon hakim sebaiknya diinformasikan kekayaannya.* Prospective judges should report on their assets.

terinformasi(kan) informed.

penginformasian providing information about, reporting on.

informatif (*D/E*) informative.

informatika (*E*) informatics.

informil (*D*) informal.

infra- (*D/E*) infra-.

inframérah infrared.

infrastruktur (*D/E*) infrastructure; → PRASARANA.

infus (*D*) to be fed intravenously, have an I.V.

menginfus to feed intravenously. *Dia terpaksa diinfus.* She had to be fed intravenously.

menginfuskan to infuse, to feed s.t. intravenously.

penginfusan intravenous feeding.

infusi (*D/E*) infusion, feeding intravenously.

ing (*Jv*) 1 of. *ratu – Madura* the King of Madura. 2 in. – *madya mangun karsa* active participation (of the military as a model). – *ngarsa sung tulada* to stand in front giving an example, direct control (by the military); → ING-ING TUT.

ingah-ingih (*Jv*) incongruous, out of step; not firm, changeable. *hakim yang –* a judge who changes his mind easily. *Jangan –!* Be firm!

inga-inga teringa-inga gaping, dazed, bewildered, puzzled, surprised.

ingar – *bangar/bingar* noise, chaos; noisy, chaotic. *di tengah – bingar* in the middle of the chaos. *seingar-bingar* as noisy/chaotic as. *mengingar-bingarkan* to upset, set s.t. on its ear. *Témpo sebulan, ia, dengan orkés Sonéta, sudah dua kali ~ Jakarta.* In the space of a month, he and the Soneta Orchestra have set Jakarta on its ear. – *tetangga* disturbance of the peace.

ingar-ingar noise, chaos, tumult; noisy, chaotic, tumultuous.

mengingari to upset/annoy/disturb by being noisy and boisterous.

mengingarkan to make (the situation) chaotic.

ingat and – *akan* 1 to remember, recall, think of, bring to mind, recollect. *Sesudah turun dari keréta api, barulah saya –, bahwa orang yang duduk di depan saya tadi adik guru saya.* It wasn't until I got off the train that I remembered that the person sitting across from me was my teacher's younger brother. *Saya tidak – akan orang itu.* I don't remember that person. *antara – dengan tidak –* and –.– *lupa* to have a vague memory of. *samar-samar saya –* I remember vaguely. *kurang –* inattentive. *memberi –* a) to warn, caution. b) to advise. c) to call s.o.'s attention (to). *menangis –* to cry over, weep when remembering s.t. 2 conscious, aware. *Anak yang pingsan tadi hingga sekarang belum –.* The child who fainted earlier hasn't regained consciousness yet. *Ketika terjatuh dari pohon itu dua jam lamanya dia tak – diri.* When he fell from the tree, he was unconscious for two hours. 3 to think about/of, be interested in. *Janganlah hanya – akan kepentingan diri sendiri.* Don't just think about your own interests. *Jika benar-benar – akan kepentingan kita bersama, masakan berbuat demikian?* If you were really thinking about our mutual interests, how could you have acted that way? *Ia sudah tak – lagi kepada tugas kewajibannya.* He is no longer interested in his duties. 4 to occur to, pass through one's mind. *Sesampai di kantor baru saya – bahwa saya belum sarapan.* Not until I arrived at the office did it occur to me that I hadn't eaten breakfast yet. 5 to intend. *Dia – hendak bertolak semalam tetapi tak sempat.* He intended to leave last night, but he didn't have the chance to. **6** to consider, take into consideration; considering. *Kalau tidak – anak, sudah lama saya keluar dari kantor saya.* If I hadn't considered my child, I would have left my job long ago. *– sebelum kena, hémat sebelum habis* look before you leap.

ingat-ingat be careful about s.t., think about s.t. before doing it.

seingat as far as ... remember. *~ saya* as far as I remember.

beringat → INGAT. *~ diri* to take care of o.s.

mengingat 1 to remember, recollect, recall. *Tanggal itu diingat-nya sekali.* He remembered that day quite well. *kalau diingat* in retrospect. **2** to think of, keep in mind. *tidak ~ haram dan halal* not keeping in mind what is forbidden and what is permitted (in Muslim law). **3** (mainly in legal documents) noting, considering, taking into consideration/account, in view of, in light of (the fact that); to advise (mainly in the passive *diingat*), as, since. *~ gelar kesarjanaan di Indonésia sekarang mémang kacau pemakaiannya* in view of the chaotic use of titles in Indonesia now. *harap diingat* please be advised. *Harap diingat bahwa anda bésok harus hadir.* Please be advised that you must appear tomorrow. *~ lagi* to think back on.

mengingat-ingat 1 to linger over (in one's thoughts), keep on thinking about, dwell on; to pay careful attention to, watch out for. **2** to try to remember/recall s.t. *Ia ~ apakah ia pernah melihat gadis itu.* He tried to remember whether he had ever seen that girl.

mengingati to be mindful of, try to remember. *Ia selalu ~ pesan ibunya.* He always tries to remember his mother's orders.

ingat-mengingati to be mindful of e.o.

mengingatkan 1 to remind s.o. of, recall/bring s.t. to s.o.'s mind, be reminiscent of. *Ia ~ bahwa harus disadari bahwa suatu perubahan sosial tidak dapat dipaksakan.* He reminded us that we should be aware that social change cannot be forced. **2** to warn, notify, inform, tell, let s.o. know about; to admonish, counsel. *Mbakyu Karto ~ suaminya, bahwa ada kemungkinan hal tadi pagi itu berékor panjang dan dapat mengakibatkan tidak baik.* Mrs. Karto warned her husband that what happened this morning might cause a number of problems and end up badly. **3** to call s.o.'s attention to (the fact that). *Présidén Soeharto ~ Pancasila dan UUD '45 menjamin persatuan dan kesatuan nasional dalam keanékaragaman kita.* President Soeharto called attention to the fact that Pancasila and the 1945 Constitution guarantee national unity and integrity within our diversity. **4** to keep s.t. in mind, think about.

memperingati 1 to celebrate. *Peristiwa penting itu meréka peringati dengan khidmat.* They celebrated that significant event solemnly. **2** to mark, note/jot down. *~ kata-kata yang sukar dihafalkan pada kartu indéks* to jot down words which are hard to memorize on index cards. **3** to commemorate. *~ Hari Sumpah Pemuda, berarti tidak melupakan sejarah!* Commemorating Youth Pledge Day means not putting history behind us.

memperingatkan to warn, caution. *Ia selalu ~ anak-anaknya supaya berhati-hati kalau menyeberang.* He always warns his children to be careful when crossing. *Apakah tiada orang yang ~nya?* Was there nobody who warned her? *~ ... agar/supaya jangan* to warn s.o. not to do s.t. *Dia ~ saya supaya jangan memukul anak itu.* He warned me not to hit the child.

ingat-memperingatkan to warn e.o.

teringat remembered/recalled suddenly, came to mind, occurred (to one), dawned on. *Saya ~ suatu kejadian yang pernah berlaku kira-kira lima tahun yang lalu.* I suddenly recalled an event that occurred about five years ago. *tidak ~ to slip (one's) mind. Sama sekali tidak ~ oléh saya.* It completely slipped my mind.

teringat-ingat be constantly reminded, be always in one's thoughts. *Meskipun sudah lama berpisah, tetapi saya masih ~ mukanya yang senantiasa tersenyum itu.* Even though we've been apart for a long time, I'm still constantly reminded of her smiling face.

ingatan 1 memory, recollection, remembrance. *~ komputer* computer memory. *Sepanjang ~ saya selama ini belum pernah dia berlaku tak jujur.* As far as I can remember, he has never acted dishonestly. *tak akan pernah hilang dari ~(nya)* still clearly

present in his mind, unforgettable. *sedikit terlintas ~ itu dari benakku* I remember that vaguely. *menurut ~ saya* as far as I remember, to the best of my recollection. **2** ability to retain s.t. that one has heard, learned, etc., retentive memory, mind. *Meskipun dia sudah tua, dia masih mempunyai ~ yang baik.* Even though he's old, he still has a good memory. *Walaupun umurnya telah lanjut ~nya masih kuat.* Even though he is old, his memory is still good. **3** what is going on in one's mind, thoughts. *mengumpulkan ~nya* to concentrate, gather one's thoughts. *~ saya hanya satu yaitu mendirikan sebuah kondominium yang serba modérn.* I have only one thing in mind, that is to build a super-modern condominium. **4** mind, ability to reason, awareness. *~nya kurang bérés* he is not quite right in the head. *sakit ~* insane, crazy. *berubah ~* be(come) crazy/insane.

ingat-ingatan 1 s.t. remembered, remembrance. *Pada masa hidup kita hendaklah membuat jasa untuk menjadi ~ dan sebut-sebutan orang di belakang hari.* During our lifetime we should perform services so as to be remembered and talked about by people in times to come. **2** souvenir. **3** to have a vague recollection.

pengingat 1 s.o. with a good memory. **2** reminder. *Biro iklan Indo Ad hanya memakai radio sebagai média ~ buat mengiklankan suatu produk yang sudah mapan.* The Indo Ad advertising agency uses the radio only as a reminder when it advertises an established product. *(alat) pembantu ~* mnemonic device.

pengingatan recalling, recollecting.

peringatan 1 → INGATAN. **2** warning; advice, reminder, admonition; lesson. *~ dini* early warning. *memberi ~ keras* to give a stern warning. *mendapat ~ keras dari* to get a stern warning from. *Ini ~ pertama dan terakhir.* This is the first and last warning (I will give you). **3** commemoration, remembrance. *buku ~* diary, journal. *tugu ~* cenotaph, commemorative column. **4** certificate. *~ Permandian* Baptismal Certificate.

ingau → IGAU I.

inger (*Jv*) **ngingerkan** to change (the direction of). *Péking berhasil ~ arah pandom politik luar negeri RI ke arahnya.* Peking was successful in changing the direction of the compass needle of the Republic of Indonesia's foreign policy in her direction.

inger-inger a pest of the teak tree, *Neotermes tectonae*.

inget → INGAT. **ngingetin** (*J coq*) → MENGINGATI, MENGINGATKAN.

inggang-inggung swaying, shaking, tottering; → INCANG-INCUT.

inggat (*Jv*) **penginggatan** *~ perempuan* abduction.

Inggeris → INGGRIS.

Inggernésia [*Inggeris dan Indonésia*] a mixture of English and Indonesian.

inggih (*Jv*) yes. *tukang –* yes man; → PENGIA. *inggih-inggih boten/ ora kepanggih* (*Jv*) to make empty promises.

inggil (*Jv*) high. *busana –* haute couture; → ADIBUSANA.

Inggris (*Port?*) **1** England, Britain. **2** English, British. *bahasa –* English (language). *negara –* England. *orang –* Englishman. *– Raya* Great Britain.

mengginggriskan to translate into English.

keinggris-inggrisan 1 Anglicism. **2** anglicized.

pengginggrisan Anglicization, translating into English.

inggriya (*Jv*) (from *ing*+*griya*) in-house. *pendidikan dan pelatihan yang diselenggarakan –* in-house education and training.

inggu I (*Skr*) asafetida, a plant which produces a foul-smelling sap and which is used for various medicines, *aka* devil's dung or food of the gods, *Ruta angustifolia/graveolens*.

inggu II *ikan –* a) a smelly coral fish, *Amphipria*. b) k.o. fish, *Holacanthus spp*.

inggung → INGGANG-inggung.

ingin to want, wish, desire, would like (to), feel like. *Saudara – menemui siapa?* Whom do you wish to see? *Sekarang ia – ketawa.* He feels like laughing now. *Saya – bertemu dengannya.* I would like to meet her. *– akan buah-buahan* to want (to eat) fruit. *– tahu* curious, inquisitive, wonder. *Saya – tahu apa yang terjadi pada meréka.* I wonder what's happened to them. *karena – tahu* out of curiosity. **keingintahuan** curiosity, inquisitiveness. *sudah lama – been meaning to. Aku sudah lama – mengatakan kepadamu mengenai hal itu.* I've been meaning to tell you about this for a long time. *– sekali* eager to, want very much to.

beringin ~ *akan* and **beringinkan** to long for, desire, wish for, crave. *beringin akan mendapat seorang anak yang pandai* wishing for a smart child.

mengingini and **menginginkan** to desire, want, wish for, long for. *tak diingini* unwanted, undesirable. *Dalam jangka panjang diinginkan supaya Bahasa Indonésia tidak saja dapat digunakan di Indonésia dan Malaysia, tetapi juga di negara-negara di luar negara-negara tersebut.* In the long run the wish is that Indonesian will be used not only in Indonesia and in Malaysia but in other countries as well.

memperingin(i) to arouse interest, tempt, make s.o. want s.t. *Radén Menteri diperingininya dengan perempuan.* They aroused Radén Menteri's interest in a woman.

teringin to have a sudden desire. *Ia ~ hendak makan telur penyu.* He had a sudden desire to eat turtle eggs.

keinginan desire, demand, wish, craving, longing, will. *di luar ~nya* against his will. ~ *berbelanja* shopping spree. ~ *tahu* curiosity. ~ *mengembang* rising demands. **berkeinginan** to have a desire/wish.

peringinan desire, want, appetite.

ing-ing (C) to move (to another site). *PBB akan – di New York?* Will the UN be moved from New York?

ing-ing tut (*Jv*) [ing ngarsa sung tulada, ing madya karsa, tutwuri handayani] providing an example from the front, willing in the middle, encouraging from behind, i.e., a description of village life.

Ingkang (*Jv*) The Honorable. *Sampéyan Dalem – Sinuhun* His Highness, title given to the Sultan of Yogyakarta and the Susuhunan of Surakarta. *- Wicaksana* His Excellency.

ingkar (*A*) **1** – *(akan/kepada)* to deny, disavow. – *(akan) janji* a) to break a promise. b) to default on/violate a contract. – *kepada sumpah* to disavow an oath. **2** denial, negation, disavowal. **3** (*gram*) negative. *kalimat –* (*gram*) negative sentence. *kata –* negation, negative word. – *ganda* double negative. **4**a) unwilling, reluctant, averse. b) unwillingness, reluctance, aversion. **5** be in breach (of contract). – *bayar* insolvent, insolvency.

mengingkari and **mengingkarkan 1** to deny, break, renege on, go back on (a promise). *Dia ~ kenyataan.* He denied the evidence. ~ *janji* to break/go back on a promise. ~ *kata* to take back one's words. ~ *sumpah* to go back on one's oath. **2** to refuse, reject, disavow, reject. *Ia ~ cinta.* He rejected the love (offered him).

keingkaran 1 disavowal, breaking (a promise), denial. **2** refusal.

pengingkar evader. ~ *pajak* tax evader.

pengingkaran 1 denial, breaking (a promise). ~ *janji* breaking a promise. **2** undermining (trust in government).

ingkel (*Jv*) **mengingkel(-ingkel)** to tease, pester.

inglo (*J*) home (in hide-and-go-seek and similar games).

ingsak → INJAK.

ingsang → INSANG.

ingsun (*Jv*) **1** I, me, my. *Niat - merdéka atau mati.* My intention is to be free or dead. **2** (the royal) we.

ingsut *jangka –* (pair of) slide compasses.

beringsut 1 to move slowly, inch/edge ahead/forward. *Pada jam sibuk, kendaraan hanya bisa ~ 20 km/jam.* In rush hours cars can only inch forward at 20 km an hour. *tak ~ mundur satu mili pun* not yield even an inch of ground. **2** to shift, move.

beringsutan (*pl obj*) to move along slowly.

mengingsut 1 = beringsut. **2** to shift, move s.t. ~ *pinggulnya* to move over.

mengingsutkan → MENGINGSUT 2.

teringsut moved/shifted over, pushed aside. *Sekolah membatik itu bernaung di bawah atap Gapura Batik Art, sehingga agaknya usaha bisnis batik tadi ~ didesak bisnis "sekolah."* The batik school is affiliated with Gapura Batik Art, so that probably the batik business was pushed aside by the "school's" business activities.

teringsutkan moveable, can be shifted.

ingsutan shift.

pengingsutan shifting.

ingus (nasal) mucus, snot. *Jika kumat, - éncér keluar terusmenerus.* When I have a relapse (of my allergy), thick mucus continually comes out of my nose. *membuang –* to blow one's nose. *sakit –* a) to have a runny nose. b) (horse) strangles.

beringus runny/running (of one's nose). *Hidungnya ~.* Her nose is running.

mengingus to blow one's nose.

mengingusi 1 to blow (one's nose). **2** to outwit, trick, deceive.

ingusan 1 still wet behind the ears, green, young and naive. *Penjudi yang masih ~ pasti kalah.* Gamblers who are still green have to lose. *anak/bocah ~* young whippersnapper. **2** runny-nosed. **3** bluetongue (a disease of cattle).

inhalasi (*D*) inhalation.

inhérén (*D/E*) inherent.

inhibisi (*D*) inhibition.

inhibitor (*E*) inhibitor.

inhuman (*D/E*) inhuman.

ini 1 this. **2** these. **3** here and now, right here/now; → NIH. *Mau ke mana –?* Where are you going (right now)? *Dan - nih, kendaraan bajaj.* And this here is a Bajaj. **4** um, uh (hesitation noise); *cp* ANU. *– dia.* Here it is. This is it. *– dia, kabar gembira.* This is it (and) it's welcome news. *bulan – dan itu* this month and that one. *– hari* (*coq*) today. *– itu* this and that, such and such. *– juga* this very. *pada waktu – juga* at this very moment. *– dari mana ya?* (over the telephone) Who is this? *– konon/pula* a) especially, the more so. b) much more. *– pula lagi!* (the same thing) again! *– itunya* the ins and outs, the whys and wherefores. *– itunya sebenarnya tak begitu jelas.* The ins and outs are actually not very clear.

ini-ini ~ *juga* always the same thing, the same thing over and over again.

inisial (*D/E*) initial.

berinisial 1 initialed. **2** with the initials ...

inisiasi (*D*) initiation.

menginisiasi(kan) to initiate.

inisiatif (*E*) and **inisiatip** (*D*) initiative; → PRAKARSA. *atas –* on the initiative of. *atas – sendiri* on one's own initiative. *mengambil – to take the initiative.

berinisiatif to take the initiative.

penginisiatif initiator.

inisiator (*D/E*) initiator; → PEMRAKARSA, PENGINISIATIF.

injak step on, tread on.

injak-injak stirrup, pedal, treadle, running board.

berinjak *tempat ~* foothold, footing.

menginjak [and **nginjak** (*coq*)] **1** to trample down on, tread on. **2** to become/get to be a certain age or status. *Sejak beberapa bulan belakangan ini, Ny. Liza yang baru ~ 30 tahun, seringkali mengeluh.* For the past few months, Mrs. Liza, who has just become 30 years old, has often been complaining. **3** to set foot (on), put one's foot on, enter. ~ *bumi Amérika* to set foot on American soil. ~ *halaman Kedubés* to enter the Embassy grounds. ~ *jaman baru* to enter a new era. **4** to step on. ~ *pédal gas* to step on the accelerator. ~ *pédal rém* to step on the brake. ~ *dua perahu* run with the hare and hunt with the hounds, i.e., to try to play two incompatible roles at the same time.

menginjak-injak to trample on, step on. ~ *hak azasi manusia* to trample on human rights. ~ *hukum* to get away with crimes.

menginjakkan to put (one's foot down on), set (foot on). ~ *kaki pada/di* to step/set foot on. *Dia tidak pernah ~ kakinya di bumi Indonésia.* He never set foot in Indonesia.

terinjak(-injak) 1 trampled on, (one's toes are) trod on. **2** totally ignored.

injakan 1 trampled down. **2** stairs; tread, step. **3** stirrup, pedal, treadle (of a sewing machine), running board (of a car). ~ *gas* accelerator pedal. ~ *kopeling* clutch pedal. ~ *rém* brake pedal.

injak-injakan → INJAKAN.

penginjak(-injak) s.o. who tramples on.

penginjak(-injak)an trampling, treading (down on).

injap mouth of fish trap which turns inward and which has bamboo spikes to prevent fish that have entered the trap from escaping again.

menginjap to install this k.o. mouth on a trap.

injéksi (*D*) injection, shot. *– beras* distribution of rice to an area to prevent a possible increase in prices due to shortages.

menginjéksi to give an injection to.

terinjéksi injected.

penginjéksian injecting.

injen (*Jv*) **menginjen** to take a look at, peek at (*esp* from the outside to the inside).

Injil (*A*) 1 the New Testament. 2 Gospel. *Kitab* – the Scriptures; the Bible. *guru* – and *pengabar* – evangelist. – *al Kudus* the Holy Gospel.

menginjil to evangelize.

penginjil evangelist.

penginjilan evangelization, missionizing.

injili evangelical. *Geréja* – the Church of God.

injin I (*E*) engine.

injin II (*C ob*) mother.

injinuitas (*E*) ingenuity. – *manusia* human ingenuity.

inkam (*E*) income.

inkar → INGKAR.

inkarnasi (*D*) incarnation.

menginkarnasikan to incarnate.

inkaso (*D*) collection (of accounts). *bank* – collecting banker.

menginkasokan to present (a check) for collection.

inklaring (*D*) (of goods, ship) clearance (inward), customs clearance.

inklinasi (*D*) inclination, dip.

inklusif (*E*) and **inklusip** (*D*) inclusive; → TERMASUK.

inkoatif (*D/E*) inchoative.

inkognito (*D/E*) incognito.

inkompatibilitas (*D*) incompatibility.

inkompetén (*D/E*) incompetent.

inkonsékuénsi (*D*) inconsistency.

inkonsistén (*D/E*) inconsistent.

inkonsisténsi (*D*) inconsistency.

inkonstitusional (*E*) and **inkonstitusionil** (*D*) unconstitutional.

inkonvénsional (*E*) and **inkonvénsionil** (*D*) unconventional.

inkorporasi (*D*) incorporation.

menginkorporasi to incorporate.

inkracht (*D ob*) /inkraht/ to be in force/effect, be valid (of a law); → BERLAKU.

inkubasi (*D*) incubation.

inkubator (*D/E*) incubator.

inkuisisi (*D*) inquisition.

inlander (*D col*) (derogatory term for a) native (Indonesian); *cp* MELAYU.

Inmas [Inténsifikasi Masal (Swa Sembada Bahan Makanan)] Mass Intensification for Self-Sufficiency in Food, i.e., an agricultural development program operating in conjunction with *Bimas*; it supplies participants with subsidized input.

inna (*A*) surely we. – *lillahi wa* – *ilaihi rajiun/rojiun* surely we come from God (said on hearing of a death and in death announcements), dust thou art and unto dust shalt thou return.

inni (*A*) surely I.

inohong (*S*) leader.

inokulasi (*D*) inoculation.

menginokulasikan to inoculate.

penginokulasian inoculating.

inong balee (*Ac*) female troops of GAM.

inosén (*E*) innocent.

inovasi (*D*) innovation.

berinovasi to innovate; innovated. *kemampuan* ~ innovated ability.

menginovasikan to innovate.

inovatif (*E*) innovative.

inovator (*D/E*) innovator.

Inpar [Industri pariwisata] tourist industry.

inpl- → also see entries beginning with **inf-, inv-, imp-**.

inplénsa (*D*) influenza.

Inprés [Instruksi présidén] Presidential Instruction; programs are *usu* for infrastructure and contain a substantial job-creating element.

menginpréskan to make s.t. into a Presidential Instruction project.

input (*E*) input; → MASUKAN.

Inréhab [Instalasi réhabilitasi] Rehabilitation Camp (on the island of Buru for *G30S/PKI* detainees).

inréyen (*D*) running-in (time of a car), road-testing (a car).

menginréyen to break in (a car, etc.).

insaf (*A*) 1 – *akan* to be(come) aware of, realize, be conscious of; to understand, comprehend, be cognizant of. – *akan dirinya* to be aware/conscious of one's own position, judge o.s. *menaruh* – to be compassionate. 2 consciousness, awareness; strong belief. 3 to reform after acknowledging one's errors. 4 fairness, justice. – *seinsaf-insafnya* to be firmly convinced.

menginsafi to realize, be aware/conscious of; to understand, comprehend.

menginsafkan 1 to make s.o. aware/conscious (of s.t.); to convince, make s.o. come to his senses. 2 to be aware of.

terinsafkan can be made to understand.

terinsafi realized, made aware.

keinsafan realization, awareness, consciousness. ~ *keadilan* sense of justice.

penginsafan awareness.

insam ginseng.

insan (*A*) mankind. – *film* s.o. from the world of film. – *pérs* members of the press, journalists. –– *prajurit* a member of the armed forces. – *téater* s.o. from the world of theater. *-(ul)kamil* the perfect man, archetype of all created things (for Muslim mystics).

insanan personification.

keinsanan personhood.

insang gills (of fish). *keras* – stubborn. *tulang* – baleen. *asal* – *ikan-lah* not choosy.

berinsang with gills, gilled.

insani(yah) and **insaniat** (*A*) human. *fitrah* – human disposition. *hubungan* – human relations. *roh* – the human spirit. *tubuh* – the human body.

insap → INSAF.

insék (*D/E*) insect; → SERANGGA I.

inséktisida (*D/E*) insecticide.

inséminasi (*D*) insemination. – *buatan* artificial insemination. *ahli* – *buatan* artificial inseminator.

menginséminasi to inseminate.

inséntif and **inséntip** (*E*) incentive.

insés (*D/E*) incest.

insét (*E*) inset. *gambar* – inserted illustration.

inseting → INSTING.

insidén (*D/E*) incident. – *Bali* the bombing of a nightclub in Kuta, Bali, on October 12, 2002.

insidénsi (*E*) incidence.

insidéntal (*E*) and **insidéntil** (*D*) incidental.

Insimal [Indonésia-Singapura-Malaysia] Indonesia-Singapore-Malaysia.

insinuasi (*E*) insinuation.

menginsinuasi to insinuate.

insinuatif (*E*) insinuating.

insinye (*D*) insignia, emblem, badge.

insinyur (*D*) [Ir.] Dutch engineering degree, comparable to M.Sc. in ... Engineering. – *éléktro* electrical engineer. – *ilmu alam* physical engineer. – *kepala* chief engineer. – *mesin* mechanical engineer. – *pembangunan kapal* naval architect. – *pertambangan* mining engineer. – *pertanian* agricultural engineer. – *séksi* superintending engineer. – *tambang* mining engineer.

keinsinyuran engineering. *prinsip* ~ engineering principles.

insipién (*D*) beginner.

insisi (*D*) incision. *pembedahan tanpa* – noninvasive surgery.

inskripsi (*D*) inscription; *cp* PRASASTI.

insolvén (*D/E*) insolvent.

insolvénsi (*D*) insolvency.

insomnia (*D/E*) insomnia.

inspéksi (*D*) inspection. – *Gajah* "Jumbo Inspection," i.e., the Income Tax Inspection Office located at Jalan Budi Utomo in Jakarta. – *Keuangan* Finance Inspection. – *mendadak* [sidak] surprise inspection.

menginspéksi to inspect.

inspéktorat (*D/E*) inspectorate.

inspéktur (*D*) inspector. – *Jénderal* [Irjén] Inspector General, the watchdog over finances and performance in a ministry. – *muda* under-inspector. – *satu* [iptu] senior inspector. – *Upacara* [Irup] Inspector of the Ceremonies.

inspirasi (*D*) inspiration.
  berinspirasi to be inspired. ~ *dari gaya balét dan busana kuno* inspired by a ballet style and antique clothes.
  berinspirasikan to be inspired by.
  menginspirasikan to inspire.
  terinspirasi inspired.

inspiratif inspiring.

inspirator inspirator.

instabilitas (*E*) instability.

instalasi (*D*) 1 installation, inauguration. – *gubernur* inauguration of a governor. 2 plant, installation, device. – *minyak* oil installation. – *muat* loading device. – *pemanas pusat* central heating installation. – *penjernihan air* water purification installation. – *réhabilitasi* rehabilitation installation, i.e., place for political detainees (on the island of Buru). – *tenaga* power plant.
  menginstalasi to install.
  terinstalasi installed.
  penginstalasian installing.

instalatir and **instalatur** (*D*) installer.

instan (*E*) instant (coffee/tea, etc.). *Udang – untuk sarapan cepat.* Instant shrimp for a quick breakfast.

instansi (*D*) 1 authority, (government) agency, body, organ; → GEDUNG/RUMAH *instansi*. – *pemerintah yang berwenang* the competent authorities, the proper agency. – *vértikal* a central government representative in a region. 2 (*leg*) instance.

insting and **instink** (*D*) instinct; → GARIZAH, NALURI.

instingtif (*E*) and **instingtip** (*D*) instinctive.

institusi (*D*) institute.
  menginstitusikan to institute.
  terinstitusi(kan) institutionalized.
  penginstitusian institutionalization.

institusional (*E*) and **institusionil** (*D*) institutional.
  terinstitusionalkan institutionalized.

institusionalisasi institutionalization.

institut (*D/E*) institute. – *Téknologi* Institute of Technology.

instruksi (*D*) instruction. – *pengapalan* shipping instructions.
  menginstruksikan to instruct.

instruksional (*E*) and **instruksionil** (*D*) instructional.

instruktif (*D/E*) instructive.

instruktir (*D*), **instruktor** (*E*), and **instruktur** (*D*) instructor.
  keinstruktoran having to do with instructors.

instrumén (*D/E*) instrument.

instruméntal (*D/E*) instrumental.

instruméntalia (*D*) instrumental music.

instruméntalis (*D*) instrumentalist.

instruméntasi (*D*) instrumentation.

insubordinasi (*D*) insubordination.

insuflasi (*D*) insufflation.

insulating (*E*) insulating material.

insulér (*D*) insular, interisland.

insulin (*D/E*) insulin.

Insulinde (*D*) the Indonesian archipelago.

insurgénsi and **insurjénsi** (*D*) insurgency.

Insus [Inténsifikasi khusus] Special Intensification (Program).
  ke-Insus-an relating to the Special Intensification Program.

insya Allah (*A*) God willing, if God wills it.

insyaf → INSAF.

Insyiqaq (*A*) *al*– "The Cleaving/Rendering Asunder"; name of the 84th chapter of the Koran.

Insyirah (*A*) *al*– "Opening Up/Field"; name of the 94th chapter of the Koran.

intaglio (*E*) intaglio.

intai spy on, observe surreptitiously.
  mengintai 1 to lie in wait for, be on the lookout for. 2 to watch surreptitiously, spy/keep an eye on.
  mengintai(-intai)kan to spy on, observe surreptitiously.
  intaian 1 surveillance. 2 look-out.
  pengintai 1 scout, spy, observer. 2 snoop.
  pengintaian spying, espionage, observation, scouting out, reconnaissance.

intan diamond. – *air beras* a snow-white diamond. – *berlian/permata* jewelry. – *jambun* a bluish diamond (found in southern Kalimantan). – *mentah* rough/uncut diamond.

intégral (*D/E*) integral.

intégrasi (*D*) integration.
  berintégrasi to be integrated.
  mengintégrasikan to integrate. ~ *diri* to integrate, assimilate.
  terintégrasikan integrated.
  pengintégrasian 1 integration, unification. 2 integrating.

integrasionis (*E*) integrationist.

intégratif (*E*) integrative.

intégritas and **intégritét** (*D*) integrity. – *bangsa* national integrity. – *moral* moral integrity.
  berintégritas having/with integrity.

intél (*E*) clipped form of **intelijén(s)**. intelligence, spying. *seorang –* a) an intelligence agent, secret service agent. b) spy. – *jalan* an employee of the highway patrol who rides public transportation disguised as an ordinary passenger and who looks for corruption, etc.
  berintél 1 to be an (intelligence/secret service) agent. 2 to be a spy. 3 to seek information, make inquiries.
  keintélan intelligence (*mod*). *bidang –* the intelligence field.

intéléjénsia (*D/E infr*) intelligentsia.

intélék (*D/E*) intellect. *kaum –* the intellectuals, intelligentsia.
  keintélékan to be too intellectual.

intéléktual (*E*) intellectual.

intéléktualisme (*D/E*) intellectualism.

intéléktualistis (*E*) intellectualistic.

intéléktualitas (*D*) intellectuality.

intéléktuil (*D*) intellectual.

intéligén (*D/E*) intelligent; → CERDAS, PANDAI I.

intéligéns (*D/E*) → INTÉLIJÉN I.

intéligénsi (*D*) intelligence (mental ability), intellect.

intéligénsia (*D/E*) intelligentsia, the intellectuals.

intélijén I (*E*) intelligence, secret service. – *yang berlaku* up-to-date intelligence.

intélijén II (*E*) intelligent; → CERDAS, PANDAI I.

intélijéns → INTÉLIJÉN I.

Intélpam [intélijén pengamanan] pacification intelligence.

Intélpampol [Intélijén dan Pengamanan Polri] Republic of Indonesia Police Pacification Intelligence.

inténdan(s) (*D*) 1 quartermaster. *Corps* – Quartermaster Corps. 2 army service corps.

inténs (*D/E*) intense.

inténsi (*D*) intention.

inténsif (*D/E*) intensive.
  menginténsifkan to intensify.
  keinténsifan intensity.
  penginténsifan intensification.

inténsifikasi (*E*) intensification.
  menginténsifikasikan to intensify.
  penginténsifikasian intensification, stepping up production.

inténsitas and **inténsitét** (*D*) intensity.

inter (in compound words) inter-; → ANTAR II, INTRA.

interaksi (*D*) interaction.
  berinteraksi to interact.

interaktif (*E*) interactive. *hubungan – agama dengan masyarakat* interactive relations between religion and society.

interdép clipped form of **interdépartemental**. *Panitia –* Interdepartmental Commission.

interdépartemental (*D/E*) interdepartmental.

interdépéndén (*E*) interdependent.

interdépéndénsi (*D*) interdependency.

interdisiplinér (*D*) interdisciplinary.

interélasi (*D*) interrelation.

intéren → INTÉRN.

interés (*D/E*) interest (in s.t.). *Saya yakin kalau meréka tidak punya – atau kepentingan lainnya.* I'm convinced that they don't have other interests.

interésan interesting; → MENARIK (*hati*). *kabar yang – sekali* a very interesting news item.

interférénsi (*D*) interference.

intergéntil (*L*) interpersonal.
interglasial (*D/E*) interglacial.
interim (*D*) interim; → AD INTERIM.
interinsulér (*D*) interisland; → ANTARPULAU.
intérior (*E*) and **intériur** (*D*) interior (decoration).
intériorisasi and **intérioritas** interiorization.
interjéksi (*D gram*) interjection.
interkom (*D/E*) intercom.
  berinterkom to use an intercom.
interkonéksi (*E*) interconnection. – *kelistrikan se-Jawa* the all-Java electrical interconnection.
interkontinéntal (*D/E*) intercontinental.
interlokal (*D*) long-distance (phone) call. *Ia menerima – dari Jakarta.* He got a long-distance call from Jakarta.
  berinterlokal to make a long-distance (phone) call. *Pemakai télepon di Belitung sulit ~.* It's hard for a telephone customer in Belitung to make long-distance calls.
  menginterlokal to make/place a long-distance (phone) call. *"Saya segera ~ mengatakan saya masih hidup dan séhat walafiat," ujarnya.* "I immediately made a long-distance call saying I was still alive and in perfect health," he said.
interlokutor (*E*) interlocutor.
intermédiasi (*E*) intermediation.
interméso (*D*) intermezzo, pause.
  berinterméso to pause.
intérn (*D*) 1 internal (affairs). 2 local (not national) examination.
intérnal (*E*) 1 internal (feelings, etc.). 2 inland (navigation, etc.), domestic. *perdagangan* – domestic trade, intratrade.
intérnalisasi (*E*) internalization.
  mengintérnalisasi to internalize.
internasional (*D/E*) international.
  menginternasional to go international.
  menginternasionalkan to upgrade to international standards (of swimming pool, etc.).
  penginternasionalan internationalization. *~ yén* the internationalization of the yen.
internasionalisasi (*E*) internationalization.
internasionalisme (*D/E*) internationalism.
internat (*D col*) boarding school.
internir (*D*) **menginternir** to intern (in a camp, e.g., during the Japanese occupation).
  interniran 1 interned. *orang* – internee. 2 internment (camp).
  penginterniran internment.
intérnis (*D/E*) internist, specialist in internal medicine.
intérogasi (*D*) interrogation. *mengadakan* – to interrogate.
  mengintérogasi to interrogate.
  pengintérogasian interrogating.
intérogatif (*D/E*) interrogative. *kalimat* – (*gram*) interrogative sentence.
  keintérogatifan interrogative (*mod*).
intérogator (*E*) interrogator.
interpélan (*D*) interpellator, questioner.
interpélasi (*D*) interpellation (in the *DPR*)
interpiu (*D/E*) interview; → WAWANCARA.
  menginterpiu to interview.
interpol [Inter(national criminal) Police Organization)] Interpol.
interpolasi (*D*) interpolation.
  menginterpolasi to interpolate.
interport [International airport] international airport.
interprétasi (*D*) interpretation.
  menginterprétasi to interpret.
  penginterprétasian interpretation, interpreting.
interprétatif (*D/E*) interpretative.
interprétir (*D*) **menginterprétir** to interpret.
intersépsi interception.
interupsi (*D*) interruption.
  menginterupsi to interrupt.
interval (*D/E*) interval.
intervénién (*D leg*) intervener (as a third party), third-party intervener.
intervénsi (*D*) intervention.
  berintervénsi to intervene.

interviu → INTERPIU.
interzone (*E*) interzonal (competition, championship, etc.).
inti 1 stuffing, filling (of cakes, etc.). 2 kernel, nucleus, center. *kabinét* – inner cabinet. 3 nuclear (*mod*). *senjata* – nuclear weapon. 4 gist, core. *orang* – hard-core people. – *persoalannya* the gist of the matter. *pada –nya* in essence. *Surat édaran itu pada –nya menyebutkan...* the circular says in essence ... – *anang* daughter nucleus. – *atom* atomic nucleus. – *batu* rock core. **penginti-batuan** coring. – *benih* (*bot*) kernel. – *beton* concrete core. – *bumi* earth's core. – *cucu* second daughter nucleus. – *hidup* what life is all about. – *pati* a) (quint)essence. b) digest, abstract. – *peledak* blasting gelatin. – *persoalan* the heart of the matter. – *plasma* kern/plasma (model: cooperation between small and middle or large businesses). – *sari* a) (quint)essence, gist (of the matter). b) digest, abstract. **mengintisarikan** to make an abstract of. – *sél* cell nucleus.
  berinti to have a core/nucleus.
  berintikan to have ... as its core/nucleus. *néo-Barisan Soekarno yang ~ sisa-sisa G30S/PKI* the neo-Soekarno Front, the nucleus of which consists of remnants of the G30S/PKI.
  menginti (*geol*) to core.
  intian core, heart, center.
  penginti corer. *~ batuan* (*petro*) corer.
intifadah (*A*) the Palestinian uprising that began on December 9, 1987 in Gaza.
Intifar (*A*) *al*– "The Splitting"; name of the 82nd chapter of the Koran.
intiha (*A*) end. – *al-kalam* finis, the end (of a book/speech, etc.).
intikad (*A*) criticism.
intil (*Jv*) **mengintil** to follow, track, shadow; → KINTIL.
intim I (*D*) 1 intimate, close (friendship). *Rus yang – dengan seorang pemuda* Rus, who was close to a young man. 2 to have sex(ual intercourse) with. *hubungan* – intimate relations, sex. *melakukan hubungan* – to have sexual intercourse. *rasa nyeri/tak énak sewaktu melakukan hubungan* – painful sexual intercourse, dispareunia. *mempunyai hubungan* – to have sexual intercourse. *menjalin hubungan – (dengan)* to have a sexual relationship (with). *berhubungan – dengan istrinya* to have sexual relations with one's wife.
  seintim as intimate as.
  berintim-intiman to have intimate relations with e.o.
  mengintimi to have sex(ual relations) with. *Bénny sudah beberapa kali diintimi Bobby meski dua-duanya sesama lelaki.* Benny has had sexual relations several times with Bobby even though they are both men.
  mengintimkan to make more intimate. *untuk lebih ~ pembicaraan* to make the conversation more intimate.
  keintiman intimacy, close connection/relations.
Intim II [Indonésia Timur] Eastern Indonesia.
intimidasi (*D*) intimidation.
  mengintimidasi to intimidate.
  terintimidasi intimidated.
  pengintimidasian intimidating.
intimidir (*D*) **mengintimidir** to intimidate.
intip I peer/peep at, spy on.
  mengintip(i) to peer at, watch secretly, spy on, snoop on, peep at.
  ngintip (*coq*) to peer at, watch secretly, spy on, snoop on, peep at. *tukang ~* peeping Tom. *~ studio* behind the scenes.
  mengintipi (*pl subj*) to spy on.
  pengintip voyeur.
  (peng)intipan surveillance, observation, spying on, reconnaissance, prying eyes.
intip II (*Jv*) scorched rice at the bottom of a pan.
intisari liaison or courier of the Communist Party of Indonesia; → INTI.
intoksikasi (*D*) intoxication.
intoleran (*D/E*) intolerant.
intoleransi (*D*) intolerance.
intonasi (*D*) intonation.
intra- (*D*) (in compounds) within, inter-, intra-; → ANTAR II, INTER-.
intra-ASEAN inter-ASEAN; → ANTAR-ASÉAN.
intrakampus intercampus.

intrakurikulér (*E*) intracurricular.

intrakutan (*E*) intracutaneous.

intramuskular (*D/E*) intramuscular.

intransitif (*D/E gram*) intransitive.

intrapartai (*E*) interparty.

intrapropinsi (*E*) interprovincial.

intrarégional (*E*) interregional.

intrasekolah interscholastic. *Organisasi Siswa* – (OSIS) Inter-scholastic Student Organization.

intrasélular (*E*) intercellular.

intrauniversitér (*E*) interuniversity.

intrawilayah (*E*) interterritorial.

intrik (*D*) intrigue.

  intrik-intrikan to carry out intrigues.

  mengintrik to carry out intrigues among. *RRC sudah langsung mencoba ~ pihak tentara.* The PRC has directly tried to carry out intrigues in the army.

intrikatif (*E*) full of intrigues.

intrinsik (*D/E*) intrinsic. *nilai-nilai* – intrinsic values.

intro clipped form of **introduksi**.

introduksi (*D*) introduction.

  mengintroduksi to introduce.

introdusir (*D*) mengintrodusir to introduce.

introspéksi (*D*) introspection; → MAWAS *diri*.

  berintrospéksi to introspect.

  mengintrospéksi to introspect. *~ diri* to introspect, think to o.s.

introver(t) (*D/E*) introvert.

introvérsi (*E*) introversion.

intrusi (*D*) intrusion. – *air laut perlu perhatian sérius* intrusions of sea water require serious attention.

intuisi (*E*) intuition.

intuitif (*D/E*) intuitive.

invalid I (*D/E*) invalid, sickly.

invalid II (*E*) invalid, not valid.

invasi (*D*) invasion.

  berinvasi to invade, invasive.

  menginvasi to invade s.t. *Negeri Paman Ho ~ Kampuchéa.* Vietnam invaded Cambodia.

invénsi (*E*) invention.

invéntaris (*D*) inventory.

  penginvéntarisan inventorying.

invéntarisasi (*D*) stock taking, taking inventory.

  menginvéntarisasi(kan) to take stock/inventory.

  terinvéntarisasikan inventoried.

  penginvéntarisasian inventorying, taking stock/inventory.

invéntarisir (*D*) menginvéntarisir to take stock/inventory, inventory.

invéntif (*D/E*) inventive.

invérsi (*D*) inversion.

invéstasi (*D*) investment. – *asing langsung* direct foreign investment.

  berinvéstasi *~ (ke)* to invest (in).

  menginvéstasikan to invest (money in); → MENANAM(KAN).

  penginvéstasian investment, investing. *~ kembali* reinvestment.

invéstigasi (*E*) investigation.

invéstigatif (*E*) investigative. *jurnalistik* – investigative journalism. *staf* – the investigative staff.

invéstor (*E*) investor; → PENANAM *modal.*

invitasi (*D*) invitation; → UNDANGAN.

invoerpas (*D ob*) /infurpas/ import license (a customs document).

invois (*E Mal*) invoice; → FAKTUR.

involusi (*E*) involution. – *kota* urban involution.

inya duenna; → INANG I.

inyéksi; → INJÉKSI.

inyiak (*M*) 1 grandfather. 2 grandmother. – *balang* Grandpa Stripe, i.e., the tiger.

inyik (*M*) → KIAI.

inyo (*M*) → IANYA.

Inza an Indonesian-manufactured antiflu medicine made by PT Konimex, Surabaya.

iodin (*E*) iodine;→ YODIUM.

iodoform (*E*) iodoform.

ion (*D*) ion.

  mengion to ionize.

  pengionan ionization.

ionisasi (*D*) ionization.

ionosfér (*E*) and ionosfir (*D*) ionosphere.

IP I (*init*) → INDÉKS *Préstasi.*

ip II (in acronyms) → INSPÉKTUR.

IPA [Ilmu Pengetahuan Alam] natural sciences.

ipar brother-/sister-in-law. *abang* – husband of elder sister, brother-in-law older than o.s. *adik* – brother-in-law younger than o.s. *kakak* – sister-in-law older than o.s. – *duai* brother-in-law. – *laki-laki* brother-in-law. – *lumai* brother-/sister-in-law. – *perempuan* sister-in-law.

  beripar 1 to have a brother-/sister-in-law. 2 to be related by marriage, be in-laws.

  ipar-beripar *~ satu sama lain* to be related by marriage, be in-laws (to e.o.).

  beriparan to be brothers-/sisters-in-law (of e.o.).

  beriparkan to have ... as one's in-law.

  periparan relationship by marriage.

IPB [Institut Pertanian Bogor] Bogor Agricultural Institute.

ipé (*sl from IV*) ngipé to shoot up, use intravenous drugs.

Ipéda [Iuran pembangunan daérah] Provincial Development Contribution; a tax on land and income-producing crops collected in cooperation with the central government. The first 10 percent is taken by the province and an additional 10 percent is for administrative costs and the balance is allotted to the *kabupatén.*

  ke-Ipéda-an and keipédaan relating to *Ipéda.*

ipik (*Jv*) k.o. fig tree, *Ficus superba.*

ipil(-ipil) k.o. large tree, *Intsia, spp.*

ipis (*S*) → TIPIS.

iprit I (*S?*) k.o. evil spirit.

  ngiprit to sell one's soul to the devil. *Meréka adalah korban ~.* They sold their souls to the devil.

iprit II (*S*) mengiprit and ngiprit to run away (out of fear, etc.).

IPS [Ilmu Pengetahuan Sosial] Social Sciences (department of a senior high school).

Ipték [Ilmu Pengetahuan dan Téknologi] Science and Technology.

Iptu [inspéktur satu] senior inspector.

ipuh 1 the *upas* tree, *Antiaris toxicaria.* 2 *getah* – vegetable poison obtained from the roots of that tree. 3 nasty, vicious.

  beripuh poisoned (of darts, arrows) with that poison.

ipuk (*Jv*) mengipuk 1 to grow, cultivate (plants). 2 to look after, cherish, take care of.

  ipukan seedling.

  pengipukan seedbed, nursery.

ipung k.o. small green snake.

IQ (*E*) [intelligence quotient] IQ.

iqra (*A*) read!

Ir I (*abbr*) → INSINYUR.

ir II (in acronyms) → INSPÉKTUR.

IR-36 name of a superior rice variety.

ira section, vein-like part (of plant, etc.). – *daging* sinews in meat. – *durian* section of durian. – *kayu* vein in wood. – *limau* section of lemon.

irab (*A gram*) declension (of nouns, etc.).

iradah and iradat (*A*) will; the will (of God).

iradiasi (*E*) irradiation.

irafah and irafat (*A*) prediction, fortune-telling, soothsaying.

irah-irahan (*Jv*) certain accessories to a male dancer's dance (hat/hairdo, etc.).

ira-ira *ikan* – k.o. yellow dolphin.

Irak Iraq.

iram to lose color, fade.

irama (*Skr*) 1 rhythm, tune, tempo, beat. 2 measure (in music). – *dadi* (*Jv*) slow rhythm. – *lancar* (*Jv*) fast rhythm. – *tanggung* (*Jv*) medium-fast rhythm.

  seirama *~ dengan* in tune/rhythm with.

  berirama rhythmic(al).

  mengiramai to add a rhythm to.

  mengiramakan to put (a song, etc.) into a certain rhythm, beat out the rhythm (of a song, etc.).

Iramasuka [Irian Jaya, Maluku, Sulawesi, Kalimantan] Irian Jaya, Maluku, Sulawesi, Kalimantan; the acronym means "Pleasant Rhythm."

iram-iram the fringe around a State umbrella.

Iran I Iran, Persia.

Iran II (*E*) [Inspect and Repair As Necessary].
  mengirankan to overhaul. *Empat Hércules TNI-AU diirankan di luar negeri.* Four Indonesian Air Force Hercules aircraft were overhauled overseas.

irap → HIRAP.

iras (*Jv*) **iras-iras** similarities.
  seiras 1 of the same (material/blood/character, etc.). **2** similar, alike.
  mengiras(-iras) 1 to form a single piece (of the same material, etc.). **2** to resemble.
  mengiras-irasi to compare two things to see whether they are the same.
  irasan a whole (of the same material, etc.).

irasional (*E*) and **irasionil** (*D*) irrational.

irasionalisme (*D*) irrationality.

irat (*Jv*) **mengirat** to split into thin strips.
  irat-iratan split piece. ~ *bambu* bamboo strips.

Irbar [Irian Barat] West Irian; → IRJA.

iréal (*E*) unreal.

Iréda [Iuran réhabilitasi daérah] Provincial Rehabilitation Revenue, i.e., a property tax on commercial objects, such as commercial businesses, industries, and markets, as well as on housing, agriculture, and fishponds; → IPÉDA.

irégulér (*E*) irregular.

irélevan (*D/E*) irrelevant.

iréversibel (*D/E*) irreversible.

iri jealous, envious. – *hati (kepada)* jealous/envious (of); → CEMBURU, DENGKI. *beriri hati* to be jealous/envious. *mengiri-hatikan* to be jealous/envious of, envy. *Bud Fox sebenarnya patut diirihatikan.* Bud Fox should really be envied.
  mengiri [and **ngiri** (*coq*)] to be jealous/envious. *Jangan sekali-kali ~ kalau temanmu mendapat kesenangan.* Don't ever be envious if your friend gets s.t. pleasant.
  mengirikan to envy/begrudge s.o. s.t.; to admire s.t. with envy.
  keirian jealousy, envy.
  pengiri jealous, envious (said of s.o.'s character). *Ia ~.* He's the jealous type.

Irian Irian, name of the former Dutch New Guinea (now renamed Papua) (said to mean "Land of Hope" in the language of Biak and in the early days of Indonesian Independence interpreted as an acronym for *Ikut Républik Indonésia Anti Nédérland*, i.e., Follow the Republic of Indonesia against the Netherlands). – *Barat* [Irbar] West New Guinea. – *Jaya* [Irja] Irian Jaya, i.e., "Victorious Irian." – *Timur* Papua and Territory of New Guinea, now Papua New Guinea.

irigasi (*D*) irrigation; → PENGAIRAN. – *téknis* mechanical irrigation.
  beririgasi irrigated. *kawasan pertanian ~* irrigated agricultural zone. *sawah ~* irrigated rice paddies.
  mengirigasi(kan) to irrigate.

irigator (*D/E*) irrigator.

irik trample, thresh.
  mengirik 1 to step on (with one's feet). **2a)** to trample (on *padi*) to separate the grains from the stalk. **b)** to thresh (*kacang*) to separate the nuts from the stalk.
  teririk trampled on.
  pengirik 1 thresher (the person). **2** threshing machine. *dataran/pelantar ~* threshing floor. *kayu/tongkat ~* a flail (used for threshing).
  pengirikan threshing.

iring I seiring 1 in a row, side by side. **2** unanimous, of one mind, at one, in harmony, concurrent. ~ *dengan* together/coupled with, along with; hand in hand with, in tandem with. *kawan ~* friend, companion, mate. ~ *bertukar jalan, seia bertukar sebut* (*M*) to differ in opinion (though the goal is the same). *menohok kawan ~* to bring misfortune to a friend. **3** along (with), accompanying. *tidak ~* in disharmony. *ketidak-seiringan* disharmony. **menyeiringkan** to attend, accompany.

beriring(an) together (with), followed (by). *Panglima tentara Bosnia Sefer Halilovic berjalan beriringan dengan Jéndral Morillon.* The Commander of the Bosnian Army Sefer Halilovic walked along with General Morillon.

beriring-iring(an) in rows, one after the other; in convoy; successively, in succession with. *Itik ~ menuju ke air.* The ducks were heading for the water one after the other. *Kira-kira seratus truk tentara ~ menuju Bogor.* About 1,000 trucks were in a convoy headed for Bogor.

mengiring(i) 1 to accompany, escort, follow in a procession. *Meréka ~ jenazah bosnya ke tempat peristirahatan.* They accompanied their boss's mortal remains to its resting place. **2** to accompany (on a musical instrument, singing, etc.), play the accompaniment for. *Upacara menaikkan bendéra diiringi dengan lagu kebangsaan.* The ceremony of hoisting the flag was accompanied by the national anthem.

mengiringkan 1 [= **mengiring(i)**]. **2** to send along s.o. or s.t. *Beberapa alasan diiringkan bersama-bersama bantahannya.* Several reasons were sent along with their refusal. *diiringkan menyépak, dikemudian menanduk* to make constant problems, be difficult.

teriring accompanied. ~ *salam kami* with our compliments.

iringan 1 row. **2** followers, suite, entourage, retinue; convoy, column. **3** accompaniment. ~ *musik* musical accompaniment.

iring-iringan procession, convoy. ~ *kapal* convoy of ships. ~ *mobil* motorcade.

pengiring follower, escort, attendant, chaperon.

pengiringan followers, suite, entourage, retinue, accompaniment.

iring II – *gemiring* (*M*) to trickle/stream down (of tears).

iris I 1 cut. **2** slice (of bread, etc.). **3** fillet (fish). **4** piece.
  seiris a slice. ~ *roti* a slice of bread.
  mengiris to slice, cut, cut in(to) slices/pieces. *bagai diiris dengan sembilu* it cuts to the heart.
  mengiriskan 1 to cut/slice for s.o. **2** to cut with s.t.
  teriris slashed, sliced.
  irisan 1 slice, cut, piece, section. **2** cut into pieces. ~ *kentang goréng* French fries.
  pengiris slicer.
  pengirisan slicing.

iris II (*D/E*) iris (of the eye).

irit I (*J/Jv*) thrifty, frugal, economical, cheap.
  seirit as economical as.
  mengirit [and **ngirit** (*coq*)] to save, economize, be frugal/cheap. ~ *biaya* to save on expenses.
  mengiritkan to make cheaper.
  pengiritan economizing, saving.

irit II → ÉRÉT I. **iritan 1** a flat-bottomed river ferry which moves along a guide rope; a sledge-like means of transportation for commodities. **2** sledge, sleigh; → ÉRÉT(AN).

iritan (*D/E*) irritant.

iritasi (*D*) irritation.
  mengiritasi to irritate.
  teriritasi (*D*) iirritated rritating.

Irja → IRIAN.

Irjén [Inspéktur Jéndéral] Inspector General.

Irlandia Ireland. – *Utara* Northern Ireland.

iron (*S*) corn porridge.

ironi (*D/E*) irony.

ironis (*D*) ironic.

irr- see entries beginning with *ir-*.

irsyad (*A*) guidance, instruction.

irung k.o. drinking glass, jar, or small cup for drinking *arak*/rice brandy.

irup I → HIRUP. **seirup** a gulp.
  mengirup to gulp, suck/draw liquid into one's mouth.
  irupan lapping, gulping, sucking (liquid into the mouth).

Irup II [Inspéktur upacara] inspector of a ceremony.

irus (*Jv*) a large ladle.

isa I → ISYA.

Isa II (*A*) Jesus. *Nabi* – the prophet Jesus; → YÉSUS. – *Almasih* Jesus the Messiah.

isa III (*coq*) → BISA II.

isak sobbing, sobs. - *tangis* sobbing and crying. ***mengisak-tangiskan*** to sob and cry over; making one sob and cry.
 isak-isak asthma.
 mengisak(-isak) 1 sobbing. 2 wheezing with asthma, asthmatic.
 terisak(-isak) = mengisak(-isak).
 isakan sob, sobbing.

isang → INSANG.

isap suck in, inhale.
 mengisap [and **ngisap** (*coq*)] 1 to suck (in), smoke (a cigarette/marijuana/opium, etc.), inhale. ~ *morfin* to smoke morphine. ~ *benak* to extort money from s.o. ~ *darah* to suck s.o.'s blood, exploit. 2 to absorb (a liquid), suck up. 3 to trick, fool.
 mengisapi to keep on sucking (on).
 mengisapkan to let s.o. suck (in).
 terisap inhaled, sucked in, absorbed.
 isapan 1 sucked (in). 2 s.t. absorbed/inhaled. ~ *darah* blood-sucking, exploitation. ~ *jempol* figment of one's imagination, invented story. 3 sucking, sucker.
 pengisap 1 suction tool, s.t. or s.o. that sucks. (*alat*) ~ *debu* vacuum cleaner. *kertas* ~ and ~ *tinta* blotting paper, blotter. ~ *darah* blood sucker, usurer. 2 smoker. ~ *candu* opium smoker. ~ *ganja* marijuana smoker, pothead. 3 suction.
 pengisapan 1 absorption. 2 extortion, exploitation. 3 suction.

isarah and **isarat** → ISYARAT.

isbat (*A*) 1 confirmation, ratification. 2 positive.
 mengisbatkan to confirm, ratify.

isén (*Jv*) 1 filling, (s.t. used for) stuffing (pillows, etc.), charge (of rifle). 2 filled up (*esp* with inferior goods), deceptive imitation. 3 stuffed (animal). 4 details inside a *batik* motif.

iseng (*J/Jv*) 1 to have nothing to do, be unoccupied, do nothing; to do s.t. to pass the time (or, out of sheer boredom); to be bored. *pekerjaan –, lumayan juga hasilnya* a job which is just a pastime, but the wages are good anyway. 2 in fun, by way of a joke. – *santai* fun. *Jangan –!* Don't bother! *mat* – joker, s.o. who likes to joke around; *cp* MAT *kodak. pria yang* – a man, *usu* already married, who fools around with girls and doesn't want to or can't make a serious commitment. *wanita* – prostitute, loose woman.
 iseng-iseng 1 to do s.t. just to pass the time, kill time. *sebagai/untuk* ~ and ~ *daripada menganggur* to pass the time, as a pastime. 2 to enjoy o.s., have a good time (rather than sit around idly). 3 when you have the time. ~ *coba kamu mampir ke rumahnya*. When you have the time, drop in at his place.
 mengisengi to treat lightly.
 isengan → KEISENGAN.
 keisengan boredom; pastime; s.t. senseless/not serious; jest, joke. ~ *tangan gatal untuk menarik picu senjata* trigger-happy. *melakukan* ~ *pada* to molest s.o. sexually.

isep → ISAP. **ngisepin** → MENGISAPI.

ishk (*A*) (mystic) love in which the lover and the beloved become one, ecstasy in love.

ishlah (*A*) compromise.

isi I 1 content(s) (of a book, etc.). 2 list of contents. 3 volume, capacity. 4 gist, main points or substance; terms (of an agreement). 5 flesh, meat (of a citrus fruit, etc.). 6 the people who live in a certain place/house, etc. 7 (*Jv*) magic power (in a kris). *memberi –* to conjure up powerful spirits in order to have them come into a kris. 8 charge (of a battery/gun, etc.). – *lemak dapat ke orang, tulang buku pulang ke kita* one man's death is another man's bread. *bagai kuku dengan* – inseparable. – *dada/hati* internal (feelings), thoughts and feelings, what is in one's heart/mind/head, what is going on in one's mind. – *durian* the meat of a durian fruit. – *kampung* inhabitants of a village, villagers. – *kawin* marriage portion, dowry. – *kota* inhabitants of a town, townspeople. – *kotor* gross tonnage. – *muatan* contents. – *negeri* population of a country. – *pantun* the third and fourth lines of a *pantun*. – *pentil* valve core. – *perut* a) intestines, bowels. b) thought(s), what is in one's mind, deep dark secrets. c) cargo, contents of a ship's hold. – *pulau* inhabitants of an island, islanders. – *rumah* household, people who live in the same house. – *senapan* charge in a rifle. – *silinder* displacement, capacity. – *tekan* supercharge. – *ulang* refillable, pre-paid (telephone card).

seisi the entire/whole, every one who lives in the same (household/village, etc.). ~ *rumah* the entire family. *Sampaikan salam saya kepada* ~ *rumah*. Give my regards to the whole family. **seisinya** and all its contents; lock, stock, and barrel

berisi 1 to have contents; loaded with, having ... in it; to feature (of a magazine). *sepucuk pistol* ~ *peluru* a loaded revolver. *cangkir* ~ *téh* a cup of tea. ~ *kapur* calcareous, chalky. ~ *zat arang* carboniferous. 2 full-bodied, plump. ~ *padat* heavy-set (of s.o.'s physique). *pemuda yang berbadan gempal* ~ a sturdily built young man. 3 to carry, have ... in it, contain, include. *Harian ini* ~ *berita dan kisah yang menarik*. This newspaper carries interesting news and stories. 4 of substance, substantive. *Saya hanya membaca artikel yang* ~. I only read articles of substance. 5 pregnant.
 berisikan to contain, hold, have ... in it. *Surat pribadi itu* ~ *keinginan Ménhan Weinberger untuk bertemu dengan Ménhankam Jusuf*. This personal letter contains Defense Secretary Weinberger's desire to meet with Minister of Defense and Security Jusuf.
 mengisi [and **ngisi** (*coq*) and **ngisiin** (*J coq*)] 1 to fill out/in. ~ *formulir* to fill out a form. ~ *Teka-Teki Silang* to do the crossword puzzle. 2 to fill (with). ~ *térmos ini dengan kopi* to fill this Thermos bottle with coffee. ~ *kembali* to replenish. 3 to stuff (with). ~ *amplop ini dengan uang* to stuff this envelope with money. 4 to fill up (the time), kill/pass (time). *untuk* ~ *waktu senggangnya* to pass his free time. ~ *kesibukan* to keep o.s. busy, fill up one's free time. 5 to charge (a battery). ~ *aki mobil ini* to charge the car battery. 6 to load (with), load (a gun). ~ *kapal itu dengan rotan* to load the ship with rattan. 7 to dub. ~ *suara film* to dub the soundtrack of a film. 8 to put (fuel into). ~ *bahan bakar* to fuel (an aircraft, etc.). 9 to fulfill, meet. ~ *adat* to fulfill one's *adat* obligations. 10 to pay for (shares).
 isi-mengisi to complement, be complementary (to e.o.). *Générasi muda dua tua saling* ~. The younger and older generations complement e.o.
 mengisikan [and **ngisiin** (*J coq*)] 1 to put (s.t. into a container). *Minyak itu diisikan ke dalam botol*. The oil was put into a bottle. 2 to fill, etc. for s.o. else.
 terisi 1 taken (of a seat); booked (of accommodations). *Réstoran itu sangat laris*. Hampir dua pertiga dari 160 *kursi* ~. The restaurant is very popular. Almost two-thirds of its 160 seats were taken. *Semua kamar hotél sudah* ~ *penuh*. All the hotel rooms were fully booked. 2 filled. ~ *dua pertiganya* two-thirds full.
 isian 1 s.t. to be filled out. *daftar/lembar/surat* ~ (blank) form, form to fill out. 2 filler (s.t. used to fill). 3 charge (of a weapon). ~ *kepala* warhead. ~ *kursi* load factor. ~ *peledak* detonating charge.
 pengisi filler. ~ *aki* battery charger. ~ *halaman* filler (in a newspaper). ~ *perut* s.t. to fill the stomach, nourishment. ~ *pojok* writer of humorous pieces in a newspaper. ~ *suara* dubber. ~ *tekan* supercharger. ~ *waktu* pastime, time killer.
 pengisian 1 filling out/in, loading, stuffing, feeding, feed. *tingkat* ~ load factor (of car). *pipa* ~ feed pipe. ~ *bahan bakar kapal* fueling a ship, bunkering. ~ *bahan bakar di udara* in-flight refueling. ~ *dana* replenishing funds. ~ *formulir* filling out a form. ~ *otomatis* autoloading. ~ *suara* dubbing (the soundtrack). ~ *tanah kosong dan jelék* landfill. 2 recharging (a battery), recharge. ~ *kembali* replenishment.
 perisian (*Mal*) software.

ISI II [Institut Seni Indonésia] Indonesian Institute of the Arts.

isim (*A*) 1 name; one of the names of God, e.g., *Yang Maha Esa*. 2 a written Arabic phrase used to ward off danger or illness; a Koranic verse or text used as a talisman. *gila* – religious frenzy.

isin (*Jv*) shy, ashamed, embarrassed. *Saya tidak* – *mundur*. I'm not ashamed to retreat.

isis (*Jv*) refreshing, cool, breezy.

isit (*J*) – *mulut* gums.

Iskandar (*A*) Alexander. – *zulkarnain* Alexander with two horns, i.e., Alexander the Great.

Iskandarmuda (*ob*) name of the Army division stationed in Aceh.

iskémik (*E*) ischemic. *penyakit jantung* – ischemic heart disease.

islah (*A*) 1 peaceful settlement of conflict. 2 efforts to improve and develop the community, nation, and people; reform.

Islam (*A*) Islam, Islamic, Muslim. *tatkala – masuk ke tanah Jawa* when Islam entered Java. *– agamaku, Ka'abah pilihanku* (the election slogan of the PPP) Islam is my religion, the *Ka'abah* my choice. *kelima rukun –* the five pillars of Islam. *masuk –* to become a Muslim. *orang –* a Muslim. *– abangan* person/people who is/are nominally Muslim but whose Islam is mixed with Javanese beliefs and customs; → ABANGAN I. *– baka* a) Muslim by descent. b) a Muslim who disobeys the religion. *– putihan* practicing Muslim; → SANTRI.
  mengislamkan 1 to convert to Islam, Islamize. *Gaddafi langsung ~ Libia ketika kedudukannya terancam.* Gaddafi immediately converted Libya into an Islamic state when his position was threatened. **2** to circumcise.
  keislaman 1 Islamic identity/feelings, Islamicity. **2** Islamic, concerning Islam. *bahasa ~* Islamic language.
  pengislaman converting to Islam, Islamization.
Islami (*A*) Islamic. *Cara-cara yang ditempuh Imran tidak –.* The methods used by Imran were not Islamic. *kelompok –* an Islamic group. *masyarakat yang –* an Islamic community. *suasana –* an Islamic atmosphere.
Islami(y)ah (*A*) Islamic.
Islamisasi (*E*) Islamization.
Islamisme (*D*) Islamism.
Islamistik (*E*) Islamistic.
islamolog (*D*) Islamologist.
islamologi (*D/E*) Islamology.
Islandia Iceland; → ÉSLANDIA.
ism → ISIM.
Ismail (*A*) (the biblical) Ishmael.
Ismailiah (*A*) Ismaili, a sect of Islam.
ismat (*A*) infallibility.
-isme (*E*) and **-isma** (*D*) -ism.
isnad (*A*) chain of authorities transmitting the words and deeds of the Prophet Muhammad.
Isnin → SENIN.
isobar (*D/E*) isobar.
isokromatik (*E*) isochromatic.
isolasi (*D*) **1** isolation. **2** (*elec*) insulation.
  mengisolasi(kan) 1 to isolate. **2** to insulate.
  terisolasi 1 isolated. *daérah-daérah yang dianggap ~* areas considered isolated. **2** insulated. **keterisolasian** isolation. *Jembatan gantung ini membuka ~ tiga désa itu.* This suspension bridge has broken the isolation of three villages.
  pengisolasian 1 isolation, isolating. **2** insulating.
isolasionisme (*D/E*) isolationism.
isolator (*D/E*) **1** isolator. **2** insulator.
isolemén (*D*) isolation. *terlepas dari –nya* freed from its isolation.
isolir (*D*) **mengisolir 1** to isolate. **2** to insulate (*elec*). **3** to cut off (outgoing telephone service for nonpayment).
  terisolir isolated. **keterisoliran** isolation.
  pengisoliran cutting off (telephone service for nonpayment).
isomér (*D/E*) isomer.
isomorf (*D*) isomorphous.
isomorfisme (*D/E*) isomorphism.
isopod (*D*) isopod.
isoprén (*E*) isoprene.
isotérm (*D/E*) isotherm.
isotop (*D/E*) isotope.
isqath al-hamil (*A*) induced abortion.
Isra (*A*) a journey; → ISRAK.
Israél Israel.
israf (*A*) waste; → PEMBOROSAN.
Israfil (*A*) Asrafel, the angel who announces the last day.
Israk (*A*) episode in which the Prophet Muhammad was brought to Al-Aqsa Mosque from Al-Haram Mosque during the night. *– Mikraj/Miraj* Muhammad's miraculous flight from Mecca to Jerusalem and His ascension to heaven.
istabrak (*A*) brocade; → ISTIBRAK.
istal (*D*) (horse) stable.
istana (*Skr*) palace. *– Bima Sakti* the name of President Soeharto's home on Jalan Batu Tulis, Bogor. *– Keprésidénan "Gedung Agung"* the presidential palace in Yogyakarta. *– Merdéka* the

"Freedom Palace," which looks south onto Jalan Merdeka Utara and Merdeka Square. *– Mersela* [Istana merdéka selatan] → ISTANA *Merdéka. – Negara* the "State Palace," which looks south onto Jalan Veteran.
  beristana 1 to reside in a palace. **2** to have/own a palace.
istanawan (*Skr neo*) palace inhabitant.
istanggi → SETANGGI.
isteri → ISTRI.
istiadat (*A*) custom. *adat –* customs and traditions.
  mengistiadatkan to make a custom of.
isti'arah (*A*) metaphor.
istibda (*A*) paternity.
istibdad (*A*) dictatorship.
  beristibdad dictatorial.
istibra (*A*) **1** woman's abstinence from sexual intercourse for three months after divorce or widowhood. **2** inquiry into the purity (of a widow or divorced woman before she can remarry).
istibrak (*A*) brocade.
istifham (*A*) inquiry, question.
istigasah (*A*) a prayer, usually asking God to ward off a disaster, etc., carried out in a large group.
istig(h)far (*A*) asking pardon. *membaca –* and
  beristighfar to pray for pardon, ask (God) for forgiveness.
istigho(t)sah (*A*) (*doa –*) communal prayer.
istihadah (*A*) menstruation; → HAID.
istihar → ISYTIHAR.
istihsan (*A*) disciplinary legal decision.
istijabat (*A*) answering a petition.
istikamah (*A*) rectitude, righteousness.
istikharah (*A*) *salat/shalat/sembahyang –* and
  beristikharah to pray for guidance.
istikhlaf (*A*) the appointment of a representative before the person concerned dies.
istikla (*A*) superiority complex.
istikomah → ISTIKAMAH.
istikra (*A*) investigation.
istikrar (*A*) ratification, confirmation.
istilad (*A*) claiming paternity.
istilah (*A*) (technical) term. *kata-kata –* terminology. *kamus –* terminological/technical dictionary. *Komisi –* Terminology Commission. *– penghalus/sopan* euphemism.
  mengistilahi to name/call s.t. by a term.
  mengistilahkan to give s.t. a term/name.
  pengistilahan coining terminology.
  peristilahan system of terminology.
istima (*A*) favorable judgment.
istimal (*A*) use.
  mengistimalkan to use, utilize.
istimbath (*A*) drawing a conclusion, deduction.
istiméwa (*Skr*) **1** special, particular, extraordinary. *Daérah – Acéh* [DIA and Dista] Aceh Special Province. *Daérah – Yogyakarta* [DIY] Yogyakarta Special Province. **2** (of dishes of food) containing more than the usual number or amount of ingredients. *nasi goréng –* special fried rice. **3** (*cla*) let alone, not to mention. *– lagi/pula* and even more (so), especially. *pandai menggésék biola – pula menyanyi* good at playing the violin and even more so at singing; (after a negative) even less (so), much less. *tidak tahu membaca – pula menulis* unable to read, much less to write.
  seistiméwa as special as.
  mengistiméwakan to make special/extraordinary, give s.t. special treatment. *diistiméwakan* (*leg*) preferred.
  teristiméwa 1 very special/extraordinary. **2** especially, in particular. *~ untuk hal ini* ad hoc.
  keistiméwaan specialty, particularity.
  pengistiméwaan making special, treating in a special way, favoring.
istimna (*A*) masturbation.
istinbath (*A*) deduction. *–ul ahkam* efforts to promulgate a law.
istinggar (*Port cla*) matchlock (of a gun).
istinja (*A*) cleansing the body with water after defecating, ablution prescribed by Muslim customs consisting of washing the anus after defecation.

beristinja to cleanse o.s. after defecating.

istiqa' and **istiqo** (A) asking for rain; → SEMBAHYANG *istiqa'*.

istiqlal (A) **1** liberty, freedom, independence. **2** name of the Mosque located at the northeast corner of Merdeka Square in Jakarta.

istirahat (A) **1** pause, break, recess, intermission, time out; to take a break/rest. **2** interval. **3** rest. *– minum kopi* coffee break; → RÉHAT *kopi. – panjang* vacation. *– sakit* sick leave. *– tahunan* annual leave.

beristirahat **1** to pause, take a break, have a rest. **2** to retire (from active service).

mengistirahatkan **1** to give s.o. a break/rest period. *~ badan* (euph) to lay s.o. to rest. *~ diri* to take a breather. **2** to postpone.

pengistirahatan **1** retiring. **2** giving s.o. a break/rest. *~ badan* laying s.o. to rest.

peristirahatan **1** vacation resort. **2** resting place. *menghantarkan ke ~nya yang terakhir* to bear s.o. to his final resting place. *balai ~* rest house. *daérah ~* rest area. *tempat ~* resting place.

istis(h)lah (A) the general good, the public interest.

istislam (A) acceptance of the Muslim faith.

istisna (A) **1** exception. **2** k.o. Islamic financing for commodity transactions.

mengistisnakan to treat as an exception.

istisqo → ISTIQA'.

istitaah (A) ability.

istito'ah (A) humiliation, insult, offense.

istiwa (A) parallel; → KHATULISTIWA.

istri (Skr) wife, spouse; cp BINI. *Présidén Soeharto dan – President* and Mrs. Soeharto. *– bungsu* → ISTRI *muda. – gelap* mistress. *– muda* younger wife (in a polygamous marriage), second wife; → TV II. *– paminggir* (Jv) concubine. *– piaraan* mistress, concubine. *– simpanan* kept woman, mistress. *– sulung/tua* first wife (in a polygamous marriage).

beristri **1** to be married (of a man). *~ dua* bigamy. *~ dua kali* to have been married twice (said of a man). **2** to get married, marry.

beristrikan to take s.o. as one's wife. *Sayang, Gunadi ~ orang lain, bukanlah Hartini.* Too bad Gunadi is married to s.o. else and not to Hartini.

memperistri to marry, take a wife.

memperistrikan **1** to marry (a son) off, find a wife for. **2** to let marry.

istri-istrian mistress.

peristrian *~ tunggal* monogamy.

istridraj (A) the ability of a sinner, with God's permission, to do s.t. extraordinary.

isu(e) → ISYU.

isut → INGSUT.

Iswahyudi name of the airbase in Madiun.

isya (A) evening. *sembahyang –* the evening prayer (at 8:00 p.m.). *waktu –* hour of the evening prayer.

isyarat (A) **1** sign, wink, nod, hint, gesture. **2** signal. *lampu –* (Mal) traffic light. *memberi –* to signal (by a sign, nod, gesture, wink, lifting the eyebrows, etc.). *~ panggilan* call sign.

mengisyaratkan to signal s.t. by nodding, etc., make a gesture of, nod to, beckon; to indicate. *Pusat Penelitian Kependudukan UGM ~ bahwa propinsi yang dinilai berhasil menekan angka kelahiran ...* UGM's Population Research Center indicated that the province considered the most successful in lowering the birth rate was ...

pengisyaratan signaling.

Isyhadu bianna Muslimin (A) (slogan used by Muslim groups during the 1977 general elections) Testify that we are Muslims.

isytihar (A) proclamation, declaration.

mengisytiharkan to proclaim, declare.

perisytiharan proclamation, declaration. *~ perang* declaration of war.

isytiraky (A) socialist.

isyu (E) **1** issue. **2** rumor.

mengisyukan **1** to make an issue of. **2** to spread rumors about.

it (in acronyms) → INSPÉKTORAT.

Itali(a) Italy.

italik (E) *huruf –* italics; → HURUF *miring*.

itam → HITAM.

ITB (init) [Institut Téknologi Bandung] Bandung Institute of Technology.

item → HITAM. ngitemin → MENGHITAMKAN.

iterasi (E) iteration.

itibar (A) **1** example, model. *menjadi –* to be(come) an example. **2** contemplation, consideration. **3** instructions, lesson, learning.

itidal (A) **1** equilibrium, symmetry, proper proportion. **2** standing upright (in praying).

itifak (A) concord, agreement (between persons, scholars, members of a body).

itik duck; → ALABIO, BÉBÉK. *bagai – pulang petang* very slow; to walk one after the other. *– berenang di laut* (or, *dalam air) mati kehausan* to suffer a lot of trouble even though one is in a good position (has a high salary/a rich spouse, etc.). *– bertali* frightening but arrogant. *seperti – (men)dengar guntur* to stare like a stuck pig; → *seperti* BÉBÉK *dengar geluduk. – tak sudu, ayam tak patuk* s.t. completely useless. *mengajar – berenang* to carry coals to Newcastle. *– air* cotton pygmy goose, *Nettapus coromandelianus*; a grebe, the masked finfoot. *– alis putih* garganey, *Anas querquedula. – ayam* poultry. *– Bali* Balinese duck. *– gunung* Pacific black duck, Australian grey duck, *Anas superciliosa. – Jawa* the Javanese duck, Indian Runner. *– kelabu* gray/Sunda teal, *Anas gibberifrons. – laut* mallard, *Anas boscas. – Manila/Menila* Mandarin duck; → ÉNTOG. *– Surati* Moscovy duck, *Anas moschata*.

itik-itikan toy duck.

itikad and **itikat** (A) **1** conviction. **2** faith. **3** determination, intent. **4** attitude. *memutuskan –* to have a firm intention (to). *salah –* to have the wrong intentions. *– untuk membina* intent to train. *– untuk menghukum* intent to punish. *– baik* good faith. *dengan – baik* in good faith. *ditandatangani oléh SK atas – baik dan inisiatifnya sendiri* signed by SK in good faith and on his own initiative. **beritikad baik** with good faith. *– buruk* bad faith. **beritikad buruk** in bad faith. *– jelék* ill-will.

beritikad **1** to be deeply convinced. **2** faithful. **3** to intend to. *~ baik* (to do s.t.) in good faith, mean well.

mengitikadkan **1** to convince. **2** to believe/have faith in.

itikaf (A) **1** praying in the mosque for some length of time. **2** (RC) religious retreat.

beritikaf to go on a retreat.

itil (J vulg) clitoris; → KELENTIT I.

itjén [Inspektorat jénderal] inspectorate general.

itlak (A) acceptance (of a theory as true without personal investigation).

mengitlakkan to generalize.

itrah (A) descent.

ittifak → ITIFAK.

ittihad (A) concord, union. *-ul Muballighin* Association of Muslim Preachers.

itu **1** that, those, that one (the one whose name I can't think of right now). **2** the. *sebab –* because of that, therefore. *sesudah/setelah – after that. untuk –* for that reason/purpose. **3** there. *– dia* a) that's it/right, exactly, precisely. b) there he/she/it is. *– juga* the same, the very. *pada hari – juga* on the same/very day. *– saja* that's all. *tidak – saja* not only that, that's not all there is to it. *-lah* a) what did I tell you! b) that's the way it is! *-lah dia!* It's your own fault. *-lah adanya!* That's it! *-pun* → ITUPUN.

itunya (euph) genitals; → ANO(NYA) 2.

itu-itu (juga) and *– ke – (juga)* (always) the same (thing/person, etc.). *yang melakukan démonstrasi orangnya ~ juga* the demonstrators were always the same people. *Orangnya ~ ke itu juga yang muncul.* The same person always shows up. *Bukan soal bosan, tapi kenapa harus punya pacar ~ juga?* It isn't a question of boredom, but why should one keep the same boyfriend? *~ saja* the same one(s) all the time.

itung → HITUNG. ngitungin → MENGHITUNGKAN.

itupun **1** that is to say. **2** with the understanding that, on condition that. *– kalau tuan suka* on condition that you like it. **3** nevertheless, in spite of that. *– tak mau datang juga* in spite of that, he didn't want to come anyway.

IUD [intrauterine device] IUD.

meng-IUD-kan to provide (people in an area) with IUDs.

iudisasi the introduction of IUDs (as part of family planning).

iur (*A?*) **beriur** to make a contribution, contribute.

iuran 1 subscription. **2** contribution. **3** collection. **4** premium (to pay for insurance, etc.). **5** dues, fee. ~ *keanggotaan* membership fee. ~ *pénsiun* contributions to a pension fund. **beriuran** to make a contribution.

iwad (*A*) compensation, indemnification.

iwel-iwel (*J/Jv*) k.o. snack made from sticky rice.

iwi (*Jv*) **ngiwi-iwi** to make faces, grimace. *Meréka berani ~, wah itu kan sudah menyinggung martabat kami.* They had the nerve to make faces at us; that alone hurt our prestige, didn't it?

iya → IA II. ~ *nggak* yes or no.

  mengiyakan to approve, agree to s.t., accept (an offer).

  pengiya yes man.

  pengiyaan approval.

iyal (*A*) dependents.

iyang deity; → YANG I.

iyuran → IURAN.

izat → IZZAH.

izhar (*A*) clearness, presentation.

izin (*A*) **1** permit, license. **2** franchise; → WARALABA. *surat* – license (allowing one to practice a profession). **3** allowance, permission, consent. – *bekerja* work permit. – *bertempat tinggal* residence permit. – *bertolak ganda* multiple exit permit. – *ékspor* export license. – *kekaryaan penata minuman* bartender's license. – *keluar* a) exit permit. b) clearance outward (paying duties on ship and goods on departure). – *kerja* work permit. – *jalan* pass, permit. – *layak huni* occupancy permit. – *masuk* a) entry permit. b) clearance inward (through customs). – *masuk kembali* re-entry permit. – *mendirikan bangunan* [IMB] building permit. – *menetap* permit to stay, residence permit. – *pemasangan* building permit. – *penempatan* occupancy permit. – *perjalanan ke luar negeri berulang kali* multiple-exit permit. – *prakték* professional license. – *tentara* military clearance. – *terbit* publication license. – *tinggal* residence permit. – *tinggalnya sudah habis* his residence permit has expired. – *usaha* business license. – *usaha tetap* permanent business license. – *usaha yang terbatas* restricted business license.

seizin *dengan* ~ with the permission of.

berizin licensed, authorized. *Dari puluhan panti pijat di Yogyakarta, hanya dua yang ~.* Of the dozens of massage parlors in Yogyakarta, only two are licensed. *tidak* ~ unauthorized.

mengizinkan and **memperizinkan** [and **ngizinin** (*J coq*)] to allow, permit. *(kalau) cuaca* ~ weather permitting. ~ *keluar* to clear outward (through customs). ~ *masuk* to clear inward (through customs).

keizinan permit, license, franchise.

pengizinan permitting, licensing.

perizinan 1 permission. ~ *berangkat ke luarnegeri* exit permit. **2** licensing, permits.

Izraél and **Izrail** (*A*) the angel of death.

izzah and **izzat** (*A*) honor, distinction.

'izzul Islam wal Muslimin (*A*) the victory of Islam and of Muslims.

J

j and J /jé/ the 10th letter of the Latin alphabet used for writing Indonesian.

ja I → SAJA.

ja II (in acronyms) → JAKARTA, JASA, JAWA I.

jaalah (A) pay.

jaat (S) /ja'at/ a climbing plant with light-blue fruit, winged/Goa/Manila bean, *Psophocarpus tetragonolobus*; → KECIPIR.

jab I (E) /jép/ jab (in boxing).

jab II (in acronyms) → JABATAN.

jaba (Bal) → SUDRA.

jabah → JUBAH.

jabal I (A) mountain. – (al-) Tarik Tarik's Mountain, i.e., Gibraltar.
menjabal to loom large (as a mountain).

jabal II (J) **menjabal** [and **njabal** (coq)] to rob, seize by force.
terjabal [and **kejabal** (coq)] seized, robbed, stolen.
jabalan gang of thieves.
jabal-jabalan gang of thieves.
penjabalan 1 robbery, stealing. 2 seizing by force.

jaban (J) **be(r)jaban** to fight.
menjabankan [and **njabanin** (J)] to fight with s.o.

jabang I – *bayi* a) (J) placenta. b) (Jv) newborn baby. c) exclamation uttered before killing a snake/insect, etc. to prevent one's unborn baby from being marked by the ugly sight. d) exclamation of astonishment, wonder, surprise. *Mémangnya asrama kami tempat gadis-gadis yang bisa diajak begituan? Huh ... Amit-amit – bayi!* Is our dormitory really a place of girls who you can ask to sleep with you? Huh... God forbid, how is that possible!

jabang II (M) → CAMBANG.

jabang III (M) forked piece of wood for supporting a cannon.
menjabang to support (a weapon).

jabar I (A) **menjabarkan** 1 (math) to reduce/simplify (a fraction to its lowest terms). 2 to simplify. 3 to analyze, formulate, explain (in detail), spell out, describe. 4 to announce, make known to the public. 5 to convert (currency, etc.). ~ *pecahan* to convert a fraction.
terjabarkan can be analyzed/explained in detail. *gejala tak* ~ unexplainable symptoms.
jabaran description, analysis in detail, detailed explanation, spelling out. ~ *tugas* job description.
penjabar s.o. or s.t. that explains.
penjabaran 1 analysis, spelling out in detail, formulation, formulating, explanation, description. *Rapuhnya struktur industri nasional disebabkan oléh rendahnya kemampuan* ~ *kemauan politik Pemerintah oléh kalangan perbankan.* The fragility of national industrial structure is due to the low level of explanatory ability of the political will of the government by banking circles. ~ *pos aktiva* (fin) postings to assets. 2 translation (of a plan into reality). 3 reduction, simplification, curtailment, conversion; → ALJABAR.

jabar II (A) omnipotent, almighty (God). *Khalik al–* Almighty Creator. *Malik al–* Almighty King, God.

Jabar III (A) Orion (constellation).

Jabar IV [Jawa Barat] West Java.

jabariah (A) 1 fatalism. 2 static.

jabarut (A) (realm of) power.

jabat – *erat dari* (at close of letter) greetings from. – *sementara* temporary placement in a post. *menjabat-sementarakan* to place s.o. in a temporary post. – *tangan* handshake.
sejabat of the same office/department/service. *kawan/teman* ~ colleague.
berjabat 1 ~ *tangan* to shake hands. 2 to change (in)to. *siang* ~ *malam* day changes to night.
berjabat(an) ~ *tangan/salam* to shake hands.
menjabat 1 to hold, grasp. *Ia* ~ *tangan Perdana Menteri dengan*

erat-erat. He clasped the Prime Minister's hand firmly. 2 to serve/function as, hold the office of. *Dia sekarang* ~ *pembantu menteri luar negeri urusan Asia Timur dan Pasifik.* He currently serves as assistant secretary of state for East Asia and Pacific affairs. ~ *jadi/sebagai* to act as, perform the duties of.
menjabati 1 (pl obj) to shake people's hands. 2 to occupy (a position).
menjabatkan to extend (the hand in a handshake).

jabatan 1 office, function, profession, occupation, job, position, post, title. *karena* ~ ex officio, by virtue of one's office. *pada waktu menerima ~nya* upon his taking office, on taking up his duties. ~ *dan kepangkatan* (mil) position and rank. ~ *fungsional* an unofficial position within an organization. ~ *guru besar* professorship. ~ *keprésidénan* the presidency. ~ *ketua* chairmanship. ~ *kunci* key position. ~ *lain yang tidak mungkin dirangkap* incompatibilities, i.e., positions that cannot be held at one time by the same person. ~ *rangkap* dual position. ~ *penting* key position. ~ *sampingan* secondary office. ~ *struktural* an official position within an organization. ~ *utama* main position. 2 shake (of the hand). 3 (Mal) government department. ~ *Negara* State Department. **sejabatan** working in the same office. **berjabatan** to hold office.

pejabat 1 officer, official. ~ *hubungan masyarakat* public relations officer. ~ *kantor lélang* auctioneer. ~ *negara* state official: includes: (a) the President and Vice-President, (b) Members of the People's Consultative Council [MPR] and Members of Parliament [DPR], (c) Members of the Fiscal Control Board [BPK], (d) the Chairman, Deputy Chairman, and Judges of the Supreme Court, (e) Members of the Supreme Advisory Council [DPA], (f) Ministers, (g) Chiefs of Mission abroad with the status of Ambassador Extraordinary and Plenipotentiary, (h) Governors/Heads of Territory, (i) Regents/Heads of Region, Mayors/Heads of Municipality, (j) Other officials set out in detail in a legislative regulation. ~ *pembuat akte tanah* [PPAT] official empowered to draw up land deeds. ~ *pendaratan* disembarkment officer. ~ *penghubung* liaison officer. ~ *penilai* official with the right to evaluate subordinates. ~ *penting* key official, dignitary. ~ *pérs* press officer. ~ *sementara* a) caretaker, s.o. in a temporary position. b) provisional official. *mempejabat-sementarakan* to make s.o. a caretaker. ~ *teras* key official. ~ *tinggi* high-ranking official. ~ *umum* public official. ~ *yang berwenang* official in charge. 2 employee. 3 acting. ~ *Présidén* Acting President.
pejabatan 1 caretakership. 2 acting.
penjabat 1 officeholder. 2 acting. ~ *kepala désa* acting village head.
penjabatan service, discharge of one's duties.

jabbar → JABAR II.

Jabekta [Jakarta, Bekasi, Tangerang] Jakarta, Bekasi and Tangerang.

jabel → JABAL II.

jabir berjabir(-jabir) (of clothes) to be baggy, hang loosely, too long and big (of clothes).

jablés (onom) knocking, rapping sound.
menjabléskan to knock/rap against.

Jabon I [Jawa Ambon] *berdarah –* of mixed Javanese and Ambonese blood.

jabon II (Jv) k.o. tree, kadamba tree, *Anthocephalus spp.*

Jabotabék [Jakarta, Bogor, Tangerang, Bekasi]. *Pengembangan Perkotaan –. Jabotabék* Urban Development.
se-Jabotabék all-Jabotabek.

Jabrail → JIBRAIL.

jabrik (S) shaggy, hairy.

Jabril → JIBRAIL.

jabu (Bat) house. – *adat* traditional house. – *talak* open house.

jabung I (Jv) k.o. glue (resin-based, esp for gluing kris blades).

jabung II (Jv) k.o. plant, flax-leaved fleabane, *Erigeron linifolius*.

jabur I → ZABUR.

jabur II jaburan (*Jv*) snacks, cookies (presented at various get-togethers, particularly at recitation evenings during the Fasting month).

jabur-jaburan (*J*) **1** leftovers, scraps (of food). **2** unimportant people, the masses.

jada → JUADAH.

jadah I (*Pers*) **1** *anak* – illegitimate child, bastard (also used as a term of abuse); → HARAMJADAH. **2** (*bio*) sport.

menjadahkan ~ *anak* to father an illegitimate child.

jadah II (*Jv*) k.o. glutinous rice cake.

jadam I a black, bitter laxative made from aloeswood.

jadam II a silverware with a blue-black filling in low relief, polished to an even surface to reveal a pattern of silver veins; the Buddhist lotus being the commonest motif on waist-buckles and small caskets.

jadam III (*A*) castrated.

Jadayat (*A*?) Capricorn; tropic of Capricorn.

Jadél [Jawa Déli] Javanese who were taken by the Dutch to Deli (Northern Sumatra, near Medan) between 1926 and 1928 as contract laborers on plantations and their descendants.

jadi I 1 thus, therefore, so, consequently, as a result, accordingly. *Saya sudah bukan ketua lagi, – jangan tanyakan saya.* I'm not chairman any more, so don't ask me. **2** to manage/get to, (emphatic) did (do s.t.); (with a negative) (not) to manage/get to, (didn't) happen, (didn't) work out. *Kami tidak – pergi ke Puncak.* We didn't get to go to Puncak. *Pertunjukan semalam tidak – karena hujan.* Last night's performance was canceled due to the rain. *Kami – pergi ke pésta itu.* We did go to the party. *Saya tidak – ke pésta.* I didn't make it to the party. **3** done, ready, successfully completed, turned/worked out. *boléh –* probably, probable. *tidak bisa –* impossible. *tidak – masalah/soal* no problem. *Potrétnya – tidak?* Did the picture turn out well? *Cacar saya tidak –.* My vaccination didn't take. *seékor burung yang sudah –* a bird that has been trained (to talk/sing, etc.). **4** will do, is all right, is OK. *Pénsil pun –.* A pencil will also do. *Kerja apa pun –.* Any k.o. job will do. *ke mana saja pun –* no matter where to. *... –, tidak pun –* (if you ...) it's OK, (if you) don't (do it) it's also OK *sedikit –, banyak apatah lagi* a little bit is welcome, but a lot is of course better. *tidak – apa* it doesn't matter. **5** it's all right, OK! *Sepuluh ribu rupiah – (lah)!* You can have it for ten thousand rupiahs. *bagaimana pun –(lah)* whatever it is is OK. **6** to come into being, be born. *ketika saya –* when I was born. *hari – a)* birthday. *b)* Christmas. **7** finished, ready-made. *pakaian –* ready-made wear. *barang-barang –* finished products. **8** (appointed) as, in(to), so as to become, into. *dipilih – présidén* to be elected president. *dibagai – dua* to be divided into two parts. *dibuat/ditumbuk – obat* to be made/pounded into a medicine. *– tidak -(nya)* whether it happens or not, in any case. **9** to be, become, come to. *– orang* to grow up to be somebody. *tidak – soal* no problem! *Saya – percaya bahwa saya salah.* I've come to believe that I was wrong. *– alas cakap* gift given to s.o. who has performed a service or done a favor. *– penghubung* s.o. who can always be depended on to help.

jadinya result, consequence, the way s.t. works out. *Begitulah ~ kalau tidak menurut nasihat orangtua.* Yes, that's about what happens if you don't follow the advice of your parents. *Apa ~ kalau meréka tidak kerja lagi?* What's going to happen if they're out of work? **sejadinya** however it turns out, whatever happens.

sejadi-jadi(nya) as hard as possible, with all one's strength, at the top of one's lungs. *bekerja ~* to work as hard as possible. *berteriak ~* to shout at the top of one's lungs. *Ia dipukuli ~.* He was beaten up mercilessly. *Ia menangis ~.* She wept with all her strength.

berjadi-jadi (*M*) → MENJADI-JADI.

menjadi 1 to become, turn, get. *Dia ~ marah.* She became angry. *kalau saya ~ saudara* if I were you. **2** to be, play the part of. **3** (after change-of-state verbs) in(to) (or no translation). *dipilih ~ présidén* elected president. *berubah ~* to turn into. *terbagi ~ dua* to be divided into. **4** to come off, succeed, go through. **5** to come to, reach the point of. *Saya ~ percaya bahwa saya salah.* I've come to believe that I was wrong. *~ air* disappeared,

turned into nothing. *~ bahan pembicaraan* to be the talk of the town. *~ begini* to work out this way. *~ berkeping-keping* (broke) into pieces. *~ hakim sendiri* to take the law into one's own hands. *~ mandi* s.t. ordinary, not unusual. *~ pikiran* became a problem to solve. *tidak ~ soal* it isn't important, it doesn't matter. *~ tahu* to find out, come to know.

menjadi-jadi to increase, lengthen, extend, grow, get worse, worsen, go from bad to worse. *Karena kehujanan demamnya ~.* Because he got caught in the rain his fever got worse.

menjadikan [and **njadiin/ngejadiin** (*J coq*)] **1** to make, use as, make s.t. (into). *Kasus itu dapat dijadikan sebab untuk menolak permintaannya.* That case could be made the reason to turn down his request. *Meréka dijadikan alat.* They were used as a tool. **2** to cause, bring about, let. *Kemarau panjang telah ~ kawasan itu kering kerontang.* The long dry season has caused the region to become bone-dry. **3** to create. *Tuhan yang ~ langit dan bumi* God who created heaven and earth. **4** to form, constitute. *Dua hal itulah yang ~ faktor penting.* Those two matters constituted a significant factor. **5** to appoint, choose, pick. *Ia akan dijadikan kadés.* He'll be appointed village head. **6** to hold (an event), execute (a contract). *Pernikahan itu hendak dijadikan sekarang juga.* They want the wedding to be held right now.

menjadi-jadikan to increase s.t., make s.t. greater, make s.t. worse, worsen.

terjadi 1 to happen, occur, take place, come about. *Kemalangan itu ~ dekat kantor pos.* The calamity occurred near the post office. *jangan sampai ~* in order to prevent. *kalau ~* in case of. *akan ~* imminent, impending. **2** to consist (of), be made up (of). *Panitia itu ~ dari tujuh wakil pengusaha.* The committee consisted of seven business representatives. **3** (over and) done (with), finished.

jadian 1 a human being who can turn him/herself into an animal. *harimau/macan ~* a human being in the shape of a tiger, were-tiger. *ilmu ~* the science (*mantra*, etc.) of transforming a human being into an animal. **2** s.t. artificial, invented, made-up. *bunga ~* artificial flowers. **3** (*gram*) derived. **4** (*BG*) to go steady (with a boyfriend or girlfriend).

jadi-jadian 1 a supernatural and invisible animal. **2** imitation.

kejadian 1 origin, creation. *hari ~* Christmas. *kitab ~* the Book of Genesis. **2** event, incident, happening, circumstances, situation. *Dia menjadi gila setelah ~ itu.* He went crazy after that event. *~ tidak terduga* unforeseen circumstances. *Masalah korupsi adalah satu ~ biasa di mana-mana di dunia.* Corruption is something that occurs all over the world. *~ alam* natural phenomenon. *~ yang tak terduga* unforeseen circumstances. **3** it takes place/occurs. *Sesudah tawar-menawar ~ juga akhirnya.* After bargaining it finally happened. **4** realization, formation. *masa kelahiran atau masa ~* the period of birth or of formation. **5** party, get-together.

pe(n)jadi (*ob*) maker, manufacturer, developer, doer.

penjadian 1 outbreak. *~ penyakit* outbreak of a disease. **2** creation, formation.

Jadi II (*A*) *bintang –* Capricorn; → JADAYAT. *garis balik –* tropic of Capricorn.

jadual (*A*) → JADWAL.

jaduk (*Jv*) **1** fighter, brawler. **2** invulnerable.

jadup [jatah hidup] basic needs allotment.

jadwal (*A*) **1** list, column, catalog. *Inilah – buku-buku yang dikeluarkan oléh penerbit itu.* This is the catalog of books published by that publisher. **2** schedule, (time)table. *– acara* program schedule. *– imsakiah* table showing when fasting starts during Ramadan. *– kegiatan* calendar of events. *– keréta api* railroad timetable. *– logaritma* logarithmic table. *– pelajaran* class schedule. *– penerbangan* flight schedule. *– perjalanan* itinerary. *– selang-seling* flextime. *– waktu* timetable.

berjadwal to be scheduled. *penerbangan ~* scheduled flight(s).

menjadwal to schedule.

menjadwalkan to schedule, make a timetable for. *~ kembali* to reschedule.

terjadwal scheduled.

penjadwal scheduler.

penjadwalan scheduling. *~ kembali* rescheduling.

jaé → JAHÉ.

jaga (*Skr*) **1** awake; to wake up, be awake. *– atau tidurkah orang itu?* Is that person awake or asleep? *– dari(pada) tidur* to wake up. **2** to watch, take care of, guard. *Pak – monitor*, housefather (i.e., a man responsible for a group of young people. *–lah barang itu baik-baik supaya tidak hilang.* Take good care of these goods so that they don't disappear. *– malam* a) to be on night guard. b) night watchman. *rumah –* guardhouse, sentry post. *tukang –* watchman, keeper. **3** take care! be careful! watch it! look out! keep ...! *–lah kebersihan* don't litter. **4** watch, guard duty (on board ship, etc). *Ali kebetulan sedang mengisi giliran –nya.* By chance, it was Ali's watch. **5** on duty/call. *dokter –* doctor on call. *– anak* baby-sitter. *– gawang* gatekeeper.

jaga-jaga *uang ~* (*ob*) reserve (funds). *~ bila* just in case.

berjaga 1 to stay awake/up (for some purpose). *~ hingga pagi* to stay awake till morning. *~ menunggu* to wait up for. **2** vigilant; to keep watch, be on guard. *Polisi sedang ~ di daérah rawan itu.* The police are on guard in that problem area. **3** to be ready, prepared. **4** to be on duty. *Siapa yang ~?* Who's on duty? **5** to be in charge.

berjaga-jaga 1 to stay awake/up all night long. **2** to get ready, prepare. *Ujian sudah dekat; baik kamu ~.* Exams are approaching; better get ready. **3** to be on standby, on alert, on one's guard, cautious. *sebagai tindakan ~* just in case.

menjaga 1 to watch over, keep an eye on, look after, guard. *Ia dijaga keras.* They keep close watch over him. **2** to take care of, pay attention to, be careful with, be responsible for, look out for, keep, maintain, preserve, protect. *Jagalah keséhatanmu.* Take care of your health. *Kita sekalian wajib ~ keselamatan dan keamanan negara kita.* We all must be responsible for the welfare and security of our country. **3** to prevent, preclude, guard against. *Tugas meréka ialah ~ bahaya api.* Their duty is to prevent the danger of fire. *~ agar/supaya* to make sure that, ensure that, keep. *~ agar kota ini bersih* to keep the town clean. *~ sungguh-sungguh supaya pengeluaran tidak melebihi pemasukan uang* to make sure that receipts do not exceed expenditures. *~ diri* to take good care of o.s., be careful. *~ hati orang* to consider s.o.'s feelings. *~ jangan sampai* to be careful not to, prevent. *~ kesopanan diri* to watch one's step. *~ ketertiban* to maintain order. *~ langkah* to watch one's step. *~ mata* to watch where one is looking. *~ mulut* to watch one's words. *~ nama baik* to maintain one's reputation. *~ perasaan orang* to consider s.o.'s feelings. *~ perkataan* to watch one's words. *~ sikapnya* to watch one's step. *~ telinga* to pay attention to what one is listening to. *~ tepi kain orang* to pay greater attention to other people's affairs than to one's own.

menjagai [and **njagain/ngejagain** (*J coq*)] to watch over/out for. *Kita tidak dapat ~ harta kita selama 24 jam penuh.* We can't watch over our property 24 hours a day.

menjagakan 1 to wake up (from sleep), awaken, rouse from sleep. *Baru pukul empat pagi sudah dijagakan.* It's just four o'clock in the morning and I'm already awake. **2** to guard/watch s.t. for s.o. else.

terjaga 1 wakened up (from sleep). *Is yang baru ~ dari tidur kagét setengah mati.* Is, who was just awakened, was frightened half to death. **2** guarded, protected, controlled. *tidak ~* out of control. **3** taken care of, well maintained. **4** protected, shadowed.

jagaan 1 protection, guard, care, surveillance. **2** s.t. or s.o. that is guarded. **kejaga-jagaan** sleepless, awake.

penjaga 1 sentry, watchman, caretaker, guard, attendant, -man. **2** s.o. who is always careful/watchful/alert. **3** ghost which haunts a house, tree, etc.. *~ anak* baby-sitter. *~ dada* (in sports) chest protector. *~ garis* (in badminton/soccer) linesman. *~ gawang* goalie, goalkeeper. *~ gerbang* gatekeeper. *~ istana* palace guard. *~ kamar* room attendant. *~ lift* elevator operator. *~ lokét* window clerk. *~ Marine* Marine Guard (in U.S. Embassies). *~ palang pintu kereta api* railroad crossing guard. *~ pantai* coast guard. *~ (parkir) mobil* parking lot attendant. *~ pintu* doorman. *~ pompa bénsin* gas station attendant. *~ ruangan* (in the Navy) quarters orderly. *~ signal* signal man. *~ stand* stand attendant (at a fair, etc.). *~ télepon* telephone operator. *~ udara* spotter (on the watch for enemy planes). **berpenjaga** to have a ghost, be haunted.

penjagaan 1 watching, guarding, security, control. *~ gerbang* gatekeeping (in communications science). *~ mutu* quality control. **2** guard post (for gatekeeper at railway crossing), station. **3** surveillance. **4** custody.

perjagaan l guarding, keeping, care, protection, defense, supervision.

jagabaya (*Jv*) village police.

jagabéla (*ob*) palace guard.

jagad → JAGAT.
   sejagad global. **kesejagadan** globalization.
   jagadan global.

jagadraya → JAGAT *raya*.

jagal I 1 retail dealer. **2** merchandise, commodities; retail trade. **3** middleman. *– keras* selling non-spoilable items. *– masak* selling food and drink. *– muda* selling spoilable items.
   berjagal to be a retail dealer, run a small shop. *~ peraih* to be a wholesaler.
   jagalan merchandise, commodities.

jagal II (*Jv*) butcher, slaughterer.
   menjagal 1 to be a butcher. **2** to butcher, slaughter.
   pejagalan abattoir, slaughter house.
   penjagalan 1 slaughtering, butchering, massacre. **2** abattoir, slaughter house. **3** murder, slaughter.

jagang I (*Jv*) support, stand, supporting pole, prop. *– sepéda* bicycle stand.
   berjagang supported, propped up.
   menjagangkan to support, prop up.

jagang II (*Jv*) ditch, moat.

jagapati bodyguard for VIP.

jagaraga bodyguard.

jagat (*Skr*) **1** world, earth. **2** universe, -cosm. *– besar* macrocosm. *– buana* the universe, cosmos. *– kecil* microcosm. *– rat/raya/semesta* the whole world, universe, cosmos.
   sejagat worldwide, global, universal. *masalah ~* global issues.

jagatraya (*Skr*) cosmos, universe.

jagawana (*Skr neo*) forest ranger, forester.

jago (*Jv*) **1** cock, rooster. *adu –* cock fight. **2** candidate (in elections), contestant. **3** champion, s.o. who fights for a cause or on behalf of others. **4** fighter, brawler, thug. **5** leader, prominent person. **6** gamecock. **7** s.o. who loves to, person addicted to. **8** s.o. who is very good at, an expert in ... *– balap sepéda* champion bicyclist. *– berenang* swimming champion. *–.– Betawi* Jakartan folk-heroes, such as, Si Pitung, Si Djampang, Si Sabeni, and others. *– bola* soccer player. *– cinta* a Don Juan. *– débat* champion debater. *– gelut* a) fighter, brawler. b) wrestler. *– gulat* wrestler. *– jotos* boxer. *– kandang* s.o. who is successful on home ground but not elsewhere. *– kapuk* has-been, s.o. who was a champion. *si – kawin* s.o. who marries many times. *– kepruk* a) strong-arm man. b) wrestler. *– kepuk* soccer player. *– kertas* paper tiger. *– luruk* a) cockcrow. b) the crack of dawn. *– makan* person who loves to eat, glutton. *(si) – mérah* fire (personified). *– nonton* inveterate moviegoer. *– politik* political contestant. *– renang* swimming champ. *– témbak* marksman. *– tinju* boxer. *– tua* grand old man (of a political party, etc.).
   sejago as expert as.
   ngejago (*coq*) cocky.

menjagoi [and **njagoin/ngejagoin** (*J coq*)] **1** to be champion of, dominate. *Pendékar itu ~ dunia persilatan.* That fighter was champion of the *silat* world. **2** to take the lead in (a match). **3** to champion, support (a candidate), back, root for.

menjagokan 1 to nominate s.o., put s.o. up; to promote, advance; to make s.o. one's favorite. *Siapa kiranya yang kita jagokan untuk ketua dan wakil ketua?* Who should we nominate for chairman and vice chairman? **2** to sponsor, back, champion.

jagoan 1 rowdy person, brawler. **2** leader, favorite; champion. **3** gamecock. *~ cabut nyawa/nyowo* (*Jv*) professional killer.
   jago-jagoan reckless, act like a champion when one really isn't.
   kejagoan 1 leadership. **2** championship. **3** supremacy, prowess.
   penjagoan brawl, fight.

jagong I (*Jv*) (in Solo) **1** to take part in voluntary, collective work. **2** to take the night watch.

jagong II (*Jv*) to attend a wedding ceremony. *Pagi itu ia bersama* *istrinya merencanakan – ke rumah Wantini.* That morning he and his wife planned to attend a wedding at Wantini's house.

jagong III (*Jv*) – *bayi* to baby-sit.

Jagorawi [Jakarta, Bogor, Ciawi] **1** the megalopolis of these towns in West Java. **2** the toll road connecting these cities. **3** (*joc*) (in the political opinion of the man in the street) [Jawa bégo raja Betawi] a stupid Javanese is king of Jakarta.

jagrak (*Jv*) easel.

jagung I corn, maize, *Zea mays. setahun/seumur* – about 100 days, three months; brief (referring to the Japanese occupation of Indonesia). *Umurnya setahun* –. He's still young and inexperienced. *belum seumur* – not long ago, recently. *(seperti) pipit menelan* – experiencing trouble due to wishing to imitate prominent persons. *habis air habislah kayu, – tua tak hendak masak* an unsuccessful job which only loses money or is exhausting. *– bakar* roast(ed) corn. *– beledug* popcorn. *– bosé* crushed corn, eaten with coconut cream or milk. *– b(e)rondong* popcorn. *– cantél* k.o. sorghum, *Sorghum vulgare. – gigi kuda* dent. *– kecil* dwarf ears. *– keprék* k.o. cornflakes. *– ledak* popcorn. *– meletus* popcorn. *– muda* dwarf ears. *– mutiara* flint. *– pipilan* husked corn with kernels stripped off. *– putri* baby corn. *– rebus* corn on the cob. *– roté* (*NTT*) k.o. sorghum, *Sorghum vulgare. – semi* baby corn. *– titik* a dish made from ground corn. *– tuak* roughly pounded corn used as food after boiling. *– tumbuk* roughly ground corn.

berjagung-jagung to keep living on corn. *baik ~, sementara padi belum masak* half a loaf is better than none.

menjagung to sprout, begin to come out (of breasts, rash, rice-grains, teeth).

jagungan corn field.

Jagung II [Jaksa agung] attorney general.

jagur 1 robust, sturdy, big for one's age, oversized (of person). **2** (*Jv*) fist. *ki/si* – or **penjagur** "The clenched Fist," the name of the sacred "male" cannon once located at Kota Inten, now Sunda Kelapa, Jakarta, a place of pilgrimage for sterile women. The cannon's breech lock has the shape of a clenched fist with the thumb placed between the index and middle finger (symbol of the male sexual organ).

jah (*Pers*) splendor, glory, grandeur, magnificence.

jaha Siamese senna, *Cassia siamea, Terminalia balerica. – keling* k.o. medicinal tree, myrobalan, *Terminalia chebula.*

jahad (*A*) apostasy.

jahan I giant marine catfish, *Arius thalassinus.*

jahan II → JOHAN.

jahanam (*A*) **1** hell. **2** damned, damn, infernal. *anak* – damn kid. **3** damn it! **4** rascal, villain, scoundrel.

menjahanami and **menjahanamkan 1** to curse, swear at, damn. **2** to bring ruin down upon, destroy.

jahang 1 dark red, crimson. **2** coarse language.

jahar (*A*) loud; aloud; *opp* ZIKIR. *ratib* – chant in praise of God; → RATIB.

jaharu (*Hind*) rascal, rogue; bad person.

jahat bad, evil, wicked, criminal, malevolent, malicious, sinful. *angin* – a bad wind. *binatang* – a harmful animal. *orang* – a person of bad character. *perempuan* – a loose woman, prostitute. *si* – *Empat* the Gang of Four. *– hati* ill-natured, malicious.

sejahat as bad as.

sejahat-jahat however bad, no matter how bad. *~ harimau tidak akan sanggup memakan anaknya sendiri.* However bad a tiger is he will not eat his own pups.

berjahat 1 to commit a crime, do s.t. wicked; to sin, seduce (a woman). **2** to gossip, say bad things about people.

menjahati 1 to do evil to s.o., wrong. *~ orang yang tidak bersalah* to wrong an innocent person. **2** to tease, say bad things about.

menjahatkan 1 to cause to become bad. **2** to slander, defame, incriminate, give s.o. a bad name. **3** to think badly of s.o.

terjahat the worst.

kejahatan 1 crime, felony; *cp* PELANGGARAN. *angka ~* crime rate. *rasa takut atas ~* fear of crime. *~ anak-anak* juvenile delinquency. *~ berdasi/berkerah putih* white-collar crime. *~ berkomputer* computer crime. *~ biasa* ordinary crime. *~ dalam dinas* malfeasance in office. *~ dengan kekerasan* [jantanras] violent

crime. *~ jabatan* abuse of office. *~ jalanan* street crime. *~ kalangan atas* upper-class crime. *~ kecil* petty crime. *~ kerah putih* white-collar crime. *~ kesusilaan* moral offense. *~ konvénsional* conventional crime. *~ korporasi* corporate crime. *~ moril* moral turpitude. *~ narkotika* narcotics crime. *~ nonkonvénsional* unconventional crime. *~ penipuan* fraud. *~ perang* war crime. *~ perbankan* banking crime. *~ perkotaan* urban crime. *~ pérs* printing-press offense. *~ tanpa korban fisik* victimless crime. *~ terhadap kesusilaan* crime against decency. *~ terhadap nyawa* a crime against s.o.'s life, homicide. *~ terorganisasi(kan)* organized crime. *~ yang bisa dihukum* punishable crime. *~ yang dilakukan di kalangan orang kantoran* white-collar crime. *~ yang sangat keji* heinous crime. *~ warungan* street crime. **2** evil, wickedness, badness, sin. *~ fitnah* defamation, slander.

penjahat criminal, malefactor, felon. *~ kambuhan* recidivist, habitual criminal. *~ kerah putih* white-collar criminal. *~ perang* war criminal. *~ ulang* recidivist. *~ ulung* master criminal.

penjahatan depravation (of morals), ruin, destruction.

jahé ginger, *Zingiber officinale. – telur* a dish of raw eggs and ginger syrup.

jahid → ZAHID.

jahil I (*A*) **1** stupid, ignorant (*esp* of Islamic teachings); → BODOH, DUNGU. *Saya sungguh – dalam hal-hal agama.* I'm really ignorant about religious matters. **2** heathen, pagan. **3** bad, wicked (people). *tangan* – thieving.

sejahil as ignorant as.

sejahil-jahil however ignorant, no matter how ignorant.

menjahili [and **ngejahilin** (*J coq*)] **1** to tease, annoy. **2** to rob. **3** to molest a woman sexually.

kejahilan 1 ignorance (of Islamic teachings). **2** stupidity. **3** badness, wickedness. **4** bad behavior.

penjahilan bad behavior.

jahil II → JAIL.

jahilia(h) (*A*) Age of Ignorance (pre-Islamic era in Arabia), paganism.

jahim (*A*) hellfire.

jahit sewing, stitching. *benang* – sewing thread. *mesin* – sewing machine. *tukang* – seamstress; tailor. *– penjahit, lalu kelindan* to be successful in one endeavor means to be successful in others. *– (sudah) kelindan putus* all gone. *– jelujur* basting, loose (temporary) stitching. *– jerumat* darning. *– lilit ubi* to sew s.t. by wrapping the thread around the edge of the area sewn. *– mati* permanent stitching. *– mesin* machine sewing. *– sembat* plain hem stitch. *– tangan* hand sewing. *– tindih kasih* counterhem.

berjahit sewn (closed), stitched (up).

menjahit 1 to sew (up). *Dia ~ pakaian sendiri.* She sews her own clothes. **2** to fix (by sewing), mend.

jahit-menjahit sewing, needlework, tailoring. *Ia membuka sebuah sekolah ~.* She has opened a sewing school.

menjahiti (*pl obj*) to sew. *~ pakaian* to sew clothes.

menjahitkan 1 to sew for s.o. *Cinderella ~ meréka baju kecil.* Cinderella sewed little clothes for them. **2** to send s.t. to (a tailor) for sewing/tailoring. **3** to use s.t. to sew with.

jahitan 1 stitch, suture, seam. *~ bersilang* cross stitch. **2** s.t. sewn, sewn item, sewing. **3** way of sewing. *~ apik* her sewing is neat.

penjahit 1 sewing needle. *mencari ~ dalam rumput* to look for a needle in a haystack. **2** sewer, tailor, seamstress.

penjahitan sewing.

jahul → JAHIL I.

jail (*A*) /ja'il/ mischievous, fond of teasing/picking on.

menjaili to tease, pick on.

kejailan naughtiness, teasing.

jailangkung → JALANGKUNG.

Jain Jain.

jaipong k.o. dance.

berjaipong(an) dance that dance.

jaipongan *tari ~* k.o. Sundanese dance.

jaitun → ZAITUN.

jaiz (*A*) a neutral action (according to God's commandments) permitted but not obligatory.

jaja hawk, sell door-to-door.

berjaja and **menjaja** to be a hawker, sell things from door to door.

berjajakan to sell from door to door. ~ *kehormatan* to prostitute o.s.

menjajakan to hawk/peddle/sell s.t. from door to door. ~ *diri* to prostitute o.s.

jajaan s.t. hawked. *barang ~nya* the goods she hawks.

jaja-jajaan merchandize, goods for sale.

penjaja hawker, seller, vendor. *perempuan ~ séks* prostitute.

penjajaan hawking.

jajag → JAJAK.

jajah well-traveled. – *désa milang kori* (*Jv*) to go from one village to another. – *milang putri* (*joc*) to go from girl to girl. – *rancah* trample. **menjajah-rancah** to trample (on), crush under one's feet.

menjajah(i) 1 to colonize. *Belanda ~ Indonésia*. The Dutch colonized Indonesia. **2** to oppress. **3** to dominate, lord it over. **4** (*bersifat ~*) domineering. **5** to travel somewhere to trade, sightsee or tour.

menjajahkan to make/turn into a colony. ~ *diri* to let o.s. be colonized.

terjajah 1 colonized. **2** oppressed, dominated.

jajahan 1 colony. ~ *Kemahkotaan* Crown Colony. **2** colonized. **3** (*ob*) district.

penjajah 1 colonizer. **2** despot.

penjajahan 1 colonialism, colonization, colonizing, colonial. *masa ~* the colonial period. **2** traveling for trade, etc. **3** suppression, subjugation.

jajak (*J/Jv*) poll. – *pendapat* poll, polling; plebiscite.

menjajaki 1 to explore. ~ *kemungkinan* to explore the possibilities. **2** to sound out, probe, fathom, take soundings, plumb.

menjajakkan to put (one's foot) down somewhere.

terjajaki sounded out, probed, plumbed.

penjajak s.t. or s.o. who sounds out, etc. ~ (*per*)*damai(an)* peace feelers.

penjajakan 1 exploration, exploratory. *pembicaraan ~* exploratory talks. **2** polling, probing, testing out, study. *studi ~ kemungkinan* feasibility study; → KELAYAKAN. ~ *perdamaian* peace feelers.

perjajakan testing, sounding out, polling.

jajal (*Jv*) **jajal-jajal** to try to, make an effort to.

menjajal to try, test. *saling ~ kekuatan* trial of strength.

jajalan test.

jajal-jajalan to keep on trying.

penjajalan testing, trying.

jajan (*Jv*) **1** snack; to snack. **2** (*sl*) to eat s.t. forbidden in secret [*esp* to have (illicit) sex]. *Suami saya tak pernah –.* My husband never cheats on me.

berjajan 1 to eat a snack. **2** to visit a brothel.

menjajankan to spend (money) on snacks, buy snacks with, use ... to buy snacks.

jajanan snack (hawked or eaten outside).

jajan-jajanan various kinds of snacks.

penjajan s.o. who has extramarital affairs. ~ *séks* sex fiend.

jajap menjajap to take on a trip. *Jepang waktu itu minta agar meréka dijajap ke Ciater.* At that time Japan asked to be taken to Ciater.

jajar I row, line, band. *berbaris 3 –* lined up in 3 rows. *– genjang* parallelogram.

sejajar 1 on the same level. **2** (to run) parallel, be in line (with). ~ *arah serat* along the grain. **3** in a row, abreast, run along. ~ *dengan* abreast of. ~ *dengan rute* abreast of the route. **menyejajari** and **mensejajari** to make parallel to. **menyejajarkan** and **mensejajarkan** to put on the same level as, equate. *lebih ~ kedua sistém pendidikan* to put the two educational systems on the same level. **kesejajaran 1** equality. **2** parallelism. **pe(r)sejajaran** parallelism.

berjajar arrayed, in a line/row, line up, abreast. *radar ~ sefasa* phased-array radar. ~ *sepuluh* ten abreast. *ditanam ~* planted in rows.

berjajaran 1 side by side. **2** lined up in rows.

menjajari to go by on the same level as.

menjajarkan 1 to put on the same level as, compare s.t. favorably with, equate. *Sebuah hotél yang kamarnya dapat dijajarkan*

dengan kamar hotél-hotél kelas setaraf. A hotel with rooms that compare favorably with rooms in hotels of the same class. **2** to line up, place in a (parallel) row. **3** (*elec*) to shunt.

terjajar placed in parallel/rows.

jajaran 1 line, row. ~ *genjang* parallelogram. ~ *komando* lines of command. **2** ranks (government/military/health services, etc.). *di antara ~ nama-nama* ranking with. *dalam ~* among the rank and file of. ~ *kantor dubés asing* embassy row. **3** (*elec*) shunt. **berjajaran** to be ranked.

penjajaran alignment, lining up, making parallel, juxtaposing, equating.

jajar II furrow. *– pasar* the ordinary person.

menjajar to plow, work (a field).

menjajarkan to drag, pull along.

terjajar dragged/pulled along.

jajaran furrow.

jajat imitation, counterfeit.

menjajat to imitate, ape (*esp* in order to mock).

jajatan an imitation, fake.

jak (in acronyms) → JAKARTA.

jaka I 1 young man. **2** young unmarried man; → JEJAKA. *– tingting* a bachelor who is a virgin.

perjaka 1 young man. **2** bachelor. **keperjakaan** virginity, bachelorhood.

pejaka virginity.

jaka II → ZAKAR.

jakal (*D/E*) jackal, *Canis aureus*.

jakar → ZAKAR.

jakaranda jacaranda, *Jacaranda filicifolia*.

Jakaria (*A*) Zacharia.

Jakarta Jakarta. *– Pér* (*coq*) the Jakarta Fair. *ke –* to Jakarta. **mengejakartakan** to send to Jakarta.

menjakartakan to Jakartanize.

kejakartaan Jakartaism.

penjakartaan Jakartanizing.

jakas k.o. plant, *Pandanus spp.* from which mats are made.

jakat → ZAKAT.

Jakbar [Jakarta Barat] West Jakarta.

jakét (*E*) jacket. *– antipeluru* flak jacket. *– pelampung* flotation jacket, lifejacket. *– penyelamat* life jacket. *– tahan api* fireproof jacket.

berjakét to wear a jacket, with a jacket.

jakgung [jaksa agung] attorney general.

jakpot (*E*) jackpot.

Jakpus [Jakarta Pusat] Central Jakarta.

jaksa (*Skr*) prosecutor, prosecuting attorney. *– agung* [Jakgung] attorney general. *– agung muda* deputy attorney general, advocate general. *– agung muda bidang tindak pidana khusus* [Jampidsus] deputy attorney general for special criminal actions. *– negeri* district attorney. *– penuntut* prosecuting attorney. *– penuntut umum* [JPU] public prosecutor. *– tentara* (*mil*) judge advocate. *– tinggi* chief prosecutor.

kejaksaan 1 prosecution. **2** District Attorney's office. ~ *agung* [Kejakgung] attorney general's office. ~ *negeri* [Kejari] district attorney's office. ~ *tinggi* [Kejati] provincial attorney general's office.

Jaksel [Jakarta Selatan] South Jakarta.

jaksi → TOPI *jaksi*.

Jaktim [Jakarta Timur] East Jakarta.

jakum and **jakun** (*A*) Adam's apple; → LEKUM.

Jakut [Jakarta Utara] North Jakarta.

jala (*Skr*) **1** (casting) net. **2** basket (in sports). *– kawat* wire netting. *– kerap* a net with small mesh. *– muatan* cargo net. *– rambang* a net with big mesh. *– serat* dragnet. *– sérét* dragnet. *– tangga* netting for climbing onto the deck of a ship.

jala-jala 1 trelliswork. **2** network. **3** net. ~ *udara* air system. **3** net. ~ *rambut* hairnet. ~ *sérét* dragnet. **4** (*med*) plexus.

menjala to throw/catch s.t. with a casting net.

menjalakan to catch with a net for s.o. else.

terjala netted, caught in a net.

penjala user of a net.

jalabria k.o. cake made of rice flour.

jalad I (*A*) frost.

jalad II (*A*) executioner.

jalak I (*Jv*) **1** (*– hitam*) starling, *Sturnupostor jalla*. **2** *ayam –* k.o. cock used in cockfighting. *– Bali* Bali mynah, *Leucopsar rothschildi*. *– bodas* black-winged starling, *Sturnus melanopterus*. *– cina* purple-backed starling, Daurian myna, *Sturnus sturnicus*. *– jantan* → AYAM *jalak*. *– putih* → JALAK *Bali*. *– surén* Asian pied starling, pied mynah, *Sturnus contra*. *– ungu* white-vented mynah, *Acridotheres javanicus*.

jalak II a bold person.

jalakan k.o. leguminous plant, beggar weed, *Desmodium gyroides*.

jalal (*A*) (in certain phrases about God) most powerful, supreme. *Allah yang –* God Almighty.

jalalah (*A*) power, majesty.

jalan l street, road, alley, path, route, trail, tract, way. **2** track, tract, course, trajectory, path. *pada – yang tepat* on the right path. **3** cause, ground, reason. *Apa –nya maka tak senang?* What's the reason that you don't feel at ease? **4** to go, run, do. *Jam ini baik –nya.* This watch keeps good time. *Arloji ini tidak/kurang baik –nya.* This clock doesn't keep good time. *Arloji ini cepat –nya.* This watch is fast. *Jam ini baik sekali –nya* This watch keeps good time. *Arloji ini tidak –.* The watch has stopped. *Kereta api itu tidak – lagi.* That train has been discontinued. *Mobil saya –nya 120 km.* My car does 120 kilometers. *Mobil ini sangat laju –nya.* This car is running very fast. **5** on the way to (a certain age), going on. *sudah – 5 bulan* going on 5 months (old). *Dia baru berumur 20 tahun, – tahun ini.* Just this year he will be 20 years old. *Umurnya – 50 tahun.* He is going on 50. **6** to pass, go. *Minta –.* Excuse me. May I pass in front of you? **7** the development or occurrence of an event (negotiation/meeting/narrative/story, etc.) from beginning to end, course. *– ceritanya kurang lancar.* The way the story goes is not flowing. **8** (*col*) to sell well, be in demand. *Barang seperti ini tidak bisa – di sini.* This type of item is not in demand here. **9** way (to do s.t.), means, manner, method, opportunity. *Tiada – lain.* There is no alternative/other way. *Rupanya tidak ada – lain menolongnya.* Apparently there is no other way to help him. *dengan –* by means of. *dengan – damai* in a peaceful manner, by peaceful means. *léwat – belakang* to do s.t. secretly, surreptitiously. *Itu tidak pada –nya.* That's not the right thing to do. *Jangan kuatir, – masih terbuka.* Don't worry, (other) opportunities are still open. **10** intermediary, go-between. *Segala itu sudah ditakdirkan Tuhan, kejadian itu hanya sebagai –.* All that was already predestined by God, the event was only an intermediary. **11** motion from one point/place to another point/place; → BERJALAN. *– kaki menelusuri – setapak menuju tempat mencétak yang gelap ini* to walk along a footpath (leading) to this clandestine mint. *Selamat –!* Have a nice trip! Bon voyage! **12** linear family relationship. *– anak* to be a nephew. *– apa orang ini kepadamu?* How is this man related to you? *menurut – bapak* on one's father's side. *banyak – kalau hendak pergi ke langgar* and *banyak – menuju Roma* all roads lead to Rome. *menempuh – yang empat* (*M*) to perform four k.o. approaches in social life, i.e., "an upward road" (with regard to s.o. with a higher social position) or *mendaki*; "a downward road" (with regard to s.o. with a lower social position). *– air* water pipe, waterway. *– aksés* access road. *– altérnatif* alternative way. *– angan-angan* way of thinking. *– angin* a) air passage. b) exhaust pipe. *– arteri* arterial road, thoroughfare. *– arteri non-tol* toll-free thoroughfare/arterial road/traffic artery. *– aspal* paved road. *– bahasa* manner/style of speech, idiom, grammar. *– baipas* (*coq*) bypass. *– bawah* underpass. *– bébas hambatan* freeway. *– belakang* a) backdoor, rear entrance. b) secret, underhanded, surreptitious. *– belantan* corduroy road. *– bentar* bypass. *– bentuk melingkar* ring road; → JALAN *melingkar*. *– berbelat-belit* winding road. *– berlubang* potholed road. *– bersayap* ramp. *– besar* a) main road. b) highway; → JALAN *raya*. *– buntu* a) dead end, blind alley. b) cul-de-sac. c) deadlock, impasse. *Tampaknya perundingan itu menemui – buntu.* It seems that the negotiations have reached a deadlock. *menjalan-buntukan* to (bring to a) deadlock. *– butulan* access road. *– cagak tiga* three-forked road. *– celaka* path of miseries. *– cukai* toll road. *– dagang* trade route. *– dalam* short cut. *– darah* bloodstream. *– darat* a) country road. b) overland route. c) travel by land. *– ékonomi* road of economic importance. *– élak* bypass. *– gelap* sneaky way of doing s.t. *– hidup* way of life. *– Ho Chi Minh* Ho Chi Minh trail. *– induk* trunk road. *– jalur kaki* sidewalk, pavement. *– kecil* lane. *– keluar* a) exit. b) way out, outlet. c) escape route. *– keluar séksual* sexual outlet. *– keréta api* railroad track. *– keréta api kabel* cable/funicular railroad track. *– keréta api lintas ganda* double railroad track. *– kerucut* funnel road for leading cattle to slaughter. *– koléktor* feeder road. *– lahir* birth canal. *– laut* seaway, sea route. *– layang* flyover, cloverleaf, overpass. *– layang Tébét* Tebet flyover (in Jakarta). *– lepas* way out. *– lingkar (lalu-lintas)* a) circuit. b) ring road. *– lingkar-dalam* inner ring road. *– lingkar-luar* outer ring road. *– lingkungan* secondary road. *– lintang* lateral road, cross street. *– lintas* short cut. *– lintas cabang* feeder line. *– lintas layang* overpass. *– Lintas Susun Jakarta* Jakarta Interchange. *– masuk* a) entrance. b) approach road. c) access road. *– masuk ke jembatan* ramp (to bridge); *cp* JALAN *bersayap*. *– mati* a) dead end, cul-de-sac, blind alley. b) an old (formerly used) street. *– meléréng* sloping road. *– melingkar* ring road. *– memintas/memotong* shortcut; → JALAN *pintas/potong*. *– mendaki* ascent, upward slope. *– mendatar* level road. *– menurun* a) descent, way down. b) "a sloping road" (with regard to s.o. still unknown) or *meléréng*, and "a level road" (with regard to s.o. of equal social standing) or *mendatar*. *– naik* ascent, upward slope. *– nafas* a) respiratory tract. b) trachea. *– negara* national highway. *– néng-nong* (*Med*) grade crossing. *– niaga* trade route. *– nontol* toll-free road. *– pelayaran* shipping lane. *– peluru* bullet trajectory. *– péndék* shortcut. *– pendekat* avenue of approach. *– penghubung* feeder road, access road. *– penglepas* escape road. *– pengumpan* feeder road. *– perairan* waterway. *– perkencingan* urinary tract. *– pikiran* train of thought. *– pintas* a) shortcut. b) bypass. *– pintas bawah tanah* underpass. *– poros* main road. *– potong* short cut. *– propinsi* provincial road. *– protokol* a) the streets in Jakarta *usu* traveled by foreign dignitaries beginning from Medan Merdeka Barat in front of the *Istana Merdéka* to Soekarno-Hatta International Airport. b) a main street in a city. *– (dengan) pungutan* toll road. *– raya* highway. *– raya berjalur empat* four-lane highway. *– raya lintas cepat* thruway, expressway, turnpike. *– Raya Lintas Sumatera* [JLS] Trans-Sumatran Highway. *– Salib* (*RC*) Stations of the Cross. *– samping* a) a street beside a house. b) a small street that runs parallel to the main road. *– searah* one-way street. *– sepéda* bike path. *– serap* beaten path, a pedestrian street. *– sérong* a) winding road. b) cunning ways. *– setapak* footpath. *– simpang* a) side street. b) feeder road. *– simpang empat* intersection, crossroads (of four roads); → PEREMPATAN, PRAPATAN. *– simpang susun* road interchange. *– simpang tiga* T-intersection. *– singkat* shortcut. *– sutera* silk road. *– tambak* roadway, embankment, causeway. *– tangga* escalator. *– tanpa hambatan* freeway. *– tembus* a) thoroughfare, through street. b) breakthrough. *– temu-gelang* (*Jv*) beltway. *– tengah* a) middle course/way. b) compromise, means of conciliation. *– terang* the honest way (to do s.t.). *– terbuka* opportunity. *– tikus* a very small footpath (in hamlets or mountainous areas), alley (in cities). *– tol* toll road. *– udara* ventilator. *– umum* public road. *– utama* arterial road. *– yang lengkung* roundabout way, detour. *– yang lurus* the honest way (to do s.t.).

jalan-jalan to (go for a) stroll, take/go for a walk/drive; → BERJALAN-JALAN. *~ bersama tetapi bayar masing-masing* to go Dutch treat.

sejalan l of/in the same direction/aim/purpose/intention/opinion. *kawan ~* a like-minded friend. **2** parallel. *dua ~* said of a question open to a double interpretation. *tiga ~* said, for instance, of a three-line proverb with two parallel lines. *saudara ~ jadi* siblings from the same mother. **3** to be in accordance/compliance/concurrence/harmony/conformity, in line (with). *Cari gadis lain yang lebih ~ untuk dijadikan istrimu.* Look for another girl who is more appropriate to be your wife. *tidak ~* incongruent. *~ dengan* in reference to (the news you just told me, etc). *~ dengan permintaan anda* in compliance with your request. *~ dengan politik kami* in line with our policy. **menyejalankan** to make ... be in accordance/compliance. *Adatnya* *disejalankan dengan perkembangan zaman.* They have adapted the traditions to changing times. **kesejalanan** 1 like-mindedness. 2 convergence.

berjalan 1 to walk, go (on foot). *orang yang ~ kaki* pedestrian. *Lebih baik ~ daripada berkendaraan.* It's better to walk than to ride in a vehicle/car. *Hanya 10 menit ~ kaki dari sini.* It's only a 10-minute walk from here. *~ dengan tangan* to walk on one's hands. *~ ke sana ke sini* to walk back and forth. *~ lambat seperti kéong* to go at a snail's pace. *~ melonjak-lonjak* to walk in an affected/arrogant way. *~ béngkok* to be dishonest. *~ beriringan* to ride in a convoy. *~ dahulu* a) to go ahead of, lead the way. b) to die prematurely. *~ darat* a) to go overland. b) to go on foot; → BERJALAN *kaki. ~ dari muka* (M) not act arbitrarily/highhandedly. *~ dari pintu belakang* to be devious/not straightforward. *~ di atas rél* to act or work according to the rules. *~ émpar* to walk with the toes turned out. *~ kaki* to go on foot. *~ lurus* a) to walk straight on. b) to follow the straight and narrow path. *~ mencakah* to take long strides. *~ mundur* to back up. *pengemudinya mencoba ~ mundur* the driver tried to back up (the car). *~ pincang* unbalanced. *~ sérong;* → BERJALAN *dari pintu belakang.* 2 (of movable parts in a watch/clock/engine/machine, etc.) to work, operate, function, go. *Wéker saya ~ baik.* My alarm clock keeps good time. *Bis itu tidak dapat ~.* The bus is not running. *ban ~* assembly line, conveyor belt. *~ stasionér* to be idle (of a motor, etc.). *sedang ~* on-going. *tidak ~* to stop working/running, go dead. 3 to move from one point/place to another point/place, go. *Keréta api itu ~ dengan lajunya menuju Bandung.* The train rushed on swiftly to Bandung. *Bis dapat ~ kencang 100 km atau lebih satu jam.* The bus can go at a speed of 100 kilometers or more per hour. *dengan ~nya waktu* over the course of time. 4 to go on, proceed, take place, be in session (of a meeting). *Kongrés GMKI [Gerakan Mahasiswa Kristen Indonésia] pada hari pertama ~ alot.* The first day of the GMKI [Congress of the Indonesian Christian University Student Movement] proceeded with some difficulty. *Segala sesuatu ~ menurut rencana.* Everything went according to plan. *~ terus* to continue, go on, survive. 5 to be getting/coming along, go. *~ baik* to go well. *~ lancar* to run smoothly. 6 to be going on (a certain age). 7 mobile. *toko ~* a mobile store. 8 (*fin*) current (account, etc.).

berjalan-jalan 1 to take a walk/drive, stroll around. *~ pada pagi hari untuk menghirup udara segar* taking a walk in the morning to inhale fresh air. *~ naik mobil* to tour (the town) in a car. 2 to go on a trip.

menjalani [and **njalanin/ngejalanin** (*J coq*)] 1 to go on, take. *~ liburan* to go on a vacation. 2 to undergo (an operation/punishment/restoration/treatment), observe. *~ masa berkabung* to observe a period of mourning. *~ operasi kecil* to have a minor operation. *~ hukuman* a) to execute/carry out a sentence. b) to serve one's sentence (in prison). *~ hukuman mati* to be executed. *~ masa percobaan* to be on probation. *~ sial* to die. 3 to go through (a period of one's life). *~ sisa hidupnya* to end one's days. *Dua tahun lalu ia ~ pénsiun sebagai Perwira menengah AD.* two years ago he retired as an Army field-grade officer. 4 to travel over/through, cover (a distance). *~ jarak 60 mil* to cover a distance of 60 miles. 5 to pass through, complete (a course/school, etc.). *Dia ~ SMA.* He graduated from Senior High.

menjalankan [and **njalanin/ngejalanin** (*J coq*)] 1 to drive (a machine/car, etc.), pilot (a plane). *Motor kujalankan perlahan-lahan.* I drove the car slowly. 2 to commit (a burglary, etc.). 3 to operate, run, work, conduct (an engine/apparatus/business, etc.), carry out. *~ perintah* to carry out an order. *~ pemerintahan* to run the government. 4 to manage/administer (the affairs), run, be in charge of, have command of. 5 to lead (one's life), go through (life). 6 to conduct (a policy, etc.). 7 to perform (an operation), say (one's prayers); to take (measures), apply (tactics, etc.), exercise (one's right). 8 to invest (money). 9 to execute, enforce. *~ hukuman* a) to execute a sentence. b) to serve/complete one's sentence. c) to undergo (a sentence). *~ akal/pikiran* to think (about), reflect (on). *~ hak* to exercise one's rights. *~ jarum (halus)nya* to carry out one's plans in a sly manner. *~ jabatannya* to take up one's duties. *~ pencarian* to

exercise one's profession. *~ pimpinan terhadap* to direct, exercise control over. *~ salat* to say one's prayers. *~ tugas* to do one's duty.

terjalankan 1 passable. 2 doable, able to be carried out.

jalanan (*J coq*) → JALAN 1. *Jangan main di ~.* Don't play in the street. *lampu ~* street lights.

pejalan walker. *~ kaki* pedestrian. *~ kaki angkasa* space walker, walker in space.

penjalan (*infr*) 1 driver (of a car, etc.). 2 (s.o. who) likes/is accustomed to walk, a confirmed hiker. 3 starter (of car). *mesin ~* (car) magnet.

perjalanan 1 trip, journey, voyage, tour, march, drive. *film ~ Présidén RI ke AS* a film about the trip of the President of the Republic of Indonesia to the United States. *dalam ~ and di tengah ~* on the/one's way (to), in transit, en route, on the move. *dalam ~ pulang* on the way home. *~ 90 menit mobil dari London* a 90-minute trip by car from London. *setengah jam ~ naik mobil* a half-hour's drive by car. *biro ~* travel bureau. *bursa ~* travel exchange. *jadwal ~* itinerary. *jawatan ~* travel agency. *orang ~* (*ob*) traveler. *surat ~* travel order; *cp* SURAT *jalan. ~ balik* homeward journey. *~ bulan madu* honeymoon. *~ dinas/jabatan* duty tour, official travel. *~ jauh* a long haul. *~ jemaah haji* the pilgrimage to Mecca. *~ kaki angkasa* space walk. *~ keliling* circle tour. *~ kembali* return trip. → PERJALANAN *balik. ~ péndel* (*mil*) shuttle march. *~ perdana* maiden voyage. *~ pulang* → PERJALANAN *balik. ~ pulang pergi* roundtrip. *~ sehari* a one-day trip. *~ tunggal* a one-way trip. *~ ulang-alik* commuter service. 2 circulation, course, tract. *dalam ~ masa* in the course of time. *~ bintang* course/motion of the stars. *~ darah* blood circulation, circulation of the blood. *~ napas* circulatory tract. 3 behavior, conduct. *Ditanyakannya kepada saya bagaimana ~ Eadir sebelum bekerja di sini.* He asked me how Eadir's conduct was before he worked here. **seperjalanan** traveling together, fellow traveler. *orang/teman ~* fellow traveler, traveling companion.

jalang I 1 wild, untamed, savage. 2 loose (of a woman). **menjalang** 1 to act/run wild. 2 to return to nature. **kejalangan** 1 wildness, savagery. 2 loose behavior.

jalang II **jalang-menjalang** to ask e.o. for forgiveness; → MAAF-MEMAAFKAN.

jalang III (M) → JELANG I.

jalangkoté (C?) k.o. cake made of flour with a bean sprout and noodle filling.

jalangkung (C) k.o. Chinese puppet used to conjure up the dead.

jalar I (in compounds) creeping. *ubi –* sweet potato.

berjalar to spread, permeate, run (through). *Api ~ sangat cepat.* The fire spread very quickly.

berjalaran and **berjalar-jalar** 1 to creep, crawl (over the ground). 2 to spread (over the ground).

menjalar 1 to creep, crawl (over the ground). 2 to spread (of a fire/disease, etc.). 3 (in compounds) creeping. 4 to be catching, contagious. *Semangatnya ~.* His enthusiasm is catching.

menjalari 1 to crawl (all) over s.t. 2 to spread (all) over/into/through. *Kesejukan luar biasa ~ urat-urat darahku.* An incredible cold spread through my blood vessels.

menjalarkan 1 to spread (disease, etc.), conduct. *~ panas* to conduct heat. 2 to disseminate.

terjalar spread. *jatuh ~* to fall flat on one's face.

jalaran stake, pole (for climbing plants).

penjalaran 1 crawling, creeping. 2 support (for supporting plants).

jalar II **jalaran** (*Jv*) because; cause, reason.

Jaraséna Naraya Naval Award for Merit.

Jalasénastri Navy Women's Association.

Jalésu Bhumyanca/Bhumyam Ca Jaya Mahé "Even on the Seas and on the Land are we Victorious", the slogan of the Marines.

Jalésvéva Jayamahé "We are Victorious on the Seas", slogan of the Navy.

jali I (*J/Jv*) k.o. plant with pea-like fruits, Job's tears. *Coix agrestis Lour/lacryma. bubur –.–* porridge made from this fruit.

jali II **jali-jali** (*J*) a popular melody played on the *gambang kromong.*

jali III (A) 1 clear, evident, obvious. *zikir –* chanted praise of God. 2 revealed, inspired.

terjali 1 clear, evident, obvious. 2 divinely inspired.

jalia (*naut*) galley.

jalibut (*E?*) galley-boat, rowboat.

jali-jali (*BG*) → JALAN-JALAN.

jalil → JALAL.

jalin 1 braid, link by winding around e.o. 2 braided, plaited. *tikar –* plaited mat. *– anyam* braiding. **menjalin-anyamkan** to braid together.

sejalin 1 a braid (of hair). 2 linked. *~ dan sejalan* hand in hand.

berjalin 1 tied together, interrelated, connected to e.o. *~ berkelindan* interconnected. 2 (to get) established (of close relations).

berjalin-jalin, berjalin-jalinan and **jalin-berjalin** 1 interconnected, intertwined, interwoven. *Mungkin terlalu banyak benang kusut yang jalin-berjalin.* Maybe there were too many tangled threads that were intertwined. 2 complex, complicated, intricate.

berjalinkan to be involved in.

menjalin 1 to tie together. 2 to establish, make (a relationship/ cooperation, etc.) closer. *~ hubungan* to establish close relations. *~ keakbraban dengan* to have close relations with. *~ kerjasama* to cooperate. 3 to braid/plait (hair, etc.).

jalin-menjalin to be intertwined/tied together.

menjalinkan and **memperjalinkan** 1 to intertwine, braid, plait. 2 to combine s.t. with s.t. else, make s.t. an integral part of. 3 to establish (a relationship). *~ hubungan budaya* to establish cultural relations.

terjalin 1 tied, related, connected. 2 involved (in). 3 established (of a relationship/love affair, etc.). **keterjalinan** involvement, entanglement; establishment (of a close relationship).

jalinan 1 braided/plaited work, wickerwork, braid (of hair), braiding. 2 concatenation, combination. 3 (*med*) plexus.

kejalinan tying together.

penjalin 1 person who or instrument that is used to weave, braid, etc. such as rope, etc. 2 s.t. that brings people closer together, tie, relationship. *~ kerjasama* the ties of cooperation.

penjalinan 1 tying together. 2 bringing closer together. 3 establishment (of a relationship). *~ kembali* reestablishment.

perjalinan cohesion, coherence.

jalinsum [Jalan Lintas Sumatra] Trans-Sumatra Highway.

jalis (*A*) companion.

jalla (*A*) Almighty.

jalma → JELMA.

jalu I (*Jv*) 1 male. 2 cock's spur.

berjalu with a spur, spurred.

menjalu to strike with the spurs.

jalu II k.o. snapper, *Lutianus sp.*

jalum [jalur umum] (in e-mail messages) sent to the entire list; *opp* JAPRI.

jalur I 1 stripe, strip (of cloth/land), band. 2 belt (an area). 3 trail, track, course, path, median, lane (of traffic), projectory. 4 lane, avenue, alley. 5 slab (of tobacco). *tembakau –* tobacco slab. 6 column, space between two lines; → LAJUR. 7 (in the eastern part of Sumatra) a surface measure of 400 m2. *– A* Armed Forces faction. *– alur* course (of a ship). *KM Minas bergéser dari – alur yang sebenarnya.* The MS Minas shifted from its actual course. *– B* the bureaucracy. *– bahan* flow line (in a factory). *– birokrasi* bureaucratic red tape. *– boling* bowling alley. *– cepat* fast lane (for fast traffic). (*jalan*) *– empat* four-lane (road). *– ganda* a) dual track (school system). b) double track (railroad line). *– Gaza* Gaza Strip. *– Golkar* Golkar tracks. *Ketiga – komponén-komponén Golkar ialah – A/ABRI, – B/ Birokrasi atau Korpri dan – G (ormas-ormas pendiri dan pendukung Golkar).* The three tracks of Golkar components are track A/ABRI or Republic of Indonesia Armed Forces, track B/ Bureaucracy or Korpri, the Republic of Indonesia Employees Corps and track G/Golkar's founding and supporting mass organizations. *– G* Golkar. *– gempa* seismic belt. *– gunung api* volcanic belt. *– hélm* lane in which motorcyclists must wear helmets. *– hias* louver. *– hijau* green belt, median (on highway). *– Ho Chi Minh* (in Vietnam) Ho Chi Minh trail. *– jalan* lane of traffic. *– jalan kaki* sidewalk. *– jalan matahari* sun's course. *–*

kabut fog bank. *– kiri* left lane. *– lalu-lintas* traffic lane. *– lambat* a) slow lane (for slow-moving traffic). b) low profile. *– landai* ramp, a sloping road joining different level. *– landasan* runway. *– lapisan* vein (of salt, etc.). *– laut* sea-lane, shipping lane. *– layang* track elevation (in railway system). *– lébar* wide band. *– léwat* aisle. *– Pantura* Java north coast road. *– pegunungan* mountain belt. *– pelayaran bébas* innocent passage. *– peluru* trajectory of projectiles. *– pemisah* median, divider (between opposing lanes of traffic). *– penahan angin* windbreak. *– pendaratan* runway. *– penerbangan* flight path, route. *– pengertian* an understanding (for paying illegal expenses). *– pengolahan* process lane. *– penyeberangan* zebra crossing. *– peradilan* legal means. *memperkarakan léwat – peradilan* to sue through the courts. *– pribadi* [japri] private response (on the internet) not disseminated to the entire list, back channel; *opp* JALUM. *– rabak* (*geol*) shear zone. *– ranjau* mine belt. *– samping* aisle. *satu spur* single track. *– sébra* zebra crossing. *– sekat* buffer zone. *– samping* aisle. *– sesar* fault line. *– suara* sound track. *– sulang* feeder line. *– suplai* supply line(s). *– susu* milk belt. *– terbang* a) runway, airstrip. b) airline, air-route. *– tambahan* contiguous zone. *– terbang* flight line. *– tunggal* single track. *– udara* airway, air lane. *– umum* [jalum] (in e-mail messages) sent to the entire list; *opp* JAPRI. *– zébra* zebra crossing.

sejalur on the same track.

berjalur 1 with ... lanes/strips. *~ empat* four-lane. 2 in columns/ rows. *~ empat* with four lanes, four-lane.

berjalur-jalur in lanes, in columns.

menjaluri to put stripes, etc. on.

menjalurkan to channel.

jaluran 1 channel, band, corridor. 2 wake (of a ship).

penjaluran routing.

jalur II (in Kuantan, Riau) k.o. dugout canoe.

jalus → JELUS.

jalusi (*D*) Venetian blind.

Jalut (*A*) (the Biblical) Goliath.

jam I (*Pers*) 1 clock, watch, timepiece. *– gelang* (wrist) watch strap (made of leather/gold, etc.). *tukang* watchmaker. 2 o'clock; → PUKUL I 4. *– lima* five o'clock. *– berapa?* what time is it? 3 hour. *lima –* five hours. *berapa –?* how many hours? *bekerja 24 – sehari* to work round the clock. 4 time/moment to do s.t. *– gini kok masih kerja!* Still working at this time (of day)? *Pada – itu juga ia berangkat.* He departed that very moment. *– absénsi* time recorder (for office personnel), time clock. *– bandul* pendulum clock. *– béker* alarm clock. *– berangkat/pulang kerja* rush hours. *– berkunjung/besuk/bezuk* visiting hours (in a hospital/penitentiary, etc.). *– bicara* consultation/visiting hours (for a physician). *– datang dan pulang kantor* rush hours. *– D* (from older spelling *Djam*) H-hour. *– digital* digital watch. *– dinding* (*listrik*) (electric) wall clock. *– Gadang* the Big Clock located in the center of Bukittinggi (Sumatra). *– istirahat* break. *– kantor* office hours. *– karét* "rubber time" i.e., the cultural habit of not being on time for meetings, parties, and the like. *– keberangkatan* time of departure. *– kedatangan* time of arrival. *– kerja* a) office hours, working hours. b) total working hours. *– komputer* (in parking lots) punch clock. *– krida olahraga* time allowed to employees for exercise. *– kukuk* cuckoo clock. *– kuliah* class hours (in an academy/university). *– kunjungan* visiting hours (in a hospital/penitentiary, etc.). *– lembur* overtime. *– main* (in theater) curtain time. *– makan* meal time. *– malam* curfew. *– mengunjungi orang sakit* visiting hours (*esp* in a hospital). *– orang* man-hour. *– padat* peak hours. *– padat kendaraan* rush hours. *– pakai gong* a striking clock. *– pasir* hourglass. *– pelajaran* lesson-hour. *– pulang kantor dan bubar sekolah* and *– pulang maupun masuk kerja* and *– puncak* rush/peak hours. *– saku* pocket watch. *– salon* grandfather clock. *– setengah ...* half-past ... *– setengah lima* 4:30, i.e., halfway to 5. *– siaran utama* prime time (on TV). *– sibuk* rush hour. *– tangan* wrist watch. *– tayang* show time. *– témbok* wall clock. *– téngok* visiting hours (in hospital, etc.). *– terbang* flying hours. *– wéker* alarm clock. *– wésminster* grandfather clock. *– yang ramai/paling sibuk* rush hours.

sejam one hour, hourly.

berjam to have/possess/own a clock/watch. *Malang sekali nasib orang tak ~ sebab ia harus bertanya atau melirik jam milik orang lain, sekedar mau tahu waktu.* Unfortunate is the person who does not have a watch, because he has to ask or steal a glance at the watch owned by another, just to know the time.

berjam-jam for hours (on end), hours and hours, hour after hour. *Kini tiba-tiba orang harus antri ~ lamanya untuk memperoléh bénsin sedikit.* Now, all of a sudden, people have to line up for hours to obtain some gasoline.

mengejami and ngejami (*Jv*) to time s.t. in hours.

jam-jaman by the hour. *Taksi itu harus dibayar ~.* Taxicabs have to be paid by the hour.

jam II → JÉM.

Jama (*A zod*) Aries.

jamaah → JEMAAH.

jamadah and jamadat (*A*) inanimate.

jamah menjamah(i) 1 to touch, feel, handle. 2 to taste (food). 3 to have sex with (a woman). *gadis yang sudah dijamah* no longer a virgin. 4 to attack.

terjamah 1 touched. 2 touchable. *belum ~* untouched. *tidak ~* untouchable.

jamahan contact, touch, feel. *~ tangannya* the touch of her hand.

jamah-jamahan female servant also used for sex.

penjamah s.o. who touches.

penjamahan 1 touching, feeling, handling, contact. 2 tasting. 3 having sex with.

Jamaika Jamaica.

jamak I (*A*) 1 plural. 2 joining two of the five daily prayers into a single prayer.

menjamak to combine two prayers into a single prayer.

menjamakkan 1 to pluralize. 2 to join two prayers into a single prayer.

kejamakan pluralizing.

penjamakan 1 pluralization. 2 combining two prayers into a single prayer.

jamak II (*A*) common, usual, normal. *sudah –* it's normal (for).

sejamaknya it's only normal.

menjamakkan 1 to consider normal. 2 to make s.t. normal, normalize.

kejamakan normalcy.

jamal I [Jawa Malaysia] Javanese-Malaysian.

jamal II (*A*) (in certain phrases and compounds) beautiful.

Jamali [Jawa-Madura-Bali] Java-Madura-Bali.

jaman → ZAMAN.

jamang I (*Jv*) diadem, frontlet; → JEJAMANG.

jamang II (*M*) sejamang a little while, a moment.

jamas (*Jv*) menjamasi to clean (a kris), shampoo (one's hair).

jambak I 1 bunch, cluster, bundle. *se– bunga* a bunch of flowers. 2 tuft, plume (on a horse/bird, etc.).

sejambak one's family/ancestors.

berjambak-jambak in bunches/clusters.

jambakan 1 bunch. 2 tuft.

jambak II (*Jv*) berjambak-jambakan and jambak-menjambak to pull e.o.'s hair.

menjambak to pull hard on (s.o.'s hair).

menjambaki (*pl obj*) to pull hard on (s.o.'s hair).

jambakan hair that has been pulled out.

penjambakan pulling out (hair).

jambak III → JAMBU.

jambal I k.o. catfish, *Wallago attu.*

JAMBAL II [Jawa, Madura, Bali, Lombok] Java, Madura, Bali and Lombok.

jamban toilet, latrine.

jambang I 1 vase, flower pot. 2 (*J/Jv*) large earthenware pot. 3 tub, trough, vat.

jambangan 1 vase, pot. 2 toilet.

jambang II → CAMBANG.

jambar I serving (of food).

sejambar a single serving.

berjambar with a serving.

jambar II temporary shelter/hut/shed.

jambat I → JABAT.

jambat II jambatan → JEMBATAN.

jambé and jambi (*Jv*) areca nut, *Areca catechu..*

jambelang → JAMBLANG.

jambian k.o. red snapper, *Lutianus argentimaculatus.*

jamblang and jambolan (*J*) k.o. tree with edible fruit, Java plum, *Syzygium/Eugenia cumini.*

jambo (*euph*) → diancuk.

jambon (*Jv*) 1 crimson. 2 pink; → JAMBU. 3 k.o. plant, *Acmena acuminatissima* and species of *Eugenia.*

jamboré (*D*) jamboree.

jambrét I (*J*) swiped, snatched, stolen.

menjambrét to snatch (s.t. from s.o. by force). *Dia ~ kalung-nya.* He snatched her necklace.

terjambrét snatched.

jambrétan s.t. snatched/robbed, loot. *hasil ~* s.t. that was snatched/robbed.

penjambrét s.o. who snatches, snatcher.

penjambrétan snatching.

jambrét II small shrimp-like fish, *Mesopodopsis sp.*

jambrong *Chévrolét* - the 1946 Chevrolet truck.

jambrud and jambrut → JAMRUD, ZAMRUD.

jambu (*Skr*) various species of rose-apples, guavas, cashews, etc. – *air* rose apple, water apple, *Eugenia aquae.* - *batu/biji* guava, *Psidium guajava.* - *bertih/bol* Malay rose apple, *Eugenia malaccensis, Syzygium malaccense.* - *dersana/darsono* → JAMBU bol. – *jamblang* → JAMBLANG. - *juwét* Java plum, *Eugenia cumini.* - *keling* → JAMBU bol. - *k(e)lutuk* → JAMBU batu. - *laut* sea apple, *Eugenia grandis.* - *manalagi* a seedless variety of rose apple. – *mawar* rose apple, *Eugenia jambos.* - *mérah* → JAMBU bol. - *mété/médé/ménté/monyét* cashew, *Anacardium occidentale.* - *Semarang* Java apple, wax apple, *Eugenia javanica.* - *susu* → JAMBU bol.

jambua pomelo, shaddock, *Citrus decumana.*

jambu-jambu tuft of hairs, tassel, feathers at the end of a spear.

jambul 1 forelock, wave (on one's forehead), crest, tuft of feathers (on bird's head). 2 crown (of a pineapple).

jambul-jambul cowlick.

berjambul with a forelock/tuft, etc.

menjambul to be like or develop a forelock/tuft, etc.

jambur 1 hut, shed. 2 guest house.

jamhur (*A*) theologian, s.o. versed in Islamic knowledge. – *dunia* world figure.

jamhuriah (*A*) republic.

jami (*A*) mosque. *mesjid –* main mosque used for Friday prayers.

jamik → JAMI.

jamil (*A*) beautiful.

jamin (*A*) guarantee, security, collateral.

berjaminkan to have s.t. as collateral.

menjamin 1 to guarantee, warranty. *dijamin* secured, guaranteed, under warranty. 2 to check, ensure. *Periksalah terjemahan saya untuk ~ ketepatannya.* Examine my translation to check its accuracy. 3 to encumber.

menjamini (*infr*) to guarantee.

menjaminkan to mortgage, use s.t. as collateral, pledge s.t. *Ia ~ rumahnya.* He mortgaged his house.

terjamin guaranteed, assured, secured. *~ aval* guaranteed party. *tidak ~* unsecured (loan). keterjaminan security.

jaminan 1 guarantee, warrantee, deposit, bond, bail, collateral, pledge. 2 security. *dijadikan ~* encumbered. *sebagai ~* as security/retainer. *~ aval* guarantee of a bill. *~ bank* bank guarantee. *~ benda* collateral. *~ cidera janji* indemnity bond. *~ hak* patent; → PATÉN. *~ hak cipta* copyright. *~ hari tua* old-age pension. *~ hukum* legal guarantee. *~ kas* cash collateral. *~ kebendaan* collateral. *~ kerja* job security. *~ kejujuran* fidelity bond. *~ kerja* job security. *~ mutu* quality assurance. *~ pascajual* express warranties. *~ pekerjaan* job security. *~ pelaksanaan* performance bond. *~ penawaran* bid bond. *~ perorangan* surety, personal guarantee. *~ sosial* social security. *~ sosial tenaga kerja* [jamsosték] workers' social security. *~ tawanan* hostage. *~ uang* bail bond. *~ wésel* guarantee, backing.

penjamin guarantor, underwriter, guarantee (*mod*). *~ aval* guarantor, accommodation party. *badan ~ dana* fund guarantee board. ~ *émisi (éfék)* (equities) underwriter. ~ *pendamping* co-maker.

penjaminan guaranteeing, underwriting, pledging.

perjaminan warranty.

jam'iyah and **jam'iyat** (*A*) organization, association.

jamiy(y)atul (*A*) association, club, union.

jamiz (*A*) sycamore.

jamjam → ZAMZAM. - *durja* facial expression; → AIR *muka.*

jamnas [Jamboré Nasional] National Scouts Jamboree.

jampal (*cla*) gold weight = 11/2 rials.

jampang → CAMBANG.

jampen k.o. Achehnese music.

jampi (*Skr*) incantation, magic spell/formula, charm, mantra.

   berjampi 1 magical. **2** under a spell. *air* ~ water over which a magic spell has been cast.

   menjampi to cast a spell/incantation on, treat s.o. with magic spells.

   menjampikan 1 to cast a spell/incantation on (for s.o. else). **2** to use s.t. to cast a spell with.

   jampian magic spell, incantation.

   penjampi s.o. who casts spells, sorcerer.

Jampidsus → JAKSA *agung muda tindak pidana khusus.*

jampuk I k.o. owl (whose screeching is a sign of an impending disaster), Asian king owl, *Bubo orientalis. bagai - kesiangan* disoriented, not knowing what to do.

jampuk II menjampuk to interrupt.

   terjampuk interrupted.

jamput (*vulg from diamput*) fuck you!

jamrah and **jamrat** (*A*) the three pillars at Mina; stoning Satan on the hajj.

jamrud → ZAMRUD.

Jamsosték → JAMINAN *sosial tenaga kerja.*

jamu I (*Jv*) traditional medicine. - *awét muda* medicine for staying young. - *bersalin* medicine for woman who has just given birth. - *géndong* traditional medicine sold by itinerant seller who carries them in a basket on her back. - *kuat* a) aphrodisiac. b) tonic. - *lempuyang* k.o. medicine prepared from ginger and given to nursing mothers. - *penambah gairah* aphrodisiac. - *sawanan* → *jamu* SAWANAN. - *singset* reducing medicine, slenderizer. - *srikaton* medicine for staying beautiful. - *temulawak* tonic prepared from a k.o. curcuma. - *tolak angin* cold medicine.

   jamu-jamu and **jamu-jamuan** various k.o. traditional medicines.

jamu II 1 guest. **2** (in compounds) meal (offered to guests), offering. - *laut* offering to the sea.

   berjamu 1 to receive guests. **2** to visit, socialize.

   menjamu 1 to receive guests and give them food and drink. *Kami dijamu dengan makanan ala Jawa.* We were received with Javanese-style food. **2** to (pay a) call on.

   menjamui to give food and drink to (guests).

   menjamukan to serve/offer (food and drink to guests). ~ *minuman* to serve drinks (to guests).

   memperjamu to serve a meal to (a guest).

   jamuan 1 s.t. served to guests. ~ *makan* dinner (party). ~ *makan malam* banquet. ~ *makan perdana* gala dinner. ~ *minum* party at which drinks are served. ~ *santap malam* formal dinner party. ~ *suci* holy communion. **2** entertainment (a deduction on income taxes).

   penjamu host.

   penjamuan serving (guests), holding a dinner party.

   perjamuan 1 feast, reception, banquet, party, event at which guests are fed. ~ *sosial* social function. **2** social call/visit. **3** (*RC*) eucharist. ~ *suci* (the Christian) Last Supper.

jamuju → JEMUJU.

jamung torch made from dried coconut fronds.

jamur (*J/Jv*) mushroom, fungus, toadstool, smut, stain, mold. *tumbuh seperti - disiram hujan* and *seperti - di musim hujan* spring up like mushrooms after a rainstorm. - *air* aquatic fungi. - *akar putih* k.o. fungus, root rot, *Rigidoporus microporus.* - *api* smut (a corn disease). - *benih* grain smut. - *biru* blue stain. - *brama* k.o. mushroom, red polypore, *Boletus/Pycnoporus sanguineus.* - *cokelat* shiitake, *Lentinus edodes.* - *hangus* smut. - *hijau* green stain (a disease of trees). - *hutan* forest mushroom. - *jelaga* sooty mold, *Capnodiaceae spp.* - *karang* moss growing on coral,

coral polyps. - *karat* rust smut, *Puccinia, spp.* - *kayu* k.o. fungus, reishi, *Ganoderma lucidum.* - *kenyal* jelly fungi, *Bacidiomycetes spp.* - *kompos* k.o. edible mushroom, button mushroom, *Agaricus bisporus/brunescens.* - *kulit* a skin disease. - *kuping (tikus)* tree ear, Jew's ear, *Hirneola auricula judae.* - *laut* sea anemone. - *lendir* slimy mold, *Myxomycetes, spp.* - *merang* k.o. toadstool, paddy-straw mushroom, *Volvariella volvacea.* - *mérah* k.o. fungus, *Boletus sanguineus.* - *muda* honey fungus, *Armillaria mellea.* - *nasi* an edible mushroom, *Hydnum fragile.* - *oncom* bakery mold, *Monilia spp.* - *padi* k.o. mushroom. - *payung* toad stool, *Agaricaceae, spp.* - *pewarna* sapstain. - *supa kincir* an edible mushroom, *Polyporus arcularius.* - *taugé* golden mushroom, enoki, *Flammulina velutipes.* - *tiram* oyster mushroom, *Pleurotus ostreatus.* - *umbi* truffle. - *upas* a whitish-red mushroom, pink limb blight, *Corticium salmonicolor.*

   berjamur moldy, mildewed.

   berjamuran to mushroom, appear suddenly in large numbers

   menjamur 1 to mushroom, appear suddenly in large numbers, grow uncontrollably. **2** to mildew.

   jamuran moldy, mildewed.

   penjamuran mushrooming, boom(ing).

jan (in acronyms) → JAWATAN.

jana (*Skr cla*) man, nation. - *bijana* birthplace.

janabah and **janabat** (*A*) impure, unclean (after ejaculation, during menstruation, etc.).

janabijana → JANA *bijana.*

janah (*A*) paradise.

janang frame. - *jendéla* window frame.

janangau → JENANGAU.

janat → JANAH.

janazah → JENAZAH.

jancok and **jancuk** → *diancuk.*

janda (*Skr*) **1** widow, widower. **2** divorce(e); → BALU I, DUDA, RANDA I. *laksana - baru bangun tidur* an attractive woman. - *béngsrat* childless widow. - *belum berlaki* a girl abandoned by her lover after he seduces her. - *berhias* a childless widow entitled to wear a bridal gown when she remarries. - *cerai* divorcee. - *kandel* a rich widow. - *kembang* a) a woman who divorced prior to consummation of the marriage. b) childless widow. - *laki-laki* widower. - *mati* widow. - *muda* a young widow. - *sekali kirai* a newly divorced woman. - *tebal* a rich widow.

   berjanda to be a widow(er)/divorce(e).

   menjanda to be/live as a widow(er).

   kejandaan widow(er)hood.

jandal-jendul bumpy.

jang (*J*) term used to address small boys.

jangak debauched, dissolute, licentious.

   menjangak to act/live in a debauched way.

   penjangak person who acts/lives in a debauched way, libertine, rake.

jangan I 1 don't! stop it! hands off! you can't have it! **2** I hope not. - *ada yang pada jahil.* I hope none of them bears a grudge. **3** don't ... too, not too! - *boléh nénék mbakyu menginap di rumah!* Don't allow your sister's grandmother to stay over at home! - *jauh-jauh!* Don't go too far away! *Sambalnya - pedas!* Don't make the chili paste too spicy. **4** (reduplicated word other than an *adj*) don't by any means! - *bilang siapa-siapa lho!* By no means tell anybody! **5** shouldn't (third-person prohibition). *Pemerintah - malu minta penjadwalan utang.* The government shouldn't be shy about asking for a rescheduling of debt. - *dikata lagi* to say nothing of, not to speak of, not to mention. - *harap* to have no chance at all: forget about it! not a hope! - *lagi* to say nothing of, not to speak of. - *lagi kita mencoba masuk ke kamar kecil di gedung-gedung jawatan pemerintah.* Not to speak of trying to enter the bathrooms in government office buildings. - *macam-macam* none of that. - *macam-macam, saya istri polisi.* None of that, I'm a police (officer's) wife. - *mau* should object to. *Kita hanya mengharapkan agar para sejarahwan Indonésia - mau dicuci otaknya.* We only expect that Indonesian historians should object to being brainwashed. - *pun* not even, let alone, much less, not to mention. *Kita tidak takut apa-apa!* - *pun gonggongan anjing!* We don't shrink from anything! Let alone the barking of dogs! – *sampai* it should not come so far that, don't let it happen that, on no account may, never, it should not go so far as to. – *sampai ketahuan si B.* By all means, don't let it be known by B. *Golongan Karya – sampai menjadi organisasi yang sifatnya tertutup.* On no account should *Golkar* become a closed organization. – *sampai merusak persatuan dan kesatuan bangsa!* It should not go so far as to destroy the unity and integrity of the nation! – *sekali-kali* in no case, not on any account, on no account. – *sekali-kali jatuh cinta pada seorang gadis, bila tidak bermaksud mengawininya.* Don't fall in love with a girl if you do not intend to marry her. – *tidak/tiada* to have to, must, not fail to. *Kalau kebetulan di Yogya, – tidak mampir.* If by any chance you are in Yogya, you must drop by. – *akan* → JANGANKAN. *biar* – and *(agar) supaya* – so that ... doesn't/wouldn't. *Bungkus makanan ini baik-baik biar – cepat mendingin.* Wrap this food up very well up so that it doesn't become cold quickly. *Dia tutup pintu mobilnya supaya – maling yang masuk.* He locked the door of his car so that a thief wouldn't get in. *–lah* (intensive). *–lah menyiarkan berita itu!* Don't (I emphasize) broadcast that news!

jangan-jangan 1 I/we hope that ... doesn't happen. ~ *ia sakit!* I hope he isn't sick! **2** perhaps, maybe, who knows (but not expected or hoped for). ~ *ia datang nanti.* Maybe he'll come later today.

berjangan-jangan to keep saying "don't."

jangankan let alone, much less, not to mention. ~ *berjalan, bergerak pun tak dapat.* He can't even move let alone walk.

menjangankan to forbid.

jangan II (*Jv*) **1** vegetable. **2** a soup-like dish made with vegetables; → SAYUR I.

janganan greens.

jangar 1 dizziness, giddiness. **2** migraine (headache).

jangat 1 skin (of human or animal body), dermis. *keras –* invulnerable (to bullets, etc.). *makan –* to be very poor. *tebal –* to be insensitive. **2** bark, rind. **3** the skin of rattan that has been smoothed (for mat making). **4** (*tali*) – rawhide (rope). *tinggal – pembalut tulang saja lagi* to be only skin and bones. *– liat kurang panggang* stubborn, unteachable. *– kepala* scalp.

menjangat 1 leathery. **2** to strip the skin off, skin, flay, peel, fleece. **3** to split (rattan or palm fronds for mat making or hides for making ropes).

menjangati to skin, flay, peel.

menjangatkan 1 to strip the skin off, skin, flay, peel. **2** to split (rattan or palm fronds for mat making or hides for making ropes), fleece.

penjangat peeler (the device), skinner, flayer.

janget → JANGAT.

janggal 1 queer, strange, odd, peculiar. *berpakaian agak –* to be rather strangely dressed. **2** clumsy, awkward, stilted. *tingkahlaku yang –* awkward behavior. **3** improper. *kelakuan –* improper behavior. **4** (*Mal*) discordant to the ear, unpleasant to the eye. *– tampak/buat dipercayai* implausible, improbable. *tak ada –nya* there's nothing odd in that.

menjanggalkan 1 to botch, spoil. **2** to consider s.t. strange. **3** to sound strange.

terjanggal the strangest.

kejanggalan 1 strangeness, queerness, oddness. **2** discordance, disharmony. **3** awkwardness, clumsiness.

Janggala name of an old Javanese kingdom in East Java.

janggel I → JANGGAL.

janggel II (*Jv*) corncob.

janggelan (*Jv*) tentative, provisional.

janggér (*Bal*) **1** Balinese dancer. **2** k.o. Balinese dance.

janggi I (*Pers*) **1** Negro, black person. **2** (*ob*) exotic, mythical. **3** (*ob*) rare, unusual, bizarre, out of the ordinary.

janggi II (in some compounds); → CENDANA I, PAUH I.

janggo (*E*) **1** cowboy. **2** tough (guy). **3** marksman.

janggol (*S*) whore.

ngejangol to prostitute o.s.

janggut I beard. *kebakaran –* in a daze. *seperti – pulang ke dagu* in the right place, where it should be. *– bauk* long beard. *– kambing* short beard on the chin, goatee.

berjanggut bearded.

janggut II (in certain compounds denoting plant names and lichens). *– duyung* k.o. lichen, Ceylon moss, *Gracilaria lichenoides*. *– kelonak* a climber, *Discorea spp.*

jangilus sailfish, *Istiophorus gladius*.

jangir → JANGGÉR.

jangka 1 range. **2** phase. **3** pair of compasses, calipers. **4** period of time, term. *dalam – seminggu* within a week. *tidak ada –nya* unlimited. *untuk – waktu tidak terbatas* for an indefinite period. **5** plan, intention. *– bagi* dividers, calipers. *– béngkok* wing compasses. *– bulat* globe calipers. *– dekat* close-range. *– gésér* sliding calipers. *– jauh* long-range. *– kaliber* calipers. *– kesalahan* range of error. *– lengkung* pair of compasses. *– menengah* medium-range. *– panjang* a) long-term. b) long-range. *– pelunasan* repayment period. *– péndék* a) short-term. b) short-range. *– sedang* medium-range. *– sorong* vernier calipers. *– tusuk/ukur* dividers, compasses, calipers. *– waktu* term (of a contract, etc.), period. *– waktu hidup* life expectancy. *– waktu pembayaran cicilan* amortization period.

berjangka 1 to measure (of space). *Lébarnya* ~ *200 méter.* It measures 200 meters in width. **2** to be spaced (in time), phased. **3** with a certain term; time (of deposits/loans, etc.), term.

menjangka(kan) 1 to measure (with calipers). **2** to plan.

penjangkaan 1 measuring. **2** planning. ~ *waktu* planning (the use of one's time), timing.

jangkah step, stride.

berjangkah to take a step, stride.

menjangkah to step/jump over s.t.

jangkang I 1 stride. **2** (*coq*) *telah –* dead.

menjangkang 1 to straddle. **2** to stand/walk with legs wide apart.

terjangkang to be wide apart (of the legs).

jangkang II (*Jv*) k.o. tree, skunk tree, *Sterculia foetida*. *– bukit* k.o. tree, *Xylopia ferruginea*. *– hutan* k.o. tree, *Polyalthia scortechinia*.

jangkap (*Jv*) full, complete (of an amount of time), exactly. *– dua tahun* a full two years.

jangkar I (*D?*) **1** anchor. **2** tie, stay. **3** armature. **4** stone (in watch). *– apung* sea anchor. *– arus* stream anchor. *– buritan* stern anchor. *– cadangan* sheet anchor. *– cermat* kedge anchor. *– darurat* spare anchor. *– garuk* drag anchor. *– haluan* bower (on boat). *– keruk* dredging anchor. *– kubah* tie anchor. *– kuku tunggal* one-armed anchor. *– lémpar* kedge anchor. *– lintang* cross-tie. *– muka* bower anchor. *– payung* mushroom anchor. *– pelat* gusset stay. *– penyalur* grapnel. *– tangkup* grapple. *– tarik* tie rod. *– terbang* grapnel. *– tongkat* cane anchor.

berjangkar and **menjangkar** to anchor.

menjangkarkan to anchor s.t.

penjangkar anchor (the fastener).

penjangkaran anchoring.

jangkar II branching aerial root (of certain trees).

jangkar III (*Jv*) to tease (*usu* by calling s.o. by his pet name).

jangkat I basket (carried on the back).

jangkat II ford (in a river), shallows, shoal, pool (in a river).

jangkau range. *– dekat* close-range.

sejangkau within reach.

menjangkau 1 to reach out for s.t. ~ *sehabis tangan* to try as hard as one can. **2** to grasp. *mudah/bisa dijangkau* affordable. **3** to reach as far as, cover. ~ *seluruh kota* it (one's view) covers the entire city.

menjangkaui to reach to, affect, infect.

menjangkaukan to reach out with (one's hands).

terjangkau reachable, affordable; achieved. *harga yang* ~ affordable price. **keterjangkauan** affordability, attainability.

jangkauan 1 range, reach. *dalam* ~ within reach. *di luar* ~ outside the reach of, beyond one's control. ~ *dekat* close range. ~ *panjang* long range. ~ *péndék* close range. **2** scope, span, domain. **3** what one wants to reach/achieve. **sejangkauan** as far as one can reach. ~ *mata (memandang)* as far as the eye can see. **berjangkauan** with a reach, -reaching. ~ *luas* far-reaching. ~ *jauh ke depan* reaching far into the future.

penjangkau sepenjangkau(an) as far as one can reach.

penjangkauan reaching.

jangkep → JANGKAP.

jangkerik → JANGKRIK I.

jangki(h) 1 strap (for attaching a basket to one's back). **2** basket (carried on the back).
menjangkih to carry s.t. in such a basket.

jangkih-mangkih 1 sticking out in all directions. **2** scattered around in all directions. *Barangnya* –. His things were scattered all over the place.

jangking → JONGKANG *jangking.*

jangkir I large nail of a bird.

jangkir II → JONGKAR-JANGKIR.

jangkit 1 contagious, infectious, catching. *penyakit* – an infectious/contagious disease. **2** (*coq*) to spread to, affect, be catching.
berjangkit 1 to be contagious, be going around, break out (of a disease). **2** to spread (of a disease/fire, etc.). **3** to be infectious (of a disease/music, etc.).
berjangkitan to spread (of a disease) in all directions.
menjangkit → BERJANGKIT.
menjangkiti 1 to infect (with a disease). **2** to afflict. *Meréka dijangkiti rasa minder.* They were afflicted with feelings of inferiority.
menjangkitkan to spread, transmit (a disease).
terjangkit [and **kejangkit** (*coq*)] **1** contaminated, infected, affected (by a disease). **2** spread (of a disease) **keterjangkitan** being contaminated/affected/infected.
terjangkiti 1 infected, contaminated. **2** smitten (by a love of s.t.).
jangkitan infection.
kejangkitan 1 contamination, contagion. **2** affected, infected, catch (a disease), smitten. *Dia* ~ *malaria.* He caught malaria. **3** to get into the (bad) habit of.
penjangkitan 1 transmission, spread (of a disease). **2** contamination, contagion.
perjangkitan outbreak (of a disease).

jangkrik I (*Jv*) **1** cricket, *Gryllus mitratus.* **2** reference to the 1942 Chevrolet truck. **3** clone (similar but not the same software or an unbranded computer). – *goréng* packet of rice filled with goat meat and spices.

jangkrik II (*euph*) → *diancuk.*

jangkung 1 k.o. heron. **2** thin and tall.
jangkungan stilts.

jangla (*Skr*) **1** jungle. **2** wild, untamed.
menjangla to roam through the forest.

janik sea urchin, *Echineis spp.*

janin (*A*) fetus, embryo.

janjang (*M*) → JENJANG I, II.

janji 1 promise. – *akan membantu* a promise to help. **2** agreement, contract. **3** oath, vow. – *kawin* marriage vow. **4** appointment, engagement, commitment, date. **5** delay, postponement, deferral. – *akhir bulan* a postponement until the end of the month. **6** condition. *dengan* – on condition that. **7** the predetermined time of one's death. *Dia sampai* –*nya.* He has passed away. – *sampai sukatan penuh* his time (to die) has come. – *sehabis bulan* words are cheap. – *berantai* perpetual clause. – *gombal* a broken promise. – *jabatan* oath of office. – *keling* false promise. – *setia* oath of allegiance. – *swajual* right-to-sell clause.
berjanji 1 to (make a) promise. *Dia* ~ *(akan)* ... He promised to ... – *bulat* to promise without reservations. **2** to agree to, reach an agreement, pledge. *Meréka* ~ *untuk saling menghormati.* They agreed to respect e.o. ~ *setia* to pledge allegiance.
menjanjikan and **memperjanjikan** [and **ngejanjiin** (*J coq*)] to promise/pledge s.t.; to make promises; promising. ~ *bantuan* to promise help. ~ *akan membantu* to promise to help.
terjanji(kan) promised. *Tanah Terjanji* The Promised Land.
janjian appointment, date. **berjanjian** to make an appointment/date.
penjanji (*infr*) promiser.
penjanjian → PERJANJIAN.
perjanjian 1 promise, agreement. **2** treaty, contract, pact, covenant, vow, Testament. ~ *atas beban* contract for valuable consideration, contract in return for payment. ~ *Baru* the New Testament. ~ *beli saham* stock subscription. ~ *beliséwa* hire-purchase agreement. ~ *berantai* perpetual clause. ~ *carter*

charter party. ~ *(dengan) cuma-cuma* contract for no consideration. ~ *di atas meterai* an official agreement over a revenue stamp. ~ *gadai* pawn agreement. ~ *Hudaibi(y)a* a treaty between the Prophet Muhammad and the non-Muslim Quraysh of Mecca in 6 A.H. which is believed to have led to the spread of Islam. ~ *hukuman* penal clause. ~ *jaminan* suretyship. ~ *jual beli* purchase agreement. ~ *kawin/perkawinan* marriage contract. ~ *karya/kerja* work contract, labor agreement, contract of work. ~ *Kerjasama Ékonomi dan Perdagangan Jangka Panjang* Agreement on Long-Term Economic Cooperation. ~ *Lama* the Old Testament. ~ *lebih pihak* multilateral agreement. ~ *lintas-batas* border-crossing agreement. ~ *menukar* barter agreement. ~ *penanggungan* contract of suretyship. ~ *perburuhan* labor contract. ~ *perdagangan* trade agreement, ~ *perdamaian* peace treaty. ~ *perpajakan* tax treaty. ~ *pertahanan* defense pact. ~ *sama tengah* compromise. ~ *sepihak* unilateral agreement. ~ *séwa beli* hire-purchase agreement. ~ *séwa guna* lease agreement. ~ *séwa pakai* rent for use agreement, rental agreement. ~ *séwa-menyéwa* rental/leasing agreement. ~ *tanpa imbalan* contract for no consideration. ~ *tidak serang-menyerang* nonaggression pact. ~ *timbal balik* reciprocal/bilateral/executory contract. ~ *untung-untungan* aleatory contract. ~ *utang-piutang* credit agreement. **3** appointment, date. **4** condition. *dengan* ~ on condition that. **5** time limit, term. ~ *selama dua bulan* a time limit of two months. **6** last will and testament. **berperjanjian** with a agreement/treaty. *negara yang belum* ~ *ékstradisi* a country which does not have an extradition treaty.

janma → JELMA. **menjanmakan** to anthropomorphize.

jannah and **jannat** (*A*) heaven, paradise.

jantan 1 male, masculine (*usu* of animals). *ayam* – rooster. **2** (in some compounds) said of things that are reminiscent of a male in shape: large, pointed. **3** bold, brave. **4** dashing. **5** virile, manly, macho. *cukup* – to be man enough to (do s.t.). *sifat* – bravery. – *teruna* dashing young man. *tidak* – cowardly, weak. **ketidakjantanan** cowardice.
berjantan 1 to have a male/partner (in a male/female pair). **2** to mate. **3** (*vulg*) to have sex.
menjantani to mount, i.e., of a male animal to mate with a female animal.
kejantanan 1 manhood, manliness, masculinity. **2** virility, machismo. **3** male organ. **4** courage, valor.
pejantan male, stud. *kuda* ~ stud horse.
penjantanan mating.
perjantanan pederasty.

jantang I (*M*) **berjantang** and **menjantang** to stand out, be prominent (of veins).

jantang II terjantang to be dazzled by bright lights.

jantang III crooked, not straight.

jantera → JENTERA.

jantik → JENTIK I.

jantingan red-throated sunbird, *Anthreptes rhodolaema.*

jantra → JANTERA.

jantuk curved, domed.
jantukan to have a domed forehead.

jantung I 1 heart. **2** the very heart/center of s.o. – *kota* the heart of the city. **3** the heart (as the seat of the emotions); → HATI II. **4** s.t. which resembles the heart in shape, *esp* the thicker part of a limb. **5** heart-shaped ornament on necklace, etc. *makan hati berulam* – very saddening. – *badak* k.o. tree, *Ervatamia hirta.* – *betis* calf (of the leg). – *hati* a) sweetheart, darling. b) the heart (as the seat of the emotions). – *mengipas* fibrillating heart. – *paha* thigh. – *pisang* banana blossom. **berjantung pisang** to be heartless. – *tangan* fleshy part of the palm (of the hand).
berjantung to have a heart. *tidak berhati* ~ to be heartless, insensitive.
jantungan 1 so nervous that one's heart is pounding. **2** to have a heart attack. **3** (*J*) awkward, clumsy.

jantung II *burung* – k.o. bird, little spider hunter, *Arachnothera longirostra.*

jantur I (*Jv*) **1** sleight-of-hand. **2** black magic, witchcraft.
menjantur to bewitch, cast a spell on.

terjantur bewitched.
penjantur 1 sorcerer, witch. **2** snake charmer.
jantur II (*Jv*) **janturan** dalang's narration during wayang performance while gamelan plays softly.
Januari (*D*) January.
janub (*A*) south.
janubi (*A*) south; → KUTUB *janubi*.
janur (*Jv*) young coconut leaf. *– kuning* ceremonial ribbons.
jap 1 enough, sufficient, complete. **2** in agreement. *Rapat sudah –.* Agreement was reached at the meeting.
 menjapkan to unify.
jap-jap(nya) complete in every detail. *jap-jap hari* every day.
japang [Jawa Padang] a child of mixed Javanese-Padang parentage.
japit (*Jv*) tongs, clamp; → JEPIT. *– dasi* tie clip.
 menjapit to pince, clamp.
 japitan tongs.
japon [Jawa Pontianak] a child of mixed Javanese-Pontianak parentage.
japrah → JERAPAH.
japri [jalur/jawaban pribadi] private response (on the internet) not disseminated to the entire list, back channel; *opp* JARUM III.
japu(k) smelt, *Osmerus eperlanus*.
japuh rainbow sardine, *Dussumiera spp.*
japut I → JEMPUT I.
japut II [Jayapura Utara] North Jayapura.
jar I (*A*) neighbor.
jar II (in acronyms) → JARAK I.
jara gimlet, auger. *– atap* large needle. *– tanah* drill for taking soil samples, earth auger.
 menjara to drill a hole.
jarab (*A*) scabies; → KUDIS.
 berjarab having scabies.
jarah I s.t. looted/stolen/looted. *tegak meninjau –, duduk meraut ranjau* said of s.o. who never stops working. *– rayah* raiding and plundering. ***menjarah-rayah*** to raid and plunder.
 menjarah to plunder, sack, loot.
 menjarahi (*pl obj*) to plunder, sack, loot.
 jarahan 1 loot. *hasil ~* spoils, booty, loot. **2** grasp. *aman dari ~ perampok* safe from the grasp of robbers. **3** looted, captured.
 penjarah 1 looter, raider. **2** poacher. **3** (*ob*) slave carried off by raiders.
 penjarahan raiding, looting, plundering.
 perjarahan plundering, looting.
jarah II → ZARAH.
jarah III (*coq*) → ZIARAH.
jarak I 1 distance. **2** range, span. *pada –* with a range of. **3** gap, space, spacing, interval, pitch. *– serasa hilang, bercerai serasa mati* if relatives or friends are together, they will quarrel; if they are far apart, they will miss e.o. *– antara* interval (between vehicles, etc.), clearance. *– bagi* pitch. *– bébas* clearance, play (in a brake pedal, etc.). *– capai* distance. *dalam – jalan kaki* within walking distance. *dalam – témbak* within shooting distance. *– dekat* close range. *– dukung* bearing. *– gandar* wheelbase. *– jangkau* visibility distance. *– jauh* long range. *– jelajah* cruising range. *– langit* as the crow flies. *– ledakan* burst range. *– pandang* visibility, sight distance. *– penglihatan* visibility. *– perjalanan* range of movement. *– poros roda* wheelbase. *– puncak* pitch (of a screw, etc.). *– roda* wheelbase. *– simpang* (*petrol*) drift (away from the vertical). *– sudut* angular distance. *– tampak* visibility. *– témbak* range (of a gun). *– terbang* cruising range. *– tempuh* radius, range. *– umur* difference in ages. *– waktu* time gap.
 sejarak at a distance of.
 berjarak 1 to be a distance of, be spaced ... apart. *~ 20 méter* spaced 20 meters apart. **2** to move away from e.o.
 menjarak to distance o.s., move away, keep one's distance. *Ia ~ dari saya.* He moved away from me.
 menjaraki 1 to move away from. **2** to put a distance between.
 menjarakkan to move s.t. away, separate, put distance between.
 terjarak far from, spaced far apart, distanced, separated.
 jarakan distance.
 penjarakan spacing.

jarak II (*– minyak*) castor oil plant, *Ricinus communis.* *– Bali* gout plant, Buddha belly plant, *Jatropha podagrica.* *– belanda/budeg/keling/pagar* physic nut, *Jatropha curcas.* *– benggala* castor oil (used as purgative). *– cina/kosta mérah/ulung* bellyachebush, *Jatropha gossypifolia/multifida.* *– kepyar* castor oil plant, *Ricinus communis.*
jaram I cold compress.
 berjaram to have/make a cold compress.
 menjaram to put a cold compress on.
 jaraman cold compress.
 penjaram cold compress.
jaram II penjaram k.o. cookie.
jarambab → JEREMBAB.
jaran I (*Jv*) horse. *– guyang* love potion. *– képang* → KUDA *képang*.
 jaranan a traditional dance of Tulungagung.
jaran II (*J*) various k.o. trees, *Lannea grandis.*
 jaranan various species of plants used as fodder, *Crataeva nurvala, Polyscias nodosa, Hiptage benghalensis.*
jarandawuk (*Jv*) a *lurik* batik pattern.
jarang I 1 rare(ly), seldom, infrequent, not often. *Saya – menonton.* I rarely go to the movies. *tidak – terjadi* it's no rare occurrence. **2** spaced far/wide apart, not dense, sparse, scanty, thin, not plentiful, few. *daérah yang – penduduknya* a sparsely populated area. **3** coarse (in texture).
 jarang-jarang rarely, infrequently. *Saudara K. ~ online.* Mr. K. is rarely online.
 sejarang as infrequently/rarely as. *~ mungkin* as infrequently as possible.
 menjarang to be widely spaced, far apart; to be rare/scarce.
 menjarangkan 1 to thin out, space wide apart. *~ kelahiran* to space out births. **2** to make s.t. happen infrequently.
 memperjarang to make rarer/thinner/less frequent, etc., space out.
 terjarang rare, spaced wide apart, infrequent.
 kejarangan rarity, being spaced wide apart, infrequency.
 penjarangan 1 thinning (cutting down of trees to improve and hasten the growth of the remaining trees). **2** spacing (of births).
jarang II ikan *– gigi* k.o. fish, tiger-toothed croaker, *Otolithes lateoides.*
jarang III (*M*) → JERANG.
jaras I bundle, bunch, bale, sheaf. *– saraf* nerve tract.
 sejaras a bunch (of long objects). *~ bawang* a bunch of leeks.
 menjaras to bundle, tie together in a bundle, arrange and tidy up.
 penjaras baler.
jaras II k.o. loosely woven bamboo basket.
jarem I (*J/Jv*) aching, still painful (of a wound), black and blue.
jarem II (*Jv*) *rumput –* k.o. grass, three flower beggarweed, *Desmodium triflorum.*
jargon (*E*) jargon.
jari 1 finger, toe. **2** spokes, tentacles. *– ampai* cat-o'-nine-tails. *– ayam* k.o. tree, *Xylopia ferruginea.* *– buaya* k.o. climbing plant, *Trichosanthes wallichiana.* *– cincin* ring finger. *– hantu* middle finger. *– jemari* fingers. *– kaki* toe. *– kelingking* pinky, little finger. *– kokat* deformed finger. *– lima* starfish. *– lipan* a) k.o. plant, *Limnophilia aromatica.* b) woven young coconut leaves used as a decoration. *– malang* middle finger. *– manis* ring finger. *– mati* middle finger. *– panjang* middle finger. *– renik* pinky, little finger. *– rimpang* splayed fingers/toes. *– syahadat* index finger. *– telunjuk* index finger. *– tengah* middle finger.
 jari-jari 1 spokes (of a wheel). **2** radius (of a circle). *~ lingkaran* radius. **3** radiating line. **4** ray (in wood). *~ empulur* (*bot*) wood ray. **5** skid (for sending logs down to a river).
 menjari 1 to stick out (like a finger), digitate. **2** to finger s.t.
jariah I and **jariat I** (*A*) slave girl.
jariah II and **jariat II** (*A*) *amal –* charitable endowment, welfare contribution.
jarig → YAREH, YARIG.
jarik (*Jv*) ankle-length wraparound skirt.
jaring 1 net, netting, grid. **2** gang, ring (of thieves, etc.). *– angkat* lift net. *– bahu* thoracic region below the shoulders. *– cincin* Danish seine. *– dasar* bottom gill net. *– dorong* push net. *– halau* drive-in net. *– hanyut* drift gill net. *– insang* gill/drift net. *– jogol*

trawl net. – *kantong* trammel net, seine net. – *lapisan tengah* mid-water gill net. – *lémpar* cast net. – *lingkar* encircling gill net. – *menetap* set net. – *payang* seine net. – *pengaman (sosial)* (social) safety net. – *perangkap* stow net. – *perawi* long line. – *permukaan* surface gill net. – *peta* grid (of coordinates on a map). – *pukat* trawl net. – *sorong* push net. – *tadongan* net seine. – *tarik* trawl, trolling. – *tetap* set gill net.

jaring-jaring net(work), system, chain. ~ *bahu* thoracic region below the shoulders. ~ *makan* food chain.

menjaring 1 to net, capture, trap. ~ *angin* to do s.t. useless. **2** to cover (an area).

menjaringi to throw a net around, cover with a net, envelop. *Hujan ~ malam.* The rain enveloped the night.

menjaringkan to net (goals in soccer or points in basketball).

terjaring [and **kejaring** (*coq*)] **1** netted, get caught. **2** tricked, fooled.

jaringan 1 network, system, grid, ring (of thieves/narcotics dealers, etc.). ~ *ikat* conjunctiva. ~ *intai* reconnaissance net. ~ *Islam Liberal* [JIL] Liberal Islamic Network. ~ *jalan* road network. ~ *kerjasama* networking. ~ *komputer* computer network. ~ *lemak* adipose tissue. ~ *listrik* power supply system, electricity grid. ~ *makan* food chain. ~ *narkotik* drug ring. ~ *rintisan* traverse net. ~ *spionase* spy ring. ~ *télepon* telephone system. **2** tissue (of body). ~ *ikat* connective tissue. *dalam* ~ *otot* intramuscular. ~ *pembuluh* vascular tissue. ~ *pengikat* connective tissue. **3** organizational chart. **berjaringan** networked.

penjaring s.o. used as a net, snare, trap.

penjaringan 1 netting. **2** sweep.

perjaringan network (of friends).

jaringau → JERANGAU.

jarit (*Jv*) long batik skirt.

jaro I (*S*) village head.

kejaroan area headed by village head.

jaro II (*Jv*) bamboo lath for making fences.

jarong k.o. tree, verbena, porter weed, *Achiranthes aspera, Stachytarpheta jamaicensis.* – *lelaki* k.o. plant, (common) snakeweed, *Stachytarpheta indica.*

jarongan various species of trees.

jarot (*J/Jv*) (fruit or vegetable) fiber.

jarotan 1 fibrous. **2** old and tough.

jaru → JAHARU.

jarum I 1 needle. **2** hand (of a gauge/watch); needle, pin (in some compounds). **3** trick, ruse. – *halus kelindan sutra* tricks often conceal a trick. – *arloji* hand of a watch. – *bantalan* bearing roller. – *beludru* cleaning pin. – *berkait* embroidery needle. – *biku* (straight)pin. – *bordir* embroidery needle. – *bundel* (straight)pin. – *cantél* safety pin. – *cocok* awl. – *detik* second hand (of a watch). – *goni* large needle for sewing sacks. – *halus* ruse, trick. – *jahit* sewing needle. – *jam* hand (of a clock). *menurut* – *jam* clockwise. – *kadut* large needle for sewing sacks. – *kait* crocheting needle. – *karung* large needle for sewing sacks. – *kompas* compass needle. – *layar* large needle for sewing sails. – *menit* minute hand (of a watch). – *neraca* balance needle, pointer. – *panjang* minute hand. – *pedoman* compass needle. – *pelampung* float needle. – *péndék* hour hand. – *penggérék* awl. – *penitik* dotting needle. – *pentol/pentul* (straight)pin. – *penunjuk* hand, pointer. – *penyemat* push pin. – *penyemprot* jet nozzle. – *rajut* knitting needle. – *sekon* second hand (of a watch). – *skép* float needle. – *suntik* hypodermic needle. – *tisik* darning needle. – *ukir* graving tool.

jarum-jarum pointer, balance needle.

berjarum 1 with a needle/pin. **2** inoculated, injected, vaccinated. **3** prickly, thorny, pointy.

menjarum 1 to stick, prick. **2** to inoculate, inject. **3** to sew. **4** to pin. **5** needle-shaped.

menjarumi to stick (a needle, etc.) into.

terjarum stuck, pricked.

jaruman 1 needlework, sewing, stitch. **2** procurer, pimp, go-between. **3** trickery, intrigue.

penjaruman 1 sticking. **2** inoculating. **3** matchmaker, go-between.

jarum II various species of plants, *Ixora spp., Andropogon aciculatus.*

jarum-jarum k.o. bush with pointy seeds, *Ixora coccina.*

jarum III [jalur umum] general, as opposed to private, channel on the internet, disseminated to the entire list; *opp* JAPRI.

jarwa (*Jv*) **1** translation from Kawi into Javanese. **2** exegesis.

menjarwakan to explain.

jarwodosok (*Jv*) folk etymology.

jas I (*D*) jacket, coat. – *berbuntut* dress coat. – *buka* open jacket with lapels. – *dingin* overcoat. – *hujan* raincoat. – *kamar* housecoat. – *kerja* work suit. – *luar* topcoat. – *mandi* bathrobe. – *minyak* slicker. – *panjang* long jacket (down to the knees). – *tutup* jacket with stiff high collar and no lapels.

berjas to wear a jacket/coat.

jas II (in acronyms) → JASA, JASMANI.

jasa (*Skr*) **1** service, contribution, favor. **2** merit. *atas* – a) on the basis of merit. b) thanks to. – *angkutan laut* freight forwarder. –.– *baik* good offices. – *bébas* freelance. – *besar* great merit. – *boga* catering services. – *guntingan* clipping service. – *kena pajak* taxable services. – *raharja* accident insurance for official government travel. – *pascajual* after-sales service. – *produksi* production bonus. – *taksiran* appraisal services. – *titipan* a) (in pawn shops) entrusted service. b) consignment service. – *turutan* ancillary services. –.– *umum* public services/utilities. – *yang tak kelihatan* invisibles, i.e., services not usually included in foreign-trade statistics.

berjasa 1 to serve, provide/render a service. **2** useful, meritorious, deserving. **3** to be the reason for, be instrumental in ...ing.

jasaboga (*Skr neo*) catering.

menjasaboga to cater.

penjasaboga caterer.

jasabogawan (*Skr neo*) caterer.

jasad (*A*) **1** body (as opposed to spirit). **2** organism. – *renik* microorganisms, microbes.

berjasad corporeal.

jasadi (*A*) bodily, physical, corporeal, carnal.

jasirah → JAZIRAH.

jas-jus (*Jv*) frivolous, not serious, slipshod.

jasmani (*A*) physical, bodily.

berjasmani to have a body, be physical.

kejasmanian materialism.

penjasmanian 1 embodiment. **2** materialization.

jasmaniah (*A*) physical, bodily, corporeal.

Jasuka [Jawa, Sumatra, Kalimantan] Java, Sumatra, Kalimantan.

jaswadi condom.

jat → ZAT.

jatah (*Jv*) **1** quota, allotment, allocation. **2** ration. **3** distribution. **4** rate. **5** (*sl*) bribe. – *guru* k.o. bribe to get one's child into a school. – *masuk* admission rate. – *saham* allotment. – *tebangan* allowable cut (in forestry). – *tebang tahunan* annual allowable cut, AAC.

menjatah 1 to allocate, allot. **2** to ration. *Segalanya dijatah.* Everything is rationed.

menjatahi to allocate (s.t.) to. *Para pengungsi tak lagi dijatahi bantuan pangan dan obat-obatan.* The refugees were no longer allocated food and medicinal assistance.

menjatahkan to allocate, allot.

jatah-jatahan ration.

penjatahan 1 allocation, allotment, appropriation. **2** rationing, distribution.

Jatayu a mythical eagle in the Ramayana.

Jateng [Jawa Tengah] Central Java.

jati I (*Skr?*) teak, *Tectona grandis.* – *belanda/londo/putih/sabrang* k.o. tree, bastard cedar, white teak, *Guazuma ulmifolia, Gmelina arborea, Peronema canescens.* – *bukit* → KAYU cina.

jati II (*Skr?*) → SEJATI. – *diri* identity.

jatian identity.

jatilan (*Jv*) k.o. horse dance in Central Java.

Jatim [Jawa Timur] East Java.

jatmika (*Skr Jv*) **1** modest, unassuming, unpretentious. **2** respectful.

kejatmikaan 1 modesty, lack of pretension. **2** respect.

Jatsiah and **Jathiyah** (*A*) *al-* "Kneeling"; name of the 45th chapter of the Koran.

jatuh 1 to fall, drop, crash (of a plane). *paling* – at the very least. – *bébas* free fall. – *pada* to fall for (a trick). **2** to fall (at/on a particular time or place). – *pada hari Minggu* it fell on a Sunday. **3** to fall [into the hands (of)]. *Kok mobil Lamborghini ini bisa – ke MS?* How could this Lamborghini fall into the hands of MS? **4** to become lower (in value/worth). *Namanya –.* His name was smeared. **5** to become, get, go, fall in. – *cinta* to fall in love. – *pailit* to go bankrupt. – *sakit* to get sick. **6** to fail (in business/school). **7** to lead to, aim at. *Ke mana -nya perkataan itu?* What do you mean by that? **8** to come down/be handed down (of a decision). *Keputusan itu sudah –.* The decision has come down. **9** relationship. *Orang itu apa -nya dengan Anda?* What's his relationship to you? *ibarat – tertimpa tangga pula* and *sudah – tertimpa tangga* bad luck on top of bad luck, to go from bad to worse. *busuk berbau, – berdebuk* the truth will out. – *di atas tilam* and – *ke kasur* to be kicked upstairs. – *bangun* to rise and fall, up and down. **menjatuh-bangunkan** to make s.o. go up and down, make or break. – *bébas* free fall. – *berkait* to get s.t. because one asks for it. – *bertindih* overlapping. – *cinta* to fall in love. **menjatuh-cintakan** to make s.o. fall in love. – *coloknya* degraded, debased, impoverished. – *di pasir* to speak to deaf ears. – *duduk* to go up and down. – *harga* to fall in price. – *hati kepada* a) to fall in love with. b) to feel sorry for. – *hujan* rainfall. – *iman* tempted. – *kasihan (pada)* to feel sorry (for). – *di pasir* and – *ke (padang) pasir* to fall on deaf ears. – *ke atas* to get lucky. – *ke bawah* to go back, retrogress. – *di/ke (atas) kasur/tilam* a) to be kicked upstairs. b) to get lucky. – *ke tanah lambuk* to fall on the ears of s.o. who likes to gossip. – *melarat/ melését* to have a run of bad luck. – *mérek* to lose one's reputation. – *miskin* to become poor. – *nama* to lose one's reputation. – *pada* to fall for, get tricked by. – *padang pasir* to speak to deaf ears. – *pingsan* to faint, pass out. – *sakit* to fall ill. – *semangat* discouraged. – *témpo* fall due, mature (of a check/loan), expire. **berjatuh témpo** to mature, fall due. – *terahap* to fall on one's hands. – *terjalar* to fall flat on one's face. – *terjerangkang* to fall on one's back with one's feet sticking up. – *tersungkur* to fall flat on one's face. – *tertangkup/tertelungkup/tertiarap* to fall flat on one's face. – *waktu* come due (of a debt).

jatuhnya the way it fits (of clothing). ~ *mahal* we'll have to pay dearly for (that).

sejatuh-jatuhnya 1 no matter how much s.t. drops/falls. **2** to fall as far as possible.

berjatuh to make a contribution, give support.

berjatuhan (*pl subj*) to fall, drop.

menjatuhi 1 to impose (sentence/sanctions, etc.) on. *Dia dijatuhi hukuman penjara.* He was sentenced to imprisonment. **2** to fall on top of, drop on.

menjatuhkan [and **njatuhin/ngejatuhin** (*J coq*)] **1** to drop, let s.t. fall, knock over. **2** to lower. ~ *harga* to lower the price. ~ *nama* to give s.o. a bad reputation. **3** to impose (a punishment/ sentence), pronounce, hand down (a ruling). ~ *hukuman* to impose sentence. ~ *pidana* to sentence (s.o. to prison). ~ *talak* to pronounce the *talak*. ~ *véto* to veto. **4** to put s.o. down. ~ *orang lain* to put other people down. **5** to topple (the government), topple, bring down, ruin, get rid of. **6** to provide (money for a government service).

terjatuh fallen down, overthrown; to fall suddenly. ~ *dihimpit jenjang* one problem after another. ~ *pingsan* to faint, fall unconscious.

jatuhan 1 (radioactive) fallout. **2** drop, fall. ~ *batu* falling rocks. ~ *udara* airdrop.

kejatuhan 1 fall, drop. **2** to get hit by a falling object. ~ *buah kelapa* to get hit by a falling coconut. ~ *bulan* to get lucky, have a windfall. ~ *ilham* to be inspired. ~ *loteré* to hit the lottery. ~ *penyakit* to get sick. ~ *rezeki* to get a windfall.

penjatuhan 1 imposition, pronouncement (of a sentence by the judge), sentencing. ~ *hukuman mati* imposition of the death sentence. ~ *putusan* ruling, handing down a decision. ~ *talak* repudiation (of one's wife). **2** dropping.

jatukrama (*Jv ob*) spouse.

jau I (*Pers*) barley.

jau II (in acronyms) → PENINJAU.

jaudi → YAHUDI.

jauh 1 far, distant, remote, far away (from the truth). *Dugaan itu*

terlalu –. That allegation is far (from the truth). *-nya* distance. *masih* – a) it's still far (away) (from where we are now). b) far from it. **2** far, by far, long, much, quite. – *lebih baik* far better. *tidak – béda dengan* not much different from. – *malam* late at night. – *sebelum itu* long before that. **3** far-reaching. *sudah – hari* for a long time. *dari* – from a distance, from afar. – *dekat* far and near. – *dicari* exaggerated. – *bumi sama laut* they are far apart. – *di mata dekat di hati* absence makes the heart grow fonder. – *di mata – di hati* out of sight out of mind. – *hari sebelum* long before. – *panggang dari api* far from the truth. – *hati* not want. **berjauh-hati** not wanting to, not feeling like, unwilling. – *malam begini* so late at night. – *pandangan/pemandangan* far-sighted. – *umur* of advanced age.

jauh-jauh 1 far away. **2** far, long. *dari* ~ long in advance, a long time ahead. ~ *hari* far in advance, long before, early on. ~ *hati* nostalgic. ~ *sebelumnya* long before then. **3** all the way. ~ *dari rumah* all the way from home. **4** no matter how far. ~ *asal selamat* it doesn't matter how far, as long as it's safe.

sejauh 1 as far as, as long as. ~ *ingatannya* as far as he can remember. ~ *mana* to what extent. ~ *mata memandang* as far as the eye can see. ~ *yang saya ketahui* as far as I know. ~ *masih ada* as long as there are. *sampai* ~ *mana* to what extent. **2** no matter how far. **3** insofar as.

sejauh-jauh 1 as far as. ~ *mata memandang* as far as the eye can see. **2** no matter how far/much. ~ "*melawan*" *dia pénsiun juga.* No matter how much he opposes it, he has to retire anyway. **sejauh-jauhnya** as far as possible.

berjauh to keep one's distance. ~ *hati* not to want to...

berjauhan far from e.o., far apart. ~ *diri* to avoid. ~ *mata* separated, far apart. ~ *tangan* not do one's share (in work).

berjauh-jauhan far from e.o., far apart.

menjauh 1 to stay (far) away, drift apart/off/away, shy away, keep one's distance. **2** to appear to be far away, disappear in the distance.

menjauhi [and **ngejauhin** (*J coq*)] **1** to keep/stay/get away from, stay off, avoid, shy away from. ~ *gula* to stay away from sugar. **2** to be/go far from, distant from.

jauh-menjauhi to keep away from e.o.

menjauhkan and **memperjauh** to remove, take away, put/keep out of the reach (of), ward off, keep s.o. away from. ~ *diri dari* a) to keep one's distance from, stay away from. b) to refrain from, avoid, abstain from.

terjauh farthest.

terjauhkan removed, taken away.

jauhan 1 distance. *dari* ~ from afar. **2** distal. **berjauhan** to be distant. *tidak* ~ *dari* not far from.

kejauhan 1 distance, remoteness. *dari* ~ from afar. **2** (*coq*) too far.

penjauhan distancing. ~ *diri dari* distancing o.s. from, refraining from, avoidance of.

jauhar (*A*) **1** jewel, gem. **2** (*ob*) sperm.

jauhari (*A*) **1** jeweler. **2** expert.

Jauza (*A*) Gemini (in the Zodiac).

Jawa I (*Skr*) **1** Java, Javanese; → JOWO. *bahasa* – Javanese. *baku* – genuine Javanese. *orang* – a Javanese. *tanah* – Java. **2** (*Jv*) knowing how to behave properly. *durung* – not yet knowing how to behave properly. **3** (in compounds) of local origin, not imported. **4** (in Jakarta and West Java refers to) Central and East Java. – *Barat* [*Jabar*] West Java. – *Tengah* [*Jateng*] Central Java. – *Timur* East Java [*Jatim*]. *jawa timuran* East Javanese.

se-Jawa all-Java.

berjawa(-jawa) to be Javanese.

nJawani (*Jv*) to have Javanese characteristics.

menjawakan 1 to translate into Javanese. **2** to Javanize.

menjawa-jawakan to Javanize.

kejawaan 1 being Javanese. **2** Javanism.

penjawaan Javanizing, Javanization.

jawa II *burung* – Blyth's hornbill, *Aceros plicatus subruficollis*.

jawab (*A*) answer, reply. *tanya dan* – question and answer, Q&A.

berjawab 1 to get a response. *panggilan* ~ a completed (telephone) call. *bak kata* ~ *gayung bersambut* in the usual way. **2** to answer, reply.

berjawab(-jawab)an to answer/respond to e.o.

menjawab to answer, reply to, respond to, react to; in response to.
menjawabi (*pl obj*) to respond/reply to, answer .
menjawabkan to answer s.t. (for s.o. else).
terjawab [and kejawab (*coq*)] answered, replied, responded to. *tidak ~* unanswerable, unanswered.
jawaban l answer, reply, response. *~ pilihan* multiple choice. 2 defense, plea. *~ tergugat* the defendant's plea.
penjawab responder, replier.
penjawaban responding, answering.
jawahir intrinsic.
jawang k.o. monitor lizard, *Varanus dumerili*.
Jawanisasi Javanization.
jawara → JUARA.
jawat → JABAT. sejawat (colleague) in the same office or the same field of work.
berjawat *~ tangan* to shake hands.
menjawat l to grasp, hold in the hand. 2 to receive, accept. 3 to hold (office); → MENJABAT.
jawatan l government office. 2 service, office (in the military), division. *~ béa dan cukai* customs and excise service. *~ géologi* geological service. *~ hukum* [Jankum] legal office. *~ imigrasi* immigration service. *~ keréta-api* the railroad. *~ keséhatan* [Jankés] health service. *~ keuangan* [janku] financial service. *- kuasa* (*Mal*) committee. *~ pajak* tax office. *~ purbakala* archeological service. *~ rahasia* secret service. menjawatankan to convert s.t. into an official office.
penjawat functionary, official; → PEJABAT.
jawawut (*Jv*) millet, *Panicum viride*.
jawén translation of the Koran (into Malay/Indonesian).
jawér (*S*) *- kotok* k.o. decorative plant used as medicine for hemorrhoids, *Coleus atropurpureus*.
jawi I (*M*) (mostly as the second member of compounds) cow, ox.
jawi II (*A*) l the Arabic script used to write Malay/Indonesian. 2 the Malayan/Indonesian homeland for Muslim pilgrims in Mecca. *~ pekan* (*Mal Sg*) an Arab or Indian Muslim.
menjawikan to translate from Arabic into Indonesian, transliterate into the Jawi script.
jawi-jawi k.o. fig tree, *Ficus benjamina/rhododendrifolia*.
jawil menjawil (*Jv*) l to touch with the finger tip. 2 to bother, annoy.
Jawza → JAUZA.
jaya I (*Skr*) l successful. 2 prosperous. 3 victory, victorious. *Dia hidup -.* He is prospering. *di masa ~ nya* in his prime. *- bumi* ground supremacy. *- jala* sea supremacy. *- kewajiban* the study of how to defeat one's enemies. *- laga* victory in combat. *- raga* bodyguard. *- sara* arms superiority. *- udara* air supremacy. *- yuda* victory in war.
sejaya as successful as.
berjaya l victorious, triumph. 2 (*Mal*) succeed, be successful.
menjayakan l to glorify, celebrate. 2 to make victorious/successful/prosperous.
kejayaan l victory. 2 supremacy. *~ udara* air supremacy. 3 glory, fame. 4 prosperity.
Jaya II [Jakarta Raya] l Greater Jakarta. 2 name of the Army division stationed in Greater Jakarta.
Jayabaya Selatan name of a train running between Jakarta and Surabaya.
jayang sekar (*Jv cla*) the name given to the cavalry recruited by Daendels from Javanese noblemen.
jayanti (*S*) k.o. forage shrub, *Sesbania sesban*.
jayarasa armament superiority.
jayéng victorious.
jayus (*BG*) not funny, stupid (of jokes).
jaza (*A*) repayment.
jazad → JASAD.
jazakumullah khairan/khoiron katsira/katsiro (*A*) may God reward you, i.e., thank you very much.
jazam (*A*) sign for apocope in Arabic writing.
jazirah and jazirat (*A*) peninsula.
jazz (*E*) /jés/ jazz.
ngejazz (*coq*) to play jazz.
menjazzkan to put into a jazz rhythm.
jeans (*E*) /jin(s)/ jeans.

jebah broad (of one's face).
jébah berjébah(-jébah) l plentiful, abundant. 2 various.
jebai berjebai to be scattered/strewn all over.
jebak trap (for animals/birds).
menjebak l to trap, capture. 2 to entrap, decoy so as to trap, lure, tempt into doing s.t. bad, frame.
menjebakkan *~ diri* to let o.s. get (en)trapped.
terjebak l trapped, snared. 2 entrapped, tricked, lured, framed.
jebakan l trap, snare, setup. *~ tank* tank trap. 2 s.t. trapped.
penjebak l trap. 2 provocateur, entrapper.
penjebakan l trapping. 2 entrapment. 3 place where s.t. is trapped.
jebang long wooden shield covered with hide.
jebar-jebur (*onom*) sound of splashing water.
jebat I (*A*) musk.
menjebat(i) to anoint.
jebat-jebatan ointments, perfumes.
jebat II → JEPAT.
jebik (lower lip) hangs down, sticks out; → CEBIK.
menjebik to hang down (or, stick out) (of lower lip).
menjebikkan to curl (the lower lip) down.
jeblak (*J/Jv*) menjeblak l to be open. 2 to tumble down.
jeblok I to sag, droop, drop, fall, decline.
jeblok II (*J/Jv*) l muddy. 2 of poor quality.
terjeblok [and kejeblok (*coq*)] stuck in the mud.
jeblos (*J*) to stop working, fail. *Rémnya -.* The brakes failed.
menjebloskan l to stick s.t. into a hole. 2 to throw (s.t., a criminal into jail). *~ para penjahat kelas kakap ke penjara* to throw the big criminals into jail.
terjeblos [and kejeblos (*coq*)] l to get stuck in a hole, fall into a trap. *~ cinta* to fall hopelessly in love. 2 cheated, tricked. 3 thrown (into prison).
penjeblosan falling (into a hole), being thrown (into prison).
jebluk (*Jv*) menjebluk to explode.
jeblus → JEBLOS.
jebobok (*Jv*) and menjebobok to stand on end (of hair), be ruffled (of feathers).
jebol (*J/Jv*) l broken down/through/into; to break down, fall apart, collapse, burst. *cepat -* falls apart quickly. 2 worn out, ruined. 3 penetrated.
menjebol l to break down, force open. *~ pintu* to break down the door. 2 to break through, penetrate. *~ pertahanan musuh* to break through the enemy's defenses. *Kakinya dijebol peluru.* His leg was riddled with bullets. 3 to destroy, tear down, demolish.
menjebolkan to break s.t. down, break through. *~ gawang lawan* to break into the opponent's goal, i.e., to score a goal.
terjebol broken down/through, into, penetrated.
jebolan l graduate (of a school or class), alumnus. *Dia hanya ~ SD kelas III.* She only got through class III of elementary school. 2 dropout. *~ sekolah* school dropout. 3 former, ex-. 4 breech, break.
penjebol s.t. or s.o. that penetrates/breaks through.
penjebolan l breaking down/through/into, incursion. 2 destruction, demolishing.
jebor roof-tile factory.
jebrét I (*onom*) clicking sound (of a stapler, etc.).
menjebrét l to make a clicking noise, click. 2 to staple.
jebrétan staple.
jebrét II scrawled, scratched.
menjebrét to scrawl, scratch.
jebrol (*J/Jv*) menjebrol l to come out all at once, erupt. *Lahar ~ dari gunung api.* Lava erupted from the volcano. 2 to be born.
menjebrolkan to produce, bring forth (young), eject (lava).
penjebrol producer, ejector.
penjebrolan producing, ejecting, ejection, expelling.
jebuh various species of marine fishes, *Dussumieria spp*.
jebul → JEBOL.
jebung I starry tiger fish, *Abalistes stellaris*.
jebung II bridge (on a prau).
jebur → CEBUR.
jeda l pause. 2 (*gram*) juncture. 3 (in poetry) caesura. 4 rest, respite, break, hiatus. *- kemanusiaan* humanitarian pause (in hos-

tilities). – *kopi* coffee break. – *larik* caesura. – *napas* breathing space. – *operasi* (*petrol*) turn-around. – *penggal* caesura. – *perang* truce.

berjeda 1 to take a break/rest. **2** intermittent. *tidak* ~ unceasing, incessant.

jedar-jedor (*Jv*) **1** again and again, over and over again. **2** loud, glaring (of colors). **3** → DAR-DOR.

jédi menjédi to indoctrinate.

jeding I (*Jv*) cistern for storing water for bathing.

jeding II (*J*) to curl upward (of lips).

jedot (*J/Jv*) **menjedotkan** and **njedotin** to bang/smash s.t. (into s.t.). **kejedot** smashed, banged.

jedul I (*Jv*) to appear suddenly.

jedul II name of a *ceki* card.

jégal (*Jv*) **menjégal 1** trip s.o. up. **2** to hamper, prevent/keep s.o. from winning, get in s.o.'s way, make s.o. fail, foil, stymie. *Posisinya sebagai Ketua MPR tidak akan digunakan untuk* ~ *pencalonannya jadi présidén.* His position as chairman of the MPR will not be used to prevent her candidacy for president. **3** to stop, intercept.

jégal-menjégal and **jégal-jégalan** to trip s.o. up, hamper, stymie.

menjégali to interfere with, stymie.

terjégal tripped up, stymied, foiled.

penjégal s.o. who hampers/trips up, etc.

penjégalan interfering with, stopping, hampering.

jegang 1 stiff, inflexible. **2** tough (of meat). **3** tense, tight.

jegat → CEGAT.

jeger (*S*) stiff, unyielding, unbending.

jéger (*Jv*) thug, young tough; → PRÉMAN.

jegil menjegil bulging, protruding (of the eyes).

terjegil bulged out.

jeglég and **jeglék** (*J onom*) clicking sound.

menjeglékkan to click, punch a hole in. ~ *kartu* to clock in (at work).

jeglékan staple.

jeglong (*Jv*) with a hole in it.

berjeglong to have holes in it.

jeglongan pothole.

jegrek (*J*) **jegrekan** build (of the body).

jegung (*naut*) sea chest (for storing ropes/rigging, etc.).

jejaban leaves or straw used as place for animals to sleep.

jejaburan → JABUR-JABURAN.

jejadian → JADI-JADIAN.

jejak I 1 track, trace, trail. **2** footprint, footstep. **3** wake (of a ship). *mencari* – *dalam air* to work hard at doing s.t. useless. – *bahu* shoulder-length. – *bara* almost touching the ground or floor. – *bumi* take-off. – *jari* fingerprint. – *kaki* footprint. – *keruh* a bad action. – *langkah* footsteps, footprint, traces. *mengikut(i)/menurut* – *langkah* to follow in the footsteps of. – *pemeriksaan* audit trail.

berjejak 1 to step foot (on), touch. *tidak* ~ *di bumi* not touching the ground. ~ *bahu* shoulder-length. **2** to leave a trace.

menjejak 1 to step (foot) on, tread on, touch. ~ *tanah* touching the ground. **2** to visit.

menjejaki 1 to step (foot) on. **2** to track (down), trace. **3** to investigate.

menjejakkan to step ... (on), put ... down. ~ *kaki* to step foot (on). ~ *roda* to land (a plane).

terjejak 1 stepped on. **2** tracked, traced.

jejakan print, footprint.

penjejak tracer, tracker. *stasiun* ~ tracking station.

penjejakan 1 stepping, treading. **2** tracking, tracing.

jejak II – *gambut* peat pot.

jejak III 1 straight, erect. **2** stable, in order.

jejaka (*J*) **1** young man; → JAKA I. **2** bachelor. – *bulukan/tua* confirmed bachelor.

jejal berjejal 1 to pack, crowd, cram, jam. **2** to be jam-packed, crowded.

berjejal-jejal 1 to throng, crowd. **2** in throngs. *Penonton* ~ *di bioskop.* The moviegoers thronged the theater.

berjejalan to throng, crowd.

menjejal 1 to patch up. **2** to stuff (full), cram.

menjejali to stuff (s.t. full of s.t.), fill. ~ *anak-anak dengan pengetahuan* to stuff children full of knowledge.

menjejalkan 1 to fill (a crack, etc. with s.t.). **2** to stuff, cram (s.t. into s.t.).

terjejal jammed, jam-packed, crowded.

jejalan throng, crowd.

penjejalan 1 thronging, crowding. **2** stuffing, patching.

jejala network; → JALA.

jejamang → JAMANG I.

jejamu → JAMU I.

jejamuan (*J*) all k.o. of *jamu*.

jejanggut awn (a cereal).

jejap (*M*) disgusting; → JIJIK.

jejari → JARI-JARI.

jejaring → JARING-JARING.

jejas (*mostly Mal*) **1** scrape, superficial wound, abrasion, lesion. **2** scraped, lacerated. *tidak* – *oléh senjata* invulnerable.

berjejas damaged, hurt.

menjejaskan to damage, harm.

jejasan damage, harm.

jejawi → JAWI-JAWI.

jejek (*Jv*) → JEJAK III. **1** straight, upright. **2** normal, standard.

jejel → JEJAL. – *riyel* chock-full, crammed, packed.

jejenang → JENANG I, II.

jejengkok small wooden stool.

jejer (*Jv*) major scene in *wayang* play.

jéjér (*Jv*) **1** series, rank. **2** standing; → JAJAR I. – *akadémik* academic standing.

sejéjér on the same line, in the same rank.

berjéjér to line up; lined up, in ranks. *berdiri* ~ to stand in a line. ~ *wayang* (*mil*) in battle array.

berjéjér-jéjér to line up. *Sehari-hari belasan mobil* ~ *menunggu pembeli.* All day long scores of cars line up waiting for buyers.

berjéjéran lined up one next to the other.

menjéjér to line up.

menjéjéri to be/get lined up with, in line with. *Ia terus melangkah* ~ *Mbak Ijah.* He kept stepping forward in line with Mbak Ijah.

menjéjérkan to line up, put in a line.

jéjéran row, line, series.

penjéjéran line-up, lining up.

jejongkong → JONGKONG II.

jejungkrak(an) razed to the ground.

jejuri (*naut*) place where a ship's helmsman stands.

jék (*E*) jack (suite of cards).

jekat → ZAKAT.

jékét (*E*) jacket.

jéksi (*D*) injection.

menjéksi to inject.

jéksian injection.

jekun → JAKUN.

jél (*E*) jail.

jéla berjéla(-jéla) to dangle, hang down and swing back and forth.

terjéla(-jéla) dangling, hanging down, sprawled (on the ground).

jelabak terjelabak to collapse, fall down.

jelabir → JABIR.

jeladan Java sparrow, *Padda oryzivora*.

jelad(e)ri (*Skr*) ocean.

jeladrén (*Jv*) dough, batter.

jelaga 1 soot, carbon black. **2** sooty (in color). – *arang* carbon deposit. – *lampu* lampblack.

berjelaga sooty, covered with soot.

jelagam ammunition.

jelagra stone cutter, sculptor.

jelah I clear; → JELAS.

jelah II vivid red.

jelai I 1 Job's tears, *Coix lacryma-Jobi*; → ENJELAI. **2** barley.

jelai II (*D*) jelly, jam; → SELAI.

jelajah I (in compounds) cruise. *peluru kendali* – cruise missile. – *alami* natural range (of fauna). – *médan* cross-country.

menjelajah to cruise, explore, travel around.

menjelajahi 1 to cruise/travel around, explore, cross (over). ~ *kepulauan Indonésia* to cruise around the Indonesian archipelago. **2** to investigate, look at closely.

menjelajahkan to look into, examine closely, investigate.

penjelajah 1 explorer. ~ *dunia* world traveler, globe trotter. ~ *hutan* forest ranger. **2** (*kapal* -) cruiser. **3** browser (on the internet).
penjelajahan 1 exploration, exploring. **2** cruising. **3** investigating.
jelajah II (*M*) **menjelajahkan** to analyze, explain in detail.
    penjelajah analyst.
    penjelajahan explanation, analysis.
jelak 1 satiated, to have had enough of s.t. **2** full (after eating); → KENYANG.
    terjelak full, stuffed, sated.
jelalat (*J*) restless, unable to stop moving or looking around.
    sejelalat ~ *mata* at a quick glance.
    jelalatan to glance/look around. *dengan mata* ~ with wandering eyes.
jelam(e)prang (*J*) *kain* - k.o. sarong with flower pattern.
jelanak menjelanak 1 to swim underwater, crawl around in the bushes. **2** to stalk, hunt undercover.
jelang I menjelang 1 approaching, prior to, just before, on the eve of, toward. ~ *akhir tahun* toward the end of the year. ~ *malam* just before nightfall. **2** to pay a call on, visit. ~ *orang tua* to pay a call on one's parents. **3** (respectful) to (in the address of a letter).
    jelang-menjelang to visit e.o.
    menjelangi to visit, go to see.
    menjelangkan just before, prior to.
jelang II (*M*) watery, thin (of liquids).
jelangak menjelangak to look upward.
jelangkung → JALANGKUNG, JAILANGKUNG .
jelantah I reused cooking oil.
jelantah II partly raw and partly cooked.
jelantik → GELATIK, JELATIK.
jelapak (*M*) **berjelapak(an)** and **terjelapak** to collapse/fall down backward.
jelapang granary, rice barn on posts.
jelar → JALAR I.
jelas 1 clear, distinct, explicit. - *dan tegas* clear and explicit. **2** cleared (of fields). **3** certain, sure, no doubt. **4** settled, resolved. *belum* - unclear. **kebelum-jelasan** lack of clarity, unclearness. *tidak* - unclear, uncertain. **ketidak-jelasan** lack of clarity, unclearness, obscurity. -*jemelas* completely clear. - *ringkas* short but clear. - *terang* clear. **menjelas-terangkan** to clarify.
    jelasnya that is to say. *hendak mengetahui* ~ wants to know the way it really is. ~ *begini* this is the way it is.
    sejelas as certain/clear.
    sejelas-jelasnya absolutely clear, as clear as clear can be.
    menjelas to become clear(er).
    menjelasi to seek clarification about s.t., look into s.t.
    menjelaskan [and **njelasin/ngejelasin** (*J coq*)] **1** to explain, elucidate, clarify, make s.t. clear, account for. *Dia harus* ~ *tindakan-tindakannya.* He has to account for his actions. ~ *secara panjang lébar* to elaborate (on). **2** to settle (debts), complete (work), resolve (a problem).
    memperjelas to make s.t. clear(er).
    terjelas clearest.
    terjelaskan *tidak* ~ unexplainable, inexplicable.
    kejelasan clarity.
    penjelas explanatory, s.t. that explains.
    penjelasan clarification, explanation, elucidation, information. ~ *belakangan* ex post facto explanation. ~ *tambahan* addendum.
jelata *si* - the man of the masses; → RAKYAT *jelata.*
jelatang 1 various species of nettles. **2** instigator, agitator. *bagai kena* - very nervous. - *di hulu air* a constant problem. - *api/gajah* (smaller and larger respectively) stinging nettle, *Laportea stimulans.* - *ayam* stinging nettle, *Laportea/Fleurya interrupta.* - *badak/rusa* k.o. climbing plant with stinging hairs, *Cnesmone javanica.*
    jelatang-jelatangan nettles.
jelatik → GELATIK.
jelau menjelau to visit unannounced.
jelawardi → LAZUARDI.
jelawat golden/maroon shark, sultan fish, *Leptobarbus hoeveni.*
jeléh (*Jv*) **njeléhi** disgusting.

jeléjéh berjeléjéhan and **menjéléjéh** to drool, dribble, slobber.
jelék (*J*?) **1** ugly, unattractive, homely. **2** bad, evil, harsh (conditions). **3** bad, of poor quality. *berpikir* - to think bad thoughts.
    jeléknya the bad thing about it is, the trouble is. *tidak ada* ~ there's nothing wrong with, there's no harm in.
    jelék-jelék it might be bad/of poor quality (but).
    sejelék as bad/ugly as.
    sejelék-jeléknya as ugly/bad as possible.
    menjeléki to sully, besmirch (s.o.'s name).
    menjelékkan [and **njelékin/ngejelékin** (*J coq*)] to sully, vilify, besmirch, denigrate.
    menjelék-jelékkan to bad-mouth, say bad things about s.o., discredit.
    memperjelék to make s.t. worse/uglier.
    terjelék the worst/ugliest.
    jelék-jelékan of poor quality.
    kejelékan 1 ugliness. **2** badness, evil. **3** poor quality, fault
jelempah menjelempah 1 to sprawl. **2** to lie scattered about.
jelengar menjelengar and **terjelengar** to be stupefied, astonished.
jelentak-jelentik to move around, not stay in one place.
jelentik (*J*) **menjelentik 1** to touch lightly with one's finger. **2** to cast aspersions on.
jeléntréh menjeléntréhkan to describe, explain.
jelepak berjelepak to abound, be plentiful.
jelepak menjelépak and **terjelépak** to fall over backward.
jelépok → JELÉPAK.
jelér (*S*) k.o. fish, barred loach, *Nemachilus fasciatus.*
jeli (*J*) **1** beautiful, ravishing, charming. *mata* - a) alluring eyes. b) the all-seeing eye. **2** observant, attentive, sharp, paying careful attention. *dengan* - carefully. *tidak* - careless. **ketidak-jelian** carelessness.
    sejeli as observant/sharp as.
    kejelian carefulness, attention paid to.
jéli (*E*) jelly, cream.
jelih protruding.
    menjelihkan to protrude, be protuberant.
jelik → JELÉK.
jelilatan → JELALATAN.
jelimet (*Jv*), **menjelimet** [and **njelimet** (*coq*)] **1** intricate, complicated, hard to understand. **2** fastidious, nit-picking.
    kejelimetan 1 intricacy. **2** fastidiousness.
jelimpat menjelimpat to go out of one's way, deviate from the normal path.
jelinap menjelinap to move furtively.
jeling menjeling to take a quick look, look out of the corner of one's eye, ogle.
    jelingan sideways glance.
jelir menjelir to stick out, protrude (of the tongue).
    menjelirkan to stick out (one's tongue).
    terjelir stuck out, protruding.
jelit I menjelitkan to insert, include.
jelit II menjelit-jelit to squirm.
jelita beautiful, pretty, lovely, charming (of women or scenery). - *juita* very beautiful.
    kejelitaan beauty, loveliness, charm.
jelma (*Skr*) **berjelmaan** to appear, manifest o.s. as.
    menjelma 1 to appear, materialize. **2** to incarnate, enter a human or animal form, transform o.s. (into). **3** to turn (into). *Sidang pléno telah* ~ *menjadi sidang istiméwa.* The plenary session turned into a special session.
    menjelmakan 1 to create, bring about. **2** to transform. **3** to (re)incarnate.
    terjelma 1 reincarnated. **2** to come about.
    jelmaan 1 (re)incarnation, metamorphosis, transformation. **2** figurehead.
    penjelmaan 1 (re)incarnation, metamorphosis. **2** formation, creation, realization, manifestation. **3** sign, indication.
jelot (*J*) **menjelot** [and **njelot** (*coq*)] to protrude, stick out.
jelotong → JELUTUNG.
jelu (*Jv*) → JELUT.
jeluak (*onom*) retching sound.
    menjeluak to retch, vomit.

jeluang bark cloth, tapa (cloth).
jeluat menjeluat to protrude, stick out (of one's tongue/eyes, etc).
jelujur I menjelujuri 1 to look into, investigate. **2** to run through. ~ *jalan-jalan* to run through the streets.
　penjelujuran 1 investigating, investigation. **2** running through.
jelujur II baste.
　menjelujur 1 to sew loosely, baste. **2** to tie/stitch things loosely together.
　menjelujuri 1 to stitch s.t. to (s.t.). **2** to tie together to (s.t.).
　jelujuran loose stitching, basting.
　penjelujuran basting, tying things loosely together.
jelujur III wooden or bamboo bar for locking a door or stable.
jeluk I deep (of plates, etc.). – *kulit* skin deep.
　menjelukkan to cup (one's hands) so as to form a hollow space.
jeluk II menjeluk to peek at.
　menjelum to wipe/bathe with a damp cloth.
jelumat menjelumat to darn.
　jelumatan darn.
jelum berjelum to wipe one's body with a damp cloth. *mandi* ~ to take a sponge bath.
jelungan (*Jv*) *bermain* – to play hide and go seek.
jelungkap menjelungkap to spring loose, recoil, rebound and straighten out again, get detached.
jeluntung and **jeluntur** chicken pox.
jelunut (*M*) sticky, viscous.
　menjelunut 1 to be sticky, glutinous, viscous. **2** to adhere, stick.
jelurai k.o. cake shaped like a net.
jelur-jelir → JELIR.
jelus (*D coq*) jealous.
　menjelusi to be jealous of.
　menjeluskan to make s.o. jealous.
　kejelusan jealousy.
　penjelus jealous person.
jelut (*J*) **menjelut 1** to have a stomach ache. **2** (*Jv*) annoyed, irritated, upset. **3** feeling low, dejected.
jelutung (– *bukit*) k.o. tree like the rubber tree, *Dyera costulata/lowii*. – *badak* k.o. shrub, *Ervatamia corymbosa*. – *laut* k.o. tree, *Euphorbia atoto*.
jém (*E*) jam, jelly.
jemaah and **jemaat** (*A*) **1** group of religious observers, congregation. **2** the public. – *haji* group of pilgrims going to Mecca. – *salaf* early Islamic times group. – *usroh* a network of Islamic study groups which urges strict implementation of Islamic law.
　berjemaah to gather together.
　menjemaahkan to bring together ... into such a group.
jemah in the future, later, in time. *di akhirat* – in the afterlife. *tidak* – will not happen, never.
Jemahat → JUM'AT.
jemajang → JAMANG I.
jemala head, skull.
jeman → JAMAN, ZAMAN.
jemang (*M*) **sejemang** a moment/short time.
jemantung → JANTUNG I.
jemari → JARI(-JARI).
jemaring → JARING-JARING.
jemawa (*cla*) **1** arrogant, conceited. **2** meddlesome.
　kejemawaan arrogance.
jemba a measure of length (*usu* two fathoms).
　menjemba to hold out the hand to grasp s.t.
　jembaan a measure of length (*usu* two fathoms).
jembak menjembak and **terjembak(-jembak)** to flutter (in the breeze).
jembalang k.o. evil spirit, gnome, or goblin that takes the form of an animal and that has the power to paralyze people.
jembar (*J*) **1** relieved. **2** (*Jv*) vast, broad, extensive.
jembatan 1 bridge. **2** connection, way of connecting two things. – *pikiran* communality of ideas. **3** (spark) gap. – *air* aqueduct. – *angkat* drawbridge. – *apung* floating bridge. – *bongkar* unloading stage. – *borstel* rocker arm. – *busur* arched bridge. – *cerocok* jetty. – *cetus api* spark gap. – *daun Semanggi* the Semanggi cloverleaf. – *emas* the best way to do s.t. – *gantung* suspension

bridge. – *gelagar* girder bridge. – *gésér* traveling platform. – *gigi tiruan* dental bridge. – *jalan* catwalk. – *jongkong* pontoon bridge. – *jungkatan/jungkit* drawbridge. – *laut* sea lift. – *layang* overpass, flyover. – *lengkung* arched bridge. – *lintas* (freeway) interchange. – *muat* loading stage. – *pelampung* pontoon bridge. – *penyalaan* spark gap. – *penyeberangan* (pedestrian) overpass. – *ponton* pontoon bridge. – *putar* swing bridge. – *rakit* floating bridge. – *saluran* aqueduct. – *semanggi* cloverleaf bridge. – *sungkitan* drawbridge. – *tali* rope bridge. – *tarik* drawbridge. – *terapung* floating bridge. – *tergenang* submerged jetty. – *timbang* weigh station.
　berjembatan with a bridge.
　menjembatani 1 to build a bridge over. **2** to bridge, act as a bridge for. ~ *jurang* to bridge the gap.
　terjembatani bridged. *sulit* – hard to bridge.
　penjembatanan 1 bridging. **2** building a bridge.
jémbél (*Jv*) very poor.
　kejémbélan poverty, squalor.
jember (*J*) dirty and humid, muddy.
jemberut → ZAMRUD.
jembiah (*Hind*) k.o. double-edged dagger.
jémblem k.o. snack made of fried cassava.
jémbrak (*J/Jv*) thick and hanging down (of facial hair or a horse's mane).
jembrana k.o. cattle disease.
jembréng (*Jv*) **menjembréng** to spread/lay out.
　sejembréng a whole bunch (of).
jembrot and **jembrut** → ZAMRUD.
jembrung (*J*) with heavy sideburns.
jembul (*J*) **menjembul** to appear, emerge.
jembung (*J*) k.o. earthen pot/mug.
jembut (*J/Jv*) pubic hair.
　berjembut with pubic hair.
jemeki (*Hind*) spangles at the edges of a garment.
jemerlang → CEMERLANG.
jemerut and **jemerud** → ZAMRUD.
jempalik → JEMPALIT.
jempalit to turn a somersault, be upside down.
　berjempalitan to turn a somersault.
　jempalitan 1 somersault. **2** topsy-turvy.
jempana (*Skr*) sedan chair, palanquin, litter.
jemparing (*Jv*) arrow. – *asmara* k.o. black magic.
jempling (*J*) **njempling** to remain silent.
jempo → JOMPO.
jempol 1 thumb. **2** first-rate, top(s), champion. – *kaki* big toe. *si* – nickname for Bank Bali.
　menjempol to fingerprint.
　jempolan 1 of top quality, first-rate. **2** with honors. *lulus* ~ to graduate with honors.
　kejempolan being first-rate/tops.
jempul → JUMPUL.
jemput I pick up. – *petugas* interview with official (in official documents).
　berjemput picked up. *datang tak* ~, *pulang tidak berantar* completely ignored.
　menjemput 1 to (go and) pick up, call for, welcome. ~ *maut* to meet one's death. **2** to pick s.t. up (from the floor, etc.), pick out, select. ~ *bola* to take the initiative. **3** to adapt. **4** to pick up, arrest.
　menjemputi to pluck/pick at s.t.
　jemputan pickup (service/car, etc.). *mobil* ~ pickup car.
　penjemput 1 s.o. who picks up or s.t. used to pick s.o. up, a pickup. *menunggu* ~ to wait for a pickup. **2** s.o. who greets and welcomes.
　penjemputan and **perjemputan 1** picking up. **2** pickup service.
jemput II sejemput a small amount of, a pinch of, a tiny. ~ *orang* a very few persons. ~ *saran* a tiny suggestion.
　menjemput to take a small amount of, pick up with the tips of the fingers.
　jemputan a pinch of.
jemput III (*M*) **berjemput** invited.
　menjemput(i) to take a man as son-in-law.

jemputan 1 invitation. **2** proposal made by female's side to male's side to be a son-in-law. **3** eligible (bachelor). *laki-laki* ~ most eligible bachelor.

jemu bored, fed up, to have had enough of s.t. *- jelak* totally fed up/bored.

jemu-jemunya *(dengan) tidak* ~ untiring.

menjemukan to bore, make s.o. fed up. *sampai* ~ *pikiran* ad nauseum.

kejemuan feeling of being bored/fed up, boredom, tedium.

jemuas smeared with dirt/filth.

jemuju caraway seed.

jemur 1 sunbathe. **2** to dry in the sun.

berjemur(-jemur) to sun o.s., take a sun bath, bask in the sun, dry in the sun.

menjemur to hang in the sun to dry. ~ *sementara hari panas* make hay while the sun shines.

menjemurkan to hang in the sun to dry for s.o. else.

terjemur [and **kejemur** (*coq*)] dried in the sun.

jemuran 1 s.t. dried in the sun, the wash, laundry. **2** drying rack. **3** staking out in the sun. *hukuman* ~ punishment by staking out in the sun.

penjemur *tali* ~ clothesline.

penjemuran 1 sunbathing. **2** drying in the sun. **3** drying rack.

jén (in acronyms) → JÉNDERAL I, II.

jenabah and **janabat** (*A*) in a state of ritual impurity.

jenaha(r) red snapper, *Lutjanus roseus/gibbus*.

jenak I moment, instant.

sejenak a few minutes/moments. *Meréka beristirahat* ~. They rested for a few moments.

berjenak-jenak for a long time.

jenak II 1 sound (asleep). **2** relaxed, at one's ease.

jenak III menjenaki to look at.

jenaka (*Hind*) humorous, amusing, funny.

berjenaka to joke, make a joke, joke around.

kejenakaan joke, humor.

jenakawan comedian, humorist.

jenakawati comedienne.

jenama (*Mal*) brand name.

jenang I uprights of door or window. *- dinding* wall post. *- pintu* door frame.

jenang II 1 aid, assistant. **2** referee (at cockfight). **3** steward (on a ship). **4** superintendent. **5** master of ceremonies. *- gelanggang* doorman. *- kapal* ship's steward.

menjenang and **menjengani** to control, oversee, supervise, referee.

penjenang 1 supervisor, foreman; adjutant. **2** referee.

jenang III (*Jv*) **1** thick porridge. **2** viscous liquid such as pudding, molten metal, wet cement. *- grendul* k.o. *kué basah* made with brown sugar, *santan*, vanilla. *- dodol* k.o. *kué basah* made with *dodol. - gula* k.o. taffy made of sticky rice, coconut, and palm sugar. *- sumsum* porridge made from rice flour and *santan*.

jenangan molten metal, wet cement, etc.

jenang IV (*ob*) **sejenang** a moment.

jenangau → CENANGAU, PIANGGANG, WALANG *sangit*.

jenasah → JENAZAH.

jenat (*Jv*) dead, deceased.

jenawi k.o. long sword.

jenayah (*A mostly Mal*) crime, criminal (*mod*).

penjenayah criminal.

jenazah (*A*) corpse, (dead) body, (mortal) remains.

menjenazahkan to bury, inter.

penjenazahan burial, interment.

jendala → CENDALA.

jendal menjendal to solidify, clot.

penjendalan ~ *darah* blood clotting.

jendal-jendul 1 not smooth on the surface, bumpy, with bumps on it. **2** to come and go.

berjendal-jendul bumpy.

jendel (*Jv*) **njendel** to become thick and solid.

jendéla (*Port*) window. *- gésér* sliding window. *- jalusi* Venetian blind. *- kisi* lattice window. *- kubah* bay window. *- kontal-kantil* flap. *- langit* skylight. *- nako* window with glass louver boards. *- pengamat* viewfinder (of camera). *- sisi* porthole. *- sorong* sliding window.

berjendéla to have a window, with windows.

jénder (*E*) gender.

jendera → CENDERA III.

jénderal I (*D mil*) **1** general. *- anumerta* posthumously promoted to general. *- berbintang 3* three-star general. **2** (*sl*) *si* – penis.

menjénderalkan to turn/hand a position over to a general. *Jabatan sipil dijénderalkan*. The civilian posts have been handed over to generals.

jénderal II (*D*) general, overall.

jendol → JENDUL.

jéndral → JÉNDERAL I.

jendul 1 protuberant, protruding. *dahi* – protruding forehead. **2** bumpy. *jalan* – bumpy road. **3** (*geol*) rise.

berjendul 1 to stick out, protrude. **2** bumpy.

menjendul to stick out, be prominent.

jendulan lump (which sticks out).

jenéla → JENDÉLA.

jeneng (*Jv*) **1** name. **2** position, status.

jenengan name.

jénéng slanting, leaning, sloping.

menjénéngkan to place s.t. in a slanting position, tilt, lean. ~ *tangga pada dinding* to lean a ladder against a wall.

jenéwer (*D*) gin, genever.

jeng (*Jv voc*) younger sister.

jengah (*J*) embarrassed, ill at ease, uncomfortable, mind. *Dia tak* – *dipanggil "mas."* He doesn't mind being called "Mas."

kejengahan embarrassment, discomfort.

jengat I → JANGAT.

jengat II (*J*) **menjengat** to surpass.

menjengatkan to stick s.t. out/forward.

jéngék I and **jengék** (*J*) **menjéngék(-jéngék)** and **menjéngéki** to ridicule, make fun of; → ÉJÉK.

jéngékan ridicule, making fun of.

jéngék II (*M*) woman who buys and sells illegal goods.

jenggala (*Skr*) forest.

jenggar (*Jv*) **1** vast, extensive, broad, roomy. **2** relieved.

jenggar-jenggur (*J*) too big (for one's age, etc.), grow up too quickly.

jénggér (*Jv*) **1** cockscomb. **2** young rooster. *- ayam* a) k.o. bush, cockscomb, *Celosia argentea*. b) a sexually transmitted disease caused by the Papiloma virus.

berjénggér to have a cockscomb.

jénggét → JÉNGKÉT.

jenggi flower parade.

jengglong (*Jv*) name of a *gamelan* instrument.

jénggot (*J/Jv*) beard; → JANGGUT I. *kebakaran* – to cry bloody murder. *- lebat* heavy beard.

berjénggot with a beard, bearded.

jénggotan 1 bearded. **2** (text) with notes written under the text; → SOROGAN.

jengguk → JENGUK.

jenggul hump, bump.

jenggur → JENGGAR-JENGGUR.

jengguut(i) to tear/pull out (one's hair); → RENGGUT.

jengit I menjengit-jengit to move up and down or back and forth (of an animal's tail/one's head).

jengit II berjengit looking startled. ~ *getir* glum-looking.

jengkal 1 span (of the hand). **2** a small quantity.

sejengkal a span. *tidak* ~ *pun* not (budge) an inch.

berjengkal-jengkal by the spans.

menjengkal(i) to measure with the palm of the hand. ~ *dada* to underestimate s.o. ~ *muka* to do s.t. useless.

jengkang menjengkang 1 to lie/fall flat on one's back. **2** (*vulg*) dead.

terjengkang and **kejengkang 1** to fall over backward, topple over. **2** (*vulg*) to die, dead.

jéngkang *- jéngkot* limping.

berjéngkang to lift one's leg.

menjéngkang 1 to stand on one leg. **2** to limp.

jengkau menjengkau 1 to reach out with the hand for s.t. **2** to touch.

jéngkék I berjéngkék(-jéngkék) 1 to jump for joy. 2 to walk on tiptoe or on high heels.

jéngkék II jig, an instrument used to separate heavy minerals from light minerals.

penjéngkékan using a jig for that purpose.

jéngkél annoyed, irritated, upset.

menjéngkéli to be annoyed at.

menjéngkélkan 1 to annoy, irritate, pester, upset. 2 annoying, irritating, upsetting.

kejéngkélan annoyance, irritation, upset.

jengkelit (Jv) menjengkelit head over heels, do a somersault.

kejengkelitan handstand, somersault.

jéngkéng I berjéngkéng and menjéngkéng to stick out, protrude.

berjéngkéngan (pl subj) to stick out.

jéngkéng II → JÉNGKÉT, JINGKAT.

jengker (J) stiff.

ngejengker (coq) to stand up straight, sit stiffly.

jengkerik → JANGKRIK I.

jengkering scarlet fever, scarlatina.

jéngkét berjéngkét, menjéngkét and ber(si)jéngkét to walk on tiptoe.

jéngki (E) (usually as the second part of compounds) Yankee, American, cowboy.

jengking I menjengking with the buttocks raised.

menjengking(kan) to turn s.t. upside down.

jengking II → KALA II.

jengkit menjengkit to curl/stand up(right), perk up.

menjengkitkan to curl/perk up (tail, ears).

jengkok (J) short bench.

jéngkol (J/Jv) k.o. vegetable, ngapi nut, Pithecolobium jiringa, which causes a bad smell in the urine of s.o. who eats it. - hutan k.o. tree with stinking edible pods, Pithecellobium ellipticum.

(ke)jéngkolan in pain when urinating from having eaten too much of this vegetable.

jéngkolét berjéngkolét, menjéngkolét and terjéngkolét to turn upside down, capsize.

jéngkot berjéngkot and menjéngkot to (walk with a) limp.

jengkrik → JANGKRIK I.

jengok → JENGUK.

jenguh → JENGUK.

jenguk berjengukan (pl subj) to peer out.

menjenguk 1 to crane one's neck to look at s.t. ~ dari jendéla to peer out the window. 2 to pay a visit (to a sick person or a condolence call).

menjengukkan to crane (one's neck) to look at s.t., stick (one's head out) to look at s.t.

jengukan visit.

penjenguk person who pays a visit to a sick person.

penjengukan visiting a sick person.

jengul menjengul to protrude, stick out. Matanya ~. His eyes protrude.

menjengulkan to stick s.t. out, make s.t. protrude.

jéni I (D) genius.

jéni II → ZÉNI I, II.

jénial (D) genius (mod).

kejénialan genius.

jénialitas genius.

jenis (A) 1 type, kind. 2 species, race. 3 (gram) gender. - darah blood type. - huruf typeface. - kata (gram) part of speech. - kelamin sex. - ragam of all sorts. berjenis-ragam of all sorts, various. - ubah variety.

sejenis of the same type/kind/species.

sejenisnya and that sort of thing, etc. dan lain-lain ~ and the like.

berjenis to be of the ... type/variety.

berjenis-jenis (of) various types/kinds/species.

menjeniskan to sort, classify into types.

kejenisan 1 sort, classification. 2 sex, gender.

penjenis classifier, s.t. that classifies.

penjenisan classification, grouping into types.

jenitri (Skr) k.o. tree, rudraksha berry, Elaeocarpus ganitrus.

jenjala (Skr) quick-tongued, talkative, bragging.

jenjam → JENJEM.

jenjang I 1 ladder, scaffolding. 2 stairs, staircase, steps. 3 stage, level, ranking, span. - pendidikan the stages of one's education. 4 gradient. 5 bench (in mining). 6 hierarchy. - kepangkatan (mil) sequence of rank. - lipat folding ladder. - organisasi table of organization. - selisih differential (of wages, etc.). - usia age level. - waktu time span.

berjenjang 1 in stages/ranks/steps/levels. 2 tiered, terraced (of rice fields). pendidikan tak ~ non-degree education. ~ naik, bertangga turun to follow the rules and regulations. 3 step by step, gradual. 4 using/with a ladder.

sejenjang a step.

berjenjang-jenjang in stages/steps/levels.

menjenjang 1 to approach (a certain age or height). Dia ~ ke usia 40. He is approaching the age of 40. 2 to hold up, support.

jenjangan 1 hierarchy. 2 span.

penjenjangan 1 grading (arranging according to difficulty). 2 staging (arranging according to stages).

perjenjangan 1 hierarchy. 2 gradation, levels.

jenjang II (Jv) long, slender (of the neck). burung - crane, brolga, Grus rubicunda.

jenjang III to hop, jump up.

jenjem calm, quiet.

jénjéng → JINJING I.

jénman /-mén/ general's yes-man.

jentai terjentai to find o.s. (in a certain position).

jentaka (Skr ob) misery, misfortune; unfortunate, miserable.

jental-jentil (J) to go up and down, in and out.

jentang mat, floor or ground covering.

jentat-jentit to stand upright.

jentat menjentat to leap, jump.

jentayu (Skr?) 1 a legendary bird in the Ramayana. 2 a legendary bird that calls for rain, a symbol of longing. seperti - menantikan hujan s.o. who longs for s.t. or s.o.

jéntelmén (E) gentlemanly, gallant, sportsmanlike.

jentera (Skr) 1 wheel, spinning wheel. 2 turbine, mill. 3 sprocket. lubang - sprocket hole. - arah hull support ring. - gigi cogwheel. - kemudi wheel (of a ship).

berjentera wheeled, with wheels.

jentét (J) menjentét to be stuck/caught; → JEPIT.

jentik I 1 pinch (of). 2 a tap (to push s.t. forward).

sejentik a pinch/small amount of.

menjentik(-jentik) 1 to pinch, tweak, nip. 2 to touch/flick lightly with the tip of the finger. 3 to scold, criticize.

menjentikkan to flick, knock off by tapping. ~ abu rokok to knock off cigarette ashes.

jentikan 1 a pinch (of). 2 reproach, criticism.

jentik II (Jv) little finger, pinky. - manis a) fleabane, Erigeron sumatrensis. b) k.o. kué basah.

jentik-jentik mosquito larvae.

jentil (J) → JENTIK I.

jenting (onom) sound of a bell.

menjentingkan to ring (a bell).

jentingan bell.

jentit → JENTIK I.

jentolak bulldozer; → BULDOSER.

jéntrét (J) row, line.

menjéntrétkan 1 to line s.t. up. 2 to stick s.t. on at the end, add s.t. on.

jentul (J) menjentul to appear, show up.

jentur I → JANTUR I.

jentur II (J) menjenturkan to smash, bang (s.t. into s.t.).

jenu (Jv) tuba (root of the Derris elliptica) used as a fish poison.

jenuh 1 to have enough/too much of s.t., fed up. 2 full. 3 saturated. tak - unsaturated. 4 burned out (of an employee). - air waterlogged.

sejenuh-jenuhnya as full/saturated as possible.

menjenuhkan 1 to satiate, make s.o. feel fed up. 2 to saturate.

jenuhan 1 sated, full. 2 saturated, waterlogged.

kejenuhan 1 leveling off, saturation. 2 fed up, had enough, overfull.

penjenuhan satiation, saturation.

jenun → JUNUN.

jepa k.o. food made from cassava.

Jepang Japan.

  men-Jepang-kan to Japanize.

jepangisasi Japanization.

jepat (*J*) and **menjepat** to come loose, get detached, be missing.

jepét → JEPIT.

jepit (*J/Jv*) 1 clip, clamp, coupling, grip, choke. 2 terminal (on battery). 3 tweezers. 4 pincers (of a shrimp). – *berpegas* spring clip. – *betina* socket (on snap fastener). – *pengaman* safety catch. – *penguat* reinforcement clamp. – *rambut* hairclip. – *selang* hose coupling. – *tekan* spring clip. – *uang* money clip.

  jepit-jepit clip, etc.; → JEPITAN.

  menjepit 1 to hold s.t. by clamping/pinching/clipping it. 2 to put s.o. in a tight spot, corner; pressing (problem).

  menjepitkan 1 to squeeze tight. 2 to clip, mount with clips/clamps, etc. 3 to put s.o. in a tight spot.

  terjepit [and **kejepit** (*coq*)] 1 squeezed, pinched. 2 in a fix/bind/tight spot, cornered, stuck, hemmed in, pinned down. **keterjepitan** being clamped, stuck in a tight spot.

  jepitan 1 clip, clamp, pin, tweezers, clothespin. ~ *dasi* tie clip. ~ *kertas* paper clip. ~ *mata ayam* grommet. ~ *rambut* hairpin. 2 (*mil*) pincer movement. 3 (*elec*) fitting.

  penjepit 1 clasp, tongs. ~ *api* fire tongs. ~ *buku* bookends. ~ *dasi* tie clasp. ~ *kertas* paper clip. 2 choke.

  penjepitan squeezing, pinching.

jeplak (*J*) **ngejeplak** to stick out (so that it can be seen).

jeprat I **jeprat-jeprét** to take snapshots.

  menjeprat to splash.

jeprat II **menjeprat** to splash.

  jepratan splash.

jeprét (*J*) 1 (*onom*) clicking sound (of taking a picture with a camera, etc.). 2 staple.

  menjeprét 1 to take a snapshot of. 2 to shoot off s.t. from a slingshot/catapult.

  menjepréti to staple.

  menjeprétkan to use s.t. to staple/take a picture/catapult.

  terjeprét [and **kejeprét** (*coq*)] taken, snapped (of a photograph).

  jeprétan 1 snapshot. 2 slingshot, catapult. 3 mousetrap. ~ *kawat* stapler.

  penjeprét ~ *kertas* stapler.

  penjeprétan 1 snapping photographs. 2 shooting off s.t. from a slingshot.

Jepun (*C? ob*) Japan; → JEPANG.

jeput I *sehari* – and *se– hari* all day long.

jeput II → JEMPUT II.

jer (*Jv*) – *basuki mawa béa* no victory without a fight, no free lunch.

jera 1 intimidated, deterred, discouraged, wary, leery. 2 to have learned one's lesson; → KAPOK I. *tiada juga –nya* incorrigible. *tidak* – unintimidated, undaunted, not put off.

  jera-jera *tidak (juga)* ~*nya* unintimidated, undaunted, not put off.

  menjera(kan) 1 to intimidate, deter, discourage, put off. *bersifat* ~ s.t. that has a chilling effect (on). 2 to teach s.o. a good lesson. 3 to be wary/leery of s.t.

  terjera intimidated, discouraged, intimidated, put off.

  penjera deterrent.

  penjeraan deterrence.

jerab → JERAP.

jerabai **berjerabai(-jerabai)** frayed, tattered.

  menjerabai to fray, tatter.

jeradik k.o. cake made from flour.

jerafah (*A*) giraffe.

jeragan → JURAGAN.

jeragih k.o. weed, *Limnophila spp*.

jerah I prevalent, in season, plentiful, abundant.

  kejerahan prevalence, being in season, being plentiful, abundance.

jerah II → JERA.

jerah III *tak –.–nya* indefatigable. – *jerih* exhausted; → JERIH.

jerahak **terjerahak** abandoned, neglected; → TERBENGKALAI.

jerahap **menjerahap** and **terjerahap** 1 to lie/fall down on one's stomach. 2 to collapse.

jerait **berjerait** to grow together/one connected to the other.

  berjerait(an) intertwined, intergrown, interwoven, tangled, climb (of a vine around a tree).

jerajak (*M*) → JERJAK.

jerak → JERA.

jeram I rapids (in a river), swift current.

jeram II **menjeram** to take a shower.

  menjerami to rain down on. ~ *musuh dengan panah* to rain arrows down on the enemy.

jeram III **jeram-jeram** k.o. fried cake.

jeram IV → JARAM I.

jeramah **berjeramah** to grab hold of and pull.

  menjeramah to grab hold of, seize, grasp.

jerambab → JEREMBAB.

jerambah open area in a house used for drying laundry, dishes.

  menjerambah(kan) 1 to use an area for that purpose. 2 to treat a woman like a servant or whore.

jerambai (*geol*) splays; → JUMBAI.

  berjerambai tasseled, fringed.

  menjerambai (*geol*) splaying out.

jerambang will-o'-the-wisp.

jerami straw, thatch, stubble.

  berjerami thatched, with straw.

jeran → JERA.

jerangau sweet flag (a medicinal herb), *Acorus calamus*.

jerangkah → CERANGGAH.

jerangkak **menjerangkak** to creep, crawl.

jerangkang **berjerangkang** 1 to stick up (of a long slender object), project upward. 2 to be stretched out with the feet sticking up.

  berjerangkangan (*pl subj*) to stick up, stretch out, project. *Tiang-tiang bendéra* ~ *sepanjang jalan.* The flag poles are sticking up along the road.

  menjerangkang to be stretched out, lie down with the limbs sticking up.

  menjerangkangkan to make s.t. stick up/out, stick s.t. in the ground so that it sticks up.

  terjerangkang fallen/standing with the limbs sticking up.

jerangkong (*Jv*) human and animal skeleton.

jerang **menjerang** to put (a pot, etc.) on the stove/fire to cook; to cook, boil (water).

  menjerangkan to heat up. ~ *air* to boil water.

  terjerang (put) on the stove/fire to cook, cooked.

  jerangan 1 cooking pot. 2 s.t. heating on the stove. *air* ~ boiling water. 3 cooked. ~ *sayur* cooked vegetables. **sejerangan** in the same pot.

  penjerangan 1 putting on the stove/fire to cook; cooking. 2 place on the stove for heating/cooking s.t.

jerapah → JERAFAH.

jerap **menjerap** to adsorb.

  terjerap adsorbed. **keterjerapan** adsorbability.

  jerapan adsorption.

  penjerap adsorbant.

  penjerapan adsorption.

jerat 1 noose, snare, lasso. 2 strap, sling. 3 trick, ruse. *pelanduk lupa akan –, tapi – tidak melupakan pelanduk* the debtor may forget about the lender but not vice versa. *tahan – sorong kepala* to get o.s. into trouble. – *halus kelindan sutera* a subtle trick. – *semua bunda kandung* a spoiled only child. *menahan – di tempat genting* to gain from another person's misfortune. – *angkat* sling. – *hukum* indictment. – *semata* favorite child.

  sejerat a bunch of. ~ *bunga* a bunch of flowers.

  menjerat 1 to snare, trap. 2 to snarl, tangle. 3 to trick, deceive. 4 to inveigle, try to bring s.o. in on s.t., entice. 5 to indict. *Ia akan dijerat dengan keterangan palsu.* He will be indicted on charges of perjury.

  terjerat [and **kejerat** (*coq*)] 1 snared, trapped, entangled. 2 tricked, fooled.

  jeratan trap, snare. ~ *pasir* sand trap (in golf).

  penjerat trapper, s.o. who entraps.

  penjeratan 1 trapping, snaring. 2 strangulation.

jerau shiny red, deep red, florid.

  menjerau to turn florid.

jeraus nimble, agile, sprightly.
  menjerauskan to make s.o. nimble/agile.
jerawat pimples, acne, pustule, rash. – *batu* large hard pimple. – *nasi* pus pimple.
  berjerawat pimply.
  jerawatan pimply, acned.
jerawut → JRAWUT.
jerba I menjerba to pounce on.
jerba II menjerba to turn (a boat) over on its side.
jerbak menjerbak flapping.
Jerbar [Jerman Barat] West Germany.
jerejak → JERJAK.
jerékét sticking together (of the eyes with sleep or due to an eye disease).
jeremak → JEREMBAK.
jeremang → JERMANG.
jerembab menjerembab to throw o.s. forward/headlong.
  menjerembabkan 1 to make s.t. or s.o. fall forward. **2** to smash s.t.
  terjerembab to fall forward/headlong.
jeremba menjeremba to put/stick one's hand out to grab hold of s.t.
jerembak berjerembak, menjerembak and **terjerembak** to run into by accident, collide with.
jerembap → JEREMBAB.
jerémbat terjerémbat to stumble, trip, get one's foot tangled in s.t., slip at the edge of s.t.
jerémbét 1 growing together to form a single one (of fingers/bananas). **2** intertwined, linked together.
jerembun terjerembun to loom up before one's eyes.
jerempak → JEREMBAK.
jerémpét → JERÉMBÉT.
jeremuk (*J*) **terjerumuk** absorbed (in thought).
jéréng I (*J*) (*ber*)*mata* – cross-eyed.
jéréng II (*Jv*) **menjéréng** to spread (cloth, etc.) out.
jerepak → JEREMBAK.
jerépét 1 linked together (such as the links in a chain), attached to e.o., tied together; → JERÉMBÉT. **2** growing together (such as fingers, etc.).
  berjerépét linked/connected together.
  jerépétan being attached to e.o., coalescence.
jeri 1 frightened, afraid (to do s.t.), nervous (about doing s.t.). *Hatinya merasa* –. He was afraid. **2** to hesitate.
  menjerikan worrisome, fearsome.
jeriau rafter, spar, joists of a house. *tiba di rusuk* – in the proper place.
  menjeriau to put up rafters, etc.
jérigén and **jériként** (*E*) jerry can.
  berjérigén with a jerry can.
jerih tired, exhausted, weary. *obat – pelerai demam* a much-loved child. – *lelah/payah* hard work; very tired, exhausted. *berjerih-lelah/payah* to exhaust o.s. (trying to do s.t.).
  berjerih-(jerih) to wear/tire o.s. out.
  menjerihkan 1 to tire/exhaust/fatigue. **2** tiring, fatiguing.
  memperjerihkan 1 to work hard at s.t. **2** to make s.o. work hard at s.t.
  kejerihan 1 weariness, exhaustion. **2** overly exhausted.
jeriji I finger. – *kaki* toe.
jeriji II → JERUJI.
jériként (*E*) jerry can.
jerimbing k.o. plant.
jering I monkeywood, *Pithecellobium jiringa/lobatum*. – *tupai/utan* k.o. tree, *Pithecellobium ellipticum*.
jering II (*onom*) sound made by a cricket.
  menjering(-jering) to make that sound.
jeringai → SERINGAI.
jeringau → JERANGAU.
jeringing → SERINGAI.
jerip → GERIP I.
jerit 1 scream, shriek, shout. **2** clamor, clamoring, complaining. – *kematian* death rattle. – *pekik* cries.
  berjeritan (*pl subj*) to scream, shriek.
  menjerit 1 to yelp, scream, screech, shriek. **2** to whine, complain.
  menjerit-jerit to yell bloody murder.

menjeritkan to scream/shout s.t. *Beliau kemudian* ~ *tiga kali slogan "Merdéka!"* Then he shouted out the slogan "Merdéka" three times.
  terjerit-jerit to scream, screech, shriek. ~ *bagai kucing biang* said of a woman who talks too loudly, to scream like a fishwife.
  jeritan 1 scream, screech, shriek. **2** whining, complaint.
  penjerit 1 screamer, s.o. who screams frequently. **2** siren.
jerjak 1 trellis, bars. **2** stud (in house). **3** bamboo stays in a basket, etc. **4** ribs. – *jembatan* railing (of a bridge).
  berjerjak barred, with bars, with a railing, ribbed, studded.
jerjat → DERAJAT.
jerkah nasty words, snarl, growl.
  berjerkah-jerkahan to snarl/growl at e.o.
  menjerkah to snarl/growl at.
jerkat young areca nut eaten with betel leaf.
jermal 1 tunnel net (k.o. fish trap). **2** off-shore fishing platform.
Jerman (*E*) German. – *Barat* West Germany.
jermang props for holding up a boat on the beach.
  be(r)jermang having/with such props. *patah tongkat* ~ never gives up (even after many failures).
jernang 1 dragon's blood, a red resin from the fruit of the dragon's blood palm, *Daemonorops draco*, which is used to make a dye. **2** fraise (in color).
  berjernang with/having dragon's blood.
jernih 1 clear (of a liquid/thinking), not cloudy/murky. **2** cloudless (of the sky). **3** shining (of countenance), not despondent. **4** calm, peaceful, not nasty (of thoughts). **5** settled, cleared up, resolved. *air – ikannya jinak* if you are prosperous, you will be kind to strangers.
  sejernih as clear as.
  menjernih to turn clear/cloudless, etc.
  menjernihkan 1 to (make) clear. **2** to calm down (one's thoughts/ the situation). **3** to clear up, straighten out (s.t. confusing). **4** to purify, cleanse.
  memperjernih to make s.t. clearer.
  kejernihan clarity, purity, being clear.
  penjernih s.t. used to purify/clarify/clear up, etc., purifier. ~ *air* water purifier.
  penjernihan 1 purification, purifying, clearing, treating (waste to purify it). ~ *air* water purification. **2** (*petrol*) decolorizing. **3** place where water is treated.
  perjernihan clearing up, becoming clear.
jeroan (*Jv*) entrails, viscera, intestines (of slaughtered animals). – *unggas* giblets.
jerobong an awning for protection of cargo on a boat.
jerohok terjerohok to sink down (into).
jerojol menjerojol and **terjerojol** to protrude, stick out (of). *Beras menjerojol dari kantongnya.* The rice was sticking out of the sack.
jerongkang – *jerongkong* to fall backwards. – *korang* to run head over heels.
  terjerongkang to lie stretched out on the ground.
jerongkés → JERUNGKIS.
jerongkok berjerongkok and **menjerongkok** to squat with the knees touching the chin.
  menjerongkok to squat.
jerongkong menjerongkong to bend down with hands on knees.
  terjerongkong to fall face down.
jerpak → JEREMBAK.
Jertim [Jerman Timur] East Germany.
jerubung → JEROBONG.
jeruji 1 trellis, bar. **2** grating, iron bars. **3** spoke.
  berjeruji barred, grated, spoked.
jeruju k.o. tidal shrub, *Acanthus ebracteatus/ilicifolius*.
jeruk citrus fruit. – *asam/asem/sitrun/sukade/tangan* citron, *Citrus medica*. – *Bali/besar* pomelo, shaddock, *Citrus grandis/maxima*. – *bodong* sour lime. – *cina* ichang lime, *Citrus ichangensis*. – *delima* pink pomelo, *Citrus maxima*. – *Garut* k.o. tangerine. – *jamblang* shaddock, *Citrus grandis*. – *jepun* kaffir lime, *Citrus nobilis*. – *katés* citron, *Citrus medica*. – *keprok/kepruk* mandarin orange, *Citrus nobilis*. – *keriput* k.o. grapefruit. – *kesturi/peres* golden lime, kalamansi lime, *Citrus madurensis/microcarpa*. – *kingkit* key lime, *Triphasia aurantifolia*. – *limau* kaffir lime,

Citrus nobilis/amblycarpa. – *macan* → JERUK *delima.* – *manalagi* k.o. pomelo. – *manis* (sweet) orange, *Citrus aurantium/sinensis.* – *nipis/pecel/tipis* lime, *Citrus aurantifolia.* – *pandan* k.o. pomelo. – *papaya* → JERUK *asam.* – *peras* tangelo. – *purut* Kaffir lime, *Citrus hystrix.* – *sambal* small citrus fruit, leprous lime, *Citrus amblycarpa.* – *siam/siyem* tangerine. – *sinas-apel* imported orange.

menjeruk(i) to pickle.

perjerukan citrus (fruit) (*mod*). *di bidang* ~ in the citrus field.

jerukun menjerukun to cover up, close.

jerukup → RU(NG)KUP.

jerum (*Jv*) **menjerum** to lie down (of animals).

jerumat berjerumat darned, mended.
  menjerumat to darn, mend.
  jerumatan 1 s.t. darned/mended. **2** darn, mend.
  penjerumat darning needle.
  penjerumatan darning, mending.

jerumbai → JERABAI, BERJUMBAI-JUMBAI.

jerumbun → JEREMBUN.

jerumbung → JEROBONG, JERUBUNG.

jerumun 1 hut used for shelter, hide-out. **2** wild pigs' lair.

jerumus menjerumuskan 1 to make s.o. or s.t. fall down, plunge. **2** to bring disaster to, disgrace.
  terjerumus [and **kejerumus** (*coq*)] **1** to fall flat on one's face, fall into a trap. **2** fallen/plunged (into sin/hard times, etc.).
  penjerumusan plunging.

jerun turtle dove, *Streptopelia chinensis tigrina.*

jerunang k.o. herbaceous plant, *Languas conchigera.*

jerung great white shark, *Carcharias dussumieri.* – *tenggiri* hammerhead shark, *Sphyrna spp.*

jerungkau menjerungkau to hang down and cover s.t. (of hair, branches of a tree).

jerungkis bent/curved upward.
  menjerungkis to break, destroy.
  terjerungkis broken, destroyed.

jerungkung menjerungkung to bow (the body or head).

jerungkup → JERUKUP, RU(NG)KUP.

jerunuk terjerunuk to fall down, collapse.

jerupih (*naut*) a board added to the side of a boat to increase its height.

jés (*onom*) puffing sound made by a locomotive.

jésbén (*E*) jazz band.

jét (*E*) jet. – *pancar gas* turbo-jet.

jéti (*BG*) from the English names of the letters *jt*, the abbreviated form of *juta*) million; → JUTA.

jetis menjetis to make a loud banging noise.

jétisasi switching over to the use of jets.

jét-sét (*E*) **1** jet set. **2** sophisticated.

jéwang menjéwang to grab, snatch, pick up quickly.

jewawut → JAWAWUT.

jéwér (*Jv*) **menjéwér 1** to box s.o.'s ear. **2** to reprimand, scold.
  jéwér-menjéwér to reprimand e.o.
  jéwéran 1 boxing s.o.'s ear. **2** reprimand, scolding.

ji I (*C*) two.

ji II (in acronyms) → PENGKAJIAN.

jiarah → ZIARAH.

jiawang k.o. monitor lizard, *Varanus dumerili.*

jib (*E*) jib.

jibaku (*Jp*) suicide attack.
  berjibaku 1 to make a suicide attack. **2** to do s.t. reckless.

jibakutai (*Jp*) suicide squadron.

jibilah, jibilat and **jiblah** (*A*) **1** nature, predisposition. **2** aptitude, talent; → BAKAT II.

Jibor Jakarta Interbank Offered Rate.

Jibrail and **Jibril** (*A*) the angel Gabriel who brings God's messages to the prophets.

jibun (*J*) lots of debts.
  berjibun 1 to pile up, teem, swarm (all over). **2** with lots of debts.

jicap (*C J*) twenty.

jicapgo (*C J*) twenty-five.

jicing (*C*) ash in a pipe from burning opium, opium dross.

jidal I (*A*) thimble.

jidal II (*A*) argue, debate.

jidar (*A*) **1** lines forming a border on a page. **2** ruler (for drawing lines). – *hitung* sliderule.
  menjidari to draw lines on.

jidat (*A J*) forehead.

jidor and **jidur** (*Jv*) k.o. drum; → TANJIDUR.

jidwal → JADWAL.

jigo (*C J*) twenty-five (rupiahs).

jigoban (*C J*) twenty-five thousand (rupiahs).

jigong (*J* C?) **1** plaque/tartar on teeth. **2** slob, dirty person.
  berjigong to have tartar, plaque, or other foreign matter on one's teeth.

jigrak menjigrak to stand up (of the hairs on one's head).

jih (*ob*) target (in certain games).

jihad (*A*) holy war, crusade.
  berjihad to wage a holy war.

jihandak [penjinak bahan peledak] *tim* – bomb squad.

jihat (*A*) side, direction.

jihin → JIN I.

jiitméh (*C*) end of the *Cap Go Méh* celebration, the 21st day of the first month in the Chinese calendar.

jijak → JEJAK I.

jijat → JIDAT.

jijay (*Pr*) disgusted; disgusting. – *bajay* very disgusting.

jijik 1 disgusting, revolting, nauseating. **2** loathsome, detestable. **3** disgusted, revolted. *Saya* – *melihat bangkai.* I felt disgusted looking at the corpse.
  sejijik as disgusting as.
  menjijiki 1 to disgust, nauseate. **2** disgusting, nauseating.
  menjijikkan 1 to disgust, revolt, nauseate. **2** loathsome, sickening.
  kejijikan 1 disgust. **2** filthiness. **3** to feel disgust(ed).

jijit → JINJIT I.

jika 1 if, in the event of, in case. **2** when (in the future or in general); → KALAU. – *dia tidak datang* if he doesn't come. – *ada* if any. – *kiranya* supposing, if … were, if by any chance. – *sekalipun* even if. – *tidak* unless, if not. **3** that. *Dia membantah keras* – *penyanyi dangdut yang lagi naik daun karena goyang ngebor-nya adalah maskot partainya.* He strongly denied that the *dangdut* singer, who has become famous due to her gyrations, is the emblem of his party.
  menjika to say "if."

jikalau → JIKA. **menjikalau** to say "if."

jikir → ZIKIR.

jil I (*E*) jail, prison.

JIL II → JARINGAN *Islam Liberal.*

jilah all gone, finished. – *kening* elated, in high spirits.

jilam (*M*) **menjilam(i)** to lick (one's lips).

jilat lick, lap up, suck.
  menjilat 1 to lick/lap up (with the tongue). ~ *bibir* a) to lick one's lips (in anticipation of good food, etc.). b) to give s.t. serious consideration. ~ *ludahnya/air liurnya* a) to eat one's words. b) to praise s.t. previously scorned. **2** to lick (at). *Api* ~ *toko di Senén.* The fire licked at the stores in Senen. **3** to curry favor. ~ *pantat* to brown-nose, kiss ass, curry favor with a superior.
  jilat-menjilat to suck e.o.
  menjilat-jilat 1 to keep on licking at. ~ *bibir* to lick one's chops. **2** to keep on ass-kissing (one's superior).
  menjilati [and **njilatin/ngejilatin** (*J coq*)] **1** (*pl obj*) to suck, lick. **2** to lick (off). ~ *periuk nasi* to lick off the bottom of the rice pot.
  jilatan 1 lick, lapping, licking. ~ *mata* glance. **2** s.t. that is licked.
  penjilat 1 licker. **2** ass-kisser. ~ *pantat* ass-kisser, brown-noser.
  kepenjilatan ass-kissing, brown-nosing.
  penjilatan 1 licking, lapping. **2** ass-kissing.

jila terjila sprawled on the ground (like a corpse); → JELA.

jilatisme ass-kissing, brown-nosing.

jilbab (*A*) Muslim woman's head covering that exposes only the face.
  berjilbab to wear such a head covering.

jilid (*A*) **1** binding. **2** a volume. *Buku ini terdiri atas dua* –. This book consists of two volumes. – *kedua* volume two. *tukang* – bookbinder. – *kawan* companion volume. – *spiral* spiral binding.
  sejilid a volume.
  berjilid bound (of a book, etc.).

berjilid-jilid in volumes, by the volume.
menjilid to bind (a book, periodicals).
menjilidkan to have s.t. bound.
terjilid bound.
jilidan 1 s.t. bound, a bound book. **2** binding.
penjilid bookbinder.
penjilidan (book)binding.
jim (*A*) name of the fifth letter of the Arabic alphabet.
jimak (*A*) sexual intercourse/relations.
  berjimak and **menjimak** to have sexual intercourse/relations.
  menjimaki to have sexual intercourse/relations with.
jimat I (*A*) → AZIMAT I.
jimat II (mostly *Mal*) → HÉMAT I.
jimbit sejimbit a pinch (of).
  menjimbit to pick up an object with the fingers.
jimbul → JEMBUL.
jimpit (*Jv*) **sejimpit** a pinch (of).
  menjimpit to take a pinch with one's fingertips.
  jimpitan a pinch (of s.t. using the thumb and two fingers).
jin I (*A*) genie, a type of spirit (between angels and humans). *tempat – buang anak* a haunted place. *– botol* alcoholic beverages. *– gundul* "bald-headed spirit," it is said that s.o. in possession of this spirit can make use of it "to obtain a treasure-trove." *– iprit* k.o. evil spirit.
jin II (*D/E*) gin.
jin III (*Hind*) saddle.
jin IV and **jins** (*E*) jeans.
jina(h) → ZINA.
jinabat (*A*) → JANABAH.
jinah (*A*) **menjinahi** to commit adultery with. *~ seorang gadis di bawah umur* to commit adultery with an underage girl. *orang yang dijinahi tersangka* the person violated by the suspect; → ZINA.
jinak 1 tame, domesticated. *Kucing adalah binatang yg –.* Cats are domesticated animals. **2** not shy/timid/bashful. *Anak itu sekarang sudah –.* That child is now no longer shy. **3** gentle, meek, docile. **4** moderate (in politics), not revolutionary. *kaum nasionalis yang –* moderate nationalists. **5** benign (of a tumor). *tumor – benign* tumor; *opp* TUMOR *ganas.*
jinak-jinak *~ lalat* s.o. who seems to be friendly but really isn't. *~ merpati* seemingly friendly and easy to get to know but actually isn't (*usu* said about women), coy. **berjinak-jinak merpati** to act coy.
sejinak as tame as.
sejinak-jinaknya no matter how tame.
berjinak-jinak(an) (*dengan*) to be on intimate terms with.
menjinaki to approach in order to get on friendly terms with.
menjinakkan and **memperjinak 1** to tame/domesticate a bird/animal, etc., housebreak. *~ gajah* to tame an elephant. **2** to restrain, subdue, curb, get under control, contain, defuse (a bomb). *~ api di sumur gas* to contain the fire in a gas well. *~ bom* to defuse a bomb.
penjinak tamer, s.t. that keeps s.t. under control. *~ singa* lion tamer. *instalasi ~ air limbah* waste water treatment plant. *tim ~ bahan peledak* bomb squad. *tim ~ bom* bomb squad, ordnance disposal team.
penjinakan 1 taming, domestication, domesticating. **2** getting s.t. under control. *~ kali Pesanggrahan* keeping the Pesanggrahan river within its banks. **3** (*euph*) imprisonment.
jinan (*A*) fairyland.
jinas (*A*) pun.
jinawi (*Jv*) fertile, prosperous.
jinayah and **jinayat** (*A*) criminal matters; → JENAYAH.
jinazah → JENAZAH.
jindra k.o. musical instrument in the *gamelan*.
jineman (*Jv*) watchman at a sugarcane plantation.
jineng rice barn.
jinerap absorbent; → SERAP.
jinganan (*J*) it's too bad (that). *wah – banget* it's really too bad that …
jingap → JINGAU.
jingau (*M*) **menjingau** to peer at.

jingga orange, reddish orange.
  menjingga to turn orange.
jingg(e)ering (*Jv*) with high heels (of shoes), with a long stem (of a glass).
jinggi red sandalwood, *Pterocarpus santalina.*
jingjing → JINJING I.
jingkat *– langkah-lompat* a hop, skip and a jump.
  berjingkat 1 to stand on tiptoe. *lari-lari ~* to run on tiptoe. **2** to jump (for joy).
  berjingkat-jingkat, bersejingkat and **bersijingkat** to stand/walk on tiptoe.
  menjingkat to stand/walk on tiptoe.
  menjingkatkan to raise (one's feet) on tiptoe.
  terjingkat(-jingkat) to walk on tiptoe.
  jingkatan jump.
jingkau → JANGKAU.
jingkék 1 tiptoes. **2** high-heeled shoes.
  berjingkék 1 to stand on tiptoe. **2** to wear high-heeled shoes.
jingkik berjingkik-jingkik to hop on one leg.
jingklak → JINGKRAK.
jingkol → JÉNGKOL.
jingkrak (*J/Jv*) **jingkrak-jingkrakan** to jump around, gambol.
  berjingkrak-jingkrak to jump up and down, jump (for joy).
  berjingkrakan (*pl subj*) to jump for joy.
  menjingkraki to jump around on, gambol on.
jingkrat (*J*) **berjingkrat** to get up, arise.
jingoisme (*D/E*) jingoism.
jinjang I 1 manager, leader, head. **2** k.o. shaman who controls evil spirits.
  berjinjang to have a manager, be managed.
  menjinjang to manage, head, lead.
  jinjangan 1 management. **2** leader, head. **3** (*ob*) person who escorts the royal herald. (*ob*) *~ raja* king's shaman who protects him from ghosts and spirits.
jinjang II tapering, tall and slender.
jinjang III → JENJANG I.
jinjing I menjinjing to carry/hold s.t. light in the hand/with the arm hanging down or stretched out. *ringan sama dijinjing, berat sama dipikul* to share the good and the bad. *bertangkai boléh dijinjing* a clear situation.
  menjinjingi (*pl obj*) to carry s.t. in the hand.
  menjinjingkan to carry s.t. light that way for s.o. else.
  terjinjing 1 carried in that way. *tas ~* a bag that is carried. **2** portable.
  terjinjingkan portable.
  jinjingan 1 s.t. light carried in the hand. **2** strap for carrying s.t.
  berjinjingan with a strap for carrying.
jinjing II *kayu –* k.o. tree used for lumber, *Albizzia moluccana.*
jinjing III → JINJIT I.
jinjit I (*Jv*) **1** to stand/walk on tiptoe. **2** with high heels (of shoes).
  berjinjit(-jinjit) to stand on tiptoe.
  menjinjit(kan) to use s.t. to stand on tiptoe.
jinjit II menjinjit to lift or carry s.t. in the hand/with the arm hanging down or stretched out; → MENJINJING.
jinjit III menjinjit 1 to box s.o.'s ear; → MENJÉWÉR. **2** to massage, pull on s.t. flexible.
jinlépis Levy jeans.
jinn → JIN I. Name of the 72nd chapter of the Koran.
jins → JEANS.
jinséng, jinsom, and **jinson** (*C*) ginsom, k.o. medicinal root;
jintan caraway seeds, *Carum carui/roxburghianum. – hitam/ireng* (*Jv*) black caraway/cumin seeds, *Nigella sativa. – manis* aniseed, *Pimpinella anisium. – putih* white cumin, *Cuminum cyminum.*
jinten → JINTAN.
jintong (*C*) → EMPÉK.
jip (*E*) jeep.
jipang I (*M*) branch, twig.
jipang II (*Jv*) bottle gourd, *Sechium edule;* → LABU *siam.*
jipang III shield covered with animal skin.
jipang IV snack made from glutinous rice and caramel or syrup, k.o. puffed rice cake.
jipang V war axe.

jipéng [tanjidor topéng] k.o. Betawi theater.

jipér (BG) scared.

jiplak (Jv) menjiplak 1 to copy, cheat by copying. 2 to plagiarize. 3 to trace (by placing one sheet of paper on top of another and tracing what is on the lower one).

   terjiplak copied, plagiarized.

   jiplakan copy, duplicate, extract; s.t. plagiarized.

   penjiplak 1 copying machine. 2 plagiarist, s.o. who copies from s.o. else.

   penjiplakan copying, cheating by plagiarism.

jiprat → CIPRAT.

jipro (D ob) ma'm, term of address for a teacher.

jir → JIH.

jirafat → JERAPAH.

jirak k.o. bush and its edible fruit, Eurya acuminata/japonica.

   menjirak ~ kelopak to bud, be in full bloom.

jiran (A mostly Mal) neighbor.

   sejiran kawan ~ close friend.

   berjiran to be neighbors, neighboring, adjacent. hidup ~ to live as neighbors.

   jiranan neighborhood.

jirangkong → JERANGKONG.

jirat I (A) grave, tomb; → ZIARAH. membuang bunga ke – to do s.t. useless.

jirat II → JERAT.

jirian leucorrhea, white vaginal discharge.

jirigén → JÉRIKÉN.

jiring (bio) loment.

jirjir (A) bean.

jirolu (Jv) [siji loro telu] one, two, three.

jirus I → DIRUS.

jirus II → TIRUS.

jis (abbr) [junctis] in conjunction with; pl of juncto.

ji-sam-su (C) two-three-four, brand name of a kréték cigarette.

jisim (A) 1 body. 2 (phys) mass. – penangkis antibody.

jismani → JASMANI.

jit (C J) seven.

jitah k.o. plant with roots that twine around supports, Willughbeia tenuiflora/apiculata.

jitak (J) blow on the head, slap on the face.

   menjitak to hit s.o. on the head, slap on the face.

jitok (Jv) nape of the neck.

jitpék (C J) seven hundred.

jitu (C?) definite, precise, accurate, exact, direct (hit).

   menjitukan to do s.t. exactly/precisely.

   kejituan exactness, precision.

jiwa (Skr) 1 soul, spirit. –nya melayang. He died. 2 the animating spirit behind s.t. 3 person, human being. 4 sweetheart, darling. –ku my darling. bertukar – dengan semangat in love. hutang – bayar – an eye for an eye and a tooth for a tooth. –nya tergantung pada seutas benang or di ujung rambut his life hangs on a thread. – budak slavishness. – (dan) raga body and soul. kejiwaragaan psychosomatic. – kecuak a) cowardly person. b) worthless person, scum. – korps esprit de corps. – ksatria chivalry. – laras bore (of a gun). – yang séhat a healthy mind.

   sejiwa with the same spirit, in the spirit of. ~ dengan perjanjian in the spirit of the agreement.

   berjiwa 1 to have a spirit, animated, spirited. 2 soulful. 3 to be alive, active, still alive. 4 to have the spirit of. Meréka yang ~ muda. The young in heart. ~ sosial sociable.

   menjiwai to animate, give life to, inspire, be the inspiration behind.

   kejiwaan 1 psychological. 2 spiritual.

   penjiwa and penjiwai (infr) inspirer.

   penjiwaan 1 inspiring, inspiration. 2 animism.

jiwani 1 spiritual. 2 psychological.

jiwasraya life insurance (from the name of an insurance company).

jiwat Java plum, Eugenia cumini.

jiwatman [jiwa atman] spirit and soul.

jiwit (Jv) menjiwit to pinch.

jizyah (A) tax levied on non-Muslims under Islamic rule.

jjs (BG) [jalan-jalan santai/soré] to hang out, take a stroll.

jl- also see entries beginning with jel-.

jlamprang → JELAMP(E)RANG.

jlegur (Jv) explosion.

jléntréh (Jv) explanation, clarification.

   menjléntréhkan to explain lucidly, expound, set forth, state, express in words.

   penjlétréhan explanation, clarification.

jlimet (Jv) 1 fastidious. 2 intricate, detailed. 3 sophisticated.

jo I (abbr) [juncto] /yungkto/ (L leg) in conjunction with, along with. Keputusan Présidén Nomor 35 Tahun 1973 – Keputusan Présidén Nomor 19 Tahun 1983 tentang Badan Perencanaan Pembangunan Nasional Presidential Decision Number 35 of 1973 in conjunction with Presidential Decision Number 19 of 1983 concerning the National Development Planning Board.

jo II (Min) personal pronoun of the second-person singular you.

joak → JUAK-JUAK.

joang → JUANG.

joan(g)lo (C) food warmer.

jobak berjobak (one's stomach) is growling/making noises.

joblos (J) terjoblos [and kejoblos (coq)] driven/stepped into a hole/ditch; → JEBLOS.

jobong I (J) whore.

jobong II and jobongan (Jv) k.o. (irrigation) aqueduct made of clay.

jodang (Jv) an oblong wooden trough for food, plates, etc. that hangs on a carrying pole, in front and at the end of which is a carrier.

jodo and jodoh (Tam) 1 mate, marriage partner. –nya telah habis to be divorced. 2 to match, be a mate. 3 intended/meant for s.o., i.e., the right one (in love, etc.). 4 to agree. tidak – not agreed on.

   sejodoh 1 a pair (of horses/husband and wife/man and woman), a twosome, a couple. 2 to be well matched. ~ bagai cincin well-matched.

   berjodoh 1 to be married. ~ dengan to be married to 2 paired off.

   berjodohan to get married to e.o.

   menjodohi to pair off (with).

   menjodohkan and memperjodohkan 1 to marry s.o. off, make a match between two people. 2 to pair (off) two things. 3 to mate (animals).

   jodohan 1 to live together as husband and wife without being married. → KUMPUL kebo, SAMENLÉVEN. 2 matched.

   kejodohan accord.

   penjodoh s.t. that matches, matching.

   penjodohan matching.

   perjodohan 1 wedding, marriage, wedlock. 2 match, pair, mate. ~ yang sumbang misalliance.

jodong to curl one's lips up (in an insulting way).

   menjodongkan to purse (one's lips).

jogan (cla) → COGAN.

jogar (Port) game of checkers.

   berjogar to play checkers.

jogét (Jv) 1 a dance. 2 dancing girl. 3 to dance.

   berjogét and menjogét to dance this dance.

   penjogét s.o. who dances this dance.

jogi (Skr) yogi.

joging (E) jogging.

jog-jogan (Jv) gratuities, handouts.

joglo (Jv) a traditional Javanese roof shape.

jogo → KACANG jogo.

jogoboyo (Jv) village police official.

jogotirto (Jv) village irrigation official.

jogrog and jogrok (J) ngejogrok and njogrok 1 to appear/emerge/turn up all of a sudden. 2 to be in the way. 3 to stand still and do nothing, not move, break down, hang out.

   ngejogrokkan and ngejogrokin to shove s.t. in front of.

   jogrokan build, physique, figure.

johan (Pers) 1 world. 2 champion, hero. Syah – King of Kings. – arifin the smartest of the smart, man of the world. – Budian Till Eulenspiegel. – pahlawan world champion, hero. – tinju boxing champion.

Johar I bintang – Venus; → ZOHRAT, ZUHARA.

johar II → JAUHAR.

johar III (*Jv*) *pohon* – k.o. tree, Siamese senna, *Cassia siamea*, that can reach a height of 20 meters, *usu* planted as a shade tree or hedge plant; the leaves are used against malaria.

johari (*A cla*) **1** jeweler. **2** (*poet*) expert, clever, specialist; → JAUHARI.

Johobu (during the Japanese occupation) Intelligence Agency.

jojing → AJOJING.

jojol barrier, palisades (in rivers), pilings.

menjojol to be projecting, jutting out, protrude.

terjojol protruding (of eyes), sticking out, protruding.

Jojon epithet for the police women in the *Sabhara* units.

jok (*C*) **1** seat (of a car/pedicab, etc.). **2** upholstery (of car). – *belakang* rear seat. – *kursi* upholstery. – *muka* front seat.

berjok with/to have a seat. *taksi* ~ *mérah* a cab with red seats. ~ *tunggal* single-seater.

joki I (*E*) jockey (in horse racing). – *disko/piringan hitam* disc jockey, D.J.

menjokikan to turn s.o. into a jockey.

perjokian jockeys' (*mod*).

joki II (*E*) **1** a State University student who takes a test for another student in the *Sipenmaru* test, ringer; → MASKOT, PEMANDU. **2** (– *three in one*) a person who waits at the side of the road until his/her service is needed as the third person needed for the high occupancy lanes in Jakarta.

perjokian taking a test for another student.

jokong → JONGKONG I.

jokul (*Pr*) to sell; → JUAL.

jolak berjolak and **menjolak** to blaze, flare up; → GEJOLAK.

jolakan a blaze. ~ *api* a sea of fire.

jolang bathtub.

jolék menjolék to wrap s.t. in banana leaves so that it doesn't wilt easily.

joli I (*Hind*) and **joli-joli** sedan (chair), palanquin.

sejoli yoke (of bullocks); team (of oxen); pair, set (of horses). *dua* ~ a couple (man and woman). *Malam itu, ketika digrebeg, kedua* ~ *itu sedang asyik berkencan.* That night, when (the house was) raided, the two lovers were still busily engaged in making love. ~ *dengan* in cahoots with.

joli II (*E Mal*) *berbuat* – and

berjoli to have a good time, enjoy o.s.

menjolikan ~ *uang* to waste money on amusements, etc.

joli-joli (*D*) yawl, jolly-boat.

jolok-jolok (*daun*) – *hantu* k.o. plant whose leaves have medicinal uses, *Arthrophyllum ovalifolium*.

jolok menjolok 1 to prod at s.t. with a pole, poke with a stick at an object above one ~ *sarang tabuhan* to do s.t. dangerous. *sarang tabuhan jangan dijolok* let sleeping dogs lie. ~ *anak* to have an abortion. **2** to probe into, make inquiries about. ~ *hati/pikiran* to sound s.o. out. **3** to pick (one's nose), poke one's nose into s.o.'s affairs. **4** to win. ~ *pertandingan* to win the match.

menjolokkan to poke with.

terjolok prodded.

penjolok 1 stake, pole, prod (for knocking fruit down). **2** person who uses that k.o. pole.

jolong I (*M*) (for) the first time. – *berkeris* to wear a kris for the first time.

jolong-jolong the very first, first-born (child), the first one to do s.t., pioneer, earlier than others. *buah* ~ early-maturing fruit. *pasang* ~ start of the tides.

jolong II menjolong 1 to project, protrude. **2** projecting, protruding, jutting out.

jolong III k.o. *jaélangkung* in the Cirebon area.

jolong-jolong *buaya* – the (false) gavial, *Tomistoma schlegeli. ikan* – garfish, halfbeak, *Hemirhamphodon spp.* → JULUNG I.

jolor (*Jv*) **menjolor 1** to creep along slowly like a child who can't crawl yet. **2** to creep, crawl, slither like a snake.

jombak → JOMPAK.

jombang (*M*) pretty, handsome, beautiful.

kejombangan beauty, good looks.

jomblang (*Jv*) go-between, pimp. *mak* – matchmaker, procuress.

jomblo and **jomlo** (*BG*) doesn't have a boyfriend or girl-friend.

jompak (*ob*) **berjompak** to prance (of horse).

berjompakan (*pl subj*) to prance/dance around.

menjompak to prance, gambol, rear (of a horse).

jomplang → JUMPLANG II.

jomplangan railroad crossing.

jompo (*J*) old, decrepit. *rumah* – nursing home.

jompong pejompongan rallying place.

jompowan an old person. *para* – the aged/old people.

jondal-jandil (*Jv*) hopping mad.

jong → JUNG.

jongang projecting, protruding, sticking out (of lips or upper teeth).

jongét menjongét curved up (of the upper lip).

jongga k.o. small deer.

jonggol (*Jv*) the responsible person, representative. – *karang* landless person.

menjonggoli to represent.

jonggolan 1 responsibility. **2** guarantee.

jongkah menjongkah to stick out, protrude (of teeth/branches). – *jangkih* sticking out all over, uneven.

jongkang I a motorized prau running between Nunukan (East Kalimantan) and Tawao (Sabah).

jongkang II to stick out, sticking/stuck out, protrude, protruding. – *jangking* and – *jangkit* to bristle with projecting points, sticking out in every direction.

menjongkang to protrude.

jongkang III – *jongkét* (*Jv*) a) to go up and down. b) seesaw.

berjongkangan (*pl subj*) to fall down.

menjongkangkan to knock down.

terjongkang fallen down with feet in the air.

jongkar-jangkir to stick out all over, completely uneven.

jongkat-jangkit seesawing, unsteady.

jongkél → DONGKÉL.

jongkét → JONGKANG *jongkét.*

jongki small basket made of rattan.

jongkit to tip up.

menjongkit to twist upward.

jongko I (*S*) stall (in market), booth (at a fair).

jongko II (*Jv*) prophesy, prediction. – *Joyoboyo* Joyoboyo's prophesies/predictions.

jongkok I (*J/Jv*) **berjongkok** and **menjongkok 1** to squat. **2** to humble/humiliate o.s.; submissive, humble, cringing.

berjongkok-jongkok to act humble, obsequious.

terjongkok squatting.

terjongkok-jongkok to walk while squatting.

jongkok II unintelligent, uneducated. *IQ* – low IQ.

jongkong I *sampan* – a) dinghy. b) longboat.

jongkong II (*Jv*) a type of cake made from rice flour and coconut milk and eaten with sugar.

jongkong III Indian rosewood, *Dactylocladus stenostachys.*

jongkotan (in Pekalongan, Central Java) to chatter.

jongos (*D col*) male domestic servant.

jongot flake, flock (of wool). – *salju* snowflake.

menjongot to pick out (as a man picks hemp or oakum).

jongsong (*E*) outboard motor (from the brand name Johnson).

jonjot 1 tuft (of hair). **2** flake, flock (of snow, soap, etc). – *salju* snowflake.

sejonjot a flake/flock/tuft.

berjonjot in flakes/tufts.

menjonjot to pluck out (hair), pick with the fingers.

jontoh folk tale about *adat.*

jontor (*J*) swollen, puffy (lips). *Bibir gadis berusia 16 tahun ini –.* The lips of this 16-year-old girl are swollen.

jon towél hoodlum, s.o. who extorts money from pedicab- and *opelét*-drivers.

jontrot I (*J/Jv*) **1** decoy, bait. **2** a person who tries to lure customers into his store, an attractive waitress in a restaurant to entice diners, etc. **3** attractive articles located in a conspicuous place to interest prospective buyers.

menjontrot to poke at.

menjontrotkan to use s.t. or s.o. as bait or decoy.

jontrot II water mill; → KINCIR *air.*

jopak berjopak and **menjopak 1** to rear, prance (of a horse). **2** to fall down.

joplang I (*J*) **menjoplang** to seesaw up and down; to lean back.
joplangan seesawing (of children).
joplang II njoplang 1 off-balance. **2** partial, biased.
joprak → JOPAK.
jora menjora to inspire.
joran fishing rod. – *ampai* divining/dowsing rod.
Jordan(ia) Jordan.
joréng 1 small strip (of fish). **2** clod (of earth). **3** shred.
sejoréng small patch/strip.
menjoréng to cut off a thin slice (of meat, etc.).
jori (*Hind*) team. *se- kuda* a team of horses; → JOLI I.
jorjoran and **jor-joran** (*Jv*) to try to outbid e.o., compete with e.o. *Meréka – berebut tempat.* They were competing with e.o. to capture a place.
jornalis → JURNALIS.
joro I (*M*) corner.
joro II (*Jv*) **menjoro** to push.
joro-joroan to keep pushing/shoving e.o.
jorok I (*J*) **1** dirty, soiled, filthy, unclean, sloppy, slovenly. *Kamar itu – sekali.* The room was very dirty. *– modal* a big messy guy. **2** bad, wicked. **3** slipshod (of work).
sejorok as filthy as.
terjorok the filthiest.
kejorokan dirtiness, filthiness.
penjorok 1 dirty person. **2** immoral person, scoundrel.
jorok II (*M*) **menjorok** to stick out, project, protrude, extend out. *Tanah yang ~ ke laut teluk itu jauh ke dalam.* The land protrudes very far into the bay.
menjorokkan 1 to stick s.t. out. **2** to shove s.t. aside.
terjorok 1 projecting, protruding. **2** fallen/pushed forward. *Ia jatuh ~.* He fell forward.
jorokan s.t. sticking out, protrusion. *~ atap* eaves.
jorong I 1 oval (of dishes, etc.), elliptical. **2** (*ob*) oval-shaped betel tray. **3** rice barn broader at the top than at the bottom. *– lintang* oblate.
menjorong to be oval/elliptical.
jorong II (*M*) part of a village, hamlet. *kepala/wali* – hamlet chief.
jorong III 1 a metal vase for betel leaves. **2** a section, division (of fruit).
jorsé (*BG*) [jorok sekali] very dirty.
jos 1 1 (*S onom*) puffing sound made by a steam engine; → JÉS. **2**a) (*sl*) to keep on going, keep going strong, full of energy. b) strong (of taste/sensations).
Jos II /yos/ naval cadet.
josé (*C*) silk crepe.
joss → JOS I 2.
josua (*C*) joss sticks.
jotakan (*Jv*) not to be on speaking terms. *Meréka lagi – karena pertengkaran.* They were still not on speaking terms because of a quarrel.
jotang (*S*) k.o. plant or vegetable, toothache plant, *Spilanthes acmella/ocymifolia*; → GETANG II.
jotos (*Jv*) a punch, blow with the fist. *beradu* – to have a fistfight.
berjotos to fight with the fist, box. *jago ~* boxing champion. *tukang ~* boxer.
berjotos-jotos to have a fistfight.
menjotos to punch, hit with the fist.
menjotoskan to punch with (the fists). *Dia ~ tinjunya ke hidung saya.* He punched my nose with his fist.
terjotos punched, hit with the fist.
jotosan 1 boxing match, prize fight. **2** blow with the fist.
jotos-jotosan fistfight, fisticuffs.
penjontosan punching.
perjotosan 1 boxing match, fistfight. **2** boxing (*mod*).
Jowo (*Jv*) → JAWA.
Joyoboyo a ruler best known for his prophesies, the Indonesian Nostradamus.
JPU → JAKSA *Penuntut Umum.*
jr- also see words beginning with **jer-**.
jrambah (*Jv*) low interior platform for sitting on.
jrang, jréng, jrung (*Jv onom*) twanging (of a stringed instrument).
jra(w)ut (*Jv*) messy, disheveled (of hair). *Rambutnya –.* Her hair was shaggy.

jréng (*Jv onom*) **1** strumming noise. *drama (musik)* – a certain rhythm characterizing a type of heavy rock music. **2** clinking (of coins). *membayar* – to pay hard cash. *Tadi ada yang beli kain tenun ikat, kontan bayar – dua juta rupiah.* A short while ago there was s.o. who bought a plaited batik woven head cloth and paid two million rupiahs in hard cash. **3** flashiness (of clothes).
ngejréng (*sl*) flashy (of clothes).
jréng-jréngan cacophonous noise.
jring-jring (*onom*) sound made by strumming guitar, etc.
jrog (*onom*) noise made by jumping.
berjrog-jrogan to make that noise.
ju (in acronyms) → JURU.
jua I 1 → JUGA. **2** only, nothing but. *empat orang* – only four people. *tidak seorang – pun* not a single person, no one.
jua II → JUAK I.
juadah (*A*) **1** a type of food made from glutinous rice. **2** cake, sweetmeat. **3** provisions, victuals.
juak I (*M*) **berjuak** to compete.
menjuak to incite (a fighting cock to fight or s.o. to do s.t.).
menjuakkan to incite, instigate.
penjuak instigator. *~ perang* warmonger.
juak II menjuak to rise, stick up.
menjuakkan 1 to lift s.t. up, hoist. *Juakkan buku itu supaya dapat dilihat oléh semua orang.* Lift that book as high as possible so that everyone can see it. **2** to stretch out (a sail as far as it will go). **3** to praise.
juak III berjuak to meet, encounter.
juak-juak (*cla*) court page/attendant.
jual sell, sales, selling. *harga* – sales price; → BERJUAL, MENJUAL. – *beli* buy and sell, deal, trade, transact. *– beli senjata* arms trading.
berjual-beli to engage in trade buy and sell. *orang yang ~ uang* moneychanger. **memperjual-belikan** to sell and buy, trade in s.t. *Dilarang ~ senjata api.* It's prohibited to trade in firearms. *Maaf tak dapat diperjual-belikan.* Sorry, it's not for sale.
penjual-belian trading. *– gadai/gadé* pledge, pawn. **menjual gadai** to pawn (at a pawn shop). *– kawin* tie-in sale, two-for-one sale. *– kosong* short sale. *– koyo(k)* a) to talk nonsense. b) to tell lies. *– lagak* arrogant, haughty. *– mahal* (speaking of girls) to play hard to get. *– muka* to show off. *– obral* marked down, fire sale. *– putus* sell outright, sell as is, a sale made with no guarantees or after-sale service. **menjual putus** a) to pawn land but the period for buying it back has passed. b) to sell s.t. with no guarantees or after-sale service, sell as is. **penjualan putus** outright sale. *– séndé* sell with the right of repurchase. *– tampang* to put on airs, show off, do s.t. to impress others. *– titip* on consignment. *– tubuh* to sell one's body, prostitute o.s. *– tunai* cash sale.
berjual 1 to deal/trade in, be a dealer in. *~ beras* to deal/trade in rice. **2** (*M*) will sell or have sold. *kambing itu ~* the goat will be or has been sold.
berjualan (*pl subj*) **1** to sell. **2** to sell things, trade, peddle.
menjual [and **ngejual** (*coq*)] **1** to sell, deal in. *dijual murah* (in ads) bargain. *dapat dijual* marketable. **2** to barter/bargain away. **3** to deceive, cheat, trick. *telah dijual, maka dibeli* look before you leap. *~ akad* to pawn, hock. *~ aksi* to show off. *~ bagus* to do nothing but sell o.s. *~ bangsa* to betray one's country. *~ bicara* to talk big. *~ calo* to sell land with the provision that the seller can buy it back. *~ cinta* to sell one's body, be a prostitute. *~ di muka umum* to auction off. *~ diri* to prostitute o.s. *~ dongkélan* (*Jv*) to sell land with the provision that the seller can buy it back. *~ galah* to gamble away all one's assets. *~ gantung* (*M*) to pawn. *~ gigi* to laugh uproariously. *~ jamu* a) to sell traditional medicine. b) to sell snake-oil, be a quack doctor. *~ kécap* to brag, talk high sounding nonsense, give s.o. a line. *~ kembali* to resell. *~ kepala* to be(come) a mercenary. *~ keras* hard sell. *~ koyok* to talk without evidence. *~ kurang* to sell land with the provision that the seller can buy it back after a certain period of time. *~ lagak* to show off. *~ lagi* to resell. *~ lalu* to sell land without the right to buy it back. *~ lélang* to auction off, sell items at an auction. *~ lembut* soft sell. *~ lepas* to sell for cash/outright. *~ mahal* a) to sell at a high price. b) (speaking of girls) to play hard to get. c) to be unwilling to do s.t., give a favor or s.t. to s.o. *~ mata* a) to flirt. b) to look around

instead of paying attention. ~ *mentah-mentah* to bamboozle, cheat. ~ *muka* to boast, brag. ~ *mulut* to talk big. ~ *mutlak* to sell without conditions. ~ *nama orang* to use s.o. else's name for one's own benefit. ~ *omong(an)* to talk big. ~ *petai hampa* to talk nonsense. ~ *rugi* to sell at a loss. ~ *rupa* to show off. ~ *sanda* to pawn land with the right to buy it back at an undetermined time. ~ *séndé (Jv)* to mortgage one's land for one season or more with the condition that the mortgagor can work the land on a sharecropping basis. ~ *sontak (dadak)* to cold call. ~ *suara* to be a professional singer or street singer. ~ *tahunan baluran* to sell land for cash for one harvest after which it is returned to the original owner. ~ *tampang* to show off, boast, brag. ~ *tandu* to sell land with the provision that the seller can continue to work the land for a certain period of time. ~ *tegak-tegak* to trick, bamboozle. ~ *titip* to sell on consignment. ~ *tunai* to sell for cash. ~ *utang* to sell on credit.

menjuali [and **ngejualin** (*J coq*)] 1 (*pl obj*) to sell. 2 to sell to.
menjualkan to sell for/on behalf of s.o. else.
terjual [and **kejual** (*coq*)] 1 sold. 2 for sale. *habis* ~ sold out. ~ *terbeli* you should be able to do whatever you ask s.o. else to do.
jualan 1 merchandise, commodities. 2 sales; → PENJUALAN. **berjualan** to earn one's living by selling. ~ *bakso* to earn one's living by selling *bakso*. *hidup dari* ~ *beberapa kilogram telur ayam* to support o.s. by selling a few kilograms of eggs. *tukang* ~ retailer.
penjual seller, vendor. *gadis* ~ salesgirl. ~ *bakmi dorongan* street vendor who uses a pushcart to sell *bakmi*. ~ *bangsa* traitor. ~ *barang-barang kuno* antiquarian. ~ *besar* wholesaler. ~ *cinta* selling sex, the sex business. ~ *dari pintu ke pintu* door-to-door salesman. ~ *écéran* retailer. ~ *ganja* drug trafficker. ~ *idé* purveyor of ideas. ~ *kécap* charlatan, con man. ~ *obat di kaki lima* quack, charlatan. ~ *partai besar* wholesaler. ~ *tikét* ticket agent. ~ *untuk masa depan* future trading. ~ *ulang* reseller.
penjualan 1 sale, selling. ~ *di muka* advance sale. ~ *di muka umum* public auction. ~ *keras* hard sell. ~ *langsung* direct sale. ~ *lélang* public auction. 2 sales, turnover. *tenaga usaha* ~ sales staff. 3 selling price.

Juanda name of the airport in Surabaya.
juandang → BUJANG *juandang*.
juang fight, combat, battle, struggle.
berjuang 1 to fight (of large animals, *usu* elephants). *biram* ~ fighting elephant. 2 to fight, combat, battle, struggle. *Indonésia telah* ~ *untuk kemerdékaannya dengan darah, air mata, bahkan nyawa.* Indonesia fought for its independence with blood, tears and even its life.
menjuang (*cla*) to attack.
memperjuangkan to fight/struggle for. ~ *kemerdékaan nusa dan bangsa* to fight for the independence of the homeland.
kejuangan readiness to fight, fighting spirit. **berkejuangan** to be ready to fight, have a fighting spirit. *Kepemimpinan masa depan adalah meréka yang* ~. The future leadership are those who have the readiness to fight.
pe(r)juang and **penjuang** 1 fighter, soldier. 2 (political) contender. **kepe(r)juangan** fighting spirit.
perjuangan 1 struggle, fight. 2 (political) contest. ~ *bersenjata yang berlarut-larut* a prolonged armed struggle. ~ *fisik* the physical struggle for independence. ~ *golongan* class warfare. ~ *hidup mati* life and death struggle. ~ *kelas* class warfare. ~ *mati-matian* fight to the death. ~ *untuk memperoléh kuasa (untuk memerintah)* power struggle. **seperjuangan** fighting for the same cause. *teman* ~ comrade in arms.
juang-juang *daun* – → LENJUANG.
juar → JOHAR III.
juara I (*Skr?*) 1 champion. 2 fighter. 3 expert in a certain field. 4 arbiter, referee (at cock fights); master of ceremonies. *adat* – *kalah menang* there's always a winner and a loser. - *bertahan* defending champion. - *buntu* (*ob*) adventurer. - *dunia* world champion. - *bal* (*J*) glutton. - *gembut* glutton. - *harapan* contender. - *judi* professional gambler. - *kedua* runner-up. - *kelas* champion in his/its class. - *makan* glutton. - *renang* swimming champion. - *ténis* tennis champ. - *tidur* sleep hound.
menjuarai to be the champion of, win (a competition/tournament), win the championship of.

menjuarakan to make a champion, let s.o. become a champion, proclaim s.o. champion.
kejuaraan 1 match, tournament. 2 championship. ~ *dunia* world championship.
pejuaraan championship.
juara II *ikan* – a river catfish, *Pangsius sp.*
juaran → JORAN.
juari → JAUHARI.
jubah (*A*) *baju* – a long robe worn by hails, cassock, (surgeon's, etc.) long gown, toga. - *mandi* bathrobe. - *putih* white gown (symbol of a medical doctor).
berjubah to wear Such a dress.
jubal → JUBEL.
jubel (*J/Jv*) **berjubel(-jubel)an** (*pl subj*) to swarm; in throngs/crowds, crammed, chock-full. *Kami berjubelan seperti ikan teri.* We were all jammed together like sardines. *berjubel kaya semut* to swarm like ants.
sejubel a lot, a huge amount.
menjubeli to pack into. *Keréta api dijubeli anak-anak.* The train was packed with kids.
menjubelkan to cram, jam, stuff (s.t. into a place).
jubelan crowd, throng. ~ *manusia* crowds.
jubi (*Pap*) k.o. spear used for fishing.
jubiléum (*D*) jubilee.
jubin → UBIN.
jubir [juru bicara] spokesman.
jubit → CUBIT.
jublek (*J*) amazed.
menjublek with a blank stare, remain utterly silent.
jubung an awning for deck-cargo; → JEROBONG.
jubur → DUBUR.
Judah (*A*) Jedda.
Judai (*zod*) Capricorn.
judas → JUDES.
judeg and **judek** (*Jv*) to be at one's wit's end; → BINGUNG. *Sudah lama saya* – *mencari padanan kata yang baik untuk mengartikan "prudence" secara persis.* I've racked my brains for a long time trying to find an exact translation for the word "prudence."
judes (*J*) 1 sharp (tongued), speaking in an angry tone, malicious, with a sharp tongue, bitchy. *Seorang sékretaris harus ramah dan tidak boléh* –. A secretary should be friendly and not bitchy. *perempuan* – a bitch. 2 cheap, stingy.
judéx (*L D*) judge. - *facti(e)* judge and appeals judge (but not the *kasasi* judge), lower court judge.
judi gambling. - *buntut* k.o. lottery. - *koprok* → KOPROK.
berjudi and **menjudi** to gamble, bet. *Dia jatuh miskin karena suka* ~. He became poor because he loved to gamble.
menjudikan 1 to gamble away. *Harta bendanya habis dijudikan.* He gambled away his wealth. 2 to bet s.t. ~ *nyawanya* to bet one's life.
memperjudikan 1 to gamble on, bet on. 2 to bet/stake s.t. ~ *nasib* to stake one's life.
pe(n)judi gambler. *Para* ~ *kakap Indonésia déwasa ini mengalihkan kegiatannya ke Las Végas, Amérika.* Big Indonesian gamblers have now moved their activities to Las Vegas, America.
pe(r)judian and **penjudian** 1 gambling den/place, 2 gambling.
judikatif (*D*) judicial.
judisial (*E*), **judisiél**, and **judisiil** (*D*) judicial.
judisium (*D*) judgment, sentence.
judo (*Jp*) judo.
pejudo judo athlete.
judoka (*Jp*) judo champion.
judokang (*Jp*) judo hall.
judul (*A*) 1 title. 2 caption. 3 (movie) credits. 4 heading. - *bawah* caption. - *berita* headline. - *perancis* title page. - *tambahan* subtitle.
berjudul 1 entitled. 2 captioned.
menjuduli to entitle, label. *Penulis itu* ~ *tulisannya ...* The writer entitled his book...
menjudulkan to enter (a title, etc.).
juék (*M*) lines stretched across a field which can be pulled and which function as a scarecrow. *menegakkan* -.- *sesudah*

menyabit (or, *sesudah padi disabit*) to lock the barn door after the horse has been stolen.

juga 1 also, too, as well. *Saya – diundang.* I too was invited. **2** (after clauses beginning with *biarpun/meskipun*, etc.) still, anyway, nevertheless. *Meskipun sudah diobati, gejala penyakitnya tidak – sembuh.* Even though he was treated, the symptoms of his illness still did not abate. *Meskipun dikatakan mogok total, tetapi – banyak kendaraan yang lalu lalang.* Even though it was said to be a total strike, many vehicles were passing by anyway. **3** rather (more than you might expect). *besar* – rather big(ger than you might expect). *belum* – still not (even though expected). *Dia belum – datang.* He still hasn't arrived. *tidak –* still not. *bila kedua surat itu ternyata tidak – dibalasnya ...* even if it turns out that those two letters still haven't been answered ... *tahu* – to know quite well. **4** (right) this/that very ... (in certain time and other expressions). *pada hari itu –* on that very day. *orang itu –* that very person. *bagaimana/siapa pun –* no matter how/who.

jugi I k.o. love potion.
menjugi to use this love potion on s.o.
penjugi s.o. who uses this love potion.
jugi II → JOGI.
jugil (*Jv*) crowbar, lever.
menjugil to force (s.t. open), pry open; → CUNGKIL.
juhi (C) dried squid.
juih curled (of lips, plate, dish).
juita (*Skr*) sweetheart.
Juja → JAUZA.
jujah (*A*) insult, disrespect, libel.
menjujah to insult, libel.
penjujah backbiter.
jujai (*ob*) continuous.
berjujai to keep on (doing s.t.).
jujat → JUJAH.
jujitsu (*Jp*) jujitsu.
jujug → JAJAK.
jujuh continuous, persistent, chronic, incessant.
berjujuh(-jujuh) and **menjujuh** to keep on, ceaseless. *Meréka berjujuh-jujuh menangis.* They cried and cried.
menjujuh continuous, unceasing, without stop.
juju menjuju to head/aim (toward). *~ ke utara* to head north; → MENUJU.
menjujukan to aim/direct s.t. toward. *~ senapan* to aim a rifle.
jujur I 1 honest, sincere. **2** candid, frank, straightforward. **3** reliable, trustworthy. *kurang* – dishonest. **kekurang-jujuran** dishonesty. *tidak* – dishonest. **ketidak-jujuran** dishonesty. *– belaka* fair and square.
sejujur as honest as.
sejujurnya honestly (speaking).
terjujur the most honest.
kejujuran 1 honesty, sincerity. **2** frankness, candor. **3** reliability.
jujur II money or property given by the bridegroom to his future in-laws, bride price. *– hilang* bride price that is not returned by the bride's family because the groom breaks off the relationship. *– kembali* bride price returned by the bride's family because the bride breaks off the relationship.
menjujuri to give that to one's future in-laws.
terjujur the most honest.
jujuran bride price.
jujuran (S) k.o. share cropping in which one party gets one-third of the crop and the other two-thirds of the crop.
jujut I berjujut-jujutan to grab hold of e.o. and pull.
menjujut to grab hold of s.t. and tug at it.
jujutan tie, connection.
jujut II berjujut one after another.
juk I ukulele.
juk II mosquito larva.
juk III (in acronyms) → PETUNJUK.
jukcong (C) Chinese junior high school.
jukir [juru parkir] parking attendant.
juklak [petunjuk pelaksanaan] operational manual, management guidelines.

juknis [petunjuk téknis] technical manual.
jukong and **jukung** non-motorized boat made from a hollowed-out log.
jukut (S) grass. *– jampang* k.o. herb, *Dicliptera chinensis*. *– laut* seaweed. *– papayungan* umbrella sedge, *Cyperus difformis*.
jula-jula (*M*) → JULO.
julab (*A*) laxative, aperient, purgative.
julai growing part of a twig.
berjulai(-julai) and **menjulai** to droop/hang down/dangle to the surface (of the water such as the roots or branches of some trees).
menjulaikan to dangle s.t.
terjulai hanging down, drooping, dangling.
julak → JOLAK.
julang I various species of hornbill, *Rhytoceros spp. – Irian* Blyth's hornbill, *Rhytoceros plicatus. – jambul coklat* wreathed hornbill, *Rhytoceros undulatus. – Sulawesi* knobbed hornbill, *Rhytoceros cassidix*.
julang II head (measure of pressure). *– hulu* head, measure of liquid pressure.
menjulang 1 to carry on one's shoulders. **2** to lift over one's head, give a boost to. **3** to tower up, rise, stick up, soar high. *gedung-gedung yang ~* the buildings which rise (up to the sky). **4** to esteem, respect highly.
julangan 1 pushing upward. **2** s.t. carried on the shoulders.
julap → JULAB.
julat I menjulat to lick at (of flame); → JILAT.
julat II (*ob*) **1** range. **2** a measurement of length. *dua –* two shiplengths.
sejulat *~ mata* as far as the eye can see.
berjulat one after the other. *~ tamu datang* guest after guest arrived. *~ datang* came one after the other.
julat-berjulat one after the other.
menjulat to get as far as, reach.
menjulat-julat to dart up. *Api ~.* The flames are darting up.
penjulat sepenjulat as far as ... can reach, as long as a ... *~ lembing* a spear-throw. *~ mata* as far as the eye can see. *~ perahu* as long as a boat.
Juli (D) July.
julig and **julik** (*Jv*) sly, cunning.
kejuligan and **kejulikan** cunning, trickery.
juling squinting. *bermata –* cross-eyed, squinting. *– air* with a slight squint. *– bahasa* with a slight squint. *– bertangkap* with a bad squint, wall-eyed. *– itik* sideways glance.
menjuling(i) to squint at.
julir two-pronged harpoon for spearing fish.
julita → JELITA.
julo (*M*) lottery played at home by a group of people; → ARISAN.
berjulo to play that lottery.
berjulo-julo to raffle off.
juluk I what one is named/called.
menjuluk(i) to dub, call, nickname.
menjulukkan to use s.t. as one's name or nickname.
julukan nickname, sobriquet, alias, label.
penjulukan naming, calling.
juluk II menjuluk to peer at, spy on.
julung I (*Jv*) child born under an unlucky star. *– caplok* born at sunset and so fated to be attacked by a tiger. *– kembang* born at sunrise and so fated to encounter a wild animal.
julung II for the first time.
julung-julung for the first time.
julung-julung various species of fish, needle fish, *Dermogenys pusillus* and *Zenarchopterus*; → JOLONG-JOLONG.
julur I to come out, stick out (of a hiding place). *– jalar* back and forth, to and fro, in and out.
julur-julur in and out, back and forth, to and fro.
berjuluran (*pl subj*) to stick out, protrude.
menjulur 1 to stick out, protrude. **2** to panhandle, beg in the streets.
menjulurkan to stick s.t. out, make s.t. protrude, crane (one's neck). *Dia ~ kepalanya dari jendéla.* He stuck his head out the window.

terjulur sticking out, jutting out, protruding.

juluran 1 s.t. that sticks out/protrudes, salient. ~ *wilayah* (*geog*) panhandle. **2** (*phys*) bore.

penjulur (~ *tangan*) panhandler, s.o. who begs in the streets.

julur II menjulur to crawl, creep (like a baby).

julur III terjulur (to fall) head over heels.

jumaah and **jumaat** → JUM'AT.

Jumadilakhir the sixth month of the Arabic calendar.

Jumadilawal the fifth month of the Arabic calendar.

jumahah and **jumahat** → JUM'AT.

jumahat (*Jv*) emerald.

jumantara (*Skr*) **1** sky, firmament. **2** air (*mod*). *angkutan* – air transport.

jumanten → JUMANTAN.

Jumat and **Jum'at** (*A*) **1** (*hari*) – Friday. **2** (the seven day) week. **3** general assembly, *esp* for praying on Friday. *salat* – Friday prayers. – *Agung/Besar* (Protestant) Good Friday. – *Berdarah* Bloody Friday; → TRAGÉDI *Semanggi*. – *Suci* (Catholic) Good Friday.

sejumat one seven-day week.

berjumat 1 to attend Friday prayers. **2** to assemble, be in a group.

jumatan and **jum'atan** to go (to the mosque) on Friday.

jumawa → JEMAWA.

jumbai tassel, fringe; frill; → RUMBAI I. – *jagung* corn tassel.

sejumbai a bunch of s.t. that dangles. ~ *kunci* a bunch of keys.

berjumbai to have tassels/fringes, tasseled, fringed.

berjumbaian (*pl subj*) fringed, tasseled.

berjumbai-jumbai tasseled, fringed.

menjumbai 1 to be a tassel or tuft in shape or form. **2** to drape (a garment).

menjumbaikan to let s.o. hang down.

terjumbai hanging down loose. *Rambutnya* ~. Her hair is hanging down loose.

jumbil wattle; → GELAMBIR.

jumblah → JUMLAH.

jumblang and **jumbleng** (*Jv*) cesspool, septic tank.

jumbuh (*Jv*) similar, almost identical.

menjumbuhkan to make two things look alike, bring two objects or concepts into line with e.o.

kejumbuhan similarity, near identity.

penjumbuhan identifying.

jumbul berjumbul-jumbul and **terjumbul-jumbul** to bob up and down.

jumeneng (*Jv*) **jumenengan 1** ascend the throne, enter office. **2** acting, temporary.

jumhur (*A*) majority (group of *ulama*s).

jumhuriyah (*A*) republic.

jumiz → JAMIZ.

jumjumah (*A*) skull.

jumlah (*A*) **1** total, amount, sum. **2** number (of), quantity. **3** overall. – *tebal* overall width. **4** (*ling*) number. – *bobot* gross weight. – *bulat* lump sum. – *cétak* a) impression (of a book). b) circulation (of a newspaper); → OPLAH. – *dan mutu* quantity and quality. – *ganjil* odd lot. – *genap* round lot. – *pokok* principal (of a loan). – *seluruhnya* sum total. – *tegakan* stock (of trees in a concession). – *terbanyak* majority (of votes, etc.).

sejumlah 1 a number of, some. **2** in the amount of.

berjumlah to total, amount to.

menjumlah 1 to add. *Anak itu belajar* ~. The child is learning to add. **2** to figure out (an amount). **3** to add up. *Harap* ~ *angka-angka ini.* Please add up these numbers.

menjumlahkan to total/add (up).

terjumlah 1 totaled, added up. **2** considered to be among; → TERGOLONG. **keterjumlahan** (*math*) summability.

terjumlahkan can be totaled. *tidak* ~ innumerable, uncountable.

jumlahan total amount.

penjumlah s.o. or s.t. that totals/adds up.

penjumlahan totaling, adding up.

perjumlahan total, addition.

jumpa meet, come across, run into. *sampai* – *bésok* see you tomorrow. – *muka* to meet. – *pérs* meet the press, press conference.

berjumpa to meet, run into, come across. ~ *muka* to meet face to face.

menjumpai 1 to meet up with, run into, find, come across. ~ *kesulitan* to run into problems. **2** to go to see.

menjumpakan and **memperjumpakan 1** to bring (s.o.) together (with s.o.), bring two things together, reconcile. **2** (*fin*) to set off. *Majikan tidak boléh* ~ *lebih dari dua perlima jumlah upah tersebut.* An employer may not set off more than two fifths of the sum of those wages.

terjumpa met up with, found.

terjumpai to be found. *Itu tidak* ~ *di sini.* That's not to be found here.

perjumpaan 1 meeting, encounter, getting together. **2** (~ *utang*) (*fin*) set-off.

jumpalit (*J*) **1** somersault. **2** quickly, suddenly. – *injak rém* to step on the brake quickly. **3** to tumble. *Harga – ke bawah.* Prices have tumbled to rock bottom.

berjumpalit to turn a somersault.

berjumpalitan (*pl subj*) to turn somersaults.

jumpalitan somersault.

jump(e)lang I 1 rocker (on a rocking chair). **2** hoop (of a wheel).

jumplang II 1 to turn upside down. **2** unbalanced, unequal.

menjumplang [**njumplang** and **ngejumplang** (*coq*)] **1** to turn upside down. **2** to become unbalanced.

jumpluk pile.

sejumpluk a pile of.

jumpotan → JEMPUTAN III 2.

jumpul grey mullet, *Mugil planiceps*.

jumput (*J/Jv*) → JEMPUT I, II. **sejumput** a small amount, pinch. ~ *garam* a pinch of salt.

menjumput to pick up between two fingers.

menjumputi (*pl obj*) to pick up between the two fingers.

jumputan → JEMPUT II.

jumputan (*Jv*) a scarf with a white floral pattern.

jumrah, jumrat, and **jumroh** → JAMRAH.

Jumu'ah (*A*) *aj*– "The Congregation"; name of the 62nd chapter of the Koran.

jumud (*A*) **1** frozen. **2** rigid, obstinate, unbending. **3** conservative.

kejumudan 1 rigidity, obstinacy. **2** conservatism.

jun (*Jv*) earthenware jug.

junai – *emas* Nicobar pigeon, *Caloenas nicobarica*.

junam dive down. – *air* downwelling (of sea).

menjunam to dive/swoop down on.

menjunamkan to immerse, plunge.

terjunam dived, plunged.

juncto (*L leg*) /yungkto/ in conjunction with; → JO I.

jundai (*M*) *si* – magician who can make people crazy.

bersijundai to go crazy through a hex.

jung (*C*) k.o. boat, junk. – *satu, nakhoda dua* two bosses. – *pecah yu yang kenyang* without leadership only bad people prosper.

jungat (*J*) **menjungat** to tilt upward at one end.

junggang → JUNGKANG-JUNGKIT.

jungjang (*J*) *tangga* – stepladder.

jungjung → JUNJUNG.

jungkal fall face down, topple. – *balik* upside down.

menjungkalkan 1 to turn s.t. upside down. **2** to overthrow, bring down (a government).

terjungkal [and **kejungkal** (*coq*)] upside down, toppled over, fallen down.

jungkalan fall, inclination.

jungkang-jungkit to bob up and down.

berjungkang-jungkit to bob up and down.

jungkar menjungkar to jut/stick out slightly.

terjungkar-jangkir to show up everywhere.

jungkat – *jangkit/jungkit* to bob up and down. ***menjungkat-jungkit*** to bob up and down.

menjungkat 1 to slant, tilt. **2** turned-up (of the nose).

terjungkat slanted, tilted.

jungkatan 1 slant, tilt. *jembatan* ~ draw bridge. **2** seesaw.

jungkel and **jungkil** → JUNGKAL.

jungkir (*J/Jv*) – *balik* a) reverse, overturn. b) turn somersaults (trying to s.t.). ***menjungkir-balik 1*** to overturn, turn around, reverse; to disorder, mess up. **2** to turn somersaults. ***terjungkir-balik*** turned over, overturned, reversed. ***penjungkir-***

balikan overturning, turning around, reversing; turning somersaults.

berjungkir fallen over backward.

menjungkir to fall over backward.

terjungkir turned over.

penjungkiran overthrowing.

perjungkiran turning over, somersault.

jungkit tilt.

menjungkit and **terjungkit** tilted up at the end.

jungkitan tilt, inclination.

jungkol decayed tooth.

jungkrak menjungkrak(kan) to tear down, raze.

jungkung → JONGKONG I.

jungur 1 snout, sword (of a swordfish); → CUNGUR. **2** bow (of a ship). – *kapal* bow of a ship.

menjungur 1 to protrude, stick out. **2** to dig around for s.t. with its snout, root out.

jungut (*M*) foreland, (mountain) spur.

Juni (*D*) June.

junior (*E*) junior.

junjang (*cla*) a measure of area.

junjung wooden pole used to support plants. – *duwur mendem jero* (*Jv*) stress the good and hide the bad within you. – *tinggi* to uphold, hold high, respect, revere. **menjunjung-tinggi(kan)** to revere.

berjunjung 1 to be carried on the head. *beban ~* a load carried on the head. **2** (*ob*) to be married (of a woman).

menjunjung 1 to carry s.t. on the head. **2** to respect, honor. *~ duli/kaki* to honor. *~ tinggi titah* to pay homage to a royal command. **3** to obey (an order, rules). *~ sangkar ayam* to be greatly embarrassed. *~ uban* to be old and experienced.

menjunjungkan 1 to carry s.t. on the head for s.o. else. **2** to put s.t. on s.o. else's head.

terjunjung carried on the head.

junjungan 1 s.o. who is respected. **2** respect. **3** s.t. carried on the head. **4** pole used to support plants. **5** (*ob*) husband. **berjunjungan** to be married.

penjunjung s.o. who respects, reveres.

penjunjungan 1 carrying on the head. **2** respecting, revering.

junta (*D*) /hunta/ junta.

juntai berjuntai *~ kaki* with feet dangling.

berjuntaian (*pl subj*) dangling.

menjuntai with feet dangling.

menjuntaikan to dangle, let (one's feet or hands) dangle.

terjuntai dangling, hanging down.

penjuntaian letting s.t. dangle, dangling.

juntrung (*J/Jv*) orderly, organized, methodical, meticulous.

menjuntrungkan to organize, put in order, arrange in an order.

juntrungan 1 order, rules. *dengan tidak (tahu) ~nya* in an unmethodical way. **2** form, shape. **3** organization.

junub (*A*) ritually impure before washing (after sexual intercourse/giving birth, etc.).

junun (*A*) **1** possessed (by a devil). **2** really, seriously.

jup (*sl*) yes, yeah.

jupang branch.

berjupang branching.

Jupitér (*D/E*) Jupiter.

jur (in acronyms) → JURUSAN.

jura(h) menjura(h) to bow down (out of respect).

juragan (*J/Jv*) **1** helmsman, skipper, captain. **2** fishing-boat owner who employs fishermen. **3** (*reg*) sir. – *darat* owner of a boat who hires others to fish. – *laut* skipper (of a fishing boat).

jurah → JURA.

jurai I 1 hanging bunch. **2** strip. **3** small group of people.

sejurai a bunch of hanging things, a strip of s.t.

berjurai-jurai and **menjurai-jurai 1** to hang down in bunches/fringes. **2** divided up into small groups.

berjuraian (*pl subj*) to hang down in many bunches.

terjurai hanging down loosely.

terjurai-jurai hanging down in bunches/fringes.

jurai II jurai-jurai k.o. tree, *Barringtonia spicata*.

jurai III (*Pal*) village head.

juran → JORAN.

jurang 1 ravine, gorge, chasm, ditch. **2** precipice, edge. **3** gap, lag. – *générasi/juriat* generation gap. – *kebudayaan* cultural lag. – *kenistaan* the depths of misery. – *pemisah* gap. – *selisih générasi* generation gap.

menjurang to open up (of a gap).

juri I (*D/E*) jury, member of the jury.

menjuri to be a member of the jury.

penjurian acting as jury, judging.

juri II → JOLI I, JORI.

juriat → ZARIAH.

juridis (*D*) juridical.

jurig and **jurik** (*J*) ghost, spook.

juring (*Jv*) section (of fruit). – *pantai* beach cusp.

berjuring to have sections, be sectioned.

juringan section, slice (of fruit).

juris (*D/E*) **1** jurist, lawyer. **2** (*infr*) law student.

jurisdiksi (*D*) jurisdiction.

jurisprudénsi (*D/E*) jurisprudence, case law.

jurit (*Jv cla*) war, battle.

prajurit and **perjurit** warrior, soldier; in the Dutch colonial period title for the native soldiers who were charged with maintaining peace and public order under the direct command of the civil administration; the European soldiers were referred to as *serdadu*; → PRAJURIT, SERDADU I.

jurkam → JURU *kampanye*. **menjurkami** to act as a campaigner for.

jurnal (*D*) **1** (in bookkeeping) journal. **2** (*naut*) logbook. **3** entry. – *berpasangan* double entry.

jurnalis (*D/E*) journalist, reporter. – *plonco* cub reporter.

jurnalisme (*D/E*) journalism. – *invéstigatif* investigative journalism. – *senang-senang* junket journalism

jurnalistik (*D*) journalistic.

kejurnalistikan to be too journalistic.

jurpen → JURU *penerang*.

juru I professional (man), craftsman (*esp* in compounds); *cp* TUKANG, AHLI, PAKAR. – *acara* master of ceremonies. – *adzan* muezzin (person who summons to prayers); → BILAL, AUDIN. – *anggar* fencer. – *api* stoker, fireman (on railroad). – *arsip* archivist, keeper of the records. – *atak* editor. – *azan* muezzin. – *bahasa* interpreter. – *batu* (*naut*) boatswain (charged with sounding and anchoring). – *bayar* paymaster, cashier. – *berita* journalist, reporter. – *bicara* [jubir] spokes(wo)man, mouthpiece. **menjuru-bicarai** to act as spokes(wo)man for. – *bisik* s.o. who gives advice behind the scenes to s.o. in a powerful position, éminence grise. – *bor* driller. – *buku* bookkeeper. – *bunuh* killer. – *cacar* vaccinator. – *cakap* spokesman. – *dakwah* proselytizer. – *damai* peacekeeper. – *dapur* cook, chef. – *film* cameraman. – *foto* photographer. – *gambar* a) draftsman. b) illustrator. – *geledah* person who conducts a body search. – *gendang* drummer. – *gudang* storekeeper. – *harta peninggalan* administrator of an estate. – *hibur* consoler, comforter. – *hikmat* s.o. who practices black magic. – *imbau* announcer. – *imunisasi* [jurim] immunizer. – *injil* evangelist. – *isyarat* signalman. – *jalan* road inspector. – *jenang* purser. – *kabar* journalist, reporter. – *kaki* gofer, s.o. who is ordered to do various tasks. – *kaméra* cameraman. **menjuru-kamérai** to film. – *kampanye* [jurkam] campaigner (for a political party). – *kasir* cashier. – *kelang* auctioneer (of confiscated goods). – *kelat* (*naut*) crewmember who runs up the sails. – *kerah* village messenger. – *ketik* typist. – *khitan* circumciser. – *khotbah* preacher. – *kira* a) bookkeeper. b) actuary. – *kirim* forwarding agent. – *kisah* storyteller. – *kuasa* proxy. – *kunci* a) cemetery caretaker; caretaker of a sacred place; → KUNCEN. b) gatekeeper. c) (in sports) the cellar, the lowest position in the relative standing of competing teams. – *laboran* laboratory technician. – *langsir* shunter. – *latih* trainer. – *layan (wanita)* steward(ess). – *lélang* auctioneer. – *lomba* racer. – *masak* cook, chef. – *(témbak) meriam/mesiu* artillerist, artilleryman, gunner. – *mesin* locomotive machinist, engineer (on train). – *minyak* greaser, oiler. – *montir udara* aircraft mechanic. – *motor* driver. – *muat* a) loading clerk. b) stevedore. – *mudi* (*naut*) helmsman. – *obat* (*ob*) a) pharmacist; → APOTEKER. b) corpsman. – *padat* stevedore. – *panggil* call boy (who calls the actors to the stage). – *pantun* storyteller. – *parkir* parking-lot attendant. – *parkir pesawat (terbang)* aircraft marshalling man. – *peledak* blaster (in salvage). – *pembahas* commentator. – *pemisah* arbiter. – *penerang* [jurpén] information officer. – *Penerang Agung* Supreme Information Officer (i.e., one of the titles conferred upon President Soekarno). – *pengacara* beadle (in England, the Netherlands, Indonesia, etc.), i.e., an official who leads university processions carrying a mace used as a symbol of authority. – *penyelesai* liquidator (of a business). – *perbekalan* purveyor. – *periksa/peréksa* a) interrogator. b) inspector. – *perum (naut)* leadsman. – *pijat* masseur, masseuse. – *pilot (naut)* pilot (to take a ship in and out of harbor). – *pisah* a) arbitrator. b) referee. – *pliat* masseur, masseuse. – *plot (mil)* plotter. – *pompa* pumper. – *potrét* photographer. – *pusaka* person who divides up an estate. – *pustaka* librarian. – *radio udara* wireless operator. – *ramal* fortune-teller. – *rancang* planner. – *rawat* nurse. – *rawat udara* flight nurse. **kejururawatan** nursing. – *résép* apothecary, druggist. – *rias* a) makeup artist, beautician. b) layout man. – *rumpaka* (music) arranger. – *runding* negotiator. – *sekar* singer. – *selam* diver. – *Selamat* the Savior, Redeemer. – *silat* expert in martial arts. – *simpan (leg)* custodian, depository. – *sita* bailiff, process server, confiscator. – *sita pajak* government-appointed tax bailiff. – *suara* soundman (in film). – *sula (cla)* executioner. – *sungging* a) painter. b) person who organizes a *wayang* performance. – *supit* circumciser. – *tagih* bill collector. – *tafsir* commentator. – *taksir* appraiser, evaluator. – *tala* (piano) tuner. – *tanak* cook, chef. – *télepon* telephone operator. – *teluh* person who utters magic formulas. – *témbak* marksman. – *tenun* weaver. – *tenung* fortune-teller. – *tera* gauger. – *terbang* (airplane) pilot. – *teriak* barker (to call people to attend a performance). – *tik* typist. – *tinggi* crew member who climbs up on the sails. – *topografi* topographer. – *tulis* office clerk, secretary. – *tunjuk* informer, stool-pigeon. – *uang* a) cashier. b) bookkeeper. – *uji kualitas* grader. – *ukir* sculptor. – *ukur* surveyor. – *ulas* commentator. – *warta* correspondent, reporter.

kejuruan 1 vocation, profession. 2 vocational, professional. *pendidikan* ~ vocational education/training. *Pusat Latihan ~ Industri* [PLKI] Training Center for Industrial Skills. *sekolah* ~ vocational school. 3 ability, capability, skill.

juru II (*S ob*) corner (of a house/table/mat/*sawah* compartment/ geometrical figure). – *angin* wind direction.

sejuru a corner, a small piece of (back)ground.

penjuru corner, direction. ~ *angin* direction of the wind, wind direction. **sepenjuru** in the same direction.

juruh (*Jv*) *air* – (thin sugar)syrup (sauce, used for Javanese cakes/ pastry).

jurung → JORONG I, II.

jurus I moment. *beberapa* – *kemudian* several moments later.

sejurus a moment, a little while. ~ *kemudian* shortly after, a little bit later.

berjurus-jurus for a while, again and again, from time to time.

jurus II straight on, direction one is headed in.

menjurus to go straight (toward), to head/go (in the direction of); to lead (to), head (toward). *Masalah ini ~ ke pencemaran nama baik.* This problem leads to defamation of character.

menjurusi 1 to head toward. 2 to look into, investigate.

menjuruskan 1 to direct. 2 to guide, push, shove toward.

jurusan 1 direction, point of view. *menuju ke ~ yang tepat* to be on the right track. 2 heading for. *keréta-api ~ Bandung* the train heading for Bandung, the Bandung train. 3 department (of university). *seorang mahasiswa ~ Bahasa Indonésia* university student in the Indonesian Language department. 4 field/area (of studies). **sejurusan** in the same department/field of studies.

penjurus directive, guideline.

penjurusan 1 dividing up into departments. 2 aiming (at), heading (in the direction of, toward).

jurus III 1 certain stances in *pencak-silat*. 2 standards, criteria.

jus I → JUZ.

jus II (*E*) (orange, banana, etc.) juice. – *tomat* tomato juice.

menjus to make juice out of.

jus III (*D?*) (in badminton/tennis) deuce, tie score.

jus IV (*onom*) puffing sound made by locomotives; → JOS.

jus-jus (*onom*) sound made by steam locomotive.

justa (*ob*) → DUSTA. *mengarang cerita* – to fabricate, make up a story.

justifikasi (*E*) justification.

justisi (*D*) justice.

justisial judicial.

justru 1 exactly, precisely, just (right). *Kenapa – sekarang ini engkau harus pergi?* Why do you have to leave right now? – *karena* just because, precisely because. – *karena aku mencintai ayahlah, maka aku tidak bisa mengabulkan permintaan abang.* It's precisely because I love father that I can't fulfill your request. 2 on the contrary, but (rather). *Sekali-kali tidak pernah saya mencaci dia, – saya pujinya.* I've never insulted him, on the contrary I've praised him. – *sebaliknya* quite the contrary.

juta (*Skr*) million.

sejuta one million. ~ *permata* k.o. black magic.

berjuta-juta by the millions.

jutaan millions. *dalam ~ rupiah* in millions of *rupiah*.

jutawan (*Skr neo*) millionaire.

jute (*D*) jute.

juték (*BG*) bad-tempered, unfriendly, hostile.

ngejutékin to put s.o. in bad mood.

juwang → JUANG.

juwéh (*Jv*) talkative, loquacious; talk, chatter; → CERÉWÉT, CERIWIS. *-nya nénék-nénék biasanya ditujukan kepada anak-anak.* Old people's chatter is usually directed at children.

kejuwéhan talkativeness.

juwét (*Jv*) k.o. plant with edible fruit, Java plum, *Syzygium cuminii*.

juwita → JUITA.

juz (*A*) one of the 30 sections or chapters of the Koran. – *amma* chapters 78 to 114 of the Koran.

K

k and **K I** /ka/ the 11th letter of the Latin alphabet used for writing Indonesian.

K II (*abbr*) → KIAI.

K III (*D*) 1,000.

K IV car license plate for Jepara/Rembang.

K4 [kemudahan, keramah-tamahan, kenyamanan, kenangan] convenience, politeness, pleasure, memories.

KA I [Keréta Api] train, railway/road. – *Liméx Sriwijaya* [Keréta Api Limited Express Sriwijaya] the fast train running between Batu Raja and Kertapati Palembang.

ka II (in acronyms) → KEPALA I.

Kaabah and **Ka'bah** (*A*) **1** the Kaaba, i.e., the cube-like stone building in the center of the mosque at Mecca. **2** the election symbol used by the Muslim-backed *Partai Persatuan Pembangunan* [PPP] in the May 1977 general election. *massa* – reference to the Muslims, particularly the *PPP*.

kab (in acronyms) → KABINÉT I, KABUPATÉN.

kaba (*M ob*) (fairy-)tale, story; → KABAR 2.

kabab (*Pers ob*) kebab, small lumps of meat roasted on a spit; → SATÉ.

kabad (*A ob*) contraction.

Kabag [Kepala bagian] Section Head.

Kabah → KAABAH.

kabair (*A*) a major sin.

kabak k.o. annual plant, New Zealand spinach, *Tetragonia expansa*.

kabal → KEBAL.

kabang-kabang dirt on the top of shelves used for storing crockery and pots, on the wall, etc.; spider webs, cobwebs, etc.

kabar (*A*) **1** news, report, account, notice. – *dibawa pikat dan langau* rumor. *indah – dari rupa* the report is nicer than the reality. *Apa –?* How are you? *tidak – tidak cerita* not say a word. *surat/ kertas* (*ob*) – (news)paper. **2** (*M*) (old) story (told in rhyme). **3** – *akan* and **kabarkan** to be conscious of. *tidak – akan dirinya* to be unconscious. – *angin/burung/selentingan/tersiar* rumor(s), gossip. (*menyiarkan*) –.– *burung* (to spread) rumors. – *cécékbocék* (*M*) scandal. – *dengkul* a canard. – *miring* rumors.

   kabarnya and ~*nya konon* they/people say, it is said. ~ *belum terang* it's not clear yet; we have to wait for further news.

   berkabar 1 to tell, speak, talk. *Ia pandai* ~. He is a clever speaker. **2** to report news.

   mengabari (*Jv*) [and **ngabarin** (*J coq*)] to get/send word to, tell, report to. *Pilot Lim C. L. dikabari.* Pilot Lim C. L. got word of it.

   kabar-mengabari to exchange information, give e.o. the news.

   mengabarkan to report, tell (about s.t.).

   terkabar spread (of news/reports), reported.

   terkabarkan reported, announced.

   pengabar ~ *Injil* evangelist.

   pengabaran 1 reporting. **2** evangelism.

   perkabaran 1 announcement. **2** news (service).

kabarét (*E*) cabaret.

kabat I (*M*) wrap, girdle, putties, scarf; → KEBAT.

kabat II (in Bengkulu, from *E*) cupboard.

kabau tree with stinking edible pods, *Pithecellobium ellipticum*; → JÉNGKOL *hutan*.

kabayan hamlet headman; → KEBAYAN I.

kabé and **Ka-Bé** [Keluarga Berencana] family planning.

   berkabé to practice birth control using condoms.

kabéh (*Jv*) all, everything.

kabéka a Manadonese welcoming dance.

kabel (*D/E*) **1** cable. – *bawah laut* submarine cable. – *tegangan tinggi* high-tension cable. **2** cord, line. *télepon tanpa* – cordless telephone. – *angkat* hoisting cable. – *antar* lead. – *bor* drilling line. – *borstel* brush holder cable. – *gulung* cable reel. – *laut* submarine cable. – *massa* ground wire. – *mati* (*petro*) deactivation.

– *pejal* solid rope. – *penerangan* power cable. – *picak* flat cable. – *sérét* tow rope. – *tarik* pull wire. – *télepon* telephone cable.

   pengabelan cabling.

kabet (*J*) (too) tight/small (of clothes).

   kekabetan too tight.

kabiku (*NTT*) landlord.

Kabil I (*A*) (the biblical) Cain.

kabil II (*coq*) treason.

kabil III berkabilan to observe cautiously. *berserah* ~ to not fully trust s.o.; to entrust s.t. to s.o. but still be cautious about him.

   mengabil to observe.

Kabilah (*A*) the Kabyle (tribe).

kabin (*D/E*) cabin, compartment (in a ship/car/truck, etc.). – *bertekanan* pressurized cabin. – *depan* fore-cabin. – *keran* crane hut. – *masinis* (in a train locomotive) engineer's cabin. – *pengemudi* cockpit (of aircraft). – *télepon* call box, telephone booth.

kabinét I (*D/E*) cabinet (of ministers). – *ahli/keahlian* business cabinet. – *bayangan* shadow cabinet. – *démisionér* outgoing cabinet. – *ékstra parleméntér* extra-parliamentary cabinet. – *inti* inner cabinet. – *keprésidénan/présidénsial* presidential cabinet. – *kompromistis* compromise cabinet. – *parleméntér* parliamentary cabinet. – *pelangi* rainbow cabinet. – *persatuan nasional* national unity cabinet. – *yang disempurnakan* revamped cabinet.

kabinét II (*D*) commode, cupboard, china closet.

kabir I (*ob*) **mengkabir** to pull up to s.t.; to row with one oar. *Baik* ~ *haluan ke tepi*. Better paddle at the bow to bring her alongside.

kabir II (*A*) great (of God, rulers). *alam* – macrocosm (of the Muslim mystic).

kabir III [kapitalis birokrat] bureaucratic capitalist, i.e., the term used by the PKI in attacking military officers who managed state companies in the early 1960s.

   kekabiran capitalist bureaucracy.

kabir IV mengabir ~ *tanah* to scrape earth toward o.s.

   kabir-kabiran dishonest; unfair; to look out for o.s. as much as possible.

kabisat (*A*) *tahun* – leap year.

kabit (*A*) pickpocket; thief.

kablatur → KARBURATOR.

kaboi k.o. beetle.

kabriolét (*D/E*) cabriolet.

kabu-kabu 1 tree cotton, kapok. **2** cotton tree, *Ceiba pentandra*. – *hutan* k.o. tree, thorny ivy-rue, *Zanthoxylum myriacanthum, Bombax valetonii*.

   berkabu-kabu fluffy, downy, cottony.

kabuki (*Jp*) kabuki (theater).

kabul (*A*) **1** answered (prayer), granted (wish), accepted, fulfilled. **2** (– *akan*) a) to consent to, agree to, accept. b) to comply with, grant, approve.

   mengabuli and **mengabulkan** [and **ngabulin** (*J coq*)] to accept, consent to, comply with, grant (s.o.'s wishes), answer (s.o.'s prayers), make (s.o.'s dreams) come true.

   terkabul accepted, granted, fulfilled, come true (of one's wish). *Mimpi saya* ~. My dream came true.

   terkabulkan to be accepted/approved/answered/granted. *Doa-doanya tak* ~. His prayers were not granted.

   pengabul s.o. who grants/wishes, etc.

   pengabulan consent, acceptance, approval, answering (s.o.'s prayer), granting (s.o.'s wishes).

kabuli → KEBULI.

kabung I (= **perkabungan**) a white mourning head-band.

   berkabung to mourn, be in mourning. *gelap* ~ heavily overcast/ cloudy/clouded over.

   mengabungi to mourn s.t.

   perkabungan 1 mourning attire/wear. **2** (the state of) mourning.

kabung II a linear measure of 4 cubits (about 1.88 meters; used for woven textiles).

kabung III sugar palm, *Arenga pinnata.*

kabung IV (*M*) piece, chunk, lump. *se-* a piece/lump/portion.

    mengabung(-ngabung) to cut into pieces, chop up.

kabupatén (*Jv*) **1** regency, i.e., an administrative area below the *provinsi*, similar to a county; → DAÉRAH *tingkat II/dua.* **2** office/residence of a *bupati/regent.*

kabupaténisme provincialism.

kabur I 1 vaguely visible (in the distance); *cp* LINDAP, SAMAR. **2** vague (of answer/sentiment, etc.), uncertain (of future plans). **3** indistinct, obscure (of a boundary, etc.). **4** faint (light), feeble (light, etc.). **5** weakening (of faith/belief/thinking). *– pikiran* not have all one's wits about one; to be a bit weak in the head. **6** hazy, misty, foggy, filmy, blurred. **7** lackluster (of one's eyes), weak (of vision). *mata sudah –* weak of vision (due to old age). **8** faded. *Warnanya sudah –.* The color has faded. **9** illegible. *Tulisannya sudah –.* His handwriting has become illegible.

    mengabur [and **ngabur** (*coq*)] to fade (away), blur, grow blurred, become indistinct/uncertain/hazy. *Bintangnya ~.* He has had a bad fate.

    mengaburi to cloud s.t. over.

    mengaburkan to cloud, dim, blur, make hazy.

    memperkabur 1 to make vaguer/less distinct. **2** to obfuscate, make s.t. unclear on purpose.

    kekaburan 1 haze, fog. **2** blurring, dimming. **3** vagueness.

    kekabur-kaburan hazy, foggy, indistinct, vague, blurry.

    pengabur s.t. that makes s.t. vague.

    pengaburan obfuscating.

kabur II (*J/Jv*) to run away, take to one's heels, bolt (of horses); → MABUR. *membawa –* to run away/abscond with.

kabur III coconut beetle.

kabus 1 hazy, misty, nebulous, indistinct. **2** dim, blurred (of sight); faint (of a distant scene). *awan yang –* vaguely visible clouds. *Matanya –.* His eyes are blurred. *hilang – teduh hujan* after rain comes sunshine; behind the clouds the sun is shining.

kabut I 1 mist, fog, haze. **2** vague, not clear, faded, blurred. *kalang/ kelam –* a) gloomy, dark, obscure. b) confused, chaotic, in disorder. **3** smokescreen. *terang –, teduh hujan →* HILANG *kabus,* TEDUH *hujan. – asap* a) smokescreen. b) smog. *– basah* humid fog. *– campur asap* smog. *– malam* evening mist. *– minyak* oil spray. *– tipis* hazy.

    berkabut 1 misty, hazy, foggy, clouded, vague, indistinct, gloomy (of thoughts); to fog up. **2** shrouded in mystery.

    mengabut 1 to become misty. **2** (of a liquid) to spray out.

    mengabuti to cover with a fine spray, mist/fog over, shroud.

    pengabut atomizer, sprayer

    pengabutan spraying.

kabut II (*ob*) **mengabutkan** to shake out (clothes); → KEBUT I 2.

kaca I (*Skr*) **1a)** glass. **b)** pane (of glass). *Jendélanya terbuat daripada –.* The window is made of glass. **2** (*- muka*) mirror; → CERMIN. **3** example. *- aman* safety glass. *- asahan* cut glass. *- bakar* burning glass. *- baur* frosted glass. *- bayangan* (*ob*) mirror, looking glass. *- benggala* a) (*ob*) a large, thick mirror. b) magnifying glass. *- bening* clear-glass (windshield); *opp* KACA *gelap. - bergambar* (in East Timor) television set. *- berlekak* stained glass. *- dasar* under-plate. *- depan* front windshield. *- duga* gauge glass. *- és* ground glass. *- gelap* tinted glass (car windshield); *opp* KACA *bening. - hias* dressing mirror. *- jendéla* windowpane. *- kasar* raw glass. *- keras* tempered glass. *- kobalt* smalt. *- kusam* opaque glass. *- lumér* enamel. *- masir* frosted glass. *- mata* and *kacamata* eyeglasses, spectacles. *dari - mata ...* from the viewpoint of ... *nilai/skor/stand - mata* (in soccer) the score is 0 to 0. *- mata baca* reading glasses. *- mata debu* goggles. *- mata hitam* dark/sun glasses. *- mata jéngkol* mod sunglasses. *- mata jepit* (pair of) pince-nez. *- mata kuda* blinders. *- mata matahari* sunglasses. *- mata pelindung* goggles, safety glasses. *- mata putih* eyeglasses, spectacles. *- mata satu* monocle. *- mata selam* diving mask. *- mata tebal* thick eyeglasses (for nearsightedness). *- mata yang berbingkai bulat lébar* mod glasses. **berkaca-mata** to wear eyeglasses. *~ minus/plus* to wear glasses to correct nearsightedness/farsightedness. *~ cukup tebal* to wear very thick

glasses. *- mobil* windshield. *- mokat* (*Pr*) eyeglasses, spectacles. *- muka* (*ob*) mirror. *- nako* leaded glass. **berkaca nako** with leaded glass/lights/panes. *- muka* mirror. *- pantul* reflecting glass. *- pembakar* magnifying or burning glass. *- pembesar* magnifying glass. *- pengaman* safety glass. *- rias* vanity, dressing table. *- sahap* cover glass. *- samping* side window (of car). *- serat* fiber glass. *- spion* outside car mirror. *- spion dalam* inside car mirror, rearview mirror. *- taméng* safety glass. *- tembus-pandang/yang tembus-penglihatan* clear glass. *- teropong* periscope. *- toko* store display window.

    berkaca 1 to use glass; a glass ..., made of glass, with glass. *Surat pujian itu diberinya ~ serta pigura.* He framed the letter of recommendation and covered it with glass. **2** (*~ diri*) to look at o.s. in a mirror. *mobil ~ gelap* a car with a tinted-glass windshield.

    berkaca-kaca to shine (with tears), to mist over (with tears). *Matanya ~.* His eyes misted over. *mata ~* teary-eyed.

    berkacakan to be mirrored in, reflect.

    mengaca 1 to look at o.s. in a mirror. *bersolék sambil ~* to dress up while looking in a mirror. **2** to take warning from, take an example from. *dalam ~ pada masyarakat Jepang* taking Japanese society as an example.

    mengacai to glaze, put glass on.

    memperkacai 1 to convince o.s. of. **2** to put s.t. under a magnifying glass.

    terkaca mirrored, reflected.

kaca II page (of a book); → HALAMAN II, MUKA, PAGINA.

kaca III *- piring* gardenia, *Gardenia augusta/jasminoides.*

kacab [kepala cabang] branch manager.

kacak I 1 handsome, smart; manly, dashing. **2** proud, conceited, haughty, arrogant.

    kekacakan 1 conceit. **2** smartness, being dashing.

    pengacak braggart.

kacak II (*M*) **sekacak** slender (of the waist).

    berkacak *~ pinggang* with arms akimbo (a defiant attitude).

    mengacak to lift, feel (weight/size, etc.) with one's hand. *~ galas* (*ob*) to try one's luck in business. *~ lengan* to lift up one's arms (to fight).

    terkacak *jangan bérang ~* don't flare up (at s.o.).

kacam k.o. climbing plant, *Embelia sp.*

kacamata I → KACA *mata.*

kacamata II *burung –* various species of white-eyes (birds), *Zosterops spp.*

kacamatan → KECAMATAN.

kacang I 1 generic name for many sorts of pulses, peas, and beans. *minyak –* groundnut oil. **2** (*vulg*) clitoris; → ITIL, KELENTIT I. **3** (*esp* in the Netherlands) a derogatory term for an Indonesian-born Eurasian. *sebatang –* quite alone; → SEBATANG *kara. - mana buang lanjaran, - nggak buang lanjaran* (*J*) and *- mongso ninggali lanjaran* (*Jv*) like father, like son. *- lupakan kulitnya* and *panas hari, lupa - akan kulitnya* a) to disavow/repudiate/deny one's origins; the man who is rich forgets his poor friends. b) not to know one's place. *bagai - direbus satu* to jump for joy. *bagai - tengah dua bulan* (*M*) to grow fast (about children). *- adas* lentil. *- arab* okra, *Hibiscus esculentus. - arcis* peas. *- asin* salted peanuts. *- atom* a snack made of fried peanuts. *- babi,* broad bean, *Vicia faba, Mucuna pruriens. - bado* lablab, *Dolichos lablab. - bandung* brown-flour coated nuts. *- banten →* KACANG *bandung. - batang* wild bean, phasey bean, *Phaseolus lathyroides. - bawang* a snack food of peanuts and garlic. *- belimbing* winged bean, Goa bean, *Psophocarpus tetragonolobus. - belut* Chinese long bean, *Vigna unguiculata. - béndi →* KACANG *arab. - béngkok →* KACANG *mérah. - bengkuang* yam bean, *Pachyrrhizus erosus/undulatus. - biduk →* KACANG *bado. - bogor* a snack from Bambara groundnuts, *Voandzeia/Vigna subterranea. - botol/botor →* KACANG *belimbing. - bulu rimau* soybean, soybean, *Glycine soja. - buncis* kidney bean, *Phaseolus vulgaris. - cina* peanut, groundnut, *Arachis hypogaea, Phaseolus lunatus. - cindai* small green peas from which *taogé* is made, *Phaseolus aureus/radiatus, Vigna radiata. - dieng* broad bean, *Vicia faba. - disco* doughnut. *- dodok* kidney beans, *Phaseolus vulgaris. - embing →* KACANG *belimbing. - ércis* a) green/garden peas, *Pisum sativum.* b) sugar pea, *Pisum arvense. - ganéfo* fried peanuts. *- gatal* → KACANG *babi. - goréng* a) a groundnut, *Arachis hypogaea.* b) roasted/fried peanuts. c) *novél - goréng* a dime novel; → ROMAN *picisan.* d) (to sell, etc.) like hotcakes. *Benda itu larisnya seperti - goréng.* That thing sells like hotcakes; → LAKU *seperti pisang goréng. - goyang* k.o. of snack made from peanuts. *- gudé* split pea, pigeon pea, *Cajanus cajan/indicus. - hantu* sword beans, *Canavalia ensiformis/gladiata. - (h)ijo* → KACANG *cindai. - iris* → KACANG *gudé. - jawa* → KACANG *bandung. - jepun* → KACANG *bulu rimau. - jeriji* bonavista, hyacinth bean, lablab, *Dolichos lablab. - jogo* white beans, *Phaseolus vulgaris. - kapri* → KACANG *ércis. - kapri muda* snow peas. *- kara(-kara)* and *- kekara* → KACANG *jeriji. - katé* k.o. ground cover, *Phaseolus trilobus. - kayu* → KACANG *gudé. - kedelai/kedelé* → KACANG *bulu rimau. - kélor* horseradish tree, *Moringa oleifera. - koro* (*Jv*) various k.o. peas, beans. *- lanjaran* → KACANG *cina. - laut* k.o. medicinal plant, bay bean, beach bean, *Vigna marina, Desmodium umbellatum/reflexa, Canavalia rosea. - lendir* → KACANG *arab. - lola* k.o. fried peanut. *- manila* Bambara groundnut, *Voandzeia subterranea. - manis* sweet pea, *Pisum sativum. - médé* cashew nut. *- mérah* a) cowpea, *Vigna sinensis/unguiculata.* b) kidney bean, *Phaseolus vulgaris. - mété* cashew nut. *- miang* a) a pea species (pulse with an itchy shell). b) troublemaker, firebrand, agitator, instigator. *- monyét* wild bean, *Phaseolus lathyroides. - nyonya* sword bean, jack bean, *Canavalia ensiformis. - oci* rice bean, *Phaseolus calcaratus. - padi* → KACANG *cindai. - panjang* cowpea, long bean, *Vigna unguiculata/sinensis/sesquipedalis. - pantai* k.o. ground cover, baybean, *Vigna marina. - parang* sword bean, jack bean, *Canavalia ensiformis/gladiata. - parang putih* jack beans, *Canavalia ensiformis. - péndék* → KACANG *buncis. - polong* sword beans, sugar pea, *Canavalia ensiformis/gladiata. - putih* garden peas, *Pisum sativum. - puyuh* rice beans, *Phaseolus calcaratus. - rebus* boiled peanuts. *- sengkuang* yam bean, *Pachyrrhizus erosus/undulatus. - sepalit* rice bean, *Phaseolus calcaratus. - sepat* → KACANG *kara. - seréndéng/serinding* lima bean, *Phaseolus lunatus. - shanghai* peanuts fried in batter (a snack food). *- sukro* peanuts fried in a flour coating. *- tanah* groundnut, peanut, *Arachis hypogaea. - tanah mérah* → KACANG *mérah. - telor* a snack food. *- tojin* roasted peanuts with garlic. *- tolo* → KACANG *belut. - tunggak* → KACANG *mérah. - uci* rice bean, *Vigna umbellata.*

berkacang to scramble (after s.t.). *~ orang* throngs of people.

mengacang to divide (up the spoils); to act as one pleases (with s.o. else's property).

ngacangin (*sl*) to look down on.

memperkacang to squander (s.o. else's money), make use of (s.o. else's property) without permission.

kacangan second-rate, small-time, petty.

kacang-kacangan leguminous plants, legumes, pulses.

kacang II *- lopék* obtuse barracuda, *Sphyraena obtusata.*

kacangan garfish, *Tylosurus, spp.*

kacang-kacangan and *ikan kacang-kacang* garfish, *Hemiramphus spp.*

kacang III *kambing* – a small goat species.

kacang IV mengacang to fight.

memperkacangkan to fight over s.t.

kacang-kacang (*M*) 1 ball bearings. 2 hail, small shot, pellet, slug. *Ini baru –nya.* This is just the beginning.

kacapi → KECAPI I.

kacapiring gardenia, *Gardenia augusta/florida.*

kacapuri (*cla*) k.o. mausoleum; inner dome of a palace.

kacar I (*ob*) *kail/pancing* – fishing rod for catching squid, cuttle fish (using feathers, etc., not a sharp wire).

mengacar to catch squid, etc. in that way.

kacar II (*M*) **mengacar** 1 to feel all around between stones (searching for fish). 2 to search, raid; to frisk.

kacar III *siput* – k.o. mollusk, *Voluta pulchra.*

kacar-kucur sprinkling water over the newlyweds (part of the wedding ceremony).

kacau 1 mixed up, disarranged, disordered, disorderly, cluttered. *Susunan kartu itu –.* The cards were all mixed up. 2 confused, disturbed, all mixed up, messed up. *Pikirannya –.* His mind was

confused. *berlari dengan* – to run away in confusion. 3 insecure, unsafe, unstable, in trouble (of one's marriage, of the political situation). *keadaan* – an unstable situation. 4 → BERKACAU. *balau* a) chaotic, mixed up, messed up. b) to be in disorder/confusion. **berkacau-balau** thoroughly mixed up. *keadaan yang ~* a completely mixed-up/messed-up situation. **mengacau-balaukan** to subvert, agitate, disturb; to cause to become disorganized. **kekacau-balauan** chaos, mess, confusion.

sekacau as chaotic, etc. as.

berkacau 1 well-mixed. *Cat itu ~ benar.* The paint is well-mixed. 2 mixed up, messed up. *Pikirannya ~.* His mind is in all mixed up.

mengacau [and **ngacau** (*coq*)] 1 to mix, stir, beat with a spoon/ladle, etc. so as to blend it. *~ air kopi* to stir the coffee. 2 to disturb, cause trouble for, mess around with, upset. *Kampanye Golkar dikacau.* The Golkar campaign was disturbed/thrown into confusion. *~ keadaan* to disturb/upset the situation. 3 to worry, trouble, make anxious. *Apa sebenarnya yang ~ hatimu itu?* What exactly is worrying you? 4 to jam, make (radio broadcasts/radar signals, etc.) unintelligible.

mengacaukan and **memperkacaukan** [and **ngacauin** (*J coq*)] 1 to mix, blend. 2 to disturb, agitate, cause trouble for, shake/churn up, upset, mess up. 3 to jam (electronic signals).

terkacau 1 shaken/mixed up, disturbed. 2 the most confused/chaotic.

terkacaukan 1 shakable. 2 to get confused (by one thing for another).

kacauan a hodgepodge, mixture, mixed up. *bahasa ~* a mixed-up language.

kekacauan 1 confusion, disturbance, disarray, disorder, chaos. *mengalami ~* to be/get (all) confused. 2 mutiny, rebellion, uprising, riot. 3 mess, confused mess, jumble, hodgepodge, mishmash.

pengacau 1 agitator, firebrand, rebel, insurgent, terrorist; a pain in the neck/ass, troublemaker. 2 mixer (a machine that mixes, such as a blender, etc.).

pengacauan disturbance, perturbation, act that causes disorder/trouble, etc.

kacau-bicau (*ob*) → KACAU *balau.*

kacau-bilau → KACAU *balau.*

kacau-birau (*ob*) → KACAU *balau.*

kacaukan (*ob*) → KACAUAN, KACUKAN.

kacék (*Jv*) 1 to differ. 2 different.

kacer (*Jv*) (*burung –*) Oriental magpie robin, *Copsychus saularis.*

kaci I (*Hind*) *kain* – white cotton.

kaci II (*ikan –*) a marine fish, painted sweetlip, *Plectorhynchus pictus;* → TEBAL II *bibir.*

kacici (*J*) right, correct.

kacici tailor-birds, *Orthotomus spp.*

kacih → KOCAH-KACIH.

kacip scissors, shears. *- ayam* poultry shears. *- kaléng* tin snips. *- pinang* betel nut scissors.

mengacip 1 to slice (a betel nut, etc. with those scissors). 2 to squeeze s.t. between the thighs.

kacir (*J*) → KOCAR-KACIR. **ngacir** to run away. *~ keluar* to run out.

kaco (*J*) → KACAU. **ngaco** 1 out of order. 2 to gas, jaw, talk. *- bélo* to talk nonsense. *- kerjanya* it's malfunctioning, it's not working.

kacoak (*J*) cockroach.

kacokan → KACUKAN.

kacu I a hard, brown substance obtained from *pinang* (*gambir*); used as an astringent in medicine and for dyeing, tanning, etc.

kacu II (*Jv*) handkerchief; a square piece of cloth used as a scarf by Boy Scouts.

kacuak → KACOAK.

kacuk hybrid, → KACAU.

kacukan hybrid, mixture, s.t. that is no longer pure. *bahasa Melayu ~* Malay mixed with words from other languages. *kelapa ~* a hybrid coconut species, a cross between the domestic *Genjah Kuning Nias* and the imported *Jangkung Afrika Barat.*

pengacukan hybridization.

kacung I *belalang* – praying mantis, *Tenodera aridifolia.*

kacung II 1 youngster, boy. **2** errand boy. – *bola* ball boy (in tennis). – *kantor* office gofer. – *koran* newsboy.

kacungan → KACUNG.

kad (*Mal*) card; → KARTU. – *koran* newsboy.

kada I (*A*) (God's) rules, (God's) decree (*esp* of one's death), one's fate.

kada II (*A*) to comply with. – *hajat kecil* to urinate. – *hajat besar* to defecate.

kada III (*A*) to perform a religious obligation outside the normal time, make up for s.t. not done. – *hajat* to relieve o.s. – *puasa* to fast in order to make up for a neglected fast. – *salat/sembahyang* to pray in order to complete neglected prayers.

mengkada → KADA III.

kadal I (*Jv*) garden lizard, skink; → BENGKARUNG. – *raksasa* Komodo dragon, *Varanus komodoensis*; → KOMODO I 1. – *terbang* flying lizard of the genus *Draco*.

kadal II a skin disease of the palms and the soles of the feet; symptoms are white spots in the affected area. *muka licin, ékor* – all is not gold that glitters. – *anjing* small leprosy spots. – *gajah* large leprosy spots.

kadal III (*Pr*) to lie, trick.

ngadal to cheat.

ngadalin (*J coq*) to cheat (on s.o.).

kadalan chestnut-breasted malkoha, *Phaenicophaeus curvirostris*.

kadaluarsa (*Jv*) → KEDALU(W)ARSA. to have expired (of a permit, etc.). *Pasportnya sudah* –. His passport has expired.

kadam I (*A*) sole (of foot). *datang menghadap ke bawah* – "to come and appear under the sole of the foot," i.e., to appear before the *raja*.

kadam II (household) slave; → KHADAM.

kadam III (*M*) box (with a convex lid) for betel-chewing ingredients.

kadang I – *kala*, **terkadang(-kadang)** and **kadang-kadang** sometimes, now and then, occasionally. **keterkadangan** s.t. rare, rarity.

kadang II (*M*) **mengadang** (*nasi*) to throw rice-water away from the cooking pot (to make the rice cook faster). *terlampau dikadang mentah* (*M*) to try to do s.t. too fast and by doing so to spoil it.

kadang III (*Jv cla*) sibling. – *kedayan/kadayan* (*cla*) relatives (of the *raja* who become his entourage).

kadar I (*A*) **1** power, might. *ala –nya* to the best of one's ability, appropriately; → SEKEDAR. *dengan –nya* as much as necessary; as well as possible; what is necessary. **2** God's will; one's destiny/fate/bad luck. **3** nature, disposition, character.

kadar II (*A*) **1** norm, standard. *Belum ada – yang tentu untuk mengatakan sah tidaknya.* There doesn't yet exist a definite norm to say whether this is legal or not. **2** content, percentage, proportion, amount, level. *Pérak ini –nya 0,800.* This silver is 800 fine (out of a possible 1,000). **3** value, price, rate. *Di situlah baru ia tahu akan – dirinya.* That's where he became aware of his own value. **4** about, approximately. *Ada – dua puluh.* There were about twenty. **5** only, merely (in order to ...), with the sole purpose of. *Kenduri itu diadakannya – jalan mengumpulkan uang.* He held the *kenduri* with the sole purpose of raising money. **6** degree, level, content, grade (of mineral). – *kesalahannya telah memenuhi kritéria untuk diberhentikan* the degree/level of his mistakes complies with the criteria for his being discharged. *kurang –nya* his standing/prestige has declined. – *air* water content, moisture – *bijih kotor* grade of crude ore. – *garam* salinity. – *gemuk* fat content. – *gula* blood-sugar level. – *kotoran* trash content. – *lengas* humidity. – *minyak* (*petro*) oil cut. – *susut* reduced grade (uranium). – *témbakan* (*mil*) rate of fire.

sekadar 1 according to, in proportion/respect to, as circumstances may require. ~ *perlu* in as far as is necessary. ~ *tenaga yang dipergunakannya* in proportion to the energy he used. **2** only, merely (in order to ...), for the sole purpose of, just for the sake of. ~ *untuk memenuhi permintaan hadirin* just to satisfy the demands of the audience. **sekadarnya** as much as is needed, sufficient. *Hal itu akan kuceritakan ~nya.* I'll tell you as much as is necessary. ~ *mengingatkan* bear in mind that, as a reminder.

berkadar to have a ... content/level. ~ *bius tinggi* to have a high narcotic content.

berkadaran proportional. *perwakilan* ~ proportional representation.

pengadaran rating.

kadar III (*ob*) *kain* – homespun cloth such as worn by Mahatma Gandhi.

kadar IV (*Jv*) **mengadar** to sleep/pray, etc. in the open (at night).

kadariah rafidi (*A*) the name of a nonorthodox Muslim sect.

kadariat (*A*) theological school.

kadas (*Jv*) – *keridas/kudis* ringworm.

kadaster (*D*) cadastre, land registration office.

kadasteral (*D*) cadastral.

kadaver (*D/E*) cadaver.

kade (*D*) quay, wharf (with facilities for loading and unloading ships).

kadelé → KEDELAI.

kademat (*ob*) → KHIDMAT.

kader (*D*) cadre, rank and file member of a party. – *pimpinan* leadership cadre.

mengaderkan to make into a cadre.

peng(k)aderan cadre formation; → KADER(N)ISASI.

perkaderan (*mod*) cadre.

kadéra (*Port IBT*) **1** chair. **2** litter or sedan chair.

kader(n)isasi 1 cadre formation. **2** any k.o. training/formation.

kaderschool (*D*) /kaderskhol/ army cadre training school.

kades seaweed.

kadés [kepala désa] village head.

kadét I (*D mil*) **1** cadet; → TARUNA, TERUNA. – *penerbangan* aviation cadet. **2** junior (level). *Kejuaraan Gulat Terbuka tingkat* – Open Wrestling Championship junior level.

kadét II (*Jv*) **1** pickpocket. **2** robber.

kadét III (*D*) k.o. bread roll.

kadi (*A*) cadi, civil judge dealing with Muslim affairs.

kadim I (*A*) **1** old, ancient. **2** antique. **3** existing from time immemorial, eternal, preexisting. *al-Kadim* the Eternal (an attribute of God). **4** indubitable, unquestionable. *manusia bersifat gawal, hanyalah Tuhan yang bersifat* – to err is human, only God is indubitable.

kekadiman eternity.

kadim II (*A*) in future, at a later date, later.

mengkadimkan 1 to predict (the future). **2** to assure, make definite (what is going to happen).

kadim III (*A*) close relative.

sekadim of the same lineage/family. *saudara* ~ sibling of the same father.

kadipatén (*Jv*) territory under the authority of an *adipati*.

kadir (*A*) powerful, mighty. *al*- (God) the Mighty.

kadit (*Pr*) no, not; → TIDAK.

kadmium (*D/E*) cadmium.

kado (*Fr D*) present, gift. – *Natal* Christmas present.

kadok I coarse leaf of long pepper, *Piper longum* used as a substitute for the betel-vine/*sirih*. – *naik junjung* to adorn o.s. with borrowed plumes; conceited, stuck-up, snobbish. – *kena air tahi* ill weeds grow apace.

kadok II *Pak* – simpleton, fool, jerk, sucker.

kadok III – *api* a bird, the red-billed malkoha, *Zanclostomus javanicus*.

Kadr (*A*) *al*- "Determination, (Night of) Power"; name of the 97th chapter of the Koran.

kadru chestnut (color).

kaduhung (*S*) repentance, remorse, compunction, contrition. *merasa* – to repent, feel sorry (for what one has done or failed to do).

kaduk → KADOK I, II.

kadung (*Jv*) **1** to miss one's mark. **2** to go too far and do s.t. that cannot be undone. *Saya sudah – cinta dengan basket dan sulit untuk dipisahkan.* I've gone too far and fallen in love with basketball and it's hard to be separated from it. (*sudah*) – (gone) too far, can't be undone.

kadut I 1 (*kain* –) sacking. **2** k.o. gunny sack; pouch.

kadut II (*M*) k.o. satchel.

kadut III (*J*) **1** a small nonpoisonous snake. **2** coward.

kaédah → KAIDAH.

kaf I (A) name of the 22nd letter of the Arabic alphabet.
kaf II (A) *ilmu* – palmistry.
kafa (A ob) sufficient.
kafalah (A) k.o. Islamic bank guarantee facilities.
kafan (A) shroud.
  berkafan shrouded.
  mengafani and **mengafankan** to shroud.
  pengafanan shrouding.
kafarah and **kafarat** (A) infidel; scoundrel.
kafé (D) café.
kaféin (D/E) caffeine.
kafétaria (D) cafeteria.
kaffah (A) complete, including food and clothing.
kafi (A) sufficient.
kafilah I (A) 1 caravan. 2 (*mil*) train, convoy.
kafilah II (A) delegation. – *Dista Acéh* the Aceh Special Region delegation to the National Koran Reciting Contest held in Aceh in June 1981.
kafir (A) non-Muslim, infidel, unbeliever, heathen. – *harbi* one who fights against Islam. – *inad* one who accepts God but does not obey His commandments. – *ingkar* atheist. – *juhud* one who accepts God internally but denies Him externally. – *kitabi* people of the book, i.e., other monotheists (Christians and Jews). – *majusi* fire-worshipper. – *musyrik* polytheist. – *nifaq* one who accepts God externally but denies internally. – *nikmat* one who misuses God's pleasures. – *riddat* apostate. – *syirik* one who doesn't deny God but puts his faith in false gods. – *zimi* an infidel who submits to Islamic rule and promises to fulfill its requirements.
  mengafiri to deny (God).
  meng(k)afirkan to consider s.o. an infidel; to abhor s.o.
  kekafiran godlessness, infidelism.
  pengkafir infidel, nonbeliever.
  pengafiran considering s.o. an infidel.
kafiri (A) unbelieving, incredulous.
Kafirun (A) al– "The Unbelievers"; name of the 109th chapter of the Koran.
kafiyah (A) rhyme.
kaftan (A) caftan.
kaftar (A) hyena.
kafur (A) camphor; → KAPUR *barus*.
kagak (J) 1 no. 2 not.
  sekagak-kagaknyé at least, in any case.
Kagama [Keluarga Alumni Gadjah Mada] Gadjah Mada Alumni Community.
ka-ga-nga South Sumatran Indic-derived scripts.
kageroh an evenhanded handling.
kagét (J/Jv) startled, stunned, surprised, taken by surprise; frightened.
  mengagét to do. s.t. suddenly.
  mengagétkan [and **ngagétin** (J coq)] 1 to startle; to scare, frighten. 2 alarming, startling.
  terkagét(-kagét) startled, surprised.
  kekagétan surprise.
kagok I (J/Jv) 1 finding it difficult to do s.t.; impeded, hampered, hindered (in doing s.t.). *Duduknya jangan terlalu dekat dengan supir, nanti ia jadi –.* Don't sit too close to the driver, or he might find it hard to drive. 2 (to feel) awkward. 3 unaccustomed. 4 strange, not usual.
kagok II (Jv) 1 different from the common language (in pronunciation/word usage, etc.). 2 (of speech) accented, dialectal. *bahasa Indonésia* – accented Indonesian.
kagol (Jv) frustrated, hindered.
  mengagolkan to frustrate, hinder.
kagum (J/Jv) amazed, astonished, surprised, impressed.
  mengagumi [and **ngagumin** (J coq)] to wonder at, be amazed at; to admire.
  mengagumkan 1 to amaze, astound, astonish, surprise. 2 amazing, awe-inspiring, awesome, astonishing.
  terkagum-kagum very amazed, astonished.
  kekaguman amazement, astonishment, surprise, wonder.
  kekagum-kaguman amazed.

pengagum admirer, fan.
pengaguman admiration, being awed by.
kagungan (Jv) 1 to possess, own. 2 possession, property.
kah I k.o. glue; → ENGKAH I.
-kah II interrogative suffix attached to word or phrase being questioned or to question word in direct or indirect question. *Sudah– makan?* Have you eaten? *Apa– dia sudah datang?* Has he arrived? *semua warganegara, Jawa– ia, Sunda– ia* all citizens, be they Javanese, Sundanese.
kahaf (A ob) cave; → GUA I, KAHF.
kahak phlegm.
  berkahak to hawk up phlegm.
kahal drought, shortage (of food).
kahan k.o. monkey.
kahanah (A) fortune-telling, divination.
kahang smelling bad.
kahar I (D) a two-wheeled, animal-drawn cart, such as a *délman, dokar, pedati,* etc.
kahar II (A) 1 all-powerful (of God). 2 tyrannical (of men), despotic. 3 unavoidable.
Kaharingan religion of the Daya ethnic group of Central Kalimantan.
kahat (A) scarce; scarcity; famine; deficient.
  kekahatan deficiency, scarcity, lack (of an element).
Kahf (A) al– "The Cave"; name of the 18th chapter of the Koran.
kahin (A) diviner, soothsayer, fortune-teller.
Kahira(h) (A) Cairo.
kahiyangan → KAYANGAN I.
kahot (S) 1 old, to have existed for a long time, time-honored. 2 experienced, veteran. *seorang yang sudah – dalam menggeluti pahit manisnya usaha* a man experienced in the ups and downs of business.
kahrab (A ob) amber. – *kuning* yellow amber.
kahwa (A ob) coffee.
kahwin → KAWIN.
kahyangan → KAYANGAN I.
kaidah (A) basis, foundation; rule, style, etiquette, system, method, principle, norm, standard. – *ganda* double standard. – *hukum* legal norms. – *ibadah* standards of worship. – *kencana* the Golden Rule. – *muamalah* standards of behavior. – *tajwid* the correct way to recite the Koran.
kaifiat (A) 1 character. 2 quality, (the right) way (to do s.t.), manner, mode. – *da'wah* the right way to preach (Islam).
kail (*mata –*) fish hook; → PANCING. *bungkuk – hendak mengena/ mendapat* to promise anything/mountains of gold. – *sebentuk, umpannya seékor, sekali putus sehari berhanyut* to act thoughtlessly/rashly. – *berladung* deep-sea weighted line. – *hambur* drift-line. – *tunda* towed line.
  kail-kail tonsillitis (feels like fishhooks in the throat).
  mengail to fish with a (fish)hook. ~ *berumpan, berkata bertipuan* to have a persuasive tongue.
  terkail hooked, caught with a hook.
  pengail 1 fisherman, angler. 2 fishing rod and line.
kailan (C) Chinese kale, *Brassica alboglabra.*
kaim (A ob) upright.
kain I 1 a length of cloth measuring approximately 2 ½ yards x 1 ⅓ yards, made of cambric-based *batik, lurik* (in Java), cotton interwoven with silk or metallic threads (in Bali), heavy silk interwoven with gold and metallic thread (in Sumatra), worn as a wraparound, ankle-length skirt. – *untuk baju* cloth for a shirt. 2 *sarong,* i.e., the principal garment of (*esp*) men and also women, consisting of a long strip of cloth sewn together at the edges, often brightly colored and printed, drooping from the hips, ankle-high. A *sarong* has sewn-together edges while a *kain* does not. *se- sebaju* very close (of friends). *(mendapat) cemar/kotor* to menstruate, have one's period; → HAID. – *basah kering di pinggang* as poor as a church mouse. – *jadi basahan* departed glory. – *dalam lipatan* designing female. – *alas bayi* baby linen. – *alas kapur* bed sheet. – *ampelas* scouring cloth. – *baju* clothing. – *ban* tire cord. – *barut* k.o. belly-belt or girdle. – *basahan* clothing worn everyday (or used for bathing). – *batik* cloth for *batik.* – *bayang* transparent cloth. – *belacu* unbleached cotton cloth. – *bendéra* bunting. – *bentangan* banner. – *bertakak* two

pieces of cloth sewn into one for use as a *sarong*. – *bulu kempa* felted cloth. – *buruk* rag. – *cadar* mattress cover; → CADAR. – *cap* printed cloth. – *cemar* → KAIN *kotor*. – *cindé/cindai* red-patterned dyed *Jv* fabric, i.e., a reticulate bandana silk fabric originating in Sind, once popular as a waist-sash. – *cita* k.o. flowered or striped cotton cloth, chintz. – *dukung* cloth slung over the shoulder for carrying a child. – *gebar* a piece of cotton, in particular enough for one *kain panjang*. – *gerusan* cotton cloth used for polishing. – *goni* burlap. – *hapus* cotton waste. – *has* gauze. – *ikat kepala* head cloth. – *ihram/ikhram* clothes worn during the pilgrimage. – *isyarat* panel. – *jarik* ankle-length *batik* wraparound skirt. – *jendéla* window curtain. – *kaci* white cotton (originally from Kachi or Kutch). – *kadut* coarse sacking, gunny cloth. – *kampuh* garment or blanket (of *kains* sewn together). – *kapur* starched white cloth. – *kasa* cambric. – *kebaya* a *sarung* and *kebaya*. **berkain kebaya** to wear those garments. – *kéci* thin white calico. – *kelarai* heavy cloth (used for sails). – *képar* twilled cloth, twill. – *kerikam* k.o. coarse linen. – *kotor* menstruation. **berkain kotor** to be menstruating. – *kulit* leather cloth. – *lajak* silk fabric. – *lap* duster. – *layang* coat/ piece of cloth that can make a person glide through the air. – *layar* a) canvas. b) oilcloth. – *lénan* linen. – *lindung* fender, screen. – *lintang* banner. – *lurik* handwoven cloth with striped design (not factory made); → LURIK. – *méja* tablecloth; → TAPLAK (*méja*). – *merikan* fabric imported from America, unbleached cotton. – *minyak* oilcloth. – *mori* white calico. – *mota* canvas. – *mréki* → KAIN *merikan*. – *murni* white calico. – *pajangan* banner. – *pakaian* material for dresses. – *pampasan (perang)* (war) reparations cloth (from Japan). – *panas* flannel. – *panjang* a *sarong* not sewn together at the edges. – *pél* mop. – *pelangi* woman's shawl worn with a *kebaya*. – *pelapis* lining. – *pelékat* k.o. striped checked *sarong*; → PELÉKAT. – *pembalut/ pembebat* bandage. – *penetap* (*ob*) towel; → (H)ANDUK. – *penggosok* scouring cloth. – *penyabun* washcloth. – *piké* piqué. – *pintu* door curtain. – *poal* voile. – *popok* baby linen. – *pual* voile. – *rahab/rahap* pall. – *rami* hemp cloth, burlap. – *randi* k.o. ribbed silk fabric used for curtains. – *rentang* advertising banner. – *salut* upholstery. – *sampaian* cloth hung out on a drying frame; → SAMPAIAN. – *saringan* filter cloth. – *sarskin* sharkskin. – *sarung* a *sarong*; → KAIN. – *serkai* filter cloth. – *songkét/sungkit* cloth interspersed with gold thread. – *taf* taffeta. – *tapis* bolting cloth. – *t(e)riko* tricot. – *terpal* tarpaulin, canvas. – *tik* mattress cover, ticking. – *tiras lénsa* lens cloth. – *upih* thick fabric using gold and silver thread.

berkain to wear a *kain* or *sarong*. ~ *dua* to be an adult (said about a woman). ~ *tiga hasta*, ~ *tak cukup sebelit pinggang* and *tak ~ sehelai benang* lacking everything, poverty-stricken.

kain-kainan various k.o. fabrics.

kain II (*Pr*) – *panjang* morphine at the street-dealer's level. – *putih* morphine at the distributor's level.

Kain III (*A?*) (the biblical) Cain.

kainat (*A ob*) the universe.

kaing I (*Jv*) **kaing-kaing** sound of a dog yelping in pain.

berkaing and **mengaing** to yelp.

terkaing-kaing to yelp in pain.

kaing II – and **kaing-kaing** (*rimba*) banded kingfisher, *Lacedo pulchella*.

Kairo Cairo.

kais **mengais(-ngais)** to just scrape by (in making a living, earning one's livelihood).

mengais to scrape, scratch for. ~ *dayung* to paddle along. ~ *dulu maka makan* to eke out one's existence, to live from hand to mouth. *dikais pagi dimakan petang* to live from hand to mouth.

mengaisi (*pl subj*) to scrape/scratch around for. *tempat meréka ~ makanannya* the place where they scratch around for their food.

mengaiskan 1 to scrape by with/on. **2** to scratch around for (food by a mother hen).

kaisan s.t. scraped up.

pengais s.o. who scratches around for s.t.

pengaisan scraping, scratching around.

kaisar (*D*) emperor.

kekaisaran 1 empire. **2** imperial.

kaison (*D*) caisson.

kait 1 hook, crook, clip. *jarum* – crochet hook. **2** complication, trouble, hitch, catch, strings. *ada –nya* there's a catch, there are strings attached. **3** serif. – *gandungan* suspension hook. – *genggam* claw hook. – *jepit* cramp. – *kaki* toe-clip. – *kemudi* rudder pintle. – *mata* eyehook. – *pegas* lock cramp (on a gun). – *pengaman* safety catch. – *tarik* draw hook.

sekait (*infr*) ~ *dengan ini* in this connection.

berkait 1 to have a hook or hooks; on the hook; hooked, furnished with a hook or hooks. **2** coherent, connected. ~ *dengan* in connection with; → BERKAITAN. ~ *tangan* arm in arm. *telunjuk lurus, kelingking* ~ to be up to some trick, have ulterior motives. **3** caught, hooked; → TERSANGKUT *pada. duri* ~ *pada bajunya* his shirt has caught on a thorn.

berkait(-kait)an 1 connected, concerning, regarding, in/with regard (to), related (to), linked (to); suitable, agreeable; → BERSANGKUTAN, BERHUBUNGAN. *Hal-hal yang* ~ *dengan keuangan* financial matters. **2** to be linked together, intertwined, related. *saling berkaitan* interrelated, related to e.o.

kait-berkait(an) to be interwoven.

mengait 1a) to hook s.t., pick s.t. (up/out/off) with a hook. ~ *mangga* to pick mangoes. **b)** to grapple a boat by using a grapnel. ~ *perahu dengan ganco* to grapple a prau with a grapnel. **2** to crochet with a crochet hook. **3** to hook onto s.t., hurt, injure, wound (by s.t. that has a hook/hooks/sharp point). *Duri itu ~ kakinya*. The thorn hurt his foot. *dikait onak* to be caught on thorns. **4** to wheedle money out of s.o., wheedle s.o. out of money. **5** → MENGAITKAN.

mengaitkan 1 to hook. **2** to connect, link, tie, peg, couple, join, associate. *Harga gas dikaitkan dengan Indéks Harga Konsumén*. The price of gas is linked to the Consumer Price Index. *dikaitkan dengan (leg)* juncto, in conjunction with. **3** to involve, implicate. *Ia meminta agar CSA tidak dikaitkan dengan perbuatan Kosék*. He requested that the CSA not be implicated in Kosek's actions.

terkait involved, relevant, related, associated, concerned. *kegiatan* ~ associated activities. **keterkaitan** linkage, interconnection, involvement, relevance, relatedness.

kaitan 1 hook, crook; crochet work, a crocheted stitch. *tali jangan putus,* ~ *jangan serkah* one should be evenhanded. **2** connection, link, linkage, bearing (on s.t.), involvement. *yang ada ~ dengan* which has a connection with. *dalam* ~ *ini* in this connection/context. ~.~ linkages, interconnections. *Tidak ada ~nya dengan kita*. It has no connection with us. **3** shady tricks.

pengait 1 hook, crook. **2** person who hooks s.t.

pengaitan linking, connecting, relating, tying, pegging.

perkaitan connection, relationship. *Apa ~ antara dua gagasan itu?* What's the connection between those two ideas?

kait-kait various k.o. climbing plants, *Uncaria spp. akar* – a climbing plant, *Zizyphus calophylla*.

kajai I *tali* – band around a horse's head, halter.

kajai II → KIJAI.

kajanah → KAZANAH, KHAZANAH.

kajang wickerwork of bamboo, palm leaves, *mengkuang*, etc. for roofing, floor- and wall-coverings, ceilings, and the like. *kertas* – a large sheet of paper (usually folded in two). *lipat* – folded in two. – *rumput* movable wickerwork.

sekajang one sheet (of such wickerwork, etc.).

berkajang to use/have such wickerwork.

mengajangi to provide s.t. with a wickerwork of bamboo, etc. *usang dibarui, lapuk dikajangi* to put a new face on s.t.

terkajang roofed, sheltered with a *kajang*.

pekajangan *kajang*-covered ship's cabin.

kajang II – *ayan* epileptic fit.

kajangan feathered river-garfish, *Zenarchopterus dispar*.

kajari [kepala kejaksaan Républik Indonésia] Attorney General of the Republic of Indonesia.

kajat → HAJAT.

kajeroan (among the Baduys of Banten) the inner *kampung*, the area forbidden to outsiders; → JERO.

kaji I 1 (Koran) recital. **2** lesson, instruction (*esp* in the religious field). **3** knowledge, teaching(s). *-nya sudah tinggi* he is at an advanced stage. *baik –nya* to have learned a lot, to have had a lot of experience. *Itu sudah – yang kedua.* That's of secondary importance. *– lama* it's the same old story (over and over again). *mengulang-ulang – lama* a) to rake up old stories. b) to put forward the same old motion again. c) to keep hammering away at the same subject. *péndék –* in short/brief. *putus –* final, nothing more can be done about it. *jangan putus – dahulu* be a tough customer (or, a stickler); be tenacious; don't give in too quickly. *ulang –* review (of judgment/decision). *Lancar – karena diulang, pasar jalan karena diturut.* Constant dripping will wear away a stone. *Sukar – pada orang alim, sukar uang pada orang kaya* (*M*). "Intelligent people only want to make a decision after careful consideration, and the rich only want to spend money if they can make a profit," i.e., look before you leap.

mengaji [and **ngaji** (*coq*)] **1** to learn to recite the Koran; → MENDARAS. **2** to read/recite the Koran. **3** to learn to read things written in Arabic. *~ agama* to study religion. *~ batang* to learn to read the Koran without spelling out the words one by one. *~ dari alif* to do things in the proper order. *~ tasawuf* to study Islamic mysticism.

mengkaji to examine and study in order to learn about, investigate. *Manusia senantiasa ingin ~ isi jagat raya.* Man always wants to study the cosmos. *tak dapat dikaji* inscrutable.

mengajikan to read the Koran (for a deceased person).

terkaji investigated, studied. *tiada ~* inscrutable, cannot be easily understood, unverifiable.

kajian (the) study (of). *~ kelayakan* feasibility study. *~ telik* critical study.

kaji-kajian studies.

pengkaji 1 research (*mod*). *lembaga ~* a research organization. **2** researcher.

pengaji and **pengkaji** (*mod*) study, research; investigator. *tim ~* study team.

pengajian a gathering at which Islam is discussed.

pengkajian 1 (careful) examination, study, analysis, review. *~ Indonésia* Indonesian studies (in a university). *~ keterlaksanaan* feasibility study. *~ menyeluruh* overall review. **2** doctrine. *~ Stratégi Angkatan Darat* Army Strategic Doctrine.

kaji II name of various fish species, sweet lips, *Plectorynchus spp.*

kajung (*Pr*) tall and thin; → JANGKUNG.

kak I clipped form of *kakak.*

kak II (*coq*) right; → HAK I.

kak III (*onom*) quack, sound made by person laughing, by a duck, etc.; → DEKAK II, KAKAK II.

kakaban palm-fibers held together by bamboo for protecting fish eggs.

kakah (*M*) **ngakah** to laugh. *suara ~nya* the sound of his laughing.

terkakah-kakah to roar with laughter.

kakak I 1 older sister. **2** (in some regions) older brother; → ABANG I. **3** form of address for older person (irrespective of sex). **4** wife's term of address for her husband; → MAS II. *– anak* placenta. *–. beradik* a pair of siblings. *Addy dan Budi adalah ~.* Addy and Budi are siblings. *empat ~* four siblings. *– ipar* sibling/cousin-in-law married to one's *kakak.* *– misan* second cousin of older lineage.

berkakak 1 to have an older sibling. *Ia tidak ~ tidak beradik.* He has no older or younger siblings. **2** to address s.o. using the word *kakak.* *Baik engkau ~ kepada anak ini.* You should address this child as *kakak.*

kakak II berkakak(an) and **mengakak** to make the sound "kak, kak," i.e., the sound that ducks make, to quack.

terkakak-kakak, ngakak and *tertawa* **ngakak** to laugh noisily, guffaw, roar with laughter.

kakaktua → KAKATUA.

kakan k.o. tree; → MERANTI *mérah.*

kakanda more respectful than *kakak* I, often used in epistolary style.

kakang (*Jv cla*) **1** older brother. **2** husband.

kakanwil [kepala kantor wilayah] regional office head.

kakao (*D*) **1** cacao. **2** cocoa.

kakap I 1 a species of marine fish, often referred to as giant perch or bass. *– batu* sea bass, *Lates calcarifer*; k.o. fish, triple tail, *Lo-*

botes surinamensis; sweet lips, *Pseudopristipoma nigra.* *– bébék* k.o. fish, *Epinephelus sp.* *– mérah* red snapper, *Lutjanus argentimaculatus.* *– putih* sea bass, *Lates calcarifer.* **2** (*mod*) big, major; *opp* TERI. *kelas –* major, big (criminal/corruptor).

kakap II *perahu –* a river boat.

kakap III mengakap to reconnoiter, patrol, observe.

pengakap 1 scout, observer, reconnoiterer. **2** Boy Scout.

pengakapan scouting.

kakap IV *sirih –* coarse and dry *sirih* leaves; → KERAKAP.

kakap V (*M ob*) **mengakap** to hold, seize; to do, perform, work, carry out; to till, cultivate (rice fields, etc.). *– jawat* activities.

kakar → KEKAR I.

kakas I (*M*) scratch (with claw). *– ayam* a scrawl.

mengakas to scratch up (food, of chickens), scrape around for food.

kakas II force. *– apung* buoyancy. *– empar* centrifugal force. *– ganduh* exchange force. *– impun* centripetal force. *– lintang* transverse force. *– pulih* restoring force.

mengakas to force, coerce, compel.

kakatua 1 cockatoo. *– hitam/palma/raja* palm cockatoo, *Probosciger aterrimus*, native to Irian Jaya and the Moluccas. *– (putih besar) jambul kuning* sulfur-crested cockatoo, *Cacatua galerita.* *– Maluku* salmon-crested cockatoo, *Cacatua moluccensis.* **2** pair of pliers, pincers. **3** (*ikan –*) k.o. parrot fish, *Callyodon spp.*

kakau → KAKAO.

kakawin (*Jv*) old Javanese poetic work and meter.

Kakbah → KAABAH.

kakeji → KEJI II.

kakék (*J/Jv*) **1** grandfather, grandpa; (*coq*) old man; → AKI I, DATUK, KAKI II, NÉNÉK. **2** (= **kakék-kakék**) a) an old man. b) very old man. *– moyang* grandparents and great-grandparents, forefathers, ancestors. *– nénék* a) grandparents. b) old folks. c) senior citizens.

berkakék to call s.o. *kakék.*

kakén (*Jv*) (being) an old man. *Semoga rukun-rukun selalu sampai –.- ninén-ninén.* May your marriage last through your very old age/till death do you part. *dari anak-anak sampai – ninén* young and old.

kakerlak (*D*) /-lak/ cockroach. *– baju hijau* thugs in military uniforms.

kaki I 1 leg, the part of the body from hip to ankle. *-nya dipalang dari belakang.* He was tripped. **2** foot, the part of the body from the ankle to the sole. **3** leg, support of a chair/table, etc.; foundation, base, pedestal. *– kursi/méja* leg of a chair/table. *– rumah* foundation of a house. **4** foot, bottom (part of s.t.). *– bukit/gunung* foot of a hill/mountain. **5** counter for objects with stems/handles, such as umbrellas, flowers, mushrooms. *lima – payung* five umbrellas. *bunga bukan sekaki* (*Mal*) "there is more than one flower," i.e., there is more than one girl in the world, there is more than one fish in the sea. **6** foot, 12 inches. *5000 – dari permukaan laut* 5,000 feet above sea level. **7** (mostly *Mal*) s.o. addicted to s.t. *– arak* drunkard addicted to toddy. *batang –* main parts of the leg: thigh and calf. *bola –* football (soccer). *ibu –* big toe. *jari –* little toe. *kura-kura –* instep. *mata –* ankle. *mesin jahit –* treadle sewing machine. *t(el)apak – sole* (of foot). *bercemar –* to go; to visit. *berjalan –* (to go) on foot, walk. *melangkahkan –* a) to leave, depart. b) *melangkahkan -nya* to stride. *sepembawa –* at random. *– sudah terlangkahkan* already done; too late to do anything about it now. *membuang –* to shift feet (at *pencak*). *berjalan peliharaan –, berkata peliharaan lidah* look before you leap. *terikat – tangan* bound/tied hand and foot. *– naik kepala turun* to bustle about. *cepat –, ringan tangan* ready and willing to help. *– untuk dipakaikan gelang* it's like a blacksmith with a white silk apron, i.e., inappropriate. *– ayam* a) drumstick. b) (*dengan*) *– ayam* to be/ go barefoot. c) name of a tree, Japanese persimmon, *Diospyros kaki Linn.* d) bar support. *– belalang* (symbol of) a beautiful leg. *– bersilang* cross-legged. *– celana* pant('s) leg. *– datar* flatfeet. *– dian* candlestick. *– dinding* plinth. *– gajah* elephantiasis. *– gigi* root of the tooth. *– hutan* edge of the forest. *– jangkar* anchor leg. *– judi* inveterate gambler. *– kuda* an herb, gotu kola,

Centella asiatica, used in traditional medicine to cure epilepsy/coughs/bronchitis/hypertension, etc. – *kuda-kuda* rafter. – *langit* horizon. – *lépér* flat feet. – *lilin* candlestick. – *lima* a) flight of steps (leading up to the front door of a house). b) five-foot-wide sidewalk. – *péndék* (*euph*) pork or pig. – *péngkor/piuh* clubfoot. – *rumah* foundation. – *seribu* to take to one's heels, run away. – *tangan* a) feet and hands. b) accomplice, henchman, stooge, running dog. c) – *tangan kerajaan* (*Mal*) government employee. – *telanjang* barefoot, unshod. – *tiang* a) pedestal. b) (*naut*) tabernacle (deck plank through which mast passes). – *tiga* tripod, trivet.

sekaki a foot (in measurements).

berkaki with feet/legs, to have feet/legs, footed. *binatang (yang)* ~ *empat* four-footed animal. *sudah* ~ *tiga* to be old and hobbling about (needing a support cane). ~ (*ke)pada* to lean on. ~ *ayam* to be/go barefoot. ~ *seribu* to run away.

mengaki 1 to be apprenticed (to), be in domestic service. 2 to kowtow. ~ *langit* horizontal. ~ *méja* (*coq*) to be left back, not promoted to a higher grade (in school).

kekakian (*geol*) footage.

pekaki ~ *layar* (*naut*) boom. ~ *lima* sidewalk vendor. **perkakilimaan** system of sidewalks, sidewalk (*mod*).

kaki II (*ob*) 1 grandfather; old man.

kaki-kaki (*Jv*) very old man.

kaki III (*D/E*) khaki.

kaki IV (*burung*) – *dian* k.o. bird, common redshank, *Tringa totanus eurhinus*. – *lébar* red-necked phalarope, *Phalaropus lobatus*. (*burung*) – *sirip* masked fin foot, *Heliopais personata*.

kakofoni (*D/E*) cacophony.

kakok (*M ob*) **mengakok**; → KAKAP III.

kakrupukan (*Jv*) 1 alarmed, nervous. 2 panic; → KEKRUPUKAN.

kaksa (*C*) layer of earth containing tin ore.

kaktus (*D/E*) cactus.

kaku 1 stiff (from cold/death/fear; of hair), unbending. 2 hard (of frozen meat, etc.). 3 tongue-tied, not fluent; too shy to speak. *Ia berasa* –. He felt tongue-tied. 4 clumsy, awkward. 5 ill at ease, uncomfortable, not (feeling) at home, as if not in one's own home. 6 spastic. *Tingkah-lakunya* –. His behavior is not gentle. – *beku* stiffened, no longer flexible. – *hati* hard-hearted, unfeeling, pitiless, cruel. – *lidah* unable to talk easily, quiet; finds it hard to pronounce foreign words. – *mayat* rigor mortis. – *mulut* lockjaw.

sekaku as stiff/awkward, etc. as.

terkaku tongue-tied.

mengaku to stiffen, become stiff.

mengakukan to stiffen s.t.

kekakuan 1 stiffness, awkwardness, clumsiness. 2 rigidity.

kakung (*Jv*) 1 manly. 2 husband. *pengantin* – groom. – *putri* husband and wife.

kakus (*D*) toilet. – *berjalan* toilet (on a bus, etc.). – *jongkok* squat toilet.

kal (*ob*) half a *cupak* or 1/8 of a *gantang*.

kala I (*Skr*) 1 time; age, period, era, epoch. *dahulu* – in former days/times, formerly, of old; → ZAMAN *dahulu*. *di/pada* – by the time that, when. *pada* – *keréta api itu* when the train arrived. *di/pada* – *itu* at that time, in those days, then. *sepanjang* – always, ever; all the time, continuously, steadily. 2 when (in the past). *wajah Tahir* – *meninjau hotél itu* ... when he looked at the hotel, Tahir's face ... *kadang* – sometimes. – *depan/keakanan* the future. – *kini* the present. – *lampau* the past. – *nanti* the future. – *tua* one's old age.

kalanya *ada* ~ at times, sometimes. *tiada* ~ continuously.

berkala 1 (*surat* ~) periodical, magazine, review; journal. 2 periodic (meetings/reports, etc.). *tiada* ~ not tied down to any fixed time, irregular.

berkala-kala from time to time, at times, occasionally.

kekalaan periodicity.

kala II 1 scorpion, *Scorpionida spp*. 2 (the constellation) Scorpio. – *bangkau* a black scorpion with wide pincers, black scorpion, Asian forest scorpion, *Heterometrus longimanus*. – *jengking* the common house-scorpion. – *mangga* (*Jv*) the common house-spider.

kala III (*ob*) snare, trap.

kala IV (*A ob*) silk material.

kala V → KADA II.

Kala VI *Batara* – Shiva as the Destroyer.

kala-kala (*naut*) sea anchor.

kalab (*A*) a star in Scorpio.

kalah → ALAH I. 1 to lose, defeated, conquered, beaten. *-nya banyak sekali* (*I*) lost heavily. *menerima/menyerah* – to accept defeat. – *dalam perang* to lose a war. – *membeli menang memakai* cheap is cheap; you get what you pay for; quality costs (money). – (*dan*) *menang* chance(s). 2 to lose (in business/gambling, etc), suffer a loss of. *Dia* – *sepuluh ribu rupiah*. He lost 10,000 rupiahs. 3 to fail (an examination). 4 less(er), lower, inferior. – *angka/biji* to be of lesser/lower value; to count for less; not to be held in high esteem. – *awu* (*Jv*) describes the relationship of the children of a younger sibling compared to the children of an older sibling in the same family. – *besar* (*dengan*) not as large (as). – *dengan* to rank below. *tidak/tak* – (*dengan*) no less (than), not less (than), not inferior to. *tak* – *dahsyatnya dengan bom atom* no less horrible than the atomic bomb. *tak* – *menang* undecided (a fight because the opponents are equally strong). *tak mau* – *dengan* is not to be outdone by. – *hati* downhearted. – *hawa/pengaruh* to be no match for. – *pintar dari/oléh* to be beaten by ... in knowledge, less clever than. – *stém* to be outvoted. **mengalah-stémkan** to outvote. – *suara* to lose an election. – *takluk* to be subjugated. **mengalah-taklukkan** to subjugate.

mengalah [and **ngalah** (*coq*)] to give in/up/way, yield (the right of way). *tidak mau* ~ (*I*) won't give up. ~ *mempersilakan yang lain jalan dulu* to yield the right of way to the other driver. ~ *pada* to succumb to.

kalah-mengalah 1 to give and take; lenient. 2 (in traffic) to yield to e.o.

mengalahkan [and **ngalahin** (*J coq*)] 1 to defeat, beat, overcome. 2 to declare s.o. the loser. *Pengadilan Negeri* ~ *instansi itu*. The District Court declared the agency the loser (in a lawsuit).

terkalahkan can be conquered. *tidak* ~ unconquerable, unbeatable.

kalahan the one defeated. *yang* ~ the underdog.

kekalahan 1 loss, defeat. *menebus* ~*nya* to recoup one's losses. 2 to lose, be defeated.

pengalah s.o. who gives in easily.

pengalahan → ALAH.

kalai I (*M*) **mengalai** to lean on, lounge against. *tikar* – sleeping mat. **mengalaikan** to let s.o. or s.t. lean against s.t., lean s.t. (on s.t.).

kalai II mengalai to scrape (rust from pots and pans for replating).

kalaidoskop → KALÉIDOSKOP.

kalaidoskopik → KALÉIDOSKOPIK.

kalajengking → KALA II.

kalak I 1 *sungsang* – topsy-turvy, upside down. – *kalik* flip-flop. 2 (*math infr*) inverse.

kalak II k.o. tree, *Mitrophora javanica*.

kalakanji → KELAKANJI.

kalakati (*M*) (a pair of) scissors (for cutting *pinang*).

kalakatu flying white ant; → LARON.

kalakemarin the day before yesterday; → KEMARIN *dulu*.

kalakian (*Skr? cla*) next, then, moreover.

kalam I (*A*) word (of God). *akhirul* – at last, eventually, finally; → AKHIRNYA. *berpanjang* – to digress, expatiate, dwell (on a subject). *tammatul* – the end (at the end of a speech/book, etc.); *cp* SEKIANLAH, TAMAT. *ilmu* – dogmatics, religious doctrine. – *Allah* and –*ullah* the word of God.

kalam II (*A*) 1 writing pen; style, stylus; → QALAM. – *batu* (*ob*) slate pencil; → ANAK *batu tulis*. – *resam* (*ob*) k.o. pen made from the rib of a fern. – *sagar* (*ob*) k.o. pen made from *sagar* fiber. 2 (*cla*) penis.

kalam III (*M*) k.o. black sand mixed with washed gold. *semiang* – a grain, whit, particle, bit.

kalam IV → KALEM.

kalamayar → KELEMAYAR.

kalambak → KELEMBAK I.

kalamdan (*A cla*) pen-case.

kalamisani k.o. *Jv* kris.

kalamkari (*A cla*) painted calico.

kalandar (*A cla*) k.o. religious mendicant.

kalang I underlayer; support; prop, stay, bracket; → GALANG I. *besar* – cowardly. *sempit* – irascible (in temper), short-/hot-/quick-tempered, has a bad temper. *terbalik* – against the grain; to be contrary, defy. – *batang* (*cla*) a fine levied on s.o. who has violated customs or religion. – *hulu* pillow. **berkalang hulu** with a pillow. – *motor* engine bracket.

  berkalang 1 to lean/recline on. **2** supported by (*dengan*). ~ *lidah* (*M*) to debate, discuss the pros and cons. *(mati)* ~ *tanah* "to have earth for one's pillow," i.e., to be dead, deceased.

  mengalang and **memperkalang** to support, uphold, prop (up).

  mengalangkan to support/prop up with. ~ *(batang) léhér* and ~ *merih* to risk one's life (for s.o.).

  terkalang 1 supported. **2** to have s.t. on one's mind, s.t. is sticking in one's craw. *Lidahnya* ~. He couldn't get a word out, he was speechless. *yang* ~ *di hatinya/matanya* what he has on his mind. ~ *di mata* visualized, in one's mind's eye. ~ *lidah* afraid to respond.

  kalangan dock, wharf; → GALANGAN *kapal*. ~ *hulu* pillow. ~ *kapal* a) dock. b) shipyard; → GALANGAN.

kalang II kalangan 1 (social) circle (of friends/politicians, etc.), group. *di* ~ *kami* in our in-group. *dari semua* ~ from all walks of life. *bahasa* ~ jargon. ~ *atas* the upper classes/echelons. ~ *pemerintah* government circles. ~ *penjahat* the underworld. ~ *pramuka* Boy Scout circles. ~ *remaja* teenagers. ~ *resmi* official sources. *dalam* ~ *terpelajar* in intellectual circles. **2** (*Jv*) population group (*esp* those with special professions, such as merchants, etc.). **3** halo, a ring of light that seems to encircle the moon, etc. ~ *bulan* halo around the moon. **4** enclosed space, arena, race track; soccer field, tennis court; → GELANGGANG.

kalang III – *kabut* dark, dim, gloomy; chaotic, confused; perplexed.

  mengalang-kabutkan to confuse.

  kekalang-kabutan confusion.

kalang IV log raft.

kalang V *ikan* – k.o. fish. *tertangkap di ikan* – to be able to stand up to smart people or the rich.

Kalang VI *orang* – the Kalang people of the Kotagedé area in Yogyakarta. Local legend says that they are the descendants of prisoners brought back by Sultan Agung from his abortive expedition to Bali in the 17th century. They manufacture articles from silver.

kalangenan (*S*) recreation.

kalangkati → KALAKATI.

kalap (*J/Jv*) **1** mad, crazy; bewitched, possessed (by an evil spirit). – *karena cemburuan* crazy with jealousy. **2** berserk. *menjadi* – to go berserk. **3** bewildered, confused.

  kekalapan 1 confusion. **2** bewilderment.

kalar (*E ob*) a collar.

kalas I tholepin, rattan rowlock.

  mengalas to put (an oar) into the tholepin.

  terkalas placed in the tholepin.

kalas II *habis* – run out, nothing is left.

kalat I saltwater parrot fish, *Callyodon fasciatus*.

kalat II smegma.

kalau 1 if, if it is. – *dia* if it were he, (*coq*) if it was him. – *keluar, harus minta izin dulu*. If you want to go out, you have to ask for permission first. – *petang* in the afternoon. **2** if, supposing that, for example; → SEANDAINYA. – *dia tidak mau membayar* ... if/supposing he doesn't want to pay ... **3** when (in general or in the future). – *pekerjaanmu sudah selesai* ... when you finish your work ... **4** as for, for one, personally. – *saya, perkara itu mudah saja memecahkannya*. Personally/as for me, that's easy to solve. **5** – *tidak* (... *tentu saja*) a) otherwise ... would/will certainly. b) (or, – *begitu*) otherwise. – *begitu* if so, in that case. **6** – ... *maka* ... whereas ... (in contrast) ... **7** (*Jv*) if, whether; → APA(KAH). *Saya tidak tahu* – *dia datang*. I don't know whether/if he's come. **8** (*Jv*) that; → BAHWA I. – *pun* even if; → JIKA ... *sekalipun*. – *pun ada, tentu mahal juga* even if there are any, they will be expensive.

  kalau-kalau 1 (to hope, etc.) that. **2** (to be afraid, etc.) that perhaps/maybe. **3** (to look/ask/listen, etc.) if by any chance, just in case. *Coba tanyakan kepada gurumu,* ~ *ia tahu*. Ask your teacher if (by any chance) he knows.

kalawarta (*Skr neo*) periodical (publication).

Kalbar [Kalimantan Barat] West Kalimantan.

kalbi (*ob*) → KALBU.

kalbu (*A*) heart (the seat of the emotions). – *zakiah* a sincere heart.

kalbud → KELEBUT.

kaldai → KELEDAI.

kaldéra (*D/E*) caldera.

kaldron (*D/E*) cauldron.

kaldu (*Port*) broth.

Kalédong (*coq*) and **Kalédonia Baru** New Caledonia.

kaléidoskop (*D*) kaleidoscope.

kaléidoskopik (*D*) kaleidoscopic.

kalelep → KELELAP.

kalem (*D*) calm. *berbuat* – to keep calm/cool.

  kekaleman calmness.

kalembak → KELEMBAK I.

kalénan (*Jv*) trench (for water).

kalénder (*D/E*) calendar. – *polos/yang bergambar wanita setengah bugil* pinup calendar.

kaléng (*Port ?*) **1** tin (box). *surat* – an anonymous letter. **2** (oil/milk, etc.) can (made of tin). **3** sheet, stamping, plate. – *tutup* covering plate.

  mengaléngi and **mengaléngkan** to can.

  kaléngan 1 canned/tinned food. **2** in cans. *dijual* ~ sold in cans.

  kaléng-kaléngan canned goods.

  pengaléng canner.

  pengaléngan canning (food).

kalérék → KELÉREK.

kaléro a dish peculiar to Central Celebes.

kali I time, occasion. *acap* – often, repeatedly, again and again. *beberapa* – several times. *(sudah) berulang* – (it happens) repeatedly. *bilang* – a) whenever. b) at any time. c) each time. *dua* – twice. *kerap* – often, frequently. *satu* – once. *sepuluh* – ten times. *sering* – often, repeatedly, again and again. *tiga* – (*sehari*) three times/thrice (a day). *untuk pertama* –(*nya*) and *untuk* – *pertama* for the first time. *buat/untuk/yang ketiga* –(*nya*) (for) the third time. – *ini* this time, for once.

  sekali 1 one time, once. ~ *pandang* at first glance/sight. ~ *sekala* once in a while, now and then. **2** one, a single. *dengan* ~ *dayung* at one pull. *dengan* ~ *guris* at one stroke (of the pen). *dengan* ~ *lihat* at first sight. *dengan* ~ *lompat* with one bound/leap. ~ *dua* once or twice. ~ *jalan* a) (all) at once. b) one way (trip). c) short time (with a prostitute), a quickie. – *lagi* a) once more. b) and nothing but. *hanya tenaga,* ~ *lagi tenaga* sheer force and nothing but force. ~ *main* short time (with prostitute), a quickie; → SOT *tém*. ~ *minum* in a (single) gulp, in one gulp. ~ *pakai* disposable, single-use. ~ *pandang saja* at first sight/glance. ~ *pukul* at a/one blow, all at the same time, simultaneously. ~ *témpo/waktu* one/some day, sometime in the future. *Kalau* ~ *waktu anda jadi penumpang kapal* ... If some day you are a passenger on a ship ... ~ ... *tetap* ... once ... always ... ~ *merdéka tetap merdéka* once free, always free. **3** every/once every (time period). *dua hari* ~ every other day, once every two days. **4**a) very (following an (*mod*), very well (following a verb). *mahal* – very expensive. *Tanggal tersebut diingatnya* ~. He remembers that date very well. *banyak* ~ very much, a great deal. b) very many, a great many. c) quite a lot. ~ *banyak* (to produce) many at the same time, mass production. **5** ~ *peristiwa* (*cla*) once upon a time (used at the beginning of a story). **6** (= **sekaligus**) a) all at once. *Utangnya dibayarnya* ~. He paid all his debts at once. b) simultaneously, at time same time. c) without delay. d) everything (without exception). *Semua yang ada dibakarnya* ~. He burnt everything. e) completely. *sama* ~ and *sama* ~ i) altogether, quite, completely, entirely, totally. ii) (all) in all, one with another. f) right at ..., at the very ... *Ia duduk di belakang* ~. He sits right at the back (or, at the very back). **sekalian 1** all. ~ *mahluk* all creatures. *Kita* ~ *wajib membantu*. All of us are obliged to help. **2** (*coq*) *kamu* – you-all, you guys. **3** (*coq*) at the same time. *Kalau pergi ke pasar,* ~ *belikan saya* ... If you go to the market, at the same time buy me ... **menyekalikan** to combine s.t., do s.t. at the same time.

sekali-kali extremely. ~ *tidak* never at all, not (even) once, under no circumstances. *jangan* ~ never, on no account. *Jangan* ~ *memperlihatkan kepandaianmu.* On no account show your skill. *Dia* ~ *tidak memikirkan keluarganya.* He never thinks about his family.

sekali-sekali once in a while, every now and then. ~ *boléh juga menonton bioskop.* Once in a while he is allowed to go to the movies.

berkali-kali repeatedly, again and again, over and over.

mengalikan and **memperkalikan** to multiply. *mengalikan dua* to multiply by two.

kalian 1 → SEKALIAN. **2** *daftar* ~ multiplication table. ~.~ → DAFTAR *kali-kalian.*

kali-kalian multiplication table. ~ *empat* the fours table.

pengali (*math*) multiplier.

perkalian 1 multiplication. **2** product (of a multiplication). **3** multiplication table. ~ *tiga* the threes table.

kali II (*J*) → BARANGKALI.

kali III (*Jv*) river; → SUNGAI. – *mati* a river that has run dry.

kali IV → KADI.

kalian (*coq*) you-all, you guys.

Kalibata the heroes' cemetery in Jakarta.

  meng-Kalibatakan to bury in the Kalibata heroes' cemetery.

kaliber (*D/E*) caliber, gauge. – *besar* large caliber. – *kecil* small caliber. – *tuang* template.

  berkaliber to be of ... caliber. *orang* ~ *besar* a man of high caliber.

kalibrasi (*D*) calibration.

kalibut (*M*) commotion.

kalicau (*M*) **mengalicau** to dodge, evade, avoid.

  mengalicaukan to turn (one's face) aside, avoid danger.

kalifah and **kalifat** → KHALIFAH.

Kalifornia California.

kaligata (*S*) nettle rash, hives, urticaria.

kaligrafer (*E*) calligrapher.

kaligrafi (*D/E*) calligraphy. *ahli* – calligrapher.

kaligrafis (*D*) calligraphic.

kalih I (*ob*) **berkalih** to move, shift. ~ *muka* to turn one's face. ~ *tidur* to move in one's sleep. *Habis tahun* ~ *musim.* Everything must be adjusted to circumstances.

kalih II (*Jv*) two.

kalik → KALAK *kalik.*

kalikanji → KALAKANJI.

kalikasar → KALIKAUSAR I.

kalikausar I (*A cla*) things, personal affects.

kalikausar II (*A*) (= *telaga kausar*) waters of Paradise.

kaliki (*M*) papaya; → BETIK I, KATÉS, PAPAYA.

kalimah (*A*) → KALIMAT. *dua* –, – *yang dua* and – *sahadat/syaha-dat* the two Arabic sentences expressing the Muslim creed: "There is no God but Allah, and Muhammed is his Prophet." – *thoyyibah* praise of Allah. – *zikir* the Arabic sentence "There is no god but God" and other sentences.

Kalimantan Indonesian Borneo.

kalimantang 1 long, white pennant. **2** white streak of light, beam. **3** luminous millipede, *Orphnaeus brevilabiatus.*

  mengalimantang 1 shining (phosphorescently, like a *kali-mayah*). **2** flashing (of lightning). **3** multicolored; beautiful (illumination/sunup/sunset, etc.).

kalimat (*A*) **1** sentence. **2** word. **3** clause. *anak* – bound/dependent/subordinate clause. *dua* – → DUA *kalimah. induk* – main clause. *perkataan (di) dalam* – a word in context. *pokok* – subject of the sentence. – *bébas* free sentence. – *berita* declarative sentence. – *bersusun* complex sentence. – *bertingkat* compound or complex sentence. – *dasar* basic sentence. – *déklaratif* declarative sentence. – *éksisténsial* existential sentence. – *ékuatif* equational sentence. – *éliptis* elliptical sentence. – *impératif* imperative sentence. – *intérogatif* interrogative sentence. – *inti* kernel sentence. – *jawaban* response sentence. – *konstituén* constituent clause. – *lengkap* full sentence. – *majemuk* compound sentence. – *matriks* matrix sentence. – *minor* verbless sentence, sentence fragment, minor sentence type. – *minor bukan klausa* non-clause structure. – *perintah* impera-

tive sentence. – *pernyataan* declarative sentence. – *persyaratan* conditional sentence. – *pertanyaaan* interrogative sentence. – *rapatan* (*ling*) a sentence in which a repeated constituent is deleted. – *sahadat/syahadat;* → KALIMAH. – *sampingan* marginal sentence. – *seruan* exclamatory sentence. – *tak lengkap* minor sentence type. – *tanggapan* response sentence. – *tanya* interrogative sentence. – *terbelah* cleft sentence. – *terbelah semu* pseudo-cleft sentence. – *terikat* dependent clause. – *Tuhan* God's word. – *tunggal* simple sentence. – *turunan* derived sentence. – *urutan* sequential sentence. – *yang dua;* → KALIMAH.

kalimatullah (*A*) the word of God.

Kalimatu(sy)syahadat *A* → KALIMAH.

kalimaya(h) I (*Jv*) luminous centipede, *Geophilus sp.*

kalimaya II *batu* – white opal.

kalimpanang (*ob*) (*akar* –) a plant with potable juice.

kaling → KOLANG-KALING II.

kalingan (*J*) hidden, concealed, the sight has been obstructed by s.t.

kalio (*M*) a k.o. Sumatran stew (not as dry as *rendang*). – *ayam* chicken curry with chilies.

kalipah and **kalipat** → KHALIFAH.

kalipso I (*D*) calypso orchid, *Calypso bulbosa*; the solitary flower has purple or yellow markings.

kalipso II (*D/E*) calypso (music).

kalis I (*A*) pure, clean; → KHALIS.

kalis II (*Jv*) **1** not shiny, dim, nonglare, frosted. **2** impervious to water, nonabsorbent, -proof. **3** invulnerable, unsusceptible/immune to disease. – *air* waterproof. – *gas* gas proof. – *jais* inattentive/not receptive (to advice). – *udara* airproof.

  mengalis to peel.

kalium (*D*) potassium.

kaliyoga the fourth and worst period of the world.

kalk (*D*) /kalek/ chalk.

kalkalah → KULKULAH.

kalkarim (*D*) a wall paint.

kalkasar → KALIKAUSAR I.

kalkausar → KALIKAUSAR II.

kalkir (*D*) tracing, calque.

kalkulasi (*D*) calculation.

  mengkalkulasikan to calculate.

kalkulatoris calculable. *penyusutan* – calculable depreciation.

kalkulus (*D/E*) calculus.

kalkun (*D*) turkey, *Meleagris galopavo.*

kalkuta Calcutta.

kalm → KALEM.

kalo I (*Jv*) a fine sieve, strainer.

kalo(k) II (*coq*) → KALAU.

kalong I (*J/Jv*) a fruit-eating flying fox, *Pterocarpus edulis/vampyrus*; → KELUANG. *bulu* – down, fine body hair.

kalong II *puasa* – (in *Jv* mysticism) to fast by eating only fruits.

kalongwéwé (*J*) vampire (bat).

kalor (*D*) heat. – *atom* atomic heat. – *bakar* heat of combustion. – *beku* heat of solidification. – *embunan* heat of condensation. – *éncéran* integral heat of dilution. – *habluran* heat of crystallization. – *ionisasi* heat of ionization. – *lebur* heat of fusion. – *listrik* electrothermal heat. – *molar* molar/molecular heat. – *pembekuan* heat of solidification. – *spésifik* specific heat.

kalori (*D/E*) calorie. *rendah* – low in calories.

  berkalori to contain calories, caloric.

kaloriméter (*D/E*) calorimeter.

kalowatan babirusa, *Sus babirusa.*

kalpataru (*Skr*) **1** arbor vitae; → POHON *hayati.* **2** annual award given by the government for environmental friendliness.

kalsifikasi (*D*) calcification.

kalsit (*D/E*) calcite.

kalsium (*D/E*) calcium. – *fluorida* fluorite.

kalu (*J*) → KALAU.

kalubu various species of bandicoots, *Echymipera spp.* and other species.

kalui (*S*) (*ikan* –) giant gourami, *Osphronemus offax.*

kaluk I → KELUK. **berkaluk** *tidur* ~ to sleep in a fetal position (because of the cold).

kaluk II (*coq*) → KALAU.

kalulus → KELULUS.

kalung I 1 necklace. – *bunga* (Hawaiian) lei. 2 halo.

berkalung to wear a necklace.

berkalungkan with … as a necklace.

mengalungi to put (a necklace, etc.) around. *Léhérnya dikalungi seutas tali.* A strand of rope was placed around his throat.

mengalungkan to put … around s.o.'s neck. ~ *Bintang Sakti kepada* to put the Bintang Sakti medal around the neck of.

terkalung be hung. *Di léhérnya ~ handuk putih berukuran kecil.* Around her neck was hung a small towel.

pengalungan hanging s.t. around the neck, wreathing. ~ *bunga* putting a wreath (on).

kalung II (*Pr*) small sickle-shaped knife.

kalurahan (*Jv*) → KELURAHAN.

kalus (*D/E*) callus.

kalut I (= berkalut) confused, chaotic. *perasaan yang* – and – *pikirannya* hopelessly lost/confused. – *malut* confused. **mengalut-malutkan** to confuse.

mengalutkan to confuse, throw out of gear; to upset (s.o.'s plans, calculations). ~ *bin kacau* extremely confused.

kekalutan confusion, disorder, disturbance, commotion, turmoil, unrest; hullabaloo.

Kalut II [Kalimantan Utara] North Kalimantan.

kam I (*D*) bridge (of violin).

kam II (*D*) camp. – *latihan* training camp.

kam III (*D*) comb; → SISIR I.

kam IV (in acronyms) → KEAMANAN.

kam V (*A*) amount.

kama I (*Skr Jv*) 1 love, passion. 2 sperm.

Kama II (*Skr*) Hindu god of love, Cupid.

kamaitan k.o. plant, *Lunasia amara*.

Kamajaya (*Skr*) (*Batara* –) Cupid.

kamal (*A*) perfect (of God).

kaman (*Pr*) to eat; → MAKAN.

Kamandanu name of a train running between Jakarta and Semarang.

Kamania Sasanagraha General Secretariat Building (in the MPR compound).

kamar I (*D*) 1 room, chamber. 2 cabin. 3 unit (in an apartment building). 4 gun chamber. – *baca* reading room. – *bakar* combustion chamber. – *balut* first-aid room. – *bedah* operating room (in hospital). – *belajar* study room/hall. – *bersalin* delivery room. – *besi* vault (in bank). – *bicara* a) consulting room (of physician). b) telephone booth. – *bilas* changing room (in public swimming pool). – *bola* a) clubhouse, casino. b) game room, pool-room. – *Dagang dan Industri* [KADIN] Chamber of Commerce and Industry. – *depan* front room. – *dalam* inner room. – *dingin* cold storage chamber. – *duduk* living room (in a house). – *és* ice house. – *gabung* adjoining room. – *ganti* dressing room. – *gas* gas chamber. – *gelap* a) prison cell. b) (photographic) dark room. – *hias* dressing room. – *induk* master bedroom. – *jenazah* morgue. – *kasak-kusuk* lobby (in Parliament). – *kecil* toilet, powder room, lavatory, restroom, bathroom (equipped with a washbowl/toilet, etc.). – *kerja* workroom. – *laras* magazine (of a firearm). – *makan* dining room. – *mandi* a) bathroom (equipped with facilities for taking a bath or shower). b) full bath. – *mati/mayat* mortuary, the morgue. – *meriam* casemate. – *mesin* engine room. – *minum* bar; → BAR I. – *motor* motor compartment. – *muka* anteroom. – *niaga* chamber of commerce. – *obat* pharmacy, dispensary. – *operasi* operating room (in a hospital). – *pas* fitting room. – *pembantu* maid's room. – *pencetusan* ignition chamber. – *pendingin* cold storage (chamber). – *penginapan* guest room (on ship). – *penjaga* guard room. – *peraga* showroom. – *perang* war room. – *perban* first-aid room. – *periksa* examining room. – *persediaan* storeroom. – *perum* sounding room (on ship). – *peta* chart room. – *petak* partitioned room. – *petang* (photographic) darkroom. – *rias* a) dressing room b) walk-in closet. – *sejuk* cold storage chamber. – *singel* a single room (in hotel, etc.). – *tahanan* deten-

tion cell. – *tamu* living room (in a house). – *(tempat) mengepas* fitting room (at the tailor's, in a department store, etc.). – *tidur* bedroom. – *tidur ganda* double bedroom. – *tidur utama* master bedroom. – *tunggu* waiting room. – *urai* dissecting room. – *wartawan* press room.

sekamar in the same room. *teman* ~ roommate. ~ *berdua* two to a room. ~ *bertiga* three to a room.

berkamar 1 to room. *Ia* ~ *di hotél itu.* He roomed in that hotel. 2 to have rooms. *sebuah hotél* ~ *30* a 30-room hotel.

berkamar-kamar partitioned off into rooms.

mengamar [and ngamar (*coq*)] 1 to room/live in (of domestic help). 2 to go to or rent a room (*usu* for sexual purposes).

Kamar II (*A*) moon. al- "The Moon"; name of the 54th chapter of the Koran.

kamar III (= kamarban) (*ob*) cummerbund, i.e., a wide sash worn around the waist.

kamariah (*A*) 1 lunar. *tahun* – lunar year. 2 a woman's name.

kamas (*Jv*) term of address for older brother.

kamasta (*A ob*) bowl.

kamat I (*A*) the call to begin prayer.

kamat II (*cla*) *kayu* – k.o. plant (the tree as well as the wood) which was used to make royal seals.

kamba bulky.

kamban mengamban to tie, bind.

kambang (*J/Jv*) floating; → AMBANG II. *bom* – sea mine.

mengambang to float (on water/in the air). *massa* ~ floating mass. *matahari* ~ the sun begins to rise.

pengambangan (the act of) floating.

kambar and kambau (*ob*) k.o. turtle.

kambéh (*M*) bitter melon, *Momordica charantia*.

kambék (*E*) 1 comeback. 2 to make a comeback, get back together again.

kambeli (*Hind*) coarse woolen fabric.

kambi (*cla*) (wooden) rib, frame for wall panels. – *pintu* door frame.

berkambi to use such a frame.

mengambi to frame; framing.

kambing I goat, sheep. – *putus tali* (to go, etc.) quickly. *kelas* – a) gallery, pit, cheapest seats in the movie, etc. b) lowest stratum of society; very low class (prostitute). *patuh seperti anak* – meek as a lamb. *bagai menghitung bulu* – to carry coals to Newcastle. *bagai* – *dalam biduk* extremely afraid. *seperti* – *diséret ke air* very reluctant. – *arab* fat-tailed sheep. – *bandot* billy goat. – *benggala* Indian goat. – *biri-biri* sheep. – *burun* wild goat. – *congék* stooge. – *domba* fat-tailed sheep. – *étawah* Indian goat. – *gibas* → KAMBING *kibas.* – *gunung* mountain goat. – *gurun/gunung* serow, *Capricornis sumatrensis.* (*si*) – *hitam* (the) scapegoat/fall guy. **mengkambing-hitamkan** to make a scapegoat of s.o. – *hutan* serow, *Capricornis sumatrensis.* – *Jawa/kacang* Hainan goat. – *kebiri* wether. – *kibas* fat-tailed sheep. – *mérah* [kamér] (in Medan) k.o. hard liquor (the "Red Goat" brand). – *perahan* milch-goat. – *putih* [kamput] k.o. hard liquor (the "White Goat" brand). – *randuk* a rank old billy goat. – *tak bertanduk* (*coq*) dog meat.

mengambing-ngambingkan to debase, degrade.

pengambing follower, participant.

kambing II *rumput* – k.o. plant used for the treatment of wounds. *akar* –.– k.o. plant, *Sarcolobus globosus.*

kambing III *ikan* –.– blue-ring angelfish, *Pomacanthus annularis.*

kambing IV *burung* – white-winged black jay, black magpie, *Platysmurus leucopterus.*

kambium (*D/E*) cambium.

Kambodia Cambodia.

kamboja I → KEMBOJA.

Kamboja II Cambodia; → KAMBODIA.

kambrat (*D*) 1 comrade. 2 accomplice (to a crime). 3 get together, party.

berkambrat to have a comrade/accomplice.

kambu k.o. game in which two or three sticks of unequal length are hidden in the hand with the ends sticking out and the player is asked to guess which is the short stick.

kambuh to have/suffer a setback/relapse, to get worse (of the sick). – *kembali/lagi* to (have a) relapse, recur; recurrence.

kambuhan relapsed. *penjahat/narapidana* ~ recidivist, habitual criminal.

kekambuhan and **perkambuhan** relapse.

kambus mengambus to bury, cover with earth, etc.

terkambus buried/covered with earth, etc.; silted up (of a river), choked up (with sand); blocked (of a drain), stuffed up (of the nose).

kambut an open-mouthed plaited bag for rice.

kamcekan (*J*) susceptible to disease.

kamcing (*C*) close friends.

kamekmek → KEMEKMEK.

kameli → KAMBELI.

kamér → KAMBING *mérah*.

kaméra (*D*) camera. – *digital* digital camera. – *ketupat* box camera. – *kompak* compact camera. – *saku* pocket camera. – *sekali pakai* disposable camera. – *téléléns* telephoto camera. – *téléskopik* telescopic camera. – *télévisi* T(ele)V(ision) camera. – *vidéo* video camera. – *vidéo rekam* camcorder.

kamerad (*D/E*) comrade.

kaméraman and **kamérawan** (*D*) cameraman.

kamérawati female cameraman.

kamerjas (*D ob*) man's dressing gown.

kamerlop (*D ob*) cannon.

Kamerun Cameroon(s).

kamerwak (*J*) orderly (the person).

kamfer (*D/E*) camphor; → KAPUR *barus*.

kamhar (*D*) **1** worsted (thread, yarn). **2** worsted (fabric).

kami 1 (exclusive) we/us/our [excludes the person(s) being spoken to]. **2** (editorial) we/us/our. **3** (the royal or presidential) we/us/our. **4** (*polite*) I, me, my.

kami-kami (emphatic) we/us/our, we and we alone. ~ *di sinilah yang akan mendapat kesulitan.* It is we and we alone who will have the problems.

kekamian individualism.

kamiat (*A ob*) quantity.

kamil (*A*) perfect, ideal. *insan* (*al.-*) the perfect/ideal man; the mystic's perfect man, in whom Allah fulfills Himself. *murid –* a student at the third stage of mysticism, when he sees only the One, the Creator, in all perfected things. – *mukamil* most perfect.

kamir → KHAMIR.

kamis I (= kamisah) (*A*) shirt.

Kamis II (*A*) (*hari -*) Thursday. – *Putih* Holy Thursday.

kamisondho (*Jv*) breast cancer.

kamisosolen (*Jv*) **1** to make a mistake in speaking, make a slip of the tongue, misspeak. **2** to stammer.

kamit → KOMAT-KAMIT.

kamitua → KAMITUWO.

kamituwo (*Jv*) **1** hamlet head, i.e., chief administrative government official of a *pedukuhan*. **2** deputy village head in Central Java.

kamkha (*A*) silk brocade embroidered with gold.

kamli → KAMBELI.

kamling [keamanan lingkungan] neighborhood safety.

kamoflase → KAMUFLASE.

kamoker (*Pr*) camera; → KAMÉRA.

kamp (*D/E*) camp; → KAM II. – *kerja paksa* forced labor camp. – *konséntrasi* concentration camp.

kampa(h) the Indonesian lettuce-tree, k.o. spinach, *Pisonia alba*.

kampai (*M*) **berkampai(an)** to lie sprawled (plural subjects), (to be) scattered all around.

mengkampaikan to sprawl against (the back of a chair, etc.).

terkampai scattered around, lie sprawled. *Sepanjang jalan ~ tubuh perusuh.* The rebels lay sprawled along the entire street.

kampak → KAPAK I.

kampanye (*D*) (election) campaign. – *bisik* whispering campaign. – *pemilihan umum* (general) election campaign. – *surat kabar* newspaper campaign.

berkampanye to campaign.

mengkampanyekan to campaign for s.t.

kampanyewan campaigner (for a political party).

kampas I (*D*) **1** canvas, (of tires) cord; → KAIN *mota/terpal*. **2** lining. – *rém* brake lining.

mengampas to canvas.

kampas II → KEMPAS I.

kampemén (*D mil*) encampment, barracks; → ASRAMA.

kamper → KAMFER.

kampil I 1 small sack made of matting (for flour/tobacco/rice/clothes). **2** (*Jv*) money bag. **3** gunnysack.

mengampil to put into a sack, bag.

pengampilan packing (in gunnysacks, etc.).

kampil II (= kampilan) (*ob*) broadsword.

kampil III → KUMPAL *kampil*.

kampiran (*Jv*) possessed by. – *bangsa lelembut* possessed by a spirit; → DISANTÉT, DIPENGGAWÉ *wong*.

kampit (*J*) k.o. sack; → KAMPIL I.

mengampit to sew up such a sack.

kampitan s.t. held in the armpit.

kampiun I (*D*) **1** champion. **2** very smart.

kampiun II (*Sumatra*) breakfast consisting of *kacang padi* and *kolak.*

kampleng (*J/Jv*) **mengampleng** and **ngampleng** to hit, beat, slap.

mengamplengi (*pl obj*) to keep on hitting, etc.

kampong → KAMPUNG.

kamprét (*J/Jv*) leaf-nosed bat, *Hipposiderus sp.*

kampse (*euph*) hick, boorish; → KAMPUNGAN.

Kampuchéa Cambodia.

kampuh I shawl, cover, ceremonial *batik* wraparound.

berkampuh to wear a shawl/cover, etc.; shrouded in a shawl, etc.

kampuh II seam, hem, strip of cloth for bookbinding, joint, suture, groove. – *berimpit* lap riveting. – *keling* riveted joint. – *lintang* cross seam. – *menumpu* butt joint. – *rapat* caulked seam. – *picak* flat seam. – *tekat* quilting seam. – *témpélan* lap joint. – *tengah* monk seam. – *tuang* burr.

berkampuh *kain* ~ a double *sarong* sewn together. *pipa baja tak* ~ a seamless steel pipe. *pisau* ~ a double-edged knife.

kampul (*Jv*) **terkampul-kampul 1** floating, drifting on the surface of water. **2** uncertain of the future.

kampung 1 a) a cluster of houses, hamlet, village or part of a village. b) a poor, semi-rural, village-like area in a town or city; (sometimes) shantytown. c) quarter, area, ward, administrative or otherwise, of a city. *anjing* – mongrel. *kepala* – village headman. *korong* – (*M*) place of birth, native village. *orang* – villager, rustic, hick. *rumah* – a simple k.o. house, such as one finds in the *kampung*. *tanah* – communal land. *tiang* – village elder; → TUA-TUA *désa*. **2** smallholder(s). *kopi* – smallholders coffee. *ayam* – a locally raised chicken; *opp* AYAM *negeri/ras*; → AYAM *buras*. – *halaman* native village, home town. – *halamanisme* provincialism. – *kota* urban village. –.– *melarat* slum areas. – *nelayan* fisherman's village.

sekampung 1 of the same *kampung*. *orang* ~ fellow villager. *yang* ~ *dengannya* those who live in the same village as he does. **2** the entire/whole village.

sekampung-kampungnya the entire village.

berkampung 1 to gather, assemble, form a group. **2** gathered. **3** together. ~ *berhalaman, bernagari berjorong* (*M*) to tell the person you are meeting for the first time the name of the village and hamlet in which you were born.

mengampung(kan) to gather into a group, assemble, bring together.

kampungan 1 country bumpkin, hick, yokel; hickish, unsophisticated. **2** broken (of a language). *bahasa Inggris* ~ broken English.

kekampungan 1 unsophisticated, having the characteristics of a *kampung*. **2** lack of sophistication.

perkampungan 1 village cluster. **2** place where a certain group of people congregate. ~ *kaum nudis* nudist colony. **3** place where a certain group of people live/work, etc. ~ *Amérika* American residential district (in Jakarta). ~ *miskin dan semrawut* slum. ~ *Négro* black ghetto/part of town. **4** housing development.

kampus (*D/E*) campus. – *Biru* reference to Gadjah Mada University in Yogyakarta. – *Ganésha* reference to the Institut Teknologi Bandung. – *Kaligrafi* reference to the *Univérsitas Islam Indonésia* in Yogyakarta. – *Kuning* reference to the University of Indonesia at Salemba. – *Romantis* reference to the University of Indonesia at Depok.

sekampus on the same campus.

kamput [kambing putih] (in Medan) trademark of a strong alcoholic drink.

kamrad → KAMERAD.

kamrat (*D*) cog-wheel.

kamsén (*D*) commission (payment); → KOMSÉN I.

kamséu (*C?*) country bumpkin, hick.

kamsia and **kamsya** (*C*) thank you.

kamso → KAMSÉU.

kamtibmas [keamanan dan ketertiban masyarakat] Community Safety and Law and Order.

kamu you (very informal; reserved for very close friends/children/people in lower social positions, etc.). – *sekalian* and *kalian* you-all, you guys. –.– *ini* you and you alone.

berkamu to use the word *kamu* (when talking to s.o.).

kamuflase (*D/E*) camouflage.

berkamuflase camouflaged. *dengan jalan* ~ under the cloak of, under cover of.

mengkamuflase to camouflage.

kamuflir (*D*) **mengkamuflir** to camouflage.

kamus I (*A*) dictionary. – *dwibahasa* bilingual dictionary. – *ékabahasa* monolingual dictionary. – *ilmu bumi* gazetteer. – *istilah* dictionary of technical terms, terminological dictionary. – *kantong* pocket dictionary. – *kecik/kecil* abridged dictionary. – *pelajar* student dictionary. – *saku* pocket dictionary. – *umum* general dictionary.

mengamuskan to include in a dictionary.

pekamus lexicographer.

perkamusan lexicography. *ahli* ~ → PEKAMUS.

kamus II (*J/Jv*) **1** tanned leather. **2** (regional) (small, outer) belt/sash (of leather/velvet, etc.; with a buckle).

mengamus to tan.

pengamusan tanning.

kamuswan (*infr*) lexicographer.

kan I → AKAN. *tak–* impossible, can't, won't.

kan II (ship's) balustrade, rail; → LANGKAN.

kan III (particle which usually appears at the beginning of the sentence or between the subject and the predicate) the speaker is asserting that the truth of the statement in which this particle occurs is or should be known to the hearer; translates as: isn't it? (don't) you know? *Kita ini – orang Timur, ya?* We are Asians, aren't we? *Aku – ibunya Dian.* I'm Dian's mother, you know?

kan IV (*D*) pitcher, can.

kan V → KANS.

kan VI (in acronyms) → KANTOR.

kana I → GELANG *kana*.

kana II (*D*) canna, *Canna orientalis/hibrida*.

kanaah and **kanaat** (*A*) satisfaction with what God provides.

Kanaan (*negeri*) – Canaan.

kanaat (*A*) satisfaction, contentment.

kanabis (*D/E*) cannabis.

Kanada 1 Canada. **2** Canadian.

kanah (*A*) **1** pleasure, contentment. **2** satisfaction.

kanakamédini (*Skr*) Pulau Mas, Island of Gold, Sumatra; → SUWARNADWIPA.

kanak-kanak infant (child under about seven); *cp* ANAK *balita. bahasa* – child language. *taman* – kindergarten. – *anyar* newborn.

kekanak-kanakan 1 childish, infantile, puerile. **2** infantilitis.

kanal (*D/E*) canal, subchannel.

kanalisasi making canals.

kanan I 1 right; *opp* KIRI. *(di) sebelah* – on the right. *kaki/tangan* – the right leg/hand. *langkah* – step off on the right foot, i.e., a lucky start. **2** (*mostly Mal*) of important or high standing, senior (officer, etc.). *tangan – saya* my right-hand man. **3** rightist, conservative or reactionary. *orang/partai* – rightist/party. – *kiri* and *kiri* – to the right and the left, on both sides. – *luar* outside right (in soccer). – *lambung* starboard.

menganan 1 (to turn) to the right. **2** dextral.

menganankan to direct/bring over to the right.

terkanan the most rightward.

kekanan-kanan leaning too much to the right.

kanan II (*Jv*) – *kirinya* about, approximately.

kanang k.o. tree, *Cordia obliqua*.

kanapé (*D/E*) canapé.

kanari → KENARI I.

kanat → KANAAH.

Kanbéra Canberra.

kanbus (*ob*) → GAMBUS.

kanca (*Jv*) friend; → KONCO. – *dolan* playmate. – *mitra* bosom friend, crony. – *wingking* "the friend in the back," i.e., wife; → WINGKING.

kancah I 1 a large pot for cooking rice, cauldron; → KAWAH. – *dapur tukang besi* forge. **2** fire center in volcano. **3** troubled situation, depths (of despair, etc.). *seperti – ditawar* (*M*) be tongue-tied, have not a word to say. – *garam* salt pan. – *informasi* mine of information. – *kehidupan/kehinaan/kenerakaan/kesengsaraan* depths of despair. – *keributan* scene of disturbances. – *penderitaan* slough of despair. – *peperangan* cauldron of war. – *perjuangan* arena of struggle. – *pertikaian* scene of disturbances. – *politik* political arena.

berkancah engulfed.

terkancah thrown into (the depths of misery).

kancah II embrace.

sekancah as much as the arms can embrace, an embrace.

terkancah seized in an embrace, i.e., in agony.

kancana → KENCANA.

kancap (*J*) level with, flush; brimful, completely full.

kancéh (*M ob*) **terkancéh** aborted (of plants), arrested in development, stunted, dwarfed.

kancéng → KAMCING

kancera k.o. fish, *Labeobarbus douronensis*.

kancil I mouse deer or chevrotain, *Tragulus ravus*, i.e., a miniature deer, a symbol of slyness and cleverness. *Sang –* the *kancil* in the *Pelanduk Jenaka* story. *si –* sobriquet for the late Foreign Minister Adam Malik.

kancil II an intelligence officer.

Kancil III [kendaraan kecil] a small vehicle powered by natural gas.

kancilan (– *emas*) golden whistler, *Pachycephala pectoralis*. – *mérah* Temminck's babbler, *Trichastoma pyrrogenys*. – *Sunda* Horsfield's babbler, *Malacocincla sepiarium*.

kancing I 1 button, hook (small metal catch inserted in a loop or eye for fastening clothes). **2** fastener, catch, latch, bolt. – *baju* shirt button. – *gigi/mulut* lockjaw. – *jeprét* a) snap fastener. b) pushbutton. – *léhér baju* collar stud. – *lengan keméja* cufflink. – *mansét* cufflinks. – *mulut* lockjaw. – *pintu* door lock. – *sorok/tarik* zipper. – *tekan* a) snap fastener. b) pushbutton. – *tutup tarik* zipper.

berkancing buttoned, fastened, bolted, latched.

mengancing 1 to button, fasten with a hook. **2** to lock.

mengancingi to sew buttons onto. *Beberapa wanita yang duduk di lantai sibuk* ~ *keméja dan celana.* Several women were busy sewing buttons onto shirts and trousers.

mengancingkan 1 to lock a door with a latch/bolt. **2** to button up, zip up.

terkancing shut, fastened, locked. *setengah* ~ partly buttoned.

kancingan lock, fastener, latch. ~ *kemudi* rudder lock.

pengancing lock, fastener, catch, bolt.

pengancingan locking.

kancing II (*sl*) the hallucinogens rohypnol or Ecstasy.

ngancing to take that pill.

kancingan Brazilian joy weed, *Alternanthera brasiliana*.

kancung long, large section of bamboo for carrying water.

kancut loincloth, G-string.

mengancut to wrap a loincloth around one's legs.

kanda I 1 → KAKANDA. **2** – *manda* playmates of an infant prince.

kanda II tradition, legend.

kandang 1 (of horses) stable, corral; (of cows) cowshed; (of pigs/hogs) pigpen; (of sheep) sheep-pen; (of chickens) chicken-house; (of dogs) doghouse, kennel; (of pigeons) loft; (of rabbits) hutch; (of automobiles) garage; (of boats) shed; (of birds) bird cage. **2** one's own backyard/home ground, stamping grounds. *Dia pulang/kembali ke -nya.* He returned to his own stamping grounds. **3** enclosed/fenced in space. **4** halo/ring (around the sun/moon). **5** margin (of a book). *di luar* – banned, ostracized. *memperlapang – musang, mempersempit – ayam* opportunity makes the thief. *masuk (ke dalam) – kambing mengembik, masuk (ke dalam) – kerbau menguak* when in Rome do as the Romans do. *– ayam* chicken house. *– anjing* doghouse. *– babi* pigpen. *– bermain* playpen. *– bibit* stud farm. *– biduk* boat shed. *– bulan* halo/ring around the moon. *– burung* birdcage. *– kapal* boathouse. *– kelinci* rabbit hutch. *– kuda* stable. *– lokomotif* locomotive shed. *– merpati* pigeon loft, dovecote. *– mobil* garage. *– monyét* guardhouse, sentry box. *– penghangat* brooder house. *– sapi* barn. *– ternak* animal pen. *– unggas* poultry house.

sekandang (in) the same stable/cage, etc. as.

berkandang with/having a stable, etc.

mengandangi (*J*) to fence in, enclose.

mengandangkan 1 to pen, confine in/put in(to) the stable. **2** (*coq*) to ground (a vehicle for infractions).

pengandangan penning up, stabling.

perkandangan cage (*mod*), caging, stabling

kandar I (*Jv*) **mengandar(kan)** to drive/operate a car, etc.; → MENGENDARAI.

kandaran 1 vehicle. **2** car; → KENDARAAN.

pengandar driver, operator, chauffeur.

kandar II → GALAS, GANDAR I. **mengandar** to carry/balance a pole on the shoulder with weights on both ends.

pengandar a pole balanced on the shoulder used for carrying things.

kandas 1 run aground (of a ship). **2** to fail, failed, frustrated, unsuccessful. *– di tengah jalan* to fail halfway through. **3** broken off (of negotiations).

mengandaskan 1 to strand, beach. **2** to frustrate, foil.

terkandas stranded, run aground.

kekandasan 1 running aground. **2** failure, frustration, fiasco, deadlock.

pengandasan 1 running aground, beaching. **2** foiling, making s.t. fail.

kandegan (*Jv*) (in the Banyumas area, Central Java) rain ceremony.

kandel (*J/Jv*) **1** thick. **2** rich. *janda –* a rich widow.

kand(h)a (*Jv*) narration. *pembaca –* narrator.

kandi I (*J*) purse, wallet, small bag, satchel.

kandi II *– putih* the white pitcher-plant.

kandidat (*D/E*) **1** candidate, nominee. **2** examinee, candidate for an examination. **2** bachelor (university degree).

mengandidatkan to nominate.

kandil (*A*) branched candlestick. *– gantung* chandelier.

kandis I a wild mangosteen, *Garcinia spp.* used instead of tamarind; → ASAM *kandis*.

kandis II (*ob*) sweets, delicacy.

kandul I (*ob*) wickerwork basket.

kandul II bunt of a casting net

berkandul with such a bunt.

mengandul to sew such a bunt into a net.

kandung uterus; bladder; purse; container. *anak/ayah/ibu –* one's own child/natural father/natural mother (not a stepchild/stepfather/stepmother). *sahabat –* a good friend. *saudara (se) –* siblings by the same parents, full brother or sister. *– empedu* gall bladder. *– jantung* pericardium. *– kemih/kencing* bladder. *– pelir* scrotum.

sekandung from the same womb. *saudara ~* siblings with the same mother.

berkandung 1 filled. **2** pregnant; with young (of animals).

mengandung 1 to carry a child in a *seléndang* or shoulder scarf; to have a child on one's lap. **2** to be pregnant. *~ anak lelaki* to be pregnant with a boy. **3** to carry along, contain, hold, have on one. *tiada ~ uang sesén jua pun* does not even have a cent on him. *awan yang ~ hujan* a rain cloud. *tak ~* free from. *tak ~ lemak* nonfat, fat-free. *hari yang ~ sejarah* an historic day. *mati dikandung tanah* dead and buried. *selama hayat dikandung badan* as long as one lives (or, is alive). *~ harapan* hopeful, promising, encouraging. **4** to cherish, nourish, foster (illusion/expectations/desires/plans, etc.). *~ hati* to bear a grudge against s.o. **5** to implicate. **6** to involve.

ngandung (*coq*) to be pregnant.

mengandungi 1 to fill with, contain. **2** to make s.o. pregnant.

mengandungkan 1 to make pregnant. **2** to carry within it. *Bumi ini ~ laut dan darat.* The earth contains the sea and the land.

terkandung implied, contained, included (in). *mencurahkan apa yang ~ dalam hatinya* to pour out one's heart, get s.t. off one's chest (by talking about it). *~ maksud* to cherish the aim of.

kandungan 1 content, contents (of a law, etc.). *masih dalam ~ niat* still under consideration. *sudah lama menjadi ~* a long-cherished ideal/desire. *~ lokal* local content. **2** womb, uterus. *masih dalam ~* still unborn, in his mother's womb. *ilmu penyakit ~* gynecology. **3** fetus. *menggugurkan ~* to have an abortion. **4** pregnancy. *~nya sudah berumur empat bulan.* She is four months pregnant. **5** (*geol*) grade. **6** (*ob*) purse.

pengandung s.t. that contains s.t. within it.

kandut I (*J*) → KANDUNG.

kandut II (*J*) **mengandut** to carry s.t. rolled up in one's lap.

Kanékés 1 the area encompassed by the hamlets of Cibeo, Cikertawa and Cikeusik (southern Banten, West Java). **2** *orang –* the Badui people of West Java.

kang I → KAKANG.

kang II a horse's bit. *tali –* reins; → KEKANG.

berkang bridled, reined in.

kang III (*C?*) large jar for bathing.

kang IV (*Jv*) short for ingkang *q.v.*

kangar *lang –* eagle, *Haliaetus leucogaster, Spizaetus limnaetus.*

kangen (*J/Jv*) **1** *– akan/dengan/kepada* to long for, miss, feel homesick for. *Saya – akan tanah air.* I miss my country. *melepaskan – * to get together after a long separation. **2** to be homesick.

mengangeni 1 to miss, long for, feel homesick for. **2** to make s.o. be homesick for s.t.

kangenan *malam/pertemuan ~* reunion.

kekangenan nostalgia, homesickness.

kangguru → KANGURU.

Kangjeng (*Jv*) title for (*Jv*) princes, high nobles and high-ranking government officials. *– Lider* a Bupati upon whom the Dutch conferred the decoration: *Ridder in de Orde van Oranje Nassau.*

kangka (*C*) *gambir* plantation.

kangkang I 1 cleft between the two thighs; space between the right and left legs when opened wide. **2** (*celah –*) perineum; → KELANGKANG. **3** crotch (of pants).

mengangkang to sit/walk with legs wide apart; to take long strides.

mengangkangi 1 to straddle, stand/sit straddling (s.o.). **2** to get between the spread legs of.

mengangkangkan to spread (s.o.'s legs).

terkangkang wide open (of door, etc.), wide apart (of legs); straddling, astride.

kangkang II (*Jv*) **mengangkangi 1** to take s.o.'s property illegally. **2** to control, take control of, have control over, hold sway over, rule over.

kangkangan s.t. taken in this way.

pengangkangan taking control of, ruling over.

kangkaréng *burung –* pied hornbill, *Anthracoceros albirostris*; → KENGKARÉNG.

kangker → KANKER I.

kangkok *– ranting* oriental cuckoo, *Cuculus saturatus.*

kangkung I swamp cabbage, water convolvulus, *Ipomoea reptans* and other species. *merayap-rayap seperti – di ulak jamban* to breed quickly. *– air* red water spinach, *Ipomoea aquatica. – darat/putih* white-flowering convolvulus, *Ipomoea sp.*

kangkung II *film –* pornographic film.

kangkung III k.o. frog, toad.

kangmas (*S*) **1** older brother. **2** (term of affectionate address for husband/fiancé) honey, darling.

kangsa (*Skr*) **1** bronze; brass. **2** (*M*) tinned iron, bell metal; → GANGSA I.

kangsar a tall tree, *Hibiscus floccosus.*

kangsén <kangsi> (*Jv*) **1** appointment. **2** to make an appointment.

kangtau(w) (*CJ*) **1** a windfall, a unexpected piece of good fortune. **2** object which can yield a profit.

kangtin → KANTIN.
kang(g)uru (*D/E*) kangaroo.
kaniaya (*Jv ob*) → ANIAYA.
kanibal (*D/E*) cannibal.
kanibalisme (*D/E*) cannibalism.
kanigara (*Skr*) sunflower, *Helianthus annuus*.
kanina canine, K-9.
kanisah (*A*) 1 synagogue. 2 temple.
kanjal (*ob*) stopped, halted (due to obstacles, etc.).
kanjang stamina, perseverance. endurance.
  berkanjang 1 to persevere, persist. 2 persevering, persistent.
  kanjangan perseverance, persistence.
kanjar I (*Pers*) broad dagger.
kanjar II berkanjar and terkanjar-kanjar (*cla*) to (put up a) fight, oppose; run amuck.
Kanjeng → KANGJENG.
kanji I (*Tam*) liquid substance obtained from cooking rice, starch (for stiffening clothes).
  menganji to starch, stiffen with starch.
kanji II (*Jap*) *huruf* – Chinese/Japanese characters.
kanji III – *rumbi* k.o. chicken dish.
kanker I (*D*) cancer. (*penyakit*) – *darah* leuk(a)emia. – *indung telur* ovarian cancer. – *paru-paru* lung cancer. – *payudara* breast cancer. – *pohon* gangrene. – *rahim* uterine cancer. – *usus besar* colon cancer.
kanker II [kantong kering] (*Pr*) broke, without money.
kano (*D*) canoe.
kanokat (*Pr*) office; → KANTOR.
kanoman (*Jv*) young people, youth (group obliged to perform services in the community).
kanon I (*D/E*) cannon, gun.
kanon II (*D*) 1 k.o. tax for land rented by descent. 2 canon (music), round. 3 canon (law).
kanopi (*E*) (parachute) canopy.
kans (*D*) chance, opportunity; → KESEMPATAN, PELUANG.
kanselaria (*D*) chancellery.
kanselir (*D*) chancellor, embassy first secretary.
  kekanseliran chancellery.
kanstof and kanstop (*D*) lace (fabric).
kanta (*Skr*) lens; → LÉNSA, SURYAKANTA. – *mata* eye-piece.
  menganta lenticular.
kantan a wild ginger, torch ginger, *Phaeomeria speciosa, Etlingera elatior*. – *hutan* a wild ginger, *Languas javanica*.
kantang (running) dry (of mud flats, etc., at low tide).
  mengantang to dry up.
  kantangan dries, dry spots in water.
kantata (*D/E*) cantata.
kantél (*J*) ngantél to be attached (to s.t.).
  kantélan place where s.t. is attached.
kanti (*Jv ob*) friend, comrade.
kantih (*S*) spin thread; → ANTIH.
kantil I → KONTAL-KANTIL.
kantil II (*Jv*) white frangipani, *Michelia champaka*.
kantil III (*sl*) a lesbian who plays the female role, fem.
kantiléver (*D/E*) cantilever.
kantin (*D/E*) PX, canteen, school cafeteria.
kantingan dry Mary, West Indian chickweed, *Drymaria cordata*.
kantonemén (*D*) cantonment.
kantong (*J/Jv*) → KANTUNG. 1 pouch, bag. 2 pocket, enclave (in garment and also *mil*), pool. *daérah* – a small area of a specified type inside another area. – *angin* wind sock. – *belakang* hip pocket. – *buah pelir* scrotum. – *empedu* gallbladder. – *jenazah* (*mil*) body bag. – *kemaluan* scrotum. – *kempés* [tongpés] broke, penniless. – *kencing* urinary bladder. – *kering* [kanker] (*Pr*) broke, penniless. – *kuning telur* yolk sac. – *luar* exclave. – *menyan* (*J*) testicle(s). – *minyak* (*petro*) oil pool. – *nasi* stomach. – *pelir* scrotum. – *pos* mailbag. – *punggung* backpack. – *sampah* trash bag. – *tebal* well-off. **berkantong tebal** well-off. – *tinta* ink sack. – *tipis* poor. **berkanton tipis** to be poor. – *udara* air bladder. – *ungkak* (*naut*) hawse bag.
  berkantong to have a pocket/pouch. *binatang* ~ marsupial. *meréka yang* ~ *tipis* the poor.

mengantongi and mengantongkan to pocket, put into one's pocket, to win (a medal, etc.).
  pengantongan bagging, packaging.
kantongisasi – *kotoran kuda* (in Klaten) putting a gunny sack on the shaft of a carriage or cart to catch the horse's manure.
kantor (*D*) office, bureau, agency. – *angin* (*coq*) weather station. – *bang* (*Jv*) and – *bank* bank. – *béa* customs office. – *berita* news agency. – *besar* main office. – *bom/bum* (*coq*) customs office. – *cabang* branch office. – *Catatan Sipil* Registry of Births, Deaths and Marriages. – *dagang* business office. – *depan* (*penerima tamu*) front office. – *kawat* telegraph office. – *Keuangan Negeri* National Treasury. – *lélang* auction hall. – *maya* virtual office. – *meterai* (*coq*) Office of Weights and Measures. – *pabéan* customs office. – *pajak* tax office. – *pasasi* passenger booking agency. – *Patén* Patent Office. – *pelancongan* (*coq*) travel agency. – *pembantu* branch office. – *pemilihan* polling place. – *Pendaftar Patén* Patent Office. – *Pendaftaran* Registry Office. – *penempatan tenaga* employment bureau. – *Pengelolaan Anggaran* Budget Management Office. – *perjalanan* travel agency. – *perjodohan* matchmaking agency. – *perwakilan* representative office. – *polisi* police station. – *pos* post office. – *pusat* main/head office. – *Pusat Perbendaharaan* Central Accounting Office. – *rédaksi* editorial office. – *stor* (in M.O. forms) office of payment. – *télepon* telephone station. – *tera* (*coq*) Office of Weights and Measures. – *Urusan Agama* [KUA] Religious Affairs Office. – *Urusan Perumahan* [KUP] Housing Affairs Office. – *wilayah* [kanwil] regional office.
  sekantor ~ *dengan* to work in the same office as.
  berkantor ~ *di* to have its offices in/at.
  ngantor (*J*) 1 to go to the office. 2 to maintain/run an office, operate. 3 (*sl*) to pickpocket (on public transportation).
  kantoran (*J*) office.
  perkantoran office (*mod*). *barang-barang kebutuhan* ~ office supplies. *gedung* ~ office building.
kantuk sleepiness, drowsiness, need for sleep; → ANTUK II. –*nya belum lepas*. He hasn't slept his fill. *sukar untuk menahan* –*nya* hard to stay awake. *menghabiskan sisa* –*nya semalam* to continue last night's interrupted sleep.
  mengantuk [and ngantuk (*coq*)] to be/feel sleepy/drowsy. **sengantuk 1** as sleepy as. **2** no matter how sleepy.
  ngantukin (*J coq*) soporific, puts you to sleep, boring.
  ngantukan (*coq pl subj*) to feel sleepy.
  terkantuk(-kantuk) nod off to sleep.
  pengantuk sleepyhead.
kantung → KANTONG. 1 pocket. 2 bag, pouch. – *air panas* hot-water bottle. – *belakang* back pocket. – *empedu* gallbladder. – *jenazah* body bag. – *kemaluan* scrotum. – *kempis* broke. – *tidur* sleeping bag.
  sekantung a bag of, a pocketful of.
  berkantung to have a pocket/bag.
  mengantungi to pocket, put in one's pocket; to get, take in (of money). ~ *warganegara Indonésia* to get Indonesian citizenship.
  mengantungkan to pocket s.t.
  pengantungan bagging, packaging.
kanun (*A*) 1 Muslim administrative law (as opposed to revealed law). 2 civil rules.
kanuragan (*Jv*) invulnerability. *ilmu* – the science of invulnerability.
kanvas (*D/E*) 1 canvas. 2 floor of boxing ring.
  berkanvas with a canvas. ~ *besar* with a large canvas.
  menganvaskan to knock to the canvas (in boxing); to ruin, destroy.
kanwil [kantor wilayah] regional office.
Kanya Virgo
kanyon (*E*) canyon.
kao name of a *ceki* card.
kaok (*Jv*) berkaok-kaok to yell and shout, cry, scream. ~ *setinggi langit* to scream one's head off. ~ *saja* to be all talk (and no action).
  mengaoki to yell after, call out to.
  mengaokkan to cackle/scream about.
  kaokan cry, yell.
  kaok-kaokan yelling, screaming.

kaoki (C) k.o. gambling game.

kaolin (D/E) kaolin, Chinese clay.

kaoliang (C?) sorghum.

kaonderan (Jv) subdistrict; → ONDERAN.

kao-pé(k) (C J) nine hundred (rupiahs).

kaos I → KAUS I.

kaos II (D) chaos.

kaotis (D) chaotic.

kap I (ob) tali – ship's cable.

kap II (D) 1 (lamp)shade. 2 cap, cover, hood. – atap roofing. – cahaya porthole. – cerobong cowl. – keréta hood (of car). – jendéla weather molding. – kepala bathing cap. – lampu lampshade. – mesin/mobil/motor hood (of automobile). – rambut hairdressing.

kapa → KAPAK I.

kapabel (E) capable.

kapah (Skr) terkapah-kapah 1 gasping for breath. 2 startled and trembling (from fear/a nightmare, etc.).

kapai → GAPAI. terkapai-kapai one's hand struggling as if to reach for s.t.

kapak I axe, adze. mata – edge (of a knife, etc.). ular – viper. habis – berganti beliung working very energetically. seperti – naik pemidangan/peminangan completely irrelevant; neither here nor there; out of place. – menelan beliung a good thing exchanged for a bad one

berkapak 1 to have an axe. 2 with an axe.

mengapak to chop with an axe, axe.

terkapak chopped with an axe.

kapak II wing; → KEPAK.

berkapak tidak ~ not to have the power.

kapak III 1 k.o. marine fish, Pellona spp. 2 moonfish, Mene maculata.

kapa-kapa ship's awning, atap shed.

kapal I (Tam) ship, boat, vessel. pengusaha – ship owner. perusahaan – shipping company. – satu nakhoda dua two captains on a ship; too many cooks spoil the broth. besar – besar gelombang high winds blow on high hills. – besar ditunda jongkong said of a person in authority who follows the orders of the man in the street. – (air) bersayap hydrofoil. – angkasa spaceship. – angkasa berawak/bermanusia manned spacecraft. – angkut minyak tanker. – angkutan freighter. – api steamship. – api baling-baling propeller ship. – apiso dispatch boat. – asap steamship. – bajak pirate ship. – bantu perambuan buoy watch boat. – bantuan support ship. – barang freighter, cargo vessel. – barang curahan bulk carrier. – bargas/barkas launch. – batubara collier. – bendéra flagship. – béngkél repair ship. – berbaling-baling screw ship. – berlunas ganda catamaran. – bermotor motorboat. – bersayap hydrofoil. – bijih tin dredger. – bijih besi iron-ore carrier. – bor hisap cutter suction-dredger. – bor penghisap lumpur [KBPL] cutter. – bulan moon ship. – cadik outrigger (prau). – capung spotter plane. – cepat speedboat, motorboat. – cepat torpédo motor torpedo boat, MTB. – curahan bulk carrier. – dagang merchant/cargo vessel. – dalam perjalanan pulang homeward-bound vessel. – dayung a) sloop. b) rowboat. – dépot untuk kapal selam submarine tender. – dérék apung floating crane. – és icebreaker. – féri ferryboat. – haji transport ship for Muslim pilgrims. – héwan cattle boat. – hidrofoil hydrofoil. – hidrografi hydrographic survey ship. – hisap lumpur suction dredger. – hoga (in North Celebes) "ghost ship," i.e., the Boeing jetfoil. – ilmiah oceanographic ship. – induk a) aircraft carrier. b) mothership. – induk kapal selam submarine tender. – induk peramuan buoy tender. – intél(ijén) intelligence-collecting ship. – jelajah cruiser. – jenis perusak destroyer. – jentera paddle-wheeler. – karantina quarantine ship. – katung hovercraft. – keduk dredger. – kelotok small motor-driven river vessel. – kepil mooring boat. – keruk dredger. – keruk bor penghisap cutter suction hopper dredger. – keruk cangkram grab clamshell dredger. – keruk penghisap lumpur trailing suction hopper dredger. – keruk timba bucket dredge. – kincir paddle-wheeler. – klinik hospital ship. – komando flagship. – kontainer/kontiner containership. – korék dredger. – laksamana (perang) flagship. – latih training ship. – laut oceangoing vessel. – layar sailboat. – liar tramp steamer. – lin liner. – lindung escort vessel. – luncur speedboat.

– Maru a vessel of the Tokyo Senpaku Kabushiki Kaisha (= Tokyo Shipping Company). – mata-mata spy ship. – mél mail boat. – menyusur coaster. – meriam gunboat. – mil mail boat. – minyak tanker. – monitor gunboat. – moring mooring boat. – motor motorboat. – motor cepat speedboat. – motor torpédo MTB, motor torpedo boat. – mualim pilot ship. – muatan freighter. – nelayan fishing boat. – niaga merchantman. – nuklir nuclear ship. – ompréngan tramp steamer. – orang sakit hospital ship. – pabrik ikan fish-factory ship. – paméran terapung floating fair. – pandu pilot ship. – panji flagship. – pantai coaster. – pasisir passenger steamer. – patroli patrol ship. – pedalaman inland craft. – pelatih training ship. – pelindung escort vessel. – pemadam tunda fire tugboat. – pemair/pemayar cruiser. – pemancing ikan fishing boat. – pembajak pirate ship. – pembantu support ship. – pembersih alur desnagging boat. – pembor minyak lepas-pantai off-shore oil drilling vessel. – pemburu destroyer. – pemburu ranjau mine hunter. – pemburu – selam submarine chaser. – pemburu torpedo destroyer. – pemecah és icebreaker. – pemimpin flagship. – pemukat trawler. – penambang ferry. – penangkap ikan paus whaler. – penarik tug(boat). – pendarat landing craft. – pendarat bulan lunar module. – pendarat tank landing ship, tank; LST. – pendingin refrigerated ship. – penempur battleship. – penempur berat battle cruiser. – pengamat survey vessel. – pengangkut freighter. – pengangkut kayu log carrier. – pengangkut lumpur hopper barge. – pengangkut pesawat (terbang) aircraft carrier. – pengangkut tentara troopship. – pengawal escort vessel. – pengejar kapal selam submarine chaser. – pengemas salvage vessel. – pengembara tramp steamer. – penggempur battleship. – penghisap lumpur [KPL] hopper. – pengiring escort vessel. – pengukur survey vessel. – penjelajah cruiser. – penjelajah peluncur peluru kendali guided-missile cruiser. – penolong lifeboat. – penumpang passenger ship. – penunjuk pilot vessel. – penyapu ranjang minesweeper. – (perang jenis) buru sapu ranjau [BSR] mine hunter. – penyebar ranjau mine layer. – penyeberangan ferry(boat). – penyelamat salvage ship. – penyeberangan ocean-ographic ship. – penyelundup smuggler's ship. – penyérét tug(boat). – penyusur pantai coaster. – perairan darat inland craft. – perang warship, man-of-war. – perbekalan supply ship. – perbekalan perambuan buoy supply ship. – peremuk és icebreaker. – peronda patrol boat. – peronda pantai coast guard vessel. – perusak destroyer. – perusak kawal destroyer escort. – pesiar excursion boat, pleasure craft, yacht. – pesisir cruise ship. – peti kémas container ship. – pompong (in Riau). k.o. small motorboat. – pos mail boat. – prah freighter. – pukat trawler. – putih a K.P.M. steamer. – radar paddle boat. – rambu beacon ship, lighthouse tender. – rampasan prize. – risét ilmiah scientific research vessel. – roda lampung a) stern-wheeler. b) paddle-wheeler. – ruang angkasa spaceship. – (rumah) sakit hospital ship. – samudera oceangoing vessel. – selam submarine. – selam bermisil/berpeluru kendali missile/guided-missile-carrying submarine. – selam bertenaga atom/nuklir atomic/nuclear powered submarine. – selam nuklir nuclear submarine. – semén bertulang baja ferro-cement ship. – sémicon /-kon/ semicontainer ship. – semi-petikémas semicontainership. – silam submarine. – suar (pandu) (pilot) lightship. – tamasya pleasure boat. – tambang ferry(boat). – tambangan ruang angkasa space shuttle. – tambat tug(boat). – tangker/tangki tanker. – tangki raksasa supertanker. – tarik tug(boat). – ténda awning-decker. – ténder headquarters ship. – tengah dua tiang schooner. – téng(ker) tanker. – terbang aircraft. – terbang bélat (coq) a Garuda Airways DC-3. – tiang dua barque. – trol a) patrol boat. b) trawler. – Tujuh the Royal Dutch Navy cruiser "Zeven Provincieen" (= Seven Provinces). – tunda tug(boat). – uap steamer. – untuk pelayaran tetap liner. – wisata cruise ship. – yang bertonase/berukuran/berbobot mati ... ton a ...-ton vessel.

sekapal ~ dengan to be a passenger on the same ship as. teman ~ shipmate.

berkapal 1 to have/own a ship. 2 to sail. 3 to go by ship, board a ship.

berkapal-kapal 1 several boats. 2 many ships. 3 by the shipload.
~ diangkut ke Éropah to be transported to Europe by the shipload.

mengapalkan to load onto a ship, ship, send by ship.

terkapalkan to be shipped.

pengapal shipper.

pengapalan 1 (act of) shipping. 2 shipment. ~ *pindahan* transshipment. *ongkos* ~ freight.

perkapalan 1 shipping. 2 navigation. 3 fleet, tonnage. 4 shipyard.

kapal II corn (on foot).

kapalan 1 corn. 2 calloused.

kapalan (*Jv*) k.o. climbing plant, *Hoya spp.*

kapan I (*A*) shroud; → KAFAN. *hantu* - a shrouded ghost.

berkapan shrouded. *mati* ~ *cindai* to die with a good reputation.

mengapan to give a shroud, i.e., to support s.o. who has lost a relative.

meng(k)apani to shroud (a corpse).

meng(k)apankan to shroud (a corpse) for s.o. else; to use (a fabric) to shroud (a corpse); to shroud with.

kapan II (*J/Jv*) → BILA I. 1 when? (in direct questions) - *ibumu pulang?* When is your mother coming home? *tahun* -? (in) what year? 2 when (in indirect questions). *Belum dapat dipastikan* - *kapal itu akan datang.* It cannot yet be determined when the ship will arrive. - *waktu saja* any time.

kapan-kapan 1 whenever. 2 sometime or other, any time. *Nantilah* ~ *saya datang.* I'll come by sometime. ~ *saja* any time (at all). ~ *pun tidak* never (will). *sampai* ~ *suka* as long as (he) likes.

kapan III isn't it the case?; → (BU)KAN. *Lu tau* - *duluan.* You knew beforehand, didn't you? - *itu sudah kauambil.* You took it, didn't you?

kapanéwonan (*Jv*) (from *ka*+*panéwu*+*an*) house/office of a *panéwu*; → KECAMATAN.

kapang I shipworm, *Teredo navalis.*

kapang II (*M*) mold, mildew. - *jelaga* sooty mold. - *lendir* slime mold.

berkapang moldy.

kapangan (*Jv*) eclipse; → GERHANA. *bulan* - lunar eclipse. *matahari* - solar eclipse.

kapar I flotsam and jetsam, wreckage, driftwood.

berkaparan (*pl subj*) to float about, lie scattered about (of dead bodies, etc.).

meng(k)aparkan to scatter, disperse.

terkapar scattered, strewn, sprawled (of a corpse). *manusia* ~ human wreckage.

kaparan 1 (neglected) rubbish. 2 flotsam and jetsam, wreckage, driftwood.

kapar II (*ob*) kaparan *pedang/parang* the back of a sword/cleaver.

kaparat I (*A*) expiatory sacrifice, peace offering (after certain offences).

kaparat II → KEPARAT I.

kaparinyo a Minangkabau melody.

berkaparinyo to sing that melody.

kapas I (*Skr*) 1 cotton plant, *Gossypium acuminatum.* 2 cotton wool, wadding. 3 gauze. *bagai/seperti* - *dibusur* snow white. - *kecantikan* cotton balls (for cosmetic purposes). - *ledak* gun cotton. - *pembalut* absorbent cotton. -.- *salju* snowflakes.

berkapas cottony, like cotton.

kapas-kapasan various k.o. cotton.

perkapasan cotton (*mod*).

kapas II - *sungai* and kapas-kapas k.o. marine fish, short pursemouth, *Gerres abbreviatus.* - *laut* k.o. fish, threadfin silver belly, *Gerres punctatus.*

kapasan pied triller, *Lalage nigra.* - *timur* white-winged triller, *Lalage suerurii.*

kapasita → KAPASITAS.

kapasitans (*D/E*) capacitance.

kapasitas (*E*) capacity. - *kursi yang ada* existing seating capacity. - *menganggur* idle capacity. - *penuh* full capacity. - *tampung* holding capacity. - *terpasang* installed capacity.

berkapasitas with a capacity of. ~ *tempat duduk* with a seating capacity of.

kapasitét (*D*) → KAPASITAS.

kapas-kapas → KAPAS II.

kapatihan → PATIH II.

kapcao → KAPSAO.

kapé 1 spatula. 2 putty knife; → PISAU *dempul.*

kapél (*D*) chapel.

kapeling (*D*) → KAPLING.

kaper I → KARPER.

kaper II (*Jv*) moth.

Kapét [Kawasan pengembangan ékonomi terpadu] Integrated Economic Development Region.

kapi I (*naut*) pulley block.

kapi II → KAPÉ.

kapialun *daun* - leaf of a wild vine, *Vitis trifolia,* used as a medicine against fever.

kapilah → KAFILAH.

kapilaritas and kapilaritét (*D*) capillarity.

kapilér (*D*) capillary.

kaping coarse weave of palm leaves; → BAGOR.

kapinis various k.o. needle tails, swifts and crakes. - *alih putih* white-browed crake, *Porzana cinerea.* - *jarum putih* silver-backed needle tail, *Hirundapus cochinchinensis.* - *laut* fork-tailed swift, *Apus pacificus.* - *rumah* house swift, *Apus nipalensis.*

kapir → KAFIR.

kapiran (*J/Jv*) 1 neglected, uncared for (of a child, etc.). 2 to go wrong, turn out badly, be in vain. *Hidupnya ternyata tidak* -. It turned out that his life was not a failure. 3 hopeless, beyond helping.

kapis k.o. scallop, *Pecten spp.*

kapisa bay (color).

kapit (*cla*) assistant, second(er), adjutant, escort.

berkapit to have an assistant/adjutant/escort, etc.; assisted, escorted.

mengapit 1 to press, crush, squeeze. 2 to escort, follow.

mengapitkan to make s.t. become squeezed/crushed.

terkapit squeezed, pressed, crushed.

kapitan 1 squeezer, press. 2 → KAPIT.

pengapit escort, adjutant, etc. ~ *pengantin* a) bridesmaid. b) best man.

kapita (*D*) 1 capita. *per* - per capita. 2 topic. - *sélékta* (a school subject) selected topics.

kapital (*D/E*) capital (money); → MODAL.

berkapital with capital.

kapitalis (*D/E*) capitalist. - *birokrat* capitalist bureaucrat (a term used by the PKI to attack army officers directing state enterprises).

kapitalisasi (*D*) capitalization; → PEMODALAN.

kapitalisme (*D/E*) capitalism.

kapitalistik (*E*) and kapitalistis (*D*) capitalistic.

kapitan (*Port*) 1 headman of an ethnic division of the population in the eastern part of Indonesia; → CAMAT. 2 (*col*) headman of the Chinese community.

kapi telaat /-lat/ gate crasher.

Kapitol (*E*) Capitol (in the U.S.A.)

kapitulasi (*D*) capitulation.

berkapitulasi to capitulate.

kapitulir (*D*) → BERKAPITULASI.

kaplar(e)s (*D*) boots.

kaplét [kapsul tablét] caplet.

kapling (*D*) lot, parcel (of land).

meng(k)aplingkan to divide into lots/parcels.

peng(k)aplingan dividing into lots/parcels.

perkaplingan division into lots.

kaplok I (*Jv*) *tukang* - claque. - *dada* to beat one's breast.

kaplok II (*Jv*) kaplokan a slap in the face; *cp* TEMPÉLÉNG, TEMPÉLING, TONJOK.

kapoce(s) (*D*) prophylactic(s), condom(s).

kapodang → KEPUDANG.

kapok I (*Jv*) to be cured, have had one's fill of s.t., to have had enough of s.t.; have been taught a good lesson. *Biar meréka* -. Let it be a good lesson for them. *Saya sudah* -! I've had it! I've learned my lesson! -*mu kapan?* When will you ever learn? *Dia tidak pernah* -! She never learns! *tidak* -.-*nya* never learned a good lesson. - *lombok* to be taught a very good lesson, but keep on making the same mistakes.

mengapokkan to teach s.o. a good lesson.

kapok II → KAPUK I.

kapol (*coq*) → KAPULAGA.

Kapolri [Kepala kepolisian Républik Indonésia] Chief, Republic of Indonesia (State) Police.

kaporal (*ob*) → KOPRAL.

kaporisasi chlorination.

kaporit (*D*) chlorine.

   mengaporit to chlorinate.

kaprah (*Jv*) common, general, customary. *salah* – established mistake, i.e., s.t. that is considered an error but is so common that it is almost accepted; → SALAH I.

kapri I *kacang* – snow peas, *Pisum sativum*.

kapri II (*Port from A ob*) a black, negro.

Kaprikornus (*L*) Capricorn.

kapsalon (*D*) hairdresser's.

kapsao coffee/teapot.

kapsel (*D*) hairdo, coiffure.

kapséti (*Port ob*) (in Manado) cockscomb, clown.

kaps(e)tok (*D*) hat-and-coat stand.

kapster (*D*) female hairdresser.

kapsul I (*E*) capsule. – *manis* capsule-shaped sweet snack.

   berkapsul with a capsule.

   mengkapsulkan to put into a capsule (of medicine).

   pengkapsulan encapsulation.

kapsul II (*E*) (space) capsule. – *komando* command capsule (of space ship).

kaptan [kapur pertanian] ground limestone.

kaptén I (*D/E*) captain (of a ship); → NAKHODA; captain (in the armed forces); commander (in the police force); leader (of a soccer team, etc.); *cp* CAPTAIN. – *angkatan bersenjata* armed forces captain. – *bermain* team captain. – *kesebelasan sépakbola* soccer team captain. – *polisi* police captain. – *tak bermain* nonplaying captain (sports). – *udara* air force captain.

   meng(k)apténi to captain (a ship).

kaptén II (pickpocket jargon) leader of a gang of pickpockets operating on Jakarta buses.

kapuk I 1 tree cotton, kapok, *Ceiba pentandra, Eriodendron anfructuosum*. **2** (*pohon* –) a tall tree yielding floss used for caulking, *Ceiba pentandra*.

kapuk II (*M*) rice barn (with bamboo-plaited wall, roofed and oval shape). *sebesar* – very large.

kapu-kapu water lettuce, *Pistia stratiotes*.

kapul (*coq*) → KAPULAGA.

kapulaga cardamom, *Amomum cardamomum*.

kapulasan a *rambutan* species, *Nephelium mutabile*; → PULASAN.

kapung float; → APUNG.

   terkapung-kapung to float.

kapung-kapung Indian trumpet flower, *Oroxylum indicum*.

kapur 1 lime. *air* – lime water. *batu* – limestone. *kain* – starched white wear. *seperti* – *di ujung telunjuk* cannot assist one's relatives. **2** calcium. **3** (*geol*) Cretaceous (time). – *air* hydraulic lime. – *barus* camphor from the *Dryobalanops aromatica*. – *batu* plaster of Paris. – *belanda* (blackboard) chalk. – *hidup/kuripan* quicklime, calcium oxide. – *karbit* calcium carbide. – *kembang* quicklime. – *mati* slaked lime, calcium hydrate. – *mentah* quicklime. – *mentah* quicklime, calcium oxide. – *naga* k.o. tree, *Calophyllum soulatri*. – *petanang* k.o. plant, *Dryobalanops oblongifolia*. – *peléster* stucco. – *pertanian* (kaptan) ground limestone. – *rawa* marl. – *sirih* lime chewed with a betel quid. – *tajam* caustic lime. – *témbok* mortar. – *tohor* quicklime, unslaked lime, calcium oxide. – *tulis* (blackboard) chalk. – *turap* stucco.

   sekapur 1 a brief preparatory note. **2** in a nutshell. **3** a few words. ~ *sirih* a betel-nut quid with the trimmings.

   berkapur containing lime, chalky, calcareous.

   mengapur 1 to calcify. **2** to whitewash. ~ *sirih* to put lime on betel leaf.

   mengapuri (*pl obj*) to whitewash.

   mengapurkan to prepare a betel quid.

   kapuran calcified.

   pekapuran 1 container for lime. **2** limekiln.

   pengapur s.o. or s.t. that plasters/whitewashes.

   pengapuran 1 calcification. **2** narrowing (of the blood vessels).

   perkapuran (*med*) calcification.

kapurancang (*Jv*) sharpened bamboo sticks in a row put on top of a wall.

   ngapurancang to clasp one's hands with fingers intertwined and thumb tips touching.

kapuspén [kepala pusat penerangan] head of the information center.

kapyok rubber mallet.

kar I (*D*) chart, map.

kar II (*D*) cart; → KAHAR I.

kara I various species of beans. – *benguk* velvet bean, *Mucuna utilis*. *kacang* –, – *gajih/putih* lablab, *Dolichos lablab*. – *pedang* sword bean, *Canavalia gladiata*.

   kara-kara k.o. bean, lablab, *Dolichos lablab*.

kara II alone, by o.s., unaccompanied. *hidup sebatang* -/*karah/ karang* to be all alone in the world, without kith or kin. *gendang* – drum with one tympanum. *udang* – a sea crustacean, unid.

kara III → UDANG *kara*.

karab → KHARAB.

karaba method of pisciculture in the Semarang area using bamboo traps in which the fish can reproduce and grow.

karabat (*A*) → KERABAT.

karabén and **karabin** (*D/E*) carbine.

karad (*A*) *akar* – a medicinal root.

karaéng (in Makassar/Ujungpandang) honorary title of Macassarese noblemen.

karaf (*D/E*) carafe.

karah I 1 (to have) tartar on the teeth. **2** stain.

   berkarah 1 to have tartar on the teeth. **2** stained.

karah II *buluh* – k.o. tall bamboo with edible roots.

karah III (*ob*) → KARA II.

karak (*ob*) → KERAK I.

Karakata → KARKATA.

Karakoram Karakoram mountain range.

karakter (*D/E*) character.

karakterdés [kader penggerak téritorial désa] Golkar cadre assigned to rural areas.

karakterisasi (*D*) characterization.

karakterisir (*D*) **mengkarakterisir** to characterize.

karakteristik (*D/E*) characteristic.

karal → KARAR.

karam 1 1 to sink, capsize, founder, be submerged. **2** to be shipwrecked, shipwreck. – *kapal* shipwreck. *orang* – *kapal* a shipwrecked person. **3** to fail, miscarry, fall through. – *di hati* overwhelmed by unrequited love. – *di darat* to have an accident in one's own place or in an unexpected place. – *berdua, basah seorang* two persons have made a mistake, but only one is punished for it, i.e., to use a double standard. – *tidak berair* to have an accident without any reason. – *sambal oléh belacan* to sustain an injury due to the actions of a close friend or loved one. *seperti Cina* – pandemonium. *telah* – *maka bertimba* to lock the barn door after the horse is stolen.

   berkaraman (*pl subj*) to be shipwrecked.

   mengaram to sink, founder. *Disangka tiada akan* ~, *ombak yang kecil diabaikan*. If you don't pay attention to a minor accident, a major one will occur, i.e., you never know when an accident will happen.

   mengaramkan 1 to sink s.t. **2** to ruin, destroy, wreck (a ship). **3** enticing/seductive (of a smile).

karam II (*A*) esteem, honor.

karam III (*A*) baseborn.

karamba (in Samarinda) fish cage. – *apung* floating fish cage.

karambol (*D*) carom (in billiards).

karamél (*D/E*) caramel.

karamunting → KEMUNTING.

karang I 1 coral. – *emas* blood coral. **2** coral reef; atoll. *bunga* – sponge. *isi* – shells, coral. *penyakit* – gravel, kidney stones. *tinjau* – seat (on bridge of ship). *tulang* – petrosal bone. *udang* – lobster. – *endapan* encrustation. – *gigi* tartar, plaque. – *mérah* organ pipe coral, *Tubipora musica*. – *pantai* fringing reef. – *penghalang* barrier reef. – *tepi* fringing reef.

   karang-karang gravel, kidney stones.

berkarang 1 (*ob*) to dive for coral. **2** with coral reefs, coralligenous. *sudah* ~ in the last stages (of a disease).

terkarang (*ob*) to run aground on a rock (of a ship).

karangan 1 rock; ore deposit, vein. **2** to have kidney stones.

karang-karangan all sorts of coral.

karang II berkarang 1 threaded, strung (e.g., pearls/coral, etc.). **2** arranged (of flowers). *bunga* – a) corymb. b) bunch of flowers. **3** set, mounted (of jewels, etc.).

mengarang(kan) [and **ngarang** (*coq*)] **1** to arrange (flowers). **2** to thread, string (pearls/beads, etc.). **3** to set, mount (jewels/stones, etc.). **4** to arrange, put in order. **5** to compose, write (a book, music, etc.). **6** to compile. **7** to contrive, devise, invent, make up (a story).

karang-mengarang 1 writing. **2** composing. *ilmu* ~ art of writing/composing.

mengarangkan 1 → MENGARANG. **2** to compose, etc. for s.o.

karangan 1 composition. **2** piece (of writing), article, paper, publication. *induk* ~ editorial; → TAJUK *rencana*. ~ *acuan* bibliography, references. ~ *ilmiah* (scientific/research) paper. **3** compiled/written by. *Kamus Déwan* ~ *Dr. Teuku Iskandar* the Kamus Dewan written by Dr. Teuku Iskandar. **4** arrangement, s.t. arranged. ~ *bunga* a) flower arrangement. b) wreath. c) bouquet; → BUKÉT. ~ *utama* masterpiece. **5** s.t. made up/invented.

pengarang 1 string, thread, etc. for threading/stringing. **2** author, writer, composer. ~ *gigi* gums. ~ *jantung* one's beloved. ~ *serta* coauthor. ~ *telur* ovary. *sidang* ~ editorial staff. **3** arranger (of music). **kepengarangan** authorship.

pengarangan composing, arranging.

karang III pekarangan 1 piece of land or yard on which a house is built. **2** yard (of a house). **3** premises, property. ~ *bertetangga* neighboring property. ~ *yang menderita/mengabdi/penerima beban* servient land.

karang IV (*Jv cla*) residence, domicile. – *keputeraan* royal children's residence. – *keputrian* neighborhood girls' association. – *taruna/Teruna* [KT] neighborhood youth association, a youth organization designed to prevent juvenile delinquency, drug abuse, etc.

karang V (*Jv*) – *abang* burning ground. *menjadi* – *abang* to be destroyed, done away with.

karang VI clipped form of **sekarang**.

karang VII → KERANG.

karang VIII *ilmu* – (*Jv*) knowledge of invulnerability; incantation, etc. causing invulnerability.

karang IX → KARA II.

karang-kitri (*Jv*) fruit trees and coconut palms.

karantina (*D*) quarantine.

meng(k)arantina(kan) to quarantine.

pengkarantinaan quarantining. *ketentuan* ~ quarantine stipulations.

karantinawan quarantiner.

karaoké (*E*) **1** karaoke. **2** (*vulg*) oral sex.

karap heddles of a weaver's loom, weaver's comb.

karapan – *sapi* (Madurese) bull race.

karar (*A*) **1** permanent, stable. **2** quiet, settled. **3** unchanging, invariant.

karas I (*kué* –), **karas-karas** and (*kué*) **kekaras** a crisp fried flour cake.

karas II a camphor-producing tree, *Aquilaria malaccensis*; → GAHARU.

karas III (*infr*) clone.

mengaras to clone.

arasan cloned.

pengarasan cloning.

karat I 1 rust; encrusting dirt. *anti-karat* and *tahan* – rustproof. *dimakan* – a) rusty. b) rusted. **2** rust brown. – *daun* leaf rust, brown rust. – *jagung* maize rust. – *kedelai* soybean rust. – *mérah* red rust (a kind of leaf spot caused by the alga *Cephaleuros virescens*).

berkarat 1 to rust; rusty; rusted; to corrode; corroded; corrodible. *tidak* ~ noncorrodable. *tidak dapat* ~ rustproof. **2** stained. **3** to get rusty (of skill or knowledge). **4** to be disgraced; depraved, morally bad, perverted. *hatinya* ~ depraved, bad.

karatan 1 rusty; corrosion; scrap iron. **2** old, long(time). **3** a deep-

rooted habit. ~ *besi* iron rust. ~ *tembaga* verdigris. **4** depraved. ~ *hati* malicious.

peng(k)aratan and **perkaratan** rusting, corrosion.

karat II (*D*) **1** carat. *emas 24* – 24-carat gold. **2** a unit of weight for precious stones and pearls, equal to 200 milligrams. **3** quality, standard, weight; → BOBOT. *yang tinggi* –*nya* of weight/importance.

karaté (*Jp*) karate.

perkaratéan karate (*mod*).

karatéka (*Jp*) karate expert.

Karatsyi Karachi.

karau berkarau well-mixed/blended.

mengarau to stir (a cup of tea, a bowl of porridge).

karavan (*D/E*) **1** caravan, convoy; → KAFILAH I. **2** (automobile) trailer, an enclosed vehicle pulled by a car or truck and designed to be lived in, mobile home.

karawang I openwork, lace, fretwork; → KERAWANG.

Karawang II the new spelling for the town in West Java formerly called Kerawang.

karawitan (*Jv*) art of the *gamelan*.

karbid and **karbit** (*D*) carbide. *gas* – acetylene. *lampu* – carbide/acetylene lamp.

mengarbit to accelerate (a training program).

karbitan quickly trained (official).

peng(k)arbitan acceleration (of a training program).

karbohidrat (*D/E*) carbohydrate.

karbol I (*D*) carbolic acid.

meng(k)arbol 1 to pour carbolic acid over, clean with carbolic acid. **2** make s.o. the object of s.o.'s rage.

karbol II air force cadet.

karbon (*D/E*) carbon. *kertas* – carbon paper. – *dioksida* carbon dioxide. – *monoksida* carbon monoxide.

pengarbonan carbonization, cementation.

karbonaci(s) (*D*) *daging* – pork chop.

karbonat (*D/E*) carbonate.

karburator (*D/E*) carburetor.

karcis (*D*) **1** (admission/train, etc.) ticket; → TIKÉT. **2** coupon (for rationed food). **3** calling card; → KARTU *nama*. – *catutan* ticket bought from a scalper. – *keréta api* railway/train ticket. – *masuk* admission ticket. – *nama* calling card, business card. – *parkir* parking ticket. – *péron* platform ticket. – *pulang-pergi/retur* round-trip ticket. – *sepur* (*ob*) railway/train ticket. – *terusan* season ticket. – *undangan* complimentary ticket.

berkarcis 1 to have a ticket. **2** which uses/requires tickets.

meng(k)arciskan to issue tickets for.

kardamunggu (*D*) cardamom, *Elettaria cardamomum*.

kardan (*D*) differential gear.

kardinal (*D/E*) cardinal (the person).

kardiograf (*D/E*) cardiograph.

kardiografi (*D/E*) cardiography.

kardiogram (*D/E*) cardiogram.

kardiol (in the Karo area, North Sumatra) gladiolus.

kardiolog (*D*) cardiologist.

kardiologi (*D/E*) cardiologist.

kardiovaskular (*E*) and **kardiovaskulér** (*D*) cardiovascular.

kardus (*D*) **1** cartridge (with gunpowder). **2** cardboard; carton, box. *kertas* – brown wrapping paper. **3** low, humble.

karé → KARI I.

karédok (*S*) vegetable salad with peanut butter sauce.

karena (*Skr*) **1** reason, cause, motive, purpose, for the sake of. *Apa* – *nya maka begitu?* Why did it turn out that way? – *apa* (= *kenapa*) what's the reason behind it, why? – *Allah* a) for God's sake. b) pro Deo, free of charge. – *kerukunan* for the sake of harmony. **2** because. *berani* – *benar, takut* – *salah* daring because it is right, afraid because it is wrong. *Ia tidak datang* – *sakit*. He didn't show up because he was sick. **3** due/owing to, because of, on account of. – *jabatan* ex officio. – *kekhilafan* due to an oversight. – *udara buruk* owing to the bad weather. (*oléh*) – *itu* (*maka*) and –*nya* (*maka*) and – *itulah* therefore, that's why, because of that. *oléh/dari* – because. *oléh* – *ia sibuk* because he is busy. *dari* – *kurang hati-hati* due to carelessness. **5** from, as a result of; → AKIBAT. *mati* – *serangan jantung* dead from a heart attack.

mengarenakan (*usu* in the passive) to cause. *mati dikarenakan serangan jantung* died of a heart attack.

karengga (*M*) *kuda –* sorrel horse; → KERENGGA.

karéo (*– padi*) white-breasted water hen, *Amaurornis phoenicurus. – kaba* common bush-hen, *Amaurornis olivaceus.*

karéséh-péséh (*M*) to chatter away in Dutch.

karésidénan → KERÉSIDÉNAN.

karét (*Jv?*) **1** (*pohon –*) rubber tree, *Hevea brasiliensis. kebun/perkebunan –* rubber estate/plantation. **2** rubber, caoutchouc; → GETAH. **3** rubber band. **4** (ink/pencil) eraser. **5** (*sl*) condom. **6a**) a piece of elastic. **b**) elastic, i.e., s.t. can be made longer or shorter or time that can be shortened or lengthened. *artikel –* an article of law that can be interpreted to one's liking. *jam –* the habit of not being on time for appointments, starting late, etc. (considered an Indonesian characteristic). *– alam* natural rubber. *– ban* rubber band. *– bongkah* crumb rubber. *– buatan* synthetic rubber. *– busa* a) foam rubber. b) sponge; → BUNGA *karang*, SEPON. *– cair* latex. *– gelang* rubber band. *– injakan* foot pedal. *– kasar/mentah* crude rubber. *– lembaran* sheet rubber. *– penghapus* eraser. *– perkebunan* estate rubber. *– rakyat* smallholder's rubber. *– remah* crumb rubber. *– sintétis/tiruan* synthetic rubber. *– spon* sponge rubber. *– tinta* ink eraser. *– tiruan* synthetic rubber.

berkarét rubberized.

mengarét to postpone.

ngarét (*sl*) **1** to postpone. **2** to be late, not on time.

kekarétan 1 elasticity. **2** postponement.

perkarétan rubber (*mod*).

kargo (*D/E*) cargo.

kari I (*Tam*) curry.

kari II (*A*) Koran reader; → QARI(AH).

kari III (*Jv*) left (over), left behind.

karia (*infr*) → KARYA.

karib (*A*) **1** (close) relative. *– (dan bait)* a) close and distant relatives. b) friends and acquaintances. **2** close, intimate. *sahabat – a* close friend. *– kepada* close to, with a close relationship to.

berkarib 1 to be (closely) related. **2** to be friends, close.

berkariban to be friends with e.o.

mengaribi 1 to be on intimate terms with. **2** to be popular.

mengaribkan and **memperkarib** to cause to become close/intimate, bring people together.

kekariban intimacy, relationship, kinship, close friendship.

perkariban → KEKARIBAN.

Karibia Caribbean (Sea).

karibu (*D/E*) caribou. *cambuk – (ob)* (riding) whip.

kariér (*D*) career.

berkariér to have a career.

kariéris (*E*) careerist.

kariérisme (*E*) careerism.

karih mengarih to stir, blend, turn (rice in the pot).

pengarih stirrer, mixer.

karikatur (*D/E*) caricature.

mengarikatur to caricature.

karikatural (*E*) caricatural.

karikaturis (*D*) caricaturist.

karil I k.o. rabbit.

karil II [karya ilmiah] scientific paper.

karim (*A*) noble, generous (by disposition), magnanimous, bountiful. *Ya –* O God, the Bountiful.

karing *ikan – garjah* a river fish, *Betta spp.*

karir (*E*) career; → KARIÉR.

berkarir to have a career.

karisma → KHARISMA.

karismatik (*E*) and **karismatis** (*D*) charismatic.

karitatif charitable.

karkas (*D/E*) skeleton, carcass.

Karkata Cancer.

karki (*A ob*) crane.

karkun (*Pers ob*) **1** clerk. **2** secretary.

karma I (*Skr*) karma, destiny, fate. *hukum –* concept that one's fate is decided by one's deeds.

karma II → KERAMA.

karmenaji → KARBONACI.

karna (*coq*) → KARENA.

Karnadhara Samiti (*Skr neo*) Consultative Committee's Hall (in the MPR Building).

karnadu (*Port ob*) k.o. scarab, long-armed chafer, *Euchirus longimanus.*

karnaval (*D/E*) carnival.

karnivor (*D/E*) carnivore.

Karo I a subgroup of the Batak ethnic group.

karo II [kepala biro] bureau chief.

karombol → KARAMBOL.

karorok (in Ujungpandang) k.o. leaf mat used as sails.

karosél (*D*) merry-go-round.

karoseri (*D*) (automobile) body, carriage work.

mengaroseri to do body work (on a car).

mengaroserikan to send (a vehicle) to the shop for body work.

karper (*D*) (*ikan –*) carp. *– rumput* grass carp; → IKAN *koan.*

karpét (*D/E*) carpet; → HAMPARAN, PERMADANI.

berkarpét carpeted. *lantai ~* a floor covered by a carpet. *sepenuhnya ~* covered with wall-to-wall carpeting.

karsa (*Skr ob*) **1** will, intention; → KEHENDAK. **2** will, to be going to; → HENDAK, MAU. *– Yudha* [KY] 72-man units within *Kopassand(h)a.*

karsinogén (*E*) carcinogen.

karsinogénik (*E*) carcinogenic.

karsinom (*D/E*) carcinoma.

karst (*D/E*) karst.

kartél (*D/E*) cartel.

karter (*D*) **1** gearcase, crankcase. **2** housing. *– minyak* oil pan.

kartéring (*E*) charting, surveying; → PEMETAAN.

kartika (*Skr ob*) **1** *bintang –* the Seven Sisters, Pleiades. **2** (film)star. *– Chandra Kirana* the name of the Army Wives Association. *– yudha* star war(s).

Kartini Indonesia's first feminist and women's emancipator. *Hari –* April 21 celebration. *– Udara* Indonesia's female commercial pilots.

kartograf (*D*) and **kartografer** (*E*) cartographer.

kartografi (*D/E*) cartography.

kartogram (*D/E*) cartogram.

karton (*D*) **1** cardboard, board. **2** carton. *– bergelombang* corrugated carton. *– berombak* corrugated board. *– témpél* mounting board.

kartonis → KARTUNIS.

kartoték and **kartotik** (*D*) card file.

kartu (*Port*) **1** card. **2** playing card. **3** index card. **4** greeting card. *main –* to play cards. *– anggota* membership card. *– as* the ace. *– Askés* [Asuransi kesehatan] Health Insurance Card; → KARTU *miskin. – Belanda/besar* playing cards used for Western card games, such as bridge, etc. *– beras* rice-ration card. *– berlubang* punch card. *– biru* the blue card issued by local authorities indicating that a certain plot cannot be built on. *– ceki* small playing cards used for Chinese card games, such as *péi, kongkin,* etc. *– domino* domino cards. *– idéntitas* identity card, I.D. *– Idéntitas Penduduk Musiman* [KIP(E)M] Season Worker Identity Card. *– Ijin Tinggal Tetap* [KITAP] Permanent Resident's Card. *– indéks* index card. *– indéks kuning* registration card for job seekers. *– isteri* wife's card. *– keluarga* [KK] family card. *– kecil* → KARTU *ceki. – kontrol* appointment card. *– krédit* credit card. *– kuning* a) the 1977 voter-registration card. b) (during the 1982 general elections) a warning from *Lembaga Pemilihan Umum.* c) a warning directed to stevedoring companies regarding their irresponsible actions in port areas. d) a playing card-sized card that a referee holds up to warn a player for dangerous or unsportsmanlike behavior (in soccer). **mengartu-kuningkan** to issue a *kartu kuning. – Lebaran* greeting card sent on *Lebaran. – magnét* magnetic card (as used by credit card companies). *– main* playing cards. *– mati* deadwood, no longer useful, over-the-hill, past one's prime; not considered (for employment, etc.). *– Mérah* a (*Mal*) k.o. alien identity card for Indonesians who plan to stay in Malaysia for longer than a brief visit. b) a playing card-sized card that a referee holds up to signal a player's removal from the game (in soccer). *– miskin* a yellow card used by the poor to cover health care expenses. – *nama* business/calling card. – *nasabah* signature card (in a bank). – *Natal* Christmas card. – *pemilihan* ballot. – *Penduduk* → KARTU *Tanda Penduduk*. – *pengenal* identity card. – *Pengenal Pengemudi* [KPP] Driver's Identity Card (a photo identity card attached to a car's dashboard). – *pengingat* tickler card. – *perekam waktu* punch card. – *pérs* press pass. – *pindah(an)* change of address card. – *pos/(ber)gambar* (picture) postcard. – *potongan harga* discount card. – *suami* husband's card. – *suara* ballot. – *tamu* calling card. – *tanda anggota* → KARTU *anggota*. – *tanda bébas* pass. – *tanda masuk* boarding pass. – *Tanda Penduduk* [katépé and KTP] Resident's Identity Card. – *tandatangan* signature card (provided with a photo; needed in Indonesian post offices to pick up registered mail, cash money orders, etc.). – *télepon* calling card. – *ucapan (selamat)* greeting card. – *undangan* invitation card.

berkartu to have a ... card.

mengartukan to card-index.

pengartuan card index (system).

perkartuan card-filing cabinet.

Kartum Khartoum.

kartun I (*E*) cartoon.

kartun II → KARTON.

kartunis (*E*) cartoonist.

karu I (*M*) → KARUT.

karu II *tiada* – (*ob cla*) → *tidak* KERUAN.

karu III mengaru to interrupt.

karuan (*J*) → KERUAN I. – *saja* it stands to reason; of course. – *saja ia menang, habis mainnya curang sih.* Of course he won; he cheated.

Karubin cherubim.

karuhun (*S*) ancestors.

karu-karu k.o. tree, *Ctenolophon parvifolius*; → MERTAS.

Karun (*A*) Korah, the enemy of Moses, believed by Muslims to have been very rich and whose treasure is now buried in the earth for wizards to find. *harta* – a) treasure-trove, hidden treasure, ownerless property. b) (*M*) wealth obtained in an unlawful way. *menjadi* – to become wealthy. *dapat harta* – to get a windfall without any effort. *mengumpulkan harta* – treasure hunt.

karung sack, bale, bag. *kain* – jute for clothes. – *anak* caul; → KARUNG-KARUNG. – *goni* gunny sack. – *rami* jute sack. – *tidur* sleeping bag.

berkarung wrapped in a sack.

berkarung-karung 1 several sacks/bales. **2** in sacks/bales.

mengarungi to (put into a) sack.

karung-karung caul (at birth).

karunia (*Skr*) **1** favor, gift, bounty (of God/kings, etc.) **2** pity, compassion, commiseration, mercy; → KURNIA.

mengaruniai 1 to favor, reward, recompense, bless (with children). *dikaruniai momongan* blessed with children. *dikaruniai* to be gifted/talented. **2** pity/commiserate with s.o.; to show mercy to s.o.

mengaruniakan to bestow a favor (up)on s.o.

terkaruniai to be blessed with.

pengaruniaan blessing. ~ *Roh Kudus* the blessing of the Holy Ghost.

karut (= **berkarut**) extremely confused/muddled/chaotic; → KALUT I. *Sangat* – *cakapnya.* He talked in a confused way. *Berkarut pikirannya.* His thoughts were confused. – *marut* completely confused, disturbed and mixed-up (in the head); entangled/enmeshed in lies. *tukang* – (*coq*) liar.

mengarut 1 to cause/create confusion, disturb, agitate. **2** to lie, make untrue statements, tell a rambling story.

mengarutkan to make a complete mess of s.t.

kekarutan disturbance, trouble.

karwan (*A/Pers*) caravan.

karya (*Skr*) work, opus (of artist/writer, etc.). – *abdi* public service work. – *agung* masterpiece. – *Artha* a token of appreciation conferred by the Department of Finance on those who performed meritorious service in printing the first O(*eng*) R(*épublik*) I(*ndonésia*). – *asil* original work (not a translation). – *baku* standard work. – *b(h)akti* pro bono work. – *besar* masterpiece. –

désa (in Central and East Java) village (compulsory, unpaid) labor. – *guna* useful work. **mengkarya-gunakan** to make s.o. or s.t. useful. – *hias* decorative work. – *ilmiah* thesis, dissertation. – *jam* timepiece. – *mat kodak* photograph(s); → *mak/mat* KODAK. – *nyata* laboratory field work. – *rujukan* reference work. – *sastra* literary work. – *Satya* award for 25 years of uninterrupted service with a government department. – *seni* objet d'art. – *siswa* trainee. **meng(k)aryasiswakan** to appoint as a trainee. – *tak berkala* occasional paper. – *wisata* field trip.

berkarya to work. ~ *bakti* to do voluntary/unpaid work.

meng(k)aryakan 1 to appoint. ~ *sebagai Dubés Luar Biasa* to appoint s.o. as Ambassador Extraordinary. **2** to use s.t. for one's own profit (illegal but tolerated); *cp* NGOBYÉK. **3** to put s.o. to work, employ. *Rudy* ~ *17 orang.* Rudy employs 17 men. *tidak* ~ to put out of operation, make not work. **4** to put s.t. to work, use, employ. ~ *24 baut baja.* It uses 24 steel bolts. **5** to assign, post (military personnel to a post outside their normal duties).

kekaryaan 1 temporary assignment (*esp* of a military officer) to a post outside one's normal duties. **2** work. **3** profession. ~ *ABRI* the posting/seconding of military personnel to civilian positions. *fungsi* ~ *ABRI* the military functioning as a sociopolitial force. **4** cadreization.

pekarya → KARYAWAN.

pengkaryaan 1 employment, assignment (to a position). **2** temporary assignment/posting of (military personnel to a post outside their normal duties).

Karyantara the mass organization of the Antara News Agency workers.

karyaseni work of art.

karyasiswa (*Skr neo*) a company employee training abroad.

karyatangan handicrafts (a school subject).

karyawan (*Skr neo*) **1** white-collar worker (as well as certain other workers such as nurses, etc.). **2** employee, personnel – *ABRI* a member of the Indonesian armed forced assigned to nonmilitary work. – *bahari* seaman. – *bank* bank employee; bank officer (in some banks). – *bulanan* monthly wage earner. – *harian lepas* a) casual worker. b) third-party employee. – *lepas* freelance worker. – *militér* → KARYAWAN *ABRI*. – *pariwisata* tour operator. – *pemerintah* government employee. – *pérs* journalist. – *perusahaan* industrial worker. – *risét* research worker. – *tambang* miner. – *tetap* permanent worker.

mengaryawankan to assign s.t. (to a job).

kekaryawanan employment, employee (*mod*).

karyawani → KARYAWATI.

Karyawanisme white-collar workerism.

karyawati (*Skr neo*) a female *karyawan*.

karyawisata (*Skr neo*) working trip/tour, field trip.

berkaryawisata to go on a working trip.

kas I (*D*) **1** pay office. – *désa/kraton/negara* village/palace/state treasury. **2** cash, funds, coffers. (*uang* –) a) cash (in hand), funds (in hand). b) (in a store/bank, etc.) ready cash. *pemegang* – cashier; (of a club, etc.) treasurer. – *kecil* petty cash. – *mobil* mobile cash. – *partai* party funds. *buku* – cashbook. *memegang* – to keep the cash. **3** cash register, cashier, cashier's window.

kas II (*D*) **1** wooden crate (for shipping goods). **2** case (of a watch). **3** armoire, wardrobe.

kas III (*ob*) → KHAS.

kas IV (in acronyms) → KEPALA *staf*.

kasa I (*Pers*) (*kain* –) gauze, muslin. *kawat* – chicken wire, wire screen, grating. *perban* – gauze bandage. – *baja* steel gauze.

pengkasaan grating.

kasa II (*cla*) sky, heaven.

kasa III (*D*) cash register; → KAS I 3.

kasa IV frame. – *acuan* frame of reference.

kasa V poppy seeds.

kasab I → KASAP II.

kasab II (*M*) k.o. gold thread.

kasad I (*A*) intention, plan, purpose.

mengasadkan to plan, intend.

Kasad II [Kepala Staf Angkatan Darat] Army Chief of Staff.

kasah I → KASA I, KHASAH.

kasah II (*cla*) rattan mat.

kasah-kosoh (*onom*) sound of s.t. being dragged.
berkasah-kosoh to make that sound.
kasai I 1 a fragrant hair lotion. **2** a skin ointment.
berkasai to smear o.s. with this ointment.
memperkasai to use s.t. as an ointment.
kasai II k.o. tree, Pacific litchi, *Pometia pinnata* and *Amoora spp.* used for building material, headache medicine and as an antipyretic. – *bukit* k.o. tree, *Pometia alnifolia.* – *talang* k.o. tree, *Aglaia cordata.* – *tembaga* k.o. tree, *Dysoxylon spp.*
kasai III various species of fish. – *janggut* scaly hair-fin anchovy, *Setipinna taty.*
kasak-kisik and **kasak-kusuk 1** whispering of voices, sound of whispering. **2** rumors. **3** plotting and intrigues on the part of bureaucrats to elicit bribes. **4** lobbying (in the legislature).
berkasak-kisik and **berkasak-kusuk** to intrigue, lobby, plot, gossip.
Kasal [Kepala Staf Angkatan Laut] Navy Chief of Staff.
kasam I (*M*) **1** grudge, spite. **2** curses. *melepaskan* – to take revenge.
mengasam to take revenge.
kasam II (*Pr*) → MASAK I.
kasanah → KHAZANAH.
kasang (*M*) → KERSANG.
kasap I rough (of bristles/leaves), course (to the touch); hairy (of bamboo stems). – *mata* roughly.
kekasapan roughness.
kasap II ship's purveyor.
kasap III – *jantan* a creeping plant, k.o. gourd, *Clerodendron villosum.*
kasar 1 coarse (of sand, etc.), rough (of surfaces). **2** shaggy, hairy, wooly, bristly. **3** stiff, rigid, tough. **4** approximate, in round figures, rough(ly). **5** material, physical, bodily, corporal. **6** rude, impolite, vulgar. **7** simple (of a manufactured article); not neatly done. **8** large (of a bird's feathers). **9** shortened number of genuflections in a daily prayer. – *mulut* dirty mouthed (always cursing). – *tangan* easy with the hands (likes to hit people).
sekasar as coarse/rough/rude, etc. as.
berkasar impolite, rough (of manners).
berkasar-kasaran to be rude to e.o.
mengasari [and **ngasarin** (*J coq*)] to be rough with, rough up, treat in a rough way.
mengasarkan to roughen, make coarse/rough, etc.
memperkasar to make rougher, roughen.
terkasar roughest.
kekasaran rudeness, roughness, impoliteness, etc.
kasasi (*D leg*) **1** appeal to a higher court in the judicial hierarchy, cassation appeal. **2** reversal of a lower court's decision.
mengkasasi to hand down a judgment in such an appeal.
terkasasi appealed. *pihak* ~ respondent (in an appeal).
kasat I doormat.
kasat II [kepala satuan] unit head.
kasatmata (*Jv*) **1** visual, can be seen with the naked eye. **2** concrete.
kasau I (bamboo/wooden) rafters, joist. – *betina* lesser rafters. – *jantan* main rafters. – *melintang* crossbeam.
berkasau with rafters.
mengasau to install rafters on.
Kasau II [Kepala Staf Angkatan Udara] Air Force Chief of Staff.
kasbi (in Ambon) cassava.
kasbon (*D*) k.o. savings certificate.
kasbuk (*D*) cashbook.
kasdu (*A*) **1** willing. **2** to want.
kaselak (*Jv*) just in time.
kasemat (*A*) **1** dispute, quarrel, controversy, conflict, feud. **2** lawsuit. **3** grudge, spite. *dendam* – rancor and enmity.
berkasemat to be in conflict.
kasemek Japanese persimmon, *Diospyros kaki.*
kasép → KASIP. – *bulan* a) delayed menstruation. b) missing menstruation. *kapsul – bulan* capsule containing drug which induces menstruation.
kaserin (*ob*) k.o. tree.

kasét (*D/E*) **1** cassette, tape. – *biang* master tape. – *vidéo* video-cassette. **2** cassette tape recorder.
meng(k)asétkan to record on a cassette, tape.
pengkasétan recording on cassette, taping.
kasi I (*J coq*) **1** to give; → BERI, KASIH II. **2** (*coq*) to cause to, let, make (often equivalent to verb with suffix *-kan* in standard language). – *keluar* to throw out, get rid of. – *lihat* to show. – *makan* to feed. – *tahu* to let know, inform. – *turun* to lower.
mengasi [and **ngasi** (*coq*)] **1** to give. *dikasi hati* given in to s.o.'s wishes. **2** (*coq*) to put.
ngasiin (*J*) to give s.t.; → MEMBERIKAN.
pengasi gift, present. ~ *tahu* informant.
kasi II (*A ob*) castrated, gelded. *ayam* – capon. *lembu* – ox.
pengasian castration.
kasi III [kepala séksi] section head.
kasian → KASIHAN.
kasiat → KHASIAT.
kasid (*A*) courier.
kasidah (*A*) Arabic poem of a religious character (recited at religious gatherings) accompanied by a *gambus.*
berkasidah to recite such a poem.
mengasidahkan to recite (such a poem).
kasidahan such a musical performance.
kasih I 1 love, affection, inclination, fondness. – *akan/kepada* to like, be fond of, be devoted to. – *yang tidak berbalas* unrequited love. – *mesra* deep love. – *sayang* love and affection. **2** to love, have tender feelings toward. *terima* – thank you. – *tidak sampai* unrequited love.
berkasih-kasihan 1 to be in love with e.o.; continually in love/on good terms with e.o. **2** to make love, court.
mengasih(i) to be fond of, love, cherish.
kasih-mengasihi to love e.o.
kekasih darling, beloved; favorite, pet.
kekasihan love.
pengasih 1 (= pekasih) love charm/potion. **2** altruistic/charitable person.
kasih II 1 to give. – *hati* to let s.o. have his/her way, give in to s.o. – *muka* a) indulgent. b) to indulge; → KASI I. **2** to cause to, make; → KASI I. – *tahu* → KASI *tahu.*
mengasih [and **ngasih** and **mengasihi** (*coq*) and **ngasihin** (*J coq*)] to give; → MEMBERI. *Siapa yang mengasih uang itu?* Who gave that money? *dikasih makan* to be fed (of a child/animal, etc.).
ngasih (*coq*) to put s.t. (on). ~ *bumbu* to season (a dish). *dikasih gelombang* to be waved (of hair).
pengasih gift, present. ~ *tahu* informant.
kasih III pity, commiseration, compassion.
mengasihani to pity, feel sorry for.
kasih-mengasihani *tidak* ~ ruthless, pitiless.
kasihan 1 pity, compassion, commiseration. ~ *akan* to have pity on. **2** disappointing! what a pity/shame! that's too bad! **3** poor thing! *jatuh* ~ to take pity on.
kekasihan pity, compassion.
pengasih the All-Merciful (a characteristic of God).
pengasihan mercy.
kasik → KOSAK *kasik.*
kasim (*A*) castrated, gelded.
mengasim to castrate.
kasima → KESIMA.
kasino (*D/E*) casino.
kasintu (*S*) jungle fowl, partridge.
kasip (*Jv*) too late.
mengasipkan to delay, postpone.
kekasipan lateness.
kasir (*D*) cashier; (in bank) teller.
kasis [kartu isteri] spouse card.
kasiterit (*E*) cassiterite (found in Bangka and Belitung).
kaskada (*D*) cascade.
kaskado I (*Port*) psoriasis.
kaskado II *ikan* – an ornamental aquarium fish species, *Glosolepis indicus*, found in Lake Sentani in Irian Jaya.
kaskaya (*Jv*) **1** power, capacity. **2** wealth, means.
kasko (*D/E*) casco, hull, body (of a ship).

kasmaran (*Jv*) *q.v.* under ASMARA. *édan* – (*ob*) madly in love.
  mengasmarani to fall in love with.
kasmir (*D*) cashmere.
kasmutik cosmetic; → KOSMÉTIKA.
kasno 1 [*kasus nomor*] case number. **2** (*joc*) [*bekas cino*] "former Chinese," i.e., a Chinese who has taken Indonesian citizenship (since the citizenship papers contain a case number).
kaso I and **kaso-kaso** (*S*) rafter; → KASAU.
kaso II (*S*) a tall reed, *Saccarum spontaneum*; → GLAGAH.
kaso III (*burung* –) chestnut-capped babbler, *Timalia pileata*.
Kasogatan a form of Buddhist teaching adhered to by ancient Indonesians.
Kassospol [*Kepala Staf Sosial/Politik*] Chief of the Social and Political Staff.
kaspé (*D*) cassava, *Manihot utilissima*; → SINGKONG I, UBI *kayu*.
Kaspia Caspian.
kasrah (*A*) a vowel point indicating *é* or *i*.
kassa → KASA III.
kasta I (*D Port*) caste (in society); → BRAHMANA, PARIA I, SUDRA, WAISYA.
kasta II (*D*) caste.
kastam (*Mal*) customs. – *dan Éksais Diraja Malaysia* Royal Customs and Excise.
kastan(y)ét (*E*) castanets.
kasténgel (*D*) cheese straw.
Kaster [*Kepala staf téritorial*] Chief of Staff for Territorial Affairs.
kasti (*D*) a ballgame played between two teams of 12 players each.
kastil (*D*) castle (in chess); → BÉNTÉNG.
kastok → KAPSTOK.
kastor (*D*) beaver hairs.
kastrasi (*D*) castration.
kastrol (*D*) casserole, stew pan.
kastroli (*D*) castor oil.
kasturi I (*Skr*) a plant, Indonesian wax ginger, *Tapeinochilus ananassae*, whose leaves are used as a remedy for wounds; a fragrant oil is extracted from the seeds; → KESTURI II.
kasturi II → KASTURI I.
kasturi III → KASTURI III.
kasuari → KASWARI.
kasub [*kepala sub*] head of the ... sub(directorate/service, etc.).
kasui *kué* – k.o. steamed cake.
kasuistik (*E*) (*secara*) – casuistic(ally).
kasum [*kepala staf umum*] chief of general staff.
kasuma (*ob*) flower; → KESUMA.
kasumat → KESUMAT.
kasumba → KESUMBA II.
kasunyatan (*Jv*) realism.
kasur (*Jv*) mattress; → BOLSAK. *jatuh di/ke* – to be kicked upstairs. *tidur di* – married to a rich woman. – *gulung* sleeping bag.
  berkasur (a bed) with a mattress.
kasuran k.o. grass, swamp millet, *Isachne globosa*.
kasus (*D leg*) **1** case, incident. – *27 Juli* reference to the attack on PDI headquarters in Jakarta on that date. **2** investigation into a case. **3** (*gram*) case.
kasut 1 sandal, slipper. **2** shoe, boot; → SEPATU I. *si* – *lurik* an orchid variety native to Sumatra, *Paphiopedilum tonsum*. – *belulang* rawhide slipper. – *bola* soccer shoes. – *getah* gumboots. – *kayu* wooden clogs. – *kuda* horseshoe. – *roda* a) roller skate. b) rim (of a wheel). – *rumput* straw slippers. – *salju* skating shoe. – *tumit tinggi* high-heeled shoe.
kas(u)wari (*Jv*) cassowary, *Casuarius spp.*
kasyaf (*A*) vision.
kasyif (*A*) the revealer (a name of God).
kasyinah (*Pers*) porridge.
Kasymir Kashmir.
kata (*Skr*) **1** word. – *demi* – word by word, verbatim. **2** expression, saying, utterance, remark, phrase. *Demikian* – *ibunya kepada saya.* That's what his mother said to me. *–nya* a) (= – *orang* and *orang* –) people/they say/said, it is said/rumored that. b) he said. c) so-called, s.t. has been alleged but in reality it is different. *orang yang –nya sakti* a people with alleged supernatural powers. *dengan* – *bulat* unanimously; by acclamation. *dengan* – *lain*

in other words. *bertinggal* – and *meninggalkan* – (*M*) to leave a message. *mengubah* – to break one's promise. *permulaan* – preface. *satu* – *satu perbuatan* to match one's words with deeds. *tertumbuk* – to get into trouble. *tutur* – old saws. – *berjawab, gayung bersambut* habit/custom becomes second nature. – *dahulu bertepati,* – *kemudian berceraian* promised must be fulfilled. *élok* – *dalam mupakat, buruk* – *diluar mupakat* (*M*) look before you leap. – *adat* traditional proverb relating to *adat*. – *akhir* final voting on an issue. – *asal* (*gram*) root word. – *asli* native/inherited word. – *awas* words of warning. – *bah* verbiage. – *batin* conscience. – *benda* (*gram*) noun. – *berimbuhan* affixed word. – *berlebihan* verbiage. – *bermula* preface. – *bersambungan* (*gram*) derivative. – *bersusun* (*gram*) derivative. – *bertimbal* (*gram*) ambivalent word (usually with two opposite meanings). – *bilangan* (*gram*) numeral. – *bilangan pangkat* (*gram*) ordinal number. – *bilangan pengganda* (*gram*) multiplier. – *bilangan pokok* (*gram*) basic numeral. –.– *bisu* just words (and no action). – *bulat* consensus. – *dasar* (*gram*) root word. – *depan* (*gram*) preposition. – *dua* ultimatum. *memberi* – *dua* to present an ultimatum. – *éjékan* term of abuse; abuse. – *ékasuku* monosyllabic word. – *ganti* (*gram*) pronoun. – *ganti diri* (*gram*) personal pronoun. – *ganti milik* (*gram*) possessive pronoun. – *ganti orang* (*gram*) personal pronoun. – *ganti penghubung* (*gram*) relative pronoun. – *ganti penunjuk* (*gram*) demonstrative pronoun. – *ganti taktentu* (*gram*) indefinite pronoun. – *ganti tanya* (*gram*) interrogative pronoun. – *hati* a) conscience. b) effusion. c) (inner) voice. – *imbuh* (*gram*) adverb. – *ingkar* breach of faith. –.– *istilah* terminology, technical terms. – *jadian* (*gram*) derivative. – *keadaan* (*gram*) adjective. – *kepala* entry, headword; → ÉNTRI. – *kerja* (*gram*) verb. – *kerja bantu* (*gram*) auxiliary verb. – *kerja réfléksif* (*gram*) reflexive verb. – *kerja resiprokal* (*gram*) reciprocal verb. – *kerja taktransitif* (*gram*) intransitive verb. – *kerja transitif* (*gram*) transitive verb. – *keterangan* (*gram*) adverb. – *kiti* gossip. – *kode* codeword. – *kunci* keyword. – *lawan* (*gram*) antonym. – *léksikal* (*gram*) lexical word. – *lelamisan* flattery. – *lontaran* expletive. – *majemuk* (*gram*) compound (word). –.– *manis* sweet talk. – *masukan* entry, headword. – *mendatang* (*gram*) derivative. – *menyusul* postscript. – *mufakat* agreement. – *muradif* (*gram*) synonym. – *mufakat* agreement. – *mutiara* words of wisdom. – *nama hissi* (*gram*) concrete noun. – *olokan* derision, mockery. – *pancung* acronym; → AKRONIM. – *panggilan* form of address. – *pasti* decisive answer. – *pembimbing* preface. – *pembuka* opening speech. – *pembukaan* preface, introduction, forward. – *pendahuluan* a) preface, introduction. b) prologue. – *pengantar* preface, introduction, forward. **mengata-pengantari** to provide s.t. with an introduction. **mengata-pengantarkan** to say s.t. in introduction, preface. – *pengecil* (*gram*) diminutive. – *pengganti* (*gram*) pronoun. – *pengganti milik* (*gram*) possessive pronoun. – *pengganti nama benda* (*gram*) pronoun. – *pengganti orang* (*gram*) personal pronoun. – *pengganti penghubung* (*gram*) relative pronoun. – *pengganti penunjuk* (*gram*) demonstrative pronoun. – *pengganti taktentu* (*gram*) indefinite pronoun. – *pengganti tanya* (*gram*) interrogative pronoun. – *penghantar* preface. – *penghubung* (*gram*) conjunction. – *pengumpul* (*gram*) collective number. – *peniru bunyi* (*gram*) onomatopoetic word. – *penunjuk* (*gram*) deictic. – *penutup* epilogue, concluding words. – *penyambung* (*gram*) conjunction. – *penyerta* (*gram*) article. – *penyusul* epilogue. – *perangkai* (*gram*) conjunction. – *perkenalan* introduction. – *perpisahan* parting words. – *persembahan* dedication. – *pinjaman* (*gram*) loanword. – *pokok* (*ling*) base form. –.– *pujian* words of praise. – *pungut* (*gram*) loanword. – *putus* a) decision (to break a betrothal, promise, contract, etc.). b) (*leg*) decision, verdict, judgment. – *sambung* (*gram*) connective. **mengata-sambungi** ... connect by the word ... – *sambutan* a) foreword (by a third person). b) welcoming speech. – *sandang* (*gram*) article. – *sandi* codeword, password. – *sapaan* term of address. – *searti* (*ling*) synonym. – *seasal* (*ling*) cognate (word). – *sebunyi* (*ling*) homophone. – *sepaham/ sepakat* agreement. – *serapan* (*ling*) borrowed word. – *seru(an)* (*gram*) interjection. – *sifat* (*gram*) adjective. – *tambahan* (*gram*) adverb. – *tanya* (*ling*) interrogative. – *tugas* (*ling*) function word. – *turunan* (*ling*) derivative. – *ulang* (*ling*) reduplication. –

utama entry, headword. – *wantahan* (*ling*) unassimilated borrowing. – *wicara* speech.

sekata 1 of the same tenor/tone as. 2 (= *seia* ~) agreed, unanimous. 3 alike, similar, of the same kind.

berkata 1 to say, tell. *Saya ~ sendiri dalam hati.* I said to myself. *tak ~ sepatahpun* didn't say a word. *~ benar* to tell the truth. *~ bohong* to tell a lie. 2 to talk. *~ yang bukan-bukan* to talk nonsense. 3 to speak. *~ dua* to speak deceitfully.

berkata-kata to tell, speak, talk, converse (of several persons).

mengata (rare except in the passive form *dikata*) to say. *jangan dikata lagi* not to mention, say nothing about, let alone. *Apa hendak dikata?* What more is there to say? *boléh dikata* it can be said (that).

mengata(-ngata)i 1 to talk/gossip about. 2 to scold, call s.o. names. 3 to reproach, cast aspersions on.

kata-mengatai to insult e.o.

mengatakan [and **ngatain** (*J coq*)] 1 to say s.t. 2 to tell, inform, assert, mention.

memperkatakan 1 to talk about, discuss. 2 to introduce/bring up (a subject).

terkata(kan) *tidak ~* indescribable.

terkata-katai (*M*) to be delirious.

perkataan 1 what has been said, remarks. *~ orang itu sangat melukai hatiku.* What that person said hurt my feelings very much. 2 word(s). *~ "syair" berasal daripada bahasa Arab.* The word "syair" comes from Arabic. *dengan ~ lain* in other words. 3 (group of) words. *Banyak ~ asing yang dilazimkan di bahasa Indonésia.* Many foreign words have become normal in Indonesian. *dengan ~ lain* in other words. 4 (*cla*) story, tale, history. *Kami péndékkan ~nya.* We cut his story short.

katabélece (*D*) → **KATTABÉLLETJE**.

katabolisme (*D/E*) catabolism.

katafalk (*D/E*) catafalque.

katagori (*D*) category.

  meng(k)atagorikan to categorize.

katah (*ob*) **terkatah-katah** hurled away, thrown down.

katai small, stunted, short (of people/fowl, etc.), dwarf. *ayam –* bantam chicken. *orang –* pygmy, dwarf. *si –* (*derog*) the Japanese. *– kedelai* soybean dwarf. *– kuning* rice yellow dwarf. (a rice disease).

  pengataian dwarfing.

katak I frog; → **KANGKUNG III**, **KODOK I**. *lompat –* leapfrog. *(seperti) – di bawah tempurung* narrow-minded. *– hendak jadi lembu* pride before a fall. *– ditimpa kemarau* make a great noise. *– bebap* k.o. toad. *– bertanduk* Malaysian leaf frog, horned frog, *Megophrys nasuta*. *– betung/hijau* Asian painted frog, *Kaloula pulchra*. *– Cina* tree frog, *Racophorus spp*. *– kuak* → **KATAK** *betung*. *– lembu* → **KATAK** *bertanduk*. *– lempung* k.o. frog, *Oxyglossus spp*. *– pisang* red-eared greenback frog, *Rana erythraea*, *Racophorus leucomystax*. *– pohon* tree frog, *Racophorus appendiculata*. *– puru* Asian black-spined toad, *Bufo melanostictus*.

  pengatak frogman.

katak II short; *opp* **PANJANG**. *meriam –* mortar (the gun).

katak III the lines on one's neck, wattles.

  berkatak-katak with those lines.

katakombe (*D*) catacomb(s).

katalis (*E*) catalyst.

katalisator (*D*) catalyst.

katalisis (*D/E*) catalysis.

katalitik (*E*) catalytic.

katalog(és) → **KATALOGUS**.

katalogus (*D*) catalog. *– induk* union catalog.

katalok (*E*) → **KATALOGUS**.

katam → **KHATAM**.

katamaran (*E*) catamaran.

katan → **KHATAN, KHITAN**.

katang-katang I a quadrangular basket, plaited from *pandan*, etc. and provided with a carrying rope.

katang-katang II a creeper, *Cynometra spp*., with itchy sap.

katapél (*D*) 1 slingshot. 2 (aircraft carrier) catapult.

  mengatapél to shoot at with a slingshot.

  pengatapélan shooting at with a slingshot.

katar k.o. sailboat.

katarak (*D/E*) cataract.

katarsis (*D/E*) catharsis.

katat (*A ob*) slander.

katawi verbatim, word-by-word.

katé (*J*) → **KATAI**.

katédral (*E*) cathedral.

kategis → **KATÉKIS**.

kategori (*D/E*) category; → **KATAGORI**.

  mengkategorikan to categorize.

  pengkategorian categorization.

kategoris (*D*) categorical.

katék I (*J*) armpit.

  mengatéki to tickle.

katék II → **KATAI**.

katekése (*E*) catechesis.

kateketik (*Jv?*) → **KATEKISMUS**.

katekis (*E*) catechist.

katekisasi (*D*) catechization.

katekismus (*D*) catechism.

katekumin (*D*) catechumen, new convert.

katél (*J/Jv*) a large, hairy, black, virulent spider that lives in a hole in the ground, Javan yellow knee, *Selenocosmia javanensis*.

katéla (*Port*) sweet potato, cassava.

katelum (*ob*) bastion, corner tower.

katépé [spelling out of KTP: Kartu Tanda Penduduk] resident's card. *razia –* (police) identity check.

  berkatépé 1 to be in possession of a resident's card. 2 to reside at/in, live at/in.

katering (*E*) /ké-/ 1 catering. 2 main power supply.

katés (*Jv*) papaya; → **BETIK I, PAPAYA**.

katéter (*D/E*) catheter.

katétong k.o. baked vanilla cake.

katholik → **KATOLIK**. *– Roma* Roman Catholic.

kati catty, unit of weight equivalent to 16 *tahil* (625 gr. or about 1 ⅓ lb).

  mengati to weigh s.t. in catties. *dikati sama berat, diuji sama mérah* of similar rank/position in society. etc.).

  katian 1 (Chinese) scale which weighs in catties. 2 by the catty.

katib I → **KHATIB**.

katib II (*A*) writer(s), scribe(s). *– aam* general secretary, rapporteur.

katibin *pl* of katib II.

katifah (*kain –*) a thick fabric used for blankets, rugs, carpets.

katik I → **KATAI**.

katik II *rumput – belalang* k.o. grass, rice grass, *Paspalum orbiculare*.

katil (*Tam*) 1 bier. 2 bed; sleep sofa.

katimaha (*Jv*) k.o. tree, *Kleinhovia hospita*, with white wood used for making kris sheaths.

katimbang (*Jv*) 1 compared to/with, (better/more useful, etc.) than. *jauh lebih unggul – meréka* fare superior to theirs. 2 rather than. *– menunggu empat jam, lebih baik ke Yogya dengan naik bis.* Rather than waiting four hours, it would be better to go to Yogya by bus; → **KETIMBANG**.

katimumul (*Jv*) corn (on foot).

katimun → **KETIMUN**.

katineung (*S*) affection, attachment.

katir outrigger.

  berkatir with outriggers.

katirah (*Jv*) a plant species with red leaves.

katlum (*Tam*) rampart, bastion; → **KATELUM**.

katode (*D/E*) cathode.

katok (*J/Jv*) underpants, (under)shorts, panties. *– kolor* shorts with drawstring.

katoka (in West Sumba) a bamboo mousetrap.

Katolik (*D/E*) Catholic. *umat –* the Catholics. *– Roma* Roman Catholic.

  mengkatolikkan to make Catholic.

  kekatolikan Catholicism.

katolika (*Port ob*) → **KATOLIK**.

katong (*IBT*) we; → **KITA**.

katot (*J*) a beating, thrashing.

  ngatot to beat up, thrash.

katréji and **katrilli** (*D*) quadrille.

katro(k) (*Pr*) **1** behind the times, conservative. **2** unmannerly, ill-bred, a hick; → KAMPUNGAN.

katrol (*D*) pulley, block. – *buka* snatch block. – *mobil* mobile crane. – *puncak* crown block.

mengkatrol 1 to lift s.t. with a pulley. **2** to lift, boost [*esp* to give a boost to a student, etc. so that he passes or is selected, etc. when he shouldn't have (been)]. ~ *diri* to work o.s. up (through boot-licking, etc.). **3** to tow (a car).

katrolan s.o. or s.t. boosted/hauled up. *orang* ~ a person who through influence or connections is appointed to a position that he is unqualified for; hand-picked.

terkatrol boosted.

pengatrol booster.

pengatrolan 1 lifting, boosting. **2** towing (a car).

kattabélletje (*D*) /katebélece/ short note to s.o. asking a favor for the bearer.

katu → KATUK I.

katub → KATUP.

katuk I (*daun* –) a shrub eaten as a vegetable, sweet leaf bush, *Sauropus androgynus*; → KETUK.

katuk II → KETUK I.

katul (– *dedek*) a by-product of milling rice, the outer bran layers of the kernel and part of the germ.

katulistiwa → KHATULISTIWA.

katumbar → KETUMBAR.

katun (*D*) cotton (fabric). – *kapas* cotton.

katung I the large leathery sea turtle, *Dermochelys coriacea. tersingit-singit bagai* – *di bawah reba* to be submissive.

katung II terkatung-katung 1 to float (on water), bob up and down (on the water). **2** to float (in the air), hover. **3** uncertain (of one's fate, etc.), pending (of a case); → TERKUMPAL *kampil/kumpal*.

katup 1 hermetically closed/sealed. **2** valve (of pump, etc.), cock, flap. – *aman* check valve. – *angin* air trap. – *atur* regulating valve. – *badai* (*petro*) storm choke. – *buang* exhaust valve. – *buluh* reed valve. – *cerat* choke, throttle. – *cuk* choke. – *dasar* bottom flap. – *gerbang* gate valve. – *hambat balik* check valve. – *(h)isap* inlet valve. – *jantung* heart/cardiac valve. – *jarum* needle valve. – *keamanan/pengaman/pengamanan* safety/relief valve. – *kontra* check valve. – *kuras* blow off. – *masuk* inlet/intake valve. – *payung* step valve. – *pelepas* release valve for s.t. – *pelepasan* release valve. – *pelonggar* crack valve. – *pemasuk* inlet valve. – *pengaman* safety valve. – *pengatur* control valve. – *pengendalian keseimbangan rém* de-accelerating sensing proportioning valve, DSPV. – *sahap* pot-lid valve. – *selérét* zipper. – *setang putar* kelly cock. – *tenggorok* epiglottis. – *udara* choke.

mengatup to close tight; tightly closed.

mengatupkan and **memperkatupkan 1** to shut/close tightly (of mouth/eyes/door). ~ *geraham* to clench one's teeth. **2** to grasp hold of.

terkatup closed, locked tightly. ~ *mulut* to be afraid to open one's mouth.

pengatupan fusing. *kegagalan* ~ *tulang belakang* failure of the spine to fuse.

katut I (*Pr*) afraid; → TAKUT.

katut II (*Jv*) to get carried along, get included. –*a banyu mili, nanging aja nganti keli* (*Jv*) swim with the stream but don't get carried away.

katwal (*Pers ob*) constable.

kau I you (usually used by elders and superiors to juniors and inferiors; also used to intimates, such as child to father); → ENGKAU.

kau II *burung* – *tuah* k.o. bird.

kau III (*C J*) nine. – *ban* ninety thousand. – *cap* ninety. – *céng* nine thousand. – *pék* nine hundred. – *tiau* nine million. – *tiau pua* nine and a half million.

kaucuk (*D*) caoutchouc.

kaukab (*A ob*) planet.

Kaukasus (*D/E*) Caucasus. *Gunung* – the Caucasus. *orang* – Caucasian.

kaukus (*E*) caucus.

kaul I (*A*) **1** opinion, view. – *yang sah* a correct opinion. **2** vow (to God). – *tak sampai* the vow was unheeded. *membayar/me-lepas* – to fulfill a vow, do what one vowed to do. **3** (*ob*) solemn promise.

berkaul to (take a) vow, vow (to).

mengaulkan to make a vow for.

kaul II (= *kawul*) sugar-palm fibers used for tinder. – *kayu* wood shavings used as tinder.

kaula (*Jv ob*) → KAWULA.

kaulanegara (*Skr*) subject (of a country).

kaum (*A*) **1**a) race. b) tribe, clan, ethnic group. *kepala* – (in W. Sumatra) clan leader. **2** (– *keluarga/kerabat*) family, (close) relatives. **3** group, class (of political associates/likeminded persons, etc.; for examples see below). **4** Islamic official who advises on religious matters and looks after the mosque; → LEBAI. **5** term used by Indonesian Chinese to refer to the *pribumi*; → WANNA. – *Adam* men, human beings. – *agama* religious persons. – *atasan* the higher-ups, the upper class, the group of senior officials/executives, etc. – *bakulan* retailers. – *bangsawan* the nobility. – *bawahan* the lower classes/strata, etc. – *bendoro* the nobility. – *Boer* the Boers; → BOER. – *buruh* the working class(es), workers. – *cerdik cendekia/pandai* the intellectuals. – *dahriah* atheists. – *galak* the hawks, hard-liners. – *gelandangan* a) the unemployed. b) the homeless. c) hooligans. – *guru* the teaching profession. – *hartawan* the wealthy/haves. – *haus-duit* the money-grubbers. – *Hawa (yang lemah)* women, the weaker sex. – *ibu* a) mothers, housewives. b) women, the fair sex. – *ilmuwan* scientists. – *intélék(tuil)* intellectuals. – *kanan* right-wingers, rightists. – *kapitalis* capitalists. – *kecil* the masses, the little people. – *keluarga* the family, relatives. – *kemajuan* the progressives. – *kepalabatu* the diehards. – *kerabat* relatives. – *kiri* left-wingers, leftists. – *ko* the collaborators (with the Dutch in 1945-1949). – *kolot* the conservatives. – *kromo* the proletariat. – *laki-laki/lelaki* men, males. – *lanjut usia* senior citizens. – *lunak* the doves, soft-liners, moderates. – *majikan* the employers. – *mapan* the well-to-do/wealthy/haves. – *marhaén* the proletariat. – *melarat* the underprivileged. – *menengah* the middle class(es). – *mérah* the Reds, Communists. – *miskin* the poor/have-nots. – *modal* capitalists. – *muda* a) youth, the younger generation. b) the modernist Muslim movement. – *murba* the proletariat, the masses. – *Muslimin* the Muslims. – *Nasrani* the Christians. – *ningrat* a) the nobility, aristocracy. b) the well-to-do. – *non* the non-collaborators with the Dutch in 1945-49. – *Packard* the rich. – *pelancong* tourists. – *pelawan* members of the resistance. – *pembangkang* dissident, the opposition. – *pemilih* the electorate. – *pemuda* youth, the younger generation. – *penarung* the opposition. – *pendéta* the clergy. – *penentang* the opposition. – *penganggur* the unemployed. – *pengkhianat* the quislings, traitors. – *pengungsi/penyingkir* the refugees, evacuees. – *pénsiunan* the retired. – *pergerakan* politically active nationalists during the Dutch colonial period. – *pertengahan* the middle class(es). – *pindahan* (*ob*) emigrants. – *plin-plan* fence-sitters, those who play both sides. – *plintat-plintut* those who lack firm loyalties. – *pria* men, males. – *priyayi* the upper middle class. – *pro-raja* royalists. – *punya* the haves. – *putar negeri* revolutionists. – *rendah(an)* the lower class(es). – *samurai* the Japanese military. – *sedang* the moderates. – *Sekutu* the Allied Powers. – *tak punya* the have-nots. – *tangan panjang* thieves. – *tani* peasants. – *tengah* middle-of-the-roaders. – *terkemuka* prominent people, VIPs. – *terpelajar* the intellectuals. – *tinggi* the higher-ups. – *tua* a) old folks. b) the traditionalist Muslim movement. – *véstin/vésted interést* those with vested interests.

sekaum allied, related.

berkaum (*dengan*) related (to). *sembahyang* ~ to say a prayer led by an *imam*.

berkaum-kaum in groups/tribes/clans.

kauman special area in the vicinity of a mosque inhabited by devout Muslims. *santri* ~ Javanese Muslims living in such an area.

perkauman 1 family (relations). **2** group, tribal, clan, racial. **3** ethnicity.

kaung (*S*) → KAWUNG I.

kaunter intélijén (*E*) counterintelligence.

kaup (*ob*) → KAUT.

kaupi → KAW PUIK.

kaur [*kepala urusan*] Head of ... Affairs.

kaus I (*Pers D?*) **1** shirt calico of loose weave. *baju* – undershirt, singlet. – *cangklék* sleeveless undershirt. – *dalam* men's sleeveless undershirt. – *kaki* sock, stocking. – *kuku* nail covering. – *kutung/péndék* short-sleeved undershirt. – *lampu* lamp wick. – *oblong* body shirt. – *pijar* incandescent mantle. – *singlét* singlet, A-shirt. – *tangan* glove. – *tubuh* body suit. **2** (*ob*) shoe; boot. *di bawah* – beneath the sovereign's foot.
  berkaus to wear a shirt. ~ *oblong* to wear a body shirt.

kaus II (*A ob*) **1** (archer's) bow. **2** Archer, Sagittarius (*zod*).

kausa (*D*) cause.

kausal (*D/E*) causal.

kausalitas and **kausalitét** (*D*) causality.

kaustik (*E*) caustic.

kaut mengkaut and **mengaut** to gather (coins/weeds, etc.) by hand-pulling them toward you, scoop s.t. up. ~ *keuntungan* to make a profit.

Kautsar and **Kauthar** (*A*) *al-* "Great Comfort"; name of the 108th chapter of the Koran.

kav 1 (in acronyms) → KAVALERI. **2** (*abbr*) → KAPLING, KAVELING.

kavaleri (*D*) **1** cavalry. **2** tank corps, armored vehicles. – *berat* heavy cavalry (such as tanks).

kaveling (*D*) → KAPLING.

kaver (*E*) → KOVER. **mengkaver** → MENGKOVER, MELIPUT.

kaviar (*D*) caviar.

kawah 1 cauldron; large, deep open pot. **2** (volcanic) crater. **3** the Buddhist hell. – *Candradimuka/Condrodimuko* a) cauldron shaped like a cow into which, according to Buddhist teachings, a man was thrown to be "boiled" in scalding water for supernatural powers and strength. b) Spartan training. c) Armed Forces Academy on Mount Tidar south of Magelang; → GUNUNG *tidar*. – *granat* shell crater. – *samping* parasitic crater. – *vulkanik* volcanic crater.

kawak (*Jv*) (very) old, longtime, veteran.

kawakan experienced, established, dyed-in-the-wool, out-and-out, of long standing. *penjahat* ~ a hardened criminal.

kawa-kawa (*Tam?*) k.o. spider.

kawal (*Tam*) **1** sentry, watchman. **2** guard, watch. – *anjur* advance guard. – *batas* border guard. – *belakang* rear guard. – *depan* advance guard. – *lambung* flank guard. **3** (*mostly Mal*) control.
  berkawal 1 to keep watch, watching, standing guard. *Empat orang prajurit* ~ *di depan istana.* Four soldiers were standing guard in front of the palace. **2** guarded, watched. *Pada ketika itu beliau tidak* ~. At that time he was not being guarded.
  mengawal(i) 1 to guard, watch (over); to escort, convoy. *Beliau dikawal oléh dua orang yang berpakaian préman.* He was escorted by two men in civilian clothes. ~ *diri (daripada)* to be on one's guard against. **2** (*ob*) to protect, look after.
  terkawal *tidak* ~ uncontrollable.
  kawalan guard. ~ *batas* a) border guard. b) guarding the border. ~ *sambang* a) night watchman. b) patrol. *hukuman* ~ imprisonment.
  pengawal 1 (body)guard, sentry, sentinel, watchman. ~ *gawang* (in soccer, etc.) goalkeeper, goalie; → PENJAGA *gawang*, KIPER I. ~ *kehormatan* honor guard. ~ *keamanan* security guard. ~ *pribadi* bodyguard. **2** chaperon(e), escort. **3** safeguard.
  pengawalan 1 guard, guarding, security. **2** escort, escorting. ~ *iring-iringan* convoy escort. ~ *udara* air escort. **3** (*ob*) control, surveillance.

kawalat → KUALAT.

kawan 1 herd, flock, swarm, school, band, group, gang, member of one's own band. **2** comrade, friend, companion, colleague, fellow-, -mate, co-, joint; → TEMAN. – *dan lawan* friend and foe. *dengan -.-nya* a) with (one's) friends/associates, etc.; → CS-NYA. b) with affiliates. **3** s.t. added to complete a whole, match, counterpart (of articles/things). – *minuman* what one eats or offers to go along with drinks. – *nasi* side dish accompanying a *rijstafel.* – *sirih* s.t. added to betel, such as *pinang, gambir, kapur,* etc. – *berbuat* accomplice, accessory. – *berdansa* dancing partner. – *berlomba* competitor, rival. – *berpiutang* joint

creditor. – *berutang* codebtor, joint debtor. – *gadis* girlfriend. – *hidup* partner for life, spouse. – *laki-laki* boyfriend. – *main* gambling buddy. – *roti* spread. – *sealmamatér* colleague from the same university. – *seanggota* fellow member. – *sebaya* peer. – *sederajat* equal partner. – *segabungan* associate. – *sehidup semati* one's partner in life, spouse. – *seimbang* equal partner. – *seiring* s.o. – *sekamar* roommate. – *sekantor* office-mate. – *sekelas* classmate. – *sekerja* colleague, s.o. who works at the same office. – *selapik seketiduran* a) spouse. b) bosom friend. – *semarga* clan-mate. – *semufakat* likeminded person. – *senasib* companion in distress. – *sepaham* likeminded person. – *separtai* political associate. – *sepenerbangan* traveling companion (on aircraft). – *seperjalanan* traveling companion (in general). – *seperjuangan* comrade-in-arms. – *sepermainan* playmate. – *persekutuan* ally. – *seperut* clan-mate. – *seprofési* professional colleague. – *seregu* teammate. – *sesekolah* schoolmate. – *setawanan* fellow prisoner. – *usaha* counterpart (in business venture).
  sekawan 1 colleague. *dua* ~ the pair/two of them. **2** (*math*) conjugate. **persekawanan** partnership.
  berkawan 1 (= **berkawan-kawan**) in groups/herds, etc. *Gajah itu biasa hidup* ~. Elephants usually live in herds. **2a**) to become friends, be/have allies. b) to mix/associate/mingle/fraternize with. *Jangan* ~ *dengan penjudi.* Don't associate with gamblers. **3** to be in the company of. **4** (*M*) (said of women) to have a husband, be married.
  mengawan (*M*) to mate, copulate, pair (of animals); *cp* KAWIN.
  mengawani to accompany, associate with, escort.
  memperkawan 1 to befriend, make friends with, ask help from. **2** (*M*) to give in marriage, marry off (one's daughter).
  kawanan 1 herd, flock, swarm, school. **2** band, group, gang.
  pengawanan accompanying.

kawang I *minyak* – vegetable oil from seeds of *Isoptera spp.* and *Shorea spp.*; → SENGKAWANG, TENGKAWANG.

kawang II (in Ambon) village police.

kawanisme cronyism.

Kawanua compatriot, fellow Manadonese. *gadis* – a Manadonese girl. *masyarakat* – the Minahasan community.

kawas berkawas (*dengan*) to border (on).
  mengawasi to border on.
  kawasan district, area, region, territory, sphere, zone. ~ *berikat* bonded zone. ~ *hawa panas* the tropics. ~ *hutan* forest. ~ *industri* industrial estate. ~ *kumuh* slum, ghetto. *Masyarakat* ~ *Pasifik* Pacific Basin Community. ~ *papa* slum. ~ *pelestarian alam* conservation area. ~ *penyangga* buffer zone. ~ *perdagangan bébas* free-trade zone. ~ *tadah hujan* catchment area/basin. **sekawasan** local, regional, in/of the same area.

kawat 1 wire, cable. *makan* – very poor. *pagar* – wire fence. *tanpa* – wireless. – *anyam* wire mesh. – *arang* carbon filament. – *baja* steel/wire rod. – *bantu* pilot wire. – (*ber*)*duri* barbed wire. – *has* screen, wire netting. – *jala* wire mesh. – *jeprét* staple (used to clip papers together). – *kasa* a) chicken wire. b) wire netting. – *listrik* electric cable. – *listrik penyambung* extension cord. – *nyamuk* screen, insect-proof gauze. – *pejal* solid wire. – *pemanas* heating coil – *penajam* (*mil*) arming wire. – *pengisi* filler wire. – *pijar* filament. – *polos* bare wire. – *rambut* fine wire. – *rantai* warp. – *sambung(an)* extension cord. – *spring* spiral metallic spring. – *tali* coil. – *télepon* telephone cable. – *tembaga* copper wire. **2** (*kabar* – and *surat* –) cable, telegram; → TÉLE-GRAM. *kantor* – telegraph office. *mengetuk/mengetok/memukul/menokok* – to send a cable.
  kawat-mengawat 1 wiring, cabling. **2** telegraphing.
  mengawat to tighten up (like a wire).
  mengawatkan to send a cable/telegram, wire, cable.
  pengawatan wiring, installing wires.
  perkawatan (*mod*) cable, telegram.

kawatir → KUATIR.

kawedanan (*Jv*) (from *ke*+*wedana*+*an*); → WEDANA.

kawentar (*Jv*) became known/famous/celebrated; (the) best (known), most famous.

kawét (*Jv*) perineum.
  mengawétkan to tie up between the legs (of a sarong).

kawi I (*Skr*) *bahasa* – a) Old Javanese. b) literary Javanese. *jaman/ zaman* – ancient times.

kawi II (*A*) strong, firm (and lasting), enduring. *adat yang* – time-honored customs.

kawi III *batu* – pyrolusite. *besi* – iron that has a supernatural power. *bisa* – magical power (such as a curse, etc.) that hits s.o. because he has violated *adat*, etc.

kawibawan (*Jv*) authority/influence held by a respected person/ group; → WIBAWA.

kawin (*Pers*) 1 to marry; → NIKAH. *isi/mahar/mas* – dowry, groom's settlement on the bride. *pésta* – wedding feast. *syarat* – marriage settlement. 2 to be married. *belum* – unmarried. *sudah* – married. *sudah – atau belum* (in application forms, etc.) marital status. 3 to copulate, have sexual intercourse, sleep together. *Meréka – sebelum nikah*. They slept together before marriage. – *sudah nikah belum* (joke based on two meanings of *kawin*) to have had sexual experiences but not be married. – *alam* natural mating (of cattle). – *andar* to marry without providing any bride price. – *batin* unofficially married. – *berencana* hand mating (of cattle). – *berpamili* inbreeding. – *campuran* mixed marriage. – *cerai* to get married and divorced. – *dengan keris/kopiah* marriage by proxy. – *emas* golden wedding (anniversary). – *gantung* officially married but not announced to the public., i.e., no wedding reception. – *kantor* (*coq*) married in a vital statistics bureau (i.e., no *adat* or religious ceremony). – *kontrak* a) cohabitation between Filipino men who are temporary workers in Eastern Kalimantan and *Daya(k)* women. b) (in the Krakatau Steel complex at Cilegon) k.o. contract between a male foreign expert working for Krakatau Steel and a local woman that they will marry for the length of his stay and then get divorced. – *lari* eloping. – *luar* outbreeding. – *masal* mass wedding. **mengawin-masalkan** to marry off en masse. – *masuk* (*IBT*) matrilocal marriage. – *mawin* various weddings. – *miskin* wedding performed without those concerned paying the usual fees. – *muda* to marry young, marriage at an earlier age than allowed by the marriage laws. – *muth'ah* a temporary marriage. – *paksa* forced marriage, shot-gun wedding. – *pérak* silver wedding (anniversary). – *rangkap* bigamy or polygamy. – *roko* (*IBT*) elopement. – *sedarah/sepamili* inbreeding. – *silang* crossbreeding. **mengawin-silangkan** (*dengan*) to crossbreed, hybridize. – *sir(r)i* a marriage performed before the religious authorities but not registered. – *sirih pinang* (*IBT*) marriage in which the newlyweds live with the bride's family until the bride price is paid off. – *slang* artificial insemination (of cattle). – *sumbang* incest. – *suntik* artificial insemination, induced breeding. **mengkawin-suntik** to artificially inseminate (of cattle). **pengawin-suntikan** artificial insemination (of cattle). – *tabrak* (*sl*) marriage because the girl is pregnant, shotgun wedding. – *tamasya* marriage with no ceremony so the couple can use the money to go on a honeymoon. – *tambalan* (*S*) marriage because the girl is pregnant by a man who is not the father. – *tunggal* monogamy. – *tunggu tunang* married by proxy. – *wali* marriage by proxy.

berkawin to be married.

mengawini 1 to marry s.o. 2 (*J*) to sleep with. 3 (of animals) to mate with.

mengawinkan [and ngawinin (*J coq*)] 1 to marry off. 2 to cross-fertilize, interbreed (plants, animals), mate.

kawinan (*coq*) wedding.

kawin-kawinan to sleep together without being married.

pengawinan cross-fertilization, interbreeding.

perkawinan 1 marriage, wedding. 2 mating, breeding. *di luar* ~ extramarital. *sebelum* ~ premarital. *menginjak jenjang* ~ to reach marriageable age. ~ *antar agama* mixed marriage (between members of different religions). ~ *campuran* mixed marriage (between members of different religions or different ethnic groups). ~ *sekerabat* marriage between close relatives, sib-mating, inbreeding. ~ *silang* crossing, crossbreeding. ~ *sir(r)i* → KAWIN *sir(r)i*. ~ *sumbang* incest.

kawiryan (*Jv*) 1 courage, bravery. 2 military (*mod*).

kawista (*pohon* –) 1 Indian wood apple, *Feronia elephantum*. – *batu* k.o. tree, *Feroniella lucida*. 2 the sacred bel-fruit tree of the Hindus, *Aegle marmelos*; → BILAK(MATA), MAJA I.

kawitan (in Bali) ancestors and origins.

Kaw Puik (*Jambi* C) nine-eight, i.e., the word used in agreeing to a deal in which the (C) broker will receive a 2 percent commission. *orang* – the commission agent.

kawruh (*Jv*) (body of) knowledge. – *hana* metaphysics. – *jiwo* psychology. – *kanuragan* occultism. – *padhuwungan* → KERISO-LOGI. – *panunggal* mysticism.

kawuk (*Jv*) a giant lizard found on the island of Nusakambangan.

kawul (*Jv*) fine fibers (*esp* of sugar palm) used for tinder; → KAUL II.

kawula (*Jv*) 1 (*ob*) servitor. 2a) I, me, my. b) we, us, our. 3 people, subject, citizen. – *Belanda* Dutch subject. 4 group. – *muda* young people. – *gusti* the patron-client pair. – *negara* (*ob*) national (of a country); → WARGA *negara*. **kekawula-negaraan** citizenship. – *swapraja* (*ob*) dependency (the state of one nation being a dependency of another). **kekaula-swaprajaan** being a dependency.

kawung I (*S*) sugar palm, *Arenga saccharifera*, from which palm wine is obtained.

kawung II (*Jv*) (dried sugar)palm leaf (used for making cigarette wrappers); → ROKOK *kawung*.

kawung III classic pattern in *batik* from Solo and Yogya.

kaya I (*Skr*) 1 rich, wealthy, well-to-do. *bahasa yang* – a language with a large vocabulary. *negara yang* – a country rich in produce. *orang* – a) a rich person. b) a high-ranking person. c) (*M*) woman whose husband has a good position in society. – *baru* newly rich, nouveau riche. *orang* – *baru* [OKB] the nouveau riche. *orang* –.– (*cla*) important persons, authorities. *cari* – to seek wealth. 2 almighty, omnipotent, powerful (God). *Tuhan yang* – Almighty God. 3 – *akan/ atas/dari(pada)/dengan/di/ kepada/oléh/tentang* rich in. – *akan anak* with many children. – *akan hutang* deeply in debt. *Allah Taala* – *daripada tiap-tiap sesuatu* God is all powerful. – *dengan protéin* protein-rich. – *hati* noble-minded, generous, liberal. – *hutang* deeply in debt. – *melangit* immensely rich. – *mendadak/muda* get rich quick, rich overnight. – *raya* immensely rich.

sekaya as rich as.

sekaya-kayanya 1 as rich as rich can be. 2 no matter how rich.

mengayakan and memperkaya(kan) 1 to make rich/wealthy. 2 to enrich. 3 to increase, improve.

terkaya 1 richest. 2 enriched. – *besar* wealthy, affluent.

kekayaan 1 wealth, assets, riches. *pajak* ~ property tax. ~ *alam* natural resources. ~ *bersih* net worth. ~ *yang dipisahkan* excluded assets. ~ *kata-kata* vocabulary; → KOSAKATA. 2 power, greatness. ~ *Allah* God's power/miracles.

pemerkaya enrichment, s.t. that enriches.

pemerkayaan enrichment.

peng(k)ayaan enrichment.

perkayaan enrichment.

kaya II (*J/Jv*) as if/though; as, like (comparison); → SEPERTI. – *apa?* how? – *gini* like this, this way. – *gitu* like that, that way. –*nya* as if/though ~ *beliau menikmati perjalanan péndék ini* as if he was enjoying this short trip.

kayai (*M ob*) mengayaikan to make an effort to stand (up).

terkayai *tidak* ~ *berjalan* unable to walk.

kayak I → KAYA II. kayak-kayaknya (it looked) as if/though. *Bapak* ~ *jadi mau sakit*. It looked as if Father was going to get sick.

kayak II (*E*) kayak, Eskimo canoe.

kayal → KHAYAL.

kayali → KHAYALI.

kayambang → KIAMBANG.

kayan I (*ob*) *kayu* – timbers (of different kinds).

Kayan II (in Bali) name indicating firstborn child.

kayang (*med*) lordosis.

kayangan I (Hindu) heaven, empyrean, abode of the gods, Olympus. *déwi dari* – a pretty girl.

kayangan II *ikan* – Asian arowana, Asian bony tongue, dragon fish, *Sclerophages formosus*; → SILUK II.

kayap various k.o. skin diseases. – *air* herpes with watery vesicles between fingers and toes. – *angin* erysipelas. – *api* k.o. small abscess on hands or feet. – *badak* boils. – *barah* carbuncle. – *tinggal* single abscess on hand or feet. – *ular* shingles.

berkayap with a skin disease.

kayau I *mengayau* [and *ngayau* (*coq*)] to behead, decapitate; headhunting; → MENGAWA-KEPALAKAN.
pengayau headhunter.
pengayauan beheading, decapitation, headhunting.
kayau II *berkayau-kayau* flooded.
mengayau to flood heavily, inundate.
kayon (*Jv*) the mountain-like figure placed in the middle of the screen before the beginning of an act in the *wayang* play; → GUNUNGAN. It depicts a small house (man's inner life), two giants (the conscience), animals (evils), and the tree of life; → KALPATARU.
kayu I 1 (*pohon* -, *pokok* -) tree, specific k.o. tree (see below for examples). *batang* - tree truck. *dahan* - tree branch. *daun* - leaf (of tree). *kulit* - bark (of tree). **2a)** wood; wooden. *Pohon ini tak berapa keras -nya.* This tree does not have very hard wood. *kapal* - wooden ship. *kursi* - wooden chair. *seberkas* - bundle of wood. *sepatu* - (Dutch) wooden shoes, clogs. *tukang* - carpenter. *ubi* - cassava; → SINGKONG I. **b)** species of wood (see below for examples). **3** timber, lumber. *pengumpulan* - log pod. - *sekeréta-api penuh* a trainload of timber. *tempat penjualan* - lumberyard. **4** stick, pole, beam. **5** instruments made of wood (see below for examples). *di mana - béngkok, di sanalah musang meniti* opportunity makes the thief. *tak - jenjng dikeping* necessity knows no law. *besar - besar dahannya* they who have plenty of butter can lay it on thick. FOR OTHER TREE NAMES BEGINNING WITH KAYU SEE THE SPECIFIC NAME. - *Afrika* k.o. tree introduced into Indonesia; provides general-purpose timber, *Maesopsis eminii.* - *alang* → KAYU *palang.* - *anduh* support, prop. - *ambon* k.o. tree, rain tree, *Enterolobium saman.* - *angin* k.o. tree, *Usnea dasypoga.* - *api* firewood. - *apu-apu* k.o. tree, water lettuce, *Pistia stratiotes.* - *apung* drift wood. - *ara* fig tree, *Ficus consociata.* - *arang* ebony, *Diospyros spp.* - *asam* tamarind, *Tamarindus indica.* - *babi* k.o. tree, *Crypteronia paniculata.* - *bakar* firewood. - *bangunan* lumber, timber. - *bapa* → MERANTI *mérah.* - *basung* a light k.o. wood (from the roots of certain trees) similar to cork. - *berat* sinker. - *besi* ironwood, *Eusideroxylon celebicum.* - *beuk* /bek/ beech wood. - *bulan* k.o. tree; → BANITAN. - *bulat/bundar* log. - *cacahan* wood chips. - *cagak* a) wooden legs of (gun, etc.) support. b) forked stick. - *cakil* toggle pin. - *celup* a wood which yields a k.o. dye. - *cendana* sandalwood, *Santalum album.* - *cina* k.o. tree, oleander-leafed podocarp, *Podocarpus neriifolius.* - *daun* hardwood. - *déwasa* mature wood. - *ében* ebony, *Cratoxylon celebicum.* - *gabus* cork-like spongy wood from the breathing roots of a tree, *Sonneratia acida.* - *gadis* → MEDANG *lesa.* - *gaharu* aloe wood, eaglewood, *Aquilaria malaccensis.* - *ganjal* chock. - *gelondongan* logs. - *gelam* k.o. *kayu putih.* - *geluga* annatto. - *gergajian* sawn timber/lumber. - *gubal* sapwood. - *gubalan* squared timber. - *hanyutan* driftwood. - *hitam* ebony, *Diospyras celebica.* - *hutan* firewood (from forest trees). - *indah* fancy plywood. - *jabon* (*Jv*) k.o. tree, kadamba tree, *Anthocephalus indicus.* - *jarum* conifers. - *jati* teak(wood), *Tectona grandis.* - *jati grajén* (*Jv*) sawn teak logs. - *jawa/jinjing* k.o. soft wood. - *kapur* various k.o. tree, *Dryobalanops spp.* - *karét* hevea pulp. - *kasar* unfinished wood. - *kemas* wale. - *kemuning* → KEMUNING II. - *kendéka* k.o. tree, black mangrove, *Avicennia officinalis.* - *keras* hardwood. - *kesturi* k.o. juniper, *Juniperus chinensis.* - *kuda* k.o. tree, wodier tree, *Lannea grandis.* - *kuda-kuda* (in Kalimantan) logs transported by human beings being used as pack horses. - *kuku* k.o. industrial tree, kuku, *Pericopsis mooniana.* - *kulit* barked wood. - *kuning* fustic. - *laka* henna, *Lausonia inermis/Emblica officinalis/Dalbergia parviflora.* - *lampung* touchwood. - *landasan* chopping block. - *lapis* veneer, plywood. - *lapis biasa* raw plywood. - *lara* (in the Celebes) k.o. ironwood, *Metrosideros petiolata Kds.* - *lasi* → LASI II. - *lat* lath. - *liat* k.o. shrub, *Litsea amra.* - *limo* a West Java wood species which has magical powers over harmful animals, such as tigers, snakes, and scorpions. - *lunak* soft wood. - *mangir* → MANGIR. - *manis/cina* cinnamon, *Cinnamomum zeylanicum, Glycyrrhiza glabra.* - *mérah* poinsettia, *Euphorbia pulcherrima.* - *meranti* various k.o. trees, *Shorea spp.* - *merbau* (in Irian Jaya) k.o. ironwood, *Instia bijuga.* - *nangka* wood of the

jackwood tree. - *olahan* plywood. - *pacat* k.o. tree, *Harpullia arborea.* - *palang* a) wooden bolt (for door). b) wooden cross. - *panél* wainscoting. - *papi* k.o. tree, *Exocarpus latifolia.* - *pelampung* flotsam, driftwood. - *pélét* k.o. tree whose wood is used for carving, *Kleinhovia hospita.* - *pemadat* dunnage. - *pemukul* bat used in sports. - *penaga* k.o. tree, *Calophyllum inophyllum.* - *pengapung* float (of canoe). - *penumbuk* tamping pole. - *penggaris* ruler. - *penunjuk* pointer. - *penyodok* tamping pole. - *peran* tie-beam. - *pinus* pinewood. - *pokok* stock wood. - *pukul* bat used in sports. - *puter(an)* wood that can be turned on a lathe. - *putih* cajaput, paper bark tree, *Eucalyptus alba, Melaleuca leucadendra.* - *ramin* k.o. wood used to make furniture, *Alchornea villosa.* - *rapat* k.o. tree, *Parameria barbata.* - *réncéh* small pieces of wood left after a tree is felled. - *réng* wood used for laths. - *rengas* rosewood, *Anacardiaceae, spp.* and other species; → RENGAS I. - *rosét* piece of wood used for electric socket or plug. - *salib* the Cross. - *sapi* k.o. tree, *Pometia spp.* - *segar* greenwood. - *semidra* k.o. shrub, *Acronychia pedunculata.* - *sepang* k.o. tree used to make dye, sappanwood, *Caesalpinia sappan.* - *sigi* → KAYU *tusam.* - *silang* a) crossbeam. b) carpenter's gauge. - *spanyol* wood that is sold without official papers. - *sula* stake (for executions). - *surén* wood from the *suren* tree (used to make house frames). - *tanduk* k.o. tree, *Roucheria griffithiana.* - *tas* wood used for frightening tigers. - *téja* → TÉJA *badak.* - *telur* k.o. tree, *Xanthophyllum excelsum.* - *teras* heartwood. - *timor* k.o. tree and tree bark from it, yellow Poinciana, *Peltophorum pterocarpum,* and other species. - *timur* bark from the *Peltophorum pterocarpum* tree used medicinally. - *topang* a) prop, support. b) crutches. - *tripléks* plywood. - *tua* ripe wood. - *tulang* k.o. tree, black she-oak, *Arytera littoralis.* - *tusam,* k.o. pine tree, *Pinus mercusii.* - *udang* k.o. shrub, *Eugenia lineata.* - *ukuran* measuring rod. - *ular* k.o. shrub, *Strychnos ligustrina.* - *ulin* (in Kalimantan) k.o. ironwood, *Eusideroxylon zwageri.*
kayu-kayu 1 (*coq*) figurehead. **2** s.o. open to bribery. **3** (*coq*) gigolo. **4** planking.
berkayu 1 wooden, made of wood. **2** to look for wood (in the forest).
mengayu 1 woody, ligneous. **2** to be(come) hard as wood.
kayu-kayuan 1 timbers (of different kinds). **2** trees.
perkayuan [and **pekayuan** (*infr*)] **1** lumber business, timber industry; logging. *Masyarakat - Indonésia* Indonesian Timber Community. **2** (wooden) framework (of house).
kayu II roll (of white cloth, etc.). *se- kain putih* one roll of white cloth.
kayuh I 1 oar (with one side), scull. **2** (*ob*) pedal (of bicycle). *sekali - dua pulau terlampaui* to kill two birds with one stone.
berkayuh to row (a boat by using oars). *~ sambil ke hilir* to kill two birds with one stone. *segan/malu ~ perahu hanyut* to miss one's chance/an opportunity, let ... slip by.
mengayuh 1 to row. **2** to pedal (a bicycle), go by bicycle.
mengayuhkan 1 to paddle, row. **2** to cycle, pedal.
terkayuh rowed.
terkayuhkan able to be rowed/paddled, able to be pedaled/cycled. *tidak ~ lagi biduk hilir* to be exhausted.
pengayuh 1 oar, scull; paddle; pedal. **2** rower, oarsman. *~ sama di tangan, perahu sama di air* well-matched.
kayuh II → KAYU II.
Kayun I name of a fashionable section of Surabaya. (*ber*)*putar* - (*coq*) to saunter, ride around, take a tour (of).
kayun II (*M ob*) in demand, much sought after.
kazab (*A*) liar.
kazaf (*A*) false accusation.
kazanah (*A*) **1** treasure. **2** treasure chamber, treasury. **3** vault, strongroom. - *kitab* (*Mal*) and - *pustaka* library. **4** lexicon, vocabulary.
KB I (*init*) [Keluarga Berencana] family planning; → KABÉ. *karét* - condom.
ber-KB to practice family planning.
meng-KB-kan to make s.o. family-planning minded, to introduce family planning to.
KB II car license plate for Kalimantan Barat.

KBRI (*init*) [Kedutaan Besar Républik Indonésia] Embassy of the Republic of Indonesia.

KDH → KEPALA *daérah*.

KDKI (*init*) [Kepala Daérah Khusus Ibukota] Head of the Capitol City Special Area (Jakarta).

ke I 1 to, toward, in the direction of. *berjalan – kantor* to walk to the office. 2 to go to. *Ia tidak – pasar.* She isn't going to the market. 3 in expressions of the type: *dari ... – ... dari hari – hari* day in and day out. *dari tahun – tahun* year by year. 4 (= *kepada*) to. *Semua mata tertuju – dia.* All eyes were directed to her. 5 (in Medan = *akan*) will. *Rasa – tampak-tampak juga.* It seems that it will be visible anyway. 6 (in Medan) ... – ... keep on. *timbang – timbang* keep on weighing. *bisik – bisik* gossiping all the time.

ke- II 1 (unproductive prefix forming nouns) person/thing who/ which is ... *ketua* chairman. *kekasih* darling. *kehendak* desire, wish. 2 (prefix with numbers forming ordinals; follows a noun) *yang kedua* the second. *yang ketiga* the third. 3 (prefix with numbers indicating a group consisting of that number; precedes a noun and follows a pronoun) *kedua gadis itu* those two girls, both those girls. *meréka ketiga* (all) three of them. *kesemua(nya)* all of (them). 4 (in some dialects) accidental or involuntary passive (= standard *ter-* and sometimes *di-*) *kepaksa = terpaksa* forced. *ketabrak = ditabrak* hit, collided with.

ké → TAOKÉ, TAUKÉ.

kéa-kéa (*Buton*) yellow-crested cockatoo, sulphur-crested cockatoo, *Cacatua sulphurea.*

kebabal young jackfruit (eaten as a vegetable).

kebacut (*Jv*) (now that it's) too late, gone too far, go past (time or place).

kebah (*ob*) dripping with sweat; (– *demam*) reaching the sweating stage of a fever.

kebaji (*M*) black magic to alienate husband and wife.

mengebaji to hate s.o.

kebal 1 invulnerable, immune. – *terhadap makian serta sumpah serapah* can withstand verbal abuse and insults. – *hukum* immune from the law. 2 armored, armor-clad/plated. *kendaraan/ keréta* – a) an armored car. b) (*mil*) tank. – *bawaan* maternal immunity. 3 thick-skinned, insensitive. 4 -proof. – *bakar* fireproof. – *peluru* bulletproof.

sekebal as immune as.

mengebal to become immune/invulnerable.

mengebalkan 1 to make invulnerable. 2 to immunize.

terkebal the most immune/invulnerable.

kekebalan invulnerability, immunity. *ahli ~ tubuh* immunologist. *~ alam* natural immunity. *~ diplomatik* diplomatic immunity.

pengebal *obat ~* immunizing agent.

pengebalan immunization.

kebal-kebul – (*dengan asap*) puffing out (smoke).

kebam I leaden-colored (of the sky).

kebam II **mengebam** *~ bibir* to close one's lips tight.

kebambam → KEBEMBEM.

kebas I 1 paralyzed, momentarily numbed (of one's foot/elbow); stiff in the legs (from fatigue), numb. 2 (all) pins and needles (of a part of the body). *membuang-buang –* to walk around to get rid of stiffness/pins and needles. *pari –* the electric ray (its sting numbs), k.o. *Torpedinidae.*

mengebaskan to numb, cause numbness.

kebas II **mengebas(kan)** 1 to shake out cloth vigorously, dust, flick s.t. with a piece of cloth to remove dust. 2 to flap (wings), wag (tail).

kebat bundle. *se- bagai sirih* (*M*) agreed. – *pegas* spring clip. – *pinggang* (*M*) (waist)band, belt, girdle.

mengebat to bandage, wrap around, tie s.t. around. *~ erat-erat membuhul mati-mati* (*M*) to make perfect regulations/contracts, etc.

mengebatkan 1 to bandage, etc. for s.o. else. 2 to use s.t. as a bandage/wrapping.

terkebat 1 bandaged, wrapped around. 2 involved (in a case).

kebatan wrapper.

pengebat bandage.

kebat-kebat (*ob*) always in motion/working, etc.; uneasy, restless, with beating heart.

kebat-kebit to jump into action.

kebaya a long-sleeved blouse worn over the *kain* or skirt-wrapping.

kebayan I (*Jv*) 1 village official whose job is to carry out errands for his superior. 2 (in Jambi) village head. 3 village messenger.

kebayan II (*S cla*) *nénék –* (old) woman who is an intermediary between two lovers.

kebek (*J/Jv*) 1 crammed (with furniture, etc.) and jumbled together in a heap. 2 frantically busy, engrossed; → RÉPOT, SIBUK II. 3 unsightly, not pleasant to look at (about clothes, use of cosmetics, etc.).

kebel I coastal tree, *Eurycoma longifolia*, whose leaves are used for medical purposes and as an aphrodisiac.

kebel II → KEBAL.

kebelangsak (*J*) to encounter/have difficulties/hardships.

kebelesek (*J*) 1 to sink into (mud, etc.), get stuck. 2 – *sampai ke huluhati* be head over heels in love.

kebelet (*J*) to have an urgent need to go to the bathroom.

kebembem (*J*) k.o. mango, *Mangifera odorata.*

keben I (*J*) bamboo-plaited basket; → BÉSÉK.

keben II (*Jv*) k.o. tree, sea poison tree, *Barringtonia asiatica Kurz*; → PUTAT.

kebendu (*Jv*) to be condemned, be an outcast.

kebes (*Jv*) wet.

kebés (*J*) somewhat peeled off; → KELUPAS.

kebét (*J*) open (of the pages of a book, etc.).

ngebét to open (the pages of a book, etc.).

kebétan 1 open (pages). 2 crib sheet (for cheating on a test).

kébin (*E ob*) (ship's) cabin; → KABIN.

kebiri 1 castrated, gelded, neutered. *ayam –* capon. 2 emasculated.

mengebiri 1 to castrate, sterilize, neuter. 2 (*J*) to shortchange, give less than is due. *~ uang* to reform currency (by cutting the value). 3 to expurgate.

terkebiri castrated.

pengebiri s.o. or s.t. that castrates.

pengebirian 1 castration, sterilization. 2 emasculation. *~ uang* currency reform.

kebit → KEBAT *kebit.*

keblangsak (*J*) *orang –* orphans, people without regular family life; indigents, bums.

keblasuk (*J*) misled, deceived, hoodwinked (said of s.o. acting in good faith).

keblinger 1 (*Jv*) walked/fallen into a trap, be trapped/caught, swallowed the bait, be taken in/tricked/fooled. 2 (*J*) absentminded, inattentive, dull-witted in one's old age. *kebat keléwat, pinter –* what is done in a hurry is seldom done well. 3 impudent, shameless.

kebluk I (*Jv*) **ngebluk** to whip, beat, knead (dough).

kebluk II (*S*) to be a sleepyhead.

kebo (*J/Jv*) water buffalo; → KERBAU. *kumpul –* a) to live together without benefit of marriage; → DAMPULAN, SAMENLÉVEN; *opp* PISAH *kebo*. b) a combination of two or more types of food on a single platter. *nasi kumpul –* rice with side dishes and vegetables on a single plate. *soto kumpul –* a combination of *soto* and rice. c) a partnership between a foreign and a privately owned Indonesian company. *– nusu gudel* (*Jv*) a) the old learn from the young. b) the children support the parents. – *pulang ke kandangnya* to return to its place of origin (said of the Dutch when they had to return to Holland, supposedly prophesied by *Joyoboyo*).

berkebo-keboan to live together without benefit of marriage; → KUMPUL *kebo*.

kebon → KEBUN.

kébot (*J*) left-handed; → KIDAL.

kebréwonggor *daun –* leaf used as a contraceptive in Irian Jaya.

kebuk cylinder for making vermicelli.

kebul (*J/Jv*) what rises/goes up/lifts, such as smoke/steam/fog; what flies up, such as dust; → KEPUL.

ngebul 1 to give off (a lot of) smoke. 2 to smoke (a cigarette, etc.). 3 done, cooked (of rice). *Nasi belum. –* The rice isn't cooked yet. 4 to talk big, boast, brag.

kebuli *nasi –* rice cooked with meat or fish, oil or butter, a sweetener, etc. and colored by turmeric.

kebun 1 garden, small field for planting vegetables, fruit trees, etc.;

cp PEKARANGAN. *perusahaan –* a) horticulture; → HORTIKUL-TURA. b) plantation. *tukang –* gardener. **2** planting; plantation, estate. *tuan –* plantation employer. **3** (*coq*) gardener. *– bibit* seed farm. *– biji* seed orchard. *– binatang* zoo, zoological gardens. *– botani* botanical garden. *– bunga* flower garden. *– cengkéh* clove tree nursery. *– karét* rubber estate. *– lada* pepper plantation. *– peraga(an)* demonstration farm. *– percobaan* experimental garden. *– Raja /raya/* (using the older spelling) Royal Park; → KEBUN *raya*. *– Raya* the Botanical Garden in Bogor. *– talun* forest garden/plantation. *– tebu* sugarcane plantation. **mengebun-tebukan** to convert into a sugar plantation. *– téh* tea estate. *– tumbuh-tumbuhan* botanical garden.
berkebun 1 to have/own a garden. **2** to lay out a garden. **3** to garden, do gardening.
memperkebuni to cultivate/raise s.t. (as a garden).
pekebun (*ob*) and **pengebun 1** planter. **2** gardener.
perkebunan 1 horticulture. **2** plantation, estate. *PN ~* Government Estates Enterprise. *~ (buah-buahan) apel* apple orchard. *~ budidaya* (rubber, tea, etc.) plantation, estate. *~ karét* rubber plantation. *~ kayu* timber estate. *~ padi* rice plantation, estate. *~ tanaman pangan* food-crop estate.
kebur (*Jv*) **mengebur** to stir/churn (up) (with force).
pengebur churner.
pengeburan stirring/churning up.
keburu 1 (*Jv*) in a hurry, hurried (because). **2** (*J*) just reached, just able to, just on time. *Saya masih –.* I just made it (to catch the train, etc.). *Saya nggak –.* I wasn't on time. I came too late. *tidak – to* have no opportunity, not to be on time (to do s.t.). *tidak – lagi* there is no time left. *– nafsu* to act rashly/thoughtlessly/impetuously. **3** (*S*) overtaken. *– subuh* overtaken by dawn. **4** too early/quickly. *Saya – menikah.* I married too soon/young.
kebut I mengebut [and **ngebut** (*coq*)] **1** to drive recklessly. **2** (for government employees) to come to the office early just to sign the attendance sheet and then to leave the office right away (usually to go to another job). **3** (for businessmen) to make profits by speculation, manipulation, bribery, etc. **4** (for stewardesses) to buy luxury items abroad and then sell them in Indonesia at a higher price. **5** to push ahead quickly, speed up. *Kini Bengkulu sedang ~ membangun.* Bengkulu is speeding up its development nowadays. **perngebutan** racing recklessly.
mengebutkan to race (a car, etc.) recklessly.
kebut-kebutan 1 reckless driving. **2** to have a race (with each other).
pengebut reckless driver, speeder.
pengebutan speeding.
kebut II (*J*) **1** fan for shooing away insects. **2** referee's signal flag (at soccer game). *tukang –* flagman at soccer game who functions as a referee.
mengebut(i) to dust off (a table, etc.) with a feather duster.
kebyar (*Bal*) Balinese solo squat dance.
kecah → KECUH-KECAH.
kecai berkecai-kecai smashed to pieces, torn to shreds.
terkecai broken into pieces, smashed.
kecak I berkecak *~ pinggan* to stand with hands on hips.
kecak II (*onom*) clicking of the tongue.
berkecak(-kecak) to click one's tongue.
mengecakkan to click (one's tongue).
kécak (*Bal*) k.o. Balinese dance, monkey dance.
kecam mengecam(kan) [and **ngecam** (*coq*)] **1** to criticize, find fault with. **2** to review (a performance, etc.).
kecaman criticism.
pengecam critic.
pengecaman criticism, criticizing.
kecambah sprout, shoot.
berkecambah to sprout, germinate.
mengecambahkan to germinate s.t.
pengecambahan germinating.
perkecambahan germination, sprouting.
kecamuk and **berkecamuk** to rage, run wild, break out (of a disease).
kecandak (*J*) caught up to, reached.
kecandan (*M*) joke, jest.

berkecandan to joke, jest.
kecantol → CANTOL.
kecap 1 (*onom*) sound of smacking the lips and tongue. **2** counter for words. *tidak se– pun* not a single word. *– kecip* smacking the lips (while eating).
berkecap 1 to smack one's lips. **2** to taste, take a bite of (food). **3** to enjoy (the pleasures of life).
mengecap 1 to taste (food by putting it on the tongue). **2** to enjoy, take pleasure in.
terkecap-kecap to keep on smacking the lips and tongue.
kecapan (after)taste, tang.
pengecap 1 tester, taster. **2** sense of taste.
kécap (*C*) **1** soy(bean) sauce. *– asin* salty soy sauce. *– manis* (Indonesian) sweet soy sauce. *– No. 1* high-quality soy sauce. **2** empty talk, nonsense.
ngécap (*coq*) to brag, talk high-sounding nonsense.
mengécapkan to babble on and on about s.t.
kecapi I (*Skr*) a boat-shaped, plucked zither of West Java. *– induk* a large version of this instrument. *– rincik* a small version of this instrument.
berkecapi to play this musical instrument.
kecapi II yellow, handball-sized fruit with slightly downy thick skin, white meat in segments, santol, *Sandoricum indicum/koetjape*.
kecap-kecip (*J onom*) **1** smacking sound (of lips). **2** to eat. *Kerjanya – melulu.* All he does is eat.
kécar (*ob*) k.o. *rujak*.
kécé (*sl*) good-looking; impressive, prominent, outstanding.
kecébong (*J*) tadpole (young of the *kodok*).
kecebur (*Jv onom*) the sound produced by s.t. falling into water: flop, plop. *Kalau tidak hati-hati, bisa –.* If you're not careful, you can flop (into the water).
kécék I (*M*) **1** talk, to talk. **2** dodges, pretexts, poor excuses, idle talk, chatter, chitchat. *banyak –* to boast, brag, talk big; be fussy, quarrelsome. *besar –* arrogant, conceited. *beralih –* to change one's tack, try another tack. *seperti – ular* (*M*) to exaggerate. *– berlauk-lauk makan dengan sambal lada* (*M*) to boast about one's nonexistent skill/wealth, etc.
mengécék 1 (= **berkécék-kécék**) **1** to chatter, babble, gossip. **2** to talk s.o. into doing s.t., persuade; to make a fool of s.o., pull s.o.'s leg. *sudah dikécék dikecong pula* (*M*) cheated twice.
mengécékkan to boast, brag, talk big about s.t.
pengécék 1 chatterbox. **2** coaxer, flatterer. *– tinggi* to talk big, brag.
kécék II *main –* a) game of dice. b) game played with coins.
kecelé (*J*) **1** do not find or obtain what one had hoped/looked for, etc., disappointed. **2** to be made a fool of, make to look foolish. **3** discomfited, crestfallen.
mengeceléi to fool, trick. *– bulé* very disappointed.
kecelik (*Jv*) → KECELÉ.
kecéng with one eye closed.
sekécéng *~ mata* in the twinkling of an eye, in no time at all. *~ mata tidak tidur* not to sleep a wink (all night long).
mengecéng(kan) 1 *~ mata* to close one eye (when taking aim, etc.). **2** to ogle.
kecéngan s.o. one has one's eye on, s.o. one likes from afar. *Ayo ngaku siapa ~ kamu di sekolah.* Come on, admit who has his eye on you in school.
kecengar-kecengir (*J*) to smile (from embarrassment).
kecengklék (*J*) sprained (from carrying a baby the wrong way).
kecentét (*J/Jv*) **1** to be emaciated due to impeded growth. **2** crushed, squeezed.
kecepak-kecepok (*Jv onom*) squishing sound.
kecépék *senapan –* a locally made gun, muzzleloader.
kecepirit (*J*) to have slight diarrhea in one's pants, make in one's pants; → MENCERÉT.
kecér (*Jv*) *gamelan* instrument resembling cymbals.
kécés-kécés (*J*) to be dripping with a liquid.
kecéwa disappointed, frustrated, sad at not getting what one hoped for; unsuccessful, failed. *– tak –* not certain whether one is disappointed or not.
kekecéwaan disappointment, frustration.

mengecéwakan [and **ngecéwain** (*J coq*)] **1** (~ *hati*) to disappoint, frustrate, cause to fail. ~ *cita-cita* to shatter one's ideals. **2** disappointing, frustrating. *tidak* ~ satisfactory. **3** detrimental, injurious, harmful; dangerously (weak, etc.). **4** to betray (the confidence of).

terkecéwa disappointed, frustrated.

keci – *beling* red ivy, crispy red flame, *Hemigraphis alternata*.

kéci I (*D/E?*) brig, ketch.

kéci II *kain* – k.o. thin white cotton for making *batik*.

keciak (*onom*) sound made by chicks and other small fowl, cheep, twitter; → CIAK, CIAP.

berkeciak to cheep, twitter.

kecibak (*onom*) trickling sound of water.

berkecibak(an) to splash around.

kecibeling name of various k.o. plants, *Desmodium gangeticum*, *Ruella sp.*, *Strobilanthes crispus*, whose leaves are used for medicinal purposes.

kecicak (*onom*) splashing sound in water.

berkecicak to splash, wade, flounder around.

kecik (*coq*) small; → KECIL.

kecik-mengecik knickknacks, small items.

kecil 1 small, tiny; *cp* KATAI, KERDIL. *anak* – a young child. *Asia* – Asia Minor. *buah* –.– small-sized fruits. *jalan* – a narrow street. *kamar* – a) (= *kamar yang* –) a small room. b) toilet, restroom, bathroom. *mak/pak* – aunt/uncle younger than one's parent. *uang* – small change; → UANG *récéh/pecah*. **2** childhood. *dari* – (*mula*) and *se(men)jak* – from childhood on, since childhood, since I was a little child. **3** little, not yet grown to full size, young. *ketika* –(*ku*) in (my) youth. *si* – a) the little man, the man in the street. b) the little one, baby. *si* – *ini* this little baby. *si* – *bulat* (*col*) the silver guilder (a *col* coin). *tuan* – a) the young master (the oldest son in a family or the youngest brother of the master of the house). b) aspirant administrator (of a plantation, etc.). *pétor* – (*cla*) deputy resident; → RÉSIDÉN. *si* – (*joc*) the penis. **4** lowercase. *huruf* – lowercase letter. **5** lacking capital, small business. *perusahaan* – a small business. **6** soft, not loud. *suara* – a soft/low voice. *dengan suara* – in a low voice, softly. *tertawa/ketawa* – a smile, a noiseless laugh. **7** insignificant, unimportant, trivial. *bagian* – an insignificant part. *bilangan* – an insignificant amount. *orang* – a) a short person. b) the masses. *perkara* – an unimportant/trivial matter. *soal-soal* – trivia. – *hati* a) annoyed, irritated, hurt (one's feelings). c) cowardly, fearful. *hati* –; → HATI II. **berhati kecil 1** limited, narrow-minded, narrow; without ideas or ideals. **2** discouraged, disheartened. – *lada api*, –.– *lada kutu* (*M*), –.– *cabé rawit* (*J*) and *sungguhpun* –, *tetapi lada kutu/cabé rawit* small but feisty. – *teranja-anja*, *besar terbawa-bawa*, *sudah tua terubah tidak* once a use, ever a custom. – *mungil* petite. – *takberhingga* infinitesimally small.

kecil-kecil ~ *cabai rawit* small but feisty.

sekecil as small as.

sekecil-kecilnya as small as possible.

berkecil ~ *hati (akan/kepada)* a) hurt/offended/piqued (at/by); to take to heart, be angry (with); annoyed/irritated (at). b) timid, shy, bashful; discouraged, disheartened; afraid, fearful; *cp* KALAH *hati*.

berkecil-kecil little by little, a little at a time.

berkecil-kecilan 1 match e.o. in smallness (to see which is smaller). **2** to mix around while still young. **3** little by little.

mengecil to become smaller, shrink.

kecil-mengecil a) to belittle/disparage e.o. b) (*benda* ~) all k.o. small things, knickknacks, bric-a-brac. *sampai yang* ~ down to the smallest/minutest details.

mengecilkan [and **ngecilin** (*J coq*)] **1** to reduce, turn down, lower (the volume). ~ *hati* to discourage, frighten. *dengan* ~ *suara* (to ask) in a low voice, softly. **2** to minimize, play down. **3** to belittle, disparage.

mengecil-ngecilkan to underestimate.

memperkecil 1 to make smaller, lessen, decrease, reduce. **2** to minimize, play down.

terkecil 1 smallest. **2** minimum.

kecilan (*J*) smaller.

kecil-kecilan petty; (on a) small scale. *berjudi* ~ small-scale gambling. *pencurian* ~ petty larceny. *serangan* ~ small-scale attack.

kekecilan 1 insignificance. **2** smallness. **3** (*J*) too small. ~ *hati* a) annoyance. b) cowardice.

pengecil *kata* ~ (*gram*) diminutive.

pengecilan 1 reducing, diminishing, belittling. **2** throttling.

perkecilan reduction.

kecimplung → KECIMPUNG.

kecimpring → OPAK I.

kecimpung I (*onom*) sound of (splashing) water.

berkecimpung(an) to make sounds by hitting water with one's hands; (of a group) to splash around in the water.

kecimpung II berkecimpung to keep o.s. occupied/busy by, to deal (in), be engaged/involved (in), be active (in). ~ *dalam urusan sépakbola* to be involved in soccer.

kecimus (*M*) mockery, derision, ridicule.

mengecimus to ridicule s.o. by sticking out one's lips; *cp* CEMOOH.

kecindan (*M*) jest, joke; → KECANDAN, KUCINDAN.

berkecindan to jest, joke.

kecing I (*Jv*) timid, not aggressive.

kecing II (*S*) reluctant (to hear or do s.t.).

kecipak (*onom*) sound of splashing (in water).

berkecipak to make that sound.

kecipang-kecipang (*onom*) sound made by more than one object/person splashing (in water).

kecipir (*Jv*) Manila/Goa/winged/asparagus bean, *Psophocarpus tetragonolobus*; → JAAT.

kecipuk → KECIPAK.

kecipung → KECIMPUNG.

keciput (*Jv*) k.o. cake made with sticky-rice flour, coconut cream, sesame seeds, etc.

kecit (*coq*) small; → KECIL.

keciut (*onom*) whistling sound (of bullet).

keciwa (*ob*) → KECÉWA.

kecoa(k) (*C? J*) cockroach.

kecoh (*Jv*) sound of spitting.

mengecohkan to spit s.t. out.

kecohan spittoon.

kécoh I (*M*) cheat(ing at cards), fraud, swindle, deceit, deception. *kena* – cheated, defrauded.

mengécoh(kan) to deceive, cheat; to make a fool of, make fun of. ~ *padan* to break a promise.

terkécoh taken in, cheated, tricked, fooled.

pengécoh swindler, cheater, sharpie.

pengécohan swindle, swindling, fraud.

kécoh II (*mass*) hysteria, tumult, uproar, hubbub, noise.

mengécoh to make a noise/uproar.

kecomak-kecimik (to eat) with one's mouth full.

kecombrang (*Jv*) k.o. tree, torch ginger, *Etlingera elatior*.

kécong → KÉCOH I, II.

kecowak → KECOAK.

kecrék I (*Jv*) pieces of metal strung on a rope which are clacked by the *dalang* to announce arrivals and departures of puppets or to accent their movements in the *wayang*.

ngecrék to beg by playing a makeshift musical instrument in the street; *cp* NGAMÉN.

kecrékan (*J*) **1** pieces of metal strung on a rope clacked by a solderer to attract customers. **2** an anchor-like device used to bring a bucket that has been lowered into a well to the surface.

kecrék II (*Jv*) handcuffs.

mengkecrék to handcuff.

kecrés (*Jv*) striking of a match.

mengecrés to strike a match.

kécu (*Jv*) robber, bandit, highwayman.

mengécu to rob.

perkécuan robbery.

kecuak → KECOAK.

kecuali 1 except (for), not including, excluding, but not. *Jam bicara pk 4-5*, – *hari Minggu* office hours from 4 to 5 except on Sundays. – *jika/kalau* except if, unless. – *itu* apart from that. **2** besides, aside from, in addition to, other than as. – *harus menjalani hukuman, harus pula membayar biaya perkara* besides being punished, one also has to pay court costs. **3** only. *– ini saja yang harus kauhafalkan.* This is the only thing you have to memorize. **4** unless. *– secara tegas disebutkan lain* unless expressly stated otherwise.

berkecuali to have exceptions. *tidak ~* without exception. *Tiada ~ semua harus disuntik.* Everyone, without exception, must be vaccinated.

mengecualikan 1 to make an exception. **2** to exempt (from), exclude.

terkecuali 1 exceptional. *dalam hal-hal yang ~* in exceptional cases. **2** with the exception of, excepting.

terkecualikan excepted, exempted. *Tidak seorang pun ~.* There are no exceptions.

kecualian exception.

kekecualian exception.

pengecualian exception; → KEKECUALIAN. *tanpa ~* without exception, exceptionless; without reservations. *Tidak ada peraturan tanpa ~.* There are no exceptionless rules. *~.~ itulah yang membentuk hukum.* Those are the exceptions that make the rule.

perkecualian exception, exemption.

kecubung I 1 plant species, datura plant, *Datura fastuosa/metel* with spiky fruit (the thorn apple) and large white or purple flowers. Flowers, seeds, and leaves are said to be poisonous. *mabuk –* a) intoxicated with thorn apple seeds. b) drugged, crazed (with love). **2** wide-mouthed (of its flowers). *– hutan/rimba* angel's trumpet (flower), *Brugmansia suaveolens. – paya* k.o. shrub, *Gardenia tentaculata.*

mengecubung [and **ngecubung** (*coq*)] to administer *kecubung* seeds to s.o. so that he will be poisoned (used by thieves when they want to break into a house).

kecubung II *batu –* and *– kasian* amethyst (believed to be a love potion).

kecuh-kecah to make a lot of noise.

kecumik berkecumik to mumble; → KOMAT-KAMIT.

kecumit → KECUMIK.

kecundang I (= **terkecundang**) conquered, defeated; → PECUN-DANG.

    mengecundangi to defeat, beat.

kecundang II (*M*) instigation, provocation; → CUNDANG II.

kecup (*onom*) smack, sound of a kiss.

    mengecup(i) to kiss by touching one's cheek to s.o. else's cheek; *cp* CIUM.

    kecupan a kiss made in that way.

kecur (*geol*) clast.

    kecuran clast. *~ gunung api* volcanoclast.

kecut I afraid, scared. *– hati* afraid, scared. *membuat – hati* to frighten, scare.

    mengecutkan to frighten, terrify, scare.

    kekecutan fear, fright.

    pengecut 1 coward. **2** cowardly. **kepengecutan** cowardice.

kecut II 1 shrunken/shriveled up (of roasted meat/planks, etc.). **2** wrinkled (of the skin, etc.). *Kulit mukanya sudah mulai –.* The skin on his face is beginning to show wrinkles. *–.– badan* to shudder, shiver, shrink.

    berkecut wrinkled.

    mengecut to contract, shrivel (up), shrink; to become wrinkled.

    mengecutkan to shrink/shrivel up s.t.

kecut III (*onom*) creaking/squeaking sound (of unoiled hinges/rusty engine parts, etc.).

    berkecut-kecut to creak, squeak.

kecut IV (*Jv*) sour (of taste/face). *menjadi –* gone sour.

keda → KEDAH.

kedabu k.o. tree, *Sonneratia ovata.*

kedadak choleric diarrhea.

kedah 1 (with) wide-open (mouth), open-mouthed. *mangkuk –* cup with wide-open mouth and with a lid. **2** wide-spread (of the legs).

kedahung and **keda(w)ung** (*pokok –*) a large tree, *Parkia biglobosa/javanica*, whose bark, leaves, and seeds are used to make medicine.

kedai (*Tam*) **1** (retail) store. **2** booth. **3** kiosk, stand, stall. *– kopi* coffee shop. *– minuman* pub, bar. *– sampah* (in North Sumatra) shop which sells miscellaneous items.

berkedai 1 to own a store. **2** to shop (at a *kedai*). **3** to keep/run a store, be a storekeeper.

mengedaikan to display (goods for sale), exhibit, decorate (a store window).

terkedai displayed, exhibited.

kedaian place where goods are displayed. *lemari ~* showcase (in store).

pekedai storekeeper, shopkeeper. *~ kopi* coffeehouse owner.

perkedaian 1 place where goods are displayed. **2** showcase (in store). **3** shop window. **4** exhibits, display, goods on display.

kedak → LINTANG *kedak.*

kedakar-kedékér → KEDÉKÉRAN.

kedak-kedok (*onom*) rumbling or rattling sound of a cart, etc.

kedal → KADAL II.

kedalon (*J*) serious (of illness), critical.

kedaluwarsa (*Jv*) → KADALUWARSA. *tanggal –* expiration date.

kedam leaden grey.

kedang I 1 outstretched (of arm). **2** extension.

    mengedang(kan) to stretch out (one's hand, etc.), raise (one's fist).

kedang II (*M*) **mengedang** to pour off (rice water to shorten the cooking time).

kedangkai plant, *Glochidion molle* whose leaves are made into a medicine.

kedangkang trigger guard, a metal ring that protects a trigger.

kedangsa *limau –* k.o. citrus fruit with green skin, citron, *Citrus medica.*

kedap 1 tight, impenetrable, impermeable, -proof. **2** *– terhadap* immune to. *– abu* dustproof. *– air* waterproof, water tight. *jas hujan – air* waterproof raincoat. *semén – air* water-resistant cement. *– angin* windproof. *– bom dan granat* shellproof. *– cahaya* opaque. *– debu* dustproof. *– getar* vibration proof. *– suara* soundproof. *– udara* airtight. **kekedapan udara** airtightness.

    mengedapkan to deaden (sound/emotions).

    terkedap tight (of a seal).

    kekedapan impermeability.

    pengedap *~ suara* a) soundproofing. b) silencer (on a gun).

    pengedapan *~ suara* soundproofing.

kedap-kedip wink (of the eye); → KEDIP.

    mengedap-ngedip to wink.

kedar → KADAR I, SEKEDAR.

kedasih (*Jv*) violet cuckoo, a cuckoo-like bird (its sound is said to predict bad luck), *Chrysococcyx xanthorhynchus. – laut* little bronze cuckoo, *Chrysococcyx minutillus.*

kedas-keridas k.o. itchy scabies.

kedat-kedut (*J*) **1** to tremble. **2** to throb.

kedaton (*Jv*) palace.

kedau (*ob*) **mengedau** to scream, cry out (for help, etc.).

kedayan (*cla*) retainer, servant, follower of a prince.

kedéblak (*J*) (*onom*) bang! thump!

    ngedéblak *jatuh ~* to fall down with a thump.

kedebluk (*Jv onom*) bang, sound made by a heavy object falling down.

kedebong (*J*) *– pisang* trunk of a banana tree.

kédék mengédék and **(ter)kédék-kédék** to waddle, waddling.

kedekai chebulic or black myrobalans, fruit of the *Terminalia chebula* used as a medicine.

kedekak-kedekuk (*J*) **1** to work one's fingers to the bone; → KEDUAT-KEDUET. **2** to be starving, live miserably.

kedékéran (*J*) to stamp one's feet, be restless (of horses).

kedeki(k) → KEDEKAI.

kedekut (*J*) stingy, miserly.

kedelai (*Tam*) (*kacang –*) soybean, *Glycine Soja, Soja hispida.*

kedelé → KEDELAI.

kedemat → KHIDMAT.

kedempung I (*onom*) plop! sound of s.t. falling into water; → PLUNG.

kedempung II wormy, worm-eaten (of fruit). *seperti buah –, di luar berisi di dalam kosong* empty barrels make more noise.

kedempung III tobacco pouch made of *mengkuang* leaf.

keden (*J*) **ngeden** to strain, press down (in defecating or giving birth).

    ngedenin *~ tahinyé* to push one's feces out.

kedengkang (*onom*) clanging noise made by empty tin cans, etc.

kedengkik skinny, emaciated. *tanah* – (agriculturally) poor/barren land.

kedengkung → KEDENGKANG.

kedér (*J*) trembling (from fear), afraid.

kéder (*J/Jv*) bewildered, dazed, completely confused; to feel lost. ngéderin to be confused about.

kedera *ikan* – 1 a small sea fish, *Holocentrum rubrum*. 2 (blue spot) gray mullet, *Valamugil seheli, Mugil sp.*; → BELANAK.

kedéra (*Port IBT*) 1 chair; → KURSI I. 2 sedan chair; → TANDU.

kederang a spiny shrub whose wood is boiled for dyestuff, *Cudrania javanensis, Hymenocardia punctata/wallichii*.

kedet (*J*) jerk, tug, pull (at the string of a kite, etc.).
  mengedet-ngedet 1 to jerk, tug. 2 to delay, put off (making payments on debts).

kedéwas butter fish, black mullet, *Stromateus cinereus/nigra*.

kedi 1 transvestite. 2 hermaphrodite (tending toward female). 3 sexually immature. 4 impotent, not virile.
  kekedian transvestism.

kédi (*E*) caddy (on golf course).

kedian (*coq*) after(ward), later; → KEMUDIAN.

kedidi various species of plovers and sandpipers. – and *si* – a) plover, *Charadrius spp.* b) wood sandpiper, *Tringa glareola*. – *besar* a) gray/black-bellied plover, *Pluvialis squatarola*. b) great knot, *Calidris tenuirostris*. – *golgol* curlew sandpiper, *Calidris ferruginea*. – *gung* sharp-tailed sandpiper, *Calidris acuminata*. – *kelicap* common sandpiper, *Tringa hypoleucus*. – *mérah* red knot, *Calidris canutus*. – *padang* Oriental pratincole, *Glareola maldivarum*. – *pantai* redshank, *Tringa totanus*. – *putih* sanderling, *Calidris alba*. – *rawa* dunlin, *Calidris alpina*.
  bersekedidi and bersikedidi to skip, hop.
  bersekedidi (in Java) to tap one's fingers, drum (on s.t.) with one's fingers.

kedik bent (slightly backward, of the body).
  mengedik 1 to bend (one's body) slightly backward. 2 to walk with one's chest stuck out.
  mengedikkan to bend s.t. back, straighten s.t. out, draw (one's body) up(right).
  terkedik 1 bent back, straightened out. 2 (*ling*) retroflex.
  pengedikan retroflexing, retroflexion.

kedikit → KEDEKUT.

kedingding (*Jv*) k.o. weed, artillery plant, *Cassia mimosoides*.

kedip 1 wink (of the eye), blink. 2 flicker; → KERDIP.
  kedip-kedip to keep on winking; to blink again and again.
  sekedip a blink of the eye. *dengan* ~ *mata* with a wink/blink of the eye.
  berkedip(-kedip), mengedip and terkedip(-kedip) to blink, wink; twinkle, flicker; to keep on opening and closing.
  mengedipkan to wink, blink. ~ *mata* to wink, blink. ~ *sebelah matanya* to wink (at).
  terkedip *tidak* ~ unblinking, with open wide (of eyes).
  kedipan 1 winking, blinking, wink, blink. 2 flicker, flickering, twinkling.

kedodoran (*J*) 1 to fit badly (of clothes); to slip off (of pants, etc.). 2 cannot serve (all the customers); *cp* KEWALAHAN.

kedok I (*J/Jv*) 1 mask; → TOPÉNG. – *gas* gas mask. 2 front, pretense, guise, cover. *dengan mengambil* – under the guise of. – *rahasianya terungkap* his secret was unmasked. 3 cover (of an intelligence agent).
  berkedok 1 to wear a mask, be masked. 2 to disguise o.s.; disguised (as), under the guise (of). *sebagai penipu* ~ *mencari sumbangan* under the guise of a collector for charitable contributions.
  memperkedok to use s.t. as a mask, use s.o. (to get s.t.).
  pengedokan masking.

kedok II (*Jv*) to cultivate/till/plant and harvest land for s.o. else with payment of part of the harvest agreed on in advance.
  kedokan 1 wages consisting of part of the harvest for tilling s.o. else's land. 2 (*Jv*) section of irrigated rice field (surrounded by small dikes); → RELUNG I.

kedok III → KADOK I.

kedombak 1 name of a forest tree, *Spondeas dulcis*. 2 name of a sea fish, *Sillago spp*.

kedombrongan (*J*) too large/big (of clothes); → GEDOMBRONGAN.

kedomprangan (*J onom*) sound made by empty cans falling.

kedondong Spanish plum, hog plum, *Spondias spp*. – *alus/batu/laut* panax, *Nothopanax fruticosum*.

kedondongan cinnamon bittern, *Ixobrychus cinnamomeus*.

kedondongisasi (encouraging the) planting (of) *kedondong* trees.

kedongdong → KEDONDONG.

kedongkok (*ob*) metal rings at the base of kris hilt; → PENDONGKOK.

kedorong (*J*) inadvertently pushed away; → TERDORONG.

kedot (*J*) strong, able to take blows.
  kekedotan strength.

keduat-keduet (*J*) to hard work, work one's fingers to the bone; → KEDEKAK-KEDEKUK.

kedubang k.o. short cutlass.

Kedubés [Kedutaan Besar] embassy (except the Indonesian embassy); → KBRI. – *AS* U.S. Embassy. – *US* embassy of the USSR.

keduduk I → DUDUK I. mengeduduki to inhabit; stay/live in.

keduduk II various species of rhododendron, *Melastoma polyanthum* and allied species; → SEKEDUDUK, SENDUDUK.

keduk (*Jv*)
  mengeduk 1 to scoop (up/out). 2 to stir around in (mud). 3 to dredge. 4 to rake in. ~ *banyak duit* to rake in a lot of money.
  mengeduki to scoop (up/out).
  kedukan a hole dug in the ground.
  pengeduk (*alat/mesin* ~) scooper.
  pengedukan digging.

kedul (*ob*) ball of wood/ivory/horn.

kedung (*J/Jv*) eddy, whirlpool, deep spot (in river), fishing hole.

kedut I fold, wrinkle (of skin), furrow (in one's forehead); crumpled (of paper/material/garment).
  berkedut wrinkled, creased; folded, crumpled.
  mengedutkan to wrinkle, crease, fold, crumple.

kedut II mengedut to snatch, take by force.

kedut III (*J/Jv*) twitch.
  berkedut to twitch.
  kedutan a nervous tick/twitch (in a part of the body such as the eyelid).
  kedut-kedutan twitching.

keduten → KEDUTAN.

kéh (in acronyms) → KEHAKIMAN.

kéham river rapids.

kéhél terkéhél 1 dislocated (of a joint/muscle), out of joint. 2 not fitting into a place; out of place. 3 off course (of a ship). 4 deformed (of a bone), scoliosis.

kehendak → HENDAK.

kehicap various species of monarch birds, *Monarcha spp.* and other species. – *ranting* black-naped (blue) monarch, *Hypothymis azurea*.

Kéibitai (*Jap*) Garrison Guards.

Kéibodan (*Jap*) Vigilance Corps.

kéilan lobster.

keja I (*J*) to make, cause; → KERJA. – *ketawa* to make s.o. laugh. – *marah* to anger, make s.o. angry.

keja II (in acronyms) → KEJAKSAAN.

kejai 1 (*pohon* –) k.o. rubber tree. 2 (*getah* –) rubber. 3 resilient, elastic. – *berlapis* very stingy, tightfisted.
  berkejai to stretch o.s. (after sleeping, etc.).
  mengejai to stretch s.t. ~ *kakinya* to stretch one's legs.

kejakgung [kejaksaan agung] Attorney General's Office.

kejam I closed tight (of eyes).
  mengejamkan ~ *mata* to close one's eyes tight.

kejam II cruel, pitiless, merciless, ruthless, unfeeling, insensitive, cold-blooded (murder). – *berbalas* – an eye for an eye, a tooth for a tooth.
  sekejam as cruel as.
  sekejam-kejamnya no matter how cruel.
  mengejami 1 (= mengejamkan) to treat s.o. cruelly/insensitively. 2 to deal firmly/severely with s.o.
  terkejam the cruelest.
  kekejaman cruelty, relentlessness; atrocity.

kejam III avaricious, miserly, tightfisted.

kejamas shampoo; → KERAMAS.

kejan → EJAN, REJAN. **mengejan** to press down (during childbirth/ in defecating); → NGEDEN.

pengejanan squeezing.

kejang 1 stiff (of a corpse/muscles from cramp). **2** to have convulsions, have a cramp. *mati –* to drop dead. *– rumput* grass tetany (a disease of cattle). *– demam* febrile convulsion. *– gagau* convulsion. *– jantung* angina (pectoralis). *– mulut* lockjaw. *–.– pada kehamilan/persalinan* eclampsia. *– terkejut* (to stand) stock-still.

berkejang(-kejang) to twitch, have a cramp, have convulsions.

mengejangkan *~ badan* to stretch out.

kekejangan 1 (muscle) cramp, convulsion, spasm, twitch. *~ sesudah mati* rigor mortis. **2** the bends.

kejap blink, wink (of the eye).

sekejap 1 (*~ mata*) a moment. **2** right away, immediate.

berkejap-kejap to blink, wink, flicker.

berkejapan (*pl subj*) to flicker, twinkle.

mengejap to wink at.

mengejapkan to blink, wink. *~ mata* to blink one's eyes.

kejapan wink, blink, winking, blinking.

kejar I *– pakét* a literacy and elementary education equivalence program.

berkejar to hurry, hasten, rush.

berkejar(-kerjar)an and **bersekejar 1** to pursue, chase, be in pursuit of. **2** to keep pace with. **3** to chase after e.o. (butterflies, people, etc.).

mengejar [and **ngejar** (*coq*)] **1** to supersede/overtake. *Berita ini kemudian dikejar oléh suatu berita héboh lagi.* This news was later superseded by another sensational news item. **2** to make up for, compensate for. *Sebagian masih dapat dikejar dengan kenaikan penerimaan dari gas bumi.* Part (of the loss) can be made up for by an increase in revenues from natural gas. **3** to catch up on (one's work, etc.). **4** to be after, pursue, hunt for, run after. *yang dikejar tidak dapat, yang dikandung bercéceran* not to throw out dirty water until one gets in clean, i.e., don't get rid of s.t. before you have a replacement. *tak lari gunung dikejar* make haste slowly. *~ keréta-api* to catch the train. *~ ke(ter)tinggalan* to catch up. *~ pencuri* to chase a thief. *~ waktu yang hilang* to make up for lost time. *Tidak dapat dikejar lagi.* There is nothing more to be done about it. **5** to be bent on ...-ing, be out for, aim at, be ...-oriented. *~ keuntungan* profit-oriented. *~ sasaran* goal-oriented. *~ uang/pangkat* to be out for money/position.

kejar-mengejar 1 pursuit. *~ waktu* time-pursuit. **2** to try to outdo e.o., chase e.o.

mengejar-ngejar to rush s.o., keep after s.o. to do s.t., nag. *dikejar-kejar waktu* to be late, be rushed for time.

mengejari (*pl obj*) to run after, pursue.

mengejarkan [and **ngejarin** (*J coq*)] **1** to pursue. **2** to pursue s.t. on behalf of s.o. else.

terkejar chased, run after.

kejaran pursuit, being run after, clutches. *lolos dari ~* escaped (from the police while being pursued). *~ hukum* the clutches of the law.

kejar-kejaran 1 chase. *adegan ~* a chase scene (in a movie). **2** tag (the game).

pengejar s.o. who pursues s.t. *~ pangkat* job-seeker, office-seeker.

pengejaran chase, pursuit, hunt. *dalam ~* under pursuit, under surveillance. *Dia sudah lama dalam ~ polisi.* He's been under police surveillance for a while.

kejar II [kelompok belajar] (*student sl*) study group.

kejari [Kejaksaan Républik Indonésia] Republic of Indonesia Attorney General's Office.

kejat 1 stiff (as a corpse). *mati –* and *mayat –* dead as a doornail. *–lah engkau!* Drop dead! **2** sturdy, strong, firm (as a fastening). *mata sabit – pada hulunya* the blade of the sickle is firmly attached to the handle. **3** close, dense.

kejat-kejat kicking.

kejati [Kejaksaan Tinggi] Chief Public Prosecutor's Office.

kejawèn (*Jv*) Javanese mysticism; everything relating to Javanese customs, traditions, beliefs.

kejeblos (*J/Jv*) **1** fallen/stepped into a hole. **2** fallen into a trap; to be tricked/taken in; → JEBLOS.

kejelog 1 to break (of a rope). **2** to shake, bump.

kejem → KEJAM II.

kején (*J/Jv*) plowshare. *besi –* pig iron.

kejengkang (*J*) fallen on one's back, fallen backwards, toppled over; → TE(R)LENTANG, JENGKANG.

kejep → KEJAP.

kejer (*J/Jv*) to keep on weeping.

keji I low, mean, abject, vulgar, despicable, infamous, scandalous. *kelakuan yang –* bad behavior. *perbuatan yang –* a foul act. *perkataan yang –* vulgar words.

sekeji as mean, etc. as.

berkeji *~ diri* to foul one's own nest; humiliate o.s.

mengeji(kan) 1 to think little of, despise. **2** to blame, find fault with, censure, disapprove (of), condemn, denounce. **3** to defame, slander, discredit, vilify.

terkeji the lowest, most abject/despicable.

kekejian vulgarity, meanness (of behavior).

pengejian meanness (of behavior).

keji II k.o. herb, *Staurogyne elongata. – beling* → KECI *beling.*

kejip 1 wink (of the eye); → KEDIP, KEJAP. **2** flicker (as an electric torch/flashlight).

mengejipkan *~ mata* to blink one's eyes.

kejoan (*Jv*) a small green pigeon.

kejolak to flare up, increase (of light, etc.).

kejora (*A?*) **1** (*bintang –*) (the planet) Venus, morning star. **2** the flag of the Papuan independence movement.

kéju (*Port*) **1** cheese. *– cédar* cheddar cheese. **2** term of abuse for a full-blooded Dutchman. *– kacang* peanut butter.

kejuju (*M?*) **mengejuju 1** ceaseless, unceasing, incessant. **2** to move towards (a target).

kejungjun charmed, enchanted.

kejur I lank, straight, stiff, bristling (of hair/fiber, etc.), inflexible, rigid, not easily bent.

mengejur to stiffen, bristle, become rigid.

kekejuran stiffness, lankness, rigidity.

kejur II a freshwater fish, large-scaled golden barb, *Acrossocheilus sumatranus.*

kejurnas [kejuaraan nasional] national competition.

kejut I 1 stiff with fear. **2** shocked, surprised, startled. **3** shying (away) (of a horse).

berkejut *~ telinga* to prick up its ears (of a nervous horse).

berkejutan (*pl subj*) to scatter with fright, run in all directions (due to alarm/fright/shock, etc.).

mengejut (*ob*) suddenly, unexpectedly. *mati ~* sudden death.

mengejuti → MENGEJUTKAN 1.

mengejutkan [and **ngejutin** (*J coq*)] **1** to shock, alarm, startle, surprise. **2** surprising, shocking, alarming.

terkejut startled, suddenly surprised, shocked. *amat ~* shell-shocked. **menterkejutkan** to startle. **keterkejutan** start, a sudden brief shock.

kejutan shock, jolt, surprise. *~ budaya* culture shock. *~ listrik* electric shock. *~ masa depan* future shock. *~ otot* muscle spasm. *~ rohani* psychic shock.

kekejutan 1 startled. **2** frightened, afraid.

pengejut 1 easily shocked/frightened/alarmed. **2** coward. **3** a horse that easily shies.

kejut II **sekejut, sikejut, si terkejut** and *rumput* **kejut-kejut** sensitive plant, *Mimosa pudica.*

kék I (*D*) /kék/ cake.

kék II 1 grandfather. **2** old man.

kék III (*J*) **1** (after each of two or more suggestions or possibilities; the speaker doesn't know or care which one is correct) whether (it's) ... or ...; I don't know/care whether it's ... or ... *apapun namanya: perploncoan –, perkenalan –, pembayatan –, kebaktian –, ...* whatever it's called: whether it's *perploncoan* or *perkenalan* or *pembayatan* or *kebaktian* ... (all words meaning 'initiation'). **2** whatever. *apa – yang lu kasih* whatever you give (me). **3** you should have just ..., why don't you just ... (in commands and suggestions).

kék IV framework of a (hand)loom.

kekabu tree-cotton, kapok; → KABU-KABU.

kekacang → KACANG-KACANG II.

kekah mitered/banded leaf monkey, *Presbytis femoralis*.

kékah I (*A*) ritual head shaving of an infant seven days after birth; → AKÉKAH.

kékah II (*Jv*) offering at a death, 1,000 days after a death, etc.; *usu* consists of a sheep or 10 pigeons.

kekal 1 everlasting, lasting (for ever), eternal, durable, perpetual, permanent, enduring, stable, imperishable, immortal. **2** to endure, last (of love, etc.). **3a**) to give/yield long(-lasting) service, will last/endure. **b**) long live, vive! viva! *alam/negeri yang* – the hereafter, the great beyond. *perdamaian yang* – lasting peace. *persahabatan yang* – eternal friendship. *tidak* – *bunga di karang* departed glory/friendship, etc. - *abadi* stable forever. **mengekal-abadikan 1** to confirm, reinforce (the belief in s.t.). **2** to tighten (bonds of friendship), draw (two thing) closer together. **3** to preserve (peace), make (a marriage) continue; *cp* KAKÉN. ~ *hajat* to become immortal. - *karar* peaceful and safe always.

berkekalan to continue, drag on, go on, be permanent. *jika perbuatannya itu dibiarkan* ~ if we let his actions continue

mengekali and **mengekalkan** to perpetuate, make lasting/permanent, maintain, keep.

kekekalan eternity, perpetuation, imperishability, permanence, durability.

kekala (*elec infr*) circuitry.

kekam scum (on water), dirt (floating on water). *balik* – the tide has turned. *mati* – slack water, neap tide.

kekandi (*cla*) (small) bag, purse.

kekang 1 (horse's) bit, clip. **2** (*tali* -) bridle, rein(s). **3** control, check, restraint, curb, inhibition, restriction. *tanpa* – unrestrained, uncontrollable. - *diri* self-restraint. - *pegas* spring clip.

mengekang 1 to adjust a bit, bridle, rein (in). **2** to (keep in) check, control, restrain, curb, inhibit. - *diri* self-control. ~ *harga barang* to control commodity prices. ~ *hawa nafsu* to restrain/repress one's passions. ~ *surat kabar* to curb a newspaper.

mengekangi to bridle, suppress.

terkekang curbed, checked.

kekangan → KEKANG 3.

pengekang restraint, depressant.

pengekangan 1 bridling. **2** checking, control, curbing, restraint.

kekap → KEKEP I.

kekapas (*burung* -) leaf-bird, green bulbul, *Chloropsis spp.*; (in Sumatra) tiger shrike, *Lanius tigrinus*.

kekar I 1 opening (of blossoms/flowers). **2** asunder, apart, separated (of rice grains). **3** (*geol*) joint.

mengekar 1 to open (of flowers). **2** to pull apart, separate. ~ *api* to rake up a fire.

mengekarkan to pull apart, separate, spread out (of rice to dry), stretch (one's muscles).

perkekaran (*geol*) jointing.

kekar II (*Jv ob*) close/tight (of weaving/wickerwork).

kekar III firm, solid, sturdy, robust, strong (physically), hefty; → KEKER.

kekara 1 → KACANG *kara*, KARA-KARA. **2** lima bean, *Phaseolus lunatus*.

Kekar Malindo [Keris Kartika Malaysia-Indonésia] name of the joint Indonesian-Malaysian Army Maneuvers.

kekaras → KARAS-KARAS.

kekas I (*ob*) **mengekas** to dig up (the soil), root around; → KAKAS I.

kekas II (*Pal ob*) a strip of land between a newly reclaimed lot and a cultivated field.

kekasih beloved, sweetheart; → KASIH I.

kekat (*ob*) foam/leaves, etc. floating on the water; → KEKAM.

kekau to be startled in one's sleep, jump up from sleep suddenly.

terkekau-kekau to keep on jumping up from sleep (as if startled).

kekawin (*Jv*) poetic epic written in Old Javanese or *Kawi*.

kéké I (*Jv*) the young of the sawfish or *cucut pedang*.

kéké II (in Manado) girl.

kéké III (in Sabah) Kota Kinabalu.

kéké IV → KÉKÉK II.

kekeb (*J/Jv*) earthen/copper lid put on a *kukusan* when the rice begins to steam; → KEKEP I.

kékéh berkékéhan (*pl subj*) to burst into laughter.

terkékéh-kékéh to roar with laughter.

kékéhan burst of laughter.

kékék I **terkekek-kekek** to giggle, snigger.

kékék II (*burung* -) a) kingfisher or halcyon, *Halcyon chloris*. b) black hornbill, *Anthracoceros malayanus*.

kekel → KEKAL.

kékél stingy, miserly.

kekélok meander; → KÉLOK.

berkekélok meandering.

kekemben (*J*) to wear a knee-length *kain*.

kekéncéng (*J*) k.o. copper pot.

kekep I (*J*) cover, lid.

ngekep to cover, put a lid on.

ngekepin 1 to cover. **2** to hide, conceal.

kekep II (*J/Jv*) **ngekepin** completely enclose in the arms, press to one's bosom, embrace, get hold of.

kekep III (*Jv?*) (- *babi*) white-breasted wood swallow, *Artamus leucorhynchus*.

keker (*J/Jv*) (of a) sturdy (build), with a good physique; → KEKAR III.

kékér (*D*) **1** binoculars. **2** telescope.

mengékér [and **ngékér** (*coq*)] to use binoculars, look with binoculars.

kekeruyuk (*Jv onom*) **1** cock-a-doodle-doo. **2** to crow, be full of beans/energy.

keketok (*J onom*) sound of the cackling of a hen. *ayam* – *bertelor* a guilty person usually talks big.

kék(h)i (*J C*) annoyed, irritated, resent(ful).

kekiprah → KIPRAH.

kekisi lattice; → KISI-KISI.

kekitir (*Jv*) land tax assessment records; → GIRIK.

kékok 1 stiff, awkward, clumsy. **2** unaccustomed; → KIKUK. **3** (*M*) (- *akalnya*) insincere.

kékol bribe, illicit commission.

mengékol to bribe.

kekondongan → KOKOKAN.

kekrupukan (*J*) **1** panic. **2** nervous, excited, upset. **3** to do s.t. with all one's might (and main).

kekucah (*Jv*) favor(s) (to inferiors).

kekuda roof truss.

kekudang (*J*) dowry given by the groom or his family to the bride based on her request.

kekudung (*J*) mantilla, scarf used as a head covering; → K(ER)UDUNG.

kelab (*D/E*) club.

kelabakan (*J/Jv*) **1** to sprawl. **2** to flounder around without knowing what to do.

kelabang I (*J/Jv*) centipede; → LIPAN.

kelabang II (*Jv*) braid, pigtail.

mengelabang to braid.

kelabangan braid of hair.

kelabat (*A?*) fenugreek, *Trigonella foenumgraecum*, used as a spice for forage and formerly in medicine.

kelabau (*ikan* -) k.o. carp, *Osteochilus melanopleura*.

kelabu gray; *cp* ABU I. *pupuk* – "gray fertilizer," an unofficial fertilizer lower in price than that fixed by the government. *putih* – off-white. - *armada* battleship gray.

berkelabuan grayish.

mengelabui (~ *mata*) to deceive.

terkelabui fooled, deceived.

kekelabuan 1 grayish. **2** deception.

pengelabuan deceiving, deception. ~ *pajak* tax fraud.

kelacam-kelécem (*J*) to smile sheepishly (due to embarrassment, etc.).

keladak dregs, lees. *si* – nickname for the youngest child. - *kulah* scum on the bottom of a *bak*. - *perut* one's last defecation before death.

mengeladak to defecate.

keladan k.o. tree, *Dryobalanops oblongifolia*.

keladasan satisfaction of greed.

keladau mengeladau to keep an eye on, watch over.

keladi I (*ubi* -) caladium, arroid; taro, *Colocasia esculenta*, *Caladium bicolor*. *air di daun* – a piece of advice that is not taken. *daun* – *dimandikan* to cast pearls before swine. *seperti birah* *dengan* – almost the same. – *babi/cina/telur/udang* k.o. taro, tannia, *Colocasia antiquorum, Xanthosoma spp.* – *bunting* water hyacinth, *Eichornea crassipes.* – *pari* k.o. thorny aroid, *Cytosperma sp.* – *ular* k.o. aroid, *Alocasia longiloba.*

keladi II *biang* – a) source, beginning, origin. b) principal person, ringleader, mastermind; → BIANG *kerok. tua-tua* – old but still vigorous/strong. *tua-tua* –, *makin tua makin (men)jadi* the older one gets, the stronger (sexually) one becomes; dirty old man. *gatal-gatal* – *semakin tua semakin jadi* a dirty old man; → TUA-TUA *kelapa.*

keladi III *belalang* – k.o. grasshopper.

keladi IV (*burung*) *pucung* – little heron, *Butorides striatus javanicus.*

kelagepan (*J*) to be out of breath, unable to breathe.

kelah I (*D*) **1** accusation, charge, complaint. **2** to complain. **3** (= **mengelah**) to sue (in court), bring suit against, charge (s.o. with a crime), accuse.

kelah II (*ikan* –) a river fish, Malaysian mahseer, *Tor douronensis/ tambroides.*

kélah (*A*) picnic.

　berkélah to (go on a) picnic.

kelahi (*Skr*) conflict, quarrel (fistfight or verbal fight). *sehabis* – *teringat silat* to be too late to be of any use.

　berkelahi to quarrel, fight (with fists, etc.). – *dalam kapuk/ kepuk* (*M*) a problem that is hard to solve. ~ *di dalam mimpi* (*M*) to fight for no good reason, expend too much energy on s.t. useless. ~ *di ékor alahan* (*M*) to argue over s.t. unimportant or already settled.

　memperkelahikan 1 to let fight (cocks), pit. **2** to fight over s.t. **3** to attack; to go against.

　pekelahi fighter. ~ *sapi* bullfighter.

　perkelahian fight, fistfight, quarrel. ~ *sangkur* bayonet charge. ~ *tanding* dueling. ~ *tinju* boxing match.

kelai (*M*) **mengelai(-ngelai)** to lean on, lounge up against; to lie around on one's back; → KALAI I.

　mengelai *tikar* ~ sleeping mat.

kelain → LAIN I. **mengelainkan** to isolate; to separate, segregate; to set apart.

kelak I in the future, later on, some day in the future. *di* – *(kemudian) hari* later, in the future. *akhir –nya* finally, at last, last of all.

kelak II → KELAH I.

kelak III (*burung* –) cuckoo-dove, *Macropygia assimilis.*

kelak IV (*J*) – *kelik* to flicker.

kelakah saltpan.

kelakanji k.o. needle grass whose seeds stick to clothing, *Andropogon aciculatus.*

kelakar 1 funny, comical. **2** jest, joke, fun. *main* – to poke fun.

　berkelakar to joke/fool around, play jokes, banter. *secara* ~ jokingly, not seriously.

　mengelakari to make fun of/ridicule.

kelakat (*J*) k.o. bamboo basket.

kelak-kelik (*J*) to flicker (of lamps); → KEDIP-KEDIP, KELIP-KELIP.

kelakkeling → KERAKELING.

kelak-keluk 1 curve, twist, coil. **2** particulars, details, ins and outs.

kelakson → KLAKSON.

kelakuk hypercorrect. *bentuk yang* – (*gram*) hypercorrection.

kelalang slender-necked earthenware decanter.

kelalap → KELELAP.

kelalawar I various species of cave-bat, horseshoe bat, *Hipposideros spp., Rhinolophus spp.*; → KELAWAR, KELELAWAR.

kelaling (*ikan* –) k.o. catfish, devil catfish, goonch, *Bagarius bagarius.*

kelam I 1 blurry, not clear, gloomy, dull, overcast, dark; → GELAP, KABUT I; *cp* BELAM II, ILAM-ILAM, SILAM II. *hari pun* – it's dark. *hari sudah mulai* – night was falling; it was getting dark. *perkara yang* – a dark affair. *suram* – hazy (of the moon due to clouds). – *alam bagi saya tentang/akan* I didn't understand a thing about, I saw no chance to. – *disigi lekung ditinjau* (*M*) each obscure case has to be investigated carefully. **2** nightfall. – *baja* iron grey. – *kabut* a) hazy, dim, dusky. b) → KALANG *kabut.* – *keciak/lebam/pekat/kelimut* (*ob*)/*membelam* pitch black. – *penglihatannya.* Everything went dark in front of him.

　sekelam as dark as.

mengelam to become dark.

mengelamkan to darken, dim, obscure, conceal.

kekelaman darkness, obscurity.

pengelaman 1 darkening, dimming, obscuring, concealing. **2** blackout. – *baja* (*ob*) about 4 in the afternoon.

kelam II (*D*) clamp, cleat. – *haluan* horseshoe clamp. – *penahan* stop cleat.

　berkelam clamped, cleated.

　mengelam to clamp.

kelamai k.o. sweet cake similar to *dodol*, made of glutinous rice, sugar and coconut milk; → GELAMAI.

kelaramin yesterday before dark; *cp* SEMALAM; → KE(LE)MARIN.

kelambai *si* – ghost, ogress with red hair.

kelambi (*Jv*) garment, dress, costume, outfit.

kelambir I (*Jv*) coconut.

kelambir II dewlap; → GELAMBIR.

kelambit fruit bat, flying fox, *Pteropus edulis.*

kelambu I mosquito net (over bed). – *kepala* balaclava.

　berkelambu to have/use a mosquito net.

　mengelambui to put a mosquito net over.

kelambu II (*ob*) *angin* – northern wind.

kelambur (*ob*) wrinkled, furrowed, rippling.

kelamdan (*Pers*) pen case; → KALAMDAN.

kelamin I 1 married pair/couple. **2** (*jenis* –) sex (male or female), gender; (having to do with) sex, sexual. *alat* – sex organ. *hidup* – sex life. *hubungan* – sexual relations. *penyakit* – venereal disease. *perhubungan* – coitus, sexual relations. *soal* – sexual problems. **3** genus. **4** genital.

　sekelamin 1 (*dua* ~) couple (of husband and wife/lovers), pair (male and female), match (man and woman). **2** forming a pair (of horses, etc.) ~ *burung* a pair of birds (male and female). ~ *kuda* a pair of horses (stallion and mare).

　berkelamin in pairs/couples; to have a husband/wife. ~ *ganda* bisexual.

　berkelamin-kelamin in couples, couple by couple.

　mengelamin to marry s.o.

　mengelamini 1 to get married to. **2** to have sex with.

　kekelaminan sex. *perubahan* ~ sex change, transvestitism.

　perkelaminan sex (*mod*).

kelamin II (*Mal Br*) family [husband, wife and child(ren)]. *kepala* – head of the family; → KEPALA *keluarga. perancangan* – family planning; → KELUARGA *berencana.*

　sekelamin the whole family.

　berkelamin to have a family. *hidup* ~ to be married and have a family.

kelamkari (*A cla*) a colored cotton cloth.

kelamun I → LAMUN. **berkelamun** and **mengelamun** to daydream, fantasize, build castles in the air.

　pengelamun (day)dreamer, brooder.

　pengelamunan (day)dream, fantasy.

kelamun II (*M*) overwhelmed.

　pengelamun sentimentalist.

　pengelamunan whim.

kelamut (*Jv*) **ng(e)lamuti** to suck on s.t.

kelana I wanderer, rover, tramp. *papa* – bum, vagrant. – *yudha* straggler.

　berkelana and **mengelana** to wander, rove, roam, tramp, ramble. *berkelana dunia* to travel about the world.

　pengelana 1 wanderer. ~ *dunia* world traveler, globetrotter. **2** tourist. ~ *yang hina papa* miserable vagrant.

　pengelanaan wandering, roving.

kelana II a Buginese noble title in Riau.

kelendara ring attaching yard to ship's mast.

kélang mill, press, factory; → KILANG I.

kelangenan (*Jv*) diversion, recreation, relaxation, distraction. *sastra* – light reading.

kelanggar (*J*) collided; → TERLANGGAR.

kelang-kabut (*ob*) **1** gloomy, dark, confused (in one's thoughts); → KALANG *kabut,* KELAM-KABUT.

kelangkan (*C? J*) balcony, balustrade; → LANGKAN.

kelangkang perineum, crotch, groin; → KANGKANG I **2**. *tulang* – sacrum.

terkelangkang with legs wide apart.

kelang-kelang go-between, matchmaker.

kelang-kelok and **kélang-kélok** twisting, twisting, bent, winding, torturous, zigzag.

kelangsa (*J*) partition or roof of woven coconut leaves.

kelanit mengelanit to open up stitches.

kelanjar I → KELENJAR.

kelanjar II (*M*) **berkelenjaran** to feel rheumatic pain (after a massage).

  mengelenjar to ricochet, bounce.

kelantang I (*J/Jv*) bleach.

  mengelantang to bleach, set out to dry (in the sun).

kelantang II (*J*) **mengelantang** to arrest and take to the police station.

kelanting k.o. tree, *Eurya acuminata*.

kelantur-lantur (*Jv*) too far off the track.

kelap – *kelip* blink. *(ber)kelap-kelip* 1 to flicker, glimmer, glitter, sparkle. 2 to twinkle (of stars).

  sekelap (~ *mata*) in a wink.

  mengelap(kan) (~ *mata*) to blink one's eyes.

  terkelap 1 winked. 2 dozed off.

kelapa (*buah* –) coconut. (*pohon* –) coconut palm, *Cocos nucifera*. *ampas* – shredded coconut after the oil has been pressed out. *gula* – (brown) coconut sugar. – *bali* → KELAPA *sawit. – cungkil* extracted coconut meat. – *dara* young coconut about to bear fruit. – *gading* a small yellow variety of coconut. – *génjah* quick-ripening coconut. – *gongséng* coconut flakes fried without oil. – *hijau* a green variety of coconut. – *kecukan* hybrid coconut. – *kering* (*Mal*) copra; → KOPRA I. – *kopyor/puan* and – *(dimakan) bulan* a coconut species with soft flesh. – *parut* grated coconut. – *sawit* oil palm, *Elaeis guineensis*.

  mengelapai to put coconut on.

  perkelapaan coconut (*mod*).

kelar I 1 notch, indentation, nick (in wood, etc.), groove. 2 rattan or metal coil or band (used on the necks of dogs or goats and attached to a rope).

  berkelar(-kelar) to have indentations/grooves, etc., notched, grooved, incised.

  mengelar to make notches/indentations, etc., incise.

  terkelar indented, notched, grooved, incised.

kelar II (*D*) 1 finished, ready, done. 2 OK, let's go (conductor to bus driver when passengers have finished getting on or off and the bus can start again).

  mengelarkan [and **ngelarin** (*J*)] to finish s.t. up.

kelara (*ikan* –) young *sembilang* fish, *Plotosus canius*.

kelarah fruit worm.

kelarai 1 diamond(-shaped) design/pattern/motif, checkered. 2 (*M*) edge, border, rim, lace. *belacu* – twill. *kain* – canvas.

  mengelarai 1 to weave a diamond-shaped design. 2 to stitch an edge.

kelari *ikan* – k.o. freshwater fish.

kelas I (*D*) 1 class, standard, rank, grade. – *lima* fifth grade (in school). 2 classroom. – *atas(an)* upper class. – *bawah(an)* lower class. – *berat* high class; heavyweight class. – *bulu* featherweight class. – *buruh* the working class. – *ékonomi* deck (class), economy class (on a ship). – *embun/India* low class. – *ikan tawes* and – *kakap* the big shots. – *kambing* gallery/pit (the least expensive class in a theater); lowest class (prostitute/hotel, etc.). – *layang* lightweight class. – *layang ringan* pinweight class (boxing). – *lélé* big shot. – *lose* box (in the theater). – *melati* at the low end of the scale. – *menengah* middleweight class; middle class. – *ningrat* the aristocracy, nobility. – *penguasa* the ruling class. – *rangkap* parallel class. – *ringan* lightweight class (boxing). – *satu* A-1, first class, the best. – *terbang* flyweight class. – *terbang mini* straw weight class (boxing). – *teri* the small fry, the unimportant (members of a group). – *yang meraja* the ruling class.

  sekelas in the same class, of its class.

  berkelas classy.

  berkelas-kelas in classes/ranks, divided up into classes.

  meng(k)elaskan to classify, rank.

  peng(k)elasan classification.

kelas II (*ob*) slack water, dead low water, neap tide.

mengelas it is the turn of the tide.

kelasa I hump (of a camel/cow, etc.).

kelasa II (*Jv*) mat, rug.

kelasa III a grass lizard.

kelasah → KELUSUH-KELASAH.

kelasak (*ob*) k.o. leather shield.

kelasam-kelésem (*J*) → KELACAM-KELÉCEM.

kelasi I (*Pers Hind*) sailor, ordinary seaman, shipmate. – *I* seaman. – *II* apprentice seaman.

kelasi II the long-nosed Borneo monkey, *Hylobates leuciscus*.

kelat I 1 (*naut*) (*tali* –) brace, sheet (of a boat's sail). *juru* – boat's crewman in charge of holding the sheet. 2 long thick rope used to pull down a tree that is being felled.

kelat II – *bahu* (*cla*) k.o. bracelet.

kelat III various k.o. myrtaceous trees, *Eugenia spp.*, *Syzygium spp.* – *api/minyak* k.o. tree, *Eugenia filiformis*. – *besar* k.o. tree, *E. pendens*. – *burung* k.o. tree, *E. macrocarpa*. – *jambu* sea apple, *Eugenia grandis*. – *jantan* k.o. tree, *E. polyantha*. – *pasir* k.o. tree, *Parastemon urophyllum*.

kelat IV (*ob*) sticky. *Matanya* –. His eyes are sticky (after sleeping). **pengelat** *jarum* – pin, fastener.

kelat V tart, slightly bitter in taste, astringent (as sour orange/unripe pineapple, etc.). *obat* – astringent (substance/drug, etc.). – *asam* the difficulties (of life).

kelati areca-nut scissors; → KACIP.

kelawan (*ob*) rattan cheek cord for buffalo; → KELUAN.

kelawar I → KELELAWAR.

kelawar II club (suit of cards).

kelawi breadfruit; → SUKUN.

kelayak (*ob*) → KHALAYAK.

kelayang (*ob*) *burung* – swallow; → LAYANG-LAYANG.

kelayapan (*J*) to wander around.

kelayu a large tree with sour fruit, *Erioglossum edule/rubiginosum*; → MERTAJAM. – *hitam* k.o. tree, *Arytera littoralis*.

keldai → KELEDAI.

kélder (*D*) cellar.

kelébat (*J*) **berkelébat** to pass/flash by. *Belum juga* ~ *bayangannya*. No sign of him could be seen.

  sekelébat ~ *mata* in passing, incidentally, at a glance. *dilihat* ~ *mata* considered superficially.

  sekelébatan (*saja*) at a glance, superficially, all at once.

  mengelébatkan to make s.t. flash by.

kelébék and **kelébét** folded back at the corner or edge (of a bed sheet/tablecloth/page of a book, etc.) so that the folded part dangles.

  mengelébékkan to turn back the corner of a page/sheet/mat; to turn up one's cuffs.

kelebon – *Cino gundulan* (*Jv*) to be cheated.

kelebu (*J*) taking in water (of a leaking boat); to sink.

  mengelebukan to sink (a ship).

kelebuk *ara* – a tree species, *Ficus Roxburghii*.

kelebur to slide down, collapse.

kelebut (*Pers*) shoe last.

kelécé (*J*) **mengelécéi(n)** to cheat.

kelécem (*J*) → KELÉSEM.

keledai (*Tam*) donkey, ass. – *tidak akan terperosok dua kali pada lubang yang sama* or *hanya* – *yang terperosok ke dalam lubang yang sama* nobody else could be that stupid. – *hendak dijadikan kuda* everyone thinks his own geese are swans.

kelédang a large tree, *Artocarpus lancifolius*, with valuable timber for household goods, coffins, etc.

keledar defensive measures or preparations in the face of danger.

  berkeledar to approach cautiously, be on one's guard, take defensive measures or preparations in the face of danger. *tali pinggang* – safety belt. *topi* – crash helmet (for drivers).

kelédék sweet potato, *Ipomoea batatas*.

kéléh (*ob*) → KELIH.

kelejet (*J*) **be(r)kelejet** to squirm around (showing signs of life).

  kelejetan squirming around (showing signs of life).

kélék I (*ob*) armpit; → KETIAK.

  mengélék to carry under the arm.

  mengéléki to put s.t. under one's arm.

kélék II and kélékan and kélék-kélékan 1 balustrade, handrail, chair arms. 2 side-gallery to a palace.

kelekap microbenthic algae.

kelekati (ob) → KALAKATI.

kelekatu flying ant. seperti – masuk api defying death, flying in the face of death. – hendak terbang ke langit wanting the impossible.

kelelap (J/Jv) drowned, sunk.
  mengelelapkan to sink s.t. under the water.

kelelawar cave bat, Hipposideros spp., Rhinolophus spp. and other species. – barong trident bat, Aselliscus tricuspidatus. – curut wrinkle-lipped bat, Chaerephon plicata. – dagu hitam black-bearded tomb bat, Taphozous melanopogon. – daun/méga Asian/Malayan false vampire bat, Megaderma spasma. – goa/gua cave bat. – gundul hairless bat, Chaeromeles torquatus. – pinang k.o. bat, Taphozous affinis.

kelelegen → KLELEGEN.

kelelesa skink, large green lizard, Lygosoma spp.

kelélot berkelélot to stick one's tongue out.
  mengelélotkan to stick out (one's tongue) (in order to ridicule s.o.).

kelem (Jv) to be shipwrecked, founder; sink (of a ship).

kelemantang → KALIMANTANG.

kelemari(n) → KEMARIN.

kelemar-kelemér (J) to take it easy, go slowly.

kelemayar luminous millipede, glow-worm, Orphnaeus brevilabiatus.

kelemayuh I k.o. herbaceous plant from which medicinal herbs are made, Homalomena spp.

kelemayuh II gangrene.

kelembahang an aroid which causes skin irritation, Alocasia ovalifolia.

kelemabai ghost depicted as a red-haired giantess; → (si) KELAMBAI.

kelembak I (Pers?) 1 Chinese rhubarb species with sweet-smelling roots, medical rhubarb root, used to make cigarettes, Rheum officinale. 2 aloeswood, agar wood, Aquilaria malaccensis; → GAHARU, KARAS II, KLEMBAK.

kelembak II k.o. large butterfly or moth.

kelémban berkelémban to hobble around, walk unsteadily/haltingly.

kelembuai large dark-shelled snail (of rice paddies), Ampulla ampullacea.

kelembubu whirlwind; → HALIMBUBU, SELEMBUBU.

kelembung (ob) (water)bubble, bladder; → GELEMBUNG.

kelempai (ob) terkelempai lying down weakly/feebly.

kelemping (J) flabby and sagging, hanging down flaccidly (of old woman's breasts or of belly).
  kelempingan to sag, be flabby (of breasts/belly).

kelemumur dandruff, scaly scurf.

kelemunting (ob) → KEMUNTING.

keléncér (J) mengeléncér [and ngeléncér (coq)] to go for a walk.

kelendara (naut) ring attaching yard to ship's mast.

kelénéng 1 sound of a bell, toll. 2 (coq) small bell (of a bicycle, etc.).
  berkelénéng to tinkle (of a bell).
  mengelénéngkan to ring (a bell).
  kelénéngan 1 (onom) tinkling sound. 2 bell.

kelengar [and kelenger (J)] to faint, pass out, become unconscious, be stunned. – matahari sunstroke.

kelenggara (ob) mengelenggarakan to manage, take care of; → SELENGGARA.

keléngkéng I (buah –) laichi/lychee fruit, Nephelium litschi; → LÉNGKÉNG.

keléngkéng II → KENGKARÉNG.

keléngkong (coq) → KONGKALIKONG.

kelenik → KLENIK I.

kelening (onom) sound of a bicycle bell, etc.

kelenjar gland. biji – lymphatic gland. buah – bubo. demam – fever with septic adenitis. sakit – inflammation of a gland. – air mata lachrymal gland. – anak ginjal adrenal gland. – beguk thyroid gland. – buntu endocrine gland. – dada mammary gland. – empedu gallbladder. – getah bening lymph gland. – gondok thyroid gland. – kacangan thymus. – kelamin gonads. – keringat salivary gland. – léhér tonsils. – liur/ludah salivary gland. – ludah perut pancreas. – minyak sebaceous gland. – palit sebaceous gland. – peluh sweat gland. – prostat prostate. – susu mammary gland.

kelentang I (onom) clanging/banging sound.
  berkelentang to clang.

kelentang II mengelentang to set out to dry in the sun; → KELANTANG I.

keléntang fruit of the horseradish tree, Moringa oleifera; → KELINTANG, KÉLOR.

kelénténg → KLENTÉNG.

kelénténg and kelenting (onom) tinkling sound of a bell, etc.

kelentit I clitoris; → ITIL.

kelentit II (bunga –) cockle (plant), butterfly pea, Clitoria ternatea. – nyamuk k.o. plant, Decaspermum paniculatum.

keléntom (D ob) and keléntong (ob) accent; stress; dialect.

kelentung (onom) sound made by cowbells, etc.
  berkelentung to tinkle.
  kelentungan wooden (cattle) bell.

kelenung 1 (onom) sound made by a small gong. 2 small gong.

kelép → KLÉP.

kelepai berkelepai and terkelepai dangling, hanging down limply (of a broken tree branch/drooping flag/head of a drunkard/s.o. dozing off).

kelepak (onom) sound of clapping (hands/s.t.), beating (wings).
  mengelepak to make that sound.

kelépak I and terkelépak dangling, hang down limply.

kelépak II – baju lapel. baju – coat open at the neck.

kelepat (Port naut) caulking.
  mengelepat to caulk (cracks in a wooden ship, etc.).

kelépék terkelépék dangling, drooping, sagging, hanging down limply.

kelépék I → TERKELÉPÉK.

kelépét II → KELÉBÉK.

kelepik (onom) 1 sound made by a small fallen object. 2 sound made by a flag fluttering in the breeze.
  mengelepik to flap (in the wind).

kelepir (ob) testicles.

kelepit-kelepai dangling (of broken fronds or branches).

kelepit (onom) the sound of branches rustling in the wind.
  mengelepit to make that sound.

kelepon (Jv) [kué(h) –] bite-sized green balls made of sticky-rice flour containing liquid brown sugar and rolled in grated coconut.

kelepuk → KELEPIK.

kelepur mengelepur to flap its wings (of a cock fighting/a chicken after its throat has been cut).

kéler Westerner who has converted to Islam and follows Indonesian ways.

kélér 1 case for liquor bottles, etc. 2 (S) large square bottle. 3 glass jar with lid, stoppered bottle.

kelerak → LERAK II.

kelérek (D) clerk (in an office).

keléréng 1 seed of the Sapindus rarak tree whose fruits are uses to make soap. 2 marble(s). main – to play marbles.

kelesa a river fish, Scleropages formosus, found in West Kalimantan.

kelésa (cla) lazy, slovenly, indolent.

kelésah (ob) restless, nervous.

keléséh-péséh (M? coq) 1 to chatter away in Dutch; → KRÉSÉH-PÉSÉH. 2 to talk nonsense/gibberish.

kelésék dried skin of banana stem (used as twine).

kelésem (J) a weak/wan smile.

kelésen (D) to chatter.

keleset-keleset (J) quietly, secretly, on the sly, stealthily.

kelesung (A ob) ocean.

kelét (J/Jv) firmly attached.
  mengelét to peel, skin.
  pengelétan peeling.

kelétah 1 affected. 2 coquettish. 3 to try to attract attention or admiration (usually said of women).
  berkelétah to act cute and coquettish.

keletak (onom) sound made by a small stone falling on board, etc.
  berkeletak to make that sound.

kelétak → GELÉTAK.

keletak-keletik (*J onom*) clacking sound made when walking wearing wooden clogs.

keletang (*onom*) sound made by a coin falling on stone, etc.

keletar to tremble, shudder, shiver; → GEMETAR.

keletas-keletes (*J onom*) sound of chewing rice which has not been cooked thoroughly.

keleték (*J onom*) sound of a key turning in a lock.

keleték (*Jv*) **mengeléték** ~ *prangko* to peel (illegally) stamps off an envelope (and then sell them).

keletik I (*onom*) **1** sound made by a small object, like a pen, falling on the floor, etc. **2** ticking (of a clock).
　berkeletik to make that sound.

keletik II to squirm (of a fish on the hook, etc.); → GELETIK II.

keleting (*onom*) tinkling sound.

keletuk I (*onom*) sound of knocking on a table, creaking.
　berkeletuk to make that sound.

keletuk II (- *kayu*) wooden rattle, castanet.

keletung (*onom*) sound made by s.t. hitting a metal can.

keletus (*J/Jv*) **mengeletus** [and **ngeletus** (*coq*)] to bite off in a single bite.

keléwang short sword (broad toward the tip; used in the Aceh war).
　berkeléwang armed with such a sword.

keléwar (*naut*) foresail.

keléwat (*J*) too, very; → LÉWAT, LIWAT I. - *berat* overweight.

keléwér (*D naut*) foresail.

keléyengan → KLIYENGAN.

keli *ikan* - river catfish, *Clarias majur/batrachus*. - *bunga* walking catfish, *Clarias macrocephalus*. - *dua selobang/selubang* two lovers of the same woman.

kéli (*Jv*) carried along by the stream.
　ngéli to have o.s. carried along by the stream.

kelian I (*Bal*) leader of a rural settlement (under the *perbekel*). - *subak* head of the *subak*.

kelian II (*ob*) alluvial mine (*esp* tin).

kelian III (*coq*) you all; → KALIAN, KAMU.

keliang (in Central Lombok) village head.

keliar - *kelior* to wander about aimlessly.
　berkeliaran [and **keliaran** (*coq*)] **1** to walk around/about (of one or more persons inside a fixed space), hang/loiter around, circle around (of aircraft), make a tour of (a town, etc.), sail around, cast one's eyes about (in search of s.t.); *cp* BERKELILING. *lari* ~ to flee in confusion, scatter. ~ *kian ke mari* to (take a) walk around. **2** to hover around (of ghosts). **3** to swarm (of ants, thugs, etc.). **4** to wander/roam/rove about (in a forest, etc.). **5** to whirl around (of thoughts in one's head). **6** to prowl (of wild animals).

keliat **mengeliat** to stretch (one's arms); → GELIAT.

kelibang **berkelibang(an)** to fly around (like flies around one's head), swarm around.

kelibat I double-headed paddle.
　mengelibat to paddle using such a paddle.

kelibat II (*J*) to be involved in; → LIBAT.

kelibat III → KELÉBAT.
　sekelibat ~ *mata* superficially. *tampak* **sekelibat(an)** visible for a brief moment.
　sekelibatan in a moment/flash, all at once. ~ *saya lihat dia jatuh*. All at once I saw him falling.
　berkelibat(an) to appear for a brief moment.

kelibet → KELIBAT II.

kelicap sunbirds, babblers, flycatchers, and similar birds. - *bakau* copper-throated sunbird, *Leptocoma calcostetha*. - *belukar* a) chestnut-naped forktail, *Enicurus ruficapillus*. b) k.o. sunbird, *Anthreptes spp*. - *berjambul* white-bellied crested babbler, *Yuhina zantholeuca*. - *bunga kantan* white-necked babbler, *Stachyris leucotis*. - *gunung* black-throated sunbird, *Aethopyga saturata*. - *jantung* little spider-hunter, *Arachnothera longirostra*. - *kunyit* common iora or leafbird, *Aegithina tiphia*. - *mérah* a) scarlet sunbird, *Aethopyga mystacalis*. b) crimson sunbird, *Aethophyga siparaja*. - *perepat* golden-bellied geryone, *Gerygone sulphurea*. - *pisang* yellow-eared spider hunter, *Arachnothera chrysogenys*. - *pucat pisang* dark-necked tailor-bird, *Orthotomus atrogularis*. - *ranting* Tickell's blue flycatcher, *Muscicapa tickelliae*.

kelici (*Tam*) **1** climber that has medicinal value, *Caesalpina crista/jayabo*. **2** (candlenut) used as marble (in a game).

kelicih → KELICIK.

kelicik **terkelicik** skidding, swerving, gliding away.

kelidai → KENIDAI.

kelih open (of the eyes), aware.
　mengelih *(mata)* to open the eyes, be able to see; to observe. *tidak* ~ *mau téngok* wanting to know about or achieve s.t. without making any effort.

kelijak (*bio*) cilia.

kelik I turn, bow; → LIKU I.
　mengelik to bow down/aside, turn the body (so as to dodge a blow, etc.).
　mengelikkan to dodge s.t. by bowing down or turning aside.

kelik II (*onom*) rumbling (of an empty stomach); → BERKERON-CONGAN.
　berkelik(-kelik) to rumble.
　terkelik (one's stomach) rumbles from hunger.

kelik III → KLIK.

kelikah and **kelikat** (*A*) character, way of behaving. *Sudah tahu bagaimana -nya*. He knows his customers.

keliki(h) **1** (*M*) papaya. **2** (*jarak -*) (*S*) castor-oil plant, *Ricinus communis*.

kelikik **mengelikik** to giggle.

kelikir I (*batu -*) pebbles; → KERIKIL. *intan disangsikan batu* - do now know the exact value (of s.t./the situation).

kelikir II rattan nose ring for cattle.

kelik-kelik (*M*) k.o. poisonous ant. - *dalam baju* nourish/cherish a viper in one's bosom; → MUSUH *dalam selimut*.

keliling **1** neighborhood, surroundings, environment, environs, vicinity. *di* - *rumah* in the vicinity of the house. **2** circumference, circuit, periphery. - *dada* the circumference of the breast. *pertanyaan* - (an agenda item at a meeting) questions from the floor. *pertunjukan* - itinerant/touring performance. *séminar* - seminar held in different places. *tujuh* - a) the seven rounds of the *Kabah* (part of the *hajj* ceremonies). b) dizzy; dizziness. - *bumi* circumference of the earth. - *kota* to look around the city. - *lingkaran* circumference.
　sekeliling all the way around, on all sides, the surrounding area. ~ *dipagar tinggi*. It was fenced all the way around. *~nya* the surroundings, all those things surrounding it.
　berkeliling **1** to circle, encircle, go around. *berjalan* ~ *candi* to walk around the temple. **2** to drive/travel around. ~ *dunia* to travel around the world.
　mengelilingi [and **ngelilingin** (*J coq*)] **1** to surround, encircle, encompass. *Anak-anak berdiri* ~ *gurunya*. The children were standing in a circle around the teacher. **2** to revolve around. *Bulan* ~ *dunia*. The moon revolves around the earth. **3** to go about, travel around, cross. ~ *dunia* to go around the world.
　mengelilingkan to take around, circulate/pass around s.t., distribute. ~ *surat undangan* to circulate letters of invitation.
　pengeliling s.o. who goes around. ~ *dunia* world traveler, globetrotter; → PELANGLANG *buana*.
　pengelilingan circumnavigating, circling.

kelilip (*J/Jv*) piece of grit in the eye.
　kelilipan to have gotten a piece of grit in the eye.

kelim **1** hem, seam. **2** (*med*) ring (on skin). - *pipih* flat hem. - *tindih kasih* counterhem.
　berkelim hemmed, seamed.
　mengelim to hem, seam.
　pengelim hemmer.

kelimantang → KALIMANTANG.

kelimat (*coq*) → KALIMAT.

kelimis → KLIMIS.

kelimpanan (*Mal ob*) → KELILIP.

kelimpungan (*J*) **1** to be at a loss. **2** embarrassed, confused.

kelimun crowd, mob.

kelimut → KELAM I.

kelin → KELIM.

kelinci (*D*) rabbit; hare, *Oryctolagus cuniculus*. *Si - Paskah* Easter Bunny. - *percobaan* guinea pig. - *Sumatra* Sumatran hare/jungle rabbit, *Nesolagus netscherii*.

kelincir → GELINCIR.
kelindan 1 newly spun thread. 2 spinning wheel's conveyor rope. 3 thread on a needle. 4 bobbin, spool. *jahit sudah, – putus* completely gone. *lalu penjahit, lalu –* and *lulus benang, lulus –* where one sheep goes another follows.
 berkelindan threaded.
kelindas [and **kelindes** (*J*)] run over, knocked down; → TERLINDAS.
Keling I (*Tam*) Coromandel Coast, the coastal region of Southeast India. *orang –* (derogatory term for) s.o. from that area. *akal –* sly, tricky. *gerantang –* empty bluff, attempt at intimidation; → GERTAK *sambal. lidah –* unreliable, deceitful, underhanded. *pusing –* to pervert words, facts, etc. *– karam* a person who is noisy/boisterous at work or speaking; → CINA *kebakaran jénggot. – mabuk todi* (*Mal*) a chatterbox. *– pelikat* Indian Muslim.
keling II (*D*) rivet.
 mengeling to rivet.
 kelingan rivet.
 pengelingan riveting.
keling III (*cla*) k.o. boat.
kelingking (*jari –*) little finger, pinky. *– kaki* little toe. *telunjuk lurus, – berkait* from a good background but of bad character.
kelingsir (*penyakit –*) rupture (of the scrotum), (scrotal) hernia; → (*penyakit*) BURUT, KONDORAN,
kelinik → KLINIK.
kelining → KELÉNÉNG.
kelinjat (*M ob*) **terkelinjat-kelinjat** to jump, start.
kelintang (*buah –*) fruit of the horseradish tree, *Moringa pterygosperma/oleifera;* → KELENTANG, KÉLOR.
kelintar (*Jv*) (**ber**)**kelintaran** to lounge/loaf/loiter/lurk around.
kelinting (*Jv onom*) sound of ringing, noise of small (handheld) bell.
 kelintingan small metal bell.
kelintung (*onom*) → KELINTING. **kelintungan** wooden cattle-bell; → KELENTUNG.
kelip I kelip-kelip 1 firefly. 2 silver or gilt paper, etc. for decoration, spangles.
 sekelip (*~ mata*) a wink, the twinkling of an eye.
 berkelip(-kelip) 1 to twinkle, glitter, sparkle, scintillate. 2 to flicker (of an oil lamp, etc.), blink, wink, open and close one's eyes.
 mengelip-ngelip to flicker.
 mengelip-ngelipkan to blink (the eyes).
 terkelip(-kelip) twinkling, flickering, sparkling.
 kelipan scintillation; → KEDIP.
 pengelip scintillator.
kelip II (*col*) (*uang –*) the former five-cent coin with a center hole.
kelip III (*E*) paper clip.
kelipar → GELIPAR.
kelipat (*M*) **berkelipat** to fold; folded (of a napkin/note paper, etc.). *tak ~ perut* cannot keep a secret.
 terkelipat folded.
kelipuk (*Pal*) → ÉCÉNG.
kelir I (*Jv*) 1 screen for *wayang* performance. 2 movie screen. 3 screen, cover (behind which one conceals s.t.). 4 backdrop.
 be(r)kelir to have such a screen/backdrop.
 mengelirkan (*infr*) to stage; → PAKELIRAN.
kelir II (*D*) color. *potlot –* colored pencil.
 mengelir to color.
keliru (*J/Jv*) 1 to make a mistake, be mistaken, commit an error. *Jangan –.* Don't misunderstand (what I'm saying). 2 wrong, false. 3 confused (with). 4 erroneous, incorrect, (*leg*) error in *persona. – anggapan* and *– tangkap* misconception, misunderstanding, misapprehension. *– tulis* typo, typographical error; → SALAH *cétak.*
 mengelirukan 1 to mislead, lead astray, delude, confuse. 2 to blame (s.o. for), declare s.t. wrong; to bring about a misunderstanding.
 kekeliruan 1 error, mistake. 2 confusion.
 pengeliruan misleading, leading astray.
kelis I **mengelis** to swerve aside, dodge; → KELIT.
kelis II **mengelis** to stick up (like unruly hair).
kelisa (*Pers ob*) church.
kelisah → GELISAH.

kelisé → KLISÉ I, II, III.
kelit **berkelit** to dodge, move quickly to one side, dart aside, evade. *Dia ~ tangkas.* He skillfully evaded (answering the question). *~ dari pajak* to dodge taxes.
 berkelit-kelit to keep on dodging.
 mengelit to dodge.
 mengelitkan to move s.t. quickly to the side.
 perkelitan evasion, dodging.
kelitak (*onom*) sound of seeds rattling inside fruit.
keliti (*naut*) tholepin, oarlock.
kelitik I (*J*) detonation, knocking (of a car engine).
 ngelitik to knock (of a car engine).
kelitik II (*Jv*) *wayang –* a *wayang* show with wooden puppets; → WAYANG *klit(h)ik.*
keliwat → KELÉWAT.
keliwer (*J/Jv*) *pating –* (*pl subj*) walk around, fly about.
 keliweran to walk back and forth.
keliyengan → KLIYENGAN.
kelobot → KLOBOT.
kelocak I (*ob*) **mengelocak** to peel off; abrade (of skin, bark).
kelocak II **berkelocak** to shake (a bottle of liquid, etc.); → KOCAK I.
keloceh → CELOTÉH.
kelodan (*ob*) 1 thunder. *panah –* a) k.o. arrow. b) legendary weapon. c) thunderbolt. 2 shooting star.
kelojotan (*J*) 1 to suffer from epilepsy. 2 to writhe (in pain/pleasure). 3 angry, furious.
kélok 1 curve, bend. 2 turn.
 berkélok and **mengélok** to turn off/aside, change direction, curve. *berkélok tajam* to make a sharp turn. *mengélok ke kanan* to turn to the right.
 berkélok-kélok winding (of a road, etc.).
 mengélokkan to turn (one's car, etc.).
 kélokan 1 turn, curve (in the road, etc.). 2 loop. **berkélokan** winding, curvy.
kelokak → KELOYAK.
kelokop (*J*) → KELOPAK.
kelola manage, supervise, organize.
 mengelola(kan) 1 to manage, supervise (a business/government operations, etc.). 2 to carry out (a job, etc.). 3 to organize (a meeting, etc.).
 terkelola managed. *kurang ~* mismanaged.
 pengelola 1 manager, supervisor, organizer. *~ rumahtangga* housekeeper, homemaker. 2 director. 3 (*port*) authority; → OTORITA.
 pengelolaan management, supervision, organization, organizing. *Pusat ~ Krisis* Crisis Management Center. *~ negara* statecraft. *~ perubahan* management of change. *~ usaha* business management. *~ waktu* time management.
kelolodan (*J/Jv*) 1 to get/have s.t. stuck in one's throat, choke. *– biji rambutan* choked on a *rambutan* pit. 2 to get too much more than one bargained for.
kelolong **terkelolong** (*cla*) to choke, swallow the wrong way.
kelom (*D*) wooden shoe/slipper. *– geulis* (*S*) woman's wooden dress slippers.
kelomang hermit crab, *Pagurus bernhardus* and other species.
kelombéng (*D*) a pastry made from egg yolks and other ingredients.
 kelombéngan a tool for making that pastry.
kelomét → KELUMIT.
kelompang (*ob*) 1 empty. 2 the empty eggshell after the chick has hatched.
kelompang II → KELUMPANG.
kelompok 1 cluster, herd, group, party, band, gang, category. 2 (*geol*) suite. *– awan* mass of clouds. *– bahasa* language subjects (in school). *– binaan* target group (for development). *– bintang* constellation. *– gerilya* guerrilla band. *– kata* (*gram*) phrase. *– 11* the group of 11 nations set up under the auspices of the International Monetary Fund to determine joint police. *– 19* the 19-nation group representing the southern nations of the world. *– 24* the 24-member IMF committee. *– 77* the developing nations, the Third World. *– Bermain* play group; → SEKOLAH *main. – Cipayung* the Cipayung Group (4 Indonesian student

organizations). – *elang* the (political) hawks. – *Empat* the four rapidly developing Asian nations (Hong Kong, Singapore, Taiwan, South Korea). – *kembang Sepatu* Hibiscus Group, i.e., the *Malari* detainees connected with the Indonesian National Party. – *kepentingan* interest group. – *keras* the hard-liners. – *kerja* shift, working group. – *mérah* (in *Maluku*) the Christians. – *merpati* the (political) doves. – *minat* interest group. – *musik* musical group, band. – *pemikir* think tank. – *pendesak/penekan* pressure group. – *pengkaji/bersama* (joint) study group. – *Pengkaji Karét Internasional* International Rubber Study Group. – *perundingan* negotiating group. – *Petisi 50* the 50 who signed a letter of protest against President Soeharto's Pakanbaru speech (May 13, 1980). – *pulau* archipelago. – *putih* (in *Maluku*) the Muslims. – *sasaran* target group. – *sebaya* cohort, peers. – *selatan* the 14 developing nations. – *suara* voting block. – *Ujung Tombak Mélanésia* the Melanesian Spearhead Group (Papua New Guinea, Solomons, Vanuatu). – *utara* the eight developed nations.

sekelompok forming a group, belonging together, a group of. ~ *penarik bécak* a group of *becak* drivers. ~ *pohon* grove of trees.

berkelompok to cluster, group/stay together.

berkelompok(-kelompok) in groups/batches.

mengelompokkan to group, sort (into groups), assemble, bring together as a group.

terkelompok put in a group, stacked up (of chairs).

kelompokan → KELOMPOK.

kekelompokan 1 cluster; clustering. 2 compartmentalization.

pengelompokan group(ing), sorting (into groups). ~ *kembali* regrouping.

perkelompokan assembly.

kelon I (*Jv*) *minta* – (*usu* said by a child to an adult) get in bed with me.

mengeloni to embrace s.o. while lying down next to him/her (may also have sexual connotations).

kelonan embrace while lying down.

kelon II (*E*) clone.

pengelonan cloning.

kelonék → KELONÉT.

kelonéng (*onom*) the ringing/tinkling of a bell.

berkelonéng(an) to ring, tinkle.

kelonét a (little) bit; → KELUMIT.

kélong I (in the Riau archipelago) a large marine fish trap consisting of several compartments.

kélong II (*ob*) a Bugis war song.

berkelong to sing that song.

kelongkong *nyiur* – a coconut so young that the shell is still soft and edible.

kelongkongan (*J*) a coconut that has been nibbled away.

kelongsong 1 husk. 2 wrapper (of paper/leaf, etc.). 3 cladding, outer casing. – *jagung* cornhusk. – *paking* packing box. – *peluru* cartridge case. – *ular* sloughed off outer skin of a snake.

kelontang (*onom*) 1 rattle of tin cans. 2 sound of scarecrow rattles.

berkelontang to make that noise.

kelontang-kelantung to loaf, drift (around the streets, etc.).

kelontok pengkelontokan dissolving, dismantling.

kelontong 1 wooden cattle bell. 2 hawker's rattle. *barang-barang* – small items for sale, sundries (toothbrushes/cups/glassware, etc.). *toko* – a store selling such wares. *tukang* – hawker, peddler.

kelontongan toy paper and bamboo clapper.

kelontongisme consumerism.

kelonyod (*J*) be(r)kelonyod and **mengkelonyod** slippery (as if oiled).

kelonyo(r) (*D*) *air/minyak* – eau de cologne.

kelop → KLOP. *kurang* – unsuitable.

mengelopkan to balance (a budget), square.

kelopak 1 thin cover/sheath. 2 (*bot*) spathe, calyx, bract. 3 (*geol*) nappe. *mengirai/menjirak* – to bud, be in full bloom. – *buluh* young bamboo sheath. – *bunga* (*bot*) sepal. – *jantung* spathe of the banana spadix. – *mata* eyelid. – *salak* calyx of the *salak*. – *tambahan* epicalyx.

berkelopak with a sheath, etc.

mengelopak to peel s.t. off.

terkelopak to peel/come off.

kélor (*Jv*) the horseradish tree, *Moringa pterygosperma/oleifera*, used for vegetables and for seasoning; → MERUNGGAI. *dunia tak sedaun* – a) with time comes counsel. b) there is more than one fish in the sea.

kelorak a climbing plant/vine. *rumput* – k.o. plant, *Lophatherum gracile*.

kelos (*D*) reel, spool, bobbin. – *terbang* shuttle.

mengelos to reel in.

kelosan reel.

pengelosan reeling s.t. in.

kelosét → KLOSÉT.

kelosok (*ob*) **mengelosok** to rub together (clothes being washed), scour; *cp* GOSOK.

keloter → KLOTER.

kelotok I (*J*) **ngelotok** 1 peeled off (of skin); → KLOTOK, NGLOTOK. 2 known by heart, memorized. *Semua pelajaran sudah* –. All the lessons have been memorized.

kelotok II *kapal/perahu* –; → KLOTOK I.

kelotokan (*J*) reckless, inconsiderate.

keloyak berkeloyak to cast off (the skin).

terkeloyak abraded/stripped off (of the skin).

keloyang (*burung* –) 1 glossy tree-starling, *Aplonis panayensis*. 2 green broad-bill, *Calyptomena viridis*. 3 stupid person.

keloyor (*J*) **berkeloyor(an)** and **ngeloyor** 1 to lounge/hang around. 2 to stagger about; *cp* KELUYUR.

Kélta Celt(ic).

kelu speechless (from fear/anxiety/shock/illness, etc.), struck dumb, mute, silent, spellbound. *dengan suara* – silently.

mengelu to become speechless.

mengelukan remain silent about, keep mum about, stonewall.

terkelu silenced, struck dumb (with surprise), dumbfounded.

kekeluan aphasia.

keluai *musang* – palm-civet, *Paradoxurus leucomystax*.

keluak k.o. tree and its fruit, *Pangium edule*; → KEPAYANG.

keluan (*M*) (buffalo's) nose rope. *bagai jawi ditarik* – obedient, docile. *menjilat* – *bagai kerbau* to make a long face.

mengeluani to put a rope in the nose (of a buffalo or cow).

keluang fruit-eating flying fox, *Pterocarpus edulis*; → KALONG I. *bagai* – *bebar petang* in swarms.

keluangsa notable family, respectable group of people.

keluar 1 to go/come out (of) (a room/house, etc.), exit. *Cacing itu* –. The worm came out (of the ground). *nomor* – outside (telephone) line. – *masuk* to go in and out (of). *Mobil* – *masuk halaman parkir.* The cars were going in and out of the parking lot. **mengeluar-masukkan** to take s.t. in and out. – *Jawa* outside Java. **mengeluar-jawakan** to relocate outside Java. – *rél* to derail; derailed. – *sidang* to walk out (of a meeting). 2 to emerge, appear, show up. – *gigi* to cut one's teeth. 3 to leave (the house), go out. *Ia tidak pernah* –. He never goes out. *Dia* – *selesai makan siang.* He left after lunch. 4 to appear, surface, (verb plus) out. *Darah* – *mencurah-curah.* The blood spurted out. *tumpah* – to pour out. 5 to be published, come out. *Bukunya akan* – *awal bulan depan.* The book will be published next month. 6 to come out (of one's mouth), be uttered/expressed. 7 to resign, retire, withdraw. *Ia* – *dari partai itu.* He resigned from the party. 8 to emerge (as winner). *PSM* – *sebagai juara.* The PSM emerged as the champion. 9 to spend (money). *kalau tiap-tiap seorang mau* – *seringgit dua* if everyone wants to spend one or two Malaysian dollars. 10 to come, have an orgasm. *Sebelum* –, *dikeluarkan.* Take it out before you come. 11 (*ob*) foreign (policy). – *tak ganjil, masuk tak genap* s.o. who is looked down on can do nothing. – *tanduknya* to get angry.

sekeluar after leaving, after getting/going out (of).

mengeluari to attack, go/come out to face (the enemy).

mengeluarkan [and **ngeluarin** (*J coq*)] 1 to take out, remove, pull out, extract. *Dikeluarkannya uang sepuluh ribu rupiah dari kantong celananya.* He pulled ten thousand rupiahs out of his pants pocket. 2 to express, utter. ~ *pendapatnya* to express one's opinion. 3 to issue, publish, release. ~ *buku* to publish a book. 4 to promulgate, enact. ~ *dékrit* to enact a decree. 5 to produce (goods, etc.). *Pabrik Goodyear tidak* ~ *ban untuk*

skuter. The Goodyear factory does not produce tires for scooters. **6** to write (a check). ~ *cék (kosong)* to write a (bad) check. **7** to export. **8** to spend (money). *Uang yang dikeluarkan sudah melebihi jumlah yang ditentukan dalam anggaran belanja.* The money spent exceeds the total stipulated in the budget. **9** to send away (from school), expel, dismiss, discharge, throw out (of a game), exclude. **10** to spit/pour out (one's feelings, etc.), spew forth, vent. ~ *isi hatinya* to vent one's feelings. ~ *unekuneknya* to spit out one's venom. ~ *angin* to pass gas. ~ *cahaya* to radiate light. ~ *darah* to draw (blood), cause (blood, etc.) to flow out. ~ *perasaan* to get it off one's chest. ~ *suara* a) to make a noise. b) to cast a vote. ~ *témbakan* to fire a shot.
terkeluar (*mostly Mal*) (~ *dari*) to go/come out of, leave.
keluaran (also see KELUARAN under LUAR) **1** product; made in/by. *sepatu ~ pabrik Bata* Bata shoes. **2** published by, a publication of. *buku ~ Balai Pustaka* a Balai Pustaka publication. **3** graduate/alumnus of. ~ *Univérsitas Nasional* a graduate of National University. **4** output; *opp* MASUKAN. **5** (in the Bible) Exodus. **6** release, edition.
kekeluaran expulsion.
pengeluar (*Mal*) producer.
pengeluaran 1 export. **2** (~ *belanja*) expenses, expenditures. ~ *tak terduga* unforeseen expenses. **3** production. **4** outflow (of water from a reservoir), discharge. **5** release, disbursement (of funds). ~ *barang dari pelabuhan* Customs clearance. **6** issuance, issuing (of stocks, bonds, etc.). **7** dismissal, expulsion. **8** removal. **9** outlet, exhaust.
keluarga (*Skr*) **1** family. *kaum* ~ (members of the) family, kin; → KELAMIN II. *kepala* – [KK] head of the family, family (in counting number of families). **2** relatives. **3** society, association. – *Mahasiswa Seni Rupa ITB* the ITB Fine Arts Students Society. – *Alumni Gadjah Mada* Gadjah Mada Alumni Association. **4** (*bio*) genus. – *batih* nuclear family. – *besar* (greater) community. – *Besar Univérsitas Krisnadwipajana* Krisnadwipajana University Community. – *berantakan* broken home. – *berencana* [KB] family planning. *Perkumpulan – Berencana* Planned Parenthood. – *bertanggung jawab* responsible parenthood. – *dekat* next of kin. – *inti* nuclear family – *prasejahtera* disadvantaged families. – *retak* broken home. – *sanak/sedarah* blood relative. – *semenda* relative through marriage, affine.
sekeluarga and family. *kami* ~ my family and I.
berkeluarga 1 (*sudah* ~) to have a family; be married. *belum* ~ a) do not have a family. b) (in want ads) unmarried, single. **2** to be related (to). ~ *semenda* to be related by marriage.
kekeluargaan 1 consanguinity, family relationship. ~ *sedarah* blood relationship. ~ *semenda* relationship by marriage. **2** family (*mod*). *suasana* ~ family atmosphere. *secara* ~ in a spirit of mutual cooperation, amicably. **3** brotherhood. **4** commonwealth (of nations). **perkeluargaan** relationship, family ties. ~ *semenda* affinity, relationship through marriage.
perkeluargaan (*mod*) family.
keluat → KHALWAT.
kelub → KLAB, KLUB.
kelubak (*M*) **terkelubak** torn, scraped (of the skin), grazed; → KELOYAK, KUBAK.
kelubi a stemless palm with edible sour fruit whose leaves are used for matting, *Zalacca conferta.*
kelubung veil, shawl.
berkelubung to wear a veil/shawl over the head and bosom; veiled, wrapped in a shawl.
mengelubungi 1 to veil. **2** to cover. *bulan yang dikelubungi méga menghitam* the moon, which was covered by a darkening cloud.
keluburan trap, pitfall (to catch large animals, etc.).
kelucak → KELOCAK I.
keluh (– *kesah*) **1** sigh. **2** lament(ation), wailing. **3** complaint, grievance. – *tidur di kasur, berkeruh di lapik penjemuran* (*M*). Living a life of luxury is not always pleasant; living a life of poverty is sometimes pleasurable. **berkeluh-kesah** to moan, groan, complain (to s.o. about s.t.), lament, grieve.
berkeluh and **mengeluh** [and **ngeluh** (*coq*)] to moan, groan, sigh, lament; to complain of. *Dia mengeluh pusing.* She complained of dizziness.

mengeluhi to moan about, bewail.
mengeluhkan [and **ngeluhin** (*J coq*)] to complain about, lament, deplore, feel sorry/bad about.
keluhan 1 sigh, lamentation. **2** groaning, groans, moaning. **3** what is said in complaint, what one complains about. ~ *mati* death rattle. ~ *sayu* lament(ation), moaning.
pengeluh s.o. who sighs/moans a lot, complainer.
pengeluhan complaint.
kelui (in Sumatra) Rhea grass, *Boehmeria nivea.*
keluih (*J*) breadfruit, *Artocarpus communis;* → SUKUN I.
keluk curve (in a kris, etc.); *cp* BÉLOK, KÉLOK, LIKU I. – *lekuk* cunning tricks.
berkeluk 1 to writhe in (pain), contort with (pain); to be ravenous with (hunger) **2** with a curl in it (of a mustache, etc.).
berkeluk-keluk and **terkeluk-keluk** curved, bent (of a tree branch, etc.).
mengeluk(-ngeluk)kan to bend s.t. (upward or downward); *cp* LENTUR I.
terkeluk *(ke kanan)* bent (to the right).
kelukan bending, buckling.
kelukup tree whose timber is used in building houses, *Shorea eximia.*
kelukur (*M*) **berkelukur(an)** abraded, grazed (of skin), scraped.
keluli (*ob*) and (*Mal*) steel; → BESI *baja.*
kelulu (*cla*) proper, appropriate, fitting. *tak* – improper, inappropriate, unbecoming.
kelulus (*cla*) a galley.
kelulut I k.o. shrub, caesar weed, *Urena lobata.*
kelulut II k.o. bee, *Melipoma sp.*
kelum → KELOM.
kelumbung → KELUBUNG.
kelumit (*J*) **sekelumit** a tiny bit, a little, a trace, a small number of. ~ *laporan* a brief report.
kelumpang tree whose timber is used for praus, etc., Java olive, *Sterculia foetida.*
kelumpuk → KELOMPOK.
kelumun (*M ob*) cover, wrapper, wrapping.
berkelumun covered/wrapped (in/with).
mengelumuni to cover, wrap (s.t.) (by putting a veil or shawl over the head, etc.).
kelun (*Jv*) **berkelun** to billow, rise (of smoke, etc.); → BERKEPUL(-KEPUL).
keluna a creeper with very small green fruit, *Smilax macrocarpa.*
kelunak *ubi* – k.o. tuber, Chinese yam, *Dioscorea oppositifolia.*
keluncur (*J*) soaking wet.
kelung 1 bent (in the center), with a deep bend in it. **2** hollow, concave.
kelungsén (*J*) it will be too late. *Lama-lama akan – jika kau tidak segera kawin.* It will be too late if you don't marry soon.
kelupak → KELOPAK.
kelupas blister.
berkelupas peeled/cast off.
mengelupas 1 peeled/cast off (of skin/bark, etc.), come off in strips/flakes. **2** to take the skin off, peel. **3** to exfoliate.
mengelupaskan to peel, take the skin off.
terkelupas peeled off.
kelupasan s.t. peeled.
pengelupas stripper. ~ *cat* paint stripper.
pengelupasan peeling, stripping.
kelupur mengelupur to leap up, flutter up, flap its wings (of a fighting cock, etc.); → GELUPUR.
keluron (*Jv*) **1** miscarriage. **2** abortion. – *menular* brucellosis, undulant fever.
keluruk to crow (of cocks).
kelurut whitlow (on finger).
kelus I peeled, stripped off.
kelus II → KELOS.
kelusuh-kelasah troubled, fitful (of sleep).
kelut(-melut) 1 commotion, confusion. **2** complicated (of a situation). **3** crisis, slump, depression (in the market); → KEMELUT.
kelutuk → JAMBU *kelutuk.*
kelutum tree whose timber is used for making furniture, etc., *Artocarpus altissima.*

kelutut a resin-collecting bee, *Melipona laeviceps*.

keluwak → KELUAK.

keluwih → KLU(W)IH.

keluyuk Chinese dish consisting of pork, sugar, etc.

keluyur (*Jv*) **berkeluyuran** and **mengeluyur** to loaf, loiter, ramble, stroll around, wander about.

kém (*E*) cam.

kémah (*A*) **1** tent. **2** camp.

berkémah 1 to camp out. **2** to put up a tent.

perkémahan camp, camping, encampment, campground. ~ *Wirakarya* (Boy Scouts) Community Service Camp.

kemak-kemik (*J*) (= **berkemak-kemik**) to mutter, mumble.

mengemak-ngemikkan to mumble/mutter s.t. again and again.

kemal I [= **berkemal(-kemal)**] **1** damp, moist, clammy, soggy. **2** dingy.

kemal II - *kemil* to keep on nibbling.

kemala → KUMALA.

kemalai → GEMALAI, GEMULAI.

kemam berkemam to mutter, mumble; muttered, mumbled.

mengemam 1 to have s.t. in the mouth but not swallow it. **2** to mutter, mumble. ~ *jari* to put and keep the fingers in the mouth.

kemamang (*Jv*) an evil spirit in the shape of a flaming human head.

kemampang (*Jv*) apt to take things too lightly.

kemampo (*Jv*) **1** to turn red, like *ampo*, (i.e., a red-colored clay), thus half ripe, *esp* of a mango. **2** become of marriageable age (of a girl).

keman (*ob*) sensitive plant, *Mimosa pudica*; → PUTRI *malu*.

kemanakan 1 nephew, niece. **2** (*M*) the relationship of a sister's descendants to her brother(s). **3** (*ob*) relatives.

berkemanakan ~ *kepada* to have as nephew, be the uncle of; → KEPONAKAN.

kemanan (*Jv*) k.o. percussion instrument used for marking rhythm.

kemandang (*Jv*) echo.

berkemandang to echo.

kemandén (*Jv*) k.o. plant, Straits rhododendron, *Melastoma malabathricum*; → SENDUDUK.

kemang I a tree which resembles the mango tree, *Mangifera caesia*.

kemang II 1 an evil spirit which attacks newborn children. **2** a female earth spirit which haunts mines and fields and which may sow tares in crops.

kemangi (various types of) (hoary) basil, *Ocimum spp.*, used to flavor meat, fish, etc. *bau cekur bau* - (in Medan) said of s.o. who is a close relative.

kementén and **kemantin** (*Jv*) → PENGANTIN.

kemantrén (*Jv*) *mantri*-ship, office of a *camat*.

kemap k.o. tree, *Ochanostachys amentacea*; → PETALING.

kémar → HÉMAR.

kemarau 1 dry (of the season/the hold a boat after it has been bailed out, etc.). **2** (*musim* -) drought, dry season, period of dry weather. - *keras* a long dry spell. **3** (*sl*) broke, without money. **4** (*naut*) bilge.

kemarén → KEMARIN.

kemari (to) here, come here.

mengemarikan bring s.t. here.

kemarin 1 yesterday. **2** (*Jv* influence) any day further back than - *dulu*, a few days ago, not long ago, recently, last (month, etc.). *di hari* - in the past. *malam* - and - *malam* last night; → SE-MALAM. *pagi* - and - *pagi* yesterday morning. *bukan anak* - (I/he) wasn't born yesterday.

kemarinnya the day before, the other day.

kemarin-kemarin earlier (than the expected or customary time).

kemaruk 1 (*J*/*Jv*) a ravenous appetite (*esp* after recovering from an illness). **2** to spend money lavishly after becoming rich suddenly or getting promoted. **3** greedy, avaricious, covetous.

kemas 1 arranged/packed, etc. neatly. **2** (*M*) clean, neat, in order; finished. *barang-barang* - valuable bric-a-brac. *peti* - shipping container. *rumah* - a neat and tidy house. *semuanya* - *dipelajarinya* he has finished studying everything. *terlalu* - *dirasa badan* physically fit. - *batuan* (*geol*) petrofabric. - *dini* early preparations. **mengemas-dinikan** to make early preparations.

berkemas(-kemas) 1 to put in order, arrange. **2** to remove, clear up/away; to clear (the table after eating). **3** to get ready, prepare (for a trip, etc.).

mengemas(i) to arrange/pack up/clear up neatly; to make preparations (to leave, etc.); to clear the clutter from, clean off. ~ *anak-anak* to take care of/look after the children. ~ *diri* to dress up. ~ *méja makan* to clear the dining room table. ~ *rumah* to put the house in order.

kemas-mengemas relating to packaging. *bisnis* ~ packaging business.

mengemaskan 1 to pack (luggage), tidy up, put in order, put s.t. away (on a shelf/in a drawer, etc.). **2** to finish up, to spend (money). *Harta orang tuanya dikemaskannya*. He spent all his parents' assets.

terkemas packaged.

kemasan 1 package. **2** container. ~ *kaléng* can (for food, etc.). *dalam* ~ packaged (food).

pengemas salvage ship.

pengemasan packing, packaging. ~ *kembali* repacking. ~ *dengan plastik* laminating.

perkemasan 1 the act/process, etc. of packing, clearing away, preparing, etc. **2** storage.

kemat I (*coq*) knowledge, wisdom; → HIKMAT.

kemat II → KEMET.

kemat-kemit → KOMAT-KAMIT.

kematu 1 *keras* - hard as a stone, stony. **2** (*geol*) hardpan.

kematus (*Jv*) tuberculosis.

kemawan *awan* - (*cla*) mass of clouds.

kemayu (*Jv*) (to act in a) cute, coquettish (way).

kembal a round, lidded wickerwork basket made of screw-pine, etc.

kembala I (*ob*) → GEMBALA I.

kembala II - *kembali* back and forth, to and fro.

kembali 1 to return, go/come back; → BALIK I, PULANG. - *ke alam asal* back to nature. - (*kepada*) *asal* to return to one's origins. - *ke rahmatullah*/*rahmat Allah* to pass away, die. - *kepada* to return to (the subject), revert to. - *kepada istri yang lama* to go back to one's wife after having repudiated her. **2** s.t. given back, change. *uang* - and -*nya* change (the difference between the price and the money offered). *Ada* -? Do you have change? *Ambil(lah)* -*nya*. Keep the change! **3** (once) again, once more, over again, a second time. - *ia bertanya kepada saya*. He asked me again. **4** (after a verb or noun) (to) re..., ... again, ... back. *hidup* - to come back to life. *membayar* - to repay, pay back. *meminta* - to ask (for s.t.) back, ask for s.t. to be returned. (*me*)*mulai* - to begin again, make a fresh start. *menarik* - to revoke, rescind, retract. *menyusun* - to rearrange. *pembayaran* - repayment, reimbursement. *permintaan* - asking back (for the return of s.t.). **5** you're welcome (after being thanked). - *aktif* reactivated. **mengembali-aktifkan** to reactivate. - *pulang* to return/go back home.

kembali-kembali *tidak* ~ *lagi* never come back again.

sekembali(nya) upon (his) return, after (he) returned, upon returning. ~ *dari kunjungan singkat* after he returned from a short visit.

mengembalikan [and **ngembaliin** (*J coq*)] **1** to return s.t., take/give s.t. back. *Buku itu dikembalikannya ke perpustakaan*. He returned the book to the library. *dapat dikembalikan* returnable, refundable. **2** to refuse to accept, return, send back, turn down. *Kadonya dikembalikannya*. She returned his present. *Ia tidak pernah/tahu* ~ *undangan*. He never turns down an invitation. **3** to restore (public order. etc.). **4** to make/have s.o./s.t. return/come/go back, get s.t. back, reintroduce (a ceremony, etc.). ~ *hak* to rehabilitate. ~ *kepada* to convert s.t. to, reduce s.t. to, go back to s.t.'s source/origin; → MENGASALKAN.

terkembali (*infr*) to return/go back (to)

kembalian *uang* ~ (small) change.

pengembali returner. ~ *sinyal* repeater.

pengembalian 1 restoration, restitution, return, recurrence. **2** repatriation, returning home. **3** changing back. ~ *asét* assets recovery. ~ *béa-masuk* drawback (i.e., a refund of import duties when the taxed commodities are later exported). ~ *dana* (*fin*) reclamation. ~ *hak* rehabilitation.

kemban (*Jv*) a long narrow sash worn at or above the waist (part of the traditional woman's dress).
 berkemban to use/wear such a sash. ~ *sarong* to wear a *sarong* as a breast cloth.
kembang I (*Jv*) **1** flower, the ... flower. – *mawar* rose. – *sepatu* China rose/hibiscus; → BUNGA I. **2** flower as a symbol of female beauty. *Salmiah adalah – désanya.* Salmiah is the (beautiful) flower of her village. *cita –* printed cotton with a flower pattern. *janda –* a beautiful younger childless widow. *kain –* k.o. starched *sarong. toko –* flower shop, florist's. FOR OTHER FLOWER NAMES STARTING WITH KEMBANG SEE THE SPECIFIC NAME. *– angin* windrose. *– api* a) fireworks. b) fireball. *– ban* tread (of a tire). *– bangkai* k.o. flower with edible tuber, *Amorphophallus variabilis. – biak* propagate. **berkembang-biak 1** to multiply in number (of population). **2** to breed. **mengembang-biakkan** to multiply, propagate, spread (the cultivation of a crop). **pengembang-biakan** reproduction, multiplication, proliferation, breeding. **perkembang-biakan** reproduction. *– bopong/ sekar* water hyacinth, *Eichornia crassipes;* → ÉCÉNG *gond(h)ok. – boreh* a flower in floral religious offerings. *– bugang* k.o. plant, *Clerodendrum calamitosum. – emas* marigold, *Stephanotis floribunda. – gula* a) (hard) candy. b) lollipop. *– gula karét* chewing gum; → PERMÉN *karét. – kembut* (*Mal*) flaring up and flickering (of a dying flame).*– kol* cauliflower. *– kuncup* → KEMBANG *kempis. – kertas* zinnia (cultivated as an ornamental plant). *– latar/ malam* whore, prostitute. *– loyang* a snack made from flour and sugar. *– matahari* sunflower. *– merak* a decorative plant, peacock flower, red bird of paradise, *Caesalpinia pulcherrima. – pacar* impatience, *Impatiens holstii. – pala* mace (the spice). *– pengantin* k.o. sweet-smelling flower, *Nyctanthes arbortristis. – semangkuk* k.o. plant, *Scaphium spp. – sepatu sungsang* Japanese hibiscus, *Hibiscus schizopetalus. – serdadu* k.o. periwinkle, *Lochnera rosea. – setaman* (*Jv*) a bunch of cut flowers for ceremonial use. *– soka* → ANGSOKA. *– soré* Indian mallow, Chinese bellflower, *Abutilon indicum. – subur* encourage growth. **mengembang-suburkan** to encourage the growth of. *– sungsang* glory lily, climbing lily, *Gloriosa superba. – susu* k.o. plant, pinwheel jasmine, *Tabernamontana divaricata. – tahu* soy cake flower. *– telang* k.o. decorative plant, butterfly pea, *Clitorea ternatea. – telon* (*Jv*) three k.o. flowers for offerings (roses, jasmine, and ylang-ylang or fragrant pandanus, frangipani, and hibiscus) or to avert calamity and ward off devils (magnolia, frangipani, and rose).
 berkembang 1 to flower, bear flowers, be in bloom/blooming. **2** flowered, with a flower pattern/design. *permadani* ~ flowered rug.
 berkembangan (*pl subj*) to flower, blossom.
 mengembang 1 like/resembling a flower, as beautiful as a flower. **2** (on the day after *Lebaran*) to clean and lay flowers on (a) family grave(s).
 mengembang(i) to draw/sew, etc. flowers on, decorate s.t. with flowers/a flower pattern. *Sampul buku ini dikembangkembangi.* The cover of the book has flowers printed on it. *Batiknya dikembangi.* She did the batik in a flower motif.
 kembang-kembangan 1 all k.o. flowers. **2a)** flowers used as decorations. b) artificial flowers, ornaments, decorations, frills, flourishes.
 pengembangan blooming, flowering.
kembang II *demam rabu –* (M) hyperpyrexia (in pneumonia). *– cuping/lubang hidung* to swell up with pride. *– kempis* a) to pant, breathe rapidly and heavily, gasp (after running, etc.). *Hidungnya – kempis.* His nostrils went up and down. b) to inflate and deflate; to expand and contract. c) diastole and systole (of the heart). *Hatinya – kempis.* His heart was pounding (in keen anticipation). d) to be at one's last gasp, at death's door. **mengembang-kempiskan** to make s.t. go up and down. *– kincup* to open and close.
 berkembang 1 to unfold (s.t. previously folded up), open (up), in (full) bloom. *parasutnya tidak* ~ his parachute did not open. *Kuncup bunga ini belum* ~. The flower buds have not opened yet. **2** to expand, rise (as of dough), spread (out). *Adonannya sudah* ~. The dough has risen. *Tubuhnya sedang* ~. Her body is

filling out, i.e., she is becoming a woman. **3** to develop, widen, grow, become better, burgeon, flourish. *Pikiran dan pandangannya mulai* ~. His way of thinking and his views began to develop. *Industri kecil* ~ *dengan pesat.* Cottage industries flourished quickly. ~ *daun telinga saya mendengar* ... I found it unpleasant to hear ... ~ *hatinya* to be elated, be in an expansive mood, be in high spirits. ~ *hidungnya* (*Mal*) to feel proud (after being complimented, etc.). ~ *sewajarnya* to take its course. **4** become animated. *Pembicaraan menjadi* ~. The conversation became animated.
 mengembang [and **ngembang** (*coq*)] to expand, spread open, open up, unfurl, opened up (of an umbrella/book, etc.); → BERKEMBANG. *dada* ~ full-breasted. *Senyumnya* ~. She smiled broadly. ~ *bakung* to let down one's hair. ~ *naik* to clear (of the weather), lift (of mist). ~ *tengkuknya* (his) hair stands on end (from fright); *cp* SERAM.
 mengembangkan [and **ngembangin** (*J coq*)] **1** to unfold, open up. **2** to spread out by unrolling, roll out (a carpet/mat, etc.). **3a)** to spread (its wings); → MEMBENTANGKAN. b) to expand one's business (into other areas). **4** to propagate (a religion, principles). **5** to open (up) (a book/one's eyes, etc.). **6** ~ *hati* to delight, please, cheer up, satisfy. **7** to increase, augment, add to; to develop; to stimulate. **8** to spread, disseminate (news/knowledge, etc.). **9** to set (sails). **10** to stretch out, extend (the arms pointing at s.t.); to spread apart (the fingers). **11** to have (offspring/descendants); to cause regret. ~ *senyum* a smile passed her lips, she smiled. **12** to lift/raise one's hand (to get a ride). **13** to make the hairs on one's neck stand on end (from fright). **14** to raise (flour); *cp* MENGAMBUNGKAN.
 memperkembangkan 1 to increase, augment, add to (one's capital). **2** to develop (a language, etc.). **3** to stimulate (the growth of s.t.).
 terkembang spread out, opened wide, open up. *dengan layar* ~ with all sails set, in full sail. *selama dunia* ~ as long as the world has existed (or, will exist).
 pengembang developer, promoter, propagator. ~ *agama* missionary. *(bubuk)* ~ *roti* baking (powder).
 pengembangan development, expansion. ~ *masyarakat désa* rural community development.
 perkembangan developments, growth, progress, expansion, course of events. ~ *ékonomi* economic development. *dengan* ~ *waktu* over time.
kembang III (*J*) s.t. which is going to happen, the seeds of. *– keributan sudah ada.* The seeds of a riot are already present.
 mengembang to gush/spurt forth/out. ~ *air mata* with tears in (one's) eyes. *dengan darah* ~ covered with blood.
kembar 1 identical, exactly alike; very similar. *Dua orang itu – namanya.* Those two have the same name. *suara –* a similar voice. **2** twin, multiple birth, i.e., triplets, etc. *– dampit/démpét* Siamese twins. *– empat* quadruplets. *– gantung* twins born some days apart. *– lima* quintuplets. *– putra/putri* male/female twins. *– siam* Siamese twins. *– tiga* triplets. **3** matching, corresponding, double, co-. *ketua –* co-chairman. *nomor –* double issue, i.e., two issues of a magazine combined into one volume. *pemerintahan –* two governments administering an area in tandem. *senapan –* double-barreled shotgun; → SENAPAN *pengantin. tali/kawat –/dua/tiga* a rope/cable twisted from two/three strands/coils. *-nya* one's double, the other (in a pair). *Dimana -nya?* Where's the other one (of a pair of items)? **4** (bananas, etc.) grown together.
 berkembar 1 combined into a pair; to form a pair. **2** to match e.o.; uniform (of clothes).
 ngembarin ~ *rupanya* (*J*) to disguise.
 mengembari 1 to complete, fight, stand up against. **2** to match, equal. *Mana boléh kamu hendak* ~ *orang sekaya itu?* How can you possibly want to be the equal of that rich man? **3** (*ob*) to accompany, escort; to assist, help.
 mengembarkan to pair, form a pair or pairs, double, duplicate.
 terkembari *tiada* ~ unable to oppose/match.
 kembaran 1 one's twin (brother or sister). **2** twinning.
 kekembaran twinning.
 pengembaran and **perkembaran** twinning.

kembara mengembara to wander, roam, rove, go from place to place without any special purpose/destination.
pengembara wanderer, traveler, explorer; vagabond. *burung* ~ migrating bird.
pengembaraan 1 wanderings, travel, exploration. **2** (in the *Pramuka* Boy Scouts) biking.
kembatu corn (on skin); → KEMATU.
Kembayat Cambay (in Gujarat, India). *kain* – a fine material produced there.
kemben → KEMBAN.
kembeng (*J*) **ngembeng** (*J*) **1** to have tears in one's eyes. **2** to overflow.
kembera helter-skelter.
kembi → KAMBI.
kembili → GEMBILI.
kembiri I gelded, castrated; → KEBIRI.
kembiri II (*ob*) *buah* – candlenut; → KEMIRI.
kemboja frangipani, a tree with fragrant blossoms often cultivated in cemeteries, *Plumiera acuminata*.
kembok(an) fingerbowl.
kémbol mengémbol to sag/bulge (as of a full pocket).
kembu a fisherman's narrow-necked wickerwork basket.
kembung I 1 puffed up with air, inflated (of a tire), puffy (of cheeks). **2** bloated (of the stomach). *katak* – a frog that inflates like a balloon; → KINTEL. – *kempis* to pant, gasp, inflate and deflate.
mengembung to become inflated/swollen/bloated, puff up.
mengembungkan to inflate, blow up, cause to swell/puff up. ~ *kantongnya* to line one's pockets. ~ *perut* to bloat one's stomach.
pengembungan inflation (of a tire, etc.), bloating (of one's stomach).
kembung II – *padi* container for storing *padi*.
kembung III *ikan* – chub mackerel, *Rastrelliger spp*. *ikan* – *lelaki* k.o. mackerel, *Scomber kanagurta*. *ikan* – *perempuan* k.o. mackerel, *Scomber neglectus*.
kembur (*ob*) *cakap* – (= **berkembur** and **mengembur**) to chatter away; to talk nonsense.
berkembur-kembur to converse, chat, talk (jokingly, etc.).
mengemburkan to chat about s.t.
kemburuan (*ob*) → CEMBURU.
kembut (*M*) open-mouthed plaited bag for carrying fruits, rice, etc., sack-shaped.
keméja (*Port*) western-style shirt; → HÉM. – *buka* sport shirt. – *buntung* → KEMÉJA *puntung*. – *dalam* undershirt. – *menurut pesanan* custom-made shirt. – *puntung* short-sleeved shirt. – *tamasya* sport shirt. – *tutup* dress shirt.
berkeméja to wear a shirt.
kemejan *yu* – k.o. shark, *Rhinobatus thonini*; → YU *kia-kia*.
kemek-kemek (*J*) to eat.
kemekmek (*J*) **1** speechless from fright. **2** have a hard time getting up due to overeating.
kemeli (*ob*) → KAMBELI.
kemelut 1 crisis (of a sickness/fever/political situation), critical stage. **2** crucial. – *naik* turn for the worse. – *turun* turn for the better.
kememek → KEMEKMEK.
kemenakan → KEMANAKAN.
kemendalam (*ob cla*) water jar.
kemendalu → BENALU, BENDALU.
kemendang (*ob*) vibration in the air, mirage, fata morgana.
berkemendang and **mengemendang** to float before the eyes; vaguely visible; *cp* TERBAYANG.
mengemendangkan to delude s.o. with false hopes, trick.
kemendikau watermelon; → MENDIKAI.
kemendir → KEMENDUR.
kemendit *tali* – → KENDIT.
kemendur (*D*) **1** commander. **2** (– *laut*) (*ob*) harbormaster. **3** → KONTE(ROL)IR. **4** → MANDOR.
kemeng (*Jv*) stiff and sore from exertion. *uang* – teacher's overtime bonus.
kemeniran a shrub used as a medicine, stonebreaker, *Phyllanthus niruri*.
kemenis → KOMUNIS.

Kemenjaya (*Skr ob*) Hindu god of love; → KAMAJAYA.
kemenjing k.o. flowering plant, *Garcinia spp*.
kementam (*onom*) booming, thundering.
berkementam to boom, thunder.
kemenyan I benjamin, benzoin, incense. *sudah/belum diasapi* – already/not yet married. *membakar* – *supaya godaan jauh* to burn incense (on Thursday evenings) to ward off evil spirits. *kayu* – the tree producing benzoin, *Styrax benzoin*. – *arab* myrrh. – *hantu* (*euph*) fart.
kemenyan II *akar* – a climbing plant, *Dioscorea oppositifolia*.
kemenyan III → YU *kemenyan*.
kemeresak (*onom*) rustling sound (of dry leaves); → KERESAK.
kemerlap glittering, twinkling; → GEMERLAP.
kemerup to vacillate, flicker.
kemerut wrinkled, shriveled, crumpled, creased; → KERUT I.
kemet (*Jv*) a magic formula, *esp* used to arouse the affections of a member of the opposite sex.
ngemet to apply such a formula.
kemeteran (*J*) to tremble, shudder (with fear); → GEMETAR.
kemi sucking fish, remora, *Echineis naucrates*; → GEMI I.
kemidi (*J*) comedy; → KOMIDI. – *bedés* traveling monkey show. – *ombak* (*J*) and – *puter* merry-go-round.
kemih urine.
berkemih to urinate.
perkemihan 1 urination. **2** urinal.
kemik 1 dented (of metal/cardboard, etc.). **2** short and turned up, pug (of one's nose). *hidung* – pug nose. **3** chapped (of the lips).
kemil I (*J*) *jato* – to be reduced to begging.
ngemil to live by begging.
kemil II (*J*) tucked in. *jatuh* – to visit at the right moment (when people are eating, etc.). *kemal* – to keep on nibbling, eat all the time.
ngemil 1 to snack between meals. **2** to hold (food) in the mouth for a long time.
kemilan 1 snacks, in-between meals. **2** food held in the mouth but not swallowed.
kemilap → GEMILAP.
kemilau flashing (of lightning); → KILAU.
keminting I → KEMIRI.
keminting II k.o. cake.
kemir (*S*) tomato; → TOMAT.
kemiri 1 candlenut, *Aleurites moluccana*. **2** macadamia nut. – *jatuh ke pangkalnya* to return to one's native place.
kemirasi encouragement to plant *kemiri* trees.
kemis I (*A*) **1** five. **2** fifth. (*hari*) – Thursday, the fifth day of the week. – *Putih* Maundy Thursday.
kemis II (*Jv*) **berkemis** and **mengemis(-ngemis)** to beg.
ngemis *orang* ~ beggar.
pengemis beggar.
pengemisan begging.
kemit (*Jv*) – *tubuh* a) garment/ornament given as a love token. b) (*gelang* – *tubuh*) name for a certain type of bracelet. – *hantar* (*ob*) a delegate.
kemladéyan (*Jv*) → BENALU.
kemlaka and **kemloko** (*Jv*) k.o. fruit, Indian gooseberry, *Phyllanthus emblica/glauca*.
kemlakaran (*Jv*) overeaten.
kemlandingan albizzia (tree with edible pods), *Leucaena glauca*.
kemocéng (*C J*) (feather) duster, brush.
kemong (*J/Jv*) a small gong.
kemongkrong (in Purbalingga, Central Java) person skilled in catching wild boars.
kemot → KEMUT I.
kempa press, clamp. *bulu* – felt (used for making hats). *cap* – Indra's thunderbolt or *vajrah*. – *air* hydraulic press. – *anggur* grape press. – *dingin* cold press. – *panas* hot press.
mengempa to press, squeeze (between the hands or knees), clamp. ~ *tangan* to clench the fists.
mengempakan to press, squeeze, compress.
terkempa pressed, squeezed, clamped.
kempaan 1 clamp. **2** clamping. **3** compressed.
pengempa press.

pengempaan compression, pressing.

kempal (*ob*) → KIMPAL.

kempang (*ob*) a river dugout.

kempang-kempis (*ob*) → KEMBANG *kempis*.

kempas I k.o. tree, *Koompassia malaccensis*.

kempas II – *kempis* to pant (from exertion, etc.); → KEMBANG *kempis*.

Kémpei(tai) the Japanese military police during the Japanese occupation.

kempék (*J*) a bag (for holding money, etc.) held under the arm.

kempelang (*J*) → KEMPLANG I.

kempén (*J*) seedless, empty (of nuts, etc.).

kempéng (*Jv*) → EMPÉNG. **mengempéng** to give the breast (to keep a child quiet).

kempés 1 sunken in, hollow (of cheeks). **2** to go flat (of tire, etc.); → KEMPIS I. **3** slack, soft. *Harapannya* –. His hopes vanished into thin air. *Kantongnya* –. He is flat broke; → TONGPÉS. *Perutnya* –. He is very hungry.

sekempés-kempésnya as flat as possible.

mengempéskan [and **ngempésin** (*J coq*)] to deflate, let the air out of.

pengempésan deflating, deflation.

kémpétai (*Jp*) secret police during the Japanese occupation.

kempih → KEMPÉS, KEMPIS I.

kémping (*E*) to go camping.

kempis I 1 shrunken, flat (of stomach). *Pipinya* –. He has hollow cheeks. **2** deflated, sunken in. **3** punctured (of tire); → KEMPÉS.

mengempis to deflate, collapse (of a lung).

mengempiskan to deflate s.t.

pengempisan deflating, deflation, collapse (of a lung).

kempis II (*J*) k.o. bottle wrapped in rattan wickerwork used as container for drinking water.

kempit I large earthenware water jar carried under the arm.

kempit II mengempit to carry/hold under the arm/between the thighs.

kempitan that which is held under the arm; → KEPIT.

kempit III (*Jv*) to sell s.t. on commission.

kempitan that which is sold on commission.

kemplang I (*J*) a blow, stroke, hit (with a stick, etc.).

mengemplang [and **ngemplang** (*coq*)] to beat, strike, hit. *Tambur dikemplang oléh M*. M. beat the drum.

kemplangan blow, hit. *kayu* ~ stick used for beating.

kemplang II (*J/Jv*) a cake made from sticky-rice flour and sugar.

kemplang III (*Jv*) **mengemplang** [and **ngemplang** (*coq*)] **1** to refuse to pay for s.t., pay less than the asking price, fail to pay what one owes. **2** to embezzle.

kemplangan s.t. embezzled.

kempléng (*onom*) twanging sound.

kemplong (*Jv*) k.o. mallet used for softening *batik*.

mengemplong to beat s.t. with that mallet.

kemplu silly.

kempos I (*Jv*) to be(come) deflated; → KEMPÉS.

kempos II kemposan killer.

kempot (*J/Jv*) **1** shrunken (of cheeks from loss of teeth), hollow, sunken in. **2** empty; to be broke, have no money.

kempu a round, lidded wooden box (for *sirih*, etc.).

kempuh (*M*) soft (of food); (*ob*) cooked, done; overripe (of fruit); putrid (of meat/fish).

kempul I (*Jv*) *gamelan* instrument consisting of five or six vertically suspended gongs.

kempul II berkempul-kempul to pant. **terkempul-kempul** panting.

kempunan 1 to be in an awkward dilemma/quandary. **2** to have a strong desire to, want to know. – *hendak mengetahui* wanting to know more about s.t. – *lapar* to have a ravenous appetite. **3** nervous; desperate, at one's wit's end.

kempung I shrunken (of cheeks from loss of teeth with age).

kempung II 1 (*Jv*) abdomen. **2** (= **kempungan**) (*J*) bladder.

kemput (*Jv*) entirely, through. *telah dibaca* – (the letter) has been read through.

kemrekes (*Jv*) feverish.

kemrungsung (*Jv*) to get excited, worry, trouble o.s.

kemu I (*Jv*) **berkemu** to gargle; gargling.

kemu II (*Jv*) **mengemu** to hold s.t. in the mouth; to suck on.

kemucak → KEMUNCAK, PUNCAK.

kemucing → KEMOCÉNG.

kemucup → KEMUNCUP.

kemudi 1 rudder, helm. *patah* – *dengan ebamnya* all hope has been abandoned. **2** steering wheel. **3** leader of a group; highest authority, reins (of government). **4** control. **5** (*ob*) twisted hairs on the crown of a horse's head. – *arah* rudder. – *bundar* whorls of hair on a horse's mane. – *cawat* European-style rudder. – *gantung* underhung rudder. – *kanan* right-hand drive. – *kiri* left-hand drive. – *mékanik* automatic pilot. – *naik turun/tinggi* elevator (of an aircraft). – *sépak* paddle used as a rudder.

berkemudi 1 to have/use a rudder/steering wheel. **2** to hold/be at the helm. ~ *dengan* to conform to, comply with. ~ *dengan haluan, bergilir ke buritan* and ~ *ke rusuk* (*M*) to be henpecked.

mengemudikan 1 to guide, steer, pilot, fly (a ship/car, etc.). **2** to manage, lead, govern. **3** to check, curb, repress, hold back.

kemudian 1 afterward, later, then. *Dia akan datang* –. He'll come later. **2** at a later time, in (the) future. *(di)* – *hari* (in) (the) future, at a later date. *Kamu harus berusaha sekarang supaya hidupmu akan senang* – *hari*. You have to work hard now to have a happy life in the future. *hari/kelak* – a) the future; → BELAKANG *hari*. b) doomsday, Last Judgment, Judgment Day. – *ini* last, finally. **3** – *daripada itu* after that, then, further, next. – *meréka itu pun pulang ke rumah masing-masing*. Then they too went to their respective homes. *keréta-api* –*nya* the next train. **4** (to notice s.t.) eventually. *(yang ter)* – *(sekali)* a) (to follow) behind/in the rear. b) (to greet, etc.) last. *sesal dahulu pendapatan, sesal* – *tiada/tidak berguna* look before you leap.

mengemudiankan 1 to postpone, delay, put off. **2** to put behind/in the rear/at the back. **3** to do s.t. at a later time. **terkemudian** last, final.

pengemudi 1 helmsman. **2** driver. **3** pilot. **4** director.

pengemudian steering, piloting.

kemudu (*Jv*) → KUDU III. *selak* – *kudu* can hardly wait until, very anxious (for s.t. to happen). *Meréka itu* – *kudu melihat musuh besarnya mati*. They can hardly wait to see their great enemy die.

kemuka → MUKA.

kemukus cubeb, *Piper cubeba*.

kemul (*Jv*) blanket, coverlet.

berkemul be covered.

mengemuli to cover, wrap, blanket.

kemulan covered with a blanket.

kemulan (*Bal*) a roofed shrine at each family temple dedicated to the ancestors.

kemumu I 1 a seaweed. **2** (*M C*) taro whose leaves and stem are made into a curry, *Colocasia esculenta*.

kemumu II (*ob*) → KELEMUMUR.

kemuncak apex, peak, top, crest.

kemuncup 1 love-grass, *Chrysopogon/Andropogon aciculatus*. **2** mimosa, *Mimosa pudica*.

kemundir (*coq*) → KEMENDUR.

kemung (*Jv*) k.o. gong which is part of a *gamelan* orchestra; → KEMONG. *mata* – large eyes.

kemungkus *telur* – addled egg.

kemuning I golden, gold-colored.

kemuning II *kayu* – Burmese boxwood, Chinese myrtle, orang jessamine, *Murraya paniculata*; the roots were used by royalty to make yellow dye for crosspieces and hilts of kris sheaths.

kemunting the rose myrtle, *Rhodomyrtus tomentosa*. *rotan* – k.o. rattan, *Daemonorops geniculatus*. – *bukit* a creeper, *Anplectrum divaricatum*. – *Cina* pink or white periwinkle, *Catharanthus roseus*.

kemut I mengemut and **(ter)kemut-kemut 1** to throb (of pulse/chicken anus/vagina, etc.). **2** stagger, sway, swing, oscillate, move from side to side.

kemut II mengemut to suck on s.t. with a chewing motion.

kemutan k.o. hard candy.

kemutul and **kemutun** a tree with hard and tough wood whose sap is used as a medicine against scruf, etc., *Cratoxylon formosum*.

Kén I (*Jv ob*) an ancient title for male or female nobles: His/Her Honor, e.g., – *Arok* Arok, the first king of Singosari. – *Dédés* a) k.o. dessert made from corn. b) Ken Arok's wife.

kén II (*Jp*) → KABUPATÉN.

kena 1 (get) hit (by), knock against. *Bagian muka mobil itu péyok – batu besar.* The front of the car was dented, hit by a large rock. **2** on target. –*!* Bull's eye! Right on target! **3** exact, accurate, precise, to the point. *Jawabannya tak pernah –.* His answers are never to the point. *tidak –* a) evasive. b) not applicable. c) didn't hit home. **4** infected, get/suffer from s.t. – *penyakit batuk kering* suffering from pulmonary tuberculosis. **5** affected by, be subject to, not excluded. – *demam* get a fever. – *pajak rumahtangga* subject to property tax. *yang –* the injured party. *yang – wajib militér* the enlistee(s). **6** to come into contact with, touch, strike. – *cat basah* touched the wet paint. – *listrik* got an electric shock. **7** becoming (of clothes). **8** effective (of medicine). **9** be realized/fulfilled, come true. *Ramalannya hampir –.* His prediction almost came true. **10** [+ *verb* (*Mal*)] have/forced to do s.t. *Pegawai itu – pergi ke kampung.* Government employees have to go into the *kampungs.* **11** (+ *noun, verbal root* or *di-/ke-*) be/get hit/struck/affected by s.t. (usually) unpleasant/bad. (for examples see below). **12** (*J coq*) to be allowed, permitted. – *apa?* What's the matter? Why ... ?; → KENAPA. – *air* to get wet. – *batunya* to get into trouble. – *berapa?* how much did it cost you? – *biaya* chargeable. – *bogem mentah* to get punched. – *bom* to get hit by a bomb. – *bubu* to get picked up (in a police raid). – *cakup* to get picked up by the police. – *cap* to be labeled/tabbed. *Ia – cap kolot.* He was labeled old-fashioned. – *cukai* dutiable. – *dakwa* to be accused. – *damprat* to get scolded. – *denda* to be fined. – *di hati* to catch the interest of, interest. – *emas* to be bribed. – *digasak* to be beaten up. – *fitnah* to be slandered. – *flu* to get the flu. – *gaét* to get tricked. – *garuk* to get stolen, get pulled in (by the police). – *gebrak* to get hit hard by s.t. bad. – *gebuk* to get beaten up. – *gempa* to get hit by an earthquake. – *getahnya* to have s.t. bad happen to one because of s.o. else's actions, to be left holding the bag. – *gogoh* to get snatched. – *gulung* to be rounded up by the police. – *gunting* to be devalued (of currency). – *gusur* to get trampled on, be dumped on. – *hama* to be infected (by a contagious disease). – *hantam* to get hit. – *hujan* to get caught in the rain. – *hujan dan panas* to be weather-beaten. – *hukum* to be affected by the law. – *imbas* to be affected. – *jaga ronda* to be on night watch. – *jaring* to be rounded up (by the police). – *jebak* a) get trapped. b) get tricked. – *jelatang* to be lascivious. – *jéwér* to be reprimanded. – *kécék* to be taken in, tricked. – *kécoh* to be gypped, swindled. – *kepotong* (*J*) to cut o.s. (by accident). – *kesrémpét* to be grazed. – *ketuk* to be rapped (on the head). – *kibul* to be tricked. – *kicu* to be deceived. – *kili* to get worked up/stimulated. – *kritik* to be criticized. – *kuliah* got a lecture. – *lecah* to have one's reputation ruined. – *listrik* to get an electric shock. – *loteré* to hit the lottery. – *marah* to be reprimanded. – *matahari* to get sunstroke. – *muka* to be disgraced. – *pajak* taxable, assessable, subject to tax. – *panas* to be exposed to the heat. – *pandang* to be stared at. – *peluru* to be shot. – *penyakit* to get sick. – *persis* direct hit. – *péstol* to be shot. – *piat* (*Mal*) to get a whipping. – *polisi* to get stopped at a red light. – *pukul* to get hit. – *rasuk* to be possessed (by a spirit). – *razia* to be rounded up (by the police). – *rongrongan* to be bled dry. – *sadap* to be bugged (of the telephone, etc.). – *sakal* to be tortured. – *sangka* to be under suspicion. – *sapu* to be pulled in (by the police). – *sembur/semprot* to get a scolding, be chewed out. – *sénsor* to be censored. – *serangan jantung* to have a heart attack. – *sétan* possessed. – *sirep/ilmu penyirep* to fall under a spell, be put to sleep by a spell. – *skors* to get suspended. – *sodok* to get pushed out of one's job. – *sogok/sorong/suap* to be bribed. – *sunat* to be devalued (of money). – *tampar* to get slapped. – *tanah* to get mud on it. – *tangkap* to be arrested. – *tebas* a) to be fired from one's job. b) to get stabbed. – *témbak* a) to be shot. b) (in Medan) to be cheated by a customer (not paid for a drink, etc.). – *témbakan meriam* to be hit by gunfire. – *tilang* to get a (traffic) ticket. – *tipu* to get cheated. – *todong* to be held up a knife-/gun-point. – *tutup* get closed down. –

umpan fooled, tricked. – *undi* a) to be drafted. b) to draw lots. – *usik* to be annoyed.

sekena-kena(nya) (*saja*) do s.t. at random, without further ado.

berkenaan 1 (~ *dengan*) concerning, regarding, with regard to; applicable to. **2** (~ *dengan*) on the occasion of. ~ *dengan ulang tahun kelima* on the occasion of the fifth anniversary. **3** to agree, be in complete agreement. *Kedua orang muda itu sudah* ~. The two young men are in complete agreement with e.o. **4** to be connected to e.o., related to e.o.

berkena-kenaan to be connected/related to e.o. *Perkataan kedua orang itu selalu* ~. The stories of those two men are always closely related to e.o.

mengena 1 to hit/strike the target, touch. *Témbakannya ~ harimau.* His shot hit the tiger. **2** to produce the desired result/effect, accomplish the task. *Jerat yang dipasang itu sudah ~.* The trap set up produced the desired result. **3** to be correct/right, hit the mark. *Rupanya témbakanku ~.* It seems that my guess was right. **4** relevant, to the point.

kena-mengena 1 to be connected with. *tidak ~* irrelevant, not to the point, have no connection (with). *tidak ~ akan* heedless, without being concerned about. **2** uncompromising.

mengenai 1 to hit/strike the target. *Senjata itu sangat berbahaya karena dapat ~ sasarannya pada jarak yang jauh.* That is a dangerous weapon because it can hit the target from far away. *dikenai* to be liable/subject to (taxes, etc.). *Penerbit minta agar penyalur tidak dikenai pajak.* Publishers have asked that distributors not be liable to pay taxes. *dikenai perampasan* subject to forfeiture. **2** to touch, come into contact with. **3** to concern, concerning, as for, in case of, regarding, in; to refer to. ~ *urusan ini, anda tak boléh turut campur.* You should not interfere in this matter. **4** (*M coq*) to have sexual intercourse with.

mengenakan 1 to dress, put/try on (clothes, etc.), be dressed in. *Dia ~ seragam hitam-hitam.* He was dressed in a pitch-black uniform. ~ *cincin pernikahan* to put on a wedding ring. **2** to fasten, secure [a (seat)belt, etc.]. *Kenakan sabuk pengaman!* Fasten your seat belts! **3** to levy/assess (taxes) on, charge. *Barang-barang itu dikenakan béa masuk.* An import duty was levied on those goods. ~ *bunga* to charge interest. **4** to put under (arrest). *Ia dikenakan tahanan kota/rumah.* He was put under city/house arrest. ~ *tahanan kepada* to put s.o. in jail. **5** to apply, consider (a legal provision) applicable. *dikenakan terhadap* to be applied to. **6** to impose, inflict (a fine, etc.). *Berapa harga yang dikenakan untuk satu ...?* What's the price of one ...? *dikenakan harga yang berlebihan* to be overpriced. *dapat dikenakan hukuman* subject to (a punishment of). ~ *denda* to impose a fine. ~ *hukuman* to condemn. *setiap negara yang ~ sanksi ékonomi* any country that imposes economic sanctions. *dikenakan sénsor* subject to censorship. *dikenakan wajib* to be obliged to, have the obligation to. **7** to hit, strike, kick.

mengena-ngenakan to deceive, fool, trick.

terkena 1 hit, struck, affected, exposed to, got, received, be subject to. *Désa itu akan ~ proyék normalisasi.* The villages will be affected by the normalization project. ~ *buku buluh* to have s.t. bad happen. ~ *getahnya* hoist by one's own petard, caught in one's own trap. ~ *skorsing* to be suspended (from one's job). ~ *kesukaran* to get into trouble. ~ *panas* exposed to the heat. ~ *peraturan* subject to the regulations. ~ *peringatan pertama* to be given a first warning. *yang ~ kejahatan* crime victim. **2** applied, inlaid, set (into), attached (to). *Beberapa butir intan ~ pada hulu kerisnya.* Several diamonds were set into the head of his kris.

pengenaan 1 application. **2** imposition. **3** assessment, levying. ~ *pajak* tax assessment. ~ *di belakang* additional (tax) assessment. ~ *di muka* advance levy.

perkenaan hit, strike.

kéna (*ob*) you.

kénaf (*E*) kenaf, *Hibiscus cannabinus,* a plant of the mallow family grown for its fiber.

kenaga k.o. bird, bronze-winged jacana, *Metopidius indicus.*

kenal and – *akan/dengan/kepada/pada/sama* **1** to recognize, recall, remember. *Saya tidak – akan suara A.* I didn't recognize A's voice. *tidak – capai* untiring. *tidak – malu* shameless, impudent; → *tidak* TAHU *malu. tak – tak sayang* and *karena tak – maka tak sayang/cinta* unknown, unloved. *tak – takut* intrepid. **2** to have had the experience of, have ever been. *éngsél pintu yang tak pernah – minyak pelumas* a door hinge that has never been greased. **3** to know, be familiar/acquainted (with). *Kita semua – akan perjuangan Bung Karno, bukan?* We all know about Bung Karno's struggle, don't we? *Sudah –?* Do you know him? *belajar –* to get to know, make s.o.'s acquaintance. *– secara dekat* to know closely. *tidak – jerih dan payah* untiring, tireless, indefatigable. *tidak – malu* insensitive, unfeeling.

berkenalan ~ *dengan* to meet, get to know, get acquainted (with). *Wanita berusia 27 tahun ingin ~ dengan pria bujangan/duda* (newspaper ad). A 27-year-old woman would like to meet a bachelor or widower. ~ *pribadi dengan* to know s.o. personally.

berkenal-kenalan to be acquainted with e.o., know e.o., get to know e.o.

mengenal [and **ngenal** (*coq*)] **1** to know, be familiar with, remember, recognize. *tak ~* to spare no (pains). *tidak ~ kawan dan lawan* not to know friend from foe. *tidak ~ jerih dan payah* indefatigable. *tak ~ kompromi* uncompromising. *tak ~ mata huruf* illiterate, uneducated. *tak ~ menyerah* unconquerable. *tak ~ takut* fearless, undaunted. *tidak dikenal* unrecognizable, unknowable. *orang tak dikenal* unknown persons. *lebih dikenal dengan nama ...* better known as ... *yang lebih dikenal dengan nama ...* more widely known as ... **2** to get to know, make the acquaintance of.

kenal-mengenal to be acquainted with e.o., well known to e.o.

mengenali to know, identify, recognize. *Para penumpang langsung ~nya.* The passengers recognized him right away. *Kami kurang ~ tulisannya.* We couldn't recognize his handwriting.

mengenalkan and **memperkenalkan** [and **ngenalin** (*J coq*)] **1** to introduce s.o., make s.o. known (to), recommend. *Perkenalkan dulu, saya Parman.* Let me introduce myself, I'm Parman. ~ *dirinya* to introduce o.s. **2** to acquaint s.o. with s.t., introduce s.o. **3** to inform, announce, notify.

pemperkenal (*infr*) introducer.

terkenal (well-)known, famous, recognized, acknowledged. ~ *akan* to be known for. *Kotagedé ~ akan kerajinan péraknya.* Kotagede is known for its silverwork. ~ *jahatnya* notorious. *tidak ~* infamous. **seterkenal** as well known as. **keterkenalan** reputation, fame.

kenalan 1 acquaintance, friend. **2** associate. **3** (*coq*) to meet, get to know. *Anda mau ~ sama dia?* Do you want to meet her?

kenal-kenalan circle of acquaintances/friends.

kekenalan 1 known, well-known. **2** found out about.

pengenal 1 identification, identifying marks/characteristics. **2** recognition. **3** (*M*) remembrance, memory, idea, notion. *ilmu ~ penyakit* diagnostics. *tanda ~* mark/sign of recognition. *zat ~* test, reagent.

pengenalan 1 introduction, introducing, making acquainted. **2** identification.

perkenalan 1 introduction, introductory. *harga ~* introductory price. *nomor ~* complimentary issue (of a magazine). **2** acquaintanceship.

kenalpot → KNALPOT.

kenan I agreement, approval; pleasure (to do s.t.)

berkenan 1 (~ *akan/pada*) (*esp* of God or of honored people) to find/take pleasure in, have the pleasure of, take delight in, approve of, agree to, be willing to. *umat memohon kepada ... untuk ~ memberikan kekuatan.* The community asked .. to please give them the power (to ...). **2** to please, suit, give satisfaction, be to one's liking. *Dia tinggal memilih perusahaan mana yang ~ di hatinya.* All that is left is for him to choose which company is to his liking. **3** to design.

memperkenankan to think fit, approve (of), permit, allow, take pleasure (in). *Tidak diperkenankan masuk!* No admittance!

perkenan(an) permit, license, approval, agreement, permission, consent.

kenan II birthmark, birth mole, strawberry mark, etc.

kenang (= **terkenang** *akan* and **terkenangkan**) to think of; to be mindful of; to remember, recollect.

mengenang(i) to remember, hold in (loving) remembrance, think back to, recall, cast one's mind back to, reminisce about, commemorate.

mengenangkan 1 to make s.t. think (of), remind s.o. (of). **2** to call to mind, remember.

terkenang suddenly remember, s.t. comes to mind.

terkenangkan long for, crave, have an unforgettable memory of.

kenangan 1 remembrance, recollection, reminiscence. *perjalanan ~* a sentimental journey. ~ *masa muda* childhood memories. **2** souvenir, keepsake, souvenir, memento. **3** certificate.

kenang-kenangan 1 remembrances, reminiscences, memoirs. **2** ideals (of the vanished past).

pengenang reminder, s.t. that reminds one of s.t.

pengenangan 1 remembering. **2** memorial service.

kenanga I ylang-ylang, a tree of the custard-apple family, *Canangium odoratum*, with fragrant greenish-yellow flowers whose oil is used in perfumes; → MINYAK *kenanga*.

kenanga II (*burung –*) bronze-winged jacana, *Metopidius indicus*.

kenantan *ayam –* a snow-white rooster; → KINANTAN.

kenap (*D*) *méja –* a small table.

kenapa (*coq*) **1** why. **2** what is the matter with?, what happened to?; → KENA *apa*.

kenari I k.o. tree, kenari-nut tree, cananga, *Canarium commune*, native to the Moluccas but now also found in Java. *– belanda* almond, *Amygdalus communis*; → BADAM I.

kenari II *burung –* canary, *Serinus canarius*.

kenari III (*ikan –*) banded wrasse, barred thick-lip, *Hemigymnus fasciatus/melapterus*.

kenas salted shellfish/scallops.

kencan (*Jv*) **1a)** a date/appointment, *esp* for a social engagement with s.o. of the opposite sex. **b)** a date (s.o. of the opposite sex with whom one has a date). **2** (*euph*) (to have) sex; → BERKENCAN. *dengan – asmara* sexual encounters.

berkencan 1 to have/go on a date. *teman ~* one's date/sexual partner. **2** to have an appointment (with s.o.). **2** (*euph*) to have sexual intercourse.

mengencani to have sexual intercourse with. *Ibunya dicumbu dan dikencani lelaki.* A man fondled and had sex with his mother.

kencana (*Skr*) gold. *– Dwipa* a poetic name for Sumatra. *– wingka* (*Jv*) always standing up for one's child/sweetheart.

kencang I 1 stiff (of breeze). *angin –* a stiff breeze. **2** strong (of tide). **3** quick, fast, speedy (of a car/s.o. running, etc.). *berlari (dengan) –* to run fast. **4** taut (of rope). **5** tight. *dipegang –* held tight(ly). **6** loud(ly). *Radio selalu distél –.* The radio was always played loudly.

mengencang 1 to become/go faster. **2** to become taut/tight.

mengencangi to tighten, make taut.

mengencangkan 1 to tighten, draw tighter, make taut, strain. ~ *ikat pinggang* and ~ *tali kursi* to fasten/tighten one's seatbelt. **2** (= **memperkencang**) to hasten, speed up, accelerate, quicken, expedite.

terkencang fastest, quickest, etc.

kekencangan 1 speed, velocity. **2** tension, tenseness (of a situation).

pengencang s.t. which tightens/makes tighter.

pengencangan tightening.

kencang II (*onom*) *– kencung* to jingle (of money), clank, bang (of an areca nut pounder); → GOBÉK), clink (of glasses).

kencar *terkencar-kencar* **1** nervous, agitated. **2** hasty, in a hurry.

kenceng → KENCANG I.

kéncéng I (*C*) (bow) drill.

kéncéng II (*C*) (iron or copper) frying pan with handles.

kencerang-kencering → KENCRANG-KENCRING.

kénci name of a *ceki* card.

kencing 1 (*air –*) urine; → AIR *seni*, KEMIH. **2** to urinate. *seperti maling kesiram air –* like a thief whom s.o. has poured urine on, i.e., not very happy, with a sour expression. *guru – berdiri, murid – berlari* the teacher urinates standing up and his pupils urinate running, i.e., pupils are apt to carry the results of their teaching to extremes. *– batu* renal calculus, kidney stone. *– darah* hematuria. *– gula/manis* diabetes. *– nanah* gonorrhea.

berkencing to urinate.

mengencingi 1 to urinate on. **2** (*vulg*) to have intercourse with, fuck.

terkencing urinate involuntary, piss in one's pants.

terkencing-kencing 1 to keep on urinating involuntarily. 2 scared stiff.

kencingan (*sl*) illegal gasoline delivered to a gas station.

pekencingan and **pengencingan** 1 bladder. 2 urinary tract, urethra.

kencit → TUYUL.

kénco (*Jp*) regent.

kéncong I (*M*) 1 awry, crooked, askew. 2 dishonest.

    mengéncong *berjalan* ~ to walk not in a straight line.

    mengéncongkan ~ *bibir* to curl (one's lip). ~ *perkataan orang* to twist/bend s.o.'s words.

kéncong II k.o. plant, *Ellipeia nervosa. akar* – woody climber, *Melodorum/Fissistigma manubriatum. asam* – k.o. plant, *Nicolaia speciosa.*

kencrang-kencring (*Jv onom*) jingling (of coins).

kencréng (*onom*) jingling sound.

kencung (*onom*) rumbling (noise).

kéncung → KÉNCONG I.

kencup → KUNCUP I.

kencur (*Jv*) reddish-brown root of a palm-like plant, greater galingale, *Kaempferia galanga*, of the ginger family used as a spice or medicine; → CEKUR. *(masih) (ber)bau* – wet behind the ears, young and inexperienced, green. *partai bau* – the new party. *jamu beras* – traditional medicine made from a mixture of uncooked rice, *kencur*, lime, brown sugar and tamarind; used as a tonic and digestive. *perawan* – a girl who has not menstruated yet and is therefore still unmarriageable.

kendaga a shell-encrusted ornamental casket.

kendak (*J*) mistress, lover, illicit sexual partner of a married man or woman; → GENDAK.

    berkendak to have an affair.

    memperkendak to (try to) make s.o. one's mistress/lover.

    kendakan lover.

kendal (*Jv*) a tree, clammy cherry, *Cordia obliqua*, whose timber is used for rafters, etc.

kendala 1 obstruction, hindrance, obstacle, difficulty. 2 constraint.

    berkendala constrained, hindered.

    mengendalakan 1 to obstruct, hinder, impede. 2 to constrain, restrict.

kendali I (*Jv*) 1 (horse's) bit, bridle, reins. *tali* – bit, bridle, reins. 2 (to be at the) helm/reins (of government). 3 guidance, influence. *proyéktil* – guided missile. *di bawah satu* – (*mil*) under one unified command. ~ *jauh* remote control.

    berkendali 1 controlled, guided. 2 to have a bridle/reins.

    mengendalikan [and **ngendaliin** (*J coq*)] 1 to bridle, curb, (keep in) check, restrain. 2 to (keep under) control (of one's emotions). *dikendalikan dari jauh* remote control. 3 to manage, guide.

    terkendali(kan) controllable. *tidak* ~ *(lagi)* uncontrollable, impracticable.

    pengendali manager, controller, attendant. *dam* ~ check dam. (*aparat*) ~ *huru-hara* riot control [PHH]. ~ *kerusuhan* riot control. **sepengendali** under common control.

    pengendalian control, management, command, restraint, check. ~ *banjir* flood control. ~ *diri* self-control/restraint. ~ *hama* pest control. ~ *harga* price controls. *Pusat* ~ *Krisis* Crisis Management Center. (*aparat*) ~ *kelahiran* birth control. (*aparat*) ~ *massa* [dalmas] crowd control (unit). ~ *mutu* quality control. ~ *nafsu* moral restraint. ~ *sungai* river control.

kendali II (*burung* –) Asian palm-swift, *Cypsiurus balasiensis.*

kendan *batu* – obsidian.

kendana (*M ob*) **mengendanai** not to lose sight of s.o.

kendang I (*Jv*) a conical-shaped drum resting on crossbeams and beaten with both hands; used to direct or conduct a group of players.

    berkendang to play that drum.

    kendangan drum music.

kendang II ream (of paper).

    kendangan *kertas* ~ a ream of paper.

kendang III (*ikan* –) k.o. fish, (spotted) scat, *Scatophagus argus.*

kéndang (*M*) *kain* **kéndang-kéndang(an)** everyday clothes, *esp* a *seléndang.*

kendara (*Skr*) **berkendara** to drive.

    mengendara driving, riding. *kenyamanan* ~ *kelas satu* first-class riding comfort.

    mengendarai 1 to drive (a vehicle). 2 to ride in (a vehicle), ride (a horse, etc.).

    mengendarakan to drive (a vehicle) for s.o.

    kendaraan 1 vehicle, conveyance. *pajak* ~ road tax. 2 car. ~ *berat* trucks and buses. ~ *bermotor* motorized vehicle. ~ *hantu* small public vehicles, such as *colt*s, driving after sunset without headlights. ~ *jenis IV* small passenger vehicles, such as *bajaj*s, *helicak*s, etc. ~ *kebal* armored car; → KERÉTA *kebal*. ~ *merta* motor hearse. ~ *niaga kategori I* small trucks, such as pickups, delivery vans, etc. ~ *panser* armored vehicle. ~ *pendarat* landing vehicle. ~ *perintis* [rantis] (police) cruiser. ~ *tempur* [ranpur] armor. ~ *udara* aircraft. ~ *umum* public transportation. ~ *yang mogok* a disabled car. **berkendaraan** to have/use/ride in a vehicle. *3 jam dengan* ~ *mobil* 3 hours by car.

    pengendara 1 driver, rider. ~ *bécak* pedicab driver. ~ *mobil* motorist. ~ *pendahulu* advance (motorcycle) escort, outrider. ~ *sepéda* cyclist. 2 horseman.

    pengendaraan drive (of a vehicle), driving (a vehicle).

kendat (*Jv*) end; break, interruption.

    ngendat to hang o.s.

kendati(pun) 1 even if, (al)though, notwithstanding. 2 let alone, not to mention. *kendati begitu* nevertheless.

kendéka (*J*) *kayu* – k.o. mangrove, *Avicennia officinalis*, whose timber is used for house poles, etc.

kendel – *kandel, jerih ketindih* (*Jv*) fortune favors the bold.

kenderi I *saga* – a small gold-weight.

kenderi II (*Tam*) *kayu* – a tree used for its timber, *Adenanthera microsperma.*

kendi I earthenware water carafe with or without a nozzle. – *maling* carafe that fills from the bottom, not through the spout.

kendi II (*burung* –) 1 whimbrel, *Numenius phaeopus.* 2 Eurasian curlew, *Numenius arquata orientalis.*

kendil (*Jv*) earthenware or copper rice cooker. *menegakkan* – to keep the home fires burning.

kendiri → SENDIRI I. **kendirian** → SENDIRIAN.

kendit 1 (*S*) a line or ring running in a circle around s.t. – *bumi* (*coq*) equator. 2 (*Jv*) a loose-hanging belt, often of silver chain or of coins.

kendo (*Jv*) loose (not tight), slack, relaxed. *stél* – to relax.

kéndo (*Jp*) stylized form of fencing using wooden poles.

kéndong → GÉNDONG. **mengéndong** to carry in a fold of a sarong or waist belt.

kendor 1 slack(ened) (of a rope/trade), deflated (of a tire), relaxed, flagged (of zeal/interest), flabby (of cheeks/character), loose, lax (of market), dull, listless (of market), sprung (of a spring). *Rezeki meréka sudah* –. Their earnings have slackened off. *Talinya* –. The rope is slack. *Ibu dari dua anak yang tak* – *semangat belajarnya.* A mother of two children with an unflagging zest for studying. *Makin tua badannya makin* –. The older he gets the flabbier he gets. *Pérnya* –. The spring has lost its elasticity. 2 to abate, die down (of a storm/wind), diminish, decrease. 3 lower (in price). 4 (to become gradually) slower (as of a horse's trot). 5 running slow (of a watch); → LAMBAT. – *lima menit* five minutes slow.

    berkendor-kendor 1 to slacken. 2 to relax.

    memperkendor to loosen, slacken.

    mengendor 1 to slacken, slow down (of speed). *Kecepatan kendaraan lalu* ~. The car then slowed down. 2 to loosen, become loose, become slack.

    mengendorkan 1 to loosen, slacken, lessen, diminish, reduce, relax. ~ *ikat pinggangnya* to loosen one's belt. ~ *semangat* to discourage. ~ *tekanan musuh* to reduce the enemy's pressure. ~ *urat-urat* to relax the nerves. 2 to lower (the volume). ~ *radio* to make a radio less loud; → MENGECILKAN.

    kekendoran slackness, looseness, relaxation.

    pengendor relaxant.

    pengendoran 1 relaxation. ~ *ketegangan* detente. 2 slowing down, slackening. – *hati* lax, listless, apathetic.

kenduduk *ubi* – k.o. tuber, *Dioscorea alata.*

kendung(an) k.o. tree, *Symplocos laurina*.
kendur → KENDOR.
kenduri (*Pers/Hind*) feast on a religious occasion, ritual feast given on a special occasion in s.o.'s honor. – *apam* feast on the occasion of Muhammad's ascension to Heaven (usually in the month of *Rejeb*). – *arwah* feast to mark s.o.'s death. – *empat puluh hari* feast held on the 40th day after s.o.'s death. – *.kendara* feasts of all kinds. – *kunut* feast held in the fasting month. – *maulud* feast held to celebrate the Prophet's birthday. – *meniga/menujuh/meratus hari* feast held on the third/seventh/hundredth day after s.o.'s death. – *moréh* feast held in the mosque during the fasting month (at breaking the fast or after night prayers). – *selamat* feast of thanks for the successful completion of some work, after s.o.'s safe homecoming, etc.
  berkenduri to have/hold/celebrate such a feast.
  mengendurikan 1 to give such a feast. **2** to use s.t. for a *kenduri*. *Daging itu pun dikendurikan.* The lamb was also used for the *kenduri*.
kéné (*Jv*) here, this place.
kenéh and **kenék** (*D*) **1** driver's assistant (of a taxi/bus, etc.). **2** assistant (to a carpenter/plumber, etc.).
kenéker (*D*) marble(s).
  berkenéker to play marbles.
kenés (*Jv*) flirtatious, coquettish.
  ngenés to flirt.
  kekenésan flirtatiousness.
kéng 1 bark, howl, yelp (of a dog). **2** call, cry (of a deer).
kéngkang bowlegged; → KANGKANG I.
  mengéngkang bowlegged. *berjalan ~* to walk bowlegged.
kéngkap → KINGKAP.
kengkaréng various species of hornbill; → KANGKARÉNG. – *hitam* black hornbill, *Anthroceros malayanus*. – *perut putih* Asian pied hornbill, *Anthroceros albirostris*.
kéngkéng mengéngkéng 1 to yelp (of a dog). **2** to whimper, whine.
kéngsél (*E*) → KÉNSÉL. *kena –* cancelled.
Kénia Kenya.
kenidai various species of trees belonging to the *Bridelia* family, such as – *babi, Bridelia stipularis*. – *hutan, Bridelia pustulata*, etc.
kenikir 1 a green with a sharp taste similar to parsley and belonging to the family of Compositae, *Cosmos caudatus*. **2** marigold, *Tagetes erecta*.
kening 1 *bulu –* eyebrows. *angkat –* wink, look of mutual understanding. *terangkat –* about 7:30 to 8:00 a.m. *belum terangkat –nya* before 7 a.m. **2** (*M*) forehead. *pelipatan –* the temples. *beradu –* to face e.o. *berkilat –nya* handsome. *jilah –* elated, in high spirits. *sempit –* touchy, easily offended.
kenini → KININE.
kenohong (*ob*) k.o. leprosy.
kenong (*Jv*) large horizontal gong.
kenop I (*D*) **1** knob, button, switch. **2** shirt button.
kenop II (*D*) bud of a flower.
kenop III rubber club, truncheon.
Kenop IV [Kebijaksanaan Nopémber] the devaluation of the rupiah on November 15, 1978.
kenor → KENUR.
kenot (*D*) → KENOP II.
kénsél (*E*) **mengéngsél** to cancel, bump (airline passengers off a flight).
kental 1 condensed (of milk). **2** thick (of a liquid/soup), viscous, solidified. **3** strong (of coffee/religious beliefs). **4** thick, strong (of accent). *Dialék Jakartanya –.* He had a thick Jakarta accent. **5** close (of friends). *sahabat –* a close friend.
  sekental as thick/strong/close as.
  mengental to congeal, coagulate, clot, curdle, condense.
  mengentalkan to thicken/clot/curdle/condense s.t.
  kekentalan 1 thickness, viscosity. **2** coagulation, congealing.
  pengental s.t. used for curdling, coagulating, thickening.
  pengentalan congealing, coagulating, condensation, curdling, thickening, concentration.

kentang (*ubi –*) potato, *Solanum tuberosum*. – *giling* mashed potatoes. – *goréng* a) fried potatoes. b) potato chips; → CRIPING *kentang*. – *jawa* k.o. herb, *Coleus tuberosus*. – *ongklok* broken boiled potatoes. – *puré* mashed potatoes.
kentar I goldsmith's weight.
kentar II (*Port IBT*) to sing (psalms).
kentara 1 visible, clear (to sight/mind), obvious, exposed, revealed, apparent, discernible. *tak –* disguised. **2** striking, conspicuous.
  mengentara to become visible.
  mengentarakan to show, give evidence of, allow s.t. to be seen/known/obvious.
kentel → KENTAL.
kenténg → GENTÉNG.
kenténg-teter (*Jv*) body repair technician; → TUKANG *ketok*.
kentit (*J*) **1** to hide s.t. **2** to steal s.t.
kentong and **kentung 1** (*onom*) resounding sound. **2** gong.
  mengentongi to signal by a warning device.
  kentongan and **kentong-kentong** a village alarm consisting of a bamboo or wooden tube which is knocked with a stick to produce warning signals.
kéntot → ÉNTOT.
kentrang (*J onom*) – *kentring/kentring/kentrung* strumming/plucking sound.
kentrung (*Jv*) singing accompanied by drumming.
kentung → KENTONG.
kentus (*Jv*) **1** a small frog that inflates and raises its forelegs when approached. **2** puffed up.
kentut I 1 gas, fart, flatus. **2** to pass gas, fart. *mengeluarkan –* to let out a fart.
  berkentut and **mengentut** [and **ngentut** (*coq*)] to pass gas, fart.
  mengentuti [and **ngentutin** (*J coq*)] **1** to fart on (s.t.). **2a)** to fool, cheat, deceive. **b)** to laugh at/off, disregard.
  mengentutkan to fart (intentionally) s.t. out.
  terkentut(-kentut) to fart suddenly and unintentionally.
kentut II *daun –* tree whose leaves are used for constipation, etc., *Poederia foetida*.
kenung 1 (*Jv*) a gong. **2** (*onom*) resounding sound of a gong.
kenup I (*D*) (collar) button; → KENOP I.
kenup II rubber club, truncheon.
kenur (*coq*) rope; rough yarn; fishing line.
kenut → KENUP II.
kenya (*Skr Jv*) **1** girl, maiden. **2** virgin.
Kénya Kenya.
kenyal 1 yielding but firm, tough, rubbery (of flesh/meat). **2** elastic, rebounding, pliable, pliant, flexible, easily bent/twisted. **3** soft (of one's voice).
  sekenyal as elastic/soft as.
  mengenyal to be elastic/resilient/rubbery/springy/rubbery.
  kenyalan elasticity.
  kekenyalan rubberiness, elasticity, flexibility, resilience, resiliency, plasticity.
  pengenyalan elasticity.
kenyam mengenyam 1 to taste, toy with s.t. with the lips. **2** to experience, undergo, have (a crisis/experience, etc.); to enjoy (a luxury), go (to school). *Dia ~ pendidikan SMA swasta.* He went to a private high school.
  mengenyami and **mengenyamkan** to experience, undergo.
kenyang 1 full, sated, gorged, not hungry anymore. **2** saturated, wet, soaked. *Tanah itu hendaknya disiram dengan air hingga –.* The soil should be watered until saturated. **3** filled to bursting. *Kasur ini sudah –.* The mattress is completely stuffed (with kapok). **4** to have had enough/one's fill (of). *Dia sudah – dengan cercaan demikian.* He's had his fill of such slander. *sudah – makan kerak* to have had lots of bitter experiences.
kenyang-kenyangnya *tak ~* insatiable.
  sekenyangnya 1 one's fill, to one's heart's content. *Makanlah ~!* Eat as much as you can! **2** as full as.
  sekenyang-kenyangnya to one's heart's content.
  mengenyangi 1 to eat one's fill of s.t. **2** to fill (one's belly). *Negara ketigalah sebenarnya yang ~ perut orang-orang di negara maju.* It's actually a third-world country that fills the bellies of people in that developed country.

mengenyangkan to satiate, satisfy one's appetite, fill s.o. up; filling (of food). ~ *perut* to eat one's fill. *Makanan itu* ~! That food is filling!

kekenyangan 1 fullness, repletion, satiation, satiety. 2 saturation. 3 (*coq*) too full.

pengenyang s.t. filling.

kenyap (*ob*) → KECAP, KENYAM.

kenyat-kenyit and **kenyat-kenyut** 1 winking, flashing (of lightning). 2 twitching (of the lips), throbbing, pulsating.

kenyi(h) (*J*) 1 sickly, susceptible to illness, gets sick easily. 2 lack of courage, cowardliness.

kenyir craving for food, desire to eat.

kenyit spasmodic (movement of the lips or eyelids); summer lightning.

mengenyit to wink.

mengenyitkan to wink (one's eye).

terkenyit-kenyit winking, flashing; twitching.

kenyitan wink.

kenyot and **kenyut** sucking movement.

kenyot-kenyot to move one's lips spasmodically.

mengenyot [and **ngenyot** (*coq*)] to suck, nurse.

mengenyoti (*pl obj*) to suck.

kenyotan rubber/plastic nipple for milk bottles.

kéok I (*onom*) cackling sound made by chicken (when afraid or caught).

berkéok-kéok, berkéokan and **mengéok** to cackle.

kéok II (*coq*) defeated.

mengéokkan to defeat.

kéong 1 snail; → SIPUT I. *berjalan lambat seperti* – to go at a snail's pace. *rumah* – snail's shell. *strategi* – Fabian strategy, i.e., slow but sure. - *emas* k.o. gastropod, golden (apple) snail, *Pomacea canaliculata*. - *laut* tiger cowry, *Cypraea tigris*. - *terompét* false trumpet shell, *Syrinx aruanus*. 2 spiral.

kep (in acronyms) → KEPUTUSAN.

kép I (*D*) percussion cap.

kép II (*D*) crest (of rooster).

kép III → KAPTÉN I.

kepada → PADA. 1 to (usually in front of pronouns and animates). *mengirim surat* – ... to send a letter to ... *meminjamkan uang* – ...to lend money to ... 2 from. *meminjam* – to borrow from. 3 to(ward). *berbuat jahat* – ... to do evil to(ward). 4 of, for. *Saya tidak ingat* – *tuan*, I don't have any recollection of you. *dia teringat* – ... he suddenly was reminded of ... *suka* – to care for, be fond of. 5 with. *marah* – to be angry with. *Saya kenal* – *nya*. I'm acquainted with him.

kepah I edible bivalve mollusks of various kinds: - *gading*, *Meretrix meretrix*, *Anodon sp*. - *gurap/kurap*, *Asaphis deflorata*. - *mérah* k.o. bivalve, *Mactra sp*.

kepah II (*Mal*) 1 to suck on s.t. (sugarcane, etc.) in the mouth. 2 to hold (tobacco, etc.) in the mouth. 3 to mumble one's words.

kepai I terkepai-kepai 1 clutching (as of one drowning or an infant), waving one's hand(s) (to departing traveler), fluttering (of flags). 2 struggling to walk (because one's leg is numb); → KAPAI.

kepai II *udang* – a small dirty-white shrimp, *Mysis*.

kepak wing (of flightless birds). – *pintu* leaf of a door.

berkepak 1 to have wings; winged. ~ *dua* folding/double doors. *pintu* ~ *dua* folding doors. 2 (= **berkepak-kepak**) to flap the wings.

mengepak-ngepak to flap the wings.

mengepak(-ngepak)kan to flap (the wings).

terkepak-kepak to flap the wings spasmodically.

kepakan flapping (of the wings).

képak I mengépak to carry on one's hip.

képak II (*ob*) **mengépak-ngépak** to flutter; fluttering.

képak III terképak broken, bent back (of a branch).

kepaksa (*Jv*) forced; → TERPAKSA.

kepal 1 lump, clod (of earth), a coagulated lump (of cooked rice). *beberapa* – *nasi* some lumps of rice. 2 counter for things at can be held in (or, gathered by) the fistful; fistful, handful. - *tangan* fist.

sekepal a fist-/handful of. ~ *nasi kunyit* a fistful of yellow rice. *tanah* ~ a handful of earth. ~ *tanah* a clod of earth. ~ *menjadi*

gunung, setitik menjadi laut a) many a little makes a mickle. b) to make a mountain out of a molehill. *diberi* ~ to be struck with the fist.

berkepal-kepal several lumps; in lumps/fistfuls; clotted (of cream).

mengepal to clutch/grasp/grasp (in the hand), knead.

mengepal-ngepal to roll up into small lumps (for swallowing).

mengepal(kan) 1 to clutch, grasp. 2 to clench (one's fists). 3 to knead.

terkepal *tangan* ~ balled-up fist.

kepalan 1 (~ *tangan*) fist. 2 s.t. rolled up into small lumps.

kepala I (*Skr*) 1 head (of the body). *batok* – skull. *batu* – a) skull. b) (humble term) head. *beras* – the best-quality whole rice. *berhitung* – to do mental arithmetic; → *hitung* MENCONGAK. *guru* – principal, head master. *keras* – to be hardheaded, stubborn. *luar* – by heart. *pajak* – (*ob*) head/capitation tax. *pening/pusing* – dizzy, giddy. *ringan* – quick-witted, smart, witty. *sakit* – to have a headache. *(arah) ke* – cranial. *garuk-garuk* – to scratch one's head. *meletakkan* – a) to go to sleep. b) to pass away, die. *memenggal* – to behead, decapitate. *menjual* – *ke dalam kompeni* to join the army, enlist. *penjual* – mercenary, soldier of fortune. *tergadar* – very shy/bashful. *telah dua* –*nya* diplopia, seeing double (from drinking too much). *ular* – *dua* a) k.o. snake, *Cylindrophis rufus*. b) a hypocrite. *untuk keselamatan* –*nya* to save one's head (or, one's own neck). 2 head, representation of a head (in painting, etc.). – *raja* (*ob*) postage stamp (with a picture of the Queen of the Netherlands on it). 3 head, leader, chief, manager. – *daérah* district head. – *jawatan* office manager, department head. – *kampung* village head. – *séksi* section head. 4 head, brains, mind. *banyak lagak dan besar cakap, tetapi* –*nya kosong* he pretends to know a lot and talks big, but his head is empty (i.e., he knows nothing). –.– *botak* a) bald persons. b) experts, professors. 5 (*ob*) head, person; → ORANG. *Tiap-tiap* – *mendapat catu beras 200 gram sehari*. Each person got a daily rice ration of 200 grams. 6 chief (executive), head. – *Daérah* [KDH] Provincial (and, Regional) Chief Executive. – *juru masak* head chef. – *negara* head of state. 7 head, the top/principal part of s.t. – *santan* coconut cream. – *surat* letterhead. – *susu* cream. 8 first digit in a number. *usia* – *tujuh* (to be in) one's seventies. – *nomor télpon* the first part of a telephone number, prefix. 9 top-quality. *beras* – top-quality rice. – *sama berbulu (hitam) pendapat (hati) berlain-lain* (so) many heads/men, (so) many minds. *diberi bahu hendak* – to want more and more, be insatiable. *tak tentu* – *ékornya* a) a vicious circle. b) fat, corpulent. *sakit* – *panjang rambut, patah seléra banyak makan* (to have a) suppressed longing for s.t. – *air* edge of flood water. – *angin* empty-headed; frivolous. **berkepala angin** to be empty-headed. – *bagian* section head. – *bahu* the part of the shoulder that joins the arm. – *ban pinggang* belt buckle. – *batok* a) stupid. b) crew cut (haircut). – *batu* obstinate. **berkepala batu** to be stubborn. **kekepala-batuan** stubbornness. – *benam timbul* roundhead countersunk (screw). – *béngkél* plant manager. – *berat* numbskull. – *berita* news headline. – *besar* a) conceited. b) hydrocephalus. – *biarawan* abbot. – *biarawati* abbess. – *Burung* Bird's Head, i.e., an area in western Irian Jaya, formerly called Vogelkop. – *busung* hydrocephalus. – *désa* village headman. – *dinas/dines* department head. – *dingin* and *dingin* – calm, cool-headed. – *dua* to make the best of both worlds. – *gudang* warehouse keeper. – *jaga* commander of the guard. – *jaksa* attorney general. – *jara* buttermilk. – *jorong* (*M*) hamlet chief. – *kain* large panel on a sarong of a different pattern. – *kampung* village headman. – *karangan* title/heading of a newspaper article. – *keluarga* [KK] head of a family; family. *200 KK* 200 families. – *keréta-api* locomotive. – *kerja* foreman; → MANDOR. – *kodi(an)/perkodian* the top-most piece of clothing, i.e., the best, in a parcel of clothes. – *lakon* principal actor, lead. – *negeri* a) (*ob*) capital of a country. b) head of state. c) (in West Sumatra) headman of a collection of hamlets, comparable to a district head in Java. – *paha* groin. – *perahu* stem (of a prau). – *Perwakilan Tahta Suci Vatikan* Nuncio, Papal Ambassador. – *pulau* a) the upstream part of an island. b) the highest part of an island. – *pusing* a) dizzy. b) not know what to do next.

– putik ovary/stigma (of a plant). *– regu* team leader. *– ringan* intelligent. *– roda* end of an axle. *– santan* cream of coconut milk. *– sari* anther (of a plant). *– sarung* large panel in a sarong of a different pattern. *– sekolah* principal. *– selubung* casing head. *– staf* (army) chief of staff. *– stasiun* station master. *– suku* ethnic chief. *– sumur* wellhead. *– surat* letterhead. *– susu* cream. *– tahun* beginning of the year. *– tiang* capital (of a column) *– tongkat* handle of a cane. *– udang* stupid. *– wanu* (in the southern Celebes) village head.

sekepala-sekepala individually; one by one *– adat →* KEPALA *suku.*

berkepala to have a head/title/leader, etc.; (en)titled. *~ besar* to be arrogant/conceited. *~ dingin* to be coolheaded. *orang ~ dua* s.o. lacking firm loyalties, available to the highest bidder. *ular ~ dua;* → ULAR *kepala dua.*

mengepala to act as head/leader, etc.

mengepalai to head, become/be the head/leader, etc. of, be in charge of.

mengepalakan 1 to appoint s.o. as head/leader, etc. 2 to drive/steer (an elephant/vehicle, etc.). 3 (in soccer) to hit the ball with the head; → MENYUNDUL. 4 (*ob*) → MENGEPALAI.

kepala II in various animal names. *– kambing* giant helmet (shell), *Cassis cornuta. – timah* k.o. fish, blue panchax, *Aplocheilus panchax.*

kepalang 1 (= *alang –*) (too, very) little, inadequate, insufficient, not so (large/high, etc.). *bukan (alang) –* not a little/few, too much, very, extraordinary, extremely. *Bukan alang – pembelanjaannya.* His expenses were very high. *kagét bukan –* a bad fright. *bukan – cantiknya* very pretty. 2 (= *– tanggung*) defective, insufficient, inadequate, not enough, halfhearted, with little enthusiasm, halfway, by halves, imperfectly, it's not enough to. *Kalau hanya seribu rupiah –.* A thousand rupiahs is not enough. *Perjalanan tak jauh lagi, – buat dibawa bermalam pula.* It's not much further; it's not worth it to stay (here) overnight. 3 (= *sudah –*) gone too far, too late (now), it cannot be helped; → *barang sudah* TE(R)LANJUR. *sudah – jauh* it has gone too far, it is too late now (to do anything about it). *– ajar →* KURANG *ajar. – basah* it's too late to go back now, to have gone too far. *– tanggung* inadequate, insufficient, incomplete.

kepam musty, moldy, stale, shopworn.

kepang (*pohon –*) k.o. tree, *Aquilaria malaccensis* from the bark of which rope is made. *akar –* a plant, *Linostoma scandens.*

képang I (C?) braid, pigtail. *– jagung* cornrows. *– képot* crumpled, rumpled; topsy-turvy, crisscross.

berképang braided, plaited. *Rambutnya ~.* Her hair was braided.

mengépang to plait, twine (rope), braid (hair). *~ rambutnya* to braid one's hair; to wear one's hair in braids.

terképang braided.

képangan 1 braiding. 2 braided, plaited.

képang II → KIPANG I.

képang III (*Jv*) woven bamboo; → KUDA *képang.*

kepangseg (*J*) to fall down in a sitting position.

kepar *ikan –* a small perch-like river fish, striped tiger wandid and other fish, *Pristolepis fasciatus, Polycanthus hasselti.*

képar (*D*) twill.

keparas → KEPRAS.

keparat I (*A*) 1 atheist, agnostic. 2 dammit!, damned. 3 rogue, scoundrel. *hidup –* to lead a miserable existence.

keparat II (*A*) → KAPARAT I.

kepau → KEPAR.

kepaya → PEPAYA.

kepayang a tree, *Pangium edule* whose seeds cause dizziness; → PUCUNG II. *gasing –* a top shaped like the seeds of this tree. *mabuk –* a) intoxicated (from eating these seeds). b) (*ob*) madly in love. *macam makan buah –* (*Med*) to be madly in love.

kepécong (*M*) cramp in the calf.

kepék I a small, flat *sirih* bag, betel pouch; → KEMPÉK.

kepék II (*Jv*) notes for cheating on a test, a crib.

ngepék to cheat on a test, do schoolwork using a crib.

kepékan crib, notes for cheating.

képék 1 dented. 2 flat (of the nose); → PÉSÉK.

képé-képé *ikan –* various species of fish, *Chelmon spp., Chaetodon spp.* and other species.

kepel I → KEPAL.

kepel II (*Jv*) k.o. tree, kepel apple, *Stelechocarpus burahol.*

kepelaga → KAPULAGA, KEPULAGA.

kepénak (*Jv*) comfortable, nice, pleasant; → ÉNAK.

kepéncong (*M*) nut of the *kepayang* tree, *Pangium edule;* → (*buah*) KELUAK.

képéng an obsolete half-cent coin with a square hole in the center; → KEPING.

kepéngén (*J*) and **kepéngin** (*Jv*) to want, desire; → INGIN.

kepépét (*J*) → PÉPÉT.

képer I → KÉPAR.

képer II → KIPER I.

keperancak (*ob*) k.o. flower.

kepergok (*Jv*) → PERGOK.

kepet (*Jv*) k.o. fan.

mengepeti and **ngepeti** to fan s.t.

mengepet-ngepetkan to shake s.t. around, manipulate.

képét I (*J*) 1 feces which sticks to one's anus after defecating. 2 (= ngépét) not cleaning one's anus and buttocks with water after defecating. 3 asshole (a term of abuse).

képét II (*J/Jv*) fin (of a fish).

kepetang (*M*) yesterday; → KEMARIN.

kepialu a severe headache. *demam –* typhoid/malaria, etc. fever.

kepiat waste matter, (coconut) refuse.

kepik I 1 dented, with a dent in it. 2 (*geol*) swale.

kepik II (*Jv*) pest, various insects harmful to crops. *– hijau* k.o. pest, green stink bug, *Nezara viridula. – mérah* k.o. pest, *Podops vermiculata. – téh* tea pest, *Helopeltis spp.*

kepil alongside, close by, side by side.

berkepil-kepil side by side (of boats/cars, etc.).

mengepil to come alongside, moor, go side by side, hug (the shoreline).

mengepilkan to moor, bring alongside (the quay), berth (a ship).

terkepil brought alongside, moored.

pengepil mooring (*mod*).

kepincut (*J*) *– (dengan)* to be swept off one's feet (by); → KEPINCUT (under pincut).

kepinding (*M*) bedbug, *Cimex rotundatus.*

berkepinding lousy, full of bedbugs.

kepindis → KEPINIS.

keping 1 (a flat and thin) piece, sheet, slice, chip, fragment, splinter, sliver, shard. *karét –* rubber sheet. *– biji* (*bot*) cotyledon. *– kayu* wood chip. *mesin –* coin(-operated) machine. *uang –* a half-cent coin. *se– hari, seonggok untuk nanti* a stitch in time saves nine. 2 coin (to pay a fare/use in a machine, etc.). 3 counter for flat and thin or wide objects. *se– album* an album. *se– gelas* a sliver of glass. *se– surat* a letter. *dua – papan* two boards. *empat – kertas* four sheets of paper. *se– tanah* a lot, plot, parcel (of land). *se– uang logam* a coin.

berkeping-keping in pieces/slices/fragments/tatters, etc.

mengeping to cut into slices (of bread/cake), cut into chips (of wood); to cut off slices, split (a piece of wood).

kepingan splinter, fragment, sliver, shard.

pengepingan splintering.

kepingin (*Jv*) → INGIN. *– muntah* to feel nauseated. *– tahu* curious.

kepinis ironwood used for tops and tool handles, *Sloetia elongata;* → TEMPINIS.

kepinjal (*Jv*) tick, flea (on dogs, etc.), *Pulex.*

kepiran → KAPIRAN.

kepiri *kain –* napery.

kepis (*Jv*) a fish basket.

kepit squeezed under one's arm/between arm and side, pressed.

berkepit *~ tangan* hand in hand, arm in arm.

berkepitan hand in hand.

mengepit 1 to carry s.t. squeezed under one's arm, hold s.t. under the armpit. *~ daun kunyit* to praise s.o. *~ kepala harimau* to frighten s.o. 2 to hold s.t. with two fingers. 3 to clench/squeeze/pinch/clasp (s.o. close to one).

mengepitkan to crimp, clench.

terkepit squeezed/pressed under the armpit/between two fingers.

kepitan 1 s.t. held under the armpit. 2 a squeeze, clasp, hold. 3 clip, clamp, pincers.

pengepit a clip.

kepiting sea crab; mangrove crab. – *bakau* mangrove crab, *Scylla spp.* – *batu* a) rock crab. b) closefisted miser. *sebagai* – *batu* miserly, stingy. – *berkaki mérah* red-legged crab. – *dasar* sand crab. – *kaki* and – *kalangkari* a poisonous crab species with four legs on each side of the body. – *kenari/kepala* coconut crab, *Birgus latro*. – *laut* sea/estuarine/grapsid crab, *Chasmagnathus granulata* and other species; → RAJUNGAN. – *putih* white crab.

keplak (*Jv*) a slap in the face.

　mengeplak to slap in the face.

képlék (*J*) one's arms hurt from hard work.

keplengek → PLENGEK.

keplését (*Jv*) skidded, slipped.

keplok (*Jv*) sound of a clap; slap with the hand; to clap one's hands; → KAPLOK I, TEPOK I. *tukang* – person in the claque.

　berkeplok to clap, applaud.

　mengeploki to clap for s.o.

　mengeplokkan to slap s.t. (against s.t. else).

　keplokan clapping; applause.

kepodang (*Jv*) → KEPUDANG.

kepoh I and kepok mengepohkan to parry/ward off and push aside.

　terkepoh pushed aside.

kepoh II → KEPUH II. – *keték* k.o. plant, *Sterculia javanica*.

képol to go away; → LIGAT.

kepompong cocoon, imago, chrysalis.

　terkepompong ~ *benar* very happy.

keponakan (*J*) nephew, niece; → KEMANAKAN.

képot 1 crumpled up, all creased; → KÉPANG *képot*. 2 disheveled, untidy.

Kepprés [Keputusan Présidén] Presidential Decision/Decree.

　mengkeppréskan to be created by Presidential Decision/Decree.

keprak (*Jv*) castanets, clacks (used in *wayang* performance).

　mengeprak to tap s.t.

kepras (*Jv*) cutting shrubbery, pruning.

　mengepras to cut back, prune.

　keprasan pruning.

képrét I (*J*) spray.

　mengépréti to spray (with water).

　mengéprétkan to spray s.t.

képrét II (*J*) mengéprétkan to beat, slap.

　képrétan slap, blow.

keprok I → JERUK *keprok*.

keprok II → KEPLOK.

kepruk I (*Jv*) *tukang* – bodyguard, hired strong-arm man.

　mengepruk 1 to hit. 2 to smash to pieces, destroy.

kepruk II → KEPROK I.

képsék [kepala sekolah] head of a school.

képsen (*E*) caption

kepudang various species of orioles, shrikes, cicada birds; black-naped oriole, *Oriolus spp.* – *hutan* black-headed/dark-throated oriole, *Oriolus xanthonotus*. – *sungu* shrike, cicada bird, *Coracina spp.*

kepuh I 1 bulging. 2 billowing (of sails).

　mengepuh bellying out, billowing (out) (of sails), swelling (because full).

　pengepuh *layar* ~ royal sail.

kepuh II mengepuh glistening white (of sails/graying hair).

kepuh III a tree whose timber is used to make crates, skunk tree, *Sterculia foetida*.

kepuk I 1 round rice bin of bark. 2 fish basket. 3 (*M*) rice barn; → KAPUK II.

kepuk II a dent; dented.

　mengepuk(kan) to (in)dent.

　kepukan indentation.

　pengepukan indenting.

kepul I 1 thick cloud (of smoke), billowing smoke, smoke cloud. 2 closely packed; clotted; → KEBUL.

　berkepul(-kepul) and mengepul(-ngepul) [and ngepul (*coq*)] 1 billowing, to give off excessive smoke, smoking, smoky; to steam. *Nasi masih mengepul*. The rice is still steaming. *kopi yang mengepul panas* steaming-hot coffee. *Tungku dapurnya bisa mengepul kembali*. There's enough money now to keep the

household running (or, to make ends meet). 2 to be closely/densely packed.

　mengepulkan to blow/puff out (clouds of smoke). *bisa ~ asap dapur* to keep the home fires burning.

　kepulan puff (of smoke).

　pengepulan puffing (of smoke).

kepul II pengepul numbers runner.

kepul III (*Mal*) a quarter of a *cupak*.

kepulaga → KAPULAGA.

kepulesan (*Jv*) to sleep soundly; → PULAS III.

kepunan *emas* – gold leaf.

kepundan 1 lava, ashes (from mountain craters). 2 (*lubang* –) mouth/crater of a volcano.

kepundung (*Jv*) a tree whose fruit is like a sour-tasting *langsat*, *Andropogon nardus* and *Baccaurea dulcis*.

kepung – *dan cari* (*mil*) cordon off and search.

　berkepung (to stand/sit, etc.) in a circle around, surrounding.

　mengepung to encircle, surround, invest (a fort, city, etc.). *tukang* ~ a beater (who drives game). *dikepung wakul binaya/buaya mangap* (*Jv*) to be in danger.

　terkepung 1 surrounded, encircled. 2 under siege, beleaguered.

　kepungan encirclement.

　pengepung s.o. who encircles/surrounds/besieges.

　pengepungan encircling, siege.

kepurun (*bubur* –) sago-gruel.

keputrén → PUTRI I.

kepuyuh quail; → PUYUH I.

kepuyuk (*M*) cockroach.

kepyar (*Jv*) lumpy (of rice).

kepyur (*Jv*) mengepyur to sprinkle (on).

　mengepyuri to sprinkle on.

　mengepyurkan to sprinkle s.t.

　kepyuran sprinkle, s.t. sprinkled.

ker- also see entries beginning with kr-.

kera I monkey, macaque, *Macacus cynomolgus*. *cengkam/genggam* – a firm grip/grasp. – *dapat bunga* and – *diberi kaca* to cast pearls before swine. – *menegurkan tahinya* to wash one's dirty linen in public. – *menjadi monyét* and *seperti* – *dengan monyét* it is all the same, it's six of one and half a dozen of the other. *sebagai/seperti* – *kena belacan* to be very restless. *sebagai/seperti* – *dapat canggung* to cling to s.o. (in distress). – *abu-abu* → KERA *hitam*. – *belanda* proboscis monkey. – *hantu* (in North Celebes) tarsier, *Tarsidiae*. – *hitam* a black long-haired and long-tailed monkey, silver langur, *Presbytis cristata*; → LUTUNG.

kera II *burung* – large green-billed malkoha, *Rhopodytes tristis*.

kera III *periuk* – pitcher plant, *Nepenthes spp.*

kerab → AKRAB I.

kerabang (*ob*) eggshell.

kerabat (*A*) 1 close relationship, affinity 2 member of the family, relative, (nearest) relatives; kinship, consanguinity. *karib/kaum/sanak* – relatives, family. – *dekat* next of kin. – *jauh* distant relative. 3 (*geol*) suite.

　sekerabat (closely) related.

　berkerabat to be allied (with), be closely related (to).

　kekerabatan 1 kinship. ~ *keluarga* family gathering. 2 (*ling*) genetic relationship.

kerabik turn apart, ripped.

　mengerabikkan to tear apart, rip.

kerabin → KARABIN.

kerabit → KERABIK.

kerabu I (*M*) a type of vegetable salad of finely cut cucumbers with salt, red pepper, dried fish and crawfish or shrimp.

　mengerabu to prepare *kerabu*.

kerabu II thin (gold) earring.

keracak I to jump for joy.

keracak II fast-sailing (of a boat), making headway.

keracak III → KRÉCÉK.

keracap a bamboo/wooden musical instrument in the *makyung* performance.

keraéng a Bugis royal title; → KRAÉNG.

kerah I 1 (*cla*) forced labor, corvée. 2 conscript, summon. *juru* – a) class village beadle/head assistant. b) (= pengerah).

berkerah mobilized, conscripted.

mengerahkan 1 (*cla*) to order, command, give orders to. 2 to summon, assemble, call together, convene. 3 to mobilize, conscript, call up. 4 to direct (to a definite point). 5 to station (soldiers, etc.), commandeer. 6 to commit, call upon the service of. 7 to exert (all efforts), devote (one's energies to). 8 to focus (one's attention on). 9 to raise (funds).

kerahan 1 summons. ~ *negeri/raja* (*cla*) summons, drafting by the state for compulsory services. 2 mobilization. 3 conscript(s). 4 committed (troops).

kerah-kerahan (*cla*) palace employees charged with correspondence with commanders, etc.

pengerah recruiter; summoner, public/town crier; foreman. *gung* ~ (*cla*) town crier's cymbal. ~ *tenaga* personnel recruiter.

pengerahan mobilization, conscription, commandeering, commitment (of troops), raising (funds). ~ *angkutan* commandeering of vehicles. ~ *tenaga* recruitment.

kerah II (*D*) collar. *memakai* – *dan dasi* to wear a collar and tie. – *biru* blue collar. – *putih* white collar. **berkerah putih** to be (a) white-collar (worker). – *lembék* soft collar.

berkerah with/wearing a collar.

kera(h)i k.o. small gherkin.

kerai bamboo blinds.

berkerai with blinds.

kerait berkerait-kerait creaky.

kerajang *emas* – gold leaf.

kerajat I (*A ob*) the fringe of hair a bride gives up at marriage. *memutuskan* – to cut off this fringe at marriage.

kerajat II (*A ob*) tax, revenue, tribute, toll.

kerak I 1 (– *nasi*) scorched rice adhering to the pot, rice crust. *balik* – to remarry the wife one has divorced previously. *keras-keras* – changeable, vacillating. *keruh-keruh* – turbid. *membesarkan* – *nasi* to spend money unnecessarily. *sudah biasa makan* – to have had a hard life. *sudah kenyang makan* – to have had a lot of experience. 2 crust (of bread, etc.). 3 rind (of cheese). 4 encrustation. – *besi* iron slag. – *bumi* earth's crust. – *coklat* a sweet made from chocolate and rice crust. – *gendar* rice chips. – *kaki* corn (on the foot). – *roti* bread crust. – *telor* a k.o. of Jakarta pizza made from rice crust, chicken eggs, shredded coconut, dried shrimps, vegetables, etc. – *terusi* verdigris.

berkerak to have a crust, be (en)crusted. *Pakaiannya* ~. His clothes are encrusted (with dirt).

mengerak to become crusty, form a crust.

terkerak 1 encrusted. 2 to want to drive a hard bargain, to the very end.

kerak II (*onom*) scratching sound.

kerak III – *basi* various k.o. reed warblers, *Acrocephalus spp.*

kerakah I k.o. ship, carrack.

kerakah II k.o. leaf monkey, *Presbytes frontata*?

kerakal (*Jv*) gravel, pebble, stones, road metal. *hukuman* – sentence to stone-breaking, hard labor.

mengerakali to metal (or, apply a layer of gravel to) (roads).

kerakap 1 old dry *sirih* leaves (symbol of a hard life). 2 (*sirih* –) the larger (and coarser) *sirih* leaves. *bagai* – *tumbuh di (atas) batu* (*hidup enggan mati tak mau*), *hidup seperti* – *di atas batu* and *macam* – *tumbuh di batu* (to have a) hard life.

kerakeling (*D*) cracknel.

kerak-kerik (*J onom*) 1 croaking sound of frogs. 2 (*onom*) snoring sound.

kerak-keruk (*onom*) cracking/crunching sound. *bersumpah* – to swear by all that's holy.

keram I (*D*) 1 cramp(-iron). 2 to have a cramp.

keram II (*D*) **mengeram** 1 to imprison, incarcerate, lock up; → **ERAM I**. 2 to stay (at home). 3 to be (in prison), be locked up. *Dia* ~ *di penjara*. He's in jail.

keraman s.o. or s.t. locked up/kept inside. *sapi* ~ cows kept in the barn.

pengeraman imprisonment.

kerama (*Skr*) curse, magic spell.

keraman (*Jv*) 1 traitor; treachery. 2 rebel; rebellion.

keramas (*Jv*) 1 shampoo. *bedak* – a rice-flour cosmetic. – *kutu* hair wash to get rid of head lice. 2 to wash after sexual relations.

berkeramas to shampoo o.s.

mengeramasi to shampoo s.o. else's hair.

keramat (*A*) 1 holiness, sanctity, holy (place/grave/tree, etc.). *tempat yang* – a holy site. 2 numinous, miracle-working (of people/ trees/graves/krises, etc.), have supernatural powers. *ditimpa* – slain by unseen powers for committing sacrilege at a sacred spot. *minta* – to ask for a blessing. 3 shrine. 4 a saint.

mengkeramatkan to treat s.t. as holy, consider sacred, respect highly.

kekeramatan holiness, sacredness.

keramba 1 woven basket for carrying or storing live fish. 2 raising fishes in cages in the water.

kerambangan (*Jv*) floating in the water.

kerambil (*Jv*) coconut, *Cocos nucifera*; → **KELAPA**. – *cungkil* copra.

kerambit a small sickle, curved knife.

keramboja (*Skr? M*) watermelon, *Citrullus vulgaris*; → **SEMANGKA I**.

kéramik (*D/E*) ceramics. *ahli* – ceramist. – *batu* stoneware.

kéramikus (*D*) ceramist.

kerampagi (*Tam ob*) 1 razor blade. 2 pocketknife.

kerampang 1 perineum. 2 crotch.

keramunting the rose myrtle, *Rhodomyrtus tomentosa*.

keran I (*D*) water faucet, tap, cock, spigot. *air* – a) running water. b) tap water. – *léding* water faucet. – *sumbat* stopcock

keran II (*D*) crane, derrick. – *laut/terapung* floating crane (in harbors).

keran III portable earthenware brazier for charcoal, chafing dish.

kerana (*mostly Mal*) → **KARENA**.

kerancang I *emas* – gold leaf.

kerancang II *baju* – open jacket; → **KERAWANG**.

keranda (*Skr*) a (bottomless Muslim) coffin.

kerandang k.o. decorative plant, karanda, *Carissa carandas*.

kerang 1 generic name for cockles, oysters, clams, mussels. 2 shell. – *bulu* ark shell, *Anadara antiquata*. – *darah* (blood) cockle, *Anadara granosa*. – *hijau* green mussel, *Perna viridis*. – *mutiara* pearl oyster, *Pinctada spp.* – *raksasa* giant clam, *Tridacna spp.* – *tahu* reticulate Venus shell, *Periglypta reticulata*. 3 (*ob*) *batu* – (coral) rock; → **BATU** *karang*. *pinggan* – a large plate.

berkerang to fish/look for shells/shellfish.

kerangan gate valve.

kerang-kerangan 1 crustaceans, mollusks. 2 path of loose stones/ rocks/bricks, etc.

pe(r)kerangan 1 cluster of shells. 2 all k.o. shellfish, crustaceans.

kérang (*IBT*) tortoise shell.

kerangga → **KERENGGA**.

kerangganggang → **GERANGGANG**.

kerangka 1 skeleton, carcass; hulk. – *harimau* carcass of a tiger. 2 frame, framework, structure. *dalam* – in the framework/context of. 3 sketch, draft, blueprint, outline, plan; → **BURAM**. *peristiwa yang masih* – an event still in the planning stages. – *hidup* a living wreck. – *jenazah* mortal remains. – *kapal* a) ship's frame. b) shipwreck. – *karangan* outline of a story. – *kekuatan* power structure. – *landasan hukum* legal framework. – *pembakaran* grate for grilling. – *pesawat* fuselage. – *rumah* house frame. – *waktu* time frame.

mengerangkai to provide with a framework, etc.

terkerangka on the drawing board.

pengerangkaan framing.

kerangkai a tree whose hard wood is used for making wheel rims, hoe handles, etc., *Quercus rajah*.

kerangkang I perineum, the fork of the body; → **K(EL)ANGKANG**, **KERAMPANG**.

kerangkang II → **SEMUT** *kerangkang*.

kerangkéng (*J/Jv*) 1 cage with iron bars (for tigers, etc.). *mobil* – *anjing pelacak* a (police) car containing a cage for tracking dogs. 2 prison cell. 3 playpen. 4 (Custom's) quarantine. *memasukkan ke dalam* – to quarantine (goods).

berkerangkéng with a cage/playpen in it.

mengerangkéng to limit.

mengerangkéngkan to quarantine (goods).

terkerangkéng jailed.

kerangkéngan → KERANGKÉNG.

kérang-kéroh and **kérang-kérot 1** higgledy-piggledy, in disarray, topsy-turvy, crisscross. **2** conniving, scheming. **3** irregular (in shape).

kerang-kerung (*onom*) sound produced by hitting tin cans, clanging noise, clattering.

kerangking(an) (*ob*) → KERANGKÉNG.

kerani (*Hind*) **1** clerk. **2** dispatcher (of a trucking company).

keranjang (rough) basket, hamper. *bola* – basketball. *mata* – s.o. who is always chasing after women. ~ *arang* basket from which charcoal is sold. ~ *kotoran/sampah* wastebasket, trash can. – *pakaian* hamper. – *sampah* wastebasket.

berkeranjang-keranjang by the basketful.

mengeranjangi to put in a basket.

keranjat (*ob*) → PERANJAT.

keranji a tree whose timber is used as building material, *Dialium spp.* – *asam* tree with sour fruit, *Dialium indicum*. – *beledu* k.o. tree, *Dialium patens*. – *lutung/tembaga* k.o. tree, *Dialium platysepalum*. – *mawa/umbut* k.o. tree, *Dialium patens*.

keranta (*ob*) louse found on (nearly) dead bodies.

kerantong and **kerantung** and – *buluh* a bamboo beaten on as an alarm.

kerantungan a small *durian* variety, *Durio oxleyanus*.

kerap I 1 – *kali* and **kerap-kerap** often, frequent(ly), many times; habitual, common. **2** closely woven (of texture). **3** frequency; repeatedly, frequently.

sekerap as frequent(ly) as.

mengerap to become more frequent.

mengerapi to repeat, do many times.

mengerapkan to weave closely.

kekerapan frequency.

kerap II (*onom*) **kerap-kerap** and – *kerup* crunching, gnawing, grating sound (of biting on a cucumber/gnawing on a bone/nibbling on a nut, etc.).

kerapai → GERAPAI.

kerapak-kerupuk (*J onom*) sound of fruits falling to the ground.

kerapan (in Madura) bull races; → KARAPAN *sapi*.

kerapis → KEROPAS-KEROPIS.

kerap-kerap and **kerap-kerup** (*onom*) munching noise.

berkerap-kerap and berkerap-kerup to make a munching noise.

kerapu grouper, *Epinephelus spp.* – *kayu* k.o. fish, *Serranus tauvina*.

keras I 1 hard, solid, firm, (*phys*) solid state. **2** (work) hard, unyielding, resolute, persistent, persevering, untiring, unflagging. *berusaha* – *untuk maju* to work hard for advancement. **3** adhering/clinging/sticking to. *berpegang* – *pada adat-adat lama* to cling to old traditions. **4** drastic, sharp. *Harga-harga barang naik* – . Commodity prices rose sharply. **5** critical, severe, serious (of an illness). *sakit* – seriously ill. **6** intensifying, escalating, mounting. **7** merciless, cruel, cold-blooded. *sikap yang sangat* – *a* merciless attitude. **8** harsh. *bersikap* – to take a harsh attitude. **9** strict, rigid, rigorous. *dilarang* – strictly forbidden. **10** close, secure. – *dijaga* securely/closely guarded. **11** strong, high (of wind). *angin* – strong wind. **12** swift (of current). – *aliran sungai ini.* This river flows swiftly. **13** loud (of voice). *bercakap dengan suara* – to talk loudly. **14** heavy (of rain). *hujan* – heavy rain. **15** strong (of cigars/liquor/desires). *minuman* – hard liquor. *obat* – strong medicine. **16** biting, caustic (of smell). **17** tight, hard to unscrew, etc. *bautnya* –, *sukar dibuka* it's hard to unscrew the tight bolt. **18** tough (of meat). **19** no longer resilient, having lost its springiness. – *batang léhér* obstinate. *berkeras batang léhér 1* to keep to the point. *2* to stick to one's guns, stand firm, insist that. – *genjur* stern (in personality). – *hati* willful, energetic. *berkeras hati* to persevere, persist, be determined, persistent. (*ber*)– *hidung* stubborn, obstinate. – *kematu* hard as a rock. – *kepala* stubborn. *kekeras-kepalaan* stubbornness. – *kerak* courage which easily abandons one. – *lidah* finding it hard to pronounce foreign words. – *makas/mangkas* hard and unripe (of fruit). – *mulut* a) hard to defeat in debate, argumentative. b) difficult to rein in (of horses). – *rahang* difficult to rein in (of horses). – *tegas* rigorous.

keras-keras **1** aloud. **2** hard. ~ *kerak* a) not permanently hard. b) unstable, changing, vacillating.

sekeras as hard/loud/strict, etc. as.

sekeras-kerasnya as hard/loud(ly), etc. as possible.

berkeras **1** to be obstinate/determined, persist (in), persevere. **2** to treat with toughness/harshness/severity, be hard (on). **3** to be firm (unyielding). **4** to insist (that/on). *Namun saya ~ untuk tetap tinggal karena waktu itu hujan deras.* But I insisted on staying since it was raining hard.

berkeras-keras to have a tug of war.

berkeras-kerasan to oppose e.o. strongly (each is unwilling to give in). ~ *mulut* to wrangle.

bersikeras to hold firmly (to a belief), insist (that). ~ *batang léhér* stubborn, unwilling to give in.

mengeras **1** to harden, become hard. **2** to become harsh. **3** to become loud(er). **4** to be unwilling to give in.

mengerasi **1** to be firm/harsh with, get tough with *Dia selalu ~ muridnya.* He's always harsh toward his students. **2** to force, compel, use force with. **3** to molest (a woman).

mengeraskan **1** to harden, make s.t. hard(er) (a road, etc.). **2** to enforce (a regulation, etc.), observe (certain rules). **3** to press the matter, pursue one's point. **4** ~ *hati* to persevere, carry on; to take heart, pull o.s. together. **5** to corroborate, bear out (a statement as a witness). **6** (to speak) louder, make (the voice) louder, amplify (sound). **7** to tighten (a screw, etc.).

memperkeras **1** to tighten/intensify (the guard/supervision/controls, etc.). **2** to compact/harden land.

terkeras loudest, harshest, roughest.

kerasan (*coq*) harder.

kekerasan **1** hardness. **2** harshness, severity, rigor, sternness. **3** loudness. **4** force, violence, assault, strife. **5** rigor, stringency. *dengan* (*jalan*) – forcibly. *tanpa* ~ nonviolence. ~ *agama* religious strife. ~ *étnik* ethnic strife. ~ *hati* determination, resoluteness, firmness. ~ *yang melembaga* institutionalized violence.

pengeras **1** a magic spell to strengthen o.s. or weaken others. **2** strengthener, hardener. ~ *otot* s.t. that makes the muscles harder. ~ *rambut* hairspray. ~ *suara* amplifier, loudspeaker.

pengerasan **1** amplification (of sound), making louder. **2** coercion, force. **3** forceful measure. **4** hardening, setting. **5** strengthening, intensification, consolidation. ~ *nadi/pembuluh darah* hardening of the arteries, arteriosclerosis.

keras II *buah* – the *kemiri* fruit, *Aleuritis moluccana*.

keras III (*akar*) – *tulang* k.o. shrub, *Chloranthus officinalis*; camphor is made from its roots and medicine from its leaves.

kerasan (*Jv*) to feel comfortable/at home; → BETAH.

mengerasankan to make s.t. feel comfortable.

kerasanisasi making (transmigrants) feel at home (in a new place).

keras-keras k.o. pastry.

kerat I piece, fragment, slice, part (of a house/road/town). *dengan tulang yang dua* – with nothing but one's two hands. *dengan tulang delapan* – with nothing but one's physical strength.

sekerat a piece cut off from s.t. larger. ~ *jalan* a part of a road. ~ *kayu* a piece of wood. ~ *roti* a) sandwich. b) single slice of bread covered with cheese, etc. c) a slice of bread. *tulang* ~ the parts of the body, the four limbs.

berkerat has been cut off. ~ *rotan dengan* to break (off) relations with.

mengerat to cut off a piece, amputate, carve (meat), cut through, sever (sugarcane/nails/umbilical cord, etc.), cut. ~ *kuku* to cut one's nails. ~ *lidah orang* to interrupt what s.o. is saying. ~ *témpél* to cut and paste.

terkerat cut, severed.

keratan part/piece/slice, etc. cut off from s.t. larger. ~ *tongkat* a piece cut off from a stick.

pengeratan cutting off, slicing.

kerat II (*ob*) **keratan** rusted (of iron), having verdigris (of copper/brass); → KARAT I.

kerat III (*A ob*) carat.

kerat IV (*onom*) sound of gnawing, munching.

mengerat to nibble at, gnaw (away) at.

pengerat *binatang* ~ rodents, rodentia.

keratau mulberry tree, *Morus indica*; → KERTAU I.

kératin (*E*) keratin.

kératitis (*E*) keratitis.

keraton (*Jv*) royal palace, court.

kekeratonan palace (*mod*).

keratu (*ob*) → KARTU.

kerau *bakul* – bamboo basket.

kerawai I a large underground wasp, *Vespa dorylloides*. *– tusam* pine sawfly.

kerawai II a climber, *Mucina pruriens* from whose leaves green manure is made.

berkerawai dangerous, s.t. to stay away from.

kerawak *tupai* – a large red-haired squirrel, *Sciurus bicolor*.

kerawang filigree, openwork (à jour), fretwork, lace.

berkerawang fretted, lacy.

mengerawang to do fretwork/openwork, pierce through. *Angan-angan ~ kepalanya.* Fantasies rushed through his head. *~ langit* to fantasize, have wild fantasies.

kerawat I band of rattan, raw leather strap (to tie around the grip/hilt/handle of a hatchet/chisel/knife, etc.). *makan –* (*M*) as poor as a church mouse. *– perdah* band tying the blade to the haft.

kerawat II *– désa* civil service.

kerawit *cacing* – pinworm, threadworm, *Enterobius vermicularis*.

kerawitan (*Jv*) 1 fine art(s). 2 a *gamelan* melody. 3 (*Jv*) gamelan. 4 overture; → KARAWITAN.

kerbang I → GERBANG I.

kerbang II (*pohon* –) a tree, *Artocarpus elastica*, from whose bark cording is made.

kerbas (*ob*) → KEBAS I.

kerbat I **mengerbat** to tie up, wrap up in folds → KEBAT. *~ mulut* to gag s.o.

kerbat II (*A ob*) k.o. leather bag for carrying water → KIRBAT.

kerbau 1 water buffalo, *Bos bubalus*. 2 numbskull, blockhead; clumsy lout. *badak –* the two-horned buffalo; *cp* BADAK I. *bunting –* ten-month pregnancy. *– punya susu, sapi punya nama* desert and reward seldom keep company. *– menandak anak* pro forma, to do as if. *– runcing tanduk* a notorious person, to give a dog a bad name and hang him. *– turun berendam* about 5 p.m. *bagai/seperti – dicocok hidung* to be henpecked, tied to one's wife's apron-strings. *membeli – bertuntun/di padang* to buy a pig in a poke. *menghambat – berlabuh* (*M*) to hamper s.t. in order to please or benefit s.o. *– balar* pink/albino buffalo. *– benuang* a huge black buffalo (in romance). *– beras* a small buffalo species. *– besi* (*coq*) a manually operated tractor used for plowing. *– bulai/bulé* a Dutchman. *– buluh seruas* a buffalo with uncloven hoofs. *– cepah* a buffalo with horns set far apart. *– dungkul* a) buffalo with horns bent downward. b) madman. *– jalang* a wild (undomesticated) buffalo. *– melukut* → KERBAU *beras*. *– péndék* (*joc*) pig; *cp* AYAM *asing*.

memperkerbau to treat s.o. like slave labor.

kerbuk (*ob*) **mengerbuk** to bore/pierce holes into. *tupai ~ nyiur* squirrels bore holes in coconuts.

kercap and kercapan (*onom*) smacking of the lips; → KECAP. *– kercip/kercup* (*onom*) smacking of the lips.

mengercapkan to smack (the lips).

kercing **mengercingkan** *~ mata* to close one's eyes.

kercit **mengercitkan** *~ mata* to blink one's eyes; → KERNYIT.

kercut 1 a common sedge/rush used in mat making and for sails, rice field bulrush, *Scirpus mucronatus*. 2 a sack made of that sedge.

kerdak 1 lees, sediment, dregs. 2 valueless things, junk. 3 modest reference to one's possessions.

kerdam (*onom*) loud thudding noise, resonance. *– kerdum* (*onom*) continuous loud thudding noise.

berkerdam and **mengerdam** to make that noise.

kerdan (*A*) → ARAS IV. *aras* – fritters.

kerdas k.o. tree, *Pithecellobium confertum*.

kerdil 1 small and short, dwarfish, stunted; stunt. *orang* – dwarf. *penyakit – rumput* grassy stunt. *pohon* – bonsai. *– hampa* ragged stunt (a disease of rice). *– rumput* grassy stunt (a disease of rice plants). 2 narrow(-minded),

sekerdil as small/narrow-minded as.

mengerdil to become stunted.

meng(k)erdilkan to stunt, dwarf (a tree). *pohon jambu yang dikerdilkan* a stunted guava tree.

kekerdilan 1 stuntedness, dwarfishness. 2 narrow-mindedness.

pengerdilan stunting.

kerdip → KEDIP. **mengerdip(kan)** to blink, wink.

kerdipan *~ mata* wink of the eye.

kerdom (*D*) **be(r)kerdom(-kerdom)** (*coq*) to curse, cuss, use abusive language.

mengerdomkan (*coq*) to curse s.o.

kerdum → KERDAM. *–.kerdam* → KERDAM *kerdum*.

mengerdum to make that sound.

kerdus → KARDUS.

kerdut 1 crease, fold, wrinkle. 2 corrugated.

keré → KERAI.

kéré I (*Jv*) (*orang*) – beggar, bum. *– dandan* (in Semarang) female bum who dresses up to become a prostitute at night.

kéré II [kelompok remaja] (*Pr*) group of teenagers.

kéré III (*Jv*) puppy.

kéré IV *– payung* Japanese fern tree, *Filicium decipiens*.

keréat-keréot (*J onom*) squeaking sound (of an unoiled bicycle chain, etc.).

kerébok **mengerébok** to tear, shred, rend; → KERABIK, KERABIT, KEROBÉK.

kerecak → KERACAK I.

kerécék → KRÉCÉK.

kerécéng repeated blinking.

mengerécéngkan *~ mata* to blink one's yes.

kerecut → KECUT III.

keredak filth (that cakes plates/dried mucus from the nose, etc.).

keredak-keredek (*J onom*) crackling sound (of static on the radio).

kerédép (*J*) **berkerédép(an)** and **mengerédép** to glitter, shine brightly.

keredip (*J*) **ngeredip** faint, weak (of light)

kerédok (*J*) k.o. *gado-gado* with uncooked vegetables.

kerédong (*J*) a sewn-together *sarong* used to cover the upper part of the body.

berkerédong to wear such a garment.

keréi → KERAI.

kerejap **berkerejap-kerejap** to keep on blinking.

kerék → KERIK I.

kérék I pulley, block, sheave. *– bor* traveling block. *– jalan/jang-gut* snatch block. *– majemuk* tackle. *– rantai* chain tackle.

mengerék to hoist, raise, ratchet up. *~ bendéra* to hoist the flag.

terkerék hoisted up.

kérékan 1 pulley, hoist, winch, sheave. 2 s.t. hoisted (up).

pengérékan hoisting, raising.

kérék II cake (of palm sugar). *se– gula* ten cakes of palm sugar.

kerekah → KERKAH.

kerékét **berkerékét** (*onom*) to make the sound of walking on a bamboo or wooden floor, squeaking.

berkerékétan (*pl subj*) to make that sound.

kerékot and kerékut 1 shriveled up into a coil (from heat or cold); deformed (of limbs/fingers). 2 bent over (from illness). 3 very miserly, stingy. 4 uneven (of a floor).

kerem I (*J/Jv*) **ngerem** 1 to sit on eggs (to hatch them). 2 to defecate. 3 to sit and brood at home.

kerem II (*J*) cramp, spasm, stiff (of muscles from a cramp); → KRAM I.

kerem III (*Jv*) to founder, be wrecked, be lost (of a vessel).

kerém (*coq*) → RÉM I.

keremak k.o. plant, *Alternathera sessilis*. *– jantan/janten* k.o. weed, false daisy, *Eclipta alba*.

kereman fatted (calf)

keremang-keremong (*onom*) tinkling sound of music.

kerémbong I (*J*) **kerémbong-kerémbong** to flutter around (of clothes that are too wide).

kerémbongan to flutter around.

kerémbong II (*J*) **ngerémbongin** to cover/wrap up in a *kain*, etc.

keréméh alligator weed, *Alternanthera philoxeroides*.

keremes (*J/Jv*) k.o. potatoes fried with sugar.

keremi → KERMI.

keremong → KEREMANG-KEREMONG.

kerémot (*ob*) puckered, wrinkled (of the face), creased.

kerempagi (*Tam? M ob*) 1 razor. 2 pocketknife.

kerempang and kerémpéng → KRÉMPÉNG.

kerémpéng → KRÉMPÉNG.

kerempung (ob) abdomen.

keremunting → KEMUNTING.

keremus (J) mengeremus 1 to beat up. 2 to gag.

kerémut → KERÉMOT.

keren (Jv) lime kiln.

kerén I (J) 1 imposing, impressive, striking, dashing. 2 handsome; beautiful. Tampangnya –. He/She is handsome/beautiful. 3 chic, stylish, fashionable, sharp. Pakaiannya –. He/She is fashionably dressed. sok – always liking to put o.s. in the forefront.

kerén II (J) high-spirited (of a horse).

kéren → KÉRN.

kerena → KARENA.

kerencang (onom) clinking/clanging noise (of coins/metal).
berkerencang to clink, clang.

kerencing → KERENCANG.

kerencung (onom) → KERENCANG.

kerenda → KERANDA.

kerendang (J) a plant, Pouzolzia zeylanica, used as fodder.

kereneng (J/Jv) 1 bag, pouch (made of pandan leaves). 2 charcoal basket (made of bamboo wickerwork).

kereng I (J/Jv) harsh, stern, gruff, brusque.

kereng II (J) pitch-black.

kereng III (J) thick, heavy (of eyebrows).

kerengga red weaver ant, Oecophylla smaragdina.

kerenggamunggu (ob) cardamom.

kerengkam a seaweed growing on coral reefs, Sargossum sp.

kerengkiang four-posted rice-granary broadening toward the steep roof; → RENGKIANG.

kerening (onom) tinkling.
kereningan tinkling sound.

kerentam → GERENTAM.

kerenting → KERENCANG.

kerenyam geranium.

kerenyau → KERNYAU.

kerenyit → KERNYIT.

kerényot mengerényot 1 to twist/distort one's mouth. 2 to grin (like a dog).

kerenyut → KERNYUT I.

kerép (J) mobil – a) ambulance. b) hearse.

kerepai → KERPAI.

kerepak → KERPAK.

kerepas I → KERPAS.

kerepas II (M) blind in one eye.
mengerepas ~ mata to blink one's eye.

kerépék → KERIPIK.

kerépés I mengerépés to grope about for s.t.

kerépés II (S) di ruang – to be buried alive.

kerépot (J) wrinkled, furrowed (of forehead).
berkerépotan (pl subj) completely wrinkled.

kerepus (J) mengerepus to swallow whole.

kerepyak (onom) pitter-patter.

kererangga → KERENGGA.

keresak and keresek (onom) sound of treading on dry leaves, rustle, crunch.

kerésék → KERISIK II.

keréséng I crevice, fissure, crack, cleft; slightly opened (of the mouth) so that what is in the mouth can be seen.
mengeréséng to open slightly.
terkeréséng mulut ~ a twisted mouth; an open mouth due to a harelip.

keréséng II bungling.

kerésé-pésé (coq) to talk Dutch continually→ KRÉSÉH-PÉSÉH.

Kéresmis and Kerésmis (D) Christmas → KRISMES.

kerésot wrinkle, furrow.
berkerésot and mengerésot wrinkled, furrowed (of one's forehead).
mengerésotkan to wrinkle.

keret → KERAT I, MENGKERET.

keréta I (Port) 1 carriage, cart, vehicle. 2 (Med Mal) car, automobile; → KENDARAAN. 3 gun carriage, (gun)mount. 4 bobbin. 5 train. – anak perambulator, pram, baby carriage. – angin (ob) bicycle. – api/asap train; steam engine → SEPUR. – api barang goods train. – api bawah tanah subway, underground railway. – api berlapis baja armored car. – api bumel local/milk train. – api cepat fast/express train. – api istiméwa special train. – api kétélan train with tank cars. – api kilat fast/express train. – api langsam (coq) local/milk train. – api listrik electric train. – api malam night train. – api monorél monorail. – api olak-alik/olang-alik commuter train. – api peluru the Japanese bullet train, Shinkansen. – api Purbaya the Purwokerto-Surabaya express train → PURBAYA. – api senja night train. – api sombong fast/express train. – api t(e)rutuk a log-fired local/milk train → SEPUR trutuk. berkeréta api to go by train. perkeréta-apian railway, railroad (mod). kondisi ~ railroad conditions. – baja armored car. – barang goods car. – bayi baby carriage. – bogi/bugi buggy. – dorong(an) pushcart. – és sleigh. – gandéngan trailer. – gantung skylift, cable car. – jenazah hearse. – kabel cable car. – kebal armored car, army tank. – kecil a mini car. – kencana (cla) golden chariot. – kuda horse-drawn cart. – léréng (in Medan) bicycle. – makan dining car. – mati/mayat hearse. – pariwisata sightseeing carriage. – pasién gurney. – pemandangan observation car. – pengiring trailer. – penumpang passenger car. – privat (Mal) private car. – rél di(e)sel [KRD] diesel train. – ruang (infr) space ship. – samping sidecar. – sétan ghost train. – séwa carriage for rent. – siram sprinkler. – sorong pushcart. – tambangan carriage for rent. – tangan pushcart. – tarik pushcart. – témpélan semitrailer. – tidur sleeping car, sleeper. – tolak handcar. – tumpangan passenger car. – udara skylift. – waja armored car.
sekeréta 1 in the same carriage. 2 a carriage-load of.
berkeréta 1 to ride in a carriage. 2 to go for a ride. ~ angin (ob) to ride a bicycle.

keréta II → GURITA II.

keretak → KERTAK.

kerétan → GERÉTAN.

kerétang → KERTANG.

keretek (Jv) bridge.

kerétek I (Jv) rokok – cigarette containing coarsely cut tobacco mixed with cloves.

kerétek II (onom) sound of burning dry leaves.

kerétek III a two-wheeled horse-drawn cart; → DOKAR.

keretik → KERTIK.

kerétok and kerétuk → KERÉKOT.

kerétot 1 deformed, gnarled. 2 uneven (of a floor, etc.).

keréwéng shards (of pottery/tile, etc.).

keri I tiny sickle for weeding.
mengeri to weed with such a sickle.

keri II (Jv) ticklish.

keria I (kuéh –) k.o. cake made from yams and sugar.

keria II eastern sarus crane, Grus antigone sharpii.

keriak (ob) outcry.
berkeriak to cry out.

keriang-keriut (onom) creaking, squeaking (of row-locks/doors, etc.).
berkeriang-keriut to creak, squeak.

keriap berkeriapan and mengeriap to swarm, assemble in large numbers (of ants, etc.).

keriat-keriut → KERIANG-KERIUT.

keriau (ob) berkeriau to yell, shout.

kerical pacal – (coq) humble slave, lowest of the low.

kericau berkericau and mengericau to chirp, twitter (of birds). punai – green pigeon, Osmotreron vernaus.

kericik I dwarf squirrel, Nannosciurus exilis.

kericik II (onom) splashing sound.
berkericik(an) to splash around.

kericit (onom) squealing sound (of car tires).
berkericit to make that sound.

keridas → KADAS keridas.

keridik various species of mole cricket, Grillotalpa spp., Brachytrypes portentosus and other species. – padang a mole cricket that sings in the evening. – pesan-pesan a k.o. poisonous insect.

keridit → KRÉDIT.

kerih I (onom) screaming sound made by monkeys.
   mengerih 1 to scream (of monkeys). 2 to groan (in pain).

kerih II (ob) with a lot of trouble, laboriously.

kerik I (onom) sound of scraping a sharp object over a mirror, etc.
   mengerik 1 to scrape/scratch s.t. off with a sharp object; to rub
   s.t. out (by scraping over it). 2 to rub s.o.'s painful back, etc.
   with a coin when he has a cold, etc.; cp MENGEROK.
   kerikan 1 scraper, scratcher. 2 the part of the body scraped/
   scratched. 3 scraping, s.t. scraped. 4 to have one's back, etc.
   scraped with a coin.
   pengerik reamer.

kerik II – api (ob) a match → KORÉK api.

kerik III (Jv) shaving and shaping the hair on a bride's forehead.

kerik IV (Jv onom) chirping sound of a cricket.
   mengerik [and ngerik (coq)] to chirp.

kerikal (cla) k.o. large brass pedestal tray.

kerikam kain – k.o. coarse linen.

kerikil 1 (batu –) gravel, pebbles, small stones. 2 obstacle.
   mengerikil(i) to use gravel to line a road, etc., cover with gravel.
   pengerikilan graveling, covering with gravel.

kerikit (Jv) mengerikit(i) to gnaw/nibble at.

kerimuk → KERUMUK.

kerimut (ob) → KERÉMOT, KERÉPOT.

kerinan (Jv ob) to oversleep. seperti maling – like s.o. who tries to
   hide a wicked deed but has been detected.

kerincing 1 (onom) sound of clinking/tinkling/jingling. 2 k.o.
   metal musical instrument.
   berkerincing(an) and mengerincing to clink, tinkle, jingle.
   mengerincingkan to tinkle s.t., make s.t. tinkle.

kerindil (J) thinning (of hair).

kering I 1a) dry, dried out. Kain yang dijemur itu sudah –. The
   cloth dried in the sun is dry. daun – dried/withered leaves. ikan
   – dried (and salted) fish. kué – k.o. pastry made from glutinous
   rice flour and eggs. musim – dry season. roti – dry bread. tanah
   – arid/dry and barren land. b) – dari running low on (supplies
   of a liquid). 2 dried up, run dry. Sungai itu sudah –. The river
   has dried up. 3 skinny, lanky. Tubuhnya – oléh batuk. He's
   skinny from coughing. 4 dry, without charm, plain, matter-of-
   fact. Novélnya yang baru itu –. His latest novel is without
   charm. 5 raw, not worked on. data-data – raw data. 6 lacking.
   Penonton yang datang tidak pernah –. There has never been a
   lack of spectators. 7 poorly paid, not lucrative (job/work). dok-
   ter/jabatan – a low-paid doctor/position; opp BASAH. 8 broke,
   to have no money. Saya – sekarang ini. I'm broke right now. 9
   to have stopped menstruating. 10 crisp(y). 11 healed completely, closed (of an open wound). béri-béri – scurvy (without
   swellings). bersifat – a dry run. pasang – ebb, low tide. tulang –
   shinbone, tibia. tidak – wet. ketidakkeringan wetness, plenty
   of rain. – darah(nya) a) terrified, bewildered, shocked, astonished, amazed. b) menopausal. – embun after the dew has evaporated, early morning. – kelontong/kerontang/lekah/lekang/
   melenting/mersik/rendang/ringkai/terik bone-dry. – mering
   skinny, as thin as a rail. – témpé soybean cake.
   kering-kering ~ air damp, moist, humid. tidak ~nya inexhaustible, never-ending.
   sekering as dry as.
   sekering-keringnya as dry as possible.
   berkering ~ air liur to waste one's breath, there's no point in,
   what's the use of.
   berkeringan (pl subj) to become dry, dry up. Air sungai pada
   ~. The rivers have all dried up.
   mengering to wither, dry up, run dry. Bunga itu ~. The flowers
   have withered.
   mengeringi to allow to be(come)/arid, dry up. ~ sawah-sawah
   to let the rice paddies become dry.
   mengeringkan [and ngeringin (J coq)] to dry, drain, evaporate.
   ~ tanah-tanah paya to drain marsh lands.
   terkering driest, etc.
   kekeringan 1 short of, for want of. karena ~ waktu for lack of
   time. ~ susu to have one's milk run dry (of a nursing mother).
   dalam ~ short of money. 2 dryness, drought, lack of rain.

Daérah itu terancam ~. The region was threatened by drought.
3 (coq) too dry.

pengering dryer. lap ~ rag used to wipe s.t. dry. ~ air dehydrator.
   ~ rambut hairdryer. ~ tinta blotter.

pengeringan 1 drying (up), desiccating. 2 drainage, draining (of
   swamps, etc.).

kering II (onom) ringing, tinkling, jingling.
   berkering(-kering) to ring, tinkle, jingle.

kering III a marine fish species, grooved razor fish, Centriscus scutatus.

keringat sweat, perspiration. memerah/memeras – to work one's
   fingers to the bone. –ku terlalu banyak yang keluar. I was
   bathed in sweat. dengan –nya sendiri on one's own, independently. biang – German measles. Keluar – keringnya. He was
   dead tired. makan – orang to exploit s.o. mandi – to sweat profusely. – buntet skin rash; heat rash. – dingin a cold sweat. – lilin
   (petro) foots oil.
   berkeringat to sweat, perspire; sweaty. basah ~ to sweat profusely. ~ dingin to be in a cold sweat, sweat bullets.
   mengeringatkan 1 (ob) to work hard for s.o. else, do s.t. with
   great trouble. 2 to sweat over s.t.
   keringatan to be sweaty.

keringet → KERINGAT.

keringkit (onom) creaking.

keringsing → GERINGSING I.

keriningan (bicycle-)bell.

kerinjal (Jv) buah – the kidneys → GINJAL.

kerinjang mengerinjang (ob) to step, stride.

kerinjing a tree whose hard wood is used for building material,
   etc., Javanese bishipwood, Bischofia javanica. – daun talang
   k.o. tree, Teijsmanniodendron coriaceum.

kerintil and berkerintil to hang in thick clusters (of fruit, etc.).

kerinting salted and dried shellfish.

kerinyit → KERNYIT.

kerinyut knitted (of brows), wrinkled; → KER(E)NYUT.

kerio (Bal) hamlet head.

kerip (onom) gnawing sound.
   mengerip to gnaw, nibble (of mice).

keripik crispy thin chips (of banana/cassava/sweet potato) →
   KRIPIK.

keriput wrinkle, a line on the forehead.
   berkeriput to be wrinkled; with lined skin (due to old age).
   mengeriput to wrinkle, furrow.
   keriputan wrinkled, full of wrinkles.
   kekeriputan wrinkling.

keris kris, creese, a wavy-bladed ceremonial dagger (a weapon and a
   cult object said to have magic powers); → TOSAN/WESI aji –
   alang/pandak/panjang a medium-sized/short/long kris. – ber
   (ke)luk a kris with a wavy blade. – Bugis kris in which the hilt
   stands out at right angles. – ganja iras kris with guard and blade
   in one piece. – meléla kris made from untempered steel. – parung
   sari a kris with seven or fewer curves in its blade. – pendarah a
   kris that has drawn blood. – pendua a kris used as a reserve. – penyalang (ob) an execution kris. – picit the oldest (Majapahit)
   type of kris with an iron figure for a hilt and thumb marks on the
   blade. – sakti magic kris. – sempana a kris with a few waves. –
   sepukal a straight-bladed kris. – sundang a long kris from Sulu. –
   terapung kris encased in gold.
   berkeris to wear/carry a kris. berkeras tidak ~ to take strong
   measures but not have the power to defend o.s.
   mengeris to stab with a kris.
   perkerisan kris (mod). kursus ~ a course on the kris.

kerisi ikan – ornate threadfin bream, Synagris spp., Nemipterus
   hexodon.

kerisik I dry old banana fronds.
   mengerisik to chip/peel off in flakes.

kerisik II (onom) rustling of dry leaves in the breeze.
   berkerisik and mengerisik to rustle.
   kerisikan rustle, rustling.

kerisik III (ob) grit, rough hard particles of sand → KERSIK I.

kerisis → KRISIS.

kerisologi the science/knowledge of krises.

Keristen → KRISTEN.
kerisut → KERIPUT, KISUT.
kerit I (*onom*) scraping/scratching/gnashing sound.
  berkerit and mengerit to make that noise.
  mengeritkan (*gigi*) to grind/gnash one's teeth.
kerit II – *dayung* and *belalang* –.- k.o. mole cricket that chirps at
  night.
keritik I (*onom*) popping sound (like corn popping).
  berkeritik to crackle, make a succession of slight, sharp, popping sounds.
keritik II → KRITIK.
keriting I curly, kinky (of hair).
  mengeriting ~ *rambut* to curl one's hair.
  mengeritingkan ~ *rambut* to have one's hair curled.
  pengeritingan ~ *rambut* permanent wave.
keriting II fluttering, fuzzy (of television picture, etc.).
keriuk berkeriuk and terkeriuk crow (of roosters).
keriut I (*onom*) creaking sound (of oars, doors, etc.).
  berkeriut to make a creaking sound → KERIANG-KERIUT.
  berkeriutan (*pl subj*) to make creaking sounds, creak.
  mengeriutkan to make s.t. creak.
keriut II (*burung* -) k.o. bird, golden plover, *Pluvialis dominica
  fulva.*
keriwil (*E*) freewheel (on a bicycle).
kerja (*Skr*) 1 work, labor; activity, what one does → KARYA. -*nya
  tak lain daripada membaca.* He does nothing but read. -*nya
  hanya makan tidur saja.* All he does is eat and sleep. *cara* – way
  of working; procedure. *hari* – weekday. *hasil* – performance.
  jam – working hours. *kata* – verb. – *upahan* paid work. 2 occupation, job. *tiada* – jobless. 3 feast, celebration (of a wedding/
  circumcision, etc.). 4 (*coq*) to work. *Hari ini ia tidak* –. He's
  not working today. *Apa* – *si Téddy?* What's Teddy doing (for a
  living)? – *dalam grup* to work as a team. – *amal* charity work. –
  badan physical work. – *bakti* community service. – *berat* hard
  labor. – *borong(an)* piecework. – *ciptaan sendiri* self-employment. – *duta* mission. (*petani*) – *ganda* part-time (farmer). –
  guru the teaching profession. – *halus* fine work, such as jewelry
  making. *pekerja halus* s.o. who does such work. – *kasar* manual
  work. – *ladang* work in nonirrigated rice paddies. – *lapangan*
  fieldwork. – *lembur* overtime. – *malam* night work. – *médan*
  fieldwork. *kuliah* – *nyata* [KKN] National Student Service
  Scheme. – *paksa* forced labor. *mengerja-paksakan* to draft for
  forced labor. – *paruh waktu* part-time work. – *raja/rodi* (*ob*)
  work for a ruler/prince, statute labor → RODI. bekerja rodi to
  do forced work. – *sama* cooperation. – *sama berganda di udara*
  canopy relative work. bekerja sama to cooperate, work together. mengerja-samakan *dengan* to cooperate with.
  peng(k)erja-samaan concerted action, teamwork. – *sambilan*
  part-time work. – *sawah* work in irrigated rice paddies. – *tempa*
  forging. – *t(e)rampil* skilled labor. – *ulang* (*petro*) workover. –
  upahan paid labor.
sekerja of the same work/profession/occupation. *kawan/teman*
  ~ colleague. *serikat* ~ labor union.
bekerja 1 to work, labor, perform, operate. *tidak ~nya* the non-
  operation of. ~ *di belakang méja* to work in an office, be a
  white-collar worker. 2 to celebrate a wedding, etc. ~ *mengawinkan anaknya* to celebrate the marriage of one's child. 3
  to be active (of a volcano, etc.). ~ *bakti* to do volunteer work.
  ~ *lembur* to work overtime. ~ *penuh* to have a full-time job.
  bisa/dapat ~ *sendiri* able to work on one's own (or, independently).
mengerjai 1 to work, work on/at, cultivate (land). 2 to manipulate.
mengerjain and ngerjain (*J coq*) 1 (*vulg*) to screw, fuck. 2 to coerce, pressure. *Petugas pengantar akan tetap dikerjain alias
  kena pungli.* Accompanying officials will continue to be pres-
  sured, i.e., to take bribes.
mengerjakan 1 to do, perform, execute, carry out, operate, run.
  Ia belum ~ *pekerjaan rumah matématika.* He hasn't done his
  math homework yet. 2 to work, work on/at, cultivate (land); to
  take care of. ~ *mayat* to take care of a corpse (i.e., bathing/
  wrapping, etc.). 3 to finish, terminate, bring to an end, perfect,

accomplish. 4 to remove; to kill, annihilate, destroy. 5 to throw
  a party for s.o.
mempekerjakan to put s.o. to work, employ, staff, hire, give s.o.
  a job. *Sebanyak 63 karyawan Pertamina menuntut dipekerjakan kembali.* Sixty-three *Pertamina* employees demanded to
  be rehired.
te(r)kerjakan 1 done, performed, carried out. 2 can be done/
  performed/carried out. *tidak* ~ impracticable. 3 employable,
  fit to be hired.
kerjaan 1 (*coq*) work. *Ia kurang* ~. He has nothing to do. 2 action (of a machine). sekerjaan of the same work, colleague.
pekerja laborer, worker, workman; employee. *jumlah* ~ *dikalikan
  hari* man-days. *badan* ~ working/executive committee. ~ *atas*
  (*petro*) derrick man. ~ *bangunan* construction worker. ~ *bawah*
  floor man. ~ *bulanan* worker on a monthly salary. ~ *cakap*
  qualified worker. ~ (*dalam pekerjaan*) *borongan* pieceworker.
  para ~ *di belakang méja* the class of white-collar workers. ~ *harian* day worker/laborer. ~ *hukuman* convict sentenced to hard
  labor. ~ *industri* industrial worker. ~ *jalan* road worker. ~ *kapal*
  longshoreman. ~ *kasar* a) blue-collar worker. b) (*petro*) rough-
  neck. ~ *konstruksi* construction worker. ~ *lapangan* a) field-
  worker. b) blue-collar worker. ~ *lepas* casual worker. ~ *logam*
  metalworker. ~ *mingguan* worker on a weekly salary. ~ *otak* s.o.
  who works with his mind. ~ *paksa* forced labor. mempekerja-
  paksakan to draft for forced labor. ~ *pelabuhan* longshoreman.
  ~ *penuh* full-time worker, full-timer. ~ *riset* researcher. ~ *sambilan* part-timer. ~ *séks* (*komérsial*) [PS(K)] sex worker. ~ *serabutan* roustabout. ~ *sosial* social worker. ~ *tangan* manual
  worker. ~ *t(e)rampil* skilled worker. ~ *terdidik* highly trained
  worker. ~ *toko* worker in a store. ~ *upahan* wage-earner.
pekerjaan 1 work, job, occupation, profession, employment,
  task, activity, assignment. *tidak mempunyai* ~ (in notarial instruments) (of) no occupation. *lapangan* ~ field of work/activ-
  ity. 2 profession, business, trade, enterprise. 3 effect (*esp* of
  medicine, etc.), action. 4 running, movement (of engine/
  watch, etc.), operation (of engine, etc.), action. 5 (almost *ob*)
  festival, celebration (of wedding, etc.). ~ *bébas* profession. ~
  belakang méja white-collar work. ~ *borongan* piecework. ~
  dagang by occupation a merchant. ~ *gonta-ganti* interaction,
  interplay. ~ *kantor* office work. ~ *kejuruan* expert work. ~
  logam metalwork. ~ *pancang* pile driving. ~ *pembetulan* repair
  work. ~ *pengairan* irrigation work. ~ *persiapan* preparatory
  work. ~ *rumah* homework (for school); → PÉ-ÉR. ~ *rumah
  tangga* housework, household chores. ~ *sambén/sambilan/
  sampingan* side/part-time job. ~ *semprot* spraying. ~ *tahunan*
  annual work. ~ *tambal-menambal* patchwork. ~ *tambang*
  mining. ~ *tanah* ground work. ~ *tangan* manual work. ~ *tuangan* cast work. ~ *tukang kayu* carpentry. ~ *tulis-menulis* administrative work. ~ *umum* public works. sepekerjaan with
  the same work. *teman* ~ fellow worker. berpekerjaan *tidak* ~
  (in notarial instruments) unemployed.
pengerjaan 1 working, executing, carrying out, performing. 2
  refining, improvement, processing, finishing, treatment. ~
  bahan mentah processing of raw materials. ~ *minyak* oil
  refining. ~ *utama* (*math*) elementary operation.
kerjang → KERAJANG.
kerjantara (*ob*) employment agency.
kerjap mengerjap(-ngerjap)kan (*mata*) to blink (one's eyes); →
  KEJAP.
kerjasama (*Skr neo*) → KERJA *sama.*
kerkah (*onom*) 1 sound of crunching/gnawing/biting to pieces. 2
  sound of cracking (of wood, bones).
  mengerkah(-ngerkah) to crunch, gnaw at, tear/rip apart, ravage.
  pengerkah gnawer, s.t. used for gnawing.
kerkak → KERKAH.
kerkap I → KERKAH.
kerkap II *sirih* - → KERAKAP.
kerkap-kerkup (*onom*) sound of crunching.
kerkas → KULKAS.
kerkau claw(like).
  mengerkau to claw, seize with a claw.
kerkeling → KERAKELING.

kérkop (*D*) (European) graveyard.
kerkup (*onom*) sound of crunching/cracking; → KERKAH, KERKAK, KERKAP I.
  berkerkup(-kerkup) to make crunching noises.
  mengerkupkan to crunch on s.t.
kerlap I – *kerlip* glittering, twinkling. ***berkerlap-kerlip*** to glitter, twinkle.
  bekerlapan and **mengerlap** to glitter, twinkle.
  kerlapan glitter, glamour.
kerlap II tekerlap doze off for a short while, take a nap.
kerling I sidewise glance. – *matanya membangkit berahi*. His glance arouses passion.
  mengerling to glance sidewise, steal a glance (at).
  mengerlingkan to make (one's eyes) glance to the side.
  kerlingan (sideways) glance.
  kerling-kerlingan ogling e.o.
kerling II mengerling to glitter, shimmer.
  kerlingan glitter, glimmer.
kerlip I 1 flickering, flashing, twinkling. **2** wink (of the eye).
  sekerlip ~ *mata* in a wink.
  bekerlip and **mengerlip 1** to flicker, flash, twinkle. **2** to wink, blink.
  bekerlipan (*pl subj*) to flicker, twinkle.
  mengerlipkan ~ *mata* to blink one's eyes.
  kerlipan twinkle.
kerlip II (*D coq*) to be/fall in love → JATUH *cinta*.
  mengerlipkan to make s.o. fall in love.
kerma → KARMA II, KERAMA.
kermak a weed eaten as a vegetable, *Alternanthera triandra/sessilis*. – *jantan* a weed, *Eclipta alba*.
kermanici → KARBONACI.
kermi (*Pers?*) *cacing* – pinworm, threadworm, *Enterobius vermicularis*.
  kermian (*J*) (*sakit*) ~ suffering from pinworm infestation, itching around the anus.
kermunting → KEMUNTING.
kérn (*D*) /kéren/ nucleus.
kerna → KARENA.
kernai mengernai to chop/cut up into small pieces.
kernék → KENÉK.
kernéli (*J coq*) vanilla.
kernét apprentice/assistant (of a taxi/bus, etc.); → KENÉK.
  ngernét (*coq*) to work as a driver's assistant.
kernia → KARUNIA.
kernu (*Port od*) ammunition box.
kernyat-kernyut (*onom*) sound of creaking/squeaking (shoes/doors, etc.).
kernyau (*onom*) sound of munching/crunching/biting down on.
kernyih grin(ning), grimacing, making faces.
  mengernyih to grin, grimace, make faces.
kernying mengernying (of animals) to show/bare its teeth/fangs.
kernyit furrow.
  berkernyit wrinkled.
  mengernyit to frown.
  mengernyitkan ~ *alis* to frown (to show displeasure/disapproval).
  kernyitan frown.
kernyut I 1 frown line (on forehead). **2** wrinkle, furrow.
  be(r)ernyut(an) furrowed, wrinkled.
  mengernyut to frown.
  mengernyutkan to frown, wrinkle.
kernyut II bekernyut to pulsate (of arteries, etc.).
kernyut III gnashing (of teeth).
kéro I *tempat tidur* – a steel bed with springs.
kéro II (in Mataram) equipment to weed paddy plants.
kéro III (*Jv*) cross-eyed, squinty.
kerobak and **berkerobak 1** with holes/rips (in it). **2** pockmarked, scarred. – *kerobék/kerabik/kerabit* a) in tatters, torn to pieces. b) badly scarred, covered with scars.
kerobék mengerobék to tear/shred/rip into small pieces.
kerobét (*onom*) squeaking.
keroco → KROCO.
kerocok 1 rattle. **2** (*onom*) rattling noise, the sound of water, etc. being shaken in a container.

kerodong → KERUDUNG. **berkerodong** to screen, cover.
  mengerodongi to cover.
keroh → KERUH III.
kéroh crooked (of morals), dishonest, deceitful, deceptive.
kerok I (*Jv*) currycomb. *biang* – troublemaker.
  mengerok to currycomb.
kerok II (*Jv*) **ngeroki** to oil and then scrape/rub the skin of a person with a cold, headache, etc. with a coin until it becomes red → MENGERIK 2.
  kerokan 1 to be oiled and then scraped. **2** a part of the body treated in this way.
kerok III scraping, curettage.
  mengerok to scrape the tongue of a talking bird (or of a person) on Thursday evening with a gold ring to make it speak better.
kerokét → KROKÉT.
kerokot → KROKOT.
kerolok (*onom*) gurgling sound.
  berkerolok to gurgle.
keromo → KROMO I.
keromong (*Jv*) a large percussion instrument consisting of 10 or 14 bronze kettles placed upside down in two rows on a low rack and beaten with two sticks. *gambang – Jakarta* a xylophone-like instrument.
kerompyangan (*J onom*) sound of breaking glass.
keron (*D coq*) (picture of a) crown (as a symbol of colonial rule).
keroncang (*ob*) → KERAJANG.
keronco → KERONCOR.
keroncong I 1 (*onom*) tinkling (of dancers' anklets with little bells). *gelang* – such an anklet. **2** rumbling, gnawing (in one's stomach).
  berkeroncongan 1 to tinkle. **2** to rumble (of an empty stomach). *Perutnya* –. His stomach is rumbling.
  keroncongan to rumble with hunger.
keroncong II (*lagu* –) a type of popular Indonesian music (originally from eastern Indonesia and influenced by *Port* music and songs).
  berkeroncong to perform *keroncong* music.
keroncong III keroncongan k.o. green manure with edible seeds, water bush, *Crotalaria striata*.
keroncong IV the deepest recess of a fish trap. *ikan di/dalam* – hopeless, past saving.
  mengeroncongkan ~ *bibir* to purse the lips.
keroncor the male king-crab, *Limulus mollucanus*. *seperti – dengan belangkas* closely associated with e.o.
keroncot (*ob*) → KERUCUT.
kerong(-kerang) (*onom*) rattling (of hard objects in a tin can, etc.).
kérong-kérong crescent perch, *Therapon argentius/jarbua*.
kerongkongan 1 gullet, throat, esophagus. **2** windpipe, trachea. **3** pharynx. *kering* – until one's throat turns dry. *kering – menasihati dia* he was advised and advised (but he ignored it). *asal* ~ *akan berair* as long as there's enough to live on.
kerongsang gold, etc. brooch attached to one's coat.
kero(n)song → KELONGSONG.
kerontang very dry, bone-dry, arid. *kering* – completely dried up. *panas* – hot and dry.
keropak (*Jv*) handwritten palm leaves (in old books found in Java and Bali).
keropas-keropis 1 small/miscellaneous items. **2** (and **berkeropas-keropis**) to carry out useless small jobs.
keropéng scab (over a wound).
  mengeropéng to peel/pick off a scab.
  mengeropéngkan to peel s.t. off.
keropes snot, dried nasal mucus.
keropok I (*M*) → KELOMPOK. **sekeropok** a group (of people).
keropok II → KERUPUK I.
keropok III (*J/Jv*) spongy, woolly, eaten away.
keropong (*J/Jv*) hollow, eaten away from the inside.
keropos 1 hollow, spongy, porous, not compact (of wood/stone, etc.); → KROPOS. -*nya tulang* osteoporosis. **2** rusted out (of a car body). **3** rarefied (of air).
  terkeropos hollowed out, not solid.
  kekeroposan ~ *tulang* osteoporosis.
  pengeroposan ~ *tulang* osteoporosis.

keropot (*J*) **ngeropotin** to eat away at little by little.
kerosak (*onom*) sound made by stepping or walking on dry leaves.
kerosang → KERONGSANG.
kerosék (*onom*) sound made by rinsing uncooked rice.
kerosi → KURSI I. **mengerosi** to give s.o. a seat (in a representative body).
kérosin (*D/E*) kerosene.
keroso I (*Jv*) → TERASA.
keroso II (*J/Jv*) k.o. bag woven from coconut leaves.
kerosok I (*onom*) → KEROSAK. – *ular di rumpun bambu* (*M*) one need not be afraid of an empty threat.
 berkerosok and **mengerosok** to rustle (of leaves when stepped on).
kerosok II *tembakau* – dried tobacco leaves.
kerosong sloughed skin (of snakes, etc.).
 mengerosong to slough skin.
kerotak (*onom*) sound of things rubbing together.
 berkerotak *bising* – to creak.
kerotot and **berkerotot** wrinkled (like the skin of certain fruits), pockmarked, shriveled up; grooved (of a file).
keroyok (*Jv*) **mengeroyok** to attack in a mob, gang up on.
 keroyokan attack en masse/in large numbers. ~ *massa* mob violence.
 pengeroyok attackers.
 pengeroyokan attack, assault, mobbing up on.
kerowak → KROWAK.
kerpai cartridge pouch.
kerpak (*onom*) sound of cracking or snapping twigs.
kerpas (*onom*) sound of people or animals going through undergrowth/bushes.
kerpik (*onom*) sound of breaking wood.
kerpis (*onom*) sound like *kerpas* but softer.
kerpu (*Jv geol*) glance, Glanz.
kerpuk (*onom*) sound of cracking twigs.
kerpus I (*Port*) cap, bonnet.
kerpus II ridge of roof.
 mengerpus to build such a ridge.
 kerpusan such a ridge.
kerpus III (*ob mil*) guardhouse.
 mengerpus to lock up in a guardhouse.
kérs (*D*) cherry.
kersai crumbly (of rice); loose (of rice that doesn't stick together), not compact (of sand).
kersak (*onom*) sound of hay or dry leaves when stepped on or when rubbing against e.o.
kersang 1 dry, barren (of land), infertile. **2** stiff, shaggy, coarse (of hair) → GERSANG.
 mengersang to dry up.
kersani (*Pers ob*) *besi* – k.o. good-quality iron (originally from Khorasan, Iran); → KURASANI.
kérsen (*D*) cherry.
kersik I fine sand, gravel, grit (of stone), silica, siliceous. *melekatkan – ke buluh* to do a hard job in vain.
 mengersik silicified.
 mengersiki to cover with gravel/fine sand.
kersik II te(r)kersik (*onom*) sound of dry leaves rubbing against e.o.
kersip → KE(R)DIP.
kérsmis (*D*) Christmas → KRISMES.
kersuk (*onom*) sound like *kersak* but stronger.
kerta (*Jv*) prosperity and peace. *tata tentrem – raharja* orderly, peaceful, and prosperous.
kertah k.o. land crab.
Kertajaya name of a train running between Jakarta and Surabaya.
kertak (*onom*) sound made by treading on wooden floor or broken branches. – *kertik* creaking sound. ***berkertak-kertik*** to creak. – *kertuk* creak and rattle.
 bekertak and **mengertak** to make a creaking sound.
 mengertakkan to make s.t. creak. ~ *gigi* to gnash one's teeth.
 kertakan gnashing (of the teeth).
kertang I soiled, dirty, foul. *Kainnya – kena darah ayam.* His cloth was soiled with chicken blood.
kertang II (*onom*) sound made by beating on empty tin cans.

mengertang to make this sound by beating on empty tin cans.
 mengertangkan ~ *perisai* to beat on one's shield.
kertang III *ikan* – a sea perch, *Epinephelus pantherinus, Piperphelus lanceolatus*
kertap (*onom*) slamming sound made by closing a poorly fitting door, crunching on food, etc.
 kertap-kertap crunching, rattling.
 bekertap and **mengertap** to crunch.
kertas I (*A*) (piece of) paper. *sebagai dawat dengan* – well-matched. – *dengan potlot* paper and pencil. *uang* – paper money. – *ampelas* sandpaper. – *aspal* tarpaper. – *atap* roofing paper. – *berharga* commercial paper. – *berlapis* coated paper. – *bernilai uang* valuable papers, securities. – *bertinta* carbon paper. – *bungkus* wrapping paper. – *buram* scratch paper. – *buyar* a) blotting paper. b) tissue paper. – *cd* k.o. coarse grade of paper. – *cétak* printing paper. – *corét* scratch paper. – *dinding* wallpaper. – *éfék* securities. – *embun* blotting paper. – *folio* paper similar in size to legal-size paper. – *fotokopi* photocopy paper. – *gambar* drawing paper. – *gésék* sandpaper. – *gosok* sandpaper. – *grénjéng* silver paper, tinfoil. – *HVS* [*Houtvrijschrijfpapier*] cellulose-free paper. – *isap* blotting paper. – *jeluang* parchment. – *jernih/jiplak* tracing paper. – *kabar* newsprint. – *kaca* cellophane. – *kado* gift wrapping. – *kakus* toilet paper. – *kalkir* tracing paper. – *karbon* carbon paper. – *karton* cardboard. – *karya* working paper. – *kembang* a) blotting paper. b) paper with pictures of flowers on it. – *kerja* working paper. – *klosét* toilet paper. – *koordinir* graph paper. – *koran* newsprint. – *kosong* blank piece of paper. – *kraft* bond paper. – *krép* crepe paper. – *kulit* parchment. – *kuning* small Chinese playing card; → CEKI. – *kwarto* letter-size paper. – *lap* blotting paper. – *lapis* coated paper. – *layangan* kite paper. – *lilin* wax paper. – *mengkilap* glossy paper. – *merang* rice paper. – *meterai* (official) stamped paper. – *minyak* wax paper. – *pak* mailing paper. – *pembersih* cleansing tissue. – *pembungkus* wrapping paper. – *penetap/penghisap* blotting paper. – *penyerap* blotting paper. – *perada* thin metallic paper used for wrapping. – *perbendaharaan* treasury bill. – *perekat* cellotape. – *pola* ruled paper. – *potrét* positive photographic paper. – *rokok* cigarette paper. – *samak* book-wrapping paper. – *sampul* wrapping paper. – *sap* blotting paper. – *saring* filter paper. – *ségel* stamped paper. – *singkong* brown wrapping paper. – *sténsil* stencil paper. – *suara* ballot. – *tapis* filter paper. – *tebal* cardboard. – *tekap* tracing paper. – *telur* a) wax paper. b) paper used for making kites. – *terlapis* → KERTAS *berlapis*. – *tik* typing paper. – *timah* aluminum/tin foil. – *tulis* writing paper. – *turap* wallpaper. – *wangi pengusap muka* towelette. – *WC* toilet paper.
 kertas-mengertas 1 various k.o. paper. **2** waste paper.
kertas II (*onom*) rustling sound of crisp paper being crumpled.
kertau I (*pohon* -) mulberry tree, *Morus indica*.
kertau II (*Jv*) k.o. evil spirit.
kertik (*onom*) **1** sound made by treading on dry leaves, etc. **2** rapping/ticking sound.
kertika *bintang* – the Seven Sisters, Pleiades; → KARTIKA.
kerting (*onom*) tinging sound.
kertip (*onom*) tapping sound (softer than *kertap*).
kertu → KARTU.
kertuk (*onom*) tapping/rapping sound.
kertup(-kertap) (*onom*) crunching sound.
kertus I (*D*) cartridge. *uncang* – cartridge case.
kertus II (*onom*) rustling sound of paper being crumpled.
keruan I (*J*) certain, clear, sure, positive, evident, obvious. – *saja* you bet, certainly, of course, definitely, positively, by all means, it goes without saying. – *saja dia marah.* Of course he's angry. *Sudah – tempatnya.* His place is clear.
keruan II (*J*) *tak/tidak* – **1** disorderly (life), in a mess. **2** precarious (living). **3** (to answer) indistinctly. **4** confused (thoughts, talk), incoherent, to make no sense. **5** tremendously, extraordinarily, exceptionally, extremely. **6** unheard-of.
kerubung I → KERUMUN. **berkerubung** and **mengerubung** to encircle.
 ngerubung to gather around.
 mengerubungi to gather around.
 kerubungan a crowd that has gathered.

kerubung II a paddy barn built of *pandan* leaves.

kerubut I (*J/Jv*) **mengerubut** to gang up.

  mengerubuti 1 to crowd around, assemble at, get/flock together at. **2** to swarm over, crawl all over (of flies/ants, etc.), mob, gang up on. **3** to make a swift sudden attack on, charge.

  kerubutan mob, gang.

kerubut II 1 a shrub with large purple flowers, *Thottea grandiflora*. **2** a plant with huge mottled crimson flowers, *Rafflesia arnoldi*.

kerubyuk (*onom*) plop, plopping sound (of a stone falling in water, etc.).

kerucil → WAYANG *kerucil*.

kerucut 1 conical leaf or paper bag (for fried peanuts, etc.). **2** cone. – *surutan* cone of depression. – *terpancung* truncated cone.

  mengerucut 1 conical. **2** to purse (the lips). **3** to truncate. **4** to get truncated, shrink in size.

  mengerucutkan to truncate.

  pengerucutan truncating.

kerudung veil. – *lampu* lampshade.

  berkerudung 1 to have a ... as a shade. **2** to wear a veil; veiled.

  mengerudungi 1 to provide (a lamp) with a shade. **2** to veil, cover (the head/face) with a veil.

keruh I 1 muddy (of water), turbid, thick (of a liquid). **2** unclean, dirty, filthy, soiled. **3** corrupt; corrupted, depraved. **4** disturbed, distracted, bewildered; restless. **5** confused (of a situation, etc.). – *hati* a) malicious. b) dirty; corrupt.

  keruh-keruh ~ *kerak* very turbid.

  sekeruh as muddy/dirty, etc. as.

  mengeruh to become muddy/turbid, etc., cloud up.

  mengeruhi to trouble, disturb, muddy (water).

  mengeruhkan 1 to muddy, make turbid, muddle. **2** to disturb, trouble. **3** to create confusion in. **4** to bewilder, puzzle.

  kekeruhan 1 turbidity, muddiness. **2** entanglement, confusion, perplexity; trouble, disturbance. **3** corruption, irregularities (in an office).

keruh II berkeruh and **mengeruh 1** to snore. **2** to purr (of a cat).

keruh III (*Hind cla*) – *bumi* and **pengeruh** linear measure of about 2 miles.

keruing a generic name for a number of trees yielding a k.o. wood-oil, *Dipterocarpus spp.*, *Vatica scortechinii*.

keruit *cacing* – thread worm; → KERAWIT.

  berkruit-keruit to wriggle/wiggle like a worm.

keruk I (*onom*) sound of scraping/scratching.

keruk II *kapal* – dredger.

  mengeruk 1 to dredge. ~ *sungai* to dredge a river. ~ *lumpur* to remove mud (from a river bottom, etc.). **2** to scrape (out). ~ *kerak* to scrape the rice crust (out of a pot). **3** to hoard, store up, reap. ~ *keuntungan yang besar* to reap huge profits.

  mengeruki (*pl obj*) to dredge, scrape out.

  mengerukkan ~ *tangan* to put one's hand (in one's pocket or somewhere searching for s.t.).

  terkeruk dredged.

  pengeruk 1 scraper. **2** exploitation (making unethical use of s.t. or s.o. for one's own gain). ~ *periuk* gourmand, glutton. ~ *uang* gold digger.

  pengerukan dredging. ~ *untuk pemeliharaan* maintenance dredging.

keruk-keruk k.o. sand fly or fruit fly.

kerukut curled, shriveled (up), warped, deformed.

  mengerukut 1 to curl up (of dry leaves), shrivel, warp, shrink. **2** to become deformed/twisted (of hands/toes).

  mengerukutkan to fold, pleat, crease, crumple, curl.

kerul (*D*) curl. *rambut* – curly hair.

  mengerul to curl/frizz s.t. *Rambutnya dikerul.* She had her hair permed.

keruma (*J/Jv*) itch-mite.

kerumit mengerumit to move the mouth while munching/nibbling.

kerumuk berkerumuk 1 crumpled (up). **2** crouched/slumped (down)

  mengerumuk(kan) to crumple (up).

  terkerumuk crumpled, creased, wrinkled.

kerumun berkerumun to swarm, throng, mill about.

sekerumun a swarm/bunch of.

  mengerumuni and **memperkerumunkan** to wander around in, come flocking to, surround, crowd/flock around, crowd.

  kerumunan crowd, mob.

  pengerumunan swarming, thronging, mobbing.

kerumus (*ob*) passionate caresses.

  mengerumus to hug, cuddle, caress.

kerumut *penyakit* – morbilli, measles.

kerun → KERON.

kerung a cylindrical hole, hole that has been hollowed out; concave, hollow, hollowed out.

kerung-kerang (*onom*) rattling of crockery.

kerunia → KARUNIA.

keruntang-pungkang (*ob*) confused, head-over-heels; entangled.

kerunting (*ob*) wooden cattle bell.

keruntung 1 bamboo money box/piggy bank. **2** fish basket.

  mengeruntungkan to put in a box or basket.

kerunyut (*M*) wrinkle, line.

  berkerunyut wrinkled, lined, shriveled.

  mengerunyut to crumple up.

  mengerunyutkan ~ *dahi* to wrinkle one's brow, frown.

  terkerunyut crumpled up, creased.

kerup (*onom*) sound made by nibbling at raw vegetables, munching noise. – *kerap* (*onom*) keep on making the sound *kerup*.

keruping scab (over a wound).

kerupuk I generic term for all k.o. of chips made from a starch base and ground shrimps, fish, or other ingredients. They come dried and are fried before eaten; → KRUPUK. – *karak* chips made from leftover rice. – *kembang Palémbang* k.o. fish chips. – *kemplang* chips made from sago flour. – *kuku macan* tiger claw-shaped chips. – *kulit/rambak* chips made from slices of cow or buffalo hide. – *legendar* crispy ground-rice chips. – *merak* k.o. fish chips made of sago flour. – *putih* cassava chip. – *sérmiyér* (red) sage chip. – *udang* shrimp chip.

kerupuk II (*J*) **kekerupukan** to be at one's wits' end.

kerus → KRUS II.

kerusi (*A Mal*) → KURSI I. **mempengerusikan** and **mengerusikan** to chair (a meeting), preside over.

  pengerusi chairperson.

kerusut → KUSUT I.

kerut I 1 wrinkle, furrow, crease, line. **2** curl (in hair). – *kemerut* wrinkles. – *kering* shriveled up. – *merut/mirut* a) wizened, shrivelled. b) rumpled. c) tangled, in a tangle, in confusion, confused. **berkerut merut** to frown, wrinkled, furrowed.

  berkerut(-kerut) 1 wrinkled, creased. **2** (*Mal*) curly (of hair), curled. *berkerut kening* to be sullen.

  meng(k)erut 1 to shrivel up, contract. **2** to wrinkle, crease.

  mengerut(-ngerut) to crease, become wrinkled.

  meng(k)erutkan to wrinkle/furrow s.t. ~ *dahi* to frown, wrinkle one's brows. ~ *gigi* to gnash one's teeth. ~ *kening* a) to frown. b) to wrack one's brains. ~ *kulit* to wrinkle one's skin.

  kerutan 1 wrinkle, crease, line, frown; wrinkling, creasing. **2** curl. **3** contraction, shrinkage.

  pengerutan contraction, wrinkling.

  pengkerutan shrinkage.

kerut II (*onom*) sound of scraping.

kerutak mengerutak to chew, crunch (of a dog on a bone, etc.).

kerutu → GERUTU I.

kerutup (*onom*) crackling sound made when wet leaves burn, etc.

  berkerutup to make that sound.

keruwek (*J/Jv*) **ngeruwek 1** to scratch with the nails, etc. **2** to envy.

keruwes → KRUWES.

keruwing → KERUING.

keruyuk I (*onom*) sound of crowing cock, cock-a-doodle-doo.

  berkeruyuk to crow.

  keruyukan rumbling (of an empty stomach).

keruyuk II → KEROYOK.

kes (in acronyms) → KESÉHATAN, KESEJAHTERAAN.

kés (*E*) cash.

kesa first; → KESATU, *yang* PERTAMA.

kesabun → MINDI.

kesad → KASAD I.

Kesada midnight ceremony of offerings made by the Tenggerese people who live near Mt. Bromo, East Java, to the God of Fire.
kesah 1 moan. **2** sigh.
  berkesah and **mengesah 1** to moan. **2** to sigh.
késah (*A*) story; → KISAH, KISSAH. *al.-* the story is. *Itu lain -.* That's another story.
kesak berkesak to move slowly/little by little, shift over.
  mengesak(kan) to move s.t. slowly, shift s.t. ~ *pantat* to move/shift over.
kesal (*- hati*) **1**a) resentful, annoyed, irritated, peevish, displeased; → DONGKOL, MANGKEL, MENGKAL, SEBAL. b) hurt, offended, disgruntled (cannot get what one wants); → BÉRANG, JÉNGKÉL, PANAS *hati*. **berkesal hati 1** resentful, annoyed. **2** fed up. **2** bored, sick (of), tired (of), fed up (with); → BOSAN, JEMU. **3** impatient, run out of patience. **4** discontented (with s.t.); to feel aggrieved at being treated in some way. **5** regretful, to feel bad.
  mengesalkan (~ *hati*) a) to annoy, irritate, get on the nerves of, displease. b) to bore.
  kekesalan 1 resentment, annoyance, irritation, being fed up. **2** boredom, weariness. **3** impatience. **4** discontent(ment), displeasure, dissatisfaction.
kesam (*ob*) → KASAM I.
kesambet (*J/Jv*) to be entered by an evil spirit, considered by many Javanese the cause of a sudden illness.
kesambi (*Jv*) (*pohon -*) Indian lac tree, *Schleichera oleosa,* used for making charcoal.
kesamping → ke SAMPING.
kesan 1 trace, mark, print (of finger, etc.); → BEKAS I, JEJAK I. **2** impression (made by s.o.), air (of looking some way). *memberi -* to give the impression. *menanam - mendalam di* to make a deep impression on. *pada - pertama* at first impression. *- kaki* footprint.
  berkesan 1 to bear a mark, marked. **2** to impress, make/leave an impression. ~ *lama* to have a lasting impression. **3** impressive, imposing, striking. **4** to get/have the impression (that s.t. is true).
  mengesan 1 to leave a mark/trace. **2** to leave an impression. *paling ~ bagi ...* what was most impressive for ...
  mengesankan and **memperkesankan 1** to leave an impression. **2** to impress, make an impression on; impressive. *berpréstasi ~* to achieve an impressive performance.
  terkesan 1 ~ (*akan*) to be impressed (by). *Ménlu Belanda ~ pembangunan Indonésia.* The Dutch Foreign Minister was impressed by Indonesian development. *tidak ~* unimpressed. **2** to give the impression of, seem. *Sering kali ~ rumit.* It often seems complicated.
  pengesanan impression, expression. ~ *kandungan hati* expression of feeling.
kesana → ke SANA.
kesandingan (*J*) **1** to suffer from a disease caused by a spirit. **2** to suffer from two ills at the same time (one as a result of the other). **3** to behave like a madman.
kesandung (*Jv*) **1** - *pada/dengan* to trip/stumble over, catch one's foot on. **2** to hit/bump up against; → TERSANDUNG.
kesang I mengesang to blow one's nose, usually by pinching one nostril with the finger.
kesang II k.o. stinking rice pest, *Acanthocoris scabrator.*
kesangsang (*J/Jv*) to be caught/stuck (of a kite in a tree, etc.).
kesap-kesip (*J*) blinking (of the eyes).
kesasar (*J*) to get lost, lose one's way, go astray; → SASAR, TERSESAT.
kesat 1 shaggy, hairy, rough (of a surface/climate, etc.). **2** weatherbeaten. **3** faded, discolored (of cloth due to exposure to the sun). **4** coarse, rude (of words). *- daun pimpin* said of s.o. who is not always weak (if necessary he can take strong measures). *bertunggal di tarah, - di empelas* (*M*) settled, made up (of a dispute).
  mengesat to wipe off (moisture, perspiration), wipe dry.
  mengesatkan to wipe s.t. off.
  pengesat ~ *kaki* doormat.
kesat(e)ria (*Skr*) **1** Kshatriya, the military caste in Hinduism. **2** knight. **3** hero.
  kekesat(e)riaan 1 nobleness, nobility, knighthood. **2** gallantry, heroism.

késbang - *dan Linmas* [kesatuan bangsa dan perlindungan masyarakat] national unity and community protection.
késéd(an) (*J*) → KÉSÉT.
késék scrub, rub → GÉSÉK.
  mengésék to scrub, rub.
kesel I (*Jv*) exhausted, tired.
kesel II → KESAL. **ngeselin** → MENGESALKAN.
késél → GÉSÉL.
keselak [and **keselek** (*Jv*) /keselek/] to choke (on a piece of food), swallow s.t. the wrong way.
keseléo (*J*) sprained; → TERGELIAT, TERPELÉCOK. *Kaki saya -.* I sprained my foot. *- lidah* to make a slip of the tongue.
  mengeseléokan to twist s.t. around.
keseliyo → KESELÉO.
kesemak (*Jv*) a tree with edible fruit, persimmon, *Diospyros kaki.*
kesemaran → KESMARAN.
kesemat → KESUMAT.
kesemek → KESEMAK.
kesemsem (*J/Jv*) and **kesengsem** (*J*) **1** to be eager for, fond of, engrossed in; to be sexually excited. **2** charmed, enchanted, fascinated. **3** always startled in one's sleep due to previous events.
kesemuan (*Med*) activity, energy.
kesepuhan (in Lampung, South Sumatra) elder; → SESEPUH.
késér(an) (*Jv*) **1** sleigh. **2** handcart, pushcart, dolly.
keseser (*Jv*) defeated.
kesét (*J*) torn; peeled off (of skin); → BESÉT I.
  mengesét [and **ngesét** (*coq*)] to tear/peel off, skin, flay; to graze/chafe/abrade one's skin. ~ *ular sawah* to peel off the skin of a python.
kesét(an) (*J*) doormat; → KÉSÉD(AN).
keseteria → KESATRIA.
kesian (*J*) pity; → KASIHAN.
kesiap (*J*) **terkesiap** (*darah*) to be frightened/startled.
kesih → KESUH-KESIH.
kesik(-kesik) (*onom*) rustling/whispering sound.
kesima (*J*) **terkesima** disconcerted, upset, confused, perplexed, tongue-tied, speechless (from amazement/embarrassment). *Saya dibuat ~.* I became confused.
kesimbukan 1 a climbing shrub, *Saprosma arboreum.* **2** a climbing plant, skunk vine, *Paederia foetida.*
kesini → ke SINI.
kesip I lacking a pip, seedless (of fruit).
  mengesip to suck (the pulp from a fruit).
kesip II (*J*) blink.
  berkesip(-kesip) to blink (one's eyes).
kesiur (*ob*) **berkesiur** to whistle; whistling, whizzing; to play the flute.
  mengesiurkan to make s.t. whiz past.
Késko [Kesatuan Komando] Commando Unit.
keskul (*Pers*) begging bowl; → SEKUL.
kesléo, keslio and **kesliyo** (*Jv*) → KESELÉO.
kesmak → KESEMAK.
kesmaran (*Jv*) *édan* - and **berkesmaran** to be head over heels in love.
kesodo a ceremony held in the Tengger region of East Java; → KESADA.
kesohor (*J*) well-known, famous; → TERMASYHUR.
kesomplok (*J*) **1** pushed, bumped; bump into (by accident). **2** broke, without any money.
késot (*J/Jv*) **berkésot, mengésot** [and **ngésot** (*coq*)] and **terkésot-késot 1** to move forward little by little, pull o.s. forward (like a baby or disabled person), bottom shuffle; → KESUT. **2** not smoothly, slowly, shuffling along.
kesra 1 [keséhatan rakyat] public health. **2** [kesejahteraan rakyat] people's welfare.
kesrakat (*Jv*) to live in misery/poverty; destitute, impoverished.
késrék (*J*) rough (of the skin).
kesruk (*J*) **ngesruk** to fall down.
  ngesrukin to throw s.t. down.
késting I (*ob*) woven material (for blouses/jackets, etc.).
késting II (*E*) casting.
kestul and **késtul** (*coq*) pistol.

kesturi I (*Skr*) **1** musk, glandular secretion of the male Asian deer. *musang* – civet cat; → RASÉ. **2** musk-shrew, *Suncus murinus*. – *mati karena baunya* to have an accident caused by one's own actions, by showing off, etc.). – *belanda* a) rabbit. b) guinea pig, *Cavia cobaya*. – *bulan* moon rat, rat-shrew, *Echinosorex gymnurus*. – *ce(n)curut* musk-shrew, *Crocidura spp*. – *gunung* marmot. – *hitam* Norwegian rat, *Rattus norvegicus*.

kesturi II various k.o. plants. *bunga* – scorpion orchid. *Arachnis flosaeris/moschifera*. *kayu* – juniper wood, *Juniperus chinensis*. *limau* – musk lime, *Citrus aurantifolia/microcarpa*.

kesturi III (*burung* –) k.o. lory, *Eos spp./Lorius spp*.

kesuari cassowary, *Casuarius galeatus*.

kesuh-kesih panting heavily.

kesu-kesi (*onom*) → KESIK-KESIK.

kesukan → KESUKAAN.

kesuk-kesik (*onom*) the sound of whispering or rustling (of bedclothes, etc.).

kesuma (*Skr Jv*) **1** (*cla*) the poetic word for flower; → BUNGA I, KEMBANG I, KUSUMA. **2** a beautiful woman. – *bangsa* the flower of a country's youth.

kesumat (*A*) dispute, quarrel, feud, lawsuit. *dendam* – rancor and enmity.

kesumba I (*Skr*) **1** anatto, Tamil safflower (yielding a red dye), *Bixa orellana, Carthamus tinctorius*. **2** *mérah* – fiery red. – *murup* bright pink.

mengesumba to paint/dye s.t. red.

kesumba II various species of trogon, *Harpactes spp*.

kesup (*onom*) sound of sucking.

mengesup 1 to suck. **2** to suck in (one's breath).

kesusu (*Jv*) hastily, in a hurry.

kesut (*ob*) **terkesut-kesut** worried and afraid.

késut berkésut-késut and **terkésut-késut** moved/shifted over slowly and quietly (to make room for another).

ketaban (*ob*) crosspiece of paddle-rudder.

ketah (*cla*) → KUTAHA.

ketai I berketai-ketai crumbled, broken into small pieces, shattered; decomposed (of a corpse).

mengetai-ngetai(kan) to crumble, shatter, cut up.

ketai II (*coq*) beaten at cards.

ketak I (*onom*) sound of rapping/tapping. – *ketik* ticking. **berketak-ketik 1** to tick (of a watch, etc.). **2** to beat, throb (of the heart); → DAG-DIG-DUG.

berketak(-ketak) and **(ber)ketuk-ketak** to cluck (of chickens, etc.), cackle.

ketak II wrinkle, skin fold (of a double chin), crease.

berketak(-ketak) folded, with/have folds, creased. *léhér berketak tiga* a) a throat with three creases (an ideal of beauty). b) the three lucky lines on Buddha's neck.

ketakar-ketékér (*Jv*) busy, occupied.

ketakong pitcher plant, *Nepenthes ampullaria*.

kétaler an anesthetic.

ketam I a crab-like nip. *bangkit* – to have/get a cramp. – *mulut* lockjaw.

berketam clenched (of teeth).

mengetam to grasp/grip/close/clasp tightly, squeeze tight. ~ *mulut* to close the mouth tightly.

mengetamkan ~ *bibir* a) to shut one's lips tightly. b) to chafe inwardly, i.e., not express one's feelings openly.

pengetam (pair of) pincers, clamp.

ketam II mengetam to harvest rice with an *ani-ani*.

ketaman the harvest.

pengetam rice harvest knife; → ANI-ANI.

pengetaman harvesting (of rice).

ketam III carpenter's plane. – *alur* router. – *betina* smoothing plane. – *boséng* grooving plane. – *bulat* molding plane. – *halus* smoothing plane. – *jantan* grooving plane. – *kasar* jack plane. – *kumai* milling plane. – *lidah* dovetail plane. – *panjang/penghalus* smoothing plane. – *perapat* dovetail plane. – *siku-siku* miter plane.

mengetam 1 to plane. **2** to trim one's fingernails.

ketaman what has been planed.

pengetam plane ~ *betina* grooving plane. ~ *panjang* smoothing plane.

pengetaman 1 planing. **2** wood shavings.

ketam IV k.o. crab; → KEPITING. – *menyuruhkan anaknya berjalan betul* when the fox preaches, beware of the geese. – *batu* a hardshell crab, mud/rock crab, *Scylla serrata*. – *galah* k.o. crab with long pincers. – *kelapa* coconut/robber crab, *Birgus latro*; → KEPITING *kelapa*. – *rénjong* swimming/flower crab, *Partunus pelagicus*.

ketam V to shrink gradually.

ketambak various species of pomfret, *Stromateus niger, Pampus chinensis*; → BAWAL.

ketampi k.o. fish owl, *Ketupa zeylonensis leschenault*.

ketan sticky/glutinous rice, *Oryza sativa*; → PULUT II. – *hitam* black sticky rice. – *srikaya* sticky rice with brown sugar and coconut milk. – *tétél* steamed sticky rice topped with brown coconut. – *urap* sticky rice with grated coconut.

ketanah k.o. tree.

ketang I (*ob*) tight(ened), taut.

ketang II a marine fish, scat, *Scatophagus argus*. – *lada* rabbit fish, *Siganidas*.

ketang III – *tanduk* k.o. plant, *Kibara sp*.

ketanggor (*Jv*) to run across/bump into s.o. by accident, run into.

ketangtang-ketinting (*J*) **1** to keep on walking back and forth. **2** wrong in every way.

ketap stopcock; → KETAM I, KATUP.

mengetap(kan) ~ *bibir* to bite/press together one's lips (from anger).

ketapak foundation.

ketapang 1 Singapore almond; its bark is used for dye, its seeds for oil, and its wood for carts and boats, *Terminalia catappa*. **2** k.o. tree, sea randa?, panao, *Guettarda speciosa*.

ketapék and **ketapik** a climbing plant, *Ventilago maingayi*.

ketap-ketap and **ketap-ketip** to wink, blink; → KEDAP-KEDIP.

ketapél (*D*) catapult, slingshot.

ketar I trembling, quivering (from excitement/fear, etc.) → GETAR. – *ketir* (*Jv*) a) to tremble. b) nervous; → KETIR-KETIR. **berketar-ketir** *hati* to be afraid, tremble with fear.

berketar-ketar and **terketar-ketar** to shiver, shake, tremble.

ketar II sour, tart, astringent.

ketara (*Jv*) → KENTARA.

ketarap (*ikan* –) parrot-wrasse, *Scaridae*.

ketat 1 tight, taut, fastened/fitting closely. **2** rigid, firm, strict, restrictive, harsh. *dijaga* – closely guarded. **3** binding (of a contract).

seketat as tight(ly) as.

seketat-ketatnya as tight(ly)/taut, etc. as possible.

mengetat to tighten, become tight.

mengetatkan and **memperketat** to tighten, make tighter/stricter/more rigid, tighten up on, beef up (security).

terketat the tightest/strictest.

keketatan tightness.

pengetatan tightening, restricting, making firm or binding. ~ *ikat pinggang* belt tightening.

ketaton <tatu> (*Jv*) to get wounded. *seperti banténg* – on the rampage, to run amok.

ketawa I (*J*) to laugh; → TERTAWA. – *ketiwi* to laugh and laugh.

mengetawai and **mengetawakan** to laugh at.

ketawaan laughter. – *gombal* to laugh out of the wrong side of one's mouth.

ketawa II – *udang* a plant, *Buchanania sessifolia*?

ketawang (*Jv*) k.o. Javanese musical form.

ketaya I a torch made of bamboo filled with resin.

ketaya II (*M*) plaited rattan collar for harnessing oxen and buffalos.

ketayap I white skullcap worn by those Muslims who have made the *hajj* → SONGKOK. – *cendawan* the umbrella-shaped top part of a mushroom.

ketayap II *kuéh* – a sweet made of cornstarch, coconut, milk, and sugar.

ketebon (*Jv*) cornstalk used as cattle fodder.

ketegar (*hati* –) stubborn, persistent, obstinate → TEGAR I.

kéték I (*onom*) clicking noise, click → KETIK I.

kéték II (*Jv*) monkey; → KERA I.

kéték I (*J*) armpit.

mengétéki to tickle s.o. under the arm.

kéték II (M) small, little.
ketel (Jv) dense, close together, thick (hair/foliage), crowded together (of persons).
ketél (J) a drop (of water, etc.). se- a drop.
berketél(-ketél) to drip; in drips and drops.
kétél (E) kettle, vessel, chamber, boiler. - angin air chamber. - kukus boiler. - uap (steam) boiler.
ketéla (Port) (ubi -) sweet potato, yam, Ipomoea batatas. - kayu/pohon cassava → SINGKONG. - manis/rambat (Jv) sweet potato.
kételpak (D ob) overalls, jumpsuit.
ketemu (J) 1 to meet, see e.o.; → BERTEMU. 2 X – X X after X, X in X out. bulan/minggu/tahun – bulan/minggu/tahun month/week/year after month/week/year. berlangsung tahun – tahun to last for years and years. 3 to find, come across. - akal rational, makes sense. - batunya (J) to meet one's match.
seketemu 1 after meeting. 2 whatever one finds/comes across.
mengetemui 1 to call on, go to; → MENEMUI. 2 to find, discover, meet with; to come across. 3 to experience (difficulties).
mengetemukan 1 (= mengetemui) 2 to cause to meet, unite, bring together.
terketemukan tidak ~ can't/couldn't be found.
kéténg (J ob) half penny → PÉSÉR, RIMIS. se- a half penny.
berkéténg-kéténg in small amounts.
mengéténg to buy retail/by the piece/little by little.
ngéténg secara ~ a) (to sell) by the piece. b) (= mengéténg-kan) to sell retail/by the piece/little by little.
mengéténgi to divide (merchandize) into piece (for sale).
mengéténgkan to sell retail.
kéténgan 1 to buy or sell retail/by the piece. 2 loose, single (copy of a magazine). harga ~ retail price. 3 discrete.
pengéténg retailer.
ketengah → TENGAH I.
ketepak-ketepuk (onom) clippity-clop.
ketepél slingshot.
ketépéng an ornamental shrub, fetid cassia, candle bush, Cassia alata/obtusifolia/tora.
ketepil → KETEPÉL.
ketepuk (onom) clattering, clickety-clack.
berketepuk to clatter.
kétering (E) catering; → JASA boga.
ketés (J) drop (of water, etc.) → TÉTÉS.
mengetés to drip.
mengetési to drip into, pour into drop by drop.
ketétér (J/Jv) 1 to fall behind, come in second. 2 to lag behind. 3 to be no match (for s.o.), not to be able to keep up (with demand, etc.).
keti I (Skr) hundred thousand. se- 100,000. dua – 200,000.
berketi-keti by the hundreds of thousands.
ketian by the thousands.
keti II anak – (ob) 1 a wooden ball. 2 heads on a battlefield.
keti III mengeti to weigh.
ketia k.o. tree which produces wood and oil.
ketiak armpit. seperti/bak – ular long-winded. di bawah – orang to be in the firm grip of. semata-mata dari – (to talk) through one's hat. mengembang – amis to wash one's dirty linen in public.
berketiak ular long-winded, tiresomely talkative, tedious
mengetiaki to carry s.t. in one's armpit.
ketial 1 fitting very tightly and so hard to remove (as a cork from the mouth of a bottle). 2 to have trouble moving about because one is obese. 3 viscous.
ketian k.o. wood sap mixed with resin.
ketiap side deck used by rowers. perahu – a houseboat used on rivers.
ketiau k.o. large tree, Ganua motleyana, with commercial timber; oil is made from the seeds.
ketib → KHATIB.
ketiban (Jv) to get fallen on (by), be struck (by). - nasib sial struck by misfortune. - nikmat ganda hit by a double pleasure. Meréka belum - rejeki/rezeki. They haven't been lucky yet. - pulung a) to get an unexpected piece of luck or award, get lucky. b) (J) to get into trouble due to s.o. else's actions. - sampur (Jv) to get one's turn (at doing s.t.).

ketibung → KETIMBUNG.
ketiding (M) large rattan basket for storing rice, fruit, etc.
ketik I (onom) sound of ticking/clicking/typing. juru - typist. mesin - typewriter.
mengetik 1 to tick (of a clock). 2 to flick, shoot (a marble) by flipping it with a finger suddenly released from the thumb. 3 (= mengetikkan) to type(write).
ketikan 1 typing. 2 s.t. typed.
pengetik typist.
pengetikan typing.
ketik II the long leg (of a cricket/grasshopper, etc.).
ketika I (Skr) 1 moment, instant. 2 (pada) - (at the moment) when. (pada) - adiknya dilahirkan when his younger brother was born. 3 while, during the time that, when, as. Ia tertidur - ia membaca buku. He fell asleep while reading a book. 4 time, period. - itu saya berada di luar negeri. At that time I was abroad. 5 (lucky) moment/day chosen by diviners. melihat - to consult primbons in order to know the lucky and unlucky days, etc. (to do s.t.). mencari - to seek the right moment (to do s.t.).
seketika 1 a moment/while/second. 2 then and there, at that very moment, at once. dengan ~ immediately, right away. ~ itu juga at that very moment/instant, on the spot. 3 at the time that, when. keseketikaan instantaneousness.
berketika at/to wait for the right time, (all) in good time. demam ~ fever recurring at regular intervals (e.g., tertiary malaria). dengan tiada ~ irregular, at no fixed time.
ketika II bintang - Pleiades; → KARTIKA.
keti-keti a small bee/wasp.
ketil sektil a pinch (of).
berketil-ketil in pinches, by bits.
mengetil to pinch off, nip. bagai belut diketil ékor (quick) as an eel whose tail has been nipped.
ketilang → KUTILANG.
ketimaha (Jv) → KATIMAHA. kayu - a tree whose timber is used for making kris-sheaths, Kleinhovia hospita.
ketimang buckle, clasp.
ketimbang (Jv) 1 compared to/with, than (in comparisons); → KATIMBANG. jauh lebih unggul - meréka far superior to theirs. "Bidang pekerjaan saya lebih besar tanggung jawabnya - wewenangnya," jelasnya. "My area of responsibility is greater than my authority," he explained. 2 rather than. - menunggu empat jam, lebih baik ke Yogya dengan naik bis. Rather than waiting four hours, it would be better to go to Yogya by bus.
ketimbir sty (on the eye).
ketimbul (J) breadfruit, Artocarpus communis.
ketimbung and ketimpung (onom) splashing (of bathers in a stream, etc.); → KECIMPUNG.
berketimbung(an) to splash around.
ketimpal a crawling mass (of maggots, etc.).
ketimpring → REBANA ketimpring.
ketimpung (onom) splashing; → KECIMPUNG I.
berketimpung to splash around.
ketimun → (MEN)TIMUN.
ketimus (J) a snack made from grated sweet potatoes and brown sugar wrapped in a banana leaf and boiled.
keting I urat - Achilles tendon.
mengeting (cla) to hamstring (as a punishment).
keting II engraved catfish, Arius caelatus.
ketingting (in East Kalimantan) a small uncovered prau used as a water taxi.
ketip I (= pengetip) nip, bite, sting (of small insects).
mengetip 1 to bite, sting. 2 to pinch slightly.
pengetip biting insect.
ketip II dime. se- a dime.
ketip III (in Central Kalimantan) one quarter of a gram (of gold).
ketiplak (onom) sound made by clogs or wooden sandals.
ketipung (Jv) a small drum.
ketirah a red-leaved shrub, bandicoot berry, Leea indica.
ketir-ketir (Jv) → KETAR-KETIR.
ketis mengetis to flick (away) (a marble/dirt off clothes, etc.) with the fingers.

ketitir(an) 1 Malay spotted dove, *Streptopelia chinensis tigrina*. **2** barred ground dove, *Geopelia striata*; → MERBUK.

ketlingsut and **ketlisut** (*Jv*) mislaid, to get lost.

ketok I (*J*) a knock(ing sound) → KETUK I. *tukang – (mobil)* (car) body repairman → KENTÉNG *tétér. – kadal* (*J*) a children's game in which a piece of wood or small bamboo strip is jerked forward by rapping on it. – *magic* a combination of body work and magic used to repair cars.
  mengetok to knock at; to bang on, rap on (s.t. with the fingers, with a small hammer, etc.), chip (paint). ~ *kawat* to (send a) cable. ~ *pintu* to knock/rap at the door.
  mengetok-ngetok to drum/keep rapping (one's fingers, etc., on s.t.).
  mengetokkan to pound (a gavel, etc.).
  ketokan 1 knock, rap(ping), banging (of a gavel, etc.). **2** knocking (sound).
  pengetok s.o. or s.t. that knocks/raps.
  pengetokan rapping, knocking, chipping (paint).

ketok II mengetok ~ *kayu* (in Riau) to levy illegal excise taxes on lumberyard owners.
  pengetok ~ *kayu* and **ketokan** *(kayu)* illegal levying of such taxes.

kétok moto (*Jv*) visual; → KASATMATA.

ketola (*Skr*) loofah, luffa, dishcloth gourd, i.e., any of the genus *Luffa* of tropical vines of the gourd family, with thin-shelled large cylindrical fruits with dense fibrous interior tissues; → PETOLA.

ketombé (*J*) → KETUMBÉ.

keton I (*col*) ringgit – ducatoon, i.e., a silver coin; → KETUN.

keton II a tree, kraton plant, *Mitragyna speciosa*, whose leaves are chewed in place of opium.

ketong → KETON I.

ketonggéng (*Jv*) large black scorpion.

ketongkéng → TONGKÉNG II.

ketopong 1 helmet. **2** caul. **3** casque.
  berketopong 1 helmeted, wearing a helmet. *lahir* ~ to be born with a caul. **2** (*– besi*) steel helmet.

ketoprak I (*Jv*) a type of modern popular play depicting stories mainly drawn from Javanese history plays, with improvised spoken dialogue in modern realistic acting and a clown who comments on current public topics.

ketoprak II (*J*) a dish consisting of bean sprouts, bean curd, red pepper, and soy sauce.

ketot (*J/Jv*) stubborn.

kétot (*E*) cutout valve.

ketrék mengetrék to try to seduce, attract (women).

ketrik mengetrik to scrape or hollow out s.t. before spackling it.
  mengetrikkan to scrape out with s.t.
  ketrikan s.t. scraped out.

ketrok (*J*) **mengetrok-ngetrok** and **ngetrok-ngetrok** to beat/strike/hit several times.
  mengetrokkan to beat s.t. (against s.t. else).

ketrucut (*Jv*) slip of the tongue.

Kéts I /kéts/ sneakers (from the brand name Keds).

kéts II dud (a bullet, etc. that doesn't explode).

ketu (*Jv*) headdress (in general); skullcap → KOPIAH. *– udeng* turban sewn in place; → BLANGKON.

ketua → TUA. **1** elder, old and experienced man in a village; head, leader. **2** chairman, chairperson, head. *– fakultas* dean. *– jurusan* department chairman (in a university). *– kelas* class monitor. *– menteri* (*ob*) prime minister, premier. *– muda* vicechairman. *– pelaksana* a) chief executor. b) executive chairman. *– pembina* promoting chairman. *– regu* team captain. *– umum* general chairman. *– wanita* chairwoman.
  berketuakan to have ... as leader/chairman.
  mengetuai to lead, head, preside over, chair.
  mengetuakan to consider/appoint/regard ... as head/chairman.
  keketuaan chairmanship.
  pengetua 1 dean (of diplomatic corps). **2** (*Mal*) head (of s.t.).

ketual → KATWAL.

ketuat wart; → KUTIL I.

ketubah → KHOTBAH.

ketuban fetal membrane, amnion, bag of waters; → TUBAN-TUBAN.

ketuir a plant used by fishermen to counteract poisons of contaminated fish, etc., glory bower, *Clerodendron inerme*.

ketuk I (*onom*) knock(ing) sound, rap, tap, beat (with the knuckles/fingertips). *– ketak* rapping sounds. *– tilu* name of a social dance popular in West Java → RONGGÉNG.
  ketuk-ketuk a wooden or bamboo cylinder with holes rapped with a stick to summon villagers to prayer or in an emergency.
  mengetuk [and **ngetuk** (*coq*)] **1** to knock at, rap on, tap at, drum on. *Jarinya* ~ *daun méja* His fingers drummed on the tabletop. ~ *hati (nurani)* to persuade, touch (one's feelings). ~ *kawat* to (send a) cable. ~ *méja* to knock on wood. ~ *pintu* to knock at the door. **2** to do body work on (a vehicle).
  mengetuk-ngetuk to keep (on) knocking.
  mengetukkan to knock with s.t., pound.
  mengetuk-ngetukkan to keep on pounding (a gavel, etc.). ~ *jari-jemarinya* to drum one's fingers.
  terketuk ~ *hati-nuraninya* to feel it in one's heart (to do s.t. for the poor, etc.).
  ketukan knock, rap, pounding.
  pengetuk hammer, knocker.
  pengetukan knocking on, rapping on.

ketuk II (*Jv*) a musical instrument in the *gamelan*, a single inverted bronze bowl or kettle.

ketuk III (*onom*) cluck, cackling, cackle (of a hen after laying an egg, etc.). *barang siapa yang –, ialah yang bertelur* the pot calls the kettle black. *– di luar sangkar, bertanam di luar pagar* to lock the barn door after the horse has been stolen.
  berketuk to cackle, cluck.

ketul I 1 clot (of dried blood), lump (of cooked rice), piece (of wood/sugarcane), chunk (of bread), clod (of earth). **2** counter for objects that are solid and in lumps/pieces, etc. *se- roti* a hunk of bread.
  berketul-ketul in clods/lumps, etc.
  ketulan lump, clod. ~ *tanah* a solid clod of earth.

ketul II contracted; (muscle) flexing.
  mengetulkan 1 ~ *kaki* to draw up one's knees (as in sleep). **2** to flex (one's muscles).
  pengetul *urat/otot* ~ adductor muscle.

ketul III (*Jv ob*) blunt, dull.

ketulah (*J*) cursed, damned; to have an accident/affliction (because one has broken a taboo/gone against the advice of one's parents, etc.).

ketumbar (*Tam*) coriander, *Coriandrum sativum*.

ketumbé (*J*) and **ketumbi 1** dandruff, scaly scurf. **2** last dregs. *– tahi ayam* riffraff, social outcast.

ketumbit medicinal herb, *Leucas zeylanica*, and other species.

ketumbu a lidded basket.

ketumbuhan 1 smallpox. **2** (*J*) boil or skin disease; → TUMBUH.

ketumpang (*Jv*) an herb, *Dysophylla auricularia*.

ketun → KETON I.

ketung (*onom*) pinging sound "tung."
  berketung-ketung to make that sound.

ketungging → KETONGGÉNG.

ketup I mengetup ~ *geraham* to clench one's teeth; → KATUP.

ketup II → KETUP-KETAP.

ketupa I a shade tree, *Baccaurea dulcis*.

ketupa II fish owls, *Ketupa spp*.

ketupat I rice-cake snack cooked in a small container of woven young coconut leaves. *belah –* lozenge-shaped. *– Bangkahulu/Bengkulu* (*coq*) a blow to the eye.

ketupat II [keadaan, waktu dan tempat] (the factor of) circumstances, time and place; → SIKON.

ketup-ketap (*onom*) sound of tapping/rapping/pattering of feet.

ketupuk buffy fish owl, *Ketupa ketupu*.

ketur I (*cla*) vase-shaped spittoon/cuspidor.

ketur II berketur to croak (of frogs).

ketus (*J*) **1** vehement, violent, impetuous, sharp; sincere, open, upright; quarrelsome, fussy. **2** bold, audacious, forward. **3** do not mince matters; to be outspoken.

Ketut (in Bali) a noncaste name element indicating fourth-born child, such as *– Lami*; → KTUT.

ketutugan (*J*) 1 covered (a hole, etc.) with, buried with. 2 to hit the jackpot. 3 not lacking a thing.

keucik (*Ac*) village head.

keutar (*S*) pungent, biting, acrid.

kewalahan (*Jv*) to be at one's wits' end, at a loss for what to do, unable to cope (or, handle the situation) (because one is overwhelmed, etc.). *Hanya ada satu hal yang membuat –!* There's only one thing that's a pain in the neck!

kéwan (*ob*) → HÉWAN.

kéwang (in the Moluccas) village police.

kewangén (in Bali) a vase made from pale-green young coconut leaves.

kewartal → KUARTAL.

kéwat (*J*) easily gets into a fight, ready with his fists.

kewatir (*J*) → KHAWATIR.

kéwéng (*J*) **dikéwéng-kéwéng** to be carried about everywhere. *Tentu saja anak itu masuk angin, habis ~ saja sih.* Of course that child has caught a cold, he was carried about everywhere, wasn't he?

kéwés (*Jv*) lovely, attractive (in speech/voice/gestures, etc.).

kéwuh (*Jv*) **mengéwuhkan** to embarrass.

kéyani → KIANI.

kéyong → KÉONG.

kg I (*abbr*) [kilogram] kilogram.

Kg II (*abbr*) [Kampung] village, city neighborhood.

kh- I also see entries beginning with **k-**.

kh. II → KHUSUS.

kha (*A*) name of the seventh letter of the Arabic alphabet.

khabal (*A*) mental disorder.

khabar → KABAR. **khabarkan** *tidak ~ diri (lagi)* a) unconscious. b) sleeping.

khabaz (*A*) baker.

khadam and **khadim** (*A*) 1 domestic servant. 2 slave. 3 wage earner. 4 clown (in *bangsawan* performances).

khafi (*A*) hidden, concealed. *zikir –* recital of liturgy to o.s.

khaid → HAID.

khaimah → KÉMAH.

khair (*A*) good. *– al-afiat* good health.

khairat (*A*) s.t. good, good deeds.

khakan (*Pers*) emperor.

khaki → KAKI III.

khalaik → KHALAYAK.

khalak (*A ob*) creature; to make, manufacture.

khalawat → KHALWAT.

khalayak (*A*) 1 God's creatures, i.e., human beings. 2 (collective plural) people, crowd, the public. *pendapat –* public opinion. *salah seorang –* a member of the public. *– muda* young people. *– pembeli* the buying public. *– ramai* the public. *– undangan* attendees, guests.

  mengkhalayakkan to make public, distribute to the public, announce publicly.

khali (*A*) 1 empty, void. 2 free (from). *tidak – dari kesalahan* not without mistakes, imperfect. *tidak – daripada* not fail to. *Tiadalah ia – daripada berdoa.* He prays all the time. *tiada – membantu A* not forgetting to help A; → SUNYI. 3 easygoing.

khalifah (*A*) caliph, successor of the Prophet Muhammad; (title of a) religious leader and ruler in a Muslim state; head of a mystic order; (in the Sunda area) representative of the *penghulu* in charge of marriage ceremonies. *– debus* leader of *debus* performances.

  kekhalifahan caliphate; empire. *~ Usmani/Usmaniyah* Ottoman Empire.

khalifatulah (*A*) the vicar of God.

khalik (*A*) the Creator. *-ul alam* creator of the universe, God. *– ulbahri* creator of the seas, God.

khalikah (*A*) 1 creation. 2 behavior, manners; → KULIKAT.

  berkhalikah to be moody, have caprices. *– raya* the universe.

khalil (*A*) friend. *– Allah* friend of God (Abraham's title).

khalis (*A*) pure, genuine.

khalkah → HALKAH.

khalkum → JAKUN, LEKUM.

khalwat (*A*) 1 reclusion, retreat, withdrawal. 2 improper behavior (said of an illicit act committed by an unchaperoned, unmarried man and woman).

  berkhalwat 1 to go into seclusion/retreat. 2 to commit an improper act.

Kham (*A*) (the Biblical) Ham.

khamar (*A*) spirits, alcoholic drink, wine, liquor.

khamir (*A*) yeast; → KAMIR.

  pengkhamiran fermentation.

khamiri (*A*) leavened.

Khamis → KAMIS II.

khanah (*Pers*) building, (store)house. *kitab –* library.

khandak (*A ob*) moat, trench; → PERANG *khandak*.

khanduri → KENDURI.

khanjar (*A*) a large curved dagger; → KANJAR I.

khaos → KAOS II.

khaotis → KAOTIS.

kharab (*A*) ruined, destroyed, perished.

kharaj (*A*) revenue, taxes.

kharanda → KERANDA.

khardal (*A*) mustard.

kharisma (*D*) charisma. *penuh –* charismatic.

  berkharisma charismatic.

kharismatis (*D*) charismatic.

khas (*A*) typical (of), special, specialty (of), specific (to), exclusive, characteristic (of), exceptional, particular. *– Jakarta* typical of Jakarta, typically Jakarta, a Jakarta specialty.

  mengkhaskan and **memperkhaskan** to reserve (for special use), earmark (for), set aside (for). *~ kamar bagi* to set aside a room for.

  kekhasan peculiarity, feature, special characteristic/feature/attraction. *Indonésia memiliki macam ~ yang mampu menarik wisatawan.* Indonesia has various special features which can attract tourists.

khasah (*ob*) → KASA I.

khasanah → KHAZANAH. *– 1001 malam* the 1,001 Nights.

khasi → KASI II.

khasiat (*A*) special virtue/property/quality (of an herb/drug, etc.). *ilmu – obat* pharmacology.

  berkhasiat to have a special virtue/quality.

  mengkhasiati to examine closely, investigate in detail.

khasis (*D*) chassis.

khasumat (*ob*) → KESUMAT.

khat (*A*) 1 line. 2 handwriting. 3 Arabic calligraphy/calligraphic writing. *– Arab* Arab style of calligraphy. *– Farsi* Persian style of calligraphy.

khatam (*A*) 1 (*cla*) seal. *– Sulaiman/Suléman* the seal of Solomon. 2 the end; final, last; ended, completed (of the reading of the Koran), concluded (*esp* of religious study), accomplished (of a difficult task). *– anbia/segala Nabi* the last of the prophets, i.e., Muhammad. *– kaji* to recite the verses of the Koran through to the end.

  berkhatam *~ kaji* to read through the Koran to the end, to have concluded reading through the Koran.

  mengkhatamkan *~ Qur'an* to complete the reading of the Koran.

  khataman a special ceremony marking the completion of reading the Koran through to the end for the first time.

khatan → KHITAN.

khatib (*A*) 1 reader (and preacher) in the mosque. 2 secretary of the *NU* organization. *– aam* general secretary.

khatifah (*A*) k.o. woven material from sheep's wool; rug, carpet.

khatimah (*A*) conclusion.

khatulistiwa (*A*) the equator. *daérah –* the tropics.

khauf (*A*) fear.

khaul (*A*) commemorating the date of (s.o.'s death/time in office, etc.); → KAUL II.

khawatir (*A*) nervous, anxious, worried, concerned, afraid, frightened, fearful, alarmed → KAWATIR, KEWATIR, KUATIR.

  mengkhawatirkan 1 to disturb, alarm; disturbing, serious, critical. 2 (= **mengkhawatiri**) to be nervous about, be afraid of, fear (that), be anxious/worried about.

  kekhawatiran worry, concern; fear, fright, anxiety. *~ ASÉAN terhadap pembangunan militér Jepang* ASEAN's fears of a Japanese military buildup. ~ *akan suatu perang nuklir* fears of a nuclear war.

khayal (*A*) **1** fantasy, hallucination, vision, imagination. **2** fantastic, imaginary, unreal, fictitious. *bilangan* – (*math*) imaginary number.

  berkhayal 1 to have hallucinations, see visions. **2** to indulge in fantasies, daydream, fantasize, imagine things.

  mengkhayal to fantasize, daydream.

  mengkhayalkan 1 to envision, imagine, fantasize s.t. **2** to visualize s.t.

  khayalan 1 fancy, hallucination, imagination, fantasy, dream. **2** image, vision.

  pengkhayal dreamer, visionary, fantasist.

  pengkhayalan fantasizing, imagining.

khayali (*A*) **1** imaginary. **2** (*cla*) drunk (in mystic reverie) (in *tasawuf* contexts).

khayat → HAYAT I.

khazanah (*A*) **1** wealth; possessions, treasure. – *kata* vocabulary, glossary. **2** treasure, treasure chamber. **3** library. **4** vault.

khélasi (*E*) chelating. *terapi* – chelation therapy.

khelembak (*ob*) → KELEMBAK I.

khémah → KÉMAH.

khéwan (*ob*) → HÉWAN.

khial → KHAYAL.

khiali → KHAYALI.

khianat (*A*) **1** betraying, traitorous, treacherous, perfidious. **2** betrayal, treason, treachery, deceit, guile. *berbuat* – and **berkhianat** (*atas/kepada*) to deceive, betray; commit treason.

  mengkhianat to be a traitor, be disloyal/treacherous.

  mengkhianati to betray, be disloyal to, deceive.

  mengkhianatkan to betray, be disloyal/traitorous to, deceive. ~ *tempatnya bersembunyi* to betray/give away s.o.'s hiding place.

  kekhianatan betrayal, treason, treachery.

  pengkhianat deceiver, betrayer, traitor.

  pengkhianatan treason/betrayal/disloyalty. ~ *bangsa* high treason. ~ *negara* treason.

khiar (*A*) optional (of a duty), freedom to complete a sale or to cancel it. – *aib* the ability of a buyer to return damaged goods. – *syarat* conditions of a sale.

khidmat (*A*) **1** respect, reverence, loyalty, submission. **2** (*Br Mal*) service(s) (rendered).

  berkhidmat 1 respectful, reverent, humble; obliging. **2** (~ *kepada*) to serve (one's country, etc.), carry out one's duties loyally, be subservient to, perform one's duties (for). *meréka yang* ~ *di Malaysia Timur* those who serve in East Malaysia.

  mengkhidmati to serve/work for, be of service to. **2** to be respectful to, respect.

  kekhidmatan 1 respect. **2** solemn reverence, solemnity.

  perkhidmatan (*Mal*) (social/military) service(s). ~ *Awam Malaysia* Malaysian Civil Service. ~ *Diplomatik* Diplomatic Service.

khik (*Pers*) bottle.

khilaf (*A*) **1** error, mistake. **2** wrong, in error, erroneous.

  mengkhilafkan to make a mistake in.

  kekhilafan 1 mistake, error, fault. **2** mistaken, fallen into error.

khilafah (*A*) matters concerning government and the state.

khilafi(y)ah (*A*) disputed, controversial.

khinat → KHIANAT.

khisit and **khizit** (*A*) envy, jealousy; envious, jealous.

khitan (*A*) circumcision; → SUNAT.

  berkhitan (to be) circumcised.

  mengkhitan to circumcise.

  mengkhitani (*pl obj*) to circumcise.

  mengkhitankan to circumcise, to have (one's son) circumcised.

  khitanan circumcision ceremony.

  pengkhitan circumciser.

  pengkhitanan circumcising.

khittah (*A*) line of action. – *nahdliyah ashliyah* basis for the *NU* organization platform.

khiyar → KHIAR.

khizanat → KHAZANAH.

khizanatulkitab (*A*) (*cla*) library.

khl- also see entries beginning with **kl-**.

khlorida (*D*) chloride.

khlorinasi → KLORINASI.

khloroform → KLOROFORM.

Khmér Khmer, Cambodian. ~ *Mérah* Khmer Rouge.

khodrat (*ob*) → KODRAT II.

khoja(h) (*Pers ob*) Muslim merchant from northern India.

khol (*A*) death. *selamatan* – an annual ceremony in observance of the anniversary of s.o.'s death.

khotbah (*A*) sermon, preaching, address, speech, talk. *bergaya* – didactic. – *nikah* marriage service.

  berkhotbah ~ (*kepada*) to preach (to), deliver a sermon/speech (to), give an address (to).

  mengkhotbati to preach to, give a lecture to, lecture.

  mengkhotbahkan to sermonize about, discourse upon, explain in a sermon, preach about.

  pengkhotbah 1 preacher, orator, speaker, sermonizer (in mosque). ~ *Injil* (Christian) minister, evangelist. **2** Ecclesiastes (in the Bible).

khotib → KHATIB.

khrom → KROM.

khronis → KRONIS.

khuatir → KUATIR.

khubz (*A*) bread.

khudu (*A*) humility.

khukum (*ob*) → HUKUM I.

khul → TALAK *khul*.

khulafaur rasyidin (*A*) the four caliphs who led the Muslim community after the Prophet Muhammad's death.

khulak (*A*) divorce granted to a woman by her husband in exchange for the return of her dowry; → TEBUS *talak*.

khuldi (*A*) *buah* – the forbidden fruit (eaten by Adam and Eve in Paradise), the apple of Adam and Eve.

khulki (*A*) natural.

khuluk I (*A*) nature, disposition, innate qualities, character, behavior.

khuluk II → KHULAK.

khunkar (*Pers*) emperor.

khunt(s)a (*A ob*) hermaphrodite, transvestite.

khurafat (*A*) fable, fiction.

khurma → KURMA.

khusmat → KESUMAT.

khusuf → KUSUF.

khusuk → KHUSYUK. *dengan* – *dan khidmat* with devotion and reverence.

  mengkhusukkan ~ *suasana* to solemnize the atmosphere.

  kekhusukan solemnity, devoutness.

khusunul khatimah (*A*) happy ending.

khusus (*A*) **1** special, exclusive, particular; → KHAS. *berat* – specific gravity. *yang* – characteristic. *pasukan* – [Pas(s)us] special forces. *Daérah* – *Ibukota Jakarta* [DKI Jaya] the Greater Jakarta Special Capital Region. **2** to make it a point to, make a special effort to. *Ia* – *datang pagi-pagi*. He made it a point to come early in the morning. – *untuk* especially/specifically/expressly for/to.

  mengkhusus specialized.

  mengkhususkan 1 to regard s.t. as special, treat s.t. in a special way, adapt for a particular purpose. **2** to set aside (for). **3** to specialize in. ~ (*diri*) *pada/dalam* to specialize in.

  terkhusus 1 especially, particularly, specifically. **2** specialized.

  kekhususan specialty, specificity, (special) feature.

  pengkhususan specification.

  khususnya *pada* ~ in particular, especially.

khus(y)u and **khusyuk** (*A*) **1** devotion, humility. **2** devoted (before God), devout. **3** conscientious. **4** engrossed/immersed/absorbed in. **5** (*J*) intention, aim, purpose. – *syahdu* religious devotions.

  berkhusyuk to be devoted (to religion/to s.t.).

  mengkhusyukkan to devote (o.s. to).

  kekhusyukan devotion, devoutness.

khutbah → KHOTBAH. – *iftitah* opening speech (such as at an *NU* congress).

ki I (*Jv*) **1** title of respect for older men, teachers and a man of religious accomplishment, e.g., – *Hajar Dewantara*. **2** title of respect for puppeteers, – *Dalang*, and people in the *gamelan* orchestra. – *yogo* a *gamelan* player. 3 title for certain venerated objects. – *Jagur* an ancient cannon located in Jakarta.

ki II (*S*) short form of *kai*, i.e., tree; prefix used in front of names of plants and trees; → KAYU I. – *putri* k.o. tree, *Podocarpus neriifolius*. – *urat* plantain, *Plantago major*.

ki III name of the letter q.

ki IV *air* – water produced from rice straw, used in preparing noodles.

ki V (in acronyms) → KOMPI I.

kia I (*Pers ob*) chain/lock stitch; → JAHITAN, SETIK I.

  bekia *menjahit* ~ to sew with that stitch.

kia II kia-kia *hiu/ikan* ~ a) a shark species, *Rhinobatus thonini*. b) k.o. guitar fish, *Rhynchobatus djeddensis*. c) two-faced.

kia III *limau* – a shrub with lime-producing fruit, *Triphasia aurantiola*.

kiah mengiah(kan) to stretch, extend, draw/pull out (gloves, etc. to enlarge the size).

  pengiah ~ *kasut/sepatu* a) shoe stretcher. b) shoehorn.

kiafah (*A*) tracking.

kiahi → KIAI.

kiai (*Jv*) 1 title given to Muslim religious scholars, e.g., – *Haji Wahid Hasyim*. 2 title for teachers of mysticism, *dukun*s, etc. 3 (in South Kalimantan) district head. 4 title used for sacred objects and animals, the venerated. – *Guntur Madu* name of the *gamelan* orchestra in the Kasunanan Palace in Surakarta. – *Tunggulwulung* the venerated flag inside the palace in Yogyakarta. – *Anggoro* the name of the elephant in the Sriwedari amusement park in Surakarta; → K(I)AYI, KI I.

  kiainya euphemistic reference to the tiger.

kia-kia I (*C coq*) to have fun/a good time, take it easy, enjoy o.s.; → KYA-KYA.

kia-kia II → YU *kia-kia*.

kiak-kiak bulldog ant, a large black biting ant that follows along trails.

kial I (ber)kial-kial and terkial-kial to shake/wrench o.s. free, get away from (or, rid of) one's pursuers. *tertawa terkial-kial* to be convulsed with laughter.

kial II (*ob*) gesture, representation.

  berkial to gesticulate, illustrate, dramatize.

  mengialkan to represent by gestures/gesticulations; to act out, illustrate, dramatize.

  perkialan dramatization, gesticulations to demonstrate an action.

kiam (*A*) to stand erect during prayer.

kiamat (*A*) 1 resurrection from the dead. *hari* – a) Judgment Day; end of the world, doomsday. b) the destruction of the world. *sampai* – *(dunia)* till the end of time. *sampai* – *tak akan dapat* will never get it in one's lifetime. *yaum al-* *di padang mahsyar* the restoration day on the plain of meeting. – *kubra* the last resurrection. 2 disaster, calamity. – *kita* we're in bad trouble. –*lah dunia* I won't survive, it's the end of the world. 3 "Resurrection"; name of the 75th chapter of the Koran.

  mengkiamat to be like the end of the world.

  mengkiamatkan to bring about the end (of the world).

kiambang water lettuce, duckweed (symbol of fleeting love), *Pistia stratiotes*. *ibarat/seperti* – drifting, unstable. *hidup seperti* – to live an unstable life. *seperti* – *dilémpar* temporarily separated and reunited later. *biduk lalu* – *bertaut* said of relatives who make up again after a short estrangement.

kiambwé(é) (*C*) dried salted plum.

kian I 1 as many/much/far as. *sepuluh* – ten times as many. *dua* – twice as much as. *bak* – *(cla)* suchlike, such as that. – ... – ... the more ... the more ...; the ...(er) the ...(er), (it gets) more and more ... – *lama* – *besar* the longer the bigger; as time goes on it gets bigger. – *lama* – *mahal* it gets more and more expensive. – *hari* – *nyata* clearer every day (or, day by day). 2 more, increase further. *Ia berlari* – *cepat dan* – *jauh dari tempat perkelahian tadi*. He ran faster and farther from the scene of the fight. – *saat* (changes) at any moment.

  sekian as much (as), to such a degree (that), so and so much, such and such an amount, (as much as) this. ~ *banyak* as many as these, so much, this many. ~ *cukuplah* as much as that is enough. ~ *lama* up to now, so far. ~ *tinggi* as tall as this, this

tall. ~*lah (dulu)*. That's all for now (often used to end a speech or letter). **kesekian** umpteenth, n'th. *untuk* ~ *kalinya* for the nth/umpteenth time. **sepersekian** [and **seperkian** (*infr*)] ~ *detik* (for) a fraction of a second, (for) a split second; in no time (at all). *dalam jangka waktu* ~ *detik* in a fraction of a second.

  berkian-kian quite a lot, a great many, so many. *perkataan yang* ~ *itu* so many words.

  memperkian to speed up.

  terkian *tidak* ~ countless, innumerable.

kian II to(ward) that place; there. – *kemari* up and down, back and forth. *berserak* – *kemari* knocked here and there (or, all over the place). *mencari* – *kemari* to search high and low. **mengiankemarikan** to send s.t. back and forth.

kianat → KHIANAT.

kiang – *kiut* (*onom*) squeaking sound made by opening and closing doors.

  kiang-kiang creaking, squeaking.

kiani (*Pers ob*) royal. *singgasana* – *(cla)* royal throne.

kiansay (*C*) son-in-law.

kiap a stand/support (for a flag mast, etc.).

kiar spray from a citrus fruit rind.

kiara (*pohon* –) a generic name for *Ficus spp.* trees.

kias I (*A*) 1 metaphor, simile, comparison, parable, lesson. *mengambil* – *(an) daripada* to draw a lesson from. 2 hint, allusion, indirect reference. 3 analogy (in Muslim theology). *ahli* – Hanafi Muslim theologians who augment tradition by analogical deductions.

  berkias to speak in metaphors.

  berkias-kias(an) to make insinuations at e.o.

  mengias 1 to make an allusion, hint. 2 criticize (in an indirect way). *Ia suka* ~ *orang*. He likes to blame others.

  mengiasi to allude to, hint at.

  mengiaskan to apply (s.t. analogically) to; to aim at, allude to, indicate/point out ironically; to compare s.t.

  kiasan 1 (reasoning by) analogy. 2 metaphor(ical language), figurative sense. 3 simile, metaphor, comparison, symbol. 4 allusion, irony, sarcasm. 5 instruction, lesson, moral. *dengan/dalam arti* ~ figuratively (speaking), metaphorically.

kias II *ilmu* – magic; → SIHIR.

kiasi (*ob*) analogous.

kiat I 1 (= **berkiat**) stiff, cramped (of one's neck/limbs, etc.); twisted, distorted. 2 (= **mengiat** and **terkiat**) sprained, dislocated.

  mengiatkan to sprain s.t.

kiat II (*M*) 1 secret (way to do s.t.), ruse, trick, knack, stratagem, special technique, way, method (to perform s.t.), means, device. *tahu* – *bekerja* to know (and follow) the right way of doing things. *ada* –*nya* there's a knack/trick to it. – *bisnis* business trick. – *komunikasi* means of communication; → AKAL. 2 hidden (meaning).

kiat III (*ob*) mengait 1 to put all one's cards on the table. 2 to take a card. 2 to shuffle the cards.

kiaupau (*C*) overseas Chinese.

kiban [kompi bantuan] auxiliary (military) company.

kibar berkibar(-kibar) to flutter, fly, wave, flap. *Bendéra yang* ~ *ditiup angin* a flag fluttering in the breeze.

  berkibaran (*pl subj*) to flutter, flap, wave.

  mengibarkan [and **ngibarin** (*J coq*)] 1 to raise/hoist/put out (a flag). 2 to fly, wave (a flag/handkerchief, etc.). ~ *dirinya* to show off.

  kibaran flutter(ing).

  pengibar s.o. who hoists/flies (a flag).

  pengibaran flying/waving (a flag). ~ *bendéra* display of flags.

kibas I → KEBAS II, KITAR II. **mengibas** 1 to flap (ears), swish (tail). *Gajah itu telinganya selalu* ~. The elephant's ears are always flapping. 2 to shake off (dust), dust. *Ibu* ~ *méja yang kotor dengan kemuncing*. Mother dusted off the dirty table with a feather duster. 3 to free o.s. of, get rid of s.t., put s.t. out of one's mind.

  mengibaskan to wag, flap, swish.

  kibasan waving, wagging, swaying, swishing, rotating.

kibas II → KAMBING *kibas*.

kibau a crab species found on the island of Krakatau.
kibernétik (*E*) cybernetics.
kibik → KUBIK II.
kibir (*A*) arrogant, haughty.
  kekibiran arrogance, haughtiness.
kiblah and **kiblat** (*A*) **1** the direction of the Kaabah in Mecca. *menghadap* – to face Mecca (when praying). **2** direction (of the wind). **3** orientation.
  berkiblat to move/face in the direction of; oriented toward. *politik yang ~ kepada kepentingan komunisme internasional* a policy directed toward international communism. *~ ke Péking* Peking-oriented.
  mengkiblat *~ ke ... ...-*oriented. *~ ke kota* urban-oriented.
  meng(k)iblatkan to cause to face, orient s.t. to, direct to(ward), move s.t. in the direction of.
kiblik (*coq*) republic.
kibriah (*A*) pride; haughtiness, arrogance, superciliousness.
kibul I (*J*) ass, backside, buttocks. *goyang* – to shake one's ass.
  mengibuli to (give s.o. a) kick in the ass.
kibul II (*J*) **ngibul 1** to lie. *tidak ~* not fake. *tukang ~* liar. **2** to talk nonsense. **3** fake.
  ngibulin (*J*) to cheat. *merasa dikibulin* to feel cheated.
  terkibuli cheated, tricked.
  pengibulan deceit, deception.
kibus [*kaki busuk*] accomplice in a narcotics syndicate.
kicak → KICAU I.
kicang-kécoh and **kicang-kicau** swindling and trickery. *– ciak* a case being investigated needs evidence.
kicap I → KICAU I.
kicap II → KÉCAP.
kicap-kicup blinking one's eyes over and over again.
  berkicap-kicup to keep on blinking one's eyes.
kicau I (*onom*) twitter, chirp, warbling.
  berkicau and **mengicau 1** to warble, twitter, chirp. **2** to chatter, engage in idle talk.
  berkicauan (*pl subj*) to warble, twitter, chirp.
  mengicaukan to babble/chatter about.
  kicauan twitter, chirping.
kicau II swindle; → KÉCOH I.
  terkicau swindled.
kicerat (*J*) **mengicerat** and **ngicerat** to spurt out/forth.
kici brig, a two-masted ship with square sails.
kicik small (in some compounds); → KECIL. *sawo* – a small *sawo* variety.
kicu I cheat, swindle, deceit, deception. *kena* – cheated, deceived, tricked; → KÉCOH I.
  mengicu 1 (= **berkicu**) to practice/commit deception/fraud, act fraudulently. **2** (= **mengicukan**) to deceive, swindle, defraud.
  terkicu cheated, deceived, swindled.
  pengicu swindler, deceiver.
  pengicuan deceiving, swindling.
kicu II → KICAU I.
kicuh → KICU I.
kicuit various species of wagtail (birds), *Motacilla spp. – kerbau* yellow wagtail, *Motacilla flava.*
kicut (*onom*) creaking sound.
  berkicut to creak (of a door).
kidab → KIDIB.
kida-kida spangles (edging a mantilla), aiglets.
kidal left-handed.
  mengidal to use the left hand (for work, etc.).
kidam (*A*) eternal (without beginning), the state of not having been created (of God), the uncreatedness (of God). *sifat* – to exist from time immemorial; → KADIM I 3.
kidamat (*ob*) → KHIDMAT.
kidang (*Jv*) → KIJANG I.
kidar (*J*) → KISAR, KITAR.
kidemat → KHIDMAT.
kider I → KÉDER.
kider II → KIDAR.
kidib (*A*) untruthful, deceitful, lying, false.

kidil (*J*) loss.
kidmat → KHIDMAT.
kidobutai (*Jp*) (during the Japanese occupation) shock troops.
kidul (*Jv*) south. *laut/segara* – the Indian Ocean south of Java.
  ngidul to go (to the) south.
kidung (*Jv*) **1** (*O Jv*) poetic work. **2** ballad, chant, lullaby, song, melody. *– Agung* Song of Songs (in the Bible). *– geréja* hymn.
  mengidung to chant verses, sing a song/ballad.
  mengidungkan to sing s.o. a song; to sing/lull (a child) to sleep.
  kidungan ballad.
kiekeboe (*D*) /kikebu/ peekaboo.
kifayat (*A*) *fardul*– Muslim collective religious obligations.
kihanat (*A*) (*ob*) fortune-telling, prophesy, prognostication, augury.
kihuru (*S*) the *huru* tree, *Quercus sp.*; the bark is used for making mosquito repellent; → KI II.
kijai I a tall tree whose timber is used as building material, *Trigonochlamys/Santiria griffithii.*
kijai II **terkijai-kijai** to shiver, shake, tremble (of an old person's hand).
kijang I barking deer with short antlers, *Cervulus muntjac. dapat – teruit* (*M*) to get a windfall. *seperti – lepas ke rimba* to look for a needle in a haystack. *– kencana* the golden deer. *– menjangan* all k.o. deer. *– mérah, Muntiacus muncak.*
Kijang II 1 k.o. Toyota jeep sold in Indonesia. **2** police patrol car.
kijap → KEJAP.
kijil (*akar –*) a climbing plant, *Smilax helferi.*
kijing I various species of edible mussels, *Tellina spp., Capsella solida, Anodonta woodiana.*
kijing II (*Jv*) tomb(stone).
  mengijing, mengijingi and **mengijingkan** to put a tombstone on a grave.
kiju → KÉJU.
kik I hand loom.
kik II → AKIK.
kik III (*E*) **1** to kick. **2** to tease s.o. in a hurtful way, say s.t. to s.o. that hurts his/her feelings.
  mengkik *~ balik* to kick back (money).
  ngekik to tease.
  kik-kikan teasing.
kik IV → KHIK.
kikih → KIKIK.
kikik (*onom*) sound of laughter/giggling; → CEKIKIKAN.
  berkikikan (*pl subj*) to giggle, chuckle.
  mengikik to giggle. *~ dengan sendirinya* to giggle to o.s.
  terkikik-kikik to giggle, snigger, chuckle.
kikil (*J/Jv*) **1** leg (of an animal or jokingly of a person). **2** dish made of cow leg skin.
kikir I file (carpenter's tool). *tahi* – filings, bits filed off. *– belah rotan* a file with a flat face and round back. *– bulat* rattail file. *– kuku* nail file. *– lurus/patar* a flat file.
  berkikir 1 filed. **2** wrinkled.
  mengikir to file, make smooth with a file.
  kikiran filings.
kikir II stingy, tightfisted. *orang* – a miser/cheapskate.
  mengikirkan to be stingy about.
  kekikiran stinginess.
kikis I 1 scraping (the paint off wood), eroding. **2** scraped.
  mengikis to erode. **kemengikisan** erosivity.
  mengikiskan to scrape off (dirt from a pan/paint from wood, etc.); to scratch out (with a knife).
  terkikis eroded, abraded; overcome, wiped out. *~ habis* totally wiped out. **keterkikisan** erodibility.
  kikisan 1 scrapings. **2** (soil) erosion, alluvium. *~ sungai* erosion.
  pengikis scraper.
  pengikisan 1 scraping. **2** eroding, erosion.
kikis II (*M*) lost, vanished. *hilang* – entirely lost/vanished/disappeared/faded away. *– habis* exterminated, wiped out. ***mengikis-habis(kan)*** to root out, exterminate. ***pengikis-habisan*** extermination.
  mengikis to eradicate, make s.t. disappear/vanish, get rid of.
  terkikis eradicated. *habis ~* cleaned up, completely gone/vanished.

pengikisan 1 loss, disappearance. **2** eradication.

kikitir (*S*) assessment notice.

kikuk awkward, clumsy.

kekikukan awkwardness, clumsiness.

kila (*M ob*) → KILAH I. **mengila** to argue against, oppose, contradict.

kilaf → KHILAF.

kilah I (*A*) **1** subterfuge, deception, stratagem, trick, ruse. **2** excuse, pretext, argument; → HELAH, HELAT. *Itu hanya – belaka.* That's nothing but a pretext. **3** to say as an excuse.

berkilah(-kilah) to give an excuse, have a lot of poor excuses, beat about the bush, talk around a subject without getting to the point; to argue, quibble, cavil; farfetched (argument).

mengilah-ngilahkan and **mengkilah-kilahkan** to twist (words), distort/pervert the facts/truth.

kilah II an edible bivalve, *Voluta sp.*

kilai reel used to keep the strands apart when making string.

kilan I (*Jv*) the span between the thumb and the index finger; → JENGKAL.

sekilan one span.

mengilan to span, measure out in spans.

kilan II (*ob*) – *di hati terkalang di mata* to be constantly dissatisfied.

terkilan hurt, offended; annoyed, irritated.

kilang I 1 a machine used for crushing/squeezing/rolling s.t., mangling machine, mangle, press, mill. – *padi* rice mill; → PENGGILINGAN. **2** mill, factory, plant, works (usually for processing raw materials). – *cerutu* cigar factory. – *(bahan bakar) minyak* hydrocracker. – *getah* rubber factory. – *gula* sugar factory. – *minyak* refinery. – *penggergajian/kayu gergajian* sawmill. – *perusahaan* industrial plant. – *serpihan* chip mill. – *tembakau* tobacco factory.

mengilang 1 to squeeze, press, mill. ~ *tebu* to press sugarcane. *sudah ~ membajak pula* to be a workaholic. **2** to manufacture, make, produce, turn out, process.

mengilangkan to manufacture, turn out, produce.

kilangan → KILANG *batu* ~ millstone. ~ *patah awak itulah mengimpitnya* to look for trouble.

pengilang manufacturer, producer, refiner. ~ *minyak Jepang* a Japanese oil producer.

pengilangan manufacture, manufacturing, producing, refining, milling. *biaya* ~ manufacturing costs.

perkilangan (*Mal*) **1** group of factories. **2** manufacturing; → PENGILANGAN.

kilang II 1 sugar water. **2** juice of the sugar palm, *Arenga pinnata*, which turns into toddy and vinegar.

kilap I 1 → KHILAF. **2** (*Jv*) I don't know; who knows.

kilap II shine (on boots), gloss (on hair), sheen, luster, flash.

sekilap ~ *mata* in a wink, in the twinkling of an eye, in no time (at all).

berkilap, meng(k)ilap (*coq*) and **terkilap** to shine, gleam, glisten, flash; shiny.

meng(k)ilapkan to shine, polish.

kilapan shine, gloss, sheen.

pengilap ~ *manikam* (*geol*) geothite.

pengilapan glazing, sateening.

kilar an edible mollusk.

kilas I 1 noose, rattan thong (for pinioning animals, etc.), rattan rings used for climbing. **2** rolls of a *sarong* around the waist.

mengilas 1 to snare, trap in a snare. **2** to tighten (knot, string, etc.).

kilas II (*M*) flash; moment in time. *untuk beberapa* – for a few minutes. – *balik* flashback.

sekilas (~ *mata/pandang*) **1** in a flash/jiffy/wink, in the twinkling of an eye, in no time (at all); → SEPERSEKIAN *detik*. **2** swift, brief. *tersirat dari percakapan* ~ implicit in the brief conversation. **3** at first (glance), on the surface, on the face of it. ~ *terdengar anéh* at first glance this sounds strange. **4** in brief, in a nutshell.

mengkilas ~ *balik* to cast a eye back on.

terkilas ~ *dalam hati* flashed through one's mind.

kilasan 1 flash. **2** glance. **3** brief, s.t. brief. ~ *Kawat Sedunia* Cable Briefs from around the World.

kilat I 1 lightning, flash (of bright light in the sky). – *sabung-menyabung* it's lightning, there's (forked) lightning (in the sky). *secepat* – quick as a flash, with lightning speed. *hilang* –

dalam kilau in brilliant company no one person stands out; to disappear in the crowd. – *dalam kilau* (his) words mean more than appears on the surface. **2** glittering, gleaming, glistening. – *mata* radiant glance/look. **3** swift, quick, fast, rapid, speedy, express, crash. *keréta api* – express (train). *kursus* – intensive/crash course. *pengumuman* – emergency announcement. *perkara* – summary process (in court). *petir* – thunder and lightning. *program* – crash program. *rapat* – urgent/emergency meeting. *siaran* – bulletin. *sidang* – urgent/emergency meeting. **4** for fast delivery (of a letter/cable, etc.).

sekilat a bit of, a flashing view of.

berkilat 1 [= *hari* -, - *berapi-api*, - *berdenyar* and *bersinar(-sinar)*] there's/it's lightning. **2** (= **mengkilat**) flashing, shiny (of metal, etc.), dazzling (of car headlights). **3** to shine, gleam, glitter, glisten. – *sahaja, haram tak makan* all that glitters is not gold.

mengilat to flash, be visible for a split second.

mengkilat flashing, shiny, dazzling.

mengilati (*pl obj*) to polish, shine.

mengkilatkan 1 [= **mengilatkan** (*ob*)] to radiate. **2** to polish s.t. until it becomes shiny, shine. **3** (= **mengilat-ngilatkan**) to allude to, hint at, refer to; to reveal, show. *Dikilat-kilatkannya hajatnya.* He keeps showing his intentions.

terkilat to flash by. ~ *ikan dalam air, aku sudah tahu jantan betina.* I knew right away that it was your doing. ~ *di/dalam hati* and ~ *di ingatan/kepala* to come to one all at once, dawn on one suddenly, flash suddenly through one's mind.

kilatan 1 flash. ~ *petir* lightning. **2** shine, polish, gleam.

pengkilat gloss.

pengilatan polishing.

kilat II – *bahu* (*ob*) armlet, bracelet.

kilat III k.o. tree, mangrove, *Rhizophora*; → BAKAU.

kilau spark, flash, shine, glare. – *kemilau* glittering, scintillating. – *kemilau/mengilau* to glitter, shine brightly, scintillate. – *ria* brilliant, glittering. **berkilau ria** to glitter.

berkilau, berkilau-kilau and **(ber)kilau-kilauan** (*pl subj*) to glitter, sparkle, shine brightly, scintillate.

meng(k)ilau to sparkle, glitter.

kilau-mengilau to sparkle.

kilauan 1 shine, glitter, sparkle. **2** (*geol*) chatoyancy.

kilau-kilauan glitter, gleam.

kiler → KILLER.

kili I (*J cla*) female hermit/anchorite.

kili II (*M*) hem.

mengili to hem.

kilik I (*ob*) – *bahu* armlet, bracelet.

kilik II (*J*) **mengilik-ngilik 1** to tickle. **2** to tamper/fiddle with, tweak. **3** to incite, instigate, stir up. ~ *jangkrik* to incite a cricket (so that it will fight).

ngilik (*sl*) to break into a building by picking the lock.

kilikan s.t. one can fiddle with or tweak.

kili-kili 1 rattan ring threaded through a buffalo's nose. **2** swivel, reel, spool. *panjang* – full of excuses. – *dayung* tholepin, oar lock. – *joran* reel on fishing pole. – *pancing* reel on a fishing rod.

mengili-ngili ~ *layang-layang* to wind up the cord in order to reel in a kite.

kilin (*C*) k.o. mythological animal in Chinese tales.

kilir I mengilir to whet, sharpen. ~ *pisau* to sharpen a knife.

kiliran 1 whetstone, grindstone. **2** sharpener. ~ *budi* sharpener of the intellect. ~ *taji* sharpened point of a cockspur.

kilir II (*M*) **terkilir** sprained; → KESELÉO. *Kakinya* ~. He sprained his foot.

kilit (*J*) **mengilit** to pluck fruit with a forked stick.

kilitan 1 forked stick. **2** plucked (fruits).

killer (*E*) (*college sl*) a college teacher who gives hard exams or is a tough grader.

killiah → KULIAH.

kilo (*D*) **1** kilogram; → KILOGRAM. **2** kilometer; → KILOMÉTER.

berkilo-kilo by the kilogram/meter.

mengiloi [and **ngiloin** (*J*)] weigh/sell by the kilogram.

mengilokan to sell s.t. by the kilogram. *Koran bekas itu akhirnya dikilokan ke tukang loak.* The old papers were finally sold to the junkman by the kilogram.

kiloan by the kilogram. *tékstil* ~ textile sold by weight (not by length).

kilogram (D) kilogram.

kilométer (D) 1 one thousand meters. 2 (*coq*) (car) speedometer.

kim I (C) k.o. bingo.

KIM II (*acr*) [Kartu Izin Masuk] entry permit (an immigration document).

kim III (in acronyms) → KEIMIGRASIAN.

kima I 1 (*siput* -) giant clam, *Tridaena gigas* and other species. 2 a large marine shell.

kima II [kompi markas] headquarters company.

kimah (A) 1 price; value. 2 approximately.

   terkimah valued. *tiada* ~ invaluable.

kimantu (*ob*) full-blooded Chinese.

kimat → KIMAH.

kimbah mengimbah to scoop up sand (like a turtle laying eggs).

kimbang mengimbang-ngimbang to circle around, hover.

   terkimbang-kimbang 1 to go back and forth/to and fro; to hover (of a bird/plane). 2 (M) to hesitate; perplexed, taken aback.

kimblo → KIMLO.

kimbul (*naut*) 1 outboard platform at ship's stern. 2 poop deck.

kimcam (C?) tuberose, *Polianthes tuberosa* (fragrant at night and used in preparing *kimlo*); → SEDAP *malam*.

kimia (A through D) (*ilmu* -) chemistry. *ahli* – chemist. – *analitik* analytical chemistry. – *anorganik* inorganic chemistry. – *fisika* physical chemistry. – *hayat/organik* organic chemistry.

kimiawan chemist.

kimiawi (A) chemical.

kim(h)a → KINGKAP.

kimis (D) chemical.

kimlo (C) k.o. vegetable soup.

kimono (*Jp*) kimono.

   berkimono to wear (or, wearing) a kimono.

kimpa → KIMPAL.

kimpal 1 welded, solid, nugget-like. 2 consistent.

   mengimpal to forge metal, beat metal, weld.

   kekimpalan consistency.

   pengimpal welder, forger.

kimplah(-kimplah) (*Jv*) to ripple (of water).

Kimpraswil [Permukiman dan Prasarana Wilayah] (Department of) Settlement and Regional Infrastructure.

kimpul I (S) a plant that produces edible tuberous roots, blue taro, *Xanthosoma violaceum*.

kimpul II (*Jv*) purse, money bag.

kimpus (M) **terkimpus** hollow, fallen in, sunken (in) (of one's cheeks).

kimput (*ob*) to be afraid, frightened.

KIMS (*acr*) [Kartu Izin Masuk Sementara] Temporary Entry Permit Card (an immigration document).

kin (*ob*) → KÉN I.

kina I (D) quinine. *pokok* – cinchona tree, *Chinchona succirubra*.

kina II the monetary unit of Papua New Guinea.

kinan right-handed.

kinang I (*Jv*) a betel quid, betel chew (betel mixed with leaves and lime).

   menginang 1 to chew betel. 2 betel-chewing.

   kinangan place for carrying betel necessities.

   penginangan set of materials, etc. for making a betel chew. *tempat* ~ (in Kalimantan) place for carrying betel necessities.

   pekinangan (*Jv*) small woven bamboo carrying bag for betel necessities.

kinang II glutinous-rice cakes.

kinantan 1 all-white (of roosters/horses, etc.). 2 extremely, unusual(ly), very (special). *bagai* – *hilang taji* like a wealthy or a wise person who has lost the people's esteem.

kinayah (A) allusion.

kinca (C) sweet syrup made from palm sugar.

kincah mengincah 1 to wash, rinse (laundry). 2 to clean (meat), dress. 3 to wash one's genitals/anus, etc. with water. 4 to stir, mix up (water to make it turbid).

kincak terkincak-kincak jumping around and gesticulating.

kincang *kécoh* – (M) sly tricks, deceit.

kincau (*ob*) **mengincau** to sir, mix.

kinces (J) 1 deflated, burst (of a boil). 2 blind (person).

kincir 1 (– *air*) a) scoop wheel (for irrigating rice fields on a higher level). b) water mill. 2 (– *angin*) a) windmill. b) propeller. 3 spinning wheel; spool, reel. – *menjahit* sewing machine. – *padi* (M) (water-powered) rice mill. – *ria* Ferris wheel.

   berkincir with such a wheel. ~ *alir* (M) to give shrewd answers.

   mengincir to sew by machine.

   kinciran → KINCIR.

kincit slight diarrhea (so that the person does not feel it come out of the anus).

   terkincit to have slight diarrhea.

kincling-kincling (*Jv*) shining, sparkling clear.

kinclong → KINCLING-KINCLING.

kincung (M) → KÉCOH I.

kincup 1 narrow (of openings). *kembang* – to palpitate, open and close. 2 (J) frightened, afraid.

   mengincup to narrow down.

kindap terkindap-kindap to look around as if searching for s.t.

kinématika (E) kinematics.

kinématis (D) kinematic.

kinepung – *wakul, binaya mangap* (*Jv*) to be in danger; → KEPUNG.

kinerja performance.

   berkinerja have a … performance. ~ *tinggi* high-performance.

kinéskop (D) kinescope, TV screen.

kinétika (E) and **kinétis** (D) kinetic.

king (E) (cards) king.

kingkap (C) kincob, gold brocade.

kingkik, kingking, kingkip and **kingkit** *jeruk/limau* – small sour citrus fruit, *Triphasia trifoliata* (used as cough medicine/massaging material and for stomach trouble).

kingkong (E) 1 great, very large, grand, enormous, huge, gigantic, colossal, tremendous. 2 a large logging truck.

kini 1 now, at the present moment. – … *nanti* … now (here) … now (there); at one time …, at another time … – *begini nanti begitu* now this way now that way. *dari* – *dan seterusnya* and *dari* – *ke atas* from now on, henceforth. *hingga/sampai* – until now, so far. 2 nowadays, at present. – *dan nanti* now and in the future, today and tomorrow. 3 modern, up-to-date; *opp* KUNO.

   kini-kini right now.

   mengkinikan to make s.t. present, bring up to the present.

   kekinian the present; contemporary. *tarian* ~ contemporary dances.

kinin (*ob*) → KINI.

kinine (D) quinine.

kinja *lompat* –, **berkinja-kinja** and **terkinja-kinja** to jump with joy, be deliriously happy, etc.

kinjat (*ob*) **terkinjat** jerked, jumped, startled.

kinjeng (*Jv*) dragonfly. – *dom* slender needle-like dragonfly.

kinrohoshi (*Jp*) (during the Japanese occupation) compulsory labor service.

kintaka (*Jv*) document, letter, archive.

   perkintakaan archives, files, records.

kintakawan archivist.

kintal I → KINTEL.

kintal II → KUINTAL.

kintal III (*Port Min*) farm; courtyard.

kintar → KITAR I.

kintel (*Jv*) a frog that can inflate itself up like a balloon.

kintil (*J/Jv*) **mengkintil** to follow, trail. ~ *di ketiak* to be at the mercy of, be left to the mercy of.

kintut (J) 1 the youngest child in a family. 2 the smallest bananas growing on the lowest bunch.

kinurang (*math*) subtrahend, minuend.

kinyam (M) → KENYAM.

kinyang rock crystal, quartz.

kinyih-kinyih, kinyis-kinyis and **kinyit-kinyit** (*Jv*) 1 to look tasty (of food). 2 to look alluring/attractive (of a woman).

kio (C) palanquin.

kioman (J) 1 hampered in growth (of a plant) due to insufficient sunlight. 2 dwarf-like person.

kiong → KÉONG.

kios (*D*) **1** kiosk, stand. **2** booth, stall. – *buku* bookstand, bookstall. – *mobil* k.o. chuck wagon, mobile foodstall. – *Santapan Malam* a 24-hour eating stall. – *tilpon* telephone booth.

kip → KÉP I.

kipa (*J*) **1** asymmetric (because one is shorter than the other). **2** one-legged.

kipai (*ob*) **mengipaikan** to wag (the tail).

kipal → KIMPAL.

Kipam [Kesatuan Intai Para Amfibi] Amphibious Airborne Recon Unit.

kipan [kompi senapan] rifle company.

kipang I (*M*) sweet made from ground sesame seeds or nuts cooked with sugar, k.o. *téngténg*. – *emping* sweet made from *emping*. – *hitam* k.o. sweet.

kipang II → KÉPANG I.

kipar → KÉPAR.

kiparat → KEPARAT I.

kipas I **1** fan. **2** propeller; → BALING-BALING. – *air (di kaca)* windshield wiper. – *angin* a) electric fan. b) ventilator. – *hujan/kaca* windshield wiper. – *radiator* radiator fan.

  berkipas 1 (equipped) with a fan/propeller. **2** to fan o.s. **3** (= **berkipas-kipas**) to wag/swish (its tail).

  mengipas 1 to throb, palpitate, flutter (of heart). **2** to fan.

  mengipasi to fan o.s. or s.t., cool (off) (with a fan, due to hot spices, etc.).

  mengipas-ngipas 1 to quiver, tremble (of the nostrils, etc.). **2** to fan, foster, stimulate, help to grow/develop.

  mengipas(-ngipas)kan [and **ngipasin** (*J coq*)] **1** to wag/swish. – *ékor* to wag its tail. **2** to wave (a handkerchief). **3** to fan.

  terkipas fanned, stirred up. *Suhu perdamaian di Éropah mulai ~ lagi.* The peace temperature in Europe has begun to be stirred up again.

  pengipas s.o. who provokes, provocateur.

kipas II (*M*) **mengipaskan 1** to nudge (with the elbow), slap. **2** to parry, ward off (a blow with the hands in *silat*).

kipas III kipas-kipas and **kipasan** various species of flycatcher and fantail, *Rhipidura spp.*; pied fantail flycatcher, *Rhipidura javanica*. – *godi-godi* willie-wagtail, *Rhipidura leucophrys*. – *mérah* rufous-tailed fantail, *Rhipidura phoenicura*. – *mutiara* spotted fantail, *Rhipidura perlata*. – *Seram* streaky-breasted flycatcher, *Rhipidura dedemi*.

kipat I (*Jv*) **mengipatkan** to shake (off), hurl away.

kipat II (*ulat -*) k.o. caterpillar, *Cricula trifenestrata*, that attacks cocoa trees.

kipé (*sl*) **ngipé** to inject (drugs).

  kipéan needle (for injecting drugs).

kiper I (*D*) goalkeeper, goalie.

kiper II *ikan* – *laut* butterfly fish, *Chaetodontidae*.

KIPM [Kartu Idéntitas Penduduk Musiman] Seasonal Worker Identity Card.

kiprah (*Jv*) **1** dance preceding a *wayang orang* performance (usually performed by a male dancer). **2** energetic and fast pace. **3** rapid movement. – *mundur* setback.

  kiprah-kiprah wildly and excitedly (dancing).

  berkiprah to perform or participate in a highly spirited activity; to take steps, act. *~ untuk melaksanakan pembangunan di segala bidang* to take steps to carry out development in every field. *~ ke barat* to move towards the west (or, become westernized).

  terkiprah to take steps, move to (do s.t.).

kiprat ngiprat 1 to squirt/spurt out. **2** to hit.

  mengiprati to splash s.o. or s.t.

kiprét (*J*) → KIPRAT.

kiprok (*Jv?*) regulator.

kipsiau (*C*) earthenware teakettle.

kipu craftsman; → KRIYAWAN.

kiputri a decorative conifer, brown pine, *Podocarpus neriifolius*.

kir (*D*) **1** examination, test. **2** inspection. – *Master* Inspector (of motor vehicles). – *mobil* motor vehicle inspection. **3** to have s.t. inspected, go (somewhere) for an inspection.

  mengkir and **mengekir 1** to inspect (trucks, etc.). **2** to examine.

  mengkirkan and **mengekirkan** to have s.t. inspected/examined.

kira 1 guess, opinion, supposition, surmise, presumption. *Pada - nya, saya yang salah.* In his opinion I was wrong. *Saya – dia pandai.* I think he's smart. **2** estimation, calculation, count, conjecture. *tidak masuk –(an)* to be of no account, deserve/get no consideration. **3** (in questions, negatives) would have thought. *Siapa yang - (bahwa) dia masih hidup!* Who'd have thought he's still alive! *juru - (ob)* accountant; → AKUNTAN. *mesin -* calculator. *salah -* miscalculation.

kira-kira 1 about, approximately, roughly, s.t. like. *~ 50 kilométer* about 50 kilometers. **2** evaluation, assessment, estimate. *Menurut ~ akan beruntung banyak.* Based on estimates there will be a big profit. **3** probably, in all probability, (most) likely, possibly, maybe, presumably, seemingly, apparently. *~ ia tidak mau menerima uang itu.* Possibly he doesn't want to accept that money. *~ masih jauh dari sini?* Could it still be far from here? **4** to guess, take a guess. *Kalau tidak tahu jawabnya akui saja, jangan ~.* If you don't know the answer just admit it, don't guess. **5** (*coq*) be reasonable, think it over first. *~ dong kalau mengambil!* Think about it first if you want to take s.t. *~ sedikit!* Mind your manners! Watch what you're doing! *~ sendiri!* (in bargaining) (pay) whatever you think is the right amount. **6** thought, idea, mind, heed. *panjang ~* crafty, not narrow-minded. *terbuka ~nya* it dawned on him (that). **7** you wouldn't mind! *~ sama* to amount to (the same thing), be tantamount to. *Tidak menjawab ~ sama dengan menolak.* Not answering amounts to refusal.

sekira-kira 1 approximately, about, in the neighborhood of. *~ lima belas hari lamanya* for about fifteen days. **2** just enough. *hanya ~ dapat memulangkan modal* just enough to recover the capital.

sekiranya if, in case. *~ perlu* if needed.

berkira *~ bicara* (*Mal*) to converse, talk, discuss.

berkira-kira 1 to calculate, reckon, estimate, figure, count, compute. *Dia ~ sebentar lalu menjawab.* He figured for a while and then answered. **2** to plan, make plans, aim, design, intend, have in mind. *Dia ~ hendak melanjutkan pelajarannya ke Jakarta.* He intends to continue his studies in Jakarta.

mengira [and **ngira** (*coq*) and **ngirain** (*J coq*)] **1** to be of the opinion (that), think, suspect, guess, imagine. *tidak dikira* a) to be of no account, exclusive of. b) to be left out of account/consideration, deserve/get no consideration. **2** to compute, calculate.

mengira-ngira to count, calculate, estimate, figure out.

mengira(-ngira)kan 1 to calculate, count, estimate. **2** to plan, make plans, consider. **3** (= **mengira-ngira**) to guess, estimate, evaluate, appraise, assess, set a value on.

memperkirakan 1 to calculate, estimate, figure out, compute. *~ bagaimana* to figure out how (to). *Diperkirakan 60 ribu pelaut Indonésia déwasa ini bekerja di kapal-kapal asing.* An estimated 60,000 Indonesian seamen are now working on foreign ships. *dapat diperkirakan* a) can be calculated. b) can count it on your fingers. **2** to consider, regard as, think, feel, care for, heed. *diperkirakan* supposedly. **3** to predict. *sulit diperkirakan* hard to predict.

terkira counted, calculated. *tak ~* immense, huge, incredibly. *tak ~ banyaknya* innumerable. *tak ~ harganya* invaluable.

terkira(-kira) describable, calculable, countable. *tidak ~* indescribable, incalculable, uncountable.

terkirakan can be calculated.

kiraan calculation.

kira-kiraan estimation, guess.

pekira enumerator, counter (the person), calculator (the person), estimator.

pengiraan (act of) counting, count, calculation, estimation, guess, surmise.

perkiraan 1 count, calculation, computation. **2** guess, estimate, assessment. **3** forecasting, forecast, prediction. *~ belanja* budget; → ANGGARAN *belanja*. *~ ongkos-ongkos* expense account. *~ kontra-intélijén* counterintelligence estimate. *~ yang sedang berjalan* (*fin*) current account. **4** consideration, judgment. **5** assumption, supposition, presumption. **6** approximation.

kiraah and **kiraat** (*A*) recitation of the Koran.

kirab (*Jv*) ritual procession, parade.

ngirab to march out (of soldiers onto the battlefield).
mengirab(kan) to carry s.t. out in a procession.
kirabat (*ob*) → KERABAT.
kirah mengirah *sayap* to stretch (out) one's wings.
kirai I mengirai(kan) 1 to shake (dust, etc.) off of s.t.; to flap [its wings (of a bird) in order to dry them] **2** to winnow (rice, etc.) by tossing it in the air in a *tampah*. **3** to spread paddy, etc. out to dry in the sun.
  terkirai-kirai 1 shaken out and (the dust, etc.) is gone. **2** hung out (of the washing).
  kiraian opening made when s.t. is spread apart.
kirai II a long strip, band. - *piuh* (*geol*) kink banding.
  berkirai banded.
kirai III (*J*) (*pohon* -) sago palm, *Metroxylon rumphii/sagus*. *atap* - roof made of sago palm leaves.
kirai V (*Mal*) *janda sekali* - a woman who has been divorced once.
  berkirai to leave, go away.
  mengiraikan to separate from (one's wife).
kirana (*Skr ob*) **1** ray/beam (of light). **2** beautiful, lovely.
kirap I 1 to hit (with its wings of an angry hen, etc.). **2** to flap, beat (the wings). **3** to flutter (of a flag). **4** to brandish (a shield).
  mengirapkan 1 to flap, spread (the wings). **2** to wave, flag down (with a handkerchief).
  terkirap spread out.
kirap II mengirap to disappear, vanish, (of illusions/ideals, etc.).
  terkirap vanished, disappeared, flown away.
kirap III → KIRAB.
kiras a tree whose timber can be used for building material, *Garcinia celebica*.
kirat (*A*) carat.
kirau half-ripe (of fruits).
kirawa → AIR *kirawa*.
kirbat (*A*) leather container (for wine, etc.). - *és* ice bag, icepack (used for medicinal purposes).
kiri 1 left, on the left. - *kanan* and *kanan* - a) both sides. b) = - *kanannya* (*Jv*) approximately. **mengiri-menganan** to waver, vacillate. *tidak* ~ point-blank, flat out, unwavering. **2** left-handed (person); → KIDAL. **3** unlucky, unfortunate, unfavorable. *langkah* - stepping out with the left foot first (a bad omen). *tangan* - the left hand (considered unclean). *maaf tangan* - excuse my left hand (said when forced to hand s.t. to s.o. with the left hand). **4** (political) leftist. *kaum* - left-winger(s). **5** (*naut*) port. **6** -! (bus passenger to driver) getting off here! - *depan!* (bus passenger to driver) getting off up ahead! - *cekar!* hard left! - *dalam* (in soccer) inside left. - *kapal* port side (of a ship). - *kemudi!* left rudder! - *luar* (in soccer) outside left. - *tengah* (in politics) left of center.
  mengiri 1 to go/move to the left. **2** sinistral.
  mengirikan 1 to take/shift/move s.t. to the left. **2** to shelve, put aside, discard, exclude. *orang yang dikirikan dari masyarakat* an ostracized person. **3** to give s.t. with the left hand (a gesture of disdain since the left hand is considered unclean).
  kekiri-kirian leftish, somewhat leftist.
kirik I (*Jv*) pup(py); → ANAK *anjing*.
kirik II (*J/Jv*) /kirik/ feel creepy (from fear), shuddering.
  mengkirik to shiver, shudder, tremble (with fear/shock).
kirik-kirik various species of bee-eaters, *Merops spp*.
kirim I send; → BERKIRIM, MENGIRIM(KAN). - *balik* send back. **mengirim-balik** to send s.t. back. - *salam (saya) kepada/sama* send my regards to.
  berkirim to send. ~ *pesan* to send a request. ~ *salam kepada* to send one's greetings/regards to. ~ *surat [(ke)pada)]* to send a letter (to), correspond (with). ~ *diri* (*cla*) to put o.s. under the protection of.
  berkirim-kirim(an) ~ *surat* to exchange letters, correspond with e.o.
  mengirim [and **ngirim** (*coq*)] **1** to send/deliver; to remit (money); to ship; to forward. **2** to send (an envoy), delegate s.o. **3** (*J*) to deposit, entrust (goods for sale/safekeeping, etc.), consign, send on consignment, put into the custody of, park. *tempat ~ sepéda* bicycle park.
  kirim-mengirim to send s.t. to e.o., exchange.
  mengirimi to send to.

mengirimkan [and **ngirimin** (*J coq*)] **1** to send off/out. **2** → MENGIRIM 1, 2.
  terkirim(kan) sent, dispatched.
  kiriman 1 dispatch, delivery, shipment. **2** [= **pekirim(an)**] consignment, s.t. forwarded/sent/dispatched. **3** (*J*) goods on consignment; deposited goods. *surat* ~ a) letter to the editor. b) pastoral letter. **4** s.t. that comes out-of-season, s.t. unexpected. *hujan* ~ out-of-season rain.
  pengirim sender. *si* ~ the sender (of a letter, etc.), consignor, shipper.
  pengiriman 1 sending (off/out), dispatch(ing), forwarding, consignment, shipment. ~ *remburs* C.O.D. shipment. ~ *uang* remittance. **2** transport, conveyance.
kirim II (*Jv*) **mengirim** to leave s.o. or s.t. for safekeeping.
  kiriman s.t. left for safekeeping.
kirinyuh Siam weed, *Eupatorium odoratum*, which has medicinal uses.
kirip *siput* - an edible shellfish.
kiris (*Min*) k.o. tree, blackberry/leopard lily, *Belamcanda chinensis*.
kirmizi (*A*) scarlet, crimson.
kirtya (*cla*) society, organization.
kiru k.o. small tree, *Mitrephora reticulata*.
kiruh (*J*) **1** turbid, thick, cloudy, full of dregs; → KERUH I. **2** (*cla*) confused.
  mengiruhkan confusing, vague.
kirut-mirut → KERUT *merut*.
kiryah and **kiryat** (*A ob*) sin.
kisa I a small dragnet.
  mengisa to catch fish in such a net.
kisa II (*Pers*) a small pouch/bag.
kisah (*A*) story, narrative, event. *Itu lain* -. That's (quite) another story. *al-* a) the story has it that ... b) serial (story) (in newspaper, etc.). - *asmara/cinta* love story. - *bersambung* serialized story. - *nyata* true story. - *para Rasul* Acts (in the Bible). - *perjalanan* travelogue. - *suksés* success story.
  berkisah to narrate, tell a story.
  mengisahkan to narrate, tell a story about.
  terkisah it is said that, the story is told that.
  pengisahan storytelling, narrating.
kisai (*M*) **mengisai** to sieve, sift. ~ *benang bulang* to disentangle/unravel the threads that attach artificial spurs to the legs of fighting cocks.
  kisaian sieve, sifter.
kisar rotation, turning (around its axis). - *bumi* the earth's rotation.
  berkisar 1 to spin, rotate, turn, revolve. **2** to shift, move, change (trains). *Duduknya sudah* ~. He has changed seats (on a train). *duduk* ~, *tegak berpaling* (*M*) to break one's promise. ~ *anginnya* to change one's position. **3** to range, vary between stated limits. ~ *antara 1.000 sampai 12.000 dolar* ranging from 1,000 to 12,000 dollars. **4** to be centered around, be concerned with, have to do with; concerning, about. ~ *pada* (the story) is about.
  berkisar-kisar variable.
  mengisar(kan) 1 to move, shift, displace (s.t.), move (a piece of furniture, etc.). **2** to pass s.t. on, hand down (a title, etc.), turn s.t. over to s.o. else. **3** to adjust (a compass, watch), make accurate by regulating. **4** (*M*) to sell (a horse, etc.). **5** (*M*) to pawn. **6** to turn (a knife while sharpening it, a wheel, etc.). **7** to husk, mill, hull. *kilang* ~ *padi* rice mill.
  terkisar ground, crushed, digested.
  kisaran 1 revolution, rotation (of a wheel, etc.). ~ *air* eddy, whirlpool. ~ *angin* whirlwind, cyclone. **2** miller; milling machine. ~ *padi* rice miller. ~ *gandum* grain-milling business. ~ *kopi* coffee mill/grinder. **3** range. **4** (*J*) the crossbreed between an *ayam alas* and an ordinary hen; → BERKISAR.
  pengisar miller; milling machine.
  pengisaran revolution, rotation, shifting, transition, replacement.
  perkisaran rotation, turning, revolution. *musim* ~ transition period.
kisas (*A*) **1** an eye for an eye, retaliation, retribution. **2** vendetta. *hukum* - lex talionis; an eye for an eye, a tooth for a tooth.
  mengisaskan to punish in kind, exact retribution.

kisat (*ob*) dry.
  mengisatkan to wipe dry, dry; → KESAT.
kiser → KISAR.
kisi I 1 grid, grill, grate, grating. *- cerobong* chimney grate. *- hablur* crystal lattice. *- pelindung* screen grid. *- polongan/riol* gully grate. **2** crack (of s.t. not tightly closed).
  kisi-kisi 1 bars, grill, lattice, trellis. **2** banister, baluster. **3** rod, pole, spokes. **4** latticework, grating. **5** crack, chink, cleft, crevice.
  berkisi 1 (= **berkisi-kisi**) to have bars/a trellis, etc., latticed. **2** ~ *kepada* to concentrate/center on.
kisi II → ULAR *kisi*.
kisik I (*J*) whisper; → BISIK.
  mengisiki and **ngisikin** to whisper to, speak softly to.
  kisikan 1 whispering. *memberi* ~ to (give a) hint. **2** incitement, instigation.
kisik II (*M ob*) **mengisik** to pound slowly.
kisma (*Jv*) **1** ground, earth, soil. **2** land.
kismat and **kismet** (*A*) **1** fate, destiny. **2** what can one do?
kismis (*A*) raisin. *roti* – raisin bread.
kisruh (*Jv*) confused, chaotic.
  mengisruhkan to confuse, upset.
  kekisruhan confusion, chaos.
kiss (*E*) kiss.
  ngekiss to kiss.
kissah → KISAH.
kista (*D*) cyst.
  mengkista to form a cyst, encyst.
kisut 1 crease, crinkle, wrinkle; → LISUT. **2** wrinkled, creased, crinkled. *- mirut* all wrinkled/shriveled up/wizened.
  berkisut wrinkled, creased, rumpled; parched (of one's lips).
  mengisut(kan) to wrinkle, rumple, crease.
kiswa(h) (*A*) the black brocaded carpet that covers the wall of the Kaaba in Mecca.
kit I (*C?*) *rumah* – opium den.
kit II (*D*) paid off (of a debt).
kit III (in acronyms) → KEBANGKITAN.
kita 1 we, us, our [includes person(s) addressed]; *cp* KAMI. **2** *- orang* (*coq*) we (not including person(s) addressed). **3** (*J*) I. **4** the editorial "we." *– menduga, faktor utama yang menghambat ...* We suspect that the main factor hampering ... **5** (*ob*) you. **6** our/this country. *nuri yang di – sudah punah itu ...* the parrot, extinct in our country.
  kita-kita only/just us (we). *Yang akan datang* ~ *saja, tidak ada orang lain.* We are the only ones coming, nobody else will come. ~ *juga yang menanggung akibatnya.* Only we are responsible for the consequences. ~ *semua* all of us. **berkita-kita** collectively, as a group. *Iklim Indonésia tidak mendorong orang Indonésia hidup beraku-aku melainkan* ~. The Indonesian climate does not encourage Indonesians to live individualistically, but instead collectively.
  kekitaan in-groupiness.
kitab (*A*) **1** book; → BUKU I, PUSTAKA. *- bacaan* reader (the object). **2** holy book, scriptures. *– Allah* the Koran. *Al–* a) the Koran. b) the Bible. **3** (legal) code. *- Bilangan* Numbers. *- hukum* code of law. *- induk* records. *- Injil* Scriptures, Bible. *- Kejadian* Genesis. *- kemitab* all sorts of books. *- kuning* the 13 books of Islamic law compiled by Muslim theologians. *- logat* (*ob*) dictionary. *- lontar/rontal* a books written on palm leaves. *- nujum* a) book of astrology. b) astrological tables. c) book of prophecy. *- Suci* a) Holy Scripture. b) the Old and New Testaments. *- Taurat* the Torah. *- Ulangan* Deuteronomy. *- ulkudus* holy books, sacred writings. *- undang-undang* statute book. *- Undang-undang Hukum Dagang* [KUHD] Code of Commercial Law. *- Undang-undang Hukum Pidana* [KUHP] Penal Code. *- Undang-undang Hukum Perdata* [KUHPerd] Civil Code. *- Undang-undang Hukum Perniagaan* Code of Commercial Law. *- Undang-undang Hukum Sipil* [KUHS] Civil Code. *- usul* book containing a treatise on the true nature of God. *- Wahyu* Revelation. *- Wasiat Baru/Lama* New/Old Testament. *- Zabur* Psalms of David, book of psalms.
  berkitab possessing scriptures. *tidak* ~ a) irreligious. b) non-Muslim, pagan, infidel, heathen.

kitab-mengitab books.
  pengitab ~ *hukum* legal code.
  pengkitaban ~ *hukum* codification of the law.
kitabi (*A*) those possessing scriptures (Christians and Jews among non-Muslims).
kitabullah (*A*) the message of God, another name for the Koran; → QUR'AN.
kitang and **kitang-kitang** *ikan* – small fish with venomous dorsal spines, *Scatophagus spp. lubuk dalam, si – yang empunya* lord and master in one's own domain.
KITAP → KARTU *Izin Tinggal Tetap*.
kitar I *sekitar* **1** proximity, vicinity, neighborhood. (*di*) ~ *kota Jakarta* in the vicinity of Jakarta. *alam* ~ surroundings, environs, environment (of a town); → KELILING. ~*nya* its environs. **2** approximately, about.
  berkitar 1 to revolve (around a center/on its axis), rotate. turn around; to orbit. **2** to travel around, go everywhere.
  mengitar(-ngitar) to go round and round.
  mengitari to encircle, move in a circle around, revolve around. *Bulan* ~ *bumi.* The moon revolves around the earth.
  mengitarkan and **memperkitarkan** to cause to revolve/rotate, turn s.t.
  terkitar-kitar to turn round and round, roll (of the eyes).
  kitaran turn, revolution.
  pengitaran rotating, revolving.
  perkitaran circulation, spinning around, turning, rotation.
kitar II mengitarkan and **memperkitarkan** (*M*) **1** to repel, push/shove away. **2** to push aside/ out of the way (to protect s.o. who is threatened by approaching danger).
kiter → KITAR I. **ngiterin** to be around (s.t.). *Meréka duduk* ~ *méja.* They sat around the table.
kitik (*J*) **mengitik(-ngitik)** to tickle.
  kitik-kitikan to tickle e.o.
kitin (*D*) chitin.
kiting I a little (bit).
  sekiting (*coq*) a tiny bit.
  mengiting to sell retail.
  kitingan retail.
kiting II (*Jv*) **mengiting** to pursue.
kitir (*Jv*) receipt; → KEKITIR.
  kitiran (*J/Jv*) small toy propeller or windmill.
kitorang (*IBT*) we; → KITA *orang*.
kitri (*Jv*) **1** fruit trees. **2** (*S*) a coconut in full bloom.
kiu (*D/E*) cue (in billiards).
kiuk I a gambling game played with dominoes.
kiuk II sprained, twisted.
kiuk III (*onom*) clucking (of a fowl).
kiu-kiu (*C*) k.o. domino card game; → GAPLÉ(H).
kiut → KIANG *kiut*, KICUT.
kiwi I (*ob*) supercargo.
kiwi II 1 kiwi (bird of New Zealand), *Apterix.* **2** kiwi (fruit). **3** reference to New Zealand. *pemuda* – New Zealand youth. *Negeri* – New Zealand.
kiwi III conspicuous consumption.
kiwir-kiwir (*Jv*) **1** almost cut through and hanging from a thread, etc. **2** common-law husband.
  berkiwir-kiwir and **terkiwir-kiwir** hanging and flapping.
kiyai title for an older male who is considered knowledgeable in Islamic matters. *- Haji* [K.H.] a *kiyai* who has made the *hajj*, e.g., *K. H. Dr. Mukti Ali*; → KIAI.
  kekiyaian kiyaiship.
kiya-kiya → KYA-KYA.
kiyek-kiyek I (*onom*) chirping/peeping (of chicks, etc.).
kiyek-kiyek II young, not full grown. *anakyna yang masih* – his young child.
kiyu (*C*) nine.
kizib (*A*) insincere, untruthful, false, lying; *opp* SIDIK III. *fajar* – the false dawn (before sunrise).
KJRI [Konsulat Jénderal Républik Indonésia] Consulate General of the Republic of Indonesia.
KK [Kepala Keluarga] head of family; family, household.
KKN I (*init*) [Kuliah Kerja Nyata] → under KERJA.

ber-KKN to work in the villages as part of the *BUTSI* program.

KKN II (*init*) [Korupsi, Kolusi dan Népotisme] Corruption, Collusion and Nepotism.

KKO (*init*) [Korps Komando] Marine Corps.

kl- also see entries beginning with **kel-**.

k.l. (*abbr*) [kurang lebih] more or less, approximately.

klab (*E*) club (for dancing/drinking, etc.). – *malam* nightclub.

klabet → KELABAT.

klaim (*D/E*) claim. – *asuransi* insurance claim. – *dengan tebusan* claim with compensation. – *jatuh témpo* due-date claim.

   mengklaim 1 to claim, file a claim. **2** ~ *dirinya* ... to claim to be a ...

   pengklaim claimant.

   pengklaiman act of claiming, filing a claim.

klakep (*Jv*) to stop talking and close one's mouth; → CEP, *klakep*.

klak-klak (*onom*) clickety-clack (of shoes, etc.).

klakson (*D*) horn (of car, motorcycle, etc.).

   meng(k)lakson to blow one's horn, honk.

klam (*D*) clamp.

klampok (*Jv*) k.o. plant, *Eugenia spp.*

klandéstin (*D/E*) clandestine, secretly.

klangenan → KELANGENAN.

klantung (*Jv*) to be out of work, unemployed (and drifting around).

klar → KELAR I.

klaras (*Jv*) a dry leaf (*esp* a banana leaf) used for wrapping; in some areas also used for the dry corn husk used in the manufacture of *klobot* cigarettes.

klarifikasi (*E*) clarification.

   mengklarifikasi to clarify.

klarinét (*D/E*) clarinet.

klaru fin whale.

klas (*D*) class, rank, grade; → KELAS I.

   menglas to class, rank.

klasemén (*D*) classification.

klash → KLÉS II.

klasi → KELASI I.

klasifikasi (*D*) classification.

   berklasifikasi classified.

   mengklasifikasikan to classify (documents).

   pengklasifikasian classifying, classification.

klasik (*D*) classic(al). *cerit(er)a* – classical story. *musik* – classical music. *tarian* – classical dance.

   keklasikan classicism.

klasikal (*D*) class (*mod*). *pengajaran* – class instruction. *secara* – class (teaching, etc.).

klassis (*D*) (Protestant) parish.

klaster (*E*) cluster.

klat (*D*) rough draft.

   mengklat to draft, draw up a rough draft of.

klausa and **klausul(a)** (*D*) clause, article, provision, stipulation (in a formal or legal document). – *sanggup/tertunjuk* order clause.

klaver (*D*) clubs (in card games); → KLAWAR.

klavir (*D*) piano.

klawar club (in card games); → KLAVER.

klawung-klawung (*Jv*) **1** to be bored (because there is nothing that one wants to do). **2** to feel weary/empty. – *karena ngganggur* weary of life because one is jobless.

klayu (*Jv*) shrubby tree used for fences, *Erioglossum rubiginosum;* → MERTAJAM.

kléang (*Jv*) dried clove leaves.

klécam-klécem (*Jv*) to smile.

kledi (in Kalimantan) k.o. mouth organ.

Kléin Ambtenaars Éxamen (*D col*) /kléin amtenars éksamen/ Clerkship Examination.

klekap plankton.

klékék mengkékék (*Jv*) to seize by the throat.

klelegen (*Jv*) to choke (on); → KESELAK. – *duri* to get a fish bone stuck in one's throat.

klelep → KELELAP.

klém I (*D*) clamp, collar, bracket. – *besi* iron strap. – *pemegang* fixing collar. – *tarik* strain clamp.

   meng(e)lém to clamp together.

terklém clamped.

klém II → KLAIM.

klemak-klemék (*Jv*) **1** to (speak with a) drawl. **2** to play/toy with one's food. **3** slow, sluggish, indolent.

klemar-klemér (*Jv*) languid, without vigor/vitality, drooping.

klembak (*Jv*) → KELEMBAK I, ROKOK *klembak kemenyan.*

klémbréh (*Jv*) **nglémbréh** to hang down, droop. *Payudara itu.* ~ Her breasts are sagging.

kléménsi (*D*) clemency.

klémsta(a)t (*D*) inventory of a forest stand.

klén (*E*) clan; → PUAK.

klenéngan (*Jv*) informal *gamelan* concert.

klenger (*Jv*) unconscious; → KELENGER. *jatuh* – to faint.

kléngkéng (*Jv*) longan (a very sweet, small, round, brown, dry-looking fruit with hard black seeds), similar to litchi fruit.

klenik I (*Jv*) black magic (inspired by *hawa nepsu/nafsu,* as opposed to *batin*). *dukun* – faith healer.

   klenik-klenikan all k.o. questionable mystical practices, pseudo-mysticism.

klenik II to talk to e.o. in a low voice; to whisper.

klentang → KELENTANG.

klenteng (*Jv*) kapok or cottonseed.

klenténg 1 Chinese temple. **2** name of a *ceki* card.

klenyem (*Jv*) fried ground-up cassava cookie.

klenyit (*Jv*) *pating* – to leave a bad taste in the mouth.

klép (*D*) valve. – *ban* tire valve. – *lekum* epiglottis. – *pengaman* safety valve.

klepek (*col*) student in the Stovia (*q.v.*).

klepon (*Jv*) glutinous rice-flower cookie filled with brown sugar.

kléptomani(a) (*D/E*) kleptomania.

klerek and **klerak** → LERAK II.

klerat rice grains used to poison rats.

klérk (*D*) /klérek/ clerk.

   nglérek (*Jv*) to work as a clerk.

   mengklérekkan to make s.o. into a clerk.

klérikal (*D/E*) clerical. *kaum* – the clericals.

klérus (*D*) clergy. – *sékulér* secular clergy.

klés I (*D*) vault, safe deposit.

klés II (*E*) **1** military clash. **2** the so-called Dutch police actions of 1947 and 1948. – *I/kesatu* first police action. *II/kedua* second police action; → CLASH.

klésot (*Jv*) **menglésot** to move in a submissive squatting posture close to the ground/floor.

   klésotan 1 to sit in this posture. **2** to sit on the floor.

kletak-kletik (*Jv onom*) clickety-clack.

kléték (*Jv*) **ngléték** to peel.

   klétékan peeled.

kletékan (*Jv*) smallholder, peasant (*mod*). *peternak* – smallholder cattle breeder.

klét(h)ék (*Jv*) a gambling game for six players similar to *macanan.*

kletuk mengletuk to nab (a thief, etc.).

kletus (*Jv*) **meng(k)letus 1** to arrest. **2** to kill. **3** to misappropriate (money).

kléwang → KELÉWANG.

kléyar-kléyor adrift.

klian (in Bali) the leadership of a *banjar;* → PEKASÉH.

kliar → KELIAR.

klién (*D/E*) **1** client (of a lawyer); → NASABAH. **2** customer; → LANGGANAN, PELANGGAN.

klik I (*D/E onom*) click, clicking sound (of a camera shutter/computer key).

   mengeklik to click.

klik II (*Fr D*) clique.

   klik-klikan cliquishness; formation of cliques.

klim → KLAIM.

klimak(s) (*D*) **1** climax. **2** to have an orgasm.

   mengklimaks to reach/come to a climax.

klimatologi (*D/E*) climatology.

klimé *ada* –*nya* it has its limits.

klimis (*J/Jv*) **1** glossy, shiny, bright, gleaming. **2** clean(-shaven). *dicukur* – clean-shaven.

klimpungan → KELIMPUNGAN.

kling (*onom*) sound of tinkling bells.

klinik (*D/E*) clinic; → POLIKLINIK. - *berjalan* mobile clinic. - *bersalin* maternity clinic. - *kesegaran jasmani* health club. - *mata* eye clinic. - *mobil* mobile clinic.

klining (*E*) cleaning.

kliningan West Javanese traditional music found in the Jabotabek area.

klinis (*D*) clinical.

klinisi (*D*) clinicians.

klintar-klinter (*Jv*) to wander about; to prowl, lurk.

klintir → GELINTIR.

klip I (*D*) (paper)clip. - *kertas* paper clip.

klip II [Kenali Langsung Idéntitas Pemanggil] caller ID (a telephone service).

kliping (*E*) clipping (cut out of a newspaper, etc.).
   mengkliping to clip (s.t. out of a newspaper).

klips (*E*) clips.

klir I (*D*) color; → KELIR II.
   mengklir to color s.t.

klir II (*E*) clear (of an issue), cleared up. *Dia ingin soalnya* –. He wants the matter cleared up.
   mengklir to become clear, clear up.
   mengklirkan to clear/finish s.t. up.

klirak-klirik (*Jv*) to look around furtively.

kliring (*E*) (bank/check) clearing.
   mengkliring(kan) to clear.

klisé I (*D*) 1 (photographic) negative; → NÉGATIF II. 2 cliché (of a printing press), plate, stereotype.
   mengklisékan to make a negative of.
   terklisé made a negative of.

klisé II (*Fr D*) cliché, a hackneyed phrase or idea. *Itu jawaban* –. That's a cliché answer.

klisé III (*D*) an imitation of the original.

klisma (*Gr*) enema.

klitoris (*D*) clitoris; → ITIL, KELENTIT I.

kliwat → KELÉWAT, KELIWAT.

kliwir clip. - *rambut* hair clip.
   kliwir-kliwir clothes hanger.
   berkliwiran (*pl subj*) to hang down loosely.

kliwon I (*Jv*) a palace employee under the *bupati* in Yogyakarta and Surakarta.

kliwon II (*Jv reg*) hamlet head under the *lurah*.

kliwon III (in Cirebon) village administration employee under the *kuwu*.

Kliwon IV (*Jv*) the fifth day of the five-day week. *Selasa* – and *Jumat* – Tuesday Kliwon and Friday Kliwon (still observed by many as sacred days).

kliyengan (*J/Jv*) 1 (to feel) dizzy, one's head is whirling around. 2 intoxicated; → TELÉR I.

KLM (*init*) [Kapal Layar Motor] motorized sailing vessel.

klo → KALAU.

klobot (*Jv*) 1 husk, bracts of the corn ear used as cigarette wrapper; → ROKOK *klobot*. 2 worn-out cliché; → KLOBOTISME.
   mengkloboti to husk.

klobotisme a worn-out cliché of an idea/opinion/teaching.

klojot (*J*) to fall down frequently, be epileptic; epilepsy.
   klojot-klojot epileptic.
   klojotan 1 to suffer from epilepsy. 2 to be convulsed with pain. 3 angry, furious; anger. *Dia ~ waktu mendengar ayahnya digampar orang.* He became furious when he heard that his father had been slapped. **berklojotan** epileptic.

klok (*D*) bell-shaped. - *rok* (*D*) bell-shaped (of a skirt).

klolodan, kloloden, and **kloloten** (*J/Jv*) 1 to choke, get s.t. stuck in one's throat. 2 to be smothered/up to one's neck in s.t. *Dia - besi tua.* He was up to his neck in scrap iron.

klomoh (*Jv*) wet, greasy.

klompen I (*D*) wooden shoes.

klompen II [kelompok pendengar] listeners, audience (of a program).

klompencapir [kelompok pendengar, pembaca dan pirsawan] listeners, readers and viewers.

klompensipedés [kelompok pendengar siaran pedésaan] Rural Broadcast Listeners Group.

klomprot (*Jv*) sloppy in personal appearance.
   nglomprot in a sloppy way.

klon and **klona** (*E*) clone.
   mengklon to clone.
   pengklonan cloning.

kloning → KLON.

klontang-klantung (*Jv*) to loaf about, hang out.

klontong → KELONTONG.

klonyo → KELONYO.

klop (*D*) → KELOP. 1 jibe, tally, square (with), agree. *kurang* – not quite right. 2 fit together, go with. 3 in balance, balanced. *membikin - (coq)* to balance.
   mengklopkan to balance (the budget), square (things), make things right.
   keklopan being right.

klor (*D*) and **klorin** (*E*) chlorine.
   berklor chlorinated.
   mengklor to chlorinate.

klorit (*D/E*) chlorite.

klorofil (*D/E*) chlorophyll.

kloroform (*D/E*) chloroform.

klos (*D*) → KELOS.

klosét (*D*) water closet, toilet bowl. - *duduk* western-style toilet. - *jongkok* squat toilet.

kloso bongko (*Jv*) a coarse mat.

klosot (*Jv*) **nglosot** *duduk ~* to sit on the ground completely relaxed; → KLÉSOT.

kloter [kelompok terbang] flight group (usually used for a *hajj* flight).

klotok I *kapal/perahu* – a water taxi with a 10 P.K. outboard motor found in Banjarmasin (Kalimantan) and Jambi (Sumatra).
   klotok-klotok (*onom*) putt-putt-putt.

klotok II *dadu* – k.o. crap game.

klotok III (*Jv*) **klotokan** a peeling, such as a part of a wall that has peeled off.

klotokan (*Jv*) genuine, authentic, real. *orang Jawa ~* a true/real Javanese. *bujangan ~* a (male) virgin.

klub (*E*) → KLAB.

kluih → KLUWIH.

klumpruk (*Jv*) heaped about in a disorderly way.

kluntang-kluntung (*Jv*) to loaf about, hang out.

kluron (*Jv*) abortion, miscarriage.

kluruk (*Jv*) to crow. *jago* – a crowing rooster.

klutuk (*Jv*) → KLOTOKAN.

kluwak (*Jv*) the seeds of the *pucung* fruit (used as a spice).

kluwih (*Jv*) k.o. breadfruit; the young fruits are eaten as vegetables, *Artocarpus communis*.

kluyar-kluyur (*Jv*) to hang out, loaf around; to wander around aimlessly.

kluyur (*Jv*) → KELUYUR. **ngluyur** to saunter around, walk around the streets.

KM [Kapal Motor] Motor Ship, M.S.

KMB [Konperénsi Méja Bundar] Round Table Conference.

KMF [Kapal Motor Ferry] motorized ferry.

KMK [Krédit Modal Kerja] Work Capital Credits, i.e., a credit program to provide working capital for small and medium-scale businesses.

knalpot (*D*) exhaust pipe, tailpipe, muffler.

knék → KENÉK.

Knésset the Israeli Parliament.

KNI [Kantorberita Nasional Indonésia] Indonesian National News Agency.

KNIL (*acr*) [Koninklijk Nederlandsch-Indisch Leger] Royal Netherlands Indies Army.

KNIP (*acr*) [Komité Nasional Indonésia Pusat] Central Indonesian National Committee, i.e., the functional equivalent of a Parliament in the Republican governmental system up to the transfer of sovereignty by the Dutch.

knol (*D*) bulb (of plant).

knop I → KENOP I.

Knop II - *15* → K(E)NOP IV.

ko I *kaum* - the cooperators (those who worked together with the Dutch during the 1945-1949 conflict).

ko II (in acronyms) → KOORDINASI, KOORDINATOR, KOMANDO.

ko III (C) title used before Chinese male names; → ENGKO.

ko IV (C) paste.

ko V → KAU I.

KO VI [Knock Out] (E) knockout (in boxing).
   meng-KO to knock out.

koa (C) k.o. Chinese card game.
   berkoa to play this game.

koaci (C) → KUACI.

koagulasi (D) coagulation.

koak berkoak-koak and **berkoak-kaok** (coq) to cry, shout, yell, moo.
   mengoak-ngoak to moo.

koalisi (D) coalition. *kabinét* – coalition cabinet.
   berkoalisi ~ *dengan* to enter into a coalition with.

koan *ikan* – grass carp, *Ctenopharyngodon idella Vall.*; → KARPER (*rumput*).

Koanda [Komando Antar Daérah] Interregional Command (during *Konfrontasi*).

koang (J) **koang-koang** to cry out, make a loud noise.
   koangan *layangan* ~ a kite equipped with a noise-making device.

koar (J) – *koér* (J) to scream, shout.
   bekoar 1 to shout, scream; to have a loud voice. 2 to be arrogant.

koas I → KUAS I.

ko-as II [ko-asistén] intern (in medicine).

koasi (economic) protection and facilities.

ko-asistén → KO-AS II.

kobah (Pers ob) kettledrum.

kobak I a tear (in s.t.).
   mengobak(kan) to peel (a fruit), tear (the skin); → KUBAK.
   terkobak peeled.

kobak II (Jv) *main* – a gambling game in which money is thrown into a small hole in the ground.
   ngobak to stand (of water), not flow.
   kobakan 1 a small hole in the ground (into which money is tossed in that game). 2 puddle, wallow, (rain)pool, mud hole.

kobal(t) (D/E) cobalt.

kobam (Pr) drunk; → MABUK.

kobang → GOBANG I.

kobar (J/Jv) flaming, in flames. – *nyala* flaming. **mengobar-nyalakan** to fire up, excite, encourage.
   berkobar 1 to catch fire, be on fire, flare up. 2 to rage, break out (of war). *semangat* ~ enthusiastic, highly motivated.
   berkobar-kobar(an) 1 to blaze, be ablaze, blaze up, flare up, rage (of a battle/revolution). 2 vehement, spirited, raging.
   mengobar(-ngobar)kan to make s.t. flare up, fire up (the imagination), rouse (courage), encourage, stimulate, stir up, inspire, excite (feelings), provoke, inflame (a situation); → MENGAN-JURKAN, MENGGELORAKAN. ~ *birahi* to get s.o. sexually excited. ~ *semangat* to motivate, encourage.
   kobaran 1 flaring up, flaming, flame. ~ *api* flaring up of a fire. 2 rage, exuberance. ~ *semangat* exuberance.
   pengobar s.o. who stirs up. ~ *perang* warmonger.
   pengobaran flare-up.

kobé (J) k.o. card game.

kobél (J) **mengobél** and **ngobél** to stick one's finger in s.o.'s anus/vagina.

kober (J/Jv) to have (enough) time (to do s.t.). *sa' koberé* whenever there's time.

kobér (Port? col) European, non-Muslim graveyard.

kobés (J) chipped, scraped.

kobis (Jv) cabbage; → KUBIS.

koboi (D/E) cowboy. – *cacing/céngéng* s.o. who likes to act tough.
   mengkoboi [and **ngoboi** (J)] to act wild, act tough.
   koboi-koboian wild actions (of stealing, etc.); to run wild, be reckless. *main* ~ to act wildly.

kobok I group (of people).
   berkobok-kobok in groups.

kobok II (J/Jv) **ngobok** 1 to wash one's hands by dipping them into water. 2 to eat using only one's hands (without utensils). 3 to touch/feel up a woman's body.
   kobokan finger bowl.

kobol (Jv) (to have a large) deficit.

kobong (S) 1 room (for a seminarian in a *pondok-pesantrén*). 2 berth (on a ship).

kobongan I (Jv) a small tent in which circumcisions are performed.

kobongan II (Jv) fire.

kobra I (D/E) cobra.

kobra II (Jv) great. *denda* – fine imposed on the village population because a murder has been committed in their village by a person or persons unknown. *Kiamat* – the Day of Judgment.

kocah-kacih to rummage around, tinker about.

kocai → KUCAI I.

kocak I shaking; shock; concussion.
   berkocak 1 to shake around; to beat. ~ *tanda tak penuh* empty barrels make more noise. 2 dull (of eyes), turbid (of a liquid).
   berkocak to shake (around), slosh around (of a liquid).
   mengocak(kan) to shake (a liquid in a bottle), shake a liquid until it ripples.
   terkocak shaken, disturbed, upset. *badan* ~ (M) emaciated. ~ *hati* shaken of one's confidence).

kocak II 1 *gagah dan* – smart, dashing, classy. 2 proud, haughty, conceited. 3 (J) funny, amusing, hilarious.
   berkocak to joke around, jest.
   berkocak-kocakan jokingly.
   mengocak (J) to clown around, speak and act in a joking way.

kocar-kacir to be in disorder, scattered around, in a mess, higgledy-piggledy.
   mengkocar-kacirkan to scatter (an army) in disorder.

kocék pocket. *menambah gembung* – *perusahaan* to line the pockets of one's company. *merogoh* – to put one's hand into one's pocket, dip into one's pocket. – *negara* state treasury.
   berkocék ~ *tebal* to have deep pockets, be rich.
   mengocéki to pocket, put in one's pocket.

koci I (*puru* – and – *lembik*) chancre. – *lambung* stomach.

koci II k.o. cake made of glutinous rice flour stuffed with coconut and wrapped in banana leaves.

kocik → KOCÉK.

kocing I (E) → GOPOH. **terkocing-kocing** hasty, hurried.

kocing II (E) → COACHING.

koclok (J) 1 stupid in an irrational way. 2 shaking.

kocoh haste.
   terkocoh-kocoh in a rush, hastily.

kocok mengocok 1 to shake (a liquid). ~ *dulu obat ini.* Shake the medicine first. ~ *perut* to make s.o. shake with laughter. ~ *telur* to beat eggs. 2 to shuffle (cards). 3 to mix up, confuse. *adat yang dikocok dengan syarak* adat a customary law that has gotten mixed up with Muslim law. 4 (coq) to incite; to stir up. 5 [and **ngocok** (coq)] (vulg) to masturbate, jerk off.
   kocokan 1 shuffling, mixing. ~ *ulang* reshuffle. 2 pump (brakes).
   pengocok shaker, beater. ~ *perut* s.t. that makes you laugh. ~ *telur* eggbeater.
   pengocokan shaking, mixing, shuffling.

kocol ngocol (coq) funny, humorous.

kocolan (J/Jv) young of the *ikan gabus*, *Ophiocephalus striatus* (used as fish bait); → ARUAN.

kocong 1 white head covering (or, hood) for a corpse or s.o. to be hanged; → SUMPAH pocong. 2 knot used to tie up a bag. *hantu* – sheeted goblin/ghost.
   mengocong 1 to shroud (a corpse). 2 (= **mengocongkan**) to tie up (a bag); to tie together.
   mengocongi to cover/envelop in such a cover.

kocor (J/Jv) → KUCUR I. **mengocor** [and **ngocor** (coq)] to flow, run (of a liquid), stream (of a river); to flow/gush out, flow down/off; outflow. *tidak ngocor* it isn't running (of water from a tap).
   ngocor(in) to water (plants).
   mengocorkan to let (a liquid) flow.
   kocoran flow.

kocuk (E) caoutchouc, rubber.

kodak I (D) camera; → (FOTO)TUSTÉL, KAMÉRA. *(orang) Mat* – (amateur) photographer; → KARYA *mat kodak. Mak* – (amateur) female photographer.
   mengodak to take a picture/photo.
   kodak-mengodak 1 photography. 2 to take pictures.

Kodak II [Komando Daérah Kepolisian] Regional Police Command.

Kodam [Komando Daérah Militér] Regional Military Command.

Kodau [Komando Daérah Udara] Regional Air Command.

kode (*D/E*) code. – *aréa* area code. – *daérah* area code (of telephone system). – *daérah pos* ZIP/postal code. – *étik* ethical code. – *komunikasi* communication code. – *Morse* Morse code. – *nomor pribadi* personal identification number, PIN. – *panggilan* (in amateur radio) call sign. – *pos* ZIP code, postal code. – *rahasia* secret code. – *télepon* area code. *alat pembuka* – *sinyal* decoder.
  berkode using code, coded. *télegram* ~ a cable in code.
  mengkodekan to encode.
  peng(k)odean (en)coding.

kodéine (*D/E*) codeine.

kodén → KODIAN.

koderat → KODRAT I.

kodi (*Hind Tam?*) a score, 20.
  berkodi-kodi by the score.
  kodian 1 by the score. **2** ready-made, mass produced. *barang* ~ mass-produced goods. **3** inferior. *Jangan menjadi pemimpin* ~. Don't be an inferior leader.

kodifikasi (*D*) codification.
  mengkodifikasikan to codify.
  pengkodifikasian codifying.

kodim I (*A ob*) → KADIM I.

Kodim II [Komando Distrik Militér] District Military Command; → KODAM.
  mengkodimkan to summon to appear before a district mil. command.

kodok I (*Jv*) frog, toad; → KATAK I. *berenang* – breaststroke (in swimming). *Fiat* – (*ob*) a small model Fiat, the "road bug." *VW* – the VW "bug" or "beetle." *mati* – to die for nothing. *seperti* – *ditimpa kemarau* to raise the devil. *laksana* – *dapat bunga sekuntum* to cast pearls before swine. – *batu* a species of frog used for frog's legs, *Rana limnocharis*. – *goréng* fried frog's legs. – *hijau/ijo* a) an edible species of green frog. b) the green pickup vans used in Bandung for city transportation. – *ngorék* stately *gamelan* music. – *pohon* tree frog. – *puru* toad. – *sapi* bullfrog, *Rana carnivora*. – *ulo* a gambling game played with dice on a revolving board.
  kodok-kodokan toy noisemaker in the shape of a frog.

kodok II (*M*) nape of the neck; → KUDUK II.

kodok III (*J*) *mas* – platinum.

kodok IV *kué* – a fried snack made of flour, sugar, and mashed banana.

kodok-kodok 1 pump piston. **2** (*naut*) cleat.

kodrat I (*A*) **1** almighty, all-powerful, having unlimited power/authority. – (*dan*) *iradat Tuhan* the power and will of God. **2** omnipotence. **3** God's will. – *Ilahi* God's will.
  berkodrat almighty, all-powerful, omnipotent. *tidak* ~ *lagi* powerless, impotent.
  mengodratkan to predestine for.

kodrat II (*Jv*) **1** nature, character. – *alam* law of nature. – *wanita* the nature of women. **2** by nature, naturally. **3** force of nature. (*letak*) *pada* –*nya* quite natural.

kodrati (*A*) to have the authority, hold the power; almighty; → ADIKODRATI.

Kodya [Kota Madya] municipality.
  se-Kodya the entire municipality.

koé (*J*) → KOWÉ.

koédukasi (*D*) coeducation.

koéfisién (*D/E*) coefficient.

koék (*onom*) quacking sound (of a duck).
  berkoék(-koék) to quack.

koéksisténsi (*D/E*) coexistence. – *damai* peaceful coexistence.
  berkoéksisténsi to coexist.

Koeln Cologne.

koérsif (*E*) coercive.

kofisién → KOEFISIÉN.

Kogam [Komando Ganyang Malaysia] Crush Malaysia Command.

kogellaher (*D*) → KOLAHER.

kognisi (*D*) cognition.

kognitif (*D/E*) cognitive.

koh → ENGKO.

kohabitasi (*E*) cohabitation.

Kohanudnas [Komando Pertahanan Udara Nasional] National Air Defense Command.

Kohanudpas [Komando Pertahanan Udara Pasif] Passive/Noncombatant Air Defense Command.

kohel (*D*) bullet; → PATRUM. – *patrum* bullets; → PELURU.

kohérén (*D/E*) coherent.

kohérénsi (*D*) cohesion.

kohir (*D*) assessment list for taxation purposes.

kohol I bracken; → RESAM I.

kohol II (*A ob*) collyrium, black-eye salve.

kohong to stink (of rotten fish/fish-paste/eggs).

kohu-kohu (*Moluccas*) smoked tuna salad.

koi Japanese carp.

koil (*E*) coil.

koin (*E*) coin (for bus/gambling, etc.).

koinsidénsi (*D*) coincidence.

koipuk (*C*) middleman in the rubber trade.

koit and **ko'it** (*J*) *mati* – to drop dead.

koitus (*D/E*) coitus, sexual intercourse. *melakukan* – to have sexual intercourse.

koja I (*Pers*) **1** earthenware bottlenecked ewer, a bottle-shaped water jar/jug with a neck. **2** (*euph*) penis. – *panggang* k.o. *kué* made with peanuts.

koja II → KHOJA(H).

kojoh flooded (of rice fields).

kojol terkojol-kojol to be convulsed with laughter.

kojor (*J vulg*) (*mati* –) to drop dead.
  ngojorin to kill, bump off.

kojur I (*Jv*) bad luck.
  sekojur-kojur *nasibnya* no matter how bad his luck.

kojur II → KUJUR I.

kok I (*E*) shuttlecock (in badminton).

kok II (*J*) **1** why? how come? (said on discovering s.t. surprising/unexpected, etc.; the speaker feels surprised at s.o.) *Lho*, – *mahal!* Hey, why is it so expensive? **2** a particle which shows disagreement with what the interlocutor has said or presumed. *Bukan dia* – *yang mengambil duit saya!* He's not the one who took my money! *Mémang* –*!* That's the way it is! *Nggak apa-apa* –*!* It's really nothing at all!

koka (*D*) coca. *pohon* – a shrub, *Erythroxylon coca*, whose dried leaves are the source of cocaine and some other alkaloids.

kokah leaf monkey, *Semnopithecus siamensis*.

kokain(e) (*D/E*) cocaine.

kokam [kontol kambing] k.o. fried cake.

kokang (*Jp*) **mengokang** [and **ngokang** (*coq*)] to cock (a rifle to fire it).
  terkokang cocked (of a rifle).

kokar (*sl*) **ngokar** to smoke (a cigarette).

kokarde (*D*) cockade.

kokas (*E*) coke, i.e., coal from which most of the gases have been removed by heating. – *minyak bumi* petroleum coke.
  mengokas to coke.
  pengokas coker, coking (*mod*).
  pengokasan coking.

kokay (*Pr*) rich; → KAYA I.

kokbrut I (*J*) **1** lousy, rotten, garbage; → BRÉNGSÉK. **2** stupid, foolish.

kokbrut II (*J vulg*) **1** to have sexual intercourse. **2** fuck you!

koker (*D*) shaft, well. – *lift* elevator shaft. – *tangga* stairwell.

koki I (*D*) cook, chef.

koki II *mas* – (*coq*) a goldfish species with large protruding eyes.

kokila (*Skr*) mynah bird; → TIUNG.

koko I (*J*) *baju* – k.o. pajama-like garment.

koko II (*C?*) elder brother; → KAKAK I.

koko III (in Serawak and Pulau Sebatik) cocoa.

Koko IV the nickname for Dr. Soedjatmoko, former Indonesian ambassador to the United States and Rector of UN University in Tokyo.

kokoh 1 tenacious; → KUKUH. **2** solid (in construction). **3** tough (can take a lot of punishment).

sekokoh as solid as.
mengokohkan 1 to confirm, corroborate. 2 to strengthen.
terkokoh the most solid/tough.
kekokohan 1 tenacity. 2 toughness.
pengokoh stabilizer.
pengokohan consolidation.
kokok I (- *petok*) crowing (of a cock). – *ayam (sekali)* very early in the morning, dawn.
 berkokok 1 to crow (of cocks). 2 to brag, boast.
kokok II – *beluk* (*Jv*) fish owl, *Ketupa ketupa.*
kokokan various species of heron and bittern. – *laut* little striated heron, *Butorides striatus.* – *sungai* black bittern, *Ixobrachus flavicolis.*
kokol I large fern, bracken (used for making baskets); → RESAM I.
kokol II mengokol to (sit, lie) hunched up/over; (to sleep, etc.) bent over, doubled over; bowed, stooping, ducking, huddled. *batuk* ~ to have a barking cough. *duduk* ~ to sit hunched over.
 terkokol-kokol shivering, trembling. *demam* ~ fever with shivers.
kokol III (*Jv*) a large signal drum made from bamboo or a hollowed-out log.
kokon (*D*) cocoon.
kokonéta k.o. cocktail (alcoholic drink).
kokop → KUKUP.
kokoro manggih mulud (*Jv*) to make use of an opportunity.
kokorselan merry-go-round, carousel.
kokosan (*J*/*Jv*) k.o. *langsat* fruit, *Lansium oleracea/domesticum.*
kokot I 1 cramp(-iron), clamp, staple, bent hook. 2 bent (of hands due to stiffness, etc.), crooked (like a claw). – *betina* gudgeon (of gate), socket (of rudder). – *jantan* pintle of rudder or gatepost, hook, clasp. – *kemudi* (*naut*) rudder socket. – *kunci* key hook. – *lentur/pelengkung* bending clamp.
 mengokot to scrape (together), to scratch out (a living, etc.), claw at.
 terkokot twisted, claw-shaped (of deformed fingers or toes).
kokot II (*J*) lock.
 mengokot to lock. *Kamarnya dikokot.* His room was locked.
kokpit (*E*) cockpit.
koktil (*E*) cocktail.
kokus (*E*) coccus.
kol I mengol 1 (*ob coq*) to calculate, estimate, reckon. 2 to tally (lists of names/pay slips, etc.).
kol II (*D*) cabbage, *Brassica oleracea.* – *banda* tree lettuce, *Pisonia alba.* – *brussel* Brussels sprouts. – *bunga hijau* sprouting broccoli. – *daun* kale. – *halus* collard. – *isi berkuah* stuffed cabbage in broth. – *kembang* cauliflower. – *mérah* red cabbage. – *putih* white cabbage. – *umbi* Swedish turnip.
kol III (*E*) (*pistol* –) Colt (revolver).
kol IV → KHOL.
kol V [*kolonél*] (*D*) colonel.
kol VI brand name of light pickup van used as a minibus for intercity transportation; → COLT, KOLT.
kola (*D*/*E*) cola.
kolaborasi (*D*) collaboration (with the enemy).
 berkolaborasi to collaborate (with the enemy).
kolaborator (*D*/*E*) collaborator (with the enemy).
Kolaga [Komando Mandala Siaga] Alert Theater Command (during *Konfrontasi*).
kolah → KULAH I.
kolaher (*D*) ball bearing; → BANTALAN *peluru.*
kolak I fruit (usually banana but also sweet potato/yam) cooked with coconut milk and brown sugar; usually eaten as an afternoon snack after the siesta. – *pisang* banana *kolak.* – *ubi* sweet potato *kolak.*
 mengolak to prepare *kolak.*
kolak II → ANAK *kolak.*
Kolakops [Komando Pelaksana Operasi] Operational Implementation Command.
kolam (*Tam*) 1 pond. 2 tank (for holding water, etc.). – *air* water reservoir. – *air putar* whirlpool bath. – *(be)renang* swimming pool. – *hias* pool (in a garden). – *ikan* fishpond. – *imbuh* recharge pit. – *induk* brood pond. – *kaca* aquarium. – *kering* dry dock. – *mandi/renang* swimming pool. – *peluncuran* pool with a water slide. – *susu* (from the title of a song) land of milk and

honey (referring to Indonesia's natural riches). – *tando* reservoir.
 mengolamkan to put in a pond.
kolang-kalik → KOLANG-KALING II.
kolang-kaling I the fruit of the sugar palm, *Arenga pinnata.*
kolang-kaling II 1 to and fro, up and down. 2 whirling around helplessly.
kolaps (*D/E*) collapse.
kolar (*D*) (*batu* –) coral; gravel; → KORAL.
kolase (*D/E*) collage.
kolasi (*D*) collation.
kolé → KOLÉK.
koléga (*D*) colleague; → REKAN I.
kolégial (*D/E*) collegial.
kolégialitas collegiality.
koléh-koléh a sweet made of granulated flour.
kolék (*Jv*) 1 k.o. canoe, dinghy. 2 (in Indramayu, Cirebon) k.o. small fishing boat.
kolékdol [koléktor-dol] art dealer.
kolék-kolék berkolék-kolék 1 to bob up and down. 2 to sway, reel (of a drunkard).
kolé-kolé (*Ambon*) dugout canoe.
koléksi (*D*) collection. – *lukisan* a collection of paintings.
 mengoléksikan to collect (publications/stamps, etc.).
kolékte (*D*) collection, a sum of money collected, *esp* for charity or church use.
koléktif (*D/E*) collective.
koléktivisasi (*D*) collectivization.
koléktivisme (*D/E*) collectivism.
koléktor (*D/E*) collector (*esp* of taxes).
kolembén (*D*) columbine.
kolembéng (*D*) a very soft pastry.
koléna *pohon* – → *pohon* GAMAL.
koléng → KOLÉK.
koléng-koléng to wander about aimlessly, be homeless.
koléra (*D/E*) cholera.
kolése (*D*) college.
kolesom and **kolésom** (*C*) (*anggur* –) a Chinese tonic, (Korean) ginseng.
kolésterol (*D/E*) cholesterol.
 berkolésterol *tinggi* with a high cholesterol content.
koli (*D*) piece of luggage, package, bale, bag, barrel.
kolibri (*D*) hummingbird.
kolik I (*Jv*) female nocturnal cuckoo (the female of the *tuhu* bird), a sign of an impending robbery.
kolik II (*D/E*) colic, griping pain.
kolin (*D chem*) choline.
koling (*E*) **mengoling** to call.
kolintang wooden xylophone of the Northern Celebes.
kolo and **ko lo** (*C*) sweet and sour (of Chinese dishes). – *bak* sweet and sour pork. – *kéé* sweet and sour chicken.
koloh *air* – waste water in which cloth has been dyed.
koloid(a) (*D*) colloidal.
kolok I → KULUK I.
kolok II (*Jv*) spoiled (of a child), indulged.
 mengolok to spoil.
 kolokan /kolo'an/ spoiled (of a child).
kolokasi (*D*) collocation.
kolokium (*D/E*) colloquium. – *doktum* colloquium doctum.
kololit k.o. shoe polish.
kolom I (*D/E*) column. – *susut* drawdown.
 sekolom a column.
 berkolom-kolom in columns.
 koloman columns.
kolom II → KULUM.
kolombi Manadonese dish made from an edible variety of snail.
Kolombia Colombia.
Kolombo Colombo. *Panca Negara* – the five Colombo countries: Sri Lanka, India, Pakistan, Burma and Indonesia. *Rencana* – the Colombo Plan.
kolomnis (*E*) columnist.
kolone (*D*) column. – *kelima* the fifth column.

kolonél (*D/E*) 1 colonel. 2 – *laut* (navy) captain.
kolong I 1 space (under s.t., such as a table/bridge, etc.). *tidur di –
jembatan* to sleep under a bridge (because one is homeless). *di
– méja* under the table. *di bawah – langit* everywhere (in the
world). *tidak ada barang baru di – langit* there is nothing new
under the sun. *pintu* – trapdoor (in floor). *rumah* – house built
on piles/stilts. 2 (coal/tin, etc.) mine, pit. *Cina* – Chinese
miner. *menggali – batu bara* to sink/dig a coal mine. – *kerja* pit
(where people work on cars, etc.). – *layar* advertising banner. –
rumah basement, cellar. – *timah* tin mine.
kolong II (*J/Jv*) **kolong-kolong** and **kolongan** a large circular rattan
ring.
kolong III – *layar* (*ob*) banner (used for advertising purposes, etc.).
kolong IV (on the island of Bangka) lake; → DANAU I.
koloni (*D/E*) colony. – *pengemis* tramp town.
kolonial (*D/E*) colonial.
kolonialisme (*D/E*) colonialism.
kolonialistis (*D/E*) colonialist.
kolonisasi (*D*) 1 (*col*) transmigration (of people from one part of
Indonesia to another). 2 colonialization.
kolonisir (*D*) **mengolonisir** to colonize.
kolonjono an alfalfa-like grass used as cattle fodder.
kolonyét k.o. perfumed tissue.
kolor I (*J/Jv*) 1 string used as a belt for trousers/underpants/paja-
mas, (with a) drawstring. 2 (under)shorts. – *anget* hot pants,
very short shorts.
kolor II ngolor to curry favor, bootlick.
Kolorado Colorado.
kolosal (*D/E*) colossal, huge, enormous, gigantic, extraordinary.
kekolosalan enormity, hugeness.
kolot (*J/Jv*) 1 old(-fashioned), out-of-date, traditional. 2 conservative, orthodox. *kaum* – the conservatives.
kekolotan conservatism, orthodoxy.
kolportase (*D*) hawking, peddling.
kolportir (*D*) hawker, peddler.
kolt → COLT.
kolumnis (*E*) columnist.
kolusi (*E*) collusion; → PERSEKONGKOLAN.
kolusi (*D*) collusion.
kom I (*D*) basin, bowl; → BASKOM. – *cuci muka* wash basin, washstand.
kom II (in acronyms) → KOMANDO.
koma I (*D*) comma. *titik* – semicolon. – *atas* apostrophe. – *bernoktah* semicolon. – *bertindik* colon (punctuation mark).
koma II (*E*) 1 coma. *dalam keadaan* – in a coma. 2 to be in a
coma. *Dia – selama 2 hari.* He was in a coma for 2 days.
komadér and **komadré** (*Port*) godmother.
komak-kamék and **komak-kamik** → KOMAT-KAMIT.
koma-koma 1 curcuma. 2 saffron.
komala → KEMALA, KUMALA.
komaliwan eating utensils (on board a ship).
koman I (*E*) common (people, etc.).
Koman II (in Bali) name element placed before personal names to
indicate the third-born child, e.g., *Dayu – Watika.*
komandan (*D*) 1 commander. – *Batalyon* [*Danyon*] Battalion
Commander. – *Korém* [*Danrém*] Military Area Commander.
– *Komando Pelaksana Operasi* [*Dankolaops*] Commander of
the Operational Administrator's Command. – *Koramil* [*Danramil*] Military District Commander. – *upacara* parade commander. 2 commandant.
mengkomandani to command, be in command of, have command over. *dikomandani oléh ...* under the command of...
pengomandanan command, commanding.
komandemén (*D*) commandment (of police force, etc.).
komanditér (*D*) sleeping/limited partner. *peséro/perséroan* – limited partner/partnership; → CV I.
komando (*D/E*) 1 command, i.e., area of military jurisdiction. 2
(*mil*) command. 3 commando, i.e., a small raiding force. 4 a
commando. – *antar daérah* interregional command. – *cadangan stratégis* strategic reserve command. – *daérah* area command. – *daérah udara* air force area command. – *distrik*
district command. – *gabungan* [*kogab*] joint command. – *gar-*

nisum [*kogar*] garrison command. – *jenis amfibi* amphibious
command. – *kerangka* skeleton command. – *Mandala* command created in 1962 to liberate West Irian. – *markas* station
command. – *Operasi Pemulihan Keamanan* [*Koopslihkam*]
Command for the Restoration of Security. – *Pasukan Khusus*
[*Kopassus*] Special Forces Command. – *patroli* patrol command. – *pemburu* destroyer command. – *pertahanan* defense
command. – *Pertahanan Udara* [*Kohanud*] Air Defense Command. – *pertempuran* combat command. – *Rakyat* or *Tri –
Rakyat* the People's Threefold Command: a) *Kibarkan Sang
Mérah Putih di Irian Barat.* Fly the Indonesian flag in West
Irian. b) *Gagalkan pembentukan "Negara Papua" oléh Belanda.* Foil the Dutch formation of a "Papuan State." c) *ABRI
siap-sedia untuk sewaktu-waktu menerima perintah bébaskan
Irian Barat.* The Armed Forces are ready to receive at any time
the order to liberate West Irian. – *séktor* [*kosék*] sector command. – *stratégis* strategic command. *Stratégis Angkatan
Darat* [*Kostrad*] Army Strategic Command. – *Stratégis Udara*
Strategic Air Command, SAC. – *wilayah* [*kowil*] territorial
command (of police force).
meng(k)omando to be in command of.
meng(k)omandokan to command, give (an order).
peng(k)omandoan act of commanding, giving a command.
Komang → KOMAN II.
komaran (*Jv*) ceremony performed on the island of Majeti by
fishermen from Cilacap at which offerings are presented to
Nyai Loro Kidul.
komat-kamit 1 to mumble, mutter, move the lips without uttering sounds. *Mulutnya sering –.* She often moves her lips
(without speaking). 2 to munch, chew.
kombala (*ob*) shepherd; → GEMBALA I.
kombali (*coq*) → KEMBALI.
kombang → KUMBANG.
kombanwa (*Jp*) 1 good night. 2 (*sl*) condom.
kombék (*E*) to come back, reconcile.
kombi (*Ger*) the Volkswagen minibus.
kombinasi (*D*) combination.
meng(k)ombinasikan to combine.
kombinir (*D*) **mengkombinir** to combine.
kombong I (*Jv*) chicken coop.
kombong II (*J*) **ngombong(in)** 1 to feed a horse in a stable from
a rack/trough. 2 (*J*) to feed (a child/s.o. else, etc.).
kombongan a wooden feeding rack/trough for horses.
kombor I (*J/Jv*) (too) wide, loose fitting. *katok* – wide, loose-fitting
shorts.
kombor II (*Jv*) **ngombor** to feed a horse with chopped grass in water.
komboran horse fodder.
komédi → KOMIDI.
komédian (*E*) comedian.
komédiawan comedian.
komédo (*L*) blackhead.
koménda (*Port ob leg*) loan.
koméndur (*D*) 1 troop commander. 2 harbormaster; → SYAHBAN-
DAR. 3 → KONTROLIR.
koméng (*J*) 1 dwarfish, stunted, undeveloped, puny. 2 congen-
itally impotent (of the male). *nyiur* – an undeveloped coconut
(without meat). *orang* – hermaphrodite.
sekoméng a little bit.
berkoméng *tidak ~ lagi* to become poor.
koméng II (*J*) cat.
koméntar (*D*) comment(ary).
berkoméntar to make a comment (on).
mengoméntar(i) to comment on, give an opinion about.
koméntator (*D/E*) commentator; → JURU *tafsir.*
komérsial (*E*) commercial, business (*mod*).
mengkomérsialkan to commercialize. ~ *jabatan* to take advantage of one's job (for one's own purposes), abuse one's office.
komérsialis (*E*) commercialist.
komérsialisasi (*D*) commercialization. – *jabatan* abuse of office.
mengkomérsialkan to commercialize.
komérsialisme (*D/E*) commercialism.

komérsialitas commerciality.

komérsi(i)l (*D*) commercial, business (*mod*).

mengkomérsilkan to commercialize. ~ *jabatan* to abuse one's office.

kekomérsilan commerciality.

pengkomérsilan commercialization.

komés I → KUMIS I, III.

komet (*Jv*) **mengometkan** to make dizzy.

komét (*D*) comet.

komfor (*D*) comfort, ease.

komfortabel (*D/E*) comfortable.

komidi (*D*) 1 comedy. 2 theater. *(ber)main* – to act/play a part/role. *gedung/rumah* – theater, opera house. – *bangsawan* stage show. – *bicara* (*col coq*) the *Volksraad*. – *gambar* (*ob*) movie theater. – *keték* a dance performance by monkeys dressed as human beings and imitating people; → KEMIDI *bedés*. – *kuda* circus. – *monyét* → KOMIDI *keték*. – *puter* (*J*) merry-go-round. – *setambul* touring stage show.

mengomidikan to make fun of s.o.

komik I (*D/E*) comic strip, comics. *buku* – comic book.

pengomikan making into comics.

komik II (*D/E*) 1 clown, comic, humorist. 2 comical, humorous.

kekomikan humor.

Kominform (*D/E*) Cominform.

kominiké → KOMUNIKÉ.

kominis → KOMUNIS.

Komintérn (*D/E*) Comintern.

komis (*D*) senior clerk.

komisariat (*D*) 1 commissioner's office. 2 (*col*) police headquarters.

komisaris (*D*) 1 commissioner. – *agung/tinggi* high commissioner. – *pemerintah* government commissioner. 2 (*col*) commissioner (of the police). – *polisi* police commissioner. – *besar polisi* chief commissioner of the police. – *jénderal polisi* police commissioner general. 3 (of a limited corporation) director. *déwan* – board of directors, member of the board of directors. – *utama* chairman of the board of directors. – *amanat* managing director. – *utama* chairman of the board of commissioners. 4 (head of any of the former commissariats in the USSR) commissar.

kekomisarisan commissariat.

komisi I (*D/E*) commission, committee (in Parliament, etc.), board; → DÉWAN, PANITIA. – *Hak Khusus* (*Sg*) Committee of Privileges. – *Kebenaran dan Rékonsiliasi* Truth and Reconciliation Commission, TRC. – *pengarah* steering committee.

komisi II (*D/E*) 1 commission, percentage, fee, charges. *barang-barang* – goods on consignment. *mendapat (uang)* – 10% to receive a 10% commission. *menerima barang-barang* – to take delivery of goods on consignment. *menjual* – to sell on a commission basis. 2 tip.

mengkomisikan to sell s.t. on a commission basis.

komisi III *pergi* – and **meng(k)omisi** to make an tour of inspection.

Komisi IV (humorous interpretation of **komisi I**) [Korupsi resmi saat ini] Corruption is Official Nowadays; → KOMISI I.

komisionér (*D*) broker.

komit → KOMÉT.

komité (*D*) committee; → PANITIA. – *Nasional Indonésia Pusat* [KNIP] Central Indonesian National Committee, i.e., the functional equivalent of a Parliament in the Republican governmental system up to the formal transfer of sovereignty. – *penaséhat* advisory committee. – *perayaan 17 Agustus* committee for celebrating August 17. – *sekolah* school board. – *tetap* standing committee.

komitmén (*E*) commitment.

komkoma turmeric, *Curcuma domestica*; → KUNIR I, KUNYIT I.

komlék → KOMUNIKASI *dan* éléktronika.

Komnas Ham [Komisi Nasional Hak-Hak Asasi Manusia] National Commission on Human Rights.

komoditi (*E*) commodity.

komodo I 1 the komodo dragon, *Varanus komodensis*. 2 Komodo Island.

komodo II *Operasi* – Operation Komodo, i.e., the codename for the 1974–75 Indonesian covert political campaign in the former Portuguese Timor.

komodor (*E*) commodore. – *Muda Udara* Junior Air Commodore. – *Udara* Air Commodore.

kompa (*Jv*) pump; → POMPA.

mengompa and **ngompa** to inflate/blow up a tire.

kompak (*D*) /kompak/ 1 compact, dense, firm. *salam – kepada ...* greetings to 2 harmonious, cohesive, with strong esprit de corps, united. *tidak* – inharmonious. **ketidak-kompakan** disagreement, lack of harmony.

sekompak as compact/cohesive, etc. as.

memperkompak and **meng(k)ompakkan** [and **ngompakin** (*J coq*)] to strengthen, reinforce, unite, make cohesive.

terkompak the most cohesive.

kekompakan harmony, solidarity, cohesiveness, agreement, unification, esprit de corps.

pengompakan compacting.

kompanyi (*mil*) company; → KOMPENI.

kompanyon (*D*) partner, (business) associate; → MITRA.

berkompanyon *dengan* in partnership with.

komparan (*D leg*) person appearing, party; → PENGHADAP.

komparasi comparative. *studi* – comparative study.

komparatif (*D/E*) comparative.

komparisi (*D leg*) personal appearance.

kompartemén and **kompartimén** (*E*) compartment, i.e., a k.o. government department under President Soekarno.

kompartemétasi and **kompartiméntasi** (*D*) compartmentalization.

kompas I (*D*) 1 compass. – *giro* gyrocompass. – *magnétik/magnit* magnetic compass. 2 (*Mal*) (pair of) compasses.

kompas II (*J*) **mengompas** [and **ngompas** (*coq*)] (*sl*) to remove the entire contents of, to steal everything. *Dia tukang ngompas orang.* He's a robber.

Kompas III Kompas, the name of a Jakarta daily newspaper.

kompatibel (*D/E*) compatible.

kekompatibelan compatibility.

kompatriot (*D/E*) compatriot.

kompék I (*J/Jv*) wallet, purse, small bag made of leather, etc. for holding money.

kompék II (*J/Jv*) *sétan* – devil who likes to hide children.

kompéndium (*D/E*) compendium.

kompeni (*D*) 1 East India Company, VOC. 2 (*col*) Dutch East Indies government. 3a) VOC soldier. b) Dutch soldier.

kompenian 1 taxes on private lands during the VOC period. 2 hard labor.

kompénsasi (*D*) compensation, indemnity.

mengkompénsasi(kan) to compensate.

kompensir (*D*) **mengkompénsir** → MENGKOMPÉNSASI(KAN).

komperang → KOMPRANG.

komperénsi → KONPERÉNSI.

komperés → KOMPRÉS.

kompés (*J*) **mengompés** [and **ngompés** (*coq*)] to exert pressure on s.o. during (a police) investigation, interrogate, give s.o. the third degree.

kompésan pressure during investigation, the third degree.

kompetén (*D/E*) competent.

berkompetén competent, reliable.

kompeténsi (*D*) competence.

kompetisi (*D*) competition (in sports).

berkompetisi (in sports) to compete, play a match.

kompétitif (*E*) competitive.

kompi I (*D mil*) company. – *berdiri sendiri* separate company. – *infanteri* infantry company. – *senapan* rifle company. – *senjata bantuan* weapons company. – *tank* tank company. – *zéni* engineers company.

sekompi 1 in the same company. 2 a company.

kompi II comfrey (used as a k.o. *jamu*).

kompie III (*sl*) /kompi/ computer.

kompilasi (*D*) compilation.

mengkompilasikan to compile.

terkompilasi compiled.

kompilator (*D*) compiler.

komping → KOMPI II.

kompit (in northern Celebes) motorized prau.

kompiuter → KOMPUTER.

kompléks I (*D/E*) complex, complicated, intricate.

kompléks II (*D/E*) (psychological) complex. – *rendah diri* inferiority complex.

komplék(s) III (*D*) complex, i.e., a group of buildings, etc., that form a unit, housing development. – *pelacuran* red-light district. – *perkantoran* office park. – *pertokoan/toko-toko* commercial center. – *perumahan* housing complex.

kompléksitas complexity.

komplemén (*D/E*) complement, supplement.

    mengkompleméni to complement, supplement.

kompleméntaritas complementarity.

kompleméntér (*D*) complementary.

komplét → komplit.

komplikasi complication.

komplin (*E*) complaint.

komplit (*D/E*) **1** complete, full. *nama –nya ialah* ... his full name is ... **2** with all the trimmings. *bécak* – (*J*) pedicab with a prostitute. *bistik* – steak dinner.

    sekomplit-komplitnya as complete(ly) as possible.

    kekomplitan completeness.

komplong (*J/Jv*) stupid, foolish.

    ngomplong to stand there with mouth wide open.

komplot (*D*) **1** intrigue(s). **2** conspiracy, plot, scheme. **3** accomplices, gang, ring. – *pencuri mobil* car-theft ring. – *penjahat* gang of bandits.

    berkomplot to plot, scheme, conspire.

    komplotan 1 gang, ring (of criminals). ~ *Empat* Gang of Four. **2** accomplice (in crime). **3** plot, scheme, conspiracy.

kompoi → KONPOI, KONVOI.

kompol (*J*) → OMPOL. **mengompol** to wet one's bed.

kompon (*E*) compound.

komponén (*D*) component, constituent part.

kompong 1 mutilated, mangled. *ayam* – a tailless chicken. **2** amputated, with only a stump left (of limbs). *seléndang* – a short *seléndang. si* – eunuch.

komponis (*D*) composer.

kompor (*D*) stove. – *gas* gas cooker. – *listrik* hot plate. *tukang* – instigator, inciter.

    mengompori [and **ngomporin** (*J coq*)] to light a fire under s.o. so that he will do s.t., instigate.

komporisasi the introduction of furnaces in brick yards.

kompos I (*D*) manure, fertilizer, compost.

    mengomposkan to transform into compost.

    pengomposan composting.

    perkomposan compost(ing) (*mod*).

kompos II mengomposkan to quarter (troops in barracks), house (prostitutes, etc.).

komposer (*E*) composer.

komposisi (*D*) **1** (literary, etc.) composition. **2** composition, compound containing several ingredients. – *kimiawi* chemical compound. **3** ingredients (of a manufactured food). – *pemain* line-up (of players on a team).

    berkomposisi 1 to have a composition. **2** to be compounded/composed of.

komposit (*D/E*) composite; → GABUNGAN.

komprador (*D*) **1** comprador. **2** supercargo. **3** official in charge of a ship's financial and passenger matters.

komprang (*J/Jv*) loose (of clothing), not tight(-fitting), roomy. *celana* – loosely fitting long pants (worn in *pencak*). *kaos* – loose shirt.

kompréhénsi (*D*) comprehension.

kompréhénsif (*E*) comprehensive.

kompréi → KOMPI II, KOMPING.

komprés (*D/E*) cold compress, ice pack.

    mengomprés to apply a cold compress to.

    komprésan a compress.

komprési (*D*) compression.

    berkomprési to have/produce compression.

komprésor (*D/E*) compressor.

kompri(ng) comfrey, a medicinal plant, *Symphytum officinalis*.

kompris (*D*) crown prince.

kompromi (*D*) compromise. – *yang tidak tenang* an uneasy compromise. *tidak kenal/mengenal* – uncompromising.

    berkompromi to (reach a) compromise.

    mengkompromikan to compromise (about s.t.).

    kompromi-kompromian all sorts of compromises.

kompromistis (*D*) compromising.

komputer (*E*) computer. *pecandu* – hacker. – *cacahan/digital* digital computer. – *jangkrik* inexpensive unbranded computer put together using a variety of components. – *pelacak penyakit* doctonics. – *pribadi* personal computer, PC. – *pribadi jinjing* laptop computer.

    mengkomputerkan to computerize.

    pengkomputeran computerization.

    perkomputeran computer system.

komputerisasi (*E*) computerization; → PENGKOMPUTERAN.

komputor and **kompyuter** → KOMPUTER.

Komrés [Komando résor(t)] District Command; police command at the *kabupatén* level.

Komrésko [Komando résor(t) kota] City District Command.

Komsat [Komunikasi satelit] Satellite Communications.

Komsék [Komando séktor] Sector Command; police command at village level.

Komséko [Komando séktor kota] City Sector Command.

komsén I (*E*) commission (payment); → KAMSÉN.

komsén II guard post that charges tolls on roads.

komsov [Komunis sovyét] Moscow-oriented Communist; *cp* KOMTIONG.

Komtabés [Komando kota besar] Metropolitan Command; police command at the city level.

komtiong [Komunis Tiongkok] Peking-oriented Communist; *cp* KOMSOV.

komunal (*D/E*) communal. *tanah* – communal land.

    mengkomunalkan to collectivize.

komunalisme (*D/E*) communalism.

komunalistik (*E*) communalistic.

komune (*D/E*) commune.

komuni (*D*) – (*suci*) **1** (Holy) Communion. **2** the bread and wine as symbols of the body and blood of Christ.

komunikan (*E*) communicator, i.e., the person who communicates.

komunikasi (*D*) communication. *ahli* – communicator. *ilmu* – communication science. – *harafiah* literal communication. – *dua arah* two-way communication. – *massa* mass communication. – *satelit* [komsat] satellite communication. – *wacana* speech communication.

    berkomunikasi to communicate. *kemampuan* ~ communicative competence.

    mengkomunikasikan to communicate s.t.

    pengomunikasian communication, communicating.

komunikatif (*D/E*) communicative.

komunikator (*E*) **1** communicator. **2** a *dalang*.

komuniké (*D/E*) communiqué. – *bersama* joint communiqué.

komunis (*D/E*) communist. *Partai* – *Indonésia* [PKI] Communist Party of Indonesia.

    mengkomuniskan to communize.

    kekomunisan state of being a communist.

    pengkomunisan communization, communizing.

komunisme (*D/E*) communism.

komunistofobi and **komunistophobi** (*D*) fear of communism.

komunitas and **komuniti** (*E*) community; *cp* BEBRAYAN, GUYUBAN, MASYARAKAT.

komutasi (*D*) commutation.

komuter (*E*) commuter; → PENGOLANG-ALIK.

Komwil [Komando Wilayah] Regional Command.

kon (in acronyms) → KONPERÉNSI, KONSUL, KONSULAT.

konak (*sl vulg*) hot, horny; erect (of one's penis).

konan (*ob*) **mengkonani** to overwhelm, attack with superior forces.

konang I (*Jv*) firefly; → KUNANG-KUNANG I.

konang II (*Jv*) **mengonangi** to find out, discover.

    konangan caught, detected, discovered, found out.

konas [Konperénsi Nasional] national conference.

konblok k.o. *batako*.

koncah rough, choppy (of water).

mengoncah to chop, go up and down.

koncahan going up and down.

konci I → KUNCI I.

konci II (sl) female friend.

konclak (J) to slosh around (of water in a container).

konco (Jv) 1 friend, buddy, comrade, crony. 2 supporter. 3 confederate. 4 accomplice. 5 satellite. negara – satellite state.

berkonco to have cronies.

konco-koncoan cronies.

perkoncoan crony (mod). sistém ~ crony system.

koncoisme cronyism.

kondai → KONDÉ, KUNDAI.

kondang I (Jv) famous, renowned, well-known, celebrated. – kuncara very well known/famous.

kondang II (Jv) companion, mate; adherent, follower.

kondang III (Jv) irrigation canal.

kondang IV (Jv) senior official. – bagian pengajaran senior official in the department of education (in Surakarta).

kondangan (Jv) invited to or be a guest at a selamatan.

kondé (Jv) hair bun, knot of hair, chignon. tusuk – hairpin. si – licin woman.

mengondé to roll up long hair, put one's hair up in a bun.

kondéktur (D) conductor, ticket-collector (on a bus, etc.).

kondénsasi (D) condensation.

mengkondénsasikan to condense.

kondénsat (D) condensate.

kondénsor (D/E) condenser.

kondisi (D) 1 condition, requirement. 2 condition, state of health. – puncak top condition.

mengkondisikan to condition, make conditional.

terkondisikan conditioned.

pengondisian conditional.

kondisional (E) conditional.

kondit → KONDUITE.

kondom (D/E) condom. Bapak – nickname for Haryono Suyono, chief of the Coordinating Committee for National Birth Control. – bertanduk a condom provided with strings. – wanita a k.o. condom for women.

mengondomi to put plastic bags on (cocoa plants to protect them from cocoa mites).

pengkondoman utilizing condoms.

kondominium (D/E) condominium.

kondomisasi (D) spreading/popularizing the use of condoms.

kondor (J/Jv) scrotal hernia, (inguinal) rupture.

kondoran to have a hernia/rupture; → BURUT.

konduite (D) efficiency report.

konék (E) to connect.

konéksi (D) (business) connection; acquaintance, esp. an influential person; → NASABAH.

terkonéksi connected.

konéksitas connection.

konéng (S) yellow. kué – name of a k.o. cake/tart. – besar zedoary, Curcuma zedoaria, used in medicines.

konféderasi (D) confederation.

konféksi (D) ready-made clothes.

konferénsi → KONPERÉNSI.

konfidénsi (D) confidence, trust.

konfidénsial (E) and konfidénsi(i)l confidential.

konfigurasi (D) configuration.

konfirmasi (D) confirmation, corroboration.

mengonfirmasi and mengkonfirmasikan to confirm, corroborate.

konfiskasi (E) confiscation; → SITA I.

mengkonfiskasi to confiscate.

konflik (D/E) conflict. – dalam diri an internal conflict.

berkonflik 1 to be in conflict (with). 2 conflicting.

konform (D/E) to conform.

konformasi (E) conformation.

konformis (E) conformist.

konformistis (E) conformist.

konfrontasi (D) 1 confrontation. 2 the Indonesian confrontation against the formation of Malaysia from 1963 to 1966.

berkonfrontasi to confront, to be in a state of hostility; to oppose. tanpa ~ dengannya without confronting her.

meng(k)onfirmasikan to confront s.t.

konfrontasionis (E) confrontationist.

konfrontatif to have a confrontational character.

konfrontir (D) mengkonfrontir to confront.

Konfusian (E) Confucian.

Konfusianisme (D/E) Confucianism.

kong I (C) 1 grandpa! 2 grandma! → ENGKONG.

kong II (C geol) barren bedrock.

kongcu (C) master, teacher.

kongésti (D) congestion.

Konggo → KONGO.

konggrés → KONGRÉS.

Kong Hu Cu and Konghucu (C) Confucius.

kongkalikong (C) 1 intrigue. 2 connivance. (main) – a) to be corrupt. b) to intrigue, plot.

berkongkalikong 1 to fool s.o. 2 to plot and scheme; conspire. 3 to swindle, cheat.

kongkang slow loris, sloth, Nycticebus tardigradus; → KUNGKANG I.

kongkau → KONGKO.

kongkin (C) k.o. Chinese card game.

kongko (C J) to gossip, chat.

berkongko and mengongko to chat.

kongkoan (C) 1 community hall. 2 (col) consultative body/council for Chinese affairs/businesses. 3 chat.

kongkol (C) intrigue, scheme, plot; → SEKONGKOL.

kongkong I 1 fetter, chain, shackle(s); → KUNGKUNG. 2 foot irons, stocks. 3 wooden neck block for cattle/criminals to prevent them from escaping.

mengongkong 1 to fetter, chain, shackle. 2 to put in irons. 3 to clog. 4 to lock up, confine.

terkongkong 1 in irons, locked up, confined. ~ pada tempat tidurnya confined to bed, bedridden. 2 surrounded, encircled.

keterkongkongan incarceration.

kongkongan 1 chains, fettles, shackles. 2 confinement, encirclement.

kongkong II loud barking (of dog); → GONGGONG II.

mengongkong to bark loudly.

kongkongan barking.

kongkong III (J) ngongkong to sit immodestly in such a way that the thighs and genitals are visible.

mengongkongkan to put (the legs) apart.

ngongkongin to dominate; to supervise.

kongkow-kongkow (C J) 1 → KONGKO. 2 lobbying.

kongkrét and kongkrit → KONKRÉT.

kongkur → KONKURS.

kongkurén → KONKURÉN, PENYAING.

kongkurénsi → KONKURÉNSI, PERSAINGAN.

kongkurs → KONKURS.

konglomerat (D/E) /kon-glomerat/ conglomerate.

Kongo Congo. – (B) Congo (Brazzaville). – (L) Congo (Leopoldville).

kongrégasi (D) congregation.

kongrés (D/E) 1 congress, convention. 2 the U.S. Congress. anggota – congressman.

kongrésis (D) conferee.

kongruén (D/E) congruent.

kongsi (C) 1 society, gang, commercial association, (trading) company, union, club. 2 (business) partner; → MITRA usaha. – dalam bisnis business partner. – hidup partner for life, spouse.

sekongsi to be in partnership (with).

berkongsi to go into partnership, be partners (with), be in collusion (with).

kongsian 1 land tax levied on tenants of private land. 2 in partnership, jointly. menyéwa rumah secara ~ to rent a house jointly (or, in a partnership).

perkongsian 1 partnership. 2 alliance.

kongsol → KONSOL I.

koni I okra, Hibiscus esculentis.

KONI II [Komité Olahraga Nasional Indonésia] Indonesian National Sports Committee.

Konidin k.o. cough medicine.

konifér (D) conifer.

konis (D) conical.

Konjén 1 [Konsul Jénderal] Consul General. 2 [Konsulat Jénderal] Consulate General.

konjugasi (D) conjugation.

konjungsi (D) conjunction.

konjungtur (D) 1 (in general) conjuncture, concurrence of circumstances. 2 (econ) economic situation, state of the market, business outlook. 3 business cycle.

konk (E) conch.

konklusi (D) conclusion; → KESIMPULAN. menarik – to draw a conclusion.
   berkonklusi to conclude.

konkologi (E) conchology.

konkologis (E) conchologist.

konkordansi (D) concordance.

konkrét (D) and konkrit (E) concrete, tangible, not abstract.
   mengkonkrétkan to concretize, give concrete form to.
   kekonkrétan concreteness.
   pengkonkrétan concretization.

konkrétisasi (E) concretization.
   mengkonkrétisasikan to concretize, give concrete form to.

konkrétisir (D) mengkonkrétisir to concretize.

konkurén (D) competitor, rival.
   berkonkurén to compete; → BERSAING.

konkurénsi (D) competition, rivalry; → SAINGAN.

konkurs (D) competition, contest; → PERTANDINGAN.

konokan (in Jember, East Java) 1 help, assistance. 2 superstitious reference to mice and rats.

konon I 1 (following an interrogative pronoun) I wonder, could possibly. Apakah – yang tersimpul dalam hatinya? I wonder what's going on in his mind? Siapakah – yang bersusah hati pada hari yang seélok ini? Who could possibly be worried on such a beautiful day? 2 demikianlah - (kabarnya) and - (kabarnya) it is said/reported/rumored that, they say; the story goes that. Demikianlah - penghabisan riwayat si garang itu. They say that it is all over with that cruel man. -, udang windu laku dijual sampai Rp 9.000 per kilo. It is rumored that tiger prawns can be sold for Rp 9,000 per kilogram. 3 presumably, probably. Itulah - maka ia berani berbuat begitu. That is probably the reason that he has the guts to do that. 4 (cla) news, report. Adapun sekarang ini patik lihat serta dengar khabar yang sah, bukan – dikarang. I'm seeing and hearing valid reports, not made-up stories. 5 (M) (sekarang) ... -kan, - pula and - lagi even ... not to mention, to say nothing of, not to speak of, let alone. Sedangkan membelanjai hidupnya sendiri tak sanggup, - pula berbini dua. He is unable to provide for himself, let alone have two wives. Saya belum kuat hati melihat segumpalan darah, - lagi membunuh sesama manusia. I can't even look at a clot of blood, let alone kill another human being. 6 (it is) because, one thinks that s.t. is true. Cantiklah dia -. She thinks that she is beautiful. tapi - (under the guise of) but actually.
   kononnya as if, (think) that. Dia pikir ~ dia dapat memikat hati gadis itu. He thinks that he can win that girl's heart.
   memperkonon to deceive/mislead s.o. by telling stories.
   mengononkan to say that s.t. is; to relate with examples or references; to deceive, delude (by telling stories). Dia dikononkan kaya. He is said to be rich.

konon II (M) not to speak of; → JANGANKAN.

konosemén (D) bill of lading, B/L.

konotasi (D) connotation.
   mengkonotasikan to connote, connect. Jika terdengar suara kritis dalam masyarakat lantas dikonotasikan dengan pemilihan umum. When critical voices are heard in the community, they are right away connected with the general election.

konpéksi → KONFÉKSI.

konpénsi → KONVÉNSI.

konperénsi (D) conference.
   berkonperénsi to hold a conference, be in conference.
   mengkonperénsikan to discuss in a conference.

konperénsisten (D) para – the conferees, conventioneers.

konpergénsi → KONVERGÉNSI.

konpoi → KONVOI.

konsékrasi (D) consecration.
   mengkonsékrasikan to consecrate.

konsekrir (D) mengkonsekrit to consecrate.
   pengkonsekriran consecration.

konsekuén (D) consistent.
   mengkonsekuénkan to make consistent.
   kekonsekuénan consistency.

konsekuénsi (D) consequence.

konsekwén → KONSEKUÉN.

konsekwénsi → KONSEKUÉNSI.

konseling (E) counseling.

konselor (E) counselor.

konsénsus (D/E) consensus.
   mengkonsénsuskan to consent; to agree on s.t. by common consent.
   konsénsus-konsénsusan so-called consensus.

konséntrasi (D) concentration.
   berkonséntrasi to concentrate, put one's mind (to). Meréka tampaknya lebih bisa ~ dalam mengajar. Apparently they were able to concentrate more on teaching.
   mengkonséntrasi to concentrate s.t.
   mengkonséntrasikan ~ diri to concentrate.
   terkonséntrasi to be concentrated.

konséntrat (D/E) concentrate.

konséntrik (E) concentric.

konséntrir (D) mengkonséntrir to concentrate (on).
   terkonséntri to be concentrated on.

konséntris (D) concentric.

konséntrisitét (D) concentricity.

konsép I (D) rough draft/copy.
   meng(k)onsép to draw up a rough draft.

konsép II (E) concept, idea, notion. – pemasaran marketing concept.
   berkonsép conceptual.
   mengkonsépkan to conceive of, imagine.

konsépsi (D) 1 concept, notion, idea. 2 the concept presented by President Soekarno on February 21, 1957, later called démokrasi terpimpin.
   mengkonsépkan to conceive of.

konsépsional (E) and konsépsionil (D) conceptional.

konséptor (E) 1 conceptor, conceiver. 2 drafter (of a plan).

konséptual (E) and konséptuil (D) conceptual.

konséptualisasi (D) conceptualization.
   mengkonséptualisasikan to conceptualize.

konsér (D) concert. – biola violin concert. – gésék string concert. – vokalia vocal concert.
   mengkonsérkan to perform (in a public concert).

konsérvasi (D) conservation. ahli – conservationist.
   mengkonsérvasi to conserve.

konsérvatif (D/E) conservative.
   kekonsérvatifan conservatism.

konsérvatisme (D/E) conservatism.

konsérvator (D/E) conservator, curator of a museum, guardian, custodian.

konsérvatori(um) (D) conservatory, school of music; → KARAWITAN.

konsérven (D) preserves.

konsési (D) 1 concession, rights. meminta – untuk pengeboran minyak to request an oil-drilling concession. 2 concession, giving up s.t. memberikan beberapa – politik to make some political concessions.
   mengkonsésikan to concede; to license.

konsetabel (E ob) constable; → KONSTABEL.

konsiderans (D leg) preamble.

konsignasi → KONSINYASI I.

konsili (D) – Vatikan (Roman Catholic) council.

konsinyasi I (D) consignment.
   mengkonsinyasikan to consign.
   pengonsinyasi consignor.

konsinyasi II (D mil) confinement to base/barracks.
   mengkonsinyasikan to restrict/confine to base; to put somewhere for safekeeping.

konsinyator (E) consigner.

konsinyéring → KONSINYASI II. mengkonsinyéring → MENGKON-
SINYASIKAN.
konsinyes types of drills on ships.
konsinyi (E) consignee.
konsinyir I → KONSINYASI I.
konsinyir II → KONSINYASI II.
konsistén (D/E) consistent. tidak – inconsistent. ketidak-
konsisténan inconsistency.
kekonsisténan consistency.
konsisténsi (D) consistency; → KEKONSISTÉNAN.
mengkonsisténsikan to make consistent.
konsitori (D) consistory.
konsol I → KONSUL I. kekonsolan consular.
konsol II representative of Muhammadiyah's Executive Board.
Konsol III (the Ford) Consul (car).
konsolat → KONSULAT.
konsolidasi (D) consolidation, grouping.
berkonsolidasi to be consolidated.
meng(k)onsolidasikan to consolidate s.t.
terkonsolidasi to be consolidated.
pengkonsolidasian consolidating.
konsolidir (D) → KONSOLIDASI. mengkonsolidir to consolidate,
become consolidated.
konsonan (ling D) consonant. – awal initial consonant. – géséran
fricative. – getaran trill. – glotal glottal consonant.
konsorsium (D/E) consortium.
konspirasi (D) conspiracy; → KOMPLOT(AN).
berkonspirasi to conspire.
konspiratif (D) conspiratorial.
konstabel (Mal) constable, a police rank lower than corporal in
Indonesia; cp KONSETABEL.
konstan and konstanta (D) 1 (math) a constant; → TETAPAN. 2
firm, staunch, loyal, constant.
kekonstanan constancy.
konstatasi (D) authentication, ascertaining.
mengkonstasi to authenticate, ascertain (the facts).
konstatéring (D) establishment (of the facts), ascertainment.
konstatir (D) mengkonstatir 1 to ascertain. 2 to establish (the
facts/s.o.'s guilt, etc.). 3 to put (a fact) on record. 4 to find,
note (a deficit of, etc.).
konstélasi (D) 1 constellation. 2 configuration, alignment. – politik
political alignment.
konstipasi (D) constipation.
konstituante (D) constitutional assembly.
konstitusi (D) constitution; → UNDANG-UNDANG dasar. tidak
menurut – unconstitutional.
berkonstitusi constitutional.
mengonstitusikan to constitute.
konstitusional (E) and konstitutionil (D) constitutional.
konstruir (D) construction.
mengkonstruirkan to construct.
konstruksi (D) construction.
mengkonstruksikan to construct.
konstruktif (D/E) constructive.
konsuél (D?) inspector.
konsul I (D/E) consul. – jénderal [konjén] consul general. – muda
vice-consul.
konsul II (D) consultation.
mengkonsul to consult.
konsulat (D/E) consulate. –jénderal [konjén] consulate general.
kekonsulatan consulate.
konsulén consultant. – pajak tax consultant.
konsulér (D) consular.
konsultan (D/E) consultant.
konsultasi (D) consultation, counseling. biro – consultation center.
mengadakan – to call (s.o.) into consultation, go (to s.o.) for
counseling. – perjodohan/perkawinan marriage counseling.
berkonsultasi to go for consultation.
mengkonsultasi to consult s.o.
mengkonsultasikan 1 to consul (s.o.) about. 2 to seek counsel for.
konsultatif (D/E) consultative.
konsumén (D) consumer; → PEMAKAI.

konsumerisme (D/E) consumerism.
konsumeristis (D) consumer (mod).
konsumir (D) mengkonsumir → MENGKONSUMSI(KAN).
konsumptif (D) → KONSUMTIF.
konsumsi (D) 1 consumption. 2 (in restaurants) food and drink,
refreshments. – méwah conspicuous consumption. – syahwat
(euph) prostitute.
mengkonsumsi(kan) to consume.
pengkonsumsi consumer.
konsumtif (E) consumptive.
kontak I (D/E) contact, communication. – Jodoh Personals (in a
newspaper). – Pembaca Letters to the Editor. – radio radio contact. – senjata (mil) firefight. – Tani (regular) face-to-face con-
tacts between farmers and government representatives.
mengontak [and ngontak (coq)] to contact (over the radio, etc.).
mengontakkan 1 to contact, get in contact/touch with, meet.
pengontak connector.
kontak II (D) 1 light switch. kunci – ignition key. (kena –) to get
an electric shock. Dia kena – listrik. He got an electric shock.
2 contact.
mengontak(kan) 1 to switch/turn on (a light/motor, etc.). 2 to
plug s.t. in (to an outlet).
kontakan (elec) switch.
kontal-kantil (Jv) (= berkontal-kantil and terkontal-kantil) 1 to
dangle, swing to and fro. 2 to go everywhere by o.s.
kontaminasi (D) contamination.
mengkontaminasi to contaminate.
terkontaminasi (to get, be) contaminated. ~ radioaktif contaminated by radioactivity.
kontan I (D) cash. uang – cash. membayar (dengan) – to pay cash.
– keras cold/hard cash.
mengontan to pay cash.
kontan II (D) 1 flatly (deny s.t.). 2 prompt, on the spot, instantly,
right away. dijawab dengan – to be answered promptly.
mengontan to answer promptly.
kontan-kontanan immediately, at that very moment, then and
there.
kontang-kanting dangle, dangling; cp KONTAL-KANTIL.
berkontang-kanting and terkontang-kanting to dangle.
konté potlot – a hard (usu black-colored) crayon of graphite and clay.
kontéks (D/E) context.
kontékstual (D/E) contextual.
kontelér and kontelir → KONTROLIR.
kontémplasi (D) contemplation.
berkontémplasi to engage in contemplation.
mengkontémplasikan to contemplate.
kontémplatif (D/E) contemplative.
kontémporér (D) contemporary.
konténer (E) container; → PETI kemas.
konténerisasi (E) containerization.
konténsius (D) contentious.
konterak → KONTRAK.
kontés (E) contest. – (adu) kecantikan beauty contest.
mengkontéskan to contest (about s.t.).
kontés-kontésan various contests.
kontéstan (D) 1 contestant. 2 contender (in an election).
kontéstasi (E) contestation, conflict.
kontét (J/Jv) small, stunted, dwarf. si – The Dwarf, i.e., a rice variety.
kontinén (D/E) continent. – Tiongkok the Chinese landmass.
kontinéntal (D/E) continental.
kontingén (D) contingent, a group of persons who represent a
place, region, country, etc. – olah raga contingent of athletes. –
tentara military contingent. 2 a group of pilgrims, consisting of
four kafilahs, going to Mecca together; → KAFILAH, KLOTER,
REGU, ROMBONGAN.
kontinjénsi (E) contingency.
kontinu (D) continuous. secara – continuously. tak – discontinuous. ketak-kontinuan discontinuity. pentak-kontinuan dis-
continuation.
kontinuitas (D) continuity.
kontinyu (E) → KONTINU.

kontinyuitas (*E*) → KONTINUITAS.
kontol I (*Jv*) **1** penis. **2** scrotum; → BURUNG, PERKUTUT, PIPIT I, TITIT I.
   ngontolin (*J*) to stick one's penis into.
kontol II short, stumpy and pendulous.
kontra I (*D*) contra-, counter-. – *mémori banding* (*leg*) appellant's counterbrief.
   mengontrai (*infr*) to oppose, go counter to.
kontra II (*D*) – *dengan* to collide with.
kontrabas (*D*) double bass.
kontradémonstrasi counterdemonstration.
kontradiski (*D*) contradiction.
   mengkontradiksi to contradict.
kontradiktif (*D*) contradictory.
kontradiktoris (*D*) contradictory.
kontradisi → KONTRADIKSI.
kontraintél(ijén) counterintelligence.
kontrak (*D/E*) **1** contract; → PERJANJIAN. *dalam* – under contract. – *bagi hasil* production-sharing contract. – *berjangka* forward/futures contract. – *jaminan* surety bond. – *karya/kerja* work contract, contract of work, a contract in which the (foreign) contractor is to conduct all stages of an operation on behalf of the Indonesian government. The contractor pays the government land rents and royalties and in exchange receives a share of the profits. *mengkontrak-karyakan* and *mengkontrak-kerjakan* to operate (a company) under a *kontrak karya*. – *kerja sama* cooperative contract. – *penyerahan* delivery contact. – *séwa-beli* hire-purchase contract. – *siap pakai* turnkey contract. **2** lease. – *séwa* lease. *persetujuan* – *séwa* a lease agreement. *mengkontrak-séwakan* to lease.
   mengontrak to lease (under a contract). ~ *rumahnya untuk 2 tahun* to lease a house for 2 years.
   mengontrakkan [and **ngontrakin** (*J coq*)] to let/rent on lease, lease. *Pelaksana itu* ~ *salah satu wismanya*. The Executive Board has leased (out) one of its houses.
   kontrakan s.t. leased (out). *rumah* ~ a leased house.
   pengontrak contracting party, party to a contract.
kontraksi (*D*) contraction. – *monétér* monetary contraction. – *otot* muscular contraction.
   berkontraksi to contract.
kontraktan (*D*) contracting party, party to a contract.
kontraktor (*D/E*) contractor. – *yang hanya sekedar nampang jual dasi* a fly-by-night contractor.
kontraktual (*E*) and **kontraktuil** (*D*) contractual.
kontramémori counterbrief.
kontraopénsip counteroffensive.
kontrapréstasi (*D*) consideration, quid pro quo.
kontraproduktif (*D*) counterproductive.
kontrarévolusi (*D*) counterrevolution.
kontrarévolusionér (*D*) counterrevolutionary.
   kekontrarévolusionéran counterrevolutionism.
kontras I (*D*) **1** contrast, opposition, antithesis. **2** to be in contrast (of colors). **3** against, contrary to, in opposition to. **4** segregation, separation (between social classes).
   mengkontraskan to contrast, oppose.
   kekontrasan contrast, opposition.
Kontras II [Korban tindak kekerasan] Victims of Violence.
kontrasépsi (*D*) contraception. *alat* – contraceptive device, IUD.
kontraséptif (*D/E*) contraceptive.
kontraspionase (*D*) counterespionage.
kontrelir → KONTROLIR.
kontribusi (*D*) contribution, donation (usually money); *cp* IURAN, SUMBANGAN.
   mengkontribusikan to contribute (money or services).
kontrol I (*D/E*) **1** control, supervision, check, inspection (of tickets). **2** self-control. *Meréka kehilangan* –. They lost control of themselves. – *jarak jauh* long-distance control. – *kemudi* vehicle control. – *panél* control panel.
   berkontrol to control o.s., control one's temper, hold o.s. in.
   mengontrol 1 to control, inspect. **2** to investigate. **3** to supervise, oversee, look after. *Gerak-gerik oknum itu terus-menerus*

dikontrol. The thug's movements are under continuous surveillance. **4** to make one's rounds.
   mengontrolkan to put (o.s.) under the control of s.o.
   terkontrol can be controlled/supervised. *tidak* ~ out of control, uncontrollable, unverifiable.
   pengontrol 1 checker, supervisor, inspector. **2** controls. ~ *rangkap* dual controls.
   pengontrolan 1 check (on), control, supervision, inspection. **2** controlling.
kontrol II (*J coq*) to loiter, loaf, stroll around.
kontrolir (*D*) **1** (*col*) a Dutch administrative officer below the rank of assistant resident; → RÉSIDÉN. **2** controller, comptroller, checker. **3** ticket inspector.
   mengontrolir to control; → MENGONTROL.
kontrovérsial (*E*) and **kontravérsiil** (*D*) controversial.
kontur (*D*) contour, outline. – *lagu* tonal contour.
   berkontur with a ... outline.
   mengkontur to appear in outline/silhouette.
konus (*D*) cone.
konvéks (*D/E*) convex.
konvéksi (*D*) ready-made clothing; → PAKAIAN *jadi*.
konvénsi (*D leg*) convention, proceedings on the original complaint.
konvénsional (*E*) and **konvénsionil** (*D*) conventional.
   kekonvénsionalan conventionality.
konvérgén (*D*) convergent.
konvérgénsi (*D*) convergence.
konvérsasi (*D*) conversation; → PERCAKAPAN.
konvérsi (*D*) conversion.
   mengkonvérsikan to convert.
   pengkonvérsian converting.
konvértibel (*D/E*) convertible.
konvértor (*D*) converter.
konvoi (*D*) convoy.
   berkonvoi to ride in a convoy.
konvokésyen (*Mal*) convocation (in a university).
konvulsi (*D*) convulsion.
konyak (*D*) cognac, brandy.
konyan (*C*) Chinese New Year's feast.
konyol (*J*) **1** rude, ill-mannered, behaving badly. **2** somewhat crazy. **3** stupid, dumb. **4** useless, in vain, a waste. **5** constantly unlucky. *mati* – to die needlessly/for nothing.
   sekonyol as stupid/dumb as.
   meng(k)onyolkan to make s.o. look foolish.
   terkonyol the stupidest/dumbest.
   kekonyolan 1 foolishness. **2** tendency towards bad luck.
konyong sekonyong-konyong all of a sudden, suddenly, all at once, unexpectedly.
konyugal (*D*) conjugal.
konyugasi → KONJUGASI.
   mengkonyugasi to conjugate.
konyungsi → KONJUNGSI.
konyungtur → KONJUNGTUR.
kookplaat (*D*) /oo as o in go and aa as a in car/ hot plate.
ko'ong (*J*) empty.
kooperasi (*D*) /ko'operasi/; → KOPERASI II.
kooperatif (*D*) /ko'operatif/ cooperative (*mod*).
Koops [Komando operasionil] Operational Command.
Koopslihkam → KOMANDO *Operasi Pemulihan Keamanan*.
koor (*D*) /kor/ choir. – *geréja* church choir.
koordinasi (*D*) /ko'ordinasi/ coordination.
   mengkoordinasikan to coordinate.
   terkoordinasikan to be coordinated.
   pengkoordinasian coordination, coordinating.
koordinat (*D/E*) /ko'ordinat/ coordinate.
koordinator (*D/E*) /ko'ordinator/ coordinator.
   mengkoordinatori to coordinate.
koordinir (*D*) /ko'ordinir/ coordinate.
   mengkoordinir to coordinate.
   pengkoordiniran coordination, coordinating.
kop I (*D*) **1** (letter)head. **2** head (of tape recorder, etc.). – *surat* letterhead. – *télepon* headphones. **3** cup.
   berkop with the heading ..., headed. *kertas* ~ letterhead.

mengkop and **mengekop 1** (~ *bola*) (in soccer) to hit (the ball) with one's head. **2** to cup, i.e., to treat medically by applying a heated glass or cup to the skin.
   kop-kopan hitting a ball with one's head.
kop II (in acronyms) → KOPERASI I.
kop III → KUP I.
kopah mass, lump, quantity, clot (of blood).
   berkopah-kopah in clots (of blood), in lumps.
kopak I → KOPOK I, KUPAK.
kopak II mengopak 1 to open, peel (a fruit); → KELOPAK. ~ *kelapa* to peel a coconut. **2** to break open/into (a box/room, etc.); → KUPAK.
kopak III small box for holding clothing.
kopal (*D*) copal → GETAH *damar*.
Kopasgat [Komando Pasukan Gerak Cepat] Rapid Action Force Command.
Kopaska [komando pasukan katak] frogmen.
Kopassandha [Komando pasukan sandi yudha] Combat Intelligence Forces Command; → RPKAD.
Kopassus → KOMANDO *Pasukan Khusus*.
kopat-kapit (*Jv*) to wag from side to side.
kopbal (*D*) header (in soccer).
Kopda [Kopral dua] → KOPRAL *dua*.
kopdar → KOPI *darat*.
kopék I flaccid, pendulous (of a woman's breasts), empty (of the breast). *mak* – a dry wet nurse.
   mengopék to suck at an empty breast.
kopék II mengopék to peel (with the fingernails). ~ (*buah*) *jeruk* to peel an orange.
kopék III small purse.
kopék IV (*D Russian*) kopeck, kopek, 1/100 of a ruble.
kopel I (*D*) → KOPELRIM.
kopel II (*D*) torque.
kopel III coupled; → RUMAH *kopel*.
   mengkopel to couple.
kopeling (*D*) **1** clutch (in car). *pédal* – clutch pedal. **2** gearbox. **3** coupling.
kopelrim (*D mil*) **1** holster belt, Sam Browne belt; → KOPEL. **2** web belt.
Kopenhagen Copenhagen.
koper (*D*) **1** trunk. **2** suitcase, bag.
   berkoper-koper by the trunkful.
koperak(an) (*J*) rattle, (bamboo) clapper (to scare away squirrels/birds, etc.).
koperal → KOPRAL.
koperasi I (*D*) coop(erative). – *among tani* farmers' cooperative. – *karyawan* [kopkar] employees' cooperative. – *pekerja* workers' cooperative. – *peternak sapi perah* [KPSP] dairy farmers' cooperative. – *peternak unggas* [KPU] poultry farmers' cooperative. – *serba usaha* all-purpose cooperative. – *Simpan Pinjam* [Kosipi] Savings and Loan Cooperative. – *unit désa* [KUD] village unit cooperative. – *Usaha Tani* [KUT] Farmers' Cooperative.
   mengkoperasikan to organize into cooperatives.
   pengkoperasian organizing into cooperatives.
   perkoperasian system of cooperatives.
koperasi II (*D*) cooperation.
   berkoperasi to cooperate.
   perkoperasian system of cooperation.
koperasiawan a member of a cooperative.
koperator (*E*) cooperator, i.e., s.o. who works together with a government, etc.
Kopertis [Koordinator Perguruan Tinggi Swasta] Private Higher Education Coordinator.
kopét I narrow (of an opening), open just a little.
kopét II (*Jv*) **1** to fail to wipe o.s. well after defecating. **2** a term of abuse.
kopi I (*A/D*) **1** coffee (the plant and the bean, etc.). **2** coffee (the drink). – *keras* a) strong coffee. b) a bawling out. – *luak* coffee beans found in the excrement of civet cats (considered excellent coffee). – *pahit* a) thick black coffee without sugar and milk. b) a scolding, bawling out. *mendapat* – *pahit/keras* to get a bawling out. – *berontak* coffee mixed with an egg. – *bubuk* pow-

dered coffee. – *hitam* black coffee. – *putih* coffee with milk. – *susu* coffee with milk. – *tok* black coffee (without sugar and milk). – *tubruk* strong coffee made by pouring boiling water over coffee grounds (usually in a glass).
   mengopi [and **ngopi** (*coq*)] to drink coffee, have a cup of coffee.
   pengopi coffee lover.
   perkopian coffee (*mod*).
kopi II (*D/E*) copy, imitation, reproduction. – *darat* [kopdar] (*BG*) to get together, meet face to face (rather than on the airwaves or on the Internet).
   mengkopi to copy, reproduce.
   pengkopian copying, reproducing.
kopi III – *andelan* coffee senna, k.o. green manure (seeds used as a coffee substitute, *Cassia occidentalis*). – *Arab* (in Sulawesi) and – *Jawa/susu* (in Java) okra, *Hibiscus esculentis*.
kopiah (*A*) k.o. cap, headdress (worn by Muslim men and as a symbol of nationalism), an untasseled fez (usually of velvet); → SONGKOK. – *stambul* fez.
kopig (*D*) stubborn; → NGOTOT.
kopilot (*D/E*) copilot.
kopiok (*Jv*) → KOPYOK I.
Kopka [Kopral kepala] → KOPRAL *kepala*.
Kopkamtib [Komando Pemulihan Keamanan dan Ketertiban] Command for the Restoration of Security and Public Order (established October 3, 1965, after the G-30-S/PKI rebellion).
koplak (*Jv*) (bus/train, etc.) stop. – *bis* bus stop.
   koplakan (*Jv*) /kopla'an/ a fixed placed where *dokars*, etc. park to wait for passengers and where drivers, hawkers, etc. spend the night.
koplamp (*D*) headlight (of car).
kopléng → KOPELING.
koplét → KUPLÉT.
kopling → KOPELING.
koplo (*Jv*) spaced out (on drugs). *pil* – tranquillizers used as narcotics such as Rohypnol and others. *générasi* – the apathetic generation.
koplok (*J*) too large.
kopo-kopo (*daun* –) various plants with edible fruit, *Physalis minima*.
kopok I (*cla*) a sounding block made of wood or metal and beaten with a drumstick.
kopok II (*Jv*) substance discharged from an infected ear.
   kopokan /kopo'an/ to have a runny ear (purulent and smelly).
kopong (*J/Jv*) **1** hollow (tree), empty (stomach). **2** pitless (of fruit).
kopor → KOPER.
Koppkalimajaktim [Koperasi Pedagang Kaki Lima (Wilayah) Jakarta Timur] East Jakarta (Area) Sidewalk Vendors Cooperative.
kopra I copra. – *asap* kiln-dried copra. – *dan bungkil* – copra and copra cakes. – *jemur* sundried copra.
   mengoprakan to make/turn into copra.
   pengopra copra producer.
   perkopraan copra (*mod*).
Kopra II [Kota Praja] (*ob*) Municipality.
koprah → KOPRA I.
koprak I (*J*) to talk and laugh loudly.
   mengoprak [and **ngoprak** (*coq*)] to proclaim s.t. loudly.
koprak II (*Jv*) bamboo clapper to scare away birds.
   mengoprak to scare away birds with such a clapper.
   koprakan (*J*) a piece of bamboo split at one end or empty cans, etc. beaten to scare away birds, squirrels, etc.
kopral (*mil D*) corporal. – *(tingkat) dua* [kopda] corporal second-class. – *kepala* [kopka] master corporal. – *(tingkat) satu* [koptu] corporal first-class. – *taruna* cadet corporal.
koprok (*J*) *dadu* – a gambling game similar to crapshooting.
koprol (*D*) to roll over. – *dan lari* to flee.
kopter (*E*) clipped form of *hélikopter*.
Koptik (*E*) Coptic.
Koptu [kopral satu] → KOPRAL *satu*.
kopula (*D*) copula.

kopur (*D*) denomination (of currency).

kopyok I (*Jv*) **mengopyok** to shake, beat, whip. ~ *telur* to beat an egg.

  kopyokan 1 s.t. used for shaking s.t. up, shaker. **2** lottery drawing.

  pengopyok beater, blender.

kopyor (*Jv*) the soft spongy meat of a certain coconut species, the *kelapa puan*, from which *és* –, a cold beverage served with syrup, is made.

koq → KOK I.

kor I → KOOR.

kor II (in acronyms) → KOORDINASI.

korah (*A*) a ball (used in various games).

korak [Komando pérak] Perak Command, i.e., a criminal, originally in the Perak port area of Surabaya, who pilfers goods from a truck by jumping onto it.

koral (*D*) **1** coral. **2** boulder; (round) cobblestone.

koralték fine coral stones.

Koramil [Komando Rayon Militér] Military District Command at the *kecamatan* level.

koran I (*D*) newspaper; → SURAT *kabar*. *orang* – reporter. – "A" newspaper for the religious groups ("A" = *Agama*). – *anak-anak* children's newspaper. – *daérah* regional paper. – *dinding* wall poster. –.– *got* gutter/yellow press. – *ibukota* Jakarta newspaper. – *kuning* yellow journal. – *masuk désa* [KMD] a rural-oriented press. – *nasional* national paper. – *pagi* morning paper. – *soré* evening paper. – *warawiri* impartial newspaper. – *Wong Li Cik* (from: *wong licik*) insulting reference to the *PKI*'s daily paper "Harian Rakyat."

  mengorankan 1 to put into the paper. **2** to spread unfavorable news about s.t.

  koran-koranan a trashy newspaper, a rag.

  perkoranan newspaper (*mod*).

Koran II (*A*) the Koran; → QUR'AN. *mengaji* – to learn to read the Koran. *mengkhatamkan* – to complete the reading of the Koran.

koran III *burung* – glossy tree starling, *Aplonis panayensis strigatus*.

Kor'an → KORAN II.

korana (in Irian Jaya) village head.

korang I to fall backward (onto one's back).

korang II (*J*) → JORAN.

koras a tree which provides timbers for ships, *Psychotria malayana*.

korat-karit dislocated, dispersed, scattered, in disorder.

Korawa → KURAWA.

korban (*A*) **1** sacrifice. **2** victim, casualty. *banyak makan* – there are a lot of casualties (of an accident/catastrophe, etc.). *menjadi* – to fall victim. *dijadikan* – to be made the fall-guy. *para* – casualties. **3** religious offering. **4** alms. – *empuk* a soft/easy touch. – *jiwa* casualties, deaths. – *kebakaran* victims of a fire. – *manusia* casualties. – *misa* communion. – *nazar* the sacrifice of an animal on Idul Adha at which the person making the sacrifice promises to give the meat to the poor. – *Pemilu* those arrested during the 1971 election campaign. – *penculikan* a kidnap victim. – *perang* war victim. – *tabrak lari* victim of a hit-and-run accident. – *témbak* a victim of a shooting/shootout. –.– *tempur* battle casualties.

  berkorban to make sacrifices/a sacrifice.

  mengorbankan [and **ngorbanin** (*J coq*)] to offer s.t. up as a sacrifice, sacrifice s.t., (do s.t.) at the expense of. ~ *anginnya* to change one's position. *dengan* ~ *rakyat* at the expense of the people.

  pengorbanan sacrifice, sacrificing. *Tidak ada* ~ *hilang terbuang*. No sacrifice is wasted.

kordén (*D*) curtain, cloth screen, drape; → GORDÉN.

kordinasi → KOORDINASI.

kordinat → KOORDINAT.

kordinir → KOORDINIR.

kordon (*D/E*) cordon. – *sanitér* cordon sanitaire.

kordoré (*E*) corduroy.

Koréa Korea. – *Selatan* [Korsél] South Korea. – *Utara* [Korut] North Korea. *Républik Rakyat Démokrasi* – Democratic People's Republic of Korea.

koréd (*J*) k.o. hoe.

  ngoréd to clear or mow grass with such a hoe.

korék I – (*api*) match(es). – *api Ronsen* Ronsen cigarette lighter. – *batu* lighter. – *gigi* toothpick. – *kayu* match. – *kuping* ear swab. *kapal* – dredger; → KAPAL *keruk*. *tukang* – hairsplitter.

  mengorék 1 to burrow, grub around (in the ground with one's fingers/paws/an object). ~ *kocék lebih dalam* to put one's hand even deeper into one's pocket (to pay for s.t.). **2** to bore (of squirrels), drill (a hole). **3** to scrape/dig around (in a garbage can/one's memory, etc.). **4** to pick (one's nose/teeth/ears). ~ *telinganya/kupingnya* to pick one's ears. **5** to dig (a tunnel under a house) (by thieves). **6** to disclose, reveal, divulge. **7** to scrutinize, examine closely. **8** to ferret/figure out, unravel, dig up (secrets). ~ *keterangan dari* to elicit information from. **9** to rake up. ~ *perkara lama* to rake up old stories. **10** to dredge (a harbor/river, etc.). **11** to make/realize (a profit).

  mengorék-ngorék ~ *rahasia* to dig up secrets.

  mengorék-korék to open up. *Kita tidak bermaksud* ~ *kembali luka lama*. We don't intend to open up old wounds.

  mengoréki to clean, scour, scrub, scrape clean. ~ *dian* to scrape an oil lamp clean.

  terkorék opened up, brought out into the open.

  korékan ~ *kuping* ear swab.

  pengorék 1 shovel, dredge, etc. **2** ~ *telinga* ear pick, ear swab. **3** excavator, digger (the person).

  pengorékan excavation, digging, burrowing.

korék II (*D*) correct. *bersifat* – *sekali* to assume a correct attitude.

koréksi (*D*) correction.

  meng(k)oréksi 1 to correct. **2** to proofread.

  peng(k)oréksian 1 correcting, correction. **2** proofreading.

  terkoréksi corrected.

  koréksian 1 material to be corrected. **2** corrected material. **3** correction.

  pengkoréksian 1 correcting. **2** proofreading.

koréktif (*D/E*) corrective.

koréktor (*D*) proofreader.

korélasi (*D*) correlation.

Korém [Komando Résort Militér] Military Area Command, i.e., the army command between the *Kodam* and the *Kodim*.

korénah (*M*) **1** disposition. **2** behavior.

koréng 1 spotted, stained. *anjing* – a spotted dog. **2** (*J*) scabies, mange, ulcerated sore, suppurating itch, scab. – *moréng* streaked all over, all covered (with soot/dirt/chalk/scabs, etc.); → CORÉNG *moréng*.

  mengoréng to scab over, develop a scab.

  berkoréng and **koréngan** (*Jv*) **1** to have many sores. **2** to suffer from (or, be infected with) scabies.

koréografer (*D*) choreographer.

koréografi (*D/E*) choreography.

korés I → GORÉS.

korés II [Komando Résor(t)] (Police) Area Command.

Korés Métro [Komando Résor(t) Métro] (Police) City Area Command.

koréspondén (*D*) correspondent. – *keliling* roving reporter.

koréspondénsi (*D*) correspondence.

  berkoréspondénsi to correspond, communicate with s.o. by an exchange of letters.

Korésta [Komando Résor(t) Kota] (Police) City Area Command.

korét I remainder, remnant, leftover(s). *nomor* – (*coq*) the very last on a list; the latter.

  mengorét to use leftovers.

  mengoréti to use (leftovers).

  korétan leftovers.

korét II (*S*) an iron object used for weeding, spud.

  mengorét 1 to clear (of weeds with such or a similar device). **2** to cut jungle grass growing between cassava trees.

korét III → KURÉT.

korét IV → KORÉK I.

korfbal (*D*) a ball game resembling basketball; the playing area is divided into three courts and the 12 players must stay within the court to which they have been assigned.

kori I (*J*) male Koran reader; → QARI.

kori II (*Jv*) door.

koriah (*J*) female Koran reader; → QARIAH.

koridor (*D/E*) corridor.

korma → KURMA.

kornéa (*D/E*) cornea. *pengambilan* – enucleation. *penderita cacat* – *corneal blind.*

kornéd → KORNÉT.

kornél I (*coq*) colonel.

kornél II (*coq*) (in soccer) corner-kick.

kornét I (*coq*) (canned) corned beef.

kornét II → KERNÉT.

koro I 1 a certain climbing vine. 2 the peanut-like fruit of this vine.

koro II → PENYAKIT *koro*.

koroh (*M*) throat, gullet.

korok I excavation, dug-out hole. – *biji* mineral vein. – *tambang* gallery (in a mine).
mengorok to hollow out, undermine.

korok II → KORO II.

korok-korok k.o. sandfly or fruit fly.

koronér (*E*) coronary, heart attack.

korong (*M*) – *kampung* surroundings of a village; village jurisdiction. **berkorong kampung** to have the atmosphere of a village (and its surroundings). *adat* ~ one's own familiar environment. *pandai* ~ to know how to behave in accordance with village customs.

korosi (*D*) corrosion.
terkorosi corroded. *logam yang* ~ corroded metal.

korporasi (*D*) corporation.

Korpri [Korps Pegawai Républik Indonésia] Republic of Indonesia Civil Servants Corps, a constituent unit of *Golkar*.
peng-Korpri-an incorporating (a group) into *Korpri*.

korps (*D*) /korep/ corps. – *angkatan darat* army corps. – *diplomatik* diplomatic corps. – *Komando (Angkatan Laut)* [KKO(AL)] (Navy) Marine Corps. – *konsulér* consular corps. – *Marinir* Marine Corps. – *médis* medical corps. – *musik* (in armed forces) (brass) band. – *Perdamaian* (U.S.) Peace Corps. – *Wanita Angkatan Darat* [Kowad] Women's Auxiliary Corps, WACs. – *Wanita Angkatan Laut* [Kowal] Women's Auxiliary Navy, Waves. – *Wanita Angkatan Udara* [Kowau] Women's Auxiliary Air Force. – *zéni* corps of (military) engineers.
sekorps in the same corps.

korpulén (*D/E*) corpulent, stout.

korpulénsi (*D*) corpulence, stoutness.

korsa *jiwa* – esprit de corps.

korsase (*D*) corsage.

korsél I (*D*) merry-go-round.

Korsél II [Koréa Selatan] South Korea.

korsét (*D*) corset.

korsi → KURSI I.

korsléting (*D*) short circuit.

korslit (*coq*) → KORSLÉTING.

kortikosteroid (*E*) corticosteroid.

korting (*D*) discount, price reduction.
mengorting 1 to (give a) discount. ~ *harga dengan 4 dolar per barel* to discount the price by 4 dollars a barrel. *harga yang telah dikorting* reduced price. 2 to reduce (a jail sentence, etc.).
pengortingan reduction (of jail sentence, etc.).

kortison (*D/E*) cortisone.

kortsléting 1 → KORSLÉTING. 2 (*coq*) misunderstanding (between speakers).

korum → KWORUM.

korup (*D*) corrupt. *orang* – → KORUPTOR.
mengkorup 1 to embezzle, misappropriate. 2 to abuse/misuse (one's power). ~ *waktu* to misuse one's time.
mengkorupkan to corrupt, make corrupt.
terkorup the most corrupt.

korupsi I (*D*) corruption. – *kakap/teri* big-/small-time corruption. *pegawai yang* – *waktu* an employee who consistently shows up late for work.
berkorupsi to be corrupt, engage in corrupt practices.
mengkorupsi to embezzle, misappropriate, steal through corruption.

Korupsi II [Keruk Oeang Rakyat Untuk Pribadi] [a humorous expansion of an invented acronym *korupsi* (using the old spelling

oeng instead of *uang*)] Scraping Money from the People for One's Own Benefit.

koruptor (*E*) 1 corruptor. 1 a corrupt person.

Korut [Koréa Utara] North Korea

korvé and **korvéé** fatigue duty.

korvét (*D*) corvette (war ship).

kos(t) (*D*) 1 to board. 2 boarder. 3 boarding house; → INDEKOS. *tempat –ku* my boardinghouse. *anak* – boarder. *bu* – landlady. *pak* – landlord; → KOSBAS. *pindah* – *dari* ... *ke* ... to change boarding houses from ... to ... *teman* – fellow boarder.
mengekosi to board at.
mengekoskan to rent out (rooms to boarders).

kosa I (*Skr*) elephant goad; → ANGKUS(A).

kosa II → PERKOSA.

kosa III *burung* – a) geat cormorant, *Phalacrocorax carbo sinensis*. b) k.o. bird, Australian darter, *Anhinga melanogaster*.

kosa IV (*Skr*) hollow cup, container; → KOSAKATA.

Kosak Cossack.

kosakata vocabulary, glossary.

kosak-kasik 1 rustling. 2 (to sit) restlessly, fidgeting.

kosambi → KESAMBI.

kosar a tree species whose wood is used for the construction of houses, etc., *Artocarpus rigida*.

kosbas (*D*) landlord, lodging-house keeper.

kosék I mengosék 1 to rinse/wash (rice) in a basket. 2 to scrub (the floor with a brush). 3 to grind (a knife) with a rotating movement of the hand.

Kosék II [Komando Séktor] (Police) Subdistrict Command.

kosél terkosél-kosél 1 to mumble, stammer, mutter. 2 to walk with difficulty.

kosén I (*J*) courageous, daring, brave.
kekosénan daring, bravery, courage.

kosén II (*D*) (door or window) frame.

koset → KOSÉK I.

Kosgoro [Koperasi Serbaguna Gotong Royong] Mutual Assistance Multipurpose Cooperative.

kosién (*D*) quotient. – *pemilihan* electoral quotient.

kosinus (*math D*) cosine.

koslét (*coq*) → KORSLÉTING.

kosmétik(a) (*E*) cosmetology, cosmetics. *ahli* – cosmetologist.

kosmis (*D*) cosmic.

kosmodrom *E* cosmodrome.

kosmogoni (*E*) cosmogony.

kosmografi (*D/E*) cosmography.

kosmolog (*D*) cosmologist.

kosmologi (*D/E*) cosmology.

kosmonaut (*E*) and **kosmonot** (*D*) cosmonaut.

kosmopolit (*D/E*) cosmopolite, sophisticated person.

kosmopolitanisme (*D/E*) cosmopolitanism.

kosmos (*D/E*) cosmos.

kosokbali (*Jv*) opposite, contrary, antonym, reverse.

kosong 1 empty, without any contents. *gelas* – an empty glass. *perutnya* – he is hungry; → PERUTNYA *keroncongan*. – *blong/melompong/melongpong* completely empty. *cék* – a bad check. *tong* – *nyaring bunyinya* empty vessels make the most noise. 2 empty, deserted, uninhabited, unoccupied, free. *Pulau itu* –. That island is uninhabited. *Tempat ini* –? Anybody sitting here? Is this seat taken? *Busnya* –. The bus is empty. *faktur* – a blank invoice. *hotel yang* – a vacant hotel. *Jalan itu* –. The road is deserted. *kertas* – blank paper. *Rumahnya* –. The house is unoccupied. *Keduanya sama-sama* –. Neither of them is spoken for (or, free to start another romantic relationship). *tanah yang* – uncultivated/wasteland. *jam* – lesson hours without a teacher. *waktu* – spare/leisure/free time. 3 vacant, unfilled (post/function). *Jabatan itu masih* –. That post is still vacant/unfilled. 4 unavailable. *Barang itu sedang* –. Those goods are not available. 5 empty, idle. *harapan* – idle hopes. *kabar* – rumor. *obrolan* – empty chatter, idle talk. *omong* – a) claptrap, nonsense. b) chatter, gossip. *beromong-omong* – to gossip, chitchat, run off at the mouth. 6 empty (heart/sentiment/idea). *hati yang* – hardhearted, unfeeling, without compassion, poker-faced. *Dia merasa* –. He feels emotionless. 7 zero, 0 (in telephone numbers/

addresses etc.). *Nomor téleponnya mengandung dua –*. His phone number contains two zeroes. **8** without results, failed, unproductive. *batuk* – a dry/hacking cough. *dengan tangan –* a) empty-handed (without results or success). b) with bare hands. *Rol film itu ternyata –*. The roll of film turned out to be unexposed. *témbakan* – blank shot. **9** grade given to a student who withdraws from a course, withdrew.

sekosong as empty as.

mengosongkan [and **ngosongin** (*J coq*)] **1** to empty, unload (the contents from a container, etc.). *bus yang ~ penumpangnya* a bus unloading its passengers. *~ anginnya* to deflate (one's tires). **2** to vacate (a house). *~ rumah secara paksa* to vacate a house by force. **3** to leave (a space) open. *daérah-daérah yang dikosongkan dari militér* demilitarized zones. **4** to abandon, give up. *Dia tidak ~ jam kuliahnya.* He did not give up his lectures.

kekosongan 1 emptiness (of feelings/a post), vacancy. *Dia merasa ~ di dalam jiwanya karena kehilangan orangtuanya.* He feels an emptiness in his life because he lost his parents. *memancing ikan untuk mengisi – waktu* fishing for pleasure (or, to while away the time). **2** vacuum. *~ kekuasaan* power vacuum. **3** insufficiency, shortage. *daérah yang sedang mengalami ~* an area suffering from shortages; *cp daérah* MINUS. **4** gap, hiatus, blank.

pengosongan 1 vacating, clearing out (a house/room, etc.), evacuation. **2** (*~ bus*) cleaning out (a letter box/mail collection). **3** liberation, discharge. *~ angkasa* atmospheric discharge. **4** depletion.

kosponser (*D/E*) cosponsor.

meng(k)osponseri to cosponsor.

kosrék (*onom*) sound made by a pedicab bell.

kost → KOS.

Kosta Rika Costa Rica.

koster I (*D*) abbot, head of an abbey.

koster II (*E*) coaster (k.o. ship).

kosthuis (*D*) /kos-hés/ boardinghouse.

kostiksoda (*D/E*) caustic soda.

kostim and **kostum** (*D*) **1** uniform, dress (for certain civil authorities). **2** costume (for formal wear).

Kostrad [Komando Stratégis Angkatan Darat] Army Strategic Command.

Kostranas [Komando Stratégis Nasional] National Strategic Command.

Kosubdahan [Komando Subdaérah Pertahanan] Defense Subregional Command.

Kosubdim [Komando Subdaérah Militér] Military Subdistrict Command.

Kosubhandamar [Komando Subpertahanan Daérah Maritim] Maritime Subdefense Regional Command.

Kosbubmar [Komando Submaritim] Submaritime Command.

Kosumbmarlanal [Komando Submaritim Pangkalan Angkatan Laut] Naval Base Submaritime Command.

Kosubmarsional [Komando Submaritim Stasion Angkatan Laut] Naval Station Submaritime Command.

Kosubsék Hansip-Hanra [Komando Subséktor Pertahanan Sipil-Pertahanan Rakyat] People's and Civil Defense Subsector Command (at the *kecamatan* level).

Kosubtrik Hansip-Hanra [Komando Subdistrik Pertahanan Rakyat] People's and Civil Defense Subdistrict Command.

kota (*Skr*) **1** city, town. *ibu* – capital (in Indonesia usually refers to) Jakarta. *orang* – townsman, urbanite, city person. *pemerintahan* – town administration, city government. *wali*- mayor. *– administratif* [kotif or kotatif] administrative town, i.e., a town that is part of a *kabupatén*, not of a *kotamadya* or municipality, and has obtained its own administrative status, e.g., Cimahi is a *kotif* as part of the *Kabupatén Dati II* of Bandung. *mengotifkan* to make (a city) a *kotif*. **2** (*ob*) fortress, stronghold, citadel. *– duduk* (*ob*) k.o. watchtower, lookout. *barang yang dikata, itulah* – an honest man's word is as good as his bond. **3** (*ob*) battlement. **4** (*M*) village, settlement. *rumah* – village house. **5** (clipped form of) *kotamadya* [kodya] and *kotapraja* [kopra]. *kekota-prajaan* municipal. *– atas* uptown. *– Anging Mamiri* Ujungpandang. *– bawah* downtown. *– besar* large city with a

population of a half to one million. *– dunia* metropolis. *– hantu* ghost town. *– kecil* small town with a population of under 200,000. *– kelahiran* hometown. *– kosmopolitan* metropolis. *– métropolitan* metropolis. *– pelabuhan* port town. *– perdagangan* commercial city. *– peristirahatan* resort town. *– raya* metropolis (with a population of more than one million). *– satelit* satellite town. *– sedang* medium-sized town (with a population of 200,000 to 500,000). *– suci* Mecca, Rome and Jerusalem. *– Vatikan* Vatican City. TOWNS AND CITIES NAMED FOR SOME CHARACTERISTIC. *– "4711"* Cologne. *– Air* Palembang. *– alam* Banda Aceh. *– Amoi/Amoy* a) Singkawang. b) Pontianak. *– Andong* Yogyakarta. *– Angin(g) Mam(m)iri* Ujungpandang. *– apel* Malang. *– Api* Banjarmasin. *– Asia-Afrika* Bandung. *– Asin* Banjarmasin. *– Asrama* Depok. *– Bandeng* a) Semarang. b) Sidoarjo. *– Banjir* Tulungagung. *– Batik* a) Pekalongan. b) Surakarta. *– Batu Akik* Punung. *– Bawang* Tegal. *– Bambu Runcing* Parakan. *– Bedah Hati* Sukabumi [Bersih, indah, séhat, tertib]). *– Bekas Ibu Kota RI yang Pertama* and *– Bekas Pusat Kerajaan di Jawa* Yogyakarta. *– Bengawan* Surakarta. *– Beras* Karawang. *– Bersaudara Médan-Pulau Pinang* the sister cities of Medan and Pulau Pinang. *– berhati nyaman* Yogyakarta. *– beriman* [bersih, indah, aman dan nyaman] Balikpapan. *– bersinar* [bersih, indah, asri dan rindang] Tasikmalaya. *– Betung* Jambi. *– Bingkuang* Padang. *– Bougainville* Kupang. *– Brambang* Brebes. *– Buah Salak* Padang Sidempuan. *– Buaya* Surabaya. *– Budaya* Yogyakarta. *– Bunga* Wonosobo. *– Clurit* Semarang. *– Daéng* Ujungpandang. *– Debu* Maumere. *– Dingin* Bandung. *– Dodol* Garut. *– Émpék/Empék-Empék* Palembang. *– Gaplék* Wonogiri. *– Gelamai* Payakumbuh. *– Gerbong Maut* Bondowoso. *– Getuk Goréng* Purwokerto. *– Gudeg* Yogyakarta. *– Hantu* a) Pontianak. b) Bengkulu. *– Hijrah Révolusi* Yogyakarta. *– Hujan* Bogor. *– Ilmiah* and *– Ilmu Pengetahuan* Bogor. *– Iman* [Indah aman dan nyaman] Bekasi. *– Indah* Singkawang. *– Indekosan* Yogyakarta. *– Industri* Malang. *– Intan* a) Old Batavia. b) Martapura. *– Jam Gadang* Bukittinggi. *– Karang* Kupang. *– Kartini* Jepara. *– Kembang* a) Bandung. b) Malang. *– Kembang Matahari* Kendari. *– Kembar* the twin cities of Telukbetung and Tanjungkarang. *– Kenari* Bogor. *– Khatulistiwa* Pontianak. *– Kréték* Kudus. *– Kripik* a) Banyumas. b) Purwokerto. *– Krupuk* Sidoarjo. *– Kumpul Kebo* Yogyakarta. *– Lima Diménsi* Sabang. *– Lulo* Kendari. *– Lumpia* Semarang. *– Mahasiswa* a) Yogyakarta. b) Depok. *– Mangga* Indramayu. *– Militér* Magelang. *– Minyak* Dumai. *– Minyak Sumbawa* Taliwang. *– Mojang Parahiyangan/Pri(y)angan* Bandung. *– Mpék-mpék* Palembang. *– Musi* Palembang. *– Nyiur* Palu. *– Oncom* Bandung. *– Pahlawan* Surabaya. *– Pajajaran* Bogor. *– Paris* a) Pariaman. b) Bandung. *– Pariwisata* a) Yogyakarta. b) Malang. *– Pata Cengké* Ambon. *– Pelajar* a) Salatiga. b) Malang. *– Pelajar/Mahawiswa* and *– Pelajar dan Mahawiswa* Yogyakarta. *– Pémpék* Palembang. *– Pendidikan* Jakarta. *– Pénsiunan* a) Salatiga. b) Bogor. c) Bengkulu. d) Pati. *– Perjuangan* Yogyakarta. *– Petis* Sidoardjo. *– Proklamasi* Jakarta. *– Réog* Ponorogo. *– Rendang* Padang. *– Resik* Tasikmalaya. *– Révolusi* a) Surabaya b) Yogyakarta. *– Romantis* Bandung. *– Rotan* Taliwang. *– Salak* Padangsidempuan. *– Sanjai* Bukittinggi. *– Sederhana* Yogyakarta. *– Sejahtera* Ujungpandang. *– Sepéda* Yogyakarta. *– Seni Budaya* Surakarta. *– Sigarét* Malang. *– Singa* Singapore. *– Singkong* Wonogiri. *– Sriwijaya* Palembang. *– Susu* Boyolali. *– Tahu Pong* Semarang. *– Taman* Bogor. *– Tambak* Sidoarjo. *– Tauco* Cianjur. *– Teduh Bersinar* [Tékad, Disiplin untuk Hidup Bersih, Séhat Indah, Nyaman, Aman dan Rapi] Ujungpandang. *– Tri Arga* Bukittinggi. *– Turis* Yogyakarta. *– Udang* a) Cirebon. b) Sidoarjo. *– Ukir* Jepara. *– yang tak pernah tidur* Surakarta.

kota-kota walking/driving around a city (for sightseeing).

sekota 1 the whole city, all-city. **2** of the same city.

berkota walled in; fortified. *siapa yang berkata harus ~* an honest man's word is as good as his bond; no sooner said than done.

mengotai to wall in, fortify.

mengotakan 1 to make into a fortress, fortify. **2** to build a fortified town. **3** (*ob*) to keep (one's promise/a treaty, etc.).

kekotaan characteristic of a town/city, metropolitan, town (*mod*).

pekotaan urban, city (*mod*). *daérah ~* urban area.

peng(k)otaan 1 urbanization. **2** urban area.

perkotaan urban, city (*mod*). *transportasi* – urban transportation.

kotah sekotah (*cla*) all, the whole, entire, total.

kotai (= **terkotai**) **1** to hang/droop down, hang from the branches, dangle by a thread. **2** to be skin and bones, all dried out. *tua* – very old. **3** dry. *nyiur* – a coconut dried and kept for seed. *pinang* – an old and dried-up areca nut.

kotak 1 compartment, cubicle, partition, section (*esp* section of a *sawah*); → PETAK. *Rumahnya disekat-sekat atas beberapa* –. His house has been subdivided into several cubicles. *sampan* – bumboat with a locker. **2** checks, checkered pattern (on fabric) (plain and level with straight sides and without flowers). **3** panel (in a cabinet/writing table, etc.). **4** locker, drawer (in a table/bureau/chest, etc.). **5** (*Jv*) wooden chest in which *wayang* puppets are stored; a set of *wayang* puppets. **6** small box, case. **7** gun housing. *télepon – uang* pay phone. *masuk* – a) on the bench (in sports). b) out of the picture, shelved. c) to be a nothing/a cipher. – *ajaib* (in some regions) television set. – *campur* mix box (*mining*). – *hitam* black box (in aircraft). – *kaca* a) glass case, display case. b) TV. – *kartu nama* business card case. – *kecantikan* cosmetics case. – *kontak* (electric) outlet. – *korék api* matchbox. – *kosong* blank space, frame, blank (of a ballot). – *makan siang* lunchbox. – *makanan otomatis* food dispenser. – *obat* (in car) first-aid kit. – *penyimpan* (in bank) safe-deposit box. – *pos* a) post office box. b) mailbox. – *sabun* soap dish. – *suara* ballot box. – *surat* a) post office box. b) mailbox. – *tampung* (in mining) drop-box. – *uang* coin box (of telephone).

kotak-kotak checks, checked. **berkotak-kotak 1** divided into compartments. **2** checkered (pattern).

sekotak a box/package/packet of.

mengotak to put in a box/case.

mengotak-ngotakkan to categorize, classify, divide into compartments, compartmentalize.

terkotak categorized, compartmentalized, classified. **keterkotakan** categorization, classification.

terkotak-kotak compartmentalized.

pengotakan 1 (re)grouping, (re)classification. **2** partitioning, compartmentalizing, categorization, categorizing.

pengotak-ngotakan segregation.

pengkotak-kotakan 1 sectioning, zoning. **2** compartmentalizing, compartmentalization. **3** segregation.

kotak-katik indications of one's presence. *tidak terdengar (lagi)* – *nya* a) no more was heard of him/her. b) he/she is not heard moving around any more.

mengotak-ngatikkan to move/sway s.t., set s.t. in motion.

kotamadya [kodya] mid-sized city (population of a half to one million), municipality.

kotamara 1 breastwork (on pirate ship). **2** parapet (of fort).

kotangén(s) (*D math*) cotangent.

kotapraja [kopra] (*ob*) municipality; → KOTAMADYA.

Kotatif → KOTIF.

kotbah → KHOTBAH.

koték I (hairy/feathery) tail.

berkoték tailed. *bintang* ~ comet. *pembagian* ~ (*math*) long division.

terkoték-koték wagging the tail.

koték II (*Mal*) child's penis.

koték III (*onom*) cackle (of hens).

berkoték to cackle. *siapa* ~ *siapa bertelur* the pot calling the kettle black; → MALING *berteriak maling*.

koték IV (*E*) Kotex, sanitary napkin.

kotéka (in Irian Jaya) penis sheath; → WALO I.

berkotéka to wear a penis sheath.

kotekelema(h) → KOTOKELEMÉH.

koténg terkoténg-koténg alone, solitary; *cp* SEBATANG *karang*.

koterék → KOTRÉK.

kotés 1 plush, shag (of fabric). **2** counter for small bits of thread/hair. **sekotés** a very small quantity, a bit.

mengotés 1 to flick off (thread/lint, etc.). **2** to bite/break a small piece off the edge of s.t.

kothékan (*Jv*) (*pl subj*) to knock rhythmically on a wooden rice pestle.

Kotif [Kota Administratif] administrative town; → KOTA *administratif*.

kotipa [Koléra-Tipus-Paratipus] *vaksin* – cholera, typhus and paratyphus vaccine.

kotok I *celana* – shorts.

kotok II (*J/Jv*) blind. *tahi* – chicken droppings. – *ayam* a) short-sighted. b) chicken droppings.

kotokan night blindness.

kotokelemém sperm whale.

kotong 1 maimed, (without finger/toe, etc.). **2** amputated, cut off, blunt. **3** short (of garment) *baju* – short sleeved or sleeveless coat. *celana* – shorts.

mengotongkan to amputate.

kotor 1 dirty, unclean, filthy, soiled. *Kaosnya* –. His socks are dirty. *lidah* – a furred/coated tongue. *putih* – off-white. – *dicuci, berabu dijentik* let bygones be bygones! **2** dirty, foul, obscene, smutty. *bercakap* – to talk dirty. *mulut* – *and* – *mulut* foul-mouthed (person). **3** dirty (sexual sense). *(mendapat) kain* – *and* – *datang* to menstruate. *penyakit* – venereal diseases. *perempuan* – prostitute. **4** vile, bad, hideous, improper. *kata-kata yang* – improper words. **5** gross (income/weight, etc.) *penghasilan* – gross income.

sekotor as dirty as.

mengotori [and **ngotorin** (*J coq*)] **1** to dirty, make/get s.t. dirty, soil, stain, foul, contaminate, pollute. **2** to bring shame/dishonor upon, besmirch, sully, defame, defile, tarnish. *Pendukungnya telah* ~ *nama baiknya*. His supporters have dragged his name through the mud.

mengotorkan to make dirty, dirty. ~ *sepatunya dengan lumpur* to dirty one's shoes with mud.

terkotor the dirtiest.

kotoran 1 impurities, filth, dirt (litter/rubbish/trash/refuse, etc.). ~ *dapur* kitchen trash. ~ *héwan* dung. ~ *manusia* human waste, feces. ~ *telinga* earwax, cerumen. ~ *tikus* sprinkles, jimmies (put on ice cream, etc.). **2** soiled linen.

kekotoran 1 dirtiness, filthiness, smuttiness, obscenity. ~ *yang ada pada luka itu hendaknya dibersihkan dulu*. Any dirt on the wound should be cleaned away first. **2** dirty, filthy, polluted, smutty, obscene.

pengotor 1 dirty fellow. **2** polluter.

pengotoran defiling, contaminating, contamination, fouling, polluting, littering.

kotrék (*D kurketrekker*) **1** corkscrew. **2** ratchet.

mengotrék to open with a corkscrew.

Kotrin [Kontra Intélijén] counterintelligence.

kotum (*D*) quota.

kover /kofer/ cover; → COVER.

mengkover (journalism) to cover; → MELIPUT.

Kovéri [Koperasi Véteran Républik Indonésia] Republic of Indonesia Veterans Cooperative.

Kowabri [Korps Wanita Angkatan Bersenjata Républik Indonésia] Republic of Indonesia Armed Forces Women's Corps.

Kowad [Korps Wanita Angkatan Darat] Army Women's Corps.

kowak I berkowak-kowak (*coq*) to argue; to chatter, jabber; to cry out, shout (with excitement, etc.); → KOAK.

kowak II – *malam* black-crowned night heron, *Nycticorax nycticorax*. – *mérah* rufous night heron, *Nycticorax caledonicus*.

Kowal [Korps Wanita Angkatan Laut] Navy Women's Corps.

Kowalpan [Komando Pengawal Pantai] Coast Guard Command.

kowan *ikan* – grass carp, *Ctenopharyngodon idellus*.

kowangan (*J*) *layangan* – a kite that has a device for making noise attached to it.

kowar (*Jv*) *jalan* – an unattended street.

Kowartég [Koperasi Warung Tegal] All-Night Food Stalls Cooperative.

Kowavéri [Korps Wanita Véteran Républik Indonésia] Republic of Indonesia Women Veterans Corps.

kowé (*Jv*) you (intimate or rude); → ENGKAU, KAU I.

mengowé to use *kowé* to s.o.

mengowé-ngowé to talk down to.

kowék *Jawa* – used by non-Javanese in West Java to refer to Javanese from Central and East Java.

kowék-kowék to cackle.

kowélo (*Port IBT*) rabbit; → TERWELU.

Kowilhan [Komando Wilayah Pertahanan] Defense Territorial Command.

Kowiltabés [Komando Wilayah Kota Besar] (Police) City Territorial Command.

koyaan (*J*) drainage ditch.

koyak 1 torn (apart), tattered, ragged, shredded, ripped. *Bajunya – sedikit.* His shirt was torn slightly. *–.moyak* torn to shreds. 2 lacerated, mangled. *kulit* – lacerated skin. *– tak berbunyi* to keep one's dirty linen indoors. *tidak mau – kulit, – kain mau juga* to run for one's life.

koyak-koyak 1 all torn, torn to shreds. 2 *–!* disperse!

mengoyak 1 to increase in size, open up (of a wound). *Lukanya ~ lagi.* His wound has opened up again. 2 to rip (up), tear, shred. *Surat itu dikoyaknya.* He ripped the letter up.

mengoyak(-ngoyak)kan to rear, rip up, shred.

terkoyak 1 torn, ripped up, shredded; lacerated. 2 (*J*) *~ bangun* risen (of prices).

terkoyak-koyak riddled (with holes), torn to pieces.

koyakan tear, rip.

pengoyak one who tears/rips.

pengoyakan tearing, ripping, lacerating.

koya-koya k.o. pest of orchids, *Pseudococcus spp.*

koyam (C) *bubur* – a porridge of glutinous rice.

koyan a measure of weight or capacity for seeds and grains, like rice (= 27 to 40 *pikuls*).

koyo(k) I nonsense, rubbish. *jual* – a) to talk nonsense. b) to tell lies.

koyo(k) II (C) a medical plaster/salve such as Salon Pas.

koyok III 1 stray dog. 2 (*Mal*) coyote. 3 (*Br*) dog.

koyok IV → KAYAK I.

Koyonif [Komando Batalyon Infanteri] Infantry Battalion Command.

Koyonpom [Komando Batalyon Polisi Militér] Military Police Battalion Command.

Koyonpur [Komando Batalyon Pertempuran] Combat Battalion Command.

Koyonzipur [Komando Batalyon Zéni Tempur] Combat Engineers Battalion Command.

KPKPN (*init*) [Komisi Pemeriksa Kekayaan Penyelenggara Negara] Commission to Investigate the Assets of State Officials.

KPM I (*init col*) 1 [Koninklijke Paketvaart Maatschappij] Royal Packet Navigation Company. 2 (humorous reference to above) [Komt Pas Morgen] Doesn't Come Until Tomorrow.

KPM II (*init*) [Krédit Pemilikan Motor] Automobile Ownership Credit, car loan.

KPP I (*init*) [Kartu Pengenal Pengemudi] Driver Identification Card.

KPP II (*init*) [Kantor Pelayanan Pajak] Tax Service Office.

KPR (*init*) [Krédit Pemilikan Rumah] Home Ownership Credit.

kr- also see entries beginning with ker-.

kraag → KERAH II.

krabu (*Port IBT*) earring.

Kraéng Buginese noble title.

krah → KERAH II.

Krakatau Krakatoa. *Anak* – a secondary crater formed after the 1883 explosion of Krakatoa.

kram I (*D*) cramp, muscular contraction.

kram II (*D*) cramp(-iron); → KERAM I.

krama → KROMO I.

kraman (*Jv*) rebellion, uprising.

kramantara (*Jv*) /kramantoro/ *kromo* style of the *Jv* language with *ngoko* references.

krama subak (in Bali) farmers.

kramat → KERAMAT.

Kramtung [Kramat Tunggak] a red-light district in Jakarta.

kran → KERAN I. *– bahan bakar* fuel gauge. *– dua arah* two-way faucet.

krandang (*Jv*) k.o. ground cover, *Pueraria phaseoloides.*

krangéyan cubeb, *Litsea Cubeba Pers.*

kranggang k.o. red ant; → RANGRANG.

krani → KERANI.

kranji k.o. medicinal plant, *Pongamia pinnata.*

kranjing (*Jv*) → KERANJINGAN.

mengranjingkan to obsess.

kranjingan obsessed (by), driven (by a mania), taken over (by a spirit).

kekranjingan mania.

krans (*D*) (funerary) wreath.

KRAP [Komunikasi Radio Antar Penduduk] CB (radio). *penggemar* – CB-er.

krapu grouper (k.o. fish).

kras karst.

krasan (*Jv*) to feel at home, feel comfortable (in a new place).

krasikan (*Jv*) k.o. cookie made of sticky rice.

kras-kres (*onom*) sound of repeated cutting/slashing.

krat (*D*) crate (containing 24 bottles). *se– bir* a crate of beer.

krating daéng (*Thai*) "red bull," an energy drink.

kratok (*Jv*) k.o. bean, *Phaseolus lunatus.*

kraton (*Jv*) royal (Sultan's) palace.

Krawang → KARAWANG II.

krawu (*Jv*) mixed with grated coconut.

krayon (*E*) crayon.

KRD [Keréta Rél Diesel] Diesel Rail Car.

kré (*J*) sunshade made of thin bamboo slats; → KERAI.

kréasi (*D*) creation.

berkréasi 1 to create. 2 to be creative.

mengkréasikan to create s.t.

kréatif (*D/E*) creative.

kekréatifan creativity.

kréativitas (*D*) creativity.

kréator (*D/E*) creator.

krécék (*Jv*) dried (buffalo) hide, cut into pieces, baked and eaten.

kréda → KRIDA.

krédénsial (*E*) credential(s).

krédép (*J*) berkrédép and mengrédép to spark, flare, flash, scintillate.

mengkrédép shiny.

krédibel (*E*) credible.

krédibilitas (*E*) credibility.

krédit (*D*) credit, loan. *bank* – credit bank. *débét dan* – debits and credits. *harga jual* – lending rate. *membeli (dengan)* – to buy on credit. *memberi* – to grant credit. *membuka* – to open a (line of) credit). *mendapat* – to obtain credit. *menjual (dengan)* – to sell on credit. *pemberi* – credit grantor. *tukang* – (*J*) s.o. who sells goods on credit. *– amanah* open credit. *– berbunga rendah* low-interest loan. *– bermasalah* nonperforming loan. *– berputar/berulang/beruntun* revolving loan. *– blanko* fiduciary loan. *– candak kulak* a loan for purchasing goods with limited capital for immediate resale at a profit. *– hipoték* mortgage credit. *– invéstasi* investment credits, i.e., medium-term investment credits available to a wider group of borrowers than those covered by *– invéstasi kecil* [KIK] small investment credits. *– modal kerja pérmanén* [KPMK] permanent working capital credit. *– jangka menengah/panjang/péndék* medium/long/short-term credit. *– komando (coq)* credit issued at the command of an influential person (k.o. illegal practice since it has no collateral and is issued over the telephone). *– lunak* soft credit. *– macet* nonperforming loan, bad debt. *– midi (coq)* a maximum credit of Rp 500,000 issued by a bank. *– mini (coq)* a maximum credit of Rp 100,000 issued by a bank. *– modal kerja* working capital credit. *– penunjang (fin)* backup line. *– rangkap* duplicate loan. *– sindikasi* syndicated loan. *– talangan* bridge loan. *– tanpa bunga* noninterest-bearing loan, interest-free loan. *– tempilan* credit taken out and signed for by one person but also partially used by s.o. else. *– topéngan* credit taken out and signed for by one person but entirely used by s.o. else. *– vérban (D)* credit lien.

mengkréditkan 1 to lend money on security. 2 to sell goods on credit.

kréditan bought on credit. *sepéda ~* bicycle bought on easy terms.

pengkréditan crediting.

perkréditan credit system, credit (*mod*).

kréditir → KRÉDITOR. **mengkréditir** to credit s.o. with s.t. ~ *ganda* to keep double entry books.

kréditor (*D/E*) creditor. *negara* – creditor state. – *akhir* creditor of last resort. – *awal* originator. – *kon(g)kurén* unsecured creditor. – *préférén/utama/yang diistiméwakan* preferred creditor.

kréditur → KREDITOR.

krédo (*D/E*) credo.

krédong (*J*) **berkrédong** wrapped up (in a blanket/*sarong*, etc.).

kréi → KERAI.

krém (*D*) 1 cream (top of milk); → KEPALA *susu*. 2 cream(-colored). 3 (cosmetic) cream. – *pemutih* bleaching cream.

krémasi (*D*) cremation.
　mengkrémasikan to cremate.

krématorium (*D*) crematorium, crematory.

kremes I (*Jv*) k.o. sweet cassava cake.

kremes II (*Jv*) **kremes(-kremes)** to crumble.

kremi → KERMI.

Krémi [Krédit Mini] Mini Credit.

Krémlinolog (*D*) Kremlinologist.

Krémlinologi (*D*) Kremlinology.

krémpéng (*J*) emaciated, thin (of figure).

kremus (*Jv*) munched (up), crunched.
　mengremus to eat bones and all.

krenék [and **krenét** (*coq*)] → KERNÉT.

krenggosan (*Jv*) out of breath, panting.

kréngséng (*Jv*) k.o. meat fried in its own oil.

krenteg (*Jv*) deep feelings.

krénten (*D*) currants.

krenyes (*Jv*) to crackle.

Kréol (*E/D*) Creole.

kréolin (*D/E*) creolin, i.e., a disinfectant resembling carbolic acid.

kréosot (*D/E*) creosote, i.e., a thick, brown, oily liquid derived from coal tar, used as a wood preservative.

krép (*D*) crêpe. *kertas* – crêpe paper.

krépdesin (*F*) crêpe de Chine.

krépot (*J*) wrinkled, furrowed.

kres (*onom*) swish, sound of cutting/slashing.

kréséh-péséh (in Sumatra) to talk Dutch all the time.

kresek (*onom*) sound of rustling/crunching of dry leaves.

krésék I (*Jv*) *kelas* – low-class, fleabag (hotel).

krésék II *penyakit* –(*krésék*) (medical) gravel, stones.

krésék III *tas* – plastic bag.

Kresna (*Skr*) Krishna.

krésten → KRISTEN.

kréstik (*D*) cross-stitch.

Kréta *Pulau* – Crete.

kréték I (*Jv*) horse-drawn cart.

kréték II (*Jv*) → KERÉTÉK I.

krétékan fastener-tape.

krétéria → KRITÉRIA.

Kretharta Karya Samuha Success Through Teamwork (motto of PT Indosat).

kreton (*F*) cretonne.

KRI [Kapal (Perang) Républik Indonésia] Republic of Indonesia (War)ship.

kria (*Jv*) craft(s); → KRIYA. *perancang seni* – crafts designer.

kriat-kriut → KERIANG-KERIUT.

kribo I (*J*) 1 curly (of hair). 2 kinky, frizzy.
　berkribo to have curly/frizzy hair.
　mengribo to curl (hair).

kribo II [kriting bohong] fake curls.

kricak (*Jv*) broken stones, rubble.

Kricika Scorpio.

krida (*Jv*) 1 activity, action. 2 (in schools) extracurricular activities. *Hari* – Day of Extracurricular Activities. *jam* – hour reserved for government workers and private agencies to engage in physical fitness activities (Friday mornings). – *lumahing asta* or *krido lumahing asto* (*Jv euph*) to beg. – *prana* → WAITAN(G)KUNG. – *wisata* study tour.
　mengridakan to put to work. *Tahanan G-30-S/PKI dikridakan untuk mencukupi pangan meréka sendiri.* The Sept. 30 Movement/PKI detainees were given work so that they could provide for their own food.

kridanirmala (*Skr neo*) epidemic control.

kridit → KRÉDIT. *tukang* – and **pengridit** man who sells small items on credit.

kriditor (*sl*) student who has to take courses over.

Krido Bekso Wiromo a Javanese dance school in Yogyakarta, the first to offer Javanese dance outside of the *kraton*.

krieek-kriaak (*onom*) crackling sound of chewing on s.t. crispy.

kriing (*onom*) ringing (of telephone).

kriir (*D*) **mengkriir** to create.

kriket (*E*) (the game of) cricket.

krim (*E*) → KRÉM. – *antiséptik* antiseptic cream. – *pembersih* cleansing cream. – *kocok* whipped cream. – *pencukur* shaving cream. – (*untuk*) *pengurut* massage cream. – *rambut* hair cream.

Krimia the Crimea.

kriminal (*E*) and **kriminil** (*D*) criminal; → PIDANA. *hukum* – criminal law. *perkara* – criminal case. *tindak* – criminal act.
　mengkriminalkan to turn (a civil case) into a criminal case.

kriminalitas and **kriminalitét** (*D*) criminality.

kriminalisasi (*D*) criminalization.

kriminolog (*D*) criminologist.

kriminologi (*D*) criminology.

kring I (*D*) an association consisting of a number of persons who form a coherent social group, a cell.

kring II → KERING II.

krio (in Muara Enim, South Sumatra) village head.

kripik (*Jv*) chips of sliced fried unripe banana, cassava or sweet potato, etc. – *gendar* rice chips. – *jagung* corn flakes. – *kentang* potato chips. – *pisang* banana chips. – *puli/putih* rice chips. – *singkong* cassava chips. – *témpé* thin slices of fried soybean cake.

kripikan acacia, *Acasia auriculiformis*.

kripto (*D/E*) crypto. –*.komunis* cryptocommunist. –*.Muslim* crypto-Muslim.

kriptografi (*D/E*) cryptography.

krisan (*D*) chrysanthemum, *Chrysanthemum*. – *putih* white chrysanthemum.

krisis (*D/E*) crisis. – *akhlak* moral crisis. – *batin* spiritual crisis. – *kabinét* cabinet crisis. – *ketenagaan* energy crisis. – *monétér* [krismon] monetary crisis.
　mengkrisiskan to cause a crisis. ~ *kabinét* to cause a cabinet crisis.

krisma (*RC*) – (*suci*) (Holy) Confirmation.

Krismes (*E*) Christmas.
　krismesan Christmas celebration.

krismon [krisis monétér] monetary crisis.

KRISNA [Partai Kristen Nasional Indonésia] Indonesian National Christian Party.

kristal I (*D/E*) crystal.
　berkristal to crystallize.
　mengkristal to crystallize s.t.
　pengkristal crystallizer.
　pengkristalan crystallization.

kristal II [krisis total] total crisis.

kristalisasi (*D*) crystallization.
　mengkristalisasikan to crystallize s.t.
　terkristalisasi crystallized.

kristalisir (*D*) **mengkristalisir** to crystallize s.t.
　terkristalisir crystallized.

kristalografi (*E*) crystallography.

Kristen (*D*) 1 Christian. 2 Protestant. *kaum* – *dan Katolik* Protestants and Catholics. *umat* – a) Christians. b) Protestants. – *Maronit* Maronite (Christians in Lebanon).
　mengkristenkan to Christianize.
　kekristenan Christianity.
　pengkristenan 1 Christianization. 2 Christianizing.

Kristenisasi (*E*) Christianization; → KRISTIANISASI.

Kristiani Christian.

Kristianisasi Christianization.

Kristus (*D*) (Jesus) Christ.

kritéria (*D pl* of *kritérium*) criteria.

kritérium (*D*) criterion.

kritik (*D*) 1 criticism. 2 critical. 2 critique. – *(yang) membangun* constructive criticism.
    mengkritik and **mengritik** to criticize.
    kritikan criticism.
    pengkritik and **pengritik** 1 critic. ~ *sastra* literary critic. 2 faultfinder.
kritikal (*E*) critical.
kritikawan critic.
kritikus (*D*) critic. – *sastra* literary critic.
kriting I → KERITING. – *daun* a filamentous fungus, *Macrophomina sp.*, a disease of the clove tree.
kriting II club (in card games).
kritis (*D*) critical.
kritisi (*D*) (plural of *kritikus*) critics.
kriuk (*J onom*) crunching sound.
    kriuk-kriuk rumbling sound produced by a hungry stomach.
    kriukan rumbling (of the stomach from hunger).
kriwikan (*Jv*) brooklet. – *dadi grojogan* (*Jv*) little strokes fell great oaks
kriya skill, craft; → KRIA, KERAJINAN.
kriyawan male craftsman.
kriyawati female craftsman.
krn (*abbr*) [karena] because.
krobongan (*Jv*) inner room in a Javanese house.
kroco (*J*) 1 low-class Eurasian/Indo. 2 low-echelon, low-ranking; → KRUCUK. 3 k.o. small snail.
    mengrocokan to look down on s.o., treat s.o. as inferior.
    kroco-kroco low-ranking, worthless people.
krocojiwa (*Jv*) inferiority complex.
kroda (*Jv*) action, behavior.
krog-krog (*onom*) crackling sound of static (over the telephone).
krokét (*D*) croquette.
krokot (*Jv*) a tall vegetable resembling purslane, *Alternantera sp.*, *Portulaca oleracea.*
krol (*D*) (artificial) curl (in one's hair).
    mengkrol to wave (hair); → KERUL.
krom (*D*) chromium.
kromat (*D*) chromate. – *seng* zinc chromate.
kromatografi (*E*) chromatography.
kromi female freshman of *Univérsitas Katolik Indonésia* [UKI].
kromium (*D*) chromium.
kromo I (*Jv*) style in *Jv* language used when speaking to a person of a higher status, an older person, a person with whom one is not well acquainted, etc. – *inggil* high kromo, references to possessions, body parts and actions of a higher or older addressee or third person.
    mengkromokan to say s.t. in *kromo.*
    kekromoan (linguistic) respect.
kromo II (*Jv*) *si* – the little man, the common people. *kaum* – the proletariat.
    kekromoan proletarianism.
kromo III *hantam* – → HANTAM *kromo.*
kromo IV male freshman of *Univérsitas Katolik Indonésia* [UKI].
kromong *gamelan* instruments tuned to a pentatonic scale.
kromosom (*D/E*) chromosome.
krompyang (*Jv onom*) crash! *suara* – a crashing sound.
kron (*D*) crown, the (Dutch) royal crown.
krona (the Scandinavian currency) crown.
kroncong → KERONCONG II.
kronik (*D*) chronicle.
kronis (*D*) 1 chronic. *penyakit* – chronic disease. 2 regular, faithful (reader of a newspaper, etc.).
kronologi (*D/E*) chronology.
kronologis (*D*) chronological. *secara* – chronologically.
kronométer (*D*) chronometer.
    berkronométer with a chronometer.
kropok (*J/Jv*) 1 decayed, putrid, worm-eaten. 2 hollow, empty. *buah yang* – a fruit without flesh. 3 decrepit, feeble, weak, powerless.
kropos (*J*) → KEROPOS. **kekroposan** hollowing out.
krosak (*Jv onom*) and **krosak-krosak** and – *krosék* sound made by crushed branches.

krosboi and **krosboy** male juvenile delinquent. – *ingusan* young thug/punk.
    ngrosboi to act like a punk.
krosgir(e)l female juvenile delinquent.
krosmama a woman who goes after young men.
krosok (*Jv*) → KEROSOK II.
krospapa a man who goes after young women.
kroto (*Jv*) 1 red ant eggs (used as a food for certain bird species). 2 young *melinjo* blossom.
krowak (*J/Jv*) with a hole in it.
kroyok → KEROYOK.
kru (*E*) crew. – *film* film crew.
krubut (*Jv onom*) noisy, confused mobbing/rushing.
    krubutan act of mobbing/overwhelming.
krucuk → KROCO.
kruis (*D*) /kres/ crotch.
kruk (*D*) crutch, crutches.
krukas (*D*) crankshaft.
krukat (*E*) crew cut (haircut). *cukur* – to get/have a crew cut.
kru-kru k.o. fried dough snack.
krul (*D*) → KERUL.
kruntel (*Jv*) **mengruntel** to roll s.o.'s hair. ~ *palsu* rolled and mingled with an artificial bun.
    kruntelan wriggling mass.
krupuk generic name for many k.o. baked or fried chips and the like made from various k.o. flour with seasonings; → KERUPUK I. – *emping* a melinjo chip. – *ikan* fish chip. – *kentang* potato chip. – *krécék/kulit* beef-skin chip. – *legendar* ground-rice chip. – *melarat* inexpensive *krupuk* made from tapioca flour. – *pati* brightly colored tapioca chip. – *sérmiyér* (red-colored) sago chip. – *udang* shrimp chip.
    perkrupukan chip (*mod*). *bidang* ~ the *krupuk* business sector.
krupukan (*J*) to be at one's wits end.
krus I → KURS.
krus II (*E*) crush, a carbonated drink; → ORANYEKRUS.
krusial (*E*) crucial.
krutuk (*Jv*) **mengrutuki** and **ngrutuki** to bombard s.t.
kruyuk → KERUYUK I.
kruwes (*Jv*) **mengruwes** and **ngruwes** 1 to scratch/claw at. 2 to pull out (hair).
ksatria (*Skr*) 1 nobleman, knight. 2 warrior. 3 noble, chivalrous, knightly; → KESATRIA. *wanita* – heroine.
    ksatrian 1 nobleman's residence. 2 place where noblemen are quartered. 3 (naval) barracks. ~ *Pangkalan Angkatan Laut Morokrembangan* [KPALM] Monokrembangan (in Surabaya) Naval Barracks.
KSO [Kerja Sama Operasi] Operational Cooperation.
    meng-KSO-kan to place under operational cooperation (with).
KT car license plate for Kalimantan Timur.
KTM I [Kartu Tanda Mahasiswa] Student ID Card.
KTM II [Konperénsi Tingkat Menteri] Ministerial Level Conference.
KTP (*init*) [Kartu Tanda Penduduk] Resident's Identification Card.
    ber-KTP with a ... resident card.
KTT [Konperénsi Tingkat Tinggi] Summit/High-Level Conference.
KTTR [Koperasi Tani Tebu Rakyat] Smallholders Sugarcane Co-operative.
Ktut (in Bali) a noncaste name element placed before personal names to indicate the fourth-born child.
ku (*C*) *kué* – a type of cake made from stuffed and steamed glutinous rice flour.
ku- shortened form of *aku* indicating first-person singular agent of a passive verb. *Rumah itu sudah –beli.* I've bought that house.
-ku shortened form of *aku* indicating first-person singular possessor, my. *rumah–* my house.
KU [Kuasa Usaha] Chargé d'Affaires.
kua I → KOA.
KUA II → KANTOR *Urusan Agama.*
kuaci (*C*) dried salted watermelon seeds.
kuadé → KUWADÉ.
kuadran (*D*) quadrant.

kuadrat (*D*) square, quadrate. *méter* – square meter.

kuah sauce, broth, gravy (usually over rice). *bakmi* – Chinese noodles cooked in broth. *– tumpah/tertuang ke nasi* refers to a marriage approved by custom or between cousins; a fitting match. *– sama diirup, sambal sama dicolék* what's sauce for the goose is sauce for the gander.

  berkuah to have a sauce/gravy on it; with sauce/gravy. *~ air mata* a) with overflowing tears. b) to experience difficulties all the time.

  menguahi to add sauce/gravy/broth to, put sauce, etc. on.

  menguahkan to pour sauce/gravy/broth over.

KUAI [Kuasa Usaha Ad Interim] Chargé d'Affaires Ad Interim.

kuai terkuai-kuai to move one's hands around in the air in excitement.

kuak I 1 low(ing), moo(ing) (of cows/buffaloes). **2** croak(ing) (of frogs). **3** quack(ing) (of ducks).

  menguak 1 to low, moo. **2** to croak. **3** to quack.

kuak II *burung –(.–)* night heron, *Nycticorax n. nycticorax. katak* – bullfrog, *Callula pulchra.*

kuak III separated, pushed aside, parted (*esp* of one part of a crowd from another to give way to s.o. entering/pushing through it or of a fence pushed aside).

  berkuak 1 to open (up) (of sail/stage curtain, etc.). **2** to widen, get bigger, enlarge (of a hole/tear, etc.), part (of joinery), step aside.

  menguak 1 to open up. **2** to break (of day). *Pagi makin ~* The day was breaking more and more. **3** to push/set aside, push out of the way, ignore. *tradisi yang sulit dikuak* a tradition that is hard to ignore. *tak dapat dikuak lagi* inseparable. **4** to open to public view, solve (a mystery/problem). *~ tabir* to raise (the curtain).

  menguakkan 1 to part (the hair/a hedge/curtains). **2** to make/ force/push one's way through (a crowd, etc.), push aside. **3** to avert (danger). **4** to open (up) (a door).

  terkuak 1 pushed aside. **2** revealed, disclosed, opened up. *Daun pintu ~.* The door opened up. **3** slotted.

  terkuakkan can be unveiled/solved.

  kuakan slot.

  penguak s.t. used to part, open up, etc.

  penguakan prying open, parting.

kuala estuary, mouth of a main river or of a tributary, confluence (of); → MUARA.

  berkuala 1 with an estuary/a river mouth. **2** to flow/empty into.

kualahan (*M*) → KEWALAHAN.

kualat (*Jv*) **1** struck by punishment from a higher authority (because one has committed an offense, sinned, etc.), hit by a calamity (due to acting badly toward older people, etc.). **2** (*coq*) accursed; cursed, damned.

kuali (*Jv?*) frying pan curved like a bowl, k.o. wok.

kualifaid (*E*) and **kualifait** qualified. *kurang* – unqualified.

kualifikasi (*D*) qualification.

  berkualifikasi to have the qualifications of; to be qualified. *guru ~ memadai* a qualified teacher.

  mengkualifikasikan to qualify.

kualita(s) (*D*) quality.

  berkualita(s) ... of ... quality.

kualitatif (*D*) qualitative.

kualitét (*D*) quality.

kualon (*J*) step-. *anak/bapak* – stepchild, stepfather.

kuang I (*burung –*) (great argus) pheasant, *Argusianus argus*; → KUAU. *mati – karena bunyi* pride goeth before a fall. *– bertam* crestless fire-back pheasant, *Lophura erythrophthalma. – bulan/ cermin/ranggas/ranting* Bornean peacock pheasant, *Polyplectron schleiermacheri. – kepala putih/raja* crested argus pheasant, ocellated pheasant, *Rheinardia ocellata nigrescens.*

kuang II (*ikan –*) a fish species, grass carp, *Ctenopharyngodon* of the *gurami* family native to China and raised in Indonesia to combat *écéng gondok.*

kuangkuit (*burung –*) cuckoo-shrike, *Lalage nigra.*

kuangwung (*J*) coconut rhinoceros beetle, *Oryctes rhinoceros.*

kuantifikasi (*E*) quantification.

  mengkuantifikasikan to quantify.

kuantita(s) (*D*) quantity.

kuantitatif (*D*) quantitative.

kuantitét (*D*) quantity.

kuantum (*D/E*) quantum, quantity, amount.

kuap yawn. *melepaskan –nya* to yawn.

  berkuap and **menguap** to yawn.

  terkuap yawned.

kuar I → KUAK I. **mengkuar(-nguar)kan** to make one's way feeling around in front of one (as a blind man with a stick).

kuar II *burung –(an)* a) a night heron, *Nycticorax nycticorax*; → KUAK II. b) white-breasted waterhen, *Amaurornis phoenicurus chinensis.*

kuar III *anak –* (*ob*) illegitimate child.

KUARI [Kuasa Usaha Républik Indonésia] Chargé d'Affaires of the Republic of Indonesia.

kuarik (*Buginese ob*) a Buginese breast-shield ornament of gold or silver.

kuarsa (*D*) quartz.

  berkuarsa quartz-bearing.

kuarsit (*D*) quartzite.

kuartal (*D*) quarter (of a year); → TRIWULAN. *– pertama* the first quarter (of the year).

  kuartalan 1 quarterly (*mod*). **2** trimester.

kuartét (*D*) quartet. *– gésék* string quartet.

kuartir (*D*) quarters, headquarters.

kuarto (*D*) quarto.

kuas I (*D*) **1** (paint/writing/shaving) brush. *– cat* paintbrush. **2** applicator. *– lém* glue applicator.

  menguas to brush.

kuas II (*D*) (lemon-)squash (a soft drink).

kuas III *– kais* to scratch around (as a fowl does); → KAIS.

kuasa I (*Skr*) **1** power, force, might, vigor. *atas – undang-undang* in accordance with the law. *pasca –* post-power. *– gaib* supernatural power. *– luas* broad powers. *– orangtua* parental authority. *– Tuhan* Divine Power. **2** concession, rights (granted by the government). *– pertambangan* mining rights/concession. **3** manager (of a hotel), chief, boss (of an office/store, etc.). *tuan – (ob*) plantation manager. **4** authority, attorney, (legal) counsel, proxy. *surat –* (*leg*) power of attorney; → OTORITA(S). *– di bawah tangan* private power of attorney. *– lisan* verbal power of attorney. *– mutlak* irrevocable power of attorney. *– penuh* full authority. **5** able, capable, having the ability to; → MAMPU, SANGGUP. *tidak –* not (being) able to, incapable of ...ing, powerless. *uang itu –* money is powerful. **6** power (state/country, etc. having influence in international affairs); → ADIKUASA. *– hukum* a) attorney, (legal) counsel. b) jurisdiction; → DAÉRAH hukum. *– kehakiman* (*leg*) judiciary. *– usaha* [KU] chargé d'affaires. *– usaha tetap* chargé d'affaires de pied.

  sekuasa as powerful as. *~ saya* as far as I am able.

  berkuasa 1 to have the power to, have authority over; authoritative, empowered. *Dia ~ memutuskan perkara-perkara seperti itu.* He has the authority to decide in such cases. *(pihak) yang ~* the authorities; → PEMBESAR. *duta besar luar biasa dan ~ penuh* ambassador extraordinary and plenipotentiary; → DUTA. **2** to be in charge/control/power/command. *Siapa yang ~ di sini?* Who's in charge here?

  menguasai [and **nguasain** (*J coq*)] **1** to have control over, dominate; to govern, rule. *dikuasai oléh istri* to be henpecked. *~ dan mengurus* to control and manage. **2** to master, acquire skills in, become proficient at. *~ tiga bahasa* to master three languages. **3** to control, contain, restrain, bottle up, keep in check. *~ hawa nafsunya* to keep one's passions under control. *~ diri* to control o.s. **4** to take charge of, manage, administer, conduct. **5** to take possession of (a house).

  kuasa-menguasai to try to dominate e.o., vie for power.

  menguasakan 1 to give the authority to, empower, authorize. *Dia dikuasakan mengurus perusahaan itu.* He was given the authority to manage the business. **2** to commission (a mine, etc.).

  terkuasa the most powerful.

  terkuasai controllable. *tidak ~* uncontrollable. *Tangisnya tidak ~.* He could not control his weeping.

  terkuasakan can be delegated/commissioned/authorized.

  kekuasaan 1 power, might, authority. *merebut ~* to make a grab for power. *kehilangan ~nya* powerless. ~ *bapak* paternal authority. ~ *berlaku* validity. ~ *bertumpuk-tumpuk* accumulated powers. ~ *éksékutif* executive powers. ~ *Hitam* Black Power. ~ *ke-4* the fourth estate, i.e., the press. ~ *kehakiman* judiciary. ~ *législatif* legislative power. ~ *orang tua* parental authority. ~ *pemerintahan* executive power. ~ *pengadilan* jurisdiction. ~ *pengampu* curatorship. ~ *penggentar* reign of terror. ~ *penuh* carte blanche. ~ *penyelenggara* executive powers. ~ *peradilan* judicial powers. ~ *tertinggi* supreme authority. ~ *perundang-undangan* legislative powers. ~ *tiada terbatas* absolutism. ~ *wali* guardianship. ~ *yang tertinggi* supreme command. ~ *yudikatif* judicial powers. 2 domination, control, power over, sway. *di bawah ~ organisasi dunia* under the domination of an international organization. 3 influence. **berkekuasaan** to have the power/authority.

penguasa 1 power, authority; one in charge/power, ruler. ~ *hukum* authorized representative, agent, proxy, person having a power of attorney. ~ *pelabuhan* port authority, harbormaster. ~ *tunggal* the regional heads (in the Ujungpandang area). ~ *yang berwenang* competent authority. 2 administrator, supervisor, manager. ~ *perang* war administrator.

penguasaan 1 command, control, mastery, authority, possession. ~ *anak-anak* authority over one's children. ~ *bahasa Inggrisnya* his command of English. *dalam ~nya* under one's control, in one's possession. ~ *(bersifat) mutlak* absolutism. 2 exploitation. ~ *sumber daya panas bumi* exploitation of geothermal resources. 3 commissioning, authorizing.

kuasa II → (ANG)KUSA.

kuasi (*D*) quasi. -.*ilmiah* quasi-scientific.

kuat (*A*) 1 strong, robust, sturdy. *obat* - tonic, fortifier, restorative (medicine). *otoritas yang* - demonstrable authority. 2a) can, be able; afford, to have the means to do s.t. *Kalau tidak - membayar seribu rupiah, lima ratus rupiah saja.* If you can't afford to pay Rp 1,000, Rp 500 will do. *Mana* –? How could I afford to (do it)? b) (*coq*) like to eat or drink a lot. *Dia – makan.* He's a good eater. c) addicted to, like to very much. *yang – menonton* movie addicts. 3a) strong (of the wind/voice). *Angin bertiup dengan –nya.* The wind blew strongly. b) loud (voice) *suara yang* - a loud voice. c) serious (sickness), vigorous (game). 4 firm, durable, not easily changed or influenced. 5 strong enough to. - *tekan* compressive strength. - *tahan payah* to have stamina/endurance. 6 – *tentang* good at, strong in. 7 well-founded/grounded (of hope/argument). 8 passionate (of love). 9 (*keras dan*) - *hati* determined, resolute. 10 strong, vigorous, energetic. 11 active, diligent, hard (working). 12 force, power. 13 backed (by), with a lot of ... at one's disposal. *yang – keuangannya* with plenty of funding. - *ketam karena sepit,* - *burung karena sayap,* - *ikan karena radai* a) to feel strong because of some superiority or advantage. b) everybody has some power/ability or other. - *beli* with purchasing power. - *garang* strong and fierce. - *gésér* shear strength. - *jua* to know better. - *kuasa* (*Sg Mal*) authority, legality; → KUATKUASA. - *majun* → MAJUN II. - *makan* to have a good appetite. - *syahwat* potent, virile. - *tekanan hawa* atmospheric pressure. - *tekan* compressive strength.

kuat-kuat 1 (to hold) tightly, firmly. 2 (to call/shout/read) aloud, out loud, loudly. 3 (to pinch) hard. 4 (to speak) up, etc.

sekuat of equal strength, as strong as; with all one's strength, as strong/loud, etc. as one can. *Aku menjerit ~ku.* I shouted at the top of my voice. ~ *suara* at the top of one's voice. ~ *tenaga* with all one's might.

sekuat-kuat(nya) with all one's strength/might.

berkuat 1 to persevere, persist, hold on/out, stick it out to the end, be firm and steadfast. 2 to hold one's own, keep one's ground. 3 to exert o.s., make every effort to do one's utmost. ~ *tulang* to work as hard as one's can.

berkuat-kuatan to test/challenge e.o.'s strength.

menguat to become stronger, appreciate, strengthen (of currency, etc.).

menguati and **menguat-nguati** 1 to do/take over/compel forcibly/by force. ~ *harta orang* to take s.o.'s possessions by force. 2 to force, coerce, compel, force, urge strongly. *Dikuati saja kalau dia tidak mau menurut.* Just force him if he doesn't want to obey. 3 to take violent action against. 4 to violate, infringe on.

menguatkan [and **nguatin** (*J coq*)] 1 to amplify, strengthen, reinforce. 2 to confirm (in general and *RC*), corroborate, affirm, support, ratify, uphold (a lower court's decision), sustain, substantiate. *Hal itu dikuatkan oléh hasil pemeriksaan dua dokter.* It was confirmed by an examination by two doctors. *Saksi kedua ~ keterangan saksi pertama.* The second witness corroborated the first witness's statement. 3 to raise (one's voice), increase (the volume). *Ia terpaksa ~ suaranya.* He was forced to raise his voice. 4 to stress, accentuate, emphasize.

memperkuat to make s.t. stronger, strengthen, reinforce, build up, amplify. *berusaha ~ kedudukannya dalam dunia bisnis* to try to strengthen one's position in the business world.

terkuat strongest, sturdiest, etc. *yang ~ yang tetap hidup* survival of the fittest.

kekuatan 1 force, forces, strength, power. *atas ~ undang-undang* under/according to the law. ~ *batin* moral force. ~ *beli* purchasing power. ~ *bukti/pembuktian* (*leg*) evidentiary value, conclusive force. ~ *cadangan* reserve forces. ~ *cahaya* candlepower. ~ *di daratan* land power (of national defensibility). ~ *di perairan* sea power. ~ *dan modal* funds and forces; → DANA *dan daya.* ~ *éksékutorial* power of enforcement. ~ *gésér* shearing strength. ~ *hidup* survivability. ~ *hukum* (*leg*) legal force. ~ *hukum (yang) pasti/tetap* final and conclusive. ~ *kedirgantaraan* aerospace power. ~ *lekat* adhesive force. ~ *lentur* bending strength. ~ *luluh* yield strength. ~ *menawar* bargaining power. ~ *mendidik* educational value. ~ *mengikat* binding force. ~ *mobil* mobile force. ~ *mulur* creep strength. ~ *mutlak* final and conclusive. ~ *pasar* market force. ~ *patah* breaking strength. ~ *pelenting* resilience. ~ *pemukul* striking force. ~ *penahanan* restraining force. ~ *pengimbang* countervailing force. ~ *pendorong* thrust. ~ *puntir* torsional strength. ~ *sembur* thrust. ~ *surut* retroactive force/effect. ~ *tarik* tensile strength. ~ *tawar-menawar* bargaining position. ~ *tekan* compressive strength. ~ *tekuk* buckling strength. ~ *témbakan* firepower. ~ *tempur* fighting force. ~ *tetap* final and conclusive. ~ *yang dilaksanakan* power of enforcement. 2 position (of strength). 3 confirmation. ~ *iman* confirmation of belief. 4 intensity (of light, etc.). 5 ability, capacity. *Dia tidak ada ~ lagi untuk mengangkat peti yang berat itu.* He no longer has the energy to lift that heavy chest. ~ *angkut* transport capacity. ~ *tekan* pressure capacity. **berkekuatan** 1 to be in force/effect, be valid, be in effect. ~ *enam bulan* to be valid for six months. ~ *hukum* to have legal force. *keputusan pengadilan yang ~ tetap* final court decision. *vonis ~ hukum* a final and conclusive sentence. ~ *hukum yang tetap* final and conclusive (about a court decision). 2 to have the strength of, be ... strong (of *mil* units), have the (electric) power of. ~ *12,000 orang* 12,000 strong. ~ *tinggi* high explosive.

penguat 1 s.t. that strengthens/amplifies/intensifies/reinforces, amplifier, booster. *bukti ~ tidak ada* (*leg*) there was no convincing evidence. ~ *sinyal* signal booster. ~ *suara* loudspeaker, amplifier. ~ *syahwat* aphrodisiac. 2 (*ling*) intensifier.

penguatan 1 strengthening, reinforcing, reinforcement, intensifying, intensification. 2 affirmation, confirmation (in general and *RC*). ~ *tandatangan* countersign. 3 amplification, (*elec*) gain. 4 excitation.

perkuatan 1 power (*mod*). *pusat ~* power center. ~ *tekan* compressive strength. 2 stiffening, bracing, reinforcement, reinforcing. ~ *lintang* cross-bracing.

kuatir (*A*) 1 afraid (that), anxious (that), apprehensive (that). 2 to worry (that); → KHAWATIR.

kekuatiran fear, anxiety.

menguatirkan 1 alarming, critical. 2 detrimental. 3 to worry about. *yang saya kuatirkan* what I am worried about.

kuatkuasa (*Mal*) to come into force, be in effect, be enforced. *Undang-undang itu akan berjalan –nya mulai ésok.* The law will be in effect as of tomorrow.

berkuatkuasa to be legal/in force.

menguatkuasakan to enforce (a law).

penguatkuasa *Bandaraya* Metropolitan Special Police.

kuau East Indian pheasant, argus, *Argusianus argus*; → (*burung*) KUANG.

kuaya (*Jv*) bile, gall; → EMPEDU.

kuayah *akar* – various species of climbing plants, *Connarus semidecandrus, Whitfordiodendron erianthum.*

Kuba Cuba.

mengkubakan to hijack and divert (a plane) to Cuba.

kubah (*A*) **1** cupola, dome, vault, arched roof; → KUPEL. – *geréja/ makam* church/grave dome. **2** turret. – *jungur* nose turret. – *kubur* small structure built over a tomb. – *meriam* (gun) turret. – *putar* (*mil*) rotary turret. – *yang tidak dapat berputar* (*mil*) cupola.

berkubah vaulted, domed, arched, turreted.

kubak berkubak and **terkubak** peeled, torn, hulled. *mendapat pisang* ~ to get a windfall; to get a sinecure.

mengubak 1 to peel (an egg/potato/shrimp, etc.). **2** to tear (the skin). **3** to hull/husk (rice). **4** to open up (a coconut/*durian*, etc.) by cutting it.

kubal → GUBAL I.

kubang I puddle, quagmire, buffalo wallow, mud hole.

berkubang 1 to wallow in a mud hole. **2** soiled, stained, covered with mud. ~ *keringat* to bathe in one's own sweat.

mengubangkan to wash cattle in medicated mud.

kubangan mud hole, buffalo wallow. *asalnya dari* ~ a dishonored person. *air lalu* ~ *tohor* easy come, easy go.

kubang II k.o. tree, *Macaranga gigantea*; → MAHANG.

kubat → KUBAH.

kubek mengubek [and **ngubek** (*coq*)] **1** (*J*) to turn s.t. around in a circle. **2** to stir (a liquid). **3** (*S*) to make the water muddy with one's hands and feet in order to bring fish to the surface.

kubik I mengubik to peel s.t. with the fingernails.

kubik II (*D*) cubic. *per–* per cubic. *séntiméter* – cubic centimeter.

berkubik-kubik in cubic tons.

kubil (*J*) **1** swollen (of eyelids). **2** (*med*) normal state of eyes, partly covered by lids.

kubin flying lizard, *Draco volans.*

kubis (*E*) cabbage, *Brassica oleracea*; → KOL II. – *daun* cabbage. – *bunga* cauliflower.

kubisme (*D/E*) cubism.

kubit (*M*?) *kena* – to be tapped.

sekubit a pinch (of salt, etc.), a tiny bit.

mengubit 1 to pinch/nip between thumb and finger. **2** to beckon (by bringing the fingers to the palm). **3** to attract s.o.'s attention by tapping/nudging him with the forefinger; → CUBIT.

mengubitkan to beckon using s.t.

kubluk (*J*) **1** too large. **2** sound (asleep).

kubra (*J*) **1** (the abbreviated form of *kiamat* –) Doomsday. **2** frustrated, unsuccessful, abortive; didn't work (out). **3** undecided, unsettled (of some matter). **4** broken/wound up (of a meeting), finished; liquidated. **5** get divorced. *Akhirnya dia – juga dengan lakinya.* She finally divorced her husband.

mengubrakan 1 to frustrate, cause s.o. to fail. **2** to keep s.t. unfinished/undecided. **3** to dissolve, liquidate; to end (a marriage).

pengubraan winding up/liquidation (of an enterprise).

Kubti (*A*) **1** Copt. **2** Coptic (language, etc.).

kubu I 1 stockade (of timber and earth), corral. **2** fort(ification), bunker, stronghold, redoubt, defense, bulwark. – *darat* ground fortification. – *gajah* elephant corral. – *meriam* gun turret. – *pertahanan* (*mil*) bunker.

berkubu to defend o.s. within a fort(ification), fortify o.s., set up fortifications.

berkubukan to use ... as a fort(ification).

mengubui to fortify.

terkubu fortified, inside a fortress.

perkubuan fortification.

kubu II *rotan* – a climbing plant which winds around trees, *Treycinetia javanica*, from whose roots rope is made.

Kubu III *orang* – Kubu, a forest tribe living in the border area between Palembang and Jambi (South Sumatra).

kubu IV small group, clique.

kubung I *burung* – lesser blue-winged pitta, *Pitta brachyura cyanoptera*. – *padi* flycatcher, *Muscicapa grandis.*

kubung II flying lemur, *Galeopithecus volans, Cynocephalus variegatus. cecak* – flying lizard, *Draco volans*; → CEKIBER.

kubung III *susu* – boil under the armpit.

kubur (*A*) **1** (*liang* –) grave, tomb. *sampai ke liang* – unto death. **2** burial place. *ahli* – the dead. *batu* – gravestone, tombstone. *bunga* – the flower of the *kamboja* plant. *tukang* – gravedigger. – *kalang* grave dating back to the Neolithic era, found in Bojonegoro (Java).

berkubur buried, entombed; to bury o.s., e.g., not come out of one's room

mengubur(kan) 1 to bury, inter. **2** to hide s.t.

terkubur buried. ~ *hidup-hidup* buried alive.

terkuburkan *tidak* ~ cannot be buried.

kuburan 1 cemetery, burial ground, graveyard. **2** tomb, grave, sepulcher.

penguburan burying, burial, interment. *perusahaan* ~ undertakers, morticians.

pe(r)kuburan cemetery, burial ground, graveyard.

kubur II *burung* – long-tailed nightjar, *Caprimulgus macrurus bimaculatus. burung* – *rimba* blue whistling thrush, *Myophonus caeruleus.*

kubus (*D*) cube. *berbentuk* – cubical.

kucai I (*C*) Chinese chives, leek, *Allium odorum/porrum.*

kucai II (*M*) → KUCIL. **mengucai** to isolate/separate o.s. (from one's friends).

terkucai isolated, separated (from the main body).

kucak I shaking fast and hard, vacillating; → KOCAK I.

berkucak to shake, move violently; shaken, moved violently. *hati* ~ upset feelings.

mengucak to shake (a liquid in a container).

terkucak 1 shaken (up). **2** *badan* ~ emaciated, (grown) thin.

kucak II → KUCEK.

kucam (*Jv*) pale, wan; gloomy (of the face); pallid (of the face).

kekucaman paleness, pallor.

kucandan (*M*) → KECANDAN.

kucapi → KECAPI II.

kucar-kacir 1 scattered, dispersed. **2** (to flee) in disorder, in a mess, turned upside down. **3** to suffer heavy losses, be hard hit. **4** irregular (of one's life), disorganized.

mengkucar-kacirkan and **mengucar-ngacirkan 1** to confuse, disconcert (a person). **2** to turn s.t. over, scatter (things) in disorder.

kekucar-kaciran disorganization, disorder.

kucek 1 (*J/Jv*) **mengucek(-ngucek)** to rub (the eyes with the hand). **2** to launder/wash clothes between the hands. **3** (*S*) to stir (a cup of tea, etc.).

ngucekin (*J*) to wash only the dirty part of a cloth.

kucel (*J/Jv*) tousled, crumpled, disheveled, rumpled; dirty, filthy.

mengucel to rumple, crumple, crease.

kucica Oriental magpie robin, *Copsychus saularis. – batu* pied bushchat, *Saxicola caprata.*

kucil mengucil(kan) 1 to squeeze out (toothpaste/glue, etc. from a tube, etc.). **2** to banish, expel, exile, remove, ostracize, excommunicate. **3** to isolate.

terkucil(kan) 1 isolated. **2** slipped off (as of a train off the rails, etc.); → ANJLOK *dari rél.*

pengucilan isolation, isolating, ostracism; expulsion, exiling, exile, banishment. ~ *diri* asceticism.

kucindan (*M*) joking (back and forth), banter; → KECINDAN, KECANDAN.

kucing I 1 cat. *mata* – a) cat's-eye (a semiprecious stone). b) a resin from *Hopea spp.* c) the green eye in older radio sets that shows that the set is warmed up and ready to use. **2** (*gay sl*) male prostitute. – *kepalanya hitam* (*Jv*) it's been stolen (remark made when s.t. is discovered missing). *bagai/seperti – dibawakan lidi* a) shy. b) scared stiff. *bagai – dengan panggang* to set the fox to watch the geese. *bagai – kehilangan anak* to lose one's bearings; → *ibarat/bagaikan* ANAK *ayam kehilangan induk. bagai – lepas senja* a) hard to find. b) to feel happy. *bagai – tidur di bantal* to be in clover. *bagai mengail – hanyut* a Sisyphean task. *ikan gantung, – tunggu* tantalizing, tormenting. *kalau – tidak bermisai, takkan ditakuti tikus lagi* when the cat's away the mice will play. *kalau/menantikan – bertanduk* when the cows come home, i.e., never. *kaya – dapur* (*J*) a) always playing in the kitchen. b) to have one's face all scratched up. *malu-malu* – coy, pretending to be shy. *(mem)beli – (di) dalam karung* to buy a pig in a poke. *seperti – dengan anjing* like a cat and dog, always at variance with e.o. – *bakau* fishing cat, *Prionailurus viverrinus*. – *batu* leopard cat, *Felis bengalensis*. – *belanda* rabbit; → **KELINCI, TERWELU**. – *bertanduk* s.t. impossible. – *biang* a "hot" woman. – *bulu* marbled cat, *Pardofelis marmorata*. – *bundel (Jv)* cat with a knotted tail. – *congkok/hutan* leopard cat, *Felis bengalensis*. – *dampak* flat-headed cat, *Prionailurus planiceps*. – *emas* golden cat, *Catopuma temminckii*. – *garong* alley cat. – *hutan* leopard cat, Bengal cat, *Prionailurus bengalensis*. – *jalang* a) flat-headed cat, *Felis planiceps*. b) a house cat that has run wild. – *kuwuk (Jv)* forest cat that eats chickens. – *marmer* marble cat, *Pardofelis marmorata*. – *negeri* house cat. – *pekak* a mousetrap with a falling arm. – *tapai* rabbit; → **KELINCI, TERWELU**. – *tua* an old hand (at s.t.). – *tuli* a mousetrap with a falling arm.

berkucing-kucing 1 to keep on pursuing/running after. **2** k.o. children's game, hide-and-go-seek. **3** immoral behavior of an unmarried man and woman. *lari ~* to walk fast.

mengucing to walk fast.

kucing-kucing(an) 1 triceps muscle in calf or arm. **2** toy kitten. **3** a hunt, chase; game of tag. *main kucing-kuncingan* to play cat and mouse with e.o.

kucing II *akar –* a shrub, *Toddalia aculeata. ékor –* a) bad-smelling herb, *Dysophylla auricularia*. b) a garden plant with catkins and ornamental foliage, chenille plant, *Acalypha hispida* from whose roots a medicine against spitting blood is made. c) a shrub, *Uraria crinita*, from whose roots an antidysentery medicine is made. *kumis –* → **KUMIS** *kucing*.

kucingan k.o. weed, touch-me-not, *Mimosa pudica*.

kucir 1 tuft of hair let grow to cover a bald spot. **2** pigtail or braid worn on the crown of the head, esp. by the *wayang* clown *Petruk*. **3** *(ob)* pigtail at the back of the head, of a Chinese male; *cp* **KELABANG** II. – *kuda* ponytail (hairdo).

nguciri to braid s.o.'s hair into a pigtail or braid.

kuco (during *Jp* occupation) village chief.

kucung → **KOCONG**.

kucup I to be closed (of s.t. that folds up).

mengucupkan to close up. *~ payung* to close up an umbrella.

kucup II → **KECUP**.

kucur I *(J/Jv)* gushing/pouring out.

berkucur and **mengucur** [and **ngucur** *(coq)*] to gush/pour out.

mengucuri 1 to pour (liquid) on(to). **2** to disburse (funds) to. *konglomerat lain yang dikucuri dana* another conglomerate to which funds were disbursed.

mengucurkan [and **ngucurin** *(J coq)*] **1** to pour s.t. out, shed (blood), break into (tears). **2** to contribute, put s.t. in. **3** to lay/put out, disburse (money by a bank).

terkucur disbursed, laid out.

kucuran 1 s.t. that gushes out, stream (of a liquid). *~ keringat* sweat (of hard work). **2** laying/putting out, disbursement (of money by a bank or lender).

pengucur disburser.

pengucuran disbursement.

kucur II *(Jv)* **1** k.o. fried cake made of rice flour. **2** stupid.

kucut conical.

KUD [*Koperasi Unit Désa*] Village Unit Cooperative.

kuda I 1 horse. *kandang –* stable. *komidi –* circus. *naik –* a) to ride on horseback. b) to mount a horse. *naik – hijau* to get drunk (and have a hangover), to see pink elephants (from drinking too much). *zaman – gigit besi* in the dim past. **2** s.o. treated like a horse, ordered to work hard. **3** unit of power, horsepower. *daya/kekuatan –* horsepower. **4** knight (in chess). *seperti – lepas pingitan* to be free as a bird. – *air* tapir, *Tapirus malayanis*; → **TENUK**. – *andalan* a sure bet (in horse races). – *anjing* a miniature two-hoofed horse. – *api* Chinese dragon lanterns. – *balap(an)* racehorse. – *Batak* Deli pony. – *beban* pack horse. – *belang* zebra. – *beraksa* Pegasus. – *beroda empat* automobile, car. – *besi* (railroad) train. – *betina* mare. – *bibit* a) broodmare. b) stud (horse). *(si) – hitam* a dark horse (in a competition). – *jantan* stallion. – *kacang (J)* pygmy horse with fat belly. – *kasi* gelding. – *kayu* stupid person. – *kebiri* gelding. – *kendaraan* riding horse, mount. – *képang* bamboo-plaited horse with

which men, imitating horses, perform a dance, usually in a trance. – *laut* seahorse. *(si) – liar* a) wild horse. b) the OV-10 Bronco aircraft. – *lomba* racehorse. – *loréng* zebra. – *lumping* a) → **KUDA** *képang*. b) leather horse. c) accomplice, lackey. – *pacu(an)* racehorse. – *pacu jarak jauh* long-distance racehorse. – *padi* a small k.o. pony. – *pejantan* stallion. – *pemacek* stud horse. – *penarik* draft horse. – *penuntun* guide horse. – *pusing* merry-go-round. – *putih* (in parts of Java and Bali) a white prostitute. – *sandel* Sumbanese horse. – *sem(e)brani* Pegasus. – *tanggung* saddle-horse. – *téji* large fast horse. – *terlatih* broken-in horse. – *Troya (E)* and – *Troye (D)* Trojan horse. – *tunggang(an)* a) riding horse, mount. b) stalking horse, decoy, the means by which s.o. gains his ends. – *unggul/yang berketurunan murni* thoroughbred. *memiliki napas –* tireless, unwearied. *seperti – lepas kandang/pingitan* be elated, overjoyed.

kuda-kuda 1 trestle. **2** easel (for a blackboard), bracket. **3** (*~ loncat*) vault (gymnastics). *~ pelana* vaulting horse. **4** sawhorse. **5** roof truss. **6** a *pencak* position. *pasang ~* to brace o.s. (by spreading the legs for an attack or defense).

berkuda 1 to have/own a horse. **2** to ride a horse, on horse(back). *orang ~* rider, horseman. *pasukan ~* cavalry.

menguda *(infr)* to ride a horse.

mengudakan to accelerate [the (argo)meter (in order to raise the fare in a taxi)].

memperkuda(-kudakan) 1 (= **memperkudai**) to ride on s.o.'s back (like a horse). **2** to exploit, work s.o. to death, drive (a horse till it drops). **3** to bully.

kuda-kudaan 1 to ride piggyback. **2** toy horse, hobbyhorse.

kekuda-kudaan equine.

pengudaan accelerating [the (argo)meter in order to raise the fare in a taxi].

pe(r)kudaan stable, horse barn.

kuda II *kayu –* a coastal tree species, *Lannea grandis*.

kuda III *ikan –* Pacific hippocampus/sea horse, *Hippocampus kuda*. – *belang/loréng* zebra, *Equus zebra*. – *laut* hippocampus, sea horse; → **UNDUK-UNDUK**. – *(sungai) Nil* hippopotamus.

kudai 1 basket made of rattan, etc. **2** round betel box made of silver, etc.

kuda-kuda 1 *burung –* rufous-fronted laughing thrush, *Garrulax rufifrons*. **2** – *laut* → **KUDA** *laut*.

kudang *(Jv)* **ngudang** to speak to a child using baby talk.

kudangan 1 *(J)* wish/request by fiancée which her future husband has to fulfill. **2** *(Jv)* loving and playful words spoken to a child.

kudap **mengudap** to eat/have a snack (not at the normal mealtime).

kudapan and **kudap-kudap** snacks or food bought outdoors and eaten at a stall.

pengudap s.o. who has a sweet tooth (or, who likes to snack between meals).

kudehél *(E)* corruption of "go to hell."

kudéhél *(J)* ridiculous words, nonsense.

kudéta *(Fr D)* coup d'état; → **KUP** III. – *tak berdarah* bloodless coup.

mengkudéta 1 to carry out a coup d'état. **2** to topple (a government, etc.) in a coup d'état. *Présidén Mauritania dikudéta pembantunya*. Mauritania's president was toppled by his aides.

kudi I *(J/Jv)* cleaver, wooden knife; → **PARANG**.

kudi II → **KODI**.

kudian *(M)* **1** at the back, behind. **2** (to come) late; later, afterward; → **KEMUDIAN**.

mengudian to stay behind, come last.

mengudiankan 1 to place s.t. second, leave behind. **2** to postpone, delay, put off.

terkudian last, final; left behind, backward.

kudidi → **KEDIDI**.

kudil → **KUDIS**.

kudis scabies, mange, scab (on plants). – *menjadi tokak* out of the frying pan and into the fire. – *anjing* mange. – *api* eczema. – *buta* itchy pussy scabies.

berkudis and **kudisan** to suffer from scabies, be mangy.

kudrat → **KODRAT** II.

kudrati → **KODRATI**.

kudrut (*J*) bankrupt.

kudu I (*Jv ob*) flower bud.

kudu II a red dye; → MENGKUDU.

kudu III (*Jv*) **1** ought to, must. *Aku – pulang.* I have to go home. **kemudu-kudu** to feel obliged to, feel strong compulsion to.

kudunya actually, strictly speaking.

kuduk I (*M*) nape of the neck.

kuduk II → NASI *kuduk.*

kudung I crippled, mutilated, maimed, missing a finger or limb. *bagai si – beroléh cincin* to get s.t. which cannot be enjoyed.

sekudung a piece, portion, section, slice, cut. ~ *limbat/lintah* an unstable attitude.

mengudung(kan) 1 to amputate. **2** to cripple, mutilate, maim, cut/chop) off.

pengudungan mutilation, amputation.

kudung II (= **kudungan**, **kekudung** and **kerudung**) (*J/Jv*) mantilla, cloth wound around the head (worn by women), veil, head covering.

berkudung to wear such a head covering.

mengudungkan to use s.t. as a head covering.

kudup → KUNCUP I.

kudus (*A*) holy, sacred. *Al.–* the Most Holy. *orang –* a saint. *roh al –* and *rohul–* the Holy Ghost/Spirit.

menguduskan to sanctify.

kekudusan sanctity.

pengudusan sanctification.

kudut (*Br*) dish, plate.

kué and **kuéh** (*C*) cake, pastry, cookie, pudding. FOR OTHER CAKES AND COOKIES SEE THE WORD FOLLOWING KUÉ(H). *– abuk* k.o. cake made from sugar-palm flower. *– acuan* k.o. cupcake. *– andapita* cake made of rice flour. *– apel* apple pie. *– apem* sweet rice fritter. *– ayas* k.o. cookie made from grated young coconut. *– bangkit* (*J*) sweet white cake made of wheat flour and no butter. *– bapél* → BAPÉL. *– basah* steamed cakes. *– bendéra* k.o. multicolored layer cake. *– biji salak* a *kolak* made of sweet potato, tapioca, and brown sugar. *– bika ambon* and *– bikambon* yellow sticky cake made of yeast, sugar, coconut milk, rice flour, sago, vanilla, salt, and eggs, sold in wedges. *– bolu* k.o. sponge cake. *– bolu kukus* steamed sweet white cake made of wheat flour. *– boter* butter cake. *– bugis* k.o. sticky rice flour cakes filled with coconut and palm sugar steamed in banana leaves. *– cang* cake made of seasoned rice and wrapped in bamboo leaves. *– Cina* cake esp prepared for the Chinese New Year. *– cincin* cake made of rice flour, candlenuts, and sugar. *– ciput* k.o. cracker. *– cohwa* cake made of agar-agar, chocolate and sweetened milk. *– cubit* finger foods sold from stalls. *– cucur* cake made of rice flour and brown sugar. *– dadar (gulung)* k.o. pancake made of wheat flour mixed with eggs, baked in a thin flat shape, filled with fresh grated coconut and brown sugar. *– dami* k.o. cake made with peanuts. *– daun* k.o. chocolate cake. *– dokok-dokok* cake made of rice flour, coconut, sugar, and bananas, wrapped in a banana leaf and steamed. *– donat* doughnut. *– gandos* → GANDOS. *– getuk* cake made of steamed cassava, etc. mixed with sugar and coconut. *– gundu* k.o. pineapple jelly cake. *– karas-karas* → KARAS I. *– kék* cake. *– kelepon* bite-sized green balls of sticky rice and brown sugar and rolled in grated coconut. *– kembang gempol* k.o. rice-flour cake. *– keranjang* → KUÉ cina. *– kering* baked cakes and cookies. *– ku* k.o. Chinese rice cake filled with mung beans. *– ladu* cookies made of rice flour. *– lepat* cake made of sticky rice, grated coconut and salt wrapped in a coconut leaf and baked. *– lapis* k.o. layer cake. *– lapis basah* sweet gelatinous mixture of rice flour, tapioca, or green bean flour. *– lapis legit* k.o. baked cake. *– lidah kucing* → LIDAH *kucing.* *– lilin* k.o. cake. *– lopis/lupis* pastry made of sticky rice eaten with grated coconut and brown sugar. *– lumpang* k.o. round cake made from sago flour and rice flour. *– lumpur* a soft cookie. *– maco* kind of fried snack made with rice flour and sticky-rice flour. *– madu* k.o. spice cake. *– makru* k.o. cake. *– mangkok* a brown, pink, green, or white cupcake made of rice flour, wheat flour, fermented cassava, brown sugar, etc. *– manis Dénmark* Danish pastry. *– Nagasari* k.o. banana cake. *– nopia* k.o. round pancake made from rice flour and coco-

nut milk. *– ondé(h)* golf ball-sized confection consisting of a mixture of brown sugar and coconut, wrapped in sticky-rice flour, rolled in sesame seeds, and fried. *– pahit* k.o. macaroon. *– pancong/pancung* k.o. cake with grated coconut. *– pancong* cake made of grated coconut, rice flour, and coconut milk. *– pasir* k.o. vanilla cake. *– pelangi* k.o. manioc cake. *– pépé* (*J*) k.o. layer cake. *– penganténs* wedding cake. *– pia* → PIA. *– pinda* k.o. peanut butter cake. *– pisang* a slice of banana in gelatin. *– pisang bolen* made of flour and containing a spiced banana. *– putu* k.o. cylindrical steamed cake. *– ranjang* → KUÉ cina. *– ruwok* k.o. cake. *– sapit* k.o. waffle. *– semprit* k.o. cookie made from sago or tapioca flour. *– semprong* rolled waffle, a crisp cylinder-shaped cookie made from coconut milk and cinnamon; → SEMPRONG. *– sénping* k.o. sweet roll. *– serabi* thick green or white pancake covered with coconut milk and brown sugar sauce. *– simping* k.o. flat cracker. *– spékula(a)s* Dutch spiced windmill cookies. *– srikaya* cake made of eggs, coconut, cassava, sugar. *– sumping talas* cake made of taro and rice flour. *– sus* cream puff. *– tahi kambing* k.o. small round cakes. *– talam* two-layered cake made of sweet potato flour or rice flour mixed with coconut milk and tapioca. *– tar(t)* tar. *– tar(t) buah apel* apple tart. *– thok* k.o. cake made from sticky rice and filled with mung-bean paste. *– tiao* rice noodles. *– ulang tahun* birthday cake.

kuék → KUIK II.

kuésionér (*E*) questionnaire. **mengkuésionér-édarkan** to circulate questionnaires.

kuétiao (*C*) k.o. rice noodles. *– siram* these noodles with broth.

kuffar (*A*) *pl* of **kafir**.

kuffiyéh (*A*) Arab men's headdress.

kufr (*A*) disbelief, heathenism.

kufu (*A*) → KUPU.

kufur (*A*) infidel, unbeliever, heathen; → KAFIR. *ilmu –* atheism. **mengkufurkan 1** to excommunicate. **2** to consider an infidel.

kekufuran heathenism, atheism.

KUHAP [*Kitab Undang-Undang Hukum Acara Pidana*] Code of Criminal Law.

KUHD [*Kitab Undang-Undang Hukum Dagang*] Code of Commercial Law.

KUHDT [*Kitab Undang-Undang Hukum Disiplin Tentara*] Code of Military Discipline.

KUHP 1 → KUHAP. **2** [*Kasih Uang Habis Perkara*] (pun on KUHP 1) Give Money and the Matter is Settled.

KUHPT [*Kitab Undang-Undang Hukum Pidana Tentara*] Code of Military Justice.

KUHS [*Kitab Undang-Undang Hukum Sipil*] Code of Civil Law.

kuhung (in Central Kalimantan) a rapid, shallow cataract; → RIAM.

kui I crucible (for smelting gold/silver).

kui II (*C*) and **berkui** to kneel down; to bow down, submit.

kuih → KUÉH. *–.muih* all k.o. of pastry.

kuik I (*onom*) rumbling in the stomach.

berkuik and **menguik** to rumble (of the stomach).

kuik II (*J*) **kuik-kuik** to shout. ~ *minta tolong* shouting for help.

nguikin (*J*) to call to (s.o.) in a loud voice.

kuil (*Tam*) (Balinese) temple. *– suci daripada jiwa* temple of the soul.

kuilu (*Port ob*) rabbit; → KELINCI, TERWELU.

kuin (*E*) queen (in a deck of cards).

kuing (*onom*) yelping (of a dog).

berkuing(-kuing) to bark, yelp.

kuini k.o. mango with a strong odor, *Mangifera odorata.*

kuintal (*D*) quintal, 100 kilograms.

kuintét (*D/E*) quintet; → KWINTÉT.

kuir (*M*) sickle used for weeding.

kuis I menguis(kan) 1 to kick/push aside (with the back of the hand); to claw at (as of a cat). **2** to scratch around for (food as of a fowl). **3** to stir up (a fire).

kuis II (*E*) quiz.

kuit jerky movement of the hand/tail. *– gamit* to beckon to s.o. by moving the hand with the knuckles up towards one's body. *– kapai* a) to scratch around for (food, as of a fowl or a person looking in a trash heap), rummage around. b) to putter about, do odd jobs.

menguit 1 to touch s.t. with the fingertips, beckon with the fingers. **2** to tap with the fingers to get s.o.'s attention. **3** to move/wag (as of an animal's tail).

menguitkan 1 to move (the hand) in gesture. **2** to paddle (a raft).

kuitansi → KWITANSI.

kuiz → KUIS II.

kuja → KOJA I.

kujang I (*S*) **1** cleaver, chopping knife. **2** name of a battalion in the *Siliwangi* Division.

kujang II k.o. plant, *Colocasia esculenta*.

kujarat (*M*) k.o. flower (in *pantuns* often used to rhyme with *melarat*).

kujur I *sekujur* over the whole (body). ~ *badan/tubuh* all over the entire body. *bekas bacokan di kepala dan* ~ *tubuh* stab wounds in the head and all over the body.

kujur II stiff (of a corpse); lank (of hair); → KEJUR I.

kujur III k.o. javelin used for spearing fish.

kujut *berkujut* to hang, strangle, or choke o.s. to death.

berkujut-kujut to be involved/implicated.

mengujut to strangle, garrote, throttle.

terkujut strangled, throttled.

pengujut hangman's rope.

kuk (C?) a single beamless yoke.

kukai k.o. fish.

kukang → KOKANG, KUNGKANG I.

kukeruyuk → KUKURUYUK.

kukila (*Jv ob*) bird.

kukis k.o. *kué basah*.

kuku I 1 nail (of finger or toe). *bunga* – lunule, the quick of the nail. *cat* – nail polish. **2** claw. – *macan* a) tiger's claw. b) staple remover. **3** hoof. – *kambing* sheep's trotter. – *kuda* horse's hoof. **4** tools or parts of equipment that resemble a nail. *hangat-hangat/ suam-suam* – lukewarm. *bergantung di ujung* – to hang by a thread. *bagai* – *dengan/dan daging/isi* inseparable (friends). *ibarat* – *jari tangan* and *ibarat* – *yang sulit dibrantas* ineradicable. *(harimau) memperlihatkan* –*nya* (s.o.) shows his power. – *bajang* the tenon that fits into the mortise in dovetailing. – *betul* the part of the nail attached to the flesh. – *Bima* a) Bima's nail; → KUKU *pancanaka*. b) (*joc*) [kurang kuat bini marah] impotent. c) the name of an aphrodisiac. – *cengkam* ingrown nail. – *jangkar* fluke of anchor. – *kaki* toenail. – *kambing* dibble stick for planting rice seedlings. – *lang* claw bent inward. – *macan* staple remover. – *pancanaka* the sharp elongated fingernails of Wrekudoro/Bima, Hanoman, and Sang Hyang Bayu (in the *wayang*). – *sauh* fluke of an anchor. – *tangan* fingernail. – *tikus* young clove plants.

kuku-kuku the clutches.

sekuku *tidak* ~ *hitam pun* and *tak* ~ *pun* not even a little/tiny bit.

berkuku 1 to have nails/claws, etc.; nailed, clawed, hoofed. **2** to be powerful. *diberi* ~ to be made powerful. *diberi* ~ *hendak mencengkam* to dominate others. *tidak* ~ (*lagi*) powerless, impotent. *mau* ~ (*J*) to stick to one's guns, stand one's ground. *bilang* ~ to maintain that ... *kekuasaannya* ~ *lagi* he became powerful again. ~ *belah* cloven-hoofed. ~ *satu/tunggal* ungulate. ~ *hendak menggaruk/mencubit* not yet having power but already wanting to exercise it.

kuku II generic name for various species of plants, for example, an ornamental garden shrub, *Nothopanax fruticosum*. – *elang* k.o. plant, *Zizyphus oenoplia*.

kuku III (*BG*) able to stand s.t. *nggak* – (the fans) went crazy.

kukuh 1 firm, tenacious (not easily changed or influenced); → KOKOH. *berhati* – to be firm of purpose, steadfast. *bersatu kita* –, *bercerai kita rubuh* united we stand, divided we fall. **2** strong, firm, sturdy.

sekukuh as strong, etc. as.

berkukuh (*pada*) and ~ *hati* to stick/cling (to), persist (in), remain firm, be staunch. ~ *kata* to make a firm promise. ~ *negeri* to maintain a country in a state of defense. ~ *pada adat lama* to cling to old customs.

bersikukuh to stick to one's guns, stand one's ground; to make a firm decision (to), insist (on). *Majelis hakim* ~ *akan melan-*

jutkan sidang. The council of judges insisted on continuing the session.

mengukuhi 1 to consolidate, strengthen, reinforce. **2** to keep (a promise), hold firmly to (a policy), stand by (a decision).

mengukuhkan and **memperkukuh 1** to strengthen. **2** to fortify, firm up. **3** to confirm (in office), install, inaugurate, swear in. *mengukuhkan kembali* to reconfirm. **4** (*leg*) to confirm, ratify, uphold.

terkukuh the strongest, etc.

terkukuhkan strengthened..

kekukuhan 1 strength, sturdiness. **2** firmness, tenacity. **3** staunchness.

pengukuh stabilizer.

pengukuhan 1 strengthening, reinforcing, consolidation. **2** confirming, installation, inauguration. *pidato* ~ inaugural speech. *upacara* ~ *guru besar* ceremony installing s.o. as a professor. **3** fortifying, strengthening. **4** (*leg*) confirmation, ratification, upholding.

kukuk I (*onom*) cock-a-doodle-doo.

berkukuk to cackle, crow; → KOKOK II.

kukuk II various species of cuckoos, *Cuculus spp.* – *besar* large hawk-cuckoo, *Cuculus sparverioides*.

kukukbeluk (*Jv*) → KOKOK II.

kukul I *mengukul* to draw the knees up close to the body, curl o.s. up; → KOKOL II.

kukul II (*Jv*) **1** blackhead, pimple on the face, acne. **2** pothole (in the street); → BOPÉNG.

kukulan to be pimply.

kukup alluvial deposit, silt (at an estuary).

mengukup to silt up.

kukupan silt.

pengukupan silting up.

kukur I (= **kukuran**) grater, rasp (for grating coconuts); → PARUT. *apa kepada* –, *nyiur juga yang binasah* easier said than done.

mengukur 1 to grate, rasp (flesh of the coconut) on a *parut*. **2** to scratch away at s.t.

kukuran grater, rasp.

pengukur 1 grater, rasp. **2** person who grates/rasps.

pengukuran grating, rasping.

kukur II (*onom*) cooing (of the *tekukur* dove).

berkukur and **mengukur** to coo.

kukuruyuk (*onom*) cock-a-doodle-doo.

kukus I 1 smoke. **2** steam, vapor. **3** (in compounds) cooked by steaming. *kué* – steamed cake. *roti* – steamed bread. – *alam* geothermal steam. – *bekas* exhaust.

berkukus 1 to smoke, steam, give off smoke/steam. **2** to purify/ refine by distillation. **3** to distill.

mengukus 1 to steam (rice, etc., until done) by putting it over boiling water. **2** to distill (arrack, etc.).

kukusan a cone-shaped bamboo basket in which rice is steamed in a *dandang*.

pengukusan steaming.

kukus II k.o. polecat, a skunk-like animal that emits a foul-smelling musky liquid when molested.

kukus III *buah* –(*an*) langsat, a type of small, round, buff-colored fruit growing in bunches, *Lansium domesticum*; → KOKOSAN.

kukut I → KOKOT I.

kukut II (*J*) adopted and raised as one's own. *anak* – adopted child, foster child; → ANAK *angkat/pungut*.

kukutan domesticated (animal).

kul I → KOL.

kul II 1 clipped form of **pukul**. **2** clipped form of **kuliah**.

kul III (*J*) to eat.

kula (*Jv cla*) I, me (in addressing a raja or sultan); → PATIK I.

kulah I (*A*) a stone, square-shaped water tank.

kulah II (*Pers cla*) (= **kulah-kulah**) k.o. helmet, headgear.

kulah III k.o. mango.

kulai I wilt (a plant disease), flagging/drooping (of a diseased tree), hanging down.

berkulai to dangle (of a damaged branch/drooping flag, etc.).

berkulaian (*pl subj*) to dangle. *Dahan-dahan kayu* ~. The branches were dangling.

mengulaikan ~ *(kepala)* to let (one's head) droop.
terkulai drooping, hanging down (of branches, the head), snapped (as of a flower).
terkulai-kulai fluttering (in the breeze).
kulai II *siput* – a univalve mollusk, green snail, *Turbo marmoratus*.
kulak I a measure for rice, etc., of about 4 *cupak* or 4 half-coconuts-full, equals about 1 *gantang*.
kulak II *(Jv)* to buy for resale, buy at wholesale (to resell at retail).
  kulakan bought (for wholesale), wholesale.
  perkulakan *(mod)* wholesale.
kulak-kulak – *tangan (M)* knuckles.
kulakasar *(A)* luggage, baggage.
kulambai → KELAMBAI.
kulan a tree, *Payena leerii*, which produces gutta percha *(getah sondék)*.
kulang-kaling → KOLANG-KALING I.
kulansing *(M ob)* a small packet of *sirih* sent to invite s.o. to a feast.
kulanuwun and **kulonuwun** *(Jv)* phrase which announces s.o.'s presence at the door of s.o.'s home; hello, anybody home?
  berkulanuwun to utter that phrase.
kulap → KULIAH *lapangan*.
kulari *(M)* a freshwater fish species, *Tylognathus spp*.
kulasentana *(Jv)* family and relatives of aristocrats.
kulat I various species of mushroom, fungus. – *cacing* ringworm.
  berkulat mildewed, moldy.
kulat II *(M)* **terkulat-kulat** to smack one's lips.
kulawangsa and **kuluwarga** *(Jv)* family; → KELUARGA.
kuldi → KHULDI.
kulem → KOLAM.
kuli I *(Tam)* coolie, unskilled laborer. – *angkat* porter, redcap (in airports). – *arit* rubber tapper. – *cemplong (Jv)* sugarcane planting worker. – *kencang* farmhand. – *klénték (Jv)* sugarcane gathering and cleaning worker. – *kontrak(an)* contract laborer. – *minterat (col)* a) unskilled city employee. b) street sweeper. – *mocok (Jv)* a) casual laborer. b) substitute (worker). – *pelabuhan* dock worker. – *pelat/pikul* porter, redcap (in railroad stations). – *pocok (Jv)* → KULI *mocok*. – *tinta* journalist; → NYAMUK *pérs*, WARTAWAN. *makan* – to work as a coolie. *uang* – coolie wages.
  berkuli and **menguli** to work as a coolie.
  memperkuli to make s.o. into a coolie; to treat s.o. as a coolie.
  kulian coolie wages.
  perkulian coolie affairs, coolie *(mod)*.
Kuli II [*Kultus Individu*] cult of the individual.
kuliah *(A)* **1** lecture (in college, etc.), course of lectures. *jam* – lecture hours. *mata* – subject matter of lectures. *memberi/mengadakan* – to give a lecture/lectures/a course. *mengikuti* – to take a course, attend a lecture. *ruangan* – lecture hall, classroom. *tahun* – academic year. *uang* – lecture fee, tuition. – *lapangan* [*kulap*] field course. – *Kerja Nyata* [KKN] National Study Service Scheme, i.e., an interdisciplinary activity which involves public service work in the villages as part of the *BUTSI* program, Community Service. – *subuh* lecture after morning prayers. **2** *(mainly Mal)* college, university; → MAKTAB. **3** → BERKULIAH.
  sekuliah to attend the same lectures/courses. *Aku* ~ *dengan dia*. I took the same courses as he did. *teman* ~ fellow student (in college).
  berkuliah to attend lectures, go to classes.
  menguliahi to lecture (s.o.), criticize.
  menguliahkan to lecture on (a subject), give a course on s.t.
  kuliahan *(sl)* classes, courses.
  penguliah lecturer.
  penguliahan curricular, classroom *(mod)*. *matéri* ~ course materials.
kulikat → KHALIKAH.
kulik-kulik female nocturnal cuckoo, *Eudynamis orientalis*; → CULIK-CULIK.
kuliling *(coq)* → KELILING.
kulim k.o. breadfruit tree that produces timber, *Scorodocarpus borneensis*.
kulimat *(M ob)* **(ber)kulimat** to curtail/reduce expenses, cut down on *(esp* food).

kulinér *(D)* culinary. *seni* – culinary art.
kulintang → KOLINTANG.
kulio *(M ob)* → KALIO.
kulir trowel.
kulis *(D)* expansion link.
kulit I 1 skin. **2** skin, peel, husk, shell (of a fruit/insect/turtle, etc.). – *apel* apple peel. – *pisang* banana skin. – *telur* eggshell. **3** hide (of an animal), pelt, leather. *sepatu* – leather shoes. **4** cover (of a magazine, etc.) – *buku* book cover. **5** crust (of the earth) – *bumi* earth's crust. **6** bark (of a tree). – *kayu* tree bark. **7** outside, exterior; superficial. *di/pada –nya saja, hanya di – saja* and *hanya yang nampak pada* – on the face of it; superficially; for the sake of appearances only. *Yang dibicarakan hanya –nya saja.* It was only superficially discussed. *jangan menilai – saja* don't judge just from appearances. *Badannya tinggal – pembalut tulang.* He was all skin and bones. *barang-barang* – leather wares. *di bawah* – subcutaneous. *kebal* – invulnerable (to weapons). *penyakit* – dermatomycosis, skin disease. *tebal* – thick-skinned. *terjemahan* – rough translation, not worked out in detail, not claiming to be exact or complete. *wayang* – shadow play with leather puppets. *tebal – muka* shameless, impudent, barefaced. *buka –, ambil isi* straight talk. – *adam* light-colored crescent at base of nail, new skin growing under the nail. – *ari* outer skin, epidermis, husk. – *atas* uppers (of shoes). – *badak* thick-skinned. **berkulit badak** thick-skinned, insensitive. – *basah* animal skin which has not yet been dried. – *batang* bark (of tree). – *benih (bot)* seed coat. – *berkikir* goose flesh. – *berwarna* colored people, people of color. – *besi* a) ferrous oxide. b) metal pads. – *biawak* lizard skin. – *buatan* imitation leather. – *buaya* crocodile leather. – *buku* book cover. – *bulu* fur pelt. – *bumi* outer crust of the earth. *(si)* – *bundar (coq)* the soccer ball. – *coklat* brown-skinned people, the Malay race. – *daging* relatives, family members. – *dalam* bast. – *gajah* thick-skinned. – *gendang* drum head. – *genjik* pigskin. – *gosok* chamois cloth. – *hitam* a) black people, Africans. b) dark-skinned. – *Inggris* moleskin. – *jangat* dermis. – *kambing* kid leather. – *kara* tortoiseshell. – *karah* tortoise shell. – *kayu* phloem. – *kebal* invulnerable. – *kelamin* foreskin. – *kepala* scalp. – *kepalan* sclerosis. – *kerang* seashell. – *khatan* foreskin, prepuce; → KULUP. – *kué* pie crust. – *lawan* → TÉJA *badak*. – *léndér/lendir* mucous membrane. – *lisut* dried-out skin (of old people). – *luar* outer skin, epidermis, cortex. – *manis* cinnamon, *Cassia vera*. – *mati* numb, insensitive. – *mentah* rawhide, untanned hide. *si – mérah* redskins, North American Indians. – *muka* front cover (of a magazine). – *mutiara* mother-of-pearl. – *odol* an empty toothpaste tube; → ODOL I. – *pari* rough skin. – *pegangan* strap (on public conveyance). – *pelindung* bark (of a tree). – *penggosok* chamois cloth. – *putih* white people, Caucasians, westerners; → BULÉ. *si – putih* the white man. – *rotan* rattan peel. – *roti* (bread) crust. – *samak* tanned leather. – *sampul* dust jacket. – *sapi* cowhide. – *sawo matang* brown-skinned people, the Malay race. – *sekam* rice husk. – *siput* snail shell. – *tanduk* horn. – *telur* eggshell. – *tiruan* imitation leather.
  sekulit ~ *sedaging* related to e.o.
  berkulit 1 to have a ... skin. ~ *hitam* to be black(-skinned). *Orang itu* ~ *hitam.* He has a black skin. ~ *badak* to be thick-skinned. **2** → MENGULIT 1.
  mengulit 1 to cast its skin, slough (off). **2** to become callous/horny. **3** to scalp, cut the scalp off.
  menguliti 1 to skin, peel (a potato, etc.). **2** to put a cover on, provide (a book, etc.) with a cover/jacket.
  pekulitan cover, jacket, wrapping.
  pengulit skinner.
  pengulitan skinning, peeling, flaying.
  perkulitan tannery.
kulit II – *lawang* a tree species, *Cinnamomum culilawan*, from whose bark a certain spice is obtained to make a medicine. – *manis* cinnamom, *Cinnamomum burmani*.
kulkas *(D)* refrigerator, icebox.
  mengkulkaskan to refrigerate.
kulkul a hollow block made out of a piece of bamboo which is beaten on to give a signal (for the hours/in emergencies/fire/theft, etc.); → KENTONGAN.

kulkulah (*A*) quavering of the voice.

kulminasi (*D*) culmination.

  mengkulminasi to culminate.

kulo'ipus (*Min*) a Manadonese dish made from a white-tailed rat.

kulon (*J/Jv*) west.

  bekulon on the west side.

  mengulon to the west, westward.

  ngulon(in) (*J*) move to the west.

kultivir (*D*) **mengkultivir** to cultivate.

  pengkultivir cultivator.

kultur (*D*) culture, civilization; → KEBUDAYAAN.

kultural (*E*) and **kulturil** (*D*) cultural.

kulturisasi (*D*) culturization.

kulturstélsel (*D*) cultivation system, i.e., system of forced cultivation of certain crops forced on Indonesia by the Dutch colonial government from 1830 to 1870.

kultus (*D*) cult. – *individu* [*kuli*] cult of the individual. *mengkultus-individukan* to deify, make a god of. *Saya tidak suka dikultusindividukan.* I don't want to be deified. – *perorangan* cult of the individual.

  meng(k)ultuskan to deify, make a god of, apotheosize.

  peng(k)ultusan deifying, deification.

kultuswan cultured man.

kulub I (*A*) heart; → HATI, JANTUNG, KALBU.

kulub II (*Jv*) **ngulub** to stew greens/leafy vegetables briefly.

  kuluban stewed greens/leafy vegetables.

kulub III → KULUP.

kuluk I (*Jv*) court headdress, a stiff white, green, or black fez without a tassel.

kuluk II – *uluk* beginning of children's chant asking for rain.

kulum I berkulum(-kulum) ~ *lidah* to French kiss (with tongues in e.o.'s mouths).

  mengulum [and **ngulum** (*coq*)] **1** to have/hold s.t. in the mouth, suck on s.t. ~ *senyum* to smirk, to smile because one doesn't want to say anything. *Lukisan Monalisa yang* ~ *senyum surgawi* the painting of the Mona Lisa with a heavenly smile on her face. *menjawab dengan suara napas dikulum* to answer with bated breath. *tersenyum* ~ to smirk, smile weakly. **2** to mumble, speak inarticulately, mutter under one's breath.

  kulum-mengulum ~ *lidah* to French kiss (with tongues in e.o.'s mouths).

  mengulumi [and **ngulumin** (*J coq*)] (*pl obj*) to suck on.

  kuluman s.t. sucked on.

  penguluman sucking.

kulum-kulum (*M*) a large millipede.

Kulunafsin zaikatulmaut (*A*) all men are mortal.

kulup (*A*) **1** prepuce, foreskin. **2** appellation for small boys (who have not yet been circumcised).

  berkulup not yet circumcised.

kulur *pohon* – breadfruit tree, *Artocarpus communis*; → SUKUN I.

kulut tree species whose wood is used for timber and boards, *Dysoxylum ramiflorum*.

kuluyuk (*C*) sweet and sour (cooking). *ayam* – sweet and sour chicken.

Kulzum *Laut* – the Red Sea.

Kum [*hukum*] **1** Legal Affairs. *Mayor (Kum) Ismét, S.H.* Major (Legal Affairs) Ismet, LL.M. **2** (in acronyms) → HUKUM I.

kumai (= **kumaian**) **1** carving(s) with milled edges or in relief (such as on picture frames/table legs, etc.). **2** raised border/edge on baskets.

  berkumai with raised edging. *sangkar ayam yang* ~ a chicken coop with a raised edge.

  meng(k)umai(kan) to provide (a picture frame, etc.) with raised carvings.

kuma-kuma 1 turmeric, *Curcuma domestica*; → KUNYIT I. **2** saffron.

kumal (*J*) **1** rumpled, crumpled, creased, dog-eared, wrinkled; → GUMAL. **2** dirty, filthy, messy. *daérah* – slum.

  sekumal as dog-eared/messy, etc. as.

  mengumalkan to rumple, crumple, crease.

  kekumalan dirt, filth; dirtiness.

kumala stone (found in snakes and dragons) that possesses magical powers. – *hikmat* magic bezoar.

kuman 1 (itch-)mite. **2** – *penyakit* parasite; bacterium, bacillus; germ, microbe. **3** particle of dust, mote, atom. *ilmu* –.– microbiology, bacteriology. *mencungkil* – *dengan alu* to carry coals to Newcastle. – *di seberang lautan tampak, gajah di pelupuk mata tidak tampak* to see the mote in the eye of others, but not the beam in one's own. – *beri bertali* to reach for the moon (or, s.t. unobtainable). – *air* (the organism responsible for) athlete's foot, *Tinea pedis*; → KUTU *air*.

  berkuman with mites, etc.

kumandang (*Jv*) echo, reverberation, resonance.

  berkumandang and **mengumandang 1** to (re-)echo, reverberate, resonate, resound. **2** to be broadcast.

  mengumandangkan 1 to cause to resound. **2** to voice (an opinion, etc).

kumanga and **kumango** *barang* – sundries (dishes/glassware, etc.).

Kumara (*Skr*) the Hindu god of war.

kumat (*Jv*) **1** attack (of asthma, etc.), bout (of the flu, etc.). **2** relapse, have a relapse; → ANGOT, BENTAN, KAMBUH.

  berkumat-kumat to keep on having relapses.

kumat-kamit → KOMAT-KAMIT.

kumayan → KEMENYAN I.

kumba I water pot. – *mayang* pot/basin decorated with palm blossoms used for ritual washing of the bride during the marriage ceremony.

kumba II (*Skr*) **1** prominent part of an elephant's forehead; ceremonial frontlet for elephants. **2** withers (of a horse).

Kumba III Aquarius (in the Zodiac).

kumbah (*Jv*) **mengumbah 1** to wash kris, launder, do the laundry. **2** to rinse (out). *Keméjanya dikumbah!* Wash your shirt.

  mengumbahi (*pl obj*) to wash/rinse. ~ *sayuran* to wash vegetables thoroughly.

  mengumbahkan to have s.t. washed, send s.o. out to be washed/laundered. ~ *pakaiannya di waserai* to have one's clothes laundered at a laundry.

  kumbahan laundry, clothing, etc., that has been or that is to be laundered. *air* ~ water that has been used to wash laundry, krises, etc.

kumbang 1 various species of bumblebee, *esp* the large gleaming-black variety. *angin* – the strong, dry wind which blows during the northeast monsoon. **2** various k.o. hard-winged insects, beetles or pests of various plants. **3** black (in color of animals). *seperti* – *dengan bunga* attracted to e.o. *seperti* – *putus talinya* gone forever. – *badak* rhinoceros beetle, *Oryctes rhinoceros*. – *(ber)tanduk* stag beetle, *Anomala cupripes*. – *hijau* chafer beetle, *Anomala cupripes*. – *janti* k.o. bee with green wings, *Lucanidae*. – *kayu* bark beetle, *Scolytidae*. – *kelapa/nyiur* coconut beetle, *Oryctes rhinoceros*, *Xylotropes gideon*. – *madu* honeybee. – *mangga* mango beetle, *Cryptorhynchus mangiferae*. – *moncong* weevil. – *nyiur* coconut beetle, *Oryctes rhinoceros*. – *orkid* (yellow) orchid beetle, *Lema pectoralis*. – *pél* scarab beetle, *Scarbaeus sacer*. – *penggérék batang* stem augur beetle, *Cosmolitus sordidus*. – *pisang* banana weevil, *Cosmopolites sordidus*. – *sagu* pest of the sago plant, *Rhynchophorus ferrugineus*. – *tahi* dung beetle, *Aphodius marginellus*. – *tanduk* atlas beetle, *Chalcosoma atlas*. – *tepung* yellow mealworm beetle, *Tenebrio molitor*. **4** beetle black in color (of panthers/dogs, etc.). *harimau/macan* – the black leopard, *Panthera pardus*. **5** (*Mal*) men that buzz around girls. *bunga diserang* – a deflowered girl. – *tidak seékor (bunga tidak sekali)* there's more than one fish in the sea.

  mengumbang to hum/buzz around (like bees around a flower). *sepéda* – moped, motorbike.

kumbar a palm with a short, thick stem and acid fruits eaten with curry, *Zalacca wallichiana*.

kumbara → KEMBARA.

kumbé (*J*) → KUMBAH.

kumbik (*pohon* -) candlenut tree, *Aleurites moluccana* and its fruit.

kumbu → KEMBU.

kumbuh *mensiang* – and *rumput* – sedges used for matting, *Scirpus grossus/mucronatus*.

kumbul (*naut*) poop.

kumel (*J*) dirty, dull (not shining).

kumi (*Port ob*) (please) eat.

kumico (during *Jap* occupation) head of a neighborhood association.

kumidi → KOMIDI.

kumilap → GEMILAP, KEMILAP.

kumin (*Mal*) particles; very small quantity.
sekumin a little bit, a small amount.

kuminiké → KOMUNIKÉ.

kuminter (*Jv*) opinionated, conceited, to pretend to be smarter than one is.

kumis I mustache. – *kepalan* mustachio.
berkumis and **kumisan** to have a mustache.

kumis II (*D*) (departmental) clerk; customshouse officer; → KOMIS.

kumis III – *kucing* a garden herb, *Orthosiphon grandiflorus* with medicinal leaves (*daun – kucing*) for treatment of renal calculus/kidney stones.

kumisi → KOMISI I.

kumit (*Mal*); → KUMIN.

kumkuma (*Pers*) turmeric, saffron, *Crocus sativus*.

kumlah *mati* – to die a natural death.

kumpai *rumput* – a) swamp grass used for candle wicks, *Hymenachne myurus*, *Lycopodium phlegmaria*. b) a grass used for fodder, *Panicum stagnium*.

kumpal I → GUMPAL. **berkumpal** to coagulate, clot.
pengumpal *bahan* ~ coagulant.

kumpal II (*J ob*) – *kampil* poor. **terkumpal-kampil** to lead a precarious existence, always struggling (of the poor); → TERKATUNG-KATUNG.
terkumpal-kumpal struggling (of the poor).

kumpar mengumpar to wind thread on a reel.
kumparan reel, spool, bobbin, coil. ~ *ciut* impedance coil.

kumpeni (*D J ob*); → KOMPENI. *téken* – (*col mil*) to enlist in the service, sign up.

kumpi (*J*) great-grandparent; → MOYANG.

kumplit → KOMPLIT.

kumpul (*J/Jv*) gather, get together. *mangan ora mangan* – (*Jv*), *makan nggak makan* – (*J*) and *makan tak makan asal* – whether we have s.t. to eat or not, the important thing is togetherness. – *kebo* to live together without being married. **mengumpul-keboi** to live with s.o. without being married. – *satu* united into a single unit. **mengumpul-satukan** to unite, bring together (into one unit).
berkumpul 1 to gather, come together (in a group), assemble, meet (as a group), (*mil*) fall into line. *hak* ~ *dan berapat* the right of assembly and public meeting. **2** together, in a group. *duduk* ~ to sit together. **3** (= **terkumpul** *kepada*) to join, unite (with), associate (with), combine/mix (together with). **4** to re-unite. ~ *kembali setelah bertahun-tahun berpisah* to reunite after many years of separation. **5** (= **berkumpul-kumpul**) to swarm, flock, mass, crowd.
mengumpul 1 converging, collective. *perdagangan* ~ collective trade. *sinar* ~ converging rays/beams. **2** cumulative.
ngumpul (*coq*) *sifatnya* ~ it has a cumulative effect. ~ *bareng* to get together.
mengumpuli (*pl obj*) to collect, gather.
mengumpulkan [and **ngumpulin** (*J coq*)] **1** to call together, convoke, convene (people). **2** to collect (coins/stamps, etc.). ~ *ingatannya/pikirannya* to collect one's thoughts; to come to one's self again (after having been unconscious). **3** to add/count up. **4** to concentrate (forces), mobilize (troops), get up (the energy to do s.t.). **5** to gather, assemble (people), bring together.
terkumpul gathered, assembled.
kumpulan 1 a collection (of things). ~ *barang anéh* curiosa. ~ *tumbuh-tumbuhan* herbarium. **2** crowd, group (of people, etc.) ~ *orang* crowd. ~ *sapi* herd of cattle. **3** assembly, gathering, meeting. **4** meeting place, place of assembly.
pengumpul collector. ~ *prangko* stamp collector, philatelist. ~ *suara* vote getter; → PEMANCING *suara*. ~ *uang* a) fund raiser. b) coin collector, numismatist.
pengumpulan 1 gathering, collecting, assembling. ~ *pendapat umum* and ~ *suara* (opinion) poll. ~ *uang* fund raising. **2** collection. ~ *prangko* stamp collection.
perkumpulan 1 club, association, society, organization, union. ~

agama congregation. ~ *amal* charitable society. ~ *dagang* chamber of commerce; → KAMAR *Dagang dan Industri*. ~ *débat* debating club. ~ *gelap* illegal organization. ~ *kematian* burial society, i.e., an organization which provides funeral services to its members. ~ *menabung* savings association. ~ *olahraga* sports club. ~ *rahasia* secret society. **2** meeting.

kumsum (*ob*) → KOMSÉN I.

kumuh (*M*) dirty, soiled. *daérah perkampungan kota yang* – and *kawasan yang* – slum.
mengumuhkan to dirty, soil, stain.
terkumuh 1 the slummiest. **2** the dirtiest.
kekumuhan dirtiness.

kumul (*ob*) → KUMAL.

kumulasi (*D*) cumulation.

kumulatif (*D/E*) cumulative.

kumulus (*D/E*) cumulus (clouds).

kumur *obat* – mouthwash.
berkumur to rinse one's mouth, gargle, rinse one's mouth.
berkumur-kumur to gargle.
mengumur to rinse (one's mouth).
kumuran mouthwash.

kumus a large tree from which timber poles for houses and bridges are made, *Shorea laevis*.

kumut (*ob*) **berkumut** to grin (like an ape, etc.).

kun I (*A*) – *fayakun* Become and it came into being! (the words by which God created the world).
mengunkan to preordain (by God).

kun II (*C*) skirt, apron.

kuna → KUNO.

kunang-kunang I 1 firefly, *Lampyris spp*. **2** ghost that hovers around a mountain, field, or *sawah* carrying a burning torch on Thursday nights. **3** will-o'-the-wisp. – *sekebun* a ring whose single gem is surrounded by a setting of many tiny diamonds.

kunang-kunang II berkunang-kunang 1 to glitter, shine, sparkle. **2** to see stars (from a blow). *Matanya* ~. He saw stars.
mengunang-ngunangkan to make one's head spin. *Minuman keras baunya mulai* ~ *kepalaku*. The smell of hard liquor made my head spin.

kunani (*M*) *si* – name of a legendary white fighting-cock; → KINANTAN.

kunarpa (*Skr*) corpse.

kunca I a small basket.

kunca II (*Jv*) train, i.e., the part of a dress, etc. that trails on the ground, lappet (of a *kain*).

kunca(h) (*ob*) **1** a bundle (of paddy), bale (of straw, etc.). **2** cubic measure of about 1,330 lbs or 160 *gantangs*.

kuncara (*Jv ob*) widely known, famous, renowned.

kuncén (*Jv*) keeper of the *kunci* or key to (or, caretaker of) (a place of worship, sacred grove, etc.); → JURU *kunci*.

Kunchantang (*C*) Communist China.

kunché a clever elephant (in the training school for elephants in Lampung, South Sumatra).

kunci I 1 lock (= *ibu* –). *tidak memakai* – doesn't have a lock, cannot be locked. *membuka* – to unlock (a padlock). **2** (= *anak* –) key, i.e., an instrument for winding a clock. *Coba putarkan jam yang mati itu dengan* – *ini*. Please wind the clock that's stopped with this key. **3** a) clue, solution. – *kecurangan-kecurangan* the key to the fraud. b) key, i.e., the answers to a set of exercises/problems. – *itu khusus untuk keperluan guru*. The key is only for the teacher. c) close, end, termination, final part (of an article/explanation, etc.). *Beberapa kesimpulan dan anjuran dicantumkan sebagai* – *karangannya itu*. The end of his article contains some solutions and suggestions. **4** key, i.e., the controlling/essential/important point. *kedudukan* – key position/employee, main (speaker). **5** (*mus*) key, clef. **6** spanner, wrench. **7** (*M*) joint. – *paha* groin. **8** (*coq*) fastened; keyed, locked. – *arloji* watch key. – *buaya* breakout tongs. – *busi* spark-plug wrench. – *cagak* fork wrench. – *dobel* duplicate key. – *duplikat* duplicate key. – *gabungan* combination lock. – *ganda* master key. – *gantung/gembok* padlock. – *gurat* pin wrench. – *induk* master key. – *ingatan* aid to memory, mnemonic device. – *inggris* monkey wrench. – *jam* watch key. – *kendaraan* ignition key. –

kesuksésan key to success. – *kontak* ignition key. – *kotrék* ratchet. – *kura-kura* padlock. – *loncéng* watch key. – *maling* master/skeleton key. – *mati* a) closely guarded secret. b) deadlock, impasse. – *pas* open-end wrench. – *pasak* tumbler lock. – *pengaman* pin (on a grenade). – *pipa* pipe wrench. – *pistol* safety pin (of a pistol). – *rantai* a) (*petro*) chain tongs. b) chain lock. – *rékening* (in Manado) in the end, finally. – *ring* box-end wrench. – *roda* lug wrench. – *sekrup* wrench, spanner. – *selubung* a) chain tongs. b) (*petro*) casing tongs. – *senapan* safety pin (of a gun). – *sok* socket wrench. – *suksés* key to success. – *tabung* pipe wrench. – *télepon* telephone locks. – *tolak* master key. – *tombol* shutter release. – *wasiat* a) secret, mystery. b) s.t. used to divulge (a secret, etc.).

kunci-kunci (*M*) joint. ~ *lutut* knee joint, patella.

berkunci 1 to use a key. **2** locked with a key.

mengunci [and **ngunci** (*coq*)] **1** to lock. ~ *mati* to lock s.t. up tight. **2** to fasten, lock s.t. *Sepéda harus dikunci.* Bicycles must be locked. **3** to end, conclude, close, wind up. ~ *pembicaraan* ... winding up his talk ... **4** to shut, zip (one's mouth). *Kunci mulutmu!* Shut your mouth!

menguncikan 1 to fasten, lock, lock in. **2** to shut (one's mouth). ~ *bibirnya* to shut one's mouth.

terkunci 1 locked. *sepéda motor* ~ a locked motorbike. **2** shut tight. *Mulutnya* ~. He was speechless. ~ *rapat* shut tight.

kuncian joint (of a bayonet).

pengunci 1 lock, clasp, bolt, hook (of a door, etc.). **2** conclusion, end, last part (of a book, etc.). **3** key, important (point).

penguncian locking.

kunci II *temu* – a tuberous plant, *Gastrochilus panduratum*, a root similar to ginger in taste and used as a spice and in folk medicine. – *fatimah* k.o. tree used to expedite labor and as a tonic after childbirth and for certain medicinal uses, *Labisia pothoina*. – *pepet* k.o. plant, narrow-leaf peacock ginger *Kaempferia angustifolia*. – *putih* round-rooted galangal, *Kaempferia rotunda*.

kuncir and **kuncit** → KUCIR.

kuncoro → KUNCARA.

kuncung I (*Jv*) **1** forelock. **2** tuft, crest (of birds); → GOMBAK, JAMBUL.

berkuncung crested.

kuncung II *burung* – green peafowl, *Pavo muticus*.

kuncup I 1 closing (of a flower), closing/shutting (of an umbrella); *opp* KEMBANG I, II. **2** bud (of flowers/leaves). – *hatinya* afraid. **menguncup hatinya** to become afraid. – *jantung* contraction of the heart. – *liar/tambahan* accessory/adventitious bud. **3** (*ob coq*) uncircumcised.

menguncup 1 to bud (of a flower). **2** to contract, shrink, close shut, shut. **2** to resemble a flower bud.

menguncupkan to shut, close, fold, furl. ~ *payung* to close an umbrella. ~ *tangan* to fold the hands (in prayer).

terkuncup furled.

kuncup II → KECUP, KUCUP I, II.

kundai (*Tam*) bun, knot of hair; → KONDÉ, SANGGUL. *tusuk* – hairpin.

berkundai to wear a bun.

mengundai to put one's hair up in a bun.

kundak [kunjungan mendadadak] sudden, unexpected visit. *mengadakan* – to make such a visit.

kundang I (*ob*) *budak* **kundangan** page who served Malay royalty; court page; → JUAK-JUAK.

kundang II (*M*) **mengundang** to take s.o. everywhere with one.

berkundang favorite.

kundangan favorite. *anak* ~ a child tied to his mother's apron strings; mother's pet.

kundang III (*J*) **1** invited guest; → KONDANGAN. **2** invitation; → UNDANG I. **3** to go to a party/feast.

kundangan invitation.

kundang IV *tali* – a) bandage for umbilical cord. b) bandage used after circumcision.

kundangan a tree, *Bouea macrophylla*, which provides wood used to make furniture and leaves for *lalap*.

kundé-kundé *ikan* – rainbow rockfish, *Stethojulis kalosoma*.

kundi (*M*) a half-red, half-black pea, rosary pea, *Abrus precatorius*; formerly used as a goldsmith's weight of 1½ to 2 grams.

kundur I wax gourd, *Benincasa hispida/cerifera*, calabash; → BELIGU. – *tidak melata pergi, labu tidak melata mari* it takes two to tango, i.e., every agreement must come from both sides.

kundur II (*Jv*) (honorific) to go home.

kunfayakun → KUN I.

kung (*onom*) **1** clanging sound (of a small gong). **2** baying (of dogs). **3**a) the sound of the *perkutut* dove. b) to have a fine singing voice (of that dove).

kungkang I slow loris, sloth, *Nycticebus tardigradus*. *agih-agih* – too generous by nature and therefore making trouble for o.s. *seperti* – shy.

mengungkang 1 to be lazy, work-shy, indolent, sluggish. **2** to nibble/gnaw at.

kungkang II k.o. large water frog or toad; → KANGKUNG I.

kungki k.o. tree, *Pometia pinnata*, whose wood is used to make wooden mortars and whose bark produces a medicine for combating suppurating wounds.

kungkum (*Jv*) sit with the body in water, take a bath by immersing the body in water; → MANDI *kungkum. tapa* – to practice asceticism by immersing one's body in a stream (the whole night for nine consecutive Thursday nights).

kungkuma → KUMKUMA, KUNYIT I.

kungkung shackles, locks (for a prisoner); → KONGKONG I.

mengungkung 1 to contain, impede, check, thwart. *Konflik Kamboja bisa dikungkung.* The Cambodian conflict can be contained. **2** to shackle, lock up. **3** to enslave, dominate.

mengungkungi to dominate, oppress, crush, govern tyrannically, keep down by force. *Rakyat dikungkungi oléh marihuana.* The people were enslaved by marijuana.

terkungkung to be enslaved/confined. *masyarakat Bengkulu yang pernah* ~ *oléh isolasi yang ketat* Bengkulu, once enslaved by a rigid isolation.

kungkungan 1 chains, fetters, shackles. **2** domination, confines, constraints. *Kawasan ini baru lepas dari* ~ *gerombolan bersenjata.* This region has just been freed from the domination of armed gangs.

pengungkung s.t. that confines, restraint.

pengungkungan confinement.

kuning I 1 yellow. **2** the color of royalty; the color associated with GOLKAR. **3** light brown (of leather). **4** warning (card in soccer); → KARTU *kuning. Keluar keringat –nya.* He broke out in a cold sweat. – *oléh kunyit, hitam oléh arang* easily falling prey to criticism or flattery. *hari* – the sky looks yellow, i.e., a sign of bad luck; → MAMBANG. *mambang* – luminous yellowish-red evening sky, i.e., spirits of sunset. *nasi* – saffron rice (served on special occasions). *Pasukan* – the Jakarta road-cleaning crews (who wear yellow uniforms). – *pucat* amber (color). *putih* – cream-colored. *sakit* – jaundice. *sirih* – a) ripe betel leaf. b) nubile girl, i.e., one ripe for love. – *bléwah* peach-colored. – *cempaka* saffron yellow. – *(e)mas* golden, gold color. *si* – *Emas* rice. – *gading* cream (colored). – *gersing* pure yellow. – *janur* greenish yellow. – *jenar* reddish yellow. – *jingga* orange (color). – *keemasan* golden yellow. – *kepodang* bright yellow; → KEPODANG. – *kunyit* chrome yellow. – *langsat/langsep* yellowish white (considered a beautiful complexion for women). – *limau* lemon yellow. – *lulur* amber-colored. – *mas* golden yellow. – *pepaya* light reddish yellow. – *telur* egg yolk.

menguning to turn/become yellow, ripen (of rice plants).

menguningkan to make s.t. yellow.

kekuningan 1 (= **kekuning-kuningan**) yellowish. **2** (*cla*) yellow regalia worn by royalty (taboo for commoners).

kuning II *akar* – a climbing plant that provides yellow dye, *Fibraurea chloroleuca*.

kuning III *burung* – black-headed bulbul, *Pycnonotus atriceps*.

kuningan brass; → KUNING I.

kuningisasi using the color yellow in public places, e.g., painting walls yellow, as a sign of support for GOLKAR.

kunir I (*Jv*) → KUNYIT I. – *asem* a *jamu* for keeping the vagina sweet smelling.

kunir II *ikan* – sulfur/yellow goatfish, *Upeneus sulphureus*.

kunit (*ob*) → KUNYIT.

kunjung I berkunjung ~ *ke* to visit, (pay a) call on, (go) see, attend (a lecture).
berkunjung-kunjungan to visit e.o.
kunjung-mengunjung to socialize, visit e.o.
mengunjungi [and **ngunjungin** (*J coq*)] **1** to visit s.o., call on, go to see s.o., look s.o. up. **2** to attend, be present at.
kunjungan visit, social call. ~ *balasan* return visit. ~ *kenegaraan* state visit. ~ *kehormatan* courtesy call. ~ *kerja* working visit. ~ *melimpah* a full house. ~ *mendadak* [*kundak*] a sudden unexpected visit (*esp* of a high-ranking official for an inspection). ~ *muhibah* (*ke*) a goodwill visit (to). ~ *pamitan* farewell visit. ~ *perkenalan* introductory visit. ~ *sehari* one-day visit. ~ *singkat* short visit. *mendapatkan* ~ to receive visitors.
pengunjung visitor. ~ *setia* loyal patron, regular customer.
pengunjungan visit, visiting.
perkunjungan visit; → KUNJUNGAN.
kunjung II (*M*) quickly, easily. *belum* – never (up to now, so far). *tidak/tak* – never, at no time, not quickly/easily. *tak* – *berubah* permanent. *tak* – *hilang* abiding, lasting. *sumber yang tak* – *kering* a never-ending source. *tak* – *padam* inextinguishable. *tak* – *puas* insatiable, never satisfied. *tak* – *tidak* a) it's inevitable, must, have to. b) certainly, of course.
kuno (*Jv*) **1** old (story, etc.). **2** ancient, antiquated, archaic. **3** dated, out-of-date, obsolete, conservative (ideas). *adat* – old and obsolete traditions. *bahasa Jawa* – Old Javanese. *barang-barang* – antiques. *jaman* – olden times. *kepercayaan* – old (and outdated) beliefs. *kesusastraan* – ancient/classical literature. *masyarakat* – primitive people.
sekuno as ancient/dated/out-of-date as.
terkuno the oldest, most ancient.
kekunoan 1 oldness. **2** antiquity, obsoleteness. **3** relic. **4** conservatism.
kunsdruk (*D*) *kertas* – fine-quality paper.
kunta (*Jv*) javelin, the spear thrown by Rawana in the Ramayana.
kuntal-kantil → KONTAL-KANTIL.
kuntau (*C*) Chinese art of self-defense. *main* – and
berkuntau to perform this art.
kuntel (*J*) **menguntel** [and **nguntel** (*coq*)] to tie s.t. up in a piece of cloth.
kuntét → KONTÉT.
kunti (*S*) a k.o. ghost; → JURIK.
kuntianak → KUNTILANAK.
kuntilanak (*J*) the spirit of a woman, who has a hole in her back, who died during pregnancy or confinement and who now wants to take possession of a woman who has just given birth or kidnap a baby in order to experience the joys of motherhood; → PUNTIANAK.
kuntit (*J*) **menguntit 1** to chase after, pursue, run after, trail, tail, shadow, follow secretly, put under surveillance. **2** to imitate, follow as an example.
menguntiti [and **nguntitin** (*J coq*)] to pursue, chase after, shadow, stalk.
penguntit 1 pursuer, tail, shadow, stalker, groupie. **2** runner-up.
penguntitan pursuit, chase, surveillance, tailing, trailing, shadowing, stalking.
kuntuan (*C*) satin-like silk.
kuntuk various k.o. egrets. – *kecil* little egret, *Egretta garzetta*. – *kerbau* cattle egret, *Bubulcus ibis*.
kuntul I tailless (of fowl). *ayam* – a chicken without a tail.
kuntul II → KONTOL I.
kuntul III (*Jv*) various species of egret and heron; (– *besar*) great white egret, *Egretta alba*. – *belang* pied heron, *Egretta picata*. – *karang/hitam* (Pacific) reef egret, *Egretta sacra*. – *kecil* little egret, *Egretta garzetta*. – *kerbau* cattle egret, *Bubulcus ibis*. – *malam* black-crowned night heron, *Nycticorax nycticorax*. – *pérak* intermediate egret, *Egretta intermedia*. – *putih besar* great white egret, *Egretta alba*. – *sedang* intermediate egret, *Egretta intermedia*.
kuntum I 1 bud, a partly opened flower. **2** a nubile/budding young girl. – *piari* clitoris. **3** virgin.
berkuntum and **menguntum** to bud, begin to develop.
terkuntum opened (of bud), in bud.

kuntum II counter for flowers. *se- bunga* a flower.
kuntung (*C*) pigtail (formerly worn by Chinese men).
kunun → KONON I.
kunut → QUNUT.
kunyado (*Port IBT*) brother-in-law.
kunyah *tablét* – chewable tablet. – *dahulu, maka telan* look before you leap.
mengunyah [and **ngunyah** (*coq*)] **1** to chew, masticate. **2** to chew on, think about. **3** digest (a lesson/knowledge). **4** to rake up (= **mengunyah-ngunyah**) old stories.
mengunyahkan to chew s.t. (for s.o. else); unfortunate. ~ *di nasi* lucky, fortunate.
terkunyah 1 chewed/masticated unintentionally. **2** digested. ~ *di batu* unlucky.
kunyahan s.t. already chewed, cud.
pengunyah s.t. that chews, chewing.
pengunyahan chewing, masticating.
kunyam (*M*) shrunken, sunken in, pinched (of cheeks).
kunyit I saffron, turmeric, *Curcuma domestica*; → KONÉNG, TEMU II. *empu/ibu* – the large underground stem of this plant. *anak* – the branches of this plant. *daun* – the leaves of this plant used in cooking. *akar* – a climbing plant which provides a yellow dye, *Fibraurea chloroleuca*; → AKAR *kuning*. *beras* – yellow (uncooked) rice sprinkled about as a sign of welcome at ceremonies. *nasi* – (cooked) yellow/saffron rice served on special occasions. *temu* – a plant, *Curcuma longa* of the ginger family whose powdered root is used as a dye, as a seasoning, and in medicine. – *jawa* anatto, Tamil safflower, *Bixa orellana*, which produces a red dye.
kunyit II *belalang* – saffron grasshopper, *Valanga nigricornis*.
kunyit III *burung* – generic term for orioles, *Oriolus spp. burung* – *besar* black-naped oriole, *Oriolus chinensis diffusus. burung* – *kecil* black-headed oriole, *Oriolus xanthornus*.
kunyuk (*J/Jv*) **1** k.o. monkey. **2** idiot, imbecile. – *keparat itu* that damn stupid ass. – *lu!* What's your problem, asshole!
kunyung (*ob*) → KONYONG.
kuorum (*D/E*) quorum.
kuo tie (*C*) k.o. boiled and then sautéed wontons.
kuota → KWOTA.
Kuoyu /gwo-yu/ Putonghua, the form of Mandarin Chinese adopted as the official national language of China.
kup I howdah (on elephant).
kup II (*D*) coupe, cut (of a dress).
kup III (*D*) coup (d'état).
mengkup to overturn the government.
kup IV (*D*) cup.
kupa various k.o. trees with edible fruit, *Eugenia spp.*
kupak 1 (*M*) smashed, broken, damaged, spoiled. **2** (*J*) when the first baby tooth falls out.
berkupak burst, broken/forced open.
mengupak to break/force open, burst.
kupakan broken pieces, fragments, shards, splinters.
kupang I 1 ancient currency which varied in value from place to place. **2** a goldsmith's weight equal to about 1/16 of a *tahil*.
kupang II various species of sea mussels, *Mytilus spp.* – *lontong* mussels inside *lontong*.
kupang III *daun* – k.o. herb, *Cassia alata*, whose leaves are used to treat skin diseases.
kupas I mengupas [and **ngupas** (*coq*)] **1** to peel (skin/fruit/coconut shell, etc.), pare (fruit), husk (rice), shell (eggs), scalp. **2** to strip, take the clothes off s.o.
mengupasi to peel/husk/shell.
mengupaskan 1 to peel/husk/shell for s.o. else. **2** to strip, take the clothes off s.o.
terkupas stripped, skinned, shelled, peeled, husked.
kupasan s.t. that has been peeled/stripped/skinned/shelled/husked.
pengupas s.o. or s.t. that peels/strips/skins/shells/husks.
pengupasan peeling, husking, shelling, stripping, depulping.
kupas II mengupas to analyze, study (problem/substance), comment on (a text), explain, criticize, review (a work).
kupasan analysis, study, etc.

pengupas analyst.

pengupasan analysis, (scientific) study, criticism, critique, commentary.

kupat (*coq*) → KETUPAT I.

kupat-kapit (*J*) 1 to flap/flutter (of an empty sack). 2 to droop, hang down loosely (of a tail).

kupé (*D*) compartment (in a train).

Kupedés [Krédit Umum Pedésaan] General Credit for Rural Areas.

kupel (*D*) dome(-shaped top), arch, cupola.

kupér [kurang pergaulan] (*BG*) antisocial.

kupét (*D*) 1 bulb (of a thermometer). 2 developing tray (in photography).

kupi I powder flask/keg.

kupi II → KOPI I.

kupiah → KOPIAH.

kupik (*ob*) → KUBIK I.

kupil mengupil to shell (peas, etc.), scale (fish), remove (bark/husk) from. ~ *jagung* to peel kernels of corn from the ear.

kuping I (*Jv*) ear; → TELINGA I. - *rasanya panas* embarrassed.
  sekuping up to one's ear, reach one's ear.
  berkuping ~ *panas* to feel embarrassed/ashamed.
  berkuping ~ *tipis* overly sensitive
  nguping (*coq*) 1 to overhear. 2 to tap (a telephone line). 3 to monitor. 4 to eavesdrop. *tukang* ~ eavesdropper. ~ *sana-sini* a) to eavesdrop here and there. b) to keep an ear to the ground. 5 (*sl*) to steal the side-view mirrors of cars.
  penguping *si* ~ eavesdropper.
  pengupingan eavesdropping.

kuping II various k.o. fungi. *jamur* - an edible fungus, *Auricularia*. - *besi* k.o. plant whose leaves are used to reduce stomach pain, *Callicarpa cana*. - *cangkir* a plant with large dark-green leaves resembling an elephant's ear. - *gajah* a) k.o. plant, *Anthurium spp*. b) k.o. cookie. - *menjangan* an herb whose leaves are used as a remedy against coughs, *Plantago major*. - *tikus* a) edible mushroom/fungus, *Auricularia Bulliard*. b) k.o. fried cassava chip sprinkled with sugar.

kuping III scab.

kupir I (*D coq*) cutter, tailor.

kupir II (*D*) **mengkupir** to cut (the cards).

kuplét (*D*) couplet.

kupling → KOPELING.

kupluk I (*Jv*) k.o. fez.

kupluk II (*sl*) stupid; → GOBLOK.

kupnat (*D*) dart (in sewing).

kupon (*D*) coupon, voucher. - *berhadiah* coupon entitling bearer to a gift. - *makanan* food coupon. - *undian* lottery ticket.

kuprum (*D*) cuprum, copper.

kupu (*A*) equal (in position/descent/due to marriage).
  sekupu of the same rank, of equal status, belonging to the same caste.
  kupuan *sama* ~ of the same origin/descent/stock.

kupui a tree, *Connaropsis sp*. whose fruit is used to prepare *sayur* (vegetable soup) or sweets.

kupu-kupu I butterfly, moth. *gaya* - butterfly stroke (in swimming). - *malam* (*coq*) prostitute. - *putih* → HAMA *sundep*. - *tamu* butterfly which enters the house (meaning there is going to be a visitor).

kupu-kupu II a small tree, *Bauhinia acuminata/tomentosa*, whose hard wood is used for making kris hilts.

kupur I → KUFUR.

kupur II (*akar* -) various k.o. shrubs, *Rubus spp*.

kupyah → KOPIAH.

kupyak (*J*) **mengupyak** [and **ngupyak** (*coq*)] to rinse, wash, bathe. *Ketika adikku perempuan melangkahiku kawin lebih dulu, aku disuruh* ~ *di kali Cimanuk, agar supaya sial yang melekat di diriku hilang*. When my younger sister got married before I did, I was told to bathe in the Cimanuk river so that the bad luck that had stuck to me would disappear.

kur I 1 (*onom*) coo of the ring-dove. 2 cluck! cluck! i.e., cry for calling fowl and birds (as well as the soul personified as a bird); → KURSEMANGAT.

kur II → KOOR.

kura I spleen. *demam* - malaria with enlarged spleen.

kura II (*Port*) 1 the wash. 2 to hang out the wash.

kurai vein (in marble/wood/kris blades, etc.).
  berkurai veined, marbled.

Kuraisy (*A*) Koreish, name of an Arab tribe in ancient Mecca to which Muhammad belonged.

kura-kura I tortoise, turtle. - *dalam perahu* to pretend ignorance (a rhyme on *pura-pura tidak tahu*). - *hendak memanjat kayu* and *seperti* - *hendak memanjat pohon kayu* it is impossible to attain. - *kali* freshwater turtle with soft carapace, *Tryonix spp*., *Pelochelys spp*. - *laut* sea turtle. - *sawah* k.o. box turtle common in rice paddies, *Cuora/Cyclemys amboinensis*.

kura-kura II *kunci* - padlock. - *jendéla* window sill. - *kaki* instep. - *tangan* back of the hand.

kurambit → KERAMBIT.

Kuran and **Kur'an** → KORAN, QUR'AN.

kurandus (*D*) ward of the court.

kurang [compounds beginning with *kurang* are found under the following root] 1 - (*dari*) less (than). - *dari sepuluh menit* less than ten minutes. *tidak* - no less, not less; no less a person than. *tidak* - *lihainya* no less sly. *tidak* - *dari Présidén Soeharto menyatakan* ... no less a person than President Soeharto stated ... 2a) not enough, insufficient. - *besar* not big enough. b) short (amount). - *500 dolar* 500 dollars short. - *tidur* not get enough sleep. 3 little, few. - *banyak* a) much too little. b) far too few. *berpengetahuan* - *mengenai* to have little knowledge of, have little acquaintance with. 4 (*makin* -) to decrease, decline; to abate, diminish. *perhatian makin* - attention (to this) is declining. *anginnya makin* - the wind is abating. 5 lacking, missing. - *beberapa halaman* some pages are missing. *tak* - (*satu*) *apa-apa* lacking nothing, all right. *Anda* - *apa? Tak* - *apa-apa*. What's wrong? Nothing, I'm fine. *tanpa* - *suatu apa* lacking nothing. *tidak* - in abundance, to be in good supply, abundant. *makanan tidak* - food is abundant. 6 to reduce, cut, lower (prices). (*Apa) tidak boléh* -? Could (the price) be reduced? 7 not, un-, under-. *serba* - underprivileged. - *bayar* underpaid. - *kuat* weak. - *senang* unpleasant. - *tahu* (I'm) not sure. 8 (*math*) minus. *enam* - *dua* six minus two. 9 to, of, before (in telling time). *pukul delapan* - *lima* (*menit*) five minutes to eight. 10 almost, about, not quite. *bekerjanya di pabrik ini 20 tahun* - to have worked in this factory for almost 20 years. *masih* - *tiga minggu lagi* still almost three weeks to go/from now. *delapan tahun* - not quite eight years. 11 to fail, fall short, not be/have enough. 12 fail (a school grade). *Dia* - *mengerti*. He doesn't quite understand. 13 (+ *adj* + *daripada*) not as/so ... as. *kota ini* - *ramai daripada Jakarta* this city is not as busy as Jakarta. 14 balance, rest, remainder. *yang dibayarnya tidak cukup, banyak juga* -*nya* what he paid was not sufficient, the balance was quite large. *paling* - a) at the very least. b) at least. *Salah-salah bisa gagal dua-duanya, atau paling* -, *salah satu tidak berhasil*. If things do not go right, both of them could fail, or at least, one of them would not succeed. - *adab/adat* a) unmannerly, impolite, rude. b) damn! - *agrésif* unaggressive. - *ajar* a) ill-bred, rude. b) exclamation of irritation or annoyance. **kekurang-ajaran** rudeness, bad behavior. - *akal* a) not very bright. b) hairbrained. - *asam/asem* (*euph* for - *ajar*). - *asin* a) not salty enough. b) (exclamation of annoyance) For heaven's sake! - *awas* negligent. - *bahasa* impolite, rude, bad-mannered. - *baik* not so/very good. - *biasa* unused (to doing s.t.), unaccustomed. - *bumbu* uninteresting. - *dalam* shallow. - *darah* anemic. - *dengar* hard of hearing. - *ékor* humorous *euph* for - *ajar*. - *garam* a) insipid, tasteless. b) inexperienced. - *hati* discouraged, disheartened; timid, shy, easily frightened. - *ingat* a) forgetful, thoughtless. b) imprudent, careless. c) indiscreet. - *ingatan* mad, insane, deranged. - *jadi* a) not grow well, do well (of a tree). b) not turn out well (of a photograph). - *jantan* weak, sissified. - *karat* of inferior quality. - *lancar* a) not go smoothly enough. b) not speak fluently. - *lebih* [k.l.] and *lebih* - [l.k.] more or less, approximately. - *makan* a) undernourished. b) (*euph*) starving. - *minum* dehydrated, desiccated. - *pandai* not very clever/smart/skillful. - *pegawai* short of staff. - *pencahayaan* underexposed (of photograph). - *pengalaman* inexperienced. – *perhatian* inattentive. – *periksa* (polite) I don't know, I haven't thought about it. – *pikir* thoughtless, inconsiderate, irresponsible. – *pikiran* stupid. – *puas* dissatisfied, discontented. – *sedikit* a little bit short. – *serasi* in disharmony. – *sesén* (*coq*) crazy, deranged. – *sopan* impolite, rude. – *terima* ungrateful. – *tidur* not get enough sleep. – *uang* short of funds. – *waras* (*otak*) crazy, deranged.

kurangnya the fault with, what's wrong with. *Apa* ~? What's wrong with it?

kurang-kurang 1 ~ ... (*lebih-lebih* ...) the less ... (the more ...). ~ *makanannya lebih-lebih lapar saya*. The less there is to eat, the hungrier I become. **2** if/in case ... fall short. ~ *sabar, tak dapat jadi* if you're impatient, it won't succeed. *tidak* ~ not any less, no less. *Tidak* ~ *kesibukan yang harus dibebankan ke pundak Menteri Keuangan*. The work loaded on the shoulders of the Finance Minister has not decreased.

sekurang *tidak* ~ not as/so.

sekurang-kurangnya at (the very) least. ~ *satu juta rupiah* at least one million rupiahs. *bagaimana bengis sekalipun meréka,* ~ *tentu mempunyai belas kasihan terhadap seorang bayi* no matter how cruel they are, at least they'll feel sorry for a baby.

berkurang to diminish, wear off, lessen, decline, abate, decrease. *Pendapatan negara semakin* ~. State revenues are declining. *Penyakitnya* ~. His illness is getting better. *hasil* ~ decreasing returns.

berkurang-kurangan to continue to decrease, keep on getting less.

mengurang to decrease, abate.

mengurangi [and **ngurangin** (*J coq*)] **1** to decrease, diminish, reduce, cut, lower, mitigate. *Kurangilah kecepatan kendaraan anda*. Please slow down. *dikurangi* minus, less. ~ *amarahnya* to calm down. ~ *berat badan* to lose weight. ~ *biaya yang tak perlu* to reduce unnecessary expenditures. ~ *produksi* to cut back production. ~ *pengeluaran* to cut down on expenses. ~ *rasa sakit* to reduce the pain. ~ *tenaga kerja* to reduce in force, RIF. *dengan tidak* ~ (*leg*) without prejudice to, with due consideration for, subject to. *dengan tidak* ~ *apa yang ditentukan dalam ayat 4 pasal 11* with due consideration for (or, subject to) what has been stipulated in paragraph 4 of article 11. **2** to mollify, calm down, soften, quiet(en), pacify.

mengurangkan 1 to reduce, diminish, curtail, alleviate. ~ *beban yang ditanggung orangtuanya* to reduce the burden borne by his parents. **2** (= **memperkurangkan**) to subtract, withdraw, take away, deduct. *Biaya itu akan di(per)kurangkan dari uang cadangan*. Expenses will be deducted from reserves.

kekurangan 1 insufficiency, shortcoming, failure, defect. *beberapa* ~ *dalam bukunya* some shortcomings of his book. **2** faulty, inadequate. ~ *gizi/zat makanan* malnutrition. **3** shortage, lack of, shortfall, deficiency, deficit. ~ *bernilai* undervalued. ~ *makanan/pangan* food shortage. ~ *oskigén* hypoxia. ~ *personil* understaffing. ~ *protéin* protein deficiency. ~ *vitamin* vitamin deficiency. **4** poverty. *hidup dalam* ~ to live in poverty. **5** (*leg*) lacuna, i.e., a missing portion of a regulation, etc. **6** to lack, not have enough of, be short of. *Saya* ~ *uang*. I don't have enough money. ~ *darah* to be anemic. ~ *modal* undercapitalized. ~ *oksigén* hypoxemia. **berkekurangan 1** to be lacking, wanting. *Hidupnya tidak* ~. He is well off. **2** to be poor, needy. *meréka yang* ~ the needy. **3** (*leg*) lacunar.

pengurang 1 (*math*) subtractor. **2** something which reduces s.t. *unsur* ~ reductions.

pengurangan 1 reduction, decrease, cut, limitation, curtailment, rollback, cutback. ~ *anggaran belanja* budget cut. ~ *bertahap* phase out, phasing out. ~ *masa hukuman/pidana* remission, pardon; → RÉMISI. ~ *senjata* arms control. **2** (*math*) subtraction. **3** restriction. **4** deduction. ~ *pajak* a tax deduction, tax deductible.

kurap I ringworm, *Trichophytosis*. *sakit* – scabby, mangy. – *anjing* mange. – *ayam* ringworm of the head, *Tinea capitis*. – *besi/bukit* Tokelau ringworm, *Tinea imbricata*. – *kain* dhoby itch, *Tinea cruris*. – *kaki* athlete's foot. – *kelongsong* → KURAP *besi*. – *susu* eczema on the cheeks of children.

berkurap 1 to suffer from ringworm. **2** false, fraudulent; treacherous, deceitful.

kurapan (*Jv*) scurvy, mangy.

kurap II *daun* – ringworm bush, *Cassia alata* used as medicine to cure ringworm.

kurapat → KHURAFAT.

kuras I *obat* – laxative. *pipa* – drain, pipe. – *otak* brainwash.

menguras 1 to drain, clean out. *Sumur itu sudah dikuras*. The well has been cleaned out. **2** (*mil*) to clear (out) (an area of enemy troops). **3** to exhaust, drain (one's energy). *Pekerjaan itu banyak* ~ *tenaga*. The job has drained a lot of our energy. **4** [and **nguras** (*coq*)] to steal, clean out. *Isi lemari itu dikuras habis*. The contents of the wardrobe were stolen. **5** to extract/elicit information from. **6** to squander, fritter away, waste (money). ~ *uang rakyat untuk pribadi sendiri* [Kurupsi] to squander the people's money for private purposes.

terkuras cleaned out, stripped. *meréka yang* ~ *kocéknya* those whose wallets have been stripped clean.

penguras drainer, s.o. who drains off assets.

pengurasan 1 draining, cleaning out. **2** giving an enema. **3** exhausting (resources, etc.), depletion.

pengkurasan draining. ~ *otak* brainwashing.

kuras II (*A*) quire (of paper), sheet (printing).

kurasani *besi* – (*cla*) good-quality iron (originally from Khorasan, Persia).

Kurasao Curaçao.

kurasi (*Jv*) *kain* – a red-flowered fabric.

kuratif (*D*) curative, remedial.

kurator (*D*) **1** (university) regent. **2** (banking) trustee, receiver, curator. **3** (museum) curator. **4** guardian (of a minor).

kurau a small edible marine fish species, *Polynemus spp*. – *manis* (in Medan) red snapper.

Kurawa the 100 brothers in the Mahab(h)arata.

kurawal curly brackets {} or square braces [].

kurban → KORBAN.

kurbuk [kurung buka] begin parentheses; open quote.

kurcaci 1 gnome, imp, goblin. **2** s.o. who likes to tease. **3** Brownie (seven- and eight-year-old Girl Scout).

kurda (*Jv*) furious, in a rage.

Kurdi (*Jv*) Kurd(s), Kurdish.

kurdin → KORDÉN.

kurét (*D/E*) curet(te).

mengkurét to curet(te).

pengkurétan curettage.

kurfa → KURVA.

kuri day-old chick, DOC.

kuria (*Bat*) **1** district. **2** parish; → PAROKI.

kuricang black-headed bulbul, *Pycnonotus atriceps*.

kurik speckled, spotted; → BURIK.

(ber)kurik-kurik *ayam* – and *ayam* ~ speckled chicken.

berkurik-kurik speckled, spotted.

kurikulér (*D*) curricular.

kurikulum (*D/E*) curriculum.

berkurikulum ... to have/use a ... curriculum.

kuring I smear, smudge, stain; speckled, marked with spots; → KORÉNG. *kelihatan* –*nya* then the cloven hoof showed itself.

kuring II (*S*) **1** servant, slave, inferior, subject. **2** I, me, mine (inferior to superior).

kuriositas (*E*) curiosity.

kuripan I quicklime; → KAPUR *tohor*.

Kuripan II an old kingdom in East Java.

kurir (*D*) courier.

kuririk (*M*) cricket; → JANGKRIK I.

kuris I (*S*) → KUDIS.

kuris II → GORÉS.

kurisi threadfin bream, *Nemipterus spp*.

kurkuma (*Pers*) **1**a) turmeric. b) saffron; → KUNIR I, KUNYIT I. **2** the symbolic representation of the clitoris in the infibulation ceremony.

kurkumin (*E chem*) curcumin.

kurma (*Pers*) date palm, date (the fruit), *Phoenix dactilifera*.

kurnia → KARUNIA.

kuro (*S*) threadfin, a fish species belonging to the *Polynemidae* family.

kurs (*D*) rate of exchange (of stocks/currency, etc.). – *bébas* free market rate. – *gelap* black-market rate. **berkurs gelap** to have a black-market exchange rate. – *konvérsi* conversion rate. – *mengambang* floating rate. – *paritas* parity rate. – *resmi* official rate of exchange. – *tengah* mean rate, middle exchange rate. – *tetap* fixed rate. – *unjuk* sight rate (of exchange). – *wésel* rate of exchange.

berkurs to have a rate (of exchange).

mengkurs ~ *ke/dengan* to convert (one currency into another).

kursani (*Jv*) k.o. medicinal plant, soma plant, *Vernonia anthelmintica.*

kursemangat 1 return, vital spirit! (said to an unconscious person or to a newborn child). 2 (an exclamation) good heavens! dear me!

kursi I (*A*) 1 chair. *angka – terbalik* (*BG*) "an inverted-chair grade," i.e., the low grade of 4. 2 seat (in Parliament), position. *menempati – to* occupy a seat. *me(mpe)rebutkan – dalam DPR* to compete for a seat in Parliament. – *ayunan* a) rocking chair, rocker. b) porch swing. – *bar* bar stool. – *basah* a lucrative position. – *bertali plastik* chair with vinyl tubing. – *beroda/dorong* wheelchair. – *duduk* chair for sitting in. – *empuk* a sinecure. – *goyang* rocking chair, rocker. – *kantor* desk chair. – *kémah* camp chair. – *lipat* folding chair. – *list(e)rik* the electric chair. – *loncat/lontar* ejection seat. – *makan* dining-room chair. – *malas* easy/lounge chair. – *méja gambar* drawing-table chair. – *pangkas* barber's chair. – *panjang* easy/lounge chair. – *pelontar* ejection seat. – *penyangga* cross hand (of a bridge). – *putar* a) (in aviation) human centrifuge. b) swivel/revolving chair. c) center support. – *rapat* meeting-room chair. – *roda* wheelchair. – *stélan* set of chairs. – *susun* stacked chairs. – *tengadah* reclining chair, recliner. *di – terdakwa* in the prisoner's dock. – *(yang bisa) rebah* and – *yang sandarannya dapat diatur* reclining chair, recliner. – *ungkang-ungkit* rocking chair, rocker.

sekursi sharing a seat (on a bus, etc.).

berkursi to have a seat. *orang ~ roda* a person in a wheelchair.

Kursi II (*A*) *ayat al.–* the Throne Verse, the Koranic verse explaining God's powers (al-Baqarah 2:255).

kursif (*D*) in italics. *huruf –* italic letter, italics.

kursis (*D*) person taking a course (of study).

kursus (*D*) short practical vocational-training course. – *bahasa Inggris* English language course. – *jarak jauh* distance learning. – *kecantikan* cosmetology course. – *kilat* cram course. – *mengetik* typing course. – *penataran (lanjutan)* (advanced) upgrading course. – *penyegar* refresher course. – *privat* private lessons. – *singkat* short course.

berkursus to take a course. ~ *kepada* (*coq*) to study under/with.

mengkursus to train.

mengkursuskan to have s.o. take a course. *Perusahaan terpaksa harus ~nya lagi.* The company was compelled to have her take a course again.

kurtup [kurung tutup] end/close parenthesis; unquote.

kurun (*A*) cycle of years; century; era; time span; → **ABAD**. – *ke-20* the 20th century. – *Maséhi* the Christian era. – *waktu/zaman* period of time, time span. *dalam – waktu yang lama* over a long period of time.

berkurun-kurun for centuries/ages. *adat yang sudah ~ dianut* a custom practiced for ages.

kurung 1 cage; s.t. similar in shape to a cage. 2 compartment (in a fish trap). *baju –* traditional Minangkabau women's long shirt without a front opening which is pulled over the head like a jumper. *beringin –* the holy banyan tree surrounded by an iron fence in front of the Kraton in Solo. – *batang* covered bier for Islamic burials. – *besar* square brackets […]. – *buka* [kurbuk] begin parenthesis; open quote. – *kurawal* curly braces {...}. – *laut* third compartment in a fish trap. – *muka* first compartment in a fish trap. – *siku* square brackets […]. – *tengah* second compartment in a fish trap. – *tutup* [kurtup] end parenthesis; unquote.

berkurung 1 to stay home; be a shut-in (of one's own free will). *perintah ~* (*Mal*) curfew. 2 to be put in brackets; bracketed. 3 (*Br*) to be dammed up, be blocked (of a stream).

mengurung 1 to put in a cage. 2 to imprison, incarcerate. 3 to surround, encircle (the enemy); → **MENGEPUNG**. *dikurung banjir* flood-bound. 4 to put in parentheses, parenthesize. *kata-kata yang dikurung* words in parentheses. 5 to stay cooped up. *Siang saya mengurung di dalam kamar.* During the daytime I stay cooped up in my room.

mengurungi (*pl obj*) to cage, etc.

mengurungkan to imprison, incarcerate, intern.

terkurung 1 to be jailed/imprisoned/confined. 2 to be a shut-in, cooped up; locked in, trapped, isolated. ~ *paham* narrow-minded; → *seperti* **KATAK** *di bawah tempurung.* ~ *salju* snow-bound. 3 narrow, restricted. **keterkurungan** isolation.

kurungan 1 cage. ~ *burung* bird cage. 2 coop. ~ *ayam* chicken coop. 3 cooped up. *ayam ~* cooped-up chicken. 4 prison; detention, lockup. *hukuman ~* detention. *diringkuk dalam ~ seumur hidup* to be imprisoned for life. 5 (*naut*) cabin (of a ship). 6 compartment in a large marine fish trap. 7 box (in a newspaper).

pengurungan 1 imprisonment, confinement, incarceration. ~ *terpisah* solitary confinement. 2 encirclement.

kurupsi [kuras uang rakyat untuk pribadi sendiri] squander people's money for private purposes (a made-up acronym, a pun on *korupsi*).

kurus 1 (of s.o.) thin, slim, slender, skinny, emaciated. *bocah itu – sekali* that boy is very skinny. – *kerémpéng/kering/lanjai* (*M*)/*tertulang* thin as a rail, all skin and bones. – *panjang* slim, slender. 2 (of a business/an office position/an airline route, etc.) unprofitable. *yang – keuangannya* backed by insufficient funds. 3 (of soil) arid, barren, dry, infertile, unfruitful, unproductive. *Tanah negeri itu sangat –.* The soil of that country is very infertile. 4 meager.

sekurus as thin/skinny as.

mengurus to become thin(ner), lose weight.

menguruskan to make thin(ner), make lean(er), emaciate.

terkurus the thinnest/skinniest, etc.

kekurusan 1 slimness, thinness. 2 (*coq*) too slim/skinny.

pengurus 1 s.t. that thins, thinning, slimming. 2 slimming drug.

pengurusan slimming, thinning.

kurut → **KERUT II.**

kuruyuk (*Jv*) to crow (of roosters).

berkuruyuk to crow.

kurva (*E*) curve (on a chart).

kus I puss! puss! → **DEKUS.**

kus II (*A Pers?*) vulva.

kusa I (*Skr*) elephant goad; → **ANGKUSA.**

mengusa to use such a goad.

kusa II *rumput –(.–)* jungle rice, marsh grass, *Echinochloa colona.*

kusal mengusal 1 to roll s.t. in the palms of the hands. ~ *rokok* to roll a cigarette; → **MENGGELINTING, MENGGULUNG, TINGWÉ.** 2 to turn a betel quid over and over in the mouth. ~ *bibir* to wipe the saliva caused by chewing betel off the lips.

kusam 1 lackluster (of the eyes). 2 dim (of light). 3 dull (of color/light/sound/mind, etc.). 4 pale, pallid, wan. 5 translucent.

mengusam to become dull/dim/pale, etc.

kekusaman dullness, pallor.

kusambi ironwood tree, gum-lack tree, *Schleichera oleosa*, whose wood is used for charcoal and whose seeds are used for oil; → **KESAMBI.** *arang –* ironwood charcoal.

kusat-kusau and **kusat-mesat** completely confused.

kusau berkusau(-kusau) 1 to be ruffled, tousled, unkempt, tangled, disheveled (of hair). *Segumpal rambutnya ~ di keningnya.* A lock of his hair was tousled on his forehead. 2 confused, mixed up.

kusén and **kusin** (*D*) (door-/window-)frame, jamb; → **KOSÉN II.** *membentur – pintu* to bump up against the doorframe.

kusir (*D*) driver, coachman (of a horse-drawn carriage). *débat –* squabbling, bickering.

mengusir to work as a coachman.

mengusiri to drive (a horse-drawn carriage).

kuskus (*A D*) cuscus, *Phalanger ursinus.*

kusruk (*J*) **mengusruk** [and **ngusruk** (*coq*)] 1 to fall forward/headlong. *jatuh –* to fall forward, overturn frontward. 2 to fall in head first. *Dia ~ di got.* He fell forward into a ditch.

kusta (*Skr*) leprosy; → **LÉPRA.** – *bangau* white leprous patches. – *bunga* colored leprous patches. – *dangkung* leprosy of the nose.

– limbung leprosy which results in the limbs, etc. having to be amputated.

kustawan (*Skr neo*) male leper.

kustawati (*Skr neo*) female leper.

kusti berkusti to wrestle.

kusuf (*A*) solar eclipse; → KUSYUFUS *syamsi.*

kusuk I → KASAK-KUSUK.

kusuk II (*M*) *daun –* k.o. leaves rubbed over the body when taking a bath.

  berkusuk to rub the body with such leaves.

  mengusuk to rub s.t.

kusuk III (*A*) devout meditation, silent reflection; → KHUSUK.

kusuka [kutipan surat kabar] press clippings (pun on *kusuka* I like it).

kusu-kusu I berkusu-kusu in throngs/crowds.

kusu-kusu II k.o. fragrant grass, vetiver grass, *Vetiveria zizanioides.*

kusu-kusu III (*ob*) **berkusu-kusu** to whisper.

kusuma (*Skr*) **1** (poetic) flower; → BUNGA I, KEMBANG I, KESUMA, SEKAR. **2** very beautiful, charming, attractive. **3** a beautiful woman; → BUNGA *désa. parang –* name of a *batik* pattern. *– bangsa* a) the youth of a nation. b) the fallen heroes of a nation, those killed in battle.

kusumawicitra (*Skr neo*) anthology.

kusur → AIR *kusur.*

kusus → KHUSUS.

kusut I 1 tousled (of hair). *Rambutnya – karena ditiup angin.* Her hair was tousled from being blown by the wind. **2** tangled (of thread, etc.). *benang –* tangled thread. *– kusau/masai/mesut/ murut/musut* all tangled up, disheveled, totally confused. **3** crumpled, rumpled, wrinkled. *Sepréi itu –.* The bed sheet was rumpled. **4** complicated, difficult, intricate, complex. **5** disturbed and confused (of one's thoughts). *hatinya –* and *pikirannya yang –* he's depressed. *– diselesaikan, keruh diperjernih* disputes have to be settled properly. *tak ada – yang tak selesai* there is no dispute that cannot be settled. *– muka* gloomy, depressed; unhappy. *– pikir* confused. *– sarang tempua* completely entangled and hard to disentangle.

  sekusut as tousled/tangled, etc. as.

  berkusut-kusut tangled, tousled.

  mengusut to become tangled, get all tangled up.

  mengusutkan 1 to entangle. *~ benang* to (en)tangle thread. **2** to confuse; to complicate. *Katakan kepadaku apa yang ~ pikiranmu.* Tell me what's confusing you. *~ perkara yang sudah hampir selesai* to further confuse s.t. which was almost settled.

  terkusut the most tangled, etc.

  kusutan 1 a kink (in thread, etc.), twist. **2** clutter.

  kekusutan 1 tangle, entanglement, ravel. **2** confusion, disturbance. **3** irregularities; corruption. **4** clutter.

  pekusutan entanglement.

  pengusutan entangling.

kusut II (*M*) **mengusut** to investigate thoroughly; → USUT II.

kusyufus syamsi (*A*) eclipse of the sun.

kut clipped form of **ikut**.

Kuta 1 name of a popular tourist beach resort in Bali. **2** [Kota Untuk Turis Australia] (pun on *Kuta*) Town for Australian Tourists.

kutaha (*cla*) possibly, probably; → KONON I.

Kutojaya name of a train running between Jakarta and Purorejo.

kutak (*M*) *– katik* **mengutak-ngatikkan 1** to act despotically/ high-handedly; to rule, reign over. **2** to fool. **3** to reshuffle. *pengutak-ngatikan* reshuffling (of the cabinet).

  mengutak to shake violently.

kutak-katik (*J*) tinkering, messing around, mixing into (what doesn't concern one).

  ngutak-ngatik 1 to repair (radios, etc.). **2** to tease, bother, intrude on/disturb, interfere with.

kutang (*Port*) **1** (strapless) brassiere, bra. **2** vest; sleeveless or short-sleeved shirt. **3** chemise. *baju –* bodice, veste-bolero. *membuka –* to undo one's bra. *– kebal peluru* bulletproof vest.

kutat I berkutat to sit around (waiting for s.t. to happen).

kutat II ber(si)kutat to struggle (to do s.t.), be busy (thinking about s.t.), concerned (with). *Meréka masih ~ pada peristiwa tanggal 1 Séptémber.* They're still busy thinking about the events of September 1.

kutat-kutet (*J*) busy, be busily engaged in s.t.

  berkutat-kutetan to be deeply involved in s.t.

kutbah → KHOTBAH.

kutéks (cutex) nail polish.

  berkutéks to use nail polish, to have … nail polish on. *Kukunya ~ mérah tua.* She was wearing dark red nail polish.

kuteni (*Tam? ob*) pimp.

kuteri (*ob*) berth (in a ship).

kutet (*J*) **be(r)kutetan 1** to fight hard, struggle (to do s.t.). **2** to be uncompromising, refuse to give in.

kuti (*M*) **menguti** to tear into small pieces.

kutik berkutik to move slightly. *tidak ~* couldn't do a thing.

  mengutik(-ngutik), mengkutik(-kutik) and **ngutik-ngutik** (*coq*) **1** to touch with the finger (to get s.o.'s attention); to move s.t. with the finger, pinch and twist a button, etc. *sebagai/seperti ular dikutik ékor* to start (with fright/anger/out of one's sleep). *~ gigi* to pick one's teeth. **2** to touch on (a question); find faults with. *Soal itu belum pernah kita kutik-kutik.* We haven't yet touched on that question yet. **3** to tinker with, make attempts to repair s.t. **4** to rake up (the past).

  kutikan nudge, hint, touch.

kutika → KETIKA I.

kutikula (*D*) cuticle.

kuti-kuti (*ob*) fault-finding; → KUTIK.

kutil I wart. *– kelamin* genital wart.

  berkutil warty.

  kutilan covered with warts.

kutil II sekutil a tiny piece, a nibble, a little bit.

  mengutil 1 to pick at (one's food).

kutil III (*Jv*) pickpocket.

  mengutil [and **ngutil** (*coq*)] to pickpocket, pilfer, shoplift. *Pimpinan proyék ~ dana proyék.* The project leader has pilfered project funds.

  pengutil shoplifter.

  pengutilan shoplifting.

kutilang (*J/Jv*) sooty-headed bulbul, *Pycnonotus aurigaster.*

kuting (*ob*) **berkuting-kuting** to trail/follow all the time.

kutip mengutip 1 to pick up little by little or in small bits, collect (money, etc.), peck at. *~ pungli* to collect illegal retributions. **2** to extract, excerpt, cite, quote, copy. *dilarang ~* copyright; → HAK *cipta.*

  mengutipkan to reproduce, copy, excerpt (for s.o. else).

  kutipan 1 quote, quotation, excerpt, citation, copy. *~ surat kabar* press clippings; → KUSUKA. **2** s.t. picked up, a collection (getting money from many people).

  pengutip quotation.

  pengutipan 1 picking up, collecting. **2** quoting, citing, copying.

kutu I 1 louse, flea, bug, tick. **2** scum, rabble. *– dalam selimut* an enemy in disguise; → MUSUH *dalam selimut. Mati -mu!* You're finished! *Mati -nya.* He's finished, his number is up. *sudah mati -nya* hopeless; powerless. *mencari – dalam ijuk* a difficult or hopeless task. *pantang – dicukur, pantang manusia dihinakan* everybody has his self-respect and does not want to be humiliated. *– air* a) athlete's foot, mycosis. b) boring shipworm. *– anjing* cat flea/tick, *Ctenocephalus felis. – ayam* chicken body louse, *Menacanthus stramineus, Menopon spp. – bayur* a) crab louse, *Phthirus pubis.* b) cad, scoundrel. *– buah* green scale, *Coccus viridis. – buku* bookworm. *– bulu putih* citrus canker, *Pseudomonas citri. – busuk* a) bedbug, *Cimex lectularius.* b) rabble, scum. *– daun* plant louse, green fly aphid, aphis, *Aphus glycines, Nyzus persicae. – dompolan* k.o. plant pest, *Pseudococcus lapellei. – ikan* fish louse, *Argulus indicus. – kapuk* k.o. whitefly, *Aleurodicus spp. – kebul* tobacco/ silverleaf whitefly, *Bemisia tabaci. – kepala* head louse, *Pediculus humanus capitis. – kerbau/lembu/ternak* cattle tick. *– loncat* a small orange-green insect that sucks the liquid from certain plants, psyllid, k.o. plant louse, *Heteropsylla spp. – pasar* thug who operates in the market. *– perisai* coconut brown scale, *Aspidiotus destructor.*

  sekutu *~ hitam* a mere nothing.

  berkutu 1 to have lice, lousy. **2** (= **berkutu-kutu**) to delouse o.s., have o.s. deloused.

berkutu-kutuan to delouse e.o.

mengutui to delouse s.o.

kutu II (*Tam ob*) trading company; → SEKUTU.

berkutu to unite, associate, federate; united, associated; federated.

kutu III (*Jv*) – *baru* k.o. woman's jacket with buttons, an open neck and a lightweight corset (without stays).

kutub I (*A*) **1** pole (of the earth). **2** axis, center. *arus* – polarization current. *bintang* – polestar, Polaris, the North Star. – *Janubi/Selatan* South Pole. – *berganda* bipolar. – *magnétik/magnit* magnetic pole. – *négatif* negative pole, cathode. – *positif* positive pole, anode. – *Syamali/Utara* North Pole.

berkutub with a pole, polar. ~ *dua* bipolar.

mengutubkan to polarize.

terkutub polarized. *cahaya* ~ polarized light.

kutuban polarization.

kekutuban polarity.

pengutub polarizer.

pengutuban polarization.

kutub II *burung* – lineated dull barbet, *Megalaima spp*.

kutuk I 1 curse. **2** bane (of one's existence), blight.

mengutuk 1 to curse. **2** to condemn.

mengutuki 1 to put a curse on. **2** (*pl subj*) to curse, condemn.

mengutukkan to condemn.

memperkutui 1 to curse. **2** to condemn.

terkutuk 1 (ac)cursed. **2** condemned.

kutukan 1 curse. *Dan bis itu jadi riuh oléh sumpah-serapah dan* ~. The bus became noisy with imprecations and curses. **2** condemnation.

pengutuk curser, s.o. who likes to curse.

pengutukan 1 cursing. **2** condemnation, condemning.

kutuk II *sekutuk* measure for rice equal to four handfuls. ~ *beras basah* useless, worthless.

kutuk III (*Jv*) baby chick, poult; → ANAK *ayam*. – *sehari* day-old chick.

kutung (*Jv*) **1** cut, chopped, hacked off, amputated (of limbs), severed. **2** to have to pay the bill/the piper.

kutup → KUTUB I.

kutut (*coq*) *burung* – → PERKUTUT.

kuud I (*A*) /ku'ut/ sitting (during prayer).

KUUD II /ku'ut/ [Koperasi Unit Usaha Désa] Village Business Unit Cooperative.

kuwaci → KUACI.

kuwadé (*Jv*) decorated seat for bride and groom at wedding.

kuwah → KUAH.

Kuwait Kuwait. –*nya Asia Tenggara* Southeast Asia's Kuwait, i.e., Brunei Darussalam.

kuwajiban → KEWAJIBAN.

kuwalahan → KEWALAHAN.

kuwalat a cosmic force that seeks retribution for disrespectful behavior toward one's elders; → KUALAT.

kuwali → KUALI.

kuwangwung → KUANGWUNG.

kuwatir → KUATIR.

kuwau → KUAU.

kuwé(h) → KUÉ.

kuwéh *ikan* – *macam* k.o. fish, golden trevally, *Gnathanodon speciosus*.

kuwel (*Jv*) **menguwel-nguweli** to crumple up.

kuwih → KUÉ.

kuwini → KUINI.

kuwu (*Jv*) **1** village head; → LURAH I. **2** village water official.

kuwuk I (*J/Jv*) *kucing* – wild cat that eats baby chicks; → KUCING I.

kuwuk II (*Jv*) cowry shell, *Cypraea annulus*.

kuwung(-kuwung) (*Jv*) rainbow; → BIANGLALA, PELANGI.

kuwur (*Jv*) troubled, confused (of thoughts).

kuya (*J*) k.o. small freshwater turtle; → BULUS II.

kuyam → KOYAM.

kuyang (in East Kalimantan) female ghost whose head and intestines fly away at night and suck the blood of pregnant women or women who have just given birth.

kuyu I dejected, low(-spirited), depressed; → LAYU. *hati* – sad,

unhappy, gloomy, depressed. **2** (of the eyes/hair) dull, lusterless; → LUYU. **3** (*M*) frightened, anxious; → TAKUT.

kekuyuan sadness, melancholy, unhappiness.

kuyuh I (*M*) urine; → KENCING.

menguyuhi to urinate on.

kuyuh II – *basah* dripping wet.

kekuyuyan to get wet.

kuyuk word used to call a dog over.

kuyung tree with commercial lumber, *Shorea eximia*.

kuyup → BASAH *kuyup*, TERJUN *kuyup*.

kuyup-kuyup soaking wet.

kV I [KiloVolt] kilovolt, kV.

KV II [Kasét Vidéo] videocassette.

kVA I [KiloVolt Ampére] kilovolt-amperes.

KVA II [Kurs Valuta Asing] foreign exchange rate; → VALUTA.

kw- also see entries beginning with **ku-**.

kw I (*abbr*) [kawan] comrade (PKI title before names). – *Aidit* Comrade Aidit.

kw II (*abbr*) [Kwartal] quarter (of a year).

kw III (*abbr*) [Kwintal] quintal, 100 kilograms.

kw IV (*abbr*) [KiloWatt] kilowatt.

kwa (*D*) qua, as; → SEBAGAI.

kwaci → KUACI.

kwadran → KUADRAN.

kwadrat → KUADRAT.

kwalat → KUALAT.

kwali → KUALI.

kwalifikasi → KUALIFIKASI.

kwalita(s) → KUALITA(S).

kwalitatif → KUALITATIF.

kwalitét → KUALITA(S).

kwangwung stag/coconut beetle; → BANGBUNG, KUANGWUNG.

kwantita(s) → KUANTITA(S).

kwantitatif → KUANTITATIF.

kwantitét → KUANTITA(S).

kwantum → KUANTUM.

Kwantung province in Southeast China. *orang* – Muslims from Yunnan, China.

kwarsa → KUARSA.

kwartal → KUARTAL.

kwarter (*E*) quarterfinal.

kwartér (*D geol*) quaternary.

kwartét (*D*) quartet. – *gésék* string quartet.

kwartir (*D mil*) quarters; → MARKAS.

kwarto (*D*) quarto.

kwas I (*D*) (paint-)brush.

kwas II (*D*) (lemon-)squash; → AIR *jeruk*.

kwasi (*D*) quasi-, pseudo-. – *ilmiah* quasi-scientific.

kwatrin (*D*) quatrain.

kwéé (*C?*) *ikan* – various species of fish. – *roméh* John Dory, *Zenopsis ocellata*.

kwéni → KUINI.

kwéstionér → KUÉSIONÉR.

kwétiau → KUÉTIAO.

kWh (*abbr*) [kiloWatt Hour] kilowatt-hour.

kwini → KUINI.

kWj (*abbr*) [kiloWatt Jam] kilowatt-hour.

kwintal → KUINTAL.

kwintét (*D*) quintet(te).

kwis → KUIS II.

kwitangsi → KWITANSI.

kwitansi (*D*) receipt (for services, goods, money, etc. received).

kworum (*D/E*) quorum.

kwota (*D/E*) quota, share.

kwt [kawat] (in government cables) cable, wire, telegram.

KWTL [Kartu Wajib Tanda Lapor] Required Reporting-in Card (for those involved in the G-30-S/PKI).

kyai 1 appellation for sacred animals; → KIAI. – *Rebo* name of an elephant in the Yogyakarta Zoo. **2** appellation for sacred *gamelans*. **3** Muslim cleric.

kya-kya to have fun/a good time.

L

l and L I /él/ **1** the 12th letter of the Latin alphabet used for writing Indonesian. **2** (abbr) liter.

L II car license plate for Surabaya.

la and laa I (A) (there) is not (in various Arabic expressions). – *ilaha illa'llah Muhammadun rasulu'llah* there is no God but Allah and Muhammad is His Prophet; → LA-BUD(DA). – *haula wala quwwata illa billahil aliyyil adzim* there is no force or power without God's permission.

la II (in response to a call) yes? what?

la III → LAH I. *Ya sudah – biarkan saja.* Just disregard this.

la IV (coq) already; → TELAH I.

la V → LHA.

la VI sixth note of the musical scale.

la VII (in acronyms) → LAMA, LAUT.

la'al (Pers) ruby.

laatbrief (D) /latbrif/ consignment note.

lab clipped form of **laboratorium**.

laba I (Skr) **1** profit, earnings, gain (in business, etc.). *tidak mencari – nonprofit*; → NIRLABA. – *tertinggal, harta lingkap* does not gain any profit and, on top of that, even one's capital has been lost. **2** benefit, advantage. – *sama dibagi, rugi sama diterjuni* (M) to share one's joys and sorrows (for instance, among friends). *menganut – dengan siku* to aim at making a profit. *kalau – bercikun-cikun, buruk diberi tahu orang* when one has obtained happiness, one shuts one's mouth, but when one is in trouble, one complains or asks favors from others. – *berkala* periodic income. – *bersih* net profits. – *bersih per saham* earnings per share, EPS. – *bruto* gross margin. – *dagang* trading profit. – *dan rugi* profit and loss. – *ditahan* retained earnings. – *fiskal* taxable income. – *istiméwa* killing. – *kena pajak* taxable earnings. – *kotor* gross profit. – *kotor penjualan* gross profit on sales. – *modal* capital gain, return on capital. – *mujur* windfall. – *per saham* earnings per share. – *perang* war profits. – *rugi* profit and loss. – *semu* paper profits. – *usaha* operating revenue, income from operations.

berlaba 1 to profit, make a profit. **2** gainful, profitable, advantageous.

melabai and melabakan 1 to be profitable, bring in a profit. **2** pays (off), advantageous, beneficial.

laba II [lapis baja] **1** armor plate. **2** armor-plated.

labah-labah spider. *akal* – smart in deceiving s.o. (se)besar – smart in concealing deceit.

labaika → LABBAIKA.

labak I → KELABAKAN.

labak II k.o. marine fish.

laban name of several trees of the genus *Vitex*; the wood is used for the construction of furniture, etc.; → LEBAN.

labang I (M) **melabang** to forge/hammer out (iron sheets).

labang II melabang to wander around aimlessly.

labang III *pekak* – hard of hearing.

labang IV (sl) marijuana, cannabis.

labas (ob) nothing is left, all used up, completely consumed.

melabaskan to use up.

labbaik – *Allahumma 'umrah* Here I am, O God, for the lesser pilgrimage; → LABBAIKA.

labbaika (A) *Allahuma* – O God, I am thy slave; Here I am, O Lord (at your service). – *Allahumma labbaik*, – *laasyariika laka*, – *innal hamda wanni'mata laka wal mulka*, – *la syariikalak* Here I am, O God, here I am, O You who have no partner, here I am, praise and grace to You and the kingdom, You who have no partner; → LABBAIK.

label (E) /lébel/ label.

berlabel labeled. *tidak ~* unlabeled.

melabeli to label.

laberak → LABRAK.

laberang and *tali* – shrouds from ship's side to masthead, rigging.

labfor [laboratorium forénsik] forensic laboratory.

labi → PELABI.

labial (D/E) labial. *bunyi* – a labial sound.

labik (Pr) reversed. *ngomong* – backwards language; → PROKÉM.

labil (D/E) labile, unstable.

kelabilan lability, instability.

labi-labi I various species of soft-shell turtles, *Trionyx cartilagineus, Pelochelys bibroni*.

labi-labi II k.o. intercity van used in Aceh.

labirin (D) **1** labyrinth. **2** the inner ear.

labkrim [laboratorium kriminal] criminal lab.

lablab (A) k.o. bean, *Dolichos lablab*.

laboran (D) laboratory chemist.

laboratoris (D) laboratory (mod). *secara* – in the laboratory.

laboratorium (D) laboratory. – *antariksa* Spacelab. – *bahasa* language lab. – *risét* research laboratory. – *(ruang) angkasa* Skylab.

labrak (J/Jv) **melabrak 1** to thrash, whack, hit, beat. **2** to reprimand, rebuke sharply, lash out at. **3** to attack, charge, storm. **4** to attack, deal with, handle, tackle (a problem).

terlabrak beaten.

labrakan 1 thrashing, beating. **2** attack, charge, assault.

pelabrakan thrashing, beating.

labrang → LABERANG.

labres (J) bald(-headed), barren (land); nothing (is) left. *dicukur* – completely defeated (in a soccer game).

labu I (Skr?) **1** bottle gourd, calabash. **2** squash, pumpkin; → WALUH. **3** flask, bottle. *tampuk* – a) tiny stalk left on cut gourd. b) (sl) clitoris. *main* – to engage in lesbian sex. – *dikerébok tikus* a deflowered girl. *seperti* – *dibenam* very arrogant. *mak* – a pregnant woman. – *air/panjang/putih* a) zucchini, squash, *Lagenaria leucantha*. b) gourd for carrying water. – *ambon/hijau/mérah/parang* musk melon, winter squash, *Cucurbita moschata*. – *didih* boiling flask. – *jepang* chayote squash. – *kendi* inedible gourd used as a bottle. – *kuning/manis/waluh* summer squash, marrow, *Cucurbita pepo*. – *siam* chayote, *Sechium edule*. – *tanah* earthenware flask.

labu-labu 1 k.o. earthenware jar with long neck used for storing water. **2** spherical ornament on top of a mosque, etc. **3** round basket hung from a pole at a port as a sign that ships may enter the port. ~ *distilasi* laboratory retort. ~ *kencing* urinal. ~ *tanah* k.o. earthen water bottle.

melabu 1 paunchy, potbellied. **2** to compress (using a *labu*). **3** (= **memperlabu**) to cheat, fool, deceive, defraud (with sweet talk).

labu II – *holiem* penis-sheath (of Irian Jaya).

labu III (ob) → LABUH I.

labuci (ob) sequins, spangles, tiny metal discs *esp* as used for ornaments on a dress, scarf, etc.; → LOBERCI.

la-bud(da) (A) necessarily, surely, certainly, undoubtedly.

labuh I 1 hanging down/trailing (like a *kelambu*/curtains, etc.); (a coat) reaches down to (the hips). **2** (ob) classifier for curtains: *tirai se-* one curtain. – *léna* demurrage.

berlabuh 1 to hang down, droop; pulled down (of curtains, etc.). **2** to anchor, moor, dock (also of aircraft). **3** (to be, ride) at anchor. *kelebihan hari* ~ (shipping term) demurrage day, day of demurrage. **4** to fall (of the night).

melabuh 1 to cast/drop anchor. **2** (M) to drop, bring forth young (of buffaloes/cows). **3** hanging down, drooping.

melabuhi to call at, touch at (of a port). *Pelabuhan itu tidak banyak dilabuhi kapal.* Ships do not frequently call at that small port.

melabuhkan 1 to lower (the mosquito net/the blinds/the curtain/one's eyes). ~ *sauh/jangkar* to cast/drop anchor. **2** to make (a ship) come to anchor, moor. **3** to put (s.o.) overboard, throw s.t. (into the water, etc.). ~ *orang* to throw s.o. overboard. ~ *pancing* to throw out a fishing line. **4** to channel, focus (one's attention). ~ *hukum* to pass/impose sentence, pass judgment.

terlabuh(kan) hanging down.

pelabuhan [and **labuhan** (mostly in place names)] and **perlabuhan 1** harbor, port, dock. ~ *alam* natural harbor. ~ *antarpulau* coaster harbor. ~ *bébas* free port. ~ *bertarif bébas* open-rated port. ~ *buatan* man-made harbor. ~ *darat* dry port. ~ *karantina* quarantine port. ~ *pantai* harbor for interisland vessels. ~ *pasang* tidal harbor. ~ *pembongkaran* port of discharge. ~ *pengapalan* port of loading. ~ *perikanan* fishing port/harbor. ~ *pertambangan* bunker harbor. ~ *punggah* port of shipment. ~ *raya* (*Mal*) highway. ~ *samudra* harbor for oceangoing vessels. ~ *tujuan* port of destination. ~ *udara* [pelud] airport. ~ *utama* main port. **2** anchorage, roads. **kepelabuhan** and **kepelabuhanan** (*mod*) harbor, port.

labuh II (*M*) street.

Labuhan (*Jv*) a ceremony that starts from the *kraton* in Yogyakarta and carries offerings and clothes to *Nyai Loro Kidul*.

labun (*ob*) **berlabun-labun** to (have a) chat, chatter, talk, converse.

labur I (*Jv*) whitewash.

berlaburkan to be surfaced with.

melabur 1 to whitewash. **2** to surface (a road, etc.).

pelaburan whitewashing, resurfacing.

labur II melabur to give food, money, etc. to workers.

pelabur and **laburan** rations (for workers).

labur III kelaburan (*ob*) pitfall.

labur IV (*Mal*) invest.

pelaburan investment.

labut (*ob*) → LA-BUD(DA).

lacak I (*Jv*) **1** track, trail, trace. ~ *balak* chain of custody. **2** call forwarding (a telephone service).

melacak 1 to trail, tail (follow surreptitiously), trace. **2** to detect.

melacaki to track, trail, trace.

terlacak [and **kelacak** (*coq*)] tracked, trailed, traced.

pelacak detector, search (*mod*). *alat* ~ *bom* bomb detector. *anjing* ~ (*narkotika*) (narcotic) sniffer dog. *tim* ~ search team. ~ *kedustaan* lie detector, polygraph.

pelacakan 1 tracing, tracking, trailing. **2** clue (to the solution of a problem).

lacak II belacak and **melacak** plentiful, abundant, more than enough; there's a glut of.

lacak III melacak to drag, glide over soft ground (of an anchor that does not grip).

laci (*D*) **1** drawer. **2** compartment (in a briefcase, etc.).

berlaci to have drawers/compartments.

lacuan (*ob*) → LOKCUAN.

lacur I (*J*) didn't work out, failed, mistaken. (*tetapi*) *apa* –? (*coq*) (but) what can one do? – *betul* what bad luck. *nasib* – an unlucky fate.

lacur II (*J*/*Jv*) immoral, indecent, lewd, lascivious, improper. *orang* – and *perempuan* – prostitute.

melacur to be a prostitute, prostitute o.s.

melacurkan ~ *diri* to prostitute o.s., sell out.

mempelacurkan to prostitute (one's art/politics, etc.).

pelacur prostitute, whore; → WANITA P. ~ *pria* gigolo.

pelacuran prostitution. **kepelacuran** prostitution.

lacut (*M*) **melacut** to whip, cane, flog; → LECUT, PECUT.

lada 1 (white or black) pepper. **2** (*M*) red pepper, *Capsicum annuum*; → CABAI I; Spanish pepper. *bisul* – small scattered boils. *kecil-kecil* – *api/padi/kutuk* small but plucky. *belum tahu di pedas* – born yesterday, i.e., innocent and inexperienced. *siapa makan* –, *ialah berasa pedas* you/he made your/his bed, so you/he have/has to lie in it. *burung terbang, dipipiskan* – to count one's chickens before they are hatched. – *api* hot pepper, *Capsicum frutescens*. – *berékor* cubebs, *Piper cubeba*; → KEMUKUS, TEMUKUS. – *burung* chili peppers. – *garam* flavoring. – *hitam* black pepper, *Piper nigrum*. – *hitam Lampong* (the commercial term) Lampung Black. – *hutan* k.o. pepper, *Piper bantamense*. – *kutuk* hot pepper, *Capsicum frutescens*. – *mérah* red pepper, *Capsicum annuum*. – *padi* (*M*) black pepper. – *panjang* a medicinal plant, long pepper, *Piper retrofractum*. – *putih* white pepper. – *putih Bangka* Munto White. – *sulah* decorticated pepper. – *tumbuk* crushed/ground pepper.

meladai to put pepper on s.t.

ladah (*M*) dirty, soiled, filthy, impure, polluted.

ladam (*Tam*) horseshoe. – *kuku* shoeing.

meladam to shoe (a horse).

ladan (*Hind*) *minyak* – resin used for caulking or joss sticks made from *damar*.

ladang 1 dry (not irrigated rice) field. *minta* – *yang berpunya* to covet a married woman. *padi* – stalk paddy from slash-and-burn farming. *tikar* – coarse-plaited mat. *lain* – *lain belalang, lain lubuk lain ikannya* other times, other manners; other countries, other customs. *menari/merentak di* – *orang* to sponge off others; to live well at s.o. else's expense. **2** a rich source of inspiration, income, etc. – *minyak* oil field. – *padi* dry (not irrigated) paddy land; newly cleared forest land; → HUMA. – *ranjau* minefield. – *sapi/ternak* ranch. – *tinggal* abandoned field (no longer cultivated).

seladang one dry field. *mati* ~ (*M*) to die having had only one wife.

berladang 1 to own/have a *ladang*. **2** to cultivate/till a *ladang*.

memperladangi to open up s.t. for a *ladang*.

memperladang(kan) 1 to plant s.t. in a *ladang*. **2** to open up s.t. for a *ladang*.

peladang farmer/cultivator. ~ *berpindah* shifting cultivator.

pe(r)ladangan 1 dry (not irrigated) fields. **2** dry-field cultivation. ~ (*ber*)*pindah/liar* shifting cultivation. ~ *ternak* ranch.

ladek (*J*) **1** not cooked through, still hard. **2** rude, brusque.

ladén (*Jv*) serve. *tukang* – a) a servant. b) (*S*) assistant cement mixer.

meladéni 1 to serve/wait on, attend to (customers); to help (customers). **2a)** to reply to (an enemy) b) to answer (questions), give an explanation. **3** to follow, act (up)on (instructions); to satisfy, comply with (s.o.'s needs), take into account/consideration, consider (ideas). **4** to resist, pit o.s. against, stand up to. **5** (do not) display interest in (an admirer); to be concerned with, have dealings with; to service, give in to (a man, sexually). **6** to look after, take care of, watch over (s.o.'s interests). **7** to entertain (guests), keep (guests) entertained; → LAYAN.

terladéni can be serviced.

ladénan service.

peladén attendant, servant.

peladénan attendance, service.

ladéng → LADINGKLÉREK.

ladi *orang* – the Sakai ethnic group of Malacca.

lading I 1 (*parang* –) a long, single-edged, curving chopper with a blade that narrows near the hilt, cleaver. **2** (*perahu* –) a long, narrow, dugout canoe. – *tak tahu akan majalnya* to be unaware of one's own situation. – *tajam sebelah* likes to get but reluctant to give. *mencenangkan* – *patah* to be proud of s.t. completely valueless. *mematuk dengan punggung* – to hurt s.o.'s feelings. *mencenangkan sesuatu* – *yang hilang* to take pride in s.t. that is past or that no longer exists.

lading-lading ~ *roda* wood curved and joined to form a wheel.

lading II (*D*) cargo, shipload, freight.

ladingk(e)lérek (*D ob*) loading clerk.

ladong → LADUNG II.

ladrang (*Jv*) k.o. Javanese musical form.

ladu I (*Hind*) *kué* – rice dumplings in syrup.

ladu II (*Jv*) mud stream from a volcanic eruption, lava.

ladung I stopped flowing (of dew on the grass/tears on the face).

be(r)ladung to collect in drops. ~ *air mata* wet with tears, tear-stained.

meladungkan (*ob*) to water, wet.

ladung II lead used as a weight for nets, etc. *batu* – plummet, plumb-line, sinker on fishing rod, sounding lead.

berladung *kail* ~ sinker.

ladung III heap of rice.

ladung IV hollow, dent; bent.

meladungkan to bend (the fingers while dancing).

laén → LAIN I.

lafal, lafat and **lafa(d)z** (*A*) **1** (correct) pronunciation (of the Koran). – *kata-kata Inggris* the correct pronunciation of English words. **2** spoken word(s). **3** term, expression, formula. **4** knockdown argument. *tamat* – *dengan makna* had finished learning to pronounce and understand. *satu* –, *dua makna* one word with two meanings. *ada* –*nya pepatah dan ada maknanya* a proverb has a literal and a figurative meaning. – *Sumpah Dokter* Hippocratic Oath.

melafal to utter s.t.
melafalkan to pronounce; to utter.
lafalan articulation, pronunciation.
pelafalan pronunciation.

laga I (*Kawi poet*) **1** war, battle, combat. **2** fight (between animals). *biar lambat* –, *asal menang* (to reach one's goal) slowly but surely; never give in.
berlaga 1 to fight (of cocks/goats/rival teams, etc.). ~ *nyawa* to risk one's life (in a fight). **2** to collide. *semua pihak yang* ~ all the belligerents. **3** to smash/wash against the side of a boat (of waves). ~ *kasih* to be in love with e.o.
berlaga-laga to knock against e.o.
melaga to set/pit s.o. against s.o. else; to confront persons (in court). *waktu dilaga* when they were confronted (in court). ~ *ayam* to hold a cockfight.
melaga-laga(kan) to have animals fight e.o., set one against the other.
mem(per)lagakan to pit (s.t. or s.o.) against, set (s.t. or s.o.) to fight(ing).
pelaga 1 fighting. (*ayam* ~) fighting cock. *ikan* ~ fighting fish. **2** combative.
pelagaan and **perlagaan 1** fight, combat; *cp* PALAGAN. **2** collision.
laga II fighting fish, *Betta splendens.*
laga III (*J*) → LAGAK. **belaga** and **berlaga-laga** to boast, brag.
laga-lagaan boastful, showing off.
lagah-laguh (*ob*) → LAGUH-LAGAH.
lagak 1 bearing, manner, conduct, action(s). **2** posture, attitude, behavior (*esp* boasting, being conceited, etc.), style. **3** bluff. – *nya seperti istri orang kaya.* She behaves like the wife of a rich man. *banyak* –*nya* to put on a lot of airs. *jual* – to boast, brag, show off; → BUANG *aksi.* – *bahasa* (*infr*) a) dialect. b) accent. – *berpidato/berkata-kata* one's way/manner of speaking. *dengan* – *yang menyakitkan hati* in a hurtful way. – *désa* rural behavior. – *kuda* (beautiful) gait of a horse. – *lagam* a) accent. b) style (of singing/writing). – *lagu* behavior. – *Padang* those bragging people from Padang.
be(r)lagak 1 to boast, brag. **2** to put on airs, be pretentious. **3** to pretend (to be what one is not), act (as if), bluff, fake. ~ *bodoh* to play the fool. *Ia* ~ *bodoh saja.* He just acts (as if he were) stupid. *belagak pilon* to play innocent.
melagak 1 to brag, boast; → BE(R)LAGAK. **2** to threaten, frighten, scare, intimidate. **3** to impress. *Ia hendak* ~ *aku.* He wanted to impress me.
melagakkan to boast/brag about, show off about, flaunt. *Dia* ~ *jam barunya.* He showed off his new watch.
pelagak 1 braggart, posturer. **2** finery, etc. worn for showing off.
lagam I (*Pers ob*) horse's bit.
lagam II (*ob*) tune, melody; → LANGGAM 3, RAGAM I 4.
lagam III *kayu* – k.o. tree, *Canarium spp.*
lagan I *kayu* – k.o. giant forest tree, *Dipterocarpus, spp.*
lagan II dinnerware (on a ship); → KOMALIWAN.
lagang melagang(kan) to set the threads or leaves (said of a weaver or basket maker beginning to make an article), take the initial steps (in work/policy, etc.).
lagi 1 still (in a given state/in the process of doing s.t.). *Ketika dia memanggil tadi, saya* – *mandi.* When he called (me), I was (still) taking a bath. *ketika* – *kecil* when (I) was (still) young. **2** in addition, additional, more, a little more (time) *sebentar* – in a minute/little while. *masih* – and furthermore, in addition. *paling penting* – most important(ly). *banyak* – many others. *Satu* – *pertanyaan saya.* I have one more question. *yang penting* – just as important. *belum* – a) still not yet (though it might be expected). *Ah, pemerintah mandiri itu belum* – *didapat dalam satu dua tahun.* Self-government cannot be achieved in one or two years. b) *belum* ... – even before. *pagi-pagi belum mandi* – early in the morning even before taking a bath. c) not to mention, still not (although should have/expected to by now), not counting, not even taking into consideration, still not having in-

cluded. *Belum* – *kerugian waktu selama menunggu di rumah sakit.* I still haven't included/counted in the loss of time waiting in the hospital. **3** (following a negative) no ... longer/more. *bukan/ tidak* ... – and *bukan/tidak* – no longer/more. *Bau keringat tidak tertahan-tahan* –. The smell of sweat could no longer be borne. *Bekerja sebagai kuli bukan* – *kerja yang mendatangkan uang.* Working as a coolie on a plantation is no longer a job that brings in money. *lebih* – even more (so). *tidak salah* – that cannot be mistaken/misinterpreted; (make) no mistake about it, without any doubt. *Tidak salah* –, *ini erat hubungannya dengan keadaan jalan di sana.* No doubt about it, this was closely connected with road conditions there. **4** again, once more. –, – *dan* – again and again and again. *Kerjakan* –! Do it again! *Begini* –! Here we go again! **5** in, from now. *dua hari* – two days from now. **6** quite, very. *baru* – quite recently. **7** also. *yang buruk* – what is also undesirable is ... . **8** the other; other (after numbers and counters). *Beri saya kesempatan* –. Give me another chance. *yang dua/tiga, etc.* – the other two/three, etc. *yang (seorang)* – the other one/person. *duanya* – the other two (people). **9** and, as well as. *mérah* – *buruk* red and horrible (of s.o.'s face). **10** while. *Satu keluarga téwas terbakar* – *tidur.* A family burns to death while sleeping.
laginya and besides that.
lagi-lagi (once) again, once more, yet again, anew. ~ *penjahat lolos.* Once again criminals have escaped.
selagi 1 as long as. ~ *bisa* for as long as one can. **2** while, during (the time that). ~ *ayah tidur* while father is sleeping.
lagian (*J coq*) besides, moreover, in addition.
lagipula and **lagipun** in addition, and what's more. – *utang saya dalam dolar.* And what's more, my debts were in dollars.
lagitu (*J*) [lagi itu] formerly, in the past.
lagiyah meaningless, futile, useless.
lago sister's husband.
lagonder (*D ob*) dragoon.
lagu 1 intonation, the rise and fall of the voice when speaking/reading, singing, etc. – *bacaan* Qari dan Qariah the intonation of the male and female Koran readers. **2** song, tune, anthem, piece (of music). – (*yang*) *lama* the same old story. *bersenandung* – *usang* it's (always) the same old song/story/thing (over and over again). *membawa* – a) to lead the singing; to sing to s.o. b) to sing (another/a different song). – *cénggéng* whining. – *daérah* regional melodies. – *hiburan* light music. – *kebangsaan* national anthem. – *langgam* western-style music with Indonesian lyrics. – *pemakaman* dirge. – *penghibur* light music. – *rakyat* folk music. – *rantau* sea chanteys. – *sériosa* classical music. **3** melody, intonation. – *keroncong* a keroncong melody. – *tanya* question intonation. **4** fashion, style, way, manner. – *lagak* behavior. –*nya seperti dahulu juga* he is/behaves the same as before; he hasn't changed.
lagu-lagu songs, carols. ~ *Natal* Christmas carols.
selagu in harmony, compatible.
berlagu 1 with songs; (to perform) by reciting; (set) to music. **2** melodious, tuneful. **3** to boast, be arrogant.
melagu to sing.
melagui to set s.t. to music.
melagukan to recite s.t. in a singing voice, intone, chant, sing.
laguan (*ob*) melody.
pelagu (*ob*) singer, vocalist.
laguh-lagah to thunder, roar, rumble (of cart).
lagundi → LEGUNDI.
-lah I (a particle suffixed to the emphatic word or phrase in the sentence) **1** softens an imperative. *Pergi* – *sekarang!* Leave now! **2** shows inversion of subject and predicate. Attached to entire predicate or part of the predicate when it precedes the subject. *Pérs* – *yang mendorong kebangkitan nasional.* It's the press which provides the impetus for national development. *Berangkat* – *dia.* And then he left. ...*pun* ...– (*cla*) and then (in narrative). *Maka permaisuripun beranak* – *seorang perempuan.* And then the princess gave birth to a daughter. – *ya* [and (*coq*) – *yauw*] (an emphasizer). *nggak* – *yauw* no way!
lah II clipped form of **telah.**
lah III *burung* – lesser blue-winged pitta, *Pitta brachyura cyanoptera.*

lahab I to flare up.

Lahab II (*A*) *al-* Lahab; name of the 111th chapter of the Koran.

lahad (*A*) (*liang -*) niche (for the body in a Muslim grave), side aperture of grave turned toward Mecca. *serasa di liang -* very sad/sorrowful.

lahak (*M*) very strong, stinking smell.

lahan I (*Jv*) **1** land. *pembukaan - baru* opening up new land. *penyiapan -* land clearing (for transmigrants). **2** land to be cultivated. **3** waste/uncultivated land. **4** soil. *- lapisan atas* topsoil. **5** location (for transmigrants). *- basah* wetlands. *- cicilan* land apportioned/set aside/earmarked. *- gundul* bare land. *- murni* virgin land. *- pertanian* agricultural land, farm. *- sawah* wetland. *- subur* fertile ground. *- tak bermanfaat* waste land. *- tandus* bare land. *- tidur* unused land. *- yang dapat diusahakan* arable land. *- yasan* real estate.

berlahan to have a ... soil.

melahan to become/turn back into soil.

melahankan to let (a liquid) run off into the ground.

lahan II (*A*) **1** melody. **2** melodious.

lahan III → PERLAHAN(-LAHAN).

lahang (*Jv*) juice of the sugar palm, *Arenga pinnata*, which turns into toddy and vinegar; → NIRA, TUAK.

lahap gluttonous, very greedy for food, ravenous. *dengan -* heartily, ravenously.

selahap-lahapnya as greedily as possible.

melahap 1 to eat greedily/a lot, guzzle. **2** to annex, grab (land).

melahap-lahap to be out of breath.

melahapi (*pl obj*) to eat up, guzzle down.

kelahapan gluttony.

pelahap 1 glutton, guzzler. **2** greedy, gluttonous.

pelahapan guzzling, eating up greedily.

lahar I (*Jv*) **1** lava. **2** volcanic mud flow.

berlahar to spout lava.

lahar II open (of land).

lahar III ravenous.

lahat → LAHAD.

laher (*D*) ball bearing.

lahip → DAIF.

lahir I (*A*) **1** external, outward, exterior, extrinsic; apparent, visible; *cp* BATIN I. *pada -nya* outwardly, on the face of it; on the surface, apparently, seemingly. *Kalau tak dapat dengan - dengan batin.* If you can't do it overtly/in the open, then do it covertly/in a sneaky way. *- (dan) batin* a) altogether, completely, entirely, all, everything. b) (honest) to the core. c) for once and for all, definitely. d) fully. e) material and spiritual, physically and mentally. **2** bodily, corporal, exoteric, worldly, material, earthly.

kelahiran (outward) appearance/aspect, exterior.

terlahirkan revealed.

lahir II (*A*) **1** (to be) born, come into the world. *dari mula -* from childhood. *hari -* birthday. *sejak -(nya)* since (one's) birth. *- dari perkawinan yang sah* (in birth certificates) born in wedlock. *- di luar perkawinan yang sah* (in birth certificates) born out of wedlock. *- dini* to be premature. *- kembali* rebirth, reincarnation. *- mati* stillbirth, stillborn. *- muda* premature birth. *- sungsang* breech delivery. **2** to come into being, be founded, originate.

berlahiran (*pl subj*) to be born.

melahirkan [and **nglahirin** (*J coq*)] **1** to give birth to (a child), bring (a child) into the world. *Kapan anak akan dilahirkan?* When is the baby due? *pada waktu ~* in childbirth. **2** to manifest/reveal itself, be manifested. **3** to express (a wish/opinion/request, etc.). **4** to create, bring about (possibilities, etc.). *~ kemungkinan-kemungkinan yang tidak dikehendaki* to create undesirable possibilities. *~ probléma* to create problems. **5** to cast (a vote). *~ suaranya* to cast one's vote. **6** to raise (hope, expectations). **7** to evoke, provoke, produce, call forth (a debate, etc.). *telah ~ perdébatan pro dan kontra* have already produced debates in favor and against.

terlahir née, born (before a married woman's maiden name).

kelahiran 1 birth. *angka ~* birth rate. *~ belum cukup bulan* premature birth. *hari ~* birthday. *tingkat ~* fertility. *tanah ~* na-

tive country, fatherland. *tempat ~* birthplace. *~ mati* stillbirth. *~ sungsang* breech birth. **2** a native of, of ... extraction. *~ Madura* of Madurese extraction. **3** to be born of/from. *~ rakyat jelata* of humble origins. **4** creation.

pelahir s.o. who gives birth to (a child), s.o. who founds s.t.

pelahiran giving birth.

lahiriah (*A*) by the look of it, from all appearances.

lahjat (*A*) dialect.

lahong a small *durian* variety, *Durio dulcis*.

lai I → HELAI.

lai II (*C*) a small *durian* variety, *Durio kutejensis*.

laici → LÉNGKÉNG, LICI.

laif (*A*) weak, feeble; → DAIF.

melaif to attenuate.

melaifkan to attenuate/weaken s.t.

pelaif attenuator.

pelaifan attenuation.

laik decent, proper, -worthy; → LAYAK I. *tidak - huni* uninhabitable. *tak - jalan* not roadworthy. *tidak -* unfeasible. **ketidak-laikan** unfeasibility. *- laut* seaworthy. **kelaik-lautan** seaworthiness. *- udara* airworthy.

kelaikan worthiness. *~ laut* seaworthiness. *studi ~ usaha* feasibility study.

Lail (*A*) *al-* "Night"; name of the 92nd chapter of the Koran.

laila (*BD*) *- rahasia* confidential secretary.

lailah and **lailat** (*A*) night. *Alfu- wa - 1,001* Nights.

la ilaha illa'llah(u) and **la ilaha illa Allah** (*A*) **1** there is no God but Allah, the first sentence of the *syahadat*. **2** exclamation of dismay, despair.

lailatulkadar, lailatulkadir, Lailatul Kadar and **lalaétulkadar** (*A*) Night of Revelation, i.e., one of the odd-numbered nights of the last 10 days of the month of *Ramadan* (the 21st, 23rd, 25th, 27th, or 29th) when the Koran was sent down to the Prophet. *mendapat malam -* to earn a very blessed night.

lain I 1 other, another, different, alternative. *tentu - kalau ...,* it would be a different story if ... *- manapun* any other. *negara Asia - manapun* any other country in Asia. *orang -* another person entirely (not the same person). *- orang* not the same person, s.o. else. *- bulan/hari/tahun* next month/day/year (not this one). *- kali* a) some other time. b) next time. c) in future, henceforth. *- lagi!* a) it's totally different! it's not that at all! b) (= *- lagi pula*) quite different (from the others). *- pula yang dilakukan pasangan Soediani dan Soeprapti.* Quite different (from the others mentioned) is what was done by Soediani and Soeprapti. *- X - (pula) Y* X and Y are different (from e.o.). *- ... - ... some ... others. - disuruh duduk, - disuruh berdiri* some were told to sit, others to stand. *- halnya dengan* it a different case/matter/business with, it's quite another thing than. *- perkara kalau* that's (quite) another thing if; that's quite a different story if. *- dari yang -* and (sporadically) *- dari(pada) yang -* a) special, peculiar, unique. b) different from others, genius. *obat flu dengan komposisi - dari yang -* a flu remedy with a unique formula. *- tidak* nothing else, nothing beyond that, that's all. *- tidak (hanyalah ...) and tak - (dan) tak bukan (ialah ...)* only, nothing else but, simply and solely. *tidak - ...* to be nothing but (or, definitely) a ..., none other than. *Benda itu tidak - ikan yulah.* It was definitely a shark. *tak - ... melainkan ...* no other ... but to ... *Tak - cita-citanya melainkan hendak jadi orang berpangkat.* He has no other aspirations but to become s.o. with a good position. *tak - karena* be only because. *dan - sebagainya* [dsb.] etcetera, etc. *yang -* the other(s), the rest. *tidak ada yang -* there was nothing (to do but ...). *Tak ada yang - dapat saya lakukan kecuali ...* There was nothing for me to do but ... *- barang - harga* different things have different prices. *- diingin - yang dapat* one gets s.t. else than what one wanted. *- di mulut - di hati, - lafaz - itikad* he says one thing but means another, insincere. *- di muka - di belakang* to be a hypocrite. *- kata - perbuatan* to say one thing but do another. *- soal - jawabnya* that is neither here nor there, irrelevant. **2** except, ... excepted, not counting/including. *harga Rp 200 - ongkos kirim* price is Rp 200, not including shipping. **3** difference. *Apa -nya?* What's the difference? *jauh -nya dari yang biasa* quite different from the usual. **4** otherwise. *kecuali apabila ditentukan* – except as determined otherwise. *jikalau tidak ditentukan cara* – if not otherwise determined. – *dulu* – *sekarang* other times, other manners, i.e., customs change over time, things are different now. – *jenis* the opposite sex. – *padang – belalang,* – *lubuk* – (*pula*) *ikannya* so many countries, so many customs, i.e., customs vary from place to place. – *orang* – *pikiran/hati* (so) many men, (so) many minds, i.e., different people have different opinions/beliefs.

lainnya 1 (said to a customer) anything else? **2** (the) other(s). *dan yang dua* ~ and the other two. *dan beberapa* ~ and several others. *jauh* ~ *dari biasa* most special/particular.

lain-lain ~ *katanya* and ~ *saja jawabnya* shuffling excuses. *dan* ~*nya* [dll.] and so forth, and so on, etc.

selain besides, in addition to, aside/apart from, except. ~ *itu* in addition to that, besides, moreover. ~ (*dari/daripada*) (*itu*) besides (that), further(more), in addition to (that), except for (that).

selainnya 1 (for) the remainder, the rest. **2** except for, besides.

berlain different. **keberlainan** variance.

berlainan 1 dissimilar. ~ *dengan* a) different from. *jauh* ~ *dengan* very different from. b) in contravention of (the rules/regulations, etc.). **2** opposite. *dua orang* ~ *jenis* two persons of the opposite sex. ~ *ibu dengan* to have a different mother from.

berlain-lainan different from e.o.

mengelainkan (*ob*) to exclude; separate from the others.

melaini (*ob*) to violate, run counter to.

melainkan 1 (= **memperlainkan**) to separate from others, segregate, isolate. **2** only. ~ *tuan yang dapat menolong saya.* Only you can help me. **3** however, instead, but (rather). *Ia tidak ke Semarang* ~ *ke Bogor.* He didn't go to Semarang but rather to Bogor.

kelainan 1 difference, dissimilarity, distinction. **2** irregularity, peculiarity, abnormality, defect, anomaly. ~ *kelamin* transsex.

pemerlain (*infr*) differentiating feature.

lain II – *porem* (*D coq*) land reform.

laip (*ob*) weak, feeble; → DAIF.

lair → LAHIR I, II.

lais I melais (*ob*) to backwater with oars, back paddle.

lais II *ikan* – glass catfish, *Cryptopterus spp.*

lais III screw pine, *Pandanus furcatus.*

lais IV (*Jv*) a religious dance danced by a man dressed as a woman.

laitul (*A*) the night of. – *bara'ah* the 15th night of *Sya'ban*, when many believe that human destiny is set. – *mikraj* the 27th of Rajab when the Prophet Muhammad's night journey took place.

laissez faire (*E*) laissez faire, noninterference of government in business.

laja (*ob*) greater galangal; → LAOS.

lajak I *kain* -, – *benang* and – *sutra* woven fabric made from yarn or silk.

lajak II (*cla*) quick, fast.

lajak III (*Mal*) too far, exceed (the limit), over; → BERLEBIHAN. *laku* – to go too far, overreact. *digertak petugas yang kadang-kadang laku* – to be intimidated by functionaries who go too far/overreact.

lajang I *orang* – an unmarried person; bachelor, spinster. *pemuda* – unmarried youth. – *tanggung* a strapping young man.

melajang to live alone, be a bachelor/spinster.

pelajangan celibacy.

lajang II (*M*) **melajang** to strike with one's legs; to spring; → LEJANG, REJANG III.

lajat I delicious; → LAZAT, LEZAT.

lajat II (*M*) severe (of illness).

lajawardi → LAZUARDI.

lajim → LAZIM.

lajnah (*A*) committee. – *tanfidziyah* executive committee.

lajo (*Jv*) **nglajo** to commute (to work).

penglajo commuter.

laju I 1 fast (of speed), swift, speedy, rapid (of driving/sailing/flying, etc.) **2** velocity. – *mula* initial velocity. – *rambat* speed of (sound, etc.). – *rimban* drift velocity. **3** to make progress, im-

prove. **4** rate. – *air* flow rate. – *cuplik* sampling rate. – *didih* boil-up rate. – *gésér* shear rate. – *inflasi* rate of inflation. – *kejahatan* crime rate. – *kematian bayi* infant mortality rate. – *malih/temah* turnover rate. – *muat* throughput. – *pengeboran* (*petro*) penetration rate. – *pertumbuhan* growth rate.

berselaju, bersilaju and **berlaju-laju(an)** to race (of praus, etc.).

melaju to race, move fast. ~ *kencang* to race by fast, dash past.

melajukan to move s.t. fast, speed s.t. up, accelerate s.t.

kelajuan speed, velocity.

perlajuan acceleration.

laju II (*J*) delicious, enjoyable.

lajuardi → LAZUARDI.

lajur 1 row. **2a**) column (in a newspaper/magazine, etc.), space between lines. **b**) (*ob mil*) line, column. **3** belt, zone. **4** strip. **5** lane (of traffic); → JALUR I. – *air* wake (of a ship). – *lunas* keel strake.

selajur 1 a row. ~ *rumah* a row of houses. **2** stripe (in pattern).

berlajur 1 with stripes, striped. ~ *mérah* with red stripes.

melajur to form a stripe.

lajuran 1 stripe. **2** neck (of land). **berlajuran** striped.

lajurwan (newspaper) columnist.

lak I (*D*) sealing wax, lac, varnish. – *emas* gold varnish. – *getah* gum lac. – *kuku* nail polish. – *kuning* shellac. – *peluru* round lac. – *sténsil* correction fluid.

melak and **mengelak 1** to seal (so that it will not be opened by the wrong person). **2** to glue, etc. with sealing wax.

pengelakan lacquering, varnishing.

lak II (*C*) six. – *ban* 60,000. – *ban go* 65,000. – *cap* 60. – *cap go* 65. – *céng* 6,000. – *pék* 600. – *pék céng* 600,000. – *pék go* 650. – *pék go céng* 650,000. – *tiau* six million. – *tiau pua* six and a half million.

lak III (in acronyms) → PELAKSANA(AN).

laka I (*D*) lacquer, red paint. *kayu* – henna, *Lausonia inermis, Emblica officinalis, Dalbergia parviflora.*

laka II [*kecelakaan*] accident. – *kerja* work accident.

lakab (*A*) title, epithet, descriptive term (for dead or deposed rulers).

melakabkan to give a title, etc. to dead or deposed rulers.

lakak (*M*) – *kucing di dapur* (*M*) to mistreat.

melakak to hit (with a hard object).

lakan → LAKEN.

lakang (*M*) → LEKANG.

lakar (*ob*) the framework of a boat.

lakban (*D*) bandage, dressing.

lakcang (*C*) Chinese sausages.

laken (*D*) felt. *topi* – felt hat. – *kelasi* sailor's cloth.

lakeri (*D*) and – *penyégel* sealing wax.

laki I husband (less refined than *suami*). – *pulang kelaparan, dagang lalu ditanakkan* to pay more attention to s.o. else's business than to one's own. *menanti* – *pulang maling* to be continually in a nervous state. – *bini* husband/man and wife, married couple. **berlaki bini** to be husband and wife. – *jemputan* a good catch/eligible bachelor. – *pengantin* bridegroom.

laki-laki 1 husband. **2** man, men. **3** very brave, bold, courageous; a brave/daring, etc. person, daredevil, hero. **4** (in some regions) male (of animals). **kelaki-lakian 1** courage, bravery, strength. **2** manliness. **3** mannish. **4** masculinity.

berlaki to have a husband, be married (of a woman). ~ *anak semang* a woman whose behavior is indecent/improper. ~ *lain orang lagi* to remarry (said of a woman).

berlaki(kan) to be married to, have ... as a husband.

memperlaki to take/have ... as a husband.

memperlakikan 1 to marry/wed (said of a woman), to take ... as one's husband. **2** to give (a daughter) in marriage, marry off (a daughter), offer a husband to a girl.

laki II – *padi* common tailorbird, *Orthotomus sutorius.*

lakin (*A cla*) still, yet; → WALAKIN.

laklak (*A*) stork.

laklakan (*J*) gullet, throat, soft palate.

lakmus (*D*) litmus.

laknat (*A*) **1** curse, malediction. **2** (ac)cursed. *si* – the cursed/damned. **3** evil spirit.

melaknati and **melaknatkan** to curse s.o.

kelaknatan cursing.

laknatullah (*A*) cursed by God.

lakon I (*Jv*) **1** play, drama(tic piece). **2** scenario, story. **3** act, episode (from the Javanized *Ramayana* or *Mahab(h)arata*, serving as the plot for a single night's *wayang* performance); role, a part/character that an actor plays in a performance. *memainkan/memegang –nya* to play one's role. *– lacak* detective story. *– pertama* the first act (of a play). *– sandiwara* (stage-)play, drama. *– tampang* line-up (in front of the police).

berlakon to act as, play the role of.

melakoni and **melakonkan** [and **ngelakonin** (*J coq*)] **1** to stage, act out; → MEMAINKAN *lakonnya*. **2** to write a play/story/drama. **3** to perform. **4** → (*cerita*) to narrate, tell the story of. *Film ini ~ seorang gadis yang ...* This film tells the story of a girl who ...

pelakon 1 → PELAKU. **2** player, actor, performer; → PEMERAN. *~ watak* character actor/player. **3** (leading) figure.

pelakonan acting.

lakon II (*Jv*) **nglakoni** to follow an ascetic regime.

lakpé (*C J*) six hundred.

Lakpus (*mil*) [Pelaksanaan Pusat] Central Executive Organs.

lakri → LAKERI.

laks (in acronyms) → LAKSAMANA, PELAKSANA.

laksa I (*Skr*) ten thousand. *empat –* forty thousand.

berlaksa-laksa tens of thousands.

laksa II (*Hind*) → MI I.

laksa III (*Pers*) crunchy rice sticks dipped in and eaten with slices of cucumbers/large onions/chilies, etc. and a specially prepared *kuah*. *– pengantin* rice noodles with baked chicken, rice cakes and yellow coconut milk.

laksamana (*Skr*) admiral. *– madya* vice admiral. *– muda* [Laksda] rear admiral. *– muda udara* lieutenant general in the Air Force. *– pertama* commander, commodore. *– tertinggi* fleet admiral. *– udara* Air Force general.

laksana I (*Skr*) **1** (typical) qualities, (distinctive/distinguishing) marks (of beauty, etc.). *– istri/perempuan* typical qualities/characteristics of a woman. *bukan –* incomparable, matchless. *– seperti* it seems to be. *– seperti benang putih* it seems to be white thread. **2** to look like, resemble. *Cincin palsu itu – cincin emas.* That fake ring looks like a gold ring.

melaksanakan 1 to carry out, put into effect/operation, effect, implement, undertake, act upon, carry through, administer (justice), exercise (one's rights). *Pemerintah akan ~ dua proyék.* The government will undertake two projects. *tidak ~* to fail to do. *tidak ~ pembayaran* to default on a payment. **2** to realize, accomplish, attain. **3** to put into practice. *tidak dapat/mungkin dilaksanakan* impracticable, not feasible, cannot be achieved. **4** to enforce (one's rights under an agreement). **5** to compare, examine to see to what extent things are similar or not. *dilaksanakan bulan dengan matahari* the moon has been compared to the sun.

terlaksana to be carried out, able to be carried out, implemented. **keterlaksanaan** feasibility.

pelaksana 1 executor, performer. **2** administrator, director. *~ bangunan* building contractor. *~ Kuasa Perang* [Pékupér] War Administrator. *~ surat wasiat* executor/executrix of a will. **3** administrative.

pelaksanaan [and (*infr*) **penglaksanaan** and **perlaksanaan**] **1** execution, implementing, putting into effect, action, performance, fulfillment, completion, administration. *dalam taraf ~* underway, in progress. *ketentuan-ketentuan ~* executory provisions. *~ dinas* status report. *~ kerja* performance (at work). *~ pidana* execution/carrying out of a sentence. *~ (ter)lebih da(hu)lu* provisional execution/enforcement. **2** enforcement (of an agreement).

laksana II sweet wattle, k.o. acacia, *Acacia farnesiana*.

laksanawan manager, executor.

Laksmi (*Skr*) **1** Vishnu's wife. **2** (*cla*) beautiful, pretty.

laksus [pelaksana khusus] Special Administrator.

laktose and **laktosa** (*D*) lactose.

laku 1 current, marketable, salable; in season; in demand/favor, sought after, favored, popular, in vogue. *kurang –* sell poorly, not be in demand/popular. *tidak – a*) (of articles) unmarketable, unsalable; out of season. b) (of people) all washed up.

sangat – and *– keras* (it is) in great demand, (it) sells readily/very well, (it is) much sought after. *– seperti kué/goréng pisang* and *– sebagai goréng pisang* to sell like hotcakes. **2** *– banyak/sedikit* yield a lot/very little, realize well/ill; pay well/poorly. **3** sold; out of stock. *habis –* sold out. **4** find favor/acceptance, be accepted, catch on (with the public), find a ready sale, find a market/an outlet for, become popular, meet with a favorable reception, be well received, be warmly welcomed. **5** (not yet) strong enough (of an oath). **6** *tidak –* it makes (no) sense (of arguments). **7** (*tingkah –*) manners, behavior, conduct, attitude, deportment, demeanor; way/manner of acting. *berbuat –* to assume an attitude, put on a good countenance. *segala salah pula –nya* he can do no good, he can do nothing right. *sebagai ... –nya/layaknya* seems to be ... *sebagai orang kaya –nya* he seems to be (a) rich (person). **8** valid, legal, in force/effect, hold (good). *Uang Indonésia tidak – di negara ini.* Indonesian currency is not legal tender in this country. *Uang kertas ini sudah tidak –.* This paper money can no longer be used (because it is no longer valid). *mulai –* goes into effect. *tidak –* invalid. *tidak – lagi* no longer in effect, expired. *– jantera hidup* life cycle. *– keras* it sells quickly/easily. *– lajak* over(re)acting. *– lampah* conduct, life, behavior. *– liku* complex. ***berlaku-liku*** intricate, complicated.

selaku 1 like, equal, similar. **2** as, in the capacity of. *~ demikian* as such. *~ présidén* as president.

selakunya *~ saja* whatever sells.

berlaku 1 to be in force/effect, be valid, be operative, be current, be in use, hold (good), apply (to); prevailing, going (rate/price); to be applicable (laws/regulations). *kurs yang ~* prevailing rate of exchange. *mulai ~* to come into force (of a law). *undang-undang yang ~* applicable law. *harga-harga yang ~ sekarang* current/prevailing prices. *kenaikan gaji yang ~ untuk semuanya* an across-the-board pay increase. *sedang ~* in operation/progress. *tidak ~* a) inoperative, in abeyance. *dinyatakan tidak ~ (lagi)* to be declared void/invalid. b) invalid, no good (of a check), void. *tidak ~ untuk menumpang* not good for passage (on a ticket). *~nya kembali Undang-Undang Dasar 1945* the reimposition of the 1945 Constitution. *dengan ~nya Undang-Undang No. 7* with the imposition of Law No. 7. *masa/waktu ~nya* term/period of validity. *telah habis masa ~nya* has expired. *~ dua pihak* it works both ways. *~ éféktif* to become effective. *~ surut* to be retroactive. *~ umum* generally accepted (standards). **2** to act (arbitrarily/high-handedly); → BERTINDAK. **3** to behave, act (in some way). *~ sebagai* to act/officiate as; representing, acting as. *~ sebagai bukti yang sah dari keputusan-keputusan yang diambil pada ...* (in notarial instruments) representing valid evidence of the decisions taken at ... **4** to happen, occur, take place, be in progress, come about. **5** to happen to, befall. **6** (to come) to be realized/fulfilled (of a wish/goal/objective), come true (of s.o.'s words). **7** to meet with success, be/prove successful. **memberlakukan** to put (regulations) into effect, impose (a law or ordinance), execute (provisions of a contract). *~ kembali* to reimpose (regulation/law). *keadaan darurat yang telah diberlakukan hari Jumat* emergency conditions imposed on Friday. *~ surut* to put into effect retroactively. **keberlakuan** validity. *~ surut* retroactive(ly).

pemberlakuan 1 imposition (of a tax/law/curfew, etc.). **2** announcement of applicability.

melakukan [and **ng(e)lakuin** (*J coq*)] **1** to dispose of, sell (articles/commodities); to introduce, put in(to) circulation, circulate (money). **2** to draw up (a report), record. **3** to guide. *hidup yang dilakukan ...* a life guided by ... **4** to conduct, carry on (a campaign), wage (war). **5** to ask/put (a question); to make/direct, address (a request) to; to carry out (a request). **6** to take/make a trip; to do (one's duty); to commit (an error), make (a mistake); to perform; to commit (a crime); to make/carry out (an experiment); to go on (a diet). *~ audit* to make/conduct an audit. *~ baiat kepada* to take an oath of allegiance to. *~ bunuh diri* to commit suicide. *~ daya upaya/ikhtiar* to make an attempt/effort, do one's utmost to, leave no stone unturned. *~ désérsi* to desert, i.e., to leave military service or one's post without permission. *~ diri seperti* to behave/act like. *~ hajat* to relieve o.s.. ~ *hubungan séks* to have sexual relations. ~ *ibadat* to fulfill/perform one's religious duties (loyally). ~ *kesukaan* to enjoy s.t. ~ *ketrampilan* to display one's skill. ~ *kudéta* to carry out a coup d'état. ~ *latih tanding* to spar (in boxing). ~ *lélang* to hold an auction. ~ *muslihat* to use tricks/guile. ~ *pelanggaran* to commit an offense. ~ *pemukulan* to beat s.o. up. ~ *penangkapan terhadap* to arrest s.o. ~ *pengawasan* to supervise, inspect, exercise control over. ~ *perintah* a) to obey/follow/carry out an order. b) ~ *perintah kepada* to give an order to. ~ *pertimbangan* to exercise one's own judgment (as to). ~ *pembunuhan atas* to murder/kill. ~ *pungli* to demand illegal levies. ~ *razia* to carry out a raid. ~ *sendiri* to manage on one's own. ~ *sikap* to take a position, adopt a policy. ~ *tindakan* to take steps. ~ *tugas* to perform one's duties. ~ *zakat atas* to impose the Muslim tithe on.

memperlakukan 1 → MELAKUKAN. **2** to treat (in a certain way), deal with, handle. *cara ~nya* the way to handle/deal with him.

terlaku the most popular.

lakuan (*infr*) action.

kelakuan 1 behavior, conduct, way of acting. **2** event, occurrence. **berkelakuan** to behave, act; to have ... character. ~ *baik* of good character.

pelaku 1 (*gram*) agent, doer. **2** perpetrator, person who has done s.t., accomplice (to a crime), associate, accessory (to a crime). ~ *kejahatan* perpetrator, criminal. ~ *peledakan* accomplice in blowing up s.t. ~ *pembangunan wilayah pedésaan* agent of rural development. ~ *pembunuhan* the killer. ~ *pencuri* accessories to a theft. ~ *penémbakan* the gunman, shooter. ~ *perampokan* robber. ~ *(pe)serta* accomplice, accessory. **kepelaku-sertaan** complicity. ~ *tabrak lari* hit-and-run driver. ~ *suruhan* s.o. who commits a crime on s.o. else's orders. ~ *tawuran* s.o. who takes part in fights (among high school students). ~ *tindak pidana* perpetrator. ~ *usaha* businessperson. **3** performer, actor, actress. ~ *utama* leading man/lady. **4** character (in a novel/play/movie, etc.). **kepelakuan** being the perpetrator.

perlakuan 1 treatment, treating. ~ *kejam terhadap anak* child abuse. ~ *tawanan* treatment of prisoners. **2** occurrence. **3** action, act. ~ *perang* act of war.

lakum wild vines, *Vitis spp.*

lakur alloyed (metals), mixed. *- baur* mixed, fused.

berlakur mixed.

melakur to alloy.

melakurkan to fuse an alloy.

lakuran alloy.

pelakuran mixing, alloying.

lala I *siput* - k.o. mollusk, *Trochus spp.*

lala II rainbow; → BIANGLALA.

lala III (*ob*) **melala** to swim on one's back.

lalab → LALAP.

lalaétulkadar → LAILATULKADAR.

lalah I gluttonous; to like to eat anything.

pelalah glutton.

lalah II (*M*) **melalah** to chase/run after. *bak menanti orang dahulu, bak ~ orang kudian* to flog a dead horse.

terlalah pursued, chased/run after; hurriedly, hastily. *- terkejar* (evidence according to Minangkabau *adat* that s.o.) was caught red-handed.

lalai I 1 inattentive, negligent, careless, inadvertent, thoughtless, absent-minded. *Manusia itu -*. To err is human. **2** unconscious, senseless; suddenly forget, preoccupied. *- membaca* (so) absorbed in one's reading (so that one forgets s.t. else). **3** careless, casual, offhanded. **4** - (*dan perlahan bekerjanya*) slow, sluggish, indolent. **5** to fail, neglect (to pay one's debts, carry out one's duties, etc.), default.

berlalai-lalai 1 dawdling. **2** to be off one's guard. **3** to be idle, loaf.

melalaikan 1 to ignore, neglect (one's duties), let matters/things take their own course, be indifferent to, forget (to provide for his requirements/needs/wants). ~ *hati (sedih)* to comfort/raise the spirits of. *untuk ~ pikiran* for/as relaxation. ~ *daripada* to divert/turn away/draw attention from (feelings of fear/a certain situation/religion, etc.). **2** to waste (one's time).

~ *hari/bulan/kesempatan* to let a good day/month/opportunity slip away/by.

memperlalaikan 1 to cause to forget/neglect/disregard, etc. **2** to postpone, put off, delay. **3** to comfort, entertain, give pleasure to.

terlalai 1 (*ob*) forgotten. **2** (*ob*) sleepy, drowsy. **3** belated/delayed (of a journey, etc.). **4** *tak - daripada beribadat* to observe/comply with/live up to one's religious/church duties regularly. **5** ~ *dari janji* (*cla*) to fail to keep one's promise.

terlalaikan neglected.

kelalaian 1 failure, error, neglect, inattention, carelessness, negligence, slovenliness. ~ *manusia* human error. ~ *berat yang sérius* gross negligence, culpa lata. ~ *dalam tugas* dereliction of duty. **2** default.

pelalai 1 s.o. who is careless/inattentive/negligent, a dawdler, lazybones. **2** (*hikmat ~*) spell which makes one forgetful/negligent/inattentive.

pelalaian the act of neglecting, ignoring (one's duties, etc.).

lalai II *tali* - (*naut*) vangs, guy ropes (from the ends of a boat's gaff to deck).

lalak (*ob*) **melalak** to burn, flare up; burnt, afire; to explode, erupt.

lalalat (*A*) wrong, deceptive.

lalang I cogon grass, *Imperata cylindrica. tanam - tumbuh padi* return like for like, give tit for tat.

lalang II (*ob*) to roam/wander about; → LANGLANG I.

lalang III (*ob*) → LALU-LALANG.

lalangasu (*geog*) hogback.

lalap 1 (*J*) relish. **2** (*Jv*) uncooked, cold vegetables as a side dish. **melalap 1** to overcome, defeat, beat. (*habis*) *dilalap api* to be burned down. *dilalap glédék* to be struck by lightning. **2** to hold up. **3** to eat *lalap*. **4** to steal, embezzle, misappropriate. ~ *daun muda* to have sex with s.o. (*usu* underage).

lalapan raw vegetables.

lalap-lalapan all k.o. cold vegetables.

pelalap ~ *mode* clotheshorse, fancy dresser.

lalar (*M*) **melalar 1** to wander around aimlessly (because one cannot stand to stay at home). **2** to spread (of fire).

pelalar s.o. who can't stand to stay home.

lalat (house) fly, *Musca domestica. kerajaan* - a densely populated country. *misai - hinggap* Hitler-moustache. *pening-pening* - (*M*) very dizzy. *tahi* - birthmark. *tak ada - langau* and *- lalaupun tak tampak* there's nobody around, nobody's here. *belum terbang* - very early in the morning. *seperti - mencari puru* greedy. *terbang-terbang* - (to do s.t.) in fits and starts. *berani* - to have courage when behind the opponent (but be scared when facing him). *- bisul* blister fly/beetle, *Procontarini mattiana. - buah* fruit fly, *Dacus pedestris. - cambium* cambium miner, *Agromyzidae spp. - kacang* bean fly, *Agromyza phaseoli. - hijau* a) bluebottle, *Calliphora vicina.* b) (*ob*) unpaid pimp. c) (and *- ijo*), (*coq*) member of the Armed Forces. *- kerbau* cattle fly, *Oestrus spp. - kuda* horsefly, *Tabanus spp. - rumah* housefly, *Musca domestica. - ternak* screw worm fly, *Chrysomya bezziana.*

lalau melalau(i) to post no trespassing signs, ward off (trespassers, etc.), obstruct the way.

pelalau 1 (*ob*) roadblock; obstruction (in the road), hindrance. **2** (*hikmat -*) k.o. charm to prevent a girl from marrying another man.

pelalauan hindrance.

laler (*J/Jv*) → LALAT.

lali I 1 insensitive (to stimuli/emotions, etc.), numb; immune (to a disease); unconscious, anesthetized. **2** (*Jv*) to forget.

melali(kan) to anesthetize, immunize, make unconscious.

pelali immunization.

pelalian 1 immunity. **2** (*Mal*) immunization.

lali II ankle bone; → BUKU *lali.*

lalim (*A*) tyrannical, unjust. *orang* - tyrant.

melalimi and **melalimkan** (*ob*) to tyrannize, oppress.

kelaliman tyranny, cruelty, oppression.

lalu I 1 to pass/go by, pass through. *tidak boléh - di jalan ini!* No thoroughfare! *beri - let* me pass. *bertukar* - exchanged without additional/further/extra payment. *hujan* - a passing/brief rain-shower. *sambil* - incidentally, casually, in passing, en passant, by the way, parenthetically. *pandang sekali/sekilas* – to look cursorily/hastily/superficially/perfunctorily. – *saja katanya* say(ing) for the sake of saying; *cp* ASBUN; → LALU-LALANG/ LANDANG, LALU-LINTAS. 2a) to let ... through; permeable, penetrable, open to passage by fluids. – *penjahit*, – *kelindan* where one sheep goes another follows; to follow like sheep. *(tidak)* – *di akal/anggan* (il)logical, (un)acceptable. *tidak* – *hujan* rainwater cannot come in. b) to succeed, be successful (of a plan, trick, etc.). 3 past, last, ago, that has passed; preceding. *sudah* – *jamannya* out of date, obsolete, outmoded. *bulan/minggu/ tahun (yang)* – last month/week/year. *tiga tahun (yang)* – three years ago. *dalam pelajaran yang* – in the preceding lesson. *tiga malam yang* – three nights ago. 4 be over/past/ended/at an end/finished, have passed. *ujian telah* – the exam is over. 5 to be redeemed. 6 to happen; → BERLALU. 7 then, after that. – *akal* reasonable. – *béa* passing through customs. **melalu-béakan** to get s.t. through customs. – *lalang* → LALU-LALANG. – *lintas* → LALU-LINTAS.

selalu → SELALU.

berlalu 1 to pass, go by (of time), pass by (of time/an opportunity/a person), pass through. 2 to expire (of terms/a contract). *sudah* ~ it's finished/all over. *yang* ~ what is past, bygones. *Kegaduhan telah* ~. The disturbance is over. *Musim tanam sudah* ~ *50 hari*. The dry season has been over for 50 days. ~ *angan* to pass through one's mind. *Wanita itu* ~ *meninggalkan warung itu*. The woman slipped away from the restaurant. *Jangan biarkan kesempatan baik ini* ~. Don't let this opportunity slip by. 4 past due, overdue. ~ *dari dunia (euph)* to die, pass away.

melalui 1 to make use of (a road/the sea/the air), pass/travel through (a town, etc.), get by (s.t. in the way). *dapat dilalui kendaraan bermotor* passable by motor vehicles. 2 via, through, by way of, over, on. *dari Jakarta ke Bandung* ~ *Purwakarta* from Jakarta to Bandung via Purwakarta. ~ *saluran-saluran diplomatik* through diplomatic channels. *disiarkan* ~ *radio* broadcast over the radio. *(ber)bicara* ~ *télepon* to talk on the telephone. 3 by means of, using. 4 to disregard, ignore, brush aside. *Jangan kaulalui perkataan orangtuamu*. Don't ignore what your parents say. 5 to infringe on (law/order, etc.), trespass, transgress, overstep. 6 to get through. *hitungan yang sukar dilalui saja* a calculation that is hard to get through. 7 *(ob)* *tiada dapat* ~ cannot escape (justice).

melalukan 1 to allow s.t. to pass, pass s.t. through, take s.t. through. 2 to admit, do, carry out. 3 to continue. 4 to pass s.t. up/by. ~ *angan* to do as one pleases. ~ *jarum* to trick, deceive. ~ *maksudnya* to accomplish/achieve one's intention/purpose.

terlalu 1 too, (to go) too far. ~ *mahal* too expensive. ~*!* That's too much/the limit! That's going too far! *mémang* ~ too much, that's really something! 2 excessively, surpassingly, overly, over-; → LAJAK III. ~ *sarat* overloaded. 3 extremely; → AMAT *sangat*. **keterlaluan** excessive, extreme, beyond all bounds, outrageous, too much. *berlaku* ~ to act outrageously. ~ *lelah* extremely exhausted.

laluan passage, thoroughfare.

kelaluan gone too far. **berkelaluan** *(M)* continuous; dragging, going on forever. *tidak* ~ limited.

pelaluan passing through, transit. ~ *angin topan* passing through the typhoon belt. ~ *planét Mérkuri* Mercury's (apparent) transit (across the face of the sun).

lalu II selalu always, incessantly, continuously.

laluasa *(ob)* → LELUASA.

laluga (on Miangas Island) k.o. taro that grows in swampy areas.

laluhur → LELUHUR.

lalu-lalang/landang 1 to pass over and over again (of passersby). *orang* – passersby. 2 uninterrupted (flow of words). 3 to please s.o., have it one's own way. 4 systemless, disorderly. 5 (extremely) indifferent, insolent. 6 indecent; to run on and on, let one's tongue get away with one. 7 to go where one pleases.

lalu-lintas 1 to and fro, vice versa, up and down. 2 to pass by (time and again/over and over again). 3 traffic. *pengawasan* – *dévisa* foreign exchange traffic control. *pengelolaan* – traffic management. *perékayasaan* – traffic engineering. *polisi* – traffic police.

– *ékamarga* one-way traffic. – *giro* (banking term) transfer business. – *giro dan kliring* (banking term) transfer and clearing operations. – *kaki* pedestrian traffic. – *langsung* through traffic. – *pembayaran luar negeri* (banking term) transfer of international payments. – *penumpang* passenger traffic. – *searah* one-way traffic. – *udara* air traffic.

berlalu-lintas traffic *(mod)*. *kesadaran* ~ awareness of traffic.

kelalu-lintasan traffic *(mod)*. *penegakan hukum* ~ traffic law enforcement.

perlalu-lintasan traffic *(mod)*. *sistém* ~ traffic system.

lam *(A)* name of the 23rd letter of the Arabic alphabet; → LAM ALIF. – *ibtida* initial *lam*.

lama 1 long (of time), prolonged (applause, etc.), protracted; (connection/friend, etc.) of long standing, longtime. – ... *baru* ... it is/was a long time before ... – *(juga)* ... *barulah/maka* ... it takes a (rather) long time before (s.o. answers, etc.), to wait a long time before. *tak tahan* – *dalam keadaan segar* perishable. *tak/ tidak* – *lagi* shortly, before long, any time now. *(me)makan tempo/waktu yang* – to take a long time. *sudah* – *benar* a long time ago. *Jangan* –. Don't take long. *Aku tak* –. I won't take long. *sudah berapa* – a) already for some time. b) how long (has it been). *belum – (ini)* recently, it hasn't been a long time. *paling* – not too exceed, at most. *sejak* – a) long ago, long before this. b) (it is) a long time since. *tak* – *antaranya/kemudian* not long afterward. *sudah* – it has been a long time. *Sudah* – *dia bisa membaca jam*. He has been able to tell time for a long time. *Sudah* – *disini?* Have you been here for a long time? *sudah* – ... *tidak* it's been a long time since ... *Sudah* – *kita tak berjumpa*. It's a long time since we met (or, We haven't met for a long time). *sekian* – all this time, all along. *setelah ditunggu-tunggu sekian* – after waiting all this time. 2 previous, ex-, former, old; → ÉKS II, MANTAN, TUA. *teman* – an old friend (i.e., a friend one has known for a long time). 3 stale (of bread, etc.); worn out (of clothes); antiquated, obsolete, outdated, no longer current, not topical (of news); → BASI I. *Berita itu sudah* –. That's old news. 4 antique; → ANTIK. 5 (of periodicals) back (number). 6 long-established.

lamanya period, duration, for (the duration of). *5 tahun* ~ for five years. *untuk berapa* ~ for some time. *tiada berapa tahun* – a few years ago. *tiada berapa* ~ not long after, soon. ~ *percobaan* duration of the test.

lama-lama gradually, in the long run, finally, in the end, after a long time. **berlama-lama** 1 for a prolonged period, for a long time; to spend a long time. *Aku tidak bisa* ~ *di sini*. I can't spend a long time here. 2 eventually, in the long run.

selama for (the duration/period) of, (for) as long as, during, in the course of, while. ~ *lima jam* for five hours. ~ ... *belum* until. ~ *pihak kedua belum membayar lunas seluruh harga* until the second party has paid the entire price in full. ~ *berlangsungnya* for the duration of. ~ *hayat di kandung badan* as long as I live. ~ *hidup* for the rest of one's life, all one's life. ~ *ini* up to/till now, so far, to date; nowadays. ~ *itu* all that time, for that length of time. ~ *lima tahun ini* (for) these last five years. ~ *perlu* as long as necessary. ~ *tiga minggu* for the (last/next) three weeks.

selamanya always, forever (after), for good. *Tak* ~ *sampah idéntik dengan kekotoran*. Trash is not always the same as filth. ~ *tidak* never (again).

selama-lamanya 1 forever, eternal, always. 2 at the most, maximum. *hukuman penjara* ~ *10 tahun* a maximum imprisonment of 10 years. *untuk* ~ forever, for good, once and for all.

lama-lamain *(J)* to prolong, extend (the time). *Saya* ~ *duduk di rumah teman*. I stayed and stayed in my friend's house.

melamakan and **memperlamakan** 1 to extend, prolong, protract (the time). 2 to delay, slacken, slow down.

memperlama to play for time, drag one's feet.

kelama-lamaan 1 too long (of time). 2 eventually, in the long run.

lama-kelamaan at last, eventually, in the long run, finally.

lamak I → LAMA.

lamak II *(Bal)* k.o. decoration on bamboo poles.

lamak III → LEMAK.

lam alif the Arabic characters lam and alif which together are pronounced *la*, meaning 'no'. An abbreviation of *la ilaha illa'llah*, there is no God but Allah. *air* – water which has had a spell cast on it (used as an antidote against hostile influences/medicine, etc.).

laman I (*coq*) the clipped form of *halaman*.

laman II (*J*) → LAMA.

lamang (*J*) a cutlass.

lamar (*J/Jv*) **melamar** [and **nglamar** (*coq*)] **1** to propose/offer marriage to, ask for a girl's hand in marriage. *Anaknya telah dilamar orang kaya*. A rich person proposed to his daughter. **2** to apply (for a job).
  melamarkan 1 to propose for s.o. **2** (~ *dirinya*) (*ob*) to surrender o.s. for employment, volunteer.
  pelamar 1 applicant. **2** suitor, wooer.
  lamaran 1 proposal (of marriage). **2** request, application.
  pelamaran applying (for).

lamat thin quilt mattress.

lamat-lamat(an) (*Jv*) **1** hardly visible; → SAYUP-SAYUP. **2** barely audible.

lambai wave, waving.
  berlambai(-lambai) to wave, flap, sway (in the wind).
  melambai(-lambai) 1 to wave (a hand/handkerchief/flag/weapon), beckon. **2** to wave = **melambai(-lambai)kan** to wave (with the hand as a sign to come over to the person waving, etc.). *(bagai) dilambai-lambai api* (*ob*) (as if he) is burning/on fire; to have a warm feeling all over.
  melambaikan ~ *harapan kuat* promising much.
  lambaian 1 waving, beckoning. ~ *bendéra* flag waving. **2** (*ob*) (a meaningless) gesture.

lambak 1 disorderly pile/heap. **2** (*Mal*) overflowing.
  berlambak(-lambak), **melambak** and **terlambak** in confused heaps (of coins/fruits/logs/nuts, etc.). *kain/tikar berlambak* double cloth/mat.
  melambakkan to pile s.t. up.

lambakan soil used to make bunds in rice fields.

lamban (*Jv M*) **1** sluggish, indolent, lazy, languid, inert, slow. **2** clumsy.
  melamban 1 to be lazy. **2** to be clumsy.
  memperlamban to slow s.t. down. ~ *kerja* to slow down (at work).
  terlamban the slowest.
  kelambanan 1 sluggishness, indolence, inertia, slowness. **2** clumsiness. ~ *méntal* mental inertia.
  pelambanan slowdown, slowing down.

lambang (*Jv*) **1** sign, symbol, emblem, mark that represents s.t. **2** badge. **3** logo. **4** decal. **5** heraldic arms/crest, coat of arms. *ilmu* – heraldry. – *dagang* brand. – *dagang pribadi* house brand. – *géngsi* status symbol (e.g., a car, in Indonesia). – *keluarga* family coat of arms. – *martabat* status symbol. – *Negara* State Coat of Arms. – *perusahaan* corporate logo.
  berlambang with the symbol ... ~ *bintang* with the star symbol.
  melambangkan to symbolize, represent, portend.
  pelambang sign, symbol.
  perlambang 1 heraldry. **2** symbolism.
  perlambangan symbolism.

lambangsari (*euph Jv*) sexual intercourse.
  berlambangsari to have sexual intercourse.

lambar (*Jv*) under layer.
  berlambar to have s.t. as a base or underlayer.
  melambari to serve as an underlayer for.
  lambaran (*Jv*) underlayer (of paper/leaves, etc. put under food on a plate); object for s.t. to rest on, such as a saucer/writing pad/doily, etc.

lambat 1 slow, not quick. *paling* – at the latest/utmost. **2** late, slow, behind time. *Dia datang – ke kantor*. He arrived at the office late. *Arloji ini – lima menit*. This watch is five minutes slow. – *sejam* an hour slow. **3** taking a long time, time-consuming. *padi yang – berbuah* slow-ripening paddy. *bekerja – sekali* to work slowly. *biar – asal(kan) selamat* a) slow but sure. b) better late than never. – *laun* a) gradually, in the long run. b) finally. c) sooner or later. – *mengeras* slow-setting.
  selambat-lambatnya at the (very) latest, not later than. ~ *pada hari Sabtu* on Saturday at the latest.
  berlambat 1 to linger, dawdle, delay. **2** unhurried, slow. *tidak* ~ immediately, without delay.

melambat to slow down.
  melambatkan to slow s.t. down. *Mobilnya dilambatkannya*. He slowed down his car. *dilambatkan dari aturan* more sluggish than usual.
  memperlambat 1 to make s.t. slow down. ~ *kemajuan* to slow down progress. **2** to delay, postpone.
  terlambat 1a) late (i.e., not on time for an appointment, etc., later than expected, etc.). *lebih baik* ~ *daripada sama sekali tidak* better late than never. ~ *bulan* late in menstruating. b) belated. *berita* ~ a belated news item. **2** delayed. ~ *banget* much delayed. **keterlambatan** delay, slowdown, lag.
  kelambatan 1 delay, slowness, inertia. **2** too late; to be overdue. ~ *tiga jam* three hours (too) late.
  pelambat delay (*mod*), delaying.
  pelambatan delay, delaying.
  penglambatan slowdown.
  perlambatan retardation.

lambau (*D coq*) agriculture.

lambé (*Jv*) **1** lip(s). **2** mouth. **3** words, talk; → ABANG-ABANG *lambé*.

lambo Buginese sailboat with one mast, peculiar to the island of Buton; *cp* PENISI.

lambu (*ob*) a ketch; → LAMBUK III.

lambuk I (*M*) friable, crumbling, loose (of earth).
  melambuk 1 to loosen (the soil). *gedang sebagai dilambuk-lambuk tinggi sebagai dijunjung* highly honored/glorified. **2** to support with money.
  pelambuk s.t. given in support.

lambuk II *celana* – (Aceh-style) loosely fitting pants made of silk.

lambuk III (*ob*) k.o. ketch.

lambung I bounce, bouncing, high (of ball). *tinggi benar* –*nya* it bounces high.
  melambung 1 to lift, be tossed about (of boat in heavy seas). ~ *dipukul ombak* tossed by the waves. **2** to jump/leap up, jump around. ~ *kegirangan* to jump for joy. *setinggi-tinggi* ~, *surutnya ke tanah juga* east or west, home is best; be it ever so humble there's no place like home. **3** to go up, soar, rise. ~ *ke atas* to skyrocket (of prices, etc.). **4** to flatter, praise, extol. **5** to fly away (of luck). *tuah* ~ *tinggi, celaka/malang menimpa badan* "luck soars away and misfortunes crush us," i.e., to have a run of bad luck, be overtaken by a series of disasters. **6** to fly s.t. high in the sky. ~ *layang-layang* to fly a kite high in the sky.
  melambung-lambung 1 to jump around. ~ *diri* to toss about restlessly unable to sleep. *dilambung-lambung angin* to be up in the clouds. **2** to flatter, praise.
  melambungkan 1 to send (a ball/kite, etc.) soaring upward, throw up(ward), toss/pitch s.t. up. **2** to praise, flatter. ~ *dada* to boast.
  terlambung bounced/thrown up.
  lambungan bounce.
  pelambung tosser, thrower, pitcher.
  pelambungan soaring, jumping up.

lambung II (*Jv*) side, flank (of a body/house). *kapal roda* – sternwheeler, paddle-wheel steamer. – *kanan* starboard. – *kiri* port. – *otot* gizzard; → REMPELA. – *selatan* (NATO's southern flank). – *timbul* freeboard.
  melambung to attack/assault s.o. or s.t.'s flank/side.
  melambungi 1 to provide a ship/boat with a flank-wall. **2** to sail on the left or right side, tack.
  lambungan side, flank.
  pelambungan (*mil*) flanking movement.

lambung III (*M*) stomach. *besar* – to eat a lot. *getah* – gastric juices. – *kosong* not having eaten breakfast; (on) an empty stomach.

Lambung Mangkurat (*ob*) name of the Army division stationed in South and Central Kalimantan.

lambur jellyfish, *Medusa spp*.

lamdukpai (*C*) k.o. liana whose roots are used for a medicine against smallpox.

lamél(a) (*D*) lamella.

laméndér (*ob*) Armenian.

lamin I (*M*) **melamin** to decorate a bridal dais.
  pelaminan altar of dais where the bride and groom sit to eat rice together in public; *cp* KELAMIN I.

lamin II (among the Daya people Kalimantan) longhouse.
lamina(h) *baju –* (*ob*) coat of mail.
laminasi (*D*) lamination.
  melaminasi to laminate.
lamis (*Jv*) **1** (to speak) softly, coaxingly, nicely. **2** lip service. *– di bibir saja* and **lamisan** lip service.
lampai (*panjang/tinggi*) – **1** tall and slender, slim, graceful, elegant. **2** slight (of build); → AMPAI III, SEMAMPAI. *liuk –* lithe/lissome and supple/flexible.
  melampai(-lampai) and **terlampai(-lampai)** sway(ing), bend(ing) from side to side gently (of leaves/branches), with swaying hips (of a girl); *cp* LÉNGGANG *lénggok*.
lampam *ikan –* k.o. freshwater carp with red and black fins, Javanese carp, *Puntius schwanefeldi/gonionotus*.
lampan wooden tray used in ground sluicing (in mining).
  melampan to wash/pan for tin (in a wooden tray), pan/sift tin.
lampang I (*M*) **1** a slap, blow (with the open hand). **2** scar.
  berlampang(-lampang) to strike e.o. with the palm of the hand.
  berlampangan scarred.
lampang II temporary shed put up to receive guests at a festival.
lampar berlampar(an) (*pl subj*) and **melampar-lampar** to be scattered (as leaves), sprawled (of human bodies); (*cla*) to spread (of news); *cp* HAMPAR. *Daun-daun berlamparan di tanah.* Leaves were scattered all over the ground.
  melampar 1 to spread out, be scattered. **2** to spread s.t. out.
  lamparan spread.
lampas I (*ob*) soft. *– suaranya* she has a soft voice.
  melampas 1 to polish (furniture). **2** (*M*) to sharpen, sandpaper, hone (a knife, etc.). **3** to train. *~ mulut/lidah* to train the tongue to become eloquent.
  pelampas s.t. used for polishing.
lampas II to speak without thinking.
lampau 1 past, ago, late. *enam belum (yang) –* six months ago. **2** over, too much. *Ia – keras bekerja.* He worked too hard. *– waktu* expired.
  melampau to overdo it, go too far. *Perkataannya selalu ~.* His remarks always go too far.
  melampaui 1a) to pass (by) (a house/person, etc.). **b)** to pass through/visit (places). *Beberapa buah negeri telah dilampauinya.* He has passed through several countries. **c)** (to feel) passed over (in favor of s.o. younger). **2** exceed, surpass, go beyond/past. *~ baris* to exceed the bounds, go too far. *yang ~ batas* excessive. *~ batas kekuasaannya* to overstep the limits of one's authority. *~ batas waktu kunjungan* to overstay. *anggaran telah dilampaui* the budget was exceeded, it went over budget. *Usianya tidak ~ ...* He has not yet turned ... (years of age). *~ cakrawala* over the horizon. *~ jangka waktu* to exceed the time limit. **3** to overcome, subdue, surmount. *tidak dapat dilampaui* insurmountable, insuperable. **4** to violate, transgress, infringe (the law). *dianggap ~ adat* considered to have violated customary behavior and law. **5** to cap, top, do better than another, outdo, outbid s.o.
  terlampau 1 too, very, extremely, exceedingly, intensely, over-. *Ia ~ penat.* He was very tired. *~ diéksploitir* over-exploited. *~ pagi* too early, premature. **2** (= **terlampaui**) to have passed/gone by, skipped. *Stasiun Karawang telah ~.* The Karawang station has been skipped. *belum/tidak akan ~ waktunya* still have the time to, not too late to.
  terlampaui passed over/by, skipped.
  kelampauan 1 too late, passed (by), preceded (by another). *Anak gadis itu sudah ~.* Her younger sibling got married before she did. *pantang ~* to always want to be the cock of the walk. *~ waktu* (*leg*) limitation, lapse of time. **2** the past.
  pelampau s.t. that goes beyond, excess.
  pelampauan excess.
lampeni (*J/Jv*) k.o. small, bitter shrub, shoe button plant, *Ardisia humilis*.
lampes (*J*) holy basil, *Ocimum sanctum*.
lampias (*J*) **1** to flow/gush easily and fast. **2** rapid, quick, swift, fast.
  melampiaskan 1 to make s.t. flow faster, speed up the flow of. **2** to give free rein to, indulge. *~ amarahnya* to fly into a rage. *~ hawa nafsunya* to give full rein to one's passions. *~ kritik keras-*

nya to criticize s.t. harshly. *~ perundingan* to initiate/establish negotiations.
  terlampiaskan indulged (of one's passion/rage, etc.).
  pelampias s.t. or s.o. that satisfies one's passions.
  pelampiasan giving full rein to, release.
lampin I 1 diaper. **2** paper or cloth used to hold anything hot, potholder.
  melampini 1 to diaper (a baby). **2** to cover the hand with paper or cloth when holding something hot.
lampin II *– budak* serrate glorybower, *Clerodendron serratum*.
lamping (*J*) slope (of a hill); → LÉRÉNG I.
lampion (*D*) paper lantern.
lampir (*Jv*) **melampiri 1** to attach to, enclose in. **2** to append to, affix to. *X dilampiri dengan Y* Y is included in X.
  melampirkan 1 to attach, enclose. **2** to annex.
  terlampir enclosed, attached.
  lampiran 1 enclosure (to a letter). **2** attachment. *~ tetap* bound attachment. **3** appendix, annex. *~ Pidato Kenegaraan* Appendices to the State Address of the President, delivered annually just before Independence Day (August 17).
  pelampiran attachment.
lampiri *mak –* (in Samarinda) k.o. spirit/ghost who bites off human beings' ears.
lampis → LAPIS I.
lampit (*Jv*) and *– rotan* a rattan mat.
lampiun → LAMPION.
lampok (*M*) pile of cut paddy.
lampor (*Jv*) roaring, howling sound heard on rivers; believed to be malevolent spirits stamping around.
lampoyang → LEMPUYANG.
lampu (*D*) lamp. *– kekurangan minyak* to be in dire straits/in a quandary. *– abang-ijo* red and green lamp [*bangjo*] (*coq*) traffic light/signal. *– antiminyak dan antilalat* a (Phillips) insect repellent lamp. *– baca* reading lamp. *– bacar* flashlight. *– belakang* taillight, rear light. *– beléncong* oil lamp (used for casting shadows in *wayang* performance). *– besar* headlights. *– besar dekat* low beams. *– besar jauh* high beams. *– blits* flashbulb. *– buritan* stern light. *– busur* arc light/light. *– coblok* lamp made from an old tin can or bottle. *– corong* a) headlight. b) oil lamp with chimney. *– dahi* miner's lamp. *– dekat* parking lights. *– depan* headlight. *– dim* parking lights. *– dinding* wall-lamp. *– duduk* a) table lamp. b) floor lamp. *– duplik* blinker. *– gantung* hanging lamp, swag lamp, drop lamp. *– gaspom* k.o. pressurized gasoline lamp. The gasoline tank is located at some distance from the lamp and is connected to it by a small wire pipe through which the gasoline flows under pressure from a pump. *– geladak* deck light. *– gembréng* k.o. hanging lamp. *– gencar* floodlight. *– hijau* green light (authorization to proceed with some undertaking). *– hijau-mérah* (*coq*) traffic light/signal. *– isyarat* directional signal. *– jalan* portable lamp. *– jalanan* street light. *– kabut* fog light. *– kaki* footlights. *– kecelakaan* warning lamp. *– kecil* parking lights. *– kerdip* turn signal, flashers. *– kerona* chandelier. *– kilat (pada kaméra)* flashlight, flash bulb. *– kom* (*J*) pressurized kerosene lamp. *– kontrol* control light (of bus or truck). *– kuning* a) fog light. b) warning signal. c) go-ahead signal, green light. *– kusam* frosted lamp. *– lalu-lintas* traffic light. *– lantai* footlights. *– limas* conical lamp. *– listrik* electric lamp. *– luar* outdoor lighting. *– malam* night light. *– menara* beacon. *– menunjuk arah* approach lights. *– mérah* a) red stoplight. b) a danger/warning signal, *esp* a red lamp, flare, etc. *– minyak tanah* kerosene lamp. *– muka* headlights, headlamps. *– néon* neon fluorescent light. *– nomer plat* license plate light. *– oto* car light. *– panggung* footlights. *– panjang* high beams. *– parkir* parking lights. *– pateri* blow lamp. *– pemantul* reflector. *– pendaratan* landing lights (on airfield). *– péndék* low beams. *– penerangan* lighting, illumination. *– pengaman* safety lamp. *– pengatur lalu-lintas* traffic light/signal. *– penyeberangan jalan* pedestrian light. *– penyorot* a) flashlight. b) projector. *– perangkap* light-trap. *– periksa* pilot lamp. *– pétromak(s)* pressurized gasoline lamp, Coleman lamp. *– pijar* incandescent light bulb; → PÉR II. *– pilot* pilot light. *– posisi* (*naut*) side-light. *– potrét* flashbulb. *– rém* brake light (of car). *– réting/richting* di-

rectional signal. – *samping* side-light. – *sekat* panel light (on car or plane). – *semboyan* blinker light. – *séin/sén* directional signal (of a car) – *sempor* oil lamp without a chimney. – *semprong* oil lamp with chimney. – *sénter/sentolop* flashlight. – *sekat* panel light. *semboyan* blinkers. – *sorot* searchlight. – *stro(e)mking/Stromking/Strongking* a pressurized gasoline lamp, a Coleman lamp. – *suar* lighthouse. – *tangan* portable lamp. – *tekan* pressure lantern. – *témpél/témplék/té(m)plok* kerosene lamp hung on walls or pillars. – *téng/ting* lantern. – *TL* fluorescent lamp. – *wasiat* Aladdin's lamp.

berlampu to have a lamp, be lighted.

melampui to illuminate, light up.

perlampuan lighting, illumination.

lampung float; → APUNG. *kayu* – touch wood.

melampung to float (on water). ~ *pukat* at one time visible, at another time invisible, appearing and disappearing.

melampungkan to set s.t. afloat, float.

pelampung 1 a float for a net/line. 2 Mae West, life jacket. 3 float, buoy. ~ *api* flashing buoy. ~ *aum* whistle buoy. ~ *bénsin* gasoline gauge. ~ *berenang/penyelamat* life belt/buoy. ~ *guntung* can buoy. ~ *jangkar* anchor buoy. ~ *kerucut* nun buoy. ~ *labuh* anchorage buoy. ~ *pengepil* mooring buoy. ~ *pengerukan* dredging buoy. ~ *pukat* pieces of wood used to keep a net afloat. ~ *runcing* nun buoy. ~ *silinder* can buoy. ~ *suar/dengan lampu* light buoy. ~ *tambatan* mooring buoy. ~ *tong* cask buoy. ~ *tongkat* spar buoy. ~ *udara* life jacket (on plane).

lampus (*Jv ob*) 1 dead. 2 to die; → MAMPUS.

lampuyang → LEMPUYANG.

lamtara and **lamtoro** (*Jv*) a small shade tree, lead tree, *Leucaena glauca/leucocephala*, also its edible seed pods; → PETAI cina. – *gung* (from *Lamtoro agung*) a useful plant for greening, lumber and cattle fodder, white lead tree, *Leucaena leucocephala*.

pelamtaraan cultivation of this tree.

lamtoronisasi encouraging the planting of *lamtoro* trees.

lamun I (*cla*) 1 (although ...) nevertheless; → NAMUN. *Biarpun hamba perempuan, – malu kubalas juga.* Although I am a woman, nevertheless I am embarrassed to take revenge. 2 even though. – *begitu ia dipenjarakan juga.* Even though that was the case, he was imprisoned anyway. 3 provided that, if. *Apatah salahnya, – patih hendak bersama-sama dengan kita?* Is there anything wrong with the premier wanting to be together with us?

lamun II melamun 1 (*M*) to stack, heap/pile up in disorder (of clothes). 2 to flood, inundate, irrigate (rice paddies), cover (as the tide). 3 to overwhelm (with grief/troubles/sorrows).

lamun III melamun and **ng(e)lamun** to daydream, to fantasize.

lamunan fancy, fantasy, daydream; → KELAMUN. ~ *kosong* wishful thinking.

pelamun daydreamer.

lamun IV sea grass, duckweed, pondweed, *Potamogeton spp.*

lamur nearsighted.

lamuran various species of grasses.

lan I (*Jv*) and; → DAN I.

Lan II shortening of various male proper names: Aslan, Dahlan, Ramelan, etc.

lan III (in acronyms)→ LANJUTAN, PANGKALAN.

lana a k.o. shrubby climbing plant, blue trumpet vine, *Thunbergia laurifolia*.

lanai (*E*) patio facing the ocean (used in Hawaii).

lanang I melanang to twist strands to make cord.

lanang II (*Jv*) 1 man. *anak* – son. 2 virile, manly.

lanang III *ular* – king cobra.

lanar I alluvium, deposit, soil brought down by rivers, ooze, slime (alluvial/on a beach/near a mine, etc.).

pelanaran (*geol*) alluviation.

lanar II *akar* – k.o. climbing plant, wild yam root, *Ipomoea digitata*.

la'nat → LAKNAT.

lanau I silt, mud, mire, ooze. 2 muddy, containing alluvial matter, silted.

berlanau silted.

lanauan silted.

lanca I (*cla*) large boat with three masts.

lanca II (*C ob*) rickshaw.

lancah maung (*S*) wolf spider, *Lycosa pseudoannulata*.

lancana → LENCANA.

lancang I 1 disrespectful, indecent, irreverent, immodest, discourteous, impolite (towards one's elders). 2 bold, audacious, forward (towards the opposite sex and in general). *terlalu* – too bold, gone too far (with a girl, without the knowledge of her parents). 3 hurriedly, hastily, quickly. – *mulut* and *mulut* – not mince one's words, get right to the point. – *tangan* a) to be light-fingered, thievish, i.e., to like to steal small articles. b) quick to hit, rough, pugnacious, combative.

kelancangan quickness (of hands/tongue). ~ *mulut* not mincing one's words.

lancang II (*Port*) 1 high-speed/fast sailboat, yacht. – *kuning* "sail boat" name of a song and dance from Riau, the symbol of Riau and also the name of a university in Pekanbaru. 2 (*cla*) warship of olden times. 3 (*M*) boat-shaped basket for betel appurtenances. 4 (*bermain –.–*) to play ducks and drakes, i.e., to throw small flat stones into water so that they skim across the surface.

lancang-lancang (to play) skipping stones over the surface of the water.

lancangan k.o. boat used in Minangkabau area.

lancang III (in Cilacap) k.o. small oyster.

lancang IV k.o. plant, asthma weed, snake weed, *Euphorbia hirta*.

lancap (*M*) smooth, slick.

terlancap slipped out (of a remark); slip of the tongue.

lancar I 1 (to run/drive/fly) fast, swiftly, quickly; fast and smooth (as of a movement, without fits and starts). 2 fluent, able to speak or read smoothly and easily (without breaks). 3 negotiable (of financial instruments). 4 current (of payments on debts). *berputar dengan* – to turn/revolve fast and smoothly (without jerks). *berjalan* – to go smoothly (of talks, etc.). *bisa membaca dengan –nya* can read smoothly. *menjawab dengan* – to answer readily/without hesitation. – *bahasa Indonésianya.* His Indonesian is fluent. *kurang* – substandard (of payments on debts). *tidak* – not smooth. **ketidak-lancaran** lack of an uninterrupted flow. – *kaji* (*M*) skillful in study. – *kaji karena diulang* practice makes perfect. – *licin* smooth and easy. – *mulut* a) to talk big, boast, brag. b) talkative, loquacious, have the gift of gab.

selancar ~ *angin* windsurfing. *papan* ~ *angin* windsurf board.

peselancar *angin* windsurfer.

berselancar and **bersilancar** 1 to play ducks and drakes, skim stones over the water; → BERMAIN *lancang-lancang*. 2 to surf (on surfboard). ~ *angin* to windsurf; windsurfing.

melancar 1 to glide by, flash by, move swiftly. 2 (*M*) to study/review (one's lessons) thoroughly.

melancarkan and **memperlancar** [and **ngelancarin** (*J coq*)] 1 to speed up, hasten, accelerate, expedite (a project/work), further (an action). ~ *jalan* to pave the way for. 2 to promote (smooth discussions/a product). 3 to start (a rumor/war), open (a campaign). 4 to launch (an attack), hurl (arrows/a spear). 5 to make (an arrest). 6 to carry out (propaganda). 7 to speed (a boat) on its way.

lancaran (*cla*) a high-speed sailing boat.

kelancaran smooth/uninterrupted flow (of goods/traffic/payments, etc.), streamlining.

pelancar s.t. used to launch, launcher.

pelancaran launching.

lancar II pelancar 1 runway (in airfield) 2 crossbeam (of Malay house).

pelancaran runway.

lancaran (*Jv*) k.o. Javanese musical form.

lancar-lancar *burung* – k.o. bird, Malay pipit, *Anthus novaseelandiae malayensis*.

lancia (*C*) rickshaw; → LANCA II.

lancing(an) (*Jv*) trousers.

berlancing(an) to wear trousers.

lancip 1 tapering and sharp, streamlined. 2 (*math*) acute. *sudut* – acute angle.

melancip to taper to a point.

melancipkan to sharpen (a pencil, etc.).

pelancip ~ *potlot* pencil sharpener.

pelancipan sharpening.

lancit melancit to squirt/spurt/slip out; → LECIT, LENCIT.

lancong melancong to go sightseeing, take a trip, go on a tour/excursion.

    pelancong tourist, sightseer. mempelancongkan to take on a sightseeing trip. perpelancongan tourism.

    pelancongan 1 tourism. 2 (orang ~) tourist.

lancung I 1 false, falsified, counterfeit, phony, fake, imitation, artificial, spurious, forged, not genuine/original. emas – imitation gold. uang – counterfeit money. 2 dishonest, deceitful, insincere, treacherous, perfidious, faithless. sekali – ke ujian, seumur orang tak percaya once a cheat/thief, always a cheat/thief.

    melancung(kan) 1 to counterfeit, forge, fake. 2 to deceive, delude, mislead.

    lancungan 1 fake, imitation. 2 forged (check, etc.). 3 impure, adulterated (of food).

    kelancungan 1 forgery, falsification, fake. 2 treason, betrayal, treachery, faithlessness, fraudulence.

    pelancung counterfeiter.

    pelancungan counterfeiting.

lancung II → LANCONG.

lancur I melancur to squirt/gush (water out of a pipe, etc.); → MEMANCUR, MEMANCAR, MELECIT.

lancur II → LELANCUR.

lancut I melancur to squirt noisily.

lancut II useless, in vain.

landa I shock, impact.

    melanda to run/knock down, overrun, strike, hit, destroy, sweep over/across/through, ravage. sebagai benang dilanda ayam chaotic, in a completely confused state. dilanda angin puyuh destroyed by a tornado. dilanda banjir flood-stricken. dilanda perang war-ravaged.

    terlanda run/knocked down, destroyed, ravaged. ~ banjir ravaged by floods.

landa II melanda to wash (gold; in a river/stream), jig (ore); → LANDAU.

    pelanda gold washer, person or implement that digs ore.

landa III 1 alkali, lye. 2 alkaline.

landahur (ob) a Giant-generation (on Ceylon).

landai I 1 sloping, slanting. lindang – completely finished, all gone (money). 2 gradient, slope. – atap pitch of roof.

    melandai sloping, slanting.

    melandaikan to recline s.t., put in a reclining position.

    landaian 1 sloping land. 2 gradient. 3 slipway, incline. ~ lintang transverse slipway. ~ muatan cargo incline.

    kelandaian slope.

    pelandaian slope.

landai II landaian (Jv) large hilt of a kris.

landak porcupine, Hystrix brachyura and other species. bunga – a thorn bush whose roots and leaves possess medicinal properties, Barleria prionitis. jari sebagai duri – fingers fine and tapering like a porcupine's quills. – Irian long-beaked/long-nosed/New Guinean echidna, Zaglossus bruijni. – laut sea/devil urchin, Diadema setosum.

landang → LALU landang.

landap k.o. plant, southern swamp lily, poison bulb, Crinum asiaticum.

landas I 1 base, foundation, substratum, bed. tingkat tinggal – take-off stage. 2 shelf. – benua/kontinén continental shelf. – meriam gun carriage. – pelana swage.

    berlandaskan (pada) to be based (on), (with) ... as its basis.

    melandas to land, touch down (of aircraft).

    melandasi to base s.t. on.

    landasan 1 foundation, basis, substratum. 2 anvil. 3 chopping-block. 4 (gun-)emplacement. ~ berpijak a) beachhead. b) foothold. ~ héli helipad. ~ hukum legal foundation/ground(s). ~ incus the middle bone in the middle ear. ~ kapal ship's bottom. ~ kata evidence. ~ kontinén/laut continental shelf. ~ menggelinding taxiway (on an airfield). ~ pacu (pesawat terbang) runway. ~ parkir apron (on an airfield). ~ peluncuran launch pad. ~ pendaratan landing strip. ~ rumput a grass strip. ~ terbang airstrip, runway. ~ turun naik pesawat runway (on

airfield). berlandasan 1 to use an anvil; anviled. 2 to be/found on.

    pelandasan basis.

landas II – bukit k.o. plant whose leaves are used as medicine and whose sap is used as glue, Malaysian ant plant, Macaranga triloba; → MAHANG.

landau (geol) secondary recovery.

    melandau 1 to wash (gold or tin). 2 to mine secondary ore.

landep (Jv) porcupine flower, Barleria prionitis.

landik (Jv) k.o. plant, hop-headed barleria, Barleria lupulina.

landing (E) landing (of aircraft).

landrad (D ob) district court.

landrat → LANDRAD.

landréform (E) land reform.

landrénte (D) land rent.

landros (D ob) (high) bailiff.

landschap (D col) and Landskap /lanskap/ self-governing district (mostly used in the outer islands as the abbreviation for "zelf-besturend landschap,") i.e., an Indonesian district under the suzerainty of the Netherlands.

Landstorm (D col) Landsturm; in the Netherlands Indies a force composed of all men liable to service but who were not already in the army, navy or reserves.

landuk various species of emperor fishes, Lethrinus spp.

landung trailing, long (of a rope/sleeve). – napas with good wind, staying power, stamina (of horses).

    melandung 1 sagging in the length. 2 to droop, hang down (of a rope, etc. which had been made taut).

landur I and melandur 1 slack (of a rope). 2 to drag o.s. along.

landur II to feel weak in the knees.

landut → LANDUR.

lang I name for various birds of pray, like hawks, falcons, eagles, etc.; → ELANG I. di tempat tiada –, kata belalang, akulah – in the kingdom of the blind the one-eyed man is king.

lang II (coq) → SELANG I.

lang III (J) kiosk/small booth where cigarettes, etc. are sold by the piece.

langah melangah and ter(be)langah open wide, agape (of mouth), ajar (of a door, etc.); → NGANGA.

    melangahkan to open (the mouth) wide.

langak (Jv) – languk/longok/lunguk (ob) to look left and right (as if looking for s.o., etc.).

    melangak to look around (for s.o.).

langau stinging horsefly. sebagai – di ékor gajah and seperti – di pantat gajah (Mal) "like a horsefly on an elephant's tail/ass," i.e., a toady. – hijau bluebottle, Stomoxydae. – kerbau horsefly. – mérah corrupt person.

    berlangau flyblown.

langca and langcia (C) rickshaw.

langen (Jv) kelangenan amusement, pleasure.

langendria (Jv) k.o. court dance.

Langen Mandra Wanara k.o. dance in which the dancers jump around from beginning to end.

langes (Jv) soot from an oil lamp.

langgai I a triangular shrimp net forced like a plow through the mud by a pole held in each hand; → SIRING I.

langgai II various k.o. ocean fishes, cutlass fish, hard tail, scabbard fish, Trichiuridae, spp.

langgam (M) 1 way, custom, style. – bahasa/kata a) accent. b) expression. c) style. 2 habits (of a people). 3 melody, tune; → LAGU.

    berlanggam in a certain style/way.

langgan subscribe.

    berlanggan (ob coq) and berlangganan to subscribe to (a magazine/newspaper, etc.), take.

    melanggani 1 to subscribe to. 2 to frequent, be a frequent customer at.

    melangganankan to take out a subscription for s.o.

    langganan 1 subscriber. menjadi ~ to subscribe to. para ~ clientele. 2 customer. 3 supplier, caterer; → PEMASOK. 4 subject to. daérah ~ banjir area subject to floods. ~ air minum water user. ~ bui (coq) jailbird, habitual lawbreaker. ~ listrik electricity user. ~ penjara jailbird, habitual lawbreaker.

pelanggan 1 subscriber. **2** customer.

pelangganan subscription.

langgang *tunggang.-* head over heels.

langgar I a hut or house which serves as a Muslim elementary school and in which students are instructed in Koranic reading or which is used as a place to pray; *cp* PESANTRÉN, SANTRI; → SURAU.

langgar II berlanggar to collide. *~ dengan* to run up against, collide with, crash into.

   berlanggaran 1 to clash, collide, ram e.o. **2** to attack e.o. **3** to contradict e.o.

   melanggar 1 to run over, collide with, ram, hit. *~ ranjau* to hit a mine. *dilanggar pélor* to be hit by a bullet. **2** to attack (a country). **3** to infringe, violate, break. *terang-terang ~* to be in clear conflict with. *~ adat* to contravene/go against a custom. *~ bahasa* to commit a breach of good manners. *~ hukum* to break/violate the law. *pekerjaan yang ~ hukum* illegal work. *~ kesusilaan* to offend against decency/morality. *~ lampu lalu-lintas* to go through/run a traffic light. *~ pantang* to violate a prohibition.

   melanggari (*pl obj*) **1** to collide repeatedly with; to attack, assault, encroach upon. **2** to violate, transgress.

   melanggarkan to ram, knock against, drive against.

   terlanggar [and **kelanggar** (*coq*)] **1** collided, hit. *~ mobil* hit by a car. **2** violated, transgressed.

   pelanggar trespasser, violator, transgressor. *~ batas kecepatan* speeder. *~ hukum* lawbreaker. *~ lalulintas* traffic offender.

   pelanggaran 1 collision, clash. **2** attack, assault. **3** violation, transgression, misdemeanor, offense, breaking (the law), infraction, infringement (of a patent); *cp* KEJAHATAN. *melakukan ~* to commit a crime/offense. *tempat terjadinya ~* scene of the crime. *~ disiplin* disciplinary infraction. *~ hak asasi* violation of human rights. *~ hukum pidana* violation of criminal law. *~ jabatan* offense committed by a public servant. *~ kekebalan diplomatik* abuse of diplomatic immunity. *~ kesusilaan* offense against decency/morality. *~ lalulintas* traffic offense. *~ ketertiban umum* offense against public order. *~ kriminal/pidana* criminal offense. *~ patén* patent infringement.

   perlanggaran collision.

langgas free, independent, without ties.

langgat (*Jv*) **nglanggati** to comply with.

langgayan (*M*) (drying) rack.

langgeng (*Jv*) eternal, lasting.

   melanggengkan to perpetuate, make eternal, preserve.

   kelanggengan 1 eternity. **2** perpetuity.

langguk I (*Jv*) proud, grand, arrogant.

langguk II very tall.

langgung melanggungkan (*ob*) to lean/put, etc. s.t. against.

langi k.o. large mackerel, *Scomberomorus, spp.*

langir 1 k.o. tree whose bark and leaves are used as hair shampoo, *Albizzia saponaria.* **2** (hair) shampoo.

   berlangir and **melangir 1** to wash with that bark and leaves. **2** to shampoo one's hair.

   melangiri 1 to wash s.o. in that way. **2** to shampoo s.o.'s hair in that way.

langis collapsed. *tumpas –* completely destroyed.

langit sky, the heavens, the upper air, space above the earth. *tidak datang begitu saja dari –* not drop from the skies/out of the blue. *beratap(kan) –* to leak like a sieve (of a house). *kolong –* the world, what is under the sky. *sawah berbendar –* rice field which depends on rainfall. *bagai/seperti – dengan bumi* as different (from e.o.) as day and night. *– runtuh, bumi telah terban* and *– runtuh, bumi cair* all his hopes were blighted. *di mana bumi dipijak, di situ – dijunjung* when in Rome do as the Romans do. *ke – tak sampai, ke bumi tak nyata* halfway or unfinished (of work, etc.). *– menyungkup kepala* the inevitable/unavoidable. *di tentang – and – di tentang bumi* to have no more means/resources. *– bersih* a clear/cloudless/unclouded sky. *– biru* a) to fly into the blue. b) sky-blue (in color).

langit-langit 1 (= **lelangit**) ceiling (of room, etc.), tester/canopy over a bed/grave, etc. **2** palate. **berlangit-langit** with a ceiling.

selangit 1 swell, terrific. **2** to reach a peak, sky high. *memuji ... ~* to praise ... to the skies.

melangit 1 to go/move skyward. **2** to soar, go sky high, skyrocket; very high. *Congkaknya ~.* He's very arrogant.

langitan palate.

langka (*J/Jv*) **1** scarce, scanty, seldom, rare, trace. *dévisa yang –* scarce foreign exchange. *élémén –* trace element. *waktu –* grace period. **2** endangered (of a species).

   melangkakan to make rare, rarefy.

   kelangkaan scarceness, rarity, scantiness.

   pelangkaan endangerment.

langkah 1 pace, stride, step. *berjalan dengan – berat* to walk with heavy/dragging steps. *dengan – lébar* with long strides. *– demi – step* by step. *kematian – (to)* come to a deadlock (in negotiations and financially). *memasang – tiga* certain steps and positions in *silat* fighting (three forward and three backward). *membawa(kan) -nya masing-masing* each goes his/her way. *mengangkat/membawakan/membuat/menarik/melepas/mengambil – seribu* to run away, leave in a hurry. *mengayun – menuju* to head toward. *mengayunkan –* to start to walk. **2** measure, action, step(s). *mengambil –* to take steps/measures; *cp* MENGAMBIL *tindakan. mengambil – pembalasan* to take countermeasures. **3** movement, stroke; → TAK II. *– ayun* elongation. *– baik* a) a good omen, propitious circumstances. b) a piece of good luck. *– balik* return stroke, backfire. *– baru* new customs and traditions. *– bébas* free travel (of pedal). *– buang* exhaust stroke. *– isap* suction stroke. *– jebakan* maneuver, stratagem, artful action. *– kanan* very lucky. *– kidal/kiri* bad luck, ill-luck; out of luck. *– laku* behavior, conduct; act, deed. *– lama* old customs and traditions. *– lanjut(an)* follow-up. *– mengena →* LANGKAH *baik. – naik* up(ward) stroke. *– pembuka* opening speech. *– penutup* closing words. *– pertama* a) initiative. b) first step. *– panjang* in a roundabout way. *– salah* misstep. *– seribu* (to run) away. *– sérong* an unfaithful/disloyal deed. *– sumbang* a false step (in *silat* fighting). *– susut* retrenchment. *– torak* piston stroke. *– turun* down stroke. **4** first step, initiative.

   selangkah *~ demi ~* step by step.

   berlangkah → MELANGKAH **1.** *~ sérong* to fool around with a person other than one's spouse, cheat on one's spouse.

   melangkah 1 to stride, move on/forward, take a step (forward). *~ maju* to proceed (of negotiations). **2** to depart, leave, set out (to walk/move along/on a voyage, etc.); to start doing s.t. **3** (*ob*) to cross, go across, wade through (a river/the ocean). *~ lautan* to cross the seas.

   melangkahi 1 to outstrip, surpass, go beyond. *~ kakaknya* to marry earlier than one's older sibling. **2** to violate, transgress. *~ suami* (*M*) to commit adultery (of a married woman). **3** to ignore, disregard (a piece of advice, etc.).

   melangkahkan [and **ngelangkahin** (*J coq*)] **1** to make preparations/get ready to go. *~ kaki kanan* to put one's right foot forward. *~ kakinya ke* to walk over to. **2** (*~ perahu*) to weigh anchor at the propitious moment. **3** (*ob*) to pass (by).

   terlangkahkan *sudah ~* it is no use crying over spilt milk; what is done cannot be undone.

   kelangkahan 1 (*M*) a man whose wife has committed adultery. **2** (*J*) overstepped. **3 →** KELAMPAUAN. **4** to have a young sibling marry earlier than one does.

   pelangkah (*ob*) gift given to older unmarried sister of a younger married sister.

   pe(r)langkahan 1 (*ob*) transgression, violation. *baik ~* a favorable/propitious day/opportunity, etc. (to take an action). **2** beginning of an activity, etc.

langkai (*M*) slim and elegant.

langkak-léngkok → LÉNGGANG *lénggok.*

langkan (*C*) latticed verandah, balcony, balustrade.

langkap I k.o. forest palm species, arenga palm, *Arenga obtusifolia/westerhouti.*

langkap II (*ob*) the container in a betel box that holds the leaf.

langkap III k.o. large fly.

Langkapura → SRI LANGKA.

langkara (*cla*) incredible, impossible; → LENGKARA I.

langkas I (*ob*) quick, rapid, swift, dexterous; active, enthusiastic, energetic.

langkas II fallen off of a tree (of ripe fruit, such as *durian*, etc.). – *buah pepaya* impossible, incredible.
  selangkas ~ *betik berbuah* a) one (short) papaya season. b) a very short time.
langkat I (*cla*) three days after today, the third day from now; → TULAT.
langkat II (sitting-mat) of several thicknesses (= *tikar* berlangkat).
langkau I skip (over). – *sehari* every second/other day.
  melangkau to skip.
  melangkaui to skip (over) s.t. ~ *empat halaman* to skip four pages; → MELAMPAUI, MELANGKAHI.
  terlangkau 1 ago. *tiga bulan yang* ~ three months ago. 2 was/got skipped (over).
  terlangkaui skipped (some pages, etc.), passed over (a competitor/schoolmate, etc.).
  langkauan skip.
langkau II ikan – k.o. halibut, spiny turbot, *Psettodes erumei*.
langking (*ob*) 1 black. 2 dark.
langkio k.o. chive, *Allium schoenoprasum*.
langkisau tornado.
langkitang (*M*) edible freshwater mollusk, *Melania spp*.
langkong *karyawan* – (in Belitung) daily worker.
langkuas (*J*) → LENGKUAS.
langkup terlangkup overturned, inverted.
langlai *lemah* – (lissome and) graceful, drooping.
langlang I (*J/Jv*) 1 wanderer, roamer, drifter. – *buana* globe-trotter. *melanglang buana* to roam about the world, globe-trot. *pelanglang buana* globe-trotter. 2 patrol, s.o. on patrol duties, watchman.
  berlanglang ~ *buana/jagat* to roam about the world, globe-trot.
  melanglang 1 to wander, roam, travel around, go from place to place without any special purpose or destination.
  pelanglang ~ *jagat* globe-trotter.
langlang II (*cla*) handsome, graceful.
langon (*Jv*) sage, *Salvia occidentalis*.
langsai I settled, paid off (of a debt, etc.).
  melangsai to settle a/one's debt(s).
  langsaian payoff, settlement.
langsai II curtain.
langsam (*D ob*) slow.
  melangsamkan to slow s.t. down, decelerate.
langsan (*C*) retail.
langsana k.o. tree, cat's whiskers, *Gynandropsis pentaphylla*.
langsar I tall and slim, slender.
langsar II melangsar to move, edge toward; to spread out lengthwise.
langsar III (*M*) lucky, successful, fortunate.
langsar IV ikan – barracuda and tylosaurus, *Sphyrena langsar*.
langsat, langseb (*Jv*) and langsep (*J*) a tasty yellow-white fruit, similar to a *duku*, *Lansium domesticum*. berkulit (*kuning*) – and *kulit putih bak – berkubah* to have a yellow-white skin color (considered a beautiful skin color).
langsé → LANGSAI II, LELANGSÉ.
langseng (*Jv*) steamer (for rice).
  melangseng to reheat by steaming.
langsep → LANGSAT.
langsi (*onom*) shrill.
  berlangsi and melangsi 1 to emit/make a shrill or humming sound. 2 to whistle past.
langsing I (*Jv*) slender (of waist), slim, svelte.
  melangsing to become slim/slender.
  melangsingkan to slenderize, make s.t. slimmer.
  kelangsingan thinness, slenderness, sveltness.
  pelangsing slimming. *klinik* ~ *tubuh* weight loss clinic. *pusat* ~ slimming center.
  pelangsingan slimming, slenderizing. ~ *badan/tubuh* weight loss/reduction.
langsing II → LANGSI.
langsir I (*D*) 1 (= melangsir) to shunt railroad cars. *tukang* – shunter, yardman. 2 (*J*) to walk up and down, to and fro, back and forth.
  langsiran shunt-yard.
langsir II (*D ob*) lancer.

langsir III (*M*) gaunt, skinny, thin.
langsuir a whinnying female banshee hostile to pregnant women, which sometimes takes the form of a night-owl.
langsung 1 direct, straight, immediate, first-hand, point-blank. *Kita tanya* –. We'll ask him point-blank. – *menuju sasaran* straight to the point. 2 at once, immediately, promptly, directly, without delay, instantly, at a moment's notice, on the spot. *luka* – *mati* died immediately from his wounds. 3 live. *disiarkan secara* – *dari stadion* broadcast live from the stadium. *démonstrasi* – live demonstration. 4 to happen, take place. *tak* – (the wedding, etc.) did not take place. 5 (with a negative) (not) at all. *tidak paham* – *tentang ...* did not understand ... at all. 6 to fail to accomplish/achieve one's purpose. – *daripada sasarannya* to fail to achieve one's purpose. 7 –! (command of bus conductor to driver) Go on! (there aren't any passengers who want to get off here).
  berlangsung 1 to happen, occur, take place. *perundingan yang sedang* ~ the negotiations taking place. 2 to persist, continue, extend, go along/on, proceed. *akan* ~ *selama seminggu* will continue/go on for a week. *yang tengah* ~ on-going. ~ *maraton* to go on and on. ~ *terus-menerus* to go on and on. 3 to elapse (of time). *waktu yang sudah* ~ the elapsed time. 4 the course. ~*nya* the course of. keberlangsungan 1 continued existence, survival. 2 persistence.
  berlangsung-langsung persistent, continuous, incessant.
  melangsung to continue, go on.
  melangsung-langsung persistent, continuous, incessant.
  melangsungkan 1 to do (work). 2 to perform, conduct (a ceremony). 3 to celebrate (a birthday, etc.). 4 to carry out, put into effect (a plan), execute (a legal instrument), conduct (a war, etc.), commit (a murder), hold (a meeting); → MENGADAKAN, MELAKUKAN. 5 to keep s.o. going, retain. ~ *akte* to execute an instrument/a deed. ~ *kehidupan* to survive. ~ *perkawinan* to perform/solemnize a marriage. *dilangsungkan dengan sepuluh catatan di pinggir* (in a notarial instrument) executed with 10 amendments in the margin.
  terlangsung 1 continued, perpetuated. 2 performed, carried out, implemented, done. 3 gone too far, exceeded; → TELANJUR, TERDORONG. *Semuanya telah* ~. It's too late to do anything about it. *Hampir saja dia* ~. He had almost gone too far.
  kelangsungan 1 continuance, continuity, continuation, duration, lastingness. ~ *hidup* survival, viability. *demi* ~ *hidup* for one's/its continued survival. 2 performance, carrying out.
  perlangsungan 1 occurrence, happening, performance, accomplishment, fulfillment. 2 continuance, persistence, perpetuation, keeping s.t. going.
langu unpleasant/rotten odor.
languh → LENGUH I.
languk → LANGAK languk.
langut melangut to have sad/melancholy feelings; to long/yearn for s.o. or s.t.
lanhir (*D col*) landlord; → TUAN tanah.
lanja (*Jv*) melanja to pay a visit to; to go visiting.
  lanja-lanjaan to go everywhere.
lanjai (*M*) (= melanjai) slender, slim and elegant, fragile, frail, as thin as a rail. *kurus* – thin (of pubescent children).
lanjak I (*Jv*) melanjak to reach, attain. *telah* ~ *usia tinggi* to have reached an advanced age.
lanjak II to rent.
lanjam (*J*) plowshare.
lanjang I small and long, slender.
lanjang II (*ob*) → TELANJANG.
lanjang III (*Jv*) unmarried (girl).
lanjar I long and pointed; stretching out far, trailing (of ropes, etc.).
  melanjar (*J*) 1 to become long. 2 to let/pay out a rope so that it becomes long.
lanjar II (*Jv*) lanjaran supporting pole for climbing plants, such as beans, vines, etc., beanpole, etc. *kacang* ~ string beans grown on climbing vines (often used as a certain side dish: *lalap*); → KACANG I.
lanjar III (*ob*) 1 after that. 2 at once, immediately. 3 all at once, all of a sudden; *cp* LANTAS, LANCAR I, LALU I, TERUS. 4 quickly finished/used up.

lanji (*Jv*) (*perempuan/sundal*) – whore.

lanjrat (*Jv*) → LANDRAD. **melanjrat** to try in court.

lanjung 1 *tebu* – a tall and slender sugarcane species. **2** (*M*) rather tall (person).

lanjur 1 (*ob*) pushed forward. **2** long-drawn-out, protracted, dragged on/out; → ANJUR II.

melanjurkan to prolong (the time, etc.), continue (the discussion, etc.), protract s.t.

kelanjur (= terlanjur) to have gone too far; irrevocable (of words/ behavior); exceed, excessive, too much. ~ *gagal di sekolah* he's failed so much in school (that he can't go on).

te(r)lanjur 1 pushed (too far forward/to the front), slipped. *Agak ~ sedikit di sempadan*. He went a bit past the finish line. **2** gone too far in doing or saying s.t. (cannot be undone). **3** too much, excessively; (to commit an offense) accidentally/by accident. *Sudah ~ kujual*. I've sold it (i.e., I can't withdraw from the deal). *pikir dulu, sebelum ~* think about it before you let your tongue run away with you/say s.t. you'll regret. *~ mulutnya* to put one's foot in it; to commit o.s. *barang sudah ~* it's too late to do anything about it. **kete(r)lanjuran** excess, too much.

terlanjur-lanjur 1 too far, beyond some limit. **2** farther and farther.

lanjut 1 long[-drawn(out)], protracted; (*panjang* –) long-winded, wordy, verbose, lengthy, detailed, circumstantial. *Amat – cerita ini*. This story is far too long. **2** (far) advanced, well on one's way, progressed, made progress/headway. *sudah – umurnya* (at an) advanced age. *orang – usia* senior citizen. *separuh/setengah* – middle-aged. *telah – kemajuannya* he has made a lot of progress. **3** further (particulars/details/information/inquiries, etc.); continuing (education), prolonged (investigations/experiments), advanced (of a course of study). *pengajaran yang –* continuing education. **4** wide/broad (view); sensible, intelligent. **5** constant, continual, persistent, incessant; continuous, continued, lasting, permanent, uninterrupted. *akan – naik* (prices) will continue to rise. *rasa benci akan –* hatred will be lasting. *telah berpikiran yang –* and *telah – pikirannya* still young but very intelligent. **6** (one) continues, goes on. *-nya* he/ she continued. *– akal/pikiran* clever (at deceiving), crafty, cunning, sly. *– ke balik* continue on the reverse.

selanjutnya 1 furthermore, besides, moreover, further. **2** then, later, in the future, from then on, after that. **3** the next (person in line), further (information). **4** the rest (you already know). *dan ~* etcetera. *untuk ~* in (the) future, hereinafter, henceforth, from now on, furthermore.

berlanjut 1 protracted, extended. **2** sustainable. *pembangunan ~* sustainable development. **3** continuing. *pendidikan ~* continuing education. *~ terus* more follows. **keberlanjutan** sustainability.

berlanjut-lanjut continuous, prolonged, protracted.

melanjut to continue; continuous, continuing. *makin ~* to increase.

melanjuti to continue.

melanjutkan [and **ngelanjutin** (*J coq*)] **1** to continue, prolong, lengthen, protract. *~ umur manusia* to prolong human life. **2** to continue, proceed/go on with, carry on, go through with, go ahead with, further (a conspiracy, etc.). *~ perjalanan* to proceed on/continue a trip. *akan dilanjutkan* to be continued (of a serial). **3** to continue speaking.

terlanjut 1 in a reckless/careless (mood); too early/far, said the wrong thing, said or did s.t. that cannot easily be withdrawn, inadvertent (proposal of marriage). *~ kesasar* wide of the mark, far off/from the mark. **2** continued, extended.

terlanjutkan sustainable. *pembangunan ~* sustainable development. **keterlanjutan** continuity. *maju ~* continuous progress.

lanjutan 1 further, in greater detail. *informasi ~* further information. **2** continued, follow-up. *persidangan ~* follow-up hearing. **3** continuation, extension. *période ~* continuing period of time. *Rapat ini ~ rapat kemarin*. This meeting is a continuation of yesterday's meeting. *sekolah ~* extended elementary school (but lower than a junior high school level). **4** consequences, outcome, sequence (to), result. *~ daripada kekeliruan-kekeliruan yang telah sudah* the result of past errors. **berlanjutan** continuing.

kelanjutan 1 follow-up, repercussion. **2** continuity, continuation,

furtherance (of a conspiracy, etc.). *~ kisah* continuation of the story. *~ nasib* survival. **3** conclusion, end, result. **berkelanjutan 1** continuous. **2** sustainable.

pelanjut 1 continuer. **2** continuator.

pe(r)lanjutan 1 (the act of) prolonging, continuing, lengthening, protracting. **2** perpetuation, propagation. *perlanjutan jenis* propagation (of a species).

Lanka Ceylon; → SRI LANGKA.

lanolin (*D/E*) lanolin.

lanréporem (*D coq*) → LANDRÉFORM.

lansai → LANGSAI I.

lansar → LANGSAR I.

lansat → LANGSAT.

lans(e)kap (*D*) landscape; → LANDSCHAP.

lansét (*D*) lancet.

lansi → LANGSI.

lansia → *orang* LANJUT *usia*.

lansing → LANGSING I.

lansir I → LANGSIR I.

lansir II (*D*) **melansir** to launch; to spread, circulate.

lanskap (*D*) landscape.

lansung → LANGSUNG.

lantah melantah to pick up and take away.

lantai 1 floor (the inside bottom surface of a room), pavement. **2** level, story, floor (of a building); → TINGKAT. *di – teratas/tujuh* on the top/seventh floor. *alas –* floor covering. *besi –* sheet iron. *tutup –* floor covering. *mencari – berjungkit/terjingkat/terjungkit* to split hairs. *– atap* top floor. *– bawah* ground floor. *– bawah tanah* basement. *– bilah* slat floor. *– bor* (*petro*) rotary (operator). *– dansa* dance floor. *– dasar* ground floor. *– dua/tiga* second/third floor. *– karét* rubber floor matting. *– perahu* ship's bottom. *– puncak* top floor. *– puncak menara* (*petro*) crown deck. *– ranap* ground floor. *– satu* ground floor. *– sisir sandar* (*petro*) monkey board. *– terbawah* basement.

berlantai with a floor/story. *~ dua* (a) two-story building.

melantai 1 to floor s.t., install a floor on s.t. **2** level (ground), perfectly flat and even. **3** to take to the floor (to give a speech or to dance). **4** to hit the floor, hit rock bottom.

melantaikan to lay s.t. on the floor.

lantaian slab.

pelantai dancer.

perlantaian *~ dansa* dance floor.

lantak ram (the tool), pile driver. *emas –* gold in bars. *luluh –* crushed, smashed, shattered. *senapan –* muzzleloader.

melantak 1 to hit hard, hammer, punch, drive (in) (a pile), clench (rivets). *~ pancang* to drive piles. *~ teguh* to ram. **2** to put down food, tuck into food. **3** (*ob*) to spend money lavishly.

melantaki (*pl obj*) to punch down.

melantakkan to ram/punch s.t. in.

lantakan → EMAS *lantak*. *senapan ~* → SENAPAN *lantak/locok*, KECÉPÉK.

pelantak ramrod for cleaning a gun barrel; pile driver/engine; piston rod; pestle of betel nut pounder; etc.

pelantakan ramming.

lantam I (of voice/sound) loud, shrill, hard, sharp; *cp* LANTANG.

melantamkan 1 to speak/utter s.t. in a louder and more stressed voice so that it can be heard. **2** to broadcast, proclaim loudly, propagate.

lantam II (*Med*) proud, conceited, arrogant, haughty, supercilious; → ANGKUH, SOMBONG.

melantamkan 1 to be proud of, feel proud because of. **2** to create a feeling of pride in s.o. (e.g., a new car). **3** to brag/boast about, vaunt.

kelantaman pride, arrogance, conceit, haughtiness, superciliousness.

Lantamal [Pangkalan Utama Angkatan Laut] Main Naval Base.

lantan (*M ob*) **melantan** to pamper, spoil, take good care of (one's body), wear a less good (*kain*) so as to spare one of better quality.

terlantan taken good care of, pampered, spoiled.

lantang 1 (= melantang) booming, loud and clearly audible, loud enough to be heard (of sounds); *cp* LANTAM I, NYARING. *menjawab dengan -nya* to answer loud enough to be heard. *bunyi* *lantung.-* confused noises. 2 noisy, boisterous, tumultuous, clamorous. 3 vivid (of colors; clearly visible/perceptible to the eye without obstacles. *kebun telah* – the yard has been cleaned, there are no longer any plants visible in it.

melantangkan to make (one's voice) loud and clearly audible.

kelantangan distinctiveness, clearness. ~ *pandangan* visual field.

lantar I melantarkan 1 (= **melantarankan**) **1** to cause, bring about/ trouble/a loss, etc. 2 to convey/deliver/present (a request).

lantaran 1 reason, motive, (immediate) cause. *mencari ~ untuk menyerang* to look for a reason to attack. 2 because/on account of, owing to, by reason of. *mati ~ sakit pés* died from the plague; → AKIBAT. ~ *ini/itu* through this/that; therefore; owing to; consequently. 3 agency, s.o. or s.t. through which power is exerted or an end is achieved. *Pada waktu ini Tuhan menggunakan ~.* God now uses an intermediary (to achieve His wishes).

pelantar 1 conveyor, deliverer, presenter (of a request). 2 middleman, intermediary/agency/medium.

pelantaran intermediary. *dengan ~* through (the intermediary/ agency/medium of), with the assistance of, via; → PERANTARAAN.

lantar II te(r)lantar 1 stretched out on the ground (of a corpse/an unconscious person); → TERGELÉTAK. 2 neglected, uncared-for, not taken care of. 3 stranded, beached (of a boat), deserted, left high and dry. 4 abandoned/left to one's fate/own devices, let down (of a person). 5 unfinished, incomplete. 6 resulting in a failure, failed, unsuccessful, abortive, reached a deadlock. 7 to be in a precarious situation. 8 duped, victimized, cheated. 9 virgin (of a forest). 10 displaced (of a person). **ketelantaran** and **penterlantaran** neglect.

men(t)erlantarkan to leave s.t. unfinished, neglect.

lantar III pelantar(an) 1 a long, hard seat for several persons, bench. 2 an unroofed elevated floor joined to the house for drying wash in the sun, porch, deck. 3 a temporary wooden framework for supporting workmen making repairs/painting walls, tall buildings, etc.; scaffold(ing).

lantari (*A M*) white undergarment.

lantas 1 immediately, directly, forthwith, right away, this very minute, at once. *tidak singgah-singgah – saja menuju pelabuhan* (the ship) did not make stopovers and set sail directly. 2 to go through (or/into s.t.) easily/readily, right, straight. – *ke dalam hatinya* went straight to his heart. – *angan* reasonable, logical. *tak – angan(nya)* a) illogical. b) that won't go down with him; he won't buy that; he cannot bring himself to do that. 3 after that, (and) then. *sesudah makan, – tidur* to eat and then go to sleep. 4 and then what, and so?

melantas 1 to go straight (to). *Dari stasiun ~ ke rumah temannya.* He went straight from the station to his friend's house. 2 (= **melantasi**) to penetrate (into). *masuk ke dalam darah ~ kulit perut besar* to enter the bloodstream through the wall of the stomach. ~ *angan* to do as one pleases. ~ *telinga* to go straight to s.o.'s heart (of advice, etc.).

melantasi to go straight through s.t., penetrate.

melantaskan to put forward (a request); to penetrate, pass through; to go on, continue. ~ *maksud/angan(-angan)* a) to try one's fate (abroad). b) to carry one's point/plans through. ~ *dendam* to take revenge.

terlantas penetrated, pierced, went through.

kelantasan berkelantasan (*ob*) continually.

pelantasan permeability.

lantéra → LENTÉRA.

lantik I melantik to install, inaugurate, appoint, swear in.

pelantik inaugurator.

pelantikan installation, inauguration, swearing in, appointment.

lantik II (*M*) → LENTIK I.

lantin (*E ob*) lamp; lantern.

lanting I (*M*) slew.

berlanting to leave, depart.

melanting 1 to throw, cast, toss. 2 to bounce, spring up (of a ball). 3 to dash away. ~ *menuju tampu, berkata menuju benar* every effort has its purpose.

melantingkan to throw (away), hurl, catapult. ~ *nota/protés* to send a note, launch a protest.

ter(pe)lanting 1 thrown/cast away (because it's no longer useful). 2 catapulted.

lantingan slew(ing).

pelanting catapult. ~ *pesawat terbang/udara* airplane catapult.

pelantingan hurling, catapulting. **berpelantingan** catapulted.

lanting II (*Jv*) **melanting 1** to take/hold s.t. at arm's length. 2 to carry s.t. in one's outstretched arm(s).

lanting III (in Banjarmasin, South Kalimantan) a floating house or small bamboo raft (on one of the large rivers).

lanting IV k.o. snack made from *singkong*, a specialty of Kebumen.

lantoro (*Jv*) → LAMTORO.

lantun (*M*) bounce.

melantun to bounce (back), rebound, ricochet, reflect, echo.

melantunkan 1 to bounce s.t., make s.t. bounce. 2 to reflect, show (an image of). *Bandar udara Jakarta ~ citra budaya alam tropis Indonésia.* The Jakarta airport reflects the cultural image of Indonesia's tropical nature. ~ *lagu* to belt out a song. *Ia ~ lagu godaan.* She belted out her song trying to tempt (a man to dance with her). ~ *mata uang* to toss a coin. ~ *suara* to sing.

lantunan 1 bouncing back. 2 delivering (a song).

pelantun s.o. who belts out (a song).

lantung I (*onom*) boom(ing sound) (of heavy guns/thunder, etc). – *lantang* tumultuous, noisy.

lantung-lantung tumultuous, noisy.

melantung to make a loud/shrill sound (like that of an explosion).

lantung II a penetrating smell (like that of rotten eggs).

melantung to smell terrible (like rotten eggs).

lantung III (*M*) **berlantung** to be in touch (contact), collide (with).

berlantung to collide (with), bump (up against).

melantung to touch, collide with.

terlantung knocked against; touched.

lantung IV (in Wonocolo, East Java) crude oil.

pelantungan crude oil source.

lantung V (*Jv*) **ng(e)lantung** to hang out.

pelantungan bum, vagabond, hobo; → LUNTANG *lantung.*

lantur melantur [and **ngelantur** (*J*)] to stray, digress (of talks/ thoughts), rambling; to deviate (from what had been planned).

melanturkan to make s.t. deviate, divert (attention), sway (thoughts).

lanturan aberration; digression.

pelanturan diversion, distraction.

lantut (*J*) delayed, hindered.

lanud [landasan udara] airport.

lanuma [landasan udara utama] principal airport.

lanun pirate (from the southern Philippines, usually operating in July and August as far south as Berau in East Kalimantan).

lanus (*ob*) **melanus** (s.t. that has been wrapped around) could be seen, sticking out.

lanyah (*M*) mud(dy), slush(y) (of roads).

melanyah to make muddy/slushy.

lanyak melanyak to knead (with the feet), tread/step on (also used about buffaloes tilling irrigated rice fields); to trample/crush under foot, tread heavily on s.t. until it is broken up or well mixed.

melanyak-lanyak 1 to trample on s.t. (e.g., soil so that it becomes watery). 2 to humiliate, insult. 3 (*M*) to thrash, trounce, wallop.

lanyau soft mud.

melanyau to play in soft mud.

lao-lao the tree kangaroo of Irian Jaya.

laos (*Jv*) galangal root, a gingery root (used as a medicine and in cooking), *Alpinia galanga*; → LENGKUAS. – *jambék/mekah* k.o. herb with edible rhizomes, Queensland arrowroot, *Canna edulis Ker*.

laoténg (*C*) → LOTÉNG.

lap I (*D*) (*kain –*) a piece of cloth used for cleaning purposes, duster, dust rag. – *keséhatan* sanitary napkin.

melap(kan) and **mengelap(kan)** to wipe, clean, dust, mop (floor/ table surface, etc.).

lap II (*E*) lap (around the track).

lap III (in acronyms) → LAPANGAN, LAPORAN.

lapad (*ob*) → LAFAL.

lapah I melapah 1 to skin, flay, fleece. **2** to chop into pieces (of slaughtered cattle), (*M*) to devour (as animals do to their prey). **3** to tear/pull apart, rip with violence. *hati gajah sama dilapah, hati tuma sama dicecat* (*M*) profits, large or small, should be divided up justly.

lapah II metal cigarette case.

lapak I (*M*) **berlapak** woven with gold or silver thread.

lapak II 1 kiosk, stall (in market). **2** (gambling) den.

lapak III junk-shop distributor who employs *pemulung* to pick up trash. *bahan* – nonorganic waste.

lapal → LAFAL.

lapan (*coq* and *Mal*) eight; → DELAPAN.

lapang I 1 wide, spacious (of a room, etc.), ample (of time), broad (of space), large (of area), roomy. *telah disediakan – untuk berolahraga* a large area has been set aside for sports. *kurang – waktunya* not to have ample time. *tanah –* a) field, plain. b) a square. **2** relaxed, easy. *bernapas dengan –* to breathe easily. *Ia merasa – di sini.* He felt relaxed and relieved here. *– dada* a) relieved. b) broad-minded. c) patient. *– pula rasa dadanya* he breathed easy, he felt relieved. *– hati* a) generous, liberal, hospitable. b) content, satisfied. *kira-kira –* not worried. *– perut* never feel full, always want to eat. *– pemandangannya* to have broad/wide experience. *– pengetahuannya* to have broad/wide knowledge. *– perasaannya/rasa* to have a feeling of relief, feel relieved. **3** free and unoccupied, not busy; leisure, spare, idle. **4** field; → LAPANGAN. *– tugas* duties.

berlapang ~ *hati* patient. *duduk seorang bersempit-sempit, duduk bersama ~* (*M*) many hands make light work.

berlapang-lapang 1 free, unrestricted, unfettered, unburdened. **2** ample, plentiful.

melapang to become roomy/spacious.

melapangi 1 to give/clear some space for, make room for, clear away for. *~ sedikit.* Make some room (for me)! **2** to (provide) help, assist, aid. *Tuhan selalu ~ meréka yang setia kepadaNya.* God always helps those who are loyal to Him.

melapangkan and **memperlapang 1** to enlarge, expand, extend. **2** to widen, broaden. **3** to loosen, relax, relieve, ease. **4** to give/provide access to. *~ dada* to provide relief; to please, satisfy. *~ jiwa* to be merciful, to receive s.t. into one's bosom/favor (of God). *Mudah-mudahan dilapangkan kuburnya.* May he be released from all the torments and punishments connected with the next world. *~ waktu* to make/spare time, take the time to, spend (time).

lapangan 1 wide area, field, open space, plain; square, (shopping) plaza/mall; court, ground, track, course. *~ belukar* brush field. *~ berbatasan* adjoining ground. *~ bermain* playing field. *~ bola* soccer field. *~ golf* golf course/links. *~ hijau* soccer field. *~ kuda* race track. *~ Mérah* Red Square (in Moscow). *~ minyak* oilfield. *~ pacu kuda* race course. *~ parkir* parking apron. *~ penumpukan kayu* log yard. *~ penumpukan peti kemas* container yard. *~ penyamakan* tan(ning)-yard. *~ perang* battlefield; → MÉDAN *bhakti/pertempuran/yudha*, PALAGAN. *~ perintis* airstrip. *~ ranjau* minefield. *~ rumput* lawn. *~ sépak bola* soccer field. *~ témbak* artillery range, practice ground. *~ ténis* tennis court. *~ terbang* airfield, airport. *~ terbang kecil* airstrip. **2** special area of study/activities, sphere, field (of study), range. *~ kerja/pekerjaan* jobs, employment, work. *~ perguruan* field of teaching. *~ usaha* a) sector (of the business world). b) sphere of action. **3** possibilities. *mendapat ~* to find room; to get a chance. *tidak mendapat ~* the chances are against it; it's unlikely.

kelapangan 1 opportunity, chance, space, room; freedom. **2** leisure, unoccupied time (for resting/relaxation, etc.). **3** spaciousness. **4** (to feel) relieved. **berkelapangan** to have the chance/opportunity.

pelapang ~ (*dada*) a relaxed person.

pelapangan relaxing.

lapang II k.o. climbing plant, *Bauhinia comifolia.*

lapar I 1 hunger. *melepaskan –* to satisfy one's hunger. **2** hungry. *perut –* an empty stomach. *merasa –* to be famished. *– gizi* undernourished. *– lahan* land-hungry. *– mata* with big eyes (for food). *– uang* greedy for money.

berlapar to be hungry.

berlapar-lapar to let o.s. get hungry.

melapari *dilapari* to be famished.

melaparkan 1 to starve (out), make s.o. hungry. **2** to long/yearn for.

kelaparan 1 hunger. *busung ~* hunger edema. **2** famine, starvation. **3** to be starving (hungry), go hungry. **4** from/of starvation. *mati ~* to starve to death.

lapar II – *kenyang* donkey's ear abalone, *Haliotis asinina.*

lapas [lembaga pemasyarakatan] penitentiary, penal institution.

lapat-lapat (*J*) vaguely, barely (audible/visible/known).

lapaz → LAFAL.

laper → LAPAR I.

lapih (*M*) **berlapih** to plait, weave; plaited, woven.

melapih to plait/weave s.t. *dilapih kelembai* all tangled up (of hair).

lapik 1 lining, layer of material added to the inside of s.t. *– duduk* mat/cushion for seat. **2** lining, anything used as a wedge, base, part of which s.t. rests on or is supported by. **3** (*geol*) basement. **4** mat. *– berlambak* a finely woven mat. *– cawan* saucer. *– kaki* slippers worn in and out of the house; shoes. *– méja* tablecloth. *– perut* breakfast; → PENANGSEL *perut*. *– sembahyang* prayer mat. *– tiang* base of a post. *– tidur* sleeping mat.

selapik ~ *seketiduran* strong, heart-felt.

berlapik 1 to use a lining, support, etc. **2** to use a lining. **3** overlaid, lined/spread with. *tidur ~ dau pisang* to sleep on a banana leaf. *~/selapik seketiduran, sebantal sekalang hulu* to be on very intimate/friendly terms.

melapik ~ *perut* (*ob*) to line the stomach, i.e., to eat in the morning so as not to be too hungry later on.

melapiki to line, put a lining/foundation/support in/under.

melapikkan to use s.t. as a lining/foundation/support.

lapir (*M ob*) to plait/weave tightly.

lapis I 1 layer, stratum. *kué – and – legit* cake made from rice flour in several green and white red and white layers; → SPÉKKOEK. *– Malang* k.o. yellow and chocolate layer cake. *– sagu* k.o. layer cake made from sago flour. *– Surabaya* three-layered cake with alternating layers of vanilla and chocolate. **2** generation. *sampai tujuh – anak buahnya* as far as the seventh generation. **3** counter for layers. *kain se-* one layer of cloth. **4** row, file. *pasukan pengawal yang diatur jadi tiga –* guard troops lined up in three rows. **5** plating, lining, coating. *– bajunya terbuat dari sutera* the lining of his coat is made of silk. *– lilin* glazing (of frozen fish). **6** (*geol*) bed, seam. *– baja* armor. *– balok* framing of joist. *– batubara* coal seam. *– cengkam* supporting layer between road surface and road-bed. *– lendir* cambium. **7** layered.

berlapis 1 plated, coated. *mobil ~ baja* armored car. *~ baja/waja* (*Jv*) ironclad. *~ emas* gold-plated. **2** layered, in rows/files/layers. *parkir ~* double parking. **3** stratified.

berlapis-lapis in rows/files/layers.

berlapiskan with a layer/plating of. *~ aspal* with an asphalt layer.

melapis 1 in layers. *susunan tanah yang ~* a layered soil composition. **2** to layer, provide with layers, arrange in layers, line. *~ baja* to armor(plate). *~ kaca* to glaze.

melapisi to layer, put a layer of ... on, coat, plate. *~ besi* to armor. *dilapisi séng* galvanized.

melapiskan to use s.t. as a lining, coating, lining, layer, etc.

terlapis layered. *~ és* frosted up.

lapisan 1 (of minerals) deposit, lode, vein. **2** layer, coat(ing), lamina. **3** level, class (in society), stratum. **4** (*petro*) formation, bed. **5** row, layer. *~ aspal* asphalt layer. *~ atas(an)* upper/top layer, superstratum, upper class. *~ baja* a) armored. b) armor(plate). *segala ~ bangsa* all classes/strata of society. *~ atas* overlay. *~ batu dasar* bedrock. *~ bawah* lower class. *~ bijih* ore deposit. *~ cabé-cabéan* mustard plaster. *~ dasar* undercoating, primer. *~ kematu* hardpan. *~ luar* outer layer. *dari segala ~ masyarakat* from all walks of life. *~ muka* surface layer. *~ olah* topsoil. *~ ozon* ozone layer. *~ padat* pan layer (of soil). *~ paling bawah masyarakat* the lowest level of society; grass roots. *~ pelindung* protective coating. *~ penciri* (*petro*) key bed. *~ penutup* (in mining) overburden. *~ rém* brake lining. *~ tanah atas* topsoil. *~ terakhir* polishing, final coat. *~ udara* air space.

pelapis lining (in clothing, etc.), coating, sheathing. *~ kopeling* facing.

pelapisan 1 lining, coating, plating. ~ *baja* iron plating. ~ *és* glazing. ~ *plastik* laminating. ~ *ulang* overlay. 2 stratification. ~ *masyarakat* social stratification. 3 buffering (in metal working). **berpelapisan** layered, stratified. *masyarakat yang* ~ a stratified society.

perlapisan stratification, layering, bedding. ~ *sejajar* parallel bedding.

lapis II (*D*) meat cut in small, flat pieces.

laplab → LABLAB.

lapo → LEPAU.

lapor (*D*) 1 school report, report card; → RAPOR. 2 to check in (at airport). 3 report. – *mata* eyewitness report. *melapor-matakan* to give an eyewitness account of. 4 (*coq*) to report to.

melapor to report, make/file a report, check in. ~ *diri* to check in, report in (at airport) ~ *ke polisi* to report to the police. ~ *kepada petugas GIA* to check in with a GIA official. ~ *keluar/masuk* check in/out (at a hotel).

melapori to report to s.o.

melaporkan [and **ngelaporin** (*J coq*)] to report s.t., state, announce, notify, inform. ~ *bahwa* to report that. ~ *diri* → MELAPOR *diri*.

terlapor s.o. reported (to have done s.t.).

laporan report, account, statement. ~ *asal-bapak-senang/ABS.* yes-sir report, i.e., a report which tells the boss what he wants to hear. ~ *awal* preliminary report. ~ *berkala* periodic reports. ~ *berpihak* biased/one-sided report. ~ *bulanan gabungan* consolidated monthly report. ~ *gabungan* consolidated report. ~ *intélijén* intelligence report. ~ *kecakapan* personnel performance record. ~ *kemajuan* (*pekerjaan*) progress report. ~ *keuangan* financial statement. ~ *keuangan gabungan* consolidated financial statement. ~ *Mingguan* Weekly Report (issued by Bank Indonesia and containing recent financial statistics). ~ (*pandangan*) *mata* eyewitness account. ~ *pemeriksaan* (*buku*) auditor's report. ~ *peninjauan* survey report. ~ *pérs* press report. ~ *polésan* (*fin*) window dressing. ~ *survéy/survai* survey report. ~ *tahunan* annual statement. ~ *usaha* operating statement. ~ *utama* [laput] lead article (in a magazine).

pelapor 1 rapporteur. 2 reporter, commentator, reporting. *perusahaan* ~ reporting enterprise. 3 whistle-blower.

pelaporan (running) commentary, reporting. *ditimbang pada bagian* ~ to be weighed in at the check-in counter. ~ *penumpang* passenger check-in.

lapud [lapangan udara] airport.

lapuk I 1 mildewed, moldy. 2 old, obsolete, antiquated, old-fashioned, out-of-date. *paham yang* – old fashioned ideas. *sudah* – behind the times. 3 rotten, decomposed, petrified (usually of wood). 4 decay. *tak – di/oléh hujan, tak lekang di/oléh panas* and *tidak – dék hujan, tak lakang dék panéh* (*M*) a) not felled by wind or rain. b) undying. c) indestructible. – *oléh kain sehelai* (*M*) to have only one wife/husband (for many, many years).

berlapuk 1 to be full of fungus, moldy. 2 obsolete, antiquated, too old, out-of-date.

melapuk 1 to weather. 2 to become moldy. 3 to decay, rot.

melapukkan to weather s.t.

lapukan weathered. *lapis* ~ weathered layer.

kelapukan (becoming) moldy, mildewed; moldiness, mildew.

pelapuk s.t. which causes decay.

pelapukan 1 weathering. 2 rotting, decaying.

lapuk II (*M*) – *lapak* (*onom*) sound of clapping.

berlapuk-lapuk (sound of people) clapping (hands).

lapun k.o. trap for birds/deer, etc. – *duduk* trap which is sprung when the animal touches it. – *tarik* trap which is sprung when the trapper pulls a trip-wire.

melapun to catch/snare birds, deer, etc. with such a trap.

lapur I → LAPOR.

lapur II (*M*) **berlapur** to leap up and flap its wings.

melapur to fight by flapping the wings (in a cockfight).

laput [laporan utama] lead article, cover story (in a magazine).

lara I 1 (*cla*) sad, sorrowful, depressing. *hidup yang* – a miserable existence. 2 (*Jv*) sick. – *wirang* (*cla*) offended/resentful and losing face. *pe(ng)lipur* – a) soother of cares, comforter. b) entertainment, amusement.

terlara-lara (*ob*) (to cry) bitterly.

kelaraan sadness, sorrow.

lara II k.o. plant, *Metrosideros petiolata*.

larah I berlarah-larahan (*cla*) in turn/succession.

melarah to take one's turn.

larah II berlarah-larah furrowed, lined.

larai (*M*) separated, disengaged, parted, weaned, set apart, divided; → TERCERAI, TERLERAI, TERPISAH.

melaraikan 1 to wean, part (persons fighting), disengage. 2 to ward off illness, etc.

terlarai separated, asunder, divided, set apart.

pelarai person who separates/breaks up a quarrel, fight, etc. ~ *demam* a) febrifuge, antipyretic. b) darling (of a child).

pelaraian disengagement (of troops).

larak I close-packed and fleshless (of pips in fruit) (e.g., *durian*).

larak II *akar* - k.o. climbing shrub, *Fissistigma fulgens*.

larak III → LERAK I.

laram affected (in manner).

melaram to behave in an affected manner.

laran k.o. tree, *Neolamarckia cadamba*.

larang I forbid, ban. – *ulang* double jeopardy, ne bis in idem.

melarang [and **nglarang** (*coq*)] to forbid, prohibit, ban, not allow s.o. to do s.t. *yang* ~ prohibitive (*mod*). *Dilarang berjualan di sini!* (signpost) No selling/trading here! *Dilarang kencing!* (signpost) No urinating here! *dilarang keras* strictly forbidden. *Dilarang mangkal di sini!* (signpost) Don't use this space for business! Don't occupy this spot for carrying out trade! → PANGKAL. *Dilarang masuk* no entrance, keep out. *dilarang masuk bagi tentara/militér!* (signpost) Off-limits/Out-of-bounds for military personnel! *Dilarang masuk untuk kendaraan!* (signpost) No thoroughfare! *Dilarang membuang sampah di sini!* (signpost) No littering/dumping here!

melarangkan → MELARANG.

terlarang forbidden, prohibited, banned, restricted. *daérah* – restricted area. ~ *untuk anggauta ABRI* off-limits/out-of-bounds for army personnel. *dinyatakan* ~ declared off-limits. *Pantai Kuta dinyatakan* ~ *bagi turis yang suka bertelanjang mandi laut.* Kuta Beach has been declared off-limits for nude bathers. *bagian-bagian* ~ the private parts (of the body).

larangan 1 prohibition, ban, restriction, interdiction, embargo. ~ *ke luar rumah* curfew; → JAM *malam*. ~ *perdagangan* trade embargo. ~ *pengasingan tanah* prohibition of land alienation. ~ (*pe*)*rangkapan jabatan* prohibition on having two different and incompatible positions/functions, incompatibility. ~ *terbang* grounded (of aircraft). 2 s.t. that is forbidden/prohibited, contraband. *benda-benda/barang-barang* ~ contraband. *hutan* ~ reserved forest. *kawasan* ~ prohibited/restricted area. *keris* ~ a holy kris, i.e., one to which certain prohibitions apply. *laut* ~ territorial waters; → PERAIRAN *téritorial. tabuh* ~ mosque drum which is only beaten on certain occasions. 3 inhibitory. 4 exclusion. 5 (*ling*) prohibitive.

pelarang prohibitor.

pelarangan 1 prohibition, ban, embargo. ~ *buku* book banning. ~ *terhadap ékspor ternak* embargo on the export of cattle. 2 s.t. that is forbidden/prohibited.

larang II (*Jv M ob*) seldom, rarely; → JARANG I.

larap I in demand, sells easily.

larap II melarapkan (*tali*) to pay/let out (a rope) gradually.

larap III (*S*) **larapan** applied. *pengetahuan* ~ applied science.

laras I 1 pitch, scale, key, tone; → TALA I. (*biola yang*) *salah* – false/off-pitch (violin). 2 [= ke(se)larasan] a) harmony, concord, accordance. – *bahasa* (*ling*) register.

selaras in accordance/agreement/concord/conformity/harmony/keeping/line (with), suit, commensurate. *tidak* ~ *lagi* out of date, old-fashioned. **me(nye)laraskan** 1 to (put in) tune, bring into agreement. 2 to adjust, adapt, synchronize; to make s.t. fit, harmonize. ~ *diri* to adapt/adjust o.s. 3 to align (the wheels of a vehicle, etc.). **keselarasan** conformity. **penyelarasan** adjustment, adaptation, synchronization. 2 alignment.

melarasi to match, go well with.

melaraskan to adjust, adapt.

kelarasan harmony.

pe(ng)larasan 1 adjustment, adaptation, harmonizing, synchronization. **2** alignment.

laras II 1 bolt upright, (as) straight (as an arrow); long and cylindrical (like a tree trunk). **2** rifle barrel. *senapan se-* rifle with one barrel. *senapan dua* – double-barreled rifle; → SENAPAN *kembar.* – *senjata api* gun barrel. *senjata api – panjang* long-barreled firearm/gun. **3** classifier (for rifles). *tiga – bedil* three rifles/guns.

laras III (*M*) **1** (an administrative) district. **2** basis of government according to *adat. tuanku* – chief of a district (this title was abolished in 1912).

laras IV *terang-terang* – dim, vague; → LARAT I.

laras V (*M*) falling (of leaves), deciduous.

melarasi to fall off (of all the leaves); → RARAS.

laras VI boots; → LARES, SEPATU *lars.*

larasetu → LOROSETU.

larat I 1 to drift, to be carried along by the current. **2** drag (of anchors), pull/drag with force along the ground, haul. **3** go far away; more and more; increasingly; always further/farther. **4** be protected. *kalau tak kuat, – jadi penyakit* gradually becoming sick. *kecepatan* – drift velocity. *kuda* – a runaway horse. *menahan/bertahan(-tahan)* – to endure s.t. with extreme patience, have lots of endurance. *orang* – a wanderer, vagabond. *sakitnya bertambah* – he became increasingly sick. *Sauhnya* –. The anchor dragged. *simpanan penahan* – a nest egg, s.t. put aside for a rainy day. *tambatan* – to keep s.t. always in mind; prevailing thoughts. *terang-terang* – dusky, somber, dark. – *hatinya mendengar perkataan anak itu.* He felt sorry hearing the child's words. – *ke negeri orang* to go abroad (to seek one's fortune). – *pikiran* a) very sad. b) thoughts which digress.

berlarat(-larat) and **melarat 1** to drag on; to move (on) slowly; to roam about (from one place to another); to deviate/stray/get away, get all mixed up. **2** to spread; be rampant. **3** further and further; (to let o.s. get) helpless, powerless; → MELARAT II.

memperlarat to enlarge on, protract (indefinitely).

larat II (*Sg*) *tiada* – unable (physically) to walk a long distance.

larat III (*akar* –) species of orchid, *Melodorum spp.*

larau I troublesome.

melarau to cause trouble for, be troublesome.

larau II (*M*) **melarau-larau** to keep on crying.

lares (*D*) boots.

lari I 1 (= **berlari**) to run, move with quick steps. *membawa* – to run away with, take s.t. and run away with it, steal; → MELARIKAN 1. – *semangatnya* he became unconscious. **2** to escape, get free/away, get out, break out/loose (as from a prison). **3** to play truant/hooky, stay away (without permission). **4** leave and go somewhere else. – *ke perusahaan lain* to join another company. **5** to flee, escape/run away (from danger). *Jangan –!* Don't run away! – *terkencing-kencing* to run away (from s.t.) with one's tail between one's legs. **6** (*coq*) the way s.t. is going, direction that s.t. is going in. *Ke mana –nya rancangan itu?* Where is this plan going to take/lead us? **7** (*J*) the length of (a piece of land, etc.). *Rumah ini –nya 12 m.* This house is 12 meters long. – *anjing* jog, jogging. **berlari(-lari) anjing** to jog, jogging. *(menghilang)* – *belakang* (to disappear) through the back door. – *berantai/beranting/berganti/beregu* relay race. – *bertemperasan* to run helter-skelter. – *bugil* streaking (run naked in public). – *cepat* sprint. – *dari kapal* to jump ship. – *éstafét* relay race. – *gawang* hurdle race. – *jarak dekat/péndék* sprint. – *jarak jauh* long-distance race. – *karung* sack race. – *kawin* to elope. – *ke barang* rush into goods. – *kencang!* on the double! – *ketakutan* to run away in fright. – *lintas alam* (*sports*) cross-country. – *lintas gawang* hurdle race. – *maju* rush (ahead). – *malam* to abscond. **melari-malamkan** to spirit/carry away in the dead of night. – *naik* (*naut*) to sail upwind. – *pagi/pelan-pelan* jogging. – *rintangan* obstacle course. – *santai* jogging. – *sekolah* to cut class, play hooky. – *serabutan* to run helter-skelter. – *seratus/ dua ratus,* etc. *méter* a 100/200, etc. meter race.

lari-lari to run about. ~ *anjing* to trot, jog. ~ *kecil* to trip.

selari (*ob*) **1** going in the same direction, parallel. **2** (= **selarian**) in accordance/agreement/conformity with; continuous.

berlari 1 to run away/off, rush (on), sprint. **2** runaway, in flight. *kuda* ~ a runaway horse. *guru kencing berdiri, murid kencing* ~

pupils are apt to carry (the results of) what they have learned to extremes. *berlari(-lari) anak* to run slowly. ~ *perut* to feel nauseated. **3** → LARI. ~ *berpontang-panting* to run away head over heels. *Pikirannya berlari-lari ke kejauhan.* His thoughts were wandering.

berlari(-lari)an 1 (*pl subj*) to run about in no fixed direction. *Orang* ~ *ke sana sini.* People were running around in all directions. **2** to run, walk quickly. ~ *datang* to come running (to). *Berjalan pun* ~ *saja karena hari hampir petang.* Walk quickly because it's almost afternoon.

melari to move to another place.

melarikan [and **nglariin** (*J coq*)] **1** to run away with, get away with, abduct, kidnap; → MEMBAWA *lari.* ~ *anak perempuan* to abduct a girl. ~ *pajak* to evade taxes. **2** to make (engines, etc.) run, put in gear and take off. *Truk itu dilarikannya.* He put the truck in gear and it took off. **3** (~ *diri*) a) to escape, get away. b) to elope. c) desert. d) to be (still) at large. ~ *nyawa* to escape from danger. ~ *untung* to go everywhere in search of a livelihood. **4** to rush s.o. (off to somewhere). *Yang luka parah dilarikan ke rumah sakit.* The seriously wounded were rushed to the hospital. **5** to run after s.t.

memperlarikan 1 to make (a car, etc.) run fast. **2** to run through. *Jarak itu diperlarikan di lorong-lorong.* The distance was run through alleys.

terlari-lari run quickly.

larian 1 → PELARIAN. **2** (~ *kuda*) (*ob*) race track.

kelarian berkelarian (*ob*) → BERLARIAN.

pelari 1 fugitive, escapee. **2** deserter. **3** runner, racer. ~ *bugil* streaker, s.o. who runs naked through a public place. ~ *cepat* sprinter. ~ *jarak dekat* sprinter. ~ *jarak jauh* long-distance runner. ~ *skat* skater. ~ *telanjang* streaker.

pelarian 1 run. **2** (= **larian**) (*ob*) (horse, etc.) race. **3** (= **larian**) footpath inside a fortress. **4** (= *orang* ~) escapee, fugitive; refugee. **5** (~ *diri*) flight, i.e., the act of fleeing; hasty departure. ~ *modal* capital flight. (*di*) *dalam* ~ in exile. *pemerintah* ~ government in exile.

perlarian seperlarian ~ *kuda* as far as a horse can run.

lari II → LARI-LARI.

larih (*Jv*) **berlarih-larih** to pour e.o. a drink.

melarih to pour out a drink into a glass, etc.

melarihi to serve s.o. a drink.

larik I melarik 1 (= **melarikkan**) to turn s.t. on a lathe, polish. **2** to bore/drill a hole.

pelarik and **pelarikan 1** potter's wheel. **2** lathe.

larik II (*Jv*) line, file, row; array. – *lurus* linear array.

melarik 1 to arrange in rows. **2** (*dengan cara* ~) scanning.

larikan 1 row (of plants). **2** groove for plants. **3** furrow, a narrow groove made in the ground by a plow.

pelarik scanner.

pelarikan scanning. ~ *dalam* deep scanning.

larik III (*D/E*) (song) lyrics.

berlarik to have ... as its lyrics.

lari-lari *rumput* – k.o. shore grass, hedgehog grass, *Spinifex squarrosus.*

laring (*D*) larynx.

laringéktomi (*D*) laryngectomy.

laris quick-selling, sells well, in demand, popular (of item). – *manis* to sell like hot cakes. – *lakunya* to sell well/briskly. – *manis* and – *seperti goréng pisang* and – *bak kacang goréng* to sell like hot cakes. *Jualannya* –. His/The goods are selling well.

melariskan to make (an article) sell well, popularize.

kelarisan 1 to be all sold out. **2** popular (of item).

pelaris 1 *hikmat/ilmu* ~ *mantra* to make an item sell well/be in demand.

penglaris k.o. charm to make goods sell well. *Buat* ~ (said by vendors of vegetables/fruit, etc. to prospective buyers) "For quick sale!" (used when the vendor tries to sell his first article at a low price, with the hope that further sales will go well; k.o. loss leader)

pelarisan putting a charm on s.t.

laron (*Jv*) **1** flying white ant. **2** (*joc*) a bunch of people.

lars (*D*) *sepatu* – boots. *bersepatu* – to wear boots.

Larte (among members of the Army Search and Rescue Group) emergency rations, i.e., an allotment of food and provisions.

laru (*Jv*) remedy against *legen* or unfermented palm wine turning sour.

melaru to mix that compound into s.t.

larung I (*Jv*) to float on the water.

melarung [and **nglarung** (*coq*)] to throw (a *sesaji*/corpse, etc.) into the water/river, etc.

pe(ng)larungan the action of throwing these items in the water, etc.

larung II k.o. coffin (open on one side, so that the deceased can touch the earth).

larut I 1 protracted, further than intended (of movement), dragging (of anchors). **2** later than agreed/usual; late (of the hour/time). *– malam* a) late at night. b) late-night (show). *malam/ siang semakin –* it became later and later in the evening/day. **3** (*Sg Mal*) *semangkin –* to get worse, take a turn for the worse (of illness). *bertambah – sakitnya* his illness got worse and worse.

selarut *~ ini* this late at night.

berlarut *~ hati/perasaan/pikiran* a) to feel unhappy/very sad/ distracted. b) brokenhearted.

berlarut-larut 1 prolonged, protracted, extended. *perang yang ~* a protracted war. **2** for a long time, go on for too long, endless, dragging on, long-drawn-out. *Pikirannya suka ~.* He likes to indulge in wild fantasies. **3** to run free/wild. *Dia membiarkan khayalannya ~.* He let his imagination run wild. **4** rambling (of a speech).

melarut 1 protracted, long and drawn out. **2** to drag on, keep going on and on.

melarutkan and **memperlarut** to prolong, drag s.t. out.

terlarut-larut prolonged.

larutan lateness.

kelarutan lateness, getting late.

larut II 1 soluble. **2** (*M*) dissolved, melted, fused; crushed (of feelings). **3** to melt (into the crowd). *– di tengah-tengah mahasiswa* melted into the (crowd of) students.

melarut to dissolve.

melarutkan to dissolve s.t.

terlarut dissolved.

terlarutkan soluble.

larutan (chemical) solution. *~ penggosok* scouring solution. *~ suspénsi* suspended solution.

kelarutan 1 solubility. **2** dissolving.

pelarut solvent. *~ yang mudah menguap* volatile solvents. **berpelarut** with a ... solvent. *~ campuran* mixed solvent.

pelarutan dissolving.

larut III (*Jv*) **1** to flow away/off, wash away. **2** to be blotted out of existence, cease to exist, be wiped out. **3** to get carried away (of feelings).

larut IV k.o. palm, k.o. arrowroot, *Maranta arundinacea.*

las I (*D*) **1** weld(ing). *pipa baja tanpa –* seamless steel pipe. *tukang – welder. – gésék* friction welding. *– kampuh* seam welding. *– karbid* carbon welding. *– lebur* fusion welding. *– listrik* electric welding. *– puncak* end-lap weld. *– sambung* butt welding. *– tembusan* root pass. *– tempa* forge welding. *– temu/tumpul* butt welding. *– titik* spot welding. **2** joint. *– menumpu* butt joint.

melas and **mengelas** to weld.

melaskan to have s.t. welded.

lasan welded.

las-lasan all k.o. of welding.

pengelasan welding.

las II *batu –* whetstone.

las III clipped form of **belas II**; → LAS-LASAN.

lasa 1 numb; paralyzed. **2** (*M*) calloused (on the soles of the feet).

lasah I melasahkan *~ badan* to work hard, wear o.s. out.

memperlasah to make s.o. work very hard.

lasah II (*M*) **pelasah** everyday clothes; worn-out clothes.

lasah III (*ob*) **melasah** to beat; to torture; → BELASAH.

lasak I everyday (cloths), casual (of clothes); for daily use; → LASAH II. *baju –* work clothes. *orang –* factotum. *tahan –* durable, lasting, enduring rough wear.

pelasak *pakaian ~* everyday clothes.

lasak II 1 unsteady, unstable. **2** has to touch everything (of a child), hyperactive, never sits still. **3** mobile, ceaselessly moving. *– berlebih* hyperactivity. *– tangan* incapable of keeping one's hands off s.t. *– tidur* do not have a permanent place to sleep. **4** aggressive.

kelasakan 1 restlessness, hyperactivity. **2** mobility.

Lasam a place in Java renowned for its *batik.*

lasana k.o. shrub, sweet acacia, *Acasia farnesiana.*

lasat (*M*) serious, severe (of illness). *Tangisnya semakin –.* His crying got worse and worse.

laser (*E*) /léser/ laser.

pelaseran lazing.

perlaseran laser (*mod*).

lasi I (*M*) afraid, scared, frightened.

melasi(kan) 1 to frighten s.o. **2** to intimidate, cow.

lasian 1 fright. **2** discouraged, disenchanted, disillusioned.

pelasi coward.

lasi II (*kayu –*) k.o. tree, *Adina fagifolia.*

lasik and **lasit** (*M*) → LESIT I.

laskar (*Pers*) **1** (*ob*) troops; army; soldier. **2** (*– rakyat*) irregular troops, irregulars, guerillas, partisans; local militia units organized as an auxiliary force. *– jihad* (Muslim) holy warriors, the name of a paramilitary Muslim group.

kelaskaran (*mod*) military affairs.

las-lasan (*Jv*) (in) the teens. *di tahun –,* in the teens (of this century).

las(s)o (*D/E*) lasso.

lastik 1 → ÉLASTIK. **2** (*ob*) catapult. **3** (tree) sap, latex (of rubber trees and banana stems).

lasuh (*M*) quick (to understand/learn), quick-study.

lasykar → LASKAR.

lat I interim, interval, intervening period; time between.

berlat to have an interval or time between, at intervals.

lat II (*D*) late; → TERLAMBAT.

selat-latnya at the latest (by); → SELAMBAT-LAMBATNYA.

lat III (*D*) lath.

lat IV (in acronyms) → LATIHAN.

lata I cascade. *– boga* herbivores.

melata to creep (of plants), crawl (of snakes/insects), crawling. *héwan ~* reptiles. *air (me)lata* waterfall, cascade (in mountain areas).

melata-lata *berjalan ~* (*Sg*) to lounge about.

lata II low, wretched, base; → LETA. *hina –* very miserable.

lata III → LATAH.

latah I 1 a psychological disorder prevalent among adult Indonesians and Malaysians (mostly women). It can be caused by a sudden noise, shock or command. In the state of *latah* the victim appears to lose awareness of him/herself and his/her surroundings and can only imitate, often accompanied by vulgar language, what he/she hears or sees. Anyone who attracts his attention can make him do any action by pretending to do that action. This condition can last for hours or until the victim drops in exhaustion; recovery to a normal state of consciousness then takes place. *ikut – + verb* or *adj* also, too. *Si suami tidak mau ikut – patah semangat.* The husband didn't also want to be brokenhearted. **2** (*coq*) any k.o. irrational and obsessive behavior involving imitation. *– mulut* can't keep quiet, keeps on talking.

berlatah-latah again and again.

melatah to go into a state of *latah.*

melatahkan to cause s.o. to go into a state of *latah.*

latah-latahan aping/imitating what s.o. else has done.

kelatahan 1 imitation. **2** nervous; → KEGUGUPAN.

pelatah s.o. in a state of *latah.*

latah II (*ob*) debris (leaves, etc.) under tree (in forests, etc.).

latah III → LATA I.

latak (*Jv*) dregs (of oil, etc.), residue.

latam compacted.

melatam to stamp down (soil), tread down (rice fields; by water buffaloes for planting); to stamp one's foot (from rage).

melatamkan to make (soil, etc.), compact/solid.

latang → JELATANG.

latar (*Jv*) **1** surface. **2** level, flat; → DATAR, RATA I. **3** background, ground, fond. *– hitam* dark background. *– putih* natural background, i.e., not dyed (of *batik*). **4** yard/grounds around a building. **5** setting. *bunga* – whore. *– belakang* background. **berlatar-belakang** with a background of. *~ politik* politically motivated. **berlatar-belakangkan** ... with a ... background/setting of. **melatar-belakangi** to constitute a background for. *dilatar-belakangi* (also has the meaning) with a backdrop of, with a ... setting. *~ daérah* with a provincial setting. *– depan* foreground. *– kasus* case history. *– pandang* backdrop. *– sélar* (*petro*) cellar deck.

berlatar with a ... background. *~ belakang* with/to have a background. *~ belakang biru tua* with a dark-blue background.

berlatarkan with a background of, have a setting in.

melatari 1 to provide s.t. with a background. *dilatari segitiga mérah muda* with a pink triangle as background. **2** to be behind s.t., be the background to s.t.

pelataran 1 background. **2** (front or inner) yard. **3** ground color (of a flag, etc.). **4** platform. *~ lapangan udara* apron. *~ parkir* parking lot. *~ parkir pesawat* apron, tarmac. *~ pengeboran* drilling platform. *~ perkémahan* campground. *~ téras* public area. *~ belakang* background, setting.

latas melatas to cut/mow grass.

latat (*ob*) **melatat-melotot** to open one's eyes wide; → MELOTOT.

latéks (*D/E*) latex.

latén (*D/E*) latent.

lateral (*D/E*) lateral.

laterit (*D/E*) laterite.

latif (*A*) fine, delicate, gentle.

latifah (*A*) elegant, pretty (of women).

latih 1 (well-)trained, experienced, skilled. **2** training. *juru –* trainer. *kapal/pesawat (pe)latih* training ship/aircraft. *– tertib* calisthenics.

berlatih 1 (*~ diri*) to train (o.s.), practice. **2** trained, exercised, in training. *~ menulis cepat* to practice shorthand.

melatih 1 to train (a dog, etc.), break (a horse), coach (athletes, etc.), groom (s.o. for a job), exercise, practice. *mengadakan ~ kembali* to take a retraining course. *~ mulut* to be careful what one says. *Saya akan ~ kau ngetik.* I'll teach you how to type. *~ ulang* to rehearse.

melatihkan to have s.o. trained/coached, etc.

terlatih 1 trained, coached, instructed. **2** practiced, skilled, veteran, elite, qualified. *sangat ~* highly skilled. *tak ~* unskilled, untrained, not practiced at. *tentara ~* trained (i.e., regular) troops. **3** exercised. **keterlatihan** training.

latihan training, exercise, practice, instruction, lesson, drill. *kurang ~* out of practice. *masuk ~* to enter military service. *pusat ~* training center. *sekolah ~* training school. *unit ~ keliling* mobile training unit. *~ darurat udara* air-raid drill. *~ dasar* basic training. *~ gerak badan* physical exercise. *~ jabatan* on-the-job training. *~ jari* (five-)finger exercise (for typing/playing the piano, etc.). *~ jasmani* physical training. *~ kemilitéran* (*mil*) drill. *~ kemilitéran pertama* (*mil*) basic training. *~ kerja* job training. *~ ketrampilan* apprenticeship training. *~ komputer* computer training. *~ lanjut* advanced training. *~ lapangan* field training. *~ menémbak* target practice. *~ menulis* writing exercises. *~ mula* primary training. *~ otak* brain teaser. *~ perang* war games. *~ perang-perangan* (*mil*) maneuvers. *~ pertempuran dengan menggunakan peluru tajam* (*mil*) live-fire exercise. *~ pola kalimat* (*gram*) sentence-pattern drill. *~ sambil bekerja* on-the-job training. *~ simak/menyimak* memorization exercises (at school). *~ swaloka* in-house training. *~ tanding* sparring. *~ tempur sambil mempertahankan hidup* combat survival training. *~ terbang* flight instruction. *~ terjun payung* jumping course. *~ ulang* rehearsal. *~ widya yudha* (*mil*) tactical field training.

pelatih 1 trainer, coach, tutor. **2** instructor.

pelatihan training. *~ kerja* job training.

Latin (*D*) Latin. *bahasa –* Latin. *huruf –* the Roman alphabet.

melatinkan to write s.t. in the Latin alphabet, Romanize.

pelatinan Romanization.

lating (*M*) **melating** to spring back.

latis (*M*) **melatis** to cut down shrub.

latu → LELATU.

latuh k.o. edible sea grass, *Enhalus acoroides*.

latuk *parang –* k.o. *parang* with curved end.

latung (*Jv*) *minyak –* crude petroleum.

latur (*M*) burnt, scalded, blistered (of one's skin). **melatur** to blister.

laturahmi → SILATURAHMI.

lau I (*A*) (*ob*) if; → JI(KALAU). *wa–* and/even if.

lau II *bunga –* an ornamental cultivated orchid, *Phalaenopsis amabilis. daun –* name of a plant species, jewel orchid. *Haemaria discolor.*

lau III (in northern Sumatra) river.

lauh I (*A*) *papan –* school slate; → LOH I.

lauh II jewfish, *Polynemus heptadactylus/sextarius?*

lauk 1 food (spiced fish/meat/vegetables, etc., except *sayur*) prepared for eating with rice. *– pauk* all k.o. of food (other than rice). *alat –* (*M*) k.o. feast on the eighth day after a marriage. **2** (*M*) meat or fish. *– sapi* beef. *lagi – lagi nasi,* the richer one is, the more friends one has; the rich get richer. *mencencang – tengah halat* (*M*) to wash one's dirty linen in public. *memberi – kepada orang membantai* help s.o. who does not need to be helped.

berlauk (*makan*) *~* (to eat) rice with side dishes.

berlauk-lauk *cakap ~ makan dengan sambal lada* to talk as if one is rich (though one is actually poor).

laukna beunang caina herang (*S*) "The fish is caught; the water isn't muddied," motto of the Siliwangi Division.

laun slow, not quick, taking a long time, at a reduced speed, slowed-down. *lambat –* gradually; → LAMBAT.

laun-laun *~ hari* a) a few days ago. b) after a few days.

berlaun to linger, loiter, dawdle, dally.

melaun-laun to slow down, delay, prolong.

laundri (*E*) /londri/ laundry.

laung a loud and clear voice (for calling/hailing/shouting, etc.).

berlaung (*cla*) to call, hail, shout.

melaung 1 to shout/cry/call out in a loud voice. **2** to call, summon.

melaungkan to call to s.o.

pelaung *gong ~* (*cla*) summoning gong. **sepelaung(an)** as far as a summoning call can be heard.

laur (*M*) **1** bent, curved, crooked. **2** classifier for curved objects, such as rings, bangles, etc. *se– gelang* a bangle.

melaur to bend, curve; curved, arched.

laut 1 sea, the continuous body of salt water covering most of the earth's surface. *di – dan di darat* on land and on sea. *– bébas/ lepas/rembang/selebu* the high seas, open sea. *angkatan –* navy. *bahasa –* language of sea nomads. *orang –* sea nomads, coastal Proto-Malay tribes. *raja –* (*cla*) admiral. *– Kidul* the Indian Ocean. *– wilayah* 12-mile zone. **2** a large undifferentiated mass like an ocean or the sea. *– api* a) a sea of fire. b) hell. *– cahaya* a beam of light. **3** (in some compounds) sea (*mod*); (in some compounds) north. *barat –* northwest. *timur –* northeast. *– budi tepian akal/ilmu* an intellectual. *– ditémbak, darat kena* to obtain s.t. unwanted. *– tak ada – yang tidak berombak* no rose without a thorn. *– mana tak berombak?* what man is without sin? *memberi garam kepada –* to carry coals to Newcastle. *diam di –, masin tidak, diam di bandar tak meniru* (*M*) unsusceptible to good manners/customs. *– Adriatik* Adriatic (Sea). *– Baltik* the Baltic (Sea). *– Cina Selatan* the South China Sea. *– Égéa* the Aegean (Sea). *– Hitam* the Black Sea. *– Jawa* Java Sea. *– Karang* the Coral Sea. *– Kaspia* the Caspian Sea. *– Kulzum* the Red Sea. *– lepas* open sea. *– Mati* the Dead Sea. *– Mérah* the Red Sea. *– Natuna/Tiongkok Selatan* South China Sea. *– pengundak* head sea. *– pinggir* marginal sea. *– Tengah* the Mediterranean (Sea).

melaut 1 like the sea. *sawah ~ hijau* the rice paddies are like a green sea. **2** to go/put out to sea, head out to sea; seafaring. **3** to splash down in the sea (of aircraft).

melauti to sail on the sea.

melautkan and **memperlaut** to send by sea mail; to make go (or, put) into the sea.

lautan 1 ocean, sea. *~ Atlantik* the Atlantic (Ocean). *~ Hindia* Ind(ones)ian Ocean. *~ Indonésia* the Ind(ones)ian Ocean. *~ Kidul* the Ind(ones)ian Ocean. *~ selebu* the open ocean. *~ Teduh* the Pacific (Ocean). **2** ocean (of fire/mud, etc.). *~ manusia* crowd (of people).

kelautan marine (*mod*). *téknologi* ~ marine technology.

pelaut 1 sailor, seaman. **2** sea nomads. **kepelautan** navigation, seamanship.

pelautan throwing s.t. overboard/into the ocean.

lava (*D/E*) lava; → LAHAR I.

lawa I (*ob*) transverse beams strengthening the sides of a *kelong* fish-trap.

melawa (*ob*) to bar the way to a bridegroom until he pays a fee for admission to his bride's house.

pelawa cross-bar.

lawa II (*Mal*) *tunjuk* – to show off.

lawa III (*Jv*) k.o. small bat.

lawa(h) vast, open/unobstructed (view over the scenery).

melawah wide open.

lawa(h)-lawa(h) (*J*) spider; → LABAH-LABAH.

lawai → LAWÉ I.

lawak I joke, jest, fun, banter. *dijadikan* – to be made fun of, ridiculed. *tukang* – clown, comedian.

lawak-lawak 1 comedy, amusing activity. ~ *main bunga tahi* joking around often leads to trouble. **2** butt of a joke.

berlawak(-lawak) and **melawak(-lawak)** to clown/joke around, do s.t. that is amusing.

melawak ~ *cabul* to crack dirty jokes.

lawakan 1 joke, gag. **2** humor.

pelawak clown, comedian, buffoon.

lawak II → TEMU *lawak*.

lawak-lawak (*M*) trough, manger, a box/trough to hold hay for horses/cattle to eat. *tinggi* – (wanting) to live/be above one's social position, i.e., arrogant.

lawalata the name of the first Indonesian to travel widely about the world on foot.

berlawalata and **nglawalata** to go on foot, hike.

lawan 1 adversary, opponent, antagonist, enemy, foe, rival, competitor, contestant, respondent (in a civil trial). – *débat* opponent in a debate. – *politik* political contender. **2** counter-, anti-. **3** person or thing that corresponds to or closely resembles s.o. or s.t. else. – *kerja* counterpart. **4** partner (in fighting/dancing/playing bridge, etc.); *cp* MITRA. *ayam yang dipilih sebagai* – sparring partner (in cock-fighting). – *latih* sparring partner (in boxing). – *(ber)bicara* interlocutor, person with whom one is conversing. – *(ber)dansa* dancing partner. **5** rival, match, parallel. *Kecantikannya tidak ada –nya.* Her beauty is unmatched/unrivalled/unequalled. **6** match, s.t. that goes well with s.t. else. *Kamu bukanlah –nya.* You're not the right person for him. *Nasi –nya lauk* rice goes well with side dishes. **7** versus, against, to. *pertandingan X – Y* a (soccer) match between X and Y. *satu – satu* one to/on one *20 suara – 6 suara* 20 votes to 6 votes. *tiga – dua* three to two (the score in a game). – *hukum* against the law, illegal, unlawful. **8** to fight/go up against. –, *bung!* (Come on and) fight, buddy! **9** opposite, antonym (*gram*) *hitam –nya putih* the opposite of white is black. – *(angin) pasat* antitrades, antitrade winds. – *asas* paradox. – *hukum* against the law, illegal. – *intélijén* counterintelligence. – *jenis* person of the opposite sex. – *kata* antonym. – *main* playmate, partner (in sex). – *pemberontakan* counterinsurgency. – *perkara* legal adversary. – *radang* antiphlogistic. – *rakitik* antirachitic. – *skorbut* antiscorbutic. – *tank* antitank.

berlawan 1 to have an opponent/rival, oppose, compete, contest. *tidak* ~ incontestable, uncontested. *kekuatan yang tidak* ~ uncontested power. **2** (~ *dengan*) to be in contradiction with/contrary to/in conflict with. *perbuatan yang* ~ *dengan keyakinan sendiri* an action contrary to one's own beliefs. **3** to have an opponent/adversary, etc.

berlawanan 1 to be contrary to, be against, be in contravention to, in violation of; contradictory, conflicting, clashing, opposing. *pandangan* ~ opposing views. ~ *dengan* ...in contrast to ... ~ *dengan undang-undang dasar* against the constitution, unconstitutional. *harga* ~ a competitive price. **2** opposite (direction). *dari arah* ~ from the opposite direction. *(datang)* ~ *arah* coming from the opposite direction, oncoming. ~ *dengan arah jarum jam* and ~ *arah (jalan) jarum jam* counterclockwise. *pasangan* ~ *jenis* a couple (man and woman). **3** to compete with e.o.

melawan 1 [and **ng(e)lawan** (*coq*)] to oppose, fight against, fight back, against. ~ *adat* to go against customs and traditions. ~ *arus* (to go) against the current, (run) against the tide. ~ *godaan* to resist temptation. ~ *dengan ingkar* to resist recalcitrantly. *dengan/secara* ~ *hak/hukum* illegal(ly), unlawful(ly), wrongful(ly). ~ *kantuk* to fight sleep, try to stay awake. ~ *kapal selam* antisubmarine. **2** to compete with, play against, challenge. ~ *berkata* to speak/listen to s.o; to invite s.o. to a talk.

melawani to treat/regard s.o. as an enemy.

memperlawankan to pit ... against e. o., cause to fight/clash, etc.

terlawan opposed. *tidak* ~ unopposable.

kelawanan 1 (*ob*) ability to oppose/stand firm/hold one's own. **2** (*elec*) resistivity.

pelawan 1 fighter, rival, opponent, opposing. *partai* ~ the opposing party. **2** disobedient, (always) in opposition. *kaum* ~ members of the resistance, rebels, insurgents. *partai* ~ opposition party. ~ *radang* antiphlogistic. **3** resistor.

perlawanan 1 resistance, opposition, defense readiness, countermeasures. *mengadakan* ~ *terhadap* to offer resistance to. ~ *nonkekerasan* nonviolent resistance. ~ *rakyat* [Wanra] civilian auxiliary forces. **2** controversy, contradiction, s.t. that is the reverse. **3** challenge, objection (in court).

lawang I (*Jv*) door, gate, (*mil*) defile. – *sekéténg* decorative gate.

pelawang 1 doorkeeper. **2** bachelor.

pelawangan grade-crossing.

lawang II (*Skr*) nutmeg tree (a *Cinnamomum*). *bunga/kembang* ~ mace; clove flowers (from the clove-tree, *Eugenia aromatica* or the star anise, *Illicium verum*. *kayu* – cinnamon, *Cinnamomum*.

lawang III *ikan* – k.o. freshwater fish, *Pangasius micronemus*.

lawar I a thin slice (of fish/meat).

melawar to slice thin (fish/meat).

lawar II *lawaran* ruthless(ly), merciless(ly).

lawar III – *putih* k.o. tree, *Elaeocarpus parvifolius*.

lawar IV (*Bal*) k.o. salad.

lawas I (*M*) clear (of view), vast, spacious (of land), wide open; → LUAS.

melawas 1 to extend (of view).

kelawasan scope.

lawas II not bearing fruit any more.

lawas III (*Jv ob*) long (in duration); long ago, old.

lawat visit, tour.

melawat 1 to pay a visit, make a trip/tour/expedition (to another country, etc.). **2** (= **melawati**) to go/come see, call on. ~ *orang mati* to pay a condolence call.

pelawat 1 visitor, caller (i.e., a person who drops in for a short visit). ~ *sekolah* and *guru* ~ (*ob*) school supervisor. **2** tourist.

(per)lawatan 1 visit (of condolence). *perlawatan kerja* work visit. **2** trip, tour, expedition, excursion. **3** mission.

lawé I (*Jv*) yarn, thread.

lawéan place where thread is woven.

lawé II (*Jv*) → SELAWÉ.

lawéan (*Jv*) a headless ghost.

lawét (*Jv*) cliff swallow, edible-nest swiftlet, *Collocalia fuciphaga*; → WALÉT.

lawi(-lawi) 1 curving tail feathers of a bird. **2** – *ayam* k.o. anchovy, *Coilia, spp.*

lawina avalanche.

lawon (*Jv*) white cotton textile (*esp Jv* hand-woven, for shrouds).

Law Puik → KAW PUIK.

layab → KELAYAPAN.

layah I flexible.

melayah to bend forward, bow, hang over, hang down.

terlayah bent (over).

layah II a long veil (the only openings are the eyeholes for women pilgrims); → BERGUK, BURKAK.

melayahkan to veil, cover with a veil.

layah III *melayah rendah* and **melayah-layah** to fly low (of aircraft); → LAYAP I.

layah IV (*M*) concave (as a soup-plate).

melayah to bend over.

melayahkan to bend s.t. over.

layak I (*A*) **1** decent, appropriate, fitting, proper, qualified, suitable, reasonable, feasible; should. *tidak –* a) inappropriate, improper. b) in poor taste, unworthy (of). *Ia mémang – memegang jawatan itu.* He is qualified to hold that position. *lahan yang – untuk dibudidayakan* land suitable for cultivation. *yang – dipercaya* reliable sources. 2 worth, worthy (of). *– beroperasi* operational. *– dicoba* worth trying. *– dipidana* punishable. *– édar* fit for circulation (of currency). *– huni* inhabitable, livable. *tak – dihuni* uninhabitable. *– krédit* credit worthy. *sértifikat – laut* certificate of seaworthiness. *– muat* publishable, fit for publication. *– pakai* usable. *– terbit* publishable, fit for publication. *– udara* airworthy. *tidak – laut* unseaworthy. 3 marginal. 4 like, in the manner of. *tidak –* improper. **ketidak-layakan** impropriety, inappropriateness.

layaknya 1 as if, as it were, properly speaking. 2 rightly; just the right/appropriate amount. *(sebagai/seperti)* ... ~ as though; much the same as. 3 qualified. *orang-orang yang bukan ~* unqualified people (occupying positions of authority).

selayaknya naturally, rightly, justly, by (all) rights, properly, reasonably, fairly, appropriately, accordingly. *diperlakukan dengan ~* to be treated fairly. *sudah ~* (entirely) as is/was to be expected. *tidak ~* improperly, inappropriately.

melayakkan to adjust, adapt, arrange, improve, consider suitable, qualify, fit.

memperlayak to make s.t. fit, adapt.

kelayakan 1 suitability, fitness, feasibility, worthiness. *studi ~* feasibility study. *– laut* seaworthiness. 2 equity, fairness. **berkelayakan** competent, qualified, capable. *tidak ~* unqualified.

layak II *ikan –* fish split down the backbone and dried (not salted). **melayak** to dry a fish that has been split down the backbone.

layam berlayam(kan) ~ *– pedang* and **melayamkan ~** *pedang* (*cla*) to brandish/swing a sword, etc. (defiantly in a dance).

layan serve, service, take care of.

melayani [and **ngelayanin** (*J coq*)] 1a) to serve, attend to (customers). b) to wait on (people at table, etc.). 2 to oblige s.o. 3 to give (a patient/an adorer) (a lot of or no attention). 4 to care for, look after, take care of, attend to (s.o.'s needs). 5 to let s.o. have his way, serve s.o. sexually, to satisfy/meet (s.o.'s needs/desires), entertain (guests), please. *~ kemauannya* to serve his sexual desires. 6 to listen/respond to; to accept (an offer, etc.). 7 to be able to hold one's own against (an enemy), be a match for s.o. 8 to be able/willing (to talk to s.o.). 9 to withstand, stand up to, resist successfully, face, confront, meet, encounter, cope with (an emergency). 10 to treat s.o. (in such and such a way). 11 to look after (interests), take care of, watch (over), protect, guard. 12 to entertain, keep (guests) entertained, keep s.o. company. 13 to supply, fill. *~ résép dokter* to fill a doctor's prescription. 14 to handle, operate, man, be in charge of. *~ senjata* to handle a gun. *~ pertanyaan* to take/answer questions. *~ télepon* to be in charge of the telephone.

melayankan to serve (up), dish (up), set out (supper, etc.).

terlayani served.

layanan (*mainly Mal* and *Sg*) service. *~ di kamar* room service (in hotel).

pelayan servant, attendant, waiter, waitress, maid; → PEMBANTU rumahtangga, PRAMUSAJI, PRAMUWISMA. *~ kabin* cabin boy. *~ kantor* office janitor. *~ lif* elevator operator. *~ meriam* gunner. *~ pompa* gas station attendant. *~ rém* brakeman (on railroad). *~ réstoran* waiter. *~ serabutan* general utility man, man who does odd jobs. *~ sinyal* railroad crossing guard. *~ télepon* switchboard operator. *~ toko* salesman; saleswoman, salesgirl. *~ wésél* switchman (on the railroad).

pelayanan 1 service, serving. *beroriéntasi pada ~* service-oriented. *~ cepat dan memuaskan* fast and satisfying service. *~ di darat* baggage handling. *~ di kamar* room service. *~ informasi keparwisataan* visitors' information service. *~ jasa bayi tabung* in vitro fertilization. *~ jasa pramusiwi* baby-sitter service. *~ keséhatan* health service. *~ lepas jual* after-sales service. *~ masyarakat* public service. *~ memuat/membongkar muatan* ramp handling service (for aircraft). *~ penuangan anggur* wine service (in a restaurant). *~ pos* postal service, mail delivery. *~ purnajual/purnaniaga* aftersales service. *~ satu atap* one-stop service. 2 (= **layanan**) treatment. *~ yang semestinya* proper

treatment. 3 supply (of requirements). 4 handling, managing. *tempat ~* counter (at airport). *~ di darat* ground handling (of aircraft).

layang I to fly, glide. *baju/kain –* coat/piece of cloth that can make a person glide through the air. *ikan –* a) flying fish, *Melalugis.* b) jack mackerel, *Decapterus. jalan/jembatan –* overpass, cloverleaf. *surat –* a letter without a return address. *– ambang* hover. **melayang-mengambang** to hover; hovering. *– gantung* hang glider. *– peluncur* hang glider.

layang-layang [= **layang-layangan** (*J*)] kite. **berlayang-layang** to fly a kite.

selayang in passing. *~ lalu/pandang/terbang/tinjau* on the surface/face of it, at first sight, roughly speaking, superficially, cursorily; overview. *cinta ~ pandang* love at first sight.

melayang [= **berlayang** (*ob*)] 1 to glide, float in/through the air (of leaves/paper, etc.), hover. *~ di atas kota* (the plane) circled over the town. 2 to float in/through the water. *lémpar ~* to skim (stones on the water). *tinju ~* flying fists. 3 to flit, pass lightly and rapidly and disappear. 4 to droop (of one's eyes from sleepiness). *pikirannya ~* a) he cannot think calmly. b) his thoughts were wandering. *~ jiwa/nyawa* to die. *kalau getah meléléh, kalau daun ~* close is the shirt, but closer is the skin.

melayang-layang to drift/float around, hover, wander (of one's thoughts).

melayangkan 1 to cause to fly/glide, set s.t. in flight. 2 to direct, dispatch, send/fire off (a letter). *~ mata/pandangan/pemandangan ke/kepada* to glance (at), shift one's eyes (over to). *pandang jauh dilayangkan, pandang dekat ditukikkan* to have seen/noticed everything. 3 to dismiss (a suit/criminal charge). 4 to dedicate (a song that one is singing).

terlayang(-layang) to glide, fly, float in/through the air. *matanya terlayang* to be half asleep, dozing off.

layangan 1 (*elec*) beat. 2 kite; → LAYANG-LAYANG.

pelayangan 1 (*ob*) crossing (a river by ferryboat). 2 ferryboat. 3 → JALAN/JEMBATAN *layang.* 4 (*ob*) → BAJU/KAIN *layang.*

layang II melayang to cut a mango so that it becomes half a sphere. *pipinya laksana pauh dilayang* with beautiful cheeks.

layang-layang *burung –* various species of swallows, swifts and martins, *Hirundinidae/Cypselidae. – api* barn swallow, *Hirundo rustica. – batu/biasa* Pacific swallow, *Hirundo tahitica. ikan –* various species of flying fish.

layap I to skim close to (surface of the sea/earth).

berlayap(-layap)an 1 to fly/swim in flocks/schools, etc. (of birds/fish, etc.). 2 to sway back and forth (of palm trees in the wind).

melayap to skim the surface (of birds looking for fish).

melayapi (*ob*) to hover over.

melayap(-layap)kan 1 to make s.t. float/hover. 2 to make s.t. move continuously (like the wind in the trees).

layap II (*J*) **ngelayap** to wander around (*esp* in the evening).

kelayapan to wander around.

layap III melayap, ngelayap (*J*) [= **layap-layap** (*Jv*)] and **terlayap** to doze off, fall asleep.

layar I 1 sail, lug. *kapal/perahu –* sailboat. *mengembangkan/membabarkan/menegang/memasang –* to set sail. *dengan – terkembang* in/under full sail, with all sails set/spread. 2 screen. *– pérak/putih* movie/silver screen. 3 roller, blind, curtain, shade. 4 scenes. *di belakang –* behind the scenes. *kain –* canvas. *sekali – terkembang, pantang perahu balik haluan* once you start to do s.t., you can't change your mind. *– timpa tiang* friends become foes. *– agung* mainsail. *– apit* batten lug. *– bahu* topsail. *– baksi* mizzen sail. *– batang* high-peaked spritsail. *– bubutan* staysail. *– bulu ayam* standing lug. *– cucur* spritsail. *– dastur* spinnaker. *– datar* flat screen (TV). *– depan* foresail. *– gap/gusi* gaff mainsail, spanker. *– gusi* gaff mainsail. *– haluan* jib. *– hujan* rain awning/screen. *– kaca* television (screen). *– matahari* sun visor. *– padau* storm canvas. *– pengaduh/penga(m)puh* topsail. *– penggiling* spritsail. *– penyorong* mizzen. *– pérak* the silver screen, the movies. **melayar-pérakkan** to film, make into a movie. *– pinggir* spinnaker. *– pucuk jala* Marconi sail. *– puncak* topsail. *– putih* silver screen, the movies. **melayar-putihkan** to make a movie out of. *~ kisah* to film a story. *– putih* silver screen, the movies. *– radar* radar screen. *– sabang* small sail laced to mast. - *sabur* top gallant sail. - *semandera/ sokong* spritsail. - *tancap/tancep* a screen driven into the ground on which movies are shown out of doors in the *kampung*. - *tan- jak/tanjung* Marconi sail. - *tembérang* staysail. - *terbang/top* large dipping lug. - *topang* foresail. - *tévé/TV* TV-screen. **melayar- TV-kan** and **melayar-tévékan** to televise, show on TV. - *utama* mainsail.

be(r)layar 1 to use a sail. **2** to run/sail. *sepekan* ~ sailing for a week. **3** to take a voyage/trip, make a sea-trip, (set) sail. **4** ~ *bilu* to sail on a reach, reach. ~ *dulu* (*cla*) to die. ~ *ke pulau kapuk/kasur* to doze off, go to sleep. ~ *mengeliling* to circum- navigate. ~ *atas angin* at the expense of. ~ *sambil memapan, merapat sambil* ~ to kill two birds with one stone. ~ *ber- nakhoda, berjalan dengan yang tua* all activities should be car- ried out under the guidance of an experienced person.

melayari to roam/sail over. *dapat dilayari* navigable.

melayarkan and **memperlayarkan 1** to navigate, steer (a ship). **2** to ship s.t.

pelayar sailor, seaman.

pelayaran 1 sea voyage, cruise. **2** navigation, sailing, shipping. *orang* ~ seaman, sailor. *sejam* ~ one-hour sail. ~ *bébas* free pas- sage (through a straits). ~ *(ber)gilir* scheduled shipping. ~ *niaga* merchant shipping. ~ *pantai* coastal shipping. ~ *pem- bajakan* privateering. ~ *percobaan/pertama* shakedown cruise. ~ *tetap* scheduled shipping. ~ *wisata keliling dunia* around-the- world cruise. **berpelayaran** skilled/competent, etc. (sailors).

layar II *ikan -(.-)* sailfish, Batavia bat fish, *Platax batavianus/ves- pertilio, Histiophorus orientalis/gladius. rotan* - name of a large rattan species.

layas I (*ob*) **melayaskan** do not take care, do not pay heed, do not care about; to reject.

layas II (*M ob*) narrow strips (of wood) fastened to rafters where the roof is installed.

layat (*Jv*) **melayat 1** to visit a bereaved family, pay a condolence call; to go to the scene of a death; → MELAWAT. **2** to attend a funeral.

pelayat s.o. who pays a condolence call.

pelayatan paying a condolence call.

layon(an) (*Jv*) corpse, dead body, mortal remains; → JENAZAH.

layu 1 wilted; faded, withered, drooping. **2** pale, faded; no longer energetic; ailing, lingering, suffering (from sickness, disease). *dianjak -, dianggur/dibubut mati* (*M*) s.t. that is already good cannot be changed again. - *bunga* already rather old but still good. - *lecuh* faded. **melayu-lecuhkan** (*ob*) to make s.t. fade/ droop/wither. - *rumput di halaman* (*ob*) the grass in the yard is withering, i.e., a sign that the king is dying.

layu-layuan 1 withered/wilted material. **2** (*padi* ~) (*M*) paddy starting to dry.

melayu to wilt, fade, droop.

melayukan to cause s.t. to fade/droop/wither.

kelayuan 1 faded, wilted. **2** wasted away; wasting away. **3** death.

pelayuan *prosés* ~ the process by which meat fibers break down.

layuh (*M*) **1** lame, paralyzed. - *kedua kaki* paraplegia. - *tangan kanan* paralysis of the right arm. **2** weak; to have no energy/ strength/power. **3** failure of function (of an organ). - *perasaan- nya* he is feeling depressed/down. - *jantung* cardiac arrest. - *zakar* impotent.

layuk (*M*) **melayuk** to sway from side to side (of branches/a girl walking).

layung (*Jv*) (= - *langit*) afterglow, sunset/evening glow.

layur I (*M*) → LAYU. **melayur 1** to roast (over a fire), to warm/ heat up. **2** to singe, scorch.

pelayur s.o. or s.t. that roasts, etc.

pelayuran roasting, warming.

layur II (*ikan* -) hairtail/scabbard ribbon fish, *Trichiurus haumela/ savala*; → SELAYUR.

layut I **melayut** to bend, bow down (of a tree heavy with fruit).

layut II **melayut** to be continuous. *bunyi sorak-sorai orang* ~ the continuous sound of people shouting.

lazat → LEZAT.

lazim (*A*) **1** usual, customary, common (practice), routine; to be in vogue/style. - *dipakai* to be in general use. - *disebut* to be usu-

ally/generally/popularly called. *jalan yang* - set/fixed/standing way/manner/fashion. **2** traditional, conventional. *tidak* - un- usual, abnormal. **ketidak-laziman** rarity, abnormality.

lazimnya usually. *seperti* ~ as (is) usual.

melazimkan to make common/usual/a habit, bring into (gen- eral) use/vogue.

kelaziman habit, usage, custom, fashion, fad. ~ *bahasa* common parlance.

lazuardi (*Hind* from *Pers*) **1** lapis lazuli, an azure-blue, opaque, semiprecious stone. **2** azure, sky-blue.

LBH [Lembaga Bantuan Hukum] Legal Aid Society.

L/C /él-sé/ Letter of Credit.

lé I (*Jv*) (little) boy! (vocative); → TOLÉ.

lé II (*J*) → LAH I.

léak (*Bali*) witch or the spirit of a living person who practices the art of black magic.

lebah (honey)bee, *Apis spp. air/manisan* - honey. *koloni* - bee colony. *malam* - beeswax. *peternak* - beekeeper, apiarist. *pe- ternakan* - beekeeping, apiculture. *sarang* - beehive. - *bergan- tung* a) bees hanging down in a swarm. b) a carved ornament under ship's figurehead; a lovely chin is compared to this. *dagu- nya sebagai - bergantung* describes the ideal shape of a woman's chin. - *betina* worker (bee). - *betul* honeybee, *Apis indica*. - *hutan* giant honeybee, wasp, *Apis dorsata*. - *jantan* drone (bee), a male honeybee. - *keram* a small honeybee. - *madu* honeybee, *Apis mellifera*. - *pekerja* worker (bee). - *ratu* queen(bee).

perlebahan (*mod*) bee, api-.

lebai (*Tam?*) mosque official; village official in charge of Muslim re- ligious affairs; registrar/keeper of records. - *malang* (*ob*) an un- lucky devil/fellow.

lebaik → LABBAIK(A).

lebak I (*onom*) the sound of a slap or of s.t. falling and hitting the ground.

berlebak to make this sound.

lebak II (*Jv*) valley.

lebak III (*ob*) family.

lebam I 1 bluish black. *biru* - black and blue (of a bruise). *hitam* - pitch black. *kelam* - pitch black. **2** lividity.

lebam II (*onom*) sound produced by a heavy object falling.

lébam k.o. marine fish. *Teuthis spp*.

leban (- *bunga/kunyit*) k.o. trees which provide wood for construc- tion; leaves and bark are used as medicines, *Vitex pubescens*.

lebang - *pinggang* (*cla*) lumbar pain (prior to childbirth).

lebap (*onom*) sound like fruits falling to the ground.

lébar 1 wide, broad. **2** width, breadth. *-nya 90 cm.* It is 90 cm wide. **3** wide-open (of mouth, door, etc.). - *ayunan* amplitude. - *ban* bandwidth. - *hadapan* frontage. - *kapal* (ship's) beam. - *laluan* width of passage. - *mulut* to talk big, brag. - *pandangan* eye- shot. - *perut* food hound. - *pita* bandwidth. - *sayap* wingspan. - *sepur* railroad gauge. - *telinga* good at picking up rumors.

selébar as wide as.

berlébar ~ *dada* to be patient.

melébar 1 to spread (of riots), become widespread, expand, broaden. **2** to become wider, broaden, widen.

melébarkan to expand, enlarge, widen, broaden (a road/sleeve, etc.). ~ *telinga* to prick up one's ears. ~ *sayap* to extend one's wings.

memperlébar to make wider, widen.

terlébar broadest, widest.

kelébaran width, broadness.

pelébar s.t. which widens, widener.

pelébaran widening, expansion, enlargement, broadening. ~ *jalan* road widening.

perlébaran broadening, widening.

Lebaran (*Jv*) day ending the fasting period of *Ramadan*; → SELA- MAT (*hari*) *lebaran*. - *Haji* (also called - *Besar, Idul Adha* and *Idul Kurban*) an important holiday falling on 10 *Zulhijah*, marking the day of the pilgrimage to Mecca. - *Idulfitri* a holi- day falling on 1 *Syawal*, often referred to as *Lebaran*. - *Sawal* (in Jakarta) one week after *Lebaran*.

ber-Lebaran to celebrate *Lebaran*.

lebas melebas (*ob*) to whip, lash.
lebat 1 dense, abundant, plentiful (of fruit). **2** bushy, thick (of a beard, etc.). **berjénggot** – with a bushy beard. **3** pouring, heavy (of rain), torrential. *hujan* – a) a heavy rain, downpour. b) to rain heavily/cats and dogs.
  melebat to become heavy/dense/plentiful/luxuriant. *Hujan turun* ~. It's raining cats and dogs.
  kelebatan abundance, profusion, luxuriance.
lebé → LEBAI.
lebéik (*J/Jv*) → LABBAIKA.
lébel → LABEL.
lébér (*J/Jv*) **melébér** to run over, overflow, flow over the brim (because the cup, etc. was too full).
lebih 1 more (than), -er (than); (*opp* KURANG). *Kamar ini* – *luas.* This room is more spacious (than the other one). *Hujan turun dengan* – *keras.* It rained harder. – *baik* preferable, better. *tidak* – *baik* (there's) nothing better than, nothing like. – *baik kamu ... you had better ...; it would be best if you ...* – *baik jangan* don't, better not. – *buruk* worse, inferior (in quality). – *dari* more than (a number). *tak* – *tak kurang* no more and no less (than). – *jauh* further, farther. – *kurang* [l.k.] and *kurang* – [k.l.] more or less, about, roughly, approximately. – *suka* prefer, would rather. **2** (after numbers) or more, more than, over. *sepuluh hari* – ten days or more, more than ten days. *setahun* – *yang lalu* more than a year ago. **3** exceeding (normal bounds), extra, more, over-. *tiga méter* – *dari yang dikehendaki* three meters more than desired. – *bayar* overpaid. **4** (in clock time) plus, and. *jam/pukul empat* – *lima menit* 4:05. **5** increasingly, more and more. – *banyak*, – *baik* the more the better, better and better. **6** remainder, rest. *yang –nya* the rest/remainder. *dahulu/dulu* beforehand, previous, earlier, prior (to). **kelebih-dahuluan** primacy. – *lagi/pula* above all, especially. – *nilai* excess value. **melebih-nilaikan** to overvalue.
lebih-lebih (*lagi*) **1** especially, particularly, mainly. *Terbitlah cemburu dalam hati kedua pengiring itu,* ~ *lagi si Togop.* The two followers became jealous, especially Togop. **2** the more so, even more so. *Sedang orang kaya demikian susahnya* ~ (*lagi*) *orang yang miskin.* The rich have such a hard time, even more so the poor.
selebihnya rest, balance, surplus, excess, remainder, leftover. *yang* ~ the remainder/rest.
selebih-lebihnya at most, at the very most.
berlebih 1 to have a surplus/remainder, abundant. *Beras* ~. There is a rice surplus. **2** excess, extra, over-. *makan* ~ overeating.
berlebihan 1 superfluous (words), wasteful, excessive, extreme, in an exaggerated way, over-, too much, beyond the normal. **2** profuse(ly). *pemakaian yang* ~ overutilization. *penangkapan ikan* ~ overfishing. *Jangan* ~ *sikap.* Don't overreact. *Tidak* ~ *kalau dikatakan bahwa ...,* It is not too much to say that ...
berlebih-lebih(an) 1 extra, remainder, leftover(s). **2** to excel, go beyond the limits, overdo it (of dressing up, etc.), exaggerate (when boasting), go too far.
melebih to be more, present o.s. as more, boast; predominantly, exaggerated.
melebihi [and **ngelebihin** (*J coq*)] **1** to exceed, in excess of, go beyond, excel, surpass. ~ *dosis* an overdose. ~ *persediaan yang ditawarkan* to exceed the available supplies. ~ *yang lain* to excell. **2** to increase, add to.
melebih-lebihi 1 to exceed, surpass. **2** to make superfluous. **3** to exaggerate.
melebihkan 1 to make s.t. more/greater. **2** to consider s.t. more/greater, favor.
melebih-lebihkan to exaggerate.
terlebih and **terlebih-lebih 1** above all, how much more so, especially (since). *pandai menggésék biola* ~ *menyanyi* good at playing the violin and so much/even more so at singing. **2** too much, excess. *Minuman kopi ini* ~ *gula.* This coffee has too much sugar (in it). **3** -est, superlative. ~ *baik* the best. ~ *da(hu)lu* a) first (of all). b) first and foremost (because ...). c) right away. *Polisi melarang karyawan masuk* ~ *dahulu.* The police didn't allow the employees to enter right away. ~ *lagi* especially.
kelebihan 1 (= **lebihan**) remainder, rest, surplus, excess. ~ *mi-*

nyak oil glut. ~ *padi* the rice surplus. **2** very much, too much, over-. *akibat* ~ *menelan pil valium* because he took an overdose of valium. ~ *berat* overweight (on an airplane). *bernilai* ~ overvalued. ~ *dosis* overdose. ~ *jumlah/bilangan* majority (in number). ~ *pasok* oversupply. ~ *permintaan beli* (*fin*) oversubscribed. **3** superiority, lead. **berkelebihan 1** to have a balance/surplus/remainder. *tempat yang* ~ *hasil panénnya* a place with a rice surplus. **2** superfluous, excessive, extreme, too much, beyond the normal. *secara* ~ too much, to too great an extent, superfluously. **3** to have s.t. more than others, have an advantage (over). *merasa* ~ *dari* to have an advantage over.
lebok (*J*) to eat fast.
lebu I (*ob*) **1** dust; → DEBU. **2** (*cla*) I; me (in answering royalty). – *duli tuanku* (*cla*) lit. "dust of royalty's feet," i.e., Your Highness; *cp* PADUKA.
  berlebu dusty.
lebu II pelebuan (*ob*) (in Bali) cremation.
lebuh (*mostly Mal*) **1** street, main road, thoroughfare. **2** boulevard. *rancak di* – (*Mal*) clotheshorse, fop, dandy. – *raya* highway.
  melebuhkan to open up a main road.
lebuk I (*onom*) sound of a thud. – *lebak* thudding.
  berlebuk to thump (of the heart).
lebuk II (*M*) friable (of soil), loose (of dug earth).
  melebuk (*tanah*) to loosen (soil).
lebum (*onom*) thud (of coconut, *durian*, etc. falling).
lebun deception, deceit, fraud.
  melebun to deceive.
lebung (*onom*) thud of drums/coconut falling, etc.
  berlebung to thud.
lebur I 1 melted (of butter), molten (of metals), dissolved. *titik* – melting point. **2** destroyed, wiped out. *sama* – *sama binasa* loyally/faithfully befriended. – *binasa* completely wiped out.
  melebur 1 to melt, fuse. **2** to merge. ~ *kesalahan* to forgive s.o.'s mistakes.
  meleburkan 1 to smelt. **2** to destroy, wipe out. **3** to be merged (into). *dileburkan menjadi satu partai* to merge with another party. ~ *diri/dalam/dengan/kepada/ke dalam* a) to merge (into). ~ *diri dengan partai lain* to merge into another party. b) to apply for naturalization, be naturalized, take out naturalization papers. *orang asing yang mau* ~ *diri dalam kebangsaan Indonésia* foreigners who want to become naturalized Indonesian citizens.
  terlebur ~ *ke dalam* merged with.
  leburan solution.
  pelebur smelter.
  peleburan and **pengleburan 1** solution. **2** dissolving s.t. in a liquid; smelting. **3** smelter, iron works. ~ *besi-baja* an iron-and-steel mill. **4** (*fin*) consolidation, merger. **5** merging, amalgamating. **6** (*ling*) coalescence.
lebur II (*ob*) **1** abyss, chasm (due to floods, etc.). **2** pitfall (for big game).
lebur III → DEBUR.
lecah 1 muddy, soggy, slushy (of roads). **2** glutinous. *kena* – to get a bad name for o.s. *dari* – *lari ke duri* out of the frying pan into the fire.
  berlecah muddy.
  berlecah-lecah to play in the mud.
  terlecah 1 sunken in the mud, fallen into a muddy place. **2** to get mud on o.s. **3** with one's reputation damaged, be discredited.
lecak muddy, slushy.
lécak (*J*) ugly, withered/faded (of face).
lecap I *basah* – drenched, soaking wet.
lecap II (*onom*) smacking sounds (of the lips and tongue).
lecat *licin* – smooth as a mirror.
lécéh 1 sticky and adhesive (as of syrup on one's lips/glue on one's fingers, etc.). **2** worthless, valueless; useless. **3** despicable, depraved. *perempuan* – prostitute. *suratkabar yang* – a worthless (news)paper, a rag. **4** troublesome, irritating, dawdling. *pekerjaan yang* – a long job that can't be hurried. – *budi* unkind.
  meléceh to flatter.
  melécéhi 1 to bootlick, flatter, butter up. **2** (= **melécéhkan**) to belittle, despise, disdain.

terlécéh stuck.
pelécéh flatterer, bootlicker, ass-kisser.
pelécéhan harassment. ~ *séksual* sexual harassment.
lecek (*J*) crumpled, creased, wrinkled; → KUMAL, KUSUT I.
lécék I soft and pulpy (of rice/mud, etc.). *akal sebagai makan nasi* – childish ideas.
  melécék to mash, crush/press to a soft consistency.
lecék II *main* – (*ob*) k.o. children's game (in which marbles are kicked away).
lécék III (*J*) worn-out.
lécér (*ob*) → LÉCÉT. (*med*) oozing.
léces → LOCO.
lécés (*ob*) *kertas* – paper made from straw, named after the place and factory where the paper was manufactured.
lécét (= **belécét**) 1 moistened; moist. 2 peeling of the skin, scratch, cut; abraded, chafed. *luka* – chafed, abraded; abrasion, scrape. 3 scraped.
  melécét 1 to chafe, scratch. 2 to suppurate, fester.
  melécétkan 1 to chafe. 2 to scratch, scuff.
léci I → LÉNGKÉNG, LICI.
léci II → LOCO.
léco (*M*) dwarf(ish); stunted.
lécok shiny, oily.
lécong → LOCO.
lecot → LECUT.
lecuh (*ob*) withered, softened (of leaves when soaked in hot water).
lécun (*C ob*) **melécun** to cheat, deceive, trick.
lecup (*onom*) sucking noise.
  melecup 1 to suck. 2 to make a sucking sound.
lecur blister, scald (on plants).
  melecur to blister (from touching s.t. hot).
  melecurkan to cause a blister on, blister s.t.
lecus → LECIT.
lecut 1 (*onom*) snapping sound. 2 whiplash.
  melecut 1 to squirt (liquid) (out of a pipe/juice out of squeezed fruit). 2 to whip. 3 to stir up, incite, encourage, prod.
  melecuti (*pl obj*) to whip.
  melecutkan 1 to squeeze in order to make (juice, etc.) squirt out. 2 to cane/whip with s.t.
  melecut-lecutkan to beat (the fist) on the palm of the other hand.
  lecutan 1 lash (of a whip), spasm. 2 incitement, encouragement.
  pelecut whip.
léda Mindanao gum tree, rainbow bark, *Eucalyptus deglupta*.
ledak (*J*) explode. *hulu* – *nuklir* nuclear (missile) warhead.
  berledakan (*pl subj*) to explode.
  meledak 1 to explode (of bombs/population/anger/laughter, etc.), blow up; *cp* MELETUS. *torpédo yang tidak* ~ a dud torpedo. ~ *urbanisasi* the urbanization explosion. ~ *tertawa* to burst out laughing. 2 to burst out (of tears). 3 to break out (of war). **semeledak** as explosive as. *tak* ~ not as explosive as.
  meledakkan [and **ngeledakin** (*J coq*)] 1 to blow up (a bridge/house/aircraft, etc.). 2 to explode, set off, cause s.t. to explode. ~ *bom atom* to explode an atomic bomb. 3 to release (emotions, etc.) in an explosion.
  ledakan 1 explosion. ~ *kompor minyak tanah* the explosion of a kerosene stove. 2 outbreak (of war/disease, etc.). 3 explosion, stream, deluge, boom. ~ *permohonan baru* the deluge of new requests. ~ *matahari* solar flare. *mengalami* ~ booming, undergoing swift and vigorous growth. ~ *perumahan* housing boom.
  peledak burster. *bahan* ~ explosive(s).
  peledakan 1 blowing up s.t., exploding. 2 blasting. 3 explosion. ~ *penduduk* population explosion.
lédang I (*cla*) shimmering white or yellowish-white color (like the clouds when the sun shines on them), cream-colored.
lédang II (*Jv ob*) **melédang** to show off.
lédék I (*J*) **melédék(in)** to tease, make fun of, nag, bait (to get s.o. to do s.t.).

mengelédék [and **nglédékin** (*J*)] to tease, make fun of.
  nglédék(-in) to irritate, anger, annoy. *Jangan* ~ *saya, ya!* Don't make me mad, OK!
lédék II (*Jv*) k.o. singer and dancer. – *keték* → KOMIDI *keték*.
ledeng and **lédéng** → LÉDING.
lédés (*J/Jv*) 1 red, inflamed (of eyes). 2 chapped (of skin).
leding meleding to sag (of plank under weight); to warp (from heat).
léding (*D*) water pipe. *air* – running water, tap water. – *umum* public tap.
ledok (*Jv*) basin (in ocean).
lédor kelédoran neglect, carelessness; → KETELÉDORAN.
ledos (*J*) **meledos** 1 to burst (of a sack). 2 collapsed (of a bridge, etc.). 3 destroyed/broken through by holes (in a wall).
  ledosan bursting, blowout.
leduk meleduk to explode, erupt.
ledung (*M*) **meledung** to sag (of a plank under a weight, etc.), warp.
  meledungkan to cause to sag/warp.
  ledungan sag, hangover (*elec*).
lega 1 spacious, roomy, open, wide. *Tegal*– name of the former race track in Bandung; meaning: open, wide and spacious field. 2 free, not busy. 3 relieved. – *dada/hati/pikiran* (to feel) relieved.
  melegakan 1 (~ *hati*) to relieve, ease, it's/what a relief! 2 to widen, expand.
  legaan clearing (in forest).
  kelegaan 1 relief. 2 at ease, relaxed.
  pelega a relief, s.t. that relieves.
légaat (*D*) /légát/ specific legacy.
legah → LEGA.
legak-legok (*J*) full of potholes, bumpy (of roads); → LEKAK-LEKUK.
légal (*D/E*) legal.
  melégalkan to legalize.
  pelégalan legalizing.
légalisasi (*D*) 1 legalization. 2 fee for authenticating a document.
  melégalisasikan to legalize, authenticate.
  pelégalisasian legalization, authentication.
légalisir (*D*) **melégalisir** to legalize, authenticate.
légalitas (*D*) legality.
legam I *hitam* – pitch black.
legam II → LEGUM.
legap I (*onom*) sound made by the tapping of clogs, blows on a floor, beating of the heart; → DEGAP I.
legap II opaque.
legar (*onom*) sound made by the slamming of a door, the beating of waves on the shore, the clapping of thunder; → DEGAR.
légar (*M*) **berlégar** 1 to rotate. 2 to go around in a circle, circle around (of aircraft); to revolve.
  melégari to circumambulate, rotate/go around. ~ *Kaabah* to circumambulate the *Kaabah*.
  melégarkan to pass s.t. around (drinks, etc.), circulate s.t.
  légaran a (one's) turn.
legarang (*Jv*) k.o. tree, Papua New Guinea wood, *Alstonia villosa*.
légar-léger to invest money everywhere.
legasi (*D*) legation.
legat straight (of course, etc.); to keep on the same course (of ship).
légataris (*D leg*) specific beneficiary. – *pemikul beban* fiduciary heir.
legawa (*Jv*) 1 lenient, good-/kind-hearted, ready to make sacrifices, magnanimous. 2 honest and straightforward, sincere and frank.
legén (*Jv*) palm wine.
legénda (*D*) legend.
  berlegénda legendary.
  melegénda to become a legend.
  melegéndakan to turn into a legend.
legendar → KRUPUK *legendar*.
legéndaris (*D*) legendary.
legénde → LEGÉNDA.
léger (*D*) ledger.
légér (*J?*) 1 the larger floor crossbeam. 2 hogshead, a large barrel or cask.
léges (*D*) administrative fees.
legetan (*Jv*) various k.o. plants including *Spilanthes acmella* the toothache plant.

legi I (*Jv*) sweet (of taste); → LEGIT I, NASGITEL.

Legi II (*Jv*) name of the first day of the five-day week.

legih (*geol*) divide (between two watersheds, etc.).

légio (*L*) legion, very many.

légionar (*D*) legionary. *penyakit* – legionnaires disease.

législasi (*D*) legislation.

législatif (*D/E*) legislative. *badan* – legislative body.

legit I (*S*) sweet, nice (of people/taste); → LEGI I.

legit II (*J*) rather hard and elastic.

légitimaris (*D leg*) forced heir.

légitimasi (*D*) 1 (legal) confirmation, legitimization.
melégitimasikan to confirm, make legitimate.

légiun (*D*) legion. – *Asing* Foreign Legion. – *Pembébas Irian Barat* West Irian Liberation Legion.

légo (*E*) **melégo** 1 to transfer, hand over. 2 to let go (of the ball in a game). 3 to sell s.t. to raise cash. 4 to drop, release. – *jangkar* to cast/drop anchor; → MEMBUANG *sauh*.
terlégo sold, disposed of (for cash).
légoan s.t. released/let go of/sold to raise cash.
pelégoan selling, disposing of.

legoja [and **legojo** (*ob*)] → ALGOJO.

legok (*J*) 1 hollow, low, spot in the ground with a hole/pit, pothole. 2 (a deep) valley.
legokan bottom land, valley.

Légong Balinese dance performed by three young girls.

legowo → LEGAWA.

legum (*onom*) boom, booming sound.
legum-legum and – *legam* bang after bang.

legu melegu to plait selvage (said of a mat maker).

legunder (*E ob*) dragoon.

legundi a shrub used for hedges, five-leaved chaste tree, *Vitex negundo/trifolia*; its leaves are used for poultices and to keep moths out of clothes and weevils out of rice.

legung I (*onom*) sound of drum beats.
berlegung to make this sound.

legung II k.o. tree, *Pinanga disticha*.

legup-legap (*onom*) sound of heart throbbing, thudding sound.
berlegup-legap to make this sound.

léha [lelaki hawa] homosexual, gay.

léhah-léhah (*J*) → LÉHA-LÉHA.

léha-léha (*Jv*) (= **berléha-léha**) to do s.t. at one's leisure (or, effortlessly), relax; a pleasant idleness, dolce far niente.

léhar (*J*) small desk for the Koran, lectern; → RÉHAL.

léhék (*S*) **léhék-léhék** to let one's head hang down.

léhér 1 neck, part of the body that connects the head with the shoulders. *sampai di* – up to one's neck (in debts). *batang* – the column/nape of the neck. *cekik* – cutthroat (tariffs). *bersetegang/ bersitegang* (*M*)/*bertegang-tegang* (*urat*) – to persist stubbornly. *memanjangkan –nya* to crane one's neck. *potong* – cutthroat (competition). 2 neck, s.t. like the neck in shape or position. *tali* – necktie; → DASI. – *angsa* gooseneck (i.e., any of various devices shaped like a goose's neck). – *baju* collar. – *botol* a bottleneck (in traffic, etc.). – *jenjang* a long and beautiful neck. – *lembut* (*ob*) sociable. – *rahim* cervix.
seléhér up to the neck, neck-high.
berléhér 1 with a neck. 2 with a collar. ~ *lembut berlidah fasih* to know how to get along with one's superiors.

leja meleja to use abusive language; to be angry at.

léja k.o. striped cotton.

lejang 1 a kick, thrust. 2 a quick motion/jump/run. 3 lap (in sports). 4 a stroke (i.e., single movement of a piston from one end of its range to the other), sweep.
selejang ~ *kuda berlari* a) the distance a horse can run. b) praise for a beautiful house, i.e., a house so big that a horse can run in it. ~ *terbang* a bird's-eye view.
melejang to kick, thrust at.
melejangkan ~ *kaki* to stretch out one's legs.
pelejang s.t. which kicks.

lejar (*ob*) very tired, exhausted.

lejat I melejat to flap, flip, flop.
melejat-lejat to flap/flip/flop around.
lejatan flip (of a coin, etc.).

lejat II → LEZAT.

lejit (*J*) **melejit** 1 to dash off/away, run/fly away. 2 to soar (of prices), jump up, skyrocket (i.e., to rise rapidly to a great height/ success, etc.).
melejitkan to make s.t. skyrocket/become successful, etc.

lek (*J*) lazy.
lek-lekan reluctant, lazy.

lék I (*Jv*) to open one's eyes, get up (out of bed); → MELÉK.

lék II (in acronyms) → ÉLÉKTRONIKA.

léka 1 negligent, careless, inadvertent; slow, sluggish, indolent; to take plenty of time (about it), (to be busy) for a long time. 2 (= **terléka**) to be absorbed in (doing s.t.), dawdle over s.t., be enthusiastic about s.t., be delighted with s.t. *tak* – [*dari(pada)*] never cease/stop (fighting/thinking about, etc.).
melékakan to absorb (s.o.'s attention).
kelékaan absorption (in s.t.), infatuation; carelessness.
terléka very enthusiastic.
peléka s.o. who is always careless.

lekah I cracked (of lips/soil), split open (of rind/pod), burst open (of buds).
melekah to crack, split open, etc. *Bibirnya* ~. His lips were cracked.
lekahan fissure.

lekah II (*ob*) *pintu* – hatchway; → PALKA.
pelekah *pintu* ~ porthole.

lekak-lekuk full of potholes, uneven, bumpy (of roads); → LEKUK.
berlekak-lekuk full of holes.

lekak-liku → LIKA-LIKU.

lekam (*ob*) **melekam** to grasp s.t. between thumb and index finger.

lekam-lekum (*onom*) noisy, groaning.

lekang 1 cracked, chapped. *tak* – *oléh panas, tak lapuk oléh hujan* and *adat tak lapuk di hujan, tak* – *di panas* (*M*) custom is not mildewed by rain nor cracked by heat, i.e., it is eternal. 2 come off easily, easily stripped off, does not stick fast, not adhering (of flesh/fruit to pit). *tidak* – inseparable. *Pakaiannya tak* – *dari badan*. He always wears the same clothes. He never changes his clothes. *tak* – *di bibir* he/she is always talking about that topic. *tak* – *dari pikiran* never out of one's thoughts, always thinking about a topic. *tak* – *memperhatikan* continuously keeping an eye on s.t. *takkan* – *dari hati* unforgettable, memorable, never to be forgotten. – *inti* nuclear fission.
melekang to crack, chap, break, come off, peel.
terlekangkan fissionable.
pelekangan cracking.

lekap cling, stick, adhere.
berlekap and **melekap 1** to stick/cleave/affix to. 2 (*M*) to cuddle up to; to sit/stand/lie very close to, cling to. *Anak itu* ~ *pada emaknya*. The child always clings to his mother. *Lemari* ~ *ke dinding*. The cupboard is very close to the wall.
melekapkan 1 to paste, put on, affix. ~ *obat ke tempat yang luka* to put medicine on the injured place. 2 to press (up against wall, etc.), bring closer together. *Kepalanya dilekapkannya ke dada ayahnya*. He pressed his head against his father's chest. 3 to wear, put on s.t. (a shirt, etc.). 4 ~ *telinga* to pay close attention to. ~ *telinga pada pembicaraan itu* to pay close attention to the conversation.
terlekap stuck, clinging, affixed.
lekapan 1 adhesion. 2 mounting.
pelekapan mounting.

lekap-lekap and **lekap-lekup** (*onom*) cracking sounds (of branches, etc.).

lekar a rattan holder/stand for holding cooking pots after they have been removed from the fire.
melekari to put (a pot, etc.) on a rattan stand.

lékar (*J*) a reading stand for the Koran, lectern; → RÉHAL.

lekas quick, fast. *paling* – at the soonest. – *marah* quick-tempered.
lekas-lekas fast, in a hurry.
selekas ~ *mungkin* and **selekas-lekasnya** as soon as possible, as fast as possible.
berlekas-lekas hastily, hurriedly.
berlekas-lekasan to race e.o.
melekaskan and **memperlekas** to quicken, hasten, speed up, expedite, accelerate.

lekasan (*coq*) hurry up! faster!

lekat 1 sticky, glutinous; → **LÉNGKÉT**. *cairan yang* – a sticky liquid. *nama itu* – a) (he) has had that (sur)name since then. b) that (sur)name suits him well. – *naik kuda* to sit firmly in the saddle, be firm in the saddle. – *pada tubuh* a) (a curse has) come over s.o. (or, begun to take effect). b) (a stick, etc.) comes down with force on (s.o.'s neck). c) to wear (clothes, etc.). d) s.t. is a good fit, (his coat, etc.) fits well, (the gown, etc.) is becoming. **2** does not come/peel off, does not easily strip off, stick fast (because it has been nailed/tied up/glued/pasted, etc.), adhere to. **3** intimate, close (of friendship). **4** permanent, not changing (of opinions, etc.). **5** used, worn (out) (of clothes, etc.). **6** interested in, attracted to. *Hatinya – kepada gadis yang berbikini itu.* He was attracted to the girl wearing a bikini. *Tuduhan itu tidak –.* The accusation didn't stick. **7** lasting, permanent (of custom), still in use. **8** closely tied (to). *Nama-nama itu – dengan isu korupsi.* Those names were closely tied to rumors of corruption. – *perut* to be pregnant. – *uri* the placenta is not coming out (during childbirth).

lekat-lekat sticky, adhesive.

berlekat 1 to stick fast, adhere. **2** sticky.

berlekatan to stick to e.o.

melekat 1 to stick, cling, adhere. *Daki ini sudah ~ benar, sukar dibersihkan.* This grime is stuck on, it's hard to clean. **2** inherent. **3** built-in. *pengawasan ~* [waskat] built-in control. **4** intimate, close (of friendship). **5** interest (in), attracted (to). **6** permanent, unchanging. **7** used, worn out. **8** to stick, be valid (of an accusation/blame). **9** (*leg*) associated. *segala apa yang ~ pada suatu kebendaan* anything associated with an object.

melekati to stick/adhere/hold to. *dilekati debu* to be covered with dust. *dilekati api* to be lit (of a cigarette, etc.).

melekatkan 1 to affix, attach s.t. (to), stick s.t. (on); to glue, paste (to). *~ label pada botol obat* to stick a label on a medicine bottle. *~ kersik ke buluh* carry coals to Newcastle. **2** to put on (a hat/glasses/coat, etc.). **3** to invest/sink/put (money) in. *Uangnya dilekatkan pada barang.* He has put his money in goods. **4** to direct (one's attention, etc.) to. **5** to utilize, make use of (a medicine, guna-guna, etc.). *berbagai obat dilekatkan* he has used various medicines. *~ kaki* to kick s.o., give s.o. a kick. *~ sifat* to consider characteristics inherent in. *~ tangan pada* to strike, hit.

memperlekat to make s.t. more permanent.

terlekat affixed, stuck.

lekatan 1 adhesion, cohesion. **2** attachment.

kelekatan sticking.

pelekat gum, glue, adhesive, paste.

pelekatan attachment.

perlekatan *~ benda* (*leg*) accession.

lékéh weak.

lekep (*J*) **melekep** and **nglekep** to feel hot because the air isn't circulating.

lekih → **LEKUH** *lekih*.

lekir streaky, with white streaks on it. *panau* – a streaky mottled ringworm, pytiriasis, *Tinea versicolor*. *ular sawa* – a streaky mottled snake, *Coluber melanurus*.

lekis k.o. tree.

lekit somewhat sticky (like glue/mud, etc.).

leklekan (*Jv*) reluctantly. *jangan pakai* – don't oppose/refuse to do it.

lék-lékan (*Jv*) to stay awake/up (usually because one has made a vow/has to watch over a dead body/has to fulfill night duty, etc.) the whole night until dawn; → **MELÉK**.

lekok (*M*) bend, curve.

melekokkan 1 to bend, curve, cause to be crooked. **2** hollow, concave.

lékong (*gay sl*) man, male.

Lékra → **LEMBAGA** *kebudayaan rakyat*.

léksik → **LÉKSIKON**.

léksikograf (*D*) lexicographer.

léksikografi (*D/E*) lexicography.

léksikologi (*D/E*) lexicology.

léksikon (*D/E*) lexicon.

lékton [kelék katon] (*Jv*) the armpit is visible.

léktor (*D*) university lecturer. – *Kepala* Senior Lecturer. – *Madya* Middle-Level Lecturer. – *Muda* Junior Lecturer.

léktorat (*D*) lectureship, readership.

léktris electric.

léktur (*D*) reading matter. – *hiburan* light reading.

leku berleku and **meleku** to lean on one's elbows; → **TELEKU**.

lekuh – *lekih* (*onom*) coughing sound.

lekuk 1 hollow, concave. **2** dent, depression. **3** pothole (in road). **4** (*bio*) fovea. – *hidung* nasal pit. – *liku* a) very bumpy, with many bumps (of street). b) tactics, devices, tricks. c) the ins and outs. – *lutut* hollow of the knee. – *mata* eye socket. – *perut* pit of the stomach. – *pipi* dimple.

lekuk-lekuk bumpy, with many potholes (in road).

berlekuk 1 to have dents; be dented. **2** dimpled. **3** with ... curves in it.

melekuk to become dented/concave/hollow.

melekukkan to dent, make a hollow in.

lekukan dent, hollow, cavity.

pelekukan dimpling, denting.

lekum (*A*) **1** throat. **2** Adam's apple.

lekum-lekam (*onom*) a rumbling noise.

lekun → **LAKON I**.

lekung sunken, hollow (of cheeks/eyes). **2** concave (of mirrors/lens, etc.).

lekup k.o. wild mango, *Mangifera odorata*.

lekup-lekap (*onom*) a rattling noise (as of dry coconut shells).

lela plain, not damascened.

léla I (*A cla*) elegant, smart, pert, perky, jaunty. *muda* – young and perky.

berléla (*keracak*) and **meléla** [teritas-titas (*ob*)] to wave a staff/drawn weapon, brandish a weapon in play.

melélakan to brandish (staff/weapon) defiantly.

léla II (*M*) caprice, whim.

seléla *~ hati* and **seléla-lélanya** according to one's wishes/desires, to one's heart's content; at leisure, at will.

berléla to have whims/caprices.

léla III (*bersi*)*maharaja* – and *meraja* – **1** to rage. **2** to rampage, operate unchecked. *maharaja* – was originally an honorific (granted by a sovereign).

léla IV (*ob*) k.o. small canon. – *rambang* long-barreled gun. – *rentaka* swivel gun.

léla V meléla *besi ~* steel. *keris ~* a steel kris.

lelabah → **LABAH-LABAH**.

lelabi → **LABI-LABI I**.

lelah I 1 tired, weary, fatigued, exhausted, worn-out; → **CAPAI**, **CAPÉ(K)**, **LETIH**, **PAYAH**, **PENAT**. *berhentikan/melepaskan/membuang* – to take a break/rest. *sesudah hilang –nya* after he has rested. *jerih/letih/penat* – and – *jerih/payah* dead-tired, tired to death. *napas* – short of breath. *obat* – payment for work. *tanpa kenal* – and *dengan tak –.-nya* untiring, untired, tireless, unwearying. **2** *batuk/sakit* – asthma(tic wheezing), spasmodic asthma. – *logam* metal fatigue. – *panas* heat exhaustion.

berlelah(-lelah) to work hard, wear o.s. out. *Tak perlu berlelah-lelah mengurus ke sana kemari.* You don't have to exhaust yourself taking care of things here and there.

melelahkan and **memperlelah 1** to cause to become tired/exhausted, tire, exhaust. **2** tiring, exhausting, wearying, fatiguing.

kelelahan 1 fatigue, tiredness, tedium, weariness, exhaustion. *~ karena perang* combat fatigue. *~ logam* metal fatigue. *~ terbang* flight fatigue. **2** very tired, totally exhausted.

lelah II (*M*) to hunt, chase, pursue, run after.

selelah *~ burung terbang* as far as a bird can fly.

lelai melelai 1 to droop, slip down, dangle, hang down (of branches/coconut leaves, etc.). **2** to pull (a branch) toward o.s. (to pick the fruits, etc.).

melelaikan to bend (a branch) to make it droop.

lelak torn to pieces, ruined (of house, etc.); → **LERAK I**, **RERAK**.

lelaki → **LAKI-LAKI**. **kelelakian** the male sex organ.

lelakon → **LAKON I**.

lélan (*M*) *ikan* – k.o. fish.

lelancur (*J/Jv*) **1** a young rooster, cockerel. **2** a young whippersnapper.

lélang (*Port*) auction, (public) sale, tender. *balai* – auction hall. *juru/tukang* – auctioneer. *melakukan* – to hold an auction. *menjual* – to sell items at an action. – *éksékusi* foreclosure sale. – *menurun* Dutch auction. – *pajak* tax sale. – *terbuka/umum* public auction.
  melélang 1 to hold an auction. **2** to buy at an auction.
  melélangkan and **memperlélangkan 1** to sell by (public) auction. **2** to auction s.t. off. **3** to invite tenders for a job.
  terlélang auctioned (off).
  lélangan having changed hands at an auction (of an item). *méja* ~ table bought/sold at an auction.
  pelélang auctioneer.
  pelélangan purchase by tender/auction. ~ *atas perintah hakim* public auction by judicial order. ~ *ulangan* retender. ~ *umum* public auction.
  perlélangan auction, (public) tender.
lelangit 1 ceiling; → LANGIT-LANGIT. **2** palate.
lelangon (*Jv*) *taman* – (*cla*) pleasure garden/ground.
lelangsé (*Jv*) (wall)paper of woven fabric for decoration, curtain, drapery; → LANGSAI II.
lélanisasi cultivation of *lélé*.
lelap 1 disappeared, gone. *Semuanya – dari pandangan,* Everything disappeared from view. **2** fast/sound asleep. **3** faint(ed); unconscious. *makan tak kenyang, tidur tak* – and *tidur tak –, makan tak kenyang* to be very restless. **4** cannot be redeemed (from the pawnshop) due to expired date. **5** (*M*) coagulated, solidified, congealed. *Minyak kelapa – kedinginan.* The coconut oil has congealed due to the cold.
  melelapkan ~ *mata* to close one's eyes (to go to sleep).
  kelelap gone under the water. *mati* ~ drowned.
  terlelap fallen asleep.
  terlelapkan can be put into a deep sleep.
  kelelapan soundness, deepness (of sleep).
lélar (*M ob*) a cliché.
  memperlélarkan to do s.t. repeatedly/over and over again/continually; to use s.t. frequently. *jangan diperlélarkan timba ke perigi, kalau tak putus genting* don't make a bad habit become second nature.
lelas 1 smooth, even, flat, level. **2** grazed, abraded, skinned. *lepas* – completely free. *mati* – to die in vain without apparent reason. *puas* – completely satisfied.
  melelas 1 to become smooth/flat. **2** peeling of the skin. **3** to abrade.
  melelaskan to smoothen. ~ *balung* to trim a rooster's comb.
  pelelas abrasive.
  pelelasan abrading.
lelat (*ob*) *sirih* – the *sirih* presented by the groom to the bride (at a wedding ceremony).
lelatang k.o. plant, three-seeded mercury, Indian nettle, *Acalypha indica* and other species.
lelatu and **lelau** (*J*) spark.
lelaunan (*S*) slow, lingering. *bermain secara* – to spin out the time.
lelawa (*J*) cave-bat; → KELELAWAR.
lelawar (*J*) fish, etc. cut into thin slices and then salted and dried.
lélé I (*Jv*) name of a fish species, walking catfish, *Clarias batrachus/melanoderma* with long, sharp tentacles on the head fins; the species lives in ponds and rivers, at the edge of the water, in mud or in holes. *kelas* – big shot, bigwig; → KAKAP I.
lélé II (= double L) Arthan (an illegal drug).
léléh 1 to melt (of wax). **2** to calm down. *Darahnya tak mau* –. He did not want to calm down. *titik* – melting point.
  berléléh(-léléh)an to ooze, flow/trickle excessively, always trickling/flowing down. *Peluhnya* ~. He's sweating a lot.
  meléléh 1 to trickle, ooze, flow in drops or in a slow steady stream (of tears/blood, etc.). **2** to melt.
  meléléhi to trickle/ooze onto.
  meléléhkan to allow to trickle/flow down; to liquefy, dissolve, dilute, melt. ~ *salju* to melt snow.
  léléhan oozing, trickling.
  peléléhan melting, meltdown. ~ *sebagian* partial meltdown.
lélék-lélék careless, slovenly.
lelembut (*Jv*) trouble-making invisible spirit.
lélénisasi the pisciculture of the *lélé* fish.

lelenjing (*J/Jv*) small rice pounder.
lelep (*Jv*) → KELELAP. **melelepkan 1** to submerge, dip. **2** to sink, scuttle (a ship, etc.).
lélér I → LÉLÉH. *tua* – very old and toothless.
  berléléran (*pl subj*) **1** to ooze, trickle. **2** to stray (of talks, thoughts), digress.
  melélér to trickle slowly (*esp* with respect to sticky substances, such as nasal mucus, saliva, etc.); → MELÉLÉH.
  keléléran scattered/strewn about.
  peléléran (*geol*) extrusion.
lélér II (*Jv*) **keléléran** to be ignored, neglected; left to take care of o.s.
lélér III (*J*) **keléléran** showing a lack of concern.
lélér IV (*cla*) naughty (*esp* of children), rude.
lelet (*Jv*) sluggish.
  ngelelet (to talk, etc.) slowly, (to speak) with a drawl.
lélét (*Jv*) **melélétkan** to smear, spread; to run (one's tongue, etc.). over s.t.
lélété and **Lé Lé Té** facetious *pron* of RRT (= Républik Rakyat Tiongkok] People's Republic of China.
leléwa (*J*) **be(r)leléwa** with much show, showy, gaudy, flashy, affected.
léli (*D*) lilly.
lélong (in East Malaysia and West Kalimantan) used clothes.
lelonobroto and **lelono-broto** (*Jv*) **1** to go from place to place seeking inspiration in God's word. **2** the journey made to gain distance from all earthly things.
leluasa 1 (to speak/act) freely/without restraint or constraint. *Ia – bergaul dengan Yakub.* She freely associated with Yakub. *dengan* – unhampered, unimpeded, undisturbed. **2** (to be allowed to enter anywhere) undisturbedly and freely/without hindrance/without impediment. **3** unlimited, without limit, lavish. **4** absolute (power/freedom).
  berleluasa to do as one pleases, act at one's own discretion.
  keleluasaan opportunity, freedom (of action/movement, etc.). ~ *gerak* freedom of movement. **berkeleluasaan** to have the freedom (to).
lelucon (*Jv*) **1** joke, anecdote; → LUCU. – *April* April Fool's joke. – *kasar* slapstick. **2** farce. **3** humor.
  berlelucon to joke around.
leluhur (*Jv*) ancestors. *negeri* – country that one's ancestors' come from (*esp* for Indonesian-born Chinese).
leluing I (*J*) k.o. fig tree, *Ficus hispida*.
leluing II → LUING II.
lélung (*ob*) → LÉLANG.
lelungit (*Jv ob*) k.o. song.
leluri (*Jv*) tradition.
lem (in acronyms) → LEMBAGA II.
lém (*D*) glue. – *aica aibon* (brand name of a) k.o. glue sniffed to get high. – *kayu* joiner's glue. – *plastik* Scotch/transparent tape. – *tikus* mousetrap in which the mouse is caught in s.t. sticky.
  melém and **mengelém** to glue.
  ngelém (*coq*) to sniff glue.
  pengeléman gluing.
lemadang dolphin, *Coryphaena hippurus*.
lemah 1 feeble, weak (of a body/argument), frail; lacking (in) energy, limp, flabby, wishy-washy; → LEMAS II. *dengan gerak yang* – with leaden feet. *alasan yang* – a weak argument/excuse. *badannya* – his body is weak/soft. *kakék yang* – a feeble old man. **2** soft, tender. **3** powerless. **4** breakable, flexible, supple, pliant, limp. – *gemalai/gemulai* graceful, swaying gracefully, willowy (as a dancer), lissome (of girls). – *hati* a) tender-hearted. b) easily influenced by people, without a will of one's own; unstable, fickle. **5** (*ling*) weak/unstressed (syllable). – *iman* easily tempted. – *ingatan* mentally retarded. – *jantung* cardiac weakness. – *jiwa* mentally retarded; → CACAT *méntal*. – *ketuaan* senility. – *lampai* slim (of line). – *langlai* feeble, weak. – *lantur* flexible, pliant. – *lembut* a) friendly, kind, gracious. b) graceful. **kelembah-lembutan 1** graciousness. **2** gracefulness. – *lentur* flexible, supple, pliant. – *lunglai* a) flexible, pliant. b) responsive, yielding. – *persendian* powerless, weak. – *pikiran* mentally retarded. – *saraf* neurasthenic. – *semangat* a)

liable to illness, of weak constitution, sickly. b) weak (of morals), spiritless, enervated. – *syahwat/zakar* impotent. **kelemahan syahwat** impotence. – *tulang* weak.

berlemah ~ *diri* to weaken.

berselemah compliant. ~ *tak patah* a) apparently accommodating/compliant. b) to adopt a go-slow policy.

melemah to weaken, become weak.

melemahkan and **memperlemah l** to weaken, enervate, enfeeble. ~ *kekuasaan* to undermine s.o.'s authority. **2** to attenuate.

lemahan s.t. that has been weakened/attenuated.

kelemahan l weakness, feebleness, frailty. **2** gentleness. **3** powerlessness. **4** weak spot, susceptibility. **5** laxness.

pelemah l attenuator. **2** s.t. that weakens.

pelemahan l weakening. **2** attenuation.

lemak l fat (of meat, fish), grease, lard. **2** fatty, greasy, oily. *nasi* – rice cooked in coconut milk. **3** (*M*) tasty, oily. – *penyelar daging* to squander the wealth of one's superior. – *babi* a) bacon; → SPÉK. b) lard. – *cair* edible oil. – *gajih* lard. – *héwani* animal fats. – *ikan* fish oil. – *jenuh* animal fats. – *kasar* ether extract. – *ketam* gray. – *nabati* vegetable oils. – *tulang* marrow (of a bone).

berlemak fatty, greasy, oily, adipose.

melemaki to put grease on, grease.

perlemakan fattiness.

léman (*Jv*) elephant.

lemang a type of food made of glutinous rice and coconut milk baked in a length of bamboo lined with banana leaf. *menyandang – hangat orang* to pull the chestnuts out of the fire for s.o. *bersandar di – hangat* to take protection (from a criminal, etc.).

melemang to bake *lemang.*

lemari (*Port*) cupboard, case, chest, box, wardrobe, cabinet, piece of furniture for keeping books, clothes, money, etc.; → ALMARI. – *arsip* filing cabinet. – *baterai* battery case. – *besi* safe. – *buku* bookcase. – *dingin/és* icebox, refrigerator. **melemari-éskan** to put s.t. on ice, table, shelve. – *és beku/mambo* freezer. – *kaca* display case. – *kedaian/kodok* (in stores) display case, showcase. – *laci* a) chest of drawers. b) filing cabinet. – *makan* food cupboard, pantry, kitchen cabinet. – *obat* medicine chest. – *pajangan/pamér* showcase. – *pakaian* wardrobe, chest. – *pecah belah* kitchen cabinet. – *pembeku* freezer. – *penghubung* switch box. – *pikiran* stifled in thought, confused. – *pintu* cupboard. – *rias* dressing table. – *sékering* fuse box. – *sudut* corner cupboard.

lemas I l suffocating, stifling, choking, having problems breathing; asphyxiated (by smoke/gas/drowning). **2** drowned. *mati* – dead from suffocation/drowning.

melemaskan to smother, stifle, suffocate.

kelemasan l suffocation. **2** suffocated, smothered, stifled.

pelemas *zat* ~ nitrogen.

lemas II l flexible, supple, pliant, limber, graceful. **2** weak, not energetic; soft, not hard; powerless; → LEMAH. **3** gentle, polite, refined, courteous, civilized, obliging.

melemas to weaken.

melemaskan l to weaken/soften s.t. **2** to make more flexible. **3** to stretch out. ~ *otot-otot kaki* to stretch and relax (one's feet). ~ *rambut* to condition one's hair. **4** (= **melemas-lemaskan**) to slow down. *Jalannya dilemas-lemaskan.* He slowed down his pace. **5** to refine.

kelemasan weakness, softness.

pelemas ~ *rambut* (hair) conditioner.

pelemasan l weakening. **2** stretching, making s.t. more flexible.

lemau l soft, supple, tender, weak, powerless; → LEMAH, LEMAS II. **2** (*ob*) moist, humid (of weather conditions).

lemba k.o. plant, unbelled pepper, *Piper umbellatum.*

lembab → LEMBAP. **pelembab l** moisturizer. **2** humidifier.

lembaga I l seed, embryo, fetus; beginning, origin. *adat* – customary laws handed down from prehistoric times. *adat diisi, – dituang* customary conditions should be complied with, for example, when one asks for forest land. **2** mold, matrix, form, shape. **3** vague outline, silhouette. – *Adam* a lump of earth made by God into the first human being. – *bisul* a) the early stages of a boil. b) the core of a boil. – *daun* the sprout of a plant. – *manusia* embryo.

lembaga II board, committee, league, society, body, institute, institution, agency, organization, group of persons carrying out a job or certain duties. – *Administrasi Negara* [LAN] National Institute of (Public) Administration. – *Alkitab Indonésia* Indonesian Bible Society. – *amal* charitable organization. – *Bahasa Nasional* [LBN] National Language Institute. – *Balai Harta Peninggalan* Probate Agency. – *Bantuan Hukum* [LBH] Legal Aid Society. – *hukuman* penal institution. – *Ilmu Pengetahuan Indonésia* [LIPI] Indonesian Institute of Science. – *inang* host institution. – *Kantor Berita Nasional* [LKBN] Antara Antara National News Office. – *Kebudayaan Rakyat* [LÉKRA] League of People's Culture. – *keuangan* financial institution. – *keuangan bukan bank* non-bank financial institution. – *kliring* clearing house. – *negara* state agency. – *nondépartemén* statutory authority. – *paksa badan* debtor's prison. – *Pemasyarakatan* [LP, lapas] penitentiary, penal institution. – *pembérésan* clearing house. – *pembiayaan* financial institution. – *pemodal* institutional investor. – *Penelitian Penduduk* Demographic Research Institute. – *penerbit* (*fin*) issuing house. – *pendidikan* educational institution. – *penyiaran* broadcasting organization. – *perantara* intermediary. – *perdagangan surat berharga* securities firm, brokerage house. – *perhitungan* clearing house. – *Pertahanan Nasional* [Lémhannas] National Defense Agency. – *Perwakilan* representative body. – *Sandi Negara* State Coding Institute. – *sosial* charitable organization. – *Swadaya Masyarakat* Non-Governmental Organization, NGO. – *Tenaga Atom* [LTA] Atomic Energy Institute. – *Tunanétra* Home for the Blind.

melembaga to become customary, be institutionalized, be a way of life.

melembagakan l to institutionalize. **2** to make s.t. into an institution.

terlembagakan institutionalized, made into an institution.

kelembagaan institutional.

pelembaga institutionalizer.

pelembagaan institutionalization.

perlembagaan (*Mal*) (political) constitution.

lembah l low-lying land (on both sides of a river), (river) valley. **2** quagmire, pits. *terjun/tersérét ke – hitam* fell/pulled down into the pits (of misery/sin, etc.). **3** hollow (of s.t.). – *kehidupan* the difficulties of life. – *kehinaan* abyss of misery.

lémbai (*M*) **melémbai** to wave (one's hand); to lick (of flames), grow bigger and begin to spread (of a fire). *dilémbai api* to be in flames; → LAMBAI.

lémbak melémbak to boil over (of water); to spill over/overflow its banks (of a river).

lembam I l inert, not energetic; inactive, languid, slow, indolent, lazy. **2** inertial.

lembaman inertia, inertial.

kelembaman indolence, languidness, inertia.

lembam II blue; → LEBAM I.

lemban (*ob*) → LEMBAM I.

lembang I l depression, depressed part/place, hollow/low place on a surface. **2** becoming depression-like/concave due to water erosion. **3** valley.

melembang to hollow out s.t.

lembangan basin.

lembang II melembang to speak in a coaxing voice.

lémbang I k.o. tree, *Grewia florida.*

lémbang II k.o. rush or cat-tail, *Typha domingensis.*

lembap l damp (of cloth/sheets/ground, etc.), moist, humid (of the climate/weather). *dingin* – cool and damp, raw (of the weather). *tembakau* – moist tobacco. *Hawanya sangat* –. The climate is very humid. *hari* – (*M*) an overcast/cloudy sky. *pasir yang* – *lembut* soft and moist sand. **2** dull-sounding. – *bunyi gendang itu* that drum has a dull sound. *suara* – listless (of voice). **3** clumsy, awkward.

melembapkan to moisten, dampen, wet.

kelembapan moisture, dampness, humidity. *alat pengurang* ~ dehumidifier.

pelembab moistener, dampener.

pelembapan moistening, dampening, wetting.

lembar I l strands (of hair/thread/strings). *tali yang tiga* – cord made of three strands. **2** classifier for objects which are long and fine, like thread.

melembarkan to twist, twine.

lembar II 1 sheet. *– isian* form to be filled out. *– jurnal (fin)* journal sheet. *– kenangan* souvenir sheet (in philately). *– lepas* loose-leaf. *– penguji* proof sheet. *– pérak* silver foil. *– percobaan* proof sheet. **2** classifier for sheet-like objects such as paper, mats, cloth. *kertas empas* – four sheets of paper. *lima puluh – kain sarung* fifty sarongs.

berlembar-lembar in sheets.

lembaran 1 page. *~ kuning* yellow pages (in a telephone directory). *~ muka* front-page (of a newspaper, etc.). *~ Putih* White Paper, criticisms of the government account of the Tanjung Priok incident of September 12, 1984. **2** sheet (of paper, etc.). *dituliskan pada ~ kertas* written (down) on a sheet of paper. *~ kayu* veneer. *~ lepas* loose leaves (not bound). *~ pembina* data sheet. *~ ukuran* size sheet. **3** leaf (of a plant). **4** issue (of a magazine), edition (of a newspaper). *~ Negara* State/Official Gazette (for public laws). *~ pagi* morning edition (of newspaper). *~ tambahan* supplementary issue. **5** copy. *~ ketikan* typed copy. **6** slab (of metal). **7** denomination (of currency).

lembayung 1 water-hyacinth, *Eichornea crassipes* with carmine-red flowers. **2** trailing plant with crimson flowers, Malabar spinach, *Basella rubra.* **3** *(mérah –)* carmine-red, crimson.

lembéga a medicinal shrub, giant milkweed, *Calotropis gigantea*; → REMBÉGA.

lembék 1 too soft (of rice/a pillow, etc.), flabby, mushy. **2** slack. **3** tender (of one's constitution). **4** effeminate, weak, feeble. *– ingatan/pikiran* mentally retarded. *– otak* stupid. *– tulang* weak.

melembék to become soft, soften, become tender, slacken.

melembékkan 1 to soften/weaken s.t. **2** to weaken, enfeeble.

kelembékan weakness, feebleness, softness, effeminacy.

pelembékan softening.

lémbéng flirtatious, coquettish, effeminate.

lémbér *(S)* → JAMUR *kuping.*

lembérgar [*lembaran bergambar*] funny pages, the comics.

lembesu hard-wood tree, *Fagraea spp.*; → TEMBESU.

lembidang flat rim of a plate/saucer; brim (of a hat).

lembiding scrambling fern, *Stenochlaena palustria.*

lembik → LEMBÉK.

lembing 1 spear. **2** javelin. *lémpar –* (in sports) javelin throwing. *tercacak bagai – tergadai (M)* struck with amazement. *menohok-kan – ke semak* carry coals to Newcastle. *– buncis* k.o. insect that attacks legumes, Mexican bean beetle, *Epilachna varivestis. – terung* k.o. insect that attacks eggplants, etc., potato lady beetle, *Epilachna sparsa.*

melembing to throw a spear at, spear.

lembir pelembir s.t. to make a car run fast.

lembok → LEMBUK.

lémbok to use or give away s.t. excessively.

lembora *(ob)* a giant marine fish.

lembu I bull, cow, ox. *– belang* spotted cow. *– betina* cow. *– dogol/dongkol* a) hornless bull. b) (his) bark is worse than (his) bite. *– hutan* wild bull. *– jantan* bull. *– kasi/kebiri* ox. *– laut* walrus. *– perahan* milch cow. *– seigu* a pair of oxen. *– tampung* piebald bull.

lembu II → BURUNG *lembu.*

lembuara *(cla)* tasseled state spear.

lembuk green-winged fruit dove, emerald dove, *Chalcophaps indica.*

lembung I swelling.

melembung 1 to swell up, bulge. **2** bulging, blown/puffed up, swollen, inflated.

melembungkan to inflate/blow up/puff up s.t. *~ dada* to throw out one's chest, be arrogant.

pelembungan 1 child's rubber balloon. **2** soap bubble. **3** bird's crop.

lembung II melembung to jump up, bounce; → LAMBUNG I.

lembur I *(J/Jv)* overtime. *kerja –* a) overtime work. b) to work overtime. *uang –* overtime pay.

melembur [and **ngelembur** *(coq)*] to work overtime.

lembur II → LAMBUR.

lémbur → LIMBUR I.

lemburu k.o. smelt; → LEMURU.

lembusir shoulder (of ox), withers.

lembut 1 tender (of meat). **2** soft (of one's skin/voice, etc.). *warna – a* soft color. **3** gentle (of behavior/manners), meek. **4** pliant, supple, flexible (of leather). **5** weak (of one's body). *– hati/perangai* a) soft-hearted, gentle, meek, friendly, kind, good. b) pliant, submissive. *– lidah* able to pronounce foreign or difficult sounds easily. *– ringkih* soft and weak.

selembut as soft/gentle as.

melembut to become gentle/mild/soft, etc.

melembuti 1 to move gently over, caress. **2** to soften.

melembutkan to soften, mitigate, refine, make soft/flexible, etc. *~ hati* to comfort, console.

kelembutan 1 softness. **2** gentleness, tenderness, meekness. **3** suppleness, flexibility.

pelembut softener. *istilah ~* euphemism.

pelembutan 1 euphemism. **2** softening.

lémék *(Jv)* underlayer. *– kasur* under-mattress, protective/mattress pad. *– kursi* seat cover.

leména *(Port) baju –* scale-armor.

leméndér *(ob)* Armenian.

lémér *(J)* fatty or gristly part of meat.

lemes → HALUS, LEMAS II. *nglemesin ~ kaki! (coq)* Let's dance! Shake a leg!

lemét *(Jv)* k.o. cake made of grated coconut steamed in leaves.

Lémhannas → LEMBAGA *Pertahanan Nasional.*

lemi *(Jv)* (vegetable) mold.

lemidang → LEMBIDANG.

lemidi k.o. climbing fern, *Stenochlaena palustris.*

Lémigas [*Lembaga Minyak dan Gas*] Oil and Gas Institute.

lemog and **lemok** *(J)* soft and bruised (of fruit), somewhat rotten (of fish, etc.).

lémon *(D/E)* lemon.

lemot [*lemah otak*] dumb, stupid.

lémot I berlémotan all smeared, smeared all over.

lémot II *(J)* good (in appearance), good-looking.

lémpah → LIMPAH.

lempai slack, drooping.

berlempaian *(pl subj)* to droop (of flowers, etc.).

melempai(-lempai) and **terlempai** to droop, hang down loosely (of a flag/banner/dog's ear, etc.).

lempam *(ob)* **melempam 1** damp. **2** languid, inert, inactive; → LEMPEM.

lempang I *(J)* **1** straight (of road, etc.); → LÉMPÉNG. *tegak – to* stand (up) straight/erect. *terus –* (to walk) in a straight line. *– hati* honest. **2** straightening (of hair).

melempang to run straight.

melempangkan to straighten out s.t. *~ ... dengan* to bring ... into agreement with, adjust ... to.

lempang II *(ob)* and **melempang** lying crosswise. *– pukang* topsy-turvy, in disorder.

lempap melempap to beat cotton.

lémpar throw, toss. *–(kan) batu, sembunyi(kan) tangan* one does not want to admit to having done s.t. wrong. *– cakram* discus throw. *– lembing* javelin throw. *– martil* hammer throw. *– melayang* skimming (stones over the water). *– peluru* shot-put. *melémpar peluru* to put the shot.

selémpar *~ jauhnya* a stone's throw away. **selémparan** *jarak ~ batu* a stone's throw away.

melémpar 1 to throw (stones, etc.), fling, toss, hurl, cast. *~ batu* to throw stones (at). *~ batu kepada anjing* to throw stones at a dog. *~ koin* to toss a coin. **2** to toss, throw away, dispose of, get rid of. *~ canda/kelakar* to crack a joke. *~ kritik* to level criticism at, criticize. *~ senyum pada* to give s.o. a smile. *~ tanggungjawab dari bahunya* to rid o.s. of the responsibility (for s.t.). *~ tuduhan terhadap* to make an accusation against, accuse.

melémpari to throw at, pelt. *Massa mulai ~ petugas dengan batu.* The mob began to pelt the officials with stones.

melémparkan [and **ng(e)lémparin** *(J coq)*] **1** to cast, throw, fling. *~ beban/kesalahan* to shift the blame/responsibility, put the blame (on). **2** to throw off (one's coat, etc.). **3** to bring up (a subject). *Soal Jaksa Agung dilémparkannya.* He brought up the subject of the Attorney General.

terlémpar [and kelémpar (coq)] 1 thrown, tossed, flung. 2 kicked/thrown (out of office, etc.).

lémparan s.t. that is thrown/flung/hurled.

lémpar-lémparan to throw at e.o. ~ tanya-jawab to hurl questions and answers at e.o. main ~ to give s.o. the run-around.

pelémpar 1 s.t. for throwing. batu ~ anjing a stone for throwing at a dog. 2 s.t. or s.o. that throws s.t. ~ bom bomber (an aircraft). ~ bola pitcher (in sports). ~ peluru shot-putter (in sports). sepelémpar ~ jauhnya a stone's throw away.

pelémparan 1 throw. 2 throwing, pelting, casting, hurling, tossing (coins). ~ produksi outlet/market for one's products. sepelémparan a ... throw. ~ batu a stone's throw.

lempari (ob) k.o. small gong.

lempaung k.o. tree with sour fruit, Baccaurea lanceolata. akar - k.o. climbing plant.

lempem (Jv) melempem 1 damp, dampened, soggy; → LEMPAM. 2 slow, weak, soft. 3 fail to go off, be a dud (of fireworks).

lempenai k.o. tree, Pimeleodendron sp.

lempeng (Jv) straight; → LEMPANG. jalan yang - a straight road. - hati straightforward, honest. berjalan - to walk in a straight line.

melempengkan to straighten s.t. (out). ~ ... dengan to bring ... into agreement with, adjust ... to.

lémpéng 1 slice (of cake), slab. 2 chunk (hunk) (of tobacco). se- tembakau a chunk of tobacco. 3 plate (of glass, etc.). 4 counter for flat plate-like objects. se- kaca a plate of glass. 5 pancake of bananas and rice flour. 6 (blood) platelet. - benua continental plate. - lempung clay pan. - rumput sod, turf, piece of turf.

berlémpéng-lémpéng in slices, chunks.

melémpéng thin and flat (as of a pancake).

lémpéngan flat piece, slab, cell. ~ kaca énérgi surya solar energy cell. ~ baja steel slab. ~ rumput a piece of turf/sod.

lemper (Jv) a croquette consisting of glutinous rice with meat wrapped in a banana leaf.

lemping → LÉMPÉNG.

lempit (J/Jv) fold; → LIPAT.

melempit to fold (newspapers/a sarong, etc.).

lempitan a fold.

lempok candied durian or similar fruit.

lempoyang → LEMPUYANG.

lempuh - daun leaf scald; → LEPUH.

melempuh swollen/blistered (due to a burn/hot water, etc.).

lempuk I delicacy made from durian or jackfruit baked with sugar. - lumpur (petro) wall/mud cake.

lempuk II (ob) berlempuk to stick a lot (of grime, etc.).

lempuk III (ikan -) k.o. small fish.

lempung I 1 soft, light, friable (of wood). kayu - light and soft wood. 2 very weak, useless.

lempung II (Jv) clay, loam. - asam acid clay. - debu silt loam. - liat clay loam.

berlempung with clay, clayey.

lempungan argillaceous.

lempur very weak.

lempuyang wild ginger plants, Zingiber spp.

lempuyangan creeping panic grass, Panicum repens.

lemukut → MELUKUT.

lemungsir → LEMUSIR.

lemuru saury, horse mackerel, Scomberesox saurus.

lemusir withers (of cattle, etc.). daging - fillet of beef. tulang - shoulder blade.

lén I (E coq) lens; → LÉNSA.

lén II → LIN I.

léna 1 (ob) deep, profound, sound (as of sleep). makan tiada termakan, tidur tiada - to be very restless. penyakit - sleeping sickness. - ayam a) a light sleep. b) afternoon between about 5:30 and 6:30. 2 absent-minded, inattentive. 3 long (of duration); → LAMA. tak - antaranya not long afterward/after that. 4 latent.

berléna(-léna) purposely dawdle/waste time, dawdling, loitering; leisurely, slowly. berjalan ke surau ~ to walk slowly to chapel.

melénakan 1 to make s.o. absent-minded. 2 to put s.o. to sleep.

terléna 1 to fall asleep, unconscious; sleepy. 2 forgotten, neglected, ignored, disregarded. 3 crazy/mad about, be engrossed in, enthusiastic about.

terléna-léna crazy/mad about, be engrossed in, enthusiastic about.

kelénaan 1 sleepiness. 2 dawdling, preoccupation, absentmindedness, somnolence. 3 latency.

lénan (kain -) → LINEN.

lencam (ikan -) spangled emperor fish, Lethrinus nebulosus.

lencana badge, insignia, metal object worn on the chest to show membership in a party/union/school, etc. - jabatan insignia of office. - perang war decoration.

lencang (M) to dress (ranks), arrange troops in a straight line or lines. - kanan (mil) right dress.

melencangkan to line s.t. up.

léncéng meléncéng to deviate, swerve, veer. prakték ~ shady practices.

keléncéngan deviation.

léncér (Jv) meléncér to walk around.

léncét (ob) → LÉCÉT.

lénci I (J) litchi, Nephelium litchi; → LÉNGKÉNG.

lénci II (coq) rabbit; → KELINCI.

lencir (Jv) 1 tall and slender (of stature), thin and shapely (of one's calf). 2 whip, a tree that cannot survive without the protection of near-by trees.

lencit melencit to squirt/slip out (of a pip squeezed from a fruit).

lencong (ob) basah - dripping/soaking wet; → BASAH kuyup.

léncong I (J) meléncong 1 to deviate, swerve; to ricochet. 2 to be lost, lose (one's way), go astray.

léncong II → BASAH léncong.

lencun (ob) → LÉNCONG.

lenda (ob) melenda to enter by force; → MELANDA.

lendaian and lendayan (ob) → LANDAIAN.

léndé (Jv) léndéan (di) to lean (against).

léndéh I to lean over (with one's head on the table, etc.).

léndéh II meléndéh to nestle up against e.o. (of boats in dock).

lendér (J) mucus, sticky discharge (from the eyes), thin pus, slime, excretion; → LENDIR. uang - money given by the owner of a she-goat to the owner of a he-goat as compensation for the cost of mating, stud fee.

lendir mucus, phlegm; → LENDÉR. kulit/selaput - mucus membrane.

berlendir 1 running/runny (nose). 2 slimy.

lendiran ooze.

pelendiran ooze, oozing.

léndot (Jv) berléndotan (di) to lean (on), hang (onto).

ng(e)léndot to lean/recline (against), hang (onto).

lendung 1 dented, bashed in. 2 curved inward. 3 bowed down.

melendung sagging, concave in shape.

lendungan deflection.

lendur → KENDOR.

lendut melendut 1 to bend, yield (of a plant/floor/rope), sag. 2 (geol) to buckle down.

lendutan (geol) down buckling.

léng a measure for grain, = ½ cupak.

lenga sesame, teel, gingili, Sesamun indicum. minyak - sesame oil.

léngah 1 inattentive, indifferent, careless. - di pay no attention to; regardless of. tak - dari careful, attentive; always. dengan tidak - lagi immediately, without delay. jangan - pay attention to what you're doing, watch where you're going, keep your eyes open. - mata take no notice of, be indifferent to. 2 to take it easy, be idle, be carefree. - bekerja to take it easy working.

berléngah-léngah 1 to dawdle, delay, postpone, waste time. 2 to enjoy, have the leisure to.

meléngah 1 (to be) negligent/inattentive. 2 (M) to make happy, solace, amuse, cheer up. 3 (M) to nurse an infant so that he won't cry. ~ waktu (M) to kill time.

meléngah-léngah 1 to while away the time, do s.t. for pleasure. 2 (= ~ waktu) to kill time.

meléngahkan 1 to neglect, ignore. dengan tiada ~ pertanian without neglecting agriculture. tidak - to keep an eye on s.o., watch s.o., look out for s.o. tidak dapat ~ waktu sebentar akan cannot find the time to. 2 to divert (s.o.'s attention). ~ hati to comfort.

meléngah-léngahkan ~ hati for amusement, as a pastime.

terléngah 1 neglected, forgotten. **2** absentminded. **3** enthralled.

keléngahan 1 negligence, carelessness, ignorance. **2** (*ob*) idleness, inactivity.

peléngah a negligent/careless/indifferent person. ~ *hati* consolation.

peléngah-léngah ~ *hati* consoler, comforter. *untuk* ~ *pikiran/ waktu* for amusement, as a pastime.

peléngahan neglecting, neglect, indifference to.

lengai 1 (*ob*) not swift; not energetic. **2** inattentive, neglectful, dawdling (at work), slow. **3** inert.

lengak (*J/Jv*) **melengak 1** to throw back one's head and look up; to raise one's head. **2** amazed, dumbfounded, flabbergasted, stunned, astonished.

lengan 1 arm, upper limb of the human body from the shoulder to the hand. *batang* – upper arm. *beradu* – to measure one's strength. *berbantal* – to have no place to lay one's head, be homeless. *besar* – powerful, mighty, influential. *pangkal* – upper arm. *Patah* –*nya*. He has broken his arm. **2** foreleg, front leg of a four-legged animal. **3** arm, sleeve, s.t. shaped like or resembling an arm, rod. **4** lever, jib. – *ayun* swing arm. – *baju* sleeve. *dengan* – *baju digulung* with rolled-up sleeves. – *bawah* forearm. – *éngkol* crank arm. – *gaya* lever. – *keran* crane jib. – *lampu* lamp bracket. – *neraca* arm of a balance. – *penggerak* push rod. – *peraba* tentacle. – *tuas* lever arm.

lengang 1 deserted, quiet. **2** (to feel) lonely. **3** empty (of a cupboard), vacant (of a home). **4** slack (of business). **5** poorly attended (of a party/show, etc.). *mulai* – there are not many people left, it's emptying out, there is nobody around. **6** uninhabited, sparsely populated (of a village, etc.).

berlengang-lengang to be deserted/quiet.

melengangkan 1 to empty, vacate. **2** to give an impression of being abandoned.

kelengangan solitude, quiet, loneliness, tranquility.

lengap tinnitus, ringing in the ears.

lengar dazed.

kelengar (*J*) and **terlengar** dizzy, with a slight headache; → (KE)LENGAR.

kelengar ~ *matahari* to have a sunstroke, get sunstroke.

lengas 1 moist (of a dog's nose/sweaty hand, etc.), damp, dank. **2** humid. *pengukur* – hygrometer.

melengas to become moist/damp.

melengaskan to moisten, make wet, dampen.

kelengasan humidity, moisture.

lengat (*ob*) steamed; (used only in) *nasi* – steamed rice, rice cooked in boiling water in a tightly closed container until done, rice cooked in a bain-marie.

melengat to cook rice in the way described.

lengau → LANGAU.

lenger → (KE)LENGER.

lenggadai k.o. tree, *Bruguiera parviflora*.

lenggak melenggak 1 to look upward. **2** to tilt upward (of the front/ end of an object).

melenggakkan 1 to cock (one's head). **2** to tilt (the end or front part of s.t.) up.

lénggak-lénggok → NGELÉNGGOK-LÉNGGOK.

lenggana (*Skr cla*) unwilling, reluctant.

lengganan → LANGGANAN.

lenggang at leisure, to rest/pause for a moment.

lénggang 1 to swing (of the hands while walking). **2** gait. *baik* – *nya* he has a good gait (doesn't limp). **3** to rock and sway (of a ship at sea). *membuang/mencampak* – to swing the arms while walking. *tak berasak* – *dari ketiak* (*M*) and *tidak akan jauh* – *dari ketiak* always the same, unchanging, invariable. – *bagai sirih jatuh, tak tahu di tempuk layu* arrogant, haughty. – *kangkung* and **berlénggang-kangkung 1** to sway gracefully like the white or pink flowered convolvulus, *Ipomea aquatica* when touched by a gentle breeze. **2** to enjoy o.s., take a rest, relax; to do s.t. leisurely or effortlessly; aimlessly. **3** easygoing. – *lénggok* to walk with swaying hips (of a girl). **berlénggang-lénggok** and **melénggang-lénggok** to sway from side to side.

berlénggang and **melénggang 1** (to walk) swaying the arms. **2** to rock from side to side (of a ship at sea). *mandi melénggang*

perut to take a ceremonial bath in the seventh month of pregnancy; *cp* SELAMATAN *mitoni*.

melénggangkan 1 to sway (the arms while walking). **2** to carry nothing, be empty-handed.

terlénggang-lénggang 1 swaying, rocking back and forth, swinging back and forth. **2** rolling (of a ship at sea).

lénggangan (*ob*) implement for washing gold or diamonds in river.

lénggang II – *goréng* cut-up pieces of *pémpék* made into an omelet.

lénggar not close to e.o., wide apart.

lenggara (*ob*) **melenggarakan** to look after, take care of, manage, organize; → SELENGGARA.

lénggék I (*M*) **1** story, floor; → TINGKAT. **2** tier; shelf.

berlénggék(-lénggék) 1 to have stories/floors, with stories, storied. **2** to have tiers/shelves, tiered. *méja berlénggék tiga* a table with three shelves (used to display goods on sidewalks).

memperlénggékkan to put things one on top of the other.

lénggék II (*ob*) **berlénggék-lénggék** to scream (of children).

lénggér (*Jv*) dance form from Banyumas.

lénggok 1 swaying/shaking/swinging movement of the body while walking, dancing, etc. **2** (*astro*) precession.

lénggok-lénggok/-lénggang swaying about (said of a fast woman). **berlénggok(-lénggok), melénggok(-lénggok)** and **terlénggék(-lénggék)** to sway/swing/move from side to side.

melénggok-lénggokkan to walk with swinging motion, have a swinging/rolling gait; to move about (of the head while peering); to bend (one's body) from side to side.

ngelénggok-lénggok (*J*) to twist from side to side (like a snake), waddle (like a duck), sway/swing one's hips (like a flirtatious woman).

lénggokan swaying, tossing, (of the head).

lenggong (*ob*) **melenggong 1** to stare open-mouthed, be plunged in thought. **2** perplexed, bewildered, puzzled, mystified.

lénggor (*J*) *langgar* – to touch repeatedly.

ngelénggor to touch (against).

lénggotbawa swaying the hips (of a girl).

lengguak (*burung* –) thick-billed green pigeon, *Treron capellei*.

lenggundi a shrub used for hedges, *Vitex negundo/trifolia*; its leaves are used for poultices and as a moth and weevil repellent.

lenggut (*J*) (*astro*) precession.

melenggut(-lenggut) and **ngelenggut(-lenggut)** very sleepy; to keep nodding (of one's head from sleepiness).

lengit I (*J*) tricky and lazy/born tired; to be up to no good.

lengit II (*ob*) a chicken disease.

lengkai (*M*) slender, graceful; → LAMPAI.

lengkak-lengkok (*J*) curvy.

lengkanas (*M*) (*si* –) instigator, s.o. who likes to put two persons at loggerheads with e.o.; traitor.

lengkang (*ob*) open at the end of a circlet that is normally closed (rings/bracelets, etc.).

lengkap 1 complete, comprehensive, everything included, nothing missing, all present, entire; full, plenary (session). *secara* – in full. *tak* – incomplete. –*nya* in full. *Surti, -nya Andi Surtiati.* Surti, or in full Andi Surtiati. – *genap/pepak/sempurna* and *cukup* – complete in every respect, lacking nothing. *tidak* – incomplete. **2** equipped, ready. – *bersenjata/persenjataannya* armed to the teeth, fully armed (*mil*). – *baju dan celananya* to be well-clothed. *kurang* – incomplete. **kekurang-lengkapan** incompleteness. *tidak* – incomplete. **ketidak-lengkapan** incompleteness.

selengkap a set of. ~ *pakaian* a complete suit of clothes (nowadays, *esp* coat and trousers of the same material). **selengkapnya** the entire/whole, in detail. *berita* ~ the entire article (in a newspaper).

selengkap-lengkapnya as complete as possible, fully complete.

berlengkap to be equipped, provided, outfitted. ~ *dengan pakaian dan makanan* to be equipped with clothes and food.

berlengkapkan to be equipped with. ~ *segala macam senjata mutakhir* equipped with all k.o. of modern weapons.

melengkapi [and **ng(e)lengkapin** (*J coq*)] **1** to equip, outfit, provide/furnish/supply with. *ruangan itu dilengkapi dengan ...* the room was furnished with ... *bersiap* ~ to prepare, make (an army/a ship, etc.) ready. **2** to complete, supplement, add to, complement. *saling* ~ to complement e.o. **3** to take care of (some problem).

melengkapkan to complete, fit out, make ready, equip, bring up to strength. *Maksudnya hendak* ~ *pegawainya.* He intended to bring his staff up to strength.

memperlengkapi ~ *diri* to equip o.s. for, prepare for.

terlengkap the most complete.

lengkapan 1 accessory. **2** device, gear, equipment, controller.

kelengkapan 1 completeness; completion, full set of. **2** equipment. ~ *tambahan* accessory. **3** paperwork, all necessary forms. ~ *kapal* (*cla*) armada, fleet (of warships).

pelengkap 1 complement, s.t. used to complete. *kata* ~ (*gram*) complement. ~ *pelaku* (*gram*) subject, agent. ~ *penyerta* (*gram*) indirect object. ~ *penderita/tujuan* (*gram*) direct object, patient. **2** accessory. **3** subsidiary, ancillary, supplement.

perlengkapan 1 equipping, supplying. **2** equipment, appurtenances, accouterments, supplies, gear, kit, furnishings, fittings, outfit, device. ~ *makanan* (*mil*) field cutlery set. ~ *mesin pengolah* processing machinery equipment. ~ *modal* capitalization. ~ *pakaian* apparel. ~ *P3K* first-aid kit. ~ *rumah tangga* household furnishings. ~ *ski* ski gear. ~ *sholat* prayer appurtenances. *dengan sekalian ~nya* lock, stock, and barrel, including all machinery.

pelengkapan [and **penglengkapan** (*ob*)] equipping, supplying.

lengkara I (*Skr cla*) impossible, very unlikely, improbable.

lengkara II (*Skr ob*) (royal) kettledrum; → NEKARA.

lengkas (*ob*) quick, fast; → LANGKAS I.

léngkéng (*C*) the litchi fruit, *Nephelium litchi*; → KLÉNGKÉNG. – *bangkok* k.o. litchi.

lengkep → LENGKAP.

lengkésa (*M ob*) **berlengkésa** to become exhausted/depleted, decrease, diminish (of rice supply in *lumbung* due to evil spirits).

léngkét (*J/Jv*) **1** attached. *Baru kenal sehari sudah begitu –nya.* He has just known her for a day and he already is attached to her. **2** close, intimate; inseparable. *kawan* – a close friend. – *berdua* inseparable. **3** sticky, adherent, glutinous.

be(r)léngkét and **méléngkét** to stick together (of eyelids/papers, etc.), cling, adhere.

berléngkét-léngketan to stick to e.o., be close to e.o.

méléngkéti 1 to stick to. **2** to smear s.t. (with).

méléngkétkan to paste s.t. (on), stick s.t. (to), make s.t. adhere (to s.t.).

terléngkét (*kepada*) become devoted/attached (to).

keléngkétan adhesion, stickiness.

peléngkétan adhesion, adhering.

léngkét-léngkét (*J*) k.o. shrub, laurel-leaf pigeonwings, *Clitoria laurifolia*, that can be used as green manure.

lengkiang (*M*) a small rice barn; → RENGKIANG.

lengking 1 (*onom*) shrill (of voices), strident/piercing sound. – *kecil* a small shriek (of alarm). **2** to say in a shrill voice.

melengking 1 to be shrill/strident. **2** to make a shrill noise, wail (of a siren).

melengkingkan 1 to utter a shrill (noise). **2** to clang out (a shrill noise).

terlengking → MELENGKING.

lengkingan shrill sound, clang.

lengkitang (*M*) edible freshwater mollusk, *Melania spp.*

léngkok curve, bend.

be(r)léngkok to curve, bend.

beléngkokan (*J*) a bend, curve. *jangan berhenti di* ~ don't stop at the curve.

méléngkok to curve.

léngkok(an) (*Jv*) **1** a curve. **2** bay, inlet.

léngkong (*J*) bend, curve.

lengkuas galingale, *Alpina galanga*; → LAOS.

lengkuk (*J*) **menglengkuk** and **nglengkuk** to bend down.

lengkung I 1 bend, curve, turn, winding. **2** arc, arch. **3** bent, curved, arched, vaulted. **4** convex, concave, hollow (and curved). – *mata* eye socket. – *mulus* smooth curve. – *saraf* neural arch.

melengkung 1 to bend, curve. **2** bent, arched, curved (like an eagle's beak). *hidung* ~ aquiline nose. *jalan* ~ a detour, roundabout way. **3** to buckle. **4** to curl (of paper).

melengkungi 1 to vault, roof (in/over). **2** to surround, encircle. *patung yang dilengkungi karangan bunga* a statue surrounded by wreaths.

melengkungkan to curve/bend/arch s.t. *besi batang yang dilengkungkan* curved iron bar/rod.

terlengkung → MELENGKUNG.

lengkungan 1 curve, arc, arch, bow, bend. **2** arch, gate. ~ *bulan* crescent moon, sickle moon. ~ *bumi* horizon, curvature of the earth. ~ *mata* eye socket. ~ *tulang punggung* curvature of the spine.

kelengkungan curvature.

pelengkung 1 (triumphal) arch, gate. **2** s.t. which makes s.t. curve/arch.

pelengkungan curving.

lengkung II (*onom*) clang (of beaten metal).

lengkung-lengkung clanging sound.

lengkur (*onom ob*) snoring; → DENGKUR.

melengkur to snore.

lengleng (*J*) somewhat crazy, loony.

lenglengan (*Jv*) k.o. herb, *Leucas spp.*

léngong (*M*) **méléngong 1** to look back; → MENOLÉH. **2** to visit, call on, come to see.

méléngongkan ~ *mukanya ke* to look back at.

lengos (*Jv*) to feel offended and become angry right away.

léngos méléngos 1 to look back; → MENOLÉH. **2** (*J*) to turn (one's head) to the side or away (in contempt/disdain/anger/to avoid seeing s.o.), look the other way.

méléngoskan to turn (one's head) to the side.

lengsar (*Jv*) (*pohon –*) k.o. tree, *Pometia tomentosa*; → TAUN II.

léngseng and **léngséng** (*D ob coq*) lecture, speech, talk, address.

léngsér I (*Jv*) to step down, abdicate. – *keprabon* to step down, abdicate.

méléngsér 1 to slide down (of a *sarong*/the sun, etc.). **2** to step down, retire, resign, withdraw (from one's position).

méléngsérkan to depose, make s.o. resign.

peléngséran 1 resignation, abdication. **2** deposing.

léngsér II baking pan, cookie sheet.

méléngsér to grease s.t.

léngsér III (*S col*) various high positions in Dutch colonial times.

léngsét berléngsét curled (of the lower eyelid), ectropium.

léngsing → LÉNGSÉNG.

lenguh I (*onom*) mooing, lowing (of cattle).

melenguh 1 to moo, low (of cattle). **2** to gasp for breath, pant (due to lack of air or to fatigue).

lenguhan 1 gasping for breath. **2** mooing.

lenguh II (*ob*) paralyzed; tired, fatigued, exhausted. – *lesu* worn-out.

melenguhkan to tire (out), exhaust.

kelenguhan exhaustion, tiredness, fatigue.

lenguk (*onom*) humming/buzzing sound.

melenguk to hum, buzz.

lengung I melengung to reflect, brood, be plunged in thought, ponder.

lengung II (*ob*) **melengung** to see, visit; → MELÉNGONG.

lengus (*onom*) barking (of dogs)

melengus to bark.

lening (*onom*) clinking sounds (of small bell).

Léninis (*D/E*) Leninist.

Léninisme (*D*) Leninism.

lenja I melenja to take liberties, behave in an improper way.

kelenjaan brazenness, behaving in an improper way.

lenja II (*ob*) hanging hoop (to hold lamp), frame (for hanging food).

lenja III (*ob*) **melenja** to dribble at the mouth, salivate.

lenjan melenjan to insult s.o. and his entire family.

lenjing (*J/Jv*) pestle (for pounding condiments).

lenjuang and **lenjuhang** name of a shrub, *Dracaena*, which is often planted on graves; the leaves are also hung in front of the entrance doors or on the top of a staircase to ward off evil spirits; the leaves and roots are also used for medicinal purposes. – *mérah* a red-leaved garden shrub, red ti plant, *Cordyline terminalis*.

lénong I (*J*) open-air folk play of the *pinggiran-Betawi* people.

lénong II (*M*) **berlénong-lénong** to rotate.

léns(a) (*D*) lens; → KANTA. – *balur* lens of the eye. – *cekung* concave

lens. – *cembung* convex lens. – *kontak* contact lens. – *laju* zoon lens. – *mata* lens of the eye, ocular. – *mata keruh* cataract. – *pembidik* viewfinder. – *putih* (colorless) eyeglass lens. – *sebar* diverging lens. – *sudut lébar* wide-angle lens. – *télé* telephoto lens.
   berlénsa with ... lens.

lénsér → LÉNGSÉR I.

lénsét → LÉNGSÉT.

lénso (in the Moluccas and Celebes) handkerchief. *tari* – handkerchief dance.
   berlénso to dance that dance.

lentam (*onom*) → DENTAM. – *lentum* clanging/banging sound (of guns/fire-crackers/things falling down, etc.).
   berlentam to clang, bang.

lentang I → TELENTANG. **melentang** to lie on one's back; → MENELENTANG.
   terlentang lying on one's back.

lentang II (*onom*) clang, metallic sound, s.t. hitting metal. –.*lentung* clanging.
   kelentangan clang.

léntang-léntok swaying the head from side to side.

lénté → PERLÉNTÉ.

lénténg (*ob*) *jalak* – a) name of a tune/song. b) beautiful, charming.

lentéra (*Port*) 1 lantern. – *jalan* street light. – *kapal* ship's lantern. – *kompas* binnacle light. – *laut* lighthouse, beacon(-light). 2 (*J*) bicycle (oil) lamp.

lentik I (= **melentik**) 1 curved upward, tilted up (of the ends of Minangkabau house roofs/fingers/bows of praus, etc.). 2 beautifully raised/arched (of eyebrows/hips). *bulu mata* – upward-curving/curled eyelashes.
   bersilentik → MELENTIKKAN *jari*.
   melentikkan to twirl (one's mustache, etc.).
   melentik-lentik(kan) ~ *jari* a) to bend (continuously) (the stretched fingertips slightly inward). b) to twiddle one's thumbs, do nothing.
   pelentik eyelash curler.
   pelentikan curling.

lentik II (*J*) small and thin (of one's eyebrows).

lenting I elastic, resilient. *daya* – power of resilience.
   melenting 1 springy, resilient. 2 curling (of dried leaves/paper).
   kelentingan elasticity, resilience.
   pelenting *kekuatan* ~ power of resilience.

lenting II (*onom*) a sharp clinking sound (of metal coins striking together), ting.
   selenting a tiny bit (of s.t. audible). *tidak* ~ *kabarpun* no news.
   berlenting to make that sound.
   lentingan ting, clink.

léntok I tilted, leaning over to one side (of the head/lamp shade, etc.). – *kulai* to sway from side to side.
   terléntok tilted.

léntok II → LÉNTANG *léntok*.

lentong (*S ob*) tone (of voice), accent, stress, pronunciation (of songs); → KELÉNTOM, KELÉNTONG.

lentuk I flexible (of fingers/hands, etc.), supple; → LENTUR I.
   melentuk flexible.
   melentuk-lentuk to sway back and forth.
   melentukkan to bend s.t. ~ *léhér* to bend one's neck.
   kelentukan flexibility.
   pelentukan warping.

lentuk II (*J/Jv*) drowsy, sleepy.

lentum I (*onom*) booming sound; → DENTUM.
   melentum to boom.

lentum II → LENTAM *lentum*.

lentun (*ob*) → LANTUN.

lentung I (*onom*) sound produced by a *tongtong*, (hand)bell, etc.
   berlentung and **melentung** to produce that sound.
   pelentung clapper of a bell.

lentung II (*M*) **melentung** to nudge, knock slightly.
   melentungkan ~ *lung* to bend/draw a bow.
   telentung knock against, strike.

lentung III (*J*) **melentung** full to overflowing.

lentur I 1 bend, curve (in long things which have been bent). 2 deflection, diffraction, refraction. 3 flexible, elastic. 4 sagging.

melentur 1 to sag (of a fishing rod/cable/rice stalks, etc.). 2 pliable, supple, easily bent without breaking. 3 to diffract (light).
   melenturkan 1 to bend, deflect, make s.t. deviate. ~ *jari* (*ob*) to twiddle one's thumbs. 2 to relax, make more flexible, flex (a muscle).
   terlentur bend, arched, curved.
   lenturan 1 bending, curving, arching. 2 curvature. 3 diffraction. 4 object that bends/arches, etc.
   kelenturan flexibility, pliancy.
   pelentur s.t. that bends, flex.
   pelenturan bending, curving, flexing.

lentur II → BENTUR I.

lenung (*onom*) bang.

lenyah (*M*) muddy, miry.

lenyai (*M*) loose, slack; weak, limp, powerless; soft.

lenyak sound (of sleep); → LENYAP 2.

lenyap 1 disappeared, gone, vanished, fade/die away. *hilang* – completely lost/vanished/disappeared/faded away. – *dari pandangan/penglihatan* to be out of sight, vanished from sight. – *seperti embun kena panas* to vanish like the morning dew. – *tak/tanpa bekas* disappeared without a trace. 2 sound, deep (of sleep). *tidur* – to be sound asleep; → LELAP, NYENYAK, PULAS III. – *daratan* confused.
   melenyap to disappear.
   melenyapkan 1 to remove, eliminate, abolish, repeal. 2 to get rid of, chase away. 3 to cause to vanish, blot s.t. out. ~ *diri* to get out of there, take to one's heels. ~ *kebiasaan buruk* to break a bad habit.
   kelenyapan disappearance, vanishing, obliteration, eradication, elimination.
   pelenyap s.o. who or s.t. which extinguishes/puts out s.t., quencher. *minuman* ~ *dahaga* thirst quencher. ~ *kesukaran-kesukaran* trouble-shooter.
   pelenyapan 1 removal. 2 disappearance.

lenyau soft with a hard crust (as of mud), crusted (mud); → LANYAU.

lenyéh to feel queasy at touching or stepping on s.t. disgusting.

lényéh melényéh 1 to knead (dough). 2 to mash (potatoes).

lényét (*ob*) soft, pulpy, mashy, squashy (of an overripe fruit, etc.).

léo I (*D*) 1 (*coq*) male lion. 2 Leo (*zod*).

léo II → LIO.

léot I (*J*) **meléot** to sag (in the middle).

léot II (*E*) layout.

lepa (*ob*) inattentive; → ALPA.

lépa I (*Skr/Hind*) plaster, stucco, mortar, caulking.
   berlépa 1 plastered. 2 to do plastering, etc. work.
   melépa(kan) to plaster, roughcast (a wall).
   lépaan plastering, stucco.

lépa II terlépa 1 lying on one's back, stretched out (on the ground). 2 to trail along the ground, extend down and hit the ground.

lépa III *perahu* – Moluccan outrigger prau made of a hollowed-out tree trunk.

lépai (*M*) weak and almost paralyzed (of a dragging leg).

lepak I (*onom*) thud (sound made by falling object hitting the ground).

lepak II (*ob*) **melepak** to (become) white. *putih* – snow white.

lepa-lepa the lowest part of a palm marrow.

lépa-lépa (*IBT*) Moluccan outrigger prau made from hollowed-out tree trunk; → LÉPA III.

lepang a tree, Bauhinia spp., Cucumis satirus. *ombak bunga* – foam-tipped waves.

lepap I terlepap fallen forward/on one's face.

lepap II a flat-bottomed prau (used for line-fishing).

lepas 1 free, loose, unbound, unchained, relieved, released. *anak panah* – *dari busurnya* the arrow was released from the bow. *Hatinya* –. He felt relieved; → PLONG I. *tertawa* – to laugh freely/in an unconstrained way. *mata* – can look around freely. *Permata* – *dari ikatannya*. The jewel got loose from its mounting/setting. *Puasanya* –. His fast was over. *Sekrupnya* –. The screw got/was loose. *angin* – a strong wind. *jalan* – a way out (of difficulties, etc.). *huruf* – unconnected letters. *hutan* – primeval/virgin forest. *kalimat/kata* – loose/unconnected sentence/word. *laut* – the open sea. *lembaran* – loose leaves (not bound). *nomor*

– loose issue, single number (of a newspaper/magazine). *pekerja* – casual worker. *surat* – a) divorce decree. b) notice of dismissal (from a job). *wartawan* – free-lance journalist, stringer. – *muda awak dulu* I would like to enjoy my youth first. – *dari* a) apart from, besides, in addition to, unconnected with. b) free from/of; exempt(ed) from, not liable/subject to; lacking, without. *Anak ini belum – dari tanggungan saya.* I am still responsible for this child. – *dari haluan* to drift off course. – *dari pensénsoran* passed the censor. – *dari perhatiannya* to escape his attention. c) escaped (from), got(ten) away/free, got(ten) away safely. – *dari bahaya maut* to escape death, get away safely from the peril of death. *tak – dari* not free from, cannot escape, always has. *tak pernah – dari rasa curiga* always is suspicious. *tak – dari tuntutan* cannot escape prosecution. *tak – dari kesalahan* not without/free from mistakes. d) (after a negative) to keep (on) ...-ing, continue ... -ing, continue to ... *tak – dari hutang* to be constantly in debt. *tak – dari memandang* to continue/keep on looking at. e) immediately after leaving. – *dari stasiun Kota* after leaving Kota Station. 2 to pass (of title to property). *Kepemilikan tanah akan – pada saat pembayaran penuh diterima.* Title to land passes when payment has been received in full. 3 unconditional, absolute. *dijual* – unconditionally sold (may not be returned). *gaji lima puluh ribu rupiah* – a salary of Rp 50,000 (with no perquisites or allowances). 4 to escape, get away, run away, quit. *Burung itu* –. The bird flew/got away. – *dari penjara* to escape from prison. – *dari kepungan* to escape from being encircled (*mil*). 5 past, ago; happened, done, carried out; finished, completed, graduated; settled (of debts). *tanggal 8 Méi 18 tahun yang telah* – on May 8, 18 years ago. *Marahnya sudah* –. He is not angry anymore. *Belum – nadarnya.* His vow has not yet been fulfilled. *Kesukaran yang satu* –, *timbul kesukaran yang lain.* Difficulty after difficulty arose. *seorang – seorang* one after another, one by one; → DEMI. *Utangnya belum – juga.* His debts have still not been settled. – *sekolah dasar* after graduating from elementary school. 6 at the end of, after (the end of). – *magrib/makan/tengah hari* after sunset/eating/midday. *bagai/seperti kucing – senja* a) looking for trouble. b) to feel happy/relieved. 7 freelance. *pekerja* – freelance worker. 8 (*ling*) released. – *bantal berganti tikar* to marry one's deceased wife's sister or relative. – *angin* to no purpose, uselessly. – *ayam/burung/unggas* a) not caged, free as a bird. b) (*cla*) liberated (of a slave). – *béa* dutyfree. – *bébas* really free/independent. – *cakap* to say whatever comes to mind. – *demam* free from fever. – *dari berbahaya* off the danger list. – *gudang* free of charges until removed from the warehouse, ex-warehouse. *melepaskan kangen* to reunite, have a reunion, get back together again. – *kendali* to give free rein to. – *landas* to take off (of an aircraft). – *landas dari ...* just past one's ... birthday. *(secara)* – *lelah* relaxed. *berlepas lelah* and *melepas-lelah* to relax. – *lelas* completely free. – *liar* released into the wild. *melepas-liarkan* to release (an animal) into the wild. – *libat* (*mil*) breaking contact (with the enemy). – *malu* circumcised. – *pabrik* ex/free factory. – *pantai* offshore (drilling, etc.). – *puasa* at the end of *Ramadan*. – *rangkai* (*petro*) to back off. – *renggang* loosened. *melepasrenggangkan* to loosen. – *sekolah* graduated. – *tangan* a) with the hands off the steering wheel (or, handlebars), no hands. b) to transfer (leadership). c) to disclaim (responsibility for). d) not interfere (in, with), not meddle (in, with), keep one's hands off. e) not implicated (in), not involved (in). *tukang – uang* moneylender; → PELEPAS *uang*.

lepas-lepas 1 to keep on getting loose/free. 2 freely. *tidak ~ dari bibir* always on one's tongue.

selepas after, when. *~nya dari SMEA* after graduating from SMEA. *~ dilantik Réktor* after having been installed by the President (of the university).

selepas-lepas as free as possible, unhampered; as far as. *~ hati* to one's heart's content. *~ mata memandang* as far as the eye can see. *(dengan) ~ suara* a) (screaming) bloody murder. b) to sing at the top of one's voice. *tertawa besar ~nya* to double over with laughter, burst out laughing.

berlepas 1 to be free/loose/independent/unbound. 2 (*cla*) to depart, leave, start, go away. *~(kan) diri dari(pada)* a) (*ob*) to refuse to carry out (an order or punishment of a *raja*). b) to escape, run away, flee. c) to exculpate o.s., clear o.s. (of wrongdoing). *~ hati* to be satisfied. *~(kan) lelah/penat* to take a break, rest, relax. *~ tangan* → LEPAS *tangan*.

bersilepas *~ diri dari tanggung-jawabnya* to disclaim one's responsibility for.

berlepasan to become free/detached from e.o.

melepas 1 to allow, permit; to see s.o. off, take leave of, say goodbye to; to start ... off (on a race, etc.). 2 to let go, release, let s.t. fly away. *~ dia pulang* to let him go home/back. *~ aku pergi ke mari* to let me come here. *Présidén dilepas.* The president was seen off. 3 to discharge, dismiss, fire; to divorce (one's wife). 4 to release, discharge (from prosecution). 5 to take off, remove (often = **melepaskan**). *mudah dilepas* comes off easily. *~ infus* to remove an IV. *~ bébas* free and independent. *~ bedil* to fire a rifle. *~ hati* to give in to one's desires. *~ jenazah* to render the last honors to s.o., bid farewell to the deceased. *~ kaul* to fulfill a vow. *~ landas* to take off. *~ langkah seribu* to run away. *~ layang-layang* to fly a kite. *~ lelah* to (take a) rest, relax. *~ lembu ke padang* to put the cows out to pasture. *~ mayat ke kubur* to bear a deceased person to his last resting place, to lay a deceased person to rest. *~ nazar/niat* to fulfill a vow. *~ pandang* to let one's eyes travel over. *~ sepatu* to take off one's shoes. *~ sérve* (in tennis) to serve. *~ tahun yang lama* to see the old year out. *~ tanggung jawab* to deny responsibility (for s.t.). *~ tawa* to let out a laugh. *~ tinja* to defecate. *~ topi* to tip one's hat. *~ tustél* to adjust/set a camera (before taking a picture). *~ uang* to lend money at interest.

melepasi 1 to redeem (s.t. from pawn); to fulfill (an obligation/promise, etc.); to settle, pay (debts, etc.). *~ hutang* to pay off/settle one's debts. *~ malu* (*M*) to marry off one's nephew/niece. *~ nadarnya* to fulfill one's vow. 2 (to be) sufficient/adequate. *Uang sekian itu tak akan ~.* That much money is insufficient. 3 = **melepaskan**.

melepaskan [and **ng(e)lepasin** (*J coq*)] 1 to let go of, let ... free, turn loose. 2 to free, liberate, release, forgive s.o. (his debt/punishment). 3 to drop (a plan), get rid of. 4 to fire/dismiss/lay off (an employee). 5 to renounce (one's rights), relinquish, abandon (assets), waive. 6 to take off, remove. *~ air mata* to cry one's eyes out. *~ anak ikan* to set fish free. *~ angan* a) to put one's mind to s.t. b) to daydream. *~ balon udara* to launch a balloon. *~ barang* a) to deliver goods for the price bid. b) to deliver on credit. *~ bedil* to shoot a rifle. *~ bersyarat* to release s.o. conditionally. *~ budel* (*leg ob*) to assign an estate. *~ cinta kasihnya kepada* to declare one's love to. *~ dahaga* to quench one's thirst. *~ dendam* to take revenge (on), vent one's resentment (on). *~ diri* a) to run away, get away. b) to abandon (a right). *~ diri(nya) dari sekolah* to drop out of school. *~ hajat* to go to the bathroom. *~ hak atas* to abandon/give up/relinquish one's right(s) to. *~ harapan* to abandon/give up hope. *~ hasil curian* to sell stolen goods/articles. *~ gurau* to crack a joke. *~ hajat* to go to the bathroom, answer a call of nature. *~ harapan* to abandon/give up a hope. *~ hati* to give (free) rein to one's passions. *~ haus* to quench one's thirst. *~ ikatan* to separate/divorce. *~ isi hatinya kepada* to unburden/pour out one's heart to. *~ istri* to divorce one's wife. *~ jiwa* to die, pass away. *~ kacamata* to take off one's eyeglasses. *~ kangen* to see e.o. again (after a long separation). *~ kaul* to fulfill one's vow. *~ kantuk* to take a nap. *~ kebiasaan* to kick a habit. *~ kecaman* to criticize. *~ kehendak* a) obliging, indulgent. b) to do what(ever) one wants. *~ kedaluwarsa* to waive a time limit. *~ keinginan* to give up a wish. *~ kepalan* to strike out with one's fist. *~ keréta* to uncouple a railroad car. *~ kesan* to get rid of an impression. *~ kesetiaan* to forswear one's allegiance. *~ ketegangan syarafnya* to unwind, relax. *~ kewarganegaraan* to renounce one's citizenship. *~ kontak* to disengage (from the enemy). *~ kritik* to criticize. *~ kuapnya* to let out a yawn. *~ lapar* to satisfy one's hunger. *~ lelah* to (take a) rest. *~ lesulelah* to relax. *~ mahkota* to abdicate. *~ maksudnya* to abandon one's intentions. *~ malu* a) to take revenge. b) to circumcise. *~ marah* to give vent to one's anger. *~ masa bujangnya* to give up one's bachelorhood. *~ masa gadisnya* to come of age (of a girl). ~ *mata* to look around (for fun). ~ *nafsu* to give (free) rein to one's passions, satisfy one's carnal desires. ~ *napas yang terakhir* to breathe one's last, die. ~ *nazar* to fulfill/ carry out a promise. ~ *niat* to fulfill one's intention. ~ *nyawa* to die, pass away. ~ *panah* to shoot (off) an arrow. ~ *pandang/ pemandangan* to look around (for fun). ~ *penat* to (take a) rest. ~ *penerjun payung* to drop parachutists/sky divers. ~ *perhatian (kepada)* to lose sight (of), forget (about). ~ *pikiran ke arah* to turn one's mind to. ~ *pukulan* to strike a blow. ~ *rém* to release the brakes. ~ *rindu* to rejoice (in seeing one's native country/home town again). ~ *sakit hati* to take revenge. ~ *sepatu* to take off one's shoes. ~ *serangan* to launch an attack. ~ *sesaknya* to get out of an awkward situation/predicament. ~ *tangisnya* to cry one's eyes out. ~ *tekanan* to put/exert pressure (on s.o.). ~ *témbakan* to fire a shot, open fire. ~ *tendangan* to give a kick. ~ *tikaman* to stab (with a dagger, etc.). ~ *tinju* to give a blow with the fist. ~ *tuduhan* to make/bring an accusation/charge (against). ~ *tuntutannya* to waive/renounce one's claim. ~ *uang* to lend money (for interest). ~ *untung masing-masing* to make everyone secure.

memperlepas 1 to liberate, release. **2** to exempt.

terlepas 1 freed, released, liberated, saved (from disaster). **2** to go free, run away. **3** (to get) loose, come out. **4** aside (from), regardless (of), in spite of. **5** set aside, separated. ~ *dari/apakah* aside from (whether). *tidak ~ dari* a) not spared. b) not separate from. **keterlepasan** blurting out. ~ *mengatakan* to blurt out, blab.

terlepaskan can be released, can be let free.

lepasan 1 graduate, alumnus, alumna. ~ *sekolah* graduate (the person). ~ *sekolah tinggi* alumnus, alumna. **2** ex-, former. ~ *pelaut* an ex-sailor. ~ *tentara/serdadu* ex-soldier, veteran. ~ *narapidana* ex-con(vict). **3** discrete.

kelepasan 1 escape, release, freedom, liberty. **2** disappearance, loss. **3** (*ob*) holiday, leave, vacation, recess.

pelepas 1 (~ *uang*) moneylender. **2** supplies, provisions (for a trip). **3** means to loosen/unwind s.t. ~ *dahaga* thirst quencher. *sebagai ~ iseng/keisengan/ketegangan perasaan* as a pastime, s.t. to make one relax. ~ *kaul* s.t. which one uses to fulfill a vow. ~ *lelah* s.t. to make one relax (after work). ~ *pahat* (*petro*) bit breaker, breakout block. **4** (*Mal*) starter, s.t. who gives the signal for a race to start.

penglepas (*Jv*) → PELEPAS.

pelepasan 1 the act of liberating, letting go, releasing, abandoning; farewell. *pésta ~* farewell party. ~ *aktiva* abandonment of assets. ~ *bersyarat* conditional release, release on parole. ~ *budel* (*leg ob*) assignment/session of estate. ~ *dari segala tuntutan hukum* acquittal from further prosecution. ~ *hak* (in notarial instruments) renunciation of rights (and titles). ~ *harta* assignment of an estate. ~ *muatan* (*elec*) discharge. **2** (*ob*) discharge, dismissal, firing (from employment). **3** release, freeing. **4** (*M*) anus.

perlepasan → PELEPASAN.

penglepasan → PELEPASAN.

lepat (~ *pisang*) a delicacy/snack consisting of sticky rice wrapped in banana or young coconut leaves and cooked in a rice steamer. *seperti/sebagai – dengan daun* inseparable; joined together; → *bagai* DAGING *dengan kuku, seperti mimi dan mintuna*.

lepau 1 (*ob*) kitchen-veranda (at rear of house). **2** food stall, small *warung*.

lépék I 1 underlayer. **2** saucer.

lépék II (*J*) drenched, dripping/soaking/sopping wet.

lépék III (*M*) **melépék** to slap/pat slowly.

lépék IV flat, flaccid.

lépé-lépé (*J*) not full/satiated.

léper → LÉVER I.

léper I flat, shallow (of dishes, etc.). *kaki –* flat feet.

léper II incorrect (of pronunciation), mispronunciation; → PELAT, TÉLOR.

léperansir → LÉVERANSIR.

léperi (*D coq*) referee.

lepet (*J/Jv*) k.o. snack made from sticky rice.

lepih folded over (the corner of a page/cloth/selvage of a mat).

melepih(kan) to fold/turn over.

lepik (*onom*) sound produced by s.t. small falling on the floor.

lepit (*J*) **berlepit-lepit** folded, in folds.

melepit to fold/bend one part of s.t. back over itself.

lepitan fold.

léplap (*J ob*) → LIPLAP II.

lépoh I (*M*) **melépoh** to plaster, besmear.

lépoh II terlépoh sprained (of a limb from a fall).

lépot (*J*) **be(r)lépotan 1** muddied, soiled, smeared. **2** to be of low repute, notorious.

melépoti to dirty, besmear, soil, stain, drag s.t. through the mud.

terlépot smeared, stained.

lépra (*D*) leprosy; → KUSTA, BODOK.

léprosari (*D*) leprosarium.

lepu *ikan –* various k.o. fishes with poisonous spines, scorpion fish, angler fish, *Pterois russelii/Antennaridae* and *Scorpaenidae*. *– angin* scorpion fish, *Scorpaenopsis sp. – ayam* common lionfish, red fire fish, *Pterois volitans*. *– tembaga* stonefish, *Synanceja spp.*

lepuh blister (raised by a burn), small swelling under the skin filled with liquid. *– kulit* blister bark. *– séminal* seminal vesicle.

melepuh 1 to blister. **2** scalded, blistered, burned.

melepuhkan to raise/cause a blister.

pelepuhan scalding, blistering, burning.

lepuk I (*onom*) "plop!"

lepuk II worn out, used up; → LAPUK I.

lepuk III (*onom*) clapping sound.

lepur I *mati –* suffocated in the mud.

melepur to sink into the mud.

lepur II melepur to attack with the wings (of fighting cocks).

lépya (*Jv*) to think no longer of/about.

lér (*J*) **melér** to spread out.

léran spread out layer.

lerah terlerah pushed/knocked out of place.

lerai separate; → CERAI.

melerai to separate, part (of people fighting), disengage.

meleraikan to separate (people fighting, etc.).

terlerai(kan) separated, asunder, put apart, divided, disengaged.

pelerai 1 s.o. who separates people who are fighting, etc. **2** medicine/object that wards off illness, etc.

peleraian 1 (*mil*) disengagement (of troops). **2** separating.

lerak I broken to pieces/bits (of house/lock/ladder, etc.).

melerak(kan) to take/pull to pieces.

lerak II *buah –* a small, hard, round fruit from a plant *Sapindus rarak*; used to produce suds for washing *batik*.

leram (*onom*) rumble (of thunder), roar (of a tiger), growl (of a dog).

lérang 1 strip, stripe (on textiles). **2** (*ob*) a half-day's sail.

lérang-lérang stretcher, litter.

lerap (*onom*) sound of walking, trotting; → DERAP.

lérap (*ob*) name of Balinese money. *main/pusing –* to play pitch and toss (a gambling game which involves spinning a coin and then covering it with the palm of the hand).

lerek → LERAK II.

léréng I 1 surface of the edge of a thin and flat object (like a coin/ wheel, etc.). *– mata uang rupiah* the edge of a rupiah coin. (*keréta*) *–* (in Medan) bicycle. **2** slope, slanting surface. *jalan –* sloping (mountain) path/road. *– balik* reverse slope. *– cekung* forward slope. *– cembung* reverse slope. *– curam* bluff. *– gunung* slope of a mountain. *– luncur* glide. *– putar* caster.

léréng-léréng casters (of a bed/table, etc.).

berléréng to cycle.

meléréng 1 to slope, incline. **2** sloping, slanting (of land, etc.).

meléréngi to follow/go along the slope of s.t.

léréngan slope, incline.

léréng II (*Jv*) (fabric which is) patterned with diagonal stripes.

lérét I row, series; → DÉRÉT. *dua – pohon kelapa* two rows of coconut trees.

seléret ~ *dengan* parallel/in one line with, on the same side of the street as.

berléret in a row.

berléret-léret in rows, in a long line.

melérét to stretch out in straight line.

melérétkan to line s.t. up.

lérétan row, chain, series.

lérét II (*J/Jv*) **melérét** and **ngelérét 1** to cut up. **2** to remove the ribs of leaves.

lérét III (*ob*) **melérét** trailing too long/loosely, dragging, trailing (of a conversation/story, etc.).

lerik → DERIK.

lérok (*Jv*) **melérok** to steal a glance at.

lérokan a sidelong glance.

lérong to run away.

lérot (*J*) **belérot** and **melérot** to walk side by side.

lerum (*onom*) crash (a sudden, loud noise, as of a falling tree/thunder, etc.).

les (*Jv*) *mak* – to drop off (to sleep), become unconscious; to disappear (quietly) from sight; → LESLESAN.

lés I (*D*) reins (for horse).

lés II (*D*) list; → DAFTAR.

lés III (*D*) **1** lesson. **2** to take lessons in. *Saya – bahasa Indonésia.* I'm taking Indonesian (lessons). *mengambil* – to take lessons. – *beramai-ramai* group lessons. – *privat/sendirian* private lessons.

meléskan to give lessons to. *Meréka diléskan piano.* They were given piano lessons.

lés-lésan lessons of all kinds.

lés IV (*D*) **1** (picture) frame; → BINGKAI. **2** trim (around windows, etc.).

lés-lésan framing.

lesa (*cla*) numb (of limbs temporarily); → LASA. – *lenyai/lesu* very tired, exhausted.

lésa paddle-rudder for rafts.

melésa to row with this rudder.

lesah → LASAH II.

lesak I (*onom*) swishing sound (of rain), rustling sound (of wind) (on grass or leaves).

lesak II melesakkan to move s.t. with force; → LASAK II.

lésan I (*Jv*) (shooting) target.

lésan II → LISAN.

lesang (*M*) **melesang** to ride (a horse/car, etc.).

lesap vanished, disappeared, gone, dissipate. *berniaga buluh kasap, ujung hilang pangkal* – to do s.t. without actually knowing how to do it (therefore doing it wrong).

melesap 1 to vanish, disappear. **2** to dissipate.

lesapan dissipation.

pelesap s.t. that makes s.t. vanish.

pelesapan disappearance, dissipation, deletion.

lesat (*J*) **melesat 1** to hurl/fling. **2** to fly along at a high speed (of cars/trains, etc.); be launched at high speed (of a missile). **3** to jump up. *Honor ~ jutaan rupiah.* Honoraria jumped up millions of rupiahs.

lesau (*onom*) swishing sound of rain drops on leaves, etc.

lésbi clipped form of LÉSBIAN.

lésbian (*D/E*) lesbian.

lésbianisme (*D/E*) lesbianism.

lésbong (*Pr*) lesbian; → LÉSBI.

ngelésbong to engage in lesbian sex.

lésbril (*D ob*) reading glasses.

léséhan (*Jv*) *duduk* – to sit cross-legged on the floor/ground. *secara* – sitting on the floor. *warung* – a small *warung* where the customers sit cross-legged on mats.

lésék (*M?*) **1** energetic. **2** restless (of sleep); → LASAK II.

lésen (*E Mal*) license.

léséng (*D*) → LÉSING.

lését melését 1 to slip/slide away. *jaman ~* depression, slump. **2** to miss, be off the mark. *~ jauh* to be wide of the mark. *jauh ~ dari* to deviate widely from (what s.o. says); → MELÉSÉT, PELÉSÉT. **3** won't do. *dugaan ~* and *~ besar* quite wrong. *~ dari jadwal* to not follow the timetable. *~ dari rél* to derail; → ANJLOK *dari rél.* **kemelésétan** depression. *~ ékonomi* (*Mal*) economic recession.

terpelését [and **kepelését** (*coq*)] → KEPLÉSÉT.

kelésétan *~ ékonomi* recession.

lesi white. *pucat* – deathly pale, anemic. *putih* – snow white.

lési 1 damage. **2** lost its function (of a part of the body). **3** lesion.

lesing (*onom*) whizzing (of bullets), buzzing; → DESING.

melesing to whiz, buzz.

lésing (*D coq*) lecture, speech.

melésing to give a lecture, deliver a speech.

lesir I (*ob*) → PELESIR.

lesir II (*ob*) *bermain* – and **berlesir** to dance a sword-dance.

lesir III → DESIR.

lesit I (*onom*) humming noise.

melesit to hum (of angry wasps/mole cricket, etc.).

lesit II melesit 1 to blow (one's nose) using one's fingers; → MEMBUANG *ingus.* **2** to squirt out; → MEMANCAR, MEMANCUR.

melesitkan *~ ingus* to blow one's nose.

lesit III melesit (*ob*) to suck (as of a *pelesit* or vampire).

pelesit k.o. blood-sucking spirit.

leslesan (*Jv*) to be drowsy.

lésnar (*D*) (reading) desk.

lésot I (*S*) to fall apart.

lésot II (*Jv*) **nglésot** to sit on the ground or floor.

lestari (*Jv*) **1** eternal, (ever)lasting, permanent. **2** continuing; continuous. **3** renewable, nondepleting. *poténsi maksimum* – maximum sustainable yield. *tidak* – impermanent. **ketidak-lestarian** impermanence.

melestarikan to make s.t. unchanging/everlasting; to protect s.t. (so that it lasts), conserve.

kelestarian continuance, conservation. *~ alam* environmental protection.

pelestari conserver, preserver.

pelestarian conservation. *~ alam* conservation of nature. *~ satwa* wildlife conservation.

penglestarian → PELESTARIAN.

lésték and **léstét** (*ob*) (elastic) catapult.

lesterung syphilis of the nose; lupus; nasal polypus.

lesu 1 tired, fatigued, weary, worn out, run down. *letih* – tired to death. **2** to not look well, look exhausted; listless. **3** (of business/the market) dull, slow, slack, sluggish, depressed. *– darah* at death's door, dying, failing (of a business).

melesukan to tire, wear out, exhaust; wearying, fatiguing.

kelesuan 1 weariness, exhaustion, fatigue. **2** slump, recession. *~ bantuan* aid fatigue. *~ ékonomi* recession, slowdown.

lesung mortar, bowl made from a hard material in which paddy, etc. is crushed or pounded. *– pinang* betel nut crusher; → GOBÉK. *menumbuk di –, bertanak di periuk* (*M*) to do s.t. in the approved manner (or, in the right way). *– mencari alu* a woman looking for a man. *antan patah, – hilang* a) a woman will leave an impotent man. b) double misfortunes. *menumbuk di priuk, bertanak di –* to do s.t. contrary to the rules, do s.t. in the wrong way. *ke mana dialih, – berdedak juga* s.t. which always involves troubles or financial loss whenever it is performed. *– kisaran* k.o. hand mill for milling rice. *– pinang* areca nut crusher. *– pipi(t)* dimple.

lesung-lesung dimple.

lesus → DESUS.

lésus (*Jv*) **1** whirlwind. **2** rush (of wind).

lesut (*onom*) swish of whip or cane.

lét (in acronyms) → LÉTNAN.

leta 1 low, wretched, base, shameful, contemptible. *orang yang hina* – a despicable/contemptuous person. **2** crippled.

meletakan and *memberi* – to despise.

letah → LETIH *letah.*

létai (*M*) very tired, worn out, totally exhausted; → LESU.

letak 1 position, situation, location, site, place. *Kota Bandung –nya di ...* Bandung is located in ... *– mesin* the positioning/location of the engine. **2** becoming, fit (of clothes). *baik –nya* fits/becomes (the wearer). **3** situation, disposition. *Bagaimana –nya perkara itu?* How do things stand? What is the present state of affairs? *– lintang* diagonal. *– sungsang* breech position.

berletakan to be located.

meletak (*M*) to put, place. *~ nasi* to put some food down (as an offering for spirits/ghosts, etc.). *~ tanda* to give a token (in the form of a ring, etc.) to the bride as evidence that the marriage has been solemnized.

meletaki to put (s.t.) on s.t.

meletakkan 1 to put, place, lay/put down. *Tolong letakkan buku-buku di atas méja saya.* Please put the books on my table. *~ batu pertama* to lay the cornerstone. *~ hipoték* to place a mortgage. *~ jabatan* to resign (one's position), quit. *~ kesalahan pada orang lain* to lay/put the blame on others. *~ lunas* to lay a keel. *~ pesawat téleponnya* to hang up the phone. *~ senjata* to lay down one's arms. **2** to put/set aside. *~ jabatan* to resign.

terletak (to be) located, placed. *Pulau Pénang ~ di ...* Penang Island is located at ... *keputusan ~ kepada Présidén* the decision is/rests with the President.

peletak s.o. who lays s.t. *~ dasar* founding father. *para ~ dasar Républik Indonésia* the founding fathers of the Republic of Indonesia.

peletakan the act of putting/placing/laying down. *~ jabatan* resignation. *~ lunas* keel laying (of ship). *~ pekerjaan* work stoppage.

perletakan the laying down of s.t. *~ senjata (sementara)* (temporary) cease-fire/truce/armistice.

létak exhausted, weak and weary (from hunger, fatigue). *- létai* tired to death, exhausted.

létal (*D/E*) lethal, mortal, deadly.

letam-letum → DENTAM *dentum*.

letang (*onom*) sound of clanking, clinking, clanging.

Létda [létnan dua/muda] Second Lieutenant.

leteh (in Bali) impure, needing a purification ceremony.

leték (*J*) **meleték** to crack open (of a pod).

létenan → LÉTNAN.

léter (*E coq*) letter, character, type.

melétér (*coq*) to mark with a letter (of the alphabet), letter.

létér → LÉTÉRAN. **berlétér** and **melétér 1** to chatter/talk incessantly, talk a lot and not say anything, talk nonsense. **2** to bleat.

pelétér chatterer, gossip.

létéran chatter, incessant/idle talk.

léterlek (*D*) literally, word-for-word.

léterséter (*D*) typesetter.

letes (*J*) **meletes** to make a soundless fart.

letih 1 weary, tired, exhausted, worn-out. **2** breathless, out of breath. *membuang -* to take a break, rest. *- lelah/lesu/letah* breathless, out of breath; tired out, exhausted; powerless, weak.

berletih-letih to tire o.s. out.

meletihkan 1 to tire, (make) weary, exhaust. **2** tiring.

meletih-letih *~ tulang saja* to knock o.s. out for nothing.

keletihan 1 tiredness, fatigue, weariness, exhaustion. **2** tired out, fatigued, exhausted.

letik (*onom*) crack, sound of cracking (usually without complete separation of parts).

meletik to crack, burst open.

letikan cracking sound.

leting I meleting to flap around (like a fish out of water).

leting II (*onom*) tinkling sound.

berleting to tinkle.

létnan (*D*) lieutenant. *- Dua* [Létda] Second Lieutenant. *- Jénderal* [Létjén] Lieutenant General. *- Kolonél* [Létkol] Lieutenant Colonel. *- Muda* [Létda] a) Second Lieutenant. b) Ensign. c) Warrant Officer. *- Satu* [Léttu] First Lieutenant.

létoi (*J*) and **letoi** (*S*) tired, exhausted, weak; → LETAI.

letok → LETUK.

letos (*J*) **meletos** (with) bulging (eyes); to open one's eyes wide.

létoy → LÉTOI.

letterlijk (*D*) /léterlek/ literal(ly); → HURUFIAH.

Lettu Pnb [Létnan Satu Penerbang] First Flight Lieutenant.

letuk (*onom*) a knocking/crackling sound.

meletuk to make that knocking/crackling sound.

letum (*onom*) a bang (of guns/firecrackers/falling objects, etc.). *- letam* banging (of guns, etc.).

letung (*onom*) a clanging sound.

letup (*onom*) sound of an explosion/s.t. blowing up; → LETUS.

letup-letup a child's toy, a blown-up rubber balloon; a small, bamboo toy rifle, etc. that can make a loud pop.

meletup to explode, detonate, burst (with a loud noise), go off (of a gun).

meletupkan to (cause to) explode/burst.

letupan 1 explosion. **2** explosive. *bahan/benda ~* explosives.

peletupan explosion, bursting.

letur I (*ob*) → LENTUR I.

letur II (*ob*) → LECUR.

letus (*onom*) sound of an explosion; → LETUP. *- atas* airburst. *- tanah* surface burst.

meletus to erupt (of a volcano/war/firecracker), explode, burst/break out with a loud noise, blow up, blow out. *ban ~* the tire burst.

meletuskan to detonate (a bomb), shoot (a bullet).

keletusan eruption.

letusan 1 explosion, eruption. **2** outburst, eruption.

peletus (*ling*) stop sound.

peletusan 1 explosion, detonation. **2** eruption, outbreak, outburst.

leuit (*S*) rice-barn.

léukémi(a) (*D/E*) leukemia.

leunca (*S*) common nightshade, *Solanum nigrum.*

léver I (*D*) **meléver** (*coq*) to supply (goods); → MEMASOK, MENSUPLAI.

léver II (*D*) liver. *penyakit -* hepatitis. *sakit -* to have a liver disease.

léveransir (*D*) supplier; → PEMASOK, PENSUPLAI.

lévis → CELANA *lévis.*

léwa meléwa to dawdle, waste time.

léwah (*ob*) **meléwah** abundant, plentiful.

léwar meléwar (*cla*) to go in schools, fly in swarms.

léwat 1a) to pass (by), go by, come past. b) passed (by), gone by, come past. *orang -* passerby. *- dari situ* passed by that place/there. *- dari itu* thereafter, then, after that, next. **2** after, past, beyond (a certain time). *- pukul 10* after/past 10 o'clock. *jam 4 -* after/past 4 o'clock. *- tengah hari* in the afternoon. *- waktu* past due. **3** (*waktu*) to expire, lapse, be over, be finished. *Musim menuai sudah -.* Harvest time is over. **4** advanced, more than, too much. *sudah agak - umurnya* rather advanced in age. **5** via, through, by (way of), over. *- darat* by land, overland. *- jalan* by road. *- jenuh* sated. *- médan* cross country. *- télepon* by/over the telephone. *- tempo* expired. *- zaman* out-of-date, outdated. **6** over-, ultra-. *- jenuh* oversatiated. *- lembayung* ultraviolet. *- mérah* infrared. *- tegang* hypertonicity. *- ukuran* an overdose. *makan aspirin - ukuran* to take an overdose of aspirin. **7** (*sl*) to die.

léwatnya *~ waktu* (*leg*) (immunity due to) lapse of time

seléwat after/past (a certain hour).

meléwati [and **ng(e)léwatin** (*J coq*)] **1** to pass/go (by/through), get past; to pass (a certain age); → MELALUI. **2** to go across, cross. **3** to exceed/surpass, be/go beyond. *~ batas* to be beyond the bounds, overstep the limits. **4** to overlook, skip, pass over. *Soal-soal yang susah-susah diléwati saja.* Just skip the difficult parts. **5** to transgress, disobey (the law).

meléwatkan 1 to allow s.t. to slip/pass/go by, miss s.t., pass up, let s.t. go by, pass/spend (time). *~ kesempatan* to miss/pass up an opportunity, let an opportunity go by. *dengan tidak ~ tempo* without any loss of time, immediately. **2** to pass s.t. around.

keléwat 1 too, excessively. *~ batas* excessive. *~ mahal* too expensive. *~ pagi* premature, too soon. *tidak ~* not too/overly. **2** exceedingly, exceptionally, extremely, remarkably, very. *Kemarau ~ panjang di sana.* The dry season is very long there.

keléwatan (*J*) → KELÉWAT. **1** to go past, pass, skip. *Kita ~ tujuan kita.* We went past our destination. *Saya ~ dua halaman.* I skipped two pages. **2** to be too much, behave outrageously.

terléwat → KELÉWAT(AN). *- jelajah* overshoot.

terléwati passed by.

terléwatkan to be overlooked.

léwatan throughput.

léyak → LÉAK.

léyat-léyot twisted.

meléyat-léyot 1 to twist around. **2** to sway, totter.

léyéh (*Jv*) **(ber)léyéh-léyéh** to lie around. *duduk -.-* to sit leaning back.

berléyéhan (*pl subj*) to lie around.

léyéhan to lie around.

leyeng (*J*) **keleyengan** disoriented.

lezat (*A*) **1** delicious, tasty. **2** sensual pleasure.
 berlezat to enjoy the pleasures of sex.
 melezatkan to flavor s.t.
 kelezatan 1 delicacy, tasty snack. **2** taste. **3** pleasure, enjoyment.
lha (*Jv pron* with breathy pronunciation of the vowel) **1** particle used to get hearer's attention. –, *kangkung saja sekarang seikat sudah Rp 50,–.* Well, one bunch of *kangkung* costs Rp 50 nowadays. **2** particle of transition from previous to next sentence. – *iya!* That's it! That's right. – *wong* that's because. – *wong perkaranya diperiksa lagi kok.* And that's because the matter is being reexamined. **3** (*infr* used in error for LAH I) – *yauw* → LAH I *yauw.*
lho (*Jv pron* with breathy pronunciation of the vowel) **1** at the beginning of the sentence expresses surprise at discovering/learning/hearing s.t. –, *sudah di sini!* What, you're here already! **2** can combine with *kok* to show surprise. –, *kok sudah ke sini lagi.* What, you've come back again! **3** at the end of the sentence used to remind s.o. that the actual situation is not as he/she might have expected or believed. *Saya tidak bawa uang, –!* Remember, I don't have any money on me! **4** placed after a word, it draws attention to a particular fact. *Ini – tempatnya!* Hey, this is the place!
li (in acronyms) → AHLI, LIAISON.
lia → ALIA.
liaison (*D/E*) liaison.
liak-liuk swaying.
li'an (*A*) a husband's accusation of his wife's infidelity.
liang I pore, hole, opening, aperture, pit. – *bulu* pore in the skin. – *dubur* rectum, anus. – *hidung* nostril. – *jarum* eye of needle. – *jimak* vagina. – *kemaluan* vagina. – *kubur* grave. *ke – kubur* to die, pass away. – *kumbang* (*naut*) scupper hole. – *lahad/lahat* niche in Muslim graves. – *luka* gash in a wound. – *mata* eye socket. – *nafas* stigmata. – *peranakan* vagina. – *renik/roma* pore in the skin. ***berliang renik*** with pores, porous. – *sanggama* vagina. – *telinga* auditory canal.
liang II (**ber)liang-liuk/liang-liut** to sway from side to side (like a snake creeping along); to stagger (as a drunk); to slink along (as a tiger).
liangliong (*C*) a Chinese dragon manipulated by several persons.
liar 1 wild, untamed, undomesticated. *binatang/bunga* – wild animal/flower. *macan* – a savage tiger. *matanya – memperhatikan céwék-céwék yang turun naik bis.* His eyes were roving about wildly looking at the girls getting on and off the buses. **2** uncivilized, uncultured, primitive, barbaric, savage, wild. *orang* – wild tribesman, primitive people. **3** illegal, unlawful, outlawed, unauthorized. *rumah* – a squatter's/illegally built house (i.e., one without the proper licenses). *taksi* – gypsy cab. *daérah permukiman* – (*Mal*) squatter area. **4** shy (of fish, etc.). **5** irregular. *kapal* – tramp steamer. *pasukan* – irregular troops, irregulars.
 berliar-liar to act wildly, be restless.
 meliar to become wild.
 meliarkan 1 to drive s.o. wild. **2** to free (a domesticated animal in the jungle in order to increase the jungle population of that species), to return (an animal) to the wild.
 liaran escape (a tree or animal that escapes disease).
 keliaran wildness.
lias (*ob*) → PELIAS.
liat I 1 tough, rubbery (of meat); clayey (of soil). *tanah* – argillaceous earth, loam. **2** lithe; elastic (of rubber), plastic. **3** sticky, clayey. **4** trying to get out of (paying back debts). **5** tough, hardened, hard to defeat (of an athlete/criminal). – *liut* twisting (of a snake), meandering (of a river).
 liat-liat twisting (of a snake).
 meliat 1 to become tough/leathery, become clayey. **2** (of a *durian*) to be almost ripe.
 keliatan toughness, plasticity.
 keliat-liatan clay-like.
liat II (*J*) → LIHAT. **meliat** → MELIHAT.
 ng(e)liatin to see, look at. ~ *aja* to stare at, eye s.o.
liau (*ob*) **meliau** to suppurate (of an abscess/wound), fester.
Libanon Lebanon.
libas (in northern Sumatra and *Mal*) *kena* – to be cheated.

melibas 1 to whip, lash, slash (of rattan). **2** to find a way to do s.t., deceive, cheat, trick.
libat selibat up to one's ... ~ *pinggang* (*J*) up to one's ass. *Utangnya* ~ *pinggang.* He's up to his ass in debt.
 berlibat-libat to be very much involved.
 melibat 1 to wrap up, bandage, dress (a wound). *Dia* ~ *lukanya pakai perban.* He dressed his wound with a bandage. **2** to wind/fold around. **3** to involve/implicate (in), draw (into), include (in).
 melibatkan and **memperlibatkan** to involve, implicate, concern, draw s.o. into, bring/call in. *Ini tidak* ~ *kamu.* This doesn't concern you. *Dia dilibatkan dalam pertentangan itu.* He was drawn into that conflict.
 terlibat [and **kelibat** (*coq*)] **1** bandaged, wrapped up. **2** ~ *dalam/dengan* to be involved/implicated/mixed up in. **3** to be rolled, coiled around. *Kabel* ~ *pada kakinya.* The cable was wound around his feet. **menterlibatkan** to involve, implicate. **keterlibatan** involvement, entanglement. **sekelibat** ~ *mata* superficially.
 pe(r)libatan involvement.
liberal (*D/E*) liberal. *kaum* – liberals.
 meliberalkan to liberalize, i.e., to free from government control.
liberalisasi (*D*) liberalization.
liberalisme (*D/E*) liberalism.
Libéria Liberia.
libero (*D*) (*in sports*) free back.
Libia Libya.
libido (*D/E*) libido.
libur (*Jv*) **1** vacation, holiday, leave, time off. *hari* – holiday. **2** to be/go on vacation/holiday/leave. **3** free time.
 berlibur to be/go on vacation/holiday/leave, take (time) off (from work). ~ *akhir-minggu* to spend the weekend away.
 meliburkan 1 to let out (school), close down (for a holiday). *Sekolah menengah diliburkan.* High school was let out. **2** to send s.o. on vacation.
 liburan 1 vacation, holiday, leave. **2** time off (from work). **berliburan** to take a vacation/holiday.
 peliburan closing down school, taking time off from school.
libut → KELEBUT.
licak I (*M*) flattened, bruised (of fruit in one spot), trodden flat.
licak II – *ria* k.o. cake.
licau shining, shiny, glossy (of one's hair), lustrous. *licin* – a) smooth and glossy. b) cleaned out (of a gambler).
lici → LÉNGKÉNG.
licik (*J*) **1** foul (play). **2** play foul (in a fight). **3** sly, tricky, cunning, crafty, wily. **4** slippery.
 berlicik-licikan to deceive e.o.
 meliciki to trick, fool.
 kelicikan 1 foulness. **2** playing foul. **3** slyness, trickery, cunning.
licin 1 smooth, slippery, slick, crisp (of paper/new currency). *Jalan ini nampaknya – setelah diaspal kembali.* The road seems to be slippery after it was repaved. – *seperti ular* slippery as a snake. *berjalan dengan* – to run smoothly. **2** glossy. **3** plain, unadorned. *nasi – saja* just plain rice (no side dishes). **4** bare, without grass, bald. **5** sly, slick, cunning, not easily fooled. **6** cleaned out, wiped out (of food/possessions after a robbery). – *langsing* streamlined. – *lecat/licau* very slippery. – *lindap/tandas* completely finished, all gone.
 berselicin ~ *lidah* to debate, discuss.
 me(ng)licin to iron (clothes).
 melicinkan and **memperlicinkan** to (make) smooth, make slippery. ~ *jalan* to pave the way.
 terlicin the smoothest, etc.
 kelicinan 1 smoothness. **2** slipperiness. **3** cunning, slyness. **4** bareness.
 pelicin 1 lubricant. **2** s.t. which smoothes (or, makes smooth). *uang* ~ bribe.
 pelicinan lubrication.
licurai welcoming dance of Timor Timur.
lid (*D ob*) → ANGGOTA.
lidah I 1 tongue. *menjilat dengan* – to lick with the tongue. *penyambung* – "extension of the (people's) tongue," i.e., (people's) spokesman, vox populi. *ujung* – a) tip of the tongue. b) (*ob*)

spokesman; → JURU *bicara.* **2** taste. *Masakan disesuaikan dengan – meréka.* The food's been adapted to their taste. *bisa membuat – menari-nari lit* "it can make your tongue dance," i.e., you can really have a great feed. **3** tongue, way of speaking. *–nya keras* and *kaku/keras –nya* (already) accustomed/used to the pronunciation of his native language and therefore he has a hard time learning how to speak another language. *lancar bersilat* – to have the gift of gab. *–nya manis* he talks sweet talk. *–nya masin* and *masin –nya* a) his speech is effective; when he speaks, things happen. b) he is influential. *diterangkan dengan* – explained verbally. *lembut/lunak –nya* can pronounce foreign words easily. **4**a) s.t. or a part of an object resembling a tongue: *– serunai/seruling* the vibrating end of the reed in a clarinet/flute. b) the part of s.t. that protrudes: *– api* tongue of fire/flame. *– dacing* tongue of scales. *– tanah* a narrow strip of land extending into the sea/river, etc. c) names of various plants, for which see LIDAH III. *berat –(nya)* reluctant to talk, keeps his mouth zipped up. *cepat* – quick-tongued; to say whatever comes into one's head. *fasih* – eloquent. *kelu –nya* his speech is defective/halting (said of the dying). *keseléo –nya (coq)* he misspoke/mispronounced. *mati –nya* no sense of taste, unable to tell what is delicious and what is not. *pahit –(nya)* his words/what he said turns out to be right. *panjang* – a) like to speak evil of s.o. else; like to blab/spread rumors. b) flatterer. *patah –(nya)* a) to mispronounce a word. b) not clever in speaking. c) silent, quiet, unforthcoming. *(doa/mantra) pematah –* (mantra) to silence s.o. (so that he will not speak). *petah* – eloquent. *putar balik –nya* to pervert/twist the facts. *ramah* – talkative; very friendly. *ringan –(nya)* a) eloquent. b) to talk big, brag. *(jadi) ujung jari sambungan –* and *(jadi) penghubung ujung –* (to be) a spokesman; (to be) a representative (during negotiations, etc.). *(hanya) di ujung –* to stick (only) to words. *selalu di ujung –* to be on everybody's tongue, be talked about constantly. *sudah di ujung –* to be on the tip of one's tongue. *kebenaran di ujung –* there is no justice. *berkata peliharakan –* to pay careful attention to one's words. *berniaga di ujung –* an untrustworthy but skillful person. *mengerat – orang* to interrupt s.o., to cut (s.o.'s words) short. *menyepitkan – ke lantai* to control one's passions/desires. *terbalik –* one's words are uncertain. *tergelincir –nya* let one's tongue run away with one; → TELANJUR. *tergigit –* a) impertinent; to pay no attention to s.o.'s criticisms. b) afraid to say things flat-out (due to moral obligations). *terkalang –nya* afraid to argue/deny/answer, etc. *–nya seakan-akan terkalang* it is as though his lips were sealed. *terlompat –nya;* → TERGELINCIR *lidahnya. terulur –* to ask for s.t. already given. *– (mémang) tidak bertulang* a) to allege s.t. without foundation, promise without further ado; also, said of an unreliable person. b) to be careful with one's words; it's easy for you to talk. c) unreliable, empty talker. d) to use double-talk. *– air* the early stages of an approaching flood. *– api* tongues of a flame. *– ayam* a small knife. *– bajak* plowshare. *– bajang* joiner's tool. *– bercabang/biawak/keling* with forked tongue, deceitful, unreliable, untrustworthy; hypocritical, sanctimonious. *– dacing* tongue of a pair of scales. *– daun* (in forestry) leaflet. *– kucing* k.o. light, soft, sweetened biscuit. *– keling* untrustworthy. *– lingkar* actinomycosis. *– ombak* a) rolling waves. b) (crest) of oncoming waves. *– papan* a) tongue, i.e., a projecting strip along the center of the edge of a board for fitting into the groove in another board. b) actinomycosis. *– pundak* shoulder strap (to hold insignia). *– serunai* reed (in a wind instrument). *– tergalang* tongue-tied.
lidah-lidah 1 anything that resembles the tongue. **2** (*bio*) ligule.
berlidah to have a tongue; to use a tongue. *~ dua* to say one thing one time and a different thing at a different time. *~ di lidah orang* to dance to s.o. else's tune. *~ ular* dishonest, two-faced.
penglidah the flat handle of a spoon.
lidah II *ikan –* sole, *Cynoglossus ssp.* and other species.
lidah III the first part of many plant names. *– anjing* k.o. plant, little ironwood, *Adenostemma lavenia, Vernonia cinerea. – ayam* an herb (used as medicine), *Polygala glomerata. – badak* a climbing aroid, *Pothos latifolius. – buaya* k.o. aloe, a succulent (from which a hair shampoo is made), bitter aloe, *Aloe ferox/vera, Al-*

lomorphia malaccensis. – gajah name of a plant, *Aglaonema oblongifolium. – kucing* an herbaceous plant, yellow alder, *Turnera ulmifolia. akar – jin* k.o. plant, *Hedyotis philippinensis. rumput – jin* k.o. plant, *Peristrophe acuminata. – katak* k.o. tree, *Pternandra coerulescens. – kerbau* k.o. plant, *Clerodendron deflexum, Pyrenaria acuminata. – lembu* an annual herb, *Aneilema nudiflorum. – mara* k.o. small tree, *Ouratea. – mertua* snake plant, mother-in-law's tongue, *Sansevieria trifasciata.*
lidah-lidah various k.o. bushes, *Bauhinia spp., Alangium ebenaceum.*
lidas itchy and sore-feeling (*esp* around the lips and mouth) after eating sour fruits.
lidi ribs/veins of coconut palm fronds/leaves. *sapu –* [and *penyapu – (Mal)*] broom made of the veins of palm leaves. *ular –* a small, thin, poisonous snake species, *Dendrophis pictus. – dupa* joss stick.
lift (*D/E*) elevator. *tukang –* elevator operator. *– barang* freight elevator. *– berkaca* capsule-like elevator. *– berkecepatan tinggi* high-speed elevator. *– sampah* trash chute, dumbwaiter.
lifter (*D*) (*– angkat besi*) weightlifter.
liga (*D*) league. *– Anti Komunis Rakyat Asia* Asian Peoples Anti-Communist League. *– Anti Komunis Sedunia* World Anti-Communist League. *– Arab* Arab League. *– Démokrasi* Democratic League. *– Sépak Bola Utama* [Ligatama] Soccer League.
ligar-léger → LÉGAR-LÉGER.
ligas canter; to canter.
  meligas to canter, amble along (of horses/bulls).
ligat rapid (of rotation), spinning.
  meligat to spin rapidly (of tops).
ligih meligih to quiver.
ligyat clever and naughty.
lihai, lihay (*C*) and **lihéi** (*J*) **1** (*coq*) pointed (weapon). **2** cunning, crafty, clever (in deceiving), shrewd. **2** witty. **3** excellent, superior.
  kelihaian cunning, craftiness.
lihat /*usu* liat/ see, look (at). *– halaman sebelah* please turn over, PTO. *salah –* a) to look at a person of the opposite sex in an improper way. b) to mistake ... for ... *sekali –* a) at first glance. b) (the facts are) on the surface (very simple), on the face of it (it seems correct).
  berlihat(-lihat)an (to get) to see e.o., exchange glances, look at e.o.
  melihat [and **ng(e)lihat** (*coq*)] **1** to see, can see (i.e., is not blind), observe, perceive, contemplate. *~ kepada* judging from (his age, etc.). *~ ke depan* a) to look ahead. b) to predict. **2** to find (s.t. or s.o. to be a certain way). **3** to look at, watch. *~ télévisi* to watch TV. *dengan tidak ~* ... irrespective of ... *dilihat orang dengan sebelah mata* to be looked askance at (with disapproval). *belum dilihat sudah terpaham* a word to the wise is sufficient. **4** in view of, considering. *dilihat dari* seen/viewed in terms of. **5** to foresee, foretell. *~ nasibnya* to tell one's future. *~ peruntungan* to have one's fortune told (by). *bagai ~ asam* attracted.
  melihat-lihat to look around, browse around/through.
  melihati [and **ng(e)lihatin** (*J coq*)] **1** to see, visit. **2** to look/stare at. **3** to observe, study, scrutinize, inspect.
  melihatkan 1 to look at. **2** to perceive, observe. **3** (= **memperlihatkan**) to show (around), display, demonstrate, exhibit. *telah diperlihatkan dan terdaftar* (in notarial instruments) exhibited and registered.
  melihat-lihat to look around (a store), shop, browse. *– étalase* to window-shop. *dilihat-lihat* to be observed, be watched.
  terlihat [and **kelihat** (*coq*)] **1** can be seen, visible, noticeable, perceived. **2** (already) seen, known, perceived, etc. *~ (ke)pada* suddenly (and unintentionally) seen. *tidak ~ mata telanjang* invisible to the naked eye.
  lihatan *pengalaman ~* s.t. one has seen and experienced. *tidak ~ mata telanjang* invisible to the naked eye.
  kelihatan 1 can be seen, visible, noticeable, perceived. *tidak ~ lagi* out of sight, cannot be seen. **2** to appear, show/turn up. *Apa dia ~?* Is he around? **3** (= **kelihatannya**) apparently, seem to be, look like. *Teman saya ~(nya) gembira.* My friend seemed to be happy. *Dia tidak ~ marah.* He didn't look angry. *tidak ~* invisible, can't be seen.
  pelihat s.o. who can foretell/forecast, prognosticator, clairvoyant.

penglihat 1 (sense of) sight, seeing. 2 perception. 3 point of view.

penglihatan 1 (sense of) sight, glance, perception, vision. *atas* ~ at sight. *secara ~ mata* visually. *berkurang ~nya* his eyesight is failing. *lenyap dari ~* to disappear/vanish from sight. 2 visibility. *jarak ~ mendatar* horizontal visibility, i.e., distance that can be seen in a horizontal direction. ~ *terbatas* limited visibility. 3 contemplation, impression. 4 point of view. 5 insight. 6 view, scenery. *suatu ~ yang cantik* a beautiful view.

lik (*ob*) excuse, pretext.
  berlik to make excuses.
lika-liku ins-and-outs, details.
likas I 1 (*daun –*) reel for newly spun thread. 2 name of a *ceki* card.
  melikas to reel in, wind on a reel.
  likasan reel.
likas II (*Pal ob*) to watch (a bathing woman) in secret.
likat I (= **belikat**) adhesive, sticky, gummy, viscous.
  kelikatan adhesion, viscosity.
  pelikat adhesive.
likat II muddy, turbid, thick, not clear. *bukat –* very muddy, etc.
likat III (*J*) embarrassed, (too) shy (to look up, etc.); → JENGAH.
like and dislike (*E*) favoritism.
liket → LIKAT I.
Likhita Bhutala Yuddha Karya (motto of the Army Topographical Corps, meaning) Cartography for the Military and for Development.
likir I plant with edible tubers, *Tacca leontopetaloides*.
likir II (*D*) liqueur.
liklik (*J*) *kelapa –* young coconut suitable for making a k.o. *sayur*. *sayur –* a *sayur* made of spinach, young coconut, etc.
liku I (*M*) curve, bend, winding (in a road/river, etc.). *– jalan* turn/curve in the road. *– lekok/lekuk* curves, ins and outs.
  liku-liku ins and outs, plot. ~ *hidup* the ups and downs of life.
  berliku complicated.
  berliku-liku 1 curvy, curvaceous, curving, winding (of a road), sinuous, rambling. 2 devious; complicated, intricate.
  kelikuan curvature.
Liku II *Paduka –* (*cla*) title for the younger wife of a Javanese prince (in the *Panji* stories).
likuida (*ling*) liquids.
likuidasi → LIKWIDASI.
likuiditas liquidity. *– wajib minimum* reserve requirements.
likur (*Jv*) in compounds with a number) twenty-: *se–* a) 21. b) blackjack (or, twenty-one) (the card game). *malam se–* (*J*) to hold a celebration on the 21st night of *Ramadan*; → SELAWÉAN (*Jv*). *dua –* 22, *tiga –* 23, *empat –* 24, *lima –* 25; → SELAWÉ. *enam –* 26, *tujuh –* 27, *delapan –* 28, and *sembilan –* 29. *tujuh –* (*Mal*) 27 nights before the final day of celebrations for the Muslim New Year.
  likuran *usia ~* in his/her twenties. **selikuran** blackjack (the card game).
likut (*M ob*) **belikut** and **melikut** to hide (behind a tree, etc.).
likwid (*D/E*) liquid.
likwidasi (*D*) liquidation.
  melikwidasi to go out of business.
  melikwidasikan to liquidate (one's business).
  terlikwidasi liquidated.
  pelikwidasi liquidator.
likwidatur (*E*) liquidator.
likwide (*D*) liquid (capital).
likwidir (*D*) **melikwidir** to liquidate.
  pe(ng)likwidiran liquidating.
likwiditas and **likwiditét** (*D*) liquidity.
likwiditur (*D*) → LIKWIDATUR.
lil I large round fish trap basket with a side entrance fitted with spikes.
lil II (*ob*) shadow; → ZILL.
lila I (*D*) lilac.
lila II (*ob*) → RÉLA.
lila III small cannon.
lilah I belilah and melilah to vomit, retch.
lilah II (*Jv*) variant form of **lila II**.

berselilah to be satisfied with, take pleasure in.
lilau I a tree species, *Xylopia elliptica*.
lilau II melilau to look around wildly.
Lilawangsa military resort command (*Korém* 011) in Lhok Seumawe.
lili (*E/D*) lily.
lilih (*ob*) → LÉLÉH.
lilin I 1 wax. 2 candle. *és –* popsicle, ice cream on a stick. *tempat –* candlestick. *nasi dimakan –* a) very sad/grieved. b) he has lost his appetite. 3 candle-power. *lampu yang nyala dengan 100 –* 100 candle-power lamp. *ke mana kelok –, ke sana kelok loyang* to trim one's sails to the wind. *– batik* k.o. wax used for batiking. *– cina* red candle used in praying. *– lebah* beeswax. *– lunak* (*petro*) slack wax. *– padat* (*petro*) scale wax. *– sambang* wax in a deserted bees' nest. *– tanah* ozokerit(e). *– tawon* beeswax. *– tétésan* (*petro*) sweated wax.
lilin II *burung –* northern pied hornbill, *Anthracoceros malabaricus leucogaster*.
lilip (*J*) kelilipan to have s.t. in one's eye.
lilipur (*S*) comfort, consolation, solace; → LIPUR II.
  melilipur to comfort, console, solace.
liliput (*D*) Lilliputian, very small, tiny. *rumah –* tiny hut.
lilir (*ob*) → LÉLÉR I.
lilit 1 a turn/twist; a coil. *Diikatnya dengan kawat empat –*. He fastened it with four twists of wire. 2 perimeter, circumference. *Bujur sangkar ini 20 cm –nya*. This rectangle has a perimeter of 20 centimeters.
  selilit 1 one twist; one coil. 2 all around (an island/table). ~ *Pulau Perca* all around Sumatra. ~ *pinggang* (so many that they are) up to here. *Anaknya ~ pinggang*. He has many children.
  berlilit 1 to wind/twist/coil around. *Ular ~ di dahan kayu*. The snake is coiled around a tree branch. 2 coiled/encircled.
  berlilitkan with ... coiled around it.
  melilit 1 to wind/twist/coil around. *Lengan tangannya dililit dengan pita hitam*. He had a black ribbon wound around his sleeve (as a sign of mourning). *jalan yang ~ gunung* road that winds around a mountain. *terlalu dililit peraturan* surrounded by too many regulations. ~ *dengan pita* to tape. *dililit utang* to be deeply in debt. *utang ~ pinggang* up to one's ears in debt. *Perutnya ~*. He has an upset stomach.
  meliliti to coil/wind/circle around (the head/neck/flag post/mountain, etc.).
  melilitkan to coil/wind/wrap s.t. around. ~ *syal di léhér* to wind a shawl around one's neck.
  terlilit [and **kelilit** (*coq*)] wound around, encircled. ~ *hutang* to be deep in debt.
  lilitan 1 perimeter, circumference. 2 winding. 3 helix. 4 coil.
  pelilitan coiling around.
liliuran (*S*) k.o. *arisan*.
lillah (*A*) *karena –* for God's sake; → LILLAHI.
lillahi (*A*) for/with/to God. ~ *ta'ala* for God's sake.
lilo-lilo there is no God but Allah.
lim (*D*) glue; → LÉM.
lima five. *minus –* below average. *Aktingmu minus –*. Your acting is below average. *seperti – belas dengan tengah dua puluh* it's all the same (to me); it's six of one and half a dozen of the other. *– belas* fifteen. *– likur* (*ob*) twenty-five. *– puluh* fifty. *pada/di tahun – puluhan* in the fifties. *– waktu* (or, *waktu –*) the five daily prayers.
  lima-lima and **berlima-lima** by fives, in groups of five.
  berlima five (in all); to make a group of five. *kami ~* the five of us.
  memperlima to divide into sets of five.
  kelima 1 the set of five. ~ *anak itu* those five children. 2 fifth. *anak (yang) ~* the fifth child.
  limaan 1 a 50-rupiah note, a five(r). 2 (*coq*) in fives.
  perlima fifth. **seperlima** one fifth. *dua ~* two fifths.
liman (*Jv* and Lampung) elephant.
limar I (*Jv*) a flower-patterned silk material (of which belts, etc.) are made.
limar II (*IBT*) (knife or rasping) file.
limas 1 dipper of palm-spathe like an inverted pyramid in shape (for water/salt, etc.). 2 pyramidal (of roofs). *rumah –* a house where the four sides of the roof meet in one point. *candi –* pyramid. *–*

ginjal renal pyramid. **3** (*math*) pyramid. – *terpancung* truncated pyramid.

selimas a pinch of. ~ *garam* a pinch of salt (held between the thumb and finger).

melimas-limas puckered up (as if about to cry).

limau (*Pers?*) lime, lemon, orange, citrus; → JERUK. *asam* – citrus acid. *seperti – masak seulas* be superior to, be in advance of. – *masak sebelah, perahu karam sekarat* discriminatory rules/ punishment, etc. geared to the person or position, etc. – *besar/ Bali/betawi* shaddock, *Citrus maximus/grandis*. – *hantu* bitter lime, Kaffir lime, *Citrus hystrix*. – *kapas* → LIMAU *nipis*. – *kedangsa* green-skinned citrus fruit, *Citrus medica*. – *kesturi* musky lime, *Citrus microcarpa*. – *kiah/kingkik/kingkit/kunci/ kursi* a shrub with fruit which can be made into glue, limeberry, *Triphasia trifolia*. – *kopék/langkat* k.o. citrus, *Citrus suhuiensis*. – *langsir* bath water containing *jeruk purut* skin and various flowers. – *manis* orange, *Citrus chinensis/nobilis*. – *nipis* sour lime, *Citrus aurantifolia*. – *purut* bitter lime, Kaffir lime, k.o. lime used as shampoo, *Citrus hystrix*. – *sundai* k.o. lime.

berlimau *mandi* ~ to take a lime-juice bath.

melimaui 1 to bathe s.o. or pour on s.o. fragrant water (mixed with the skin of *jeruk purut*). **2** to say bad things about others, denigrate, vilify

pelimau (*ob*) bath house.

limbah 1 waste (product). **2** by-product. **3** [= **pelimbah** and **(pe)limbahan**] cesspool, drain. *membuang* – to sway while walking/dancing. – *B3* toxic and hazardous waste. – *beracun* toxic waste. – *beracun dan berbahaya* [B3] toxic and hazardous waste. – *industri* industrial waste. – *nuklir* nuclear waste. – *ong- gok* (tapioca) pulp waste. – *padat* solid waste. – *pertanian* com- post heap. – *rumah tangga* household waste. – *terigu* pollard, coarse wheat flour.

melimbah (= **melimbahkan**) to sway (one's arms) back and forth.

kelimbahan and **pelimbahan** ditch for waste.

limbai swaying (of the arms).

melimbai to sway.

melimbaikan to wave (one's arms while walking), move (one's arms while dancing)

limbak I melimbak to boil over (of water), overflow; → MELÉM- BAK, MELUAP.

limbak II (*ob*) **berlimbak-limbak** in confused heaps (of coins/ fruits/logs/nuts); → LAMBAK.

limban and **pelimban** gangway, catwalk, footbridge.

limbang I 1 to wash for gold dust by using a *dulang*. **2** to wash rice before cooking.

pelimbang 1 large wooden platter for panning ore. **2** gold-washer.

limbang II (*cla*) to loiter/lounge/saunter around.

selimbang an entire (area).

limbang III – *tengah hari* (*ob*) noon; → REMBANG I.

limbat (*ikan* –) walking catfish, *Clarias nieuhofi*.

limbing outer part of the ear (in fowl).

limbubu (*M*) whirlwind; → HALIMBUBU, SELEMBUBU.

limbuhan black-naped fruit dove, *Ptilinopus melanospila*.

limbuk(an) emerald dove, *Chalcophaps indica*.

limbung I 1 inner harbor. – *pelabuhan* basin. **2** area of beach par- titioned off and used for bathing.

limbungan dock.

pelimbungan inner harbor. ~ *kapal* dock, slipway.

limbung II (*J*) **1** unstable, unsteady. *berdiri* – unbalanced, shaky. **2** to vacillate. **3** confused, bewildered.

melimbung to shake s.t.

limbur I *sambur* – dimly visible, dusky; → KABUR I, SAMBUK II.

limbur II (*M*) **melimbur** to inundate, flood; → MEMBANJIRI, MENGGENANGI. *dilimbur bah/pasang* to be flooded.

limfa → LIMPA.

limit (*D/E*) limit.

limnologi (*D/E*) limnology.

limolas (*Jv*) fifteen; → LIMA *belas*.

nglimolasi to charge 15 percent interest on a loan.

limonade (*D*) lemonade; → LIMUN II.

limosin (*D/E*) limousine.

limpa 1 spleen. **2** (in some regions) liver; → HATI I. – *kecil* pancreas. **3** lymph.

berlimpa with a spleen. *tidak* ~ (*coq*) insensitive, harsh.

limpah 1 abundant(ly), plentiful(ly), ample, amply. – *minyak* oil glut. **2** lavish(ly), rich(ly). **3** generous(ly). **4** affluent(y). **5** pro- fuse(ly). – *méwah* luxurious. **kelimpah-méwahan** luxury, pro- fusion. – *ruah* abundant, overflowing, full. **melimpah-ruah** to overflow. **kelimpah-ruahan** affluence, boom, affluent times.

berlimpah-limpah 1 to overflow. **2** overflowing, abound, abun- dant, in abundance.

berlimpahan abundant, much.

melimpah 1 to overflow (of rivers/rage/fury), run over; full to overflowing, chock-full (of a glass/mailbox, etc.); over(popu- lated). *air* ~ *dari sungai* and *sungai* ~ the river is overflowing; → MELUAP. **2** abundant, plentiful, copious, profuse; lots/plenty of (money, etc.). **3** to flock (to). *beribu-ribu orang* ~ *ke* ... thou- sands of people flocked to ... **4** to spread (and become a revolt/ insurrection, etc.). **5** to pass on (of qualities to descendants).

melimpah-limpah in abundance. *pasar(an)* ~ a) the market is overstocked (with) (labor/commodities, etc.). b) overbusy (the market, etc.).

melimpahi 1 to confer upon, give s.o. the benefit of, be generous to. *Tuhan* ~ *hambaNya dengan* ... God confers ... upon His servants. **2** to overflow onto s.t., deluge, inundate.

melimpahkan 1 to fill s.t. to overflowing. **2** to give (abundantly/ plentifully), grant (s.o. pardon, etc.), confer, show/extend/give full confidence. ~ *gelar dokter HC kepada* to confer the title of Doctor Honoris Causa upon. ~ *air mata* to weep copiously. **3** to turn over (a case to a court), delegate (authority).

melimpah-limpahkan to increase/enlarge, make abundant (of exports/production, etc.).

terlimpah bestowed (of blessings).

limpahan 1 s.t. bestowed. **2** flow, stream. ~ *penduduk* stream of residents. **3** abundance. **4** overflow.

kelimpahan 1 affluence, luxury. **2** abundance, plentifulness. (*masa*) ~ *minyak* oil boom. **3** profusion.

pelimpah spilling. *bangunan* ~ spillway (as from a reservoir).

pelimpahan delegation, delegating. ~ *kewenangan* delegation of authority.

limpang-limpung (*Jv*) baked sweet potatoes.

limpap berlimpap(-limpap) 1 piled one on top of the other. **2** too much (about money).

limpapas and **limpepas** (*M ob*) k.o. moth, butterfly.

limpas (*J*) to run off (of liquid). *jembatan* – run-off bridge.

melimpas to be wet with rainwater.

melimpaskan to let a liquid run off (or, overflow).

limpasan (*mining*) runoff. ~ *air tanah* groundwater runoff.

pelimpas overflow. *saluran* ~ spillway.

pelimpasan running off, overflowing.

limpit (*M*) lamina, layer; → LAPIS I.

berlimpit-limpit in layers/sheets.

memperlimpitkan to put one layer on top of another.

limpoh (*M ob*) heap, pile (of rice/fruits, etc.).

limpung I (*Jv cla*) k.o. javelin.

limpung II to run back and forth.

kelimpungan to run back and forth not knowing what to do.

limpung III (*Jv*) baked banana; *cp* LIMPANG-LIMPUNG.

limpung IV (*S*) **kelimpungan 1** paralyzed, crippled; → KELUMPUHAN. **2** lost (subscribers to a magazine).

limpung V wren-babbler, *Napothera macrodactyla*.

limpungan k.o. weed, Joe Pye weed, *Eupatorium spp*.

limun I invisible. *ilmu* – (*Mal*) *doa* – spell to make o.s. invisible.

limunan invisibility.

limun II (*D?*) a bottled, citrus-flavored and carbonated soft drink; → LIMONADE. – *jahé* a soft drink flavored with ginger. – *skuas* lemon squash.

limur → LIMBUR I.

limusin (*E*) limousine.

limut melimut abundant.

lin I (*D*) (geometry) line; → GARIS.

lin II (*D*) ribbon; → PITA.

lin III (*D*) (of a tramcar/bus, etc.) route, line (number); → JALUR I

3. *dengan bis* – 4 by bus number 4. – *yang ke Kebayoran* the Kebayoran bus, the bus which goes to Kebayoran. – *gemuk* (in
shipping and aviation circles) profitable routes. – *kurus* unprofitable routes (domestic routes used only for prestige and
politics). – *penerbangan* airline, air-route.

lin IV (in acronyms) → LINTASAN.

linakini (*gay sl*) boyfriend.

linan → LINEN.

linang berlinang(-linang) and **melinang 1** to shimmer; shimmering (as velvet). **2** to trickle (down), drip, fall in drops (of tears,
sweat).

    melinangkan to shed (tears).

    linangan ~ *airmata* tears; weeping.

linau nibong palm, *Oncosperma filamentosa*.

lincah 1 fidgety, restless. **2** not permanent, inconstant, always
changing, fickle (as of minds/job/dwelling/wife, etc.); fluctuating, shifting, unreliable. **3** active, energetic, quick-moving, agile,
dynamic, mobile, lively, brisk.

    berlincah (*pl obj*) to make energetic movements.

    melincah-lincah and **terlincah-lincah 1** constantly changing/
moving, restlessly, always shifting. **2** to jump/skip from one
subject to the next.

    melincahkan to animate.

    kelincahan 1 restlessness, fidgetiness. **2** activity, agility.

lincak I (*Jv*) low bamboo bench.

lincak II → LINCAH.

lincam (*M*) **melincam 1** to flash (of lightning/weapon). **2** to stab
quickly. **3** (to disappear) in a twinkling, as quick as a flash.

    selincam (~ *kerling*) a brief moment.

lincin (*ob*) → LICIN.

lincip (*Jv*) sharp, pointed.

lincir 1 slippery, smooth. **2** to go/run smoothly, without a hitch. **3**
lubricating. *minyak* – lubricating oil. **4** fluent (of speech). **5**
slide, sliding. – *lidahnya*. He has the gift of gab. – *mulut* a) glib.
b) smooth talking, misleading.

    melincirkan to smooth (out), lubricate (the running of a ma-
chine, etc.).

    kelinciran 1 slickness, slipperiness. **2** oiliness.

    pelincir 1 lubricant. *uang* ~ bribe. **2** slider (k.o. control knob).

    pelinciran lubrication.

lincun (*ob*) *basah* – soaking wet; → BASAH *kuyup*.

lindak (*M*) **berlindak-lindak** in confused heaps (of coins/fruits/
logs, etc.); → BERLAMBAK-LAMBAK.

lindang (*M*) finished, gone, used up, consumed; vanished. *lenyap*
– vanished into thin air. – *landai/tandas* all gone.

    melindang *lenyap* ~ vanished into thin air.

    melindangkan 1 to run low on, run out of. **2** to cause to vanish/
disappear, squander, dissipate.

lindap (*M*) **1** lee; shade. *di bawah* – *pohon kurma* in the shade of a
date tree. *berdiri di* – *di belakang orang* to remain in the background. **2** vaguely (visible); → SAMAR. **3** indistinct, unclear, obscure (utterance, etc.). *pertanyaan yang* – an unclear question.
4 (*hari*) – overcast (day); → MENDUNG. **5** extinguished, over (of
a fire/lamp/riot/life/anger/lust), quenched (of thirst). **6** subdued (light). **7** underexposed.

    lindap-lindap ~ *layu* died away (of footlights).

    melindap 1 to become blurred, dim (of light); → MENGABUR. **2**
to cool down (of the heat), go down (of a fever, etc.). **3** disappeared slowly; → LINDANG.

    pelindapan quenching.

lindas crush.

    melindas 1 to crush. **2** to run over. **3** to suppress.

    melindasi (*pl obj*) to run over, crush.

    terlindas [and **kelindas** (*coq*)] crushed, run over.

    pelindas mortar.

lindes → LINDAS.

lindi lye, lixivium; alkaline.

    melindi to leach.

    pelindi s.t. that leaches.

    pelindian leaching.

lindih (*Jv M*) **melindih** to level *sawah* land with a board, press
down firmly on.

lindis (*M*) **1** → LINDIH. **2** to suppress, subdue, overpower and crush,
defeat.

    pelindis roller.

lindu (*Jv*) earthquake.

lindung I protective cover, concealment, protection, protective. –
nilai (*fin*) hedging.

    berlindung 1 (= **berselindung**) to take cover/shelter; to hide, be
in hiding, conceal o.s., lie low. *tempat* ~ sanctuary. **2** to seek
protection from s.o. else's power.

    melindung 1 to form a shelter/protection from, protect(ed),
guard(ed)/against. **2** to be under the wing/aegis of (refers to
privately owned ships under the aegis/patronage of *Pélni*).

    melindungi [and **ngelindungin** (*J coq*)] **1** to shelter/protect/
shield from; protective. *dilindungi oléh* under the aegis of. **2** to
protect against. **3** to safeguard. ~ *dari* to guard/save from. **4**
to hide, cover up, conceal (ugly qualities/fear). **5** to hide (s.t.
behind s.t. else, for example moonlight hidden by clouds).

    memperlindungi to shelter s.t. from.

    me(mper)lindungkan 1 to conceal/hide s.t. **2** to protect, safe-
guard, save. ~ *nyawa* to save one's life. **3** to take into protective custody.

    terlindung 1 hidden, concealed, sheltered. **2** protected, safe-
guarded. **3** restricted.

    terlindungi protected.

    lindungan 1 s.t. protected. **2** hide-out; → PERLINDUNGAN **2**. **3**
protection; → PERLINDUNGAN **1**. – *tinjau* protection.

    kelindungan 1 overshadowed, surpassed. **2**a) s.t. has been re-
moved from one's sight. b) one's view was impeded by s.t. **3**
protected, sheltered. *tempat yang* ~ a protected spot. **4** toned
down, subdued (of color). *ungu* ~ subdued violet.

    pelindung 1 s.o. who protects, protector. **2** patron. **3** guard, s.t.
which protects, protective, cover. *lapisan* ~ protective coating. ~ *kepala* head guard. ~ *mata* goggles. ~ *nilai* (*fin*) hedge,
hedging. ~ *picu* trigger guard. ~ *tangan* hand guard. ~ *terik
matahari* sun visor.

    pelindungan (*ob*) toilet, water closet. **2** protection.

    perlindungan 1 protection, cover. *di bawah* ~ under the aegis
of. ~ *alam* nature preservation. ~ *binatang* prevention of cruelty to animals. ~ *hukum* legal protection, safeguarding of
legal rights. ~ *masyarakat* civil defense. ~ *sosial* social pro-
tection/security. ~ *udara* air cover/umbrella. **2** (*tempat* ~)
hiding place, hide-out, dugout, shelter. **3** protectionist (barriers, etc.).

lindung II (*J*) eel.

lindung III k.o. climber, snake gourd, *Trichosanthes anguina*.

lindur (*J/Jv*) **melindur** [and **ngelindur** (*J*)] to sleepwalk; to talk in
one's sleep; → MENGIGAU.

linen (*E*) linen (material). – *ampelas* scouring pad.

linés (*gay sl*) lesbian.

ling I a measure of ½ *chupak*.

ling II (in acronyms) → LINGKUNGAN.

lingar melingar (to keep looking around) restlessly.

lingga I (*Skr*) **1** memorial, monument. – *alam* nature preserve, nature park.

lingga II – *api* k.o. tree, *Dysoxylon dumosum*.

lingga III (*Skr*) **1** phallus. **2** the phallic symbol used in the worship of the Hindu god Siva.

linggam red lead; → SEDELINGGAM.

linggata k.o. stinging nettle.

linggayuran (*M ob*) tall and slender (of palm trees).

linggi and **linggi-linggi** the covered/decked portions at the prow
and stern of a boat. – *muka* cutwater.

linggis I (*Jv*) crowbar, long hoe, jimmy; → ALABANGKA.

    melinggis to break open (or, dig up) with a crowbar.

linggis II **linggisan** ~ *dayung* (*ob*) a long pole fixed alongside a
boat's gunwale as a rest for oars.

lingir arris.

lingkah → TELINGKAH.

lingkap (*cla*) cleaned out; spent (of money).

lingkar 1 band, coil (of a rope/rattan/snake's body), roll (of wire). **2**
(– *roda*) (wheel)rim. **3** hoop (of a barrel). **4** circumference. –
bumi circumference of the earth. – *dada* chest size. – *inti* inner

circle, core. – *luar* outer ring (road). – *ular* coils of a snake. – *usia* service life (of material).

selingkar *di* ~ in the surrounding(s).

berlingkar 1 to roll up, wind around, twine, twist. **2** curved, coiled. *duduk* ~ to sit in a circle. *tidur* ~ *sebagai ular* to sleep all coiled up like a snake.

melingkar 1 twisted, coiled; to go round and round, circular. **2** to roll up (a cable, etc.). **3** to coil, wind, twist, curl (around). *Seékor ular* ~ *di badannya.* A snake coiled around her body.

melingkari 1 to coil/twine/twist/spiral/wind around s.t. ~ *dahan nangka* spiraling around the jackfruit branch. **2** to encircle, surround. *dilingkari* to be surrounded (by hills, etc.). *berjalan* ~ *rumah* to walk around the house.

melingkarkan 1 to coil s.t., bend s.t. into a circle. ~ *tubuh* to curl up. **2** to bend s.t. around (s.t. else).

terlingkar 1 in circles/coils, coiled. **2** (hair) wound (around the head).

lingkaran 1 circle, (of a) circular (form); cycle, circuit; coil, spiral. **2** circumference, perimeter. **3** territory, district, area. ~ *arus* (*elec*) circuit. ~ *arus terpadu* integrated circuit. ~ *buta/gila* vicious circle. ~ *haid* menstrual cycle. ~ *inti/keliling* inner circle, core. ~ *Kutub Selatan* Antarctic Circle. ~ *Kutub Utara* Arctic Circle. ~ *mimang/sétan/tak berujung* (*ber*)*pangkal/yang jahat* vicious circle/cycle. ~ *putar* turning circle. ~ *sosial* social circles. ~ *tumbuh* growth ring (of trees).

lingkas (*ob*) → RINGKAS.

lingkis (*Jv ob*) **melingkis(kan)** to roll up (one's sleeves).

lingkun (*J*) penis.

lingkung 1 circle. **2** perimeter. *sambal –* (in Palembang) k.o. *sambal*.

selingkung: *di* ~ a) (and *dalam* ~) all over, everywhere in (that area/building, etc.). b) all around (a table, etc.); → LINGKUP I, LIPUT. ~ *kampung* all around (the village).

melingkung to fence (in).

melingkungi 1 to surround. **2** to enclose; ringed in with, walled in by. **3** to envelop, encircle. **4** to include, cover.

terlingkung 1 surrounded, enclosed. **2** included.

lingkungan 1 concentric ring, circle. **2** circles. ~ *sosial* circle of acquaintances. ~ *yang mengetahui* well-informed circles. **3** domain. **4** circumference, perimeter. **5** the earth, environment, (natural) setting, surroundings. *ahli* ~ environmentalist. *aktivis pecinta* ~ environmental activists. *ilmu-ilmu* ~ environmental studies. *pendidikan* ~ eco-education. *sesuai dengan* ~ adaptable to the environment. ~ *alam* environment. ~ *hayat* biosphere. ~ *hidup* a) environment. b) (*sistém* ~) ecosystem. ~ *hunian* residential area. ~ *industri* industrial estate; → KAWASAN *industri*. ~ *keluarga* within the family. ~ *kerja* work environment. ~ *pemukiman* residential area. ~ *pengaruh* sphere of influence. ~ *peradilan* jurisdiction. ~ *peruntukan* zoning. ~ *sewajarnya* natural setting. ~ *umur* age bracket. ~ *waktu* time zone. **6** (in Lombok) → DÉSA.

lingkup I 1 scope. **2** covered/veiled at the top. *tudung –* veil; *cp* KUDUNG II. *bertudung –* to wear a veil. **3** area. *– pengaruh* area of influence.

berlingkup to have a(n) ... scope. ~ *nasional* to have a national scope.

melingkupi 1 to cover s.t. **2** to embrace, surround, encompass, enclose, envelop, overwhelm. **3** to overlap. **4** to envelop, overcome, overwhelm. *dilingkupi damba* to be overcome by desire. *dilingkupi kepelikan* to be overwhelmed/inundated with problems.

lingkup-melingkupi to overlap e.o.

terlingkup screened, covered, sheltered, enveloped, veiled.

pelingkupan scoping.

lingkup II (*M*) (to go somewhere/attack/gather) in large numbers.

linglung 1 dazed, stunned. **2** preoccupied, absent-minded, lost one's memory, confused.

melinglungkan to upset, confuse.

lingsa (*Jv*) nits.

lingsang (*Jv*) k.o. otter or related animal such as weasel, marten, *Prionodon gracilis*.

lingsem (*Jv*) ashamed, embarrassed.

lingsir (*Jv*) to be slanting, be low in the sky (of the sun/moon). –

kulon when the sun is low in the west. – *wétan* when the sun is low in the east. *menjelang –* just before sunset.

melingsir to set (of the sun).

melingsirkan to let slide, pull down. ~ *lengan baju* to pull down one's sleeves.

lingual (*E*) lingual.

linguis (*E*) linguist.

linguistik (*E*) linguistic(s); → ILMU *bahasa*, WIDYABASA. *Lembaga –* Linguistics Institute.

linguistis (*D*) linguistic.

lini (*E*) **1** line. **2** run (aircraft). *– belakang* back line. *– depan* front line. *– Manado-Jakarta* the Jakarta-Manado run. *– pendukung* backup line. *– produk* product line. *– rakit* assembly line. *– tengah* center line.

Li Niha the language of the island of Nias.

linimén (*E*) liniment.

linjak melinjak to trample on.

linjang (in South Sumatra) **berlinjangan** and **selinjang 1** to flirt. **2** to court, try to get ... to love one.

linoléum (*E*) linoleum.

linsang → LINGSANG.

lintabung (*M*) a grass species used as fodder for cattle, *Panicum palmifolium. ilmu –* proud but silly (person).

lintadu (*ob*) mantis; → SENTADU I.

lintah leech. *– darat* bloodsucker, profiteer, usurer, loan shark. **melintah darat** to lend out money at exorbitant rates. *– melong* leech that swells out into a pear-like shape, *Chthonobdella sumatrana. – padi* k.o. leech, *Hirundo vittata. – paya/ perca* buffalo leech, *Hirundinaria javanica.*

lintahan k.o. medicinal plant, *Desmodium latifolium.*

lintang I 1 width, breadth; *opp* BUJUR. *-nya empat méter* it's four meters wide. **2** along the width, across, crosswise. **3** (degree of) latitude. *garis –* degree of latitude. *kayu –* crossbeam. *letak –* transverse. *sanggul –* knot of hair positioned crosswise. *– angkasa* celestial latitude. *– batang* barrier placed across a river. *– bujur* a) diagonal. b) (to go/run) every which way (or, in all directions). *– bumi* terrestrial latitude. *– kapal* abeam. *– kedak* topsy-turvy. *– kencono* k.o. magic which protects one from harm. *– pukang* a) topsy-turvy, in disorder, in a mess. b) (to run) helter-skelter. c) from all sides. *– selatan* southern latitude.

melintang 1 to lie across/diagonally/in the way, transverse. *dicocok* ~ to be drilled through transversely. **2** to prevent, hamper; → BELINTANG. **3** to block, obstruct. *aral* ~ unforeseen circumstances; hindrance. *malang* ~ an unexpected hindrance/accident, etc.

melintangi 1 to prevent, hinder, impede, obstruct. **2** to oppose, contradict.

melintangkan to place across, intersect.

terlintang 1 placed crosswise, put athwart. **2** obstructed, blocked, impeded.

lintangan s.t. that goes across, obstruction, obstacle, hindrance; → RINTANG(AN).

lintang II (*Jv*) star; → BINTANG. *– kemukus* comet.

lintap stack, pile.

lintar → HALILINTAR.

lintas 1 pass (by) (quickly). *tak – di akal* illogical; unacceptable; not plausible. *– pintas* back and forth, to and fro. *hak – damai* innocent passage (for foreign ships through the Straits of Malacca, etc.). *lalu –* traffic; → LALU I. *program –* crash program. **2** cross. *tim – départemén* cross-department team. *psikologi – budaya* cross-cultural psychology. **3a)** line, route, track, path, trajectory. b) stretch, leg, section (of a route), way. *– Panjang-Merak* the Panjang to Merak leg. **4** trans-. *– nasional* transnational. **5** -borne. *– air* airborne. *– alam* cross-country. *– batas* border-crossing. *– bébas* free passage; → HAK *lintas damai*. *– budaya* cross-cultural. *– cabang* feeder line. *– édar* orbit. *– élak* evasive action. *– jarak jauh* trunk line. *– laut* seaborne. *– léwat* overpass. *– médan* cross-country. *– Nusantara* "Crossing the Indonesian Archipelago," i.e., the name of the travel program for prospective and young diplomats to give them an understanding of their country beyond Jakarta. *– peluru* trajectory of projectile. *– pintas* heavy traffic. *– raya* overpass. *– sébra/zébra* zebra crossing (at intersection). – *tapal batas* border-crossing. – *udara* airborne. – *utama* trunk line. – *utara* northern route (across Java). – *wahana* transient (visitor). – *waktu* time line.

selintas at a glance; (to be heard just) for a moment. ~ *lalu* a) at first sight; by ear. b) at once, in a flash. c) at first (... and then ...). d) on the face of it, superficially.

melintas 1 to pass quickly (in front of s.o.). ~ *masuk di* to ride into (a train, etc.). **2** to take a shortcut. **3** to cross (a street). **4** to flash through one's mind for a moment. ~ *wajah mendiang ibunya dalam angan-angannya.* His late mother's face flashed through his mind.

melintas-lintas to keep on passing/occurring.

melintasi 1 to flash (by), pass (by); by way of, via, by; → MELALUI. ~ *udara* by air. **2a)** to cross (a street/river); → MENYEBERANGI. b) to cross (s.t.) diagonally. *"headline" yang* ~ a banner headline. **3** to overcome, surmount, get over (obstacles/difficulties); → MENGATASI.

terlintas pass/flash (through) (s.o.'s mind). *tak pernah* ~ *di benaknya* never passed though her mind (that), never occurred to her (that), never dreamt (that). ~ *dalam pikiran* to cross/ pass through one's mind, occur to one.

lintasan 1 a flash. **2** road, course, track, path, pathway, lane. ~ *atas* overpass. ~ *jalan kereta api* grade crossing. ~ *lurus* straight path. ~ *suara* sound track. **3** place one goes through. *kota* ~ transit town (on the way to somewhere else). ~ *laut* sea route. ~ *proyéktil* trajectory. ~ *udara* air route. **4** a traverse. **5** orbit.

kelintasan passed, surpassed, overtaken, late. *(ber)pantang* ~ do not want to be passed/surpassed/overtaken, i.e., to want to be the cock of the walk. *Ia* ~ *adiknya.* His younger sibling has married before he did.

pelintas s.o. who crosses. ~ *batas/perbatasan* border-crosser. ~ *kendaraan* those who cross (a bridge) by car.

perlintasan 1 transfer, transition. ~ *jaman* transition period. **2** (*Pal*) present from the groom to the bride's unmarried older sister. ~ *pesawat* taxiway (on airfield).

linter (*J*) **selinter** and **melinter** to wander around.

melinteri and **nglinterin** to wander around s.t.

linterik name of a *ceki* card.

lintibang (*M*) millipede; → LIPAN.

lintih (*ob*) → PERLINTIH.

linting I (*Jv*) rolled up (a cigarette), in the form of a roll; counter for handmade cigarettes. *empat* – *rokok ganja* four marijuana cigarettes/joints.

selinting a cigarette. ~ *gélé* a (marijuana) joint.

melinting to roll (a cigarette); → TINGWÉ.

lintingan rolled. *rokok* ~ a rolled cigarette.

pelinting device for rolling cigarettes.

pelintingan rolling (cigarettes).

linting II (*J*) wick of an oil lamp.

lintir (*Jv*) **melintir 1** to roll (a cigarette). **2** to spin, skid, roll.

pelintiran (in table-tennis) spin.

lintuh (*M*) soft, gentle, flaccid, weak.

pelintuh charm to make a woman fall in love with you.

lintup completely covered, closed (of doors), all covered (with veils).

melintup(i) to cover completely and carefully.

linu I smarting/shooting pains (in one's teeth/nerves, etc.), sharp pain (from hearing the sounds of sawing/sharpening metal, etc.).

linu II (*J*) earthquake.

Linud [*Lintas Udara*] Airborne.

linuhung (*Jv*) **1** lofty, exalted. **2** sophisticated; → CANGGIH I.

linyak (*M*) flat (of trampled or pressed-down objects).

berlinyak to quarrel.

melinyak to trample/step on (s.t. until it becomes flattened), flatten; to grind, crush, run over.

linyap → LENYAP.

linyar melinyar to glide over the water.

lio (*C J*) **1** brickyard. **2** tile works. *berusaha* – to be in the brick/ tile business.

liong (*C*) paper lion carried around at processions.

liontin (*E*) medallion, locket, pendant.

lipai small screen used as an umbrella in a sudden storm.

lipa-lipa → LÉPA-LÉPA.

lipan centipede, *Chilipoda/Lithobius/Scutigera spp.* – *sama kala* when Greek meets Greek.

lipas cockroach, *Periplaneta spp.*; → CORO I, KAKERLAK, KECOA(K), KEPUYUK. *ékor* – (*Mal*) curls at the nape of the neck. *mata* – a) colorless eyes (as of a horse). b) dull (eyes). – *kudung* a) brown cockroach, *Periplaneta orientalis.* b) (*Mal*) metaphor for s.o. who works very fast. *seperti* – *kudung* a) always in motion (of hands, etc.). b) apparently busy. – *air* water beetle.

lipat 1 s.t. folded; folded, folding, collapsible. *kajang* – awning folded in two. *kursi* – folding chair. *pisau* – pocketknife. *tempat tidur* – folding/foldaway bed. **2** multiple, -fold. – *dua/empat kali* two/fourfold. **3** ... times as much/many. *dua/tiga/empat kali* – twice/three times/four times that much. – *dua* twofold, double. ***melipat-duakan*** to double. – *empat* fourfold. ***melipat-empatkan*** to multiply by four. – *ganda* doubled, multiplied. ***berlipat ganda*** doubled, multiplied, manifold, many times over. ***melipat-gandakan*** and ***memperlipatgandkan*** to multiply, increase (again and again). ***pelipat-gandaan*** augmentation, increasing. – *kajang* folded in two. – *paha* groin. – *pandan* style of hairdo with a bow across the back of the head. – *tiga* threefold. ***melipat-tigakan*** to triple.

selipat folder.

berlipat 1 folded. *kain yang* ~ *pada tepinya* a piece of cloth folded at the edges. **2** to multiply by, (become) ... times as much. *hasilnya* ~ *tiga* the result is three times as much (as earlier). ~ *perut* able to keep a secret. ~ *ganda* multiple.

berlipat-lipat 1 in layers/many folds. **2** multiple; → BERLIPAT ganda.

melipat 1 to fold. *Jangan dilipat!* (printed on envelopes containing photographs, etc.) Do not fold! ~ *surat* to fold a letter. ~ *dua/tiga/empat* to fold in two/three/four. **2a)** to embezzle, misappropriate (money). b) to round up (criminals), break up (a gang). c) to arrest (gamblers/thieves, etc.). d) to sell off s.t. *Dia terpaksa* ~ *méja kursinya.* He was forced to sell off his furniture. e) to disregard, ignore. f) to tuck away (food). *Makanan sebanyak itu dilipatnya habis-habis.* He tucked away that much food. ~ *flénsa* to flange. **3** (*coq*) to become ...-fold (double/triple, etc.). *Harga barang-barang itu* ~ *dua.* The price of those goods has doubled. **4** to bend (ones' knee). **5** (*coq*) to beat, defeat. ~ *bendéra* a) to fold a flag. b) to surrender, give up.

lipat-melipat 1 to fold (paper, etc. into fancy shapes). **2** (*coq*) to manipulate s.t. in a deceptive way. *Prakték* ~ *uang negara itu merajaléla.* The practice of manipulating state funds is raging.

melipatkan 1 to fold together. **2** to multiply; → MELIPAT-GAN-DAKAN. ~ *dua* to double.

memperlipatkan to increase, increment.

terlipat folded.

lipatan 1 s.t. that is folded, fold, crease. **2** pack of playing cards, set of cards. **3** fold, folding. ~ *condong* (*geol*) inclined fold. ~ *kelopak* nappe fold. **berkelipatan** → BERLIPAT 2.

kelipatan (*math*) multiple. *15 ialah* – *5* 15 is a multiple of 5. ~ *persekutuan terkecil* least common denominator.

pelipat ~ *lutut* hollow of the knee.

pelipatan 1 fold, folding. **2** multiplication.

perlipatan 1 folding. **2** multiplication.

lipen(setip) (*D ob*) lipstick.

lip(p)enstip lipstick.

liperi → LÉPERI.

lipet → LIPAT. **kelipet** → TERLIPAT.

lipir → LÉPÉR I.

lipis → PELIPIS(AN).

lipit (= **pelipit** and **lipitan**) hem, crenulation.

melipit to hem, crenulate.

lipitan crenulation.

liplap I tidbit, delicacy.

liplap II (*E ob*) *Belanda* – a derogatory term for a Eurasian of Dutch-Indonesian descent. *anak* – child of a mixed-race marriage.

liplap III in thin layers (of different colors). *emas* – imitation/ Dutch gold, tinsel, brass foil.

liplip → LIP-LAP II.

lipstik (*E*) lipstick; → GINCU.

lipu (*ob*) **melipu** tarnished, lost its brightness/shine, dull, lackluster.

lipur I (*M*) lost, disappeared. *tak dapat kita – saja* cannot be ignored.

melipur(kan) 1 to cause to disappear, make disappear. **2** to remove/obliterate/efface/wipe out (traces/marks, etc.). **3** to avoid (feelings of fear/shame) (by looking away).

lipur II (*J/Jv*) consoled, quieted down (after being angry); → LILI-PUR.

melipur(kan) 1 to console, soothe, comfort, solace. **2** to entertain.

lipuran comfort.

pe(ng)lipur comfort(er). *memberi ~ hati* to bring relief, ease the strain/pain. *pembacaan ~* light/recreational reading. *~ lara* consolation, comfort, s.t. that consoles/comforts.

liput (*M*) cover. *~ dua* double. *meliput-duakan* to double.

berliput covered, enveloped, flooded, inundated.

meliput to cover (a story/situation, etc.).

meliputi 1 to cover s.t., encompass. **2** to inundate, flood. **3** to comprise, include. **4** to overshadow, overcome, dominate (one's thoughts); to seize, take over, haunt (one's feelings). *diliputi ketakutan* (to be) fear-stricken. *diliputi ombak* awash. *masyarakat yang diliputi suasana korupsi* a corruption-ridden society. *diliputi perasaan resah* haunted by an uneasy feeling.

terliput 1 covered, flooded, blanketed. **2** enclosed, included. **3** overwhelmed, dominated.

liputan 1 cover. *~ awan* cloud cover. *~ udara* (*mil*) air cover. **2** coverage, reporting. *mendapat ~* be covered (of events). *~ ilmiah* scientific reporting. *~ menyelidik* investigative reporting.

peliput 1 (in journalism) coverage. *wartawan ~ perang* war correspondents. *wartawan ~ SU MPR* correspondents covering the MPR General Session. **2** s.o. who covers (the news). *~ resmi* official reporters.

peliputan (in journalism) coverage. *~ berita* news coverage.

lir I (*Jv*) like. *sang – sari* flower-like goddess (said of a beautiful woman). *– angkasa kang angemu dahan* like the sky burning with fire. *– gabah dén interi* "like winnowed paddy grains," i.e., scattered.

lir II (*D*) winch. *– jangkar* windlass.

lira I (*D*) lyre.

lira II (*D/E*) lira (Italian currency).

lirak *– lirik* to look around.

liran k.o. giant palm tree, *Pholidocarpus majadum*.

lirih (*J/Jv*) low, soft (of sound). *katanya –* (he) said softly. *tertawa –* to laugh softly.

lirih-lirih softly (of sounds).

melirihkan 1 to lower (one's voice). **2** to turn down (the radio, etc.).

lirik I melirik to drill (a hole); to bore into s.t. (of squirrels).

lirik II a stealthy glance.

selirik at a glance.

melirik to look at, eye.

melirik(-lirik)kan *~ ke* to look stealthily at.

lirikan glance.

pelirikan glancing.

lirik III (*D/E*) (song) lyric.

berlirik ... with the lyrics ...

liris I *corak –* name of a batik design.

liris II (*D*) lyrical, emotional.

liron reciprocation.

pelironan reciprocating.

liru → KELIRU.

lis I (*D*) → LÉS IV **1** rail(ing). **2** welt (on clothes). **3** trim. *– atas* cornice. *– cuaca* weatherstripping. *– jendéla* window molding. *– karét kaca mobil* weatherstripping (for car). *– lukisan* picture frame. *– tétés* drip rail.

lis II → LÉS II.

lisa → LINGSA.

Lisabon Lisbon.

lisah I → GELISAH.

lisah II (*ikan –*) k.o. fish, goby, *Periophthalmus schlosseri/koelreuteri*.

lisan (*A*) **1** tongue. **2** oral, verbal, spoken (language). *bahasa –* spoken language. *dengan –* orally. *dengan – atau tulisan* orally or in writing. *keterangan –* (*leg*) oral testimony. *ujian –* oral examination, orals.

melisankan to put into words, express, utter, recite.

lisani (*A*) oral. *huruf –* (*ling*) linguals.

lisénsi (*D*) license, permit.

melisénsikan to license.

perlisénsian licensing.

lisnar (*ob*) → LÉSNAR.

lisol → RISOL.

lisong (*C J*) cigar.

lisplang (*D*) molding.

listerik → LISTRIK.

listrik (*D*) **1** electricity. *sudah masuk/dimasuki –* has been electrified. *Dirjén – dan Énérgi* Director General of Electricity and Energy. *konsumén –* electricity consumer. *Perusahaan – Negara* [PLN] National Electricity Company. **2** electric. *bangunan pembangkit –* powerhouse. *daya –* electric power. *gardu –* powerhouse, generating plant. *sambungan –* electric connection. *tenaga –* electric power. **3** electrical. *hubungan péndék –* electrical short circuit. *– mati* blackout, power outage.

berlistrik to have electric power, be electrified.

melistriki to electrify, provide with electricity.

terlistiki electrified.

kelistrikan electricity, electrification. *pembangunan ~* electricity development.

pe(r)listrikan 1 electricity (*mod*). *bisnis perlistrikan* the electricity business. **2** electrical.

listris (*ob*) electrical.

lisu (*geol*) rift.

lisut 1 wrinkled, furrowed; flattened (after being swollen). *Bengkaknya –.* The swelling receded. **2** wilted, faded. **3** withered, atrophied. **4** senile, wizened.

melisut to become wrinkled/flattened out.

melisutkan to wrinkle, furrow, wizen.

kelisutan wrinkling, flattening.

pelisutan atrophy.

lit (in acronyms) → PENELITIAN.

litah (*– mulut*) garrulous, talkative, blabber-mouth.

litak (*M*) **1** exhausted, worn-out, tired. **2** hungry; → LÉTAK. **3** deprived (of oxygen, etc.).

litani (*D/E*) (Roman Catholic) litany.

litenan → LÉTNAN.

liter (*D*) liter.

berliter-liter by the liter.

literan 1 liter (measure). **2** by the liter.

literal (*D/E*) literal.

literator (*D*) literary man, litterateur.

literatur (*D/E*) literature.

literér (*D*) literary.

litigasi (*D*) litigation.

litium (*D/E*) lithium.

litnan → LÉTNAN.

litografi (*D/E*) lithography.

litotés (*D*) litotes.

litsus [penelitian khusus] special investigation for security purposes, clearance.

litup tightly covered so that s.t. cannot be seen. *berselimut –* bundled up.

melitupi to cover/seal up.

liturgi (*D*) liturgy.

liuk (= **meliuk**) to bend aside (of a tree, etc., due to the wind). *– lampai* swaying (like a snake/dancer, etc.); supple, flexible.

meliuki to pick s.t. up (from the ground) by bending over.

meliukkan 1 to swing (one's body) aside to evade (a blow), dodge. **2** to wriggle s.t.

terliuk(-liuk) bent over.

peliuk bend over. *sepeliuk ~ jauhnya* as far as one can reach by bending over.

liuk-liuk k.o. flute made from a paddy stem.

liung-liung k.o. marine fish.

liur *air –* saliva, spit; → LUDAH. *menerbitkan/menimbulkan air –* to make one's mouth water, make one salivate. *Menitik air –nya.* His mouth watered. *air – basi* a) the unpleasant taste in one's mouth on getting up from sleep. b) empty talk, drivel. *menjilat air –nya* to eat one's words.

be(r)liur and **meliur** to salivate.

terliur to long/yearn for.

liurai (in East Timor) village chief.

liut tough, leathery; → LIAT I.

liver (D) → LÉVER II.

liwa (A) flag; standard.

liwaat(h) → LIWAT II.

liwat I past; → LÉWAT.

liwat(h) II (A) sodomy; to have sexual intercourse with an animal or anal intercourse.

liwet (Jv) cooked in water until all the water is gone.
   meliwet to cook rice that way.

liyak → LIHAT.

liyer-liyer (Jv) to doze.

l.k. (abbr) → LEBIH kurang.

LN [luar negeri] foreign.

lo I (J) → LHO.

lo II (Jv) pohon – k.o. tree, Ficus glomerata.

loa (C) → LOAK I.

loak I (C) bakul – rag basket. pasar – flea market, old-clothes market. tukang – a) rag dealer, junkman. b) secondhand dealer.
   meloakkan to sell s.t. old/secondhand. ~ pakaian to sell used clothes.
   loakan used. barang ~ junk, rubbish, rags, used articles. 2 flea market. di ~ at the flea market.

loak II (J) civet cat; → LUAK I, MUSANG.

lob (E sports) lob.

loba (Skr) greedy, selfish, covetous, ravenous, avaricious. – (akan) uang money-grubbing. – tama(k) greedy. **keloba-tamakan** greed, greediness, covetousness, avarice.
   melobakan to covet.
   kelobaan covetousness.

lobak (C) 1 (– putih) white/Chinese radish, daikon, Raphanus sativus/caudatus. minyak – rape-seed oil. – asin salted white radish. – cina radish, Raphanus sativus. – mérah beet, carrot. 2 (M) cabbage, Brassica oleracea.

loban I → LUBAN.

loban II k.o. marine fish, gray mullet, Mugil dussumierii, Liza macrolepsis.

lobang (J) → LUBANG. yang – digali, yang gunung diurug (J) the poor get poorer and the rich get richer.
   ngelobangin (J) to make/pierce a hole in, perforate; → MELUBANGI.
   pelobang hole maker. ~ karcis ticket-punch. ~ kertas hole punch.

loberci (D) spangles.

lobi (D/E) 1 lobby, foyer (to a hall). 2 lobby (a group of lobbyists). mengadakan/melakukan – to lobby (for).
   melobi to lobby for s.t.
   pelobi lobbyist.

lobiing (E) lobbying.

lobi-lobi tree with edible fruit, batoko plum, Flacourtia inermis.

lobster (D/E) lobster.

locah → LUCAH.

locak → KOCAK I.

locéng (C) → LONCÉNG.

loco (J/Jv) **meloco** [and **ngeloco/ngloco** (coq)] to masturbate. **loco-locoan** mutual masturbation.

locok melocok 1 (a long object, such as a gun barrel/pump, etc.) moves in and out of a hole. 2 to pound a pestle up and down on (rice, etc.). 3 to masturbate.
   locokan piston.
   pelocok 1 pestle. 2 piston rod. 3 nozzle (of hose).

locot I (J) blister (from a burn).
   melocot to blister (from a burn).
   melocoti [and **ngelocotin** (J)] 1 to skin. 2 to unsheathe (a machete, etc.).

locot II (J) **melocoti** to take off, remove (one's clothes/glasses, etc.).

loda [lotto daérah] regional/provincial lottery.

lodan (J/Jv) ikan – whale.

lodéh (Jv) sayur – a (Central Javanese) coconut milk and vegetable soup or stew.

lodoh, ngelodoh and **melodoh** to become very soft because it has gotten rotten/overripe/overcooked.

lodong (J/Jv) 1 large bamboo cylinder. 2 glass jar with stopper.

lodrok (J) → LUDRUK.

loe /lu/ → LU I.

log (in acronyms) → LOGISTIK.

logam (Tam) metal. uang – coin(s). – adi/mulia precious metal. – biasa nonalloy. – campur alloy. – hitam ferrous metal. – kasar crude metal. – panas (sl) hot lead, i.e., a bullet. – putih babbit. – tidak berkarat noncorrodable metal. – tua scrap metal. – warna nonferrous metal.

logaritma (D) logarithm.

logat (A) 1 word. terjemahan menurut – a word-by-word/literal translation (of the Koran; one not based on the meaning of the whole). ilmu – philology. 2a) a regional language or dialect. – Jakarta the Jakarta dialect. b) slang. 3 accent; pronunciation. 4 vocabulary. kitab – dictionary.
   berlogat to speak with [a certain (regional, etc.)] accent.

loge → LOSE.

logika (D) logic.

logis (D) logical, reasonable.
   melogiskan to make s.t. logical/reasonable.
   kelogisan logicality, reasonableness.

logistik (D/E) logistics.

logo (D/E) logo(type).
   berlogo with the logo of, having ... as its logo. kotak makanan ~ Garuda food boxes with the Garuda logo on them.

loh I (A) (writing) tablet. papan – school slate, blackboard. – catur chessboard; → PAPAN catur.

loh II (Jv) fertile (of land, due to adequate water supply). – jinawi a well-watered and fertile area. gemah ripah – jinawi a well-watered, fertile, prosperous and populous area.

loh III → LHO.

loha (A) forenoon (about 10:00 a.m.) sembahyang – forenoon prayer (not obligatory).

lohmahpul → LUH'ULMAHFUL (under LUH).

lohok (ob) rotting (soft), overripe; → LODOH.

lohong (M) gap, opening.

lohor (A) noon. sembahyang – noon prayer. waktu – noon (12:00 to 1:00 p.m.).

loji I (D col) 1 a lodge (the meeting place of a local chapter of a trading company, etc.). 2 office of the Dutch East India Company (1602–1800).

loji II → ARLOJI.

lojikal (E) logical.

lok (coq) (clipped form of **lokomotif**) locomotive, engine. – adhési adhesion locomotive. – bergigi cog locomotive. – lansir shunting engine. – uap steam engine.

loka (Skr) 1 (ob) world. 2 (= meloka) (ob) to see. 3 location.
   seloka in the same location.
   meloka and **memperloka** to locate.

lokah → LUKAH.

lokakarya (Skr neo) workshop.
   berlokakarya to workshop, hold a seminar or series of meetings for intensive study, work, discussion, etc.
   melokakaryakan to hold a workshop about/on.

lokal (D/E) 1 local; → SETEMPAT. 2 Local, i.e., an army captain may have a Lokal rank of major when he occupies a post to which this rank is assigned; he loses the rank when reassigned. 3 stated after a university degree, it means that the degree holder has not yet taken the State examination for his field of study, such as Sarjana Muda – and Sarmud – Local B.A.

lokalisasi (D) 1 localization. 3 confining certain activities (e.g., prostitution) to a specific area.
   melokalisasi 1 to localize. 2 to confine certain activities to a specific area. 3 to contain (a fire).
   terlokalisasi located.
   penglokalisasian localization.

lokalisir (D) **melokalisir** to localize.
   terlokalisir localized.

lokalitas locality.

lokan an edible bivalve, Polymesoda spp., found in muddy estuaries and mangrove swamps. – laut conch.
   berlokan with a ... valve.

lokananta (*Jv*) *gamelan* music from heaven.

lokap (*E*) lockup (in police station).

    melokap to lock up (a prisoner).

lokaripta operations room.

lokasi (*D*) location, site. – *judi* gambling den. – *transmigrasi* place to which people transmigrate, transmigration site – *WTS* brothel; red-light district.

    berlokasi to be located.

    melokasikan to locate.

lokat loose (of wallpaper/plaster); → LUKAT.

Lokawirasabha Member's Office Building (in *MPR* compound).

lokawisata tourist attraction.

lokcan and lokcuan (*C*) silk crepe used for men's belts.

lokék mean, stingy, miserly. *si* – the miser.

lokét (*D*) 1 box office, ticket window. 2 (in a post office/bank, etc.) window, counter. *penjaga/penunggu* – a) (in station) ticket clerk. b) (in a bank) cashier, teller. – *imigrasi* immigration counter. 3 pigeonhole.

loki (*C*) prostitute.

lokio (*C*) chives, *Allium schoenoprasum*, used as an ingredient of *asinan*.

lokir (chess) castling.

loklok (*A ob*) pearl.

loklokbungaok → PELESIT I.

lokomotif (*D/E*) locomotive, engine; → LOK. – *diesel* diesel locomotive. – *listrik* electric locomotive. – *uap* steam locomotive.

lokos 1 bald (of head). 2 bare (of land), denuded.

    melokos to denude.

    pelokosan denuding.

    lokosan denudation.

lokro (*Jv*) too loose/slack (of a button/rope, etc.).

    nglokro hopelessly.

loksék (*J*) ruined, destroyed, bankrupt, insolvent.

loksok → PELOSOK.

loksun (*C*) consumptive and spitting blood.

loktong (*C*) prostitute.

lokuttara (*Skr*) supramundane.

lola [lonté lanang] male prostitute.

lola → KELOLA.

lolak *siput* – k.o. topshell, trochus, *Trochus niloticus*.

lolak-lolok (*sl*) to look around.

loléba thin-walled bamboo, *Bambusa atra*.

loléng (*C*) 1 Chinese (paper) lantern. 2 Chinese pronunciation of the word *loréng*. *Cina* – (*J*) a Chinese speaker who substitutes l for r in Indonesian words, e.g., says *selatus lupiah* instead of *seratus rupiah*.

loli(pop) (*D*) lollipop.

loloh I (*Jv*) 1 food. 2 medication. – *balik* (*infr*) feedback; → UMPAN *balik*.

    meloloh (*J*) to feed (a baby/sick person, etc.), stuff.

loloh II (*M*) loosely fitting (of garment).

loloh III (*J*) terloloh-loloh in a hurry, hurriedly.

lolohan canal.

lolok (*ob*) melolok to watch/observe surreptitiously, spy on, scout out; → MELULUK.

lolong howling (of a dog).

    berlolongan (*pl subj*) to howl.

    melolong to yelp, howl (of dog; *esp* a long-drawn-out howl at night). memekik ~, menjerit ~ *panjang*, and menangis melolong(-lolong) to cry and shriek.

    melolongi to howl at.

    terlolong-lolong 1 to yell out unnecessarily. 2 to howl continuously.

    lolongan howl, yelp. ~ *anjing* a dog's howling/yelping.

lolopis kuntul baris (*Jv*) ho-heave-ho.

lolos 1 slipping off (as a finger-ring). 2 to slip away, escape, get away (from a cage/encirclement/jail); → LEPAS and *cp* LULUS. – *dari lobang/lubang jarum* to have had a narrow escape. (telah) – *dari maut* escaped from death. 3 passed (an exam/course). *Dia – pengujian ini*. He passed this test. – *sénsor* passed by the censor. *dilolos-sénsorkan* released/passed by the censor (of a film, etc.).

    melolos to take out, draw (a knife, etc.).

    meloloskan 1 to remove (a ring/bracelet, etc.). 2 to release, free.

~ *diri* a) to flee, escape. b) to get o.s. out of doing a task. 3 to let slip, leak (an undesirable news item, etc.). 4 (*J*) to sell s.t. off (when in need of money).

    terlolos released, escaped. ~ *dari kematian* cheated death.

    kelolosan escape, breakout.

    pelolos escapee.

    pelolosan escape, escaping.

lolot (*J*) ngelolotin to look at s.o. angrily; → MELOTOT.

lomak (*M*) → LEMAK.

lomba race, competition (in speed), contest. – *daya tahan* endurance race. – *dayung* rowboat race. – *ketahanan* endurance race (for automobile racing). – *lintas médan* cross-country race. – *berkuda* jumping competition (on horseback). – *pacu rintangan* steeplechase. – *tunggang serasi* dressage.

    berlomba to race. ~ *dengan waktu* to race against time.

    berlomba(-lomba) and berlomba(-lomba)an to race (e.o.), compete in a race (with e.o.). *Pémda berlomba-lomba mengeluarkan aturan pelaksanaan*. The provincial governments competed with e.o. in issuing implementing regulations.

    melombakan and memperlombakan to cause/have/allow to race/compete (with e.o.).

    pelomba runner, racer, competitor, contestant.

    perlombaan 1 race, contest, competition. ~ *beranting* relay race. ~ *bersambung* relay race. ~ *bersenjata* arms race. ~ *kendaraan berbunga* pageant of flowers. ~ *perahu layar* yacht race. ~ *persenjataan* arms race. ~ *renang* swimming match. ~ *ruang angkasa* space race. ~ *senjata* arms race. 2 racecourse, race track, track.

lomban (*Jv*) tradition observed on every *bada kupat* at Kartini Beach, Jepara (Central Java), for a good catch and safe return of the fishermen.

lombar (*M*) melombar 1 to pay/let out (a rope/cable, etc.); → MENGULUR. 2 to yield/give in to (a child's whims, etc.).

    lombar-melombar accommodating, obliging.

lombok several varieties of red pepper, *Capsicum*; → CABAI I. *sambal* – hot-pepper sauce. – *ijo/mérah* green/red pepper. – *belis* cayenne pepper, *Capsicum frutescens*. – *rawit* small very hot pepper, bird pepper.

lombong I 1 deep and concave (of a bowl/basin/plate). 2 (*mostly Mal*) (tin/coal/gold) mine, pit, quarry; → TAMBANG I. 3 crater. 4 chasm, cleft. *anak* – miner. – *arangbatu/batubara* coal mine. – *emas* gold mine. – *gunung berapi* volcanic crater. – *hidup* active mine. – *timah* tin mine.

    melombong to dig (in search of tin ore), operate a mine.

    pelombong miner.

lombong II (in Samarinda) a long prau which can hold 40 to 60 oarsmen and can achieve a speed of 30 to 40 kilometers per hour. It is made from a tree trunk (generally from the *pohon meranti* or the *kayu kapur*).

lomi (*C*) a noodle dish, lo mee.

lomot (*J*) nglomot to stick s.t. big into one's mouth, suck s.t. into one's mouth.

lompa *ikan* – a fish species which lives in estuaries in the Central Moluccas and Ambon, *Trissina baelama*.

lompat 1 leap, jump. – *galah* pole vault. *sekali* – in a single bound. – *sekali – sampai ke seberang*; – (ber)galah pole vault. – *berjingkat* skip. – *jauh* broad jump. – *katak* a) leap-frog. b) squat jumping. – *kijang* a hop, skip, and a jump. – *kinja* to jump for joy. – *langkah-berjingkat* and *jingkat langkah* – a hop, skip, and a jump. – *pagar* "to leap over the hedge," i.e., to boost s.o. who otherwise would have failed in a screening so that he can pass anyway; → KATROLAN. – *tiga* a hop, skip, and a jump. – *tinggi* high jump. 2 to skip (over), every other (period of time). – *sehari* every other day. – *dua hari* every two days.

    selompat ~ *hidup*, ~ *mati* in danger of death, to be in a life and death struggle.

    (ber)lompat-lompat to jump/skip around. *Omongnya* ~. He skips from one subject to another.

    berlompat(-lompat)an (*pl subj*) to jump (around).

    melompat 1 to jump, leap. ~ *keluar* to bail out (of an aircraft). ~ *menganjur* (*Med*) to take a preliminary run (before jumping). 2 to bypass, go over the head of (one's superior).

melompat-lompat to hop up and down.

melompati [and **ng(e)lompatin** (*J coq*)] **1** to jump over. ~ *pagar/parit* to jump over a fence/ditch. **2** to swoop down on, pounce on, attack, assault.

melompatkan to cause to jump, let jump; carry s.t. along while jumping, jump with.

terlompat 1 to jump suddenly/unintentionally. **2** (= **terlomat-lompat**) ~ *dari* a) (*mulut*) inadvertently let drop (or, say). b) to fall (out of one's hand). c) to jolt, bump (of a *bécak* over cobbles, etc.). d) to jump up and down for no reason.

lompatan 1 jumping off place. **2** s.t. over which one jumps, hurdle. **3** length/height of a jump. **4** the act/way, etc. of jumping, vaulting. ~ *dengan galah* pole vaulting. ~ *listrik* (*elec*) flashover.

pelompat jumper (*esp* in sports). ~ *jangkit* steeplechaser. **sepelompat** as far as a jump.

pelompatan a jump, leap. **sepelompatan** as far as one can jump.

lompok aggregate.

berlompok-lompok heaped/piled up, stacked; in piles/heaps/stacks, in clumps (dirt).

melompok to aggregate.

lompokan aggregated.

pelompokan aggregation.

lompong I empty; → KOSONG.

melompong: *janji* ~ an empty promise. *kosong* ~ a) completely empty. b) meaningless, senseless.

lompong II (*M*) *kué* – a pastry made from sago and banana. – *sagu* k.o. sweet made from boiled sago.

melompong to make that k.o. pastry.

lomprot → NGLOMPROT.

lonan(g) *buah* – custard apple, *Annona reticulata*; → BUAH *nona*.

loncat I jump, hop, move by leaping or springing on both/all four legs at the same time (as a bird/frog, etc.). – *jauh* broad jump. *melompat jauh* to make a broad jump. – *jongkok* squat jump. – *tinggi* high jump. *melompat tinggi* to make a high jump. *peloncat tinggi* high jumper. – *tiga* hop-step-and-jump.

berloncat to hop and jump.

berloncat(-loncat)an (*pl subj*) to jump, jump around.

meloncat 1 to hop, jump. *ikan* ~ the fish are jumping (out of the water). *katak* ~ the frogs are hopping. *Harga* ~ *naik*. The price soared. **2** (in sports) to jump (up), leap, spring. **3** to snap, release, let go. *Pérnya* ~. The spring snapped. **4** to move (from one job to another). *Ia* ~ *ke perusahaan swasta*. He moved to a private company. **5** to defect, desert. ~ *ke pihak musuh* to defect to the enemy.

meloncati 1 to jump over. **2** to rush/jump on (a prey), make a swift sudden attack on.

meloncatkan 1 to let/cause to jump, have jump. **2** to jump with.

terloncat to jump suddenly/unintentionally. *Ia* ~ *ketika mendengar letupan itu*. He jumped when he heard the blast.

terloncat-loncat jumping up and down, hopping about. ~ *bagai ulat pinang* to be very restless/nervous.

loncatan 1 jump, leap, bound, sudden change. ~ *Jauh Ke Depan* The Great Leap Forward (in the PRC). ~ *urut* successive bounds. **2** the distance/height of a jump. ~ *setinggi dua méter* a 2-meter-high jump. *batu* ~ stepping-stone, foothold.

peloncat jumper, leaper.

peloncatan jumping, hopping.

loncat II (*M*) frog.

loncéng (*C*) **1** bell, chimes. – *geréja* church bell. – *kematian* death knell. **2** large clock (on wall, etc.). – *angka* digital clock.

meloncéng to ring a bell, play the chimes.

loncér (*J*) loose (of a screw), does not fit any longer (due to frequent use, etc.).

meloncér to become loose, loosen.

lonco (*J*) **meloco(-lonco)** to stroll around.

loncong → LUNCUNG.

loncor tapering, pointed.

loncos tapering upward, coming to a point. *telanjang* – stark naked.

londang shallow stagnant pool, mudhole.

londar (*Mal*) locus.

londi (*M ob*) → LUNDI.

londo (*Jv*) **1** Dutch(man). *di jaman* – during the Dutch/colonial period. **2** any Westerner. – *bulé* European or American, Westerner. – *durung jowo wurung* (*Jv*) (said about a Eurasian) "not yet a Dutchman and failed at being a Javanese," i.e., neither Dutch nor Indonesian but s.t. in between.

londoisme favoring western over Indonesian tourists.

londong (*M*) **melondong(kan) 1** to carry along, drive/wash away. **2** to plunge s.o. into misery; to destroy, devastate, ruin.

londot (*Jv*) loose (of a screw), stripped (of the threads of a screw).

lonéng (*D J*) railing (of a bridge, etc.), balustrade, banisters, low wall in front of house.

melonéng [and **nglonéng** (*J*)] to loiter, sit/loaf around, get some fresh air.

long I (*C J*) k.o. large firecracker.

long II (*cla*) bottomless Malay coffin.

long III nickname for oldest child; → SULUNG I.

longak-longok (*J*) – and **melongak-longok** to look around (idly).

longderés (*D J*) LONGRÉS.

longgar 1 (to feel) relieved, relaxed, not oppressed. **2** loose, not tight (of nails/screws/sewing, etc.). *Jahitannya* – *dan kasar*. The sewing was loose and coarse. *Sekrupnya sudah* –. The screw is loose. **3** flexible, not rigid, lax. **4** not binding (of regulations), lax. **5** loose (in sexual matters). **6** free (of time). **7** free and easy, not lacking anything. – *ulir* (in mining) breakout.

melonggari 1 to add s.t. in order to widen s.t. else. *Bajunya dilonggari sedikit*. His coat was made looser (by adding material and resewing). **2** to slacken. **3** to make room for.

melonggarkan and **memperlonggar 1** to make (a tie/bond/button/screw, etc.) looser, loosen, slacken (s.t. that was taut). ~ *katup* to crack a valve. **2** to make (time). **3** to facilitate, make easier (conditions/terms of payment), relax/make less strict or severe (regulations/rules). **4** to mitigate, alleviate, soften (regulations/laws, etc.).

terlonggar the loosest, slackest.

kelonggaran 1 too big/loose (of clothes/pegs/masts, etc.). **2** dispensation, release, exemption (from an obligation), loosening, slackening, relaxation (of rules), allowance. *Empat kapal penumpang diberi* ~ *mengangkut penumpang melebihi kapasitas biasa*. Dispensation was granted to four passenger ships to carry excess passengers. ~ *tarik* unused drawing rights (to a committed but unused loan). ~ *pajak* tax holiday. **3** margin, elbowroom, ample/extra room, enough space, opportunity, leeway, Lebensraum. ~ *keselatan* safety margin. **4** leisure, ease. **5** privilege (as opposed to a right). **6** laxness, laxity.

pelonggaran granting relief, mitigation, relaxing.

longgok heap, pile (of rice/fruit/grass, etc.), stack.

berlonggok(-longgok) 1 to accumulate, pile up, collect, gather. **2** in heaps/piles/stacks; heaped/piled/stacked up.

melonggok(kan) to accumulate/pile up s.t.

terlonggok piled/heaped/stacked up.

longgokan 1 heap, pile, stack, accumulation. **2** deposit. ~ *bijih* ore deposit. ~ *cebakan* ore deposit. ~ *uranium* uranium deposit.

pelonggokan accumulation.

longgor (*J/Jv*) shot up, grown rapidly. *Anak ini* – *benar*. This child has really gotten big.

longkak (*J*) **melongkaki** to deal with first, give priority to.

longkang canal, ditch, drain.

longkap → LONGKAK.

longkong (*J*) chance, opportunity.

longo (*J/Jv*) **melongo** openmouthed, bewildered, blank, agape; to stare (into space), gawk, have a blank look on one's face.

terlongo-longo with mouth agape.

longok (*J/Jv*) a look, glimpse, view (from around the corner).

melongok to look at/see s.o. or s.t. (from around the corner), peep into s.o.'s house, see through (the window, etc.), stick one's neck out (of a window, etc.), look out (the door, etc.) (to see s.t.), rubberneck. ~ *(pandang)* to have/take a look around. *tak hentinya dilongok petugas* to be under the continuous surveillance of officials.

melongokkan ~ *kepala* to stick out/crane one's neck to see s.t.; → PANCALONGOK.

longong (*J/Jv*) dumbfounded. *dibuat* – to be dumbfounded.

melongong and **terlongong(-longong)** to gape; to be openmouthed, amazed, startled, dumbfounded, perplexed, astonished.

longpong (*J*) empty.

    melongpong *kosong* ~ and ~ *kosong* completely empty.

longrés (*D*) a long dress.

longsér (*S*) a Cirebon folk art.

longsong I (*M*) **terlongsong 1** slid down (a tree/chute/banisters). **2** gone too far.

longsong II melongsong to peel (fruit).

longsor to slide down, slip down (as of earth in a landslide). *tanah* – landslide.

    melongsor to slide/slip down, collapse.

    melongsorkan to make s.t. slide down, erode.

    longsoran 1 soil erosion. **2** landslide.

    pelongsoran erosion, eroding.

lonjak a move to jump up (with the two legs lifted simultaneously). *cakap* – to boast, talk big. *si* – the kangaroo. *seperti alu penumbuk padi* to walk with vigorous or arrogant steps. – *sebagai labu dibenam* and –*nya seperti labu terbenam* arrogant, haughty. – *anjlok* ups and downs, fluctuations.

    berlonjak(-lonjak)an (*pl subj*) to jump/bounce around.

    melonjak 1 to jump up (with both legs) to reach for s.t. *Ia* ~ *hendak menangkap bola*. He jumped up to catch the ball. **2** to jump/shoot up, skyrocket (of prices). **3** to bounce (as of a ball). **4** to sprawl (of a child). **5** ~ *ria* to jump for joy; to give a startled jump. **6** to shake/shudder (with sobs). **7** to plop down

    melonjak-lonjak to jump repeatedly (with joy, etc.), bounce/jump around. *berjalan* ~ to walk in a jerky way.

    melonjakkan to cause to jump/leap/spring up, provide an impetus for s.t. ~ *badannya* to withdraw, pull back.

    terlonjak 1 to jump suddenly (with joy, etc.). **2** to sit down with a plop. *hati* ~ feeling up/elated. ~ *dari duduknya/kursinya* to jump up from one's seat/chair. ~ *oléh kedudukannya yang tinggi itu*. His high position has gone to his head. ~ *rasa semangat* to feel up/elated/delighted.

    lonjakan 1 jump, leap, bump (on a plane flight). **2** sudden increase.

    pelonjakan jump, increase, rise.

lonjong 1 long and straight (of trees). **2** (*Jv*) tapering, oval (face); elliptical, oblong; → BULAT *bujur*.

lonjor I (*Jv*) bar (of soap); a classifier for long objects. *se–* a bar.

    lonjoran wholesale.

lonjor II extend, stick out; → LUNJUR. **berselonjor** ~ *kaki* with legs extended.

    selonjor menyelonjorkan to stretch/sprawl out.

    melonjor to stretch. *meletakkan kakinya dengan* ~ *pada sebuah kursi kecil* to stretch one's legs out onto a small chair.

    melonjorkan to stick s.t. out, extend s.t.

    lonjoran s.t. stuck out, extended, long stretch of s.t. ~ *kayu* timber.

lonsong → LONGSONG I.

lonta → LUNTA. **terlonta-lonta** to always be in trouble/a fix (said of the poor).

lontai (*ob*) **melontai** bent, not straight (of a line).

lontang I (in Ujungpandang) a roadside stall where people can drink *tuak*; → BALLOK.

lontang II – *lantung* to go around and around with no set goal.

lontar I throw, hurl. – *martil* (in sports) throwing the hammer.

    selontar 1 a single shot/throw. **2** a little bit, a few.

    berlontaran to throw/hurl at e.o.

    melontar to throw.

    melontari 1 to throw at, pelt. **2** (*pl obj*) to throw, toss.

    melontarkan 1 to hurl, fling, throw. ~ *gas* to spew forth gas (of a volcano). ~ *hinaan* to hurl insults. ~ *kecaman* to criticize. ~ *pertanyaan* to pose a question. ~ *tuduhan* to accuse, level an accusation. **2** to come up with/broach (an idea), put forward. *gagasan yang dilontarkan Adam Malik* an idea broached by Adam Malik. ~ *diri dengan alat otomatis* to eject (from an aircraft). **3** to present. *jaminan yang dilontarkan kepada pérs* the guarantees presented to the press.

    terlontar 1 hurled, thrown. **2** come up with, broached. *matanya* ~ *ke* his eyes alighted on.

    lontaran throw, toss.

    pelontar 1 sling, implement, etc., s.t. that hurls, throws or flings. **2** thrower, hurler (the person). ~ *granat* grenade launcher. ~ *rokét* rocket launcher. **3** s.o. who broaches (an idea). ~ *gagasan* an idea-man. **sepelontar(an)** as far as s.t. can be hurled. ~ *batu* a stones throw.

    pelontaran coming up with (an idea).

lontar II 1 the Palmyra palm, *Borassus flabellifera*; → SIWALAN I. – *utan gebang* palm, *Corypha utan*. **2** the leaf of the Palmyra palm, used for writing before the introduction of paper. **3** (*ob*) an old manuscript (written on *lontar* leaves).

lontarak (in the Buginese-Makassarese area of South Celebes) old manuscripts originally written on *lontar* leaves.

lonté (*Jv*) prostitute, whore, loose woman. – *lanang* male prostitute.

    melontékan ~ *diri* to prostitute o.s., sell o.s.

lontok short and thick (as a bottle), stumpy. *tua* – old and stumpy.

lontong (*Jv*) **1** a rolled package of cooked rice wrapped in a banana leaf, giving the rice a slightly greenish color; the banana leaf is peeled off when the *lontong* is eaten. **2** (*euph*) penis.

lontos straight (as a plain pillar).

    pelontos → PLONTOS.

lop (*D*) → LUP I.

lopak I a puddle, pool (of water), sump. – *jadi perigi* to go from rags to riches.

    berlopak-lopak full of puddles.

    lopakan (*J*) puddle.

lopak II (*M*) section of a wet rice field.

    selopak ~ *sawah* one such section.

lopak-lapik vacillating, inconsistent.

lopak-lopak pouch of screw pine leaf used for holding tobacco, *sirih*, etc.

lopék a small prau.

loper (*D*) **1** (bank) messenger. **2** delivery boy/man. – *susu* milkman. **2** newspaper boy/man. – *koran* newspaper boy.

lopés and **lopis I** clown knife-fish, *Notopterus chitala*.

lopis II a delicacy of glutinous rice, palm sugar and grated coconut.

lopong → LOMPONG I.

lopot → LÉPOT.

lor (*Jv*) north.

lorah (*ob*) tackle, pulley.

lorat (*ob*) **1** worried, confused. **2** annoying, troublesome.

lorék stripes, bands, long lines; striped, banded, marked with long lines; → LORÉNG, LURIK.

    berlorék-lorék marked with such marks.

loréng striped. *berpakaian (macan)* – (*mil*) to wear/wearing a camouflage uniform.

    berloréng-loréng 1 striped. **2** camouflaged (fatigues).

lori I (*D/E*) lorry, i.e., a flat wagon without sides fitted to carry sugar and to run on rails in sugar factory compounds. – *gantung* overhead cableway.

lori II (*burung* –) parakeet.

lornyét (*D*) (pair of) pince-nez.

Loro Jonggrang (*Jv*) name of the main temple of the *Prambanan* complex on the road from Yogyakarta to Solo.

loro-loroning atunggal (*Jv*) lit. "the two we see is actually one," two in one (*esp* in mysticism).

lorong I 1 path, lane, alley, course. **2** shaft. **3** (*naut*) corridor. **4** trail. – *Ho Chi Minh* Ho Chi Minh Trail. – *angin* wind tunnel.

    melorongkan 1 to open a way, guide. **2** to grant (a request).

lorong II (*M*) about, concerning, in connection with.

lorong III (in Tebing Tinggi) *kepala* – deputy village chief.

Lorosaé and **Loro Sa'e** the new name of independent Timor Timur (the former Portuguese Timor).

lorosetu and **loro setu** (*Jv*) lavender, k.o. fragrant grass, vetiver, *Andropogon zizanioides*.

lorot melorot 1a) to slide down, slip off. **b)** to decline, sink, fall, become lower (of income/profits, etc.), drop. – *tajam* to decline sharply. **c)** to wane, become weaker/worse (of health, etc.). **d)** to fall/drop (of pants/temperature, etc.). *Harga beras mulai* ~. Rice prices began to decline. *Seluarnya* ~. His trousers fell down. *suhu* ~ the temperature dropped. **2** to be demoted. *Bukannya naik pangkat, melainkan* ~. It was not a promotion but rather a demotion. **3** (*Jv*) in the batik-making process to remove wax from a batik cloth after dyeing.

melorotkan [and melorotin (*J*)] to lower, drop, decrease, lessen.
  memeloroti to drop, lower.
  memelorotkan to dry up.
los I (*D*) pilot, pilot-ship (a ship that guides another safely into a harbor).
los II (*D*) a shed, booth, stand (in the market, etc.). – *bawang mérah* onion stand. – *loko* roundhouse. – *pakaian* clothes booth. – *pasar* stall in the market.
los III (*A*) almond.
los IV (*D*) 1 free, loose. 2 slack, loose (of rope) 3 permissive.
  mengelos to let loose, let run free.
  meloskan to release, free, allow to run free.
  los-losan to play rough, no holds barred.
lose (*D*) 1 lodge. 2 loge, first class seats (in a theater/cinema, etc.).
losé (*D*) lodger, (paying) guest.
losin → LUSIN.
losion (*D/E*) lotion.
losmén (*D*) lodgings, a (cheap) place to stay, inn, (cheap) hotel, hostel. – *remaja* youth hostel.
loso (*J*) meloso and ngeloso 1 to creep (like a snake). 2 to crawl (with the chest touching the ground). 3 to lie sprawled (from pain).
losong I *kurap* – k.o. skin disease, ringworm.
losong II – *kosong* and *kosong* – completely empty; *cp* KOSONG *melompong*.
lot (*D*) lottery ticket.
  mengelot (*coq*) to raffle off.
lota to become soft (of s.t. that was hard).
lotar → LONTAR I.
loték 1 (*C ob*) putty. 2 (*J/Jv*) k.o. salad made from mixed vegetables and fruits with bean cake.
loténg (*C*) 1 attic, loft, top floor. 2 ceiling. 3 story, floor.
  berloténg with an attic, etc. *rumah* ~ a multistory house.
loteré (*D*) 1 lottery, raffle, pool. 2 lottery ticket. 3 lottery prize. *kena/menang/menarik/putus* – a) to win the lottery. b) to get a windfall. – *buntut* pool in which people try to guess the final digit of the winning lottery number.
  meloteré to gamble on the lottery.
  meloterékan 1 to raffle s.t. off. 2 to supply a lottery prize.
lotis (*Jv*) k.o. snack of fruit dipped in hot sauce.
lotok (*Jv*) melotok peels easily, separates out easily (of fruit from its stone).
lotong I 1 k.o. monkey, *Presbytis spp.*; → LUTUNG. 2 black (of dogs/scorpions).
lotong II → LOKTONG.
lotong III → SANGGA *lotong*.
lotot (*J*) melotot open/staring (of one's eyes).
  melototi to state at.
  melototkan to open wide (one's eyes).
lotré (*D*) → LOTERÉ.
lotus (*D/E*) lotus; → TERATAI.
lowa k.o. fig tree, cluster fig, *Ficus glomerata Roxb*.
lowak → LOAK I.
lowo (*Jv*) k.o. large fruit-eating bat.
lowong (*J/Jv*) vacant, blank, empty, void, free, unoccupied.
  melowongi to vacate, empty out.
  melowongkan to make empty/vacant, vacate. ~ *jabatan* to vacate a position.
  lowongan vacancy, job opening.
  kelowongan 1 vacancy. 2 gap.
loya I (= meloya) nauseated, about to vomit, to feel sick/squeamish. *Perutnya meloya*. He feels sick (to his stomach); → NEK.
loya II (in West Kalimantan) k.o. *dukun* and soothsayer.
loyak soft from being wet.
loyal (*D/E*) loyal.
  keloyalan loyalty.
loyalita(s) (*D*) loyalty.
loyang I brass. (*badan*) – *disangka emas* aiming too high; overestimating o.s. 2 (*J*) k.o. large brass or bell-metal tray. 3 a cake mold. *kembang* – (*ob*) rice-flour porridge mixed with sugar.
loyar I (*J*) liberal, generous, openhanded; → ROYAL.
loyar II (*E*) lawyer.

loyo I (*J/Jv*) 1 lethargic, inert, listless, sluggish, slow, lazy. 2 in a slump, bad (of business), in bad shape. 3 in a bad mood. 4 tired, fatigued, exhausted. *dengan* – in an exhausted way.
loyo II → LOYA I.
loyong meloyong to walk stooping over and tottering; *cp* HUYUNG.
loyor → KELOYOR, KELUYUR.
LP I (*init*) [Lembaga Pemasyarakatan] penitentiary.
LP II (*init*) long playing record.
  meng-LP-kan to record on an LP.
LS → DLS.
lu I (*C J*) you (singular). *siapa* – *siapa gua* and –.– *gua-gua* to live in a selfish way; every man for himself; → ELU III.
lu II (in acronyms) → LUAR *negeri*.
luah discharge.
  meluah 1 (to be) sick (to one's stomach), feel like vomiting. 2 to vomit, throw up.
  meluahkan to vomit/throw up s.t., belch forth.
  luahan discharge.
  peluahan discharging, discharge.
  perluahan spittoon.
luak I (*Jv*) k.o. civet cat, marbled cat, *Pardofelis marmorata. kopi* – coffee beans discharged in the dung of civet cats: considered excellent coffee.
luak II (*M*) (an administrative) district; → LUHAK.
luak III decreased, lessened.
  meluak(i) to decrease, lessen, reduce.
luak IV (*ob*) meluak to retch, wanting to vomit.
luak V (*M*) a dug well.
luan → HALUAN I.
luang I vacant (of space or time). *dalam waktu –nya* in his spare time.
  berluang *pikiran* ~ *sedikit* calmed down, relieved.
  meluangkan to vacate (a place, etc.). ~ *waktu* a) to make time available, make time, set aside time. b) to spend time.
  terluang 1 vacant (of a post), empty. 2 free/spare/extra/leisure (time). *waktu* ~ spare time. 3 clear, free from any impediment; cleared (of a road).
  keluangan opportunity, chance, occasion. *tidak* ~ to have no chance/spare time to. berkeluangan to have the time.
  peluang 1 time (to do s.t.), opportunity, chance. ~ *emas* golden opportunity. ~ *hidup* life expectancy. 2 lull. 3 leisure. 4 uncovered part of the body (in *silat*).
luang II meluang stiff all over the body, feeling of malaise.
luap boil over, overflow.
  meluap 1 to boil over (of a liquid), overflow. 2 to flood (of a river), to run/spill over, pour out, flare up (of anger). 3 to rise. *Semangatnya* ~ His spirits flared up.
  meluap-luap 1 to boil over. 2 to rise, flare up, pour out. 3 fiery (of a speech).
  meluapi to overflow onto.
  meluapkan 1 to cause to overflow. 2 to cause to boil over.
  luapan 1 bubbling over. 2 (over)flow, outpouring. ~ *semangat* an outpouring of high spirits. 3 (*elec*) discharge.
  peluapan outpouring.
luar outside (of); outer place/part; external. *datang dari* – to come from the outside. *dari* – *kota dan gunung-gunung* from far and wide. *di* – a) outside, outdoors. *di* – *negeri* abroad, overseas. *di* – *rumah* outside the house. b) on the free/black market. c) beyond, without. *di* – *batas-batas kesusilaan* immoral. *di* – *harapan* beyond one's expectations. *di* – *kebiasaan* outside the norms, unusual. *di* – *keharusan* unnecessarily. *di* – *kendali* beyond the control (of). *di* – *pengetahuan* without the knowledge (of). d) excluding. *di* – *téks* ad lib, without a text. *ke* – outward; *cp* KELUAR. *ban* – tire casing. *negeri* – foreign countries. *obat* – embrocation, medicine for external use. *orang* – a) a foreigner; a stranger. b) another person. c) an outsider. *penyakit* – external disease. – *batas* (to be) out of bounds, off limits. – *biasa* a) extraordinary, wonderful. b) abnormal, anomalous. c) associate, temporary/acting. **keluar-biasaan** peculiarity. – *bicara* excluding. – *dalam* a) physically and mentally, in every way. b) inwardly and outwardly. – *dinas* honorably discharged. **meluar-dinaskan** to honorably discharge. – *dugaan* beyond expectations, unexpected. – *dunia* other worldly. *di* – *hadirnya*

in the absence of. – *janji* outside/not included in the agreement. – *kampus* off campus. – *kanan* (in soccer) right wing. – *kawin* extramarital. – *kelas* extracurricular. – *negeri* foreign, overseas. *di* – *kemampuan* beyond one's ability/powers. – *kepala* (to learn) by heart. – *kiri* (in soccer) left wing. *di* – *kota* out of town. – *negeri* foreign, abroad, overseas. *Départemén* – *Negeri* Ministry of Foreign Affairs. – *rencana* unplanned, unscheduled. – *ruang* outdoor. – *siar* off the record.

keluar *q.v.*

meluar to appear, show, stick out (part of a handkerchief, etc.), come to the fore.

meluarkan to exclude, segregate, separate, alienate, isolate, ask to go out; *cp* MENGELUARKAN.

luaran 1 foreign. *orang* ~ a foreigner; another person. *negeri* ~ foreign countries. 2 environment, ambiance.

keluaran → KELUARAN. 1 a graduate of. 2 issue, edition. 3 product; make. 4 (in the Bible) Exodus. 5 external. *orang* ~ (*cla*) s.o. outside palace circles. 6 output.

peluaran *dunia* ~ another world/country, outer regions (outside the town); *cp* PEDALAMAN.

luas 1 wide, broad, vast, roomy, spacious, extensive, capacious. *masyarakat* – the general public. 2 area, extent, surface area. *suatu* – *laut* a body of water. 3 wide-ranging, far-reaching, widespread, comprehensive, broad, sweeping. *orang yang* – *pengetahuannya* a person with broad knowledge. – *hutan* woodland area. – *lingkaran* area of a circle. – *pergaulannya* with a wide circle of friends. – *tanah* surface area.

luasnya 1 width. 2 extent, spread. ~ *ayunan* (*elec*) amplitude. ~ *lingkungan* scope. ~ *sayap* wing spread.

seluas an area of, to the extent of. *dunia ini tidak* ~ *daun kélor* there are many other fish in the sea.

berluas-luas to feel at ease because there's enough room, not feel cramped.

meluas to extend, spread, widen, broaden, be(come) widespread. ~ *melintasi* to spread/spill over (an area).

meluaskan and **memperluas(kan)** to broaden, enlarge, expand, extend, widen, improve (one's knowledge of).

keluasan 1 area. 2 opportunity, chance, occasion, leeway. 3 extent, width, breadth, spread. 4 spaciousness.

peluas 1 (*petro*) step-out (well). 2 expander. 3 (*Mal*) s.t. that enlarges, expands, etc.

pe(ng)luasan and **perluasan** expansion, enlargement, extension, spreading, widening. *perluasan arti* (*ling*) generalization of meaning.

luasa (*ob*) → LELUASA.

luat **meluat** to hate, be disgusted to (see/hear s.t.). ~ *saya dengar*. I'm disgusted to hear it.

luba k.o. sago palm, *Eugeissona spp.*

luban (*A*) a resin, gum benjamin. – *jawi* incense.

lubang 1 hole, opening (in a solid body), eye (of needle). 2 hole, hollow (in the ground), cavity. 3 perforation. 4 (in moonlighting terminology) a buyer, purchaser. *menggali* – *menimbun* – and *gali* – *tutup* – to borrow from Peter to pay Paul. *barang siapa menggali* –, *ia juga terperosok ke dalamnya* he who digs a pit for others may fall into it himself. – *air* water pipe. – *angin* ventilation. – *angin jujut* vent hole. – *batubara* coal mine. – *béha* cup of a bra. – *Buaya* "Crocodile Hole," i.e., a well into which six generals and a soldier were thrown after they were killed during the abortive Communist coup of September 30, 1965. – *céngkok* dogleg (of an oil well). – *dubur* anus. – *éngkol* crank slot. – *érong* (*naut*) scupper hole. – *gérék* burrow (made by an insect in a tree, etc.). – *gigi* cavity, caries (in a tooth). – *gotri* shot hole (a disease of plants). – *hawa* ventilator. – *hidung* nostril. – *hukum* loophole. – *intip* peephole. – *jarum* a) eye of a needle. b) pinch hole (made in leaves by a disease or insect). – *kancing* buttonhole. – *keluar* discharge opening. – *kepundan* crater. – *kering* dry hole. – *kulit* skin pore. – *kunci* keyhole. – *kuping* ear hole. – *kuras* (*naut*) scupper hole. – *ledak* blast-hole. – *lengan* armhole (on a shirt, etc.). – *lénsa* aperture. – *masuk* a) manhole. b) inlet. – *meriam* muzzle. – *orang* manhole. – *palka* hatch(way). – *pantat* anus. – *pasak* cotter hole. – *pelihat/periksa* peephole. – *penjebak téng* tank pit, antitank trap. – *per-*

lindungan a) shelter. b) foxhole. – *sanggama* vagina. – *silinder* cylinder bore. – *sumbat* bunghole. – *tali* eyelet. – *tap* mortise. – *telinga* cavity of the ear. – *tubrukan* rupture, breach. – *ungkak* hawse hole.

berlubang with a hole, perforated, with a cavity.

berlubang-lubang perforated, full of holes.

melubang to get the ball in the hole (in golf).

melubangi to make a hole in, pierce, perforate, punch a hole in.

melubang-lubangi to riddle/punch s.t. full of holes.

melubangkan to perforate, punch a hole in.

pelubang perforator, borer, perforating (*mod*), s.t. that punches a hole.

pelubangan 1 pitfall, a hole made in the ground to trap animals. 2 perforating.

lubér I (*Jv*) to overflow.

melubér to overflow.

melubéri to fill to overflowing.

pelubéran overflowing (of liquid), spill(age).

lubér II [Langsung, Umum, Bébas, Rahasia] direct, public, free, private.

lubi-lubi → LOBI-LOBI.

lubuk 1 depths, i.e., the deepest part (of a sea/river/lake), abyss. 2 deep pool found in a stream. 3 deep; → JELUK I, LEKUK. *piring/pinggang* – soup plate. – *akal lautan/tepian ilmu/budi* all-round, versatile. *tahu di dalam* – to be thoroughly conversant with. *batu jatuh ke* – vanished into thin air, disappeared without a trace. – *menjadi pantai, pantai menjadi* – nothing lasts forever. *dari* – *hati/jiwa* from the bottom of one's heart. *lain* – *lain ikannya* so many countries so many customs.

lubur (*ob*) → KELUBURAN.

lucah 1 (*ob*) very humble/low, despicable. 2 indecent, pornographic; filthy (of language); → CABUL. 3 shameless (of women), brazen.

kelucahan 1 humiliation, disgrace, shame. 2 obscenity, smuttiness.

lucan a *batik tulis* of Pati.

lucu 1 funny, amusing, comical, witty; → LELUCON. 2 burlesque. 3 cute. 4 roguish, arch.

selucu as funny as.

berlucu (*ob*) and **melucu** to joke/clown around, be amusing.

terlucu the funniest.

lucu-lucuan joke, humor. ~ *menggigit* satirical, biting humor. *program/acara* ~ comedy show.

kelucuan 1 joke, jest, comedy; clowning around, banter, humor. 2 cuteness. 3 roguishness, archness.

pelucu joker, wit, amusing person.

lucup sunken (beneath the surface of the water/soft ground, etc.).

melucup to sink (beneath the surface).

lucur → LUNCUR.

lucuria humor.

lucut I **melucut** to slip, drop, fall (because not held firmly or not on tight).

melucuti to strip/take/slip off, remove. ~ *pakaian* to undress. ~ *senjata* to disarm, take a weapon away from.

melucutkan 1 to release s.o. (from), let s.o. get away (from), loosen s.t. 2 to take off, remove.

terlucut slipped off/away.

lucutan (*elec*) discharge.

pelucutan stripping, removing.

perlucutan stripping. ~ *senjata* disarmament.

lucut II **melucut** chafed, abraded (of skin).

lucut III (*M*) disappeared, vanished.

melucutkan 1 to make s.t. disappear, cause to vanish. 2 to ruin, injure, harm, spoil.

ludah (*air* –) saliva, spit(tle). *belum kering* – *di bibir membicarakan* ... not yet finished talking about ... – *sirih* betel-nut spittle.

berludah and **meludah** to spit. *sudah diludah dijilat balik* to eat one's words, take back one's words. *meludah ke langit (muka juga yang basah)* to attempt to do the impossible.

meludahi 1 to spit s.t. 2 to spit on s.t.

meludahkan to spit s.t. out.

pe(r)ludahan cuspidor, spittoon.

ludang I *perahu/sampan* – a narrow rowboat; → SELUDANG 2.

ludang II (*S*) exhumation, disinterment.

ludas → LUDES.

ludat (*api-api* -) k.o. tree, *Avicennia officialis*.

ludes (*J/Jv*) all gone/finished (of money); destroyed, kaput. *terbakar* - burned to the ground. - *di méja judi* gambled away.

luding *tenggiri* - k.o. mackerel, *Scomberomorus spp*.

ludruk (*Jv*) /ludruk/ folk drama of East Java, acted by an all male cast, dealing with the daily lives of the lower classes and also some heroic stories of opposition to Dutch domination during the colonial period.

lugas (*Jv*) **1** without any adornment, unadorned, simple, plain; → LUGU I. **2** bare, plain (facts). **3** to the point, pertinent, relevant. **4** businesslike. **5** objective, impersonal, without any ulterior motive.
  melugaskan to simplify.
  kelugasan businesslike character, matter-of-factness, objectivity.

lugat → LOGAT.

luget (*J*) clumps easily.

lugu I (*Jv*) unadorned, without ornament, real, true, genuine, not pretentious, sincere, simple; bald, bare (facts); → LUGAS, POLOS.
  keluguan unadornedness, simplicity.

lugu II satisfied, satiated, full. *tak* - dissatisfied.

lugut (*Jv*) fine hair of the nettle and bamboos; → MIANG.
  selugut (to have) a grain (of sense), a little bit, an iota.

luh I (*A*) → LOH I. - *mahful*, -'*ulmahful* and *suratan* - *Tuhan* the Muslim tablet on which the fate of mankind and that of the world until Doomsday has been written.

luh II → LU I.

luh III → LHO I.

luhak (*M*) one of three central regions of the Minangkabau area in Sumatra. - *50 Kota*, - *Tanah Datar dan* - *Agam* the nucleus of the Minangkabau region.

luhung (*Jv*) **1** supreme, noble. **2** superb, magnificent
  keluhungan **1** supremacy, nobility. **2** magnificence.

luhur (*Jv*) exalted, grand, noble, glorious, high, sublime; *cp* LELUHUR. *bercita-cita* - to have high ideals.
  meluhurkan to glorify, exalt, honor. ~ *nusa dan bangsa* to glorify the country and the nation.
  keluhuran magnificence, state, pomp, glory, grandeur, sublimity, solemnity.

luih (*Jv ob*) more.

luik meluik 1 to drip, trickle. **2** to spit s.t. out of the mouth, retch.

luing I k.o. tree, *Ficus hispida*.

luing II centipede; → LIPAN.

luk curve (in kris); → KELUK.

luka 1 break in the skin, wound, cut, injury. *si* - the wounded. **2** injured, wounded, hurt. *siapa* - *siapa menyiuk* people who live in glass houses shouldn't throw stones. - *bacok* stab wound. - *bakar* a burn, burns. - *baring* bedsore. -.- *berat* trauma. - *borok* ulcers. - *dalam* deep wound. - *di kantung nasi* stomach/gastric ulcer. - *hati* insulted, wounded (one's feelings), offended. - *lécét* chafed, abraded, scrape. - *luar* superficial wound. - *memar* bruise, contusion. - *parah* seriously wounded. ***meluka-parahi*** and ***meluka-parahkan*** to injure s.o. seriously. - *robék* abraded, chafed; abrasion. - *sipi* flesh wound. - *témbak* gun-shot wound. - *tempur* wounded in action. - *tetak* slash wound. - *tikam* stab wound.
  berluka injured, wounded.
  melukai to injure, hurt, harm, wound. ~ *hati* to offend s.o., hurt (s.o.'s feelings). *tanpa dilukai* unhurt, unscathed.
  melukakan to hurt, injure. ~ *hati* to hurt s.o.'s feelings.
  terluka 1 to get wounded, be injured. **2** offended, hurt.
  kelukaan to get hurt/injured.

lukah (*M*) a fish trap made of bamboo. -*nya mengena* his tricks were successful. *menahan* - *di penggentingan* to misuse an opportunity. *menyandang* - *tiga* to perform a difficult job with ease.
  melukah to catch fish with a *lukah*.

lukat (= **melukat**) to come loose/detached of things that had been stuck together.
  terlukat detached.
  pelukatan detachment.

lukéh k.o. shrub, pia plant, *Tacca pinnatifida*.

lukék (*J*) belukékan to vomit, throw up.

lukis draw, paint. *pandai* - (*ob*) painter, artist. *seni* - (art of) painting.
  berlukiskan painted with, with a picture of … on it.
  melukis 1 to engrave, carve (out). **2** (= **melukiskan**) to paint, portray, represent, depict, picture, draw, illustrate, describe.
  melukisi to paint, illustrate, decorate.
  melukiskan 1 to paint for s.o. else. **2** to depict.
  terlukis painted, pictured, described, appearing on the surface.
  terlukiskan describable. *tak* ~ indescribable.
  lukisan 1 sketch, picture, drawing, picture, image, painting; diagram, reproduction. ~ *dinding* mural. **2** depiction.
  pelukis painter, artist.
  pelukisan 1 painting. **2** description, describing.

lukita (*Jv*) literary work. *juru* - man of letters.

luks (*D*) luxury. *barang* - luxury article/item/goods.

Luksemburg Luxembourg.

luku (*Jv*) plow; → BAJAK I.
  berluku to plow.
  meluku to plow s.t.
  pelukuan plowing.

luk-uluk → KULUK II, ULUK.

lukup → TELU(NG)KUP.

lukut duckweed and, in general, all the fine verdure that grows in water or along the water's edge on rocks, *Symplocos fasciculata*. **2** k.o. fern, *Platycerium spp*.

lulai k.o. tree, *Garcinia spp*. - *paya* k.o. tree, *Baccaurea wallichii*.

luli I 1 cotton held in the hand when making yarn. **2** (*M*) spindle on which cotton for making yarn is wound.
  meluli to wind cotton on a spindle/reel.

luli II (*ikan* -) Bombay duck, *Harpodon nehereus*.

lulo a social dance of the southeastern Celebes.

lulu I → LULUR I.

lulu II → MELULU.

luluh 1 crushed to pieces, pounded, pulverized, smashed. - *diamuk api* razed to the ground by a fire. - *lantak* and *hancur* - crushed to pieces, etc. (stronger than - alone). **2** to be merged into (one large organization); to be absorbed in (one's work, etc.). **3** (*ling*) (phonetically) assimilated. *Hatinya* -. He was won over/persuaded. *hatinya* - *menjadi satu dengan* to become of one heart and mind with. - *cair* liquefied. - *lantak* pulverized, smashed.
  meluluh-lantakkan 1 to pulverize, raze, smash. **2** to destroy (an enemy tank, etc.).
  meluluh to smash, pound.
  meluluhkan 1 to pulverize, smash, pound. **2** to dilute, melt, dissolve, liquefy. ~ *hatinya* (*J*) to calm s.o. down.
  peluluhan pulverizing, pounding.

luluk I (*M*) mud, mire.
  be(r)luluk (to be) muddy. *tidak* - *mengambil cekarau* be thrown into s.o.'s lap.
  berluluk-luluk to grub around in the mud.
  terluluk loosened from soil and mud (of rice plants ready to be transplanted).

luluk II (= **peluluk**) (*cla*) a spy.
  meluluk to spy on.

lulum → KULUM. **melulum** to suck (with the tongue and lips), hold in the mouth (chewing gum, etc.).

lulung (*ob*) to yelp, whine, howl, moan; → LOLONG.

lulur I melulur 1 to slip down (of food). **2** to devour, swallow whole without chewing, choke down.

lulur II (*Jv*) a yellow rice-powder cosmetic.
  berluluran (*pl subj*) to be all powdered, covered with this cosmetic.
  melulur to rub (the body with this powder).
  melulurkan to apply (this powder).
  luluran to apply this powder.

lulur III (beef) tenderloin.

lulus 1 to go/get through, penetrate; to slip off (a ring from the finger); to stumble (into a hole). **2** to sink (into the mud). *tak* - *pada/di/akan pikiran* illogical, unacceptable, incredible. **3** to pass (an examination, etc.); to succeed; to be permitted/allowed. – *dari* to graduate from. – *dari psikotés* to pass a psychological test. – *purna* passed all subjects (in a university). 4 vanished, disappeared, gone. 5 permeable. – *jarum*, – *kelindan* where one sheep goes follows another. *sudah – maka hendak melantai* (*M*) to lock the barn door after the horse is stolen. – *tidak berselam, hilang tidak bercari* to be in trouble but nobody wants to help.

selulus (*ob*) always; often.

selulusan (*M*) 1 (~ *pakaian*) a suit (of underwear). 2 (*saudara* ~) siblings with the same mother but different fathers.

melulusi 1 to take off (one's clothes, etc), remove. 2 to accept, accede to (s.o.'s request).

meluluskan 1 to approve, grant, permit. 2 to pass s.o., let s.o. pass (an examination). 3 to allow to penetrate/go through, yield (to s.o.'s wishes). ~ *diri* to run away, flee, desert. 4 to release, let go. 5 to remove, take off.

terlulus permeable. **keterlulusan** permeability.

lulusan a graduate/alumnus/alumna of. *surat* ~ license.

kelulusan 1 (to have a) miscarriage/abortion. 2 passing. *angka* ~ passing grade. 3 acceptance. 4 permeability.

lulut I sweet-smelling powder used for body cleansing, a cosmetic.

berlulut to rub o.s. with this cosmetic; to have a massage with this cosmetic.

melulut to rub s.o. with this cosmetic; to massage s.o. with this cosmetic.

melulutkan to rub (this cosmetic) onto.

pelulut 1 masseur, masseuse. 2 liniment.

lulut II (*J/Jv*) devoted, deeply attached (to s.o.).

lum (*ob*) *masak* – overripe.

lumai k.o. herb, *Blumea lacera*.

lumang smear.

berlumang stained, smeared, daubed.

melumangkan to soil, stain.

lumar (*M*) dirty, soiled.

berlumar dirtied, smeared, all covered with dirt, stained.

melumari to soil s.t.

pelumaran 1 smearing. 2 soiling, polluting.

lumas (*J?*) grease.

melumas to smear (with oil), lubricate; to coat (with whitewash).

melumasi to lubricate, grease, smear oil on.

melumaskan to lubricate.

pelumas lubricant.

pelumasan lubricating, lubrication.

lumat 1 fine powder. 2 pulverized, fine. 3 destroyed, smashed to pieces. – *dalam air* dissolve in water.

melumat(kan) to pulverize, crush fine.

terlumat(kan) pulverized, crushed.

lumatan crushed, pulverized.

pelumat ~ *tulang* bone crusher (reference to a boxer).

pelumatan pulverizing, crushing. ~ *tanah* soil liquefaction.

lumayan (*J/Jv*) 1 reasonable, enough but not too much (of food), moderate, better than nothing. 2 (pretty) fair, not bad, so-so, adequate, OK. 3 profitable. 4 equitable. – *juga* substantial, pretty big. *perbédaan yang – juga* a pretty big difference. *jarak yang – juga* a good distance.

lumba → LOMBA.

lumba-lumba (*ikan* –) dolphin, *Delphinus spp*. – *air tawar* → PESUT.

lumbrah → LUMRAH.

lumbu – *jawa* a climbing plant, *Willughbeia coriacea*.

lumbung rice barn/granary. – *désa* rice barn for the entire village. – *padi periuk nasi* source of income, livelihood.

lumer (*Jv*) (to feel) fine and smooth (of texture).

lumér 1 (*Jv*) fluid, melted; to liquefy. 2 (*J*) accommodating, yielding, complaisant, submissive.

melumér to liquefy, turn to liquid, melt.

melumérkan to liquefy s.t.

peluméran liquefying.

lumi-lumi (*ikan* –) phosphorescent smelt, *Harpodon nehereus*.

lumintu <lintu> (*Jv*) continuous, uninterrupted.

kelumintuan continuity.

lumpang 1 wooden bowl for pounding rice. 2 (*M ob*) mortar and

pestle (for pounding betel). 3 (*cla*) cannon barrel. 4 cup (for catching sap from a tree).

lumpia (*C*) egg roll. – *basah* spring roll. – *goréng* fried egg roll.

lumping I (*J/Jv*) (made of) leather. *kuda* – a horse made of leather (thin, not stuffed) hung over the shoulders; → KUDA *képang*.

lumping II *kué* – a pastry made from rice flour, sugar, etc.

lumpis → LUPIS II.

lumpuh 1 paralyzed, crippled, lame. *penyakit* – a) paralysis. b) polio(myelitis) 2 crippled, neutralized (of the enemy's power/one's chances, etc.), immobilized. – *saraf* palsy.

melumpuhkan 1 to paralyze. 2 to disable, incapacitate, neutralize, disarm, put out of action/commission. ~ *bom* to disarm a bomb.

kelumpuhan stroke, paralysis. *penderita* ~ paraplegic. ~ *separo badan* hemiplegic. ~ *saraf* palsy.

pelumpuh s.t. which paralyzes.

pe(r)lumpuhan 1 paralyzing. 2 disabling, disarming.

lumpuk I (*ob*) **melumpukkan** to collect (articles), gather (people).

lumpuk II (*ob*) → LUMPUH.

lumpur mud, slime, sludge, slurry. *beroléh – di tempat yang kering* to run into unexpected trouble. *takut akan –, lari ke duri* out of the frying pan and into the fire. – *batu bara* coal slurry. – *bor* drilling mud. – *dasar minyak* (*petro*) oil-base mud. – *karter* engine sludge. – *keminyakan* (*petro*) oil cut mud. – *ketam* mud on the shore/bank/above the high-water mark. – *laut* ooze, slime. – *minyak asam* (*petro*) acid sludge. – *pemboran* (*petro*) drilling mud. – *salju* slush.

berlumpur muddy.

melumpur to turn muddy, silt up.

melumpuri to make s.t. muddy, fill with mud, muddy.

pelumpuran 1 muddy place, mudhole. 2 silt.

lumrah (*Jv*) 1 common, normal, usual, ordinary, customary, general. 2 reasonable (not strange in any way). *tidak* – unusual. *ketidak-lumrahan* being unusual.

lumrahnya usually, ordinarily.

melumrahkan to make s.t. customary.

kelumrahan customary practice.

lumuh → RAPAK *lumuh*.

lumur smear, smudge.

berlumur(an) smeared, covered in/with (blood/mud, etc.), soiled with (paint/soot, etc.), stained with.

melumur to become smeared, soiled.

melumuri to smear. ~ *dengan sabun* to smear soap on (a child).

melumurkan to smear, dirt, stain. ~ *bedak ke muka* to smear powder on one's face.

lumuran 1 smear, stain. 2 s.t. smeared/stained.

pelumuran smearing, staining.

lumus smeared, soiled, stained; → LUMURAN. *tungkus* – overwhelmed/flooded/inundated with work, debt, etc.

berlumus stained, smeared.

lumut 1 moss, green-colored coating (in bottles/kettles, etc.). 2 mildew; duckweed. 3 algae. – *daun* moss. – *ékor kuning* a water-weed with yellow flowers, k.o. bladderwort, *Utricularia flexuosa*. – *karang* sponge. – *kerak* lichen. – *laut* kelp, sea lettuce, *Ulva lactuca*.

berlumut(an) mossy, moss-grown, covered with moss/lichen/algae. 2 mildewed, moldy.

lumutan 1 mossy, moss-grown. 2 (*J*) (to have lived/worked/studied, etc.) for a very long time, to have been (in some place) for ages and ages. 3 (*Jv*) green-colored coating (in a glass/pitcher, etc.). 4 (*Jv*) grown gray (in the service of s.t. or s.o.).

lunak 1 tender, soft. *pinjaman* – soft loan. 2 gentle, moderate, meek. 3 lenient, permissive, pliable, easygoing. – *di sudut, keras ditakuk* tit for tat. – *gigi dari lidah* gentle. – *hati* flexible, not stubborn. – *lidah* finding it easy to pronounce foreign words. – *mulut* obedient (of horses, etc.).

melunak to become tender/gentle, soften.

melunaki to be gentle/tender to; to persuade, coax.

melunakkan 1 to soften (up). 2 to soften, tenderize. 3 to moderate, ease up on. ~ *hati* to comfort s.o.

memperlunak(kan) to make s.t. softer, tenderize; to moderate.

kelunakan 1 softness, tenderness, gentleness. 2 moderation.

pelunak softener, tenderizer. ~ *cucian* laundry softener.
pelunakan softening, tenderizing.
perlunakan (*leg*) emancipation.
lunas I (*J/Jv*) paid in full, paid up, settled (of a debt).
melunasi and melunaskan [and ng(e)lunasin (*J coq*)] 1 to pay up/in full, settle, discharge. *yang belum dilunasi* outstanding (debts). 2 to heed (the call of one's fatherland). 3 to accomplish (a task), do (one's duty). 4 to mend (one's ways), expiate (a sin). 5 to satisfy (one's passions).
terlunasi paid up, paid in full, discharged.
pelunas s.t. which pays off, discharges (a debt).
pelunasan full payment, paying off (one's debt), discharge, redemption. *jangka* ~ term of redemption, i.e., point when the debt is paid off. ~ *béa ékspor* clearance out. ~ *impor* customs clearance. ~ *dan pemindahbukuan* redemption and transfer. ~ *obligasi* bond call. ~ *sebagian* pay-down.
lunas II keel, bottom. – *dalam* apron (on ship). – *panci* the bottom of a cooking pan. – *pokok/utama* main keel. – *samping* bilge keel.
lunau (*M*) slimy mud (at the bottom of a river), silt; → LANAU.
pelunauan grinding down ore.
luncai (*ob*) with a big/distended belly. *si* – Mr. Potbelly, Fat-guts.
luncas 1 wrong, amiss. 2 to miss, fail, fall short. 3 to escape; → LUPUT I.
keluncasan error.
luncip 1 tapering, pointed; → LANCIP. 2 (*elec*) peak.
peluncipan (*elec*) peaking.
luncung (*M*) 1 short and protruding (like a hog's nose). 2 tapering to a point (like a pyramid). 3 slightly protruding (of the mouth when gossiping in a whisper). *dientak alu* – defeated by a stupid person.
meluncungkan to protrude, stick out, purse (the lips).
luncur 1 to slip down, (let s.o.) slide away, glide, skim; to zoom (of a fast motorcycle/car, etc.), to soar off, to rush past. – *darat* ground launched. 2 slipped (from), escaped; lost, forfeited (of pawned items); invalid (of a promise, etc.). 3 to leave the slipway. 4 (words) come (out of one's mouth) smoothly.
berseluncur and bersiluncur to slip/slide down on a smooth/slippery surface; to slide down into the mud.
meluncur 1 to slip down, slide/glide away, zoom by fast. ~ *gantung* hang-gliding. 2 to head off (for/toward).
meluncuri to move quickly by, glide past, slide by/on, roll along on/along. *Sédan itu* ~ *jalan.* The sedan was rolling along the road.
meluncurkan to launch, shoot off, make s.t. roll out smoothly.
terluncur [and keluncur (*coq*)] 1 slipped/slid away. 2 pushed out (of one's position).
luncuran (*ling*) glide, semivowel.
peluncur 1 glider. *pesawat* ~ (an engineless) glider. 2 launcher. ~ *rokét* rocket launcher. ~ *torpédo* torpedo tube. 3 guide, slide (on weapons).
peluncuran 1 slip(way). 2 slide (on weapons). 3 blastoff (of spaceship), launch(ing). ~ *rokét* rocket launching, launch.
luncus → LONCOS.
lundang I → AKAR *lundang.*
lundang II (*M*) section (of fruit).
lundi grub, beetle larvae.
lundu I a river catfish, *Macrones gulio.*
lundu II k.o. tree, *Antidesma coriaceum.*
lung I 1 curve, bend; a curved line. 2 archer's bow. *melentungkan* – to bend/draw a bow.
melungkan to bend into an arch.
lung II (*C*) a Malay coffin (bottomless).
lung III (clipped form of *sulung*) eldest (child).
lung IV firecracker; → LONG I.
lungguh I melungguh (*cla* and *Jv*) to sit (at one's ease).
lungguh II (*J cla*) lungguhan appanage, i.e., land enjoyed free by officials in lieu of pay; *cp* BENGKOK, TANAH *pelungguh.*
kelungguhan position, job.
lungguk I heap, pile; → LONGGOK.
lungguk II (in Tapanuli Utara) hamlet.
lungkah (*ob*) easily loosened.
lungkang → LONGKANG. – *gén* gene pool.
lungkrah (*Jv*) 1 exhausted, weary. 2 inability, powerlessness.

lungkum dome-shaped, vaulted; → MUNGKUM.
lungkup terlungkup upside down; capsized (of a boat), inverted (of cups/bowls).
lunglai (*lemah*) – feeble, limp and powerless. *lemas* – a) (with) dragging steps, (with) leaden feet. b) (to feel) powerless.
lunglit (*Jv*) [balung kulit] emaciated, abnormally lean. *bangsa* – a nation of skin and bones.
lunglung (*S*) k.o. tree, *Aromadendron elegans.*
lungsé (*Jv*) too late.
lungsin warp (in a loom).
lungsur I → GELONGSOR II, LONGSOR, LUNCUR.
lungsur II melungsurkan and ngelungsur to hand s.t. down (to another user).
lungsuran (*Jv*) used, second-hand (article); cast-off clothes, hand-me-down.
lunjak (*J*) → LONJAK. nglunjak 1 to jump up. 2 to behave improperly.
lunjung → LONJONG.
lunjur berlunjur to stretch one's legs (when sitting); → LONJOR II, UNJUR.
melunjur to protrude, stick out.
melunjurkan to extend/stretch out (one's legs).
lunta (*hidup*) terlunta(-lunta) 1 to lead a miserable existence; to struggle (of the poor); → MELARAT I. 2 to have bad luck all the time.
luntang I (= peluntang) a floating fishing rod.
meluntang to (catch) fish with such a rod.
peluntang s.o. or s.t. used to catch fish with such a rod.
luntang II – *lanting/lantung* a) to dangle, bob up and down, drift about. b) to loiter about, loaf, hang out on the streets, be unemployed. *orang* – *lantung* loafer, drifter.
luntas → BELUNTAS.
luntur I (*J/Jv*) 1 to fade (away), lose color, discolor (of fabrics), wear off (of stains), not fast/lasting (of colors). *Niatnya itu* –. His intention has faded away. *tahan* – washable, won't fade (of clothes). *Sudah* – *namanya.* He has a bad reputation. *Sudah* – *tembaganya.* His bad character has come to light. 2 to be watered down (of a regulation, etc.). 3 to change one's stand/position/opinion, etc., become unfaithful/disloyal. 4 to flag, wane, weaken, decrease. *cinta kasih yang tak akan* – *selama-lamanya* an undying love. 5 no longer effective (a spell, curse, etc.); broken (of an oath), outdated (of a theory, etc.). –*lah sumpah jabatannya.* He broke his oath of office. 6 to drop in rank/position, etc.
meluntur to fade away, decrease.
melunturi to run and affect other clothes in the wash, run onto.
melunturkan to make s.t./cause s.t. to fade/discolor/run, discolor, bleach. ~ *kepercayaan rakyat kepada* to shake the people's confidence in. ~ *semangat* to diminish one's enthusiasm.
kelunturan 1 outdated, obsolescent, fading. 2 affected by running colors.
peluntur bleach.
pelunturan fading away.
luntur II relaxed/emptying easily (of the bowels).
meluntur to take a laxative.
peluntur relaxant. (*obat*) ~ laxative.
luntur III *burung* – (*gunung*) k.o. bird, blue-tailed trogon, *Harpactes reinwardtii.*
lunuk (in Palangka Raya) *pohon* – banyan tree.
lunyah melunyah 1 (for buffaloes) to trample fields soft for rice-planting. 2 (*M*) to have a fist-fight; to beat, strike.
terlunyah trampled (for rice-planting).
lunyai crumpled (of clothing).
lup I (*D*) barrel (of rifle).
lup II (*D*) magnifying glass.
lupa 1 (– *akan/kepada/pada*) forget, fail to recall; slipped one's mind. *saya* – a) I've forgotten (it). b) I've overlooked it; it slipped my mind. *Ia* – *mengunci lacinya.* He forgot to lock his drawer. *jangan* – don't forget to, make sure to. – *akan dirinya* a) faint(ed) away. b) unconscious. – *kepada orangtuanya* to forget one's parents. – *diri* a) to forget o.s., go too far (in behavior). b) to be unconscious. 2 (– *oléh*) do not strike s.o., do not

flash into one's mind; cannot recall, cannot call to mind. *Mungkin ada sesuatu yang - oléhnya.* There might be s.t. that he cannot recall. **3** to fail, neglect; to be indifferent (to). *- akan kewajibannya* to neglect (one's duties), forget (one's obligations). *panas hari, - kacang akan kulitnya* a) to forget one's origins/friends who have helped in the past, etc. after one has become happy or rich; the man who is rich now forgets his former friends. b) ungrateful. *- daratan* a) to forget o.s., lose one's head. b) to walk on air (after s.t. good happened). c) bewildered, beside o.s. d) reckless.

lupa-lupa *~ ingat* a) no longer sure about s.t., vaguely remember s.t. b) to have a poor memory. *lakunya sudah ~ ingat* to suffer from a poor memory. *dilupa-lupa-ingatkan* not recalled perfectly, only vaguely remembered.

me(nge)lupai *(ob)* to forget s.t.

melupakan [and **ng(e)lupain** *(J coq)*] **1** to forget (about), to put out of one's mind (purposely), get over (s.t. bad that happened). *Dia tidak bisa ~ peristiwa itu.* He can't put that event out of his mind. **2** to neglect, disregard; to lose sight/track of s.t. **3** (= **memperlupakan**) to cause to forget, wipe/put out (of s.o.'s mind). *Lupakanku dari ingatanmu.* Forget about me.

terlupa(kan) 1 forgotten accidentally. **2** (it has) slipped one's mind. **3** neglected. *tidak ~* unforgettable.

lupa-lupaan pretend to forget; apt to forget, forgetful. *tak bisa tidak ~* just cannot get it out of one's mind.

kelupaan 1 forgetfulness, aptness to forget. **2** to forget, let slip from one's mind. *~ apa engkau?* What have you forgotten? *~ minum.* I forgot to have a drink.

pelupa 1 to be forgetful, absent-minded. *sifat ~* aptness to forget, forgetfulness. **2** forgetful person.

pelupaan disregard, neglect, lack of attention, forgetfulness.

lupak → LOPAK I.

lupa-lupa fish maws of the threadfin, *Polynemus spp.*

lupas → KELUPAS, KUPAS I.

lupat *(siput) -* a gasteropod mollusk, *Hippopus maculatus.*

lupi *papan -* *(naut cla)* fore and aft decking (in boat).

lupis → LOPIS II.

lupuh melupuh to flatten out bamboo (for flooring/fencing/walls); *cp* PELUPUH, PUPUH I.

pelupuh flattened-out bamboo. *dinding ~* wall made of this material.

lupuk k.o. climbing plant, *Adenia acuminata.*

lupung *(- jantan)* k.o. tree, *Antidesma velutinosum.*

luput I 1 vanished, disappeared, gone. *- di/dari mata* out of sight, no longer visible. *- di/dari hati* out of one's mind, no longer remembered; *cp* JAUH *di mata, jauh di hati.* **2** escaped, got away, cleared. *- dari(pada)* a) escaped from. *- dari tuduhan* cleared (of an accusation). b) without. *- dari keinsafan/keyakinan* without realizing/conviction. **3** *tak/tidak - (dari)* a) not free (from), cannot escape. *tak - kena sadap* (his telephone) did not escape from being bugged. b) to keep (on) ...-ing, continue ...-ing, continue to ... *tidak - dari memikirkan* keep on thinking about. *tidak - dari memperhatikan* always paying attention to.

meluputkan 1 *~ dari* to put out of one's mind, forget; to take away (the chance to ..., control over ...). **2** to make (one's) escape from, get away from. *~ diri dari* to withdraw from; to shirk (a task); to back out of (an obligation). **3** to dodge, evade, avoid (being a target).

terluput *~ dari* a) free from. *Tiada seorangpun ~ dari kesalahan.* Nobody is free from making mistakes. b) secured against, protected from, guaranteed against. c) escaped from, avoided. *~ dari bencana yang lebih besar* avoided a greater catastrophe.

luput II *(J/Jv)* to fail, not succeed, missed, didn't hit the mark, wrong.

Luqman *(A)* the name of the 31st chapter of the Koran.

lurah I *(Jv)* **1** village head, i.e., the chief administrative official of a *kelurahan.* **2** *(coq)* boss. *- kota* head of a ward (in a town). *- polisi* assistant for security matters.

kelurahan village/ward, subdistrict, i.e., the administrative unit below a *kecamatan,* often the same as a *désa;* → NAGARI, PERBEKALAN. *~ kota* a *kelurahan* in a town. *~ pinggiran* a *kelurahan* on the edge of a town.

lurah II *(M)* valley, ravine, canyon. **2** groove. *bukit sama didaki, - sama dituruni* and *ke bukit sama mendaki, ke - sama menurun* unanimous, of one mind. *- hidung* groove in upper lip, philtrum.

berlurah *~ di balik pendakian* there is s.t. going on behind it, there is a snake in the grass, there's a catch in it somewhere.

lurai (in East Timor) a lower, local sovereign.

lurik *(Jv)* **1** hand-woven cotton with a striped pattern from Yogyakarta. **2** *(geol)* stringer.

lurikan to wear *lurik.* **2** *(geol)* striation.

luru meluru to chase, pursue, run after.

lurub *(J/Jv)* → LURUP. cloth over a bier, pall.

melurubkan [and **ngelurubin** *(J)*] to cover the entire thing or body with a cloth/blanket.

luruban cloth over a bier, pall.

lurug *(Jv)* **nglurug 1** to fight, be up in arms. **2** to make an expedition, take a trip.

lurugan (to go on an) expedition.

luruh I 1 to drop, fall (of flowers), fall out (of one's hair), molt, scale off (of a scab). **2** deciduous. **3** *(- hatinya)* touched (of one's feelings). **4** breaking (of one's voice).

berluruhan *(pl subj)* to drop, fall, etc.

meluruh 1 to fall off (of leaves, etc.). **2** to molt, shed (its feathers). **3** *(phys)* to disintegrate.

meluruhkan *(phys)* to make s.t. fall off, molt, etc.

peluruh s.t. which makes s.t. drop/fall off, etc. *~ kencing* medicine for making a kidney stone come out. *~ muntah* emetic.

peluruhan 1 shedding, falling off, dropping off. **2** disintegration.

luruh II *(cla)* area, district, dependency.

luruk meluruk to assault, attack.

lurup *(J)* **lurupan** *~ mayat* winding sheet, shroud.

lurus 1 straight, without curves, not crooked. *- kanan!* *(mil)* right dress! **2** right. *belum -* not yet right (of command of a language). **3** upright. *- tegak* bolt upright. **4** *(- hati)* straightforward, candid, honest. **5** literal, word-by-word. *terjemahan yang -* a literal/verbatim translation. **6** linear (relationship). **7** (in mining) swaging. *- akal* straightforward, honest. *- lempeng* straight, direct.

selurusan directly facing, opposite; → SETENTANG.

selurusnya actually; the reality is.

berselurus to do s.t. honestly.

melurus 1 to stretch out straight, go straight ahead. **2** to straighten out.

melurusi to go straight along s.t., follow s.t. faithfully.

meluruskan and **memperluruskan 1** to straighten (out), correct. *kekeliruan yang harus diluruskan* an error that must be corrected. **2** to make a correction by saying what is correct. *~ bahwa dia seorang Muslim* made a correction saying that she is a Muslim. **3** to stretch out (one's legs). **4** to align, line up.

lurusan *(geol)* lineament.

kelurusan 1 straightness. **2** honesty, sincerity, straightforwardness.

pelurus 1 straightener. *~ selubung (petro)* casing swage. **2** *(math)* supplement(ary); → SUDUT *pelurus.*

pelurusan 1 straightening (out), correcting. **2** streamlining.

lurut I to fall out, fall (of flowers/leaves), fall out (of one's hair); to drop off prematurely (of fruits/hair/a fetus that dies in the womb).

lurut II melurut 1 to massage (a swollen hand, etc.) with the fingers. **2** to slip s.t. off with the fingers (a ring, etc.). **3** to smooth s.t. out with the fingers (cigarette paper, etc.). **4** to separate seeds or leaves from the stalks. **5** to flow (of water).

melurutkan to take s.t. off, strip off.

lus → ELUS.

lusa the day after tomorrow. *bésok (atau) -* a) one/some day (in the future). b) before long, soon, in a day or two. c) two days from now. *pada hari Minggu -* on Sunday (the day after tomorrow). *pada -nya* two days later/from then.

lusi warp (in weaving).

lusin *(D)* dozen, a set of 12. *cangkir empat -* four dozen cups.

berlusin the/per dozen.

berlusin-lusin dozens of.

lusinan 1 about a dozen. **2** by the dozen.

luslas darting, flashing by rapidly.

luslus (*J*) **ngeluslus** → MENGELUS(-ELUS).

lustrum (*D*) lustrum, a five-year period; → PANCAWARSA.

lusuh 1 crumpled (of clothes, etc.). **2** worn-out, discolored, faded (of fabric); shabby (of clothes).

 melusuh to crumple, become crumpled.

 melusuhkan to crumple (up), crease; to wear out, discolor.

 kelusuhan crumpling.

 pelusuhan fading.

lusur → LUNCUR.

lut I penetrable, translucent (to light), permeable (to a liquid). *tidak* – invulnerable, impenetrable; → KEBAL, MEMPAN. *tidak* – *oléh senjata* invulnerable to weapons.

 telut penetrated. *tidak* ~ invulnerable.

lut II *batu* – plummet.

Lut(h) III (*A*) (the Biblical) Lot (Abraham's nephew). *Bahar* – The Dead Sea.

lutar → LO(N)TAR.

lutcahaya (*Mal*) translucent.

luti crumpled (of cloth, paper), wrinkled. – *lusuh* all crumpled up.

 meluti to crumple s.t.

lutsinar (*Mal*) transparent.

lutu I melutu (*cla*) **1** to hit out at, pitch into (them), attack furiously, go for (s.o.). **2** to fall down.

lutu II (*M*) dirt.

 berlutu dirty, filthy.

lutung and – *berbulu hitam* leaf monkey, a black, long-haired, long-tailed monkey, *Presbytis spp.*; → KERA *hitam.* – *Jawa* silver leaf monkey, *Trachypithecus spp.* – *Kasarung* a Sundanese literary work.

lutut knee. *berdiri* – to sit on the floor or on a bench with one knee pulled up (a position often used when eating at a *warung*). *bergoyang* – to sit and move one's legs. *bersaksi ke* – a) to make a friend/relative one's witness. b) to take advice from a stupid person. *bertegak* – → BERDIRI *lutut. bertekuk* – a) to bend the knees, kneel. b) to surrender. *bertemu* – to sit with one's knees brought together. *bertindih* – (to squat on the ground) with knees touching (of people sitting in a crowd). *bertongkat/bertopang* – to sit with the elbows/hands resting on the knees. *melipat(kan)/menekuk* – to bend one's knees. – *belakang* stiffle (of a horse).

 selutut up to the knees, knee-high, knee-length.

 berlutut 1 to kneel. **2** to surrender, give up.

luwak → LUAK I.

luwang (*Jv*) pit, hole (in the ground).

luwé (*J*) *uler* – centipede; → LIPAN.

luweng (*Jv*) cavern, cave, sinkhole; → LUWANG.

 meluwengkan to put s.t. into a cave.

luwes (*Jv*) **1** free and easy (in one's movements and manners), supple, flexible, smooth. **2** elegant, stylish, charming, pleasant (of manners), graceful.

 meluweskan to smooth s.t. out.

 memperluwes to make s.t. smooth(er).

 keluwesan 1 smoothness. **2** suppleness, flexibility. **3** elegance, grace, gracefulness.

luwing (*Jv*) k.o. centipede; → LIPAN.

luwuk → ULAR *gadung.*

luyu sleepy. *mata* – so tired one's eyes are drooping; → RUYUP.

luyur → KELUYUR.

luyut meluyut 1 (= **berluyutan**) to droop (of tree branches under the weight of fruit). **2** → LUYU.

lw (*abbr*) [lawan] against, versus.

M

m and **M I** /ém/ the 13th letter of the Latin alphabet used for writing Indonesian.

m II (*abbr*) **1** [méter] meter (= 39.37 inches). **2** [menit] minute.

m III /ém/ (*euph* for *ménstruasi*) to have one's period.

M IV (*abbr*) [Maséhi] **1** A.D. – *1987* A.D. 1987. **2** Christian.

M V car license plate for Madura.

3M [Masak-Macak-Manak] (*Jv*) Cooking-Dressing Up-Giving Birth (the duties of a perfect woman).

4M [Masak-Macak-Manak-Mlumah] (*Jv*) Cooking-Dressing Up-Giving Birth-Sex; → **3M**.

ma I (*A*) water. – *ul-hayat* water of life.

ma II (*A*) who, which, what. –*sya Allah* what God wishes; → **MASYA ALLAH**.

ma III (*Timor D*) but. *Béta bukan orang Timor, – béta pernah tinggal di sana.* I'm not a Timorese, but I have lived there.

ma IV (in acronyms) → **MAJELIS I, MARKAS.**

ma V clipped form of **ama II**.

ma' → MAK I.

M.A. 1 [Master of Arts] Master of Arts; in Indonesian: S(arjana) S(astra). **2** [Mahasiswa Abadi] eternal college student (derogatory epithet for a student who has been at the same level for some time).

Maab (*A*) Moab.

maaf (*A*) **1** forgiveness, pardon, excuse, apology. *Tidak ada – bagi anggota Polisi yang terlibat narkotika.* There's no excuse for members of the police force who are involved in narcotics. *minta –* a) to apologize. b) to ask permission to leave. **2** Excuse/pardon me. I'm sorry. **3** sorry (said to a beggar to whom one does not want to give anything). **4** excuse the expression (used before saying something improper).

bermaaf-maafan to forgive e.o. at the end of the fasting month or *puasa* (for mistakes made to e.o.); → **MINALAIDIN WALFAIZIN.**

memaafi to forgive s.o.

memaafkan to forgive s.t. or s.o. *~ diri dengan mudah* to let o.s. off the hook. *dapat dimaafkan* forgivable, excusable. *~ tapi tidak melupakan* to forgive but not forget.

maaf-memaafkan to forgive e.o. *~ dan melupakan* to forgive and forget.

termaafkan excusable. *tidak ~* inexcusable, unforgivable.

kemaafan forgiveness, pardon.

pemaaf 1 forgiver (person or thing). **2** forgiving, inclined to forgive. **kepemaafan** forgivingness.

pe(r)maafan forgiving.

maag (*D*) /makh/; → **MAG.**

maal hayat → MAULHAYAT.

maalim → MUALIM. *– fil tariq* (*A*) milestone.

maani (*A*) meaning; → **MAKNA.**

maap → MAAF. *dimaapin* (*J coq*) to be excused/forgiven.

maarif (*A*) education.

Maarij (*A*) al– "The Steps"; name of the 70th chapter of the Koran.

MAB [Memayu Ayuning Buwana] → **MAMAYU HAYUNING BUWONO.**

mabés [markas besar] headquarters.

mabir → TABIR I.

mabit (*A*) to sleep over at certain places during the *hajj.*

mabok → MABUK.

mabruk (*J*) bad, in a bad state.

mabrur (*A*) accepted by God. *haji –* a haji accepted by God; → **HAJI mabrur.**

mabuk 1 drunk, intoxicated. *dalam keadaan setengah –* tipsy. **2** to be crazy about, love s.t. *– di enggang lalu* highly attracted to a person one doesn't know yet. *sebagai orang – gadung* deathly pale. *– andan* intoxicated with the idea of getting married. *– angan-angan* intoxicated on one's own fantasies. *– asmara* head over heels in love. *– baca* loves to read. *– bayang* to wish for the impossible. *– berahi* head over heels in love. *– berhias*

loves to dress up. *– bunga raya* flushed from drinking. *– bunga selasih* dead drunk. *– cendawan* madly in love. *– (akan) darah* a) can't stand the sight of blood. b) run amok at the sight of blood. c) bloodthirsty. *– darat* carsick. *– empat tiang* dead drunk. *– ganja* stoned, high. *– gunung* altitude sickness. *– harta* materialistic. *– kayal* lightheaded, intoxicated. *– kebesaran* suffer from megalomania. *– kecubung* intoxicated from datura poisoning. *– kekenyangan* suffer from having eaten too much. *– kemenangan* flushed with victory. *– kendaraan* (suffer from) motion sickness. *– kepayang* a) madly in love. b) somewhat tipsy. c) high on drugs; → **FLAAI.** *– kesenangan* drunk with happiness. *– khayal* lightheaded, intoxicated. *– laut/ombak* seasick. *– pangkat* crazy about one's position or rank. *– perbuatan* audacious(ly). *– (dengan) pikiran* lost in thought. *– pukulan* punch drunk. *– rasa* ecstasy. *– rupa* deceived by appearances. *– selasih* dead drunk. *– uang* money hungry. *– udara* airsick.

bermabuk-mabuk to act like a drunken person.

bermabuk-mabukan (*pl subj*) drunk.

memabuk only in passive form *dimabuk. dimabuk angan-angan* to be lost in thought. *dimabuk bayang-bayang* wanting to do the impossible. *dimabuk cinta* to be head over heels in love. *dimabuk kenangan* to be lost in thought. *dimabuk kekuasaan* to be power-hungry. *dimabuk nasib yang malang* to be in trouble, be troubled. *dimabuk sayang* to be love sick.

memabukkan 1 to intoxicate, make s.o. drunk. **2** intoxicating.

mabuk-mabukan to go on a drinking spree.

kemabukan drunkenness.

pemabuk drunkard, a drunk.

pemabukan drunkenness. **sepemabukan** *rekan/teman ~* drinking buddies.

mabul(-mabul) (*Jv*) scattered, dispersed.

mabur (*J/Jv*) to fly/run away.

ma'bud (*A*) worshipped.

mac (*D*) /mak/ → **MÉK.**

macak (*Jv*) to dress up; → **3M.** *– diri biar cantik* to dress up to look pretty.

macam 1 sort, kind, species, quality, type. *kain dua –* two kinds of cloth. *Orang – apakah dia?* What kind of a person is he? *– apa sih meréka?* What will they be like? **2** model, pattern, design. *pakaian – sekarang* fashionable/stylish clothes. **3** manner, way, method. *– mana?* in what way? *Bagaimana –nya ia mengajar kuda kita?* How is he training our horses? **4** as, like, resemble, look like. *– ini/itu* like this/that. *– dia* like him, as he does. *– mana besar anakkau?* How big is your child? *Bukan – dia.* Not his kind of thing, not what he does. *bukan –mu ini, orang yang ...* you're not (the kind of) man to... *kalau begini –nya* if this is how the matter stands (or, how things are). *– ragam* diverse. **memacam-ragamkan** to diversify.

macam-macam *~ ada saya lihat* it is as if I had seen s.t. *~ saja* always s.t. new/different. *Jangan ~.* a) Don't be a wise guy, don't get any bright ideas, don't do anything stupid, don't try anything with me. b) Get off my back! Stop bugging me! c) Don't keep making excuses. *Tuan ini ~ saja.* You've always got s.t. to say.

semacam 1 of the same kind/sort. **2** like, as, resembling. *yang ~ itu* like that one *atau yang ~nya itu* or that sort of thing, or s.t. like that. *dan ~nya* and the like. **3** a k.o., a sort of.

bermacam various, several, diverse.

(ber)macam-macam miscellaneous, mixed, diverse, assorted, several, of various types, all kinds/sorts/types of. *Apa saja yang dibicarakan tadi? ~.* What was discussed earlier? All sorts of things.

mempermacam-macamkan 1 to treat s.t. differently. **2** to try all k.o. things on s.o.

macan I (*Jv*) tiger; → **HARIMAU I.** *membangunkan – tidur/turu* to awaken sleeping dogs. *– makan tuan* it backfires; → **SENJATA** *makan tuan. – Bali* Bali tiger, *Panthera tigris balica. – dahan* clouded leopard, *Neofelis nebulosa*. – *gadungan* were-tiger. – *hitam* black panther. – *kertas* paper tiger. – *kumbang* black panther. – *loréng* a) the striped royal tiger. b) camouflage (clothing). – *ompong* paper tiger. – *sima* (in Central and East Java) the striped royal tiger. – *tutul* spotted leopard, *Panthera pardus*.

memacani to intimidate, scare, frighten.

macan-macanan 1 toy tiger, plaything. **2** k.o. game of siege.

macan II *ikan* – tiger barb, *Barbus tetrazona* found in Sumatra and Kalimantan.

macan III *rambutan (si)* – an oval, sweet, dark-red rambutan variety.

macang (*ob*) → EMBACANG.

macapat (*Jv*) **1** meter, verse. **2** reading of Javanese literary works in verse form, singing them without musical accompaniment.

macat → MACET.

maceki (*Bal*) to play *ceki*.

macet (*J*) **1** stuck, not run(ning) smoothly, come to a halt. *-lah pembuatan film itu*. Production on that film has come to a halt. **2** clogged (of pipe, etc.), blocked (of traffic), jammed (of street). *Lalulintas menjadi –*. There was a traffic jam. *– total* totally blocked. **memacet-totalkan** to block (traffic) completely. **3** frozen (up), seized up. **4** to jam, jammed (of a weapon). **5** non-performing (of a loan).

macetnya *di mana letak* ~ where the shoe pinches.

semacet as jammed as.

memacetkan 1 to block, hold up. ~ *lalulintas* to block/hold up traffic. **2** to jam (the streets).

kemacetan 1 deadlock, stalemate. **2** shutdown. **3** stagnation. **4** jam. ~ *lalulintas* traffic jam, bottleneck.

pemacet jammer. ~ *radar* radar jammer.

pemacetan jamming.

mac(h)iok → MAHYONG.

machtsaanwénding (*D ob*) /makhts-/ use of power.

machtsvorming (*D ob*) /makhstforming/ formation of power.

ma'ci' → MAKCIK.

maci kwé (*C*) k.o. pastry filled with fried sesame seeds.

maciok → MACOK.

macis (*E esp* in Bangkahulu) matches.

macok (*C*) mahjong.

mad(d) (*A*) mark for lengthening (of vowel) in Arabic script.

mada I (*M*) stupid, dull, feeble-minded.

mada II (*Skr*) **1** furious. **2** must (of male animal).

ma'da → MAK I.

Madagaskar Madagascar.

madah I (*A*) **1** eulogy, high praise. **2** stanza.

bermadah 1 to praise; to recite. **2** to speak, talk.

memadahkan 1 to express, pronounce, recite. **2** to relate.

madahan eulogy.

pemadah a religious person.

madah II (*A*) long-vowel mark in Arabic writing; → MAD(D), MADDAH.

madali (*cla*) k.o. musical instrument.

madaliun (*D*) medallion, locket.

madam (*D*) madam.

ma'dan → MAKDAN.

madang I → MEDANG. – *kapas* (*S*) k.o. tree, *Litsea chinensis*.

madang II (*J*) to eat (*esp* rice); → MAKAN.

madani I (*Jv*) *saling* – mudslinging.

madani II (*J*) → PERMADANI.

madani III (*A*) civic, civil; → MASYARAKAT *madani*.

madap → MADEP.

madar (*M ob*) → MADA I.

madarat (*A*) **1** loss (in business), detriment, damage, injury, harm; → MUDARAT. **2** abuse.

madarsah → MADRASAH.

madat I (*A*) **1** prepared opium; *cp* CANDU I. *minum* – to smoke opium. *rumah* – opium den. **2** mania; excessive, persistent enthusiasm, obsession; craving; obsession; craze; -mania. *di kalangan yang belum – seni* in circles which are not yet art-crazy.

bermadat 1 to smoke opium. **2** with opium in it.

madatan ~ *lelaki* nymphomaniac(al).

pemadat 1 opium smoker/addict. **2** addict. **3** (*coq*) crazy/deranged/obsessed person.

pemadatan 1 smoking opium. **2** opium den.

madat II (*J*) a jobless person who begs for cigarettes, money, etc.

madat III 1 turret, watchtower. **2** battlements, scaffolding.

madd → MAD.

maddah → MAD(D), MADAH II.

maddi (*A*) material, not spiritual. *hukum* – material law.

madep (*J*) → MENGHADAP.

madet I (*J*) → PADAT.

madet II → MADAT.

madhab → MAZHAB.

madi – *pita* banded broadbill, *Eurylaimus javanicus*.

madia → MADYA.

madidihang yellow-fin tuna, *Thunus macropterus*.

madik (*Pal*) marriage broker.

madikipé (*J*) (rude term of abuse). Damn it/you; → MADIPANTAT. *"–, mahal banget, cing!"* "Damn it, that's too expensive, man!"

Madinah Medina.

madipantat (*J*) → MADIKIPÉ.

madon (*Jv*) to chase after women.

madona (*D*) Madonna.

Madrali [Madura-Australi] crossbreed between a Madurese and Australian cow.

madrasah (*A*) (Muslim religious) school, usually privately owned, though some receive a subsidy from the Department of Religious Affairs; → ALIYAH, IBTIDAIYAH, TSANAWIYAH. – *jamiah* theological university.

madu I (*Jv*) **1** co-wife, one's husband's other wife; for instance, A has two wives, B and C; B is the *madu* of C and vice versa. **2** competition in love; *cp* MADON.

bermadu to have a co-wife, share one's husband with another wife.

memadu to be made a co-wife. *Dia dimadu*. Her husband has taken another wife.

memadui to take another wife.

memadukan and **mempermadukan** to give one's wife a co-wife.

permaduan polygamy; polygyny.

madu II (*Skr*) **1** honey. **2** as sweet as honey. **3** very sweet (of a smile). *di luar bagai –, di dalam bagai empedu* all that glitters is not gold. – *air* watermelon honey. – *labu* melon honey.

madu III *burung* – plain-throated sunbird, *Anthreptes malaccensis*.

madu IV joined, linked, united; → PADU. – *mancung* joining at a sharp point.

madukara (*Skr*) **1** bee. **2** *kain* – silk with gold-thread pattern.

madya (*Skr*) **1** medium, average, intermediate, mid-level. **2** form of the Javanese language between *kromo* and *ngoko*.

madyapada (*Skr*) place of human habitation; earth.

madz(h)ab → MAZHAB.

madznun → MAJENUN.

maédah (*A*) table.

maem (children's language) to eat.

maén (*coq*) → MAIN. – *cap keliling* to goof off.

maéngkét a Minahasan dance.

maésan → MÉSAN, MISAN I.

maéstro (*D*) maestro, master (eminent composer/painter/musician/dancer, etc.). *sang – seni lukis Indonésia ini* this Indonesian master painter.

mafela (*ob*) shawl.

mafhum (*A*) to know, understand, comprehend, be familiar (with).

memafhumi to know about, understand, be familiar with.

mafia (*E*) mafia; → BERKELEY MAFIA. – *jati* mafia-like elements operating in teakwood sales on the island of Muna (Southeast Celebes). – *peradilan* mafia-like elements which control court decisions through various institutions in several places in Indonesia.

mafiaisme mafia practices (carried out by gangs who extort money from hotels and nightclubs).

mafiosi (*D/E*) mafiosi, gangsters.

mag (*D*) stomach; → MAAG. *sakit* – stomach/gastric pains.

magal k.o. tree, *Sarcocephalus hirsutus*.

magang I (*Jv*) **1** trainee. **2** candidate for a position. **3** apprentice, on-the-job learner. *guru* – student teacher with license.

bermagang and **memagang** to work as an apprentice.

pemagang apprentice.

pemagangan and **permagangan** apprenticeship.

magang II overripe, ripe and rotten (of fruit), turning sour (of fermented liquor).

magasén and **magasin** (*D*) magazine, warehouse.

magbub (*A?*) minced lamb saté.

magel (*J/Jv*) **1** half-ripe. **2** not fully cleaned, still has spots on it. **3** not full-fledged, without sufficient knowledge. **4** hard, tough. *urat* – penis.

magersari (*Jv*) **1** s.o. who owns and occupies (with permission) a home on the land of a wealthy person. **2** tiller, farmer, cultivator. **3** person who helps prospective transmigrants to settle in another area.

magfirah, magfirat, and **maghfiroh** (*A*) forgiveness.

maggi /magi/ (a brand name) bouillon cubes.

maghlub (*A*) conquered, defeated.

maghrébin (*A*) inhabitants of the Maghreb, i.e., the Arabic name for the northwest part of Africa; included are Morocco, Algeria, Tunisia, and sometimes Libya.

maghrib → MAGRIB.

magi (*D*) magic(al power).

magis (*D*) magical.

magistér (*D*) magistrate, master, i.e., the latest version of the *sarjana* degree. – *Manajemém* Masters in Management. – *Pendidikan* Master of Education, M.Ed. – *Sains* Master of Science, M.Sc. – *Téknik* Masters in Engineering.

magistik (*D*) majestic. *imprési* – a majestic impression.

magistra(a)t (*D*) → MAGISTER.

maglub (*A*) defeated.

magma (*D/E*) magma.

magnésium (*D/E*) magnesium.

magnét (*E*) and **magnit** (*D*) magnet.
  bermagnét magnetic.
  memagnétkan to magnetize.
  kemagnétan magnetism.

magnétik (*D/E*) magnetic.

magnétograf (*D/E*) magnetograph.

magnétométer (*D/E*) magnetometer.

magrib (*A*) **1** the west (*esp* as viewed from Arabia). **2** sunset. *waktu* – at sunset. *salat/sembahyang* – sunset prayer. *orang-orang yang usianya sudah menjelang* – the elderly. **3** Morocco.

magribi (*A*) **1** western. **2** Moroccan; Moorish.

magrong (*Jv*) immensely large, sizable, looming.

magrur (*A*) proud, arrogant.

magun fixed (of awnings/ventilators on ships, etc.), built-in, permanent. *kajang* – fixed awning. – *angin* ventilator, skylight, porthole.

mah I shortening for *maha*, e.g. *mahraja* → MAHARAJA.

mah II (*SJ*) shows that the previous or new information is stressed. *Kalau saya* – *tidak salah.* As far as I'm concerned, it isn't wrong. *Itu* – *peraturan!* That's (what you call) a regulation!

mah III (in acronyms) → MAHKAMAH.

maha- (*Skr*) (in compounds) high, superior; extreme, great, very.

mahaasih All-Loving (of God).

Mahab(h)arata (*Skr*) "Great Epic of the Bharatas," the second of the two great Hindu epics in Sanskrit adopted by the Javanese, believed to be based on the war between the two families of the Bharata clan, the *Pandawa*s and the *Kurawa*s, in the 13th or 14th century B.C.

mahabintang superstar.

mahadahsyat tremendous, dreadful, awful. *gempa* – a tremendous earthquake.

Ma'had Atta'lim Allughat Al'Arabiyah Bi Indunisia (*A*) Institute for the Teaching of Arabic in Indonesia.

Mahadéwa (*Skr cla*) Siva, the Supreme God.

Mahadéwi (*Skr cla*) **1** Durga, wife of Siva. **2** title for a second queen.

mahaduta (*Skr ob*) ambassador.
  permahadutaan embassy.

mahaesa omnipotent. *Tuhan yang* – God, the Omnipotent.

mahaguru professor.

mahajana I (*Skr*) (*ob*) a great/famous man, an important person.

mahajana II (*Skr*) the public. *di* – in public.

mahajutawan (*Skr neo*) multimillionaire.

mahakarya (*Skr neo*) masterpiece.

mahakeramat most sacred.

Mahakuasa the Almighty.
  kemahakuasaan almightiness.

mahal 1 expensive, high-priced, dear. **2** scarce, hard to find. – *dibeli, sukar dicari* expensive and very hard to find. – *mencari orang sebaik itu.* It's hard to find a person as good as that. – *ketawa* does not laugh easily, always serious. – *rezeki* it's hard to make a living. – *senyum* doesn't smile easily.

semahal as expensive as.

semahal-mahalnya 1 no matter how expensive. **2** at the most expensive, no more expensive than.

memahalkan 1 to raise the price of. **2** to (over)value, (over)estimate.

termahal the most expensive.

mahalan (*coq*) more expensive.

kemahalan 1 tightness, scarcity. **2** (*coq*) too expensive. **3** very expensive. *tunjangan* ~ cost-of-living allowance.

mahalama very long (of time). *waktu yang* – a very long time.

mahalezat extremely tasty/delicious.

mahaligai → MA(H)LIGAI.

mahaluas vast.

mahamenteri (*cla*) chief minister (below the *bendahara*).

Mahaméru (*Skr*) the World-Mountain which reaches from Heaven to Earth. At its peak the gods have their abode. The Javanese identify it with *Gunung Seméru*, in East Java. The Sumatrans believe it was located in Sumatra; the Indonesian Olympus.

mahamulia (*Skr neo*) **1** most exalted, most illustrious. **2** *Yang* – His Highness (term of address for sovereigns).

mahang various species of soft-wood trees, *Macaranga spp.* – *bayan* k.o. tree, *Macaranga javanica.* – *kukur* Malaysian ant plant, *Macaranga triloba.*

mahap → MAAF.

mahapencipta (*Skr neo*) the Almighty Creator.

mahapenting most important.

mahapialang top broker.

mahar (*A*) dowry (given by the groom to the bride). *membayar* – to give a dowry.

maharaja (*Skr*) **1** great raja. **2** once a title for a nobleman; then became *seri* –.
  kemaharajaan empire.

maharajaléla (*cla*) chief minister who was responsible for the execution of prisoners.
  bersimaharajaléla 1 to do as one pleases without fear of anyone else, act mercilessly, go on a rampage, operate unchecked/tyrannically. **2** to rage.

maharana (*Skr cla*) the great war (of the *Mahabharata*).

maharani (*Skr cla*) princess, queen.

maharesi (*Skr cla*) a great Hindu sage.

maharupa (*Skr cla*) extremely beautiful.

Maha Sabha (in Bali) Grand Conference (of the Parisada Hindu Dharma).

mahasayang all-merciful (of God).

mahasiswa (*Skr neo*) male college/university student. – *abadi* eternal college student (derogatory epithet for a student who has been at the same level for some time). – *fotokopi* college student who mostly studies from photocopied lecture notes. – *kedokteran* premed. – *pendengar* auditor. – *tingkat I/Satu* freshman. – *pindahan* transfer student. – *tingkat II/Dua* sophomore. – *tingkat III/Tiga* junior. – *tingkat IV/Empat* senior. – *tingkat sarjana* graduate student at the master's level (i.e., for the Drs., S.H., or other degree equivalent to the master's).
  kemahasiswaan 1 student (*mod*). **2** student affairs.

mahasiswi female college/university student.

Mahasuci the Most Holy (God).

mahatahu all-knowing, omniscient (of God).

mahatinggi exalted.

mahatma (*Skr*) exalted soul (title for the late Gandhi, India's leader).

mahatur *paduka* – (*cla*) junior queen in ancient Java.

Mahawas Mahaya Swajama Parajama the motto of the Immigration Directorate, meaning: Protect and Supervise Citizens and Aliens.

Mahayana form of Indian Buddhist religion adopted by some ancient Indonesian dynasties.

mahbub (*A*) beloved, sweetheart (of men).

mahbubah (*A*) beloved, sweetheart (of women).

mahdi (*A*) *al*- and *imam* – the leader, who, Muslims believe, will come to the earth before the Last Day and slay the Anti-Christ; the Muslim Messiah.

mahérat (*ob*) to disappear, vanish; to go away; → MAIRAT II, MÉRAT.

mahésa (*Skr*) class buffalo; an old Javanese honorific.

Mahéswara class Supreme Lord (Siva).

mahful (*A*) 1 memorized, learned by heart. 2 memory.

   memahfulkan to memorize.

mahing (*M ob*) to give off a strong, unpleasant smell, stink.

mahir (*A*) skilled, well-versed, intelligent, clever.

   semahir as clever/skilled as.

   memahirkan to practice, learn, acquire.

   mempermahir to perfect.

   kemahiran skill, know-how.

mahisa → MAHÉSA.

mahkamah (*A*) court (of justice), tribunal. – *Agung* [MA] Supreme Court. *Ketua* – *Agung* Chief Justice of the Supreme Court. – *Banding* Court of Appeals. – *Kehakiman Internasional* International Court of Justice. – *Militér* [Mahmil] Court Martial, Military Court. – *Militér Luar Biasa* [Mahmilub] Extraordinary Military Tribunal. – *Militér Tinggi* [Mahmilti] High Military Court. – *Pelayaran* Merchant Shipping Tribunal. – *Tentara* Court Martial. – *Tinggi* High Court.

mahkamat → MAHKAMAH.

mahkota (*Skr*) → MAKOTA. 1 crown. *putra* – crown prince. 2 corolla (of a flower). – *alhajat* the afterlife. – *gadis/kegadisan* hymen, maidenhood, virginity. – *jiwa* sweetheart. – *kekayaan* crown of glory. – *tajuk* canopy. – *tambahan* corona.

   memahkotai to crown, give a crown/award to.

   kemahkotaan crown (*mod*). *jajahan* ~ crown colony (Hong Kong).

   pemahkotaan crowning, coronation.

mahligai → MALIGAI. – *cita-cita* castles in the air.

mahluk → MAKHLUK.

Mahmil [Mahkamah Militér] Military Tribunal.

   me-Mahmil-kan to summon before a Military Tribunal.

Mahmilti [Mahkamah Militér Tinggi] High Military Court.

Mahmilub [Mahkamah Militér Luar Biasa] Extraordinary Military Tribunal.

   me-Mahmilub-kan to bring before the Extraordinary Military Tribunal.

mahmud (*A*) praised, lauded.

mahnit → MAGNIT, MAKNIT.

mahoni I (*BG*) to have nothing to do.

mahoni II (*D*) mahogany, *Swietenia macrophylla*.

mahout instructor at the *Sekolah Gajah Way Kambas* at Tanjungkarang.

mahraj point of articulation.

mahram (*A*) immediate/close relative (whom one cannot marry).

mahrib → MAGRIB.

mahsar → MAHSYAR.

mahsul (*A*) 1 product (of a country). 2 production. *hasil* – products, produce, yield.

   memahsulkan to produce.

   pemahsul producer.

mahsyar (*A*) gathering place (where all the Dead are judged on the Last Day). *hari* – Day of Resurrection. *padang* – Place of Resurrection.

mahtab (*Pers*) moonlight.

mahu → MAU.

mahung → MAUNG I.

mahyong (*C*) mahjong.

mahzi (*A*) genuine, pure.

mai (*J*) 1 → PUKI *mai*. 2 (*reg*) woman.

Maidah (*A*) *al*– "The Feast"; name of the fifth chapter of the Koran.

maido → PAIDO II.

maimun (*A*) lucky, fortunate.

main 1 to play (a games/musical instrument, etc.). *bukan* – extraordinary, enormous. – *kartu* to play cards for money. 2 to play/screw/fool (around). 3 to fuck, screw, do. – *yook* Come on, let's do it. *sekali* – short-time (one sex act with a prostitute). 4 to go out (with), have a romantic relationship (with). *Karyawati ada* – *dengan atasannya*. Some female employees go out with their superiors. 5 to start, go on. *Bioskopnya* – *jam tujuh*. The movie starts/goes on at seven o'clock. 6 (*Jv*) to visit, stop by; → DOLAN. *Silakan* – *ke rumah saya*. Please, come and visit me. 7 play, game, sport. – *témbak* gunplay. 8 to do s.t. corrupt. *ada yang* – there are people who take advantage of the opportunity to acquire material gains through corruption. *Meréka ada* – *dengan toko itu*. They were in cahoots with the store. 9 to be unfaithful (to one's spouse). *suaminya ada* – *dengan ...* her husband had an affair with ... 10 (*coq*) to run a (taxicab/pedicab, etc.) business. 11 followed by certain (verbal) roots— sometimes accompanied by *saja*—forms a phrase meaning at random, indiscriminately, without careful plan, unjustifiably; to make a practice of doing s.t. deplorable, for one's own pleasure, etc. – *akrobat* a) to be an acrobat (as a livelihood). b) to do odd jobs on the side for extra income. c) to engage in vigorous sex. – *ambil rokok* to take s.o. else's cigarettes (without asking permission). – *anggar* to fence. – *angin* to be inconstant, unpredictable. – *api* to play with fire. – *api dengan lelaki/pria lain* to have an extramarital affair. – *atur* to break the rules, disobey the regulations. – *backing/béking* to back up s.o. unthinkingly. – *bak-bak-bur*; → BERWOKWOK KETEKUR. – *barangkali* to say/use "perhaps, maybe" a lot. – *begituan* to fuck, screw. – *belakang* to do s.t. in an underhanded way. – *belakang dengan lelaki/pria lain* to have an extramarital affair. – *berjantan* to commit homosexual acts. – *beslah saja* to seize (smuggled goods) without reason. – *biola* to play the violin. – *bola* (*coq*) to play soccer. – *bola gelinding* to go bowling, bowl. – *bola gulir* to play golf. – *bola sodok* to shoot pool. – *bom* to bomb recklessly. – *bowling* to go bowling, bowl. – *burit* to engage in anal intercourse, commit sodomy. – *cari-carian* to play hide-and-(go-)seek. – *catur* to play chess. – *ceki* to play *ceki*. – *cinta* to flirt. – *comot* to be a kleptomaniac. – *culik* to kidnap. – *curang* to play dirty. – *dam* to play checkers. – *dil* (*ob*) to play hockey. – *ding-dong* to play video games/slot machines. – *domino* to play dominoes. *ikut-ikutan* – *dorong* just follow (the crowd) blindly, push one's way through blindly. – *duit* a) to bribe. b) to accept a bribe. c) to misappropriate government funds. – *gajah* to play chess. – *galan-galanan* to be chivalrous. – *gampang-gampangan* and – *gampang saja* to take it easy, play it the easy way. – *gant(h)ol* to play dirty. – *gaplé* to play dominos. – *gasak* to play rough. – *gayung* to fence (stolen goods). – *gelap-gelapan* to act in an illegal way. – *gila* a) to act arrogantly. b) to joke, fool around. c) to engage in extramarital sexual intercourse. – *gituan* to fuck, screw. – *golf* to play golf. – *hakim sendiri* to take the law into one's own hands. – *hoki* to play hockey. – *hutang* to borrow money left and right. – *jahat* to play dirty tricks. – *jalan belakang* to do s.t. under the table. – *judi* to gamble. – *judo* to engage in judo. – *jujur* to play fair. – *karaoké* (*vulg*) to engage in oral sex, give s.o. a blow job. – *karét* to be delayed; → JAM *karét*. – *kartu* to play cards. – *kartu terbuka* to lay one's cards on the table, be frank. – *kasak-kusuk* to do s.t. under the table. – *kasar* to act like a boor. – *kayu* a) to play rough/dirty. b) unfair play. – *kejar-kejaran* to play tag, play cat and mouse. – *kelah* to complain indiscriminately. – *keléréng* to shoot marbles. – *kelinci* to go whoring. – *kenéb* to play a certain children's game which uses rubber bands. – *keroyok* to gang up on s.o. – *kitik-kitikan* to tickle s.o. for fun. – *komidi* a) to put on (or, perform in) a stage play, act in a play. b) to pretend. – *kongkalikong* a) to fool s.o. b) to carry out intrigues. c) to swindle. d) to be in cahoots (with). – *kucing-kucingan* a) to play cat and mouse. b) to avoid s.o. – *layang-layang* to fly a kite. – *limau nipis* to commit homosexual acts. – *mata* to flirt. – *mata sérong-sérongan* to play dirty. – *muda* to flirt, court, neck, pet. – *menang-menangan omong* to be a matter of winning a war of words. – *nrimo saja* to be a fatalist. – *pajak* to play the tax game. – *paksa* to use coercion/force, use one's power. – *pancang* (*ob*) a game similar to bowling. – *panco* to arm-wrestle. – *pantat* to engage in anal intercourse. – *pasal* to be glib, argue legal niceties. – *pencak* to engage in pencak. – *peran* role playing. – *peras* to extort (money). – *perempuan* to run after girls, run around with women. – *petak-sembunyi* to play hide-and-(go-)seek. – *pinjam* to borrow from everybody. – *pintu belakang* to do s.t. in an underhanded way. – *pompa* (*vulg*) to fuck, screw. – *pukul (saja)* to lash out with the hand arbitrarily, hit at random. – *rebutan* "pole-climbing," a popular game and contest in which prizes are attached to the top of a pole covered with soap so that it is very difficult to climb. – *renggang* to maintain a distant relationship (with). – *rolét* to play roulette. – *sabun* a) to fix (a game). b) to masturbate (using soap). – *salip-salipan* to keep on passing e.o. (in cars). – *sandiwara* a) to put on (or, perform in) a stage play, act in a play. b) to put on an act. – *sapu rata* to make a clean sweep. – *selundup* to do s.t. under the table. – *semburit* to commit sodomy. – *serampangan* (to play for) all or nothing. – *serobot* to commit a crime. – *sérong* to fool around with another woman or man (than one's spouse). – *sikat* to be tricky. – *sikut* to elbow one's way (through). – *silap* a) to juggle. b) to conjure. – *simbang* to play jacks. – *sip* to play it safe. – *ski* to ski, go skiing. – *serobot* to grab things that don't belong to one. – *suap* to throw bribes around. – *sulap* a) to juggle. b) to conjure. – *suntik* to vaccinate without reason. – *tampuk labu* (*Mal*) to engage in lesbian intercourse. – *tangan* a) to hit with the fists. b) to gesticulate. – *tangan panjang* a) to touch a woman improperly. b) to like to steal things. – *tatakrama* to pull rank. – *tayang* k.o. children's game. – *tédéng aling-aling* to play hide-and-(go-)seek. – *télepon* to use the telephone without reason. – *témbak* a) gunplay, shootout; to shoot-'em-up. b) to shoot without provocation/reason. c) to bribe (explained as *ntar saya kasih* "I'll give you s.t. later"). – *témpél* to try to get s.t. out of s.o. rich or powerful. – *tendang* to kick out indiscriminately/without reason. – *tinggi* to have influence with higher-ups. – *tonjok* to punch, hit with the fist, box. – *top* to gamble. – *tunjuk saja* to appoint (people) without careful consideration. – *tutup mata* to play blind man's buff. – *udik* to play a children's game played with balls or hard seeds. – *umpet-umpetan* to play hide-and-(go-)seek. – *undi* to gamble.

main-main 1 not serious, in fun. *Ia mulai ~ dengan kata-kata sanjungan.* He began jokingly by using words of praise. *Bermula ia hanya ~ dengan busur dan anak panah.* At first she only played with bow and arrow. *buat ~ saja* a) just for fun, in play. b) to pass the time of day. *cuma ~* (I was) only joking. *Itu bukan ~.* It's not a joke. *jangan ~* no kidding! stop kidding around! *tidak ~* serious. *Polisi tak ~ dengan disiplin.* The police are serious about discipline. *~ jadi sungguhan* what was originally meant to be casual or not serious turned out to be very serious. **2** (*Jv*) to drop by for a visit.

bermain 1 to play, have fun, amuse o.s., be having a good time (also in a negative sense). *kelompok ~* play group (for children). [also look under **main**] *~ air basah, ~ api letup, ~ pisau luka.* If you play with fire, you'll be burned. *~ api* to play with fire. – *akal* to play tricks. – *akrobatik* to perform acrobatics. – *bola* to play ball/soccer. – *bola gelinding* to bowl, go bowling. – *budi* to play tricks, cheat. – *drama* to play (around). – *gila* to commit adultery. – *gundu/keléréng* to play marbles. – *hakim* to take the law into one's own hands. – *kepala* (in soccer) to hit the ball with one's head; → MENGKOP, MENYUNDUL. – *lancang-lancang* to play ducks and drakes, i.e., the game of throwing a small, flat stone so that it will skim or skip along the surface of a body of water. – *mata* a) to make eyes at s.t. (between men and women), flirt. b) to wink at s.o. (not limited to between men and women). c) to come to an illegal agreement. – *muda* to be unfaithful to one's spouse; → MUDA. – *piano* to play the piano. – *ranjang* to have sexual intercourse. – *tangan* to gesticulate with one's hands, make gestures. – *tangan panjang* to touch a woman lasciviously. – *tidak bersih* to sabotage. *Bila ~ dengan api hangus, ~ dengan air basah.* if you play with fire,

you'll be burned, i.e., everything has its consequences. **2** to flutter (of a flag). **3** to be manipulative.

bermain-main 1 to have fun (playing). **2** (just) for fun, all in fun, in play, playful(ly), joking(ly), not serious(ly). *Jangan ambil marah, saya hanya ~ saja.* Don't be angry, I did it just for fun. *Ah tidak apa, cuma ~ saja.* Oh, it's not serious; it's all in fun.

memaini to play (around) with.

memainkan [and **ngemainin** (*J coq*)] **1** to play (an instrument/ melody). *~ biola* to play the viola. *~ piano* to play the piano. **2** to play (a role, etc.). *~ kembali* to play back. *~ lakonnya* to play one's role/part. *~ mata* to flirt. *~ peranannya/rolnya* to play one's role. *~ waktu* to play for time. **3** to perform/give/put on (a play), stage. **4** to show (a film). *~ gas* to step on the gas.

mempermainkan 1 to perform, act. *~ lakon sedih* to stage a tragedy. **2** to play/fool around with. *Jangan suka ~ harta benda orang.* Don't play around with s.o. else's wealth. *~ ular* to play (for fun) with a snake. **3** to make fun/a fool of, tease. *suka ~ orang* to like to tease/make fun of. **4** to manipulate, victimize, give s.o. the runaround. *~ lidah* to cajole, sweet-talk.

mainan toy(s), plaything; toy- ..., play-... *~ perusahaan ~* a) toyshop. b) a phony company. *~ alat memasak* play cooking set. *~ anak-anak* children's toys. *pistol ~* toy pistol.

main-mainan toy.

pemain player, actor, performer. *~ anggar* fencer. *~ belakang* (in soccer) fullback, center back, behinds. *~ biola* violist. *~ bola baskét* basketball player. *~ cadangan* (in soccer) reservist. *~ depan* (in soccer) forwards. *~ drama* dramatist. *~ gitar* guitarist. *~ golf* golfer; → GOLFER, PEGOLF. *~ klarinét* clarinetist. *~ musik rock* rock musician. *~ orgel geréja* church organist. *~ rugby (prof)* (professional) rugby player. *~ sélo* cellist. *~ sépakbola* soccer player. *~ ténis* tennis player. *~ tunggal* soloist. *~ wanita* actress. *~ watak* character actor.

permainan 1 play, toy. *hujan panas ~ hari, senang susah ~ hidup* the ups and downs of life, the good and the bad (in life). *bola ~ para oknum* a plaything of thugs. *~ hati* favorite child. *~ kembali* replay (of a video cassette). **2** performance, show. **3** hanging ornament (for girls/women; such as a locket/pendant, etc.). **4** (*M*) acting. **5** game, sport. *~ asmara* the courting/dating game. *~ bola gelinding* bowling. *~ kucing-kucingan* game of cat and mouse. *~ pat-gulipat* manipulations (in the bad sense). *~ petak-sembunyi* hide-and-(go-)seek. *~ sabun* point shaving, fixing a game. *~ tebak-tebakan* guessing game. *~ umpet* hide-and-(go-)seek. *~ untung-untungan* game of chance. *~ vidéo* video games. **6** (*coq*) woman as a sex object, plaything. **sepermainan** *kawan/teman ~* playmate, childhood friend.

mair MAHIR.

mairat I (*A*) → MIKRAJ.

mairat II (*coq*) **1** disappeared, gone (away). **2** dead.

mairilan (in West Sumatra) the homosexual relationship between *santris* in a *pesantrén*.

maiséna (*D*) cornstarch, maizena (a proprietary brand of cornstarch/cornflower).

maisir and **maisyir** (*A*) gambling, pure speculation (forbidden under Islam).

mait → MAYAT.

maitan (*Jv*) k.o. plant which produces an essential oil, *Lunasia amara.*

maizéna → MAISÉNA.

maja I (*Jv*) /mojo/ a generic name for a number of kemiri-like plants, such as *majakani, majapahit,* etc. – *batu/(h)ingus* belfruit tree, *Aegle marmelos.*

maja II clipped form of **remaja.**

majakani oak-galls imported for medicinal use or to be made into coal for blackening the teeth, *Quercus lusitanica.*

majakaya in one piece (of poles/sticks).

majakeling a hard fruit (for medicinal use), *Terminalia arborea.*

majal 1 blunt, dull, not sharp (of knives). **2** dumb, not smart.
  memajalkan to blunt, dull.

majalah (*A*) magazine, journal, periodical. – *bergambar* illustrated magazine. – *berita* newsmagazine. – *berkala* periodical. – *bulanan* monthly magazine. – *dwimingguan* biweekly magazine. – *hiburan* light-reading magazine. – *ilmiah* science magazine. –

kanak-kanak children's magazine. – *kejuruan* trade/professional journal. – *mingguan* weekly magazine. –*niaga* trade journal. – *remaja* young people's magazine, teenagers' magazine. – *wanita* women's magazine.

majamuju → JEMUJU.

majapahit 1 the sacred (Asian) Indian bel-fruit tree, *Aegle marmelos* of the Hindus and the calabash, *Crescentia cujete*. 2 the name of the Hindu-Javanese empire in East Java (1292–1522).

majas (*A*) 1 figuratively. 2 figure of speech, metaphor.

majasi (*A*) figurative, metaphorical.

majedub (*A*) religious mania.

majegau k.o. tree, *Dysoxylum caulostachyum/densiflorum*.

majelis I (*A*) 1 council, board, committee, panel. 2 group of people. – *penonton* (in movie theaters) the spectators/audience. 3 assembly, meeting. 4 meeting chamber. – *Musyawarah Agama* (*Br*) Religious Council – *geréja* a) church council. b) (Christian-Protestant) consistory. – *hakim* judicial tribunal, panel of judges. – *luhur* high council. – *Luhur Taman Siswa* Taman Siswa Supreme Council. – *Musyawarah Di-Raja* (*Br*) Privy Council. – *Musyawarah Menteri-Menteri* (*Br*) Council of Ministers. – *Musyawarah Negeri* (*Br*) Legislative Council. – *musyawarat perang* council of war. – *Permusyawaratan Rakyat* [MPR] People's Consultative Assembly. – *Pengurusan Harta Peninggalan* Probate Court. – *Rakyat Papua* [MRP] Papuan People's Council. – *Tahkim* National Congress (of the Syarikat Islam). – *taklim* Islamic study group (usually of women). – *Tarjih* (*A*) Council of Legal Consideration. – *Tinggi* (*Mal*) Senate. – *Tinggi dan – Rendah* House of Lords and House of Commons (in Great Britain).

majelis II (*M*) (= **mejelis**) 1 beautiful, lovely. 2 neat (and nice), in order, orderly, clean.

majemat (*A*) assembly.

majemuk (*A*) 1 compound (of sentences/words), complex, composite. *cahaya* – composite light (consisting of several rays). *kalimat* – a compound sentence. *kata* – a compound (word). 2 mixed (of oils). *minyak* – mixed scented oil. 3 pluralistic, multiple. *masyarakat yang* – a pluralistic society.

kemajemukan 1 complexity. 2 pluralism.

pemajemukan compounding.

majenun (*A*) possessed, insane, crazy, frantic.

kemajenunan being possessed.

majer → MAJIR.

majikan (*J/Jv*) employer, boss.

majikanisme bossiness.

majilis (*M*) clean; → MAJELIS II.

majir (*J/Jv*) childless, barren, sterile.

kemajiran sterility.

ma'jizat → MUKJIZAT.

Majlis (*A*) the Iranian Parliament; → MAJELIS I.

majong (*C? J*) oakum, cotton waste (to clean engines); → MAJUN I.

maju to go/move forward, advance, progress; → AJU. –! (Come) forward! *lebih dahulu – daripada* and *telah – lebih dahulu* be ahead of, have an advantage over. – *hidupnya*. He's doing well. – *jalan* Forward march! – *loncat katak* to advance by leaps and bounds. – *mundur* a) to go back and forth, go to and fro. *tidak – tidak mundur* to reach a stalemate. b) to vacillate, have ups and downs (of an enterprise). – *terus, pantang mundur!* Onward, no retreat! –*lah Singapura!* "Let Singapore flourish!" i.e., the official translation of Singapore's national anthem, which also appears as a motto in the State Coat of Arms. – *penuh* full speed ahead. 2 to pass (an examination). 3 to thrive, progress, succeed, be successful (in business). 4 progressive, forward-looking. *bersifat/berhaluan* – progressive.

memajukan [and **ngemajuin** (*J coq*)] 1 to advance (troops/a country, etc.), improve. 2 to propose, suggest. 3 to press. 4 to forward, proceed. 5 to further, promote, encourage, put forward (a cause/industry, etc.), bring (s.o./a question) to the front. 6 to face, confront. 7 to advocate, propagate (a holy war, etc.). 8 to lodge, present, file, submit (a request, etc.). 9 to bring up (for discussion) (objections/a matter, etc.). 10 to develop (a country). 11 to deploy (army/tanks, etc.). 12 to fix (a curfew) at an earlier hour, advance the time for s.t. 13 to move

the clock/the date forward. ~ ... *jadi* to nominate s.o. as. ~ *diri* to apply (for a job). ~ (*di hadapan*) to summon (before). ~ *perkara* to conduct a case (in court). *dimajukan ke dalam* to be indented (of a line).

kemajuan progress, advance(ment), development, success (of troops/policies, etc.), improvement. ~ *sosial* social advances. ~ *téknologi yang pesat* swift technological advances. *kaum* ~ the progressives. *mendapat* ~ to make progress.

pemaju (*Mal*) developer.

pemajuan advancing, improving, promoting, etc.

majuh gluttonous, greedy.

Majuj (*A*) (the Biblical) Magog.

majun I (*C*) k.o. dust cloth, oakum (for caulking), cotton waste; → MAJONG.

majun II (*A*) k.o. medicine for body strength and health made from various ingredients, usually spices; aphrodisiac, tonic.

majung (*M*) oakum (for caulking).

majusi (*A*) magician, fire-worshiper (in Iran).

mak I 1 mother; → EMAK. – *angkat* foster mother. – *bapak* parents. – *bungsu/busu* father's or mother's youngest sister. – *buyung* a) matchmaker, procuress. b) (jokingly) a pregnant woman. – *cik* aunt younger than one's father or mother. – *comblang* matchmaker, go-between. **memakcomblangi** to broker, be a matchmaker for. – *da* → MAK *muda*. – *éték* aunt. – *jomblang* matchmaker, go-between. – *kandung* birth mother. – *kecik/kecil* aunt younger than one's father or mother. – *kopék* foster mother. – *lung* aunt older than one's father or mother. – *mentua/mertua* mother-in-law. – *muda* a) aunt younger than one's father or mother. b) second wife, concubine. – *ngah* middle aunt. – *nyai* a) (*Jv*) grandmother. b) effeminate. – *saudara* aunt. – *su* father's or mother's youngest sister. – *sulung* aunt older than one's father or mother. – *susu/téték* wet-nurse. – *tiri* stepmother. – *tua/ua* a) father's or mother's older sister. b) first wife. – *uda* aunt younger than one's father or mother. 2 term of polite address to all women of one's mother's generation.

mak II → MAMAK.

mak III (*Jv*) a particle indicating that the following word(s) represent(s) the impact of the action. *Sang Kancil kecemplung – blung!* The Mouse deer plunged in with a splash. – *brol* to come out in large quantities. – *cep klakep* to stop talking suddenly. – *nyus* it hits the spot (about certain kinds of food).

maka 1 and, further, next, then. – *terjadilah perkelahian yang hébat*. Then a violent fight occurred. 2 (= **makanya**) (opening a clause) therefore, and so, thus, hence, consequently, accordingly. *Selalu diusik – menangis*. He was teased all the time and so he was crying. 3 (following a word or sentence stating a reason) that. *Apa mulanya – ia tidak datang?* What is the reason that he didn't come? 4 (introducing a main clause following certain subordinate clauses, often no translation) *Sebagai tercantum dalam Anggaran Dasar Yayasan Mitra Budaya Indonésia, – maksud dan tujuan Yayasan ialah...* As stated in the Articles of Association of the Yayasan Mitra Budaya Indonesia the object and purpose of the Foundation is (namely)... – *itu* and that, and for that reason.

makadam (*D*) macadam. *jalan* – a macadamized road.

makalah (*A*) 1 newspaper article. 2 working paper.

pemakalah s.o. who delivers a paper.

makam I (*A*) 1 (holy) grave; cemetery, graveyard. 2 shrine, tomb (usually for respected persons). – *kelompok* mass grave. – *Pahlawan* National Cemetery.

bermakam buried (at), enshrined, entombed.

memakamkan to bury, enshrine, entomb.

pemakaman burial, interment. ~ *ulang* reburial.

makam II (*A*) place, abode, residence.

bermakam to dwell, reside.

makan 1 a) to eat, have a meal. b) (= **memakan**) to eat s.t. – *tak/ nggak – asal(kan) kumpul* and – *ataupun tidak asalkan tetap bisa berkumpul* (a Javanese attitude) "whether we eat or not, the important thing is to be together/in a group," i.e., the important thing in life is not prosperity but togetherness. 2 to eat (up), consume, devour, swallow. *Kurangi – garam* Decrease your salt intake. – *sepuas perut* to eat one's fill. 3 to chew. – *sirih* to chew betel nut. **4** to take (a pill). – *pil* to take a pill; → MINUM *pil*. – *aspirin léwat ukuran* to take an overdose of aspirin. **5** to smoke (opium). – *candu* to smoke opium. **6** a living, one's livelihood. *mencari* – to earn one's (daily) bread, make a living. **7** to penetrate, go in, make a way into/through, cut. *Diketuknya paku pada tiang itu tapi tidak* – *karena terlalu keras*. He drove the nail into the pole, but it did not go in/penetrate since the wood was too hard. *pahat tidak* – a dull chisel. – *ke* (a cog-wheel) gears into (a cog railway). *Pisau tidak* –. The knife won't cut. *sudah* – *(delapan orang)* (this gun) has already killed (eight people). **8** to take (time), require (money). *Perbaikan jalan itu akan* – *biaya setengah juta rupiah*. The road improvements will cost/require half a million rupiahs. – *tempo tiga hari* to take/require three days. *banyak* – *uang* it takes/runs into a lot of money (to do that), it's expensive. – *korban* to claim victims, cost the life (of). **9** to occupy (an area). – *tanah seluas ...* to occupy an area of ... **10** to affect. *Obat ini* – *pada kulit*. This medicine affects the skin. **11** to function, hold (of brakes), bite (of a tool). *Rém tidak* –. The brakes failed/did not hold. **12** to set well in a breeze (of sails). *Layarnya tidak* –. The sails did not set well. **13** to draw (of a ship). *Kapal itu* –*nya dalam air 5 méter*. The ship draws five meters. **14** (*sl*) to sleep with. *alat* – tableware. *bayar* – to board with s.o. *ibu tempat saya bayar* – my landlady. *kasi* – to feed, give s.o. s.t. to eat. *kurang* – undernourished. *pulang* – to go home for lunch (*esp* when the employee's home is not far from his office). *tempat* – *jangan dibéraki* "don't shit where you eat," i.e., don't bite the hand that feeds you. – *sudah terhidang, tamu belum juga datang* said about a marriageable girl with no suitors. *sudah* – *bismillah* to do things according to the rules. – *ampun* to beg one's pardon. – *anak uang* to get interest. – *angin* to get a breath of fresh air. – *arwah a selamatan* to commemorate s.o. who has died. – *asam* experienced. – *ayapan* to eat leftovers. – *bawang* to be furious, very angry. – *benak* to have a windfall profit. *tidak* – *benang* doesn't make sense, isn't logical. – *beradat* to attend an official dinner. – *berpantang* to (go on a) diet. – *berulam* married. – *besar* a big party. *telah banyak* – *budi* (in Medan) to be under a lot of moral obligation to s.o. – *cepat* to have a light meal, eat some fast food. – *daging* meat eater, carnivorous. – *darah a)* to make a large profit. b) to fret. – *daun muda* to have relations with young girls, rob the cradle. – *dawai/dedak* to be very poor, impoverished. – *di akal* good (of a piece of advice). – *diam-diam* secretly spread (influence, etc.). – *diri a)* to worry s.o. sick. b) to become moth-eaten. – *duit* to take a bribe. – *éksprés* to have a light meal, eat some fast food. – *emas* to take a bribe. – *gaji* to work for wages. – *gaji buta* to have a soft job. – *gaji kecil* to earn a low salary. – *garam* experienced. – *hak* to trespass/infringe on s.o.'s rights. – *hati a)* to displease, disappoint. b) to sadden. c) to suffer from s.o. else's actions. d) to eat one's heart out. – *jalan* (*coq*) buffet, smorgasbord. – *jangat/kawat/kerawat* very poor, impoverished. – *kacang kulit* (*vulg*) to perform cunnilingus on s.o. – *keringat orang* to profit from s.o. else's labor. – *korban* to claim victims, result in casualties. – *kuli* to work as a day laborer. – *malam a)* dinner, supper. b) to have/eat dinner/supper. – *malam prasmanan* buffet dinner. – *minum* to eat and drink. – *modal* to eat into one's capital. – *obat* to take medicine. *banyak* – *ongkos* expensive, costly. – *pagi a)* breakfast. b) to have/eat breakfast. – *pancing* to take the bait. – *péna* to make one's livelihood by writing. – *pénsiun* to be retired; → DIPÉNSIUNKAN. – *pokok* to eat into one's capital. – *riba* to lend money at usurious rates. – *risiko* to be risky. – *rumput* to graze. – *sabun* to fix (a game). – *sehidangan* to eat together. *sudah* – *sekolah* to have gone to school, to be educated. – *sepinggan* to eat from the same plate. – *siang a)* lunch. b) to have/eat lunch. – *siku-siku* to talk in an indirect way, beat around the bush. – *sogok/sorong/suap* to take a bribe. – *sumpah* to perjure o.s. – *tali* to have to sell everything in order to live. – *tanah a)* very poor; to starve. b) (*tertangkup/tersungkut*) – *tanah* to bite the dust, fall forward onto the ground. – *tangan a)* to come to blows. b) to make a profit (on). c) to profit by, be lucky, hit the jackpot. – *tempat* to take up space. – *tempo (tiga minggu)* it takes (three weeks). – *tenaga* to make a lot of trouble (for s.o.). – *tidur saja* to do nothing but eat and sleep. *tidak* – *tua* ageless. – *tulang* to

drive o.s. hard, work hard. – *ulam* to have a mistress. – *upah a)* to work for wages, be a wage-earner. b) to be open to bribery. – *waktu (dua jam)*. It takes (two hours).

makannya the way s.t. works/does its job. *Bagaimana* ~ *mortir itu?* How does that mortar work? *halus* ~ (s.t.) which works in a very subtle way. *jauh* ~ long-range (guns). ~ *dalam air* draft, the depth of water that a ship draws. ~ *(senang saja)* to eat at one's leisure/completely relaxed. ~ *ke sungai* (in Medan) to have a picnic.

makan-makan to have a relaxed meal (usually in great numbers at a party).

memakan 1 to eat, consume, use up, destroy, etc. (in general has the same meanings as *makan* but is more formal or active than *makan*; must be used when followed by the object -*nya*, i.e., *memakannya* to eat it). *saling* ~ dog-eat-dog. **2** [*usu* passive in the following meanings] a) to consume, hit, affect, strike. b) to capture (a chess piece). *Gajah dimakan bidak*. The castle was captured by a pawn. *tidak lalu dimakan* cannot be swallowed. *Uang itu dimakannya sendiri*. He used the money for his own benefit, he embezzled the money. *dimakan api* catch/be consumed by fire. *mudah dimakan api* highly combustible, inflammable. *dimakan berdua* (money) enough to feed two people. *tak dimakan besi* to be invulnerable. *dimakan guna-guna* to be a victim of black magic. *dimakan hari* to be weather-beaten. *dimakan karat* to be corroded by rust. *dimakan keparat a)* to be cursed. b) to be hit by a disaster (due to marrying a *janda raja* or from sacrilege, etc.). *dimakan keréta api* to be run over by a train. *dimakan masa* timeworn; to be out of date. *dimakan pakaian benar-benar* to wear clothes that fit like a glove. *dimakan (cahaya) panas* to be weather-beaten. *dimakan peluru* to be hit by a bullet. *mati dimakan penyakitnya* to die from one's illness. *tidak dimakan senjata* to be invulnerable. *tidak dimakan siku-siku* dishonest, deceitful. *dimakan sumpah a)* to forswear s.t. b) to meet with an accident because one has committed perjury. *dimakan tikus* to be stolen. *dimakan umur/usia/zaman* timeworn, dilapidated, to be out of date.

memakani 1 (*pl obj*) to eat frequently, feed on, eat up. **2** to feed, give food to.

memakankan 1 to allow to eat. **2** to give (s.o.) s.t. to eat. **3** (benefactive) to eat for.

termakan [and **kemakan** (*coq*)] **1** can be eaten, edible. *Tidak* ~ *oléh para tetamu*. The guests could not (manage to) finish (up the food). **2** to be devoured, eaten up. *Sabarnya* ~. He calmed down. ~ *di/ke(pada) akal* plausible. ~ *di haram* violated God's commandments. ~ *di sadah* (*M*) to look sheepish/foolish (due to being deceived, etc.). **3** to fall for s.t., fall a victim to, be taken in by. ~ *guna-guna* fall a victim to black magic. ~ *isyu* to fall a victim to evil rumors. ~ *lumpur* swallowed up by/stuck in the mud. ~ *ketuaan* suffer from the ravages of time. ~ *mode (rambut péndék)* succumb to the (short hair) fad/fashion. ~ *propaganda* fall victim to propaganda. ~ *provokasi* fall victim to (a) provocation. **4** to eat/consume by accident. ~ *racun* to swallow poison by accident.

makanan 1 food, nourishment; *cp* PANGAN. **2** cuisine. ~ *khas Indonésia* typical Indonesian cuisine. *bukan* ~ *aku* this does not suit me. *bahan* ~ *(tak tecerna)* (indigestible) food. *barang* ~ food, things to eat, comestibles. *pemasukan* ~ food-taking. *sisa* ~ leftovers. ~ *baku* staple food(s). ~ *bergizi (tinggi)* (highly) nutritious food. ~ *berpantang a)* diet. b) food one is not allowed to eat. ~ *berserat* high-fiber foods. ~ *biasa* habitual, a habit. *Masuk dan keluar tahanan telah menjadi* ~ *biasa baginya*. He's always in and out of jail. ~ *cepat (siap)* fast food, snack, light meal. ~ *cuci mulut* dessert. ~ *daging* meat dishes. ~ *éksprés* fast food, light meal, snack. ~ *empuk* easy prey/target. *Skuter Véspa merupakan* ~ *empuk*. Vespa scooters are an easy target (for thieves). ~ *héwani* animal food. ~ *jadi* processed food. ~ *kaléng* canned food. ~ *kecil* hors d'oeuvres, snacks. ~ *Jepang* (*sl*) methyl amphetamine. ~ *lembu* fodder, food for animals. ~ *mentah* raw/uncooked food. ~ *nabati* vegetable/non-meat food. ~ *pembuka* appetizer; → UMPAN *tekak*. ~ *pencuci mulut* dessert. ~ *pokok* staple foods. ~ *ringan* snacks. ~ *rombéng* junk food. ~ *séhat* health food. ~ *siap santap* catered food, catering; → JASA *boga*. ~ *ternak* cattle fodder. ~ *utama* main course. ~ *yang (tergolong) cepat membusuk* perishables.

makan-makanan various foods.

kemakanan completely eaten up/destroyed/consumed/finished/corroded/decayed.

pemakan 1 eater. ~ *bawang* hothead, s.o. quick to anger. *bangsa* ~ *bawang* hothead. ~ *daging* carnivore. ~ *daun-daunan* herbivore. ~ *gaji* wage earner. ~ *nabatah* vegetarian. ~ *orang* maneater, cannibal. ~ *rumput* herbivore. ~ *segala* omnivore. **2** feeder. **sepemakan** the time that it takes to eat s.t.

pemakanan 1 eating. **2** (*mostly Mal*) diet.

makantar-makantar (*Jv*) **1** to blaze up; to glow, burn bright. **2** to run/rise high, be at a fever pitch. *Semangatnya* ~. He has a fiery temperament. *pembangunan* ~ *terutama bagi daérah Jawa Tengah yang baru* ~ *di segala bidang* development, especially for Central Java, which has been exploding in every field.

makanya → MAKA.

Makao Macao. *benang* ~ gold or silver thread. *wayang* ~ k.o. Chinese puppet show (from Macao).

makao-po (*C*) Chinese prostitute.

makar I (*A*) **1** deception, cheating, trickery. **2** stratagem, scheme, plan (for a coup/to commit a crime, etc.), revolt. *berbuat* ~ to scheme, plot, plan a mutiny.

makar II unripe (of fruit). **2** tough (of fruits and vegetables).

makara I (*Skr*) **1** ornamental design in the form of a ferocious animal in sculptures, temples, etc. **2** mythological creature that causes eclipses.

Makara II Capricorn.

bermakara cancerous.

makaroni (*D/E*) macaroni. ~ *kruntel* curlicue macaroni. ~ *skotel* macaroni casserole.

Makarti Karya Tama (*Skr*) (motto of the Department of Transmigration and Cooperatives; meaning) Work Hard to Achieve Prosperity.

makarya 1 to have the will to work. **2** practical.

makas (*cla*) hard; → MANGKAS I. ~ *keras* ~ very hard.

makasi(h) (*coq*) contraction of *terima kasih*.

Makassar Makassar, also known for a period as Ujung Pandang.

makatana (in Minahasa) traditional folk medicine to cure hypertension; consists of celery plus its roots and stalks, boiled in water.

Makau → MAKAO.

Makbét (*coq*) Shakespeare's Macbeth.

makbud (*A*) worshipped, adored (of God). *Allah al-* Allah who is adored/worshipped.

makbul (*A*) **1** approved, answered, heard (of prayers); → KABUL. **2** efficacious, effective (of drugs).

memakbulkan 1 to approve, answer, hear (prayers). **2** to realize (one's dreams, etc.).

termakbul approved, answered, heard (of prayers).

makcik 1 auntie. **2** aunt (youngest sister of father or mother).

makcomblang → COMBLANG.

makda (from *mak muda*) auntie.

makdan (*A*) mine (minerals).

makdikipé → MADIKIPÉ.

makelar (*D*) broker, middleman. ~ *éfék* stock broker. ~ *mobil* automobile dealer. ~ *pengganti* contra-broker. ~ *penjualan sawah-sawah* broker in selling rice fields. (*sang*) ~ *pertandingan tinju* matchmaker, s.o. who arranges boxing or wrestling matches. ~ *rumah/tanah* real estate broker, realtor.

memakelari to act as a middleman for, act in the capacity of broker for.

makelaran and **kemakelaran** brokering.

makena(h) → MUKENA(H).

makepung 1 (in Bali) water buffalo race, using four-wheeled carts running over dry land. **2** (in Sumbawa) ditto, using wheelless carts running over muddy land.

makeruh → MAKRUH.

makét (*D*) (scale) model, mock-up.

makhdum → MAKHUDUM.

makhluk (*A*) creature, all the creatures created by God. ~ *halus* supernatural creature.

makhudum (*A*) sir (honorific, generally used for people well-versed in religion, for Muslim pundits).

maki *hamun (dan)* ~ (*M*), ~ (*dan*) *nista, caci/cuci* ~ and ~ abusive words, invective, insults and curses. *kena* ~ suffer abuse, be insulted and abused. *mencaci/mencuci* ~ to heap abuse on s.o.

maki-maki to use abusive language to s.o., call s.o. names.

memaki(-maki) to use abusive language to s.o., call s.o. names. *Dia harus puas dimaki-maki petugas.* He had to swallow the curses piled on him by the (police) officer.

makian (term of) abuse, abusive words, cursing, scolding.

pemaki reviler, curser.

makin word indicating an increasing or decreasing degree. ~ ... ~ ... the more/less ... the more/less. ~ ... *tambah* ... the more ..., the more ... ~ *lama tambah banyak* the longer the time the greater the amount. ~ *hari* ~ *bertambah kurus badannya.* Day by day he is getting thinner. *Tua-tua keladi, ~ tua ~ jadi.* "As old as a taro, the older it grows the better it becomes," reference to "a dirty old man."

semakin to keep on, do s.t. more and more. *Bila* ~ *menunda-nunda, maka akan* ~ *ketinggalanlah kita.* If we keep on postponing things, we will get further and further behind. ~ *hari* ~ (*kalah*) more and more (defeated). ~ *tahun* increasingly over the years.

makjizat → MUKJIZAT.

makjun (*A*) tonic for strengthening the body.

Makkah Mecca.

maklaf (*A*) a trough (for animal fodder).

maklum (*A*) **1** (well-)known; to know (about), understand, be aware. *demikian agar* ~ and *agar* ~ *adanya* for your information. *pulang* ~ *kepada* it is left to (the reader). **2** you know how it is. ~*lah, kami orang kota.* We're city folk, you know. ~*lah* that's the way it is.

memaklumi to know, understand, have an understanding of. *harap dimaklumi bahwa* please be advised that.

mem(per)maklumkan 1 to announce, inform, publish. *Di(per)maklumkan dengan hormat bahwa ...* It is respectfully announced that ... **2** to declare (war). **3** to issue (a prohibition), promulgate (a law). **4** to proclaim. ~ *damai kepada* to offer peace to.

pe(r)makluman announcement, declaration, proclamation, statement.

maklumat (*A*) announcement, declaration, proclamation, communiqué, information.

memaklumatkan to announce, declare, proclaim, inform.

maklun (*D coq*) charge for making, cost of making (clothes).

makmal (*A mostly Mal*) laboratory.

makmum (*A*) **1** the congregation which repeats prayers after their *imam*/leader in the mosque. **2** (*coq*) to follow. ~ *masbuk* congregant who does not have to say the *fatihah* because he is late. ~ *muafik* congregant who does not complete the *fatihah* because the *imam* has continued.

bermakmum to follow a leader in prayer.

makmur (*A*) **1** prosperous (and populous), rich, wealthy, successful, flourishing, having good fortune or a lot of profit. **2** luxurious, lavish, very abundant.

semakmur persemakmuran commonwealth.

memakmurkan to improve, enrich, develop, make prosperous/wealthy, etc.

kemakmuran 1 prosperity. **2** luxury. **3** abundance.

pemakmuran enriching.

makna (*A*) meaning, purport, sense, importance. ~ *ganda* dual, ambiguity. **bermakna ganda** to have two meanings, be ambiguous. **kemakna-gandaan** dualism, ambiguity. ~ *kabur* ambiguous. **kemakna-kaburan** (*gram*) ambiguity.

semakna synonymous, with the same meaning.

bermakna to have a meaning, be meaningful, significant, important. ~ *berbilang* to be ambiguous, have more than one meaning. **kebermaknaan** significance.

memaknakan to explain, elucidate.

pemaknaan understanding.

maknawi (*A*) **1** esoteric, spiritual. **2** essential, important.

maknawi(y)ah (*A*) figurative.

maknit (*D*) /maknit/ magnet.
  memaknitkan to magnetize.
  kemaknitan magnetism.
  pemaknitan magnetizing.
Mako → MARKAS *komando*.
makota (*Skr*) → MAHKOTA. **1** crown. **2** to be a king/ruler, have power/authority. *putra* – Crown Prince. *wakil* – viceroy. *– alam* crown of the world. *– negeri* ruler of the state, monarch, sovereign, king. **3** title for high-ranking persons; in Aceh, North Sumatra, once a royal title. *– hatiku* and *– jiwaku* beloved, sweetheart.
  bermakota crowned.
  memakotai to crown s.o.
makramat (*A*) holiness, sanctity.
makramé (*D*) /makramé/ macramé (lace).
makrifat (*A*) **1** wisdom, knowledge. **2** (in *ilmu tasawuf*) mystical knowledge of the Godhead.
  bermakrifat 1 to meditate, be plunged in thought. **2** to really know.
makro (*D/E*) /makro/ macro-. *ékonomi* – macroeconomics; → MAKROÉKONOMI.
makroékonomi (*D*) macroeconomics.
makrokosmos (*D*) macrocosm.
makroni (*D*) macaroni; → MAKARONI.
makroskopik (*D/E*) macroscopic.
makruf (*A*) **1** well-known, good. **2** merit, good deeds.
makruh (*A*) objectionable, odious, improper, reprehensible (but not forbidden).
maks clipped form of **maksimum**.
maksi (*D/E*) /maksi/ maxi, woman's skirt or coat extending to the ankles; *cp* MAKRO, MIDI, MINI.
maksiat (*A*) immoral act, sin.
  kemaksiatan vice, sin, wickedness, immorality.
  pemaksiat sinner.
maksim (*D/E*) /maksim/ maxim.
maksimal (*D/E*) /maksi-/ maximal. *secara* – maximally.
  semaksimal ~ *mungkin* as much as possible, to the greatest degree possible.
  memaksimalkan to maximize.
maksimum (*D/E*) /maksi-/ maximum.
  semaksimum ~ *mungkin* to the maximum.
  memaksimumkan to maximize.
maksud (*A*) /maksut/ **1** purpose, aim. *untuk – damai* for peaceful ends. *untuk – khusus ini* for this special purpose, ad hoc. *untuk – tersebut* for that purpose, to this end. **2** wish, intention, aim, plan. *–nya tak mau diubah*. He does not want to change his plans. *– baik* goodwill. *dengan – baik* with the best of intentions. *dikandung –* it is our intention to ... **3** meaning. *–nya (apa)?* What do you mean? **4** tendency. *– tujuan* objective, aim.
  maksudnya 1 they/people mean; one means; I mean. **2** that is to say. **3** with the intention of, with a view to. **4** meaning. ~ *apa?* What do you mean (I didn't understand you?)?
  bermaksud 1 to intend, plan, mean, have in view, wish. **2** with a tendency.
  memaksud (only in passive *dimaksud*) to be meant, referred to, intended. *ketentuan dimaksud dalam pasal 7* the provision referred to in article 7. *yang dimaksud dengan penghasilan bersih adalah/ialah* by net income is understood/meant.
  memaksudkan to have in mind, intend. *yang dimaksudkan dengan X ialah* by X is understood/meant.
  termaksud meant, intended.
maksum I (*A*) **1** apportioned, allotted; separated, divided. **2** free from/of.
maksum II (*A*) dirty (of clothes/person, etc.), filthy.
maksur (*A*) shortened.
maktab (*A*) **1** writing school. **2** (elementary) school. **3** college. **4** office.
maktub (*A*) **1** recorded. **2** (*al-*) the Holy Book, the scriptures.
  memaktubkan to write down.
  termaktub written down, specified in writing. *ketentuan yang ~ dalam pasal 14 ayat 4 anggaran dasar perséroan* (in notarial instruments) the stipulation embodied/laid down in article 14 paragraph 4 of the bylaws of the corporation.

makua k.o. African gorilla.
ma'kul (*A*) intelligible, reasonable, logical, acceptable.
ma'kulat (*A*) metaphysics.
Makutarama the military resort command (*Korém* 073) in Salatiga.
makyong and **makyung** (theatrical) play (with dancing and singing) popular in the northern part of Western Malaysia.
makzul (*A*) dethroned, deposed.
  memakzulkan to depose. ~ *diri(nya)* to abdicate.
  pemakzulan deposing, dethroning.
mal I (*A*) topmost portion (of a pillar), top (of a kris blade); bottom (of a spear blade, i.e., away from the point). *– datang* a kris in which the blade and the guard are made separately and welded together later.
mal II (*A*) property, possessions, chattel, goods; → BAITULMAL. *– waris* estate.
mal III (*E*) (shopping) mall.
mal IV (*D*) gauge, curve, form(er), mold. *– menggambar* French curve.
mal V (in acronyms) → MALUKU.
mala I (*Skr ob*) (= *termala*) withering (of flowers/youth).
mala II (*A*) **1** accursed, unlucky. *– petaka* a) born under an evil star. b) misfortune, disaster. **2** spot, stain, flaw, blot on one's reputation.
mala III (*M*) fluid from a corpse. *harum semerbak mengandung –* the end justifies the means.
malaékat → MALAIKAT.
Malagasi Malagasy.
malagizi malnutrition.
malah I and **malahan 1** on the contrary, instead. *Dia tidak kelihatan marah, – dia sangat gembira.* He doesn't seem to be angry; on the contrary, he is very happy. **2** what is more, and even, in fact (even). *Saya mengizinkan itu, – menggalakkannya.* I allowed it, in fact I encouraged it. *Hujan yang kelihatan reda sebentar tadi – lebih lebat sekarang.* The rain, which seemed to be abating, has, in fact, increased. **3** moreover, further(more), besides, in addition (to this). **4** at that. *dan – murah* and cheap at that (or, and in fact it was cheap).
malah II (*M*) **1** (shortened form of *marilah*) a) go ahead! b) let's ... *– kita pergi!* let's go! **2** if, when. *– hendak dimandikan, anak itu mesti menangis.* When the child is bathed, he will cry. **3** provided that. *– akan dipulangkan bésok* provided that it will be returned tomorrow.
malai I (*Tam? bio*) panicle, spire. *– rata* corymb. *– sulur* shoot.
  memalai panicle-/spire-like, to decorate with panicles/spires.
malai II **malai-malai** name of a tree with oil-seeds, *Litsea sebifera*.
malaik → MALAK II.
malaikat (*A*) angel. *– Israfil* the angel who will blow the last trumpet. *– Izrail* the angel of death. *– Jibrail/Jibril* the messenger of God. *– Malik* the angel who guards Hell. *– maut* the angel of death. *– Mikail* the angel of rain and sun. *– Mungkar dan Nakir* → MUNKAR, NAKIR. *– pelindung* guardian angel. *– pembalas* avenging angel. *– pencabut nyawa* angel of death. *– penolong* angel of mercy, guardian angel. *– Ridwan* the angel who guards Heaven.
malaikatul (*A*) *– maut* the angel of death.
malaise (*D*) /malése/ depression, slump.
malak I (*A*) → MALAIKAT.
malak II (*J*) **memalak** to pilfer, steal.
  malak-memalak pilfering, stealing.
  pemalak pilferer, thief.
  pemalakan pilfering, stealing.
malaka name of a tree and its fruit, Indian gooseberry, emblic, *Phyllanthus emblica*. *– buah* a) the fruit of this tree. b) the name of a delicacy.
malakama and **malakamo** (*M*) *buah si –* a proverbial fruit, fatal whether one eats it or not; Hobson's choice, damned if you do and damned if you don't. *bagai/seperti makan buah si –, dimakan bapak mati, tidak dimakan ibu mati* or, *bagai/seperti makan si –, dimakan mati ibu, tak dimakan mati bapak* and *bagai bertemu buah si –, dimakan mati bapak, tidak dimakan mati ibu* damned if you do, damned if you don't; lack of an alternative.

malakulmaut → MALAIKATULMAUT.

malakut (*A cla*) 1 (*alam* –) the world of angels and spirits. 2 kingdom.

malam I 1 the night and evening (from sunset) preceding a given day and included in that day, eve (of). In this meaning *malam* precedes the name of the day in which it is included. – *Minggu* Saturday evening. – *Senin* Sunday evening. 2 the night and evening of the day that has just passed. In this meaning *malam* follows the name of the day in which it is included. *Minggu* – Sunday evening. *Senin* – Monday evening. 3 night, the dark hours between sunset and sunrise. *sepanjang* – all night long. – *hampir mendekati pagi.* Day was breaking. *setiap* – *jam 03.00* every (night at) 3 o'clock in the morning. *di/pada* – *buta* in the dead of night. *di/pada* – *hari* in the evening, at night. *hari* –*lah* night is falling. *Hari sudah* –. Night has fallen, it is night now. *sampai jauh/larut* – until the early hours of the morning, far into the night. *pada suatu* – a) some night (in the future). b) one night (in the past). *tengah* – a) midnight. b) the dead of night. – *akhir tahun* New Year's Eve. – *amal* charity ball. – *ber(inai)* two days before a wedding when the bride's nails are painted with henna. – *buta* a dark night. – *gembira* an evening party. – *harinya* in the evening (of that day). – *kemarin* the other evening/night. – *larangan* (*Mal*) curfew. – *mat-matan* a social/relaxing evening. – *Natal* Christmas Eve. – *panjang* a) Saturday night. b) any holiday evening when one can stay up late. – *pertama* wedding night. – *pertemuan* evening get-together. – *silaturahmi* a social evening. – *Sunyi*, – *Kudus* Silent Night, Holy Night. – *Tahun Baru* New Year's Eve. **bermalam tahun baru** to spend New Year's Eve. **malam tahuh baruan** to celebrate New Year's Eve. – *takbiran* the night of the last day of Ramadhan. – *tirakatan* vigil.

malamnya in the evening (of that day).

malam-malam late at night. ~ *begini* so late at night, at this hour.

semalam: 1 ~ (*ini*) tonight. 2 ~ *suntuk* and **semalam(-malam)an** the whole night, all night long. 3 last night. 4 one night, overnight. *tak bisa merubah dalam* ~ cannot change overnight.

bermalam 1 to spend the night. ~ *di jalan* to spend the night en route (to a certain place). 2 to stay for the night. 3 to keep (certain dishes) overnight. ~ *Minggu* to spend the weekend/Saturday night. ~ *pertama* to spend one's wedding night; → MALAM *pertama*. **membermalamkan** to lay (a body) in state. *Jenazahnya akan dibermalamkan.* The mortal remains will lie in state for one night.

bermalam-malam for nights and nights, night after night.

memalami (*M*) to spend the night at the bedside of.

mem(per)malamkan to keep/leave s.t. overnight.

kemalaman overtaken by night, out after dark.

pe(r)malaman overnight stop, place to spend the night (hotel, etc.).

malam II (*Jv*) wax, paraffin (in particular, that used for making *batik*).

malan (*M*) 1 intoxicated (from betel chewing). 2 to feel uncomfortable (from slight intoxication/sadness/bewilderment, etc.), feel anxious.

malang 1 (– *melintang*) transverse, (to lie) across/athwart, be in the way; *cp* PALANG. – *melintang di jalan* lying across the road. **(ber)malang-melintang** to have it all one's own way. 2 unfortunate, unlucky. 3 to go around (doing s.t.). *Kelompok ini* – *melintang melakukan pembantaian terhadap saingannya.* The group went around butchering their rivals. *jari* – middle finger. – *nasibnya.* He had bad luck. – *yang timbul* and – *akan tumbuh* as fate would have it, he ...; unfortunately, he ... – *tak boléh ditolak, mujur tak boléh diraih* bad luck cannot be avoided, good luck cannot be grasped, i.e., nobody can escape his fate. – *kerik* with arms akimbo. – *migung* crisscross. – *mujur* fate, luck, chance.

malangnya 1 as ill luck would have it ..., unfortunately. 2 what bad luck!

malang-malang ~ *mujur* misfortune is always accompanied by some luck.

semalang as unfortunate/unlucky as.

semalang-malangnya if worse comes to worst.

bersimalang ~ *bersimujur* (*M*) at random, haphazardly.

memalangi to bar (a door, etc.).

memalangkan to use ... as a bar, bar with s.t.

kemalangan 1 bad luck, calamity, adversity. 2 struck by a disaster. 3 disadvantage, harm. 4 (*Mal*) accident.

malangbang a large dugout canoe.

malangkamo → MALAKAMO.

malangkerik both arms akimbo.

malap 1 dim (of a lamp/place), flickering (of a light). 2 smoldering (of a fire).

malapari Indian oilseed tree, *Pongamia pinnata*.

malapetaka catastrophe. – *Limabelas Januari* → MALARI.

malaprakték and **malapraktik** malpractice.

malar 1 continuous, constant, nonstop. 2 (= malar-malar) on the contrary; the more so.

bermalar continuing. **kebermalaran** continuousness.

memalarkan to continue s.t.

termalar continued. **ketermalaran** continuability.

termalarkan continuable.

malaran 1 (*ling*) continuant. 2 (*math*) continuum.

kemalaran continuity.

Malari [Malapetaka 15 Januari] The January 15 Disaster, i.e., the anti-Japanese riots in Jakarta during Prime Minister Tanaka's visit on January 15, 1974.

malaria (*D*) malaria. *kena* – to get malaria. – *hitam* black-water fever.

malarindu tropikangen (*BG*) brokenhearted (pun on "malaria tropicana"; and KANGEN, RINDU).

malas I 1 lazy, idle, indolent, unwilling to work. 2 not feel like (doing s.t.), not be up to s.t., reluctant. – *bekerja* work-shy. – *berbicara* to be silent.

semalas as lazy as.

bermalas ~ (*diri*) and **bermalas-malas(an)** to loaf around, lounge around, take it easy.

memalaskan to cause s.o. to become lazy, make one lazy/inactive/sluggish.

mempermalas to make s.o. lazy.

malas-malasan (to come/arrive) at one's leisure/when it pleases one.

kemalasan 1 idle. 2 laziness, idleness, sluggishness.

pemalas lazybones, to be born lazy.

malas II *burung* – nightjar, *Caprimulgus spp.*

malas III various species of trees, *Parastemon spp.*

malau → EMBALAU.

malaun (*A*) 1 cursed by God, accursed. 2 wicked (people), evil.

Malawi Malawi (the former Nyasaland).

Malaysia Malaysia.

memalaysiakan to Malaysianize.

maléan k.o. *karapan sapi* on the island of Lombok.

Maledéwa the Maldives.

malem → MALAM I. **maleman** (*Jv*) *selamatan* held on the five odd-numbered nights, starting with the 21st, in the fasting month of *Ramadan*.

maléo maleo, bird resembling a chicken, blackish colored with dark brown chest feathers and white belly, *Macrocephalus maleo*.

males → MALAS I.

malése (*D*) (trade or industrial) depression, slump; → MALAISE.

maligai (*Tam*) princess's bower in the upper story of a palace.

malih (*Jv*) to alter, change/metamorphose (into).

malihan 1 metamorphosed. 2 turnover.

pemalih (*elec infr*) converter.

pemalihan metamorphosis.

malik (*A*) 1 king, monarch. 2 owner, proprietor. *Al*– king of kings, i.e., God. 3 the angel who guards the doors of Hell.

Maliki (*A*) adherents of the religious sect of Malik ibn Anas (one of the four sects of Muslim law).

Malikuljabbar (*A*) the Mighty King, i.e., God.

malim (*A*) 1 religious/holy person, religious leader. 2 leader, guide. 3 navigator, pilot. 4 (in Sumatra) shaman.

memalimkan to treat s.o. as one's religious leader/guide.

kemaliman being a religious leader/guide.

ma-lima (*Jv*) → MO-LIMO.

mali-mali k.o. shrub, *Leea spp.*

malin → MALIM.

Malindo [Malaysia-Indonésia] Malaysia-Indonesia.

maling (*Jv M?*) 1 thief. 2 (*coq*) to steal. *kunci* – master/skeleton key. *pintu* – back/side entrance. – (*ber*)*teriak* – the pot calls the kettle black. – *amatiran* amateur thief. – *curi* all k.o. thefts. – *dapat* (in Palembang) to keep found articles. – *hujan* a thief who operates in the rainy season. – *jalan* s.o. who takes your lane on the road, road-hog. – *prof* professional thief.

   memaling to steal.

   memalingi to steal from, rob.

   kemalingan 1 to be/get robbed. *Meréka ~.* They got robbed. **2** theft, robbery.

   pemaling thief, robber.

malinjo → BELINJO, MELINJO.

malis 1 pale, washed out, light, faint (of color/smell); discolored. 2 vague, vaguely sensed.

malnutrisi (*E*) malnutrition.

malprakték (*D*) malpractice. *melakukan* – to engage in malpractice.

malpraktik (*D*) → MALAPRAKTÉK.

Malteng [Maluku Tengah] Central Moluccas.

maltose (*D*) maltose.

malu I 1 shy, bashful, embarrassed, be/feel ashamed. *tuntut* – to take revenge. *penuntut* – s.o. who takes revenge. *tidak ada –nya* (he) has no shame, is shameless. 2 respectful. 3 humble. 4 shame. *dengan tidak tahu* – and *tidak kenal* – shameless. – *bertanya sesat di jalan* (– *berdayung perahu hanyut*) one should not be shy about asking advice from others. – *diri* ashamed. – *besar* to die of shame, be very embarrassed.

   malu-malu *tidak ~nya* and *tidak ~ lagi* shameless. *tidak usah ~* there is no need to be embarrassed. *Jangan ~!* Don't be shy! *~ bahasa* very bashful. *~ kucing* pretend(ing) to be shy, coy.

   semalu *sehina ~* of one destiny, to share the same fate.

   semalu-malunya as embarrassed as one can be.

   bermalu shy, bashful, ashamed. *~lah sedikit!* Behave yourself!

   memalui (= **mengemalui**) 1 to embarrass, shame. 2 (*cla*) to respect. *supaya tuanhamba dimalui oléh raja lain-lain* so that you will be respected by other kings.

   memalukan 1 to be ashamed of. **2** embarrassing. **3** (= **mempermalukan**) to embarrass, make s.o. ashamed. **4** disgraceful, shameless.

   termalu-malu quite shy/bashful/timid.

   kemaluan 1 private parts, genitals. **2** (feel) ashamed. **3** shame.

   kemalu-maluan 1 feel very shy, shyly. **2** slightly timid. **3** due to shyness, shyly.

   pemalu 1 a shy person. **2** shy, timid.

malu II *puteri* –, *rumput si* – and *si* – mimosa, a type of plant or shrub with a thorny stem and feathery leaves, *Mimosa pudica*.

malu III [Mantri Kehutanan dan Lurah] the official in charge of forestry and the village head.

Maluku the Moluccas, Maluku. – *Tengah* [Malteng] Central Maluku. – *Utara* [Malut] North Moluccas.

ma'lul (*A*) defective.

ma'lum → MAKLUM.

ma'lumat → MAKLUMAT.

malun (*A*) /mal'un/ cursed, damned.

malung conger eel, *Muraenesox spp.*

malur the part above the inner ear.

Malut [Maluku Utara] North Moluccas.

Malvinas the Argentine name for the (British) Falkland Islands.

mam I (*D*) mom.

mam II (children's language) to eat.

mama I → MAMAK.

mama II (*D*) mother.

mama III (*IBT*) mamma.

mamah I 1 to chew, masticate. 2 to munch (of toothless child). – *biak* cud chewing. **memamah biak** to chew the cud. **pemamah biak** ruminant.

   memamah to chew.

   memamahkan to chew for s.t. or s.o.

   mamahan cud, s.t. chewed.

   pemamah chewer. *~ biak* ruminant.

mamah II mother, mamma.

mamai 1 wandering about (of an old/sick/drunk person). 2 talking in one's sleep.

   bermamai to talk in one's sleep.

mamak (*M*) 1 uncle (on the mother's side), mother's older brother. 2 a polite form of address by rulers to, for example, aged chiefs. – *bendahara* the treasurer. 3 (*Mal*) a form of address for Indian Muslims or Malays of Indian descent. *ninik* – and – *ninik* the chiefs. *bersaudara beranak* – to be cousins.

   bermamak *aturan ~ kemanakan* matriarchate (also referred to as *adat kemanakan* or *adat semenda*).

mamalia (*D*) mammals.

mamam (children's language) to eat; → MAM II.

maman a generic name given to some medicinal plants.

mamanda polite form of *mamak*.

mamang I 1 confused, absent-minded, mixed up, bewildered, at a loss for what to do. 2 one's eyes grow dim (before fainting). – *gopoh* hastily, hurriedly.

mamang II (*Jv*) uncle (younger brother of father or mother).

mamang III (*M*) proverb, adage.

mamang IV a plant whose leaves are sometimes used in pickling and for medicinal purposes, bastard mustard, African spider flower, *Gynandropsis gynandra*. – *besar* spider flower, *Cleome spinosa*.

mamar → MAMANG I.

mamas(-mamas) k.o. tree, *Sapium baccatum*.

mamayu hayuning buwono (*Jv*) to leave the world a better place; to make life worth living.

mambang 1 k.o. spirit (red, yellow, green, white or black, the colors of lower deities). 2 (*M*) (sometimes identified with) *bidadari* (or, with their colors). 3 evening glow in the clouds. – *kuning* ominous yellowish-red evening sky. – *soré* and – *cahaya* dusk; → SENJA.

mambeg (*Jv*) stagnant, dead (water), clogged. *rawa yang berair* – backwater.

mambo (*D*) mambo (dance).

mambruk (*IBT*) crowned pigeon, *Goura spp.* – *biasa* western crowned pigeon, *Goura cristata*.

mambu (*J/Jv*) rotten (of odors).

mambung dry and empty of contents (of fruit, etc.); → MAMPUNG.

mami I 1 (children's language) mamma, mommy, mother. 2 aunt. 3 madam (of a house of prostitution), female pimp.

mami II (in Lombok) one of the two highest titles of Sasak nobility.

mamiisme (*D*) momism.

mamik gone bad in taste (of food/fruit), becoming tasteless.

mamlakat (*A ob*) sovereignty.

mammie (*D*) mommy, mummy.

mammouth (*D*) mammouth.

mampan → MEMPAN.

mampang (*Jv*) – *mumpung* to take advantage of a situation (*usu* to do s.t. bad); → MUMPUNG.

mampat I 1 compact, solid, compressed. 2 clogged up (of ditches, etc.), stuffed up (of nose). *hidung* – stuffed-up nose.

   memampatkan 1 to compress. **2** to stanch (bleeding).

   termampatkan compressible. **ketermampatan** compressibility.

   mampatan compression.

   pemampat compressor.

   pemampatan compression.

mampat II excellent, fine.

mampet → MAMPAT I.

mampir (*Jv*) 1 to call at, drop in, come by. 2 (of a ship) to moor, touch down at.

   memampiri to visit, stop off at.

   memampirkan to drop s.o. off.

   kemampiran a brief visit, stopover.

   pemampiran stop, place to stay.

mampu (*J/Jv*) 1 (cap)able. – *hukum* legally competent. **kemampulabaan** profitability. **2** well-off, wealthy. **3** can/be able to afford. *kurang* – can't pay (one's bill, etc.). **kekurang-mampuan** inability to pay. *tidak* – a) indigent. b) incapable, unable, unable to pay. **ketidak-mampuan 1** inability, inability to pay, indigence. **2** disability.

semampu 1 within one's reach, what one can afford. 2 as best one can, to the best of one's ability.

kemampuan 1 (cap)ability, competence, skill; performance. *hal-hal di luar ~nya* circumstances beyond one's control. *~ berbicara* speaking ability. *~ berdwibahasa* bilingual ability. *~ bertanggungjawab* culpability. *~ membaca* ability to read. *~ menerjemahkan* ability to translate. *~ mengerti* ability to understand. *~ menulis* ability to write. *~ meramal* predictability. *~ pukul* strike capability (of the air force). *~ tukar* interchangeability. 2 wealth, riches, means. **berkemampuan** to have the ability/capability. *~ pancar sejauh ... kilométer* to have a(n) ... kilometer broadcast range.

mampung 1 light and hollowed out (of bread); → MAMBUNG. 2 (*geol*) vesicular.

mampus 1 (*J vulg*) dead, croaked. *boléh* – and – *lu!* and *-lah kamu!* Drop dead! Go to hell! 2 damn it! (reaction to a piece of bad luck). – *ini, uang habis semua*. Damn it, all the money's gone!

ma'mum → MAKMUM.

ma'mur → MAKMUR.

mamut (*D*) mammoth.

man I (*A cla*) unit of weight, about 80 pounds.

man II 1 clipped form of *paman*. 2 (*sl*) man!

mana 1 which (of a number of choices)? *Tuan mau buku –?* Which book do you want? – *buku anda?* and *Buku anda –?* Which book is yours? *yang –?* which one (of a number of choices)? *–nya* which part of it. 2 from where/which country? *Tuan orang –?* What country are you from? 3 (= *di mana*) where? – *kantornya?* Where's your/his/her office? *dari* – from where? *di* – where (location), wher(ever). *di – ada asap disitu ada api*. Where there's smoke there's fire. *di – mungkin/perlu* where possible/necessary. *ke* – where (direction)? **mengemanakan** to bring/take where? *Dikemanakan pembunuh itu?* Where was the killer taken? **mengemana-manakan** to take/bring to some place or other. – *lagi* and – *pula* and also, furthermore, moreover, in addition, and what is more. *Dia pandai – lagi dia punya uang*. He is intelligent and he also has money. – *... – ...* both ... and ..., whether ... or ... – *tua – muda* both old and young. – *mahal – murah, belilah*. Buy it, whether it's expensive or cheap. – *panas – berdesak-desak*. It was warm as well as crowded. – *saudara jauh, – istri meninggal, – badan sakit, saya jadi kebingungan*. Whether it's because my brother was far away, or because my wife died, or because I felt sick, I became confused. 4 how could (one possibly) ...? – *saya tahu?* How could I possibly know? – *bisa (jadi)*, – *boléh* –, *dapat*, – *mungkin* (*J*). 5 from which part of? *Jakarta –?* From which part of Jakarta (are you)? *–kah* a) how is it possible? *–kah boléh jadi* and *–kah bisa?* How is it possible? How could that be? – *saja* a) whichever, any at all. *yang – saja kausuka* whichever you like. b) which (plural). c) (= *yang mana*) the one(s) that... – *tahu* who knows? – *tahu dia seorang tukang sikut*. Who knows, maybe he's a con-man.

mana-mana 1 whichever. *Ambillah ~ yang kamu suka*. Take whichever you like. 2 wherever. 3 whoever, whosoever. – *di antara kamu*. whoever among you. 4 everywhere. *di ~* everywhere. *di ~ (tempat)* in all/every (places). *ke ~* (to) everywhere. *~ yang perlu* what is strictly necessary. *~ yang bersekolah* all those going to school. *~ yang terpanggil namanya* all those whose names are called.

ma'na → MAKNA.

Manado the city of Manado in North Celebes.

management (*E*) → MANAJEMÉN.

manah I clipped form of *amanah*.

manah II (*M*) (*harta* –, *mas* –) wealth, riches, property (inherited from one's ancestors), heirlooms.

bermanah to have wealth, property, owning possessions.

manah III (*cla*) heart, feelings.

manai lack of blood, anemia. *pucat* – deathly pale from loss of blood.

manajemén (*D/E*) management. *pembinaan* – management development. *pendidikan* – management training. – *bawah* low-level management. – *kepegawaian* personnel management. – *kerja* work management. – *keuangan* financial management. – *konflik* conflict management. –

madya middle management. – *muatan* cargo management. – *operasi/produksi* operations and/or production management. – *pemasaran* marketing management. – *pembangunan* development management. – *pembelanjaan* purchasing management. – *penyimpanan* inventory management. – *perusahaan* corporate management. – *produk* product management. – *program doktor* Ph.D.-program management. – *proyék* project management. – *puncak* top management. – *risiko* risk management. – *sumber daya manusia* human resources management. – *tenaga kerja* manpower management. – *tengah* middle management; → MANAJEMÉN *madya*. – *teras* top management. – *terpadu* integrated management. – *wirakarya* business management.

memanajeméni to manage (a business, etc.). *~ sumber daya manusia* to manage human resources.

manajér (*D*) manager. *asistén* – assistant to the manager. – *kepegawaian* personnel manager. – *keuangan* financial manager. – *madya* middle manager. – *pemasaran* marketing manager. – *pembantu* assistant manager. – *pengembangan usaha* business development manager. – *penjualan* sales manager. – *percétakan* printing manager. – *periklanan* advertising manager. – *pérsonalia* personnel manager. – *perusahaan* corporate manager. – *produk* product manager. – *profesionél* professional manager. – *proyék* project manager. – *puncak* top manager. – *téknik arsitéktur dan sipil* technical manager for civil and architectural engineering. – *tim* team manager. – *umum* general manager. – *wilayah* district/regional manager.

manajérial (*D/E*) managerial. *berkeahlian* – with managerial skills.

manak name of a *ceki* card.

manakala 1 when(ever), in case. – *saya pergi* whenever I go. 2 as soon as, when. *Pencurian itu baru diketahui – pintu gerbang nampak jebol*. The crime was discovered when the entrance door appeared to be broken into. *Komisi itu akan segera dibubarkan – tugasnya selesai*. The board will be dismissed as soon as its tasks have been completed.

manakan I → MANA.

manakan II clipped form of **kemanakan**.

manalagi I → MANA.

manalagi II *jeruk (si)* – → JERUK *manalagi*.

manasik (*A*) ceremony. – *haji* ceremonies relating to the pilgrimage to Mecca.

manasuka as you like it, voluntary, optional. *acara* – free time (at a meeting). *jam* – optional subjects (in school).

manat (*M ob*) agreement, concurrence (reached at a meeting).

manau (*rotan*) – the largest of rattans, manau rattan, *Calamus manau*, used for polo sticks, basket ribs, etc. *seperti maksud* – wanting the impossible. *seperti mengilang* – a very difficult problem.

memanau 1 to block off a road with a leafy rattan rope as a prohibition. 2 to whip with rattan. 3 to gather rattan.

ma'nawi → MAKNAWI.

manazil (*A*) phases of the moon.

mancan(an) (*J*) improper.

mancanegara (*Jv*) 1 originally the former eastern and western border districts of Surakarta. 2 foreign (country). *penyanyi* – a foreign singer. *sapi* – an imported cow. *wisatawan* – foreign tourists.

mancawarna multicolored; → PANCAWARNA.

manci (*Jv*) 1 pan. 2 iron frying pan; → PANCI.

mancis (*D*) – *api* match; → MACIS.

memancisi to light up with a match.

memanciskan to light (a match).

mancit (*M*) mouse; → MENCIT.

mancrang (*Jv?*) bulbul, *Pycnonotus spp*.

mancrot and **mancrut** (*J/Jv*) to spurt out.

mancung I high and sharp (of the nose). *hidung* – an aquiline nose.

memancungkan to make s.t. sharp.

mancung II (*Jv*) dried sheath of coconut-palm blossom. *perahu* – a spathe-shaped boat.

mancur to spout, gush, spray; → PANCUR.

manda I short for *mamanda*.

manda II (*Jv*) can bear/stand to do s.t., not be so particular (about ...), can put up with.

manda III → MANDI *manda*.

manda IV → KANDA I.

mandah I leaves or husks put in a mortar (for padding).

mandah II → MANDA II.

mandah III to flee, run away.

mandai k.o. tree.

mandala (*Skr*) **1** a magic circle or shrine built for meditation. Borobudur, for example, is one. **2** name of a small, army-run airline. **3** (*mil*) theater of operations. – *Bhakti Wanita* name of the women's center in Yogyakarta. – *Krida* name of the stadium in Yogyakarta. – *Wisata* tourist information center. – *Yudha* command, i.e., a military district under s.o.'s authority (during the 1945 revolution).

mandalika I monkey-jack tree with edible fruit, *Artocarpus rigida*.

mandalika II (*Skr ob*) provincial governor of Sriwijaya and medieval Malacca.

mandam (= **termandam**) drunk, intoxicated. – *berahi* drunk with love.

mandana hysterical.

mandang k.o. bird.

mandar I *burung* – various species of grackles, moorhens, crakes, coots, and rails. – *batu* moorhen, *Gallinula chloropus*. – *besar* purple swamp hen, *Porphyrio porphyrio*. – *hitam* common coot, *Fulica atra*. – *kelam* dusky moorhen, *Gallinula tenebrosa*. – *padi* slaty-breasted rail, *Gallirallus striatus*. – *Sulawesi* snoring rail, *Aramidopsis plateni*.

Mandar II an ethnic group of Sulawesi.

Mandarin (*D/E*) (a dialect of) Chinese, in various compounds, such as *bahasa* – Mandarin Chinese.

mandarsah → MADRASAH.

mandat (*D*) **1** mandate; authorization. **2** government pay order.

mandataris (*D*) mandatory (person to whom a mandate has been given).

mandau sacred decapitating knife of Kalimantan.

mandeg → MANDEK.

mandéh (*M*) maternal aunt.

mandek (*J/Jv*) **1** to stop, get stuck, stall. **2** to stagnate. **3** to come to a halt/standstill (of traffic, etc.).

    memandekkan to bring s.t. to a halt.

    kemandekan halt, standstill. ~ *penyelesaian masalah Kamboja* a standstill in settling the Cambodian problem.

mandeng (*Jv*) to watch, keep an eye on.

mandering → MIND(E)RING.

mandi I 1 to take/have a bath, take/have a shower. **2** to swim, go swimming (in the sea or ocean) for relaxation. *banyak orang – di laut* many people went swimming in the ocean. **3** to be drenched, spattered; to be showered (with); to be rolling in (money, etc.). *(mati-mati) – biar basah* don't do things by halves. *bagai – dalam cupak* said of insufficient help. *Kita – uang*. We were rolling in money. – *ala koboi* (to take a) sponge bath. – *angin* to be exposed to a lot of wind. – *bakal* to bathe a corpse immediately after his/her death. – *balai* to bathe s.o. to chase away evil spirits. – *barat* to wash one's face. – *basah lantai* to bathe forty days after childbirth. – *bébék* to wash one's face. – *berendam* (to take) a tub bath. – *bersiram* (to take) a shower. – *bunting* to bathe in the seventh month of pregnancy. – *burung* (to take) a splash bath. – *damai* to take a bath after a marriage has been consummated. – *darah* a) to be bathed in one's blood. b) bloodshed. – *duduk* (to take) a hip/sitz bath. – *gubah* → MANDI *bakal*. – *guyur* to take a bath using a *gayung* or water dipper. – *hadas* to bathe after sexual relations. – *haid/hail* to bathe after menstruation. – *janabat/junubat* to wash after sexual relations. – *keringat* soaked in sweat. – *kubat* → MANDI *bakal*. – *kucing* to a) take a quick bath. b) to lick s.o.'s body all over, tongue bath. – *kungkum* (to take) a bath during which the body is dipped/immersed in water. – *laut* to go swimming in the sea/ocean. – *layang-layang* to bathe by splashing o.s. with water. – *lénggang perut* → MANDI *bunting*. – *luas* → MANDI *hadas*. – *mait* → MANDI *bakal*. – *manda* all k.o. of baths/ablutions, various ways to bathe. – *matahari* to take a sunbath, sit out in the sun. – *mayat* to bathe a corpse (in the Muslim way). – *nifas* → MANDI *basah lantai*. – *ombak* washed by the waves (when taking an ocean bath). – *peluh* bathed in sweat. – *rendam* → MANDI *kung-*

kum. – *Safar* a festival held on the last Wednesday of the month of *Safar* to purify o.s. so as to avert future disasters (in practice, an excuse for a bathing party). – *sauna* (to take) a sauna bath. – *sudah* to bathe a corpse for the last time (before it is wrapped in a shroud). – *tian* → MANDI *bunting*. – *tobat* repentance ritual through bathing. – *Turki/uap* (to take) a steam/Turkish bath. – *wajib* → MANDI *janabat*. – *wiladah* → MANDI *bunting*.

    bermandi 1 to bathe, take/have a bath, wash o.s. **2** to be bathed in. ~ *keringat/peluh* to be bathed in sweat. *jalan* ~ *warna* streets bathed in colors.

    bermandikan bathed in, covered with, drenched with (sweat/oil, etc.). ~ *air mata* to drown in tears. ~ *cahaya lampu* to be bathed in light. ~ *darah* to be covered with blood. ~ *keringat/peluh* to be bathed in sweat.

    memandikan [and **ngemandiin** (*J coq*)] **1** to bathe/wash s.o. ~ *(anak) bayi* to bathe the baby, give the baby a bath. **2** to wash (a corpse) with water. **3** to submerge, immerse, dip (a kris in a liquid to get rid of corrosion, etc.). **4** to shower (with), bestow (s.t. on), give abundantly. *Anak-anak itu mau dimandikan dengan kasih sayang ibunya*. Maternal love will be showered on those children.

    mempermandi(kan) 1 (*cla*) to bathe with. **2** to baptize. **3** to bathe s.o. according to a certain ritual.

    pemandi 1 s.o. who washes. ~ *mayat* mortician. **2** baptizer. *Yohanes* ~ John the Baptist.

    pemandian bathing place. *bapak* ~ godfather. *ibu* ~ godmother. *tempat* ~ bathing place.

    permandian 1 bathing/seaside resort. **2** baptism, christening.

mandi II (*Jv*) strong, powerful.

    memandikan to make (a fighting cock, etc.) powerful.

mandiang the late; → MENDIANG.

mandil (*A ob*) coverlet; tablecloth; handkerchief.

mandir *mondar* – (*Jv*) to and fro, up and down, back and forth.

mandiréng (*Jv*) contraction of *mandiri ing*.

mandiri (*Jv*) **1** independent. *belajar* – to study by o.s. (without a teacher). *belajar hidup* – to learn to stand on one's own two feet/to be independent. *berpikir* – to think independently. *Menuju Hidup* –. Toward Independent Living. – *sebagai partai* to become an independent party. *secara* – independent(ly), self-sustaining. **2** autonomous, self-governing. *pemerintah* – autonomy, self-rule.

    bermandiri to stand on one's own two feet, be independent.

    memandirikan to make self-reliant/able to live etc. on one's own. ~ *tunanétra* to make the blind able to live on their own. – *ing pribadi* (*Jv*) self-reliant.

    kemandirian 1 independence. **2** self-reliance. ~ *dalam pangan* self-reliance in food. **3** autonomy; sovereignty.

    pemandirian making s.t. or s.o. independent.

mandolin (*D*) mandolin.

mandor (*Port*) **1** foreman, overseer (of workmen). **2** headwaiter (in a hotel, etc.). **3** employee (with some power, in hospitals/libraries, etc.). **4** Superintendant (in prison). – *angin* (*infr*) assistant policeman. – *jalan* a) Superintendant of roads. b) vagabond, bum, loiterer.

    memandori 1 to have ... work under one. *dimandori* to work under, be headed by. *tim juru bicara yang dimandori WW* a team of spokesmen working under WW. **2** to supervise (s.o.'s work). **3** to give s.o. orders, order/boss s.o. around.

mandraguna (*Skr*) invulnerable.

Mandrax (trade mark) k.o. imported barbiturate containing derivatives of quinazolone and diphenhydramine.

Mandrin → MANDARIN.

mandu (*M*) thesis, proposition.

mandub (*A*) recommended.

mandul infertile, barren (of women/animals), sterile.

    memandulkan to sterilize, spay.

    kemandulan sterility, infertility.

    pemandulan sterilization, spaying.

mandulika → MANDALIKA I.

mandung I cock, fowl.

mandung II *kemenyan* – *jati* white incense.

mandur → MANDOR.

manejér (D) → MANAJÉR. memanejéri → MEMANEJEMÉNI.

manekin (D/E) mannequin, model.

manfaat (A) 1 use, benefit, advantage. untuk – for the use of. – pasti fixed benefits. 2 profit, gain. – dan mudarat and melarat dan – a) profit and loss. b) advantages and disadvantages, pros and cons. c) joys and sorrows. tidak ada – there's no point in.
  bermanfaat 1 useful, beneficial. 2 profitable. 3 advantageous. 4 to avail, gain advantage.
  memanfaati to be beneficial to, be of use to.
  memanfaatkan 1 to use, utilize, make use of, resort to. 2 to take advantage of, capitalize on, abuse (one's position), exploit. ~ kesempatan to avail o.s. of an opportunity. ~ keuntungan to take advantage of (an opportunity). kurang dimanfaatkan under-utilized.
  mempermanfaatkan to make use of, utilize.
  termanfaatkan usable, could be used.
  kemanfaatan usefulness. ~ umum public utilities.
  pemanfaat 1 user; → PENGGUNA. 2 appliance. ~ listrik electric appliance.
  pemanfaatan use, utilization, application. ~ tenaga kerja labor utilization.

mang 1 → MAMANG II. 2 term of address for Sundanese men. – Ihin the affectionate term of address for the former Governor of West Java Solihin G(autama) P(oerwanegara).

mangan I → MANGGAN.

mangan II (Jv) to eat; → MAKAN. – ora – angger/nék/waton kumpul and – ora – sing penting ngumpul (a cultural attitude) whether we have s.t. to eat or not, the main thing is to be together (or, to associate); → MAKAN tidak makan asal(kan) kumpul.

mangap (J) agape, with the mouth wide open (in surprise/amazement, etc.).
  termangap (mouth) agape.

mangas k.o. tree, Memecylon acuminatum.

mangau termangau-mangau agape with amazement, taken aback.

mangga I (Tam) mango (the tree as well as the fruit, Mangifer indica. – arumanis medium-size type of mango, dark green and reddish or yellowish when ripe, very sweet. – daging small round type of mango, yellow when ripe, sweet-sour tasting. – dodol k.o. mango. – gedong medium-small round type of mango, orange skin when ripe, distinctive odor. – golék long yellow-green type of mango with orange meat. – Indramayu large roundish type of mango, green-yellow when ripe; sweet tasting. – kuéni/kuini roundish yellow type of mango, green when ripe, sweet sour strong-tasting, Mangifera odorata. – madu medium-small roundish type of mango, green when ripe. – si manalagi large and sweet type of mango.

mangga II sakit – swelling in the groin, usually with pus.

mangga III (S) [and (Jv) /monggo/] 1 please (go ahead and ...). 2 (Jv) (as a response to kulo nuwun) come in! 3 come on!

mangga IV padlock.
  memangga to lock (a door, etc.).

manggah 1 asthma. 2 short-winded.

manggala I (Jv) commander of the Kraton guards in Yogyakarta. – Karya Kencana "Leader of Work Redeemable in Gold," i.e., the highest title of appreciation for family planning development. – Wanabakti "Commander of Forest Devotions," i.e., the name given to the Main Forestry Building in Jakarta.

manggala II the highest level upgrader for P4; → PENATAR.

manggan (D) manganese.

manggar 1 coconut palm blossom. 2 (M) base of (a palm tree, etc.) frond.

manggis(tan) mangosteen, Garcinia mangostana, i.e., a segmented fruit with hard purplish skin.

manggul tanah – highland.

mangguli (in Sumatra) molasses.

manggung I (Jv) continuous cooing (esp of the perkutut).

manggung II → PANGGUNG I.

manggustan → MANGGIS(TAN).

manggut (Jv) to nod (in approval); → ANGGUK I, ANGGUT.
  manggut-manggut to keep nodding one's head (considered a token of respect).
  memanggut(-manggut)kan to nod (one's head).
  termanggut-manggut kept on nodding.

mangir (J) k.o. powder used to lighten the skin.

mangka (ob) → MAKA.
  mangkanya → MAKANYA.

mangkah → MANGKAR.

mangkak I (J) proud, haughty.

mangkak II (J/Jv) dirty(-looking), dingy, (become) dirty white (of clothes), yellowed, discolored.

mangkal I → MANGKEL I.

mangkal II → PANGKAL.

mangkar 1 hard (of fruit, esp durians, or of cooked potatoes). 2 not done, raw.

mangkara → MAKARA II.

mangkas 1 hard (of rice so that dry pounded grains break instead of being crushed). keras – hard as a rock.

mangkas II → BANGKAS.

Mangkasar → MAKASSAR.

mangkat (respectful) to pass away, die.
  kemangkatan passing away, dying.

mangkel I (J/Jv) 1 annoyed, irritated. 2 resentful.
  kemangkelan annoyance, irritation.

mangkel II → PANGKAL.

mangkih sticking out, as a cigar from the mouth or a pencil from behind the ear; bristling, spiky.

mangkin → MAKIN.

mangkir (D) 1 to be out/absent (from work/school, etc.), cut class. kebiasaan – absenteeism. 2 to fail (an examination). 3 to be missing, lacking.
  kemangkiran absenteeism.
  pemangkir absentee.

mangkok I (J) → MANGKUK. mangkokan hip joint.

mangkok II mangkokan → DAUN mangkok.

mangkrak (J) 1 spotted (with dirt). 2 in a disorderly pile.

mangkring (J) stubborn, obstinate.

mangku → PANGKU I.

mangkubuana (Jv) a title of the Sultan of Yogyakarta.

mangkubumi (cla) 1 minister in charge of government property, finance minister. 2 prime minister.

mangkuk bowl, cup, crucible. kué – k.o. cupcake (not the same as an American cupcake). pinggan – a) cups and saucers. b) china, crockery. – baja kibble (in mining). – bekam cupping glass. – sabun soap dish.
  memangkukkan to cup (one's hands).

mangkus (M) efficacious, effective; → MANJUR, MUJARAB, MUSTAJAB. tindakan – effective measures.
  kemangkusan efficacy, efficaciousness, effectiveness.

mangoni → MAHONI.

mangro (Jv) 1 (to be able to go) in two directions. 2 dual. –.tingal a) two-faced. b) to serve two masters, divide one's loyalties.
  kemangroan dualism, duality.

mangsa (Skr) 1 prey (of animals), bait. 2 victim.
  memangsa(i) to prey on. Dua sapi dimangsa harimau. Two cows fell victim to a tiger. 13 toko dimangsai api. Thirteen shops fell victim to a fire.
  pemangsa predator, of prey.
  pemangsaan predation.

mangsai → MASAI.

mangsét → MANSÉT.

mangsi (Skr) 1 ink. ikan – cuttlefish. 2 (ob) black tooth-stain. 3 (M) indigo-blue, dark-blue, black.

mangu termangu(-mangu) 1 confused, dazed. 2 taken aback. 3 thoughtful. ketermanguan confusion.
  kemanguan confusion, daze.

Manguni I a legendary bird in the coat-of-arms of the Minahasa area (of the North Celebes).

Manguni II a dissident organization which attacked the cavalry center in Bandung and the Presidential Palace in Jakarta on March 30, 1960.

mangupa antidote.

mangut I 1 daydreaming, confused, dazed. 2 to doze off.
  bermangut in a daze.
  termangut confused.

mangut II – ikan fish cooked in coconut milk.

mani (*A*) semen. *pemancaran* – ejaculation (of semen). – *éncér* premature ejaculation.

mania (*D/E*) mania.

maniak (*D/E*) maniac.

manifés (*D*) manifest (of ship). – *penumpang* passenger manifest.

manifést (*D/E*) 1 → MANIFÉS. 2 manifesto.

maniféstasi (*D*) manifestation.

  memaniféstasikan to manifest.

manifésto (*D/E*) manifesto. – *Kebudayaan* → MANIKEBU.

manik (*Tam/Hind?*) 1 jewel, precious stone, gem. 2 Adam's apple. – *mata* pupil (of the eye). *Éksprési muka bisa berdusta, – mata tidak.* The facial expression can lie, (but) the pupil of the eye cannot.

  manik-manik (*Skr*) beads, small objects of glass, wood, etc. with holes through them for threading on a string.

  bermanik-manik 1 to wear a necklace, etc. made of beads, bead-like. 2 drops of water/sweat.

manikam (*Tam*) 1 precious stone, jewel, gem. *ratna mutu* – gems of all kinds. – *sudah menjadi sekam* to have lost its value/power (after a secret has been revealed). 2 (*ob*) sperm, semen. 3 essence. 4 embryo. *jauhar juga yang mengenal* – it takes a jeweler to judge a gem. *mengembalikan – ke dalam cembulnya* to rethink s.t. said earlier.

Manikebu [*Maniffésto Kebudayaan*] Cultural Manifesto, a manifesto issued on August 17, 1963, protesting political interference with the arts and opposed to Lekra.

Manikebuis supporter of *Manikebu*.

Manikebuisme the *Manikebu* philosophy.

manikur (*D/E*) manicure.

  bermanikur to get a manicure.

manikuris (*D*) manicurist.

manila I *bébék/itik* – Muscovy duck, *Anas moschata*.

manila II *bunga/kembang* – an ornamental shrub, crepe jasmine, *Tabernaemontana divaricata*.

Manipol [*Maniffésto Politik*] Political Manifesto (President Soekarno's Independence Day address of August 17, 1959). – *usdék* Manipol and Usdek. *memanipol-usdékkan* to retool/reorganize in accordance with this doctrine.

  bermanipol to profess this manifesto.

  kemanipolan this doctrine (*mod*).

Manipolis supporter of *Manipol*. – *munafik* fake/hypocritical supporter of *Manipol*.

manipolisasi conforming s.t. to this doctrine.

manipulasi (*D*) 1 manipulation. 2 graft.

  memanipulasikan 1 to manipulate. 2 to embezzle. *~ uang rakyat* to embezzle the people's money.

manipulator (*D/E*) manipulator (the person). – *pajak* tax evader.

manipulir (*D*) **bermanipulir** to manipulate.

  memanipulirkan to manipulate s.t.

manira (*Jv cla*) I, me, my.

manis 1 sweet (of sugar/fruits/face/manners). *si* – sugar. – *jangan segera ditelan, pahit jangan segera dimuntahkan* take it with a grain of salt. *mulut* – affable, sweet talk. 2 dear, pretty, cute, charming. 3 honey, sweetie. *Selamat malam, –!* Good evening, sweetie! 4 friendly, kind, nice. *muka* – a pleasant face. 5 engaging, captivating; attractive, interesting. 6 smooth. *berhenti dengan* – to stop smoothly (of a car/plane). *habis – sepah dibuang* to take advantage of s.o. or s.t. and then throw him/her/it away. – *budi* friendly. – *hati* kind, likable. – *muka* sweet expression. – *mulut* sweet talk.

  semanis as sweet as.

  semanis-manisnya as sweet(ly) as possible.

  bermanis to act in a sweet way.

  bermanis-manis to use flattery. *~ kepada* to kowtow to, flatter.

  memanis 1 to become sweet. 2 (= **memanis-manis**) to decorate (a table, etc.), adorn.

  memanisi 1 to add sugar to, sweeten. 2 to adorn, embellish.

  memaniskan and **mempermanis** to sweeten, make sweeter, make nicer. *memaniskan muka* to make one's face look pleasant, act sweet in front of others.

  termanis the sweetest.

(manis-)manisan sweets, preserved fruit, candy. *~ belimbing*

carambola candy. *~ cokelat* chocolate bar/candy. *~ hati* likable, kindly. *~ lebah* honey.

  kemanisan 1 sweetness. 2 beauty. 3 (*coq*) overly sweet.

  pemanis 1 sweetener. *bahan ~ (buatan)* (artificial) sweetener. *sekedar ~ kalimat/tutur saja* to say s.t. just out of politeness, a formula of courtesy. 2 (*~ muka*) cosmetics. 3 decoration.

  pemanisan sweetening.

manisjangan (*Jv*) cinnamon.

manja I 1 spoiled, pampered (of child, young woman). 2 attached (emotionally). 3 intimate, familiar, confidential.

  semanja as spoiled as.

  bermanja to coax, cajole, court.

  bermanja-manja 1 to be on intimate terms with s.o., be friendly. 2 to romp around.

  memanja 1 to be(come) spoiled. 2 to try to get on intimate terms (with).

  memanjakan and **mempermanjakan** to spoil, coddle, pamper, baby, over-indulge (a child).

  termanja-manja spoiled, pampered.

  kemanjaan familiarity, intimacy, over-indulgence.

  kemanja-manjaan very spoiled, pampered.

  pemanja *~ wanita* playboy.

  pemanjaan pampering, spoiling.

manja II (in compounds) → MAJA I.

manjakani → MAJAKANI.

manjapada (*Skr*) this world; → MARCAPADA.

manjau and **bermanjau** to pay a visit (of a young man to a young woman); to cruise (in search of girls).

manjung I a torch (used for catching fish).

manjung II **manjungan** prau, boat; → ANJUNG, MANCUNG II.

manjung III **permanjungan** mezzanine room (next to the house; its floor is higher than the house floor).

manjur (*J/Jv*) 1 efficacious, effective (of medicine). *rumusan yang* – magic formula. 2 potent (of poison). 3 powerful. *dukun yang* – a powerful *dukun*. *Doanya* –. His prayers are powerful.

  semanjur as effective/efficacious as.

  kemanjuran efficacy, effectiveness.

manol (*Jv*) 1 janitor. 2 (in Muncar, Banyuwangi) person who works transporting fish from fishing boats to the fish auction or processing site.

manométer (*D/E*) manometer.

manpaat → MANFAAT.

mansét (*D*) 1 cuff of a sleeve. 2 cufflinks. 3 bushing, packing, ring.

mansiang (*M*) a sedge used for mat-making, greater club rush, *Scirpus grossus*; → MENSIANG.

mansub (*A*) subjunctive.

mansuh and **mansukh** (*A mostly Mal*) 1 abolished. 2 expired, annulled, cancelled, abrogated. 3 the abrogated, i.e., a part of the Koran which has been abrogated by another part of the Koran; *cp* NASIKH.

  memansuhkan 1 to abolish. 2 to cancel, annul, abrogate.

mantab → MANTAP.

mantan (*Basemah*) ex-, former. *kedua – Kaskopkamtib* two former *Kaskopkamtib* Chiefs of Staff.

mantakan that's the reason, that's why.

mantang (*S*) sweet potato, *Ipomoea batatas*.

mantap I 1 stable, stabilized, constant, firm, solid. 2 well adjusted. 3 resolute, determined, steady. *bertékad* – to make a determined effort to. 4 sure, skilled. *Ia menjadi – dalam mempermainkan beberapa gending.* He became skilled at playing various instruments. *tidak* – unstable. *ketidak-mantapan* instability.

  semantap as firm/stable as.

  memantapkan 1 to reinforce. 2 to shore up. 3 to (make) steady. 4 to put s.t. on a firm footing, provide a firm foundation for s.t.

  kemantapan 1 stability, solidity. 2 steadiness, firmness.

  pemantap stabilizer.

  pemantapan stabilization, consolidating, consolidation. *~ harga* price stabilization. *~ peruntukan tanah* land consolidation.

mantap II (*M*) stolid, calm; → ANTAP II. "*Wah senang ya, Bu?*" "*Ya tentu,*" *jawabnya* –. "Well, you must be happy, aren't you?" "Sure," she answered calmly.

mantari (*M*) sun; → MATAHARI I.

manték → MANTIK I.

mantel (*D*) 1 coat, cloak. – *bulu* fur coat. – *bulu musang* mink coat. – *hujan* raincoat. 2 mantle. – *kehormatan* (*euph*) condom.

mantelpak (*D*) lady's (tailored/two-piece) suit, coat and skirt.

mantén → KEMANTÉN.

mantep → MANTAP I.

mantera → MANTRA.

manteri → MANTRI.

manterus → MAT(E)ROS.

manthuk-manthuk (*Jv*) to nod one's head again and again. *cara bicara kalau –, pegang manuk* to talk while nodding one's head again and again and holding one's hand in front of one's genitals, a Javanese attitude of respect and submissiveness towards one's superiors.

manti (*M*) k.o. civil official; → MENTERI.

mantik I (*A*) *ilmu* – logic; → LOGIKA.

mantik II (*M*) tidy, orderly.

mantiki (*A*) logical. *penalaran* – logical reasoning.

manting (*Jv*) → UBAR I.

mantiqi (*A*) region, district.

mantol → MANTEL. *organisasi* – undercover organization.

mantongan (*Jv*) (in Surabaya) salt-pan worker.

mantra (*Skr*) mantra, magic formula/spell/incantation. *membaca* – to recite mantras.

  memantrai to charm, cast a spell on s.o., put a curse on.

  memantrakan to cast a spell on s.t. *Abu dan tulang-tulang dimantrakan oléh pedanda.* The (Hindu-Balinese) priest has cast a spell on the ashes and bones.

mantram → MANTRA.

mantri I (*Skr*) 1 a title for a number of low-level positions. 2 (*cla*) (in older documents and stories) minister or counselor of the sovereign (subordinate to the *patih*), first official of the *paséban*; – *jero* chamberlain, or also valet, personal servant. – *air* irrigation officer. – *belasting* (*ob*) → MANTRI *pajak*. – *cacar* smallpox vaccination officer. – *candu* head of the opium control division. – *garam* salt trade official. – *guru* headmaster, school superintendant. – *héwan* officer in charge of livestock. – *hutan* forestry official. – *jaga* warden, jailor. – *jalan* loafer, idler. – *kabupatén* first clerk of a *bupati*. – *keséhatan* paramedic. – *klinik* paramedic (often also functions as a doctor and as clinic head). – *lanbau* foreman of the agricultural information service. – *pajak* tax officer. – *pamong praja* head of a local district in a city. – *pasar* market supervisor (collects fees for market space). – *polisi* police detective. – *Polisi Pamongpraja* [MPP] Civil Service Police Officer (in a *kecamatan*). – *suntik* vaccination officer. – *ukur* land registrar, surveyor. – *ulu* water distribution officer.

  kemantrén (*Jv*) area under the control of a *mantri*.

mantri II → MENTERI.

mantu (*J/Jv*) 1 son-(daughter-)in-law. *abang* – older brother-in-law. 2 (to hold) a wedding for one's child (or, by extension, s.o. else's child); → MENANTU.

mantuk I (*A ob*) the literal meaning (of a word).

mantuk II (*Jv*) to go back home.

manual (*D/E*) 1 manual, i.e., by hand. 2 manual, i.e., book of instructions for operating a piece of equipment.

manufaktur (*D*) manufacture.

  pemanufaktur manufacturer.

manuk (*Jv*) 1 bird. *dada* – pigeon breast. – *déwata* bird of paradise. 2 (*coq*) penis.

manula [*manusia usia lanjut*] senior citizen. *kaum* – the elderly, the seniors.

manunggal (*Jv*) 1 to become one with *gusti* (the master) or *Allah* (God). 2 to integrate. 3 integrated. – *Empat* the four-in-one unit consisting of the three fighting forces: Army, Air Force, and Navy; plus the Police. *–ing kawula-gusti* and *–ing kawula lan gusti* the unity of the subjects and the king, i.e., the king (or, president) can do no wrong. – *ajur-ajer* to become completely one with.

  memanunggalkan 1 to unite s.t. (with s.t.), integrate s.t. 2 to associate o.s. (with s.t.).

  kemanunggalan becoming one, amalgamation.

panunggalan becoming one with *gusti* or *Allah*.

manusia (*Skr*) 1 human being, man, mortal; mankind. 2 human (*mod*). – *angkasa* spaceman, cosmonaut. – *Indonésia seutuhnya* the perfect Indonesian (man); *cp* INSAN *ul-kamil*. – *katak* frogman. – *kera* ape-man, anthropoid (ape). – *loka* the earth, world. – *mesin* apathetic person. – *mini* midget. – *pekerja* homo faber. – *pemain* homo ludens. – *pemikir* homo sapiens. – *penganalisa* analytic man. – *pinggiran* marginal person. – *purba* prehistoric man. – *Salju* the Abominable Snowman. – *tiga jaman* a person who experienced the Dutch colonial period, the period of the Japanese occupation and the present period of independence.

bermanusia with men, manned.

memanusiakan and mempermanusia to humanize.

kemanusiaan 1 humanity. 2 human nature. 3 humanitarianism. 4 humanism; → PERIKEMANUSIAAN

manusiawi human (*mod*). *tidak* – inhuman, inhumanely. *ketidakmanusiawian* inhumanity.

manuskrip (*D/E*) manuscript.

manuswantara (*Skr neo*) anthropomorphic. *paham serba* – anthropocentrism.

manut (*Jv*) 1 to follow; according to (the rules, etc.). 2 to obey, follow orders, be obedient. 3 a yes-man.

  manut(an) and – *lutut* obedient, docile.

manuver (*D/E*) maneuver, i.e., a planned and controlled tactical or strategic movement of troops, planes, etc.; exercise.

bermanuver to maneuver.

manuvra and manuvre → MANUVER.

manyala (*J*) 1 swell, terrific, great. 2 bright (of colors), flashy. – *Bob!* Terrific! Groovy.

manyar (*Jv*) streaked weaver bird, *Ploceus manyar*.

manyun (*S*) to do nothing but sit around and pout.

  bermanyun ~ *diri* to pout.

  termanyun-manyun sitting around and pouting.

manyung (*ikan*) k.o. sheath-fish, giant cat-fish, *Arius spp.*

manzil(ah) (*A*) halting-place, rest house, place to spend the night when on a trip.

manzum (*A*) orderly.

mao → MAU.

maoni → MAHONI II.

Maoisme (*D/E*) Maoism.

map (*D*) file for keeping papers in order, file folder. – *gambar* portfolio. – *snélhechter/snélhékhter* binder with clips.

mapak (*J*) – and memapak to meet s.o., welcome; → PAPAK II.

mapalus (in the Minahasa area) (compulsory) mutual assistance (in farming/house building, etc.), under the leadership of one of the members of the group.

mapan (*Jv*) established. *kaum* – the well-to-do/wealthy/haves. *dengan* – firmly.

  semapan as established as.

  memapankan to establish. ~ *kembali* to reestablish.

  kemapanan the establishment, i.e., the haves and those in power in a particular society.

  pemapanan establishment, establishing.

mapatih (*Jv ob*) chief minister (of the *Majapahit* empire).

mapela (*D*) muffler (of a car).

Maperma [Masa Perkenalan Mahasiswa] college-student initiation period.

Maphilindo the cooperative association of Malaysia, the Philippines, and Indonesia formed in 1963 at the suggestion of Philippine president Macapagal.

mapitu → MO-PITU.

Mapram [Masa Prabakti Mahasiswa] → MAPERMA.

mar (*A cla*) check to the queen (in chess).

mara I (*Skr cla*) danger, disaster, peril. – *jangan dipukat, rezeki jangan ditolak* don't look for trouble and don't reject good fortune. – *bahaya* (all k.o.) dangers, disasters, perils.

bermara 1 dangerous, hazardous, perilous. 2 endangered.

memarakan to endanger, imperil.

mara II 1 to advance, move forward. 2 to approach.

memarakan to advance, move forward.

kemaraan 1 advancement, progress. 2 approach.

mara III → KOTAMARA, SANGGAMARA.

mara IV → MARAH I. ngemarain → MEMARAHI.

marabunta 1 k.o. ant. 2 name of the 512th battalion.

marah I 1 angry, mad. 2 anger, fury. 3 to become angry. – *akan/kepada* to be angry at/with. – *besar* very angry. – *yang tiada sampai* angry for a very short time.
  marah-marah to keep on being angry, being angry. *Jangan* ~. Don't be angry.
  semarah as angry as.
  semarah-marahnya no matter how angry, however angry.
  bermarahan to be angry at e.o.
  memarahi [and ngemarahin (*J coq*)] to be angry at/with, scold, reprimand. *Saya dimarahinya.* He was angry at me.
  memarahkan 1 to make angry, anger, infuriate. *Ucapan itu* ~ *kaum keluarganya.* That statement made his relatives angry. 2 to become angry/upset at s.t. or about s.t.
  termarah too/very angry.
  marahan → BERMARAHAN.
  kemarahan fury, rage, anger.
  kemarah-marahan very angry, furious, enraged.
  pemarah 1 hothead, i.e., person who becomes angry easily. 2 hot-tempered.

marah II (*M*) (in Padang) title for *Sutan*'s son with common wife or daughter with common husband; the title is lower than *Sutan*.

maraja and marajo short for *maharaja*.

marak 1 shine, gleam, glow. *Namanya naik* –. His esteem is growing. 2 (= memarak) to flare up (of flame/rebellion/tension, etc.), explode. 3 striking (of a color). 4 luster.
  semarak 1 shine, gleam, glow. 2 blooming, in the full bloom of youth, nubile. bersemarak convivial, enjoyable (of a party, etc.). kesemarakan 1 conviviality. 2 being in the full bloom of youth. 3 growing (esteem, etc.). penyemarak s.o. or s.t. that shines, etc.
  memarak to flare up, glow, explode.
  memaraki to add luster to.
  memarakkan to brighten/light up (a room, etc.). ~ *api* to stir up the fire. ~ *semangat* to enliven.
  kemarakan flaring up.
  pemarak s.t. that stirs up (a fire).
  pemarakan brightening up.

marakas maracas, a k.o. South American musical instrument.

marambung (*M*) ironweed?, beach naupuka, *Veronia arborea*, *Vitex vestita*.

maranta prayer plant, banded arrowroot, *Marantha leuconeura/bicolor*.

marapulai (*M*) bridegroom.

maras (*Jv*) 1 afraid, scared, frightened. 2 very anxious/worried.

maratib (*A*) grades.

maraton (*D/E*) marathon. *berjalan* – marathon race. *berlangsung* – to go on and on at great length.

marawis (*A J*) a Betawian art form consisting of drumming and chanting; → MARWAS.

marbodat (in Tapanuli) person who raises and trains a monkey to pick coconuts for a fee.

marbut 1 (*A*) marabout. 2 (*J*) caretaker and drumbeater at a mosque.

marcado /markado/ (in Timtim) market.

marcapada (*Jv*) the earth.

mardan (*Pers ob*) human beings.

Mardijker (*D ob*) descendants of Portuguese-speaking freed slaves living in Jakarta in the 17th century; → MERDÉKA.

mardud (*A*) doubtful (of a *hadits*).

marem (*Jv*) satisfied, content, complacent.

maréng (*Jv*) transition period between the end of the rainy season and the beginning of the dry season (March, April, and May).
  maréngan → MUSIM *maréngan*.

Maret (*D*) March.

marga I 1 Batak kinship group (an exogamous clan). Membership in a *marga* is determined by descent in the male line, and no member is allowed to marry a woman of his own *marga*. A woman becomes a member of her husband's *marga* after her marriage. 2 (in Palembang, South Sumatra) a village, i.e., an administrative unit below the *kecamatan*, often the same as a *désa*; → LURAH I.
  kemargaan belonging to a *marga*.

marga II 1 genus. 2 plant family. *masih satu* – *dengan* to be a member of the same family as.

marga III (*Skr*) wild (animals); → MARGASATWA.

marga IV (*Skr*) 1 road. 2 highway.

margarin(e) (*D*) margarine.

margasatwa (*Skr*) 1 wild animals, beasts. 2 wildlife. – *besar* big game. 3 fauna.

marge (*D*) /marsye/ margin. – *keuntungan* profit margin.

margin (*E fin*) margin.

marginal (*D*) marginal.

margub (*A*) enjoyable.

marhaban (*A*) k.o. song of praise for the Prophet Muhammad.
  memarhabankan to serenade with religious melodies.

marhaén 1 a fictitious man-of-the-people, John Doe (term first used by Soekarno in 1930 and then later when he was president). 2 proletarian. 3 the have-nots.
  kemarhaénan protelarianism.

marhaéni female *marhaén*.

marhaénis support of *marhaénisme*.

Marhaénisme populism, an ideology which eulogizes the wise and hard-working peasant.

marhum (*A*) that which has found mercy; → ALMARHUM.

marhumah (*A*) the (female) deceased, the late. e.g., – *Sitti Juwariah. atas nama* – on behalf of the deceased. *jenazah* – the mortal remains of the deceased.

mari I 1 –*!* (–*!*) a politeness formula used in inviting s.o. to do s.t. 2 please (take some, in offering s.t.), help yourself. 3 in leave-taking after a visit; good-bye (in this meaning usually reduplicated, i.e., *mari-mari*). 4 (in agreeing to a price after bargaining; okay, take it (at that price). ke – (and *kemari*) to here, hither. *ke sana ke* – go to and fro/back and forth. *gampang dibawa ke sana-kemari* easily transportable. – *sini, ke* – *dulu,* – *dulu ke sini,* – *ke* – *sebentar, coba* – *ke sini* come here for a moment, come over here. **mengemarikan** to bring over here. "*Kemarikan jambu itu. Cepat.*" "Bring those guavas over here and be quick about it."

mari(e) II (*D*) *roti* – biscuit.

mariara (in the Northern Celebes) k.o. black magic.

marifat and ma'rifat (*A*) 1 (perfect, mystical) knowledge, gnosis. 2 wisdom. *berjumpa dalam* – to call s.o. to mind. – *putus* (mystical) concentration of thoughts (to obtain s.t.).
  bermarifat 1 to meditate, immerse o.s. (in); to philosophize. 2 to have intuitive knowledge. 3 to be convinced (of s.o.'s death).

marihuana (*D*) marijuana.

marika (*coq*) → MERÉKA I.

marikan (*coq*) American; → MERIKAN. *kain* – (*M*) unbleached cotton cloth.

Marikh (*A*) (the planet) Mars.

marin (*coq*) → KEL(E)MARIN, SEMALAM.

marine (*D*) navy.

marinir I (*D*) marine (the person).

marinir II (*D*) memarinir to marinate.

marinyo and marinyu 1 k.o. military police. 2 (in the Moluccas) messenger (of a *raja*).

maritim (*D/E*) maritime.
  kemaritiman maritime (*mod*). *lingkungan/pendidikan* ~ maritime circles/training.

marijuana (*D*) marijuana.

marjan → MERJAN.

marjik (*A*) return (to God).

marjinal (*D/E*) marginal.

marjuh (*A*) outweighed (a legal term).

marka(h) (*D*) mark, sign, symbol, indication. – *jalan* road markings.

markas (*A mil*) 1 post. 2 station, office. – *besar* [MABÉS] headquarters, HQS. **bermarkas besar** *di* to be headquartered in. – *komando* [Mako] command quarters.
  bermarkas to be quartered.
  pemarkasan quartering (of troops).

markis (*D*) awning (against the sun).

markisa(h) (*Port*) passion fruit, *Passiflora quadrangularis*; a plumlike, greenish-purple fruit; → ÉRBIS.

markonigram (*E*) marconigram.

markonis (*D*) (ship's) radio operator.

Marksis (*D/E*) Marxist.

Marksisme (*D/E*) Marxism.

marmar (*A*) → MARMER. *(batu)* – marble.

marmer (*D*) marble.

marmot (*E*) and **marmut** (*D*) marmot, *Arctomys marmotta*.

marning (*Jv*) k.o. snack made of coated and toasted corn kernels.

maro (*Jv*) → PARO. – *tingal* to keep two things in sight at the same time; two-faced, insincere, hypocritical; to serve two masters.

Maroko (*D*) Morocco.

Maronit (*D*) Maronite. *Kristen* – (in Lebanon) Maronite Christian.

marquisa → MARKISA.

mars I (*D*) **1** marching tune. **2** a march. – *tertutup* close column.

mars II (in acronyms) → MARSEKAL.

Mars III (*D*) (the planet) Mars.

Marsekal (*D*) Chief Air Marshal. – *Madya* [Marsdya] Air Marshal. – *Muda* [Marsda] Air Vice Marshal. – *Pertama* [Marsma] Air Commander.

marsekalak → MARSEKAL.

marsepén (*D*) marzipan.

Marso (*ob*) → MARET.

marsosé (*D col*) military police, constabulary.

martabak (*A*) a crispy pancake made from a sheet of dough with various fillings. – *manis* a sweet stuffed pancake. – *telor* deep-fried beef, eggs, and vegetable pancake.

martabat (*A*) **1** rank, degree. **2** high rank, prestige, status. **3** value. – *kemanusiaan* human values.

  bermartabat 1 worthy. **2** dignified.

  kemartabatan dignity, prestige.

martandang (in Tapanuli) (a young man) visits a potential marriage partner or partners, the first visit of a young man to a girl he likes.

martani I to notify.

martani II (*Jv*) bringing salvation, consolation.

martél → MARTIL.

martelar and **martelaar** (*D*) martyr. *kaum* – martyrs.

martélu (*IBT*) → MARTIL.

martil (*Port? D*) hammer.

  memartil to hammer s.t.

martir (*D*) martyr.

  kemartiran martyrdom.

martumba (in the Toba Batak area) girls' dance after the harvest.

maru k.o. ghost that likes to disturb people.

maruah (*M*) **1** bravery, courage, valor. **2** self-esteem.

maruas → MARWAS.

maruf and **ma'ruf** (*A*) **1** (well-)known. **2** merit; → MAKRUF.

marus (*Jv*) clotted blood (eaten as a food).

marut → CARUT *marut*.

marwah (*A*) **1** pride, dignity. **2** manliness.

marwa-suta (*Jv*) to be overjoyed, very happy.

marwas (*A*) k.o. two-headed drum.

Marxisme (*D/E*) Marxism.

Maryam (*A*) **1** (The Virgin) Mary. **2** "Mary"; the name of the 19th chapter of the Koran.

mas I → EMAS I. *kemasan* goldsmith. – *belanda* 18-carat gold. – *kodok* platinum. – *terus* pure gold. – *tua* 24-carat gold.

mas II (*Jv*) **1** respectful term of address or reference for (mostly a Javanese) man not a great deal older than the speaker; → PAK I, SAUDARA, etc. **2** respectful title before male names. – *Hamdan* Mr. Hamdan. **3** term of address used by wife to husband, girlfriend to boyfriend, or to men of status equal to their husband. **4** term of address for one's older brother or male about the same age as the speaker. **5** term used by domestic servants to male children in the house. **6** term used to call a waiter in a restaurant or for bus/colt driver, etc. **7** term of address used among Javanese male friends to e.o. – *galak* reference to Governor General Daendels. – *geluntungan* (*J*) term of reference for a Javanese.

mas III (*S*) title of semi-nobility.

mas IV *ikan* – carp, *Cyprinus carpio*. – *koki* goldfish species with protruding eyes.

mas V (in acronyms) → MASSA, MASYARAKAT.

masa I (*Skr*) **1** (a period of) time, a long period of time, period, era, epoch. *dari* – *ke* – from time to time. – *datang/depan* the fu-ture. *di* – *datang* and *pada* – *depan* in the future. *pada* – *depan yang dekat* and *di* –.– *nanti* in the near future. *pada* – *itu* at that time, in those days. *salah* – anachronistic. **2** the proper/suitable time, a good time (for doing s.t.). **3** phase, stage. – *penyakit* stage of a disease. – *perkembangan* stage in development. – *azali* time immemorial. – *bakti* term of office/service. – *balik modal* payback period. – *baru* a new era. – *bébas bayar/bunga* grace period, period during which one does not have to pay interest on a loan. – *bébas pajak* tax holiday. – *belajar* study period. – *berhentinya haid* menopause. – *berkabung* period of mourning. – *berlaku* → MASA *laku*. – *birahi* mating season. – *bunting* period of pregnancy. – *cuti* leave. – *dinas* period of service. – *dini* early maturing. – *gencat* down time. – *genting* critical phase. – *giliran* tour (of duty). – *jabatan* term of office. – *kanak-kanak/kecil* childhood. – *kembali modal* pay-back period. – *kerja* a) length of service. b) duration of effect. – *kesempitan* depression, slump; → MALAISE. – *kini* nowadays, now, contemporary. *lukisan* – *kini* a contemporary painting. **kemasa-kinian** contemporaneousness. – *kosong* period between pregnancies. – *laku* duration, period of validity, valid for (a certain period of time). – *lalu/lampau* the past, the old days. – *manfaat* useful life. – *menganggur* free time. – *muda* childhood. – *mula* at the beginning, formerly. – *mulai pembayaran cicilan* grace period. – *nifas* postnatal period, the 40-day period after childbirth during which a woman may not observe certain Muslim rituals. – *pajak* tax period. – *pancaroba* change of season. – *panén* harvest time. – *Pencerahan* the Enlightenment. – *peralihan* period of transition. – *perang* wartime. – *percobaan* probationary/trial period (at a job), probation. – *Persiapan Pénsiun* [MPP] Retirement Preparation Period. **me-MPP-kan** to prepare s.o. for retirement. – *pertunangan* period of engagement. – *perubahan* period of transition. – *prabakti mahasiswa* [MAPRAM] college student initiation period. – *purba* antiquity. – *putar* (in a movie theater) screening time, show time. – *remaja* puberty, adolescence. – *selam/silam* the past. – *senggang* period between planting and harvesting. – *subur* fertile period. – *subur pengangguran* period of high unemployment. – *tanaman* growth time of a plant. – *ténggang (waktu) pembayaran* grace period. – *tenggat* time limit, deadline. – *tidur* dormancy. – *tinggal* stay (in a hotel). – *transisi* transition period. – *tua* old age. – *tunas* incubation period. – *tunggu* waiting period. – *tular* communicable stage. – *waktu* a) chronology. b) periodization.

  masanya his/its time. *ada* – sometimes. *dapat* – a) to take place. b) to get the right chance, see one's chance to (do s.t.).

  semasa during, while, when, at the time of, from the time stated, at the same time. ~ *kecil di kampung* when I was a youth in the village.

  semasa-masa at any time, timely, from time to time.

  bermasa with a ... time. ~ *depan suram* with a bleak future.

masa II (= *masakan*) used to express the speaker's doubt or disbelief about s.t. that he or she has just heard, learned, or noticed. How can that be? It's hard to believe that ... – *iya*? a) Is that so? Are you kidding? b) oh, no; impossible! *Ah,* –! Come on, you must be kidding! – *(be)gitu*! I can't believe it! – *begitu caranya bikin pantalon*! I can't believe that's the way pants are made! – *bodoh* (shortened to *booodoh*) I don't care. *Kamu ikut apa tidak,* – *bodoh*! I don't care whether you join us or not. – *bodoh saya tidak mengerti*. I don't know and I don't care. *bersikap* – *bodoh* don't care one way or the other. **memasa-bodohkan** a) to leave s.t. up to s.o. else; to take no responsibility for s.t. b) to be indifferent to. **kemasa-bodohan** indifference.

masa III mass, the masses; → MASSA. – *mengambang* floating mass.

masaalah (*A*) → MASALAH I.

masai *kusut* – entangled, tangled up (of string/hair/thread); → MANGSAI.

masail diniyah (*A*) problems relating to religious law.

masak I **1** done (of meat, etc.), cooked (of food), ready. **2** ripe (of fruit); → MATANG I. **3** boiled (of water). **4** thoroughly, vigorously, (to consider s.t.) maturely/thoroughly. *sudah menjadi* – *ikhtiar* to have come to an agreement about a plan. *paham yang sudah* – a foregone conclusion, an established truth. – *sekolahnya* he has had enough schooling. **5** experienced, accustomed to. **6** to be well-versed (at s.t.). – *di luar mentah di dalam* all that glitters is not gold. – *malam, mentah pagi/siang* to change one's mind. – *air* completed, fully done. – *ajar(an)* courteous, polite, correct in behavior. – *akal* mature in thinking. – *dini* early maturing. – *habang* a k.o. cooking style found in Banjarmasin. – *lambat* late maturing. – *mangsai* overripe. – *masai* experienced. – *niat* fully intentioned. – *tebang* maturity (of trees ready to be cut down).

masak-masak carefully, deeply, maturely, thoroughly. – *ma(ng)sai* a) overripe. b) dyed-in-the-wool. *dipikirkan* ~ thought about carefully.

semasak as done/thoroughly as.

semasak-masakan (think/consider) as thoroughly as possible.

bermasak-masak to be in the process of cooking.

bermasakan (*pl subj*) **1** to cook. **2** all ripe.

memasak 1 to cook, prepare food. **2** ~ *air* to boil water.

memasak-masak (= **masak-memasak**) cooking; matters connected with cooking.

memasakkan 1 to cook for s.o. *Ibu* ~ *saya sesuatu yang énak.* Mother cooked s.t. delicious for me. **2** to cook.

termasak 1 cooked. **2** too cooked.

masakan 1 food, cooking. ~ *bungkus* carry-out/take-out food. ~ *paripurna* one-dish meal. **2** cuisine (of a country/region, etc.); style of cooking.

kemasakan maturity.

pemasak 1 cook. **2** cooking utensil, cooker. *alat* ~ *Présto* a "Presto" pressure cooker. **3** (*M*) spices, seasonings. **4** still. ~ *minyak bumi* (*petro*) crude still. ~ *rengkah* cracking still.

pemasakan (the act of) cooking.

masak II → MASA II.

masakan → MASA II.

masakat (*A*) difficult, troublesome; → MASYAKAT.

masakini → MASA *kini.*

masal (*D*) wholesale, massive, mass. – *kawin* mass marriage. *memasal-kawinkan* to marry off in a mass marriage.

pemasalan making s.t. massive.

masala (*A*) prayer mat; → MUSALA, MUSYOLLA.

masalah I (*A*) **1** enigma, problem, issue. **2** question. – *pokok* basic question.

bermasalah to have a problem, problem (*mod*). *remaja* ~ problem teenager.

me(mper)masalahkan 1 to make a problem/issue of s.t., raise (an issue). **2** to discuss, argue about.

permasalah problem.

pemasalahan and **permasalahan** problem.

masalah II (*coq*) → MASYA ALLAH.

masam 1 sour, acid. *muka* – a sour face; sour-faced. **2** sullen, surly.

bermasam ~ *muka* sour faced.

memasam to turn/become sour.

memasamkan 1 to make sour, pickle. **2** to acidify.

kemasaman 1 sourness, acidity. ~ *tanah* soil acidity. **2** sullenness, unfriendliness.

kemasam-masaman sourish, rather sour.

pemasaman acidity.

masap (*ob*) **memasap** to steam, evaporate; → ASAP.

masarakat → MASYARAKAT.

masase (*D*) massage.

masbuk (*A*) → MAKMUM *masbuk.*

masdar (*A gram*) infinitive.

Maséh (*A*) (= Almaséh); → MASIH II.

Maséhi (*A*) **1** Christian. *tahun* – Anno Domini, A.D. **2** Protestant.

memaséhikan to Christianize.

pemaséhian Christianization.

masem → MASAM.

masgul → MASYGUL.

mashab → MAZHAB.

mashaf (*A*) the handwritten notes taken down by Muhammad's companions that constitute the Koran.

mashét (*E*) masthead (in newspaper).

ma'shum (*A*) free from sin.

ketidak-ma'shum-an not being free from sin.

mashur → MASYHUR.

ma'siat → MAKSIAT.

masif (*D/E*) massive. *pembalasan* – massive retaliation.

masih I 1 still, (even) now; remaining (in a certain condition), continue to. – *ada separuh* there's still half left. *Dia* – *muda.* He is (still) young. *Entah sudah mati, entah* – *hidup.* I don't know if he's dead or alive. – *ada juga orang yang* ... even now there are people who ... – ... *lagi* still ... available/on hand. *Uangnya* – *sepuluh rupiah lagi.* He still has ten rupiahs (left). **2** (*Jv* influence) related, can be considered a relative. *Dia* – *saudara saya.* He's related to me.

semasih while. ~ *saya kecil* when I was a child. – *témpo* (*IBT*) there is still time.

Masih II (*A*) (= Almasih) (the) Messiah.

mas'ilah → MASALAH I.

masin I salty, briny, brackish. – *lidah/mulut* and *lidahnya* – he speaks effectively. He has the gift of gab. *belum tahu di* – *garam* inexperienced. *Garam kami tidak* – *padanya.* Our words were not well received by him. – *perkataannya.* His words were complied with.

kemasinan salinity.

masin II → MESIN.

masinal (*D*) mechanical.

masing masing-masing 1 each. ~ *meréka akan merobah sikap meréka sebagai* ... each of them will change his attitude as ... **2** respective(ly). ~ *pada tempatnya* in their respective places. ~ *maupun bersama-sama* jointly and severally.

masing-masingan everybody stays to himself, nobody knows his neighbors.

masinis (*D*) **1** engineer, s.o. who operates an engine (on board a ship). – *satu* first engineer. **2** railroad/locomotive engineer. – *kapal* engineer. – *pabrik gula* s.o. who runs a sugar-processing plant.

masir (*Jv*) granular, crumbly. *kaca* – frosted glass.

masjid (*A*) mosque (mostly serving a larger area; *cp* MUSHOLLA) – *Agung Al Azhar* the mosque in Kebayoran Baru, Jakarta. *-ilaksa* and – *il Aqsha* the mosque on the Temple in Jerusalem. – *il-haram* and *-il Haram* the main mosque in Mecca. – *Istiqlal* the mosque on Jalan Pintu Air, Jakarta, the largest mosque in Southeast Asia. – *jamik* chief mosque for divine services on Friday. – *nonterjemah* "a nontranslating" mosque, i.e., a mosque at which sermons are given in Arabic without Indonesian translations.

permasjidan (*mod*) mosque.

maskan(at) (*A*) poverty (chosen by mystics).

maskapai and **maskapé** (*D*) company, (business) enterprise, firm. – *anak* subsidiary (company).

maskar → MASKER.

maskara (*D/E*) mascara (cosmetic for the eyes).

maskat *baju* – k.o. waistcoat (crossed over the chest).

masker (*D*) **1** (gas, etc.) mask, facial mask (in beauty parlor). – *oksigén* oxygen mask. **2** face-guard.

maski → MESKI(PUN).

maskoki goldfish, *Carrasius auratus*. – *tosa* veiltail (fish). – *tosakin* peacock tail (fish).

maskot (*D/E*) mascot, emblem.

maskulin (*D/E*) masculine.

maskumambang (*music*) form of *macapat.*

maslahat (*A mostly Mal*) use, benefit, advantage, profit.

bermaslahat to gain advantage.

kemaslahatan use, benefit, advantage, profit.

masmédia (*D/E*) mass media; → MÉDIA *massa/khalayak.*

memas-médiakan to put in the mass media.

masmur → MAZMUR.

masnawi (*A*) k.o. poetic form.

masohi (in Ambon) mutual aid; → GOTONG *royong.*

masoi → MESUI.

masoyi (*Jv*) massoyi plant, *Massoia aromatica.*

masrik → MASYRIK.

masrul → MASYGUL.

masrum (*D/E*) mushroom.

massa (*D*) **1** the masses, the people; → MASA III. – *aksi* mass action. – *apung/mengambang* the floating mass (of people in the villages). – *ontslah/ontslag* mass layoff. – *produksi* mass production.

2 supporters (of a political party, etc.). - *PDI* PDI supporters. **3** mob.

massal (*D*) mass (unemployment, etc.). *kuburan* – mass grave.

mastaib → MUSTAID.

mastautin (*A mostly Mal*) **bermastautin** to reside, live, maintain a home in.

mastépé (*Jv*) reference to a male member (*mas*) of the *Tentara Pelajar* [TP] Student Army during the guerrilla war against the Dutch (1945–49).

mastik (*D/E*) mastic.

mastika → MESTIKA. – *Hadis* the precious sayings of the Prophet.

mastodon (*D/E*) mastodon.

mastuli a thick silk fabric with gold thread.

mastur (*A*) veiled.

masturbasi (*D*) masturbation.

   bermasturbasi to masturbate.

   memasturbasikan to masturbate s.o.

masuk 1 to enter, go into. – *ruang kelas* to enter the classroom. – *dalam* to fall under (a provision of the law). *dapat – mobil* (in classified ads) accessible by car. *membawa –* to bring (the dog, etc.) inside. – *kuping* to come to the attention of. – *sekolah* a) to go to school. b) to enter a school building. c) to enroll in school. **2** to check in (to a hotel, etc.). **3** to set, go down below the horizon (of the sun/moon, etc.). *Bulan –.* The moon is setting. *Matahari telah –.* The sun has set. **4** to be present at or go to a certain place. – *(be)kerja* a) to go to work. b) to start working, assume one's duties. *tidak –* a) absent (from school/the office, etc.). b) not present (at a certain place). *tidak – bekerja* do not go to work. **5** to enter, join, become a member of. – *tentara* to join the army. **6** (already) reached (the time/age, etc.). *Sudah – hari yang kelima.* It has lasted/been on for 5 days. *Umurnya telah – 17 tahun.* He is in his 17th year. *sudah – 3 hari ditanamkan* to have been in the grave for less than 3 days. – *waktu* the time has come (for prayers, etc.). **7** inclusive, ... included. *Tip pelayan sudah –.* The waiter's tip is included. **8** to convert to (a religion), become a member of (a religion). – *Islam/Melayu* to become a Muslim. – *Serani* to become a Christian. **9** to participate, take part in. – *perang* to go to war, take part in the war. **10** incoming. *surat-surat yang –* incoming letters. **11** to go (to court). *Perkara itu sudah – ke Pengadilan Negeri.* The case has gone to District Court. – *lima keluar sepuluh* and – *tiga keluar empat* expenditures are higher than revenues. – *ajar* willing to listen to advice. – *(dalam) akal* reasonable, plausible, makes sense. *tidak – akal* makes no sense, illogical. – *angin* "a draft or wind has entered (the body)," i.e., to have a slight cold. – *asuransi* to insure o.s. – *asuransi jiwa* to buy life insurance. – *Belanda* become a naturalized Dutch citizen. – *bilangan* a) to belong to, be reckoned among, be under the jurisdiction of. b) *tidak – bilangan* to be of no/little account. – *buta* to get in without paying. – *daftar hitam* to be blacklisted. – *daun* to get a good opportunity/chance. – *golongan* to belong to, be reckoned among. – *kandang* (of a sports team) to lose. – *kelambu* to go to bed. – *keluar* to go in and out. **memasuk-keluarkan** to move s.t. in and out. – *koran/suratkabar* to get into the papers. – *kotak* a) (in sports) on the bench, out of the game. b) to be out of the picture. c) to be a nothing/a mere cipher; *cp tidak* MASUK *bilangan.* – *latihan militér* to enter military service. – *menjadi* to belong to. – *milisi/militér* to enlist. – *mulut buaya* in a dangerous position. *tak – nasihat* pig-headed, stubborn. – *paksa* to force one's way in. – *perangkap* to walk into a trap. – *peti és* put on ice, postponed, tabled. – *serdadu* to enlist. – *setéling* (*mil*) to emplace. – *suluk* to go into seclusion. – *tahanan* to be under arrest. – *télévisi* to be on television. – *tempias* it's raining in. – *tentara* to enlist. – *tidur* to go to sleep. – *ujian* to go in to take an examination. – *ulur* to become a slave.

   bermasukan (*pl subj*) to enter.

   memasuki [and **(nge)masukin** (*J coq*)] **1** to enter, go into, join, become a member of (the army, etc.). *dalam ~ tahun 1981* ... at the beginning of 1981 ... – *jenjang perkawinan* to enter the bonds of matrimony. ~ *masa purnawira* to reach retirement age (for army personnel). ~ *pasaran* to be put on the market (of a product). ~ *ruang lapor* to check in (at the airport). ~

ulur (*ob*) to be enslaved. ~ *usianya yang ke-* ... to enter one's ...th year (of age), to become ... years old. ~ *... tahun* to enter one's ... year. *sudah ~ hari ke-*... to have lasted for ... days. ~ *perkara orang lain* to meddle in other people's affairs. **2** to penetrate, force one's way into (a house, etc.).

   masuk-memasuki to influence e.o.

   memasukkan [and **(nge)masukin** (*J*)] **1** to take s.t. inside. ~ *jemuran ke rumah* to take the wash inside. **2a**) to put (s.t. or s.o.) into, insert. ~ *barang ke dalam lemari* to put the things in the cupboard. b) to place (on the agenda). **3** to import (goods from abroad or from another part of the country). **4** to invest (capital), put (money) into. **5** to reckon among, group with, class with/under, include among. **6** to introduce (a proposal), file/present a petition, submit (a proposal/claim, etc.). **7** to include in (a committee, etc.), admit s.o. as a member of. **8** (in soccer) to rack up (a certain number of goals). ~ *kembali ... dalam wilayah* ... to re-annex ... into the territory of ... ~ *nama untuk* to enter/register one's name on ...; to enroll in/for ... ~ *peluru* to enchamber (a bullet in a gun). ~ *préventif* to keep s.o. in custody.

   termasuk 1 to belong to, fall under, fall into (a certain category/group). **2** inclusive of, including. ~ *di dalamnya* ... included in it is ... ~ *kekurangan* as is. ~ *kemungkinan* not ruled out, not out of the question. *tidak ~* excluding, exclusive of, not including.

   masukan input. *memberikan ~* to furnish/provide s.o. with information.

   kemasukan 1 possessed (by bad spirits). ~ *sétan* possessed by the devil. **2** get entered accidentally. *Matanya ~ debu.* Dust got in his eyes. **3** entered. *Rumahnya ~ pencuri.* A thief entered his house. **4** infected, adulterated (with a foreign substance, such as impure blood). **5** to get (a shot).

   pemasuk s.o. who imports/introduces/files/submits.

   pemasukan 1 introduction (of s.t. into s.t.). ~ *bahan* feeding (material into a machine, etc.). **2** introducing, filing, presenting, submitting. **3** registration, entering. ~ *air ke waduk* the inflow of water into the reservoir. **4** import(ing). **5** immigration. **6** income.

mas'ul (*A*) person responsible/accountable.

masup (*J*) → MASUK. **masupin** → MEMASUKKAN.

masupang → MESUPANG.

masya Allah (*A*) **1** God forbid! **2** terrible! It's the will of God! Heavens! (used as an exclamation of surprise/pity or after hearing bad news, etc.). *Masya Allah, nasi begitu banyak kok habis!* My God, what a lot of rice you ate! *Masya Allah, sungguh mengerikan!* My God, that's really horrible!

masyaf (*A*) handwritten sections of the Koran.

masyaikh (*A*) elders.

masyakah and **masyakat** → MASAKAT.

masyarakat (*A*) **1** society, community. **2a**) inhabitant. *ribuan ~ Ibukota* thousands of Jakartans. b) citizenry, the public, members of society. *sikap ~ terhadap kejahatan* the public's attitude toward crime. **3** public (*mod*) *keséhatan –* public health. – *belajar* learning society. – *désa* rural community. – *Ékonomi Éropah* [MEE] European Economic Community. – *gotong-royong* communal society. – *kota* urban community. – *madani* civil society. – *majemuk* pluralistic society. – *pedésaan* rural community. – *pembaca* reading society. – *pemodal* investment community. – *pendengar* listening society. – *ramai* the public. – *sekolah* school community. – *tanpa uang tunai* cashless society. – *tembéréng* fringe society. – *terasing* isolated community; → PRADÉSA. – *terbuka* open society. – *yang bersifat tunggal* monolithic society. – *yang komunal* communal society. – *yang majemuk* pluralistic society.

   bermasyarakat in communities, with a society/community.

   memasyarakat to become common, customary (in a society). *Bahasa Indonésia belum ~.* The (use of) Indonesian has not yet become customary.

   memasyarakatkan to return (prisoners) to society, release from prison. ~ *saham* to go public (of a closely held corporation to offer shares for sale to the general public).

   kemasyarakatan social, public (*mod*). *jasa-jasa ~* public/social services. *keadaan ~* social conditions. *soal-soal ~* social problems.

pemasyarakat s.t. which makes s.t. customary. ~ *penggunaan brikét batu bara di Indonésia* making the use of coal briquettes customary in Indonesia.

pemasyarakatan 1 the return(ing) of prisoners to society. *lembaga* ~ penitentiary, correctional institution. 2 (making s.t.) public knowledge (or, known to the public).

masyawarat → MUSYAWARAT.

masygul (*A*) 1 sad, troubled, depressed, worried, unhappy, anxious, concerned. 2 displeased, resentful.

memasygulkan 1 to be worried about. 2 to displease, arouse anxiety, arouse resentment.

kemasygulan 1 anxiety, concern, solicitude. 2 grief, sorrow. 3 resentful. 4 sad, discontented.

masyhadat (*A*) meeting place, rendezvous.

masyhur (*A*) 1 (= **termasyhur**) (become) famous, well-known, known widely. *Dia – ke mana-mana.* He's known everywhere. *tempat yang –* a well-known place. 2 a *hadis* recounted by three different *sanad*.

semasyhur as famous as.

memasyhurkan 1 to spread the fame of, make s.o. famous/celebrated/eminent. ~ *diri* to make a name/reputation for o.s., gain a reputation as (a *dukun*, etc.). 2 to announce, proclaim.

termasyhur reputed. ~ *berani* to have a reputation as a brave person. ~ *jahatnya* to be infamous, be a notorious villain.

kemasyhuran fame, eminence, notoriety.

pemasyhuran proclamation, declaration.

masyrik (*A*) East, Orient.

masyuarat → MUSYAWARAH.

masyuk (*A*) beloved; → ASYIK (*dan*) *masyuk*.

Masyumi [Majelis Syuro Muslimin Indonésia] Consultative Council of Indonesian Muslims.

mat I (*Pers*) check, announcement that one's opponent's king is about to be captured (in a chess game). *syah –* checkmate, announcement that one's opponent's king cannot escape and therefore that the game is over.

mat II (*Jv*) delicious, pleasant, nice

mat-matan to enjoy o.s., have fun.

Mat III truncated form of Muhammad.

mat IV (*D*) rhythm, tempo.

mata I eye (the organ of sight in man and animal). *melihat dengan – kepala sendiri* to see with one's own eyes, witness s.t. o.s. *melihat/memandang dengan sebelah –* to look askance/with disdain at s.t. *dengan – tidak sedap* with regret. *di bawah empat –* privately, just between the two (of us, etc.). *sudah di depan –* to be just around the corner, coming up soon. *– ditutup dengan kain* blindfolded. *berjauhan –* to be far apart (of persons). *jadi – (dan) telinga* to become an accomplice/informer. *tidak kelihatan – hidungnya* he was nowhere to be seen, neither hide nor hair of him was seen. *memasang –* a) to make good use of one's eyes, keep one's eyes wide open for s.t. b) to (be on the) watch. *Pasang –!* Keep your eyes open! Pay attention! *membuang-buang –* to make good use of one's eyes, keep one's eyes open for. *mengangkat –* to look/gaze at. *menutup –* a) to close one's eyes. b) to pass away, die; → TUTUP *usia. rembang –* ladies' man, philanderer, wolf. *terbuka –nya* begin to know/understand. – *mu!* (rude) Do you have eyes? Can't you see? *– ganti –, gigi ganti gigi* an eye for an eye, a tooth for a tooth. *– tidur bantal berjaga* to be unfaithful (of a woman, when her husband is not paying attention). *silap – pecah kepala* if you're not alert, you'll have an accident; pay attention to what you're doing! *biar (ber)putih tulang, jangan (ber)putih –* death before dishonor. *tentang – dengan –* privately, in private. *jika tiba di – tidak dipicingkan, tiba di perut tidak dikempiskan* one should not have eyes but be unable to see, one should not be blind with one's eyes wide open. *– awas* sharp eyes. *bermata awas* sharp-eyed. *– bakup* a black eye (from a blow with the fist). *– bayar –* an eye for an eye. *si – biru* a European, westerner. *– buaya* a man who is always looking for women. *– bugil* the naked eye. *– cemperling* red-eyed. *– dekat* nearsighted, myopic. *– elang* eagle eyed. *– jauh* farsighted, presbyopic. *– kemung* big eyes. *– kepala sendiri* one's own eyes. *– lipas* colorless eyes. *– majemuk* compound eye. *– malam* night blindness, nyctalopia. *– mérah* with blood-shot eyes. *– ragum* cross-eyed. *– sipit* slanty-eyed. *– telanjang* the naked eye.

bermata with eyes/an eye, with ... eyes, with a ... jewel.

termata-mata very clearly visible, as clear as daylight.

mata II 1 center (of a pimple). 2 jewel (in its setting). 3 rung (of a chair/ladder, etc.). 4 cutting edge, point. 5 point (on a graduated scale of a thermometer, etc.). 6 compartment, partition. 7 objective. 8 eyelike object/thing/article. 9 knot in wood. 10 first part of the name of some animals and plants. *– acara* agenda item. *– acara iklan* (TV) commercial. *– acara musik* a musical (TV) program. *– air* spring, well, source. *– alamat* target, bull's-eye, aim. *– anggaran* budget allocation/line/item. *– angin* point(s) of the compass. *– awas* a sharp eye, keen sight. *– ayak* holes in a sieve. *– ayam* a) (*J*) eyelet (of shoes). b) nearsighted. *– bajak* plowshare. *– bakup* black eye. *– bantal* pillow end made of stiff embroidery or thin silver plate. *– batin* innermost feelings. *– bedil* bead (of a gun). *– belanja* budget allocation/line. *– beliung* the cutting edge of an adze/hoe/ax. *– benda* valuables. *– besar* big-eye tuna, *Thunnus obesus*. *– betung* dumb, uneducated, ignorant. *– bisul* the core of a boil. *– bola* arc-lamp. *– bor* cutting edge of a drill. *– buatan* glass eye. *– buhu* → BUHU. *– buku* knuckle. *– bulan* a) dimly visible moon. b) k.o. gastropod, *Turbo marmoratus*. *– cincin* stone in a ring. *– dacing* the stripes which mark weights on a scale. *– dadu* die. *– dagang(an)* commodity; → KOMODITI. *– duitan* craving for money, money-hungry. *– gawé* (*Pal*) helper, assistant. *– gelap* amok, in a rage. *– gobék* pestle. *– gunting* the sharp edge of a pair of scissors. *– hari* the sun. *– hati* the mind's eye. *– hidup* livelihood. *– huruf* character, letter (in a writing system). *tidak mengenal – huruf* illiterate. *– ijo* (*coq*) green with envy. *– ikan* a) a corn on the foot or toe. b) (*Jv*) scar from a wound. c) (*Jv*) duckweed. *– ikanan* (*J*) small pimple containing pus. *– imbal* unbalanced. *– itik* reinforcement around a buttonhole or similar hole. *– jala* mesh (of a net). *– jalan* road observer, watchman, scout. *– jaring* mesh (of a net). *– jarum* eye of a needle. *– jeli* a) alluring eyes. b) All-seeing Eye, the Big Eye. *– kail* fishhook. *– kain* the design on a *sarong*. *– kait* hook eye. *– kakap* (*naut*) plughole. *– kaki* ankle. *semata kaki* ankle-length. *– kayu* a) knot in wood. b) illiterate. *– keranjang* ladies' man, woman-mad, a man who runs after women (sometime explained as *– ke ranjang*). *– kérék* knots on a pulley. *– keris* blade of a kris. *– kucing* a) the magic (green-colored) eye (in some older radio sets indicating the radio is warmed up). b) semiprecious stone, cat's eye. c) damar (resin used in making *batik*). d) k.o. plant, *Nephellium malaiensa*. *– kuliah* school subject. *– kuncup* bud. *– luka* orifice of a wound. *– mata* → MATA-MATA. *– mérah* ruddy-breasted crake, *Porzana fusca*. *– mobil* headlights (of a car). *– nurani* innermost feelings. *– pajak* (*Pal ob*) taxpayer. *– panah* arrowhead. *– pancing* → MATA *kail*. *– pangkur* the blade of a hoe. *– parang* blade of a small sickle. *– pedang* sharp edge of a sword. *– pedoman* → MATA *angin*. *– pelajaran* subject of instruction/study. *– pelajaran tambahan* minor subject. *– pelajaran utama* major subject. *– pelanduk* a) k.o. plant, shoe-button plant, *Ardisia elliptica*. b) k.o. shrub, *Ixora anguta*. *– peluru* percussion cap. *– pencarian/penghidupan* livelihood, living. *– perang nuklir* nuclear warhead. *– perdagangan* commodity. *– petir* flash of lightning. *– piano* piano key. *– pintal* spindle. *– pisau* knife blade. *– pukat* mesh. *– pulpén* nib of a fountain pen. *– rantai* link (in a chain). *– rantai yang terputus* the missing link. *– Rumah Oranye* The House of Orange (in the Netherlands). *– sangkur* bayonet. *– sapi* fried egg, sunny-side-up. *– sapi balik* fried egg over. *– sasaran* bull's-eye (of a target). *– sebelah* a flatfish, peacock sole, *Pardachirus pavoninus*. *– surat* character, letter (in a writing system). *tidak tahu di – surat* illiterate. *– susu* nipple (of the breast). *– tangga* rung (of a ladder). *– telinga* intimate friend, confidant(e). *– timbangan* → MATA *dacing*. *– tombak* the sharp point of a spear, spearhead. *– tong* bung-hole. *– tutup* blinder(s). *– uang* currency. *– uang acuan* anchor currency. *– yuyu* crybaby, tending to cry easily.

bermatakan with ... stones/jewels. ~ *zamrud* with emerald stones.

mata III *semata wayang* (*J*) the only one, only. *mobil ~ wayang*

yang ada di kantornya the only car at his office. *anak perempuan ~ wayang* (his) only daughter; → SATU-SATUNYA. **semata-mata** [and **sematanya** (*infr*)] **1** exclusively, solely, purely. *Burung itu hidup ~ dari ikan.* That bird lives exclusively on fish. **2** merely, nothing but. *~ hendak mengganggu saja* just wanting to tease. **3** entirely, completely, wholly, throughout, altogether, utterly. *kesalahanmu ~* it's all/completely your fault.

mata IV 1 1/100 of a tahil (of opium = 0.386 grams). **2** unit of weight for morphine, etc.; internationally it equals 4 *cekak* but dealers in Jakarta convert it into 18 *cekak*.

matab (*Pers ob*) fireworks.

matabélo k.o. herring, *Clupea kanagurta*.

matahari I the sun. *cahaya –* sunlight, sunshine. *dekat –* perihelion. *(di) sebelah – hidup/naik/terbit/timbul* eastward. *di sebelah – masuk/mati/tenggelam/terbenam/turun* westward. *– masuk ke peraduannya* the sun set/went down. *menengadah/menentang – to* oppose a powerful/clever, etc. person. *penyakit hangus –* sunstroke. *penyentuh –* sun-grazer. *– beralih* about 5 p.m. *– berayun* approximately 3:30 p.m. *– di puncak kepala* noon, when the sun is overhead. *– gelincir* 4:30 p.m. *– hidup* a) sunrise. b) the east. *– léngsér* 4:30 p.m. *– masuk/mati* a) sunset. b) the west. *– naik* a) sunrise. b) the east. *– sepenggalah tingginya* around 7 a.m. *– tengah naik* around 9 a.m. *– tengah turun* around 3 p.m. *– tengah mengayun* around 4.30 p.m. *– tenggelam/terbenam* a) sunset. b) the west. *– terbit/timbul* a) sunrise. b) the east. *Pintu(nya) – Terbit* "The Gate to Sunrise," i.e., *Nusa Tenggara Timur* the Eastern Lesser Sundas. *– turun* a) sunset. b) the west.

matahari II *bunga/kembang –* sunflower, *Halianthus annuus*.

matahari III *burung –* k.o. sunbird, spotted crocias, *Crocias albonotatus*.

matalamat (= *mata alamat*) target; bull's-eye; objective.

mataliur → MITRALIUR, MITRALYUR.

mata-mata 1 spy. **2** (*mostly Mal*) policeman, agent. **3** detective. *– gelap* detective. *– rangkap* double agent. *– ulung* master spy.

memata-matai to spy on, watch, keep an eye on s.o.'s movements.

matan I knot in wood.

matan II (*A*) **1** meaning of a sentence. **2** original text; gist, purport (of a speech). **3** (original) copy/manuscript, text (for a lecture/speech/sermon). **4** the exact words of a *hadis*.

matan III firm. *janji –* a firm pledge.

matang I (*J*) **1** ripe (of fruits). **2** mature (of thoughts/sense/debt), well thought out. **3** cooked, done. *setengah –* rare, parboiled. **4** definite, certain. **5** finished, completed, developed. *mébel –* finished furniture. *setengah –* partly developed (of land). *belum – the* preparations were still not completed. *– biru* (beaten) black and blue; → BABAK *belur.*

mematangkan 1 to let ripen. **2** to cook. **3** to make s.t. final.

mempermatang to let s.t. mature.

kematangan 1 overripe. **2** ripeness. **3** maturity.

pematangan 1 ripening. **2** maturing, maturation. **3** preparing. **4** improvement, improvements (on land).

matang II → PEMATANG.

matari → MATAHARI I.

Matarmaja name of a train running between Jakarta and Malang.

matelase (*D ob*) mattress.

matématika (*D*) mathematics. *– tinggi* higher mathematics.

matématikawan mathematician.

mateng → MATANG I.

matera → MATRA.

materai → METERAI.

materi → PAT(E)RI. **termateri 1** affixed, stuck. **2** written (in one's heart), imprinted (on one's mind).

matéri (*D*) (subject) matter, substance. *dari segi –* substantively.

matérial (*D*) **1** material(s). **2** stock.

matérialis (*D*) materialistic.

matérialisme (*D/E*) materialism.

matérialistis (*D*) materialistic.

matériil (*D*) material, i.e., pertaining to the physical rather than the spiritual aspects of s.t., substantive, tangible.

materos → MATROS.

mati I 1 to die; to be dead, perish; died. *dibawa –* carried to the

grave. *– aku!* Oh me, oh my! (mild exclamation). **2** to close up, be liquidated (of a firm/business). **3** fixed (of prices). *harga –* fixed price (not subject to bargaining). **4** numb, unfeeling, insensible. *Kaki saya –*. My legs are numb. **5** to stop (of an engine/watch, etc.), out of order, broken, stopped working. *Teléponnya –*. The phone is out of order. *Jam tangan saya –*. My watch stopped working. *jalan –* a) an old/unused road. b) a dead end. **6** to go out, be extinguished (of a light/flame/fire/lamp/radio, etc.). *Apa radionya sudah –?* Is the radio (turned) off? *Apinya belum –*. The fire isn't out yet. *gunung berapi –* an extinct volcano. **7** closed, shut (of faucet). **8** expired (of a passport/permit/visa, etc.). *– masa berlakunya* it is no longer valid, it has expired. **9** deserted, unfrequented (of a street). **10** dried up (of a well). **11** to be slow (of a business/trade). **12** to calm down, abate (of the wind). **13** inflexible, solid (not pneumatic). *ban –* a solid (not pneumatic) tire. *Karét itu sudah –*. The rubber has lost its elasticity. **14** (*ling*) syllable final (of a consonant). *anak berkalang bapak, – bapak berkalang anak* father and child are required to defend/help e.o. *– dicatuk katak* a powerful person has been defeated/humiliated by a humble/weaker one. *– sawiji bangkit sekethi* (*Jv*) if one dies, a thousand arise in his place (a PKI slogan). *–.– mandi biar basah* and *–.– berdawat biar hitam* when you do s.t., do it well. *– andar* dead of no apparent cause, to die without being slaughtered (of animals). *– angin* a) feeble, weakly. b) impotent. c) (*naut*) headwind. *– anjing* to die like a dog, die for nothing. *– ayam* to die (like an animal), croak. *– bebang* stillbirth. *– beku* to freeze (or, frozen) to death. *– beragan* apparent death, suspended animation. *– beranak* to die in childbirth. *– berangai* swoon, faint away. *– bersebab* dead from an obvious but unnatural cause (accident/murder/drowning, etc.). *– bongkong* → MATI *konyol. penyakit – bujang* a) dead before one has married. b) "Sumatra disease," i.e., a disease affecting clove plants, *esp* in West Sumatra. *– digantung* die on the gallows, hanged. *– diracun* poisoned to death. *– disalib* crucified. *– disambar listrik* electrocuted. *– garing* to starve to death. *– haid* menopause. *– hanyut* drowned. *– hukumulah/hukum Allah* dead from natural causes. *– jalan* hopeless. *– jangkang* dead as a doornail. *– kagét* to die of fright. *– katak* died like a frog, i.e., to die unnoticed. *– kebebangan* → MATI *bebang. – kejang* have rigor mortis. *– kekam/kekat* neap tide. *– kelelap* to drown. *– konyol* to die in vain. *– kumlah* to die (or, dead) from natural causes. *– kutu* powerless, impotent. *– kutumu!* you're finished! *– langkah* (in chess/badminton/soccer) unable to move, checkmated. *– lelas* to die in vain. *– lemas* to asphyxiate. *– lepur* to die buried in mud. *– lidah* unable to taste. *– mampus* a) to die right off. b) the hell with you! go to hell! *– mawai* to sprawl on the ground dead. *– mendadak* sudden death. *– modar* a) to die on the spot. b) the hell with you! Go to hell! *– muda* to die young. *– napas* apnea. *– oléh kekerasan* to die a violent death. *– organ* dieback. *– pengap* to asphyxiate. *– percuma* to die in vain. *– pucuk* a) dead as a doornail. b) impotent. c) dieback. *– raga* deep in meditation. *– rasa* a) insensitivity, anesthesia. b) unfeeling, insensible. *– sabil* to die (or, dead) in the course of a religious duty, as one killed in a *jihad* or during the *hajj. – sahid* to die in a holy war. *– seajal* to die a natural death (due to sickness/old age). *– seladang* to die (of one of a faithful married couple). *– sematimatinya* as dead as a doornail. *– semu* apparent death, suspended animation. *– separuh* semi-paralyzed. *– sesat/sirik* to die a sinful death (e.g., a suicide/an atheist, etc.). *– suri* apparent death, (in a state of) suspended animation. *– syahid* to die a martyr's death. *– teraniaya* tortured to death. *– tersalai* asphyxiated.

mati-mati *takkan ~* immortal.

semati-mati *~ angin* a) most unfortunately. b) at least.

bermatian (*pl subj*) to die en masse/in large numbers.

bermati-mati(an) to do all in one's power, exert o.s. to one's utmost.

bermatikan *~ diri* to pretend to be dying.

mematikan [and **(nge)matiin** (*J coq*)] **1** to kill, murder. **2** to extinguish, turn/put out, switch off (a light, etc.). *~ mesin* to stop/turn off the engine (of a car, etc.). **3** deadly, lethal.

mati-matian 1 to pretend to be dead. **2** with all one's effort, as hard as possible, tooth and nail, to the death (of a fight), stubbornly.

kematian 1 death. ~ *bayi* perinatal/prenatal death. ~ *ibu* a) maternal mortality. b) death of one's mother. **2** lose s.o. (to death), bereft of, to have one's ... die. *Saya ~ ibu.* My mother died. I lost my mother. ~ *angin* to die down (of the wind), to encounter a drop in the wind.

kemati-matian 1 with all/every possible effort, as hard as possible. **2** to appear dead.

pemati killer, kill. *saluran ~ (petro)* kill line.

pematian killing off, extinction.

mati II (*burung*) – *anak* a) banded bay cuckoo, *Penthoceryx sonneratii malayanus.* b) brain-fever bird, plaintive cuckoo, *Cacomantis merulinus threnodes. burung – sekawan* bushy-crested hornbill, *Anorrhinus galeritus carinatus.*

Matias (the biblical) Matthew.

matik clipped form of **otomatik**.

matiné (*Fr D*) matinee.

matitulang caries.

matlab (*A*) end of the paragraph.

matlamat (*Mal*) target, objective; → **MATALAMAT**.

mat-matan and **matmatan** (*Jv*) (*berbuat*) – to sit around and enjoy life, live a life of pleasure. *tarian untuk* – a dance done for the sheer pleasure of it.

Matoa → **ADIL** *Matoa*.

maton (*Jv*) reasonable.

matra (*Skr*) **1** dimension. **2** (in music) measure, bar. **3** (*gram*) meter. **4** guidelines. **5** component, element. *keempat* – the four military forces (Army, Navy, Air Force, Police). *sapta* – seven guidelines. *Penataran – Laut* Naval Upgrading (Course). – *keagamaan* the religious complement. – *lengkap* acatalectic, complete in the number of syllables (in a line of poetry).

    bermatra and **kematraan** dimensional.

matran (*A*) bishop.

matras (*D*) mattress; → **KASUR**.

matré (*BG*) materialistic, greedy; → **CÉWÉK** *matré*.

matriarkat (*D*) and **matriarki** (*E*) matriarchy.

matriks (*D/E*) matrix.

matrikulasi (*D*) matriculation.

matrilinéal (*D/E*) matrilineal.

matrimoni (*D/E*) matrimony.

matrimonial (*D/E*) matrimonial.

matris (*D*) matrix.

matros (*D*) sailor.

matu (*Tam*) troy (weight); carat; → **MUTU III**. (*emas*) *sepuluh* – 24-carat (gold).

    mematukan to determine the gold content.

Matusalakh (*A*) Methuselah.

matur I (*Jv*) *paduka* – (*cla*) term of address for the fourth wife of a Javanese prince (for instance, in the Panji stories); → **MAHATUR**.

matur II (*Jv*) to say s.t. politely, inform, tell (a socially higher person). – *nuwun* thank you very much.

maturasi (*D*) maturation.

mau 1 will, shall, be going to. *Dia – pergi ke New York.* He's going to go to New York. *Dua hari – Lebaran.* In two days it's going to be *Lebaran. -mu* (*coq*) as you like. b) wouldn't you like that, I'd bet you'd like that! *-nya* (*coq*) a) as he likes it. b) wouldn't he like that! I bet he'd like that! **2** to be going to, be about to. – *hujan* a) it's going to rain. b) it looks like rain. **3** to be ... -ing. – *ke mana (ini)?* Where are you going (now)? **4** willing, want. *hidup segan, mati tak* – work-shy but unwilling to die (said of the lazy). – *tak* – a) willing or not, willy-nilly, in spite of o.s. b) have to, must. – *tidak/ndak?* (are you) willing or not? Do you want to or not? *tidak – tahu dengan* not to want to have anything to do with. **5** can bring o.s. to do s.t. *tidak* – to refuse (to do s.t.). **6** [+ *di-* form of verb (*coq*)] wants or needs to be ... *Anduk ini – dijemur.* This towel needs to be dried/drying. – *apa?* What can we do (about it)? – *saja dong* I sure will! – *tahu urusan orang* (*coq*) (you) like to poke your nose into other people's business. *kalau* – ... If you're interested/willing. *jangan* – you should refuse, don't do it. *Jangan – memperkenalkan meréka.* Don't introduce

them. – *tahu saja* (just) nosy. – *sama* – by mutual agreement, without coercion. *-pun* a) although, in spite of the fact that. b) → **BAIK II**. *-(pun)* ... *-(pun)* ... both ... and ... *-pun* ... *tetapi* ..., *baik* ... *-pun* ..., *-(pun)* ... *ataupun* ... a) either ... or ... b) whether ... or ...

maunya 1 one wants s.t., what one wants. ~ *apa?* What does he want? ~ *sih* "prom night" *kita jadi suatu peristiwa yang asyik dikenang.* We want our prom night to be s.t. memorable. *Ada ~.* There's s.t. he wants. **2** one wants s.t. but gets s.t. else, to want (to) (but it doesn't happen). ~ *républik tapi kelakuan présidén dan para pejabat pada waktu itu seperti raja.* They wanted a republic, but the president and officials at that time behaved like kings. ~ *membantu malah bikin rakyat sengsara.* They wanted to help but instead they made the people suffer. **3** you should ..., it would be better to ..., (you) should have ... ~ *siapa?* (on the telephone) Who did you want to talk to? *banyak ~* a) exacting, hard to please, fastidious. b) characteristic (word).

mau-maunya (after a negative) *tak* ~ still don't want to, continue not to. *Buah-buahan ini tak ~ matang.* These fruits just aren't getting ripe (no matter what we do to them).

semau ~ *gué* (*J*) at my (own) discretion, as I see fit, just as one pleases. *Pengemudi jangan* ~ *gué di jalan raya.* Drivers shouldn't just drive the way they feel like on the highway. ~ *sendiri* at will.

semau(-mau)nya 1 at will, as one likes, whatever one would like (to do). **2** arbitrary, arbitrarily.

memaui and **mengemaui** [and **ngemauin** (*J coq*)] (usually in the passive: *dimaui/dikemaui/dimauin*). *sangat dimaui* a) to be in great demand, much sought after. b) (*J*) *dimauin* to be after (my money, etc.).

memau-mau and **memau-maukan** to force s.o. to do s.t. *hati itu dimau-maukan* to do s.t. perfunctorily.

kemauan the will, wish, desire. *kalau ada ~ ada jalan* where there's a will there's a way. *~nya pulang-pergi* he has no firm will, he vacillates. ~ *baik* goodwill. *atas ~ sendiri* of one's own accord/free will. *di luar ~ sendiri* against one's will.

berkemauan to have the will/wish/desire/willingness to. ~ *keras* to be determined to.

maujud (*A*) **1** existing, extant. **2** tangible, concrete, real.

    memaujudkan to realize, bring about.

    kemaujudan existence.

maujudat (*A*) all that has been created, the universe.

maukif (*A*) the waiting place on the plain of *Arafat.*

maul (*A*) lord.

maulai (*A*) O, Lord! (God!)

maulana (*A*) **1** our Lord. **2** my lord (term of address for prominent Muslim scholars). – *Yusuf* the military resort command (*Korém* 064) in Serang.

maulhayat (*A*) elixir of life.

Maulid (*A*) **1** birthday (*esp* of the Prophet Muhammad). **2** birthplace.

Maulud (*A*) **1** anniversary. **2** the Prophet Muhammad's birthday. *bulan* – Rabiulawal, the third Muslim month.

mauludan 1 *Maulud* celebration, i.e., a religious festival on Muhammad's birthday. **2** to celebrate *Maulud*; → **GAREBEK**. **3** to play tambourine music to celebrate Muhammad's birthday.

    Mauludan → **SEKATÉN**, but celebrated in the month of *Masulud* in the *kraton*s of Cirebon.

ma'un (*A*) *al-* "Things of Common Use"; name of the 107th chapter of the Koran.

ma'unah (*A*) the ability of an ordinary person, with God's permission, to do s.t. extraordinary.

maung I bitter and smelly, musty, unpleasant (in taste), nasty (of flavor). *pahit* – a) bitterness of life. b) bitter and smelly taste. *telah merasai pahit -nya* to have experienced all k.o. trouble.

maung II (*S*) **1** tiger. – *lodaya* (in West Java) the striped royal tiger. **2** reference to members of the Siliwangi Division.

maupun → **MAU**.

Mauritius Mauritius.

mauruts (*A*) estate, what is left after all funeral expenses and debts have been paid.

maut (*A*) **1** (the hour of) death (for humans). *kedatangan* – to die.

dijemput – to die. *membawa* – to cause s.o.'s death. **2** (*sl*) terrific! great! **3** fatal. *tabrakan* – fatal collision.

memautkan to kill.

pemautan mortality.

mauz (*A*) banana; → PISANG.

mawa (*A*) abode.

mawad(d)ah (*A*) romantic love, affection. *sakinah* – *dan rahmah* tranquil, loving, and compassionate (of life/a family).

mawai (*ob*) *mati* – sprawled on the ground dead.

mawar I (*A*) rose. *air* – rose water.

mawar II *tawar* – utterly tasteless.

mawas I orangutan, *Pongo pygmaeus, Simia satyrus* of Kalimantan and Sumatra.

mawas II (*Jv*) to watch attentively. – *balik* retrospection. – *diri/ pribadi* a) introspection. b) to introspect.

memawas ~ *diri* to introspect.

kemawasan ~ *diri* introspection.

pemawasan ~ *diri* introspecting.

mawin → KAWIN *mawin*.

mawut (*Jv*) turned upside down at random; → AWUT I.

maya (*Skr*) **1** phantom, vision, illusion, hallucination. **2** virtual. *kantor* – virtual office.

bermaya illusory, hallucinatory.

kemayaan illusion.

mayam weight for gold (= 1/16 *bungkal*).

maya-maya I clear, transparent.

bermaya-maya clear.

Maya-Maya II name given to the ethnic Malays of Eastern Sumatra; → PENDUDUK *pesisir*, SUKU *déli*.

mayam (*ob*) measure of weight for precious substances, such as gold, = 1/16 *bungkal*.

mayang I 1 (*bot*) palm-blossom, spadix, flower-cluster, *ikal* – curly (hair). – *mengurai* unfolding palm-blossom. **2** (*poet*) abundant hair. – *menolak seludang* to forget the person who has raised one from childhood. *seludang menolak* – to boast, brag. *bulu* – (*S*) pubic hair. *buluh* – name of a bamboo species. *kué* – *pinang* k.o. cookie. *putu* – a rice-flour cake filled with brown sugar. – *mengurai* describes curly hair.

mayang II *perahu* – (= **pemayang**) traditional seagoing sailboat.

Mayang III (*zod*) (*bintang* –) Virgo.

mayangda (*cla*) the world.

mayapada (*Skr*) the earth; the abode of mortals.

mayar → KELEMAYAR.

mayas (in Kalimantan; → MAWAS I.

mayat (*A*) dead body, corpse; *cp* BANGKAI I. *seperti* – *ditegakkan* emaciated and pale. *pucat seperti* – white as a ghost, ghostly pale. *langkahi dulu -ku* (*coq*) over my dead body! *mukanya seperti* – as pale as a ghost. – *berjalan* the walking dead, describes s.o. near death. – *kering* mummy.

mayau absent-minded.

mayeur → MAYOR IV.

mayit → MAYAT.

mayogyog (*J*) completely destroyed, wrecked.

mayonés (*D*) mayonnaise.

mayong → MAHYONG.

mayor I (*D*) **1** (army) major. **2** lieutenant commander. **3** (*coq*) head of foreign communities in Java, appointed by the Dutch government; higher than, for instance, *kaptén Cina*. – *genderang* drum major. – *udara* (air force) major.

mayor II k.o. *délman*, peculiar to the Cibadak area of West Java.

mayor III (*Jv*) to feast.

mayor IV (*D*) major (key in music).

mayorat (*D leg*) entailed estate. – *pria* eldest son of the deceased. – *wanita* eldest daughter of the deceased.

mayorét (*D*) – *genderang* drum majorette.

mayoritas (*D*) majority. – *bungkam/diam* silent majority.

mayoritét (*D*) → MAYORITAS.

mayung I a marine catfish, *Arius sp.*, usually dried.

mayung II → DAYUNG *mayung*.

mayur I → MAYOR I.

mayur II → SAYUR *mayur*.

mazab → MAZHAB.

mazaz (*A*) synonym.

mazbah (*A*) altar (for sacrificing).

mazhab (*A*) **1** religious sect, denomination. **2** school of thought concerning the interpretation of Islamic law. The four schools are: Hambali, Hanafi, Maliki, and Shafii (Syafi'i). Most Indonesian Muslims subscribe to the last of these. **3** (economic) doctrine.

mazi (*A*) semen, seminal flow.

mazkur (*A cla*) **termazkur** written, recorded. *seperti yang* ~ as stated.

mazlum (*A*) injustice, tyranny.

mazmur (*A*) psalm.

bermazmur to sing a psalm.

mb- for words starting with **mb-** also look for entries starting with **b-** and **emb-**.

mbah (*Jv*) **1** grandparent (of either sex). **2** respectful term of address or title for s.o. in grandparents' generation. **3** (in certain areas, a taboo word) term of address for a tiger (when meeting it in the jungle).

mbak (*Jv*) term of address for young woman. – *ayu* and –*yu* a) older sister. b) (in some regions) middle-aged woman. – *ayu bakul jamu* door-to-door female seller of traditional Javanese medicinal herbs. –*yu di belakang* the cook, domestic help in the kitchen.

mbarang (*Jv*) to tour (of a troubadour).

mbarep-lanang (*Jv*) the oldest/first-born male.

mbau-reksa (*Jv*) *sing* – the guardian spirit of a house, tree, etc.

mbék → EMBIK I.

mbeling (*Jv*) **1** disobedient; insubordinate. **2** to offer passive resistance. **3** unconventional; → BELING III.

mberot (*Jv*) to attempt to free o.s. from restraint.

mblandrék → MEMBLANDRÉK.

mblenger (*Jv*) to be disgusted with, be sick of.

mbludak (*Jv*) **1** to overflow, boil over (full to overflowing of a vessel, etc.). **2** (*reg*) to overflow its banks (of a river). **3** to protrude, bulge (can no longer be kept in). **4** cannot be kept in check (of talkativeness, recklessness). **5** full (of generosity).

mbludus (*Jv*) → MENYELUNDUP.

mbok I (*Jv*) **1** mother. **2** term of address for woman of lower and middle classes. *si* – the female servant who supervises the household chores. *ayam mBok B(e)rék* a chicken dish (usually ordered out); the chicken is simmered in spiced coconut milk and then fried. – *bakul* female vendor who carries her wares in a basket. – *emban* nursemaid.

mbok II (*Jv*) please do. – *iya!* please do (so). – *sudah/wis jangan menangis!* do stop crying. – *ya ada pengertian* good gracious, have some understanding.

mbok-mbok well, well! (surprised, astonished).

mbuh (*Jv*) I don't know.

MCK (*init*) [Mandi, Cuci dan Kakus] public bath, wash place and toilet.

mdleming (*Jv*) to rave, be delirious; to talk to o.s.

Mébéa-Bingo a three-wheel passenger car which uses a 50-cc motor.

mébel (*D*) furniture.

permébelan furniture (*mod*).

mébelér (*D*) furniture.

mecin methamphetamine; → SHABU-SHABU.

mécis → MACIS.

mécky /méki/ → MÉMÉK II.

medali I (*D*) medal.

medali II flute.

medalion → MADALIUN.

médan I (*A*) **1** field, plain, square. **2** terrain. – *berombak* rolling terrain. – *bhakti* battlefield, field of honor. – *dharma* field of honor. – *gaya* magnetic field. – *jurit* (*cla*) battlefield. – *laga* battlefield. – *listrik* electric field. – *magnét* magnetic field. – *orang pandai-pandai* society of learned people. – *peperangan/perang/ pertempuran* battlefield. – *ramai* the public. – *ranjau* minefield. – *yang berat* rough terrain. – *yudha* battlefield.

Médan II city in North Sumatra, near the Strait of Malacca.

medang laurel-like trees with commercial timber used for furniture and planks, *Lauraceae spp. batu* – *sila* gypsum, hydrous calcium sulfate imported from China. – *air* k.o. commercial tree, *Alseodaphne umbelliflora*. – *api-api* k.o. tree, *Adinandra dumosa*. – *asam* k.o. shrub, *Ixora pendula* and other species. – *batu* k.o. commercial tree, *Dehaasia caesia*. – *belanak* k.o. tree, *Gironniera subaequalis*. – *bunga* k.o. tree, *Litsea sp.* – *bunut* k.o. tree, *Anisophyllea sp.* – *gajah* k.o. tree, *Randia anisophylla*. – *gelugur* k.o. tree, *Pyrenaria acuminata*. – *harum* k.o. commercial tree, *Litsea odorifera*. – *hitam* k.o. tree, *Gironniera nervosa*. – *kuning* k.o. commercial tree, *Dehaasia cuneata*. – *lesa* k.o. commercial tree, sarsaparilla wood, *Cinnamomum parthenoxylon*. – *padang* bollywood, *Litsea sp.* – *padi* k.o. commercial tree, *Litsea firma*. – *paya* k.o. tree, *Lindera malaccensis*. – *pungut* k.o. commercial tree, *Phoebe opaca*. – *telur* k.o. tree with white wood, *Eugenia griffithii*. – *wangi* k.o. tree, *Erythroxylon sp.*

medang-medangan laurel-type trees.
médé → *kacang* MÉTÉ.
médebewind (*D*) the power of a local government to perform duties delegated to it by the central government or by a higher level of local government.
medel (*Jv*) coloring; dyeing with a blue color.
medeli → MEDALI II.
média (*D/E*) media. – *cétak* print media. – *massa* mass media (both singular and plural). – *khalayak* mass media.
médian (*D*) *huruf* – (printer's) type of medium size.
médiasi (*D*) mediation.
médiator (*D/E*) mediator.
médik (*D/E*) medic.
médikal (*D/E*) medical.
medil (*ob*) → BEDIL.
médio (*D*) mid-. *(pada)* – *Januari* (in) mid-January.
médis (*D*) medical.
medit (*Jv*) mean, stingy, cheap.
méditasi (*D*) meditation.
  berméditasi to meditate.
Méditérania (*D*) Mediterranean.
medok I (*J/Jv*) 1 thick (of a regional accent). 2 too thickly applied (of spices/makeup/fertilizer, etc.). 3 done, finished, cooked.
medok II (*J*) 1 porous, with lots of holes in it. 2 dirty, filthy.
medu uneasy feeling in the bowels. – *hati* dyspeptic, with food rising up into the throat.
meduk → MEDOK II.
méerwinst (*D*) excess profit.
meg (*J*) nausea from overeating.
méga I (*Skr*) cloud. – *berarak* drifting clouds. – *mendung* rain cloud. – *Mendung* name of a small vacation village near Bogor.
méga II (*Jv*) grayish-blue; cloud-colored.
mégafon (*D/E*) megaphone.
megah 1 proud, haughty, arrogant, aloof; → GAGAH. 2 distinguished; refined (taste), chic. 3 elevated, exalted, lofty. 4 famous, famed, glorious, renowned, eminent.
  bermegah 1 to show off. 2 to shine, glitter. 3 (still) in the prime of life.
  bermegah-megah 1 to boast, brag. 2 to win notice, get a name for o.s.
  bermegah-megahan to do s.t. in a grand style.
  memegahkan to brag about. ~ *diri* to pride o.s. on.
  kemegahan 1 pride. 2 glory. *abad* ~ Golden Age. 3 greatness. 4 honor.
  pemegahan ~ priding o.s.
megak bold, daring, disrespectful.
mégalit (*D/E*) megalith.
mégal-mégol (*Jv*) to wiggle one's hips/behind provocatively.
mégalomania (*D/E*) megalomania.
mégan a dessert made of glutinous rice with coconut milk and sugar; → DODOL I.
megap-megap (*J/Jv*) to pant, gasp. – *kepedasan* (mouth) is on fire (from eating spicy food).
megar (*Jv*) 1 to bud, flower. 2 to stand wide apart and upright (of hair after washing); → MEKAR.
  memegarkan 1 to develop s.t. 2 to make s.t. stand wide apart and upright.

kemegaran development, budding, flowering.
  pemegaran flowering, development.
megat I (*Skr cla*) hereditary title for men of royal descent on the mother's side.
megat II → MEJAM I.
mégaton (*D*) megaton.
megeg-megeg (*Jv*) to sit/stand motionless; to be firmly in the saddle.
megibung (*Bal*) a Hindu-Balinese religious ceremony consisting of a joint meal.
megol → MEGAL-MEGOL.
megrék and **mégrék** (*J*) 1 sickly; to be ailing, have a chronic illness. 2 overworked.
méh (*C*) pulse.
méhé flat(-nosed),
  méhék terméhék-méhék out of breath.
Méhfil-E-Qirat (*A*) Koranic reading contest.
Méi (*D*) (month of) May.
méja (*Port*) 1 table, board (in some compounds). *daun* – table leaf. *uang* – court costs. – *abu* Chinese ancestral altar. – *angkat* raising platform. – *bilyar/bola* billiard table. – *bundar* round table. – *cuci muka* washstand. – *dengan laci* chest of drawers. – *gambar* drawing table. – *hias* dressing table. – *hijau* the bench, court. **meméja-hijaukan** to summon s.o. to appear in court. – *goyang* wobbly table. – *kedai(an)* counter (in a bar/shop, etc.). – *kerja* workbench. – *kursi* furniture. – *makan* dining-room table. – *periksa* doctor's examination table. – *perundingan* conference table. – *peta* map table. – *putar* rotary table. – *susun* nested tables. – *tarik* table with leaves. – *tinta* ink board. – *tulis* desk. 2 dummy (in card games).
  seméja ~ *dengan* (to eat) at the same table as s.o.
  berméja-méja tablefuls.
mejam I apparently motionless (of a swiftly moving top or engine).
mejam II (*air* –) latex.
mejan → MEJEN.
méjan (*M*) tombstone; → MÉSAN, NISAN I.
mejana (= *semejana*) average, medium, median.
méjar (*Mal*) (army) major. – *jénderal* major general.
mejelis (*M coq*) pretty, beautiful.
mejen (*J/Jv*) 1 dysentery. 2 to fail to explode, be a dud.
méjéng (*J sl*) to hang out and show off.
méjrék (*J*) heavily damaged, destroyed.
mék (*D*) /mék/ Mac, buddy, man. *Hébat, –!* Great, man!
Mekah (*A*) Mecca.
mekangkang *duduk* – to sit with legs straddling s.t./spread apart; → TERKANGKANG.
mékanik (*D/E*) 1 mechanic. *gaya* – mechanical power. *ilmu* – → MÉKANIKA. 2 mechanism, gear, device. – *katup* valve gear.
mékanika (*D*) mechanics. *gaya* – mechanical power. – *kuantum* quantum mechanics. – *tanah* soil mechanics. – *téknik* structural mechanics. – *téorétis* theoretical mechanics. – *terapan/terpakai* applied mechanics.
mékanis (*D*) mechanical.
mékanisasi (*D*) mechanization.
  memékanisasi to mechanize.
mékanisme (*D*) mechanism. – *keuangan* financing mechanism.
mekantar-mekantar → MAKANTAR-MAKANTAR.
mekar (*Jv*) 1 to open up, blossom, unfold (of a palm-blossom). *pembuluh* – varicose veins. 2 to rise (of dough). 3 to spread out.
  bermekaran (*pl subj*) to open up, blossom, etc.
  memekar → MEKAR.
  memekarkan 1 to make s.t. blossom, develop. *untuk* ~ *bakat générasi muda ke tingkat setinggi-tingginya* to develop the talents of the younger generation to the highest possible level. 2 to break (up) (s.t. into). *rencana pemerintah* ~ *Irian Jaya menjadi tiga provinsi* government plans to break Irian Jaya up into three provinces. 3 to open up, spread (out). ~ *payung* to open up an umbrella. ~ *sayap* to spread one's wings. 4 to make (dough) rise.
  kemekaran opening up, expanding, efflorescence.
  pemekar expander, s.o. who develops/opens up.
  pemekaran 1 blossoming, development. 2 expansion, expanding. 3 opening up, spreading out. – *darat* land reclamation. ~

kota Jakarta the development of Jakarta. ~ *pribadi* the expansion of the self toward others. **4** breaking (up) (s.t. into). ~ *Papua* breaking Papua up (into a number of provinces).

mekasi (*J coq*) → TERIMA *kasih*.

mekepung (*Bal*) water buffalo racing.

mekidung (*Bal*) k.o. classical verse.

méki → MÉMÉK II.

mekik → PEKIK.

mekis → MENGKIS.

Mékkah (*A*) → MEKAH.

mékmék (*J*) **memékmék** to grab hold of.

mekobok k.o. gambling game in Bali.

Méksiko Mexico.

mél I (*D*) **1** to report. **2** illegal highway toll. *bayar* – to pay a tax to an illegal post.

  ngemél (*coq*) to take that k.o. bribe.

mél II (*D/E*) mail. *kapal* – mail boat.

melabuai a large tree, *Dyera costulata*; → JELUTUNG.

melah(an) → MALAH(AN).

melainkan only, but, however; except (that); → LAIN I.

melak (*J/Jv*) **melak-melak** openly, clearly, obviously.

Melaka I Malacca.

melaka II (*Skr*) k.o. tree and its fruit, Indian gooseberry, *Phyllanthus emblica*.

melambang → MALANGBANG.

melambing → MALANGBANG.

Mélanésia Melanesia. *orang* – Melanesian.

melang anxious, restless.

melangbang → MALANGBANG.

melangbing → MALANGBANG.

mélankolis (*D*) melancholic.

melapari → MALAPARI.

melapetaka → MALAPETAKA.

melar (*Jv*) **1** to stretch, expand, rise. **2** extendable. **3** expansion. *berhaluan* – eager for expansion. **4** elastic. *tak bisa* – has lost its elasticity, inelastic.

  kemelaran elasticity.

melarat I (*A*) **1** loss, detriment, injury, harm; – *dan manfaat* the advantages and disadvantages; → PAHIT *getir*. **2** poor, miserable, needy. **3** impoverished, destitute.

  memelaratkan to plunge into misery, impoverish.

  kemelaratan 1 disadvantage. **2** misery, poverty.

melarat II → LARAT I.

melas I → BELAS I.

melas II (*D*) molasses.

melati (*Skr*) **1** jasmine, *Jasminum sambac*. – *gambir* downy jasmine, *Jasminum pubescens*. – *utan* glory bower, *Clerodendron inerme*. – *tongkéng* k.o. climber, Chinese violet, *Telosma cordata*. **2** → HOTÉL *melati*.

melawah k.o. Buginese prau (from the southern Celebes).

Melayu 1 Malay. *bahasa* – Malay, the Malay language. *tanah* – Malacca. **2** Malayan. **3** (*Mal*) the Malaysian, a *pribumi* Muslim. *masuk* – to become a Muslim. **4** (lower-case) a derogatory term used by Indonesians about themselves. – *jati* (*Mal*) the true Malay (one born and raised a Muslim and not converted). – *Polinésia* Malayo-Polynesian (languages). – *Raya* Greater Malaysia (a nation suggested by Sukarno).

  memelayukan to translate into Malay; to Malaysianize.

  kemelayuan Malay identity.

  kemelayu-melayuan Malayish.

melék (*Jv*) **1** to stay/keep awake. **2** to open one's eyes. *begitu saya* – as soon as I opened my eyes. **3** to be able to see, (his eyes) are open. *Matanya belum* –. His eyes aren't open yet. **4** to know, understand, be aware of, -minded, have the use of. *belum* – don't know yet, don't understand yet, still ignorant/unaware. *masyarakat* – *obat* a medicine-minded/-conscious society. – *aksara* literate. – *hukum* ignorant of the law. – *huruf* literate.

  memelék-hurufkan to make literate, teach how to read and write. **kemelék-hurufan** literacy. – *télepon* to have a telephone.

  memelékkan to open (one's eyes).

  melék-melékan to stay up (late at night), burn the midnight oil (said of gamblers, etc.).

mélek → MÉLK.

meléla plain, not damascened. *besi* – undamascened iron. *pasir* – laterite (bluish colored).

melelet (in Bali) to put a dead body into a coffin.

melempem (*Jv*) **1** not up to standard in some respect. **2** soggy (of *krupuk* left out too long, etc.). **3** to misfire. **4** inactive, slow. **5** gone out (of fighting spirit).

meléncéng (*Jv*) to deflect, divert; → MÉNCÉNG, MÉNCONG. ~ *dari aturan* to deviate from the rules and regulations.

meleng (*Jv*) with all one's attention concentrated on it.

meléng (*J*) **1** to take no notice of, be indifferent, look aside, be inattentive, absent minded. **2** careless, negligent, sloppy, untidy.

  memeléngkan to divert s.o.'s attention (to another object or in a different direction). ~ *orang* to turn one's attention away from people and not notice them; *cp* MEMALINGKAN.

meléngken (*coq*) → MELAINKAN.

mélér (*J/Jv*) to keep running (of nose). *hidung* – a running nose.

melesek (*J*) to collapse.

melesét (*D*) **1** to misfire (of a shot), be off target. *jauh* – *dari* to be entirely off the mark/off target. – *besar, dugaan* –, *persangkaan* –, *taksiran* – and *terkaan* – to be completely off the mark, be mistaken/wrong. – *dari rél* to derail, be derailed. **2** to fail (of an enterprise/a venture/calculations). *jatuh* – went downhill fast. **3** do/does not match. **4** slump, slack, decrease, depression (in business). *zaman* – period of depression, a slump; → MALAISE.

  memelesétkan to cause s.t. to be off target, cause a slump.

  kemelesétan depression, slump. ~ *ékonomi* recession.

meliat → MELIHAT.

mélik (*Jv*) would like to have, to cast covetous eyes on. – *nggéndong lali* (improper) desire frequently turns into neglect. – *pangkat tinggi* to covet a high position.

  kemélikan greed, (improper) cravings.

Melindo [*Melayu-Indonésia*] Malay-Indonesian (spelling of 1959).

meling → MELÉNG.

melinjo → BELINJO, MLINJO.

melionér → MILYUNÉR.

melirang → BELÉRANG.

melit (*J*) inquisitive, curious. *tanya dengan* – wanted to know the ins and outs of s.t.

  kemelitan curiosity.

meliwis (*Jv*) → BELIBIS.

mélk (*D*) /mélek/ canned milk.

mélodi (*D/E*) melody.

  bermélodi melodious, tuneful.

mélodrama (*D/E*) melodrama.

melompong → KOSONG (*melompong*).

melon a) a k.o. melon; the outer shape of this fruit is similar to that of the *semangka*/watermelon. b) reference to a prostitute in the Bogor-Puncak area of West Java.

melongo (*Jv*) taken by surprise, bewildered.

melongok (*J*) to look up, hold the head up, go see, sit down to look at; → LONGOK.

melongpong → KOSONG (*melongpong*).

mélor a two-wheeled vehicle.

melotot → LOTOT.

meluang to feel stiff in one's limbs; to suffer from rheumatism; → LUANG II.

mélu handuwéni (*Jv*) sense of belonging.

melukut broken rice-grains, rice-dust. *seperti* – *di tepi gantang* of little importance. – *tinggal*, – *melayang* the good remains, the bad disappears.

melulu (*J*) all one does is, nothing but, merely, only, simply, solely, exclusively. *Kerjanya tidur* –. All he does is sleep.

melur 1 (*bunga* –) jasmine, *Jasminum Sambac*; → MELATI. **2** *pohon* – k.o. tree, coffin wood oil, *Dacrydium elatum*.

mém (*Mal*) (British) lady.

memal to become violent.

memang to beg s.o. who is unwilling to give you s.t., importune.

mémang 1 (agreeing with what previous speaker has said) yes, that's so; (predicate) is (indeed) the case. **2** indeed. **3** (such-and-such) is true; to be sure, but ... **4** of course, certainly. **5** actually, the case is (such-and-such), but ...

mémangnya 1 inherently, by nature. **2** of course. **3** Do you think that ...? What do you think, ...? (slightly angry). *~ aku ini buta?* Do you think I'm blind? What do you think, I'm blind?

semémangnya 1 indeed, of course (more emphatic than *mémang* alone), naturally. **2** should.

memar 1 bruise, contusion. **2** bruised. *– bagian muka* bruises on the face. *luka –* bruise, contusion.

memata k.o. shrub, sweet-leaf bush, *Sauropus androgynus.*

membacang horn mango, *Mangifera foetida;* → (EM)BACANG.

membal (*J*) rebound, spring back.

membang → MAMBANG.

membasir → MUBASIR.

memberang otter, *Lectra sumatrana* (sometimes beavers and weasels are also included here); → BERANG-BERANG.

mémblé (*Jv*) **1** to have the lips drawn back (ready to cry). *Raut mukanya agak – di sebelah kiri.* His face was twisted to the left. **2** discouraged, disappointed, frustrated. **3** lousy, poor (quality), trash(y). **4** hopeless, beyond hope. **5** cowardly.

mémbran (*D*) membrane.

memedi (*J/Jv*) ghost, spook.

mémék I bermémék-mémék to whine, whimper.

mémék II (*vulg*) cunt, pussy.

memelas → BELAS I, WELAS.

memerang → MEMBERANG.

memet (*Jv*) close to, pressed up against. *terlalu – dengan jalan* too close to the street.

memetri (*Jv*) → PETRI. **1** to keep s.t. carefully. **2** to honor, revere, worship, venerate.

mémo (*D*) memo(randum). *– pelengkap* deficiency letter. *– saling pengertian* memorandum of understanding.

mémoar (*D*) memoir(s).

mémorandum → MÉMO.

mémori (*D leg*) brief. *– banding* appeal brief. *– kasasi* cassation brief.

mempan (*J/Jv*) **1** to be penetrated (by a bullet/knife, etc.); to be injured (by a shot, etc.). **2** to be effective, efficacious. *secara –* effectively. **3** to catch fire, get burnt. **4** to understand. **5** to be affected (by criticism/propaganda). *tidak –* a) impenetrable. b) unaffected, invulnerable, immune. c) didn't work, ineffective.

memparat k.o. ebony tree, *Maba buxifolia.*

mempaung k.o. tree, *Baccaurea lanceolata* and other species; → RAMBAI I.

mempedal → EMPEDAL.

mempelai (*Tam*) **1** (*– perempuan*) bride. **2** (*– laki-laki*) bridegroom. *kedua – and – berdua* the newlyweds, bride and groom. *naik –* to marry, get married.

mempelam (*Tam*) mango, *Mangifera caesia.*

mempelas I **a** fig tree, *Ficus ampelas, Tetracera indica.* **2** the leaves of this tree (which are used for scouring); → AMPLAS, EMPELAS.

mempelasari (*ob*) → PULASARI.

mempening various species of trees, *Quercus spp./Lithocarpus spp.*

mémper (*Jv*) *– (dengan/kepada)* to be/look like, resemble. *masa – that* is as bad as bad can be.

mempisang k.o. tree, *Polyathia longifolia pendula.*

mempitis a tree species used for timber, *Cratoxylon formosum;* → MERPITIS.

memplak dead white.

mempoyan k.o. tree, silverback, *Rhodamnia cinerea.*

mempulur → EMPULUR.

mempurung (*ikan –*) k.o. herring, saber-toothed thryssa, *Lycothrissa crocodilus.*

memur → MEMAR.

memutah k.o. tree, milky mangrove, *Excoecaria agallocha*, the root of which has medicinal properties; it provides strong but lightweight timber.

mén (in acronyms) → MENTERI, RÉSIMÉN.

mena (*Skr*) *tidak* **semena-mena** (and frequently nowadays without *tidak* or *tiada*). **1** (to do) an injustice (to), (to treat) unjustly, (to beat) arbitrarily, in a high-handed fashion, without motive/motivation; → SEMAU-MAUNYA, (SE)WENANG-WENANG. *dengan tiada ~* without any motive. **2** without a good/valid reason, for no good reason. **3** rude.

Ménag [Menteri Agama] minister of religion.

menaga a tree, *Callophyllum inophyllum*, the leaves and bark of which have medicinal properties.

menak → KEMENAKAN.

ménak I (*Jv*) noble, aristocratic, distinguished, prominent. *Sekolah – OSVIA* [Opleidingsschool Voor Inlandsche Ambtenaren] Training College for Natives (read: Indonesian) (Civil Service) Officers.

Ménak II (*Jv*) stories about the Muslim hero Amir Ambyah, depicted in *wayang golék* dramas.

Ménakertrans [Menteri Tenaga Kerja dan Transmigrasi] Minister of Manpower and Relocation.

menalu → BENALU.

menampun (*ob coq*) contraction of *minta ampun* (I beg your) pardon; excuse me.

menang 1 to win, succeed, be successful; to gain. *Singapura – 3-1 atas Malaysia.* Singapore beat Malaysia 3 to 1. *yang –* the winner, victor. **2** gain, profit. **3** not to be second to, not be inferior to. *– gak kondan, kalah wiran* (*Jv*) if you win you will not become famous, but if you lose you will lose face. *– asal –* victory at any cost; to want to win at any cost. *– angka* to win on points (in sports). *– berjuang* to win the fight. *– derajat* to be held in high esteem. *– hati* cheerful, brave, valiant. *– loterai* to win the lottery. *– mapan* to have the advantage (over). *– mutlak* overwhelming victory. *– pangkat* to be held in high esteem. *– pengaruh* to dominate (over). *– perang* to win the war. (*ingin/mau*) *– sendiri* self-righteous, always consider o.s. right. *– telak* clear victory. *– tipis* narrow victory. *– ujian* to pass an exam.

memenangi 1 to win. *usaha memenangi hati rakyat* efforts to win the hearts of the people. **2** to win in. *Dia memenangi kategori Pop Rock.* He won in the category of Pop Rock. **3** (*pl obj*) to defeat, beat s.o.

memenangkan [and **ngemenangin** (*J coq*)] **1** to win (a prize, etc.). **2** to make/help s.o. win. **3** to declare s.o. the winner.

mempermenangkan 1 to make s.o. win s.t., help s.o. win s.t. **2** to declare s.o. the winner. **3** to win s.t.

kemenangan 1 victory, superiority. *~ melimpah/mutlak* a landslide, overwhelming victory. *Ia mendapat ~ tanpa tanding* (in sports), He was the undisputed victor. **2** victorious. **3** (margin of) profit.

pemenang 1 winner, victor. *~ dengan angka* winner on points (in boxing). *~ hadiah Nobél* Nobel laureate/Prize winner. **2** profit.

pemenangan winning. *~ pemilihan* winning the election.

Menangkabau → MINANGKABAU.

menantu 1 son-/daughter-in-law. **2** (a non-blood relative) considered a relative by marriage (by all blood relatives whom he or she has married).

bermenantu to have as one's son-/daughter-in-law.

bermenantukan to take ... as one's son-/daughter-in-law.

menapaat → MANFAAT.

menara (*A*) tower, minaret. *– air* water tower. *– api* lighthouse. *– bor/pemboran/pengebor* oil rig, derrick. *– gading* ivory tower. *– kontrol lapangan terbang* air control tower. *– pengawas* a) (in general) watchtower. b) (in airport) control tower. *– peninjau* observation tower. *– radio* radio mast. *– sentak* flash tower. *– suar* lighthouse.

menasabah → MUNASABAH.

menase (*D mil*) meal serving.

menasik procedures for the religious services of aspirant *hajis;* → MANASIK.

ménat → MINAT.

menatu laundryman, bleacher.

mencak → PENCAK. **bermencak** to do *pencak.*

memencak *~ lidah* to debate, discuss.

memencak-mencak and **mencak-mencak** to be furious, jump around in rage.

mencanegara → MANCANEGARA.

méncang-méncong twisted, contorted.

mencelat (*J*) to jump up.

ménceng (*J*) askew, skewed.

keméncéngan skewness, slant.

mencerét (*J*) (to have) diarrhea; → CIRIT.

mencil (*coq*) isolated; → (TER)PENCIL.

mencit (*M*) mouse. – *seékor penggada seratus* to face superior forces. – *sawah* field mouse, *Mus caroli.* – *rumah* house mouse, *Mus musculus.*

méncla-ménclé (*Jv*) unreliable, inconsistent.

ménclok (*J*) 1 to perch, alight. 2 to land a job (at).

méncok (*Jv*) to perch; → MÉNCLOK.

méncong (*J/Jv*) 1 askew, skewed, aslant. 2 directionless, aimless.
   meméncongkan to twist s.t.
   keméncongan skewedness.

méncos (*J/Jv*) not to go straight to the point, deviate from the right path, miss the target.

mencrét → MENCERÉT.

méncrok → MÉNCLOK.

mendadak *dengan* – suddenly; → DADAK I.

Mendagri [Menteri Dalam Negeri] Minister of the Interior/Home Affairs.

mendak 1 silt, sediment. 2 to settle, precipitate.

mendala (*geol*) province, a broad area with its own special characteristics.

mendali → MEDALI I.

mendalika → MANDALIKA I.

mendalu mistletoe; → BENALU, BENDALU.

mendam (*Jv*) drunk, intoxicated; → MENDEM. – *berahi* drunk with love, head over heels in love. – *durian* having a headache and stomachache from eating too many *durian*s. – *minuman* drunk. – *tembakau* feeling poorly from smoking too much.
   kemendaman drunkenness, intoxication.

mendap 1 to sink, settle. 2 sediment, deposit.

mendapa → PENDAPA I, PENDOPO.

mendek (*J/Jv*) to bend over/down.
   mendek-mendek 1 to bend down so as not to be seen. 2 to hide.

mendeléka and mendelika monkey-jack tree with edible fruit, *Artocarpus rigida.*

mendem (*Jv*) 1 in a trance. 2 → MENDAM.

méndéng → SÉNDÉNG *méndéng.*

mendera (*manis* –) gentle and charming (of a woman).

mendéra I (*Skr?*) banyan tree, *Ficus benjamina.*

mendéra II → BENDÉRA I.

menderang → BENDERANG I.

mendhem – *jero mikul dhuwur* (*Jv*); → MIKUL DUWUR MENDEM JERO.

mendiang 1 the late, deceased, dead; → ALMARHUM. – *suaminya* her late husband. 2 defunct, no longer in existence. *grup musik yang sudah* – the now-defunct music group.

mendikai watermelon, *Citrullus vulgaris.*

Méndikbud [Menteri Pendidikan dan Kebudayaan] Minister of Education and Culture.

Méndiknas [Menteri Pendidikan Nasional] Minister of National Education.

mending(an) (*J/Jv*) (*masih*) – tolerable, passable, it will do; average; fairly/pretty well.; to some degree/extent; preferable, it would be better to. *belum dapat dikatakan* – not enough yet, by no means sufficient.

mendira → MENDÉRA I.

mendonan (*J*) 1 immigrant. 2 stranger.

méndong (*Jv*) k.o. grass whose stalk is used for weaving mats, etc., Asiatic pipewort, *Fimbristylis globulosa.*

mendora a Malayo-Thai dramatic performance.

méndréng and méndring → MINDRING.

mendu stage play from Pontianak, West Kalimantan.

mendung cloudy, overcast, lowering (of clouds as a sign of imminent rain). *setelah* – *jalipun tiba* after rain comes sunshine.
   memendungi 1 to cloud over. 2 to cast a cloud over.
   memendungkan to cloud s.t. over.
   kemendungan cloudiness.

mendura → MENDORA.

mendusin (*J*) 1 to be awake. 2 to be aware/conscious of (s.o.'s intentions).

mendut (*Jv*) k.o. cake made from sticky-rice flour.

ménéjemén → MANAJEMÉN.

ménéjér → MANAJÉR.

meneng (*J/Jv*) to be silent.

menepaat → MANFAAT.

menér (*D ob*) sir, Mr.

méng 1 word used to call a cat, here puss, puss! 2 cat.

mengangah (*Jv ob*) glowing, flaming.

mengah *sakit* – 1 asthma. 2 bronchitis.
   termengah-mengah panting (from illness or exertion), gasping, out of breath.

mengap (*J*) agape, openmouthed.
   mengap-mengap panting, gasping for breath.

mengangah → API *mengangah.*

mengapa 1 what are you doing? 2 why?; → APA. *tidak* – never mind! it doesn't matter!

mengecat → CAT.

mengéh → MENGIH.

mengenai → KENA.

mengepas → PAS II.

mengepél → PÉL I.

mengerawan a species of tree which provides timber, *Hopea spp.*; → MERAWAN.

mengerib (*coq*) → MAGRIB.

mengerna (*cla*) 1 bright(-colored), cheerful, gay. 2 (*poet*) darling, beloved.

mengerti [in contemporary Indonesian this derivative has become a root on the analogy of (*Jv*) *ngerti*]; → ARTI, ERTI. (= me-mengerti) 1 to understand, comprehend, conceive (of), grasp, realize, be aware (of). *-lah ia* it dawned on him, he realized. – *tak* – to understand only half of it. *lambat* – slow to understand. *sudah* – tamed, domesticated (of a bird, cat, etc.). 2 – *sendiri* reference to "bribing." 3 (*Jv*) a) to understand. b) to know, learn, be informed. *Saya tidak/belum* –. a) I don't understand. b) (polite) I don't know. *Saya tidak* – *namanya.* I don't know his name. *Benar saya* –. OK, I get it. *kurang* – to misunderstand, not quite understand. **kekurang-mengertian** misunderstanding, lack of comprehension.
   memengerti (usually in passive *dimengerti*) to understand. *sukar dimengerti* hard to understand. *Harap* ~ *keadaan saya.* Please, understand my situation.

mengetahui → TAHU I.

ménget → SÉNGÉT.

mengga (*J*) semengga-mengga simply and solely.
   semengga(-mengga) *tidak* ~ defective, damaged.
   semengga-mengga in its entirety, as a whole.
   mengga(h) semengga(h)-mengga(h)nya individually, singly.

menggala I (*cla*) a good omen, bringing good luck.

Menggala II Bengal.

menggerib (*J*), menggerip and menggirip → MAGHRIB.

menggusta mangusta, mangosteen, *Garcinia mangostana.*

mangiang (*M*) (*ular* –) rainbow.

mengi(h) 1 to pant, have difficulty in breathing, asthmatic, shortwinded, wheezy. 2 (*penyakit* –) bronchial asthma.

mengirat → MAIRAT II.

mengkal 1 not completely ripe yet (of fruits). 2 (– *hati*) annoyed, vexed, irritated, offended, peevish. 3 discontented/dissatisfied with, displeased at; to sulk, nurse a grievance. 4 impatient (due to waiting too long); → KESAL.
   bermengkal ~ *hati* to be annoyed, irritated.
   memengkalkan ~ *hati* 1 to irritate, annoy. 2 annoying, irritating.
   kemengkalan irritation, annoyance.

mengkali (*J*) → BARANGKALI.

mengkar → MEKAR.

mengkara (*Skr*) (*bintang* –) Cancer (in the Zodiac); → MAKARA II. *udang* – crawfish.

mengkaras name of a tree with light wood, *Aquilaria malaccensis.*

mengkarung skink, large green lizard, *Lygosoma spp.*; → BENGKARUNG.

Mengkasar Makassar, renamed Ujungpandang for a few years.

mengkawan 1 roof-lath. 2 classifier for kinds of *atap.*

mengkel → MENGKAL.

mengkelan termengkelan swallowed and stuck in one's throat (of food). *tercekék* ~ choking from food stuck in one's throat. ~ *di hati* resented, repellent.

mengkerang a climbing plant, *Urceola brachysepala*.

mengkerat and **mengkeret** (*J*) 1 to shrink, huddle up, double up (in pain). 2 afraid.

memengkeretkan to make s.o. or s.t. shrink/double up.

mengkerut → MENGKERET.

mengkilap (*J*) to shine, glitter, flash; → KILAP II.

memengkilapkan to shine s.t.

mengkilat (*J*) to sparkle, glitter; → KILAT I.

mengking to shiver from fright, tremble with fear. *cengking* – to yell.

mengkirai k.o. tree, *Trema orientale*, *Ilex cymosa*, whose bark is used for coloring fishing nets, etc.

mengkirap to shake out (a tablecloth/clothes, etc.); → KIRAP I.

mengkirik to make one's flesh creep/crawl, hair-raising, terrifying.

mengkis (= **memengkis**) 1 to deride, mock, taunt. 2 to insult, call s.o. names. 3 to defy, challenge.

mengko gék (*Jv*) to doubt.

mengkuang screw pine, *Pandanus atrocarpus* and other species of pandanus; leaves are used for making mats. – *duri/laut* k.o. screw pine, *Pandanus fascicularis*. – *hutan* k.o. pine, *Pandanus hulletii*.

mengkudu a shrub whose roots and bark provide red, purple, and brown dyes, Indian mulberry, awl tree, *Morinda citrifolia/elliptica*. – *Siam* lettuce tree, *Pisonia alba*.

méngméngan (*J*) ailing, sickly, in poor health.

méngok awry, crooked; → MÉNGOT.

mengolkol and **mengolkon** (*J*) to cough.

méngot awry, crooked.

méngsol and **méngsong** (*J*) slanting.

mengung (= **termengung**) 1 to ponder, muse on. 2 pensive, brooding; → TERMENUNG.

Ménhan [Menteri Pertahanan] (the U.S.) Secretary of Defense.

Ménhankam [Menteri Pertahanan dan Keamanan] Minister of Defense and Security.

ménhir (*D*) menhir.

Ménhub → MENTERI *Perhubungan*.

méni (*D*) red lead, anticorrosive red paint.

meniaga (*Skr*) to trade; → BERNIAGA.

menidih to boil (water); → MENDIDIH.

menikam → MANIKAM.

menila *bébék/itik* → MANILA I. *sawo* – the chiku, sapodilla, *Achras zapota*.

meninjau tree with edible seeds, *Gnetum gnemon*; → BELINJO, M(E)LINJO.

meninting white-crowned forktail, *Enicurus leschenaulti*.

menir I (*Jv*) broken rice grains; → MELUKUT.

menir II (*D*) sir, gentleman.

menira → MANIRA.

meniran I a medicinal plant (for bladder trouble), stonebreaker (because of its strong roots), *Phyllanthus niruri*.

meniran II (*J/Jv*) and **meniren** tired around the mouth (due to speaking too long).

menit (*D*) minute (of time).

menitan about … minutes.

menjak (*ob*) (**se**)**menjak** since (of time).

menjana (*Skr ob*) **semenjana** medium, average.

menjangan (*Jv*) deer.

menjarum (*mérah*) a shrub whose bark is used for making walking sticks, etc., *Ixora concinna*.

ménjé (*Jv*) young *kluwak*.

menjelai a cereal, Job's tears, *Coix lachryma Jobi*; → (EN)JELAI, JELAI I.

menjelis → MEJELIS II.

ménjep (*J/Jv*) with a bitter mocking smile.

Ménkés [Menteri Keséhatan] Minister of Health.

Ménkésra [Menteri Kesejahteraan Rakyat] Minister of Public Welfare.

Ménkéu [Menteri Keuangan] Minister of Finance.

Ménkimpraswil [Menteri Permukiman dan Prasarana Wilayah] Minister of Settlement and Regional Infrastructure.

Ménko [Menteri Koordinator] Coordinating Minister. – *Ékuin* Coordinating Minister for the Economic, Financial, and Industrial Sector. – *Kesra* Coordinating Minister for Public Health. –

Kesra Taskin Coordinating Minister for Public Health and the Reduction of Poverty. – *Polkam* [Menteri Koordinator (Bidang) Politik dan Keamanan] Coordinating Minister for the Political and Security Sector.

me-Ménko-i *di-Ménkoi* X headed by coordinating minister X.

Ménkop [Menteri Koperasi] Minister of Cooperatives.

Ménkopolkam [Menteri Koordinator Politik dan Keamanan] Coordinating Minister for the Political and Security Sector.

Ménkumdang [Menteri Hukum dan Perundang-undangan] Minister of Justice and Laws.

Ménlu [Menteri Luarnegeri] Minister of Foreign Affairs, Secretary of State.

Ménlugri → MÉNLU.

Ménmud [Menteri Muda] Deputy/Junior Minister.

Ménmud Séskab [Menteri Muda Sékretaris Kabinét] Deputy Minister/Cabinet Secretary.

Ménnaker [Menteri Tenaga Kerja] Minister of Manpower.

Ménnég [Menteri Negara] Minister of State.

Ménnégsus [Menteri Negara Khusus] Special Minister of State.

ménong *gajah* – a) a fabulous animal. b) a palanquin (in the shape of an animal).

ménor (*J*) 1 dressed in colorful/bright clothes. *dengan dandanan* –. wearing bright clothes. 2 glossy, shiny (new). *si raja* – fire, conflagration.

Ménpan [Menteri Negara Penertiban Aparatur Negara] Minister of State for the Control of the State Apparatus.

Ménparpostél [Menteri Pariwisata Pos dan Télékomunikasi] Minister of Tourism, Post and Telecommunications.

Ménpén [Menteri Penerangan] Minister of Information.

Ménperbu [Menteri Perburuhan] Minister of Labor.

Ménperdag [Menteri Perdagangan] Minister of Trade.

Ménperhub [Menteri Perhubungan] Minister of Communications.

Ménpora [Menteri Negara Pemuda dan Olahraga] Minister of State for Youth and Sports.

Ménristék [Menteri Risét dan Téknologi] Minister of Research and Technology.

méns [clipped form of *ménstruasi*] to have one's period.

Ménséknég [Menteri Sékretaris Negara] Minister/State Secretary.

Ménsésnég [Menteri Sékretaris Negara] Minister/State Secretary.

mensiang a sedge used for making mats, *Scirpus spp.* and *Cyperus procerus*. – *agam* k.o. sedge, rice field bulrush, *Scirpus mucronatus*. – *mancik* k.o. tall grass, *Fimbristylis globulosa*.

mensiu → MESIU.

Ménsos [Menteri Sosial] Minister of Social Affairs.

ménstruasi (*D*) menstruation; → HAID.

menta (*Skr*) rutting, in rut, rogue (bull elephant); → META.

mentah 1 uncooked (of meat/rice/vegetables, etc.), not yet ready to be eaten. 2 unfinished, incomplete, raw, unrefined, crude, draft (of a resolution). *bahan* – raw material(s). *mébel* – unfinished furniture. *Sekolahnya masih* –. He has not finished school yet. 3 unripe (of a mango/banana, etc.). 4 undeveloped (of land). – *pék seadanya* exactly what was there (nothing cut or removed).

mentah-mentah 1 raw, uncooked, fresh. *Daging itu dimakannya* ~. He ate the meat raw. 2 blunt, straightforward, unconditional(ly), categorically, flatly; → BLAK-BLAKAN. *Usulnya ditolak* ~. His proposal was flatly refused. *menyerah* ~ to surrender unconditionally.

sementah as crude/raw as.

mementahkan to foil, counter, dampen (spirits), break into (s.o.'s daydreams), destroy (speculations), overturn (a ruling). ~ *kembali* to redo s.t. from scratch.

kementahan rawness, unripeness.

pementahan foiling, countering, overturning. ~ *kembali* redoing s.t. from scratch.

mentak (*J/Jv*) probable. *tak* – improbable.

kementakan probability.

mental I (*J/Jv*) 1 resilient. 2 glancing off (of a weapon). 3 to bounce off, rebound. – *mentul* bouncing back and forth. 4 to backfire. 5 be launched (of a missile or vessel).

mental II (*S*) *tak* – 1 useless. 2 of no effect (of medicine).

méntal (*D/E*) 1 mental, connected with the mind. 2 mental attitude, mentality. – *budak* slave mentality. – *Jawa/Jowo* a Javanese mentality. – *témpé* a spineless, lazy, weak mentality.

berméntal with a ... mentality. ~ *amplop* bribable.

méntalitas and **méntalitét** D mentality.

méntalisme (*D/E*) mentalism.

Méntan [Menteri Pertanian] Minister of Agriculture.

mentang mentang-mentang, sementang(-mentang) and **sementangkan** (just) because, all because (sometimes contains element of boasting, taking pride in s.t. or an unjustified cause from an effect). *Dan jangan angkuh mentang-mentang orang tua kalian mampu membiayai kalian.* And don't be arrogant just because your parents can afford to pay for all of you. *mentang-mentang kami miskin pemadam kebakaran datang malas-malasan.* Just because we're poor the firemen came when they felt like it. *Dia itu sombong sementang-mentang anak orang kaya.* He is proud of himself just because he is the son of rich people.

mentangur → BENTANGUR.

mentaos → MENTAUS.

mentara → SEMENTARA I.

mentari I → MATAHARI I.

mentari II prepaid Satelindo card.

mentaruh a tree with various medicinal uses, milky mangrove, *Excoecaria agallocha.*

mentas (*Jv*) (*sudah* –) well provided for, one's future is provided for.

mentaus (*akar* –) k.o. tree (wood used for carving), *Wrightia javanica.*

ménté → KACANG *mété.*

mentéga I (*Port*) butter. *surat* – (*D ob*) walking papers, pink slip, employer's notice of termination of employment. – *buatan* margarine. – *kacang* peanut butter. – *yang tidak asin* unsalted/sweet butter. – *tiruan* margarine.

bermentéga buttered.

meméntégai 1 to spread butter on s.t. **2** (*coq*) to bless/endow richly with s.t. **3** to butter up, flatter (to get s.t.).

mentéga II *buah* – breadfruit, *Dispyros discolor.*

menték (*Jv*) a disease that attacks the roots of rice plants; → TUNGRO.

mentelah → SEMENTELAH(AN).

ménténg I (*J*) k.o. tree, *Baccaurea racemosa* and its fruit.

Ménténg II 1 a residential area in Central Jakarta. **2** telephone exchange in Jakarta.

ménténg-ménténgan to act highfaluting.

méntér k.o. fern, vine spike moss, *Selaginella willdenowii.*

mentera → MANTRA.

menterajam a tree with edible fruit.

mentéréng I (*J*) **1** conspicuous, catches the eye, showy. **2** dignified, formal. **3** magnificent, smart (in outer appearance), luxurious, splendid.

sementéréng as conspicuous/splendid, etc. as.

kementéréngan outward splendor, pomp, luxury, magnificence.

mentéréng II (*D*) new outfit of clothes, uniform (provided by one's office, etc.); dressed up.

menteri (*Skr*) **1** minister (head of a government department/ministry. *Perdana* – Prime Minister. – *Agama* [Ménag] Minister of Religion. – *Besar* (in Malaysia) governor of a state. – *Dalam Negeri* [Méndagri] Minister of the Interior/Home affairs. – *Hukum dan Perundang-Undangan* [Ménkumdang] Minister of Justice and Laws. – *Kehakiman* [Ménkéh] Minister of Justice. – *Kehutanan* Minister of Forestry. – *Keséhatan* [Ménkés] Minister of Health. – *Keuangan* [Ménkéu] Minister of Finance. – *Koordinator* [Ménko] Coordinating Minister. – *Koordinator Bidang Ékonomi, Keuangan Industri dan Pengawasan Pembangunan* [Ménko Ékuin Wasbang] Coordinating Minister for the Economic, Financial, Industrial, and Development Supervision Sector. – *Koordinator Bidang Kesejahteraan Rakyat* [Ménko Kesra] Coordinating Minister for the People's Welfare Sector. – *Koordinator Bidang Politik dan Keamanan* [Ménko Polkam] Coordinating Minister for the Political and Security Sector. – *Koperasi* [Ménkop] Minister of Cooperatives. – *Luar Negeri* [Ménlu] Minister of Foreign Affairs. – *muda* [Ménmud] deputy minister. – *Muda Sékrétaris Kabinét* Deputy Minister/Cabinet Secretary. – *Muda Urusan Peningkatan Penggunaan Barang*

Produksi Dalam Negeri Deputy Minister for the Increase in the Use of Domestically Manufactured Goods. – *Muda Urusan Peningkatan Produksi Pangan* Deputy Minister for Increasing Food Production. – *Muda Urusan Peternakan dan Perikanan* Deputy Minister for Increasing Cattle and Fishery Products. – *Muda Urusan Peningkatan Produksi Tanaman Keras* Deputy Minister for the Increase in Perennial Crops. – *Negara* [Ménnég] State Minister. – *Negara Kependudukan dan Lingkungan Hidup* [Ménnég KLH] Minister of State for Population and Environmental Affairs. – *Negara Pemuda dan Olahraga* [Ménpora] Minister of State for Youth and Sports. – *Negara Pendayagunaan Aparatur Negara* Minister of State for the Efficiency of the State Apparatus. – *Negara Perumahan Rakyat* [Ménpra] Minister of State for People's Housing. – *Negara Risét dan Téknologi* [Ménristék] Minister of State for Research and Technology. – *Negara Urusan Khusus* Minister of State for Special Affairs. – *Negara Urusan Peranan Wanita* Minister of State for Women's Role. – *Pariwisata, Pos dan Télékomunikasi* [Ménparpostél] Minister of Tourism, Post, and Telecommunications. – *Pekerjaan Umum* [Mén PU] Minister of Public Works. – *Pendayagunaan Aparatur Negara* [Ménpan] Minister for the Supervision of the State Apparatus. – *Pendidikan dan Kebudayaan* [Méndikbud] Minister of Education and Culture. – *Pendidikan Nasional* [Méndiknas] Minister of National Education. – *Penerangan* [Ménpén] Minister of Information. – *Perdagangan* [Mén(per)dag] Minister of Trade. – *Perdagangan dan Transmigrasi* [Ménperdagkop]. – *Perencanaan Pembangunan Nasional* Minister of National Development Planning. – *Perhubungan* [Mén(per)hub] Minister of Transportation. – *Perindustrian* [Ménperin] Minister of Industry. – *Permukiman dan Prasarana Wilayah* [Ménkimpraswil] Minister of Settlement and Regional Infrastructure. – *Pertahanan dan Keamanan* [Ménhankam] Minister of Defense and Security. – *Pertanian* [Méntan] Minister of Agriculture. – *Pertambangan dan Énérgi* [Ménpertam, Méntambén] Minister of Mining and Energy. – *Sékretaris Negara* [Ménséség] Minister/State Secretary. – *Sosial* [Ménsos] Minister of Social Affairs. – *téknis* the minister responsible for the matter under discussion. – *Tenaga Kerja* [Ménaker] Minister of Manpower. – *Transmigrasi* [Méntrans] Minister of Transmigration. – *Transmigrasi dan Koperasi* [Méntranskop] Minister of Transmigration and Cooperatives. **2** bishop (in chess); → GAJAH, WAZIR.

mementerikan to make a minister.

kementerian ministry, department. ~ *Pendayagunaan Aparatur Negara* [PAN] Ministry for the Supervision of the State Apparatus.

menteros → MATROS.

mentibu k.o. tree, Indian rosewood, *Dactylocladus stenostachys*; → JONGKONG III.

mentigi a small tree whose wood is used for making kris hilts, *Pemphis acidula.*

mentika (*ob*) a bezoar; → MESTIKA.

mentiko (in Medan) showoffiness.

mentilau a bird species.

mentimun I cucumber, *Cucumis sativus. seperti* – *dengan durian* and [(*Jv*) *timun mungsuh durén*] can't be compared, such as a small/weak opponent of a strong, powerful rival. *anak-anakan* – to adopt a girl who becomes one's wife when she grows up. – *Belanda* granadilla, *Passiflora quadrangularis.*

mentimum II *ikan* – sea-perch, *Lutianus spp.*

ménto k.o. cake made from rice.

mentog and **mentok** (*J*) **1** to be bumped (against); → PENTOK. **2** to clash with e.o. **3** to be unable to go on, get stuck, reach a deadlock/dead end, go as far as it can go.

méntog (*Jv*) manila duck; → ÉNTOG. – *rimba* white-winged duck, *Cairina scutulata.*

mentok (*Jv*) *dada* – breast of chicken.

méntol (*D*) menthol, mint, *Mentha arvensis.*

mentolo (*Jv*) to be able to endure, stand, bear. *Meréka tidak* –. They couldn't stand it.

méntor (*D/E*) mentor.

mentora (*ob*) *balai* – reception room in palace.

Méntrans [Menteri Transmigrasi] Minister of Transmigration.

mentua I mother-/father-in-law; → MERTUA.

mentua II (*burung*) - *pelanduk* gray wagtail, *Motacilla cinerea melanope.*

mentul (*Jv*) elastic, springy.

  mentul-mentul bouncy, springy.

mentung (*J*) full to overflowing.

menturung bear-cat or bear-civet; → BINTURUNG.

menu (*D*) menu.

menung bermenung(-menung) 1 contemplative, pensive, meditative. **2** to ponder, meditate, muse; absorbed in thought.

  memenungkan to consider, meditate on.

  termenung *duduk* ~ to be lost in thought. ~ *memikirkan* to brood about s.t.

  termenung(-menung) → BERMENUNG(-MENUNG).

  (ke)menungan meditation, reflection, musing.

  pemenung dreamer, ponderer.

  permenungan contemplation, musing.

Menur Putih Snow White.

menur I circular design at the center of s.t.

menur II Arabian jasmine, *Jasminum sambac.*

ménwa [résimén mahasiswa] student regiment.

menyampang → (SE)NYAMPANG.

menyan → KEMENYAN I.

menyawak (*Jv*) water monitor, *Varanus salvator*; → BIAWAK.

menyényé (*J*) pussy and suppurating.

ményep (*J*) **1** to smile sourly. **2** to mock s.o. by wrinkling one's mouth.

menyolok obvious, conspicuous; → COLOK II.

méong I (*J*) **1** cat. *memegang ékor* – (*coq*) to get nothing. **2** (*onom*) sound made by a cat, meow. **3** (*S*) tiger. *ketempuhan buntut* – to pay the piper. – *congkok* leopard cat, a panther variety that likes to eat *durian, Felix bengalensis.* – *gedé* the striped royal tiger. **4** (*gay sl*) to have sex; → MAIN.

mepandes (*Bal*) tooth filing.

mépér → PÉPÉR I, II.

mépés → PÉPÉS.

mépét (*J*) → PÉPÉT.

mer (in acronyms) → MERIAM.

mér name of a *ceki* card.

merabu (*burung* –) lesser adjutant, *Leptoptilus javanicus.*

meracang → MRACANG.

meragi (*burung* –) painted snipe, *Rostratula capensis/benghalensis.*

merah an old Sumatran term for chief, still extant in Naning; → MARAH II.

mérah 1 red. *anak/bayi* – newborn (baby). *besi* – red-hot iron. *kaum* – the Reds, leftists, left-wingers. *Palang* – Red Cross. **2** brown. *gula* – brown sugar. **3** the colors of the PDI. **4** the color associated with Christians (in Maluku); *cp* PUTIH I. – *anggur* wine-red. **5** bad (of school reports); *cp* HITAM. **6** ejection (card in soccer); → KARTU *mérah.* – *api* flame red. – *bata* brick red. – *bawang* violet red. – *bungsu/bungur* light lilac. – *dadu* pale red. – *daging* flesh colored. – *darah* blood red, scarlet. – *delima* purplish pink. – *gincu* carmine. – *hati* reddish brown color of liver. – *hijau* traffic light. **memérah-hijaukan** to provide with a traffic light. – *jadam* reddish violet. – *jambu* pink, rose. – *kesumba* pastel pink. – *lembayung* magenta, crimson. – *manggis* maroon. – *manyala/menyala* fiery red, scarlet. – *marak* scarlet. – *mengkudu* madder red. – *merang* scarlet. – *merjan* coral red. – *merona* vermillion. – *muda* light red, pink. **memérah muda** to turn pink. – *muka* a) to blush. b) blushing. – *murup* bright/fiery red. – *padam* bluish red, crimson. – *pijar* red hot. (*Sang*) – *Putih* the Indonesian flag. – *saga* bright red. – *samar* subdued red, reddish, sandy (hari), ruddy (glow). – *semérah-mérahnya* as red as red can be. – *senduduk* mauve. – *sepang* dull red. – *serah* carmine. – *tedas* bright red. – *telinga* angry. – *telur* egg yolk, yellow of an egg. – *tembaga* copper colored. – *terang* cherry red. – *total* [métal] total support of the Indonesian Democracy Party-Struggle (PDI-P) (who wore red jackets during the general elections). – *tua* dark red, maroon.

semérah as red as.

memérah to redden, become red, blush.

memérahi to rouge (one's lips/cheeks).

memérahkan 1 to make red. **2** to cover with the (red) colors of the PDI.

mérahan *tanggal* ~ official holiday (marked red on the calendar).

kemérah-mérahan 1 reddish. **2** (he) got red in the face.

pemérah reddener. ~ *bibir* lipstick. ~ *kuku* nail polish. ~ *pipi* rouge.

merak I peacock, *Pavo muticus.* – *hijau* peafowl, *Pavo muticus.* – *kerdil* Bornean peacock-pheasant, *Polyplectron schleiermacher.* – *pungsu* k.o. peacock-pheasant, *Polyplectron malaccensis.*

merak II (*Jv*) – *hati* sweet and friendly, attractive (in appearance), winsome, affable.

merak III (*naut*) – *simpir* outboard galley (on a ship).

merak IV (*bunga* –) k.o. plant with red and yellow flowers, dwarf Poinciana, *Caesalpina pulcherrima.*

  merakan a tall grass, *Andropogon amboinicus, Heteropogon concortus.*

meram → MEREM.

merambai k.o. tree, *Melanochyla?*

merambung various k.o. trees, *Scaevola frutescens, Ardisia lanceolata,* and *Vernonia arborea.*

merana → RANA I.

merang I *mérah* – bright red.

merang II (*J/Jv*) rice-stubble.

merangsi k.o. plant, *Carallia suffruticosa.*

merangu (*ob*) k.o. flute.

meranti 1 a large tree, *Shorea, spp.* with timber used for boards, etc. **2** a mahogany-like wood. – *kawan;* → MERSAWA. – *mérah* → TENGKAWANG. – *merkujang* k.o. tree, *Shorea leptocladus.* – *paya/seraya* k.o. tree, *Shorea curtisii.* – *rawang* k.o. tree, *Shorea hemsleyana.* – *tembaga* k.o. tree, red lauan/meranti, *Shorea leprosula.*

merasi (*M*) (short for *merarasi*) the falling of leaves.

mérat (*J*) **1** to disappear, escape, flee. **2** (*infr*) to die; → MAIRAT.

Merauké name of a town in Irian Jaya. *dari Sabang ke* – from Sabang to Merauke (indicating the entire territory and integrity of the Republic of Indonesia).

merawal a small and long flag; a triangular ceremonial flag, (*mil*) colors. – *memulang bukit, cerana menengah kota* a ceremonial announcement should not be misunderstood.

merawan k.o. timber-producing tree, *Hopea mengerawan.*

merbah various species of bulbuls, shrikes, and babblers. – *berjang-gut* crested bulbul, *Criniger ochraceus sacculatus.* – *ékor gading* paradise fly-catcher, *Tersiphone paradisi affinis.* – *gila* fantail flycatcher, *Rhipidura javanica longicauda.* – *jambul* red-whiskered bulbul, *Pycnonotus jocosus pattani.* – *kapur* yellow-vented bulbul, *Pycnonotus goiaver personatus.* – *kelabu* ashy bulbul, *Microscelis flavalus cinereus.* – *kunyit* stripe-throated bulbul, *Pycnonotus finlaysoni.* – *rimba* wood shrike, *Tephrodornis gularis fretensis* and brown-headed tree-babbler, *Malacopteron magnirostre.* – *tanduk* black-and-white bulbul, *Pycnonotus melanoleucos.*

merbak (*ob*) → SEMERBAK.

merbau Moluccan ironwood (used for furniture/railway sleepers, etc.), *Intsia spp.* – *paya* k.o. ironwood, *Afzelia palembanica, Intsia bakeri.*

merbaya (*coq*) danger, risk, peril; → MARA *bahaya.*

merbot → MARBUT 1.

merbuan k.o. plant, *Albizia saponaria.*

merbuk 1 spotted dove, *Streptopelia chinensis tigrina.* **2** barred ground-dove, *Geopelias striata.* – *gila* pied fantail fly-catcher, *Rhipidura javanica longicauda.*

merbulan name of a tree with soft wood, usually used for firewood, *Endospermum mallacanse.*

merca → MURCA.

mércado (*Port* in East Timor) /mérkado/ market.

mercak-mercik (*ob*) splashing in water.

mercapada (*Skr*) the earth.

mercon (*J/Jv*) fireworks.

  memercon to set off fireworks.

mercu 1 highest peak, top, highest point (of a mountain, etc.), summit. **2** tower. – *api* lighthouse. – *gunung* mountain peak. –

minyak oil rig. – *pulau* highest point of an island. – *suar* a) lighthouse. b) prestigious. **kemercu-suaraan** prestige.

memercu to reach the peak.

mercun → MERCON. – *bumbung* k.o. bamboo cannon.

mercupada (*ob*) → MERCAPADA.

Mércy (*coq*) /mérsi/ the Mercedes automobile.

merdangga (*Skr*) k.o. long drum.

merdéhéka → MERDÉKA.

merdéka (*Skr*) 1 free (of persons), independent (of nations), liberated, having freedom from any control. *majalah* – an independent newspaper, i.e., not the organ of a political party or group; *cp* INDÉPÉNDÉN. –*!* Freedom! (a greeting used by Republicans around the time of the 1945 Revolution; used when meeting e.o., when opening or closing letters/speeches, etc.) – *ayam/bébas* completely free, free as a bird. 2 (*ob*) name of the Army division stationed in North and Central Sulawesi.

semerdéka as free as.

memerdékakan 1 to (set) free, liberate, release, grant independence to, give freedom to. 2 to acquit, exonerate, absolve.

kemerdékaan freedom, independence, liberty. ~, *persamaan dan persaudaraan* liberté, égalité, fraternité. – *beragama* religious freedom. ~ *berkumpul* freedom of assembly. ~ *berpolitik* political freedom. ~ *berserikat* freedom of association. ~ *orang* personal freedom.

pemerdéka liberator.

pemerdékaan 1 liberating, freeing, emancipating. 2 emancipation, liberation.

merdésa 1 good (of roads/manners); beautiful. 2 correct (of behavior/words, etc.). 3 choosy, picky, fussy. 4 well-bred, refined. 5 contented, happy.

merdu (*Skr*) melodious, sweet (of voice/music).

semerdu as melodious as.

kemerduan melodiousness, tunefulness, sweetness (of voice).

merduk 1 (*ob*) junk, trash. 2 (*geol*) gange.

merebung k.o. tree; → JONGKONG III.

mérek (*D*) 1 trademark, brand (name). *sédan biru – Pontiac* a blue Pontiac sedan. 2 nameplate, superscription. *papan –* signboard. 3 quality, name-brand. 4 make, manufacture. *Mobilnya – apa?* What make is your car? 5 good name. *jatuh/turun –* to lose one's good name. – *air* watermark. – *dagang* trade mark. – *jasa* service mark. – *perniagaan* trademark. – *perusahaan* industrial trademark. – *terdaftar* registered trademark.

bermérek branded, with a (well-known) brand, designer.

meréka I 1 they, them, their. – *itu* those persons.

meréka-meréka they, them (emphatic). ~ *juga* the same ones all the time. – *ini* these people.

meréka II → RÉKA.

merékan → MERIKAN.

merem (*Jv*) shut tight (of the eyes), with eyes closed.

memeremkan ~ (*matanya*) to close (one's eyes).

méréng (*J*) → MIRING.

mérés (*J*) level, even.

mergat sugar palm, *Arenga saccharifera*; → ARÉN, ENAU.

merguk (*A*) pilgrim's veil, showing only the eyes; → BERGUK.

mergul k.o. otter.

méri (*Jv*) to be envious; → IRI.

meriah → RIAH I.

meriam cannon, gun. – *air* water cannon. – *beroda* mounted gun. – *buluh* toy cannon. – *gerak sendiri* self-propelled gun. – *gunung* mountain artillery. – *katak/kodok* mortar. – *mobil yang dapat bergerak sendiri* self-propelled gun. – *penangkis (bahaya udara)* antiaircraft gun. – *penémbak cepat* rapid-fire gun. – *sapu jagat* heavy artillery. – *sundut* muzzle-loader cannon. – *tanpa tolak-belakang* recoilless gun.

memeriami to shoot at.

meriang (*J*) feverish, subfebrile. – *kemelut* fever which reaches a crisis.

merica I (*Skr?*) (black or white) pepper. – *bulat* peppercorns.

merica II (*Jv*) clubs (in suit of playing cards).

méridian (*D/E*) meridian.

merih throat, windpipe. *bercekik –* (*M*) to debate fiercely.

merik k.o. owl.

merikan (*coq*) American. *kain –* a) American material. b) twill, unbleached cotton.

merinci → PERINCI.

mering *kurus –* thin as a rail.

meringis (*J*) to grin.

merinyu → MARINYU.

mérit (*E BG*) marriage, to get married.

merjan (*A*) red coral beads for making necklaces.

mérjer (*E*) merger.

mérk → MÉREK.

merkah → MARKA(H).

mérkantilisme (*D/E*) mercantilism.

mérkantilistis (*D*) mercantilist.

merkosa with force; to rape (a woman); → PERKOSA.

mérkuri (*D/E*) mercury. *lampu –* mercury lamp. – *klorida* mercuric chloride.

merlilin I k.o. tree, *Vernonia arborea*.

merlilin II (*burung –*) northern pied hornbill, *Anthracocerus malabaricus leucogaster*.

merlimau various k.o. trees, *Gelonium glomerulatum*, *Phyllochlamis wallichii*, *Aglaia odoratissima*, *Atalantia spinosa*, *Paramignya monophylla*.

merongos (*Jv*) protruding (of teeth/lips). *gigi –* buckteeth.

merosot 1 to fall, decline (of morale/prestige/price, etc.). 2 to decrease. 3 to deteriorate (of health). 4 to suffer a slump/recession (of business). 5 to slip off (of pants, etc.); → ROSOT.

kemerosotan 1 fall. 2 decline, drop, setback. 3 degradation, deterioration. ~ *akhlak* degeneration (of character).

pemerosotan fall, decline, deterioration.

meroyan (*sakit –*) ill after childbirth; → ROYAN.

merpati (*Skr*) pigeon, dove, *Columba domestica, Geopelia striata*; → JINAK-JINAK *merpati.* – *jambul* crested dove. – *laut* seagull. – *mahkota* crown pigeon, *Goura cristata.* – *mas* Nicobar pigeon, *Caloenas nicobarica.* – *pos* carrier/racing pigeon, *Columba livia.*

merpaud (*coq*) a lot, more than one *belum ada –nya* not yet married, still single.

merpelai (*M*) → MEMPELAI.

merpitis k.o. tree, pink mempat, *Cratoxylon formosum Dyer*.

mersawa various species of a k.o. plant, *Anisoptera marginata Korth*.

mérsi → MÉRCY.

mersik I shrill (of voice), piercing (of violin).

mersik II crisp (of *krupuk*, etc.), dried (of fish).

mersik III *kurus –* skinny/thin as a rail; → KURUS *kering*.

mersik IV *badar –* (*ob*) a k.o. fish.

mersinga k.o. tree, freshwater mangrove, *Carallia brachiata*.

mersuji k.o. fish, black marlin, *Makaira spp*.

merta I *dengan serta –* immediately.

merta II (*Skr*) *air – jiwa* water of life, aqua vitae.

mertabak → MARTABAK.

mertabat → MARTABAT.

mertajam k.o. large tree, *Erioglossum rubiginosum*.

mertamu (*J*) to visit, call at; → TAMU.

mertapai and **mertapal** k.o. tree, *Ochanostachys amentacea*; → PETALING.

mertas k.o. tree, *Ctenolophon parvifolius*.

mertéga (*Jv*) → MENTÉGA.

mertelon (*Jv*) to divide into three. *sistim –* farming system in which the crop is divided into two parts for the landowner and one part for the farmer.

mertua (*J/Jv*) parent(s)-in-law. – *laki-laki/lelaki* and *bapak –* father-in-law. – *pak guru* the teacher's in-laws. – *perempuan* and *ibu –* mother-in-law.

meruah (*A*) self-respect; → MARWAH.

merual → MERAWAL.

meruap 1 to steam, evaporate; → UAP I. 2 to bubble up.

merubi (*keris –*) a kris with a knobby potato-shaped hilt.

merunggai horseradish tree, *Moringa oleifera/pterygosperma*.

merut → KERUT *merut*.

més (*E mil*) mess.

Mésa (*Skr*) Aries.

mésan (*A M*) gravestone; → NISAN I.

mesara (*A*) allowance, pay; → SARA I.
mésem (*J/Jv*) to smile.
  bermésem-mésem to keep smiling.
mesera → MESRA.
méses → MÉSYES.
mesigit → MASJID.
mesin (*D*) **1** machine, engine. **2** apparatus, appliance. *dengan* – a) mechanized. b) mechanical. *juru* – machinist (s.o. who operates a machine). – *absén(si)/absén karyawan/pegawai* time clock, attendance time recorder. – *bagian luar* outer engine (of an aircraft). – *bakar* combustion engine. – *bantu* auxiliary motor. – *bicara* phonograph. – *bor* drill. – *bubut* (turning) lathe. – *cacah* perforating machine. – *cétak* printing press, printer. – *cétak tangan* hand printing press. – *cuci (pakaian)* washer, washing machine. – *cuci piring* dishwasher. – *cukur listrik* electric shaver. – *dérék* derrick. – *dikté* Dictaphone. – *ding-dong* (*coq*) pinball machine. – *frais* milling machine. – *gali* excavator. – *ganda* twin engine. – *garuk* scraper. – *gergaji* chainsaw. – *gijig* jigsaw. – *gilas/giling jalan* (road)roller. – *hisap* piston engine. – *hitung* calculator. – *jahit (kaki)* (treadle) sewing machine. – *jangkar* (*naut*) capstan. – *kapal* ship's engine. – *kas* cash register. – *kembar* twin engines. – *keping* coin/slot machine. – *ketik* typewriter. – *kira* calculator. – *las* welding machine. – *mata ayam* eyelet punch. – *ngomong/nyanyi* (*ob*) phonograph. – *pembangkit* lifter. – *pelapis plastik* laminator. – *pemancang* pile driver. – *peledak* exploder. – *pemanén* harvester. – *pembekalan air* water supply system. – *pembeli rokok otomatis* cigarette vending machine. – *pembukuan* bookkeeping machine. – *pemecah batu* stone crusher. – *pemotong kertas* paper cutter, trimming board. – *pemotong rumput* lawn mower. – *pemusnah sampah kertas* paper shredder. – *penambah* adding machine. – *pencuci piring* dishwasher. – *penetas* incubator, brooder, hatcher. – *pengeram* → MESIN *penetas*. – *pengering* dryer (machine for drying clothes). – *pengering rambut (pakai listrik)* (electric) hair dryer. – *penggabah* (rice) huller. – *penggerak barang* cargo winch. – *penggerak jangkar* anchor capstan. – *penggilas jalan* road roller. – *penghalus* grinder. – *penghancur* shredder, crusher. – *penghancur batu* stone crusher. – *penghancur dokumén* shredder. – *penghitung uang* cash register. – *pengolah kata* word processor. – *penjaja barang* vending machine. – *penjawab* answering machine. – *penyemprot* blower. – *perata* grader. – *permainan keping* coin/slot machine. – *perontok padi* paddy thresher. – *pons* punching machine. – *potong kertas* paper cutting machine. – *potong rumput* lawn mower. – *réken* calculator. – *ronéo* mimeograph machine. – *témpél* outboard motor. – *tenaga* power machine. – *terbang* airplane. – *tik/tulis (listrik)* (electric) typewriter. – *timbris* tamper. – *tunu* combustion engine. – *uap* boiler. – *waktu* time machine.
  bermesin with a machine, motorized. ~ *ganda* twin-engine (plane). *pesawat* ~ *hisap* piston-engine plane.
  mempermesin(kan) to mechanize.
  pemesinan and **permesinan 1** engineering (*mod*). **2** machinery.
Mesir (*A*) Egypt.
mesiu saltpeter used for making gunpowder and reddening gold filigree. *garam* – gunpowder.
mesjid → MASJID.
meskat → MASKAT.
meski(pun) (*Port*) **1** (al)though, even though. **2** in spite of. *meski ... sekalipun* however much, much as. *meski ... begitu* nevertheless, although that's the case, even so. *meskipun begitu* nevertheless.
mésolitikum (*D*) mesoliticum.
mesoyi (in Irian Jaya); → PASAK *bumi*.
mesra (*Skr*) **1** intimate, closely united, absorbed (of emotions/affections, etc.). *dengan segera menjadi – pengajaran* the teaching were quickly and fervently absorbed. *kasih* – heartfelt love. *serap* – deep affection. **2** closely united together (of countries, etc.). **3** well mixed (up). *dengan* – lovingly, with affection. – *dalam hati* taken to heart, heartfelt.
  semesra as intimate as.
  bermesra 1 completely mixed. **2** to interfere.
  bermesra(-mesra)an to be (usually sexually) intimate with e.o.

  memesrakan 1 to mix fervently. **2** to assimilate, absorb.
  termesra deeply pervaded. ~ *dalam darah* it runs in the blood.
  mesra-mesraan romantic.
  kemesraan 1 affection, intimacy. **2** closeness, familiarity.
  permesraan 1 interference. **2** absorption, pervasion.
mesta → SEMESTA.
mestari and **mesteri** (*ob*) master, skilled worker.
méster I (*D*) **1** (*ob*) teacher. **2** [Mr.] Master of Laws. **3** lawyer.
Méstér II (originally Meester Cornelis, now) Jatinegara, i.e., a section of Jakarta.
mesti (*Jv*) **1** must, without fail, have to, inevitable, be obliged to, predictable. *Kau – makan.* You must eat. *tidak* – and *enggak* – (*coq*) need not, not necessarily, don't have to. *tidak – sama dengan* it doesn't have to be the same as. *orang – mati* man is mortal. *Pesan bapak – saya sampaikan.* I'll certainly convey your message. *Masa itu – datang.* That time must come. – *harus* to have to, must (emphatic). **2** certain, sure(ly). *Kalau kauturut nasihatku ini, – tercapai maksudmu.* if you follow my advice, you'll surely achieve your goal. *Tidak – perut ini kemasukan nasi.* We were not sure when we could eat rice. **3** always.
  mestinya 1 as a natural consequence of (the foregoing). **2** was supposed to (but didn't). ~ *tidak usah demikian* this should not be the case. *Jadi bagaimana* ~? So, how should it be? ~ *kau tak perlu menceritakan itu.* You shouldn't tell about that. *sebagaimana* ~ a) as it should. b) as required/needed. *bekerja sebagaimana* ~ to function as it should. **semestinya 1** should, actually, ought, appropriate, (as it) should (be), proper, fitting, inevitable. *Tidak ~ kita datang duluan.* We shouldn't come first. **2** properly speaking, naturally; really, actually. *sudah* ~ naturally, as was to be expected.
  memestikan 1 to compel, require, make compulsory. *Tiap-tiap orang Islam dimestikan berpuasa.* Every Muslim is required to fast. **2** to determine, fix. *Pendapatan sekian itu tidak boléh kita mestikan.* We may not determine such-and-such an outcome. *tidak dimestikan* to be optional.
  kemestian 1 certainty, assurance. **2** a must, necessity, obligation.
mestika (*Skr*) **1** bezoar, talismanic stone, often mentioned in old Malay literature. – *embun* a talisman of "petrified dew" (= a large crystal) that can revive the dead; *cp* WIJAYA *kesuma*. **2** beautiful jewel (describing a woman). **3** extremely beautiful. *seperti – gamat* very beautiful. – *hati* sweetheart.
mesuarat → MUSYAWARAT.
mesui *kayu* – aromatic massoil bark used for flavoring food and cigarettes (from the *Massoia aromatica* tree).
mesum (*J*) **1** dirty, filthy. **2** improper, indecent, immoral, obscene. *berbuat* – to commit adultery. **3** mean, shabby, lousy.
  memesumi to fornicate with, have sex with.
  kemesuman 1 dirt, filth. **2** indecency, immorality, obscenity. **3** meanness, shabbiness, lousiness.
  permesuman 1 filthiness. **2** indecency.
mesupang *meranti* – k.o. tree, *Shorea pachyphylla*.
mesut → KUSUT *mesut*.
mésyes (*D*) sprinkles, jimmies; → KOTORAN *tikus*.
met clipped form of **selamat**.
meta (*Skr*) **1** mad, drunk, in a rage, fierce (of large animals/man). **2** rut (of elephants).
métabolisasi (*D*) metabolization.
  memétabolisasikan to metabolize.
métabolisme (*D/E*) metabolism.
métafisik(a) (*D*) metaphysics.
métafisis (*D*) metaphysical.
métafor(a) (*D*) metaphor.
metah *baru* – brand-new. *putih* – snow white. *muda* – very young.
metai (*Tam ob*) cushion, mat.
métajén (*Bal*) gambling on cockfighting.
metal (*D*) bushing, brass. – *batang penggerak* connecting rod bushing.
métal I (*D/E*) metal; → LOGAM.
métal II → MÉRAH *total*.
métalik (*D/E*) metallic. *coklat* – metallic brown.
métalografi (*D/E*) metallography.
métalurgi (*D*) metallurgy.

métamorfosa, métamorfose, and métamorfosis (D) metamorphosis.
métan(a) (D) methane; → GAS *métan*.
métanol (D/E) methanol.
metari (*coq*) → MATAHARI I.
métastasis (D/E) metastasis.
métatésis (D) metathesis.
mété cashew; → KACANG *mété*.
meténgkréng (*Jv*) 1 to be silent and motionless, continuously remain sitting (without getting up from one's seat). 2 to be passive, inactive.
metengteng (*Jv*) 1 tense (of feelings). 2 to take a (firm) stand.
météo (D) *jawatan* – meteorological service.
météor (D/E) meteor.
météorik (D/E) meteoric, ascending rapidly.
météorit (D/E) meteorite.
météorologi (D/E) meteorology.
méter (D) 1 meter, the unit of measurement in the metric system. – *firkan* square meter, m². – *gas* gas meter. – *persegi* square meter. 2 meter (device for measuring).
  seméter a meter. ~.~ meter by meter.
  berméter-méter by the meter.
  meméterkan to convert to meters.
  méteran 1 meter, i.e., instrument for measuring and recording. ~ *air* water meter. ~ *parkir* parking meter. ~ *taksi* taximeter; → ARGOMÉTER. 2 by the meter.
meterai seal, stamp, postage, gauge, verification, and stamping of weights and measures, revenue/duty stamp (on documents). *kertas* – stamped paper (for notarial instruments/contracts, etc.). – *surat* postage stamp. – *témpél* seal on money orders/checks, etc., receipt-stamp. – *upah* tax seal/stamp.
  bermeterai sealed (of a document).
  memeterai(kan) to stamp, put a seal on.
  termeterai stamped, sealed. ~ *(di) dalam hati* heartfelt.
méterstand (D) meter-reading.
metetet (*Jv*) too tight. *celana* – (a pair of) very tight pants.
métil (D/E) methyl. – *alkohol* methyl alcohol.
métode (D/E) method. – *angsuran* installment method. – *garis lurus* straight line method. – *harga peroléhan* cost method. – *perséntase penyelesaian* percentage of completion method. – *saldo menurun* declining balance method. – *sediaan pokok* base stock method.
métodik (E) → MÉTODOLOGI.
métodis I (D) methodical.
Métodis II (D) Methodist.
métodologi (D/E) methodology.
métodos → MÉTODE.
mét of zonder (D *ob*) with or without (approval).
métonimi(a) (D) metonymy, i.e., the use of the name of one thing for that of another associated with or suggested by it, e.g., *Cendana* for *Présidén*.
metri memetri (*Jv*) to honor, respect, venerate, revere.
métrik (E) metric. – *ton* metric ton.
Métro a variety of corn first grown in South Sumatra.
métrologi (D) metrology, science of weights and measures. *ahli* – metrologist.
métromini small passenger van used in cities/towns.
métropolis (D/E) metropolis.
métropolitan (D/E) metropolitan.
  memétropolitankan to make into a metropolis. ~ *Médan* to make Medan into a metropolis.
  kemétropolitanan metropolitan character.
  métropolitanisasi incorporating certain areas into the Jakarta metropolis.
métrui k.o. gambling peculiar to Bali.
meubel (D) → MÉBEL.
meubilair (D) furniture; → MÉBELÉR.
meunasoh (*Ac*) a small Muslim chapel; → SURAU.
mevrouw (D *ob*) /mefro/ Mrs., madam.
méwah 1 luxurious, deluxe, extravagant. 2 abundant. 3 chic (of attire, etc.). *barang* – article of luxury. *barang-barang* – luxury goods. *hidup (dengan)* – to live in luxury. *limpah* – (to live) in luxury.
  seméwah as luxurious as.

berméwah-méwah luxurious, flashy.
  terméwah the most luxurious.
  keméwahan 1 luxury, extravagance. 2 abundance, profusion, prosperity.
méwék (*J*/*Jv*) 1 pursing up the mouth to cry, pouting (ready to cry). 2 wide open.
mezbah (A) altar (for sacrificing); → MAZBAH.
mi I (C) noodles; → BAKMI. – *basah* noodles in broth. – *godok* parboiled egg noodles. – *goréng* pan-fried noodles. – *instan* instant noodles. – *kering* dried noodles. – *kocok* soup with noodles and other ingredients. – *kuah* noodles in broth. – *pangsit* noodle soup with wontons. – *rebus* → MI *godog*. – *tékték* noodles sold by a street vendor.
mi II (E) third note in the musical scale.
miak → CIAK *miak*.
mial *ciak* – chirp (of bird); → CIAK I.
miana k.o. plant, *Coleus atropurpureus* whose roots are used as medicine for stomach pains.
miang 1 fine hair of the nettle or bamboos. 2 (= – *gatal*) a) itching from a sting. b) sexually excited, horny. – *jelatang* a) hair of the stinging nettle. b) instigator.
  semiang (~ *kalam*) an iota, the least little bit. *tidak takut barang* ~ to be not a bit afraid. *habis* ~ *karena bergésér* practice makes perfect.
  bermiang with such fine hairs.
miap → TIAP *miap*.
miara → PELIHARA.
micara (*Jv*) 1 articulated. 2 to speak in a deliberately provocative way; → WICARA.
micin (C? *J*) monosodium glutamate, MSG, vetsin.
midar (*Jv*) to circulate, move around.
middenstand (D) 1 middle classes. 2 trades people, petit bourgeois.
midi (D) mediocre, moderate, midi (skirt, etc.). *hasil* – a mediocre income; *cp* MINI.
midik I → SIDIK *midik*.
midik II memidik to look at carefully.
midodaréni (*Jv*) the night before a wedding (for the bride).
mie → MI I.
migal-migul (*Jv coq*) to wiggle; → MÉGAL-MÉGOL.
Migas [Minyak dan Gas (Bumi)] (Department of) Petroleum and Natural Gas.
migran (D) migrant. – *musiman* seasonal migrant.
migrasi (D) migration. – *keluar* out-migration.
  bermigrasi to migrate.
mihrab (A) niche in a mosque wall indicating the direction toward Mecca.
mihun Chinese vermicelli; long, slender strips made from a flour paste, like fine noodles.
mijah (*Jv*) memijah to spawn.
  pemijahan spawning.
miju(-miju) lentil, *Lens esculenta*.
mik I (C *ob*) pulsation (of the pulse).
mik II clipped form of mikropon.
mika I you (to intimates).
mika II → mica; → ABRAK.
Mikaél and Mikail (E) the Archangel Michael.
mikania climbing hemp vine, mile-a-minute weed, *Mikania micrantha/scandens*.
mikér [minuman keras] alcoholic beverage.
Mikha (the Biblical) Micah.
Mikimus (D) Mickey Mouse.
mikin (*J*) (= semikin) → MAKIN.
mikol [minuman beralkohol] alcoholic beverage.
mikolog (D) mycologist.
mikologi (E) mycology.
mikrab → MIHRAB.
Mikrad and Mikraj (A) Muhammad's ascension to Heaven; → MI'RAJ.
  mikradan the commemoration of Muhammad's ascension to Heaven.
mikro (D) micro. *ékonomi* – microeconomy. *gelombang* – microwave. *neraca* – microbalance.

mikroba and **mikrobe** (*D*) microbe.
mikrobiologi (*D/E*) microbiology. *ahli* – microbiologist.
mikrobiologiwan male microbiologist.
mikrobiologiwati female microbiologist.
mikroéléktrika (*D*) microelectronics.
mikrofilm (*D/E*) microfilm.
  memikrofilmkan to microfilm.
  pemikrofilman microfilming.
mikrofon (*D/E*) microphone.
  bermikrofon with a microphone. *~ ganda* to have a dual micro-
    phone system.
mikrolét k.o. microbus which has replaced the *op(e)lét*.
mikron (*D/E*) micron.
Mikronésia (*D/E*) Micronesia.
mikroorganisma and **mikroorganisme** (*D*) microorganism.
mikul duwur mendem jero (*Jv*) to respect one's parents while they
    are alive and after their death; parents' message to and expec-
    tation from their children.
mik up (*E*) makeup.
  memik-up to make up.
mil I (*D*) mile. *– laut* nautical mile.
mil II (*D*) mail. *kapal* – mail boat.
mil III (in acronyms) → MILITÉR.
milad (*A*) anniversary.
milangkori (*Jv*) 1 to make house-to-house visits. 2 to travel widely.
milat [Militér Atasé] military attaché; → ATMIL.
mili (*D*) milli-, a 1000th part of a unit in the metric system. *–detik*
    millisecond. *–liter* milliliter. *–méter* millimeter.
milik (*A*) 1 property, possession, ownership. *Rumah itu – saya*.
    The house belongs to me. *terlepas dari* – lose possession of, slip
    out of one's hands. *hak* – proprietary right, title. *tanah* – heredi-
    tary lands. *tanah – raja* crown lands/estates. 2 fate, good luck,
    fortune. *belum* – not fated. *– bersama* joint tenancy. *– mutlak*
    sole ownership. *– negara* a) state property. b) nationalized. *–
    orang* s.o. else's property. *–pribadi* private property.
  bermilik propertied.
  memiliki 1 to possess, own, have. *dimiliki hingga jatuh témpo*
    held to maturity. 2 to take possession of, appropriate, annex.
    3 to seize.
  termilik taken possession of, appropriated.
  kemilikan possession, ownership. *~ kembali* repossession.
  pemilik possessor, owner, proprietor. *~ angkutan laut* ship-
    owner. *~ bersama* joint tenant. *~ guntai* absentee landlord. *~
    manfaat* beneficial owner. *~ mutlak* sole owner. *~ tanah* land-
    lord. *~ tanah secara guntai* absentee landlord. *~ terdaftar* reg-
    istered owner. **kepemilikan** ownership, title. *~ manfaat*
    beneficial ownership. *~ terdaftar* registered ownership. *~
    tunggal* sole ownership.
  pemilikan possession, ownership. *~ bersama* joint ownership. *~
    intéléktual* intellectual property. *~ tunggal* sole proprietorship.
milionér → MILYUNÉR.
milir (*J*) downstream; → HILIR. *– mudik* to go back and forth.
milis (*E*) mailing list.
  pemilis member of a mailing list.
milisi (*D*) 1 militia. 2 military man. 3 military service. *terpanggil
    –* called up for (first compulsory) military service.
militan (*D*) militant.
  memilitankan militant.
militansi (*D*) militancy.
militér (*D*) military. *kaum –* the military clique. *– atasé* [milat] mil-
    itary attaché. *– sukaréla(wan)* volunteer. *– wajib* conscript; →
    WAJIB *militér*.
  memilitérkan to militarize.
  kemilitéran military (*mod*).
  kemilitér-militéran paramilitary, military-like.
militérisasi (*D*) militarization.
  memilitérisasikan to militarize.
militérisme (*D/E*) militarism.
militéristis (*D*) militaristic.
miliun → MILYUN.
miliunér → MILYUNÉR.
mil-milan (*Jv*) snacks. *jajan –* to eat a snack.

milo (*coq*) → MULO.
milu (*ob*) maize, corn, *Zea mays*.
milyar(d) (*D*) billion.
  milyaran 1 billions of. *~ dolar* billions of dollars. 2 in/by the bil-
    lions.
milyardér (*D*) billionaire.
milyonér → MILYUNÉR.
milyun (*D*) million.
  bermilyun(-milyun) by the million(s).
  milyunan millions.
milyunér (*D/E*) millionaire.
mim (*A*) name of the 24th letter in the Arabic alphabet.
mimang *akar* – aboveground intertwined roots, usually of the
    banyan, k.o. magic roots; → LINGKARAN *mimang*.
mimba nim tree, *Azadirachta indica*.
mimbar (*A*) podium, forum, pulpit, speaker's platform, rostrum.
    – bébas free speech platform.
mimi (*Jv*) king-crab, *Limulus moluccanus*; → BELANGKAS. *kaya/
    seperti – dan mintuna* inseparable (of lovers); → MINTUNA.
miméograf (*D/E*) mimeograph.
mimik I (*D*) mimicry, mimicking.
mimik II (*Jv*) to drink (children's word).
mimik III *makan* termimik-mimik to smack one's lips while eating.
mimis (*J/Jv*) small shot.
mimisan (*J/Jv*) (to have a) nosebleed.
mimpi a dream (literal meaning; *cp* IMPIAN). *– basah* wet dream.
  bermimpi to dream. *Ibu ~ bertemu dengan ayah*. Mother dreamt
    that she met father. *~ berjalan* sleepwalk(ing). *~ di siang
    bolong* to daydream.
  bermimpikan to dream of/about. *Saya ~ saudara saya*. I dreamt
    about my brother.
  memimpikan 1 to dream of/about. *~ syahwat* to have erotic
    dreams. 2 to hope/wish for s.t. *Saya ~ sebuah dunia yang
    damai*. I dream of a peaceful world.
  termimpi-mimpi 1 keep on dreaming. 2 to dream, imagine.
  mimpian dream.
  pemimpi 1 dreamer. 2 sleepwalker.
min I (in acronyms) → ADMINISTRASI.
min II → MINUS 1.
mina I (*Skr*) *gajah* – whale, walrus.
mina II *burung* – myna bird.
Mina III (*Skr*) Pisces (*zod*).
Mina IV (*A*) a place on the *hajj* where pilgrims stone the *Jamrah*.
Minah proper name associated with a lower-class Indonesian
    woman. *si* – petroleum → PERTAMINA.
minalaidin walfaizin (*A*) "from those who have celebrated their
    victory for keeping the fast," i.e., the phrase used on *Lebaran*
    to congratulate those who have kept the fast.
Minang short for *Minangkabau*.
Minangkabau ethnic group in West Sumatra. *alam* – the west
    coast of Sumatra.
Minang-kiau the insulting transformation of *Minangkabau* into a
    Chinese-sounding name to point out their similarity in entre-
    preneurial spirit to the Chinese.
minantu (*M*) son/daughter-in-law.
Minas name of a small village located 30 km from Pekanbaru,
    Central Sumatra; a trademark for a crude oil with a low sulfur
    content.
minat interest, liking, desire, attention (paid to s.t.), tendency.
    tidak ada – untuk bekerja not to feel like working. *menaruh –
    kepada* to pay attention to; → MEMINATI. *menjadi – dunia*
    known throughout the world. *– baca* interest in reading.
  seminat with the same interests as.
  berminat to be interested (in), have an interest (in), have a lik-
    ing (for). *Sedikit yang ~*. Few are interested. *kurang ~ ter-
    hadap* to have little interest in.
  meminati to be interested in. *Sténografi: Mengapa kurang di-
    minati?* Shorthand: Why so little interest in it?
  peminat devotee, amateur, fan, admirer, supporter, interested
    person. *~ baca* a reader.
  peminatan (in higher education) concentration, major.
minatu (*S*) laundryman; → BINATU, MENATU.

minaut problem solving and decision making.

minbar → MIMBAR.

mindah → PINDAH.

minder (*D*) inferior. *merasa* – to feel inferior. *rasa* – subservience, feeling of inferiority.

keminderan feelings of inferiority.

minderhéitsnota (*D*) minority report (in MPR).

mindering → MINDRING.

mindi (*Jv*) and – *kecil* Chinaberry, nim tree, a tree with a bark that can be used to cure skin diseases and as a pesticide and anti-dandruff shampoo, *Azadirachta excelsa*.

mindik(-mindik) (*J/Jv*) to spy on secretly, do s.t. secretly; → INDIK.

mindo (*J*) to eat rice at lunch mixed with rice left over from a previous meal.

mindring (*D*) to sell things from town to town on the installment plan. *Cina* – itinerant (Chinese) moneylender and hawker who makes small short-term loans at high interest rates. *hidup* – to buy everything on the installment plan, live on credit.

mineral (*D/E*) mineral.

mineralisasi (*D*) mineralization.

mineralogi (*D/E*) mineralogy.

mineur (*Fr D*) (*pron* as in French) 1 somber, depressed, downcast. 2 minor (key).

minggat (*J/Jv*) to flee, run away, escape.

peminggatan fleeing. ~ *cendekiawan* brain drain.

minggir (*J/Jv*) 1 to move to the side/curb; → PINGGIR. –*!* (Get) out of the way! 2 (request to stop at the side of the road) stop! – *di dekat mesjid* –*!* Stop near the mosque!

meminggirkan to push aside.

minggu (*Port*) 1 (*hari* –) Sunday. – *malam* Sunday night. 2 (7-day) week; *cp* PEKAN II. – *Palma* Palm Sunday. – *tenang* a) cooling-off week, i.e., the week before the general elections in which the contesting parties are not allowed to campaign. b) the week before final exams, when classes are not in session.

seminggu a/one week.

seminggu-mingguan all week long, throughout the week.

berminggu-minggu for weeks (and weeks).

mingguan 1 weekly. 2 a weekly (periodical). *dua* ~ biweekly. *se*~ once a week.

mingkin (*J*) → MAKIN. **mingkinan** extreme, excessive.

mingser (*Jv*) to get out of place, shift.

minhaj (*A*) path, way.

mini (*D/E*) 1 small, miniature, mini-. 2 (– *rok*) miniskirt. **ber-mini-rok** to wear a miniskirt.

bermini to wear a miniskirt. – *Éksprés* (in West Sumatra) the Honda pickup (truck).

meminikan to minimize.

miniatur (*D/E*) miniature.

miniaturisasi (*D*) miniaturization.

minicar (*D/E*) a jitney-like, three-wheeled vehicle propelled by a four-stroke Honda S-110 engine.

minim (*D*) 1 minimal, minimum. 2 marginal.

seminim ~ *mungkin* and **seminim-minimnya** as minimal/little as possible.

meminimkan to minimize.

peminiman minimizing.

minimal (*D/E*) minimal.

meminimalkan to minimize.

peminimalan minimizing.

minimi k.o. small machine gun.

minimum (*D/E*) minimum. *upah* – minimum wage.

miniskirt (*E*) miniskirt; → MINI.

minister (*D/E*) minister, i.e., a diplomatic officer of a foreign nation sent to represent his government; ranks below an ambassador; in Indonesia referred to as *duta*. – *counselor* minister counselor (a title used in all Indonesian embassies).

minit (*D*) 1 → MENIT. 2 original (document). *diletakkan pada* – *akta ini* (in notarial instruments) attached to the original of this document.

minor → MINEUR.

minoritas (*D*) minority.

meminoritaskan to count as a minority (group).

minoritét → MINORITAS.

minsua temple guard.

minta 1 (= **meminta** *kepada*) to ask for, request, beg; → PINTA I. 2 to say (one's prayers). 3 (*coq*) please. – *bicara dengan/sama* ... may I please speak to ... (on the telephone). – *tunggu sebentar* please, wait a minute; → HARAP. – *berdiri sebentar*. Please, stand up. 4 please give me, I'd like some. – *kopi susu*. Please give me coffee with milk. 5 (= *diminta*) to be proposed to, to be asked for one's hand in marriage. *Sudah beberapa kali ia diminta orang*. She has been proposed to several times. 6 to need, require. *Soal ini* – *perhatian kita*. This matter needs our attention. *seperti* – *tanduk kepada kuda* to ask for s.t. from s.o. who doesn't have it. – *adik* he/she is asking for a younger sibling (said of a crying child). – *akal* to ask for a way to do s.t. – *ampun* a) to ask pardon, beg one's pardon, apologize. b) O, my God! Unbelievable! c) extremely. *susah* – *ampun* extremely difficult. – *banding* to appeal to a higher court. – *belét* to request a letter of appointment. – *berhenti* to tender one's resignation. – *bicara kepada/sama* ... (on the telephone) May I please speak to ... – *cerai* to sue for divorce. – *damai* to ask for an armistice/settlement out of court. – *dilawan* just asking for a fight. – *diri* a) to take one's leave, depart. b) to ask to be excused. – *disambung dengan* ... (on the telephone) please, connect me with ... – *doa* to pray, say one's prayers. – *hati* to seek attention. – *izin* to request permission. – *jalan* to request permission to pass (on the street/road). – *janji* to ask for more time. – *kasih* to beg for mercy. – *keramat* to ask blessings at a holy place. – *korban* to claim victims. – *lepas* to resign (one's position). – *libur* to take off (from work). – *lihat* let me see it. – *maaf* pardon me, to apologize. – *musyawarah* to request/ask for a consultation. – *nyawa* to beg for mercy, beg for one's life. – *pergi* to ask permission to go. – *perkara* to appeal to a higher court. – *permisi* to say good-bye. – *pisah* to sue for divorce. – *sambung* please connect me (with). – *selamat* to ask God for protection. – *tabik* (*ob*) to say good-bye, depart. – *terima kasih* to thank. – *tolong* to ask for help, summon s.t. to one's aid.

minta-minta 1 ~ *saja* ... let's hope that ... will happen (but it probably won't). ~*lah jangan hujan hari ini*. Let's hope it doesn't rain today. ~ *luluslah saya*. Let's hope I pass. 2 to beg. *orang/tukang* ~ beggar. **berminta-minta** to ask for s.t. earnestly/repeatedly, beg for, insist. **meminta-minta** to ask/beg (for alms). **peminta-minta** beggar.

berminta to be requested/asked for (not bought). *licin karena minyak* ~ strut in borrowed feathers.

meminta 1 → MINTA. ~ *keluar/berhenti* to tender one's resignation. ~ *korban* to claim victims. 2 to decide on (life or death, etc.). *tanah Mekah* ~ he will die in Mecca.

memintai 1 to ask s.o. for s.t. 2 to question, interview. *Dia dimintai keterangannya*. He was questioned (by the police). 3 to ask repeatedly or a lot.

memintakan [and **mintain** (*J coq*)] 1 to request/ask for s.t. for s.o. *Aku akan memintakan ampun bagimu kepada Tuhanku*. I will ask God for mercy for you. 2 to ask s.o. to do s.t. *Aparat gabungan memintakan agar seluruh aparat brimob meletakkan senjata*. The joint forces asked the entire mobile brigade to lay down their weapons. 3 to ask for s.t. *Tidak dapat dimintakan banding terhadap putusan itu*. No motion for appeal can be filed against that decision.

peminta 1 petitioner. 2 destiny, fate (determined by God). 3 (*cla*) request; petition.

permintaan 1 request. *atas* ~*nya* at his request. *atas* ~ *sendiri* at one's own request. ~ *memaksa* extortion by a public servant. ~ *penawaran* call for tenders. ~ *suaka* request for asylum. 2 demand (for goods). ~ *dan penawaran* supply and demand. 3 application, petition, motion. ~ *krédit* application for credit. *mengajukan* ~ *paliseménnya* to file one's petition (for bankruptcy). *péndék/singkat* ~ to die soon, will die soon.

mintak I → MINTA.

mintak II (*A*) girdle, belt.

mintakat (*A*) zone. – *dingin* cold zone. – *pasang* tidal zone. – *penyangga* buffer zone. – *tropika* topical zone. – *ugahari* temperate zone.

permintakan zoning.

mintakulburuj (*A*) Zodiac.

mintal and **mintel 1** chubby, stumpy, plump (of babies). **2** full and large (of breasts).

minterat (*coq D*) municipal council. **kuli** – city street cleaner.

mintuna 1 female sea crab; → MIMI. **2** the Twins (in the Zodiac), Gemini; → MINTAKULBURUJ.

minuét (*D*) minuet.

minum 1 to have a drink. *Ia belum* –. He has not yet had a drink. **2** (= **meminum**) to drink s.t. – *air* to drink water. *–nya apa?* (waiter to customer) What will you have to drink? *pelangi* – rainbow. **3** to swallow s.t. (such as a pill) with liquid, inhale (into one's lungs). – *hawa* get some fresh air. – *madat* to smoke opium. – *pil* to take a pill. – *air sambil menyelam* and *sambil menyelam* – *air* to kill two birds with one stone. – *air terasa duri, air diminum rasa duri* and – *serasa duri* (*M*) listless, apathetic; to be spiritless. – *aspirin* to take an aspirin. – *madat* to smoke opium. – *obat* to take medicine; → MAKAN *obat*. – *rokok* to smoke a cigarette.

minum-minum 1 to sit around drinking. **2** to drink (alcoholic beverages). *Di suka* ~, *kadang-kadang sampai mabuk.* He likes to drink, sometimes until he gets drunk.

meminum to drink s.t. *Diminumnya sekali teguk habis.* He drank it down in one gulp.

meminumi 1 to water, give water to. ~ *ternak* to give water to the cattle. *Ia ~ku sejenis jamu.* He gave me a k.o. medicine to drink. **2** (*pl obj*) to drink.

meminumkan 1 to give s.t. to drink. *Minumkan padanya air.* Give him some water to drink. **2** to water, give water to (animals).

terminum 1 drunk accidentally. **2** potable, drinkable.

minuman 1 drink(s of all sorts). **2** beverage. ~ *botolan* bottled drink. ~ *campuran* mixed drink. ~ *keras* liquor, alcoholic beverage. ~ *lembut/lunak* soft drink. ~ *meruap* aerated water. ~ *pelenyap dahaga* thirst quencher. ~ *ringan/segar* soft drink. ~ *selamat datang* welcoming drink.

minuman-minuman drinks, beverages.

peminum 1 drinker. **2** drunkard. ~ *candu* opium smoker. ~ *rokok* smoker.

peminuman 1 drinking. ~ *obat* taking medicine. **2** s.t. used for taking medicine with. **sepeminuman** the time it takes to drink (a cup of tea, etc.).

minus (*D*) **1** minus. **2** grade, strength (of eyeglasses used for short-sightedness). – *berapa kaca(mata)mu?* How strong are your glasses? **3** poverty-stricken because short of food. *daérah* – an area suffering from a food shortage. – *beras* suffering from a shortage of rice.

keminusan poverty (because of a shortage of food).

minut and **minuta** (*D*) valid original; → MINIT 2.

minyak 1 oil, grease, fat, lubricant. **2** petroleum. *akar* – various species of climber, *Limacia velutina, Hypserpa cuspidata. damar* – resin-producing tree, *Agathis alba. sebagai* – *dengan air* like cats and dogs. *seperti menating* – *penuh* handling s.t. with kid gloves. – *adas* fennel oil. – *akar wangi Jawa* Java vetiver oil. – *angin* a medicinal oil used as a liniment against various ailments. – *antrasén* anthracene oil. – *asihan* love potion. – *atar* perfume. – *atsiri* volatile/essential oil. – *babi* lard. – *bakar* fuel oil. – *bakar berat* heavy fuels. – *bakar campur* blended fuel oil. – *bakar sulingan* distillate fuel oil. – *basah* cut oil. – *batu bara* coal oil. – *batu tulis* shale oil. – *bekas* used oil. – *belian balik* buy-back crude. – *bénsin* gasoline. – *berat* heavy oil. – *bijan* sesame oil. – *bilas* flushing oil. – *buangan* waste oil. – *bubut* cutting oil. – *bulus* (*Jv*) turtle oil, used to eliminate wrinkles due to old age and to strengthen breasts. – *bumi* petroleum, crude oil. – *bumi tercampung* topped/reduced crude. – *bungker* bunker oil. – *cat* linseed oil. – *céréran* abandoned oil. – *cenduai* (*ob*) k.o. love potion. – *cétak beton* form oil. – *cor* core oil. – *cuci* mineral spirits, white spirit. – *dan gas bumi* [migas] oil and natural gas. – *dasar* (*petro*) base stock. – *dian* illuminating/burning oil. – *diesel* industrial diesel oil for low r.p.m engines. – *énapan* clarified oil. – *étéris* etherical oil. – *gas* kerosene. – *gelap* black oil, industrial diesel oil, IDO, hot oil. – *gérék* drilling oil. – *goni* batch oil. – *goréng* cooking oil. – *hidup* live oil. – *hitam* black oil. – *ikan* a)

fish oil. b) cod-liver oil. – *industri* industrial oils. – *Istambul* rosewater. – *jagung* corn oil. – *jarak* castor oil. – *jelantah* coconut oil left after frying. – *jernih* white product. – *kacang* peanut oil. – *karbol* carbolic oil. – *karter* crankcase oil. – *kasar* crude oil. – *kasrén* (*petro*) sweet crude. – *kasti* sour crude. – *kayu putih* cajeput oil. – *kelapa* coconut oil (for frying). – *kelonyo* eau-de-cologne. – *kenanga* essential oil. – *keruh* pale oil. – *kerul* pomade; → KERUL. – *kopok gajah* oil used to bathe/wash krises. – *kruing* oil from a Dipterocarpaceae. – *kuku* neat's-foot oil. – *ladan* ladanon, fuel made from damar resin. – *lagam* copaiba balsam. – *lampu* kerosene, illuminating oil. – *lapis* slushing oil. – *latung* → MINYAK *tanah*. – *liar* wild oil. – *lincir* lubricating oil. – *lobak* rapeseed oil. – *lumas* lubricating oil. – *lumas mérah* red oil. – *lumas untuk kendaraan* automotive oils. – *macan* a liniment (Tiger Balm). – *majemuk* a mixture of oils, perfumes. – *Makassar* oil made from the seeds of the *Schleichera trijunga* used for its aroma. – *mati* dead oil. – *mawar* rose oil. – *média* mineral seal oil. – *mentah* crude (oil). – *(mentah) berat* heavy crude. – *(mentah) médium* medium crude. – *(mentah) ringan* light crude. – *mesin* engine oil. – *minéral* mineral oil. – *misik* oil used to bathe/wash krises. – *motor* engine oil. – *nabati* vegetable oil. – *nétral* neutral oil. – *nilam* patchouli oil. – *nyaman* a) perfumed hair oil. b) k.o. rubbing oil. – *oncor* illuminating oil. – *pajan* weathered oil. – *pala* nutmeg oil. – *palem* palm oil. – *patra* kerosene. – *pedar* oil made from coconut dregs and used in lamps. – *pekat* bright stock, ointment. – *pélét* love philter. – *pelikan* mineral oil. – *pelincir* a) lubricating oil. b) bribes. – *pelita* illuminating/burning oil. – *pelumas* lubricating oil. – *pemanas* heating oil. – *penat* ointment. – *pengéncér* petroleum spirit. – *pengéncér cat* paint thinner. – *penghangat* heater oil. – *penyu* → MINYAK *bulus*. – *penimbul* liniment. – *permén/pépermin* peppermint oil. – *poko* a peppermint oil that is used to treat pain. – *putih* white oil, premium/super grade gasoline. – *raksi* perfume. – *rambut* brilliantine, hair oil. – *rapa* rapeseed oil. – *rengas* varnish. – *resap* penetrating oil. – *ringan* light oil. – *ringan Arab* Arabian Light Crude, ALC. – *roda gigi* gear oil. – *samin* suet from a goat/camel, etc. – *sapi* suet, beef fat. – *sarat* (*petro*) rich oil. – *sari wangi* fragrant oil. – *sawit* palm oil. – *sawit kasar/ mentah* crude palm oil, CPO. – *sayur* vegetable oil. – *segar* live oil. – *semir* lubricating oil. – *semprot* spray oil. – *serai/seréh* citronella oil. – *serpih* shale oil. – *silinder* cylinder oil. – *singa laut* an aphrodisiac. – *solar* automotive diesel oil for high r.p.m. engines, HSD. – *songgo langit* (*Jv*) coconut oil for bathing/washing the revered heritage of the ancestors of Sunan Kalijogo at Demak and for the heirloom at the Kraton in Solo. – *suci* chrism. – *tanah* a) petroleum. b) kerosene. – *tampungan* slop oil. – *tangis duyung* k.o. water that is believed to come from the *dugung* and is used to seduce women; → DUYUNG. – *tanah* kerosene. – *tawon* k.o. oil used on insect bites, etc. – *telon* a liniment containing three oils: cajaput, fennel, and olive, used for rubbing on babies and for sprained muscles. – *tér* tar oil. – *terbang* volatile oil. – *tesala* a panacea against all k.o. of diseases. – *tumbuh-tumbuhan* vegetable oil. – *tung* oil from the seeds of the *Aleurites cordata* used in making paint and varnish. – *tungku* furnace oil. – *wangi* perfume. – *wijén* sesame oil. – *zaitun* olive oil.

berminyak oily, greasy, greased. ~ *air* a) to toady (to). b) to flatter, cajole, wheedle, to butter s.o. up. c) to put on an act. ~ (*air*) *mukanya* to show that one is happy. *licin* ~ smooth as silk.

meminyaki to oil, grease, lubricate.

keminyakan oil (*mod*).

perminyakan [and **peminyakan** (*infr*)] **1** lubrication. **2** (*mod*) oil. *politik* ~ oil policy. *sakramén* ~ (*RC*) chrism, extreme unction. **3** petroleum/refinery matters.

miom(a) (*D med*) myoma.

mipan (*C*) pastry with sweet sauce.

mipil (*J/Jv*) to buy or collect little by little.

mipis → NIPIS.

Miqat and **Miqot** (*A*) "boundary" where the *ihram* is put on during the *hajj*.

mirah (*Jv*) ruby.

mirai → TIRAI *mirai*.

Mi'raj and Miraj (Nabi Muhammad) (A) the Prophet Muhammad's miraculous ascension from Jerusalem to the throne of God. The site is now the Dome of the Rock; *cp* ISRA.

miras [minuman keras] alcoholic beverages, hard liquor.

mirat (A) /mir'at/ mirror.

Miriam → MARYAM.

mirih (M) 1 to trickle, drip. 2 to melt.

mirik memirik to pulverize.

miring (Jv) 1 at an angle, aslant, askew, inclined, oblique, tilted. 2 to bank. *Pesawat – ke kanan.* The plane banked to the right. 3 to lie on one side (of persons). 4 to keel, list (over to one side) (of boats). 5 to swerve (of cars). 6 cursive (of handwriting), in italics (of printed letters). *tulisan –* running hand. 7 cheap, competitive (of prices). *Tarip lebih –.* The prices are competitive. 8 biased. *keputusan –* a biased decision. *– kepada* inclined to. *– otaknya.* He is crazy.

memiring to slant, slope.

memiringkan to incline/tilt s.t, put s.t. at an angle, angle.

kemiringan incline, dip, slope, tilt. *~ dasar* base tilt. *~ léréng* acclivity.

pemiringan italicizing.

mirip (J) to resemble, bear a likeness/resemblance to, look like. *– (dengan/sebagai/seperti)* to resemble. *– benar dengan ayahnya.* He really looks like his father.

bermiripan to resemble e.o., look like e.o.

mirip-miripan sort of resemble, look vaguely like.

kemiripan resemblance, similarity.

pemirip double, i.e., a person who closely resembles another person.

pemiripan similarity.

miris I (Jv) 1 fear; timid; afraid. *– hati* timid, afraid. 2 anxious, concerned; alarmed; discouraged.

miris II → TIRIS *miris.*

miroso (Jv) tasty.

miru → MEWIRU.

mirunggan (Jv) 1 extra, additional. 2 special.

mirut → KERUT *merut/mirut.*

mis (E) Miss (young lady).

mis-misan *pemilihan ~* contest for Miss this and Miss that.

mis. (abbr) [misalnya] e.g.

Misa (D) *– Kudus/Suci* the Holy Mass.

misai moustache. *– kucing* whiskers. *– lalat hinggap* a tiny moustache.

bermisai with a moustache.

misal (A) 1 example, instance. *diambilnya – …* he took as an example … 2 parable. *– kata* by way of speaking.

misalnya for example/instance, e.g.

semisal like, resembling, similar to.

memisalkan 1 to compare with. 2 to follow s.o.'s example, take/use as an example. 3 to consider/regard as. 4 to suppose, assume, take it (that). 5 to represent (a picture). *dimisalkan* assuming/supposing that. *dimisalkan (kepada)* a) to be compared with, be meant figuratively, be alluded to. b) (can be) taken/considered as.

misalan (infr) emblem, symbol.

pemisalan 1 assumption; → PERUMPAMAAN. 2 sampling.

misan (J/Jv) cousin.

misbah (A) lamp, light, lantern.

misbar (J) [kalau gerimis, penonton bubar] (when it drizzles, the moviegoers scatter) open-air cinema;→ BIOSKOP *misbar.*

misi (D) (Roman Catholic) mission. *sekolah –* Catholic mission school. *– muhibah* goodwill mission. *– pencari fakta, – penjajagan* and *– siasat hakikat* fact-finding mission. *– perdagangan* trade mission. *– suci* sacred mission. *– tempur* combat mission.

misih (coq) → MASIH I.

misik (coq esp C) → MASIH I.

misil (D) missile; → PELURU. *– antarbenua* intercontinental missile. *– antibalistik* antiballistic missile. *– antimisil balistik* antiballistic-missile missile. *– balistik* ballistic missile. *– balistik antarbenua* intercontinental ballistic missile, ICBM. *– balistik jarak menengah/sedang* medium-range ballistic missile. *– berkepala perang nuklir* missile with a nuclear warhead. *– darat-darat* ground-to-ground missile. *– darat-udara* surface-to-air missile,

SAM. – (di)kendali guided missile. *– jarak jauh* long-range missile. *– jarak sedang* medium-range missile. *– kendali nuklir* nuclear guided missile. *– nuklir* nuclear missile. *– nuklir jarak sedang* medium-range nuclear missile. *– penangkis* interceptor missile. *– pertahanan* defensive missile. *– udara-darat/permukaan* air-to-surface missile. *– yang berpangkalan di darat* ground-based missile. *– yang diluncurkan dari kapal selam* submarine-launched missile.

misionaris (D) missionary.

Misir → MESIR.

miskal (A) goldsmith's weights, approx. 4.2 grams, shekel.

miskalkulasi (D) miscalculation.

miskin (A) poor, miserable, destitute, needy. *rumah –* poorhouse. *– papa* very poor. *– ruh* poor in spirit.

miskin-miskin very poor.

memiskinkan 1 to impoverish, make poor. 2 to reduce to poverty.

kemiskinan poverty, misery, indigence. *di atas garis ~* above the poverty line.

pemiskinan impoverishment.

miskol (E BG) a missed call (on a mobile/cell phone).

miskram (D) miscarriage.

misluk(t) (D) 1 to be botched, badly made. 2 unsuccessful.

mismanajemén (E) mismanagement.

mismis (J) 1 very stingy. 2 wanting to go into every detail, meticulous.

misoa (C) long slender threads made from flour; vermicelli.

Misri (A) Egyptian.

misro (J) k.o. snack made of fried cassava filled with brown sugar.

Missa → MISA.

missi → MISI.

missionaris → MISIONARIS.

mistar (A) 1 ruler, rule, line, measure, lath. *– hitung* slide rule. 2 post. *– gawang* (in soccer) goal post. 3 veil.

mistér (E) term of reference or address for Caucasian male (sometimes also used to women).

mister (D) [Mr] → MÉSTER I, SH.

mistéri (D) mystery.

mistérius (D) mysterious.

kemistériusan mystery.

misti (coq) → MESTI.

mistik (D) 1 mysticism. 2 system for predicting lottery winners.

memistik to do numerology.

kemistik-mistikan numerology, mystical things.

mistisisme (E) mysticism.

mistri (naut) ship's carpenter.

misuh (Jv) → PISUH. to curse, revile, abuse, use abusive language; → MEMAKI.

misuh-misuh to curse/abuse s.o., use abusive language.

misykil → MUSKIL.

mit (D) mid-. *ujian – séméster* midterms, midsemester examinations.

mitasi I → IMITASI.

mitasi II → MUTASI.

mite → MITOS.

miting I (Jv) 1 to grip, grasp. 2 to hold s.t. in the crook of one's arm; → PITING I.

miting II (E) meeting.

memiting to hold a meeting.

mitnaitsyo (E) midnight show.

memitnaitsyokan to put on as a midnight show.

mitoha (J) parents-in-law.

mitologi (D/E) mythology.

mitoni (Jv) ceremony held for a woman in the seventh month of pregnancy; → SELAMATAN *mitoni.*

mitos (D) myth.

memitoskan to mythicize.

mitra (Jv) 1 friend. 2 partner. *– dagang* trading partner. *– kerja* work partner, counterpart. *– pendiri* founding partner. *– Perempuan* Women's Crisis Center. *– sejajar* equal partner. **kemitrasejajaran** equal partnership. *– tanding* opponent. *– usaha* business partner. **kemitrausahaan** and **kemitraan usaha** partnership. *– wicara* dialogue partner. *– Wisata* "Tourist Partner," i.e., a doorless automobile manufactured in Indonesia by PT Garuda Mataram Motor Co. for short-distance transportation of tourists.

bermitra 1 to befriend, act as a friend, be friendly with. 2 to act as/be a partner ~ *dengan* in partnership with. ~ *tanding* (in boxing) sparring.

memitrakan to join in partnership.

kemitraan partnership.

pemitraan partnering.

mitraliur and **mitralyur** (*D*) machine gun.

memitraliur to machine gun.

mitsal → MISAL.

Miwon → AJI-NO-MOTO.

miyang (*Jv?*) to make a living at sea.

miyar-miyur (*Jv*) undecided, wavering, hesitant.

miyos (*Jv*) to be born. – *dalam* (*Jv*) born on (reference to the birthday of s.o. exalted, such as the birthday of Sri Sultan Hamengkubuwono IX).

miyosi (*Jv*) to commemorate one's birthday falling on a *Sabtu-Pahing*.

mizab (*A*) a water spout in the Kaabah.

mizan (*A*) 1 Libra (*zod*). 2 scales.

MKGR [Partai Musyawarah Kekeluargaan Gotong Royong] Mutual Assistance Familial Deliberation Party.

ML (*E BG init*) [make love] to have sex.

mlaka-mlaku (*Jv*) to keep walking back and forth.

mlandingan (*Jv*) → KEMLANDINGAN.

mligi (*Jv*) 1 (simply and) solely, only, nothing but. *bukan – ilmu* not only science. *benar-benar – mengajar* only serious about teaching.

mlinjo (*Jv*) k.o. tree with edible seeds. – *muda* small clusters of these seeds; they look like immature dates (*emping* is made from the meat of the seed of the mature *mlinjo* or *mlinjo tua*); → BLINJO.

mlinting (*Jv*) to roll (cigarettes). ~ *rokok* to roll a cigarette; → TINGWÉ.

mliwis → BELIBIS.

mlongo → MELONGO.

mo → MAU.

moa → MUA.

mo'alaf → MUALAF I.

mob (in acronyms) → MOBIL.

mobat-mabit (*Jv*) to toil, exhaust o.s.

mobét (*J*) (probably the *abbr* of Motor Bétjak, in the pre-1972 orthography) motorized *bécak*.

mobil (*D*) 1 (motor)car, automobile; → KENDARAAN. *satu – dengan* to sit/be in the same car as. *berkendaraan –* to ride in/drive a car. 2 mobile. *bersifat –* transportable. – *acuan* racing car. – *ambulans* ambulance. – *baja* armored car. – *balap(an)* racing car. – *ban baja bergigi* caterpillar tractor. – *barang* motor truck. – *beban* truck. – *berkaca gelap* car with tinted window glass. – *berp(e)lat hitam* a privately owned car. – *bis* bus. – *boks* van. – *bréngsék* jalopy. – *cicilan* financed car. – *dérék* tow truck. – *dinas* staff car, official car. – *gerobak* truck. – *jip* jeep; → JIP. – *jenazah* hearse. – *keran* crane truck. – *kerangkéng* cattle car, paddy wagon (used for transporting prisoners). – *mérah* a government-owned car. – *panser* armored car. – *pemadam kebakaran* fire engine. – *pembersih* cleaning truck. – *pengangkut personil lapis baja* armored personnel carrier. – *(pengangkut) sampah* garbage truck. – *pengangkutan* motortruck. – *pengantén* wedding limousine (used for carrying bride and groom from the church to the reception). – *pengintai* police van. – *penumpang* passenger/private car. – *penyelamat* rescue vehicle. – *penyerkap* paddy wagon. – *perecik* sprinkler. – *séwa* (taxi)cab. – *siram* sprinkler. – *tahanan* paddy wagon. – *tangga* ladder-truck (of the fire department). – *tinja* honey truck/wagon (for collecting human excrement). – *yang separuh pakai* and – *yang sudah dipakai* (previously) used car.

semobil ~ *dengan* to share a ride with, ride in the same car as.

bermobil to drive a car, motor(ing). *Dia* ~ *ke Gdansk.* He drove to Gdansk.

bermobil-mobilan to drive around.

permobilan 1 automotive. 2 car business/matters.

mobilér → MÉBELÉR.

mobilét (*D*) a moped of the "Mobylette" trade mark.

mobilisasi (*D*) mobilization.

memobilisasi(kan) to mobilize.

pemobilisasian mobilization.

mobilisir (*D*) **memobilisir** to mobilize; → MEMOBILISASI(KAN).

mobilitas and **mobilitét** (*D*) mobility.

moblong I (*Jv*) 1 full, round, white, and beautiful (of a woman's face); also: heavily made-up with face powder. 2 clear, cloudless (of sky).

moblong II (*J*) open (of clothes).

mobnas [mobil nasional] the national automobile.

mobyor (*Jv*) (dressed) sparklingly, conspicuously.

mocok (*Jv*) to substitute/fill in for s.o. temporarily in a job.

mocok-mocok casual (laborer).

mocopat → MACAPAT.

moda (*D*) mode, means. *menurut – angkutan* according to the means of transport.

modal (*Tam*) (financial) capital (to be invested), equity. *barang-barang –* capital goods. *kaum –* capitalists. *menanamkan –* to invest capital. *padat –* capital-intensive. *penanam –* investor. *penanaman –* investment. – *lari ke luar negeri* and *larinya –* capital flight. – *bayar* paid-in capital. – *bekerja* working capital. – *belum disetor* unpaid capital. – *belum ditempatkan* unissued capital. – *bergerak* a) personal estate. b) floating capital. – *berisiko* venture capital. – *berwujud* tangible net worth. – *cadangan* capital reserve, reserve fund. – *dan poténsi/tenaga* funds and forces. – *dasar* initial/original/authorized capital/stock. – *dengkul* goods received from others to be sold on a commission basis. **bermodal dengkul** to make money (without capital of one's own) by receiving goods for sale on a commission basis. – *(yang) disetor* paid-up/-in capital. – *ditempatkan* issued/subscribed capital. – *doméstik* domestic/national capital. – *doméstik asing* "foreign domestic capital," i.e., capital coming from indigenous foreign groups, particularly Chinese. – *kerja* working capital. – *kursi* money acquired through graft and corruption. – *lancar* circulating capital. – *masuk* capital inflow. – *obligasi* debenture capital. – *pelengkap* supplementary capital. – *pemilik* owner's equity. – *pemula* initial capital. – *penyertaan* equity capital. – *persekutuan* share/authorized/registered/nominal capital, capital stock. – *perséroan* corporate equity. – *perusahaan* business capital. – *pinjaman* borrowed capital. – *saham* capital stock. – *saham (ditempatkan dan disetor penuh)* capital stock (subscribed and fully paid up). – *saham diterbitkan* issued capital stock. – *sendiri* (owner's) equity. – *séro* authorized capital. – *setoran* paid-in capital. – *statuta/statutér* capital stock. – *sumbangan* donated capital. – *(dengan) – swadaya* owner's equity. – *tertanam* invested capital. – *tetap* fixed capital, real estate. – *uang kas* liquid capital. – *usaha* capital employed. – *véntura* venture capital.

semodal to enter into a financial partnership. *orang* ~ (co)partner; *cp* MITRA.

bermodal to have capital, be capitalized. ~ *kuat* financially strong.

bermodalkan with ... as capital.

memodali to finance. *proyék yang dimodali invéstasi asing* projects financed by foreign investments.

kemodalan 1 capitalism. 2 capitalistic.

pemodal 1 investor. 2 capitalist.

pemodalan capitalization.

permodalan financing. – *ékuitas* equity financing.

modalitas and **modalitét** (*D*) modality.

modalwan 1 capitalist. 2 financier.

modar (*J//Jv*) *mati –* a) not ritually slaughtered; dead without having the throat cut, as Islam requires. b) (*sl*) to die, kick the bucket.

mode (*D*) (in) fashion/style/vogue. *tidak menjadi – lagi* out of fashion.

modél I (*D*) 1 model, i.e., (a) an example to be followed; (b) a small-scale representation of s.t. – *étalasi* dummy. – *matriks* die pattern. 2 make (of a car). 3 fashion, style. 4 to be in fashion.

modél II (*Pal*) k.o. soup.

moderasi (*D*) moderation.

moderat (*D*) moderate.

moderator (*D/E*) moderator.
  memoderatori to moderate.
modér(e)n (*D/E*) modern, up-to-date.
  semodér(e)n as modern as, no matter how modern.
  memodérnkan and **mempermodérnkan** to modernize.
  kemodérnan modernity.
  termodérn most modern.
  pemodéren modernizer.
  permodérenan modernization.
modérnisasi (*D*) modernization.
  memodérnisasi to modernize.
  pemodérnisasian modernization.
moderok (*J*) 1 soft, mushy (because rotten). 2 damaged, unhealthy.
modifikasi (*D*) modification.
  memodifikasikan to modify.
modin (*A*) 1 muezzin, the caller to prayer. 2 (at the village level) the person who leads the prayer at a *selamatan, kematian*, etc.
modis (*D*) stylish.
modiste (*D*) (female) dressmaker.
modol I (*J/Jv*) messy, in disorder. *jorok* – a big messy guy.
modol II (*J*) to kill.
modong k.o. black magic. *tukang* – practitioner of black magic.
  memodong to cast a spell on.
modul (*D*) module.
modulasi (*D*) modulation.
modulir (*D*) **memodulir** to modulate.
modus (*L*) 1 modus. – *operandi* mode of operation, way of doing s.t., procedure. 2 (*ling*) mood.
moga, semoga, and **moga-moga** may (it be), I hope that, hopefully.
Mogadon k.o. tranquilizer.
mogok (*J/Jv*) 1 to (go on) strike (of workers). 2 to stall, stop, break down (of a car), stop working. 3 to jib (of a horse). 4 to turn at bay (of animals). – *belajar* (in high schools and universities) to boycott classes or lectures. – *duduk* sit-down strike. – *ginjal* anuria. – *lapar/makan* hunger strike. – *solidér* sympathy strike.
  memogoki to (go on) strike against.
  memogokkan to stop (work, etc.). *Kapan krisis yang telah ~ aktivitas pertanian itu akan berakhir?* When will the crisis which stopped agricultural activities end?
  pemogok striker. ~ *makan* hunger-striker.
  pemogokan strike, work stoppage. ~ *liar* wildcat strike.
mogol (*Jv*) 1 immature, uncooked. 2 to fail. 3 unsuccessful, only partly finished. *murid* – a (school) dropout.
mogor (*S*) to go whoring.
  pemogor Bluebeard, Don Juan.
  pemogoran prostitution.
moh (*Jv*) (I) don't want to! → EMOH. – *tumbuh* won't grow.
Moh. (*abbr*) → MOHAMAD.
mohalil → MUHALLIL.
Mohamad the Prophet Muhammad (also as a proper name); → MUHAMMAD. – *Rasul(l)ol(l)ah* Muhammad the Prophet of Allah.
Mohammadiyah a modernizing Islamic movement established on November 18, 1912, in Yogyakarta; the main force behind it was Kiyai Haji Ahmad Dahlan.
mohon 1 to ask (politer than *minta*), request, beg; → POHON III. – *akta* (*leg*) to request that s.t. be entered into the records. – *izin kepada yang berwajib* to request a license from the proper authorities. 2 (in Old Malay literature) to ask (a superior) to be excused from. – *patik beristri* I beg to be excused from taking a wife. 3 to implore, beseech.
  bermohon to present a petition, (make a) request. ~ *diri* to take one's leave (from a superior), ask leave to withdraw, say goodbye.
  memohon to ask for, request, plead for.
  memohonkan to ask for s.t. for s.o.
  termohon respondent, petitionee. ~ *kasasi* appellee/respondent in cassation. ~ *pailit* respondent in bankruptcy.
  pemohon 1 applicant, petitioner. ~ *banding* appellant. ~ *kasasi* appellant in cassation. ~ *pailit* petitioner in bankruptcy. 2 supplicant.
  permohonan 1 request, appeal, petition. ~ *ampun* appeal for a

pardon. ~ *banding* appeal. ~ *kasasi* petition for cassation. 2 application. ~ *krédit* loan application.
mohor (*Pers*) (royal) seal. *cap* – royal seal. *cincin* – royal signet ring. – *Kerajaan* (*Br*) State Seal.
moi (*J*) → AMOI.
mojah (*Pers ob*) socks, stockings.
mojang (*S*) girl. – *Priangan* a beauty from the Preanger, West Java, area.
mojeng (*J*) k.o. tree, ngapi nut, *Pithecolobium lobatum*.
Mojopahit → MAJAPAHIT.
moka (*D*) mocha (coffee).
mokaha not worth while.
mokal I → MUHAL.
mokal II (*Pr*) shy; → MALU I.
  mokal-mokalan (*pl subj*) to be shy.
moké k.o. arrack made from sugar palm.
moko [mobil toko] mobile shop/store.
mokoyong (*C*) dog meat.
mokak-malik (*Jv*) 1 to keep turning one way and then the other. 2 opportunistic.
moko (*ob*) k.o. drum.
moksa (*Skr*) (in Buddhism) free from reincarnation; *cp* MUKSA.
moksai I (*C*) Pekingese dog.
moksai II a *silat* movement.
molar (*D/E*) molar.
molé (only used in) *bako* – (Preanger) locally grown tobacco.
molék beautiful, pretty (of girls), cute, attractive.
  mempermolék to beautify, make more beautiful.
  kemolékan beauty, charm, attractiveness.
  pemolékan beautification. ~ *jalan-jalan* the beautification of the streets.
molekul (*D/E*) molecule.
molen (*D*) cement mixer.
molér (*Port J*) whore, prostitute.
molig (*D*) /molekh/ pleasingly plump.
  kemoligan plumpness.
mo-limo (*Jv*) the five sins whose names start with *mo* (the name of the *m* in Javanese script): *madat* (addicted to opium), *minum* (drinking alcohol), *main* (gambling), *madon* (playing around with women), and *maling* (stealing).
molong a snack made of lumps of dough in syrup.
molor I (*S*) to go to bed/sleep.
molor II (*Jv*) to extend, stretch (rubber/time/fabric), become longer (in time); → MEMUAI.
  memolorkan to stretch out (time), extend. *Dia ~ batas waktu.* He extended the deadline.
molos (*S*) 1 to slip in. 2 can enter (a hole, etc.). 3 (*sl*) to slip out without paying.
moluska (*D*) mollusk.
momén I (*D*) moment. – *gerak/kakas/puntir* torque. – *lembam* moment of inertia.
momén II on-the-spot administration of justice for a traffic violation. – *tilang* a speed-trap.
moméntum (*D/E*) momentum.
momok I bogey(man), spook, ghost often mentioned to scare children, imminent danger. *Ada –!* Watch out, there's a ghost!
  memomoki to haunt.
  memomokkan to set s.t. or s.o. up as a bogeyman.
momok II (*J vulg*) cunt, pussy; → MÉMÉK II.
momol (*Jv*) the soft, tender top of the sugarcane.
momong (*J*) **memomong** to care for, attend to, look after, take care of (a child, etc.), guide (a child). ~ *anak* to raise a child. ~ *penduduk désa* to provide guidance for the villagers.
  pemomong children's caretaker.
  momongan child/young animal to be taken care of; *cp* PAMONG.
momot (*Jv*) to load (goods in a van, etc.).
  memomoti to load s.t. with. ~ *sayuran* to load down with vegetables.
Monako Monaco.
monarki (*D/E*) monarchy.
Monas [Monumén nasional] National Monument (in Jakarta).
monat-manut (*Jv*) to obey/follow habitually.

moncér (*Jv*) excellent, skilled (at s.t.), skillful.

moncong (*Jv*) **1** snout (of a fish/pig). **2** beak (of bird). **3** muzzle (of a cannon/gun). – *bedil* rifle muzzle. – *meriam* cannon muzzle. – *pistol* pistol muzzle. **4** nozzle (of a pump/hose). **5** spout. – *cérék* spout of a kettle. **6** projecting (of pouting lips). **7** (– *peluru*) warhead (of a missile). **8** face/front part. – *bis* the front part of a bus. **9** (*vulg*) mouth. *sekeras -nya* at the top of his lungs.
  bermoncong 1 to have a projecting mouth. ~ *nuklir* with a nuclear warhead. **2** (rude) to speak.
  memoncong to jut/stick out.
  memoncongkan to stick s.t. out, make s.t. protrude, pucker up (one's lips).

moncor (*J*) **1** to flow out. **2** to suffer from diarrhea.

mondar-mandir (to walk) up and down (aimlessly), (to move) to and fro, (to go) back and forth (repeatedly); to shuttle between ... and ...

mondial (*D*) worldwide.

mondok I short and thick, squat, fat. *parang* – k.o. short cleaver. *tikus* – Norway rat, *Mus decumanus*.

mondok II (*Jv*) **1** to stay, live/board with s.o. temporarily. – (*indekos*) to board/lodge. – *dirumah sakit* to spend time in the hospital. **2** to live in a subleased room; → PONDOK.

mondokaki (*Jv*) wax flower plant, grape gardenia, *Ervatamia divaricata*.

mondolan (*Jv*) cloth knot at the back of a fabric headdress (common in Yogyakarta).

mondong I (*Jv*) to carry (away) one's bride in one's arms, symbolizing that she is a prize being carried off.

mondong II → CONDONG.

monél stainless steel.

monetér monetary. *bidang* – monetary sector.

mong (*onom*) sound of a gong.
  mong-mong a small gong.

monggo (*Jv*) (response to *kulo nuwun* or similar phrase to announce one's presence as a visitor) Come in! Hello!; → MARI I, MANGGA III, SILAKAN.

monggok → MONGKOK.

monggol knotty, gnarled (of trees).

mongki bisnis (*E*) monkey business.

mongkok (*J*) (= **bermongkok**) **1** to stick out. **2** to tower above. – *dada* for the chest to stick out in pride; to feel flattered/delighted.
  memongkokkan to stick s.t. out, make s.t. protrude. ~ *hati* to make s.o. proud.

mongkor k.o. sedan chair, palanquin.

mongmong (*Jv*) to take care of (a child); → MOMONG.

Mongol (*D*) Mongol(ian).

monitor (*D/E*) monitor; → PANTAU II.
  memonitor to monitor.
  termonitor monitored.
  pemonitoran monitoring.

monodualisme (*D/E*) monodualism.

monoftong (*E ling*) monophthong.

monoftongisasi (*E ling*) monophthongization.

monogami (*D/E*) monogamy.

monografi (*D*) monograph.

monogram (*D/E*) monogram.

monoksida (*D*) monoxide.

monokultur (*D/E*) monoculture.

monolitik (*E*) and **monolitis** (*D*) monolithic.

monolog (*D/E*) monolog.

monologis (*D*) monologist, a talk or lecture (rather than a discussion).

monoloyalitas (*D*) monoloyalty.
  bermonoloyalitas to have a single loyalty.

monon (*Pr*) homosexual; to engage in homosexual sex; → HOMO.
  memonon and **mononin** to sodomize.

monopoli (*D/E*) monopoly.
  memonopoli to have a monopoly, monopolize.
  pemonopolian monopolization.

monopolisir (*D*) **memonopolisir** to monopolize.

monopsoni (*D/E*) monopsony, market situation in which there is one buyer and a large number of sellers

monorél (*E*) and **monoril** (*D*) monorail.

monosakarida (*D*) monosaccharide.

monosok (*D/E*) single shock (absorber).

monotéisme (*D/E*) monotheism.

monotipe (*D/E*) monotype.

monoton (*D/E*) monotone.

monsinyur (*Fr D*) monsignor.

monster I (*D*) monster.

monster II (*D*) merchandise sample.

monsun (*D/E*) monsoon.

montang-manting to run headlong.

montase (*D*) **1** assembly; → RAKITAN. – *mobil* automobile assembly. **2** montage.

monté → MOTÉ.

montéring (*mil*) uniform.

montir (*D*) **1** mechanic. **2** fitter. **3** to make repairs, repair things.

montit (*Jv*) plantation railway.

montok (*J/Jv*) **1** plump; → SINTAL, SINTAR I. **2** large and shapely (of a woman's breasts). – *banget!* really stacked!
  semontok as plump/big as.
  memontok to be(come) plump, well built, etc.
  kemontokan shapeliness.

montong (*S*) auxiliary word used for prohibiting and dissuading: it is not necessary to, don't.

montor → MOTOR.

montur (*D*) frame, setting, mounting.

monumén (*D/E*) monument. – *alam* natural landmark. – *Gajahmada* the Gajahmada Monument at Police Headquarters in Jakarta. – *Nasional* [Monas] the National Monument in Jakarta. – *Pancasila Sakti* the Sacred Pancasila Monument at Lubang Buaya where the seven heroes of the revolution were kidnapped and killed in 1965.

monuméntal (*D*) monumental.

monyét 1 monkey. **2** ape. **3** a term of playful contempt. **4** a term of abuse. *baju* – a male infant's suit (of joined coat and trousers). *cinta* – puppy love. *kandang* – (*J*) sentry box. *rumah* – sentry box. *kera menjadi* – it is six of one and half a dozen of the other. – *keluar dari lengan baju* then he showed the cloven hoof.

monyong (*J/Jv*) **1** muzzle, beak, spout, snout. – *dowér* protruding mouth. **2** a somewhat offensive term of address but may be used jokingly between male friends.
  memonyongkan to stick out (the lips and mouth).

monyos (*ob*) (very) bashful.

mop → APRIL *mop*.

mopéd (*E?*) moped.

mopela → MAFELA.

mopit (*C*) k.o. pencil (used for writing Chinese characters).

mo-pitu (*Jv*) = *molimo* plus gluttony and false witness.

mor (in acronyms) → BERMOTOR.

morak-marik → MORAT-MARIT.

moral (*D*) moral.
  bermoral moral.

moralisasi (*D*) moralization.

morat-marit messy, scattered around, confused, disorganized. *hidup* – to lead a precarious existence.

moré (in Irian Jaya) woman's loin cloth.

moréng mottle; → CORÉNG *moréng*.

morés a fabric; → MURIS I.

morfém (*D ling*) morpheme.

morfin (*D/E*) morphine.

morfinis (*D*) morphine/drug addict.

morfologi (*D/E ling*) morphology.

mori white cambric, i.e., a basic material for making batik.

moril (*D*) moral. *bantuan* – moral support. *Rusak -nya* He is demoralized.

moorkop (*D*) /morkop/ chocolate éclair.

Mormon (*D*) Mormon.

morong I → MURUNG.

morong II can (kettle) for boiling tea water.

morotin → POROT.

morpin → MORFIN.

morpinis → MORFINIS.

mortalitas and mortalitét (D) mortality; → ANGKA *kematian.*

mortél (D) mortar (for building purposes).

mortir (D) mortar (a short-barreled gun).

mosa (S) in folk belief a large, long-living eel which can be invaded by spirits.

mosaik (D/E) mosaic.

mosalaki (in Ende, East Nusa Tenggara) ethnic/*adat* chief.

Mosambik (D) Mozambique.

mosao a Manadonese war dance.

mosi (D) motion, vote. – *kepercayaan* vote of confidence. – *tidak percaya* vote of no confidence.

mosin (*sl*) crazy.

Moskou and Moskwa Moscow.

mosok (*Jv*) → MASA II.

mosoléum (D) mausoleum.

mostard and moster I (D) mustard. – *basah* prepared mustard.

moster II → MONSTER II.

mota (*Hind*) 1 purple nutsedge, flowering sedge with medicinal tubers, *Cyperus rotundus.* 2 *kain* – canvas. *balé-balé* – canvas cot.

motcin [*motor cina*] Chinese car.

moté (*Jv*) coral bead.

motékar (S) dynamic, inventive.

motél (D/E) motel.

motif I (D) motive, object, aim.

   bermotif to have a motive, be motivated. ~ *politik* politically motivated.

   bermotifkan ... with ... as its motive, motivated by ...

motif II (D) motif, design.

   bermotif to have a ... motif.

motip → MOTIF I, II.

motivasi (D) motivation.

   bermotivasikan to be motivated by.

   memotivasi to motivate.

   termotivasikan motivated.

   pemotivasian motivation, motivating.

motivator (D/E) motivator.

moto I (D) motto.

moto II → AJI-NO-MOTO.

motokar (*Mal*) (motor)car, automobile.

   bermotokar 1 to have a car. 2 to travel by car.

motong → POTONG.

motor (D) 1 motor, engine. – *2 tak* a two-stroke engine. 2 motorcycle, scooter. 3 (motor)car, automobile. 4 the impetus behind s.t., motivating force. – *air* (in Jambi) speedboat. – *bakar* internal combustion engine. – *balap* speedboat. (*sepéda*) – *bébék* → SEPÉDA *motor bébék.* – *duduk* inboard motor (of boat). – *gandéng* motorcycle and sidecar. – *kéték* motorized prau. – *pompa* fire engine. – *sangkut* outboard motor. – *tambang* (in West Kalimantan) a barge used for passengers and freight. – *témpél* outboard motor (of boat).

   bermotor 1 motorized. 2 to go by car; → BERMOBIL.

   memotori 1 to be the motivating/driving force behind s.t., motivate, drive. 2 to motor on, go by car on. 3 to provide s.o. with a car.

motorbot (E) motorboat.

motoris (D) 1 motorist. 2 engineer, motorman.

motorisasi (D) motorization.

   memotorisasikan to motorize.

motorkap convertible roof (of car).

motorpit (D) motorcycle.

motosikal (E *Mal*) motorcycle.

motto (D/E) motto.

moyang 1 great-grandparents. 2 ancestor, predecessor. – *asal* common ancestor.

   bermoyang to have ... as one's ancestor.

mozah → MOJAH.

mp- also see entries beginning with emp-.

mpet (*J*) annoyed, irritated.

mpét-mpétan (*J*) 1 paper cone. 2 whistling balloon.

mpok (*J*) 1 (older) sister. 2 title of address for older women; *cp* BIBI.

mpot → EMPOT II.

MPP [Masa Persiapan Pénsiun] Retirement Preparation Period.

me-MPP-kan to retire s.o.

MPR (*init*) [Majelis Permusyawaratan Rakyat] People's Consultative Assembly.

MPS [(Sistim) (Menghitung, Menetapkan dan) Menyetor Pajak Sendiri] Self-Assessment (System) (in taxation).

mpu (*Jv*) 1 master craftsman; → EMPU I. 2 armorer. 3 term of address for those who have attained high distinction in literature, philosophy, etc. 4 honorary degree (once) conferred by the Universitas Nasional when a professor reached the age of 60.

mracang (*Jv*) *pedagang* – retailer in seasonings/flavorings, such as salt, etc.

mrengkal (*Jv*) to stick to s.t. stubbornly.

mrétéli → MEM(P)RÉTÉLI.

mrongos (*Jv*) with teeth that are too large and protruding so that the mouth cannot be closed; → MERONGOS.

MRP [Majelis Rakyat Papua] Papuan People's Council.

MS [Magister Sains] Master of Science, M.S(c).

MTQ(N) [Mushabaqah Tilawatil Qur'an (Nasional)] (National) Koran-Reading Contest.

mua I (*C J*) *ikan* – eel, *Apodes spp.*

mua II spoiled, poorly behaved.

muaci (C) pastry filled with fried sesame.

muadin → MODIN.

muafakat → MUPAKAT.

muafik (A) → MAKMUM *muafik.*

muahal very expensive; → MAHAL.

muai 1 to rise (of dough, paste), swell (of boiled rice grains). 2 to spread, expand. *daya* – expansive power. 3 to ferment. 4 expansion. – *panjang* linear expansion.

   memuai to rise, expand, swell up.

   pemuai expander, expansion. *sambungan* ~ expansion joint.

   pemuaian expansion (of heated metals, etc.).

   permuaian fermenting, brewing.

muak 1 to be fed up, have enough of s.t., be bored; → JEMU. 2 nauseated, sick, wanting to vomit, feel queasy. 3 to feel sick (on hearing s.t.).

   muak-muak *tiada* ~ to keep on (promising without delivering).

   memuakkan 1 to sicken, disgust, nauseate, bore. 2 loathsome, disgusting, nauseating, repugnant, boring, tiresome.

   kemuakan nausea.

mual 1 queasy. 2 to loathe s.t. 3 to vomit. 4 to feel nauseated/ squeamish/revolted.

   memualkan 1 to sicken, disgust, nauseate, bore. 2 sickening, loathsome, disgusting.

   kemualan disgust, loathing, repugnance.

mualaf I (A) convert (to Islam).

mualaf II (A) published (of a book).

mualap → MUALAF I.

mualamat (A) science.

mualim (A) 1 (religious) teacher. 2 pilot (of a ship), steersman. 3 (– *kapal*) mate, deck officer. – *Pelayaran Besar* [MPB] Deck Officer with Ocean License. – *Pelayaran Indonésia* [MPI] Deck Officer with Local Trade License. – *Satu* Chief/First Officer/Mate (on board a ship).

mualamah and mualamat (A) social intercourse/life, association (with others).

mualip (A) writer.

muallafien (A) foreigner.

Muangthai Thailand.

muara 1 estuary, mouth (of a river). *hidup dua* – to wear two hats. 2 outcome. 3 opening, orifice.

   bermuara 1 ~ *ke* to empty/flow (into). 2 ~ *pada* to lead up (to), end up by, result in.

   memuarakan to empty s.t. (into s.t.).

muarikh → MUWARIKH.

muas (*ob*) dissolved, fused, melted.

muasal (A) = *asal.*– from of old, from ancient/remote times; the origin, beginning. – *bertebarnya keturunan Cina* the beginning of the spread of the Chinese.

Mua(s)sasah (A) the Saudi Arabian Council, which takes charge of pilgrims bound for Mecca.

muat 1 (able) to contain, have (s.t. in it). *Suratkabar ini* – *banyak*

iklan mini. This newspaper has a lot of classified ads. **2** to hold, accommodate (people or furniture in a room, etc.). *Mobil sport itu – hanya dua orang.* This sports car only holds two people. *Ruang itu – tiga puluh orang.* That room accommodates thirty people. **3** to include. **4** to insert, place (an ad in a newspaper, etc.). *– ulang* reprinting. **memuat-ulang** to reprint.
bermuat 1 to contain, be loaded with. *Lori itu ~ tebu.* The truck is loaded with sugarcane. **2** to have/with ... as cargo. *kapal ~ minyak* a ship with a cargo of oil. **3** to be charged with. *besi yang ~ listrik* iron charged with electricity.
memuat 1 to hold, contain. **2** to accommodate, be able to hold. **3** to load (a ship). **4** to carry (a news item).
memuati [and **muatin** (*J coq*)] **1** to fill (a container). *Peti itu dimuatinya dengan barang-barang gelap.* He filled that chest with contraband. **2** to load (a vessel). *~ perahu* to load a prau.
memuatkan 1 to load s.t. (into). **2** to insert, place (in a newspaper). *~ adperténsi di suratkabar* to place an ad in a newspaper.
termuat *~ dalam/di* contained/placed in. *berita yang ~ dalam/ di suratkabar* the news (contained) in the newspaper.
muatan 1 cargo. *Ékspedisi ~ Kapal Laut* [EMKL] Oceangoing Cargo Forwarders. *~ guna* payload. *~ kapal* cargo. *~ udara* air cargo. *~ umum* general cargo. **2** load, contents. *sarat ~* fully loaded. *~ curah* break-bulk. **3** capacity. **4** charge. **bermuatan 1** loaded. *~ penuh* fully loaded. **2** to carry (a load of), be loaded with. **3** to be charged with (electricity).
pemuatan loading, shipment. *~ barang* cargo loading. *~ penumpang* embarkation.
permuatan load, shipment.
muazam (*A*) great, exalted (of rulers).
muazin (*A*) the caller to prayer; → MODIN.
mubad(z)ir → MUBAZIR.
mubah (*A*) s.t. allowed by religion, but not considered meritorious; neither good nor bad.
mubahalah (*A*) an oath taken by two parties who differ in opinion asking God to curse the one who is lying; malediction.
mubalig(h) (*A*) preacher, local religious teacher who actively teaches Islam to adults by giving lectures in offices.
mubalighat (*A*) female preacher.
muballigh → MUBALIG(H).
mubarak (*A*) blessed. *Id –!* Happy Id; → ID.
mubarat (*A*) divorce at the wife's request (dowry not returnable).
mubasir (*coq*) and **mubazir** (*A*) **1** redundant, extravagant, overly generous. **2** to waste.
    memubasirkan to waste.
    kemubasiran 1 a waste. **2** redundancy.
mubasyir (*A*) announcer.
mubaya'ah (*A*) homage.
mubéng trypanosomiasis.
mubtadi (*A*) beginner, novice.
mubut fragile, weak, brittle.
    memubutkan to grind, crush, pound.
mucah (*Pers*) eyelash.
mucikari → MUNCIKARI.
mud (in acronyms) → MUDA.
muda 1 young (in age). *mati –* to die young. *(ber)main –* to run after the girls; to be unfaithful to one's wife. *kaum –* the younger generation. *orang –* a young man. *orang-orang –* youth, young people, the younger generation. *– belia* in the prime of life, youthful. *– léla* young and beautiful. *– mentah* a) very young, early/tender (of years/verdure). b) inexperienced. *– mudi* youth, young people. *– remaja* to be in the bloom of youth, be at that awkward age. *– teruna* youthful (and still unmarried). **2** unripe, green (of fruit). *mangga –* a green, unripe mango. *tulang –* cartilage. **3** light, pale (of color). *(e)mas –* gold of a low alloy (less than 18 carats). *mérah –* light red, pink. **4** deputy, junior, vice-. *Menteri –* [Ménmud] Vice-Minister, Deputy Secretary. **5** young, new, of recent origin. *negara yang masih –* a young country.
    semuda as young as.
    bermuda (*M*) to commit adultery, have an extramarital affair. *~ diri* to take a new wife (or, concubine) again.
    bermuda-muda to enjoy o.s. like a young person, behave like a young person.

memudakan to make o.s. appear younger, rejuvenate.
mempermuda to make younger.
termuda the youngest.
kemudaan 1 youth. **2** early age.
kemuda-mudaan youthful behavior.
pemuda 1 youth, young man. **2** chap, lad. *~ belasan tahun* a teenage boy. *~ gagal sekolah* a (school) dropout. *~ Peuyeum* "Yeast-Sweetened Cassava-Bun Youth," i.e., the derogatory epithet given to the youth of Bandung when they made an unsuccessful stand against the Japanese in 1945. *~ putus-sekolah* a (school) dropout. *~ Rakyat* People's Youth, i.e., the youth arm of the now banned Communist Party of Indonesia. *~ tanggung* teenager, adolescent. *~ teruna* adolescent. *~ tempé* a good-for-nothing kid. *~ pemudi* young people; → MUDI II. **kepemudaan** youth (*mod*).
pemudaan making young, rejuvenating. *~ kembali* rejuvenation.
permudaan regeneration. *~ alam* natural regeneration. *~ kembali* rejuvenation.
mudah I 1 easy, simple. *– bergaul* easy to get along with. *– berteman* congenial, makes friends easily. *– dibujuk* susceptible to flattery. *– busuk* spoils easily, perishable. **kemudah-busukan** perishability. *– dicapai* accessible. *– dicari* easy to find (in stores, etc.). *– didapat* readily available, easy to get. *– di mulut* easily said. *– diserang* vulnerable to attack. *– kena* susceptible (to disease), vulnerable. *– lupa* forgetful. *– meledak/meletup* explosive. *– menerima* receptive. *– (me)nyala* inflammable. *– pecah/retak* fragile. *– rusak* perishable. *– saja* nothing could be easier. *– sakit* gets sick easily. *– terbakar* flammable. *– terkena* → MUDAH *kena. – tersinggung* easily offended. **2** hasty, rash, thoughtless. **3** (*coq*) light, frivolous, flippant, without morals. *perempuan yang – an* easy woman. **4** easygoing, gets along with people.
mudahnya *untuk ~* for convenience's sake.
semudah as easy/simple as. *~ berdiang* nothing could be simpler. *tidak ~ membalik tangan* it's not all that easy.
bermudah-mudah(an) to take things easy, take casually/lightly. *Jangan ~ menghadapi masalah itu.* Don't take things for granted in facing this problem.
memudahan [and **ngemudahin** (*J coq*)] **1** to simplify, facilitate, ease. *untuk ~* for convenience('s sake), for (the sake of) convenience, as a matter of convenience. **2** (= **mempermudah**) to make easy, make easier, facilitate. **3** (= **mempermudahkan**) to consider easy/unimportant/valueless, etc., belittle, take s.t. lightly.
termudah the easiest/simplist.
mudah-mudahan *bukan ~* it's not a trifle/nothing.
kemudahan 1 ease. *~ hubungan* accessibility. *~ masuk* accessibility, ease of entrance. *~ tersedianya krédit* ease with which credit is made available. **2** amenities, facilities, convenience(s). *~ rékréasi* recreational facilities. *untuk ~ saya* for my convenience. **3** rashness.
pemudah 1 person who likes simplicity. **2** easygoing person. *~ hidup* convenience.
pemudahan *~ dalam tindak pidana* (*leg*) obstructing justice.
mudah II mudah-mudahan 1 one hopes that, it is to be hoped that, hopefully, may! *~ kita dapat bertemu lagi kelak.* Let's hope we meet again soon. **2** in the hopes that. *Ia belajar sungguh-sungguh, ~ dapat maju di ujian penghabisan ini.* He is studying hard in the hopes that he can pass this final examination. **3** (at the end of a sentence) amen, may it happen, hopefully.
mudai (*A*) plaintiff.
mudaraba (*A*) k.o. Islamic banking in which one partner (the *rabb al-mal*) provides the capital and the other (the *mudarib*) manages the enterprise. Profits and losses are shared in an agreed ratio with no predefined rate of return.
mudarat and **mudharat** (*A*) **1** disadvantage, detriment, drawback, damage, injury, harm, loss (in business); → MADARAT. **2** failure; not successful/profitable, to have a run of bad luck. **3** to fail, take a loss. **4** harmful, dangerous, useless. *memberi –* to damage, harm, do harm to. *– dan manfaatnya* a) advantages and disadvantages, profit and loss. b) pros and cons. c) joys and sorrows.
kemudaratan disadvantage, drawback, detriment, injury, harm.
mudarib (*A*) the manager of an enterprise; → MUDARABA.

mudarsah (*A*) public lecture.

mudasir (*A*) *dasar* – that's part of his nature/character.

mud(d)at → MADAH II.

mudharabah → MUDARABA.

mudharib (*A*) entrepreneur, user of the capital (in an Islamic loan transaction); → MUDARIB.

mudharobah → MUDARABA.

mud(d)athir (*A*) *al*– "The Enfolded"; name of the 74th chapter of the Koran.

mudeng (*Jv*) to understand.

mudi I *juru* – helmsman, quartermaster.

    kemudi steering wheel. **berkemudi** ~ *di haluan* to be under the thumb of, be henpecked. **mengemudikan 1** to command. *tidak dapat dikemudikan* not under command. **2** to drive, steer. **pengemudian** driving.

mudi II *muda* – a) young men and women. b) a new Indonesian-style form of social dancing.

    pemudi young girl/woman. ~ *belasan tahun* teenage girl. ~ *teruna* adolescent girl.

mudigah (*A*) embryo, fetus.

mudik 1 (to go) upstream, (go) upcountry. **2** (*Jv*) to go back/ home to one's native village, hometown, or country; to repatriate, go back to one's native village at *Lebaran*.

    semudik *sehilir* ~ in agreement.

    memudiki to sail upstream on. ~ *sungai* to go up the river.

    memudikkan to sail (a prau) upstream, navigate (a boat) upstream.

    pemudik s.o. who is going home to his native village, particularly to celebrate *Lebaran* with his family.

mudin → MODIN.

mudlarat → MUDARAT.

mudraj (*A*) gloss.

mudun I (*A*) **bermudun** cultured, civilized; → TAMADUN.

mudun II (*J/Jv*) to come down. **2** to slope downward (of a road).

mudun-leumah (*S*) a joint (religious) meal held when a child is seven months old.

Mudzalifah (*A*) a place on the *hajj* where one collects rocks for the stoning at *Mina*.

mudzarakah → MUZARA'AH.

mudzarat → MELARAT I.

mufaham (*A*) to understand; → PAHAM.

mufakat → MUPAKAT.

mufakham (*A*) emphatic.

mufarik (*A*) separated, disentangled.

mufasal (*A*) separated, detailed, detached, particularized.

mufasir (*A*) commentator (*esp* of the Koran).

mufid (*A*) profitable.

muflis (*A*) bankrupt.

    kemuflisan bankruptcy.

muflisi (*A*) insolvency.

mufrad (*A*) singular, one.

mufti (*A*) Muslim consultant jurist.

mughayat (*A*) supreme (in titles).

muhabah and **muhabat** (*A*) love, affection. *utusan* – goodwill mission; → *misi* MUHIBAH.

muhadis (*A*) a specialist in the *hadis*.

muhajat (*A*) dispute, quarrel, misunderstanding.

muhajir (*A*) **1** term used for the people who fled with the Prophet Muhammad to Medinah. **2** exile, fugitive.

muhajirin (*A*) **1** the plural of *muhajir*. **2** immigrants.

muhal (*A*) **1** impossible, unbelievable, out of the question. **2** absurd. **kemuhalan 1** impossibility. **2** absurdity.

muhallil (*A*) man who marries a divorced wife in order to make it lawful for her to remarry her former husband (if they want to); → CINABUTA.

muhami (*A*) lawyer.

Muhammad 1 the Prophet Muhammad. **2** name of the 47th chapter of the Koran.

Muhammadiyah → MOHAMMADIYAH.

muharaf (*A*) corrupt.

Muharam (*A*) the first month of the Muslim year.

muhasabah and **muhasabat** (*A*) introspection; to account for one's emotions and thoughts on a daily basis (a duty of the mystic).

muhib (*A*) lover.

muhibah and **muhibat** (*A*) **1** sympathy. **2** goodwill. *misi* – goodwill mission.

    bermuhibah to go/be on a goodwill mission.

muhit (*A*) *al*– the All-Embracing (God). *laut* – the ocean surrounding the world.

muhkamat (*A*) of clear and established meaning (of verses of the Koran).

muhrim (*A*) those who are forbidden to marry because they are too closely related but are allowed to associate with e.o., close relatives.

    kemuhriman having that relationship.

muhsan (*A*) married man.

muhsanah (*A*) married woman.

muhsin (*A*) virtuous, honest, pure.

muhsinat (*A*) a pure and honest woman.

muhtadar (*A*) dying.

muhtamil (*A*) probably.

muhtasyam (*A*) **1** highly respected, dignified, reverend. **2** sublime, majestic, august.

muhtasyim (*A*) bashful, shy.

muhun → MOHON.

muih → KUIH *muih*.

mujadid (*A*) reformist. – *agama* religious reformer.

Mujadilah (*A*) *al*– "The Disputant"; name of the 58th chapter of the Koran.

mujahadah and **mujahadat** (*A*) **1** struggle for Islam, holy war. **2** a mystic's war against his passions.

mujahid (*A*) warrior who fights for Islam.

mujahidin (*A*) the plural of *mujahid*.

mujaib [*mujarab dan ajaib*] effective and wonderful (of medicine).

mujair I cichlid fish, *Tilapia mossambica*.

mujair II (in moonlighter's jargon) small, minor, less lucrative.

mujalah → MAJALAH.

mujamal (*A*) summarized.

mujang (*Jv*) slave, servant; → BUJANG I 6.

mujanasah (*A*) category.

mujarab (*A*) efficacious, effective (of medicine), tested.

    kemujaraban efficiency, effectiveness.

mujarabat (*A*) remedy.

mujarad (*A*) abstract, stripped down. *hati* – the naked heart of the mystic who thinks only of God.

    pemujaradan abstraction.

mujarap → MUJARAB.

mujari (*M*) k.o. plant whose leaves are very fragrant and which are chewed as betel.

mujidat → MUKJIZAT.

mujir (*A*) the lessor in an *ijarah* transaction.

mu'jizat → MUKJIZAT.

mujtahid (*A*) Muslim legal specialist, founder of a school of religious law; the *ulama* of the *Shi'a*.

mujtamak (*A*) society, community.

mujur 1 fortunate, lucky, in luck. *kalau sedang* – as luck would have it. *malang* – at random, haphazardly. **2** luck. **3** straight, not askew. – *tidak dapat diraih* luck is not thrown into one's lap.

    kemujuran luck.

    pemujur a lucky person.

muk (*J*) cup.

muka (*Skr*) **1** front (side). *di* – a) in advance. *membayar di* – to pay in advance/up front. b) ahead. *jauh di* – far ahead. c) front (part of a contract). d) before (the court). *di* – *pintu* at/in front of the door. *di* – *puasa* just before the fast. *di* – *umum/orang ramai* in public, publicly. *di* – *sekali* right in front. *dari* – from the front, frontally. *ke* – to the front, (move) forward, advance. **mengemuka** to come up, come to the fore, appear. **mengemukakan 1** to suggest, offer, propose, put/bring forward. **2** to utter, express. **3** to confront s.o. ~ *diri* to thrust o.s. forward. **terkemuka** prominent. *orang yang* ~ prominent person/people. **pengemukaan** the act of bringing forward/suggesting, etc. *sejak sekarang ke* – from now on, henceforth. *lain di* –, *lain di belakang* hypocritical. *kulit* – front page (of a book). *uang* – advance/down payment. **2** face, countenance. *air* – facial expression. *beralih* – to look away from, disregard. *berjumpa/bertemu* – to see e.o., run into e.o., come across e.o. *berminyak –nya* happy, contented. *kehilangan* – to lose face. *memberi/kasi* – to be indulgent. *membuang* – to look away from, disregard. *membuang – kepada orang tua* to disregard one's parents. *membuat* – to get praise/appreciation. *menarik* – to turn the face away. *mencari* – to be in favor with s.o. *mengambil* – to be in favor with s.o., flatter, coax, cajole, wheedle. *mengangkat* – to look up (in wonder). *menjual* – to show off; → MENJUAL *tampang. menyembunyikan* – to hide one's face. *Mérah padam –nya.* He was furious. *merasa –nya tebal* to lose one's prestige. *meratakan* – to level. *perataan* – leveling. *perbédaan* – difference in levels. *raut* – (facial) features. *(waktu) samar* – late twilight or early daybreak. *tarik – dua belas* very disappointed; to put on an unhappy face. *terpecah peluh di* – very embarrassed. *tunjuk* – to show o.s. (in order to pay one's respects to s.o.). 3 page (in a book). 4 aspect, facet. 5 facade, front. *– rumah* house facade. 6 next. *bulan/minggu* – next month/week. 7 heads (of a flipped coin). 8 (*Mal*) page. *buruk – cermin dibelah* to blame s.o. else for one's mistakes. *– licin, ékor penuh kudis* looks rich but is in debt. *– nak naik kepala* "the face wants to meet the top of the head," i.e., an absurd idea. *– air* water surface/level. *– badak* shameless, brazen. **bermuka badak** to be shameless, brazen. *– ban* tread (of a tire). *– bantal* embroidered end of a pillow. *– batu* a blank face. *– berkerut* showing signs of anger. *– bujur* an oval face. *– bumi* earth's surface. *– disapu arang* "a face smeared with charcoal," i.e., grossly insulted. *– dua* hypocrisy. **bermuka dua** hypocritical, double crossing. *– kecut* a sour face. *– laut* sea level. *– manis* a pleasant face. **bermuka manis** to be friendly. *– masam* a sour face. *– papan* a) face of a board. b) brazen-faced, impudent, shameless, audacious. **bermuka papan** to be shameless. *– polos* an innocent expression (on one's face), (with) a straight face. *– rata* flush (up against). *– sengkalan* unashamed. *– tebal* and *tebal* – unashamed. *dengan –nya tebal* bare-faced, impudent, shameless. *– tembam* a puffy face. *– témbok* → MUKA *papan.*

muka-muka 1 sanctimonious, hypocritical. 2 superficial friendship. *bukan ~* sincere, not false.

semuka confronting. **bersemuka** 1 vis-à-vis, face-to-face, privately. *komunikasi ~* face-to-face communication. 2 opposed (to), confronted (with). **menyemukakan** to confront.

bermuka ... to have ... as its face/front/surface, etc. *tidak ~* embarrassed, shy. *~ asam* sullen, grouchy. *~ dinding/kayu/papan/tebal/témbok* to be impudent, insolent.

bermuka-muka 1 to pretend, feign. 2 face to face. 3 frank, sincere, outspoken, (to tell s.o.) to his face. 4 hypocritical, sanctimonious.

termuka responsible party, guarantor.

pemuka 1 leader, leading/important figure, promoter. *~ masyarakat* community leader. 2 foreman (in charge of a group of prisoners). 3 (Christian) pastor.

permukaan 1 surface. *di ~* on the surface, superficially. *yang ~nya terbuat dari* ... surfaced with ... *~ air* water surface. *~ air laut rata-rata* mean sea level, m.s.l. *di bawah ~ air sewaktu surut* lowest water standard, LWS. *~ bumi* earth's surface. *~ jalan* (road) surface. *~ laut* sea level. 2 face.

mukabalah (*A*) contrast; comparison.
mukadam (*A*) first, leading.
mukadamah → MUKADIMAH.
mukadas (*A*) holy, sacred, consecrated; → BAITULMUKADAS.
mukad(d)imah and **mukad(d)imat** (*A*) introduction, preface.
mukadin (*A*) assistant to the *imam.*
mukadis (*A*) holy, sanctified.
mukah 1 fornication, adultery; → ZINA. 2 illicit lover (of either sex).
   bermukah 1 to fornicate, commit adultery. 2 to have an illicit affair.
   pemukah fornicator, adulterer.
   permukahan fornication.
mukalaf and **mukalap** (*A*) adult, of age.
mukara (*A*) a section of the Koran.
mukaram (*A*) revered (of rulers).
mukasyafah (*A*) revelation.
mukatabah (*A*) contract, contractual liberation of a slave.

mukena(h) the white veil worn by women when performing the *salat.*
muker [*musyawarah kerja*] working meeting.
mukhabarat (*A*) intelligence.
mukhalaf (*A*) heresy.
mukhalafah (*A*) contravention, transgression, infringement; opposition, resistance.
mukhlis (*A*) sincere.
mukhrim → MUHRIM.
mukhtasar (*A*) outline, summary, résumé. précis, condensation.
mukhtasyam → MUHTASYAM.
mukibat a large type of cassava and by extension anything larger than ordinary.
mukim (*A*) 1 to stay/live somewhere (*esp* in Mecca, for longer than the normal period needed for a *hajj*) for study or other purposes. 2 permanent resident. 3 residence, abode, home, dwelling. 4 parish, area served by a mosque. 5 territorial subdivision for administrative purposes. 6 (in Aceh) administrative unit one step higher than a *désa.*
   bermukim 1 to reside, live, stay, be established. 2 to take up one's station, encamp (of army troops).
   memukimi to stay at, live in, reside at.
   memukimkan to settle, put (people as residents in an area). *~ sekitar 5.000 pengungsi* they settled about 5,000 refugees (in the area). *~ kembali* to resettle (transmigrants).
   pemukim settler.
   pemukiman 1 settlement. *tempat ~* settlement. *~ kembali* resettlement. *~ perkotaan* urban settlement. 2 habitat.
   permukiman 1 residence, living place, residential area. 2 residential (*mod*).
mukimat (*A*) female resident of a *pesantrén.*
mukimin (*A*) 1 inhabitants, residents. 2 male resident of a *pesantrén.*
mukin → MUNGKIN.
mukir → MUNGKIR.
mukjijat and **mukjizat** (*A*) miracle.
   bermukjizat miraculous.
mukmin(in) (*A*) the faithful, devout (of Muslims).
mukosa (*D*) mucous membrane.
muksa and **mukso** (*Jv*) to disappear in a mysterious way, cease living by vanishing in body and soul rather than by dying.
   kemuksaan *jagad ~* heaven.
muksir (*A*) impoverished.
muktabar (*A*) honored, respected.
muktabis (*A*) person who quotes.
muktadi (*A*) follower.
muktamad (*A*) 1 (person) who can be trusted, is reliable. 2 final (of a decision/measure taken, etc.), peremptory, conclusive; → TUNTAS.
muktamar (*A*) congress, conference.
muktamirin (*A*) conferees.
mutashabihat (*A*) of allegorical meaning (of verses in the Koran).
muktazilah (*A*) heresy.
mukti (*A*) to be well off.
mukun a bowl/cup with a lid.
mula (*Skr*) (= *asal* –) origin, beginning, start; first. *pada –nya* originally, at first. *– pertama* (to see/do, etc.) for the first time. *dari* – from the beginning/start/outset. *dari – hingga akhirnya* from beginning to end/start to finish. *huruf* – initial letter. *dari kecil* – from (one's) childhood. *– pertama* the very beginning.
mula-mula 1 (= *mula-mulanya*) first of all, (at) first, at the (very) beginning, to begin with. *yang ~ mendarat di Indonésia* who first landed in Indonesia. 2 original.
semula 1 from the beginning, again. *Bacalah ~.* a) Read it from the beginning. b) Read it again, please. *dari ~* from the (very) beginning/start, all along. 2 since (the time that) *dari ~ jadi/lahir* and *sejak ~* since birth, from childhood; inherited, hereditary. *dari ~ insaf* from the moment that he/she became conscious. 3 in the beginning, at first/the outset. 4 (again as) before/formerly, as it was at first. *balik/kembali ~* as before again. *tetap sebagai ~* still like before. *badannya pulang ~, kebuatannya telah timbul sebagai ~* and *séhat kembali sebagai ~* to regain one's health and fitness. **semulanya** 1 original,

initial, first. **2** at first, initially. **menyemulakan** to start from … again.

bermula 1 to have a beginning. **2** to begin, start, commence. *gaji* ~ beginning/initial salary. **3** (= **bermula-mula**) first, for the first time. *Beliaulah yang ~ mendirikan sekolah kebangsaan.* It was he who first set up a national school. **4** originally, in the beginning. **5** (= **sebermula**) to begin with, at the beginning (an opening phrase used in Malay classical literature).

memulai 1 to begin, start, commence. **2** to open (an assembly/meeting). **3** from, since, as of. **4** → MULAI.

memulakan 1 to commence, begin, start to do s.t., originate, do from the start, allow to start/begin. **2** to cause, bring about, occasion. **3** to have … begun.

pemula 1 beginner, novice, tyro, apprentice, originator. **2** Cub Scout. **3** starter (any device used to start s.t.).

permulaan 1 beginning, start, onset, the first part (of a speech), opening (of a letter). *dari ~ sampai akhir* from start to finish. ~ *kalam/kata* preface, foreword. **2** flag-fall. **3** early (in a time period). ~ *tahun ini* early this year.

mulai 1 → MEMULAI. to begin/start – *berjalan* to begin walking. – *bekerja* to start work(ing). – *berkuasa* to assume control. – *berlaku* to go into effect, come into force. – *sembuh* to be getting better, recuperate. **2** from the beginning, from, as of. *dari – itu* (*coq*) from that time on, from then (on). – *dari baris pertama* from the first line. – *hari ini* as of today; → MULA. – *tanggal 1 sampai tanggal …* from the first to the … – *dengan …* beginning with …

mulajadi (*mostly Mal*) origin, original.

mulakat (*A*) meeting, encounter, gathering.

mulas 1 – *perut* colic, upset stomach; *cp* PULAS II. **2** *daun* – plant name, *Desmondium triflorum*; makes good fodder and the leaves are used for medicinal purposes, *esp* against dysentery.

memulaskan to upset (one's stomach), cause indigestion.

mulat (*Jv*) – *sarira/sariro* to introspect. – *sariro hangroso wani* to have the will to introspect.

Mulawarman (*ob*) name of the Army division stationed in East Kalimantan.

mulbéri (*D/E*) mulberry, *Morus alba*.

mulek (*Jv*) to pervade, characterize.

mules → MULAS.

mulhid (*A*) **1** to go astray. **2** heretic, freethinker.

mulia (*Skr*) noble, sublime, lofty, honorable, illustrious, distinguished. *logam* – precious metal. *orang* – noble person. *yang* – a) respected (of commoners). b) *Yang* – His Excellency (of royalty); the Honorable, Your Honor (of judges/members of Parliament). – *biak* breed. **pemulia-biakan** breeding. ~ *ternak* animal breeding. – *raya* supreme.

semulia as noble as.

mempermulia 1 to make more exalted. **2** to honor, ennoble.

memuliakan 1 to honor, glorify, exalt, observe (a holiday). ~ *Hari Kemerdékaan* to celebrate Indonesian Independence Day (August 17). **2** to maintain, uphold (traditions). **3** to improve the breed of s.t.

mempermuliakan to honor, glorify, exalt.

termulia the noblest, etc.

kemuliaan glory, honor, grandeur, mark of distinction, magnificence, pomp.

pemulia breeder. ~ *tanaman* plant breeder.

pemuliaan breeding (to improve the stock). ~ *tebu* (sugar)cane breeding.

muliawan (*Skr neo*) **1** noble. **2** noble person.

mulih → PULIH.

Mulk (*A*) *al-* "The Kingdom"; name of the 67th chapter of the Koran.

Mulo and **MULO** [Meer Uitgebreid Lager Onderwijs] (*coq*) junior high school grades 8, 9, and 10 for Dutch and native children.

mulok [muatan lokal] local content.

mulsa (*E?*) mulch.

pemulsaan mulching.

multi- (*D/E*) multi-.

multibahasa multilingual.

kemultibahasaan multilingual (*mod*).

multibahasawan multilingual person.

multibisa can do a lot of things, jack-of-all-trades.

multifasét multifaceted.

multifungsi (*D*) multifunctional.

multijutawan multimillionaire.

multijutawati female multimillionaire.

multikompléks (*D/E*) multicomplex.

multilateral (*D/E*) multilateral.

multilingual (*D/E*) multilingual.

kemultilingualan multilingual (*mod*).

multimilyunér multimillionaire.

multinasional (*D/E*) multinational.

multipléks (*D/E*) multiplex.

multirasial (*D/E*) multiracial.

multiwajah multifaceted.

mulu (*J*) → MELULU.

Mulud (*J/Jv*) **1** anniversary. **2** the Prophet Muhammad's birthday. *bulan* – Rabiulawal, the third Muslim month.

muludan 1 *Mulud* celebration, i.e., a religious festival celebrated on Muhammad's birthday. **2** to play tambourine music to celebrate Muhammad's birthday. **3** to celebrate *Mulud*; → GAREBEK.

muluk I (*A*) kings; → MALIK.

muluk II (*J*) **1** to fly high (of pigeons/kites, etc.). **2** high-pitched (of voices), loud (of salutes). **3** (= **muluk-muluk**) bombastic, pompous, stilted, high-sounding (promises, etc.), unrealistic; magnificent, splendid, glorious.

bermuluk-muluk to dream about getting s.t. (without making any effort to).

kemulukan bombast, pomposity.

mulur 1 elastic, extendable; *cp* ULUR I. **2** to be extended (of time). *waktunya* – his hours have to be extended; he has to work overtime. – *dua bulan* extended two months. **3** flexible. **4** to creep (of trees to cover an area).

kemuluran and **pemuluran** elasticity.

mulus (*J/Jv*) **1** clean, pure, flawless, in undamaged condition. *dalam keadaan* – (in ads selling cars) in good running condition. **2** sincere, honest. **3** immaculate. **4** smooth. *berlangsung* – to proceed/run smoothly/without a hitch. **5** soft. *pendaratan* – soft landing. *putih* – soft white.

semulus as smooth/sincere, etc. as.

memuluskan and **mempermulus** to make s.t. run smoothly.

termulus perfect, flawless.

kemulusan perfection, flawlessness.

pemulusan smoothing, making s.t. run smoothly.

mulut 1 mouth (of persons/animals/birds/fishes/bottles/rivers, etc.). *kering* – after the mouth became dry (talking about s.t.), after talking and talking. **2** muzzle (of cannon/firearm). **3** opening, hole, entrance (to a cave/street, etc.). *buah* – talk, gossip, topic (of conversation). *besar* – (= **bermulut** *besar*) to like to brag. *gatal* – talkative. *lébar* – to like to brag. *rapuh* – unable to keep a secret, blabbermouth. *tutup* – close-/tight-lipped. *dari ke mulut* mouth-to-mouth. – *bau madu, pantat bawa sengat* beware of Greeks bearing gifts. *gula (di) dalam* – an easy job, a piece of cake. *hanya di* – insincere. – *disuapi pisang, pantat dikait dengan onak* (= – *manis hati berkait*) said of a two-faced person, of a person who talks out of both sides of his mouth. – *telanjur/terdorong emas tentangannya/padahannya* in for a penny, in for a pound. *murah di – mahal di timbangan* to promise a lot but deliver nothing. *karena – binasa* don't let your mouth get you into trouble; be sure brain is in gear before engaging mouth. – *manis mematahkan tulang* speak softly but carry a big stick. – *manis jangan percaya, lepas dari tangan jangan diharap* you get what you pay for; there is no free lunch. *lain di –, lain di hati* saying one thing but doing another. *lepas dari – buaya masuk ke – harimau* out of the frying pan into the fire. – *satu lidah bertopang* watch out for the geese when the fox preaches. – (*ber*)*bisa* sharp-tongued, sarcastic. – *besar* braggart. – *busuk* bad breath. – *daun* pore (of leaves). – *gang* entrance to an alley. – *gatal* talkative, verbose. – *gawang* goal mouth. – *gunung* crater. – *harimau* dangerous situation. – *jalan* road entrance. – *knalpot* muffler exhaust. – *kotor* dirty mouthed. – *kulit* pore (of the skin). – *kunci* keyhole. – *lokét* counter window. – *lunak* easy to tame. – *manis* gentle in speech. – *murai* very talkative. – *perigi* well opening. – *pukat* the opening in a seine net. – *rambang/ringan* talkative. – *sumbing* harelip. – *sumur* wellhead. – *sungai* estuary; → KUALA. – *tangki* hatch. – *terdorong* to put one's foot in one's mouth. – *usil* likes to meddle in other people's affairs.

semulut in agreement.

bermulut 1 to have a mouth/an opening. **2** to talk, chat. ~ *di* – *orang* to echo s.o.'s words. ~ *asin* s.o. who always says what is true. ~ *besar* to talk big, be a big mouth, show off. ~ *keras* to be stubborn/obstinate, like to oppose. ~ *manis* to sweet talk, speak gently.

memuluti to put one's mouth around s.t.

mulut-mulutan ~ *orang* the subject of gossip.

mulya → MULIA.

mulyawaras and **muryawaras** (*Jv*) an informal ceremony at which all lights are turned off and the gamelan plays.

mumai(yi)z (*A*) to have attained/arrived at the age of discretion/reason (seven years old).

mumbang the young, green, unripe coconut. *menanam* – to undertake a hopeless task. – *jatuh, kelapa jatuh* death keeps no calendar. *coba-coba menanam* –, *kalau tumbuh sunting (= suri, turus) negeri* slow and steady wins the race.

mumbul (*J/Jv*) to go up into the air, take off (of a balloon, etc.), rise, soar.

mumbung (*ob*) packed to overflowing, full to bursting, crammed full; piled high (of a plate/cargo, etc.).

mumet (*J/Jv*) **1** dizzy. **2** (to have a) headache. **3** confused. *tidak ambil* – (*pada*) (*coq*) doesn't give a damn about.

mumi(e) (*D*) mummy.

memumi to mummify.

mu'min → MUKMIN.

mumkin → MUNGKIN.

mumpung (*Jv*) **1** as long as (it is possible to take advantage of the opportunity), while (it is still possible); → MAMPANG. *Minumlah kopimu.* – *masih hangat!* Drink your coffee while it's still hot! – *ada kesempatan* when the opportunity arises. – *énak*, – *ono* (*Jv*) while still available, it's nice. *aji* – (*Jv*) to indulge one's fancies/whims. **2** before it is over/too late. *Pulanglah sekarang saja,* – *belum gelap.* Go home before it gets dark. **3** opportunistic.

mumpungisme opportunism.

mumpuni (*Jv*) highly skilled, professional. *yang berkualitas* – professional (*mod*).

Mumtahanah and **Mumtahinah** (*A*) *al*– "The Woman Tested"; name of the 60th chapter of the Koran.

mumuk (*M*) moldering, worn away.

mumur (*Jv*) *hancur* – smashed, shattered, crushed to bits.

mumut worn away, moldering; → MUBUT, MUMUK.

mun (*Jv*) (clipped form of *lamun*) provided that, if.

muna → MUNO.

munafik (*A*) **1** hypocrite. **2** hypocritical (in religion).

kemunafikan hypocrisy.

Munafiqun (*A*) *al*– "The Hypocrites"; name of the 63rd chapter of the Koran.

munajat (*A*) the secret communion of the mystic's soul with God in prayer; private devotions; supplication.

bermunajat to pray (to God).

munajim (*A*) **1** astrologer. **2** astronomer.

munakid (*A*) contradictory.

munang k.o. tree; → KENDAL.

munaqasah (*A*) discussion.

Munas [*Musyawarah Nasional*] National Conference/Congress.

ber-Munas to hold a national congress.

munasabah (*A*) **1** probable, possible, credible, consistent. **2** relationship, kinship. **3** similarity, agreement. **4** to fit, be suited.

munawarah (*A*) radiant.

muncah abundant, plentiful.

muncak clipped form of *kemuncak*.

muncang (*S*) candlenut, *Aleurites moluccana Wild.*

muncang-muncang to walk up and down.

muncar (*ikan* –) whale.

muncerat → MUNCRAT.

munci (*J/Jv*) **1** concubine. **2** prostitute.

muncikari (*M*) **1** madam (in a brothel). **2** pimp, procurer, procuress.

kemuncikarian pandering.

muncrat (*Jv*) **1** to spurt up/out. **2** (*vulg*) to come, have an orgasm.

memuncratkan to spray, squirt.

muncuk (*J*) sprout.

muncul (*Jv*) to emerge, appear, make an appearance, show/turn up. *Kepala negara akan* – *di TV malam ini.* The president will appear on TV tonight.

bermuncul → MUNCUL.

bermunculan (*pl subj*) to appear, take place.

memunculkan 1 to show s.t., display, make s.t. appear, bring out into the open, set (a scene at a certain time), put forward, feature. *Masukkan nilai yang ingin dimunculkan pada title bar.* Enter the value that you want to appear on the title bar. *Acara ini* ~ *seniman-seniman baru.* The show featured new artists. **2** to make s.t. come/rise to the surface.

termuncul arose, appeared suddenly.

kemunculan 1 emergence. **2** ascent.

pemunculan 1 debut. **2** appearance. **3** roll-out (of aircraft). ~ *kembali* comeback.

permunculan appearance, emergence. ~ *kembali* resurgence.

muncung 1 snout (of a dog/pig/fish, etc.). **2** beak (of bird). **3** (*Min*) mouth; → MONCONG.

muncus (*M*) ineffective, inefficacious.

mundam (*Ac? cla*) a metal bowl with a lid for water.

mundar-mandir → MONDAR-MANDIR.

munding (*S*) water buffalo. (*ber*)*turut* – to follow blindly.

mundu tree whose bark provides a dye, *Garcinia dulcis.*

munduk-munduk (*Jv*) to walk by s.o. in a stooped-over position so as not to be higher than they are.

mundur 1 to retreat, retire, withdraw, recede, back up, go backward, turn back; *opp* MAJU; → AT(E)RÉT, UNDUR. *memukul* – to repulse, repel, drive back. *menarik* – to withdraw (of troops). *pantang* –*!* never retreat! – *perlahan* (*naut*) easy aft. – *teratur* to retreat in an orderly fashion/as planned. **2** backward, unprogressive, underdeveloped (of countries). **3** to decline, decrease, deteriorate. (*bersikap*) – *maju* (constantly) vacillating, hesitating.

memundurkan [and **ngemundurin** (*J coq*)] **1** to cause to retreat/decrease, etc. **2** to set back (the clock, etc.). **3** to move/push s.t. back.

termundur 1 to back up, step back. **2** the most backward.

kemunduran 1 retreat, deterioration, decline, decrease. **2** setback. ~ *kehidupan* setback in life. **3** cutback (in production). **4** slowdown. **5** lag. ~ *kebudayaan* cultural lag.

pemunduran pulling/drawing s.t. back.

mung sound of a gong; → MUNGMUNG.

mungaré (in Ambon) young man.

munggah → PUNGGAH.

munggu(k) mound, hillock.

munggur (*Jv*) rain tree, name of a tree whose leaves and pods are used for cattle fodder, *Enterolobium Saman Prain.*

mungil (*J*) **1** nice, sweet, cute. **2** dainty.

mungkam → BUNGKAM.

mungkar I (*A*) **1** denied. **2** ignored. **3** sinful. **4** to go against God's will, disavow one's faith in God, disobey (authority).

memungkari 1 to deny, disavow, repudiate. **2** to ignore. **3** to disobey (God's word). – *mangkir* to deny repeatedly.

kemungkaran 1 denial, disavowal, refusal, repudiation, disloyalty. **2** disobedience (to God's word).

Mungkar II one of the two angels of death; → MUNKAR.

mungkeret → MUNGKRET.

mungkin (*A*) **1** possible; *cp* MENTAK. **2** could/may be, possibly. *tidak* – out of the question, impossible. *bukan tidak* – not impossible, not out of the question. **3** as ... as possible *sedapat* – as well as possible; → SEDAPAT-DAPATNYA. *selekas* – as soon as possible. – *sekali* probable.

mungkin-mungkin quite possible.

memungkinkan 1 to enable, make possible. **2** probable. *sebab yang paling* ~ a probable cause. **3** feasible.

kemungkinan 1 possibility. *termasuk* ~ not ruled out, not out of the question. *tertutup* ~ the possibility has been excluded. **2** eventuality. **3** it's possible that.

mungkir (*A*) **1** to deny, disavow, disclaim, renounce, repudiate; → INGKAR. **2** does not apply (or, is not applicable) (of a method), to produce/have no result. **3** to miss (of a gunshot). *tidak ada - nya* never misfires, reliable (of a firearm). **4** – *daripada* a) to desert, abandon, turn one's back on (a leader, etc.). b) does not adhere/stick to, does not comply with. **5** to rescind, cancel, break (one's promise). **6** to refuse to acknowledge (that one has done s.t.), deny. *Dia* ~ *mengambil uang*. He denied that he took the money. **7** to go against (a sound piece of advice), disobey (a regulation). **8** to be opposed to. *tak* – a) to come/prove true, prove correct (of a suspicion, etc.). b) working/functioning well, unfailing (of a compass, God's will). *tiada pernah* – without fail, infallibly. c) regularly, without fail. *Tidak – ia datang*. He always comes without fail. d) approved, tried, efficacious, effective (medicine).

memungkiri and **memungkirkan 1** to deny. **2** to ignore, not to pay attention to, fail to comply with. **3** to neglect/fail in one's duties, shirk (one's duties).

mungkiran denial.

pemungkir s.o. who always breaks his promises.

pemungkiran breaking (promises), neglecting.

mungkret (*Jv*) to shrink, contract; → MENGKERET, MENGKERUT.

memungkretkan to fold up (a bicycle).

mungkum 1 deep (of bowls/plates), concave. **2** convex, dome-shaped.

mungkur I (*cla*) → MONGKOR.

mungkur II → PUNGKUR.

mungmung (= **mungmungan**) crier's cymbal, a small gong.

mungpung → MUMPUNG.

mungsi wild caraway, Ajwain seed, *Carum copticum* whose fruit has medicinal qualities.

mungsing *ikan* – k.o. shark.

mungsret (*Jv*) too short.

mungut (*ob*) **1** unstable. **2** staggering (of a drunk).

munib (*ob*) widow(er).

munisi (*D*) ammunition, ammo.

munjuk – *atur* (*Jv*) to report, notify.

munjung (*J/Jv*) **1** a lot, a large quantity. **2** full to the brim, full/filled to overflowing. *nasi sepiring* – an overflowing plate of rice.

Munkar (*A*) – *wa/dan Nakir* the two angels who interrogate the deceased to determine if he/she is truly a Muslim; → NAKIR.

Mun-Mén [Muntah dan Mencrét] "vomiting and having diarrhea," i.e., gastroenteritis.

muno (*M*) to keep silent. (*sakit* –) silent and without willpower due to sorcery.

munsang → MUSANG.

munsyi (*A*) language teacher.

muntab (*S*) to seethe with rage.

muntabér [muntah dan bérak] "vomiting and defecating," i.e., gastroenteritis.

muntah 1 to vomit, throw up. – *api* (*coq*) to spit fire (of a volcano). **2** to fade, run (of colors). **3** (= **muntahan**) vomitus, vomited matter. – *bérak*; → MUNTABÉR. – *bocor* gastroenteritis. – *darah* to spit up blood.

memuntahi to vomit on.

memuntahkan to vomit up s.t., spew forth, bring up. ~ *peluru* to spit out bullets. ~ *unek-unek* to spew forth one's anger.

muntahan 1 vomitus, s.t. vomited. **2** overflow.

pemuntahan vomiting (up).

muntaha (*A*) the end, final stage (in mysticism).

muntahi (*A*) a mystic who has reached the stage where he stands in the very presence of God.

muntap (*Jv*) to pour out forcefully.

pemuntapan outpouring. ~ *unek-unek* outpouring of one's anger.

muntir → MONTIR.

muntu (*Jv*) wooden *sambal* crusher; → ULEK(-ULEK).

muntul (*J*) dull, blunt (of knives, etc.).

muntup (*J/Jv*) to appear, be visible, show up.

munyeng (*Jv*) dizzy.

mupaham (*A*) to understand.

mupakat (*A*) **1** to agree, consent, be of the same opinion, vote for (a proposal/motion, etc.). – *dengan ketuanya* to agree with the chairman. *kata* – agreement, consensus, arrangement, understanding. *dengan* – *orang tuanya* with the consent of his parents. *mengadakan kata/kebulatan* –, *membulatkan* – and *mendapat kata* – to reach/come to an complete understanding, come to terms. – *jahat* conspiracy. **2**a) discussion, deliberation, consultation. b) point of discussion, (an important) matter (still) to be discussed. **3** to discuss, deliberate, consult. **4**a) harmonious, unanimous. b) harmony, unanimity.

semupakat in agreement. *dengan* ~ a) to be in agreement. b) unanimously. **menyemupakati** to agree to (a proposal), be in agreement with, approve. **kesemupakatan** agreement.

bermupakat and *dibawa* – **1** to meet together to discuss, make an agreement, deliberate, confer, agree. **2** to plot, conspire.

memupakati to agree to (a proposal), be in agreement with, approve s.t.

memupakatkan to talk about s.t. with, discuss s.t. with; to bring into agreement, reconcile. *susah dimupakatkan* hard to reconcile. *boléh dimupakatkan* (conditions) to be agreed (up)on.

kemupakatan agreement, arrangement, consultation, discussion. ~ *jahat* conspiracy.

permupakatan 1 meeting, discussion. **2** agreement. ~ *bulat* unanimity. **3** plot, conspiracy. ~ *jahat* conspiracy, collusion.

muparik → MUFARIK.

MU PBB [Majelis Umum Perserikatan Bangsa-Bangsa] U.N. General Assembly.

mupéng (*BG*) [muka péngén] to stare.

muqaddimah → MUKAD(D)IMAH.

muqarada (*A*) k.o. Islamic bonds.

mur I (*A*) myrrh.

mur II (*D*) nut (for a bolt). – *antar* guide nut. – *baut* bolt. – *flénsa* flange nut. – *gelang* ring nut. – *jepit* locknut. – *kontra* locknut. – *kupu-kupu* wing nut. – *lawan* locknut. – *luncur* sliding nut. – *mahkota* castle nut. – *pucuk* cap nut. – *sayap* wing nut. – *selongsong* sleeve nut. – *sokét* sleeve nut. – *sungkup* cap nut. – *terpasak* locknut.

Mur III (*D*) Moor.

mura *ular* – a poisonous spitting snake, *Lachesis purpureo-maculatus*; *cp* BURA. *bertemu* – *dengan tedung* of equal strength/intelligence, etc.

murabahah (*A*) a form of Islamic banking in which the bank buys or finances the purchase of goods from a third party and sells them to a customer for a pre-agreed price to be paid back at a specified point in the future.

murad (*A*) **1** intention, aim, purpose. **2** meaning, significance.

muradif (*A*) synonym.

murah 1 cheap, inexpensive, low in price. *dijual* – to be sold for a song. **2** generous, ready to give freely. **3** plentiful, abundant. **4** easy; → MUDAH I. *Tidak* – *mengajak ia pergi*. It isn't easy to take her out. *lagi* –, *lagi menawar* (= *makin* –, *makin menawar*) give him an inch and he'll take a mile. – *dimulut mahal di timbangan* quick to promise, slow to perform. – *hati* generous (by disposition), magnanimous. *bermurah hati 1* to be generous. **2** tolerant. *kemurahan hati* generosity. – *kata* likes to talk. – *meriah* dirt cheap. – *mulut* a) affable, amiable, amicable, jovial, cordial, friendly, genial, intimate. b) informal. – *rejeki* full of luck. "*Panjang umur,* – *rejeki*" (a birthday wish) "long life and lots of luck." – *senyum* always ready to smile. – *tangan* liberal, generous (in giving), openhanded. – *tawa/tersenyum* always ready to laugh/smile.

semurah as cheap/inexpensive as.

semurah-murahnya as cheap(ly) as possible.

memurahkan to reduce/lower the price, make s.t. cheaper.

mempermurah to make s.t. cheaper.

termurah the cheapest, the least expensive.

murahan 1 of low quality. **2** (*coq*) cheaper. **3** cheap, easy, sluttish.

kemurahan 1 cheapness, inexpensiveness. **2** generosity, liberality. **3** kindness. **4** facilities. ~ *belanja* to live cheaply because of low prices.

pemurah 1 kind (and helpful), benevolent, generous. **2** a generous person.

murai various species of birds. *burung* – the magpie-robin, *Copsychus saularis*. *bunyi* – at dawn/daybreak. – *air* fork-tail. – *bakau* mangrove flycatcher shrike, *Pachycephala cinera butaloides*. – *bangau* resident paradise flycatcher, *Tersiphone paradisi affinis*. – *batu* the white-rumped shama, *Copsychus malabaricus*. – *belanda* dusky thrush, *Turdus obscurus*. – *belukar* common brown babbler, *Turdoides spp*. – *ékor gading* → MURAI *bangau*. – *gajah* fairy bluebird, *Irena puella malayensis*. – *hutan* k.o. shama, *Copsychus malabaricus mallopercnus*. – *padi* k.o. flycatcher, *Muscicapula westermanni*. – *rimba* various k.o. bulbuls and babblers, *Pycnototus spp*. – *sampah* a) common nunthrush, k.o. fulvetta, *Alcippe poiocephala cinerea*. b) great reed-warbler, *Acrocephalus arundinaceus*.

murak (*S*) to eat, consume.

murakkab (*A*) compound, composite. *jahil* – dense ignorance.

muram sad, gloomy, depressed. *cita-cita* – for ideas to become clouded over or lost sight of.
  semuram as sad/gloomy as.
  bermuram sad. ~ *durja* to look depressed/sad, with a sad expression on one's face.
  memuramkan to sadden, make sad, depress.
  kemuraman sorrow, gloom, dejection, depression.

murang (*Port cla*) fuse, match for cannon.

muraqabah (*A*) introspection.

muras → PEMURAS.

murat-marit → MORAT-MARIT.

murba (*Skr*) 1 common, plain, ordinary. *kaum* – the masses, common people, proletarians. *rakyat* – the proletariat. 2 a prole(tarian man).

murbai and **murbéi** (*D*) mulberry, *Morus alba*.

murbi (*Skr neo*) a proletarian woman.

murca (*Skr cla*) 1 swooning, fainting, unconscious. 2 to vanish in a mysterious way.

murdan → MARDAN.

muri I (*A cla*) k.o. metal flute.

muri II → MORI.

murid (*A*) 1 pupil, student. – *mogol* a (school) dropout. 2 disciple.

muring-muring (*J/Jv*) grumbling, irritable, in a bad mood.

muris I a fabric.

muris II (*J*) greedy, close-fisted, covetous.

Murjangkung (*J coq*) (the Dutch Governor General) Jan Pieterszoon Coen (1611–29).

murka I (*Skr*) 1 (*cla*) wrath (of God/ruler, etc.), anger, fury. 2 angry.
  memurkai to be angry at/with s.o.
  memurkakan to anger, make s.o. angry, infuriate.
  kemurkaan anger, fury, rage.

murka II (*angkara* –) greedy.
  kemurkaan greed.

murni (*Jv*) pure (of young women/ideals, etc.), clean, sweet, beautiful (of arts), genuine, unadulterated. *divonis bébas* – exonerated/cleared/acquitted of any wrongdoing. *tidak* – impure.
  ketidak-murnian impurity.
  semurni as pure as.
  memurnikan 1 to purify, clean. 2 to purge. 3 to refine (oil, etc.).
  termurni the purest.
  kemurnian purity, cleanliness, genuineness.
  pemurni cleanser, purifier. ~ *air* water purifier.
  pemurnian 1 cleansing, purification. 2 purge. 3 refining.

mursal I (*A*) 1 name of s.o. referred to by the Muslims as *nabi/prophet* but not further specified. 2 apostle.

mursal II (*Jv*) 1 to get out of hand/control, become unmanageable. 2 disobedient, badly behaved, recalcitrant. *orang yang* – opponent, reactionary.

mursalat (*A*) *al*– "The Emissaries"; name of the 77th chapter of the Koran.

mursid (*A*) male guide.

mursidah (*A*) female guide.

mursyid (*A*) 1 pious. 2 spiritual guide, leader, religious teacher.

murtad (*A*) apostate, renegade.
  memurtadkan to excommunicate.
  kemurtadan apostasy.
  pemurtadan conversion (to another religion).

murti (*Skr*) form; → TRIMURTI.

murung (– *hati*) dejected, gloomy, sad, depressed, in low spirits, down, in a bad mood.
  bermurung-murung depressed, down.
  kemurungan 1 melancholy, depression. 2 hypochondria.
  pemurung melancholic, person who is always depressed.

murup (*Jv*) to flame/flare up. *mérah* – fiery red.

murus (*Jv*) discharge of liquid feces, loose bowel movement.

murut → KUSUT *murut*.

murwakala (*A*) calamity preventer.

mus (in acronyms) → MUSYAWARAH.

Musa (*A*) Moses. *Jabal* – Sinai.

musadah (*A*) aid, assistance.

musabab (*A*) reasons; → SEBAB *musabab*.

musabaqah and **musabaqoh** (*A*) competition, contest. – *Tilawatul Qur'an* [MTQ] Koran Reciting Contest.

musadah (*A*) help, aid.

musafar → MUSAFIR.

musafir (*A*) 1 traveler, tourist. 2 wanderer.

musaharah (*A*) in-law.

musakah (*A*) share cropping.

musakat (*A*) trouble, torment.

musal(l)a → MUSHOLLA.

musang civet cat, polecat, *Paradoxurus spp*. – *terjun, lantai terjungkat* every thief (etc.) leaves a trace. – *berbulu ayam* a wolf in sheep's clothing. – *air* otter civet, *Cynogale bennettii*. – *akar* a small, white-whiskered species of civet cat, *Arctogale spp*. – *bulan*, *Viverricula spp*.; → RASÉ. – *dédés* → MUSANG *tenggalaung*. – *jebat/kesturi* civet cat, *Viverra zibetha*. – *keluai* various species of palm civets, *Paradoxurus*. – *pisang* Malayan weasel, *Mustela nudipes*. – *tenggalung* small Indian civet, *Viverricula malaccensis*. – *keluai* marten, *Paradoxurus spp*.; → LUAK I.

musapir → MUSAFIR.

musara (*A*) 1 salary, allowance. 2 ration(s); → SARA I.

musawah (*A*) equality.

musawamah (*A*) bidding.

musbat (*A*) confirmed.

muséum (*D*) museum.
  memuséumkan to put in a museum.
  permuséuman museum (*mod*).

mushaf → MASHAF.

mushobaqah → MUSABAQAH.

musholla (*A*) prayer house, place where people can say their prayers; not used for Friday services; found in any small residential or office area.

musi → MUNGSI.

musibah and **musibat** (*A*) 1 calamity, disaster. 2 disastrous.

musik (*D*) music. – *cadas* rock-'n-roll. – *kamar* chamber music. – *klasik* classical music. – *lembut* soft music, easy listening (music). – *lutut megal-megol* the twist (dance). – *ngak-ngik-ngok/nguk* rock-'n-roll. – *pop* pop music. – *remaja* teenager music. – *rok* rock-'n-roll. – *tiup* woodwind music.
  bermusik to play music.
  musikan 1 to play music. 2 a musical.
  pemusik musician. ~ *jalanan* street musician; → PENGAMÉN.

musikal (*D/E*) musical.

musikalisasi (*D*) putting s.t. to music.

musikan (*D*) 1 musician. 2 to make music.

musikolog (*D*) musicologist.

musikologi (*D/E*) musicology.

musikus (*D*) musician.

musilago (*D*) mucilage.

musim (*A*) 1 season, period (of time). 2 *sedang* – a) in season. b) a fad, in. – *angin gombal* the lean season for fishermen (August through December). – *bah* flood time. – *barat* west monsoon. – *berburu* hunting season. – *buah-buahan* the season in which many varieties of fruit are available on the market. – *bunga* spring(time). – *dingin* winter. – *durian* the durian season. – *gelora* period of stormy/nasty weather. – *giling* (sugarcane) harvest season. – *gugur* fall, autumn. – *haji* the time of year when pilgrims go to Mecca. – *hujan* the rainy season, wet monsoon. – *hujan mulai turun* the start of the rainy season. – *kawin* mating season. – *kemarau/kering* dry season. – *labuh* (in Semarang) the period of changeover from the dry to the rainy season. – *liburan sekolah* school vacation. – *maréngan* the end of the rainy season. – *paceklik* period of food shortages before the harvest. – *panca-roba* transitional period between seasons. – *panén* a) harvest season/time. b) peak time of year (for an industry or business). – *penghujan* rainy season, wet monsoon. – *perjodohan* mating season. – *ramai* peak/high season. – *rambutan* the rambutan season. – *rendeng* (*ob*) rainy season, wet monsoon. – *rontok/run-tuh* fall, autumn. – *salju* winter. – *semi* spring(time). – *sepi* off season. – *tanam/tandur* planting season. – *timur* season in which winds come from the East (April-September). – *wisata* tourist season (July, August, December, January).

musimnya *sudah* ~ it's time to.

semusim 1 a season. *perkawinan* ~ "marriage for a season," i.e., a "marriage" between an Indonesian woman from East Kaliman-tan and a foreign (mostly Filipino) worker; after the foreigner has completed his contract, he returns to his country and aban-dons his "wife" and any children they may have had; → KAWIN *kontrak*. 2 seasonal.

bermusim 1 to be in season. 2 seasonal.

musiman seasonal.

musim-musiman seasonal.

musir (*A*) wealthy.

musisi (*D*) 1 (plural of *musikus*) musicians. 2 (frequently also) musician.

musium → MUSÉUM.

muskil (*A*) 1 difficult (to solve), precarious, critical. 2 delicate. – *hati* worried, perplexed.

memuskilkan to consider s.t. difficult.

kemuskilan 1 difficulties. 2 difficulty, precariousness.

muslihat (*A*) plan, trick, conspiracy. *penuh* – tricky. *tipu* – tricks and devices, arts and wiles. – *perang* military/war tactics.

memuslihati to trick, deceive.

Muslim I (*A*) a Muslim.

muslim II (*E*) muslin, a k.o. white cloth for sheets/pillowcases, etc.

Muslimat (*A*) a Muslim woman.

Muslimin (*A*) Muslims. – *mazhab Hanafi* the Hanafi Muslims, Hanafis.

muslin → MUSLIM II.

musna (*coq*) → MUSNAH.

musnad (*A*) a collection of hadiths arranged on the first authority of its *isnad*.

musnah (*O Jv*) destroyed, shattered (of hopes/plans, etc.), anni-hilated, annihilation. – *dimakan api* went up in flames, was destroyed by fire. – *hama* sterilized. **memusnah-hamakan** to sterilize.

memusnahkan to destroy, annihilate.

kemusnahan destruction, extinction, annihilation. *skénario* ~ doomsday scenario.

pemusnah agent for destroying s.t., eradicator.

pemusnahan annihilation, eradication (of weeds, etc.), destruc-tion. ~ *hama* antisepsis. ~ *masal* genocide.

muson (*D*) monsoon.

Muspida and **MUSPIDA** [*Musyawarah Pimpinan Daérah*] Regional Executive Conference. – *Daérah* regency-level MUSPIDA. – *Se-tempat* district-level MUSPIDA. – *tingkat I* provincial-level MUSPIDA. – *tingkat II* regency-level MUSPIDA. – *tingkat ke-camatan/kacamatan* district-level MUSPIDA.

Muspika [*Musyawarah Pimpinan Kacamatan*] District-Level Ex-ecutive Conference.

muspra (*Jv*) in vain, for nothing, redundant.

Mussabaqah Tillawatul Qur'an → MUSABAQAH.

mustabid (*A*) dictator.

mustadh'afun and **mustadh'afin** (*A*) the oppressed.

mustafa (*A*) chosen.

mustahadah (*A*) woman.

mustahak (*A*) important, vital, urgent, in need.

memustahakkan to need, require.

mustahaq (*A*) person entitled to receive the *zakat*.

mustahil (*A*) 1 incredible, impossible, ridiculous. *misi* – mission impossible. 2 nonsense.

semustahil as impossible as.

memustahilkan to make s.t. impossible.

kemustahilan 1 incredibility, impossibility, absurdity, the im-possible. 2 nonsensicality.

mustahiq (*A*) the poor and needy.

mustaid (*A*) 1 in working order, ready to use, prepared, ready, settled.

memustaidkan to prepare, get/make ready.

mustajab (*A*) effective, sure-acting (of a medicine), efficacious.

kemustajaban effectiveness.

mustajir (*A*) the lessee in an *ijarah* transaction.

mustak (*A*) derived (of words).

mustakim (*A*) straight, upright, honest, sincere; → SIRATul-mus-takim.

mustakmal (*A*) s.t. (water/soil) that has been used for ritual cleans-ing.

mustami (*A*) (in university) auditor, person who audits classes.

mustasyar (*A*) adviser (of *NU*); → MUSYTASAR.

musti → MESTI.

mustika → MESTIKA. – *delima* bezoar, magic jewel used as a rem-edy and which gives its owner a certain position in society.

musuh 1 enemy, adversary, foe. 2 opponent, rival, competitor, con-testant (in games). 3 (moonlighter's slang) purchaser. – *dalam selimut* a) an enemy in disguise, a wolf in sheep's clothing, a viper in one's bosom. b) (*Mal*) a nagging wife. – *alam* natural enemy. – *bebuyutan* traditional foe. – *masah* various enemies. – *negara* State/public enemy. – *nomor satu* arch-enemy.

bermusuh(an) 1 to be/act like enemies, fight/quarrel with e.o. 2 hostile.

bermusuh ~ *dengan* to be at odds with.

memusuhi [and **musuhin** (*J coq*)] to regard/treat as an enemy/ adversary/opponent, be antagonistic toward, oppose, compete with. *tidak* ~ to have no quarrel with s.o.

permusuhan hostility, rivalry, enmity, animosity.

musut → KUSUT *musut*.

muswil [*musyawarah wilayah*] regional conference.

musyabah (*A*) resemblance.

musyafir → MUSAFIR.

musyahadah (*A*) vision.

musyala → MUSHOLLA.

musyammas (*A*) water.

musyarakah and **musyarakat** 1 (*A ob*) partnership, association, corporation, league, union; → SERIKAT. 2 society, community. 3 capital participation (in Islamic banks), a joint business en-terprise or partnership in which the partners (the bank and the customer) share the profit or loss in an agreed ratio.

musyarik (*A*) partner.

musyawarah and **musyawarat** (*A*) 1 meeting, conference. 2 discus-sion, deliberation, consultation, negotiation; a meeting leading to consensus. *minta* – to call for consultations. – *kerja* work-shop; → LOKAKARYA. – *majelis* deliberations. – *mufakat* mutual agreement/consensus. – *nasional* [Munas] national conference. – *Nasional Luar Biasa* [Munaslub] Extraordinary National Conference. – *pimpinan daérah* [Muspida] regional leaders conference. – *wilayah* [muswil] regional conference.

bermusyawarah 1 to hold a meeting. 2 to consult, deliberate, ne-gotiate.

memusyawarahkan to discuss, talk about/over, deliberate about, negotiate.

pemusyawarah negotiator.

permusyawarahan 1 conference. 2 consultation, discussion, de-liberation, negotiation. *Majelis* ~ *Rakyat* [MPR] People's De-liberative Council, People's Consultative Assembly.

musykil (*A*) delicate, difficult (to do/solve, etc.); → MUSKIL.

kemusykilan difficulty (in doing s.t.).

musyollah → MUSHOLLA.

musyrik (*A*) polytheist.

kemusyrikan polytheism.

musyrikin (*A*) *pl* of *musyrik*.

musytarak (*A*) inherited share.

musytari (*A*) (*bintang* –) (the planet) Jupiter.

musytasar (*A*) adviser (of *NU*). – *aam* general adviser (of the *NU* at the Executive Board level).

mut → KEMUT I.

mu'tabar → MUKTABAR.

mu'tabarah (A) honored, respected.

kemu'tabarahan honor, respect.

mu'tabir → MUKTABAR.

mutaf(f)ifin (A) al– "The Defrauders"; name of the 83rd chapter of the Koran.

mutah I k.o. plant whose roots have medicinal uses, Excoecaria agollocha; → MEMUTAH.

mutah II → MUNTAH.

mutah III (A) kawin – trial marriage.

mut'ah (A) enjoyment.

mutahir → MUTAKHIR.

mutakadim(in) (A) 1 former, earlier, previous. 2 preceding, foregoing.

mutakalim(in) (A) theologian(s).

mutakhir (A) recent, up-to-date, latest, modern.

memutakhirkan to bring up to date, update.

mutaki (A) devout, pious.

mutalaah (A) study, reading.

memutalaah(kan) to study s.t.

mutalak → MUTLAK.

mu'tamad → MUKTAMAD.

mu'tamar (A) conference.

mutan (D) mutant.

mutanakid (A) antonym.

mutar → PUTAR I.

mutaradif (A) synonymous.

mutarjim (A) translator.

mutasi (D) transfer (of government employees, etc.) to a new post, reassignment. – horisontal parallel move (to a new position at the same level).

memutasikan to reassign/transfer to a new post.

pemutasian reassignment/transfer (of military/diplomat, etc.) to a new post.

mutawarrik (A) pious.

mutawasid (A) intermediate.

mutawatir (A) traditional, handed down from generation to generation, the traditions of the Prophet that were transmitted through the first several generations. – amali the deeds of the Prophet. – lafzi the words of the Prophet.

mutawif → MUTHAWWIF.

mu'tazilah (A) rational, a school of thought in Islam that emphasizes the importance of rational thinking.

muté → MOTÉ.

muter → PUTER I.

muthaqqafin (A) intellectuals.

muthawwif and muthowif (A) licensed guide for Muslim pilgrims visiting the Prophet's grave in Medina.

muthrafun (A) the haves, the well-to-do.

mutia (Skr) pearl, mother-of-pearl; → MUTIARA. intan – diamonds and pearls. siput – mother-of-pearl shell.

mutiara I (Skr) 1 pearl. indung – mother-of-pearl, oyster that contains a pearl. ayam – guinea fowl. 2 mixture of corn/maize and soybeans.

Mutiara II – Selatan night express train which runs between Bandung and Surabaya (via Yogyakarta and Surakarta). – Utara night express train which runs between Jakarta and Surabaya via Semarang.

mutih → PUTIH.

mutla'ah → MUTALAAH .

mutlak (A) 1 absolute, total, unlimited, unconditional, non-negotiable, imperative. hak – natural rights. syarat – conditio sine qua non, indispensable condition. tanggung jawab – strict liability. wakil – plenipotentiary. wujud – absolute (as opposed to phenomenal) being. 2 general. 3 a necessity, a must. Pelajaran agama – di Perguruan Tinggi. Religious instruction is a must in colleges.

memutlakkan to make s.o. an indispensable condition.

kemutlakan an absolute, absoluteness. ~ perlu prerequisite.

pemutlakan making s.t. absolute/unconditional.

mut-mutan (Jv) to suck and chew (candy, etc.; like children or toothless old people).

mutrib (A) delightful.

muttabi (A) follower.

mutt(h)ahidah (A) united (mod).

mutu I 1 dumb, mute, speechless. 2 anxious, solicitous. berhati – doleful, sad, gloomy. 3 stalemate (in chess).

termutu struck dumb.

mutu II (Tam) pearl; → MUTIARA. ratna – manikam jewels of all kinds.

mutu III (Tam) 2.4 carats. mas sepuluh – 24-carat gold.

mutu IV (Tam) 1 quality, grade, value. 2 level, standard. di bawah – below standard, substandard, not up to the mark. – pengelolaan good governance.

semutu with the same value, of equal value.

bermutu to be of good/high value/quality, be of high quality. ~ rendah inferior, be of low quality. ~ tinggi high-quality. sebermutu of the same quality.

mutung I (J) 1 brokenhearted, frustrated, discouraged. 2 to sulk, pout, nurse a grievance.

mutung II (in South Sumatra) burned up, destroyed in a fire.

mutzasyar (A) adviser. – Aam General Adviser (of the NU's Executive Board).

muwah(h)id (A) monotheist.

muwakal (A) representative, agent; → WAKIL. kamus yang – a representative dictionary.

muwarikh (A) historian.

muwari(t)s (A) testator.

muwark(k)al (A) agent, representative, proxy.

muwarikh (A cla) 1 historian. 2 historiograph.

muyeg (Jv) characterized by complicated activity, action-packed/filled.

muzah → MOJAH.

muzakar (A) masculine.

muzakarah (A) discussions of a problem, exchange of thoughts/views/ideas.

muzakirah (A) memorandum.

muzalah → MAJALAH.

muzara'ah (A) crop sharing.

muz(z)m(m)il (A) al– "The Enwrapped"; name of the 73rd chapter of the Koran.

muzawir (A) escort/guide for Muslim pilgrims when circumambulating the Kaabah in Mecca.

muzhab → MAZHAB.

muzik → MUSIK.

mu'zizat → MUKJIZAT.

MX [MandraX] → MANDRAX.

N

For verbs beginning with n- also look under roots beginning with t-, e.g., **nabrak** → TABRAK.

n and N I /én/ the 14th letter of the Latin alphabet used for writing Indonesian. – *gelung* eng [ŋ]. – *tilde* enye [ñ].

N II car license plate for Malang.

na (exclamation to indicate joy) ha. – *itu dia ayah baru pulang!* Ha, there he is, father has just come home! – *lu,* – *lu!* (children's language) I got you there!

naam (*A*) /na'am/ **1** yes. **2** certainly. **3** so it is.

naar (*A*) /na'ar/ Hell, Hades; → NERAKA.

naar boven (*D*) /naar bofen/ to go to the mountains (*usu Puncak* with the implication of for relaxation or sexual fun).

naar eiland (*D*) /nar élan/ to go to one of the islands of *Kepulauan Seribu* (with the implication of for relaxation or sexual fun).

naas I (*A*) /na'as/ **1** bad luck. **2** unlucky, ill-omened. *bulan* – (the month of) *Safar,* the second Muslim month.
  menaaskan 1 to bring misfortunes to. **2** to consider unfavorable.
  kenaasan bad luck, calamity.

naas II → NAS II.

naba' (*A*) *an-* "News"; name of the 78th chapter of the Koran.

nabatah and nabatat (*A*) *alam* – flora, the vegetable kingdom/world.

nabati (*A*) vegetable (*mod*). *lemak* – vegetable fat. *minyak* – vegetable oil. *nyawa/roh* – plant/vegetable life. *sakar* – vegetable sugar.

nabe → NAF.

nabi (*A*) (religious) prophet; → ANBIA. – *Adam* Adam (the first man). – *Isa* Jesus. – *Muhammad* the Prophet Muhammad. – *Musa* Moses. – *palsu* false prophet. – *Zulkifli* Ezekiel.
  menabikan to glorify (as prophet).
  kenabian 1 prophethood. **2** prophetic.
  nabi-nabi k.o. starfish.

nabiah (*A*) **1** prophetic. *agama yang* – a prophetic religion. **2** prophetess.

nabtun (*A*) grass, plant.

nabu (*M*) seed, pip, stone (of a *durian/nangka/empedak*) with meat.

nabuat → NUBUAT.

naco /nako/ → NAKO.

NAD → NANGGROE ACÉH DARUSSALAM.

nada (*Skr*) **1** (musical) tone, tone (of voice), note. **2** intonation. **3** pitch, key. – *bawah* undertone. – *bawah rujuk* conciliatory undertone. – *bicara* busy signal. – *dasar* fundamental. – *mayeur* major key. – *menaik/menurun* rising/falling pitch. – *mineur* minor key. – *pakai* busy signal. – *pilih* dial tone. – *rendah* low key. – *sela* call waiting (a telephone service). – *sibuk* busy signal. – *sumbang* off-key note. – *tambahan* overtone. – *utama* keynote. – *warna* hue.
  senada 1 unanimous. *ungkapan* ~ expression of the same tone/tenor. **2** harmonious. **3** to say the same thing, be in agreement, similarly. **bersenada 1** to be unanimous. **2** to be harmonious. **3** to be similar. *hal* ~ something similar. **4** monotonous. **persenadaan 1** unanimity. **2** harmony. **3** similarity. **4** monotony.
  bernada 1 to smack of, sound like. **2** to sound, ring. ~ *sumbang* to be off key.
  bernadakan to have the tone of, sound like, smack of. *Tulisan itu ada yang* ~ *mengundang belas kasihan.* Among those articles there are some that sound as if they're asking for pity.
  penadaan intonation.

nada-nadanya there are indications, to all appearances, judging from appearances. ~ *kurang baik* the symptoms are unfavorable.

nadapol → NAPOL.

nadar (*A*) vow (to God), solemn promise to do s.t. if a wish is fulfilled. *melepas/membayar/memenuhi/menunai(kan)* – to fulfill one's vow, keep one's promise.
  bernadar to (make a) vow, promise.
  menadarkan to vow, make a solemn promise about.

nadasela call waiting (a telephone service).

nadi (*Skr*) **1** pulse (the regular beat of the arteries). *meraba/memeriksa* – to take one's pulse. *batang* – aorta. **2** artery. *pembuluh* – artery. *urat* – artery. – *bersikeras* arteriosclerosis. – *cepat* rapid pulse. – *ketiak* axillary artery. – *lambat* slow pulse. – *lengan* brachial artery. – *mengeras* arteriosclerosis. – *paru(-paru)* pulmonary artery.
  bernadi *tidak* ~ *lagi* dead, lifeless

nadim (*A*) confidant, close friend.

nadir I (*A*) rare, unusual. *buku* – rare books.

nadir II (*A*) nadir.

nadir III a Malacca type of large sea-going fishing boat.

nadir IV (*A cla*) supervisor, inspector (of *wakaf*).

nadirat (*A*) *barang* – rarity, curiosity; → NADIR I.

nadzar → NADAR.

nadzir → NADIR IV.

naf (*D*) hub (of a wheel).

nafakah → NAFKAH.

nafas → NAPAS I.

nafi (*A mainly Mal*) **1** denial, refusal, repudiation, rejection. **2** negative, negation. **3** to not want.
  menafi to repudiate.
  menafikan 1 to deny, refuse, reject. *Penobatan bahasa Melayu-tinggi sebagai bahasa Indonésia dengan serta-merta* ~ *karya sastra yang sudah berkembang dalam bahasa daérah.* The establishment of High Malay as the Indonesian language simultaneously rejected the literary works already developing in the regional languages. **2** to be opposed.
  penafian rejection, denial. ~ *agama* denial of a religion. ~ *secara mutlak* absolute denial.

nafilah (*A*) good works.

nafiri (*Pers*) a long valveless trumpet used in royal ceremonies.
  bernafiri to sound such a trumpet.

nafkah (*A*) **1** livelihood, living, subsistence, (source of) income; → REZEKI. *mencari* – to earn one's living. **2** expenses, money used/needed for s.t. – *batin* conjugal rights. – *cerai* alimony, maintenance.
  bernafkah to have a source of income.
  menafkahi to support (financially), maintain, give alimony/maintenance to.
  menafkahkan to spend, disburse, pay out (money). ~ *hartanya* to use one's money/wealth for (one's subsistence or in the public interest).

nafkhatan (*A*) the blowing of the trumpet by the angel Israfil on the last day.

nafs (*A*) **1** soul; spirit; psyche. *ilmu* – psychology. **2** personal identity, self (used for the reflexive pronoun).

nafsi I (*A*) self-centered, thinking only of o.s., selfish.
  nafsi-nafsi individual, private, not social, not caring about others, selfish. *hidup* ~ individual life. *sikap* ~ individualism.
  bernafsi-nafsi individual; private; egoistic(al); every man for himself; → LU-LU *gua-gua.*
  pernafsi-nafsian individualism.

nafsi II (*J*) anger, fury, wrath.

nafsu (*A*) **1** desire, lust, yearning. **2** (*hawa* –) passion. *obat penekan* – *makan* appetite suppressant. *patah* – to have no appetite. – *besar, tenaga kecil/kurang* the spirit is willing, but the flesh is weak. – *nafsi, raja di mata, sultan di hati* to do whatever one pleases. – *alami* natural appetites. – *amarah* a) anger. b) wickedness. – *bejat* depravity. – *beli* urge to buy things. – *binatang* irrational action. – *birahi* sex drive, lust. – *dukana* lust. – *iblis* desire to do s.t. immoral. – *kebendaan* material desires. – *kuda* passion. – *lawamah* vicious passion (in mysticism). – *makan* appetite. – *makan bertambah kurang* to have no appetite. – *merusak* vandalism. *memuaskan* –*nya* to give free rein to one's passions. – *mutmainah* strong drive to avoid immoral actions. –

nafsi desires. – *radiah* strong desire to do s.t. looked on favorably by God. – *séks* libido. – *séksnya tak pernah terpuaskan* his insatiable sex drive. – *séks yang berlebihan* oversexed. – *sétan* desire to do s.t. immoral. – *syahwat* sex drive. – *tabiat* instinct; → GARIZAH, NALURI. – *yang tak tertahan* unbridled/unrestrained passion.

bernafsu 1 to be passionate, lustful. ~ *hidup* to have a lust for life. 2 to be eager to, have a strong wish to (buy/eat, etc.); want to, be in the mood for.

bernafsukan to have a strong desire for s.t.

menafsui to have a desire for, want (sexually).

menafsukan to arouse desires/one's appetite (*esp* sexual).

nafta (*D/E*) naphtha.

naftalén(a) and **naftalin** (*D*) naphthalene.

naftol (*E*) naphthol.

naga (*Skr*) 1 dragon. *rakyat – mérah* the PRC Chinese. *si – besar* the People's Republic of China. *empat – kecil Asia* the four little dragons of Asia, i.e., South Korea, Taiwan, Hong Kong, and Singapore. 2 (*Jv*) a fabulous serpent about which superstitions exist with regard to the directions of the wind in which one should not go or sit. *cacing menjadi ular –* a poor/stupid man has become a rich/smart person. *buah –* → BUAH *naga*. – *ditelan ular lidi* when nobility marries a commoner. – *antaboga* (appellation for a) whale. – *balun* dragon which kills with a swipe of the tail. – *berapi* fire-breathing dragon. – *bura* fire-breathing dragon. – *gentala* dragon with deadly breath (painted on vehicle wheels). – *hari* dragon which guards the points of the compass and shifts daily. – *kecil* the newly industrialized nations of Asia. – *rahu* a dragon which encircles the world. – *sekuik* a dragon depicted on a woman's dress worn to win back her husband's affections. – *setala* k.o. batik pattern. – *tahun* dragon which guards the points of the compass and shifts annually. – *umbang* sea monster.

naga-naga 1 Chinese paper dragon. 2 dragon figurehead on a boat. 3 (*cla*) high dais in the palace/audience hall.

naga-nagaan s.t. similar to a dragon.

nagam I (*A*) string of pearls, pearl necklace.

nagam II (*A*) harmony of tone.

naga-naga (*J*) omen.

naga-naganya (*J*) it seems as if ..., to all appearances ..., by the look of things ..., apparently, seemingly. *Kalau begini ~ dia tidak akan datang.* To all intents and purposes he won't come; → NADA-NADANYA.

nagara I (*ob*) – *bukit* mountaintop, summit.

nagara II → NAKARA.

Nagarakertagama (*Jv*) a sacred hymn composed in 1365 by *Prapanca*, the poet to the court of Majapahit.

nagari (*M*) a Minangkabau community. *kepala –* village head; → *kepala* NEGERI.

nagasari I ironwood, Indian rose chestwood with white showy flowers, *Mesua ferrea*.

nagasari II (*Jv*) /nogosari/ delicacy made from banana with flour and sugar steamed in a banana leaf.

nah 1 (interjection inviting s.o. to accept s.t.) here! take it! –, *ini uang sepuluh ribu untuk membeli sesuatu!* Here, here's ten thousand (rupiahs) to buy s.t.! 2 well (opening a new topic/expressing one's opinion). –, *ini baru lagu!* Well, this is what you call a song! –, *selesai sekarang!* Well, it's done now! – *lu* serves you right!

nahak (*ob*) **ternahak** overcome by desire (for food, etc.).

nahas (*A*) inauspicious, doomed to failure, unlucky, ill-fated, portending evil; → NAAS I. *hari –* an unlucky day.

menahaskan to see s.t. as ominous/unlucky.

kenahasan bad luck, misfortune.

nahat (*A*) coining of words.

Nahd(l)atul Ulama [NU] "Renaissance of Muslim Clergy," i.e., a Muslim organization.

nahd(l)i follower of the *NU* party.

nahd(l)iyat female members of the *NU* party.

nahd(l)iyin male members of the *NU* party.

nahi (*A*) forbidden (by Islam or in general); prohibition, interdiction. – *mungkar* prohibitions imposed by Islamic law.

nahl (*A*) "(the) Bee"; name of the 16th chapter of the Koran.

nahnu (*A*) we. *Ada dua sebab mendasar mengapa –, umat Islam Indonésia, begitu terlibat dalam masalah Politik di Timur Tengah.* There are two fundamental reasons why we, Indonesian Muslims, are so involved in Middle Eastern political issues.

nahu and **nahwu** (*A*) *ilmu –* grammar, *esp* syntax. – *bentuk* morphology. – *saraf* grammar.

naib (*A*) 1 deputy, assistant; representative. 2 head of mosque personnel, (Muslim) government religious official empowered to legitimize and register marriages, *talak*, and *rujuk*; → PENGHULU. – *kadi* deputy marriage registrar. – *ketua* deputy/vice chairman. – *laksamana* (*ob*) rear admiral; → LAKSAMANA *muda*. 3 (*Mal*) vice-.

kenaiban low-level office of religious affairs.

naif (*D*) naive.

naifnya as ill-luck would have it, unfortunately.

senaif as naive as.

menaifkan to treat s.t. naively. *cita-cita yang dinaifkan* ideals which couldn't possibly be reached.

kenaifan naiveté.

naik 1 to go up, rise, mount. *Adonannya sudah –.* The dough has risen. *Karirnya – lebih cepat.* His career is rising to greater heights. *Asap – ke udara.* Smoke goes up into the air. *bulan – a* waxing moon, from the first through the fifteenth of the month (from crescent moon through full moon). 2 to climb, enter a house (after having gone up the stairs; in the Minangkabau area), get on board (a ship). *Ia tidak dapat – tangga.* He can't climb a ladder. *Tamu itu dipersilakan – ke rumah.* The visitor was invited up into the house. 3 to travel by. – *keréta api* to travel by train. – *lift ke tingkat tujuh* to take the elevator to the seventh floor. – *mobil ke Bogor* to go by car to Bogor. – *sepéda* to ride a bike. 4 to increase, go up, rise, gain/put on (weight). *Kejahatan –.* Crime is on the rise. *Pengangguran –.* Unemployment is increasing. *Berat badannya –.* He has put on weight. *Semua harga barang –.* All commodity prices went up. – *dari ... menjadi ...* to rise/increase from ... to ... 5 to become, turn. *Ia tidak mau – saksi.* He didn't want to be a witness. *Air mukanya dan mendadak – mérah padam.* All of a sudden his face turned fiery red (from anger). 6 to take off (aircraft); → LEPAS *landas*, MENGUDARA. *kecepatan – udara* take-off speed (of aircraft). 7 (*reg*) to mount, mate (with a female animal). 8 to be promoted (from one grade to the next). 9 (in various compounds) to flare up. – *melompat, turun terjun* pride goes before a fall. *bulan –, matahari –* to get lucky. – *dari janjang, turun dari tangga* to proceed systematically. – *angin* (*naut*) on the wind. – *apél* to appeal to a higher court. – *api* to catch fire. – *banding* to appeal to a higher court. – *benang* to get the opportunity, have the pleasure. – *bertabal* to crown, install (s.o. as king). – *benar* to grow up (of children). – *besar* to get older. – *cétak* to go to press (of a newspaper). – *dango* an *adat* feast celebrated in the Pontianak Regency after the harvest. – *darah* to become/get angry. – (*ke*) *darat* to disembark, go ashore, land. – *daun* a) to be lucky. b) flourish, be prosperous, be doing well. c) to become well known. – *derajat* to be promoted. – *déwasa* to become an adolescent. – *dok* to go into dry dock. – *gaji* to get a raise (in salary), get a pay hike. – *gembira* to get excited. – *geram* to become excited/angry. – *haji* to go on the pilgrimage to Mecca. – *harga* to go up in price. – *hati* a) happy, glad. b) proud, arrogant, conceited. – *jabatan* to get promoted, go up in rank. – *kaki* on foot. – *kapal* a) to embark, board (a ship). b) by ship. – *kartu* to have a stroke of good luck. – *kelas* to be promoted (to the next higher grade in school). – *ke surga* to ascend to heaven. – *kuda* to ride a horse. – *kuda hijau* to be drunk. – *lift* to take the elevator. – *marah* to become angry. – *marak* a) to start to glow. b) to be at her best (said of a girl). c) to become famous. – *mempelai* a) to get married. b) to sleep with one's husband for the first time. – *mérek* (*coq*) to have a good reputation, rise in rank. – *mesin* a) to go to press (of a newspaper). b) to install an engine. – *mimbar* a) to mount the pulpit. b) to take the stage. – *mobil* a) to get into a car. b) to go by car. – *nilai* premium. – *nobat* a) to get married. b) to be installed as a ruler. – *ompréngan* to hire a car as a group. – *pan* to get angry. – *panggung* to appear on stage. – *pangkat* to be promoted. – *pasang* rising tide. – *pelak* a) to get angry. b) to be fed up, displeased. – *pelamin(an)* to get married. – *pentas* to appear on the stage, come on. – *penuh* (flag) at full mast. – *perkara* to appeal to a higher court. – *pesawat (terbang)* to board a plane, enplane. – *pitam* a) to get angry, become enraged. b) to become dizzy. – *raja* to become king. – *ranjang* to marry an older sibling of one's former wife/husband. – *rejeki* to get lucky. – *ring* to enter the ring (in boxing). – *rumah baru* (M) to hold a housewarming party. – *saksi* to take the witness stand. – *setengah* (flag) at half mast. – *setum* to become enraged. – *sorga* to go to heaven. – *stum* to become enraged. – *suara* to raise one's voice. – *takhta* to ascend the throne. – *tangan* to get lucky. – *tidur* to go to bed. – *tinggi* to get high (on drugs). – *tubuh* to be growing fast (of a child). – *turun* a) to fluctuate; fluctuation. b) to go up and down. c) to nod. *Kepalanya – turun.* He nodded. **menaik-turuni** to go into and come out of (a pit, etc.). **menaik-turunkan 1** to cause to fluctuate. **2** to pick up and drop off (passengers). **3** to load and unload (cargo on and off a ship).

menaik to rise, increase (of prices/salaries, etc.). *Hasil panén ~.* The crop yield is increasing.

menaik-naik to keep on rising/increasing /heightening.

menaiki 1 to go up (stairs), go up (the stairs). *Dia ~ tangga.* He went upstairs. **2** to climb. ~ *pohon* to climb a tree. **3** to ride on, take on board. ~ *kuda* to ride on horseback. ~ *lift* to take the elevator. *Meréka ~ lift ke lantai tiga.* They took the elevator to the third floor. *Pesawat Concorde itu dinaiki oléh anggota-anggota MEE menuju Éropa.* The Concorde was boarded by members of the EEC bound for Europe. **4** to begin to live in (a new house).

menaikkan [and **naikin** (*J coq*)] **1** to raise, hoist, boost, lift, hike. ~ *bendéra* to hoist/fly the flag. ~ *darah* to make s.o. angry, anger. ~ *doa syukur* to send up prayers of thanks. ~ *gajinya* to boost his salary. ~ *harga-harga* to jack up prices. ~ *pangkat* to promote s.o. ~ *séwa apartemén* to raise the rent of the apartment. **2** to load on, take aboard. ~ *peti kémas ke atas truk* to load a container on the truck. *Seorang yang tenggelam dinaikkan ke atas kapal.* The drowning person was taken aboard the ship. *Sebuah bis antarkota ~ penumpang di jalan tol.* An intercity bus was taking on passengers at the toll road. **3** to promote. ~ *menjadi kepala séksi* to promote to section head.

menaik-naikkan to keep on raising, etc.

naikan 1 mount, what one rides. **2** rise, riser.

naik-naikan promotion time (at school).

kenaikan 1 rise, increase, hike, boost. ~ *gaji* pay raise. ~ *harga* price increase. **2** promotion. ~ *kelas* promotion (at school). ~ *pangkat* promotion (at work). **3** ascension. ~ *Nabi Isa* the Ascension of Jesus. **4** (*ob*) mount; vehicle; vessel.

penaik 1 driver, person who ... ~ *darah* hothead. ~ *haji* pilgrim. ~ *mobil* motorist. ~ *sepéda* cyclist. ~ *sepéda motor* motorcyclist. **2** passenger. ~ *bis* bus passenger.

penaikan 1 rising, increasing. **2** raising. *upacara ~ bendéra* flag-raising ceremony.

naim (*A*) /na'im/ pleasant, delightful, delicious. – *Allah* the grace of God.

naitklab (*E*) nightclub.

najam (*A*) star, celestial body.

najar → NADAR.

najasah and **najasat** (*A*) filth, pollution; → NAJIS.

najat (*A*) prayer, devotions; → MUNAJAT.

bernajat to pray.

najib (*A*) **menajibkan** to topple. *Seolah-olah dia akan ~ Pak Présidén.* (It is) as if he is going to topple the president.

najik (*A*) diamond (in cards).

najis (*A*) **1** filthy, (ritually) unclean. **2** feces, (animal) droppings. **3** (*BG*) yuk, gross, (it's) disgusting! *membasuh – dengan malu* to cover up mistakes or shame with still greater insults. – *berat* filthy (according to Islam), such as pigs and dogs. – *besar* feces. – *kecil* urine. – *ringan* not serious filth, such as a child's urine.

bernajis filthy, covered with filth.

menajisi to make dirty, soil.

menajiskan 1 to make dirty, soil. **2** to consider s.t. dirty. ~ *segala*

yang bau popular to consider everything dirty that reeks of the popular.

kenajisan dirt, filth, squalor.

penajisan contamination (with filth).

najm (*A*) *an*– "The Star"; name of the 53rd chapter of the Koran.

nak I → ANAK I.

nak II → HENDAK.

nakal 1 naughty, mischievous, play practical jokes. *Jangan –.* Behave yourself. **2** loose (of morals), wanton. *perempuan –* loose woman, prostitute, whore. **3** delinquent, bad, fresh (of behavior).

menakal to be mischievous, behave in a mischievous way.

menakali 1 to be mischievous toward, tease. **2** to assault sexually.

ternakal the naughtiest, loosest, most delinquent, etc.

nakal-nakalan 1 in a teasing/naughty way. **2** to act badly. **bernakal-nakalan** (*dengan*) to tease, nag, pester, irritate.

kenakalan 1 naughtiness, mischief. **2** looseness (of morals). **3** delinquency, hooliganism. ~ *jalanan* ruffianism. ~ *remaja* juvenile delinquency.

naka-naka bernaka-naka to sing by turns (of a *pantun*, etc.).

nakar → AYAM nakar.

nakara (*Pers*) royal kettledrum.

naker [*tenaga kerja*] worker, manpower. *Banyak – Indonésia menyelundup ke Malaysia.* Many Indonesian workers have snuck into Malaysia.

nakerwan [*tenaga kerja wanita*] female worker.

nakhoda (*Pers*) ship's captain, skipper. – *Agung* fleet admiral.

bernakhoda to have a pilot. *tidak ~* without a pilot, pilotless.

menakhodai to captain s.t., be the captain of. *KM 207 yang dinakhodai oléh Péltu Pol Minwan.* MS 207, which was captained by Police Sublieutenant Minwan.

Nakir (*A*) one of the two angels of death; → MUNKAR, MUNGKAR II.

nako glass louver board. *jendéla –* window with glass louver boards.

nakoda → NAKHODA.

nakokaké (*Jv*) the way a man, through his elders, tries to find out whether or not a girl is still available for marriage.

nal I (*D*) wad (in a gun).

nal II (*A*) horseshoe.

nala (*M*) **bernala-nala** to ponder, consider.

nalam (*A*) (traditional) poem.

bernalam to recite poetry.

menalamkan to compose (poetry), tell a story in verse.

nalar I (*A*) – *wajar* common sense, sound judgment, native intelligence.

bernalar to reason, argue; to be rational. *tidak ~* irrational. **kebernalaran** logic, reasoning, argumentation.

penalaran logic, reasoning, argumentation. ~ *berputar* confused thinking. ~ *moral* moral reasoning.

nalar II always, often, regular.

naléh and **nali(h)** (*ob*) measure for rice (16 *gantang*, 1/50 *koyan*).

nalo [*nasional loteré*] National Lottery.

naloka [*betina lokal*] (in the Asahan Regency, northern Sumatra) a domestically raised chicken.

naluri instinct; → INSTINK. – *bisnis* business instinct. – *keibuan* maternal instinct. – *purba* primitive instinct. – *untuk membunuh* killer instinct.

naluriah instinctive.

nam clipped form of **enam**.

nama (*Skr*) **1** name. **2** (*hanya*) *-nya saja* nominal, formal, (only) in name. **3** fame, renown. *Sophia Sciolone yang kemudian merubah – akhirnya jadi Lorén* Sophia Scicolone who later changed her last name to Loren. *atas –*; → ATAS *nama. daftar –* nomenclature. *dengan –* in the name of, under the name of. *bersumpah dengan – Allah* to take/swear an oath in the name of Allah. *di bawah – bersama* under a joint name. *memberi –* to name, entitle; to christen (a ship). *mempunyai – baik* to have a good reputation. *mempunyai – buruk* to have a bad name/reputation. *mencari –* to seek one's own advantage. *mendapat –* to make a name (for o.s.). *menjual –* to make use of s.o. else's name to obtain s.t. – *saja balik ke rumah* he passed away. – *akhir* last name. – *baik* good reputation, good will. – *batang tubuh* real name. – *belakang* last/family name. – *benda* noun. – *besar* (*Min*) family/last name. – *buruk* a bad/poor reputation/

name. – *daérah* vernacular name. – *dagang* trademark. – *daging* surname, family name (given at birth or baptism). – *depan* first name. – *diri* proper noun. – *éjékan* nickname. – *ilmiah* scientific name. – *jelas* printed name (as opposed to signature). – *jenis* common noun. – *julukan* nickname. – *kaum* family name. – *kecil* given name, first name. – *kelahiran* name at birth. – *keluarga/keturunan* last/family name, surname. – *kimia* chemical name (of pesticides, etc.). – *kumpulan* generic name. – *lahir* name at birth, maiden name. – *muka* first/Christian name. – *niaga* trademark. – *panggilan* a) nickname. b) call sign. – *panggilannya Gendut* his nickname is Gendut, people call him Gendut. – *pédéngan/samaran* pseudonym, pen name. – *sandi* a) code name. b) alias. – *sepuh* adult name. – *sindiran* nickname. – *tambahan* subtitle. – *tempat* toponym. – *tengah* middle name. – *tepat* (*bio*) correct name. – *terang* name written in block letters (as opposed to a signature). – *timangan* pet name. – *tjé-tjé-an / cé-cé-an/* Dutch diminutives, like Mientje, Saartje, etc. – *tubuh* name given at birth/baptism. – *turunan* family name, surname. – *umum* common name, shortened name of the active ingredient in a pesticide, etc.

namanya 1 so-called, in name, nominally, what you might call. ~ *saja Pegawai tinggi*. He is only a senior employee in name. *Itu pemborosan* ~. That is what you might call squandering. 2 his/ her name. ~ *siapa?* a) what is his name? b) what is your name? (facing the person spoken to). *Apa* ~? What is it called? 3 that's the way s.t. is, that's the nature of s.t. *Itu* ~ ... *and* ~ *juga* ... that's the way it is with, that's the way that ... is/are. *Itu* ~ *mesin.* That's the way machines are. ~ *juga anak-anak.* That's the way children are/behave.

senama 1 of the same name. 2 (*math*) having the same denomination (of fractions). 3 similar.

bernama 1 with/to have a name, be called/named, be known as. *Anak itu* ~ *Hasan.* The child is called Hasan. 2 famous, renowned, well-known. *pengarang yang* ~ a well-known author.

menamai to name, call, give a name to. *Ia* ~ *anaknya Pamela.* He named his child Pamela. *Kapan orok itu dinamai?* When will the baby be given a name?

menamakan 1 to name, call, christen (a ship). *Karena timpang jalannya, orang* ~*nya si Pincang.* Because he limps, people call him the Cripple. 2 consider, regard as. *Ia* ~ *orang seperti itu kejam.* He considers such a person cruel. ~ *diri* a) to claim (to be); → MENGAKU. *Ia* ~ *diri spésialis.* He claimed to be a specialist. b) to call o.s. *Kami* ~ *diri kami orang Jawa.* We call ourselves Javanese.

ternama fame, renown, notability.

kenamaan 1 fame, renown. 2 famous, well-known. **berkenamaan** famous, renowned, well-known.

penamaan 1 naming, christening, labeling. 2 appellation.

namad (*Pers*) felt (cloth).

nambat (*M*) don't.

nambi sore on soles or palms of hands from yaws.

naml (*A*) *an–* "The Ant"; name of the 27th chapter of the Koran.

nambor (*D*) nameplate, name board.

namék (*BIT*) friend.

namnam a fruit tree, namnam, *Cynometra cauliflora*, the fruit of which grows on the stem and which when stewed tastes like stewed pears.

nampak 1 to see, observe, notice. *Meréka tidak* – *siapa yang mengambil surat kabar itu tadi.* They did not see who took the newspaper. 2 visible, can be seen, seen, in sight; evident, clear. *Rumahnya tidak* – *dari sini.* His house cannot be seen from here. – *bahwa anak itu senang.* It is clear that the child is happy; → KELIHATAN, TAMPAK I. – *belangnya* one's true character appears. – *sekali* conspicuous, obvious. – *sekali bahwa ia mencintai gadis itu.* It is obvious that he loves the girl.

nampaknya apparently, seemingly; it looks like; → KELIHATANNYA, RUPA-RUPANYA. ~ *tidak ada.* It looks like there isn't any. ~ *dia tidak akan datang.* It looks like he won't show up.

nampak-nampak ~ *apung* to appear and disappear.

menampak to see, watch. *Para pelakon di belakang cermin ini boléh dinampak oléh penonton.* The spectators were allowed to see the actors behind the mirror.

menampakkan to show, display, exhibit. ~ *diri* to show o.s., show up.

ternampak saw; (could be) seen, visible. *Dia* ~ *temannya yang sedang berjalan.* He saw his friend walking.

kenampakan visible, seen, obvious, noticeable.

penampakan appearance (of spirits), vision.

nampal → NAPAL.

nampan (*J*) tray; → TETAMPAN.

namun 1 however, but, yet. *Tun Abdul Razak telah lama meninggalkan kita,* – *jasa dan baktinya tetap hidup dalam ingatan seluruh bangsa.* Tun Abdul Razak left us a long time ago, but his services and devotion still live in the memory of the entire nation. – *apa (juga)* no matter what. – *begitu/demikian* nevertheless. *Ahmad seorang yang miskin,* – *demikian dia tidak pernah minta bantuan orang lain.* Ahmad is a poor person, but he has never asked for help from others. – *begitu dia tetap tabah.* Nevertheless he remained determined. 2 provided that. *Apa kehendakmu akan kuberi,* – *jangan juga aku engkau bunuh.* I'll give you what you want, provided that you don't kill me.

nan (*M poet*) which, that, who; → YANG II. *kawan* – *setia* a faithful friend. – *Ampék Jinih* "The Four Kinds (of persons)," i.e., a k.o. village Cabinet. – *lurah jua dituruti air* the rich get richer.

nanah pus, suppuration. *kencing* – gonorrhea, the clap.
bernanah to be pussy, full of pus.
menanah to suppurate.

nanak-nunuk (*Jv*) with weak sight, so that one has to walk to and fro like a blind person looking and groping for s.t.; also, for instance, looking for a way out.

nanang (*M*) to meditate.

nanap 1 staring, wide open, gazing (of one's eyes). 2 to be startled. 3 (*J*) to be woken up from sleep.
menanap to stare at.

nanar 1 confused, dazed (from an injury/sickness/drink, etc.), giddy, bewildered. 2 in a rage, mad, angry.
menanarkan 1 to confuse, daze. ~ *otak* to puzzle one's brain. 2 to drive s.o. mad/wild.
ternanar confused, bewildered, perplexed, dazed.

nanas pineapple, *Ananas comosus*. – *belanda* agave, *Agave cantala*. – *goréng* fried pineapple. – *kerang* k.o. plant, oyster plant, *Rhoeo spathaceae*. – *kista* agave, *Agave cantala*. – *mérah* k.o. pineapple, *Ananas comosus*. – *sabrang/seberang* sisal hemp, *Agave cantala/rigida*. – *tali* agave, *Agave cantala*.
pernanasan banana (*mod*).

nanda → ANAKANDA.

nandung I *tupai* – giant squirrel, *Ratufa bicolor*.

nandung II gizzard shad, *Dorosoma chacunda*.

nang I (*Jv*) in, at, on. – *kéné* here, in this place. "*Sudah lama nggak lihat montor bagus, tiba-tiba muncul montor* – *kéné,*" *ujar orang-orang désa.* "It's been a long time since we've seen nice cars and suddenly a car shows up here," said the villagers.

nang II → YANG II.

nangak k.o. *nipah* palm.

nanggroe (*Ac*) nation; → NEGERI. *Daérah Otonomi Khusus* – *Acéh Darussalam* [NAD] the Darussalam Aceh Nanggroe Special Autonomous District.

nangka I jackfruit, *Artocarpus integra/heterophylla*. *kalau takut kena getah, jangan makan* – if you can't stand the heat, get out of the kitchen. *orang makan* –, *awak kena getahnya* to pull s.o.'s chestnuts out of the fire. *siapa makan* – *ia kena getahnya* (or, *dialah kena getahnya*) as one sows, so shall one reap. – *belanda/londo/manila/sabrang* soursop, *Annona muricata*. – *cina* → CEMPEDAK. – *kera* k.o. plant, monkey nut, *Artocarpus rigidus*.

nangka II *burung* – golden oriole, *Oriolus sp.*; → KEPODANG.

nangkoda → NAKHODA.

nangkring (*J*) 1 to sit (perched on a high place, e.g., on a branch). 2 to sit (at the top). *Ia kini* – *di peringkat teratas pencétak gol terbanyak.* He now sits in the top ranking of the top scorers. 3 to sit (down) at (the table). *Salah seorang sopir langsung* – *di méja makan.* One of the drivers immediately sat down at a dining table. 4 to be parked (of cars). *Beberapa buah mobil méwah di antaranya berplat B* – *di halaman.* Several luxurious cars, among them some with B-license plates, were parked on the premises. **5** to be a wallflower.

nang-ning-nong/nung (*onom*) sounds produced by a *gamelan* orchestra. *bahasa* – the Indonesian language. *masyarakat* – the Indonesian community.

nangoi and **nangui** k.o. small, wild pig, bearded pig, *Sus barbatus*. *menggeriak bagai anak* – s.o. who has a lot of children but is too lazy to look for work.

naning a large, yellow-colored wasp, giant honeybee, *Apis dorsata*.

nano-nano 1 k.o. candy. **2** s.t. in which a lot of different things are mixed into one producing a strange result (often has a negative connotation).

nansuk (*D*) nainsook, a fine, soft cotton fabric, *usu* white.

nanti I 1 later (*usu* the same day but may be later). *malam* – and – *malam* (later) this evening, tonight. *petang/soré* – and – *petang/ soré* (later) this afternoon. *bulan Novémber* – next November. *akhir Agustus* – at the end of August (coming up). *Itu perkara/ soal/urusan* –. That's a matter for later concern. *Sampai* –! See you later. *di hari* – in the future. *-lah saya kemari* and *-lah kapan-kapan saya datang* I'll drop by one day, i.e., Don't call me, I'll call you. *pada suatu waktu* – some day (in the future). **2** (implying a warning/concern/encouragement) or else, otherwise. *Awas,* – *jatuh!* Watch out or you'll fall! *Hati-hati,* – *terbakar!* Be careful, you'll burn it! – *ibu gusar!* Mother might get angry! *Baik-baik belajar,* – *dapat menjadi dokter*. Study hard so that you can become a doctor. **3** (*coq*) will surely, likely. *Jika dia tahu akan perkara ini* – *héboh sekampung*. If he knows this matter, the whole village will be in a commotion. *tak* – will never. *Pasukan Itali tak* – *mampu untuk membendung invasi Sekutu*. The Italian forces would never be able to dam up the Allied invasion.

nanti-nanti ~ *saja* soon.

nanti II wait a second (on the analogy of Javanese *kosik*); → TUNGGU I. – *dulu!* Wait a moment! – *dulu, belum ada témpo!* One moment please, I don't have the time!

nantinya afterward, later.

bernanti to wait for, await.

bernanti-nanti and **menanti-nanti** to wait for a long time, wait and wait.

bernanti(-nanti)an to wait for e.o.

menanti to wait for. ~ *nasi disajikan ke lutut* said about s.o. who just waits for s.t. to happen to him.

menantikan [and **nantiin** (*J coq*)] to wait for, await. *tinggal* ~ *takdir* (we'll) just wait and see what our fate is. ~ *kucing bertanduk* to wait for s.t. impossible. ~ *laki pulang maling* very nervous.

ternanti-nanti anxiously waiting.

nanti-nantian to wait for s.t. that one hopes will happen.

penanti 1 receptionist, person who receives visitors. **2** hostess.

penantian 1 waiting, anticipation. **2** waiting room.

pernantian waiting place.

nantiasa → SENANTIASA.

nanting to sound s.o. out.

Nanyang (*C*) South China Sea.

nap → NAF.

napa (*J*) clipped form of **kenapa**.

napak tiles (*Jv*) to follow in s.o.'s footprints; → TAPAK *tilas*.

napal edible earth, marl. *batu* – k.o. hard marl. *gemar* – geophagy. – *kapur* lime marl.

napalan marly.

napas I (*A*) **1** breath. **2** breathing, respiration. *alat* – respiratory organs. *Orang yang sakit parah itu susah menarik* –. The severely sick person has difficulty breathing. *-nya telah menjadi péndék dan tersekat-sekat sebelum ia meninggal*. His breathing became short and obstructed before he died. *jalan* – windpipe, trachea. *menahan* – to hold one's breath. *menarik/menghéla* – to breathe. *menarik* – *panjang* to take a deep breath. *menghembuskan* – *penghabisan* and *menghembuskan -(nya) yang terakhir* to breathe one's last, die. *sakit* – asthma. *-nya senén kemis* he's on his last legs. *sesak* – tight in the chest. *Kasi dia* – *dulu!* (*coq*) Give him some breathing space! **3** inspiration. – *akhir* last breath. – *baru* second wind. – *kuda* a breath that is held for a

long time. – *lelah* short-winded. – *panjang* a deep breath. **bernapas panjang** to take a long breath (of relief). – *penghabisan* last breath. *-(nya) satu dua* (he) is dying/at death's door. – *sudah putus* dead. – *terakhir* last breath. – *tinggal satu-satu/ separo-paro* to be dying/at death's door.

senapas 1 (mentioned) in the same breath. **2** similar, agreeing, conforming, in harmony, similarly inspired. *Kalimat-kalimatnya sejenis dan* ~. The sentences are of one type and similar to e.o. ~ *dengan ajaran Islam* to conform to Islamic doctrine. **menyenapaskan** to conform s.t. (to), make s.t. conform (to), make s.t. congruent (with).

bernapas 1 to breathe. **2** to sigh. **3** to catch one's breath. ~ *lega* (to breathe) to be relieved. ~ *dengan lapang* relieved. ~ *ke luar badan* to trust other people's opinions more than one's own.

bernapaskan to breathe (the spirit of), be inspired by. *cerita-cerita yang* ~ *keislaman* stories breathing the spirit of Islamism.

menapasi 1 to breathe new life into. **2** to apply artificial respiration to, give mouth-to-mouth resuscitation to, revive, resuscitate.

menapaskan to exhale/breathe out s.t.

napasan breathing.

pernapasan breathing, respiration. ~ *buatan* artificial respiration.

napas II reddish yellow color (of fur); → NAPES.

napekah → NAFKAH.

naper [nama dan peristiwa] names and events (rubric in newspaper).

napes (*Jv*) sorrel, bay. *kuda* – a bay/sorrel horse.

napi I [nara pidana] **1** prisoner, inmate. **2** criminal.

napi II → NAFI.

napol [narapidana politik] political prisoner.

Napoli Naples.

napsi → NAFSI.

napsu → NAFSU.

napuh (larger) dwarf musk deer of Java, *Tragulus napu*; *cp* KANCIL I.

napza, Napza and **NAPZA** [narkotika, alkohol, psikotropika dan zak adiktif (lainnya)] narcotics, alcohol, psychotropic drugs, and (other) addictive substances.

naql (*A*) textual. – *dan aql* textual and contextual (regarding the Koran).

nara (*Skr*) man, person, human being (in compounds). – *pertama/ kedua/ketiga* (*gram*) first/second/third person.

naracoba guinea pig.

naradakwa the accused, defendant; → TERDAKWA.

naraindra king.

naraka → NERAKA.

narakarya (*Jv*) worker, laborer.

naram (*Pers*) bass (voice).

narapati (*Skr ob*) king.

narapidana [napi] **1** prisoner, inmate. **2** criminal. – *politik* [napol] political prisoner.

menarapidanakan ~ *diri* to imprison o.s. ~ *diri di dalam sél-sél penjara matérialisme* to imprison o.s. in the prison cells of materialism.

narapraja (*Jv*) government official.

narasetu → NARWASTU.

narasi (*E*) narration.

narasumber resource person, i.e., a person who provides information about a certain topic.

menarasumberkan to resource.

naratif (*E*) narrative.

narawangsa race.

narawastu → NARWASTU.

narayana (*Jv*) **1** one's youth. **2** a boyhood name of Krishna.

naréndra (*Jv*) king.

narestu → NARWASTU.

narkoba [narkotik dan bahan berbahaya] narcotics and dangerous substances.

narkose (*D*) narcosis, anesthesia.

narkosis (*D/E*) narcosis.

narkotik(a) (*D*) narcotics.

narkotik-narkotikan addicted to drugs.

narsis (*D*) narcissus, daffodil, *Amarylidaceae*.

narsisisme (*D/E*) narcissism.

narsisistik (*E*) and **narsisistis** (*D*) narcissistic.

narwastu 1 vetiver, *Andropogon zizanioides*. 2 perfume (prepared from its roots), spikenard oil.

nas I (*A*) 1 authoritative quotation from the Koran or the Traditions
that settles a point of Islamic law or theology. 2 text, thesis. –.–
yang suci Koranic verses requiring careful interpretation.

   menaskan to authorize by quoting the Koran or *Hadis*.

nas II (*A*) *an*– "Human Beings"; name of the 114th chapter of the
Koran.

nas III (in acronyms) → NASIONAL.

nasab (*A*) family, lineage (*esp* on the male side). – *orangtua* parents' patrilineal family.

   menasabkan 1 to count as a member of the family. 2 (*geol*) to
correlate.

   nasaban (*geol*) correlation.

   penasaban (*geol*) correlating.

nasabah (*A*) 1 relation, connection. 2 customer, client (of a bank/
insurance company, etc.). – *bank* customer/depositor. – *utama*
best client.

   pernasabahan customer, client (*mod*).

nasakh (*A*) abrogated; abrogation.

   menasakhkan to abrogate.

Nasakom [Nasionalisme, agama, komunisme] Nationalism, Religion, and Communism, i.e., the unity proposed by President
Soekarno.

   menasakomkan to bring into *Nasakom*.

   penasakoman bringing s.t. into the *Nasakom* spirit.

Nasakomis supporter of *Nasakom*.

Nasakomisasi Nasakom-ization.

nasal (*D/E*) nasal.

nasalisasi (*E*) nasalization.

nasar (*A*) vulture.

nasarani → NASRANI.

nasèhat → NASIHAT.

nasgitel [panas, legi dan kentel] (*Jv*) hot, sweet, and thick (*esp* for
tea or coffee).

nashr (*A*) "Assistance"; name of the 110th chapter of the Koran.

nasi I cooked rice. *makan* – to eat (in general). *mencari sesuap* – to
look for a livelihood. *kalau belum makan* – *belum makan* rice is
essential to every meal. – *sudah (men)jadi bubur* what is done
cannot be undone; it's no use crying over spilt milk. – *habis budi
bersua* a friend in need is a friend indeed. – *tersaji di lutut* s.t.
good that is gotten easily. – *adap-adapan* k.o. rice dish served
at ceremonies. – *angkatan* rice served at banquets. – *begana*
rice and vegetables. – *belantah* rice that hasn't been cooked
enough. – *beriani* rice cooked in Indian spices. – *berkuah laksa*
rice cooked with noodles. – *besar* rice cooked for ceremonial
purposes. – *biji limau* rice that hasn't been cooked enough. –
bubur rice porridge. – *bungkus* rice wrapped in banana leaves. –
damai rice cooked for a wedding. – *dan lauk-pauknya* rice and
the accompanying side dishes. – *datang* rice boiled in a leaf. –
detus rice that hasn't been cooked enough. – *didang* steamed
rice. – *godak* rice cooked with vegetables. – *goréng* fried rice. –
gudangan rice mixed with vegetables, half an egg, etc. – *gudeg*
cooked rice with young jackfruit and chicken prepared with coconut milk (a specialty of Yogyakarta); → GUDEG. – *gurih* rice
cooked with coconut milk. – *hadap-hadapan* rice cooked for
ceremonies. – *jagung* ground corn. – *jaha* k.o. rice cakes from
Manado. – *jamblang* (in Cirebon) cooked rice wrapped in
leaves of the teakwood tree with various side dishes. – *jelantah*
rice that hasn't been cooked enough. – *jemah* rice cooked/boiled
in water. – *kabuli* rice cooked with mutton or goat curry. –
kapan rice plus hot peppers, meat wrapped in a leaf. – *kapau*
k.o. Minangkabau rice dish. – *kebuli* → NASI *kabuli*. – *kepal*
clotted cooked rice. – *kerak* the rice crust which adheres to the
pot. – *ketupat* rice wrapped in coconut leaves. – *kucing* small
portion of rice with tempeh and vegetables. – *kuduk* rice
cooked in coconut milk. – *kukus* steamed rice. – *kuning/kunyit*
rice boiled in coconut milk and colored yellow with turmeric. –
lamak creamed glutinous rice. – *langgi* coriander rice. – *lécék*
smashed up rice to be fed to an infant. – *lemak* boiled rice and
side dishes. – *lemang* glutinous rice with coconut milk boiled in
bamboo tubes. – *lengat* steamed rice. – *léngko* k.o. rice dish. –

lepat sticky rice boiled in a leaf. – *liwet* a) rice cooked until it has
absorbed all the water placed in the pot with it (a specialty of
Surakarta). b) (outside Central Java) rice cooked in coconut
milk. – *megono* k.o. rice dish from Pekalongan, contains young
jackfruit. – *mentah* rice that hasn't been cooked enough. – *minyak* rice boiled in water and some oil. – *papak* rice premasticated by mother. – *pelabur* rice ration in prison, etc. – *pulan*
rice that has been perfectly cooked. – *pulau* rice cooked in
broth. – *pulut* cooked glutinous rice. – *putih* white/steamed rice
(without anything added). – *ramas/rames* (*Jv*) rice mixed in
with the accompanying dishes. – *ransum* rice ration in prison,
etc. – *rawon* (*Jv*) cooked rice eaten with dark brown beef soup
with fresh bean sprouts and hot sauce. – *sega* (*J*) rice and spices
mixed together. – *tambah* seconds of rice. – *tanak* rice boiled in
water. – *thiwul* dried tapioca rice. – *tim* rice cooked in a pan of
water (au bain-marie). – *timbel* (*S*) cooked rice rolled in a banana leaf. – *tingkas* cooked white rice with a border of colored
rice. – *tiwul* dried cassava used as a substitute for rice. – *tuai*
glutinous rice with a creamy sauce. – *tumpeng* (*Jv*) a cone of rice
surrounded by various dishes; the yellow color signifies happiness and is served at wedding anniversaries, birthdays, etc. –
uduk rice cooked with coconut milk. – *ulam* steamed rice eaten
with raw vegetables and *sambal*. – *wuduk* → NASI *uduk*.

   bernasi with/to have rice. – *di balik kerak* there is s.t. going on
here, there is s.t. behind this; → ada UDANG *di balik batu*.

nasi II *jamur* – an edible mushroom, *Hydnum fragile*.

nasi III (*D*) nation.

nasiah (*A*) credit in financial transactions.

nasib (*A*) fate, destiny, lot (in life). *membawa/mencoba –nya* to try
one's luck (somewhere). *menentukan – sendiri* self-determination. *hak menentukan – sendiri* right of self-determination. –
saya belum sampai di situ my time hadn't come yet (to die).
menerima –nya to accept one's fate (uncomplainingly). *mengadu –nya* to try one's luck (somewhere). *menjalani –nya* to
fulfill/carry out one's destiny. *terdesak oléh keadaan – yang malang* (to have to accept s.t.) forced by necessity. *sudah – it* is
one's fate to, one is destined to. *sudah untung –* it has been one's
fate. *–nya sedang terang* he's lucky. – *baik* (good) luck, fortune.
– *bedebah/buruk/celaka/(ditimpa) malang/sial* bad luck.

   senasib of one destiny, having the same thing happen. *kawan/
saudara ~* a fellow-sufferer, one sharing the same fate. *~
sepenanggungan* sharing another's trials and tribulations.

   bernasib to have the fate of, have the same thing happen (as
happened to s.o. else). *~ baik/buruk* to have good/bad luck.
Nur yang tinggal di Tanah Abang juga ~ sama. Nur who also
lives at Tanah Abang shared the same fate. The same thing
happened to Nur, who also lives in Tanah Abang.

   menasibkan to destine, predestine; to foreordain (to any fate).

   nasib-nasiban haphazardly, at random.

nasihat (*A*) 1 (words of) advice, counsel; moral. *atas –* on the advice of. *memberi –* to give advice, advise. – *hukum* legal advice/
counsel. 2 admonition, warning, reprimand. *tak masuk –* not
receptive to advice, to be pigheaded/opinionated.

   menasihati 1 to advise s.o., give s.o. a lecture *~ anaknya supaya
belajar dan rajin* to advise one's child to study hard. 2 advisory. *kekuasaan ~* advisory power.

   menasihatkan to advise; to suggest. *Dokter ~nya supaya berhenti merokok.* The doctor advised him to stop smoking.

   penasihat 1 adviser, counselor, consultant. *~ hukum* legal coun-
sel/advisor. *~ perkawinan* marriage counselor. *~ politik* political adviser. 2 advisory. *déwan ~* advisory council.

   penasihatan advisement, advising.

nasikh (*A*) the abrogator, i.e., a part of the Koran which abrogates
another part of the Koran; *cp* MANSUKH.

nasi-nasi a plant whose roots are used to treat stomachaches, *Callicarpa longifolia*.

nasion (*E*) nation. *pembangunan ~* nation building.

nasional (*D/E*) national.

   menasional to be(come) national.

   kenasionalan 1 nationality. 2 nationalism.

   penasionalan nationalization.

nasionalis (*D*) nationalist.

nasionalisasi (*D*) nationalization.
  menasionalisasikan to nationalize.
nasionalisir (*D*) **menasionalisir** to nationalize.
nasionalisme (*D/E*) nationalism.
nasionalistik (*E*) and **nasionalistis** (*D*) nationalistic.
nasip → NASIB.
naskah (*A*) **1** (original) manuscript. **2** copy (to appear in newspapers/magazines/books, etc.). **3** draft, rough copy (of a treaty, etc.). **4** transcript. – *berita* copy. – *ceramah* script. – *cétakan* hard copy. – *digital* soft copy. – *film* scenario, (movie) script.
  senaskah a single copy.
  penaskah draft (*mod*). ~ *panitia* draft committee.
nasofaring (*E*) nasopharynx.
Nasr (*A*) *an-* "Assistance"; name of the 110th chapter of the Koran.
Nasrani (*A*) **1** Nazarene, Christian (formerly only referring to Roman Catholics; the Protestants were known as *Maséhi*; now used for either). *agama* – Christianity. *orang* – (*usu* shortened to *serani*). **2** (*ob*) Eurasian of mixed Asian and Portuguese descent.
  menasranikan to Christianize.
  kenasranian Christianity.
nastar [*ananas tar*] a *lebaran* pineapple pie.
nasut (*A*) mankind, human beings.
nasyid (*A*) antiphonal singing (by mystics), a capella group that sings songs with Islamic lyrics.
nata (*Skr*) king, majesty.
Natal (*Port*) Christmas. *Hari* – Christmas Day. *Selamat Hari* – Merry Christmas.
  bernatal(an) to celebrate Christmas.
  Natalan 1 to celebrate Christmas. **2** Christmas celebrations.
  pernatalan (*mod*) Christmas.
Natali Christmas (*mod*).
natalitas (*D*) birthrate. *angka* – birthrate.
natang (*cla*) a small window, aperture. *pintu* – side entrance.
natar (*Jv*) background/primary color of *batik* cloth. – *kuning* with a yellow background.
  penataran yard.
natijah (*A*) **1** alternative. **2** conclusion (of an act or event). **3** results, consequences, aftermath.
natirlek (*D ob*) of course.
nato I [*naskah asli ditepatkan oléh*] certified to be a true copy by.
NATO II North Atlantic Treaty Organization.
Nato III [*Nasution dan Soeharto*] (General) Nasution and (President) Soeharto.
natrium (*D*) sodium.
natur (*D*) nature.
natura (*D*) **1** natural. *dalam bentuk* – in a natural state. **2** in kind. *pembayaran dalam* – payment in kind.
natural (*D/E*) natural.
naturalis (*D*) naturalist.
naturalisasi (*D*) naturalization.
  menaturalisasi(kan) to naturalize.
naturalisir (*D*) **menaturalisir** to naturalize.
naturalisme (*D/E*) naturalism.
naturalistik (*D/E*) naturalistic.
naturalistis (*D*) naturalistic.
naturél (*Fr*) having its natural color or form, plain.
nau → ENAU.
naud(z)ubillahi (*A*) **1** God forbid! save us! (an expression uttered on seeing s.t. horrible). **2** terrible. *bau durian yang – harumnya* the incredibly fragrant smell of the *durian*.
naung 1 shadow, shade. **2** protection, shelter.
  bernaung 1 to seek/take shelter; sheltered, shaded. *duduk ~ di bawah pohon waringin* to sit and take shelter under a banyan tree. **2** to seek protection; protected. **3** to be under the (aegis, flag) of, affiliated (with). *Kapal tangker itu ~ di bawah bendéra Panama*. The tanker was under the Panamanian flag.
  menaungi 1 to shade, cast a shadow over. **2** to protect, shield, shelter, put under the aegis of.
  menaungkan to place (under the aegis of). *dinaungkan di bawah Ménko Kesra* to be placed under the aegis of the Coordinating Minister of Public Health.

ternaungi sheltered, protected.
naungan 1 shelter, protection. *di bawah* ~ under the aegis/auspices/wing of. *di bawah* ~ *Comecon yang pusatnya di Moskwa* under the aegis of Comecon whose headquarters are in Moscow. *Sebanyak 140 kapal lokal selama ini dioperasikan di bawah* ~ *perusahaan-perusahaan pelayaran Nusantara*. Up to now, as many as 140 ships for coastal shipping have been operating under the wing of Indonesian shipping companies. **2** shade. **3** under the sign (of the Zodiac) of. *Ia dilahirkan di bawah* ~ *Vrisaba*. He was born under the sign of Taurus.
  penaung 1 shelter. **2** patron.
  penaungan 1 patronage. **2** shelter. **3** shading.
  pernaungan shelter, protection.
nautik (*E*) nautical.
nautika nautical science. *Dinas* – Nautical Service.
nautis (*D*) nautical.
nau(d)zubillahi → NAUDUBILLAHI.
nav (in acronyms) → NAVIGASI.
navigasi (*D*) navigation. – *udara* aerial navigation. *alat* – navigational instruments.
  kenavigasian navigational. *kapal survéi* ~ navigational survey ship.
navigator (*D/E*) (Air Force) navigator.
nawa (*Skr*) nine (only in compounds).
nawab (*A*) viceroy.
nawafil (*A*) commendable, though not obligatory, prayers.
nawaitu (*A*) I intend.
Nawaksara [*Nawa + aksara*] Nine Points, i.e., the title of President Soekarno's speech to the MPRS on June 22, 1966, in which he was supposed to give an accounting for G30S/PKI.
nawala (*Jv*) **1** letter, writing. **2** ID card. – *patra* a) letter, writing. b) deed, instrument.
Nawalapradata (*Jv*) name of a book of laws in the Javanese Sultanates of Yogyakarta and Surakarta.
nawastu → NARWASTU.
nayaga 1 (*Jv*) *gamelan* player. **2** (*S*) player in *debus* performance.
nayaka (*Jv*) (cabinet) minister, advisor to the king.
nayam plowshare.
nayap (*Jv*) to steal s.t. (in broad daylight).
nayl (*A*) attainment, achievement. – *al-awthar* achievement of one's desires.
nayuban → TAYUB.
NAZA [*narkotik, alkohol dan zat adiktif*] narcotics, alcohol, and addictive substances.
nazak (*A*) **1** on the point of death. **2** unusable, worn out, in poor condition.
nazam → NALAM.
nazar (*A*) → NADAR.
Nazi (*D*) Nazi.
Nazi'at (*A*) *an-* "Those Who Pull and Withdraw"; name of the 79th chapter of the Koran.
nazim (*A*) poet, composer.
nazir → NADIR IV.
N.B. [*Nota Béné*] nota bene, note well, take notice.
nc- also see entries beginning with enc-.
nd- for words starting with nd- also see entries beginning with d- and end-.
ndableg and **ndablek** (*Jv*) stubborn, obstinate.
ndadak (*Jv*) → DADAK I. *Hujannya* –. All of a sudden it began to rain.
ndak I (*Jv coq*) no; not; → ENDAK II, NGGAK.
ndak II → HENDAK.
ndalem (*Jv*) room, hall.
ndang-ndut → DANGDUT.
ndara → NDORO.
ndérék (*Jv*) to accompany. – *béla sungkawa* my condolences.
Ndik (in Ujungpandang) the clipped form of *Andi(k)*, a title of nobility.
ndilalah (*Jv from A*) and fate would have it that, it so happened that, chance would have it that. – *masuk bersamaan dan pengaruh hippies, ganja, free sex dan sebagainya*. It so happened that this entered (the Third World) at the same time as the influence of hippies, marijuana, free sex, and the like; → DILALAH.

ndoblé (*Jv*) to be flabby and protruding (of one's lower lip). *kenalan saya yang bibirnya* – my acquaintance who has a flabby protruding lower lip.

ndoro (*Jv*) **1** sir, ma'am. **2** master, boss, employer; mistress. – *kakung* the master of the house. – *kanjeng* the *bupati*. – *mas* the son of the master. – *putri* the wife of the master. – *tuan/toewan* (*ob*) title of respectful address (for Arabs and Dutch). **mendoro-tuani** to use respectful titles in speaking to. **kendoro-tuanan** using respectful titles for people.

   mendorokan to call s.o. *ndoro*.

   ndoro-ndoroan to call (everybody) *ndoro*.

ndoroisme obedience, submissiveness (a feudal attitude).

ndto (*abbr*) [naskah ditandatangani oléh] draft copy signed by.

ndué gawé (*Jv*) to celebrate/have a (family) party (*esp* circumcision/wedding).

nduk → GENDUK.

ndut (*Jv*) go up and down.

   ndut-ndutan (*coq*) to pulsate, throb (with pain, etc.).

né (*C*) mother!

nébéng → TÉBÉNG II.

nébula (*E*) nebula.

nebus weteng (*Jv*) a joint (religious) meal in commemoration of the fact that an expectant mother is seven months pregnant.

néces and nécis (*D*) neat, smart, spruce, trim.

Néderlan(d) (*D*) the Netherlands.

Nederlandsche Handel Maatschappij → NMH.

Néfo(s) [New Emerging Force(s)] New Emerging Forces.

néfrologi (*E*) nephrology.

negara (*Skr*) the state, the government of a country; country, nation; *cp* NEGARI, NEGERI. *ahli* – statesman; → NEGARAWAN. *alat* – state apparatus. *bank* – national bank. *ibu* – *Indonésia* a) Fatmawati Soekarno. b) Tien Soeharto. *tamu* – state guest. – *adalah saya* l'état c'est moi. *empat* – *adidaya/adikuasa* superpower. – *agung* the hinterlands controlled by Mataram. – *anggota* member nation. – *Arab* Arab country. – *Arktik* Arctic country; the eight Arctic countries are: the U.S.A., Canada, Russia, Finland, Sweden, Norway, Denmark, and Iceland. – *As* Axis Powers (during WWII). – *asal* country of origin. – *bagian* (partition) state, i.e., any of the territorial and political units that together constitute a federal government, as in the U.S.A., Australia, etc. – *Bahari* Indonésia. – *bangsa* nation-state. – *bawah Sahara* sub-Saharan countries. – *bébék* satellite state. – *belahan Utara* countries of the Northern Hemisphere. – *berhaluan keras* hard-line countries (in the Arab world: Libya and Syria). – *beriklim tropis* tropical country. – *berkembang* developing country. – *bertetangga* neighboring country. – *beruang (mérah)* Russia. – *birokratik* bureaucratic state. – *bonéka* puppet state. – *débitur* debtor nation. – *Dunia Ketiga* Third World countries. – *4 musim* the West, i.e., the U.S.A. and its noncommunist allies in Europe and the Western Hemisphere. – *fédéral* (in the defunct RUSI or RIS) federal (partition) states, such as NIT, Pasundan, and Madura. – *féodal* feudal state. – *G-7* the "group of seven" leading industrial nations: the U.S.A., Japan, the United Kingdom, Canada, Italy, West Germany, and France, which meet occasionally to discuss economic matters. – *Gajah Putih* Thailand. – *Ginséng* Korea. – *gundal* satellite state. – *hukum* constitutional state. – *Indonésia Timur* [NIT] State of East Indonesia established by the Dutch in 1946 and constituted as a state of the Republic of the United States of Indonesia [RUS] (1949–50). – *induk* mother country (of a colony). – *industri baru* newly industrialized countries, NIC, such as Korea, Taiwan, Hong Kong, Singapore, Brazil, and Mexico. – *industri maju* advanced industrial nations. – *Islam* Islamic state. – *Islam Indonésia* [NII] Indonesian Islamic Nation. – *jiran* neighboring country (*usu* refers to Malaysia or Singapore). – *Kangguru* Australia. – *kapitalis* capitalist state. – *kekuasaan* totalitarian state. – *kekuatan raksasa* superpower. – *kepolisian* police state. – *kepulauan* archipelagic/island state. – *kerajaan* monarchy. – *kesatuan* unitary state. – *Kesatuan Kalimantan Utara* Unitary State of North Kalimantan, Sabah (under President Soekarno). – *Kesatuan Républik Indonésia* [NKRI] Unitary State of the Republic of Indonesia. **bernegara kesatuan** to have a unitary state. – *kesejahteraan*

welfare state. – *kincir angin* the Netherlands. – *kiwi* New Zealand. – *koboi* the United States. – *konco* satellite state. – *konfédérasi* confederated state. – *kota* city-state, i.e., Singapore. – *kréditor* creditor nation. – *Mabuhay* the Philippines. – *Macan Asia* the (emerging) four, East Asian Tigers. – *maju* developed/advanced countries. – *Masyarakat Éropa* [ME] European Community. – *matahari terbit* Japan. – *mitra dagang* trading partner country. – *multirasial* multiracial country. – *musang* the U.S.A. – *nasional* nation state. – *naungan* protectorate. – *Néfo(s)* Newly Emerging Force(s) nations (under President Soekarno). – *nonblok* nonaligned countries. – *nonkomunis* noncommunist countries. – *Oldefo(s)* Old Established Force(s) nations (under President Soekarno). – *palu-arit* Communist country. – *Paman Sam* the United States. – *Pancasila* Pancasila-based nation, i.e., Indonesia. – *pantai* coastal state. – *pascakolonial* postcolonial country. – *penampung pertama* first-asylum country, i.e., a nation which initially took in Indochinese refugees. – *pengékor* client state. – *pengékspor* exporting country. – *penyangga* buffer state. – *perusahaan* corporate state. – *polisi* police state. – *Poros* Axis Powers (during WW II). – *pulau* island-state, e.g., Singapore. – *raksasa* superpowers. – *républik apartheid* South Africa. – *sahabat* friendly nation. – *sakura* Japan. – *satelit* satellite state. – *sejahtera* welfare state. – *sékulér* secular state. – *sekutu* an ally. – *serikat* confederated state. – *sesaudara* sister countries, such as North and South Korea. – *Sirikit* Thailand. – *Skandinavia* Scandinavian countries. – *Stars and Stripes* the U.S.A. – *suapan* satellite state. – *super(kuat)* superpower. – *Syi'ah* reference to Iran. – *tak/tidak berpantai laut* landlocked country. – *Teluk (Persia)* (Persian) Gulf States, i.e., the oil-producing countries bordering on or located near the Persian Gulf. – *ter(ke)belakang* underdeveloped countries. – *terkunci daratan* landlocked country. – *terkurung daratan* land-locked nation. – *Timur Tengah* [TimTeng] Middle East(ern) countries. – *tirai bambu* the Peoples Republic of China. – *tirai batik* Indonesia. – *tirai besi* the Soviet Union. – *totalitér* totalitarian state. – *tropik/tropis* tropical country. – *tuan rumah* host country. – *tujuan* country of destination. – *Yahudi* Israel. – *yang berdaulat* sovereign state. – *yang cinta damai* peace-loving country. – *yang lebih berkembang* more developed countries. – *yang sedang berkembang/membangun/tumbuh* developing nations. –.– *yang sudah maju* developed countries. – *yang suka berperang* bellicose country. – *yang terkunci dan tidak berpantai* landlocked country. – *yang baru tumbuh* newly emerging countries. – *yang kurang berkembang* less developed countries, LDC. – *yang kurang maju* underdeveloped countries. – *yang lebih berkembang* more developed countries. – *yang sedang berkembang/membangun/tumbuh* developing nations. – *yang sudah maju* developed countries. – *yang suka berperang* bellicose country. – *yang terkunci dan tak berpantai* landlocked country.

   senegara of the same country, compatriot.

   bernegara 1 to be in the framework of a state. **2** state (*mod*). **3** as a state, with a state. **kebernegaraan** statehood.

   menegara to be(come) a state.

   menegarakan 1 to create a state. **2** to make s.t. state property.

   negara-negaraan a would-be state.

   kenegaraan state (*mod*), matters of state. *pidato* ~ Presidential address, State of the Nation message. *urusan* ~ state affairs.

   penegaraan state making.

negarawan (*Skr neo*) statesman; → AHLI *negara*.

   kenegarawanan statesmanship.

negari (*M*) **kenegarian** township, subdistrict.

négasi (*D*) negation.

   menégasi to negate.

   penégasian negating.

négatif and négatip I (*D*) negative; a word, phrase, etc. that denies, rejects, or refuses. *menjawab* – to answer in the negative. *nilai/pengaruh* – negative value/influence.

   menégatifkan to negate.

   kenégatifan negativity.

négatif and négatip II (*D*) negative, i.e., an exposed and developed photographic film.

négativisme (*D/E*) negativism.

Néger (*D*) Negro, a black.

negeri (*Skr*) **1** land, country. *Orang itu di mana –nya?* What is that person's native country? *ayam* – a species of chicken raised for its eggs and meat. *dalam* – a) domestic. b) internal (affairs). *ibu* – capital/city; → IBU *kota. kepala* – local chief. *kucing* – domestic cat. *luar* – a) abroad. b) foreign affairs. *Départemén Luar* – [Déplu] Department/Ministry of Foreign Affairs. *sekolah/universitas* – state school/university. *pengadilan* – district court. **2** (*ob*) town, city. *Kerapatan ini diadakan pada tanggal 27 dan 28 Oktober 1928 di – Jakarta.* This congress was held on October 27 and 28, 1928, in the city of Jakarta. **3** state; → NEGARA. **4** civil (servant), public (school). **5** (*M*) a cluster of hamlets or villages under a *penghulu* → NEGARI. **6** (*col*) the Netherlands. *pergi ke* – to leave (Indonesia) for the Netherlands (referring to a repatriated Dutchman); → PULANG *negeri Belanda. – akhirat* the hereafter, afterworld. *– antah-berantah* never-never land, fairyland. *– asing* a foreign country. *– atap dunia* Tibet. *– awak* one's native country. *– yang baka* the hereafter. *– Belanda* the Netherlands. *ke – cacing* to pass away. *– Cina* China. *– di atas angin* a) (originally) Arabia, Persia, and India. b) (by extension) Europe. *– dingin* the Netherlands. *– Embun Pagi* Korea. *– Gajah Putih* Thailand. *– Hang Tuah* Malaysia. *– jajahan* colony. *– jiran* neighboring country, reference to Malaysia. *– Kangguru* Australia. *– kekal* the hereafter. *– kembang tulip* the Netherlands. *– Kincir Angin* the Netherlands. *– kiwi* New Zealand. *– Kuda Semberani* North Korea. *– Lancang Kuning* reference to Riau. *– leluhur* ancestral country. *– luaran* foreign country. *– Mabuhay* the Philippines. *– matahari terbit* Japan. *– Oshin* Japan. *– orang* foreign country. *berada di – orang* to be abroad/in a foreign country. *– Paman Ho* Vietnam. *– Paman Sam* the United States. *– para datuk* Malaysia. *– Persemakmuran* Commonwealth country. *– Ramal* Saudi Arabia. *– Sakura* Japan. *– samba* Brazil. *– sauna* Finland. *– sendiri* one's own country. *– seribu candi* Burma. *– Singa* Singapore. *– Sirikit* Thailand. *– tetangga* neighboring country, reference to Malaysia or Singapore.

senegeri from one's own country. *orang* ~ compatriot, (fellow) countryman.

menegerikan to nationalize, transfer control of a university, etc. to the national government.

penegerian nationalizing.

négo(s) clipped form of *négosiasi*.

négosi (*D*) business, trade.

négosiasi (*D*) **1** (*ob*) trade, commerce. **2** negotiations. *melakukan* – to negotiate. *menolak melakukan – dengan para téroris* refusing to negotiate with the terrorists. *tidak memiliki posisi dalam bernégosiasi dengan pengusaha* do not possess a position in negotiating with the businessmen. *– perdagangan multilateral* multilateral trade negotiations. *– keringanan hukum* plea bargain.

bernégosiasi to negotiate.

menégosiasikan to negotiate about.

penégosiasian negotiating.

négosiator (*E*) negotiator; → PERUNDING.

Négro (*E*) Negro.

Négus → NIJAS.

néhé → BULUH *néhé*.

nek (*J/Jv*) **1** sickening, nauseating, disgusting; → ENEK. **2** sick to one's stomach, feel queasy. *rasa* – vertigo, dizziness, nausea. **3** irritated, annoyed. *Melihat mukanya saja saya sudah* –. Just seeing his face I become irritated.

nék clipped form of *nénék*.

néka → ANÉKA.

nékad I (*Jv*) → NÉKAT.

Nékad II [Negara kita pertahankan, ékonomi kita sosialisasikan, keamanan kita selenggarakan, agama kita muliakan, démokrasi terpimpin kita jalankan] the nation we defend; the economy we socialize; security we maintain; religion we honor; guided democracy we practice, slogan used by President Soekarno when installing members of the National Front on September 8, 1960.

nekara (*Pers*) large bronze drum.

nékarawan determined person.

nékat (*J?*) → TÉKAD. **1** determined, resolute, unwavering, firm of

purpose. *Kalau dilarang, saya akan – dan kabur.* If prohibited, I'll disappear. *Dan – dia mengakhiri hidupnya.* Unflinchingly he put an end to his life. **2** daring, rash, bold, headstrong, reckless. *Sudah – dan hilang malunya.* He is capable of anything. He will stop at nothing. *Akhirnya –nya menyebabkan matinya.* Finally his recklessness caused his death.

menékat to become determined (to do s.t.).

nékat-nékatan at all costs; (to do s.t.) regardless of the costs/difficulty involved, by any means required.

kenékatan recklessness, willful disregard of consequences; persistence in a course of action.

penékat s.o. who is determined.

nékel → NIKEL.

néker (*D Jv*) marble(s).

Nékolim [Néokolosme, kolonialisme dan impérialisme] Neocolonialism, Colonialism, and Imperialism (slogan launched under President Soekarno).

néko-néko (*Jv*) **1** various k.o. things; → (A)NÉKA. **2** to play games, fool around. *Kalau ada aparat Pemerintah yang – rakyat tidak akan sabar.* If there's a government apparatus that's playing games, the people won't be patient.

nékrofilia (*D/E*) necrophilia.

nékrolog (*D*) necrologist.

nékrologi (*D*) obituary (in newspaper).

nékromansi (*D/E*) necromancy.

nékropolis (*D/E*) necropolis.

nékrose (*E*) necrose, affected with necrosis.

néktar (*D/E*) nectar.

nelangsa (*Jv*) heartbroken, crushed with grief/hardship, miserable, pitiful, wretched.

kenelangsaan frustration.

penelangsaan feelings of grief/heartache.

nelayan (*Tam*) fisherman. *– andon/boro* (in Muncar, Banyuwangi, East Java) fisherman from outside the Muncar area who comes and stays in this area only during the fishing season. *– pendéga* a fisherman who works for a *juragan*.

kenelayanan fisherman's (*mod*).

penelayanan **1** fishing matters. **2** fisherman (*mod*). *Mendagri akan membicarakan soal* ~. The Minister of the Interior is going to discuss fishermen's problems.

nelongso (*Jv*) → NELANGSA. *serba* – deplorable, regrettable.

nem I shortening of various female names, such as, *Parsinem*.

nem II → ENAM.

NÉM [Nilai Ébtanas Murni] "pure Ébtanas evaluation," i.e., final examination grade on national exams.

nembé (*J/Jv*) the first(born). *Kalau anak – biasanya harus diruwat.* In case it's a firstborn child *usu* a ceremony should be held (giving a shadow-play performance).

nempil I <tempil> (*Jv*) **1** to participate in (a large purchase). **2** to buy little by little or in small quantities.

nempil II <tempil> (*J*) a small item among large ones. *Rumahnya – di tengah-tengah gedung-gedung besar.* His house is located among large buildings.

nempiri → NAFIRI.

némplok → TÉMPLOK.

némprak (*J*) to lie down on the floor.

nenar → NANAR.

nenas → NANAS.

nénda → NÉNÉNDA.

nendatan (*S*) **1** debris, detritus. **2** slump.

kenendatan slump.

penendatan slumping.

nénék **1** grandmother. **2** old woman. **3** granny. **4** (in certain areas) grandfather, great-uncle. **5** (*euph*) *si – loréng* the tiger; → KIAINYA. *– kebayan* (in fairy tales) a messenger, *usu* an older or married woman, between lovers. *– mamak* (*M*) elders. *– moyang* ancestors, forefathers; → KARUHUN, LELUHUR. **bernénék-moyangkan** to have as one's ancestors. *– saudara* great-aunt. *– sihir* an old sorceress.

nénék-nénék (of women) **1** very old. **2** a very old woman.

kenénék-nénékan to behave like a very old woman.

senénék with the same grandmother. *saudara* ~ first cousins.

bernénék to call s.o. *nénék.*

nének(an)da and **nénénda** (in correspondence) grandmother.

nénén (*J*) to breastfeed, nurse.

nénér young (freshly caught) milkfish; → BANDENG I.

nénés ooze.

bernénés and **menénés** to ooze out, be pussy (of a wound).

néng I (*onom*) tinkling (of a bell).

néng II (*J*) **1** appellation for a young woman. **2** term of endearment to one's little daughter.

Nengah (*Bal*) name element placed before personal names to indicate the second-born child, such as, *I – Widia.*

neng-nengan (*Jv*) not on speaking terms with e.o.

néng-nong 1 a bell. *pintu –* railway crossing bell. **2** (*onom*) sound of a bell ringing.

néngtét (*J*) **1** petite. **2** peeking out, partly visible (of one's body because the greater part is hidden behind a door, etc.).

néo- (*D/E*) neo-.

néofasis (*D*) neofascist.

néofit (*D*) neophyte.

néoimpérialisme (*D/E*) neoimperialism.

néoklasik (*D/E*) neoclassic(al).

néokolonialis (*D*) neocolonialist.

néokolonialisme (*D/E*) neocolonialism.

néolit (*E*) neolith.

néolitik (*E*) Neolithic.

néolitis (*D*) Neolithic.

néolitium (*D*) the Neolithic period.

néologisme (*D/E*) neologism.

néomodérnis neomodernist.

néomodérnisme (*D/E*) neomodernism.

néon (*D*) neon (light). *lampu –* neon lamp. *memasang – buat jalan-jalannya* to install neon lighting for the streets.

bernéon to have neon lighting.

menéonkan to convert (street lighting) to neon lighting.

penéonan illumination with neon.

néonisasi the introduction of neon lighting to replace older street lights.

nepakah → NAFKAH.

nepi (*Jv* → SEPI.

penepian place of asceticism.

népotis (*D*) nepotist.

népotisme (*D/E*) nepotism.

neptu (*Jv*) k.o. numerology.

Néptunus (*D*) **1** Neptune, the God of the sea. **2** Neptune, a planet in the solar system.

neraca (*Tam*) **1** (pair of) scales; → BALANS, DACIN(G). *membuat –* to draw up the balance sheet. **2** Libra (*zod*). **3** balance (of power), equilibrium. **4** account. *– akhir* closing balance sheet. *– awal* opening balance sheet. *– barang* trade balance. *– baskul* bascule. *– dagang* trade balance. *– dagang aktif* favorable trade balance. *– gabungan* consolidated balance sheet. *– kekuatan* balance of power. *– konsolidasi* consolidated balance sheet. *– modal* capital account. *– niaga* trade balance. *– pembayaran* balance of payments. *– percobaan* trial balance. *– perdagangan* trade balance. *ketekoran – perdagangan* unfavorable balance of trade. *– permulaan* opening balance sheet. *– renik* small pair of balances. *– saldo* trial balance. *– singkat* condensed balance sheet. *– utang-piutang* balance sheet.

nerak (*Jv*) to infringe, violate (the law). *– sarak* against regulations.

neraka (*Skr*) **1** hell. *isi –* people in hell. *siksa –* tortures of hell. **2** all k.o. sufferings and misery (e.g., poverty/sickness, etc.). **3** a bad person. *–, nyah di sini!* Beat it, you rat. *– dunia* unbearable torment. *– jahanam* the most hellish part of hell where infidels are put.

menraka 1 to become like hell. **2** to become all the rage. **3** to fly into a rage.

menerakai to make s.o.'s life a hell.

menerakakan to make s.t. into a hell, cause disaster, bring ruin upon. *~ derajatnya* to throw away one's reputation.

kenerakaan hell, calamity, disaster; place/condition of great suffering/misery.

néralgia → NÉURALGIA.

nerawang → NRAWANG.

nerétét (*J*) (to talk) nonstop.

nerimo → NRIMA.

néritis → NÉURITIS.

nerocos → NROCOS.

nérologi → NÉUROLOGI.

nésan → NISAN I.

nestapa (*Skr*) *duka –* sad, sorrowful, miserable; → SEDIH.

kenestapaan and **penestapaan** sadness, grief, sorrow, misery.

nét I (*D*) **1** net (in tennis/badminton, etc.). **2** (hair)net.

nét II (*D*) neat, clean, clear, fair; *opp* rough (of a copy/draft).

menétkan to make a fair/neat copy.

netiasa → SENANTIASA.

néting (*E*) **1** play (tennis, etc.) in front of the net. **2** hitting (the ball) into the net.

néto (*D*) net (profit/weight, etc.).

nétra (*Jv*) eye (in compounds only); → TUNANÉTRA.

nétraksara literate.

nétral (*D*) **1** neutral. **2** nonaligned. **3** (*gram*) neuter. *tidak –* nonneutral. *ketidak-nétralan* nonneutrality.

menétralkan 1 to keep neutral/nonaligned. **2** to neutralize. *~ racun dalam tubuh* to neutralize the poisons in the body.

kenétralan 1 neutrality. **2** nonalignment.

penétralan neutralizing, neutralization.

nétralis (*D*) neutralist. *golongan –* the neutralists.

nétralisasi (*D*) neutralization.

menétralisasikan to neutralize.

nétralisir (*D*) **menétralisir** to neutralize.

nétralisme (*D*) neutralism.

nétralitas and **nétralitét** (*D*) neutrality.

nétron → NÉUTRON.

nét(t)o (*D*) net (of price/weight, etc.); → BERSIH. *berat –* net weight. *gaji –* net salary, take-home pay. *laba –* net profit.

néuralgia (*D/E*) neuralgia.

néuritis (*D/E*) neuritis.

néuroanatomi (*D/E*) neuroanatomy.

néuroanatomis (*D*) neuroanatomical.

néurobiolog (*D*) neurobiologist.

néurobiologi (*E*) neurobiology.

néurolog (*D*) neurologist.

néurologi (*D/E*) neurology. *ahli/dokter –* neurologist. *– klinis* clinical neurology.

néurologis (*D*) neurological.

néurosis (*D/E*) neurosis.

néurotik (*E*) and **néurotis** (*D*) neurotic.

néutrino (*D/E*) neutrino.

néutron (*D/E*) neutron. *bom –* neutron bomb.

néven (*D ob*) branch, subsidiary.

ng- For verbs beginning with **ng-** also look under roots beginning with the following vowel or with **k**, for example, **ngalong** → KALONG; for verbs beginning with **nge-** also look under roots beginning with the following consonant, for example, **ngebagusin** → MEMBAGUSKAN.

ngabé(h)i (*Jv*) **1** official of middle-level rank. **2** police chief (in a rural area). **3** s.o. of lower nobility; title of lower nobility.

ngabektén (*Jv*) showing respect to an older person by kissing his/her knee on *Lebaran* day (in the *kraton*).

ngabekti (*Jv*) to show respect to an older person by kneeling and kissing his/her knee on *Lebaran* day.

ngabet (*Pr*) very.

ngabuburit to wait to break the fast.

ngaceng (*J*) → ACENG. **1** to have an erection. **2** to be erect.

ngaco → KACAU.

ngadak-ngadak (*J*) → MENDADAK.

ngadi-ngadi (*J*) recalcitrant, making it hard for others, stubborn. *Anaknya – benar, susah dinasihatkan.* His child is really stubborn and hard to give advice to.

ngah I (*J*) **1** conscious, aware. **2** to understand, know. *tidak –* don't know; → ENGAH I. *Beberapa pengamat ékonomi agaknya – bahwa mahalnya harga mobil sédan di sini karena pengaruh pajak.* It seems that some economic observers understand that the high cost of sedans locally is due to the effect of taxes.

ngah II clipped form of *tengah* in designations for siblings or parents' siblings. *abang* – an uncle between the eldest and youngest brothers of a parent.

ngahari → GAHARI.

ngah-ngah and **ngah-ngih** panting, gasping (for breath); → ENGAH-ENGAH, TERENGAH-ENGAH.

ngai (C) I (the personal pronoun).

ngajéni (*Jv*) to rate at its true value, appreciate at its proper value. – *pemimpin* to rate a leader at his true value.

ngak-ngik-ngok and **ngak-ngik-nguk** (*onom*) a discordant noise, out of tune. *kebudayaan* – a) imperialist/colonialist culture (so-called by President Soekarno). b) rock culture. *musik* – rock(-'n-roll) music; → MUSIK *cadas*.

ngalau (*M*) (natural) cave, grotto; → GUA I.

ngalor (*J/Jv*) to go north; northward; → LOR. *Terbangnya* –. It flew north. – *ngidul* a) (to differ) widely, immensely; on opposite sides. b) here and there, all over. c) wild (stories). *sambil cerita* –.*ngidul* while telling crazy stories.

ngambing a prickly perennial herb, *Lasia spinosa.*

ngamén → AMÉN. *tukang* – street musician.

ngan → DENGAN.

ngana (*Min*) you (personal pronoun *sg*).

nganga open-mouthed, gaping, wide open (of the mouth/door, etc.).
  senganga-nganganya as wide open as possible.
  menganga to be wide open, gape open, gaping.
  mengangai to gape at.
  mengangakan [and **ngangain** (*J*)] to open (one's mouth) wide. *Mulutnya dingangakannya atas permintaan dokter.* He opened his mouth wide at the doctor's request. *Ngangain mulutnya!* Open your mouth wide!
  ternganga l gaping, wide open. *Pintu rumah itu ~ walaupun tak seorang pun yang berada dalam rumah.* The house door stood wide open though nobody was home. **2** surprised, flabbergasted. *Dia ~ mendengarkan adiknya hendak menikah lagi.* He was flabbergasted to learn that his younger brother wanted to get married again.

ngangat → NGENGAT.

ngangen (*Jv*) to collect, gather, store up. – *kawruh* to gather wisdom.

ngangrang (*Jv*) a large red tree ant; → RANGRANG.

ngangsa eager, ambitious. *Dalam mengejar sesuatu kita tidak usah terlalu* –. In pursuing s.t. we shouldn't be too ambitious.

ngangu mengangu to roar.

ngangut mengangut to mutter inaudibly, mumble.

nganjal (*J*) to loaf around, stroll about without purpose.

ngantek (*Jv*) as far as, till, until, up to.

ngantol (*J*) to rest, take a break (from work/walking, etc.).

nganyep (*Jv*) to use no salt in one's food as a form of self-denial.

ngap ngap-ngap(an) l tired, panting. **2** to gasp for breath; → ENGAP-ENGAP, MENGAP.

ngapa (*J*) why? → MENGAPA.

ngapain (*J coq*) to do what; → MENGAPAKAN. *~ dia?* What's he doing?

ngaprah (*J*) to be found in large quantities. *Rambutan – di sana.* There are a lot of *rambutan* over there.

ngaprin (*J*) to be boyfriend and girlfriend.

ngarai (*M*) gorge, ravine, narrow pass, chasm, canyon.

ngarep → HARAP.

ngarsa (*Jv*) /ngarso/ in front. *ing* – *sung tulad(h)a* in front, providing with an example (part of an often quoted description of village life); → TUTWURI *handayani.* – *dalem* His Highness (the Sultan of Yogyakarta).

ngarti → ARTI.

ngas (*J*) body odor after having worked or played in the sun; → ENGAS.

ngasé (*IBT*) levies by the village administration.

ngas-ngasan (*Jv*) in a great hurry. *Jangan* –, *duduklah!* Don't rush around so much; sit down!

ngatang-atang (*Jv*) to lie stretched out on one's back.

ngatok (in East Java) bootlicking.

ngaung (*onom*) reverberating sound made by sirens, etc.
  mengaung to reverberate (as an empty house, etc.), echo.

ngawai (*Jv*) personal, (to do s.t.) personally, in person. *Saya sendiri tadinya acuh – terhadap kesembronoan pembangunan yang*

merugikan warga masyarakat. I myself used to pay personal attention to the frivolity of developments that inflict financial losses on the community.

ngawur (*J/Jv*) l to chatter (maliciously). **2** (to do a thing) without any reason or at random, act wildly; → AUR II.

ngayab and **ngayap** (*J*) to lounge around, saunter, hang out aimlessly.

ngayawara (*Jv*) l to talk incoherently. **2** made-up, invented. *Itu bukan cerita yang* –. That's not a made-up story. *kabar* – unconfirmed reports; → KABAR *angin/burung.*

nge- also look under entries beginning with **e** or **k** or with the consonant immediately following the **e.**

ngéak (*onom*) sound made by a crying baby.
  mengéak-ngéak [and **ngéak-ngéak** (*coq*)] to cry, scream (of a baby).
  terngéak-ngéak to keep on screaming.

ngebadeg and **ngebadek** (*J*) everywhere, quite a lot. *Utangnya – di mana-mana.* He's in debt everywhere.

ngébér (*gay sl*) to hang out.

ngebet I (*J/Jv*) l to hurt, ache, smart (of a wound). *Bisul* –. The abscess was aching. *Hati Bang Kojan sudah empot-empotan* –. Kojan's heart was beating so hard that it hurt. **2** to have a strong desire (for). *kalau céwék – sama cowok* if a girl hankers after a boy. *Dia – betul untuk mengunjungi Tanah Toraja.* He has a strong desire to visit Toraja Land. **3** horny, to feel sexy.

ngebet II tired of waiting. – *menyedot duit* to be out to hoard up money.

ngebleng (*Jv*) neither eat nor drink for certain days (in Javanese mysticism); *cp* PUASA *mutih.*

ngeblong (*Jv*) to overtake (a car).

ngebrit → IBRIT.

ngebrok <brok> (*Jv*) l to live together without being married. **2** to settle (down) in, take up one's residence.
  ngebroki to occupy, live in. *Balatentara Jepang ~ Jakarta.* The Japanese Forces occupied Jakarta.

ngebul l to puff, blow out clouds of smoke. **2** done, cooked (of rice). *Nasi belum – jangan diangkat dulu.* The rice has not yet cooked, don't remove it from the fire yet. **3** to talk big, boast, brag. *Tidak boléh – di tempat umum!* Don't smoke in public places!; → KEBUL.

ngebut (*J*) and **ngebutin** l to dust off (furniture). **2** to chase away mosquitoes (from a bed with a *kelambu*, etc.) using a *sapu lidi*; → KEBUT I.

ngecam (*sl*) to shoot up (with narcotics). *Meréka kepergok* –. They were caught in the act of shooting up.

ngécap → KÉCAP (*J*) to brag about o.s.

ngécéng (*BG*) l to show off. *Anak muda yang berkebiasaan – dengan Mércy.* Youngsters who are accustomed to show off in a Mercedes. **2** to draw attention to o.s. **3** to hang out.

ngeces <ces> (*Jv*) fizzle out. *Namanya kok* –? How come his name just fizzled out?

ngecrét (*sl*) to come, ejaculate; → CRÉT.

ngeden (*J*) to strain during a bowel movement or when giving birth.

ngedul (*J*) to act indifferently, intentionally unwilling to obey a command.

ngegetget (*J*) to tremble. *Dengkulnya – karena takut.* His knees trembled in fear.

ngegongi(n) <gong> (*J*) to agree to/with. *Seolah-olah saya – mendukung dia.* It was as if I agree with and support him. *Kalau orang itu berbicara, jangan – saja.* If that person talks, don't just agree with him.

ngeh (*BG*) to understand; → ENGAH I, MENGERTI. *nggak* – not understand, be out of it, not with it.

ngéhé I (*J*) to be cured of a habit, learn one's lesson. *-mu kapan?* When will you learn your lesson?

ngéhé II (*euph for ngéntot*) fuck s.o., fuck you.

ngejot (*J*) l to send food, etc. to one's parents, neighbors, etc. in the fasting month; → PUASA. **2** to send food to s.o. in order to win his/her heart.

ngék-ngék (*J*) crying (of a baby).

Ngéksigondo (*Jv*) (the former kingdom of) Mataram.

ngéli <kéli> (*Jv*) – *ning ojo keli* to give in. –, *nrimo*, *sabar* giving in, passive/uncomplaining/acquiescent and patient.

ngeliat → MELIHAT.

ngélmu (*Jv*) knowledge (usually esoteric); → ILMU. – *kadigdayan* knowledge of magical powers. – *katuranggan* physiognomy.

ngelotok <kelotok> come/peel off easily.

ngelu (*Jv*) aching and heavy (feelings in head).

ngembat <embat> (*J*) 1 to attack (food). *Sudah nyaplok ketupat tiga biji, kok sekarang – tiga biji lagi.* You've already swallowed three *ketupats*, how come you're attacking three more? 2 to take, steal. – *jemuran orang* to steal s.o.'s laundry. 3 to accelerate, increase the speed of.

ngemot and **ngemut** to hold s.t. in one's mouth.

ngemplang → KEMPLANG I, II.

ngendek <endek> (*J/Jv*) 1 to reside, live, stay. *Tiga hari saya – di rumah janda itu.* For three days I stayed in that divorcee's house. 2 to live together without being married.

ngendek-ngendek <endek> (*J*) 1 to come or go surreptitiously. *Dia – masuk ke rumah kami.* He clandestinely entered our house. 2 to walk/move with head bent over (so as not to be noticed).

ngendog <endog> (*sl* in Bandung elementary schools) to flunk.

ngenes (*J/Jv*) deeply saddened.

    mengeneskan pitiful, pitiable, sad. *Populasi jalak Bali di habitat aslinya sangat ~.* The population of the Bali mynah in its original habitat is most pitiable.

ngéngang (*J*) to walk with (one's) legs apart (for instance, due to having a pimple on the thigh).

ngengap <ngap> (*J*) to pant, gasp for breath.

ngengat (*J?*) various species of moth.

    berngengat with lots of moths in it.

ngéngék → RÉNGÉK.

ngéngér (*Jv*) 1 to live in s.o.'s home as a servant. 2 (of a child) to live in the home of a relative, to serve him and to learn proper manners and become educated. *menghindarkan sikap méntal – seperti pembantu zaman dulu* to avoid the servile attitudes of the past.

ngenget → NGENGAT.

ngentit (*J*) to pilfer s.t. *Seorang kondéktur bis PPD mengakui setiap bertugas, bersama rekannya serta pengemudi berhasil – uang hasil penarikan ongkos bis sampai Rp 15.000,-.* A conductor of a bus of the Jakarta Transportation Company admits that every functionary, together with his colleagues and the driver, can pilfer up to Rp 15,000.00 from the proceeds of a bus ride.

ngenyék (*J*) to humiliate, ridicule.

ngéong (*onom*) meow.

    mengéong to meow.

ngepék <kepék> (*Jv*) to cheat on a test, do schoolwork dishonestly by using a crib.

ngepér → PÉR VI.

ngépét → KÉPÉT I, BABI *ngépét*.

ngepia too much, to overdo.

ngepiah and **ngepié** (*J*) sincere, open, honest.

ngéréng (*J*) fragrant, aromatic.

ngeres 1 to have s.t. in one's eye. 2 dirty. 3 to feel sad.

ngeri 1 horrible, terrible. 2 afraid, scared, frightened, terrified.

    mengerikan 1 terrifying. 2 horrifying. 3 to scare, frighten. 4 eerie, it gives one the chills.

    kengerian 1 terror, fear. 2 horrified. 3 terrified.

ngeriap → RAYAP II.

ngerong-ngering very noisy.

nges (*Jv*) 1 sensitive. 2 moved. 3 emotional. *kurang* – apathetic.

ngésot → KÉSOT.

ngetnget → NGENGAT.

ngétngot (*J*) accordion.

ngg- for verbs starting with **ngg-** also look for entries beginning with **g-**.

nggak (*J*) no, not; → NDAK I, ENGGAK.

nggo pék → GO PÉK.

ngiang (*onom*) buzz, whistle, hum, whining sound. *si ngiang-ngiang* k.o. ghost.

    mengiang(-ngiang) to buzz, whistle, whine.

    mengiangi to buzz in (one's ears), whistle.

    terngiang(-ngiang) to buzz, whistle, whine. *Dia selalu ~ nasihat ayahnya.* He's always whining about his father's advice.

ngiau → NGÉONG.

ngidem – *gawé* (*Pal*) to hide the evidence of one's crime.

ngih (*onom*) sound of s.o. blowing his nose.

ngikngik (*J*) 1 out of breath. 2 sickly.

ngilu 1 gnawing pain. 2 setting one's teeth on edge. –.– *kuku* lukewarm, tepid.

nging (*onom*) whistling noise.

ngipé → IPÉ.

ngitngit (*onom*) buzzing sound of mosquito.

ngiung-ngiung (*onom*) sound of a racing engine.

'ngkali clipped form of **barangkali**.

ngko → ENGKO.

ngkong → ENGKONG.

ngliat → MELIHAT.

nglokro (*Jv*) hopeless, desperate.

nglomprot (*Jv*) sloppy (*esp* about dress).

ngo (*C*) I, me.

ngohiang and **ngohiong** (*C*) five-spice powder.

ngok-ngik (*onom*) sound of cacophonous musical instruments.

ngoko (*Jv*) low level (of Javanese language).

ngom clipped form of **ngompol**.

ngombé (*J*) to be a free-loader.

ngorok snore. *penyakit* – septicemia, a disease of cattle.

    mengorok to snore.

    ngorokan snoring.

    pengorok snorer.

ngos to run out of steam, be without any energy.

    ngos-ngosan 1 to pant. 2 to be near death.

ngot-ngotan (*Jv*) irregularly, recurrent.

ngoyang post-partum blues.

ngoyo (*Jv*) to exert o.s., take the trouble to. *tak* – not interested, unenthusiastic.

Ngr (*abbr*) [Ngurah] Ngurah, a name element in Balinese names.

ngrasa → MERASA.

nguing (*onom*) sound of a siren.

nguk and **nguk-nguk** (*onom*) sobbing sound.

ngulét (*J*) 1 to stretch after waking up. 2 to turn around in one's sleep. 3 to warp (of wood in the sun).

ngung (*onom*) snoring sound.

ngungap → NGAPNGAP.

ngungu (*onom*) sobbing sound.

    mengungu-ngungu to sob.

    terngungu to sob.

ngurek eel.

ngurtak (*sl Med*) to do drugs.

ngutngit (*onom*) 1 gnawing sound. 2 sound of harmonica.

ngutngut I 1 to mumble. 2 to move one's lips while eating.

ngutngut II in doubt, hesitant.

ni I (*J*) clipped form of *ini*; can precede the noun. – *buku sangat baik.* This book is very good.

ni II clipped form of **nini**, **noni**, **uni**.

ni III (*C*) you.

ni IV → NYAI.

Ni V (*Bal*) a caste-indicating title placed before female personal names to indicate that the persons who hold this title belong to the Sudras, such as – *Nyoman Puri*, – *Wayan Mariani*.

NI VI [Negara Islam] Islamic State.

nia (*C*) collar (of shirt, etc.).

niaga I (*Prakrit*) 1 commerce, trade, business. – *Ékasari* the women's association of the Department of Commerce and Cooperatives. – *jasa perjalanan* travel bureau. 2 commercial (vehicle) (as opposed to a passenger vehicle).

    berniaga to conduct/do business.

    meniaga (*infr*) → BERNIAGA.

    meniagakan and **memperniagakan** to trade in s.t.

    terniaga traded, sold.

    keniagaan business, trade (*mod*).

    peniaga merchant, trader, dealer, businessman. *bangsa ~* a trading nation.

    perniagaan trade, commerce. *~ budak* slave trade. *~ éceran/rincih* retail trade.

niaga II → NIYAGA.

niagawan trader, businessman.

nian (*M*) **1** very, really, truly; → BANGET, SANGAT, SUNGGUH. *benar* – very true. *besar* – very large. **2** (word to emphasize or stress the meaning of the preceding word). *apa* –? what? *sebentar* – just a minute.

niat (*A*) **1** intention, aim, plan; → MAKSUD. – *baik* good intentions. – *hati* firm intention. *mengubah* –*nya* to change one's plans. *sudah bulat* – determined, convinced. **2** vow (to God) *melepas* – to fulfill a vow. *memasang* – to vow; → BERKAUL, BERNADAR. *membayar* – to fulfill a vow. **3** wish, desire, the will to do s.t. – *tak sampai* my devout wish was not fulfilled. *kaul (di)* –, *lain (di) takdir* man proposes, God disposes.
  berniat to intend, hope/expect to.
  berniat-niat to keep intending/hoping.
  meniati to want s.t., intend to get s.t.
  meniatkan 1 to intend, plan, aim. **2** to make a vow (for s.o.'s benefit). **3** (*M*) to pray for; to hope for.
  meniat-niatkan to have a strong wish to do s.t.
  terniat 1 intended, meant. **2** s.t. for which a vow was made.
  niatan intention, aim, s.t. intended.

niaya → ANIAYA.

nibung a tall tufted palm whose thorny stem is used for flooring, fishing stakes, and wash-strakes of boats; nibong palm, *Oncosperma filamentosum* and giant fish-tail palm, *Caryota rumphiana*. – *bangsai bertaruk muda* an old person trying to behave like s.o. young.

NICA /nika/ [Netherlands Indies Civil Administration] Netherlands Indies Civil Administration, i.e., the Dutch civil administration at the early stages of its attempts to recapture Indonesia (August 1945).

nich → NIH.

nick (*E*) **1** user name (in an Internet website). **2** nickname.

nidera (*Skr*) **1** sleepy. **2** asleep. **3** sound, deep (of sleep).

nifak (*A*) hypocrisy; → MUNAFIK.

nifas (*A*) childbirth, confinement. *darah* – lochia. *demam* – puerperal/childbed fever. *mandi* – cleansing 40 days after childbirth. *masa* – period of confinement. *perempuan* – a woman in labor.

nigong (*J*) tartar, plaque; → JIGONG.

nih (*coq*) → NI I. – *yé* it's this one, right?

nihil (*D*) nothing, zero.
  kenihilan nothingness.

nihilis (*D*) nihilist.

nihilisme (*D/E*) nihilism.

NII [Negara Islam Indonésia] Indonesian Islamic Nation.

nijas (*A*) the King of Ethiopia; → NÉGUS.

nik I term of address for young girl, miss; → NONIK.

nik II term of address for nénék.

Nik III [Nomor Induk Kepegawaian] ID number for BUMN employees.

Nik IV [Nomor Induk Kependudukan] Resident's ID Number.

Nik V [Nomor Idéntifikasi Kendaraan] Vehicle Identification Number, VIN.

Nika → NICA.

nikah (*A*) **1** marriage; → KAWIN. **2** to get/be married. *akad* – marriage contract. – *agama* wedding performed before a religious official. – *bedol* wedding performed at home. – *campur* mixed marriage. – *gantung* legally married but waiting for the marriage to be consummated. – *kantor* wedding performed before a government official. – *mut'ah/mutah* trial marriage. – *sirri* Islamic but unregistered marriage. – *taklik* to marry with the stipulation of divorce if the husband deserts. – *tambelan* marriage with a pregnant woman so that the child has a legal father.
  bernikah to marry, get married.
  menikah to marry, get married. ~ *tamasya* a wedding after which there is no reception; the couple leaves for their honeymoon immediately.
  menikahi to get married to.
  menikahkan to marry s.o. off.
  nikah-nikahan (*coq*) to get married again and again.
  pernikahan 1 marriage. **2** wedding.

Nikaragua Nicaragua.

nikel (*D*) nickel.
  pernikelan nickel (*mod*).

nikmat (*A*) **1** delightful, nice, pleasant, comfortable. **2** comfort, luxury. **3** gift, grant (from God), grace.
  senikmat as pleasant as.
  menikmati 1 to enjoy, taste (food). ~ *hidup* to enjoy life, have fun. **2** to benefit from (a privilege, such as a tax holiday, etc.).
  menikmatkan to enjoy, relish.
  ternikmat enjoyed, relished.
  kenikmatan 1 pleasure, enjoyment, happiness, bliss, comfort, joy. ~ *duniawi* worldly pleasures. ~ *rohani/ruhani* spiritual pleasures. **2** privilege. **3** a benefit (enjoyed). ~ *di daérah terpencil* remote/hardship allowance.
  penikmat 1 lover, aficionado, s.o. who enjoys s.t., fan. ~ *musik* music lover. **2** (*fin*) beneficiary.
  penikmatan enjoying, enjoyment, relishing, benefiting.

nikotin (*D/E*) nicotine.

nil I → NIHIL.

Nil I the Nile.

nila I (*Skr*) **1** indigo; *Indigofera spp.* **2** blue. – *setitik rusak susu sebelanga* and *sebab* – *setitik rusak santan/susu sebelanga* one rotten apple spoils the whole barrel. – *kecil* k.o. groundcover, birdsville indigo, *Indigofera linnaei*.

nila II *ikan* – parrot fish, *Pseudodax, spp.*; → BECUK.

nilai 1 value. **2** cost, worth, price. **3** rate. **4** appraisal, estimate, assessment, rating, grade (in school). **5** standard, quality, rank. **6** (school) grades, marks. *kemunduran* – depreciation. *kenaikan* – appreciation. *dengan* – *sebesar* to the value of. – *agunan* loan value. – *bakar* combustion efficiency. – *batas* cut-off point. – *batas lulus* passing grade. – *beli* purchase price. – *berwujud* tangible value. – *budaya* cultural value. – *buku* book value. – *campur* (*petrol*) blending value. – *dinyatakan* declared value. – *dugaan* estimate. – *Ébtanas Murni* → NÉM. – *gizi* nutritive value. – *hidup* moral values in life. – *jaminan* collateral value. – *jual kembali* resale value. – *keagamaan* religious value. – *jual objék pajak* [NJOP] taxable item market value. – *kapitalisasi pasar* market cap. – *kecerdasan* IQ. – *lalai* default value. – *lawan* rate (when exchanging one currency for another), equivalent, countervalue. – *lebih* a) advantage. b) value added. c) surplus value. – *luhur* core/ancestral values. – *mérah* low grade, low rating, caution, disclaimer (on an accountant's report). – *modal* assets. – *nominal* face/nominal/par value. – *pakai* use value. – *pari* par value. – *pasar* market value. – *patokan* (*fin*) check rate. – *pelunasan* redemption price. – *pengembalian* refund value. – *pengganti(an)* replacement value. – *penghargaan* award for achievement. – *penguangan* surrender value. – *perdagangan* commercial value. – *perkenaan* (*mil*) percentage of hits. – *peroléhan* (acquisition) cost. – *pertumbuhan* growth rate. – *rata-rata* average value. – *réalisasi bersih* net realizable value. – *sastra* literary value. – *sisa* salvage/scrap/recovery value. – *tambah* value added. – *tebusan* redemption price. – *tengah* mean. – *tercatat* carrying value. – *tukar* exchange rate. – *tunai* cash value (of an insurance policy), surrender value. – *uang* monetary value. – *wajar* fair value.
  senilai worth, for the amount of, with a value of. ~ *12 ribu dolar* worth $12,000.
  bernilai 1 to be worth, cost. *Barang-barang ini* ~ *jutaan rupiah.* These goods are worth thousands of rupiahs. **2** valuable, precious. ~ *sejarah* of historical value. *tidak* ~ invaluable, priceless.
  menilai(kan) 1 to evaluate, put a value on, appraise, assess, judge. **2** to believe, think, consider.
  ternilai 1 evaluated. *tidak* ~ (*harganya*) invaluable, priceless. **2** believed, thought to be.
  nilaian value, price, worth.
  penilai 1 evaluator, assessor, appraiser. **2** grader, judge (in a contest).
  penilaian 1 appraisal, evaluation, assessment, rating. ~ *kemampuan dan kepatutan* fit and proper test. ~ *krédit* credit rating. ~ *pegawai* personnel evaluation. **2** opinion, belief, judgment. ~ *dari jawaban-jawaban* judging from the replies.
  pernilaian rating, evaluation, appraisal.

nilajada dark grey.

nilakandi (*Skr*) **1** azure, royal blue. **2** (*batu* –) sapphire.

nilam I (*Tam*) patchouli, *Pogostemon patchouli/heyneanus*.

nilam II *burung* – k.o. bulbul, *Pycnonotus aurigaster*.
nilangsuka dark cyan blue.
nilau k.o. tree whose bark is used for fiber, brown kurrajong, *Commersonia bartramia*.
nilem → NILAM I.
nilon (*E*) nylon.
NIM [Nomor Induk Mahasiswa] Student ID Number.
ni'mat → NIKMAT.
nimba and **nimbo** → MINDI.
nimbrung → TIMBRUNG.
nimfa (*D*) nymph.
nin (*cla*) → INI.
ninabobok lullaby.
   meninabobokkan to sing a lullaby to, rock to sleep.
   terninabobok(kan) lulled (to sleep).
   peninabobokan lullabying, rocking to sleep.
ning (*onom*) ringing or tinkling noise.
ningnéng and **ningnong** (*onom*) ringing noise.
ningrat (*Jv*) noble, aristocratic.
   meningratkan 1 to ennoble. **2** to treat s.o. as a noble.
   ningrat-ningratan feudal.
   keningratan nobility, aristocracy.
   keningrat-ningratan to act like nobility, snobbish.
ningratisme feudal thinking and behavior.
nini (*J/Jv*) term of address to old woman; → NÉNÉK. – *towok/towong* female puppet made from coconut shell attached to a stick.
ninik – *mamak* (*M*) *adat* chief, clan head.
nini-kemang dwarf.
ninon-ninon – *gunung* indigo flycatcher, *Muscicapa indigo*.
NIP [Nomor Induk Pegawai] Civil Service ID Number.
nipah mangrove tree, *Nipa fruticans*.
nipas → NIFAS.
nipel (*D/E*) nipple.
nipis → JERUK *nipis*.
Nippon Japanese.
nir- I (*Skr*) prefix used in neologisms meaning without, -less, non-.
nir II (*coq*) kidney.
nira (*Skr*) juice of the sugar palm (*Arenga pinnata*), which when fermented turns into toddy and vinegar.
nirabjadi illiterate.
nirair anhydrous, waterless.
nirakal senseless.
nirakhlak characterless.
niraksara illiterate.
   keniraksaraan illiteracy.
niraksarawan illiterate person.
niranta endless, infinite. – *kecil* infinitesimal.
nirarti meaningless.
nirasa → NIRRASA.
niratap roofless.
niratma inanimate.
nirbahaya safe, without danger.
nirbait homeless.
nirbangun amorphous, shapeless, formless.
nirbarat non-Western.
   menirbaratkan to dewesternize.
   penirbaratan dewesternization.
nirbau odorless.
nirbentuk amorphous, shapeless, formless.
nirbusana without clothes, undressed, naked. *orang* – nudist.
nircék checkless.
niréléktronik nonelectronic.
nirfisik nonphysical. *kualitas* – nonphysical qualities.
nirgelar nondegree.
nirgema anechoic.
nirgerak motionless.
nirgésékan frictionless.
nirguna useless.
nirhawa without air, airless.
nirhenti ceaseless, nonstop.
nirinti non-nuclear.
nirjana unpopulated.

nirkabel wireless.
nirkarat stainless (steel), rustproof.
nirkelamin agamous.
NIRL [Nomor Induk Régistrasi Lulusan] Graduate Registration ID Number.
nirlaba nonprofit. *organisasi* – nonprofit organization.
nirlaras disharmonious.
nirléka prehistoric.
NIRM [Nomor Induk Régistrasi Mahasiswa] Student Registration ID Number.
nirmakna meaningless.
nirmala pure, stainless.
nirmana (*infr*) – *ruang* interior design.
nirnalar unreason.
nirnama anonymous.
nirnoda spotless, stainless, immaculate.
nirnyawa lifeless, inanimate.
nirrasa apathetic.
nirseni artless.
nirsuara voiceless.
nirtata disorderly.
   kenirtataan disorderliness.
nirtropis and **nirtropik** nontropical.
niru → NYIRU.
nirwana (*Skr*) Nirwana.
nirwarganegara stateless.
nirwarna colorless, achromatic.
nirwarta off the record, non-notification.
Nisa (*A*) *an*– "The Women"; name of the fourth chapter of the Koran.
nisab I (*A*) → NASAB.
nisab II (*A*) the smallest amount of assets subject to the *zakat*.
nisa(a)k → NISA.
nisan I (*Pers*) gravestone, tombstone. – *batu* gravestone.
nisan II (*Pr*) marijuana.
nisbah I (*A*) **1** ratio, quotient. – *gas minyak* [NGM] (*petro*) gas oil ratio [GOR]. – *laba terhadap aktiva* return on assets [ROA]. – *utang* debt ratio. **2** relationship, tie. – *tunai* reserve requirement. **3** share of the profits or losses.
   bernisbah to be related (to).
   menisbahkan to relate s.t. (to).
nisbah II (*A*) **1** family relationship. **2** a single generation.
nisbi and **nisbiah** (*A*) relative.
   menisbahkan to make s.t. relative (to).
   kenisbian relativity.
niscaya (*Skr*) certain(ly), sure(ly).
   keniscayaan certainty.
nisf sya'ban and *malam* **nisfu** (*A*) – the night of 15 *Sya'ban* when the angel Gabriel spoke to the Prophet Muhammad.
nishab → NISAB.
niskala (*Skr*) **1** abstract. **2** immaterial.
   meniskalakan to abstract.
   keniskalaan abstraction.
   peniskalaan abstracting.
nista (*Skr*) **1** shame, stigma. – *yang tidak terhapuskan lagi* indelible shame. **2** humiliation, insult, abuse. **3** humiliated. **4** mean, base, low, vile, contemptible, rotten, unethical. *durjana* – base, vile.
   menista to revile, insult, humiliate, defame.
   menistai to revile, insult, humiliate.
   menistakan to revile, insult, humiliate.
   ternista reviled, humiliated.
   nistaan insult.
   kenistaan 1 insult. **2** feelings of humiliation.
   penista defamer.
   penistaan insulting, humiliating, defaming, defamation, stigmatizing, defamation, libel. ~ *lisan* oral defamation. ~ *tulis* written defamation, libel.
niti (*Skr*) policy.
nitrat (*D*) nitrate.
nitrifikasi (*D*) nitrification.
nitrit (*D*) nitrite.
nitrogén (*D/E*) nitrogen.
Niugini New Guinea; → NUGINI.

niur → NYIUR.

nivo (F) level.

niyaga and niyogo (Jv) performers in a *gamelan* orchestra.

niyah → NIAT.

niyahi → NYAI.

nizam (A) regulations.

njawani → JAWA.

njlimet → JLIMET.

NJOP → NILAI *jual objék pajak.*

NKK → NORMALISASI *Kehidupan Kampus.*

NKRI [Negara Kesatuan Républik Indonésia] Unitary State of the Republic of Indonesia.

NMH [Nederlandsche Handel Maatschappij] Netherlands Trading Company, created in 1824 as the colonial government's monopoly trading company.

Nn (abbr) [Nona] Miss.

no I (C J) two (in money values).

no II (J/Jv) over there. –, *di kamar belakang!* over there, in the back room!

no III (Jv) Do it that way!

no IV (IBT) respectful term of address to man.

No V (abbr) [Nomor] number.

noban (C J) 20,000 (rupiahs); → NO I.

nobat (Pers) 1 a large drum (beaten in homage of the sovereign during accession to the throne). 2 audience. *Baginda tiada –.* His Excellency does not grant audiences. *naik –* a) (M) to marry; to become a bride(groom). b) inaugurated as the sovereign.

bernobat to hold an audience.

menobatkan to install, inaugurate, crown.

penobatan installation, inauguration, coronation.

nobra braless.

nocap (C J) 20 (rupiahs).

nocéng (C J) 2,000 (rupiahs).

noda (J?) 1 stain, blot, spot, speck, dirt (on clothes, etc.), blemish, patch (on flora or fauna). *obat –* stain/spot remover. 2 disgrace, stain on one's reputation. 3 rape. 4 infamy, ignominy. – *matahari* sunspot.

bernoda 1 to have spots/stains; besmirched, soiled, stained. 2 to have a bad name, dishonored, disgraced. 3 to be raped. *tidak ~* a) unsullied. b) immaculate, spotless. c) saintly.

menodai 1 to foul, defile, soil, make dirty. 2 to deflower (a virgin). 3 to dishonor, disgrace. 4 to rape.

ternoda 1 defiled, soiled, sullied. 2 dishonored, disgraced. 3 raped.

penodaan 1 staining, soiling. 2 disgrace. *~ darah* incest.

nodari → NODA *matahari.*

nodék (Med) *tidak diambil –* not take notice of it, not heed it.

nodul (D/E) nodule.

nogat (D) nougat.

no go (J C) 2,500 (rupiahs).

noh I (J/Jv) there. *Pacar gué – nonton!* My sweetie there is watching!; → NO II.

Noh II (A) (the biblical) Noah.

noja I plant that produces a substance for dyeing fabrics, *Peristrophe bivalvis.*

noja II mosque official who beats the drum for prayers.

nok clipped form of denok.

noken – *as* camshaft.

nokén (Pap) crocheted or knitted basket.

noktah (A) 1 dot, point, vowel point (in Arabic). 2 period, full stop. – *bertindih* colon. – *koma* semicolon. 3 (bio) pit.

bernoktah to have a dot/period. *koma ~* semicolon.

menoktahi to dot, put dots on.

nol (D) 1 (numeral) zero, naught, 0. *4508 dibaca sebagai empat, lima, nol, delapan.* 4,508 is read as four, five, zero, eight. *0,5 dibaca sebagai nol koma lima.* 0,5 is read as zero comma five. *Meréka yang sama sekali – bahasa Jepang, kini sudah bisa menulis dan berbahasa Jepang.* Those who had not the slightest knowledge of the Japanese language can now write and speak the language. *titik –* zero. 2 lowest grade (in school classification system with a preparatory class) *murid kelas –* a kindergarten pupil. *naik kelas – besar* to be promoted to the second level of kindergarten. *kelas – kecil* class for three- and four-year-olds. 3

(starting from) scratch/zero. *memulai usahanya dari –* to start his business from scratch. 4 without (any) result, unsuccessful. *Dia sudah berusaha, tetapi hasilnya –.* He has already tried hard, but without success. – *besar* total zero, nothing at all.

menolkan to put (the needle) back to zero. *Angka belum dinolkan kembali.* It hasn't been set back to zero.

kenolan nullity.

nolina pony-tail plant, *Beaucarnea recurvata, Nolina recurvata.*

nomad (D/E) *orang –* a nomad.

nombor (coq) → NOMOR.

noméi → IKAN *noméi.*

noménklatur (D) nomenclature.

nomer → NOMOR.

nomina (D gram) noun(s). – *majemuk* compound noun.

nominal (D) nominal, face. *nilai –* face/nominal value. *saham tanpa nilai –* no par (value) share, share of no par value.

nominalisasi nominalization.

nominasi (D) nomination. *masuk –* to be nominated; → PENCALONAN.

nominatif (D/E) nominative.

nomor (D) 1 number. 2 numeral. – *atom* atomic number. – *berikut* serial number. – *berturut-turut* consecutive number. – *bewés* driver's license number. – *bukti* assigned number (k.o. receipt). – *bulat* whole number. – *buncit* a) finally. b) last of all. – *buntut* the last three digits in a k.o. lottery. – *catatan* register number. – *depan* (of a magazine) next issue. – *dua* number two. **menomor-duakan** to put in second place, subordinate, consider inferior. **penomor-duaan** subordinating. – *éceran* (of a magazine) a single number, loose number. – *ganjil* odd number. – *Idéntifikasi Kendaraan* [Nik] Vehicle Identification Number, VIN. – *indéks warna* color index number, CI number. – *induk* a) student registration number, student ID number. b) serial number. – *Induk Kepegawaian* [Nik] BUMN employee ID Number. – *Induk Kependudukan* [Nik] Resident's ID Number. – *induk mahasiswa* [NIM] student ID number. – *induk pegawai* [NIP] civil servant's ID number, government employee ID number. – *jabatan* service number. – *kembar* (of magazine) double issue, two volumes of a magazine combined into one – *korét* the latter, the last one – *lama* back issue. – *lambung* a) hull number (on a ship). b) vehicle number (on the side of a vehicle). – *lepas* (of a magazine) a single number, loose issue. – *lingkungan wilayah pos* ZIP, postal code. – *motor* engine number. – *panggil* call number. – *pelat* license plate number. – *pelat CD* C(orps) D(iplomatic) license plate. – *pencatatan* registration number. – *pendaftaran* registration number. – *penerbangan* flight number. – *pengenal* ID number. – *percontohan* (of a magazine) introductory issue/number. – *perdana* premiere issue (of a newly published magazine). – *perkenalan* (of magazine) complimentary issue. – *petunjuk* reference number. – *pintu* medallion number (of a taxi). – *pokok (régistrasi)* [nrp] main (registration) number. – *pokok wajib pajak* [NPWP] taxpayer's ID number. – *polisi* tag number (of vehicle). – *Régistrasi Personil* [NRP] Personnel Registration Number (used before the serial number of army officers). – *rumah* house number. – *satu* a) number one in priority. **menomor-satukan** to give top priority to. *Ternyata 462 orang réspondén ~ hiburan.* It turned out that 462 respondents gave top priority to entertainment. b) the best/first. *yang nomor satu* the first one. – *séri* serial number. – *tarikan* (in the lottery) the winning number. – *télepon* telephone number. – *terus* consecutive number. – *tukar* (of a newspaper/magazine) exchange number. – *tunggal* (of a magazine) composite number. – *undian* lottery number. – *urut(an)* consecutive number. – *utama* the best. – *wahid* a) the best/first. b) top priority.

senomor per issue (of a magazine).

bernomor numbered, with a number on it. *kartu ~* a numbered card.

menomor(i) to give a number to, number.

menomorkan to number s.t.

penomor numbering (machine).

penomoran numbering. *~ rumah* numbering houses with house numbers.

nomorbewés (D) (car) license number registration card.
nomplok → TOMPLOK.
non I 1 miss (to telephone operator). **2** (coq) → NONA.
non II clipped form of noncooperator. *kaum* – the noncooperators, i.e., the so-called (Indonesian) republicans who did not cooperate with the Dutch during the Dutch-Indonesian clashes (between August 1945 and December 1949).
non III (E) prefix meaning "not," used to give a negative force to nouns; → BUKAN. *-mahasiswa* not a college student.
non IV (D) nun.
nona I (Port) *buah* – a) sweetsop, sugar-apple, *Anona squamosa*. b) custard apple, *Anona reticulata*. *– makan sirih* glory bower, a woody climber, *Clerodendrum thomsonae*.
nona II (D Port?) **1** young girl, miss. **2** Asian mistress of a European.
nonagama nonreligious.
nonagrési (D) nonaggression.
nonaktif (D) inactive.
  menonaktifkan to put on inactive duty.
  penonaktifan inactivation, putting s.o. on inactive duty.
nonanggota nonmember.
nonbaku nonstandard.
nonbank nonbank.
nonbelajar nonstudy. *kegiatan* – nonstudy activities.
nonberas nonrice. *bahan makanan* – nonrice foodstuffs.
nonbintang nonstar, nonluxury. *250 hotél* – 250 nonstar hotels.
nonbis nonbus. *kendaraan angkutan* – nonbus transportation vehicles.
nonblok nonaligned. *negara-negara* – nonaligned countries.
nonbonorowo nonmarsh (land).
nonbujétér nonbudgetary, off-budget.
nonbulé nonwhite (as a racial identification).
noncina non-Chinese.
noncurah nonbulk. *angkutan barang curah dan* – the transportation of bulk and nonbulk articles.
nondépartemén nondepartmental. *Lembaga pemerintah –, misalnya, adalah Mabés ABRI, Bakin, Kejaksaan Agung, Mabés Polri, BP 7.* The nondepartmental government institutions are, for example, the Armed Forces (of the Republic of Indonesia) Headquarters, State Intelligence Coordinating Agency, Office of the Attorney General, Police (of the Republic of Indonesia) Headquarters, and the Management Board for the Educational Implementation of the Guidelines for Experiencing and Applying *Pancasila*.
nondévisa nonforeign exchange. *bank* – nonforeign exchange bank.
nondiplomat nondiplomat.
nondiplomatik nondiplomatic. *anggota staf* – nondiplomatic staff member.
nondiskriminatif nondiscriminative, nondiscriminating. *idéologi Pancasila yang sejak semula bersifat terbuka dan* – the ideology of *Pancasila* which from the beginning has had an open and nondiscriminating character.
nondolar nondollar. *impor bahan baku dari negara-negara* – the import of raw materials from nondollar countries.
non-Dolog [non-Dépo Logistik] non-Logistics Depot.
noné I (J) → NONA II. *– Betawi* and *– Jakarté* Miss Jakarta (in beauty contest); *cp* ABANG *Jakarté*.
noné II (J) → BUAH nona.
noné III (J) *– Betawi* name of a white orchid variety.
nonékonomi(s) noneconomic. *faktor – yang mendorong inflasi* noneconomic factors that have pushed up inflation.
nonéksakta nonexact sciences, i.e., those dealing with humanities and social sciences.
nonéselon nonechelon. *Para birokrat – pénsiun pada usia 55 tahun.* The nonechelon bureaucrats retire with a pension at 55.
nonétis nonethical.
nonfakultas *– kedokteran* nonschool of medicine.
nonfasilitas nonfacility.
nonfiguratif nonfigurative; → ACITRA.
nonfiksi nonfiction.
nonfisik nonphysical, nonmaterial.
nonformal (E) and **nonformil** (D) informal.
nongelar nondegree; → NIRGELAR. *diploma/fakultas* – nondegree diploma/faculty.

nongnong (J) prominent, protruding. *Biar jidatnya –, tapi orangnya cakap.* Even though he has a protruding forehead, he is smart.
nongtot (J) to protrude. *– bo'ol* hemorrhoids.
nonguru nonteacher. *pendidikan* – nonteacher education.
nonharfiah nonliterary.
nonhayati vegetable (as opposed to animal) *sumber daya alam, baik hayati maupun* – natural resources both animal and vegetable.
noni 1 young girl; miss. **2** a white girl. *– panggilan* call girl.
nonik (Jv) → NONI.
nonilmiah nonscientific.
nonilmuwan nonscientist.
nonindustri nonindustrial.
noninféksi noninfectious. *penyakit inféksi dan* – infectious and noninfectious diseases.
noninprés nonpresidential instruction.
nonintervénsi nonintervention. *– asing* nonforeign intervention.
non-Islam non-Islamic. *di lingkungan* – in non-Islamic surroundings.
nonis(y)u nonissue, quasi-issue.
nonius (D) vernier.
nonjaksa nonpublic prosecutor.
nonjob inactive (service).
  menonjobkan to put on inactive service.
nonjurnalistik nonjournalistic.
nonkaféin noncaffeine.
nonkalori noncaloric. *makanan* – noncaloric food.
nonkarir noncareer. *jabatan* – a noncareer function.
non-Katolik non-Catholic. *tokoh-tokoh agama* – non-Catholic religious figures.
nonkatrolan not based on family relations and connections; → KATROL.
nonkayu nontimber. *ékspor* – exports of nontimber.
nonkekerasan nonviolence. *perlawanan* – passive resistance.
nonkepala-sekolah not a headmaster/head of school.
nonkependidikan noneducational. *program studi* – a noneducational study program.
nonkolestérol noncholesterol.
nonkomando noncommand.
nonkomérsial noncommercial.
nonkomputer noncomputer.
nonkomunis noncommunist.
nonkonselor noncounselor. *pérsonil – di sekolah* noncounselor personnel in schools.
nonkonvénsional unconventional.
nonkooperatif uncooperative.
nonkooperator a noncooperator; → *kaum* NON.
nonkosmétik noncosmetic.
nonkulit putih nonwhite (as a racial identification).
nonkuota nonquota.
nonkurikulér noncurricular.
nonlahiriah nonphysical.
nonmagnétik nonmagnetic.
nonmahasiswa nonuniversity student. *di lingkungan* – in nonuniversity student circles.
nonmakanan noncomestibles. *Selain bahan makanan, ada juga barang – yang dimasukkan ke dalam bungkusan.* In addition to articles of food, there are also noncomestibles put in the package.
nonmanajér nonmanagerial.
nonmanusia nonhuman.
nonmatéri nonmaterial. *Kebutuhan-kebutuhan –, seperti séks, dapat diperoléh dengan mudah.* Nonmaterial needs, such as sex, can easily be obtained.
nonmazhab nonsect.
nonmékanis nonmechanical.
non-Melayu non-Malay. *orang Islam* – non-Malay Islamic people.
nonmigas nonoil and natural gas. *Ékspor – Indonésia tahun 1985 kurang cerah.* Indonesian nonoil and natural gas exports in 1985 were bleak.
nonmilitér nonmilitary. *Industri militér RRC memproduksi barang-barang –.* PRC's military industry produces nonmilitary goods.
nonminyak nonoil. *Dalam usaha meningkatkan ékspor – hendaknya kita tidak terpaku pada persoalan résési ékonomi dunia.* In the

effort to step up nonoil exports we should not be pinned down by the issue of a world economic recession.

nonmobilisasi nonmobilization.

non-Muslim non-Muslim. *umat* – non-Muslims.

nonneraca off-balance sheet.

non-niaga noncommercial.

nonnuklir nonnuclear. *senjata* – nonnuclear weapons.

nonobat nonmedicine.

nonoh → SENONOH.

nonok (*J/Jv*) young girl's vagina.

nonol (*Jv*) pest on coffee plants, *Zeazera coffia*

nonong I menonong to hurry straight ahead without noticing one's surroundings, walk like a drunken person with back erect and legs wobbling.

nonong II (*Jv*) protruding (of forehead).

non-Ortodok(s) non-Orthodox. *Yahudi* – non-Orthodox Jews.

nonpadi nonrice.

nonpahlawan nonhero's. *kuburan pahlawan dan* – heroes' and nonheroes' graves.

nonpajak nontax.

nonpakan nonfodder (for cattle).

nonpalu → HAKIM *nonpalu.*

nonpanti nonhome (dealing with senior citizens homes or *sasana tresna werdha*).

nonpasang surut nontidal.

nonpatogénik nonpathogenic.

nonpemangsa nonpredatory. *ikan* – nonpredatory fish.

nonpemerintah nongovernmental. *organisasi* – nongovernmental organization, NGO.

nonpengajar nonteaching.

nonpengion nonionizing.

nonpenyebaran nonproliferation.

nonperang noncombatant. *Jepang akan mengirimkan personél – ke kawasan Teluk.* Japan will dispatch noncombatant personnel to the Gulf region.

nonperawat nonnurses (in a hospital).

nonperbankan nonbanking.

nonpermanén nonpermanent.

nonperokok nonsmoker.

nonpérs nonpress. *pengusaha percétakan pérs dan* – entrepreneurs of printing houses for the press and nonpress.

nonpertanian nonfarm.

nonpetani nonfarmer. – *penunggak krédit* nonfarmers who are in arrears on their payments.

nonplasma nonplasma; → PLASMA II.

nonpolar nonpolar.

non-Polri non-Police members.

nonpri(bumi) nonnative (*esp* referring to the Chinese minority group).

nonpribumisasi nonnativization, i.e., non-Indonesianization. *Beberapa anggota DPR mencela keras kegiatan – oléh pimpinan sebuah perusahaan bir.* Several MPs have strongly criticized the non-Indonesianization activities by the management of a beer brewery.

nonprioritas nonpriority.

nonproduktif nonproductive.

nonprodusén nonproducer. *petani* – nonproducing farmer.

nonproliferasi nonproliferation. *perjanjian – nuklir* nuclear nonproliferation treaty.

nonpsikologis nonpsychological.

nonputra daérah not a native son from the area.

nonrasional irrational.

nonrawan trouble-free. *daérah* – a trouble-free area.

nonrégular irregular. *penerbangan* – irregular flights.

nonrém nonbrakes.

nonresmi unofficial. *pungutan* – unofficial levies.

nonrokok nonsmoking.

nonrombongan not belonging to a group.

non-RRI non-Republic of Indonesia Radio.

nonsastra nonliterary.

nonsawah unirrigated rice field.

nonséks nonsexual.

nonséktarianisme nonsectarianism.

nonsembako non-staples.

nonsén (*D/E*) nonsense.

nonseni antiart.

nonstaf nonstaff.

nonstandar nonstandard.

nonstéroid nonsteroidal. *obat anti-inflamasi* – a nonsteroidal anti-inflammation medicine.

nonstop (*D/E*) nonstop.

nonstratégis nonstrategic.

nonstruktur nonstructural. *komponén* – nonstructural component.

nontebu nonsugarcane.

nontéknis nontechnical.

nonterjemah nontranslating. *masjid* – a mosque which delivers sermons in Arabic without an Indonesian translation.

nontésis nonthesis. *Lulusan IKIP jalur – tak diterima menjadi dosén negeri.* IKIP graduates of the nonthesis course are not accepted to become government lecturers.

nontol nontoll. *jalan* – not a toll road.

nonton → TONTON.

nontradisi nontradition.

nontradisional nontraditional. *mengékspor barang-barang* – to export nontraditonal commodities.

nonvakséntral nonaffiliated (labor party).

nonvérbal nonverbal. *komunikasi* – nonverbal communications.

nonya → NYONYA I.

nonyodium uniodized. *garam* – uniodized salt.

nonyuridis nonjudicial.

noot (*D*) /not/ (musical) note; → NOT II.

nopék and nopé' (*C J*) 200 (rupiahs). – *go* 250 (rupiahs).

Nopémber → NOVÉMBER.

nopia k.o. cake, a specialty of Purwokerto.

nopol [nomor polisi] (police) vehicle registration number.

norak (*J*) **1** uncivilized, unrefined, unsophisticated, awkward, uncouth. *orang* – countryman, bumpkin, hick. **2** vulgar, tacky, flashy, lacking in good taste. *Dua penyanyi rock yang sudah kondang, Madonna dan Tina Turner, dinilai – oléh Blackwell dalam hal busana pentas.* The two well-known rock singers, Madonna and Tina Turner, were considered vulgar in their stage costumes.

senorak as uncouth/tacky as.

ternorak the most unsophisticated.

noraka → NERAKA.

Nordik (*E*) and **Nordis** (*D*) Nordic. *wilayah* – the Nordic region, Scandinavia.

norit (*D*) a powder used against stomachaches.

norm(a) (*D*) norm, standard. – *hukum* legal norms/standards. – *kerja* labor standards. – *sosial* social norms.

normal (*D/E*) normal. *tidak* – abnormal. **ketidak-normalan** abnormality.

menormalkan to normalize.

kenormalan normality.

penormalan normalization.

normalisasi (*D*) normalization. – *hubungan diplomatik Indonésia-RRC pada 8 Agustus 1990* the normalization of Indonesian – PRC diplomatic relations on August 8, 1990. – *kehidupan kampus* [NKK] restoration and maintenance of order in universities.

menormalisasikan to normalize.

penormalisasian normalization.

normalisir (*D*) **menormalisir** to normalize.

normalisten (*col*) students at a normal school.

normalitas normality.

normalschool (*D*) /normalskol/ teacher training school.

normatif (*D/E*) normative.

menormatifkan to make normative.

Norwégia Norway.

nosel (*E*) nozzle.

nostalgia (*D*) nostalgia.

bernostalgia to be homesick.

nostalgis (*D*) nostalgic.

not I (*D*) short for Dutch *banknoot* (banknote).

not II 1 (*D*) (musical) note. **2** (*E*) note, annotation. – *angka* numerical notations (in music). – *balok* staff, i.e., the five horizontal lines and four intermediate spaces on which music is written or printed. – *musik* musical note.

not III (*D*) short for footnote.

nota (*D*) **1** note, notice. **2** statement of account. **3** memorandum. – *anggaran* budget message. – *béda pendapat* → MINDERHÉIDSNOTA. – *débit* debit note. – *dinas* service report. – *kesepahaman* memorandum of understanding. – *kesepakatan* letter of intent. – *keterangan* cover note. – *Keuangan* Financial Note presented with the Annual Budget which provides details of Budget proposals. – *krédit* credit note. – *pengiriman* packing note. – *penjelasan* aide-mémoire. – *penutup* contract slip. – *penutupan pertanggungan* (*insur*) cover note. – *perubahan* written amendment. – *protés* protest note. – *Saling Pengertian* Memorandum of Understanding, MOU.

nota béné (*D*) nota bene, N.B., important.

notariat (*D*) notary's office.
  kenotariatan notarial.

notariil (*D*) notarial.

notaris (*D*) notary. – *perangkap* substitute notary.
  kenotarisan notarial.

notasi (*D*) **1** (musical) notation. **2** special system of signs or symbols. **3** a note, jotting, annotation, marginal note.
  bernotasi annotated.

notés (*D*) notebook.

notifikasi (*E*) notification.

notula (*D*) minutes (of a meeting).

notulen (*D*) notes (of a meeting, etc.), minutes of proceedings. *membuat* – to draw up the minutes.

notulis (*D*) person who takes the minutes.

notun (*C J*) two (rupiahs).

novasi (*D leg*) novation, renewal (of a debt agreement).

novél (*D*) novel.
  pernovélan (*mod*) novel.

novélis (*D*) novelist. – *wanita* female novelist.

Novémber (*D*) November.

novis (*D*) novice.

novisiat (*D*) novitiate.

novum (*L leg*) new evidence.

NPWP → NOMOR *pokok wajib pajak*.

nracak (*Jv*) to touch when one shouldn't, e.g., s.o.'s head.

nrawang (*Jv*) transparent.

nrecel (*Jv*) dense (of population).

NRI [Negara Républik Indonésia] Republic of Indonesia.

NRII [Negara Républik Islam Indonésia] Islamic Republic of Indonesia.

nrima (*Jv*) to be passive, uncomplaining, fatalistic. – *ing pandum* to accept one's lot, be satisfied with what one has. (*main*) – *saja* to acquiesce. *sikap serba* – *dengan dalih cari selamat* being completely passive and uncomplaining.

nrimo → NRIMA.

nrimois passive, uncomplaining person.

nrocos → CROCOS.

nrp (*abbr*) [Narapidana] criminal.

NRP [Nomor Régistrasi Pérsonil] Personnel Registration Number (used before serial numbers of army officers).

NT Nusa Tenggara.

NTA [Negara Tuhan Acéh] Theocratic State of Aceh.

'ntar (*J*) → SEBENTAR.

NTB [Nusa Tenggara Barat] West Nusa Tenggara.

NTCR [Nikah Talak Cerai dan Rujuk] Marriages, Repudiations, Divorces, and Reconciliations.

NTT (*init*) [Nusa Tenggara Timur] East Nusa Tenggara.

NU (*init*) [Nahdlatul Ulama] "Awakening of Muslim Clergy," i.e., the name of a Muslim mass organization.
  ke-NU-an Nahdlatul Ulama's. *pandangan dunia* ~ NU's world vision.

nuansa (*D*) nuance. – *warna* shade/hue (of color).
  bernuansa nuanced.

nubari → SANUBARI.

nubika (*acr*) nuclear, biological, chemical.

nubuat (*A*) **1** (the gift of) prophecy. **2** a mole on the shoulder blade of Muhammad, the sign that he is a Prophet.

bernubuat to prophesy.

menubuatkan to prophesy s.t. *Dua puluh lima abad yang lalu, Ézékiél* ~ *"perang hari akhir" antara anak-anak Israél dan "tanah Magog" di utara.* Twenty-five centuries ago, Ezekiel prophesied the last day's war between Israelites and Magogs in the north.

nubuatan prophecy. ~ *Bibel* biblical prophecies.

nudis (*D*) nudist.
  kenudisan 1 nudism. **2** nudist (*mod*).

nudisme (*D*) nudism; → BUGILISME.

nugerah(a) → ANUGERAH.

Nugini → PAPUA NUGINI.

nugrah(a) → ANUGERAH. – *Sakanti* order of merit for the police.

Nuh (*A*) **1** (the biblical) Noah. **2** name of the 71st chapter of the Koran.

nuhun (*J coq*) thanks.

nujum (*A*) **1** astrology. *ahli* – astrologer; soothsayer. *ilmu* – astrology. *melihat* – to forecast. **2** horoscope.
  menujum and **mempernujumkan 1** to consult the stars. **2** to forecast.

menujumkan to prophesy, predict.

nujuman prophecy, prediction, forecast.

penujum horoscopist, fortune-teller.

penujuman prediction, prophecy, fortune-telling.

pe(r)nujuman astrology.

nukhter (*D*) matter-of-fact, down-to-earth.

nukil (*A*) **1** citation, quotation, extract. **2** summary, abstract.
  menukil 1 to cite, quote, extract. *Dia* ~ *bagian itu dari syair terkenal.* He quoted that part from a well-known poem. **2** to summarize, abstract.

menukilkan 1 to cite, quote, extract s.t. *"Antara "* ~ *berita itu dari Associated Press.* "Antara" quoted that news item from the Associated Press. **2** to summarize, abstract s.t.

ternukil cited, quoted, extracted.

nukilan 1 citation, quote. **2** summary.

penukil quoter.

penukilan quotation.

nukléus (*D/E*) nucleus.

nuklir (*D*) nuclear. *senjata* – nuclear weapons.

nuklirisasi (*E*) nuclearization.

nuktah → NOKTAH.

nul → NOL.

numéralia numerals.

numérik (*D*) numerical.

numismatik (*D/E*) numismatic.

nun I (*cla*) yonder, over there. – *di sana itu kilang getah.* Over there is the rubber factory. – *jauh* far away.

nun II (*A*) *ikan* – a legendary fish which carries the universe on its back.

nun III (*A*) **1** name of the 25th letter of the Arabic alphabet. **2** alternative name for the 68th chapter of the Koran.

nunak-nunuk (*Jv*) **1** to walk slowly like a blind man feeling his way. **2** to snoop around.

nung I (*onom*) bong, sound made by large clock.

nung II aristocratic title in Riau.

nunsius (*D*) (*papal*) nuncio.

nunut (*Jv*) to occupy space (in s.o.'s vehicle/bed/house, etc.). *Saya pulang – mobil teman saya.* I got a lift home with a friend of mine. *swarga/suwargo – neraka katut* to share the good and the bad (between married couples). – *neda* to eat in s.o. else's house. – *tidur* to sleep in s.o. else's bed.

menunut to get a ride from s.o. *Saya* ~ *Wirono.* Wirono gave me a ride.

menunuti to get a ride with s.o. *Saya* ~ *Wirono.* I got a ride with Wirono.

menunutkan to get a ride for s.o. *Anaknya dinunutkan ayahnya.* He got his son a ride with his father.

nunutan s.t. put in s.o.'s vehicle, etc. *Barang yang dalam tempat bagasi mobil itu* ~ *saya.* The stuff in the car trunk is mine.

Nupiksa Yana (*Jv*) (Government) Research Institute.

nuqson (*A*) not meet the target (referring to collecting money for Islamic charities).

nur (*A ob*) **1** light of the sun. **2** the light with which God lit up chaos at the creation. **3** the light of truth revealed from God to the prophet Muhammad. **4** "Light"; name of the 24th chapter of the Koran. – *kalong* aureole. – *kutub* aurora borealis.

nuraga (*Skr*) sympathy.

nurani I (*A*) luminous, bright, shining; clear.

nurani II (*A*) *hati* – consciousness, the depths of the heart; a heart so enlightened that it can see what to the eyes is invisible. *suara hati* – *rakyat* the voice of the people's consciousness.

  bernurani to be conscious.

nurbisa (*Skr*) antidote (to a venom).

nuri I (*A*) blue-crowned parroquet, *Loriculus galgulus*; vernal hanging parrot, *Loriculus vernalis*; blue-rumped parrot, *Psittinus cyanurus*. – *paruh besar* great-billed parrot, *Tanygnathus megalorhynchos*. – *Sulawesi* ornate lory, *Trichoglossus ornatus*.

nuri II a marine fish, *Callyodon spp.*

nuriah (*A ob*) bright.

nurmala → NIRMALA.

nurun (*Jv*) to cheat (on an exam).

nus *ikan* – k.o. cuttlefish, *Sepia spp.* – *comék* small cuttlefish.

nusa I (*Skr*) **1** island (in names). **2** birthplace, native land. *guna/untuk* – *dan bangsa* for country and nation. – *cendana* Lesser Sundas [NTT]. – *dan bangsa* Indonesia. – *Ina* Ceram. – *Indah* Nusakambangan. – *Nipa* Flores. – *Lontar* Lesser Sundas. – *Tenggara* [Nusra and Nusteng] Lesser Sundas.

nusa II 1 – *indah* a decorative plant, *Mussaenda philippica*. **2** greenish white.

Nusakambangan name of an island off Java's south coast where certain well-known criminals are imprisoned.

  menusakambangkan to deport s.o. to that island.

Nusantara (*Skr*) **1** the Indonesian Archipelago. **2** (in Malaysia) the Malay Archipelago. **3** Indonesia, Malaysia, the Philippines, Brunei, and Singapore. *Tokoh-tokoh sastra dari kelima negara* – *mengemukakan pendapat dan pokok-pokok pikirannya*. Literary figures from the five Nusantara nations put forward their views and basic ideas. *bahasa-bahasa* – the regional languages of Indonesia. *negara* – an archipelagic state. *perairan* – archipelagic waters. *wilayah* – archipelagic region. *wilayah* – *yaitu Indonésia, Singapura, Brunéi, dan Malaysia* the archipelagic region, i.e., Indonesia, Singapore, Brunei, and Malaysia.

Nusra [Nusatenggara] Nusatenggara, Lesser Sunda Islands.

Nusrabar [Nusatenggara Barat] West Nusa Tenggara.

Nusrateng [Nusatenggara Tengah] Central Nusa Tenggara.

Nusratim [Nusatenggara Timur] East Nusa Tenggara.

Nusteng [Nusatenggara Tengah] Central Nusa Tenggara.

Nustengbar [Nusatenggara Barat] West Nusa Tenggara.

Nustengtim [Nusatenggara Timur] East Nusa Tenggara.

nusus and **nusyus** (*A*) refusing to follow one's husband's lawful wishes, *esp* refusal to have sex with one's husband.

nut (*Jv*) (to act) in accordance with.

nutfah (*A*) **1** sperm, seed of life. **2** germ. *bank plasma* – germ plasma bank. *pilihan* – seminal choice. **3** gene.

nutrisi (*E*) nutrition.

nutrisionis (*E*) nutritionist.

nuwun (*Jv*) **1** to request/ask politely (of s.o. of a socially higher rank). **2** thank you! with your permission. *kulo* – a) please allow me, may I be permitted, permit me; (said when entering a home and seeing nobody) anybody in? *"Saya kulo* – *dulu kepada anda-anda ..."* "I first have to make myself known to you all ..." b) to report to s.o. *Waktu itu ia hanya diperingatkan, kalau beroperasi di daérah lain agar kulo* – *kepada aparat setempat*. At that time he was reminded that when operating in another area, he had to report to the local state apparatus. **mengulonuwuni** to ask permission of. *Majikan bukanlah orang yang selalu harus dikulonuwuni oléh karyawan*. The employer is not s.o. who always has to be asked for permission by the employees. – *séwu* a thousand thanks. *tanpa bilang* – *séwu* without a word of thanks.

Nuzul = **Nuzulul Qur'an** (*A*) the day commemorating the handing down of the Koran on Ramadan 17.

NV I (*init*) [Naamloze Vennootschap] /namlose fenotskap/ (*D*) Inc., Ltd.

NV II [nieuwe vrouw] (*joc D*) new wife.

NW [Nahdlatul Wathan] "Awakening of the Fatherland," a mass organization.

For verbs beginning with *ny*- also see entries beginning with c- or s-.

Ny. (*abbr*) [Nyonya] Mrs.

-nya 1 his, her, its, their. *buku*- his/her/its/their book. **2** your (indirect second person). *"Kampung*- *di mana?"* "Where is your kampung?" *Nama*- *siapa?* a) What is his/her name? b) What is your name? **3** form of the third-person pronoun used after prepositions or meN- verbs. *bertamu dengan*- to visit her. *memberitahu kepada*- to inform him. *Mobil itu terbeli oléh*-. He could afford to buy that car. *melihat dari jauh*- to see her from far away. **4** *alangkah (betapa/bukan main)*- how ...! *Alangkah mahal*- *kamus ini!* How expensive this dictionary is! *Betapa seremnya film itu!* How terrifying the film was! *Bukan main pintar*- *mahasiswa itu*. How smart that college student is! **5** *yang* + noun + *-nya* whose, of which. *Rumah yang jendélanya hijau sangat bagus*. The house whose windows are green is very nice. **6** the other (of a pair or series). *yang satu*- *lagi* the other (one). *yang satu biru, satu*- *mérah* one is blue, the other is red. **7** per, each, a(n). *satu pon*- 70 cents a pound. **8** *bukan*- a) in a statement it suggests "to my mind ... not." *Bukan*- *besar rumah yang dibelinya*. To my mind, the house he bought was not large. b) it's (not that). In a contradictory statement it expresses "not that ... ," usually followed by another sentence preceded by the conjunction *tetapi* or *melainkan*. *Bukan*- *dia bodoh melainkan dia malas saja*. It's not that he is stupid; he's just lazy. **9** (anaphoric) the (aforementioned). *Koran*- *di mana?* Where's the newspaper? **10** forms nouns from intransitive or passive verbs or adjectives. *tinggi*- the height. *berat*- the weight. *pergi*- (s.o.'s) going away, leaving. *Ketemunya di mana?* Where did they meet?

nya(h) → NYONYA(H).

nyabu → SHABU.

nyadik (*Jv*) addicted to.

nyah go away! beat it! → ENYAH.

  menyahkan and **mengenyahkan** to drive/chase away.

nyaho (*J*) **1** to know, be aware. **2** a) to give s.o. a lesson he will not forget. b) to learn from bitter experience, find out the hard way.

nyai 1 (*col*) a mistress of a European or Chinese man. **2** grandmother. **3** (*Jv*) older woman of some social status or of religious accomplishment or the wife or daughter of a *kiayi*. – *Loro Kidul* the goddess controlling the Indian Ocean around whom so many traditional stories are told. – *Nyonyah* Chinese lady. – *Srinaulbi* an expert in traditional medicine or health potions. **4** (*S*) girl! → NÉNG II, UPIK.

nyak (*J*) mother; → ENYAK II, IBU. *Babé dan* – *Nolly* Mr. and Mrs. Nolly.

nyaknyuk (*J*) senile, forgetful.

nyala 1 flame, fire, glow. **2** flaming, flaring up, blazing. **3** to be ablaze (of a house, etc.), be on fire, on (of an electric appliance). *dalam posisi* – in the on position. – *api* spark, flame, torch. – *balik* backfire. – *mata* the light in one's eyes. -.– *hidup* flickers of life, keeps going on and off. – *sendiri* autoignition. – *sisa* afterglow. – *terendam* smoldering fire.

  bernyala to flame, flare up, ignite.

  bernyala-nyala 1 to get set on fire, be kindled. **2** to catch fire. **3** to burn (with patriotism).

  menyala 1 to burn, flame, ignite, be on fire, flare up, light up. **2** to run (of a machine).

  menyala-nyala to flare up, burn brightly, be red hot (of anger, etc.). *Semangatnya* ~. His enthusiasm was red hot.

  menyalai to set fire to, light, ignite.

  menyalakan 1 to light, ignite. ~ *korék* to light a match. **2** to start up (a machine), switch/turn on. **3** to stir up, inflame.

  menyala-nyalakan to provoke, incite.

  penyala s.t. that ignites, igniter. ~ *mula* ignition.

  penyalaan 1 ignition, lighting up. **2** start up, firing up. ~ *mati* misfiring. ~ *susulan* delayed firing.

nyalang (*M*) with (eyes) wide open. *Matanya* –. His eyes are wide open.

  senyalang-nyalangnya as wide open as possible.

  menyalangkan to open (one's eyes) wide.

nyalar always, ceaseless.

nyalawadi (*Jv*) mysterious, arousing suspicion.

nyalé sea worm.

nyali (*J*) 1 bile, gall. 2 courage, bravery, pluck. *pecah –nya* to lose one's courage. 3 feelings. *besar* brave, courage. (*punya*) *– kecil* afraid, cowardly.

bernyali to have the nerve to. *Meréka pun ~ melawan polisi.* They had the nerve to oppose the police. *~ besar* brave, courageous. *~ kecil* cowardly.

nyalin k.o. tree, *Xanthophyllum spp.*

nyaman 1 pleasant, comfortable. *– didengar* pleasant to listen to. *– dipandang mata* and *– ditentang* nice (to look at). 2 fresh, invigorating (of air). 3 in good shape. *badan kurang –* not in good shape, not feel well. *bertambah –* to recuperate. *tidak – pikirannya* not in one's right mind. 4 delicious, tasty. *hati tidak – peevish*, crabby. *tidak –* uncomfortable, unpleasant. **ketidak-nyamanan** discomfort, displeasure.

menyamankan 1 to make comfortable. 2 to please, make s.o. happy. *~ perasaan* to put s.o. in a good mood.

ternyaman the most comfortable.

nyamanan comfort.

kenyamanan 1 comfort, pleasure. 2 coolness, freshness.

penyaman s.t. that makes one comfortable.

nyambing k.o. marsh plant, *Lasia spinosa.*

nyamen → ÉKSAMEN.

nyamikan (*Jv*) /nyami'an/ 1 snacks. 2 mistress. 3 a loose woman.

nyamleng (*Jv*) → NYAMAN.

nyamnyam (*sl*) delicious.

nyampang (just) in case, if by chance.

nyampang-nyampang if by chance.

senyampang 1 supposing that. *~ usaha penstabilan nilai tukar dilakukan* supposing that attempts are made to stabilize the exchange rate. 2 while … (still). *Makanlah bakso itu ~ lagi hangat.* Eat the *bakso* while it's still hot. 3 (*cla*) although.

nyampé(k) → SAMPAI I.

nyamping (*Jv*) batik garment.

nyamplung a coastal tree from which an oil is extracted, tamanu, *Calophyllum inophyllum.*

nyamuk 1 mosquito. 2 gnat. *– mati gatal tak lepas* to take revenge against s.o. who has already been punished, do s.t. unnecessary. *– gajah* a large species of mosquito. *– harimau/loréng* tiger mosquito, *Aedes stegomyia albopictus.* *– pérs* reporter, journalist, paparazzi. *– serampang* anopheles mosquito, *Anopheles spp.*

nyamur (*M*) dew.

nyana (*Jv*) think, believe. *tidak –* unsuspected.

menyana (*usu* in passive) to think, believe. *tidak dinyana tidak diduga* completely unsuspected.

menyanakan to suspect.

ternyana expected. *tidak ~* unexpected.

nyang → YANG II.

nyantrik → SANTRI.

nyanya (*J*) **menyanya** to fry without oil.

nyanyah menyanyah to mumble.

nyanyang (*M*) nervous, restless, upset.

nyanyar to become soft, overripe (of fruits).

nyanyi sing.

bernyanyi 1 to sing. 2 to rat/sing (to the police).

menyanyi 1 to sing. 2 to rat/sing (to the police).

menyanyikan to sing s.t.

nyanyian song. *~ bersama* choir. *~ fajar* aubade. *~ Natal* Christmas carol. *~ rakyat* folksong.

penyanyi singer.

penyanyian singing (of a song). *setelah ~ lagu kebangsaan* after the singing of the national anthem.

nyanyu → NYANYAH.

nyanyuk senile, talk nonsense like an old person.

menyanyukkan to make s.o. drunk.

nyapang friend, comrade.

nyap-nyap (*J*) to natter, chatter away (angrily).

bernyap-nyap to natter away (angrily).

nyarang k.o. medicinal plant, devil's horsewhip, *Achyranthes aspera.*

nyarik → NYARING.

nyaring 1 loud and clear (of sound), shrill, strident. 2 (*ling*) strident (sound).

menyaringkan to make s.t. louder and clearer. *~ telinga* to prick up one's ears.

ternyaring loudest and clearest.

kenyaringan 1 clarity. 2 too shrill/loud. 3 (*ling*) stridency.

nyaris almost, nearly.

nyaru → SARU II.

nyasar → SASAR I.

nyata (*Skr*) 1 clear, plain, distinct, obvious. 2 real, tangible, concrete, solid (evidence). *keadaan yang –* reality. *nilai –* real value. *perhitungan yang –* real matter-of-fact plans, etc. *sebesar – life-size.* 3 striking, conspicuous, heavy (losses), evident. *dari sépak terjangnya* it is evident from his behavior. *secara – obviously*, unequivocally.

nyatanya 1 it is obvious that. 2 actually, what actually happened.

nyata-nyata 1 (to look at s.o.) keenly, (to look) straight (at s.o.). 2 obvious(ly), public(ly), open(ly).

senyatanya → NYATANYA.

menyata to become clear(er).

menyatai to be(come) a reality to/for. *Belum dinyatai kok sudah sambas.* It hasn't even happened to you yet, and you're already complaining.

menyatakan [and **nyatain** (*J coq*)] 1 to state, express, show. *~ diri sebagai* to proclaim/declare o.s. to be s.t. *~ kembali* to restate, reiterate. *~ minat* to express interest. *~ kesanggupannya* to promise, pledge. *Dia ~ kesanggupannya untuk melaksanakan instruksi itu.* He promised to carry out the instruction. *~ lalai* to give notice of default. 2 to find (of the court), declare, pronounce, stipulate. *~ bersalah* to declare guilty, convict. *~ bertanggung-jawab* to hold s.o. responsible. *~ bubar* to declare dissolved (of a contract). *~ s(y)ah dan berharga* (*leg*) to declare valid, uphold, validate. *~ tergugat telah melakukan perbuatan melawan hukum* to find the defendant guilty of having committed an illegal act. *~ berlakunya jam malam* to declare a curfew. *Dia dinyatakan téwas.* He was pronounced dead. *~ tidak bersalah* to declare not guilty, acquit. *~ tidak sah* (*leg*) to set aside (a finding), nullify (a decision). *dinyatakan tidak sah* invalid. 3 to reveal (in Christianity).

mempernyata(kan) to make s.t. clear/obvious.

ternyata 1 it turned out that. *~ kami pergi ke tempat yang keliru.* It turned out that we went to the wrong place. 2 evident, evidently. *~ dari* as appears/will be seen from, as shown by. *~ kepada* it is evident to.

ternyatakan 1 expressed. 2 can be proven/explained.

kenyataan 1 reality, fact. *~nya* the truth is, in fact. *pada ~nya* in fact. *menjadi ~* to come true. 3 found to be true. *aku dapat ~* I have noticed.

penyataan 1 (religious) revelation. 2 expression, statement.

pernyataan statement, declaration, proclamation, expression, notice, notification. *~ di bawah sumpah* affidavit. *~ gugatan* statement of claim. *~ kapal* manifest. *~ keadaan darurat perang* proclamation of martial law. *~ kehendak rakyat* plebiscite. *~ lalai* notice of default. *~ pailit* declaration of bankruptcy. *~ pembatalan* nullification, revocation. *~ pendapat* reasons given for one's vote (in politics). *~ penolakan* disclaimer. *~ perdamaian* declaration of settlement. *~ perélaan* (*leg*) consent form. *~ perang* declaration of war. *~ pikiran* state of mind. *~ politik* political platform. *~ resmi* official declaration/notification/statement. *~ riwayat hidup* curriculum vitae. *~ sah dan berharga* validation. *~ sarju* expression of sympathy. *~ selamat* congratulations. *~ simpati* expression of sympathy. *~ terimakasih* expression of appreciation. *~ tertulis di bawah sumpah* affidavit. *~ turut berdukacita* condolences. *~ utang* liability certificate.

nyatoh and **nyatuh** various species of trees which produce a k.o. sticky liquid called *getah –, Palaquium scholaris* and other species.

nyatut → CATUT II.

nyawa 1 (physical) life (of persons/animals/plants). *tak ada –nya lagi* dead. *hendak melepas –* to be dying. *–nya sudah melayang/terbang* he has passed away. *taruhannya ~* to risk one's life. *Kecelakaan itu meminta – 3 orang.* The accident claimed three lives. *membuang/mempertaruhkan/menyabung –* to risk one's life. *minta* – to beg for one's life. *mengambil/menghilangkan/memadamkan/mencabut* – to kill. *meminta* – to beg for mercy. *ketika* – *sampai tenggorokan* to be at death's door. **2** soul, spirit of life. *satu* – *dua badan* to be faithful to e.o. in life and in death. **3** life, livelihood, subsistence. **4** sweetheart, darling. *ada* – *ada rezeki* the future will look after itself, God will provide. *ada* –, – *ikan* almost dead, there's still a spark of life (left in s.o.). – *bergantung di ujung kuku* to be in a precarious state. *hutang* – *dibayar* – *and* – *ganti* – an eye for an eye, a tooth for a tooth. – *pergi* – *datang* life is precarious. *satu* – *dua badan* very close to e.o. – *ayam* unimportant. – *ikan* breathing one's last. – *rangkap* (with) two lives. – *rapuh* on the point of death.

senyawa 1 of one mind, unanimous. **2** forming a unit, united, combined. *kata* ~ (*gram*) compound word. *sudah* ~ *sudah sebadan* to go through thick and thin together. **bersenyawa 1** to agree completely, see eye to eye. **2** to become a chemical compound, compounded. *Hidrogén dan oksigén kalau dicampur* ~ *menjadi air.* When hydrogen and oxygen are mixed they become the compound water. **mensenyawakan** and **mempersenyawakan** to unite, combine, compound. **tersenyawa** entered into a chemical compound. **senyawaan** and **persenyawaan 1** chemical combination/compound. **2** (*gram*) compound word.

bernyawa animate, alive, living, live. *tak* ~ inanimate, lifeless, dead. ~ *rangkap* to have more than one life, have nine lives.

nyawang (*Bal*) cremation of effigy.

nyedar sound (asleep); → NYENYAK.

nyelang → NYALANG.

nyelekit (*J/Jv*) to hurt s.o.'s feelings; biting/sharp (remark).

nyeleneh (*Jv*) odd, different, eccentric. *Pemikirannya dianggap agak* –. His way of thinking is considered rather eccentric.

nyelimur inattentive, bored. *dengan nada* – in a bored tone of voice.

nyelonong → SELONONG.

nyem (*J*) tasteless, insipid, not salty enough.

nyemek, nyemék, and **nyémék** (*Jv*) neither too moist nor too dry. *Bakminya* –. The noodles are just right.

nyemil → CEMIL. **nyemilan** snacks.

nyemplung → CEMPLUNG.

nyemprat-nyemprit to keep on blowing on a whistle; → SEMPRIT I.

nyengék (*Jv*) to torment s.o. and make him cry.

nyéntrik (*D*) eccentric, abnormal.

nyenyai loosely woven.

nyenyak to be sound (asleep). *tidur dengan –nya* to sleep soundly; → LELAP, NIDERA, NYEDAR, NYENYEP, PULAS III. *Tantawi membangunkan Syamsuddin yang sedang* – *tidur.* Tantawi woke up Syamsuddin who was sound asleep. **menyenyakkan** to put s.o. sound asleep. **kenyenyakan** soundness (of sleep).

nyenyat very quiet.

nyényéh (*J J*) **menyényéh** to fester (of a wound).

nyenyek → NYENYAK.

nyenyén menyényén to insult, humiliate, stick one's tongue out at.

nyenyep (*Jv*) sound, deep (of sleep). *tidur* – to be sound asleep.

nyenyet (*Jv*) still, quiet. *sepi* – deadly quiet.

Nyepi (*Bal*) the Balinese New Year according to the Saka calendar (a day of absolute silence without lights/work/traffic, etc.); → SEPI.

nyepit → SEPIT II.

nyerénggés (*Jv*) to grin (to o.s.).

nyeri sharp pain, stinging pain, ache, cramp. – *haid* menstrual cramps. – *persendian* joint pains. – *otot* muscle pains. – *pinggang bagian bawah* lower back pain. – *syaraf* nerve pain, neuralgia. – *tulang* arthritis. **kenyerian** ache, twinge, shooting pain.

nyerowok (*J*) **1** to bark (of dogs). **2** to scold.

nyes (*Jv*) chilly, cool.

nyesep (*J*) to enter into, penetrate, infiltrate.

nyetrékin → CETRÉK.

nyi (*Jv*) title of address to older women; → NÉNÉK, NYAI.

nyiat-nyiat k.o. bush.

nyilih (*Jv*) borrow(ing). – *tangan* to hire s.o. to do the dirty work (while remaining behind the scenes).

nyilu → NGILU.

nyingnying (*J*) pencil-tailed tree mouse, *Chiropodomys gliroides.*

nyinyik (*M*) – *mamak* clan head.

nyinyir (*M*) **1** whining, nagging. *orang tua* – an old bore. **2** chatterbox, tattler. **nyinyiran** drivel, nonsense. **kenyinyiran** drivel, sniveling.

nyirih various k.o. coastal trees, *Xylocarpus granatum* and other species; *Carapa moluccensis*, pussur wood, whose bark is used for tanning fishing nets.

nyiru a tray made from bamboo for winnowing rice. *bak* – *bak tampian, bak guru bak anak siswa* students imitate their teachers.

nyit go away, beat it!; → NYAH.

nyiur coconut palm, *Cocos nucifera.* – *bawang* a coconut with an edible husk. – *dara* coconut palm before it bears fruit. – *gading* a small palm with pale-yellow coconuts, Queen palm, *Cocos plumosa*; → KELAPA. – *hijau* coconut whose fruit is green when young, used as a medicine. – *kelongkong* young coconut with soft edible flesh. – *kesumba* a coconut with red-colored fruit. – *melambai* reference to the Minahasa area (at the northern tip of Sulawesi). – *pagai* k.o. short coconut tree. – *puyuh* k.o. coconut with pale-green nuts. – *sungkuran* young coconut.

Ny Jd (*abbr*) [Nyonya Janda] the widow ...

nyok I a kiss. **menyok** to kiss.

nyok II (*J*) come on! let's go! → AYO, MARI I. – *sekarang kita ke Puncak.* Come on, let's go to Puncak now.

nyokap (*Pr*) mother; *cp* BOKAP.

nyokor (*J*) barefoot.

nyolnyolan (*J*) nagging, fussy, quarrelsome, hard to please, faultfinding.

nyolo (*C*) censer, place for burning incense.

nyolong → COLONG.

nyolot → COLOT.

Nyoman (*Bal*) name element placed before personal names to indicate the third-born child.

nyong (in Ambon) young man. – *dan Noni* (*Min*) (in contests) title awarded to the "best" male and female adolescents from their area.

nyonya I and **nyonyah** (*Port C?*) **1** Mrs., Madam. **2** lady, woman. *Tuan-Tuan dan Nyonya-Nyonya!* Ladies and Gentlemen! – *Amérika* an American lady. **3** wife, lady of the house. "*Ayo, kuénya ini dimakan, nanti* – *saya bisa marah kalau jamuannya tidak dimakan.*" "Come on, have some of these cookies, otherwise my wife will be angry if you don't touch her treat." – *besar* the boss's/patron's wife. – *Menteri* the Minister's wife. – *rumah* a) hostess. b) lady of the house. c) housewife. **4** wife, spouse.

nyonya II *si* – a type of *rambutan.*

nyonyéh old and toothless.

nyonyol (*J*) **nyonyolan 1** talkative. **2** irritated, hurt (of feelings). **3** coarse behavior.

nyonyong menyonyong to stick out (of a tooth/swollen face), pout (of one's lips), protrude (of one's teeth). **ternyonyong** stuck out (of the mouth unintentionally).

nyonyor (*Jv*) to purse one's lips, swollen (of one's lips).

nyonyot menyonyot to pull (on) with the mouth.

nyora (*Port IBT*) madam.

nyunyut I menyunyut to suckle.

nyunyut II (*Jv*) soggy.

nyunyut III menyunyut to throb; → NYUT.

nyut (*J*) throb (of pulse, boil, etc.); → DENYUT. **bernyut(-nyut)** to throb. **nyut-nyut** and **nyut-nyutan** a beating/pulsating/throbbing pain (in one's head/tooth, etc.).

O

o and **O I** the 15th letter of the Latin alphabet used for writing Indonesian.

o II 1 (interjection) o, oh. **2** (to express surprise/fear/amazement/pain, etc.). *–, engkau rupanya yang bersembunyi di situ!* Oh, it looks like you were the one hiding there! *–, begitu.* Oh, I see. *–, tidak.* Oh, it's not so. **3** (in direct address) *Mak, – Mak, di manakah Mak berada?* Mommy, oh mommy, where are you? *– ya* a) by the way, incidentally; → OMONG-OMONG. *–, ya apakah sudah kauterima surat itu?* By the way, have you received that letter yet? b) Is that so? c) Are you kidding? No kidding? *– ya? Meréka menang?* Are you kidding? They won? **4** (interjection to get s.o.'s attention) hey!

O III [clipped form of *orgasme*] to have an orgasm.

oalaah Oh my God!

oase (*D*) and **oasis** (*E*) oasis; → WAHA(H).

obah → UBAH.

Obaja (the biblical) Obadiah.

oban → UBAN I.

obar (*ob*) to flare up; → KOBAR.

obat 1 medicine, remedy, cure. *ahli –* pharmacist. *anak –* (*ob*) patient. *rumah/toko –* pharmacy. *tukang –* (*ob*) chemist. *jual –* charlatanism. *Daun ini sering kali dibuat – penyakit perut.* These leaves are often made into a medicine for a stomachache. **2** therapy, treatment. *– terbaik ialah dicintai orang di sekitar kita.* The best therapy is being loved by the people around us. **3** -icide, repellent, poison against ... *– nyamuk* mosquito killer. *– serangga ini sungguh mujarab.* This insecticide is really effective. **4** (chemical) agent. **5** ammunition. *membuang –* (*infr*) to fire a warning shot. **6** charm, spell, occult force; philter; → GUNA-GUNA. **7** (*sl*) various k.o. of forbidden drugs, such as Rohypnol. *– jauh penyakit hampir* to be in a difficult spot. *– jerih pelerai demam* loving words for one's sweetheart. *kehabisan – dan peluru* powder and shot/lead are all gone/used up. *– ajaib* wonder drug. *– angin* an ointment to cure a cold. *– antibiotika* antibiotics. *– antidiaré* medicine for diarrhea. *– antimabok kendaraan* motion sickness pills. *– antipanas* antipyretic, fever-reducing medicine. *– asah(an)* abrasive. *– aspirin* aspirin. *– awét muda* youth-preserving medicine. *– basah* a) a medicinal powder mixed with water, such as, *boréh.* b) unreliable news. *– batuk* cough medicine, antitussive. *– bébas* over-the-counter drug. *– bébas terbatas* limited unrestricted drug. *– bedil* gunpowder. *– bius* a) anesthetic. b) (addictive) drugs, narcotics. *– cacar* vaccine. *– cacing* deworming medicine, vermifuge, anthelmintic. *– dahaga* thirst quencher. *– dalam* for internal use only. *– demam* antipyretic (such as quinine), fever-reducing medicine. *– dukun* magic charm. *– G* [from Dutch *gevaarlijk*] dangerous medicine, the use and dosage of which must be carefully controlled by a doctor. *– génerik* generic drug. *– gosok* a) liniment. b) scouring powder. *– gosok gigi* toothpaste; → ODOL *gigi. – gula* artificial sweetener used for medicinal purposes. *– guna* (love) philter, charm. *– hati* consolation, balm. *– haus* thirst quencher. *– isap* lozenge. *– jerih* a) tip. b) sweetheart, darling. *– jadi* medicinal drug. *– jalan* outpatient treatment. ***berobat-jalan*** to be treated as an outpatient. *Salah seorang penderita kanker payudara harus ~.* A breast-cancer patient has to be treated as an outpatient. *– jarum* serum. *– jiplakan* me-too drug. *– kampung* folk medicine prepared from all k.o. herbs by ordinary people (not by pharmacists). *– kangen* a cure for homesickness. *– kejang* antispasmodic. *– kelantang* bleaching powder. *– keluron* abortifacient, aborting agent. *– keramas* powdered shampoo. *– keras* prescription drug. *– ketiak* deodorant. *– kimia* chemotherapy. *– kinakrin* medicine to cure and prevent malaria. *– kopi* (*petro*) quebracho. *– koyok* medicated plaster. *– kuat* a) tonic. b) aphrodisiac. *– kuat badan* restorative. *– kuat lelaki* aphrodisiac for men. *– kumur* mouthwash, gargle. *– lali* anesthetic. *– lawan-*

asam antacid. *– ledak* (*ob*) gunpowder. *– lelah* a) tip. b) refreshment. *– luar* for external use only. *– mata* eye drops, collyrium. *– mérah* (*coq*) mercurochrome, tincture of iodine. *– minum* potion. *– mujarab* effective/efficacious remedy. *– nyamuk* mosquito coil/repellent. *– O* [from Dutch *opium*] narcotic, illegal drug. *– pasang* (*ob*) gunpowder. *– patén* patent/proprietary medicine. *– pekasih* love philter. *– pelancar* lubricant, Vaseline. *– pelawan serangga* insecticide. *– peledak* explosive. *– pelindung tanaman* pesticide. *– peluntur* laxative, purgative, aperient. *– pembasmi ... ...icide. – pembasmi cendawan* fungicide. *– pembasmi serangga* insecticide. *– pembasmi lipas* cockroach poison. *– pemberantas hama* pesticide. *– pemucat* bleach. *– pemusnah hama* antiseptic, disinfectant. *– penahan batuk* cough suppressant. *– penahan darah* styptic. *– penangkal* remedy. *– penangkal buang air* medicine against diarrhea. *– penangkis* prophylactic. *– penawar* antidote. *– penawar sakit* analgesic. *– pencahar* laxative, aperient. *– pencegah kehamilan* contraceptive. *– pencuci perut* laxative, aperient. *– penenang* tranquillizer. *– pengasih* love philter. *– pengelat* astringent. *– penghapus hama* disinfectant. *– penghenti ingus* mucolytic. *– penghilang noda* spot remover. *– penghilang rasa nyeri/sakit* analgesic. *– penghilang rasa sakit dan penurun panas* antipyretic analgesic. *– penguat* tonic. *– penguat jantung* heart medicine, cardiac strengthener. *– penidur* sleeping pills. *– penurun demam/panas* antipyretic, fever-reducing medicine. *– penyegar* tonic. *– penyemprot* aerosols. *– penyiang rumput* herbicide, weed-killer. *– perangsang* a) stimulant. b) aphrodisiac. *– perangsang ludah* expectorant. *– perangsang séks* aphrodisiac. *– pereda (rasa) nyeri* analgesic. *– potrét* chemicals used in photography. *– puru* medicine for boils. *– rambut* depilatory. *– rindu* a cure for homesickness or for s.o. who is missed. *– rumah* home/household remedy. *– sayuran* a preparation used to rid vegetables of germs. *– sedingin* antipyretic. *– semprot hidung* nasal spray. *– senapan* ammunition. *– sendawa* gunpowder. *– serasi* tested medicine. *– serbuk* medicine in powder form; → PUYER. *– sétan* hard drugs. *– sinsé* Chinese folk medicine. *– stimulansia* (*infr*) stimulants. *– suntik(an)* serum. *– telan* oral medicine. *– telan kontraséptik* oral contraceptive. *– témpél* plasters. *– tétés* drops. *– tétés hidung* nose drops. *– tétés mata* eye drops, collyrium. *– tidur* sleeping pill. *– tradisional* traditional medicine. *– urus-urus* laxative.

berobat 1 to take medicine. *Bagaimana bisa sembuh kalau tidak ~.* How can you recover if you don't take your medicine? **2** *~ ke/kepada dokter* to see a doctor, be under a doctor's care. *Pada dokter mana engkau mau ~?* Which doctor do you want to see? **3** to be treated, be under treatment. *Sesudah lama ~ baru dia sembuh.* After a long period of treatment he has recovered. *~ hati* to be happy, satisfied. *~lah hatinya* he was very pleased/happy/glad to hear/see ...

mengobati [and **ngobatin** (*J coq*)] to treat (s.o. or s.t.), provide medical care for. *~ hati* to comfort, console. *~ luka* to dress a wound.

mengobatkan 1 to treat, cure. *Daun ini dapat dipakai untuk ~ penyakit kulit.* These leaves can be used to treat skin diseases. *~ diri sendiri* to treat/medicate o.s. **2** to cure/treat (s.o. or s.t.) with/by using.

memperobatkan to cure/treat (s.o. or s.t.) with/by using.

terobat(kan) 1 treated, cured. **2** reduced, tempered, decreased.

terobati 1 cured, treated. **2** comforted, consoled, relieved. *Hatinya yang sedih dapat ~ oléh kata-kata sahabatnya.* His friends' words were able to relieve his sadness. **3** treatable, can be treated. *penyakit yang tidak ~* an incurable disease.

obat-obatan 1 all k.o. medicines. *ilmu ~* pharmacology. *~ penurun berat badan* slimming-down/reducing medicines. **2** ingredients.

pengobat 1 medicine, s.t. used to treat s.o. medically. *~ hati* consolation, balm. **2** therapist, healer. ~ *tradisional* traditional healer, practitioner of folk medicine.

pengobatan therapy, (medical) treatment. *balai* ~ (poly)clinic. ~ *alamiah* physiotherapy. ~ *ceplok* treatment of a cold or headache by cupping and sucking. ~ *diri sendiri* self-medication. ~ *jarak-jauh* telemedicine. ~ *keséhatan darurat* emergency medical treatment. ~ *kimiawi* chemotherapy.

perobatan treatment, health care.

obat-abit (*Jv*) swaying.

mengobat-abitkan to brandish (a sword, etc.).

obduksi (*D*) obduction, autopsy, post-mortem.

obéd (from the name Robert; *Maluku*) Christian; → *cp* ACAN IV.

obéng I (*Jv*) screwdriver. - *belimbing/bintang/kembang/plus* Phillips screwdriver. - *minus/pipih* flat-tip screwdriver. - *sok* Robertson-tip screwdriver.

obéng II (*Jv*) **mengobéng** to work in a *batik* factory.

pengobéng worker in the *batik* industry.

oberal → OBRAL I.

obésitas (*E*) obesity.

obét → OBÉD.

obi (*Jp*) a long, broad sash tied about the waist of a Japanese kimono.

obituari (*E*) obituary.

objék → OBYÉK I.

oblak (*J/Jv*) **1** wide, spacious. **2** wobbly, shaky.

oblasi (*D*) offering, sacrifice, oblation.

oblék (*J*) tremble.

obligasi (*D fin*) bond, debenture. - *abadi* annuity bond. - *angsuran* installment bond. - *anuitas* annuity bond. - *atas nama* registered bond. - *atas unjuk* bearer bond. - *bagi-hasil* profit-sharing bond. - *bébas pajak* tax-exempt bond. - *berhak suara* voting bond. - *berséri* serial bond. - *boléh alih* negotiable bond. - *bunga* interest-bearing bond. - *daur ulang* recycled bond. - *dalam perédaran* outstanding bond. - *emas* gold bond. - *gombal* junk bond. - *instansi* agency bond. - *jaminan induk* joint bond. - *kekayaan* property bond. - *kekal* permanent bond. - *konvérsi* convertible bond. - *kupon* coupon bond. - *lindung nilai* hedge bond. - *niragun* debenture. - *pangkalan* terminal bond. - *pelanggan* client bond. - *pemerintah* treasury bond. - *pendapatan* income bond. - *perdana* refunding bond. - *persetujuan* assented bond. - *perusahaan* corporate bond. - *sampah* junk bond. - *sementara* interim bond. - *swasta* corporate bond. - *tanpa jaminan* debenture bond. - *tebus* callable bond. - *terdaftar* registered bond. - *terjamin* collateral trust bond. - *tertunda* extended bond. - *tukar* convertible bond. - *tunda (bunga)* deferred bond. - *unggul* gilt-edge bond. - *unjuk* bearer bond. - *yang bisa dikonvérsikan* convertible bond.

obligat (*D*) obligate.

obligatoir and **obligatoris** (*D leg*) obligatory.

obligor (*D leg*) liable/responsible party.

oblik (*D*) oblique, indirect (angle).

oblok-oblok (*Jv*) **1** k.o. food made from leftovers. **2** children from a mixed marriage.

oblong (*E*) *kaos* - T-shirt. **berkaos oblong** to wear a T-shirt.

obo (*E*) oboe.

obok obok-obok (*Jv*) **mengobok-obok 1** to put one's hand in water and splash around. **2** to dig up (dirt on or information about s.o. or s.t.). **3** to rummage around (in).

pengobok-obok s.o. who digs around (in).

pengobokan 1 splashing/digging around in. **2** digging up dirt on s.o.

obong (*J/Jv*) **mengobong** to put s.t. near a source of heat, set s.t. on fire.

obor (*Jv*) **1** torch. **2** guide, adviser. **3** oracle. - *bléncong* (lights on the outskirts of an airstrip) gooseneck.

berobor with torches, using a torch.

mengobor [and **ngobor** (*coq*)] **1** to smoke out (with a torch). **2** to incite, instigate. **3** (*ngobor*) to hunt for swamp eels at night using a torch. *ngobor kodok* to catch frogs at night using a torch. *tukang ngobor kodok* frog catcher.

mengobori 1 to illuminate, shed light on, light up. **2** to stimulate, inspire, fire up.

pengobor ~ *kodok* frog catcher.

pengoboran 1 smoking, fumigating, fumigation. **2** instigation, incitement. **3** information, education, guidance.

obrak-abrik (*J/Jv*) **mengobrak-abrik 1** to overturn, destroy, put in total disorder. **2** to rummage/go through.

terobrak-abrik destroyed; overturned, turned upside down. ~*nya sistém nilai* the destruction of the system of values.

pengobrak-abrikan destruction, breakup, overturning.

obral I (*Jv*) (clearance) sale. *lebih murah dari* – dirt cheap. *harga* - sale price. - *besar* super/giant sale. - *murah* big sale.

mengobral to sell at a reduced price, sell off, clear. *Apa barang-barang ini diobral?* Are these items on sale? ~ *pengaruh* influence peddling.

mengobralkan to sell s.o. cheaply.

obralan merchandise to be sold at a reduced price, items on sale.

pengobral s.o. who sells items at a reduced price.

pengobralan sale, selling at a reduced price.

obral II (*Jv*) quick to do s.t., easily … - *ketawa* easily amused, likes to laugh.

mengobral to distribute in large quantities, waste/squander (in large quantities). *Banyak gadis yang suka* ~ *cinta.* Many girls like to throw their love around lavishly. ~ *janji* to make a lot of promises. ~ *senyum* to smile a lot. ~ *tenaga* to waste a lot of manpower.

obras (*D*) overcast, the sewing over an edge with loose stitches so as to prevent raveling. *mesin* – machine for making such stitches.

mengobras(kan) to sew stitches in this way.

obrasan overcast.

obrigado (*Port*) (in East Timor) thank you.

obrol (*J/Jv*) chat, talk.

mengobrol [and **ngobrol** (*coq*)] to chatter (away), gossip. *Lagi énak ngobrol, datang Saéchon dan menjambak rambut perempuan 25 tahun ini.* While chattering away pleasantly, Saéchon showed up and grabbed the hair of this 25-year-old woman. *Meréka ngobrol-ngobrol dengan teman-temannya.* They were chattering away with their friends. *tukang ngobrol* chatterbox, gossip. *ngobrol di kedai/warung kopi* to talk idly in the coffee shop. *ngobrol ngalor ngidul* to chat, talk about this and that.

mengobroli [and **ngobrolin** (*J coq*)] [*pl obj*] to talk/gossip about.

mengobrolkan to chatter/talk/gossip about. *dingobrolkan* to be chattered about.

obrolan chattering, gossiping. ~ *warung kopi* idle talk around the coffee table.

pengobrolan chatting, chatter. ~ *kosong* idle chatter.

obros and **obrus** (*D ob*) lieutenant-colonel.

obsérvasi (*D*) observation.

mengobsérvasi to observe.

obsérvatori (*E*) and **obsérvatorium** (*D*) observatory.

obsérvir (*D*) **mengobsérvir** to observe.

obsési (*D*) obsession.

berobsési to be obsessed.

mengobsésikan to be obsessed about s.t.

terobsési to be obsessed.

obsésif (*E*) obsessive.

obsidian (*D*) obsidian.

obsolét (*E*) obsolete.

obstétri (*D*) obstetrics.

obstétrikus (*D*) obstetrician.

obstruksi (*D*) obstruction.

obyék I (*D*) **1** object, thing, item; → BENDA. *Meréka tidak boléh memperlakukan petani sebagai* –. They shouldn't treat farmers as objects. - *pajak* taxable item. **2** (*gram*) object. **3** object, objective, aim, goal; → SASARAN. - *pariwisata* tourist attraction. **mengobyék-pariwisatakan** to make s.t. into a tourist attraction. *Istana Bogor diobyékpariwisatakan.* The Bogor (Presidential) Palace has been made into a tourist attraction. - *penyelidikan* object of study/research. - *turisme* tourist attraction. - *vital* vital object.

obyék II (*D*) source of extra income (often illegal) from one's principal job, object for earning extra money (by moonlighting), side-earnings.

mengobyék [and **ngobyék** (*coq*)] **1** to earn extra money by moonlighting (usually by acting as a middleman in a sale). **2** to earn extra money by selling at a profit s.t. that one has bought at a bargain price, buy low and sell high. **3** to earn extra money by offering for sale the services or goods one gets for free as part of one's job, k.o. bureaucratic graft or corruption, e.g., by renting out the house one is allowed to live in because of one's government position; *cp* OMPRÉNG II. **4** to support o.s. with difficulty.

mengobyékkan to sell/trade/do business with s.t. for a profit. ~ *arloji digital Sicura* to sell a Sicura digital watch for a profit. *Pembébasan film Amérika kini banyak diobyékkan.* The release of American films is now a big way of making extra money.

obyékan object used for earning extra money.

pengobyék s.o. who makes extra money by moonlighting or selling s.t. for a profit, etc.

pengobyékan moonlighting, earning extra money by selling s.t., etc., for a profit.

obyéktif (*D*) **1** objective, unbiased. **2** objective, goal.

mengobyéktifkan to make objective/unbiased.

keobyéktifan objectivity, lack of bias.

obyéktivisme (*D*) objectivism.

obyéktivitas (*D*) objectivity.

ocak-ocak (*Jv*) **mengocak-ocak** to shake. *Obatnya diocak-ocak dahulu sebelum diminum.* Shake the medicine well before taking it.

océh (*Jv*) **mengocéh** [and **ngocéh** (*coq*)] **1** to chirp, cheep, twitter (of birds). **2** to chatter, gossip (of people). *terlalu banyak ngocéh tapi sedikit yang dikerjakan* a lot of talk and no action.

mengocéhkan to chatter/gossip about.

océhan gossip, small talk, idle chatter.

pengocéh chatterbox, gossip.

odalan (*Bal*) community prayer (by adherents of the *Hindu Dharma* religion).

ode (*D*) ode.

odeklonyo and **odekolone** (*D*) eau-de-cologne.

odha [orang dgn HIV/AIDS] HIV/AIDS patient.

odiénsi → AUDIÉNSI.

odim → UDIM.

oditif (*D*) auditive.

oditir → ODITUR.

oditorium (*D*) auditorium.

oditur (*D leg*) judge advocate. – *jénderal* judge advocate general. – *militér* [odmil] military prosecutor. – *militér pengganti* alternate military prosecutor. – *militér tinggi* [odmilti] supreme military prosecutor.

keodituran the function of judge advocate.

oditurat (*D leg*) judge advocate's office.

odmil → ODITUR *militér*.

odmilti → ODITUR *militér tinggi*.

odoh 1 ugly. **2** stupid.

odoklonyo → ODEKLONYO.

odol I (*D*) (- *gigi*) toothpaste.

odol II (*J*) **ngodol** to take apart, take to pieces, strip, dismantle, slit open, rip up. ~ *saku/kantong* to reach into one's pocket.

ngodolin to take advantage of s.o., fleece. *tukang* ~ sponger, parasite, freeloader.

odol III (*Jv*) **mengodol** to remove, extract (kapok) from (the husk/ a mattress, etc.).

odolan 1 removed, extracted (of kapok). *pengusaha* ~ *terbesar* the largest kapok-extracting entrepreneur. **2** retail.

odol-odolan (*J*) pulling/tugging at s.o.

pengodol (kapok) extractor, s.o. who processes unhusked kapok into marketable kapok.

pengodolan removing, extracting.

odométer (*E*) odometer.

odontologi (*D/E*) odontology. – *forénsik* forensic odontology.

odo-odo (*Jv*) the *dalang*'s singing (in a *wayang* performance).

odoran (*E*) odorant.

oék (*onom*) neighing.

mengoék to neigh.

ofénsif (*D/E*) offensive, attack. – *balas* counteroffensive.

oférte (*D*) offer, bid (in business).

Officier van Justitie (*D col*) public prosecutor.

ofisial (*E*) **1** official, formal. **2** (in sports) official.

ofisiil (*D*) official, formal.

ofsét I (*E*) offset. *cétak* – offset printing. *dicétak* – printed in offset. *percétakan* – offset printing office.

mengofsét 1 to make an offset of. **2** to print by offset lithography.

ofsét II (*E*) compensation (for orders placed abroad).

ofsét III (*E*) off-side (in soccer).

oftalmologi (*D/E*) ophthalmology.

oga (*A*) → HOKAH.

ogah I (*J/Jv*) reluctant, unwilling, averse to, not wanting to. *pasién yang – dioperasi* a patient who doesn't want to be operated on. *Agaknya meréka ingin numpang, tapi – bayar karcis.* It seems they wanted to get a ride, but they were unwilling to pay for the tickets. *pak* – s.o. who unofficially directs traffic and asks for a fee from drivers.

ogah-ogahan (*secara* ~) reluctantly, unwillingly, grudgingly, not wanting to. *Dua dékade setelah ditetapkan untuk berubah ke sistém pengukuran métrik, Inggris kini berada di pertengahan jalan dan masih* ~ *dengan perubahan itu.* Twenty years after deciding to change to the metric system, England is halfway there but is still unwilling to make the change.

keogahan aversion, unwillingness, not wanting to. ~ *berobah* inertia.

ogah II – *agih* shaky, loose.

mengogah to loosen by shaking (a tooth/pole/stake, etc.).

ogah III → HOKA.

ogak-ogak (*cla*) clown, buffoon, jester.

berogak-ogak to clown/joke around.

pengogak-ogak clown, jester, jokester.

ogal-agil and **ogal-ogél** → OGÉL-OGÉL.

ogal-ogalan → UGAL-UGALAN.

ogam mengogam to put s.o. into a trance through magic.

pengogam a charm or drug to do this.

ogé whore.

ogél-ogél (*J/Jv*) **1** to keep moving back and forth, wag back and forth. *Buntutnya – terus.* Its tail kept on wagging. **2** rickety.

mengogél-ogélkan to wag s.t. back and forth.

ogoh mengogoh to shake s.t.

ogoh-ogoh (*Bal*) k.o. large *ondél-ondél*.

ogok I (*M*) **mengogok-ogok 1** to totter, stagger (from fatigue). **2** to breath with difficulty (after hard work).

ogok II → OKOK.

ogok III (*M*) **mengogokkan** to display s.t. for sale.

Ogos (*Mal*) August.

ogot jagged (of a knife edge).

ogut and **og'ut** (*Pr*) I, me; → GUA II.

oh → O II.

ohir (*D J*) **1** old man. **2** to be weak (due to old age), be no longer useful/fit for use, unusable, worn out (from use). *Sepatu yu sudah –, mendingan yu buang.* Your shoes are worn out, you better throw them away.

ohm (*D*) ohm (unit of electrical resistance).

oi hi! hello! (calling s.o.).

oikoméné and **oikumené** (*D*) (o)ecumenism.

oikuménis (*D*) (o)ecumenical.

oja(h) mengoja(h) 1 to incite, instigate, pit (fighting cocks/animals) against e.o. **2** to encourage, inspire.

ojahan (in Bengkulu) corner. *batu* – cornerstone.

ojék (*J*) bicycle or motorcycle put to use as an inexpensive means of hired transportation; the passenger sits behind the driver and is driven to his destination for a fee.

mengojék [and **ngojék** (*coq*)] to transport a paying passenger on a bike or motorcycle.

mengojékkan to use (a bike or motorcycle) as a hired vehicle.

ojékan bike or motorcycle used as a hired means of transportation.

pengojék driver of an *ojék*.

ojékwan driver of an *ojék*.

ojo (*Jv*) don't. – *duméh* Don't get on your high horse (just because you ...), i.e., don't lord it over others. – *gumun* don't be amazed so easily. – *kagétan* don't be startled so easily. – *ngoyo* take it easy!

ojok I (*M*) **mengojok** to grope one's way slowly while stooping over, walk in a stooped-over position.

ojok II (*Jv*) ojok-ojok to instigate, incite, urge; → OJA.
  mengojok-ojoki to instigate, incite, urge.
  pengojok instigator.
ojok III → ÉJÉK.
ojok-ojok (*J*) directly, without an intermediary.
OK and O.K. /oké/ → OKÉ.
OKB (*init*) → ORANG *kaya baru*.
oké (*E*) 1 okay/OK. 2 to agree, say okay.
  mengokékan to okay/OK s.t. *Praktek disko diokékan*. Running of discos has been okayed.
  keokéan being okay, excellence.
okém (*J*) private person; outsider, person not belonging to the in-group. "*Calo-calo meminta pungli dengan mengancam, sementara –.– hanya duduk-duduk mengawasi kita, ujar supir jurusan Jakarta-Labuan*. "The bus touts asked for a *pungli* using threats, while the outsiders just sit around watching us," said a driver on the Jakarta-Labuan route.
oker (*D*) ocher.
OKI [(Kabupatén) Ogan Komering Ilir] the (Regency) of the Lower Course of the Ogan Komering (River).
oklusif (*E ling*) occlusive.
OKM (*init*) → ORANG *kaya mendadak*.
oknum (*A*) 1 shady character, bad person, rogue; thug. – *DLLAJR* thugs of the Highway Traffic and Transportation Service. – *Kamtib* thugs of the Security and Public Order Service. – *Polri* rogue cop. 2 person. *Allah satu tiga* – Holy Trinity. 3 individual.
  keoknuman personality.
okok (*ob*) miserly, stingy, closefisted, tight.
okol(-okolan) (*Mad*) k.o. wrestling in which two opponents try to push e.o. back with their outstretched arms.
oksalat (*D*) oxalate. *asam* – oxalic acid.
oksid(a) (*D*) oxide. – *tembaga* cupric acid.
  mengoksid(a) to oxidize.
  pengoksid(a) oxidizer.
  pengoksid(a)an oxidizing, oxidation.
oksidasi (*D*) oxidation. – *tidak sempurna* partial oxidation.
  mengoksidasi to oxidate.
  mengoksidasikan to oxidize. *Melalui prosés ini, kandungan sulfur dalam pétroléum dioksidasikan, kemudian terpisah dengan sendirinya*. Through this process the sulfur contained in the petroleum is oxidized and then it automatically separates itself out.
  teroksidasi oxidized. *Asam askorbat mudah ~ menjadi asam déhidroaskordat*. Ascorbic acid is easily oxidized into dehydroascorbic acid.
  pengoksidasi oxidizer.
  pengoksidasian oxidizing.
oksidator oxidizing agent.
oksigén (*D/E*) oxygen.
  beroksigén containing oxygen, oxygenated.
oktaf (*D*) octave.
oktan(a) (*D*) octane.
  beroktan(a) -octane. *bénsin yang ~ 94* 94-octane gas. *~ tinggi* high-octane.
oktét (*D/E*) octet.
Oktober (*D*) October.
  Oktoberan commemoration of the events of 30 September/1 October 1965.
oktroi (*D*) patent.
OKU [(Kabupatén) Ogan Komering Ulu] the (Regency) of the Upper Course of the Ogan Komering (River).
okular (*E*) ocular.
okulasi (*D*) grafting.
  mengokulasikan to graft s.t.
  pengokulasian grafting.
okulér (*D*) ocular, visual lens(es).
okulis (*D*) oculist, ophthalmologist.
okultis (*D*) occult.
okultisme (*D/E*) occultism.
okupansi (*D*) occupancy. *Tingkat – hotél rata-rata mencapai 75%*. Hotel occupancy rates have reached an average of 75%.
okupasi (*D/E*) 1 (illegal) occupation (of land), squatting. 2 occupation, employment, job; profession, career.

olah I 1 method, fashion, way, manner (of acting); → ULAH. 2 whim, caprice, mood. *membuat* – to joke. 3 trick, prank. – *gerak* maneuver (of a ship). *mengolahgerakkan* to maneuver. – *rasa* sensitivity. *mengolahrasakan* to sensitize. *pengolahrasaan* sensitizing. – *yudha* war games.
olah-olah (not) seriously, jokingly, playfully. *bukan ~* no kidding. seolah-olah as if/though, like. *~ menjual diri* as though selling out.
berolah and mengolah 1 to behave in a ridiculous way; to be capricious/whimsical. 2 to use tricks/pranks. 3 (*Jv*) to be engaged in, practice. *Kaum wanita di dalam berolah séks umumnya lebih banyak menerima dari memberi*. When women have sex they usually get more than they give.
  memperolahkan to tease, make fun of; to deceive, trick, cheat.
  olahan whim.
olah II process. – *serap* absorption. *pengolahserapan* absorption process. – *ulang* recycle. *mengolah ulang* to recycle, reprocess. *olahan ulang* recycled. *pengolahan ulang* recycling.
  mengolah 1 to prepare, manufacture. 2 to till, work, cultivate (the land). *~ tanah* to work the land. 3 to process, i.e., take a raw material and turn it into a processed product. *belum diolah* unprocessed, crude, raw. *~ bahan mentah* to process raw materials. *~ kata* word processing. 4 to treat. *~ limbah* to treat waste. 5 to work on (a plan).
  olahan 1 processed. 2 a preparation.
  pengolah 1 manufacturer. 2 tiller, worker (of the land), cultivator. 3 processor. *mesin ~ karét remah* crumb-rubber processor. *(mesin) ~ kata* word processor. *unit ~ terpusat* (in computers) central processing unit, CPU.
  pengolahan 1 preparation, manufacture, manufacturing. *industri ~* manufacturing industry. 2 tilling, tillage, working (the land). *~ lahan* land clearing. 3 processing, treatment, refining, currying (leather). *~ air (kotor/limbah)* (waste)water treatment. *~ cerita* scenario. *~ data* data processing. *~ kapas (berbiji menjadi serat kapas)* ginnery. *~ pelarut* solvent refining.
olahraga 1 sports. 2 physical exercises (as a sport). *kelab* – sports club. *- arus deras* [orad] white-water rafting. *- dan keséhatan* [okés] sports and health. *- dayung* rowing (as a sport). *- hidup baru* [orhiba] new life physical exercises. *- kuda* equestrianism. *- udara* aerosports.
  berolahraga to engage in sports/physical exercise.
  mengolahragakan to make s.o. sports-minded. *~ masyarakat* to make the community sports-minded.
  keolahragaan 1 sports. 2 sportsmanship.
  pengolahraga 1 sportsman. 2 athlete.
olahragawan 1 sportsman. 2 athlete.
olahragawati 1 sportswoman. 2 female athlete.
olahwedar (*Jv*) berolahwedar *~ dalam* to be active in.
olak I whirling, eddying, turning. *arus* – rotary/eddy current (electrical). *- air* whirlpool, eddy. *- angin* whirlwind.
  berolak to turn, twirl, whirl, eddy.
  mengolak to turn, twirl, twist around.
  mengolakkan *~ janji* to put off doing s.t. promised.
  olakan eddy. *~ air* whirlpool. *~ angin* windstorm. *~ kemudi* wake of a ship.
  perolakan turn(ing), circulation.
olak II (*M*) 1 downstream, lower reaches. 2 to return, go back. *membayar* – to repay, refund, pay back.
  berolak 1 weakening (of the body, etc.). 2 no longer effective/efficacious (of medicine).
  mengolak 1 to reverberate. 2 to not want to (eat s.t.).
olak-alik to and fro, back and forth; vacillating (of talk, etc.); → BOLAK *balik*, ULANG-ALING. *pesawat* – *Challenger* the Challenger space shuttle.
  mengolak-alikkan 1 to move s.t. to and fro/back and forth. 2 to deal cleverly with (money, etc.).
olak-olak *burung* – brown booby, *Sula leucogaster plotus*; → ITIK *laut*.
Olanda (*ob*) → BELANDA I.
olang-alik commuting, commuter (*mod*); → ULANG-ALIK. *pelayanan* – commuter service.
  pengolang-alik commuter.

olang-aling 1 to swing (back and forth). **2** to roll (of a ship).
  mengolang-alingkan to (let) swing.
  terolang-aling swing back and forth.
old and new (*E*) **berold-and-new** to celebrate New Year's Eve.
old crack (*E*) /olkrék/ old hand (at s.t.).
Oldefo(s) [Old Established Force(s)] Old Established Forces, i.e., the first- and second-world nations.
oléander (*D*) oleander, *Nerium oleander.*
oléat (*mil*) overlay.
oléfin (*D*) olefin(e).
oléh 1 by (with passive verbs with the prefixes *di-* or *ter-* and certain other verbs with passive meaning), i.e., precedes the person or thing which performs the action or is the cause of the action, *usu* used only with third-person agents but occasionally with first- or second-person agents. *Buku itu dibawa – ayah.* Father took the book. *Anak itu digigit – anjing.* The child was bitten by the dog. *Buku itu terbawa – saya/anda/dia/-nya.* I/you/he accidentally took the book. *Seorang pengendara sepéda motor Selasa pagi téwas seketika setelah tertindih – sebuah truk.* A motorcyclist was killed on the spot Tuesday morning after being struck by an overturned truck. *Tampak –nya seorang tua berjalan di tengah-tengah sawahnya.* He could see an old man walking in his rice fields. *Ada seorang ibu guru kena tonjok – salah seorang anak laki yang tidak lulus.* There was a female teacher who got hit by a student who didn't pass. **2** to (after certain adjectives). *tak jelas – saya* it wasn't clear to me. **3** (after certain adjectives) with. *Keméja lengan panjang yang melekat di tubuh meréka kuyup – keringat.* The long-sleeved shirts, which were sticking to their bodies, were soaked with sweat. *Mata Ani sudah basah – air mata.* Ani's eyes were wet with tears. *Halaman rumah Gubernur penuh sesak – orang.* The yard of the Governor's mansion was chock-full of people. *Mukanya penuh – jerawat.* His face was covered with freckles. **4** (*M*) of (indicating a family relationship). *Ia anak yang satu-satunya – paman saya.* He is my uncle's only child. *Ia pun sepupu juga – tuan.* He's also your cousin.
  beroléh 1 to get, receive (implies passive reception by the subject). *Tidak ~ uang sesén juga.* Didn't get even a penny. *~ hidung* to be embarrassed. *~ telur busuk* to be embarrassed. **2** (*cla*) may, might. *supaya segera ~ kembali* that he might return soon.
  memperoléh to get, acquire, obtain (implies active effort on part of the subject), have (children), secure (a loan). *Usia yang baik untuk ~ keturunan adalah yang putri 20 tahun.* The best age for a woman to have offspring is when she is 20 years old. *Keuntungan yang diperoléhnya adalah berlipat ganda.* The profit she obtained was double. *diperoléh dengan jalan tidak halal* ill-gotten. *~ kemajuan* to make progress. *~ kembali* to regain, get back.
  memperoléhi (*mostly Mal*) to obtain, get.
  terperoléh obtained. **keterperoléhan** availability.
  pemeroléhan [formed from a hypothetical form *memeroléh*] acquisition. *~ bahasa* language acquisition.
  peroléhan 1 acquisition. *~ bahasa* language acquisition. *~ balik* trade-off. *~ dengan imbalan* acquisition for a consideration. *~ suara* (number of) votes (gotten). **2** (*petrol*) recovery, yield. *~ kedua* secondary recovery.
oléh-oléh 1 small presents, souvenirs (brought back from a trip). **2** (*euph*) bribe(s).
  mengoléh-oléhi to bring s.o. back a present from a trip.
oléin (*D*) olein(e).
olék → OLÉT I, ULÉT. **mengolék** to hush (a child).
oléng 1 swinging, rocking (of a boat). **2** shaky, not firm. *– kemoléng* rolling from side to side.
  beroléng-oléng and **mengoléng-oléng** to swing, rock, shake.
  mengoléng to shake one's head from side to side. *Ia ~ sebagai tanda tidak setuju.* He shook his head as a sign of disagreement.
  teroléng-oléng swung, rocked, shaken.
  oléngan and **keoléngan** swinging, rocking.
olés (*J*) **beroléskan** rubbed/smeared with (a salve, etc.).
  mengolés to grease, lubricate.
  mengolési to smear a substance on s.t. *~ roti dengan mentéga* to butter bread.

mengoléskan to smear, grease with s.t. *Wanita itu ~ minyak kelapa ke rambutnya.* The woman smeared coconut oil on her hair.
  olésan ointment, s.t. smeared on. *Secara keseluruhan wanita terpilih itu harus diakui menarik, meskipun ~ cat bibirnya berlebihan.* One must admit that on the whole the woman selected was attractive although she used an excessive amount of lipstick.
  pengolés s.t. used for smearing, etc.
  pengolésan smearing, rubbing s.t. on.
olét → OLÉK.
oli (*D*) oil, *usu* lubricating oil. *– campur* mixed oil. *– mesin* engine/machine/lubricating oil. *– oplosan* adulterated oil. *– samping* 2-cycle engine oil.
olia (*coq*) → AULIA.
olibol (*D*) k.o. fritter.
olie → OLI.
oligarkik (*E*) and **oligarkis** (*D*) oligarchic.
oligopoli (*D/E*) oligopoly, i.e., a market situation in which a small number of producers influence but do not control the market.
oligopolistik (*E*) oligopolistic.
oliman (*D*) oiler (on a ship).
Olimpiad (*E*) and **Olimpiade** (*D*) Olympics.
Olimpik (*E*) Olympic.
olnait (*E*) all night (use of a prostitute).
olok I olok-olok mockery, ridicule, derision. *gambar ~* caricature, (political) cartoon. *main ~* to mock, speak in fun.
  berolok-olok to mock, joke around.
  mengolok-oloki to mock, deride, laugh/jeer at, ridicule, make fun of.
  mengolok-olokkan and **mem(p)erolok(-olok)kan** to make fun of, make a fool of, pull s.o.'s leg, deride, mock, ridicule.
  olok(-olok)an jesting, banter, mockery, ridicule. *bahan ~* laughingstock.
  pengolok-olok 1 clown, jester. **2** s.o. who likes to ridicule people.
olok II chain stitch (in sewing).
olong-olong (*Jv*) larva species in teakwood, bee hole borer, *Xyloites cermaicus.*
oloran (*Jv*) new land that results from sedimentation which protrudes into the sea.
olrait (*E*) all right.
om I → OOM.
om II (*Hind Bal*) holy syllable, om.
oma (*D*) grandma, grandmother; granny, i.e., appellation for an older woman of one's grandmother's generation.
omah-omah (*Jv*) **1** to live (in a house), make one's home (in). **2** to marry, set up housekeeping; to run one's own household.
ombak wave (in the sea, of hair), undulation, surf. *– kedengaran, pasirnya tidak kelihatan* much ado about nothing. *– yang kecil jangan diabaikan* a small leak will sink a ship; small beginnings make great endings. *– balik* backrush (of the waves). *– bunga lepang* whitecaps. *– galur* waves pounding on cliffs. *– gemulung* rolling waves. *– memecah* breakers. *– pengundak* head sea. *– selebu* rollers.
  berombak 1 to have waves, be wavy/choppy. *Laut mulai ~.* The sea began to become choppy. **2** to be waved, wavy (of hair). *Rambutnya ~ air.* Her hair was waved by water. **3** to heave. *Dadanya ~.* His chest heaved. **4** undulating, rolling (terrain), wrinkled (of skin).
  berombak-ombak in waves, waving, undulating.
  mengombak to wave, undulate. *rambutnya yang ~ lembut* his soft wavy hair.
  ombakan 1 wave(s). **2** flood, stream. *~ nafsu* a flood of desire.
  ombak-ombakan wave motif (on cloth).
ombang-ambing berombang-ambing to toss about.
  mengombang-ambingkan 1 to toss, toss about/to and fro. *Kapal itu diombang-ambingkan ombak selama tiga jam.* The ship was tossed about by the waves for three hours. **2** to swing s.t. to and fro. *Tak dapat meredakan hatinya yang diombang-ambingkan oléh asmara.* They couldn't calm him down, he was swung to and fro by love. **3** to give s.o. the run-around. *Saya diombang-ambingkan waktu mengurus paspor saya.* I got the run-around when I tried to arrange for my passport.

terombang-ambing 1 tossed/tossing about, bobbing up and down. *Kapal itu ~ di tengah lautan.* The ship tossed about in the open sea. 2 to wander about aimlessly. 3 be uncertain (of life, etc.). *Hidupnya ~ keadaan ékonomi.* His life was uncertain due to the economic situation. 4 to get the run-around.
keterombang-ambingan uncertainty. *dalam ~ yang melanda dua pihak yang berurusan langsung* in the uncertainty which struck the two sides which were dealing directly with e.o.
ombang-ambingan vacillation.
ombaykuk (*D*) k.o. honey cake.
ombé (*J*) ngombé to ask/beg (for s.t.).
omblad (*D*) → DÉKBLAD.
ombol (*J/Jv*) pile, heap.
ombyok (*Jv*) ombyokan 1 bunch, cluster. *kunci se~* a bunch of keys. *Jakarta bak ~ bangunan, sarana, dan penyempurna.* Jakarta is like a bunch of buildings, means of communication, and perfectionists. 2 *secara ~* in great numbers. *Perampok itu datang secara ~.* The bandits came in great numbers.
omél (*J/Jv*) mengomél [and ngomél (*coq*)] to grumble, complain, grouse. *tanpa ~* without a murmur/word (of complaint)]. *Jika saya mandi lebih dari lima gayung, ibu kos saya akan ~ panjang.* If I use more than five scoopfuls (of water) to take a bath, my landlady complains the whole day long. *tukang ngomél* grumbler, complainer.
mengoméli [and ngomélin (*J coq*)] to be angry at, reprimand, rebuke, admonish. *Anak jangan ~ ortunya.* Children shouldn't reprimand their parents.
omélan grumbling, complaining, grousing.
Omiba (*col*) [Obyék Militér Baturaja] Baturaja Military Object, i.e., the former Dutch combat training area in Baturaja.
omisi (*D*) omission.
omnibus (*D*) (omni)bus.
omnivora (*D*) omnivore, omnivorous animal; → PEMAKAN *segala.*
omo (*Jv*) → HAMA.
omong (*J/Jv*) speech, way of speaking/pronouncing; parlance; dialect. *banyak –nya* he talks a lot. *–nya lompat-lompat* he jumps from topic to topic. *pasang ~* talk, chat, gossip. *lagak Padang, – Betawi* unjustified boasting. *– besar* boasting, bragging, big talk. **mengomong-besarkan** to boast/brag about. *P-4 untuk diamalkan, bukan diomong-besarkan.* P-4 is for putting into practice, not for bragging about. *– Betawi/Jakarta* the Jakarta dialect, Jakartanese. *– jorok* to talk dirty. *– kosong (melompong)* empty talk. **beromong kosong** to talk idly. *– kotor* to talk dirty. *– punya –* by the way.
omong-omong 1 to talk, chat. *~ santai* to chat in a relaxed way. 2 by the way, incidentally. *~, Anda punya ...?* By the way, do you have a ...? ngomong-ngomong 1 to come/get to the point. 2 by the way, incidentally. *~, saudara sudah beristri apa belum?* By the way, are you married or not?
beromong(-omong) to chat, talk (idly), gossip.
mengomong to speak, talk. *pagi ngomong tahu, soré ngomong tempé* unreliable, inconsistent.
ngomong to talk, chat, converse. *~ doang/saja* all talk (no action); to boast. *~ ngelantur* to talk idly, chew the fat. *Sejak tengah malam sampai sekitar pukul 03.00 pagi tetap ~ ngelantur.* From midnight to about 3 in the morning they continued to talk idly.
mengomongi to speak to.
mengomongkan [and ngomongin (*J coq*)] to talk/chat about.
omongan 1 gossip. 2 talk. *~ yang terloncat dari mulut begitu saja* a slip of the tongue. *jadi ~ orang* to be the talk of the town. *~nya ngaco.* He blathered away.
pengomong a talkative person.
ompang-ompang (*Mal*) → OLÉH-OLÉH.
omplok (*J*) mengomplok [and ngomplok (*coq*)] to assemble, gather together, hang out. *Jangan ~ di situ, nanti dimarahi ayah.* Don't hang out over there, father will be angry.
ompol (*J/Jv*) bed-wetting, enuresis.
mengompol [and ngompol (*coq*)] to wet one's bed/pants. *tukang ngompol* bed wetter, s.o. who frequently wets his bed. *Anak-anak balita masih mengompol dan bérak di celana.* Children under the age of five still pee and shit in their pants.

mengompoli [and ngompol (*coq*) and ngompolin (*J coq*)] to pee (inadvertently) on. *Lolly ditaruhnya kembali setelah mengganti alas yang diompoli oléh Lolly.* She put Lolly back (in her cot) after changing the diaper that Lolly had peed on.
ompong (*J/Jv*) 1 toothless, with missing teeth. 2 missing (of issues of a magazine/steps in stairs, etc.). *Saya punya persediaan TÉMPO 1975-1983, meski ada nomor-nomor – sekitar April-Agustus 1977.* I have a collection of TEMPO magazines from 1975 to 1983, though some issues from around April to August 1977 are missing. *Jembatan penyeberangan di Jl Matraman Raya di depan pasar Jatinegara tampak – anak tangganya.* Apparently the pedestrian overpass at Jl. Matraman Raya in front of the Jatinegara market is missing a step. 3 gap, lacuna.
mengompongi to knock s.o.'s teeth out (in boxing).
ompréng I (*J*) 1 (thin) eating trough. 2 multiple unit container, metal food carrier, stackable picnic pack; → RANTANG I.
ngompréng to carry food in such a container; to eat from such a container.
ompréng II (*J/Jv*) ngompréng 1 to use one's car (private or government-owned) as an illegal taxi. 2 to ride in such an illegal taxi. *Kalau mau ke Grogol lebih énak ~ daripada naik taksi.* If you want to go to Grogol, it's more comfortable to ride in an illegal taxi than in a taxi. 3 to live like a parasite, benefit from s.t. without paying for it. 4 to be a prostitute, sell one's body (of a married woman). *Kalau suaminya tidak ada di rumah wanita itu suka ~.* When her husband's not at home, that woman works as a prostitute.
mengompréngkan 1 to lend out (a vehicle) for illegal use. *Bus kota itu diompréngkan kepada supir lainnya.* The city buses have been rented out to other drivers. 2 to use (a vehicle) as an illegal taxi or truck. *Truk sampah diompréngkan mengangkut kayu jati balokan.* The garbage truck was used (illegally) to transport teak logs.
ompréngan 1 (passengers) picked up illegally by a bus. 2 (vehicle) used as an illegal taxi or truck. *kapal ~* tramp. *truk ~* truck used to transport passengers illegally.
pengompréng s.o. who uses a car he doesn't own to transport passengers or freight.
omprong (*Jv*) cured with smoke. *tembakau ~* smoke-cured tobacco.
mengomprong to dry tobacco leaves by smoking/fumigation.
omprongan dried tobacco. *los ~ tembakau* tobacco drying shed/house.
pengomprong tobacco fumigator.
pengomprongan drying (tobacco by smoking).
ompu (*Bat*) an honorary title.
omsét (*D*) turnover, sales.
beromsét to have a turnover of ... *Sarang perjudian yang ~ Rp 2,5 miliar per hari dibongkar resérse Polda Métro Jaya.* The gambling den with a turnover of 2.5 billion rupiahs a day was broken up by the Greater Jakarta Regional Police Force detectives.
omslah (*D*) cover (of a book).
mengomslahkan to put a cover on (a book).
omzét → OMSÉT.
on → ONS.
onak 1 thorn, prickle. 2 a thorny rattan, *Plectocomia griffithii.* 3 the difficult parts of life.
onak-onak thorny bushes.
onani (*D*) masturbation, onanism.
beronani to masturbate.
mengonani to masturbate s.o.
onanis (*D*) masturbator, onanist.
onar I (*Pers*) 1 noisy, loud, boisterous. 2 commotion, stir, tumult, upheaval. *berita yang menimbulkan –* news which caused a big commotion. *membuat –* to make a scene, make trouble. *tukang bikin –* troublemaker, rioter.
mengonarkan to cause a commotion about, agitate about.
keonaran 1 confusion, sensation, commotion. 2 disturbance, riot. 3 quarrel, brawl.
onar II (*Pers M*) dirty/nasty trick, fraud. *membuat –* to perpetrate a fraud.
beronar fraudulent, scandalous (of conduct/news).

oncang Welsh onion, *Allium fistulosum.*
oncat (*Jv*) to make one's escape.
oncék (*Jv*) mengoncék(i) to peel, shell.
oncén (*Jv*) string (of flowers, etc.); → RONCÉN.
oncér (*J*) loose (of a screw). *Sekrupnya sudah –.* The screw is loose.
oncés (*Med*) young prostitute, slut.
onclang (*Jv*) mengonclang 1 to toss, flip. 2 to transfer s.o. against his will.
oncok-oncok (*J/Jv*) directly, without stopping any place else.
oncom (*Jv*) k.o. fermented beans. *– gejos* these beans mixed with shredded coconut from which the milk has been squeezed.
oncor I (*Jv*) bamboo torch.
  mengoncori to light s.t. with a torch.
oncor II (*Jv*) mengoncori to irrigate, inundate.
  oncoran irrigated; irrigation. *~ sawah* rice-paddy irrigation. *sawah bukan ~* unirrigated rice paddies.
oncor-oncoran (*Jv*) 1 to make a higher bid, try to bid up, outbid, try to outdo. 2 competition, rivalry; → JOR-JORAN.
ondéh (*M*) (interjection) too bad!
ondék I *pedagang –* small citrus dealer.
ondék II (*E*) on deck.
ondél-ondél (*J*) a giant puppet moved by a person inside it, *usu* used in the marriage procession.
ondé-ondé (*J*) polka-dot. *motif –* polka-dot pattern.
ondé(h)-ondé(h) (*Tam?*) and *kué –* sesame balls made of fried sweetened rice flour, potato, water, sugar, green beans, sesame seeds, oil.
onder (*D Jv ob*) assistant *wedana.*
  (ke)onderan subdistrict.
onderbouw (*D*) /onderbau/ subparts, branches (of a political organization or party).
onderdil (*D*) 1 spare part(s) (of a car/bicycle, etc.); → SUKU *cadang.* 2 (*euph*) penis.
onderdistrik (*D*) subdistrict.
onderhoud (*D*) /onderhaut/ maintenance.
ondernéming (*D*) estate, plantation. *– karét/kopi* rubber/coffee plantation/estate.
onderok (*D*) petticoat, slip.
Onderos (*D*) *pulau –* Onrust, an island in the Bay of Jakarta formerly used as an internment camp; → PULAU *Seribu.*
understand (*D*) assistance, relief, maintenance; → BANTUAN.
ondersten (*D mil*) financial support payments (for retired soldiers). *– sementara* financial support payments for five to seven years for those with fewer than eight years service. *– terus-menerus* financial support payments for life for those with 8–14 years service.
ondo I (in Central Sulawesi) a tuber; → UMBI *hutan.*
ondo II (*Jv*) ladder.
ondoafi (*Pap*) ethnic chief.
ondofolo (*Pap*) *adat* chief.
ondoh (*M*) berondoh-ondoh to jostle e.o.
  mengondoh to push s.t. along.
  terondoh shoved around, jostled.
ondok berondok to hide o.s.
  mengondok(kan) to hide/conceal s.t. or s.o. *~ diri* to hide/conceal o.s.
ondos-ondos a dish consisting of pounded glutinous rice with young coconut.
ondrok → ONDEROK.
onéng-onéng great-great-grandchild; → PIUT.
ong (*ob*) holy syllable, om; → OM II.
ongah-angih to wobble; wobbling.
ongéh arrogant.
onggak-onggak and mengonggak-onggak to go to the left and then to the right, zigzag.
onggél (*J*) loose and almost falling out.
onggok I heap, pile, stack (of rice/fruit/grass).
  seonggok a pile/stack, etc. of. *~ cucian* a heap of laundry. *~ rumput kering* a stack of hay.
  beronggok in a heap/pile.
  beronggok-onggok 1 in heaps/piles/stacks. *mengumpulkan batu ~ banyaknya* to gather piles of stones. 2 to gather together in a

crowd. *Murid-murid ~ untuk mendengarkan pidato kepala sekolah.* The pupils gathered to listen to their principal's speech.
  mengonggok to pile up.
  mengonggoki to pile up on s.t.
  mengonggokkan to pile/stack s.t. up. *Rezeki itu tidak akan dionggokkan di hadapan kita tanpa bekerja.* Fortune will not be piled up before us unless we work.
  teronggok piled/stacked up.
  onggokan accretion.
onggok II pulp (of tubers/fruits). *makan –* to have nothing to eat, starve.
onggol-onggol (*J/Jv*) k.o. gelatin-like food eaten with shredded coconut.
onggrok (*Jv*) mengonggrokkan to leave s.t. unattended to.
ongji (*C*) permit, license.
ongka → UNGKA.
ongkah-ongkah restless (in one's sleep).
ongkak wheelless timber truck.
ongkang-angking (*J*) and ongkang-ongkang (*Jv*) *– (kaki)* and berongkang-ongkang 1 (to sit) with one's legs dangling. 2 to laze (about), do nothing, take it easy. *Keberhasilan ini bukan dari kerja ~ saja tetapi dari kerja keras.* This success comes not just from loafing about but from working hard.
ongkep (*Jv*) 1 oppressive, close, sultry, stifling. 2 to feel uncomfortable/uneasy/ill at ease. *NU merasa – dalam rumah PPP.* The NU feels uncomfortable in the PPP party.
ongklét (*burung –*) crested jay, *Platylophus galericulatus.*
ongklok (*Jv*) boiled (peeled vegetables). *kentang –* boiled peeled potatoes.
ongko (*Jv*) → ANGKA I.
ongkok (*M*) mengongkok-ongkok to walk with a stoop.
  mengongkoki to approach s.o. in a crouching position (to attack).
ongkos (*D*) 1 expense, expenditures, charges, cost, price. *Semua – ditanggung oléh negara.* All expenses are borne by the state. *berapa pun –nya* and *dengan – berapa pun* at all costs, at any cost. 2 pay, wages, fees; → BIAYA. *– administrasi* service/handling charges. *– angkutan* transportation charges. *– balik nama télepon* cost of transferring telephone service. *– damai* an unofficial financial agreement between two people, by mutual consent. *– éksploatasi* working expenses. *– hidup* cost of living. *– inklaring* customs fees. *– kirim* freight, postage. *– lelah* reward. *– makan* food expenses. *– Naik Haji* [OHN] cost of making the pilgrimage to Mecca. *– pemasangan* initial cost. *– perbaikan* cost of repairs. *– perkara* costs of the proceedings, court costs. *– perusahaan* operating costs. *– pindah* moving expenses. *– produksi* cost of production. *– sendiri* (at) one's own expense. *– siluman* hidden costs. *– tambang* freight. *– tetap* fixed costs, overhead.
  mengongkosi and memperongkosi [and ngongkosin (*J coq*)] to finance, pay for, support. *Permerintah akan ~ proyék ini.* The government is going to finance this project. *Ia dapat mengongkosi keluarganya.* He can support his family.
  pengongkosan financing, paying for, defraying the cost of, supporting; capitalization.
  perongkosan charges, expenses, costs.
ongok (*M*) stupid, dull.
ongol-ongol (*J*) k.o. sweet eaten with shredded coconut.
ONH → ONGKOS *Naik Haji.*
oniks (*D*) onyx.
onjén fish lure.
onkolog (*D*) oncologist.
onkologi (*D/E*) oncology. *ahli bedah –* oncological surgeon.
onom (*S*) evil spirit, ghost.
onomatopé (*D*) onomatopoeia.
onrechtmatige overheidsdaad (*D leg*) unlawful government act.
ons (*D*) 1 100 grams. 2 ounce.
onslah (*D*) dismissal (from one's job).
  mengonslah to dismiss, fire.
onta (*Skr Jv*) camel; → UNTA I. *burung –* ostrich.
ontang-anting (*Jv*) only child.
ontél (*Jv*) 1 crank(shaft). 2 to crank (a car to start it). *sepéda –* a non-motorized bicycle.
ontogénésa, ontogénése, and ontogénésis (*D*) ontogenesis.

ontogéni (*E*) ontogeny.

ontologi (*D/E*) ontology.

ontologis (*D*) ontological.

ontong (*Jv*) **1** corn/maize crib. **2** counter for corn. *jagung se-* one ear of corn. **3** the (single, red) blossom of a banana tree.

ontorejo (*Jv*) figure in the *Mahabharata* who lived under the ground.

ontoséno (*Jv*) figure in the *Mahabharata* who lived under the sea.

ontowacono (*Jv*) dialogue; → ANTAWACANA.

ontran-antran (*Jv*) disturbance, riot(s).

   ontran-antranan small-scale rioting.

onvang (*D*) receipt issued by the police each time a driver's license or automobile registration is confiscated.

onyah-anyih wobbly.

onyak-anyik (*Jv*?) to thrust/force (a present/goods, etc. on s.o.), slip s.t. into s.o.'s hand, throw s.t. in s.o.'s teeth.

onyok (*M*) **mengonyokkan** to hand over, offer up s.t.

onyo-onyo (*Jv*) **mengonyo-onyo** to criticize. *Ketika harga minyak turun, dia dionyo-onyo sebagai pihak yang salah.* When oil prices dropped, he was criticized as the party at fault.

onyot → NYONYOT.

oom (*D*) /om/ **1**a) uncle. b) term of address or reference for one's own uncle or an adult friend of the family. **2** term of address or reference to a male person of higher status or education or an older foreigner, e.g., a *bécak* driver to his passenger, younger man to slightly older man in a higher status, a salesperson to a prospective customer, wife to husband, prostitute to customer. *"Ayo dong – masuk. Minum-minum atau mau santai," katanya.* "Come on in, Mister. Do you want to drink or have a good time?" she said. **3** term of address or reference used by children to any male person to whom they wish to show respect. **4** humorous term of address to a male person. *Ah, si - nih, gimané sih, ngelamun ajé.* Hey, what's with you, buddy, daydreaming all the time? *– senang* a married man who chases after young girls, dirty old man; *cp* TANTE *girang*.

op(s) (in acronyms) → OPERASI.

opa (*D*) **1** grandpa. **2** old man.

opah → UPAH.

opak I (*J/Jv*) a cracker, such as *kerupuk* or *emping* made from cassava, etc.

opak II **mengopak** to rekindle a dying fire, stoke (a fire)

   mengopakkan to instigate, stir up; → MENGGALAKKAN.

   pengopakan stoking (a fire).

opal (*D*) opal.

opas (*D*?) **1** messenger, attendant. **2** policeman. *– pos* mailman.

OPÉC (*E*) /opék/ Organization of Petroleum Exporting Countries; → ORGANISASI *Negara-Negara Pengékspor Minyak.*

opelét 1 a small urban bus. **2** the C-46 Dakota aircraft. *– kosong* a woman who chases after men.

   mengopelétkan to use (a vehicle) as an *opelét.*

open → OVEN.

opén (*J*) attentive, careful.

   mengopéni to pay careful attention to, be attentive to.

   keopénan, kopén, and **kopénan 1** to be treated in an attentive manner. **2** attention.

openkap (*D*) open hood. *bioskop –* drive-in, open-air movie. *mobil –* convertible (automobile). *pakaian –* décolleté/low-cut garment.

oper (*D*) (to take/carry, etc.) over. *mengambil –* to take over (a business).

   mengoper 1 to take s.t. over. **2** to hand over, pass s.t. over. *~ bola* (in soccer) to pass (the ball to a teammate). **3** to shift (gears), transfer. *Persnéléngnya dioper dua.* He shifted into second.

   mengoperkan to transfer, pass down.

   operan s.t. transferred to s.o. else, pass (in sports).

   oper-operan (in soccer) passing (the ball). *~ jauh* long pass. *~ péndék* short pass.

   pengoper 1 s.o. who takes over, takeover (*mod*). **2** passer (in sports).

   pengoperan 1 taking over (a business). **2** transfer, transferal. **3** delegation. *~ kekuasaan* delegation of power.

opera (*D*) opera. *– picisan/sabun* soap opera.

operasi (*D*) **1** (surgical) operation. *menjalani –* to undergo an operation, be operated on. **2** operation, maneuver (*mil*). *– bantuan* support operation. *– bersama* joint operation. *– bhakti* (1963–65) Indonesian military civic action program. *– cermat* precision operation. *– diam-diam* clandestine/undercover operation. *– gabungan* joint operation. *– jantung* heart surgery. *– ganti kelamin/alat vital* sex-change operation. *– karya* civic/civil action. *– Khusus* [Opsus] Special Operations (Staff). *– Komodo* Operation Komodo Dragon; code name for covert political campaign in Portuguese Timor in 1974–75. *– lawan gerilya* counterinsurgency operation. *– militér* military operation. *– pasar* market operation. *– Pasar Terbuka* [OPT] Operation Open Market. *– penyelamatan* rescue operation. *– plastik* plastic surgery. *– politik* political maneuver. *– sandi yudha* secret warfare operation. *– Seroja* reference to military operations against separatists in East Timor. *– sésar* Caesarian (section), C-section; → SÉKSIO *sésaréa. – tepat* (*mil*) surgical strike. *– terselubung* covert operation. *– usus buntu* appendectomy. *– Woyla* the military operation retaking the hijacked Garuda aircraft Woyla in Bangkok in April 1981.

   beroperasi to operate, maneuver, take action, conduct an operation. *mulai ~* to become operative, start to operate.

   mengoperasi to operate on (a patient or part of the body), perform an operation on.

   mengoperasikan to operate s.t., put s.t. into operation/service. *siap ~ 175 bus baru untuk trayék jarak jauh* ready to operate 175 new buses on long-distance routes. *Tangga berjalan belum lagi dioperasikan.* The escalator has not been put into service yet.

   pengoperasi operator, surgeon.

   pengoperasian putting s.t. into operation, operating.

operasional (*E*) and **operasionil** (*D*) operational.

   mengoperasionalkan to make s.t. operational. *~ semua sila dari Pancasila* to make all the principles of the *Pancasila* operational. *~ idéologi* to make the ideology functional.

   pengoperasionalan operationalizing, making s.t. operational.

operasionalisasi (*D*) process of putting s.t. into operation.

   mengoperasionalisasikan to put s.t. into operation.

operatif (*E*) operative, effective.

operator (*E*) operator. *– lantai bor* rotary helper. *– menara bor* derrick man. *– radio* radio operator. *– télepon* telephone operator.

operbelas (*D*) overloaded, overcrowded (with passengers).

operét (*D*) operetta.

opini (*D*) opinion, point of view.

   beropini to have the opinion (that).

   mengopinikan to consider, view, have the opinion (that).

opior (*IBT*) k.o. bird, bicolored dark-eye, *Tephrozosterops stalkeri.*

opisil → OFISIAL.

opium (*E*) opium.

opla(a)h and **opla(a)g** (*D*) **1** run, number of copies printed (of a book). **2** circulation (of a newspaper/periodical); → TIRAS I.

   beroplah with a circulation of ...

oplét → OPELÉT.

oplos (*D*) **mengoplos 1** to dissolve (in a liquid). *Péstisida cair dioplos lagi.* The liquid pesticide is redissolved. **2** to adulterate (by mixing with lower-grade gasoline).

   oplosan 1 dissolved. **2** adulterated.

   pengoplos adulterator.

   pengoplosan 1 dissolving. **2** adulteration, adulterating

OPM (*init*) → ORGANISASI *Papua Merdéka.*

opmak (*D*) layout (of a newspaper/magazine, etc.); → TATA *letak.*

opmaker (*D*) layout man.

opnaisel (*D*) tuck (a sewed fold in a garment, for shortening, etc.).

   beropnaisel tucked, with a tuck (in it). *gaun ~* tucked-up gown.

   mengopnaisel to tuck up, sew with a tuck/fold in it.

opname I (*D*) admission (to a hospital), hospitalization.

   mengopname to admit (to a hospital), hospitalize; → MENGHOS-PITALKAN, MERUMAHSAKITKAN. *Anak saya diopname di rumah sakit.* My child was hospitalized.

opname II (*D*) (photographic) picture, photo, shot.

   mengopname to shoot (with a camera), take a picture of.

opname III (*D*) → STOK *opname.*

Opo (*Min*) chief, head. *– Lao* Village Head.

oponén (*D/E*) opponent.

opo-opo (*Min*) medicine man, shaman; → DUKUN.

opor I (*J/Jv*) dish consisting of chicken and coconut milk, generally classified as a curry, but it has a white sauce that clings to the meat and does not overwhelm the taste of the chicken.

opor II → OPER.

oportunis (*D*) opportunist.

oportunisme (*D/E*) opportunism.

oportunistik (*E*) and oportunistis (*D*) opportunistic.

oportunitas (*D*) opportunity.

oposan (*D*) opponent.

oposisi (*D*) opposition.

   beroposisi to be opposed, be/act in opposition.

   mengoposisikan to oppose s.t.

OPP (*init*) → ORGANISASI Peserta Pemilu.

oprak (*Jv*) oprak-oprak ~ terus always play the same tune.

oprék (*Jv?*) mengoprék [and ngoprék (*coq*)] to change, modify.

   oprékan modified.

oprit (*D*) ramp, access (road).

ops (in acronyms) → OPERASI.

opsén (*D*) surcharge, surtax.

opsét I (*D*) tukang – taxidermist.

   mengopsét to stuff (animals/birds, etc.).

   pengopsétan taxidermy.

opsét II (*E*) → OFSÉT I.

opsét III (*E*) (in sports) offside.

opséter I (*D*) supervisor, overseer.

opséter II (*E*) typesetter.

opsi (*D*) 1 option. 2 (– jual) (*fin*) put option.

opsihter → OPSÉTER I.

opsin(d)er (*D*) inspector, overseer.

opsir (*D col*) (military or government) officer; → PERWIRA I. – Justisi Officer of Justice.

Opspék [Oriéntasi Program Studi dan Pengenalan Kampus] Study Program and Campus Orientation Program.

opsporing (*D*) search, investigation.

opstal (*D*) buildings. hak – building rights.

Opstib [Operasi Tertib] anticorruption operation.

   mengopstibkan to apply anticorruption methods to s.t. within the framework of the Opstib operation.

   pengobstiban apply anticorruption methods to s.t. within the framework of the Opstib operation.

Opsus → OPERASI Khusus.

optatif (*D/E*) optative.

optie → OPSI.

optik (*D*) 1 optic. ilmu – optics. 2 optical. cakra – optical disk. 3 optician.

optimal (*D/E*) optimal, maximal.

   seoptimal as optimal as.

   mengoptimalkan to optimize, maximize.

   teroptimal the most optimal.

   pengoptimalan optimization.

optimalisasi and optimasi (*E*) optimization.

   mengoptimalisasikan to optimize.

optimis (*D*) optimist(ic). Saya –. I'm optimistic.

   mengoptimiskan to make s.o. optimistic.

   keoptimisan optimism.

optimisme (*D/E*) optimism.

optimistis (*D*) optimistic.

optimum (*D*) optimum.

   mengoptimumkan to optimize.

   pengoptimuman optimizing.

optis (*D*) optic.

optisién (*D*) optician.

Opu a Bugis title of nobility.

opus (*D*) opus.

opyak (*Jv*) opyak-opyakan a noisy roundup (of animals to the slaughter).

opyok (*J/Jv*) s.t. wet (applied to the head).

   mengopyok-opyoki to apply moisture to, wet (the head). Anaknya panas, kepalanya diopyok-opyoki air. Her child is feverish; she's putting moist cloths on his forehead.

or (in acronyms) → ORGANISASI.

ora I (*J/Jv*) not. – adé (*J*) and – ana (*Jv*) /ono/ not available, not present, nonexistent. yang malu – keduman a timid person doesn't get his share. – pantes improper, undignified. – tedas tapak paluné pandé and – tedas sisané gurindo (*Jv*) to be invulnerable to weapons.

ora II (in Nusa Tenggara Timur) the komodo dragon; → KOMODO II.

orad white-water rafting; → OLAHRAGA arus deras.

   ber-orad to go white-water rafting.

orader s.o. who goes white-water rafting.

orak I mengorak to open up, uncoil, unfold, untie. ~ janji to renege on a promise. ~ pura to discharge one's debts. ~ selimut to unfold a blanket. ~ senyum to smile. ~ sila to get up, stand up from a sitting position. ~ simpul to untie a knot.

   terorak opened up, uncoiled, untied.

orak II mengorak to bail/scoop water out of a boat.

orak III (*J*) mengorak 1 to shake s.t. hard. 2 to make a mess out of s.t.

orakel (*D/E*) oracle.

orak-arik (*Jv*) 1 mixed up, confused. 2 stir-fried cabbage and eggs.

   mengorak-arik to mix up, confuse.

oral (*D/E*) oral.

ngoral [and ngoralin (*J coq*)] to lick.

orang I 1 person, human being (man or woman); someone. Tadi ada – datang kemari. Someone just came here. – lain a) another person. b) others. per – per person. Per – penumpang bis itu harus mengeluarkan uang péron Rp 50.–. The bus passengers have to pay Rp 50.00 per person for a platform ticket. 2 (in general) people, they, you, one. Daunnya dibuat – untuk obat. People make the leaves into medicine. Kadang-kadang – harus pergi juga. Sometimes one has to go anyway. kata – people say, it is said; → KATAnya. disenangi – popular. si –, bukan si mesin the man behind the machine. 3 classifier for human beings/people. tiga – perwira and perwira tiga – three officers. Ada dua – suami istri. There was a (married) couple (or, a husband and wife). Berapa – yang datang kemarin? How many people came yesterday? 4a) people, staff, subordinate. Mana –mu? Where are your people? Where is your staff? – Pak Lurah belum datang. The village head's staff isn't in yet. b) dependents, belonging to a certain group of people. bukan – saya not one of my people. 5 member of a certain race or ethnic group, etc. – Ambon Ambonese. – Batak a Batak. – bulé(k) a white person, European or American. – Cina Chinese (person). – Melayu Malay. – Jawa a Javanese. 6 a person from a certain place. – New York a New Yorker. – Surabaya a Surabayan; → ARÉK Suroboyo. 7 of/belonging to s.o. else. anak – s.o. else's child. kesalahan – another person's mistake. kucing – s.o.'s cat. negeri – s.o. else's country, foreign country; → MANCANEGARA. – itu he, she, they. – itu-itu juga always the same person. (men)jadi – to become s.o., i.e., a person of consequence. 8 (*ling*) person. – ketiga third person. – berdendang di pentasnya, – beraja di hatinya to fulfill one's respective desires. – tua diajar makan pisang and jangan diajar – tua makan dadih don't teach people who are already clever. seperti menanti – dahulu, mengejar – k(em)udian to carry coals to Newcastle. – abangan Javanese who is nominally Muslim but who adheres to pre-Islamic Javanese beliefs. – alih kelamin transsexual. – am the public, the masses. – amanah delegate. – Amérika an American. – antun a dandy, fop. – Arab an Arab. – Asia an Asian. – asing a) foreigner. b) stranger. – asli a) a native (of a place), an aborigine. b) the real person (not an imposter). – atas(an) a) superior. b) upper-class person. – awak a) fellow countryman. b) a Minangkabau, a West Sumatran. – awam a) the public, the masses. b) lay person, nonprofessional. – ayan epileptic. – baik-baik respectable people. – balar albino. – bambungan vagrant, bum, tramp. – banci hermaphrodite. – bangsawan nobleman. – banyak the public, the masses. – baru newcomer, recent arrival. – bawah(an) a) ordinary person/people. b) subordinate, underling. – bekerja workman, working person/people. – belakang wife. – Belanda Dutchman, Netherlander. – berbangsa nobleman. – berjusta liar. – berdosa sinner. – berilmu scholar. – berkuda rider, horseman. – berkunjung visitor. – berpiutang creditor. – bersalah culprit, wrongdoer, delinquent. – bertapa hermit. – besar a) a grown-up. b) an important/high-ranking person, dignitary, VIP. – biasa commoner. – bodoh blockhead, stupid person. – *Bombai/Bombay* (somewhat obsolete now) an (Asian) Indian. – *bongkok/bungkuk* a hunchback. – *buangan* an exile. – *bukit* hillbilly, bumpkin. – *bulai* albino. – *bulé(k)* a white person, European or American. – *bumi* native (of a place), aborigine. – *buta* a blind person; → TUNANÉTRA. – *cacat tubuh* a physically handicapped person; → TUNADAKSA. – *daérah anu* a person from you-know-where, i.e., the system of hiring a person who happens to know a big shot who comes from the same region. – *dagang* a) merchant, tradesman. b) foreigner. c) out-migrant. – *dalam* insider; *opp* ORANG *luar*. – *dapur* wife. – *datang* a) newcomer, recent arrival. b) foreigner. – *désa* a) villager. b) boor. c) rustic. – *dip* [displaced Indonesian person] s.o. taken out of Indonesia by the Japanese during World War II. – *dompléng* freeloader. – *durhaka* mutineer. – *durjana* wretch. – *dusun* (country) bumpkin. – *Éropa(h)* a European. – *gajian* wage earner. – *gedé* a) a tall person. b) a big shot, important person, VIP. – *gedongan* occupant of a brick or concrete building located in an elite section of town, i.e., well-off person. – *gelandangan* vagabond, bum, tramp. – *gunung* s.o. who lives in the mountains. – *halimun* spirit, ghost, apparition. – *halus* a) spirit, ghost. b) scholar. – *hanyut* drifter, vagrant. – *helat* visitor/guest (at a celebration, etc.). – *hina dina* poor person. – *hobat(an)* witch, sorcerer, magician. – *hukum* (*leg*) natural person. – *hukuman* offender, convicted person. – *hulu* (country) bumpkin. – *hutan* a) forest dweller. b) aborigine of East Sumatra. c) orangutan, *Pongo pygmaeus*. – *jauh* a) person who comes from another area, stranger. b) merchant, tradesman. – *kampung* villager, country fellow (often derogatory). – *kasim* eunuch. – *kaya* a) rich man, wealthy person. b) person of rank. c) (*rang kaya*) (*M*) form of address to the spouse of a high-ranking or highly respected person. – *kaya baru* [OKB] nouveau riche. – *kaya mendadak* [OKM] nouveau riche. – *kebanyakan* the public, the man in the street. – *kecil* a) small-sized person. b) small fry, unimportant person. – *kelinci* bunny (of the Playboy Club). – *kemit* (*Jv*) (night) watchman, guard. – *kepercayaan* confidant. – *ketiga* third person/party. – *koméng* hermaphrodite. – *kota* city/town-dweller, townsman, urbanite. – *kuasa* agent, mandatory. – *kurungan* prisoner, inmate. – *lama* old-timer. – *lasak* handyman, jack-of-all-trades. – *laut* sea nomad, sea gypsy. – *luar* outsider; *opp* ORANG *dalam*. – *makan gaji* wage earner. – *makhluk* genie, spirit. – *mampu* a well-to-do person. – *muda* youth, young person. – *nakal* a) prostitute. b) promiscuous/loose woman; → PEREMPUAN *nakal*. – *nguler kambang* s.o. who takes life easy. – *nomor dua* number two man, second in command. – *numpang* outsider. – *papak* hermaphrodite. – *pasak kampung* a) settled village population which doesn't leave its village. b) country bumpkin. – *patut-patut* respectable people. – *pedalaman* a) a person from the hinterlands, backwoodsman. b) (during the Indonesian revolution) a person who comes from an area not occupied by the Dutch forces but still under the control of the RI. – *pendatang* foreigner, outsider. – *pendatang baru* newcomer, recent arrival. – *perahu* boatpeople (Vietnamese refugees). – *perorang* (*infr*) individual. – *pertandang* a) traveler. b) visitor. – *perutang* (*ob*) creditor. – *pesakitan* prisoner, inmate. – *pidak pedarakan* the downtrodden. – *ramai* the public, the masses. – *pribadi* individual (as opposed to a legal entity). – *rantai/perantaian* prisoner, inmate. – *ronda* night watchman. – *rumah* member of the household. – *sabun* albino; → ALBINO, BULÉ. – *sakit* [os] patient. – *sangiang* (in Palangka Raya) *dukun* for spirits. – *sebelah* (next-door) neighbor. – *sedapur* the family. – *semodal* (business) partner; → MITRA. – *seorang* an individual; personal. – *séwaan* hireling. – *tahanan* prisoner. – *talang* yokel, country bumpkin. – *tidak dikenal* unknown person(s). – *terlantar* (*ob*) displaced person. – *titipan* s.o. put in a certain position because he knows a VIP or an insider, not because he is qualified for the job. – *tua* (written as two words) a) rich person. b) (in Teluk Cilacap) shaman. –*tua* (*usu* written as one word) parent(s) [ortu]; → IBU *bapak*. -*tua angkat* adoptive parents. –*tua asuh* foster parents. –*tua kandung* biological parents. **berorang tua** to have parents. *yang tidak* ~ parentless. **keorangtuaan** parenthood. – *tua-tua désa* village elders. – *turutan* a) fellow traveler (of a political party). b) hanger-on. – *tutupan* prisoner,

inmate. – *udik* country bumpkin. – *utangan* (*ob*) debtor. – *utas* artisan, craftsman. – *Wajo* coastal people of Malay descent. – *yang belum déwasa* minor. – *yang indekos/menumpang tinggal* boarder. – *yang punya* the haves. – *yang sudah berganti jenis kelamin* a transsexual. - *yang tidak punya* the have-nots.

orangnya 1 the person in question (or, under consideration), he, she. ~ *cantik*. She was pretty. ~ *bagaimana?* What's he like? ~ *tidak ada*. He/she/the person you're asking for isn't in/at home, etc. ~ *sendiri* the person himself. **2** (as a) real person. *Apakah gadis ini mémang ada* ~? Does this girl (in the painting) really exist? **3** the k.o. person to/who is. *Saya* ~ *mau tidak percaya begitu saja*. I'm the k.o. person who doesn't easily believe things. *Pak Soewono* ~ *diam*. Mr. Soewono is a quiet kind of guy.

seorang 1 a man, a person. ~ *demi/lepas* ~ one by one, one at a time. *tak* ~ *dua* (to have) more than two (children). ~ (*pun*) *tak* (*ada yang*), *tidak* ~*pun*, – *tak ada* ~ *juga*, and *tidak* ~ *juga* nobody at all. -*nya cuma* ~ *juga* and -*nya yang* ~ *itu juga* one and the same person. **2**a) ~ *diri* alone, all by o.s. *Dia datang* ~ *diri*. He came all by himself. b) (to feel) lonely. **orang-seorang** individual. **seorang-seorang** one by one, one at a time. **seseorang 1** this, a (known to the speaker but not to the hearer). ~ *dokter* a/ this doctor. **2** a certain individual/person. ~ *yang bernama Jakson* a certain Mr. Jackson. **3** individual, personal. **berseorang(an)** (all) alone, (all) by o.s. *Dia suka duduk* ~ *di dalam kamarnya*. He likes to sit all alone in his room. **keseorangan** solitary, lonely. *Sumitro merasa* ~ *karena teman karibnya baru-baru ini tutup usia*. Sumitro felt lonely because his close friend passed away recently. **perseorangan 1** individual. **2** individualism.

berorang to have/be with people. *tiada* ~ there isn't anybody. *tidak* ~ *di air* no longer a virgin.

orang-orangan 1 doll, puppet. ~ (*pengusir burung*) scarecrow. **2** dummy. ~ *mata* pupil (of the eye).

perorangan personal, private, individual. *pajak* ~ individual tax.

orang II (by analogy to *Jv wong*) since, the reason is, because. *Mana dapat membayar, – belum gajian*. How can I pay since I haven't gotten my salary yet. – ... *kok* (implies surprise at hearing or learning s.t.) – *sudah besar kok masih nangis!* You're a big boy now and you're still crying? – *mobil begini kok bagus!* You call such a car a nice car?

orang-aring (*J*) name of various plants, such as *Tridax procumbens*, *Maoutia diversifolia*, *Pouzolzia zeylanica*; → URANG-ARING.

oranye (*D*) orange(-colored).

oranyekrus (*D*) orange crush, i.e., an orange-colored, carbonated sweet-tasting beverage resembling orange juice.

orasi (*D*) oration, public speech. – *ilmiah* scientific presentation.

orat → AURAT.

orat-arét graffiti; → ORÉT.
   mengorat-arét to make graffiti, scribble on.

orator (*D/E*) orator, demagogue, speaker; → PEMBICARA.
   keoratoran oratory, the art of eloquent speech.

oratoris (*D*) oratorical.

oratorium (*D*) oratorio.

Orba 1 [Orde Baru] the New Order, i.e., the period from March 11, 1966, until the time that President Soeharto stepped down in 1998. **2** [Orde Batak] (jokingly) the Batak Order, so called because many Bataks have held high office during the period of the New Order. **3** [Ora Bayar] (*Jv*) (jokingly) *lit* he doesn't pay, i.e., whispered about an army man not paying his fare on public transportation.
   meng-Orbakan to impose the New Order upon s.t.
   peng-Orbanan imposition of the New Order. ~ *aparatur Départemén Dalam Negeri* orchestrating the Ministry of the Interior into the New Order.

orbit (*D*) orbit. – *tetap di angkasa luar* geostationary orbit.
   berorbit to be in orbit.
   mengorbit to orbit, be in orbit.
   mengorbiti to orbit (around).
   mengorbitkan to put s.t./s.o. into orbit.
   terorbit orbited.
   orbitan orbit.
   pengorbit launching pad.

pengorbitan putting into orbit.
orbita (*L*) orbit, eye socket.
orbital (*D/E*) orbital.
orde (*D*) 1 order (structure or administration). 2 order (a group of plants or animals classified as similar in many ways). – *primata* the primates. 3 order of knighthood (a Dutch decoration). – *Baru* → ORBA. **peng-ordebaruan** making s.t. conform to the *Orde Baru*. – *Lama* → ORLA.
ordening (*D*) arrangement, planning, regulation.
order (*D*) 1 order (for merchandise, etc.); → MEMESAN. 2 command, order, instruction; → MEMERINTAHKAN. 3 (*col*) forced labor.
  orderan s.o. who can be ordered around.
ordi I (*Port*) order, command.
ordi II (*ob*) forced labor; → RODI.
ordinal (*D/E*) ordinal.
ordinat (*D*) (co)ordinate.
ordinér (*D*) ordinary, common.
ordner (*D*) ring binder.
ordo (*L*) 1 (monastic) order. 2 (in natural history) order. *Wereng coklat termasuk – Hemiptera.* The brown *wereng* belongs to the order of Hemiptera.
ordonan(s) (*D mil*) orderly, messenger.
ordonansi (*D*) ordinance.
ordonatur (*mil*) representative with rights of *ordonansi*.
orék-orék → ORAT-ORÉT.
orén (*E ob*) orange.
oréng (*M*) philtrum, the groove between the nose and the lips.
orét → CORÉT I. **mengorét-orét** to scribble, scratch.
  orét-orétan 1 graffiti. 2 scribble, scratch.
organ (*D*) 1 organ (of the body). – *penerima* receptive organ. 2 organ, i.e., magazine or newspaper used to express the opinions of an organization, party, etc.
organda [Organisasi Pengusaha Angkutan Darat] Land Transportation Business Organization.
organik (*D/E*) 1 organic, of the bodily organs, vital. 2 organic, supported by or resulting from the constitution or, at least, a legal regulation of higher order. *undang-undang* – an organic law. 3 (*mil*) in one administrative unit.
organis (*D*) organis.
organisasi (*D*) organization. – *kebudayaan* [orkéb] cultural organization. – *kembar* sister organization. – *mantel* (*D*) front/cover organization. – *massa* [ormas] mass organization. – *massa keagamaan* religious mass organization. – *massa nonagama* nonreligious mass organization. – *nir-laba* not-for-profit organization. – *nonpemerintah* [ornop] nongovernmental organization. – *Papua Merdéka* [OPM] Free Papua Organization, i.e., a secessionist movement during the pre-Irian Jaya period. – *Pembébasan Paléstina* Palestine Liberation Organization, PLO. – *perangkat* the government and its various agencies. – *perjanjian* treaty organization. – *Peserta Pemilu* [OPP] Organization of Participants in General Elections. – *politik* [orpol] political organization. – *profési/fungsional dan kemasyarakatan* [orsinalmas] professional and/or functional and community organization. – *seazas* subsidiary organization (of a political party). – *sosial* [orsos] social organization. – *sosial/kemasyarakatan dan profési/fungsional* [orsosmasinal] social and/or community and professional and/or functional organization. – *sosial-politik* [orsospol] sociopolitical organization. – *tanpa bentuk* [OTB] Formless Organization. – *tanpa tujuan laba* [OTTL] not-for-profit organization. – *tata laksana* [ortala] managing organization. – *terlarang* [OT] prohibited organization.
  seorganisasi in the same organization.
  berorganisasi 1 to organize. 2 to be organized. *pasukan yang ~* organized troops.
  mengorganisasi(kan) to organize s.t. *~ kaum tani* to organize the farmers.
  terorganisasi organized. *sebuah béngkél keséhatan yang ~ secara éfisién* an efficiently organized health shop. **keterorganisasian** being organized, organization.
  organisasi-organisasian all k.o. organizations. *Tidak perlu ~; cukup niat dan kemauan.* You don't need all k.o. organizations; all you need is the intention and the desire.

keorganisasian organizational; organizing (powers/talents). *iklim ~* organizational climate.
pengorganisasi organizing. *alat ~ yang paling utama* a key organizing device.
pengorganisasian organizing; organization. *~ kembali* reorganizing.
organisator (*D*) organizer.
organisatoris (*D*) 1 organizational. 2 organization-oriented.
organisir (*D*) **mengorganisir** to organize.
  terorganisir organized. *kejahatan yang ~* organized crime.
  pengorganisiran organizing.
organisme (*D/E*) organism.
organsa (*D*) organdy.
orgasme (*D/E*) [O] orgasm.
orgel (*D*) organ (musical instrument); harmonium. – *geréja* church organ. *pemain – geréja* church organist. – *putar* hand organ.
orhiba → OLAHRAGA *hidup baru*. **berorhiba** to engage in these exercises.
ORI (*ob*) [Oeang Répoeblik Indonésia] Money of the Republic of Indonesia, issued on October 30, 1946, to replace the money of the Netherlands Indies, money of the Javasche Bank, and Japanese occupation money.
Oridab (*ob*) [ORI Daérah Banten] Money of the Republic of Indonesia for the Province of Banten.
oriéntal (*D/E*) oriental, eastern.
oriéntalis (*D*) orientalist.
oriéntalisme (*D/E*) orientalism.
oriéntalistik (*D/E*) orientalistic.
oriéntasi (*D*) orientation. – *Studi dan Pengenalan Kampus* [Ospék] Study Orientation and Getting Acquainted with the Campus (a program for college freshmen).
  berorién tasi to have an orientation, be oriented (towards). *~ ke luar* outward-oriented. *~ ke masa depan* future-oriented, forward-looking. *~ kepada pasar* market-oriented. *~ pada kehidupan* life-oriented. *~ pada keuntungan/laba* profit-oriented. *~ pada pekerjaan* job-oriented. *~ pada pemakai* user-oriented. *~ pencapaian hasil* results-oriented.
  berorién tasikan (*kepada*) to be oriented (towards). *~ pemecahan masalah* problem-solving-oriented. *~ rumah tangga* home-oriented. *~ kepada kekuasaan* power-oriented.
  mengoriéntasi to reconnoiter.
  mengoriéntasikan *~ diri* to orient o.s., take one's bearings.
Oril (*ob*) [Oeang Répoeblik Indonésia Lampung] Money of the Republic of Indonesia for Lampung (South Sumatra).
Orion (*D*) Orion.
Orips (*ob*) [Oeang Répoeblik Indonésia Propinsi Sumatra] Money of the Republic of Indonesia for the Province of Sumatra.
  meng-Oripskan to state in *Orips* money. *Harga 1 bambu beras (kira-kira 1 1/2 kilo) f. 80, uang Djepang; kalau di-Oripskan mendjadi f. 0,80.* The price of one bamboo container of rice (about 1 1/2 kilos) is f. 80 in Japanese money; in *Orips* money it's f. 0.80.
orisinal (*E*) and **orisinil** (*D*) original. *idé –* an original idea.
  keorisinalan originality.
orisinalitas (*D*) originality.
orkéb → ORGANISASI *kebudayaan*.
orkés I (*D*) orchestra. – *dangdut* a *dangdut* orchestra. – *filharmonis* philharmonic orchestra. – *gésék* string orchestra. – *kamar* chamber orchestra. – *Kamar Nusantara* [OKN] Nusantara Chamber Orchestra. – *simfoni* symphony orchestra. – *tiup* wind orchestra.
orkés II → OLAHRAGA *dan keséhatan*.
orkéstrasi (*D*) orchestration.
Orla [Orde lama] the Old Order, ancien régime, under President Soekarno (prior to 1965).
orloji → ARLOJI.
ormas mass organization; → ORGANISASI *massa*.
  keormasan mass organization system.
orna → RONA.
ornamén (*D*) ornament. – *pohon Natal* Christmas tree ornament.
ornaméntal (*D/E*) ornamental.
ornitolog (*D*) ornithologist.
ornitologi (*D/E*) ornithology.

ornitologik (E) and ornitologis (D) ornithological.
ornop → ORGANISASI nonpemerintah.
orografi (D) orography.
orografik (E) and orografis (D) orographic.
orok I (J) newborn (baby), infant.
orok II (J/Jv) → DENGKUR. mengorok [and ngorok (coq)] to snore, make a droning noise.
  pengorok snorer.
orok-orok I (Jv) a plant, crotalaria, Crotalaria striata, that produces a pea-like vegetable used as a green-manure crop.
orok-orok II k.o. rattle used to attract fish.
  mengorok-orok to use this rattle to attract fish.
orong cancelled, failed, null and void; → URUNG I.
orong-orong I (cla) vent of (archaic) cannon (where the match is applied).
orong-orong II (Jv) mole cricket, Gryllotalpa africana.
orong-orong III (in Surabaya) petty thefts.
oro-oro (Jv) (pronunciation of ara-ara) large field, uncultivated grassland.
orot (Jv) to dissipate, squander.
  pengorotan wastefulness, dissipation.
Orpadnas [Oriéntasi kewaspadaan nasional] National Vigilance Orientation.
orpol → ORGANISASI politik.
orsi (clipped form of orisinil) original.
orsidé (D) orchid; → ANGGRÉK.
orsinalmas → ORGANISASI profési/fungsional dan kemasyarakatan.
orsos → ORGANISASI sosial.
orsosmasinal → ORGANISASI sosial/kemasyarakatan dan profési/fungsional.
orsospol → ORGANISASI sosial-politik.
ortala → ORGANISASI tata laksana.
ortodok(s) (D) orthodox; old-fashioned.
  keortodoksan orthodoxy.
ortodoksi (D/E) orthodoxy.
ortodonsi (D) orthodontics.
ortografi (D/E) orthography.
ortografik (E) and ortografis (D) orthographic.
ortopédagogi (D) orthopedagogics.
ortopédi (D) orthopedics.
ortopédis (D) orthopedic(al). ahli – orthopedist.
ortu → ORANG tua.
os (init) the patient; → ORANG sakit.
osak (Jv) mengosak-osak to mess up, turn upside down, clutter.
osaka (in Southern Tapanuli) a four-wheeled pushcart, two meters long and one meter wide, with a steering wheel at the rear end.
Oscar (E) /oskar/ Oscar (movie industry award). pemenang piala – winner of the Oscar award.
osé I (Jv) kacang – shelled pulses/leguminous plants.
osé II (in Ambon) you. "– mau apa?" tantang si pemuda. "What do you want?" challenged the young man.
oséan (D/E) ocean; → SAMUDRA.
oséania (D/E) Oceania.
oséanografi (D/E) oceanography. sarjana – oceanographer.
oséanolog (D) oceanologist.
oséanologi (D/E) oceanology.
oséng (Jv) mengoséng-oséng to sauté.
  oséng-oséng sautéed.
osifikasi (D) ossification.
osilasi (D) oscillation.
  berosilasi to oscillate.
osilator (D/E) oscillator.
osiloskop (D/E) oscilloscope.
Osing bahasa/orang – the language (a dialect of Javanese) and people of the easternmost tip of Java (the Balambangan, Banyuwangi area).
osio → WÉSIO.
osis → ANAK osis.
Oskar → OSCAR.
oskultasi (D) auscultation.
osmosa, osmose (D) and osmosis (E) osmosis.
osmotik (E) and osmotis (D) osmotic.

osog I (J/Jv) mengosog [and ngosog (coq)] to grind small fruits, such as cermai, lobi-lobi, etc. until soft (for making candy).
  osogan ground-up fruits.
osog II (J) mengosog [and ngosog (coq)] to instigate, encourage.
ospék → ORIÉNTASI studi dan pengenalan kampus.
osténtasi (D) ostentation.
ostéoporosis (E) osteoporosis.
Osvia (D col) [Opléidingsschool voor Indische Ambtenaaren] Training School for Indies Civil Servants.
OT I (init) → ORGANISASI terlarang.
ot II (init) [orang tahanan] prisoner.
otak 1 (– benak) the brain, brains (the organ). Kepalanya pecah dan –nya bercéceran. His skull was fractured and the brains scattered around. 2 brains (as substance or intelligence). memecahkan/memerah/memutar –nya to rack one's brains. 3 brains (behind s.t.), mastermind. Empat orang pengédar morfin diringkus setelah –nya ditémbak kakinya. Four morphine traffickers were captured after the mastermind was shot in the leg. tajam – acute, sharp, smart. waras – (mentally) normal. tidak waras – mentally ill. – ayam silly, foolish. – besar/depan cerebrum. – éncér smart, clever. – kecil cerebellum. – kera monkey brains (considered to be an aphrodisiac by the Chinese). – minyak smart, clever. – miring crazy. – pelaku/perbuatan instigator, brains behind s.t. – telur silly, foolish. – udang a) stupid, foolish. b) a tree species, Norrisia malaccensis. berotak udang very stupid.
berotak brainy, clever, bright. ~ terang intelligent. tidak ~ stupid. ~ tajam clever, intelligent.
mengotaki to mastermind, be the brains behind. Uang PT KS dirampas pengawalnya, diotaki bekas pegawainya. The money of KS, Inc. was stolen by their guard, masterminded by their former employee. Komplotan pemeras atas pelajar diotaki mahasiswa. A college student was the brains behind the conspiracy to extort (money) from high-school students.
otak-otakan 1 bragging, boasting. 2 braggart, boaster. 3 to brag, boast. 4 (J) show-off, s.o. who likes to do daring and dangerous things.
pengotakan cerebralization.
otak-atik (J) mengotak-atik to putter around, busy/occupy o.s. in a leisurely/casual/ineffective manner, tinker; to try to get s.t. loose, etc.
otak-otak I dish made from fish, prawns, etc. mixed with spices, wrapped in coconut leaves and roasted.
otak-otak II a decorative plant, pigtail tree, Desmodium pulchellum.
otar (ob) small round metal shield.
otarki → AUTARKI.
OTB → ORGANISASI tanpa bentuk.
otda [otonomi daérah] regional autonomy.
oté → OT I.
oték I a marine fish species, Arius/Tachysurus utik.
oték II (Jv) and otél (J) loose, almost falling out (of teeth).
oték III (Jv) grain, millet.
oténg (J) to be averse/unwilling (to); → OGAH I.
oténg-oténg (J) ladybird (beetle), a small, yellow insect often found in bottle gourds.
oténsitas (D) authenticity.
oténtik (D/E) authentic.
  keoténtikan authenticity.
oténtikasi (E) authentication.
oté-oté k.o. filled fritter.
othak-athik gathuk (Jv) to fiddle around with s.t. until you make it fit/work.
oto I automobile, car. – balap racing car. – gandéngan car and trailer. – gerobak (infr) truck; → TRUK I. – pengangkut orang sakit ambulance; → AMBULAN(S).
  beroto 1 to drive a car. 2 to ride in a car, by car.
oto II (C Jv) protective cloth placed on a baby's chest for warmth.
oto- (in many modern compounds) auto-, self-; → AUTO-, SWA-.
otoaktivitas (E) autoactivity.
otobiografi → AUTOBIOGRAFI.
otobis (D) (city) bus.
otodidak (D) autodidact, self-taught person.

otogén (*D*) autogenous.

otog-otog (*Jv*) toy noisemaker made of bamboo, string, and a piece of tin can.

otoklaf (*D*) autoclave.

otokrasi (*D*) autocracy.

otokratik (*E*) and **otokratis** (*D*) autocratic.

otokratisme (*E*) autocratism.

otokritik (*D*) self-criticism.

otolét (*D*) → OP(E)LÉT.

Otoman (*D*) Ottoman; → USMANI(YAH).

otomasi (*E*) automation.

otomat (*D*) automatic. *télepon* – automatic telephone. – *minuman* vending machine for beverages.

  mengotomatkan to automatize.

  keotomatan automatism.

  pengotomasian automating.

otomatik (*E*) and **otomatis** (*D*) automatic(ally). *senapan* – automatic weapon.

otomatisasi (*E*) automation.

  mengotomatisasikan to automatize.

otomatisitas automatism.

otomatisme (*D*) automatism.

otomobil (*D*) automobile.

otomotif (*E*) automotive. *dunia/industri* – automotive world/industry.

oton (*Bal*) 210 days. *pada usia tepat tiga – atau 3x210 hari (hampir dua tahun)* at the age of almost two years.

otonan birthday.

otonom (*D*) autonomous; → SWATANTRA. *daérah/pemerintah* – autonomous area/government.

  keotonoman autonomy.

otonomi (*D*) autonomy. – *daérah* [otda] regional autonomy.

  berotonomi to have autonomy, be autonomous, with autonomous power(s).

  keotonomian autonomy.

otonomisasi granting of autonomy. – *rumah sakit* granting autonomy to a hospital.

oto-oto (child's) bib.

otopét (*D*) scooter.

otopsi → AUTOPSI.

otorisasi (*D*) authorization. *alat – kartu krédit* credit-card authorization machine.

  mengotorisasikan to authorize.

  pengotorisasian authorizing.

otorisator (*mil*) official with the right to issue authorizations.

otorisir (*D*) **mengotorisir** to authorize.

otorita(s) (*D*) authority. – *sementara empat kelompok* quadripartite interim authority.

otoritér (*D*) **1** authoritarian (regime/state, etc.). **2** authoritative (air/manner/tone).

otoritérisme (*E*) authoritarianism, authoritarian system.

otoritét (*D*) authority.

otoséntralitas (*E*) autocentricity.

otot (*J/Jv*) **1** muscle. *besar* – muscle size. *daya tahan* – muscle endurance. *kekencangan* – muscle tone. *kekuatan* – muscle strength. *ketidakseimbangan* – muscle imbalance. **2** tendon, sinew. **3** (*sl*) penis. – *bokong* gluteus muscle. – *dada* pectoral muscle. – *dubur* anal sphincter. – *halus* smooth muscle. – *kawat balung wesi* (*Jv*) and – *kawat tulang besi* as strong as steel, as hard as nails. – *kulit* cutaneous muscle. – *kedang* extensor muscle. – *kunyah* masticatory muscle. – *lingkar* sphincter. – *lurik* striated muscle. – *perut* abdominal muscle.

  berotot muscular, sinewy, brawny.

  mengotot 1 to talk so loudly that the muscles stand out in one's

neck. **2** to persist. **3** persevering, tenacious. **4** to be obstinate/adamant/stubborn.

  ngotot (*coq*) **1** to exert o.s. **2** to be stubborn/obstinate. ~ *lawan* ~ to want to have the last word. ~.~ to have an argument/dispute with e.o. **kengototan** obstinacy, stubbornness.

  otot-ototan 1 musclebound. **2** strong-arm. **3** to have a fistfight. **ngotot-ngototan** to have a dispute/fight.

otsus [otonomi khusus] special autonomy.

OTTL (*init*) → ORGANISASI *tanpa tujuan laba.*

out (*E*) /awt/ (thrown) out, left, quit; → AUT II, KELUAR. *Saya – dari partai itu.* I left the party.

outlét (*E*) /awt-/ outlet.

output (*E*) /awt-/ output.

oval (*D/E*) oval.

  mengovalkan to make s.t. oval-shaped.

  keovalan ovalness.

ovari(um) (*D*) ovary.

ovasi (*D*) ovation.

oven (*D*) **1** oven, kiln. *langsung dari* – fresh from the oven. **2** stove. – *bakar* kiln. – *gas* gas stove. **3** (in the tobacco industry) dehydration.

  mengoven to bake in an oven.

  pengoven dehydrator (in an oven). ~ *kopra* copra maker.

over- (*D/E*) (a prefix meaning) above, too much, excessive(ly), very.

over (*D?*) to change gears.

overaktif (*E*) overactive.

overakting (*E*) overacting.

overdosis (*D*) overdose.

overste (*D ob*) lieutenant-colonel; → LÉTNAN *kolonél*, OBROS.

overzak (*D ob*) to pour (cheaper grade cement) from its original bag into a (higher grade cement) bag (in order to increase its selling price).

ovulasi (*D*) ovulation.

  mengovulasikan to ovulate.

ovum (*D*) ovum.

owa-owa Javan silvery gibbon, *Hylobates moloch*.

owé(h) (*C J*) (used by men) I, me; yes; → SAYA.

owel (*Jv*) reluctant (to be separated from s.t.), unwilling (to lose s.t.). *Tetapi meréka bersikap – melepaskan uangnya guna meninggalkan produksi kapas.* But they were reluctant to lay out their money to increase cotton production.

owengan (*E ob*) Owen-gun.

oyak I (*M J*) shaky, unsteady.

  mengoyak(-oyak)kan to shake, vibrate.

oyak II (*Jv*) **mengoyak** to chase, pursue, run after.

oyan (*C?*) black Chinese painting powder.

oyék (*Jv*) dried, grated cassava, boiled and then eaten.

oyod (*J/Jv*) **1** root (of a plant); vine stem, stalk, creeper (fodder for goats). **2** snake (taboo word). **3** period in which the rice plant ripens, about six months. – *munding* k.o. pulse, *Padbruggea dasyphylla*. – *santenan* k.o. medicinal plant, *Ficus aurantiaca Griff, F. callicarpa Miq.*

oyok (*J/Jv*) **mengoyok** [and **ngoyok** (*coq*)] to pursue, chase after, hunt down.

  ngoyok-ngoyok to race. ~ *waktu* to race against time.

oyong I shaking, trembling, swaying, moving.

  mengoyongkan to shake, make s.t. tremble.

oyong II (*J*) a creeping plant, angled luffa, strainer vine, *Luffa acutangula*, whose edible fruit resembles the bitter gourd; → GAMBAS.

oyot I → OYOD. *kena – mimang* bothered by invisible creatures.

oyot II → OYOD **ngoyot** to drink straight from the bottle.

Oz (*sl*) Australia.

ozon (*D*) ozone. *lapisan* – the ozone layer.

ozonisasi (*D*) ozonization.

P

p and P I /pé/ the 16th letter of the Latin alphabet used for writing Indonesian.

p II (*abbr*) [Pagina] (*D*) page.

P III [Paduka] Excellency.

P IV (*abbr*) [Pangéran] Prince. *P. Diponegoro* Prince Diponegoro.

P V [(Wanita) Pelacur] prostitute; → WTS.

P VI (*abbr*) [Pulau] Island. *P. Jawa* the Island of Java.

P VII (*abbr*) [Putu] (*Bal*) name element placed before personal names to indicate the firstborn child in a family, such as P(*utu*) *Setia*.

P VIII car license plate for Besuki.

P IX *lima* – [Perut, Pakaian, Perumahan, Pergaulan, dan Pengetahuan] The people's five needs according to President Soekarno: Stomach, Clothing, Housing, Intercourse (social or sexual), and Knowledge.

P4 (*init*) → PEDOMAN *Penghayatan dan Pengamalan Pancasila*.

P5 (*init*) an umbrella initialism referring to five types of Army regulations: **PBB-PPM-PDT-PUD-PDG**, respectively expanded to: Peraturan Baris-Berbaris Drill Regulations; Peraturan Penghormatan Militér Military Honors Regulations; Peraturan Disiplin Tentara Military Discipline Regulations; Peraturan Urusan Dalam Domestic Affairs Regulations; Peraturan Dinas Garnisun Garrison Service Regulations.

pa I (*S*) clipped form of **bapak**.

pa II (in acronyms) → PERWIRA.

PA III (*init*) → PAKU *Alam*.

PA IV (*init*) → PANGKALAN *Armada*.

PA V (*init*) → PENGADILAN *Agama*.

PAA (*init*) → PANGÉRAN *Adipati Ario*.

PAAD → PERWIRA *Administrasi*.

paal I /pa'al/ → FAAL I.

paal II (*D*) /pal/ about 1507 meters; → PAL I.

Paasbrood (*D*) /pasbrot/ hot cross bun; → ROTI *Paskah*.

pabéan (*Jv*) 1 customs house/office. 2 customs; → BÉA (*dan*) *cukai* [BC]. *kantor* – customs office. *pegawai* – customs officer. *Surat Keterangan* – Customs Declaration.

  kepabéanan (*mod*) customs. *Aparat ~ di Pelabuhan Udara Internasional Cengkaréng*. Customs at Cengkareng International Airport. *pelayanan ~* customs service. *peraturan ~* customs regulations.

paberik → PABRIK.

pabian → PABÉAN.

pabila clipped form of **apabila** when(ever). *barang –* (at) any time. *– pun tidak* never.

pabrik (*D*) factory, plant, works. *buatan –* make, manufacture. *cap –* trademark. *kepala –* production manager. *manajér –* factory manager. *pengusaha –* maker, manufacturer. *– baja* steel mill. *– baja canai dingin* cold rolling mill. *– baja lembaran panas* hot strip mill [HSM]. *– batik* batik plant. *– bekas* not a brand-new factory, secondhand factory. *– berskala besar dan menengah* large- and medium-scale factories. *– besi* ironworks. *– bijih tembaga* copper smelter. *– bir* brewery. *– botol* bottle works. *– cat* paint factory/works, dye works. *– cétak uang* (*coq*) mint, i.e., the place where coins/paper currency, etc. are produced under government authority. *– farmasi* pharmaceutical plant. *– gelas* glassworks. *– gula* [PG] sugar plant/refinery. *– gurem* (*Jv*) an insignificant/unimportant factory. *– kapal* shipyard; → GALANGAN *kapal*. *– kapok/kapuk* cotton mill. *– kapur* limekiln; → PEMBAKARAN *kapur*. *– kertas* paper mill. *– kertas koran* newsprint factory. *– kimia* chemical plant. *– kopi* coffee mill. *– kulit* tannery. *– mesin* engine works. *– minyak* oil refinery. *– mobil* automobile factory. *– nuklir* nuclear plant. *– oto* automobile factory. *– pakaian jadi* garment factory. *– panduan* pilot plant. *– papan* lumber mill. *– peleburan aki bekas* factory for recycling used storage batteries. *– peleburan besi* iron foundry. *– pemaduan* assembly plant. *– pemasak minyak* oil refinery. *– pemasangan (mobil)* (automobile) assembly plant. *– pemintalan* [patal] spinning mill. *– pengaléngan* cannery. *– pengecoran* foundry. *– penggergajian kayu* sawmill. *– pengolahan* processing plant. *– perakitan* assembly plant. *– percobaan* pilot plant. *– pétrokimia* petrochemical plant. *– rajutan* knitting mill. *– roti* bakery. *– semén* cement plant. *– senjata* arms factory. *– spiritus* distillery. *– susu* dairy plant. *– tékstil* textile mill. *– tenun* textile mill.

  berpabrik to own a factory/mill, etc.

  memabrikkan to manufacture, produce. *rumah yang bahannya sudah dipabrikkan lebih dulu* a prefab(ricated) house.

  pabrikan 1 manufactured goods. 2 manufacturer.

  kepabrikan factory (*mod*); factory system.

  pemabrikan manufacturing, producing.

pabrikan (*D*) manufacturer.

pabrikasi (*D*) manufacture, production.

pabukoan (*M*) sending food to the homes of members of the family and close relatives in connection with the end of the fasting month; → BERBUKA *puasa*.

pabum [panas bumi] geothermal.

Pacad → PERWIRA *cadangan*.

pacai sandalwood scraped and sprinkled over a corpse.

pacak I skilled (in), skillful (at/in), expert (at/in), adept (at), proficient (in/at/-ing), accustomed (to doing s.t.).

  kepacakan skill, skillfulness, expertise, ability, capability, competence, proficiency.

pacak II 1 (roasting) spit, skewer. 2 stake, pile, pole, anything pointed at one end. *daging –* roast beef. *– kuala* mooring post.

  memacak 1 to skewer meat or fish on a (roasting) spit. 2 to drive (a pole) into the ground.

  memacaki to fix upon, drive (s.t.) into.

  memacakkan to drive (a pole) into the ground.

  terpacak 1 spitted, skewered, pierced. 2 nailed, pinned, affixed (to the wall, etc.), stuck (into the ground), put up. *Semuanya harus tunduk pada peraturan yang ~ di dinding bangunan.* Everybody must obey the regulations affixed to the wall of the building. 3 planted (in) (of spearhead, etc.), stuck (to). *~ menjadi* raised/elevated to. *~ saja* stand/sit stock-still, as if nailed to the floor.

pacak III (*M*) sprinkle; → PERCIK.

  memacak-macak to splash, splatter, sprinkle, scatter.

  terpacak *~ peluh* to break out in sweat.

pacak IV (*Jv*) memacaki to wear, put on (clothes). *Dia suka sekali ~ celana panjang saya.* He likes to wear my trousers.

pacak V → PACEK.

pacal I (*cla*) humble slave (of a sovereign). *– kerical* all the subordinates, the lowest of the low. *– Tuanku* Your humble servant, i.e., I, me (the humblest way of referring to o.s. when speaking to the ruler). *patik – Tuanku yang hina ini* Your must humble servant.

pacal II *ikan –* wolf herring, *Chirocentrus dorab*; → ikan PARANG-PARANG.

pacangan (*Jv*) fiancé(e).

  berpacangan to be engaged/affianced to e.o.

  memacang(kan) to engage (a couple), affiance.

  pacangan fiancé(e).

pacar I *– air/banyu* (*Jv*) balsam, *Impatiens balsamina*. *– cina/culan* plant whose flowers are used to scent tea and clothes, mock lime, Chinese perfume plant, *Aglaia odorata*. *– kuku* henna plant, *Lawsonia inermis*; the leaves are squeezed to produce a red nail polish; → INAI.

  berpacar (*BD*) to use the red dye made from the henna plant to varnish the fingers and toes of the bride in Malay weddings.

  memacar to apply this dye to (fingernails, etc.).

pacar II (*J/Jv*) 1 boyfriend, girlfriend. *Gadis remaja lagi ngam-*

beki –nya. The teenage girl was still pouting at her boyfriend. **2** beloved, sweetheart. *- gelap* secret boy-/girlfriend.

berpacar(-pacar)an to have a boyfriend or girlfriend, go out with a boy or girl, go steady, be seeing e.o., go out with e.o., be having an affair; → NYOSOT. *Martina berpacaran dengan Ramoz selama sembilan tahun.* Martina and Ramoz have been seeing e.o. for nine years. *Menurut kabar selentingan, suaminya berpacaran dengan sékretarisnya.* Rumors have it that her husband has been having an affair with his secretary.

memacari [and **macarin** (*J coq*)] **1** to go steady with. **2** to have sex with, make love to. *Dia mémang tipe perempuan yang pantas untuk dipacari semata-mata.* She's really the type of woman just to have sex with.

pacaran 1 to go out (on a date). **2** to make out, have sex.

pacar-pacaran 1 to make love, make out. *Sampai larut malam kedua remaja ini asyik ~.* The young couple were making out till late at night. **2** to have a boy or girlfriend.

perpacaran (*mod*) relations between the sexes. *étik ~* the ethics of boy-girl/male-female relations.

pacar III *tikar –* and **pacaran** a high-quality mat made from colored layers of screw pine.

pacat I land leech, jungle leech, *Haemadipsa javanica; cp* LINTAH. *- hendak menjadi ular* to pretend to be rich; to have an unrealizable desire. *seperti - kenyang* to eat and run; → SMP II. *- daun* a leech species that sticks to plant leaves. *- kenyang* a) (an object) which is large around the middle. b) *cincin - kenyang* a large thick ring used to protect the finger when using a kris.

memacat to attach itself (to), be attached (to).

pacat II *burung -* lesser blue-winged pitta, *Pitta brachyura cyanoptera.*

pacat III → KAYU *pacat.*

pacau 1 a smelly scarecrow used to frighten away birds. **2** a talisman hung on fruit trees to make anyone who steals the fruit become sick.

pacé I (*J*) → MENGKUDU.

pacé II → PAKCIK.

pacek (*Jv*) **berpacek** to mate, mount (of animals); *cp* KAWIN.

memacek 1 to penetrate into the ground (*esp* of roots); to take root. **2** to pair, mate, copulate (of animals).

pemacek stud (for breeding). *kuda ~* stallion, stud horse. *sapi ~* stud bull.

pemacekan mating, copulating.

paceklik (*Jv*) **1** famine. **2** scarcity/insufficiency/lack of food, etc. *musim -* hard times, a difficult period economically. *tahun-tahun -* lean years. **3** (*J*) to be hard up, broke, short (of money); → TONGPÉS. *Pinjamkan saya uang lima ribu rupiah, saya sedang - sekarang ini.* Lend me five thousand rupiahs; I'm short of money right now. *- listrik* electric failure, power outage; → BYAR-*pet.*

pacet → PACAT I.

pachinko the Japanese form of pinball.

paci (*J*) section (of *jeruk* or other fruit); → PANGSA.

pacik (*M*) **memacik** to hold (on to).

Pacinan → PECINAN.

pacing I (*S*) *- (tawar)* name of a plant with a frail stalk, crepe ginger; *Costus speciosus;* → SETAWAR.

pacing II (*burung -*) scaly-breasted bulbul, *Pycnonotus squamatus.*

pacinko → PACHINKO.

paci-paci (*J*) k.o. bush, *Leucas spp.*

Pacitan a coastal area on the Indian Ocean in the Madiun regency, Central Java, known for its *jeruk.*

pacok (*J*) → PATUK I.

pacombéran (*Jv*) open sewage ditch, drain; → COMBÉR.

pacu 1 spur (worn on the heel). *Koboi itu menggertak kuda dengan -nya supaya berlari lebih cepat.* The cowboy spurred the horse on with his spurs to make it run faster. *kuda -* racehorse. *kuda - jarak jauh* stayer. **2** a (horse/boat, etc.) race. *jalur/landas(an) -* runway (on an airfield). *- jalur* (in the Kuantan area, Indragiri Hulu Regency, Riau) a traditional canoe race; → JALUR II. *(alat) - jantung* pacemaker (for the heart).

berpacu 1 with a spur, wearing spurs. *sepatu ~* spurred shoes. **2** to race. *Pembangunan di Acéh ~ dengan waktu.* Development

in Aceh is racing against time. *~ mendahului saat datangnya kemacetan lalu-lintas* to leave home/the office early to avoid traffic jams. *~ Dalam Mélodi Name That Tune* (a TV show based on the American version). *~ dengan waktu* to race against time. *~ kuda* to race on horseback, have a horse race. *~ lari* to (run a) race, have a foot race. *~ mengejar ketinggalan* to catch up.

berpacuan to race e.o.

memacu 1 a) to spur on (a horse to make it run faster), make (a horse/car, etc.) speed up/run faster, accelerate. *~ (mobilnya)* to accelerate/speed up (one's car). *Dipacunya sepéda motornya dengan laju.* He made his motorcycle go faster. *~ perékonomian* to spur the economy. b) to (want to) overtake (by running fast). **2** to spur, encourage (s.t. or s.o. to work hard, etc.); → MENGGALAKKAN. *Belum jelas kenapa mékanisme kedelai sampai ~ penyakit itu.* It's not clear yet why the soybean mechanism encourages that illness. *~ semangat* to keep up one's spirits. **3** (of aircraft) to taxi; taxiing. *~ di landasan* to taxi on the runway.

memacukan to spur on, encourage (s.t. or s.o. to work hard, etc.).

terpacu-pacu *lari ~* to run as fast as one can.

pacuan race. *anak ~* jockey; → JOKI I. *kuda ~* racehorse. *~ kuda* a) horse racing. b) race track. *Bekas ~ kuda di Pulo Mas akan dijadikan lapangan olahraga terbuka.* The former race track in Pulo Mas will be turned into an open sports ground. *~ persenjataan/senjata* the arms race.

pemacu accelerator (the person or the substance), promoter. *alat ~ jantung* pacemaker (for the heart). *faktor ~* accelerating factor, impetus. *~ réaksi* catalyst; → KATALISATOR.

pemacuan 1 accelerating, speeding up. *~ persenjataan* the arms race. **2** acceleration.

perpacuan a race. *telah dicanangkan ~ sesama negara ASÉAN* a race among fellow members of ASEAN has been announced.

pacuk (*J*) **memacuk** to peck (of birds), bite (of snakes/fish); → PATUK I.

pacul I (*Jv*) hoe, pickax, spade.

memacul to hoe, spade.

terpacul hoed.

pacul II memacul to squeeze (pus out of a boil/seeds out of a fruit). **terpacul** squeezed out; pulled out (of a tooth); emerging (from behind a bush/scrub, etc.).

PAD I (*init*) → PENDAPATAN *Asli Daérah.*

pad II (in acronyms) → PADUAN.

pada I 1 (preposition of location) in, on, at; *cp* DALAM II, DI I. *Dia meletakkan buku - méja.* He put the book on the table. *Dia menggantungkan topinya - paku.* He hung his hat on a nail. *Kapal itu singgah - pelabuhan Tanjung Priok.* The ship called at the port of Tanjung Priok. **2** (preposition of time) at, in, on. *- masa itu* at that time. *- abad kedua puluh* in the twentieth century. *- tahun 1992* in 1992. *- tanggal itu* on that date. *- hari Jumat* on Friday. **3** (clipped form of **kepada**) to. *Dia melaporkan hal itu - majikannya.* He reported that matter to his employer. **4** (preposition used in various adverbial phrases) in, to, etc. *- hakékatnya* in fact, actually. *- pendapat saya* in my opinion, to my mind. *- sangkanya* in his opinion. *- umumnya* in general, generally. *- waktunya* in a timely fashion. **5** (other prepositional meanings) of, with. *Rakyat sudah muak - kekejamannya.* The people are already sick of his atrocities. *Buruh Jepang gandrung - pekerjaan.* Japanese workers are in love with their work. **6** in the possession of, in the care of. *ada -nya/-ku/-mu* with him/me/you. **7** (*cla*) (in order) to. *- menerangkan arti berbagai-bagai mimpi* to explain the meaning of various dreams; → AKAN, BUAT II, UNTUK.

pada II 1 enough, sufficient, adequate, satisfactory. *Sekian itu belum - juga.* That much is still not enough. **2** satisfied. *Belum - hatinya.* He is not satisfied yet. *asal ada kecil pun -* better s.t. than nothing.

berpada-pada 1 not overdo s.t. *Buat baik ~, buat jahat jangan sekali.* Do a fair amount of good, but do no wrong at all. **2** to be sufficient but not too much.

memadai 1 to satisfy, be satisfactory, suffice, reasonable, be enough/adequate; to reach the level of, be up to, equal. *Hasilnya belum ~ keinginannya.* The results haven't reached what he wished for. *Ganti rugi yang diberikannya dianggap belum ~.* The compensation he gave was considered not satisfactory. **2** to measure up to (expectations, etc.). **kememadaian** sufficiency, satisfactoriness, acceptability, adequacy.

memada-madai to do s.t. just enough and not to excess. *Kerja baik pada-padai, jangan badan diperpayah.* Work well and just enough, don't work yourself to death.

memadakan to satisfy (one's needs/desires). *untuk ~ hatinya* to satisfy him. *~ dirinya dengan gaji yang sedikit itu* to content o.s. with a low salary.

memada-madakan to make s.t. be adequate/sufficient. *Duit dipada-padakan.* They made the money go far enough to satisfy their needs.

terpada equaled, matched, paralleled. *tidak ~* unequaled, unprecedented, unparalleled. *Gempa bumi itu tidak ~.* The earthquake was unprecedented.

pada III (*J/Jv*) (located at beginning of the predicate marks plural subjects) (they) all. *Memfotokopi pun membutuhkan cukup banyak uang. Pada umumnya mahasiswa yang kurang mampu – mengeluh kekurangan buku.* Even making photocopies requires a lot of money. In general, poor university students all complain that they don't have enough books. *Burung-burung sudah – resah menunggu pangannya.* The birds are all restless waiting for their food.

pada IV (*Skr*) **1** foot (of royalty); *cp* **PADUKA**. *di bawah – Batara* under the rulers of Majapahit. **2** (*cla*) (in compounds) clipped form of **marcapada** "place of humans," i.e., the earth.

pada V end of a stanza.

padah warning sign, indication, omen, premonition.

padahan presage, omen, warning (that appears in dreams, etc.). *tidak baik –* that's a bad sign/omen.

padahal (*A*) however, (and) yet, still, all the same, in fact, even though, notwithstanding the fact that, while (at the same time), whereas. *Kenapa dia ditangkap, – dia tidak bersalah?* Why was he arrested even though he isn't guilty?

padahan (*M*) **1** consequence, result, what one deserves (to get). *emas –nya* he had to pay dearly for that. *Mulut terdorong, emas –nya.* He opened his mouth and he had to pay dearly for that. *Inilah –nya.* It serves him right. **2** sanction. *PP 10/1983 juga menetapkan suatu pidana bagi laki-laki dan wanita pegawai negeri yang melanggar ketentuan tentang perkawinan dan perceraian dengan diaturnya dengan – administratif berupa pemberhentian dengan hormat tidak atas permintaan sendiri (pasal 16).* Government Regulation Number 10/1983 also stipulates that an administrative sanction of honorable discharge not at the employee's request (article 16) will be imposed on male or female government employees who violate the marriage and divorce regulations.

padak I (*Jv*) salt pan.

padak II deaf.

padaka → **PEDAKA**.

Padaleunyi [Padalarang dan Cileunyi] the toll road between Padalarang and Cileunyi; → **PANCI II**.

padam I 1 extinguished, (put) out, dead (of fire); → **PET**. *Lilin yang bernyala tadi telah – ditiup angin.* The candle which was lit a minute ago was blown out by the wind. *gamelan – a muted gamelan. – hayatnya/nyawanya* he has died/passed away. **2** quelled, crushed, stamped out, put down. **3** calmed down, relaxed, unwound, cooled off, quenched (of one's spirit/desire, etc.). **4** ended. *tak kunjung –* endless, unending, inextinguishable. *api nan tak kunjung –* the eternal flame. **5** extinct. *di mana api –, di sanalah puntung tercampak* and *– nyala tarik puntung* one is buried where one dies.

padam-padamnya (only in the following expressions) *takkan ~* and *tak mau ~* will never die, endless, unending. *usaha yang tak ~* an untiring effort.

memadam to become extinguished, go out.

memadami and **memadamkan 1** to extinguish, put out. *~ api* to extinguish/put out a fire. *~ semangatnya* to deaden/dampen one's enthusiasm. b) to turn/switch off. *~ lampu listrik* to turn off an electric light. **2** to tranquilize, calm (down), quiet(en), pacify, appease. *~ amarahnya* to calm down. *~ hawa nafsunya*

to control one's passions. **3** to quell, stamp out, put down, suppress, put an end/stop to, bring under control. *~ pemberontakan* to put down a rebellion. *~ perkelahian* to put an end to the fighting. **4** to quench, satisfy, slake. *~ dahaganya* to quench one's thirst.

terpadam extinguished, put out.

terpadamkan extinguishable.

kepadaman 1 extinguishing, putting out. **2** cooling off, calming down. **3** quenching. **4** extinction.

pemadam 1 extinguisher. *~ api* fire extinguisher. *Setiap rumah harus punya ~ api portabel.* Every house must have a portable fire extinguisher. *~ kebakaran* [PK] firemen. *jawatan ~ kebakaran* fire department. *mobil ~ kebakaran* fire engine. **2** firefighter, fireman.

pemadaman 1 extinguishing, putting out. *~ listrik* blackout. **2** extinction.

padam II *mérah –* fiery red, scarlet.

padan I 1 match, equal, equivalent. *bukan –nya* matchless, unequaled. **2** right, suitable, well-suited, fit(ting); matching, corresponding, harmonious. *Pemuda itu – menjadi suaminya.* That young man is the right man for her. *–lah anda dipilih menjadi ketua.* You are the right choice for chairman. *sama –* matching, harmonizing.

sepadan (*dengan*) **1** to match, correspond, go (well) together, suit e.o.; commensurate (with), in accordance/conformity/line (with), equivalent (to). *Gajinya tidak ~ dengan tenaga yang dipakainya.* His salary is incommensurate with the energy he puts out. **2** to be in harmony. **3** to agree, correspond. *secara ~* corresponding. *Peningkatan suku bunga tersebut tidak diikuti oléh peningkatan suku bunga déposito secara ~.* An increase in that interest rate was not followed by a corresponding increase in the interest rate on deposits. *~ dengan kesusahan* corresponding to the difficulties. *(tidak) ~ dengan* (not) to be worth (the time/the money/trouble, etc.). *tidak ~* inharmonious, not in agreement. **ketidaksepadanan** disagreement, lack of correspondence; inadequacy. **bersepadanan** to be in harmony, go together (with e.o.). **kesepadanan** agreement, correspondence, equivalency, fungibility.

berpadan to be a match (for).

berpadanan → **SEPADAN** 1, 2. *~ dengan* commensurate with.

memadan(i) and **memadankan** to compare, correlate, set two or more objects next to e.o. to look for their similarities and/or differences. *~ ayam* to compare two cocks which are going to be pitted against e.o.

memadan-madan to weigh, consider, take into consideration. *tidak ~ perasaan orang* not take other people's feelings into consideration.

padanan 1 comparison, correlation. **2** (*~ kata*) synonym, equivalent. *~ kata yang baik* the right word/synonym. **berpadanan** proportional; → **PROPORSIONAL**.

pemadan s.o. or s.t. that compares, etc.

pemadanan matching, comparing.

padan II (*M*) **1** boundary stone. **2** boundary, border line. **3** starting point (in a competition, etc.).

padan III (*J*) unfair, dishonest.

memadani to treat unfairly.

padan IV promise. (*M*) agreement, contract, promise. *mengécoh – to break a promise;* → **KÉCOH**. *syarat dan – bersabung* the conditions and rules agreed on for cockfighting.

berpadan to (make a) promise.

padang 1 field, plain, ground. *– perahu di lautan, – hati di fikiran* look before you leap. *di – orang berlari, di – sendiri berjingkrak* to want to take but not to reciprocate. *lain – lain belalang (lain lubuk lain ikannya)* so many countries, so many customs. *tersérak – ke rimba* everything has been tried and there are no resources left. *– belantara* desert. *– golf* golf course/links. *– gurun* desert. *(perlombaan) – luas* (*ob*; in sports) cross-country. *– lumut* tundra. *– mahsyar* the place where the dead assemble on Judgment Day. *– minyak* oil field. *– pasir* sandy desert. *– pembidikan* rifle/shooting range. *– penggembalaan/peternakan* ranch. *– ragut* pasture (land). *– rumput* a) meadow. b) prairie, grassland. *– tandus* desert. *– tekukur* waste/uncultivated land. – *témbak* rifle/shooting range. – *(kapal) terbang (ob)* airfield. – *tiah* desert; the Arabian desert in which the Biblical Jews wandered. – *usaha* field of work.

berpadang with/to have a field/plain, etc. *memberi ~ luas* to give s.o. a free hand.

padas *(Jv)* pan, various k.o. hard, stony soils, tuff; → CADAS. – *liat* clay pan.

padasan *(J/Jv)* large-bellied water jar with a spout (for ritual cleansing).

padat 1 compact, solid, packed/squeezed together, crowded, stuffed, chock-full, crammed, overflowing, filled to the top/to capacity. *bahan bakar* – solid fuel. *berbahan bakar* – using solid fuel. *ban* – solid/nonpneumatic tire. *benda* – solid(s). *jam* – peak hour. *pakeliran* – a compressed show/performance. *zat* – solid(s). *negara yang paling* – *senjata nuklir di dunia ini* the country with the most nuclear weapons in the world. *Orang sudah* – *di bioskop*. The movie theater was chock-full of people. *Koper itu kecil tapi isinya* –. The suitcase was small but tightly packed. *Gas itu dipompa* –.– *ke dalam silinder besi baja yang tebal*. The gas was compressed into a thick steel cylinder. 2 shapely, having a pleasing or graceful shape, well-shaped. *tubuh yang* – a shapely body. 3 full figured, chubby. 4 dense, packed closely together; congested, tight (schedule). *daérah yang* – *penduduknya* a densely populated area. *dunia yang* – a congested world. 5 full, complete, entire, whole. 6 (in compounds) intensive, full of, requiring or having a high concentration of a specific quality or element. *acara* – (to have) a full schedule. *sudah* – *hatinya (M)* determined. *rundingan telah* – *(M)* to be in full agreement. – *berisi* a) plump, fully developed (of a girl). b) short but complete. – *dana* capital intensive. – *gizi* full of nutrients. – *karya* labor-intensive. **memadat-karyakan** to carry out (an endeavor) in a labor-intensive way. *Pengerjaan 148 km saluran térsiér di NTB dipadatkaryakan*. The 148-km tertiary canal in the Western Lesser Sundas was dug by labor-intensive methods. – *modal* capital intensive. – *pengetahuan dan keterampilan* knowledge- and skill-intensive. – *tangkap* overfishing.

sepadat as solid/compact/full, etc. as.

memadat 1 to cram, stuff, pack full. *~ kasur* to stuff a mattress (with kapok/feathers, etc.). *~ perut* to stuff o.s. full of food. 2 to become crammed/stuffed/packed full.

memadati 1 to cram, stuff, fill (up) (to overflowing). *Pasangan demi pasangan mulai ~ lantai dansa*. Couple after couple began to fill the dance floor. *Bom meledak di dua kafétaria yang sedang dipadati pengunjung*. Bombs exploded in two cafeterias which were full of visitors. 2 to condense, summarize, abstract, write a précis of. *~ isi majalah* to summarize the contents of a magazine.

memadatkan to stuff, pad, cram, fill full, make s.t. solid. *~ jadwal* to fill up one's schedule. *~ kantongnya* to line one's pockets.

memperpadat to (make s.t. more) compact.

terpadat most densely populated. *Jawa, pulau ~ sedunia* Java, the world's most densely populated island.

padatan 1 *(phys)* solid (matter). *~ terlarut* dissolved solids. 2 compression, compactness, density, denseness, solidification. *~ gas* compression/density of a gas. 3 solidified.

kepadatan 1 congestion, jam. *~ daya-tampung* congestion (in harbors). *~ lalu-lintas* traffic congestion/jam, bottleneck. 2 density. *~ penduduk* population density. *~ tidak terhingga* infinite density. **berkepadatan** to have a density of.

pemadat rammer, stuffer, compressor. *(alat) ~ (jalan)* roller. *(alat) ~ sampah* (garbage) compactor.

pemadatan cramming, stuffing, compressing, compacting. *~ jalan* road metaling/surfacing.

padau *layar* – *(naut)* storm sail.

padema → PADMA.

padépokan <dépok> *(Jv)* 1 a holy man's shrine. 2 complex (groups of associated buildings).

paderi *(Port)* 1 Roman Catholic priest; pastor. 2 Protestant minister. – *tentara* chaplain (of the armed forces). *perang* – (1821-1837) the war on Sumatra's West Coast between orthodox Muslims and those who upheld *adat* law, who were backed by the Dutch.

padet → PADAT.

padewakang a Bugis-Makassarese sailing boat.

padi I 1 the rice plant, *Oryza sativa*. 2 (to sell/buy, etc.) rice in the husk. 3 *(butir* –) grain of rice. *ilmu* – the modesty that comes from wisdom. *kian berisi kian rendah/runduk/tunduk* the wiser one is, the more modest one is. – *segenggam (dengan senang hati), lebih baik daripada* – *selumbung (dengan bersusah hati)* a bird in the hand is worth two in the bush. *menyisip* – *dengan ilalang* one rotten apple spoils the whole barrel. – *sekepuk hampa, emas seperti loyang, kerbau sekandang lalang* all that glitters is not gold. – *basah* wet-stalk rice plant. – *berat* late-bearing rice plant. – *betina* (in the Kendari Regency, Southeast Sulawesi) ordinary rice; → PADI jantan. – *cerai/ceré* a variety of long-grained rice. – *dalam* late-bearing rice plant. – *dodokan* a fast-growing rice plant variety. – *gadu/gadon* rice grown in a rice paddy during the dry season. – *gaga/gogo* mountain rice plant, rice plant grown on unirrigated land. – *gora* [gogo rancah] rice grown on unirrigated land; → RANCAH I. – *génjah* early-bearing rice plant. – *huma* stalk rice plant from shifting slash-and-burn agriculture. – *jantan* (in the Kendari Regency, Southeast Sulawesi) alang-alang, *Imperata cylindrica*; → PADI betina. – *jero* late-bearing rice plant. – *kering* dry-stalk rice plant. – *ketan* rice plant which yields sticky rice. – *ladang* stalk rice plant from shifting slash-and-burn agriculture. – *lambat* late-bearing rice plant. – *lekas* early-bearing rice plant. – *PB-5 dan PB-8* [(padi) Peta Baru 5 dan Peta Baru 8] high-yielding rice varieties known as "miracle rice." – *pulut* a rice plant with sticky *beras*. – *radin* early bearing swamp rice plant. – *ranap* overripe rice. – *rendeng(an)* rice plant grown during the rainy season. – *ringan* early-bearing rice plant. – *sawah* stalk rice plant from wet cultivation. – *séntra* rice from rice-plant centers. – *sipulut* a rice plant variety with sticky *beras*.

berpadi to have rice plants.

padian grain.

padi-padian cereals, grains; → SÉRÉALIA.

perpadian rice situation. *Begitu runyamkah ~ kita?* Is our rice situation so precarious?

padi II (in certain expressions) very small, tiny. *lada* – tiny pepper.

sepadi *(tidak) ~* (not) a bit.

PADI III → PARTAI Aliansi Démokrat Indonésia.

padma *(Skr)* 1 (red) lotus, *Nelumbium nelumbo/speciosum*. 2 deep magenta; → PADAM II.

padma-padmaan various types of Rafflesiaceae.

padmasana *(Bal)* a stone throne for the sun god Surya. It stands in the upper right-hand corner of the temple with its back toward *Gunung Agung*. The base of the throne represents the universe, which rests ultimately on the mythical turtle *bedawang*, which has two serpents coiled around his body.

padmi *(Jv)* principal, leading, first, highest. *garwa* – the first wife in a polygamous marriage, the mother of the legal successor(s); queen.

padmosari *(Jv)* the *Rafflesia zollingeriana* plant; → RAFFLÉSIA.

padol 1 → PEDULI. 2 *(J)* please, go ahead; → SILAKAN.

padpinder *(D ob)* boy scout; → PANDU I , PRAMUKA.

padri → PADERI.

padsyah *(Pers)* sultan, ruler.

padu 1 solid, compact, substantial. *Cincinnya dibuat daripada emas* –. Her ring was made of solid gold. 2 combined, united, harmonious. *Segala lapisan masyarakat* – *dalam satu perarakan*. All social classes were united in one procession. *kurang* – uncoordinated. **kekurang-paduan** lack of coordination. – *hati* resolute.

sepadu *(Mal)* in harmony, harmonious. **tersepadu** united, integrated. *ékonomi yang mempunyai jaringan industri yang mantap lagi ~* an economy with a permanent and integrated network of industries.

berpadu 1 to combine, unite, mix together. *Oksigén ~ dengan hidrogén untuk membentuk air*. Oxygen combines with hydrogen to form water. 2 to unite/join into one whole. *Seluruh rakyat Indonésia ~ menentang penjajahan*. The entire Indonesian people united to oppose colonialism. *kalau cinta ~* if love is reciprocated. *emas ~* solid gold. 3 to go hand and hand, combine.

Suka dan duka ~ *mengharu hati Surtinah.* Happiness and sorrow combined to trouble Surtinah. **4** to clot, coagulate, curdle. *Darahnya* ~. The blood has clotted.

berpadu-padu 1 truly united. **2** to be of one mind, unanimous. *Ketua RT mengajak warganya* ~. The chairman of the neighborhood association asked the members to be unanimous in their opinion.

berpadu-paduan 1 to gather together and become one. **2** to discuss and reconcile opinions.

memadu 1 to purify (gold). **2** to mix, blend (two solids into one). **3** to match (up), harmonize. *Kali ini ia berpelekat biru tua yang dipadu dengan kaos oblong kuning dan jas batik kehitaman.* This time he wore a checked dark-blue sarong matched with a yellow singlet and black batik coat. **4** to knead, mix together. **5** to conclude/make/enter into an agreement, agree on. **6** to combine/unite/join with. **7** to forge, weld, merge (voices). ~ *suara* to sing in harmony/unison. **8** to raise (capital). ~ *adonan (tepung terigu dengan telur)* to knead (a batter of wheat flour and eggs). ~ *bicara* to consult. ~ *cinta (antara A dan B)* to tighten the bonds of love (between A and B). ~ *hati (dengan)* to confer/discuss (with). ~ *janji* to reach/come to an agreement. ~ *kasih (dengan)* to love, take up (with). ~ *kebutuhan séks* to fulfill sexual needs. ~ *modal* to get capital together. ~ *pakaian* to fit/try on clothes. ~ *pendapat* to reconcile opinions. ~ *perkataan* to form a compound (word). ~ *satu* to unite, consolidate, make one ~ *suara* to sing in harmony/unison. ~ *warna* to match colors.

mem(perp)adukan 1 to unite, join, ally, combine, match, blend, integrate. *Kemampuan untuk mengerti dan* ~ *téknologi masih kurang.* The ability to understand and integrate technology is still insufficient. ~ *paham semua manusia* to integrate all human understanding. **2** to consolidate, strengthen, reinforce.

terpadu 1 integrated, fused, coordinated. ~ *(bulat-bulat/menjadi satu)* to become one, fused, merged, integrated, united. *pendekatan* ~ integrated approach. *transmigrasi* ~ [transterpadu] integrated transmigration. ~ *sepenuhnya* fully integrated. **2** firm (in ideology). *kurang* ~ unintegrated. **kekurang-terpaduan** short on cohesion/integration, not cohesive enough. **ketidak-terpaduan** lack of cohesion/integration, disunity. *Perbédaan persépsi, kebijaksanaan dan* ~ *antardépartemén dalam pemanfaatan hutan di Indonésia sering terjadi di masa lalu.* In the past there have often been differences in perception and in policy and disunity among the ministries concerning the utilization of Indonesian forests. **seterpadu** in harmony/keeping (with). *Pelajaran agama di perguruan tinggi umum tidak* ~ *yang diberikan di IAIN.* Religion courses in public universities are not in harmony with those given in State Institutions for Islamic Studies. **keterpaduan** integration, cohesiveness, unity, homogeneity. ~ *seluruh masyarakat* total civil unity. *prinsip* ~ integrative principle. ~ *berbagai instansi untuk mengerjakan masing-masing proyéknya masih kurang.* The integration of various agencies to carry out their respective projects is still inadequate.

paduan 1 mixture, mix, combination, alloy, blend, anything that results from a mixing together of elements. ~ *hijau* a salad made of avocado and oranges. ~ *logam* alloy. ~ *logam besi yang terdiri dari timah, antimon dan tembaga* an alloy consisting of tin, antimony and copper, i.e., pewter. ~ *suara* choir, chorus. ~ *warna* color combination. ~ *yang selaras* a harmonious mixture. **2** unity, solidity, firmness. **3** harmony; agreement, concurrence. **4** unification. **5** outfit, set of clothes. **berpaduan** joint and several.

kepaduan unity, solidity, firmness.

pemadu mixer, blender (the person or the implement), integrator. ~ *sistém* systems integrator. ~ *suara* mixer (the electronic device used for broadcast or recording).

pemaduan 1 blending, mixing together. ~ *gambar* film mixing. **2** unifying, harmonizing.

perpaduan 1 harmony; agreement, concurrence. **2** blend, mixture; unification. *Dalam Tokyo Motor Show '89 ditampilkan* ~ *produk Jepang dengan seléra Éropa.* In the '89 Tokyo Motor Show a mixture of Japanese products and European taste was shown. ~ *padat modal dan padat karya* a mixture of capital-intensive and labor-intensive.

paduda (in South Sulawesi) a welcoming dance, *usu* for VIPs.

padudan (*Jv*) **1** opium pipe. **2** (foreign-made) pipe (used for smoking).

paduk (*ob*) starting line (in sports), baseline.

paduka (*Skr*) **1** shoe, sandal. **2** honorific appellation for high dignitaries. – *liku* title of a princess in the *Panji* tales. – *Tuan* [PT] Your Excellency. – *Yang Mulia* [PYM] His Excellency.

padukuhan <dukuh> (*Jv*) hamlet.

padusan <adus> (*Jv*) **1** bathing place. **2** the day before the beginning of the fasting month, when people cleanse themselves ritually.

padusi (*M*) **1** woman. **2** wife.

paduta → UPADUTA.

paédah → FAÉDAH.

paés (*Jv*) bridal makeup and ornamentation, *esp* for the forehead. **memaés** to make up, put cosmetics on. ~ *pengantén* to make up the bride. **paésan** makeup, cosmetics.

paga (*Jv*) kitchen shelf/rack for dishes, glassware, and food.

pagan 1 strong, powerful, vigorous. **2** solid, firm, tough; → KUAT, KUKUH, TEGUH.

paganisme (*D/E*) paganism.

pagar 1 fence, palisade, railings. *Meréka mendirikan sebuah* – *di sekeliling kebunnya.* They erected a fence around their yard. **2** hedge. **3** (the) # (sign). *di luar* – a) (to live) on the fringes of society. b) cast out; no longer honored. – *makan padi/tanaman* a) to nourish/cherish a viper in one's breast. b) the expenses exceed the proceeds; the disadvantages outweigh the advantages. *"Anjing kan lebih bisa dipercaya daripada mempekerjakan orang untuk jaga gudang. Salah-salah – makan tanaman," kata Rudy.* "Isn't it true that a dog is more reliable than a person hired to guard your warehouse? It could turn out badly and the disadvantages could outweigh the advantages," said Rudy. *Bagai melompati – tiga hasta, akan dilompati rendah, akan dilangkahi tinggi.* It's hard to make s.t. fit exactly (or, be exactly suitable). – *adat* traditional stipulations/regulations; traditional law; customs and traditions. – *alam* natural barrier, such as, mountains. – *anak* palings leading to an elephant corral. – *Ayu* the charming young girls who formed a k.o. fence at weddings and in welcoming foreign dignitaries disembarking from their aircraft. – *bagus* wall of good-looking boys. – *bambu* bamboo hedge. – *batas* demarcation/boundary fence. – *batu* a brick wall erected around a yard or town. *Jawa dahulu disebut Japa; kota utamanya ada 4, semuanya tanpa – batu.* Java used to be called Japa; it had four main towns, all without brick walls around them. – *Baya* the Jakarta village police; → POLISI *Pamong Praja.* – *bedil* mopping-up operation (*mil*). – *besi* iron fence. – *betis* a cordon of volunteer servicemen for combating banditry in villages. **berpagar betis** to have a cordon of volunteer servicemen for combating banditry in villages. **memagar betis** to cordon off, block. *Abang-abang bécak yang jumlahnya ratusan orang itu serentak mengepung términal dan* ~ *jalan keluar.* Hundreds of pedicab drivers encircled the terminal and blocked the exits. – *bulan* halo around the moon. – *buluh* bamboo hedge. – *buritan* (*naut*) taffrail. – *caling* barbed fence for keeping out wild boars. – *dék* (ship's) deck railing. – *désa* village guard/militia. – *duri* barbed-wire fence. – *gedék* braided-bamboo wall. – *hidup* hedge consisting of growing plants. **berpagar hidup** with such a hedge. – *indukan* brooder guard. – *jaro* (*J*) bamboo hedge. – *kapal* railing, guard rail. – *kawat* wire fence. – *kawat berduri* barbed-wire fence. – *kisi-kisi* lattice fence. – *lambung* bulwark. – *listrik* electrified fence. – *mati* fence made of wood, brick, or wickerwork. – *musang* (*naut*) stern taffrail. – *negeri* protector of the nation. – *papan* boarded fence. – *péron* platform barrier. – *pemisah (jalan)* (road) divider fence. – *Praja* one of the names given to the Jakarta village police. – *putar* turnstile. – *sasak* wickerwork fence. – *sua* partition between two water buffalos which are to be pitted against e.o.; → BERSUA. – *témbok* a brick/masonry partition/dividing wall. – *tenggalung* (*naut*) stern taffrail. – *tiang* pile fence. – *tutup* demarcation/boundary fence.

berpagar 1 with/to have a fence, fenced. **2** to be fenced (in). *Rumahnya* ~ *besi.* His house has an iron fence around it.

berpagarkan to have ... as a fence. *Jalan raya itu ~ pinus.* The highway is fenced in with pine trees.

memagar to make a fence, plant a hedge. *~ diri* to look after o.s. *~ diri bagai aur* (*M*) only thinking about o.s., selfish.

memagari 1 to put a fence around, fence in. **2** to protect o.s. (against danger, etc.); to isolate. **3** to demarcate. *Bunderan Hotél Indonésia dipagari oléh Plaza Indonesia, Wisma Nusantara, Hotél Mandarin Oriéntal, dan Hotél Indonésia.* The Hotel Indonesia traffic circle is demarcated by Plaza Indonesia, Wisma Nusantara, Hotel Mandarin Oriental, and Hotel Indonesia.

memagarkan 1 to use ... as a fence. *~ buluh* to use bamboo for a hedge. **2** to (put a) fence (around s.t.). *Tukang-tukang itu ~ kebun sayuran.* The workers put a fence around the vegetable garden.

terpagar fenced; protected.

pagaran fence, railings, etc.

pemagar s.t. that fences (in) s.t.

pemagaran hedging, fencing.

pagarisasi government program to provide fences.

pagas → PANGKAS.

pageblug (*Jv*) epidemic. *diterjang* – to be hit by an epidemic. – *pés* an epidemic of the plague.

pagelar (*Jv*) **mempagelarkan** to stage, perform; → GELAR II.

pagelaran I performance, show. *~ busana* fashion show. *~ musik aliran keras* hard rock concert. *~ séks* sex show; → GELAR II.

pagelaran II the front part of the *kraton* in which officials jointly pay their respects to the sultan; → GELAR III.

pager I → PAGAR.

pager II (*E*) /péjer/ pager.

pagi 1 morning. *bangun pukul lima* – to get up at five in the morning. **2** the early part of the day from sunup to about 10–11 a.m. *Selamat pagi!* Good morning! **3** early; → DINI. *hari masih* – it's still early (in the morning or in the evening). *terlalu/terlampau* – too early, too soon, premature. *dapat – habis petang* easy come, easy go. *sebentar –, sebentar malam* to be fickle, changeable, have an unstable point of view. *– hari* in the morning. *– ini* this morning (said during the morning). *– tadi* this morning (said later in the day). *– soré* a) morning and evening. b) *kembang – soré* a species of flower that blooms twice a day, *Mirabilis jalapa.* c) (*Jv*) batiked with a different pattern on each side. *Ikat kepalanya – soré.* His headband had a different batik pattern on each side. *-nya* a) the same morning. b) the next/following morning.

pagi-pagi 1 very early in the morning. *~ buta/hitam* before daybreak, at dawn. **2** at the very outset, early on. **3** so soon, so early. *Jangan pulang ~.* Don't go home so soon.

sepagi 1 so early, as early as. *~ itu, Selasa 12 Séptémber 1989, SD Negeri, Labuhanbatu, Sumut masih lengang.* So early on Tuesday September 12, 1989, the Labuhanbatu, North Sumatra, Government Elementary School was still deserted. *~ mungkin* as early as possible. **2** (= **sepagian**) the whole/entire morning, all morning. *jalan yang licin oléh hujan ~* a road made slippery by an all-morning rain. **sepagi-paginya** as soon/early as possible; → SELEKAS-LEKASNYA.

terpagi the earliest in the morning. *Seperti biasa ia bangun yang ~.* As usual, he woke up earliest/first.

kepagian too early, too soon, ahead of time.

pagina (*D*) page (of a book).

paginasi paging, pagination.

pagini → PAGI ini.

pagoda (*D*) pagoda.

pagon (*S*) to remain (where one is); to stagnate (of water).

pago-pago (in Simalungun, Tapanuli) k.o. compensation, indemnification; → PANJAR I.

pagu (*M*) **1** rack, shelf (above the kitchen fireplace). **2** loft, k.o. attic above the ceiling (used only for storage). **3** ceiling (of a room). **4** ceiling, cap, the highest limit. *– krédit* credit limit, line of credit. *– pembayaran* payment cap. *– produksi* production limit/line.

memagu to put a ceiling on.

pagun → PAGAN.

pagupon <gupu> (*Jv*) dovecote.

paguron <guru> (*Jv*) educational institution. *Taman Siswa merupakan – (tempat berguru) dan pusat budaya masyarakat sekelilingnya.* Taman Siswa is an educational institution (where one goes to learn) and cultural center for the surrounding community.

pagut I peck, bite. *kena – ular berbisa* to be bitten by a poisonous snake.

berpagut *~ mulut* to bill and coo.

berpagutan to peck at e.o.

memagut 1 to peck (of birds), bite (of snakes/fish); *cp* PATUK I. *~ lutut* to sit around and do nothing. **2** to clutch at, try to grab hold of.

memaguti (*pl obj*) to peck at.

memagutkan to bite at with s.t., use s.t. to bite at.

pagutan peck, bite.

pagut II (*M*) embrace.

berpagut to embrace; → BERPELUK. *~ lutut* to sit around idly.

berpagutan to embrace e.o.

berpagut-pagut to sit idly with the arms around one knee.

memagut 1 to embrace. *~ mata yang melihat* to catch the eyes of the bystanders. **2** to surround.

terpagut to be gripped, fascinated, enthralled.

pagutan grip, hug, embrace. *Bibirnya tak lepas dari ~ lawan mainnya.* Her lips could not escape from the grip of her fellow actor (in a film). **sepagutan** and **sepemagutan** as much as the arms can embrace, an armful.

paguyuban <guyub> (*Jv*) association, club, union, society. *– Ilmuwan Penjelajah* The Scientific Explorers' Society. *– kulawarga* family circle. *– Widiyani/Widyani* Civitas Academica, community of scholars; → SIVITAS AKADÉMIKA.

pah (*coq*) → PAK I.

paha I thigh. *kunci/lipat* – groin. *pangkal* – hip. *tulang* – femur. *bergendang* – to feel schadenfreude, malicious pleasure in s.o. else's troubles. *cubit – kanan, – kiri pun sakit* to hang one's dirty linen outside. *diberi betis, hendak* – give him an inch and he'll take an ell. *ditaruh di bawah* – paid no attention to. *– ayam* drumstick (of fowl). *– belakang* a) a woman's shapely curving thigh. b) safety pin. c) (metal, spiral) spring.

sepaha 1 (*cla*) quarter, one fourth. **2** thigh-high.

paha II *burung – kelati* bronzed drongo, *Dicrurus aenus malayensis.*

pahala (*Skr*) reward from God for good works; award, merit. *Kelembagaan – Amal* University Awards Board (of the Bogor Agricultural Institute). *tanpa* – without expecting anything in return. *– Amal Kebaikan* merit earned for good deeds. *– Amal Mayang* award for merit in human relations and information. *– Amal Melati* an award for scientific research. *– Amal Seroja* award for research in conception.

berpahala to merit an award; meritorious.

paham (*A*) **1** comprehension, understanding; → FAHAM. *pengetahuan banyak, -nya kurang* to know a lot but understand little. **2** opinion, view. *– majikan itu mengenai perkara ini sangat berlainan dengan – para pekerjanya.* The employer's views on this matter differ from those of the employees. *menurut/pada – saya* in my opinion. **3** to be well versed in, skilled or learned, know, understand. *Dia – dalam bahasa Indonésia.* He is well-versed in Indonesian. *Saya sendiri tidak berapa – akan perkara itu.* I myself don't know too much about the matter. *kurang – akan* not understand. *salah* – misunderstanding. **kesalahpahaman** misunderstanding. **4** school of thought, -ism. *angan lalu, –.- tertumbuk* a) almost helpless. b) when it comes to the point, nothing happens. *kurang* – to fail to understand s.t. **kekurang-pahaman** misunderstanding, failure to understand s.t. *– démokrasi borjuis* liberalism. *– hidup berdampingan secara damai* peaceful coexistence. *– nasional* nationalism. *– (serba) naskah* conceptualism.

sepaham 1 of the same opinion/view, in agreement, eye to eye. **2** likeminded. *teman ~* congenial soul/spirit; (political) supporter, sympathizer. *tidak ~* in disagreement. **ketidak-sepahaman** disagreement. **kesepahaman** understanding.

berpaham 1 to have a notion/conception of. *Rakyat tempat itu lebih ~ kedaérahan daripada ~ kenegaraan.* The people there have a greater conception of regionalism than of nationality. *masyarakat kita yang ~ panutan* our paternalistic society. **2** to be intelligent/experienced. *Ia sangat ~ dan disegani oléh masyarakat*. He is very intelligent and is respected by the community.

memahami [and **mahamin** (*J coq*)] **1** to understand, know. *Saya tidak ~ percakapan orang asing itu karena meréka bercakap dalam bahasa Rusia.* I didn't understand the foreigners' conversation because they were speaking Russian. *Saya ~ maksud anda.* I know what you mean; I get it. *Dia ~ perasaanmu.* He sympathizes with your feelings. **2** to be aware of. *Meréka ~ keadaan anda.* They are aware of your situation. **3** to make sense out of, figure out. *Tidak dapat dipahami apa yang dikatakannya.* They couldn't make sense out of what he said. *mencoba ~ arti kata itu* trying to figure out the meaning of the word.

memahamkan 1 to study carefully, understand fully/completely. *Seorang pengemudi mobil harus ~ tanda-tanda lalu-lintas.* A driver has to understand the traffic signs completely. **2** to interpret, explain the meaning of, make s.t. understandable. *Jangan salah dipahamkan adat itu.* Don't misinterpret that custom.

terpahami and **terpahamkan** comprehensible, can be understood. *Khotbah itu tidak terpahamkan para jemaah karena diucapkan dalam bahasa Latin.* The sermon couldn't be understood by the congregation because it was delivered in Latin. **keterpahaman** understandability, comprehensibility, intelligibility. *~ kata dan istilah* the intelligibility of words and terms.

pemahaman comprehension, conception, understanding. *~ bahasa sumber dan bahasa sasaran sangat penting bagi penerjemah.* Understanding the source language and the target language are of primary importance for the translator.

pahang (*S*) to smell bad, emit/give off an offensive odor (e.g., the smell emitted by the leaves of the sweetsop fruit). *pahit – →* PAHIT *getir*.

pahar a large copper or bronze pedestal tray for serving food.

pahargyan (*Jv*) celebration. *– jumenengan* celebration of ascension to the throne, coronation ceremony of a Sultan or Sunan.

pahat 1 chisel. **2** (drill) bit. *– alur* anvil/bolt chisel. *– bangku* bench chisel. *– blok* block chisel. *– bor* flat-ended chisel. *– bulat* round chisel. *– gérék (buntu)* (blind) plain-chisel. *– jantan* tapering sharp chisel. *– ketam* plane iron. *– kuku* gouge. *– lekuk* hollow chisel, gouge. *– pating* blunt/stonemason's chisel. *– perapat* blunt chisel. *– picak* flat chisel. *– potong* anvil chisel. *– serombong* hollow chisel. *– tembus* punch. *– tetak* file chisel. *– ulir sekrup* chaser.

berpahat chiseled, chipped, carved.

memahat to chisel, gouge, carve, cut (stone).

pahat-memahat carving. *~ dan bentuk-membentuk* modeling.

memahatkan to engrave.

terpahat engraved.

pahatan carving, sculpture, s.t. carved/chiseled. *~ batu* lithography. *~ lino* linocut.

pemahat carver. *~ patung* sculptor.

pemahatan carving, chiseling.

pahé (*sl*) [*pakét hémat*] value package: a small quantity of illegal drugs or fast food.

paheman (*Jv*) organization, association.

Pahing (*Jv*) the second day of the five-day market week.

pahit 1 bitter, acrid, biting. *Minuman keras itu rasanya sedikit –.* The hard drink tasted somewhat bitter. *pengalaman –* a bitter experience. **2** unsweetened, natural (of drink). *téh –* plain/unsweetened tea. *mendapat kopi –* a) to get black/unsweetened coffee. b) to get a sharp reprimand. **3** to hurt (s.o.'s feelings). *Semua perkataannya –.* Everything he said hurt (people's feelings). **4** unpleasant, hard, difficult. *Betapa –nya kehidupan orang kampung.* How hard life is for villagers. **5** (*ob*) bitter drink, bitters. *– dahulu, manis kemudian* look before you leap. *–darah* to live a long life. *– getir* the ups and downs (of life). *– getirnya kehidupan* life's hardships. **kepahit-getiran** unpleasantness. *– lidah* a) a sharp tongue. b) what one says is true or effective, one's prayers are answered. *– manis* the good and the bad. **sepahit-semanis** (to live through) the good and bad together, for better or worse. *– maung* a) very bitter. b) unpleasantness, bitterness. *– meninggal* a) to leave a bitter taste (in one's mouth). b) his insincerity became obvious right away. *– pahang* a) acrimony. b) the ups and downs (of life).

sepahit as bitter as.

berpahit-pahit 1 to suffer hardships. **2** to act/speak in a frank and outspoken way, recognize the difficulty of s.t. (before doing it).

memahiti to make bitter, embitter.

memahitkan to make bitter, embitter, exasperate.

terpahit the most bitter.

pahitan (*Jv*) carpet grass.

pahit-pahitan all k.o. bitter things.

kepahitan 1 bitterness, embitterment, exasperation. **2** trouble, suffering.

kepahit-pahitan somewhat bitter.

pahlawan (*Pers*) **1** hero. *Hari –* Heroes' Day (November 10). **2** patriot. **3** champion, advocate. *– bakiak* henpecked husband. *– bulutangkis* badminton champion. *– dunia balapan mobil* world champion drag racer. *– Islam dan Kemerdékaan* Hero of Islam and Independence, i.e., the title conferred on President Soekarno by the Afro-Asian Islamic Conference. *– kebenaran* martyr. *– kemerdékaan* hero of independence. *– kesiangan* a "hero" after the danger has passed. *– Réformasi* the students killed on May 13, 1998, at Trisakti University. *– setia* loyal retainer. *– tak dikenal* the unknown soldier. *– tak kenal takut* intrepid hero. *– tanpa tanda jasa* an unsung hero.

mem(p)ahlawankan to declare a hero. *~ meréka yang masih bernafas* to honor as heroes those still alive.

kepahlawanan heroism, bravery, courage, valor.

pahlawati heroine.

pahtar (in Samarinda) lessee, leaseholder (of small island where turtle eggs are found); → PAKTER I.

pahter → PAKTER I.

pai I (*Port Min*) **1** father. **2** big, fat.

pai II (*M*) to go.

pai III (*E*) pie.

pai IV (*Mal*) still not yet; → BELUM *lagi*.

paidah → FAÉDAH.

paido I (*J*) fussy, hard to please, faultfinding, quarrelsome.

paido II (*Jv*) **1** doubt, disbelief. **2** distrust.

maido to disparage, belittle.

paidon (*Jv*) cuspidor.

pailit (*D*) **1** to fail, go bankrupt. **2** broke. *jatuh –* to go bankrupt.

mem(p)ailitkan to declare bankrupt. *Perséroan ini dipailitkan setelah ketakmampuan membayar.* The corporation was declared bankrupt after it was unable to pay its debts.

kepailitan bankruptcy.

pemailitan bankrupting, bankruptcy.

Paing → PAHING.

paip (*E mostly Mal*) (system of) pipe(s); → PIPA.

pair I *perahu* – patrol boat.

berpair-pair to cruise, patrol.

memairi to cruise (around) s.t.; to patrol.

pemair 1 patrol boat. **2** cruiser.

pair II not function as it should (of a part of the body). *– jantung* heart block.

pais seasoned fish cooked in banana leaves; → PÉPÉS.

memais to cook seasoned fish in banana leaves.

pait → PAHIT.

paitua 1 (*IBT*) → BAPAK. **2** (*Pap*) → BUPATI.

pajak I tax. *Dia belum membayar –nya.* He hasn't paid his taxes yet. *menghitung sendiri –nya (yang terutang)* self-assessment. *hukum –* tax law. *kena –* taxable, assessable. *dikenai/dikenakan –* be taxed/assessed. *Setiap anjing milik warga Jakarta akan dikenai –.* Every dog owned by a resident of Jakarta will be taxed. *Pemilik sepéda juga dikenakan – sepéda tahunan.* Bicycle owners will also have to pay an annual tax on their bikes. *masa bébas –* tax holiday. *menarik –* to collect taxes. *obyék –* taxable item. *pembayar –* taxpayer. *penarik –* tax collector. *pengelabuan –* tax fraud. *penggelap –* tax dodger. *Surat Pemberitahuan Tahunan – Penghasilan* [SPTPPh] Annual Income Tax Return. *tatacara menghitung – sendiri* self-assessment tax system. *– anjing* dog tax. *– atas Bunga, Dividén, dan Royalti* [PBDR] tax on interest, dividends, and royalties. *– badan* corporate tax. *– Bangsa Asing* [PBA] foreigners tax. *– berganda* double taxation. *– bulé* (*joc*) the "extra charges" that foreigners have to pay. – *Bumi dan Bangunan* [PBB] tax on land and the buildings erected on it. – *daérah* state and local taxes. – *dividén dan tantiéme* tax on dividends and tantiemes. – *ganda* double taxation. – *hasil bumi* tax on produce. – *jalan* road tax. – *kekayaan* wealth tax. – *keluaran* output tax. – *kendaraan* vehicle tax. – *Kendaraan Bermotor* [PKB] motor vehicle tax. – *kendaraan tidak bermotor* nonmotorized vehicle tax. – *kepala* capitation tax. – *keuntungan* profits tax. – *kohir* assessment register tax. – *langsung* direct tax. – *masukan* input tax. – *meterai* stamp duty. – *modal* capital levy. – *pembangunan* development tax. – *Pendapatan* [PPd] income tax. – *penggunaan jalan* road use tax, toll. – *penghasilan* [PPh] income tax. – *penghasilan badan* corporate income tax. – *penghasilan orang pribadi* personal income tax. – *Penjualan* [PPn] sales tax. – *Penjualan atas barang-barang Méwah* [PPnBM] sales tax on luxury items. – *peralihan* transitional tax. – *perponding* ground tax. – *perorangan/ perseorangan* personal tax. – *perséroan* corporate tax. – *pertambahan nilai* [PPN] value added tax, VAT. – *pertambahan nilai barang dan jasa* value added tax on items and services. – *perusahaan* corporate tax. – *potong* slaughter tax. – *réklame* advertising tax. – *rumah tangga* household tax. – *sepéda* bicycle tax. – *tanah* land tax. – *tersembunyi* hidden tax. – *tidak langsung* indirect tax. – *tonggak* tax on electric poles. – *Tontonan* [PTo] entertainment tax. – *upah* pay-as-you-earn income tax. – *warisan* estate tax.

pajak-memajak having to do with taxation. *bidang* ~ taxable sector.

memajaki 1 to assess, levy a tax on. *Pemerintah* ~ *perusahaan setiap tahun.* The government levies an annual tax on his enterprise. **2** to pay a tax on. *Petani itu belum* ~ *sawahnya.* The farmer has not yet paid a tax on his rice paddy.

memajakkan to tax, levy a tax on. ~ *anjingnya* to levy a tax on one's dog.

kepajakan tax system.

pemajakan taxation, levying a tax on. ~ *bunga déposito dimulai 14 November 1988.* Taxation on the interest on deposits began on November 14, 1988.

perpajakan 1 tax system. **2** tax (*mod*). *hukum* ~ tax law. *RUU itu mémang merupakan terobosan untuk menembus kepincangan-kepincangan* ~ *yang berlaku sekarang ini.* The draft law is a real breakthrough in breaking through the tax loopholes currently in effect.

pajak II 1 lease, rent, monopoly. **2** (*ob*) market section. **3** market stall/stand/shop licensed by the government. – *candu* a) monopolistic right on opium sales (by paying a tax to the government). b) (*ob*) official opium den. – *gadai* a) (*ob*) the right to open a pawnshop (by paying a tax to the government). b) pawnshop. – *ikan* fish section (in the market). – *judi* gambling den. – *kopi* coffee shop in the market. – *sayur* vegetable section in the market.

memajak 1 to lease, rent, assume a lease. **2** to pawn. ~ *barang-barang emas* to pawn gold articles.

memajaki to lease, rent, take out a lease (for collecting birds' nests, for marsh land, etc.).

pemajak lessee, leaseholder.

pajan (*M*) exposed, weathered.

memajankan to expose.

terpajan exposed.

pajanan exposure.

pajang memajang 1 to decorate, adorn, array, deck out. **2** to display, exhibit, hang out and show off. *sebuah truk yang* ~ *gambar Bung Karno* a truck displaying a picture of President Soekarno. ~ *diri* to show off; → MÉJÉNG, NGÉCÉNG. *Sembari mengisap rokok dan makan-minum, meréka itu* ~ *diri alias ngécéng, sampai dinihari.* Smoking cigarettes and eating as well as drinking, they showed off till dawn.

memajangi to decorate s.t. with (flowers, etc.).

memajangkan to display, exhibit, show.

terpajang displayed. *tumpukan barang* ~ *rapi* a pile of neatly displayed goods.

pajangan decoration; show, window display.

pemajang 1 decorator. **2** decoration.

pemajangan bridal apartment/bed.

pajar (*A*) → FAJAR. – *buta* still pitch dark. – *menyingsing* day is breaking. – *sidik* about 04:00 in the morning.

paji (*J*) wedge; peg.

paju I (*Jv*) **1** wedge. **2** angle, corner.

berpaju angular. *bintang* ~ *lima* 5-pointed star/medal.

paju II (*ob*) **memajukan** to put forward, advance; → (M)AJU.

pajuh (*ob*) gluttonous.

memajuh to guzzle, gobble down.

pak I (clipped form of **bapak**) **1** appellation for older man. *Apa kabar,* –? How are you, Sir? –! (in restaurant, etc. to older man) Waiter! **2** title before the name of an older man. – *Sanusi* Mr. Sanusi. – *cik* younger uncle. – *Kadok/Pandir* a simple but honest person. – *lurah* term of address or reference for village head. – *ogah* → *pak* OGAH. – *pos* mailman, postman. – *su* youngest uncle. – *uda* uncle (younger than father or mother). – *wa* older uncle.

pak II (*D*) **1** package, parcel. *menerima kiriman barang tiga* – to receive a consignment of goods in three packages/parcels. **2** pack. *Rokoknya berapa se*–? How much is a pack of cigarettes?

berpak-pak by the pack.

mempak and **mengepak** to pack (up), package, wrap (up).

mengepaki to package.

pak-pakan by the pack, packs and packs of.

pengepak packer. *mesin* ~ packing press.

pengepakan packing; packaging.

pak III (*D*) lease, rent (of land). *uang* – *dan uang lisénsi* money for leases and licenses. – *temurun* hereditary tenure, long lease.

mempak and **mengepak** to lease, rent. **2** (*coq*) to buy up, corner the market on. *Karcis semuanya sudah dipak tukang catut.* All the tickets have been bought up by black-marketers.

mempakkan and **mengepakkan** to lease, rent out (land).

pempakan and **pengepakan** leasing, renting out.

pak IV (*D*) pact; → PAKTA.

pakai 1 (*coq*) to wear. *Ia* – *baju safari.* He is wearing a safari jacket. *wartawan* – *jakét antipeluru* a reporter wearing a bulletproof jacket. *Meréka tidak* – *sepatu.* They were barefoot. **2** to use. *sekali* – single use (of a hypodermic syringe). *alat suntik plastik sekali* – *(dibuang)* a disposable syringe. *siap* – ready to use. **3** (*coq*) to go around doing s.t., do things in a certain way. *Bulog tak akan* – *nunjuk-nunjuk.* Bulog is not going to go around appointing people. – *dalam* for internal use only. – *hasil* usufruct. – *luar* for external use only. – *ulang* to reuse. **4** (provided) with, with ... in it, using; → DENGAN. – *susu* with cream/milk. *Saya biasa minum kopi* – *susu.* I usually have cream in my coffee. *Kopi ini* – *apa?* What's in this coffee? (sugar/cream, etc.). *téh tidak* – *gula* unsweetened tea. **5** by means of, with, using. *mobil yang* – *radio* a car with a radio. *Sehabis bacok istri dan seorang hostés, laki-laki berdarah dingin bunuh kawan* – *clurit.* After stabbing his wife and a hostess, the cold-blooded man killed a friend with a *clurit. Bapak datang* – *apa?* – *mobil.* How/by what means of transportation did you come? By car. *tidak* – *perantaraan* without the intermediary of.

berpakai 1 (*ob*) to get dressed. **2** (*M*) to be valid/in effect/in force. *Hingga kini adat itu masih* ~. Up to now that tradition is still in effect.

berpakaikan to wear, have ... on. *Ia* ~ *sarung.* He is wearing a sarong, he has a sarong on.

memakai 1 to wear (shoes/a hat, etc.). ~ *sepatu/kacamata/jas* to wear shoes/eyeglasses/a coat. **2** to use, employ for some purpose. *mulai dipakai* began to be used, come into use. *untuk dipakai sendiri* for private/personal use, not public. ~ *bahasa Inggris* to use English. ~ *pisau untuk memotong roti* to use a knife for slicing bread. **3** to bear/have (a title, etc.). ~ *gelar/ nama/sebutan* to bear a title/name/designation. **4** to stick to, abide by. ~ *aturan permainan* to abide by the rules of the game. **5** by, on, by means of. ~ *pesawat terbang* by plane. **6** to require, call for. *Pembangunan pasar swalayan bertingkat itu* ~ *biaya yang besar.* The construction of that multistory supermarket requires a large sum of money. **7** to follow, adhere to. *Suku itu masih* ~ *adat lama.* That ethnic group still adheres to old traditions. ~ *baju hitam* to go into mourning. **8** to use for. *Bolsak itu saya* ~ *tidur.* I for one used that mattress for sleeping. *gampang* *dipakai* user-friendly. *Komputer itu akan semakin bersifat gampang ~.* Computers will become increasingly user-friendly.

memakaii (*J*) to dress s.o. *Maria lalu dipakaii orang dengan pakaian yang amat bagus.* Then they dressed Maria in very beautiful clothes.

memakaikan 1 to dress s.o. or s.t. *Ia dipakaikan pakaian pengantén.* He was dressed in groom's clothing. **2** to apply, put into practice. *Kita tidak boléh ~ aturan ini pada golongan yang berpendapatan rendah.* We are not allowed to apply this arrangement to low-income groups.

terpakai [and **kepakai** (*coq*)] **1** to be used unintentionally. *Jas hujan saya ~ oléh orang lain.* My raincoat was used by s.o. else by mistake. **2** to be fit for use, usable. *tidak ~* unfit for use, unserviceable, useless. *kapasitas yang tidak ~* idle capacity (for aircraft, etc.). **3** canceled, void (of a passport/visa, etc.). **4** applied. *ilmu-ilmu pengetahuan ~* applied sciences.

pakaian 1 clothes, clothing, dress, apparel, attire, suit, uniform. *~nya diseterika licin lagi rapi.* He was dressed in neat, freshly ironed clothes. *kain ~* fabric, materials (for making into clothing). **2** harness. *~ adat* traditional costume. *~ adun-temadun* fancy dress. *~ angkatan* a) (*mil*) service uniform. b) state robes, gala dress. c) Sunday best. d) pilgrim's attire. *~ antiapi* fireproof clothes. *~ atas* outerwear. *~ basahan* (*Mal*) everyday clothes. *~ bébas* casual wear. *~ bekas* used clothing. *~ biasa* everyday dress. *~ daérah* local costume. *~ dalam* underwear, underclothes. *~ dinas* (*mil*) uniform. *~ dinas harian* (*mil*) daily uniform. *~ dinas lapangan* (*mil*) battle dress. *~ dinas upacara* (*mil*) dress uniform. *~ dunia* traditions of the world. *~ hamil* maternity clothes. *~ hidup* traditions of life. *~ ihram* special attire, consisting of two pieces of white cloth, worn during the pilgrimage to Mecca. *~ jadi* ready-made garment. *~ kebangsaan* national dress/costume. *~ kebesaran* (*mil*) full dress/uniform. *~ korvé* (*mil*) fatigues. *~ kuda* harness. *~ lapangan* (*mil*) battle dress/fatigues. *~ lengkap* coat and tie. *~ loréng* (*mil*) camouflaged uniform. *~ luar* outerwear. *~ malam* evening dress. *~ mandi* bathing/swimsuit. *~ ngepop* mod clothing (jeans, etc.). *~ olah-raga* athletic clothes. *~ panas* sexy clothing. *~ panggung* stage dress. *~ pas badan* body suit. *~ pelasak* everyday clothes. *~ pelindung antisenjata kimia* antichemical-weapons protective clothes. *~ pengantin* bridal attire. *~ préman* civilian clothes, civvies. *~ rajutan* knitwear. *~ renang* bathing/swimsuit. *~ resmi* official dress, formal attire. *~ senam* sportswear. *~ seragam* (*mil*/school) uniform. *~ sipil* civvies. *~ taruhan* Sunday clothes/best. *~ tekanan* pressurized suit. *~ terbuka separuh dada* low-cut dress, dress that shows a lot of cleavage. *~ tidur* nightclothes. *~ tradisonal* traditional costume. **berpakaian** to be dressed. *Teman-teman sebayanya waktu itu biasa ~ perlénté.* At that time his contemporaries usually dressed stylishly. *~ seénaknya* to be dressed casually. **memakaiankan** to dress in, put ... on. *Bonéka itu lalu dipakaiankan kain kebaya dan dikalungi untaian bunga-bungaan tertentu.* The puppet was then dressed in a woman's blouse and a necklace of flowers was put around its neck.

pemakai user, consumer. *~ akhir* end user. *~ hasil* usufructuary. *~ jalan* road user. *~ jasa angkutan laut* shipper. *~ narkotika yang ketagihan berat* a narcotics addict. *~ terdahulu* first inventor.

pemakaian 1 use, consumption. *~ bahan bakar* fuel consumption. *~ sendiri* own use. **2** application, use. *memperkenalkan ~ alat yang canggih itu* to introduce the use of those sophisticated devices. **sepemakaian** a complete set of clothes, suit, outfit.

pakaja drift-fish pot (a floating fish trap).

pakal caulk.
   memakal to caulk.
   pemakal 1 caulker. **2** caulking tool/device.

pakam → PAKEM I.

pakan I woof, weft.
   berpakan(kan) to have ... as its woof; interwoven (with). *sarung berpakankan emas* a sarong with gold thread woven into it.
   memakankan to interweave with. *Pada lungsin itu dipakankan benang sutra.* Gold thread was woven into the warp.
   pakanan s.t. that is used as woof.

pakan II various species of climbers and trees, *Vitis spp.* (*pohon*) –

jantan k.o. shrub, *Kibara coriacea*. *– paya* Sumatran ironwood, *Fagrea racemosa*. *– rimba* k.o. shrub, *Allomorphia malaccensis*.

pakan III (*M*) → PEKAN II.

pakan IV (*Mal*) *obat* – ointment for invulnerability (smeared on fighting bulls).

pakan V (*Jv*) animal food, feed, fodder, diet (of domesticated animals); → MAKANAN *ternak*. *– burung/udang*, etc. bird/shrimp, etc. feed. *– tambahan* feed additive.

pakanira (*O Jv ob*) you/sir.

pakansi (*D*) vacation; → VAKANSI.
   berpakansi to go on vacation.

pakar expert, specialist; → AHLI. *– antropologi ragawi* physical anthropologist. *– agraria* agrarianist. *– arsitéktur* architect. *– astrofisika* astrophysicist. *– bahasa* linguist, language expert. *– cuaca* meteorologist. *– ékonomi* economist. *– éléktronika* electronics expert. *– épidémologi* epidemiologist. *– fisika* physicist. *– futurologi* futurologist. *– géologi* geologist. *– hukum* jurist, lawyer. *– ilmu komunikasi* communications expert. *– masa depan* futurologist. *– médis* physician. *– pajak* tax expert. *– parfuman* perfumer. *– pendidikan* educator. *– pertahanan* defense expert. *– robotika* roboticist. *– sejarah* historian. *– solék* (*Mal*) beautician. *– sosiologi* sociologist. *– stratégi bisnis* business strategist. *– téknologi* technologist. *– viktimologi* victimologist.
   kepakaran expertise, skill.

pakarti (*Jv*) behavior, actions.

pakarya <karya> (*Jv*) (white-collar) worker, (handi)craftsman; → PEKERJA. *Kepada – diberikan tunjangan Rp 10.000 per bulan.* An allowance of Rp 10,000 per month is given to workers.

pakaryan <karya> (*Jv*) **1** (art)work. **2** (handi)craft.

pakasi (*D*) *uang* – attendance fee.

pakat I (*A*) **1** agreement, consent; → MUPAKAT. **2** discussion, conference.
   sepakat *q.v.*
   berpakat 1 to agree. *Ada yang ~ akan pergi mandi di pulau itu.* Some agreed to go swimming at that island. **2** to discuss, confer.
   memakati 1 to agree with (s.o.), agree on (a price, etc.). **2** to advise.
   pakatan (*ob*) pact, agreement; → SEPAKAT.

pakat II (*M*) → PEKAT I.

pakau I (*C*) a Chinese card game in which a hand consists of three cards; → TIGA *lai*.

pakau II (*ob*) k.o. reinforcing hem or trimming (of rattan, etc.); crosspiece/handle of bucket.

pakau III (*M*) **terpakau** bewildered, perplexed, dazed, aghast.

pakaw (*sl from pakai*) to use drugs (intravenously).

pakbon (*D ob*) trade union.

pakcik clipped form of **bapak kecik**, uncle (parent's younger brother); → PAKLIK.

pakdé 1 clipped form of **bapak gedé**, uncle (parent's older brother). **2** "Big Daddy" (= President Soekarno).

pakdés [pakét Désémber] the package of regulations of December 1987.

pakdéwakang (*ob*) k.o. Buginese-Makassarese sailing boat.

paké → PAKAI.

pakeliran <kelir> (*Jv*) show, performance.

pakem I (*D*) holding well (of brakes). *Rém mobil itu sangat –.* The car has good brakes.
   memakem [and **makem** (*coq*)] to take hold (of brakes).

pakem II (*Jv*) **1** *dalang*'s handbook, scenario for a *wayang*. **2** norm, rule.

Pakem III [Pengawas aliran dan kepercayaan dalam masyarakat] Committee for the Supervision of Trends and Beliefs in Society.

pakenira → PAKANIRA.

paket → SEPAKAT.

pakét (*D*) **1** (postal) parcel. **2** package, a set of programs for a certain purpose, sold as a unit. *– dengan ketentuan harga tanggungan* insured parcel. *– kelistrikan désa* rural electrification package. *– Lebaran* presents for Lebaran. *– pos* parcel post. *– tur(is)/wisata* tour package. *secara –* as a package, not separately, bulk (sale), wholesale.
   memakétkan to make s.t. into a package. *Khusus sarung dari Présidén, ia pakétkan kepada istrinya dengan pesan agar disim-*

pan baik-baik, agar bisa dipakai setiap sholat Ied. He specially packaged the sarong from the President for his wife with the request that it be kept carefully so that it could be used every Ied prayer.

pemakétan packaging.

pakéwuh (*Jv*) **1** reluctant, unwilling. *menyebabkan bawahan rikuh atau – (sungkan) terhadap atasan* making a subordinate feel awkward/ashamed or reluctant to act towards a superior. *Jangan –, silakan duduk di situ.* Make yourself at home; have a seat over there. *éwuh –* ill at ease, (to feel) uncomfortable/awkward/embarrassed. *Orang Timur umumnya masih besar rasa éwuh –nya.* Asians, in general, still feel awkward. *jaman –* an era full of challenges. **2** shyness, timidity, bashfulness. *Meréka sering diliputi perasaan – menampilkan dan mengakui karyanya sendiri.* They are often enveloped by a feeling of embarrassment at displaying and acknowledging their own work.

pakih → FAKIH.

pakihang (among certain groups in Kalimantan) small bottles filled with a special k.o. oil that has been given magical power.

pakihi (*A*) *ilmu –* Islamic canon law. *kitab –* code, body of law.

paking (*D*) **1** gasket, joint. **2** packaging, packing. *– asbés* asbestos gasket. *– flénsa* gasket. *– karét* rubber joint. *– minyak* oil seal.

pakir → FAKIR.

pakis (*Jv*) various species of ferns; → PAKU II. *– angkrik* (*Jv*) k.o. fern, *Diplazium proliferum. – hias* k.o. fern, *Cyras revoluta. – pohon* tree fern, *Cyathea/Alsophila.*

pakjan [*pakét Januari*] the packet of regulations of January 1990.

paklik (*Jv*) /pa'li'/ (clipped form of **bapak cilik**) uncle (parent's younger brother); → PAKCIK.

pakma (*Skr*) a parasitic plant with flowers to which magical powers are ascribed, *Rafflesia patma/hasselti.*

pakné (*Jv*) term of address used by a wife to her husband after they have children.

pakno /pakno/ [*pakét Novémber*] the packet of regulations of November 1988.

pakpui (*C*) **1** fortune-telling in Chinese temple. **2** Chinese fortune-teller.

pakpung I cigarette containing morphine.

Pak Pung II brand name of a well-known peppermint oil used against colds and other illnesses.

paksa I (*Skr*) /paksa/ **1** compulsion, coercion, pressure, necessity. *secara –* by coercion. **2** forced, coerced. *menjalankan – terhadap* to bring pressure (to bear) on. *kawin –* forced wedding, shotgun wedding. *keadaan –* (state of) emergency. *kerja –* forced labor. *sakit – (M)* seriously ill. *surat –* a search/arrest warrant. *uang –* penalty.

memaksa [and **maksa** (*coq*)] to force, compel, make (s.o. do s.t.), coerce. *Kalau tidak mau ikut jangan dipaksa.* If he doesn't want to come, don't force him. *keadaan yang ~* state of emergency, force majeure. *suatu kekuatan ~* a coercive power, an overwhelming force. *~ masuk* to force one's way in(to). *Empat lelaki ~ masuk mobil.* Four men forced their way into the car.

memaksa-maksa to press/urge/exhort again and again.

memaksakan [and **maksain** (*J coq*)] to force/press upon, drive, compel. *~ kehendaknya* to force one's wishes on another. *terlalu ~ diri* to overstrain, overdo s.t. *~ keputusan* (*leg*) to enforce a ruling.

terpaksa [and **kepaksa** (*coq*)] **1** forced, compelled. **2** to be certain to, have no choice but to, can't help but. *Dia ~ meninggal dunia setelah kepalanya ditembus peluru.* After the bullet penetrated his skull, death was inevitable. **3** involuntary; *opp* SUKARÉLA. **keterpaksaan** compulsion, constraint, coercion.

paksaan force, pressure, coercion, duress. *dalam keadaan ~* under duress. *~ badan* (in notarial instruments) imprisonment for debt.

pemaksa compulsory, mandatory.

pemaksaan 1 pressure, force; forcing. **2** *~ keputusan* enforcement of a ruling.

paksa II /pa'sa/ favorable opportunity, good chance; *cp* PELUANG, KESEMPATAN. *menantikan – yang baik* to wait for a favorable opportunity. *angin –* a favorable wind. *– belayar* favorable time to start a voyage/trip. *– tekukur padi rebah, – tikus lengkiang/*

rengkiang terbuka "fallen down rice plants and open granaries are a godsend to a turtledove and mouse respectively," i.e., a blessing, boon; to come at the right moment.

paksa III (*Skr ob*) wing; party; side. *Swa Bhuana –* (motto of the Indonesian Air Force) With Wings We Are Masters in Our Own Country.

Paksebali → GALUNGAN.

paksi I (*Skr*) bird. *– déwata* bird of paradise.

paksi II /paksi/ **1** peg (of a top); → PANGSI I. **2** axis. *– inti* core bar. *– jangkar/kapal* capstan. *– mata* eye axis. *– putar* pin. **3** spindle.

paksina (*Skr ob*) /paksina/ north.

pakta (*D*) /pakta/ pact, treaty. *– militér* military pact. *– nonagrési* nonaggression pact. *– persahabatan* treaty of friendship. *– Pertahanan Atlantik Utara* North Atlantic Treaty Organization; → NATO II. *– Warsawa* Warsaw Pact.

pakter I (*D*) /pakter/ lessee, leaseholder.

mempakterkan to lease, let (out) on lease, put (out) to lease.

pakter II (*D*) /pakter/ kiosk. *– tuak* toddy stall (k.o. bar where alcoholic beverages are served).

paktir (*D mil*) /paktir/ messenger.

pakto /pakto/ [*pakét Oktober*] the packet of regulations of October 1988.

paktur (*D*) /paktur/ → FAKTUR.

paku I 1 nail. **2** (*coq*) silver-colored pip on colonial army uniform (for rank immediately below second lieutenant). **3** (*mil*) shrapnel, fragment (of a shell). **4** name of a *ceki* card. *harga –* fixed price; → HARGA *mati. – Alam* [PA] "Nail of the Universe," i.e., a princely title in Yogyakarta. *– Belanda* obstinate. *– bumi* a large pole of reinforced concrete for high-rise buildings. *– buta* rivet. *– cabut* dowel. *– cengkam* clasp nail, cut nail. *– jamur* thumbtack. *– keling* rivet. *– lekat* binding rivet. *– mati* an unextractable nail. *– mistar* lath nail. *– pasak* brad. *– payung* thumbtack. *– pegas* spring pin. *– pinés* thumbtack. *– rapat* nail in tight. **memaku-rapatkan** to nail down. *– rebana* tack. *– sekrup* screw. *– serat* a nail that is hard to remove. *– siar* jointing nail. *– sumbat* rivet. *– ulir* screw.

berpaku 1 with a nail, with nails. **2** spiked. *sepatu ~* spiked shoes. *~ kepada* to adhere/cling to.

memaku 1 to nail. **2** to captivate, enthrall, fascinate, grip (the audience), grab (one's attention); → MEMESONA.

memakui to stud (a door, etc.) with nails, put nails into.

memakukan to nail down/up.

terpaku 1 nailed (down). **2** captivated, fascinated, gripped, fixated (on). *Masyarakat selama ini hanya ~ pada pemanggilan para jénderal.* Society has been fixated on calling the generals. **3** stuck (in). *Aparat pemerintah jangan ~ pada pola kerja tradisional.* The government apparatus should not be stuck in traditional work patterns. **4** struck dumb.

pemaku *alat ~* nailer.

pemakuan nailing.

paku II 1 fern, bracken. *betapa pun lurus –, ujungnya berkelok juga* a rogue always betrays himself. *– aji* → PAKU *haji. – air* water gladiolus, a floating aquatic plant, *Azolla pinnata,* which hampers the growth of certain plants. *– aji* fern-like plant, bread/sago palm, *Cycas rumphii. – andam* bracken, *Gleichenia linearis. – buah* (*S*) k.o. fern, *Diplazium proliferum. – ékor kuda* horse-tail fern, *Equisetum debile. – gajah* tree fern, *Angiopteris evecta. – haji* an elegant tree with edible leaves, bread palm, *Cycas Rumphii/revoluta. – hias* k.o. fern, sago palm, *Cycas revoluta. – ikan* fish fern, *Blechnum orientale. – kélor* maidenhair fern, *Adiantum cuneatum. – laut* a coarse fern species whose leaves are used as roof covering, coastal/golden leather fern, *Acrostichum aureum. – payung* k.o. fern, *Helminthostachys zeylanica. – pelanduk* slender brake fern, *Pteris ensiformis. – pohon* tree fern, *Cyathea, Alsophila spp. – resam/rotan* (*J*) bracken fern, *Dicranopteris linearis. – tanjung* a species of marsh fern used as a vegetable, vegetable fern, *Diplazium esculentum. – udang* k.o. herb, climbing fern, *Stenochlaena palustris. – ular* k.o. fern, *Pleopeltis phymatodes. – uncal* staghorn fern, *Platycerium bifurcatum.* **2** name of a *ceki* card.

paku-pakuan all k.o. ferns.

pakuak (in Padang) (*M*) → POTONG. *tukang –* killer, slaughterer.

Pakuan the center of the Pajajaran kingdom in West Java at the beginning of the 16th century.

Paku Buwana state name of the *Sunan* of Surakarta; *cp* HAMENGKU BUWANA.

pakuh *burung* – helmeted hornbill, *Rhinoplax vigil*; → BURUNG *tebang mentua*.

pakuk (*M*) **memakuk** to hack (with an axe/hoe/pick).
  pemakuk 1 hacker. 2 axe, hoe, pick (for hacking).
  terpakuk hacked.

pakum (*D*) vacuum; → VAKUM.

pakuncén <kunci> (*Jv*) (lodge of the) caretaker (of a revered cemetery or grave).

pakus (*D ob*) warehouse; → GUDANG.

pakusarakan *semangat* – patriotism.

pakwa clipped form of **bapak tuwa**, uncle (parent's older brother).

pakyu (*C*) k.o. gambling game. *Judi gelap adu ayam dan* – *meresahkan masyarakat.* Illegal gambling on cockfighting and *pakyu* disturb the community.

pal I (*D*) a marker placed along a road; the interval between two markers indicates a distance of about 0.93 miles = 15077 meters (about one kilometer) from the previous marker.
  berpal-pal several kilometers (long or far). *Kita sebagai bangsa yang ~ jauh tertinggal di belakang.* We are a nation who have been left far behind.

pal II (*D? naut*) sheet, i.e., a rope attached to a lower corner of a sail. *membuang* – and
  berpal-pal to tack (in sailing).

pal III → FAAL I.

pal IV (in acronyms) → PERALATAN.

PAL V [Penataran Angkatan Laut] Naval Station.

PAL VI [(Jurusan) Pengetahuan Alam] (Department of) Physics (in Senior High Schools).

PAL VII (*init*) → PERWIRA *Angkatan Laut*.

pala I *buah* – nutmeg. *bunga* – mace (of nutmeg). *manisan* – nutmeg candy. *pohon* – nutmeg tree, *Myristica fragrans. – laki-laki* k.o. tree, Samoan nutmeg, *Myristica fatua.*

pala II (*J*) clipped form of **kepala**. *– gué digetok polisi.* The cop hit me on the head.

pala III fruit, reward, award; → PAHALA.

palagan (*Jv*) battlefield, battleground; → MÉDAN *laga. bertempur ke* – to go into battle.

palai k.o. dish grilled on a pandanus leaf.
  memalai to stew until tender.

palaikat → PELÉKAT.

palak I → FALAK.

palak II (*M*) 1 stifling, muggy, sultry, oppressive. 2 passionate, quick-tempered, angry; excited. 3 adventurous. *– dan bergajul/ nékat* fierce, vicious. *naik* – to get angry; → NAIK *darah.*
  palak-palak ~ *dingin* lukewarm.
  memalak 1 to stir up trouble, make s.t. difficult. 2 [and **malak** (*coq*)] (*J*) to mug s.o.
  pemalak 1 a hot-tempered person, hothead. 2 adventurer. 3 mugger.
  pemalakan mugging.

palak III broke, out of money.

palaka manger.

palakiah → FALAKIAH.

Palaksana → PERWIRA *Pelaksana.*

palam I plug, stopper, cork.
  memalam to plug (up) (a hole, etc.).
  pemalam plug, stopper, cork.

palam II (*D*) palm; → PALEM.

palamarta (*Jv*) merciful, good-natured, kind.

palanangan <lanang> (*Jv*) penis.

palang 1 crossbeam/bar. 2 bolt (of a door, etc.), pawl. 3 cross. *– atap* crossbeam on roof. *– Hitam* a funeral home in Jakarta. *– jalan* roadblock, barrier. *– (jalan) KA/keréta api* (railroad) grade crossing. *– Mérah (Internasional)* (International) Red Cross. *– Mérah Indonésia* [PMI] Indonesian Red Cross. ~ *kepalang-mérahan* Red Cross (*mod*). *merupakan suatu bentuk kepahlawanan* the Red Cross is a form of heroism. *kegiatan ~ Red Cross* activities. *– picu* slide bolt. *– pintu* crossbar used

to reinforce doors from the inside in older Indonesian houses. *mendapat – pintu* to get hell from one's wife for staying out late. *– roda* wheel axle. *– sejajar* parallel bars.

memalang 1 to block/close off (a road). 2 to bolt with a crossbar. *Tiap-tiap malam dia ~ pintu itu.* Every night he bolted the door with a crossbar. 3 to trip s.o. *Kakinya dipalang dari belakang.* He was tripped from behind.

memalangi to block/close off (a road).

memalangkan 1 to block/close with. 2 to crucify.

kepalang (*Jv*) obstructed, blocked, impeded. *Bisnya ~.* The bus was blocked. *~ tanggung* not worth the trouble.

terpalang blocked, obstructed.

palangan crossbar.

pemalang s.t. used to bar/bolt.

pemalangan blocking, obstructing.

Palapa 1 *Amukti* – "Final Blissfulness," the name of the *Sumpah* – or Palapa Oath, pronounced in 1334 by Majapahit's Prime Minister Gadjah Mada (1319–1364) to Queen Tribhuwanatunggadewi to the effect that he did not want to receive any reward until *Nusantara* had been defeated and *Majapahit* is united. 2 Indonesia's first domestic communications satellite, launched in 1976.

pala-pala and **sepala-pala** (in a few proverbs) if really, in case. *(se)pala-pala nama jahat, jangan kepalang* better to hang for a sheep than a lamb. *sepala-pala menipu, baik menipu betul* better to deceive thoroughly than part way. *sepala-pala mencuri jangan tanggung-tanggung* and *sepala-pala mandi biar basah* better to hang for a sheep than a lamb.
  memala-malai at least try to.

palar memalar(kan) 1 to depend/rely/count on. 2 to consent/ agree to, be content/satisfied with. *daripada tak ada, sedikit pun dipalar juga* a bird in the hand is worth two in the bush.

palas I small fan palm, *Licuala spp. – padi* k.o. small fan palm, *Licuala glabra.*

palas II ship's deck (including the outboard, raised platform at the stern of a Malay boat). *– bujur* (*naut*) bow deck. *– lintang* (*naut*) ship's bridge.
  palas-palas 1 clothes rack. 2 observation post.

palasik (*M*) k.o. spirit; → PELESIT I 2.

palat I (*ob*) *kayu* – stocks formerly used to chain and hold up disobedient slaves for caning.

palat II penis. *main* – to commit sodomy. *tahi* – smegma.

palatal (*D ling*) palatal.

palatalisasi (*D ling*) palatalization.

palau scar, cicatrice.

palawija (*Jv*) nonstaple food crops, subsidiary or secondary to rice, such as KACANG *(h)ijau/kedelai/tanah*, JAGUNG *pipilan*, and UBI *jalar/kayu. bunga* – short-lived blossoming nonperennials.

palé I (*J*) *tukang* – gambling chief (in cockfighting). **memalé** 1 to take good care of and strengthen a fighting cock by giving it a massage, good food, etc. 2 to work on s.t. in order to change it, transform. *dipalé menjadi* to be turned into.
  paléan *ayam* ~ a fighting cock which has been put into that condition.

palé II (*J*) → KEPALA I.

palélé middleman; → PAPALÉLÉ.

palem (*D*) 1 palm (tree). *Ahad* – Palm Sunday; → MINGGU *Palma*. 2 (*naut*) tide gauge. *– botol* bottle palm, *Mascarena lagenicaulis. – dop* Fiji fan palm, *Pritchardia pacifica. – ékor rubah* foxtail palm, *Wodyetia bifurcata. – hitam* black palm, *Normanbya normanbyi. – jari* Lady palm, *Rhapis excelsa. – Jepang* Japanese palm. *– kipas* Fiji fan palm, *Pritchardia pacifica. – kuning* yellow palm, *Chrysalidocarpus sp. – mérah* red/sealing wax palm, *Cyrtostachys lakka. – phoenix* Phoenix palm, pygmy date palm, *Phoenix roebelenii. – putri* Christmas/Manila palm, *Veitchia merrili. – raja* royal palm, *Roystonea regia. – sadeng* footstool palm, *Livistona rotundifolia.*

palén (*Jv*) *barang* – sundries, small items, all k.o. cheap household articles, small hardware, etc. *toko* – a store which sells such items. *tukang* – s.o. who sells such items.

paléoantropologi (*D/E*) paleoanthropology. *ahli* – paleoanthropologist.

paléobiologi (*D/E*) paleobiology.
paléobotani (*D/E*) paleobotany.
paléograf (*D*) paleographer.
paléografi (*D/E*) paleography.
paléolitik (*E*) and **paléolitis** (*D*) Paleolithic.
paleolitikum (*D*) paleolithicum, the Paleolithic period.
paléontografi (*D/E*) paleontography.
paléontologi (*D/E*) paleontology.
paléozoologi (*D/E*) paleozoology.
pales (*D infr*) out of tune; → FALS.
palét (*D*) (painter's) palette. *médali – emas* the golden palette prize.
pali I taboo; → PEMALI.
Pali II the Pali language in which some Buddhist scriptures are written.
paliatif (*E*) palliative.
palilah <lilah> (*Jv*) permission, approval. *pemohon asli yang diberi - (ijin) oléh kraton* the original applicant given permission by the *kraton*.
palindrom (*D*) palindrome.
paling I (*J/Jv*) **1** (- + *adj* and some intransitive verbs) -est, most, highest degree of. *- kecil/mahal* the smallest/most expensive. *badan yang – berkuasa di negeri ini* the most authoritative agency in this country. *yang – berbahaya* the most dangerous. *yang – terkemuka* the most prominent, the leading. **2** far, extreme, very, due. *berdiri – kanan* to stand to the far/extreme right. *tercantum – bawah* mentioned at the very bottom (of the list). *terletak – utara Pulau Timor* located due north of Timor. **3** (- + transitive verb) most, best. *- disukai* most favored. *Ford menekankan rasa puasnya pada status negara – disukai bagi Romania dalam urusan-urusan perdagangan dengan AS.* (President) Ford emphasized his satisfaction with Romania's most-favored nation status in matters of trade with the U.S. *Yang – dapat memahami sikap Mesir dan menyetujui persetujuan itu adalah Saudi Arabia dan Yordania.* Those who can best understand Egypt's attitude and agree to the treaty are Saudi Arabia and Jordan. *- atas* uppermost. *tanah - atas* topsoil. *- banter/cuma* at most. *Yang tinggal – cuma 40 persén* At most 40 percent remained. *- hanya* at most, not exceeding. *Sehari dia hanya bisa menjaring rezeki Rp 1.000 bersih.* Every day he was able to earn at most Rp 1,000 net. *- malam* not later than (in the evening). *- sedikit* a (the) least, not less than. *- sedikit sepuluh* at least ten. *- sial* under the most adverse circumstances, if worst comes to worst, at worst. *- tidak* at least, in any event, at any rate; anyhow, anyway. *Buah durian merupakan buah musiman. – tidak di negeri kita.* The durian is a seasonable fruit, at least in our country. *- untung* at (the) best.
paling-paling 1 extremely, exceedingly, at most, at best. *Saya ~ hanya dapat memberi nasihat.* At best, I can only give advice. **2** very bad/naughty. *Anaknya mémang ~, masa orang lagi berjalan dilémpari dengan tahi kuda.* His child is really incorrigible; can you imagine that he hurls balls of horseshit at passersby.
sepaling sole, just that one. *kata yang ~ itu* just that one word.
paling II berpaling 1 to turn one's head to the side, look to the side. *Dia tidak ~ apabila namanya dipanggil.* He didn't turn his head when his name was called. *Sebelum menyeberang, ia ~ ke kiri dan ke kanan.* Before crossing the street, he looked left and right. **2** to turn away (from). *~ dari agamanya* to abandon/turn away from one's religion. **3** to change. *~ haluan* a) to change course. b) to switch to another subject. *~ hati* to have a change of heart. *~ ke dalam* to look inward; inward-looking. *Kedua negara adikuasa terpaksa menganut politik ~ ke dalam.* The two superpowers were compelled to adhere to an inward-looking policy. *~ sembah* to be disloyal (to the king, etc.). *~ tadah* to become an apostate.
memalingkan [and **malingin** (*J coq*)] to turn s.t. (away), divert, make s.o. turn (his head). *~ haluan* to change course. *~ muka* to turn one's head. *Ia ~ mukanya ke arah lain.* He looked in the other direction. *Fatimah ~ mukanya karena tidak mau terkena cahaya matahari.* Fatimah turned her face aside because she didn't want to get the sun on her face. *~ pandangan ke* to (cast a) glance at. *~ pandangan ke belakang* to look back(wards). *~*

pendiriannya to turn away from one's point of view, change one's opinion. *~ percakapan* to switch subjects (of conversation).
palingan that which is changeable, that which is easily turned. *hati ~ Allah, mata ~ sétan* and *neraca ~ bungkal, hati ~ Tuhan* one's thoughts are changeable/can easily be changed.
pemalingan turning aside (one's face).
palinologi (*D*) palynology.
palis I berpalis and **memalis** to glance out of the corner of one's eye, cast a sideways look, avert (one's eyes). *~ muka* to turn one's face aside, avert one's eyes.
palis II (*J*) **berpalis(kan)** polished with.
memalis 1 to polish, shine. **2** to touch lightly with the fingertip.
memaliskan 1 to spread on evenly (of polish). **2** to touch lightly with the fingertip.
terpalis involved in (a dirty business), gotten a bad reputation, smeared.
palis III (*D ob*) palace; → ISTANA.
palismén → KEPAILITAN.
palit I 1 ointment (for eyebrows). *si – gila* a love philter that is smeared on and will drive a girl crazy with love. **2** sebum (skin oil). *sudah calit, jangan –* don't make matters worse than they are.
sepalit a dab of.
memalit to smear on (rouge/eye shadow, etc.).
memalitkan to spread on evenly (of ointment).
terpalit 1 smeared (on). **2** involved in (a dirty business).
pemalit *~ bibir* lipstick; → LIPSTIK, PEMÉRAH *bibir*.
palit II → PAILIT.
palka (*Port naut*) hold (of a ship).
palkon (*sl*) [kepala kontol] head of the penis.
pallu butung (in South Sulawesi) fried banana fritters.
palm /palem/ and **palma I** (*D*) palm (tree); → PALEM.
Palma II [(Ilmu) Pengetahuan Alam dan Matématika] Natural Sciences and Mathematics.
palmarosa k.o. grass; the oil produced from the flowers is a substitute for *minyak kenanga*.
palmistri (*E*) palmistry.
palontara (in Sidrap, South Sulawesi) s.o. who can read lontar writing in the old Buginese language, a local historian and agricultural advisor.
pal-palam (*J*) to act crazy.
palsabet (*J*) **dipalsabet 1** on (the) average. **2** to be equally divided. *~ saja seorang seribu rupiah* divided up so that each person gets one thousand rupiahs.
palsu (*Port*) **1** false, counterfeit, forged. **2** phony. **3** unfair, dishonest. **4** not pure (of the voice).
sepalsu as fake as.
memalsu(kan) [and **malsuin** (*J coq*)] **1** to counterfeit, falsify, forge. *Meréka sengaja memalsukan nomor casis dan nomor mesin sehingga tidak mudah diketahui kepalsuannya.* They purposely falsified the number of the chassis and engine so that the forgery could not easily be traced. **2** to adulterate.
palsu-memalsu counterfeiting. *soal ~ paspor* counterfeiting passports. *bidang ~* the field of counterfeiting.
kepalsuan counterfeit, forgery, falseness.
pemalsu counterfeiter, forger, adulterator.
pemalsuan 1 falsification. **2** counterfeiting, forging. *~ (mata) uang* counterfeiting of money. **3** adulteration.
paltu (*Hind Port?*) **1** deputy, assistant. **2** acting, temporary (holder of position or office).
palu I 1 hammer, mallet. **2** gavel. **3** blow. *sebelum mengetuk – vonis* before pronouncing the verdict. *- arit* hammer and sickle. *- angin* pneumatic drill. *- besar* sledgehammer. *- bor* hammer drill. *- bulat* ball hammer. *- genggam* claw hammer. *- godam* club, bludgeon, sledgehammer. **memalu-godamkan** to hammer out s.t. *- pemutus (arus)* (*elec*) breaker arm. *- pimpinan* gavel. *- tangkai* sledgehammer.
berpalu (*cla*) to dash against. *ombak ~ pantai* waves dashed against the beach.
berpalu-palu(an) to hit e.o.
memalu 1 to hit (with a stick). **2** to beat (a drum/gong, etc.).
palu-memalu to hit e.o.

paluan blow with a hammer.

palu II berpalu-palu to barter goods.

paluh 1 eddy, whirlpool. **2** deep pool (after a high tide/rain storm), puddle.

palun (*M*) **berpalu-palun** to embrace/hug e.o.
  memalun to clench, clasp in one's arms, hug, embrace.
  memalunkan to put (one's arms) around.
  palunan grip, grasp, embrace.

palung 1 pool; bed, watercourse. **2** manger. **3** (*geol*) trough, basin. – *ikan* aquarium; → AKUARIUM. – *ikan* fishbowl. – *kuku* nail bed. – *laut* sea trough. – *Pasifik* Pacific Basin. – *sungai* river bed.

palungan 1 crib, manger (of Jesus in the stable at Bethlehem). **2** trough.

palut wrapper, covering, envelope. *élok* –, *pengebat kurang* all is not gold that glitters.
  berpalut(kan) to be wrapped in/with. *buku* ~ *plastik* a book wrapped in plastic.
  memalut(i) to wrap, cover, envelope.
  memalutkan to wrap with/around.
  terpalut wrapped.
  palutan covering.
  pemalut wrapper. *tinggal kulit* – *tulang* be only skin and bones.

palwa [penjualan dan penyéwaan] (video) sales and rentals.

PAM I (*init*) → PERUSAHAAN *Air Minum*.

PAM II → PARTAI *Adil Makmur*.

pam III (in acronyms) → PENGAMANAN.

Pama I → PERWIRA *pertama*.

pama II [perwira pertama] officers from second lieutenant to captain.

pamah (*cla*) lowland.

pamajikan <pajik> (*S*) wife, spouse.

pamali → PEMALI.

paman (*Jv*) **1** uncle (younger brother of parent); → (O)OM, PAKCIK. – *Sam* Uncle Sam (symbol of the United States). **2** younger cousin of parent
  berpaman to call s.o. "uncle".

Pamardisiwi (*Jv*) name of the Juvenal Detention Center in Jakarta [*pamardi* (*Jv*) = education; *siwi* (*Jv*) = child].

pamarta (*K*) savior, redeemer.

pambakal (in Central Kalimantan) village head.

pambek (*Jv*) pride; proud.

pamegat and **pameget** (*S*) *juragan* – sir, master (of the house).

Pamén → PERWIRA *menengah*.

paméo (*M*) **1** proverb, saying. **2** slogan, catchphrase, buzzword.
  mempaméokan to make into a slogan, use as a catchphrase.

pamér (*J/Jv*) **1** show, exhibition. **2** to show off. *naluri* – exhibitionism. *Mungkin di sini, naluri* – *diri yang bicara.* Probably exhibitionism is what speaks here. *ruang* – showroom. – *kekuatan* show of force. – *tongkrongan* social display.
  berpamér ~ *diri* to show off, make an exhibit of o.s.
  mem(p)améri to model (clothes).
  mem(p)amérkan 1 to exhibit, show, display. **2** to show off, make a display of. ~ *kepandaiannya* to show off one's cleverness.
  terpamér exhibited, displayed.
  paméran exhibition, show, performance. *untuk* ~ for show, as a demonstration. ~ *bendéra* showing the flag. ~ *buku* book exposition/exhibit. ~ *busana* fashion show; → PAGELARAN *busana*. ~ *dagang* trade fair. ~ *dirgantara* air show. ~ *foto* photography exhibit. ~ *ilmiah* scientific exhibition. ~ *kekuatan* show of force. ~ *keliling* traveling exhibition. ~ *lukisan* art exhibit. ~ *makanan* food festival. ~ *mode batik* batik fashion show. ~ (*modél*) *pakaian* fashion show. ~ *sandang murah* inexpensive clothing show. ~ *senjata* military review. ~ *tunggal* one-man show. **berpaméran** to put on an exhibition.
  pemamér exhibitor, displayer.
  pemaméran display(ing). ~ *dagangan* commodities display.

pamerih → PAMRIH.

pamflét (*D*) pamphlet. – *gelap* clandestine pamphlet.

pamili → FAMILI.

paminggir <pinggir> (*Jv*) *istri* – concubine.

pamit (*Jv*) **1** permission to leave/be absent. **2** to ask permission to leave; to say good-bye. *minta* – to ask permission to leave; to say good-bye. *Ternyata Bagio juga minta* –. It appears that Bagio also said good-bye. *tanpa* – without saying good-bye. – *pada* to say good-bye to.
  berpamit(an) ~ *dengan/kepada*, **memamiti** and **pamitan** to ask permission to leave; to say good-bye, take one's leave. *Duta Besar Singapura Othman Wok kemarin berpamitan kepada Ménko Polkam M. Panggabéan.* Yesterday Singapore's Ambassador Othman Wok said good-bye to Coordinating Minister for the Political and Security Sector M. Panggabean. *A. pamitan gurunya.* A. said good-bye to the teacher. *Ia memamiti temannya.* He said good-bye to his friend.
  pamitan good-bye, farewell.

pamong (*Jv*) **1** guardian, caretaker. **2** (in the *Taman Siswa* school structure) teacher. – *désa* village officials, i.e., the executive part of village administration. – *Praja* Civil Service.
  kepamongan Civil Service matters, having to do with the Civil Service. *Gubernur untuk DKI dengan setumpuk problémnya, seharusnya orang yang mengerti* ~ *serta menghayati arti sebuah kota métropolitan dan perkembangannya.* The Governor of the Special Capital Region (of Jakarta), with its many problems, should be a man who understands Civil Service matters and who can fully understand the meaning of a metropolis and its development. *sikap* ~ *aparat* the civil service attitude of government agencies.

pamor 1 whitish stripes or flames in steel weapons, such as krises, which become visible when they are cleaned, a proof of excellence. **2** power, authority, influence. **3** glory, splendor, fame, prestige, popularity. – *Singapura buat orang Indonésia sebagai tempat belanja entah sampai kapan rasanya takkan padam.* Singapore's prestige as a place for Indonesians to go shopping will not die down for who knows how long. *gejala redupnya* – *Taman Siswa* symptoms of a decline in Taman Siswa schools. *Sejak itu –nya makin bersinar.* Since then, its splendor has continued to sparkle. *–nya mulai suram.* Its splendor has started to become dull. *Sedikit demi sedikit pudar –nya.* Little by little its splendor has faded. *kehilangan* – to have lost its splendor, become tarnished.
  berpamor 1 to be damascened. **2** to have prestige.

pampa *kayu* – k.o. tree, New Guinea rosewood, *Vitex cofassus*.

pampan anchor pocket.

pampang memampang(kan) to unfold, display.
  terpampang 1 to be displayed, be on view, be spread out. *Gambarnya* ~ *di mana-mana.* His picture was displayed everywhere. **2** striking, notable.
  pemampangan unfolding, displaying.

pampas 1 compensation, indemnification; → GANTI *rugi*. **2** satisfaction, reparation.
  memampas to indemnify/compensate s.o.
  pampasan indemnification, compensation. *kain* ~ cloth sent to Indonesia as part of Japanese war reparations. ~ *perang* war reparations.
  pemampas s.t. that serves as compensation/indemnification.
  pemampasan indemnification, indemnifying, compensation, compensating.

pampat 1 stopped up (of pipes/drains), clogged. **2** to stand still, stagnate (of water).
  memampat 1 to press, squeeze, compress. **2** to stop up, plug up; → MAMPAT I.
  memampatkan to clog up (a drainpipe, etc.). *Segundukan sampah yang dibuang ke selokan itu ~nya.* The pile of trash thrown in the drain has clogged it up.
  terpampat compressible. **keterpampatan** compressibility.
  pampatan compression.
  pemampat press, compressor.
  pemampatan compressing.

pampet → PAMPAT.

pamplét (*D*) → PAMFLÉT.

pampung (*geol*) vesicle.

pamrih (*Jv*) **1** intention, purpose, aim. **2** ulterior motive, self-interest. **3** ambition. *bekerja tanpa* – to work without ulterior motive, without expecting anything in return. *sifat ilmu yang tanpa* – scientific disinterestedness.

berpamrih to have an ulterior motive.

kepamrihan self-interest, personal interest, ulterior motive.

pamukti (*Jv*) substitute housing/dwelling place. *-nya lebih baik, ada listrik dan jalanannya beraspal.* The substitute housing was better; there was electricity and the roads were asphalted.

pamulang (*Jv*) instructor.

pamungkas <pungkas> (*Jv*) **1** latest, most recent. **2** deadly, fatal. *senjata* – a) deadly weapon. b) one's special "weapon" (such as an effective smash in tennis). **3** the military resort command (*Korém 072*) in Yogyakarta.

pamur → PAMOR.

pan I (*D*) comprising, embracing, or common to all or every, pan-. *Pan-Amérika* Pan-American. *Pan-Arabisme* Pan-Arabism. *Pan-Islamisme* Pan-Islamism. *Pan-Asia* Pan-Asian.

pan II (*D*) (cooking) pan.

  mempan and **mengepan** to cook (in a pan).

pan III (*J*) indicates surprise that a hearer doesn't know s.t.; → KAN III, KAPAN. *– rumahnya di Jalan Madura?* His house is on Madura Street, isn't it?

pan IV (in acronyms) → PANITIA.

PAN V → PARTAI *Amanat Nasional.*

pana I terpana(-pana) to be amazed/dumbfounded/stupefied. *Aku hanya – dengan darahku mengencang bergelora karena takut.* I was just stupefied and my pulse was racing from fear.

pana II → FANA.

panah 1 (*anak* –) arrow. **2** (*ibu* –) bow. **3** (*tanda* –) arrow (in typography: → = see, *vide*). *kepala* – arrowhead. *melepaskan* – to shoot an arrow. *– Amor/Asmara* Cupid's dart. *– api* rocket, roman candle. *– arah* blinker. *– kelodan* a) thunderbolt. b) shooting star, meteor. c) k.o. (archer's) bow (a legendary weapon). *– liang* k.o. hornet. *– matahari* the sun's rays. *– petir* thunderbolt.

  berpanah arrowy.

  berpanah-panahan to shoot arrows at e.o.

  mamanah to shoot an arrow at.

  memanahi (*pl obj*) to shoot many arrows at.

  mamanahkan to shoot (s.t. like an arrow). *~ api asmara* to shoot Cupid's dart.

  terpanah hit by an arrow.

  panahan archery.

  pemanah archer. **sepemanah** as far as an arrow will fly.

panai a wooden tray.

panakawan (*Jv*) **1** court jesters (in *wayang*). **2** follower, adherent, servant.

panar (*M*) amazed, astonished, dumbfounded, stupefied.

panas 1 a) hot, warm. b) heat; → BAHANG. **2**a) (*sakit* –) (to have) a fever, (high) temperature. b) feverish; → KEMREKES. *Kalau -nya meninggi, dia mengigau yang bukan-bukan.* When his fever was high, he was hallucinating. *Sudah tiga hari anak saya – badannya tinggi serta batuk pilek.* My child has had a high fever for three days and has had flu-like symptoms. **3** fierce (of heat, etc.), heated, flushed; hot-blooded; passionate. *Sepasang wisatawan dari Australia sedang – beradu bibir.* A couple of Australian tourists were kissing e.o. passionately. **4** vehement, violent, tense, explosive (of the atmosphere, etc.), critical (of the situation). *Suasana menjadi –.* The atmosphere became tense. *derajat* – temperature. *dingin-dingin* – now cold now hot. *hujan* – sun shower (according to folk belief a Chinese is dying). *laki-bini* – a couple having marital problems or who are incompatible with e.o. *pengukur* – fever/clinical thermometer. *rumah* – a haunted house; → RUMAH *angker. timbang* – a full measure. *– setahun dihapuskan hujan sehari* one quarrel will destroy a long friendship. *– tidak sampai petang* prosperity doesn't last. *sudah – berbaju pula* when it rains it pours. *– bara* a) burning/baking hot, glowing heat. b) pent-up wrath/anger. *– berdenting* suffocating/stifling heat. *– bumi* [pabum] geothermal. *kepanas-bumian* geothermics, geothermal. *– dingin* a) to be on pins and needles. b) ups and downs. c) cold and hot by turns (a symptom of malaria). *Rasmani pernah digigit seékor ular. Badan rasanya – dingin.* Rasmani was once bitten by a snake. He felt hot and cold by turns. d) malaria. *– embun* "heat and dew". *dipanasembunkan* to be weather-beaten. *– hati* easily irritated, cross, annoyed, exasperated, cranky. **memanas hati**

annoying, exasperating, irritating. **pemanas hati** hot/quick-tempered, irascible. *– jenis* specific heat. *– keras* suffocating/stifling heat. *– kuku* lukewarm. *– kuping* to be angry/resentful; anger, resentment, hard feelings. *– kupingnya mendengar ...* he got angry when he heard ... *– matahari* solar, the heat of the sun. *– mendenting* suffocating/stifling heat. *– pijar* red hot. *– sengangar* noonday heat. *– tangan* a) (about a doctor or midwife) who provides poor service. b) (about a farmer) whose crops don't grow well, he has a black thumb. *– terik* suffocating/stifling heat. *– tis* malaria. *– tubuh* body temperature.

  panas-panas 1 glowing (hot). **2** brand new. **3** when it is hot. *~nya minum és* to drink iced drinks when it's hot. *~ hendak ...* unable to stop o.s. from doing s.t., hot to do s.t. *~ tahi ayam* a) short-lived enthusiasm, flash in the pan. b) trendy, fashionable.

  sepanas as hot as.

  sepanas-panasnya 1 as hot as ... is. **2** as hot as it can be.

  berpanas 1 to sit in the sun; endure the heat. **2** to heat up.

  berpanas-panas to warm o.s. in the sun.

  memanas 1 to be(come) hot/warm. **2** (*Jv*) to sunbathe.

  memanasi to make s.t. hot, heat s.t. up. *Tolong panasi sop saya.* Please heat up my soup.

  memanas-manasi [and **manas-manasin** (*J coq*)] to instigate, incite.

  memanaskan 1 to heat (up), warm (up). **2** to encourage, inspire, stimulate. *~ hati* annoying, exasperating, irritating.

  memanas-manaskan to incite.

  memperpanas to warm s.t. up some more, raise the temperature of, heighten (a conflict).

  terpanas the hottest.

  panasan a warm place, warmth. **berpanasan** to sunbathe.

  kepanasan 1 heat. **2** (to feel) too hot, suffer from the heat. **3** to get the heat/warmth of.

  pemanas 1 heater, heating (*mod*) (*alat* ~) heating apparatus; couveuse, incubator. *alat ~ air* hotwater-heater. *~ air yang menggunakan sistém panas matahari* solar-powered water heater. *tukang kompor ~ kericuhan* instigator, inciter. *~ sajian* food warmer. *~ surya* solar heater. **2** hothead.

  pemanasan 1 heating, warming. **2** heating up, warming (up). *~ awal* preheating. *~ bumi/global* global warming. *~ ulang* reheating.

panasaran → PENASARAN.

panatik → FANATIK.

panau ringworm, *Tinea versicolor* or *T. flava*, which causes pale patches on brown skins. *– besi, Tinea nigra,* which causes small black patches, *esp* on the face. *– bunga,* which causes light patches. *– lekir,* which causes light, streaky patches. *– mengkarung,* which causes light hair-covered patches. *– tekukur,* which causes small, light patches.

Panawanganisasi a nation-wide system for land and water conservation through integrated efforts of farmers; the system started in the Panawangan-Ciamis subdistrict.

panca I (*Skr*) (the five fingers of) the hand. *main –* and **berpanca** to clasp an opponent's fingers and to try to press down his forearm, a k.o. arm-wrestling.

panca II (*Skr*) five (in compounds).

panca III (*Skr*) multi-, poly-.

Panca Agama (*Skr neo*) the Five National Religions officially recognized as compatible with 'a belief in God': Islam, Catholicism, Protestantism, Buddhism, and Hinduism.

Pancabalikrama and **Pancawalikrama** (*Bal*) a ceremony worshiping God in His manifestation as Shiva asking that the state and nation be protected from disasters, that He remit human sins and lead the way to good deeds; it takes place once every 10 years at the Pura Besakih.

panca bersaudara The Pan Brothers (in PT Pan Brothers Textiles). *Nama Pan Brothers itu sendiri diambil dari kata Panca Bersaudara alias lima bersaudara.* The name Pan Brothers itself was taken from the words *Panca Bersaudara,* i.e., the five brothers.

pancabicara (*Skr*) **1** (*ob*) a five-pronged pendant worn by rulers at their installation and by bridegrooms at their marriage. **2** (a mixture of) five oils, flowers, etc.

pancab(h)uta (*Bal*) the five elements: *pertiwi* (earth), *apah* (water), *téja* (fire), *bayu* (air) and *akasa* (ether).

Panca Cinta (*Skr neo*) The Five Loves, i.e., the educational policy adopted by the nonreligious and communist-oriented educational institutions under President Soekarno.

pancadharma (*Skr neo*) five obligations.

Panca Dharma Bhakti (*Skr neo*) The Five Obligations of University Students.

Panca Dharma Wanita (*Skr neo*) The Five Obligations of a Woman.

Panca Gatra (*Skr neo*) a social system with the following aspects: ideological, sociopolitical, socioeconomic, sociocultural and national defense and security.

pancaind(e)ra (*Skr*) the five senses.

pancak (*Jv*) – *suji* railing(s), trelliswork, fence made of laths or trellis.

pancaka (*Skr*) crematorium, funeral pyre.

pancakara (*Jv*) **1** to fight, be at odds with e.o. **2** to wage a war.

Panca Karsa/Karya Husada (in *Pelita IV*) The Five Health Goals: a) increase and consolidate health efforts; b) increase the number of health workers; c) control, procure and supervise medicine, food and substances dangerous to health; d) improve nutritious substances and increase environmental health; e) enhance and reinforce legal management.

pancakembar quintuplets.

Panca Krida (*Skr neo*) The Five-Point Working Program of the First *Kabinét Pembangunan* (formed on July 5, 1968).

pancal I (*Jv*) *sepéda* – push-bike.
  memancal to pedal (a bike forward).
  pancalan pedal.

pancal II delay.

pancalima k.o. forecast or prediction made with the fingers.

pancalipat fivefold.

pancalogam (*Skr + Tam*) **1** alloy of five metals. **2** veined marbles, varicolored beads, etc.

pancalomba pentathlon (five sports events, such as running/long jump/high jump/discus throwing/javelin throwing).

pancalongok (*J*) petty thief; → LONGOK, PANCA I.

pancamarga (*Skr neo*) The Five Roads (of leadership).

pancamuka (*Skr neo*) The Five Aspects contained in the *Supersemar*: historic, ideological, political, juridical, and spiritual.

pancanegara (*Skr neo*) five nations, *usu* the five nonaligned nations which sponsored the *Konperénsi Afrika-Asia*: Indonesia, Ghana, India, the United Arab Republic, and Yugoslavia.

pancang I 1 pole, stake, post, pile, a length of wood or metal driven into the ground. *mesin* – pile driver. **2** boundary pole, border line. **3** sapling. *bagai – digoncang arus* to trim one's sails according to the wind.
  berpancangan (*pl subj*) stuck in, implanted, rammed in.
  berpancangkan to be implanted into s.t.
  memancang 1 to drive (a stake/pole, etc.) into the ground, ram. *Kayu itu dipancang di tengah-tengah gelanggang*. The pole was driven into the middle of the arena. **2** to stake out. ~ *gelanggang* a) to stake out an arena (for cockfighting, etc.). b) to throw a party (for a wedding, etc.). ~ *rumah* to begin to construct a house. ~ *tiang* to pile drive. **3** straight up, standing upright (like a stake driven into the ground).
  memancangkan 1 to drive/plant a stake/pole, etc. into the ground. **2** to insert/place/put (an article in the newspaper). **3** to establish (power/influence, etc.).
  terpancang 1 driven into the ground. **2** demarcated by stakes. **3** put/stuck up, erected. **4** rooted to the spot. *Ia ~ melihat pemandangan yang indah itu*. He was rooted to the spot looking at the beautiful view. ~ *bagai patung* struck dumb. **5** well-grounded, established (of reputation/attitude, etc.).
  pancangan 1 stake, post, pole, pile, s.t. driven into the ground. ~ *hidup* firm beliefs. ~ *kaki* foothold. ~ *kaki pantai* beachhead. ~ *tonggak* a) milestone. b) landmark. **2** place where s.t. is driven into the ground.
  pemancang pile driver.
  pemancangan 1 pile driving. *melakukan ~ tiang pertama* ground breaking. **2** insertion (of an article in the newspaper). **3** establishment (of power/influence, etc.). **4** pegging down (of a tent).

pancang II – *bendéra* a marine fish, ocellated coral fish, six-spined butterfly fish, *Parachaetodon ocellatus*.

pancaniti (*Jv*) conference hall (in the *kraton*).

pancapersada (*Skr*) **1** a tiered elevated floor on which prominent persons sit during official ceremonies. **2** a many-tiered bathing place. **3** (*cla*) k.o. house of pleasure.

Panca Prabawa Manunggaling Citra (*Skr neo*) The Motto of the Directorate General of Immigration, meaning: *Dari Setiap Warga Imigrasi Dituntut Adanya*: a) *Sikap Tangguh*; b) *Tanggon*; c) *Tanggap*; d) *Trampil, dan* e) *Wibawa*. From Each Member of the Directorate General of Immigration is demanded that he/she: a) stand firm; b) be trustworthy; c) be smart; d) be skilled; and e) be authoritative.

pancar 1 descendant, offspring, scion. **2** transmit, relay. *menara/stasiun* – *ulang* relay tower/station. (*pesawat terbang*) – *gas* jet (plane). – *luas* far and wide. – *Melayu* a Malay; of Malay descent. – *luas* transmission. **memancar-luaskan** to transmit (a radio broadcast). *dipancarluaskan oléh 48 stasion RRI di seluruh tanah air* broadcast by 48 stations of the Republic of Indonesia Radio all over the country.
  sepancar of the same kind/origin/descent, kindred, related, have a common source/origin.
  berpancar 1 to spout, spray, gush (out), flow out quickly. *Air memancar ke luar dari pipa yang bocor itu*. The water gushed out of the leaking pipe. **2** to shine brightly, give out bright light. *Matahari ~ cahayanya ke atas bumi*. The sun shines brightly onto the earth.
  berpancar-pancar scattered all over, dispersed.
  berpancaran (*pl subj*) **1** to spread everywhere. **2** to gush forth, spout (out). *peluh* ~ bathed in sweat. **3** to shine in every direction, brilliant.
  memancar → BERPANCAR.
  memancarkan 1 to spout (forth), gush, spurt out, squirt, send forth. *Di sana sini mata air ~ air yang jernih*. Here and there the well spouted out clear water. **2** to radiate (light). **3** to broadcast, send out. *Pidato Présidén Soeharto dipancarkan oléh RRI*. President Soeharto's speech was broadcast by the Republic of Indonesia Radio. **4** to give birth to. *Brawijaya ~ raja-raja Majapahit*. Brawijaya gave birth to the kings of Majapahit.
  terpancar 1 spurted (out), squirted (out), emitted, sent forth. ~ *rata* spread out evenly. **2** born, sprouted. **3** broadcast.
  pancaran 1 ray, flow, stream, jet. **2** descendant. **3** image, reflection. **4** broadcast, emission, (radio) signal. ~ *air* fountain. (*sastra ialah*) ~ *kehidupan* (literature is) the image of life. ~ *kembali* reflection. ~ *mani* ejaculation. ~ *mata* (bright) glance (of the eye). ~ *pasir* sandblast. **sepancaran** homologous.
  pemancar 1 radiator. **2** transmitter. ~ *air* fountain. – *induk* main radio station. ~ *pengulang* repeater, i.e., a device capable of receiving and sending radio signals. ~ *radio* radio transmitter. – *télévisi* television transmitter.
  pemancaran broadcasting, transmitting, sending out. ~ *mani* ejaculation. ~ *ulang* relay.

pancaragam (*Skr + Tam*) **1** various, motley, all k.o. **2** band, orchestra. *seperangkatan* – a troupe of musicians. – *tentara* military music.

pancaraja – *diraja* (*cla*) royal bier.

pancarangkap quintuplet(s).

pancaroba 1 turn of the tide, transition (period); showers. *musim* – change of season. **2** difficult period; puberty.

pancarona → PANCAWARNA.

pancarutan (*Jv*) a homemade firearm. *Biasanya para peladang sambil mengerjakan ladang selalu membawa senjata api buatan sendiri yang dinamakan* –. Farmers usually carry a homemade firearm called a *pancarutan* when they work their fields.

Panca Setia Five Pledges of Loyalty, a loyalty oath taken by government employees.

Pancasila (*Skr neo*) The Five Principles of National Ideology proclaimed by President Soekarno on June 1, 1945: (following is the official Ministry of Information English version): belief in the one and only God; a just and civilized humanity; the unity of Indonesia; democracy guided by the inner wisdom in the unanimity arising out of deliberations among representatives; social justice for the whole of the Indonesian people.
  berpancasila to adhere to/based on *Pancasila*. *kehidupan bermasyarakat yang* ~ a community life based on *Pancasila*.
  mempancasilakan to bring s.t. under *Pancasila*, pancasilize.

"Saya ingin ~ dunia," katanya. "I want to pancasilize the world," he said.
kepancasilaan Pancasilism. *~ kita dan kesetiaan kita kepada UUD 45* our Pancasilism and our loyalty to the 1945 Constitution.
Pancasilais supporter of *Pancasila*, pancasilist.
  mempancasilaiskan to make s.o. into a supporter of *Pancasila*.
Pancasilawan *(infr)* → PANCASILAIS.
pancasona magical saying that can bring back the dead.
pancasuara *(Skr neo)* medley of voices.
pancasuda forest *gambir* plant, *Jasmianum pubescens.*
pancatantra five fables in the form of a series of stories; they originated in India.
Panca Tunggal Quintumvirate, the five-member group of local officials under President Soekarno *usu* composed of the head of the local government, military and police commanders, public prosecutors, and a representative of the National Front; → MUSPIDA.
Panca Usaha *(Skr neo)* The Five Efforts, i.e., the system used to provide agricultural guidance to farmers. At the initiative of the *Institut Pertanian Bogor*, it comprises: a) the use of superior seeds; b) the use of artificial fertilizers; c) an adequate irrigation system; d) a well-regulated irrigation system, and e) a good method of soil conservation.
pancawarna *(Skr neo)* 1 multicolored, of many colors. 2 brightly colored.
pancawarsa *(Skr neo)* five-year period, lustrum, quinquennium.
pancawindu forty years (five eight-year periods).
pancén *(S)* a percentage of agricultural yield given to a *lurah* as compensation for service rendered to the community.
pancer I *(J/Jv) akar – → AKAR tunggang.*
pancer II → PANCAR.
panci I *(D)* cooking pot, pan. *wajan dan* – pots and pans. *– tekan* pressure cooker. *– tétésan* drip pan. *– tuang* casting ladle.
Panci II [Padalarang dan Cileunyi] the Padalarang-Cileunyi toll road in South Bandung; → PADALEUNYI.
pancing 1 fishing rod. 2 fishing hook. *tukang* – and – *mancing (Jv)* fisherman, angler. 3 fishing. *– biasa* pole and line. *– kacar* fishing for octopus without a hook. *– rawai* fishing line strung with many hooks. *– tunda* a fishing hook tugged behind a prau. *– ulur* hand line.
  memancing [and **mancing** *(coq)*] 1 to fish/go fishing, catch (fish with bait). *lomba ~ di laut dalam* deep-sea fishing competition. *Tiap-tiap minggu banyak orang ~ ikan di laut.* Every week many people go fishing at sea. 2 to prime (a pump). 3 to do some action in order to get s.t., provoke, invite (questions). *~ dalam belanga* like shooting fish in a barrel (s.t. very easy). *~ di air keruh* to fish in troubled waters. *~ hati* to appease s.o. *~ jawaban* to try to get an answer out of s.o. *~ kehéranan* to cause surprise. *~ keinginan* to tempt. *~ kesalahan* to find fault. *~ minat* to arouse interest. *~ musuh* to draw out the enemy. *~ pembeli* to tempt buyers. *~ pertempuran* to provoke a fight. *~ rahasia* to ferret out a secret. *~ seléra* mouthwatering. *~ suara* to get votes (at an election). *~ tawa* to draw laughter. *~ tepuk tangan* to elicit applause, get applauded.
  terpancing [and **kepancing** *(coq)*] 1 get caught (of fish). *Tak satu pun dari enam ékor ikan yang ~ merupakan hasil pancingan Soeprapto.* Not one of the six fish hooked were caught by Soeprapto. 2 provoked, incited. 3 tempted. 4 taken in. *Masyarakat jangan ~ isu.* The community should not be taken in by rumors.
  pancingan 1 bait, testing the waters (to see if s.o. will rise to the bait). 2 provocation. 3 catch, trick. *~ sapu tangan* a trick used by pickpockets: one of them drops a handkerchief, another yells "Who dropped a handkerchief?" and in the ensuing uproar another one steals s.t. from the victim.
  kepancingan sore throat, pharyngitis, laryngitis (it feels like there are fishhooks in the throat); → KAIL-KAIL.
  pemancing 1 *(~ ikan)* fisherman, angler. *~ nafsu makan* appetizer; → PEMBANGKIT *seléra/nafsu makan. ~ suara* vote-getter (in an election). 2 instigator, inciter.
  pemancingan *~ tindak pidana* incitement.

pancir front part of a procession, etc.
pancit memancit to spout/squirt out bit by bit.
  memancitkan to squirt s.t. out bit by bit.
  terpancit squirted out.
panco *(J)* arm-wrestling. *adu* – arm wrestling. *bertanding/main –* to arm wrestle.
pancoléng → PENCOLÉNG.
pancong I *(J) kué* – a cake made of grated coconut, rice flour, and coconut milk.
pancong II *(J)* vulva, vagina.
pancong III k.o. mahjong game.
pancong IV domino. *penjudi* – domino player.
pancor pancoran → PANCURAN.
pancung I 1 train (of dress), tail (of shirt), flap (of coat). 2 sharp, pointed, angular; → MANCUNG. 3 decapitation. *hukum gantung dan* – punishment by hanging and decapitation.
  memancung 1 to behead, decapitate. 2 to cut s.t. at an angle, truncate. *~ telang* to cut on the bias.
  memancungkan to make s.t. sharp. *~ hidung* to bob one's nose.
  terpancung truncated.
  pancungan a cut with a sharp weapon.
  pemancung 1 hangman, executioner. 2 axe, hatchet.
  pemancungan 1 beheading. 2 cutting down on.
pancung II *boat – (bermotor)* a certain type of (motorized) prau found in the Riau archipelago; about five meters long and one meter wide.
pancur berpancur and **memancur** to spout (forth), pour out, gush (forth). *air (me)mancur* fountain (in a park/yard, etc.).
  pancuran 1 jet of water. 2 *(~ mandi)* shower. 3 tap, faucet.
pancut memancut to spout/squirt/spurt up (of water under pressure).
  terpancut *(mostly Mal)* 1 to squirt. 2 to come, have an orgasm.
  pancutan spout, spurt, squirt.
  pemancut tool for squirting, spray.
pandai I 1 clever, intelligent, bright, smart. *Anak itu – di kelasnya.* That child is smart in school. *– hajilah* you know yourself best. *hanya mau – sendiri* pigheaded, obstinate. *segala – ia* and *ia – segala hal* he is well-rounded/a jack of all trades. 2 expert/skilled/skillful in, excellent at. *Ia – berbahasa Indonésia.* His Indonesian is excellent. 3 able, capable. *belum – menggambar kepala orang* not yet able to draw human heads. 4 knowledgeable, scholarly, erudite. *orang – scholars. – belanja* knowing how to make ends meet. *– berkarang kampung* able to adapt o.s. to village life and customs. *– bergaul* to have good manners, know how to get along with people. *– berminyak air* good at cajoling/wheedling. *– bersiasat* prudent. *– bersilat lidah* good at arguing. *– hidup* a) to know how to make both ends meet. b) easy to get along with. *– jatuh* a) to know how to get out of a tough situation. b) good at finding pretexts/excuses. *– membawa diri/tabiat* easy-going. *– menanam* to have a green thumb. *– mencari muka* clever in asking people for favors. *– menegur orang* easygoing. *– merayu* to have a way with words. *– meréka-réka* resourceful. *– obat* pharmacist. *– pidato* eloquent.
sepandai as clever as.
sepandai-pandai however/no matter how smart. *~ membungkus, yang busuk berbau juga* murder will out. *~ tupai melompat sekali akan gagal/gawal/terjatuh juga* it is a good horse that never stumbles.
berpandai-pandai and **memandai** *diri (M)* to make s.t. for s.o. without asking him beforehand.
memandai-mandai to pretend to be smart, know-it-all; opinionated, pigheaded.
memandaikan 1 *(cla)* to work with skill. 2 to teach s.o., impart knowledge to s.o., make s.o. intelligent.
terpandai the cleverest/smartest.
kepandaian cleverness, intelligence, skill. *angka ~* school grades. *sekolah ~ putri* girls' high school that specializes in home economics. *~ menémbak* marksmanship. **berkepandaian** to be skilled/competent.
pandai II 1 craftsman; → TUKANG I. 2 skilled worker. *– api* stoker. *– besi* blacksmith. *– bubut* turner. *– emas* goldsmith. *– keris* krismaker. *– obat (ob)* pharmacist. *– turap* plasterer.

memandaikan (*cla*) to make s.o. into a craftsman, etc.

pandak (*Jv*) short; → PÉNDÉK I.

memandakkan and **memperpandak** to shorten, abridge, abbreviate.

pandam I k.o. resin used for sticking a knife, etc. into its sheath. **memandam** to fasten with resin.

pandam II (*M*) → PENDAM. - *pekuburan* cemetery. **memandam** to bury, inter.

pandan I pandanus, a plant with long sweet-smelling leaves whose thorns are used for weaving hats/mats, etc., screw pine. *tikar –* mat made from pandanus thorns. *topi –* k.o. Panama hat made from pandanus thorns. - *bidur* giant pandanus, *Pandanus bidur.* - *darat* a pandanus with hairy leaves. - *duri* k.o. pandanus, *Pandanus atrocarpus.* - *laut/podak/pudak* k.o. screw pine, *Pandanus tectorius.* - *raja* giant pandanus, *Pandanus bidur.* - *tikus* k.o. pandanus, *Pandanus ridleyi.* - *wangi* k.o. screw pine, *Pandanus amaryllifolius/odorus.*

pandan II red (as a color of dogs).

pandan III (*ikan –*) k.o. bream, short purse mouth, *Gerres abbreviatus.*

pandang 1 glance, look. *Keduanya saling tertumbuk –.* They glanced at e.o. *sekali –* at first glance, at a glance. *selayang –* in passing, at a glance. *sekali –* at first glance. **2** (*coq*) → MEMANDANG. *tidak – bulu* without respect of persons, not caring who it is, not discriminating against. *tidak – lawan* to fear no one. *tak – uang* regardless of whether one is rich or poor. - *jauh dilayangkan, - dekat ditukikkan* (*M*) to examine carefully. *lihat anak, - menantu* to weigh the pros and cons in choosing a son- or daughter-in-law. - *dengar* audiovisual.

berpandang(-pandang)an [and **bersipandangan** (*infr*)] to exchange glances, glance at e.o. *Meréka ~.* They looked at e.o. *~ mata* to meet face to face.

memandang 1 to look at and notice. *sejauh-jauh mata ~* as far as the eye can see. **2** to consider, regard. *Kami ~nya sebagai anggota keluarga sendiri.* We consider him a member of the family. *~ bahwa* to be of the opinion that. *~ bulu* to show partiality. *tidak ~* irrespective of, regardless of, without taking into consideration. *~ énténg/gampang/réméh/ringan/tak penting* to underestimate, disregard, take s.t. lightly. *~ hina/rendah* to look down on. **3** (*usu* with a negative) to pay attention to, take into consideration. *dengan tidak ~ bangsa/bulu/orang* without respect of persons/race, etc., without prejudice. *tidak ~ lawan* to fear no one, shrink from nothing. **4** to respect. *Dia dipandang masyarakat karena jasa-jasanya.* He is respected because of his services to the community. *~ sebelah mata* to underestimate, to look askance at, shut one's eyes to.

pandang-memandang 1 to look at e.o.; → BERPANDANGAN. **2** to respect e.o. *dengan tidak ~* regardless of who it is.

memandangi [and **mandangin** (*J coq*)] to gaze/look/stare at. *Senang hati ~nya.* He's nice to look at.

memandangkan to fix one's eye (on), stare (at).

terpandang 1 to be visible, can be seen. *Baktéri itu tidak ~ oléh mata telanjang.* Those bacteria are invisible to the naked eye. *tidak ~ muka lagi* doesn't have the guts/nerve to face people any more. **2** to catch sight (of), spot. *Baru saja duduk di kursi, ~lah ia kepada seorang gadis remaja.* He had just sat down in a chair when he caught sight of a teenage girl. **3** only paying attention (to), only caring (about). *~ kepada gaji dan pangkat* only paying attention to salary and position. **4** to be respected, highly regarded. *Ia termasuk orang ~ di kampungnya.* He is among those respected in his village. *keluarga ~* a highly regarded/respected family. **seterpandang** most highly respected. *majalah ~ "Témpo"* Tempo, the most highly respected magazine. **keterpandangan** being highly respected, a high level of respect.

terpandang-pandang to be in one's mind, pictured in one's mind. *~ selalu wajah bakal istrinya.* The face of his fiancée was always in his mind.

pandangan 1 view. *Bangunan itu mempunyai ~ muka ke sebelah Utara.* The building faces north. **2** viewpoint, outlook. **3** look, glance, sight. *jatuh cinta pada ~ pertama* to fall in love at first sight. *~ tajam menusuk sumsum* a sharp, piercing/penetrating look. **4** knowledge. *meluaskan ~nya* to broaden one's knowl-

edge. **5** opinion, judgment. *~ dunia* philosophy, world view. *~ hidup* philosophy of life, world view. *~ kemudian* afterthought. *~ Marksis/Marxis (yang kuno)* (old-fashioned) Marxism. *~ mata* visibility. *(laporan) ~ mata* eyewitness (report). *~ orang ketiga* third-party viewpoint. **berpandangan** to have a certain viewpoint, be . . . -minded. *pimpinan yang ~ jauh ke muka* leadership with a far-sighted vision. *kurang lebih ~ sama* more or less like-minded. *~ luas* broad/open-minded. *~ picik* narrow-minded.

pemandang spectator, onlooker, observer, viewer. **sepemandang** at a glance.

pemandangan 1 (eye)sight, vision. *tajam ~nya* he has good eyesight/vision. **2** appearance. *memberi ~ tidak sedap* to present a hideous appearance. **3** panorama, scenery, view. *Di Bali banyak ~ yang indah.* There is a lot of beautiful scenery in Bali. *~ putus* interfered-with view. **4** knowledge. *Ia hendak meluaskan ~nya ke luar negeri.* He wants to go abroad to expand his knowledge. **5** (general) view, overview, review, explanation, discussion. *~ dalam dan luar negeri* domestic and foreign review. *~ umum* (in the DPR/MPR, etc.) general debate. **sepemandangan** as far as the eye can see. **berpemandangan** to have a . . . viewpoint. *~ jauh* far-seeing.

pandau marsh, swamp.

Pandawa (*Jv*) (*- Lima*) the five brothers who are the heroes of the *Mahabharata* epic: Yudhistira (Puntadéwa), Bima (Brataséna/Wrekudara), Arjuna (Janaka), and the twins Nangkula and Sadéwa.

pandégo (in East Java) coastal pond worker.

pandémi (*D*) pandemic.

pandir stupid, foolish; → PAK *Pandir.* **sepandir** as stupid/foolish as. **berpandir** *~ diri* to play dumb, act stupid. **kepandiran** stupidity, foolishness. **kepandir-pandiran** stupidly, foolishly.

pandit (*Skr*) pundit, pandit, scholar. - *Ratu* (*Jv*) the ideal Javanese ruler.

pandita (*Skr*) Hindu priest; → PENDÉTA.

pandom (*Jv*) **1** compass needle. **2** compass.

pandratari [pantomim, drama, dan tari] Pantomime, Drama, and Dance; *cp* SENDRATARI.

pandu I 1 guide. **2** ship's pilot. **3** scout. - *Ansor* an Islamic scouting movement. - *bandar* harbor pilot. - *kapal* ship's pilot. - *kurcaci* (in scouting) cub scout (younger than 10). - *laut* a) sea scout. b) pilot. - *pariwisata/wisata(wan)* tour(ist) guide. - *putra* Boy Scout. - *putri* Girl Scout. - *udara* air scout. - *tentara* military scout. - *wreda putra* ex-Boy Scout. - *wreda putri* ex-Girl Scout.

berpandu(kan) to use a guide/pilot, guided (missile); navigated.

memandu to moderate, preside over, direct, guide. *Diskusi itu dipandu oléh seorang dokter.* The discussion was moderated by a physician. **2** to pilot (a ship). **3** (*Mal*) to drive (a car).

memandui to guide, be a guide for. *Turis itu memisahkan diri dari rombongan yang dipandui penduduk setempat.* The tourists detached themselves from the group guided by people from the local population.

memandukan to pilot (a ship into port).

terpandu guided.

panduan 1 guidance. **2** piloting. **3** (*Mal*) (telephone) directory/book. *buku ~* guidebook. *proyék ~* pilot project.

kepanduan 1 scouting. **2** pilotage.

pemandu 1 guide, pilot. **2** ringer, s.o. who takes an exam for s.o. else for payment; → JOKI II, MASKOT. *kapal ~* pilot boat. *~ acara* a) master of ceremonies, emcee. b) moderator. *~ irama* disk jockey, D.J. *~ pesawat* marshaler. *~ piringan hitam* disk jockey, D.J. *~ supir* (in rally) navigator. *~ udara* air traffic controller. *~ wisata* tour(ist) guide. **3** (*Mal*) driver.

pemanduan 1 guiding, piloting. **2** scouting. *~ bakat* talent scouting.

pandu II memandu to try, attempt, endeavor to.

panekuk (*D*) k.o. pancake.

panél I (*D*) panel (of speakers). *diskusi –* panel discussion.

panél II (*E*) wooden panel.

panéli → VANILI.

panélis (*E*) panelist.

panembahan (*Jv*) **1** a man of high nobility. **2** title for a highly esteemed person, *usu* a holy hermit.

panén (*Jv*) **1** harvest. *cepat* – quick-yielding. *musim* – a) harvest time. b) peak time (of the year). **2** to be booming, be doing well financially. **3** to have a field day. *Pedagang écéran pun* –. Even retailers were having a field day. – *berganda* multiple cropping. – *susulan* follow-up harvest. – *uang* a paying proposition, be doing well financially. *Sandiwara itu betul-betul* – *uang.* The play was doing very well.

memanén to harvest.

memanéni to take (the crop) from a rice field.

panénan 1 harvest. **2** profit, gain. ~ *anggur* vintage. ~ *nanas* pineapple harvest. **3** heyday, boom.

pemanén harvester, reaper (the person or machine). *mesin* ~ harvester, reaper (the device).

pemanénan harvesting.

panerus (*Jv*) a *gamelan* instrument.

panéwu (*Jv*) assistant district chief (in Yogyakarta and Surakarta).

pang I (*Jv*) branch (of tree).

Pang II boy's name (= *Dutch Frans* and *English Francis* or *Frank*).

pang III (in acronyms) → PANGLIMA.

pang IV (*onom*) bang (of a drum).

Pangab → PANGLIMA *Angkatan Bersenjata.*

pangabekti and **pangabektén** (*Jv*) respectful homage; → BAKTI.

Pangad → PANGLIMA *Angkatan Darat.*

pangah memanga to open one's mouth wide.

terpangah (with) open (mouth).

Pangal → PANGLIMA *Angkatan Laut.*

pangalungan <alung> (*S*) money that the audience throws to the actors or dancers in certain shows.

pangan (*Jv*) food, feed, fodder, s.t. to eat. *ilmu* – food science. *sandang* – food and clothing. *sandang,* –, *dan papan* food, clothing, and housing (the basic necessities of life). – *burung* bird food. – *cepat* fast food. – *dalam bentuk setengah prosés* semiprocessed food. – *dalam bentuk yang telah diolah* processed food. – *ternak* cattle fodder, forage.

panganan delicacies; → PENGANAN.

Pangarmabar → PANGLIMA *Armada (RI) Kawasan Barat.*

Pangarmatim → PANGLIMA *Armada (RI) Kawasan Timur.*

Pangau → PANGLIMA *Angkatan Udara.*

pangayo <kayo> (in Palu, Celebes) headhunter.

Pangbés → PANGLIMA *Besar.*

Pangdam → PANGLIMA *Daérah Militér.*

pangék (*M*) a Padang style of cooking. – *ayam Padang* a dish of beans and fried chicken. – *bungkus* a wrapped fish dish. – *ikan* a sour-sharp fish dish.

pangéran (*J/Jv*) **1** prince. **2** Lord. **3** (*BG*) boyfriend. *Setiap malam Sabtu dan malam Minggu, -ku datang bertamu. Seperti biasa kami berkencan.* Every Friday and Saturday evening my boyfriend comes to see me. As usual we go out on a date. **4** (in Java) title for a prince. **5** (in BD) title for a noble (*usu* spelled **pengiran**). – *adipati anom* and – *pati* crown prince. – *Adipati Ario* [PAA] Prince, Venerable Sovereign; title conferred during the Dutch colonial period on feudal lords, such as the *Mangku Negara* of Surakarta, and the *Paku Alam* of Yogyakarta. – *Cendana* (*joc*) the Prince of Cendana, reference to Hutomo ("Tommy") Mandala Putra.

pangéstu (*Skr Jv*) blessing, good wishes, prayers.

panggah (*Jv*) **1** to stand firm. **2** unchanging, consistent, constant. *tidak* – inconsistent. **ketidak-panggahan** inconsistency. ~ *logis* logical inconsistency.

memanggahi to stand up against, make a stand against.

kepanggahan consistency.

panggak (*M*) proud; → BANGGA.

memanggakkan to be proud of, pride o.s. on, boast of; to create a feeling of pride in.

panggal → PENGGAL.

panggang roasted, grilled, toasted, baked, barbequed. *roti* – toast. *jauh* – *dari api* neither here nor there, off center, far from where it should be. *terlampau* – *jadi angus* pride goes before a fall. *bagai kucing dengan* – to set the cat to watch the cream. – *ayam* and *ayam* – broiled/barbequed chicken.

memanggang [and **manggang** (*coq*)] to roast, toast, bake. ~ *di (dalam) oven* to bake in an oven. *dipanggang panas matahari* to be sunburned. *dipanggang tidak angus* had a narrow escape.

terpanggang [and **kepanggang** (*coq*)] roasted. *hangus* ~ burned up. *Hari itu, ada lima mayat yang hangus* ~. That day there were five bodies burned up.

panggangan 1 grill, toaster. ~ *roti listrik* electric toaster. **2** grilled, s.t. roasted.

pemanggang toaster (the person). *(alat)* ~ *roti* toaster (the device).

pemanggangan 1 grill, barbecue, spit. **2** toaster.

panggar I and **panggau** platform for drying fish, etc.

panggar II [panitia anggaran] budget committee.

panggeng (*J/Jv*) constant, unchanging, consistent.

panggih (*Jv*) – *temanten* to meet one's bride(groom). *upacara* – the marriage ceremony during which the bride and groom meet e.o.

memanggihkan to bring the bride and groom together.

panggil memanggil [and **manggil** (*coq*)] **1** to call (for), hail. *Dia* ~ *taksi.* He hailed a taxi. ~ *kembali* to reinstate (in a previous position), call back. **2** to ask, invite, summon, convoke. *Meréka hanya* ~ *teman-temannya yang karib.* They only invited their close friends. ~ *paksa* to subpoena. **3** to name, call. *Panggil saja nama saya Mia.* Just call me Mia.

memanggil-manggil to call repeatedly.

panggil-memanggil to call e.o.

memanggili [and **manggilin** (*J coq*)] **1** (*pl obj*) to call, hail. **2** to call out to s.o. **3** to call, summon.

memanggilkan 1 to call for s.o. else. ~ *dokter untuk si sakit* to call a doctor for the sick person. **2** to address s.o. as. *Ia tidak* ~ *ayah kepadanya.* He didn't call him father.

terpanggil called, summoned, called upon. *merasa* ~ *untuk* to feel/be called (up)on to. *Angkatan bersenjata* ~ *untuk membela negara.* The armed forces are called on to defend the country. **keterpanggilan** calling, vocation. *Seorang pemimpin muncul oléh prosés* ~. A leader comes forth because he has a calling.

panggilan 1 call, summons, invitation. ~ *resmi* official summons, subpoena. **2** title, nickname. ~*nya apa?* What's your nickname? What should I call you? **3** person who is called/summoned. *sudah* ~ *darahnya* it is in one's blood. **4** call (girl, etc.). *surat* ~ convocation. *tanda* ~ call sign. *tidak terima* ~ not on call (on signboards in front of doctor's residences). ~ *yang tak terjawab* no answer (when telephoning). ~ *ilahi* divine call. ~ *suci* sacred mission.

kepanggilan vocation, calling. ~ *dan profésionalisme adalah dua hal yang harus dimiliki oléh setiap pekerja sosial.* Every social worker should have a calling and be a professional.

pemanggil caller, s.o. who calls/summons. **sepemanggil** as far as one's voice can reach, calling distance.

pemanggilan 1 call, summons (to register, etc.). ~ *dinas tentara* recruitment. **2** to convene (a meeting).

panggonan (*Jv*) place, spot.

panggu 1 portion, share. **2** fraction.

panggul pelvis, hip; → PINGGUL. – *senjata!* shoulder arms!

sepanggul hip-length, down/up to the hip.

memanggul 1 to (carry on one's) shoulder, bear, take up (arms). ~ *senjata* to bear arms. **2** to shoulder (responsibilities). *Ini merupakan tugas pertama yang harus dipanggulnya sebagai diplomat muda yang baru jebol dari bangku kuliah.* This is the first assignment that he had to shoulder as a young diplomat who had just graduated from college.

terpanggul carried (on the hip or back).

pemanggul bearer, carrier, porter (who carries things on his shoulder). ~ *bedil/senapan* gun bearer.

pemanggulan carrying on the shoulder.

panggung I 1 scaffolding, stage. *seri* – star of stage, prima donna. **2** platform, dais. **3** grandstand, tribune. **4** the public. – *kehormatan* dais of honor, i.e., a raised platform for honored guests. – *politik* the political stage. – *terbuka* open stage. – *wayang* (*Mal*) movie theater. *ke* – (to go) on stage. **mengemanggungkan** to (put on the) stage.

sepanggung on the same stage as.

berpanggung to have a stage/platform/dais.

memanggung [and manggung (*coq*)] to appear on stage, perform on the stage. *Direncanakan New Kids on the Block manggung di Istora Senayan.* Plans were for New Kids on the Block to perform at the Senayan Sports Palace.

memanggungkan to (put on the) stage. ~ *kepala* to raise one's head.

panggungan 1 lookout, watchtower. 2 the public.

pemanggungan performance (of a play), performing, staging. *mengadakan ~ di gedung-gedung untuk dikarciskan* to put on performances in buildings in order to sell tickets.

panggung II memanggung to chirp (of certain birds, such as the turtledove, etc.).

pangi k.o. tree, *Pangium edule.*

pangirak (in Kalimantan) deputy village head.

pangjeujeuh (*S*) compensation, indemnity, repayment/reimbursement for loss/damages, etc.; → GANTI *rugi.*

pangkah I 1 Hindu caste mark, *usu* on forehead. 2 sign of conjuration (cross on forehead) to ward off evil spirits.

memangkah to put such a sign on the forehead with charcoal, lime for chewing with betel leaves, or turmeric.

pangkah II memangkah 1 to throw a top at another top (in playing with tops). 2 to trump an opponent in a card game, defeat a rival in a debate.

pangkai bertikai – → BERTIKAI *pangai.*

pangkal 1 a) (thick) lower end (of a tree); *opp* UJUNG I. b) foot, base (of a tree). 2 (*elec*) pole. 3 starting point (of a tramline, etc.). *dari* – from the beginning/outset. 4 cause (of a misfortune/quarrel, etc.), instigator of. 5 origin (of news), source (of wealth/existence). 6 necessary prerequisite (for becoming smart, etc.). 7 principal points, essentials. *si* – (*helat*) (*M*) host. *pulang* – *jalan* to return to the starting point. *uang* – a) initial capital. b) admission fee. – *air* source of water. – *bahu* top of shoulder. – *batang* caudex (of tree). – *bedil* rifle butt. – *bertolak* starting point. – *cerita* main point of a story. – *ékor* base of the tail. – *hidung* bridge of nose. – *jalan* point of departure, starting point. – *kaki* tarsus. – *kata* a) base/root of a word. b) topic of conversation. – *kata kerja* (*gram*) infinitive. – *kerongkongan* throat. – *léhér* lower part of the neck. – *lengan* upper arm. – *lidah* root of the tongue. *takbir di* – *lidah* to be dying, be at death's door. – *mata* corner of the eye. – *musim* start of the season. – *nama* first name. – *paha* hip, haunch; groin. **sepangkal paha** hip-length. – *pedang* hilt of a sword. – *pikir* premise. – *pohon* foot/base of a tree. – *pokok* gist, essence. – *rumah* part of a house above the stairs. – *senapan* gunstock. – *tangan* a) underarm. b) the part of the hand nearest the wrist. – *tekak* pharynx. – *telinga* base of the ear (where it joins the head). – *tenggorok* larynx. – *tikai* cause of a quarrel. – *tolak* point of departure, starting point.

berpangkal ~ (*pada*) a) to originate (in), have its roots (in). b) to be founded (on), be based (on). ~ *tolak dari* to have one's starting point at. *tempat* ~ home base. *tidak* ~ unfounded. *tidak berujung, tidak* ~ it makes no sense, you can't make heads or tails of it; → UJUNG.

berpangkalkan to be based on/in. *seorang perantara yang* ~ *London* a London-based broker.

memangkal [and mangkal (*coq*)] to stay temporarily at a certain place (in order to work/trade/harvest/wait for passengers, etc.), base o.s.

memangkalkan 1 to unload, discharge, put (passengers) ashore. 2 to station, place, post.

terpangkal with a cost price of. *dijual* ~ sold at cost.

pangkalan 1 landing stage, pier, moorage, anchorage, quay. 2 bridgehead. 3 storage/discharge place. 4 (*mil*) base. 5 base camp. 6 stand, place, location, site. (*M*) *si* ~ host. ~ *aju udara* air-head. ~ *angkatan laut/udara* naval/air base. ~ *Armada* [PA] Fleet Base. ~ *bis* bus station. ~ *data* data base. ~ *induk* home base. ~ *jembatan* abutment. ~ *peluncur* launch site. ~ *pendaratan* jetty. ~ *perawatan* maintenance base. ~ *rokét* rocket base. ~ *taksi* taxi stand. ~ *tolak* departure base. ~ *utama* [lantama] main base.

pemangkalan (*mil*) ~ *depan* forward base echelon for logistic support.

pangkas pruning, cutting, shearing. *toko* – barbershop. *tukang* – barber; trimmer, cutter, shearer.

berpangkas 1 cut, trimmed. 2 to get/have a haircut. ~ *péndék* to have/get a crew cut.

memangkas 1 to trim (hair, trees), prune (trees/bushes). *Setiap pohon dipangkas terlebih dahulu di bagian atas.* First, the top of each tree is pruned. 2 to cut (hair/costs/salaries, etc.), reduce (the number/amount of). ~ *biaya produksi* to cut production costs. ~ *harga obat antara 10% dan 25%* to lower the price of medicine between 10% and 25%. ~ *kata* to summarize, recapitulate. 3 to deduct (income illegally). 4 to file (teeth in Bali). ~ *gigi* to file the upper front teeth.

memangkasi (*pl obj*) to cut, trim, etc.

terpangkas 1 cut, trimmed. 2 (*elec*) limited.

pangkasan 1 hairdo, hair style, coiffure. 2 trimming.

pemangkas 1 barber. 2 trimmer, cutter, shearer. *gunting* ~ pruning shears. ~ *gigi* tooth filer (in Bali). 3 (*elec*) limiter.

pemangkasan 1 barbershop. 2 cutting (hair), pruning/trimming (trees/costs, etc.).

pangkat I rank, position, degree, grade. *naik* – to be promoted (in school), get a promotion (at work). *tanda* – insignia, chevrons. – *anumerta* posthumous rank. – *kaptén/nakhoda* captaincy, captainship.

sepangkat 1 of the same rank/position/grade, equal in rank, etc. 2 of the same age, coeval; → SEBAYA.

berpangkat 1 to have a rank/position/grade. 2 distinguished, noble, ranking, high-ranking; to have a senior (position). *Suaminya orang* ~. Her husband is a distinguished person.

berpangkat-pangkat tiered, graduated.

memangkati to give the rank of. *Lama pendidikan satu tahun, setelah itu dipangkati Brigadir Polisi tingkat II.* Training is for one year; after that, (the graduate) is given the rank of Police Brigadier Second Class.

memangkatkan 1 to appoint s.o. 2 to promote s.o.

kepangkatan rank, position, grade, ranking. *sistém* ~ system of ranking.

pemangkatan 1 appointment. 2 promotion.

perpangkatan (*mod*) promotion, rank.

pangkat II (*math*) power. – *dua* to the second power, squared. *empat* – *dua sama dengan enam belas* four squared is sixteen, $4^2 = 16$. – *naik* ascending power. – *tiga* cubed.

memangkatkan to raise to a power. ~ *18 dengan 3* to raise 18 to the 3rd power, cube 18.

pangkat III 1 rung, step. 2 raised floor (of *pancapersada*). 3 floor, story (in building).

berpangkat-pangkat terraced, tiered, at/with various levels.

pangkék (*S*) memangkék 1 to bind cut rice-stalks together into sheaves. 2 to catch (and kill), lynch (during the *Pétrus* period). *Édi Joni, jégér Pasar Johar, Karawang, ditemukan téwas dipangkék dengan tali plastik.* Edi Joni, a habitual criminal from Johar Market, Karawang, was found dead, lynched with a plastic rope.

pangkéng → PANGKING.

Pangkep [Pangkajéné kepulauan] the Pangkajene Archipelago (in South Sulawesi).

pangking (C) 1 bed, k.o. wooden sleeping platform, place to sleep. 2 bedroom.

Pangkolakops → PANGLIMA *Komando Pelaksanaan Operasi.*

pangkon I (*Jv*) set of *gamelan* instruments.

pangkon II (*Jv*) to hold bride and groom on one's lap (part of the wedding ceremonies); *cp* PANGKUAN.

Pangkoopsau → PANGLIMA *Komando Operasi Angkatan Udara.*

Pangkopkamtib → PANGLIMA *Komando Pemulihan Keamanan dan Ketertiban.*

Pangkorps Brimob → PANGLIMA *Korps Brigade Mobil.*

Pangkostranas → PANGLIMA *Komando Stratégis Nasional.*

Pangkowasmar → PANGLIMA *Komando Kawasan Maritim.*

Pangkowil → PANGLIMA *Komando Wilayah.*

Pangkowilhan → PANGLIMA *Komando Wilayah Pertahanan.*

Pangkowilu → PANGLIMA *Komando Wilayah Udara.*

pangkréas (*D/E*) pancreas.

pangku I lap, the front part of the human body from the waist to the knees when one is in a sitting position.

berpangku to sit on s.o.'s lap. *Anak itu ~ di haribaan ibunya.* The child sat on his mother's lap. *~ tangan (saja)* to (sit around and) do nothing, be idle. *Jangan ~ tangan melihat kesulitan orang lain.* Don't sit around and do nothing when you see other people's hardships.

memangku to put/hold s.o. on one's lap.

mangku (*Jv*) to put/hold s.o. on one's lap. *~ Negara* (*Jv*) title of the Prince of Surakarta. *~ temanten* putting the bride and groom on one's lap (part of the marriage ceremony).

memangkukan to put/hold s.o. on one's lap.

pangkuan lap. *tidur di ~ ibunya* to fall asleep on his mother's lap. *~ ibu pertiwi* the lap of the fatherland.

pemangku holder. *~ kepentingan* stakeholder. **sepemangku** the amount of space one can reach one's arms around.

pemangkuan putting/holding s.o. on one's lap.

pangku II memangku 1 to manage, administer, take care of, look after, hold (a position). **2** to represent s.o.

pemangku administration, management. *~ hutan* forest administration. *Kesatuan ~ Hutan* [KPH] Forest Administration Unit. *~ jabatan* installation in office.

pemangku 1 guardian, administrator, manager, management. *~ adat* head of *adat*. **2** functionary. *~ jabatan* acting, in charge, pro tem. *~ kehutanan* forest ranger.

pemangkuan management. *~ Hutan* Forest District.

pangku III (*Bal*) **pemangku** Balinese priest.

pangkung memangkung to beat with a cudgel/stick.

terpangkung beaten.

pangkur I 1 pickaxe. **2** hoe, rake, spade. *meraih – ke dada* a) to come to one's senses. b) to be touchy, be quick to take offense.

memangkur to till/work the soil.

terpangkur tilled, worked.

pangkur II (*Jv*) a classical verse form.

Pangla → PANGLIMA *Mandala.*

panglima commander. *– Angkatan Bersenjata* [Pangab] Commander of the Armed Forces. *– Angkatan Darat* [Pangad] Army Commander. *– Angkatan Laut* [Pangal] Navy Commander. *– Angkatan Udara* [Pangau] Air Force Commander. *– Armada (RI Kawasan) Barat* [Pangamarbar] Commander of the Western Area Armada of the Republic of Indonesia. *– Armada (RI Kawasan) Timur* [Pangamartim] Commander of the Eastern Area Armada of the Republic of Indonesia. *– Besar* [Pangbés/Pangsar] commander-in-chief. *– Burung* (in Kalimantan) a semi-mythical Dayak figure. *– Daérah Militér* [Pangdam] Military Region Commander. *– kaum* (*Ac*) clan head. *– Komando Kawasan Maritim* [Pangkowasmar] Commander of Maritime Area Command. *– Komando Pelaksanaan Operasi* [Pangkolakops] Commander of Operations Command. *– Komando Operasi Angkatan Udara* [Pangkoopsau] Commander of Air Force Operations Command. *– Komando Pemulihan Keamanan dan Ketertiban* [Pangkopkamtib] Commander of the Command for the Restoration of Security and Order. *– Komando Stratégis Nasional* [Pangkostranas] Commander of the National Security Command. *– Komando Wilayah* [Pangkowil] Commander of Territorial Command. *– Komando Wilayah Pertahanan* [Pangkowilhan] Commander of the Defense Territory Command. *– Komando Wilayah Udara* [Pangkowilu] Commander of Air Zone Command. *– Korps Brigade Mobil* [Pangkorps Brimob] Commander of the Mobile Corps (of the National Police). *– Mandala* [Pangla] Theater Command. *– pangkalan* (*ob*) harbor master, port officer. *– Pasukan* [Pangpas] Troop Commander. *– perang* warlord. *– santé* (among the Baduy in Banten, West Java) security chief. *– sagi* (*Ac*) province head. *– Téritorial* [Pangter] Territorial Commander. *– Tertinggi* [Pangti] Supreme Commander.

kepanglimaan commander (*mod*).

panglimunan <limun> (*Jv*) charm that makes one invisible.

pangling (*Jv*) to fail to recognize, no longer recognize.

kepanglingan failure to recognize.

panglingsir <lingsir> (*Jv*) elder; → SESEPUH.

panglong (*C*) lumber mill.

pangon (*Jv*) shepherd.

pangonan pasture, meadow.

pangot (*S*) (*pisau –*) a small knife or pin, completely made of iron, formerly used to write or engrave on bamboo or on *lontar* leaves.

pangpang (*– manis*) k.o. rectangular-shaped flour-based snack.

Pangpas → PANGLIMA *Pasukan.*

pangpet (*J*) clogged (up); → MAMPAT I.

memangpet and **mangpet** (*coq*)] to get clogged up.

pangpung (*Jv*) dry (tree) branch.

pangrawit <rawit> (*Jv*) *gamelan* player.

Pangréh Praja (*Jv*) Civil Service, name now replaced by **Pamong Praja**.

pangrok (*E*) punk rock.

pangsa 1 segment, section (of a *durian*/orange, etc.). **2** share. *– ékspor* export market share. *– pasar* market share. *– waktu* time share/sharing. *menumbuhsuburkan – waktu* to make time sharing grow and prosper. *– menunjukkan bangsa* a tree is known by its fruit.

berpangsa(-pangsa) in segments/sections, segmented.

memangsakan to divide into segments/sections, section.

pemangsaan compartmentalizing, segmenting, segmentation.

pangsan fainted; → PINGSAN.

pangsapuri (*Mal*) apartment. *bangunan –* apartment building.

pangsar → PANGLIMA *Besar.*

pangsek (*J*) **kepangsek** fallen/landed deep in a hole, to fall on one's ass.

pangsi I peg (of top), pivot, (*naut*) winch.

pemangsian pivoting.

pangsi II (*C*) k.o. black silk.

pangsit (*C*) wonton. *– kuah* wonton soup.

pangsiun → PÉNSIUN.

Pangter → PANGLIMA *Téritorial.*

Pangti → PANGLIMA *Tertinggi.*

pangul ricochet.

pangula-ula (*Bat*) s.o. who has the power of black magic.

pangur 1 (*M*) rasp, file. **2** tooth file.

memangur to file down evenly (of teeth).

pangus I graceful, neat, good-looking, dashing.

pangus II memangus to spout (of a whale/porpoise).

panguyuban → PAGUYUBAN.

panik (*D*) **1** panicky. **2** panic-stricken.

kepanikan 1 panic. **2** to be in a panic.

paniki (*Min*) a dish made from bat meat.

panil (*D*) panel (of speakers and wood panel); → PANÉL II.

panili (*D*) vanilla (the shrub and its product), *Vanilla planifolia*.

paningset (*Jv*) engagement present; → PENINGSET.

panir I (*D*) breadcrumbs. *tepung –* breadcrumbs; → BUBUK *roti*.

panir II (*Pers ob*) cheese; → KÉJU.

paniradia and **paniradya** (*Jv*) → PANIRADYO.

paniradyapati (*Jv*) (in Yogyakarta) department head.

paniradyo (*Jv*) department. *– racana lan pencawara* Department of Information and Propaganda (of the Yogyakarta *Kraton* under the Japanese occupation).

panitera (*Skr Jv*) secretary, clerk (*esp* of the court), registrar. *– fakultas* registrar (of a university department). *– pengadilan* clerk of the court. *– pengganti* alternate court registrar. *– utama* [panitrama] chief secretary.

kepaniteraan secretariat. *~ pengadilan* office of the court clerk.

paniterama → PANITRAMA.

panitia (*Skr Jv*) committee, board. *seorang –* a committee member. *– ad hoc* [PAH] ad hoc committee. *– anggaran* [panggar] budget committee. *– angkét* board of enquiry. *– bersama* joint committee. *– kecil* subcommittee. *– kepangkatan* promotion board. *– kerja* [panja] working committee. *– kerja tetap* [panjatap] standing working committee. *– khusus* [pansus] special committee. *– Koordinasi Bantuan Luar Negeri* Coordinating Committee for Foreign Aid. *– pelaksana* executive committee. *– pembantu* relief committee. *– pemilihan daérah* [PPD] regional election committee. *– penaséhat* advisory committee. *– penaskah* draft committee. *– pendaftaran pemilih* [pantarlih] voter registration committee. *– pengarah* a) steering committee. b) watchdog committee. *– pengawas pelaksana daérah* [panwaslakda] regional executive oversight committee. *– pengawas* *pelaksana pusat* [panwaslakpus] central executive oversight committee. – *penguji* examining board. – *penolong* relief committee. – *penyelidik* enquiry committee. – *perumus* formulating committee. – *Penyelesaian Perselisihan Perburuhan* [P4] Committee for the Settlement of Labor Disputes. – *Penyelidik Persiapan Kemerdékaan* Independence Preparations Investigation Committee (March 1, 1945). – *perumus* formulating committee. – *sénsor* censorship board. – *tetap* [pantap] standing committee.

kepanitiaan committee (*mod*). *dalam bentuk* ~ in a committee format.

panitikismo (*Jv*) cadastre.

panitra → PANITERA.

panitrama → PANIT(E)RA *utama*.

panja I → PANITIA *Kerja*.

panja II (*Pers ob*) hand. *mengarak* – (*M*) to carry in procession the five fingers (of a brass hand) in an ark decorated with flowers (at the Hasan-Husain celebrations); → PANCA I.

panjak (*Jv*) gamelan player (sometimes, at the same time, a singer or dancer).

panjang long (of distance and of time). *–nya* length, distance. *jari* – middle finger. *persegi* – rectangle. *waktu lebih* – more time. – *tidak* – of medium length. *hendak* – *terlalu patah* pride goes before a fall. – *langkah singkat pinta/permintaan* to die, pass away. – *kalau* – *beri beruas, kalau péndék beri berbuku* look before you leap. *mendapat* – *hidung* to be ashamed. *sama* – *dengan urat perut/belikat* a damn lie. – *akal* a) crafty, sharp, astute. b) full of ideas. – *belit* tricky, crafty. – *bentang* span. – *bibir* a) always complaining about others. b) always slandering/backbiting. – *bulat* cylindrical. – *gelombang* wavelength. – *ingatan* to have a good memory. – *jalan* the distance (to be covered). – *jimat* (*Jv*) the public display of *kraton* heirlooms in *Maulud*, the month of the Prophet's birth. – *kili-kili* full of excuses. – *kira-kira* smart, clever, bright, intelligent, wise. – *lampai* tall and slender; → SEMAMPAI. – *langkah* a) dishonest, roundabout, not straightforward. b) to die, pass away. – *lanjut* prolonged, protracted, verbose. *dengan* – *lébar* in detail, at length. **memanjang-lébarkan** to explain at great length. – *lébarnya isi kata* the full import/meaning/effect (of one's words). – *léhér* a) to like to cheat on exams. b) tired of waiting too long. – *lidah* a) backbiting, slandering. b) bootlicking. c) nagging, grumbling. d) indiscreet. – *mata* lewd, lascivious (about women). – *mulut* tattletale, gossip(monger). – *muncung* talking about others. – *napas* full of stamina. – *panjang lébar* detailed, circumstantial. – *péndék* long or short. **memanjang-péndékkan** to make s.t. either longer or shorter. – *permintaan* a long life. – *pikiran* a) smart, clever, bright. b) intelligent, wise. – *pinta* long-lived. – *sayap* wingspread. – *sedikit* not so long. – *tangan* a) to finger everything, not be able to leave things alone. b) thievish. *si/yang* – *tungkai* (*M*) rain. – *tunjang* long-legged. – *umur* (having/reaching) a long life, long-lived. – *umur tanpa prosés penuaan* longevity-without-aging. – *untung* living together as husband and wife for a long time. – *urat belikat* lazy, indolent. – *usia* (having) a long life. – *usus* patient.

panjang-panjang too long, long-winded, tedious.

sepanjang 1 as long as, (for) the length of, during, throughout, for the (length of) time of, (for) the whole. – *hari/malam/tahun* all day/night/year long; → *sehari/semalam/setahun* SUNTUK. ~ *hayatnya/hidupnya* all his life. ~ *masa* forever, always, continually; (combined with negative) never. ~ *saat* for a/the moment. ~ *sejarah* throughout history. ~ *umur zaman* for many years to come. ~ *waktu* always, forever, continually. 2 as far as, insofar as, to the extent that. ~ *apa yang kita ketahui* as far as we know. ~ *ingatanku* as far as I remember, to the best of my recollection. ~ *pengetahuan saya* as far as I know, to the best of my knowledge. ~ *pikiran saya* in my opinion. 3 as long as, provided that, on condition that. 4 *-long. luka* ~ *4 cm* a 4-cm-long wound.

berpanjang 1 to describe in detail. 2 to talk a lot. ~ *kalam* to relate at length, expatiate. ~ *madah* to talk a lot.

berpanjang-panjang too long, tedious.

berpanjang(-panjang)an 1 in the long run. 2 for a long time. *kemesraan yang berpanjangan* eternal love.

memanjang 1 to lengthen, become longer. *Antrian di depan lokét mulai* ~. The line in front of the ticket window started to become longer. 2 prolonged, lengthy (negotiations, etc.). *tepuk tangan yang* ~ prolonged applause. 3 longitudinal, across, cross-wise

memanjangi to go along the length of.

memanjangkan [and **manjangin** (*J coq*)] to make s.t. long(er), extend s.t. to its full length. ~ *kaki* to stretch one's legs. ~ *léhér* to crane one's neck, *esp* to see better. ~ *rambutnya* to let one's hair grow long(er).

memanjang-manjangkan to keep on protracting/stretching out (the time). ~ *témpo/waktu* to gain time.

memperpanjang(kan) to extend, renew, prolong, stretch (out). *tidak perlu diperpanjang lagi* needs no further argument.

terpanjang the longest. *Sungai yang* ~ *adalah sungai Kapuas*. The longest river is the Kapuas.

panjangan 1 extension. 2 extension.

kepanjangan 1 length. 2 duration. 3 too long. 4 expansion (of an abbreviated form), in full. *Apa ~nya ...?* What is ... in full? *A ~ dari B.* A is the expanded form of B. ~*nya adalah ... in full* (it is) ... 5 continuation, s.t. that is an extension of s.t. else, arm. ~ *pemerintah pusat* an arm of the central government. **berkepanjangan** prolonged, protracted. *perang yang* ~ a protracted war. *Hujan* ~ *mencemaskan petani kapas*. The prolonged rains have alarmed cotton farmers. *Rasa sesal itu tidak* ~. The regret did not last long (or, was short-lived).

pemanjangan lengthening, protraction.

perpanjangan renewal (of a passport/subscription), extension, rollover (of a deposit). *tidak mendapat* ~ *penahanan lagi di pengadilan* does not obtain an extension from the court. ~ *tangan* extension, arm. ~ *utang* refunding of debt.

panjar I (*Jv*) earnest money; payment in advance, cash advance, down payment, deposit; imprest; → UANG *muka*. – *pesangon* first payment of severance pay.

memanjari to give s.o. a cash advance.

panjaran down payment.

panjar(an) II bias.

panjarwala (*Hind ?*) sailor whose job it is to roll up or unfold the sails.

panjat – *pinang* k.o. game involving climbing a slippery pole to get the prizes at the top. – *tebing* rock climbing (*sports*).

memanjat [and **manjat** (*coq*)] 1 to climb, get up (a tree/pole, etc.). 2 to ascend, climb (up) (a mountain, etc.). 3 ~ *pengadilan* to appeal to a higher court. 4 to mount, rise. *Air* ~ *sampai 1 1/2 m dari ketinggian biasa*. The water rose to 1 1/2 meters above its normal height. *dipanjat kaya* to become rich overnight. ~ *bersengkelit* inexperienced. ~ *dedap* to be brave under pressure. ~ *tebing* (to do) rock climbing (sports). ~ *terkena seruda* to go through many adversities, have a lot of bad experiences.

memanjati 1 to climb up (a tree) using hands and feet. 2 to mount (for mating).

memanjatkan to make s.t. go up, raise. ~ *doa* to say a prayer, pray. *Kami panjatkan doa ke hadirat Allah*. We prayed to God. ~ *kaki (pada tangga)* to set foot on (the stairs to climb up). ~ *perkara* to appeal to a higher court. ~ *puji* to praise (God). ~ *syukur* to say a prayer of thanks.

terpanjat climbed, climbable.

panjatan 1 place for climbing/going up/ascending, climb, ascent. 2 step.

pemanjat climber.

pemanjatan praying, sending up (prayers). ~ *doa* saying prayers.

panjer → PANJAR I.

panjergala look-out (on ship).

Panji I name of the legendary prince of Janggala or Kahuripan.

panji II (*Jv*) title of nobility in Java higher than *Radén*, but lower than *Radén Mas*. – *Klantung* comic reference to an unemployed person; → KLANTUNG.

panji III standard, banner. *di bawah* – *révolusi* under the banner of revolution. – *kebesaran* banner. – *Pengayoman* the Banner of Protection, which is placed to the left of the judge's chair in Indonesian courts.

panji-panji banner, standard, pennant.

panjing (*Pal*) servant in the house of a village head (an unmarried pregnant woman who does not want to reveal the name of the father).

memanjingkan to employ s.o. in the house of the village head.

panjonan → PANJUNAN II.

panjul (*J*) bulging (at the back of the head).

panjunan I (*S*) potter, pottery maker.

panjunan II (*Jv*) brothel.

Panju Panjung the military resort command (*Korém* 102) in Palangkaraya.

panjut I (*Jv*) torch (made of resin wrapped in leaves, etc.).

panjut II white spots or white color (at the extremity of a kris or the tail of a dog).

panjut III memanjut(-manjut) to spout, gush (out), spurt (out); → PANCUT.

memanjutkan to make s.t. spurt out.

pankréas (*D*) pancreas.

pankromatik (*D/E*) panchromatic.

pano → PANAU.

panorama (*D/E*) panorama.

berpanorama with a ... panoramic view. *pemukiman ~ indah* a residence with a beautiful panoramic view.

panoramik (*D/E*) panoramic.

panser (*D*) armored car/vehicle (which uses rubber tires); *cp* TANK. *- pengangkut pasukan* armored personnel carrier, APC.

pansiun → PÉNSIUN.

pansus → PANITIA Khusus. **mampansuskan** to discuss in a special committee (of Parliament).

pantai 1 (sea)shore, beach, coast(al zone). **2** (*M*) sloping, slanting (down to the coast). *lepas* – offshore. *menyusuri* – to follow the coast(line)/seashore. *orang* – people who live along the shore/coast. *- Barat* a) West Coast (of the U.S.A.). b) Military Resort Command (*Korém* 023) in Sibolga. *- belakang* back shore. *- depan* foreshore. *- Emas* Gold Coast. *- Gading* Ivory Coast. *- sawar* barrier beach. *- Timur* a) East Coast (of the U.S.A.). b) Military Resort Command (*Korém* 022) in Pematang Siantar.

berpantai 1 with/to have a beach. **2** to be bordered by a beach. *~ laut* on the sea(shore), with a coast. *negara tak ~ laut* a landlocked country.

berpantaikan to have ... as its coastline. *lautan yang ~ sebagian Kepulauan Indonésia* the sea which borders on part of the Indonesian Archipelago.

memantai 1 to (move toward the) beach, get to the shore. *Meskipun yang digunakan kapal Alut Baru jenis LST, namun di pulau-pulau itu tak mungkin melakukan ~ karena faktor alamnya.* Although the Alut Baru of the LST-class was used, it was impossible to approach the shore due to natural factors. **2** beaching. **3** to skirt/keep close to the shore. **4** to set (of the sun).

pantak invasion. *- botol* cork.

memantak to penetrate, stick (a sharp object) into; *cp* LANTAK.

memantakkan to drive in (nails/stakes, etc.).

pantalon (*D*) long trousers; → CELANA *panjang*.

pantang 1 prohibition, action or thing that is forbidden according to custom or beliefs, prohibitive regulation; abstinence, refraining from. **2** forbidden, prohibited; taboo (by custom). **3** cannot stand, do not want to; to abstain/refrain from, avoid (doing s.t.). *melanggar* – to go against a prohibition. *- berjudi* ban on gambling, no gambling allowed. *- berkala* periodic abstinence. *- berubah* invariable, unchangeable. *- dan larangan* all k.o. taboos and restrictions. *- dibantah* pigheaded, obstinate. *(diet) - garam* salt-free (diet). *- di hutan* to observe certain prohibitions when in the forest, such as to use the word *datuk* instead of the taboo word for tiger. *- kerendahan* a) high-spirited. b) do not want to be surpassed, hates to be surpassed by s.o. *- larang* various k.o. prohibitions. *- mengalah* no defeat! *- mengeluh* no complaining. *- menyerah* never give up, never say die. *- mundur* no retreat! *Maju terus, - mundur!* Ever onward, no retreat! (President Soekarno's slogan during *Konfrontasi*). *- patah di tengah* persevering. *- pemali* various taboos and restrictions. *- surut* adamant, doesn't give in easily. *- tersinggung* touchy, quick to take offense, thin-skinned.

berpantang to be prohibited from, banned, tabooed. *hidup ~* to live under a (certain) prohibition. *makan ~* to (be on a) diet.

makanan ~ prohibited food. *~ dilawan/(k)alah* invincible, cannot be defeated, never admits defeat. *~ kelintasan* to be the cock of the walk, refuse to be inferior to anyone. *~ makan daging* to be a vegetarian, do not eat meat. *sebelum ajal ~ mati* nobody dies before his time. *~ patah di tengah* to persevere, press on to the end, see it through. *~ surut* to be adamant/uncompromising.

memantang(i) to abstain from, avoid.

memantang(kan) to refuse to, not yield an inch on, abstain from (smoking, etc.), despise, disdain, scorn. *tak pernah ~ lawan* not yield to anybody. *tidak memantang kerja* to accept any k.o. work. *~ minuman keras* to abstain from alcoholic beverages.

pantangan 1 prohibition. **2** forbidden (food, etc.), s.t. taboo. *Menangkap ikan hiu merupakan ~ bagi pelaut.* It is taboo for fishermen to catch sharks.

pantang-pantangan forbidden thing, taboos.

kepantangan abstinence, s.t. disliked/avoided; taboo. *Tiadakah engkau tahu bahwa yang kauperbuat itu ~ku?* Didn't you know that you did s.t. that I dislike?

pemantangan avoiding, abstaining (from).

pantango (in Gorontalo) about one-fourth of a hectare.

pantap → PANITIA *tetap*.

pantar (*J/Jv*) **pantaran** and **sepantaran** *dengan* of the same age as. *Ia pantaranku/sepantaran dengan aku.* He is my age.

Pantarlih → PANITIA *pendaftaran pemilih*.

pantas I 1 proper, suitable, adequate. *Beberapa harian memberikan honorarium yang –.* Several dailies give an adequate honorarium. *tidak –* improper, in poor taste. **2** agree, match, go well with, fit, correspond to. *Gaun itu – dengan potongan tubuhnya.* That gown goes well with her figure. **3** appropriate, fitting. *Kita harus berpakaian yang –.* We should be dressed appropriately. **4** it goes without saying, naturally, of course. *– tiap-tiap pegawai yang pulang ke negeri Belanda kaya-kaya belaka.* It goes without saying that every government employee who repatriates to the Netherlands is rich. *tidak –* inappropriate. **ketidakpantasan** inappropriateness, impropriety.

sepantasnya properly, accordingly, appropriately, naturally, fitting, as is proper. *Sudah ~ kita menghargai jasa-jasanya.* Naturally, we appreciate his services. *Dia kurang ajar. Perlakukanlah dia ~.* He's rude. Treat him accordingly.

berpantas-pantas to get o.s. all dressed up (to go to a party, etc.).

memantas(-mantas) to adorn, decorate so as to be appropriate (look beautiful, etc.). *~ diri* to adorn o.s. (with nice clothes).

pantasan (*coq*) no wonder, of course, it figures.

kepantasan fairness.

pemantas attire, array, trimmings (to look appropriate/beautiful, etc.).

pantas II 1 fast, speedy, quick; → CEPAT, KENCANG I, LEKAS. *Langkahnya – dan péndék-péndék.* He takes quick, short steps. **2** adroit, deft, adept, agile. *Meréka lebih pandai, lebih cakap, lebih –.* They are smarter, more skillful, and more adroit. *- mulut* silver-tongued, good at talking. *- pangus* (*cla*) fast and adroit. *- tangan* thievish, prone to stealing.

sepantas as fast as. *~ kilat* lightning fast.

berpantasan to race e.o.

memantaskan to speed up, accelerate, hasten. *Langkahnya pun dipantaskan.* He even hastened his steps.

terpantas the fastest.

kepantasan speed, velocity.

pantasi (*D*) fantasy, fancy, for show; → FANTASI. *saputangan –* fancy handkerchief.

pantat I 1 behind, backside, buttocks, posterior; → BIRIT, BOKONG I, KIBUL I. *– meréka tetap melekat di bangku.* They stayed on the bench as though glued to it. *menendang –* to give s.o. a kick in the behind. *(meng)adu –* (*J*) a) with their behinds against e.o. b) they went their separate ways. *(meng)angkat – dari sini* to get out of here. **2** anus, ass; → SILIT. *main –* to engage in anal intercourse. *menjilat –* to kiss s.o.'s ass. *penjilat –* ass-kisser. **3a)** vulva, female pudenda. b) (*Mal*) sex organ (of either sex). **4** base, bottom. *– botol* a) bottom of a bottle. b) alcoholic (person), drunkard. *– jarum* eye of needle. *– kuali* bottom of a saucepan. *– kuning* stingy, miserly, cheap.

– *mabuk* drunkard. – *mobil* rear of a car. – *periuk* bottom of a saucepan. – *truk* back of a truck.

sepantat down/up to one's behind.

berpantat to have a bottom, etc.

memantat to have sexual intercourse with.

memantati 1 to turn one's behind on. **2** not give a damn about s.t.

pantat II memantat ~ *getah* to tap rubber; → MENORÉH *getah.*

pantau I (*M*) a small freshwater fish.

pantau II monitor(ing). – *harga* price monitoring.

memantau 1 to observe, watch, examine. **2** to monitor, record. *satelit mata-mata mutakhir yang mampu* ~ *ujicoba rudal-rudal Soviét* the latest spy satellites which can monitor Soviet guided missiles.

terpantau (to be) monitored.

pantauan (results of) monitoring. *Dari hasil* ~ *itu dipilih satu wakil dari satu propinsi.* One representative from each province is chosen from the results of monitoring.

pemantau 1 observer, examiner. **2** monitor. *komisi* ~ *genjatan senjata* cease-fire monitoring commission. ~ *jantung* heart monitor.

pemantauan 1 observation, examination. **2** monitoring, recording. *Kejaksaan ditugasi untuk melakukan* ~ *tentang perkembangan kriminalitas.* The attorney general's office has been assigned the task of monitoring the growth of criminality. *memperketat* ~ *kelakuan pasar* to tighten the monitoring of market behavior.

pantéis (*D*) pantheist.

pantéisme (*D/E*) pantheism.

pantéistik (*E*) and **pantéistis** (*D*) pantheistic.

panték (*Jv*) pin, peg, dowel; shim, wedge driven into a space to make s.t. fit tighter. *sumur* – a drilled/artesian well.

memanték 1 to peg, pin, put a wedge/shim into. **2** to pierce, drill (a well).

memantékkan to drive (a wedge/shim) (into s.t.).

terpanték (to be) pegged/pinned/shimmed.

pantékan s.t. drilled.

Pantekosta 1 Pentecost. **2** Whitsuntide. **3** Pentecostal sect.

panteng (*J*) **manteng** to stabilize.

pantéon (*D/E*) pantheon.

panter (*D*) panther.

pantes → PANTAS I.

panti (*Jv*) **1** house, dwelling, residence, home. **2** institution. *anak* – foster child. – *asuhan* orphanage. – *cukur* barbershop. – *derma* charitable institution. – *Husada* Medical Unit (in MPR Building). – *jompo* senior citizens home, old age home. – *karya* (*infr*) workshop; → LOKAKARYA. – *pembenihan* hatchery. – *pengetahuan umum* university extension courses. – *perwira* officers mess. – *pijat/pijit* massage parlor. – *réhabilitasi penyandang cacat nétra* [PRPCN] institution/home for the blind. – *rékréasi* amusement center. – *Résosialisasi* Rehabilitation Center (for prostitutes). – *suka ria* amusement center. – *tatarambut* hairdresser's salon, beauty parlor. – *usada* pharmacy, drugstore. – *werd(h)a* senior citizens home, old age home.

memantikan to put s.o. into a nursing/old-age home.

pantik I memantik 1 to light a fire (using a match/flint, etc.). **2** to snap (one's fingers).

memantikkan to light (with/using).

pantikan ignition.

pemantik 1 flint stone. ~ *api* cigarette lighter. **2** trigger, s.t. that ignites or sets s.t. off. *program oriéntasi studi yang menjadi* ~ *munculnya mégalomania* a study orientation program which becomes a trigger for the emergence of megalomania.

pantik II (*Jv*) peg, nail, dowel; → PANTÉK.

memantik 1 ~ *darah/urat (nadi)* to bleed (a vein). **2** to peck at. **3** to drill.

pantikan s.t. drilled.

pemantikan ~ *darah* blood letting.

panting (*J*) particle that precedes a verb or adjective and gives it a meaning of plural and disorganized. *Anak-anak sudah* – *nguyek di tegalan depan rumah Gatot.* The children were swarming all over Gatot's lawn.

berpantingan to throw/hurl away; → BERPELANTINGAN.

terpanting to dart off/away.

terpanting-panting on and on. *perkataan* ~ to talk/run on and on.

pantis mascara. *menarikkan* – (*pada alis*) to put mascara on one's eyebrows.

memantis to apply mascara.

panto (*M ob*) annual/growth rings (in wood).

pantofel (*D*) slippers (with closed toes).

pantok (*Jv*) (to have reached) the end, (have gone) as far as possible; → MENTOG. *seorang pelajar yang belum* – *sekolahnya* a school dropout.

pantomin (*D*) pantomime.

pantopel → PANTOFEL.

pantul reflection, ricochet. *témbakan* – ricochet shot. *titik* – point of reflection.

berpantul(an) to be reflected (of light/sound/heat), reverberate, reverberant (of sounds).

memantul 1 to bounce (back/off), reflect, ricochet. **2** to rebound (of balls). *Detak jantungnya terasa seperti suara genderang yang* ~ *pada bantal yang mengganjal kepalanya.* The beating of his heart felt like the sound of a large drum bounced off the pillow supporting his head. ~ *balik* to bounce back, reverberate.

memantul-mantul to bounce back and forth.

memantulkan to reflect s.t., express s.t. *wajah yang* ~ *kegembiraan* a face expressing/radiating happiness.

terpantul to be reflected, bounced back. *Ketakutan* ~ *kuat dari ribuan penduduk yang menghambur menghindari tempat kejadian.* Fear reflected strongly off (the faces of) thousands of residents scattering all over to avoid the scene (of the disaster).

pantulan 1 reflection. *Tiba-tiba terdengar suara ledakan hébat disertai* ~ *cahaya api.* The sound of an enormous explosion was suddenly heard accompanied by the reflection of a glare from the fire. **2** backlash, recoil. **3** reaction, reflex action.

pemantul reflector, astragal.

pemantulan reflection, bouncing back.

pantun I 1 quatrain, old poetry form consisting of verses of four lines each, k.o. epigrammatic style (*esp* in Sumatra). **2** saying, expression, fixed phrase. **3** answer, reply, rebuttal, rejoinder. *Apa* – *tuan?* What is your response? *balik* – reversal. *Keadaan perkara ini mesti balik* –. In this case there will certainly be a reversal of plaintiff and accused. – *berkait* sets of quatrains. – *kilat* two-line couplet. – *rantai* set of quatrains. – *sindiran* epigram. – *teka-teki* a pantun containing a riddle.

sepantun *tidak* ~ *pun* not even a single, not one.

berpantun to recite a quatrain.

berpantun-pantun(an) to recite quatrains in turn to e.o.

memantuni to tease/make fun of s.o. with quatrains.

memantunkan to compose quatrains on the subject of, say s.t. in the form of a quatrain.

pantunan quatrain contest.

pemantun composer or reciter of quatrains.

pantun II like, as if; → SEPERTI.

pantung k.o. tree, *Dyera costulata*; → JELUTUNG.

pantura [pantai utara] the north coast (of Java).

panu (*Jv*) a ringworm, *Tinea versicolor/flava*, which causes pale patches on brown skin; → PANAU. – *besi* a ringworm, *Tinea nigra*, which causes small black patches (*esp* on the face).

panuan to suffer from ringworm.

panunggalan (*Jv*); → MANUNGGAL.

panus I (*A*) candle-holder.

panus II dark, lowering clouds.

panut (*Jv*) → ANUT. **memanuti** to adhere to, follow, keep to. *Ria melanggar hubungan sosial yang selama ini dipanutinya.* Ria violated the social relationships she had adhered to up to now.

panutan s.t. or s.o. to be followed, leader, exemplar. *Di masyarakat Indonésia, terdapat tiga kelompok* ~, *yaitu umara (pemerintah), ulama dan zuama (tokoh masyarakat).* In Indonesia there are three groups of exemplars, i.e., the government, the theologians, and important figures in society.

panyecep (*S*) present, gift (*usu* in the form of money).

panyembrana (*Bal*) welcoming dance accompanied by *gamelan* music and strewing of yellow rice or flowers.

panyipuhan <nyipuh> (*S*) purification, cleansing.

paohi → PAUHI.

paok various species of pitta, *Pitta spp.* – *delima* black crowned pitta, *Pitta granatina.* – *ékor biru* banded pitta, *Pitta guajana.* – *Halmahéra* ivory-breasted pitta, *Pitta maxima.* – *hijau* hooded pitta, *Pitta sordida.* – *hujan* blue-winged pitta, *Pitta moluccensis.*

pao-pao (C) k.o. leather purse (worn on belt).

paos (*Jv*) tax; → PAJAK I.

pap I (*onom*) popping sound.

pap II (*D*) pap.

papa I (*Skr*) (very) poor, destitute, penniless. – *sengsara* miserably poor. **kepapa-sengsaraan** miserable poverty, destitution, misery.

  terpapa the poorest of the poor

  kepapaan poverty.

papa II (*D*) papa, daddy. *Selamat ulang tahun, –!* Happy birthday, daddy! – *Boot* sobriquet for President Soeharto during his visit to Timor Timur in July 1978.

  sepapa with the same daddy.

pa-pa (*coq*) → APA-APA.

papacang (*S*) fiancé(e).

papah I berpapah to be supported while walking (of s.o. sick, etc.). ~ *atas* to lean on.

  berpapahan to support e.o.

  memapah to support (s.o. sick, etc. in walking).

  pemapah support.

  papahan support.

papah II (*Jv*) leaf stalk of a palm/banana, etc. tree.

  memapah and **mampah 1** resembling a leaf stalk. **2** to make use of a leaf stalk.

  papahan leaf stalk.

papah III → PAPA II.

papain (*D*) papain, an enzyme found in *papaya.*

papak I (*J/Jv*) flat, level, smooth. *ayam –* a combless rooster without tail feathers. *burung –* thick-billed shrike, *Lanius tigrinus. gedung/rumah –* a house with a flat roof.

  memapakkan to flatten, level.

papak II (*Jv*) **berpapak(an)** to meet (in the street coming from opposite directions).

  memapak and **memapaki 1** to come/go to meet, meet/pick up (at the station, etc.). **2** to receive, welcome, greet, look forward to. *Guru besar sejarah itu mulai pekan ini memapaki masa pénsiun, pada usia hampir 67 tahun.* The history professor was looking forward to his retirement at the age of almost 67 starting this week. **3** to intercept, get in the way of.

  papakan 1 meeting, running into. **2** welcome, looking forward to, reception.

  pemapakan greeting, welcoming, salutation.

papak III palm-wine, toddy.

papak IV (*J*) **mapak** to chew.

papakerma (*ob*) **1** wicked, cruel, bad. **2** unlucky, unfortunate (in life).

papalélé 1 (in Kupang, Timor) peddler, hawker. **2** (in South Sulawesi) broker, middleman (in fish-collecting and cattle centers).

papan I 1 plank, plate, board. **2** shelf. **3** (road) sign. **4** (*sl*) strip (of illegal pills). – *arah* route marker/sign. – *asbés* asbestos plate. – *batu* school slate. – *beroda* skateboard. – *besi* steel plate. – *betina* grooved plank. – *bidai* keyboard (of computer terminal). – *catur* chessboard. – *congkak* a boat-shaped board with 12 small holes and one large home hole (= *rumah*) at the end; the player who gets the most shells or seeds into the home hole wins the game. – *cuci* washboard, scrubbing board. – *cuki* board for a checker-like game. – *dam* checkerboard. – *dék* deck planking. – *hubung(an)* switchboard (of telephone). – *hubung utama* main switchboard. – *induk* mother board (in a computer). – *jamban* toilet seat. – *jantan* tongued plank. – *jantan betina* clench building. – *jepit* clipboard. – *jungkat-jungkit* seesaw. – *ketik* keyboard (of computer terminal). – *kol* call board. – *kunci* keyboard. – *lahad* boards placed at the head and foot of a grave. – *lapis* plywood; → KAYU *lapis.* – *lis* eaves board. – *lompatan/loncatan* springboard. – *luncur* surfboard. – *lupi* thick boards attached to the stern and bow sides of a boat for protection. – *mérek* signboard. – *nama* a) name/door plate. *Perguruan tinggi – Nama* an institution of higher learning

actively engaged in enrolling students but which has not yet submitted its name to the proper authorities for processing of its status. b) name tag. – *nisan* → PAPAN *lahad.* – *pantul* backboard. – *pelancar/peluncur* surfboard. – *penémpélan* billboard. – *pengumuman* bulletin board. – *penunjuk préstasi* scoreboard (in sports). – *penyesah* board for beating laundry. – *perkenaan* (*infr*) target (for rifle practice). – *plot* plotting board. – *réklame* billboard (for advertising). – *sakelar/sambung* switchboard. – *sasaran* target (for rifle practice). – *selancar/silancar* (*angin*) (wind) surfboard. – *serat* fiber board. – *seterika* ironing board. – *suara* sound(ing) board. – *tangga* gangplank. – *tongkah* k.o. sledge used for crossing mudflats or marshy ground. – *tulis* blackboard, chalkboard. – *tuts* keyboard.

  memapan(i) to provide (a floor/wall, etc.) with planks. *berlayar sambil* ~ (*M*) to kill two birds with one stone.

  pemapan plank.

  pemapanan planking.

papan II housing, shelter; dwelling, home, residence. *–ku* my home. – *Sejahtera* [PS] the institution which finances housing development for the upper middle class. *Tahun – Internasional bagi Kaum Tunawisma* International Year of Shelter for the Homeless. *Cukup sandang, pangan, dan – merupakan kebutuhan hidup manusia.* Sufficient food, clothing and shelter are the necessities of human life.

papan III (*Jv*) place, position. – *andrawina* (in the Surakarta *Keraton*) place where the Sultan organizes parties or entertains his guests. – *atas* leading, top, first-class/-rate; important person, VIP. *tiga mérek mobil – atas adalah Mercédes Benz, Volvo, dan BMW* the three first-rate brands of cars are Mercedes Benz, Volvo, and BMW. *bank – atas* a top-rated bank. *Instansinya itu telah mengorbankan – bawah dan melindungi – atas.* His agency has already sacrificed the unimportant persons and protected the important persons. – *bawah* low-ranking, of poor quality. *tim – bawah* a lousy team, low-ranking team (in sports); low-ranking person. – *klangenan* Sultan's place of recreation. – *klangenan sangnata* recreation place for the Sultan's family. – *tengah* mid-level (in quality, etc.).

  mapan established, having found its place, settled. *kaum* ~ the establishment. **kemapanan** complacency.

  pemapanan adaptation (to), fitting (in).

papan IV (*S*) classifier for pods (of *petai*, etc.). *harga petai se–* the price of a pod of *petai.*

papar I flat, level, smooth. – *parang* the blunt side of a blade.

  memapar 1 to extend, stretch. **2** to flatten, level (out), smooth, spread out, expand, fold out.

  memapari to expose s.o. (to s.t.). *Meréka dipapari rangsangan audio dan visual.* They are exposed to audio and visual stimuli.

  memaparkan 1 to explain, set forth/out a case. **2** to expose, spread out for all to see. ~ *kegiatan* to expose s.o.'s activities. **3** to flatten, level/smooth out, spread out.

  terpapar exposed, spread out for all to see.

  paparan 1 flat side (of a knife, etc.). **2** explanation, statement, exposition. ~ *para pakar tadi juga didukung dua pakar dari Pusat Penelitian dan Pengembangan.* The statement made by those experts was also supported by two experts from the Center for Research and Development. **3** exposure (to nuclear radiation, etc.). **4** shelf, platform. ~ *benua* continental shelf.

  pemaparan 1 flattening. **2** explanation, exposure, spreading out for all to see.

papar II (*ob*) **memapar** to recruit (soldiers/manpower, etc.); → MEWÉRAK.

  pemapar recruiter.

papas I memapas 1 to take/strip off, remove. **2** to take/steal s.t. (from s.o.). **3** to cut off (part of the body), amputate. **4** to peel (off). ~ *kajang* to roll up a mat.

  terpapas [and **kepapas** (*coq*)] taken away, cut off, amputated, peeled (off).

papas II (*J*) **(ber)papasan** to cross by e.o., pass e.o. (going in opposite directions). *Mobil kami ~ dengan sebuah mobil lain.* Our car passed another car (going in opposite directions).

  memapas(i) to meet, run into, come to meet; to go (up) against. ~ *angin* to make headway against the wind.

terpapas met (up) with, encountered, crossed (going the opposite way), confronted (by).

papasan meeting, encounter.

kepapasan (coq) run into, met up with.

papasan k.o. climber, ivy gourd, Coccinia cordifolia.

papat → PEPAT.

papatong (S) dragonfly. - ageung helicopter.

papaya buah - papaya, Carica papaya; → BETIK I. getah - latex of the papaya tree used an anthelmintic for worms. - semangka a tasty red-fleshed papaya.

papayungan umbrella sedge, Cyperus halpan.

papéda (IBT) sago porridge.

paper (E) /péper/ paper, essay.

papi (D) daddy.

papil (D) papilla.

papilyun → PAVILYUN.

papinyu (Port IBT) cucumber.

papirus (D) papyrus.

papras (Jv) memapras to cut off, prune, make smaller.

paprika (D/E) paprika.

Papua Nugini [PNG] Papua New Guinea.

pa'pui (C) fortune-telling in a Chinese temple using sticks.

par (in acronyms) → PARTAI I.

para I (Jv) 1 (k.o. collective plural article for human beings) the (plural). - hadirin a) the audience, those in attendance. b) Ladies and Gentlemen! - Hemingway the Hemingways. - pembaca readers. - pemirsa télévisi the television audience, televiewers. - pendengar listeners. 2 entire, whole, complete, total. - pelaku the cast (of a play, etc.). - pengurus SPSI/Serikat Pekerja Seluruh Indonésia the entire/whole executive board of the All-Indonesia Workers Union. - tentara the entire army. 3 - yang the (plural). - yang berwenang the authorities, those in authority. - yang berkepentingan those concerned/interested. 4 (in phrases and sentences containing words indicating plurality, such as, banyak, meréka, pada III, seluruh, semua) all (those), many, they all, all of them. banyak - peternak many poultry-farmers. - meréka yang mengaku petani all those who say they are farmers. Di saat itulah - penumpang berloncatan ke dalam sungai tanpa memikirkan risiko akan tenggelam oléh arus sungai yang begitu kuat. At that moment all the passengers jumped into the river without thinking of the risk of being drowned by the river's strong current. seluruh - peserta Munas most of the participants in the National Conference. semua - utusan all the delegates. 5 (preceding an adjective) the ones who are, the group of people who are ... - pintar the smart people, the intelligentsia. 6 (infr used to pluralize inanimates) - organisasi parpol dan golkar the political party organizations and functional groups. meréka (- agency) yang bermutu they (the agencies) which are qualified.

para II rubber. kebun - rubber plantation.

para III (D) clipped form of paratrooper.

keparaan paratroop (mod).

parab (Jv) nama paraban nickname, epithet.

parabel (D/E) parable.

parabol(a) (D) 1 parabola. 2 satellite dish.

parabolik (E) and parabolis (D) parabolic.

paradam (D coq) damn(ed).

paradam-paradam and - paradom to keep on cursing.

memaradam to swear at, curse.

parade (D) parade. - kemenangan victory parade. - laut sailing pass. - perpisahan passing out parade. - resmi ceremonial parade. - senja a flag-lowering ceremony held three times a year at the presidential palace. - udara fly-past, flyby.

berparade to parade, assemble in military formation for show.

paradigma (D) paradigm.

paradigmatis (D) paradigmatic.

paradoks (D/E) paradox.

paradoksal (D) paradoxical.

paradom → PARADAM.

paraf (D) initials.

memaraf to initial, mark with one's initials.

pemaraf s.o. who initials.

pemarafan initialing.

parafin (D/E) paraffin.

parafrase (D/E) paraphrase.

mem(p)arafrase(kan) to paraphrase.

paragnos (D) clairvoyant.

paragog (D) paragoge.

paragraf (D/E) paragraph, section; → ALINÉA.

parah serious (of a wound/illness/situation, etc.), enormous (difficulties), in difficulty; → GAWAT, TERUK. Jakarta Barat yang tampaknya paling - mengalami luapan air. It seems that West Jakarta suffered most from the flooding. luka - seriously wounded. sakit - gravely ill.

separah as serious as.

memarahkan and memperparah to worsen, make worse, aggravate. Untung tidak ada angin kencang yang akan memperparah keadaan. Fortunately, there wasn't a strong wind to make the situation worse.

terparah the most serious, the worst.

keparahan seriousness, graveness.

Parahiyangan (S) 1 the West Java region. 2 name of the express train between Jakarta and Bandung.

paraid → FARAID.

para-ilmu jiwa parapsychology.

paraji (S) midwife; → DUKUN beranak.

memarajikan to use a midwife when giving birth.

parak I (A) 1 spacing, interval, intervening space. 2 separation, division; partition. 3 different; difference.

berparak to part, separate.

mamarakkan to leave room/a space between, distinguish between, differentiate, separate s.t.

terparakkan tak ~ undifferentiated.

pemarakan differentiation.

parak II approaching (a time/a time of day, etc.). - déwasa entering adulthood. - pagi at dawn/daybreak. - siang late morning.

parak III (M) 1 garden; → KEBUN. 2 field; → LADANG.

perparakan area covered by fields.

parako (S) bamboo shelf for storing kitchen utensils.

Paraku [Pasukan Rakyat Kalimantan Utara] North Kalimantan People's Force (during Konfrontasi).

paralayang (sports) hang-gliding.

paralél (D) 1 parallel. 2 extension (phone).

memparalélkan to make s.t. run parallel with s.t. else.

paralélisasi (E) making s.t. run parallel with s.t. else, paralleling.

paralélisme (D/E) parallelism.

paralélogram (D/E) parallelogram.

paralisis (E) paralysis.

param medical embrocation or ointment (used by women on their feet after giving birth). minyak - an ointment applied to the skin. - kocok k.o. hot liniment that must be shaken before application.

memarami to apply param to (a part of the body).

paramanusia (infr) human race.

paramarta (Jv) good, noble; → AMBEK paramarta.

paramasastra (Jv) grammar.

paramasastrawan grammarian.

paramédik (E) and paramédis (D) paramedic.

paramén (D) vestment.

paramésuari → PERMAISURI.

paraméter (D) parameter.

paraméx a patent headache medicine.

paramilitér paramilitary.

paramita (Skr) perfection. - Jaya Intermuseum Association of the Greater Jakarta Capital Special Region.

paramitra crony; → KONCO.

parampara (Jv) 1 spokesman; chairman. 2 political advisor.

paran I (J/Jv) direction; aim, goal. Ke mana -nya? Which way are you going? - jujugan a) a place/person visited frequently. b) place of consultation.

memarani to direct one's course; to aim at.

paranan (elec and naut) homing.

paran II (M) ridgepole.

paranada (mus) staff.

parang I chopping knife, cleaver. – *gabus menjadi seperti* – *besi* a weak person becomes strong and holds power. *punggung* – *sekalipun jika selalu diasah akan tajam juga* constant dripping wears away a stone. *seperti – bermata dua* a) to wear two hats. b) it cuts both ways. – *cangkuk/latuk* bill hook.
  memarang 1 to cut with a *parang*. 2 to cross/strike out.
  memarangkan 1 to chop/cut with s.t. 2 to cross/strike out.
parang II (*Jv*) classic *batik* pattern from Solo and Yogya. – *baris* k.o. batik design. – *rusak* (*cla*) "broken blade," *aka* "the princely pattern," traditionally worn only by members of the royal house of Yogya and its retainers; this design is *esp* associated with Central Java.
parang III parang(an) *sakit* ~ to have a certain skin disease on the nape of the neck or on the nose.
parang-parang (*ikan* –) wolf herring, *Chirocentrus dorab*.
paranima paranymph.
paranoia (*D/E*) paranoia.
paranoid (*D/E*) paranoid.
paranormal (*D/E*) paranormal.
paranti I (*Jv*) ancestral customs/institutions.
paranti II → PERANTI.
parap I berparap to fight with weapons.
  memarap to hammer, pound. ~ *dada* to strike one's breast.
  pemarap s.t. used for pounding.
parap II → PARAF.
para-para 1 bamboo rack (for crockery and pots), shelf. 2 attic. *arang* – soot (in kitchen).
parapati (*M*) pigeon; → MERPATI.
parapik (*M*) trap for tigers.
paraplégia (*D*) paraplegia. *penderita* – paraplegic.
parapsikolog (*D*) parapsychologist.
parapsikologi (*D/E*) parapsychology.
paras I face, countenance, physiognomy, look. – *jalan* road surface.
  berparas to have a (beautiful, etc.) face/look. *seorang wanita muda ~ dan berbodi melangit* a young woman with a fantastic face and body. *Diberitakan tenaga kerja wanita Indonésia – cantik dan séksi tidak diizinkan bekerja di negara itu.* It is said that beautiful sexy Indonesian female workers are not allowed to work in that country. ~ *lumayan* good-looking.
paras II smooth, level, even. – *laut* sea level.
  separas equal (in height), (a)like, as ... as; proportional. *tingginya ~ lutut/pinggang* as high as the knee/waist, knee-/waist-high.
  memaras 1 to level (off) (a bushel measure) ~ *cupak/gantung* to level out the excess (hulled) rice in a *cupak/gantung* (so as to sell exactly the right amount of rice). 2 to plane, shave. ~ *janggut* to shave one's beard.
paras III (*ob*) *batu* – k.o. sandstone, tuff.
paras IV → FARJI.
Parasamya Purnakarya Nugraha (*Skr neo*) the highest presidential award for a province, etc. which excels in realizing the Five-Year Development Plan; → PELITA II.
parasil (*E*) parasail, i.e., a type of parachute used in sport of sailing through the air towed by a powerboat.
parasit (*D*) 1 parasite, an organism that lives on another species; → BENALU. 2 (human) parasite, freeloader.
parasitér (*D*) parasitic.
parasitis (*D*) parasitic(al).
parasitisme (*D/E*) parasitism.
parasitolog (*D*) parasitologist.
parasitologi (*D/E*) parasitology.
parasut (*D/E*) parachute, chute. – *cadangan* reserve parachute. – *penarik* extraction parachute.
parasutis (*D*) parachutist.
parataksis (*D/E*) parataxis.
paratifoid (*E*) paratyphoid. *demam* – paratyphoid fever.
paratifus (*D*) paratyphus.
parau hoarse (from a cold/talking too much, etc.); → SERAK I.
  memarau to become hoarse.
  keparauan hoarseness.
parawisata → PARIWISATA.
parbaringan (*Bat*) shaman, medicine man; → DATU, DUKUN.
pardon (*D*) pardon, clemency. *tanpa* – without clemency.

paré → PERIA I. – *anom* (*Jv*) the green and yellow flag of the Mangkunegaran in Solo. – *welut/uler* snake gourd, *Trichosanthes cucumerina*.
paréban sibling.
paréi (*Ban*); → PADI I.
parek → PARK.
parem → PARAM.
paréman → PRÉMAN.
parénkim (*D*) parenchyma.
paréntal (*E*) parental.
paréntésis (*E*) parenthesis; → TANDA *kurung*.
paréwa (*M*) → PERÉWA.
parfum (*D*) perfume. *bau bir,* – *murahan* the smell of beer and cheap perfume.
  perparfuman perfume (*mod*). *pakar* ~ perfumer.
Parhalado (*Bat*) k.o. central parliament in the *HKBP* structure.
pari I *ikan* – various species of rays and skates, *Hymanturae, Trygonidae, Torpedinae, Myliobatidae* and others. – *ampai* spotted numbfish, *Narcine timlei*. – *bunga*, k.o. ray, *Astrape dipterygia*. – *burung* eagle ray, *Aetobatus maculata/narinari*. – *daun* cowtail ray, *Trygon sephen*. – *dedap* thornback, *Urogymnus spp.* – *kamprét* short-tailed butterfly ray, *Gymnara spp.* – *kelapa* cowtail ray, *Trygon sephen*. – *kembang* blue-spotted stingray, *Taeniura lymma*. – *nyiru* pale-edge stingray, *Dasyatis zugei*. – *pasir* k.o. stingray, *Hymantura/Trygon uarnak/bleekeri*. – *tohok* k.o. skate.
pari II *bintang* – the southern cross (constellation near the southern celestial pole).
pari III fairy; → PERI III.
pari IV par value (of stocks, etc.).
  keparian parity.
pari V (*Jv*) rice (only used in certain compounds); → PADI I. – *jero* late-bearing rice plant. – *gaga/gogo* rice cultivated in non-irrigated rice fields.
pari VI (*Skr*) a prefix meaning: plenary, full; complete, entire, total.
pari VII → PERIA.
PARI VIII → PARTAI *Rakyat Indonésia*.
paria I (*D*) pariah, outcaste, low-caste person.
paria II → PERIA I.
pariban (*Bat*) the daughter of one's mother's brother (an ideal marriage partner).
parih memarih to shoot/throw dice; to deal (playing cards); to cast (lots); to predict the future (using playing cards).
pariharta (*Jv*) (in Yogya) finance.
Parijs (*D*) /paris/ → PARIS I.
parik I → PORAK-PARIK.
parik II in line, in a line/queue.
parikan (*Jv*) /pari'an/ a chanting song, consisting of a senseless string of words containing repeated syllables, made up by children to ridicule or taunt s.o.
parikena (*Jv*) *guyon* – apparently in fun but, in fact, in all earnestness. *guyon/sembrana* – to ask for s.t. in a joking way. *Masih ingat model guyon – dalam Obrolan Pak Besut di RRI Yogyakarta?* Do you still remember the joking way of asking for s.t. in Mr. Besut's talk show on Yogyakarta Republic of Indonesia Radio?
paring (*Jv*) a gift from a higher to a lower status person.
  keparingan *kemerdékaan* ~ given/granted independence.
paripurna 1 complete (set of ...). 2 plenary (session, etc.). *pertemuan/sidang* – plenary session. 3 perfectly.
  keparipurnaan perfection. ~ *hidup* life's ideal.
Paris I Paris. *-nya Java* Bandung. *-nya Sumatra* Bukittinggi. *-nya Timur Tengah* Beirut. – *Club* Group of Indonesia's main industrialized, noncommunist creditors who held talks in Paris about Indonesia's debts following the fall of Soekarno.
Paris II *cita/kain* – half-silk, artificial silk, rayon. – *goyang* brocade.
Parisada Hindu Dharma (*Bal*) Supreme Council of Balinese Hinduism.
pariskot (*ob*) → PERSEKOT.
parit I 1 ditch, trench, drain, moat, fosse. 2 groove, slot, channel, rabbet. – *batu* quarry. – *kapur* lime pit. – *keling* moat. – *pengalir* drainage ditch, drain. – *pertahanan* defense trench. – *Sunda* the Sunda Trough (west of Java). – *témbak* (*mil*) trench.

berparit grooved, furrowed.
berparit-parit with/to have ditches, etc.
memarit to dig a ditch, dredge, entrench.
pemaritan entrenchment.
parit II (*ob*) mine, charge. – *laut* sea mine, depth charge.
memarit to drag for s.t. in the ocean.
paritas and paritét (*D*) parity.
pariwara I (*Jv*) 1 advertisement, advertising. 2 announcement (in a newspaper).
pariwara II followers, retinue.
pariwisata tourism. *obyék* – tourist attraction. *mengobyékpariwisatakan* to turn s.t. into a tourist attraction. – *untuk kebudayaan* cultural tourism. – *untuk rékréasi* recreational tourism.
berpariwisata to be a tourist.
kepariwisataan 1 tourism. 2 tourist (*mod*). 3 tour. ~ *yang bersifat khusus* special-interest tours.
pariwisatawan tourist; → WISATAWAN.
parji → FARAJ.
park (*D*) park; → TAMAN I.
parkét I (*D*) Public Prosecutor's Office.
parkét II (*D*) parquet.
Parkindo [Partai Kristen Indonésia] Indonesian Christian Party.
Parkinson *penyakit* – Parkinson's disease.
parkir (*D*) parking (of vehicle). *juru/petugas* – parking lot attendant. *tempat* – *pesawat* apron (for airplane). *tempat* – *susun* parking structure. *tempat* – (*umum*) public parking. *tukang* – parking lot attendant. *tukang* – *pesawat* marshaler (of airplane); → PEMANDU *pesawat*. – *bawah tanah* underground parking. – *di badan jalan* on-street parking. – *paralél* parallel parking.
mem(p)arkir 1 to park (a car, etc.). 2 to take a position/job. *wartawan yang* ~ *di kantor Humas* a reporter who took a job in the public relations office. 3 to deposit (money in a bank). *modal orang Indonésia yang diparkir di bank-bank luar negeri* Indonesian capital deposited in foreign banks. 4 to place/put s.o. in a department or office. *Mungkin ia akan diparkir menjadi petugas bagian administrasi.* He might be put in the administration department.
parkir-mem(p)arkir parking (*mod*). *masalah* ~ parking problems.
mem(p)arkirkan to moor (a boat). *Sebuah sampan kecil diparkirkan di muka gubug meréka.* A small *sampan* was moored in front of their bungalow.
terparkir parked. *Di luar* ~ *mobil-mobil méwah.* Luxury cars were parked outside.
parkiran parking lot.
pemarkir s.o. who parks (a car).
pemarkiran parking.
perparkiran parking (*mod*). *keadaan* ~ the parking situation.
parkit (*D*) parakeet, *Melopsittacus undulatus*.
parlemén (*D*) parliament. *anggota* – member of parliament, MP. *sidang* – parliamentary session.
berparlemén to have a parliament, with a parliament. *Indonésia* ~ Indonesia with a parliament (slogan during colonial times).
parlemén-parleménan a would-be parliament.
parleméntaria parliamentary affairs.
parleméntarisme (*D/E*) parliamentarism.
parleméntér (*D*) parliamentary. *démokrasi* – parliamentary democracy.
parmasi pharmacy; → FARMASI.
PARMI → PARTAI *Rakyat Miskin Indonésia*.
parmitu (*Bat*) boozer, heavy drinker.
Parmusi → PARTAI *Muslimin Indonésia*.
paro (*Jv*) half, middle; → PARUH II. *penyanyi sintal* – *baya Waljinah* the plump middle-aged singer Waljinah. – *waktu* part-time. *tenaga penjual* – *waktu* part-time salesman.
paro-paro half-and-half, half-hearted.
separo a/one half. *lebih* ~ *dari wisatawan asing yang berkunjung ke Indonésia* more than half of the foreign tourists visiting Indonesia. menyeparokan to divide in half/two.
memaro and maro 1 to divide in half/two. 2 to cultivate a field on a métayage/sharecropping basis.
maron sharecropped (field). *sistém* ~ system in which the crop

is divided in two; one half is for the landowner and the other half for the cultivator.
paron sharecropping, métayage.
paroan half. ~ *bumi* hemisphere.
pemaro sharecropper.
parodi (*D/E*) parody, travesty, farcical skit.
parodom → PERDOM.
paroh half; → PARO.
separoh a/one half. *hampir* ~ *dari orang-orang Amérika di Singapura* almost half of the Americans in Singapore.
paroki (*D*) parish.
paron (*Jv*) anvil. – *tanduk* beak iron.
parpol [partai politik] political party.
berparpol to be a member of a political party.
keparpolan party (*mod*). *sistém* ~ system of political parties.
Parpostél [Pariwisata, pos dan télékomunikasi] (Department of) Tourism, Post, and Telecommunications.
Parsi I (*Pers*) 1 Persia. 2 Persian. *orang* – Persian.
parsi II *akar* – asparagus, *Asparagus officinalis*.
parsial (*E*) and parsiil (*D*) partial. *intégrasi* – partial integration (*math*).
parsubang (*Bat*) Muslims and those who don't eat pork.
partai I (*D*) (political) party; → PARPOL. – *Adil Makmur* [PAM] Prosperous Just Party. – *Aliansi Démokrat Indonésia* [PADI] Indonesian Democratic Alliance Party. – *Aliansi Rakyat Miskin Indonésia* [PARMI] Indonesian Poor People's Party. – *Al-Islam Sejahtera* [PAS] Welfare Islamic Party. – *Amanat Nasional* [PAN] National Mandate Party. – *Amanat Penderitaan Rakyat* [AMPERA] People's Suffering Mandate Party. – *Bhinéka Tunggal Ika* [PBTI] E Pluribus Unum Party. – *Bulan Bintang* Crescent and Star Party. – *Buruh Indonésia* [PBI] Indonesian Labor Party. – *Buruh Nasional* National Workers Party. – *Cinta Damai* Peace-Loving Party. – *Daulat Rakyat* [PDR] People's Sovereignty Party. – *gurem* a minority/underdog party. – *Démokrasi Indonésia* [PDI] Indonesian Democracy Party (which represents the former *PNI, Partai Katolik, Parkindo, IP-KI,* and *Partai Murba*; formed in 1973). – *Démokrasi Kasih Bangsa* [PDKB] Love the People Democracy Party. – *Démokrat Katolik* [PDK] Catholic Democrat Party. – *Hijau* Green Party. – *Indonésia Baru* [PIB] New Indonesian Party. – *Islam Démokrat* Democratic Islamic Party. – *Islam Indonésia* [PII] Indonesian Islamic Party. – *Karya Peduli Bangsa* [PKPB] Concern for the Nation Functional Party. – *Katolik* Catholic Party. – *Keadilan* [PK] Justice Party. – *Keadilan dan Persatuan Indonesia* [PKPI] Indonesian Justice and Unity Party. – *Keadilan Sejahtera* [PKS] Prosperous Justice Party. – *Kebangkitan Bangsa* [PKB] National Awakening Party. – *Kebangkitan Muslim Indonésia* [KAMI] Indonesian Muslim Awakening Party. – *Kebangsaan Merdéka* Free Nationality Party. – *Kedaulatan Rakyat* [PKR] People's Sovereignty Party. – *Kesejahteraan Umat* [PKU] Community Welfare Party. – *Komunis Indonésia* [PKI] Communist Party of Indonesia; established in 1934 and banned in 1966 as a result of *G30S-PKI.* – *Kristen Indonésia* [Parkindo] Christian Party of Indonesia. – *Kristen Nasional Indonésia* [PKNI/KRISNA] Indonesian National Christian Party. – *kuning* reference to Golkar. – *Masyumi Baru* New Masyumi Party. – *MKGR* → MKGR. – *Muda Pembangunan Indonésia* [PMPI] Indonesian Development Youth Party. – *Muslimin Indonésia* [Parmusi] Indonesian Muslim Party; established in 1968, fused with other Muslim parties in 1973 into the *PPP.* – *Nahdlatul Ulama* [PNU] Muslim Scholars Party. – *Nasional Démokrat* Democratic National Party. – *Nasional Indonésia* [PNI] Indonesian National Party. – *Patriot Indonésia* [PPI] Indonesian Patriots Party. – *PDI Perjuangan* Indonesian Democracy Party-Struggle. – *Pekerja Indonésia* [PPI] Indonesian Workers Party. – *Pelopor* Vanguard Party. – *Pembaharuan Indonésia* [PPI] Indonesian Renewal Party. – *Persatuan Pembangunan* [PPP] United Development Party, q.v. – *Pilihan Rakyat* [PILAR] People's Choice Party. – *Rakyat Bersatu* [PRB] United People's Party. – *Rakyat Démokratik* [PRD] Democratic People's Party. – *Rakyat Indonésia* [PARI] Indonesian People's Party. – *Rakyat Miskin Indonésia*

[PARMI] Indonesian Poor People's Party. – *Réformasi Indonésia* [PRI] Indonesian Reformation Party. – *Républik* [PR] Republic Party. – *Solidaritas Pekerja* [PSP] Workers Solidarity Party. – *Syarikat Islam Indonésia* [PSII] Indonesian Islamic Union Party. – *Tionghoa Indonésia* [Parti] Indonesian Chinese Party. – *Ummat Islam* Islamic Community Party. – *Uni Démokrasi Indonésia* [PUDI] Indonesian Democratic Union Party.

separtai in the same party (as).

berpartai partial. *tidak* ~ impartial; nonparty.

kepartaian party (*mod*).

partai II (*D*) parcel, lot, quantity. *dalam – besar* in bulk.

berpartai-partai lots of, in large quantities.

partai III (*D*) game (of badminton/billiards/tennis, etc.). – *ganda* doubles.

Parti → PARTAI *Tionghoa Indonésia.*

particuliere landerijen (*D col*) private estates or latifundia particularly given or sold to Chinese and Europeans.

partikel (*D ling phys*) particle. *papan* – particle board. – *ingkar* negative particle. – *pementing/penegas/penentu* emphatic particle. – *radioaktif* radioactive particle.

partikelir (*D*) 1 private individual (in notarial instruments). 2 (of) no occupation, independent. 3 private (not government); → SWASTA. *sekolah – dan pemerintah* private and government schools.

mempartikelirkan to privatize, convert into a private enterprise (of a State Trading Corporation, etc.).

partikularis (*D*) particularist.

partikularisasi (*E*) particularization.

partikulir (*D*) → PARTIKELIR.

partisan (*D*) partisan.

partisi (*E*) partition.

partisip (*D gram*) participle.

partisipan (*D*) participant.

partisipasi (*D*) participation.

berpartisipasi to participate.

partisipatif participating.

partitif (*D gram*) partitive.

partitur (*D*) musical score.

partner (*D/E*) partner.

berpartner to have a partner; as a partner.

partus (*L*) delivery, confinement, giving birth.

partuturon (*Bat*) kinship, family relationship.

paru lung. *ahli penyakit* – pulmonologist. – *molor* emphysema.

paru-paru lung(s). *penyakit* ~ lung disease (tuberculosis, etc.). *radang* ~ pneumonia. ~ *basah* pleurisy.

parud (*Jv*) scrape, grate; → PARUT.

parudan 1 grated. *kelapa* – grated coconut. 2 grater. ~ *kelapa* coconut grater.

paruh I beak/bill (of a bird). – *serangga* rostrum (of an insect).

berparuh 1 to have a beak. 2 beaked.

memaruh to peck at, pick up in small pieces (as a bird does with its bill).

paruh II half, middle, partial; → PARO. *lelaki – baya* a middle-aged man. *pada – pertama tahun 1990* in the first half of 1990. *pada – kedua abad ke-20 ini* in the second half of the 20th century. – *daya* half power.

separuh 1 a/one half. 2 partially. ~ *baya* middle-aged. ~ *harga* half price. (*di*) ~ *jalan* halfway (there), at the halfway point. *Kita sudah berada di* ~ *jalan menuju cita-cita bangsa.* We are halfway to (achieving) the nation's aspirations. ~ *hati* halfhearted. ~ *mati* half dead; → SETENGAH *mati.* ~ *tanah* half the land. ~ *umur/usia* middle-aged. **separuh-separuh** half and half, fifty-fifty, divided equally. *Sisanya ditanggung* ~ *oléh BNI dan BRI.* The rest is accounted for on a fifty-fifty basis by the *BNI* and the *BRI.*

berparuh to share fifty-fifty.

memaruh to halve, divide in half/two.

paruhan half. *Selama beberapa jam aliran listrik padam untuk* ~ *utara Pulau Luzon.* For several hours the electricity was cut off for the northern half of Luzon.

paruik (*M*) k.o. sausage filled with duck eggs.

paruman (*Bal*) council. – *Agung* a) Council of Balinese Rulers. b) Balinese council consisting of representatives from each *swapraja.* – *Negara* Advisory Council (in Bali).

parun (*M*) **memarun** to burn rubbish; → PERUN.

parunan burnt items.

pemarun rubbish burner.

pemarunan the burning of rubbish.

parung I sinuous. *keris* – (*sari*) kris with a wavy, snake-like blade.

parung II *pokok* – k.o. plant, *Dysoxylon cauliflorum.*

parut 1 scrape, grate. 2 scratch, scar, cicatrice. 3 grated. *kelapa* – *kering* desiccated grated coconut.

berparut with scratches/scars, scratched, scraped, scarred.

memarut 1 to scrape, grate. ~ *kelapa* to grate coconut. 2 to scratch, graze.

parutan 1 grater. ~ *kéju* cheese grater. 2 s.t. grated. *kéju* ~ grated cheese. *kelapa* ~ grated coconut.

pemarut grater. ~ *kelapa* coconut grater.

pemarutan grating, flaking.

parvenu and **parvinu** (*Fr D*) parvenu.

parwa (*Skr*) part of an old (*Jv*) literary work, such as, *Adiparwa*, and *Wirataparwa*, which are parts of the book of *Mahabharata.*

pas I (*D*) 1 clipped form of **paspor**. 2 (*surat* –) pass, travel, etc. document. – *jalan* travel permit. – *kapal* certificate of registry. – *lintas batas* border pass (required to cross border between Irian Jaya and Papua New Guinea). – *naik ke pesawat* boarding pass (for airplanes). – *pengantar* way bill. – *Perjalanan Haji* [PPH] Haji Travel Permit (travel document for Indonesian citizens on the pilgrimage to Mecca).

pas II (*D*) 1 accurate, hits the mark. *Kenyataannya, jam DKI lebih banyak ngaco daripada –.* The fact is that the clocks in Jakarta are more often inaccurate than accurate. 2 to fit (of clothes), be the right size. 3 (the) exact (amount). *harga* – fixed price. *uang* – exact change. *Bayar dengan uang –!* No change given! *khasiat yang paling* – the most appropriate quality. 4 exactly, precisely, right. – *depan hidung anda!* right in front of your nose! *tak* – *bunyinya* out of tune (of a musical instrument). 5 just enough. *penghasilanmu* – you earn just enough. 6 in line/compliance. *Menyajikan isi yang* – *dengan keinginan dan kebutuhan para éksékutif kita.* It (the magazine) offers contents in line with the needs and desires of all our executives.

mempas and **mengepas** to try on (clothes).

mempaskan and **mengepaskan** 1 to have s.o. try on (clothes). 2 to equalize, level off, put s.t. in line with s.t. else. ~ *pendapatan dengan pengeluaran* to make income equal to expenditures.

ngepas (*coq*) to be just enough.

pas-pasan just enough (no more and no less). *harga* ~ break-even point. *hidup* ~ to live from hand to mouth, have just enough to live on. *keuntungan* ~ marginal profit. *kaum yang berpenghasilan* ~ people who live at the subsistence level/who earn just enough to live on.

pas III (*E*) (mountain) pass.

pas IV (*E*) pass (in bridge).

pas V (*D*) step, a movement made with the foot/feet in dancing; *cp* LANGKAH.

pas VI (form of address for **opas**) janitor!

pas VII (*sl*) when(ever). *Mereka bagi-bagi stiker ke penonton* – *manggung.* They pass out stickers to the audience when(ever) they appear on stage.

pas VIII (*E Mal*) to pass (an examination).

pas IX (in acronyms) → PASUKAN.

PAS X → PARTAI *Al-Islam Sejahtera.*

pasa (*Jv*) the fast; → PUASA.

pasah I (*A*) (– *nikah*) divorce, annulment of a marriage granted by a religious court judge at the request of the wife on grounds that the *taklik* was broken (desertion or lack of maintenance). *minta* – to request such a divorce.

memasah to divorce one's wife after she has filed for divorce on those grounds.

memasahkan to divorce s.o.

pasah II (*M*) **terpasah** to land/arrive somewhere which was not the goal of the trip, end up somewhere.

pasah III (*Jv*) carpenter's plane.

memasah 1 to plane, smooth with a plane. 2 to shave ice, chip ice from a cake of ice by moving it across a stationary plane.

pasahan shavings.

pasai (*M*) tired/sick of, bored, fed up with.

pasak 1 nail, (wooden) peg, wedge, cotter, bolt. **2** spindle, axis. *besar – dari tiang* to live beyond one's means. *– aman* (*Mal*) safety pin (on a gun). *– baut* cotter bolt. *– bumi* a plant, *Eurycoma longifolia*, found in Central Kalimantan, k.o. aphrodisiac; → STRONG-PA. *– datar* joint tongue. *– ganda* fox wedge. *– kampung* a) villagers who never leave their village. b) hick, country bumpkin. *– kayu* dowel. *– kuku* a black, longitudinal stripe on fingernails and hooves. *– kemudi* tiller. *– kunci* the authorities, s.o. in power. *– negeri* person considered the "backbone" of a country, one often asked for advice. *– tetap* crank pin.
  memasak to nail (down).
  memasakkan 1 to fasten (with a peg/wedge). **2** to hammer s.t. into s.t., insist (that). *~ ke telinga* to give sincere advice.

pasal (*A*) **1** paragraph, article, section; → FASAL, PARAGRAF. *satu – dari UUD 45* an article of the 1945 Constitution. *–.- karét* (*coq*) articles 154, 155, and 156 of the *KUHP* about stirring up enmity and hatred. *– pelengkap* addendum. *–.- penutup* closing articles (in notarial instruments dealing with incorporation). *– demi –* article by article (in government regulations). **2** reason, cause, motive; → LANTARAN, SEBAB. *apa –* why, what's the reason? *Apa – sampai Bandung ikut aturan Jakarta?* Why is Bandung following Jakarta's regulations? *mencari –* to look for a pretext/reason for a quarrel; → MENCARI *gara-gara/penyakit. – nya* the reason is that. *–nya, ia tidak setuju dengan syarat itu.* The reason is that he did not agree to that condition. *–nya, para pengemudi bécak aslinya penduduk pinggiran kota Solo.* That's because the pedicab drivers are all originally from Solo's perimeter. **3** due to, because of, on account of. *Terkenalnya nama Radén Awang bukan – kuat.* Raden Awang's name became well known not because of his strength. **4** about, concerning, regarding, as for. *– itu* as for that. **5** matter, concern, affair, business. *Itu lain –!* That's another matter!
  berpasal 1 to have paragraphs/articles. **2** article by article. **3** to have a reason/motive.

pasaléwa (*ob*) multicolored, parti-colored.

pasamuan (*Jv*) gathering, meeting, assembly. *– suci* the Catholic community.

pasang I 1 couple, two persons/things which go together. **2** counter for things that come in pairs. *dua – burung merpati* two pairs of pigeons. *empat – sepatu* four pairs of shoes. *sekitar 800 – kacamata* about 800 pairs of glasses. **3** set, number of things of the same kind or complementary to e.o.
  sepasang 1 a pair (of persons/animals), couple. *~ kerbau* a yoke of water buffaloes. *~ mata bola* two-man patrol. *~ pengantin* bride and groom, newly married couple. *~ remaja* a young couple. *~ suami-istri* a married couple, man and wife. **2** to suit, match, go well with, complement. *Pakaiannya ~ benar dengan badannya.* The dress fits her well. **3** to constitute a set or complementary pair, be one of a pair (with). *Subang ini ~ dengan itu.* This earring is one of a pair with that one.
  sepasang-sepasang in pairs/couples.
  berpasang-pasang 1 many/several pairs/sets. *~ pakaian* many sets of clothes. **2** in pairs/couples. *berjalan ~* to walk in pairs. *~ tangan* hand in hand.
  berpasang(-pasang)an 1 to form a pair, be the counterpart/mate of. *Gelang ini ~ dengan gelang itu.* This bracelet forms a pair with that one **2** to team up with e.o. *berpasangan tangan* hand in hand.
  memasangkan 1 to make into a pair, pair up. **2** to mate (animals), join in marriage, couple off. *Rasanya kena juga kalau kuda ini kupasangkan dengan kudaku.* I think it will be just right if I mate this horse with mine.
  pasangan 1 pair, partner, counterpart, mate. *Gadis itu patut jadi ~mu.* That girl is the one for you. *~ afiks* (*ling*) simulfix. *~ asyik-asyoi* a pair of lovers. *~ ganda-putra* men's doubles (in badminton/tennis). *~ kerja* counterpart. *~ setaraf* equal partners, partnership. *~ suami-istri* [pasutri] a married couple, husband and wife. *wanita dan ~ tanpa nikah* an unmarried woman and her companion. *~ yang dimabok cinta* and *~ yang sedang asyik dilanda cinta-kasih* lovers. *judi ~nya tipu* gambling and deceit go together. **2** running mate (in an election).

Mondale memilih ~nya untuk pemilihan présidén. Mondale has chosen his running mate for the presidential election. **3** bond. **4** pairing.
  perpasangan coupling.

pasang II 1 to rise (of the tide or a river), wax (of the moon). *– surut* ups and downs, vicissitudes. *– surut kehidupan nelayan Riau* the vicissitudes of life of Riau fishermen. *ada – surutnya* it has its ups and downs. *air – incoming tide. air – ripples of a tide.* **2** tide. *adat – berturun naik, air pun ada – surutnya, takkan – selalu, di mana surut senantiasa* an uncertain situation, such as, wealth, a position, etc. *ibarat – masuk muara* words that can no longer be stopped from leaving the mouth. *Kalau takut dilimbur –, jangan berumah di tepi pantai* if you can't stand the heat, get out of the kitchen. *Tidak mengenang – surut.* Don't worry about problems that might arise in the future. *– bah* flood tide. *– besar* waxing moon. *– bulan* lunar tide. *– kering* low tide, ebb. *– mati* neap tide. *– mérah* red tide. *– naik* high tide. *– perbani* waxing moon, neap/spring tide. *– purnama* high/spring tide (at the full moon). *– surut/turun* low tide, ebb tide. *– surut gundah* neap tide. *– surut purnama* spring tide.
  memasang *~ rasa iba* to arouse s.o.'s pity, make s.o. feel sorry for one.

pasang III (*coq*) *– aksi* a) to show off. b) to put on one's best behavior.
  memasang [and **masang** (*coq*)] **1** to put on, sew/pin on. *~ ban/dasi/kacamata/pakaian/sepatu* to put on a tire/a tie/glasses/clothes/shoes. *~ bintang di dada* to pin a medal on s.o.'s chest. *~ kancing* to sew on a button. *~ tanggalkan* to put on and take off. **2** to turn/switch on, light. *~ gérétan* to light a match. *~ lampu* to turn on the light. *Dia ~ warta berita pukul 23.00 di TV.* He turned on the 11 o'clock news on TV. **3** to put on. *~ piringan hitam yang lain* to put on another record. **4** to install, put in, put up, lay, build (in a spot), construct. *~ jalan keréta-api* to lay a railroad track. *~ pagar* to put up/build a fence. *~ jembatan* to build a bridge. **5** to stake (in a game). *~ satu sén* to stake one cent. *~ tikaman* to stake one's money. **6** to put, insert, place, plant. *~ bom* a) to place a bomb. b) to set off a bomb. *~ guna-guna* to cast a spell (on s.o.). *~ iklan* to run/place/insert an ad. *~ mata-mata* to plant a spy. *~ orang-orangan* to put up a scarecrow. **7** to set. *~ harga* to set/fix a price. *~ harga tinggi* to ask a high price. b) to make great demands. *~ layar* to set sail. *~ perangkap* to set a trap, stake out. *~ tarif/tarip* to set the fare. *~ wéker* to set the alarm. *~ uuwu* to set out a fish trap. **8** to hoist, raise, hang out. *~ bendéra* to raise the flag. **9** to cock, prick up (ears), use (eyes for watching). *~ kuping/telinga* to prick up one's ears. *Sopir itu rupanya diam-diam ~ kuping mengikuti dengan cermat percakapan M dengan S.* The driver seemed to prick up his ears quietly to follow M and S's conversation. *~ mata terhadap* to keep an eye on. *~ mata dan telinga* to keep one's eyes and ears open. *~ mata tajam-tajam* to watch closely. **10** to lower (horns of an animal in preparation for an attack). *Kerbau itu ~ sungunya.* The water buffalo lowered its horns (to attack). **11** to play, take part in, participate in. *~ loteré* to play the lottery. **12** to offer (for sale). *Sepéda perempuan dipasang untuk Rp 25.000. Ladies'* bicycles were offered for Rp 25.000. *~ badan* (*Jv*) a) to serve time, do time (in prison). b) to defend o.s. (against criticism). *~ bicara ini dan itu* to talk about this and that. *~ kuda-kuda* → KUDA-KUDA. *~ pelana* to saddle up (a horse).
  berpasang-pasangan and **pasang-memasang** to fire at e.o. *~ mercon/petasan* to let off fireworks.
  memasangi to put/install in, set. *suatu ruangan yang dipasangi alat perekam* a room in which a bugging device had been installed.
  memasangkan [and **masangin** (*J coq*)] to install/set up/fix/assemble, etc. for s.o. else. *Aku ~ juga kipas angin di depan ibu.* I also set up an electric fan in front of mother.
  terpasang [and **kepasang** (*coq*)] fixed, installed, fastened, posted.
  pasangan 1 s.t. fixed/installed/set up, etc., assembly. **2** stake (in gambling). **3** installing. *– batu bata* masonry. **4** wooden ox yoke.
  pasang-pasangan to place bets.
  pemasang fitter, installer, etc. *~ iklan* advertiser. *~ pipa* pipefitter.

pemasangan fixing, setting up, assembling, installation.
pasang IV various species of oak, *Quercus/Lithocarpus spp*. – *batu* k.o. tree, *Lithocarpus sundaicus*. – *poh* (*Jv*) k.o. tree, *Lithocarpus javensis*.
pasanggerahan → PASANGGRAHAN.
pasanggiri (*Jv*) prize contest. *mengadakan* – to hold a prize contest.
pasanggrahan (*Jv*) rest house, *usu* government-owned.
pasar I (*Pers*) **1** market, marketplace. *pergi ke – untuk membeli daging* to go to the market to buy meat. *buaya* – pickpocket. *ékonomi* – market economy. *harga* – market price/quotation. *(bahasa) Melayu* – bazaar Malay. *mékanisme* – market mechanism. *nilai* – market value. *pangsa* – market share. *pembukaan* – market access. *pemimpin* – market leader. *pialang – uang* money broker. **2** (*Jv*) five-day week (consisting of the days *Legi, Paing, Pon, Wagé,* and *Kliwon*). – *amal* charity bazaar. – *bébas* free market. – *berjangka* futures market. – *bersama* common market. – *Bersama Éropa* [PBE] European Common Market. – *bursa* stock market. – *dalam negeri* domestic market. – *derma* charity bazaar. – *éceran* retail market. – *ékonomi bébas* free economy market. – *élite* elite market, i.e., market catering to the Indonesian elite. – *galak* market rally. – *gelap* black market. – *grosir* wholesale market. – *induk* central distributing market for one commodity, food station. – *inprés* market built with special funds made available through *inpres*. – *jengék* (in Aceh) market that sells luxury goods; → JENGÉK. – *kagét* small market without permanent location. – *kendaraan niaga* market for commercial vehicles. – *kerja* job market. – *komérsial* commercial market. – *laris* seller's market. – *lesu* slack/depressed market. – *loak* flea market. – *lokal* local market. – *lopak* (in Jambi) market where pork is sold. – *luar bursa* over-the-counter market. – *malam* a) evening market. b) an outdoors fair held in the evening. – *maling* k.o. flea market. – *mapan* mature market. – *Masyarakat Éropa* [Pasar ME] European Common Market; → MASYARAKAT *Ékonomi Éropa*. – *modal* capital market. – *naik* bull/rising market. – *nonswalayan* not a supermarket. – *pembeli* buyer's market. – *penghambat* curb market. – *penjual* seller's market. – *penyerahan kemudian* futures market. – *perdana* primary market. – *poténsial* potential market. – *raya* supermarket. – *sampingan* fringe market. – *sayur(an)* vegetable market. – *sékundér* secondary market. – *sénggol(an)* the market at Kramat Tunggak, Jakarta Utara (so-called because the shoppers bump into e.o.). – *séntral* central market. – *sepi* dead market. – *serba ada* (*infr*) supermarket. – *spékulasi* futures market. – *surut* declining market. – *swalayan* supermarket. – *swalayan keuangan* financial supermarket. – *tahunan* annual fair. – *tenaga kerja* labor market. – *terapung* floating market (found along some rivers in South Kalimantan). – *tunai* spot market. – *tunggal* single/common market. *Masyarakat Éropa dan – Tunggalnya* the European Community and its Common Market. – *turun* bear/falling market. – *uang* money market. – *utama* core market. – *uang* money market. – *uang antar-bank* [PUAB] inter-bank money market. – *yang sedang berkembang* emerging market. – *yang sedang lembék* bear/falling market.
sepasar (*Jv*) a/one five-day market.
memasarkan to market, sell on the market.
terpasarkan marketed. *belum* ~ not yet marketed. *tak* ~ unmarketable, cannot be marketed. *Bawang putih tak* ~. Garlic couldn't be marketed.
pasaran 1 market, outlet. *Belanda masih tetap merupakan* ~ *terbesar bagi krupuk ikan, terutama krupuk udang Indonésia*. The Netherlands is still the largest market for Indonesian fish chips, especially shrimp chips. *Istilah lokal yaitu "kumpul kebo" akhir-akhir ini memasuki* ~ *bahasa nasional Indonésia*. Recently the local term "kumpul kebo" (shack up) made its way into the marketplace of the Indonesian national language. *siap turun ke* ~ ready to be marketed. ~ *Bersama Éropa* European Common Market, ECM. ~ *dunia* world market. ~ *ékspor* export market. ~ *jarak-jauh* telemarketing. ~ *memikat* captive market. ~ *mobil* automobile market. ~ *pembeli* buyer's market. ~ *penjual* seller's market. ~ *sepi* slack market. ~ *tunai* spot market. ~ *yang pasti* captive market. **2** inferior/low quality, cheap. *arloji* ~ a cheap watch. **3** common(place), ordinary.

Pokoknya, nama Mini itu sudah out of date. ~! In short, the name Mini is out of date. It's common! **4** (*hari* ~) (*Jv*) a day of the five-day market week. **5** (*Jv*) to hold a market.
pemasar 1 marketer. **2** (insurance) agent.
pemasaran marketing. *badan* ~ marketing agency. *déwan* ~ marketing board. *kebijakan* ~ marketing policy. *koperasi* ~ marketing cooperative.
pasar II (*M*) slippery (of a path going to and from the market). – *jalan karena diturut, lancar karena diulang* experience is the best teacher.
pasara 1 (*M*) grave; → PUSARA I. **2** market; → PASAR I.
pasaraya supermarket; → PASAR *raya*.
pasaréan (*Jv*) grave, cemetery.
pasase (*D*) passage (in navigation).
pasasir (*D*) **1** passenger. – *gelap* stowaway; → PENUMPANG *gelap*. **2** (*J*) customer of a *warung*.
pasat (*D*) *angin* – trade wind.
pasca- (*Skr*) (used in many of the following neologisms) post-, after. – *45* post-1945.
pascabayar postpaid.
pascabedah postoperative. *pengobatan* – postoperative care.
pascadoktor postdoctoral.
pascaéra politik the postpolitical era.
pasca-G30S/PKI *masa* – the period after the *G30S/PKI*.
pasca-industri postindustrial.
pascajual aftersale. *pelayanan* – aftersale service.
pascakawin postnuptial.
pascakekuasaan *sindrom* – postpower syndrome.
pascakoloni postcolonial. *negeri-negeri terbelakang* – postcolonial backward countries.
pascakolonial postcolonial. *ciri* – postcolonial characteristics.
pascakomunisme postcommunist.
pascakonsénsus postconsensus.
pascakuasa *sindrom* – postpower syndrome.
pascakudéta post-coup (d'état)
pascalahir postnatal, postpartum.
pascalebaran post-Lebaran.
pascalokakarya after the workshop.
pasca-Majapahit post-Majapahit.
pascamati postmortem, necropsy.
pasca-migas post–oil and gas; → MIGAS.
pascaminyak postoil. *surutnya ékonomi* – the decline of the postoil economy.
pascamodérnisme postmodernism.
pascamortem postmortem, rigor mortis.
pascanasional postnationalistic.
pasca-operasi postoperative. *inféksi – pada pasién* patient's postoperative infection.
pascapanén after-harvest, postharvest.
pascapemasaran postmarketing. *pengawasan* – postmarketing surveillance.
pascapemilu postelection. *masa* – after the period of the general elections.
pascapendidikan post ... education. – *doktor* postdoctoral.
pascapengapalan postshipment. *pembiayaaan* – postshipment financing.
pascaperang postwar. – *dingin* post–cold war. – *Teluk* after the Gulf War.
pascaperkosaan postrape.
pascapersalinan postpartum.
pascaproduksi postproduction.
pasca-Ramadan post-Ramadan.
pascarawat posttreatment.
pasca-révolusi postrevolution.
pascarézim after the ... regime. – *Komunis* after the Communist regime.
pascasalin postpartum.
pascasarjana postgraduate.
pascasunting postediting.
   mempascasunting to postedit.
pascatahun after the year ... – *1991* post-1991.
pascaterima postreceptive.

pascatransplantasi posttransplantation.
pascatrauma posttrauma. – *korban perkosaan* rape victim's post-trauma.
pasca-UU after the law on ... – *Perbankan* after the banking law was put into effect.
pascavaséktomi postvasectomy.
pascawacana postscript.
pascawaktu after hours.
pascayuwana postjuvenal.
paséban (*Jv*) audience hall.
paseduluran <sedulur> (*Jv*) **1** blood relationship. **2** friendship.
paséh → FASIH.
paselin (*D*) vaselin; → VASELIN.
pasemén (gold or silver) braid; → PASMÉN.
paser I (*D*) (pair of) compasses.
paser II (*Jv*) dart.
pasét (*D/E?*) **1** k.o. diamond. **2** facet (of diamond).
paséwakan <séwa> (*Jv*) audience hall in royal court.
pasfoto (*D*) passport photo.
pasgab → PASUKAN *gabungan.*
pasi (*M*) *pucat* – deathly pale.
   kepasian paleness, pallor.
pasién (*D*) (medical) patient. – *titipan* an indigent patient admitted to a hospital for free treatment by an *RT/RW*. – *yang berobat jalan* outpatient.
pasif (*D*) passive, not active.
   memasifkan to make passive, passivize.
   kepasifan passivity, inaction.
Pasifik Pacific (Ocean). *Cekung* – Pacific Basin; → PASU *Pasifik.* – *Selatan* the South Pacific.
pasifikasi (*D*) pacification.
   mem(p)asifikasi(kan) to pacify.
pasifis (*D*) pacifist.
pasifisme (*D/E*) pacifism.
pasih I → FASIH.
pasih II memasihkan to work on (the land). *Éntis yang mewakili teman-temannya, mengadukan soal tanah 85 ha yang dipasihkan oléh TNI-AU.* Entis, who represented her friends, brought up for trial the issue of the 85 hectares worked on by the Air Force.
pasik (*A*) **1** criminal, sinful. **2** crazy, mad.
   memasikkan to declare sinful, consider wicked.
   kepasikan sin, criminality.
pasilan (*Jv*) **1** arboreal parasitic plant, epiphyte. **2** freeloader, parasite; → PENDOMPLÉNG. – *kelapa* a parasite from which medicines are made, *Drynaria rigidula.*
pasilitas (*D*) facility; → FASILITAS.
pasinaon (*Jv*) course (of study); institute of learning.
pasindén (*Jv*) female singer with a *gamelan* orchestra.
pasip (*D*) → PASIF.
pasir 1 sand. – *dan batu* [sirtu] sand and stones. –, *batu dan tanah* [sirtunah] sand, stones, and soil. *bejana* – sandbox. *busung* – dune, sand hill. *emas* – gold dust. *gula* – granular sand. *gurun* – sandy desert. *ibu* – gravel. *jam* – hourglass, sandglass. *padang* – sandy desert. **2** sandy beach. **3** (*M*) sea. **4** granular (in compounds). *gula* – granular sugar. *tepi* – seashore. *jatuh di/ke (padang)* – (his words) fell on deaf ears. – *ambang/apung* quicksand. – *awukir* hilly sand dunes. – *besi* iron-bearing sand. – *beton* sand used to make concrete. – *gunung* pit sand. – *hanyut/hembus/hidup* drifting sand. – *kersik* gravel. – *kuarsa* quartz. – *meléla* laterite. – *minyak* oil sand. – *produktif* pay sand. – *tambang* pit sand. – *tér* tar sand.
   berpasir sandy; to have sand in it.
   memasir to silt up, choke up with sand.
   pasiran sandy, arenaceous.
   kepasiran (*petro*) sanded up.
   perpasiran sand (*mod*). *berusaha di bidang* ~ to operate in the sand business.
pasirah (*Pal*) head of a *kampung/marga.*
pasir-pasir (*ikan* –) sea bream, *Scolopsis spp.*
Pasis → PERWIRA *siswa.*
pasisir I coastal area, *esp* the north coast of Java, *esp* the area between Cirebon and Surabaya.

pasisir II passenger; → PASASIR.
pasit (*J*) sticking together (of eyelids).
pasiva (*D*) (financial) liabilities; *opp* AKTIVA. – *lancar* current liabilities.
paska- (*infr*) post-; → PASCA-.
paskabayar postpaid.
Paskah (*A*) Easter. – *Yahudi* Passover.
Paskhasau → PASUKAN *Khas Angkatan Udara.*
Paskibraka → PASUKAN *Pengkibar Bendéra Pusaka.*
pasmat (*D*) Spanish dollar.
pasmén (*D*) (gold or silver) braid.
paso (*J/Jv*) earthenware vessel used as water container; → PASU.
pasogit (*Bat*) ancestors; → LELUHUR. *bona* – ancestral land.
pasok (*Jv*) **memasok** to supply. ~ *sayuran langsung ke pasar konsumén* to supply vegetables directly to consumer markets.
   terpasok supplied.
   pasokan supply. *sewaktu-waktu* ~ *dari penghasil terganggu atau terputus* now and then the supply from the producers is disturbed or cut off.
   pemasok supplier. *perusahaan* ~ *makanan* catering business.
   pemasokan supply(ing). *kepastian* ~ certainty of supplies.
pasompé a Buginese migrant to Sumatra or Malaysia.
Pasopati 1 name of *Arjuna's* invincible magic arrow. **2** the code name given by the *G30S/PKI* to the *Cakrabirawa* troops.
pasowan (*Jv*) (in Yogyakarta and Surakarta) assembly/meeting place.
PasPal [(Ilmu) Pasti dan Pengetahuan Alam] Mathematics and Natural Sciences (in Senior High Schools).
Paspamprés → PASUKAN *Pengamanan Présidén.*
paspor (*D*) passport. -*nya sudah lama mati.* His passport expired a long time ago. – *biasa* ordinary passport. – *cokelat* passport issued to those going on the pilgrimage. – *dinas* official passport. – *diplomatik* diplomatic passport. – *biru* non-diplomatic official passport. – *haji* passport issued to those going on the pilgrimage. – *hijau* ordinary passport. – *hitam* diplomatic passport. – *konsulér* consular passport. – *nonpri(bumi)* (*coq*) nonnative-born Indonesian's passport. – *Orang Asing* [PORA] Foreigner's Passport. – *pri(bumi)* (*coq*) native-born Indonesian's passport.
   berpaspor to hold a passport. *orang yang* ~ *diplomatik* holder of a diplomatic passport.
pasrah (*Jv*) **1** to surrender to, give up to another's power. **2** (= **berpasrah**) to surrender, hand over. *Sekarang ini banyak orang tua* – *bongkokan (menyerahkan seluruhnya) kepada sekolah.* Nowadays many parents hand everything over to the schools. *bersikap* – *kepada nasib* to be fatalistic. **3** to be resigned (to s.t. bad).
   memasrahi to hand over to, entrust to. *yang dipasrahi mengopén rumah* the one entrusted with the care of the house.
   memasrahkan to entrust, delegate, give over. *S* ~ *putranya kepada A.* S put his son in A's hands (for education, etc.). ~ *diri* to surrender.
   kepasrahan 1 surrender, handing over. **2** acquiescence, resignation. *Ada* ~ *yang bulat dalam diri perempuan itu.* That woman was completely resigned.
   pemasrahan 1 surrender, handing over, delegation, delegating. **2** surrendering, submission.
passiva → PASIVA.
pasta (*D*) paste. – *gigi* toothpaste, dentifrice.
pastél I (*D*) pastel, drawing chalk. *warna* – pastel shade/tint.
pastél II (*D*) paté, meat-and-vegetable pastry.
pastéurisasi (*D*) pasteurization; → PASTURISASI.
pasti 1 certain, sure, precise, positive, determined, proven (reserves). *Saya* –. I'm sure. *belum* – not sure yet, uncertain. *ilmu* – mathematics. *tidak* – uncertain, unsure, in doubt, doubtful. *ketidak-pastian* uncertainty, doubt, dubiousness. ~ *hukum* legal uncertainty. ~ *pasar* market uncertainty. **2** (impersonal) for sure, surely, no doubt, certainly, without doubt, of course. – *namanya akan harum.* He will certainly become famous.
   sepasti as certain/sure as.
   memastikan [and **mastiin** (*J coq*)] **1** to assure, guarantee, confirm, make sure (that), see to it that, make sure of. *Pastikan semua pintu ke luar dijaga.* Make sure that all outer doors are

guarded. **2** to ascertain. *tidak bisa dipastikan* there's no telling (whether).

terpasti the surest, the most certain.

kepastian l certainty, sureness. ~ *hukum* legal certainty. **2** assurance, confirmation. ~ *mutu* quality assurance.

pemastian determination, making sure, ascertainment, confirming.

pastil (*D*) → PASTÉL II.

pastiles (*D*) pastille(s), lozenge(s).

pastir (*D*) **mem(p)astir** to pasteurize; → PASTURISASI.

pastor (*D*) (Catholic) priest. – *militér* military chaplain. – *paroki* parish priest. – *praja* diocesan priest.

pastoran presbytery, parish house.

kepastoran pastorate; pastorship.

pastoral (*D*) pastoral. *déwan* – pastoral council.

pastori (*D*) presbytery, parish house.

pastur (*D*) (Catholic) priest; → PASTOR.

pasturalis (*D*) pastoral. *masyarakat* – a pastoral society.

pasturisasi (*D*) pasteurization.

mem(p)asturisasi(kan) to pasteurize. *Susu murni yang berédar perlu dipasturisasikan.* Pure milk for distribution must be pasteurized.

pasu l bowl, tub, washbasin, washbowl, basin, earthenware pot. – *bunga* a large flower vase. – *Pasifik* Pacific Basin. **2** the inner part of the groove running around the surface of a gong.

berpasu-pasu bowlfuls.

pasuk berpasuk(-pasuk) and **berpasuk(-pasuk)an** in troops/ groups/force.

pasukan l troop(s), force(s). **2** team (of players). ~ *pemain bola keranjang yang kuat* a strong basketball team. **3** unit in the *Pramuka* Boy Scout Movement consisting of four *regu*: 40 members. **4** formation. *se*~ *pesawat terbang* a formation of aircraft. ~ *agas* raiding parties consisting of children in Maluku. ~ *amfibi* amphibious formation. ~ *anti-huru-hara* riot troops. ~ *bayaran* mercenaries. ~ *Bela Diri (Jepang)* (Japanese) Self-Defense Force. ~ *berani mati* suicide troops. ~ *berkaki* infantry; → INFANTERI. ~ *berkuda* cavalry. ~ *cadangan* reserves. ~ *gabungan* [pasgab] combined troops (taken from various forces). ~ *Gerak Cepat (Angkatan Udara)* (Air) Commandos, (Air Force) Shock Troops, Rapid-Deployment Forces, RDF. ~ *gerilya* guerilla troops. ~ *induk (mil)* main force. ~ *jalan* infantry; → INFANTRI. ~ *jibaku* suicide squad. ~ *katak* frogman forces. ~ *kawal belakang* rear guard. ~ *kawal depan* advance guard. ~ *keamanan (setempat)* (local) security forces. ~ *kehormatan* honor guard. ~ *kerangka* troops stationed in a region to combat guerrilla forces. ~ *Khas Angkatan Udara* [Paskhasau] Air Force Special Forces. ~ *khusus (antitéroris)* special (anti-terrorist) forces. ~ *KKo/KKO* (Indonesian) Marines. ~ *kuning* the street sweepers and other sanitation employees of various Indonesian cities who dress in yellow uniforms. ~ *Lapis Baja* [Laba] armored troops. ~ *laut* navy. ~ *linggis* raiding parties consisting of children in Maluku. ~ *lintas udara* airborne troops. ~ *marinir AS* U.S. marines. ~ *meriam* artillery. ~ *musik* band. ~ *Paman Sam* U.S. troops. ~ *panser* armored troops. ~ *para/payung* paratroops, airborne forces. ~ *pemadam api/kebakaran* fire brigade. ~ *Pembela Keadilan (Mal)* Team for the Defense of Justice. ~ *pemberontak* rebel forces. ~ *pembidas* shock troops. ~ *pemelihara(an) perdamaian (multinasional)* (multinational) peace-keeping forces. ~ *pemukul (yang mobil)* (mobile) strike force. ~ *penahan* holding force. ~ *pangkal nuklir* nuclear deterrent forces. ~ *pendamai* peacekeeping forces. ~ *pendarat* landing force/troops. ~ *pengamanan Pemilu* elections security police. ~ *pengamanan Présidén* [Paspampres] Presidential Security Guards. ~ *pengawal* guards, guard platoon. ~ *penggempur* shock forces. ~ *Pengkibar Bendéra Pusaka* [Paskibraka] Flag Hoisting Unit. ~ *penjaga belakang* rear guard. ~ *Penjaga Pantai AS* U.S. Coast Guard. ~ *penjaga perdamaian* peace-keeping force. ~ *penyangga* support troops. ~ *penyerbu* shock troops. ~ *perdamaian* peace-keeping force. ~ *perhubungan* signal corps. ~ *pilihan* élite troops. ~ *Polis Hutan* [PPH] *(Mal)* Forest Police Force; → BRIMOB. ~ *sandi yudha* special mission forces. ~ *sekutu* allied forces. ~

sukaréla volunteer troops. ~ *tempur* combat troops. ~ *teras* elite corps. ~ *terpilih* crack/élite troops. ~ *tugas* task force. ~ *udara* air force. **sepasukan** in the same military force.

pasumendan (*M*) bridesmaids.

Pasundan Sundanese area; → SUNDA I.

pasung l stock, pillory. **2** wooden block for a mentally disturbed person, k.o. straitjacket. **3** incarceration. *rumah* – prison, jail.

berpasung pilloried, in the stocks.

memasung(kan) l to put s.o. in the stocks, pillory. **2** to put a mentally retarded person in a *pasung*. **3** to incarcerate, imprison. **4** to ban (a book), suppress. *Buku-buku karangan Pramudya dipasung.* Books by Pramudya are banned.

terpasung l s.o. put in a *pasung*. **2** incarcerated, imprisoned, jailed.

pasungan → PASUNG.

pemasungan l putting s.o. in a *pasung*. **2** incarceration, imprisonment. **3** banning, suppression.

pasu-pasu cheekbones.

pasut [pasang-naik pasang-surut] tides, tidal.

pasutri → PASANGAN *suami istri.*

pat I clipped form of **tempat**. – *tidur* bed.

pat II clipped form of **empat**. – *ratus* four hundred.

pat III (*J*) (*permainan*) *–.gulipat* **l** a children's game, k.o. hide-and-go-seek. **2** hanky-panky, shady dealings; → KONGKA-LIKONG. *main* –.*gulipat* to engage in shady practices. *pembongkaran prakték gelap* –.*gulipat yang dilakukan oléh banyak perusahaan kakap* the disclosure of illicit practices and shady dealings carried out by many large-scale businesses.

berpat-gulipat to have shady dealings (with).

mempatgulipatkan to embezzle, misappropriate.

pat IV a draw (in a game).

pat V (*E*) putt.

patah I l broken, fractured. *Pénsilnya* –. His pencil is broken. *Kakinya* –. He broke his leg. **2** to be interrupted. *Pelajaran saya* – *di tengah jalan.* My studies were interrupted half-way. – *dahan tempat bernaung,* – *lantai tempat berpijak* there's no place to fall back on for help. – *lidah alamat kalah,* – *keris alamat mati* not smart enough to defend a case means defeat. – *tumbuh hilang berganti* "the broken grows, the lost is replaced," i.e., chiefs die but not their office; the King is dead, long live the King. – *sayap bertongkat paruh* never say die. – *arang* a) broken off irreparably (of a marriage/dispute, etc.). b) to break (with the past). **berpatah arang** to break with the past. **mematah-arangkan** to conclude definitively, sever forever. – *batu (hatinya)* do not want to work again. – *cengkih* a) (formerly) to harvest cloves. b) to have fun, have a good time. – *cinta/hati* broken-hearted. – *di tengah (jalan)* stopped in the middle, not completed. – *dua* broken in two. **mematah-duakan** to break s.t. in two. – *hati* a) discouraged. b) heart-broken. – *lesu* broken-hearted. *tidak lekas* – *hati* adamant. – *lidah* a) speech impediment. b) speechless, tongue-tied. – *mayang* wavy (hair). – *nafsu* to lose one's appetite. – *pucuk* interrupted (of a journey, etc.), unfinished (of work). – *riuk* displaced (of a broken limb). – *seléra* to lose one's appetite; not feel like ...ing. – *semangat* to lose one's enthusiasm, be discouraged/demoralized. – *siku* a) an acute angle. b) powerless, defenseless. – *seterika celana* to lose the pleat in one's pants. *Tidak pernah* – *seterika celananya.* His plants are never without pleats. – *tulang* a) fracture (esp of the leg). b) (*M*) indulgent, permissive, lenient. – *tulang (ber)himpit* depressed fracture. – *tulang sederhana* closed fracture. – *ulet* ductile fracture.

patah-patah broken (use of language). *Dia berkata dalam bahasa Inggris yang* ~. He spoke in broken English.

berpatahan (*pl subj*) broken into pieces.

mematah-matah ~ *jari* to crack one's knuckles.

mematah, mematahi and **mematahkan l** to break, rupture, fracture. ~ *tiang* to break a pole. *mematahkan tuduhan jaksa* to nullify the public prosecutor's accusation. **2** to foil, cause to fail, defeat. *Invasi ke Haiti dipatahkan.* The invasion of Haiti was foiled. – *langkah* to dishearten. *Sempitnya dan mahalnya kesempatan untuk memperoléh pendidikan tinggi* ~ *langkah dari banyak pemuda Indonésia.* The limited opportunities and the expense of higher education have disheartened many young Indonesians. **3** to stamp out, destroy, put down, repulse.

terpatah(-patah) broken.

terpatahkan breakable. *tidak* ~ unshakable.

patahan l fracture. **2** broken fragment. ~ *kayu* splinter. **3** (*geol*) fault.

pematah l breaker. **2** means of breaking.

pematahan l breaking off. **2** fracture, fracturing.

patah II classifier for words. *se– kata* a) a single word. b) preface (to a book). – *dua (patah) kata* (to say) a few words.

patah III – *kemudi* a) a medicinal shrub, k.o. golden weed, *Senecio sonchifolius*. b) red tassel flower, *Emilia sonchifolia*. – *tulang* milk bush, a shrub with very tiny leaves and poisonous milky sap used to cure skin diseases, pencil bush/tree, *Euphorbia tirucalli*.

patah IV → FATHAH II.

pataka (*Skr*) banner, standard.

patal [pabrik pemintalan] spinning factory.

patam ornamental edging to garment. – *kemudi* pintle strap.

berpatam to be edged with. ~ *emas* edged with gold.

patang (*Jv*) four.

patar rasp, a large rough file used for smoothing wood.

mematar to file.

patarangan <tarang> (*Jv*) nesting place, *esp* for poultry.

patas [cepat dan terbatas] express service (of city bus and train).

patatas → BATATAS.

patéhah → FATIHAH.

paték I framboesia, yaws.

patékan to suffer from yaws.

paték II → PATIK III.

patembayan <tembaya> (*Jv*) appointment.

patén (*D*) patent. *obat* – patent medicine.

mem(p)aténkan to patent, take out a patent on s.t.

pematénan patenting.

pater (*D*) father (in a religious order).

patera (*cla*) leaf.

pateram (*cla*) → PETARAM.

pateri (*Hind*) → PATRI.

paternalis (*D*) paternalist.

paternalisme (*D*) paternalism.

paternalistik (*E*) and **paternalistis** (*D*) paternalistic.

pateroli → PATROL.

patet (*Jv*) key/mode of *gamelan* music; that part of the shadow play in which this mode is played.

patétis (*D*) pathetic.

patfinder (*D ob*) boy scout; → PANDU I, PRAMUKA.

patgulipat → PAT III.

pathol (*Jv*) (in Rembang, Central Java) traditional fishermen's wrestling sport similar to *Japanese* sumo wrestling.

pati I l starch. **2** essence. **3** core, basic substance, essential attribute. *dikté* – the essence of a dictation (spelling, in schools). – *arak* spirits.

pati-patian starches.

pati II (*Jv*) *denda/hutang* – blood money. *kerap* – assassination.

pati III [perwira tinggi] General Officer (officer with the rank of general), high-ranking officer.

pati IV – *geni* (*Jv*) one may not eat, drink or see the light of the sun or of a fire on certain days.

pati V (*M*) → PATRI.

patiang (*Jv*) various species of plants, *Euphorbia etc*.

patidur → TEMPAT *tidur*.

patih I l docile, meek, submissive. **2** obedient.

kepatihan l obedience, discipline. **2** submissiveness.

pematih meek/submissive person.

patih II (*Jv*) **1** grand vizier, chief minister to a king. **2** high-ranking government official.

kepatihan l residence/office of one of these officials. **2** area headed by one of these officials.

patih III (*Jv*) queen (in chess).

patihah → FATIHAH.

patik I l slave. **2** I, me (humble form).

berpatik to use the word *patik* to refer to o.s.

patik II mematik to touch; → PETIK I.

patik III (*J*) poisonous dorsal fin or spine (of certain fish).

patikan → PATIANG.

patikim k.o. plant, Asian pennywort, *Hydrocotyle sibthorpiodes*.

patil I pole, (carpenter's) adze.

mematil to use a pole.

patil II (*Jv*) stinger, barbel (of certain fish).

mematil to sting.

pematil barbel.

patin (*ikan* –) a large catfish, *Pangasius nasutus/ponderosus*.

pating I l a large peg (used for climbing trees). **2** hook for hanging clothing.

memating to drive such pegs into a tree trunk.

pating II (*J/Jv*) particle which precedes the verb, which often contains an infix *-er-* or *-el-*; it indicates that the subject is plural and/or that the action is repeated, multiple, or chaotic. – *belasur* confused, chaotic. – *seliweran* to cruise around (of many cars, etc.).

pating III → PAHAT *pating*.

patirasa (*Jv*) immune.

patis pematisan the drawing of a rope through the nose of a cow.

patiseri (*D*) patisserie.

Patko → PATROLI *kota*.

patma → PADMA.

patogén (*D*) pathogen.

patogénésis (*D/E*) pathogenesis.

patok I (*Jv*) **1** pole, stake, peg. **2** measurement for rice paddies (*app* 2,300 square meters). – *labrang* (*petro*) dead man. – *tapal-batas* boundary marker, i.e., a pole marking the boundary of a country, etc. **3** (*mining*) bench. – *atas* upper bench.

berpatok marked by such a pole or stake.

mematok 1 to stake out, mark out boundaries. **2** to lay out. *Perumtél* ~ *rencana*. The Telecommunications Public (State) Corporation is laying out plans. **3** to put one's mark on. *Bahkan meréka juga mematok sejarah, sekalipun itu dianggap kecil*. They put their mark on history, even though it is thought to be minor. **4** (*fin*) to peg/fix (the value of currency). ~ *namanya* to make a name for o.s. – *tékad* to reach a firm decision, be firm.

patok-mematok 1 staking out. **2** setting standards.

mematokkan 1 to drive (poles/stakes) into the ground for purposes of demarcation. **2** to set, fix (a date for some event). *Meréka* ~ *pésta perkawinannya 6 Juni tahun ini*. They set the date of their wedding for June 6 of this year.

terpatok fixed, fixated (on), riveted (on). *Pihaknya sudah mengimbau para alumni untuk tidak* ~ *pada pangsa kerja di Jakarta*. His people told the alumni not to be fixated on market share in Jakarta. *Perhatianku 100%* ~ *pada siaran berita di TV*. My attention was 100% riveted on the news on TV.

patokan l pole, stake. **2** definition. **3** rule, line of action. **4** norm, standard, criterion, benchmark, guidelines. *harga* ~ base/benchmark price. *Selama ini minyak ringan Arab ditetapkan sebagai harga* ~ *keseluruhan minyak OPEC*. Thus far, Arabian Light Crude was set as a benchmark for all of OPEC oil. **berpatokan** ~ *pada* to base o.s. on, use ... as a criterion, postulate. *melacak kejahatan dengan* ~ *pada dialék si tersangka* to track down a crime by using the suspect's dialect as a criterion. *Meréka* ~ *pada pertumbuhan pengunjung yang berkisar 15% setahun*. They are postulating a growth in visitors of about 15% a year. ~ *duga* hypothesis. ~ *harga* price fixing. ~ *masyarakat* social values.

pematok s.o. who stakes out (land).

pematokan l staking out, surveying. **2** (*fin*) pegging (the value of one currency against another).

patok II – *may* yellow-breasted sunbird. – *muda* brown-breasted sunbird.

patok III (*J*) bill, beak; → PATUK I.

mematok 1 to peck (of birds). **2** to bite (of snakes).

patola *kain* – k.o. sash worn around the waist.

patolog (*D*) pathologist.

patologi (*D/E*) pathology. *ahli* – *forénsik* forensic pathologist. – *klinik* clinical pathology. – *wicara* speech pathology.

patologik (*E*) and **patologis** (*D*) pathological.

patorani (*IBT*) a species of flying fish found in the waters of Eastern Indonesia.

patos (*D*) pathos.

patrap (*Jv*) application; → TERAP I.

  pematrapan application; → PENERAPAN.

patraséli → PÉTERSÉLI.

patri (*Hind*) solder. *tukang* – solderer. *kaca* – stained glass. – *pérak* silver solder.

  mematri(kan) 1 to solder. **2** to fix, establish; to seal (closed). *Surat ini dipatri lalu dicap.* This letter was sealed and then a seal affixed to it.

  terpatri 1 to be soldered. **2** to be fixed/established. *keputusan yang telah kuat* – ~ a firm decision. ~ *dalam ingatan* etched in one's memory. **3** hypnotized, mesmerized, transfixed. *Meréka ~ pada kenyataan yang terjadi di depan mata meréka.* They were transfixed by the reality that unfolded before their very eyes.

  patrian solder.

  pematri solderer, soldering iron.

  pematrian soldering.

patriark (*D*) patriarch.

patriark(h)al (*D*) patriarchal.

patriark(h)at (*D*) patriarchy.

patrilinéal (*D*) and **patrilini** patrilineal. *kebudayaan* – patrilineal society.

patrimonial (*D/E*) patrimonial.

patriot (*D/E*) patriot.

  kepatriotan patriotism.

patriotik (*E*) and **patriotis** (*D*) patriotic.

  kepatriotikan patriotism.

patriotisme (*D/E*) patriotism.

patrol (*E*) and **patroli** (*D*) patrol. *mengadakan* – to patrol. – *Jalan Raya* [PJR] Highway Patrol. – *kota* [patko] city patrol.

  berpatroli to patrol. *tentara ~ di jalan-jalan* the troops are patrolling the streets.

  mematroli to patrol s.t.

patromak → PÉTROMAK(S).

patron I (*D*) pattern, design (for making dresses).

patron II and **patrum** (*D*) cartridge, shell. – *kosong* blank shells.

pattas → PATAS.

Pattimura (*ob*) **1** name of a national hero from Maluku. **2** name of the Army division stationed in Maluku.

patuh 1 obedient, loyal, faithful. **2** docile, submissive, disciplined. – *hukum* law-abiding. *rakyat yang* – *hukum* law-abiding citizens. – *janggal* fake/sham loyalty. – *kebenaran* faithful. – *kepada undang-undang* law-abiding. *tidak* – disobedient. **ketidak-patuhan** disobedience.

  berpatuh to be obedient/loyal (to).

  mematuh (*ob*) to bend to one side.

  mematuhi to submit to, be obedient to, follow, obey, comply with; to respond/reply to. *Dia tidak ~ panggilan saya.* He didn't respond to my call. ~ *diri* to adjust o.s. (to).

  kepatuhan 1 loyalty, obedience, faithfulness. *Saya meragukan ~nya.* I doubt his loyalty. ~ *adalah gerbang masuk untuk mencapai kebébasan.* Obedience is the gateway to freedom. **2** compliance.

patuk I 1 beak, bill (of a bird). **2** (*coq*) penis, cock.

  mematuk 1 to peck (of birds). **2** to bite (of a snake, fish); → MEMAGUT. **3** to cock (a gun). **4** to grab hold of succeed in getting.

  patuk-mematuk to peck e.o.

  mematuki (*pl obj*) to peck at.

  mematukkan to peck with s.t.

  patukan 1 peck, bite. **2** bill, beak.

patuk II *daun* – *tuan* k.o. climbing plant, liana, *Thunbergia laurifolia.*

patun (*J ob*) fifty cents.

patunda name of a South Sulawesi dance.

patung I 1 image, statue, dummy. *anak* – doll. *perajin* – sculptor. *seni* – sculpture. *seniman* – sculptor. **2** effigy. *membakar* – *présidén* to burn the president in effigy. **3** sculpture. – *dada* bust (sculptured). – *Kemerdékaan* Statue of Liberty (in New York City). – *Pembébasan Irian Barat* West Irian Liberation Statue

(located in Banteng Square, Jakarta). – *salib* crucifix. – *Selamat Datang* Welcome Statue (located in the circle in front of the Hotel Indonesia, Jakarta). – *setengah badan* bust (sculptured).

  mematung to keep still and silent like a statue. *berdiri ~* to stand stock-still/perfectly motionless.

  patung-mematung (art of) sculpture, sculpturing.

  mematungkan 1 to make s.o. or s.t. into a statue, sculpt (s.o. or s.t.). *Tiga pahlawan dipatungkan.* A statue was made of three heroes. **2** to consider a statue.

  pematung sculptor.

  pematungan sculpting, sculpturing.

patung II → SIPATUNG.

patung III a freshwater perch-like fish, striped tiger wandid, *Pristolepis fasciatus.*

patung IV (*J/Jv*) **berpatungan** to do s.t. as a group, each person chipping in for that purpose, chip in to pay for s.t., be involved in a joint venture (with). *Ketiga pengusaha itu lebih banyak ~ dengan invéstor dari Éropa dan AS.* The three businessmen are more involved in joint ventures with European and American investors.

  mematung(kan) to join in a venture together.

  patungan 1 to chip in to pay for s.t. *Para wartawan telah ~ untuk memberikan bukét kepada Ibu Tien.* The reporters chipped in to give a bouquet to Mrs. Tien (Soeharto). **2** joint. *perusahaan ~* joint venture. ~ *kerja* job sharing.

patur → PERWIRA *Instruktur.*

paturasan <turas> (*Jv*) **1** urinal. **2** toilet.

paturay tineung (*S*) *acara* – farewell program.

patusan <tus> (*Jv*) discharge, outflow.

  pematusan drainage.

patut 1 of good social standing/reputation, respectable. *orang-orang* – and *orang* –.– decent/respectable people. **2** appropriate, in line, advisable, makes sense; reasonable (of prices/behavior). *Saya akan memeriksa arti kata-kata itu dan bagaimana – dipakainya.* I'll look carefully at the meaning of those words and how to use them appropriately. *ucapan/kata-kata itu tidak* – an ill-advised remark. *Pada hémat saya tuntutan meréka itu tidak boléh dikatakan tidak* –. In my opinion it can't be said that their demand makes no sense. *harga-harga di sini* – prices around here are reasonable. *tujuan yang* – a reasonable objective. **3** (+ passive verb) worth(y), deserving. – *diduga* worthy of consideration. – *dihukum* punishable. – *dilihat* worth seeing. – *dipuji* praiseworthy, commendable, admirable. **4** suitable, proper. *Ini tidak – untuk peristiwa itu.* That's unsuitable/improper for the event. *dengan* – properly, fairly. **5** must, ought to, should. *Penjahat itu – dihukum seumur hidup.* The criminal should be sentenced to life imprisonment. **6** naturally, it goes without saying. – *ia tidak sanggup membayar utang karena uangnya habis.* It goes without saying that he's unable to pay his debts since his money is all gone.

  sepatutnya *dengan ~* a) as it should be, as is proper, properly, fittingly, appropriately. *Meréka menerima kedatangan kami dengan ~* they received our arrival as was proper. b) accordingly. *Ia akan menghukum orang yang bersalah dengan ~.* He will sentence the guilty person accordingly.

  berpatutan to be commensurate (with). *Gajinya yang besar ~ dengan kepandaiannya.* His high salary is commensurate with his skills.

  mematut to adjust, make fit, arrange, repair, adapt. *Ia berdiri di hadapan cermin besar sambil ~ topinya.* She stood in front of the mirror and adjusted her hat. ~ *diri* to dress o.s. up. *Untuk menghadiri suatu résépsi, Srintil sudah lama ~ diri dengan seabrek kombinasi.* To attend a reception, Srintil had already dressed herself up in an outfit.

  patut-mematut to put one's affairs in order, settle one's affairs.

  mematut-matut 1 (*M*) to observe, investigate s.o., take a hard look at. ~ *bakal menantunya* to take a hard look at one's prospective son-in-law. **2** to consider s.t. *Dia lantas ~ dan menduga-duga keadaan masa depannya.* He then considered and made an estimate of his future situation. **3** to adjust, set right. ~ *diri* to adjust (one's clothes). **4** to get dressed up.

  mematutkan 1 to fit, adjust; to put s.t. into proper order, to tidy up, straighten out/up. **2** to decorate, deck (with flowers, etc.).

3 ~ *diri* to adjust one's clothes. 4 to bring s.t. into line (with), adjust s.t. (to). *Seorang istri harus dapat ~ pengeluaran dengan gaji suaminya.* A housewife has to be able to bring expenses into line with her husband's salary.

terpatut the most proper/respectable.

patutan view, opinion, judgment.

kepatutan 1 view, opinion, judgment. 2 suitability, compatibility; propriety. *Segala yang kita lakukan hendaknya sesuai dengan batas-batas ~.* Everything we do should be in accordance with the limits of propriety. 3 reasonableness, equity, fairness. *~ dan keadilan* reasonableness and fairness.

patwa → FATWA.

paugeran <uger> (*Jv*) regulation(s).

pauh I *pohon* – a wild mango species, *Mangifera indica*; → MANGGA I, MEMPELAM. *pipi seperti* – *dilayang* smooth and round cheeks (of a woman). – *janggi* the double coconut, *Lodoicea maldivica.* – *kijang* dika tree, *Irvingia malayana.*

pauh II a rice measurement equal to ¼ *cupak.*
berpauh-pauh ~ *padi* to measure uncooked rice by the *pauh.*

pauhi and **pau hie** (*C*) abalone.

pauk I *lauk* – all k.o. side dishes; → LAUK.

pauk II k.o. hook; → GANCU.
memauk to draw s.t. closer to o.s. with a hook.
memaukkan to hook in, draw in with a hook.
pemauk (fire)hook.

paul I (*J*) improper, indecent; unfit, inept, unfit for use.

paul II (*Jv*) light blue.

paun (*E*) pound (sterling).

paung (*Port*) k.o. rusk.

paus I *ikan* – whale, *Physeter macrocephalus* and other species. – *pilot* pilot whale, blackfish. – *bongkok* humpbacked whale, *Megaptera novaeangliae.*

Paus II (*D*) pope. *Sri* – the Pope. – *Sastra Indonésia* the Pope of Indonesian Literature, the honorific title bestowed upon H. B. Jassin.
kepausan papacy.

pause (*D*) intermission, interval.

paut I clinging, attached.
berpaut 1 to cling (to), hold on (to), hang on to. 2 to close again (of the valve of mollusks). 3 coherent, holding together. *idéntitas nasional yang ~* a coherent national policy. *tempat ~* a) handhold. b) what one depends on, source of support. *~ tidak bertali* in the in-between state of having been sued for divorce but not having been granted it yet.
berpautan to hold on/cling to e.o. *Tangan meréka ~.* They held e.o.'s hand.
memaut 1 to cling to, hold on to. *Tangannya ~ kedua-dua lututnya itu.* His hands held firmly onto his knees. 2 to connect, link. 3 to tie up, tether. *~ perhatian* to attract attention.
paut-memaut 1 to hold e.o., cling to e.o. 2 connected, related.
memautkan and **memperpautkan** 1 to attach, tie up, tether. 2 to hook s.t. on to, tie, fasten.
terpaut 1 tied, fastened, tethered. *~ hatinya.* He's in love. *~ kasih* deeply in love. *hatinya/cintanya ~ kepada* he is in love with. 2 bound to, affixed/stuck to. *Ujung tambang itu ~ pada tonggak di tepi dermaga.* The end of the rope was fastened to a pole at the edge of the dock. 3 located. *Ia harus memacu sepéda motornya menuju Désa Selimeum, ~ 48 km di luar kota.* He had to race his motorbike toward the village of Selimeum, located 48 kilometers outside of town. 4 apart, separated by, away (from s.t. else). *~ 15 hari* 15 days apart.
keterpautan 1 connection, linkage. *saling ~* interconnection. *~ hati* love. 2 separation, being apart from e.o. *~ lima poin* a separation of five points (between the scores of two teams).
pautan 1 tethering post. 2 origin, source. 3 s.t. or s.o. that one clings to or depends on. *~ hati* darling, dearest. 4 perch (where a chicken perches). *seperti ayam pulang ke ~* it's fitting.
pemautan fusing, fusion.
perpautan connection, linkage, relation, coherence.

paut II terpaut [and **tepaut** (*J*)] different, discrepant.

pauze → PAUSE.

pavilyun (*D*) pavilion, an annex to a main house.

pa'wa contraction of **bapak tuwa** uncle/parent's older brother.

pawagam [panggung wayang gambar] (*Mal*) movie theater.

pawah I *rempah* – all k.o. spices; → REMPAH II.

pawah II sharing of profits between tenant and absentee landlord.
memawahkan to lease out land or loan cattle with an agreement to share profits.

pawai (*Tam*) procession, parade, show, review. – *alégoris* allegorical procession. – *hias* carnival. – *kesenjataan* show of force. – *mobil berhias* parade with flower-bedecked floats. – *obor* tattoo, an outdoor military pageant or display. – *taaruf* getting-acquainted procession. *Sebelum MTQ dibuka, diselenggarakan* – *taaruf keliling kota* before the Koran Reading Contest was begun, a get-acquainted procession around town was organized. – *17 Agustusan* Independence Day Parade.
berpawai 1 to hold a procession. 2 in procession.

pawaka (*Skr cla*) fire.

pawana (*Skr cla*) wind.

pawang 1 s.o. who practices a traditional industry, such as hunting, fishing or agriculture with the aid of black magic. 2 a witch doctor, shaman. 3 s.o. who combines magic and skill in the exercise of his or her profession (animal-trainer/hunter, etc.). – *anjing* dog handler. – *belat* expert in deep-sea fishing by using *belat* or large traps. – *buaya* s.o. who has the skill of catching or taming crocodiles, crocodile handler. – *buru* master hunter. – *darat* a *pawang* who carries out his profession on shore. – *gajah* elephant handler. – *hujan* k.o. of sorcerer who claims to have power over the rain. – *hutan* s.o. who is knowledgeable about the forest. – *jermal* expert in deep-sea fishing by using *belat* or large traps. – *laut* (in Aceh) expert in fishing (catching or guiding others). – *lebah* apiarist, bee raiser. – *pukat* expert in catching fish with a *pukat* or seine net. – *ular* snake handler. – *uteuen* (*Ac*) s.o. who is knowledgeable about the forest.
memawangi to handle/guide/train (dogs and other animals). *Dipawangi Sérsan Satu Sumadi, Jakaria disuruh mengendus tumpukan batu di pinggir tanggul Kampung Cirampo.* Guided by First Sergent Sumadi, Jakaria was told to sniff a pile of stones at the edge of the Cirampo Village embankment.
kepawangan the art of being a *pawang, esp* in training animals.
perpawangan relating to a *pawang.*

pawiyatan <wiyata> (*Jv*) 1 educational institution; → WIYATA. 2 school for *wayang* performances. – *Jawi* course of study relating to Javanese language, literature, and culture.

pawon (*Jv*) → PAWUHAN.

Pawonsari [Pacitan, Wonogiri, Wonosari] the development area of Pacitan, Wonogiri, Wonosari which crosses administrative boundaries.

pawuhan (*Jv*) 1 kitchen. 2 fireplace, hearth. *Ada satu anjuran yang belum saya kerjakan, yaitu tidur di* –. There's one suggestion I haven't acted on yet, that is, to sleep in the kitchen. 3 combustion chamber.

pawukon <wuku> (*Jv*) a Javanese k.o. astrology.

paya marsh, swamp.
berpaya(-paya) marshy, swampy.

payah 1 tired, fatigued, exhausted, overworked. 2 difficult, not easy, hard, arduous. *jerih/susah* – with difficulty; wearisome, hard. 3 to be in trouble/a fix. 4 severe (of illness), critical. *sakit* – seriously ill. 5 *tak* – (*Mal*) unnecessary, it's not necessary, don't have to; → *tidak* USAH. – *jantung* heart trouble. – *sesak* trouble breathing.
payah-payahnya *tidak ~* indefatigable.
sepayah as difficult/hard as.
berpayah-payah to wear o.s. out, work o.s. to death/the bone, go to a lot of trouble to; → JERIH, SUSAH.
memayahkan 1 to tire, weary, fatigue, exhaust. 2 tiring, wearying, exhausting. 3 to cause trouble, bother.
memayah-mayahkan ~ *diri* to work o.s. to death.
terpayah the most difficult, the hardest.
kepayahan 1 tiredness, fatigue, weariness, exhaustion. 2 difficulty; to be in great difficulty. *~ uang* to be in financial straits.

payang I seine/drag net. *perahu* – fishing boat equipped with a seine net.

memayang to fish with a seine net.

pemayang seine/drag net.

pemayangan seining.

payang II (*J*) **memayang** to support s.o. in walking. *Saya ~ babé dari langgar ke rumah.* I supported father from the prayer house to home.

payar → PAIR I. *perahu* – patrol boat.

berpayar(-payar) to cruise, patrol

memayar to scan.

pemayar 1 patrol boat. 2 cruiser. 3 scanner.

pemayaran 1 patrolling. 2 scanning.

payas – *agung* (*Bal*) full traditional dress.

payau 1 brackish (water). 2 salty, briny. – *tekaknya* nothing tastes right to him.

payét (*D*) paillete, spangle, sequins.

payir → PAIR.

payit (*coq*) → PAILIT.

payo (in Jambi) swamp, morass.

payon (*Jv*) 1 roof. 2 shed. 3 shelter.

payu (*Jv*) 1 amount of an offer; value. 2 to sell (well), be in demand (of goods), sought-after. *sudah* – already sold.

berpayu to bargain, haggle.

memayukan to fix the price (of goods).

terpayu *tidak* ~ priceless, invaluable.

payudara (*Skr*) (female) breast. *puting* – nipple. – *subalan* falsies.

payung 1 umbrella. 2 parachute. *tentara* – a) parachute troops, paratroopers. b) parachutist. *(ber)sedia* – *sebelum hujan* prevention is better than cure. – *agung/ageng* (*Jv*) large red ceremonial umbrella. – *berapit* (*cla*) two umbrellas held over dignitary. – *Cina* oiled-paper parasol. – *iram* (*cla*) fringed umbrella used by royalty. – *(kekuatan) nuklir* nuclear umbrella. – *kebesaran* umbrella of state. – *kuning* royal umbrella (held by a servant who did not allow the king to step on his own shadow). – *lawa/mota* (*Jv*) European black sailcloth umbrella. – *pradan* (*Jv*) the gilt umbrella (of the *kraton* in Yogyakarta). – *putih* umbrella of Muslim clergymen. – *rém pendarat* breakchute. – *ubur-ubur* fringed umbrella. – *udara* parachute; → PARASUT.

sepayung under the same umbrella.

berpayung 1 to use an umbrella/parachute. 2 with an umbrella/parachute. *tentara* ~ parachute troops. ~ *sebelum hujan* prevention is better than cure.

berpayungkan with ... as an umbrella. ~ *daun pisang* using a banana leaf as an umbrella.

memayung umbrella-like in shape.

memayung(i) 1 to screen. 2 to cover (like an umbrella). 3 to shelter, shield, cover, protect from sun or rain (with an umbrella). 4 to drape s.t. over. *dipayungi awan mendung* under cloudy skies.

memayungkan to use s.t. as an umbrella.

terpayungi protected, under the protection of.

payungan toy umbrella.

PB (*init*) → PENGURUS *Besar*.

PB-5 dan PB-8 → PADI *PB 5 dan PB 8*.

PBA (*init*) → PAJAK *Bangsa Asing*.

PBB I (*init*) → PAJAK *Bumi dan Bangunan*.

PBB II (*init*) → PERSERIKATAN *Bangsa-Bangsa*.

mem-PBB-kan to bring up for discussions in the United Nations.

PBDR (*init*) → PAJAK *atas Bunga, Dividén, dan Royalti*.

PBE (*init*) → PASAR *Bersama Éropa*.

PBH I (*init*) [Pemberantasan Buta Huruf] Eradication of Illiteracy.

PBH II (*init*) [Pengurus Besar Harian] Day-to-Day Board of Directors.

PBI → PARTAI *Buruh Indonésia*.

PD (*init*) → PÉDÉ I.

PD-I (*init*) → PERANG *Dunia pertama*.

PD-II (*init*) → PERANG *Dunia kedua*.

P dan K (*init*) → PENDIDIKAN *dan Kebudayaan*. *Départemén* – Ministry of Education and Culture. *Menteri* – Minister of Education and Culture.

PDB (*init*) [Produk Doméstik Bruto] Gross Domestic Product, GDP.

PDI (*init*) → PARTAI *Démokrasi Indonésia*.

PDI II (*joc*) [penurunan daya ingat] a senior moment.

PDIN-LIPI (*init*) [Pusat Dokuméntasi Ilmiah National – Lembaga Ilmu Pengetahuan Indonésia] National Scientific Documentation Center – Indonesian Scientific Council.

PDIP (*init*) → PARTAI *Démokrasi Indonésia Perjuangan*.

PDK I (*init*) [Pejabat Diplomatik Dan Konsulér] Diplomatic and Consular Corps.

PDK II → PARTAI *Démokrat Katolik*.

PDKB → PARTAI *Démokrasi Kasih Bangsa*.

pdkt [pendekatan] approach (to get to know s.o.).

PDN (*init*) → PERUSAHAAN *Dagang Negara*.

PDR (*init*) → PARTAI *Daulat Rakyat*.

PDRI [Pemerintah Darurat Républik Indonésia] Emergency Government of the Republic of Indonesia, in existence from December 22, 1948, to July 1949.

PDS [Penguasa Darurat Sipil] Civil Emergency Authority (in Maluku).

Pdt. (*abbr*) → PENDÉTA. *Pdt. Hendro Soewarno, S.Th.* Minister Hendro Soewarno, Master of Theology.

pé I (*Jv*) (*ikan* –) ray (the fish); → PARI I.

pé II → WANITA *P*.

péang (*J*) 1 oval (in shape). 2 (of the shape of the head) deformed, distorted, misshapen, knocked out of shape. 3 rugged, bumpy. *Kendaraan itu jalannya – sebab roda depan dan belakang tak menginjak jejak yang sama.* The ride in the car was bumpy because the front and rear wheels didn't touch the ground at the same time.

terpéang-péang to be worn-out/-down, threadbare. *Sol sepatunya sudah* ~. The soles of his shoes were all worn down.

pebahu *layar* – yardarm, i.e., either of the outer portions of the yard of a square sail.

pebéan → PABÉAN.

pebila → PABILA

peboler and **peboling** bowler; → BOLING.

Pébruari → FÉBRUARI.

pecah I 1 to break, be broken into small pieces; broken, defective, out of order. *Telur itu jatuh* –. The eggs fell and broke. *plastik yang tak bisa* – unbreakable plastic. *Pesawat DC-9 Garuda pada saat mendarat di Ngurah Rai – menjadi tiga.* The Garuda DC-9 broke into three pieces when it landed at Ngurah Rai Airport. *uang* – small change. – *berkeping-keping* smashed to pieces. 2 cracked, chapped (of the skin, lips); → MEREKAH. *Bibirnya* –. His lips were chapped. – *karena matahari* suncracked. *suara* – a cracked voice. 3 curdled (of milk); → MENGENTAL. *Susu ini sudah* –. The milk is curdled. 4 spread (of news); → TERSIAR. *sas-sus cepat* – rumors spread fast. 5 leaked, become known (of a secret). *Tidak* – *rahasia itu.* The secret didn't leak out. 6 to break out (of war); to burst (into tears/laughter). *Perang* –. War broke out. *Tangisnya akan* –. He will burst into tears. – *tertawanya.* He burst into laughter. 7 to burst (of a sore/boil). 8 to hatch, burst open (of a shell). *Telur itu belum juga* –. The egg hasn't burst yet. 9 punctured (of a tire). *mengalami ban* – to have a flat (tire). 10 to break up (of a relationship). *Persahabatan meréka sudah lama* –. Their friendship broke up a long time ago. 11 to be killed (in action/battle). – *sebagai ratna* to be killed in action, fall in battle. – *buyung, tempayan ada* there is a wide choice of mates; there is more than one fish in the sea. – *berantakan/berderai* shattered into pieces. – *menanti belah* just waiting for the final breakup. – *belah* a) earthenware, pottery, crockery. b) to be scattered around, be dispersed. **berpecah-belah 1** to be scattered around, be dispersed, in scattered pieces. **2** in disorder/a mess; confused, disorganized. **memecah-belahkan** to smash to pieces, smash up. **terpecah-belah** shashed up, split up, disintegrated. **pemecah-belah** divisive/disintegrative force, fissiparous tendency. *Tetapi sebaliknya agama juga dapat menjadi ~ yang dahsyat.* But on the other hand religion can be a terrible divisive force. – *hati* a) lost courage/heart. b) broken-hearted; → PATAH *hati*. – *kabar.* The news broke. – *kepala* skull fracture. – *kepercayaan* lost confidence. – *keringatnya* sweat poured off him. *beras* – *kulit* husked brown rice. – *nyalinya* to lose courage/heart. – *perang* a) war broke out. b) (*cla*) to lose the war. – *riak* breakers, surf. – *rumah* housebreaking. – *rumah* *terjadi pada waktu siang dan malam.* Burglaries occurred during the day and at night. *tukang - rumah* housebreaker.

berpecah divided/split up/broken up into several groups/pieces. ~ *dua/tiga* split up into two/three parts.

berpecahan (*pl subj*) to split into pieces.

memecah 1 to break (of waves). *Ombak ~ di pantai.* The waves broke on the beach. **2** to crack open (a wall, etc.). *berusaha ~ témbok* to try to crack open a wall. **3** to divide, break up into parts, break (money) into smaller denominations. *Jawa dipecah menjadi tiga provinsi.* Java has been divided into three provinces. **4** to drive away, break. ~ *kesepian* to drive away loneliness. ~ *kesunyian* to break the silence. **5** to solve (a problem). ~ *masalah* to solve a problem, problem solving.

memecahi to smash s.t. to pieces. *Saya pecahi kepalanya nanti!* I'll knock your brains out!

memecahkan [and **memecahin** (*J coq*)] **1** to smash into pieces, smash up, break, shatter. ~ *gelas* to smash a glass into pieces. ~ *kepala* to puzzle one's head (over s.t.). ~ *telinga* deafening. *letusan yang ~ telinga* a deafening explosion. **2** to divide (up) into separate parts. *Keuntungan sebanyak itu dipecahkan jadi tiga.* Such a large profit was divided into three parts. **3** to break (news, a record). *Siapa yang ~ kabar itu?* Who broke the news? ~ *rékor dunia* to break the world's record. **4** to disrupt. ~ *persatuan* to disrupt the unity. **5** to solve/cope with (a problem). *tidak dapat dipecahkan* insolvable. **6** to surpass. **7** to parse (a sentence).

terpecah to be divided into parts/groups. *Rombongan itu ~ menjadi dua.* The group was divided in two. **keterpecahan** discord, division. *Mungkin bangsa Indonésia yang majemuk ini masih berada dalam ~ dan tidak seperti wujudnya sekarang.* The pluralistic Indonesian nation might still be fragmented and not in its present form.

terpecah-pecah in pieces, fragmented, all broken up.

terpecahkan solvable (of a problem), soluble (of a substance). *Berbagai kekurangan dan masalah yang tak kunjung ~ harus meréka hadapi.* They have to face various shortcomings and problems which never can be solved. *Belum ~ masalah lalulintas dan angkutan umum.* The traffic and public transportation problems have not been solved yet.

pecahan 1 piece, fragment, splinter, shard. ~ *batu* stone chips. ~ *beling* shards, pieces of broken glass. ~ *ombak* breakers. **2** (*math*) fraction. ~ *berulang* repeating decimal, repeater. ~ *biasa* common fraction. ~ *lancung* improper fraction. ~ *murni* proper fraction. ~ *persepuluhan* decimal fraction. ~ *sempurna* proper fraction. **3** denomination (of money). *uang dolar (América) ~ seratus* an (American) 100-dollar bill.

kepecahan breakage. ~ *telur sebutir* a meaningless profit or loss.

pemecah 1 breaker, smasher. ~ *aksi mogok* strike breaker. ~ *atom* atom smasher. ~ *frékuénsi* equalizer. ~ *gelombang* breakwater. *alat ~ gumpalan* disintegrator. ~ *rékor* record breaker. **2** solver (of problems). ~ *masalah* problem solver.

pemecahan 1 solving, solution. ~ *masalah* problem solving. **2** smashing into pieces. ~ *atom* atom smashing. **3** breakup.

perpecahan 1 split, division into parts/groups, rift. ~ *intérn* internal schism. ~ *kepribadian* personality split. ~ *partai* split in the party. *Tidak terjadi ~ yang merugikan.* No harmful split occurred. **2** breakdown, breakup. **3** feud, dissension.

pecah II - *beling* k.o. plant, *Strobilanthes crispus*.

pécai (*C*) Chinese cabbage, kale, *Brassica chinensis*; → KAILAN.

pécak 1 damaged, dented; flat, flattened; → PESUK. **2** blind in one eye; → PÉCÉ; *cp* TOJI. - *boléh dilayangkan, bulat boléh digulingkan* to be in complete harmony/accord.

memécakkan to flatten.

pecal I → PECEL.

pecal II memecal to massage, pinch, squeeze.

pecara ancient objects of the Cirebon *Kraton* which are exhibited on Muhammad's birthday.

pecat *main -* to fire people right and left. *- iman* (*S*) s.o. who has lost faith. *- nonaktif* suspended with pay. **memecat-nonaktifkan** to suspend with pay.

memecat(kan) 1 to fire, discharge. *dipecat dengan hormat* honorably discharged. *dipecat tidak dengan hormat* dishonorably discharged. **2** to expel. ~ *sementara* to suspend, discontinue.

memecati (*pl obj*) to fire.

pemecat s.o. who dismisses.

pemecatan 1 dismissal, discharge, firing. ~ *atas permintaan sendiri* dismissal at one's own request. ~ *dengan mendapat hak pénsiun* dismissal with pension rights. ~ *dengan hormat* honorable discharge. ~ *dengan tidak hormat* dishonorable discharge. ~ *seketika* immediate dismissal. **2** expulsion. **3** suspension, discontinuance.

pécé (*C? J*) blind in one eye, one-eyed.

peceklik → PACEKLIK.

pecel (*Jv*) a cooked vegetable salad with peanut dressing.

péci (*D*) untasseled fez, *usu* made of black velvet; → KOPIAH.

berpéci to wear such a fez.

pecicilan (*Jv*) **1** to stare about rudely. **2** to demonstrate.

Pecinan Chinatown, Chinese quarter of town.

pecing → PICING.

pécok I (*J*) dented; → PÉCAK.

pécok II (*Jv*) a hoe-like farm implement for loosening soil; → PACUL I.

pécong I (*J*) careless, not watching out.

pécong II (*Pr*) boy-/girlfriend; → PACAR II.

pecuk I various species of cormorants. *burung - (kecil/padi)* little cormorant, *Phalacrocorax niger*. - *cagakan* great cormorant, *Phalacrocorax carbosinensis*. - *hitam* little black cormorant, *Phalacrocorax sulcirostris*. - *ular* oriental darter, *Anhinga melanogaster*.

pecuk II (*ob*) a mixture of Dutch with a local language.

pécun I [possibly from <u>pérék culun</u> or from <u>pérék cuma-cuma</u>] young slut/whore.

pécun II (*C*) Chinese dragon-boat festival.

pecundang I (*J*) the loser. *Dia akhirnya jadi -.* In the end he was the loser; → (KE)CUNDANG I.

mem(p)ecundangi 1 to defeat, conquer, vanquish. **2** to swindle, cheat, defraud. *Ketika itu, S. Y. bersama seorang temannya sudah berada di Palémbang dan ~ petugas di Bank Bumi Daya.* At that time, S. Y. and a friend were already in Palembang and cheated an employee of the Bank Bumi Daya.

pecundang II instigator, provocateur; → CUNDANG II.

pecundang III grip (in karate, etc.). *Héllie berputar, dan dengan satu - karaté Yahya terpental ke pinggir tempat tidur.* Hellie turned and with one karate grip Yahya was thrown to the edge of the bed.

pecus (*ob*) *tidak -* incapable, incompetent; → BECUS.

pecut whip. - *kuda* k.o. medicinal plant, blue porter weed, snakeweed, *Stachytarpheta jamaicensis*.

memecut 1 to whip. **2** to whip on, urge on, instigate.

pecutan whip, lash.

pemecutan whipping, lashing.

peda I salted and dry-smoked sea fish (*kembung* or *layang*); a side dish. *ikan -* fish prepared in that manner.

memeda to pickle fish in brine.

peda II (*M*) short machete; → PARANG I.

pedada *pohon -* a large beach tree, *Sonneratia spp.*, with a knob-like fruit (= *buah -*) which gives its name to the knob at the apex of a boat's mast; → BEREMBANG.

pedadah medicine chest; → CERAKIN I.

pédagog (*D*) pedagogist.

pédagogi (*D/E*) pedagogy.

pédagogik (*E*) and **pédagogis** (*D*) pedagogical.

pédah → FAÉDAH, PAÉDAH.

pedak I (*J*) salted sea fish; → PEDA I.

pedak II (*cla*) k.o. legendary poisonous animal.

pedaka (*Skr cla*) collar with pendants; → AGUK, DOKOH I.

pedal I gizzard; → EMPEDAL, REMPELA.

pedal II memedal to toss s.t. down hastily, wolf down.

pédal (*D*) pedal. *mengayuh -* to pedal. *- gas* gas pedal, accelerator. *- kopling* clutch pedal. *menekan/menginjak - kopling/rém* to step on the clutch/brake pedal.

berpédal with a pedal.

memédal to step on the pedal of.

pedanda (*Bal*) Buddhist high priest (belonging to the Brahman caste) of the Bali-Hindu religion.

pedandé (*NTB*) caretaker of a holy well.

pedang 1 sword. *main* – to cross swords. *menghunus* – to draw one's sword. *kena* – *bermata dua* highly irritated/offended. *menepik mata* – to oppose those in authority. – *Allah* epithet for Khalid al-Walid, an early supporter of Islam. – *beladau* a tiny curved dagger. – *bermata dua* double-edged sword. – *ékor belangkas* a sword with a triangular blade. – *ékor pari* sword with triple edge. – *jenawi* a long sword held with both hands. – *kerajaan* royal ceremonial sword. – *lurus* a sword used for fencing. (*ilmu*) – *pari* sword with a triangular blade. – *pekir* k.o. black magic in which the soul of a sleeping victim is conjured up so that his or her face appears in a dish of water and the *dukun* can stab it with his *belati* (in Nusa Tenggara). – *péndék* cutlass. – *pora* k.o. sword worn by naval cadets. – *serunai* a sword used for fencing. – *setiabu* a) a sword with a triangular blade. b) a bayonet; → SANGKUR. – *terhunus* a drawn sword. 2 (*sl*) penis.

berpedang to have a penis. *Céwék melécéhkan cowok yang maaf ~ kecil itu.* Girls despise the boy who has, excuse the expression, a small penis.

pedang-pedangan 1 toy sword. 2 swordplay.

memedang to stab/slash/strike with a sword.

pédantik pedantic.

pedapa twig.

pedar 1 rancid (of oil). 2 (– *hati*) in a bad mood, dejected, out of sorts.

memedarkan to make s.t. good turn into s.t. bad.

kepedaran 1 displeasure, discontent, dissatisfaction. 2 out of sorts, dejected.

pedarakan *pidak* – (*K*) the downtrodden, those of the lowest social order.

pedas 1 spicy, hot, peppery. *telur dadar* – omelet with hot sauce. 2 sharp, severe, harsh, biting. *kritik yang* – sharp criticism. 3 burning, smarting. *Mata kami terasa* –. Our eyes were burning/smarting. – *perih* great problems/difficulties. *Apakah anda mengerti* – *perihnya hidup di mancanegara?* Do you understand the great problems of living in a foreign country?

pedas-pedas too hot. *Sambalnya jangan ~!* Don't make the sauce too hot!

sepedas 1 as spicy/sharp as. 2 [and **sipedas** (*M*)] ginger; → JAHÉ.

memedaskan 1 to make (food) hot/spicy, spice. 2 to hurt, inflict pain on. *Perkataannya ~ hati saya.* His words hurt my feelings.

terpedas the spiciest/sharpest.

kepedasan 1 very highly spiced. 2 to suffer from eating s.t. that is too spicy.

pedat compact; → PADAT.

pedati (*Skr*) a horse- or ox-drawn two-wheeled car, *usu* provided with a tilt; → CIKAR I, GEROBAK I, KAHAR I. – *dorong* pushcart.

berpedati to have or ride in such a cart.

pedato → PIDATO.

pedat-pedot frequently broken/interrupted; → PEDOT-PEDOT.

pedauw and **pedaw** (*sl*) to get the rush (from heroin).

pédé I and **pé-dé** (*BG*) [percaya diri] self-confident.

pédé II [pendidikan jasmani] (following the old spelling) physical education, phys. ed.

pédél I (*D*) a university official who has ceremonial duties such as marshal in an academic procession.

pédél II (*J*) flat(tened); → PIPIH.

pedena (*ob*) large earthenware pot.

pedendang I gold or silver braid.

pedendang II (*burung* –) masked finfoot, *Heliopais personata.*

pedendang III – *gagak* k.o. climbing plant, *Trichosanthes wallichiana.*

pédéngan (*J*) 1 curtain, cover, screen. 2 cover-up, s.t. used for hiding one's real intentions. *nama* – pseudonym.

pedes → PEDAS.

pédéstrian (*E*) pedestrian.

pédéstrianisasi the construction of special strips of pavement for pedestrians.

pedét (*Jv*) calf, heifer; → SAPI I. – *jantan* steer.

pedéwakan → PADÉWAKANG.

pediah → FIDYAH.

pediang (*Jv*) to warm o.s. over a fire (the custom for a woman nearing childbirth); → (BER)DIANG.

pédiatri (*D*) pediatrics.

pédiatrik (*D*) pediatrics.

pédiatris (*D*) pediatrician.

pedih smarting, stinging (of a cut/one's eyes), feel a stinging pain. – *hati* very sad, sorrowful.

sepedih as stinging as.

memedih to smart, sting.

memedihi and **memedihkan** 1 to sting s.t. 2 to sadden, distress, be painful.

terpedih the most stinging.

kepedihan 1 smarting/stinging pain. 2 sadness, distress, poignancy.

pemedih s.t. that smarts/stings.

pédikur (*D/E*) pedicure.

pedis I smarting; → PEDIH.

pedis II → PEDAS.

pediyan (*BD*) a floating market in which female peddlers sell fish, vegetables, etc.

pedoman (from *Jv dom*) 1 compass; → DOM I. – *gasing* gyrocompass. 2 guideline(s). *harga* – pilot price. *tanggal* – target date; → *tanggal* ANCER-ANCER. – *Penghayatan dan Pengamalan Pancasila* Guidelines for Instilling and Implementing Pancasila. 3 criterion. 4 guidance, instruction(s), orientation. 5 (*buku* –) guidebook, set of directives, directory, manual, code. – *prilaku* code of conduct. 6 leadership, board, executive committee.

berpedoman 1 to use a compass. 2 ~ (*ke*)*pada* to be guided by.

berpedomankan to be guided by. ~ *kaidah bahasa* guided by grammatical rules.

mem(p)edomani to provide guidance to. *Kita jangan dipedomani pihak lain tentang hidup kita sendiri.* We should not be guided by others about our own lives.

mem(p)edomankan to guide, orient, orientate.

pedongkang lighter (a boat); → TONGKANG.

pedot (*Jv*) 1 broken, broken loose. *Layangannya* –. The kite broke loose. *Talinya* –. The rope broke into short pieces. 2 interrupted.

pedot-pedot spasmodic, frequently broken off. *Penerbitannya* ~. Publication of it was spasmodic.

memedotkan 1 to break for s.o. 2 to break off, interrupt, cause s.t. to be discontinued.

pedotan 1 broken (off). *benang* ~ a piece of thread. 2 interrupted. 3 a pause in singing (by a *waranggana*).

pedu → EMPEDU.

pedukang *ikan* – k.o. catfish, *Arius spp.*

peduli (*A*) 1 care, heed; interested in, paying attention to. – (*akan/dengan/terhadap*) to care (for), pay attention (to), take s.t. to heart. *tak* – *apa(kah)* it doesn't matter whether. *tak bakal ada yang* – nobody will care. *Dia tidak* – *dengan saya.* He doesn't care about me. *tidak* – *terhadap* do not care about, pay no attention to. *membangkitkan* – to interest s.o. (in s.t.). *tidak mengambil* – to ignore, pay no attention to. *tidak* – do not care, be indifferent. *ketidak-pedulian* indifference. ~ *secara menyeluruh* total indifference, overall passivity. 2 (*I*) don't care! – *amat!* Who cares! I could care less, I don't give a damn.

mem(p)edulikan to care about, pay attention to.

kepedulian involvement, concern, caring about. *Pemerintah tidak melarang mahasiswa untuk menunjukkan ~ meréka terhadap masalah-masalah sosial.* The government does not prohibit university students from showing their concern about social matters. **berkepedulian** to care (about), be concerned (about).

pedupan → DUPA.

pedusi (*M*) woman; wife. *dilangkahi* – to be tied to one's wife's apron-strings.

pedut (*Jv*) fog, mist.

peduta (*Skr*) ambassador; → DUTA.

pé-ér homework; → PR VI.

peg. I (*abbr*) [pegawai] government employee.

peg. II (*abbr*) [pegunungan] mountainous area.

pegaga and **pegagan** (– *tekukur/ular*) various species of pennywort, creeping herbs used for many medicinal purposes, Indian pennywort, *Hydrocotyle asiatica, Centella asiatica*; → PENGGAGA. – *embun* k.o. pennywort, *Hydrocotyle sibthorpiodes.* – *hutan* k.o. herb, *Merremia emarginata*. - *gajah* k.o. creeping herb, *Hydrocotyle javanica*. - *tikus* k.o. herb, *Geophila reniformis*.

pegah (*ob*) **terpegah** famous; → MEGAH.

pegal 1 stiff and sore from strain or exertion. **2** (- *hati*) annoyed, irritated, fed up; → DONGKOL I, KESAL. - *linu* sore. - *urat* stiff tendon.

pegal-pegal ~ *kejang* stiff as a board.

memegalkan 1 to stiffen, make rigid. **2** exasperating, irritating.

pegalan 1 to feel stiff and sore. **2** to tend to feel annoyed or irritated.

kepegalan 1 stiffness, rigidity. **2** peevishness, grumbling disposition.

pegan (*ob*) **terpegan** silent and bewildered.

pegang [and **pégang** (*coq*)]. **berpegang** [(*ke*)*pada*] **1** to hold on to, rely completely on, cling to. ~ *kepada haknya* to assert one's rights. ~ *pada pendiriannya* to stick to one's opinion. ~ *tangan* to hold hands. ~ *teguh pada* to cling desperately/firmly to. **2** to be guided (by). ~ *kukuh pada adat dan agama.* to be firmly guided by *adat* and religion.

berpegangan 1 to hold on to e.o. *Kami* ~ *menyeberangi jalan itu.* We held on to e.o. crossing the street. ~ *tangan* a) to cooperate. b) to help e.o. c) hand in hand. **2** (*pl subj*) to hold on to s.t.

memegang [and **megang** (*coq*)] **1** to hold, grab hold of. *Pegang saya erat-erat!* Hold me tight! *Jangan dipegang.* Don't touch. Stay away. ~ *seikat bunga dalam tangan kanannya.* He had a tied-up bunch of flowers in his right hand. **3** to hold/have in one's grasp. *Dia* **4** to drive (a car, etc.). *Untuk* ~ *mobil orang harus punya SIM.* To drive s.o. else's car you must have a driver's license. **5** to arrest (a thief, etc.). **6** to handle, use (a weapon). **7** to have control over (power); to run (a corporation, etc.). ~ *jabatan kunci* to occupy a key position. **8** to carry out, perform (one's duty), play (a role). *tetap* ~ *perintah dan aturan* to keep on fulfilling orders and regulations. **9** to favor, think is going to win. *Pegang Holmes atau Tyson?* Do you favor Holmes or Tyson? (names of boxers). **10** to rely on. *Mereka tidak tahu kata pemimpin atau aparat pemerintah yang mana yang bisa dipegang omongannya.* They don't know which leader's or government apparatus's words they could rely on. **11** to root for (an athletic team). ~ *adat* to live in accordance with the *adat.* ~ *batang* a) to be in charge of an important task. b) to be a driver (of a *bécak/bémo*, etc.). ~ *batang léhér* (*cla*) to grab s.o. by the neck, i.e., to arrest s.o. ~ *besi panas* to do a job that is full of anxiety. ~ *buku* to keep the accounts/books. ~ *cemput-rit* to pull the strings (from behind the scenes); → TUTWURI *handayani.* ~ *ékor* to have s.o. under one's thumb. ~ *gelar* to have a title/name. ~ *kartu* to hold the cards (i.e., have everything under control). ~ *kas* to be the treasurer (of an association, etc.). ~ *kekuasaan* to be in power/charge. ~ *kemudi* to be at the wheel (of a vehicle), drive a car. *Saya merasa gugup melihat anak di bawah umur* ~ *kemudi.* I'm nervous when I see an underage child at the wheel. ~ *kewajiban* to shoulder a task. ~ *Kitab* to abide by the Scriptures/Holy Scripture. ~ *lidah/mulut* to rely on s.o.'s promises/words. ~ *nasihat* to take a piece of advice to heart. ~ *paspor* ... to hold a ... passport; → BERPASPOR. ~ *peranan* to play a role. ~ *peraturan permainan* to play by the rules of the game. ~ *pesawat* to fly a plane. ~ *pisau* to carry a knife. ~ *puasa* to keep the fast. ~ *rumah tangga* to run a household. ~ *senjata* to hold the power, have the authority. ~ *s(e)tir* to drive a car. *Wanita itu belum berani* ~ *s(e)tir mobilnya di jalan raya.* That woman is still afraid of driving on highways. ~ *tampuk* to manage, run. *Dia* ~ *tampuk perusahaan itu.* He runs that company. ~ *tampuk negeri* to govern a country. ~ *teguh* to obey, follow. *Sejak dulu kami* ~ *teguh aturan ini.* We have followed this rule for a long time. ~ *toko* to run a store. ~ *uang* a) to manage the finances (of an enterprise, etc.). b) to be powerful because one is rich.

memegangi [and **megangin** (*J coq*)] **1** (*pl obj*) to hold. *Gadis-gadis kurus malu-malu* ~ *rok panjang meréka dari gangguan angin.* The skinny girls shyly held their long dresses because of the gusts of wind. **2** to hold on to s.t. *dipegangi erat* to listen to (advice). *Nasihat itu harus* ~ *erat kalau ingin selamat.* One has to listen to that advice if one wants to be safe.

memperpegangi to hold/adhere to.

memegangkan to hold s.t. for s.o.

terpegang [and **kepegang** (*coq*)] held on to, grasped. ~ *di abu dingin* don't get a thing (from one's family, etc.). ~ *di bara hangat* (to have) bad luck. *Di tangannya* ~ *sebuah bungkusan berisi kain yang baru dia beli.* In his hand he grasped a package containing the cloth he had just bought. *bisa* ~ manageable.

pegangan 1 s.t. that is held. **2** handle, grip, holder, cinch, hilt, lever. ~ *pintu* door bracket. **3** directory. (*buku* ~) directory. **4** s.t. that has become the basis for determining s.t. else, guide(line), standpoint; favorite. *Massa yang datang ke tempat kampanye telah mempunyai* ~. The masses that came to the rally already have their political favorite. **5** rule-of-thumb. *Misalnya Tsurumi mengatakan bahwa sebagai* ~ *para énginer di pabrik-pabrik memperkirakan pekerja-pekerja Indonésia mengerjakan hanya 50-60 persén dari yang sama di Jepang, Koréa dan Singapura kalau dilihat kerjanya dari waktu dan interaksi pekerja yang sama.* For example, Tsurumi said that as a rule-of-thumb factory engineers estimate that Indonesian workers only work 50-60 percent as much as those in Japan, Korea and Singapore from the point of view of time and interaction with fellow workers. **6** specialty, s.t. one is good at. **7** function, office. **8** amulet. *Apa mungkin Samiun punya* ~ *semacam Jaran Goyang, tidak ada yang tahu.* Is it possible that Samiun has an amulet like a love potion; nobody knows. **berpegangan 1** to have a handle. *Alat ini diberi* ~ *supaya mudah memakainya.* This tool has been provided with a handle so that it will be easy to use. **2** to stick fast (to).

pemegang 1 handle, grip. **2** holder, bracket. **3** holder, s.o. who holds s.t. ~ *adat* s.o. who adheres to *adat.* ~ *andil* (*ob*) shareholder. ~ *arsip* archivist. ~ *buku* bookkeeper. ~ *gadai* pledgee. ~ *gelar* title holder. ~ *hak* (*leg*) person entitled to s.t. ~ *hak cipta* copyright holder. ~ *hak manfaat* usufructuary. ~ *hipoték* mortgagee. ~ *izin* concessionaire. ~ *jujur* bone fide holder. ~ *karcis* ticket holder. ~ *kas* cashier, teller. ~ *kekuasaan* power holder. ~ *konsési* concessionaire. ~ *kuasa* (*leg*) mandatary, agent, authorized representative. ~ *lisénsi* licensee. ~ *obligasi* bond holder. ~ *patén* patentee, patent holder. ~ *peluru* cartridge holder, clip. ~ *polis* insurance policy holder. ~ *prokurasi* attorney-in-fact, holder of a power of attorney. ~ *rékening* account holder. ~ *rékor* record holder. ~ *saham* shareholder. ~ *saham tercatat/terdaftar* stockholder of record. ~ *saham utama* substantial shareholder. ~ *s(e)tir* driver. ~ *surat mandat* mandatory. ~ *surat utang* note holder.

pemegangan 1 s.t. to hold on to, grip. **2** holding on to, keeping. **3** function, office. **4** detention, custody. ~ *buku* bookkeeping.

pegar *ayam/burung* - crested fireback pheasant, *Lophura ignit/rufa.*

pegari visible.

kepegarian visibility.

pegas 1 (spiral) spring. **2** (*M*) a rattan beater (for carpets/mattresses, etc.). **3** suspension. *gaya* - elasticity, resilience. - *daun* leaf spring (of car). - *jam* watch spring. - *jepit* clip. - *kemudi* rudder stay. - *lawan* counterspring. - *rambut* hairspring. - *ulir* coil spring.

berpegas elastic, resilient, supple.

memegas 1 to be elastic/springy; to spring. **2** to flap the wings in order to fly. **3** to beat (a carpet/mattress, etc.).

kepegasan elasticity, resilience.

pemegasan 1 resilience, elasticity, springiness. **2** suspension (in a car, etc.).

pegat (*J/Jv*) **memegat 1** to intercept (a car/the enemy, etc.). **2** to sever, break (a tie), block, cut off (communications/supplies/relations, etc.).

pegatan 1 ~ *dengan* blocked/cut off from. **2** (*Jv*) divorced.

pemegatan 1 interception, interdiction. **2** blockade.

pegau k.o. red shellac used for dying silk.

pegawai 1 official, employee, officer; worker. **2** (-.- and *para* -) employees, staff, personnel. *Kantor Urusan* - [KUP] Personnel Office. *kelebihan* - overstaffed. *urusan* - personnel affairs. - *administrasi* administrative officer, clerical worker. - *arsip* file clerk. - *atasan* executive officer. - *biasa* ordinary/regular employee; *cp* PEGAWAI *luar biasa.* - *bulanan* monthly wage earner.

– *catatan sipil* registrar of births, deaths, and marriages; registration officer. – *darat* (in the shipping business) shore staff. – *duane* customs officer. – *fédéral* federal employee. – *harian* daily wage earner. – *honorér* temporary employee. – *kantor* office/white-collar worker. – *keséhatan* health officer. – *kotapraja* municipal employee. – *lama* former employee, ex-employee. – *latihan* training officer. – *lepas* piece worker, contract employee. – *lini* line employee. – *luar biasa* extraordinary employee; *cp* PE-GAWAI *biasa*. – *méja* (*infr*) white-collar worker. – *menengah* middle-grade employee. – *mingguan* weekly wage earner. – *negeri* civil servant, government employee (includes civilian employees of the central and regional governments and members of the Indonesian Armed Forces). **mempegawai-negerikan** to convert s.o. into a government employee. *prosés ~ karyawan "honda" dalam penyelesaian masalah pegawai "honda"* the procedure of converting regional honorarium workers into civil servants. – *nonproduksi* nonproductive employee, dead wood. – *operatif* operative employee. – *pelaksana* executive employee. – *pemerintah* government employee. – *pendaftaran warga* registrar of births, deaths, and marriages. – *percobaan* probationary employee. – *PGP(N)* employee whose salary is based on the Civil Service Pay Scale; → PGP(N). – *pérsonalia* personnel officer. – *rendah* low-level civil servant. – *satuan* pieceworker. – *sementara* temporary employee. – *serikat sekerja* unionized employee. – *staf* staff member. – *tatausaha* administrative employee. – *téknik* technician. – *teladan* model employee. – *teras* key/senior/top employee. – *tetap* permanent employee. – *tinggi* high-ranking official. – *wanita* female employee.

berpegawai to have employees; with personnel.

kepegawaian 1 officialdom, civil service. 2 personnel (*mod*). *kepala bagian ~* head of the personnel department. *urusan ~* personnel affairs.

pegel I → PEGAL.

pegel II [pengusaha golongan ékonomi lemah] Businessmen from the Economically Weak Group.

Pégépé [Peraturan Gaji Pegawai] Civil Servant Salary Regulations.

pegi (*coq*) → PERGI.

pegimana (*coq*) → BAGAIMANA.

pégoh pearl oyster.

pégon (*Jv*) Javanese or Sundanese written in Arabic script; → HURUF *pégon*.

pegonin (*J*) **dipegonin** to be tortured/chided.

pégot → PAGUT I.

peguam (*Mal*) lawyer, attorney. – *negara* attorney general; → JAKSA *agung*.

peguambéla (*Mal*) advocate, lawyer for the defense.

peguamcara (*Mal*) solicitor. – *negara* solicitor general.

pegun stationary.

terpegun struck dumb, speechless.

péh (*D infr*) bad luck.

péhai (an initialism for PHI) Indonesian Hajj Association.

péhak → PIHAK.

péhaka termination of employment, dismissal; → PHK.

mempéhakakan to dismiss/fire.

péhcun → PÉCUN.

péhong (*C J*) k.o. venereal disease; syphilis.

péhu a side dish of *témpé* and *tahu* (considered poor man's food).

péi (*C*) k.o. Chinese card game.

péil (*D*) level, grade (of a building).

pejajaran (*J*) evil spirit (often in the shape of a crocodile/tiger, etc.); Satan, devil (also used as a curse word), villain.

pejaka time limit.

pejal 1 solid, massive, firm (of flesh). 2 hard (of stone/timber, etc.), chewy (of meat). *batu –* granite.

memejalkan to solidify, press/tamp down tight (of earth).

pejalan (*geol*) massif.

pejam closed, shut (of the eyes).

memejam to close one's eyes.

memejamkan to close/shut (one's eyes). *Kami sukar ~ mata.* We couldn't sleep a wink.

terpejam 1 closed, shut (of the eyes). 2 to revolve rapidly so as to seem motionless. 3 to disappear from sight.

Pejambon a street in Jakarta, the location of the Foreign Ministry.

pejatian (*ob*) regarding s.t. as genuine/authentic/true, etc.; → JATI II. – *awak, kepantangan orang* to stand alone (in one's opinion), fight a lonely battle.

pejem → PEJAM.

péjer (*E*) *radio –* beeper, pager.

pejera the sighting bead of a gun.

péjét (*Jv*) pinching; → PIJAT.

meméjét(i) to push/press down on/exert pressure with the thumb.

péjétan pushbutton.

pejompongan → JOMPONG.

peju(h) (*J/Jv*) (*air –*) (human) semen.

pék I (*D*) pitch, tar, asphalt; → ASPAL I, TÉR I. – *kokas* pitch coke.

pék II clipped form of **empék**.

pék III → PIK.

peka and **péka** 1 sensitive, thoughtful, considerate. *kurang/tidak –* insensitive, impervious, inconsiderate. 2 attentive, paying attention. *Anda harus ~ terhadap perasaan orang lain.* You should pay attention to other people's feelings. 3 alert. *keadaan rélaks yang –* an alert relaxed situation. 4 allergic. *kurang –* not sensitive enough. **kekurang-pekaan** insensitivity, lack of consideration. *tidak –* insensitive. **ketidak-pekaan** insensitivity – *jejas* vulnerable.

sepeka as sensitive as.

memeka 1 to be sensitive. 2 to take care not to be offensive.

terpeka the most sensitive.

kepekaan 1 sensitivity. *~ yang berlebih-lebihan* hypersensitive, overly sensitive.

pekaca (*Skr*) lotus; → PEKAJA. *adiratna –* pure jewel (term for one's sweetheart).

pekah → NAFKAH.

Péka-i (*pron* of **PKI**) Communist Party of Indonesia.

pekaja (*cla*) 1 lotus. 2 sweetheart

pekak 1 deaf, hard of hearing; → TULI. 2 dull (of sound/coins jingling, etc.). *kucing –* k.o. mousetrap. *penuh –* chock-full. *tabung –* a closed cylinder used as a money box. – *pembakar meriam* everyone is useful. – *badak* a) stone-deaf. b) pretending to be deaf. – *batu* stone-deaf. – *bunyi* sound-deadening. – *labang* hard of hearing.

pekak-pekak *~ badak* a) stone-deaf. b) pretending to be deaf.

berpekak-pekak *~ diri* to pretend not to hear.

bersipekak (*ob*) to turn a deaf ear to.

memekak(kan) deafening, ear-splitting, stunning (of noise). *Iringan musik yang tersembul dari alat perekam pita cukup ~ telinga.* The musical accompaniment that emerged from the tape recorder was completely ear-splitting.

terpekak deafened.

pekakak I *burung –* various species of kingfishers: brown-winged kingfisher, *Pelargopsis amauroptera*, chestnut-collared kingfisher, *Halcyon concreta*. – *bukit* blue-banded kingfisher, *Alcedo euryzona peninsulae*. – *cicit* Indian common kingfisher, *Alcedo atthis bengalensis*. – *rimba* banded kingfisher, *Alcedo pulchella*.

Pekakak II an ethnic group of the Riau Archipelago.

pekakas → PERKAKAS.

pekam 1 safety/hand brake. 2 → PAKEM I.

pekan I market; → PASAR I. *hari –* market day. – *Ahad* the Sunday market in Payakumbuh. – *Raya* (Industrial) Fair. – *Sabtu* the Saturday market in Bukit Tinggi.

berpekan to (put on the) market.

pekan II 1 week (seven successive days, *usu* from Sunday through Saturday); → MINGGU. – *depan* next week. 2 (*Jv*) week (five successive days, i.e., *Legi, Pahing, Pon, Wagé, Kliwon*). *akhir –* weekend. **berakhir minggu** to spend the weekend. *dua –* two weeks, a fortnight. 3 (often capitalized) a period of seven or fewer successive days devoted to a certain event. – *Budaya* Culture Week. – *Film Anak-Anak* Children's Film Week. – *Olahraga Nasional* [PON] National Sports Week. – *Oriéntasi Studi Mahasiswa* [posma] Student Study Orientation week. – *Seni Flora dan Fauna* Flora and Fauna Arts Week.

sepekan 1 one week (of seven days); → SEJUMAT. *warta ~* a weekly magazine. 2 (*Jv*) one week (of five days).

berpekan-pekan for weeks and weeks, for weeks on end, lasting for weeks.

pekan III *bunga* – jasmine, *Jasminum grandiflorum*; → MELATI.

pekarang (S) weapon.

pekasam a strong-smelling preserve (of fish/meat/vegetables).

pekaséh (*Bal*) leader of a *subak*.

pekasin brine, pickle; → ASINAN.

pekat I 1 thick (of a liquid), viscous. *penuh* – chock-full, crowded. 2 strong (of coffee/tea, etc.), bitter (of cold); → NASGITEL. *cinta* – madly/head over heels in love. *musim dingin yang* – a bitter cold winter. 3 concentrated. *susu* – condensed milk. *tanah* – clay. 4 troubled, turbid (of water). 5 dark. *buta/hitam/kelam* – pitch black. *malam* – dark night. – *hati* firm, determined, resolute.

   sepekat as thick/dark, etc. as.

   memekat 1 to congeal, coagulate, curdle. 2 to become dark.

   memekatkan to thicken, condense.

   pekatan concentrate.

   kepekatan density, thickness, concentration, darkness (of color).

pekat II (*A coq*) agreed, in agreement; → (MU)PAKAT.

pekatu (*cla*) *bedil* – an old type of cannon.

pekatul flour from broken grains of rice (used for cooking gruel).

pekau yell, scream; → PIKAU I, PINGKAU.

   memekau to yell, scream.

pékcun (C) Chinese dragon-boat race (held on the fifth day of the fifth Chinese month).

pekéh → FIQIH.

pekek → PEKAK.

pekerti (*Skr*) 1 (*budi* –) character, temperament, disposition. 2 conduct, behavior.

   berpekerti with a ... character.

pekéwuh → PAKÉWUH.

pékgo (*C J*) one hundred and fifty (*usu* used in counting money).

pekih → FAKIH.

pekik yell, scream; → PEKAU. – *pekau* yells and screams. – *pekuk* screams and screams.

   berpekik and memekik to yell, scream, shout.

   berpekikan (*pl subj*) to yell, scream, shout.

   memekik to yell, shout.

   memekikkan to yell/scream/shout s.t.

   terpekik yell/scream/shout out suddenly.

   terpekik-pekik to yell incessantly.

   pekikan yell, scream, shout.

peking I memeking to whine, howl (of dogs).

   terpeking-peking to howl.

peking II *burung* – k.o. finch or sparrow, *Calornis feadensis*..

peking III part of a *gamelan sekaten*, i.e., a *kraton* gamelan played by eight persons (in Cirebon).

Péking Peking (now Beijing).

pekir I → FAKIR.

pekir II (*J*) rejected as unfit; → APKIR.

pekis (*onom*) defiant scream.

   memekis to scream defiance (at a game/cockfight, etc.).

pekiwan (*Jv*) restroom, toilet.

pekojan quarter of town in which Indian merchants live and work; → KHOJA(H).

pekoléh 1 efficient. 2 efficiency.

pékong → TEPÉKONG.

pékpék (*C J*) eight hundred (*usu* used in counting money).

péksi → PAKSI I, INSPÉKSI.

péktai (C) *penyakit* – discharge, leucorrhoea.

péktin (*D/E*) pectin.

peku (*J ob*) a thousand *képéng*.

pekuk I deformed (of a limb).

pekuk II (*M*) memekuk to hack at.

pekuk III → PEKIK *pekuk*.

pekulun (*Jv cla*) your Highness, sire; → TUANKU.

pekung cancerous tumor, canker, foul-smelling ulceration (cancerous or syphilitic). *meraih* – *ke dada* asking/looking for trouble; → MENCARI *gara(-gara)*. – *bubuk* a dried-up nonpurulent pustule. – *melayang* superficial canker.

   berpekung to have a cancerous tumor.

pekur (*A*) memekur to muse, meditate; → TEPEKUR.

pél I (*D*) 1 mop, swab.

   mempél and mengepél [and ngepél (*coq*)] to mob, swab (the floor, etc.). *Ia sedang mengepél lantai di rumah majikannya.* She was mopping the floor in her boss's house.

   pélan mopping, swabbing.

pél II (*D*) pill; → PIL I.

pél III (*D*) field, plain.

   pélan (*J*) a field.

pél IV (*D*) 1 a sheet (of paper). 2 a sheet (consisting of 8 or 16 printed pages).

pél V (in acronyms) → PELABUHAN.

péla harmless drifter. *daérah/masyarakat* – an area/community of drifters.

pelabaya → PELBAYA.

pelabi (*Jv*) 1 trick, ruse. 2 excuse, alibi. 3 (for the sake of) appearance(s), not (meant) seriously.

pelabur (*cla*) ration, portion; → LABUR IV.

pelaga cardamom, *Amomum cardamomum*; → KAPULAGA, KEPULAGA.

péla gandung (*Ambon*) system of traditional alliances between villages of different faiths.

pelagra (*D*) pelagra, a disease which causes the skin to become coarse and scaly.

pelah – *lidah* speech impediment.

pelahan → PELAN.

pelaju [petik, olah dan jual] pick, process and sell.

pelak I hot (of one's body); → PALAK II.

pelak II → FALAK.

pelak III tired.

pélak I evil spirit (also used as a curse word); → PILAK I.

pélak II mistaken; wrong; false. *tak* – *lagi* (there can be) no doubt about it, certainly. *Tidak* – *lagi bahwa upaya pemukiman kembali penduduk membutuhkan serangkaian kegiatan terencana yang tepat.* There is no doubt that efforts to resettle the population require a series of well-planned actions.

pélak III → PÉLEK.

pelakat (*D*) placard, poster.

pelalah glutton; → LALAH.

pelambang → LAMBANG.

pelamin(an) bridal dais/bed. *naik* – to marry.

pelampang (*J*) k.o. temporary covered shed (at festivals), festive tent.

pelampung I buoy, float (of a fishing line); → LAMPUNG.

pelampung II a coastal shrub, *Scaevola frutescens*, whose pith is made into artificial flowers and dyed.

pelampung III various k.o. barbs (fish), *Puntius spp*.

pelamur (*J*) *uang* – money given by people to a newborn baby (*esp* to a firstborn child).

pelan (*coq*) 1 slow. 2 soft(ly) (of speaking voice); → PERLAHAN. *dia berkata* – *sekali* he said very softly.

   pelan-pelan 1 slowly. 2 soft (of sound). *distél* – turned down (of a radio).

   memelankan to reduce the speed of, slow down. *Saya pelankan mobil saya.* I slowed down my car. *Langkahku sengaja kupelankan.* I purposely slowed down.

   pelanan (*coq*) take it easy!

pelana (*Pers*) saddle.

   berpelana to use a saddle; saddled.

   memelanai to saddle, put a saddle on (a horse).

pelanangan → PALANANGAN.

pelancar beams supporting the girders that support joists to which floorboards are attached (in houses on stilts).

pelanduk I the smaller chevrotain, *Tragulus kanchil*. *(se)bagai* – *di dalam cerang* like a fish out of water.

pelanduk II *mata* – a small shrub, Christmas berry, *Ardisia crenata*.

pelanél → FLANÉL.

pelang I striped; → BELANG.

pelang II (*D*) 1 board. 2 road sign, street sign.

pélang (*cla*) a royal boat with oars and sails.

pelangah terpelangah wide open.

pelangai → PELANGI.

pelanggi → PELINGGAM.

pelangi rainbow. *kain* – a silk *kain* of various colors. *selaput* – iris.

pelangkah (*J*) a gift from the groom to the older brother of the bride because he has been "stepped across," i.e., his younger sister is getting married sooner than he is; → LANGKAH.

pelangki and **pelangkin I** → PELANGKING.

pelangkin II tar, pitch.

pelangking (*Port*) palanquin; → PELANGKI(N) I.

pelangpang → PELAMPANG.

pelanin → FLANÉL.

pelantar 1 gangway between house and kitchen outbuilding. **2** jetty for tying up boats, k.o. pier with a hut. **3** landing on staircase. **4** long bench in the front yard or at the back of a house.

pelantaran an unroofed platform attached to a house.

pelantik spring gun.

pelanting falling and rolling.

berpelantingan (*pl subj*) to tumble over the ground, scatter all over. *Buah-buahan yang dibawanya ~ di lantai waktu ia terjatuh.* When she fell down, the fruit she was carrying scattered all over the floor.

memelantingkan to hurl, fling all over, knock down all over.

terpelanting flung, thrown, hurled; → TERPENTAL.

pelapah → PELEPAH.

pelas I memelas to splice (the two ends of ropes).

pelas II → EMPELAS.

pelasah (*M*) every-day clothing, worn-out and faded clothing; → LASAH II.

pelasari → PULASARI.

pelasik → PELESIT I.

pelaspas (*Bal*) **memelaspas** to inaugurate.

pelastik → PLASTIK I.

pelasuh lazybones, sluggard, idler.

pelat → PLAT.

pélat having a speech defect.

pelata (*ikan* –) herring travelly, *Scomber microlepidotus, Alepes kalla.*

pelataran (*J*) lawn, yard.

Pelatnas → PEMUSATAN *Latihan Nasional*. **mem(p)elatnaskan** to put s.o. into the National Training Center.

pelatuk I *burung* – crimson-winged woodpecker; *Picus puniceus;* → BELATUK. – *bawang* common flameback woodpecker, *Dinopium javanense.*

pelatuk II 1 (– *bedil*) trigger. *menarik* – to pull the trigger. **2** rocker-arm.

pelawa crossbar. *membuang* – to invite s.o. to enter the house or a prohibited place.

mempelawa to invite/call over respectfully.

pelawaan invitation.

pelawan various species of trees, *Tristania spp.*

pelayon (*Pal ob*) a fine for eloping with a woman.

pelbagai a variety of, an assortment of, all kinds/types of. – *ragam* various kinds, multifarious. ***mempelbagairagamkan*** to diversify.

kepelbagaian diversity, variety.

pélbak (*D*) garbage dump.

pelbaya (*cla*) executioner; → ALGOJO.

pélbéd (*D*) cot, field cot.

pelbegu pagan, animist.

Példa → PEMBANTU *Létnan Dua.*

pelebaya → PELBAYA.

pelécéh flatterer, bootlicker, ass-kisser

memelécéh to flatter, ass kiss.

pelécét (*J*) **memelécéti** to trick, deceive.

pelecing a way of cooking chicken, etc. using *sambal pelecing.*

pelécok terpelécok sprained, twisted (or ankle, wrist).

pelék (*D*) stain, spot; → VLÉK.

pélek (*D*) wheel-rim. *tutup* – hubcap; → VÉL(E)G.

pelekat I (*D*) placard, poster.

pelekat II → PEREKAT.

Pelékat name of the town of Pulicat on the Coromandel coast (east coast of India), the origin of the *kain/sarung* –, which has a striped and checked motif.

pelékok terpelékok bent, sprained (of ankle, wrist).

pelekuh terpelekuh humped (of the back), crooked.

pelekuk (*M*) twisted, bent.

pelélé (*J*) person who buys fish (at fish markets) for resale.

pélem → FILM I.

pelembaya → PEL(E)BAYA.

pelempap sepelempap a hand's breadth.

pelencit terpelencit 1 to be made to spurt/squirt out by squeezing. *cat yang ~ dari tube* paint squirted out of a tube. **2** flipped (with the finger).

pelengak (*J*) **terpelengak** dumbfounded (from fear/amazement), surprised and shocked, astounded, stunned.

péléngan (*J*) temples (of the forehead).

pelengkung → LENGKUNG I.

peléngsét → BELÉNGSÉT.

peléngsong (*J*) **meléngsong** to deviate so as not to hit the target, go off target.

perénjak → PRÉNJAK.

pelepah frond (of a banana/palm, etc., tree), sheath (of leaf). – *bawah lurus, – atas jangan gelak* all living things must die.

sepelepah one frond.

pelér → PELIR I.

pelés (*D*) (glass) jar, bottle, flask.

pelesat terpelesat to dart off/away.

peléset terpeléset [and **kepeléset** (*coq*)] slipped, skidded; → TERGELINCIR. *~ lidah* made a slip of the tongue.

pelesir (*D*) **1** pleasure, amusement. **2** to take a trip for pleasure, go for an outing/picnic.

berpelesir(an) to take a trip for pleasure, go for an outing/picnic.

pelesiran 1 to take a trip for pleasure, go for an outing/picnic. **2** sexual pleasure. *wanita ~* a promiscuous woman.

kepelesiran pleasure.

pelesit I 1 (*belalang* –) cricket (the insect). **2** a spirit controlled by a sorcerer to suck the blood of a person or eat a child's corpse; it often appears in the shape of a blood-sucking cricket. – *dua sejinjang* and *sejinjang dua* – two men who share one woman. *~ kudung* such a spirit which has only a head but no body.

pelesit II a small flute.

peléster (*D*) **1** plaster. **2** adhesive plaster, band-aid.

mem(p)eléstér 1 to plaster. **2** to put an adhesive plaster/band-aid on a wound.

pélét I a veined wood used for kris hilts, *Kleinhovia hospita.*

pélét II (*Jv*) **1** bird lime. **2** toadyism, flattery. *ilmu* – love magic. *minyak* – a love charm (oil from a *dugong*'s tears).

memélét 1 to catch birds using lime. **2** to attract a girl using magic or sweet talk.

terpélét [and **kepélét** (*coq*)] **1** to be caught with bird lime. **2** to be made to fall in love with s.o.

pélétan 1 bird lime. **2** seduction by magic. **3** sweet talk. **4** s.t. caught by using bird lime.

peletak-peletik (*J onom*) crackling sound.

peletak-peletok (*J onom*) knocking sound.

peletik (*onom*) crackling sound; → PELETAK-PELETIK.

peleting *buluh* – bamboo shuttle (of a loom).

peleton (*D*) platoon.

peletongan garbage pail.

peliaran → PEMELIHARAAN.

pelias (*cla*) magic formula that makes one invulnerable.

peliboi (*E coq*) playboy.

pelih liver.

pelihara (*Skr*) → PIARA. **memelihara(kan) 1** to take care of. *~ tiga orang anak* to take care of three children. **2** to raise (animals, etc.), grow (plants). *~ ayam itik* to raise fowls. **3** to be careful about, watch. *~ dirinya* to be careful about one's behavior, mind one's p's and q's. *~ hati/perasaan* to consider s.o.'s feelings. *~ kumis* to grow a moustache. *~ lidah/mulut* to watch one's tongue/language; to behave modestly. *~ mata* to be careful not to look at s.t. forbidden by Islam. *~ lidah* to watch one's tongue, be careful about what one says. **4** to protect. *~ dari* to shelter/screen s.t. from. *~ keamanan* to watch over security. *~ nyawa (dari bahaya)* to rescue (from danger). **5** to keep up the level of, uphold, maintain. *~ bahasa Inggrisnya* to keep up one's English. ~ *nama baik* to uphold one's reputation. ~ *pangkatnya* to live up to one's station in life.

terpelihara 1 to be taken care of, be maintained, watched over. *tidak* ~ neglected. **2** to be observed, respected (of feelings, etc.).

peliharaan 1 a kept woman, mistress, concubine; → GULA-GULA, TV II. **2** domesticated (of an animal).

pemelihara 1 provider, caretaker. **2** breeder, nurseryman. ~ *lebah* apiarist, bee-raiser. **3** protector. **4** careful, tender.

pemeliharaan 1 care, treatment. **2** maintenance, upkeep. ~ *keséhatan* health maintenance. ~ *pencegatan* preventive maintenance. ~ *perbaikan* maintenance and repair. ~ *rumah* housekeeping. **3** breeding, raising, growing, cultivation, culture. ~ *héwan* animal husbandry. ~ *pohon* arboriculture. **4** safeguarding, protection.

pelik I peculiar, remarkable, curious, striking. **2** complicated, intricate. **3** crucial.

sepelik as complicated as.

terpelik the most complicated.

kepelikan 1 curiosity, peculiarity. **2** complication.

pelik II pelikan mineral. *ilmu* ~ mineralogy.

pelik III 1 (*cla*) k.o. ear stud. **2** name of a *ceki* card.

pélikan (*D*) (*burung* -) pelican.

peliket (*J/Jv*) sticky.

pelimun (in Tanah Karo, North Sumatra) k.o. black magic that can make s.o. invulnerable to *guna-guna*, and make him disappear.

pelinggam multicolored marble.

pelintat-pelintut → PLINTAT-PLINTUT.

pelinteng (*Jv*) catapult, slingshot.

pelintir (*Jv*) **memelintir(kan) 1** to turn around, rotate. **2** to twist, distort, put a spin on s.t. *Wartawan itu* ~ *berita.* The reporter put a spin on the news.

terpelintir 1 to be turned around, be rotated. **2** to be twisted, distorted out of shape.

pelintiran 1 turned, rotated. **2** twisted, distorted out of shape.

pelintut → PLINTAT-PLINTUT.

pelipir (*Jv*) side. - *jalan* roadside.

pelipis(an) temple (of the forehead). - *kepala* side of the head near the ears.

pelipit (*Jv*) hem.

memelipit(i) to hem s.t.

pelir I penis. *batang* - penis. *buah* - testicles, testis. - *itik* screw thread.

pelir II (the first part of certain plant names) - *anjing* k.o. shrub, *Chailletia griffithii.* - *kambing* a low-country shrub, *Lepionurus sylvestris, Sarcolobus globosus.* - *musang* k.o. tree, *Anaxagorea scortechinii, Fagraea auriculata.* - *tikus* k.o. tree, *Drypetes spp.*

pelisir (*D*) pleating.

berpelisir pleated.

memelitir(i) to pleat.

pelisit (*J*) **memelisit** to brush fish or animal intestines with the hand to clean them.

pelit (*J/Jv*) **1** stingy, cheap, miserly; → KIKIR II. **2** (too) economical, not providing enough, too little. *Dia selalu berhasil berwawancara dengan sumber yang biasanya* - *berita.* He always succeeds in interviewing sources which usually provide little in the way of news.

sepelit as stingy as.

terpelit the stingiest.

pelit-pelitan to pinch pennies. *Dia* ~ *supaya dapat memborong oléh-oléh.* He pinches pennies so that he can buy as many gifts as possible.

kepelitan 1 stinginess, cheapness. **2** economy, thriftiness.

pelita I (*Pers*) **1** lamp. **2** light. - *hati* the light of one's heart.

Pelita II [Pembangunan Lima Tahun]. Five-Year Development [Plan]. - *I* the 1969–74 plan. - *II* the 1974–79 plan. - *III* the 1979–84 plan. - *IV* the 1984–89 plan. - *V* the 1989–94 plan.

Pelita III [Pelajar, Industri, dan Pariwisata] Students, Industry, and Tourism. *Kota* - Malang.

pelitur (*D*) (furniture) polish, varnish; → PERNIS.

berpelitur finished (of furniture). *tidak* ~ unfinished.

mem(p)elitur to polish, varnish.

terpelitur to be polished/varnished.

pelituran polished, varnished.

Pélnas [Pelayaran Niaga Swasta] Private Commercial Shipping Company.

Pélnawaksara [Pelengkap Nawa Akarsa] Supplement to the Nine Points, i.e., the name of the report about the *G30S* submitted by President Soekarno on January 10, 1976, to the *MPRS*; → NAWAKSARA.

Pélni [Pelayaran Nasional Indonésia] Indonesian National Shipping Company.

pélo (*Jv*) with a speech impediment, faulty pronunciation (of old/sick/foreign people); → PÉLAT, TÉLOR.

pélog (*Jv*) seven-tone scale with uneven intervals.

peloh (*Jv*) impotent; → IMPOTÉN, MATI *pucuk*, PELUH I.

pelojok and **peloksok** (*J*) corner, nook; → PELOSOK, POJOK.

pelok (*bio*) drupe.

pelompong (*Jv*) hole; → LOMPONG I.

pelonci female freshman.

pelonco I freshman. *kepala* – crew-cut (haircut).

mem(p)elonco 1 to haze, initiate. **2** to shave s.o. bald.

perpeloncoan hazing, initiation.

pelonco II 1 (*Jv*) young watermelon. **2** still very young, inexperienced, naive. **3** boll weevil (inexperienced worker in the oil field).

pelong bike fender.

pelontos → PLONTOS.

pelopak → KELOPAK.

pelopor (*D*) **1** forerunner, vanguard, advance guard. **2** pioneer, trailblazer; → CAKAL-BAKAL. **3** shock troops. **4** scout, ranger, advance (troops). **5** champion, advocate. – *perubahaan* agent of change.

mem(p)elopori 1 to lead the way, be at the forefront of. **2** to pioneer (a movement, etc.), be a pioneer in, crusade in.

kepeloporan pioneering. ~ *ABRI* with *ABRI* in the forefront.

pemelopor pioneer, the first one to do s.t. *Pak Sosroreksoko* ~ *yang memberikan kursus perkerisan* Mr. Sosroreksoko who gave the first courses in the science of the kris.

pemeloporan first steps/moves, initiatives.

pélor I (*Port*) bullet. – *kesasar* stray bullet. – *melempem* a dud.

pélor II ball bearing.

pelorot memelorotkan to pull off (clothing).

pelorus (*naut*) dummy compass.

pelosok (*Jv*) **1** corner, nook; → POJOK. **2** remote spot, outlying district/area. *di segenap* – *Nusantara* in all the corners of the Indonesian Archipelago. *dari segala* – from every nook and cranny. *sampai ke* -. – and *sampai segala* – to the four corners of the earth.

memelosokkan to push into a corner; *cp* MEMOJOKKAN. *Meréka tidak mau dipelosokkan dari kota ke désa.* They don't want to be pushed from the city into a village.

pelosot (*S*) **terpelosot** to fall, go down (of prices); → ANJLOK.

pélota jai-alai.

pélotaris jai-alai player.

peloton → PELETON.

pelotot (*J*) **memelotot** [and **melotot** (*coq*)] with eyes (bulging) wide open.

memelototi to stare at. *Mobil Jaguar yang méwah itu saya pelototi saja.* I just stared at the luxurious Jaguar.

memelototkan to open wide. ~ *mata* to stare. *Marah boléh saja, tapi jangan* ~ *mata.* It's OK to get angry, but don't stare at me.

pelpén (*D Jv*) fountain pen.

pélpén (*D*) plummet (used by carpenters to get a straight line).

pélplés (*D*) canteen, water container.

pélpolisi (*D col*) rural constabulary trained by the Dutch to carry out military functions in plantation areas.

péls (*D*) fur coat.

pélt (*E*) pelt.

Péltu → PEMBANTU *Létnan Satu.*

Péltu Pol → PEMBANTU *Létnan Satu Polisi.*

peluang 1 calm (at sea, of the wind), lull (after a storm). *musim* – monsoon of calm. **2** free time, leisure. **3** exposed spot on opponent's body (in *silat*). **4** chance, opportunity. *membuka* – to give/afford s.o. an opportunity. *memetik – bagus* to seize the opportunity. *– emas* a golden opportunity. *– kerja dan berusaha* employment and business opportunities.

berpeluang to have/get the chance/opportunity to. *~ besar* to have a good opportunity.

mempualangi (*infr*) to give s.o. an opportunity.

Pelud → PELABUHAN *Udara*.

peluh I → PELOH.

peluh II sweat, perspiration. *biring* – German measles. *– berpancaran* sweat poured off (him). *mandi* – bathed in sweat. *– dingin* cold sweat, the sweat of fear.

berpeluh 1 to sweat, perspire; sweating, perspiring. **2** to work hard, sweat and toil.

berpeluh-peluh to work hard, sweat and toil.

peluit (*D*) whistle, siren. *– bahaya* alarm signal, siren. *– lokomotif* locomotive whistle.

peluk 1 hug, embrace. *bantal* – a bolster, Dutch wife type of pillow; → GULING. *tinggal – tangan saja* not willing to lift a finger. **2** arms' breadth, a measurement of length *app* equal to one fathom; → DEPA. *– cium* a) tender embrace. b) a hug and a kiss (an affectionate salutation at the end of a letter). *berpeluk-ciuman* to hug and kiss e.o. *– dengkul* to do nothing, be idle.

berpeluk to hug, embrace. *~ dada* with one's arms around one's knees. *~ tangan* a) with folded arms. b) to do nothing, be idle. *~ lutut/tubuh* to do nothing, be idle, laze about.

berpeluk-peluk and **berpeluk(-peluk)an** to hug/embrace e.o. *Meréka berpelukan dan berciuman.* They embraced and kissed e.o.

memeluk 1 to hug, embrace, put one's arms tightly around. *~ dada/lutut* to do nothing, be idle. *dipeluk sengsara* in a state of misery. **2** to adhere to, follow. *~ agama* to be a follower of (a religion).

memeluki to hold in one's embrace. *Anak itu ~ bonékanya.* The child is holding the doll in her embrace.

memelukkan and **memperpelukkan** to put ... around in an embrace. *~ kedua belah tangannya* to fold one's arms.

terpeluk accidentally embraced/hugged.

pelukan hug, embrace. *di dalam ~ kegaiban malam itu* in the embrace of that mysterious night.

pemeluk follower, adherent (of a religion). *~ agama Islam* adherent of Islam. *sepeluk(an)* as much as the arms can embrace, the distance around which one can hold one's arms.

peluluk *pohon* – k.o. sugar palm, *Arenga pinnata*.

pelumpung and **pelungpung** (*Jv*) **1** a tall reed growing in swampy areas. **2** whitish yellow.

pelupuh flattened bamboo (used for a floor covering, etc.).

memelupuh to flatten bamboo.

memelupuhi (*pl obj*) to flatten bamboo.

pelupuk thin cover/sheath; → KELOPAK. *– mata* eyelid. *di bawah – mata* in one's presence, right in front of one. *tidak berani menegakkan – mata* afraid to look up.

peluran mortar.

peluru (*Port*) **1** (rifle) bullet, ball, cartridge; → PÉLOR I. *dari – ke pemungutan suara* from the bullet to the ballot. **2** projectile, missile. **3** shot-put (in sports). *tolak* – shot-put (in sports). *– cahaya* tracer bullet. *– dacha* (*mil*) irritant gas grenade. *– garis pertama* first-line ammunition. *– gotri* pellets, shot. *– jelajah* cruise missile. *– karét* rubber bullet. *– kendali* [rudal] guided missile. *– kendali antarbenua* intercontinental ballistic missile. *– kendali antibalistik* antiballistic missile. *– kendali berbedorkan/berkepala nuklir* nuclear warhead missile. *– kendali bumi-ke-udara* ground-to-air missile. *– kendali dari udara ke darat* air-to-ground missile. *– kendali jarak menengah/sedang* medium-range missile. *– kendali jelajah* cruise missile. *– kendali penyergap* intercept missile. *– kendali udara-ke-udara* air-to-air missile. *– kosong* blank ammunition. *– nyasar* stray bullet. *– payar* cruise missile. *– penembus baja* armor-piercing bullet. *– pengarah* tracer bullet/shell. *– suar* (signal) flare. *– tajam* live ammunition.

peluruh emetic. *– dahak* phlegm emetic, expectorant.

pelus → SIDAT.

pélvis → PANGGUL.

pém (in acronyms) → PEMERINTAH.

pemajikan → MAJIKAN.

pemali 1 prohibition, act or thing that is forbidden (*usu* forever), taboo; → PANTANG(AN). *adalah – melangkahi bakul nasi* it's taboo to step over a rice basket. **2** forbidden, prohibited, sacred.

pemangku (*Bal*) temple priest.

pemarip (*cla*) person who sings lullabies to royal infants to put them to sleep.

pemarit grapnel, such as an anchor, used for recovering sunken objects.

pematah → PEPATAH.

pematang 1 dike (in a rice paddy), bund; → GALENGAN, GILI-GILI. **2** long, sharp ridge (in hills) along which one can walk. **3** high and dry path through or along marshland or shoreline. *– empang* edge of a fishpond. *– jalan/lebuh* pavement. *– sawah* dike (in a rice paddy), bund.

pematusan (*Jv*) drainage.

pembangunanisme (*infr*) developmentalism.

pembayan (*M*) brother/sister-in-law; → BIRAS I.

berpembayan to be in a brother/sister-in-law relationship to e.o.

pembekal (in Kalimantan) village head; → PERBEKEL.

Pembesrév → PEMIMPIN *Besar Révolusi*.

pembokat (*sl*) domestic help, servant.

pembringsongan raid, roundup, razzia, mopping-up operation (of prostitutes, etc. by the police).

Pémda → PEMERINTAH *Daérah*. **mem-Pémdakan** to have s.t. arranged by a Provincial Government.

peméo → PAMÉO.

pemerajan (*Bal*) family place of worship in every household.

pemidang stretching frame; → PEMBIDANGAN.

pemihutang → PEMIUTANG.

pemilu → PEMILIHAN *umum*. *– kilat* snap election. *– raya* full general election. *– sela* (*Mal Sg*) by-election.

pémkab [pemerintah kabupatén] regency government.

pémkot [pemerintah kota] municipal government.

pémpék fish cake with tamarind sauce; → EMPÉK-EMPÉK II.

pémprop and **pémprov** [pemerintah propinsi] provincial government.

pemréd → PEMIMPIN *rédaksi*.

pemudi young woman, girl; → MUDI II.

pemuras (*cla*) blunderbuss, muzzleloader.

pen (in acronyms) → PENERANGAN.

pén I (*D*) **1** peg, dowel (for joining wood/bamboo, etc.). **2** (grenade) pin; → PÉNA *penyelamat*.

pén II (*D*) pen. *– atom* ballpoint pen (used shortly after WWII); → BOLPÉN, BOLPOIN.

pén III (in acronyms) → PENERANGAN.

péna (*Port*) **1** (writing) pen. *buah* – writing. *makan* – to live from one's pen/writing. *mata* – pen point, nib. *perang* – polemic. *sahabat* – pen pal. *tangkai* – penholder. **2** pin. *– isi* (*infr*) fountain pen; → PULPÉN. *– kodok* special k.o. pen with blunt end used for writing Arabic. *– pemukul* firing pin. *– penyelamat* safety pin (of hand grenade).

penad I relevant.

Penad II [Penerangan Angkatan Darat] Army Information Office.

penaga and *– laut* k.o. tree with medicinal and other uses, *Callophyllum inophyllum*. *– lilin/putih* ironwood tree, *Mesua ferrea*, which produces a k.o. oil used for skin disease.

pénak → PINAK.

penaka 1 supposing. **2** like, resembling. **3** as though, (as) if, as it were.

penakawan → PUNAKAWAN.

Penal [Penerangan Angkatan Laut] Naval Information Office.

pénalti (*E*) penalty (in sports).

penampan presentation tray; → TETAMPAN.

penanggah buffet, salad bar.

penanggahan palace kitchen; kitchen house. *jung* – a junk fitted up as a kitchen for a fleet.

penanggalan vampire with severed head and hanging entrails.

penanjung → SEMENANJUNG. *– Tanah Melayu* The Malay Peninsula.

penaram k.o. meat or fish patties.

penasaran (*J*) **1** curious, inquisitive; eager for knowledge, inquiring.

2 disturbed, troubled, worried, ill-at-ease. 3 indignant, annoyed, angered, irritated, embittered.

kepenasaran(an) 1 curiousity. 2 anger, rage, fury, frenzy.

penat tired, fatigued, exhausted. *melepaskan/membuang* – to take a break, relax for a while. – *jerih/lelah* very tired/exhausted.

penat-penatnya *tak* ~ indefatigable, unwearying.

sepenat as exhausted as.

berpenat-penat to toil away (at s.t.).

memenatkan 1 to tire, weary, fatigue. 2 tiring, wearying, exhausting, fatiguing.

memenat-menatkan ~ *tubuh* to work hard with no result.

kepenatan 1 tired, weary, exhausted, fatigued. 2 tiredness, weariness, exhaustion, fatigue.

penatarama drum major.

penatu (*Jv*) 1 laundryman; → BINATU. 2 the laundry/wash. – *kimia* dry cleaner's.

memenatukan to have s.t. laundered/washed.

penatuan laundry (where the wash is done).

penatua I elder. – *geréja* church elder.

penatua II (*IBT*) village priest.

Penau [Penerangan Angkatan Udara] Air Force Information Office.

penca → PENDERITA *cacat.*

pencak martial art. – *kembang Minang* a Minangkabau art of self-defense. – *silat* the art of self-defense.

berpencak and **memencak** to perform/practice the art of self-defense. *memencak lidah* to debate, discuss.

memencak-mencak [and **mencak-mencak** (*coq*)] 1 to make *pencak* movements. 2 to jump on s.o., flare up at s.o.; to be very angry/furious.

pencaka → PANCAKA.

pencalang a Bugis trading ship, k.o. large cargo ship.

pencar scatter, disperse; → SEBAR, SÉRAK.

berpencar to scatter, disperse. *Meréka* ~ *setelah membagi hasil rampokan.* They scattered after sharing the loot.

berpencar-pencar and **berpencaran** 1 to be dispersed/scattered; disseminated. 2 (to go/run, etc.) all over (the place) (not in groups), run away helter-skelter. *Mendengar bunyi témbakan itu, meréka lari* ~. Hearing the shots, they ran away helter-skelter.

memencar to disperse, scatter. *Pasukan* ~. The troops scattered.

memencarkan to disperse, scatter; to disseminate, send out. *Tenaga-tenaga dipencarkan ke daérah dalam kampanye.* Personnel were sent out to the provinces during the campaign. ~ *diri* to scatter, disperse.

terpencar(-pencar) scattered, dispersed; disseminated, be/sent out all over. *Keluarga saya tinggal* ~. My family lives scattered all over.

pencaran dispersion.

pemencaran dispersion, scattering; dissemination.

perpencaran dispersion, distribution.

péncéng (*Jv*) lopsided, skewed.

méncéng to be lopsided, skewed.

pencét (*Jv*) squeezed, pressed, pushed.

memencét [and **mencét** (*coq*)] 1 to squeeze. 2 to push (a button, etc.), step on/apply (the brakes); → MENGINJAK. ~ *knop* to push the button. *Terpaksa rém dipencét dan menunggu giliran lampu hijau selanjutnya.* We were forced to step on the brakes and wait until the next green light.

memencét-mencét to keep on pushing, push repeatedly. ~ *tombol komputer* to keep on pushing the computer buttons.

memencéti [and **mencétin** (*J coq*)] (*pl obj*) to squeeze, push, step on.

memencétkan to push with s.t.

terpencét [and **kepencét** (*coq*)] squeezed, pressed, pushed.

pencétan 1 knob. 2 pressure, squeezing.

pencil 1 secluded, isolated. 2 remote.

memencil 1 separated, isolated, secluded. 2 distant, remote, outlying, out-of-the-way. *sebuah rumah yang* ~ *ditengah-tengah hutan* a house isolated in the middle of the woods.

memencilkan 1 to isolate, segregate, seclude. *hidup dengan* ~ *diri dari pergaulan* to live isolated from society. 2 to keep away from (out of dislike, etc.). *Ia dipencilkan oléh keluarganya.* His family kept away from him.

terpencil isolated, remote, secluded, set apart, out-of-the-way. *Ia*

lahir di sebuah désa yang ~. He was born in an isolated village.

keterpencilan isolation, seclusion. ~ *désa ini menimbulkan keterbelakangan masyarakat.* The isolation of this village has produced a social backwardness.

kepencilan isolation, seclusion.

pemencilan isolation, isolating, secluding, withdrawing.

pencit (*Jv*) a young mango.

pencok (*Jv*) burnt and pounded *kacang hijau* with *sambal* as a side dish to rice.

péncong awry, askew, off center/target. – *méncong* higgledy-piggledy, in disorder.

meméncongkan to make s.t. crooked/slanting, cause s.t. to be off center/target.

kepéncongan skewness.

pencu the boss of a gong.

pencuk boiled vegetable salad.

péncut (*Jv*) → PINCUT. **kepéncut** (*ke*)*pada* fallen in love (with), captivated/attracted (by); → KEPINCUT.

penda (*mostly Mal*) **memenda** to correct, improve, remedy, alter (for the better).

pendaan correction, improvement, remedy, alteration.

pendaga (*Skr*) shell-encrusted ornamental box (for clothes, etc.).

pendahan (*ob*) javelin.

pendak I (*S*) a ring around the lower end of a kris hilt.

pendak II (*Jv*) 1 every, each. – *hari Rabu* every Wednesday. 2 (a week/month/year) from, hence. – *manak* after one year of marriage they have a child.

pendam **memendam** to bury, hide s.t. in the ground, conceal; to repress. *Dia tidak tahan lagi* ~ *rasa ingin tahu.* He can no longer stand to suppress his curiosity. ~ *rindu* to conceal one's desires/yearnings.

memendamkan 1 to bury, hide, disguise, conceal. ~ *diri* to hide (o.s.), conceal o.s., lock o.s. up. 2 to cherish (plans/feelings), keep (one's feelings, etc.) to o.s., (know how to) conceal (plans, etc.); to swallow (one's anger), keep one's feelings inside one; to keep (a secret). ~ *cinta pada Rima* to conceal his love for Rima. ~ *dendam kesumat dalam hatinya* to harbor a grudge. *Enam pelaut asing terpaksa* ~ *rindu anak istri.* The six foreign sailors had to suppress their homesickness for their wives and children. *Ia* ~ *perasaan dalam batinnya ketika diberitahu bahwa saraséhan soal penyu yang sedianya dilaksanakan hari itu ditunda tanpa kepastian waktu.* He kept his feelings to himself when he was told that the conference on turtles which was to be held that day had been postponed indefinitely.

terpendam [and **kependam** (*coq*)] 1 kept hidden/buried. 2 cherished (in one's heart). 3 disguised, kept to o.s., locked up, concealed, kept secret. ~ *dalam hati* s.t. bottled up inside one.

pendaman s.t. hidden (away), s.t. kept to o.s., etc.

pemendam s.o. who keeps things inside himself/herself.

pemendaman 1 burial, hiding away. 2 cherishing, harboring, keeping s.t. to o.s. 3 concealment.

pendamén → FONDAMÉN.

pendap pickled.

memendap to pickle (fish).

pendapa I (*Jv*) large open pavilion-like veranda at the front of a big house where guests are entertained and *wayang* performances to celebrate family events are held.

pendapa II (*ob*) a young shoot.

pendar 1 fluorescence, luminescence. 2 (*petro*) cast, bloom.

berpendar(-pendar) 1 fluorescent, phosphorescent, luminous (of sunlight on water). 2 to see stars (after being hit on the head, etc.).

pendaran and **kependaran** fluorescence, luminescence.

péndar (*M*) **berpéndar** to whirl (around), rotate, go round and round.

berpéndaran (*pl subj*) to whirl around.

meméndar-méndarkan to turn s.t. around, rotate. ~ *perkataan* to twist words for one's own purposes.

pendaringan (*J*) a big-bellied earthenware bowl used for rice storage. – *kosong* broke, penniless; → SEPÉSÉR *buta pun tak punya* .

Pendawa → PANDAWA.

pendéga I a member of the *Pramuka* Boy Scout Movement aged 21 to 25.

pendéga II fisherman who works for a *juragan.*

péndék I short, brief; → PANDAK. *celana* – shorts. *cerita* – [cerpén] short story. *waktu yang* – a short time. – *akal* narrow-minded. – *ingatan* narrow-minded. – *kaji/kata/madah* in short, in a word, to put it briefly. – *kira-kiranya* narrow-minded. – *napas* short of breath, short-winded. – *permintaan* will die soon. – *pikiran* narrow-minded. – *pinta* short-lived. – *tali* poor. – *umur* to have a short life, die young.

péndéknya in short, in a word, in brief.

sependék as short/brief as.

meméndék to become short, shorten.

meméndékkan and **memperpéndék 1** to shorten s.t., curtail, cut short. **2** to abbreviate (a word, etc.).

terpéndék the shortest. *Gué cowok ~ di dunia?* Am I the shortest guy in the world?

kependékan 1 shortness, briefness, brevity. **2** abbreviation, shortening, abridgement. **3** (*coq*) too short.

peméndékan shortening, curtailing, abbreviating.

perpéndékan shortening, curtailment, reduction. *~ waktu* reduction in the amount of time.

péndék II *orang* – (in the forests at the foot of Mt. Kerinci, Jambi) refers to a hard-to-catch race of pygmies with round faces, long beards, 80–100 centimeters high, with hairy bodies; → BIGAN.

pendékar 1 champion, advocate. **2** fighter. **3** fencing instructor. **4** cock of the walk. **5** s.o. who engages in *silat*. – *kata/lidah* a) eloquent, silver-tongued. b) a good debater. – *péna* skillful writer.

kependékaran championship, advocacy.

péndel (*D*) shuttle.

pendem (*Jv*) → PENDAM. *topo* – to live as an ascetic by burying o.s. underground like a corpse.

penderah → PENDARAH.

pendét (*Bal*) ritual dance of offering and welcoming.

pendéta (*Skr*) **1** scholar. **2** clergyman, minister, (Lutheran) pastor. *kaum* – the clergy. – *armada/angkatan laut* navy chaplain. – *tentara* army chaplain. – *Yahudi* rabbi.

kependétaan 1 clergy. **2.** clerical, minister (*mod*). *pendidikan ~* clerical education.

pending lady's belt.

pénding (*E*) pending.

mem(p)énding(kan) to postpone (a decision), table.

pendita → PENDÉTA.

pendok I → PENDAK I.

pendok II [penerimaan dokumén] acceptance of documents.

pendongkok metal rings at the base of a kris hilt.

pendopo → PENDAPA I.

penduk metal casing for the straight part of a kris sheath.

pendul spur (small round bone protrusion).

penduta (*ob*) envoy, ambassador; → DUTA.

penembahan (*Jv*) ruler to whom a *sembah* is made.

péneng (*D*) tag. – *anjing* dog tag.

pénés pinnacle, k.o. light sailing ship.

pénétrasi (*D*) penetration.

mem(p)énétrasi to penetrate.

penéwu → PANÉWU.

pénfriend (*E*) /-frén/ pen pal; → SAHABAT *péna*.

pengak (*J/Jv*) penetrating odor of urine.

pengalasan (*ob*) k.o. courtier.

pengambek (*Jv*) moneylender (in the fisherman trade).

pengampuh → PENGAPUH.

penganak k.o. musical instrument.

penganan between-meal snack.

pengang (*J*) numbed (due to noise).

pengangsu (*Jv*) → PENGÉCÉR.

pengantén and **pengantin I 1** bride. **2** bridegroom. *adat-adat* – wedding customs. *kué* – wedding cake. *kursi* – bridal chair (occupied by the bride and groom during the wedding). *malam* – wedding night. *senapan* – double-barreled rifle; → SENAPAN *laras kembar*. – *baru* to go newlywed(s). **berpengantén baru** to be/go (on one's) honeymoon. – *laki-laki* bridegroom. – *perempuan* bride. – *sarimbit* (*Jv*) bridal couple. – *sunat* child who is going to be circumcised.

berpengantén 1 to become a bride(groom). **2** to celebrate one's wedding.

pengantin II *kembang* – shrub with sweet-smelling flowers, night/coral jasmine, *Nyctanthes arbortristis*.

pengap 1 close, stuffy, airless, musty. **2** tight in the chest, stifled.

sepengap as stuffy/airless as.

memengap 1 to close (up) tightly. **2** to choke/suffocate s.o. **3** to preserve (fish) by putting it in an airtight container.

memengapkan 1 to oppress, stifle, choke, suffocate. **2** oppressive, stifling, choking, suffocating.

kepengapan 1 tightness in the chest; lack of fresh air, stuffiness. **2** to suffocate, suffer from stuffiness.

pengapa → MENGAPA.

pengapuh *layar* – (*naut*) topsail.

pengar 1 to have a hangover. **2** to feel that one's brain isn't working right, dull. **3** to have an aftertaste (of food or drink).

pengaron (*Jv*) earthenware pot for cooking rice, etc.

pengaruh 1 influence, power (over). *ruang lingkup* – sphere of influence. **2** distinction, respectability. *mencari – di kalangan orang dusun* to seek distinction in rural circles. **3** effect, impact. – *lingkungan* environmental impact. – *samping(an)* side effect. **4** (*S*) ominous, propitious.

berpengaruh 1 to have influence (over), have power (over). **2** influential. *komisi trilateral* – influential trilateral commission.

memengaruhi to influence, affect, have an effect on.

pengaruh-mempengaruhi (*saling*) *~* to interact with e.o., affect e.o., have influence over e.o.; → BERINTERAKSI.

terpengaruh influenced, under the influence of. *mudah ~* susceptible, gullible. **keterpengaruhan** being influenced.

pengasi (in the interior of Kendari in Sulawesi) a traditional alcoholic drink made from husked rice.

pengat a k.o. flan containing yam, etc. cooked in coconut milk and sugar.

memengat to prepare *pengat*.

pengatu (*ob*) *bedil* – k.o. antique rifle.

pengawinan halberdiers.

pengelingsir (*Bal*) leader of a *pura III*.

péngén (*J*) to want, desire, wish, long for; → (KE)PINGIN. "*Saya belum tahu mau ngapain. –nya sih kerja. Tapi kerja apa?*" *ujar Wiwik.* "I don't know what I'm going to do. I'd like to get a job. But, what k.o. job?" said Wiwik.

pengeng 1 a splitting headache. **2** → PENGANG.

pengepul collective trader/merchant, i.e., s.o. who collects certain commodities in order to sell them at a profit.

pengéran → PANGÉRAN.

pengerih k.o. fish trap; → LUKAH.

pengetua 1 elder. **2** (*infr*) dean (of diplomatic corps); → KETUA.

pengga deep (of a bowl, basin); → JELUK I.

penggaga a creeper whose leaves are eaten as a vegetable, Indian pennywort, *Hydrocotyle asiatica*; → PEGAGA(N).

penggah glorious; → MEGAH.

penggak (*Jv*) **memenggak** to deter, restrain, keep back.

penggal 1 piece, lump, chunk (of wood/meat). **2** fragment, portion, part (of s.t. larger). – *waktu* part-time; opp PURNAWAKTU. *mahasiswa – waktu* part-time student. *penerjemah – waktu* part-time translator. *tenaga (secara)* – part-time help.

sepenggal a part (of s.t. larger), half. *~ hari* half a day.

berpenggal-penggal in pieces/sections/chunks/portions/parts.

memenggal 1 to cut off/to pieces/into sections; to lower (a highrise building). **2** *~ kepala* to behead, decapitate. **3** to break up (a sentence), syllabify (a word), divide (up) into syllables. *~ lidah* to interrupt.

terpenggal cut off, decapitated, beheaded.

penggalan 1 piece, bit, section, portion, part (of s.t. larger); (*elec*) partial. **2** sectioning (of trees). **berpenggalan** decapitated.

pemenggal *tanda – (gram)* syllable break.

pemenggalan 1 cutting, slashing. **2** decapitation, beheading. **3** syllabification, syllabifying. *~ kata (gram)* syllabification of a word. **4** lowering (a highrise). *Sudah disepakati prosés ~ Istana Plaza.* The process of lowering the Istana Plaza has been approved.

penggang → PEGANG.

penggar → PENGAR.

penggawa → PUNGGAWA.

penggérék 1 a natural enemy of a crop. – *pucuk tebu* sugarcane sprout borer, *Scirpophaga nivella*. **2** (*sl*) an older woman who wants to have sex with a younger man.

Penggolékmah [Pengusaha golongan ékonomi lemah] Businessmen from the economically weak group.

penggolér (*Jv*) shrimp catcher during the harvest.

penggulu (*Jv*) second in age (of a child in a family).

penggunting various species of shearwaters. – *laut* wedge-tailed shearwater, *Puffinus paificus*. – *putih* streaked shearwater, – *Calonectris leucomelas*.

penghulu 1 headman; → HULU. **2** priest (in general). **3** head of mosque personnel. **4** government official appointed by the *bupati* to perform such duties as the supervision of marriages, divorces, and inheritance. **5** (*M*) *adat* head. – *hakim* authority, for example the *penghulu*, appointed by the court, who acts as a *wali* (in marriages, etc.) in the absence of an appropriate male relative. – *hutan* forester. – *kampung* village headman. – *kawin* official who unites bride and groom in marriage. – *landrat* (*col*) member of the tribunal. – *muda* deputy head of mosque.

kepenghuluan *penghulu*ship.

péngin to want, desire, wish, long for; → PÉNGÉN, (KE)PINGIN. *Sejak semalam saya penasaran – lihat tampang tertuduh*. Since last night I've been anxious to see the face of the accused.

pengiran (*BD*) → PANGÉRAN.

pengkal → (TER)PINGKAL-PINGKAL.

pengkal(an) → PANGKAL(AN).

péngkar crooked (of legs). – *ke dalam* bowlegged. – *ke luar* knock-kneed.

pengki (*C J*) dustpan-shaped basket.

pengkis memengkis to challenge, defy; → PEKIS.

péngkol (*J/Jv*) crooked, curved.

  meméngkol to turn aside.

  péngkolan curve, bend (in the road).

péngkor (*J*) maimed, mutilated; crippled, disabled; fractured (of one's leg/foot); lame.

pengluru → PELURU.

péngok (*J*) dented.

péngos (*Jv*) **1** slanting, sloping. **2** obtuse (angle).

pengpengan (*Jv*) notable, noteworthy, celebrated, renowned, outstanding. *dokter-dokter* – outstanding physicians. *orang* – *dalam dunia permalingan* a notorious person in the world of thieves.

penguam → PEGUAM.

penguin (*D*) /pingwin/ penguin.

pengulun (*ob*) His Highness.

péni I code word among Jakarta thieves for a member of the *Tékab*.

péni II (*Jv*) fine, rare, splendid.

  péni-péni fine things; valuables.

peniaram a pastry made from rice flour and sugar.

pening 1 dizzy. **2** to lose one's head. – *kelam* vertigo with a migraine headache. – *kepala* dizzy, giddy.

  pening-pening ~ *lalat/pikat* to feel a bit dizzy, have a slight headache.

  memening to be dizzy/giddy, have a dizzy fit.

  memeningkan ~ *kepala* a) to make dizzy/giddy. b) dizzying. c) difficult.

  kepeningan (to be subject to fits of) dizziness.

péning (*D*) bicycle tax plate; dog-license tag.

peningset → PANINGSET.

pénis (*D/E*) penis.

penisi two-masted Buginese sailboat; *cp* LAMBO.

pénisilin (*D/E*) penicillin.

péniténsi (*D*) penitence.

peniti (*Port*) pin. – *aman/cantél* safety pin. – *dasi* tie clip. – *kebaya* brooch to pin a *kebaya* together.

penitian *pohon* – a shade tree.

penjajab and **penjajap** (*ob*) a Buginese warship.

penjalin (*Jv*) rattan. *kursi* – a rattan chair. *Kemudian seorang lelaki muda itu dipersilakan duduk di kursi* – *yang di sana sini sudah jebol*. Then the young man was invited to sit down in a rattan chair which was worn out in spots.

penjara (*Skr*) jail, prison, detention center; → BUI I, KURUNGAN, LEMBAGA *pemasyarakatan*, TERUNGKU, TUTUPAN. *hukuman* – imprisonment.

sepenjara in the same prison. *napi* ~ fellow inmates.

memenjara(kan) to imprison, jail, put in jail/prison. ~ *hawa nafsu* to restrain one's passions.

terpenjara imprisoned, jailed, locked up. **keterpenjaraan** captivity, imprisonment. *membébaskan orang dari* ~ to free s.o. from captivity.

kepenjaraan prison affairs, prison (*mod*).

pemenjaraan incarceration, imprisonment. *kesalahan* ~ wrongful imprisonment.

pénjol (*J/Jv*) bump, swelling.

pénjor (*Bal*) eight-meter-high bamboo poles festooned with bamboo decorations which are put over roadways or pathways during *Galungan* or other important religious occasions.

penjunan potter.

penjurit 1 soldier; warrior. **2** courageous, brave; → PRAJURIT.

penjuru 1 corner. *empat* – four corners. **2** angle. – *angin* points of the compass.

  berpenjuru angular, having angles/points. *bintang* ~ *lima* five-pointed star.

pénmés (*D*) penknife.

Pénmot [Penerangan dan Motivasi] Information and Motivation.

pénologi (*D/E*) penology.

penomah *raja* – gift given to one's parents-in-law.

penoména → FÉNOMÉNA. – *kebudayaan* cultural phenomena.

Pénprés [Penetapan Présidén] Presidential Decree.

pénsét → PINSÉT.

pénsi (*M*) k.o. small shell.

pénsil 1 (*E*) pencil. – *alis* eyebrow pencil. – *isi* mechanical pencil. – *kopi* penciled in. – *tinta* indelible pen. **2** (*D*) artist's brush.

pénsion (*D*) boardinghouse.

pénsiun (*D*) **1** pension, retirement. *Ketika* – *turun, 25 tahun silam, tubuhnya masih kekar*. When he retired, 25 years ago, he was still sturdy. *kelebihan* – excess pension. *sebelum menjalankan masa* – before reaching retirement age. **2** to retire. *Ayah akan* – . Father is going to retire. *makan* – to be retired/pensioned off. *penerima* – retiree. – (*sebagai jaminan*) *hari tua* old-age pension. – *dini* early retirement. – *janda* widow's pension. – *muda* early retirement. *mengajukan/minta* – *muda* to ask for early retirement.

  berpénsiun to retire; retired.

  meménsiunkan 1 to pension off, retire s.o. *Yang sudah waktunya pénsiun dipénsiunkan*. Those who have reached retirement age are made to retire. *Singapura* ~ *présidén*. Singapore has pensioned off its president. **2** to discontinue the use of, discard. *Malaysia* ~ *pesawat tempur Skyhawk A-4-nya karena sering jatuh*. Malaysia retired its Skyhawk A-4 fighters because they crashed frequently.

  pénsiunan 1 to retire, be retired. *Uang itu untuk membeli rumah bésok kalau sudah* ~. The money is for buying a house when he retires. ~ *pegawai negeri* retired civil servant. **2** retirement (*mod*). *gaji* ~ annuity, pension. *Meréka antré mengambil gaji* ~. They stood in line to pick up their pension. **3** retiree, retired person. ~ *dokter/guru* a retired physician/teacher. ~ *negeri* government retiree.

  peménsiunan pensioning off, retiring, retirement.

pénstrép (*D coq*) penicillin-streptomycin.

péntab [pendahuluan tahun ajaran baru] beginning of the new academic year.

Péntagon (*E*) the Pentagon; → DÉPARTEMÉN *Pertahanan AS*.

pental (*J/Jv*) **memental** to fall down (into s.t.).

  mementalkan to bounce s.t.

  terpental [and **kepental** (*coq*)] thrown/fallen into a sprawling position, flung.

péntan definite, certain, established; → NYATA.

pentang I → BENTANG. **mementang** to open, deploy, unfold, spread (a net), bend (a bow). ~ *busur* to bend a bow. ~ *jari* to spread one's fingers.

  mementangkan to release, shoot. ~ *panah* to shoot an arrow.

  terpentang opened, deployed, spread (out).

pentang II (*Jv*) **mentang** to draw a bow(string). *Tangannya kaya gendéwa pinentang*. His arms are like drawn bows, i.e., the classical ideal shape.

pentar weak, low, soft (of the voice).

pentas 1 stage, raised platform/floor (in a bedroom/kitchen). – *busana* fashion show. – *dapur* raised platform in the kitchen. **2** appearance on stage, performance.

berpentas and **mementas** [and **mentas** (*coq*)] to perform, appear on stage; to be performed/put on *Srimulat kini ~ di Senayan.* Srimulat is being performed at Senayan.

mementaskan to stage, perform, put on (a performance/play/show, etc.). *~ karya para komponis Indonésia di negeri tercinta ini* to perform the works of Indonesian composers in our beloved country.

pementas performer; stage manager, producer.

pementasan 1 stage show, performance, presentation. *~ hidup* live show. **2** performing, putting on.

péntatonik (*E*) and **péntatonis** (*D*) pentatonic (scale).

penténtang-penténténg (*J*) → PETAN(G)TANG-PETÉN(G)TÉNG.

pentét (*Jv*) species of predatory bird, *L. Laniidae.*

pentil I 1 (– *susu*) nipple. **2** valve. – *limpah* overflow valve. **3** (*Jv*) bud.

pentil II mementil to touch lightly, tap; → SENTIL I.

mementil-mentil to strum (a guitar).

pentilan touch, tap.

péntil (*D*) valve. – *ban sepéda* bicycle-tire valve.

péntilasi → VÉNTILASI.

penting I 1 important, vital, significant, of interest, momentous. *tidak – * unimportant, insignificant. *rasa – berlebih* over-importance. *merasa –* (*infr*) to need, be in need of, want, require; → KEPENTINGAN 2. **2** (*ob*) critical; → GENTING I. *musim yang –* critical period.

sepenting as important as.

mementingkan [and **mentingin** (*J coq*)] **1** to emphasize, put more importance on, consider/regard as important, give priority to. *~ diri* to pursue one's own interests. *– diri sendiri* selfish. **2** to take into account/consideration, consider, reckon with.

terpenting most/particularly important.

kepentingan 1 importance, meaning, significance, value, weight. **2** interest, benefit. **3** purpose(s), sake. *demi ~* in favor of. *untuk ~* a) in the interest of, for the benefit of. b) on behalf of, for the sake of, for … purposes. *untuk ~ negara* for the well-being of the nation, in the public interest. *untuk sesuatu ~* for a well-defined/specific purpose. *mempunyai ~ atas* to be interested in, be concerned about, have an interest in. *mempunyai ~ yang pantas* to have a suitable purpose in mind. *~ kebendaan* material interest. *~ hukum* legal interest. *~ langsung* direct interest. *~ manusiawi* human interest. *~ melekat* vested interest. *~ nasional* national interest. *~ negara* a) national interest. b) government holding (in a business). *~ pajak* tax purposes. *~ pribadi* individual/personal interest, personal affairs. *~ publik* public interest. *~ sendiri* self-interest. *~ sesaat* a short-term interest. *~ sesungguhnya* essential interest. *~ sosial* social purpose/aim/goal. *~ umum* public interest. *demi ~ umum* in the public interest. *~ yang tertanam* vested interest. **4** (*infr*) necessity, need. **berkepentingan** to have an interest, be concerned. *~ terhadap* to have an interest in. *~ untuk* to be interested in ...-ing. *yang ~* a) interested party/person, party/person concerned; those concerned/interested. *kepada yang ~* to whom it may concern. *Yang tidak ~ dilarang/tidak boléh masuk.* Employees only (on signboards). b) complainant. *pihak yang ~* those who have a stake in the matter, the parties concerned.

pementing s.t. which gives special importance, emphatic.

pementingan *~ diri sendiri* self-interest.

penting II berpentingan to shoot away in all directions; → PELANTING.

penting III (*onom*) metallic sound, clink(ing).

mementing to (cause to) make clinking sound, clink (money), pluck (guitar strings).

pentok (*J*) → BENTOK.

pentol I (*J/Jv*) knob, handle; flap at the back of a *blangkon* worn by Javanese nobility; head (of a pin). *jarum –* pin.

pentol II pentolan (*coq*) a dab.

pentol III mementoli to head, lead.

pentolan prominent leader, distinguished/important people.

pentol IV pentolan hothead.

pentolat-pentalit → PLINTAT-PLINTUT.

pentopan gambling house.

pentul → PENTOL I.

pentung (*Jv*) night stick, truncheon, cudgel, billy-club.

berpentung with a club.

mementung to club, cudgel.

mementungi (*pl obj*) to club again and again.

mementungkan to club/cudgel with.

pentungan cudgel, billy-club.

penuh 1 full, full of, fully packed, filled completely, packed, crowded; well-lined (of one's wallet); full-time. *Hotél-hotél sudah – semuanya.* All the hotels are full/fully booked. *berdiri – di belakang* to stand fully behind (s.o.). *berisi – dengan* loaded with. *dibayar –* fully paid up, paid up in full. *surat kuasa –* full powers. *Rakyat masih – di pekarangan.* A big crowd was still on the premises. *seorang apotéker yang bekerja –* a full-time pharmacist; → PURNAWAKTU. *– dengan/oléh/berisi* full of, filled with, with many. *Bis itu – dengan penumpang.* The bus was full of passengers. *Lembaga ini mempunyai kampus yang sepi dan dikelilingi oléh bukit yang – oléh pohon cemara.* This institute has a peaceful campus and is surrounded by hills with many eucalyptus trees. **2** numerous, much, many, a lot of, in large amounts/quantities, in great numbers. *mendapat – perhatian* to draw a lot of attention. *Orang – naik turun berebut tempat.* Many people getting on and off were jostling for seats. *Di mana-mana pemuda sudah – menantikan perintah.* Everywhere the young people were waiting in great numbers for orders. **3** complete, entire, whole (day/week, etc.). *sehari –* a whole/entire day; → *sehari* SUNTUK. *Waprés Umar Wirahadikusuma selama sehari – Kamis lalu mengadakan kunjungan kerja ke daérah Jawa Timur.* Vice President Umar Wirahadikusuma made a working visit to East Java last Thursday for a full day. **4** charged (of a battery). **5** (*math*) whole (of a number). *– akal* ingenious, resourceful (person). *– arti* meaningful, significant, full of meaning. *Sorot matanya – arti.* He gave a meaningful look. *– émosi* emotional. *– gaya* stylish. *– hormat* respectable, venerable, honorable. *– madet* crowded, chock-full. *– montok* shapely. **kepenuh-montokan** shapeliness. *– padat/papak/pekak/pekat/pepak/ruah/sarat* crammed, crowded, full to the brim. *– pengabdian* dedicated. *– risiko* risky, chancy. *– sesak* filled/jammed to capacity. **memenuh-sesaki** to fill/jam to capacity. *– tepat/terak/tumpat* crammed, crowded, packed, etc. *– tepu* full, brimming.

penuh-penuh fully, completely.

sepenuh complete, entire, whole, total, all. *~ jalan/kampung* the whole/entire street/village. *dengan ~ minat/perhatian* with full attention, fully attentive. *dengan ~ hati* a) heartily, with all one's heart, whole-heartedly. b) (in adoption documents) (to give up one's child for adoption, abandon all claims on one's child) forever, for good, permanently.

sepenuhnya fully, completely. *Saya mengerti ~.* I fully understand.

sepenuh-penuhnya (to realize, etc.) fully; completely (free, etc.).

memenuh to be(come) full/crowded/jammed, fill up.

memenuhi [and **menuhin** (*J coq*)] **1** to fill (a glass/page of a newspaper, etc.). *~ halaman suratkabar* to fill the page of a newspaper. *~ lowongan* to fill a (job) vacancy. **2** to grant/comply with (a request). *~ permintaan* to comply with a request, meet a demand. **3** to fulfill, keep (one's promise). *~ janjinya* to keep one's promise, meet one's obligations, keep an appointment. *~ kata yang sudah terkatakan* to keep one's word, be as good as one's word. *~ kewajibannya* to carry out one's obligations, discharge one's duties. *~ perikatan* to fulfill an agreement. **4** to satisfy, fulfill, meet, comply with (requirements/obligations/conditions, etc.), settle. *cukup ~* satisfactory/satisfying. *~ kebutuhannya* to satisfy the requirements/needs of. *~ ketentuan pemerintah agar agén tunggal secara bertahap menggunakan komponén bikinan lokal* to comply with government stipulations that sole agents use locally manufactured components in stages. *~ persyaratannya/syarat* to meet the requirements, be eligible, qualify. *~ utang* to settle a debt. **5** to keep/stick to (the schedule). *~ jadwal* to stick to the schedule. **6** to accept (an offer). *Tawarannya saya penuhi.* I accepted his offer.

memenuhkan 1 to make s.t. full, fill up s.t. **2** to fulfill, meet (a demand, etc.).

terpenuh the fullest.

terpenuhi fulfilled, satisfied, complied with, met, able to be carried out. *Dengan demikian ~ pula keinginan orang.* In this way the people's desires were also satisfied.

kepenuhan 1 fullness, entirety, totality. **2** (*coq*) overfilled, filled too full.

pemenuh 1 filling. **2** filler.

pemenuhan 1 fulfillment, fulfilling. *~ rasa ingin tahu* fulfilling one's curiosity. **2** settlement, settling. *~ utang* settlement of a debt. **3** compliance with. **4** keeping (one's promise).

penuju (*J*) to approve, agree with; to be agreed on; → SETUJU.

penukut k.o. starter made from rice for making cakes.

penyakap laborer who tills the land, farmhand.

penyang (in Kalimantan) little stones, pieces of wood, small bottles filled with a magical oil, animal tusks, etc. worn around the waist or neck as an amulet.

penyap (*ob*) → LENYAP.

penyaram (*M*) → PENIARAM.

penyék and **pényék** → PENYÉT.

penyét and **pényét** flattened, squeezed flat, crushed (flat); → PENCÉT.

memenyét *~ tombol* to press/push the button/bell.

terpenyét hard pressed, in a corner/tight place.

pényok (*J/Jv*) to have a dent in it, dented; → PÉNYOT. *penyak.-* full of dents.

pényot dented; → PÉOT.

penyu 1 sea turtle; *cp* KURA-KURA I. *telur –* turtle eggs. **2** tortoise shell. *– agar* green turtle, *Chelonia mydas. – belimbing* leatherback turtle, *Demochelys coriacea. – hijau* green turtle, *Chelonia mydas*, found along the south coast of West Java; its meat is used for turtle soup. *– lekang* k.o. large sea turtle, *Lepidochelya olivacea. – sisik* Hawksbill turtle, *Eretmochelys imbricata.*

péok (*Jv*) dented; → PÉOT.

péot (*Jv*) awry, twisted, distorted; dented, with a dent in it (of a fender, etc.); → TUA *péot. péat.–* a) full of dents. b) bumpy (of a road).

pepadang (*Jv*) **1** light, brightness. **2** guidance, wisdom.

pepagan (tree) bark.

pepah stick, lath (used for beating).

memepah to beat/lash out with a stick.

pepai *udang –* species of small shrimp.

pepak full, complete, plenary (session). *penuh –* chock-full, crowded, jammed.

sepepak all, the whole/entire.

memepaki and **memepakkan** to complete, bring s.t. up to a full complement.

pepak-pepak (*Jv*) etiquette, good manners; → BASA *basi.*

pepaku *burung –* red-wattled lapwing, *Lobivanellus indicus atronuchalis.*

pepali (*Jv*) prohibitions.

peparé → PERIA I. *– welut* snake gourd, *Trichosanthes anguina.*

peparu lungs; → PARU-PARU.

pepas fish hook.

memepas to catch fish using a fly, fly-fish. *~ dalam belanga* to depend on one's own resources and those of one's relatives.

pepat 1 flattened, leveled out, flat, smooth, oblate. **2** (*M*) exact (amount of time). *tiga hari –* exactly three days. *– bumi* flattening of the earth. *– gigi* tooth filing. *– di luar, rancung/pancung di dalam* hypocritical, fake.

memepat 1 to pollard, trim (trees). **2** to file (teeth to make them level). *~ gigi* to file one's teeth. *~ kuku* to cut one's nails. **3** to blunt (of arrows).

kepepatan flatness.

pepatah saying, proverb, adage, aphorism, maxim, old saw. *– (dan) petatih* various proverbs/sayings; → PETATAH-PETITIH.

berpepatah-petitih to use various proverbs/sayings/adages/aphorisms. *Orang Minang tak hanya jago ~ sebagai éksprési lisan, tapi juga léwat tulisan.* Minangkabau people are not only champions in using various proverbs as verbal expressions, but also in their writings.

memepatahkan to turn s.t. into a proverb/aphorism.

pepaya papaya, *Carica papaya. – jantan* a papaya which flowers but bears no fruit.

pépé I (*J*) (*kué –*) cake made of bananas and flour (in layers).

pépé II *kain –* khaki drill.

pépé III (*Jv*) to lie out in the sun.

mépé to dry s.t. in the sun.

pépéan sun-dried. *tembakau ~* sun-dried tobacco.

pepeda (*Ambon*) sago porridge.

pepejal (*Mal*) solid; → PEJAL.

pépék I to take part in a game (said of spectators who bet on the game).

pépék II (*Jv*) vulva; vagina. *– bolong/disodok* said of a deflowered girl; → MÉMÉK II.

pépél (*J*) **mépél** to make and form dough.

pepéling (*Jv*) warning.

péper (*E*) scientific paper.

péper I (*cla*) **mémépér** to deviate from its course, veer off course (of a boat, etc.).

terpépér veered off course.

pépér II mépér 1 (*J*) to clean one's dirty hands by wiping them on a piece of cloth. **2** (*Jv*) to clean o.s. after defecating without using water, i.e., with toilet paper/tissue/leaves.

pepérék pony fish, *Leiognathus spp.*

pepérétan water chestnut, *Heleocharis dulcis.*

pépermin (*D/E*) peppermint.

pépés (*J/Jv*) food (mostly fish) that has been wrapped in banana leaf, spiced with *serai, kunyir, lombok, kemiri, bawang, salam*, etc., and roasted over hot coals. *– oncom* spiced mixture of fermented peanuts or soybeans rolled up in a banana leaf.

mépés to prepare this dish (as part of a *rijstafel*).

terpépés wrapped/stuffed in this manner.

pépésan (fish, etc.) roasted in such a way. *~ ikan mas* (a Sundanese specialty) freshwater carp roasted in banana leaves (said to be an aphrodisiac). *~ kosong* lies, bluff.

pepet I (*Jv ling*) the schwa, reduced vowel; the breve mark formerly used to mark this vowel.

memepet to write an e with this mark.

pepet II (*Jv*) stuffed up (of the nose). *pikiran yang –* to be at one's wit's end.

pépét (*J/Jv*) dead end, there's no way out.

memépét [and **mépét** (*coq*)] **1** pressed/pushed up against/to. *Méja tulisnya ~ témbok.* His desk is pushed up against the wall. **2** tight, pressed to the limit, pressed for money. *Waktu/uang saya ~.* I'm pressed for time/money. *Kenaikan kurs yén sejak Séptémber "sudah cukup besar mengurangi laba kami, sekarang sudah ~," katanya.* The rise in the value of the yen since September, "has reduced our profits a lot; we're now pressed to the limit," he said. *Kalau sayalah, bisa dipépét-pépét, tapi rekan-rekan saya yang sudah kawin, mana bisa hidup?* Me, I can be short of money, but my friends who are married, how can they live? **3** right next (to), right up (against). *Rumahnya ~ dengan rumah saya.* His house is right up against my house.

memépéti to press (up) against. *Motor itu ~ mobil yang ditumpangi si korban.* The motorcycle pushed up against the car in which the victim (of the robbery) was sitting.

memépétkan 1 to push s.t. against s.t. else. *Pépétkan kursi ini pada lemari.* Push this chair up against the cupboard. **2** to put s.t. or s.o. under pressure. *Dia ~ saya.* He argued me into a corner.

terpépét [and **kepépét** (*coq*)] **1** to be cornered/trapped/driven into a corner. *Orang yang ~ mau buang air harus bersabar sampai ia tiba di rumahnya.* A person who has to urinate must be patient until he has gotten home. **2** broke, penniless; in trouble/a tight spot. *~ pembayaran séwa rumah* to be having a hard time paying one's rent. **3** to be pressed close up against. *Mobil kami kepépét dan dibuntuti.* They were following close behind our car.

pepetek (*Jv*) **1** a small marine fish, salted and dried. **2** small-time, petty. *pengusaha –* small-time businessman (on the sidewalk or door to door).

pepetri → PETRI.

pepindan (*Jv*) metaphor, figure of speech; → MAJAS, PIGURA *bahasa*, TROPE.

pepisang (*Mal*) bananas.

pepohonan → POHON I.

pépsin (*E*) pepsin.

péptida (*E*) peptide.

péptidase (*D*) peptidase.

péptidisasi (*D*) peptization.

pépton (*D/E*) peptone.

pepuju (*J*) womb, uterus.

pepundén and **pepundi** (*Jv*) 1 object of respect and reverence. 2 amulet.

pepura → PURA-PURA.

peputut (*ob*) pupil/disciple of a holy hermit.

per I (*D*) 1 per, each. – *menit* per minute. 2 by. – *pon* by the pound. *satu* – *satu* one by one; → SATU *demi satu*.

per II divided by (in fractions). *lima -delapan* five-eighths, 5/8.

per III → PR-.

per IV (in acronyms) → PERATURAN, PERHIMPUNAN, PERSATUAN.

pér I (*D*) spring (of watch, etc.). – *kéong* spiral spring. – *rambut* (very fine) watch spring.

  berpér with a spring, with springs.

pér II (*D*) (electric) light bulb.

pér III (*D coq*) (trade) fair, festival. *Jakarta* – Jakarta Fair.

pér IV (*D*) as of. – *1 Juli* as of July 1.

pér V (*D*) pear.

pér VI (*Jv*) dogcart, i.e., a small, two-wheeled horse-drawn cart.

pér VII (*J*) **ngepér** to be afraid.

pera (*Jv*) granular, dry (rice).

perabis *jualan* – clearance sale.

perabot (*Jv*) 1 tools, utensils, equipment, supplies, accessories. 2 (*coq*) penis. – *di kelangkang pahanya yang paling berharga itu* the most valuable "tool" between his legs. – *dapur* kitchen utensils. – *kantor* office supplies and equipment. – *mobil* automobile parts. – *rumah (tangga)* furniture, house furnishings. – *sekolah* school supplies. – *tukang* workman's tools. – *tukang kayu* carpenter's tools.

  memperaboti to furnish (a house).

  perabotan tools, utensils, equipment, furnishings.

perabu (*Skr*) monarch; → PRABU.

  keperabuan 1 monarchy. 2 palace.

perabung ridge (of palm-leaf house). – *lima bentuk* pyramid-shaped (house).

perada I (*Port*) 1 gold leaf, tinsel. 2 tin coating.

  berperada with gold leaf. *gaun malam* ~ *yang berkesan élégan serta méwah* an evening gown with gold leaf which makes an elegant and luxurious impression.

perada II (*E mil*) parade, review; → PARADE. – *buku* (*ob*) book review; → TINJAUAN *buku*.

Peradin → PERSATUAN *Advokat Indonésia*.

peraga → RAGA IV. *alat* – teaching aid.

  berperaga(kan) and **mem(p)eragakan** to exhibit, display; to show off (one's clothes).

  peragaan show. ~ *busana* fashion show.

  keperagaan *Balai Pendidikan* ~ Teaching Aid Center.

  pemeraga mannequin, (fashion) model.

  pemeragaan exhibiting, displaying.

peragat (*M*) 1 regalia. 2 attribute.

peragawan male (fashion) model, mannequin.

peragawati female (fashion) model, mannequin.

  keperagawatian modeling (skills). *ujian tingkat dasar keluwesan dan* ~ a basic-level examination of elegance and modeling skills.

perah I squeeze, press; → PERAS I.

  memerah 1 to squeeze (juice out of a fruit), press out. 2 to milk (a cow). 3 to exploit, take advantage of. ~ *keringat* to work one's fingers to the bone. ~ *otak* to rack one's brains. ~ *santan di kuku* to do s.t. the hard way. ~ *tenaga* to use one's powers.

  perahan 1 s.t. squeezed out (of juice/milk, etc.). 2 animal which is milked. *kambing/sapi* ~ a) milch goat/cow. b) cash cow.

  pemerah 1 ~ *susu* milker. 2 extortionist, blackmailer.

  pemerahan 1 squeezing, pressing out. 2 milking. 3 exploiting, exploitation.

perah II k.o. tree, *Elateriospermum tapos*; → TAPOS III.

perahu 1 (*naut*) prau, boat, ship. *menginjak dua* – to have the best of both worlds. *segan kayuh* – *hanyut* to miss one's chance. – *balang* double-masted sailboat. – *bandung* houseboat. – *bermotor témpél* (in Samarinda) longboat. – *dayung* rowboat. – *golékan* medium-sized sailboat. – *gubang* sailing canoe. – *guntung* a stripped-down prau. – *jolong-jolong* long-nosed boat. – *karét* dinghy. – *lading* longboat. – *lanun* pirate ship. – *layar* sailboat. – *lesung/lépa-lépa* dugout (canoe). – *lombong* k.o. barge with deep draft and wide beam. – *mancung* prau shaped like a sheath. – *mayang* seagoing fishing boat. – *motor* motorboat. – *motor cepat* (in Pekanbaru) speedboat. – *nelayan* fishing boat. – *(Nabi) Nuh* Noah's Ark. – *pendarat* landing craft. – *pesiar* pleasure boat. – *penisi* Buginese prau with two main masts. – *pukat* → PERAHU *mayang*. – *rakit* raft. – *sasak* pontoon ferryboat. – *sérét* barge. – *tambang* ferry(boat). – *tarik* canal boat. – *terbang* flying boat. 2 name of a *ceki* card.

  berperahu (to go) by boat, on a ship.

perai I loose, fallen apart.

  berperai-perai scattered/spread everywhere, dispersed; to fall apart.

  memerai to shatter to pieces, disintegrate.

perai II (*D*) 1 off (duty), on vacation. *hari* – a day off. *mendapat* – *seminggu* to have a week off. – *bekerja* to have a day off, be off (duty). 2 free, gratis. 3 vacant, empty (of a chair). 4 unobstructed, unhampered.

  mem(p)eraikan to give s.o. time off. *Sekolah-sekolah diperaikan seminggu lamanya*. Schools were given a week off.

perai III *bawang* – and *daun* – spring onion, leek, chives, *Allium porrum*.

perai IV *membuang* – and

  berperai-perai to tack (of a sailing vessel).

  memeraikan ~ *perahu* to sail a boat on the tack.

perai V *kain* – black silk cloth with a flower motif.

peraja → PRAJA I.

peraji midwife.

perajurit → PRAJURIT.

perak → PARAK II.

pérak 1 silver. *berambut* – silver-/gray-haired. 2 (*col*) the silver guilder. 3 (*coq*) rupiah, rup(s). *lima puluh ribu* – *per bulan* fifty thousand rups a month. – *bakar* black-enameled silver made in Kotagede, Yogyakarta. – *daun* silver foil.

  sepérak 1 (*col*) a (silver) guilder. 2 (*coq*) a rupiah, one rup.

  memérak white as silver.

  pérakan (*coq*) a rupiah coin or note. *lima* ~ a five-rupiah note.

  kepérakan and **kepérak-pérakan** silvery.

peraka ship's deck (emptied for cargo, etc.); ship's hatch; → PALKA.

perakték and **peraktik** → PRAKTÉK, PRAKTIK.

peraktis → PRAKTIS.

peram I memeram to coo (of pigeons).

peram II berperam 1 to be shut off from society, isolate o.s. ~ *di rumah/dalam kamarnya* to stay (cooped up) at home/in one's room. 2 to be kept in a pile to ripen.

  memeram 1 to keep (fruits) (in a pile of *beras*, etc.) to ripen them artificially, make ... ferment. 2 to seclude/confine/isolate (a marriageable girl at home). 3 to brood about, keep s.t. bottled up. ~ *dendam/perasaan/perhatian* to keep one's grudge/feelings/interest bottled up (inside o.s.). ~ *di hati* to keep s.t. locked up inside o.s. and not tell anybody about it.

  memerami (*pl obj*) → MEMERAM.

  memeramkan ~ *mata* to keep one's eyes fixed (on a spot).

  terperam kept locked up inside. *segala rupa bentuk ketidakpuasan yang* ~ *sekian lama* all kinds of forms of dissatisfaction that had been locked up for so long.

  pemeram 1 artificially ripened (fruit). 2 secluded. 3 pent-up (feelings/rage, etc.).

  pemeraman fermentation.

perambut *tali* – the catgut between fishing line and hook, the strong silk line immediately above the fishhook.

peran I 1 (stage) actor. 2 character (in a novel/play, etc.). 3 (*Mal*) clown/jester in *makyung* and *menora* shows. 4 (theatrical/political, etc.) role. *modél* – role model. – *figuran* an extra. – *serta* participation, taking part (in). *Pembangunan kota menuntut – serta seluruh masyarakat.* Urban development demands the participation of the entire community. **berperan-serta** to participate, take part. *empat negara yang ~ dalam pasukan pemelihara perdamaian multinasional* four countries which are taking part in the multinational peace-keeping force. **keperan-sertaan** participation. *Keluarga Berencana sangat ditunjang oléh ~ para alim ulama dalam memberi motivasi pada umat Islam umumnya.* Family Planning was greatly supported by the participation of Muslim scholars in motivating the Muslim community in general. **pemeran-serta** participant. *– utama* leading man/woman. *– watak* character actor.

berperan (and **main ~**) to play a role, act/play a part. *Penari kawakan Sentot ~ sebagai Adam.* A seasoned dancer Sentot played the role of Adam. *~ besar dalam* to play an important role in. *T. banyak ~ dalam kemajuan pelajaran saya di sekolah.* T. played an important role in the improvement of my learning in school.

memerani to play the role/part of, play a role in. *ujar Mér selepas ~ Éva* said Mer after playing the part of Eve. *film yang diperani kelompok ini* a film in which this group plays the roles.

memerankan 1 to play the role of. **2** to stage, perform (on stage). *~ kembali* to reenact.

peranan (theatrical/political, etc.) role; part, task. *~ advokat tidak bisa diabaikan dalam menegakkan hukum.* The role of lawyers cannot be ignored in enforcing the law. *~ bertujuan* purposeful role. *~ memimpin* leading role. *~ penentu* determining role. *~ utama* lead/principal role. **berperanan** to play a role, act/play a part. *"Ibu kelihatan ~ sekali dalam perlombaan ini," kata Salomé.* "Mother seems to have played an important role in this race," said Salome.

pemeran player, actor. *~ pembantu* supporting actor/actress. *~ pengganti* stuntman, double.

pemeranan acting, role-playing.

peran II rooftree, tie beam (of roof).

perana (*J/Jv*) clitoris; → ITIL, KELENTIT.

peranakan I (*Jv*) a long-sleeved dark blue cloth jacket worn by officials at the Court of Yogyakarta.

peranakan II → ANAK I.

perancah I skeleton framework of a wooden house; scaffolding, temporary structure. *– bor* drilling rig.

perancah II (*M*) *– gulai* flavoring for *gulai.*

Perancis → PRANCIS.

perancit → PANCIT.

peranda porak-peranda → PORAK-PARIK.

perandah → PERAGA (under RAGA IV).

perang 1 war, warfare, battle, combat, hostilities, armed conflict. **2** fight (against illiteracy, etc.). *– melawan kejahatan* fight against crime. **3** (*coq*) to wage/be at war, battle, fight. *pergi – to* go to war. *adat –* rules of war. *akal –* stratagem, ruse (in a war). *bahaya –* danger of war. *berpengalaman –* battle-seasoned/hardened. *hukum –* martial law. *ikat(an) –* a) battle line. b) order of battle. *imam –* war leader. *kalah/kéok –* to lose a battle, lose the war. *kejahatan –* war crimes. *keletihan –* battle fatigue. *kerugian –* war damage. *mati –* killed in action. *médan –* battlefield; → MÉDAN *bhakti/laga/pertempuran/yudha;* → PALAGA. *menang –* to win a battle, win the war. *mengikat –* to send into battle. *pampasan –* war reparations. *pecah –* a) war broke out. b) (*ob*) to lose a battle. *undang-undang –* war regulations. *– bermalaékat, sabung berjuara* man proposes, (but) God disposes. *– adu pintar* battle of wits. *– angkasa* space war. *– antargéng/antarkelompok penjahat* gang war. *– antariksa/antarplanét* star wars; → KARTIKA *yudha. – asabat* psywar, war of nerves. *– asap* mock/phony war. *– Badar/Badr* an early victorious battle of Islam. *– batu* rock-throwing war. *– bicara* war of words. *– bintang* star wars. *– dingin* cold war. *– dunia* world war. *– Dunia Pertama* World War One, WWI. *– Dunia Kedua* World War II, WWII. *– éléktronika* [Pernika] electronic warfare. *– fi sabilillahi* a) Holy War. b) Aceh war against the Dutch. *– gerak* mobile warfare. *– gerilya* guerrilla warfare. *– harga* price war. *– kecil-kecilan* skirmish(es). *– kembang* "flower battle" (in the *wayang kulit*). *– kemerdékaan* war of independence. *– khandak/khan-*

daq battle of the trench, a Muslim victory in 627. *– kilat* blitz-krieg, lightning war. *– kota* urban warfare. *– kucing-kucingan* game of cat and mouse. *– meletihkan* war of attrition. *– mendada* hand-to-hand combat. *– Muktah* an early Islamic battle against the Romans. *– mulut* verbal battle, shouting match. *– nuklir* nuclear war. *– paderi* the war from 1821 through 1837 between the orthodox Muslims and those on the West Coast of Sumatra (supported by the Dutch) who upheld *adat* law. *– panas* hot/shooting war. *– panjar* make-believe war. *– parit* trench warfare. *– partisan* partisan war. *– péna* paper war, war of words, polemics. *– pijar* (*ob*) maneuvers. *– pijat* knop push-button war. *– psikologi* psywar. *– putih* → PERANG *paderi. – sabil* (*Allah*) a) Holy War. b) Aceh war against the Dutch. *– salib* crusade, the Crusades. *– saraf* psywar. *– saudara* civil war. *– semak* bush war (in South Africa). *– sinu* war of nerves. *– suci* holy war. *– tanding* a) duel, hand-to-hand combat. b) polemics. *– tanding artileri/meriam* artillery duel/exchange. *– tanpa diumumkan* undeclared war. *– Teluk* Gulf War. *– terbuka* open warfare. *– terselubung* covert war. *– udara* aerial warfare/combat. *– Uhud* an early defeat of Islam in 625. *– urat saraf* war of nerves. *– watang* jousting. *– Yarmuk* a Muslim victory in 637.

berperang to wage/be at war, battle, fight. *~ dingin* to wage a cold war.

berperang-perangan 1 to fight against e.o., clash with e.o. **2** to hold (training) maneuvers, wage a mock war.

memerangi to fight, battle (against), combat, wage war on. *~ segala bentuk keterbelakangan dan kemiskinan* to combat all types of backwardness and poverty. *Pemerintah ~ mercon.* The government waged war on fireworks.

memerangkan and **memperperang(kan) 1** to incite a war. **2** to fight/stand up for.

terperangi 1 can be waged (of a war). **2** can be defeated (of a bad habit). **3** can be eliminated (of poverty, etc.).

perang-perangan mock warfare, (training) maneuvers.

pemerang s.t. or s.o. that battles against s.t.

pemerangan battling, fighting; battle, fight.

peperangan battle, war, warfare, combat, struggle. *~ bukan konvénsional* unconventional warfare. *~ kimia* chemical warfare. *~ tanpa disengaja* inadvertent war.

pérang 1 blond. **2** brunette. **3** dark brown (of hair); reddish-black/-yellow; → PIRANG. *– perus/pucat* wan, pale (of complexion).

perangah terperangah dumbfounded, perplexed. *duduk – to* sit dumbfounded. *Anak-anak itu ~ sebentar.* The children were perplexed for a while.

perangai character, disposition, temperament, nature. *laku –* behavior, way of acting, attitude. *lembut – a)* soft-hearted, gentle. b) pliant, submissive.

berperangai 1 to have a ... character/temperament/nature/disposition. *~ jahat* to have a bad character. **2** temperamental.

perangas-perongos (*J*) quick to take offense, touchy.

perangas-peringus (*J*) with a sour expression on one's face.

peranggang *ayam –* roaster, i.e., a tender chicken big enough to roast.

peranggi → PERENGGI.

peranggo → PERANGGU.

peranggu set. *Bahasa ialah – ungkapan.* Language is a set of expressions.

seperanggu(an) a set of (buttons/studs, etc.), a suit (of clothes of the same fabric).

perangkap 1 trap (for birds, animals, criminals, etc.). *pertanyaan – trick question.* **2** ambush.

memerangkap to trap, (capture by a) trick, cheat, deceive.

terperangkap trapped, captured, caught (in a trap), cheated, tricked. *Dua orang ~ di lumpur kotoran binatang.* Two persons were trapped in a pool of animal droppings.

pemerangkap s.t. that traps, trap.

pemerangkapan trapping.

perangkat 1 apparatus, tool, instrument, equipment, rig; → ANGKAT V, PIRANTI. **2** the government, functionaries, officials; → APARAT. *– bahan bakar* fuel assembly (in atomic energy plant). *– daérah* local/regional government and officials. *– désa* village government and officials. – *keras* (computer) hardware. – *lunak* (computer) software.

seperangkat a set (of samples, etc.), pair. ~ *alat musik* a band. *Penggolongan sastra dan nonsastra tidak ditentukan oléh ~ ciri ragam, tetapi kwalitas.* The classification of literature and nonliterature is not determined by a set of diverse characteristics, but by quality. ~ *shalat* prayer paraphernalia (a common dowry).

perangko → PRANGKO.

perangsang incentive, stimulus, spur; → RANGSANG I.
  memerangsang to stimulate.

peranjak terperanjak to fall down on one's behind.

peranjat mem(p)eranjatkan to startle, surprise, shock; to frighten. **te(r)peranjat** startled, surprised, shocked. **keterperanjatan** feeling of surprise.

peranti (*J/Jv*) **1** device, tool, equipment, instrument, appliance; → PERANGKAT, PERAWIS, PIRANTI. – *keras* (computer) hardware. – *listrik* electrical equipment. – *lunak* (computer) software. – *rumah* household furniture. – *télepon* telephone (instrument). – *tulis* writing materials. **2** means, remedy. **3** for, in order to.
  memerantikan to prepare, make ready.

peranyak (*M ob*) **te(r)peranyak** flopped down (into a chair) (from astonishment, etc.).

peranye (*D ob*) fringe.

perap I (*ob*) **memerap 1** to flap (the wings). **2** to flutter (of a fowl struggling after its throat has been cut). **3** to get all excited, become aggressive.

perap II (*ob*) **terperap 1** piled up, stopped, not forwarded (of the mail). **2** fixed (of one's gaze).

perapatan → PRAPATAN.

peras I squeeze, press; → PERAH I. *tukang* – blackmailer, extortionist **memeras 1** to squeeze out (juice/fruit), press. ~ *kantong* to spend a lot of money. ~ *keringat* to slave away, work hard, work one's fingers to the bone. ~ *otak/tenaga* to rack one's brains. **2** to extort (money), extract (money by threats), blackmail. **3** to exploit (the poor/the people).
  memerasi (*pl obj*) **1** to squeeze. **2** to blackmail, extort.
  perasan extract, s.t. squeezed out.
  pemeras 1 extortionist, blackmailer. **2** squeezer. *pesawat ~* squeezer, (juice, etc.) press. ~ *jeruk* juicer, citrus-fruit squeezer.
  pemerasan extortion, blackmailing.

peras II (*M*) smooth; → PARAS II.

perasat I → FIRASAT.

perasat II trick, artifice. *persalinan* – forceps delivery, induced labor.

Perasman (*D*) Frenchman. *negeri* – France; → PRASMAN I, P(E)RANCIS.
  perasmanan *makanan* – buffet, smorgasbord.

peras-perus to laugh to o.s.

perasukan (*ob*) → PASUKAN.

perat 1 rancid (of oil); → TENGIK I. **2** sour. *terung* – a small k.o. eggplant.

perata berperata to nullify the prohibition against the marriage of two persons whose marriage, based on *adat*, would have been considered incestuous.

Peratun → PERADILAN *tata usaha negara*.

peratus percentage; → PERSÉNTASE, PERSÉNTASI, RATUS I.

perawan 1 virgin; maiden, girl, young unmarried woman. *daérah/ hutan yang masih* – virgin area/forest; → HUTAN *lepas*. *Santa* – *Maria* the Virgin Mary. *tanah* – virgin land. **2** (in Islamic marriage licenses) unmarried woman, single. *membuka* – to deflower, take away the virginity/maidenhood of. *tidak* – no longer a virgin, deprived of her virginity. **ketidakperawanan** no longer being a virgin, deprivation of virginity. – *aspal* girl who has had sexual intercourse before marriage and who has undergone an operation to restore her hymen to its original state; → ASPAL II. – *kencur/sunti* girl entering puberty. – *suci* "pure" virgin. – *tin(g)ting* "pure" virgin. – *tua* [pertu] a) old maid, spinster. b) –.– *tua* reference to the three-wheeled motorized vehicles dating back to 1931–33, known by their registered trademarks, such as the *démmo, Masco,* and *Masca.* – *yang tak bercela* the Holy Virgin.
  memerawani 1 to deflower, take away the virginity/maidenhood of. **2** to inaugurate, initiate.

keperawanan maidenhood, virginity. *kesucian* ~ feminine purity.

perawas a plant whose aromatic leaves are used as medicine, *Litsea odorifera.*

perawira → PERWIRA.

perawis ingredients, component materials; → PIRANTI. – *keras* (computer) hardware. – *lunak* (computer) software.

perbagai → PELBAGAI.

perbahasa → PERIBAHASA.

perbal (*D*) summons, subpoena; → PROSÉS *vérbal*, TILANG II.
  mem(p)erbal to summons, subpoena.

perban (*D*) bandage, dressing. – *kasa* gauge bandage.
  mem(p)erban to bandage, dress (a wound).

Perbanas [Perhimpunan Bank Nasional Swasta] Association of Private National Banks (established May 25, 1952).

perbani I *air* – neap tide, dead (of tides at their highest or lowest); slack water.

perbani II *bulan* – crescent moon, waxing moon. – *akhir* last quarter (of the moon).

perbasa → PER(I)BAHASA.

perbatin 1 (title of) *adat* chiefs in Jambi, Lampung, and Palembang. **2** head of a *kuria* in Tapanuli. **3** (*Mal*) head of a Malaccan proto-Malay clan.

perbawa (*Jv*) **1** prestige. **2** influence. *Karena – minuman keras, ia menjadi beringas.* Because he was under the influence of liquor he became furious. **3** authority.

perbegu heathen(ish).

perbekel (*Bal*) village chief.

perboden (*D*) forbidden, prohibited. *memasuki jalan* – to enter a prohibited road.
  memperboden to forbid, prohibit.

perca I (*Pers*) rag, remnant (of fabric).

perca II *getah* – gutta-percha. *Pulau* – Sumatra.

perca III → LINTAH *perca*.

percak memercak to make the sound of rushing water.

percasis [perkenalan calon siswa] initiation.

percaya (*Skr*) belief, trust, confidence, hope, expectation. – *akan/ (ke)pada* a) to believe in. b) to rely on. *Hingga kini masih ada yang – kepada hantu.* Up to now there still are those who believe in ghosts. *boléh – tidakpun tak jadi apa* and – *boléh tidak juga boléh* believe it or not. *lantas* –, *mudah* – *saja* and *main* – credulous. – *tak* – (can) only half believe it. *pembangunan sikap saling* – mutual confidence building. *tidak* – distrustful, disbelieving, suspicious. **ketidakpercayaan** distrust, disbelief, suspicion, lack of confidence, credibility gap. – *angin* vain/idle hope. – *angin lalu* belief in rumors. – *diri* self-confidence. – *habis* total trust.
  mempercaya (only in passive *dipercaya*) *dapat dipercaya* trustworthy, dependable, authoritative (sources).
  percaya-mempercayai to trust e.o.
  mempercayai to believe in, trust, rely on, have faith in. *yang dapat dipercayai* reliable, trustworthy (sources, etc.).
  mempercayakan to entrust (s.t. to s.o./s.o. with s.t.). ~ *rahasia kepada seseorang* to entrust s.o. with a secret.
  te(r)percaya 1 reliable, trustworthy. *mengutip sumber-sumber yang* – quoting reliable sources. **2** *bona fide. tak* ~ in bad faith.
  kete(r)percayaan reliability, trustworthiness, credibility.
  kepercayaan 1 faith, creed, belief. **2** trust, confidence. **3** religious belief, faith. *secara* ~ fiduciary. ~ *akan/(ke)pada diri sendiri* self-confidence. ~ *yang diterimanya* the trust placed in him. *memperoléh* ~ *yang tebal dari* to enjoy the full confidence of. *surat* ~ credentials, letter(s) of credence. *orang* ~ confidant.

percik 1 spot, stain, speck. **2** splash, spatter. –.– *kaca pecah* splintered glass, shards of broken glass.
  sepercik – *api* a spark. ~ *darah* a small amount of blood. ~ *sinar* a thin ray of light.
  be(r)percikan (*pl subj*) **1** to splash/spatter about. **2** splashed/ spattered about, sprinkled all over.
  memercik 1 to splash, spatter/splatter (water or other liquid). **2** (of perspiration) to pour off one's face. **3** to suddenly appear/arise.
  memerciki to splash, spatter, sprinkle, splatter.
  memercikkan 1 to splash/sprinkle/splatter s.t. (on s.t.). *Dia ~ cat ke mana-mana.* He spattered paint everywhere. **2** to spark.

~ bunga-bunga api kebencian politis tertentu to spark certain political hatreds.

te(r)percik splashed, splattered, sprinkled; got splashed on, splattered. *Air itu ~ ke atas baju saya.* The water splashed on my shirt.

percikan 1 splash, sprinkle, sprinkling, drops (of sprinkled water). *~ air* a splash of water. **2** sputtering. **3** spark. *~ api* spark. *~ cerita* fragment (of a story).

pemercik sprinkler.

pemercikan sprinkling, splashing, spattering. *Peresmian penerbangan pertama Amérika-Indonésia itu ditandai dengan upacara adat ~ tirta atas badan pesasat DC-10 "Irian Jaya".* The inauguration of the first America-Indonesia flight was marked by the traditional ceremony of sprinkling water over the body of the DC-10 aircraft "Irian Jaya".

percil (*Jv*) young frog that is no longer a tadpole.

percis (*D coq*) precisely, exactly; → PERSIS. *- seperti* exactly/just like.

percit memercit and **tepercit 1** to spurt out (like pus from a squeezed carbuncle). **2** to splash, spatter; to come out bit by bit.

percul tepercul protruding (as animal's head from a hole or cage); *cp* PACUL II.

percuma → CUMA.

Perda [*peraturan daérah*] Provincial Regulation.

perdag (in acronyms) → PERDAGANGAN.

perdah I handle of adze.

perdah II (*Pers*) k.o. curtain/screen.

perdam-perdom memperdam-perdom to curse roundly/up and down; → PERDOM.

perdana (*Skr*) **1** prime, primary, principal. **2** first, initial, inaugural, maiden. *ékspor – nenas kaléngan dari Subang* the first exports of canned pineapples from Subang. *kuliah –nya* his first/maiden lectures. *nomor –* first issue (of a magazine). *penerbangan –* inaugural/maiden flight. *penerbitan –* first publication (of a book). *pengapalan –* first shipment. *pergelaran –* premiere. *perjalanan –* maiden voyage (of a ship). *pertunjukan –* premiere, first night (of a play), first run (of a film); → PEMUTARAN *pertama. siaran –* maiden broadcast (of a TV program). *– menteri* [PM] prime/first minister, premier. **keperdana-menterian** prime minister's, prime ministerial, premier's. *Ia menghendaki tetap menduduki kursi ~nya yang akan berakhir Oktober mendatang.* He wishes to hold on to his prime minister's position which will end next October. *– pertunjukan* gala performance, preview.

memperdanakan to preview (a film).

perdata I (*Skr Jv*) **1** civil; *opp* PIDANA. *hukum –* civil law. *Kitab Undang-Undang Hukum –* [KUH Perdata] Civil Code. *perkara –* civil suit/case. *tindak –* civil act. **2** (*ob*) civil court.

memperdata to take civil action against, sue. *~ para koruptor dan manipulator setelah dipidana* to take civil action against corruptors and manipulators after they have been sentenced in criminal court.

keperdataan (*mod*) civil law.

perdata II (*J*) **1** to be attentive/careful, be on one's guard. **2** to pay attention to, mind.

perdéo and **perdio** → PRODÉO.

perdi → PERIDI.

perdikan (*Skr? Jv*) exempt from the obligation to pay taxes and tribute to the ruler (granted to certain *désa*s before 1962).

perdiping (*D*) story, floor (of a building).

perdom (*D coq*) damn(ed).

mem(p)erdom(i) to curse, rage at.

perdu I 1 shrub, stool. *jalan sempit yang ditumbuhi semak –* a narrow street overgrown with underbrush. **2** base of tree trunk. *pohon –* shrub. *tanaman –* shrubs, brush. *– bambu* bamboo stool.

seperdu a clump (of bamboo).

perdu II → PERLU.

perduli → PEDULI.

peré → PERAI II.

peredus terperedus 1 pot-bellied. **2** pregnant; → BERDUS.

péréh terpéréh-péréh dead tired (after athletics); tottering, staggering.

peréi I → PERAI II.

peréi II → PRÉI II.

peréi III (*coq*) broke, penniless.

perék (*D coq*) to hell with you!

pérék → PEREMPUAN *ékspérimén.*

perékik (*E*) **1** free kick (in soccer). **2** against the rules (of the game); improper, indecent.

pérékisme being a slut/loose woman, sleeping around. *Kita juga mendengar banyak gejala anak sekolah yang terlihat dalam –.* We have also heard about many symptoms in school children which can be seen in that they are sluts.

peréksa → PERIKSA.

pérélék (*S*) rice grains which have fallen through holes in bags during transportation. *béras –* (uncooked) rice contributed by the community (for residents of an area hit by a food shortage).

perem → PERAM II.

peréman → PRÉMAN.

perempuan 1 woman. **2** female (of human beings), feminine, womanly; *cp* BETINA. **3** girl. **4** (*orang –*) (*J*) wife, spouse. *– ayé lagi ke pasar.* My wife has gone to the market. *anak –nya* his/her daughter. *bunyi – di air* very noisy. *– bergelandang/cabul* prostitute. *– éksperimén* [pérék] "experimenting woman," i.e., a teenage girl who likes to go out *usu* with older men for money, an easy lay. *"Mau ikut?" "Ke mana?" "Cari pérék!"* "Would you like to come along?" "Where to?" "Looking for *pérék*"! *– galak* aggressive woman. *– geladak* (*ob*) whore. *– jahanam* wicked woman. *– jahat/jalang* prostitute. *– jangak* loose woman. *– nakal* loose woman, woman of easy virtue. *– P(elacur)* prostitute; → WANITA *P. – pengérét(an)* gold digger. *– piaraan* mistress, kept woman; → GULA-GULA, TV II. *– yang masih gadis* virgin.

keperempuanan femininity.

keperempuan-perempuanan 1 feminine, female. **2** womanliness, femininity. **2** effeminate. *Suaranya agak ~.* His voice is somewhat effeminate.

perencah *– gulai* seasoning for *gulai.*

perenggan I (*cla*) border, boundary, frontier, front (between two weather systems, etc.); → HINGGA.

perenggan II (*Mal*) paragraph.

Perenggi (*Pers cla*) **1** European. **2** French(man). **3** Portuguese; → FERINGGI.

peréngkat → PERINGKAT.

perenjak → PRENJAK.

perenyak (*M*) **terperenyak** dropped/flopped down with a thud (in a chair, etc.). (due to surprise, etc.).

perenyuk and **perenyup** (*ob*) **terperenyuk** and **perenyup** toothless.

perepat I tall mangrove-swamp tree, *Sonneratia alba* Smith, *Cambreto carpus rotundatus*, whose wood is used for making ribs for boats.

perepat II (*Pal ob*) **1** friend, comrade. **2** companion, mate.

perepat III → KELICAP *perepat.*

perepet (*J*) dawn or dusk.

peres → PERAS I, PERAH I.

pérés leveled off, level. *seséndok makan –* a level tablespoon.

memérés to level off, smooth out (rice in a measure).

peresat → FIRASAT.

peresih (*cla*) clean, pure-white.

péréstroika (*Russian*) restructuring; → RÉSTRUKTURISASI.

berpéréstroika to restructure.

peret (*Jv*) no longer slippery/slimy, dry, dried out (also said of the vaginal canal).

perétél → PRÉTÉL.

peréwa (*M*) **1** courageous/reckless person, adventurer. **2** reckless, inconsiderate, thoughtless.

péréx (*infr*) → PÉRÉK.

pérfék (*D*) perfect.

pérféksi (*D*) perfection.

pérféksionis (*D*) perfectionist.

pérféksionisme (*D/E*) perfectionism.

pérféksionistik (*E*) perfectionistic.

pérféktif (*D gram*) perfective.

kepérféktifan perfectivity.

pérforasi (*D*) perforation.

pérforator (*D/E*) perforator.

performa, pérformansi and **pérformens** (*E*) performance; → KINERJA. *Tapi sayangnya – politiknya kurang cantik.* But unfortunately his political performance was not too great.

pergajul → BERGAJUL.

pergam 1 various species of pigeons, *Carpophaga* and *Ducula spp.* **2** (*- hijau*) green imperial pigeon, *Ducula aenea. - bodas/laut/putih* pied imperial pigeon, *Ducula bicolor. - bukit/gunung* mountain imperial pigeon, *Ducula badia. - raja* Christmas Island imperial pigeon, *Ducula whartoni. - tarut* blue-tailed imperial pigeon, *Ducula concinna.*

perganda → PROPAGANDA.

pergandering (*D ob*) meeting; → RAPAT II.

pergat (*D*) frigate.

pergedél (*D*) minced meat. *- daging* minced meat patty. *- jagung* corn fritter.

pergi 1 to go (away). *-!* go away! **2** to depart, leave. *Silakan - dulu; saya akan menyusul.* Please leave first; I'll catch up to you. **3** to go out, leave the house, be away from the house. *sudah -* gone, left; not at home, out. **4** (*euph*) (*- untuk selama-lamanya*) to pass away, die. *- balik* a) (to go) to and fro, back and forth. b) to come and go. *- berbelanja* to go shopping. *- datang* a) (to go) to and fro, back and forth. b) to come and go. *- duduk* to go and sit. *- haji* to make the pilgrimage to Mecca; → NAIK *haji. - ke darat* to go to Jakarta (said by inhabitants of islands near the port area of Jakarta). *- kerja* to go to work. *- lés* to take lessons (with/from), study (with). *- liburan* to go on vacation. *- makan* to go to eat. *- mandi* to go for/to take a bath. *- melihat* to go and see. *- mencari* to go and get. *- menghindar* to run for safety, take to one's heels. *- mengikut* to go with, follow. *- merantau* to migrate to another place (to seek one's fortune, etc.). *- minum-minum* to go out for a drink. *- perang* to go to war. *- pulang* round trip; → PULANG *pergi. - ronda* to (go on) patrol. *- tak kembali* to pass away. *- turné* to make a tour of inspection.

sepergi after/upon leaving/departing. *~nya* after he/she left.

bepergian to go on a trip, travel, be away (from home). *- ke Hongkong untuk urusan bisnis* to be away on business, go on a business trip to Hong Kong.

memergikan 1 to send away; to discard. **2** to drain (water).

kepergian 1 departure. **2** trip, journey. **3** (*euph*) death.

pemergian (a lengthy) trip, tour, journey.

pergok (*J/Jv*) **bepergok(an)** to meet (by accident).

memergok(i) [and **mergokin** (*J coq*)] **1** to detect, find out, discover. **2** to meet (by accident), run into. *Di Fiji dipergokinya sebutan angka dari satu sampai sepuluh yang serba mirip dengan yang terdapat dalam bahasa Jawa.* In Fiji he discovered that the numbers from one to ten are similar to those found in Javanese.

tepergok [and **kepergok** (*coq*)] **1** caught (red-handed)/in the act, discovered. **2** met by accident. **ketepergokan** being caught red-handed.

pergol and **pergul** (*D*) gilding, gilt; silver-plated.

memergol to gild to silver-plate.

pergola (*E*) pergola.

pergul → PERGOL.

perhadering(an) (*D ob*) meeting; → RAPAT.

perhal → PERIHAL.

perhub (in acronyms) → PERHUBUNGAN.

peri I 1 condition, nature, character(istic), disposition; → PERIHAL. *menceritakan – kemanusiaan* to tell s.t. about mankind. **2** way, manner, fashion, behavior, -wise. *betapa -(nya)?* how, in what way? *Betapa -nya membuat kué ini?* How does one make this cake? *- yang layak bagi manusia* proper human actions. **3** (*cla*) event, affair, occurrence, happening, incident. *jika tuan sesuatu – (ob)* if s.t. should happen to you. *- hidup* living conditions. *- jam* clock-wise. *- kehidupan* life. *- kelakuan* line of conduct. *- kemanusiaan* humanity; human history. *- laku* behavior. *- loncéng* clockwise.

peri II (*cla*) word.

berperi to speak.

memerikan 1 to describe, depict, tell. *Dia ~ ranjau itu terbuat dari 186 gram bahan peledak dan pecahan-pecahan logam yang tajam.* He described the mine as made of 186 grams of explosives and sharp metal shrapnel. *tidak dapat diperikan lagi* indescribable, beyond description. **2** to define.

terperikan *tidak ~* inexpressible, indescribable.

perian description. *Dalam buku ini terdapat ~ mengenai sifat dan kebiasaan pribadi beberapa tokoh terkenal.* In this book are found descriptions of the characteristics and personal habits of several well-known figures.

pemerian description, definition.

peri III (*Pers*) fairy, benevolent spirit.

peria I (*- pahit*) a bitter gourd, i.e., a type of edible gourd with a bitter taste and a slightly nubbly skin, *Momordica charantia. sudah tahu – pahit* to have learned from bitter experience, have learned s.t. to one's cost.

peria II → PRIA.

periai → PRIAYI.

perian large section of bamboo (used to carry water). *mengisi - bubus* a useless job, fruitless task. *Suaranya seperti - pecah.* He has a harsh/grating voice.

periang auspicious moment/season for carrying s.t. out.

peribadi → PRIBADI.

peribahasa proverb, saying, adage.

peribudi (*cla*) virtue, goodness.

peribumi → PRIBUMI.

peridi (*Skr*) prolific, fertile (of animals).

périfér (*D*) peripheral.

périferal (*E*) peripheral; → PINGGIRAN.

périféri (*D/E*) periphery.

perigel → PRIGEL.

perigi well, shaft (usually lined with bricks or stone, for obtaining water from an underground source). *lupak jadi -* to achieve (a great) success (such as, a poor man who becomes rich), be a great hit. *- mencari timba* the girl does the courting. *- buta* dried-up well (one which no longer produces water). *- wakaf* a well made available to the public.

perih (*Jv*) smarting, a sharp and stinging pain; → PEDIH.

memerihkan to smart, cause a sharp and stinging pain.

keperihan 1 smart, sting, sharp pain. **2** affected by pain, (to cry out) in pain.

perihal 1 event, circumstances, incident, happening. **2** condition, nature, character(istic). **3** concerning, regarding; (in letterheads) re, as to, about.

perihatin → PRIHATIN.

périkarditis (*D/E*) pericarditis.

perikeadilan justice. *citarasa -* sense of justice. *- pidana* criminal justice. *- politik* political justice. *- sosial* social justice.

perikemanusiaan humanity; → PERI I. *berdasarkan -* humanitarian. *perbuatan di luar -* inhumane act.

berperikemanusiaan human, humanitarian, humane. *perbuatan yang ~* human/humane act(ion). *tidak ~* inhuman, inhumane.

periksa (*Skr*) **1** examination, inspection, investigation; (scientific) research; (legal) hearing. *datang untuk - (coq)* to come for a medical examination. **2** (*Jv*) to know, understand. *kurang - a)* I don't know for sure, not that I know of. b) inconsiderate, without motivation. *salah -* improper, unbecoming. *usul -* investigation, examination, check. *tidak dengan usul -* without proper investigation. *- mayat* post-mortem, autopsy, coroner's inquest. *- silang* cross-check.

memeriksa 1 to check, inspect. *~ kembali* to recheck. **2** to examine/study/look at carefully in order to learn about/from, look over. **3** to investigate, inquire into, question (a witness), hear (a case). *~ pesakitan dan saksi-saksi* to question the accused and the witnesses. *diperiksa sebagai saksi* questioned as a witness. *sedang diperiksa* being questioned, under investigation. **4** to control, observe, watch. **5** [at the beginning of a sentence/judgment in a civil suit] taking cognizance of (the fact that). **6** to audit.

memeriksai (*pl obj*) to check, inspect, examine, etc.

memeriksakan 1 to examine/check, etc. for s.o. else. *Tolong periksakan karangan ini, saya tidak sempat.* Please check this composition for me; I don't have the time. **2** to have (o.s. or a part of the body) examined. *Si anak itu sebaiknya diperiksakan pada seorang dokter anak-anak.* It would be a good idea to have the child examined by a pediatrician. *Ibu ~ adik di rumah sakit.* Mother had my younger sibling examined at the hospital. Mother took my younger sibling examined to be examined. *Ia ke hospital hendak ~ matanya.* He went to the hospital to have his eye examined. *~ diri ke dokter* to have a medical examination, get a check-up. *Suzzana sudah ~ diri ke dokter ahli kandungan, konon masih bisa membuahkan anak.* Suzzana has been examined by a gynecologist; it's said that she can still bear children.

terperiksa s.o. under examination, the one investigated.

pemeriksa 1 (*~ buku*) auditor. *~ intéren* internal auditor. *~ keuangan* comptroller. **2** investigator, examiner, inspector. *~ ayat* coroner. **3** controller (in certain contexts). **4** (*leg*) cross-examiner.

pemeriksaan [and **peperiksaan** (*Jv*)] **1** examination, inspection, assay. *~ balik* counter check. *~ buku* audit, auditing. *~ dengan sinar tembus* X-ray examination. *~ kendaraan* check-up of cars (in slalom test). *~ korupsi* investigation into corruption. *~ minyak bumi* (*petro*) crude assay. *~ pendahuluan* (*leg*) preliminary investigation; → PRAPERIKSA. *dalam ~* under investigation. *guna menjalani ~* in order to be investigated, for investigation. *hasil ~* examination result(s). **2** cross-examination, interrogation, questioning. **3** check, check-up. *~ badan sebelum terbang* preflight check. *~ keséhatan (secara) menyeluruh* general check-up. **4** audit. *~ akhir* postaudit. *~ akuntan* accountant's investigation. *~ awal* preaudit. *~ buril* desk audit. *~ mayat* autopsy, postmortem. *~ pembukuan* auditing. *~ perkara* (*leg*) hearing. *~ saksi* examination of witnesses. *~ lapangan/setempat* field audit. *~ ulang* reexamination.

periksawan (*Skr neo*) inspector, investigator.

perilaku behavior. *~ mandiri* self-reliance. *~ profésional* professional behavior.

berperilaku to have (a certain) behavior, conduct o.s. *Bagaimana ~ yang baik pada rakyat, ini penting.* How to conduct o.s. before the public is important. *pribadi yang ~* a well-behaved person.

perimbon → PRIMBON.

périméter (*D*) perimeter.

perimpen → PRIMPEN.

perimpin (*naut*) bolt-rope; rope edging on sails.

périnatologi (*E*) perinatology.

perinci detailed, specified; → RINCI.

memerinci to itemize, detail, specify/spell out (in detail), break down, go into details.

terperinci itemized, detailed, specified (in detail), broken down, complete. *secara ~* in detail. **keterperincian** itemization, specifying (in detail), breaking down.

pemerincian and **perincian 1** details, items. *~ lebih lanjut* further particulars/details/information. **2** description, breakdown. *~ tugas* job description.

perincis (*J/Jv*) **memerinciskan** to specify.

perincisan specification(s), specs.

perincit sun-bird; → KELICAP.

perindu *buluh* – a piece of bamboo with slits cut in it so that when hung in trees it emits a musical tone, k.o. aeolian harp, wind chime. *seperti buluh –* charming, sweet (voice).

pering I stinking, to stink (like *petai* or a urinal).

pering II (*Jv*) bamboo; → AUR I, AWI, BAMBU, BULUH. *– tali* k.o. bamboo, *Gigantochloa apus. – ori* k.o. bamboo, *Bambusa bambos. – tutul* spotted weavers' bamboo, *Bambusa textilis.*

peringgan (*cla*) border, frontier, limit; → HINGGA.

Peringgi → FERINGGI.

peringgitan (*Jv*) to show/bare one's teeth.

peringkat 1 stage, grade, level, standard. **2** rank, rating. *ditentukan oléh –* to be determined by ranking. *Anwar Anas bukanlah figur – atas.* Anwar Anas is not a top-ranking figure. *menduduki – kedua* to be the runner-up; → *menduduki* URUTAN *kedua. pembicaraan – atas* summit talks. *– kehidupan* standard of living. *– krédit* credit rating.

berperingkat in stages, phased.

memeringkatkan to divide up into stages; to categorize.

pemeringkat rating. *perusahaan ~* rating agency.

pemeringkatan ranking, rating, categorizing.

perintah 1 order, command, instruction. *atas –* a) by order of. b) warrant. *surat –* warrant. **2** (religious) instruction, direction. **3** rule, regulation (from higher-ups). *– administrasi* administrative order. *– éksékusi* (*leg*) writ of execution. *– hakim* court order. *– halus* a gentle hint (from a higher-up). *– harian* (*mil*) order of the day. *– jabatan* administrative/official order. *– jalan* marching orders. *– lanjut* further orders. *– pembatalan* countermand. *– pembayaran* payment instruction/order. *– pembayaran blanko* clean payment instruction. *– pembayaran kepada bank yang ditunjuk oléh pihak penjual* payment order to the bank designated by the sellers. *– penangkapan* warrant for (s.o.'s) arrest. *– penegasan* confirmatory order. *– pengusiran* expulsion order. *– pindah* marching orders. *– témbak di tempat* order to shoot on sight. *– tetap* standing order. *sepuluh – Tuhan* the Ten Commandments.

seperintah to obey all the rules/laws (of one's parents, etc.).

memerintah 1 to (give an) order, command, order s.o. around. **2** to govern, rule. *meréka yang ~* the rulers, those who govern. *meréka yang diperintah* the ruled/governed. *~ adalah melihat ke depan* gouverner, c'est prévoir.

memerintahi 1 to govern, rule (a country). **2** to give instructions to.

memerintahkan 1 to order, command, instruct. **2** to rule, govern, administer.

terperintah subjected, dominated.

keperintahan (*Min*) government (as an institution).

pemerintah government, administration (in particular, the officials who make up the executive branch of the government and their policies and principles; often capitalized in this meaning). *~ Agung dan Badan-badan ~ Tertinggi* Supreme Government and Highest Government Agencies. *~ bayangan* shadow government. *~ berdaulat* sovereign government. *~ bonéka* puppet government. *~ daérah* [Pémda] Provincial Government. *~ dalam pengasingan* government in exile. *~ darurat* emergency government. *~ gotong-royong* mutual-aid government, i.e., a national coalition government (as was suggested by the *PKI*). *~ interim* interim/caretaker government. *~ kediktatoran* dictatorial government. *~ konco* satellite government. *~ kota* [Pémkot] municipal government. *~ lokal* local government. *~ mandiri* self-government. *~ negara* national government. *~ pelarian* government in exile. *~ peralihan* interim government. *~ provinsi* [pémprop] provincial government. *~ Pusat* the Central Government (of the Republic of Indonesia) seated in Jakarta, (in the U.S.) the federal government. *~ setempat* local government. *~ sipil* civil authorities (as opposed to the military). *~ tandingan* counter-government. *~ yang berdasarkan démokrasi* a democratic government. *~ yang berkuasa di dalam negeri* home government. *~ yang bersih* a clean/noncorrupt government. **kepemerintahan** (*mod*) government.

pemerintahan 1 government (as an institution), system of government. **2** the administration. *sewaktu ~ Présidén Johnson* during the Johnson administration. *tokoh-tokoh di luar ~* nongovernmental leaders/figures, leaders outside the administration. *~ dalam negeri* civil service, the bureaucracy. *~ umum dan otonomi daérah* [PUOD] general administration and regional autonomy. *~ yang bersih dan berwibawa* a clean and authoritative administration.

période (*D*) **1** period (of time). **2** term (of political office). *– lanjutan* continuing period of time. *– setelah perang dingin* post-cold war period.

pemériodean periodization.

périodik (*D*) periodic(al). *secara –* periodically.

périodisasi (*E*) periodization.

périodisitas (*D*) periodicity.

périodontal (*D/E*) periodontal. *penyakit –* periodontal disease.

périodontologi (*D/E*) periodontology.

perioritas → PRIORITAS.

perirana (*cla*) music; sounds.

perisa delicious.

perisai (*Tam*) **1** shield. **2** armor, i.e., the metal plating on guns, vehicles, etc. **3** peltate. **4** scutellum. *- baja* steel armor. *- diri* self-defense. *- gulung* (*euph*) condom.
    berperisai iron-clad, armored.
Periska Tani and **Periskatani** [Persatuan Istri Karyawan (Départemén) Pertanian] Association of Employee Wives of the Department of Agriculture; the acronym means: To develop the welfare of farmers' communities.
périskop (*D/E*) periscope.
peristiwa (*Skr*) **1** episode, event, happening, affair, historical fact. *sekali –* (it happened) once, one day (it happened that ...). **2** phenomenon. *– 5 Augustus '90* the August 5, 1990 Affair: Bandung Institute of Technology student demonstrations to prevent Interior Minister Rudini from giving a lecture on the *P4 II* to freshmen on campus; six students were imprisoned as a result. *– Cikini* the unsuccessful attempt to assassinate President Soekarno in Cikini, Jakarta in 1957. *– 17 Oktober '52* The October 17, 1952 Affair, a show of force by the army with the aim of exerting pressure on Parliament. *– hukum* (*leg*) juristic fact. *– Ketapang* interethnic rioting that took place in Ketapang, Jakarta on November 22, 1998. *– Madiun* The Madiun Affair: September 1948 armed rebellion by the *PKI* against the government in Madiun, East Java. *– Sambas* interethnic conflict between Dayaks and Madurese in Sambas, West Kalimantan beginning on January 19, 1999. *– Semanggi* demonstrations on November 11, 1998, in Semanggi, Jakarta against the MPR's *Sidang Istiméwa* [SI]. *– Tiga Selatan* The Three Souths Affair: in 1960 the regional war authorities [Peperda] of South Sumatra, South Kalimantan, and South Sulawesi ordered the suspension of all *PKI* activities in their respective provinces. *– Trisakti* the incident on May 12, 1998, in which four students were shot by members of the military outside Trisakti University. *– yang tidak dapat disingkiri* unavoidable circumstances.
    berperistiwa historic, eventful.
    mem(p)eristiwakan to phenomenalize.
    pemeristiwaan case (*mod*). *cara ~* case method.
perit I (*J*) *burung –* a finch species; → PIPIT I.
perit II → PRIT *jigo*.
perit III sudden stinging pain; → PEDIH, PERIH.
péritonitis (*E*) peritonitis.
periuk (cooking) pot, a type of round earthenware, metal or glass (cooking) vessel; → KUALI. *besar – besar keraknya* those who have plenty of butter can lay it on thick. *– mengumpat belanga* the pot calling the kettle black; → MALING *berteriak maling. – api* (explosive) shell, bomb, mine, hand grenade. *– api laut* sea mine. *– belanga* earthenware. *– gandar* ball bearing. *– nasi* rice bowl as a symbol of livelihood. *– tiris* s.o. who can't keep a secret.
periwil → PRIWIL.
perjaka (*J*) **1** young/unmarried man. **2** virginity (of a man).
    keperjakaan virginity (of a man).
Perjan → PERUSAHAAN (*Negara*) *Jawatan*.
perji → FARAJ.
perjurit → JURIT, PRAJURIT.
perjuta [perjuangan bersenjata] armed struggle.
perkakas 1 apparatus, tools, implements, utensils, instruments; → ALAT I, INSTRUMÉN, PERABOT. **2** (*joc*) (male or female) sex organ; → ALAT *kelamin. – bedah* surgical instruments. *– cap/cétak* printing equipment. *– dapur* kitchen utensils. *– makan* dinnerware. *– menulis* writing materials. *– perang* munitions. *– perbéngkélan* shop tool sets. *– rumah* furniture, household goods. *– tenun* loom.
    be(r)perkakas equipped; provided with tools, etc.
    memperkakasi to provide with equipment, equip.
    perkakasan all k.o. equipment/tools, etc.
pérkamén (*D*) parchment.
perkansi → PAKANSI.
perkapita (*E*) per capita.
perkara (*Skr*) **1** affair, matter, concern. *Lupakan saja dulu – hutangnya yang belum selesai itu.* Just forget about his unsettled debts. **2** (*leg*) lawsuit, case. *dapat –* to be involved in a lawsuit. *habis –!* that's it, no problem! *Saya tahu duduknya –.* I know

the ins and outs of the matter. *Letaknya – begini.* It's like this. This is the way it is. **3** because of, on account of, concerning. *– wanitalah meréka berdua itu berkelahi.* It was because of a woman that they fought. *– bandingan* (*leg*) an appeal. *– belakang* a) unimportant. b) a matter for later concern, s.t. that can be put off until later. *– dagang* business matters/affairs. *– gugatan* (*leg*) civil action, lawsuit. *– pemerasan* extortion. *– perdata* (*leg*) civil case. *– pidana* (*leg*) criminal case. *– sengkéta* civil action. *– sepélé* s.t. trivial/unimportant. *– sipil* (*leg*) civil case.
    be(r)perkara 1 to litigate, go to court. *~ pada zaman sekarang ibarat memasuki jalan tanpa ujung.* To go to court nowadays is like going on a road without end. *kedua belah pihak yang ~* (*leg*) the two litigating parties, the litigants. *~ perdéo/tanpa biaya/secara cuma-cuma* (*leg*) to sue in forma pauperis, sue as an indigent person. **2** litigating. *pihak-pihak ~* the litigants.
    memperkarai (*leg*) to bring a case about, sue over.
    memperkarakan 1 to bring (a matter) before the court. **2** to make a case of (an issue). **3** to sue s.o.
    terperkara to be sued.
    pemerkaraan indictment.
perkasa (*Skr*) **1** brave, valiant, courageous. **2** powerful, mighty. **3** violent, forcible. *gagah –* courageous, brave, bold; strong, powerful, forceful.
    memperkasai to rape, molest.
    keperkasaan 1 courage, spirit. **2** power, might. **3** force, violence. **4** virility.
perkat → PEREKAT.
perkedél (*D*) minced-meat ball; → PERGEDÉL. *– daging* minced-meat patty. *– jagung* corn fritter. *– kepiting* crab cake.
perkejut (*cla*) → (TER)KEJUT.
perkelang (*cla*) Siamese title.
perkéwuh → PAKÉWUH.
perkici rainbow lorikeet, *Trichoglossus haematodus*.
pérkolasi (*D*) percolation.
pérkolator (*D/E*) percolator.
pérkoper (*D ob*) salesman; → SALESMAN.
perkosa 1 violent. **2** force, violence.
    mem(p)erkosa 1 to rape (a woman). **2** to violate/transgress (a law).
    perkosaan 1 rape (of a woman). *pelaku ~* rapist. *~ dengan rayuan* seductive rape, rape by seduction. *~ karena adanya dominasi* domination rape. *~ sadis* sadistic rape. **2** (*~ hukum*) violation (of a law), transgression.
    pemerkosa [derived from a hypothetical form *memerkosa*] **1** rapist. **2** violator, transgressor.
    pemerkosaan [derived from a hypothetical form *memerkosa*] rape, raping. *melakukan ~ terhadap korban* to rape the victim.
pérkusi (*D*) percussion.
pérkusionis (*E*) percussionist.
perkutut 1 turtledove, *Geopelia striata*. **2** (*coq*) penis.
perlahan slow; → PELAN. *dengan –* slowly, softly.
    perlahan-lahan 1 easy! steady! **2** little by little. **3** soft (of the voice).
    memperlahankan 1 to slow down. **2** to turn down (the volume), lower (one's voice).
perlak I (*D*) varnished (of shoe leather), lacquered. *kain –* lacquered/varnished canvas. *kulit –* patent leather.
perlak II (*M*) garden.
perlak III rubber sheet put under bed sheet.
perlan → PELAN.
perlaya (*Jv*) **1** dead. **2** to die.
perlemén (*Mal*) parliament.
perléng (*D J*) **memperléng** to extend. *Kartu penduduk lu udé diperléng apé belon?* Has your resident's card been extended yet?
perlénté chic, stylish, elegant. *Dia mémang seorang –.* He's a real clotheshorse.
    keperléntéan elegance, stylishness, chic.
perléntéh and **perlintih 1** loafer, idler, tramp. **2** criminal; thief.
perli 1 playful, sportive; ironical, wry. **2** teasing, flirting.
    memerli to flirt; to tease.
    perlian teasing.
perlina (*Skr?*) vanished into thin air, gone, lost.

perling I various species of starling, *Aplonis spp. burung* – glossy tree starling, *Aplonis strigatus.*

perling II teperling shining (of the eyes), glittering, sparkling.

perlintih → PERLÉNTÉ.

perlip (*D coq*) 1 in love, enamored. 2 sweetheart, darling, one's love.

  perlip-perlip and **perlipan** to flirt.

  perlipan flirting.

perlit (*D*) perlite, a volcanic glass.

perlonco → PELONCO.

perlop (*D*) 1 leave, furlough. 2 to be on leave.

  memerlopkan to give s.o. a leave, furlough.

perlu (*A*) 1 must, should, have/ought to. *Mau tidak mau kita – menunggu di sini sampai ia datang.* Whether we like it or not, we have to wait here till he comes. *– diingat bahwa ...* it should be remembered/borne in mind that ... *tidak –* there's no need to, one doesn't have to. *beliau tidak – ...* he doesn't have to ... 2 necessary, needed, required, important (for some purpose). *Surat keterangan ini dibuat untuk dipergunakan di mana –.* This document has been drawn up to be used where needed/required. *Ini tidak –, jangan kaubawa.* This is unimportant/not needed; don't bring it. *tak ada –nya* there's no point in, it serves no useful purpose. 3 – (*akan/dengan*) to require, need, want, be in need of. *Ia – (akan) uang.* He needs money. *Peraturan ini – (dengan) penjelasan.* This regulation requires clarification. *– di sini* (*coq*) I need it myself. It's for me. *– untuk* for (the purpose of), earmarked/destined for. *Pemungutan derma itu – untuk mendirikan mesjid.* The collection of donations is earmarked for building a mosque. 4 (in Islam) compulsory, obligatory; *opp* SUNAH. *sembahyang lima waktu itu –* it is compulsory to pray five times (a day).

  perlunya *Apa ~?* and *~ apa?* Why? For what reason? For what purpose? Why bother?

  perlu-perlu urgently needed. *perabot rumah yang ~* urgently needed furniture.

  seperlunya in so far as needed, as far as there is need, to the extent necessary. *Ia bersedia memberi bantuan ~.* He was prepared to give help to the extent necessary.

  seperlu-perlunya *yang ~ saja* the (barest) necessities.

  memerlukan 1 to need, require, call for. *Pada umumnya meréka tidak ~ bantuan uang, melainkan bantuan tenaga ahli.* In general, they don't need financial aid but rather help in the form of experts. *Meréka lebih ~ pakaian daripada makanan.* They need clothing more than food. *Ini ~ tindakan cepat.* This calls for quick action. 2 to consider/think it necessary/important/useful, feel the need to. *Banyak orang yang ~ datang untuk melihat gerhana matahari.* Many people felt the need to come and watch the solar eclipse. 3 to consider necessary, make s.t. compulsory/obligatory. 4 to make compulsory/obligatory, require. *~ pelajaran bagi anak-anak meréka* to make education compulsory for their children.

  keperluan 1 a must, an obligation. *Cinta kepada tanah tumpah darah suatu ~ bagi bangsa yang merdéka.* Love for one's native soil is a must for an independent nation. 2 importance, interest. *~ bersama* collective/joint interest. *bagi/buat/untuk ~ in/on* behalf of, in the interest of. 3 need, necessity. *Ada ~ apa?* What do you need? How can I help you? *barang-barang ~ hidup sehari-hari* necessities of life, everyday needs. *~ kantor* a) office supplies/equipment. b) stationery. 4 s.t. intended; intention, plan. *Saya ada ~ lain.* I have other things to attend to.

perlup I (*D coq*) engaged (to).

perlup II (a screw that) won't bite.

perlus teperlus stepped into (a hole), sank into (the mud, etc.). *– baru menutup lubang* to bolt/lock the barn door after the horse is stolen.

permadani (*O Jv*) carpet. *disambut dengan – mérah* to be given the red carpet treatment. *– yang menutupi seluruh lantai (kamar)* wall-to-wall carpeting.

permai I beautiful, pretty, nice, charming.

  kepermaian beauty, charm.

permai II (*cla*) queen, princess; → PERMAISURI.

permaisuri (*Skr*) queen, princess.

permak (*D*) altered.

mempermak 1 to alter (clothes). 2 to rebuild (a house), convert (one type of building into another); to reorganize. 3 to beat s.o. up/black and blue. 4 to transform. *Euis harus bersedia dipermak ...* Euis had to be willing to be transformed into a ... (in a film shooting).

  permakan s.t. which has been altered/rebuilt.

  pemermakan [derived from a hypothetical *memermak*] alteration (of clothes).

perman → FIRMAN.

permana I (*Skr*) number; amount.

  tepermanai calculable, countable. *tidak ~* incalculable (of numbers), limitless. *kekayaan matérial yang tidak ~ yang tersimpan di puncak-puncak gunung hingga dasar lautan* incalculable amounts of material wealth hidden from the mountain tops to the bottom of the sea.

permana II (*Jv*) careful, circumspect.

pérmanén (*D*) 1 permanent, everlasting. 2 permanent wave, perm.

  mempérmanénkan to give s.t. a permanent character, make s.t. permanent. *Pasar Seni Rupa Ancol akan dipérmanénkan.* The Ancol Art Fair will be made permanent.

pérmanénsi (*D*) permanence.

pérmanganat (*D*) permanganate. *– kalium* potassium permanganate.

permasan (*cla*) nobility, aristocracy; → KAUM *ningrat*.

permata I (*Skr*) jewel, gem. *seperti cincin dengan –* to be well matched. *– lekat di pangkur* out of place. *– belantara* (*lit*) "jewels of the jungle," i.e., a poetic reference to orchids. *– hati/mata* the apple of one's eye. *– nila* sapphire.

permata II [Pertemuan Melalui Télepon Anda] conference call (a telephone service).

permatang bund, mountain ridge, dune, sand hill; → PEMATANG.

permati 1 vital, key, critical. 2 absolutely final.

  memermati(kan) to finalize, make s.t. final.

pérméabel (*E*) permeable (to a fluid).

pérméabilitas (*E*) permeability.

permén I (*D*) peppermint (lozenges) (packed in a long narrow tube), candies. *minyak –* peppermint oil. *– batuk* cough (suppressant) tablets/drops. *– karét* chewing gum. *– strong* strong peppermint.

Permén II and **Per-Mén** → PERATURAN *Menteri.*

Perméndagri [Peraturan Menteri Dalam Negeri] Minister of the Interior Regulation.

Perménkés [Peraturan Menteri Keséhatan] Minister of Health Regulation.

Perménpén [Peraturan Menteri Penerangan] Minister of Information Regulation.

Permésta [Perjuangan semesta] Charter of Universal Struggle, signed by 51 local leaders in Sulawesi demanding full autonomy for the four eastern provinces in the late 1950s, linked with the *PRRI*; the movement which followed this charter.

Permias → PERSATUAN *Mahasiswa Indonésia di Amérika Serikat.*

permil (*E*) per mil/thousand, pro mille.

permili → FAMILI.

permisi (*D*) 1 consent, permission, leave. *Saya minta – ...* I asked permission to ... 2 with your permission; pardon me, excuse me (asking permission to say s.t. or to leave). *–, Bu, boléhkah saya duduk di sini?* Excuse me, ma'am, may I sit here? *–, saya mau pulang dulu, ya.* I'm sorry/Excuse me, I'm leaving now. 3 *minta – to* say good-bye, take one's leave. *Minta – dulu, Pak.* I have to leave now. 4 absent (with permission). *Yang tidak masuk lima orang, mangkir dua dan – tiga orang.* Five persons didn't come in: two failed to show up (without previous notification), and three were absent with permission.

  mempermisikan 1 to ask for (annual/sick, etc.) leave. 2 to permit, allow.

permisif (*E*) permissive. *masyarakat –* a permissive society.

permosi (*coq*) → PROMOSI.

pernah I 1 (in an affirmative sentence) (at least) once (in the past), used to, have/has (plus past participle). *Ia – ke sana.* He has been there. *Saya sudah – ke Pulau Bali.* I've been to Bali. 2 (in negative sentence and in questions) ever. *belum –* never yet, not yet up to this point. *tidak –* never. *tak – tak tekor* to suffer from a chronic shortage of money.

pernah II (*J/Jv*) (family) relationship, kindred. – *apanya?* what's his relationship (to you)? – *paman* to have s.o. as one's uncle, to be a nephew to.

   kepernah to be related to s.o. (as brother/nephew, etc.).

pernak-pernik → PERNIK-PERNIK.

pernama → PURNAMA.

pernékel → PERNIKEL.

pernél → FLANÉL.

perni (C) k.o. vessel for water.

pernik (*J*) **1** little things. **2** little beads. *banyak* – and **pernik-pernik** fussy things, do-dads, gewgaws, nonsense. *Givenchy selalu membuat skétsa yang to the point tanpa banyak* – *tetapi toh berkesan anggun.* Givenchy always made sketches to the point without a lot of fuss but yet making an elegant impression. *Mahasiswa itu enggan bergelut dengan not balok dan* –*.–nya.* Students are reluctant to wrestle with musical notes and all that nonsense. –*.–* *kehidupan di rumah susun* all the little problems of living in an apartment building. *Penyanyi rock ini rupanya sudah meninggalkan pernik-pernik yang menggantung di léhér, lengan, dan kepalanya.* It seems that rock musicians have given up the do-dads that used to hang on their necks, arms and heads. *tanpa banyak* – *lagi* without further ado.

pernika → PERANG *éléktronika.*

pernikel (*D*) coated with nickel, nickel-plated.

pernis (*D*) varnish. – *kuku* nail polish.

   mem(p)ernis to varnish, apply varnish to. *kursi yang dipernis* a varnished chair.

   pernisan varnished.

perogol memerogol to rape (a woman).

perohong hole (in wall).

   terperohong gaping (of holes).

peroi crumbly, brittle.

péroksida (*D*) peroxide.

péron (*D*) station platform. *karcis* – platform ticket (permitting one to go onto the platform).

peronyok terperonyok 1 crumpled (of cloth/paper). **2** (sat/slept) hunched over.

perop (*D*) **1** cork (of bottle); stopper (of bottle). **2** *topi* – safari hat.

peropot → PROPOT.

perosok mem(p)erosokkan to plunge (s.t. into).

   terperosok [and **keperosok** (*coq*)] to sink rapidly, plummet, plunge; sunken/plunged/plummeted. *Indéx Saham Gabungan terperosok 18 poin.* The Composite Stock Index plummeted 18 points. ~*nya pesawat Airbus A-300 ke dalam lumpur* the plunging of an Airbus A-300 into the mud.

perosot (*J*) **memerosot** [and **merosot** (*coq*)] **1** to drop, fall. **2** to decline, decrease, become low(er); → ROSOT. *Harganya merosot.* Prices fell. *Moralnya anak-anak zaman sekarang ini agak merosot.* Young people's morality have fallen somewhat nowadays.

   memerosotkan 1 to cause/make s.t. drop/fall. **2** to decrease, lower/reduce/cut prices.

pérot (*Jv*) (of the mouth) awry, twisted to one side; → ÉROT I.

   memérot [and **mérot** (*coq*)] to twist (the lips) to one side (a gesture of dislike/contempt/disbelief).

perotés → PROTÉS.

perpati → MERPATI.

perpatih (*cla*) **1** chief. **2** the legendary founder of Minangkabau law.

perponding (*D*) *pajak* – property/real estate tax. *tanah* – land handed down from (Indonesian) fathers to sons.

pérporasi (*E*) **mempérporasi** to perforate, punch (a hole in a ticket).

Perprés [Peraturan Présidén] Presidential Regulation.

Perpu [Peraturan (Pemerintah) Pengganti Undang-Undang] (Government) Regulation in Lieu of Law.

perpus clipped form of **perpustakaan.**

pérs (*D*) the press (newspapers/magazines, etc.). – *asing* foreign press. – *delik* offense made by the press against press laws. – *got* yellow/gutter press. – *mahasiswa* student press. – *réaksionér* reactionary press.

persaben (*S*) (common in Bandung, when brushing off beggars) sorry (I can't give you anything).

persada 1 (*Skr? cla*) platform, dais. **2** delightful place, pleasure ground; garden of Eden; → PANCAPERSADA. **3** center, rallying point. *di* – on the altar (of the fatherland). – *tanah air* native soil/country. **4** group (of nations).

Persagi [Persatuan Ahli-Ahli Gambar Indonesia] an arts organization (1938–42).

persangga (*Pers cla*) **1** parasang, an ancient Persian measure of length, about 3¼ miles. **2** limit (of the earth).

persasat (*Jv*) **1** like, as. **2** as if/though.

Persatwi [Persatuan Tenaga Wanita Indonésia] Indonesian Women's Labor Association.

persegi square; → SEGI. **2** *méter* – 2 square meters. *empat* – *panjang* oblong.

   pemersegi squaring.

persekot (*D*) **1** down payment, cash advance, deposit. **2** prepayment.

   mem(p)ersekoti 1 to give an advance to, pay s.o. in advance. **2** to have sex with before marriage.

   mempersekotin (*J*) to have sexual intercourse with s.o. before marriage. *Nonong sudah dia persekotin.* He had sex with Nonong before they were married.

perselah (*D*) result(s); a report of the result(s).

persén I (*D*) **1** present, gift, reward (given to a subordinate). **2** tip.

   mem(p)erséni to give s.o. a present/tip, reward s.o.

   persénan present, tip; gift.

persén II (*D*) percent, %. *seratus* – 100 percent. *dinyatakan dalam jumlah* – proportionally.

   persénan percentage.

   kepersénan percentage.

perséntase and **perséntasi** (*D*) percentage.

persépsi (*D*) **1** perception. – *ancaman* feeling of being threatened. **2** collection (of a debt).

perséptif (*D*) perceptive.

perséro I → SÉRO I.

Perséro II → PERUSAHAAN (*Negara*) *Perséroan.*

persétan (*coq*) go to hell!, damn it! (exclamation to denote anger or hatred).

   mempersétan(kan) to damn, send to hell.

persetua → PERISTIWA.

persih (*cla*) clean, neat; → BERSIH.

pérsik (*D*) peach.

persil te(r)persil protruding, sticking out (of one's eye/a kernel from a fruit which has burst open/a tooth from the gum/one's breast from a dress), bulging.

pérsil I (*D*) lot, parcel (of land), plot; premises.

Pérsil II (*D*) bleaching powder (from the brand name of a Dutch bleaching powder).

persis (*D*) exactly/precisely (like); (a) perfect (fit). *Anaknya* – *ibunya.* The child is exactly like her mother; → MIRIP. *jam tiga* – exactly three o'clock, three o'clock on the dot.

   sepersis as precise(ly) as. ~ *mungkin* as precisely as possible.

   persisnya to be precise/exact.

Persit KCK → PERSATUAN *Istri Tentara Kartika Chandra Kirana.*

perslah → PERSELAH.

persnéléng and **persnéling** (*D*) gear, transmission (of car). *ganti/oper* – to change gears. *masuk (ke)* – *tiga* a) to be in high gear. b) in a state of high efficiency, at top speed. *pegangan* – shifting knob. *pindah* – *ke rendah* to shift down. *tungket* – (*J*) reverse (gear). – *atrét/mundur* reverse (gear). – *otomatis* automatic transmission. – *satu/kedua/ketiga* first/second/third gear.

person (*D*) (private) person. *berjumpa secara* – to meet in person/face to face.

persona I (*L*) **1** (*gram*) person. – *kedua/ketiga/pertama* second/third/first person; → NARA. **2** person, individual. – *nongrata persona non grata.* **mempersona-nongratakan** to declare s.o. persona non grata.

persona II → PESONA.

personal (*E*) personally.

personalia (*D*) **1** personal data/information/details. **2** personnel. *kepala* – head of personnel.

personalitas (*D*) personality.

persona non grata (*L*) persona non grata.

mempersonanongratakan to declare s.o. a persona non grata.

personawi (*infr*) personal. *unsur* – personal element.

personél and **personil** (*D*) personnel, staff. *urusan* – a) personnel affairs. b) personnel department.

personifikasi (*D*) personification.

mempersonifikasikan to personify.

pemersonifikasian personification.

pérspéktif (*D*) perspective. *dalam – historis* in historical perspective.

perstèk → VERSTÉK.

pérsuasi (*D*) persuasion.

mempérsuasi to persuade.

pérsuasif (*E*) persuasive.

pertal (*D ob*) **memertal** to translate.

pertalan translation.

pertala (*cla*) magic steed.

pertama (*Skr*) 1 (the) first. *cétakan* – first edition. *untuk – kali(nya)* and *untuk kali* – for the first time. 2 primary. *yang* – the former (*opp* of the latter). *yang – sekali* the very first. *kerugian* – primary damages.

pertama-tama first of all; first(ly), in the first place; above all. ~ *di waktu pagi* first thing in the morning.

mempertamakan to give s.t. first priority.

Pertamina → PERUSAHAAN *Pertambangan Minyak dan Gas Bumi Negara.*

pertanda I executioner, hangman.

pertanda II → TANDA.

Pertasikencana [(*hari*) Pertanian, koperasi, dan keluarga rencana] Farmers, Cooperatives and Family Planning Day.

pertepél (*D*) portfolio.

Pertiwi (*Skr*) 1 the earth. *Déwi* – the earth goddess. *Ibu* – motherland, fatherland, native soil/country. 2 name of the women's association of the Department of the Interior.

pertu → PERAWAN *tua.*

pertua (*ob*) elderly people (held in high esteem); → TUA.

pertusis (*E*) pertussis, whooping cough.

peruak (*ob*) **terperuak** wide open (of one's mouth/a wound, etc.).

peruan (*Hind naut*) yard arm (of a mast/flagpole). – *gema* sonic depth finder.

peruang I *ilmu* – (*cla*) magic art of creating a cavity of air around one's body and thus escaping from drowning; → RUANG.

peruang II (*cla*) torture of sentence to death by fastening the prisoner to a pole and pouring boiling oil over his head until he is dead.

pérubalsem (*D*) Peruvian balsam, i.e., resin from the Peruvian balm tree used as an emollient for skin wounds.

perudang *burung* – redshank, *Totanus calidris.*

perugul rapist; → PEROGOL.

memerugul to rape.

perui → PEROI.

peruk memeruk(kan) to stuff s.t. (into).

terperuk (*J*) stumbled (into a hole).

perum I (*naut*) sounding lead. *membuang* – to sound, fathom. – *arus* drift lead. – *berat* deep-sea lead. – *gema* echo sounder. – *tangan* hand lead.

memerum to sound, fathom.

pemeruman sounding.

perum II [*perumahan*] housing.

Perum III → PERUSAHAAN *Negara Umum.* **mem-Perum-kan** to convert ... into a Public/State Corporation.

Perum Asabri → PERUSAHAAN *(Negara) Umum Asuransi Sosial ABRI.*

Perum Astèk → PERUSAHAAN *(Negara) Umum Asuransi Sosial Tenaga Kerja.*

Perum Husada Bakti → PERUSAHAAN *(Negara) Umum Husada Bakti.*

Perumisasi conversion into a *Perum*. – *PJKA akan lebih luwes*. The conversion of the *PJKA* into a state corporation will be smoother; → PERUMKA.

Perumka → PERUSAHAAN *(Negara) Umum Keréta Api.*

Perum Pegadaian → PERUSAHAAN *(Negara) Umum Pegadaian.*

Perumpél → PERUSAHAAN *(Negara) Umum Pelabuhan.*

Perum Perumnas → PERUSAHAAN *(Negara) Umum Perumahan Nasional.*

Perum Peruri → PERUSAHAAN *(Negara) Umum Percétakan Uang Républik Indonésia.*

Perum PFN → PERUSAHAAN *(Negara) Umum Perusahaan Film Negara.*

perumpung → GLAGAH *prumpung.*

Perum Taspén → PERUSAHAAN *(Negara) Tabungan Asuransi Pegawai Negeri.*

Perumtél → PERUSAHAAN *(Negara) Umum Télékomunikasi;* (now replaced by *PT Télkom Indonésia*).

perun heap of trash/waste matter, etc. for burning. *puntung* – charred wood.

memerun 1 to burn for the second time the trunks and branches left charred after the first burning in preparing a newly felled area of jungle. 2 to burn trash.

pemerunan 1 burning of trash. 2 place where trash is burned.

perunggu bronze.

perungus passionate, quick/short-tempered, fiery.

perunjung seperunjung(an) the distance from the tips of the fingers of the arms stretched high above the head down to the toes.

perupuk I a k.o. rush, *Lophopetalum spp., Hemigyrosa longifolia.*

perupuk II wooden cymbals.

Peruri [Percétakan Uang Républik Indonésia] Indonesian National Mint.

perus I stern, grim.

perus II → PERAS-PERUS.

perusa (*Skr*) willful, domineering, headstrong.

memerusa (*cla*) 1 to compel, force; → MEMAKSA. 2 to rape (a woman); → MEMPERKOSA. 3 to annoy, disturb; → MENGGANGGU.

perusda → PERUSAHAAN *daérah.*

perusi → TERUSI.

perut I 1 abdomen, belly. 2 fuselage, ramp. *Ratusan penerjun bagaikan lebah-lebah nampak keluar dari – Hércules C-130.* Hundreds of paratroopers like bees were seen coming out of the belly of the Hercules C-130. 3 stomach. *mengisi* – to fill one's belly. – *nya keroncongan* his stomach is rumbling (with hunger). *–nya bertambah besar*. She's pregnant. *membawa* – to visit s.o.'s house just to eat. 4 intestines, entrails. 5 (*M*) uterine family, tracing descent from the same maternal grandmother. *buruk* – to be sick, sickly, ailing. *buta* – a stomach so insensitive that one can eat lawful and unlawful food (such as pork). *cuci* – a) laxative. b) to open one's bowels. *duduk* – pregnant. *dengan seénak* – to do whatever one pleases/likes; → *dengan seénak* UDEL. *isi* – a) intestines, bowels, guts. b) character, nature, disposition. c) contents (of a truck, etc.). *Truk sampah menuangkan isi –nya di tempat pembuangan sampah*. Dump trucks were unloading their contents at the dumping grounds. *Lapar –nya*. He's hungry. *mandi lénggang* – ceremonial bathing of pregnant woman in the seventh month of pregnancy. *tali* – intestines, viscera. – *panjang sejengkal* to feel disappointed. *tak berkelipat* – (*M*) cannot keep a secret. *tiba di* – *dikempiskan, tiba di mata dipicingkan, tiba di dada dibusungkan* (*M*) unjust treatment, double standard (treating one person harshly but another person leniently). *tepuk* – *tanya seléra* look before you leap. *seperti* – *rotan* said about s.o. useless. – *ayam* k.o. small round cakes. – *besar* a) stomach. b) (*coq*) pregnant. – *betis* calf (of leg). – *bumi* bowels of the earth. – *buntu/buta* appendix. – *gembung* swollen stomach (due to intestinal gas). – *gendut* potbelly. – *jala* tripe. – *kaki* calf (of leg). – *kapal* hold (of ship); → PALKA. – *karét/karung* (*coq*) to be a glutton. – *laut* bottom of the sea. – *meloya* queasy. – *memilin-milin* (to suffer) from indigestion/gastric upset. – *muda* intestines. – *pulas* indigestion. – *padi* ear of rice. – *panjang* intestines. – *pesawat* cargo hold of aircraft. – *rotan* a useless person. – *sapi* tripe.

seperut (*M*) of the same maternal grandmother. *"Saudara-saudara ~-sedarah, selamat datang!"* "Ladies and Gentlemen, Kinsmen and Kinswomen, of the same maternal grandmother, welcome!"

berperut 1 to have a belly/stomach. 2 big-bellied, potbellied. *Padi sudah ~.* The ears of rice are already filled. *~ karét* to be a big eater, glutton.

memeruti to remove the entrails of, gut.

perutan entrails of slaughtered animals; → JEROAN.

perut II small reel of thread.

pérvérsi (D) perversion.

Perwalan → PERSATUAN *Wanita Lembaga Administrasi Negara.*

perwangsa (in Lombok) nobility.

perwara (*Skr ob*) *biti* – ladies-in-waiting of queen or princess. *candi* – auxiliary temple.

Perwari → PERSATUAN *Wanita Républik Indonésia.*

perwatin (*Pal*) (title of) *adat* chief; → (PER)BATIN.

perwira I (*Skr*) [Pa] (army) officer. *–Administrasi* [PAAD] Administration Officer. *– Angkatan Laut* [PAL] Naval Officer. *– Angkutan* [Paang] Transport Officer. *– Angkutan Daérah Militér* [Paangdam] Military Provincial Transport Officer. *– Bawahan* Junior Officer (of the Merchant Marine). *– Cadangan* [Pacad] Reserve Officer. *– Geladak* Deck Officer (of the Merchant Marine). *– Instruktur* [Patur] Instruction Officer. *– Intél(ijén)* Intelligence Officer. *– intéchans* quartermaster officer. *– Jaga* Duty Officer. *– Kamar Mesin* Engine room Officer (of the Merchant Marine). *– Keséhatan* [Pakés] Health/Medical Officer. *– mancanegara* overseas officer. *– Menengah* [Pamén] Field-grade Officer (colonels, lieutenant-colonels, and majors). *– Pelaksana* [Palaksa] Executive Officer. *– Pembantu* [Paban] aide. *– Penghubung* Liaison Officer. *– pengukur* surveyor officer. *– Penyerah Perkara* Officer who turns a case over to the court when ready for trial. *– Perbekalan* Supply Officer. *– Perhubungan* [Pahub] Communications Officer. *– Pertama* [Pama] Company-grade Officer (captains and lieutenants). *– Petugas* Duty Officer. *– Pikét* Sergeant of the Guard. *– Polisi* Police Officer. *– Provos* Provost Marshall. *– Remaja* Junior Officer. *– rohani* chaplain. *– samapta* stand-by officer. *– Satu* a) [Pa-I] First Officer. b) chief Officer (of the Merchant Marine). *– Séksi* [Pasi] Section Officer. *– Sénior* Senior Officer. *– siaga* stand-by officer. *– Siswa* [Pasis] Officer in Training. *– Staf* [Pas] Staff Officer. *– Staf Umum* [Pasu] General Staff Officer. *– Téritorial* [Pater] Territorial Officer. *– Tinggi* [Pati] General-grade Officer (generals, lieutenant generals, and brigadier generals). *– Topografi* [Patop] Topographic Officer. *– Utama* [Patam] Main Officer, high-ranking officer. *– Zéni* [Pazi] Engineer Officer.

keperiwiraan (*mod*) officer.

perwira II (*Skr*) brave, courageous, valiant, heroic. *orang yang* – a courageous person. *gagah* – dauntless. *– perkasa* dauntless.

keperwiraan heroism, courage, bravery, valiance.

pes. (*abbr*) [pesawat] (telephone) extension.

pés I (D) *penyakit* – (bubonic) plague, pestilence. *– ayam* → PENYAKIT *tetélo.*

pés II (E) piece (of cloth).

pesa beam in loom for the woven cloth.

pesagi (*Jv*) → PERSEGI.

pesai berpesai-pesai (to fall) apart/to pieces; crumbling, scaling off; to be separated.

memesai to tousle s.o.'s hair.

pesak (*J*) husk, chaff, hull (of rice).

pésak gusset, gore, piece of cloth sewn in a garment to strengthen or enlarge it.

pesaka → PUSAKA.

pesakéh (*Bal*) head of a *subak* board.

pesam tepid, lukewarm.

pesam-pesam ~ *kuku* lukewarm.

memesamkan to heat until lukewarm.

pesamuan (*Bal*) conference; *cp* PASAMUAN. *– agung* working conference. *– sulinggih* conference of Hindu priests.

pesan I 1 order, command, instruction. **2** message. *– sponsor* a message from our sponsors. **3** order, commission. **4** testament, (last) will. *– terakhir* last will and testament. **5** appeal. *– pengiklanan* advertising appeal.

berpesan 1 to instruct, tell (s.o. to tell s.o. else), send a message. **2** to have an order put in. **3** to make/draw up a will. **4** to advise.

memesan 1 to (place an) order, book, reserve. *habis dipesan* to be (fully) booked up (of a hotel). *Kamar-kamar yang ada di Yogya seluruhnya telah habis dipesan untuk tiga hari sebelum dan sesudah gerhana terjadi.* Hotel rooms in Yogya were all

booked up for three days prior to and after the solar eclipse. **2** to instruct, order. ~ ... *agar* ... s.o. to ...

memesani to give an order/instruction to s.o., order from s.o., deliver a message to s.o.

memesankan 1 to place an order for; to make a request for delivery of; to send for. ~ *hotél* to make hotel reservations. ~ *tempat* to book/reserve a seat/place. **2** to order s.o. (to do s.t.).

terpesan ordered. ~ *habis* fully booked up, reserved.

pesanan 1 order, commission. *atas – pesanan* on request, custommade. *kapal-kapal* ~ *dalam negeri* domestic order of ships. ~ *melalui pos* mail order; to order through the mail. ~ *percobaan* trial order. ~ *tertunggak/tunda* back order. **2** message. ~ *pribadi/tertulis* a personal/written message. **3** the goods ordered, the order, s.t. ordered. ~ *saya belum datang* my order hasn't arrived yet.

pemesan 1 booker (of films). **2** the person/party ordering/placing an order, ordering agent. **3** purchaser, buyer, customer.

pemesanan ordering (of goods). ~ *tempat* (advance) booking. ~ *tikét* ordering tickets. *mengadakan* ~ *60 kamar* to reserve 60 hotel rooms.

pesan II → PESAN-PESAN.

pesanggem (*Jv reg*) **1** forest farmer. **2** one who buys forest produce wholesale or in large quantities.

pesanggrahan → PASANGGRAHAN.

pesangon (*Jv*) lump sum (paid to s.o. who does not receive a pension), severance pay. ~ *pindah* moving expenses.

pesan-pesan a poisonous centipede, *Poecilotheria sp.*

pesantrén (*Jv*) Islamic boarding school (mostly located in rural areas). *pondok* – Islamic boarding school; → PONDOK, SANTRI.

pesara I (*M*) graveyard, cemetery.

pesara II → PASAR I.

pesasir (D) **1** passenger (of a ship); → PASASIR. **2** (*J*) theatergoer; customer of a *warung*; → PASASIR.

pesat I quick, fast, speedy, swift, rapid. *dengan sangat –nya* at full speed.

pesatnya suddenness, speed.

memesat to make rapid progress/headway, speed up.

memesatkan 1 to hurry up with, proceed with, get on with. **2** to hasten, speed up.

kepesatan speed, headway, swiftness, rapidity.

pesat II k.o. boat.

pesawat 1 apparatus, appliance, tool, machine, device. *dijalankan dengan* – machine-operated. *ilmu* – mechanics (as a science). **2** (air)plane, aircraft. *Tiga – Afghanistan membom sebuah désa Pakistan.* Three Afghani planes bombed a Pakistani village. **3** (telephone) extension. *– 250* extension 250. **4** (radio/television) set. *– dua méter* (CB sl) amateur radio. *– sebelas méter* (CB sl) citizen's band radio. **5** an endless strap or band made of leather or other material for transferring motion from one wheel/pulley to another. *tali* – transmission belt. *– akrobatik* stunt plane. *– amulan(s)* ambulance plane. *– ambifi* amphibious plane. *– angkasa (luar)* space ship/vehicle. *– angkut* transport plane. *– angkut prajurit* troop carrier. *– antariksa ulang-alik* space shuttle. *– antariksa yang bersenjata/tak berawak* armed/unmanned space vehicle. *– antikapal selam* antisubmarine aircraft. *– baling(-baling)* piston/propeller plane. *– bécak* (*coq*) the DC-3 plane. *– berbadan lébar* wide-bodied plane. *– bermesin dua/ganda* twin-engine aircraft. *– bermesin satu* single-engine aircraft. *– bersayap putar* helicopter. *– bis/bus udara* airbus, i.e., a short- or medium-range subsonic jet passenger aircraft. *– bolak-balik antariksa* space shuttle. *– buru sergap* fighter interceptor. *– cabang* extension (the device). *– Capung* the Beachcraft (airplane). *– capung dom* (*coq*) helicopter. *– darat* land plane. *– darat air* amphibious plane. *– férry/féri angkasa* space shuttle. *– foto* camera. *– halo-halo* a) telephone. b) loudspeaker. *– induk* command module. *– intai* reconnaissance plane. *– jét* jet plane. *– kapal induk* carrier-borne aircraft. *– komérsial* commercial aircraft. *– kristal* crystal receiver. *– langsung* (of a telephone) main number. *– latih(an)* trainer, training plane. *– latih dengan dua kursi duduk* two-seat trainer. *– layang* glider. *– layang gantung* hang glider. *– mata-mata* spy plane. *– non-Garuda* an aircraft used by *Merpati* or *Sempati* Airlines, exclusively used for domestic flights. – *pancargas* jet plane. – *patroli antikapal selam* antisubmarine patrol craft. – *pelatih* trainer, training plane. – *pelémpar bom (penyelundup)* dive bomber. – *peluncur* glider. – *pembom* bomber. – *pembom berawak/jarak jauh/malam/selundup/supersonik antarbenua/ tempur* manned/long-distance/night/dive/supersonic intercontinental/fighter plane. – *pemburu* fighter plane. – *pemutar* (laserdisk, etc.) player. – *pencegah/pencegat* interceptor. – *pendarat* landing vehicle. – *pendarat di bulan* lunar module/landing vehicle. – *penempur* military aircraft. – *penerima* receiver, radio set. – *pengangkut* transport aircraft. – *pengebom* bomber. – *pengeras* amplifier. – *pengintai (tanpa pengemudi)* (pilotless) reconnaissance plane. – *penggerak* driver. – *pengisap debu* vacuum cleaner. – *penumpang* passenger plane. – *penumpang jét berbadan lébar* wide-bodied jet plane. – *penumpang komérsial* commercial airliner. – *penyerang* attack plane. – *penyergap* interceptor. – *radio* receiver, radio set. – *ruang angkasa* space ship/vehicle. – *ruang angkasa berawak* manned space ship. – *ruang angkasa bola-balik* space shuttle. – *sayap putar* helicopter. – *sayap tetap* fixed-wing aircraft. – *sayap tunggal* monoplane. – *sekoci* outrigger plane. – *serang* interceptor. – *siluman* stealth plane. – *stasiun angkasa luar* outer-space station. – *Stol* STOL, Short Take-Off and Landing aircraft. – *supersonik serbaguna* multipurpose supersonic aircraft. – *tak berpilot* and – *tanpa penerbang* pilotless plane, drone. – *tambangan/tambang ruang angkasa* space shuttle. – *télepon* telephone (the device). – *télepon pencetan* pushbutton phone. – *télepon tanpa kabel* cordless phone. – *télévisi* TV set. – *télévisi berwarna* color television set. – *télévisi hitam-putih* black-and-white television set. – *télévisi warna* color television set. – *tempur* fighter (plane). – *tempur baling/yang berpangkalan di daratan* propeller/land-based fighter (plane). – *tempur dalam keadaan siap terbang* combat-ready fighter (plane). – *tempur jenis Mirage/Phantom* a Mirage/Phantom fighter (plane). – *terbang* (plane). – *terbang air* seaplane. – *terbang bermesin dobel/ganda* twin-engined aircraft. – *terbang bersayap/dengan sayap tetap* fixed-wing airplane. – *terbang bersayap putar* rotary-wing airplane. – *terbang carter(an)* charter plane. – *terbang pengangkut* transport plane. – *terbang pengintai* reconnaissance plane. – *terbang penumpang* passenger plane. – *terbang radar pemberi peringatan dini* and – *terbang dengan radar pengintai* AWACS. – *terbang supersonik* supersonic aircraft. – *terbang untuk membawa bom atom* plane carrying an atomic bomb. – *tinggal landas tegak lurus* STOL, Short Take-Off and Landing aircraft. – *turboprop bermesin dua* twin-engined turboprop plane. – *uap* steam engine. – *udara* airplane. – *udara sipil* civil airplane. – *ultraringan* ultralight aircraft. – *wésel* railroad switch.

peséban (*Jv*) audience hall, i.e., the place where visits to high officials take place. – *agung* main audience hall.

pesegi → PERSEGI.

peséh → KELÉSÉH-PÉSÉH.

pések (*Jv*) pug, flat (of nose).

pesemendan (*M*) all the wives of the men who belong to the same tribe.

pesemuan (*Jv*) *adat* house.

pesen → PESAN.

pésér a copper coin worth half a cent.
  sepésér a half-cent coin. ~ *buta pun tak punya* to be penniless/ broke. *tidak mempunyai ~ (buta) pun* to be completely broke.

peséro → PERSÉRO I, SÉRO I.

pését → PÉSÉK.

pesi (*M*) **1** too cool. **2** very pale, anemic.

pesiar to take a trip, go on a trip/an excursion. *kapal* – excursion ship, tourist ship. – *pengantén baru* honeymoon.
  berpesiar to (have a) picnic, eat outdoors/in the open air.

pésimis (*D*) **1** pessimist. **2** pessimistic.
  kepésimisan pessimism. *perundingan Jenéwa di tengah ~ dunia* the Geneva talks amid worldwide pessimism.

pesimisme and **pésimisme** (*D/E*) pessimism.

pésimistis (*D*) pessimism. *Sajak-sajak itu menggambarkan ~*. Those poems depict pessimism.

pesindén (*Jv*) female singer with the *gamelan* orchestra.

pesing stinking/smelling (e.g., the smell of urine). *bau* – smelling of urine.

pesirah (*Pal*) headman of a *marga*.

pesisir I (*Jv*) **1** sands, shore, coast, beach. **2** coastal, coastal region.
  pesisiran 1 shoreline. **2** coastal region.

pesisir II → PASASIR.

pésmol k.o. fish dish with *acar* on top.

péso (*Sp*) peso (the unit of currency).

pésok I dent; → PESUK.
  memésokkan to dent.

pésok II (*Jv*) sagging (of a woman's breasts).

pesona (*Pers*) **1** love potion, philter. **2** incantation, charm, magic spell, words used as a magic charm. *ilmu* – black-magic lore. *kena* – charmed, *tukang* – a) practitioner of black magic. b) (*ob*) demagogue.
  mem(p)esona(kan) 1 to chant/cast a spell over, enchant. **2** to have s.o. cast a spell on s.o. else. **3** to attract, enchant, allure, fascinate. **4** fascinating, enchanting.
  terpesona and **tepesona 1** spellbound, fascinated, enchanted. **2** attracted, captivated. **keterpesonaan** fascination, attraction, being attracted.

pésong I (*J*) slanting, sloping; wry.

pésong II (*M*) turning (to the left or right).
  berpésong to turn, revolve.
  memésong to turn (to the left or right), move/edge toward.
  terpésong 1 changed direction, deflected, off course. **2** deviated, turned aside (from a topic), missed the mark.

pésta (*Port*) party, feast. – *bulan Oktober* Oktoberfest (in Munich). – *dansa* ball, dance. – *gila* masked ball. – *karya* work camp (of *taruna bumi*). – *kawin/nikah* wedding party. – *maskara* masked ball. – *pora* orgy, bacchanal, wild party. **berpésta pora** to have a wild party. – *séks* orgy. – *taman* garden party.
  berpésta(-pésta) to have a party (feast), celebrate.
  meméstai and **mempéstakan** to celebrate s.t., give a party for.
  pésta-péstaan feasts and festivities, parties.

pestaka (*Skr*) **1** divining manual; → PRIMBON. **2** *ilmu* – black magic, voodoo; → GUNA-GUNA. **3** (*cla*) (blessed or ominous) magic power (in an inanimate object).

pesti → PASTI. **memestikan** inevitable; → MESTI.

péstipal → FÉSTIVAL.

péstisida (*E*) pesticides.

péstol → PISTOL.

pesuk hole, dent, hollow space; perforated (of cloth/mats/roofs), dented (of a hat, etc.).
  berpesuk-pesuk to have holes/dents in it; full of holes/dents; dented, perforated.
  memesukkan to dent, make a dent in, make a hole in, perforate, pierce.

pesuruhjaya (*Mal*) commissioner. – *Tinggi* High Commissioner.

pesut k.o. freshwater dolphin, *Orcaella brevirostris/fluminalis*.

pet (*Jv onom*) sudden blackout (of electricity), sudden darkness; *opp* BYAR.
  pet-petan (it becomes) dark (before one's eyes).

pét (*D*) cap (with a visor).

peta [and **péta** (*coq*)] I (*Skr*) **1** map. **2** chart, plan. **3** picture. – *angin* weather chart. – *bagan* chart, outline map. – *bumi* geographic chart. – *buta* outline map (names omitted). – *dasar* base map. – *kadaster* cadastral map. – *laut* nautical chart. – *pendaftaran tanah* cadastral map. – *penyelidikan* coverage map. – *tanah* soil map. – *timbul* topographical plan (of clay), relief map. – *udara* air photographic map.
  memetakan 1 to draw/make map (of), map (out). **2** to draw a picture/diagram. *dipetakan dalam angan-angan* imagined in one's mind/thoughts.
  terpeta 1 mapped, charted. **2** pictured.
  pemeta mapmaker, cartographer; → KARTOGRAFER.
  pemetaan mapping, mapmaking, cartography.
  perpetaan weather chart.

peta II (*J*) (= **petaan**) motion (of the hand, etc. in signaling, etc.)

péta I → PETA I.

Péta II [Pembéla Tanah Air] Defenders of the Homeland, i.e., the name given to the Indonesian auxiliary troops during the Japanese occupation.

pétah 1 (– *lidah*) fluent, eloquent (of speech). **2** witty.

memétah(kan) ~ *lidah* a) to practice speaking fluently/eloquently. b) to practice reciting Arabic.

kepétahan (~ *lidah*) **1** eloquence, fluency. **2** wittiness.

petai a smelly, edible bean, *Parkia speciosa. sebagai – sisa pengait* completely useless. *menjual – hampa* to boast, brag. *– belalang* k.o. *petai, Pithecolobium spp. – cina/sélong* lead tree, *Leucaena glauca. – laut* k.o. *petai, Desmodium umbellatum.*

petak (*J*) (*main*) *– asin* (to play) hide-and-go-seek. *– kadal* children's game played with bamboo laths; → KETOK *kadal.* (*main*) *– sembunyi/umpat/umpet* (to play) hide-and-go-seek.

pétak I 1 sector of irrigated rice field (marked out by *pematang* or small dikes). *se– sawah* a rice-paddy sector/section. **2** flowerbed, seedbed, garden bed. **3** compartment, partitioned-off space. **4** cubicle (in a house or office). *rumah –* a large house divided up into separate apartments, tenement. **5** (*infr*) (sailor's) cabin. *– dinding* wall panel. *– gunung* children's game similar to hopscotch; → ÉNGKLÉ. *– percobaan* test plot. *– péta* map grid. *– tilik* check plot.

berpétak with compartments, etc.

berpétak(-pétak) 1 divided up into compartments, compartmentalized, partitioned, sectioned, in sections. **2** checkered.

pétakan parcel/plot (of land), section.

perpétakan *rencana ~* site plan (of a town or city).

pemétakan 1 breaking up into parcels, parceling out (into lots). **2** lot, parcel (of land).

pétak II (*Jv*) **1** a white blaze on a horse's forehead. **2** a hairless spot on s.o.'s skull resulting from a scar.

petaka (*Skr cla*) disaster, accident, calamity; → BENCANA. *mala –* disasters, calamities.

petakil (*Jv*) **petakilan 1** to clamber/scramble about. **2** fidgety, fidgeting. **3** full of tricks. **4** overacting.

petal (*Jv*) **memetalkan 1** to press s.t. (onto s.t.). **2** to remove/take off by pressing down on it.

petala (*Skr*) stratum, level. *tujuh – langit* the seven tiers of heaven. *tujuh – bumi* seven tiers of the earth (in Muslim cosmology).

petaling a hardwood tree, *Ochanostachys amentacea*; its wood is used for house poles and its fruits are edible.

petam bridal headband.

berpetam to wear such a headband.

petamari (*ob*) a fast ship with one or two masts.

pétan (*Jv*) to look for lice (in s.o.'s hair).

métani 1 to look for lice (in s.o.'s hair; often done by rural women sitting in a line, with each working on the hair of the woman in front of her). **2** to look closely at, examine closely. *Meréka memang sengaja ~ DPP.* They really were purposely looking closely at the Central Executive Council.

pétanan looking for lice. *perempuan yang ~* a woman looking for lice (in s.o.'s hair).

petanang (*kapur –*) k.o. plant, *Dryobalanops oblongifolia.*

petang I afternoon (originally meant from noon to sundown, but due to *Jv* influence this word is used by some to cover the time from noon until midnight); → SORÉ. *Jumat – jam 16.45* Friday afternoon at 4:45. *Hari sudah pukul 7 ketika kami tiba di San Diégo.* It was 7 p.m. when we arrived in San Diego. *sejak jam 22.30 –* since 10:30 p.m. *hari semakin – juga* it was getting late in the day. *bésok –* tomorrow afternoon. *bésok –nya* and *– ésoknya* the next afternoon. *– ésok* the next afternoon (after this day). *– hari* a) afternoon. b) late in the afternoon. *– Senin (malam Selasa)* Monday evening. *duduk-duduk minum téh – hari* to sit around drinking afternoon tea.

petangnya the afternoon/evening (of that day); *cp* NANTI *petang.*

petang-petang toward evening.

sepetang ~ *itu* that afternoon.

sepetang-petang ~ *hari ini* before dark, before evening falls. ~ *hari masih belum nampak jua.* He still hasn't shown up even though it's already dark.

sepetang-petangan the whole afternoon/evening, throughout the afternoon/evening.

memetang-metangkan ~ *hari* (*M*) to waste/kill time (chatting, etc.).

pemetang-metangkan ~ *hari* (*M*) time killer.

kepetangan to be overtaken by the afternoon, or (*Jv*) caught (out) after dark.

petang II kepetangan 1 (*cla*) k.o. secret agent, detective. *orang ~* policeman in charge of the night watch. **2** (*cla*) sly, cunning.

petang III kepetangan *ilmu ~* the art of making s.o. invisible.

pétang (*J*) divination. *ilmu –* the art of this k.o. fortune-telling. *tukang –* clairvoyant, fortune-teller.

pétangan a way of fortune-telling or clairvoyance which can tell where s.t. was lost, who the thief was, etc. *kartu ~* cards used in this k.o. fortune-telling.

petan(g)tang-petén(g)téng [and **petan(g)tang-petin(g)ting** (*J*)] to walk around/back and forth. *Banyak importir dan saudagar – menawarkan barangnya.* Many importers and merchants walked around excitedly offering their goods.

petaram (*cla*) a small woman's kris.

petarang *pukat –* a large fishnet used for fishing from a *perahu payang.*

petarangan (*J*) nest of a broody hen.

petari → PATRI.

petas I *beras –* all k.o. rice; → BERAS.

petas II petasan fireworks, firecrackers.

petas III bubbling movement in water.

petatah-petitih (*M*) (to speak in) proverbs and sayings. *Masyarakat awam Indonésia merupakan masyarakat yang –.* Indonesian society is a society that speaks in proverbs and sayings.

petatang-petiting (*J*) **1** to give o.s. airs. **2** to strut about in a provocative manner. *Meréka pada – di mulut gang seraya berkaok-kaok: "Hai, Aslan, keluar lu!"* They were strutting around at the entrance to the alley shouting: "Hey, Aslan, come out, you!"

petatas sweet potato.

peté 1 → PETAI. **2** (*sl*) methyl amphetamine.

pété and **pé-té** → PUTAU(W).

peték (*Jv*) guess [only in the compound **nyolong –** (*q.v.*)].

peték-peték *ikan –* sea perch, *Ambassis spp.*

petél (*Jv*) k.o. adze.

petenah → FITNAH.

peteng (*Jv*) → PETANG II.

petengan (*Jv*) dried cassava; → GAPLÉK. *nasi –* dried cassava rice.

peténtang-peténténg (*J*) → PETAN(G)TANG-PETÉN(G)TÉNG.

peténténgan I (*Jv*) to put on airs.

peténténgan II (*J*) to run around making a big fuss about s.t. *Mengapa lu yang jadi – melihat orang yang ketiban rezeki?* Why did you get all excited when you saw s.o. hit the jackpot?

pété-pété (in Ujungpandang/Makassar) mini light trucks and minibuses, *mikroléts, bémos, opeléts.*

peterah → FITRAH I.

peteram → PETARAM.

peterana (*Skr cla*) **1** platform for princes in ruler's audience chamber. **2** dais for bride and groom. *kamar –* bridal chamber.

péterséli (*D*) parsley, *Petroselinum vulgare.*

peterum (*ob*) cartridge; → PATRUM. *obat –* cartridge powder.

pétés (*M*) to talk fluently (*esp* said of children). *– mulut* eloquent (of speech).

petét (*Jv*) **memetéti** to snap the finger lightly against (a songbird to make it sing). *Jalak berbunyi bila ingin bernyanyi. Bukan karena dipetéti atau diperintah meniru si pemerhati.* The starling makes a noise when it wants to sing, not because one snaps one's finger against it or because it is ordered to imitate the observer.

pethet (*Jv*) to graft a cutting (onto). *buruh –* cigarette-paper cutter (the person).

pethok (*Jv*) k.o. land ID card, document in support of land ownership.

peti (*Tam*) case, box, trunk, casket. *– ajaib* (*infr*) a television set. *– balut* ambulance medical kit. *– besi* a safe. *– bicara* (*ob*) phonograph. *– dingin* refrigerator. *– és* refrigerator; → KULKAS. *mem(p)eti-éskan* to shelve, put aside, freeze, put on ice. *pemeti-ésan* shelving, putting aside/on ice. *– jenazah* coffin, casket. *– kémas* container (in shipping). *memeti-kémaskan* to ship by container. *– mati/mayat* coffin. *– menyanyi (ob)* phonograph. *– mesiu* powder keg. *– ngomong/nyanyi* phonograph. *– pendingin* freezer, deep freeze. *– pengering* dehumidifier. *– Perjanjian* Ark of the Covenant. *– sejuk (Mal)* freezer; → RUANG *pembekuan. – suara* ballot box. *– uang* cash/money box.

berpeti-peti by the boxful, many boxes full.

memetikan to crate, put into boxes.

pemetian crating, putting into boxes.

petia *(ob)* attention.

    memetia(kan) to pay attention to.

petik I pluck, pick. *tanda –* quotes, quotation marks. *"dihémat" dalam tanda –* "economized," in quotes. *uji –* random sample, test sample.

    memetik 1 to pick, pluck (flowers/fruits, etc.). *~ daun muda* to "pluck" a young girl. **2** to extract, select (out of), quote, copy out (passages from a book, etc.), borrow. **3** to pluck (the strings of a guitar, etc.), strum (on), play (a guitar). *~ senar gitar* to strum on a guitar. **4** to pull (the string of a bow, the trigger of a gun, etc.), cock (a rifle). *~ picu pistol* to pull the trigger of a pistol. **5** to snap (one's fingers). **6** to switch/turn on or off (the electric current). **7a)** to light up (a cigarette). **b)** to draw on, puff (a cigarette, etc.). *~ cerutu* to smoke a cigar. **8** to strike (a match); → MEMANTIK. **9** to take (instructions) from. **10** to reap (profit). *~ untung puluhan juta rupiah* to reap a profit of tens of thousands of rupiahs. **11** *(sl)* to filch, steal. *~ sebuah bunga,* to find one's life partner. *boléh ~ angin* to hell with him! *~ bola* to jump up and catch or deflect a ball (in sports). *~ kumis* to twist one's moustache. *~ rezeki* to try one's luck. *Tapi jika musim hujan mulai tiba seperti sekarang, tiba pula saat penjual jas hujan ~ rezeki.* But when the rainy season begins, as now, the moment also arrives for the raincoat vendors to try their luck.

    memetiki *(pl obj)* to pick/pluck, etc.

    memetikkan 1 to pick/pluck, etc. for s.o. else. **2** to pick/pluck, etc. with s.t. **3** → MEMETIK.

    terpetik picked, plucked; quoted, extracted, copied out, etc. *Tidak ada ~ berita.* No news was spread; → TERBETIK.

    petikan 1 the thing picked/plucked/quoted, etc., quote; → KUTIPAN, NUKILAN. **2** trigger (of a firearm). **3** piece (of music). **4** electric switch; → SAKELAR.

    pemetik 1 picker, plucker, harvester (the machine). **2** player (of a stringed instrument). *~ gitar* guitar player. **3** trigger (of a firearm). **4** cigar-lighter. **5** electric switch. **6** *(sl)* thief.

    pemetikan picking, plucking, quoting, etc.

Petik II *– Laut* traditional ceremonial event in fishermen's communities to thank God for bestowing the blessings of the sea.

pétikut *(E)* petticoat.

petilan *(Jv)* fragment (of a *wayang* play), episode. *– wayang wong* episode from a *wayang orang.*

petiman → TIM II.

peting *(M)* device used for separating cotton from the seeds.

    memeting to separate the seeds from cotton using this device.

petinggi village head; → LURAH I. *– negara* high government official.

petir 1 thunder, thunderclap. **2** *mata –* flash of lightning. *disambar/ditémbak –* struck by lightning. *bagai – di siang bolong* and *bagaikan – di terik matahari* like a bolt out of the blue, like a bombshell. *– tunggal* a violent thunderclap.

    memetir-metir to thunder.

petis *(J/Jv)* congealed fish, shrimp or meat paste. *– udang* shrimp-paste.

    memetis to make (fish/shrimp/meat) into a paste.

petisi *(D)* petition. *– 50* the petition signed on May 5, 1980, by 50 persons, including some prominent people, which was critical of the Soeharto regime.

petitih *(M)* maxim, saying, proverb; → PETATAH-PETITIH.

    berpetitih to use a proverb.

petitum *(D leg)* relief sought.

petisiwan petitioner.

petola I *(Malayalam?) kain –* a reticulate silk fabric originating in Sind, once popular for waist-sashes.

petola II *– buntal/manis* loufah, dishrag gourd, *Luffa cylindrica.*

petopan gambling den/house.

pétor *(Port cla)* government official in out-stations, k.o. *kontrolir* or *asistén résidén.*

petri *(Jv)* **memetri** to honor. *upacara ~* (in the *Universitas Sarjana Wiyata* of the *Taman Siswa,* Yogyakarta) initiation ceremony consisting of sprinkling water from a *kendi* over the heads of the freshmen, after which they wear a *péci* and uniform.

pétrodolar *(D/E)* petrodollar. *negara-negara –* petrodollar countries.

pétrografi *(D/E)* petrography.

pétrokimia petrochemical. *industri –* petrochemical industry.

pétrol *(E)* gasoline.

pétroléum *(D)* petroleum.

pétrologi *(D/E)* petrology.

Pétromak(s) *(E)* Petromax pressurized kerosene lamp, like the Coleman lamp.

Pétruk a character in the *wayang* play with a high, long nose who serves the *Pandawa. mbah –* Javanese designation for Mount Merapi, a volcano in Central Java; the top of the mountain resembles a head with a pigtail like that of Petruk. *– menjadi Raja* to go hog-wild.

pétrus I [*penémbak mistérius*] mysterious killers, i.e., the secret marshals charged with the extrajudicial murders of the so-called *gali-gali* or habitual lawbreakers, etc., starting around 1983, mainly in the Yogyakarta area.

    mempétrus(kan) to kill. *Terdakwa A (34) dalam keributan itu mengancam ~ wartawan kalau foto dirinya dimuat di koran.* The accused A, 34, in those riots, threatened to kill reporters if his picture was put in the paper.

Pétrus II (the biblical) Peter.

pétsai *(C)* vegetable similar to mustard greens, *Brassica chinensis*; → PÉCAI.

petua(h) *(A)* **1** religious information; explanation, interpretation. **2** (stern) admonition; advice; → FATWA.

    berpetua(h) to advise on religious matters.

    mempetuai and **mem(p)etua(h)kan** to admonish; to advise.

petuk I *(Jv)* land tax receipt, document dealing with land tenure; → GIRIK.

petuk II *(Jv)* k.o. *gamelan* instrument.

petulak large wood shrike, *Tephrodornis gularis.*

petulo *(Jv)* cook made of glutinous rice flour strands.

pétungan *(Jv)* calculation.

petunia *(D) bunga –* petunia.

peturasan <turas> *(Jv)* restroom.

peturun *harimau –* black panther; → HARIMAU *kumbang.*

petus *(J)* → PETIR. *sebagai – tunggal* like a bolt out of the blue.

petut *(ob)* paralyzed, lame.

peusing *(S)* anteater.

peuyeum *(S)* fermented cassava or glutinous rice.

    peuyeuman *nenas ~* a pineapple artificially ripened with carbide; → KARBIT.

Pewarta [*Perhimpunan Wartawan (Radio dan Télévisi Indonésia)*] Indonesian (Radio and Television) Reporters Association.

péwat *(A)* difference.

    berpéwat differential.

péyang → SILUK II.

péyék *(Jv)* clipped form of **rempéyék**. *– kacang* peanut fritters, k.o. peanut brittle.

péyok and **péyot I** → PÉOK, PÉOT.

péyot II *(Jv)* twisted, awry (of edges/lines).

PGRI *(init)* → PERSATUAN *Guru Républik Indonésia.*

Pgs *(abbr)* [*Pengurus sementara*] caretaker, acting head.

ph *(init)* [*piringan hitam*] /pé-ha/ (phonograph) record.

    mem-PH-kan to record, make into a record.

Philindo [*Philippines-Indonésia*] reference to the joint Filipino-Indonesian naval maneuvers.

phinisi → PINISI. *– Nusantara* the motorized sailboat that successfully made the voyage from Indonesia to Vancouver, Canada in 1986.

phio *(C)* illegal paper currency in the form of a piece of paper on which Chinese characters and certain codes are written; widely circulated for business transactions and gambling in Chinese circles in Tanjungpinang, Riau archipelago; → PI II.

PHK *(init)* → PEMUTUSAN *Hubungan Kerja,* PÉHAKA. lay-off.

meng-PHK(-kan) to lay off (a worker).

PHK-wan dismissed laborer, s.o. laid off.

pi I clipped form of pergi.

pi II (C) stake, bet (in gambling); → PHIO. main – gambling in which the money bet is paid afterwards.

pi III (C J) 1 freshwater tortoise. 2 tortoise meat.

pi IV (D math) pi.

pia (C) k.o. flat round cake.

piadah (Pers cla) pawn (in chess).

piagam (Jv) 1 charter. 2 contract, deed. 3 record, certificate (of appreciation/participation, etc.). – Atlantik Atlantic Charter. – Jakarta Jakarta Charter; the preamble to the June 22, 1945 document which stipulated that Muslims must obey Islamic laws. It was removed from the final draft of the 1945 Constitution. – Kekaryaan Certificate of Achievement. – Penghargaan Certificate of Merit.

memiagamkan to record in a charter.

piah rempah – all k.o. spices; → REMPAH II.

piai leather fern, Acrostichum aureum.

piak I warped (of a board).

piak II side; → PIHAK.

piak III (col) a colonial coin worth 10 cents.

pial 1 cock's wattles. 2 gills (of hens and other birds).

piala (Pers) 1 a (prize) cup. 2 a glass phial/vial, goblet. – bergilir a) challenge cup, trophy. b) a girl who goes from man to man, a slut. – citra the highest honor for a national film. – ginjal a) pelvic calyx. b) calyx (of the kidney). – Thomas Thomas Cup (in badminton).

pialang agent, broker. perusahaan – brokerage firm. – asuransi insurance broker. – saham stockbroker.

berpialang to make use of a broker.

mem(p)ialangkan to buy s.t. through a broker.

pialing k.o. parakeet, Psittinus cyanurus/incertus.

pialu demam (ke)– high fever/temperature.

piama I (D) pajamas; → PIYAMA.

piama II musim – the season for starting to plant.

piancang (C) warrior.

piandel k.o. talisman.

piang I mother (of animals); → BIANG I.

piang II pastry made from sweet glutinous (white) rice.

memiang to prepare such pastry.

pianggang green, stinking rice-bug, gundhi bug, Leptocorisa varicornis; → CENANGAU, WALANG sangit.

pianggu various species of trees, Clerodendron nutans and other species. – pipit k.o. tree, Knema laurina.

pianis (D) pianist.

kepianisan piano virtuosity.

piano (D) piano. pemain – pianist.

memianokan to play s.t. on the piano.

perpianoan piano playing. negeri yang lebih maju dalam ~ a country more advanced in piano playing.

pianola (D) pianola.

piansui and pianswie (C) apoplexy, stroke.

piantan (cla) auspicious or usual time (for s.t. to occur); (period of) 24 hours, a 24-hour day, circadian; → SEHARMAL. – demam expected/usual time for intermittent malaria to recur; → PIALU. – hujan usual time for the monsoon.

piao (C) dart.

piar terpiar combed (of the hair).

piara (variant of pelihara). anak – foster child.

memiara 1 to bring up, raise. 2 to protect; → MEMELIHARA. ~ ayam to raise chickens. ~ kumis to have/grow a mustache or beard.

piaraan 1 domestic (animal). 2 bini ~ mistress, concubine; → TV II.

piarit 1 k.o. harpoon, a double-barbed fish spear. lurus sebagai – treacherous (but nice to look at). 2 antenna of an insect.

pias I a strip (of cloth/sail/land); pieces of a pandanus mat sewn together into a sail.

pias II splash, drip (of rainwater, etc.).

pias III ikan – gizzard shad, Dorosoma chacunda.

pias IV (S) pale.

pias V margin, line. – alir flow chart.

piasan marginal.

piat I 1 twisted. 2 awry; bent, crooked. – besi iron sheet.

memiat to twist (fiber/string/threads into a cord).

terpiat twisted.

piat II descendant (of the fifth or sixth generation). –.piut remote descendants.

piat III one quarter of a carat. Empat – sama dengan satu karat. Four piats equal one carat.

piatu 1 parentless; in some regions a difference is made between piatu, meaning a child both of whose parents have died, an orphan, and yatim, meaning a child one of whose parents has died, a motherless or fatherless child. 2 alone in the world, without relatives/family. anak – a parentless child, orphan. dagang – alone in a foreign place. rimba – jungle, primeval/virgin forest. rumah – orphanage. yatim – a parentless child.

kepiatuan 1 orphaned. 2 without relatives/family.

piau (C) commission agent (in Palembang).

piawai (M) 1 correct, precise, accurate, finely calibrated (of a scale). 2 clever, expert, skilled, capable. orang – an expert; → AHLI, PAKAR.

sepiawai as expert as. ~ apa pun no matter how expert.

kepiawaian 1 correctness. 2 skill, expertise. Dengan ~ seorang akuntan itu, pemerintah akhirnya bisa menyelamatkan APBN 1985-1986 itu berimbang pada angka Rp 22.825 milyar. Using that accountant's expertise, the government was finally able to balance the 1985–86 budget at Rp 22,825 billion.

PIB → PARTAI Indonésia Baru.

pica (M) take no notice of, indifferent, careless, dawdling, inattentive, negligent.

memicakan to disregard, neglect, pay no attention to.

terpica negligent.

picah → PECAH I.

picahbeling an herb, Strobilanthes crispus, whose leaves are used as a medicine for renal calculi.

picak 1 dented. 2 blind in one eye; → PÉCAK.

memicak(kan) to flatten.

pemicakan flattening.

picek (Jv) blind in one eye; → PÉCAK.

pici fez-shaped cap usu made of (black) velvet.

berpici to wear such a cap.

picik 1 narrow (of space), not wide; → SEMPIT. 2 narrow-minded. 3 (J) economical, thrifty. – memakai uangnya thrifty in the use of money.

sepicik as narrow(-minded) as.

memicikkan and memperpicik 1 to narrow, make narrower. 2 to narrow, make narrow-minded. Penghidupan di désa itu ~nya. Village life made him narrower.

kepicikan 1 narrowness. 2 narrow-mindedness. 3 lack of knowledge, ignorance. 4 to be hard up, have financial problems.

picing (M) wink, brief closing of the eye.

sepicing a wink. ~ (pun) tidak tertidur and tidak tidur ~ jua couldn't sleep a wink.

berpicing ~ mata to close one's eyes.

memicing to close (of one's eyes).

memicingkan ~ mata to close one's eyes (in sleep).

terpicing with closed eyes, fallen asleep. Matanya tiada ~ sedikit juapun. He couldn't sleep a wink.

picis I (col) 10-cent silver piece/coin.

sepicis 10-cent silver coin.

picisan 1 dimes. 2 of low level/quality, small-time. novél/roman ~ dime novel.

picis II picisan various species of ferns, Cyclophorus spp.

picit → PIJAT. keris – the Majapahit (Dongsonian) kris.

memicit to massage (by squeezing), pinch. 2 to oppress.

terpicit squeezed.

picu (Port) trigger, cock, hammer (of gun). harga – trigger price, i.e., a minimum fair price for imported goods. menarik – senjata to pull the trigger of a weapon. memetik – senapan to pull the trigger of a rifle. – semangat encouragement.

picunya the trigger, s.t. that starts the ball rolling. ~: berita penahanan 48 imigran dari Sumatera Barat. The trigger: the news about the detention of 48 immigrants from West Sumatra.

memicu to trigger, start. ~ *pecahnya peristiwa Tanjungpriok*. It triggered the outbreak of the Tanjungpriok incident.

pemicu trigger, initiator, start. *Makin kuatnya mata uang Éropa dan Jepang bisa dianggap salah satu ~nya*. The increasing strength of European and Japanese currency can be considered one of the triggers. ~ *ledak* detonator.

picung (*Jv*) breadfruit, *Pangium edule*.

PID [Politieke Inlichtingendienst] (*D col*) Political Information Service.

pidada → PEDADA.

pidak pedarakan (*Jv*) of the lowest social order. *orang-orang* – the lowest of the low, the downtrodden.

pidana (*Skr Jv*) **1** criminal. *hukum* – criminal law. **2** penalty, punishment, conviction, sentence, condemnation (for a criminal offense). – *bersyarat* suspended sentence, probation. – *badan* corporal punishment. – *denda* fine. – *hilang kemerdékaan* imprisonment. – *kurungan* detention. – *mati* death sentence/penalty, capital punishment. – *penjara* imprisonment, incarceration, prison term. *Ia dijatuhi – penjara*. He was sentenced to prison. – *penjara seumur hidup* life imprisonment. – *perampasan kebébasan/kemerdékaan* imprisonment. – *pokok* principal punishment. – *ringan* misdemeanor. – *tutupan* confinement, detention.

mempidana to condemn, convict, find guilty, sentence (a criminal). ~ *mati* to sentence s.o. to death. *dapat dipidana* punishable.

mem(p)idanakan to prosecute/bring to justice/arraign. *dapat dipidanakan* punishable, can be prosecuted, actionable.

terpidana 1 condemned/sentenced (to). **2** the condemned/convicted person, convict. ~ *mati* a person who has been condemned to death, a prisoner on death row. *Menurut sumber di Jepang, masih banyak ~ mati yang sudah lama dalam penjara menunggu éksékusinya*. According to Japanese sources, there are still many persons sentenced to death who have been in prison for a long time waiting to be executed.

terpidanakan punishable.

kepidanaan (*mod*) criminal.

pemidanaan 1 sentencing, punishment, punishing (of criminals), conviction. **2** criminalization.

pidanawan (*Skr neo*) offender, wrongdoer, criminal.

pidari → PADERI

pidato 1 speech, address. *dalam –nya tanpa téks* in his impromptu speech. **2** talk. **3** lecture. – *kampanye* campaign speech (during general elections). – *kenegaraan* state-of-the-nation address, state-of-the-union speech. – *mahkota* address from the throne (in the Netherlands), royal speech. – *pelantikan* inaugural address (of the president). – *pembélaan* defense plea. – *penerimaan* acceptance speech (of a professor). – *pengarah* briefing. – *pengarahan* key-note speech. – *pengukuhan* inaugural speech (of a professor). – *perpisahan* farewell address. – *purnasantap* after-dinner speech. – *sambutan* welcoming speech.

berpidato to make/give a speech.

mem(p)idatoi to give a speech to.

mem(p)idatokan to make a formal speech about.

pidato-pidatoan speechifying, all k.o. speeches.

pidi (*J*) **memidi** [and **midi** (*coq*)] **1** to shoot (a marble), aim. **2** to draw lots (in playing marbles).

pidia → PEDIAH.

pidsus [pidana khusus] special crimes.

pidum [pidana umum] common crimes.

pié – *kéju* cheese stick.

Piet Hitam /pit/ (a direct translation from Dutch *Zwarte Piet*) Black Peter, i.e., the black man who accompanies *Sinterklaas*.

pigi (*coq*) → PERGI.

pigimana (*coq*) → BAGAIMANA.

pigmén (*D*) pigment.

berpigmén to be pigmented.

pigméntasi (*D*) pigmentation.

pigola (*D ob*) pergola.

pigura (*D*) **1** figure, picture. **2** painting, print. **3** (picture-)frame. – *bahasa* (*gram*) figure of speech; → MAJAS, TROPE.

berpigura to be framed, have a frame around it. *lukisan ~ a* framed painting.

memigura to frame (a painting/diploma, etc.). *Di antara gambar yang dipigura itu, terdapat lukisan Pangab Jénderal Benny Moerdani*. Among the pictures already framed is a painting of Armed Forces Commander General Benny Moerdani.

pihak (*A*) **1** side, part. *Présidén Républik Islam Pakistan, Zia Ul-Haq, menegaskan –nya tidak menerima pesan dari manapun untuk disampaikan kepada Indonésia*. The President of the Islamic Republic of Pakistan, Zia Ul-Haq, explained that his side (i.e., Pakistan) had not received any message to be delivered to Indonesia. *dari satu* – one-sided; partial; unilateral. **2** one (of two or more opposing/competing groups/parties/people, etc. in a war/game/politics), (*leg*) party; (to belong to) a certain group/party, etc., be on a certain side. *Dalam perang dunia ini – yang menang dan – yang kalah sama-sama menderita kerusakan*. In this world war the victors and the losers all suffered damage. *Supaya nyata siapa-siapa – kita dan siapa-siapa – majikan...* So that it is clear just who is on our side and just who is on the side of the bosses. – *kedua* the second party. – *lawan* the opposing party. – *pertama* the first party. **3** line, side (of a family). **4** (from ...) direction(s). *Seakan-akan angin datang dari segala –*. It's as though the wind was coming from all directions; cp PENJURU. **5** viewpoint, point of view, standpoint, angle. *dari – saya* from my point of view. *di satu – ... di lain –, di satu – ... di – lain, di – satunya ... di – lainnya* and *pada suatu – ... pada – yang lain* on the one hand ... on the other hand. *Situasi seperti itu, di satu – mendorong petugas memungli, di lain – mendorong warga untuk menyogok*. Such a situation, on the one hand encourages officials to collect illegal retributions, on the other hand it encourages citizens to offer bribes. **6** *pada –* a) take the side of, side with, belong to. b) with regard to, as for, concerning. *Pada – agama meréka itu bersikap nétral*. As for religion, they take a neutral position. **7** quarters, people, office, the people in a social institution, plural indicator for human beings who work in a certain place, the ...; → KAUM. – *polisi* the police. *Malam itu pukul 21.00 beberapa – Kedubés Uni Soviét menghubungi Dirjén Protokol dan Konsulér*. That evening at 21:00 hours some staff members of the Soviet Embassy contacted the Director General of Protocol and Consular Affairs. – *atas* upper side, top (side), upper part. – *atasan* superiors. *dari – atasan* on the part of the authorities, from/on the part of the government, on high authority. – *bawah* underside, lower side, bottom. – *ibu* maternal line. – *kanan* right side. – *keamanan* security people/personnel. – *keamanan yang hilir-mudik* security people walking back and forth. – *kedua* (in a contract) the party of the second part. – *kesatu* (in a contract) the party of the first part. – *ketiga* third party, outsider, i.e., the one or those not involved in a contract. *bantahan/perlawanan – ketiga* (*leg*) opposition made (or, objection taken) by a third party. – *kiri* left side. – *kolot* a) old-fashioned people. b) the conservatives. – *lawan* the other side/party, the opposition, adversary. – *pertama* (in a contract) the party of the first part. – *ramai* the people, the masses. *mendapat persetujuan – ramai* to enjoy popular approval, to get the approval of the masses. – *sana* (*col*) the Dutch (as seen from the viewpoint of the Indonesian nationalists). – *sini* (*col*) the Indonesians (as seen from the viewpoint of the Indonesian nationalists). – *situ* (*col*) the Indos/Eurasians (as seen from the viewpoint of the Indonesian nationalists). – *teraniaya* the injured party. – *terkait* stakeholder. – *yang berperang* the belligerents. – *yang berperkara* (*leg*) a) a party to a lawsuit. b) the litigant(s). – *yang bersangkutan* the party/parties/person/persons concerned, the party/person in question, the one/persons involved. – *yang bersengkéta/bertikai* the disputants, the disputing parties. (*dari*) – *yang berwajib* (from) an authoritative source, on good authority. – *yang berwenang* the competent authorities. – *yang dirugikan* the injured/aggrieved party. – *yang dikalahkan* the losing side, the one losing (the match/suit, etc. – *yang memberi amanat* principal, mandator. –.– *yang mempunyai hubungan istiméwa* related parties. –.– *yang mengadakan kontrak* the contracting parties. – *yang terkena* the affected party. –.– *yang tidak senang kepada* ... those dissatisfied with ...

sepihak one-sided, unilateral. *aksi ~* unilateral action. *dengan ~* unilaterally. **kesepihakan** one-sidedness.

berpihak 1 to side (with), take the side (of), support one (side/party/group, etc.). ~ *kepada tanah air, salah atau benar* my country, right or wrong. **2** to go over (to one side), defect. ~ *kepada lawan* to defect to the enemy. **3** partial, biased, one-sided, tendentious. *laporan-laporan* ~ tendentious reports. *negara tidak* ~ a nonaligned country. **keberpihakan** partiality, bias. ~ *pérs pada suatu OPP merupakan langkah mundur* the press's partiality toward one of the participants in the General Election is a step backward. ~ *kepada yang benar* siding with justice, on the side of justice. *tidak* ~ impartial, unbiased, neutral. **ketidak-berpihakan** impartiality, lack of partiality.
berpihak-pihak to be divided into several parties/groups, etc.
memihak 1 to side with, be on the side of, back, support. ~ *partai yang sedang berkuasa* to back the ruling party. **2** partial, biased, tendentious. *berita* ~ a biassed news report. *tak* ~ impartial. ~ *sebelah* one-sided; partial, biased. **3** to go over/defect (to). *Ia* ~ *kepada lawan.* He defected to the enemy.
memihakkan 1 to divide into several groups/parties/factions, etc. **2** to put/lay aside; to segregate. **3** to class s.o. with (a particular party/group, etc.).
pemihakan choosing sides, siding (with), favoring. *dalam segi hiburan pun sudah terdapat* ~ *pada nilai Barat* even in the entertainment area the favoring of Western values can already be seen.
pihutang → PIUTANG.
PII I → PARTAI *Islam Indonésia*.
PII II [*Pelajar Islam Indonésia*] Indonesian Islamic Students
PII III [*Persatuan Insinyur Indonésia*] Indonesian Engineers Association.
piil → FIIL I.
pijah berpijah and **memijah** to spawn, deposit eggs or sperm directly into the water.
memijahkan to spawn s.t., hatch, bring forth (young from eggs). *Keuntungan lainnya, ikan air tawar bisa dipijahkan.* Another advantage is that freshwater fish can be spawned.
pemijahan 1 spawning, hatching. **2** spawning/hatching place, fish nursery. *tempat* ~ *bagi udang dan ikan* nursery for shrimp and fish. *Balai Budidaya Laut Lampung berhasil melakukan* ~ *ikan kakap mérah.* The Lampung Pisciculture Agency succeeded in spawning red snapper.
pijak step/trample on, put one's foot down.
pijak-pijak pedal, treadle, stirrup. ~ *kaki* doormat. ~ *pelana kuda* stirrups.
berpijak 1 to step/stand (on). *tempat* ~ foothold. *Artinya, kalau Irak kalah, ia tidak akan mempunyai lagi tempat* ~ *untuk melanjutkan perang.* That is to say, if Iraq loses, it will no longer have a foothold for continuing the war. **2** to stand firmly (on). *ABRI selalu* ~ *pada aspirasi rakyat.* ABRI always takes its stand firmly on the desires of the people.
memijak 1 to step/stand on; to set foot on. **2** to trample on. ~ *kepala* to humiliate.
memijaki to put one's foot down on, walk on.
memijakkan to put (one's foot) down on, set (foot on), trample down on. ~ *tanah* to touch the earth for the first time (a ceremony in a child's life); → TEDAK *siti*.
terpijak accidentally stepped/trod on. *matahari* ~ and ~ *bayang-bayang* midday, noon.
pijakan 1 step, tread. ~ *kaki* pedal. **2** platform, position, stepping-off point. *Dapat kita gunakan sebagai* ~ *untuk melompat lebih jauh lagi dalam pembangunan télkom di tanah air.* We can use it as a stepping-off point to jump even further in developing telecommunications in our country.
pemijak footrest, stirrup, pedal, place to step/tread on. ~ *kaki* pedal.
pemijakan trampling, stepping/treading on.
pijam → PEJAM.
pijar 1 glowing (of burning metal), blazing, red-hot. *besi* – red-hot iron. *lampu* – electric bulb, incandescent light. *mérah* – fiery red (of an angry face, etc.). **2** very hot, sizzling (of oil).
pijar-pijar borax (used by goldsmiths for melting solder).
berpijar to glow, blaze with heat.
berpijar-pijar 1 to glow; glowing. **2** to be red-hot.

memijar 1 to heat a metal till it becomes soft. **2** to glow (of s.t. heated).
memijarkan 1 to temper (steel), burn off (a mantle). **2** to glow (green and red) (of flames), burning (of a fever, hands from touching hot chilies, etc.).
pijaran ~ *api* glare, hot flames. *Gunung Soputan mengeluarkan* ~ *api.* Mt. Soputan spat out hot flames.
pemijaran annealing.
pijat to get/have a massage. *Dia langsung menawarkan kepada kita apa mau – saja atau – plus.* She immediately asked us whether we would like just a massage or a massage plus (i.e., plus sex). *tukang* – masseur, masseuse. – *(buah) dada* to get/have a body massage. – *knop* pushbutton.
memijat [and **mijat** (*coq*)] 1 to massage (with the fingers by squeezing). *Kaki saya yang keseléo itu dipijat Pak Ali.* Mr. Ali massaged my sprained foot. **2** to pinch, press, push, knead (with the fingers). ~ *bél/knop/tombol* to press/ring the bell. ~ *klakson* to blow the horn (of a vehicle).
pijat-memijat massages, massaging. *Dunia* ~ *konon kabarnya mémang telah ada sejak dahulu kala.* They say that the world of massaging has existed for a long time.
memijat-mijat to keep (on) massaging.
memijati (*pl obj*) and **memijat-mijat** to keep on rubbing, massage repeatedly.
memijatkan to massage, knead.
terpijat 1 squeezed, pinched. **2** massaged.
pijatan massage.
pemijat masseur, masseuse; → PIJITWATI.
pemijatan massage, massaging. *melakukan* ~ to massage. *Biasanya lalu dilakukan* ~ *untuk menghilangkan pegal pada otot itu.* Usually then a massage is given to relieve the stiffness of the muscle.
pijat-pijat bedbug.
pijet → PIJAT.
pijin (*E*) pidgin (language).
pijit → PIJAT. **mijitin** → MEMIJATKAN.
pijitran water bush, *Crotolaria striata.*
pijitwati masseuse, hostess in a massage parlor.
pik (*C*) eight. – *ban* 80,000. – *ban go* 85,000. – *cap* 80. – *cap go* 85. – *céng* 8,000. – *pék* 800. – *pék céng* 800,000. – *pék go* 850. – *pék go céng* 850,000. – *tiau* 8 million. – *tiau pua* 8,500,000.
pika (*E*) pica.
pikah → FIKIH.
pikap (*E*) 1 pickup truck. **2** phonograph, hi-fi.
pikat I stinging horsefly, *Tabanidae*; → CATAK. *pening* – rather dizzy. *seperti* – *kehilangan mata* desperate, at one's wits' end.
pikat II decoy(-bird); bait, lure. *daya* – attractiveness, attraction.
memikat 1 to bait, lure, decoy, catch/snare/trap birds (by using a decoy or a domesticated bird or animal as bait). **2** to allure, attract, captivate, entice; to tempt; to seduce.
terpikat 1 trapped, snared, caught, captured. ~ *hati* enchanted (with), in love (with), enamored (of); seduced, attracted, captivated. **2** attracted, interested. **keterpikatan** captivation, enchantment, interest. *Sanggupkah* ~ *anak-anak dipalingkan pada seguntingan boneka kulit bernama wayang?* Can the children's interest be turned to a cut-out leather puppet called a *wayang*?
terpikat-pikat misled, misguided, seduced.
pikatan 1 bait, lure, decoy. **2** enticement, trick to lure s.o., allurement, attraction, interest.
pemikat 1 bird-catcher, fowler. **2** bait, decoy(-bird). ~ *hati* enticement.
pemikatan enticement.
pikau I berpikauan (*pl subj*) to scream/cry out loudly in fear.
terpikau(-pikau) startled, screaming with fright.
pikau II blue-crested/Chinese button-quail, *Excalfactoria chinensis.*
piké (*D*) (*kain* –) pique (a soft fabric).
pikét (*D*) 1 picket (in a strike). **2** guard duty (*mil*). *perwira* – officer of the guard.
memikét to guard s.t.
pikir (*A*) 1 opinion, idea. **2** to think, reflect, consider. –*ku* I thought to myself. *ahli* – thinker, philosopher. *jangan banyak* – don't

worry too much. *kurang* – thoughtless, inconsiderate, rash. *pada – saya* in my opinion. *tanpa –(.-) panjang* without thinking very long about it, without a moment's thought. *– punya –* after careful consideration, after much thought. *tak habis –* can't understand/figure out. *tak habis – mengapa* ... can't stop puzzling out why ... *saya –*... I believe (that) ... *– dahulu pendapatan, sesal kemudian tidak berguna* look before you leap.

pikir-pikir to think more than once. ~ *dulu* think twice (about it)! ~ *kembali* second thoughts. *Berkurangnya dukungan internasional, terutama karena krisis yang berkepanjangan, menimbulkan ~ kembali pada pihak negara-negara yang terlibat.* Diminishing international support, especially because of the protracted crisis, has caused the countries involved to have second thoughts.

berpikir to think, reflect, meditate, ponder, muse, mull (over), be absorbed in thought, weigh, consider, figure out. ~ *12 kali* to give serious thought/consideration to s.t. *asyik ~* deep in thought. *jalan ~* train of thought. *pola ~* way/pattern of thinking. *Perlu adanya pola ~ yang filosofis.* One should have a philosophical way of thinking. *Lama ia ~ sebelum menjawab pertanyaan itu.* He thought for a long time before answering the question. ~ *masak-masak* to give some thought, think s.t. over. ~ *selayaknya* to think straight.

berpikir-pikir to weigh the pros and cons, think over. *Silakan ~ dahulu, saya sediakan waktu dua hari.* Think it over, I'll give you two days.

memikir (*usu* in the passive) *tanpa dipikir* without thinking, on impulse.

mikir (*coq*) to think. *Jangan ~ yang nggak-nggak.* Don't think about nonsense.

memikir-mikir to weigh the pros and cons.

pikir-memikir *dengan tidak ~* thoughtless(ly), inconsiderate(ly).

memikiri to think about, reflect on, ponder. *Pikiri dulu baik-baik.* Think about it carefully first.

memikirkan [and **mikirin** (*J coq*)] **1** to think about/over, concentrate on, ponder over, rack one's brains over, have s.t. in (one's) mind. *Dia ~ soal itu sebelum membuat keputusan.* He thought about that matter before making a decision. *Kaum bapak jangan hanya ~ kenikmatan séksual saja.* Men shouldn't only think about sex. *Nénék itu merasa sedih ~ nasib dirinya yang malang itu.* The old lady felt sad thinking about her bad fortune. ~ *diri sendiri* to be selfish. ~ *dalam-dalam* to think (things) through. **2** to care/bother about, take into consideration. *Tindakan itu diambilnya tanpa ~ kepentingan anak-anaknya.* He took those steps without considering his children's interests.

terpikir [and **kepikir** (*coq*)] thought (about). *Tidak ~kah oléhnya akibat-akibat apa saja dari tulisan itu?* Didn't he think about the possible consequences of that article? **2** it occurred (to s.o.), it dawned (on s.o.). *Tiba-tiba ~ oléhnya bahwa ia lupa membawa KTP-nya.* All of a sudden it occurred to him that he had forgotten to bring his Resident's Identity Card.

terpikirkan could be imagined/thought. *tak ~* unimaginable, unthinkable. *Sungguh tak terbayangkan jika perang nuklir pecah, akibatnya, kata para ahli, tak akan pernah ~ karena belum ada présédénnya.* It's really unimaginable what would happen if a nuclear war broke out; the consequences, say the experts, will never be imagined because there hasn't been a precedent.

pikiran 1 thought, idea. ~ *ini timbul dalam kepalanya.* The thought crossed his mind. *Saya mendapat suatu ~.* I have an idea. **2** opinion, reflection. *sepanjang ~ saya* in my opinion. **3** intelligence, mind. *berbalik ~* to change one's mind. *Akankah Sabry berbalik ~ sebelum dihadapkan ke méja hijau?* Will Sabry change his mind before he is brought before the court? *kacau ~* incoherent, delirious. *hilang ~* to be confused. *tajam ~* sharp, bright, smart, intelligent. *Pakailah ~mu!* Use your brains! *Tapi satu hal yang menjadi ~ yaitu* ... But one thing to think about is ... ~ *bercabang* vacillation. ~ *kusut* confused ideas. ~ *péndék* narrow-minded. ~ *séhat/waras* sound judgment/thinking, good ideas. *Kami perbuat surat keterangan ini dengan ~ yang waras.* We drew up this certificate on the basis of sound judgment. ~ *Pembaca* Letters to the Editor. *bulat ~* unanimous. *lemah/lembék ~* half-witted, mentally defective.

kurang ~ foolish, silly, stupid. *menaruh ~* to be interested (in), consider. *mencari ~* to seek a solution. *panjang ~* intelligent, sensible, wise. *pertukaran ~* exchange of ideas; debate, discussion. *sakit ~* insane, mad, crazy. *pada ~ selanjutnya* on second thought. *déwasa dalam ~* old and wise enough. ~ *tumpul* stupid. **sepikiran** to have the same opinion, be of the same opinion; → SEPAHAM, SEPENDAPAT. **berpikiran** to use one's brains, have ideas, think. *tidak ~* thoughtless. *paling tidak ~ maju* the most backward-thinking, least progressive.

kepikiran 1 to happen to think about s.t., comes to one's mind. *Saya belum ~ mau apa.* I haven't thought about what I'm going to do. **2** to worry about. *Ibu ~ anaknya pulang malam-malam.* Mother was worried about her child coming home late at night.

pemikir thinker, philosopher.

pemikiran thinking, pondering, consideration; idea, thought. *masih dalam ~* still under consideration. *pertemuan ~* meeting of minds. *Buang jauh-jauh ~ bahwa Pancasila mengancam agama.* Get rid of the idea that Pancasila threatens religion. **berpemikiran** to have ... thinking, who thinks ... *PDI harus dipimpin oléh orang ~ séhat.* The Indonesian Democracy Party should be led by s.o. with sound judgment.

pikmén → PIGMÉN.

piknik (*D/E*) **1** picnic. **2** to go on a picnic.
berpiknik to go on a picnic.

pikolo (*D*) piccolo.

piksel (*D*) low-quality coffee beans.

piktograf (*E*) pictograph.

pikuk → HIRUK *pikuk*.

pikukuh rules of the Baduy community in Banten on nature conservation.

pikul 1 load carried over the shoulder on either end of a pole. **2** unit of weight equal to 100 *kati* or about 133 pounds. *tukang – water carrier.*

berpikul-pikul several *pikuls*, by the *pikul*.

memikul 1 to carry (a load, etc.) on the shoulder. **2** to shoulder, bear, support, endure. ~ *ongkosnya* to bear the costs. ~ *risiko bersama* risk sharing. *tangan menetak/mencencang bahu ~* you have to take responsibility for the errors that you have committed. ~ *tanggung-jawab* to assume/take/take on the responsibility.

mikul ~ *duwur mendem jero* (*Jv*) to respect one's parents and ancestors, remembering the good things and burying the bad things.

memikulkan 1 to load s.t. (on an animal). **2** to make (a country) pay (reparations, etc.). **3** to apportion (expenses) (among). **4** to blame s.t. (on s.o.). **5** to impose s.t. on s.o. **6** to bear for s.o. else.

terpikul(kan) portable; bearable. *tak ~(kan)* unbearable.

pikulan 1 carrying pole, yoke. **2** load, burden.

pemikul carrier, bearer, porter. ~ *kekuasaan/prabawa-praja* person in authority.

pemikulan carrying/bearing, loading, etc.

pikun (*C J*) **1** forgetful (of an old person), senile. **2** very old.
kepikunan 1 dementia. **2** senility, old age, dotage.

pikup → PIKAP.

pikutus name of a *ceki* card.

pil I (*D*) pill, tablet. *menelan – pahit* to swallow a bitter pill. *– antidisénteri* antidysentery pill. *– antihamil* birth control pill, the pill. *– gedék* ecstasy. *– KB* birth control pill. *– kina/kinine* quinine (as a medication). *– kontraséptif* birth control pill, the pill. *– MX* a tranquillizer. *– pelangsing tubuh* diet pill. *– perangsang séks* sex pill, aphrodisiac pill. *– tidur* sleeping pill.

pil II [*pria idaman lain*] boyfriend, lover (of a married woman).

pilah (*Jv*) arranged, sorted.
pilah-pilah selective.
memilah 1 to arrange, sort, divide into groups/sections/compartments. **2** to separate, split up.
terpilah selected, set aside.
terpilah-pilah (to be) separated/divided up (into groups), (to be) split up. *Unsur staf pengajar, mahasiswa, tenaga administrasi dan alumni ~.* Elements of the teaching staff, university students, administrative employees, and alumni have been divided up into groups. *Negeri itu bagaikan ~.* It looks as if that country is splitting up.
pilahan sorting, arranging, dividing up.

kepilahan selectivity.

pemilahan 1 sorting. **2** separation, separating, splitting up. *memperbaiki cara perontokan dan ~ gabah dari kotoran* to improve the way of threshing paddy and of separating unhulled paddy from impurities.

pemilah-milahan separation, splitting up.

pilak I (*cla*) evil spirit; accursed, harbinger of evil (of people).

pilak II → PILEK.

pilang (*Jv*) a tall tree that provides timber and fodder, *Acacia leucophloea*.

pilar I (*D*) pillar, post.

  berpilar pillared, with pillars.

pilar II (in Muara Petai, Riau Province) "Caterpillar" bulldozer.

PILAR III → PARTAI Pilihan Rakyat.

pilas (*M*) *ayam* – black-beaked fighting cock with black feet and yellow-speckled feathers.

pilau (*cla*) k.o. Indian ship.

pileg and **pilek** (*Jv*) **1** (to have a) cold, (to have the) flu. **2** (*coq*) gonorrhea, the clap.

pilem → FILM.

pileuleuyan (*S*) good-bye!

pilih choose, select, pick. *boléh* – optional, elective, it's one's choice. – *bulu* to consider/take into consideration race and descent in making a selection. *dengan tidak – bulu* irrespective/without respect of persons, indiscriminately. – *kasih* a) favoritism. b) partial, biased. *tidak – kasih* a) to be unbiased/impartial. b) to stop at nothing. *tidak pilih(-pilih)* a) irrespective of (race, etc.). b) no matter what (subject, etc.), it doesn't matter (at all).

pilih-pilih 1 to choose, select, pick/single out. **2** picky, fastidious, choosy. *~ ruas, terpilih pada buku* grasp all, lose all, i.e., to try to get everything and so to lose everything.

berpilih-pilih 1 to choose/select carefully. *Dia ~ gadis untuk dijadikan istrinya.* He carefully chose a girl to become his wife. **2** to be choosy/fussy/particular/picky. **3** not (just) anyone; it's hard to find (a person) who. *~ orang yang bersedia menjadi ketua perkumpulan itu.* Not just anyone is willing to be chairman of the club.

memilih [and **milih** (*coq*)] **1** to choose, pick/single out, select, opt for. *~ bulat* to choose unanimously/without any dissenting votes. *~ kawan hidup* to pick a marriage partner, one's partner for life. *Ia minta tolong ~ hadiah.* He asked for help in selecting presents. *tidak ~* a) not shrink from (an adversary). b) not choosy, accepting (any k.o. work, etc.). *tidak ~ bulu* irrespective/without respect of persons. *banyak yang dapat dipilih* many to choose from. *kirim untuk dipilih* send (books/stamps, etc.) on approval (or, for inspection). **2** to vote (in an election, etc.). *berhak ~* entitled/qualified to vote. *yang berhak ~* the franchised (to vote), those who have the right to vote. *hak ~ dan dipilih* active and passive suffrage/franchise. *dapat dipilih kembali* eligible for reelection, re-eligible. **3** to vote for, elect. *Meréka ~nya menjadi ketua RT.* They elected him chairman of the Neighborhood Association.

memilih-milih 1 to be too choosy/picky/fastidious. **2** to select/pick some out of many.

memilihi to choose, select.

memilihkan [and **milihin** (*J coq*)] to choose/select for s.o. else. *Suami itu berusaha ~ warna yang cocok bagi istrinya.* The husband tried to choose the right color for his wife.

terpilih [and **kepilih** (*coq*)] **1** selected, chosen, picked. *Bengkulu ~ sebagai lokasi program pertukaran pemuda Indonésia-Kanada tahun 1986.* Bengkulu was chosen as the site of the 1986 Indonesian-Canadian youth exchange program. *Namanya ~ paling tinggi.* He was held in high esteem. *~ paling cantik* to be a well-known beauty. **2** elected; elect, i.e., elected to office but not yet sworn in (*usu* following the title of the office). *Présidén ~* President elect. **3** eligible (for an office, etc.). *Ia tidak ~ untuk menjadi anggota.* He was not eligible for membership. **keterpilihan** eligibility.

pilihan 1 choice, selection, pick. **2** selected, handpicked. *Anda tidak ada ~.* You have no choice. *yang diundang hanya orang-orang ~* only selected/handpicked persons were invited. *Disinilah tersedia berbagai macam buah-buahan, silakan mengam-*

bil ~. Various k.o. fruit are available here; please take your pick. *atas ~ sendiri* by choice, of one's own choosing. *Suami-istri itu tidak mempunyai anak atas ~ sendiri.* That couple is childless by choice. *Calon penatar-penatar P4 orang ~.* Prospective P4 upgraders are a select few. *~ (ber)ganda* multiple choice. *~ karangan* selected works. *~ yang tak salah lagi* the right choice. *~ lain* alternative, option. *tidak ada ~ lain, kita harus berangkat sekarang ini juga* there is no alternative; we must leave right away. *~ kosong/titik nol* zero option. *orang ~* favorite. *pemain ~* (in sports) player's player. *~ raya* (*Mal*) general elections.

pemilih 1 voter, elector. *para ~* constituency. *~.~nya* the electorate. *pendaftaran ~* voter registration. *panitia pendaftaran ~* [Pantarilih] voter registration committee. *~ perkotaan* urban voter. **2** choosy, picky, fussy. *Anak itu ~ benar.* That child is really choosy.

pemilihan 1 election. *~ babak kedua* run-off election. *~ bertingkat/berjenjang* indirect elections, elections at two removes. *~ kembali* reelection. *~ kepala daérah* regional-head elections. *~ kepala désa* [pilkadés] village-head elections. *~ langsung* direct election. *~ pendahuluan* primary (election) (in the U.S.). *~ présidén* presidential election. *~ tak langsung* indirect election. *~ umum* [pemilu] general election(s). **2** choice, choosing, selection, selecting. **3** vote, voting.

pilihanraya (*Mal*) general election(s); → PILIHAN raya. – *kecil* by-election; local election. – *negeri* state election (in Malaysia).

pilin spiral. *piuh* – twisted; twisted words, prevarication. *tangga* – spiral staircase.

berpilin 1 to turn and twist. **2** twisted (of rope), winding, spiral (of stairs). **3** distorted, crooked. *~ bagai kelindan* inseparable, cannot be separated.

berpilin-pilin distorted; crooked.

memilin 1 to twist (fiber/string/threads into cord). *~ rokok* to roll a cigarette. *~ telinga* to pull/box s.o.'s ear. *perut ~(-milin)* (to suffer from) stomach cramps (or, gastric upset). **2** to twist s.t. off.

memilin-milin 1 to keep on twisting s.t. **2** to keep on twisting/turning.

pilin-memilin to twist e.o.

terpilin twisted, turned.

pilinan twisted fringe/cord.

pemilin 1 roller. *~ rokok* cigarette roller (the person). **2** roller (the device).

pemilinan turning, twining, twisting.

Pilipina → FILIPINA.

pilis (*Jv*) **1** powder put on forehead as a pain reliever. **2** mark smeared/stuck on forehead to ward off disease.

berpilis to apply such a powder or mark.

memilis to apply this powder to s.o.

pilkada → PEMILIHAN kepala daérah.

pilkadés → PEMILIHAN kepala désa.

pilm → FILM.

pilon (*J*) ignorant, stupid. *be(r)lagak* – to play dumb, pretend ignorance.

pilong (*Jv*) blind; → BUTA I.

pilot I (*D*) pilot (of an aircraft). – *héli(kopter)* helicopter pilot.

berpilot piloted, with a pilot. *tak ~* pilotless, drone; → PESAWAT tak berpilot.

memiloti to pilot (an aircraft). *Di awal tahun 1978, Donald sempat kepergok saat membawa sejumlah narkotik dalam pesawat yang dipilotinya.* At the beginning of 1978, Donald was caught carrying narcotics in the small plane he was piloting.

pilot II (*E*) pilot, serving as an experimental or trial undertaking prior to full-scale operation or use. – *proyék* pilot project. **memilotproyékkan** to run/set up as a pilot project. *Oléh I S, temu karya yang dipilotproyékkan di Yogyakarta, tahun depan akan diperluas ruang lingkupnya di propinsi lain.* Next year I. S. will expand the scope of the working meeting set up as a pilot project in Yogyakarta to other provinces.

pilu I 1 (very) sad, moved, touched, affected, sorrowful, unhappy; *opp* RIANG. **2** anxious, troubled; → SEDIH, TERHARU. – *hati* melancholy.

memilukan 1 moving, affecting, touching. **2** sad, pitiable, deplorable. **3** to sadden, make sad. *peristiwa yang ~ a* sad event.

kepiluan sadness, sorrow; anxiety; tenderness (of a lover's feelings).

kepilu-piluan to feel sad, be moved/touched/affected.

pilu II → PILAU.

pilun → PILON.

pilus (*Jv*) a sweetmeat of glutinous rice eaten with syrup.

pimpang → PINGPONG.

pimpin *salah –* mismanaged.

berpimpin to be guided/led/directed. *~ tangan* to be led by the hand, go hand in hand.

memimpin [and **mimpin** (*coq*)] **1**a) to lead/conduct/take by the hand. b) leading. *peranan/posisi ~* a leading role/position. **2** to lead, be ahead. **3** lead, head, manage, be at the head/top of, preside over, chair. *Ia diserahi tugas ~ rapat itu.* He was entrusted with the task of presiding over the meeting. **4** to guide, train, educate, teach. *~ para calon pegawai negeri* to train prospective government employees. **5** to take care of. *dalam ~ keselamatan seluruh keluarga* in taking care of the well-being of the entire family.

memimpinkan to give orders to s.o.

terpimpin guided. *Démokrasi ~* Guided Democracy (part of President Soekarno's doctrine 1959–65).

pimpinan 1 leadership, guidance. *di bawah ~* under the leadership of. **2** led/guided (by). *partai ~ Datuk Onn* the party led by Datuk Onn. **3** management; → MANAJEMÉN. *di bawah ~* under the management of. *pucuk ~* a) top/general management. b) supreme leadership. **4** leader, director, manager, executive, presidium; mastermind, brains (behind). *Déwan ~ Pusat* [DPP] Central Executive Board, Executive Committee (of a political party, etc.). *memegang ~ "Radio Surakarta"* to manage "Radio Surakarta." *menjalankan ~ terhadap* to direct, manage. *Tersangka Srd merupakan ~ perampokan.* The accused Srd was the brains behind the robbery. *~ pelaksana* [pinlak] managing director. *~ penémbakan* (*mil*) fire control. *~ proyék* [pimpro] project leader. *~ rombongan* team leader (of a group of bridge players, etc.), chef de mission. **5** manual, guide(book).

berpimpinan *~ tangan/jari* to be led by the hand/finger, go hand in hand.

kepimpinan leadership. *~ melalui teladan* leadership by example.

pemimpin 1 guide, leader. *~ acara* master of ceremonies, M.C. *~ Besar Révolusi* [Pembesrév] Great Leader of the Revolution (one of the titles conferred upon President Soekarno). *~ cilik* a small wheel, i.e., an unimportant leader. *~ filial* branch head. *~ massa* demagog. *~ oposisi* opposition leader. *~ perjalanan keréta api* [PPKA] stationmaster. *~ politik* political leader. *~ rakyat* demagog. *~ rapat* chairman. *~ rédaksi* [pemréd] chief editor, editor-in-chief. *~ sidang* moderator. *~ tertinggi* top leader. **2** manager; → MANAJÉR. *~ madia/madya* mid-level manager. *~ proyék* [pimpro] project manager; → PIMPINAN *proyék*, PROYÉK. **3**a) guide, key. b) manual, guide(book).

kepemimpinan leadership, authority.

pemimpinan leading, the act/action of a leader.

pimping k.o. tall grass that grows along ditches, k.o. reed, *Themeda gigantea*, whose culma are used for pen handles, fishing rods, bars of birdcages. *(se)bagai – di léréng* to set one's sail to every wind, blow hot and cold.

pimpong → PINGPONG.

pimpro 1 → PIMPINAN *proyék*. **2** → PEMIMPIN *proyék*.

pin (*D*) pin, peg.

pinak *anak –* a) children and grandchildren. b) descendants. **beranak pinak 1** to have children and grandchildren. **2** to have descendants.

pinaka baladika (*mil*) (principle of) becoming a complete soldier.

pinalti → PÉNALTI.

pinandita (*Jv*) **1** (Hindu) priest. **2** pundit.

pinang I *buah –* areca nut, betel nut. *pohon –* (*sirih*) areca palm, betel palm, *Areca catechu, Pinanga kuhlii. (menyerupai) seperti/sebagai – dibelah dua* like two peas in a pod; to be hand in glove with e.o.; symmetrical. *Mahathir dan Musa tidak lagi se-*

bagai – dibelah dua. Mahathir and Musa are no longer hand in glove with e.o. *seperti – pulang ke tampuknya* to be in the right place, fit. *darah baru setampuk –* still very green/inexperienced. *– tua mérah ékor* (*M*) a middle-aged woman who acts like a young girl; → TANTE *girang. – jerkat* the young areca nut. *– kotai* old dried areca nut. *– masak* a) ripe *pinang* fruit. b) orange- or apricot-colored. *– mérah* lipstick palm, *Cyrtostachys lakka. – monyét* k.o. plant, *Areca vestiara. – raja* a *pinang* species, ceiling-wax palm, *Cyrtostachys lakka. – sebatang* to have no relatives, be all alone in the world; → *hidup sebatang* KARA. *– sirih* a) betel palm, *Areca catechu.* b) mixture for chewing betel. *– tutul* k.o. decorative plant, *Pinanga densiflora.*

peminang (*ob*) *sirih ~* box/plate (with gifts presented at a marriage proposal).

pinang II *– muda* a) pimp, procuress. b) matchmaker, go-between.

meminang 1 to woo, court, propose to, ask for s.o.'s hand (in marriage). **2** to apply for (a job, etc.).

meminangkan to propose to a girl for s.o. else.

pinangan 1 proposal, courtship, courting, wooing. *melakukan ~* to propose to, ask for s.o.'s hand (in marriage). **2** application (for a job, etc.). **3** s.o. proposed to, s.o. whose hand is asked for.

peminang 1 suitor. **2** applicant, candidate.

peminangan 1 courtship, proposal, courting, wooing. **2** applying, application.

pinang III (*M*) **meminang-minang** to spoil, coddle; to dandle, move a child up and down in one's arms.

pinang IV *pipit –* k.o. bird, spotted munia, *Munia acuticaudia/punctulata.*

pinang-pinang pig-faced bream, *Sparus spp.*

pina-pina I *akar/pohon –* creeper, trailer, *Pterococcus corniculatus.*

pina-pina II escargot, edible snail, *Pinna spp.*

pinar *– emas* gold decoration.

berpinar *~ emas* embroidered with gold thread.

berpinar(-pinar) 1 to shine, be radiant. **2** fluorescent, phosphorescent.

pinas cargo ship.

pinatua church elder.

pinawéténgan (*Min*) → BATU *pinabéténgan.*

pincang I 1 lame, limping, crippled. *si – the* Cripple, Limpy. **2** wobbling, wobbly (of a table, etc.). **3** unequal (of a treaty/contract, etc.), one-sided; inharmonious. **4** defective, faulty; insufficient. *– pincut* irregular, not in a straight line.

memincang off-balance, lopsided, unstable, leaning in one direction.

memincangkan to cripple.

terpincang-pincang haltingly. *Dia berjalan ~.* She walked haltingly.

kepincangan 1 lameness. **2** defect, fault; evil. *~ berpikir* faulty thinking. **3** imbalance, inequality.

pemincangan laming, crippling.

pincang II (*J*) *sepincang* (*ob*) (a copper coin worth) one-and-a-half cents.

pincara raft.

pincuk I a fruit salad mixed with sugar, hot red peppers, and fish paste, etc.

pincuk II (*Jv*) a small, shell-shaped food container made from a piece of banana leaf by folding it down and fastening it with a bamboo pin.

sepincuk one such container. *~ rujak* one such container filled with *rujak.*

memincukkan to make a leaf into such a container. *daun yang sudah dipincukkan* a leaf that has been made into a *pincuk.*

pincuk III → PINCUT.

pincut (*J*) **memincut** to charm, enchant.

terpincut [and **kepincut** (*coq*)] to be charmed, enchanted; fallen in love (with). *~ dengan/pada* charmed by, fallen in love with. *Gadis-gadis bisa ~ dengan wajah-wajah manis.* Girls can be swept off their feet by attractive faces.

pinda I (mostly *Mal*) **meminda 1** to alter, amend, correct. **2** to improve.

pindaan 1 alteration, amendment, correction. **2** improvement.

pemindaan correcting.

pinda II (*Jv*) **meminda** to imitate; to assume the guise of.

pindaan imitation.

pemindaan a figure of speech; to represent figuratively. *Hidupnya ~ kebo nusu gudel.* His way of life is an example of the expression "the water buffalo calf suckles the parent," i.e., the (grown) children look after their parents.

pindah 1 to move. *– kantor dari ... ke ...* to move one's office from ... to ... **2** to change. *– agama* to change religions, convert (to another religion). *Subandi ikhlas anaknya – agama.* Subandi accepted his son's conversion. *– alamat* to change one's address, move. *– bahasa* change of language. **memindah-bahasakan** (*ke/dalam*) to translate (into). *– bekerja* to change jobs. *– bis* to change buses. *– bola* to change serve. *– buku* transfer from one account to another. **memindah-bukukan** to transfer from one account to another. **pemindahbukuan** transfer from one account to another, transfer accounts. *– darah* transfusion. *– duduk* to move to another seat, change seats. *Zul yang masih bujangan itu – duduk di bangku belakang menemani Wat.* Zul, who is still a bachelor, changed seats on the (*mikrolét*) bench to sit next to Wat. *– haluan* to change course. *– iman* change of faith, conversion. **berpindah iman** to change religions, convert. *Ferry sudah ~ iman memeluk agama Islam.* Ferry has converted to Islam. *– jalur* change of lanes (on a road by cars). **berpindah jalur** to change lanes. *si penabrak berusaha menjauh dengan ~* the person who caused the collision tried to get away by changing lanes. *– kapal* transshipment. **memindahkapalkan** to transship, transfer from one ship to another. **pemindah-kapalan** transshipment. *– keréta (api)* to change trains. *– kerja* to change jobs. *– muat* to transship. *– muatan* transshipment. *– nama* to transfer title. *– negeri* to move from one place to another. *– parpol/partai (politik)/perahu* to cross party lines, go over to the other party. *– partai merupakan bagian dari prosés pengembangan démokrasi* crossing party lines is part of the process of democratic development. *Mantan ketua DPD PDI Acéh – perahu.* The former chairman of the Aceh Regional Executive Council of the Indonesian Democracy Party crossed party lines. *– rumah* to change address. *– silang* crossover. *– tanam* transplantation (of a heart, etc.). **memindah-tanamkan** to transplant. *– tangan* to pass into the hands of, change hands/ownership, be transferred to. *Dompét ~ tangan.* The wallet was snatched (by a pickpocket). **berpindah tangan** to change hands, pass from one owner to another. **memindah-tangankan** to transfer ownership. *kendaraan bermotor yang dipindahtangankan* the motor vehicles which changed hands (or, were sold). **pemindah-tanganan** transfer of ownership. *Harus diusut, ~ rumah dinas kepada yang tak berhak.* Transferring the ownership of an official residence to a person not entitled to it should be investigated. *– tempat* to move. **memindah tempatkan** to move s.t. *– tidur* to sleep in a different place every night (out of fear of begin kidnapped, etc.). *– tuang darah* blood transfusion. **berpindah tuang** *darah* to transfuse blood, give a blood transfusion. *– tugas* transfer to a new post (of army personnel, etc.). **memindah-tugaskan** to transfer to a new post, transfer. *Saya dipindahtugaskan ke Bandung.* I was transferred to Bandung. *– tukar* relocation and replacement. **memindah-tukarkan** to relocate and replace. *Di Jakarta banyak asrama tentara dipindahtukarkan.* In Jakarta many army barracks have been relocated and replaced.

pindah-pindah → BERPINDAH-PINDAH.

berpindah 1 to move. *~ dari negeri/dunia yang fana yang negeri/dunia yang baka* and *~ ke rahmatullah* to pass away, die. *~ negeri* (*ob*) to emigrate. *~ randah* to wander (as a nomad). *burung-burung yang ~* migrating birds. **2** to change, shift. *Sesampai ke Cikampék meréka ~ keréta jurusan Purwakarta.* Upon arrival at Cikampek they changed trains for Purwakarta. *~ hak* to change title. *~ haluan* to change one's mind. *~ jenis* to change sex.

berpindah-pindah 1 to infect, contaminate; to spread (of a disease). *Penyakit pés ialah penyakit yang mudah ~.* The plague is a disease which spreads easily. *~ gelombang* to keep on changing the wavelength (of a radio/television, etc.). **2** to keep on moving/shifting, move from place to place, move around.

memindah (*Jv*) **1** to change, shift, transfer. *Koper-koper itu dipindah ke pesawat terbang lain.* The luggage was transferred to another plane. **2** to move/spread from one place to another.

mindah (*coq*) to change. *~ gelombang* to change the wavelength (of a radio/television, etc.).

pindah-memindah and **mindah-mindah** to infect, contaminate; to spread (of a disease). *Mula-mula anaknya yang tertimpa penyakit itu, kemudian pindah-memindah ke segenap penghuni rumah.* At first it was the child who was struck by the disease; later, it spread to all his housemates. *dipindah-pindah* mobile, movable. *stasiun bumi yang dapat dipindah-pindah* a mobile earth station.

memindahi 1 (*ob pl obj*) to move s.t. **2** to contaminate, infect, spread (of a disease).

memindahkan [and **mindahin** (*J coq*)] **1** to move, transfer, change, switch (channels on television). *Meréka dipindahkan ke tempat yang lebih aman.* They were moved to a safer place. *Ia ~ lemari itu ke kamar lain.* He moved the wardrobe to another room. *~ hak* to transfer title. *~ perhatian* to distract. *~ persnéling* to shift/change gears. **2** to translate, render. *lelucon yang dipindahkan ke Indonésia* a joke translated into Indonesian. **3** to infect, contaminate; to spread (a disease). *Ada sejenis nyamuk yang ~ penyakit kuning.* There's a k.o. mosquito which spreads jaundice.

terpindahkan transferable. *tak ~* nontransferable.

pindahan 1 s.t. that is moved/transferred (like furniture). *~ dari* came/transferred from. *barang-barang ~* furniture being moved. *kartu ~* change-of-address card. *kaum ~* (*ob*) emigrants; → ÉMIGRAN. **2** (in bookkeeping) brought forward (an item or amount).

kepindahan 1 moving (house), transferring, move, transfer. *~nya diundurkan* his transfer was postponed. **2** contaminated, infected.

pemindah conveyor. *~ panas* heat exchanger. *~ torsi* torque converter.

pemindahan 1 transfer, shift, assignment (of rights, etc.), transplant(ing) switch(-over). *~ tempat kedudukan perséroan* change of domicile of the corporation. *~ telepon dari sistém manual ke sistém otomat* switch-over from a manual to an automatic telephone system. *~ bahang* heat transfer. *~ gigi* gearshift. *~ hak* transfer of title. *~ jantung* heart transplant. *~ nama* transfer to s.o. else's name. *~ nama saham* transfer of shares (to s.o. else's name). *~ tanah* transfer of land. *~ tangan* transfer of ownership. **2** transport, conveyance, movement. *~ pasukan* troop movement(s). *~ tanah* ground movement/sliding. **3** displacement. *~ air* water displacement (of ship).

perpindahan 1 change, transition. *~ alamat* change of address. **2** transfer, removal, move, displacement. *~ besar-besaran* exodus. *~ dari jabatan* removal from office. *~ dari désa ke kota-kota besar* urbanization. *~ hak milik* transfer of ownership. *~ kekuasaan* transfer of power. *~ panas* heat transfer. *~ penduduk* movement of population, population displacement.

pindai (*M*) **memindai 1** to gaze, stare. **2** to scan, scrutinize.

pemindai scanner, scrutinizer.

pemindaian scanning, scrutinizing.

pindakaas (*D*) /-kas/ peanut butter.

pindang a process for preparing eggs, meat, or fish using salt, tamarind juice and other ingredients; a dish prepared in this way. *seperti – saja* and *seperti – dalam kuali* like sardines in a can. *– bandeng* salted milkfish prepared as above. *– daging* k.o. braised beef. *– seruni* k.o. soup made of lamb ribs.

memindang to prepare fish, meat, etc. as above.

pemindang s.o. used for preparing *pindang*.

pemindangan salting of fish, meat, etc. as above.

pinding → KEPINDING.

pinentang → PENTANG I.

pinés (*D*) thumbtack; → PAKU *payung*.

pinga terpinga-pinga dumbfounded, bewildered; → TERCENGANG.

pingai 1 cream-colored. **2** white. *burung –* white crow; the bird of life.

pingat (*Mal*) medal.

pinggah bellows, current (of wind, air); → EMBUSAN.

pinggala apricot-colored.

pinggan (*Tam*) (porcelain/earthenware) plate, dish, saucer. – *batik* colorful dish. – *cépér* dinner plate. – *dalam* soup plate. – *kerang* platter. – *lingkar* plate without a lip. – *mangkok/cawan* crockery, china. – *sup* soup bowl.

   sepinggan a plate(ful). *nasi* ~ a plate(ful) of rice.

pinggang 1 waist, loins, hip. 2 (*M*) – *bukit/gunung* slope of a hill/mountain. *buah* – kidneys. *ikat* – waistband, belt. *penyakit* – backache; nephritis. *sakit* – kidney trouble. *bercekak/berkacak/bertekan/bertolak* – to stand with arms akimbo. *meluruskan-nya* to draw o.s. up to one's full height. *anaknya selilit* – he has a lot of children. *utang selilit* – to be up to one's ears in debt. – *bukit* mountain slope. – *genting* the narrow part of an oar. – *celana* waist of trousers. – *keran* large platter.

   sepinggang as far down as/up to/down to the waist. *Rambutnya* ~ *panjangnya*. Her hair came down to her waist. *(tinggal) sehelai* ~ came away empty-handed due to a theft or business losses.

   berpinggang *tidak* ~ (*coq*) stout, stocky, heavy-set, portly.

   peminggang amidships, central nave. *dayung* ~ oars amidship.

pinggir 1 edge, side, rim, brim, outskirt, border (of country). –! pull over (to the side of the road) (bus conductor's command to driver). – *depan* pull over ahead (to the side of the road) (bus conductor's command to driver). 2 hem. *ke* – to the edge. *mengepinggirkan* to move s.t. over to the edge, edge out s.o. or s.t.

   berpinggir with a hem/rim/brim, etc.

   meminggir [and **minggir** (*coq*)] 1 (to go over) to the side/edge/rim. *minggir!* move over, get out of the way! 2 to go along the edge. 3 to give the right of way (to a passing car).

   meminggiri to edge, put an edge on s.t.

   meminggirkan [and **minggirin** (*J coq*)] 1 to move s.t. over to the edge/side, move s.t. away. ~ *mobil* to move a car over to the side of the road. 2 to eliminate, put/set aside.

   terpinggir(kan) pushed aside/to the side.

   pinggiran edge, boundary, border, outskirt. ~ *Betawi* perimeter of Jakarta: the areas of Palmerah, Kebayoran Lama, Tangerang, Kramat Pulo, Klender, and Pasar Rebo. *orang* ~ marginal person. ~ *kota* a) city limits. b) outskirts of the city. ~ *miring* bevel. **berpinggiran** with borders/edges.

   peminggir ~ *jalan* shoulder (of a road).

   peminggiran *orang* ~ marginal person.

pinggul (*M*) 1 hip. 2 seat, behind, rear. *berat* – (*M*) a) lazy. b) lazybones. *bergoyang* – to swing one's hips.

   sepinggul down/up to the hips, hip-length, hip-high.

pingin (*J*) **kepingin** to want; → INGIN.

pingit berpingit to be locked up, isolated, secluded (of a marriageable girl at home).

   memingit 1 to lock up, cage. 2 to isolate, seclude (of a marriageable girl at home).

   pingitan 1 k.o. purdah, secluding (s.o. at home). 2 confined, secluded. *ayam/dara* ~ a hen/virgin put in confinement/seclusion. 3 cage.

pingkal (*Jv*) **terpingkal-pingkal** *tertawa* ~ to laugh uproariously.

pingkau → PIKAU I. **terpingkau-pingkau** to scream, cry out.

pingkel → PINGKAL.

pingpong (*D*) Ping-Pong, table tennis. *bermain* – to play Ping-Pong.

   memingpong ~ *ke sana kemari* to send s.o. from pillar to post. *Ia dipingpong oléh pejabat-pejabat yang bersangkutan.* The officials concerned sent him all over the place. ~ *kesalahan pada orang lain* to put the blame on s.o. else.

pingsan (epileptic) fit, fainting spell, unconsciousness. *jatuh* – to faint, fall unconscious.

   memingsangkan to make s.o. faint.

   terpingsan to faint, become unconscious.

pingser (*J*) **mingser** to be pushed aside, swerve. *Mobilnya* ~. The car swerved (out of the driveway).

   mingserin (*J*) to push aside. *Tapi pingserin dulu tu ... tahi temen!* But just push that stuff aside ... it's real shit!

pingsut 1 to draw lots to see who goes first by throwing out one's fingers. 2 to take a chance, try one's luck; → SUTEN.

pinguin (*D*) /pingwin/ penguin, *Aptenodytes forsteri*.

pingul 1 blunt (of edge), not squared off. 2 wane (in forestry).

pinhong (*C*) screen.

pinis I (*D*) pinnace.

pinis II ironwood used for tops and tool handles, *Sloetia elongata*; → TEMPINIS.

pinisepuh (*Jv*) 1 one's elders. 2 elders (of a village/organization, etc.).

pinisi Buginese cargo sailboat.

pinjak (*M*) → PIJAK.

pinjal – *penusuk* sticktight flea, *Echidnophaga gallinacea*.

pinjam lend, loan, borrow. *kasih/memberi* – to loan. *minta* – *dari(pada)* to ask s.o. for a loan, borrow from. – *pakai* loan (for use). *kontrak* – *pakai* loan agreement. **meminjam-pakaikan** to loan (for use). – *pakai habis* loan for consumption. – *paksa* commandeering. – *séwa* hire-purchase. – *tangan* to hire s.o. to do one's dirty work; → NYILIH *tangan*.

   meminjam [and **minjam** (*coq*)] 1 to borrow, make use of s.t. belonging to s.o. else. ~ *kepada* to borrow from. ~ *mulut* to ask s.o. to say s.t. that one is afraid to say o.s. ~ *uang sepuluh ribu rupiah daripada/kepada bank* to borrow 10,000 rupiahs from the bank. ~ *télepon* to use s.o.'s telephone. 2 to be derived from, take (one's name) from. ~ *nama dari seorang sahabatnya, orang Bali* to use the name of his friend, a Balinese. 3 (*math*) to borrow (in subtracting).

   pinjam-meminjam 1 borrowing. *perjanjian* ~ loan agreement. 2 to borrow from e.o.

   meminjami to lend to. *Anak itu dipinjami sarung.* The child was lent a sarong.

   meminjamkan [and **minjamin** (*J coq*)] 1 to lend. *Mobilnya dipinjamkan kepada temanya.* He lent his car to his friend. 2 to borrow for s.o. else. *Ini lho, saya pinjamkan sepéda.* Here, I borrowed a bike for you.

   memperpinjamkan to lend out s.t. that one has borrowed from s.o. else.

   pinjaman 1 (*uang* ~) loan, debt. ~ *angsuran* installment loan. ~ *jangka péndék/singkat antarbank* call money. ~ *bébas bunga* non-interest-bearing loan. ~ *berjaminan* collateralized loan. ~ *berjangka* term loan. ~ *bersyarat* term loan. ~ *cerukan* overdraft loan. ~ *dari luar negeri* offshore/foreign loan. ~ *dari pemegang saham* subordinated loan. ~ *dari pemerintah kepada swasta* loan G to P, government loan to the private sector. ~ *diragukan* doubtful loan. ~ *dua tahap* two-step loans. ~ *hari ini dan kembali bésoknya* overnight loan. ~ *jangka panjang/péndék* long/short-term loan. ~ *kol* call loan. ~ *lunak* soft/concessional loan. ~ *nirkala* evergreen loan. ~ *obligasi* secured note. ~ *penyelesaian* workout loan. ~ *ragu-ragu* doubtful loan. ~ *sebrakan* loan that has to be repaid within one month. ~ *semalam* overnight loan. ~ *siaga* standby loan. ~ *sindikasi* syndicated loan. ~ *singkat* call money. ~ *subordinasi* subordinated loan. ~ *tak terikat* uncommitted loan. ~ *tidak berbunga* non-interest-bearing loan. ~ *untuk keperluan penyesuaian* adjustment loan. ~ *yang disediakan untuk diambil sewaktu-waktu* and ~ *yang siap disalurkan* stand-by loan. *mendapat* ~ *mobil penumpang* to obtain passenger cars on loan (during the Soekarno regime; the cars were used to transport dignitaries participating in mass demonstrations). 2 borrowed. *barang* ~ s.t. borrowed, a borrowed item. *kata* ~ (*gram*) loanword.

   peminjam borrower, obligor. ~ *tangan* perpetrator, henchman.

   peminjaman loan, lending.

pinjem (*J*) → PINJAM.

pink (*E*) pink. *warna* – pink color.

pinlak → PIMPINAN *pelaksana*.

pinsan → PINGSAN.

pinsét (*D*) (pair of) tweezers, pincers.

pinsil → PÉNSIL.

pinta I question, request; → MINTA. "*Tahan dirilah. Tidak usah macam-macam,*" – *istri Kalil.* "Control yourself. You don't have to come up with all k.o. excuses," begged Kalil's wife.

   berpinta to ask (s.t. for o.s.). *Saya* ~ *kepada Tuhan agar kesehatan saya pulih.* I asked God to restore my health.

   meminta(i) to make a request of s.o.

   pintaan question, request.

pinta II destiny, (allotted) term of life. *buruk* – to have bad luck. *singkat* -(*nya*) to die (at a) young (age).

meminta to predestine.

terpinta predestined, fated (to), allotted.

peminta destiny, (allotted) term of life.

pintak → MINTA, PINTA I.

pintal twisted (of strands of thread/rope/wires, etc.). *cincin – tiga* ring made of twisted gold wires. *mata –* spindle. *tali –* twisted rope/cord.

berpintal twisted.

berpintal-pintal tangled (of hair), twisted, matted.

memintal 1 to spin, twine, form thread by twisting wool, etc. **2** to twist into a rope, make a rope by twisting a number of strands.

terpintal twisted, spliced.

pintalan 1 splice. **2** s.t. twined. *~ kabel* strand.

pemintal 1 spindle, spinning wheel. *pabrik ~* spinning mill. **2** spinner (the person).

pemintalan 1 spinning. *~ benang* yarn spinning. **2** spinning wheel.

pintang *hilang –* completely lost; → HILANG *lenyap.*

pintar (*Jv*) **1** capable, competent, able, clever, intelligent, good (at some task). *Istrinya – pegang uang.* His wife is good at managing money. *orang –* a) a clever person. b) shaman; → DUKUN. **2** skillful, expert. *paling – dari yang lain-lain* to excel. *Dia – bicara.* He has the gift of gab. He speaks fluently. **3** smart, shrewd, cunning. *– busuk* sly, crafty.

sepintar as capable, etc. as.

terpintar very skillful, most able/clever.

kepintaran cleverness, capability, skill, intelligence, smartness.

pintas to pass (by). *jalan –* shortcut. *mengambil jalan –* to take a shortcut. *saluran –* bypass.

sepintas 1 glance, glimpse. **2** brief (of explanation, etc.). *~ kilas/lalu (saja)* a) at first sight, at a glance, on the surface. *~ kilas nampaknya DPR kita mémang mengalami kemajuan yang cukup berarti.* At first glance, it seems that our Parliament has made significant progress. b) hasty, cursory, in no time at all. c) just for a moment. *kalau kita pandang ~ lalu, terus ...* if we look at it briefly, we immediately (understand that ...). **3** (at) first (but then ...). **4** on the face of it, on the surface, roughly speaking. **5** in brief, in short. *pemandangan/tinjauan ~ lalu* brief observations; → SEKAPUR *sirih.* **6** by the way; → NGOMONG-NGOMONG. *~, Persetujuan Moskow tahun 1963 itu tidak mempunyai nilai historis apapun.* By the way, the Moscow Agreement of 1963 has no historical significance whatsoever.

memintas 1 to take a shortcut, cut through, bypass. *jalan ~* the straightest/most direct road (to). *~ ke kanan/kiri* to turn off to the right/left. *tidak dapat dipintas lagi* there is not much we can do (to cure the disease). **2** to interrupt, cut off. **3** to cut across, go through. **4** to cut short.

memintasi 1 to cut straight across. **2** to bar/block s.o.'s way, cut off; to shut the door on; to intercept s.o. **3** to cut s.o. off, interrupt. **4** (*M*) to rescue (a drowning person, etc.). *~ kesukaran/penyakit* to overcome/surmount difficulties/a disease. *~ maksud* to avoid, elude; to beat about the bush.

pintas-memintasi *~ maksud* to talk/be at cross purposes with e.o.

memintaskan to intercept, cut off.

pintasan 1 shortcut. **2** street crossing. **3** bypass.

kepintasan 1 intercepted; interrupted, stopped. **2** cut short/off. **3** surmounted, overcome. *Akalnya ~.* His tricks are well known. *Tak mungkin akan ~ lagi.* There's not much we can do (to cure the disease).

pemintasan 1 cutting short, barring (the road, etc.). **2** (*M*) place where tigers show up.

pintau *burung –* weaverbird, *Ploceus sp;* → MANYAR.

pinter → PINTAR.

pintil I bundle, skein (of thread).

pintil II → PÉNTIL.

pintir **memintir** to turn.

pintit *ikan –* (*Ban*) catfish.

pinto(o) (C) Buddhist priest.

pintu I 1 door. *uang –* bribe, illicit commission. **2** gate. **3** hatch. **4** wing (of a door). *Siapa yang mengetuk – itu?* Who knocked at the door? **5** classifier for houses/buildings. *Lima – rumah petak habis dimakan api.* Five row houses were destroyed by fire. **6**

grade crossing. *Rumahnya tak jauh dari – keréta api Cikini.* He lives not far from the Cikini grade crossing. **7** door, the means of obtaining/approaching s.t.. *Kalau kita tekun belajar – kejayaan akan terbuka bagi kita.* If we study hard, the door to success will open up for us. *terlepas dari – dunia, ke – kubur* to die, pass away. *sempit – rezekinya* luck was against him. *bagai – tak berpasak, perahu tak berkemudi* s.t. dangerous. *– air* sluice, locks, floodgate. *– angin* a) swinging doors (to protect against drafts). b) air sluice. c) porthole, vent. *– api* fire door. *– ayun* swinging door. *– bahaya* emergency exit. *– bayar* checkout point (for paying for purchases, as in a supermarket). *– bawah* tailgate. *– (yang menembus ke) belakang* backdoor. *– belakang* a) the back door. b) an irregular way which bypasses the rules. *– butulan* side door. *– darurat* emergency exit. *– depan* front door. *– dorong* sliding door. *– gapura/gerbang* main gate/entrance. *– geladak* hatchway. *– gerbang masuk* gate entrance. *– gésér* sliding door. *– gua* cave entrance. *– gulung* roll-a-door, rolling door. *– jalan ke* gateway to. *– jendéla* casement window. *– kecelakaan* what caused the bad luck. *– Kecil* the street of Chinese moneylenders and merchants in Jakarta; it has the connotation of New York's "Wall Street" or London's "The City". *– ke kubur* to die. *– keluar* exit. *– keréta api* grade crossing. *– khasanah* strong door (of a safe). *– kolong* trapdoor. *– kota* city gate. *– kubu* hatchway. *– kubur* the grave. *– kupu-kupu* swinging door. *– lantai* trapdoor. *– lawang* main gate. *– lintas jalan* and *– lintasan keréta api* grade crossing. *– limpah* overflow pipe. *– lipat* bi-fold door. *– maling* back/side entrance. *– masuk* entrance. *– mati* a sealed door (cannot be opened). *– monyét* double door (with upper and lower halves). *– muka* front door. *– pabéan* (ob) tollgate. *– pagar* fence door. *– pelekah* (naut) porthole. *– pelintasan jalan keréta api* and *– perlintasan keréta api* grade crossing. *– perlintasan (keréta api) otomatis* automatic grade/railroad crossing. *– putar* revolving door, turnstile. *– rangkap* folding doors. *– rezeki* means of subsistence/support. *– salah* (ob) k.o. window in palace wall. *– samping* side door. *– sekat* isolating door. *– sorok/sorong* sliding door. *– sorong lipat* accordion door. *– tani* main gate outside the palace. *– tarik* sliding door. *– terbuka* open-door. *menyelenggarakan – terbuka* to organize/hold an open house. *politik – terbuka* open-door policy. *– turun* trapdoor. *– utama* main gate.

sepintu *~ sedulang* motto of Bangka/Belitung: "one door one tray" mutual help; → GOTONG-ROYONG.

pintu II (in Pontianak) commission agent.

pinus pine (tree).

pinusisasi encouraging the planting of pine trees.

pio(h) (C) **1** k.o. (land) tortoise. **2** turtle soup.

pion (*D*) pawn (in chess).

pionir (*D*) pioneer (a type of military engineer).

mempionirkan to be a pioneer in, pioneer.

kepioniran pioneering.

pioniria (*infr*) female pioneer.

piopo (C?) water parsley, *Oenanthe javanica;* → SELUM.

pipa (*Port*) **1** pipe, line. *merokok –* to smoke a pipe. **2** (*– pabrik*) chimney, smokestack. **3** tube, tubing. **4** (pant's) leg. *– air* water pipe. *– air balik* (*petro*) runback line. *– baja tanpa kampuh/sambungan* seamless steel pipe. *– balik* (*petro*) return bend. *– besi* iron pipe. *– bor* (*petro*) tubular goods. *– buang* outlet/exhaust pipe. *– celana* trouser leg. *– gas buang* (car) muffler. *– halus/kapilér* capillary tube. *– isi* filler neck. *– jepit* choke line. *– kaca* glass tube. *– karét* rubber tubing. *– keluar* exhaust pipe. *– keras* pipe. *– kuras* drainpipe. *– lébar* wide pants legs. **berpipa lébar** with wide pants legs. *– lédéng* plumbing. *– lentur* flexible hose. *– limpah* overflow pipe. *– logam* metal tube. *– loncéng* bell-bottoms. **berpipa loncéng** bell-bottomed. *– lurus* straight legs (on pants). **berpipa lurus** with straight legs. *– masuk* inlet pipe/tube. *– minyak tanah* oil pipeline. *– naik* riser, stand pipe. *– napas* trachea. *– peluncur* launching tube (for torpedoes). *– pengisap* suction pipe. *– pengisi* filler tube. *– pengisian* feed pipe. *– penyalur* discharge/outlet pipe. *– penyambung* fitting. *– pernapasan* snorkel. *– pindah* syphon. *– pralon/PVC* a plastic pipe made from PVC/polyvinyl chloride resin. *– rambut* capillary tube. *– rokok* cigarette holder. *– saluran* duct, pipeline. *–*

selubung casing. *– sembur* tubing. *– siku* square elbow. *– talang* down spout. *– tanpa las* seamless pipe. *– tanpa sambungan* seamless pipe. *– tegak/tekan* stand pipe. *– tembakau* tobacco pipe. *– tempaan* wrought-iron pipe. *– uap* steam pipe. *– union* conduit.

pemipaan piping, discharging through a pipeline. *~ luruh* straight piping.

perpipaan (system of) pipelines; piping, pipe (*mod*).

pipanisasi installation of pipelines. *– bahan bakar minyak* installation of pipelines for fuel oils.

pipét (*D*) pipette.

pipi cheek. *lesung –* dimple. *– témpél –* cheek to cheek. *tulang –* cheekbone. (*bersdansa*) *– lekat –* (to dance) cheek to cheek. *– licin* (*J*) a beautiful woman. *– péot* flabby cheeks.

pipih 1 thin and flat (as of a coin/paper/seam, etc.). 2 snub, stumpy, flat (of one's nose/breasts). *bulat –* round and flat (like a coin). *cacing –* tapeworm. *hidung –* flat nose. *– asahan* thin section of s.t.

memipihkan to flatten, level (out).

pemipih s.t. which flattens s.t.

pemipihan flattening.

pipik memipik to become thin, thin out.

pipil I (*Jv*) → GIRIK.

pipil II (*Jv*) **memipil** to husk, shell (corn/soybeans, etc.).

pipilan s.t. shelled, pulled/torn off (kernels of corn from the cob, etc.). *Ny Sinah tetap merebus – jagung sebagai sarapan keenam anaknya.* Mrs. Sinah kept on boiling the corn kernels for breakfast for her six children.

pipis I grind, pound.

memipis to pound, grind, turn into powder.

memipiskan to pound, etc. for. *burung terbang dipipiskan lada* to count one's chickens before they are hatched.

pipisan grinding stone.

pipis II (*coq*) to pee, urinate; → (BER)KENCING.

pipit I various species of small birds, such as finch, sparrow, munia, etc. *yang – sama –, yang enggang sama enggang* birds of a feather flock together. *seperti – menelan jagung* to live beyond one's means. *– pekak makan berhujan* extremely industrious. *– anggerék* white-belled crested babbler, *Yuhina zantholeuca interposita*. *– benggala* red avadavat, *Amandava amandava*. *– genting/geréja* sparrow, *Passer montanus*. *– gunung* brown bullfinch, *Pyrrhula nipalensis waterstradti*. *– padang* Richard's pipit, paddy-field pipit, *Anthus novaeseelandiae malayensis*. *– padi/uban* white-headed munia, *Munia maja maja*. *– pinang* spotted munia, *Munia punctulata*. *– rumah* a) house sparrow, *Passer montanus*. b) stay-at-home, homebody. *– tuli* sharp-tailed munia, *Munia striata subsquamicollis*.

pipit II mouthpiece, embouchure (of a wind instrument).

pipit III (*Jv*) **memipit** to press.

pipitan oil-press.

pipit IV baby's penis.

pipuhunan <puhun> (*S*) offerings for the rice goddess; → POHACI *Sang Hyang Sri*.

pir I (*D*) spring (of watch, etc.); → PÉR I.

pir II (*D*) light bulb; → PÉR II.

pir III (*D*) pear, *Pyrus communis*; → PÉR V.

pir IV (*E*) pier.

pir V (in Tegal, Central Java) → DOKAR, PÉR VI.

PIR VI [Perkebunan Inti Rakyat] People's Nuclear Plantations, i.e., nucleus agricultural enterprises to which smallholder undertakings are attached.

pirai gout, rheumatism (*esp* of the hands).

piramid(a) and **perimide** (*D*) pyramid.

piramidal (*D*) pyramidal.

pirang I brown, tea-colored (of hair/eyes). 2 blond. *wanita berambut –* blond girls. 3 russet. *– perus* sallow. *– tibarau* rosy buff.

kepirang-pirangan off-white (the color of *beras*).

piranti → PERANTI.

pira-pira (*Jv*) it's amazing that. *Sudah – anakmu sudah ada yang membiayai.* It's amazing that your child has found s.o. to pay for his studies.

pirasah and **pirasat** → FIRASAT.

pirat (*D*) pirate.

pirau I 1 grey, dark brown (cigar color). 2 (*M*) dim.

pirau II (*M*) **berpirau(-pirau)** and **memirau** 1 to zigzag, make a detour. 2 to tack (of a boat). 3 to shunt.

Piraun → FIRAUN.

pirdaus and **pirdus** → FIRDAUS.

piréks U.S. trademark of heat-resistant glassware, such as, plates, cups, etc., Pyrex.

pirid (*Jv*) **piridan** example, analogy.

pirik I **memirik** to pulverize, crush to powder (of pepper/spices).

pirik II (*M*) **memirik** to pinch, squeeze.

pirik III driving fish into traps.

piring 1 plate; saucer. *se–* a plate(ful), plate of. *tari –* Sumatran dance in which plates containing lit candles are placed on the hands and then inverted during the dance. 2 (*daun –*) leaf-blade. 3 section of a wet rice field; → PÉTAK I. *– alas* saucer. *– cangkir* dinner set, dishes. *– cépér* dinner plate. *– dalam* soup plate. *– hitam* (phonograph) record. **memiringhitamkan** to record (onto a phonograph record). *– kelung* soup plate. *– makan* dinner plate. *– mangkok* dinner set, crockery. *– sepéda* cogwheel (of bicycle). *– terbang* a) flying saucer. b) (*J*) merry-go-round, carousel. *– vidéo* videodisk.

piring-piring 1 cogwheel. 2 face (of timepiece).

piringan disk. *~ hitam* (phonograph) record. *memutar ~ hitam* to play a record. *~ putar* rotary dial. *~ terbang* flying saucer. *~ vidéo* videodisk.

pirit I (*D*) pyrites.

pirit II (*Bal*) k.o. card game.

pirman → FIRMAN.

Pirngon → FIRAUN.

piroman (*D*) pyromaniac.

piromani (*D*) pyromania.

pirométer (*D*) pyrometer.

pirotéhnik (*D*) pyrotechnics.

pirsa (*Jv*) to see.

pemirsa 1 televiewer. 2 onlooker, spectator.

pirsawan 1 televiewer. 2 onlooker, spectator.

pirsidér (*D*) refrigerator.

piru (*Port ob*) guinea fowl, turkey.

piruét (*D*) pirouette.

piruk → HIRUK *piruk*.

pirus (*Pers*) turquoise (stone).

piruzah → PIRUS.

pis I (*coq pron* i as in kiss) to piss.

pis II (*E pron* i as in meet) piece (of textile).

pisah separation, disengagement. *ilmu –* (*ob*) chemistry. *juru –* arbiter, referee, umpire. *– batas* cut-off. *– kebo* cancellation of a consensual marriage, k.o. legal separation; *opp* DAMPULAN, KUMPUL *kebo*, SAMENLÉVEN. *– makan/méja dan ranjang/tempat tidur* separation from bed and board. *– pasukan* troop disengagement. *– ranjang* separation from bed and board. *acara – sambut* transfer and acceptance ceremony. *acara – sambut Pangdam VI/ Tanjungpura* transfer and acceptance ceremony for the post of Commander of the VIth Military Region of Tanjungpura.

berpisah 1 to be separated. *Untung, nyawa dan badan S tidak ~.* Fortunately, S's body and soul were not separated (i.e., he didn't die). 2 to part, separate. *~ jalan* to go their separate ways. *~ ranjang* judicial/legal separation, separation/divorce a mensa et toro. *Tidak terasa hari telah siang membuat meréka harus ~.* Unexpectedly, the lateness of the day made them (the lovers) have to part. *hidup ~* separated from bed and board. *mengucapkan selamat ~* to say good-bye, bid farewell.

berpisah-pisah scattered, separated from e.o.

berpisahan to separate from e.o. *~ jalan* to go their separate ways; to drift apart.

memisah to separate. *gerakan ~* separatism.

memisahkan [and **misahin** (*J coq*)] 1 to separate, break up (a fight between). *~ orang yang berkelahi* to break up a fight between the people fighting. 2 to keep s.o. away (from). 3 to separate, isolate. *~ penderita penyakit tébésé dari yang lainnya* to isolate the person with TB from the others. *tidak dapat dipisahkan* inherent. 4 to separate, make a boundary between.

Pagar hidup itu ~ kedua rumah yang baru. The hedge separates the two new houses. **5** to differentiate, draw a distinction between, tell apart, tell the difference between. *Ia belum dapat ~ mana yang buruk mana yang baik.* He can't tell the difference between good and bad yet.

memisah-misahkan to separate, divide, split up. *tidak dapat dipisah-pisahkan* inseparable. *tidak ~ mata dari* don't keep one's eyes off of.

terpisah [and **kepisah** (*coq*)] **1** separated, apart, segregated, isolated. *berjalan ~ dua* to walk in two separate groups. *orangtuanya hidup ~* his parents live apart. *dengan ~* under separate cover. **2** free from, inseparable. *Perjuangan menegakkan bahasa Indonésia sebagai bahasa kebangsaan ialah perjuangan yang tidak ~ daripada perjuangan kemerdékaan negara kita.* The struggle to uphold the Indonesian language as the national language is a struggle that is inseparable from our country's struggle for independence. **keterpisahan** segregation, separation. *~ kekayaan* separation of assets.

terpisah-pisah separated, dispersed, isolated, fragmented. *bagian-bagian yang ~* knocked-down parts (of imported cars). *tak ~* inseparable, inherent, integral.

terpisahkan *tidak/tak ~* inseparable, inherent, integral, cannot be separated.

pemisah 1 partition, separator. *~ air/minyak/tér* water/oil/tar separator. *~ aliran air* watershed. *garis ~* dividing line. **2** arbiter, referee, umpire. *badan ~* arbitration board. *juru ~* arbitrator.

pemisahan 1 separation, division, splitting up, isolation, segregation. *~ antara geréja dan negara* the separation of church and state. *~ diri* separation. *~ harta kekayaan/peninggalan* partition of an estate. *~ kekuasaan* separation of powers. *~ perkara* division of a case. **2** arbitration.

perpisahan 1 separation. *~ kekayaan* separation of property, separate (ownership of) property. *~ méja dan ranjang* separation from bed and board. **2** leave-taking, parting, farewell. *malam ~* farewell evening (i.e., ceremony and party to bid farewell to s.o.). **3** discord, dissension, disunion.

pisak → PÉSAK.

pisan (*J/Jv*) very, completely; (after a negative) at all. *di depan hidungnya ~* under his very nose. *gedé ~* very large. *nggak adé reraméan ~* (*J*) there isn't any party at all.

pisang banana, *Musa, spp.* **2** (*euph*) penis. *"Kalau suami saya berani main perempuan, saya tidak takut meremas-remas ~nya,"* ditambahnya. "If my husband dares to fool around with women, I'm not afraid to squeeze his penis," she added. *jantung ~* the red-purple flower of the banana plant. *tandan ~* the entire stalk of bananas. *keplését kulit ~* slipped on a banana peel. *tak akan dua kali ~ berbuah* and *~ tak akan berbuah dua kali* once bitten twice shy. *mendapat ~ terbuka/terkubak* to have a stroke of good luck. *~ mas di luar, onak di dalamnya* all is not gold that glitters. *mengenalkan diri bagai ~ lebat* pride goes before a fall. *menopang ~ yang berbuah* to do s.t. useless. *ia bukan budak-budak makan ~* he wasn't born yesterday; → ANAK *kemarin. laku sebagai ~ goréng* and *laku sebagai goréng ~* and *laris seperti ~ goréng* to sell like hot cakes. *~ ambon* a large dessert banana, gros michel, *Musa paradisiaca. ~ abu* ashy plantain, *Musa acuminata. ~ badak* dwarf banana, *Musa nana. ~ bali* a banana species with a pink skin. *~ barangan* a sweet, aromatic banana species from Medan. *~ batu/biju/klutuk* a banana variety with acid, sour, bitter seeds; white when young, black when ripe, skin fibers are made into yarn or rope, *Musa brachycarpa. ~ benang* → PISANG *manila. ~ calvanis* a banana variety imported from the Philippines and grown in Halmahera. *~ démpét* two bananas growing in one skin. *~ goréng* and *goréng ~* fried banana. *~ hijau* banana similar to *pisang Ambon*; skin green when ripe. *~ kapas* a type of squat, angular banana. *~ kapok/kepok* cooking banana. *~ klutuk* seed-filled banana whose leaves are made into wrappers, *Musa brachycarpa. ~ lampung* a very small, sweet finger-sized banana. *~ manila* k.o. banana tree whose fibers are made into yarn or rope, abaca, Manila hemp, *Musa textilis. ~ mas* a very small, sweet finger-sized banana. *~ molén* banana fried in a batter made from flour, egg and salt. *~ montél* cavend-

ish, *Musa acuminata. ~ nangka* a large banana variety, green when ripe, jackfruit banana, . *~ pidak* k.o. wild banana, *Musa glauca. ~ raja* a large variety of banana. *~ raja serai* a short, thin banana variety with red/yellow and brown spots. *~ salé* (*Jv*) sun-dried banana slices. *~ serai* an inferior variety of banana. *~ seribu/séwu* (*Jv*) the smallest species of banana, *Musa sapientum/chiliocarpa*, thumb-sized. *~ siam* a banana variety with splotchy skin. *~ susu* small, plump sweet banana variety. *~ tadah embun* (*Mal*) top comb in a bunch of bananas. *~ tanduk* a long, horn-shaped banana variety, horn banana, *Musa paradisiaca sapientum. ~ uli* a banana species which is green when ripe.

pisangga brownish red.

pisango name of a *ceki* card.

pisang-pisang I various species of wild plants.

pisang-pisang II (*ikan ~*) sun bream, rainbow runner, fusilier *Caesio spp., Elagatis bipinnulata.*

pisang-pisang III (*naut*) rubbing strakes, (tusk-like) ribs of a boat.

pisau I knife, cutter. *bangsa ~ dua belah mata* a hypocrite. *~ bedah* scalpel. *~ belati* small dagger-like knife. *~ bermata dua* a two-edged sword. *~ cukur* razor. *~ dapur* kitchen knife. *~ daun padi* lancet. *~ dempul* putty knife. *~ karton* cardboard cutter. *~ kertas* letter opener. *~ lémpar* throwing knife. *~ lipat* pocketknife, folding/clasp knife. *~ makan* dinner knife. *~ méja* table knife. *~ péna* pen knife. *~ raut* (*S*) knife used to peel/cut bamboo or rattan. *~ roti* bread knife. *~ sadap* (rubber) tapping knife. *~ sayat* split knife. *~ silét* a) (originally) a Gillette razor blade. b) (now) any razor blade. *~ wali* small, sharp carving knife.

berpisau with a knife; to carry a knife.

pisau II (*ikan ~*) razor fish, *Aeoliscus strigatus.*

pisgor [*pisang goréng*] fried banana.

pisik I (*D*) physical; → FISIK. *kekuatan ~ dan kekuatan batin* physical and spiritual strength.

pisik II (*M*) plump, chubby.

pisika (*D*) *ilmu ~* physics.

pisin (*S*) saucer.

pisit I → PISIK II.

pisit II memisit 1 to squeeze, press. **2** to massage. **3** to force (s.o. to confess/reveal s.t., etc.), interrogate (as of the police); → KOMPÉS.

piskal → FISKAL.

pispot (*D*) chamber pot.

pistol and **pistul** (*D*) pistol, revolver. *mencabut ~* to draw/pull out one's pistol. *moncong ~* the barrel of a pistol. *~ air* water pistol, squirt gun. *~ air mata* tear-gas pistol. *~ angin* air pistol. *~ benaran* a real pistol (not a toy). *~ bius* tear-gas pistol. *~ genggam* handgun. *~ las asétilin* acetylene torch. *~ mainan* toy pistol. *~ mitralyur* machine gun. *~ peredam* pistol (equipped) with a silencer. *~ sungguhan* a real pistol (not a toy).

berpistol to carry a pistol; (armed) with a pistol.

memistol to shoot with a pistol.

pistol-pistolan toy pistol.

piston (*D*) piston.

pisuh (*Jv*) **memisuh** [and **misuh** (*coq*)] to curse, use abusive language.

memisuhi to revile s.o., curse s.o., use abusive language toward.

pisuhan 1 insult, insulting language, slander. **2** farce, mockery.

pisungsung (*Jv*) present/gift (honoring s.o.). *pengukuhan gelar ~ selaku Maharsitama pada Univérsitas Saraswati di Surakarta, September 1971* the confirmation of an honorable degree as "Maharsitama" at Saraswati University in Surakarta in September 1971.

pit I (*D*) (*pron* i as ee in meet) bicycle.

pit II (*C*) (*pron* i as in kiss) brush-pen; → MOPIT.

pit III (*E*) (*pron* i as in kiss) burner. *kompor 2 ~ plus oven* a stove with two burners and an oven.

pit IV (*E*) (*pron* i as in kiss) pit, i.e., an area at the side of a (race)track for servicing and refueling the cars.

pita (*Port*) **1** ribbon. **2** tape (used in tape recorders, etc.); → PITA *suara cacing ~ tapeworm. gelondong ~* tape reel. *kasét ~* tape cassette. *perekam ~ (vidéo)* (video) tape recorder. **3** legulate (form of plant leaves). *~ cukai* cigarette revenue stamp, tax tape. *~ digital sarat data* high-density digital tape. *~ film* movie film. *~ isolasi* insulating tape. *~ kasét* cassette tape. *~*

kosong blank tape. – *magnétis/magnétik* magnetic tape. – *mesin* drive belt. – *mesin tik/tulis* typewriter ribbon. – *méteran* measuring tape. – *penggerak* drive belt. – *penutup* poster stamp. – *rekaman* recording tape. **memita-rekamkan** to tape. *Pengakuan yang dipitarekamkan oléh B telah diperdengarkan kembali.* The confession taped by B was replayed. – *rekaman* recording tape. – *rekaman bergambar* videotape. – *suara* a) vocal cords. b) recording tape. **memita-suarakan** to tape. – *ukur* measuring tape. – *vidéo* videotape.
  berpita with a tape/ribbon, which uses a tape/ribbon.
pitah → PÉTAH.
pitak → PÉTAK I.
pitam 1 dizzy, giddy. 2 dizziness, vertigo. 3 (apoplectic) fit, stroke. *penyakit* – stroke. *naik* – a) to become dizzy. b) to get angry, fly into a rage. – *babi* epilepsy. – *otak* stroke.
pitamin → VITAMIN.
pitanggang (*M*) *doa/mantra* – (*hati nurani*) magic formula that makes s.o. take an aversion to eating, making love, etc.
pitar (*Port*) **memitar** (*cla*) to point/aim (a gun).
  pemitar gun-sight.
pitarah (*cla*) ancestors.
pitawat (*M*) (official religious) advice, explanation, instruction.
pitaya (*Jv*) → PERCAYA.
Pitekantropus Pithecanthropus (erectus).
pitenah → FITNAH.
piterah → FITRAH I.
piterséli → PÉTERSÉLI.
pites (*Jv*) **memites** ~ *kutu* to pinch/crush a louse to death with the fingernails of one's thumbs.
  memitesi (*pl obj*) to pinch, etc.
pitet (*J/Jv*) scar.
Pit Hitam → PIET HITAM.
piti (*Jv*) small bamboo basket.
pitih (*M*) money; → PITIS. *bakirim* – (*M*) to send/remit money.
pitik (*Jv*) chicken.
  sepitik small.
piting I (*J/Jv*) **berpiting-pitingan** to clasp e.o.
  memiting 1 to grip, clasp. 2 to hold s.o.'s head in the crook of one's arm, hold s.o. tightly with arms and foot to prevent him from escaping.
  memitingi (*pl obj*) to grip, clasp.
  pitingan stranglehold, clinch.
piting II (*E coq*) fitting (of an electric bulb).
  pitingan (*elec*) fitting.
piting III → KEPITING.
pitis (*C*) 1 (*ob*) very small coin with a hole in the center, worth less than a half-penny. 2 money (in general).
  sepitis *tidak mengeluarkan* ~ *garis* do not spend a cent.
pitnah → FITNAH.
piton (*D*) python (snake); → ULAR *sanca/sawa*.
pitpit (*burung* –) brain-fever bird, *Cacomantis merulinus threnodes*.
pitrah → FITRAH I.
pitrun [(to) pit (and) run] name given by U.S. Highway Engineers to mixture of soil and sand used for the roadbed at Citeureup (West Java) in building the Jakarta Bypass (now called *Jalan Raya Jos Sudarso*) because all one has to do is dig a "pit" and "run" away with the material.
pitu (*Jv*) seven.
pituah → PETUA(H).
pitulasan (*Jv*) the August 17 celebration of Indonesian independence; → TUJUHBELASAN.
pitulikur (*Jv*) 1 twenty-seven. 2 *tumpuk* – very. *hostés yang hayunya tumpuk* – a very beautiful hostess.
pitulungan (*Jv*) assistance, aid, help.
pituo (*M*) → SESEPUH.
pitut (*ob*) bent, crooked (of one's legs, etc.).
pitutur (*Jv*) what s.o. says; (words of) advice, guidance. *Wasiat nénék moyang untuk mencapai keberhasilan harus melalui 5 prosés:* – (*naséhat*), *pituduh* (*petunjuk*), *pitulungan* (*bantuan*), *pitukon* (*modal*), *pituwas* (*hasil*). Our ancestors' injunctions on how to achieve success has to pass through five processes: advice, hints, assistance, capital, and rewards.

pituwas (*Jv*) 1 reward, compensation. 2 wages.
piuh distorted, twisted. – *pilin* twisting words, prevarication.
  piuh(-piuh) to twist one's hand.
  berpiuh to turn; twisted, twined (around).
  berpiuh-piuh 1 to wring (e.o.'s necks, like fighting cocks). 2 (nervous) quivering (of the lips). *ikal* ~ curls falling in strands (over one's cheeks).
  memiuh to twist (rope), twine (around); to distort. *perut* ~ to have the gripes. ~ *lengan orang* to twist s.o.'s arm. ~ *telinga* to pull s.o.'s ear.
  terpiuh twisted, distorted; plaited.
  terpiuh-piuh ~ *hatinya* to be touched (by emotion). *Khalayak Amérika* ~ *hatinya melihat bagaimana keluarga kaya Ewing kehilangan putra tercinta Bobby.* America's masses were touched to see how the rich Ewing family lost their beloved son Bobby.
  piuhan distortion.
  pemiuhan distortion, distorting.
piun → PION.
piung (*Port cla*) k.o. policeman.
piut descendant of the fifth generation, child of a *cicit*; → PIAT II.
piutang loan/debt/money that is owed to one, receivable; *cp* UTANG. *utang* – debits and credits. – *bawa* bearer debt instrument. – *dagang* accounts receivable. – *dengan hak didahulukan* preferred debt. – *karyawan/pegawai* loans to employees. – *macet* bad debt, non-performing loan. – *penjualan* sales draft. – *ragu-ragu* doubtful accounts. – *usaha* trade receivables. – *yang diakui* allowed claim. – *yang diberi hak mendahului* and – *yang berhak mendahului* preferred creditor.
  berpiutang to have money owed, to have a claim (on), be a creditor. *si* ~ the creditor.
  memiutangi to lend money to, be involved in a debtor-creditor relationship with.
  memiutangkan to sell on credit.
  pemiutang creditor.
piwulang (*Jv*) lesson, teaching.
piyama → PIAMA.
piyik (*Jv*) baby chick.
Pj (*abbr*) [Pejabat] acting. – *KHD* is appointed (not elected) to serve as *KDH*.
PJK (*init*) → PENYAKIT *Jantung Koronér*.
PJKA (*init*) → PERUSAHAAN *Jawatan Keréta Api*.
PJR (*init*) → PATROLI *Jalan Raya*.
Pjs (*abbr*) [Pejabat Sementara] Provisional, Acting.
PK I (*init*) → PEMADAM *Kebakaran*.
PK II (*init*) → PARTAI *Keadilan*.
PKB → PARTAI *Kebangkitan Bangsa*. – *Batutulis* a faction of the PKB with offices on Jl. Batutulis, Jakarta. – *Kuningan* a faction of the PKB with offices in Kuningan, Jakarta.
PKI (*init*) → PARTAI *Komunis Indonésia*.
PKP I (*init*) → PARTAI *Keadilan dan Persatuan*.
PKP II → PENDAPATAN *Kena Pajak*.
pk(l) (*abbr*) [pukul] o'clock.
PKR → PARTAI *Kedaulatan Rakyat*.
PKS (*init*) → PARTAI *Keadilan Sejahtera*.
PKU (*init*) → PARTAI *Kesejahteraan Umat*.
pl- also see entries beginning with **pel-**.
plaak (*onom*) slapping sound; → PLAK I.
pladaran a bamboo rack for drying fish.
plafon (*D*) ceiling. – *anggaran* budget ceiling. – *gantung* drop ceiling. – *kaca* glass ceiling, i.e., a level in a corporation or the government beyond which certain groups cannot go. – *krédit* line of credit, credit line; → PAGU *krédit*.
plafondéring (*D*) crediting interest on loans in arrears as principle.
plagak-plegok and **plegak-pleguk** (*Jv*) (to speak) haltingly, stammering, with difficulty; to stutter. – *di depan yang hadir* to speak haltingly in front of the audience.
plagiat (*D*) plagiarism.
  memplagiat to plagiarize, pirate (of books, etc.); → MEMBAJAK.
plagiatisme plagiarism.
plagiator (*D*) plagiarist.
plaiboi (*E*) (in the Kuta-Legian area in Bali) playboy.

plak I (*onom*) sound of a blow made with s.t. flat or with the flat of the hand. – *plok* sound of several slaps. *pipinya panas diterpa kaplokan: – plok* his cheeks became hot because of several slaps in the face.

plak II (*E*) plaque (on teeth).

plakat (*D*) placard, wall poster.

plakét (*D*) small plaque (*esp* as a souvenir).

plakségel (*D*) an official stamp, somewhat larger than a postage stamp, affixed to the right-hand bottom corner of a bill or invoice.

plambing (*E*) plumbing.

plamir → PLAMUR.

plampang (*J*) temporary bamboo or iron platform with a roof made of palm leaves or canvas added to a building to function as a seating area for spectators.

plamur (*D*) putty, spackle.

plan (*D*) plan.

pengeplanan planning.

planél → FLANÉL.

planét (*D*) planet.

keplanétan planetary. *sejumlah informasi yang selama ini menjadi teka-teki* ~ some data that up to now have been a planetary puzzle.

planétarium (*D*) planetarium.

plang (*D Jv*) signboard/-post, placard, board.

plangi (*Jv*) → PELANGI.

plangkan (*Jv*) wooden stand holding *gamelan* instruments.

plangton → PLANKTON.

planimétri (*D/E*) planimetry, plane geometry.

planit I → PLANÉT.

Planit II a red-light district in Jakarta.

plankton (*D*) plankton. – *héwani* zooplankton. – *nabati* phytoplankton.

planning (*E*) planning; → PENGEPLANAN.

plano (*D*) broadsheet.

planologi (*D/E*) planology.

planologis (*D*) planologic.

plan-plan → PERLAHAN-LAHAN.

plantar → PELANTAR.

plasa → PLAZA.

plasanisasi the transformation of Pasar Johar in Semarang into a plaza.

plasébo (*L*) placebo.

plasénta (*D*) placenta.

plasma I (*D*) plasma. – *nutfah* germ plasm. **keplasma-nutfahan** having to do with germ plasm.

plasma II [pengembangan lahan dan sumber daya alam] *petani* – a farmer who produces a commodity and supplies it to a factory. *perkebunan* – *téh* a tea plantation which supplies its product to the factory.

plas-plosan → CEPLAS-CEPLOS.

plastik I (*D*) plastic(s). *bahan* – s.t. made from plastics. *bahan pembuat* – polystyrene.

plastik II (*E*) and **plastis** (*D*) plastic. *operasi* – plastic surgery. *seni* – plastic arts.

keplastikan and **keplastisan** plasticity.

plastisitas (*D*) plasticity.

plastron (*D*) plastron.

plat (*D*) 1 (phonograph) record, disk, album. 2 zinc plating. 3 plate. 4 nameplate, doorplate. 5 slab. 6 flat (of a concrete roof, etc.). 7 automobile license plate, vehicle tag number; → PLATNOMOR. – *arloji* face of a watch. – *baja* steel plate. – *beton bertulang* reinforced concrete slab. – *buaya* (*naut*) apron plate. – *ésér* (*D*) iron sheet. – *hitam* the black-colored license plate issued to non-government and non-public transportation vehicles. **berplat hitam** with such a license plate. **memplat-hitamkan** to provide a car with such a license plate. – *jarum* dial. – *kuning* the yellow-colored license plate (for public vehicles). **berplat kuning** with such plates. **memplat-kuningkan** to provide a car with such a license plate. – *mérah* the red-colored license plate issued to government-owned cars. *bank* – *mérah* a government-owned bank. *perguruan tinggi téhnik* – *mérah* a state-owned education institution of higher technical learning. **berplat mérah** with

such plates. **memplat-mérahkan** to provide a car with such a license plate. – *nomor* license plate. – *pembungkus diskét* floppy disk. – *timah* tin plate.

berplat with ... plates.

platat-plétot (*J*) bent, curved, tortuous.

platform (*D/E*) platform (of a political party); *cp* KHITTAH.

platina I (*D*) platinum.

platina II distributor contact; point set (in an automobile).

platnomor license plate number.

plato (*D*) plateau; → DATARAN *tinggi*.

platonis (*D*) platonic. *cinta* – platonic love.

platuk (*Jv*) 1 trigger (of a gun). 2 hammer for cocking a gun.

plausibilitas and **plausibilitét** (*D*) plausibility.

playboy → PLAIBOI.

plaza (*E*) plaza.

plébisit (*D*) plebiscite.

memplébisitkan to decide by plebiscite.

plécét (*J*) *uang* – bribe (in the form of money).

plédoi → PLÉIDOI.

plegak-plegok and **plegak-pleguk** → PLAGAK-PLEGOK.

pléidoi (*D*) (counsel's) speech, (legal) argument. *HRD gagal membacakan –nya.* HRD failed in reading out his argument.

plek (*Jv*) exactly like (s.t. else).

plék (*D*) stain, spot; → FLÉK, VLÉK.

plékat → PELÉKAT I.

plembungan (*Jv*) balloon.

plempeng (*Jv*) large drain pipe.

plengek (*J*) **keplengek** struck dumb, dumbfounded.

plengkung (*Jv ob*) → LENGKUNG I.

pléngos (*Jv*) **mlengos** to avert one's eyes.

pléngséngan (*Jv*) 1 talus, slope. 2 embankment latrine.

pléngséran (*Jv*) waterway to a *tambak*.

pléngsong (*J*) **dipléngsongin** to be turned aside, be diverted.

pléno (*D*) plenary, full. *rapat/sidang* – plenary session.

memplénokan to introduce in a plenary session. *Tujuh RUU Pembentukan Pengadilan Tinggi diplénokan DPR.* Seven bills on the formation of Appellate Courts were introduced in the plenary session of Parliament.

plentong (*Jv*) electric light bulb.

pléonasme (*D*) pleonasm.

plés (*D*) bottle; *cp* STOPLÉS.

pléséd → PLÉSÉT II.

pléset I (*J/Jv*) **keplését** skidded, slipped (by accident).

pléset II (*Jv*) **memplését(-plését)kan** to pun, make a play on words. *Mobnas: mobil nasional diplésétkan menjadi mobil dinas.* Mobnas: national car has been turned by a play on words into service car.

plésétan to be a punster, make plays on words habitually; → PLÉSÉT II.

plesir (*D*) **plesiran** to go somewhere for fun; pleasure-seeking.

plésong (*Pr*) police; → POLISI. *Jangan takut ama –.* Don't be afraid of the police.

pléster I (*D*) 1 adhesive tape, Scotch tape. 2 (medical) dressing. – *obat* medicated dressing.

mempléster 1 to gag. *Mulutnya dipléster.* He was gagged. 2 to dress (a wound).

pléster II (*D*) concrete mixture for making floors, plaster.

mempléster to plaster.

plésteran plastering, stucco.

Pléstosin (*D*) Pleistocene. *kala* – the Pleistocene.

pletak (*onom*) sound of a hard object hitting a firm surface, click. – *pletuk* clicking noises.

plétat-plétot (*Jv*) bent, not straight.

pletik (*onom*) sound made by a small ejected object, pop.

pletikan small ejected object. ~ *api* spark.

pléyat-pléyot (*Jv*) 1 shaky, wobbly. 2 bent.

plh (*abbr*) [pelaksana harian] duty manager.

pliket (*Jv*) sticky.

plin (*E*) (air)plane.

plinkoto and **plinkut** (*E*) Flint Coat.

plin-plan (*Jv*) not straightforward (in one's dealings), devious, opportunistic; shilly-shally; → PLINTAT-PLINTUT. *Mata uang yén* *masih* –. The yen is still flopping around. *orang* – a wishy-washy person. – *diplomatik* diplomatic flip-flop.

berplin-plan to act in an opportunistic way.

keplinplanan lack of firm loyalties, deviousness.

plinplanisme deviousness.

plintat-plintut (*Jv*) not straightforward (in one's dealings), devious, opportunistic.

plinteng (*Jv*) slingshot, catapult.

plintir (*Jv*) **mlintir** to spin, twirl, twist around.

plintiran twisted around.

pliosén (*D*) Pliocene.

plisir → PELISIR.

plit → FLIT.

plitur → PELITUR.

PLLU (*init*) → PENGATUR *Lalu Lintas Udara*. **ke-PLLU-an** Air Traffic Controller's matters. *pengetahuan* ~ air traffic controller's knowledge.

PLM (*init*) [Perahu Layar Motor] Motorized Sailboat.

PLN (*init*) → PERUSAHAAN *Listrik Negara*.

ploi (*D*) pleat.

berploi pleated. *rok* ~ pleated skirt.

memploi to pleat.

plokis (*Pr*) police; → PLÉSONG.

ploksok (*J*) 1 corner; → PELOSOK. 2 pipe socket.

plombir (*D*) 1 filling (of a tooth). 2 lead tax sticker for a vehicle, *usu* for a bicycle.

memplombir 1 to fill (a tooth). 2 to plug up (a leak).

plonci 1 female novice, neophyte. 2 female college freshman who is undergoing hazing.

plonco I (*Jv*) male college freshman who is undergoing hazing (his head is usually shaved).

mlonco to initiate, haze.

perploncoan hazing.

plonco II (*Jv*) young watermelon.

plonco III (*Jv*) *kepala* – bald, clean-shaven; → PLONTOS.

plonco IV (*Jv*) still wet behind the ears, green, inexperienced.

plong I (*Jv*) relieved. – *rasanya* and *merasa hatinya* – to feel relieved.

plong II a 3x3-meter kiosk.

plonga-plongo (*Jv*) (to stare) with open mouth, open-mouthed gaping (in astonishment); → MELONGO.

plontos (*Jv*) 1 bald. 2 (close-)shaven. 3 freshman of the Armed Forces Academy at the Gunung Tidar in Magelang, Central Java.

memplontos to defeat (in soccer).

memplontosi to shave s.o. bald.

memplontoskan to shave bald. *Ia* ~ *rambutnya*. He shaved his hair off.

keplontosan baldness.

plorak-plorok looking this way and that with eyes wide open.

plosok → PLOKSOK.

plot (*D*) plot (of a story); → ALUR *cerita*.

plotot (*J*) **mlotot** open wide (of the eyes).

PLTA (*init*) → PEMBANGKIT *Listrik Tenaga Air*.

PLTD → PEMBANGKIT *Listrik Tenaga Diesel*.

PLTG (*init*) → PEMBANGKIT *Listrik Tenaga Gas*.

PLTGU (*init*) → PEMBANGKIT *Listrik Tenaga Gas dan Uap*.

PLTN (*init*) → PEMBANGKIT *Listrik Tenaga Nuklir*.

PLTP(B) (*init*) → PEMBANGKIT *Listrik Tenaga Panas (Bumi)*.

PLTU (*init*) → PEMBANGKIT *Listrik Tenaga Uap*.

plug (*D*) /pluh/ shift (group of employees who work a certain time of day or part of the workday). – *malam* night shift.

pluit → PELUIT.

plumbum (*L*) lead.

plumbumisasi *prosés* – plumbization process.

plung (*onom*) *mak* –! plop! the sound of s.t. falling into water; → PUNG.

plungker (*Jv*) curling up. *hama* – (folk term) a pest which attacks the young leaves of the *lamtorogung* which then become dry and curled up.

mlungker to curl up.

plung-lap 1 (*onom*) sound of s.t. falling into the water and then sinking, plop. 2 to defecate in a river.

pluntir (*Jv*) **mempluntir** and **mluntir** to twist.

plur (*D*) floor (of a room/hall, etc.)

memplur to floor/pave, provide with a floor or pavement. *Gang-gang désa diplur dengan semén pasir*. The village lanes have been paved with a mixture of sand and cement.

pluralis (*D*) plural.

pluralisme (*D*) pluralism.

pluralistik (*E*) and **pluralistis** (*D*) pluralistic.

pluralitas (*D*) plurality.

pluriform (*E*) pluriform.

pluriformitas (*E*) pluriformity.

plus (*D*) 1 plus, with, and. *jumlah uang* – *bunga* the money plus interest. *Ia memboyong patung garuda* – *satu sét kursi ukiran*. He carried off a garuda statue and a set of carved chairs. 2 (the arithmetic sign) +. *3 plus 5 = 8*. – *minus* plus or minus, more or less, approximately. *budaya Sunda* – *minus* more or less Sundanese culture. 3 excess, surplus; with enough food left over to feed itself and still have some left over. *daérah* – an area with a food surplus. 4 and more. *Kréativitas bukan hanya kemampuan tetapi kemampuan* –. Creativity is not only capability but capability and more. 5 (in some compounds) super-, a more complete and therefore more expensive version of something (more than what is usual for that category).

plutokrasi (*D*) plutocracy.

plutokrat (*D*) plutocrat.

plutokratis (*D*) plutocratic.

plutonium (*D*) plutonium.

PM I (*init*) → PERDANA *Menteri*.

PM II (*init*) → POLISI *Militér*.

PM III [Pro Mémori] (in budgets, etc.) for your information. *mata anggaran* – proforma entry.

PMA (*init*) → PENANAMAN *Modal Asing*.

PMDN (*init*) → PENANAMAN *Modal Dalam Negeri*.

PMI (*init*) → PALANG *Mérah Indonésia*.

PMPI (*init*) → PARTAI *Muda Pembangunan Indonésia*.

PMS (*init*) → PENYAKIT *menular séksual*.

PN (*init*) → PERUSAHAAN *Negara*. **mem-PN-kan** to convert into a State Corporation.

Pnb [penerbang] flight, air (*mod*).

pnématik → PNÉUMATIK.

pnémonia → PNÉUMONIA.

pnéumatik (*D/E*) pneumatic.

pnéumonia (*D/E*) pneumonia.

PNG (*init*) → PAPUA *Nugini*.

PNI (*init*) → PARTAI *Nasional Indonésia*.

PNU (*init*) → PARTAI *Nahdlatul Ulama*.

po (*C*) k.o. card game. *main* – to play that card game.

poad → FUAD.

poal (*D*) voile (k.o. of fabric).

poatang (*C J*) discovered, caught (red-handed/in the act). *Baru dia mau nyopét sudah* –. He was just about to pickpocket s.o. when he was caught red-handed.

pocap (*Jv*) **mem(p)ocapkan** to have (*wayang* puppets) speak on the stage.

pocés (*J*) *main* – to play a game with marbles using a very small pot into which the marbles are to be rolled.

poci (*D*) earthenware receptacle for boiling coffee or tea; teapot; coffeepot.

pocok (*Jv*) **mocok-mocok** *bekerja* ~ to work at a lot of different jobs. *Orang itu bekerja* ~ *alias serabutan di Kota Binjai*. That person has too many irons in the fire on Binjai (North Sumatra).

memocoki to fill a place/post/position temporarily.

memocokkan to fill in for s.o. else temporarily.

pocokan /poco'an/ 1 casual/temporary laborer. *Dia mengakui bahwa meréka adalah supir* ~ *yang sering disuruh mengambil kayu di lélangan*. He admitted that they were temporarily employed drivers who were often told to pick up logs at auctions. 2 filler (newspaper article that fills in).

pocong I (*Jv*) 1 harvested rice tied in bundles. 2 a unit of weight for raw rice (15 of them make an *agem*).

sepocong a bundle of harvested rice, about a handful.

pocong II (*Jv*) a winding sheet, burial shroud. *hantu* – a ghost wrapped in a winding sheet. *sumpah* – an oath to prove one's innocence, the person taking the oath is wrapped in a winding sheet and takes the oath before a judge in a mosque. **bersumpah pocong** to take such an oath.

memocong(i) to wrap s.o. who is taking the oath in a winding sheet.

pocongan a shrouded corpse.

poco-poco (*Min*) k.o. Manadonese song and dance.

berpoco-poco to dance this dance.

podak *pandan* – a *pandan*-like epiphyte, *Pandanus tectorius*.

podang → KEPUDANG.

podemporem (*D Jv*) iodoform.

podéng (*D*) pudding. – *roti* bread pudding.

podi dust (of precious stones).

poding (*D*) → PODÉNG. – *waluh kuning* pumpkin pudding.

podium (*D*) podium, platform.

podomoro (*Jv*) k.o. stir-fried beef in coconut milk.

podsol (*E*) podzol.

podsolik (*E*) podzolic.

poen /pun/ marijuana; → PUN II.

poési (*D*) poetry.

pof (*D*) (*usu* a part of the name of a garment) bouffant, puffed out (of a garment/article of clothing). *celana* – plus fours. *lengan* – puff sleeves.

poffertje (*D*) /poferce/ tiny buttered and sugared pancakes.

pogo kitchen shelf; kitchen rack for dishes/glassware/food. *Ada seékor harimau tutul di atas – di rumah Gimin.* There was a panther on the kitchen shelf in Gimin's house.

pogrom (*D*) pogrom.

Pohaci (*S*) name of a female deity, goddess. – *Sang Hyang Sri* or *Nyi Seri* the consort of the god Wishnu and the patron of the rice plant.

pohon I 1 tree. 2 plant. 3 origin, source, cause, root. – *segala kejahatan* the root of all evil. *ketela* – cassava. *pulang* – commemoration of s.o.'s death at one year, two years, etc. after the person's death. *bagaimana – tiada akan tumbang dipanah halilintar, sebab baluhan kulit ada di batangnya* if you play with fire, you'll get burned. *seperti – beringin ditiup angin* it was pull-devil-pull-back. *ada angin ada –nya* everything has its source. – *beringin* banyan tree. – *buah(an)* fruit tree. – *hayati* arbor vitae; → KALPATARU. – *jaran* k.o. tree whose leaves are used for goat fodder. – *jarum* conifer. – *kayu* (wild growing) tree. – *kehidupan* arbor vitae; → KALPATARU. – *kelapa* coconut tree. – *mérah* poinsettia, *Euphorbia pulcherrima*. – *natal plastik* artificial Christmas tree. – *peneduh/perindang* shade tree. – *pisang* banana tree. – *rebahan* downed tree. – *Terang* Christmas tree.

pohon-pohon [and **pepohonan** (*J*)] 1 a cluster of various k.o. tree species. 2 a heavily wooded area. 3 trees (in general). 4 place where plants grow luxuriantly. 5 an artificial Christmas tree.

sepohon one tree(ful). *monyét* ~ a) a tree full of monkeys. b) all the monkeys on a tree.

berpohon *hujan* ~, *panas berasal* everything has its source.

pohon-pohonan trees, vegetation.

pohon II 1 s.t. that resembles a tree. 2 basis, principles. – *angin* thick, dark rain clouds on the horizon (presaging a storm). – *bahasa* the basis of (or, principles behind) a language. – *mata* inner canthus of the eye. – *sejarah* family/genealogical tree, genealogy. – *telinga* part of the ear that joins the head.

pohon III **memohon** to request, ask nicely/respectfully; → MOHON and *cp* PINTA I.

memohonkan to ask for nicely/respectfully.

poin(t) (*E*) point, *naik dua* – to increase by two points.

pojok (*J/Jv*) 1 corner (of a room/street, etc.). 2 (newspaper) column. *isi* – short, sharp criticism (on government measures/politics, etc.) written in a humorous way and published in the newspaper.

memojok to (go) sit in the corner.

memojokkan [and **mojokin** (*J coq*)] to corner, force into the corner (or, into a difficult position). *Ménko Polkam Sudomo tidak bermaksud ~ réktor.* Coordinating Minister for the Political and Security Sector Sudomo did not intend to corner the deans.

terpojok(kan) cornered, backed into a corner, forced into a difficult position, in a bad spot. **keterpojokan** being forced into a corner/difficult position.

pojokan corner.

pemojokan cornering, forcing into a difficult position.

pok (*J*) (older) sister; → (E)MPOK.

poka **memoka-moka** to gouge out. *Kunci lemari dipoka-poka.* The wardrobe lock was gouged out.

pokah broken (of branches, etc.), ruined, irreparable.

pokal (*Jv*) trick, ruse.

pokang leg, quarter (of a slaughtered animal).

pokat *buah* – avocado; → *buah* ADPOKAT/ADVOKAT II/ALPUKAT/ APOKAT.

pokay (*Pr*) difficult; → PAYAH.

poken (*D*) *sakit* – smallpox.

pokéng tailless (fowls).

poker (*D*) poker.

pokét (*E*) 1 pocket (in a coat). 2 pocket (an isolated group of soldiers).

pokja → KELOMPOK *kerja*.

poko and **pok-o** (*C*) /po'o/ *minyak* – peppermint oil, mentholatum ointment (to help relieve cold symptoms, etc.), such as Vick's Vaporub, etc.

pokok I 1 *kayu* tree (trunk). 2 plant. 3 stem (of trees, from base to top), stalk. *Pada – pohon karét itu terdapat banyak toréhan.* Many notches can be found on the stem of the rubber tree. 4 (*Mal*) tree. – *beringin* banyan tree, *Ficus benjamina* – *bunga* flowering plant. – *eru* casuarina tree, *Casuarina equisetifolia*. – *nyiur* coconut palm, *Cocos nucifera*. – *padi* rice plant, *Oryza spp*.

sepokok a/one tree; of the same tree.

pokok II 1 (– + noun) topic, subject, point. 2 cause, source, reason, tenet; basic, fundamental. 3 origin, beginning, starting point, center (of one's attention). 4 capital, stake, pool. 5 base, main ingredient, essentials, principal. 6 main/lower part of s.t. 7 root, radical, etymon. *inilah yang – buat saya* this is the fundamental thing for me. *Keperluan – orang Indonésia hanyalah beras dan pakaian.* The only essential needs of Indonesians are rice and clothing. *dijual di bawah* – sold below cost. *mahal – nya* a) purchased at a high price. b) great initial costs. *(terus) menuju* – to the point. – *belum sampai* hasn't recovered the cost price yet. – *acara* main point. – *acuan* itemized list. –.– *ajaran agama* tenets, dogmas. – *amal* funds. – *bahasan* topic/subject under discussion. – *cerita* main story, plot line; → ALUR *cerita*. – *dasar* main point/thing. – *hidangan* main course. – *hujan* rain cloud. – *hukum* judicial basis. –.– *hukum Islam* the foundations of Islam. – *kalimat* (*gram*) subject of a sentence. – *kata* (*gram*) root, stem, radical, etymon. *menghendaki – katanya ialah kehendak dan kehendak – katanya ialah hendak* the stem of *menghendaki* is *kehendak* and the stem of *kehendak* is *hendak*. – *kehidupan* source of livelihood. – *lampu* light fixture. – *lukisan* a) drawing motif. b) the main features, (sketchy) outline, draft. – *masalah* the gist of the problem. – *nama* surname, family name. – *pajak* principal of the taxes. – *pangkal* main point. – *pekerjaan* source of income. – *pembicaraan* topic of conversation. – *pencaharian/penghidupan* source of income. – *peperangan* cause of war. – *perasaan* (*hati*) (inner) motives. – *perkara* (*leg*) substance of the case. – *perlawanan* pocket of resistance. – *perselisihan* matter in dispute, cause of conflict, bone of contention. – *persengkétaan* feud, enmity. – *persoalan* the gist of the matter. – *perundingan* topic of discussion. – *pikiran* basic idea, leading thought. – *pinjaman* principal (of a loan). – *tentara* main force/body of the army.

pokoknya the main thing. ~ *ialah* ... the main thing is that ..., the primary consideration is that ..., the heart of the matter is that ..., it boils down to this ... ~ *kepada Anda* it's in your hands. *pada* ~ in principle, fundamentally, basically, essentially, in effect; → *pada* ASASNYA.

sepokok 1 same as the cost. *dijual* ~ to be sold at cost. 2 the most basic/important.

berpokok 1 ~ *[(ke)pada]* to be based/founded (on), have as a basis. *masyarakat yang* ~ *kepada kemajuan ilmu dan téknologi* a society based on scientific and technological advancement. 2 to come/derive/emanate/proceed (from). **3** to have capital. **4** with cause/reason. **5** starting from (the assumption that).

berpokokkan ~ *[(ke)pada]* to be based on, have as a basis. *Bahasa Indonesia ~ (pada) bahasa Melayu.* Indonesian is based on Malay.

memokoki to finance, provide the capital for, subsidize.

mem(p)okokkan 1 to center on. **2** to concentrate (all one's strength) on. *Dia ~ diri pada pelajaran sekolah.* He concentrated on school subjects.

memperpokokkan to use as capital. *~ uang yang dipinjam dari bank* to use the money borrowed from a bank as capital (to carry on a business).

terpokok 1 most important, foremost. *Maksud kongrés yang ~ ialah ...* the foremost goal of the congress was to ... **2** fixed (price). **3** to cost, be worth. *~ oléhnya 80 hari bekerja.* It cost him 80 days of work. *Itu ~ mahal buat saya.* It's worth a lot to me.

pokok III cloud (token of bad luck). *- angin/hujan/ribut* black rain clouds (presaging a "Sumatra" gale, as viewed from the Malaysian side).

pokrol (*D procureur*) **1** lawyer, attorney. **2** (*coq*) s.o. who has the gift of gab. *- bambu* a) small-time/shyster lawyer. b) able debater. ***mempokrolbambukan*** to distort (the truth), twist (the facts around). ***perpokrol-bambuan*** hairsplitting, arguing for the sake of arguing.

memokrolkan to have (a *pokrol*) represent one.

pokrol-pokrolan to twist words around, split hairs.

poksai and **poksay** (*C*) *- kuda* rufous-fronted laughing thrush, *Garrulax rufifrons.*

pokta (*Pers*) perfect, paramount, preeminent.

pol I (*D*) **1** full (of a bus, etc.). *Bisnya sudah -.* The bus is full (of passengers). *paling - at most, maximum. Gedung itu hanya didatangi paling - 100 atau 125 orang.* The building was visited by at most only 100 or 125 people. **2** at top volume, full blast. *Radionya dipasang -.* He turned the radio up full blast. **3** (paid) in full. *saya sudah membayar - harganya* I've paid the price in full.

sepol-polnya as full as possible.

mempolkan 1 to floor (the gas pedal of a car). **2** to fill up (a car).

pol-polan (to play) at top volume, full blast.

pol II (*D*) volt(age). *lengkap -.-nya* totally lit up.

pol III (*J*) /poul/ rendezvous point, place where people, cars, etc. meet.

mempol to meet (mostly in passive *dipol*). *Semua yang mau ikut dipol di stasiun.* Everyone who wants to go along should meet at the station.

pol IV (*E*) (public opinion) poll; → JAJAK *pendapat.*

pol V (in acronyms) → KEPOLISIAN, POLISI, POLITIK.

pola (*Jv*) **1** pattern (for sewing). **2** model, pattern. **3** structure. **4** blueprint, outline, plan. *Gedung -* Blueprint Hall (Jl. Pegangsaan Timur 56 in Jakarta); the site of the proclamation of Indonesian independence on August 17, 1945. *- baju* pattern (for sewing). *- berpikir* mindset. *- bunyi* phonology. *- dasar* basic pattern. *- gelar* (*mil*) deployment pattern. *- hidup* lifestyle. *- induk* master plan. *- kalimat* (*gram*) sentence structure. *- kebudayaan* cultural pattern. *- pembangunan* development plan. *- pengobatan* plan of therapy. *- tataniaga* marketing plan. *- tidur* sleep pattern.

sepola with the same pattern as.

berpola to have a pattern/model.

mem(p)ola to form a pattern.

mem(p)olakan to take as one's pattern, fashion. *~ hidup sederhana* to fashion a simple life.

terpola taken as a pattern, patterned after. *Banyak orang Islam di Teluk, khususnya di negara itu, sudah ~ oléh pemikiran Barat.* Many Muslims in the Gulf, especially in that country, pattern themselves on Western ways of thinking.

pemolaan model, pattern.

polah I (*M*) affluent.

berpolah-polah 1 extravagant, luxurious. **2** plentiful, abundant.

polah II (*Jv*) way of acting, manner.

polam → PUALAM.

polan (*A*) *si -* John Doe, Mr. So-and-so, what's his name; → DADAP II.

Polandia Poland.

polang-paling to sheer (of the wind), whirl.

polang-poléng (*J*) **1** checkered. **2** painted in camouflaged colors.

Polantas → POLISI *Lalu-Lintas. - udara* (*coq*) air traffic controller.

polar (*D/E*) polar.

Polaris *bintang -* polestar, Polaris.

polarisasi (*D*) polarization.

berpolarisasi to be polarized.

mem(p)olarisasikan to polarize. *Tugas pria dan wanita masih dipolarisasikan dengan tajam.* The duties of men and women are still sharply polarized.

terpolarisasi(kan) polarized.

polaritas (*D*) polarity.

polas-polés smeared; → POLÉS.

Polda → KEPOLISIAN *Daérah.*

Polda Métro Jaya → KEPOLISIAN *Daérah Métropolitan Jakarta Raya.*

poldan (*D*) fully paid (of debt).

polder (*D*) polder.

Polék → POLISI *Ékonomi.*

Poléksosbudhankam [Politik, Ékonomi, Sosial, Budaya, Pertahanan dan Keamanan] Politics, Economics, Social, Cultural, Security and Defense.

Poléksosbudmil [Politik, Ékonomi, Sosial, Budaya dan Militér] Politics, Economics, Social, Cultural and Military.

polémik (*D*) polemic.

berpolémik to carry on a controversy.

mem(p)olémikkan to carry on a debate over.

polémis (*D*) polemic(al), controversial.

polémologi (*D/E*) polemology.

poléng (*Jv*) check (in pattern); → POLANG-POLÉNG.

berpoléng-poléng checked, checkered.

polentér (*D*) **1** (practical) trainee, unsalaried clerk. **2** volunteer.

polés (*D*) polish, s.t. used for polishing. *- muka* face cream.

memolés(i) 1 to polish, apply polish/wax, etc. to. **2** to make up (one's face/nails, etc.). **3** to improve, polish.

polés-memolés ~ *muka* facial makeup.

memoléskan to smear with.

terpolés polished.

polésan 1 s.t. polished. **2** makeup, s.t. smeared on.

pemolés s.o. or s.t. that polishes.

pemolésan polishing.

polét I (*D*) **1** epaulette. **2** (*coq*) blaze, a broad, colored line or incision made on a tree trunk as a sign or token.

polét II (*Jv*) guard/watchman at the village head's house.

Polgab [Polisi Gabungan] Joint Police (Force).

Polhuttér → POLISI *Hutan Téritorial.*

poli → POLIKLINIK.

poliandri (*D*) polyandry.

berpoliandri to practice polyandry, polyandrous. *Wanita ~ akhirnya berurusan dengan pengadilan.* In the end the polyandrous woman had to deal with the court.

poliéster (*D/E*) polyester. *benang -* polyester yarn.

poligam (*D*) polygamous.

poligami (*D*) polygamy.

berpoligami to practice polygamy, be a polygamist.

poligamis (*D*) polygamist.

poligini (*D/E*) polygyny.

poliglot (*D/E*) polyglot.

poligon (*D/E*) polygon.

poliklinik (*D*) (poly)clinic. *- gigi* dental clinic. *- spésialis* specialist clinic. *- umum* general clinic.

poliklinis (*D*) polyclinical.

polimér (*D*) polymer.

pemoliméran polymerization.

polimérisasi (*D*) polymerization.

Po Limo (*Jv*) the Five P's (President Soeharto's pun on *Mo Limo*; 1959). *Perut, Pakaian, Perumahan, Pergaulan dan Pengetahuan,* i.e., Stomach, Clothing, Housing, Social Intercourse, and Knowledge.

polimorfonukléar (*E*) polymorph nuclear.

polinasi → PENYERBUKAN.

Polinésia (*D/E*) Polynesia.

polio I (*D*) polio(myelites).

polio II (*D*) foolscap-size paper; → FOLIO.

poliol (*E*) polyol.

polip (*D*) 1 polyp, an organism of which coral is composed. 2 polyp, an abnormal growth projecting from a mucous membrane.

polipropilén (*E*) polypropylene.

polis I (*D*) (insurance) policy. – *asuransi* insurance policy. – *bersusut* floating policy. – *pausal* blanket policy. – *terbuka* open policy.

polis II → POLÉS.

polis III (*Mal*) police. – *Hutan* similar to Indonesian Mobile Brigades. – *Marin* Marine Police. – *tentera* military police, MP.

polisakarida (*D*) polysaccharide.

polisémi (*D/E*) polysemy.

polisi (*D*) 1 police. 2 policeman. *agén* – policeman. – *antihuru-hara/antikerusuhan* (*infr*) riot police. – *berkuda* mounted police. – *cepék* → PAK ogah. – *Ékonomi* [Polék] Economy Police. – *gadungan* bogus/fake policeman. – *Hutan* Forest Rangers; → JAGAWANA. – *Hutan Téritorial* [Polhuttér] Territorial Forest Rangers. – *Kehutanan* Forest Rangers. – *kesusilaan* vice squad. – *Khusus* [Polsus] Special Police. – *Khusus Keréta Api* [Polsuska] Special Railway Police. – *Khusus Kehutanan* [Polsustan] Special Forest Rangers; *cp* JAGAWANA. – *Lalu Lintas* [Pol(an)tas] Traffic Police. – *Lalu Lintas Swasta* [Poltas Swasta] Private Traffic Police, i.e., individuals posing as traffic police and pocketing fines, "donations," etc. – *Militér* [P(O)M] Military Police, MP. – *Pamong Praja* Jakarta's Village Police. – *Pariwisata* [Polpar] Tourist Police (in tourist areas, such as Yogyakarta, Bali, etc.). – *pengendali huru-hara* (*infr*) riot control police. – *perairan* a) coast guard. b) harbor police. – *Perairan dan Udara* Sea and Air Police. – *rahasia* secret police; detective. – *Sahabat Anak* a police program to introduce traffic laws, etc. to schoolchildren. – *susila* vice squad. – *tidur* (*coq*) speed trap, traffic bump. – *udara* sky marshal. – *Wanita* [Polwan] policewoman.

mempolisii to be the police for, to police. ~ *kualitas kehidupan bangsanya* to police the nation's quality of life.

mempolisikan to police/regulate/control, keep order over (by means of the police). ~ *birokrasi* to police the bureaucracy.

polisi-polisian bogus/fake policeman; → POLISI *gadungan*.

kepolisian 1 police (*mod*). 2 police (force). *aksi* ~ police action. *angkatan* ~ police force. – *Daérah* [Polda] Regional Police; has jurisdiction over a province and supervises *Polrés* and *Polwil*. ~ *Daérah Métropolitan Jakarta Raya* [Polda Métro Jaya] Greater Jakarta Metropolitan Regional Police. ~ *Kota Besar* [Poltabés] Large City Police (in Semarang, Padang, etc.). ~ *Negara Républik Indonésia* [Polri] Republic of Indonesia State Police. ~ *Résort* [Polrés] Subregional Police; has jurisdiction over a *kebupatén* or *kota madia* and is one level above a *Polsék* and one level under *Polwil*. ~ *Résort Kota* [Polrésta] City Subregional Police. ~ *Résort Métropolitan* [Polrés Métro] Metropolitan Subregional Police. ~ *Séktor* [Polsék] Sector Police; has jurisdiction over a *kecamatan* and is one level under a *Polrés*. ~ *Séktor Kota* [Polsékta] City Sector Police, precinct. ~ *Wilayah* [Polwil] Territorial Police, one level above *Polrés* and one level under *Polda*. ~ *Wilayah Kota Besar* [Polwiltabés] Large City Territorial Police (the only one which exists at present is for Surabaya).

pemolisian policing.

polisilabik (*D gram*) polysyllabic. *kata* – polysyllabic word.

polisionil (*D*) (and sporadically **polisional**) police (*mod*); → KEPOLISIAN. *aksi* – police action, i.e., the two police actions launched by the Dutch against the *de facto* Republic of Indonesia in 1947 and 1948.

Politbiro (*D*) Politburo.

politéis (*D*) polytheist.

politéisme (*D/E*) polytheism.

politéknik (*D/E*) polytechnic.

politik (*D*) 1 (= *ilmu* –) political science. 2 politics. 3 political. *tahanan* – [tapol] political prisoner. 4 policy. *menjalankan* – a) to participate actively in politics. b) to pursue a policy. c) to be in power. – *antropologi* anthropological politics. – *banting harga* dumping policy. – *berdampingan secara damai* policy of peaceful coexistence. – *bermuka dua* two-faced policy. – *(ber)tetangga baik* good-neighbor policy. – *berunding-terbang-kiankemari* shuttle diplomacy. – *burung unta* ostrich policy. – *dagang sapi* horse-trading, jobbery. – *dalam dan luar negeri* domestic and foreign policy. – *dekat-mendekati* policy of rapprochement. – *dua-Cina* two-China policy. – *ékonomi* economic policy. – *ekspansionis* expansionist policy. – *impérialisme* imperialist policy. – *kepungan* policy of containment. – *keuangan* financial policy. – *keuangan ketat* tight-money policy. – *luar negeri bébas aktif* and – *luar negeri yang aktif dan bébas* nonaligned foreign policy. – *menentang* aggressive policy. – *mengalah demi perdamaian* appeasement policy. – *monétér* monetary policy. – *nasional* national policy. – *pat-gulipat* manipulatory policy. – *Pemerintah* Government policy. – *pengepungan* policy of containment. – *pintu terbuka* open-door policy. – *praktis* action-oriented policy. – *Putih Australia* White Australia Policy. – *satu-Cina* one-China policy. – *témpél-menémpél* patchwork policy. – *tidak berpihak* nonaligned policy. – *uang* financial policy. – *uang seret* tight-money policy.

berpolitik 1 to take an active part in politics, be an active member of a political party. 2 to have a ... political character.

mem(per)politikkan to politicize.

politik-politikan tomfoolery. *Dagang sapi sungguhan (dan bukan ~) di Bondowoso cukup ramai.* Real cattle trading (and not fooling) around was quite animated in Bondowoso.

kepolitikan 1 politics; political (*mod*). 2 political affairs.

pemolitikan politicization, politicizing.

perpolitikan 1 politicizing. 2 political (*mod*).

politikawan (*infr*) politician.

politikolog (*D*) political scientist.

politikus (*D*) politician.

politis political. *tujuan* – political goals.

politisan politician.

politisasi (*E*) politicization.

mempolitisasikan to politicize.

politisi (*D*) 1 (*pl* of *politikus*) politicians. 2 (used as *sg*) politician.

politisir (*D*) **mem(per)politisir** to politicize. *Hentikan sikap ~ bahasa Melayu.* Stop the policy of politicizing the Malay language.

politur (*D*) polish, varnish, shine.

mem(p)olitur to polish, varnish, shine.

polituran polished, varnished, shine.

poliurétan (*D/E*) polyurethane.

polmah (*D*) 1 power of attorney; → SURAT *kuasa*. 2 proxy.

Polmas [(Kabupatén) Poléwali Mamasa] Mamasa Regency (in South Sulawesi).

polo (*D*) polo (a game played on horseback). – *air* water polo.

polok memolok to swallow, gulp down, gorge o.s. on (rice and side dishes).

polonés (*D*) polonaise.

polong I 1 a bottle imp, familiar spirit in the form of a cricket. 2 nervous breakdown, k.o. hysteria (attributed to black magic/witchcraft/sorcery, etc.). *seperti – kena sembur* a) submissive, docile. b) to be off like a shot.

polong II *kacang* – green peas, *Pisum sativum. tumbuhan* – legume.

polong-polongan leguminoceae.

polong III – *angin* k.o. skin bump.

polong IV k.o. clove (the spice).

polong V (*M*) **memolongkan** to lay outlet pipes.

polong(-polong)an outlet (pipe), waste pipe, drainpipe, sewer, culvert.

polontér unsalaried clerk.

polorogo (*Jv*) illegal retribution on the transfer of a lien on land, on the slaughter of cattle, on house transactions, etc.

polos (*J/Jv*) 1 simple, solid (of color), unpatterned (of fabrics, etc.), blank. 2 uncovered, naked, bare. 3 single, unmarried. 4a) unbiased. b) honest, straightforward, calling a spade a spade, not mincing one's words, matter-of-fact. 5 innocent. 6 smooth. 7 (*Jv*) plain, unadorned. 8 pure, impeccable, immaculate. *telanjang/dalam keadaan* – stark-naked. *Pengakuan-pengakuan – dari Déwi.* Dewi's straightforward admissions. *pikiranku yang masih* – I'm not aware of any wrongdoing. *cincin* – a plain ring.

pandangan hidup yang – a straightforward/uncomplicated way of looking at life. *pintu* – a flush door. *tarif* – bus fare which excludes extras, such as a reclining chair, air-conditioning, refreshments, passenger insurance, toilet, etc. *warna* – solid color.

sepolos as simple/honest, etc. as.

berpolos-polos uncovered, bare, naked.

memoloskan to blank.

polosan blanking.

kepolosan 1 honesty, straightforwardness. **2** smoothness. **3** naturalness, unadorned nature.

pemolosan blanking.

polowijo (*Jv*) nonstaple food crops, subsidiary or secondary to rice.

Polpar [Polisi Pariwisata] Tourist Police.

Polrés(ta) → KEPOLISIAN *Résort (Kota)*.

Polri → KEPOLISIAN *Negara Républik Indonésia*.

Polsék(ta) → KEPOLISIAN *Séktor (Kota)*.

Polsus → POLISI *Khusus*.

Poltabés → KEPOLISIAN *Kota Besar*.

Poltas → POLISI *Lalu Lintas*, POLANTAS.

Poltas Swasta → POLISI *Lalu Lintas Swasta*.

polusi (*D*) pollution; → PENCEMARAN. *– udara* air pollution.

   berpolusi polluted. *industri semén merupakan industri ~ berat* the cement industry is a heavily polluted industry. *tidak ~* pollution-free, unpolluted. *industri tidak ~* pollution-free industry.

   terpolusi polluted.

polutan (*E*) pollutant.

polutif (*E*) polluting.

Polwan → POLISI *Wanita*.

Polwil(tabes) → KEPOLISIAN *Wilayah (Kota Besar)*.

pom I (*D*) pump; → POMPA. *– bénsin* gas station. *Pada jam 21.30 WIB –.– bénsin sudah tutup*. The gas stations have closed by 9:30 p.m. West Indonesia time.

POM II (*init*) → PERSATUAN *Orangtua Murid*.

POM III (*init*) → POLISI *Militér*.

pomade (*D*) pomade.

pomang (in West Kalimantan) *pawang* for *adat* ceremonies, hired when opening up new land for prospective transmigrants.

poma-poma (*Jv*) **1** emphatically. **2** (in negative sentence) in no case, on no account. *– jangan sampai memakai siasat mundur teratur*. On no account should we use a tactic of orderly retreat.

pompa (*D*) **1** pump. **2** squirt, syringe, hose. *rumah –* (water) pumping station, pump house. *– air* water pump. *– angin* air pump. *– asi* breast pump; → ASI V. *– bahan bakar* fuel pump. *– ban* tire air pump. *– bantu* auxiliary pump. *– benam* submerged pump. *– bénsin* a) gas station. b) fuel pump. *– bolak-balik* reciprocating pump. *– hidro-éléktrik* hydroelectric pump. *– hisap* suction pump. *– infus* intravenous pump. *– isap* suction pump. *– isi* charging pump. *– kaki* foot pump. *– kebakaran* fire engine. *– kincir* winding pump. *– lénsa* bilge pump. *– minyak* oil pump. *– pemadam api* fire engine. *– pemadam api pakai slang* hose fire engine. *– pendingin* coolant pump. *– pengisi* charging pump. *– pusingan* centrifugal pump. *– putar* rotary pump. *– perangkap* sump pump. *– semprot* injection pump. *– sepéda* bicycle pump. *– sérét* draw pump. *– tangan/tusuk* hand pump. *– udara* air pump.

   memompa 1 to pump, inflate (a tire, etc.); to inflate, pump up, jack up. *Sekarang secara buatan harga kopra dipompa ke atas*. Nowadays the price of copra has been jacked up artificially. *Tapi semangat tampaknya tetap dipompa*. But it seems as if his spirits were constantly being pumped up. *~ kehidupan* to support life. **2** (*vulg*) to fuck; to move s.t. in and out (as in sex).

   memompakan 1 to pump/inflate s.t. for s.o. else. *~ adiknya (ban) sepéda* to inflate the bicycle tires for his younger sibling. **2** to pump (into). *Sejak tahun itu, sewaktu negara itu berdiri, Amérika telah ~ 23,8 milyard US $ ke negara itu*. Since that year, when that country was founded, America has pumped $23.8 billion dollars into it. *~ semangat* to inspire. **3** to cram s.t. into s.o. *Pengetahuan yang dipompakan kepada kita, hilang semuanya*. All the knowledge crammed into us has disappeared.

   terpompa pumped.

   pompaan 1 s.t. that has been inflated. **2** pumping movements.

   kepompaan pumpage.

   pemompa s.o. or s.t. that pumps, pumper, pump.

pemompaan 1 pumping (water, etc.) up. **2** inflating (tires, etc.).

pompanisasi (the introduction of a) system of pumps (for irrigation).

pompom (*E*) pompom, i.e., a rapid-firing automatic weapon.

pompong I a small inedible cuttlefish.

pompong II → KEPOMPONG.

pompong III (*M*) kepompongan restless, worried.

pompong IV memompong to honor/love s.o.

pompong V (*ob*) memompong **1** to carry in both arms. **2** to carry on the hip or waist (in a scarf or piece of cloth).

pompong VI nail protector (for a nail that has been allowed to grow long).

pompong VII a small tree with white flowers, erberus tree, *Cerbera manghas*.

pompong VIII *perahu –* (in the Riau archipelago) a wooden riverboat.

pon I (*E*) pound (the measure of weight), about half a kilogram.

   pon-ponan by the pound.

pon II (*E*) pound sterling (the monetary unit of the United Kingdom); → PAUN.

pon III (*Jv*) nephew; niece; → KEMENAKAN, KEPONAKAN.

pon IV (*Jv*) the third day of the five-day market week.

PON V (*init*) → PEKAN *Olahraga Nasional*.

ponakan (*Jv*) nephew; niece; → KEMENAKAN, KEPONAKAN.

ponco (*D/E*) poncho.

poncol I small market.

poncol II (*J*) bud, sprout; young leaf.

poncol III (*J/Jv*) swelling, projecting outward; slight lump/swelling, bulge on the forehead.

pondamén (*D*) foundation (of a building). *– beton* concrete foundation.

pondan (*Mal*) hermaphrodite who passes as a female; → PONÉN.

pondar (*M*) short and fat.

pondasi (*D*) foundation (of a building). *– cakar ayam* "chicken-claw foundation" a road construction technique invented by Dr. Sedyatmo.

pondik (*M*) conceited, proud.

pondoh (*Jv*) edible palm pith, palm cabbage.

pondok (*A?*) **1** cottage; bungalow (in the mountains). **2** one's humble abode (irrespective of size). **3** (*J*) cabin, shed, hut, hovel. **4** (*M*) Muslim religious boarding facility/school; → PESANTRÉN. *– Bambu* the Pondok Bambu Penitentiary in East Jakarta. *mem-Pondok Bambukan* to incarcerate at the Pondok Bambu Penitentiary. *2.444 gelandangan di-Pondok Bambukan*. 2,444 homeless people were incarcerated in the Pondok Bambu Penitentiary. *– Bersalin Pedésaan* [Polindés] Rural Maternity Station. *– boro* temporary housing. *– pamér* stand, booth. *– wisata* home stay, pension. *– wisata pemuda* youth hostel.

   berpondok with a boarding facility/house.

   memondok [and **mondok** (*coq*)] to live in a rented room away from home, board.

   memondoki to rent a room in (s.o.'s house). *Rumahnya dipondoki para mahasiswa*. University students rented rooms in his house.

   memondokkan to board s.o., have s.o. live in s.o.'s house as a paying guest.

   pondokan 1 place to stay when away from home. **2** lodgings. **3** rented room. *menerima ~ untuk dua karyawati* to accept two female employees as paying guests. *Untuk membayar ~ kamar dicari yang semurah mungkin dan yang disesuaikan dengan penghasilan yang diterima sepekan sekali*. In order to pay for a rented room one has to find as cheap (a place) as possible commensurate with one's weekly income. *anak ~* boarder; → ANAK *kos. tempat ~* housing accommodations. **sepondokan** in the same boarding facility/house. *seorang teman perempuan yang tinggal ~ dengan saya* a female friend who lives in the same boardinghouse as I do.

   pemondok boarder.

   pemondokan accommodations, boardinghouse. *mencari ~* looking for accommodations (or, a boardinghouse) (in advertisements). **sepemondokan** in the same boardinghouse. *kawan ~* fellow boarder.

pondong I shelter to protect young plants.

berpondong with such a shelter.
memondong(i) to provide plants with such a shelter.
pondong II (*Jv*) **memondong** to carry (a child or s.t.) in both arms.
memondong-mondong to carry s.t. on one's back. *orang yang ~ ransel* a backpacker.
pondongan (during a wedding) the ceremony of carrying one's bride in one's arms; if the groom is unable to do this, he can be helped by s.o. else (similar to the best man at Western weddings).
ponén (*Mal*) hermaphrodite who passes as a female.
pong (*C*) *tahu* – small pieces of fried soybean cake eaten with a spicy hot soy sauce.
pongah I conceited, arrogant, cocky (in words and in actions), snobbish.
berpongah(-pongah) and **berpongah** *diri* to boast, brag.
memongahkan to boast/brag about.
kepongahan conceit, arrogance, cockiness, boasting, bragging. *~ kekuasaan* arrogance of power.
pongah II (*J/Jv*) stupid, dull.
memongah to cheat.
pongang → SIPONGANG.
ponggawa I (in the southern Celebes) middleman; → TENGKULAK.
ponggawa II → PUNGGAWA.
ponggok I tailless, stumpy. *ayam* – tailless chicken.
ponggok II owl; → PUNGGUK I.
ponggok III (*M*) **terponggok 1** to squat on one's haunches. **2** to loom.
pongkol (*J*) bulb(root).
pongo (*Jv*) (to be a) simpleton.
pongpong I (*J*) **1** empty. *Kelapanya sudah pada – dimakan bajing.* The coconuts were all empty because the insides had been eaten by squirrels. **2** hole (in coconut husk).
memongpongi [and **mompongi** (*coq*)] **1** to eat the contents of a coconut until it is empty. **2** to gnaw a hole in (a coconut husk).
pongpong II *burung* – fluffy-backed babbler, *Macronous ptilosus*.
pongsu (ant)hill.
poni I (*E*) *rambut* – bang, fringe (of hair). *potong* – and
berponi to wear one's hair in a bang.
poni II (*E*) *kuda* – pony (type of horse).
ponis (*D*) verdict, sentence; → VONIS. *menjatuhkan* – to sentence, pass verdict (on).
ponok 1 (fleshy) hump (of cattle/camel); → PUNUK. **2** dome. – *uap* steam dome.
berponok with a hump, humped.
ponokawan → PUNAKAWAN.
ponoso (*Port Min*) clogged/stuffed up (of the nose).
ponpés [*pondok pesantren*] Islamic boarding school.
pons (*D*) punch (the device). *mesin* – punch press.
pontal (*Jv*) **kepontal-pontal** to have difficulty keeping up. *Kita bisa ~, sebab infrastrukturnya belum siap.* We might have difficulty keeping up because the infrastructure isn't ready yet.
pontang k.o. *rebab*.
pontang-panting (*J*) **1** scattered/strewn all over. **2** rolling over and over. **3** to run very fast, run around. *tidak kurang dari 726.000 orang tenaga kerja mungkin akan – mencari lapangan kerja selama Pelita V* no fewer than 726,000 workers will probably have to run around looking for work during the Fifth Five-Year Development Plan. *Ketiadaan kepala keluarga itulah membuat Ny Sinah harus – menghidupi anaknya.* The absence of a head of family is what made Mrs. Sinah have to run around trying to feed her children.
berpontang-panting rolling over and over.
memontang-pantingkan 1 to scatter/strew. **2** to make s.t. roll around.
terpontang-panting to run very fast, run around (like crazy trying to do s.t.). *Ini rékor baru yang, apa boléh buat, membuat Garuda ~.* This new record is s.t. that (and what could they do about it?) made Garuda run around like crazy (trying to meet the demand).
ponten (*D*) **1** marks, grades. **2** points (in a game).
berponten have a grade of…
memonten to grade (papers/exams).
pontén (*D*) fountain.

pontianak I vampire ghost of a woman who died in childbirth, banshee; → KUNTILANAK, PUNTIANAK.
Pontianak II capital city of Kalimantan Barat.
pontoh large armlet in the shape of a dragon worn on the upper arm or higher than the wrist.
berpontoh to wear such an armlet.
ponton (*D*) pontoon. *jembatan* – pontoon bridge.
pontong maimed; → PUNTUNG.
ponyar (*D*) poniard, dagger (worn by naval cadets).
po'o → POKO.
pop I (*E*) **1** pop, popular (music, etc.). *lagu-lagu* – pop songs. *penyanyi* – pop singer. **2** popularly. *Surakarta, Solo nama –nya.* Surakarta, popularly known as Solo.
ngepop 1 to sing pop music. **2** to be popular, mod. **3** to be informal. *"Hai" terasa lebih ~ dibanding "Selamat Pagi" yang terdengar klasik itu.* "Hi" feels more informal than "Good Morning," which sounds classical. *berpakaian ~* to wear mod clothing (jeans, etc.).
mempopkan to convert into pop music. *Dia lebih banyak menyanyi lagu-lagu tradisional yang dipopkan.* She more often sings traditional songs which have been converted into pop music.
pop II (*D*) doll (a child's toy); → POPI I.
popbruk (*D J*) plus-fours; → CELANA *pof*.
popelin → POPLIN.
popi I (*C*) **1** doll (a child's toy). **2** puppet.
popi II (*C*) to protect (of idols protecting worshippers).
poplin (*D*) poplin.
popok I (*Jv*) *kain* – diaper. – *sekali pakai* disposable diapers.
memopoki to diaper, put a diaper on, change (a child's) diaper.
popok II (*S*) ointment made from powder mixed with water.
memopokkan to apply such an ointment to.
popokan ghost, spook; → MOMOK I.
popor (*J/Jv*) – *senjata* rifle butt. *dipukul dengan – senjata/senapan* to be beaten with a rifle butt.
memopor to strike/hit with a rifle butt.
popos → PUPUS I.
popular (*E*) **1** popular. **2** easily understood by the masses (or, by ordinary people), not special(ized). *kamus* – a dictionary for the man in the street. *kuliah* – lecture aimed at the general public. *tidak* – unpopular. **ketidak-popularan** unpopularity.
mempopularkan 1 to popularize. *~ ilmu* to popularize the sciences. **2** to promote (a product).
terpopular most popular. *salah seorang Jurkam Nasional Golkar ~* one of the most popular *Golkar* National Campaign Leaders.
kepopularan popularity, fame.
pemopularan popularization.
popularisasi (*D*) popularization.
popularitas (*D*) popularity.
populasi (*D*) population.
populér (*D*) → POPULAR. **sepopulér** as popular as.
populir (*D*) *pohon* – poplar (tree).
populis (*D/E*) populist.
populisme (*D/E*) populism.
popwé (*C*) talisman, charm, amulet.
pora I (*J*) generous, liberal; lavish, wasteful, prodigal. *pésta* – bacchanal, feast, orgy. **berpésta** – to celebrate lavishly, have a feast. *Biasanya apabila panén berhasil para petani berpésta –.* When the harvest is successful, the farmers usually celebrate with a feast.
PORA II → PASPOR *Orang Asing*.
porah (*M*) liberal, generous, lavish; → PORA I. *berpésta* – and
berporah-porah to celebrate lavishly, have a feast.
memorahkan to waste, dissipate, squander.
porak-parik, **porak-peranda**, and **porak-poranda** messy, in a mess, chaotic, disorganized, topsy-turvy.
mem(p)orakparikkan, **mem(p)orak-perandakan** to turn upside down; to make a mess of, destroy. *Gunung Merapi di Jawa Tengah telah memporak-porandakan Kerajaan Mataram dan menyebabkan Raja Érlangga menyingkir ke Jawa Timur.* Mt. Merapi in Central Jawa destroyed the Kingdom of Mataram and forced King Erlangga to move to East Java; → PERLAYA.
porang (*S*) marl; → NAPAL.

pordéo → PRODÉO.

porek → POROK II.

porga (cla) laxative, purgative.

pori (D) pore.

  berpori-pori to have pores, be porous. ~ dengan to have pores filled with.

  keporian porosity.

porkas (E forecast) k.o. soccer pool set up on December 28, 1985. uang – soccer pool money.

  memporkaskan to bet one's pool money on (a team). kesebelasan yang diporkaskan the soccer team bet on.

porman (D coq) guard, chief.

pormil → FORMAL.

pormulir → FORMULIR.

pornés (D) oven. - gas/listrik gas/electric oven.

porno (D/E) 1 porno(graphy); pornographic; → PORNOGRAFI. 2 immoral. 3 erotic. - lunak soft porn.

  kepornoan 1 pornography. 2 pornographic.

pornografi (D/E) pornography.

pornografis (D) pornographic.

porok 1 half a coconut shell used in a child's game.

porok II (D) fork (of bicycle which holds the front wheel between the two prongs); → PENGAPIT roda.

porong congenital black patch on the skin.

poros 1 axis, pivot. 2 axle (of a wheel), shaft, spindle. 3 point (of spearhead). – angker armature spindle. – ayun oscillating axle. – baling-baling pesawat aircraft propeller hub/shaft. – belakang rear axle. – bénjol camshaft. – bor drill rod. – bubungan camshaft. – bumi earth's axis. – cagak fork shaft. – depan front axle. – éngkol crankshaft. – halang (in soccer) center half. – hubung coupled axle. – kardan crank shaft. – laras senapan axis of the bore. – lawan countershaft. – mata axis of the eye. – pemutar (roda) crankshaft. – penggerak drive shaft. – perut anus. – putar pivot. – rém brake shaft. – Tengah a political grouping headed by Amien Rais. – tombol spindle (of a lock). – tusuk hub spindle. – usus rectum. – utama main shaft.

  seporos 1 centered. 2 allied. menyeporoskan 1 to center around. 2 to ally with.

  berporos to have an axis, with an axis.

  berporoskan to be centered around.

porosésing (E infr) processing; → PEMROSÉSAN, PENGOLAHAN.

porositas (D) porosity.

porot (J) memorot 1 to make a hole in s.t. by gnawing, gnaw a hole in. 2 to steal; to trick s.o. out of s.t.

  memoroti [and memorotin/morotin (J coq)] 1 to cut into, gnaw away at (a sack of rice, etc.); to steal bit by bit. Perempuan itu ~ duit lelakinya. That woman is stealing her husband's money bit by bit. 2 to trick s.o. out of (his money). 3 to pull off (clothing).

porsekot → PERSEKOT.

porselén and porselin (D) porcelain, china. tégel – porcelain tile.

porsén → PERSÉN I.

porsés → PROSÉS.

porsetél (D) proposal.

  mempors(e)télkan to propose.

porséter (D ob) head, chairperson.

porsi (D) 1 portion. 2 order, serving. satu – nasi goréng one order of fried rice.

  seporsi a portion.

  memporsikan ~ bagi to portion out to.

porsidér (ob) → FRISIDÉR.

porsir → FORSIR.

porstél → PORSETÉL.

portabel (E) portable (typewriter/computer, etc.).

portal 1 (D) porch, hall; (iron) roadblock. 2 (E) (Internet) portal.

  pemortalan putting up roadblocks.

portalisasi the installation of (iron) roadblocks.

portefolio (E) portfolio; → PORTEPÉL. menteri tanpa – minister without portfolio.

portepél → PORTEFOLIO. - kehakiman justice's portfolio.

porterét → PORTRÉT.

portéro (Port Min) office boy, doorman, porter.

portik (D) portion.

portir (D) porter.

porto I (D) postage.

Porto II (in Timtim) orang – a Portuguese.

portofolio → PORTEFOLIO.

portrék and portrét → PORTRÉT.

Portugal (Port) Portugal.

Portugés and Portugis (Port) Portuguese.

pos I (D) 1 the postal service, post. kantor – post office. keréta – post chaise. 2 mail, post (letters, etc. delivered by the postal service). 3 post, i.e., a position or duty to which one is appointed. 4 (ob) station, one of series of stations along a postal route for furnishing relays of men and horses for carrying the mail. 5 (police) station. 6 (mil) post, station. 7 checkpoint. Dia juga mendirikan -.- yang terus memeriksa keluar-masuk ternak di Jawa Timur. He also set up checkpoints which constantly inspect incoming and outgoing cattle in East Java. buku harian – mail log. cap – postmark. kantong – mailbag. kartu – postcard. (nomor) kode wilayah/daérah ZIP code, postal code. kotak – post-office box, P.O. box. Pak – mailman. pegawai – postal clerk. tukang pengantar – mailman. warkat – aerogram, air letter. dikirim dengan – delivered by mail. tidak dapat disampaikan – undeliverable (by the mailman). dengan – yang berikut by return mail. dengan perantaraan – by mail, through the mail. - ABRI Armed-Forces mail. – anjur (mil) forward post. - cepat antaran kota [poscanta] special delivery within city limits. - cepat antarkota terbatas [pospatas] limited intercity special delivery. - dan télékomunikasi [postél] post and telecommunications. - dengar listening post. - depan outpost. - diplomatik diplomatic post. – éksprés express mail (now superseded by – kilat). – éléktronik electronic mail, E-mail. – gombal junk mail. – keamanan lalu lintas traffic safety post. – keséhatan kecelakaan lalu lintas traffic accident first-aid post. – kilat express mail. – kilat khusus registered express mail. – komando [posko] command post. – laut sea mail. – pelayanan terpadu integrated service station, i.e., centers for pre- and postnatal health care and information for women and for children under five; → BALITA. – pemeriksaan check post. – penjagaan guardhouse, sentry post, checkpoint. – pertemuan rahasia (intelligence term) safe house. – pertolongan first-aid station. – polisi police station. – réstan poste restante, i.e., instructions written on mail to indicate that it should be held at the post office until called for by the addressee. – tercatat registered mail. – udara airmail. – wésel → POSWÉSEL.

  berpos to have a post (at); to be posted. 700 orang diplomat yang ~ di Perancis 700 diplomats posted in France.

  memposkan, mengeposkan and memperposkan 1 to mail/post (a letter). Diposkan hari ini sampai ke alamat bésoknya. Mailed today, delivered tomorrow. 2 to send s.t. through the mail. 3 to post (s.o. to a position).

  pos-posan guard-post.

  pengeposan mailing, posting.

  perposan postal. Sebagian jasa ~ yang dapat dipercayakan pada swasta. Some of the postal services that could be entrusted to private enterprise.

pos II (D) (in bookkeeping) item, entry. – anggaran budget item. – luar biasa extraordinary item. – peralihan (in balance sheet) item running into the following year.

pos III (infr) post-; → PASCA-. – doktoral postdoctoral; → PASCA-DOKTOR.

poscanta → POS cepat antaran kota.

posdok [posdoktoral] postdoctoral, post-doc.

pose (D) 1 pose, posture. Riko memintanya bergaya dalam beberapa – untuk dibidik kaméranya. Riko asked her to pose in different ways for his camera. 2 build, physique.

  berpose to adopt a pose, strike an attitude.

posésif (E) possessive.

posir (D) poaching (eggs).

posisi (D) position. - beragam (fin) spread. - depan forward position. - kunci key position. - menyeluruh overall position. - tawar-menawar bargaining position. Iklim demikian memungkinkan lahirnya - tawar(-menawar). Such a climate enables the creation of a bargaining position.

berposisi to hold a position.
memosisikan to position.
terposisikan positioned.
posisional (*E*) positional.
posita (*leg*) allegations.
positif and **positip** (*D*) positive, favorable, constructive (criticism).
mempositifkan to make positive, affirm.
kepositifan positivity.
positivistis (*D*) positivistic.
positivitas (*D/E*) positivism, positivity.
positum (*leg*) allegation.
posiyandu (in Central Sulawesi; pun on *posyandu*) to act immorally.
poskar (*E*) postcard; → KARTU *pos*.
posko → POS *komando. satuan* -.- command post units.
Posma → PEKAN *Oriéntasi Studi Mahasiswa.*
poso (*ob*) part of a loom.
posologi (*D*) posology (science of administering medicine).
posong sandbar.
pospakét (*D*) parcel-post package.
pospat → FOSFAT.
pospatas → POS *cepat antarkota terbatas.*
pospor → FOSFOR.
post-audit (*E*) postaudit.
Postél → POS *dan Télékomunikasi.*
postéma (*Port Min*) repulsive face, ugly, loathsome.
poster (*E*) poster.
mem(p)osterkan to make a poster of. *menonton film yang diposterkan* to watch a film about which posters have been made.
posting (*E*) posting (on the Internet).
mempostingkan to post s.t. (on the Internet).
postmodérn (*E*) postmodern.
postmodernisme (*E*) and **postmodérnitas** postmodernism.
postulat (*D*) postulate.
mempostulatkan to postulate.
postur (*D*) posture, build. *Ini akan memberi warna kepada kedudukan dan* – *Angkatan Bersenjata kita dalam tahapan sejarah nanti.* This will give color to the position and posture of our Armed Forces in the historical phase to come.
berpostur to pose (as), impersonate. *Meréka ~ seperti tentara.* They impersonate military men.
poswésel (*D*) (postal) money order; → WÉSELPOS.
memposwéselkan to remit via (postal) money order.
posyandu → POS *pelayanan terpadu.*
pot I (*D*) 1 pot. 2 chamber pot; → PISPOT. – *bunga/kembang* flowerpot.
pot II (in acronyms) → POTÉNSI.
pota and **po'ta** excellent; → POKTA.
potas (*D*) potash.
potéhi (*C*) Chinese *wayang* performance using wooden puppets and based on Chinese stories, performed by Chinese-Indonesians in Chinese-flavored Javanese and Indonesian; → WAYANG *golék.*
potél (*Jv*) broken, chipped.
memotéli to break, chip.
memotélkan to break.
potelot → POTLOT.
poténsi (*D*) 1 potency. 2 potential. – *ékonomi* economic potential.
berpoténsi to have the potential (to). *Irian Jaya ~ sebagai penghasil migas yang cukup besar sekitar 25 ribu barel/sehari.* Irian Jaya has the potential to develop into a rather large producer of oil and natural gas, about 25,000 barrels a day. *Kain kita ini ~ untuk memodiskan penampilan.* Our fabrics have the potential of making a presentation stylish.
poténsial (*E*) and **poténsiil** (*D*) potential.
kepoténsialan and **kepoténsiilan** potentiality.
poterét → POTRÉT.
potia (*C*) supervisor, foreman.
potisasi the introduction of pots and vases containing bougainvillea, etc.
potlot (*D*) pencil; → PÉNSIL. – *alis* eyebrow pencil, eyeliner. – *isi* mechanical pencil. – *tinta* copying(-ink) pencil.

poto → FOTO.
potol (*J/Jv*) 1 cut off. 2 broke, hard up.
potolan broken-off piece. *anak ~ SD* an elementary school dropout.
poton (*geol*) mud volcano.
potong 1 slice, piece, chunk, lump, bit (of s.t.), fragment. 2 classifier for various items made of fabric that are seen as having been cut off a larger piece of cloth, such as, a blouse, shirt, pants, etc. *Waktu saya buka tas pakaian itu, ternyata celana panjang saya tidak ada tiga* –. When I opened the suitcase, it turned out that three pairs of my pants were missing. 3 (*coq*) to cut/chop off. *pajak* – slaughter tax. *rumah* – abattoir, slaughterhouse. *sapi* – slaughter cattle. *tukang* – a) butcher. b) one who performs circumcisions; → TUKANG *béngkong. tukang* – *rambut* barber, hairdresser. – *hidung rusak muka* to cut off one's nose to spite one's face. – *ayam* a) to slaughter a chicken. b) k.o. oath used for by Chinese (accompanied by slaughtering a chicken); → SUMPAH *potong ayam.* 4 cut, slash, reduce. – *bawah* bottoming (of trees). – *harga* reduce prices. – *kalimat* to interrupt. – *kambing* a) to slaughter a goat. b) (*coq*) a big party with lots of drinking and eating (accompanied by slaughtering a goat). – *kompas* a shortcut. – *léhér* a) to cut the throat. b) to lose one's livelihood intentionally, cut one's own throat. *harga* – *léhér* cut-throat prices. – *rambut* to get/have a haircut. – *tahanan* reduce a prison sentence.
sepotong one slice/piece/bit, etc. ~ *daging* a slice/hunk of meat. ~ *ikan* ~ *ular* two-faced, dishonest. ~ *jalan* (in a negative context) half-heartedly. ~ *kain* a piece of cloth. ~ *roti* a slice of bread. ~ *sabun* a cake of soap.
sepotong-potong fragmented, in bits and pieces, a piece at a time, piece by piece. *menggunakan ayat-ayat Qur'an dan hadis* ~ to use verses of the Koran and the Hadits one piece at a time.
berpotong-potong in slices/pieces/portions/parts, etc.
berpotongan to cut across e.o.
berpotong-potongan to cut across e.o.
memotong [and **motong** (*coq*)] 1 to cut (off), cut/chop into pieces, divide up/separate with a knife. *meminjam gunting/pisau untuk* ~ *tali* to borrow scissors/a knife to cut a rope. ~ *bola* (in soccer) to intercept the ball. 2 to slice (bread, etc.). 3 to amputate (an arm, a leg, etc.). 4 to fell (a tree). 5 to slaughter/kill (an animal or person). ~ *ayam* to slaughter a chicken. ~ *léhér* to cut s.o.'s throat. 6 to cut, slice. ~ *rambut* to get a haircut. ~ *kartu* to cut (cards). ~ *pusat* to cut the umbilical cord. ~ *roti* to slice bread. 7 to tap (rubber). ~ *getah* to tap rubber. 8 to cut out (a dress from a pattern). 9 to reap (a rice crop). 10 to operate on (s.o.'s stomach, etc.). 11 to deduct (from wages, etc.), withhold (taxes), discount (a price), reduce (a sentence). *dipotong 25%* reduced 25%. 12 to abbreviate, shorten (a word/name, etc.), crop (a photograph). 13 to take a shortcut, cut corners. ~ *jalan* a) to take a shortcut. b) to block s.o.'s way. 14 to interrupt (s.o.'s words), cut off. ~ *bicara* to interrupt, butt in. ~ *lidah* to shut s.o. up. *Ia mémang tidak suka orang* ~ *percakapannya.* He really doesn't like people to interrupt him. 15 to cut across/off/in front of. *Mobil itu* ~ *di depan kami.* The car cut in front of us. ~ *mobil* to cut off a car. *landasan yang* ~ *angin* a crosswind runway. 16 to punch. ~ *karcis* to punch tickets.
motong (*sl*) ~ *ayam* to have a gang bang (sex between one woman and a group of men).
potong-memotong cutting (of clothes).
memotong-motong 1 to abbreviate/clip/shorten. 2 to cut up, cut into pieces, dice. 3 to mutilate.
memotongi [and **motongin** (*J coq*)] (*pl obj*) to cut up, etc.
memotongkan 1 to cut, etc. for s.o. else; to instruct in cutting, etc. 2 to use s.t. to cut, cut with. 3 to deduct, subtract.
memperpotongkan to deduct, subtract.
terpotong 1 cut (into parts/pieces), sliced. *mayat* ~ *lima itu* the body cut into five pieces. 2 cut, reduced. 3 accidentally cut.
terpotong-potong cut up (into small pieces), segmented. *Mayatnya ditemukan terpotong-potong dalam tujuh bagian.* His body was found cut into seven pieces.
potongan 1 share, part, piece, bit, slice. *dijual* ~ sold by the piece. 2 (trade) discount, deduction. *mendapat 10%* ~ to get a 10%

discount. ~ *gaji/harga* wage/price cut. **3** s.t. cut (off/up), deduction. *ayam* ~ fryer (chicken). *dengan* ~ *waktu tahanannya* minus the time spent in custody. ~ *pajak* tax deduction. **4** cut, model, build, shape, form, look, figure. ~ *badan* build, stature. ~ *celana* style/cut of pants. ~ *mobil* car model. ~ *muka* profile, features. *Lihat dulu dong* ~ *orang.* Take a look first at the cut of his jib. *Ia* ~ *tukang catut.* He has the cut/look of a black marketer. *Ia tidak ada* ~. He has no personality. ~ *rambut* haircut. ~ *sikat/ tentara* crew cut (haircut). *seorang bapak berambut* ~ *sikat* an older man with a crew cut. **5** abbreviation, shortening, short form of s.t.. ~ *kata/nama* abbreviation of a word/name. **6** leg, one of the stretches or sections of a flight. *pada* ~ *terakhir ini* in this last leg (of the route). **berpotongan** to have the body/figure/look of.

potong-potongan cuts, parts of a whole, bits and pieces.

pemotong 1 cutter (the device), clipper. ~ *kuku* nail clippers. **2** cutter, slaughterer. **3** (tax) withholder.

pemotongan 1 cutting, chopping. ~ *uang* currency reform, reorganization of the currency. **2** deduction, reduction, withholding (of taxes). ~ *pajak* tax withholding. **3** stoppage (of wages). **4** slaughter(ing), butchering.

perpotongan secant, intersecting line.

potpuri (*D*) potpourri.

potrék (*Jv*) photograph, picture, snapshot; → POTRÉT.

potrét (*D*) photo(graph), picture, snapshot. *alat* – *pakai lampu jeprét* (*coq*) a camera with a flash. – *diri* self-portrait.

berpotrét 1 to have one's picture taken, pose for a picture. **2** pictured, photographed. ~ *bersama Ni Polok* photographed with Ni Polok.

memotrét [and **motrét** (*coq*)] to take a picture/photo(graph) of. *Adam Malik bersedia untuk duduk dipotrét.* Adam Malik was willing to sit for his photograph.

potrét-memotrét photography.

pemotrét photographer. *alat* ~ camera.

pemotrétan photography, photographing, picture-taking. ~ *udara* aerial photography.

perpotrétan photography.

poya → FOYA.

poyang I → LEMPUYANG.

poyang II 1 *datuk* – ancestors. **2** forefathers. **3** (*M*) great-grandparents. **4** medicine man, shaman; → DUKUN, PAWANG.

poyok (*Bal*) not quite right in the head.

poyokan (*Jv*) /poyo'an/ *nama* – a) pet name. b) trademark.

poyot great-great-grandparent, parent of a *poyang*.

pp and **PP I** (*init*) → PERATURAN *pemerintah*.

PP II (*init*) [*pimpinan pusat*] central executive committee.

p.p. III (*abbr*) [*Pulang Pergi*] **1** round trip. **2** vice versa. **3** to and fro, back and forth.

PPD (*init*) → PANITIA *Pemilihan Daérah*.

PPh [*Pajak Penghasilan*] income tax.

PPH (*init*) → PAS *Perjalanan Haji*.

PPI (*init*) → PARTAI *Pembaharuan Indonésia*.

PPLH [*Pembinaan dan Pelestarian Lingkungan Hidup*] (Minister of State for) Promotion and Preservation of the Environment.

PPN → PAJAK *Pertambahan Nilai*.

PPn BM (*init*) → PAJAK *Penjualan Barang Méwah*.

PPP I (*init*) → PANITIA *Pendaftaran Pemilih*, PANTARLIH.

PPP II (*init*) → PARTAI *Persatuan Pembangunan*.

PPPK (*init*) → PERTOLONGAN *Pertama Pada Kecelakaan*.

P4 and **PPPP** (*init*) → PEDOMAN *Penghayatan dan Pengamalan Pancasila*, P4.

pr- also see entries beginning with **per-**.

PR I [*Palangkaraya*] Palangkaraya, the capital of Central Kalimantan Province; → PRAYA.

PR II [*Pajak Radio*] Radio Tax.

PR III [*Pastor*] (Catholic) priest.

PR IV [*Pegawai Rendah*] Lower-level (government) Employee.

PR V [*Pekan Raya*] (Industrial) fair.

PR VI /pé'ér/ [*Pekerjaan Rumah*] homework.

PR VII [*Pembantu Réktor*] Assistant Dean (in a university).

PR VIII [*Pemuda Rakyat*] People's Youth, an arm of the now defunct Communist Party of Indonesia.

PR IX [*Pengajaran Rendah*] Elementary Education.

PR X [(*Kapal*) *Penyapu Ranjau*] minesweeper.

PR XI [*Perang Rakyat*] People's War, the war waged by the now defunct Communist Party of Indonesia.

PR XII [*Perguruan Rakyat*] People's Educational Institute.

PR XIII [*Pertahanan Rakyat*] People's Defense.

PR XIV [*Perusahaan Rokok*] cigarette factory.

PR XV (*E*) /pi'ar/ [*Public Relations*] Public Relations; → HUMAS.

pra- I also see entries beginning with **pera-**

pra- II 1 prefix meaning pre- (used in neologisms). **2** in Indonesian newspapers occasionally used as an equivalent of *menjelang*. *menjelang Lebaran* (*pra-Lebaran*) during the period before *Lebaran*.

pra III [*prajurit*] private (soldier).

pra IV [*perlawanan rakyat*] People's Resistance.

praada preexistence, preexisting.

Pra-Adhyaksa Assistant Public Prosecutor.

praak (*onom*) sound made by s.t. big, such as a building, collapsing.

praakhir (*gram*) penultimate. *sukukata* – penultimate syllable.

pra-AMN before/prior to the National Military Academy.

praang (*onom*) sound of breaking glass.

praanggapan prejudice, bias; → PRASANGKA.

berpraanggapan 1 to prejudice, bias. **2** prejudiced, biased.

pra-apotéker prepharmacist.

pra-autopsi preautopsy.

prabakti hazing, initiation (of university freshmen); → PRAMA, PRAMI. *masa* – hazing/initiation period.

prabawa (*Jv*) **1** influence, prestige. **2** induction. **3** authority. **memprabawa 1** to influence. **2** to induce.

prabayar pre-paid.

prabedah preoperative.

prabot → PERABOT(AN).

prabu (*Skr*) **1** king, sovereign. **2** title for a king. *Sang* – His Majesty. – *anom* a) crown prince. b) title for a crown prince.

keprabuan 1 majesty. **2** empire.

pracerita preamble, introduction, opening statement/remarks, overture.

pracétak 1 preprint. **2** prepress (center). **3** precast (of concrete).

pracimoyono (*Jv*) part of the *Kraton* where the princess has her private chambers.

pracipta s.t. created ahead of time.

prada → PRAJURIT *dua*.

pradah (*Jv*) generous.

pradaksina (*Skr*) circumambulation of the Borobudur temple by Buddhist priests.

pradana (*Skr*) the material body.

pradérégulasi prior to deregulation.

pradésa home of certain isolated ethnic groups (the so-called *masyarakat terasing*); → DÉSA.

pradéwasa preadult.

pradini premature (baby).

mempradinikan to make s.t. ripen early.

pradisain predesigned.

praduga presumption. – *bersalah* presumption of guilt. – *tidak bersalah* presumption of innocence. – *hubungan sebab-akibat* presumption of cause and effect (or, causation).

berpraduga to have a presumption. *lekas* ~ to jump to a conclusion.

praésés → PRÉSÉS.

pra-évangélisasi preevangelization.

prafabrik prefabricated.

praga- also see entries beginning with **peraga-**.

pragata (*Port IBT*) frigate.

pragawan → PERAGAWAN.

pragawati → PERAGAWATI.

pragmatik (*E*) and **pragmatis** (*D*) pragmatic (sanctions, etc.).

pragmatisme (*D*) pragmatism.

prah (*D*) freight, cargo.

Praha Prague.

prahaid premenstrual. *gejala* – premenstrual syndrome, PMS.

prahara (*Jv*) **1** wind-and-rain storm, tempest. **2** hurricane. *Rumah tangganya dilanda* –. His house was struck by a hurricane.

prahoto (*D*) truck.

prailmiah prescientific.

praindustri preindustrial. *masa* – preindustrial times.

prainterogasi preinterrogation.

pra-Islam pre-Islam(ic).

praja I (*Jv*) **1** the State; principality. **2** seat of the sovereign. **3** capital (city). *pamong* – civil service, bureaucracy. – *Kejawén* → VORSTENLANDEN.

praja II (*Jv*) student of the *Akadémi Pemerintahan Dalam Negeri* (APDN), the Academy of Public Administration.

Pra-Jaksa → PRA-ADHYAKSA.

Praja Wira Braja the military resort command (*Korém* 173) in Biak.

Praja Wira Tama the military resort command (*Korém* 171) in Sorong.

Praja Wira Yakthi the military resort command (*Korém* 172) in Abepura.

prajaya (*Jv*) **memprajaya 1** to defeat. **2** to kill.

prajilid prebound. *édisi* – prebound edition (of a book).

prajurit (*Jv*) **1** soldier, service/military man; *cp* SERDADU I. **2** private (soldier). **3** (*col*) designation for the indigenous soldiers whose function was to keep peace and order and who were placed under the direct command of the Civil Service. **4** (since Indonesian Independence) any soldier not engaged in colonialist or imperialistic practices. **5** warrior. **6** heroic. – *cadangan* reservist. – *dua* [prada] private second class. – *kepala* [praka] master private, private in charge. – *Kraton* Palace soldier; formerly the soldiers of the Yogyakarta Palace made up one battalion, divided into several units, each wearing different uniforms and carrying different standards. – *péna* journalist. – *satu* [pratu] private first class. – *sukaréla* volunteer. – *tak dikenal* the unknown soldier. – *tangkas* [pratangkas] specialist (title in the military). – *taruna* [pratar] cadet private. – *udara dua* airman second class. – *udara satu* airman first class. – *tua tak pernah mati, ia hanya surut* old soldiers never die, they just fade away. – *wajib* conscript.

   keprajuritan 1 military (*mod*). *latihan* ~ military training. *Muséum* ~ *Indonésia* Indonesian Military Museum. **2** heroism, bravery.

praka → PRAJURIT *kepala*.

prakala before, prior to. – *Perang Dunia II* prior to World War II.

prakapitalisme precapitalism.

prakarsa initiative, first move. *atas* – on the initiative of. *atas* – *sendiri* on one's own initiative. – *membuka kesempatan kerja* employment-generating initiative. – *Pertahanan Stratégis* Strategic Defense Initiative, SDI, *aka* Star Wars.

   mem(p)rakarsai and **mem(p)rakarsakan** to initiate, take the initiative in, sponsor. *ikut* ~ to cosponsor. *Ketua MPR* ~ *pertemuan orsospol...* The chairman of the MPR sponsored the meeting between the ... sociopolitical organizations.

   pemrakarsa 1 initiator, promoter, sponsor, originator. **2** self-starter, s.o. who works on his own initiative without being given directions.

   pemrakarsaan initiating, sponsoring, sponsorship.

prakarya (in schools) handicrafts and other vocational subjects.

prakasa → PERKASA.

prakata preface, foreword, introduction (by the author); → KATA *pendahuluan*.

   memprakatai to provide with an introduction, introduce.

prakeberangkatan predeparture.

prakekuasaan prepower. *sindrom* – prepower syndrome.

prakemerdékaan pre-Independence.

prakilang prefabrication.

prakira (weather) forecast, prediction.

   memprakirakan to forecast, predict, expect, project. *Jamu asli Indonésia diprakirakan memiliki masa depan cerah.* Indonesian traditional medicines are expected to have a bright future.

   prakiraan (weather) forecast.

   pemprakiraan forecasting.

prakirawan weather forecaster, weatherman.

praklinis preclinical.

prakondisi (*E*) precondition, prerequisite; → PRASYARAT. *Waspada terhadap upaya menciptakan* – *yang membahayakan masyarakat.*

Watch out for efforts to create preconditions which can endanger society.

prakonsépsi preconception.

prakték (*D*) and **praktik** practice. *meletakkan* –*nya* (of a physician) to retire from practice. *dalam* – in practice, in reality. *kurang* – out of practice. – *gelap/meléncéng* shady practices. – *umum* general practice.

   berprakték to practice (of a medical doctor).

   memprakttékkan 1 to practice, put into practice. **2** to apply (teachings). ~ *ajaran Buddha* to apply the teachings of the Buddha.

praktikabilitas (*E*) practicability.

praktikan (*D*) practitioner.

praktikum (*D*) practical work (in laboratory).

praktikus (*D*) practitioner, s.o. who practices s.t. specified.

praktis (*D*) **1** practical, convenient. **2** mobile. *tidak* – impractical, inconvenient.

   kepraktisan practicality.

praktisi (*D*) **1** (*pl of praktikus*) practitioners. **2** (used as *sg*) practitioner. *P. X. Harsono,* – *seni rupa baru dan rédaktur majalah Dialog Seni Rupa.* P. X. Harsono, practitioner of the new art movement and the editor of the magazine Dialog Seni Rupa.

prakualifikasi and **prakwalifikasi** prequalification. *Surat Izin* – *Perusahaan Pemborong Bangunan* Building Contractors Company Prequalification License.

prakudéta pre-coup d'état.

pralahir prenatal.

pralaksana pre-audit.

pralambang (*Jv*) **1** profound simile. **2** prediction, prophesy.

pralaya (*S*) dead. *Kiai Rata* – the hearse which belongs to the Keraton of Yogyakarta; → KIAYI. *bantuan* – death benefit.

pra-Lebaran pre-*Lebaran*; → PRA- II.

pralon *pipa* – hard plastic pipe made from polyvinyl chloride.

prama 1 male freshman. **2** [(masa) prabakti mahasiswa] university student predevotional period; → PRAMADARA, PRAMARIA.

pramadara female freshman.

pramana I (*Jv*) sharp, clear (of vision).

pramana II norm, standard.

pramandiri (in family planning) pre-independent.

pramaria male freshman.

pramaséhi pre-Christian.

Prambors [Prambanan, Mendut, Borubudur, dan Sekitarnya] Prambanan, Mendut, Borubudur and Surroundings, i.e., a cluster of streets and their surroundings in Jakarta.

prambos (*D*) raspberry, *Rubus rosaefolius.*

pramanénstruasi premenstrual.

pramésuari → PERMAISURI.

prami 1 female freshman. **2** [(masa) prabakti mahasiswi] female university student predevotional period.

pramobilisasi premobilization.

pramodérn premodern.

pramu- first element in words referring to people who provide a service.

pramubakti room boy (in hotel). – *pakaian* valet.

pramubalita and **pramubayi** baby-sitter.

pramubar bar man.

pramubhakti → PRAMUBAKTI.

pramugara steward, attendant (on board an aircraft/bus/train). – *geréja* male usher (in church). – *udara* flight attendant.

pramugari stewardess, attendant (on board an aircraft/bus/train). – *angkasa* airline stewardess. – *darat* ground stewardess. – *geréja* female usher (in church). – *laut* stewardess on board ferryboats running between Surabaya and Kamal on Madura. – *udara* flight attendant.

   kepramugarian stewardess (*mod*), steward, stewarding. *pendidikan* ~ *internasional di Hong Kong* an international stewarding course in Hong Kong. *pengetahuan* ~ stewarding (a subject taught in the *Institut Pramugari-Pramugara Bandung* [Ipraba].

pramugayani (*infr*) hairdresser.

pramuirama disc jockey, D.J.

pramujasa s.o. who renders service, agent.

Pramuka [Praja Muda Karana] **1** the Indonesian Boy Scout

Movement (*Gerakan Pemuda*) founded by presidential decree in 1961. **2** Boy Scout. **3** Girl Scout. **4** vanguard, pioneer. – *Ad(h)i* Super Scout. – *Bahari* Sea Scout. – *Bhayangkara* Police Scout. – *Dirgantara* Air Scout. – *Garuda* Boy Scout who has received the highest award within the *Gerakan Pemuda* system. – *Putra* Boy Scout. – *Putri* Girl Scout. – *Tarunabumi* Agriculture Scout. – *Teladan* Exemplary Scout. – *Wanab(h)akti* Forest Scout. – *Wirabumi* Rural Scout.

mempramukakan to turn s.o. into a Boy Scout.

kepramukaan scouting (movement). *memajukan* ~ to promote scouting.

pramukamar room boy (in a hotel).

pramukawati Girl Scout.

pramuktama preconference.

pramulayan nightclub hostess.

pramunas pre-national conference.

pramuniaga salesman; → **SALESMAN**. – *wanita* saleswoman.

pramuniagari (*infr*) and **pramuniagawati** (*infr*) saleswoman; → **SALESGIRL**.

pramunikmat 1 female entertainer. **2** (*joc*) prostitute.

pramupijat 1 masseur. **2** masseuse.

pramupintu 1 concierge. **2** doorman.

pramuria nightclub hostess. – *mandi uap* steam bath attendant.

pramusaji 1 waiter, server. **2** waitress.

pramusiswi baby-sitter.

pramustand girl who stands in a booth/stall/stand at a trade fair, etc.; → **STAN(D)** II.

pramusyahwat sex worker.

pramutama – *tamu* bell captain.

pramutamu 1 receptionist. **2** bellboy.

pramuwicara announcer, M.C.

pramuwidya museum guide.

pramuwisata tour(ist) guide.

kepramuwisataan tour(ist) guide (*mod*).

pramuwisma domestic help, servant (in the house); → **PEMBANTU** *rumah tangga*, **PRT**.

kepramuwismaan domestic help (*mod*). *Kesepakatan tentang* ~. Agreement on Domestic Help (a labor contract).

pranakan → **PERANAKAN** (*Jv*).

pranala (*Skr*) link(s) (on the Internet).

pranata <tata> (*Jv*) **1** (– *cara*) protocol; master of ceremonies, M.C. – *mangsa* astrological calculation according to the season in the Javanese calendar. **2** infrastructure; → **PRASARANA**.

pranatan regulation, ordinance, rule.

pranatal 1 ceremonies and religious services organized prior to Christmas; → **NATAL**. **2** prenatal; → **PRALAHIR**.

Prancis (*Port*) French. *bahasa* – French (language). *pemakai bahasa* – Francophone, French speaker. *negeri* – France. *orang* – Frenchman, Frenchwoman.

keprancisan French (*mod*). *pencinta* ~ Francophile.

prang (*onom*) sound made by a falling object hitting the ground.

prangas-pringis (*J*) to grin, make a face; → **PRINGAS-PRINGIS**.

prangko (*D*) **1** (postage) stamp. **2** postage paid. – *1000 rupiah* a 1,000-rupiah stamp. – *amal* charity stamp. – *balasan* return postage. – *berlangganan* prepaid postage.

berprangko to be stamped/prepaid (of letters), franked. *tidak* ~ unstamped, postage due.

memprangkoi to stamp, put postage on. *Koenen sudah berjanji akan* ~ *surat itu dan memposkannya*. Koenen has promised to put a stamp on the letter and mail it.

pemrangkoan prepayment (of postage).

perprangkoan philately. *sejarah* ~ philatelic history.

pranikah premarital; → **PRAPERKAWINAN**.

pra-Olimpiade pre-Olympics.

praolimpik preolympic.

prapabrik prefabricated. *matérial* – prefabricated material.

Prapanca the poet to the court of *Majapahit* at the height of its glory.

prapanén preharvest.

prapatan 1 crossroads. **2** name of a residential area in Central Jakarta. – *10* address of the dormitory for students of the Medical School where Eri Sudewo read out the Proclamation of In-

dependence at the same time that President Soekarno was reading it out at Pegangsaan Timur 56. This building is now used by the Department of Health.

pra-Pelita pre-Five-Year Plan (period), i.e., prior to 1970; → **PELITA II**.

prapemilihan (pre-election) primaries (in the U.S.A.).

prapén (*Jv*) fireplace; place for an open fire, e.g., a blacksmith's forge.

prapendaftaran preregistration.

prapendapat prejudice.

prapendinginan prechilling.

prapengapalan preshipment.

prepénsiun preretirement.

prapenuntutan preprosecution.

prapenyunting pre-editor.

praperadaban precivilization. *masa* – *manusia* the period of human precivilization.

praperadilan pretrial hearing.

mempraperadilankan to try preliminarily.

praperang prewar.

prapercobaan pretesting. *masa* – pretesting period.

prapereksa preliminary investigation; → **PEMERIKSAAN** *pendahuluan*.

praperistiwa precedent.

praperkawinan premarital.

prapertunjukan preview.

Pra-Piala *Turnamén* – *Dunia* Pre-World Cup Tournament.

praproduksi preproduction.

prapromosi pre-examination (for university promotion).

prapubér prepuberty.

prapupa cocoon.

prapustaka preliterary.

pra-Rapim preliminary meeting of *Rapim*.

prarasa preference, partiality.

prarekaman prerecording.

prarencana preplanning.

prasaja (*Jv*) **1** simple, not ornamented. **2** straightforward, modest.

prasaji → **PRAPERTUNJUKAN**.

prasamak wet blue.

prasangka prejudice, bias. – *bangsa/ras* racial prejudice, racism.

berprasangka and ~ *buruk* (*terhadap*) to be prejudiced, biassed (against).

prasantap appetizer, aperitif; → **PEMBANGKIT** *seléra/nafsu makan*.

prasaran (working) paper.

memrasarani to provide an introductory or working paper for.

memrasarankan to use s.t. as a working paper.

pemrasaran 1 keynote speaker. **2** reader of such a paper.

prasarana 1 infrastructure, improvements. **2** public utilities. – *untuk kepentingan umum* public utilities.

prasarat precondition.

prasarjana → **PRASYARAT**.

Prasarlub [*Prasekolah dan Sekolah Dasar Luar Biasa*] Kindergarten and Elementary School for Exceptional Children.

prasasti 1 record/carvings/inscription written on stones, copper, etc. **2** stone tablet. **3** commemorative plaque on building.

prasejahtera (*euph*) underprivileged, disadvantaged.

prasejarah prehistory. *ahli* – prehistorian.

prasekolah preschool; → **TAMAN** *kanak-kanak*. *anak* – preschooler. *pendidikan* – preschool education.

praséléksi preselection.

praséminar preparatory seminar.

prasetia and **prasetya** (*Jv*) pledge of loyalty. – *perwira* officer's oath, swearing-in of military officers. – *Ulah Cakti/Sakti Bhakti Praja* (motto of the province of Central Java) Pledge of Loyalty and Firm Will to Behave as an Example for Serving the State.

prasikap 1 prevention. **2** bias.

praskripsi prethesis, B.A. thesis.

prasman I (*D*) Frenchman.

prasmanan *makanan* ~ meal served buffet style, smorgasbord. *menghidangkan secara* ~ to serve a meal buffet style.

prasman II k.o. plant, ayapana, *Eupatorium triplinerve*.

prastudi preliminary research.

prasunting preediting.

prasyarat precondition, prerequisite.

memprasyaratkan to make s.t. a precondition/prerequisite (for).

prataman – *kanak-kanak* prekindergarten.

pratanak *prosés* – parboiling.

pratanam preplanting.

pratanda (*Jv*) **1** sign, indication. **2** forerunner.
  berpratanda foreboding, indicating in advance.

pratanggal predated.

pratangkas → PRAJURIT *tangkas*.

pratar → PRAJURIT *taruna*.

prategang prestressed. *beton* – prestressed concrete.

pratekan prestressed. *beton* – prestressed concrete. – *melingkar* circumferential prestressing.

pratéknologi pretechnology. *masyarakat* – pretechnological society.

pratelaah prestudy.

pratérsiér pretertiary.

pratidina (*Jv*) every day, daily.

pratijangkit antiseptic.

pratinjau preview.

pratirasa antipathy.

pratisabda echo.

pratiwi → PERTIWI I.

prat-prit (*onom*) sound of repeated whistle blowing; → PRIT *jigo*.

pratransisi pretransition.

pratu → PRAJURIT *satu*.

prauji pretesting.

praunivérsitér preuniversity (from Kindergarten through High School).

pra-Upakarti pre-Upakarti; → UPAKARTI.

prausul preliminary advice.

pravokasional (*E*) and pravokasionil prevocational. *pilihan* – (in diplomas) chosen with a view to a future profession.

prawacana introduction, preface.

prawan → PERAWAN.

prawira → PERWIRA I.

Praya [Palangkaraya] Palangkaraya (the airfield).

prayitna (*Jv*) **1** vigilant. **2** cautious.
  keprayitnan **1** vigilance. **2** caution.

prayoga (*Jv*) advisable, recommended.

prayojana motivation, motive, purpose, intention, grounds.

prayudha **1** prewar, prebelligerent. **2** 13-man units within *Kopassandha*.

Pra-Yuwana pro juventute, for youth.

PRB (*init*) → PARTAI *Rakyat Bersatu*.

PRD (*init*) → PARTAI *Rakyat Démokratik*.

pré → PERAI I.

préambul (*D*) preamble; → MUKADIMAH.

Préanger (*ob*) the highlands of West Java.

prédator (*E*) predator; → PEMANGSA.

prédikat (*D*) **1** designation, notation, citation. *dengan* – *cum laude* cum laude. – *kelulusan* pass category. **2** (*gram*) predicate.
  berprédikat **1** to have a certain title/designation. **2** titled, designated.
  memprédikati to designate/call.

prédikatif (*D*) predicative.

prédiksi (*E*) prediction.

prédiktif (*E*) predictive. *pendekatan* – prediction approach.

preessss (*onom*) sound made by a knife slashing into s.t.

préfab (*E*) prefabricated.

préfék (*D*) prefect. – *apostolik* apostolic prefect.

préféktur (*D*) prefecture.

préferénsi (*D*) preference.

préferénsial (*E*) and préferénsiil (*D*) preferential.

préfiks (*D gram*) prefix.

préh (*Jv*) *pohon* – k.o. banyan tree, *Ficus Ribes*.

préhistori (*D/E*) prehistory; → PRASEJARAH.

préhistoris (*D*) prehistoric.

préi I → PERAI II.

préi II (*D*) leek.

prék (*D coq*) damn (it)! damn you!

prekéwuh (*Jv*) (to have) difficulties; (to feel) discomfort; → PAKÉWUH, PERKÉWUH.

prékondisi (*E*) precondition; → PRASYARAT.

prékursor (*E*) precursor.

prélat (*D*) prelate.

préliminér preliminary.

prélud (*D/E*) prelude.

prém (*D*) plum.

préman (*D*) **1** hoodlum, thug, petty criminal; → GALI II, JÉGER. **2** (dressed) in plain clothes, in civvies. *seorang agén polisi yang berpakaian* – a plainclothes policeman. *secara* – incognito. **3** private (not public). *mobil* – private car. **4** exempted (in particular from compulsory service in the village). **5** retired (soldier, etc.) *lurah* – retired village head. **6** civilian; *opp* of military. **7** (in Central and East Java) a field worker.

prémanisme hooliganism, thuggery.

prématur (*D*) premature.

prématuritas (*E*) prematurity.

prémi (*D*) **1** premium. – *asuransi* insurance premium. – *tebusan* redemption premium. **2** bonus, award.

prémiér (*D*) premiere, first night (of a play), first run (of a film).
  memprémiérkan to premiere s.t.

prémis (*D/E*) premise.

prémisi → PERMISI.

prémium premium (gas).

prémolar (*D/E*) premolar.

prénatal (*D/E*) prenatal, antenatal; → PRALAHIR.

prenesan (*Jv*) appealing and light-hearted.

prengutan (*Jv*) looking at e.o. with a sour expression or with a frown.

prenjak bar-winged wren-warbler, *Prinia familiaris* (according to folk belief if this bird sings loudly in your yard, you will be receiving guests). – *belalang* Pallas's warbler, *Locustella certhiola*. – *belalang lurik* lanceolated warbler, *Locustella lanceolata*. – *coklat* brown prinia, *Prinia polychroa*. – *daun* mountain leaf warbler, *Phylloscopus trivirgatus*. – *gunung* Javan ground warbler, *Cettia vulcania* (*fortipes*). – *Jawa* bar-winged prinia, *Prinia familiaris*. – *kuning* yellow-bellied warbler, *Abroscopus superciliaris*. – *kutut* Arctic warbler, *Phylloscopus borealis*. – *mahkota* eastern crowned warbler, *Phylloscopus coronatus*. – *puncak* Javan scrub warbler, *Bradypterus montis* (*seebohmi*). – *sikatan Sunda* Sunda flycatcher warbler, *Seicercus grammiceps*. – *sisi mérah* tawny-flanked prinia, *Prinia subflava*. – *perut kuning* yellow-bellied prinia, *Prinia flaviventris*. – *sayap garis* bar-winged prinia, *Prinia familiaris*.

préparat (*D*) (blood) preparation.

prépéntif and prépéntip → PRÉVÉNTIF.

préposisi (*D gram*) preposition.

prérogatif (*D*) prerogative.

prés I (*D*) *mesin* – press, machine for pressing (clothes, etc.).
  memprés and mengeprés to press (clothes) with a presser.
  ngeprés **1** to press. **2** pressing, urgent. *Dananya* ~. Funds are limited.
  pengeprésan pressing (of clothes).

prés II (*D*) prize; → PRIS.

prés III (in acronyms) → PRÉSIDÉN.

Présdir → PRÉSIDÉN *Diréktur*.

présedén (*D*) precedent.
  berprésedén precedented, with a precedent. *fakta yang tak* ~ an unprecedented fact.

présénsi (*D*) presence.

préséntasi (*D*) presentation. *memberikan* – to give a presentation. – *tentang keadaan perusahaan* presentation on the state of a company.
  mempréséntasi(kan) to present, display, demonstrate.

préséntatif (*E*) presentative.

présentir (*D*) mempresentir to present, display.

présérvasi (*E*) preservation.

préses (*L*) chairman, president (of *HKBP*).

présidén (*D*) president (of a college, society, country, etc.). – *tidak dapat diganggu gugat* the president can do no wrong. *bakal* – president elect. *wakil* – [Waprés] vice-president, VP. – *Diréktur* [Présdir] President-Director (of a company). – *Komisaris* [Préskom] president/head of the board of commissioners. – *Seumur Hidup* [Présmurhi] President for Life. – *terpilih* president elect.

memprésidénkan to keep on as president. *selama dua tahun Soekarno ~ Soekarno* was kept on as president for two years.

présidénan presidency.

keprésidénan 1 executive. 2 president's palace/residence. 3 presidential. *mobil ~* the presidential car.

présidénsi presidency, chairmanship.

présidénsial (*E*) and présidénsiil (*D*) presidential. *kamar présidénsial* presidential room (in the Grand Hotel Preanger, Bandung).

présidium (*D*) presidium.

présipitasi (*E*) precipitation.

présipitat (*E*) precipitate.

presis (*D*) precise; → PERSIS.

présisi (*D*) precision.

Préskom → PRÉSIDÉN *Komisaris*.

préskripsi (*D*) prescription.

mempréskripsikan to prescribe.

préskriptif (*D gram*) prescriptive.

Présmurhi → PRÉSIDÉN *Seumur Hidup*.

préspéktif → PÉRSPÉKTIF.

préstasi (*D*) achievement, performance. *seorang yang -nya di bawah taraf kemampuannya* underachiever. *pendekatan –* achievement approach. *- kerja/karya* performance; → KINERJA. *- kerja kurang* unsatisfactory performance. *- kerja memuaskan* satisfactory performance. *- kerja standar* standard performance.

berpréstasi to perform, achieve.

mempréstasikan to perform, achieve.

préstise (*D*) prestige.

préstisius (*D*) prestigious. *daérah/jabatan –* a prestigious area/position.

présto (*D*) presto.

présumsi (*D*) presumption. *- adanya keteraturan administratif* presumption of administrative regularity.

prétél (*Jv*) to become detached.

mem(p)rétéli 1 to molt, fall off (of a bird's feathers). *Bulu burung itu pada ~.* The birds molted. 2 to break and fall off (of leaves/fruits). 3 to pull apart, take apart, dismantle, demolish. *Gedung itu sudah diprétéli.* The building has been demolished. 4 to fleece, plunder, rob, strip (of possessions).

prétélan dismantled, demolished. *dalam bentuk ~* knocked down (of an imported car, etc.).

pemrétélan 1 dismantling, demolishing. 2 plundering, robbing.

Prétélin (*coq*) joking reference to Frétélin, *q.v.*

préténsi (*D*) pretension, claim.

berpréténsi 1 to have pretensions, pretend (to be s.o. other than what one is). 2 pretentious.

préténsius (*D*) pretentious.

prévalénsi (*E*) prevalence.

prévénsi (*D*) prevention.

prévéntif (*D/E*) preventive.

préview and prévyu (*E*) preview.

mempréviewkan to preview (a film, etc.).

préwangan (*Jv*) medium, witch. *dukun –* female medium.

pri I → PERI I.

pri II clipped form of pribumi.

pri III (in acronyms) → PRIBADI.

pria (*Skr*) 1 man. 2 men, gentlemen (on door of men's public restroom). *- (dan) wanita* man and woman; men and women. *- homoséks* gay. *- loyo* impotent man. *- pemuas wanita* gigolo.

priagung [pria agung] (*Jv*) 1 person of noble birth. 2 high dignitary. *para – Jawa* Javanese notables/celebrities.

priai → PRIAYI.

Priangan (*S*) *Tanah –* the heartland of the Sundanese in West Java, the interior highlands of West Java.

priayi (*Jv*) 1 upper-class man. 2 snobbish.

pribadi (*Jv*) 1 personal(ly), individual; own, self. *Saya – tidak apa-apa.* Personally it's OK with me. 2 person, individual. 3 private. 4 in person. *bakat/milik/pendapat/pengawal –* personal aptitude/property/opinion/body-guard. *mobil –* private car. *sékrétaris –* [sékpri] private secretary. *perusahaannya –* his own business. *- hukum* corporate body. *- yang terpadu* integrated self.

berpribadi to have a ... personality.

mempribadi to be private/personal.

mempribadikan to personify.

terpribadikan personalized.

kepribadian 1 (individual) personality. 2 personhood. 3 individuality. 4 identity. *~ Indonésia* Indonesian identity. *~ prajurit* soldierly consciousness. *~ terbelah* split personality. berkepribadian to have a ... personality.

pemribadian 1 personalization. 2 embodiment. 3 personalism. 4 characterization.

pribahasa → PERIBAHASA.

pribumi (*Jv*) earth, land. (*orang*) – a) native, indigene; indigenous. b) (in some parts of South Sumatra which have Javanese transmigrants) the natives of the area. (*orang*) *non-* a) the nonnative, i.e., an Indonesian of foreign extraction (*esp* refers to Chinese). b) (in some areas of South Sumatra which have Javanese transmigrants) Javanese transmigrants whom the local population considers to be treated favorably by the central government, because most of the transmigrants are members of the armed forces.

mempribumikan to nativize, indigenize.

terpribumi native. *Penghuni ~ yang tak dibunuh, terusir mengungsi ke Indonésia Timur.* The native inhabitants who were not killed were forced out into the eastern part of Indonesia.

kepribumian indigenous, native (*mod*).

pemribumian nativization, indigenization.

pribumisasi nativization, i.e., assimilation to Indonesian customs (of the Catholic rite, etc.).

prigel (*Jv*) skillful, expert, competent.

keprigelan skill. *~ tangan* handicrafts.

prihatin (*Jv*) 1 sad, deeply afflicted, grieved, depressed, dejected. *turut –* to share s.o.'s grief. 2 worried, concerned, anxious, disturbed, alarmed. *Kelompok Warga –.* Concerned Citizen's Group. *Ibunya sangat – karena bayinya sakit.* The mother is very worried because her baby is sick.

berprihatin 1 seriously striving after or trying to achieve one's goals. *Kalau begitu, marilah kita ~.* If that's the case, let's try to achieve our goal. 2 to be concerned. *~ terhadap* to be concerned about.

memprihatinkan to cause alarm/concern/anxiety/worry; alarming, worrisome. *Remaja hamil semakin ~.* Pregnant adolescents are causing more concern.

keprihatinan anxiety, concern, worry. *pegawai negeri ber-Lebaran dalam ~* government employees anxiously celebrated Lebaran. *hidup dalam ~* live in anxiety, all but dead; → KEMBANG *kempis*.

prikik (*E*) 1 (in soccer) free kick. 2 to act in a disrespectful way.

prilaku → PERI I.

priléns (*E*) freelance.

priloka (*geol*) autochthonous.

prima (*D*) first-rate/class, prime, number 1, excellent.

primadona (*D*) 1 prima donna. 2 the first/most important (item/principal/commodity, etc.).

primair → PRIMÉR.

primakuin (*E*) primaquine (used in the treatment of malaria).

Primaniyarta a trophy awarded by the government to exporters who have increased nonoil and gas exports.

primat I (*D*) primate (an archbishop, the highest ranking archbishop in a province, etc.).

primat(a) II (*D*) primate(s) (apes/monkeys, etc.). *ahli –* primatologist.

primatologi (*D*) primatology.

primbon (*Jv*) handbook which contains predictions, calculations of unlucky days etc.

primér (*D*) 1 primacy. 2 *uang –* base money.

primitif (*D*) primitive.

keprimitifan primitiveness.

primitifisme (*D/E*) primitivism.

primordial (*D/E*) primordial, atavistic (beliefs/attitude, etc.).

primordialisme (*D/E*) primordiality, atavistic views. *- dapat menghambat pembangunan bila tidak lentur.* Atavistic attitudes can obstruct development if they are not flexible.

primordialistik primordialistic, having atavistic views. *masyarakat – a* society with an atavistic viewpoint.

primpen (*Jv*) secure(ly put away).
memprimpeni to keep/store safely, put in safe keeping.
primpén (*Jv*) **memprimpéni** to appear to s.o. in a dream.
prin (in acronyms) → PERINTAH.
pring → PERING II.
prin(g) (*mil*) "friend" (in answer to Who's there?).
pringas-pringis (*Jv*) to sneer, grin.
pringgitan (*Jv*) section of a traditional-style house [located between the front veranda (the *pendapa*) and the main family section] on which shadow plays are performed for guests.
pringis (*Jv*) → PRINGAS-PRINGIS.
pringisan grin.
pringsilan (*Jv*) 1 testicles. 2 scrotum.
prinjak → PRENJAK.
prinsés (*D*) princess.
prinsip (*D*) principle, tenet. *pada –nya* basically, in principle, fundamentally. *– akuntan yang berlaku umum* generally accepted accounting procedures. *– pembédaan* distinction principle.
berprinsip 1 to have principles. 2 principled.
prinsipal (*D*) principle.
prinsipiil (*D*) in principle. *hal-hal yang –* matters of principle.
printing (*E*) printing, impression (on fabric). *batik –* hand-blocked batik made by using a copper stamp, *usu* of low quality.
prioritas and **prioritét** (*D*) priority, preferential treatment. *memberikan – jalan* to yield the right of way. *– pertama* first/top priority.
memprioritas-pertamakan to give the highest priority to.
memprioritaskan to give priority to, earmark.
pemrioritasan granting of priority, earmarking.
pripih (*Jv*) amulet, talisman, charm, mascot.
pris → PRÉS II.
prisidér → FRISIDÉR.
priskoran (*D*) price list.
prisma (*D*) prism. *– nama* desk marker, nameplate (on desk).
prit I /i as ee in meet/ (*onom*) sound made by a whistle. *– jigo* a way of extorting bribes (the traffic policeman blows on his whistle and you have to pay him 25 rupiahs; → JIGO, SEMPRIT I.
memprit to stop (of a traffic policeman who then extorts a bribe). *Banyak sekali mobil-mobil yang diprit.* Many cars were stopped by the traffic police.
prit II clipped form of **emprit**.
privasi (*D*) privacy.
privat (*D*) private. *lés –* private lesson(s).
keprivatan privacy.
privatisasi (*E*) privatization.
privé (*D*) private. *urusan –, bukan urusan kantor* private business, not office business.
keprivéan privacy.
privilése (*D*) privilege.
berprivilése to be privileged.
priwil (*D*) freewheel.
priya → PRIA.
priyagung → PRIAGUNG.
priyayi (*Jv*) 1 s.o. of the upper class, aristocrat. 2 (traditional) functionary; government employee; → PRIAYI.
kepriyayian aristocracy, priyayi mentality.
priyayisme aristocracy, *priyayi* mentality.
pro I (*D*) 1 pro. 2 (in compound word) pro-. *– Indonésia* pro-Indonesia. *– dan kontra* pros and cons; those for and those against. *Polémik antara yang – dan kontra senjata nuklir semakin luas.* The polemics between those for and those against nuclear weapons keep on increasing.
pro II (in acronyms) → PROGRAM.
probabilitas (*D*) probability.
problém(a) (*D*) problem.
seproblém *– dengan* to have the same problem as. *Adakah pembaca yang ~ dengan saya?* Is there a reader who has the same problem as I?
problématik (*E*) and **problématis** (*D*) problematic.
problim → PROBLÉM(A).
pro bono publico (*L*) for the public good, pro bono.
procot (*Jv vulg*) to be born.
memprocotkan to give birth.

Proda [Projék Daérah] Regional Project. *– Akte Kelahiran* Regional Project for Birth Certificates.
prodénia a type of worm that attacks soybean crops, among others, in the area around Jombang, East Java.
prodéo (*D*) 1 in God's (Allah's) name. 2 free, gratis, without having to pay. *hotél –* (*euph*) prison.
produk (*D*) product. *pembuat –* producer. *– Doméstik Bruto* [PDB] Gross Domestic Product, GDP. *– ikut-ikutan* me-too products. *– samping(an)* by-product. *– Nasional Bruto/Kotor* Gross National Product, GNP. *– tambahan* by-product.
memproduk to produce.
produksi (*D*) production. *kelebihan –* overproduction. *prosés – yang komérsial* commercial manufacturing process, commercial process of production. *– berkesinambungan* sustainable production. *– bersama* joint production. *– massal* mass production. *– pangan* food production. *– ruah* (*petro*) flush production. *– sekali banyak* mass production.
berproduksi 1 to produce. 2 to be in production.
mem(p)roduksi(kan) to produce s.t., manufacture. *memproduksi motif yang lagi ngetrénd* to produce a trendy batik pattern.
produksian product (*mod*).
pemroduksi producer, manufacturer. *perusahaan –* manufacturing company.
produktif (*D/E*) productive, pay (*mod*).
keproduktifan productivity.
pemroduktifan productivity.
produktivitas and **produktivitét** (*D*) productivity.
berproduktivitas to have a ... productivity. *~ tinggi* to have a high level of productivity. *menghasilkan tenaga kerja ~ tinggi* to create a high-productivity labor force.
produsén (*D*) → PRODUSER.
produser (*E*) producer. *– film* film producer.
produsir (*D*) **memprodusir** to produce.
prof prof, clipped form of **profésor**.
profan (*D*) profane.
memprofankan to profane.
profanisasi (*E*) profanation.
profési (*D*) profession.
seprofési in the same profession, does the same kind of work.
berprofési 1 to have the profession (of). *~ sebagai seorang manol* to have the profession of redcap. 2 professional.
keprofésian professionalism.
profésional (*E*) professional. *perilaku –* professional behavior. *kurang –* unprofessional. **kekurang-profésionalan** lack of professionalism, unprofessional behavior. *tidak –* unprofessional. **ketidak-profésionalan** lack of professionalism.
memprofésionalkan to professionalize.
keprofésionalan professionalization.
profésionalis a professional.
profésionalisasi (*E*) professionalization.
profésionalisme (*D/E*) professionalism.
profésionil (*D*) professional.
profésor (*D/E*) (university) professor. *– madya* (*Mal*) associate professor. *– tamu* guest professor.
keprofésoran professoriate. *sejarah ~ di Univérsitas Indonésia* the history of the professoriate at the University of Indonesia.
profétik (*E*) and **profétis** (*D*) prophetic; → KENABIAN.
profil (*D*) profile. *– kriminalitas* crime profile. *– skolastik* scholastic profile.
memprofilkan to profile. *~ Nancy léwat mingguannya* to profile Nancy in his weekly paper.
profilaksis (*D/E*) prophylaxis.
profisiat (*D*) congratulations!
profit (*E*) profit; → LABA I.
berprofit to profit (by); to take advantage (of).
profitabilitas *E* profitability.
pro forma (*L D*) pro forma, for the sake of form. *Prosédur pembelian kapal Tampomas II hanya –.* The purchase procedure for the Tampomas II was just pro forma.
prog (in acronyms) → PROGRAM.
progésteron (*E*) progesterone.

prognosa, prognose (D) and **prognosis** (E) prognosis.
program (D) program, plan. – *diploma* certificate program. – *jangka péndék* crash program. – *kesederhanaan* austerity program. – *kilat* crash program. **memprogramkilatkan** to give priority to, run as a crash program. *Penambahan peralatan Dinas Kebakaran diprogramkilatkan.* A crash program has been instituted to increase Fire Department equipment. – *politik* platform (of a political party). – *terpadu* integrated program. – *yang kurikulumnya disesuaikan dengan kebutuhan* in-house program.
  berprogram with a program; programmed.
  mem(p)rogramkan to program.
  pemrogram programmer.
  pemrograman programming. *bahasa* ~ programming language.
programa (D) → PROGRAM.
programatik (E) and **programatis** (D) programmatic.
programatir and **programatur** (D) software; → PERANGKAT *lunak*.
programer (E) programmer; → PEMROGRAM.
progrés (E) progress.
progrésif (D) progressive.
  keprogrésifan 1 progressiveness. **2** progressivism.
Prokasih → PROYÉK *Kali Bersih*.
prokém 1 (*usu* spelled with an upper-case P) disguised youth language, a kind of Pig Latin, in which words are formed from ordinary words by several different processes, for example, the syllables are reversed, or the word is truncated and an -ok- is inserted into the word; the word *prokém* itself is formed from *préman* by this process. **2** street kid. *Dulu senantiasa ada – yang minta uang dari meréka.* There used to be street kids who begged money from them.
  memprokémkan to make into a *prokém* word. ~ *bahasa* to turn one's words into *prokém*.
proklamasi (D) proclamation.
  memproklamasikan to proclaim, announce.
proklamator (E) proclaimer (of Indonesian independence) (refers to Soekarno-Hatta).
proklamir (D) **memproklamir(kan)**→ to proclaim.
proksi [perang proksi] proxy war.
prokurasi (D) procuration, power of attorney.
proletar (D) proletarian.
  memproletarkan to proletarianize.
  keproletaran proletariat.
proletarisasi (E) proletarianization.
proliferasi (D) proliferation.
prolifik (E) prolific. *pengkritik yang handal dan –* a well-known and prolific critic.
prolog (D) prologue.
prolongasi (D) prolongation.
prombéngan (*Jv*) junkman, dealer in second-hand goods.
promenade (D) promenade.
promés (D) promissory note. *yang menandatangani/mengeluarkan –* promissory. – *atas/kepada pengganti* promissory note to order. – *atas tunjuk, – bawa, – kepada/untuk pembawa* bearer promissory note. – *kepada tertunjuk* promissory note on order.
prominén (D) prominent, outstanding, distinguished.
promiskuitas (D) promiscuity.
promosi (D) **1** promotion (advancement in rank or position). **2** (sales) promotion. *Pusat – Perdagangan* Trade Promotion Center. *tenaga – penjualan* sales promotion person. **3** graduation (for a doctoral/Ph.D. degree). *berhak menempuh –* to be entitled to take one's doctoral/Ph.D. degree. **4** degree ceremony, commencement. – *penjualan* sales promotion. – *pinjaman* lending promotion.
  berpromosi 1 to be promoted (to a higher office), rise to a higher position; to stimulate, boost, encourage. **2** to advertise, publicize, promote (a product). *"Lumpia kami mempunyai sejarah paling tua," timpal Ny. Ida ~.* "We've been making egg rolls for the longest time," responded Mrs. Ida, promoting them.
promotif (E) promotive, promotional.
promotor (D) **1** promoter. **2** dissertation advisor, professor who presents the graduating Ph.D. candidate.
  mempromotori 1 to promote, be the promoter of/for. ~ *pertandingan ulang* to promote a rematch. **2** to be the dissertation ad-

visor for, be the professor who presents (the Ph.D. candidate). *promovéndus dipromotori oléh Prof. Ahmad Sadali* the Ph.D. candidate was presented by Prof. Ahmad Sadali.
  kepromotoran promotion.
promovénda (D) female Ph.D. candidate.
promovéndus (D) male Ph.D. candidate.
pron → FRONT.
Prona → PROYÉK *Operasi Nasional Agraria.* **mem-Prona-kan** to make (a region) into an agrarian national operation project.
prongkol (*Jv*) lump.
  prongkolan in lumps.
pronomén (D *gram*) pronoun.
pronomina *pl* of *pronomen*.
pronominal (D *gram*) pronominal.
prop I (D) **1** cork (of bottle), stopper. **2** cork (the material). *topi –* topee, pith sun helmet.
prop II clipped form of **propinsi**.
prop III clipped form of **propadéus**.
propadéus (D) preparation for entering (a course/profession, etc.).
propaganda (D/E) propaganda.
  berpropaganda to propagandize, make propaganda.
  mempropagandai to propagandize s.o.
  mem(p)ropagandakan to propagandize for, make propaganda for.
propagandis (D) propagandist.
Propan → PROYÉK *Pandu*.
propana (D/E) propane.
Propéda [Program Pembangunan Daérah] Regional Development Program.
propélan (E) propellant.
propéler (D) propeller.
Propenas [Program Pembangunan Nasional] National Development Program.
properti (E) property. *bisnis –* business property (land and buildings).
propésor → PROFÉSOR.
propinsi (D) province → DAÉRAH *(Swatantra) tingkat I.*
propionat (D) propionate.
propisi → PROVISI.
propokasi → PROVOKASI.
proporsi (D) proportion. – *yang sebenarnya* true proportion/perspective.
  berproporsi to have ... proportions; proportioned.
proporsional (E) and **proporsionil** (D) proportional; balanced, unbiased, appropriate. *secara –* correspondingly, in a corresponding way.
proposal (E) proposal.
proposisi (D) proposition.
propot (*Jv*) *mak –* procuress. *pak –* pimp.
propulsi (E) propulsion.
prorata (D) prorata. *harga –* prorata price.
prorogasi (D) prorogation.
prosa (D) prose. – *berirama* rhythmic prose.
prosais 1 prosaic. **2** prose writer.
prosaisme (E) prosaism.
prosédé (D) process, procedure.
prosedur (D) procedure, (working) method.
prosedural (E) and **proseduril** (D) procedural.
prosén (D) percent; → PERSÉN II.
proséntase (D) and **proséntasi** percentage.
proséntuil (D) on a percentage basis.
prosés (D) **1** process. **2** lawsuit, (legal) proceeding. – *akulturasi* acculturation process. – *kemerosotan* drifting/sinking/declining process. – *lanjutan* secondary process. – *malih* metamorphic. – *pem-Baratan* westernization process. – *penuaan* senescence, growing old. – *dalam – persidangan* (*leg*) in procedure. – *vérbal* minutes, police officer's report, (official) report of an infraction drawn up by the investigator, by the police or by the *penyidik*.
  berprosés 1 to proceed, continue, go on. **2** to be engaged in a lawsuit (with), be involved in litigation (against).
  memprosés to settle; to process (information/gases into ammonia, etc.); to manufacture; to develop (film).

pemrosés processor. ~ *data* data processor. ~ *kapas berbiji menjadi serat kapas* ginnery.

pemrosésan processing. ~ *data (éléktronik)* (electronic) data processing.

prosési (*D*) procession.

prosésing (*D*) processing.

prosésor (*E*) processor. – *kata* word processor.

prosiding (*E*) proceedings.

prosodi (*D*) prosody.

prosodis (*D*) prosodic.

prospék (*E*) prospect, perspective. *memiliki – yang cerah* to have bright prospects. *– bisnis* business prospects. *– hari depan* future prospects.

berprospék to have prospects/perspectives. *Walaupun jamur ~ baik tetapi cara penanaman masih tradisional.* Although mushrooms have good prospects, planting methods are still traditional.

prospéksi (*E*) prospection (result), prospecting (action).

prospéktif (*E*) prospective.

prospéktus (*D*) prospectus.

prostaglandin (*E*) prostaglandin.

prostat (*D*) prostate. *kelenjar* – prostate gland.

prostitusi (*D*) prostitution.

memprostitusikan to prostitute. ~ *diri* to prostitute o.s.

protagonis (*D*) protagonist.

protap [prosédur tetap] standard operating procedures, SOP.

protéin (*D*) protein. *– héwani* animal protein (such as, fish, meat, milk, and eggs). *– nabati* plant protein.

berprotéin containing protein, protinaceous. *makanan ~* food containing protein.

protéksi (*D*) (industrial) protection.

memprotéksi to protect (an industry).

protéksionis (*D*) protectionist.

protéksionisme (*D/E*) protectionism.

protéktif (*E*) protective.

protéktorat (*D*) protectorate.

protés (*D*) 1 a protest. 2 to protest. *– duduk* sit-down strike.

protés-protésan all k.o. protests.

berprotés to protest.

mem(p)rotés to protest s.t.

protésan a protest that has been made.

pemrotés protester. *tujuh orang ~* seven protesters.

pemrotésan protesting, a protest action.

protése and **protésis** (*D*) prosthesis.

Protéstan (*D*) Protestant. *umat* – Protestants. *– Anglosakson Putih* White Anglo-Saxon Protestant, WASP.

protokol I (*D*) protocol. *jalan-jalan* – the main, well-kept streets in a city. *– Kesepakatan* Protocol of Understanding.

protokol-protokolan various k.o. (annoying) protocols. ~ *birokrasi* what one has to go through in dealing with the bureaucracy, red tape.

keprotokolan protocol (*mod*), according to protocol.

protokol II master of ceremonies (at formal assemblies).

protokolér (*D*) according to protocol, protocol (*mod*).

protol (*Jv*) to snap/break/come off.

mrotol (*Jv*) to drop out.

memrotoli 1 to pull to pieces. **2** to rob, hold up. *Penumpang otobis diprotoli.* The bus passengers were robbed.

protolan (school) dropout.

proton (*D*) proton.

Proton Saga trademark of the first Malaysian national automobile manufactured by the *Perusahaan Otomobil Nasional* in cooperation with the Japanese Mitsubishi Company.

protoplas (*D*) protoplast.

protoplasma (*D*) protoplasm.

prototip(e) (*D*) prototype.

memprototipkan to prototype, create a prototype or experimental model. *Kita ingin ~ hasil kerja seorang perancang muda.* We would like to create an experimental model of the performance of a young designer.

prov (*abbr*) [provinsi] province.

provinsi (*D*) province.

provinsial (*D*) provincial.

provinsialis (*D*) provincialist.

provinsialisme (*D/E*) provincialism.

provinsialistis (*D*) provincialistic.

provisi (*D*) **1** (stock) provisions, supplies. **2** (*bank*) commission. **3** (*leg*) provisional (decision/action), application for interim relief.

provokasi (*D*) provocation.

memprovokasi(kan) to provoke.

terprovokasi provoked.

provokatif (*E*) provocative.

provokator (*E*) provoker, provocateur.

provos (*D*) provost. *regu* – internal affairs (in the police department).

provosir (*D*) **memprovosir** to provoke.

provost (*D*) **1** provost, military police in the air force or navy. **2** soldier's detention room, brig.

proyék (*D*) project. *– cikal* pilot project. *– Javanologi* Javanology project. *– Kali Bersih* [Prokasih] Clean Rivers Project. *– Mandataris/Mercusuar* Mandatory/Lighthouse Projects, i.e., a number of large-scale construction projects in Jakarta under President Soekarno. *– MHT/Mohamad Husni Thamrin* the *Kampung Improvement Program* in Jakarta, named after one of the leaders in the *Volksraad* during colonial times. **mem-proyék-MHT-kan** to improve a *kampung* as part of this program. *– Operasi Nasional Agraria* [Prona] Agrarian National Operations Project. *–.– padat karya* labor-intensive projects employing the otherwise unemployed labor force. *– Pandu* [Propan] Pilot Project. *– pelopor* pilot project. *– Penelitian dan Pengembangan Jawa* Javanology project. *– Pengembangan Kebun Karét Rakyat* [PPKKR] Smallholders Rubber Development Project, SRDP. *– percobaan/percontohan* pilot project. *– perindustrian* industrial project. *– perintis/pola* pilot project. *–.– prasarana* infrastructure projects. *– rintisan* pilot project. *– tekan tombol* and *– terpakét* turnkey project.

seproyék (working) on the same project.

memproyékkan to make s.t. into a project.

proyéksi (*D*) **1** projection. **2** plan.

memproyéksikan to project; to design, lay/set out.

terproyéksi projected.

proyéktil (*D*) missile, projectile. *– bakar yang digerakkan tenaga rokét* fin-stabilized rocket-propelled incendiary missile. *– balistik antarbenua* intercontinental ballistic missile. *– kendali* guided missile.

proyéktir (*D*) **memproyéktir** to project; to design.

proyéktor (*D/E*) projector.

PRRI (*init*) [Pemerintah Révolusionér Républik Indonésia] Revolutionary Government of the Republic of Indonesia, proclaimed on February 15, 1958, in Bukittinggi, became the *Républik Persatuan Indonésia* Federal Republic of Indonesia in Bonjol, West Sumatra on February 8, 1960, dissolved on August 17, 1961.

PRT (*init*) → PEMBANTU *Rumah Tangga*.

pruf (*D*) proof (sheet), printer's proof. *– bersih/halaman* page proof. *– kotor* galley proof.

prufrit (*D*) test drive (an automobile).

pru(u)k (*onom*) sound of s.t. collapsing with a thud.

prusi (*D?*) verdigris.

Prusia (*D*) Prussia.

PS(K) [Pekerja Séks Komérsial] sex worker.

psalm (*D*) psalm.

pséudo- false, pretend, unreal.

pséudonim (*D*) pseudonym.

pséudosains (*D*) pseudoscience.

PSII → PARTAI *Syarikat Islam Indonésia*.

psiké (*D*) psyche.

psikedélik (*D/E*) psychedelic. *lampu* – psychedelic lights used in disco dancing.

psikiater (*D*) psychiatrist.

psikiatri (*D/E*) psychiatry.

psikiatrik (*E*) and **psikiatris** (*D*) psychiatric.

psikis (*D*) psychic.

psikoanalis (*D*) psychoanalyst.

psikoanalisa and **psikoanalisis** (*D*) psychoanalysis. *ahli* – psychoanalyst.

psikodinamika (D) psychodynamics.
psikofarmako (E) *térapi* – psychopharmacotherapy.
psikofisiologis (E) psychophysiological.
psikogénik (E) psychogenic.
psikolinguistik (D/E) psycholinguistics.
psikolog (D) psychologist.
psikologi (D/E) psychology. – *massa* mass psychology.
psikologikal (E) and psikologis (D) psychological.
psikologisme (E) psychologism.
psikomotorik (E) psychomotoric.
psikoneurosa (D) psychoneurosis.
psikopat (D) psychopath.
psikose (D) psychosis. – *ketakutan* psychosis of fear. – *yang tidak umum* atypical psychosis.
psikoséksual (E) psychosexual.
psikosis (E) psychosis.
psikosomatik (E) and psikosomatis (D) psychosomatic. *penderita* – s.o. who suffers from psychosomatic symptoms.
psikososial (E) psychosocial.
psikotéknik psychotechnics, industrial psychology.
psikotérapi (D/E) psychotherapy.
psikotés (E) psychotest.
  mempsikotés to subject s.o. to a psychotest.
psikotik (E) and psikotis (D) psychotic.
psikotropika (E) psychotropic. *obat* – the patent medicines: rohypnol, mogadon, and lexotan.
psk (*abbr*) [pasukan] army troops.
PSK Patrol Ship Killer.
psoriasis (E) psoriasis.
PSP [Persenjataan Sasaran Panser] Antitank Weapons.
PSPB [Pendidikan Sejarah Perjuangan Bangsa] Course in the History of the National Struggle (for Independence; a school subject).
pst ... pst ... pst pst, psst (exclamation used to attract s.o.'s attention, a call for silence, etc.).
PSU [Persenjataan Sasaran Udara] Antiaircraft Weapons.
Pt. (*abbr*) [Pendéta] Protestant clergyman, Rev.
PT I [Pengadilan Tinggi] Appellate Court.
PT II (*init*) → PERGURUAN *Tinggi*.
PT III (*init*) → PERSÉROAN *Terbatas*.
PT IV (*init sl*) → PÉTÉ, PUTAU(W).
PTDI (*init*) → PERGURUAN *Tinggi Dakwah Islam*.
PTF [Patrol (Boat) Torpedo Fast] Fast Torpedo Patrol Boat.
PTIK (*init*) → PERGURUAN *Tinggi Ilmu Kepolisian*.
PTKP → PENDAPATAN *Tidak Kena Pajak*.
PTL (*init*) → PAJAK *Tidak Langsung*.
PTN (*init*) → PERGURUAN *Tinggi Negeri*.
PTP (*init*) [Pos, Télékomunikasi, Pariwisata] Post, Telecommunications, and Tourism.
PTRI [Perwakilan Tetap Républik Indonésia] Republic of Indonesia Permanent Mission (to the United Nations).
PTS I (*init*) → PERGURUAN *Tinggi Swasta*.
PTS II [Pria Tuna Susila] gigolo, male prostitute; *cp* WTS.
PTT (*init*) [Pos, Télegrap dan Télepon] Post, Telegraph, and Telephone Agency.
PTW (*init*) → PUTAU(W).
PU I (*init*) [Pekerjaan Umum] Public Works.
  ke-PU-an Public Works (*mod*). *tajuk tentang masalah* ~ an editorial about Public Works problems.
PU II [Pembantu Utama] Principal Assistant.
puad → FUAD.
PUAD [Pangkalan Udara Angkatan Darat] Army Air (Force) Base.
puadai (*Tam J*) rug/carpet/cloth mat spread for rulers/VIPs/brides and grooms to walk/sit on.
puah I (A) spiritual power; → AFUAH.
puah II (*onom*) 1 sound made when spitting out between the lips (expressing disgust/disdain), a Bronx cheer. 2 shame on you!
puah III (children's language) berpuah to walk.
puak 1 ethnic group; tribe, class, race, clan. *Tiap* – *mempunyai cara perkawinan yang diatur rapi.* Every group has its well-organized wedding customs. 2 party, group. *Ada dua* – *yang besar pengaruhnya dalam pemerintahan Inggris.* There are two parties which are highly influential in British government. – *kiri* leftist group.

berpuak-puak in groups/parties.
  kepuakan (*mod*) group.
puaka 1 *hantu* – guardian spirit/sprite. – *air* water sprite. – *hutan* wood sprite. – *tanah* earth sprite. 2 haunted.
  berpuaka haunted.
puaké (in Kalimantan) evil spirit.
pual I (D) voile.
pual II eddy (of wind/water), vortex.
  berpual(-pual) 1 to bubble up, eddy. 2 to be in a whirl (of one's head).
pualam (*Tam*) *batu* – 1 marble; → MARMAR. 2 alabaster.
  memualam to be/turn white (like marble or alabaster).
puan I gold/silver plate (for betel) (*usu* used by queens or brides).
puan II (*Mal*) clipped form of perempuan. 1 lady (title, form of address to royalty). 2 female title, Miss, Mrs., Ms.
puan III (*J?*) *kelapa* – coconut with soft, loose pulp.
puang 1 "God Father" of the Indonesian workers at the plantations of Tawau and Eastern Malaysia. 2 (in Tana Toraja) descendant of royalty.
puanjang (*coq*) very long.
pua-pua casuarina tree.
puar various species of cardamom, such as, *Alpina malaccensis;* → LENGKUAS. *condong* – *ke uratnya, cinta manusia kepada bangsanya* charity begins at home. *tercengang* –, *tergerak andilau* (*M*) one rotten apple spoils the whole barrel.
puas 1 satisfied, contented, pleased, happy. "*Bila Anda* –, *beritahu kawan. Bila kecéwa, beritahu saya.*" (slogan in some restaurants) "If you're satisfied, tell your friends; if you're disappointed, tell me." 2 tired of, no longer eager/keen, fed up. *sudah* – *bertanya-tanya* to have asked again and again until one is tired of asking. 3 quenched (of thirst). *tidak* – dissatisfied, discontented, displeased. ketidak-puasan dissatisfaction, discontent, displeasure. – *apa adanya* to let well enough alone, make the best of things. – *diri* self-satisfied. – *hati* satisfied. sepuas hati until one is satisfied, to one's heart's content. berpuas hati to be satisfied/contented. – *lelas* completely satisfied.
  puas-puas until one is satisfied, to one's satisfaction. *Anak-anaknya dapat* ~ *memutar lagu kesayangannya.* His children could play their favorite tunes as much as they wanted.
  sepuas as satisfied as. ~ *mungkin* (sleep, etc.) to one's heart's content.
  sepuas(-puas)nya until one is satisfied, until one has had enough of it, to one's heart's content. *Makanlah* ~! Please eat as much as you like.
  berpuas ~ *diri* to feel satisfied/pleased with o.s., complacent. *Pemerintah jangan cepat* ~ *diri dengan adanya organisasi-organisasi kemasyarakatan yang berpacu untuk mencantumkan Pancasila sebagai satu-satunya asas dalam anggaran dasarnya.* The government should not content itself quickly with social organizations that move swiftly to insert *Pancasila* as the one and only principle in their statutes.
  berpuas-puas to do s.t. to one's heart's content.
  memuas to become satisfied.
  memuasi to satisfy.
  memuaskan [and muasin (*J coq*)] 1 to satisfy; satisfactory, rewarding, fulfilling. *tidak* ~ unsatisfactory, unsatisfying. *meraih gelar doktor dengan prédikat* ~/*sangat* ~ to obtain a Ph.D. with a citation of satisfactory/very satisfactory. ~ *dagaha* to quench one's thirst. ~ *hawa nafsunya* to give free reign to one's passions, satisfy one's carnal urges. ~ *lapar dan dahaga* to satisfy one's hunger and thirst. ~ *mata melihat* to keep one's eyes wide open. ~ *tangisnya* to weep one's eyes out. *Kubiarkan ibu* ~ *tangisnya.* I let mother weep her eyes out. *Kekayaan dan keméwahan tidak dapat* ~ *hatinya.* Wealth and luxury cannot give him satisfaction. *Hasil ujian tahun ini sangat* ~. This year's examination results have been very satisfactory. *tidak mungkin dipuaskan* impossible to please, insatiable. 2 to give into one's ..., indulge one's ... ~ *nafsu* to indulge one's baser instincts.
  terpuaskan *tidak* ~ insatiable.
  kepuasan 1 satisfaction, contentment. 2 saturation. ~ *diri sendiri* self-satisfaction. ~ *hati* complacency. ~ *klién* customer/client

satisfaction. ~ *konsumén* customer satisfaction. *sampai pada puncak ~ séks* to the point of orgasm.

pemuas satisfier, s.t. that satisfies, s.t. that quenches (thirst). *Wanita kita hanya berfungsi sebagai bahan ~ hawa nafsunya orang asing.* Our women only serve as objects to satisfy the carnal passions of foreigners. ~ *dahaga* thirst quencher.

pemuasan satisfying, quenching (thirst), satiation, gratification.

puasa (*Skr*) **1** to fast (to abstain from all food). *bulan* – the fasting month of Ramadan. *hari mangkat* – the day before the beginning of the fast. *membuka* – to break the fast. **2** abstinence from sexual intercourse (due to husband's impotence, etc.). *Nyonya M menahankan – hampir setahun penuh.* Mrs. M abstained from sexual intercourse for almost a full year. – *apit* fast on one's birthday plus the previous and following days. – *bedug* fasting from dawn till noon and then again till evening. – *biologis* abstinence from sexual intercourse. – *Daud* fasting every other day. – *fardu* obligatory fast during the month of Ramadan. – *haram* forbidden fast on *Idul Fitri, Idul Adha,* and *Tasyrik* days, i.e., the three successive days of *Zulhijah* 11, 12, and 13. – *makruh* (uncommendable) fasting almost continuously for one year. – *mutih* fasting by eating only rice and tuberous plants, without salt, for 40 days (an ascetic regimen). – *sanggama* abstinence. – *Senin Kemis* to fast on Monday and Thursday. – *sunnah/sunat* (commendable) fast often performed by the prophet Muhammad; fasting on Mondays and Thursdays; fasting each 13th, 14th, and 15th of the month; fasting six days in the month of *Syawwal*; fasting on *Zulhijah* 9 (one day before the *Idhul Adha*) and on *Muharam* 10. – *wajib* obligatory fasting.

berpuasa to fast. *Meréka yang ~ akan menjadi muda kembali.* Those who fast will become young again.

puasawan (*Skr neo*) s.o. who fasts.

puatang (*C*) **1** failed, unsuccessful. **2** foiled, baffled.

puawang → PAWANG.

pub (*E*) /pab/ pub. *pengusaha* – pub owner, publican.

puber and **pubér** (*D*) pubescent. *masa* – puberty.

pubertas and **pubértas** (*D*) puberty.

publik (*D/E*) public. *opini* – public opinion.

publikasi (*D*) publication.

mem(p)ublikasikan to publicize. ~ *diri* to advertise/promote o.s.

terpublikasi publicized. *kurang* ~ insufficiently publicized, underpublicized.

pemublikasian publication, publishing.

publikatif *secara* – through publication.

publisir (*D*) **mempublisir** to publicize.

publisis (*E*) publicist.

publisistik (*D*) communications science.

publisitas and **publisitét** (*D*) publicity.

pucak → PUNCAK.

pucang (*Jv*) areca nut palm; → PINANG I.

pucat pale, washed out, faded. – *benihan/bagai mayat/kesi/ kelabu/kuam/kusam/lesi/lesu/manai/pasi/pudar* a) deathly pale, as white as a ghost/sheet. b) anemic.

sepucat as pale as. ~ *kertas/mayat* as white as a ghost/sheet.

memucat to become/grow/turn pale.

memucatkan 1 to bleach. **2** to make s.t. or s.o. turn pale.

terpucat-pucat to turn pale.

kepucatan 1 paleness. **2** somewhat pale.

kepucat-pucatan somewhat pale.

pemucat bleach, bleaching agent.

pemucatan bleaching, making s.t. fade.

pucet → PUCAT.

pucik the two main posts at the entrance to large marine fish traps; → JERMAL.

pucuk I **1** bud, sprout, shoot. *mati* – a) dead as a doornail. b) impotent. c) to die back. *Tanaman yang terus-menerus terserang penyakit tak pernah berdaun lebat dan secara berangsur mengalami mati* –, *sehingga akhirnya tanaman mati.* Plants which are continuously attacked by disease will never have abundant leaves, will gradually die back and the plant will finally die. **2** sharp-pointed tapering tips (of a flame/tree, etc.). *Daun-daun masih terlekat di* – *pohon.* The leaves at the top of the tree are

still stuck together. **3** the highest, the most important, the highest point (in s.t.), the leading edge (of s.t.); the one authorized. *ditanam* – (*M*) to be erected by a *penghulu. harganya kini berada di* – *pohon cemara* prices are sky-high nowadays. **4** a budding feeling. – *dicinta, ulam tiba* and *hendak ulam* – *menjulai* and *bak* – *dicinta* unexpected luck; to get a piece of unexpected luck, get a windfall. *tak (ber)* – *di atas enau* (*M*) conceited, cocky. *seperti* – *eru* to trim one's sails according to the wind. *minta* – *pada alu, menghendaki* – *alu* to cry for the moon, i.e., ask for the impossible. *bagai* – (*enau*) *dilancarkan/diluncurkan* (to go off) like a shot, as swift as an arrow. – *layu, disiram hujan* it's hard to be pleased. – *api* tongues of flames. – *bulat* (*M*) the highest authority. – *cinta* love in bloom. – *enau* shoots of the young *enau* used for cigarette wrappers. – *jala* the center of a (cast) net. (*di*) – *kekuasaan* (at) the height of power. – *lembaga* plumule. – *lembing* spearhead. – *nipah* young leaf of the marsh palm, *Nipa fruticans,* used for cigarette paper. – *nuklir* nuclear warhead. – *ombak* crest of a wave. – *pemerintahan* the supreme government. – *pimpinan* a) supreme leadership, supreme command (of an army, party, etc.). b) general management (of a company). c) central/governing board. **memucuk-pimpinan** to become a member of the governing board. – *pisang* greenish yellow. – *rebung* a) young bamboo shoot. b) a V-shaped pattern common on the "head" of the *batik* sarong. – *surai* mane (of a horse).

berpucuk 1 to sprout, bud. **2** to have a sprout/bud/shoot. *kata tak* ~ the last word. *rudal nuklir* ~ *ganda* nuclear missile with a multiple warhead.

memucuki to stand at the head of, be the leader of.

pucuk II classifier for letters, fire arms, needles. *se– surat* a letter. *jarum dua* – two needles. *beberapa* – *senapan* several rifles.

pucuk III 1 an herb, costus root, *Saussurea lappa;* the oil from the dried root (Costus root oil) is used as a medicine. **2** gebang palm, *Corypha gebanga.*

pucuk IV *ular* – a green-colored snake, short-nosed vine snake, *Dryophis prasinus.*

pucuk V belt fish, ribbon fish, hair tail, *Trichiurus haumela/savala.*

pucung I *burung* – gray heron, *Ardea cinerea.* – *keladi* little green heron, *Butorides striatus javanicus.*

pucung II (*Jv*) k.o. tree, *Pagium edule* and its fruit; → KEPAYANG, MÉNJÉ.

pucung III (*Jv*) k.o. song form.

pudak → PODAK.

pudar 1 pale (in color), dull (of eyes), faded (of clothes/colors/ complexions), dim (of light), burned down (of fire); discolored, faded. **2** weakened, watered down, dispirited.

sepudar as dim/dim/pale, etc. as.

memudar 1 to fade, fading. **2** to weaken, become weaker, recede. *Déwasa ini masalah tata krama dan unggah-ungguh di kalangan masyarakat Jawa, tampak ~ dan bahkan tidak lagi memperhatikannya.* Nowadays matters of etiquette and good form in social intercourse in Javanese society seem to be weakening and, what's more, no one pays any attention to them anymore.

memudarkan 1 to dim, dull, make pale. **2** to dispirit. **3** to weaken, attenuate.

kepudaran 1 paleness. **2** slackness, weakness.

pemudaran 1 fading (of colors), dimming, dulling. **2** bleaching. **3** weakening. **4** attenuation.

pudat filled to overflowing, full to the brim.

pudék [pembantu dékan] assistant dean.

pudel (*D*) *anjing* – poodle.

pudéng (*D*) pudding.

puder (*D*) (face) powder; *cp* PUYER.

pudi I diamond dust, diamond fragment. *intan* – tiny diamonds.

memudikan to crush (diamonds) into dust.

PUDI II → PARTAI Uni Démokrasi Indonésia.

puding I crotons, colorful plants or bushes *usu* planted in gardens, *Codiaeum variegatum.*

puding II → PUDÉNG.

pudot (*M*) a bird, similar to the *bangau,* somewhat smaller than the *kuntul II,* which lives near swampy areas and feeds on frogs, etc.; → AYAM-AYAMAN.

pudur (M) 1 extinguished, put out (of fire). 2 extinct (volcano).
  memuduri and **memudurkan** to extinguish, put out; → MEMA-
  DAMKAN. ~ *hawa nafsu* to dampen one's passions.
  kepuduran extinction.
puf (D) pouf.
pugak berpugak-pugak and **memugak** to do s.t. seriously, work
  hard at s.t.; → PUGAR II.
pugar I *segar* – in good health, perfectly healthy; → BUGAR.
  memugar(i) to restore, rehabilitate, repair, renovate, mend; to
  renew, refresh. *memugar hutan* a) to reforest. b) to clear a forest, deforest.
  memugarkan to maintain, rehabilitate.
  pemugar s.o. or s.t. that repairs/renovates.
  pemugaran restoration, renovation; restorative. ~ *candi* temple
  restoration.
pugar II (M) **memugar** to do s.t. seriously, work hard at s.t. ~
  berjalan to walk fast. ~ *minum* to drink a lot.
pugas (Jv) **memugas** to finish s.t. up, complete.
  pugasan s.t. added to make it complete.
  pemugasan finishing s.t. up to make it complete.
puguh 1 (J) certain(ly), sure(ly). – *saja* of course. – *saja saya mendongkol* of course I was angry. *tidak* –. to be completely nonsensical. 2 (Jv) to stand firm, hold one's ground, stick to one's
  point. *Présiden IOC Juan Samaranch mendapatkan jawaban
  tegas dari pihak Soviét yang tetap – untuk tidak ikut Olimpiade
  Los Angeles.* The president of the IOC Juan Samaranch got a
  firm answer from the Soviets who stuck to their position of not
  participating in the Olympic Games in Los Angeles. *sikap* – a
  firm stance.
  kepuguhan certainty. *Saya lihat sudah tidak* ~. I saw that it
  was already uncertain.
puh exclamation of feeling hot, wheew!
puhi → REPUT *puhi*.
puhun → POHON I.
puih → REPUT *puhi*.
puik (C) ten.
puing (D) debris, ruins.
  memuing to become ruins, crumble. *Penghuni terpaksa dengan
  susah payah menyelamatkan diri ke sudut-sudut rumah yang
  ~.* The occupants were forced to go to a lot of trouble to save
  themselves by going into the corners of their crumbling houses.
  memuing(kan) to turn s.t. into ruins, ruin.
puisi (D) 1 poetry. 2 poem.
  berpuisi to write poems. ~ *untuk pahlawan révolusi* to write
  poems for the heroes of the revolution.
  mem(p)uisi to write/compose poetry.
  memuisikan to turn s.t. into a poem, compose in the form of a
  poem.
  kepuisi-puisian doggerel, would-be poetry.
  pemuisi poet.
  perpuisian poetic. *pengintérpretasian* ~ poetic interpretation.
  puisiwan poet.
puitik (E) and **puitis** (D) poetic.
puitisasi turning s.t. into poetry.
puja (Skr) veneration, worship (of gods), adoration; → PUJI. – *puji*
  all k.o. words of praise, encomium, eulogy. *Buku pengantar
  Ali Audah ini bukan semata – puji.* This introductory work of
  Ali Audah is not merely words of praise. *memuja-muji* to flatter, praise (repeatedly).
  memuja(kan) 1 to worship (an object of religious veneration,
  such as a grave or the deity, with offerings). 2 to idolize, deify;
  to worship, adore. 3 (Jv) to make/create s.t. with magic in-
  cantations/charms/sacred formulas. *Dipetikkannya sekuntum
  bunga, lalu dipujanya menjadi gadis remaja.* He plucked a
  flower and then magically turned it into a teenage girl.
  memuja-mujai to worship, venerate.
  pujaan 1 worship, adoration, veneration; offering. 2 worshipped,
  venerated; idol. ~ *hati* one's darling/sweetheart. *Dia gadis* ~
  saya. She's the girl I adore. *petinju* ~ favorite boxer.
  pemuja worshipper, adorer.
  pemujaan 1 worship(ping), veneration. ~ *lelaki* male chauvinism. ~ *nénék moyang* ancestor worship. ~ *pada segala masukan*

luar negeri worship of everything that comes from abroad, xe-
  nomania. 2 place of worship, temple. 3 cult. *Meréka itu percaya
  akan* ~. They are followers of a cult.
Pujagalana [Pusat jajanan segala ana] (in Cirebon) supermarket
  selling all k.o. handicrafts and foods peculiar to Cirebon.
Pujakekal [Putra Jawa kelahiran/keturunan Kalimantan] Javanese born in Kalimantan or of Kalimantan descent.
Pujakesuma [Putra Jawa kelahiran/keturunan Sumatra] Javanese
  born in Sumatra or of Sumatran descent.
pujangga (Skr) 1 literary man, man of letters, author, poet. –
  Baru literary school of the 1930s. – *kraton* court poet; → BU-
  JANGGA. 2 linguist, philologist.
  kepujanggaan literature; authorship.
Pujasera [Pusat jajan serba ada] Snack Food Center.
puji (Skr) praise, eulogy, commendation.
  memuji 1 to praise, laud, commend; to speak highly of, extol. 2
  to glorify, eulogize, idolize; to celebrate in song. *selayaknya
  dipuji* commendable, laudable, praiseworthy. ~ *setinggi langit*
  to praise to the skies.
  memuji-muji to heap praise on. *Meréka* ~ *juara dunia itu.* They
  heaped praise on the world champion.
  memujikan to recommend, commend highly.
  terpuji 1 laudable, highly recommended, praiseworthy. *tidak* ~
  unethical, unscrupulous. *Meréka dipersalahkan berbuat tidak
  ~ karena mengutip uang suap Rp 2 juta dari kliénnya.* They
  were declared guilty of unethical behavior because they stole 2
  million rupiahs from their clients. 2 praised, extolled, com-
  mended.
  pujian 1 praise, flattery, compliments, eulogy. 2 recommendation. 3 (in the university) *lulus dengan* ~ graduated cum laude.
  lulus dengan ~ *tertinggi* graduated summa cum laude. *melémparkan* ~ to trumpet forth praises, be loud in one's praises. *surat
  ~* letter of recommendation/introduction. ~ *Untuk Sultan
  Brunéi Darussalam* the national anthem of Brunei Darussalam.
  puji-pujian praise; compliments, commendations. *dapat* ~
  praiseworthy.
  kepujian laudable, praiseworthy, commendable.
  pemuji flatterer, s.o. who praises.
  pemujian recommendation, praising, extolling.
pujuk coax; → BUJUK I.
  memujuk to coax, wheedle, flatter, persuade, get s.o. to do s.t. by
  coaxing.
  pujukan flattery, coaxing, persuasion.
pujur (A) dissipated, dissolute, profligate.
pujut strangulation; → KUJUT.
  memujut(kan) to strangle s.o. (as punishment for a crime).
pukah broken, cracked; → PATAH I.
  memukah to break, crack, snap.
  terpukah to break, snap; broken, snapped.
pukal block (of metal), lump.
  sepukal *keris* ~ a) a kris with blade and crosspiece in one piece;
  → GANJA *iras*. b) a straight kris (without curves). *mas* ~ a lump
  of gold; native (forged) gold.
  memukal to make into a block (of metal).
pukang I 1 thigh, shank, femur. *sela* ~ perineum. 2 angle (of compass, etc.).
  memukang-mukang 1 to cut up into joints, tear apart. 2 (coq)
  to divide (into), split up (an area into sections).
pukang II → LINTANG *pukang*.
pukang III sloth; → KUKANG, KUNGKANG I.
pukang-pukang k.o. ghost only the feet of which are visible.
pukas vulva, female genitals; → PUKI I.
  berpukas to be naked (of a woman).
  berpukas-pukas(an) to insult e.o. using obscene words.
pukat I dragnet, seine net; → PAYANG I. *mata* – mesh of seine.
  pawang – a person skilled in using a seine. *perahu/sampang* –
  fishing boat which uses a seine. – *terlabuh ikan tak dapat* carry
  coals to Newcastle, to do s.t. wholly useless/unnecessary. –
  Cina seine with beads. – *cincin* Danish/purse seine. – *dogol*
  Danish seine. – *hanyut* drift net. – *harimau* trawl, large trawling
  net. – *ikan* fish net. – *Jepang* seine dragged by a motorboat. –
  kantong seine net. – *lengkung* pocketless seine. – *payang* large

seine net. – *tahan* seine set up between coral reefs at sea; the fish are driven into the net by beating or by yelling. – *tangguk* a net with a rim around it so that it can be stood up in a ditch and the fish driven into it. – *tarik* dragnet, seine.

memukat to catch fish with a seine, trawl.

pemukat 1 fisherman who catches fish with a seine. **2** fishing boat, trawler.

pemukatan netting.

pukat II avocado; → POKAT, ADVOKAT II.

pukau a powder (made from the poisonous *kecubung* plant) which is used to intoxicate or cause s.o. or s.t. to sleep soundly (also used by thieves), k.o. anesthetic. *kena* – a) to be intoxicated in that way. b) confused, upset, bewildered, dazed.

memukau 1 to drug, anesthetize in that way, to put s.o. or s.t. to sleep. *Orang itu dipukau dan dirampok.* That person was drugged and robbed. **2** to deceive, trick, fool. **3** to fascinate, mesmerize; fascinating. *Pertunjukan itu ~ para penonton.* The show fascinated the audience. **4** astonishing, admirable.

terpukau 1 caused to fall asleep (out of one's control), intoxicated/drugged by *kecubung* powder. **2** tricked, deceived, fooled, swindled. **3** spellbound, in a trance, astonished, mystified.

pukauan charm.

pemukau s.t. that spellbinds/entrances.

pukes → PUKAS.

puki I vulva, female genitals. – *mai/mak* "your mother's cunt," i.e., an insult similar to "mother fucker."

puki II – *anjing* a tree with edible fruit, namnam, *Cynometra cauliflora*; → NAMNAM.

pukis k.o. cake, a specialty of Banyumas.

pukta excellent.

pukul I 1 blow, hit, stroke (with a hard or heavy object; also used figuratively). *kena* – a) got hit. b) suffered a loss, deceived. c) angered. *salah* – a) to strike out but to miss. b) to misunderstand. c) to accuse wrongly. *sekali* – a) at one blow, straight away. b) to do s.t. once. *tukang* – hatchet man, strongman, bouncer, goon. *tukang-tukang* – goon squad. **2** (*coq*) to hit, strike. *jangan asal* – don't just strike out wildly. **3** take. – *dulu, bayar belakang* buy now, pay later. – *anak, sindir menantu* beat a daughter as a hint to a daughter-in-law. – *besar* windfall. – *besi* hammer. – *dan menghilang* (*infr*) hit-and-run; → TABRAK *lari.* - *rata* [*purata*] on the average, mean. - *rata kisaran mean range.* **memukul-rata(kan) 1** to average. **2** to generalize. *kalau dipukul rata* on (the) average. – *terus* move ahead/on! **4** hour (of the day), o'clock; → JAM. – *berapa?* What time is it? – *enam pagi* six o'clock in the morning. – *dua malam* two o'clock at night. **5** position of the hour hand on a clock face. *posisi* – *lima* the five-o'clock position.

berpukul-pukulan, bersipukul (*infr*) and **pukul-memukul** to beat/hit/strike e.o.

memukul [and **mukul** (*coq*)] **1** to beat/hit/strike (with a hard or heavy object); to beat (a percussion instrument, such as, a drum, etc.). *Kepalanya dipukul dengan besi.* His head was hit with a piece of iron. ~ *besi* to forge iron. ~ *cap* to stamp, mark (with a stamp). ~ *denda* to impose a fine. ~ *gong* a) to beat a gong in a *gamelan* orchestra. b) to open a meeting (by striking a gavel, etc.). c) to take the lead in. *Pertamina telah ~ gong swastanisasi SPBU. Pertamina* has taken the lead in privatizing gas stations. ~ *habis* to wipe out. ~ *kawat* to (send a) cable. ~ *kentongan* to beat the tom-tom, usually as an alarm or signal, but now also used to signal the beginning of an event. ~ *knock-out* to knock s.o. out. ~ *mati* to beat to death, kill. ~ *méja* to hit the table. ~ *mundur* to push/beat/force (the enemy) back, repulse. *dipukul pajak* to be hit hard by taxes. ~ *stémpel* to stamp, mark (with a stamp). ~ *telur* to beat eggs; → MENGOCOK *telur.* **2** to attack; to defeat, beat; to repulse, drive back. – *angin* (in boxing) to shadowbox. *para petinju berlatih ~ angin* the boxers were practicing shadowboxing. ~ *mundur* to repulse, drive back. ~ *musuh* to defeat the enemy. *dipukul ombak* driven back by the waves (of a boat). ~ *roboh* to knock s.o. down. ~ *sansak* (in boxing) to spar. **3** to hit hard. *Keputusan itu ~ banyak daérah.* That decree hit many regions hard. **4** to take, capture (in chess/checkers, etc.). *bidak* ~ *kuda* the pawn captured/took the knight. ~ *rata* to generalize.

pukul-memukul to hit/beat e.o.

memukul-mukul [and **mukul-mukul** (*coq*)] to keep (on) hitting.

memukuli [and **mukulin** (*J coq*)] **1** (*pl obj*) to beat/hit/strike frequently/again and again, beat up. **2** to teach s.o. a lesson he won't forget.

memukulkan 1 to beat/hit/strike/bang with. *Dia ~ palunya.* He struck a blow with his hammer. **2** to beat/hit/strike for s.o. else. **3** to multiply. ~ *empat dengan lima* to multiply four by five.

memperpukulkan to beat/hit/strike frequently/again and again.

terpukul [and **kepukul** (*coq*)] **1** beaten, struck, hit; defeated (in a debate, etc.); discomfited. **2** to get hit hard. *Dia sangat ~ mendengar berita kematian ibunya.* He was hit hard by the news of his mother's death. ~ *mundur* to be beaten back. ~ *nasib* struck by fate. ~ *oléh pajak ékspor yang tinggi* hit by high export taxes. ~ *rubuh* to get knocked down.

pukulan 1 blow, beating, hitting, striking. ~ *yang bertubi-tubi itu selalu ditangkisnya.* He kept on warding off the repeated blows. **2** attack, strike. *menerima ~ yang hébat daripada angkatan bersenjata* to take a tremendous attack from the armed forces. ~ *1 bis* (in softball) base hit. ~ *balik* a) (in tennis) backhand (shot). b) counterblow (in boxing). ~ *berat* a heavy blow. ~ *mati* death-blow. ~ *mematikan* (in boxing) knock-out punch. ~ *rancung* (in tennis) drop shot. ~ *tanah* (in tennis) ground stroke. ~ *terobosan* (in tennis) passing shot. **3** (*sl*) cocaine, blow.

pemukul 1 beater, person who beats, hits. **2** beater. *alat* ~ beater, device/tool used for beating. ~ *besi* hammer, mallet. ~ *drum* drummer. ~ *karpét* carpet beater. ~ *kasur* mattress beater. ~ *lalat* fly swatter.

pemukulan beating, hitting, striking, attacking, etc. ~ *gong* beating the gong; opening a meeting.

pukul II – *empat* the marvel-of-Peru, the four-o'clock, *Mirabilis jalapa*; → SEDAP *malam.*

pukul III – *lima* monkey pod, rain tree, *Samanea saman.*

pukur meter.

pul I (*D*) pole (of the earth); → KUTUB I.

pul II (*E*) pool (of cars, etc.).

mengepul to pool.

pengepul fence, s.o. who receives and disposes of stolen goods; → PENADAH.

pul III (*Jv*) gong stroke; → KEMPUL I.

pula 1 again, once more, over again. *Minggu yang lalu sudah pergi, minggu ini hendak pergi* –. Last week you went out, and this week you want to go out again. **2** also, too; furthermore, besides, in addition. *Saya tidak membeli barang itu, tambahan – uang saya tidak cukup.* I didn't buy those articles, and besides I didn't have enough money with me. **3** yet, still. *Walaupun dia dibenci orang, ada – yang suka padanya.* Even though people hated him, there still were some who did like him. **4** (following question words) ... in the world/could possibly? *Apa – yang membuat ayah begitu marah?* What could possibly have made father so angry? *Siapa – yang datang malam-malam begini?* Who in the world could be coming so late at night? *demikian –* also, as well, likewise. *lagi –* moreover, besides, in addition. *sebagai –* so much the more, so much more so.

pulai devil's tree, stool wood, *Alstonia angustiloba/scholaris/spatulata*, whose soft bark and foliage are used for medications. – *pandak* serpent wood, a plant whose roots are used as a medication against hypertension, *Rauwolfia serpentina (Benth.), Ophioxylon serpentinum (Linn.).*

pulak → PULA.

pulan I 1 well-cooked but not soft (of rice). **2** not well-cooked (of a yam/tapioca). **3** mellow (of one's voice).

pulan II → FULAN.

pulang 1 to return/go back (home or to where one started from), come/go back to one's starting point/home/office/room/country of origin, etc.; → KEMBALI. – *kepada istrinya yang pertama* reconciled with his first wife; → RUJUK I, TALAK I. **2** to boil down (to), be traceable back (to), be up (to) (s.o. to do s.t.). *Semuanya itu – kepada soal ...* It all boils down to ... *Hal itu – kepada anda.* It's up to you. – *asal* a) to return to one's origins. b) to return to its original state/condition. c) to die, pass away. *tidak* – not come back/home. ***ketidak-pulangan*** not returning home, absence from home. *Ia melaporkan kepada polisi ~ putranya.* He reported to the police that his son had not come home. *- balik* a) vice versa. b) to and fro, back and forth. c) round trip; → PULANG *pergi. - basamo* (*M*) to return in a group to one's *kampung* to celebrate *Lebaran* with one's family. *- bermain* a) to go back (home) after the game. b) to go back (home) after gambling. *boléh* – dismissed, you may leave now. *- girang* (for Jakartans) to go out into the country on *Lebaran* day (after having worked in the city for the rest of the year). *- haji* to come home after having gone to Mecca on the pilgrimage. *- hari* to get back to the same day of the week (such as Thursday to Thursday of the following week). *- ingatan* to regain consciousness. *- kampung* to return to one's *kampung*/region after having been away for a while or after celebrating *Lebaran* with one's family. **memulang-kampungkan** to send s.o. back to his *kampung*/region (to become a prominent person, etc. there). *Selain itu juga ada dirjén, sékjén dan dubés yang dipulangkampungkan menjadi gubernur.* Besides that, there were also several directors general, secretaries general and ambassadors who were returned to their regions to become governor. *- kandang* to go back to one's country/native land. *- kantor* to come home from work/the office; *opp* PULANG *ke kantor* to go back to work/the office. *- ke alam baka* and *- ke hadirat/haribaan Tuhan* to die, pass away. *- ke hulu* to return/go back to the country(side). *- ke negeri cacing* (*joc*) to die. *- kepada ... it's up to ... - ke rahmat Allah* to die, pass away. *- ke tanah air* to go back to one's country/native land. *- kerja* and *- dari pekerjaan* to come home from work. *- maklum (kepada)* left (up to) (the reader, hearer, etc.), judge for yourself. *- mudik* to go home to the country (*usu* to celebrate *Lebaran* with one's family). *- nama* to die abroad/en route to somewhere, in a war, etc., i.e., only one's name and not one's body comes home). *- (negeri Belanda)* to return to the Netherlands (for Dutch people living in Indonesia). *- paling* (*infr*) to and fro, back and forth. *- pangkal* to return to the starting point. *- pergi* [p.p.] a) round trip. b) to and fro, back and forth. *kemauannya – pergi* he vacillates. c) vice versa. d) passing by again and again. *- pokok (saja)* a) to break even, i.e., not make a profit. b) to be even/quits, accounts are squared. *- pulih* to recover completely. *- punci* (*C J*) to break even, i.e., not make a profit. *pembikinan karét sintétis sampai sekarang dijual dengan – punci* synthetic rubber products haven't been profitable up to now. *- sekolah* to come home from school. *- semangat* to come to (after fainting). *- semula* to return to its original state/condition. *- tambah* to give gifts (delicacies, etc.) to a *dukun*, etc. after successful treatment of an illness. *- tongsan* to go (back) to one's ancestral country, return to the country of one's ancestors; → TONGSAN. *- udik* to go (back) to the country(side).

pulang-pulang *belum ~* still hasn't come home (even though expected).

sepulang after/upon returning/coming back. *~ dari kantor dia terus ke rumah kawannya.* After returning from the office, he went right to his friend's house. *~nya dari sekolah* after coming home from school.

berpulang 1 to die, pass away; died, dead. *~ ke (alam/negeri) yang baka* and *~ ke asalnya/rahmatullah/rahmat Allah* to die, pass away; → MENINGGAL, TUTUP *usia. Pak Adam Malik ~ ke rahmatullah.* Adam Malik has passed away. 2 to be up to (s.o. to do s.t.). *Kini ~ pada M untuk membuat sintésis yang pas.* It's now up to M to achieve the right synthesis.

berpulangan (*pl subj*) to return, go home, etc.

memulangi 1 to return/go back to (one's ex-wife), remarry (one's former wife). 2 (*M*) to marry (one's first cousin).

memulangkan [and **mulangin** (*J coq*)] 1 to send back (home/to one's place of origin), return, bring/give s.t. back. *Rekannya dipulangkan ke Indonésia sekitar pertengahan Séptémber lalu.* His colleague was sent back to Indonesia about the middle of last September. *~ buku ke perpustakaan* to return the books to the library. *~ kembali* to deport/expel s.o. from a country. *~ pertanyaan kepada* to turn a question back to s.o. 2 to repatriate. 3 to restore (to its original state). *~ keamanan* to restore (public) order. *~ napas* to take a break/breather/rest. 4 to

refer to, leave up to. *Soal perubahan kabinét dipulangkan kepada DPR.* The issue of revamping the cabinet was referred back to Parliament. 5 to trace s.t. back to. *Ada yang ~ permainan catur itu kepada bangsa India kuno.* Some trace chess back to the people of ancient India.

terpulang 1 left up to. *Keputusannya ~ kepada anda.* The decision is up to you. 2 goes back to, can be traced back to. *Kisah orang Amérika di tanah Cina ~ jauh ke awal abad ini.* The history of Americans in China goes way back to the beginning of this century.

kepulangan 1 return, going back home, etc. *~ kehormatan* rehabilitation. 2 repatriation. 3 deportation, extradition, expulsion.

pemulangan sending home, repatriating, repatriation, extradition. *Pemerintah Filipina telah melakukan ~ terhadap meréka.* The Filipino government has extradited them.

pulangan (*naut*) seat for oarsmen.

pulas I (*Jv*) **sepulas** a dab.
  berpulas made up.
  memulas 1 to paint, lacquer, varnish. 2 to cover with a layer of color, color (over). 3 to retread, vulcanize (a tire). *~ pipi/bibir* to apply color/rouge to one's cheeks/lips; → MEMÉRAHI.
  memulasi to spread/smear (s.t.) on.
  memulaskan to spread s.t.
  pemulas *~ bibir* lipstick.
  pulasan 1 s.t. painted/lacquered. 2 retreaded, vulcanized. 3 fraudulent, deceptive, phony; (purely) symbolic. *penarikan ~* the symbolic withdrawal (of troops from an occupied country). 4 smear.

pulas II mulas to have the colic, have an upset stomach.
  memulas(kan) 1 to wring (s.o.'s neck). *Dia diempaskan ke tanah lalu dipulaskan léhérnya.* He was flung to the ground and then his neck was wrung. 2 to screw down. 3 to wring (out) (laundry/wash, etc.). 4 colicky, upset (stomach). *perut/usus ~* colicky stomach/guts. 5 to tweak (s.o.'s ears).

pulas III (*Jv*) fast/sound asleep.
  kepulasan to feel very sleepy, fall asleep from exhaustion (involuntarily).

pulasan a fruit, *Nephelium mutabile*, which closely resembles the *rambutan* but with a spiky skin.

pulasari liana which smells like woodruff and whose bark is used for flavoring medicine, *Alyxia stellata*.

pulasi (*D*) (in Yogya, Central Java) a retribution/fee levied by the village administration for each sale or purchase of land, in which a percentage of the purchase price is paid by the buyer; → UANG *pulasi.*

pulau island. *berlayar di – kapuk* (*coq*) to sleep. *- sudah lenyap, daratan sudah tenggelam* hopeless, total failure. *berlayar menentang/mengandang/menuju -* every effort must have its goals. *berlayar sampai ke -, berjalan sampai ke batas* keep on making an effort until one's goal has been reached. *seperti batu di -* a lot, innumerable. *- Agama* Bali. *- Andalas* Sumatra. *- Antah-Berantah* Never-never Land, Fantasy Island. *- bébas-béa* bonded/duty-free island. *- cacing* (*euph*) the grave. *- Déwata* Bali. *- Garam* Madura. *- Harapan* Sumatra. *- Hippies* Bali. *- Kapal* Onrust Island, one of the islands in the *- Seribu* in the Bay of Jakarta. *- karang* coral island, atoll. *- Ka(h)yangan* Bali. *- Kerapan* Madura. *- Kota* Java. *- Mutiara* (*Mal*) Penang/Pinang. *- Panaitan* formerly called Princen Eiland, off the west coast of Java. *- Paska* Easter Island. *- Perca* Sumatra. *- Seribu* a district in the Bay of Jakarta consisting of about 110 islands. **memulau seribukan** to isolate on Pulau Seribu (of drug addicts). *- Timah* Bangka and Belitung.

sepulau 1 the entire island. 2 (from) the same island.

berpulau with islands, islanded.

berpulau-pulau looking like small islands are on it, i.e., bumpy.

memulau to become isolated.

memulaukan 1 to isolate, segregate. 2 to boycott.

terpulau 1 isolated, segregated. 2 boycotted.

kepulauan archipelago; → GUGUSAN *pulau. ~ Riau* Riau Archipelago.

pemulauan 1 isolation, isolating, segregation, segregating. 2 boycott(ing).

pulauisme insularity.
pulé → PULAI.
pulen (*Jv*) (of rice) cooked just right (not mushy and not dry).
pulén (*S*) soft, smooth and easy to eat (of rice).
pules I → PULAS II.
pules II → PULAS III.
puli (*E*) pulley; → KATROL.
pulih 1 restored (to its original condition), return to normal, repaired, remedied, reconditioned, fixed up. *Keadaan di ibu kota telah – kembali.* The situation in the capital has returned to normal. **2** to be cured, recover, get well, get over (an illness). *Keséhatannya mulai – kembali.* His health has begun to return to normal. *Dia berangsur-angsur – daripada sakitnya.* He is gradually recovering from his illness. *simpul* – slipknot. *dapat – ke asal sebelumnya* reversible. *tak dapat – kembali seperti sebelumnya* and *tidak bisa –* irreversible. *tidak –* not return to its original state. **ketidakpulihan** irreversibility, not being able to return to its original state. *– asal* recovery, return to normal. *Diperlukan waktu untuk – asal.* Recovering takes time.
mulih (*Jv*) *~ nalar* realistic. *Keterangan itu rasanya membawa orang untuk ~ nalar dalam memikirkan kemerdékaan.* It seems that the explanation has lead people to think realistically about independence.
memulihkan 1 to repair, restore, return to normal. *~ status* to reinstate. *tak bisa dipulihkan* irreversible. *~ kembali* to rehabilitate, restore, normalize (relations). **2** to cure, heal.
terpulihkan can be restored/repaired, returned to normal.
pemulih 1 restorer, recuperating valve. **2** restorative, s.t. which restores s.o. to health, etc.
pemulihan restoration, rehabilitation, recovery, recuperation. *pusat ~* rehabilitation center. *ruang ~* recovery room (in hospital). *secara ~* rehabilitative. *~ hak* restoration of rights. *~ kembali* restoration, normalization (of relations), recovery. *~ kewarganegaraan* restoration of citizenship. *~ nama baik* restoration of one's good name. *~ tertib hukum* restoration of law and order.
pulik equally strong, well matched.
puling k.o. parakeet; → PIALING.
pulir (*J/Jv*) **memulir** [and **mulir** (*coq*)] to twist/turn s.t. around.
pulisi → POLISI.
pulitik → POLITIK.
puljut [puluhan juta] tens of millions.
pulkanisir (*D*) → VULKANISIR.
pulover (*D*) pullover, sweater.
pulp (*D/E*) (wood) pulp; → BUBUR (*kayu*).
pulpén (*D*) fountain pen; → VULPÉN. *– atom* (used for a short time after WW II) ballpoint pen.
berpulpén to have a fountain pen.
pulper (*E*) huller.
pulsa pulse/message unit, electric pulse used to time telephone calls. *denyut –* pulse beat.
pulsasi (*D*) pulsation.
pulu *– mara* k.o. boiled fish from Ujung Pandang.
pulubalang *– kuta* (*Bat*) guardian spirit of a village.
puluh tens digit. *se–* ten. *dua–* twenty. *tiga–* thirty.
sepuluh ten. *~ yang terbaik* the top ten. **bersepuluh** set of ten, the ten of (plus pronoun). *meréka ~* the ten of them. **kesepuluh 1** (in front of the noun) ten, set of ten. *~ kursi itu* those ten chairs. *~ meréka itu* the ten of them. **2** (after the noun) tenth. *kursi (yang) ~* the tenth chair. *untuk ~ kalinya* for the tenth time. **kesepuluh-sepuluhnya** all ten of them. **sepuluh-sepuluh** by/in tens. *Murid itu berjéjér ~.* The pupils sat in rows of ten. **sepuluhnya** ten of them. **persepuluh** tenth, divided by ten. *se~* one tenth, 1/10. *dua~* two tenths, 2/10. *~nya* a tenth of it, 10 percent. **persepuluhan** decimal. *pecahan ~* decimal fraction.
berpuluh-puluh 1 in tens, by the tens. **2** several, dozens/scores of. *~ abad* scores of centuries. *~ tahun yang lalu* several decades ago.
puluhan 1 tens, dozens, scores. **2** ten-rupiah note. *~ ribu* a) tens of thousands. b) 10,000-rupiah note. c) the years of a particular decade. *pada/di tahun lima ~* in the fifties/50s.
pulun I berpulun-pulun 1 in columns (of smoke). **2** (*kain*) *~* a sarong gathered up in folds; crumpled (of cloth).

pulun II (among the Tengger who live near Mt. Bromo in East Java) magic incantation.
pulung I (*J*) a small ball, pill, pellet.
memulung to roll (a cigarette/s.t. into a pellet).
memulungi (*pl obj*) to roll cigarettes/things into pellets.
pulungan s.t. rolled into a pellet.
pemulungan pelleting.
pulung II (*Jv*) **1** shaft of light descending on s.o. from heaven as a sign that he destined for great things. **2** lucky star; *cp* WAHYU. *kejatuhan/ketiban –* to luck out, get lucky.
pulung III (*Jv*) *tukang –* rag picker, s.o. who picks up rags and other discarded material off streets, refuse heaps, etc. for a living, scavenger.
memulung to pick up rags, etc. for a living. *~ barang-barang yang telah dibuang oléh orang-orang lain* to pick up items discarded by other people.
pemulung rag picker, scavenger.
pemulungan rag picking. *bisnis ~* the rag picking business.
pulur pith or soft core of palm trees; → EMPULUR.
pulus → FULUS.
pulut I k.o. gum/lime (prepared from the sap of certain trees) used for catching birds.
memulut 1 to catch (birds) using this k.o. gum. **2** to entice, tempt, lure, induce.
terpulut 1 caught (of birds trapped with this k.o. gum). **2** charmed, enchanted.
pulut II 1 *si –* (*M*) and *beras –* (sweet) glutinous/sticky rice; → KETAN. **2** the first part of a compound name for various k.o. sweetmeats made from this glutinous rice, such as, *– apit* k.o. biscuit made from sticky rice. *– hitam* black sticky rice. *– panggang* crushed sticky rice and coconut in a leaf wrapper. *– udang* glutinous rice with shrimp. *– urap* k.o. dessert of sticky rice mixed with shaved coconut and spices. *dilihat – ditanak berderai* don't judge a book by its cover, appearances are deceiving.
pulut III pulutan k.o. shrub, caesar weed, *Urena lobata*.
pulut-pulut various species of mucilaginous plants, *Triumfetta rhomboidea, Mallotus spp., Fimbristylis spp.*, and other species.
pumigasi → FUMIGASI.
pumpun I (*M*) focus. *– angin* wind focus. *– angin yang diikuti liputan awan dan angin kencang berulang terjadi hampir di seluruh wilayah Indonésia.* The wind focus followed by the cloud cover and by fast-moving winds are repeated over almost every area of Indonesia.
berpumpun to assemble, gather, flock together. *~ abu* there is evidence of an error. *~ pada* to be focused on.
memumpun 1 to focus. **2** to gather, collect.
terpumpun 1 gathered, collected. **2** centralized, concentrated, focussed.
pumpunan 1 center, gathering/meeting place, rendezvous point, focus. **2** collection, assemblage, gathering. *pusat jala ~ ikan* the gathering/rendezvous point; center of government.
pemumpunan focusing.
pumpun II a marine worm used as bait, *Perinereis nuntia, Sipunculus spp.*
pumpung (*Jv*) while one has the opportunity, as long as, until (with negative). *– matahari belum ditelan oléh entah gunung itu namanya, nun di Sumatra sana* (to continue to take pictures) until the sun has been swallowed up by who-knows-what that mountain is called over there in Sumatra; → MUMPUNG.
pun I 1 (particle following the subject, sometimes reinforced by *juga* at the end of the predicate) also, too, as well, in addition, moreover. *Dia – hendak pergi.* He also wants to go. *Dia – hendak pergi juga.* He also wants to go as well. **2** even. *Yang kaya – tidak mampu membeli itu.* Even the rich can't afford to buy that. *kenal – tidak* didn't even know, hardly knew. *jangankan menyapa, melihat – tidak mau* not to speak of greeting you, he doesn't even want to look at you. *– sekiranya* even if. **3** (preceding the subject) besides, in addition. *– perkara pencurian berkurang juga dalam bulan ini.* Besides, thefts have decreased this month. **4** (with *juga* at end of predicate = anyway) (even) though, although, nevertheless. *Mahal – dibelinya juga.* Even though it was expensive, he bought it (anyway). **5** (with question

word, sometimes reinforced with *juga* or *jua* at end of predicate) any, every. *Apa – dimakannya (jua)*. He eats anything and everything. **6** (with *–lah* after verb) indicates that the action is about to begin. *Hari – malamlah*. Evening is falling. **7** (with *–lah* after the verb) and then. *Sesudah minum, ia – berangkatlah lagi*. After having a drink he (then) left again. **8** (as a suffix on various words) though, although; → ADAPUN, BIAR *pun*, KENDATIPUN, MESKIPUN, SEKALIPUN, SUNGGUHPUN, WALAUPUN.

pun II (*Pr*) marijuana; → POEN.

ngepun to smoke marijuana, do drugs.

punah I 1 destroyed, ruined, wrecked. *habis – dimakan api* destroyed by fire. **2** extinct, died out, disappeared from the face of the earth. *Badak jangan sampai –*. The rhinoceros should not become extinct. **3** vanished (into thin air). *telah – harapannya* all his hopes have vanished. **4** (*S*) settled, paid off (of a bill or debt).

memunah to become extinct, be wiped out, destroyed, annihilated.

memunahkan **1** to annihilate, exterminate, destroy, wipe out. **2** (*S*) to pay off, settle (a debt/bill).

kepunahan **1** annihilation, destruction. **2** extinction, disappearance, extermination.

pemunah destroyer, eradicator, exterminator. *obat ~ racun* antidote.

pemunahan destroying, destruction, annihilating, annihilation, exterminating, extermination, eradicating, eradication.

punah II → PUNAK.

punai *burung –* various species of green pigeons and doves. *mata –* open-work (in mats). *mengharap burung di udara, – di tangan dilepaskan* a bird in the hand is worth two in the bush. *– ara →* PUNAI *kericau. – bakau* cinnamon-headed green pigeon, *Treron fulvicollis. – berkuk lengguak* larger thick-billed green pigeon, *Treron capelli magnirostris. – besar* large green pigeon, *Treron capellei. – bukit* wedge-tailed pigeon, *Sphenurus sphenurus robinsoni. – dada jingga* orange-breasted green pigeon, *Treron bicincta. – ékor baji,* wedge-tailed green pigeon, *Treron sphenura. – ékor panjang* yellow-bellied green pigeon, *Treron oxyura. – gading/jambu* pink-headed fruit dove, *Ptilinopus jambu. – gunung* Seimund's pintail pigeon, *Sphenurus seimundi. – kecil* little green pigeon, *Treron olax. – kericau* lesser thick-billed green pigeon, *Treron curvirostra. – léhér mérah* pink-necked pigeon, *Treron vernans. – lembu* little cuckoo dove, *Macropygia ruficeps malayana. – manten* gray-headed green pigeon, *Treron griseicauda. – paruh tebal* thick-billed pigeon, *Treron curvirostra. – salung* k.o. dove, *Treron oxyura. – siul* little green pigeon, *Treron olax. – tanah* emerald dove, *Chalcophaps indica.*

punak k.o. tree, *Tetramerista glabra*.

punakawan (*Jv*) attendants (in the *wayang* play), the small group of comics who are the male companions of the main heroes; → GARÉNG II, PÉTRUK, SEMAR.

punar (*elec*) etch.

memunar to etch.

punaran electric etching.

pemunaran electric etching.

punat 1 core of a boil. **2** the root (of all evil).

punca I (*Skr*) **1** end, extremity, furthermost point (of rope/coiled thread, etc.); leading edge, prominence. **2** tail, flap (of a shawl/ scarf, etc.), corner (of a piece of cloth). **3** beginning, first step, start, introduction, first level, elementary. **4** basis, foundation, cause; topic, subject. **5** source, place from which s.t. emanates/is derived. *– bulat* ball peen (of hammer). *– kekuasaan* the reins of power. *– pembicaraan* subject under discussion. *– pengetahuan* elementary knowledge. *– perselisihan* cause of conflict. *– politik* prominent politicians. *– sebai* the flap of a shawl that hangs loose. *– tali pancing* the end of a fishing rod (the part held in the hand). *kitab – usuluddin* a primer of basic concepts of Islam; → USUL IV. *–.– yang akan membawa hidup* sources of welfare. *– yang layak dipercaya* dependable/unimpeachable source.

punca II (*M*) *angin – beliung* cyclone, whirlwind; → ANGIN *puyuh*.

puncak 1 top, summit, peak, ridge. *konperénsi –* summit conference. *pertemuan –* summit meeting. **2** zenith, apex, acme, climax, high point, highlight. *masa –* peak season. *pengalaman –*

peak experience. **3** top (leadership). **4** (*petro*) crown. *éksékutip –* top executive. *– és* the tip of the iceberg. *– gigi* crown (of a tooth). *– Gunung Merapi* the peak of Mt. Merapi. *– harapan* the last hope. *– hidung* the point of one's nose; a person. *Sedangkan biang rusuh tak tampak – hidungnya.* But neither hide nor hair was seen of the brains behind the unrest. *– karir* the high point of one's career. *– kejadian* highlight. *– nafsu/nikmat* orgasm. *– paru* upper part of lung. *– pematangannya* the height of his powers, the peak of his experience.

memuncak **1** to taper, come to a point, become narrower and narrower. **2** to reach a climax, be at its peak, intensify, mount. *Ketakutan ~ di benaknya.* Fear mounted in his brain.

memuncaki to reach a high point, end with. *Perselisihan dipuncaki dengan adu jotos.* The quarrel ended in a fist fight.

memuncakkan to raise s.t. to a peak, intensify.

terpuncak highest, peak (*mod*).

pemuncak **1** summit, high point. **2** (*M*) champion.

pemuncakan raising s.t. to a peak, intensification.

punci (*ob*) what luck!

puncrat (*J*) muncrat to splash, spatter, sprinkle, spurt out in different directions (as of drops of water, etc.).

puncratan drops, sprinklings. *~ ludah menyongsong wajahnya waktu ia baru saja mau naik bis.* Drops of saliva landed on his face as he was about to get on the bus.

puncung (in Riau province) a motorized prau.

pundak (*J/Jv*) shoulder. *tertanggung/terpikul di atas –nya* (the responsibility) lay on his shoulders. *angkat –* to shrug (one's shoulders).

pundén (*Jv*) **1** holy site, place to worship the souls of one's ancestors or the guardian spirits of the village. **2** place where villagers take a vow. *– berundak* a terraced gravesite that is revered.

pundi (*Jv*) memundi-mundi(kan) to honor.

punding tangled (of string/thread); kink (in rope).

pundi-pundi purse, bag. *–.– sampai terkerak* to spend all one's money. *– udara* air pocket.

punduh (*Jv*) an old woman who acts as a *dalang*.

pundung I (*Jv*) discouraged, disheartened, disappointed, saddened. *Jangan lantas menjadi – apabila ternyata anugerah itu tidak jatuh ke Provinsi Jawa Barat.* Don't be discouraged if it turns out that the award is not given to West Java.

pundung II (*Jv*) anthill.

punel (*Jv*) soft and tasty; thick (neither loose nor stiff). *beras yang lebih –* a softer and tastier rice; → PULEN.

pung (*onom*) plop!; → PLUNG-LAP.

pungak-pinguk (*S*) embarrassed.

punggah *tukang –* stevedore.

memunggah to unload (from a ship/truck, etc.), discharge (cargo); → MEMBONGKAR, MENURUNKAN.

punggahan **1** dock, place where cargo is unloaded, port of discharge. **2** cargo that has been unloaded/discharged.

pemunggahan unloading, discharging (cargo).

punggai k.o. tree with reddish wood, *Coelostegia griffithii*.

punggal (*J*) cut-off tip.

memunggal to cut/break/slice off (the tip or end).

punggawa (*Skr*) **1** k.o. army officer. **2** (*Bal*) district head. **3** (*Jv*) kraton official. *– marga* (*Pal*) subdistrict head.

punggel (*J/Jv*) cut off at the top.

memunggel to cut off the top (of a plant). *Pucuk tanaman dipunggel pada usia sekitar 95 hari.* The top of the plant is cut off at the age of about 95 days.

pungguk I *burung –* hawk-owl, *Ninox scutulata malaccensis. seperti – merindukan bulan* to wish for the moon, wish for s.t. impossible.

pungguk II tailless; → PONGGOK I.

punggung 1 back (the part of the body behind the chest). **2** backside, buttocks, rear(end). **3** back/top part of s.t. *buah –* kidneys; → BUAH *pinggang. gaya –* backstroke (in swimming). **4** (*– bukit*) ridge. *– buku* spine of a book. *– gunung* ridge of mountains. *– kaki* instep. *– parang* dull side of a cleaver. *– pisau* back of a knife. *– tangan* back of the hand.

berpunggungan and punggung-memunggung back to back, with backs to e.o.

memunggung 1 (*M*) to turn one's back (on s.o.); to show one's back (to).

memunggungi to turn one's back on. *Jangan ~ orang tua kalau duduk.* Don't turn your back on old people when you sit down.

punggungan ridge, margin (of sea and land). *~ benua* continental margin.

punggur 1 dead tree stump. **2** block (the tool). *- rebah belatuk menumpang mati* retainers suffer along with their master.

pungkah I lump, large piece; → BONGKAH.

berpungkah-pungkah in lumps.

pungkah II (in Balikpapan) k.o. bribe.

pungkas (*Jv*) **1** finished. **2** end, conclusion. *yang - sendiri* the very last o., the one at the very end.

memungkas to destroy.

memungkasi to bring to an end; to finish up.

pungkasan conclusion, termination. *kesimpulan ~* final conclusion.

pemungkas 1 final (agreement/decision). **2** end(ing), close, termination, conclusion; → PAMUNGKAS. *senjata ~* lethal weapon, one's best weapon.

pungki (*J?*) k.o. wastebasket; → PENGKI.

pungkir → MUNGKIR. **memungkiri 1** to deny. **2** to ignore.

terpungkiri 1 denied; ignored. *tidak ~* undeniable. **2** deprived. *~ oléh pendapatan* deprived of income, without resources.

pemungkiran denial.

pungkis k.o. flat open basket.

pungkur 1 (*ob*) buttocks, rear(end), behind. *tulang -* pelvic bone; pubic bone. **2** rest, remainder, residue (of *sagu*, etc.).

mungkur with one's back turned.

memungkiri to turn one's back on.

pemungkur rest, remainder, residue (of *sagu*, etc.).

pungli [*pungutan liar*] illegal fee/tax/retribution (on services, such as being allowed to park one's car without getting a parking ticket, etc.).

memungli [and **mungli** (*coq*)] to collect *pungli* from s.o.

perpunglian illegal fees/taxes.

pungliwan collector of *pungli*.

pung nak pung no [*mumpung kepénak mumpung ana* (*pron* /ono/)] (*Jv*) just as long as life is comfortable and you have enough money (an attitude toward spending one's money).

pungsa [*pungutan paksa*] illegal fee/tax/retribution with the threat of force; *cp* PUNGLI.

pungsi → FUNGSI.

pungtuasi (*D*) punctuation.

punguan association.

pungut I pick up, collect. *- hasil* usufruct.

memungut [and **mungut** (*coq*)] **1** to pick (up). *~ penumpang* to pick up passengers. **2** to harvest. **3** to take in (the profits). **4** to collect (donations/taxes, etc.). *~ bayaran* to charge (a fee). *tanpa ~ bayaran* free of charge. **5** to quote, cite. *Laporan itu mengandung beberapa kutipan yang dipungut dari sumber yang baik.* The report contains several quotes taken from good sources.

memunguti [and **mungutin** (*J coq*)] (*pl obj*) to collect, pick up, etc.

memungutkan to collect/pick up s.t. for s.o. else.

terpungut picked up, collected.

pungutan I fee, tax, revenues, charge, levy. *~ liar* [*pungli*] illegal fee/tax/retribution. *~ pelabuhan udara* airport tax. *~ penelitian* research charge. *~ peremajaan* replanting charge. *~ tambahan* surcharge. **2** quotation, quote. **3** harvest, plucking, picking (crop). **4** collection (in church, etc.). *~ suara* voting.

pemungut I collector. *~ pajak* tax collector. **2** plucker, picker. *~ barang bekas* rag picker; → PEMULUNG. *~ bola* golf caddy. *~ tanaman kapas* cotton picker. *~ puntung rokok* collector of used cigarette butts.

pemungutan 1 harvest. **2** collection. *~ pajak* tax collection. *~ suara* voting. *~ suara kasar* straw poll.

pungut II adopted. *anak/saudara -* adopted child/sibling.

memungut to adopt (a child, etc.). *~ anak terlantar* to adopt a neglected child. *~ sebagai anak asuh* to adopt s.o. as a foster child.

pungutan adopted (child).

pemungutan adoption. *~ anak* adopting a child.

punjin (*M*) k.o. money belt.

punjul (*Jv*) **1** outstanding. *klas yang - sendiri* the highest-ranking class. **2** plus an extra, with an excess of. *Kursinya jumlahnya seratus - lima.* There are 100 chairs plus 5 extra.

kepunjulan excellence. *orang-orang yang punya ~ dalam bidang itu* those who are outstanding in that field.

punjung I lath work (made of bamboo for plant to climb on); arbor, bower.

punjung II (*M*) **memunjung(i)** to honor.

punjungan gift of honor.

punjung III memunjung to project, jut out, protrude.

punjut k.o. bag made from a handkerchief.

memunjut to tie the four ends of a piece of cloth together to form a bag.

punk (*D/E*) punk. *gaya rambut -* punk haircut.

ngepunk to act punk.

punokawan → PUNAKAWAN.

puns (*E*) punch (the machine).

punsu (*C*) clever, smart, bright.

punt (*D*) /pén(t)/ that's it! period!

puntal berpuntal-puntal 1 to undulate, roll (of waves); rolled up, coiled. **2** several rolls (of thread, etc.), by the roll. *rambutnya ~* her hair was waved.

memuntal 1 to roll, wind (thread around a pole, etc.). **2** to shorten (a case/affair, etc.).

terpuntal-puntal rolling around.

puntalan 1 ball (of yarn, string), spool, coil. **2** shuttle (on sewing machine).

pemuntal roller, winder (the person and the device).

pemuntalan rolling, winding.

puntang-panting head over heels, helter-skelter.

punten (*S*) **1** anybody home? **2** excuse me.

puntén (*D*) mark, grade (in school); → PONTÉN I.

punti I banana species, *Musa paradisiaca*; → PISANG *raja*.

punti II 1 *ikan -* a marine fish. **2** *ular -* cat snake, *Dipsadomorphus dendrophilus*.

puntianak the ghost of a woman who died in pregnancy or childbirth and who now tries to possess a woman in that condition in order to enjoy the motherhood that was denied her; it is said that this ghost has a hole in her back.

punting I thin pointed end (hilt).

punting II *pohon kelapa* **memunting** a coconut tree which does not bear fruit.

puntir (*J/Jv*) torsion.

memuntir to twist together firmly; → PLUNTIR.

puntiran twist(ing), torsion. *kabel ~* twisted cable.

pemuntiran twisting, torsion.

puntrén (*Jv*) baby. *jagung -* baby corn.

puntuk (*Jv*) mound; hill, bluff.

puntul (*J*) blunt, dull, obtuse.

puntung 1 anything remaining after the main part has been burned (a cigarette butt/piece of wood, etc.). **2** classifier for short pieces of wood. **3** maimed, crippled, mutilated. **4** stump, stub. *- api* glow on burning wood. *- berasap* s.t. impossible. *- rokok* cigarette butt.

seputung a/one piece. *~ kayu api* a stick of firewood. *~ sekerat* some sticks.

memuntung to become a stump.

memuntungkan to cut off, mutilate.

keputungan become a stump, leaving a stump.

pemuntungan mutilation. *~ alat kelamin* genital mutilation.

punuk hump (on the back), lump (on the neck of cattle).

punya 1 to have, possess, own. *Gua tidak - bapak lagi.* I no longer have a father. *- kerja* to hold a celebration (*esp* of a marriage or circumcision). **2** (in certain phrases starting with *yang*) *yang -* and *si -* the owner, possessor. *Pungut uang itu dan kembalikan kepada yang -.* Pick up the money and give it back to the person it belongs to; → *yang* EMPUNYA. *yang - sah* the rightful/legitimate/legal owner. *yang - perintah* the one in charge/command). *yang - perjamuan* the host(ess). **3** (+ noun or personal pronoun) is ...'s, belongs to ... *buku ini - saya* this book belongs to me. *Sepéda ini -nya.* This bicycle is his. *(di) mana - pak* *guru?* Where's the teacher's? **4** *ada yang* – to have a boy/girlfriend; be spoken for. *Perempuan itu belum ada yang* –. That woman isn't spoken for yet. **5** (*coq*) (personal pronoun or noun + *punya* + noun) possessive. *saya* – *bini* my wife. *mobil* – *ban* the car's tire. **6** (adjective + *punya* + synonymous adjective) high degree of the quality. *ganjil* – *ajaib* very odd; → BIN I. **7** [verb(al root) + *punya* + the same verb(al root)] (after) long-drawn-out/repeated/intense action. *bekerja* – *bekerja* after persistent efforts, after working and working. *beli* – *beli* buying one thing after another. *bicara* – *bicara* all that talk. *cari* – *cari* after long searching. *Cari* – *cari kagak ketemu*. Even though they looked for it for a long time, they couldn't find it. *cerita* – *cerita* to make a long story short. *fikir* – *fikir* after having thought about it for a long time. *Fikir* – *fikir akhirnya diterimanya juga tawaran itu*. After thinking about it for a long time, he finally accepted the offer. *hitung* – *hitung* no matter how many times he counted it. *jalan* – *jalan* after wandering about all over the place. *kongkow* – *kongkow* after a long chat. *ngomong* – *ngomong* finally, at last; → OMONG. *putar* – *putar* after turning it over and over. *selidik* – *selidik* after thorough investigation. *tak* – *darah* to be weak, ineffective. *tunggu* – *tunggu* after a long wait. *usul* – *usul* after many suggestions. **8** (*euph*) penis.

berpunya 1 to have an owner; there is s.o. who owns it; already owned; → BERTUAN. *yang/si* ~ the haves, the well-to-do. *orang* ~ a wealthy person. *yang tak* ~ the have-nots, the poor. *tak* ~ whose owner is unknown. *harta tak* ~ unattended/ownerless assets. *rusa* ~ a deer which is taboo, the property of an *orang* BUNIAN, etc. *kursi-kursi yang sudah* ~ occupied seats. **2** (already) engaged (to be married), (already) married, spoken for. *Gadis itu sudah* ~ *jangan diganggu*. That girl is already engaged/married; don't bother her.

mempunyai [and **mengepunyai** (*infr*)] to have, possess, own. *orang yang* ~ *hak* rightful claimant. ~ *kebébasan* to be free (to do s.t.). ~ *status/kedudukan diplomatik* to hold diplomatic status.

mempunyakan 1 to turn s.t. into one's property, take possession of s.t. **2** ~ *untuk diri sendiri* to use (money) for one's own purposes; to arrogate s.t. for o.s.; to usurp (power). **3** to have, possess, own. **4** to consider s.t. one's own property.

kepunyaan 1 possession, property, ownership. *Kebanyakan tanah ini* ~ *orang kampung*. Most of this land belongs to the villagers. **2** (*euph*) thing, penis.

pupa (*E*) pupa.

pupil (*D*) pupil (of the eye); → ANAK *mata*.

PUPN [Panitia Urusan Piutang Negara] State Debts and Claims Committee.

mem-PUPN-kan to inspect (of this committee).

pupu degree of affinity/kinship/family relationship. *saudara dua* – second cousins.

sepupu *anak* ~ nephew, niece. *saudara* ~ first/full cousins.

pupuh I *ayam* – gamecock (without spurs). *berperang* – (*ob*) war games. *perang* – (*Jv*) hand-to-hand combat.

berpupuh 1 to fight, compete, clash; to come together suddenly (of fighting cocks). **2** to make (cocks) fight e.o. **3** ~ (*-bertinju*) to come to blows.

memupuh 1 to beat, batter; to pound (with one's fist). **2** (*M*) to do s.t. frequently. *dipupuhnya makan* he eats a lot. *dipupuhnya bekerja* he is a workaholic.

memperpupuhkan to have (cocks without spurs) fight e.o.

pupuh II (*Jv*) a stanza.

pupuk I manure, fertilizer. – *alam/asli* natural/organic fertilizer. – *bawang* a) (to be) a nothing/cipher. b) figurehead. c) a hanger on, s.o. who cannot contribute his fair share to a game/venture (*usu* a small child playing with adults). *menjadi* – *bawang* to keep mum. – *buatan* artificial/chemical fertilizer. – *daun* leaf compost. – *fosfat alam* rock phosphate. – *hijau* compost. *pemupuk-hijauan* green manuring. – *kandang* manure (from horses and sheep). – *kompos* compost. – *subur* good (healthy) fertilizer. *memupuk-suburkan* to apply good fertilizer to. – *uréa* nitrogen fertilizer.

memupuk 1 to fertilize, apply fertilizer to. **2** to till the soil. **3** to foster (the growth of), promote. **4** to fill (the coffers of a party, etc.).

memupuki (*pl obj*) fertilize, promote, etc.

terpupuk fertilized, promoted.

pemupuk enricher, cultivator, manurer.

pemupukan 1 fertilizing, manuring. **2** filling the coffers of (a party, etc.). *bagi* ~ *kas partai* to fill the party's coffers. **3** promoting, cultivating, fostering. ~ *modal* capital formation.

pupuk II plaster, poultice (made of pounded herbs and placed on a child's head above the forehead to ward off illness). *masih berbau* – *jerangau* (*coq*) still wet behind the ears; → *masih bau* KENCUR.

memupuk to put a poultice on a cut, etc.

pupun → PUMPUN I.

pupur I (*J?*) face/body powder (used for cosmetic or therapeutic purposes), rice powder used as a cosmetic.

berpupur 1 to powder o.s. **2** powdered.

memupur(i) [and **mupur(i)** (*coq*)] **1** to powder, apply powder to, put powder on. *Dua juga tak suka kalau saya pupuri*. She didn't like it if I put powder on her. **2** to spruce up, make s.t. old look better. *Kami tidak cuma mupuri, atau sekedar modifikasi*. We didn't just spruce it up or merely modify it.

memupurkan to powder, apply powder to, put powder on.

pupuran face powder.

pupur II – *ayam* place where fowl roll in the dust.

memupur to roll in dust or sand (of fowl).

pupuran place where (fowl) roll in the dust or sand.

pupus I 1 wiped out, erased, obliterated; → HAPUS. **2** disappeared, gone, vanished, come to nothing, fade away. *Harta bendanya telah* –. His wealth is gone. *Dan –lah sudah harapan*. All hope has vanished into thin air. *Keinginannya* – *kembali*. His desires have come to nothing again. *Percikan darah di bajunya tak* – *oléh air*. Applying water didn't make the bloodstains on her blouse disappear. *Tokoh-tokoh légéndaris seperti Hang Tuah, Hang Nadim, Tun Téja, dll. merupakan warisan kebanggaan yang tidak* –. Legendary figures like Hang Tuah, Hang Nadim, Tun Teja, etc. are a proud inheritance which won't fade away.

memupus(kan) to wipe out, erase, obliterate, exterminate. ~ *malu* to wipe out/away the shame.

terpupus wiped out, disappeared, erased. *Nama A sudah* – *dari hati B* A's name has been erased from B's heart.

pupus II (*Jv*) young leaf (at the top of a tree). *hijau* – leaf-green.

puput I (*M*) **1** a flute-like wind instrument (made from rice stalks/coconut palm leaves, etc.), reed-whistle. **2** to blow (of the wind/bellows). – *angin sejuk* a cool wind was blowing. **3** to blow on a *puput*.

berpuput 1 to blow (of wind, bellows). ~ *angin sejuk* a cool wind was blowing. **2** to blow on a *puput*.

memuput 1 to blow on a *puput*. **2** to blow s.t. about (by wind). *diputput angin ribut* to be blown about by a hurricane.

memuputi to make s.t. whistle, make a whistling sound with s.t.

puputan 1 ~ *angin* blast of wind. **2** (pair of) bellows.

puput II (*J*) crowbar.

memuput to break open (with a crowbar or similar tool).

puput III (*Jv*) **1** to (come to an) end. **2** dead, deceased.

puputan 1 undaunted, intrepid, bold. **2** (*Bal*) a suicidal fight to the death when the only alternative is defeat. *perang* ~ all-out war (frequent way of referring to the battle against the British during the war for Independence in Surabaya in 1945).

puput IV (*Jv*) – *puser* dropping off of a newborn's umbilical cord; → PUSAR II, PUSER I.

puputan ceremony at the dropping off of a newborn's umbilical cord; *usu* coupled with giving the child a name; → SELAMATAN *puput puser*.

puput V pemuputan blowing smoke into a mouse hole to suffocate the mice.

pura I (*Skr*) (mostly used as the second part of compound city names) city, town (such as, Singapura, Jayapura, etc.).

pura II 1 waistband, money belt. *membuka* – to loosen one's purse strings, spend money. **2** stock exchange. **3** funds. *membuka* –, *utang langsai* when you do s.t., do it right! – *hati* what is in one's heart.

pura III (*Bal*) village temple. – *balai agung* the great council temple. – *dalem* the temple of the dead. – *désa* the great council temple.

– *laba* rice paddies whose yields are earmarked for maintaining the temples. – *puséh* the original temple.

pura-pura pretending, feigning, making believe, pretense, simulation; → SEOLAH-OLAH. *Jangan – alim!* Don't be hypocritical! *menangis* – to shed crocodile tears. *penuh* – phony, fake.

berpura-pura 1 to act as if; to pretend to, make believe. *Dua orang ~ membeli melakukan perampokan.* Two people pretending to buy s.t. carried out the robbery. *dengan ~ sebagai* under cover of. **2** hypocritical, false (smile), put-on.

mempura-purakan to pretend, feign, simulate, falsify.

kepura-puraan feigning, pretense, pretending, falsity, falseness, dissembling.

purak (*J*) **memurak** [and **murak** (*coq*)] **1** to fall off (of fruit from a tree after it is shaken). **2** to break up into scattered parts (of an aircraft that has been shot down, etc.). **3** (cooked rice) doesn't stick to the pot.

puras (*cla*) blunderbuss; → PEMURAS.

purata → PUKUL *rata*.

purau → PARAU.

purba (*Skr*) very old, ancient, antique. *masa/zaman* – the (good) old days, olden days.

kepurbaan ancientness; primeval age.

purbakala (*Skr neo*) ancient times, olden days. *ahli* – archaeologist; → ARKÉOLOG. *ilmu* – archaeology; → ARKÉOLOGI. *jawatan* – archaeological service.

kepurbakalaan archaeological.

purbakalawan (*Skr neo*) archaeologist; → ARKÉOLOG.

purbani → PERBANI I.

purbasangka (*Skr neo*) bias, prejudice.

berpurbasangka biased, prejudiced.

Purbasari (*S*) the attractive, decorous, and intellectual *Mojang Priangan*.

purbawara k.o. one-act drama relating the story of ancient times.

purbawisésa (*Jv*) authority, control.

Purbaya [*Purwokerto-Surabaya*] the express train running between those cities.

purdah (*Pers*) **1** purdah, the system in some Muslim or Hindu countries of keeping women out of sight of men to whom they are not related. **2** a screen, curtain, or veil used for this purpose.

puré (*D*) purée.

mempuré to mash, make into puree.

purék [*Pembantu Réktor*] Vice-President (of a University); → RÉKTOR.

Purél [*Public Relations*] public relations; → HUMAS, PR XV.

puret I (*Jv reg*) to die.

puret II (*Jv*) leave! beat it!

puret III (*Jv*) do not flourish/thrive well (of plants).

purgatif (*D*) purgative, laxative.

puri (*Skr*) **1** fortress/bastion/rampart surrounding by a ditch/moat. **2** royal palace, castle. **3** (*Bal*) temple.

purifikasi (*D*) purification.

purik (*Jv*) to leave one's husband and go back to one's family after a quarrel.

puring I a species of marine fish, *Clupea variegata*.

puring II (*J?*) Bombay laurel, *Codiaeum variegatum*. – *benggala* poinsettia, *Euphorbia pulcherrima*.

puring III → VURING.

puris (*D*) purist.

purisme (*D/E*) purism.

puritan (*D/E*) puritan.

puritanisme (*D/E*) Puritanism.

Purn. (*abbr*) ret.; → PURNAWIRAWAN.

purna (*Skr*) **1** perfect, finished, complete, accomplished; → SEM-PURNA. *lulus* – passed all subjects (in a university). *pembuatan* – (*infr*) full manufacturing. **2** (as a prefix) post- (used in many of the following neologisms); → PASCA. **3** (as a prefix) full-.

purna-angkasawan former, retired announcer of *Radio Républik Indonésia*.

purnab(h)akti retired (from the Army). *tunjangan* – pension of retired Army personnel.

purnabirokrasi postbureaucratic. *période* – postbureaucratic period.

purnacandra full moon.

purnadévaluasi postdevaluation. *langkah-langkah* – steps taken after a devaluation.

purnajual after-sale. *layanan* – after-sale service.

purnakarya retired from the civil service. *orang-orang yang sudah* – people retired from the civil service.

berpurnakarya to be retired from the civil service.

mempurnakaryakan to retire s.o. from the civil service.

purnakaryawan civil service retiree.

purnakata 1 last words. **2** conclusion. **3** postscript.

purnakebijakan postpolicy. *dunia perbankan – uang ketat* the post-tight-money policy of the banking world.

purnalaksana postaudit.

purna-Lebaran post-Lebaran.

purnam (*D*) **1** first name, Christian name. **2** (*J*) nameplate, *usu* made of cardboard and put up in front of s.o.'s residence or on a pole at the entrance to the alley leading to his house when a wedding ceremony or other party is held there.

purnama (*Skr*) full (of the moon). *bulan* – full moon.

purnamaraya full moon.

purnamasidhi (*Bal*) totally full moon.

Purnantara [*Purnawirawan Antara*] s.o. who has retired from the Antara news agency.

purna-Pemilu post–General Elections; → PEMILU. *sindrom* – post-election syndrome.

purnapemugaran total restoration.

purnapenerbangan postflight. *analisa data* – postflight data analysis.

purna-Perang post-War. – *Dingin* post–Cold War. – *Dunia II* post–World War II. *tahun – Dunia II* post–World War II years.

purnapugar total restoration. *Candi Borobudur selesai –nya tanggal 23 Fébruari 1983.* The restoration of Candi Borobudur was completed on February 23, 1983; → PURNAPEMUGARAN.

purnarévolusi postrevolution(ary). *période – fisik* the period following the physical revolution.

purnasantap after-dinner.

purnasarjana Ph.D., doctor.

mempurnasarjanakan *orang yang dipurnasarjanakan* Ph.D. candidate.

purna-Shah and **purna-Syah** post-Shah (of Iran). *di masa* – in the post-Shah era.

purnaswasta person retired from the private sector.

purnatak [*purna+atak*] comprehensive layout.

purnatambang postmining. *mencegah kerusakan ékosistém hutan tropis kawasan – harus dihijaukan* to prevent destruction of the ecosystem tropical forests in postmining regions must be replanted.

purnatugas to retire/be retired from a private enterprise.

purnaungu ultraviolet.

purnavérbal postverbal.

purnawaktu full-time; *opp* PENGGAL *waktu*. *penterjemah* – full-time translator.

purnawirawan (*purn.*) retired from the Armed Forces. – *mayor jénderal* a retired Major General.

mempurnawirawankan to retire from the Armed Forces.

kepurnawirawanan retirement from the Armed Forces. *~ merupakan meterai dari ketanggukan moral meréka selaku pejuang* retirement is the seal of their moral strength as fighters.

purser (*D/E*) purser.

puru 1 yaws, *Framboesia tropica*. **2** blastomycosis, saccaromycosis. **3** tumors, ulcers, abscesses. *bunga* – white spots on skin (forerunner of yaws). *katak* – toad. – *bidai* k.o. skin disease. – *bunga* secondary stage of yaws. – *jahat* malignant tumor. – *koci* Cochin-China sore, sclerotizing granuloma of the pudenda. – *sembilik* hemorrhoids, piles.

berpuru to have/suffer from yaws. *orang yang ~ selalu hendak menggaruk* a guilty person will be nervous for fear of being found out.

puruk (*M*) **memuruk** to sink down.

memurukkan 1 to sink s.t. *~ kapal ke laut* to sink a ship. **2** to put s.t. (into). *~ badannya di bawah longgokan kain* to hide one's body under a heap of clothes.

terpuruk 1 disappeared, went down, set. *Matahari ~ di balik pegunungan.* The sun set behind the mountains; → TERBENAM.

2 to sink (down) into an abyss. *Kakinya ~ ke dalam lubang.* His foot sank into a hole. **3** depressed (of economic conditions), depreciated (of the value of a currency). *Mata uang itu makin ~.* The currency depreciated even more. **menerpurukkan** to cause depression or depreciation. **keterpurukan** abyss, depression (of economic conditions).

puruk-puruk scattered all over, in a mess, in disorder (policies, economics, etc.); → PORAK-PERANDA.

purun k.o. rush, *Lepironia mucronata* used for making baskets/mats/ropes, etc.

purus I (*Jv*) axis, pivot, shaft; → POROS.

purus II diarrhea.
   memurus [and **murus** (*coq*)] to have/suffer from diarrhea.

purus III (*Jv*) the spot where the urinary tract exits the body.

purusa (*Skr*) **1** man, person. **2** the soul. **3** (*Bal*) family relationship in the male line. **4** (*Bal*) adult, of age.

purut tough-skinned. *jeruk/limau* – dark-green lime species used for cooking, washing the hair, as a medicine, etc., *Citrus hystrix.*

purwa (*Jv*) ancient; → PURBA. *wayang* – → WAYANG *purba.*

Purwa Adhyaksa an award for retired Public Prosecutors and administrative staff of the Office of Prosecuting Attorneys.

purwadaksina origin, descent.

purwaka in the beginning.

purwakanti (*Jv*) repetitious use of syllables as a poetic device (similar to scat singing). – *swara* assonance. – *wanda* paronomasia. – *wyanjana* alliteration.

purwaning dumadi (*Jv*) the Creation (of life in the universe).

purwarupa (*Skr neo*) prototype.

Purwasuka the development area of Purwakarta, Subang and Karawang.

purwocéng *tanaman obat* – the plant *Pimpinella pruatjan* used as an aphrodisiac.

Purwojaya name of a train running between Jakarta and Cilacap.

pus I (in acronyms) → PUSAT I.

pus II here puss, puss (calling a cat).

pusa I urge, impulse.

pusa II → PUSO II.

pusa III momentum. – *sudut* angular momentum.
   memusa to force (s.o. to do s.t.).

pusaka (*Skr*) **1** heirloom. **2** inheritance, anything received from the *saka* of one's ancestors. *adat* – (*Mal*) customary law regulating inheritance. *bendéra* – inherited flag; → PASKIBRAKA. *harta* – a) estate (of a deceased person). b) inheritance. c) bequest, legacy. *keris* – family kris (handed down from one generation to the next). *tanah* – inherited land, land handed down from one generation to the next. – *guntung* unowned heirlooms which fall to the state.
   berpusaka to have/receive a *pusaka.*
   memusakai 1 to inherit, become heir to. **2** to leave/pass down (a legacy).
   memusakakan to leave/pass down (a legacy).

pusakawan (*Skr neo*) male heir/inheritor.

pusakawati (*Skr neo*) female heir/inheritor.

pusang – *hati* worried, anxious. **2** *perut* – swollen/distended belly (due to disease).

pusar I *pusar-pusar* and – *kepala/rambut* crown of the hair.
   berpusar(-pusar) to revolve, turn. *Adat-istiadat Batak sebagian besar mémang berpusar pada perkawinan.* For the most part Batak customs revolve around marriage.
   memusar 1 to turn, revolve. ~ *cat* to stir paint. ~ *obat* to crush a drug. ~ *tepung* to sift flour. **2** to roll up (a betel leaf/cigarette, etc. pressed between the palm of the hand and the fingers of the other hand).
   pusaran 1 rotation. **2** crank, handle. **3** centripetal. ~ *air* eddy, whirlpool. ~ *angin* cyclone, whirlwind, turbulence. **4** vortex.
   kepusaran vorticity.
   pemusar s.o. or s.t. that turns.

pusar II (*Jv*) *titik* – center; → PUSAT I.

pusara I (*M*) cemetery; gravesite. – *pahlawan* heroes cemetery; → TAMAN *pahlawan.*

pusara II (*Jv*) **1** bond, tie, link. **2** (*memegang*) – *negara* (to hold) the reins of government; → TAMPUK *pimpinan/negeri.*

pusat I 1 center, focus. **2** head, main. *kantor* – head office (of a company). *Masjid Istiqlal letaknya di* – *Jakarta.* The Istiqlal Mosque is located in the center of Jakarta. **3** (with an uppercase P) the Central Government in Jakarta. *pemerintah* – central government. – *berat* center of gravity. – *Bina Hipérkés dan Keselamatan Kerja* National Center for Industrial Hygiene, Occupational Health and Safety. – *gempa bumi* epicenter of an earthquake. – *hiburan* amusement center. – *jala* center of a fishnet. – *kebugaran* fitness center. – *kediaman* legal residence. – *kesegaran jasmani* physical fitness center. – *Keséhatan Masyarakat* [Puskésmas] Public Health Center. – *keunggulan* center of excellence. – *laba* profit center. – *pembangkit tenaga listrik* power house. – *pemerintah* center/seat of government. – *Pengkajian Masalah-Masalah Stratégis dan Internasional* Center for Strategic and International Studies, CSIS. – *Pendidikan dan Latihan* [Pusdiklat] Training and Educational Center. – *Pendidikan dan Latihan Pertempuran* [Pusdiklatpur] Center for Combat Training and Education. – *Pendidikan Marinir* [Pusdikmar] Marines Education Center. – *Pendidikan Pasukan Khusus* [Pusdikpassus] Special Forces Educational Center. – *Pendidikan Persandian Angkatan Darat* [Pusdiksandiad] Army Cryptography Education Center. – *Penerangan* [Puspén] Information Center. – *Penerangan Masyarakat* [Puspénmas] Public Information Center. – *Penitipan Anak Siang Hari* Day Care Center. – *perbelanjaan* shopping center. – *perdagangan* trade center, emporium. – *perhatian* center of attention/interest, cynosure. – *pertokoan* shopping center. – *Réhabilitasi Narkotik* Drug Rehabilitation Center. – *roda* wheel hub. – *telur* embryo in an egg. – *jala pumpunan ikan* oracle, person to whom one turns for answers to difficult questions.

sepusat concentric, having a common center. *bulatan* ~ concentric circle.

berpusat ~ *(ke)pada* to center/be centered/concentrate on. ~ *pada inisitif manusia* people-centered initiative.

berpusatkan to have a center at, have as its center.

memusat to be centered. *Sekarang pertempuran* ~ *di Khorramshar.* The fighting is now centered on Khorramshar.

memusatkan 1 to concentrate/focus s.t. ~ *pikiran* to concentrate on s.t. *Meréka hendaknya* ~ *perhatiannya terhadap soal yang sangat mendesak ini.* They should focus their attention on this very pressing matter. **2** to assign s.t. to a central location (*usu* the central government).

terpusat centrally positioned.

pemusatan concentration, centralization. ~ *Latihan Nasional* [Pelatnas] National Training Center. ~ *tentara* troop concentration.

pusat II navel; → PUSAR II, PUSER I. *tali* – umbilical cord.

Pusdikandiad [Pusat pendidikan persandian Angkatan Darat] Army Code Education Center.

Pusdiklat → PUSAT *Pendidikan dan Latihan.*

Pusdiklatpur → PUSAT *Pendidikan dan Latihan Pertempuran.*

Pusdikmar → PUSAT *Pendidikan Marinir.*

Pusdikpassus → PUSAT *Pendidikan Pasukan Khusus.*

Pusdiksandiad → PUSAT *Pendidikan Persandian Angkatan Darat.*

puser I (*Jv*) **1** navel. **2** center; → PUSAR II. – *bumi* the center/pivot of the world. *Menurut beberapa dongéng orang Jawa menganggap Tanah Jawa sebagai* –*ing bumi.* According to various legends the Javanese consider Java to be the center of the world. *seénak* -*nya* and *semau* -*nya sendiri* (to act) as one pleases (without concern for others or for appropriate behavior); → seénak UDEL-*nya* (*sendiri*). *nggak punya* – (*coq*) a) stupid, brainless. b) tireless, never gets tired. *Ya dia nggak pernah capé kok, orang nggak punya* –. Well, he's never tired, he's a tireless person.

puser II pusher, tug boat; PUSYER.

push up (*E*) push up. – *sampai 50 kali* 50 pushups.

pusing 1 to be concerned about, trouble about, get involved in. *Pihak hotél tidak mau* – *mengurus hilangnya mobil tamunya.* The hotel management doesn't want to get involved in handling the disappearance of the guest's car. *Saya tidak* –, *itu bukan urusan saya.* I'm not concerned, it's none of my business. *tidak (meng)ambil* – *mengenai* and *tidak diambil* – *kepada/atas* don't make a fuss about, don't get excited about. **2** cannot think straight, at a loss for what to do, not know what to do. *Saya sam-*

pai – menghadapi soal itu. It got to the point that I didn't know what to do about that problem. **3** (*- kepala*) a) dizzy, giddy. b) to have a headache. *Dia merasa –.* a) He feels dizzy. b) He has a headache. *Saya – sekali.* I have a splitting headache. **4** (*coq*) to rotate, turn around. *Baling-baling hélikopter itu mulai –.* The propeller of the helicopter started to rotate. *– belit* not straightforward, dishonest. *– keling* to twist (s.o.'s words). *– kepala sebelah* migraine (headache). *– separuh kepala* migraine (headache). *– tujuh keliling* to get totally confused, end up with a splitting headache. *Saya sempat – tujuh keliling menentukan pilihan program D-3.* I ended up with a splitting headache in making a choice for the 3-year diploma program.

pusing-pusing to make a big effort to do s.t., go crazy trying to do s.t.

berpusing(-pusing) l to rotate, turn, spin. *Propéler pesawat terbang itu ~ apabila pilotnya menghidupkan énjin.* The propellers of the aircraft rotated when the pilot started the engine. *~ dan berkitar* spinning and rotating. **2** to revolve, turn/go around. *Bumi ~ pada sumbunya dari barat ke timur.* The earth revolves on its axis from west to east. **3** to go around (sightseeing, etc.). *~ kota Jakarta* to go around Jakarta. **4** to circle, go around in circles. *Pesawat itu ~ selama setengah jam sebelum mendarat.* The plane circled for half an hour before landing.

berpusingan (*pl subj*) to turn.

memusing to turn, fasten, tighten. *~ dadu* to shoot dice. *~ sekrup* to turn/tighten a screw.

memusingkan [and **musingin** (*J coq*)] **l** to rotate, cause s.t. to turn around. *~ baling-baling* to make the propellers rotate. **2** to make s.o. dizzy, make s.o.'s (head) swim, make s.t. spin. *Baunya ~ kepala.* The smell makes you dizzy. **3** to embarrass, upset. *berbagai tuntutan kaum buruh itu mémang ~ para manajér* some of the workers' demands really are embarrassing for the managers. **4** to rack one's brains about, worry about, trouble o.s. about. *jangan ~ perkara itu* don't worry about that matter. **5** to circulate (money for investment, etc.), put into circulation.

terpusing-pusing l drifting about, carried along aimlessly by the current. **2** rotating.

pusingan l spin(ning), rotation. *~ gasing itu semakin perlahan* the spinning of the top kept slowing down. **2** centrifugal. **3** round (in sports). *Petinju itu mengalahkan lawannya dalam ~ yang kedua.* The boxer defeated his opponent in the second round.

kepusingan dizziness, giddiness; headache. *menimbulkan ~ baru* to cause a new headache.

pemusing centrifuge, spinner. *~ sekrup* screwdriver (the tool).

pemusingan rotation, rotating, turning (around), revolving; circulation.

perpusingan l rotation, turning (around), revolving, revolution; circulation. **2** worries, upsets.

Puskésmas → PUSAT *Keséhatan Masyarakat.*

puso I 1 (as of rice plants which do not bear grains due to a disease) empty, without grains. **2** (of rice fields) dried up. **3** (as of transmigrant houses which have been standing empty for a long time) unoccupied; damaged, dilapidated, worthless. *rumah – an* unoccupied dilapidated house.

memusokan l to neglect, fail to pay attention to, (of transmigrant houses) leave unoccupied/empty. *Seorang menteri dikecam karena akan ~ 16.000 rumah yang sudah dibangun.* A minister was criticized because he left unoccupied 16,000 houses that had already been built. **2** to dry s.t. up.

puso II urge, impulse.

puspa (*Skr*) **1** flower. **2** (as a prefix) a collection of (for examples see below). **3** (as a prefix) promotion (for examples see below). *– juita* darling, dear. *– lestari* (*Bal*) a welcoming dance; → PANYEMBRANA. **4** (*Jv*) k.o. tree, *Schima spp., Canna orientalis.*

puspadanta (*Skr*) carved ivory.

puspakala spring.

puspaniaga (*infr*) sales promotion.

mempuspaniagakan to promote the sale of.

puspapajangan bed covered with flowers.

pusparagam multicolored, colorful, of many colors/shades.

kepusparagaman varied coloration.

puspas (*D*) hodgepodge, mishmash.

puspawarna multicolored; → PUSPARAGAM.

puspawisata tourism promotion.

Puspén → PUSAT *Penerangan.*

Puspénmas → PUSAT *Penerangan Masyarakat.*

puspita (*Skr*) **1** full of flowers. **2** flower. *– hati* (*Mal*) sweetheart, darling.

pus-pus cry for calling cats, here pussy!

pusta (*Port naut*) lighter, barge.

pustaka (*Skr*) **1** book. *Balai –* Institute of Belles-Lettres, a publishing house established in 1908. *daftar –* bibliography, list of references. **2** divining manual. **3** astrology book. **4** horoscope. *– Raja* "Book of the Kings," the name of a voluminous quasi-historical work by R. Ngabehi Ranggawarsita/Ronggowarsito.

berpustaka with books, having books.

mempustakakan to set down in writing, record.

kepustakaan l literature, literary works. **2** (*daftar ~*) bibliography.

perpustakaan l library. **2** belles-lettres. *~ Daérah* Regional Library. *~ keliling* mobile library. *~ Kongrés* Library of Congress (in the U.S.). *~ mobil* mobile library. *~ Nasional* National Library.

Pustakaloka (*Skr neo*) Library Room (in the *MPR* building, Jakarta).

pustakawan (*Skr neo*) male librarian.

pustakawati (*Skr neo*) female librarian.

Pustu [Pusat Keséhatan Masyarakat Pembantu] Auxiliary Puskesmas

pusu I anthill; → BUSUT.

pusu II (*M*) group, band; → KELOMPOK.

berpusu-pusu in groups/crowds/large numbers/throngs; crowding (to get in or out).

pusu III (*M*) **1** tuft (of hair), tangle. **2** confused.

berpusu-pusu tangled, in a tangle. *lari ~* run around in confusion.

pusung (*M*) stupid, foolish, silly; → BODOH, TOLOL.

pusut (*J*) awl, tool for punching holes.

memusut to drill a hole in, bore into, pierce.

pusyer (*E*) pusher, tug boat.

putah → PUTAT.

putahi (*C*) marionette play.

putak k.o. sago gruel made from the bark of a tree.

putao → PUTAU.

putar I turning, rotation, revolving, spinning; → PUSING, ROTASI. *– balik* a) to and fro, back and forth. b) magic spell to make s.o. who has left come back. c) constantly contradicting o.s. *Dia ngomong – balik.* He keeps contradicting himself. **memutar-balikkan l** to turn s.t. around in the opposite direction. **2** to twist/distort the meaning of (words, etc.). *~ fakta* to twist the facts around. **terputar-balikkan l** turned around (in the opposite direction). **2** twisted, distorted (the meaning of words, etc.). **pemutar-balikan l** turning in the opposite direction. **2** twisting, distorting (the meaning of words, etc.). *– belit* intrigues, tricks, tricky tactics. *– kayun* to tour, drive around. *– kunci* turnkey (*mod*). (*télepon*) *– langsung* direct-dial (telephone). *– lawang* (*naut*) capstan. *– negeri* coup, coup d'état; revolution. *kaum – negeri* revolutionaries. *– paksi/poros* spindle turn. *– penerangan* misinformation. *– pengayuh* to run around for fun. *– (tukang) – piringan hitam* disc jockey, DJ. (*tukang*) *– rolét* the person who turns the roulette wheel. *– sauh* (*naut*) capstan.

putar-putar (*coq*) to go around sightseeing. **mutar-mutar** to go around and around, wander about (without any fixed destination). *membawa ~* to take s.o. around. *Saya dibawa ~ kota Los Angeles.* I was taken around Los Angeles.

seputar (*J*) **1** around, through(out); → SEKELILING, SEKITAR. *di ~ negeri* throughout the country. *sungai-sungai yang mengalir di ~ Métropolitan Jakarta* the rivers which flow through Metropolitan Jakarta. *daérah ~nya* the surroundings, environs. **2** concerning, about.

berputar l to rotate, revolve, move/turn around, change; rotating, revolving. *waktu cepat ~* time flies. *~ belit* to be insincere/unfaithful. *~ cakap* to change the subject, talk about s.t. else. *~*

haluan a) to change/take another direction. b) to follow another policy. ~ *kécék* to change the subject, talk about s.t. else. ~ *lidah* to beat about the bush. ~ *pikiran* to change one's mind, think better of it. *–lah pikiranku.* I've changed my mind. **2** to circulate, be in circulation (of money). *Uang yang baru sudah* ~. The new currency is already in circulation. **3** to circle (of aircraft). *dua kali* ~ *di atas kota* circling twice above the city. **4** to equivocate, hem and haw. *dapat* ~ revolvable. ~ *dari kanan ke kiri* counterclockwise. *Angin sudah* ~ *dari kanan ke kiri.* The wind has shifted. ~ *ke kanan* turning clockwise. ~ *pada asasnya* to rotate/turn on its axis.

berputar-putar to go round and round, revolve (around), beat around the bush, go around in circles.

berputar-putaran to go around (and around).

memutar [and **mutar** (*coq*)] **1** to turn, dial (a telephone number), wind (a watch), throw (dice), show (a film), play (records/cassette tapes), turn/switch on (the light/ignition, etc.), make s.t. revolve, spin, rotate, twist s.t. around. *Sekarang silakan anda* ~ *563014.* Please dial 563014 now. ~ *arloji/jam tangan* to wind one's watch. ~ *balik* to replay, play back. *Kami tidak dapat* ~ *balik jarum jam.* We cannot turn back the clock. ~ *dadu* to play dice, shoot craps. ~ *film* to show a film. ~ *kasét-kasét lagu-lagu Hawai* to play cassettes of Hawaiian songs. ~ *kayun* to go around sightseeing. ~ *kécék* to change the topic. ~ *knop lampu listrik* to turn on the electric light. ~ *kunci kontak* to turn on the ignition. ~ *lidah* to twist s.o.'s words around. ~ *modal dalam* to invest money in. ~ *nomor télepon* to dial a telephone number. ~ *otak* to rack one's brains. ~ *pikiran* to think hard. ~ *poros éngkol mesin* to crank a car. ~ *sekrup* to turn/tighten a screw. ~ *sepédanya* to ride a bike, cycle. ~ *télepon* to (make a) call, phone. ~ *uang dalam* to put one's money into. ~ *uang negeri untuk kepentingan pribadi* to use public money for personal gain. **2** to turn s.t. (in another direction). *Ia* ~ *perahunya ke arah sebuah pulau yang kecil.* He turned his boat toward a small island. **3** to twist/distort s.o.'s words. **4** to move (plants/graves, etc.), transplant. *Pohon itu baik diputar ke tempat lain.* It would be a good idea to transplant the tree to another place. **5** to stir. *Adonan telur dengan air susu diputar lalu dikocok.* The egg batter is stirred with milk and then beaten. **6** to put (money, etc.) into a business.

memutar-mutar to twist s.t. around. ~ *matanya* to roll one's eyes.

memutari to tour, travel around. ~ *Kota Kinabalu tidak perlu waktu lama.* Touring Kota Kinabalu doesn't take long.

memutarkan 1 to turn, change the direction of, put money into a business, etc.; → **MEMUTAR**. **2** to turn, etc. for s.o. else.

memperputarkan to circulate (money/commodities, etc.).

terputar turned (around), turned (in another direction).

terputar-putar to keep on turning around and around.

putaran 1 spin, rotation, revolution, twirl, swirl. ~ *motor* revolutions of a motor. *seiring dengan* ~ *waktu* as things evolve. **2** (in politics/sports, etc.) round. ~ *Uruguay* Uruguay Round (of negotiations). *dalam* ~ *akhir* (in sports) in the last round. *kampanye* ~ *kelima* the fifth round of the (election) campaign. **3** an object that turns (such as a turn-table). ~ *air* whirlpool, eddy. ~ *angin* a) whirlwind. b) wind shear. c) cyclone. ~ *dadu* roll of the dice. ~ *jangkar* capstan, device used to raise and lower an anchor. ~ *pertama* first run (of a film in a movie theater). ~ *sikat* brush displacement. *– tinggi* high-revolution (engine).

pemutar 1 screwdriver. **2** s.o. who turns or causes s.t. to turn. **3** rotator, spinner.

pemutaran 1 rotation, rotating, revolution, revolving, showing (a film). **2** turntable. *alat* ~ *balik kasét* (cassette) rewinder. ~ *film* film showing. ~ *perdana/pertama* first run (of a film). ~ *kembali* rerun, replay.

perputaran 1 turn, twist. **2** revolution, rotation, gyration. **3** change, turn (of events). ~ *alamat* change of address. **4** turnover; → **OMSÉT**. ~ *dagang* a) turnover, sales. b) trade, business dealings. ~ *dana* cash flow. **5** circulation. ~ *uang* money circulation. **6** cycle (of life and death); → **DAUR**.

putar II Javan turtledove, a variety of dove kept as a pet, *Streptopelia bitorquata* and other species, *Tortora.*

putarwali a woody climber with medicinal uses, *Tinospora crispa/tuberculata*; → **BRATAWALI**.

putat various species of trees. *– ayam* k.o. tree, *Barringtonia spicata*; → **PUTAH**. *– darat* k.o. tree, *Barringtonia macrostachya*. *– gajah/gunung* k.o. tree, *Planchonia valida*. *– laut* k.o. tree, *Barringtonia asiatica*; → **BUTUN(G)**.

putat-putatan Lecythidaceae.

putau (C) Chinese rice wine.

putau(w) (*Pr from putih*) low-grade heroin.

  mutau(w) to get high on such drugs.

puter I (*Jv*) → **PUTAR II**.

puter II → **PUTAR I**.

putera → **PUTRA**. *– Allah* the son of God, Jesus.

puteri → **PUTRI I**.

putet → **PUTAT**.

puti I (*M*) princess; title for a royal or aristocratic girl or woman; *cp* **PUTRI**.

puti II → **PUTIS**.

puti III *burung –* a crossbreed between the Javan turtledove and a pigeon.

putih I 1 white. *bangsa kulit –* the white race, Caucasians, white people. *orang (kulit) –* a white person, Caucasian; → **ORANG** *bulé(k)*. *bawang –* garlic. *kain –* white cloth. *mukanya –* he looks pale. *perang –* the *Paderi* war (1821-1837) in the Minangkabau area; so called because the followers of *Imam Bonjol* wore white. **2** pale-skinned, fair-skinned. **3** pure, clear, immaculate. **4** gray (of hair). *rambut –* gray hair. **5** the color associated with Muslims in Maluku; *cp* **MÉRAH IV**. **6** (*si –*) (*sl*) heroin. *– di luar kuning di dalam* appearances are deceiving. *– kapas boléh dilihat, – hati berkeadaan* you can't tell a book by its cover. *(ber)– tulang, jangan (ber)– mata* and *lebih baik (ber)– tulang daripada (ber)– mata* death before dishonor. *suruh – hitam datang* to be awarded with ingratitude. *– dikejar, hitam tak dapat* and *lepas –, hitam tak dapat* don't count your chickens before they've hatched. *– Pak Harto, – Rakyat.* What is good for Soeharto is good for the nation. *tidak membilang – maupun hitam* didn't say a word. *belum tentu hitam –nya* the outcome is still up in the air. *– bahana* dull white. *– bersih* bright white. *– bron* silver-colored. *– hati* a) sincere. b) kind-hearted, helpful. c) pure, immaculate. *– hitam* black-and-white (television). *– kapur* chalk white. *– kuam* beige. *– kuning* a) cream-colored (stereotype of Chinese skin color). b) yellow-white colored (considered a beautiful complexion); → **KUNING** *langsat.* c) darling, sweetheart. *– lembaga* albumen. *– lesi(h)* very pale, whitewashed. *– mangkak* dirty white. *– melepak* snow white. *– metah* dead white. *– murup* shining white. *– mutiara* pearl gray. *– pérak* silvery. *– pucat* pale white. *– timah* washed-out white. *– uban* hoary, grayish white.

putih-putih sparkling white. *mengenakan setélan* ~ to wear a sparkling white suit.

seputih as white as.

berputih ~ *mata* a) to be disgraced, in disgrace, lose face. b) to be annoyed at having to wait for a long time. ~ *tulang* (*euph*) to die.

memutih 1 to turn white/pale; to fade away. *ombak* ~ whitecaps. **2** swarming (with people). ~ *kelihatan orang berkumpul di alun-alun* the town square was swarming with people. **3** to grow/turn gray (of one's hair). ~ *seperti kapas* to turn white. *Rambutnya mulai* ~. His hair is turning gray. *Kerudung hitam pun tak sanggup lagi menyembunyikan rambutnya yang* ~ *rata.* Even a black veil could no longer hide her evenly graying hair.

mutih (as an ascetic practice) to eat small amounts of unsalted steamed white rice taken in the cup of the hand without any side dishes, drink a few sips of water, stay awake, practice religious meditation for three days and three nights; → **PUASA** *mutih.*

memutihi to whitewash.

memutihkan [and **mutihin** (*J coq*)] **1** to whitewash. **2** to bleach. **3** to examine closely, look at carefully. **4** to legalize, clear, grant clearance to, launder (money). *Tunggakan iuran télévisi akan diputihkan jika pemiliknya bulan Agustus ini mendaftar ke kantor pos.* Unpaid television fees will be cleared if the TV owner reports to a post office in August. *1.551 orang karyawan Dépkés sudah diputihkan.* 1,551 Department of Health employees have been cleared (for promotion). ~ *mata* a) to irritate s.o. by making him wait too long or by treating him as a passive onlooker. b) to embarrass.

terputih the whitest.

putihan pious people, those who follow religious observances.

keputihan 1 whitish. 2 (*coq*) too white. 3 (*med*) leucorrhoea.

keputih-putihan whitish.

pemutih bleach, whitener; person who bleaches. ~ *cucian* laundry bleach.

pemutihan 1 whitewashing, bleaching. 2 close examination. 3 legalizing (foreign workers), laundering (money), granting clearance to. *program* ~ *40.000 TKI yang berada di Sabah* the program legalizing 40,000 Indonesian workers in Sabah. 4 purification, making immaculate, improving the quality of. ~ *sapi Jawa* improving the quality of Java cattle (though crossbreeding local cattle with *sapi putih*, i.e., white cows from Sumba.

putih II a freshwater fish, common little cyprinid, *Puntius binotatus*.

putih III *kayu* – cajeput, *Maleleuca leucadendron*, of the myrtle family with papery bark and yielding a greenish aromatic oil.

putihan kingfish, *Caranx sexfasciatus*.

putik 1 bud. 2 pistil. 3 nipple.

berputik to bear fruit.

memutik to burgeon, bud.

puting 1 tang, the part of a knife blade that is inserted into the hilt or handle. 2 stalk. 3 nipple. 4 clitoris. *angin – beliung* a) whirlwind, tornado. b) waterspout. – *cepu-cepu* (*naut*) the foot of a mast, which fits into a socket. – *damar* the handle of a torch made of *damar*. – *rokok* cigarette butt; → PUNTUNG *rokok*. – *susu/téték* nipple (of breast).

memuting *lari* ~ (to run) as fast as the wind.

putir – *mandi* k.o. *kué basah* made with *pandan* leaves.

putis (*E*) puttees.

putra (*Skr*) 1 boy. 2 child. *Berapa –nya?* a) How many boys do you have? b) How many children do you have? 3 (in sports) mens. *ténis* – mens tennis. 4 (*ob*) prince. – *daérah* (the policy of supporting) a local person (for civil service positions in that area). – *mahkota* crown prince. – *putri* sons and daughters. – *remaja* adolescent boy.

berputra 1 to have a child/...children, have a sons/sons. *Jénderal A. K.* ~ *dua orang yaitu seorang laki-laki dan seorang wanita.* General A. K. has two children, a boy and a girl. 2 to be confined with child.

memutrakan to give birth to.

keputraan birth. *hari* ~ birthday; → HARI *ulang tahun*, ULTAH.

putranda my child/son.

putri I (*Skr*) 1 girl, lady, woman. *guru* – female teacher. 2 (in sports) women's. *lompat tinggi* – women's high jump. *ténis* – women's tennis. 3 (*ob*) girl of royal descent, princess. *tuan* – a) princess. b) prince's spouse. – *duyung* mermaid. – *Hijau* the express train running between Medan and Tanjung Balai. – *Indonésia* a) the Daughters of Indonesia. b) Miss Indonesia. – *Mawar* Princess of the Briar Rose (folktale). – *Salju* a) Snow White. b) k.o. cake.

kaputrén (*Jv*), **keputrén** and **keputrian** k.o. harem, a building inside the *Keraton* complex where the *raja* keeps his wives and their servants, forbidden to men.

keputrian women's (*mod*), womanhood.

putri II – *malu* mimosa, *Mimosa pudica*; → KEJUT-KEJUT, SIMALU II. – *ngendat* k.o. orchid, *Platanthera susannae*.

putri III *sepah* – orange-bellied flowerpecker, *Dicaeum trigonostigma*.

Putu I (*Bal*) noncaste name element placed before personal names to indicate the firstborn child, such as, – *Setia*.

putu II (*Tam*) *kué* – rice-flour cake filled with brown sugar and eaten with grated coconut. – *ayu* a dish made with eggs, sugar, and *santan*. – *buluh* rice and palm sugar steamed in a section of bamboo. – *mayang* k.o. wreath-shaped cake made from rice noodles. – *tegal* k.o. cake made from sticky-rice flour, bananas, and grated coconut.

putus 1 broken off, snapped off (of a chain/rope, etc.); to break, snap. *Kabel itu –.* The cable snapped. 2 cut (off), severed. *Per-* *hubungan keréta api – disebabkan karena banjir.* Railway connections were cut due to the floods. 3 fleeced, relieved of one's money. *Para penjudi itu tidak ada yang menang di Las Végas. Meréka – semua!* None of the gamblers won in Las Vegas. They were all fleeced! 4 finished, ended, over, settled/decided (of a case). *Tali persahabatan kami telah –.* Our friendship is finished. *Sampai sekarang perkara itu belum – juga.* The case hasn't been settled so far. *aktivitas yang tidak pernah –* never-ending activity. 5 disrupted, broken (off), dissolved. – *cinta biasa, – rém matilah kita* breakups are common in love, but brake failures are fatal. *Perkawinan Férry dan Margarétha harus –.* The marriage between Ferry and Margaretha must be dissolved (by Court decision). 6 as is (of a sale), with no guarantees; → JUAL *putus*. 7 definite, decisive. *kata –* the last word, the final say. – *akad* (an agreement, etc.) is no longer in force/effect. – *akal* at a loss, at one's wits' end. – *arang* irreparable, beyond repair (of a marriage/love affair). – *asa* hopeless, desperate. *Gadis itu – asa dan mungkin akan berbuat sesuatu yang tidak dapat diramalkan.* That girl is desperate and might act in an unpredictable way. **seputus-asa** as desperate as. **berputus-asa** to be hopeless/desperate. *Jangan mudah ~!* Don't give up easily, don't give in to despair. **memutus-asakan** to lose hope of, give in to despair about. **keputus-asaan** despair, (feelings of) hopelessness. – *benang* (a relationship that has been broken off) can still be patched up again. – *bicara* a) at one's wits' end. b) (to reach a) settlement in a legal case. – *cinta* to break up (with a boyfriend or girlfriend). – *harapan* hopeless, desperate, give up hope. *Jangan – harapan!* Don't give up! – *harapannya* he felt hopeless. – *harga* a) fixed price. b) to agree on a price. – *hati* in despair. – *hubungan* a) to lose contact (with), lose track (of). b) to break up (of a relationship), break off (relations). c) to be interrupted (of communications). – *ikhtiar* to be at one's wits' end. – *janji* agreed! done! – *jiwa* dead. – *kaji* definite, final (agreement/decision that cannot be changed). *sudah – kaji* settled. – *kata* a) ended, finished. b) agreed. – *kuliah* a) to drop out. b) school dropout. *Ia – kuliah.* He dropped out (of college). – *loteré* to win the lottery. – *mufakat* to have reached an agreement. – *napas* a) out of breath, exhausted. b) dead. – *niat* a) determined, resolute, firm. b) to have reached one's goal. – *nyawa* dead. – *pacaran* to break up with one's boyfriend or girlfriend. – *rasa* no longer interested. – *rezeki* to be without a source of income, lose one's livelihood. – *runut* to get off the track. – *sambung* on and off (again). – *sekolah* a) to drop out. b) to be a school dropout. – *tali gantung* sad, touched. – *umur* dead.

putus-putus 1 to keep on breaking. 2 intermittent(ly), on and off. *Suaranya ~.* He spoke in fits and starts. (*dengan*) *tidak ~nya* unceasingly, constantly, continuously. *dengan tiada ~* continuously, uninterruptedly, incessantly.

(ber)putus-putus broken, disjointed, hesitating.

memutus 1 to cut in half, sever, break. 2 to interrupt. *"Lebih baik kau diam saja dulu. Dengarkan baik-baik. Ayahmu belum selesai bicara," ibunya ~ dengan suara tinggi.* "It would be better for you to be quiet. Listen carefully. Your father hasn't finished speaking," her mother interrupted in a high-pitched voice. 3 to turn off (electric current), cut off, disconnect (telephone service). ~ *aliran listrik* to turn off the electric current. *Télepon saya diputus kawatnya.* My telephone service has been disconnected. *Tigapuluh lima kontraktor diputus kontraknya.* Contracts with 35 contractors were terminated. 4 to break (a contract), settle (a case). *tanpa perkaranya diputus* without the case's being settled. – *nyawa* to die. – *hidupnya* to put an end to one's life. 5 to decide, declare. *Terdakwa diputus bébas.* The accused was declared innocent. ~ *pidana* to convict. 6 to cut across (a road, etc.).

memutusi (*pl obj*) to break, etc.

memutuskan [and **mutusin** (*J coq*)] 1 to cut/break off, sever, disrupt. *Indonésia ~ hubungan diplomatik dengan RRC.* Indonesia broke off diplomatic relations with China. *Dia diputuskan sama cowok.* Her boyfriend broke up with her. 2 to decide, come to a decision/make up one's mind, decree, reach a verdict (on). *Sebagai penyeling, aku ~ untuk mencari banyak kesibukan.* For a change, I've decided to look for a lot of activity. *Sidang kabinét ~ akan menyerahkan mandatnya kepada Présidén.* The cabinet meeting decided to hand its mandate over to the President. *Kamu harus ~ apakah kamu mau menerima tawaran itu atau tidak.* You have to decide whether to accept that offer or not. **3** to cancel, terminate, breach (a contract); to break (a promise); to give up (hope). *~ segala pengharapan* to give up all hope. *mempunyai hak untuk ~ perjanjian ini dengan terlebih dahulu mendapat persetujuan tertulis dari Menteri Pertambangan dan Énérgi* to have the right to cancel this agreement by obtaining prior approval from the Minister of Mining and Energy. *Kedua belah pihak berjanji tidak akan ~ perjanjian dengan tiada berunding lebih dahulu.* Both parties agreed not to terminate the contract without prior discussion. *~ sekolah* to drop out of school. *~ nyawa* a) to kill. b) to die. *~ umur,* to topple, make an end of s.t. *~ umur kabinét* to topple a cabinet.

terputus [and **keputus** (*coq*)] interrupted, broken/cut (off), disrupted, disconnected. *daérah ~* cut-off area (due to floods, etc.). *keadaan yang pecah, tidak lengkap dan ~* a broken up, incomplete, and disconnected situation. *pembicaraan itu ~ karena* discussions were interrupted because. **keterputusan** discontinuity.

terputus-putus **1** disintegrated. **2** broken, disjointed, hesitating, on and off.

terputuskan to be cut (off). *tidak ~* indissoluble, inseparable, unbreakable.

putusan **1** s.t. that has been broken/cut off s.t. bigger, piece. *~ tali* a broken-off piece of rope. **2** (*leg*) decision, judgment, verdict, finding/ruling (of a court), resolution (of a determinative body). *Sidang akan dilanjutkan pada 15 Januari mendatang guna mendengarkan ~ hakim.* The session will be continued on January 15 next to hear the judge's verdict/decision/ruling. *mengambil ~* to make/take/reach a decision *menjatuhkan ~ tanpa hadirnya terdakwa* to sentence the accused in absentia. *~ antara* provisional decision/ruling. *~ bébas/lepas* acquittal. *~ gugur* cancellation, annulment, declaration of lapse. *~ imbal* unfair/biased decision. *~ pengadilan* court ruling, sentence. *~ sela* provisional/interlocutory decision/ruling. *~ yang tetap* final decision. **3** fracture, break. **seputusan** *~ perut* with the same parents.

keputusan **1** end, conclusion. *~ bicara* at one's wits' end. **2**a) decision, directive, decree. *Bapaklah yang harus mengambil ~.* It's father's decision. *pengambilan ~* decision making. b) directive, decree, edict. *~ kementerian* ministerial directive. *~ présidén* [Kepprés] presidential decree. *~ raja* royal decree. c) verdict. *menurut ~ pengadilan negeri ia harus membayar ganti rugi kepada pemilik rumah* according to the district court's verdict, he has to pay compensation to the owner of the house. **3** green-light, go-ahead. *Meréka sedang menunggu ~ dari atasannya.* They're waiting for the go-ahead from their superiors. **4** results (of an examination/investigation, etc.). *~ ujian tidak lama lagi akan diumumkan.* The examination results will be announced shortly. **5** interruption, cut off (of service/funds, etc.). *Banyak pedagang yang ~ modalnya* many businessmen whose capital has been cut off. **berkeputusan** to make the decision to, resolve to. *tidak ~* a) unresolved. b) endlessly, without interruption.

pemutus **1** person or instrument that breaks, interrupts, cuts off;

decisive. *sumpah ~* decisive oath. **2** breaker. *~ arus* (circuit) breaker. *~ gelombang* breakwater. *~ kontak* circuit breaker.

pemutusan cancellation, severance, cutting off, interruption (of service), termination. *~ hubungan kerja* [PHK] termination of employment, laying off, dismissal. *~ hubungan diplomatik* severance of diplomatic relations. *~ momén* (*elec*) momentary trip. *~ perjanjian* breach of an agreement/contract.

perputusan breaking/cutting off.

putut → PEPUTUT.

puun I /pu'un/ tribal chief of the *Badui* people in Banten Province.

kepuunan the area ruled by such a chief.

pu'un → POHON I.

puyan (*J*) grime, dirt (that sticks to the skin); → DAKI I.

berpuyan grimy, dirty (of the skin).

puyang → LEMPUYANG.

puyen → PUYAN.

puyeng (*J/Jv*) dizzy, groggy, headachy. *Saya ini dibuat – tujuh keliling, dia kira saya ini punya gaji banyak.* He drove me crazy because he thought I earned a lot of money.

berpuyeng-puyeng to whirl around.

memuyengkan to make s.o. dizzy/groggy.

kepuyengan dizziness, vertigo.

puyer (*D*) (medicine in the form of) powder.

puyonghai → FU YONG HAI.

puyu I → PUYUH II.

puyu II *ikan –(.-)* climbing perch, a fish that shuffles along in the mud, *Anabas scandens.* *bagai – di air jernih* in clover, in a situation that makes one very happy.

puyu III **memuyu-muyu** to rub (one's eyes).

puyuh I various species of quail. *burung –* (Japanese) quail, *Turnix spp.;* → GEMAK. *demam –* subfebrile. *demam-demam –* s.o. who seems sick but if offered s.t. that could make him better, suddenly feels better again. *nyiur –* a coconut species with small green fruits. *bagai – lega* to talk incessantly. *mati – hendaknya ékor* to ask for the impossible. *bagaikan burung – merindukan matahari* to have an unrealized desire. *– batu* blue-breasted quail, *Coturnix chinensis.* *– gonggong* various species of quail, *Arborophila spp.* *– mahkota* crested wood partridge, *Rollulus roulroul.* *– pepekoh* blue-breasted quail, *Coturnix chinensis.* *– tegalan* buttonquail, *Turnix spp.*

puyuh II *angin –* whirlwind, cyclone.

puyuh III *bintang –* the Pleiades. *– berlaga* the two stars in the tail of the constellation Scorpio.

puyunghai → FU YONG HAI.

PV [Personéél Verzorger/Verzorgster] (*D*) Personnel Affairs Assistant (approved by immigration officers to look after personnel matters so that the persons concerned need not appear before immigration officers in person).

PW (railway term) electric generator car (in train formation).

PWI (*init*) [Persatuan Wartawan Indonésia] Indonesian Journalists Association.

PYM [Paduka Yang Mulia] His Excellency.

pyuh-pyuh exclamation of surprise.

pyurpyuran (*Jv*) aghast (with fear/anxiety/concern).

Q

/q/ is usually pronounced /k/. Words beginning with a Q not found under this letter should be looked for under K or KH.

q and Q /ki/ or /kiu/ the 17th letter of the Latin alphabet used for writing Indonesian (used only for words borrowed from Arabic).

qaadi → KADI.

Qabil (A) (the biblical) Cain.

qadha → KADA.

qadhil qudhah (A) chief justice.

qadim → KADIM I.

qadzaf (A) allegation.

qaf (A) name of the 21st letter of the Arabic alphabet.

Qalam (A) al– "The Pen"; name of the 68th chapter of the Koran.

qalb (A) heart; → KALBU.

qard(h) (A) k.o. loan that is acceptable to Islamic beliefs.

qari (A) male Koran reader.

qariah (A) female Koran reader.

qas → KHAS.

qashar (A) to shorten a prayer.

qasidah → KASIDAH. berqasidah to sing religious melodies in Arabic or Indonesian.

qasirah (A) s.t. beneficial for o.s. (as opposed to for society).

Qatar (A) Qatar.

qath'i (A) authoritative; clear, distinct.

qawm → KAUM.

qiah → KIAS I.

Qiblatullah (A) direction to which Muslims turn in praying (toward Allah; read: the Kaaba); → KIBLAT.

qidam (A) from eternity without beginning, uncreatedness (of God); cp BAKA.

qimar (A) (the Islamic principle forbidding) uncertainty based on luck, gambling.

qiradah (A) ape; monkey.

qiradh (A) to lend money to carry on a business and get paid back with a share of the profit or of the loss, lend money (with or without interest).

qishas (A) lex talionis, the law of revenge; an eye for an eye, a tooth for a tooth; → KISAS.

berqishas to take revenge.

qital (A) war, battle; slaughter, massacre.

qiyas (A) 1 hint, inkling, innuendo, allusion. 2 analogy, comparison; → KIAS.

qobladdukhul (A) before consummation (of a marriage).

qori → QARI.

qoriah → QARIAH.

Qous (A) Sagittarius (zod).

QS [Qur'an Suci] the Holy Koran (precedes chapter and verse references).

qudrah and kudrat (A) → KUDRAT.

Qulil haq walau kaana muuro (A) Tell the truth though it be bitter for you.

qunbulah (A) bomb. – dimugrafiyah demographic bomb, i.e., a reference to the Palestinians living in the occupied areas of Israel.

qunut (A) to pray in the middle of the second rakaat in the shalat subuh. doa – prayer recited in the qunut. – nazilah to pray for guidance when about to take a difficult examination.

Quraisy 1 kaum – Koreish, name of an Arab tribe in ancient Mecca, Muhammad's tribe. 2 al- name of the 106th chapter of the Koran.

Qur'an and Quran (A) the Koran, the Muslim holy book. mengaji – to learn to recite the Koran, study religion.

qurani (A) Koranic.

qurban (A) a sacrifice; → KORBAN.

R

r and **R I** /ér/ the 18th letter of the Latin alphabet used for writing Indonesian.
R II (*abbr*) [Radén] title for Javanese nobility.
R III car license plate for Banyumas.
ra. I (*abbr*) [radiallahu an(hu)] → RADI.
ra II (in acronyms) → RAKYAT, RAPAT II.
ra III (*A*) the name of the 10th letter of the Arabic alphabet.
R.A. I [Radén Ajeng] title for unmarried Javanese female aristocrats.
R.A. II [Rasul Allah] the Prophet Muhammad.
R.Ay. [Radén Ayu] title for married Javanese female aristocrats.
raad I (*D col*) /rat/ court; → RAD. - *van Justitie* /rat fan yustisi/ [RvJ] Court of Justice.
Raad II (*A*) *ar-* "Thunder"; name of the 13th chapter of the Koran; → RA'D.
Rab and **Rabb** (*A*) Lord. - *al-mal* person who provides the capital in a business enterprise; → MUDARABA.
raba I raba-raba the feel of s.t., how s.t. feels.
  meraba l to feel (one's way), grope around. *Orang buta itu ~ jalan dengan tongkatnya.* The blind man was feeling his way with his cane. **2** to search (a suspect, etc.), frisk, search around in. *Dia ~ saku orang yang dicurigainya.* He searched the suspect's bag. **3** to guess at, take a guess at, try to figure out. *Kami tidak dapat ~ isi hatinya.* We couldn't figure out what he had on his mind. *~ tulang iga sendiri* to be introverted. **4** to grope, touch, feel, fondle.
  meraba-raba [and **ngeraba-raba** (*coq*)] **1** to look/search around for. *Cabang renang, tinju, dan judo masih ~ siapa atlétnya yang pantas diusulkan masuk Pelatnas.* The swimming, boxing, and judo branches are still looking for the right ones to propose for the National Training Center. **2** to touch, grope/feel (around), feel (one's way). *Dengan tangannya ia ~ mencari tombol lampu.* With his hand he felt around for the lamp switch. **3** to caress, fondle, run one's hands over. **4** to guess (at), figure out. *Melihat gerak-geriknya, orang dapat ~ maksudnya.* Seeing his behavior, people can figure out his intentions.
  merabai (*pl obj*) to grope, touch/fondle/caress repeatedly (frequently with sexual overtones). *Ia ~ tubuh pacarnya.* He fondled his girlfriend's body.
  teraba 1 touched. **2** felt, noticed. **keterabaan** sense of touch.
  teraba-raba groping, fumbling (about).
  rabaan 1 feeling, touching, touch. **2** grope, groping. **3** guess, surmise, estimate, hunch. **4** grasp, comprehension, understanding. *agar supaya para siswa mempunyai ~ internasional tentang masalah-masalah internasional* in order for students to have an international grasp of international problems.
  peraba (sense of) touch/feeling. *alat ~* organ of touch, tentacle.
  perabaan feeling (around), palpating.
raba II raba-rubu (*J*) (running around) in a hurry.
raba III (*M*) **meraba** to be angry/annoyed.
  peraba hothead.
rabah a bird species found in small forests, k.o. shrike, *Criniger tephrogenys.*
rabak I 1 (with a) large rip (in it). *koyak - and rabik -* all ripped/torn up, with large rips in it. **2** (*geol*) shear.
  merabak to tear, rip.
rabak II (completely) burned down.
  terabak burned down, destroyed by fire. *Kampung itu ~.* The village was completely burned down.
raban 1 confused. **2** babbling. *bahasa -* jabbering, gibberish.
  meraban 1 to mumble, jabber (away), stammer, mutter. *masa ~* babbling period (in child's language development). **2** to be delirious, rave; → MENGIGAU, MERACAU. **3** ecstatic.
rab(b)ana (*A*) our Lord (in prayers).
rab(b)ani (*A*) concerning God, divine. *hati -* a heart which belongs wholly to God. *Tuhan -* Lord God.

rabarber (*D*) rhubarb, *Rheum rhabarbarum.*
raba-rubu → RABA II.
rabas (*M*) **1** water that drips from leaves after rain. *hari -* it's drizzling. **2** drizzle. **3** to fall, drip (of tears, water, etc.; → REBAS. **4** discharge.
  rabas-rabas *hujan ~* drizzle.
rabat (*D*) rebate, discount.
rabet (*J?*) **merabet** to beat up.
Rabi and **rabbi** (*A*) my Lord, oh Lord. *Ilahi -* Lord God.
rabiés (*D*) rabies; → GILA *anjing.*
  ber-rabiés to have rabies, rabid. *anjing yang ~* a rabid dog.
rabik → RABIT.
Rabingulakir (*Jv*) → RABI(')ULAKHIR.
Rabingulawal (*Jv*) → RABI(')ULAWAL.
rabit torn at the edge, torn (of an ear by an earring). *bibir -* harelip. *telinga - dipasang subang, kaki untuk dipakaikan gelang, jari kudung dimasukkan cincin* it suits you as a saddle suits a sow.
  merabit 1 to tear at the edge. **2** (*M*) *~ muncung* to scream at the top of one's lungs.
rabit(h)ah (*A*) association, alliance, federation, league.
Rabithah-al Alam-al Islami (*A*) International Muslim League.
Rabithah Ma'ahid Islami (*A*) Association of Muslim Seminaries.
Rabi(')ulakhir (*A*) the fourth month of the Muslim calendar.
Rabi(')ulawal (*A*) the third month of the Muslim calendar.
rabu I (*A*) fourth. (*hari -*) Wednesday (the fourth day of the week). *- akhir* the last Wednesday in the month of Sapar.
rabu II (*M*) lungs. *besar -* stupid, foolish, dull. *penyakit/sakit -* tuberculosis.
rabuk I k.o. mushroom; → CENDAWAN, JAMUR.
rabuk II (*Jv*) **1** tinder made out of palm-tree fibers; → KA(W)UL. **2** cause of a quarrel. *seperti - dengan api* a) catches fire easily. b) spoiling for a fight. c) don't set the fox to watch the geese. *sehabis - sehabis putaran* easy come, easy go.
rabuk III (*Jv*) fertilizer, manure, dung; → PUPUK I. *- buatan/garam* artificial fertilizer. *- hijau* compost, green fertilizer. *- kandang* dung, stable/farmyard manure. *- TSP* trisodium phosphate fertilizer.
  merabuk(i) to fertilize with manure, dress.
  perabukan manuring, fertilizing with manure.
Rab(b)ul (*A*) Lord of.
Rab(b)ulakwan (*A*) Lord of the Universe.
rab(b)ulalamin (*A*) Lord of Mankind.
rab(b)ulgafar and **rab(b)ulgafur** (*A*) Lord, the All-Forgiving.
rab(b)uliz(z)at (*A*) Lord, the All-Merciful.
rab(b)uljalil (*A*) Lord, the All-Serene.
rabun I smoke (from burning leaves/rubbish/incense, etc.) used to fumigate (a house/room, etc.), drive away (mosquitoes), exorcise (evil spirits, etc.).
  merabuni to smoke, fumigate.
  merabunkan to burn (leaves/incense, etc. to drive away mosquitoes, etc.).
  perabun leaves, etc. burned to drive away mosquitoes/evil spirits, etc.
  perabunan smoking, fumigating.
rabun II blurred, dim. *buta -* near-sighted (objects look blurry). *- ayam* a) near-sighted, myopic. b) dusk, twilight. *- dekat* near-sighted, myopic. *- jauh* far-sighted, presbyopic. *- senja* (*M*) night blindness.
  berabun-rabun to play blind-man's buff.
  merabunkan to weaken s.o.'s vision, blind.
  kerabunan nearsightedness, myopia.
rabung 1 ridge of a roof. **2** high (of the tide). *air -* high tide. **3** big talk, boasting (of words). *bercakap -* to talk big, brag, boast.
  merabung 1 to ascend, rise, swell up. **2** to rise (of the tide). *(air) pasang ~* spring tide.

perabung(an) ridge of a roof. *perabung limas* pyramid-shaped roof ridge.

rabut get loose, come undone; → CABUT I.

merabut 1 to tear/pull out, extract (teeth). **2** to pull hard at s.t.

racak (*M*) **meracak** ~ *kuda* to ride horseback, horseback-riding.

racana the smallest unit (maximum membership is 10) in the *Pramuka* Boy Scout Movement consisting of *pandéga*.

racau I 1 delirious, raving. **2** delirium.

meracau to rave (in a nightmare/delirium), hallucinate.

racauan delirium, hallucination.

racau II (*M*) restless, fidgety.

racek (*J*) pockmarked.

racik I bird trap/snare (made of horsehair).

meracik to snare birds using such a trap.

racik II seracik a thin slice (of cucumber, etc.).

meracik to cut up into thin slices; → MENGIRIS, MERAJANG.

racikan 1 finely sliced (vegetables/tobacco, etc.). **2** thin slice.

racik III (*Jv*) medicinal preparation made of herbs. *tukang* – s.o. who makes such preparations.

meracik 1 to compound (medicines), blend ingredients together. **2** to make the necessary preparations to do s.t. **3** to eat mixed foods.

racikan medicinal mixture/compound.

peracikan compounding (medicine).

racuk meracuk 1 to try to pick up (a girl). **2** to bother, annoy, tease.

racun 1 (chemical) poison, toxin, agent (used for chemical warfare); *cp* BISA I. *gas* – poison gas. *ilmu* – toxicology; → TOKSIKOLOGI. *mati karena termakan* – accidentally poisoned. **2** s.t. harmful/destructive (to one's happiness/welfare, etc.). *Banyak film yang menjadi* – *bagi jiwa masyarakat.* Many films are bad for the community. – *api* extinguisher (the substance). – *cekik* choking agent. – *hama* insecticide. – *kimia* chemical agent. – *lepuh* blister agent. – *serangga* insecticide. – *syaraf* nerve agent. – *tikus* rat poison.

beracun poisonous, poison (*mod*), toxic, poisoned. *bahan* ~ toxin. *panah* ~ poison(ed) arrow.

meracun 1 to poison s.o., put poison into s.t. *secara sengaja* ~ *dirinya sendiri* to poison o.s. intentionally. **2** ~ *hati* seductive, enticing; to seduce. *senyum yang* ~ *hati* a seductive smile. ~ *sukma* to corrupt.

meracuni [and **ngeracunin** (*J coq*)] **1** to poison, give poison to. **2** to drug.

meracunkan 1 to use ... to poison. **2** to poison for s.o. else.

teracuni poisoned. *orang yang* ~ s.o. who has been poisoned.

keracunan 1 intoxicated, drugged; poisoned. **2** intoxication, poisoning, toxicity. ~ *darah* blood poisoning, septicemia. ~ *jamur* mycotoxicosis. ~ *kehamilan* eclampsia, toxemia. ~ *makanan* food poisoning. ~ *sendiri* autointoxication. ~ *zat arang* asphyxiation.

peracun 1 poisoner. **2** s.t. that poisons.

peracunan 1 poisoning. **2** intoxicating.

racut multiple pimples or abscesses.

rad (*D col*) council; → DÉWAN, MAJELIS I. – *agama* religious council.

Ra'd (*A*) *ar*– "Thunder"; name of the 13th chapter of the Koran.

rada (*J* [from *E*?]) rather, fairly, somewhat; → AGAK I. – *gila* somewhat crazy. – *pahit* rather bitter.

rada-rada rather, fairly, somewhat (more emphatic than **rada**).

radah (*M*) **meradah** at random, wildly; to do s.t. on a large scale.

radai I (*M*) fin (of fish).

radai II (*M*) **1** to ask for alms. **2** to carry an idol in a procession.

radak I stab (from the same level or below, *usu* with a spear).

beradak to stab e.o.

beradakan and **radak-meradak** to stab e.o.

meradak to stab (from below with a spear).

meradakkan to stab with (a weapon), poke at with s.t.

radakan stabbing, blow.

radak II (*M*) attack.

beradak to attack.

meradak 1 to attack s.t. **2** to break in.

radang 1 fever(ish), hot; → DEMAM, PANAS. **2** inflammation, -itis. *naik* – to get very angry, flare up. – *amandel* tonsillitis. – *ambing* mastitis. – *beku* frostbite. – (*buah*) *ginjal* nephritis. – *busuk ber-*

gas k.o. sore on the leg. – *gusi* gingivitis. – *hati* hepatitis. – *kandung empedu* cholecystitis, inflammation of the gallbladder. – *kandung kencing* cystitis, inflammation of the bladder. – *kandung telor* inflammation of the ovaries, salpingoophoritis. – *kelenjar susu* mastitis. – *kerongkongan* sore throat. – *kulit* dermatitis. – *kura* anthrax. – *lambung* gastritis. – *léver* hepatitis. – *liang peranakan* vaginitis. – *limpa* anthrax. – *ludah telinga* parotitis. – *mag* gastritis. – *mata* conjunctivitis, pinkeye. – *mulut* stomatitis. – *paha* blackleg (a cattle disease). – *panggul* pelvic inflammation. – *paru(-paru)* pneumonia. – *paru-paru dan bronkus* bronchopneumonia. – *saluran pencernaan* gastroenteritis. – *selaput otak* meningitis. – *selaput perut* peritonitis. – *sendi* arthritis. – *sumsum* myelitis. – *susu* mastitis. – *telinga* otitis. – *tenggorokan* bronchitis. – *tonsil* tonsillitis. – *umbai cacing* and – *usus buntu* appendicitis.

meradang 1 to become feverish. **2** to become inflamed. **3** to flare up, get angry/excited.

meradangi to inflame.

meradangkan 1 to get very angry at. **2** to make s.o. angry, anger. **3** to inflame.

peradang hothead, bad-tempered person.

peradangan inflammation, infection, -itis. ~ *ginjal* nephritis. ~ *kelopak mata* blepharitis. ~ *otot* tendonitis. ~ *payudara* mastitis. ~ *persendian* rheumatism. ~ *seludang perut* gastritis. ~ *usus besar* colitis. ~ *vagina* vaginal infection, vaginitis.

radar (*D/E*) radar. – *atmosfér* atmospheric radar. – *jajar-sefasa* phased-array radar. – *pelayaran* navigational radar.

beradar to have a radar (system). ~ *kasatmata* to have a visual radar system.

radas instrument, apparatus; → PERKAKAS.

radén (*Jv*) [R] title for Javanese nobility (often in combination with other qualifications). – *adipati* title for the *Patih* of Surakarta or Yogyakarta. – *adipati arya* an honorary title for the regent. – *ajeng* [R.A.] title for an unmarried female aristocrat. – *aria/ arya* title higher than *radén*. – *aria/arya adipati* title for regents. – *ayu* [R.Ay.] title for a married female aristocrat. – *bagus* title higher than *radén*. – *mas* [R.M.] and – *panji* title for male nobility. – *ngabéhi* title for a married male or female aristocrat. – *rara/roro* [R.R.] title for an unmarried high-status girl. – *tumenggeng* title for regents.

rader (*D*) small knife or (India-)rubber to erase pencil or ink marks from paper.

radés (*D*) radish, *Raphanus sativus*; → LOBAK.

radi (*A*) pleased, may (God) bestow favor on. – *Allah anhu* and – *Allahuanhu* may God bestow favor on him, may God be pleased with him.

radial (*D/E*) radial. *ban* – radial tire.

radian (*D/E*) radian (of a circle).

radiasi (*D*) radiation. – *atom* atomic radiation. – *éléktromagnétik* electromagnetic radiation. – *gelombang radio* the radiation of radio waves. – *nuklir* nuclear radiation. – *nuklir lanjutan* residual nuclear radiation.

meradiasi to radiate.

peradiasian radiation.

radiator (*D/E*) radiator.

radif (*A*) rhyme; → RIMA.

radikal (*D/E*) **1** radical. **2** (political) radical, extremist.

keradikalan radicalism.

radikalisasi (*E*) radicalization.

radikalisir (*D*) **meradikalisir** to radicalize.

radikalisme (*D/E*) radicalism.

radin I → RADÉN.

radin II *padi* – k.o. rice variety, *Oryza sativus*.

radio (*D*) radio. *berita* – radio report. *léwat/liwat* – via the radio, radiographic. *pesawat* – wireless set. *siaran* – radio broadcast. – *amatir* amateur/ham radio operator. – *antar penduduk* [RAP] citizens band radio, CB radio. – *canting/dengkul* rumors. *menurut siaran* – *dengkul* rumor has it that. – *gelombang péndék* shortwave radio. – *kasét* pretaped messages. – *kontak* (*infr*) beeper. – *mobil* car radio. (*dengan*) – *mulut* (by) word of mouth. – *panggil* pager. – *portabel* portable radio. – *salon* console radio. – *transistor* transistor radio.

beradio with a radio, to have a radio.

meradiokan to broadcast over the radio/air. ~ *berbagai instruksi* to broadcast various instructions over the air.

peradioan radio *(mod)*. *téknologi* ~ radio technology.

radioaktif *(D)* radioactive.

beradioaktif radioactivated, radioactive. *air* ~ radioactive water.

meradioaktifkan to radioactivate, make radioactive.

keradioaktifan radioactivity.

radioaktivitas and **radioaktivitét** *(D)* radioactivity.

radiobiologi radiobiology.

radiodiagnostik radiodiagnostic.

radiofotografi radiophotography.

radiograf *(E)* radiograph.

radiografi *(D/E)* radiography.

radiogram *(D/E)* radiogram.

radio-isotop *(D/E)* radioisotope.

radiolisis *(E)* radiolysis.

radiolog *(D)* radiologist.

radiologi *(D/E)* radiology. *ahli* – radiologist.

radiologis *(E)* radiologist.

radiométer *(D/E)* radiometer.

radiotéléfoni *(D/E)* radiotelephony.

radiotélégrafi *(D/E)* radiotelegraphy.

radiotélégrafis *(D)* radiotelegrapher.

radiotérapi *(D/E)* radiotherapy.

radiowan radioman.

radis → RADÉS.

radium *(D)* radium (the chemical element).

radius *(D)* radius. *dalam* – *empat kilométer* within a radius of four kilometers.

radla'ah *(A)* a woman whom a man may not marry because she suckled him.

radli → RADI.

radmolen *(D infr)* Ferris wheel.

radu completed, finished. *Ia baru saja* – *makan*. He's just finished eating.

beradu 1 to stop. *Kendaraan itu* ~ *di tepi jalan karena mogok*. The car stopped at the side of the road because it broke down. 2 to (take a) rest. 3 *(rev)* to sleep. *Sang Raja dan Permaisuri sedang* ~ *di peraduan*. The King and Queen were sleeping in the royal bed.

meradukan to finish, complete.

peraduan 1 resting place. 2 *(rev)* royal bed.

Ra'du → RAAD II.

Radyapustaka a museum in Surakarta containing *wayang bébér*, the prau of Rajamala, and many books on the city.

rafa(k) *(A)* 1 rise, lift. 2 elevation.

merafakkan 1 to raise, lift. ~ *surat* to present a letter to s.o. 2 to elevate.

rafaksi *(D)* allowance for damage or moisture in the rice trade.

rafal → LAFAL.

rafé *(naut)* raffee.

rafi *(A)* 1 honored, respected. 2 exalted, noble, sublime, lofty.

rafia *(D)* raffia, i.e., a soft fiber from the leaves of a k.o. palm tree, *Raphia ruffia/pedunculata*, used for tying up plants and for making mats, etc. *tali* – rope made from raffia fiber, plastic rope.

rafidhah and **rafidi** *(A)* 1 *(lit)* "forsakers," the name used by Sunni Muslims for Shi'ite Muslims. 2 schismatic, Muslim heretic.

rafi'i *(A) ar.*– the Exalter (one of God's names).

rafik *(A)* close friend.

rafinasi refined. *gula* – refined sugar.

rafinat *(D/E)* raffinate.

rafizi → RAFIDI.

Rafflésia (Arnoldii) a giant insectivorous flower found in Sumatra, one of the national flowers of Indonesia, and named after Sir Thomas Stamford Raffles. - *patma* k.o. Rafflesia found in Meru Betiri Botanical Gardens in East Java, *Rafflesia zollingeriana*.

rafraf *(A)* smooth brocade cloth.

raga I a coarse creel, (wooden or wicker) basket, (straw or wicker) beehive.

meraga 1 like a basket. 2 coarse, rough to the touch. *Rambutnya* ~. His hair is all tangled up.

raga II a ball plaited from rattan. *(ber)main sépak* – and **beraga** to play a k.o. game with such a ball.

meraga to make or play with such a ball.

raga III *(Jv)* the body; → OLAHRAGA, JIWA *dan raga*. - *(dan) jiwa* body and soul. *Yang mati hanya* –*nya saja, jiwanya tetap hidup*. Only his body died; his soul still lives on.

raga IV **beraga** and **meraga** 1 to show off, parade o.s., display o.s., exhibit o.s.; → MÉJÉNG. 2 to boast, brag.

meragakan to display, show, demonstrate. *Dengan* ~ *pelajaran, anak-anak lebih cepat mengerti*. By demonstrating the lesson, children will understand more quickly.

memperagakan 1 to show off, brandish, brag about. 2 to display, model. *Ia akan* ~ *pakaian batik*. She'll model batik dresses.

keragaan *(infr)* performance. ~ *yang dicapai dalam pengusahaan perkebunan* the performance achieved in plantation management.

peraga 1 braggart, boaster. 2 fop, dandy. 3 model, mock-up, s.t. displayed. *alat* ~ *anatomi* anatomical model. 4 mannequin, (fashion) model; → PERAGAWAN (-WATI). 5 display, screen.

peragaan 1 demonstration, presentation, show, display, modeling. ~ *busana/mode/pakaian* fashion show. ~ *laju kapal* sail-by (of ships). 2 ostentation, showing off.

ragad *(Jv)* expense(s), cost (of s.t.).

ragam I *(Hind)* 1 way (of acting), manner, mode. 2 whim, caprice, prank. *menahan* – *(M)* a) patient, tolerant, forbearing. b) endurable. 3 kind, sort, type. *Berbagai* – *barang yang digunakan sehari-hari dijual di toko itu*. Various goods for everyday use were sold in that store. 4 tune, melody. *ahli* – musician. *puspa* – potpourri. 5 color, design, pattern, motif. *Pedagang itu memperlihatkan saya kain yang sungguh cantik* –*nya*. The merchant showed me a piece of cloth with a really beautiful design. 6 *(gram)* voice, mood; speech, language; register, style. 7 *(stat)* variance; multiple. *banyak orang banyak* –*nya* so many men, so many minds; so many countries, so many customs. – *akrab* intimate language. – *aktif (gram)* active voice. – *baku* standard language. – *cara* multimodal. – *gramatikal (gram)* grammatical voice. – *lisan* spoken language. – *pasif (gram)* passive voice. – *perintah (gram)* imperative mood. – *resmi* official language. – *santai* informal speech. – *terikat (gram)* finite (form of the verb). – *tulis* written language.

seragam uniform, of one kind, alike. ~ *sebau* of one mind (husband and wife, etc.). *pakaian* ~ a uniform. *remaja dengan* ~ *sekolah* youngsters in school uniforms. *tidak* ~ not uniform, diverse. **ketidak-seragaman** lack of uniformity, diversity. ~ *ketrampilan di antara para jaksa dan menangani perkara* the lack of uniformity in capabilities and in handling lawsuits among public prosecutors. **berseragam** in uniform, uniformed (army men/police, etc.). **menyeragamkan** to make uniform, uniformize, standardize. ~ *peraturan tentang pajak kendaraan di seluruh Indonésia* to make the tax regulations for vehicles uniform all over Indonesia. **keseragaman** uniformity. **penyeragam** equalizer, equalizing. **penyeragaman** uniformizing, making uniform, standardization, equalization.

beragam *(ob)* to sing.

beragam(-ragam) of all sorts/kinds, of various types, varied, variegated, diversified, diverse, heterogeneous; multi-colored. *Di kelas yang berisi 40 murid dengan usia* ~ *(belasan sampai 50-an tahun)* *itu hanya terdapat 6 murid perempuan*. In a classroom containing 40 students of various ages (from teenagers to 50-year-olds) only six female students were found. *masyarakat* ~ pluralistic society. *ramai beragam, rimbun menyelara* everyone talks after his own fashion. **seberagam** as varied as.

meragam 1 to sing. 2 to color, tinge. 3 to vary.

meragamkan to vary.

keragaman 1 variation, variety, diversity; heterogeneity, pluralism. ~ *hayati* biodiversity. ~ *kehidupan* biodiversity. ~ *perasaan* emotional nuances. ~ *struktural* structural heterogeneity. *massa yang percaya pada* ~ the masses that believe in pluralism. 2 condition, state. ~ *jiwa* mental state, state of mind.

peragam variant.

peragaman diversification.

ragam II (*Hind*) unanimous, in complete accord, harmonious, of one mind.

meragamkan to tighten the bonds/ties of friendship.

keragaman unanimity, unison, concord, harmony. *Kepala désa dapat memelihara ~ di kampungnya.* The village head was able to maintain harmony in his village.

ragang I meragang 1 to climb (while holding on to s.t. with one's hands and knees), clamber up. *Ia jatuh ~ témbok.* He fell while clambering up the wall. **2** to assault, attack (a fortress). *~ gawé/gawai* (*Pal ob*) to rape a woman.

ragang II (*J/Jv*) **ragangan** (wooden) scaffolding; framework, frame (of house/kite, etc.).

ragas I meragas 1 (*cla*) to tear/pull out (hair/grass, etc.). **2** (*ob*) to cut, trim (hair); to prune, trim (trees).

ragas II meragas to creep up (of plants).

ragas III information; sign, token; proof, evidence. *-nya bahwa ia mencuri ialah barang itu ternyata di rumahnya.* The proof that he was a thief is that the goods turned out to be in his house.

ragawi physical; → RAGA III. *antropologi* – physical anthropology. *aspék* – physical aspects.

ragbol (*D*) ceiling mop (a feather duster on a long pole).

ragem (*J*) → RAGAM II.

ragi I (*Hind*) **1** yeast (for bread/*tempé/tapai*) starter. **2** ferment.
beragi 1 with yeast. *roti yang tidak ~* unleavened bread, unrisen bread. **2** to ferment; fermented. *ketan itu mulai ~* the sticky rice began to ferment.
meragi to add yeast to. *~ ketan* to add yeast to sticky rice.
meragikan 1 to add yeast to. **2** to make yeast for. **3** to ferment.
peragi s.t. that ferments. *~ téh* tea fungus.
peragian fermentation; brewing.

ragi II color (of fabric); *batik* pattern.
seragi with a single design/color.
meragi to color (fabric).

ragi III → DÉNDÉNG *ragi.*

ragib (*A*) absorbed in. *membaca Qur'an dengan* – to be absorbed in reading the Koran.

ragil (*Jv*) last-born, youngest (child in a family); → BUNGSU. *si* – the last-born (child), Benjamin. *kangen dengan anak -nya* to miss one's youngest child.

ragom gawi (in Lampung, South Sumatra) mutual aid, solidarity, cooperating; → GOTONG *royong.*

ragu I – (*akan*), – *hati* and **ragu-ragu 1** hesitating, wavering, indecisive, uncertain, dubious, doubtful, in doubt, indecisive, hesitant. *Saya ragu akan kejujurannya.* I have doubts about his honesty. *sikap yang ragu-ragu* a wavering attitude. *Jangan ragu-ragu melanjutkan pekerjaanmu.* Don't hesitate to finish your work. *dengan tidak – lagi* undoubtedly, without a doubt, certainly. **2** wishy-washy. **3** confused, embarrassed, worried. *Saya jadi ragu setelah mendengar kejadian yang sebenarnya.* I felt embarrassed after hearing what really happened.
beragu to hesitate, have doubts about, be uncertain/undecided, waver. *~ mengajukan pertanyaan* to hesitate to ask questions.
meragu to be in doubt, uncertain, unsure. *Hatinya ~.* He's uncertain.
meragui to call into question, have doubts about. *Cinta seorang ibu tak layak diragui.* It's not right to have doubts about a mother's love.
meragukan [and **ngeraguin** (*J coq*)] **1** to doubt, have doubts about, be suspicious of. *Kejujuran orang itu masih diragukan.* That person's honesty is still in doubt. **2** suspicious, suspect. *Kepribadiannya sangat ~.* His character is very suspicious. **3** to be doubtful, in doubt, uncertain. *Hasil pemilihan masih ~.* The election results are still in doubt. *diragukan* doubtful (of payments on debts). *tidak dapat diragukan* without doubt, beyond question.
meragu-ragukan to cast doubts on.
teragukan suspect. *tak ~ lagi* undoubtedly, without a doubt, certainly. *Ras Melayu secara keseluruhan tak ~ lagi sangat mirip dengan penduduk Asia Timur.* The Malay race on the whole shows undoubted similarities to the population of East Asia.
ragu-raguan doubtful.

keragu(-ragu)an uncertainty, doubt, hesitation, faltering, wavering; suspicion(s), reservations (about s.t.). *membangkitkan/menimbulkan ~ kepada masyarakat* to raise doubts in the community.
peragu doubter.
peraguan doubt, doubting.

ragu II meragu (*M*) to disturb, bother, irritate.

ragu III (*D*) ragout.

raguk → REGUK.

ragum vise, clamp. *– bangku* bench screw, jaw vise. *– jajar* parallel vise.
raguman (*infr*) joint; → GABUNGAN.

ragung teragung run into, collided with.
teragung-ragung collided with e.o.

ragut → RENGGUT.

rah (in acronyms) → DAÉRAH, PENGERAHAN.

rahab → RAHAP.

rahak (*M*) → DAHAK.

raham → RAHIM II.

rahang jaw. *tulang* – jaw bone, mandible. *– atas* upper jaw, maxilla. *– bawah* lower jaw, mandible.

rahap I *kain* – shroud.
merahap 1 to cover a corpse with a shroud. **2** to cover (with a blanket, etc.).
merahapi to cover (with a blanket, etc.). *Ia ~ tubuhnya dengan kain basah.* He covered his body with a wet cloth.
merahapkan to cover/wrap with s.t.
perahap covering.

rahap II merahap 1 to alight, get down. **2** to throw o.s. down.
terahap fallen down prone. *jatuh ~* fallen face down.

raharja and **raharjo** (*Jv*) prosperous, successful; lucky; → RAHAYU.

rahasia (*Skr*) **1** secret, classified. *agén* – secret agent. *membocorkan – negara* to leak state secrets; → MENYANYI. *membuka* – to reveal/disclose a secret. *memegang* – to keep a secret. *bukan menjadi – lagi bahwa* it's no longer a secret that. **2** mysterious. **3** confidential, private. *– dipegang teguh* strictest confidentiality assured, held in strict confidence. *– alam* secrets of nature. *– dagang* trade secret. *– dinas/jabatan* a) official secret. b) professional confidentiality (of a doctor, etc.). *– negara* state secret. *– surat* privacy of correspondence. *– umum* open secret.
berahasia to have/keep a secret.
merahasiakan to keep s.t. secret/confidential, keep s.t. under wraps, keep s.t. to o.s., cover s.t. up. *tidak ~* to make no secret of s.t.
kerahasiaan 1 secrecy. **2** privacy. **3** confidentiality.
perahasiaan secrecy, keeping s.t. confidential, confidentiality.

rahat I spinning wheel (for winding thread) with a metal axle.

rahat II (*A*) → ISTIRAHAT.

rahayat → RAKYAT.

rahayu (*Jv*) **1** welfare, prosperity, good luck; prosperous, lucky, fortunate. **2** salvation.
kerahayuan welfare, good luck, prosperity.

rahi the flat area on the surface of a gong.

rahib (*A*) Christian monk or nun.

rahim I (*A*) **1** compassion, pity; → BELAS *kasihan.* **2** merciful, compassionate; → PENGASIH, PENYAYANG. *Allah yang* – God, the Merciful.
merahimi to have mercy on, take pity on.
kerahiman mercy, pity.

rahim II (*A*) womb, uterus; → KANDUNGAN. *bayi masih dalam* – an unborn child, fetus. *– bunga* ovum.

rahimahullah (*A*) may God have mercy on him.

rahin (*ob*) → RAHIM I.

rahmah (*A*) love and affection.

rahman(i) (*A*) merciful, compassionate (of God).

rahmat (*A*) **1** mercy (*esp* the mercy of God), pity. *pulang/kembali ke – Allah* to return to the mercy of God, pass away, die. **2** God's blessing. *– Ilahi* God's grace. *– pengudus* (*RC*) God's blessing which purifies the soul. *– terselubung/tersembunyi/ tidak langsung* a blessing in disguise.
merahmati to be merciful to, have mercy on, take pity on.
rahmatan (*A*) *– lil 'alamin* pity for the entire world.

rahmatullah (*A*) God's mercy. *pulang/kembali ke* – to return to the mercy of God, i.e., pass away, die.

rahn(u) (*A*) k.o. Islamic pawn-broking or collateralized borrowing services .

rahsia → RAHASIA.

Rahu (*Skr*) a monster or dragon which is believed to swallow the moon during a lunar eclipse. *bulan dimakan* – eclipse of the moon.

rahuh big sigh of relief.

   merahuh to let out a big sigh with relief.

rahul (*J*) **ngerahul** to bluff.

rai I shepherd, herdsman.

rai II (*onom*) sound of rain falling on a window, etc.; → DERAI III.

rai III (in acronyms) → BATERAI I.

rai IV → RAHI.

raiat → RAKYAT.

raib (*A*) vanished, disappeared, gone; → GAIB. – *ditelan bumi* disappeared as if swallowed up by the earth.

   meraibkan to make s.t. disappear/vanish.

raigedék (*Jv*) shameless, impudent.

raih I pull (towards o.s.); *opp* TOLAK. *tolak/menolak* – a) give and take, push and pull. b) bid back and forth, bargain, buy and sell. – *pangkur ke dada* self-assured. – *pekung ke dada* to go out of one's way to look for trouble.

   meraih 1 to pull (towards o.s.). *Ia ~ anaknya ke dalam rangkulannya.* She pulled her child into her arms. *~ dayung* to row. **2** to seize, grasp, catch hold of, snatch, catch sight of, perceive. *Mataku tak dapat ~ orang yang kuharap datang menjemput kami.* My eyes couldn't catch sight of the person I expected to pick us up. *Mujur tak dapat diraih (malang tak dapat ditolak).* Good luck cannot be seized (bad luck cannot be avoided) (a fatalistic view of life). **3** to entice, charm, tempt, win over. *~ hati* to win over to one's side. *~ dengan uang/pemberian* to tempt with money/gifts. *~ perhatian* to get s.o.'s attention. **4** to achieve, manage to obtain, attain (with much effort), walk away with. *~ gelar Doktor* to get one's Ph.D. *Aku gunakan séks sebagai alat ~ cinta.* I use sex as a tool to get love. *~ suara* to get votes.

   meraih-raih to keep on reaching for.

   teraih can be achieved/obtained/reached out for; achieved, reached. *tidak ~* unattainable, unreachable, beyond the reach of. *Harga-harga sudah tidak ~ lagi oléh rakyat.* Prices are beyond the reach of the people.

   raihan (what is) gotten, achieved. *hasil ~ suara* votes gotten.

   peraih s.o. who manages to get s.t., winner of. *~ médali emas* winner of the gold medal.

   peraihan getting, obtaining.

raih II meraih to buy wholesale.

   peraih 1 middleman, wholesale dealer who sells his goods at retail. *berjagal ~* (*M*) to trade wholesale. **2** a trading *sampan. ~ suara* vote-getter.

raimuna 1 (in Papua) get-together of the wise leaders of the Ambay ethnic group to discuss problems. **2** *Pramuka* get-together/activities, such as a jamboree of *penegak* and *pandéga*.

rainproof (*E*) /rénpruf/ rainproof, waterproof. *Listrik kami tidak –, bila akan/sedang hujan, listrik sering mati.* Our electricity isn't rainproof; when it's going to rain or is raining, it often goes off.

rairat → GAIRAH.

rais I (*A*) **1** head, chair(man), leader. **2** president. – *a(a)m* general chairman (of the *NU*). – *akbar* great leader (of the *NU*). – *awal* first chairman (of the *NU*). – *din* religious leader. – *Jumhuriyah* President of the Republic (of Indonesia/Egypt, etc.). – *salis* third chairman (of the *NU*). – *syuriah* advisory chairman (of the *NU*). – *tsani* second chairman (of the *NU*).

rais II merais to sweep off (trash/food crumbs, etc.).

raiser (*E*) riser.

rait (*onom*) screeching sound.

   merait to screech.

raja I (*Skr*) **1** king, monarch, sovereign; royal. – *Brunéi Darussalam Sultan Hassanah Bolkiah* the monarch of Brunei Darussalam Sultan Hassanah Bolkiah. – *Inggris pada masa ini ialah seorang perempuan.* The present sovereign of England is a woman. *keluarga* – royal family. **2** sultan. *Di Malaysia Barat delapan dari-*

pada –.-nya bergelar sultan. In West Malaysia eight of the kings bear the title of sultan. **3** (*IBT*) village head. *Di seantéro Seram Utara tercatat ada 49 orang – atau kepala désa.* Forty nine sovereigns or village heads have been registered all over North Seram. **4** magnate, baron, s.o. with great power or influence (in business/financial circles, etc.). – *tékstil* the textile king. **5** s.o. who does a lot of some activity. **6** an animal/ spirit/human being considered to dominate members of the same species or profession. – *binatang* the lion or tiger. – *copét* master pickpocket. **7** the king (in chess/in the deck of cards/ the name of a *ceki* card). – *akhirat* king of eternity, God. – *badar* k.o. white fabric. – *bola* superior soccer player. – *brana* wealth, riches. – *bunga* peony. – *di* – king of kings, the Shah of Iran. *(si)* – *hutan* the tiger. – *jenang/jejenang* s.o. who takes care of everything in cockfighting. – *jin* king of the spirits. – *kunci* master key; → KUNCI *ganda/induk/maling.* – *laut* (*ob*) admiral. – *makan* a big eater. – *minyak* oil baron/sheikh. – *muda* a) crown prince. b) king's representative (in a colony). – *penomah* a gift presented to one's parents-in-law. – *putih* leukorrhea. – *putra* prince. – *putri* princess. – *rimba* king of the forest: the lion or tiger. – *sehari/sari* (*coq*) bride and/or groom. – *siang* the sun. – *singa* syphilis. – *tidur* sleep hound. – *uang* millionaire.

   beraja 1 to act like a king/monarch/sovereign. **2** to have a king, etc., be ruled by a king. *Negeri itu tak ~ lagi.* That country is no longer a monarchy. **3** to be a slave to, be enslaved by, submit to. *~ kepada duit/uang* to serve Mammon. *~ di hati, bersultan di mata* and *~ di mata, bersultan di hati* opinionated, pigheaded.

   beraja-raja (*cla*) to move in court circles. *Baiklah anakku supaya engkau tahu ~.* It's good, my child, for you to know how to move in court circles.

   meraja 1 to act like a king, etc. **2** (*coq*) → MERAJALÉLA.

   merajai 1 to be(come) a king over, rule (over), govern. *Sultan Muzaffar Shah mula-mula sekali ~ negeri Pérak.* At the very beginning Sultan Muzaffar Shah ruled the State of Perak. **2** to control, have control over, influence. *Hati akan ~ seluruh jiwa.* The heart controls the entire psyche. *~ dirinya sendiri* to control o.s.

   merajakan 1 to name as king, etc. *Anakanda yang akan dirajakan di sana.* You, my child, will be named as king there. **2** to consider s.t. or s.o. most important, worship. *Meréka ~ harta benda.* They worshiped wealth.

   kerajaan 1 kingdom, empire, monarchy. *~ absolut* absolute monarchy. *~ Bersatu* United Kingdom (of Great Britain and Northern Ireland). *~ Inggris* the British Empire. *~ Ketiga* the Third Reich. *~ konstitusional* constitutional monarchy. *~ mutlak* absolute monarchy. *~ parleméntér* parliamentary monarchy. *~ Persekutuan Tanah Melayu* (*ob*) the Central Government of Malaya in Kuala Lumpur; *cp* PUSAT I. **2** royal. *payung ~* royal umbrella. *takhta ~* royal crown. **3** royal rank/grade/status. **4** area under the control of a king, etc. **5** characteristics of a king, etc. **6** to become a king, ascend the throne. *Jika ia ~, tiada akan sempurna negeri ini.* If he ascends the throne, this country will not be perfect. **7** (*Mal*) government. **berkerajaan** to be ruled by a monarch, be a monarchy.

raja II various species of kingfisher, *Halcyon* spp. – *udang*: a) blue-eared kingfisher, *Alcedo meninting.* b) stork-billed kingfisher, *Halcyon capensis.* c) common kingfisher, *Alcedo atthis bengalensis.* – *udang ékor panjang* long-tailed kingfisher, common paradise kingfisher, *Tanysiptera galatea.* – *udang kalung putih* white-collared kingfisher, *Halcyon chloris.* – *udang kerdil* Sulawesi kingfisher, *Ceyx fallax.* – *udang sungai* Indian common kingfisher, *Alcedo atthis.*

raja III *kayu* – a Moluccan resin-producing tree, golden shower tree, *Cassia fistula. pisang* – a banana variety; → PISANG *raja. rumput* – k.o. orchid, *Dendrobium calcaratum.* – *tawi* → PISANG *Ambon.*

raja'ah (*A*) to return to one's divorced wife.

Rajab (*A*) the seventh month of the Muslim year.

rajaberana (*Skr Jv*) treasures, jewels.

rajagung *bulan* –. → ZULKAÉDAH.

rajah I 1 (magic) sign, rune, figures used as a charm/talisman (to ward off sickness, etc.). **2** lines on the palm of the hand (used for palmistry), grain (in wood). – *tangan* the lines on the palm of the hand. *ahli – tangan* palmist, palm-reader. **3** tattoo marks. **4** figures. **5** grain (of wood, leather).

berajah tattooed.

merajah 1 (*M*) to make signs on the body of a sick person to cure him. **2** to tattoo. **3** to plot, draw lines for plotting.

rajahan tattoo.

perajah s.o. or s.t. that tattoos.

perajahan tattooing.

rajah II merajah to stab with a sharp object/javelin/spear/etc.

rajakula (*Skr*) dynasty.

rajaléla merajaléla 1 to act arbitrarily/in a tyrannical way/in a high-handed way. **2** to run rampant, increase rapidly. *Belakangan ini penyelundupan narkotika ~ di seluruh dunia.* Lately narcotics smuggling has been running rampant all over the world. **3** to rage (of an epidemic), rampage, go unchecked; → MAHARA-JALÉLA. **kemerajalélaan** a rampage, rampaging.

rajalélé a rice variety.

rajam (*A*) physical punishment for an adulterer (by the whip/sword/stoning).

merajam 1 to stone to death. **2** to punish/torture for transgressing Islamic law. *dirajam cambuk* to be whipped/lashed. *dirajam paku* to be rolled in a barrel full of nails. *~ di air* to drown s.o.

merajamkan to punish with s.t.

terajam physically punished/tortured.

rajaman torment, punishment, torture; stoning.

perajam s.o. who stones, tortures, etc.

perajaman stoning.

rajang (*Jv*) → RACIK II. **merajang** to cut into thin or small slices, mince, slice up fine (of tobacco).

terajang chopped (up), minced.

rajangan (s.t.) sliced/cut (up) fine. *berambang ~* sliced shallots. *~ bawang mérah* minced onions. *~ kayu* wood chips. *tembakau ~* cut tobacco, cuts.

perajang chopper.

perajangan mincing.

rajapati (*Jv*) manslaughter, homicide.

rajawali (*Skr*) **1** kite, sparrow hawk, *Haliastus indus intermedius* and *Accipiter virgatus gularis* or *A. badius poliopsis*. **2** black-thighed falconet, *Microhierax fringillarius*. *- coklat* brown falcon, *Falco berigora*. *- totol* Moluccan/spotted kestrel, *Falco moluccensis*. **3** pilot; → PENERBANG.

rajawardi → LAZUARDI.

rajéh (*Jv*) and **rajét** (*S*) in shreds, broken/torn to pieces.

raji → TALAK *raji*.

rajih (*A*) legal opinion.

rajim (*A*) stoning (to death); → RAJAM.

rajin 1 industrious, diligent, hardworking. **2** to do s.t. habitually. *orang-orang yang – mengunjungi nite club* people who habituate nightclubs. *-nya!* how hardworking (you, etc., are)!

merajin to do handicrafts.

merajinkan to cause s.o. to be diligent/industrious/hard-working. *~ diri* to do one's utmost.

kerajinan 1 industry, diligence. **2** handicrafts, handmade. *barang ~* handmade goods. *~ kayu* woodworking. *~ rumah tangga* home industry. *~ tangan* handicraft. **3** too industrious/hardworking).

pe(ng)rajin craftsman, artisan.

pe(ng)rajinan crafts.

rajuk I merajuk 1 to sulk, act up, show an unwillingness to do s.t., be an impossible person to deal with. *Orang itu ~ dan enggan bergaul dengan kami.* He was sulking and didn't want to associate with us. **2** to grumble, complain, fret. *Anaknya yang manja itu ~ karena ia tidak dapat barang yang dikehendakinya.* That spoiled child was fretting because he didn't get what he wanted.

merajuki 1 to reprimand, rebuke. *Istrinya ~nya karena ia terlambat pulang.* His wife reprimanded him because he came home too late; *cp mendapat* PALANG *pintu*. **2** to sulk over/toward.

perajuk 1 sulky person. **2** grumbler.

rajuk II (*M*) demarcation stake made from live wood.

rajul (*A*) man, male person.

rajungan k.o. edible small black crab, *Portunus pelagicus*. *- angin* sentinel crab, *Podophthalmus vigil*. *- batu* k.o. marine crab, *Charybdis lucifera*. *- bintang* three-spot crab, *Portunus sanguinolentus*. *- hijau* swimming crab, *Thalamita crenata*. *- karang* swimming crab, *Charybdis natator*.

rajut 1 net(ting), mesh. **2** texture. *- rambut* hair net, snood.

serajut a basketful, a netful.

merajut 1 to make a net. **2** to knit, crochet. *~ badan (sendiri)* (*M*) to make (one's life) hard. *~ léhér* to hang o.s. *~ perut* (*M*) to deny s.o. food. *~ tali cinta/kasih dengan* to fall in love with.

rajut-merajut *karya ~* knitting.

merajutkan to put s.t. into a net.

terajut 1 can be netted. **2** to get into trouble.

rajutan 1 knitting, crochet-work, crocheting, mesh, knit (*mod*). *bahan ~* knitted material. **2** snood. **3** texture.

perajut 1 knitter. **2** *mesin ~* knitting machine.

perajutan knitting.

rak I (*onom*) sound of cracking; → DERAK.

rak II (*D*) rack, stand. **2** shelf. *- buku* (open) bookshelf. *- piring* plate rack, dish rack. *- pengering(an)* drying rack.

raka I broken, cracked, with a tear in it; → PATAH I, RETAK.

raka II 1 (*Jv*) older brother. **2** senior male university student.

raka III (*ob*) king.

rakaat (*A*) the series of ritually prescribed movements and attitudes of a prayer. *sembahyang subuh dua –* morning prayer consisting of two such movements, etc.

rakah merakah to laugh.

rakak → RANGKAK. **merakak** to crawl.

rakam (*Mal*) → REKAM.

rakan (*Mal*) stock, type from which a group of animals is derived; → REKAN I. *- héwan* livestock. *- lembu* cattle stock.

rakanita female senior university student.

rakap I merakap to cringe with humility.

rakap II (*A*) stirrup.

rakat I (*Jv*) closely (related).

rakat II (*Mal ob*) a masked dance with clowning around. **merakat** to perform that dance.

Rakata the volcanic island of *Krakatau*, Krakatoa.

rakawan 1 male senior university student. **2** tutor.

rakawati female tutor.

rakbol → RAGBOL.

Raker → RAPAT *Kerja*.

Rakerda → RAPAT *Kerja Daérah*.

Rakerkornas → RAPAT *Kerja dan Koordinasi Nasional*.

Rakerna → RAPAT *Kerja Paripurna*.

Rakernas → RAPAT *Kerja Nasional*.

Rakernis → RAPAT *Kerja Téknis*.

Rakertas → RAPAT *Kerja Terbatas*.

raket (*Jv*) → RAKAT I.

rakét (*D*) **1** racket. *- ténis* tennis racket. **2** rocket; → ROKÉT.

rakhim → RAHIM II.

rakhman(i) → RAHMAN(I).

rakhmat → RAHMAT.

Rakib (*A*) *al-* The Preserver (a name of God).

rakik deep-fried. *- pisang* deep-fried banana.

rakit I raft; → GÉTÉK II. *naik -* to travel by raft, go rafting. *- bambu* bamboo raft. *- kayu* lumber-raft/-float. *- penolong* life raft. *- penyeberangan* ferry (boat). *- penyelamat* life raft. *- penyelamat dari karét* inflatable life raft. *- penolong* life raft. *- pisang* (*M*) a snack made of young bananas sliced and arranged in the shape of a raft.

berakit to ride on a raft, use a raft. *~ menuju kampung* to raft home.

berakit-rakit *~ ke hulu, berenang-renang ke tepian (bersakit-sakit dahulu, bersenang-senang kemudian)* after rain comes sunshine.

merakit to build/make a raft.

rakit II (*Jv*) pair, team, span. *kerbau dua –* two pairs of water buffaloes.

serakit *~ kerbau* a pair of water buffaloes. *~ kuda* a set of horses. *~ sapi* a team of cows.

rakit III merakit 1 to assemble (cars, etc.). **2** to invent, devise, contrive; → MERÉKA(-RÉKA). *siap dirakit* prefab(ricated). *rumah siap dirakit* a prefab(ricated) house.

rakitan 1 assembled. *sédan* ~ assembled sedan. **2** homemade. *bom* ~ a homemade bomb. **3** arrangement. **4** assembly.

rakit-rakitan spare parts; → ONDERDIL, SUKU *cadang*.

perakit [and (*infr*) **pengrakit**] **1** assembler (of cars, etc.). *perusahaan perakit kendaraan bermotor* automotive assembly plant. **2** arranger, planner, designer.

perakitan assembling, assembly (*mod*). *garis* ~ assembly line. *perusahaan* ~ assembling plant.

rakit IV perakit clerk (in category C of the Government Employees Scale). ~ *télékomunikasi penerbangan* radio flight operator.

rakit V *burung* – **1** black-and-red broadbill, *Cymbirhynchus macrorhyncos malaccensis*. **2** banded broadbill, *Eurylaimus javanicus pallidus*.

rakitanisasi assembling (of parts).

rakitis (*D*) rachitis.

rakna (*ob*) → RATNA I.

rakor → RAPAT *Koordinasi*.

rakorbang → RAPAT *Koordinasi Pembangunan*.

raksa I (*Skr*) /ra'sa/ *air* – quicksilver, mercury. – *urai* native mercury.

raksa II (*Jv*) – *bumi* member of the village civil service, irrigation overseer.

raksamala → RASAMALA.

raksasa (*Skr*) /rak-/ **1** monster, giant, ogre, goblin; → BUTA III. **2** like a giant, gigantic, of great size/strength, etc., enormous, mass. *kekuatan* – Herculean strength/power. *kran* – gantry crane. *perusahaan* – gigantic enterprise. *proyék* – enormous/macro- project. *tank* – (*mil*) monster tank.

meraksasa 1 to become gigantic/enormous. **2** to resemble/be like a giant. *kekuatan ékonomi yang tumbuh* ~ an economic force which has been growing enormously.

keraksasaan gigantic size/stature, gigantism; demonic. *sifat* ~ demonic character.

raksasi (*Skr*) ogress, giant.

raksi I (*Skr*) /rak-/ **1** scent(s), perfume(s), perfumery. **2** fragrant, aromatic, sweet-smelling; → HARUM, WANGI. *minyak* – perfumed water, perfume.

meraksi 1 to perfume, scent. ~ *kain batik* to scent a batik cloth. **2** to brighten/cheer s.o. up.

peraksi fragrance, s.t. used to perfume/scent.

raksi II → RASI I.

rakuk (*M*) notch, nick, indentation (in a tree); → TAKUK. *Dia membuat beberapa* – *pada batang pohon kelapa itu sebagai tempat berpijak ketika memanjat.* He made several notches in the coconut tree trunk as points of support when he climbed the tree.

berakuk with/to have notches/nicks/indentations; notched, nicked, indented. *membuat titian* ~ to lay/set a trap for s.o.

rakungan (*M*) **1** throat. **2** pharynx; → KERONGKONGAN.

rakus 1 greedy, gluttonous, ravenous, voracious; → LOBA, SERAKAH, TAMAK. **2** having a strong desire for more. – *duit* money-grubbing; mercenary.

kerakusan 1 gluttony, greediness, greed. **2** eagerness for more, avarice, rapacity. *Karena ~nya, ia tetap korupsi.* Because of his avarice he kept on being corrupt.

perakus glutton, greedy person.

rakut merakut 1 to set a trap. **2** to deceive, mislead, cheat.

rakyat (*A*) **1** people, nation. *Déwan Perwakilan* – [DPR] People's Representative Council, Parliament. *kedaulatan* – sovereignty of the people. *Amanat Penderitaan* – [Ampera] Message of the People's Suffering. **2** population, populace, inhabitants; → PENDUDUK. *Dalam perang gerilya* – *turut serta.* The populace took part in the guerrilla warfare. **3** the public; → MASYARAKAT, UMUM. *keséhatan* – public health. **4** folk, folkloristic. *musik* – folk music; → MUSIK *pop.* **5** citizens, citizenry. *Lurah harus melindungi ~nya.* The village head has to protect his citizens. **6** smallholder. *hasil* – smallholders' produce. *kopi* – smallholders' coffee. *Proyék Pengembangan Karét* – Smallholders' Rubber Development Project. **7** (*ob*) troops, a body of soldiers. *Maka baginda pun berangkat diiringkan oléh seluruh* – *lengkap dengan senjatanya.* Then His Majesty departed accompanied by

all his fully armed soldiers. – *biasa* common/ordinary people. – *gémbél* (*J*) vagabonds, beggars, bums. – *Indonésia* the Indonesian people/nation. – *jelata* the masses. – *jémbél* the poor, underprivileged. – *kecil* the common people, the man in the street. – *kelas bawah* the lower classes, the grass roots. – *marhaén/murba* the proletariat, masses. – *pemilih* the electorate. – *terlatih* national guard.

merakyat 1 to be(come) popular (among the mass of the population). *Senam keséhatan sekarang sudah* ~. Health gymnastics have now become popular. **2** to be popular, appeal to the people. *jadilah pemimpin yang* ~ to become a popular leader. *tidak* ~ does not appeal to the people, does not strike the imagination of the people, unpopular.

merakyatkan to turn s.t. over to the people. ~ *seluruh aréal tebu, pabrik, dan produksinya* to turn the entire acreage of sugarcane, the factories, and production over to the people.

kerakyatan 1 democratic, populist. *kesadaran* ~ democratic awareness. **2** citizenship.

perakyatan turning s.t. over to the people.

rakyatisme populism.

rakyu (*A*) mind, intellect.

ralat (*A*) **1** error, mistake. **2** typographical error, typo, misprint. **3** errata (in script, print), correction, rectification.

meralat to correct, rectify. *Dia* ~ *keterangannya.* He corrected his statement.

rali → RÉLI.

ralip I (*A*) **meralip** catnap, short nap, dozing.

peralip sleepyhead.

ralip II → GALIB. *pada –nya* normally.

ralli → RÉLI.

ralliwan → RÉLIWAN.

ram I (*onom*) a rumbling/roaring noise; *cp* DERAM.

ram II (*D ob*) window. *tingkap* – louvers.

ram III → ERAM I, II.

rama (*Jv*) father (a respectful term for priests/ministers, etc.); → ROMO.

perama primate (of a religious order).

Ramad(h)an and **Ramadlan** (*A*) the fasting month, the ninth Muslim month; → PUASA. – *Mubarrak* Success in carrying out the fast.

ramah 1 cordial, warm and sincere, hearty, affectionate. *Gadis itu menyambut tetamunya dengan* –. The girl greeted her guests cordially. **2** friendly, amicable, amiable. *Kami suka bergaul dengan orang yang* – *lagi periang.* We like to associate with friendly and happy people. *tidak* – impolite. **ketidak-ramahan** impoliteness. – *layan* courteous in service. **keramah-layanan** courteous service. – *lidah* talkative. – *lingkungan* environment-friendly. – *tamah* amiable, affable, courteous, kind, cordial, jovial. *malam* – *tamah* an amicable reunion. **beramah-tamah** (*dengan*) to talk in a friendly way (to), get together (with). **keramah-tamahan** amiability, affability, friendliness.

beramah-ramahan (*dengan*) to be on friendly/familiar terms (with).

meramahi to treat in a kind/friendly/affable/amiable way. *Dia selalu diramahi orang.* People always treat him kindly.

meramahkan to cause to be friendly, make amiable. *Ia menyambung omongannya dengan suara yang diramahkan.* He continued his conversation in an amiable tone.

teramah the friendliest.

keramahan friendliness, amiability, cordiality.

peramah 1 friendly, hospitable, kind. **2** a friendly/amiable/cordial person.

ramai 1 with many/lots of people, thronged (with people), crowded (with people), busy. – *orang menonton* the show was thronged. – *pasién* busy (of a doctor's office), with many patients. **2** full of action/noise, noisy, exciting. *Suara témbakan itu* – *sekali.* The sound of shooting was very loud. *Perkelahian anak sekolah itu sangat* –. The fight among the schoolchildren was noisy. **3** showy, flashy. *Gadis itu suka berpakaian yang* –. The girl likes to wear flashy clothes. **4** lively, cheerful, talkative, animated, bustling. *Péstanya* –. The party was lively. **5** active, busy, lively, heavy (of traffic). *jalan yang* – *dilalui kendaraan* a road with heavy traffic. *jam-jam yang* – peak/rush hours. **6** public; → UMUM I. *di mata* – in the eyes of the public. *di muka (khalayak)* – in public, in front of everybody. *kegemaran/kemauan* – public amusements/wishes. *khalayak/masyarakat* – the public, populace. *orang* – the public, masses. *suara* – public opinion, vox populi. – *beragam, rimbun menyelaras* tastes differ; there's no accounting for taste. *tidak* – quiet, light (of traffic), not busy.

ramai-ramai by many people acting together, in a group, in droves. *Sala Kabiran secara ~ telah dianiaya oléh para awak kapal.* Sala Kabiran was mistreated by the entire ship's crew. *Ada apa ~?* What's up? What's happening?

ramai-ramainya with lots of activity/people. *Sekarang ini jalan sedang ~.* It's rush hour now.

seramai as busy as.

beramai-ramai to do s.t. together/in a group, throng. *~ meréka pergi ke sawah.* They thronged to the rice fields. *Ia diperkosa ~.* She was gang raped.

meramaikan and **memperamai 1** to brighten/cheer/liven up, enliven. *Meréka datang untuk ~ pésta itu.* They showed up to enliven the party. **2** to engross, absorb, keep busy.

meramai-ramaikan to perform/do/carry out in great numbers (or, en masse).

teramai very busy.

keramaian 1 rush, noise, bustle. *~ membeli uang kertas asing* the rush to buy foreign money. **2** festivity. *~ untuk para pria* stag party. **3** crowd, gathering. *puncak ~* peak season/time. *Dikatakan, keadaan itu makin berat lantaran kini puncak ~ kunjungan wisatawan asing ke Bukittinggi semakin panjang.* They said that the situation had gotten worse because the peak season for foreign visitors to Bukittinggi was getting longer now.

ramal I (*A*) **1** (*ob*) sand. *negeri* – Arabia. **2** the marks on sand used to predict the future. *membilang/membuka/membaca* – to predict the future (by consulting a book of prophesy, etc.). *juru* – a) forecaster. b) fortune-teller. *tukang* – fortune-teller.

meramal to predict/foretell the future, prophesize; to tell s.o.'s fortune.

ramal-meramal prophesying, predicting the future.

meramalkan [and **ngeramalin** (*J coq*)] to predict, forecast, prognosticate, portend. *dapat diramalkan* predictable. *sulit untuk diramalkan* unpredictable. *Hasilnya mémang sudah dapat diramalkan.* The result was predictable in advance. *Seorang dokter sekali-sekali dapat ~ keadaan keséhatan pasiénnya.* A doctor can sometimes predict the future health of his patient.

teramal predicted. **keteramalan** predictability.

teramalkan predictable.

ramalan prediction, forecast, prognosis, prophecy. *~ Joyoboyo telah menyebutkan akan datangnya bangsa yang berkulit kuning.* Joyoboyo's prophecies mentioned the coming of a yellow race. *~ bintang* horoscopy, reading the stars. *~ cuaca* weather forecast; → PRAKIRAAN *cuaca.* *~ lalu lintas* traffic report. *~ tokék* prediction based on the sounds made by a gecko. For example, s.o. makes a wish and to know whether this wish will come true, he has to say "yes" or "no" after each sound made by a gecko; if the series of sounds is followed by a "yes," the wish will come true; if followed by a "no," it will not come true. *~ yang memenuhi sendiri menjadi kenyataan* self-fulfilling prophecy.

peramal fortune-teller, forecaster, soothsayer.

peramalan fortune-telling, predicting the future, forecasting.

ramal II (*Pers cla*) handkerchief, face towel.

Ramalan → RAMAD(H)AN.

ramanda (*Jv*) reverent father.

ramang → REMANG I.

rama-rama a large butterfly variety; → KUPU-KUPU I. *– kuda* atlas moth, *Attacus atlas.*

ramas I → REMAS. **meramas 1** to press, knead (dough, etc.). *perut ~* colic, gripes. *~ bibir* to beat up. *~ jantung* to be resentful, regrettable. *~ kerupuk* to crush *kerupuk* to bits with one's fist. *~ léhér* to wring s.o.'s neck. *~ mulut* to beat up. *~ perut* to be resentful, regrettable. *~ santan di kuku* to seek the impossible. **2** to squeeze the liquid out of (a fruit/breast/udder). *Ibu ~ kelapa yang sudah diparut itu untuk mengeluarkan santannya.*

Mother squeezed the scraped coconut to extract its milk. *~ santan di kuku* to do s.t. useless. **3** to wring (cloth) (out). **4** to massage, press, and rub the body with the palms of one's hands to lessen pain or stiffness.

meramasi (*pl obj*) to press, squeeze, etc.

ramas II mixed together (of foods). *nasi* – rice mixed in with accompanying dishes.

meramas to combine/mix together (foods).

meramasi to prepare *nasi* – for s.o.

Ramayana (*Skr*) the Hindu epic, said to have been composed by Valmiki, narrating the life and adventures of Rama, Vishnu's seventh incarnation, how his wife Sita is kidnapped by the demon Rawana and carried off to the island of Sri Lanka and then rescued by Rama and the monkey king *Anoman/Hanuman*; it forms the basis for many Indonesian *wayang* stories, art, and references.

rambah merambah 1 to cut down, fell (trees). *Meréka ~ pokok-pokok kecil.* They cut down small trees. **2** to clear/open up a forest/jungle, cut a narrow path through the forest/jungle. *~ hutan* to clear the forest. *~ jalan* to cut a path, pave the way. **3** to exterminate, destroy, cut down (soldiers by machine-gun fire, etc.). *Musuh berhasil dirambah.* The enemy was successfully destroyed.

merambahi (*pl obj*) **1** to fell. **2** to clear/open up a forest.

terambah 1 cleared. **2** able to be cleared.

rambahan 1 remains of ground clearing. **2** brush(wood), herbage.

perambah *~ hutan* s.o. who clears the forest. *~ jalan* a) pioneer, trailblazer. b) promoter, originator.

perambahan clearing (forest). *~ hutan* forest clearing.

rambai I 1 *buah* – a salmon-buff-colored fruit which grows in long strings from a tree, *Baccaurea motleyana.* **2** various species of plants, *Baccaurea spp. pohon* – k.o. tree, mangrove apple, *Sonneratia caseolaris.*

rambai II 1 saddle-hackles of a cock; beard (of a goat, etc.). **2** hanging roots (of trees).

berambai 1 to hang down (of roots, feathers, etc.). **2** hairy, shaggy, hirsute.

rambaian 1 tail feathers. **2** hairy, shaggy, hirsute.

rambak I merambak 1 to spread in all directions (of creepers). **2** to increase in number, multiply.

merambakkan to cause to develop/spread/multiply. *~ uang* to lend out money (at a certain rate of interest).

rambak II (*Jv*) k.o. *krupuk* made from dried buffalo skin.

rambak III *– cina* k.o. bird.

ramban (*J/Jv*) **meramban** to search/look for leaves for goat-fodder, browse.

merambani (*pl obj*) → MERAMBAN.

rambanan leaves, grass, and herbs used for goat-fodder.

rambang I (*M*) arbitrarily, aimlessly, at random, randomly. *menebar jala* – to throw out a wide-casting net looking for information. *mulut* – talkative, saying whatever comes into one's mind. *– mata* sensual, lascivious, always on the lookout for women.

rambang-rambang → RAMBANG I.

merambang at random.

merambang-rambang to saunter about aimlessly.

rambangan at random.

kerambangan randomness.

rambang II → REMBANG I.

rambang III (*math*) to the power of. *dua – tiga* two cubed, two to the power of three.

rambas I merambas to wave/flap s.t.

rambas II → RAMAS I.

rambat I spreading, propagating. *– nyala* (*petro*) flame propagation.

merambat 1 to spread (out), propagate. *Mode batik tidak saja digandrungi masyarakat Indonésia sendiri tetapi ternyata juga sudah ~ sampai keluar negeri.* Batik fashions are not only in vogue among Indonesians themselves but it appears that they also have spread overseas. **2** to spread (of a fire/news/a disease, etc.). *Berita sudah ~ ke semua tetangganya.* The news had already spread to the neighbors. **3** to creep along and spread. *~ lamban* to creep along slowly. *Beratnya beban truk-truk pengangkut menyebabkan truk-truk itu harus ~ lamban.* The weight of the loads of the transport trucks made them creep along slowly. **4** (*Jv*) to climb (a tree) (of creepers/snakes), clamber up. *Tanaman itu ~ di dinding.* The plant is creeping up the wall. *~ naik* to creep up.

merambati to creep up on, spread out over, overgrow. *Lima kecamatan di Lamongan dirambati banjir.* The flood has spread out over five districts in Lamongan. *Pohon itu dirambati benalu.* The tree is overgrown with parasites.

merambatkan to make (creeping plants, etc.) spread/creep up over. *Tanaman itu dirambatkan di bambu.* S.o. made the plant creep up over the bamboo pole.

rambatan spread, propagation.

perambat (physical/electrical) conductor. *~ panas* heat conductor.

perambatan spread(ing), propagating, propagation. *ancaman ~ agrési komunis* the threat of the spread of communist aggression.

rambat II dais, platform raised above the floor (inside a house for guests of honor).

rambat III (*BD*) casting net.

rambaté raté hayo (*J*) and **rambatira hayo** to do s.t. with united strength, with a united effort, yo-heave-ho; → HOLOPIS *kuntul baris.*

rambia → RUMBIA.

rambih merambih to go (on a religious pilgrimage/excursion, etc.) in large numbers.

Rambo /rém-/ s.o. who, like the movie character Rambo, advocates or carries out violent acts of retribution.

merambo to act like Rambo.

rambu I berambu(-rambu) fringed, tasseled. *tirai berambu-rambu* a fringed curtain.

rambu-rambu fringes, tassels, hairs (hanging from the hem of shawls/shoulder scarves/curtains, etc.). *tombak ~* ceremonial lance with tassels. *~ ketiak* armpit/axillary hair.

rambu II 1 a short post/pillar (used for mooring boats/attaching traffic signs, etc.). **2** beacon. *béa –* beaconing. **3** guideline, framework. *– jalan* road signs. *– lalulintas* traffic signs/signals. *– larangan parkir* no-parking sign. *– rintangan* hazard beacon. *– sinar* flashing buoy. *– suar* light beacon/buoy. *– ukur* measuring rod.

merambu to mark out (an area with posts, etc.).

perambuan 1 beaconing, signaling. **2** beacons.

rambun I undergrowth or low shrubs.

rambun II → HUJAN *rambun.*

rambung Indian rubber tree, *Ficus elastica.*

rambusa k.o. vine, love-in-a-mist, *Passiflora foetida.*

rambut 1 hair (of the head); *cp* BULU, JEMBUT, ROMA I. *anak –* lock of hair, ringlet. *belah –* parting (of the hair). *berpotong –* to have one's hair cut short, have short hair. *cat –* hair coloring. *minyak –* hair tonic. **2** mane. **3** filament. *pér –* a very fine watch spring. **4** s.t. very small. **5** (*coq*) body hair; → BULU. *tidak seujung – pun* not the tiniest bit, not the slightest. *ia tidak menduga seujung – pun* he wouldn't have dreamed/imagined (that). *Saya tidak pernah ada niat seujung – pun menemui Bung Karno.* I had not the slightest intention of meeting Bung Karno. *– jangan putus, tepung jangan tersérak* disputes should be settled fairly so that both parties are satisfied. *– sama hitam, hati masing-masing berlainan* so many countries, so many customs. *bagai – dibelah tujuh/seribu* a) a little bit, an extremely small amount. b) rare as hen's teeth. *jiwanya bergantung pada/di – sehelai* his life hangs in the balance. *sakit kepala panjang –* to pretend to have a headache. *termakan di –* to be in trouble/great difficulties/a fix. *– buatan* wig. *– dipotong péndék* crew cut. *– getar* cilia. *– gondrong* bushy/long hair. *– hiasan* wig. *– ikal* curly/wavy hair. *– jagung* auburn/reddish brown hair. *– jangkit* bristling hair. *– kalong* fuzz, down. *– kejur* bristle. *– kelamin* pubic hair. *– keriting* curly/wavy hair. *– konita* wig. *– kribo* a) curly/wavy hair. b) kinky hair, Afro-style hair. *– kusut* tangled hair. *– madul-madul* disheveled hair. *– palsu* wig. *– pangkas péndék* crew cut. *si – panjang* women, females. *– pembantu* hairs growing in the ear. *si – péndék* men, males. *si – pirang* the blond. *– potongan péndék* crew cut. *– remang* bristling hair. *– sasak* bouffant hairdo, teased hair. *– terurai* disheveled hair.

serambut very small/fine, as large/fine as a hair. *Tidak ada suatu kejadian yang betul-betul sempurna tanpa ada sebarang cacat walau ~ juga.* Nothing is perfect. *~ dibelah tujuh* a) not even the tiniest bit. b) as rare as hen's teeth.

berambut hairy, with ... hair, hirsute. *seorang gadis manis ~ ikal* a sweet girl with curly hair. *~ lurus* with lank hair. *~ panjang* to wear one's hair long. *~ pérak* gray-haired. *seorang laki-laki ~ putih* a man with gray hair.

merambut 1 fibrous, thready, stringy, hair-like, capillary. **2** to become like hair. **3** to catch in a k.o. net. **kerambutan** capillarity.

perambut the lower end of a fishing rod.

rambutan I fruit with a hairy *usu* reddish integument, *Nephelium lappaceum. ibarat mencari – di musim* like mushrooms after a spring rain, popping up everywhere. *– cilebak* round, meat easily separated from seeds, reddish, sweet and sour taste. *– léngkéng* sweet, dry, reddish, round, not much hair, small. *– melotok* one whose meat separates easily from the skin. *– si macan* oval, sweet, dark red. *– si nyonya* dark red, long hair, round, difficult to separate fruit from seeds, juicy, sweet and sour, cheap. *– rapiah* short hair, small, greenish, very sweet, cheap, tastes like *keléngkéng.*

rambutan II *– laut* sea urchin.

rambuti (*ob*) *kain –* woolly cloth.

ramé I → RAMI I.

ramé II → RAMAI.

Ramelan (*Jv*) → RAMAD(H)AN.

rames → RAMAS II.

rami I 1 a shrub, *Boehmeria nivea*, which yields a fiber used *esp* in making textiles, ramie; → RUMPUT *Tiongkok.* **2** the fiber ramie. *kain –* sack cloth. *tali –* string made from ramie. *– halus* flax.

rami II (*D*) rummy (the card game).

ramil → RAYON *militér.*

ramin I loop work (in basketry).

beramin in loops, looped.

meraminkan to twist into loops, loop.

ramin II *kayu/pohon –* a tree that grows in swampy areas and is used for timber, *Gonystylus bancanus.*

rampai mixed, various. *bunga –* a) bouquet, bunch of flowers, posy. b) potpourri, medley. c) anthology (of stories, poems, etc.).

rampai-rampai mixture, variety; miscellaneous.

merampaikan to mix different k.o. flowers together, make a bouquet out of. *~ kabar* to spread news.

rampaian a collection of various things, miscellany. *~ kalangan* collection of writings, anthology.

rampak I 1 *– rindang* foliage, leafage, leaves. **2** *– rampai* wide-stretching (forest, etc.). **3** in full dress/uniform. *berpakaian –* to be in full dress.

serampak → REMPAK I.

berampak (to grow/spread out) broadly.

merampak to storm, rush, assault.

rampak II (*Jv*) **1** in equal rows/files/lines; in step. **2** to walk together in step, march past in single file or by files, defile; → REMPAK I. **3** all the same.

merampak to do s.t. in a row.

rampak III (*M*) fallen down, collapsed.

merampak to knock down.

rampak IV berampak wearing layers of clothing or lots of jewelry.

rampang I angry, furious.

merampang to get angry, flare up, rage.

perampang hothead.

rampang II *– rempus* uncertain, unpredictable.

rampang-rampang *dengan ~nya* uncertain.

rampang III → SERAMPANG(AN).

rampas seize, snatch.

merampas 1 to seize, snatch (away), grab, take by force, violate (one's rights), confiscate. *Uang saya dirampas.* My money was snatched. *Ia ~ surat itu dari tangan saya.* She grabbed the letter out of my hand. *~ kekuasaan negara* to take over power. *~ kemérdékaan* to deprive s.o. of his/her liberty. *~ nyawa* to take s.o.'s life, murder. **2** to hold up, rob; to steal. *Kopornya dirampas kawanan penjahat.* His suitcase was stolen by a gang of criminals. **3** to monopolize, take over, usurp, expropriate. *Kun-*

jungan Présidén ~ perhatian umum. The president's visit has monopolized public attention.

merampasi (*pl obj*) to assail, assault, rob, plunder, loot.

terampas taken away by force, seized, confiscated.

rampasan loot, plunder, booty. *~ perang* spoils of war.

perampas bandit, robber, looter.

perampasan 1 robbery, plunder, holdup. **2** seizure, confiscation, attachment, forfeiture, appropriation. *~ kebébasan/kemerdékaan* a) false imprisonment. b) deprivation of liberty. *~ kekuasaan negara* coup d'état, power grab. **3** violation (of rights).

rampat generalized. *– papan* equal treatment. **merampat papan** to treat in the same way, generalize. *Kita semua dirampat papan.* We were all treated the same. **merampat-papankan** to generalize, treat in the same way.

merampat to mow/cut/hack down (at one blow). *~ papan* to strike out at everyone. *~ tanaman* to cut down plants.

merampatkan to generalize, treat all cases the same way. *Penulis tidak ingin membahas masalah itu hanya dari satu kasus, yang kemudian dirampatkan.* The author didn't want to discuss the matter from only one case, which was then generalized.

kerampatan generalization.

rampatan 1 general (*mod*). **2** generalized. *dengan sikap ~* in a general way.

perampatan generalization, generalizing.

ramping I slender, slim, thin, narrow (of waist). *Pinggangnya –.* She has a narrow waist. *pinggang – bagai ketiding* (M) jokingly said of a fat woman who has no waistline.

meramping to thin out. *Pohon di kanan kiri jalan itu mulai ~.* The trees on both sides of the road began to thin out.

merampingkan 1 to cut down on, reduce. *~ jumlah pegawai negeri* to reduce the size of the bureaucracy. **2** to downsize.

kerampingan slenderness, thinness, slimness.

peramping *~ badan* corset.

perampingan 1 streamlining, thinning out, reducing, cutting down on. *~ pohon-pohon itu memerlukan dana cukup besar.* Thinning out the trees requires a large amount of money. **2** downsizing.

ramping II 1 disfigured, mutilated. **2** pierced (of ears); → TINDIK.

meramping to be in tatters/rags, be dilapidated/worn/tattered, frayed at the edge.

ramping III (*M*) → DAMPING I, SAMPING I.

rampis (*M*) → RAMPING I.

rampit conglomerate.

rampog (*Jv*) → RAMPOK.

rampok (*M/Jv*) robber, housebreaker, bandit, brigand; → BÉGAL. *– bertangan satu* one-armed bandit, slot-machine; → BANDIT *bertangan satu.*

merampok to rob, plunder, burglarize, stick/hold up.

merampoki (*pl obj*) to steal, rob (several places), burglarize, break into (a house), hold up.

terampok robbed.

rampokan s.t. stolen, loot. *barang-barang ~* loot, stolen goods, booty. *Mobil itu hasil ~.* That's a stolen car.

rampok-rampokan (to play) cops and robbers.

kerampokan to be/get robbed. *Tetangga kami sudah dua kali ~.* Our neighbor's been robbed twice.

perampok robber, bandit, thief, burglar, looter. *~ jalan raya* highway robber.

perampokan robbery, theft, looting. *terlibat dalam ~ sebuah mobil* involved in car theft.

rampuh (*ob*) ready, all settled.

rampuk → RAMPOK.

rampung I (*Jv*) finished, ended, completed, concluded, terminated. *Karya itu – diterjemahkan.* The translation of that work has been completed. *proyék yang diborongkan sampai –* turnkey project.

merampungkan to finish, complete, bring to a successful conclusion. *Meréka ~ bangunan itu.* They put the finishing touches on that building.

terampungkan finished, completed.

kerampungan completion, termination, finish. *Gedung itu mendekati ~nya.* The building is nearing completion.

perampungan 1 completion, completing, finishing, final. **2** (*petro*) flange up.

rampung II → ROMPONG I.

rampus and **ramput** (*ob*) gross, vulgar, indecent, improper, obscene; → KASAR.

berampus to call names.

merampus to call s.o. names, use abusive language to.

ramput meramput to talk through one's hat, talk boastful nonsense.

ramsum → RANSUM.

ramu meramu to gather/collect ingredients that will be needed (for construction/firewood/medicine, etc.). *~ rumah* to look for timber to build a house. *seperti api yang ~* like wildfire.

ramuan 1 materials, ingredients. **2** concoction.

peramu collector. *~ irama* disc jockey.

peramuan concocting.

ramunia a tree with edible fruit, *Bouea macrophylla*; → GANDARIA(H).

ramus 1 (superfluous) hair. **2** hairy, hirsute.

beramus hairy (of face), shaggy.

meramus to become hairy.

ran (in acronyms) → KENDARAAN, RANCANGAN, RANSUM.

rana I long-suffering.

merana 1 to languish, be ailing, waste away, be in a bad state. **2** lingering/chronic (of a disease, etc.). *inflasi/sakit ~* chronic inflation/disease. **3** nervous, worrying. **kemeranaan** languishing, chronicness.

rana II (*Skr cla*) **1** battle. **2** battlefield. **3** bellicose. *seorang raja yang –* a bellicose king. **4** daring.

rana III (*Jv*) **1** folding screen. **2** shutter (of a camera). *bukaan –* diaphragm (of a camera). *waktu bukaan –* exposure time.

rana IV (*ob*) → RATNA I.

rana V (*Skr*) joyful.

ranah (*M*) **1** low-lying plain, lowland; → DATARAN *rendah.* **2** valley; → LEMBAH. **3** marshland. **4** domain, realm, field (of study). *– Minang* the Minangkabau area. *23 makalah – bahasa* 23 papers in the field of language. *– publik* public domain.

ranai (*M*) moist (from tears/perspiration); → RENYAI.

meranai to trickle down (of tears), drizzle (of rain).

ranak (*ob*) **meranak** to give birth; → BERANAK.

ranap I leveled to the ground (of a house, etc.). *lantai –* ground floor.

meranap 1 to raze/level to the ground. **2** (*ob*) to float about level ground (as of an island in the sea, etc.).

ranap II (*M*) quiet; lonely.

ranca (*ob*) **meranca** to consider s.t. easy.

rancah (*M*) **1** swampy soil, bog. **2** marshy; → RENCAH.

merancah to walk through swampy ground.

perancah 1 tracer. **2** scavenger.

perancahan scaffolding.

rancak I (*M*) **1** beautiful, handsome, good-looking. *gadis nan –* a beautiful girl. **2** quick, fast, lively, energetic, cheerful (of songs/music/dance, etc.). *– di labuah/lebuh* a dandy, clotheshorse in public but messy in private; → PESOLÉK.

merancakkan to liven up, enliven.

kerancakan good looks.

kerancak-rancakan conceited (because one is good-looking).

rancak II (*J/Jv*) **merancak** to hack, cut off. *tukang –* and **perancak** s.o. who makes his living by collecting and selling teakwood remnants.

rancak III (*J/Jv*) **serancak** one set of *gamelan* instruments.

rancakan wooden rack for the *bonang* in *gamelan* performances.

rancam (*ob*) **merancam** to mix, concoct.

rancaman various mixtures/blends.

rancang I pointed pole, stake, post.

merancang 1 to stake out, place stakes. **2** protruding.

merancangkan to stake out for s.o. else.

rancang II *– bangun* design; to design, engineer; → RÉKAYASA. *– satelit* design for a satellite. **merancang-bangun** to design. *~ komponén éléktronik* to design electronic components. **perancang-bangun** designer.

berancang with/to have a plan; planned in advance, premeditated; → BERENCANA. *pembunuhan ~* premeditated murder.

merancang to plan, arrange, design; → MERENCANAKAN. ~ *mode* to design fashions.

merancangkan to plan out, make arrangements for.

rancangan 1 plan, program. *masih berada dalam* ~ still in the planning stage. ~ *induk* master plan. ~ *pola* blueprint. **2** draft. ~ *Anggaran Pendapatan dan Belanja Negara* [RAPBN] draft national budget. ~ *Anggaran Pendapatan dan Belanja Daérah* [RAPBD] draft provincial budget. ~ *keputusan présidén* draft of a presidential decision. ~ *ketetapan* [rantap] draft resolution. ~ *peraturan pemerintah* [RPP] draft government regulation. ~ *skétsa* rough draft. ~ *undang-undang* [RUU] bill, draft law (proposed but not yet enacted into law).

perancang planner, drafter. ~ *busana* fashion designer. ~ *gambar* draftsman. ~ *huruf* type designer. ~ *mode* fashion designer. ~ *tata ruang* interior designer. ~ *tékstil* textile designer. ~ *undang-undang* legislator.

perancangan planning, drafting, designing. ~ *kembali* redrafting. ~ *undang-undang* legal drafting.

rancap I (*J*) masturbation (of males).

merancap to masturbate (of males).

perancapan masturbation.

rancap II (*Jv*) sharp, pointed; → RUNCING. *tukang* ~ grinder, sharpener (of knives, etc.).

merancap to sharpen (weapons/knives, etc.).

ranch (*E*) /rénsy/ ranch.

rancu 1 confused (in thought). **2** careless (in language usage/word or sentence form), poorly worded.

merancu 1 to be confused, in confusion. **2** to be careless (in language usage).

merancukan to confuse, misword.

kerancuan 1 confusion. **2** careless use of language, miswording. **3** (*ling*) contamination (of one linguistic form by another).

perancuan miswording, careless use of language.

rancung with a sharp point, pointed, acute; → PANCUNG I.

merancung 1 to sharpen to a point. **2** to cut at an angle. **3** to be pointed.

perancung (pencil) sharpener.

randa I (*Skr Jv*) widow (and regionally also widower); → RANGDA I. ~ *gadis* old maid, spinster. ~ *kembang* young childless widow. ~ *tua* a) old maid, spinster. b) elderly bachelor. **meranda tua** to remain a spinster till one's death.

meranda 1 to live as a widow. **2** to still be unmarried.

randa II → RUNDU-RANDA.

randa III ~ *midang* → KENIKIR.

randah 1 (*ber*)*pindah* ~ to keep moving (of nomads). **2** portable.

randai I merandai to ford/wade across (a river/swamp/grassy plain, etc.), traverse.

randai II (*M*) k.o. round dance performed by a group of dancers who sing and clap hands.

berandai-randai in succession/a row, continuously.

perandaian relating to that dance.

randajawa (*Jv ob*) → JAWAWUT.

randang → RENDANG I.

randa-rondo (*J*) to walk in a stooping position looking from side to side (as if searching for s.t.).

randau berandau mixed (of food). *nasi* ~ *ubi* rice mixed with edible tubers.

merandau to mix food with other foodstuffs to make it tastier or to increase the quantity. ~ *beras dengan jagung* to mix rice with corn.

merandaukan to mix in. ~ *sayur-mayur* to mix in vegetables.

randek (*J*) **merandek** to stop, come to a halt, stand still, halt. *Saya* ~ *jéngkél*. I stood still with irritation.

randemén → RÉNDEMÉN.

randi dotted, speckled. *kain* ~ variegated tie-dyed silk fabric.

randih → RONDAH-RANDIH.

random (*E*) random. *secara* ~ at random.

randomisasi (*E*) randomization.

randori (*Jp*) (in *Kempo* self-defense sport) free fight.

randu I (*J/Jv*) kapok (tree), *Ceiba pentandra, Eriodendron anfractuosum.*

randu II roger (message received and understood, in radio communications).

randuk I meranduk to wade through bushes, swamp, or water.

randuk II 1 with long hair. *kambing* ~ bearded old billy goat. **2** old roué, dirty old man.

randung → SERANDUNG. **merandungkan 1** to strike/bump up against. **2** to trample. **3** to violate, infringe.

rané(h) 1 spreading selaginela, spike moss, a decorative plant. *Selaginella plana/willdenovii.* **2** k.o. fern, club moss, *Lycopodium cernum.*

rang I plan, design, draft, outline; → RANCANGAN, RANGRANGAN.

rang-rangan draft, outline.

rang II (*onom*) sound of a *genderang*; *cp* DERANG I.

rang III (*M*) clipped form of **orang**. ~ *kaya* k.o. Minangkabau *adat* title; → ORANG I.

rang IV (*D*) rank, position; → PANGKAT I, TINGKAT. -*nya apa?* what's his position?

perangan ranking.

rang V (in acronyms) → PENERANGAN, PERANG.

rangah proud, conceited, haughty.

merangah (to be) proud/conceited/haughty.

rangai (*ob*) **merangai 1** to clear weeds from a rice field. **2** to search through.

rangak I gastropod mollusk with an ornamental shell. ~ *betul* (common) spider conch, *Lambis lambis.* k.o. mollusk, ~ *cekang* orang spider conch, *Lambis chiraga.*

rangak II (*M*) loud, noisy, boisterous, tumultuous, uproarious; → RAMAI.

rangam k.o. tomato, *Solanum lycopersicum.*

rangas I (*J/JV*) white ants; → ANAI-ANAI, RAYAP I.

rangas II stripped of its leaves, defoliated, deciduous. *tak* ~ evergreen.

merangas 1 to be deciduous. *hutan* ~ deciduous forest. **2** to become dry and yellow and about to fall off (of leaves). *Daunnya sebagian hijau dan sebagian* ~ *kuning seperti hendak rontok.* The leaves are partially green and partially yellow as if they were about to fall off.

perangas defoliant.

rangda I → RANDA I.

rangda II (*Bal*) character in Balinese dance-play; looks like a witch and represents evil.

rangga I tine of an antler. ~ *gunung* crest/ridge of a mountain.

berangga tined (of antlers), with antlers. *Rusa betina tidak* ~. The female deer has no antlers.

merangga to look like tines/antlers.

rangga II → RUNGGU-RANGGA.

rangga III (*M*) alternating.

berangga-rangga alternating.

perangga alternator.

rangga IV (*Jv*) a title granted by the Netherlands Indies government to Indonesian local leaders, such as *patih, wedana,* etc.

rangga V (*ob*) **merangga** to work too hard.

meranggakan ~ *diri* to exhaust o.s.

ranggah I meranggah to strip a tree of fruit by breaking the branches. ~ *kumis orang* to insult s.o.

ranggah II (*M*) cock's comb; → JÉNGGÉR.

ranggah III → RANGGA I.

ranggak meranggak(kan) (*naut*) to haul (a boat) ashore.

ranggas → RANGAS II.

ranggéh (*J/Jv*) to reach (out) for s.t.; → MENGGAPAI, MENJANGKAU.

ranggi (*Hind/Tam*) handsome, dashing; → GAGAH.

meranggikan to boast, brag.

ranggit hook.

meranggit(kan) to hook on, hang (s.t.). ~ *lampu ke plafon* to hang a lamp on the ceiling.

ranggu k.o. tree which produces good timber, *Koordersiodendron pinnatum.*

ranggul meranggul to pitch up a little (as of a car running over a brick).

ranggung I straddling. (of one's legs/two pieces of wood which form an angle); → RANGKUNG I.

meranggung 1 to bend down while resting on both the hands and legs. **2** to sit on the knees with the legs wide apart and the arms extending supporting o.s. *duduk* ~ to sit with legs straddling s.t.

meranggungkan to reach for s.t. and get hold of it.

ranggung II *batu* – a plummet with branching arms from which catgut and bait are hung. *(pandai) memainkan* – (clever) at looking for an opportunity.

ranggung III *burung* – a nickname for a tame heron, *Ardea spp.*; → RANGKONG.

rangin a long shield used in war dances.

rangka I 1 skeleton, carcass; → KERANGKA. 2 frame(work). *dalam* – in the framework/scope/context of, as part of (the effort to), within the scope of, in order to. *dalam* – *meningkatkan kesempatan kerja* in order to increase employment opportunities. *dalam* – *perjanjian ini* under (the terms of) this agreement. *Saudara di Indonésia dalam* – *apa?* For what purpose are you in Indonesia? What are you doing in Indonesia? 3 draft, sketch, outline, plan; → RANCANGAN, RENCANA. 4 truss. – *bakar* grate. – *bawah* trestle, underframe. – *bogi* bogie. – *cétak* molding box. – *dada* chest, thorax. – *dasar* basic/fundamental structure. – *kaku* rigid frame. – *karangan* outline. – *layangan/layang-layang* kite frame. – *manusia* human skeleton. – *pekerjaan* working plan. – *pesawat* airplane frame. – *rumah* house structure. – *tubuh* skeleton. – *utama* head frame.

berangka with/to have a skeleton. *Binatang bersél satu itu tidak* ~. One-celled animals have no skeleton.

merangka(-rangka) to frame, construct, sketch.

merangkakan to design, plan, arrange, organize; → MERÉKA(-RÉKA). *Dia* ~ *program yang akan diisinya kelak.* He designed a program the details of which he'll fill in later.

rangka II → RENGGA, RENGKA.

rangkah (*M*) → RENGKAH.

rangkai bunch, cluster. – *hati/jiwa* sweetheart. – *jangkar* anchor cable.

serangkai 1 a bunch/cluster. *bunga* – a bunch of flowers. 2 joined, linked, connected. *ditulis* ~ written as a single word (without a space in between). *empat* ~ (during the *Jp* occupation) foursome consisting of Soekarno, Hatta, Ki Hajar Dewantoro, and K.H. Mansoer. *tiga* ~ triumvirate. **menyerangkaikan** to connect, link up, (re)unite, join together (into one).

berangkai(-rangkai) 1 to be attached/connected/linked up/united. 2 one after another, in a series. *cerita yang berangkai-rangkai* story that appears in episodes, serial.

merangkai 1 to arrange (flowers), make bouquets. *Ia sekolah* ~ *bunga.* He took a course in flower arranging. 2 to compose.

merangkaikan 1 to coordinate with. *Tindakan swasta dirangkaikan dengan rencana pemerintah.* Private measures have been coordinated with government plans. 2 to join/hook/connect two things together, dock (a space ship).

rangkaian 1 bouquet. ~ *melati* bouquet of jasmines. 2 combination, arrangement, assembly. ~ *bunga* floral arrangement. ~ *lagu* medley of songs. 3 series, chain, string. ~ *pembunuhan/peristiwa/pertanyaan* a series of murders/events/questions. ~ *hotél* hotel chain. *satu* ~ *peluru mitralyur berisikan 150 butir peluru* a 150-bullet machine gun cartridge belt. ~ *pipa bor* (*petro*) drill stem. ~ *selubung* (*petro*) casing string. ~ *selubung minyak* (*petro*) oil string. 4 composition, set, group. ~ *kalimat* a set of sentences. ~ *perkataan bohong* a tissue of lies. 5 collection, selection, anthology. ~ *tulisan* a collection of articles. 6 (*elec*) circuit. ~ *arus* electric circuit. ~ *akor* chord progression. ~ *peledak* igniter. ~ *terpadu* integrated circuit. **serangkaian** a set, string, number of. ~ *sidang* a number of sessions.

perangkai s.o. who puts things into bunches, connector, coupling. *ahli* ~ *bunga* flower arranger. *kata* ~ (*gram*) preposition. ~ *khusus* sequencer. ~ *rém* brake coupling.

perangkaian 1 connection, chain. 2 (*petro*) stabbing.

rangkak crawl. *si* – nickname for animals which crawl, creepy-crawlies.

merangkak 1 to crawl on hands and knees (like an infant). *Anak kecil itu* ~ *ke arah ibunya.* The small child crawled toward his mother. ~ *naik* to crawl up(ward). 2 to move along slowly, move slowly towards. *Hari mulai* ~ *petang.* It was getting toward evening.

merangkak-rangkak 1 to crawl (along), creep (along); slow, not fluent, stumble (in speaking). *Dalam kelas saya, ada murid*

yang tidak tahu membaca langsung dan ada pula yang ~. In my class there's a student who cannot read a long stretch and there's one who just crawls along. *dengan jalan* ~ creeping along. *Dia* ~ *datang pada bosnya.* He reluctantly went to his boss. 2 to cringe. 3 to stoop so low as to as to.

merangkaki to creep along/over to. *Landrover kami* ~ *jalan curam dan berliku-liku.* Our Landrover crept along the steep and winding road. *Dia* ~ *perempuan itu.* He crept over to the woman.

merangkakkan to have/let s.o. crawl/creep. *Ia* ~ *anaknya di atas balé-balé.* She let her child crawl on the bamboo couch.

rangkakan crawl, creep, way of crawling.

perangkak crawler, creeper.

perangkakan crawling, creeping.

rangkam (*M*) **serangkam** a handful.

merangkam 1 to clutch, (take) hold of s.t. with all of the fingers.

rangkap I (*J*) → RANGKAK.

rangkap II (*M*) forked branch.

rangkap III religious training center for advanced Islamic studies.

rangkap I double, dual. *baju* – lined coat. *kelas* – parallel class. *pajak* – double taxation. *pengontrol* – dual controls. *pintu* – a) folding door. b) two-layer door. *spasi* – double-spaced. *tugas* – double function. – *dua* duplicate, twofold, double. *Surat itu diketik (dalam)* – *dua.* The letter was typed in duplicate. *dibuat dalam* – *dua* drawn up in duplicate. – *jabatan* two positions/functions. – *tiga* in triplicate. – *lima* in quintuplicate.

serangkap a pair, set of two.

berangkap to be doubled, be coupled.

berangkap-rangkap(an) in pairs/couples. *menari* ~ to dance in couples.

merangkap 1 to put one over the other, double up. *Tiga helai kertas dirangkap untuk membungkus kado ini.* Three sheets of paper were put over e.o. to wrap up the present. 2 to also function/serve as, have a double function as, double as; to wear two hats, have two jobs, serve concurrently. *kamar duduk* ~ *kamar makan* a sitting room which also doubles as a dining room. *Wakil Perdana Menteri* ~ *(menjadi) Menteri Pertahanan* Deputy Prime Minister concurrently Minister of Defense. *Rockefeller akan* ~ *dua jabatan.* Rockefeller is to wear two hats. *tidak dapat dirangkap dengan* to be incompatible with (of a position or job).

merangkap-rangkap to take on concurrent (responsibilities, etc.).

merangkapkan 1 to put one thing over another, combine, join together, unite. ~ *baju yang tipis dengan baju tebal* to put a thick coat on over a thin coat. 2 to do concurrently (of jobs). ~ *jabatan bendahara dengan sékrétaris* to do the jobs of treasurer and secretary concurrently.

rangkapan 1 combined, joined. *kalimat* ~ (*gram*) complex sentence. ~ *kedua* duplicate. 2 lining (of a coat, etc.). 3 combining.

perangkap s.o. who has two jobs concurrently.

perangkapan 1 combining, combination, putting together. 2 holding two (jobs) at the same time.

rangkap II merangkap 1 to cover with the palm of the hand. 2 to catch in the palm of the hand, *esp* an insect/bird, etc. so that it doesn't die. 3 to catch with both hands.

perangkap 1 trap, pitfall. *masuk* ~ to walk/fall into the trap, get trapped. *memasang* ~ to set a trap. ~ *tikus* mousetrap. 2 ambush.

rangkas (*ob*) → RANGAS II.

rangkaya (*M*) → ORANG *kaya.*

rangkep → RANGKAP.

rangkét (*J/Jv*) **merangkét** to cane, beat (with a piece of rattan as punishment), thrash. *B dirangkét petugas.* B was beaten by an official.

rangkiang (*M*) → RENGKIANG.

rangkik a shellfish, univalve mollusk with ornamental shell, *Conus spp.* – *belang sawa* k.o. large shellfish, *C. bandanus.* – *rintik* mollusk with spotted shell, *C. capitaneus.*

rangking I lidded basket.

rangking II (*E*) ranking (in sports); → RANKING.

merangking to rank.

rangkit → RANGKÉT.

rangkok (*Jv*) and rangkong (*S*) various species of hornbill. *burung –* and *– badak* rhinoceros hornbill, *Buceros rhinoceros*. – *Buton* red-knobbed hornbill, *Buceros cassidix*. – *dompét* plain-pouched hornbill, *Aceros subruficollis*. – *gading* helmeted hornbill, *Buceros vigil*. – *jambul* hornbill. – *kecil* oriental pied-hornbill, *Anthracoceros albirostris/malabaricus*. – *papan* great hornbill, *Buceros bicornis*. – *Sulawesi* Sulawesi hornbill, *Penelopides exarhatus*. – *Sumba* k.o. hornbill, *Aceros everetti*.

rangkuh → RENGKUH.

rangkul (*J/Jv*) embrace. – *pukul* (slogan of the former Communist Party of Indonesia) embrace and hit.

berangkul(-rangkul)an [= rerangkulan (*Jv*)] 1 to embrace e.o. 2 to act/work together closely. *Meréka berangkul-rangkulan dalam berusaha.* They worked hand in hand in business.

bersirangkulan to embrace e.o.

merangkul 1 to embrace, clasp, hug. *Ia ~ istrinya di depan umum.* He hugged his wife in public. 2 to win s.o. over, gain s.o.'s support; to put one's hand on s.o.'s back. *Petugas béa cukai justru dirangkul, diberi hadiah-hadiah.* The customs officials were actually won over by being given presents. ~ *lawan* (in boxing) to clinch.

merangkulkan to put/twine (one's hands, etc.) around. *Tanganku kurangkulkan pada pinggangnya.* I put my hands around her waist.

terangkul embraced, hugged.

rangkulan embrace, accolade. *Dia lari ke ~ku.* He rushed into my arms.

perangkul embrace. seperangkul an armful, such that it can be surrounded by one's outstretched arms.

perangkulan embracing.

rangkum serangkum an armful. ~ *pakaian kotor* an armful of dirty clothes. menyerangkumkan to collect (by the armfuls).

merangkum 1 to carry in one's arms. *Dirangkumnya setumpuk buku.* He carried a pile of books in his arms. 2 to embrace. *Sebelum pergi ke kantor suami itu ~ istrinya.* Before leaving for the office, the husband embraced his wife. 3 to embrace, adopt, choose and adhere to. *Dia ~ aliran pemerintah.* He adopted government policy. 4 to embrace, comprise, encompass, include. *Kawasannya ~ daérah hutan.* The territory includes a forest area. *Sebagian tulisan-tulisannya dirangkum dalam buku ini.* Some of his writings are included in this book. 5 to seize. *Selama perang orang-orang selalu dirangkum rasa khawatir.* In wartime people are always seized by feelings of anxiety.

merangkumi to embrace, put one's arms around.

merangkumkan 1 to stretch (the arms) out (to embrace). *Dia ~ kedua belah tangannya memeluk kekasihnya.* He stretched out both his arms to embrace his sweetheart. 2 to gather up (in one's arms), collect. 3 to wrap up, make a résumé/summary of s.t., summarize. ~ *hasil rapat* to summarize the results of the meeting.

terangkum 1 collected. 2 summed up, summarized.

rangkuman 1 embrace. 2 grip. 3 summary, résumé. 4 series. 5 scope.

perangkuman pooling. ~ *risiko* risk pooling.

rangkun integration.

merangkun to integrate.

rangkunan integration, integrated.

perangkunan integration.

rangkung I merangkung to squat down, crouch, stoop down.

rangkung II (*M*) rangkungan throat. *nafas sudah di ~* to be dying.

rangkung III bow for a *rebab*.

rangkup hollow (between the two closed hands).

merangkup 1 to form a hollow (with the two hands as in scooping up uncooked rice, etc.). 2 to embrace. 3 to cover (up), hide, conceal. *Malam ~ sekitar lorong belakang.* Night covered the back alley.

merangkupkan to scoop up (with the two hands).

terangkup embraceable. *tak ~* unembraceable.

rangkupan coverage.

rangkus merangkus to gather up, take everything there is.

rangkut (*J*) merangkut to seize s.o. else's property believing it's yours.

ranglis (*D ob*) list of candidates.

rango-rango *pohon –* a tree with a curved trunk, *Voacanga foetida*.

rangrang (*J/Jv*) weaver ant, *Oecophylla smaragdina*; → KERENGGA.

rangrangan idea, plan, project, concept; → RANG I.

rangsang I 1 pungent, sharp, biting (of smells). *Kari yang dimasaknya itu – baunya.* The curry she was cooking had a pungent odor. 2 stimulating, s.t. that arouses strong feelings. *Politikus itu telah menyampaikan pidatonya yang –.* The politician delivered his stimulating speech. 3 stimulant, drink, etc. that unleashes bodily or mental activity. *Obat itu adalah suatu – yang biasa digunakan oléh dokter.* That medicine is a stimulant *usu* employed by physicians. *kena –* stimulated, excited.

berangsang to be angry/annoyed.

merangsang 1 to stimulate, encourage, arouse; → MENGGALAKKAN. *Bagaimana éskpor bisa dirangsang?* How can exports be encouraged? ~ *seléra* to tickle the palate, make one's mouth water. 2 to excite, turn on. 3 sexually stimulating, arousing, erotic, sexy. *adegan yang ~* an erotic scene (in a film). *dengan pakaian yang ~* wearing sexy clothes.

merangsangi to stimulate/excite s.o.

merangsangkan to stimulate, excite.

terangsang [and kerangsang (*coq*)] stimulated, excited, animated, incited. *Ia tidak ~ oléh goyang pinggulnya.* He wasn't excited by her swaying hips.

rangsangan 1 stimulus, incentive, stimulation, impulse. ~ *asmara/ séks* sex drive. ~ *invéstasi* investment incentive. ~ *membeli* impulse buying. ~ *méntal* mental stimulation. ~ *pendahuluan* prestimulation. 2 stimulating effect. ~ *minuman keras itu cepat sekali.* The stimulating effect of the alcoholic drink was very rapid.

kerangsangan stimulant.

perangsang 1 stimulant, stimulus, excitement. *naik ~nya* he became angry/furious. *obat ~* stimulant, aphrodisiac. *penggunaan obat ~* doping, using stimulants. 2 incentive, boost. *Dalam pertemuan itu Menteri Murata tidak menyinggung soal pemberian ~ oléh pihak Indonésia untuk penjualan minyaknya kepada Jepang.* At the meeting Minister Murata did not touch on the granting of incentives by Indonesia for the sale of its oil to Japan. ~ *rasa* taste potentiator. 3 rage, fury, anger. *membangkitkan ~* to annoy, irritate, anger.

perangsangan 1 stimulation, excitement. ~ *birahi* sexual excitement. ~ *sumur* (*petro*) well stimulation. 2 irritation. ~ *kulit* skin irritation. 3 activation.

rangsang II (*J*) merangsang 1 to oppose. *Anak itu walaupun masih kecil berani ~ saya.* Though still small that child is brave enough to oppose me. 2 to attack, storm (a fort).

perangsang attacker. *pasukan ~* shock troops.

rangsang III 1 dry, fallen branches. 2 girdle of thorns put around tree trunks to prevent thefts.

rangsek (*J*) *main bola –* a) to play volleyball. b) to push forward at any price.

merangsek to push forward/ahead. ~ *maju* to thrust forward. ~ *masuk* to force one's way into.

rangsekan assault, thrust.

rangsel → RANSEL.

rangsuk (*J*) → RASUK I.

rangsum → RANSUM.

rangu *cendawan –* an edible mushroom species, *Schizophyllum alneum*.

rangum (*ob*) merangum to snatch away.

rangup crisp (as dry leaves/biscuits/grain), brittle, easily breakable.

rani I (*Hind cla*) 1 queen; *cp* MAHARANI. 2 king's consort.

rani II (*A*) tone (of music), melody.

rani III → GANI.

rani IV (*ob*) clipped form of berani.

ranjah (*J*) meranjah to rob, plunder, pillage, loot.

peranjah robber, looter, plunderer.

ranjam (*Jv*) → RAJAM.

ranjang 1 (iron) bed(stead); → TEMPAT *tidur*. *Ia tergolék di –.* He was sprawled on the bed. *adegan –* sex scene (in a bed/film). 2 berth, bunk. – *bayi* baby's crib. – *dorong* gurney (in a hospital).

– *kéro* steel-pipe bed with springs. – *lipat* folding bed/cot. – *pengantin/perkawinan* marriage/nuptial bed. – *pér* steel-pipe bed with springs. – *sakit* hospital bed. – *susun* bunk bed.

seranjang one/the same bed. (*tidur*) ~ to sleep in the same bed. *Angan-angan untuk* ~ *dengan gundiknya yang di Cibinong buyar.* His hopes of sleeping in the same bed as his mistress, who is in Cibinong, went up in smoke. ~ *dan sebantal dengan* in bed with.

beranjang with/to have a bed. *Aku dibawa ke dalam sebuah kamar* ~ *dua.* I was taken into a room with two beds.

ranjau 1 caltrop of iron/bamboo (set up on a path/in a pit, etc. to trap enemies), trap. 2 (land or sea) mine, depth charge. 3 deceit, trickery. *kena* – to get tricked. *duduk meraut* –, *tegak meninjau jarak* and *duduk meraut* –, *berdiri melihat musuh* to be continually on one's guard. – *apung* floating mine. – *berduri* spiked mine. – *bicara* act restricting s.o.'s freedom of speech in public. – *cacak* a mine laid erect. – *darat* land mine. – *dasar* seabed mine. – *hanyut* floating mine. – *jangkar* anchor mine. – *jebatan* booby trap. – *kerang* auster mine. – *kontak* contact mine. – *lapuk* intrigues. – *laut* sea mine. – *melayang* drifting mine. – *pérs* act restricting freedom of the press. – *sentuh* contact mine. – *tajam* activated mine. – *tekan* pressure mine. – *yang terikat dengan dasar laut* anchored mine.

beranjau mined.

keranjauan mining (*mod*).

peranjauan mining. *Sénat Amérika menolak* ~ *di perairan Nikaragua.* The U.S. Senate has rejected the mining of Nicaraguan waters.

ranjing keranjingan 1 possessed (by evil spirits), haunted. 2 addicted to, -manic, passionately fond of, mad/crazy about. ~ *main judi* addicted to gambling. ~ *menonton sépakbola* addicted to watching soccer games.

ranjo → RANJAU.

ranju (*Jv*) → RANJAU.

ranjul bumpy (of a road).

ranjungan k.o. shellfish.

ranking (*E*) /réngking/ ranking. *menurut* – (in sports) seeded.

   meranking to rank.

   perankingan ranking.

ranmor → KENDARAAN *bermotor.*

Ranperda [Rancangan Peraturan Daérah] Draft of a Provincial Regulation.

ranpur (*acr*) [kendaraan tempur] armor.

ransel (*D*) knapsack. – *para* paratrooper's field bag. – *punggung* backpack.

   beransel to carry a backpack.

ransum (*D*) 1 ration, allowance; → BAGI II, CATU. *tukang* – food distributor. 2 starter (in animal husbandry). – *anak* creep feeding (in raising animals).

   meransum to ration, put on rations.

   ransuman ration, allowance.

rantah → RUNTUH *rantah.*

rantai 1 a) chain. *memakai roda* – tracked. b) chain, i.e., a number of shops, hotels, etc. owned by the same company. – *réstoran* restaurant chain. 2 necklace. – *emas* gold chain worn as a necklace. 3 bond, tie. *memutuskan* – *pertunangan* to break off an engagement. 4 fetters, handcuffs, manacles, shackles (of wood or iron). 5 chain, a connected series/sequence. *baju* – coat of mail, hauberk. *mata* – link (of a chain). *mata* – *yang hilang* missing link. *orang* – convict. *surat* – chain letter. 6 → RANTÉ. – *babi* k.o. magical substance which, it is said, can make its owner invulnerable to bullets in a war; it is allegedly found in the tusks of wild boars which live alone. – *besi* iron chain. – *dingin* cold chain. – *distribusi* distribution chain. – *éngsél* sprocket chain. – *hukuman* chains (worn by a prisoner). – *kangkang* shackles. – *komando* chain of command. – *makanan* food chain. – *pembatas* barrier. – *pemutar* (*petro*) spinning chain. – *pengait* (*petro*) bridle chain. – *pengejut* tickler chain (attached to a trammel net used for catching shrimp). – *penggerak* drive chain. – *perkawinan* the bonds of marriage. – *rak* truss pendant. – *sepéda* bicycle chain. – *tangan* bangle, bracelet.

   berantai 1 with a chain, chained, in chains. *arloji* ~ watch with a

chain. *surat* ~ chain letter. 2 in sequence, successive, chain. *serangan* ~ successive attacks. *dampak* ~ multiplier effect. 3 (*sports*) in relays; → LARI *beranting.*

berantai-rantai connected to e.o., in a chain.

merantai(kan) 1 to chain, put in chains. *Pencuri itu dirantai(kan).* The thief was put in chains. 2 to sequence, put into a sequence.

   terantai (en)chained, in chains. *Asal ada sama di hati, gajah* ~ *boléh dilepaskan.* Where there's an agreement, all obstacles can be overcome.

   rantaian series, sequence.

   perantaian 1 convict. 2 chaining (a prisoner).

rantak → RENTAK I, BERANTAKAN.

rantam berantam to do s.t. collectively/in a group; → HANTAM.

rantang I 1 basket (with a lid/cover/cap, for food). 2 stackable picnic pack, multiple-unit container with a top handle for transporting food. 3 meal delivered in such a container from a restaurant or from home.

   merantang 1 to order one's food from a restaurant/caterer which specializes in preparing food for others. 2 to deliver food in a *rantang.*

   rantangan ordered meal, meal delivered in a *rantang. Selama kami tidak mempunyai koki, kami ambil* ~ *dari Ibu S.* While we don't have a cook, we'll order our meals in from Mrs. S. *mengusahakan makanan* ~ to run a catering business which delivers food in *rantang*s.

rantang II → RENTANG I.

rantang III – *manggut* (*Jv*) puppet derived from Chinese culture used to conjure up the spirits of the dead, k.o. ouiji board.

rantap [rancangan ketetapan] draft resolution (of the government or the authorities).

   merantapkan to turn s.t. into a draft resolution, make a draft resolution on s.t.

rantas (*Jv*) 1 broken off; → RAWÉ-RAWÉ *rantas, malang-malang putung.* 2 cut down, cleared (of bushes and shrubs). 3 frayed, threadbare, worn-out. *Bajunya* – *karena tua.* His shirt is frayed from age. 4 (*geol*) suture.

   merantas 1 to break off. 2 to cut down, clear bushes and shrubs. *Rumput dirantas dengan tajak.* The grass was cut down with a hoe.

   merantaskan to break off.

rantau 1 the part of a beach along a bay or river. *berkelana sepanjang* – to roam alongside a river. *anak* – a) s.o. who lives at the coast/seashore. b) trader. c) foreigner. *ceruk* – every nook and cranny. *teluk* –, *teluk dan* –, and *daérah* – a) area, territory. b) dependency. c) bights and reaches. 2 the areas not belonging to the Minangkabau or Achehnese homelands, abroad. *di* – (*orang*) (to live) abroad, in foreign parts, in a foreign country (*esp* outside the Minangkabau homeland). *sampai di segala pojok* – to the ends of the earth. 3 colony, settlement; → JAJAHAN. 4 (*Mal*) region. – *jauh tidak terulangi,* – *dekat tidak terkendanai* wealth, whether near or far, should be kept safe. – *jajahan* a) area, territory. b) dependency. c) bights and reaches.

serantau 1 of the same region/part of the country. *teman* ~ fellow countryman. *Segan bergalah hanyut* ~. If you don't try, you'll face a disaster. 2 (*Mal*) regional.

merantau 1 to go along the coast (to earn one's living). 2 to travel toward the coast, sail along the reaches of a river. 3 to emigrate, out-migrate (*esp* away from the Minangkabau homeland). ~ *cino* (*M*) to emigrate for once and for all. ~ *ke sudut dapur* and ~ *ke ujung bendul* to seek one's fortune not far away. ~ *pipit* (*M*) to emigrate seasonally.

perantau 1 wanderer, vagabond, tramp. 2 s.o. who lives outside his country or home region, emigrant. *Anak* ~ *selalu merindukan tanah kelahirannya.* Emigrants always miss their native land.

perantauan 1 journey, travel; emigration, out-migration (*esp* away from the Minangkabau homeland). *Moga-moga kau akan selamat dalam* ~*mu.* Have a safe trip. 2 settlement (abroad). 3 sojourn outside of one's home region, time spent abroad. *Cina* ~ overseas Chinese. *di* ~ (to live) abroad/in foreign parts. *orang* ~ a) wanderer, vagabond, tramp. b) s.o. who lives outside his country or home region, foreigner.

ranté I (in Tapanuli Utara) a unit of land measure which varies in size from place to place.

ranté II → RANTAI.

ranti black nightshade, k.o. herb with fruit like tiny tomatoes, *Solanum nigrum*.

ranting I 1 twig, small branch. **2** branch (of an office, etc.); subsection. **3** bronchiole. *di mana – dipatah, di situ air disauk* when in Rome, do as the Romans.

  beranting 1 with/to have twigs. *Pohon itu ~ kecil-kecil*. That tree has very small twigs. **2** (by) relay. *lari/perlombaan ~* relay race. *secara ~* by relay, relayed. *Surat itu disampaikan secara ~.* The letter was relayed. **3** to involve others. *Skandal ini ~.* The scandal involved others.

  meranting 1 to have the form of a twig, twig-like, dendritic. *Badan pecandu dadah itu kurus ~.* The drug addict was as thin as a rail. *Dalam musim kemarau, pokok-pokok getah mulai ~.* In the dry season rubber trees begin to lose their leaves. **2** to prune, trim (the twigs off). *~ gawé (Pal ob)* to try to seduce a girl. **3** (*ob*) to shed leaves.

ranting II → RONTANG-RANTING.

rantis → KENDARAAN *perintis*.

ranto → RANTAU.

rantuk (*ob*) **merantuk(kan) 1** to transgress/violate (the law/regulations, etc.). **2** to collide with, come in contact with; → ANTUK.

rantus I (*ob*) completely severed; → RANTAS. *harapan tak putus sampai jerat tersentak –* hope is not lost until the last moment, hope springs eternal in the human breast.

rantus II (*M*) infected, contaminated.

rantus III [rancangan keputusan] draft decision (of the government/authorities, etc.).

ranum [and **ranun** (*infr*)] **1** overripe (of fruit). *Pisang itu sudah –.* The bananas are overripe. **2** plump, fleshy, full (of lips/breasts, etc.). *bibir yang –* full lips. *payudara yang –* full breasts.

  meranum to become overripe.

ranyah I meranyah 1 to pick the best pieces of food out of a dish. **2** greedy, covetous, grasping.

ranyah II (*M*) difficult, restless, fidgety (of a child).

  meranyah to be difficult/restless.

ranyang (*M*) **1** lively, animated, restless, active. **2** capricious, whimsical.

  meranyang 1 to be lively, etc. **2** to be capricious, etc. **3** to eat before others do.

ranyau to rave (in a nightmare/delirium).

ranyuk (*M*) → RENYUK II.

ranyun meranyun to rave (in a nightmare/delirium).

raon → RAWON.

rap I (*onom*) sound of wood rubbing over wood, sound of footsteps; *cp* DERAP.

rap II (*E*) /rép/ rap (music). *konsér –* rap concert.

rapa *biji –* rapeseed.

rapah merapah 1 to trample on (plants, etc.). **2** (*ob*) to roam, wander around, cruise around. *Beberapa bulan lamanya sudah ia ~.* He has been wandering around for several months. **3** (*ob*) to clear away weeds.

rapai I (*ob*) **merapai** to hold up the hand to grasp s.t.; → MENGG(ER)APAI.

rapai II k.o. tambourine covered with goatskin.

rapak I (*A*) (*– lumuh*) request for divorce (by a woman because of abandonment by her husband).

rapak II (*M*) **berapak** and **merapak** visible, publicly; collectively.

rapal (*Jv*) **1** saying, aphorism, maxim. **2** incantation, spell, charm, magic formula; → LAFAL.

  mengerapal [and **ngerapal** (*coq*)] to read/speak a magic formula.

  merapali to read a magic formula over, cast a spell on.

  rapalan magic formula, incantation.

rapang *ikan –* gray mullet, *Mungil planiceps/bleekeri*; → BELANAK *rapang*.

rapa-répé (*J*) to grope around in the dark. *Tangannya sekarang sudah berani – ke kanan ke kiri.* Now he had the nerve to grope around from right to left.

rapat I 1 very near, close (to). *Kapal dapat berlabuh – pada pangkalan.* The ship was able to anchor close to the quay. **2**

thick, tight, close, dense, not loose/far apart, heavy. *daérah yang – penduduknya* a heavily populated area. *Tikar itu dibuat daripada daun kelapa yang dianyam –.* The mat was made from tightly plaited coconut leaves. **3** closed tight(ly), fast. *Tikus dapat memasuki lemari itu karena tidak ditutup dengan –.* Mice could enter the cupboard because it wasn't closed tightly. **4** closely related, intimate, familiar. *Perhubungan antara Malaysia dengan Indonésia sangat –.* Relations between Malaysia and Indonesia are very close. **5** closely/strictly (guarded). *Pelabuhan dijaga –.* The harbor was closely guarded. **6** density; → KERAPATAN. **7** -tight, -proof; → KEDAP. *– angin* windproof. *– daya* (*geol*) energy density. *– erat* close and tight. **merapat-eratkan** to make closer, close up. *– minyak* oil-tight. *– massa* (*phys*) density. *– permusyawaratan* deliberative meeting. *– uap* vapor density. *– udara* air-tight.

rapat-rapat tightly. *menutup pintu ~* to close a door tightly.

merapat 1 close/next to. *Ia duduk ~ ayahnya.* He sat down next to his father. **2** to draw close to, close in on. *Pihak polisi mulai ~ tempat persembunyian garong itu.* The police began to close in on the robbers' hideout. **3** to get close to e.o., settle differences. *Keluarga yang berselisih itu mulai ~.* The family which was not on speaking terms began to settle their differences. **4** to moor, dock. *Perlahan-lahan motorbot itu pun ~lah.* Slowly the motorboat docked. *~ sambil belayar* to kill two birds with one stone.

merapati 1 to approach, come/draw nearer to. *Ia ~ rumah itu.* He approached the house. **2** to become intimate with, get close to (s.o.). *Tiada orang yang berhasil ~nya.* Nobody was able to get close to him.

merapatkan 1 to pull/draw up. *~ kursi ke méja* to pull/draw a chair up to the table. **2** to draw tighter, tighten. *~ barisan* to close ranks. **3** to strengthen (relations/friendship, etc.). *~ barisan* to close ranks. *~ diri dengan/kepada* a) to sit next to s.o. b) to make/political, etc. overtures toward, seek closer relations with. *~ tali silaturahim* to strengthen the bonds of friendship. *~ telinga ke* to put one's ear up close to (a wall, etc.).

memperapat 1 to close tighter, tighten, move s.t. closer. *~ sila* to cross one's legs tighter, sit more neatly.

rapatan 1 s.t. that causes closeness/nearness. **2** s.t. made closer.

kerapatan density. *~ lindak* bulk density. *~ penduduk* demographic density.

perapat 1 densifier. **2** seal. *~ bocoran (petro)* oil saver.

rapat II meeting, session, gathering, assembly. *– akbar* mass meeting. *– anggota* membership meeting. *– darurat* emergency meeting. *– désa* rural meeting. *– gabungan* joint meeting. *– gelap* illegal meeting. *– Kerja* [Raker] Working Meeting. *– Kerja Daérah* [Rakerda] Regional Working Meeting. *– Kerja dan Koordinasi Nasional* [Rakerkornas] National Working and Coordinating Meeting. *– Kerja Logistik* [Rakerlog] Logistical Working Meeting. *– Kerja Nasional* [Rakernas] National Working Meeting. *– Kerja Panglima* Commanders Call. *– Kerja Paripurna* [Rakerna] Plenary Working Meeting. *– Kerja Téknis* [Rakernis] Technical Working Meeting. *– Kerja Terbatas* [Rakertas] Limited Working Meeting. *– kilat* emergency meeting. *– Komando* Commanders Call. *– Koordinasi* [Rakor] Coordinating Meeting. *– Koordinasi Pembangunan* [Rakorbang] Development Coordinating Meeting. *– lengkap* plenary meeting. *– paripurna* plenary meeting. *– permusyawaratan* deliberative meeting. *– Pimpinan* [Rapim] Leadership Meeting (of chiefs of staff, Kodam commanders, representatives of the Armed Forces under Hankam, in corporations and ministries). *– raksasa* mass meeting. *– rutin* routine meeting. *– samudera* mass meeting. *– terbatas* closed-door meeting. *– terbuka* public/open meeting. *– tertutup* closed session. *– Umum Anggota* General Membership Meeting. *– Umum (Luarbiasa) (Para) Pemegang Saham/Andil* [RUPS] (Extraordinary) General Shareholders' Meeting. *– Umum Tahunan Para Ahli Peserta* and *– Umum Tahunan Para Pemegang Saham/Andil* Annual General Shareholders' Meeting. *– vérifikasi* (first) creditors' meeting.

berapat 1 to hold/have a meeting. **2** to meet, assemble, attend a meeting.

merapatkan to hold/have a meeting about.

kerapatan meeting. ~ *besar* congress, conference. ~ *nagari* (M) meeting of the elders and leaders of the village; → REMBUG *désa*.

rapat III *kayu* – a climbing plant with medicinal bark, *Parameria barbata/bata*.

RAPBD (*init*) → RANCANGAN *Anggaran Pendapatan dan Belanja Daérah*.

RAPBN (*init*) → RANCANGAN *Anggaran Pendapatan dan Belanja Negara*.

rapél (D) 1 retainer. 2 (*uang* –) arrears, back pay, outstanding debts. – *gaji* back pay.

rapélan (~ *gaji*) back pay.

rapet → RAPAT I.

rapi (J/Jv) 1 clean, neat, well-cared-for, well-groomed, tidy. *Kita harus berpakaian – bila ke kantor.* We have to dress neatly when we go to the office. *Kamarnya –.* His room is tidy. 2 well taken care of, done well. *Semua kerja diselenggarakan dengan – dan memuaskan.* All the work was done well and satisfactorily. 3 strict, well-guarded. *Rumah Présidén RI dikawal – siang dan malam.* The residence of the president of Indonesia is well-guarded day and night. 4 well-kept/maintained, sturdy, strong. *perpaduan yang teguh dan –* a firm and well-kept integration. 5 accurate, precise, punctilious. *Suatu penyelidikan yang – harus dijalankan.* A precise investigation has to be carried out. *Perkumpulan itu tidak – keuangannya.* The financial situation of that organization was a mess. – *jali* (J) it's all settled/cut and dried, in perfect order, neat. *Tidak berarti keadaan sudah – jali.* It doesn't mean that it's all settled. – *ramping* all neat and slender.

merapikan [and **ng(e)rapiin** (J *coq*)] to tidy up, straighten out, put in order, make (a bed). ~ *diri* to straighten one's clothes, neaten o.s. up.

kerapian neatness, orderliness, tidiness, neat appearance.

perapi 1 s.o. who straightens up or puts s.t. in order. ~ *rambut* hairdresser. 2 s.t. which puts s.t. else in order. ~ *rambut* hair cream.

rapiah → RAMBUTAN *rapiah*.

rapih I → RAPI.

rapih II → REPIH.

rapik I nonsense, claptrap.

merapik to talk nonsense/through one's hat.

rapik II → ROPAK *rapik*.

Rapim → RAPAT *pimpinan*.

rapkol (D) kohlrabi, *Brassica napus*.

rapor (D) 1 school report, report card. – *hitam* a good report card. – *mérah* a bad report card. 2 official report; → LAPOR.

meraporkan to report on/about.

raporan report.

rapsodi (D) rhapsody.

rapu (*ob*) **merapu** to pick up (discarded or useless items); to ask for alms.

rapuh 1 fragile, brittle, crunchy; crumbles/breaks easily, fluid (of a situation). *Ranting kayu itu sangat – dan mudah dipatahkan.* The branches of that tree are very brittle and break easily. 2 delicate, weak, tender (of the heart). 3 subtle. 4 frail, weak. *nyawanya –* a) he is frail. b) he's near death. *penyakit – daun karét* South American leaf blight. 5 sensitive. – *hati* a) thin-skinned, easily offended. b) tender-hearted. c) easily discouraged/disappointed. – *imannya* wavering in faith. – *mulut* unable to keep a secret, blabber-mouth.

merapuh 1 to become brittle/fragile. 2 to crumble.

merapuhkan to weaken, soften, make weaker.

kerapuhan fragility, brittleness. ~ *tulang* osteoporosis.

perapuh *ilmu* ~ magic to paralyze the enemy or to make enemy weapons brittle.

perapuhan making brittle. ~ *tulang* osteoporosis.

rapun I (M) 1 broken, cracked; destroyed; → HANCUR, REMUK. 2 collapsed.

merapun to collapse.

merapun(kan) to smash, crush; to destroy.

rapun II puckered hem.

berapun to have/use a puckered hem.

rapung → APUNG. **merapung** to float on the water.

merapungkan to make s.t. float, keep s.t. afloat/above water.

rapus merapus to tie the legs of an animal before slaughtering it.

Raqib (A) 1 the name of an angel who records all the good actions of human beings. 2 one of God's names (= the vigilant).

rarai (M) separate; → LARAI, LERAI.

merarai to separate.

perarai arbiter.

rarak → RERAK.

raras to fall (of leaves, etc.).

merarasi to shed (leaves, etc.).

raron (J) → LARON.

ras I (*onom*) sound made by dry leaves when swept, rustling sound.

ras II (D) 1 race, ethnic origin. *diskriminasi –* racial discrimination. 2 thoroughbred, pedigreed. *anjing –* pedigreed dog. *bukan –* [*buras*] nonpedigreed, mongrel. *ayam buras* barnyard chicken; → TRAH. – *kuning* the yellow race.

ras III (*Hind*) reins.

ras IV (A) headland.

rasa I (*Skr*) 1 taste, sense. *mati –* apathetic, insensitive, unfeeling. *tanpa –* a) insensitive (to feelings), apathetic. b) tasteless. *tidak ada –nya* tasteless, bland. 2 (physical) feeling. –*nya sakit* it hurts. 3 (emotional) feeling/experience, inner meaning. *gerak dan –* presentiment. –*nya kok senang kalau bepergian membawa uang.* It feels good to travel when you take some money with you. *tidak menimbang/bertimbang –* heartless, unfeeling. *dapat/tahu menimbang –* a) sensitive, delicate. b) helpful, ready to help. *timbang –* a) flexible, supple, elastic; flexibility, suppleness, elasticity. b) (*Mal*) sympathy; sympathetic. *tiada mengenal – tenggang-menenggang* inexorable, relentless, unyielding. 4 opinion, notion, idea, view. *saya –* and –*nya* I think, in my opinion, to my mind. 5 to think, feel. *sama – sama rata* what's sauce for the goose is sauce for the gander. – *akal* intellectual sense. – *asin* salty taste. – *benci* hatred, resentment. – *berita* nose for news. – *budaya* cultural sense. – *demam* feverish. – *énak* pleasant feeling, ease, comfort. – *gelisah* (feelings of) unrest. – *gondok* (feelings of) discontent. *menimbulkan – gondok* makes one feel discontented/unhappy. – *harga diri* (sense of) self-esteem/self-respect. – *hati* state/frame of mind, mood, disposition. – *hormat* (feeling of) respect, sense of honor. – *ikut berperan serta* sense of participation. – *ikut memiliki* sense of belonging. – *ingin tahu* a) (feeling of) curiosity. b) need to know. – *kasihan* (feelings of) commiseration. – *kebersamaan dalam manfaat* (sense of) mutual benefit. – *kehormatan* (feeling of) respect, sense of honor. – *keindahan* sense of beauty, esthetic sense, good taste. – *kekhawatiran dan waswas* (feelings of) fear and anxiety. – *kesatuan bangsa* sense of national unity. – *kesusilaan* ethical sense. – *ketakutan* (feeling of) fear, anxiety. – *keterikatan* (feeling of) being committed. – *kurang (harga diri)* feelings of inferiority. – *lega* sense of relief. – *malu* (feeling of) embarrassment, sense of shame. – *manis* sweetness, sweet taste. – *marah* anger. – *masa bodoh* indifference, apathy. – *menyendiri* (feelings of) alienation. – *ngantuk* drowsiness, sleepiness. – *nikmat* pleasant sensations, (feelings of) pleasure. – *nyaman* feeling good/healthy, comfortable. – *nyeri* ache. – *pahit* bitterness, bitter taste. – *panas* heat sensation. – *pedih* biting/caustic taste. – *pirasa* feelings. – *rendah diri* inferiority complex, feelings of inferiority. – *rendah hati* sense of humility. – *risi* a feeling of irritation. – *sakit waktu haid* menstrual cramps. – *salah* feelings of guilt. – *saling menghormati* (feelings of) mutual respect. – *senang* pleasantness, snugness, comfort. – *senasib-sepenanggungan* sense of belonging. – *séntimén* sentimental feelings. – *suci* sanctity, pureness. – *sukur* (sense of) gratitude, thankfulness. – *susila* ethical sense. – *tak suka* distaste. – *takut* (feelings of) anxiety, fear, -phobia. – *takut terhadap kusta* leprophobia. – *tanggung-jawab* sense of responsibility. – *tawar* neutral feeling. – *teraniaya* (feelings of) peevishness, querulousness. – *terima kasih* gratitude, thankfulness.

rasanya, **rasa-rasa(nya)**, **serasa**, **(se)rasa-rasa**, **rasakan** it seems that, most likely; it feels as if, it feels/looks like, it's as if/though. *Rasanya hari ini ia tidak dapat datang.* It seems that he can't come today. *Rasa-rasanya akan berhasil juga usaha kita ini.* It looks like our efforts will be successful. *Rasa-rasa hendak ditinggalkannya pekerjaannya yang berat itu.* It looks like he wants to quit his difficult job. *Rasakan pecah anak telinga.* It looks like the eardrum is broken. *serasa bayang(-bayang)* unconscious, insensible.

berasa 1 to have the feeling, feel (pain/sick/happy, etc.). *Saya ~ lelah/sakit.* I feel tired/sick. *Punggungnya ~ pegal.* His back is stiff. *Mana yang ~ sakit?* Where does it hurt? 2 to taste. *Karena bercampur dengan kinine tentu saja ~ pahit.* Of course it has a bitter taste; it was mixed with quinine. 3 (*M*) to feel like, seem to be. *Rumahku ini tidak ~ rumahku lagi.* This house doesn't feel like my house any more.

merasa 1 to feel, experience a stimulus through one of the sense organs, parts of the body or the mind, have a feeling (that). *Setelah ia ~ pahit, obat itu diludahkannya.* After he tasted the bitter taste, he spat out the medicine. *~ dirinya kurang* to have an inferiority complex. *~ lega* to feel relieved, breathe easy again. *~ ria-derita* to feel schadenfreude/pleasure at s.o. else's misfortune. 2 to weigh/lie heavy on one's heart. *~ hati* a) to take s.t. to heart. b) to feel hurt/offended. c) to feel s.t. amiss, resent. *~ bersalah* a) to feel guilty. b) to feel bad (that s.t. happened). *~ perlu* to feel the need (for s.t.), feel obligated to. *yang dirasanya dalam hati* what weighs heavily on him, what depresses him. *tidak ~ apa-apa* (*I*) feel no emotions.

merasai 1 to taste, savor. *Rasai dulu masakanmu sebelum dihidangkan.* Taste your cooking first before you serve it. 2 to experience. *Belum pernah ia ~ hidup senang seperti orang-orang lain.* He has never had a pleasant life as others have. 3 to feel around with hands or feet to find out s.t. *Rasa-rasai dengan kakimu dalam atau tidak sungai itu.* Feel around with your feet to see whether the river is deep or not. 4 (*M*) to figure out, ferret/sound out. *Dari air mukanya kita dapat ~ apa yang terkandung dalam hatinya.* From his facial expression we could figure out what was in his heart.

merasa-rasai to feel with hands or feet to find out s.t.

merasakan 1 to experience, go through, encounter, have/get a taste of; to suffer, endure. *Rakyat belum ~ nikmat kemerdékaan secara merata.* The people have not yet experienced the pleasures of freedom in an even-handed way. *Ia dapat ~ penderitaan yang menimpa keluarganya.* He was able to endure the sufferings that hit his family. 2 to feel, realize, be aware of. *Rupanya ia tidak mau ~ pahit getir yang diderita istri dan anaknya itu.* It seems that he doesn't want to be aware of his family's sufferings. *~ akibat* to face the consequences.

ngrasain (*J*) to feel s.t. *Rasain lu!* Serves you right!

memperasakan to experience, encounter; to suffer, endure.

terasa [and **kerasa** (*coq*)] 1 to feel (of s.t. inanimate or a part of the body) *~ dingin* it feels cold. *Kaki saya ~ pegal.* My foot feels stiff. *Sengatan terik mentari dalam perjalanan pulang sekolah tadi membuat badan Andi ~ penat.* The heat of the sun on the trip home from school made Andi's body feel tired. 2 to be felt/noticed/experienced, one feels that. *Setelah berkeliling-keliling melihat Ngarai Sianok, kebun binatang, dan muséum, tak ~ waktu sudah menunjukkan pukul 16.00.* After going around to see Ngarai Sianok, the zoo, and the museum, it wasn't noticed that it was already 4 in the afternoon.

terasakan felt, sensed, noticeable. *Alat angkut KA milik negara, mungkin salah satu angkutan termurah, ~ sekali peranan besarnya.* The role of the state-owned train, perhaps one of the cheapest means of transportation, is very noticeable.

kerasaan 1 to have a feeling, able to feel. 2 → K(E)RASAN.

perasa 1 (*alat ~*) feeler, palp, tentacle; sensor. 2 sense of feeling/ touch. *~ lidah* sense of taste. *~ kulit* sense of touch. 3 easily susceptible, overly sensitive/sentimental. *Jiwanya terlalu ~.* He's too sentimental. *~ angin* easily hurt/offended, touchy. *~ aral* not too happy. 4 flavoring, s.t. added to food to season/ flavor it.

perasaan 1 feeling, sensation, sense, impression, perception. *~ bersalah* guilty feeling. *sangat tajam ~nya* his perception is very acute. *bangsa yang lembut ~nya* a gentle nation. *Ada ~ iba menyelinap di hati Syarief.* A feeling of sadness overcame Syarief. *tanpa ~* apathetic. 2 sentiment. *Itu hanya berdasarkan*

~ belaka, bukan berdasarkan pikiran. That's only based on sentiment, not on judgment. 3 view, opinion. *Dapatkah anda memberitahu kami ~ anda mengenai soal ini?* Can you tell us your opinion about this problem? *~ agama* religious feelings. *~ budaya* cultural sense. *~ diri tertekan dan terpojok* terrifying psychosis (feeling oppressed and cornered). *~ halus* sensitivity, delicacy. *~ hidup* sense of life. *~ hina diri* inferiority complex. *~ kebudayaan* cultural sense. *~ kehormatan* sense of honor. *~ kemasyarakatan* public spirit, sense of community. *~ mulia* noble feelings. *~ nikmat* sense of pleasure. *~ waktu* sense of time. **berperasaan** to have a/the feeling of; feeling, sensitive, compassionate. *orang yang tidak ~* an unfeeling/insensitive person.

rasa II → RAKSA I.

rasai (*M*) **merasai** to endure, undergo, suffer through.
   merasaikan → MERASAI.
   perasaian suffering, enduring a painful or sad experience.

rasak → RESAK.

rasakan → RASA I.

rasaksa → RAKSASA.

rasalat (*A*) apostleship.

rasam (*A*) 1 custom. 2 customary; → RESAM II. *- minyak ke minyak, - air ke air* birds of a feather flock together.
   serasam (*dengan*) in agreement (with).

rasamala a forest tree, *Altingia excelsa*, which produces fine, durable wood and whose sap is made into incense.

rasan I (*M*) → RASAM.

rasan II (*Jv*) **berasan** to have a meeting between two people.
   merasan(i) to discuss the bad side or shortcomings of another person, gossip about.
   perasanan a private discussion between two persons.

rasan III spoiled, stale. *Nasinya sudah –.* The rice is spoiled.

rasau I the wild screw pine, *Pandanus helicopus*.

rasau II (*onom*) the sound made by dense foliage or trees blown about in a strong wind; → DESAU.

rasau III merasau to talk in one's sleep.

rasbéri (*E*) raspberry; → ARBÉI.

rasé (*Jv*) lesser Oriental civet, small Indian civet, *Viverricula indica*.

raseksa (*Jv*) → RAKSASA.

raseksi (*Jv*) → RAKSASI.

rasi I (*Skr*) 1 constellation, astrological sign. *tinggi -* a) (born) under a lucky star. b) (supernaturally) powerful. *orang yang lahir di bawah – Libra* a person born under the sign of Libra. 2 horoscope. *- pari* the Southern Cross. *- perahu* Ursa Major.
   serasi harmonious, matching, well-matched, compatible, congruent. *obat yang ~* a medicine which cures an illness instantly; → CESPLENG. *Pasangan itu ~.* The couple is compatible. **keserasian** congruity, compatibility, harmony. **keserasian-pasangan** compatibility (of a couple).
   merasi(kan) to calculate cabalistically whether a couple are well matched (by giving the letters of their names certain numerical values).
   perasian constellation, horoscope.

rasi II (*M*) **rasian** an ominous dream. **berasian** to dream.
   merasi to dream.

rasi III → SERASI.

rasia I → RAHASIA.

rasia II → RAZ(Z)IA.

rasial (*D/E*) racial.

rasialis (*E*) racist, racialist.

rasialisme (*E*) racism, racialism.

rasian → RASI II.

rasio (*D*) 1 reason, reasoning. 2 ratio. *- aktiva lancar* quick-asset ratio, acid-test ratio. *- cepat* (*fin*) acid-test ratio. *- dividén* (*fin*) pay-out ratio. *- kecukupan modal* (*fin*) capital adequacy ratio, CAR. *- laba modal* (*fin*) return on investment. *- pembayaran utang* (*fin*) debt service ratio. *- utang dan modal* (*fin*) debt to equity ratio.
   berasio reasonable.
   kerasioan rational.

rasional (*E*) and **rasionil** (*D*) rational, showing reason(ing). *tidak – irrational.* **ketidak-rasionalan** irrationality.

kerasionalan rationality, reasonableness.

rasionalis (D) rationalist.

rasionalisasi (D) 1 rationalization. 2 reduction in force, rif, layoff. *Ia kena -.* He was laid off.
   merasionalisasikan to rationalize.

rasionalisme (D/E) rationalism.

rasionalitas (D) rationality.

rasis (D) racist, racialist.

rasisme (D/E) racism, racialism.

raskin [rakyat miskin] the poor, the underprivileged.

rasmi (A Sum Mal) → RESMI I.

rasta (E) Rastafarian. *rambut a la –* dreadlocks.

raster (D) 1 lath. 2 grill. 3 screen.

rasuah (A Mal) 1 bribe. 2 graft, corruption. *Badan Pencegah –* Anti-corruption Agency.

rasuk I possessed. *kena –* possessed by an evil spirit.
   merasuk 1 to possess, take possession of. *dirasuk hantu/sétan* possessed by an evil spirit. *dirasuk mimpi* to have a dream. *Semalam ia dirasuk penunggu pohon beringin itu.* Last night he was possessed by the guardian of the banyan tree. 2 to permeate, penetrate, pervade, soak in. *Pengaruh daérah Sumatra Barat juga ~ dalam sajian makanan, umumnya sama dengan citarasa makanan Padang.* The influence of West Sumatra also pervades the food offered to guests; it is in general similar to Padang-style food. *~ hati/jiwa/kalbu* to disturb, stick in one's mind. *Ia terus-menerus termenung seolah-olah ada sesuatu yang ~ kalbunya.* He remained absorbed in thought as though s.t. was stuck in his mind. *~ iman di dada* enchanting, charming.
   merasuki to penetrate, enter into, pervade, obsess.
   merasukkan to let s.t. take possession of, let s.t. obsess one.
   terasuki possessed, invaded (by).
   kerasukan 1 possessed by an evil spirit, etc.; → KEMASUKAN, KESURUPAN. *orang ~* a medium, intermediary between the natural and the supernatural world. *~ sétan* possessed by the devil. 2 addicted. *Ucok ~ alkohol.* Ucok is an alcoholic.
   perasukan penetration.

rasuk II (floor) crossbeams. *– rakit* crosspieces of a canoe. *– rangka* framework.

rasul (A) 1 messenger, apostle, prophet (*usu* but not necessarily Islamic). 2 the apostles (of Jesus). *kisah segala –* the New Testament. *– Allah, –ilahi, –(l)ol(lah),* and *–ullah* the apostle of Allah, Muhammad. *– Pétrus dan Paulus* the apostles Peter and Paul.
   merasul to proselytize.

rasulan 1 a ceremony exalting Muhammad. 2 (in West Java) a ceremony announcing an intended marriage. 3 (in Central and East Java) a post-harvest festival.

   kerasulan 1 apostolate, apostleship. 2 apostolic. *karya ~* apostolic work. *~ awam* laity.

rasuli (A) apostolic.

rasyid (A) 1 (s.o. who follows) the right path. 2 justice. *Al.–* the one who shows the right way (one of God's names). 3 *sudah –* adult. 4 of sound mind.

rasywah → RASUAH.

rat I → ERAT.

rat II (Jv) world. *jaya(di)ning– (* part of many personal names) conqueror of the world.

rat III → RAD.

rat IV (in acronyms) → DARAT, SURAT I.

rata I 1 flat, level, smooth, horizontal. *Tanah yang – adalah sangat cocok untuk penaman padi sawah.* Flat land is highly suitable for cultivating irrigated rice. *tapak –* flatfoot(ed). *Jalannya –.* The road is smooth. *Kota itu dibikin – dengan tanah.* The city was razed to the ground. *sama –* a) all at the same level, equally flat. b) equality of rights and solidarity. 2 everywhere, all over (the place). *sudah – mencari* to have searched all over (the place). 3 equally, evenly, fairly (all receiving the same amount). *pusaka itu dibagi –* the heirlooms were divided up equally. *sama – sama rasa* equality and solidarity; what's sauce for the goose is sauce for the gander. *– kanan/kiri* right-/left-justified. *– tanah* leveled/razed to the ground. **merata-tanahkan** to level/raze to the ground.

rata-rata 1 evenly, equally. *Kaveling itu harus dibuldoser dahulu ~.* The lot has to be leveled evenly first. 2 in general, on (the) whole; → PADA umumnya. *Bawahannya ~ segan dan hormat kepadanya.* In general his subordinates showed him proper respect and honor → PURATA. 3 on (the) average; average, mean. *Pertambahan penduduk Indonésia ~ 2,5%.* On the average the annual population growth in Indonesia is 2.5%. *kecepatan ~* average speed. *~ tertimbang* weighted average. *umur ~* mean life.

serata 1 as high as, up to. *Air sudah ~ hidung.* The (flood) water was nose-high. 2 the entire/whole, all over. *Poster-poster tertampak di témbok-témbok di ~ kota.* The posters could be seen on walls all over the city. *di ~ dunia* all over the world. **menyeratakan** to spread throughout/all over/everywhere.

merata 1 to be(come) even/flat/level, be evenly/equally (balanced/distributed, etc.). *Keséhatan ~.* Health for All. *tidak ~* unequally distributed, nonegalitarian. *struktur masyarakat pedésaan yang tidak ~* nonegalitarian rural social structure. **ketidak-merataan** nonegalitarianism, unequal/uneven distribution, unevenness. **meredam** *~ yang implisit dalam kebijaksanaan pemerintah itu* to reduce the implicit nonegalitarianism of government policy. **memeratakan** to distribute evenly/equally/fairly. *~ keadilan* to distribute equal justice. 2 to be common practice, widespread, prevalent, spread all over (the place). *Sebentar saja berita kejadian itu ~lah ke seluruh kota.* In a split second the news of the event spread all over town. *tidak merata* inequitable. **kemerataan** egalitarianism, equal/even distribution. **pemerataan** equality, equity, equalization. *~ kesempatan* equal opportunity. 3 steady (of rain). *tidak ~* patchy (of rain).

merata-rata 1 to average. *jika dirata-rata selama tahun ini* if averaged over this year. 2 to spread everywhere/throughout/all over.

meratai to cover, engulf, include (all). *Tidak mungkin rasanya peraturan itu ~ seluruh lapisan rakyat.* It seems impossible for the regulation to cover all strata of the population.

meratakan 1 to flatten, level (off). *Seluruh kawasan itu diratakan untuk dijadikan tapak kawasan perindustrian.* The entire area was leveled and turned into an industrial park. *diratakan dengan tanah* leveled/razed to the ground. 2 to distribute/divide up evenly. *~ kemakmuran kepada seluruh rakyat* to distribute prosperity evenly among the people. *~ jalan* a) to pave the way. b) to provide an opportunity.

merata-ratakan to distribute evenly.

memperata to level off.

rataan flats, reef flat.

kerataan flatness.

perata (elec) rectifier. *~ arus* current rectifier.

perataan equalization, equalizing, equal/equitable distribution, leveling. *~ tanah* ground leveling.

rata II (Skr) 1 (ob) chariot (for Hindu demigods). 2 (Jv) carriage.

ratah plain, unmixed with other things (such as side dishes with rice).

   meratah to take only one thing (not mix it with other things).

ratak (in northern Sumatra) raft. *menyeberang dengan –* to cross (a river) by raft.

rataka (A leg) a woman who has an obstruction in the vaginal opening making intercourse difficult; marriage with such a woman may be annulled without payment of the marriage settlement.

ratap mourning, lamentation, wailing. *– tangis* wailing and weeping, mourning.

   meratap to lament, mourn.

   meratapi to mourn/cry for, lament, weep for/over, bemoan. *Hatinya ~ nasibnya.* In his heart he bemoaned his lot.

   meratapkan to mourn, lament.

   ratapan 1 lament, mourning sounds, cries of mourning. *~ tangis* mourning, lamentation, wailing. *~ tangis dan jerit ketakutan, tiap sebentar terdengar.* Lamentations and cries of terror were heard from time to time. 2 Lamentations (a book of the Bible).

ratas (M) → RETAS I.

ratib (A) k.o. *zikir*, continuous praise of God, often in unison, reciting: *Lailahaillallah, Allahu akbar.* There is no god but God; Allah is great.

meratib to recite a *ratib*.

meratibkan to recite a *ratib* for (a deceased person).

peratib reciter.

ratifikasi (*D*) ratification.

meratifikasi(kan) to ratify.

peratifikasian ratification.

ratifisir (*D*) **meratifisir** to ratify.

Ratih [Rakyat terlatih] k.o. militia.

ratio → RASIO.

ratna I (*Skr*) precious stone, jewel, pearl; → INTAN, PERMATA I. – *cempaka* topaz. – *dwipa* name given to West Kalimantan due to its many diamond deposits. – *kencana* topaz. – *kendi* precious stone. – *mutu manikam* all k.o. jewels. – *wilis* ruby. – *wiraswasta* (*infr*) businesswoman.

ratna II (*Skr*) hero, the best/cream of. *gugur/pecah sebagai* – killed in action. – *déwi* beautiful lovely princess. – *juita* darling, dear. – *pekaja* darling, dear; → JANTUNG *hati*.

ratna III – *pakaja/pekaja* a plant whose leaves are eaten as a vegetable, *Gomphrena globosa*.

ratu I a) queen, princess. *Seri* – Her Majesty. b) queen bee. c) beauty queen. **2** king, monarch, prince. **3** king (in chess). – *Adil* Just King, messianic leader. – *Amérika* Miss America. – *Anggabaya* title of power holder. – *Ayu* Beauty Queen. – *Batik* Batik Queen. – *Dangdut* Queen of *Dangdut* singing. – *dunia* "Queen of the World," i.e., the press. –.– *Halim* beautiful young ladies who offer sexual favors to customs officials at Halim Perdanakusuma International Airport in exchange for having the import duties on their merchandise reduced. – *Juliana/Yuliana* Queen of the Netherlands. – *Kecantikan* Beauty Queen. – *Kecantikan Dunia/Sejagat* Miss Universe. – *lebah* queen bee. – *Majapahit* King of Majapahit. – *malam* "queen of the night," i.e., the moon. – *Pariwisata* Queen of Tourism. – *rumah tangga* "queen of the household," one's wife. – *Sejagat* Miss Universe.

meratui 1 to be superior in beauty, etc. to. **2** to reign as queen of.

meratukan to consider a queen, make s.o. into a queen, regard as superior to others.

ratu-ratuan 1 a fake queen. **2** queens (in contests).

keratuan 1 principality; → K(E)RATON. **2** royal.

ratus I hundred. *tiga* – three hundred.

seratus a/one hundred. **menyeratus** [and **meratus** (*infr*)] to do s.t. related to one hundred. ~ *hari* to hold a religious feast on the hundredth day after s.o.'s death. **keseratus 1** a group of a hundred. ~ *ini* this group of a hundred. **2** hundredth. *yang* ~ the hundredth. *hari yang* ~ the hundredth day. **perseratus** hundredth (the fraction), divided by a hundred. *dua* ~ two hundredths, 2/100. **seperseratus** one one-hundredth, 1/100.

beratus-ratus by the hundreds, hundreds and hundreds. ~ *orang* hundreds of people.

ratusan 1 (*Jv*) the digit occupying the hundreds place, e.g., the 7 in the number 756. **2** denomination of 100 (rupiahs, etc.). **3** (by the) hundreds. ~ *ribu rupiah* hundreds of thousands of rupiahs. ~ *tahun yang lalu* hundreds of years ago. **4** about (one/two, etc.) hundred. *se*~ about one hundred. *dua* ~ about two hundred, a couple of hundred.

peratus hundredth. *tujuh* ~ 7/100, 0.07. *sembilan* ~ 9/100, 0.09.

ratus II meratus 1 to chirp, twitter, warble (of birds). **2** to chatter, talk nonsense.

ratus III (*Jv*) a mixture of incense and other fragrant substances. **meratus** to apply such a mixture. ~ *rambut* to scent one's hair with that mixture.

rau I (*onom*) swishing sound of heavy rain; → DERAU.

rau II *pohon* – New Guinea walnut?, *Dracontomelon mangiferum*; → *pohon* RAWA.

raudah (*A*) garden.

raudatulatfal and **raudlatul atfal** (*A*) kindergarten.

Rauf (*A*) *ar.*– one of God's names, the All-Pitying.

raum roar, growl (of tiger); → AUM.

meraum to roar, growl.

raun (*E*) to make a tour of ... (in a car); rounds (of the police/a watchman, etc.).

raun-raun to take a stroll (window-shopping, walking around, etc.).

meraun to ride/drive, etc. around.

merauni to ride/drive, etc. around s.t.

raung (*onom*) howl, roar, loud weeping. – *ratap* cries and laments.

meraung to howl, roar, weep loudly. *tangis berkepanjangan* ~ prolonged weeping and wailing.

meraung-raung to cry and scream.

meraungi to howl at.

meraung-raungkan to announce loudly. *tidak jemu-jemunya* ~ *cita-citanya itu* to trumpet forth one's ideals tirelessly.

raungan roar. ~ (*bunyi*) *siréne* the wail of sirens.

raup I (*Jv*) to wash one's face. *Saya bangun pagi dan ingin* –. I got up in the morning and wanted to wash my face. *air* – water for washing one's face.

raup II scoop up.

seraup as much as both hands can hold, two handfuls. *beras* ~ a handful of uncooked rice.

meraup 1 to scoop up with the two cupped hands. *Beras itu disukatnya dengan tangan* ~. He measured out the uncooked rice in his cupped hands. **2** to procure, get, earn (a profit). ~ *rupiah dari kapur* to get rupiahs from lime. **3** ~ *kaki* to kiss s.o.'s feet (to show respect). **4** to grab, steal. *Perhiasan emas di dalam kaca étalase seharga Rp 700.000 diraup.* Seven hundred thousand rupiahs worth of gold jewelry was stolen from the display case.

meraupkan ~ *tangan* to pass the palms downward over the face after praying.

raupan handful.

raut I whittle, sharpen. *pisau* – a razor-sharp knife.

seraut and **siraut** (*M*) knife.

meraut to smooth (rattan, etc.) with a knife, sharpen (a pencil, etc.) with a knife, hone, whittle.

merauti (*pl obj*) to hone, whittle, etc.

rautan 1 sharpener. ~ *pénsil* pencil sharpener. **2** s.t. that has been sharpened. **3** whittling. ~ *halus*. His whittling is fine work.

perautan whittling, smoothing.

raut II 1 (– *muka/wajah*) facial expression, profile, looks. **2** form, cut. – *badan* figure. – *bumi* landform.

seraut (*ob*) features.

rautan ~ *muka/wajah* facial expression.

raut III *burung* – Eurasian curlew, *Numenius arquata orientalis*. *burung pisau* – whimbrel, *Numenius phaeopus variegatus*.

rawa I and **rawa-rawa** marsh, swamp, bog, morass. – *asin* salt marsh. – *gambut* peat marsh. – *nonpasang surut* nontidal marsh. – *pasang* tidal swamp. – *payau* salt marsh.

berawa(-rawa) marshy, swampy, boggy.

merawa *berjalan* ~ to make one's way through a swamp.

merawakan to turn into a marsh/swamp.

rawa II *burung* – pied imperial pigeon, *Ducula bicolor*.

rawa III k.o. plant, *Mangifera microphylla*. *pohon* – → RAU II.

Rawa IV a district in Sumatra. *kain* – a bright tie-dyed mantilla; → KAIN *pelangi*.

rawah I → RAWA I.

rawah II (*M*) a large pan; → KAWAH 1. *telinga* – s.o. who won't listen to advice.

rawah III partnership in which one supplies the capital and the other supplies the labor.

rawai moor lines of unbaited hooks strung across an estuary to catch fish. – *dasar* bottom long line.

merawai to fish with such lines.

rawak haphazard, random; → ACAK I, AWUR II, RAMBANG I. *menémbak* – to fire random shots (at s.t. unseen). – *rambang* to do s.t. at random.

merawak to do s.t. at random, throw s.t. at s.t. unseen. ~ *rambang* to do s.t. in a slapdash way.

rawan I 1 affected, moved, touched; melancholy, downcast; → PILU I, SAYU I, TERHARU. **2** critical, crucial, serious, grave. **3** problematic, difficult, prone (to problems), vulnerable (of species, etc.), crisis-prone, unstable, fragile (situation), easily subject to (s.t. bad). *tempat* – hardship post. *usia* – a difficult age. – *gempa* subject to earthquakes. – *kecelakaan* (place/street) subject to accidents. – *kejahatan* crime-ridden (area). – *pangan* a) food shortage; → KEKURANGAN *pangan*. b) (*euph*) famine, hunger.

berawan ~ *hati* moved, touched.

merawan(i) moving, touching, pathetic.

merawankan ~ (*hati*) to move, affect, touch. *suara yang sangat sedih dan* ~ *hati* a sad and touching voice.

terawan the worst, the most seriously affected.

kerawanan 1 grief, sorrow; emotion. *Kebimbangan dan* ~ *hatinya terbayang pada mukanya yang murung.* Anxiety and grief were etched on his downcast face. **2** critical situation, hazard, crisis. ~ *pangan* food crisis. ~ *sosial* social tensions.

perawan s.t. that moves/touches/affects one; → PERAWAN.

rawan II (*tulang* – a) cartilage, gristle; → TULANG *muda*. b) breastbone, sternum.

rawan III classifier for things that occur in a small series/sets/suits. **serawan** one set. ~ *jala* one casting net. ~ *kancing baju* a set of shirt buttons.

rawan IV (*cla*) k.o. vehicle. *takhta* – k.o. litter, a vehicle mentioned in old romances.

rawan V merawan to be in the clouds; → (BER)AWAN.

rawang I (*M*) swamp, marsh, peat bog, fen; → RAWA I.

rawang II (*M*) **merawang 1** to take random aim (with a gun), make a haphazard choice (from a number of equally attractive items). **2** to be confused, unfocused.

rawat treat, take care of. *juru* – nurse, hospital attendant. – *jalan* outpatient. – *gabung* rooming in (in a hospital). – (*ng*)*inap* inpatient. **merawat (ng)inap** to treat s.o. as an inpatient. *Terdakwa dirawat nginap untuk menjalani operasi.* The accused was an inpatient for an operation. – *panas* (*petro*) hot oil treatment. – *purna* overhaul.

berawat to be treated, get treatment.

merawat 1 to take care of, look after, attend to, nurse, treat, groom (a pet). *Ia dirawat di hospital.* He was treated in the hospital. ~ *diri* to take care of o.s., look after o.s. ~ *rambut* to take care of one's hair. *Ia* ~ *rumah kami dengan baik.* She took good care of our house. **2** (*ob*) to resume one's original form (of a god after appearing as a human).

merawati (*pl obj*) to treat, take care of (s.o. who is ill, etc.). *Ia* ~ *tanaman saya dengan baik.* She took good care of our plants.

merawatkan to take s.o. for treatment.

terawat taken care of, looked after, treated, maintained, attended to, nursed. *Keadaannya* ~ *baik.* The situation was well taken care of. *Jalannya rusak tak* ~. The streets were broken up and not well maintained.

rawatan 1 nursed, taken care of. **2** treatment. ~ *kejutan* shock treatment.

perawat 1 baby-sitter; → PRAMUSISWI. **2** caretaker, nurse. ~ *udara* flight nurse. **3** s.t. or s.o. that treats/takes care of, maintenance engineer. ~ *rambut* (hair) conditioner. **keperawatan** caretaking, nursing (*mod*). *ilmu* ~ nursing science.

perawatan 1 treatment, treating, therapy. **2** nursing. **3** care, maintenance, management. *mudah* ~*nya* easy to maintain. ~ *badan* physical care. ~ *benih* blending seeds with fungicides and insecticides prior to testing or storing. ~ *gigi* dental care. ~ *jantung* cardiac care. ~ *kaki* pedicure. ~ *kecantikan* beauty treatment. ~ *keluarga* home nursing. ~ *kuku* manicure. ~ *kulit* skin care. ~ *lanjutan* aftercare. ~ *mandi lulur* treatment with a yellow-rice powder bath. ~ *muka* a) facial. b) makeup. (*rumah*) ~ *orang tua* senior citizens home, nursing home. ~ *purna* overhaul. ~ *rambut* hair conditioning. ~ *rohani* spiritual care. ~ *sebelum kelahiran* prenatal care. ~ *seluruh tubuh pesawat* airframe overhaul. ~ *Sepanjang Hari* Day Care. ~ *tanah* soil treatment. ~ *tangan* manicure. ~ *wajah* facial.

rawatib (*A*) (*pl* of **ratib**) (recommended but optional) prayer.

rawé (*Jv*) k.o. plant whose leaves cause stinging and itching, velvet bean, *Mucuna pruriens*.

rawé-rawé (*Jv*) hanging down, dangling (of tassels/fringes, etc.). – *rantas, malang-malang putung* (preindependence nationalist slogan) "the tassels will be broken off, obstacles will be snapped," i.e., all obstacles will be overcome.

rawi I (*A*) **1** narrator of the *hadits*. **2** narrator, storyteller.

merawi to narrate, tell a story, relate s.t.

merawikan to narrate, tell, relate.

perawi narrator.

rawi II (*K ob*) the sun.

rawis (*burung* –) Nicobar pigeon, *Caloenas nicobarica*.

rawit I (*J/Jv*) *cabai* – a very small but hot chili pepper; → CABAI I. *kecil-kecil cabai* – small but plucky.

rawit II (*Jv*) **karawitan** and **kerawitan 1** overture to a *wayang* performance. **2** *gamelan* music in general. *ahli* ~ expert in *gamelan* music. *seni* ~ music (of the *gamelan*).

rawit III merawit to implicate, drag (s.o. else into a dispute).

rawon (*Jv*) boiled beef prepared with spicy hot *kluwak* sauce. *nasi* – rice and that beef eaten plain or with bean sprouts.

rawuh (*Jv*) to come. *Menteri akan* – *ke sini juga.* The minister will also come here.

rawun (*S*) *upacara* – a ceremony, performed when the *padi* is 40 days old to ask for blessings from the goddess of rice for an abundant harvest; incense is burned and people make rice porridge and offerings of cooked rice straight from the basket in which the rice was steamed.

ra'y (*A*) **1** rational. **2** a legal opinion based on someone's judgment and not on the Qur'an or Sunnah.

raya 1 large, great; very; full (not partial). *alam* – cosmos. *badak* – large one-horned rhino, *Rhinoceros sondaicus*. *bunga* – hibiscus, *Hibiscus rosa sinensis*; → BUNGA *sepatu*. *gendang* – a large mosque drum. *hari* – a) holiday. b) feast day. *hari* – *besar* → LEBARAN. *hari* – *haji* → LEBARAN *haji*. *hari* – *Idulfitri* feast at the end of Ramadan. *jagat* – cosmos. *jalan* – highway. *kaya* – very rich. (*bulan*) *purnama* – full (moon). *rimba* – virgin forest. **2** greater. *Indonésia* – Greater Indonesia, i.e., the Indonesian national anthem. *Jakarta* – [Jaya] Greater Jakarta.

merayakan to celebrate, observe. ~ *hari kemerdékaan* to celebrate independence day. ~ *hari Natal* to celebrate Christmas. *untuk* ~ in honor of.

perayaan celebration, festival, festivities. ~ *Ékaristi* Feast of the Eucharist. ~ *hari kemerdékaan* independence day celebration. ~ *perkawinan* wedding feast.

Rayagung (*Jv*) the 12th month of the Arabic calendar.

rayah (*Jv*) **merayah** to plunder, rob, loot.

merayahi to raid frequently. ~ *jalan raya siang-malam* to raid the highways day and night.

rayahan booty, spoils, loot, plunder.

rayan (*M*) **rayan-rayan 1** to rave, be delirious. **2** to dream of s.t. that has been preoccupying one during the day.

terayan-(r)ayan 1 between sleeping and waking, dozing. **2** continually seeing in a dream.

rayang reeling (from a blow, etc.).

merayang to reel (from a blow/drink/dizziness).

perayangan reeling, head-spinning.

rayan-royon (*J*) to wander about.

rayap I 1 white ants, termites. *seperti* – packed in like sardines in a can; → ANAI-ANAI. **2** a corrupt person; embezzler. –.– *uang negara* embezzlers of state funds. **3** freeloader, moocher.

merayap to be like termites, swarm.

rayap II crawl, creep.

merayap 1 to crawl, creep (across). **2** [and **mengerayap** (*Jv*)] to move slowly/stealthily. *Pasukan gerilya itu* ~ *memasuki pertahanan musuh.* The guerilla forces moved stealthily into the enemy's defense lines. **3** to creep; to grow along the ground (of plants); → MELATA. *Tumbuhan-tumbuhan yang menjalar akan* ~ *di tanah.* Creepers will creep along the ground. ~ *naik* to creep up.

merayapi 1 to crawl/creep in/on/over/along. *Kerangga* ~ *bajuku.* Big red ants crept up my jacket. **2** to come over (of feelings). *Perasaan takut* ~ *hati saya.* A sense of anxiety came over me.

terayap-rayap crawling, creeping. *Dari jauh kelihatan ia* ~. From a distance he was seen crawling along.

rayapan 1 slow motion, creep. **2** slow landslide. **3** creeper (of plant).

rayau merayau(-rayau) 1 to roam/wander/travel over (looking for s.t.). *Hutan itu dirayau.* The jungle was roamed over. **2** (to move around) restlessly. **3** to grope one's way (through).

rayon I (*D*) area, district, precinct. – *militér* [ramil] military district.

perayonan districting, dividing into districts/zones/precincts.

rayon II (D) rayon.

rayonisasi dividing up into districts.

rayu I 1 (sayu -) sad, melancholy; → BERAWAN hati.

merayu to move, touch, affect; ~ belas kasihan moving one to pity, touching, affecting.

merayukan to move, touch, affect.

rayu II flattery, excessive compliments; seduction, sweet talk. - nya sering memikat. His sweet talk is often seductive. cumbu - compliments, sweet talk.

merayu(-rayu) 1 to charm, captivate; pleasing. suara merdu yang ~ a sweet and pleasing voice. mudah dirayu easily charmed/seduced. 2 to court, seduce, sweet talk. Ia ~ gadis itu dengan kata-kata manis. He seduced that girl with sweet talk. 3 to (file a) request, petition. Meréka ~ supaya yang berwajib mengambil tindakan tegas. They requested that the authorities take firm steps.

rayuan flattery, excessive compliments, sweet talk; seduction. ~ gombal empty sweet talk. ~ maut deadly seduction.

perayu flatterer, seducer.

rayun → RAYU I.

Razaq (A) ar.- one of God's names, the Provider, Sustainer.

razi → RADI.

raz(z)ia (D) /rasia/ razzia, police raid/sweep; → GELÉDAH, GEREBEG II. Tadi pagi ada - surat keterangan. This morning there was a check on ID cards. kena - to be swept up in a raid. mengadakan/melakukan - terhadap to make a clean sweep of.

meraz(z)ia to (carry out a) raid/sweep.

RBg (D leg) [Rechtsreglement Buitengewesten] → RÉGLEMÉN Daérah Seberang.

RCTI [Rajawali Citra Télévisi Indonésia] name of an Indonesian television channel.

RDIP (init) → RUMAH Déténsi Imigrasi Pusat.

ré I (D) ré, the second note in the musical scale.

ré II (in acronyms) → REGU, RENCANA.

réagéns (D) reagent.

réagénsia reagents.

réak → RIAK I.

réaksi (D) reaction. - balasan backlash. - balik reaction. - berantai chain reaction. - kimia chemical reaction. - silang cross reaction.

be(r)réaksi and meréaksi to react.

meréaksikan 1 to cause a reaction. 2 to react with.

peréaksi reagent; → RÉAGÉNS.

réaksionér (D) reactionary.

réaktif (E) reactive.

réaktivasi (E) reactivating.

réaktor (D/E) reactor. - air tekan pressurized water reactor. - atom atomic reactor. - nuklir nuclear reactor. - pembiak cepat fast breeder reactor. - pembibitan nuklir nuclear breeder reactor.

réaktualisasi (E) reactualization.

réal I → RIAL.

réal II real (value).

real estate (E) /ril éstéit/ real estate. perusahaan - real estate company. - Indonésia [REI] Indonesian Real Estate.

réalis (D) realist.

réalisasi (D) 1 realization, bringing about, completion (of a project), (real) results. 2 actual (as opposed to projected). - anggaran actual budget.

meréalisasi(kan) to realize, bring about, actualize, complete (a project).

teréalisasi(kan) realized, brought about, completed, actualized; settled (of a legal question), provided (of loans). Pusat pendidikan setingkat SMA ini diharapkan ~ dalam Pelita V. It's hoped that this SMA-level education center will be completed in the Fifth Five-Year Development Plan. belum teréalisasi unrealized.

réalisir (D) meréalisir to realize, bring about, actualize.

réalisme (D/E) realism.

réalistik (E) realistic.

meréalistikkan and mengréalistikkan to make realistic.

réalistis (D) realistic.

meréalistiskan and mengréalistiskan to make realistic.

réalita(s) and réalitét (D) reality.

Réalpolitik (D) Realpolitik.

Réaumur temperature scale in which 0 is the freezing point and 80 is the boiling point.

réasuradur (D) reinsurer.

réasuransi (D) reinsurance.

réat-réot (J onom) sound of squawking; → KERÉAT-KERÉOT.

reba (cla) brush, a heap/pile of branches and trees which have been cut down.

rebab (A) a musical instrument with two or three strings, k.o. violoncello, spike fiddle.

berebab to play this instrument.

rebah I to fall down, collapse, fallen (of trees). dapat tebu - to get a windfall/stroke of good luck; → (dapat) durian RUNTUH. sokong membawa - to bring ruin on s.o. by trying to help. - haluan to let a boat fall off the wind. - pingsan to fall down in a faint. - rémpah to stumble and fall. - semai damping off (a disease of the rice plant). - tersungkur/tertiarap/tertumus to fall face forward, fall flat on one's face.

rebah-rebah(an) to relax, lie around. Meréka ~ di bawah pohon itu. They were lying around under the tree.

berebahan (pl subj) to fall down.

merebah 1 to fall/drop (down), collapse. 2 to lie down.

merebahi to fall down on s.t.

merebahkan 1 to fell/cut down, knock down, topple. ~ pohon to cut down trees. ~ pemerintah to topple the government. ~ rumah-rumah to demolish houses. 2 to put (to bed). ~ anak di tempat tidur to put the children to bed. 3 to throw down, lay down. Dia ~ dirinya di atas rumput untuk melepaskan lelah. He threw himself down on the grass to rest. 4 to slaughter (animals).

terebah fallen down, sprawled.

rebahan 1 s.t. which has fallen down/collapsed. ~ pohon fallen trees. 2 place where one lies down (bed, etc.) 3 (coq) to lie around.

rebah II - bangun mimosa, Mimosa pudica/invisa; → PUTRI malu.

rébah (ob) belt.

rebak merebak to be teary (of the eyes). Matanya ~. He had tears in his eyes.

rébak I deep (of wound), gashed, torn (of sails).

merébak to have a deep cut in it.

rébak II spread, bloom (of algae); → RÉWAK I.

merébak to spread (of fire/news/war/skin disease/epidemic). ~ ke berbagai daérah to spread to several areas.

perébakan spread, spreading.

rébak III diamond-shaped design (on a fabric).

reban pen (for poultry) under a house built on stilts.

merebankan to pen (up).

réban meréban to toss/hurl aside.

teréban tossed/hurled aside.

rebana (Hind) tambourine. - ketimpring this instrument with bells attached to it.

berebana to play the tambourine.

rebas (M) drizzle; → RABAS, REBAH I.

rebas-rebas drizzle; drizzling.

rebat merebat 1 to block/close off (a road). 2 to protect (a tree) by fencing (it in).

rébéh I torn or broken and hanging down on one side (of an ear, wing, leg, etc.).

rébéh II 1 in tatters, ragged; → COMPANG-CAMPING. 2 worn out, decrepit.

rébék (J) 1 dirty, foul, not cleaned, unwashed. 2 (Jv) mucus in the corners of the eye. 3 bad, evil. 4 disorganized, disorderly.

rébékan dirty, unwashed.

rebéli (D) rebellion, mutiny.

rébén (E) kacamata - Ray Ban sunglasses (once considered a luxury item).

rebes berebesan missing (of teeth). Giginya ~. He's missing some teeth.

rébét I → RÉMBÉT II.

rébét II → RIBUT.

rébewés (D) driver's license; → (RÉ)BOWÉS, BUWÉS.

berébewés to have a driver's license.

Rebo (*J*) (*hari*) – Wednesday; → RABU I. – *pungkasan/wekasan* the last Wednesday in the month of *Sapar*.

réboasasi and **réboisasi** reforestation, retimbering, regreening. **meréboasasi** and **meréboisasi** to reforest.

rébok-robék in tatters.

rebon I (*J/Jv*) *udang* – a very small species of river shrimp, *Mysis spp.*; → UDANG *geragau*.

Rebon II (*Jv*) every Wednesday.

rebong I → REBUNG.

rebong II (*BG*) thousand; → RIBU.

rébowés (*J*) → RÉBEWÉS.

rebu merebu to stream/flow/pour in.

rebuk a wound filled with pus, suppuration. **merebuk** to suppurate, ooze pus.

rebung young edible bamboo shoot. *pucuk* – acute-angled chevrons, a common pattern on the *kepala* of *sarung batik*. – *tidak jauh dari rumpun* like father, like son. **merebung 1** to sprout (of a bamboo shoot). **2** like a bamboo shoot.

rebus boiled in water, cooked in boiling water. *kacang* – boiled peanuts. *telur* – *setengah matang* soft-boiled egg. – *tidak empuk* unchanging (of one's opinion/behavior). – *kacang* boiled peanuts. – *kol* boiled cabbage. **merebus** to boil in water. ~ *air* a) to boil water. b) very poor. ~ *kacang* to boil peanuts. ~ *tak empuk* steadfast, firm, resolute, unchanging. **terebus** boiled. **rebusan** s.t. boiled in water. *air* ~ decoction. ~ *pisang* boiled bananas. **perebus** s.t. to make things boil. *alat* ~ boiler. **perebusan** boiling.

rebut compete, fight over. – *rampas* various k.o. robberies/holdups. **berebut 1** to fight, compete for. ~ *kata* to quarrel. ~ *kedudukan* to fight for a position. *bertengkar* ~ *mulut* to wrangle, quarrel. ~ *jabatan/nama/pangkat* to vie for fame, position, or popularity. ~ *petai hampa* to fight over s.t. worthless or that doesn't exist. ~ *rezeki* to fight to stay alive, struggle to survive. ~ *tua* to fight for supremacy. **2** to go from (one part of the day into another). *pada waktu hari* ~ *senja* when it began to get light (in the morning). *senja* ~ *dengan malam* and *siang* ~ *senja* and *di kala malam* ~ *senja* the transition from twilight to dark. **berebut(-rebut)** to race e.o. to do s.t., scramble. *Pelajar-pelajar itu* ~ *naik bus sekolah.* The high school students scrambled into the school bus. **berebut(-rebut)an** to fight over, grab/seize from e.o. *Anak-anak itu senang sekali makan* ~. Children love to fight over food. **merebut 1** to seize/take/grab s.t. by force (of arms), capture, corner (the market), win (an award), secure. *Ia berhasil* ~ *pisau belati dari tangan penjahat itu.* He managed to grab the dagger from the criminal's hand. *berjuang* ~ *kemerdékaan* to struggle for one's independence. **2** to obtain with the utmost difficulty. *Belum ada yang dapat* ~ *hati gadis itu.* No one has succeeded in capturing/getting that girl's love. **me(mpe)rebutkan** [and **ngerebutin** (*J coq*)] **1** to seize, grab, take by force. **2** to fight/battle/compete over/for. *Kedua peserta itu berlomba-lomba antara satu dengan lain untuk merebutkan tempat pertama.* The two participants competed, among other things, for first place. *memperebutkan kursi perdana menteri* to fight for the prime minister's seat. *yang diperebutkan* at stake. **terebut** fought over, seized, obtained. **rebutan 1** s.t. that is contested/fought over. *Céwék cantik itu menjadi* ~ *cowok di kampungnya.* The beautiful girl became the object of competition for the boys in their village. **2** struggle, fight. ~ *kekuasaan* a) coup d'état. b) power struggle. ~ *pangkat* job hunting. ~ *pekerjaan* the struggle for jobs. **3** a Chinese celebration combined with a religious meal. **4** contest to climb a pole smeared with grease to obtain the items hung at the top. **perebutan** [and **pengrebutan** (*Jv*)] **1** fight, struggle, s.t. contested for. *menjadi* ~ to be a bone of contention. **2** grab(bing), seizure. ~ *kekuasaan* power grab. **3** a struggle for.

reca (*Jv*) → ARCA.

recak I (*Jv*) pockmarked; → BOPÉNG.

recak II *beras* –(-*recak*) broken rice grains.

recak III (*M*) **merecak** to sit on s.t. with the legs apart, straddle; to ride (a horse). ~ *kuda* a) to ride on a horse. ~ *tengkuk orang* to ride piggy-back. b) to benefit from s.o. else's efforts.

recall (*E*) /rikol/ **merecall** to recall and force members of Parliament to give back their mandate.

récéh (*J?*) *uang* – small change. **récéhan** *uang* ~ small change.

recék (*E*) /ricék/ recheck. *Selalu saya lakukan cék dan* –. I always check and recheck.

récéng diced, cut up into small pieces. **serécéng** a small piece.

récét to burst out crying/shouting; to make a big fuss.

réchtswége (*D*) *van* – (*leg*) lawfully, legally, *ipso jure*.

recik sprinkle, small drop; → PERCIK. **merecik(-recik)** to sprinkle, splash, splatter. *bunyi air merecik-recik* the sound of splashing water. *peluh merecik* sweat stood in drops. **mereciki** to sprinkle on. **merecikkan** to sprinkle s.t. **recikan** sprinkle, sprinkling. **perecik** sprinkler.

récok (*J*) **1** excitement, trouble, fuss, noise; loud, noisy. *Surat-surat kabar itu bikin* – *saja.* The newspapers just make a big fuss. *Sudah diberi uang masih* – *saja.* We've given you a lot of money and you're still making a fuss. **2** restless, fidgety. **récok-récok** ~ *di belakang* (unpleasant) aftermath (of a revolution, etc.). **merécok** to get excited, make a fuss. **merécoki** to get excited about, make a fuss over. **merécokkan** [and **ng(e)récokin** (*J coq*)] **1** to make a fuss over. ~ *hal-hal yang sepélé* to make a fuss over trivial matters. **2** to make trouble for. **kerécokan 1** fuss, commotion. **2** quarrel, brawl. **perécok** noisy fellow, rowdy, troublemaker. **perécokan** making a fuss, making trouble.

récot → RÉCOK.

recup just sprouting. **merecup** to bud, sprout, burgeon.

réd clipped form of either **rédaksi** or **rédaktur**.

reda 1 to calm down, quiet down, abate, subside, become calm (of storms/wind, etc.). *Hujan lebat mulai* –. The downpour began to subside. **2** to decrease, lessen, calm down (of anger/heat/illness, etc.). *Bunyi bising itu sudah mulai* –. The noise has begun to decrease. **3** almost finished/over/vanished. *Kendaraan yang lalu-lintas di jalan raya sudah mulai* –. Vehicles going back and forth over the highway have almost disappeared. **reda-redanya** *tiada* ~ incessantly. **bereda 1** to calm down, abate, lessen. **2** to take shelter, hide o.s.; → BERTEDUH. **mereda** to abate, wane, lessen, decrease, calm down. *Tangisan anaknya sudah* ~ *sedikit.* His child's crying has abated a bit. **meredai** and **meredakan** to reduce, lessen, soothe, calm/quiet (down), cool off. *Dia berhasil* ~ *kemarahan ayahnya.* He succeeded in calming down his father's anger. *meredakan suhu perékonomian yang cenderung memanas* to cool off an economy that is tending to heat up. **keredaan** abatement, calm, calming down, relaxation. ~ *hati* calming down. ~ *ketegangan* détente, relaxation of tensions. **pereda** suppressor, suppressant, s.t. that relieves. ~ *batuk* cough suppressant. ~ *ketegangan* depressant, s.t. that calms down tensions. **peredaan** calming/slowing/quieting down, easing. ~ *ketegangan* relaxation of tensions, détente.

réda → RÉLA.

redah I → REDA.

redah II (*M*) **meredah** to fell (trees); → MENEBANG.

redah III **meredah** to traverse, pass (a limit), go beyond.

rédaksi (*D*) **1** editorial staff (of a newspaper, etc.). – *luar negeri* foreign editorial staff. **2** wording (of text). **merédaksi** to edit. **kerédaksian** editorial (*mod*). *di bidang* ~ in the editorial sector/field. *kerja* ~ Board of Editors activities.

perédaksian editing.

rédaksional and **rédaksionil** (*D*) editorial (*mod*); → KERÉDAKSIAN.

rédaktris (*D*) female editor.

rédaktor and **rédaktur** (*D*) editor. – *film* film editor. – *kota* city editor. – *malam* night-shift editor. – *naskah* copy editor. – *olahraga* sports editor. – *pelaksana* managing editor. – *penyunting* copy editor.

merédakturi to edit. *Mas Nug waktu itu belum ~ cerita.* At that time Mr. Nug wasn't editing stories yet.

redam I 1 vague, faint, dim. 2 muffled, hushed.

redam-redam 1 faintly (audible or visible). 2 muffled, hushed; → REDUP, SAYUP. *Suara saksofon dari klub malam itu kedengaran ~.* The sound of the saxophone was faintly audible from the nightclub.

meredam 1 to dull, make faint. *Masa empat tahun telah ~ sebagian dari daya penariknya.* Four years has dulled part of her charm. 2 to reduce, damp.

meredamkan to muffle, deaden (a sound), damp.

teredam damped, muffled, deadened, attenuated.

redaman damping, attenuation. *faktor ~* damping factor.

peredam 1 reducer, absorber, suppressor. *~ bunyi* silencer (of a pistol). *~ getaran/guncangan/kejut* shock absorber. *~ ketukan* knock suppressor. *~ letus/suara* muffler. 2 silencer. **berperedam** (equipped) with a silencer. *senjata ~* a weapon equipped with a silencer.

peredaman damping, reduction, muffling, deadening.

redam II crushed, shattered. *remuk –* crushed, pulverized. – *padam* a) completely extinguished/out. b) destroyed.

meredam(kan) to crush, shatter.

rédan → RIDAN.

redang 1 → RADANG. 2 lukewarm.

rédang a deep marsh/morass/swamp/bog.

redap I meredap kept inside (as of anger), not appearing on the surface.

keredapan keeping/being kept inside.

redap II (*A*) k.o. tambourine.

redap III meredap to spread (of diseases, etc.).

redas I redas to make a beeline for, head directly for.

redas II → REDAH II.

réde (*D naut*) roads. – *transport* roads transport (motorboats/praus, etc. for passengers embarking and disembarking on a ship that cannot moor due to lack of mooring facilities).

rédéh row, line.

merédéh(kan) to line s.t. up.

rédenasi (*D*) reasoning.

rédha, rédho → RÉLA.

rédi I (*E*) ready.

rédi II (*Port ob*) 1 large fishing net. 2 hammock.

redih rice seedlings.

meredih to plant rice seedlings.

peredih plant out rice seedlings.

redik 1 scolding, snarling. 2 snappish, acrimonious; → HARDIK.

meredik 1 to snap at. 2 to scold, dress down.

rédistribusi (*E*) redistribution. – *tanah* land reform.

merédistribusikan to redistribute.

rédoks (*E*) redox.

rédpél (*acr*) → REDAKTUR *pelaksana*.

réduksi (*D*) reduction.

meréduksi(kan) to reduce.

peréduksi reducing agent.

peréduksian reducing.

réduktif (*E*) reductive.

réduktor (*E*) reductor.

redum I (*onom*) the sound made by a large object dropped into the water, plop!

redum II gloomy, dull; → REDUP.

rédunansi (*D*) redundancy.

redup 1 cloudy, overcast (of the sky before a storm), hazy (sky); → MENDUNG; *opp* TERANG *cuaca*. 2a) lackluster/dull (of the eyes). b) glassy, lifeless (of the eyes of a dead body). 3a) – *dan sejuk* (afternoon) coolness (after a hot day). b) the lee(side) of a tree; → LINDAP. c) to abate/die down (of a storm or of love). d) wan-

ing (glory). 4 fading (away), dying away (light of the setting sun or moon, sound). 5 burning dimly/faintly (of a fire or lamp), almost dying out, flickering (of a lamp when the fuel is almost gone).

redup-redup *~ alang/bahasa* barely visible (in the dark), faint.

meredup to become faint (of light, sound). *Nyala pelita itu makin lama makin ~.* The light of the lamp is becoming fainter and fainter.

meredupkan to dim, turn down (the lights, etc.).

keredupan overcast (of the sky).

peredup dimmer.

réduplikasi (*D ling*) reduplication.

rédusir (*D*) **merédusir** to reduce.

redut (*M*) annoyed, irritated; disillusioned.

meredut to feel resentful. *hatinya ~* he felt hurt/insulted.

réédukasi (*E*) reeducation.

réékspor (*E*) reexport.

meréékspor to reexport.

réévaluasi (*E*) reevaluation.

meréévaluasi to reevaluate.

réferat (*D*) report, lecture.

réferéndaris (*D*) referendary, an advisor (*esp* to the royal palace).

réferéndum (*D*) referendum. – *fakultatif* optional referendum.

réferénsi (*D*) 1 reference. *buku –* reference book. 2 certification in writing about s.o.'s work experience, letter of referral/reference, confirmation. – *bank* bank reference.

réferénsial (*D*) referential.

référs (*D*) reverse.

référte (*D*) reference.

réflasi (*D*) reflation.

réfléks (*D*) reflex.

berfléks to show a reflex.

réfléksi (*D*) reflection.

berfléksi to reflect.

merfléksikan 1 to cause a reflection. 2 to reflect, mirror s.t. *Ucapan seseorang biasanya ~ isi hatinya.* What s.o. says usually reflects his state of mind.

terfléksikan reflected.

réfléksif (*D*) reflexive.

rérléktif (*D*) reflective.

rérléktor (*D*) reflector.

réform (*E*) reform.

réformasi (*D*) reformation, reform.

meréformasi(kan) to reform.

réformir (*D*) **meréformir** to reform.

réformis (*D*) reformist.

réformisme (*D*) reformism.

réformulasi (*D*) reformulation.

réformulir (*D*) **meréformulir** to reformulate.

réfraksi (*D*) refraction.

réfréin (*D/E*) refrain, chorus.

réfri (*E*) referee (in sports).

réfrigerator (*E*) refrigerator.

réfungsionalisasi (*E*) refunctionalization.

meréfungsionalisasi(kan) to refunctionalize.

rega (*Jv*) → HARGA.

regah meregah to break lengthwise and open up (of the skin of a fruit/palm of the hands, etc.); cracked (of the soil); budding (of a flower).

regak (*Ac*) k.o. mackerel.

régan (*M*) sash, the wooden upper and lower parts of a window frame.

regang taut, tight, tightly stretched (of ropes, etc.). *Tali yang dahulu itu – sekarang telah menjadi kendur.* The rope that was taut has become loose. – *kain* banner.

seregang tense. **berseregang** and **bersiregang** to quarrel, dispute; to take a firm stand (against). *~ mulut* to wrangle, squabble. **keseregangan** tension.

beregang-regang to stretch the limbs of the body (in preparation for fighting, etc.).

meregang 1 to become taut/tight. *Kabel télepon mengendur pada waktu panas dan ~ pada waktu sejuk.* Telephone cables become loose in hot weather and tight in cool weather. **2** to tug, pull. *merebut* ~ (*M*) to take by force. ~ *badan* to have convulsions. ~ *diri* to stretch (in pain, etc.). ~ *hidupnya* to lead a miserable life. ~ *jiwa/nyawa* to die, be on the point of death; → SEKARAT. ~ *telinga* a) to pull s.o.'s ear. b) to admonish.

meregangkan to tighten, make taut (of cord/net/sails/muscles), stretch, strain. *Karena angin bertiup dengan kencangnya, meréka meregangkan tali kémah.* Because there was a strong wind, they tightened the tent ropes. ~ *urat* to pull a muscle.

regangan 1 tautness, tightness, tension, strain. **2** elongation, extension.

keregangan tension, strain.

peregang strainer, stretcher, tightener.

peregangan stretching (of muscles). ~ *nyawa* s.o. life threatening.

regas meregas to cut (grass/hair, etc.).

regat meregat to cut straight across (a street/river, etc.); to take a shortcut through.

regatan (*elec*) short circuit, by-pass.

régat(t)a (*D*) regatta, boat race.

régel (*D IBT*) **1** (the upper edge of a) veranda wall; fence. **2** shelf (attached to a wall). **3** ruler, measuring stick.

regén (*D*) regent; → BUPATI.

keregénan 1 regency, area headed by a regent. **2** residence/office of a regent; → KABUPATÉN.

régenerasi (*D*) **1** changing of the guard, replacement of the old by the new. **2** regeneration.

régénérator (*E*) regenerator.

régés (*J/Jv*) **1** defoliated, leafless. **2** to fall (of leaves).

régi (*D*) state monopoly. – *garam* salt monopoly.

régim (*D*) → RÉZIM.

régiméntasi (*E*) regimentation.

merégiméntasikan to regiment.

régional (*D*) regional, local. *kerjasama* – regional cooperation.

régionalisasi (*E*) regionalization.

régionalisme (*D/E*) regionalism.

régisir (*D*) (stage or film) director; → SUTRADARA.

régister (*D*) register; → DAFTAR.

merégister to register.

régistrasi (*D*) registration.

merégistrasi(kan) to register.

régisur → RÉGISIR.

réglemén (*D leg*) regulation. – *Acara Perdata* (= Reglement op de rechtsvordering [Rv]) (*col*) Code of Civil Procedure. – *Daérah Seberang* [RDS] (*col*) Regulations for Outer Areas (= Rechtsreglement Buitengewesten [RBg]). – *Indonésia yang diperbarui* [RIB] (*col*) Revised Indonesian Regulations (= Herziene Indonesisch Reglement [HIR]).

réglemèntasi, réglemèntéring (*D*) regulation.

réglemèntér (*D*) regulation (*mod*), prescribed (by the rules).

régol (*Jv*) (covered) outer gateway.

régrés (*D*) regress, recourse. *hak* – right/power of regress. – *melompat* regress to a remote party.

régrési (*D*) regression.

régrésif (*D*) regressive.

regu → GU I. **1** company, smallest tactical unit of the *TNI*, consisting of 12 to 14 men. **2** smallest unit of the *Pramuka* Boy Scout Movement, consisting of *penggalang* (maximum membership 10). **3** squad, party, team, unit. **4** (day/night) shift. **5** (soccer) team; → KESEBELASAN. **6** crew (of rowing boat). **7** (botanical) species; → SPÉSIÉS. – *bantuan* (*mil*) support group. – *Béla Diri* Self-Defense Squad (of the *PKI*). – *belakang* (*mil*) rear party. – *bunuh diri* suicide squad. – *malam* night shift. – *muat* loading hands. – *pelopor* (*mil*) advance. – *penémbak* firing squad. – *pengintai* (*mil*) reconnaissance party. – *penolong/penyelamat* rescue squad. – *provos* internal affairs (in the police). – *siang* day shift. – *témbak* firing squad.

seregu on the same team.

beregu in squads/groups/shifts/teams, etc.

meregukan to divide up into squads, shifts, etc.

kereguan (*mod*) squad, relating to squads, etc.

reguk (*M*) **sereguk** a gulp/swallow/slug (of a drink), sip. ~ *air* a gulp of water.

mereguk 1 to gulp down. **2** to finish (a certain amount of education). *Dia hanya* ~ *bangku SD 6 tahun.* He only finished six years of elementary school. **3** to taste. ~ *liur* to want s.t. very much.

tereguk gulped down.

regukan gulp.

régular (*E*) regular.

merégularkan to regularize.

régularisasi (*E*), **régulérisasi** (*D*) regularization.

régularitas (*E*) regularity.

régulasi (*D*) regulating, adjusting.

merégulasi(kan) to regulate, adjust.

régulatif (*D*) regulative.

régulator (*E*) regulator, governor.

régulér (*D*) regular.

merégulérkan to regularize.

regup meregup 1 to drink. **2** to taste; → REGUK.

regut → RENGGUT.

réh (*Jv*) rule, regulation.

ngréh to govern, rule.

réhab clipped form of **réhabilitasi**.

meréhab to rehabilitate, repair. *Sebagian jalan-jalan bopéng dan sedang diréhab.* Some of the streets are potholed and are being rehabilitated.

réhabilitasi (*D*) **1** rehabilitation, recovery. **2** reparation. **3** reeducation.

meréhabilitasi(kan) 1 to rehabilitate. **2** to repair. **3** to reeducate.

teréhabilitasi rehabilitated.

peréhabilitasian rehabilitating.

réhabilitir (*D*) **meréhabilitir 1** to rehabilitate. **2** to repair. **3** to reeducate.

réhal (*A*) a small desk or reading stand for the Koran, Koran rest/lectern. *kena* – to be reviewed (of a book).

meréhalkan to review (a book). *Bila buku menarik dan memenuhi kritéria kami, tentu kami réhalkan.* If a book is interesting and meets our criteria, of course we'll review it.

réhan (*A ob*) dream life.

réhat (*A*) **1** rest, break; → ISTIRAHAT. **2** dormant. – *kopi* coffee break.

beréhat(-réhat) to relax, take a break.

meréhatkan to give s.o. a rest/break.

réhidrasi (*E*) rehydration.

REI (*init*) Real Estate Indonesia.

réindoktrinasi (*E*) reindoctrination.

meréindoktrinasi to reindoctrinate.

réinkarnasi (*D*) reincarnation.

beréinkarnasi to reincarnate.

réintegrasi (*E*) reintegration.

réinterprétasi (*E*) reinterpretation.

réinvéntarisasi (*E*) reinventorization.

réinvéstasi (*E*) reinvestment.

réislamisasi reislamization.

réja (*A?*) scraps, leftovers, remains, remnants.

réja-réja ~ *ayam* inedible chicken parts. ~ *kain* scraps of cloth, remnants. ~ *kayu* wood chips. ~ *kertas* scraps of paper. ~ *nasi* leftovers. ~ *roti* breadcrumbs.

Rejab → RAJAB.

rejah merejah to charge/dash forward recklessly; intrude on, gatecrash.

merejahkan to crash/ram into.

perejah intruder, gate-crasher; → DAYAK.

rejam → RAJAM.

rejan intense physical strain (from coughing/dysentery). *batuk* – whooping cough. *sakit* – dysentery.

merejan to strain (when coughing, etc.).

rejang I k.o. horoscope or divination based on days of the month symbolized by different animals.

rejang II merejang to break up soil with a crowbar.

perejang crowbar.

rejang III gallop (of a horse); → LEJANG.

serejang as far as (a horse) can gallop. ~ *kuda berlari* the distance a horse can run.

rejang IV k.o. tree, milkwood, *Alstonia spathulata.*
Rejang V an ethnic group in Sumatra.
rejap leaking.
rejasa I (*ob*) tin.
rejasa II (*Jv*) a tree whose bark is used for medicine against a suppurating skin disease and the leaves as a remedy for exhaustion, *Elacocarpus grandiflora.*
rejat → REJAP.
rejeb → RAJAB.
réjéh bloodshot (of eyes). *sakit* – suffering from conjunctivitis/pinkeye.
rejeki → REZEKI.
rejeng (*J/Jv*) **merejeng** to seize and hold (by several persons). *Kalau tidak direjeng bersama-sama, anak itu sukar disuruh minum obat.* If he isn't grabbed hold of by several persons, it's hard to get that child to take his medicine.
réjim → RÉZIM.
rejuk merejuk to spring/jump up, pounce (of a cat/tiger, etc.).
rék I (*onom*) scratching sound made by a knife scraping over a board.
rék II (*D*) rack, bookshelf.
rék III (in East Java) clipped form of **arék**, i.e., a term of address to young males; → ARÉK *Suroboyo.* "*Gampang – cari duit di Jakarta,*" *katanya.* "It's easy, kid, to make a living in Jakarta," he said.
rék IV to bet on each number in a series (in the lottery).
rék V (*Jv*) (clipped form of **korék**) 1 match. 2 cigarette lighter (with a flint).
réka (*Skr*) 1 composition; fiction; → RÉKAAN. 2 (*ob*) arrangement; measure, step; → RÉKA-RÉKA. *Orang banyak –nya untuk mencari uang.* People have many different ways of making money. – *ulang* reconstruction, reenactment.
réka-réka (*ob*) arrangement; measure, step. *mengambil ~ untuk menyelamatkan keluarganya* to take steps to safeguard his family.
meréka(-réka)(kan) 1 to compose (a poem, etc.), write. *~ sajak yang élok* to compose a beautiful poem. 2 to look for (ways, etc.). *Ia tidak jemu-jemunya meréka-réka jalan yang manakah yang harus ditempuhnya kelak.* He doesn't stop looking for what he should do in the future. 3 to plan, think up, devise, invent, contrive. *meréka-rékakan undang-undang baru* to think up new laws. 4 to fantasize, imagine, picture in one's mind. *meréka-réka apa yang akan terjadi* to imagine what is going to happen. 5 to consider, weigh, think over, contemplate. *Kami sudah meréka bahwa ia akan terpilih menjadi présidén.* We think that he's going to be elected president.
rékaan 1 coinage. 2 invented, made-up, fictional. *cerita ~* fiction. *Cerita seumpama ini adalah semata-mata ~.* A story like this is pure fiction. 3 (*mod*) dummy.
réka-rékaan 1 composition, tale, story. 2 invention, artifact, creation. 3 idea, plan, program.
peréka inventor, creator, designer.
perékaan inventing, designing.
rekaat /-ka'at/ → RAKAAT.
rékabaru analogy.
rékabentuk design.
merékabentuk to design.
perékabentuk designer. *~ pesawat terbang* aircraft designer.
rékacipta (*Skr neo*) invention.
merékacipta to invent.
perékacipta inventor.
rekah cracked. – *pecah* shatter and crack.
merekah 1 cracked, chapped (of lips/fingers/soil); split open (of a rind/pod), burst open (of buds/shell of fruit). 2 to break (of daylight, etc.), crack (a smile). *seperti delima ~* cracked/burst open (said of a beautiful mouth and teeth). *~ fajar* the day is breaking. *fajar ~* daybreak. *~ jantung* to be heartbreaking.
merekahkan to crack/split s.t. open.
rekahan 1 crack, break. 2 (*geol*) cleat.
perekahan fracturing.
rékal → RÉHAL.
rékalkulasi (*D*) recalculation.

rékalsitran (*D*) recalcitrant.
rekam (*A?*) 1 (im)print, impression. 2 embroidery. 3 sound groove (on record or tape). *– sumur* (*petro*) well logging. 4 (medical) records.
berekam recorded, taped. *musik yang sudah ~* recorded/taped music.
merekam 1 to record, tape (sound on records or tapes), log. 2 to print, color (woven material, etc.). 3 to embroider (with gold or colored thread), batik. 4 (*M*) to stick to (one's body or article of clothing).
merekamkan 1 to record (sound on records or tapes), log. 2 to paint (a picture/letters from a mold in white paint on suitcases, etc.), engrave. *Novél itu ~ kehidupan masyarakat secara keseluruhannya.* The novel paints a picture of social life in its entirety. 3 to embroider. 4 to leave an impression of.
terekam [and **kerekam** (*coq*)] recorded, taped, painted, impressed. *~ 160 kali goncangan* 160 tremors were recorded. *~ dalam kotak hitam* recorded on the black box (of airplanes).
rekaman 1 recording, taping. *~ bunyi* sound recording. *~ médis* medical records. *~ pita* tape recording. *~ suara* sound recording. 2 copy. *~ dikirimkan kepada* (typed under a letter in Sumatra) copy sent to, cc. 3 log, logging (in). *~ sumur* well log.
perekam recorder (the person and the device). *alat ~* (*suara*) tape recorder. *alat ~ penerbangan* flight recorder. *~ kasét vidéo* video cassette recorder. *~ pita* tape recorder. *~ pita vidéo* video tape recorder.
perekaman (tape)recording, logging.
rekan I 1 associate, (business) partner; → MITRA. 2 friend, companion, colleague; fellow-, -mate, co-. *dengan -.-nya* a) with his friends/associates; → C.S., CUM SUIS. b) with affiliates. *– dialog* interlocutor. *– kental* a close friend. *– penebus* (*RC*) coredeemer (= Mary). *– penumpang* fellow passenger. *– seasrama* dorm mate. *– sefraksi* person in the same (political) faction. *– sejawat* colleague. *– sekamar* roommate. *– sekelas* classmate. *– sekerja* office colleague. *– selatihan* training partner. *– semobil* fellow passenger (in a car). *– seperguruan* schoolmate. *– sepondokan* fellow boarder. *– seprofési* professional colleague. *– setahanan* fellow prisoner. *– sewartawan* co-reporter, fellow journalist. *– sponsor* co-sponsor.
berekan to associate (with). be associated (with).
merekan to associate with, befriend.
rekanan partner. *~ untuk Kemajuan* Partners for Progress. **berekanan** to be partners with.
kerekanan partnership.
rekan II market, emporium.
rekanan supplier.
perekanan supplier; → PEMASOK, PENYUPLAI.
perekanan supplying. *~ makanan* catering; → JASABOGA.
rekanita female colleague.
rékap (clipped form of **rékapitulasi**) recap.
rékapitalisasi (*E*) recapitalization.
merekapitalisasi to recapitalize.
rékapitulasi (*D*) recapitulation.
réka-réka an annual grass, *Setaria laxa.*
rekasa (*Jv*) to live in poverty.
rekat cement, glue. *– tanaman* vegetable glue.
merekat to glue (two things together), affix.
merekatkan to stick, attach, affix. *Jangan lupa ~ perangko pada sampul surat.* Don't forget to put a stamp on the envelope.
terekat glued, cemented.
rekatan 1 gluing, affixing, attaching. 2 two things glued together. *~ kertas* two pieces of paper stuck together.
kerekatan adhesion, adhesiveness.
perekat 1 glue, adhesive. *daya ~* adhesive strength. *~ gigi palsu* denture adhesive. *~ kayu* joiner's glue. *~ pita* self-adhesive tape, Scotch tape. 2 cement, mortar. **berperekat** with an adhesive.
perekatan 1 sticking, gluing, cementing. 2 consolidation. *~ pasir* (*petro*) sand consolidation.
rekata 1 scorpion; → KALA. 2 Scorpio (*zod*).
rékatéknik engineering.
rékayasa 1 engineering; → TÉKNIK. *ahli –* engineer. *ilmu – génétika*

genetic engineering. *proyék* – engineering project. **2** machinations, manipulations, skulduggery. – *angkutan* transportation engineering. – *bio* bioengineering. – *génétika* genetic engineering. – *kebaharian/kelautan* naval/ocean engineering. – *keuangan* financial manipulation. – *lalu lintas* traffic engineering. – *lepas pantai* off-shore engineering. – *molékulér* molecular engineering. – *penanaman* plant engineering. – *pesisir* coastal engineering. – *politik* political manipulation. – *sosial* social engineering.

merékayasa 1 to engineer. **2** to manipulate, doctor (the books, etc.).

kerékayasaan engineering. ~ *lalu lintas* traffic engineering.

perékayasaan 1 engineering. ~ *industri* industrial engineering. ~ *kendaraan bermotor* automotive engineering. **2** manipulation, skulduggery, doctoring.

rékayasawan engineer.

réken (*D*) **beréken** (*IBT*) to calculate, figure out.

meréken 1 to calculate, figure out, compute. **2** to count, reckon. *sudah diréken* already included/taken into account.

rékenan calculation, counting.

rékening (*D*) **1** bill, check, invoice. *Dia dikenakan – sebesar 2.500 dolar.* He was presented with a bill for $2,500. *tukang –* bill collector. **2** (bank) account. *membuka – pada sebuah bank* to open a bank account. – *administratif* off balance sheet. – *air* water bill. – *berjalan* current account. – *bernomor* a numbered account. – *bersama* joint account. – *bersama dengan tandatangan ganda* joint account with two signatures required. – *bersama dengan tandatangan tunggal atau ganda* joint account with one or two signatures required. – *déposito* deposit account. – *dibekukan* blocked account. – *gabungan* joint account. – *gas* gas bill. – *giro* demand deposit account. – *koran* a) statement of accounts. b) current account. – *listrik* electric bill. – *penampungan* escrow account. – *penjualan* account sales. – *Rupiah Bukan Penduduk* Nonresident Rupiah Account. – *tabungan* savings account. – *tagihan* statement of an account. – *télepon* telephone bill. – *terkendali* zero-balance account. – *titipan* escrow account.

rekés (*D leg*) **1** request, petition. **2** letter of application. *membuang –* to send out letters of application at random.

merekés to petition, file/lodge a petition.

rékisitoar → RÉKUISITOR.

réklamasi (*D*) reclamation.

meréklamasi(kan) to reclaim (land).

réklame (*D*) **1** (*leg*) complaint, claim. **2** advertising. *papan – raksasa* giant billboard, ballyhoo. – *berjalan* k.o. sandwich board (advertising carried around on a board slung over s.o.'s shoulders); → WAWAR.

me(ng)réklamekan to advertise.

réklaséring (*D*) discharged prisoner's aid, aftercare of prisoners, probation.

réklasifikasi (*E*) reclassification.

rékognisi (*E*) recognition.

rekol (*E*) /rikol/ recall.

merekol to recall (force members of Parliament to give up their mandate).

rékoléksi (*E*) recollection, reflection.

rékomendasi (*D*) recommendation. *surat –* letter of recommendation.

merékomendasikan to recommend.

perékomendasian recommending, referring.

rékoméndir (*D*) **merékomendir** to recommend.

rékondisi (*E*) recondition.

rékonpénsi → RÉKONVÉNSI.

rékonsiliasi (*E*) reconciliation; → RUJUK. *melakukan –* to reconcile. – *nasional* national reconciliation.

berékonsiliasi (*dengan*) to reconcile (with).

merékonsiliasikan to reconcile.

rékonstruir (*D*) **merekonstruir** to reconstruct.

rékonstruksi (*D*) **1** reconstruction (of events). **2** reorganization.

merékonstruksi(kan) to reconstruct.

rékonstruktif (*E*) reconstructive.

rékonvénsi (*D leg*) reconvention, counterclaim proceedings.

rékor (*D*) record. *memecahkan –* to break a record. *memegang –* to

hold a record. *menumbangkan –* to break a record. *pemegang –* record holder. – *dunia* world record. – *nasional* national record.

rékréasi (*D*) recreation. *ruang –* recreation room.

berékréasi to take some recreation.

rékrék k.o. fish, bald glassy, *Ambassis gymnocephalus*.

rékrut (*D*) recruit, draftee.

merékrut to recruit, draft. *Cathay Pacific telah ~ 80 awak pesawat warga negara Indonésia.* Cathay Pacific has recruited 80 Indonesian crew members.

perékrutan recruitment, drafting.

rékrutir (*D*) **merékrutir** to recruit, draft.

rékrutisasi recruitment, drafting.

reksa (*Jv ob*) /-so/ **1** to guard, watch over. **2** police.

reksabumi (*Jv*) /-so-/ member of village administration.

reksadana and **reksa dana** (*Jv + Skr*) mutual fund, investment fund, unit trust. – *campuran* balanced fund. – *saham* equity fund. – *terbuka* open-end investment fund. – *tertutup* closed-end investment fund.

rékstok (*D*) horizontal bar (for gymnastics).

rékta *wésél –* nonnegotiable bill.

réktifikasi (*D*) rectification.

réktor (*D*) **1** president (of university and some academies). **2** dean (of a university).

keréktoran 1 presidency (of a university). **2** deanship.

réktorat (*D*) **1** presidency (of a university). *gedung –* president's building. **2** deanship.

réktum (*D/E*) rectum.

rékuiém (*D/E*) requiem.

rékuisisi (*D*) requisition.

rékuisitor and **rékuisitur** (*D*) public prosecutor's closing statement.

rekurs (*D*) to repeat a course.

rekut convulsion during epileptic attack.

rél (*D*) rail(s), railway track. *keluar (dari) –* a) derailed, off the rails. b) off the subject. c) out of control. – *ganda* double track. – *gerigi* a) cog railway. b) the cog railway between Jambu and Gemarang station in Central Java. – *lawan* guardrail. – *penuntun* guide rail. – *silang* crosspiece.

ber(r)él with a track/rails. ~ *satu* monorailed. *keréta api listrik ~ satu* monorail electric train.

réla (*A*) **1** to be ready/willing (to do s.t.). – *mati membéla tanah air* willing to die to defend one's country. **2** permission, approval. *dengan – hati* with pleasure, wholeheartedly. *Saya memberikan ini kepada anda dengan – hati.* I give you this with pleasure. *dengan suka –* voluntarily, freely (without expecting recompense). *menyerahkan dengan suka – sebagian dari pendapatannya* to hand over part of his income voluntarily. *pasukan suka –* volunteer troops; → SUKARÉLAWAN. – *dan ikhlas* freely and sincerely.

seréla(nya) at will, just as one pleases. *memberikan sedekah ~ saja* to give alms at will.

merélai to grant/give permission to, agree with, be kindly disposed towards, bless. *perbuatan yang dirélai Tuhan* an act permitted by God.

merélakan [and **ngerélain** (*J coq*)] **1** to permit, allow, let. *Rélakan saya pergi merantau.* Let me emigrate. **2** to cede/renounce/relinquish/give up/surrender. *Wanita yang taat beribadah harus ~ tiga kerbaunya yang tersisa.* The woman who was a loyal worshiper had to relinquish her three remaining buffaloes. ~ *waktu* to give up (or, volunteer) time. **3** to accept/suffer, etc.

kerélaan 1 willingness, readiness. **2** permission. **3** favor, blessings.

perélaan relinquishment.

rela(a)s (*D leg*) (official) report, account.

relai I k.o. pearl shell.

relai II (*reput –*) crumbling (*esp* of wood), falling to pieces.

relai III k.o. tree which provides varnish

rélai (*E*) relay; → RILÉ. *stasiun –* relay station.

merélai to relay.

rélaks → RILÉK(S).

rélaksasi (*D/E*) → RILÉKSASI.

relang I merelang to glitter, flash.

relang II ring (of rattan or wire).

relap merelap to glitter, flash (of gems/silver plate/fish in water, etc.).

relas I merelas 1 to peel (skin/fruit/coconut shell). **2** to husk (rice). **3** to shell (eggs). **4** to strip (s.o. of his possessions).

relas II merelas to break s.t. up into small pieces.

rélasi (D) **1** relation, connection. **2** acquaintance. **3** subscriber. **4** customer (of a bank), client.

rélatif and **rélatip** (D) relative(ly). *dalam waktu yang – singkat* in a relatively short time. **kerélatifan** relevativeness.

rélativis (D) relativist.

rélativisasi (E) relativization.

rélativisme (D/E) relativism.

rélativitas (D) relativity. *– kultural* cultural relativity.

relau furnace for tin smelting, smelter.

rélawan volunteer; worker. *– sosial* social worker.

rélban (D) railroad.

rélék(s) (E) to relax, take it easy; → RILÉK(S).

rélévan (D) relevant. *kurang –* irrelevant. **kekurang-rélévanan** irrelevance.

rélévansi (D) relevance.

rélevir merélevir (D) to make s.t. relevant, bring s.t. to the forefront.

réli (E) rally, i.e., a competitive automobile race over a fixed route. *– mobil kuno* antique car rally. *– sepéda* bicycle rally. **peréli** participant in a rally.

réliabilitas (E) reliability.

réliéf (D) relief (in sculptures, etc.). **ber(r)éliéf** with reliefs. *guci-guci antik yang ~* antique jars with reliefs.

réligi (D) religion.

réligiositas (D) religiosity.

réligius (D) religious. **keréligiusan** religiousness.

rélikui and **rélikwi** (religious) relic.

réling (D/E) railing.

rélis (E) release. **merélis** to release.

réliwan participant in a rally, rallier; → PERÉLI.

rélokasi (E) relocation. **merélokasi(kan)** to relocate.

reluk curve, bend. **bereluk** with curves/bends.

relung I 1 hollow (in the ground/on mountain slopes, etc.), niche, recess, alcove. **2** ins and outs. *–.– politik* the ins and outs of politics. **3** the innermost part, depths. *Suara itu begitu lembut masuk ke –.– hatiku.* The voice was so soft that it entered the depths of my heart. *– empasan* cove. *– hati* subconscious. *– langit* airspace. **merelung 1** to be coiled up. **2** to be dome-shaped. **relungan** niche, recess, alcove.

relung II (ob) a land measure of *app* 1⅓ acres.

rém I (D) brake(s). *Mobil itu mengalami kecelakaan karena –nya blong.* The car had an accident because the brakes failed. *menginjak –* to step on the brake, brake to a stop. *tukang –* a) (railroad) brakeman. b) person whose task it is to corner a victim (in pickpocket jargon on Jakarta city buses). *– angin* air brake. *– bahaya* emergency brake. *– cakra/cakram* disk brake. *– dalam* expansion brake. *– darurat* emergency brake. *– féli* rim brake. *– hidraulik* hydraulic brake. *– kaki* foot brake. *– sepéda* bicycle brakes. *– tangan* handbrake. *– t(e)romol* drum brake. *– torpédo* coaster/back-pedaling brake.

merém and **mengerém** to brake, put on the brakes. *~ cepat-cepat* to slam on the brakes. *~ hawa nafsu* to control one's passions. *~ diri* to restrain o.s. *Ia bisa ~ diri untuk hanya menelan pil penenang tiap tiga malam.* He was able to limit himself to taking sedatives only every third evening.

réman *bekas ~* skid/tire mark.

pengerém brake (on).

pengeréman braking. *Sebuah as keréta api "Sriwijaya" rusak akibat terjadinya ~ mendadak.* One of the Sriwijaya railroad axles broke because of the sudden braking.

rém II (in acronyms) → RÉSORT *militér*.

réma (Jv) hair (on the head); → RAMBUT.

rémah I crumbs (of bread, etc.). *karét –* crumb rubber. **merémah-rémah 1** to crumble; crumbly. **2** (= merémah-rémahkan) to make crumbs of s.t., crumble up.

rémah II (M) crumpled, rumpled, friable.

remai aching (of the bones), k.o. rheumatism.

remaja (Skr) **1** adolescent, of marriageable age, nubile. *dalam usia – put(e)ra/put(e)ri* a) at a marriageable age. b) in the prime of life, in one's youth. *masa (pancaroba) –* puberty, adolescence. *Pada masa -nya ia seorang penyanyi dan penari.* In his youth he was a singer and dancer. *put(e)ra –* adolescent, teenager. **2** young, youthful, juvenile, teenage, in one's teens. *golongan –* the teenage set, teenagers. *kejahatan –* juvenile delinquency. **3** junior. *– kedua* second childhood, Indian summer. *– kencur* a) minor. b) inexperienced. *– put(e)ra* a) manhood. b) teenage boy. *– put(e)ri* a) womanhood. b) teenage girl.

meremaja to become young again, rejuvenate.

meremajakan 1 to rejuvenate s.o. **2** to replace older persons/things by younger/newer ones, update. *Perusahaan Penerbangan Garuda akan tetap ~ armada pesawatnya.* Garuda will continue to replace its fleet of older planes with new ones. **3** to renovate, (urban) renew, refurbish.

keremajaan youth(fulness).

peremaja rejuvenator.

peremajaan 1 rejuvenation. **2** renovation, renewal, replacement of old by new, updating. *~ kota* urban renewal.

remajawati (Skr neo) teenage girl, young lady.

remak (it would be) better (to), (it would be) preferable (to).

remang I fine body hair. *kacang –* k.o. hairy-skinned bean. *– tegak* stand on end. **meremang tegak** to stand on end. **meremang tegakkan** to make s.t. stand on end. **meremang** *~ bulu roma* it makes one's hair stand on end, gives one goose flesh. **meremangkan** *~ bulu (kuduk)* to make one's hair stand on end; horrible, horrifying.

remang II meremang 1 to flow out slowly (of tears/perspiration). **2** to be drenched (in sweat).

remang III cloudy, overcast; dim, vague, obscure; vaguely visible. **remang-remang 1** dim, dusky. *tampak ~* vaguely visible in the dark. **2** shady. *tokoh ~* a shady character. **keremang-remangan 1** dimness. **2** somewhat dim. **meremang 1** to get to be dusk (in the evening). **2** (to be/become) dimly visible. **keremangan 1** twilight, dusk; darkness. **2** faint glow.

remang IV yellow pike conger, *Muraenesox talabon*.

remang V meremang to hum (of insects).

remas knead, squeeze. **meremas 1** to knead, squeeze. *~ tepung* to knead flour. **2** to wring out. *~ kain basah* to wring out wet clothes. **3** to crumple (up). *Ia ~ surat itu, lalu dibuangnya ke keranjang sampah.* She crumpled up the letter and threw it into the wastepaper basket. **4** to massage. *Ia ~ kakinya yang keram itu.* He massaged his cramped leg. *perut ~* to have a stomachache, have the gripes. *~ bibir* to beat up. *~ santan di kuku* to do s.t. that cannot be profitable. *~ jantung* a) to be angry, irritated. b) heartrending. *~ mulut* to beat up. *~ perut* a) to be angry, irritated. b) heartrending. **5** to crush by pressing.

meremas-remas to keep on kneading/squeezing.

meremasi (pl obj) to squeeze.

meremaskan to squeeze (one's hand).

teremas squeezed out.

remasan squeezing, kneading.

peremasan kneading.

remat → REMAS.

rématik (D) rheumatism. *terserang –* to have an attack of rheumatism.

rématisme (D) → RÉMATIK.

rématologi (D) rheumatology. *ahli –* rheumatologist.

remba a pair. **beremba-remba** in pairs.

rembah I *– rembih* a) to trickle/stream down (of tears). b) sloppily dressed (one's sarong isn't straight, etc.).

rembah-rembah pouring out (of tears, etc.).
    merembah to trickle down (of tears).
rembah II → RAMBAH.
rembak right, precise. – *itulah.* That's it/right.
rembang I 1 (at the) highest point, (at the) zenith/apex. *sebelum –
tengah hari* before noon. *matahari –* and *– tengah hari* noon,
midday. **2** the exact moment in time. *Segala takwin kitab dibuka, –lah saat dengan seketika.* All the Koranic explanations
were opened and all of a sudden it was the precise moment. –
petang a) toward late afternoon, past three o'clock in the afternoon. b) getting dim. – *petang partai politik Islam.* Dark clouds
began to loom over the Muslim parties. – *senja* toward evening.
3 apex, apical. – *mata* philanderer, wolf.
    berembang and **merembang** *hari sudah ~ petang* it's late after-
noon.
rembang II a green vegetable used in *lalapan.* – *panas* coastal tea-
tree, *Leptospermum laevigatum.*
rembas ruined, spoiled. *habis –* finished, all gone, completely
wrecked/ruined.
    merembas to seep out.
    rembasan seepage.
    perembasan seepage.
rembat to shake from side to side.
    merembat 1 to move from side to side. **2** to hit from left to right
and then from right to left.
rémbat and **rémbatan** (*ob*) crossbar (of a door), long pole along
gunwale of a boat.
    merembati to provide s.t. with a crossbar (for strengthening).
rembau (*M*) *adat –* matriarchy.
rembéga a medicinal shrub, madar, giant milkweed, *Calotropis gigantea.*
rémbés and **rembes I** (*J/Jv*) **merémbés 1** to ooze out, leak. *Keringatnya ~ keluar ke sekujur badannya.* His whole body oozed
perspiration. **2** to seep (in/through), penetrate, permeate. *Air
hujan dapat ~ masuk ke dalam kamar tidur.* Rainwater could
seep into his bedroom. **3** to trickle (in), spread (into), infiltrate.
~ ke bawah to trickle down. *"Ganja" barang terkutuk itu
sekarang mulai ~ ke segala ceruk-rantau.* "Ganja," that cursed
thing, has started to spread to every nook and cranny. *Gerom-
bolannya ~ ke kota.* The rebels have infiltrated the city.
    merémbési 1 to ooze/leak into. **2** to penetrate into. **3** to
infiltrate into.
    merémbéskan to make/cause s.t. to leak into, infiltrate s.t.
    terémbés penetrated, infiltrated. **keterémbésan** permeability.
    rémbésan infiltration, seepage. *~ gas* (*petro*) blow-by. *~ masuk*
influent seepage.
    perémbés infiltrator.
    perémbésan 1 oozing, leakage, seepage. *~ air laut masuk ke
darat* the leaking of sea water into the land. **2** infiltration.
rémbés II (*Jv*) bloodshot and irritated (of the eye). *Matanya –.*
He has pinkeye/conjunctivitis.
rémbét I hampered, hindered, impeded, obstructed.
    merémbét to hinder, hamper, impede, obstruct.
rémbét II (*Jv*) **merémbét 1** to spread; → MENJALAR. *Dengan pesat
api ~ ke rumah tetangganya.* The fire spread quickly to the
neighboring house. **2** to bring in, involve, include, implicate.
Jangan ~ nama saya dalam perkara itu. Don't bring my name
into that case. *Bukan anak-anak saja yang dicaci-makinya, melainkan ~ ke orangtua meréka.* He not only heaped curses on
the children, but he also included their parents. **3** to proceed/
move slowly/by fits and starts. *Suara mobil ~ di jalan berbatu
itu.* The sound of a car moved slowly along the rocky road.
    merémbétkan 1 to involve/implicate, bring in. *Pembicaraan
kita biarlah terbatas pada soal pokok saja, jangan ~ soal pribadi.* Let's limit our discussion to the basic problem, don't
bring in personal matters. **2** to spread s.t.
    kerémbétan to get involved/implicated.
    perémbétan involvement.
rembia → RUMBIA.
rembih merembih to trickle/drip down, flow.
rémbong (*Jv*) **berémbong(-rémbong)an** (*pl subj*) tattered, frayed.
rembuk and **rembug** (*Jv*) deliberation, consultation, discussion,

conference. – *désa/kampung* a meeting of the elders and leaders of a village. –*nasional* national deliberations.
    berembuk to discuss, hold discussions, confer, deliberate, con-
sult. *Ia akan ~ dulu dengan kawan-kawannya.* He'll hold discussions with his friends first.
    me(mpe)rembukkan to discuss s.t.
    rembukan discussions. *Sebelum DPR mengembalikan RUU ke-
pada Pemerintah terlebih dulu diadakan ~ antara pimpinan
fraksi dan pimpinan déwan.* Before Parliament returns the
Draft Bill to the Government, discussions are first held between leaders of the factions and Parliament leaders.
    perembukan discussions, deliberations, conference, consulta-
tion.
rembulan (*Jv*) moon.
rembunai 1 (*cla*) average (of a person's size or height). **2** (*bio*) low-
growing.
rembunia → REMENIA.
remburs (*D*) **1** cash on delivery, COD. **2** reimbursement.
rembus → EMBUS I.
rembut I terembut-rembut to flicker, glitter, twinkle. *Pelita-pelita
itu menyala ~.* The oil lamps were flickering.
rembut II (*J*) **berembut-rembut** to struggle to get a glimpse of
s.t.; → REBUT.
rémédial (*E*) remedial. *kursus –* remedial course.
réméh trivial, unimportant, insignificant, negligible. *soal yang tidak
dapat dipandang –* a problem that cannot be considered trivial. –
céméh/téméh worthless, unimportant. **meréméh-téméhkan** to
consider insignificant, trivialize, neglect, ignore. *Kecenderung-
nya memegah-megahkan satu pihak dan ~ pihak lain.* His tendency is to brag about one party and to consider the other party
insignificant.
    seréméh as simple/unpretentious as. *Persoalannya tidak ~ itu.*
The matter is not as simple as that.
    meréméhkan to consider insignificant/trivial/unimportant,
think nothing of, underestimate; to ignore. *Jangan ~ bersin,
karena bersin dapat berubah menjadi flu.* Don't ignore a cold
because a cold can turn into the flu.
    keréméhan unimportance, insignificance, triviality. *~ hati* pet-
tiness.
    peréméhan trivializing, treating as unimportant, neglect, ne-
glecting.
remen (*Jv*) to like.
remeng (*Jv*) → REMANG III.
remenia a tree with edible fruit which provides timber for building materials, *Bouea burmanica/macrophylla.*
rémét merémét to chatter away, ramble on, talk nonsense.
    perémét chatterbox.
remetuk (*burung –*) golden-bellied gerygone, *Gerygone sulphurea.*
remi and **rémi** (*D*) rummy (the card game).
remiak → RIAK *remiak.*
rémigran (*E*) remigrant.
rémigrasi (*E*) remigration.
rémiling (*E*) remilling.
réminisénsi (*E*) reminiscence.
remis I and **remise** (*D*) (in chess) a draw, tie. *bermain –* to draw,
tie. *ditahan –* held to a draw.
remis(e) II (*D*) remittance (of money).
remis III a small, edible, sand-dwelling bivalve, *Corbicula spp.*
remis IV (*D*) depot (of a tramway, etc.).
remis V (*col*) a half-cent coin.
rémisi (*leg*) remission.
rémoh (*M*) crumpled (up), rumpled.
rempa (*cla*) **merempa** to hit.
rempah I merémpah 1 to run through trampling on (plants, etc.).
2 to roam, rove, wander. **3** to clear away (weeds/undergrowth,
etc.).
rempah II 1 spices (as a commercial object). – *aromatik* a blend of
peppermint, lavender, cloves, and thyme. – *pawah/perawis/
piah* all k.o. spices. **2** ingredients (in medicinal drugs). – *ratus*
various ingredients (of a medicine, etc.).
    rempah-rempah all k.o. spices.
    merempah to spice s.t.

merempah(-rempah)i 1 to season, spice, flavor. *Ia pandai ~ berbagai masakan.* He's good at flavoring various dishes. 2 (*ob*) to embalm.

perempah 1 seasoning, flavoring. *Lada hitam ~ daging.* Black pepper is a seasoning for meat. 2 (*ob*) embalmer.

rempah III (*Jv*) beef and coconut patties.

rempah IV to collapse and fall down; → REBAH *rémpah.*

rempak I berempak in rows/files/lines.

serempak(-serempak) altogether, all at once, in unison, simultaneously. menyerempak a) to overpower, overwhelm, crush, subdue. b) to attack in unison. menyerempakkan to synchronize. keserempakan unison, synchronization. ~ *kerja* teamwork. terserempak overpowered, overwhelmed, etc.

merempak to run toward the same goal.

rempak II → RAMPAK I.

rémpak chipped (of a blade).

rempang eccentric.

rémpang-rémpok and rémpang-rémpong tattered, ragged, jagged, wounded.

rémpat merémpat to run aground (of a boat).

rempela (*Jv*) gizzard.

rempelas sandpaper (leaf); → EMPELAS. *akar* – k.o. shrub (leaves are used as an abrasive), stone leaf, *Tetracera scandens.*

rempelu and rempelo gall; → EMPEDU. *dikéi ati ngrogoh rempelo* (*Jv*) give him an inch and he'll take an ell.

rempenai a small tree whose leaves are made into a remedy against scabies, shoe button, *Ardisia humilis.*

rémpét tender (a boat for carrying passengers, etc. to and from a large ship anchored close to shore).

rempéyék (*Jv*) 1 peanuts fried in spiced batter, k.o. peanut brittle; → PÉYÉK *kacang.* 2 fritter. *– jagung* corn fritter. *– udang* shrimp fritter.

remplas → REMPELAS.

rémpong → RIMPUNG.

rempu → REMUK *rempu.*

rempuh merempuh to rush against, force a way through/into, jostle → MENEMPUH. *Oléh karena tikét telah habis terjual, beberapa orang telah mencoba ~ masuk ke dalam stadion.* Because the tickets were sold out, some people tried to force their way into the stadium.

rempuk → REMBUK.

rempus → RAMPUS.

remujung a plant whose leaves can be used as a medicine against diabetes, cat's whiskers, *Orthosiphon grandiflorus*; → KUMIS *kucing.*

remuk 1 crushed, smashed, broken into very small pieces. 2 to make small, reduce in size, diminish (by hauling/pressing, etc.). *– hati* to fall apart (emotionally/mentally). *– redam* smashed to bits, shattered. meremuk-redamkan to smash to bits. *– rempu* smashed to bits. *– rengsa* to suffer, feel miserable.

remuk-remuk totally crushed/smashed.

meremuk(kan) to crush, smash to bits.

remukan s.t. crushed.

keremukan destruction, breaking up into pieces.

peremuk crusher (the device).

peremukan crushing, smashing to bits, shattering.

remunai → REMBUNAI.

rémunerasi (*E*) remuneration.

remunggai horseradish tree, *Moringa oleifera.*

remuni → REMBUNAI.

rén I (*D*) (chicken) coop.

rén II (in acronyms) → RENCANA.

rena (*ob*) → RONA, WARNA.

réna (*M*) glitter.

renah (in Jambi) village; → DÉSA.

renai (*M*) *hujan –(.-)* drizzle; → RENYAI.

rénaisans (*D*) renaissance.

renang (in compounds) swim(ming), stroke. *kolam –* swimming pool. *pakaian –* bathing suit, swimsuit. *perlombaan –* swimming match. *– (gaya) bébas* freestyle. *– (gaya) dada* breaststroke. *– indah/keindahan* synchronized/exhibition swimming. *– katak/kodok* breaststroke. *– (gaya) kupu-kupu* butterfly stroke. *– menelentang/punggung* backstroke.

berenang to swim, go swimming, take a swim. *mengajar itik ~* to carry coals to Newcastle. ~ *gaya dada* and ~ *kodok* to swim using the breaststroke. ~ *te(r)lentang* to swim using the backstroke.

berenangan (*pl subj*) to swim.

merenangi 1 to swim across/over/to. ~ *selat sepanjang setengah kilométer* to swim across a half-kilometer-long strait. ~ *orang yang tenggelam itu* to swim over to a drowning person. 2 to experience, go through. ~ *liku-liku kehidupan* to go through the ups and downs of life.

merenangkan 1 to let/have swim. 2 to carry s.o. while swimming. *Ia ~ anak yang hanyut itu.* He swam with the child who was carried away in the current.

perenang swimmer.

rencah I – *jebak* quagmire.

merencah 1 to wade through. *Ia tidak mau ~ lumpur jalan itu.* He didn't want to wade through the mud in the street. 2 to defy, dare, face (up to), brave. ~ *bahaya dan kesukaran* to face dangers and hardships. 3 to break up the soil or rice fields by having buffaloes trample on them. *Sawahnya baru-baru ini direncah dengan beberapa kerbau.* His rice fields were recently broken up by buffaloes.

terencah (*M*) 1 overstepped, transgressed. 2 trodden (upon).

rencah II merencah 1 inconstant, fickle. 2 to skip from one subject to another; to try to do so many things that nothing gets done, to flit from job to job.

rencah III spices, ingredients.

merencah to season, flavor, spice.

perencah seasoning, flavoring.

rencak I a large pan.

rencak II (*ob*) merencak to paddle.

rencam (*Skr*) merencam ~ *mata* confusing (to the sight).

rencana (*Skr*) 1 plan, schedule, program; proposal. *sesuai dengan –* on schedule. *tinggal dalam – saja* is still in the planning stage. *"Kapan – nikah?" "Tak tahu, entah kapan."* "When do you plan to get married?" "I don't know when." *dengan – lebih dahulu* with premeditation. 2 draft, rough copy (of a letter, etc.). *– surat itu disimpan di dalam map.* The rough copy of the letter was kept in a file folder. 3 story. *– kuno* an old story. 4 account, report. 5 agenda. *Usul yang tercantum dalam – itu akan dibicarakan malam ini.* The suggestion placed on the agenda will be discussed this evening. 6 article, working paper. *tajuk –* editorial. 7 dictation; → DIKTÉ, IMLAH. *– tinggal – saja* plans just remained plans. *– anggaran belanja* budget proposal. *– babon* master plan. *– buta* a not-too-carefully-thought-out plan. *– induk* master plan. *– kerja* work program/schedule. *– lima tahun* five-year plan. *– kota* urban planning. *– operasi* [rénop] operational plan. *– pekerjaan* a) work program/schedule. b) tender documents, specifications. *– pelajaran* curriculum. *– Pembangunan Lima Tahun* [Répélita] Five-year Development Plan. *– Pembangunan Tahunan* [Répéta] Annual Development Plan. *– perjalanan* itinerary. *– rapat* agenda of a meeting. *– rinci* detailed plan. *– stratégis* [rénstras] strategic plan. *– surat* contents of a letter. *– tapak* site plan. *– terinci* detailed plan. *– Umum Tata Ruang* [RUTR] general plan for spatial planning. *– Undang-Undang* [RUU] bill (in parliament), Draft Bill. *– urgénsi* urgency program. *– usaha tani* farm program. *– usul* draft proposal. *– waktu* time schedule.

berencana with a plan; planned, premeditated. *keluarga ~* family planning, planned parenthood. *pembunuhan ~* premeditated murder. *secara ~ dan sengaja* premeditated, with malice aforethought.

merencana 1 (*ob*) to narrate, relate. 2 to arrange, plan. *Pada sékrétariat itu pula kegiatan direncana pelaksanaannya.* At the secretariat actions for implementation were also arranged.

merencanakan [and ngerencanain (*J coq*)] 1 to draft/write a report/letter. ~ *surat* to draft a letter. 2 to plan. ~ *pembangunan kota* to plan city development. 3 to report, tell, relate. 4 to have in mind, intend (to use); allocate, appropriate. ~ *uang ini untuk membeli beras* to allocate this money for purchasing rice. 5 to arrange, design, schedule, plot. *direncanakan tiba* estimated time of arrival, ETA. *direncanakan dibuka* scheduled to open. 6 to propose. 7 to dictate.

terencana planned, premeditated. *pembunuhan* ~ premeditated murder. keterencanaan planning.

perencana planner, designer. ~ *kota* city planner. ~ *lingkungan* environmental planner.

perencanaan planning, design. *Badan* ~ *Pembangunan Nasional* [Bap(p)enas] National Development Planning Board. ~ *dan penerangan* planning and information. ~ *dari bawah* bottom-up planning. ~ *keluarga* family planning, planned parenthood. ~ *ketenagakerjaan nasional* national manpower planning. ~ *koridor transportasi secara terpadu* integrated transportation-corridor planning. ~ *kota* city/town planning. ~ *pengembangan wilayah sungai* river-basin development planning. ~ *penggunaan tanah* land-use planning. ~ *secara badan usaha* corporate planning. ~ *secara meningkat* incremental planning. ~ *sumber daya manusia* manpower planning. ~ *sumber daya otak* brain-power planning. ~ *tangkal* contingency planning. ~ *tataguna tanah* land-use planning. ~ *tenaga kerja* manpower planning.

rencang (*onom*) clanging.

rencat (*ob*) → BENCAT, GENCAT. terencat stopped, halted, held back. *Kerjanya* ~ *karena air pasang.* His work was halted by the high tide.

rénceh I 1 small (in names of fishes, amounts of money); → RÉCÉH. 2 shriveled.

rénceh II excess, surplus, remainder.

réncék (*J/Jv*) small branches or twigs used for firewood. meréncék(kan) to prune, lop off small branches. réncékan pruned branch.

rénceng I 1 slender/slim (of one's body); spindly-legged. 2 to have no calves (of the legs).

rénceng II (*J*) seréncéng(an) a string (of beads/fireworks/medals of appreciation, etc.). *Semua anggota ABRI memasang* ~ *bintang penghargaan di dada meréka.* All the members of the Indonesian Armed Forces put strings of medals on their chests. beréncéng on a string, stringed. *merjan* ~ beads on a string. meréncéngkan to string things together. réncéngan a string (of fireworks, etc.), line of things one after the other.

rénceng III – *mulut* talkative, loquacious, garrulous.

réncét row, series, file, line; → RÉNTÉT. beréncétan in a row/series, etc., in succession. meréncét piece by piece, little by little.

rencik → RECIK.

rencis merencis to sprinkle (with water, etc.); → RENJIS.

réncong an Acehnese dagger with a curved handle (often used as a symbol of Aceh). *Tanah* – Aceh.

rénda (*Port*) lace(work). berénda with lace. meréndra 1 to crochet, make lace. 2 to sketch out. *Tékad keduanya untuk* ~ *hari depan.* The two of them determined to sketch out their future. meréndai to provide with lace.

réndabel (*D*) profitable, remunerative.

rendah I 1 low (off the ground), low-hanging, short. *Ia tidak dapat memetik buah mangga yang – itu.* He couldn't pick the low-hanging mangos. 2 low/soft (of sounds). *Ia berbicara dengan suara yang –.* He spoke in a low voice. 3 humble, modest. *Ia tetap – hati.* He remained humble. 4 cheap, inexpensive, low in price. *Pada masa dahulu komoditi ini harganya sangat –.* In the past these commodities were low in price. 5 low (in amount or price), little, under-. *meréka yang berpenghasilan –* those with low incomes. *–nya penggunaan/pemanfaatan* underutilization. 6 primary, low-level. *sekolah –* elementary school; → SEKOLAH *dasar.* 7 low (of humble rank or position). *Dari pangkat yang – ia cepat naik ke pangkat yang tinggi sekali.* From a low rank he quickly climbed to a very high rank. 8 low (in quality), inferior. *barang-barang yang bermutu –* low-quality goods. *memandang –* a) to disparage, have a low opinion of. b) to underestimate, undervalue, underrate. – *budi* immoral, of low morals. – *diri* inferior (feelings). – *harapan* hopeless. – *hati* humble, modest, unassuming, not arrogant. *kerendah-hatian* modesty, humility. – *pengawakan* small of stature. – *rezeki* it's easy to make a living.

merendah 1 to descend, come/go down; to get lower (in volume). *Dengkurnya* ~. The sound of his snoring got lower. *Pesawat terbang itu* ~. The airplane descended. 2 to be humble, humble o.s., act modest. *Sifatnya yang selalu – itu mendatangkan banyak kawan kepadanya.* His modest attitude brought him many friends. *bersikap* ~ to be humble, modest, low-key.

merendahkan 1 to bring down, lower, reduce, make lower. 2 to humble, downgrade, humiliate, scorn, put down. ~ *diri* a) to lean forward so as not to be higher than s.o. else. b) to humble o.s., demean o.s., stoop so low as to.

rendahan subordinate, lower (personnel/staff, etc.), low-ranking. *pegawai* ~ low-ranking employee.

kerendahan 1 lowness. 2 low-lying (land). ~ *budi* immorality. ~ *hati* modesty, humility. *dengan segala* ~ *hati* with all due respect.

perendahan humiliation, mortification; lowering.

rendah II noisy, uproarious. *riuh* – uproar, din; noisy, boisterous.

rendam immerse, soak.

berendam 1 to bathe, immerse, immerse o.s. in water; be immersed/submerged/soaked in a liquid, wallow. *Kerbau itu suka* ~ *dalam lumpur.* Buffaloes like to wallow in mud. ~ *sesajak air, berpaut sejengkal tali* to get into hot water, be in a fix. 2 to stay in one place all the time.

merendam to soak, put s.t. into a liquid for some time. ~ *baju-nya yang kotor di dalam air sabun* to soak one's dirty shirt in soapy water. *direndam tak basah* a) very cunning/sly. b) a decision hasn't been reached yet. c) miser, skinflint.

merendami to flood, put water on s.t. ~ *sawah* to flood rice fields.

merendamkan to immerse, soak in a liquid; to inundate, flood with water. ~ *sawah* to inundate a rice field.

terendam [and kerendam (*coq*)] 1 soaked, immersed, submerged (in water, etc.). 2 stayed somewhere for a long time. *Ia* ~ *di rumah orangtua saya.* He got stuck in my parents' house. 3 absorbed (in). *Ia sedang* ~ *dalam novélnya.* He was absorbed in his novel. ~ *sama basah, terampai sama kering* to share one's joys and sorrows; → RINGAN *sama dijinjing, berat sama dipikul.*

rendaman 1 s.t. that has been soaked (in a liquid). 2 bath, place for soaking s.t. ~ *pencuci* developing bath.

perendam soaking agent/device. *larutan* ~ soaking agent solution.

perendaman soaking, hydrocooling.

rendan → KÉRÉ *dandan.*

rendang I dish made of beef (or other ingredients) cooked in chilies and coconut milk until dry. *pisang* – (*Mal*) fried banana fritters; → PISANG *goréng. sagu* – pearl sago.

merendang to prepare *rendang.*

perendangan k.o. frying pan.

rendang II shady (of trees).

rendap → RENDAM.

rendem → RENDAM.

réndemén (*D*) 1 yield, profit (margin), return, output. 2 conversion rate, e.g., percentage of milled rice left after processing stalk paddy.

rendeng I (*Jv*) *musim* – west monsoon, the rainy/wet season in Java (December through January.).

rendengan west monsoon. *padi* ~ paddy grown during the rainy season. *panén* ~ harvest (of a crop planted during the rainy season).

rendeng II (*J*) merendeng to grumble, mutter, complain.

réndéng I (*J*) beréndéng(-réndéng) to be one behind the other, be in (a) row(s). beréndéngan to be in line with. *Idéalisme itu* ~ *dengan kemauan-nya menerima réalitas.* This realism is in line with his desire to accept reality.

meréndéngi and meréndéngkan to place in a row, line things up in rows, align.

réndéng II (*Jv*) leaves of the peanut plant (used for fodder).

rendet (*Jv*) 1 slow, behind (of a watch). *Jam saya – sampai sepuluh menit.* My watch is 10 minutes slow. 2 not smooth, not working smoothly.

kerendetan s.t. that doesn't go smoothly, screw-up.

réndévu(s) (*Fr D*) rendezvous.

réndong (*M*) *terbawa* – involved.

teréndong involved (in), implicated (in), mixed up (in). *Dalam perkara korupsi itu namanya* ~. His name was implicated in the case of corruption.

rénégosiasi (*E*) renegotiation(s).

merénégosiasikan to renegotiate.

rénéh meréneh almost boiling; to simmer, poach.

rének merének to quaver (of the voice), tremble, vibrate.

réng I (*Jv*) (bamboo/wooden) lath (used for roof construction); → RÉNGRÉNGAN. *- kayu* wooden lath.

réng II k.o. vulture-like bird.

rengadéan a small tree whose wood can be used for the construction of houses, etc., *Ploiarum alternifolium.*

rengah → ENGAH.

rengang merengangkan to prick up (one's ears).

rengap shortness of breath.

berengap and **merengap** to pant (with exhaustion), huff and puff; → ENGAP.

rengas I a generic name for trees which yield timber and a sap that produces lacquer varnish, *Gluta velutina* and other species. *minyak* – lacquer. *- air/burung/manuk* k.o. tree, *Melanorrhoea wallichii. - api* a) k.o. tree, *Melanochyla tomentosa.* b) k.o. tree, *Gluta elegans. - ayam* k.o. tree, *Buchanania sessilifolia.*

merengas 1 to varnish. **2** to shine up, make s.t. gleam.

perengasan vitrification, glazing.

rengas II (*J*) mite.

rengat I (*J/Jv*) crack, cleft, split. *- hati* aggrieved, angry.

merengatkan to crack/split open.

rengatan crockery.

rengat II (*M*) **merengat** to ooze out, trickle out; to sweat.

rengat III colic, shooting pain (in one's stomach/teeth/ear).

merengat to have shooting pains.

réngéh meréngéh to neigh, whinny; → MERINGKIK.

réngék whining, wheedling.

meréngék(-réngék) 1 to whine, wheedle (of children), nag. **2** to squeak.

meréngékkan to blare out (a song, etc.).

réngékan whining, wheedling. ~ *kanak-kanaknya* his children's whining.

peréngek whiner, tiresome person.

rengeng (*Jv*) **rengeng-rengeng** and **rengrengan** to hum or sing softly; → BERSENANDUNG.

rengengan humming.

rengga (*cla*) seat on an elephant, saddle for a howdah.

renggam small knife for reaping grain; → TUAI.

renggang I 1 come apart, parted (of joinery). **2** distant (of relations). *Persahabatan meréka menjadi* –. They have become estranged. **3** spaced far apart. **4** loose (of a knot). **5** (to act) aloof.

merenggang to part, come apart, split open.

merenggangi to keep s.o. at a distance from, avoid.

merenggangkan and **memperenggang 1** to separate (what was joined together), keep/push apart, widen (a gap), keep at a distance, space. ~ *hubungan* to break up a relationship. **2** to loosen (a knot/tie).

terenggang with the widest distance between them.

renggangan 1 space; cleft, crack, crevice, slit. **2** thinning, rarefaction.

kerenggangan parting, estrangement.

perenggang ~ *waktu* pastime.

perenggangan loosening.

renggang II (*Pal*) **merenggang** ~ *gawai* to rape a woman.

renggat corrugations (on horns), (annual) rings (on tree trunks).

rénggék merénggék(-rénggék) to keep urging; → RÉNGÉK.

rénggés stripped (of fruit/leaves), almost bare (of feathers), bald; → RANGGAS, RÉGÉS.

merénggés to become bald, stripped.

rengginang a fried sweet cookie made from glutinous rice.

renggut pull, tug, jerk.

merenggut 1 to pull at/away, tug at, snatch, take away by force. *Pencopét itu* ~ *jam tangan teman saya.* The pickpocket snatched my friend's wristwatch. ~ *jiwa suaminya* to take her husband's life. ~ *kegadisan/kehormatan/mahkota (anak) gadis* to deflower a maiden. *Kegadisannya direnggut.* Her maiden-

hood was taken by force. ~ *nyawanya* to take s.o.'s life, kill. *Penyakit léver akhirnya* ~ *nyawanya.* The liver disease finally killed him. *tidak bisa direnggut* inalienable. **2** to obtain through great effort.

merenggut-renggut to keep on pulling at, snatching, etc.

merenggutkan to tear s.t. off/down, pull toward o.s. (of oars). ~ *diri dari* to tear o.s. away from. ~ *dayung* to pull the oars towards o.s. ~ *kaki hendak mati* to be near death in convulsions.

terenggut snatched, taken. ~*nya keperawanannya* the snatching away of her virginity.

renggutan jerk, tug, pull.

perenggut snatcher. ~ *nyawa* killer. *Di Indonésia PJK (penyakit jantung koronér)* ~ *nyawa nomor tiga.* Coronary heart disease is the number three killer in Indonesia.

perenggutan snatching at.

rengit (*S*) gnat, sandfly, a pest of the tobacco plant.

rengka → RENGGA.

rengkah cracked/split (open), broken/burst open; → REKAH. *- dua* split in two.

merengkah to crack open, split apart, burst open.

terengkah cracked open, split apart.

rengkahan crack, cracking, split.

perengkah (*petro*) cracker, cracking still.

perengkahan (*petro*) cracking. *prosés* ~ *itu* the cracking process. ~ *hidro* hydrocracking. ~ *katalik* catalytic cracking. ~ *panas* hot cracking.

rengkam k.o. seaweed, *Sargossum spp.*

réngkat one limb is shorter than the other.

réngkéh bent down, stooping.

meréngkéh to stoop (under a burden), bend (of heavily laden boughs).

teréngkéh(-réngkéh) stooped (under a burden), bent (of laden boughs).

rengket (*Jv*) tightly spaced, too close to e.o., cramped.

réngkét (*J*) **meréngkét** to tremble, quake (with fear). ~ *ketakutan* to tremble with fear.

rengkiang (*M*) rice barn built on four poles.

rengkinang a laurel-like tree with commercial timber used for furniture and planks, *Elaeocarpus floribunda.*

réngking (*E*) ranking.

rengkit (*M*) stiff (of bones and joints).

réngkot (*Jv*) portable set of nesting food containers; → RANTANG I.

rengkudah loaded down.

rengkuh 1 greedy, glutinous. **2** tearing at, pulling toward o.s.

merengkuh to drag toward o.s., tear at s.t. to get at it, pull down (boughs), tug at, eject (cartridges from the breech).

rengkuhan pulling toward o.s., embrace.

perengkuhan grasping for s.t.

réngréng (*Jv*) **meréngréng** to draw up a draft/plan/scheme.

réngréngan (*Jv*) **1** plan, project. **2** blueprint, design. **3** draft, rough copy; → RANCANGAN. **4** scheme.

réngsa I weak, apathetic, indolent, energyless. *- sengsara* beaten down.

meréngsa to take it easy, be idle, be unwilling to work.

keréngsaan listlessness, apathy.

réngsa II intractable (of illness). *- sengsara* and *remuk -* miseries, hardships.

réngsék → RINGSEK.

rengus merengus surly, grumpy, sullen.

merengus to sulk, be sullen.

perengus 1 gruff/surly person. **2** peevish, cross.

rengut → RUNGUT. **berengut** and **merengut(-rengut) 1** to grumble, complain. **2** to be sullen.

perengut sullen person, grumbler.

renik 1 small (of persons, etc.), tiny. *jasad –* microorganisms, microbes. *liang –* pore. *neraca –* microscales. **2** fine (of rain/writing, etc.). *– pernik rumahtangga* everyday household chores.

renik-renik fine, delicate, small (of stature). *hujan* ~ drizzle; drizzling; → *hujan* RINTIK-RINTIK.

berenik-renik 1 drizzling. **2** dotted, speckled.

merenik-renik 1 drizzling. **2** fine(ly). *Berasnya ditumbuk* ~. The rice was pounded very fine. **3** speckled, dotted, spotted.

kerenikan fineness, delicateness.

renjak merenjak 1 to walk with a spring in one's walk. **2** to trample on.

perenjakan saltation.

renjam → RUNJAM.

renjana (*Skr*) strong emotion, longing, desire, love.

berenjana emotional.

kerenjanaan emotionality.

renjang normal; → NORMAL.

renjat renjatan (*mostly Mal*) (electric) shock. *membuat* – to shock, cause an electric shock. *sindrom* – *déngué* dengue shock syndrome.

rénjéng (*M*) **merénjéng** to lift up, raise. ~ *lidah* to begin to speak, take the floor.

rénjer (*E Mal mil*) ranger.

renjis spot, stain, speck.

merenjis to sprinkle, spatter.

merenjisi to sprinkle/spatter on.

merenjiskan to sprinkle, spatter.

rénjong I k.o. swamp crab, *Goniosperma sp.*

rénjong II (*M*) **merénjong** to lift up, raise high; → MERÉNJÉNG. ~ *lidah* to begin to speak, take the floor.

renjul 1 rugged, uneven, bumpy. *jalan-jalan yang – dan berlubang-lubang* the bumpy potholed roads. **2** incoherent.

renminpiao (*C*) currency of the People's Republic of China.

renop (*acr*) → RENCANA *operasi*.

rénovasi (*D*) renovation, repair, renewal.

merénovasi to renovate, repair. *sedang dirénovasi* under repair.

ren-ren-ren (*onom*) sound made by revving a motorcycle engine.

rénstras (*acr*) → RENCANA *stratégis*.

renta I → RENTAK I. **merenta-renta** to speak in a loud and angry voice, raise one's voice, stamp one's feet in anger.

renta II and **rénta** *tua* – very old, decrepit, worn out with age.

réntabilitas and **réntabilitét** (*D*) remunerativeness, profitability.

rentak I 1 stamp(ing) (of the feet); → ENTAK. *dengan –nya* angrily. – *sedegam, langkah sepijak* (*M*) unanimous, in harmony, together, united. **2** beat, rhythm.

berentak ~ *kaki* to stamp one's feet (in anger).

merentak to stamp one's feet (in anger). ~ *di ladang orang* to eat the food or use the assets of others.

merentakkan to stamp. ~ *kaki* to stamp one's foot.

rentak II and **réntak** pull, tug, jerk, wrench; → RENGGUT I, SENTAK.

merentak(kan) to pull, tug, jerk. ~ *lengan baju saya untuk menarik perhatian.* (He) pulled at my shirt-sleeve to get my attention.

terentak pulled, tugged, jerked.

rentak III serentak at the same time, simultaneously, all. *Meréka ~ meninggalkan rapat itu.* They all walked out of the meeting.

menyerentakkan to do s.t. at the same time/simultaneously.

rentaka (*cla*) revolving artillery/guns.

réntal (*E*) rental. *vidéo* – video rental.

rentan 1 vulnerable, sensitive, susceptible to (illness), subject (to), fragile, allergic. *Para éksékutif tergolong orang yang – terhadap strés yang kronis.* Executives belong to the class of people subject to chronic stress. *Séktor ékspor sangat –.* The export sector is very vulnerable. – *hati* irritable.

merentan ~ *hati* quick-tempered, irascible, irritable.

merentankan to make s.t. more fragile, put s.t. in a vulnerable position.

rentanan susceptibility.

kerentanan susceptibility, sensitivity, vulnerability. *poténsi ~* vulnerability potency.

rentang I the distance between ends/supports, span (of a bridge), band (of values, etc.). *jembatan lima* – a five-span bridge. – *cakupan* range. – *hidup* life span. – *ira* across the grain. – *kendali* what one has control over, scope of control, jurisdiction. – *keséhatan* health span. – *pengawasan* scope of supervision. – *sayap* wingspan. – *umur* life span. – *waktu* time span.

serentang 1 a span (of time, distance). *setelah ~ perjalanan* (*M*) after having walked for a while. **2** ~ *pukat* a seine/dragnet. **3** ~ *ayam* while pitting fighting cocks against e.o.

merentang 1 to extend, stretch. *Tugas hidupku ~ di depanku.* My

life's work stretches out before me. **2** to become tense. **3** to place (a bridge across a gap). ~ *panjang* to relate s.t. in detail, go into s.t.

merentangi 1 to stretch, go over a distance. *kabel télepon yang ~ dari rumah ke rumah* a telephone cable that stretches from house to house. **2** to stretch out, make pass. *untuk merentang-rentangi waktu* to make the time pass.

merentangkan 1 to stretch s.t. out, spread, extend. ~ *tangan kanan ke muka* to stretch the right hand forward. **2** to relate (in detail). *pandai ~ cerita* good at telling a story. **3** to build s.t. that spans s.t. ~ *jalan/jembatan* to build a road/bridge, etc. **4** to unravel, disentangle. *benang kusut yang sulit direntangkan* a tangled thread which is hard to unravel. ~ *antap* (*ob*) to take a shortcut.

terentang 1 stretch, stretched (out). *Antara Jakarta dengan Bandung ~ jarak 180 km.* The distance between Jakarta and Bandung is 180 km. **2** to span.

terentangi 1 stretched, extended. **2** spanned.

rentangan span (of a bridge), stretch, range.

perentang stretcher. ~ *rél* rail tie bar.

perentangan stretching out.

rentang II → RINTANG I. **merentangi** to place obstacles in s.o.'s way, thwart.

terentang blocked, obstructed.

réntang (*ob*) **merentang-réntang** to snap at, bawl out.

rentap → RENTAK I.

rentas → RETAS I. **merentas 1** to take a shortcut, cut through. **2** to pioneer, break new ground. ~ *jalan* to clear a way, beat a path (through).

rénte (*D*) interest (on a loan). *tukang* – s.o. who lends money at interest.

meréntekan to lend (money at interest).

rénten (*D*) **merénteni** to pay interest on.

me(mpe)réntenkan to lend (money at interest).

rénténg (*J/Jv*) row, range, series. *tanggung* – collective (responsibility/guarantee). *Tanggung-jawab dari pendiri-pendiri adalah secara tanggung –.* The liabilities of the founders are collective.

serénténg a string (of fireworks).

berénténg(-rénténg) one after the other, in a row.

berénténgan connected to e.o. in a row.

merénténg ~ *mercon* to set off a string of firecrackers.

rénténgan row, chain, series.

réntenir (*D*) **1** rentier, person who lives off the interest or rent on real estate/bonds, etc. **2** loan shark, moneylender.

réntét (*J/Jv*) row, series; → RÉNTÉNG.

seréntét a series of. ~ *diplomat* a parade of diplomats.

beréntént(-réntét) one after the other, in a row.

berénténtan one after the other.

rénténtan 1 series. ~ *peristiwa* a series of events. **2** sequence, row, run. ~ *témbakan* salvo, burst of gunfire. **serénténtan** a row, string, series, convoy (of vehicles).

renti (*J*) clipped form of *berenti*; → HENTI.

merentikan → MENGHENTIKAN.

rentik (*J*) **merentik 1** to have a pain/ache. **2** to feel sick.

rénumerasi renumbering.

renung I merenung 1 to stare at. *Ia berasa tersinggung jika orang ~nya.* He felt insulted if s.o. stared at him. **2** to look out (at s.t.) by craning the neck. *Saya ~ ke luar jendéla.* I looked out of the window.

merenungi to look fixedly at, stare at. *Pria itu ~ kekasihnya.* The man stared at his sweetheart.

renung II daydreaming, thought. *Dia lagi dihanyut –nya.* She was lost in thought.

merenung 1 to think about s.t. intently. **2** to daydream. *Ahmad berbaring di atas sofa dan ~ tentang hari depannya.* Ahmad lay down on the sofa and thought about his future.

merenungkan to muse over, dwell on, think about, daydream about. *Ia selalu ~ nasibnya yang malang itu.* He always mulls over his unlucky fate.

terenung daydreaming.

renungan meditation, daydreaming.

perenung daydreamer.

perenungan meditating, daydreaming.

rénvo(o)i (*D leg*) marginal note/alteration.
renyah I restless, uneasy; → RENYANG.
renyah II careful concentration, requiring concentration.
  berenyah to work slowly and precisely.
  merenyah to take pains over s.t., work carefully on.
renyah III (*J/Jv*) 1 soft and crunchy, crispy but easy to eat (of cucumber, etc.). 2 pleasant (of voices). – *canda mahasiswa-mahasiswi* the pleasant joking around of the college students.
  kerenyahan crispiness.
  perenyah *minyak ~* (animal or vegetable) shortening.
renyah IV → RANYAH I.
renyai (*M*) drops (of rain/sweat). *hujan* – drizzle.
  renyai-renyai drops, in drizzles. *hujan ~* drizzle.
  berenyaian 1 drizzly, drizzling. 2 to come out in small drops (of perspiration).
  merenyai to lessen, abate, slow down, become less.
  merenyai-renyai slightly, a little (bit).
renyak (*Jv*) **merenyak** to squeeze, twist.
renyam 1 itchy. 2 to be upset. 3 to feel uncomfortable.
renyang (*M*) 1 restless, uneasy. 2 out of order, not as it should be.
renyau k.o. smelt, *Atherina spp*.
rényéh I merényéh to whimper, whine, complain.
rényéh II berényéh muddy, slippery (after the rain).
renyek (*J/Jv*) crumpled.
  merenyek to crumple.
renyem → RENYAM.
renyok and **renyuk I** crumpled (up), crinkled.
  merenyuk to crumple up, crinkle.
renyuk II (*M*) pull, tug, jerk. *Dengan – ia bangkit.* He got up with a jerk.
  merenyuk to stand up quickly (with one movement).
  merenyukkan 1 to tug/pull out. 2 to hand over/present s.t. with a jerk.
renyuk III merenyuk to pout, sulk.
renyut to throb; → DENYUT.
  merenyutkan to shrug (the shoulders).
réog (*Jv*) a comic performance of a group of three to five comedians who dance in a circle, each carrying a different-sized drum tied to his waist by a sash.
réok (*J*) to cackle.
réol → RIOL.
réorganisasi (*D*) reorganization. *– dan rasionalisasi* [réra] reorganization and rationalization.
  meréorganisasi(kan) to reorganize.
  peréorganisasian reorganizing, reorganization.
réorganisir (*D*) **meréorganisir** to reorganize.
réoriéntasi (*D*) reorientation.
  meréoriéntasikan to reorient.
réostat (*D/E*) rheostat.
réot (*Jv*) ramshackle, broken-down, decrepit, dilapidated, falling apart, worn out. *sebuah gubuk* – a ramshackle hut.
repah → RAPAH.
repak → REPAS I.
repang evened off (of a hedge/one's teeth, etc.), clipped.
  merepang to cut even, clip. *~ gigi* to cut the teeth to an even level.
réparasi (*D*) repairs.
  meréparasi to repair.
  meréparasikan 1 to repair. 2 to have s.t. repaired.
  peréparasi repairman, repairer.
repas I crisp, brittle, friable.
  terepas brittle, friable. **keterepasan** friability.
repas II (*Ac*) list of gamblers who take part in *judi buntut*.
répatrian (*D*) repatriate, i.e., s.o. who has returned to his homeland.
répatriasi (*D*) repatriation.
  merépatriasi(kan) to repatriate.
répéh-rapih (*S*) be on good terms with e.o.
répék merépék to talk nonsense, chatter away.
Répélita (*acr*) → RENCANA *Pembangunan Lima Tahun.*
répértoar (*D*) 1 repertory. 2 list.
répés I merépés to do odd jobs.
répés II merépés to shake (from illness or old age).

répét merépét(-répét) to talk nonsense, chatter away.
  répétan chatter.
  perépét chatterbox.
Répéta [Rencana Pembangunan Tahunan] Annual Development Plan.
répetén (*D ob*) repetend, recurring decimal (in arithmetic).
repetir (*D*) to repeat. *senapan* – repeating rifle.
répétisi (*D*) rehearsal, repetition.
  berépetisi to repeat itself. *~ dalam bentuk* to repeat itself in shape/form.
répétitif (*E*) repetitive.
repetitor (*D*) private tutor, coach.
repih breakable, fragile. crumbly.
  serepih a piece (of s.t. crumbly like bread).
  merepih to crumble.
  merepihkan to crumble s.t.
  repihan crumb.
repis → REPIH.
répitalisasi → RÉVITALISASI.
réplik (*D leg*) rejoinder, reply, counterplea, replication.
réplika (*D*) replica, facsimile.
  meréplika to replicate.
réplikasi repetition.
répolpér → RÉVOLVÉR.
répolusi → RÉVOLUSI.
répolusionér → RÉVOLUSIONÉR.
répormir (*D*) reformed, i.e., Calvinist. *Kristen* – Reformed Christian (Calvinist).
report (*E*) report.
reportase (*D*) commentary, reportage.
  mereportasekan to report on.
réporter (*E*) reporter.
repot (*ob*) to report (on).
  merepotkan to report, announce.
répot (*Jv*) 1 occupied, busy. *Ia – mengurus pajaknya.* He is busy taking care of his taxes. 2 overburdened, overloaded, preoccupied. *Ia agak – waktu-waktu ini.* He's been overburdened with work these days. 3 complication, difficulty. 4 tedious, full of details. 5 it's a bother to, it's a lot of trouble to. *Saya capék rambut panjang, – ngurusnya.* I'm tired of long hair; it's a lot of trouble to take care of it.
  répotnya the problem is ... *~ jumlah tenaga kerja ilégal di Malaysia terus bertambah.* The problem is that the number of illegal workers in Malaysia continues to increase.
  répot-répot to get all excited; to worry, bother, go to some trouble (to do s.t.). *Jangan ~!* Don't go to any trouble. Please, don't bother. *Mau minum apa? Ah, jangan ~!* What would you like to drink? Oh, don't go to any trouble.
  merépotkan [and **ng(e)répotin** (*J coq*)] 1 to cause trouble/a fuss, make work/difficulties/problems for, cause inconvenience for, bother, impose on. *Ia tidak mau ~ adiknya.* He didn't want to bother his younger brother. *~ diri* to worry. 2 bothersome, troublesome, a bother.
  kerépotan 1 stir, bustle, activity. 2 trouble, difficulty. 3 overwhelmed (by work, etc.), have a hard time, be unable to handle s.t. *Dia ~ menghadapi peraturan lalu lintas baru itu.* He's having a hard time with the new traffic regulations.
reprep (*J*) full of holes, in shreds.
répréséntasi (*D*) representation.
  merépréséntasikan to represent.
répréséntatif (*D*) making a good impression, prepossessing, presentable.
  kerépréséntatifan good impression.
répréséntir (*D*) **merépréséntir** to represent.
réprési (*D*) repression.
réprésif (*D*) repressive.
répro clipped form of **réproduksi**.
réproduksi (*D*) reproduction. *– aséksual* asexual reproduction. *– séksual* sexual reproduction.
  meréproduksi(kan) to reproduce.
réptil(ia) (*D*) reptile.
républik (*D*) republic. *– Démokrasi Jerman* German Democratic

Republic, East Germany. – *Démokrasi Rakyat Koréa* Democratic People's Republic of Korea, North Korea. – *Démokrasi Viétnam* Democratic Republic of Vietnam. – *Dominika* Dominican Republic. – *Indonésia* [RI] Republic of Indonesia. – *Persatuan Arab* [RPA] United Arab Republic. – *pulau* (*coq*) island republic, i.e., Singapore. – *Rakyat Cina/Tiongkok* [RRC/RRT] People's Republic of China, PRC.

républikan (*E*) and **republiké(i)n** (*D*) /républiké(i)n/ republican (*mod*). *orang* – a republican. – *boncéngan* republican fellow traveler, i.e., s.o. who pretended to be for the Indonesian republic but who sympathized with the Dutch-created federal system.

kerépublikanan and **kerépublikénan** republican (*mod*).

répudiasi (*D*) repudiation (of nationality); → PENANGKALAN.

repuh I – *muda* young scrub.

repuh II merepuh to padlock.

repuh-repuh padlock.

repui crumbly, loose (of pastry/cakes, etc.), friable.

reput rotten, decayed (of wood, etc.), putrefied, friable. – *hitam* black rot. – *puhi* crumbling to the touch. – *relai* rotten, decayed (of wood/textiles, etc.).

mereput to putrefy.

reputan s.t. that has rotted/decayed.

pereputan putrefaction.

réputasi (*D*) reputation.

réputatif (*E*) reputative.

requisitoir → REKUISITOR.

réra → RÉORGANISASI *dan rasionalisasi*.

rerainan (*Bal*) ceremony, ritual.

rerak broken; → LERAK I.

bererakan broken into pieces.

mererak to break into pieces.

rerambut capillary, thin-walled blood vessel which connects arteries and veins.

reramuan ingredients; → RAMUAN.

rerangka framework; → RANGKA I.

rerantingan all k.o. twigs; → RANTING I.

reras (*M ob*) **mereras** to drop, fall (of fruit, etc.).

pererasan decay. ~ *radioaktif* radioactive decay.

rerasanan (*Jv*) subject/topic (of discussion).

rerata average; → RATA-RATA. – *tertimbang* weighted average.

rerep (*J*) better, recovered (from an illness).

rérét (*onom*) squeaking sound.

berérétan (*pl subj*) to squeak.

reribu → RIBU-RIBU.

reridu (*Jv*) trouble.

ngreridu to make trouble.

rerimbunan foliage. – *daun* foliage.

rerintih → RINTIH.

rerompok (*Jv*) → ROMPOK I.

rerongkong(an) (*Jv*) skeleton.

rerongsokan → RONGSOKAN.

rérot (*J*) **berérot(-rérot)** to follow in each other's footsteps (of a group); → BERDÉRÉT-DÉRÉT, BERUNTUN-RUNTUN.

merérot one after the other, in a row.

rérotan row, line.

rerotian *produk* ~ bakery products.

rerugi → RUGI.

reruk → GARAM *reruk*.

rerumpunan cluster. – *padi* paddy cluster.

rerumputan grassy area, lawn; → RUMPUT.

reruntuh and **reruntuk** ruins, debris, wreckage. – *dunia* prostitute; → SAMPAH *masyarakat*, SUNDAL I.

reruntuhan 1 ruins, debris, wreckage. 2 subsidence.

rés (in acronyms) → RESÉRSE, RÉSOR(T).

resa 1 movements made by a baby at birth. 2 peristalsis. – *hati* heart's desire.

resah to fidget, fidgety, restless, tossing and turning (in one's sleep); upset, disturbed, alarmed, anxious, agitated. *pembuat* – troublemaker. *rusuh* – all k.o. of unrest; disturbed; irregularities; → RUSUH I, II.

beresah-resah to feel restless/troubled, etc.

meresah to become restless.

meresahkan to upset, disturb, alarm, perturb. *Impor ban selundupan* ~ *produsén ban dalam negeri*. The importation of smuggled tires has upset domestic tire producers.

keresahan 1 restlessness. 2 upset, unrest. 3 frustration. ~ *terhadap* grievances against.

resak 1 various species of trees which produce good timber, *Shorea glauca/Vatica sp./Cotylelobium*. 2 Java cardamom, *Amomum maximum*.

resam I a large fern, bracken (used for basketry/making fish traps, etc.), *Gleichenia linearis*. – *gajah* k.o. fern.

resam II (*A*) customary usage, natural habit, mode, constitution. – *minyak ke minyak*, – *air ke air* birds of a feather flock together. – *tubuh* physique, build, body.

seresam (*dengan*) to agree (with), be in accordance (with).

resan offended.

meresan(kan) to take s.t. to heart; → RASA I.

peresan s.o. who is easily offended, thin-skinned.

resap seep, percolate, penetrate.

meresap 1 to penetrate, spread (into), break (into), make inroads on, encroach (on), sink (into). *Jawanisasi sudah* ~ *ke mana-mana*. Javanization has encroached on everything. 2 to ooze (through), percolate (into), soak/seep (into), break out (into a sweat). 3 to disappear, vanish (from sight). 4 to become deeply rooted, take root.

meresapi to penetrate, pervade, enter/go deeply into.

meresapkan 1 to cause s.t. to penetrate, make s.t. spread. 2 to ooze. 3 to make s.t. disappear/vanish from sight. 4 to digest (information).

teresap penetrated, pervaded.

resapan absorption. ~ *dalam* resorption. ~ *buatan* artificial recharge.

peresap absorber.

peresapan impregnation, penetration, pervasion, absorption.

résbang (*D*) couch, lounge.

résdés (*acr*) → RÉSÉTELMEN *désa*.

résé to be annoying; → RISI II.

resek (*Jv*) messy, cluttered.

résék (*J M*) → RISIK II. **merésék(-résék)** 1 to grope one's way. 2 to make inquiries about/into, inquire about. *Orang itu dirésék-résék oléh polisi*. The police made inquiries about that person. 3 (*BG*) *saling* ~ to neck, make out.

réséksion (*D*) locating (on a map).

resén (*D/E*) recent, new, fresh.

resénsén (*D*) (book) reviewer, critic.

resénsi (*D*) (book) review.

meresénsi(kan) to write a (book) review about.

peresénsi (book) reviewer.

peresénsian (book) reviewing.

résénsor (book) reviewer.

resep I → RESAP.

resep II (*S*) enjoyable.

resép (*D*) 1 (cooking) recipe. 2 (drug) prescription. *tanpa* – over the counter, nonprescription. *Sekarang obat itu dapat dibeli tanpa* – *di apotik*. That medicine can now be bought over the counter at drugstores. 3 formula, plan, recipe. – *mengatasi inflasi* a recipe for overcoming inflation.

meresépkan to prescribe (a medicine).

peresépan prescribing (medicines).

resép-resépan all k.o. of prescriptions. *Kau dapat membeli obat di pinggir jalan tanpa* ~. You can buy medicines at the side of the road without all k.o. prescriptions.

resépsi (*D*) 1 reception. 2 front desk (in a hotel).

beresépsi to hold/give a reception.

meresépsikan to hold a reception for.

resépsionis (*E*) receptionist.

reséptif (*D*) receptive.

reséptor and **reséptur** 1 (*D*) dispensing (of medicines). *ilmu* – pharmacology. 2 (*E*) receptor.

resérse (*D*) (police) criminal investigation department. *seorang* – plainclothesman (or, detective); → RESÉRSIR. – *kriminal* [réskrim] criminal investigation (squad). – *mobil* [résmob] mobile investigation (squad). - *narkotika* [<u>réstik</u>] narcotics investigation (squad).

keresérsean relating to criminal investigation.

resérsir (*D*) plainclothesman/detective.

résérvasi (*D*) reservation.

résérvat (*D*) reserve, preserve (for animals), sanctuary (for birds), reservation (for an ethnic group).

resérve (*D*) 1 reserve (troops). 2 substitute. 3 stand-in (in sports).

réservir (*D*) **meréservir** to reserve.

réservoar (*D*) reservoir, container, tank.

resés (*D*) recess.

    ber(r)esés to be in recess (of Parliament).

    mereséskan to recess. ~ *parlemén* to recess Parliament.

resési (*D*) (economic) recession.

résételmen (*E*) resettlement. - *désa* [<u>résdés</u>] village resettlement.

resi I (*Skr*) religious ascetic and mystical leader.

resi II (*E?*) (*surat -*) receipt (for s.t. received at the post office, etc.), luggage check. - *gudang* warehouse receipt.

resi III → RAKSI I.

resia → RAHASIA.

résidén (*D col*) resident, i.e., a Dutch administrative officer who had authority over a residency or part of a *propinsi*; the present officeholder is called *pembantu gubernur*.

    kerésidénan residency, area administered by a *résidén*. The former residencies have been split up into various *kabupatén*.

résidif recidivist (*mod*).

résidivis (*D*) recidivist, repeat offender. - *kawakan* hardened criminal.

résidivisme (*D/E*) recidivism.

résidu (*D/E*) residue; → AMPAS.

resik I 1 (*onom*) shrill, piercing sound. 2 (*onom*) rustling/whispering sound. 3 blistering (of the heat).

    meresik 1 to make a shrill sound. 2 to rustle (of leaves, etc.). 3 to be blistering (of the heat). 4 to whisper; to spread rumors.

resik II (*J/Jv*) 1 clean; pure, without fault or flaw. 2 clean, cleaned up/finished. *Nasi sepiring kok bisa -*. Wow, he cleaned up a plateful of rice.

    keresikan cleanness; pureness.

resiko → RISIKO.

résim → RÉZIM.

résimén (*D mil*) regiment. - *induk* main regiment. - *mahasiswa* [<u>ménwa</u>] student regiment. - *pelopor* scout regiment.

résin (*E*) resin.

résintél [<u>Résérse dan Intélijén</u>] Investigation and Intelligence.

résipién (*E*) recipient (of a transplant).

résiprok (*D*) and **résiprokal** (*E*) reciprocal.

résiprokatif (*E*) reciprocative.

résiprositas and **résiprosité** (*D*) reciprocity. - *diplomatik* diplomatic reciprocity.

résistan and **résistén** (*D*) resistant.

résistansi (*E*) resistance.

résital (*E*) (musical) recital.

résitasi (*D*) recitation.

    merésitasi(kan) to recite.

résitatif (*D*) recitative.

réskrim (*acr*) → RESÉRSE *kriminal*.

résléting → RITSLÉTING.

resmi I (*A*) official, legitimate (government), formal. *pakaian* - formal attire. *pemberitahuan* - public announcement. *dengan* - on the record, in public, officially, formally (dressed, etc.). *tidak* - unofficial. *ketidak-resmian* being unofficial.

    meresmikan [and **mengresmikan** (*infr*)] 1 to make s.t. official, inaugurate, dedicate, open an event officially, announce s.t. formally. 2 to certify, authenticate, make official. 3 to execute (a legal instrument).

    resmi-resmian semi-official.

    keresmian 1 official (*mod*); officialdom. 2 official recognition/announcement.

    peresmi inaugurator, person who officially opens a ceremony. ~ *selamatan adalah Gubernur*. The person opening the *selamatan* is the governor.

    peresmian [and **pengresmian** (*infr*)] 1 inauguration, dedication.

~ *pemutaran (film)* (film) premiere. 2 certification, authentication. 3 execution (of a legal instrument).

resmi II (*M*) character.

résmob (*acr*) → RESÉRSE *mobil*.

résolusi (*D*) resolution.

    merésolusi(kan) to make a resolution about.

résonan (*E*) resonant.

résonans (*D*) resonance.

résonansi (*E*) resonance.

Résopim [<u>Révolusi, Sosialisme (Indonésia) dan Pimpinan (Nasional)</u>] Revolution, Indonesian Socialism, and National Leadership, title of a speech given by President Soekarno on August 17, 1961.

résor(t) (*D*) 1 subarea, district, precinct. - *militér* military district. 2 jurisdiction. 3 sphere of activity.

résosialisasi (*D*) resocialization.

réspék (*D*) respect, regard.

réspirasi (*D*) respiration.

réspon (*D*) respond.

réspondén (*D*) respondent.

réspons (*D*) response.

    beréspons and **merépons** to give a response.

résponsif (*D*) responsive.

réssort (*Bat*) (in HKPB terminology) regency, county (an area smaller than a province).

réstan I (*D*) excess, remainder, leftover. - *makanan* leftovers, food remains.

réstan II → POS *réstan*.

restik (*acr*) → RESÉRSE *narkotik*.

réstitusi (*D*) 1 reimbursement to a government employee for travel expenses, medical expenditures, etc. 2 back/retroactive (payment), refund. - *kenaikan gaji bulan Januari akan dibayar bersama-sama dengan gaji bulan Fébruari*. Back pay for January will be paid together with February's pay. - *pajak* tax refund.

résto clipped form of *réstoran*.

reston (*Jv ob*) **merestoni** to bless; → RESTU.

réstoran (*D*) restaurant; → RUMAH *makan*. - *kaki lima* roadside eating stall.

    peréstoran restaurateur, restaurant owner.

    peréstoranan restaurant business.

réstorasi I (*D*) restoration, renovation.

    meréstorasi(kan) to restore, renovate.

réstorasi II (*D*) dining. *gerbong* - dining car (on a train). *petugas* - dining-car staff.

réstorir (*D*) **meréstorir** to restore, renovate.

réstriksi (*D*) restriction.

    meréstriksi to restrict.

réstrukturisasi restructuring.

    merestrukturisasi(kan) to restructure.

restu [and **réstu** (*less frequent*)] (*Skr*) 1 blessing, good wishes, prayers for, benediction. *minta/mohon (doa)* - to ask for s.o.'s blessings. 2 enchantment.

    merestui [and **merestoni** (*Jv*)] to bless, give s.t. one's blessings. *Seorang calon kepala daérah "direstui Bapak Présidén"*. One of the candidates for provincial head "was given the President's blessings."

    restu-restuan so-called blessings.

réstul (*D*) wheelchair.

restung syphilis of the nose; lupus; nasal polypus.

resu → RESI I.

résultan(te) (*D*) resultant.

résumé (*D*) summary, résumé.

    merésumé(kan) to make a summary of, summarize.

résumir (*D*) **merésumir** to make a summary of, summarize.

résurjénsi (*E*) resurgence.

rét (*D*) diamonds (in deck of cards).

reta (*ob*) → HARTA.

réta meréta-réta to talk nonsense, chatter away.

retai → RETAK *retai*.

retak 1 crack, split, line where s.t. is broken but not into separate parts, fissure, fracture, chink. - *pada piring itu* the crack in the saucer. *kepribadian yang* - split personality. *mudah* - fragile. 2

flaw, shortcoming; → GADING I. *Kamus itu masih banyak -nya.* That dictionary still has many shortcomings. **3** chapped (of lips). **4** breakup (of love/marriage, etc.). *Dia tidak mau kasih sayang meréka menjadi -.* He didn't want their love to break up. *Perkawinannya -.* Their marriage broke up. **5** cracks in certain places on krises and plates (considered lucky). *tak ada gading yang tak -* no rose without a thorn, nothing is perfect. *sumbing melukai, - melampaui tara/garis* (M) a big mistake, blunder. *- menanti/mencari/tanda akan pecah/belah* a) make a mountain out of a molehill. b) on the brink, just waiting for s.t. bad to happen (such as a death, etc.). *-.- mentium* (M) to have only fine cracks externally, not seriously damaged. *- bandut* cracks on a kris (considered lucky). *- batu* damaged beyond repair (of relations). *-.- bulu ayam* easily settled (of differences). *- inti* chink. *- retai* many cracks, cracked a lot. *- tangan* a) the lines on the palm of the hand, lifelines; → RAJAH/SURATAN *tangan.* b) fate, destiny.
  meretak to begin to crack, crack open.
  meretakkan to crack, break; to break up, ruin, destroy. *~ hidup rumahtangga* to cause a breakup of family life.
  retakan crack, cleft. *~ és* crack in the ice.
  keretakan split, crack, rift; breakup (of a love affair). *~ kepribadian* split personality. *~ dalam rumah tangga* broken home.
  peretakan (*petro*) fracturing.
retal → HARTAL.
rétaliasi (E) retaliation; → TINDAKAN *balasan.*
rétardasi (E) retardation. *- méntal* Down syndrome. *- néuromotorik* neuromotoric retardation.
retas I opened up (of stitches).
  meretas 1 to break open/through, open up (stitches). **2** to slit/cut open. *Orang gila itu ~ perutnya sendiri.* The crazy man slit open his own stomach. **3** to cut/chop down, fell (trees). *~ jalan* to clear a path. **4** to trespass on.
  peretas 1 trespasser. **2** a device used for opening up stitches, slitting envelopes, etc. *~ jalan* pioneer.
  peretasan preliminary treatment of softening or thinning the skin of seeds.
retas II dike, dyke.
retas-retas k.o. cake made of flour.
rétéh to crackle.
réték (M) **meréték** to shiver (with cold).
réténsi (D) **1** retention. **2** fee.
rétét I (*onom*) sound of rattling (of rifle fire).
  berététan to rattle (of gunfire).
rétét II → RÉNTÉT.
retetet-tetet rattling, rat-ta-tat-tat-tat-tat.
reti → ARTI.
retih I meretih to stand in beads (of perspiration).
retih II (*onom*) crackling sound of frying rice/wet leaves burning, etc.
  meretih to crackle like frying rice, etc.
rétikular (D/E) reticular.
rétina (D/E) retina.
retir → RETUR.
retna → RATNA I.
rétok → RÉCOK.
retool → RITUL.
retooling → RITULING.
retor (D) retort. *dapur -* furnace retort.
rétorik (E) and **rétoris** (D) rhetorical.
rétorika (D) rhetoric.
rétorsi (D) retortion.
rétrét (D) (religious) retreat.
  ber(r)étrét to go on retreat.
rétrétisme (E) retreatism.
rétribusi (D) **1** repayment of money advanced for a specific purpose from the proceeds of that purpose. **2** fee, payment for the use of government services or facilities, includes light and sewer bills.
rétro- (D) back(ward).
rétroaktif (D) retroactive.
rétrofléksi (D) retroflexion.
rétrogrési (D) retrogression.

rétrogrésif (E) retrogressive.
rétrolingual (E) retrolingual.
rétromamal (E) retromammal.
rétromandibular (E) retromandibular.
rétrosipasi retroprocity.
rétrospéksi (D) retrospection.
retul → RITUL.
retuling → RITULING.
retur (D) return (ticket).
  meretur to return s.t.
retus (D) retouching (a photograph).
reuay (S) many, in great numbers, numerous. *Semoga bahagia selalu sampai - putra dan - incu* (in wedding announcements). May your marriage always be happy and blessed with many boys and girls.
réuni (D) reunion.
  ber(r)éuni to hold a reunion.
réunifikasi (E) reunification.
révaksinasi (E) revaccination.
révaluasi (E) revaluation.
  merévaluasi to revaluate.
revans (D) revenge. *mengambil -* to take one's revenge.
révindikasi (D *leg*) recovery, revindication.
révindikatur (D) revindicatory.
révisi (D *leg*) revision, retrial on the basis of new evidence.
  merévisi to revise.
révisionis revisionist.
révisionisme (D/E) revisionism.
révisir (D) **merévisir** to revise.
révitalisasi (E) revitalization.
révival (E) revival.
révolusi (D) **1** revolution. **2** (with an upper-case R) the Indonesian Revolution of August 17, 1945. *- dua babak* two-stage revolution. *- fisik* the physical revolution, i.e., that part of the Indonesian Revolution which took place from 1945 to 1950. *- hijau* green revolution. *- industri* industrial revolution. *- istana* palace revolution. *- séks* sexual revolution.
  berévolusi 1 to revolt, bring about a revolution. **2** (usually with an upper-case R) to revolt against the Dutch colonial system.
  merévolusikan to revolutionize.
révolusionér (D) revolutionary.
  merévolusionérkan to revolutionize.
  kerévolusionéran revolutionariness.
  pengrévolusionéran revolutionizing.
révolusionérisme an outlook based on revolutionary principles.
révolusionisasi revolutionizing.
  pengrévolusionisasian the process of revolutionizing.
révolvér (D) revolver.
réwak I → RÉBAK II. **merewak** a) to spread (of a disease); → MENJALAR. *Dalam musim hujan, penyakit malaria mudah ~.* Malaria spreads rapidly in the rainy season. b) to spread (of news); → TERSIAR. *Berita itu ~ ke seluruh kota.* The news spread all over town. c) to spread (of a fire, etc.); → MELUAS. *Api yang membakar hutan itu telah ~ ke rumah-rumah di pinggirnya.* The forest fire has spread to the houses at the edge of the forest.
réwak II there is s.t. one wants to communicate.
réwan (*ob*) → RAWAN I.
réwanda (*Jv*) monkey.
réwang I yaw.
  meréwang 1 (*naut*) to yaw, sheer. **2** to swing back and forth. **3** unstable, changeable.
réwang II (M) **meréwang** to do s.t. at random/haphazardly. *Témbakannya ~.* He fired shots at random.
réwang III (*Jv*) **1** servant, domestic help. **2** mutual help.
  peréwangan helping e.o.
réwél (*J/Jv*) **1** fussy, choosy, picky, finicky, hard to please, crabby (of behavior). *tukang -* fussbudget. **2** troublesome, giving a lot of trouble, to give s.o. a hard time, act up. *Mesin tik yang baru ini - sekali.* This new typewriter is giving a lot of trouble.
  meréwél to be(come) fussy, troublesome.
  meréwéli to make trouble for s.o.

meréwélkan 1 to cause/give s.o. trouble, troublesome. 2 to make a fuss about.

keréwélan fussiness, choosiness.

réwés (*Jv*) **meréwés** to mind, heed. *tidak (me)réwés* to ignore, pay no attention to.

réwét meréwét to spread rapidly. *Si jago mérah terus ~ ke gedung-gedung di sekelilingnya.* The fire kept on spreading to the neighboring buildings.

réyal → RIAL.

réyog → RÉOG.

réyot → RÉOT.

rezeki (*A*) 1 basic necessities of life, daily food. *Itu bukan – saya.* That is not for me. *memberi –* a) to give food (to). b) to bring good luck (to). 2 income, earnings. *kehilangan –* to lose one's livelihood. *membagi –* to share s.o.'s good fortune. *mencari –* to earn one's daily bread. *mendapat –* a) to get food/one's liveli-hood. b) to be fortunate/in luck. *mengais –* to make a living, get income. *banyak mendapat –nya* to earn a lot. *putus –* to lose one's livelihood. 3 opportunity to obtain food, etc.; luck, good fortune. *banyak anak banyak –* many children, much fortune. *berebut –* to struggle to survive. *bukan –* not s.o.'s luck. *Ini bukan – saya.* It's not my lucky day. *dekat –nya* easy to have good luck. *jauh –nya* difficult to have good luck. *kalau ada –* if we're lucky. *karena – di pihak S* because luck was on the side of S. *kecipratan –* to get lucky, luck out, get a stroke of good luck. *Mudah-mudahan dimurahkan –nya.* May he have a lot of luck. *murah –* to have good luck and fortune come to one easily. *naik –nya* he got luckier and luckier. *pembagian –* distribution of wealth. *perebutan –* struggle for life. *terbuka –nya* he stands a good chance. *ada nyawa/umur ada –* with time comes counsel. *– elang tak akan dapat/dimakan oléh musang/burung pipit* every dog has his day. *– batin* spiritual nourishment; → SANTA-PAN *rohani.* *– harimau* at all times there are various k.o. food. *– jangan ditolak* don't let any opportunity pass you by. *– mahal* hard to make a living. *– mata* s.t. that strikes the eye. *– me-limpah* a glut. *menikmati – melimpah minyak* to enjoy an oil glut. *–nya meninggi* (*M*) fortune smiles on him. *– merendah* (*M*) everything he tries brings him luck. *– murah* luck always favors him. *– musang* an unprotected or stupid girl (and there-fore an easy prey). *– nomplok/nonjok* (*J*) a windfall, an unex-pected piece of good luck. *– yang halal* "allowed" fortune (not obtained through corruption, etc.).

kerezekian good luck, prosperity.

rézim (*D*) 1 regime. 2 scheme, plan. *– dévisa bébas* free foreign-exchange regime. *– militér* military regime. *– nilai tukar tetap* fixed exchange-rate regime. *– nuklir* nuclear regime. *– totalitér* totalitarian regime.

RI → RÉPUBLIK *Indonésia* (also used in acronyms).

ria I 1 glad, happy, cheerful, merry. *berhati/berpésta/bersuka –* to have fun/a good time. 2 noisy, loud (of voices of people enjoy-ing themselves). 3 (as the second part of many compounds) (to do the action) for fun, for enjoyment. *bersenam –* to exercise for fun. *bercanda –* to joke around. *main sepéda –* to ride a bike for fun. *– derita* schadenfreude, happiness at s.o. else's unhap-piness. *– gembira* extraordinarily happy. *– jenaka* fun and jokes. *– riuh* hustle and bustle and cheerfulness.

beria-ria to have a good time, celebrate.

keriaan 1 happiness, gladness, cheerfulness. 2 feast celebrating a wedding or circumcision, etc. *– khitanan anaknya diramai-kan dengan orkés dangdut.* The circumcision feast of his child was enlivened by a *dangdut* orchestra.

ria II (*A*) proud, haughty, arrogant.

riadah and **riadat** (*A*) the ascetic exercise of controlling one's pas-sions (abstaining from eating certain foods, etc.).

riadiat (*A ob*) *ilmu –* mathematics.

riah I *meriah* 1 merry, cheerful; → RIA I. *Meréka merayakan ke-menangan dengan ~.* They celebrated the victory joyfully. 2 grand, majestic. *Perayaan menyambut Hari Kemerdékaan tahun ini lebih ~ dari tahun-tahun yang sudah-sudah.* This year's Independence Day celebrations were grander than in previous years. *Murid-murid sekolah itu menyanyi lagu ke-bangsaan dengan ~ dan penuh semangat.* The pupils of that

school sang the national anthem cheerfully and enthusiasti-cally. **kemeriahan** grandeur, majesty.

memeriahkan 1 to put on (a concert, etc.). 2 to celebrate s.t. 3 to cheer up, enliven.

keriahan festivity, merry-making, rejoicing, luster, splendor.

riah II → RIA II.

riak I → RIA I.

riak II 1 ripples (in water). *pecahan –* and *– yang berdebar-debar/me-mecah di (tepi) pantai* breakers, surf. 2 vibration (of the air). 3 trace, sign. *–nya belum tampak* no trace of it can be seen yet. *– tanda tak dalam, bergoncang tanda tak penuh* empty vessels make the most sound. *– air* ripples in the water. *– gelombang* a) wavelength. b) rippling water. *– ikan* vibration of water due to the motion of a fish. *– mata* the evil eye. *– remiak* to ripple; ripples. *– udara* air waves (radio).

beriak(-riak) 1 to move in ripples, ripple. 2 to fail (of breath). *air beriak tanda tak dalam, air berguncang tanda tak penuh* still waters run deep.

meriak 1 to ripple. *sececah ~* to ripple for a short time. 2 to spread, bloom.

riakan and **ria-riakan** ripples, etc.

riak III phlegm, mucus; → DAHAK.

beriak to cough up phlegm.

rial (*Port*) 1 real (a former coin worth about 2 guilders). 2 Saudi Arabian currency. 3 a weight of *app* 20 grams. 4 money. *jika tiada – di pinggang, saudara yang rapat menjadi renggang* a friend in need is a friend indeed.

rialat → RIADAT.

riam rapids, cataract, cascade; → JERAM I.

riaman cascading.

rian skein of thread: 1/16 *tukal.*

riang I very happy, joyous, glad. *– gembira* overjoyed. *– hati* elated, in high spirits, in a good mood. *– mulut* talkative.

seriang as happy as.

beriang(-riang) to be happy/joyful/glad, enjoy o.s. *~ hati* to be elated, be in high spirits.

meriangkan to cheer up, make s.o. happy.

keriangan cheer(fulness), happiness, joy.

periang cheerful (person), s.o. who is always happy. *Ia seorang yang ~ dan peramah.* He is a happy and amiable person.

riang II *meriang* (*~ semangat*) dizzy. *sakit ~* feverish, not feeling well. *~ kemelut* the fever is peaking.

riang-riang I and **reriang** cicada.

riang-riang II 1 a tree with beautiful flowers and hard wood, *Ploiarum sp.* 2 (*rumput –*) a grass variety, *Themeda gigantea.*

riang-riang III (*biawak –*) a large lizard species, water monitor, *Varanus salvator.*

riap growth, proliferation (of children/plants/animals), incre-ment (of tree growth).

meriap 1 to thrive, prosper, flourish, multiply, proliferate. *Rum-put di depan rumahnya ~.* The grass in front of his house is thriving. 2 (*J*) to have one's hair hanging (down) loose. *Kalau ada tamu, kamu jangan keluar ~.* When we have guests, don't come out with your hair hanging down loose.

riapan increment.

periapan proliferation.

rias I (*Jv*) → HIAS. *kamar –* dressing room. *méja –* dressing table. *tata –* makeup; making o.s. up. *tukang –* beautician, makeup art-ist. *– kepala* headdress. *– panggung* theatrical makeup. *– rupa* makeup.

berias to freshen up.

merias to make/dress up, fix (one's hairdo). *~ muka* to make up one's face, apply makeup. *~ pengantin* to make up the bride(groom). *~ rambut* to do s.o.'s hair.

rias-merias cosmetics, makeup. *~ wanita* women's makeup.

meriasi to apply makeup to, makeup.

riasan 1 makeup; → HIASAN. 2 decoration, ornament.

perias 1 makeup artist, bridal makeup artist, beautician. *~ ram-but* hairdresser. 2 makeup. *~ mata* eye makeup.

periasan makeup.

rias II the pith of a banana tree.

Riau Riau. *– Daratan* Mainland Riau (located on Sumatra).

riba I lap; → PANGKU I.
  beriba to sit on s.o.'s lap.
  meriba to take s.o. on one's lap. *Istrinya ~ anaknya.* His wife took her child on her lap.
  ribaan lap.
riba II (*A*) usury, moneylender's interest. *makan –* a) to practice usury. b) to live by lending out money at a high interest rate. *tukang –* usurer, loan shark. *– nasiah* credit involving usury. *– qiradh* borrowing involving usury. *– salaf* lending involving usury.
  periba usurer, loan shark.
ribak → RÉBAK II.
ribang (*ob*) to long for.
ribatat (*A*) (family, etc.) bond, tie.
ribawi usurious (of interest rate).
ribén (*E*) Rayban. *kaca –* tinted glass. *kacamata –* Rayban sunglasses.
ribet impractical, hard to put into practice, hard to find.
ribon (*E sports*) rebound.
  meribon to rebound.
ribu thousand. *lima –* five thousand. *ratusan –* hundreds of thousands.
  seribu 1 a/one thousand. 2 very many, lots of. *dengan ~ daya* in lots of ways. *diam/membisu (dalam) ~ bahasa* to be totally silent, as silent as the grave. *membuat/mengambil/mengangkat langkah ~* to take to one's heels, take off. *retak ~* a) cracked into many splinters (of a plate, etc.). b) k.o. Malaysian *batik* motif. **menyeribu** to do s.t. related to one thousand. *– hari* to hold a religious feast in memory of s.o. on the thousandth day after his death. **keseribu** 1 a group of a thousand. *~ ini* these thousand. 2 thousandth. *yang ~* the thousandth. **perseribu** divided by a thousand, thousandth. *satu ~* 1/1,000. *seperseribu* one one-thousandth.
  beribu thousands of. *~ kali* a thousand times. *~ maaf* a thousand pardons. *~ terima kasih* a thousand thanks.
  beribu-ribu by the thousands, thousands and thousands of. *~ orang* thousands of people.
  ribuan 1 denomination of 1,000 (rupiahs). *mencétak uang ~* to print thousand-denomination notes. 2 (by the) thousands, thousands and thousands. *~ kilo* thousands of kilometers.
ribu-ribu a genus of ferns, *Lygodium spp.*, used for cordage and basketry.
ribut I *angin –* hurricane, storm, gale. *pokok –* a tree-shaped cloud that precedes a "Sumatra." *turun –* a) a stiff breeze, strong wind. b) it's blowing up a storm.
  beribut and **meribut** to storm, be stormy.
ribut II 1 with a lot to do, be busy; → SIBUK I. *Ia terlalu – untuk mendengarkan kata-kata bosnya.* He was too busy to listen to what his boss was saying. 2 noisy, tumultuous, clamorous. *Di pelabuhan sangat – bunyi berbagai-bagai truk dan sorak-sorai pekerja.* The sounds of all k.o. trucks and the loud cheering of workers in the harbor was very tumultuous. *Jangan –.* Don't make so much noise. 3 excited. 4 to make trouble, cause problems. 5 to make a fuss about. *– mulut* squabble, verbal fight. *Rupanya yang ditegur tidak senang, hingga terjadi – mulut, disusul kemudian dengan perkelahian.* It seems that the person reprimanded was unhappy, so that a squabble occurred followed by a fight.
  ribut-ribut to make a big fuss (about s.t.).
  meributi to make a fuss/big deal about s.t.
  meributkan [and **ng(e)ributin** (*J coq*)] 1 to make a fuss about, bother about, worry about. 2 to cause/make a stir, be controversial. 3 to be upset about s.t. *Mengapa diributkan?* What's the big deal? What's all the fuss about?
  keributan 1 noise. 2 stir, bustle, excitement. 3 confusion, disorder, disturbance, riot.
  peribut 1 noisy fellow, fussy person. 2 thug, hoodlum.
rica (*ob*) small Spanish pepper; → MERICA I.
rica-rica a Manadonese specialty prepared with peppers, tomatoes, etc.
ricau mericau 1 to twitter (of birds); → KICAU I. 2 to babble, mumble incoherently.
  mericaukan to babble out s.t.
rices (*D*) (drinking) straw.
ricih → RICIK I, RICIS.

ricik I (*onom*) murmuring/rushing sound (of water).
  mericik(-ricik) to murmur (of a stream/flowing water).
ricik II (*Jv*) **ricikan** 1 spare parts; → ONDERDIL, SUKU *cadang*. 2 (*Jv*) the particular instruments in a *gamelan* orchestra, such as *rebana*, etc.
ricis (*J*) **mericis** to cut up (cucumbers, etc.) into fine pieces, dice; → RACIK II, RINCIS.
ricu(h) (*J*) in a mess, chaotic, confused.
  kericu(h)an chaos, confusion.
rida → RÉLA.
ridai meridaikan to hang s.t. up to dry.
ridan 1 *pohon –* k.o. tree with *rambutan*-like fruit, *Nephelium glabrum/Mischocarpus lessertianus*. 2 a tree from whose wood planks are made, *Nephelium maingayi/Aglaia cordata*.
rid(d)at (*A*) apostasy; → MURTAD. *kafir –* apostate.
ridha → RÉLA. **meridhai** to bless. *Insyah Allah, upaya kami ini diridhai-Nya* God willing, may He bless our efforts.
ridi I (*A*) → RÉLA. *sudi dan –* ready and able.
ridi II → PERIDI.
ridi III → RÉDI I.
riding I (*cla*) a long line of rattan nooses used for catching deer.
riding II meriding to stick out a little bit from the water.
ridip I 1 dorsal fin (of sharks). 2 ridge of a crocodile's back.
ridip II (*J*) **meridip** to like to touch things (like a child), can't keep one's hands off.
ridla, ridlo(h), and **rido** → RÉLA.
Ridwan (*A*) an angel who guards the doors to heaven.
riél (*D*) real.
rigai (*M*) *– ringan* skinny.
rigi-rigi (*M*) tooth, cog; → GERIGI.
  berigi milled (the edge of s.t.).
  berigi-rigi to be indented, toothed, cogged.
  merigi to mill (the edge of s.t.).
  merigi-rigi(kan) to indent, notch.
rigu → TERIGU.
rih (*A*) wind.
rihal → RÉHAL.
rihat → RÉHAT.
riil (*D*) /riyil/ real.
  meriilkan to make s.t. a reality.
  keriilan reality.
rijal (*A*) (*pl* of **rajul**) men, males.
rijalulgaib (*A*) the invisible spirits of saints who protect mankind.
rijang (*geol*) flint, flint stone, chert.
rijs (*A*) 1 disgraceful action. 2 pollution, dirt. 3 punishment.
rijsttafel (*D*) /rés-/ Indonesian smorgasbord consisting of white rice with a large variety of side dishes.
rik I (*onom*) sound of rustling, rustle; *cp* DERIK.
rik II (*A ob*) slavery.
rikaz (*A*) found/dug-up treasures.
rikétsia (*D*) rickets, rickettsia.
rikik → RAKIK.
rikisitor (*D leg*) requisitory.
rikosét (*D*) ricochet.
riksa and **riksya** (*C*) rickshaw.
rikuh (*J/Jv*) 1 awkward, ill at ease; ashamed, embarrassed. *Jarang ada pegawai negeri yang berani menélepon atasannya, karena hal ini menimbulkan perasaan –, tidak sopan.* It is rare that government employees have the courage to telephone their superiors because this causes a feeling of embarrassment. 2 reluctant, unwilling. 3 impolite, rude.
  merikuhkan to embarrass; embarrassing. *merasa dirikuhkan* to feel embarrassed.
  kerikuhan shyness, timidity, bashfulness.
ril → RÉL.
rila(h) → RÉLA.
rilalegawa (*Jv*) wholeheartedly willing.
rilé (*E*) relay.
  merilé to relay. *Anténa parabola ékspérimén mahasiswa Éléktro ITS berhasil ~ pertandingan itu.* The experimental parabolic antenna of Surabaya Institute of Technology's electrical engineering students succeeded in relaying the match.

rilék(s) (*E*) to relax, take it easy; relaxed.
    berilék(s) to relax, take it easy.
    merilékkan to relax, make s.t. relaxed.
riléksasi (*D/E*) relaxation.
    meriléksasi to relax. *Adalat juga berfungsi ~ otot polos pembuluh darah tepi. Adalat* also functions as a relaxant for the smooth muscles of the peripheral blood vessels.
rilis (*E*) release (of an album, etc.).
    merilis to release (an album, etc.).
rim I (*D*) ream (of paper).
rim II (*D*) military style leather belt for ammunition, etc., Sam Browne belt.
rima (*D*) rhyme. *- akhir* end rhyme. *- dalam* internal rhyme.
    berima to rhyme, rhyming.
    merimakan to rhyme, make s.t. rhyme.
rimah → RÉMAH I.
rimas to feel uncomfortable due to the heat (causing one to perspire). *Kebanyakan orang muda sekarang kurang gemar lagi memakai pakaian kebangsaan, - kata meréka.* Most of the younger generation no longer likes to wear their national dress; they say it's uncomfortable.
    berimas to feel uncomfortable due to the heat, break out in sweat.
    merimaskan to cause discomfort, make s.o. feel uncomfortable.
rimau → HARIMAU I, II.
rimba I forest. **2** jungle. *hukum* – law of the jungle, mob law. *hutan* – jungle. *raja* – a) tiger. b) (*coq*) forest ranger. **3** (in certain expressions) whereabouts. *hilang tak tentu –nya* and *hilang lenyap tak ketentuan –nya lagi* disappeared without a trace. *Tak pernah diketahui di mana –nya.* His whereabouts are never known. *– belantara* primeval/virgin forest. *– beton* the concrete jungle, i.e., the city. *– larangan* forest preserve. *- piatu* (*cla*) desolate jungle. *- raya/sawang* (*M*) wilderness.
    merimba 1 to turn into jungle, become overgrown. *Ladangnya sudah ~.* His dry field has become overgrown. **2** to go (work) in the forest/jungle. *Setiap hari ia ~ mencari kayu bakar.* Every day he goes to the forest looking for firewood.
    perimba s.o. who makes his livelihood from the forest.
rimban side (of a boat).
rimbang collyrium.
rimbas (cooper's) adze.
    merimbas 1 to cut wood with an adz. **2** to clear weeds from, work or cut s.t. with an adz. **3** to mow down (with a machine gun).
rimbat → RÉMBAT.
rimbawan forestry expert; sylviculturist, forester.
    kerimbawanan forestry (*mod*).
rimbit I hampered, impeded; → RÉMBÉT I.
    rimbitan impediment, hindrance.
rimbit II to spread; → RÉMBÉT II.
rimbu → RIMBA.
rimbun 1 leafy, having many leaves. *Pohon-pohonnya –.* The trees have a lot of leaves. *- rampak/rindang* shady. **2** thick and bushy (of hair). **3** having a lot of. *perahu yang - layarnya* a prau with many sails. **4** wearing many (clothes or adornments).
    merimbun to become leafy, with lots of leaves. *Rumah itu terlindung oléh bebungaan yang ~.* The house is concealed by many leafy flowers.
    merimbuni to cover s.t. with dense foliage.
    rimbunan s.t. which is leafy. *~ daun* foliage, leaf cover.
    kerimbunan overgrown with leaves, covered over with leaves.
rimis (*M*) half a cent.
    serimis (*col*) a half cent (coin). *tidak berharga ~* worthless.
rimpang trailing/finger-shaped roots (of ginger/turmeric, etc.), rhizome. *akar –* ramification (of branches). *jari –* fingers or toes that are not close to e.o., splayed fingers or toes. *- kuning* zedoary, *Curcuma zedoary/xanthorrhiza,* used in medicines; → TEMULAWAK.
    serimpang a shred (of ginger/turmeric, etc.).
    berimpang trailing, with such roots.
rimpel (*D*) **1** wrinkle (of the skin). **2** ruffle (of water).
    berimpel 1 wrinkled. **2** ruffled.
    merimpel to ruffle, pleat.
rimpi dried (fruit, such as banana); → PISANG *salé.*

rimpu traditional head-dress of Bima women on Sumbawa (leaves only the eyes and nose uncovered).
rimpuh exhausted, weary, tired.
    merimpuhkan to exhaust s.o. *~ lawannya* to exhaust one's opponent.
rimpung with pinioned legs.
    merimpung to pinion the legs (of animals for slaughter).
rinai I merinai to hum.
    merinaikan 1 to hum s.t. **2** to hum for s.o.
rinai II (*M*) drops, sprinkles; → RENYAI. *hari –* it's drizzling. *hujan - drizzle,* light rain; → HUJAN *rintik-rintik.*
    merinai(kan) to drip, sprinkle.
rinci detail; detailed, itemized. *secara –* in detail. *lebih –* in greater detail. *penjelasan yang lebih –* a more detailed/itemized explanation. *- serinci-rincinya* down to the smallest detail. *menjelaskan secara – tindakan-tindakan yang harus diambil* to explain in detail the measures to be taken.
    merinci 1 to explain in detail, go into the details of. *~ program nasional Keluarga Berencana* to explain in detail the Planned Parenthood national program. **2** to specify, detail, itemize. *~ pengeluaran uang belanja* to itemize housekeeping expenses.
    pemerincian specification.
    memperincikan to detail, itemize, break down (into specific items). *Mohon agar ongkosnya diperincikan.* Please itemize expenses.
    te(pe)rinci(kan) itemized, specified in detail, broken down. *jika dihitung secara terinci isi keranjang Lebaran* if we calculate in detail the contents of a *Lebaran* basket.
    rincian details, specifications, breakdown, items (in a list). *–nya* this breaks down into. *–nya, 5 hari pada permulaan puasa dan 10 hari pada sekitar Hari Raya Idul Fitri.* This breaks down into 5 days at the beginning of the fast and 10 days around Lebaran. *dengan ~* itemized as follows. *~ tugas* job description.
    keperincian details, breakdown.
    perinci s.o. who details, etc. *panitia ~* drafting committee.
    perincian specification, detailed analysis/description, details, breakdown. *~ tugas* job description.
rincih very small parts/slices, etc.; → RÉNCÉH I.
    merincih to cut into small parts/pieces, etc.
rincik small (as the second element in some compounds).
rincis merincis to slice thin.
    rincisan slice.
    perincis s.t. or s.o. that slices thin.
rincu(h) → RANCU, RICU(H).
rindang I shady, leafy. *beristirahat di bawah pohon yang –* to rest under a shady tree. *- daunnya* dense foliage.
    merindang to become shady.
    merindangi to shade, conceal behind dense vegetation.
    rindangan dense shady vegetation.
    kerindangan shade. *di ~ pokok-pokok palem* in the shade of palm trees.
    perindang shade (*mod*). *pohon ~* shade tree.
rindang II (*J*) happy, joyful.
rinderpést (*E*) bovine pleuropneumonia.
rinding I (*Jv*) Jew's harp; → GERINDING I.
rinding II (*J*) **merinding** (one's hair) stands on end, have gooseflesh; → NGERI. *Ia ~ mendengar suara mahluk itu.* His hair stood on end when he heard the creature's voice.
    merindingkan to make (s.o.'s hair) stand on end, horrify.
rindu 1 longing, yearning, desiring. *melepaskan –nya* to indulge one's fantasies. **2** homesickness (for), nostalgia (for); → NOSTALGIA. *nafsu - negerinya* to be homesick, nostalgic. *- akan/ke/ (ke)pada* long(ing) for. *- akan tanah airnya* to be homesick, be nostalgic. *- ke kampung, - (akan) kampung (dan) halaman* and *- kembali ke désanya* to be homesick, feel nostalgic. *- berahi* to be passionately in love. *- dendam* a) deep yearning/longing. b) head over heels in love. *- rawan* a) deep yearning. b) head over heels in love.
    merindu 1 to yearn, long, desire. **2** to feel homesick. **3** to hum due to homesickness.
    merindui to long for, hanker after; to be homesick for.

merindukan 1 to long for, hanker after; to be homesick for, miss. *seperti pungguk ~ bulan* to wish for the moon, want s.t. that is impossible. *Warga désa Purwodadi ~ listrik.* Purwodadi villagers long for electricity. **2** to cause s.o. to long for. **3** to make s.o. feel homesick.

rinduan s.t. longed for.

kerinduan 1 longing, yearning. **2** homesickness. **3** person who is longed for, lover.

perindu 1 person who longs for. **2** love/magic potion; → GUNA-GUNA. *buluh ~* wind harp/chime.

ring I (*onom*) sound of ringing.

ring II *gelang –* k.o. round bracelet.

ring III 1 (*D*) rings (used in gymnastics). **2** (*E*) (boxing) ring. *naik – to* enter the (boxing) ring. **3** (*E*) syndicate. *– tinju* boxing ring.

ringan 1 light (in weight); not serious, minor, superficial; → ÉNTÉNG. *luka –* not seriously injured. **2** unimportant, insignificant, of no account. **3** easy, not hard. *dengan –* easily, without any trouble. **4** abated, alleviated (of pain, etc.). **5** inexpensive, moderately priced. *dengan harga –* at a reasonable price. *– di lidah berat di langkah* easier said than done. *– sama dijinjing, berat sama dipukul* and *berat sepikul, – sejinjing* to share one's joys and sorrows. *– kaki* to like to go visiting, go around visiting people. *– kepala* a) smart, quick-witted. b) relieved. *– langkah* to like to frequent/visit. *– lidah/mulut* a) friendly, amicable, cordial; talkative, loquacious. b) carping, nagging, hard to please. *– pelatuk* trigger-happy. *– tangan* a) helpful, willing to help, neighborly, cooperative. b) prone to thieving, light-fingered. c) fast with the fists, likes to hit people. *– tulang* adroit, adept, agile, hardworking.

meringani to bring relief to, reduce.

meringankan [and **ngeringanin** (*J coq*)] **1** to lighten, ease, reduce (a judicial sentence, etc.), alleviate, relieve. *~ hukuman* to reduce a sentence. *keadaan yang ~* (*leg*) mitigating circumstances. **2** to make light of, take lightly, consider unimportant. *~ langkah* to come willingly, pay a social visit (to).

memperingan 1 to consider easy/simple, disregard. *~ pekerjaan yang diwajibkan kepadanya* to consider the work required of him to be easy. **2** to lighten (a load or burden), relieve.

teringan the lightest.

keringanan 1 ease, lightness. **2** clemency, leniency, relief. *mohon ~ dalam pembayaran pajak* to request a relief in tax payments. *~ hukuman* leniency/commutation of a sentence. *~ pajak/perpajakan* tax relief. *~ utang* debt relief. **3** too light/easy, etc.

peringan lightener. *ilmu ~ tubuh* the art of reducing body weight (in boxing, etc.).

peringanan easing, making light, relief, simplification. *~ utang* debt relief.

ringga → RENGGA.

ringgik → RÉNGGÉK.

ringgit I 1 (*col*) the two-and-a-half silver guilder. **2** (*ob*) 2½ rupiahs. **3** the Malaysia and Brunei dollar, equal to 100 cents.

ringgit II notch (in rim of coin), serration (at the edge of a knife, etc.).

beringgit notched, serrated.

meringgit to notch, serrate.

meringgiti to make notches/serrations in (iron, etc.). *besi baik diringgiti* to do s.t. more than is necessary; to make s.t. that is nice even nicer.

ringgit III (*Jv*) shadow-play puppet.

peringgitan the space in a house behind the front veranda (where shadow play performances are held).

ringgit IV name of a *ceki* card.

ringih meringih to neigh, whinny.

ringik (*J/Jv*) to whine, whimper; to moan, groan; → RÉNGÉK.

ringin I (*cla*) *main sapu-sapu –* k.o. hop-scotch, a children's game in which they squat, hop and sing.

ringin II (*Jv*) banyan tree; → BERINGIN.

ringis meringis 1 to grin (like a monkey), make faces. *Tokoh kita yang terkenal itu jadi ~.* Our famous figure grinned. **2** to grimace, turn the corners of the mouth down (from pain, etc.). **3** to look sour (from disappointment, etc.).

meringiskan to turn up (the corners of the mouth in a grin).

ringisan grin.

ringkai shriveled (up), dried up (of leaves, etc.). *– ringan* dry and light.

meringkai to dry out, shrivel up.

meringkaikan to dry, desiccate. *Nelayan ~ ikan hasil tangkapannya.* The fisherman dried his catch.

ringkas short, brief, succinct, concise (of an essay, etc.). *secara –* briefly, concisely. *– kata* in short.

ringkasnya in short/brief/a word; to put it briefly, in a nutshell, to sum up; → PÉNDÉKNYA.

meringkas(kan) 1 to shorten, make brief/concise, condense. **2** to abbreviate. **3** to summarize, recapitulate.

ringkasan 1 shortened form, résumé, summary, précis, abstract. *~ cerita* an abridged version of a story. *~ tésis* dissertation abstract. **2** abbreviation.

keringkasan 1 succinctness. **2** résumé, abstract.

peringkas s.o. who summarizes.

peringkasan 1 shortening, abridgment. **2** abbreviation, abbreviating.

ringkel (*Jv*) **meringkel** to roll o.s. up, (to sleep) hunched over.

ringkih (*Jv*) weak, frail, lacking strength/firmness/stamina, etc.

meringkih to become weak/frail.

keringkihan weakness, frailness, feebleness.

ringkik (*onom*) neigh, whinny; neighing, whinnying.

meringkik to neigh, whinny.

ringkikan neigh, whinny.

ringking yell, shriek, scream.

meringking to yell, shriek, scream.

ringkok (*J*) deep bowl (for eating).

ringkuk (*Jv*) **meringkuk 1** to sleep/sit, etc. all hunched up/over. **2** to be incarcerated/imprisoned; → MENDEKAM. *Lelaki berusia 41 tahun itu kini ~ di balik terali besi Sukamulia Médan.* The 41-year-old man is now behind bars in Sukamulia jail in Medan.

meringkukkan 1 to bend (one's back). **2** to imprison, incarcerate.

ringkukan 1 hunched over. **2** *dalam ~* in confinement, imprisoned.

ringkul (*ob*) → RINGKEL.

ringkus (*J/Jv*) **meringkus 1** to bind head and feet or the feet alone together (for an animal to be slaughtered), pinion. **2** (*coq*) to arrest, capture; → MEMBEKUK, MENAHAN. *Seorang gembong pemalsuan cék wisata di Asia diringkus Polri di Bandara Soekarno-Hatta.* A ringleader of the traveler check forgeries in Asia was arrested by the Republic of Indonesia Police at the Soekarno-Hatta Airport. **3** (*Mal*) to embezzle.

meringkusi (*pl obj*) to arrest.

teringkus arrested.

ringkusan arrest, custody. *dalam ~* in custody, under arrest.

peringkus captor.

peringkusan arrest, apprehension.

ringsek (*J*) completely demolished/in pieces, broken into pieces, totally damaged, a total loss. *Sepédanya – ditubruk mobil.* His bike got hit by a car and was completely demolished.

meringsek to destroy, demolish. *~ maju/masuk ke* to break (one's way) in(to).

ringsekan in bad shape, of bad/poor quality. *wantunas ~* low-class prostitute.

ringsing (*ob*) **meringsing** to furrow, wrinkle. *Bertambah tua kulitnya mulai ~.* With age his skin began to wrinkle.

ringsut decline, go down.

meringsut to decline, go down.

meringsutkan to decrease, make s.t. go down.

rini (*col*) half a cent; → RIMIS.

rinjing (*Jv*) a large hamper of bamboo wickerware which is carried on the back or as a pair on a horse.

rintak → RENTAK I.

rintang I block, obstruct, hamper.

merintang(i) 1 to block, close off, barricade. *Pohon yang tumbang di jalan raya itu merintangi arus lalu-lintas.* The tree that fell across the highway has blocked the flow of traffic. **2** to hamper, hinder, impede, obstruct, stop (s.o. from doing s.t.). *tidak dirintangi* unimpeded, unhampered. *Ada beberapa faktor sosial yang merintangi kemajuan kaum tani kita.*

There are several social factors which impede our peasants' progress.

merintangkan to block with, use ... to block. *Polisi ~ sekatan-sekatan di jalan.* The police blocked the road with obstructions.

terintang hampered, obstructed, impeded, blocked. *Perjalanan kami ~ oléh cuaca yang buruk.* Our trip was hampered by bad weather.

rintangan 1 hindrance, impediment, obstruction, obstacle, handicap. *tanpa ~* unimpeded, unhampered, unobstructed. *Kalau tidak ada ~, saya pasti datang.* If all goes well, I'll certainly come; → *kalau tidak ada* ARAL *melintang. ~ kawat* entanglement. **2** barrier, barricade, roadblock. *~ bahasa* language barrier. *~ bunyi* sound barrier. *~ penutup (mil)* sea-mine barrier to close off a harbor. *~ pohon* abatis. *~ usus (anat)* ileum.

perintang 1 hindrance, obstacle, impediment. **2** obstructionist, s.o. who gets in the way.

perintangan obstacle.

rintang II 1 occupied, busy, engaged, absorbed in. **2** addicted to (a bad habit).

merintang *~ anak* to amuse a child (to make it stop crying), keep a child occupied. *~ diri* to keep busy (with s.t.). *~ hati* to console, comfort. *~ lelah* to rest up, relax. *~ mata* to rest one's eyes by looking at s.t. beautiful. *~ payah/penat* to rest up, relax. *~ pikiran* to seek amusement/diversion. *~ waktu* to kill time, pass the time.

merintang-rintang 1 to do s.t. to overcome a difficulty. *Dengan bekerja keras kesusahan dalam rumah dapat juga dirintang-rintang.* Through hard work miseries at home could be overcome. **2** to entertain, keep occupied, seek amusement.

terintang(i) diverted, distracted.

perintang(-rintang) diversion, distraction, amusement. *perintang hati* consolation, solace. *bernyanyi-nyanyi akan ~ hati* singing to forget one's grief. *~ waktu* pastime.

rintas merintas to take a shortcut (by land or by sea), cut across; → LINTAS, PINTAS.

rinték → RINTIK.

rintih groan, moan.

merintih 1 to groan, moan. *seorang laki-laki yang sedang ~ kesakitan* a man groaning with pain. **2** to complain. *Meréka selalu ~ karena kesusahan.* They always complain about difficulties.

merintihkan to moan about, bemoan.

rintihan 1 groan(ing), moan(ing). **2** complaint.

perintih mourner.

rintik 1 spot, speck(le), stain. *kuda – a* spotted/speckled horse. **2** drop (of water). *hujan –* drizzle; → HUJAN *gerimis/renyai. bapak borék anak –* like father, like son. *– embun* dew drop.

rintik-rintik small drops. *hujan –* drizzle.

berintik(-rintik) spotted, speckled, blotched.

merintik(-rintik) to drip, appear in droplets (of water/dew, etc.). *Embun pagi mulai ~.* The morning dew began to appear in droplets.

rintikan *~ hujan* drizzle.

rintis (*Jv*) a narrow path cut through the forest/jungle.

merintis to cut a path through the jungle/forest. *Setelah beberapa hari ~ hutan, barulah meréka tiba di perkampungan terpencil itu.* After cutting through the forest for several days, they arrived at that isolated group of villages. *~ jalan* a) to plant stakes in the ground to mark out (a road). *Meréka sendiri yang membuat pekerjaan ~ jalan baru ke kampung meréka.* They themselves planted stakes to mark out a new road to their village. b) to pioneer, break new ground, lead the way, open the way to (s.t. new), set the stage for. *Kartini telah ~ jalan untuk memajukan kaum wanita.* Kartini broke new ground for the advancement of women. *Dana Inprés telah berjasa besar ~ jalan ke arah pemerataan ékonomi.* The Inpres funds have served greatly to open the way to economic equality.

merintiskan to cut a path for s.o.

rintisan 1 path through the forest/jungle. **2** pioneer work, pilot (*mod*). *proyék ~* pilot project.

perintis 1 pioneer, trailblazer, groundbreaker; → PELOPOR. *~ Pérs Indonésia* Pioneer of the Indonesian Press, i.e., an award given to an outstanding member of the Indonesian press corps. **2** maiden, first-time, made/tried for the first time, pilot (*mod*).

penerbangan ~ ke daérah-daérah terpencil maiden flights to isolated areas. *proyék ~* pilot project. **3** one of a group of foot soldiers detailed to make roads, bridges, etc., in advance of the main body of troops. *~ kemerdékaan* freedom fighter. **keperintisan** pioneering.

perintisan pioneer work, pioneering.

rinyai → RENAI, RENYAI.

rinyau k.o. fish used as bait.

rinying name of a *ceki* card.

rio(o)l (*D*) sewer, drain.

rioléring (*D*) sewer/drainage system.

ripit (*M*) crispy banana/taro, etc. chips.

ripot I (*E*) report.

ripot II → RÉPOT.

ripta meripta to design.

Riptaloka (in the *Bina Graha*, Jakarta) Operations Room.

ripu (*J*) and **ripuh** (*S*) **1** occupied, busy, engaged; → RÉPOT, SIBUK I. **2** in disorder, confused; → RIBUT. **3** to be in a fix, in trouble (due to financial problems, illness, etc.); → KEJEPIT.

ripuk → RUNTUH *ripuk.*

riqab (*A*) slave who wants to redeem his freedom; → HAMBA *sahaya.*

ririk → LIRIK I.

ri ri ri a cry for calling ducks.

ririt (*M*) row, line series; → DÉRÉT, LÉRÉT I.

RIS [*Républik Indonésia Serikat*] Federal Republic of Indonesia (from December 27, 1949, until August 17, 1950), when it was replaced by the *Negara Kesatuan Républik Indonésia*); → RUSI.

risa callus. *– lendir* callus with liquid under it.

risafel (*E*) reshuffle.

merisafel to reshuffle (a government cabinet).

risak merisak 1 to tease. **2** to annoy, bother.

risalah (*A*) **1** (*cla*) letter, message. **2** circular (letter); brochure, leaflet. **3** treatise, (scientific/research) paper, essay. **4** minutes, proceedings. *– rapat* minutes of a meeting. *– ujian* (*ob*) dissertation, thesis; → DISÉRTASI, TÉSIS.

risalat → RISALAH.

risau I bad (of behavior/attitude), like to cause problems, causing disturbances. *orang –* vagabond, tramp, bum.

merisau to live an irregular life; to roam/wander about without any fixed address, be a drifter from place to place.

perisau vagabond, tramp, bum.

risau II 1 restless, anxious, apprehensive, disturbed, concerned, worried; → CEMAS, KHAWATIR, RESAH. *Meréka merasa – mengenai anaknya yang sakit beberapa hari.* They're worried about their child who's been sick for a few days. *Penerbang itu merasa – mengenai keselamatan penumpangnya dalam penerbangan yang berbahaya itu.* The pilot felt anxious for the safety of his passengers during the dangerous flight. *Saya – mendengar kematiannya.* I'm disturbed to hear of his death. *Jangan-jangan meréka – saya lambat pulang.* I hope they won't be worried about my coming home late. **2** unsafe, insecure. *Keadaan dalam negeri masih – dan kacau.* The domestic situation is still insecure and confused.

merisau (*~ hati*) to alarm, disturb, perturb, worry.

merisaui and **merisaukan 1** to upset, disturb, worry, bother. *Berita buruk itu ~ saya.* The bad news upset me. **2** to make unsafe/insecure, disturb (safety/tranquility).

kerisauan worry, concern, anxiety, apprehension, nervousness. *Sebagian orang menghadapi masa depan yang tidak pasti dengan ~.* Some people face an unknown future with anxiety.

perisau 1 agitator, disturber (of the peace), troublemaker. **2** worrier, anxious person.

risbang → RÉSBANG.

risét (*E*) research. *ahli –* researcher. *mengadakan –* to do/carry out research (work). *– dan téknologi (nasional)* [risték(nas)] research and technology. *– atom* atomic research. *– ilmiah* scientific research. *– khalayak* audience research. *– pasar* market research. *– terpakai* applied research.

merisét to do/carry out research (work), do scientific research.

perisét researcher.

risi I and **risih I** (*J/Jv*) **1** to shudder, have the creeps, feel one's flesh creep, feel one's hair stand on end. *Melihat tampangnya yang* *bopéng-bopéng saya –*. Seeing his pockmarked face gives me the creeps. **2** not be up to par, not fit. *Badan saya terasa – sehabis ronda semalam.* I don't feel up to par after making the rounds last night. **3** to feel uneasy/uncomfortable/ill at ease, not feel at ease. *Bali sekarang mémang lain dengan 20 tahun silam, ketika kaum berada di mancanegara – tinggal di penginapan ala kadarnya.* The fact is, nowadays Bali is different from the Bali of 20 years ago when rich foreigners felt uncomfortable staying in modest lodgings.

risi II and **risih II** (*Jv*) irritated. *rasa –* a feeling of irritation. *Aku jadi – dibuatnya.* He irritated me. *Ditatap begitu Ruminten agak risih juga.* Ruminten felt irritated when stared at like that.
  merisikan 1 to cause one to feel irritated, etc. **2** to irritate, repel. *Hiruk pikuk orang di pasar dirasakannya seperti ~ hatinya.* The confused clatter of people in the market irritated her.

risik I merisik to grope/feel one's way for s.t. *Dalam gelap itu ia ~ knop lampu.* He groped in the dark for the light switch.

risik II 1 (surreptitious) efforts to find out about s.t., secret investigation. *Dari – yang dibuat ternyata kekuatan musuh lebih besar daripada yang diduga semula.* On investigation it turned out that enemy strength was greater than had been thought. **2** information/proof obtained in a surreptitious manner. *Ia memperoléh – bahwa rencananya telah diketahui orang.* He found out that people knew of his plans.
  merisik 1 to investigate secretly/surreptitiously/in a confidential manner. **2** to go or have s.o. find out whether a marriage proposal has been successful or not; to send a matchmaker.
  risikan secret investigation.
  perisik investigator.
  perisikan investigation.

risik III 1 (*onom*) sound of rustling. **2** whisper(ing), rumors, gossip. *ada pula –.– yang mengatakan ia telah menikah lagi.* There were also rumors that he had gotten married again. *belum ada –.–nya* there is still no sign of him.
  berisik and **merisik 1** to rustle, make rustling noises. **2** to whisper, gossip.
  merisikkan 1 to cause (leaves, etc.) to rustle. **2** to spread by gossip. *Berita burung itu dirisikkan kepada seorang wartawan.* The rumor was spread by gossiping to a news reporter.
  risikan rustling.
  kerisikan rustle, rustling noises.

risiko (*D*) risk, chance. *mengambil –* to take/run a risk. *mengambil – yang diperhitungkan* to take/run a calculated risk. *penuh –* risky, chancy. *apapun –nya* at all costs. *– keamanan* security risk. *– sendiri* deductible. *– yuridis* legal risk.
  berisiko to be risky. *~ tinggi* high-risk. *olahraga yang ~ tinggi* a high-risk sport.
  merisikokan *~ dirinya* to take a risk/chance.
  kerisikoan risk (*mod*). *manajemén ~* risk management.

risit (*E*) receipt.

riskan (*D*) risky.
  keriskanan risk.

riskir (*D*) **meriskir** to risk.

riskol (*J*) a Jakarta *batik* headdress for men, permanently sewn in shape.

riso → RISAU I.

risol (*D*) rissole, i.e., minced meat mixed with bread crumbs, eggs, etc. enclosed in a thin pastry and fried.

rispot (*D*) a Dutch specialty consisting of mashed potatoes, carrots, and onions with meat.

risték → RISÉT *dan téknologi*.

ristéknas → RISÉT *dan téknologi nasional*.

ristung → RESTUNG.

risuh embarrassed.

rit I (*onom*) creaking sound.

rit II (*D*) run (of a bus/truck), trip (made by a bus driver). *satu –* one haul.

rit III → RICES.

ritél (*E*) retail.
  peritél retailer.

ritme (*D*) rhythm. *– biologis* biorhythm.

ritmik (*E*) and **ritmis** (*D*) rhythmic(al).

ritsléting and **ritsliting** (*D*) zipper, zip fastener; → KANCING *tarik*.

ritual (*E*) and **rituil** (*D*) ritual.
  meritualkan to turn s.t. into a ritual, make a ritual out of.

ritul (*E*) **meritul 1** to reorganize, reeducate ideologically. **2** to replace civil servants of doubtful loyalty with others more sympathetic to the regime.
  peritulan reorganization, retooling, purge.

rituling (*E*) → PERITULAN.

ritus (*D*) rite.

riuh noise, uproar; loud, noisy, boisterous, tumultuous. *– rendah/ miuh* (*ob*) noisy, boisterous, tumultuous. **meriuh(-rendahkan)** to make noisy/boisterous, make (a sound) louder.
  meriuh to become noisy.
  meriuhkan to make noisy.
  keriuhan din, tumult, hubbub.

riuk 1 sprained, wrenched (of one's ankle), twisted; → TERKILIR, TERPELÉCOK, TERGELIAT. **2** distorted, deformed. **3** deformation.
  meriuk to deform.
  riukan deformation.
  periukan deformation.

riung I (*J*) to get together (with). *– mumpulung* (*S*) to get together (of university students, etc.). *mengadakan acara – mumpulung* to organize a get-together program. *– gunung* mountain chain.
  meriung and **mereriung 1** to come/get together, gather, meet, assemble. *Ibu tua itu senang direriung anak dan cucunya.* The old woman was happy when her children and grandchildren got together with her. **2** to hold a ritual gathering involving a common meal, such as a *selamatan. Datanglah ke rumah saya, kita akan ~*. Come to my house, we're holding a *selamatan*.
  (re)riungan 1 gathering, get-together. *~ saung* get-together in a small guard hut built in the rice paddies. **2** to get together. *Dia reriungan bersama saya.* He got together with me.
  riung-riungan to celebrate a (collective religious) meal, such as a *selamatan*.

riung II *– anak* k.o. tree, *Captanopsis javanica*.

riut I meriut to be bent/folded over.
  meriutkan to bend, fold over.

riut II (*onom*) creaking sound.
  meriut to creak.
  meriutkan to make s.t. creak.

rival (*D/E*) rival. *– bebuyutan* sworn/traditional/hereditary enemy.

rivalitas (*D*) rivalry.

riwan (*S*) (to have a) dream.

riwaq (*A*) patio.

riwayat (*A*) **1** story, account, narrative, tale; → CERITA. **2** history; → SEJARAH. *habis –nya* he's done for, he's about to die. **3** transmitting reports concerning the Prophet Muhammad's words. **4** (Christian) sermon. *– hidup* biography, curriculum vitae, résumé. *– hidup (yang ditulis) sendiri* autobiography. *– kerja* work history. *– singkat* brief account, précis.
  beriwayat 1 to tell a story, narrate. **2** historic. *hari ~* a historic day. **3** to deliver a (Christian) sermon, preach.
  meriwayatkan to tell, narrate.
  keriwayatan 1 origins of a story. **2** life-story (*mod*).
  periwayat 1 storyteller. **2** s.o. who narrates the *hadis*.

riweng (*Jv*) and **riwing** to be at one's wits' end, be at a loss for what to do.

riya → RIA II.

riyaya *– undhuh-undhuh* (*Jv*) thanksgiving ceremony among some Javanese Christians thanking God for the harvest and for good fortune over the past year.

riyep-riyep (*J*) to flicker. *lampu pijar yang ~* flickering light bulbs.

riz(e)ki, rizqi → REZEKI.

RM (*init*) [Ringgit Malaysia] Malaysian *ringgit*.

RMS (*init*) [Républik Maluku Selatan] Republic of the South Moluccas.

ro (in acronyms) → BIRO, RODA.

roa I → RUWAH.

roa II (*Port*) street (in *– Malaka*, name of a street in Jakarta).

roba (in compounds) → RUPA.

robah change; → RUBAH, UBAH II.
  merobah 1 to change. **2** to alter, amend, modify. *sebagaimana*

telah dirobah dan ditambah (i.e., a set phrase in regulations, etc.) as amended and supplemented.

perobahan 1 change. **2** alteration, emendation. ~ *kabinét* cabinet shake-up.

robak-rabik and **robat-rabit** in tatters/rags.

Robbi → RABBI.

robék (*J*) **1** torn, in shreds, ripped; torn off, ripped down. *Keméjanya* - *kena paku*. His shirt got torn on a nail. **2** tattered, ragged (of mats, etc.).

robék-robék torn to shreds.

merobék 1 to tear (up). *Dirobéknya semua surat itu*. He tore up all the letters. **2** to rip down, tear off. **3** to rend. ~ *hati* heart-rending. **4** to dig into (one's pocket). *Seorang amatir radio yang ingin memiliki peralatan ini tidak perlu* ~ *kantong terlalu besar*. An amateur radio buff who wants to own this equipment need not dip deeply into his pocket. *Harga makanan dan ongkos angkutan* ~ *kantong*. The cost of food and transportation are digging deep into people's pockets.

merobék-robék to shred to pieces.

merobéki (*pl obj*) to tear up.

merobékkan to tear up.

terobék-robék torn to shreds.

robékan fragment, scrap, stub (of a ticket). ~ *kertas* scrap of paper.

perobék s.o. who tears/cuts up.

perobékan tearing/cutting up. ~ *bendéra* tearing up a flag.

robewés → RÉBEWÉS.

robo a perennial grass, *Digitaria wallichiana*.

roboh 1 to fall (down), collapse, cave in, uprooted (of trees), topple. *Beberapa rumah di tepi pantai telah* - *akibat angin ribut*. Several houses at the seashore have collapsed as a result of the typhoon. **2** to fall, collapse (of a power/government, etc.). *Kerajaan itu sudah lama* -. That kingdom collapsed a long time ago. *batu* - a) avalanche, landslide. b) roaring (success/laughter, etc.). **3** to fail (of one's faith/a business), go bankrupt. - *semai* a disease of the cabbage plant.

merobohkan 1 to cause s.t. to collapse/fall, tear down, demolish. ~ *pohon* to fell/cut down trees. **2** to topple, overthrow (the government), overturn (the ruling party, etc.). **3** to beat, defeat, knock down, floor.

teroboh (*infr*) collapsed.

(ke)robohan 1 ruins. **2** collapse.

perobohan overthrow, pulling down, ruin(ing).

robok I merobok to bubble, burble (of water). *hati* ~ boiling with anger.

robok II merobok 1 to be affected on the inside and not visible externally (of a disease). **2** pent up (anger).

robok III bersirobok to meet e.o.

robok-robok (among the Malay ethnic groups in Sumatra) an annual traditional ceremony held on the last Wednesday of the month of Syafar to ask God for well-being, to pray for a good harvest, for successful cattle breeding, and for good fishing.

robot I (*J onom*) crackling sound of fireworks, etc.

merobot to crackle, make crackling sounds.

robot II (*D*) **1** robot. **2** a person who seems to act like a machine. *masyarakat* - a society of robots. - *hidup* a living robot.

robotasi the replacement of human workers in nuclear-power plants by robots.

robotika (*E*) robotics.

robur k.o. motorized pedicab.

Robusta the coffee made from the seeds of the coffee plant, *Coffea canephora*.

robyong (*Jv*) decorative chandelier.

rocét (*S*) chaotic, in a mess, in disorder.

kerocétan chaos, confusion, disorder.

rock (*E*) /rok/ clipped form of **rock 'n' roll**. *grup* - rock group. *lagu* - rock tune. *musik* - rock music. *pemusik* - rock musician.

ber-rock ('n' roll) 1 to dance to or play rock music. **2** to have the driving beat characteristic of rock music.

merock to dance to rock music. *ketika Ikang* ~ *Melayu* when Ikang danced to Malayan rock music.

merockkan to turn into a rock song.

rocker male rock star or fan.

rockerwati female rock star or fan.

rocok (*J*) **1** to flow forcefully (of liquids). **2** to leak.

roda (*Port*) **1** wheel, disc. - *terbalik* the tables are turned. **2** carriage, vehicle; (in Ujungpandang) pedicab; → BÉCAK. **3** tire. *mengempéskan* - *pesawat* to deflate the tires of an aircraft. **4** wheel, animating force(s), mechanism. *menjalankan* - *pemerintah* to turn the wheels of the administration. *hidup/untung bak/sebagai* - *pedati (sekali ke bawah, sekali ke atas)* the ups and downs of life, the vicissitudes of life. - *air* water wheel. - *angin* bicycle; → SEPÉDA. - *angka* indexed roller. - *belakang* rear wheel. - *berkaki ulat* caterpillar tread/wheels. - *ciduk* paddle wheel. - *depan* a) (of car, bike, etc.) front wheel. b) (of aircraft) nose wheel. - *dua* bicycle, (motor)bike. - *empat* car. *Nasib pasar si* - *dua ternyata tidak lebih baik dari si* - *empat*. It turns out that the market fate of bicycles is no better than that of cars. - *gaya* flywheel. - *gendeng* flywheel. - *gigi* a) cogwheel. b) caterpillar treads. **beroda gigi** with caterpillar treads. - *gila* flywheel. - *giling* mangle wheel. - *gotri* ball bearing. - *hambat* ratchet wheel. - *hubung* coupled wheel. - *jalan* traversing wheel. - *kapal* ship's wheel. - *kemudi* steering wheel. - *kemudi (di sebelah) kanan/kiri* /left-hand drive. - *kumai* milling wheel. - *lambung* paddlewheeler. - *palang* ratchet wheel. - *pedati* cartwheel. - *pembangunan* mechanism of development. - *pendarat* landing gear (of aircraft). - *penggerak* drive wheel. - *penghidupan* wheel of fortune, fate. - *pengimbang* balancing wheel. - *penyiksa* the wheel (on which people are tortured). - *pilih* telephone dial. - *rantai* track (of a tank, etc.). - *setir* steering wheel. - *takal* hoist. - *tiga* a) a three-wheeled vehicle. b) pedicab (in Ujung Pandang); → BÉCAK. - *tinta* inking wheel. - *tirus* mitre wheel.

beroda to have wheels, wheeled. *truk* ~ *delapan* an eight-wheeler truck.

merodai to put a wheel on.

rodaan (in the Karawang area, West Java) a *padi* or unhulled rice grains dealer who carries his goods on an oxcart.

rodan (*cla*) injury in a tender spot; agonizing, tender, painful.

rodapaksa → RUDAPAKSA.

rodat (*A*) Arabic religious song (with tambourine accompaniment).

rodéntisida (*E*) rodenticide.

rodi (*Port col*) (*kerja* -) forced/statute labor; → KERJA *paksa*. *menjalankan* - to carry out forced labor. *orang* - forced labor.

berodi and **merodi** to perform forced labor.

rodok I merodok 1 to thrust upward, stab, prod. **2** (*vulg*) to fuck, screw. *Dirodok lu!* Fuck you!

rodok II 1 (*M*) to run with the neck stretched forward (like a swan). **2** to act rashly/recklessly, do s.t. without thinking about it first.

rodok III (*Jv*) → RADA.

rodong I close (friends). *sahabat* - a) traveling companion. b) a close friend.

berodong to be on friendly relations (with).

merodong 1 to come across, encounter, bump into s.o. **2** to bump up against s.t.; to collide with s.t.; to penetrate.

merodongkan to make intimate, bring two things close together.

terodong to run into (a friend).

rodong II merodong to wander/roam about.

rofel (*D*) roll (of a drum).

merofel to beat (a drum/tambourine) with rapid, continuous strokes.

roga (*acr*) → RODA *tiga*.

rogo(h) (*J/Jv*) **merogo(h) 1** to put one's hand into s.t. to feel s.t. in it or take s.o. out of it. ~ *duit* to reach into one's pocket for money. ~ *kantong/saku* to reach into s.o.'s pocket for his/her purse. ~ *kocék lebih mendalam* to dip one's hand deeper into one's pocket. **2** (*Jv*) to sound out, pump s.o. for information. **3** to nab, nip.

merogohi (*pl obj*) to grope around for, etc.

rogoh-merogoh groping around.

rogoh-rogohan groping around.

perogo(h) s.o. who likes to feel up women by putting his hand into their clothes.

rogok merogok to prod with a long stick.
rogol merogol and **memperogol** to rape (a woman); → PEROGOL.
roh (*A*) **1** spirit of life. *terbang* – "life flew away," i.e., he fainted. *Semua mendoakan –nya diberkati Tuhan.* Everyone prayed that God would bless his spirit. **2** spirit. – *malaikat bunda itu* mother's ghostly spirit. – *(ul)kudus* a) the Holy Spirit. b) Gabriel, the angel of revelation and the intermediary between God and Muhammad. **3** soul, spirit. – *héwani* the life force in animals. – *insani* the human spirit. – *pelindung* guardian spirit of a house, tree, etc. – *suci* Holy Spirit.
rohani (*A*) spiritual. *nyawa* – the world soul that dwells in all souls.
  kerohanian spirituality. *préstasi* ~ spiritual achievement.
rohaniah (*A*) spiritual.
  merohaniahkan to spiritualize.
rohani(a)wan spiritual leader, (male) ecclesiastic.
rohani(a)wati female ecclesiastic.
rohim → RAHIM I.
rohmat (*ob*) → RAHMAT.
rohulkudus → ROH (*ul*)*kudus*.
roi (*D*) *garis* – building alignment.
rois (*A*) → RAIS I.
roisul ma'had (*A*) monitor, housefather (i.e., a man responsible for a group of young students living in a dormitory attached to a *pesantrén*).
roja (*Port ob*) garland of roses.
rojabiyah (*A*) pertaining to the month of *Rajab. mengadakan pidato* – to make a *Rajab* speech.
rojéng (*Jv*) **merojéng** to steal rice plants from the field.
  rojéngan stolen rice plants.
  perojéng rice-plant thief.
rojer (*E*) roger: message received and understood, a response to radio communications; → RANDU II.
roji → RUJI II.
rojiem → RAJIM.
rojog and **rojok I** (*J*) **merojok** to flow (of liquids).
rojok I → RUJUK I.
rojok II (*J*) **merojok 1** to poke at. **2** to stick s.t. into (frequently with sexual connotations).
  merojok-rojok to keep on poking at.
  merojokkan to stick (s.t.) (into s.t.).
rojol merojol to jut out, protrude, emerge (of one's head from a hole/window, etc.).
rojolélé a rice variety.
rok I (*D*) **1** skirt. **2** dress, gown. – *balon* flared skirt. – *dalam* underskirt, slip. – *hamil* maternity dress. – *jadi* ready-made skirt. – *jéngki* tight skirt. – *ketat* straight/tight skirt; → SPAN-ROK. – *kembang* flared skirt. – *klok* full skirt. – *lurus* straight skirt. – *maksi/midi/mini* maxi-/midi-/miniskirt. – *mini serba kelihatan* see-through miniskirt. – *plisir* pleated skirt. – *span* straight/tight skirt. – *terusan* sheath skirt.
  be(r)rok to wear a skirt. *wanita* ~ *ungu* a woman wearing a purple skirt.
rok II (*E*) rock; → MUSIK *rok/cadas*.
rokaat → RAKAAT.
rokade (*D*) **1** castle, rook (in chess). **2** castling (in chess).
roker (*E*) rock star/musician.
rokét (*E*) rocket, missile. *meluncurkan* – to launch a rocket. – *antitank* antitank rocket. – *berkepala perang nuklir* rocket with a nuclear warhead. – *berpengendali* guided missile. – *bertingkat* multistage rocket. – *dua tingkat* two-stage rocket. – *kendali* guided missile. – *peluncur* booster rocket. – *penangkis* defense/interceptor rocket, antimissile missile. – *pendorong/penggerak* booster rocket. – *penyokong berbahan bakar padat* solid-fuel rocket booster. – *terkendali* guided missile.
  merokét to shoot/rocket up. *Harga tanah* ~. The price of land is shooting up.
  merokétkan to make s.t. shoot up. ~ *kariérnya* to make one's career shoot up.
  perokétan rocketry.
rokh → ROH.
rokhani → ROHANI.
rokhaniah → ROHANIAH.

roki (*D*) dress suit/coat.
rokok I cigarette (wrapped in paper or in straw). *daun* – cigarette paper. *meng(h)isap/minum* – to smoke a cigarette. *menyulut sebatang* – to light up a cigarette. *pecandu* – cigarette addict. *uang* – a tip, gratuity. – *berfilter* a filter cigarette. – *berméntol* a mentholated cigarette. – *cengkéh* a clove-flavored cigarette. – *cerutu* cigar. – *daun* cigarette wrapped in *nipah* leaves. – *hokah* water pipe, hookah. – *jengking* cigarette made from butts collected off the street. – *jontal* (in Sumbawa) a long cigarette wrapped in *lontar* leaf. – *kawung* cigarette wrapped in dried sugar palm leaves. – *klembak kemenyan* cigarette filled with rhubarb and incense (popular in Kedu and Banyumas). – *klobot* cigarette wrapped in the bracts of the corn ear. – *krétek* cigarette with clove-flavored tobacco wrapped in corn leaves of the corn ear. – *lima-lima* the State Express 555 cigarette. – *linting* a hand-rolled cigarette. – *polos* cigarette without an excise tax strip of paper affixed. – *putih* an ordinary cigarette (not filled with any special filler). – *rakitan lokal* foreign cigarettes assembled in Indonesia. – *ringan* mild cigarettes. – *serutu* cigar. – *siong* factory-produced cigarettes containing incense or aloeswood that produce a unique, strong pungent aroma. – *tingwé* (*Jv*) hand-rolled cigarette.
  berokokan to smoke (*pl subj*).
  merokok [and **ngerokok** (*coq*)] to smoke (a cigarette). *Dilarang* ~. No smoking. ~ *pipa/serutu* to smoke a pipe/cigar. ~ *terus sambung-menyambung* and ~ *sigarét beruntun* to chain-smoke, be a chain-smoker. *orang-orang yang* ~ *dan tidak* ~ smokers and nonsmokers.
  perokok smoker. ~ *berantai* chain smoker.
rokok II (in Ujungpandang) code word for a detonator used in fishing.
roko-roko glossy ibis, *Plegadis falcinellus.*
rokrak (*S*) debris, small pieces of wood, cut-off ends of small sticks, waste matter, twigs, etc. found in the street.
rol I (*D*) part, role (of an actor in a film, etc.), character; → PERANAN. *memegang* – *jagoan* to play the leading role, be the leading man/lady. *memegang* – *penting* to play an important role.
rol II (*D*) **1** a roll, rolled object, such as a film/toilet paper, etc. *film se-* a roll of film. *menghabiskan dua* – *film* to use up two rolls of film. **2** roller, cylinder, cylindrical piece of wood, iron, etc. used as a roller, ruler, press (machine), platen, etc. – *gilas* mat roller. – *kumai* knurling tool. – *mesin tulis* typewriter platen. – *rambut* hair rollers. – *sisir* stripper. – *tinta* ink roll.
  merol and **mengerol** to roll (hair, etc.). *Rambutnya dirol.* She rolled her hair.
  rol-rolan hair rollers.
  pengerolan rolling.
rol III (*E*) roll (k.o. small bread).
rolade roulade, collared beef, rolled roast.
rolét → RULÉT.
roling (*E coq*) moving from place to place.
rolprés (*D*) a press for printing stamps.
roltar(t) (*D*) a cylindrical-shaped cake served in slices.
rom → RUM II.
roma I (*Skr*) **1** *bulu* – fine body hair. *liang* – pores. *tegak (berdiri) bulu –nya* his hair stood on end. **2** (*geol*) pore.
roma II (*Skr*) appearance, look (of persons); → MUKA, ROMAN I. *Meréka tidak boléh bertemu* –. They can't get near each other (without a quarrel erupting). – *muka* features (of the face).
  seroma ~ *dengan* to be like, resemble, look like; → MIRIP (*dengan*).
roma III (*acr*) → ROMBÉNGAN *Malaysia.*
Roma IV Rome. *banyak jalan menuju* – all roads lead to Rome. – *Kuno* Ancient Rome.
Rom(a)don → RAMAD(H)AN.
romal a black and bluish headdress worn by *Baduy* males.
roman I appearance, look, countenance. – *cilik* petite. – *muka* features (of the face).
  seroman ~ *dengan* to resemble, look like; → MIRIP (*dengan*).
  peroman (*ob*) appearance, look (of persons); → ROMA II.
roman II (*D*) novel (a genre of fiction). – *berangsur* serial, feuilleton, continued story; → CERITA *bersambung,* CÉRBÉR. – *berténdéns* novel with a tendentious theme. – *détéktif* detective

novel. – *kodian* dime novel. – *masyarakat* novel with a social theme. – *obralan/picisan* dime novel. – *sejarah* historical novel. – *setalénan* dime novel.

roman III (*coq*) romance.

roman-romanan l romantic, full of romance. **2** *main* ~ to have a love affair. *Oom, kalau si Boby main* ~, *asyiiik déh.* Sir, if Bobby has a love affair, he really falls hard.

roman IV (rice) husk, straw (of the rice plant).

roman V Roman, Latin. *huruf* – Latin alphabet; → RUMAWI.

Romanis (*D*) Romanist, Romanticist.

Romanistik (*E*) Romanistic.

romans(a) (*D*) romance.

romantik (*E*) romantic.

beromantik-romantikan to be romantic. *Ini sudah bukan saatnya* ~ *lagi.* This is no longer the time to be romantic.

romantika romance, romantics. – *kehidupan* romance of life.

romantikus (*D*) romanticist.

romantis (*D*) → ROMANTIK.

meromantiskan to romanticize.

keromantisan romanticism.

romantisasi romanticization.

meromantisasi to romanticize.

romantisi (*D*) romanticists.

romantisir (*D*) **meromantisir** to romanticize.

romantisisme romanticism.

Romawi → RUMAWI. *gulat gaya* – Greco-Roman-style wrestling.

rombak demolished, destroyed, wrecked.

merombak l to demolish, wreck (buildings). ~ *gedung-gedung yang tua itu* to demolish those old buildings. **2** to abolish, destroy, nullify. ~ *adat/aturan/perjanjian* to abolish customs/regulations/treaties. **3** to reorganize, reshuffle. ~ *susunan kabinét* to reshuffle the cabinet. **4** to alter, make alterations in. **5** to overhaul (an engine, etc.). **6** to fall apart, disintegrate.

(ke)rombakan materials of demolished building, rubble, debris, ruins, wreckage. *rombakan léréng* scree, talus.

perombak l demolisher. **2** reorganizer.

perombakan l demolition. **2** reshuffle. ~ *kabinét* cabinet reshuffle. **3** falling apart, disintegrating. **4** reorganization, shake-up. ~ *kembali* restructuring. **5** overhaul(ing). **6** alteration.

rombang-rambing tattered and torn, in rags; → ROMPANG *ramping*.

rombé → RUMBAI I.

rombéng (*J*) l torn up, tattered, in tatters/rags. **2** (*Jv*) worn (out), the worse for wear, secondhand. *pakaian* – old clothes, rags.

merombéng to deal in used clothing, etc.

merombéngkan l to sell (secondhand items) to a ragman. **2** to sell as a used item/as is.

rombéngan l (old) junk, secondhand clothes, rags, rubbish; the worse for wear, worn (out). ~ *Malaysia* [roma] (in Pontianak) used clothes (from Malaysia) sold in Pontianak. *tukang* ~ ragman, secondhand clothes dealer. **2** worthless. *Kau busuk* ~. You're rotten and worthless.

romboida rhomboid.

rombok I (*M*) thick, dense (of foliage/forest, etc.), shady; → RAMPAK I, RIMBUN

rombok II k.o. gold or silver jewelry.

rombong I l a large rice basket. **2** pushcart.

rombong II berombong and **merombong** l to be a group; to gather together in a group. **2** in piles/stacks, piled high.

rombongan l group; → GRUP. *secara* ~ in groups. **2** gang. **3** troupe, team, party, entourage. **4** a set of (musical) instruments. ~ *gubernur* the governor's party. ~ *haji* group of pilgrims. ~ *pelajar* student group. ~ *pemain bola* soccer team. ~ *sandiwara* theatrical group. **berombongan** in groups/a party.

rombus (*D*) rhombus.

romel and **romel-romel** (*coq*) junk.

romét I merométt to putter around, tinker, do odd jobs.

romét II → RUMIT.

romhorn (*D*) puff pastry filled with cream and coated with sugar.

Romli (*A*) – *dan Juli/Zubaédah* Romeo and Juliet.

romo (*Jv*) (Roman Catholic) priest, father; → RAMA. – *préfék* assistant to the rector in a seminary.

romo-romo(nya) ~ *pembangunan* the founding fathers of the Republic of Indonesia: Soekarno, Hatta, Ali Sastroamidjojo, Sartono, Soekiman, Leimena, Achmad Soebardjo, Haji Agoes Salim, and Moh. Yamin.

romok meromok and **teromok** l to look scrawny (of chickens). **2** to look depressed (of people).

romol (*D*) junk.

romong (*J*) old clothes/things, junk, rags.

rompak I merompak to commit piracy.

perompak pirate.

perompakan piracy. *Aksi* ~ *kapal dagang dan kapal tangker pernah terjadi di Selat Malaka.* There were once acts of piracy against trading ships and tankers in the Straits of Malacca.

rompak II (*M*) destroyed.

merompak to destroy, break s.t. to pieces. ~ *pagar* to break with customs. ~ *pintu* to break down a door.

rompal (*J/Jv*) to fall out (of teeth, etc.). *Dua buah lampu pijar yang* – *diganti.* Two broken electric light bulbs have been replaced.

rompang → RUMPANG. – *ramping* tattered and torn, with holes in it (of baskets/thatched roofs), in shreds; → ROMBANG-RAMBING.

rompéng chipped at the edge (of one's teeth), gnawed away (of fruit by birds).

rompés jagged (of the edge of an ear).

rompi (*D*) l singlet, undershirt. **2** waistcoat, vest. – *antipeluru* bulletproof vest, flak jacket.

ber(r)ompi wearing a waistcoat.

rompiok bundle.

berompiok in bundles.

rompoh → ROMPONG I.

rompok I (*Jv*) hut, hovel; → PONDOK.

rompok II hem, edging (of cloth).

rompong I l mutilated (of one's ear/nose by accident/disease, etc.), with the tip cut off, broken at the edge (of teeth), truncated. **2** (*M*) broken into, violated (of a girl). **3** (*bio*) truncate.

merompong(kan) to mutilate, cut the tip off, perforate.

rompong II (fish) lure.

rompyok → ROMPIOK.

romsus and **romsusyes** (*D*) cream puff (pastry).

romus → RUMUS.

romus(h)a and **romusya** (*Jp*) forced labor (compelled to do hard labor during the Japanese occupation).

meromusyakan to put s.o. to work as a forced laborer.

rona (*Skr*) l color, tone; → WARNA. **2** beauty. **3** outer appearance, features (of land). *hilang* – *karena penyakit, hilang bangsa tidak beruang* s.o. who is poor is not respected. – *awal* baseline. – *lingkungan* environmental setting. – *muka* face; facial expression.

berona l to have a color. **2** colored.

merona l to color s.t. **2** colorful. *mérah* ~ bright red.

meronai to color s.t.

perona ~ *mata* eye shadow. ~ *pipi* rouge, blush; → PEMÉRAH *bibir*.

roncé I (*J/Jv*) **meroncé** to steal, rob, loot, plunder; → MERAMPOK.

peroncéan robbery, looting, plundering.

roncé II (*Jv*) l string (of beads, etc.), wreath (of flowers).

meroncé to string (beads, etc.), arrange (flowers). *Ia mencari tambahan penghasilan dengan* ~ *abakus.* He got additional income by stringing abacuses.

teroncé strung (beads, etc.), arranged (flowers).

roncéan wreath (of flowers).

roncén I (*Jv*) (variant form of **roncé II**).

roncén II l string (of beads), wreath (of flowers). **2** details (of a story).

meroncéni l to string (beads), wreathe (flowers). **2** to tell (a story) in detail.

peroncén *segala* ~ *pengalaman* empirical, experimental.

roncét beroncét-roncét l to advance/progress gradually/bit by bit/little by little. **2** to be of various sorts; varied.

meroncét to do s.t. little by little.

ronda (*Port*) l rounds, patrol, beat. **2** guard, watchman. *orang* – night watchman. **3** (in Ambon) to take a walk. – *kampung* village patrol. – *malam* night watch. – *ték-ték* traditional night watch accompanied by beating on a *kentongan*, or bamboo or wooden drum.

meronda to be/go on patrol, make one's rounds.

merondai to patrol in/around.

rondaan patrol, watch.

peronda watchman, patrol. ~ *malam* night watchman.

perondaan patrolling, (making the) rounds.

rondah-randih deranged, disordered, confused.

ronde (*D*) 1 a round (in sports); → BABAK I. 2 rounds; → RONDA.

rondé (*Jv*) small, round, glutinous-rice balls, sometimes containing peanut and/or palm kernels. *wedang* – hot ginger-flavored drink containing *ronde*.

rondes (*D*) rounders (the sport).

rondo I (*D*) rondeau, roundel.

rondo II (*Jv*) – *gulung* sweetmeat peculiar to Surakarta, made from flour mixed with bananas, jackfruit, or cacao and made into an omelet. – *royal* fritters made with fermented manioc.

rondo III → RANDA I.

rondok (*ob*) **berondok** and **merondok** to hide, conceal o.s. *Sesampai di situ, meréka berondok di balik pohon.* When they got there, they hid behind a tree.

merondokkan to hide s.t.

ronéo (*D*) mimeograph; → STÉNSIL.

meronéo(kan) to mimeograph.

rong I (*Jv*) hole (in the ground). – *tikus* mousehole.

rong II (*D*) stake, stanchion, upright.

rongak I 1 full of holes, with gaps (of a fence/teeth). *bergigi* – gap-toothed. 2 spacing.

rongak II → RONGGANG.

rongéh (*Jv*) restless, can't stand still, moving all the time.

rongga 1 hollow space, cavity, hole (of the ear/mouth/nose/pore/in a tree), opening (between leaves), antrum. 2 ullage. – *benih* (*bot*) loculus. – *bulu* skin pore. – *dada* chest/thoracic cavity. – *hidung* nasal cavity. – *insang* gill opening. – *kayu* hole in tree. – *mata* eye socket, orbital cavity. – *mulut* oral cavity. – *perut* abdominal cavity. – *timpani* hole in eardrum.

berongga with/to have a hole/cavity in it, hollow. *batu-batu* ~ hollow stones. *gelang itu* ~ *tidak padat* that bracelet has hollow spaces in it, it isn't massive. *patung* ~ hollow (not solid) statue.

merongga to form a hollow space.

meronggakan to hollow out.

ronggang → RENGGANG I.

ronggéng (*Jv*) girl who dances and sings for payment along with guests at a party. – *gunung* (in the Pangandaran area in West Java) a traditional art form accompanied by a hot rhythm and lots of humorous remarks. – *kunyuk* (in Cirebon and Tegal); → KOMIDI *keték*.

meronggéng to dance (of a *ronggéng*).

keronggéngan the art of *ronggéng. Ia sadar pada stéréotipe berpikir yang menganggap keagamaan tepat berhadapan dengan* ~. He was aware of the stereotyped way of thinking which considers religion the direct opposite of the art of *ronggéng*.

peronggéngan place where a *ronggéng* performs.

ronggoh → RUNGGUH I.

ronggok → LONGGOK.

ronggot (*J*) **meronggot** to climb a tree.

ronggoh → RUNGKUH.

rongkok merongkok to walk stooped over.

rongkol I cluster (of fruit).

serongkol a bunch. ~ *kunci* a bunch of keys.

berongkol clustered, bunched.

rongkol II (*J*) **merongkol** 1 to sleep with a blanket pulled up around o.s. 2 to shiver from the cold.

rongkong I windpipe, throat, larynx. – *menghadap mudik* easy to do well. – *menghadap hulu* hard to do well.

(ke)rongkongan 1 windpipe, trachea. 2 throat, Adam's apple. 3 gullet, esophagus. *Makanan itu masuk ke dalam* ~ *lalu ke perut.* Food enters the esophagus and then goes down into the stomach. *rongkongan menghadap mudik/hilir* (*M*) to have an easy/hard time making a living. *berair rongkongan* (*M*) to be successful/lucky. *pembuluh rongkongan* a) lucky person. b) means of livelihood.

rongkong II (re)**rongkongan** (*J*) skeleton.

rongong (*M onom*) buzzing sound.

merongong to buzz, hum, drone, whirr (like the sound made by flies, etc.).

rongos I merongos to be short-tempered, hot-tempered, get angry easily, irritable, peevish.

perongos s.o. who is quick to anger/short-tempered/irascible/irritable/touchy.

rongos II (*J*) **merongos** to turn one's face to the side.

rongot → RUNGUT.

rongrong (*J*) **merongrong** 1 to gnaw/nibble (away at). 2 to bother s.o. (for money, etc.). *Belum apa-apa sudah* ~. Nothing's happened yet and he's already bothering (us). 3 to undermine, sap, eat away at (one's capital/a budget). *Musuh-musuh negara berusaha* ~ *pemerintah.* The enemies of the state are making efforts to undermine the government.

merongrongi to gnaw/nibble away at.

rongrongan gnawing away at, undermining, harassment. ~ *séksual* sexual harassment.

perongrong s.o. who nibbles away at, s.o. who attempts to destroy s.t.

perongrongan gnawing away at, undermining, harassing.

rongséng 1 peevish, crabby, testy; gruff, surly. *Orangnya* –, *sukar diajak bicara.* He's surly, it's hard to get him to talk. 2 annoyed, irritated, fed up.

merongséng to grumble, nag, grouse.

merongséngkan to upset s.o., make s.o. surly.

kerongséngan peevishness, crabbiness, surliness.

perongséng grumbler, complainer.

rongsok (*J/Jv*) spoiled, damaged, impaired, broken down; → ROMBÉNG. *Moralnya sudah* –. His morals are damaged. *piano* – a broken-down piano.

rongsokan junk. *barang* ~ s.t. worn out or no longer usable. ~ *logam* metal waste.

ronsel (*D*) crimp.

ronsen → RONTGEN.

ronta meronta(-ronta) to struggle (against), struggle to free o.s. (from attack/arrest/an abductor, etc.); to oppose, resist. *Wau-wau itu takut pada kaméra. Itu sebabnya, ketika kami mau memotrétnya, ia* ~ *dan berusaha merebut kaméra foto.* The gibbon is camera-shy. That's why, when we wanted to take a picture of him, he resisted and tried to grab the camera. *pikiran meronta* restless.

merontakan to make s.o. struggle.

rontaan struggle.

rontak → RONTA.

rontal → SIWALAN I.

rontang-ranting (*Jv*) torn, tattered.

ronték a pennoned lance.

rontgen (*D*) X-ray. *gambar* – X-ray picture, radiograph.

merontgen to X-ray, take an X-ray (picture) of.

rontok (*Jv*) 1 to fall/drop off, shed (leaves/twigs, etc.). *Angin kencang membuat daun pepohonan* –. A strong wind made the leaves of the trees fall off. *musim* – fall, autumn. 2 to fall out (of one's hair). *Rambutnya jadi* – *setelah ia melahirkan anaknya yang kelima.* Her hair fell out after she gave birth to her fifth child. *penyakit* – *rambut* sickness which causes the hair to fall out. 3 to peel off (of paint, etc.). *Cat pintu itu sudah* –. The paint on that door has peeled off. 4 to get loose, loosen (of one's teeth). *Giginya* –. His teeth got loose. 5 shot down (of an aircraft). – *jantung* dejected, downcast.

berontokan (*pl subj*) to fall, drop off, etc.

merontok to fall off, drop.

merontokkan 1 to cause to shed/fall out, shake down. 2 to defeat, overthrow, bring down. *Kesebelasan itu berhasil* ~ *lawannya.* The soccer team succeeded in defeating its opponent. 3 to shoot down (an aircraft). 4 to miss (a chance). *Peluangnya dirontokkan.* He missed his chance.

rontokan s.t. which has fallen off/out by itself. *durian* ~ a *durian* fruit that has fallen off the tree because it was ripe. *dapat durian* ~ to get a windfall/a stroke of luck; → DURIAN *runtuh*.

perontok thresher. *alat* ~ *padi* thresher for unhusked rice. *alat* ~ *pedal* pedal thresher. *mesin* ~ power thresher.

perontokan away from, de-. ~ *industri* deindustrialization.

ronyak → RENYUK I.

ronyéh meronyéh 1 to chatter away, natter, babble. **2** to talk nonsense/drivel.

peronyéh chatterbox.

ronyok rumpled, crumpled, crinkled, full of wrinkles. *Mukanya – dimakan usia.* Her face was wrinkled with age.

meronyok(kan) to crumple (up), rumple. *Ia mengumpulkan kertas yang sudah dironyokkannya.* He gathered up the papers that he had crumpled up earlier.

roofbouw (*D col*) /rofbaw/ **1** wasteful exploitation, premature exhaustion (of mines). **2** exhaustive cultivation (of the soil).

room → ROM II.

roos → ROS I.

ropak untidy. – *rapik* untidy, disorderly.

ropak-ropak untidy, disorderly.

ropel → ROFEL.

ropoh (*S*) very old, aged, far advanced in years.

roréhé (*IBT*) a motorless boat (used for catching tuna).

rorod (*J*) **merorod 1** to slip off (of clothes), come off (of dirt). *Celananya ~.* His pants slipped off; → MELOROT. **2** (*J*) to remove the wax layer of *batik* by dipping the cloth in hot water.

merorodkan to remove the husk.

Roro Kidul → NYAI *Loro Kidul.*

rorot → ROROD.

ros I (*D*) rose; → MAWAR I.

ros II (*D*) bull's-eye (in target shooting).

ros III (*Jv*) → RUAS.

rosak (*Mal*) → RUSAK.

rosario (*Port*) rosary. *berkalung –* to wear a rosary around one's neck. *Ada yang berjilbab, ada yang berkalung –.* Some wore a *jilbab*, others had a rosary around their necks.

rosbang → RÉSBANG.

roséla (*D*) roselle, Jamaican sorrel, *Hibiscus sabdariffa*, a plant belonging to the mallow family which is mainly used for its fibers.

roséng → RONGSÉNG.

rosét (*D*) rosette.

roskam (*D*) currycomb (for horses).

rosok I (*M*) **merosok** to grope (one's way or in one's pocket/bag, etc.). ~ *ikan* to look for fish by groping between rocks, etc. ~ *saku* to put one's hand into one's pocket; to dip into one's purse (for money).

merosokkan to put s.t. (into a hole/one's pocket). *Ia segera ~ saputangannya ke dalam saku.* He immediately put his handkerchief into his pocket.

perosok stumble. **teperosok** stumbled (into a hole, etc.); → PEROSOK.

rosok II (*Jv*) run-down, dilapidated, worn out. *main – (coq)* to act arbitrarily/at random.

rosokan junk, rubbish, trash.

rosot (*J*) **merosot 1** to slip off (of a garment), fall down. **2** to fall, decline (of morale/prestige/price, etc.), sink, drop, go down. **3** to deteriorate (of one's health). **4** to suffer/be in a recession (of business), contract (of the economy). **kemerosotan 1** drop, setback, decline. **2** degradation, deterioration, degeneration. ~ *akhlak* degeneration. ~ *moral* moral degeneration. **pemerosotan** decline.

merosotkan and **memerosotkan** to lower, let drop, let decline. ~ *diri* to drop down, lower o.s.

rosotan (*hydro*) recession.

roster I (*D*) roster, timetable (of classes).

roster II → RASTER.

rosul → RASUL.

rotan 1 rattan, cane. **2** punishment by flogging with a cane, caning. *ada – ada duri* no rose without a thorn. *kerat –, patah arang* irreparably broken. *tiada – akar pun berguna/jadi* half a loaf is better than none. – *asalan/bulat* round rattan (not processed). – *asam* k.o. rattan which bears fruit, devil shrub, *Daemonorops acidus*. – *cacing* k.o. rattan, *Calamus javanicus*. – *cincin* k.o. prickly palm, *Daemonorops melanochaetes*. – *gelang* k.o. rattan, *Daemonorops geniculatus*. – *getah* various species of rattan, *Daemonorops spp*. – *jernang* red rattan, *Daemonorops hygrophi-*

lus. – *kubu* a climber, *Freycinetia javanica*. – *kemunting* → ROTAN *gelang*. – *layar* a thick white rattan. – *lilin* k.o. rattan, *Calamus javanicus*. – *manau* manau rattan, *Calamus manau*. – *relang* k.o. rattan, *Plectocomiopsis geminiflorus*. – *sega* a rattan species with a fine and shiny skin, *Calamus caesius*. – *semambu* Malacca cane, *Calamus scipionum*. – *semut* k.o. rattan, *Korthalsia spp*. – *setengah jadi* partly processed rattan, webbing. – *tikus* a small reddish rattan, *Flagellaris indica*. – *udang*, shrimp rattan, *Korthalsia echinometra*. – *ulur* a strong rattan, *Calamus ulur*.

berotan to collect/look for rattan.

merotan 1 to collect/look for rattan. **2** to cane (s.o./furniture).

perotan person who collects/looks for rattan.

Rotari (*E*) *Perkumpulan –* Rotary Club.

rotasi (*D*) **1** rotation. **2** crop rotation. – *bumi* rotation of the earth.

berotasi to rotate, gyrate.

roti I (*Hind*) (a loaf of) bread. *sepotong –* and – *sepotong* a slice of bread. *mentéga di antara dua tangkap –* a bread and butter sandwich. *kéju di antara dua potongan –* a cheese sandwich. *ibu –* yeast. *panggangan –* toaster (the appliance). – *Amérika* sliced white bread. – *bakar* (*J*) toasted bread, toast. – *blok-blokan* bread cut into large cube-like portions wrapped in plastic bags; sometimes the bread is spread with chocolate or pineapple jam. – *bola* roll (of bread). – *bolu* → KUÉ *bolu*. – *bulan sabit* croissant. – *capati* chapati, an (East) Indian bread. – *gerobakan* bread sold from a pushcart. – *goréng* crouton. – *hitam* brown/dark bread. – *jala* lacy bread which resembles a net, eaten with sauce. – *kabin* salt crackers. – *kadét* French roll (of bread). – *kaléng* crackers. – *kalong/kalung* brass knuckles, knuckle-duster. – *kering* biscuit. – *kismis* raisin bread. – *kukus* steamed cupcakes. – *manis* sweet/sugared bread. – *mari* k.o. cracker. – *mentéga* bread and butter. – *meriam* (*J*) k.o. pancake. – *Natal* Christmas bread. – *panggang* toasted bread, toast. – *Paskah* Easter bread. – *Prancis* French bread, baguette. – *putih* white/sandwich bread. – *setangkap* (*Jv*) sandwich. – *sobék* bread cut into large cube-like portions and wrapped in plastic bags; sometimes spread with chocolate or pineapple jam. – *sisir* k.o. sweetened bread. – *sumbu* (in Java humorous term for) cassava. – *tanduk* croissant. – *tawar* white/sandwich bread. – *waluh kuning* pumpkin scone.

roti-rotian various k.o. breads.

perotian 1 (*mod*) bread. **2** bakery.

roti II (*Jv*) a female high school or college student who prostitutes herself.

rotok I (*onom*) crack (of explosions/rifle fire).

merotok 1 to grumble, mutter under one's breath. **2** to crack (the sound of a rifle).

rotok II merotok to grumble.

rotok III (*J*) **merotok** to sprout (of leaves/pimples on the skin, etc.).

rotor (*D*) rotor.

rotsoi (*D coq*) **1** disorderly, chaotic, messy. **2** rotten, lousy.

rowa (*Jv*) bulky.

rowah → RUWAH.

rowot merowot to abstain from eating rice.

roya (*D*) **1** cancellation, reconveyance. **2** disbarment. – *hipoték* cancellation of a mortgage.

meroya 1 to cancel (a mortgage). **2** to disbar.

royak meroyak to spread, extend. *Penyakit kapitalisme bisa ~ jauh dari sana dengan menggerogoti sendi-sendi sosialisme yang sedang meréka bangun.* The disease of capitalism can spread from there (i.e., Vietnam) and gnaw away at the very foundations of the socialist system they are constructing.

royal (*D*) **1** generous, extravagant. **2** (*sl*) to be sexually promiscuous. *Secara terus-terang Pak Béi pernah bilang, bahwa dia paling tidak suka dengan orang yang senang main, minum, – perempuan.* Mr. Bei once said frankly that he most dislikes people who like to gamble, drink, and play around with women.

beroyal-royal to spend money (for fun). *waktu ada uang hidup ~, sesudah uang habis menangis* when there's money, one lives to spend it, when there's none, one cries.

meroyalkan to waste, squander, spend extravagantly.

royal-royalan to overdo it, exceed the bounds, live high off the hog. *Janganlah ~ pada waktu negara menghadapi résési.* Don't live high off the hog when the country is facing a recession.

keroyalan extravagance, waste, generosity, spending extravagantly.

peroyal profligate, playboy, roué.

royalis (D) royalist.

royalti (E) royalty.

royan cramp, postnatal complications. – *beranak* labor pains. – *haid* menstrual cramps. – *tahi* diarrhea after childbirth.

meroyan 1 to have labor pains. 2 to go up and down, fluctuate tremendously (of prices).

royat → RUKYAT.

royemén (D) expulsion (from a political party).

royér (D) **meroyér** to expel (from a party).

royir → ROYÉR.

royokan (Jv) /royo'an/ working, fighting in a group; → K(E)ROYOK.

royong (Jv) → GOTONG-ROYONG.

rozijn (D) /rozén/ raisin.

Rp (abbr) → RUPIAH.

RPA (init) → RÉPUBLIK *Persatuan Arab*.

RPH (init) → RUMAH *Pemotongan Héwan*.

RPI (init) [République Persatuan Indonésia] Federal Republic of Indonesia (established by PRRI in Bonjol, West Sumatra on February 8, 1960, and dissolved on August 17, 1961).

RPP (init) → RANCANGAN *Peraturan Pemerintah*.

RRC (init) → RÉPUBLIK *Rakyat Cina*.

RRI (init) RADIO *Républik Indonésia*.

RRT (init) → RÉPUBLIK *Rakyat Tiongkok*.

RS (init) [Rumah Sakit] Hospital; → RUMKIT.

RSAB (init) → RUMAH SAKIT *Anak dan Bersalin*.

RSAD (init) → RUMAH SAKIT *Angkatan Darat*.

RSAL (init) → RUMAH SAKIT *Angkatan Laut*.

RSAU (init) → RUMAH SAKIT *Angkatan Udara*.

RSI (init) → RUMAH SAKIT *Islam*.

RSJ (init) → RUMAH SAKIT *Jiwa*.

RSKO (init) → RUMAH SAKIT *Ketergantungan Obat*.

RSPAD → RUMAH SAKIT *Pusat Angkatan Darat*.

RSU (init) → RUMAH SAKIT *Umum*.

RSUP (init) → RUMAH SAKIT *Umum Pusat*.

RT (init) → RUKUN *Tetangga*.

RTM (init) → RUMAH *Tahanan Militér*.

ru I → ERU.

ru II (in acronyms) → PELURU, REGU, RUMAH.

ru III a measure equal to 14.49 square meters.

rua I wide, big, large, spacious; loose.

merua 1 to grow, increase in size. 2 to extend, expand, spread; → MERUAK.

rua II → ROA II.

ruadat (A) ceremony of homage/honor/respect.

ruah I 1 chock-full, crammed, packed, full to overflowing. (ber)tumpah/(me)limpah – overflowing. 2 (petro) flush. *produksi* – flush production. 3 bulk.

meruah bulky.

meruah(kan) to pour out/empty (solids, such as grains/sand/flour, but not liquids).

keruahan overflow.

peruahan bulking.

ruah II (cla) **meruah** to call, hail; to summon, send for.

se(pe)ruah and **seruahan** within calling/hailing distance.

ruah III (A) souls; → ARWAH. *bulan* – *Syaban*, the eighth month of the Muslim calendar; → RUWAH.

ruai I loose (of fittings, rope, mast); weak, shaky (of limbs/structures).

ruai II – *gajah* k.o. small tree, *Gonocaryum longeracemosum*.

ruak meruak to spread (of a cobra's hood/fire, etc.); to break open and its contents all spread out (of eggs), be scattered.

ruak-ruak (*burung* –) white-breasted water hen, *Amaurornis phoenicurus chinensis*. – *bangkai* k.o. heron, adjutant.

ruam rash, tiny red spots on the skin. – *saraf* shingles, *Herpes zoster*; → SINAGA.

meruam to break out in a rash.

ruan → ARUAN.

ruang I 1 the space between two (rows of) pillars or between four pillars (of a Sumatran house built on poles). – (*tiang-tiang*) *itu* *dua méter lébarnya* the space (between the pillars) is two meters wide. 2 (math) the hollow space limited or encircled by planes. – *yang berbatas enam segi empat* a cube. *ilmu ukur* – solid geometry. 3 space, i.e., the unlimited great three-dimensional realm in which all objects are located and all events occur. – *dan waktu sejak dahulu kerap diperbincangkan oléh para ahli pikir* space and time have often been discussed by philosophers. 4 a spacious place, a (large) room (in a house), hall, ward. *Gedung ini mempunyai dua – tidur yang besar*. This building has two large bedrooms. *pembatas* – room divider. 5 section (of a fruit, such as *durian/jeruk*, etc.). 6 (ship's) hold; → PALKA. *air* – bilge water. *Barang-barang itu dimasukkan ke dalam – kapal*. The goods were loaded into the ship's hold. 7 column (in the press). 8 cavity, chamber, compartment. – *andrawina* banquet hall. – *angkasa/antariksa* outer space. – *antara* a) anteroom. b) interstice. – *baca* reading room. – *bakar* combustion chamber. – *bangkét* banquet room. – *barang* cargo hold. – *bawah-tanah* basement. – *belajar* study (the room), classroom. – *belakang* back room. – *ber-AC* an air-conditioned room. – *berhias* dressing room. – *bernapas* breathing space. – *bertekanan* pressure chamber. – *dada* breast, thorax. – *dalam pesawat* airplane cabin. – *darurat* emergency room. – *duduk* living room. – *éksékusi* (Mal) execution chamber (for those under death sentence). – *gandéng* adjoining rooms. – *ganti* changing/dressing room. – *gantung baju* cloakroom, closet, wardrobe. – *gawat darurat* intensive care unit, ICU. – *gerak* room to maneuver. – *hidup* living space. – *huruf* space between letters. – *Jepara* a room in the presidential palace furnished with wood carvings from Jepara. – *jinem* (Jv) private chambers. – *juruterbang* cockpit; → KOKPIT. – *kaca* greenhouse. – *kaki* legroom (in a car). – *kantor* office space. – *kapal* (ship's) hold. – *keberangkatan* departure hall (at airport). – *kedatangan* arrival hall (at airport). – *kelas* classroom. – *keluarga* family room (in a house). – *kerja* a) office (in a building). b) workshop (where work is done). – *komprési* combustion chamber. – *konperénsi* conference room. – *krukas* crankcase. – *kuburan* tomb. – *kuliah* classroom. – *lambai penumpang* waving gallery (at airport). – *lingkup* scope. – *lingkup berlakunya undang-undang* areas of application of a law. – *lingkup pengaruh* sphere of influence. – *Lonjong Gedung Putih* the Oval Office (in the U.S. White House). – *main* clearance, tolerance. – *makan* dining room. – *mandi uap* steam room. – *masuk* entrance hall. *di* – *mata* before one's eyes; in sight. – *mesin* engine room. – *muat(an)* cargo space, tonnage. – *niaga* economy class (in airplane). – *nirgema* anechoic chamber. – *olahraga* sports column (in a newspaper). – *operasi* operating room. – *pajang(an)* and – *pamér(an)* showroom, exhibition room. – *pariwisata* tourist class (in an airplane). – *pas* fitting room. – *pasién* ward (in a hospital). – *pembakaran* (di dalam) (internal) combustion chamber. – *pembekuan* freezer compartment. – *pemberangkatan* departure lounge. – *pemulihan* recovery room (in a hospital). – *penampungan* holding tank. – *pengadilan* courtroom. – *pengantar* waving gallery (in an airport). – *pengeram telur* brood chamber. – *penghidupan* living space. – *penumpang* (passengers') cabin (in an airplane); → KABIN. – *penyadaran* recovery room (in a hospital). – *perawatan* ward (in a hospital). – *perawatan khusus* intensive care unit, ICU. – *perkantoran* office space. – *pérs* press room. – *persidangan* assembly hall. – *pertama* a) first class (in an airplane). b) first column (in a newspaper). – *pertunjukan* showroom. – *peturasan* rest room. – *pola* operations room (in the *Balai Kota*, Jakarta). – *prakték* consulting room (of a doctor, etc.). – *proyéksi* projection room (in a movie theater). – *rékréasi* recreation room. – *rugi* a) (in barrels, etc.) ullage. b) (in an engine) clearance (space). – *rumah sakit* ward. – *sari* (bio) theca. – *saji* pantry. – *séwaan* rental space. – *sidang* a) meeting room, assembly hall. b) courtroom. – *sidang meninggalkan* – *sidang* to walk out (of a meeting). – *sidang pengadilan* courtroom. – *sidang pléno* plenary-session hall; → GRAHA *Sabha Paripurna*. – *siksaan* torture chamber. – *susu* cleavage, the space between the two breasts. – *tahanan* detention room. – *tamu* reception room. – *tanpa bobot* weightless room. – *tempat duduk pesawat* airplane cabin. – *tengah* middle room (in a house). – *terbuka* a) outdoors.

b) gap. – *transit* transit lounge (in an airport). – *tunggu* waiting room (in a doctor's office/at an airport). – *uap* steam chamber. – *udara* a) air space. b) air chamber. – *Udara Bertekanan Tinggi* [RUBT] recompression chamber. – *untuk menunggu sebelum naik pesawat terbang* boarding lounge (at an airport). – *VIP* VIP lounge. – *waktu* space of time, period. – *waktu yang sempit* a narrow space of time. – *wartawan* pressroom. – *yang serba putih* a hospital ward with pure-white walls. – *Yudha* War Room (*esp* in Army Headquarters, Jakarta). – *Yudha Sésko ABRI* War Room in the Republic of Indonesia Staff and Command School.

seruang in/of the same room. *teman* ~ *kerja* office-mate.

ruangan room, booth, chamber. (frequently = **ruang**). *pendingin* ~ room air conditioner. *pengharum* ~ room freshener. ~ *darurat* emergency room. ~ *gawat darurat* emergency room. ~ *jurubahasa* interpreter's booth. ~ *juruterbang* cockpit (in an airplane); → KOKPIT. ~ *kuliah* lecture hall (in a university). ~ *operasi* operating room (in a hospital), OR. ~ *Pancasila* the area in the Foreign Office in Jakarta where the *Pancasila* was proclaimed on June 1, 1945. ~ *pemungutan suara* voting booth. ~ *sidang* assembly hall, meeting room. ~ *Sidang Ampera* the *Ampera* Meeting Hall in the Department of Public Works and Electric Power. ~ *tempat duduk* seats, seating accommodation (on a bus). ~ *tunggu* waiting hall (in a station, etc.). **seruangan** in the same room. *rekanku* ~ my roommate.

keruangan spatial. *penglihatan* ~ spatial visualization.

ruang II (*cla*) **meruang** ~ *mayat* to clean a human corpse for burial.

ruap foam, froth, lather, scum. – *(dan) ampas* and – *(dan) sampah* scum of society. – *bibir* foam(ing) at the mouth. – *bir* head on beer. – *sabun* soap scum.

meruap 1 to froth, foam. *Sabun* ~. Soap foams. **2** to evaporate. *Air anggur* ~. Wine evaporates. **3** to bubble, froth; to seethe, boil. ~ *darahnya* his blood was boiling. **4** to show off, boast, brag. *Janganlah kamu sering* ~ *begitu, kurang baik*. Don't brag so much; it isn't nice. **5** to pervade, spread (through)out (of smell, etc.). *Dari dapur* ~ *bau saté kambing yang membuka seléra*. The smell of lamb satay spread out from the kitchen and made one's mouth water.

meruap-ruap to well up.

ruas 1 section between joints (of bamboo/fingers, etc.), node. **2** stretch, spur. *bertongkat* – to lean on one's elbows; → BERTELEKU. *bertemu/berjumpa* – *dengan buku* and *bertemu/berjumpa buku dengan* – a) they are well matched. b) to go hand and glove. *terentak* – *ke buku* (*M*) to be at one's wits' end. **3** (*math*) parts of an equation. – *bambu* internodes of bamboo. – *jalan* road (between two points), stretch of road. – *jari* phalanx of a finger. – *tulang belakang* vertebrae.

seruas one section. *sebagai betung* – honest, straightforward. *penerbangan* ~.~ point-to-point flight. ~ *tebu yang berulat* the scapegoat of the family.

beruas(-ruas) 1 with joints, jointed. **2** several joints. **3** segmented.

meruas to be jointed. *bambu* ~ jointed bamboo. *batang betung* ~ very honest.

peruasan the system of joints (of the body).

ruat I 1 shaky, loose (of tooth). **2** unstable, inconstant.

ruat II → RUWAT I.

ruat III → RUWET.

ruaya (*Jv*) migration (of flocks of birds/schools of fish). – *harian* diurnal migration.

beruaya to migrate (of birds/fish, etc.).

peruaya migratory (birds, fish, etc.).

ruba (*acr*) → RUMAH *bawah tanah*.

rubah I (*Pers*) fox, *Canis vulpes*.

rubah II → UBAH.

rubai I (*A*) quatrain; → RUBAIAT.

rubai II k.o. herbaceous plant, *Pouzolzia zeylanica*.

rubaiat (*Pers*) Old Malay *pantun* whose form is derived from Arabic literature.

ruban (*ob*) *air* – water found in coconut oil (when making oil). **meruban** to get rid of that water.

ruba-ruba (*Jv*) **1** present, gift (from a boat captain to port authorities). **2** bribe in the form of a gift.

Rubayyat (*Pers*) Rubaiyat. *stansa* – a stanza of the Rubaiyat.

rubel (Russian) ruble.

rubéla (*E*) rubella.

rubiah (*A*) **1** nun. **2** a pious woman. **3** female teacher (*esp* in Koran recital).

rubik (*M*) delicacy made from *keripik*.

rubin (*D*) ruby.

rubing I ravine.

rubing II (*naut*) temporary top-strake in a Malay sailing ship.

rubrik (*D*) column, section, rubric (in a newspaper).

rubrikasi (*E*) rubrication.

RUBT (*init*) → RUANG *Udara Bertekanan Tinggi*.

rubu I merubu merubu-rubu and ~ *raba* **1** (*M*) to wander aimlessly. **2** to grope around, fumble around; → RABA I.

rubu II a traditional device used to figure out the phases of the moon in calculating the year of the Islamic calendar.

rubu III and **rubuh** → ROBOH.

rubung (*Jv*) **merubung(i)** to approach in a large group; → KERUBUNG I. *Bank itu dirubungi orang*. There was a rush on the bank. *Berpuluh-puluh tukang becak tahu-tahu merubungi aku*. Scores of *becak* drivers suddenly rushed over to me.

rubungan encirclement, rushing in a large group.

rubut kerubutan gang.

rucah (*Jv*) **1** common, ordinary. **2** dirty.

rucat (*Jv*) **perucatan** scrapping (of old equipment, etc.). *Delapan lokomotip bertenaga uap akan memasuki tahap* ~ (*pembesituan*) *di Cilegon*. Eight steam locomotives will be scrapped (turned into scrap iron) in Cilegon.

rucita (*A*) concept, conception, idea.

rucut → LUCUT I.

rudah (*ob*) → RUADAT.

rudal (*acr*) → PELURU *kendali*. – *antibalistik* antiballistic missile, ABM. – *antilapis baja* armor-piercing guided missile. – *darat-udara* ground-to-air missile. – *jelajah* cruise missile. – *jelajah luncur udara* air-launched cruise missile. – *pamungkas* deadly/lethal missile. – *pelacak pancaran radar* antiradiation missile, ARM. – *penangkal* interception guided missile. – *udara-keudara maju jarak menengah* advanced medium-range air-to-air missile. – *yang dipangkalkan berpindah-pindah* and – *yang tempat peluncurannya dapat dipindahkan* mobile missile.

merudal 1 to launch a missile attack on. *Iran* ~ *términal minyak Kuwait*. Iran launched a missile attack on a Kuwaiti oil terminal. **2** to shoot down with a missile. *AS* ~ *pesawat Airbus A-300 Iran Air di Teluk Pérsia*. The US shot down an Iran Air Airbus A-300 in the Persian Gulf.

rudapaksa (*Skr Jv*) **1** (*med*) trauma. **2** force, coercion.

rudat traditional dance with Islamic elements.

rudi (*M*) Achilles tendon/heel.

rudimén (*D/E*) rudiment(s).

rudiméntér (*D*) rudimentary.

rudin (*J*) impoverished, poverty-stricken, poor, needy.

merudin to become impoverished/poor.

merudinkan to impoverish, make poor.

rudra (*Bal*) guardian spirits of the eleven points of the Balinese compass.

rudu I 1 sleepy, drowsy. **2** drooping (of eyelids from sleepiness).

rudu II merudu (to walk) stooped over (from age).

rudu III swift.

merudu to shoot forward (over the surface of the water).

rudus k.o. Achehnese cutlass.

merudus to hit with that weapon.

ruet → RUWET.

rugbi (*E*) rugby.

rugi 1 (*Skr*) (to sell) below cost price, lose money (on a sale). *Apa gunanya berdagang kalau selalu* –. What's the use of being in business if you always lose money. *jatuh/menanggung/menderita* – unprofitable, not lucrative. *dijual* – sold at a loss. –.– *untung* even though it's not profitable, it has its good side. *untung* – the advantages and disadvantages, the pros and cons. *untung* – *Bursa Swasta* the pros and cons of the Private Stock Exchange. **2** a (financial) loss. *Jika dijual Rp 2500,00* –*nya Rp 100,00*. If it's sold for Rp 2,500.00, there will be a Rp 100.00 loss on the sale. – *barang/uang* material/financial loss. – *tenaga/waktu* loss of energy/time. **3** useless, not worthwhile. *Ia merasa – mengikuti kursus itu, karena apa yang diajarkan di kursus itu sudah dipelajarinya beberapa tahun yang lalu.* He thinks it was useless to take that course because he learned what is taught in that course several years ago. **4** harm. *tidak* – there's no harm (in ...ing). *Tidak ada –nya kita mengunjungi rapat itu.* There's no harm in attending that meeting. *ganti/silih* – compensation, indemnification. **5** (it's) too bad, it's a shame/pity. – *kamu tidak datang ke pésta.* It's too bad you didn't make it to the party. *mengganti* – to pay back the cost of, reimburse. *Wali Kota Bengkulu dituntut mengganti – 64.000 kaléng gabah kering.* The mayor of Bengkulu was sued for reimbursement of the cost of 64,000 cans of dried unhulled rice. – *menentang laba, jerih menentang boléh* nothing ventured, nothing gained. – *bersih* net loss. – *bruto* gross loss. – *daya* (*elec*) energy loss. – *kurs* loss on foreign exchange. – *selisih kurs* loss on foreign exchange, foreign exchange losses.

berugi to suffer a loss/losses. *sudah* ~ to have gone to great expense. *tak mau berugi/merugi* do not want to spend money for no purpose.

merugi to suffer a loss/losses, lose money. *dijual dengan* ~ sold at a loss. *Pélni masih terus* ~. Pelni is still losing money.

merugikan [and **ng(e)rugiin** (*J coq*)] **1** to harm/hurt/damage/injure (financially, etc.), be detrimental to, cost (money to), cause loss to. *Banyak penduduk yang telah dirugikan oléh gerombolan-gerombolan itu.* Many residents have been harmed by those gangs. *Perbuatan-perbuatan yang* ~ *kepentingan umum harus diberantas.* A stop should be put to actions that are detrimental to the public interest. *Dia* ~ *negara sekitar Rp 154 juta.* He cost the nation about Rp 154 million. **2** to inconvenience, bother, take advantage of. *Saya tidak senang* ~ *orang.* I don't like to inconvenience people. **3** to sell at a loss intentionally. *Karena perlu uang, banyak pedagang yang* ~ *barang-barangnya.* Due to lack of funds, many traders had to sell their goods at a loss.

kerugian 1 to suffer a (financial) loss. *Akhirnya kita juga yang* ~ *besar.* In the end, we too suffered a heavy loss. **2a**) loss; *opp* **PROFIT.** b) damages. ~ *benda* material damages. ~ *dalam sebulan ini sama dengan keuntungan setahun yang lalu.* This month's loss is equal to last year's profit. ~ *imatériil* nonmaterial/emotional damages. ~ *kedua/ketiga* secondary/tertiary damages. ~ *laut* average, i.e., loss incurred by damage to a ship at sea or to her cargo. ~ *matériil* material damages. ~ *pertama* primary damages. ~ *total* total loss, write-off (of a car/plane, etc.). – *yang berwujud matéri* material loss. ~ *yang sudah diperhitungkan* calculated loss. *Pemboman itu menimbulkan* ~ *besar kepada musuh.* The bombing caused great damage to the enemy. **3** compensation, damages. *diharuskan membayar* ~ *Rp 5000,00* Rp 5,000.00 has to be paid in compensation. **4** disadvantage. *keuntungan dan* ~ advantages and disadvantages.

rugos (*D*) lettering sheet.

rugul merugul to rape; → **MEROGOL.**

ruh → **ROH.**

ruhak (*S*) embers.

ruhani → **ROHANI.**

ruhaniah → **ROHANIAH.**

ruhban (*A*) (Christian) monk.

ruhbanat (*A*) (Christian) nun.

ruhbaniat (*A*) (religious) order; celibacy.

ruhul → **ROH.**

ruilslag (*D*) /réĺslah/ exchange, swap.

meruilslag to swap.

ruing the first reel (of a weaving loom).

meruing to reel, wind up.

ruit I barbed hook.

beruit barbed.

teruit hooked.

ruit II → **RÉT.**

rujah merujah to stab downward (into a hole, etc. to drive out whatever is hiding inside).

rujak unripe fruit salad seasoned with vinegar, chilies, sugar, etc. –

bébék this salad in which the ingredients have been pulverized. – *buah dingin* rujak whose fruits have been precooled. – *cingur* rujak with slices of tender meat. – *gobét* unripe shredded fruits eaten with *petis*. – *juhi* rujak with peanut sauce, *tahu, mie,* and potatoes. – *loték* fruits dipped in sweet and hot sauce as they are eaten. – *manis* fruit salad in a sweet sauce. – *pengantén* vegetable salad, cucumbers, hard-boiled eggs with peanut sauce. – *serut* → **RUJAK** *gobét.* – *tumbuk* → **RUJAK** *bébék.*

ruji I (*Pers cla*) (daily) ration, staple food.

ruji II and **ruji-ruji 1** spokes, trellis work. **2** radius. **3** muntin (in a window). – *ligat* radius of gyration.

beruji with a trellis, trellised.

meruji radial.

rujit (*S*) ugly; → **JELÉK.** – *ningalina* ugly/unpleasant to look at.

rujuk (*A*) **1** return (*esp* to a wife after a first or second annullable divorce), recall (after repudiation). **2a**) reconciliation. b) reconciled. – *kembali* settlement (of a dispute). – *masyarakat* social settlement (of a conflict). – *nasional* national reconciliation.

merujuk(i) 1 to remarry (the same woman one had previously divorced), take back (a wife when the divorce is not yet final). **2** to become reconciled with.

rujukan reconciliation.

perujukan reconciling.

rujuk II reference. *sistém* – reference system. – *silang* cross-reference. **merujuk-silangkan** to cross-reference, make a cross-reference to.

merujuk ~ *pada* to refer to.

merujuki to refer to.

rujukan reference, referral. *buku/pusat* ~ reference book/center. ~ *silang* cross-reference.

perujuk mediator. *tim* ~ mediating team.

perujukan reference, referencing. *sumber* ~ reference source.

rujung 1 cone. **2** outer portion of a palm trunk.

rujungan coning.

ruk (*onom*) cracking noise.

rukaat → **RAKAAT.**

rukam many varieties of small trees with edible berries, Indian prune, *esp Flacourtia inermis/rukam.*

rukan → **RUMAH** *perkantoran.*

rukem (*Jv*) → **RUKAM.**

rukh (*Pers*) castle (the chess piece).

rukhani → **ROHANI.**

rukhsah (*A*) dispensation from fasting when one is sick, or allowing one to shorten a prayer when on a journey.

rukiah and **rukiat I** (*A*) sorcery, witchcraft.

rukiat II → **RUKYAT.**

ruko (*acr*) → **RUMAH** *toko.*

ruku I (*onom*) roocoocoo, i.e., the sound made by the turtledove.

meruku to make this sound.

ruku II → **RUKUK.**

ruku III → **RUKU-RUKU.**

rukuh (*A*) women's all-white prayer clothing worn over the head with only the face and palms showing.

rukuk (*A*) bow in prayer, prostration during prayer.

merukuk (*duduk*) ~ to prostrate o.s. in prayer.

rukun I (*A*) support, pillar, cornerstone, foundation, basic/fundamental principles, directives, articles of faith. *lima* – Islam and – *agama/Islam* the five obligatory Muslim duties, the five pillars of Islam which every good Muslim tries to observe: a) the declaration of faith; → **LA ILAHA ILLALLAH.** b) the five daily prayers; → **SALAT I.** c) fasting during the month of fasting; → **RAMAD(H)AN,** *bulan* **PUASA.** d) the obligation to give alms; → **ZAKAT.** e) the pilgrimage to Mecca; → **HAJJ.** *tidak* – discordant. *ketidak-rukunan* discordance. – *iman* the six basic beliefs of Islam (God, angels, holy books, prophets, Day of Judgment, predestination). – *salat* the elements of prescribed prayer. – *syarak* basic Islamic principles and Islamic law. – *syarat* a) principle, basis, foundation. b) (*M*) s.t. that has to be done based on *adat* law.

perukunan (*J*) regarding the basic principles of Islam. *kitab* ~ a book which contains instructions on worshipping, the fast, etc.

rukun II (*A*) **1** harmonious, in harmony, peacefully; like-minded, unanimous. *hidup* – to live in harmony. – *agawé santoso* (*Jv*) in union is strength; → **BERSATU** *kita teguh*. – *(dan) damai kepada* (to associate/live) in peace and harmony with. **2** to be(come) friends again, make up. **3** to get along with e.o.

serukun unanimous, of one mind, in harmony.

merukunkan to appease, reconcile, bring about peace.

kerukunan 1 harmony, concord, unison. **2** reconciliation. ~ *nasional* national reconciliation.

perukunan ~ *kembali* reconciliation.

rukun III (*A*) association. – *Kampung* [RK] village association, association of sections of town. – *Isteri Ampera Pembangunan* association of cabinet ministers' wives. – *kematian* burial association. – *kerjasama* cooperative association. – *layon* (*Jv*) burial society. – *tani* farmers' association. – *Tetangga* [RT] neighborhood association. – *Warga* [RW] citizens association (formerly called – *Kampung*).

Rukunegara (*Mal*) Five-point State Ideology proclaimed 31 August 1970 (comparable to Indonesia's *Pancasila*): a) Belief in God; b) Loyalty to the *Raja* and the State; c) Glory of the Constitution; d) Sovereignty of the Laws; e) Respect and Decency.

kerukunegaraan peaceful harmony, amity, friendship, concord. *Perjanjian* ~ *Kerjasama di Asia Tenggara* Southeast Asia Treaty of Friendship and Cooperation.

rukup → **RUNGKUP**.

ruku-ruku and **reruku** basil, *Ocimum spp.*; → **SELASIH I**. – *hutan* a medicinal herb, *Hyptis suaveolens*.

rukyah, ru'yah, and **rukyat** (*A*) sight, observation. *tanda* – the signal (by *bedug*, etc.) that the moon has been seen in determining the beginning and end of *Ramadan*. – *hilal*, – *al-hilal*, and –*ul-hilal* sighting the new crescent moon to determine the beginning and end of *Ramadan*.

rulét (*D*) roulette. *bermain-main* – *Rusia* to play Russian roulette.

ruli [rumah liar] squatter's shack.

rum I (*onom*) sound of a low rumble; → **DERUM II**.

rum II (*D*) cream; → **KEPALA** *susu*.

rum III clipped form of **harum**.

rum IV (*D*) rum (the drink).

rum V (*A*) **1** (*negeri*) – Byzantium (now Istanbul). **2** Rome; → **ROMA IV**. **3** roman. *geréja* – Roman (Catholic) church. **4** *ar*– "The Romans"; name of the 30th chapter of the Koran. – *Katolik* Roman Catholic; → **KATOLIK** *Roma*.

rum VI (in acronyms) → **rumah**.

rumah 1 house, dwelling, residence, home, building. *Di dalam* – *itu ada/terdapat tiga kamar tidur.* That house has three bedrooms in it. *Meréka ada di* –. They're home. *Ia senang tinggal di* –. He likes to stay home. *Ia tidak di* –. She's out/not home/not in. *dari* – *ke* – (from) door to door. **2** public facility. – *bilyar* billiard hall. – *komidi* theater. **3** housing (a box, etc. for holding a part, etc.), case, casing, box. – *gérétan* matchbox. – *kancing* buttonhole. **4** the large hole in a *papan congkak*. *ahli* – the family, housemates; → **AHLULBAIT**. *nyonya* – a) lady of the house, hostess. b) housewife. *perabot* – furniture. *tahanan* – (under) house arrest. *tuan* – a) head of the family; → **KEPALA** *keluarga*. b) host. *bagai* – *di tepi tebing* to live on a volcano. – *buruk disapu cat* an ostentatious person. *dalam* – *membuat* – pursuit of personal gains (while working for s.o. else). – *gedang ketirisan* a woman who brings bad luck to her husband. – *sudah, tukul berbunyi* it's too late to be of any use; too late for the fair. – *sudah tokok berbunyi* to raise s.t. that is already over and done with. – *adat* traditional house; → **BALAIRUNG**. – *Allah* mosques; → **RUMAH** *Tuhan*, **BAITHULLAH**. – *angker* haunted house. – *api* lighthouse. – *asap* smokehouse (used in processing rubber). – *atap* penthouse. – *atap genting* house roofed with palm fronds. – *bagonjong* (*M*) West Sumatra's Governor's Office. – *batang* button hole. – *batu* brick/concrete/stone house. – *bawah (tanah)* [ruba] a) underground tunnel built for fugitive communist leaders after the abortive 1965 coup. b) bunker. – *bentang* k.o. Dayak longhouse. – *berhala* house of worship (mosque, church, temple, etc.). – *berkelompok* (*Mal*) housing complex. – *berloténg/bertingkat* multistory building; high-rise (if a large number of stories and provided with elevators). – *bersusun* multistory building. **pengrumah-bersusunan** moving people into

multistory buildings. – *besar* main building. – *bicara* town hall. – *bilik* house with woven bamboo walls. – *bilyar* billiard hall, poolroom. – *bola* (*ob*) clubhouse. – *bongkar-pasang* prefab house. – *bordil* bordello, brothel. – *botang* buttonhole. – *buruh* laborer's house. – *busana* fashion house. – *buta* home for the blind. – *cicilan* house with a mortgage. – *contoh* model home. – *dansa* dance hall. – *démpét* duplex house. – *Déténsi Imigrasi Pusat* [RDIP] Central Immigration House of Detention. – *di atas rakit* (in interior of Central Kalimantan) floating house made of boards build over a raft; → **LANTING III**. – *dinas* agency's house (occupied by an employee of the agency). – *duka* house of mourning. – *gadai* pawnshop. – *gadang* (*M*) family house. – *gadang bergonjong* (*M*) *adat* house of a *kaum* or *suku*. – *gambar* picture gallery. – *gandéng* row house. – *gedék* house with woven bamboo walls. – *gedongan* full-brick house (considered middle-class housing). – *gedung* a brick house. – *génsét* generator set housing. – *genténg* tiled house. – *gérétan* a) matchbox. b) a small and very simple house. – *gila* insane asylum. – *hantu* haunted house. – *ibadat* house of worship (mosque, church, temple, etc.). – *idaman/impian* dream house. – *indekosan* boarding house. – *induk* main building. – *instansi* agency house (occupied by an employee of the agency). – *inti* core house (built by the government to be occupied immediately and further developed by the occupant). – *jabatan* official residence. – *jadi* prefabricated house. – *jaga* a) guardhouse, sentry post. b) (*petro*) doghouse. – *jagal* abattoir, slaughterhouse. – *joglo* traditional Javanese house with a steeply pitched top section. – *jompo* senior citizens home; → **PANTI** *jompo*. – *judi* gambling den; → **PETOPAN**. – *kaca* greenhouse. – *kaki seribu* k.o. *adat* house among the Arfak group in Irian Jaya. – *kampung* (*usu*) a house built from planks and woven bamboo wall with an elevated floor and a thatched roof. – *kancing* buttonhole. – *kayu* house with wooden walls. – *kebun* garden house. – *kecantikan* beauty parlor; → **SALON I**. – *kedai* a small shop with a residence (*usu* at the rear), shop-house. – *kediaman* residence. – *kemanakan* (*M*) house for an extended family. – *kematian* a) morgue. b) residence at death. – *kembar* duplex house. – *kemudi* wheelhouse. – *kenikmatan* house of pleasure. – *kéong* a) snail's shell. b) tiny, ramshackle hut along the riverside occupied by bums. – *ketam* stock of plane (the tool). – *kétel* boiling house. – *kit* opium den. – *kolong* house built on stilts. – *komidi* theater. – *kongsi* company housing. – *kontrakan* contracted house. – *kopel* duplex house. – *kosong* unoccupied house. – *kotangan* house with half-brick walls. – *kréditan* a house bought on a loan. – *kuning* brothel, bordello. – *lamin* longhouse of the Dayak people in Kalimantan. – *lélang* auction house. – *lepas* detached house. – *liar* [ruli] squatter's shack. – *liliput* tiny, ramshackle hut along the riverside occupied by bums. – *limas* (in Sumsel) a house whose four sides run up to a single point. – *loténg* multistory building; high-rise (if a large number of stories and provided with elevators). – *madat* opium den. – *makan* restaurant; → **RÉSTO(RAN)**. – *mandi* bathhouse. – *maya* home page (on Internet). – *mayat* morgue. – *minim* low-cost/-income house. – *minum* pub, tavern, bar; → **PUB**. – *miskin* almshouse. – *mode* fashion house. – *monyét* guardhouse, sentry post; → **GARDU**. – *murah* low-cost housing. – *negeri* official residence (of a civil servant). – *obat* pharmacy; → **APOTÉK**. – *paku* house made of planks and nails. – *pala-pala* a room with railings instead of walls, observation post. – *panas* a house which brings bad luck. – *panggung* house built on stilts. – *pangkas* barbershop. – *pangsa* (*Mal*) apartment building. – *panjang* a) brothel, bordello. b) longhouse (among Dayaks of Kalimantan). – *papak* (*J*) house with a flat roof; → **GEDUNG** *papak*. – *papan* house with wooden walls. – *pasung* a) police station. b) jail. – *pedoman* compass housing. – *pelacuran* brothel, bordello, whorehouse. – *pelesiran* brothel, bordello. – *pemasyarakatan* penitentiary; → **LEMBAGA** *Pemasyarakatan*. – *pembangkit* powerhouse. – *Pemotongan Héwan* [RPH] abattoir, slaughterhouse. – *Pendidikan Anak Negara* State Orphanage. – *Pendidikan Paksa* House of Correction. – *penginapan* hostel, inn. – *penginapan kecil* home stay. – *peranginan* rest house. – *percontohan* model home. – *perdéo* prison, jail. – *peribadatan* house of worship (mosque, church, temple, etc.). – *peristiraha-*

tan rest house, bungalow. – *perkantoran* [rukan] office building with residential quarters. – *persalinan* maternity house. – *persinggahan sementara* halfway house (for the rehabilitation of criminals). – *pétak* row house, cubicle house. – *piatu* orphanage. – *pijat/pijet/pijit* massage parlor. – *pompa* pump housing. – *pondokan* boardinghouse. – *potong* slaughterhouse. – *prodéo* prison, jail. – *Putih* (*Mal*) U.S. White House; *cp* GEDUNG *Putih*. – *puli* pulley block. – *rakit/rangka* prefab house. – *rangka bersusun* apartment building. – *rumbia* house with a roof made of *rumbia* leaves. – *sakit* [Rumkit, RS] hospital. – *sakit Anak dan Bersalin* [RSAB] Children's and Maternity Hospital. – *sakit Angkatan Darat* [RSAD] Army Hospital. – *sakit Angkatan Laut* [RSAL] Navy Hospital. – *sakit Angkatan Udara* [RSAU] Air Force Hospital. – *sakit bantu* auxiliary hospital. – *sakit berjalan* mobile hospital (equipped with medicines and paramedics). – *sakit bersalin* maternity hospital. – *sakit héwan* [RSH] veterinary hospital. – *sakit Islam* [RSI] Islamic Hospital. – *sakit jiwa* [RSJ] insane asylum. – *sakit Ketergantungan Obat* [RSKO] Drug Dependency Hospital. – *sakti lépra* leprosarium. – *sakit mata* ophthalmologic hospital. – *sakit milik pemerintah* government-owned/public hospital. – *sakit N(ahdlatul) U(lama)* NU Hospital (in Surabaya). – *sakit petirahan* convalescent hospital. – *sakit Pusat Angkatan Darat* [RSPAD and Rumkitpusad] Army Central Hospital. – *sakit Pusat Angkatan Udara* [Ruspau] Air Force Central Hospital. – *sakit rujukan* referral hospital. – *sakit swasta* private hospital. – *sakit Umum* [RSU] general/public hospital. – *sakit Umum Pusat* [RSUP] central general hospital. **merumah-sakitkan** to hospitalize, send to the hospital. **kerumah-sakitan** and **perumah-sakitan 1** hospital (*mod*). *di/dalam bidang* ~ in the hospital field/sector. **2** (the field of) hospitals. *menaruh modal baik asing maupun dalam negeri bagi* ~ to invest foreign and domestic capital in hospitals. – *samping* annex. – *sangat sederhana* [RSS] low-income housing. – *sederhana* [RS] basic housing – *sékering* fuse box. – *sekolah* school building. – *selérét* a) row of houses. b) (*Mal*) a small, long house. – *seribu* k.o. *adat* house among the Arfak group in Irian Jaya. – *sesebuah* (*Mal*) privately owned house; *cp* RUMAH *sebuah* one (detached) house. – *sétan* Freemason Lodge. – *séwa* rented house. – *siap pasang* prefab house. – *singgah* halfway house (for street children). – *sinyal* signal box. – *siput* a) a snail's shell. b) cochlea (of the ear). – *sub inti* very simple housing for people with irregular income. – *susun* [rusun] high-rise. – *susun empat belas* a fourteen-story high-rise. – *swadaya* house built with one's own means (not government supported). – *tahanan* [rutan] house of detention. – *Tahanan Militér* [RTM] Military House of Detention. – *tancap* house on stilts (of the Suku Laut). – *tangga* a) the home and its affairs, household. *mengurus* – *tangga* to manage the household, run the house/home, keep house. b) family. – *tangga dengan dua pendapatan* two-income family. – *tangga Keprésidénan* Presidential Household. – *tangga retak* broken home. – *sékering* fuse box. **serumah tangga** and his family. **berumah tangga 1** to keep house. **2** to have a family, set up one's own household. *Penghasilan dan umurnya sudah cukup untuk* ~. He makes enough money and he is old enough to set up a household. **3** to be married. *Saya ingin melihat kau* ~ *dulu.* I would like to see you married first. **kerumah-tanggaan** and **perumah-tanggaan** (*mod*) household, household affairs. *soal-soal* ~ household matters. – *tawon* beehive. – *terapung* floating house (found on rivers in Riau). – *tikelan* (*Jv*) apartment building. – *tinggal* dwelling. – *tinggal berlantai empat* a four-story house/dwelling. – *toko* [ruko] store with a residence on top of it, shophouse. – *Tuhan* House of God (church/synagogue/temple/chapel, etc.). – *tumbuh* a) a smaller house that is going to be renovated into a larger house. b) houses of aboriginal people living on the edge of transmigration areas; they are fixed up at government expense. – *tumpangan* a) boardinghouse. b) (*Mal*) small hotel used by prostitutes. – *tunggal* detached house. – *tusuk saté* a house located at a T-intersection (brings bad luck in Feng Shui). – *tutupan* jail, prison. – *Versluis* /ferslés/ (*ob*) government official's house. – *vértikal* multi-story building. – *warisan* house which is part of a legacy. – *welit* (*Jv*) a very simple windowless village house made of bamboo

with a roof of dried leaves. – *yang ber-AC* an air-conditioned house.

rumah-rumah 1 houses. **2** (= **rumah-rumahan**) toy house(s). **3** casing, case.

serumah 1 the entire house. **2** the entire family. *Meréka enggan berbagi rasa dengan orang* ~. They were reluctant to share their feelings with the entire family. *Salam ke(pada) orang* ~. My regards to the whole family. **3** to be under one roof, be in the same house. *Kedua-dua céwék itu hiduplah* ~, *seorang di atas loténg dan seorang di bawah.* Both girls live under one roof, one on the top floor and one downstairs. *hidup* ~ *dengan* to live in the same house as, to live together with. **4** married. **menye-rumahkan** to put in the same house.

serumah-rumahnya the entire family.

berumah to own a house. *Orang itu* ~ *besar.* That person has a large house. ~ *tinggal di* to live in/at. ~ *dua* dioecious, unisexual. *Bunga Rafflésia adalah bunga* ~ *dua, yaitu bunga jantan dan betinanya terpisah.* The Rafflesia flower is dioecious, i.e., it has separate male and female flowers.

berumah-rumah to have a family (i.e., wife and children).

berumahkan to use s.t. as a house. ~ *kémah* to use a tent as a house.

merumahi to accommodate, lodge, house, put up. *Pada dasarnya manusia wajib* ~ *sesamanya.* In principle, mankind is obliged to provide housing for his fellow man.

merumahkan 1 (*euph*) to place s.o. under house arrest. **2** (*euph*) (~ *sementara*) to send s.o. home temporarily (due to participation in a strike, etc.); to lay off, furlough.

memperumahkan to marry off. ~ *anaknya yang bungsu* to marry off one's youngest child.

rumahan 1 housing, casing, case, cage, box (in which some instrument is located). **2** (*mod*) home, house. *anak* ~ homebody (s.o. who likes to stay home).

rumah-rumahan toy house.

perumahan 1 housing. *perusahaan pembangun* ~ (*infr*) real estate company. ~ *murah/rakyat* low-cost/-income housing. ~ *layak huni* livable housing. ~ *yang layak* suitable housing. **2** (*mod*) housing, accommodation, lodging. *kesukaran* ~ *di kota-kota besar semakin memuncak* the housing problem in big cities is becoming more and more difficult. **3** for housing. *disediakan tanah* ~ *land for housing is available.* **4** (*plane*) stock. **5** (*euph*) house arrest. **6** (*M ob*) standpoint, viewpoint; intention, purpose. ~*mu sudah diketahuinya.* He already knows your viewpoint.

rumal → RAMAL II.

rumat maintenance. *dosis* – maintenance dose.

Rumawi Roman. *angka* – Roman numerals. *hukum* – Roman law. *huruf* – Latin/romanized letters of the alphabet. *kaisar* – Roman Emperor.

rumba rumba (the dance).

rumbah (*Jv*) uncooked leaves eaten with rice.

rumbai I tassel, fringe, etc. hanging down from s.t. as an ornament.

berumbai-rumbai tasseled, fringed; dangling.

berumbai-rumbaikan fringed with.

terumbai dangling (an arm, etc.).

rumbai II and – *latah* a plant that grows in marshland, *Scirpodendron ghaeri*; its leaves are used for wickerwork.

rumbang-rombéng (*J*) shabby, tattered, in tatters.

rumbia 1 sago palm, *Metroxylon sagu.* **2** the thatch made from its leaves used for roofing/a roof-covering. *sebuah pondok beratap* – a hut covered with a sagopalm roof.

rumbing I (*M*) dented, chipped; → SEMPAK, SUMBING. *pisau* – a knife with a jagged/serrated edge.

rumbing II *ikan* – k.o. angelfish, *Holocanthus sp.*

rumboter (*D*) creamery butter.

rumbu I fish trap; → BUBU.

rumbu II (*M*) **1** improper. **2** aimless.

merumbu 1 to act improperly. **2** to walk around aimlessly.

rumbu III merumbu overflowing (of a liquid, etc.).

rumbu IV (*Port ob*) money.

rumbun merumbun to pile firewood on a fire.

rumdin (*acr*) → RUMAH *dinas.*

rumen (*E*) rumen, the first stomach of ruminating animals which is located next to the reticulum.

rumenia → REMENIA.

Rumi → RUMAWI.

rumin (*M*) ramie.

ruminansia (*E*) *ternak* – ruminants.

ruminansi (*E*) mastication.

rumit (*M?*) **1** difficult, tough, hard. **2** complex, complicated, intricate, complex, elaborate.

   merumit to become difficult, etc.

   merumitkan to complicate, make complex/difficult.

   memperumit to make s.t. complicated, make things difficult.

   kerumitan 1 difficulty. **2** complexity, intricacy. *tingkat* ~ degree of complexity.

   perumit complicating.

   perumitan complication.

Rumkit → RUMAH *sakit*.

Rumkitpusad → RUMAH *sakit Pusat Angkatan Darat.*

rumongso (*Jv*) **1** to have a sense of, be conscious/aware of. – *handarbéni* sense of belonging; → RASA *ikut memiliki.*

rumpakan (*Jv*) a poetic narrative.

rumpang (*M*) **1** gap-toothed. **2** with gaps/breaks (a fence, etc.). *Kambing itu bisa masuk melalui pagar yang* –. The goats can enter through openings in the fence. *Tiada –nya ia berpuasa setiap Senin dan Kemis.* There's no gap when he fasts every Monday and Thursday. **3** (*geol*) fissure, break, gap. **4** vacancy (empty area on plantation where plants have died).

   merumpangkan to hollow out.

   rumpangan recess, hole. ~ *bingkai* frame hole.

rumpi I (*sl*) gossipmonger; gossip.

   merumpi [and **ngerumpi** (*coq*)] **1** to get together. **2** to chat, gossip.

   rumpian gossip, s.t. to gossip about.

rumpi II → ROMPI.

rumpil (*J/Jv*) barely passable (of street).

   kerumpilan difficulties.

rumpon (*Jv*) **1** fish trap in the form of a small diversion in a river or covered with reeds, rush, and similar water plants. **2** place for fish to breed made up of objects discarded into the water.

   merumponkan to throw discarded objects, such as *bécak*s, trucks, etc. into the sea as a place for fish to breed.

   perumponan throwing discarded objects into the sea as a place for fish to breed.

rumpun I clump (of trees), cluster; → PERDU I. – *aju* (*mil*) advance force. – *bambu* stand of bamboo. – *bunga* cluster of flowers. – *tangki* (*petro*) tank farm. – *telinga* cavity of the ear.

   rerumpunan clusters, clumps.

   berumpun 1 to have clumps/clusters, clumped, clustered, in clusters. **2** to regroup/reassemble, get together.

   berumpun-rumpun in clusters, clustered.

rumpun II group, family. *(ter)masuk/(dalam) bagian* – to belong to one (language) family, be related (linguistically); be of the same race/kind. – *kata* (*gram*) part of speech, syntactic class.

   serumpun to belong to one (language) family, be related (linguistically); of the same race/kind. *Bahasa Indonésia dan Bahasa Malaysia itu* ~. Indonesian and Malaysian belong to the same language family. *kerjasama kejiranan* ~ cooperation of neighbors belonging to the same race. ~ *bahasa* language family. ~ *Sebalai* reference to the Bangka-Belitung region. **keserumpunan** of the same origin, relatedness.

   berumpun to belong to a group.

   perumpunan classification.

rumpun III subject of study. – *boga* the study of catering. – *busana* the study of fashion.

rumpung → ROMPONG I.

rumput 1 grass, weed, herb. *kebun* – grass farm. *padang* – steppe; grassland. **2** (*sl*) marijuana, grass. – *mencari kuda* a woman looking for a man, i.e., s.t. unusual. *embun di ujung* – volatile. *ibarat* – *yang sudah kering, ditimpa hujan segar kembali* every cloud has a silver lining; sunshine follows the rain. *bicarakan* – *di halaman orang, di halaman sendiri* – *sampai ke kaki tangga* to see the mote in the eye of others, but not the beam in one's own. *mencari penjahit dalam* – to look for a needle in a haystack. FOR NAMES OF OTHER GRASSES SEE THE WORD FOLLOWING RUMPUT. – *air* a) swamp grass, annual grass used as cattle fodder, *Poa annua.* b) ditch moss, *Naias graminea, Enhyrdrias angustipetala.* – *angin* rolling grass, *Spinifex littoreus.* – *anting* annual grass used as food for livestock, little quaking grass, *Briza minor.* – *babi* wild heliotrope. – *bahia* bahia grass, *Paspalum notatum.* – *bambu* wild perennial grass, miniature bamboo, *Pogonatherum paniceum/ Panicum montanum/notatum.* – *bébék* shama millet, jungle rice, an annual grass cultivated as fodder for livestock, *Echinochloa colonum.* – *belulang* goose/wire grass, *Eleusine indica.* – *benggala* guinea grass; perennial grass, cultivated as pasturage, *Panicum maximum.* – *bérak kambing* herbaceous plant, its young leaves are eaten as *lalap, Synedrella nodiflora.* – *betung* horsetail grass, *Equisetum arvense.* – *daru* perennial grass, its young leaves are used as food for livestock. – *ékor* wild perennial grass, seeds are used as food for birds, *Microlaena micranthera.* – *ékor kucing* pearl/cattail millet, yellow foxtail, seeds are used as food for birds, cultivated as pasturage, dried leaves and flowers are used in dried flower decorations, *Setaria glauca.* – *embun* perennial grass, cultivated as cover crop, used in traditional medicine for beri-beri, *Polytrias amaura.* – *gajah* Napier/elephant grass; perennial grass, cultivated as pasturage, *Pennisetum purpureum.* – *gangsiran* k.o. grass, *Digitaria sp.* – *gatang* Hilo grass, *Spilanthes ocimifolia.* – *geganjuran* koda millet; perennial grass, grows as a weed, used as forage grass, *Paspalum commersonii.* – *gelagah* → GLAGAH. – *grinting* k.o. weed, Bermuda grass, *Cynodon dactylon* and other species. – *gunung* a perennial grass, *Tripogon exiguus.* – *jajagoan* k.o. grass, *Oplismenus compositus.* – *jarong* k.o. grass. – *jarum* → BAJANG-BAJANG. – *jejarongan* a perennial grass, swollen finger grass, *Chloris barbata.* – *jepang* seaweed, algae, from which isinglass is made. – *karang* rockweed (brownish marine plants that cling to rocks). – *kawat* Bermuda grass, perennial grass, used as food for livestock, grows as a weed in tea and cinchona gardens, *Cynodon dactylon.* – *kejut-kejut* → PUTRI malu. – *kemaluan/kejut-kejut* sensitive plant, *Mimosa pudica;* → SEMALU. – *kembang goyang* → RUMPUT *jejarongan.* – *kening* hay. – *kerbau* k.o. grass, *Paspalum conjugatum.* – *kering* hay. – *kumbar* sedges used for matting, *Scirpus grossus/mucronatus.* – *lapangan* carpet grass, *Axonopus compersus.* – *lari(-lari)* → RUMPUT *angin.* – *laut* edible seaweed used to make gelatin; → AGAR-AGAR. – *lidah lembu* k.o. herb, *Aneilema malabaricum.* – *maléla* para grass, *Brachiaria mutica.* – *manila* k.o. spongy grass used on athletic fields and lawns, turf grass, *Zoysia matrella.* – *manis* honey grass, sweet weed, *Stevia rebaudiana Bertoni.* – *muda* young woman (*esp* as sex object). – *natal* natal grass, *Rhynchelytrum roseum.* – *pahit(an)* carpet grass; perennial grass, cultivated as pasturage, sour grass, *Axonopus compressus.* – *pengganggu tanaman* weeds. – *raja* a) king grass, a crossbreed between *Pennisetum purpureum/typoides.* b) k.o. orchid, *Dendrobium calcaratum.* – *rantai* all k.o. grasses. – *sarang puyuh* k.o. grass, *Panicum sarmentosum.* – *sarang semut* short-leaved panic grass, *Panicum brevifolium.* – *sarang tikus* a perennial grass, *Panicum brevifolium.* – *sepon codium.* – *sétan* a) witch weed, *Striga lutea.* b) Siam weed, *Chromolaena odorata.* – *siak-siak* a plant whose roots are used against intestinal worms, *Dianella spp.* – *solo* → CAKAR *ayam b).* – *sunduk gangsir* pangola grass; perennial grass, cultivated as forage, *Digitaria decumbens.* – *surga* marijuana, grass; → GANJA II. – *tapak burung* k.o. herb, *Aneilema malabaricum.* – *teki* nut grass, coco grass; perennial herb with an edible tuberous root; → EMPING *teki.* – *telur ikan* k.o. grass, *Panicum repens.* – *turi* k.o. weed, *Clitoria laurifolia/cajanifolia.* – *udang* Chinese love grass, *Eragrostis unioloides* – *Uganda* Napier/elephant grass, perennial grass cultivated as pasturage, *Pennisitum purpureum.*

berumput grassy, overgrown with grass. *Halamannya* ~ *tebal.* His garden is overgrown with thick grass.

merumput 1 to weed grass. **2** to eat/feed on grass, graze (of cattle). **3** to gather grass.

merumputi 1 to weed, to remove grass (from a garden, etc.). **2** to plant grass in patches, seed with grass.

rumputan grasses, Gramineae.

rumput-rumputan and **rerumputan** various species of grasses/weeds, herbage. *Meréka beristirahat sejenak sambil berbaring di ~.* They relaxed for a minute lying down on the grass.

perumputan pasture, meadow, grasslands, lawn.

rumrum (*Jv cla*) **merumrum** to coax (a girl) by flattering her.

rumuhun (*K*) first. *jaman* – ancient times; → ZAMAN *baheula. sang* – the first sovereign.

rumuk → ROMOK. **merumuk** huddled, curled up, crouched.

rumung (*J*) **merumung** to crowd around. *Jangan ~ di pinggir jalan.* Don't crowd around at the side of the road.

rumus (*A*) **1** formula, scientific formulation; → AKRONIM, KEPÉNDÉKAN, SINGKATAN. *- aljabar* algebraic formula. *- bangun* structural formula. *- kimia* chemical formula. *- sidik jari* fingerprint formula. **2** (*ob*) abbreviation, a shortened form of a word.

merumuskan 1 (*ob*) to abbreviate. **2** to formulate, express in/reduce to a formula, describe, lay out. *Hak-hak pegawai negeri sudah dirumuskan dalam undang-undang kepegawaian.* The rights of government employees have been formulated in the civil service laws.

terumuskan formulated. *Belum ~ pemecahannya.* A solution has not yet been formulated.

rumusan 1 formulation. **2** description.

perumus formulator. *panitia ~* steering committee.

perumusan 1 formulation, formulating. **2** description. *~ delik* description of the offense. **3** (*ob*) abbreviation.

runcing 1 pointed, sharp, sharpened to a point, acute, peaked. *bambu* – bamboo lance/spear (symbol of the struggle for Indonesian independence). **2** to become critical/tense, reach a climax (of a dispute/quarrel, etc.). *Pertentangan itu semakin ~.* The controversy was becoming more and more tense. *- tanduk* his wickedness is well known.

meruncing 1 to taper off, come to a point, decrease in width toward one end. *Benua India ~ ke arah selatan.* The Indian continent comes to a point in the south. **2** to become critical/aggravated. *Perselisihan itu bertambah ~.* The dispute became more and more tense. **3** to sharpen. *~ pénsil* to sharpen a pencil.

meruncingi to sharpen.

meruncingkan to aggravate, make sharper/worse/tenser/more critical, sharpen. *Ia ~ telinganya.* He pricked up his ears.

memperuncing 1 to make s.t. sharper. **2** to exacerbate, make things worse.

keruncingan 1 sharpening; sharpness. **2** criticality, tenseness (of a situation).

peruncing s.t. that aggravates (a problem).

peruncingan extremism.

runcit → RONCÉT. (*Mal*) retail.

runding 1 (*cla*) calculation, computation. **2** discussion, deliberation. *tidak berbanyak* – not to talk a lot. *merentang* - to draw out (a conversation/talks). *juru* – negotiator.

berunding to have a conversation/discussion; to converse, discuss, hold talks, confer, consult with e.o. *membawa ~* to bring/involve s.o. in a conversation/discussion. *~ kembali* to renegotiate.

merunding (*cla*) to calculate, count, estimate.

runding-merunding calculation, estimation.

merundingkan and **memperundingkan** to discuss, debate, dispute, argue about, negotiate, consult about. *dapat dirundingkan* negotiable. *sedang dirundingkan* under discussion. *setelah dirundingkan dengan* upon consultation with.

rundingan talks, deliberations, (items of a) discussion. *~ telah putus* the talks have ended and an agreement reached. *segan menurut ~ orang lain* reluctant to follow s.o. else's advice.

perunding negotiator, participant (in discussions).

perundingan negotiations, talks. *~ dua-pihak* bilateral negotiations. *~ Pembatasan Persenjataan Stratégis* Strategic Arms Limitations Talks, SALT. *~ Pengurangan Senjata Stratégis* Strategic Arms Reduction Talks, START. *~ perdamaian* peace talks. *~ segi tiga* tripartite conference.

runduk merunduk to bend down (of a rice plant). *penémbak* – sniper. *sebagai ilmu padi, kian/makin berisi kian/makin ~* the modesty of wisdom is the wiser the more modest; → ILMU *padi*, PADI I.

merunduk-runduk (to walk) stooped over.

merundukkan to bow (one's head). *Kepalanya dirundukkan.* He bowed his head.

rundukan s.t. bowed/bent down.

rundung merundung 1 to pester, harass, bother, give s.o. a hard time. *~ suaminya dengan meminta terus-menerus membelikan kalung emas.* She gave her husband a hard time by continually asking him to buy her a gold necklace. **2** to strike, hit, afflict, haunt, ravage. (*usu* passive in this meaning). *dirundung cinta* to be head over heels in love. *dirundung duka* to be full of sorrow. *dirundung hutang* to be over one's head in debt. *dirundung kesulitan* to be having a hard time, have a lot of problems. *dirundung malang* to be struck by misfortune/bad luck). *dirundung perang* to be ravaged by war. *~ rindu* to be very homesick.

perundungan harassing. *~ séksual* sexual harassment.

rundu-randa (*J*) **1** to follow in crowds. **2** to wander about with all one's belongings; → RANDA-RONDO.

rung → BALAIRUNG.

runggas I merunggas to uproot, extract, pull out; → MENCABUT, MENYENTAK.

runggas II berunggas-runggas with many gems on it. *cincin yang ~* a ring with many gems.

runggau (*ob*) sleep deprived.

runggu → RUNGGUH II.

rungguh I (*M*) **merungguh** to squat, sit on one's haunches/heels.

rungguh II 1 pledge, guarantee. **2** (*leg*) security.

merungguhkan to pawn, mortgage.

rungguhan pledge, item pawned.

perungguhan pawning, mortgaging.

runggu-rangga spiky, pointy (of deer antlers, etc.).

runggut → RENGGUT.

rungkai → UNGKAI.

rungkas merungkas to open by force.

rungkat windthrow (knocking down of trees by the wind).

rungkau merungkau 1 to hang down and cover (like hair over the face). **2** to overspread/spread over, overgrow/grow over, cover; → JERUNGKAU.

rungkuh very old, aged, elderly, decrepit, feeble (with age).

merungkuh to decay (with age), become dilapidated/decrepit.

kerungkuhan decrepitude, feebleness, old age, senility.

rungkun (*J*) cluster (of bamboo/bananas, etc.); → RUMPUN I.

rungkup 1 covering, sheltering. *atap* – a wide, low roof over a house, almost covering the whole house. *kajang* – two pieces of *kajang* arranged so as to function as a sunshade. **2** hanging down low. **3** almost completely covered.

merungkup(i) to cover up almost totally.

rungrum → RUMRUM.

rungsing (*J*) fretful, worried, irritable; troubled, unhappy; → RONGSÉNG.

merungsing to grumble, complain, fret.

merungsingkan to worry, trouble, irritate; to make s.o. feel worried/uneasy.

kerungsingan a troubled state of mind; worry, irritation. *mengalihkan ~ pikiran dalam menghadapi beban kehidupan* to shift away from a troubled state of mind in facing life's burdens.

rungsum → RUMRUM.

rungu (*Jv*) (the sense of) hearing, audibility; auditory. *rupa -* (*infr*) sound-slide (slides backed up by a cassette player; used as an audiovisual aid).

rungus (*M*) **merungus** to rumble (of thunder), make a loud noise.

rungut berungut to grumble, mumble, mutter.

berungutan to complain.

merungut to mutter/mumble (as a sign of discontent), grumble. *Ia ~ karena pelayanan yang diterimanya sungguh tidak memuaskan.* He grumbled because the service he had received was really unsatisfactory.

merungut-rungut to grumble, complain.

merungutkan to complain about, grumble because of.

rungutan grumbling, mumbling, muttering, complaining.

perungut grumbler, complainer.

runjak → LONJAK.

runjam stick/force into. → HUNJAM.

merunjam(kan) to stick/force into the ground;
terunjam stuck/forced into the ground.
runjang merunjang l to knock s.t. down with a long pole. **2** to grope around, feel one's way.
merunjangkan to use s.t. to knock s.t. down or grope around. ~ *tongkat ke lubang* to use a stick for poking around in a hole.
perunjang long pole.
runjau (*ob*) **merunjau** tall and lanky.
runjung cone, conical. *hantu* – ghost which starts off small and then grows bigger.
berunjung and **merunjung l** conical. **2** piled high in the shape of a cone.
runjungan coning.
runjut (*M*) **merunjut** hanging loose (like the skin of old people).
runsing → RONGSÉNG.
runtai bunch, cluster; → UNTAI.
seruntai a bunch/cluster.
meruntai to hang down loosely, dangle.
runtaian bunch, cluster.
runtak → RONTA.
runtang-runtung (*Jv*) always (going out) together, be the closest of friends. *Ia mendapat penggilan akrab Black Sam, dan sering kelihatan – bersama céwék kulit putih sepanjang Malioboro.* His nickname was Black Sam and he was often seen with white girls on Malioboro Street.
runtas meruntas l to pull with a jerk. **2** to snatch away.
runti (*cla*) **merunti** to remove the rough skin from cane (*esp rotan sega*), polish cane.
runtih (*M*) torn off.
meruntih to tear off.
runtihan shred, tatter.
runtuh l to collapse, disintegrate, fall apart. *Banyak bangunan yang – akibat angin kencang.* Many buildings collapsed because of the strong wind. **2** to fall off (before ripening). *(dapat) durian* – to get a windfall or an unexpected piece of good luck. **3** to slide down (of land/hillsides), cave in. **4** fall, collapse; fallen, toppled, ruined, destroyed. *–nya Mojopahit* the fall of Mojopahit. *Impiannya –.* His dreams fell through. **5** shot down (of a plane). **6** caving. *– rantah/ripuk* completely collapsed, in ruins.
meruntuh l to collapse. **2** to fall off. *musim durian* the *durian* season (when the fruit falls off the trees). **3** (*ob*) to infiltrate.
meruntuhi to collapse onto.
meruntuhkan l to demolish (a house), destroy. *Gempa bumi itu telah ~ beratus-ratus bangunan sekaligus.* The earthquake destroyed hundreds of buildings all at once. **2** to bring down, overthrow (the government, etc.), overcome. *Segala usahanya untuk ~ pertahanan musuh gagal.* All his efforts to overcome the enemy's defenses failed. ~ *hati* to capture the heart of. ~ *iman* a) to destroy s.o.'s faith/beliefs. b) tempting, alluring.
runtuhan l ruins, debris. **2** caving. ~ *salju* avalanche.
reruntuhan ruins, debris.
keruntuhan l fall, downfall, collapse, overthrow, breakdown. *Struktur perékonomian kolonial sudah mendekati ~nya.* The structure of the colonial economy was approaching collapse. ~ *batin* mental breakdown. **2** hit by s.t. which collapsed, have s.t. collapse on one *Banyak yang mati ~ rumah-rumah dan gedung-gedung.* Many died, hit by collapsing houses and buildings.
peruntuh destroyer, overthrower.
peruntuhan destruction, overthrow.
runtuk → RONTOK.
runtun I run (in testing); → RÉNTÉT. *– konsonan* (*gram*) alliteration. *– vokal* (*gram*) assonance.
beruntun(-runtun) l one after the other, in a row, chain (accident). *Dan tawaran film pun datang beruntun.* And film offers came one after the other. **2** linked together. **3** in succession, successively, consecutively, in a row. *dua tahun ~* for two years in a row. *Untuk menutupi kegelisahan ia merokok sigarét ~.* To cover up his nervousness he smoked one cigarette after another. *témbakan ~* volley (of gunfire). **4** sequential.
meruntunkan to link/join together.
runtunan series, row, file, sequence.

peruntunan sequence.
runtun II meruntun(kan) to pull/tug down (a branch/rope, etc.).
runtung → RUNTUN I. **runtungan** (*geol*) reworked.
runtut (*Jv*) harmonious, coherent. *tidak* – a) disharmonious. b) incoherent. **ketidak-runtutan l** disharmony. **2** incoherence.
beruntut in a row.
runtutan row, series.
keruntutan harmony, coherence.
runtuyan (*S*) cluster (of bananas).
runut l trace, track, trail, rut (in a road). *mendapat* – to be on the track (of), get information (about a case). *putus* – to get off the track. *songsong* – (*M*) k.o. witchcraft for predicting the future. **2** furrow.
merunut(i) l to track, follow the tracks/trail of, shadow s.o., trace. *Jika dirunut, ungkapan di atas mémang pancaran dari jiwa Titik.* If we trace it to its source, the expression above comes from Titik's soul. *Meréka dirunutinya dari belakang.* He shadowed them from behind. **2** to investigate, look into (a crime/the history of s.t.).
runutan l trace. *unsur ~* trace element. **2** tracer.
perunut trace, tracer.
perunutan tracing, tracking down.
runyai → UNYAI.
runyam and **runyem l** difficult, hard, problematic; complicated. **2** to fail. *Kalau begitu, tentu akan – usaha kita ini.* In that case, our efforts will surely fail.
merunyam to become difficult.
merunyamkan l to hamper, hinder, thwart, make difficult. **2** to cause to fail.
memperunyam to make s.t. more difficult, complicate.
kerunyaman difficulty, complication. *cara mengatasi ~ masalah budidaya cengkéh* the way to overcome the difficulties of cultivating cloves.
perunyam s.t. which complicates.
runyut (*M*) **merunyut** furrowed, wrinkled, creased.
ruok (*M*) **meruok l** to foam, fizz, bubble up. **2** to boil over; to rage/storm (at s.o.).
rupa (*Skr*) **l** (outward) appearance, aspect, looks. *Anak harimau itu –nya seperti kucing.* A tiger cub looks like a cat. *tidak memandang* – not considering the outward appearance of s.t. *mabuk –mu!* Who the hell do you think you are? *begitu/sedemikian* – in such a way. *Rute-rute penerbangan pesawat Merpati Nusantara Airlines sejak April 1983 diatur begitu – sehingga tidak paralél dengan rute penerbangan pesawat Garuda.* Since April 1983 Merpati Nusantara Airlines routes have been set up in such a way that they are not parallel to Garuda's routes. **2** (*– muka*) countenance, face, profile. *Dua bersaudara itu bagai pinang dibelah dua –nya.* The two siblings look like two peas in a pod. **3** shape, form. *berubah* – to change shape. *Menara itu –nya seperti rokét.* The tower looks like a rocket. **4** sort, kind. *tersedia segala – makanan* all k.o. food are available. *– boléh diubah, tabiat dibawa mati* the leopard doesn't change its spots. *– harimau, hati tikus* to look courageous but to be a coward. *indah kabar dari –* all that glitters is not gold. *– rungu* (*Jv*) audiovisual (of a slide).
rupa-rupa (*coq*) all k.o. *Dibelinya ~ barang méwah.* She bought all k.o. luxury items.
rupanya l → RUPA. **2** obviously, apparently, it seems, it looks like, in view of the circumstances. ~ *hari akan hujan* it looks like rain. *Anak ini ~ sakit malaria.* This child seems to have malaria. ~ *akan gagal juga perundingan itu.* It looks like those negotiations will also fail. **3** could, probably, maybe. *Siapa pula ~ yang mengambil buku saya?* Who could have taken my book? **4** instead, but in fact, actually. *Kusangka ia sedang membaca dalam kamarnya, ~ tidur.* I thought he was reading in his room, but in fact he was sleeping.
rupa-rupanya it looks like, by the looks of it, on the face of it. *perang dunia yang ketiga tak dapat dihindari lagi.* It looks like World War III cannot be avoided.
serupa l similar, of the same kind/type. *Mobilnya ~ dengan mobil saya.* He has the same kind of car that I do. **2** alike, in the same way. *berpakaian ~* to be dressed alike. **3** similar, like, re-

sembling closely. *Petunjuk yang baru itu ~ saja dengan yang mendahuluinya.* The new guidelines are just like the preceding ones. **4** like, as, as if (one were). *Perbuatannya ~ orang yang tidak sabar.* He behaved just like an impatient person. **5** of the same form/shape, similar in form/shape. *~ dan sebangun* congruent. *dua paralélogram yang ~* two similar parallelograms. **berserupa** to be alike, resemble, look alike. **menyerupa** (*M*) to pretend to be, act as if, disguise o.s. as. **menyerupai** I to be like, resemble, look like, take after. *Batu yang hitam dan keras ~ besi.* The hard black rock is like iron. **2** to equal, be the equal of, match. *Mustahil anda dapat ~ dia.* You couldn't possibly be his equal. **3** (*J*) to imitate, mimic. *Kelakuannya ~ orangtuanya.* His behavior is just like his parents'. **menyerupakan** I to make s.t. the same (as s.t. else), make equal (to s.t. else). *Syarat dan aturan ujian itu telah diserupakan untuk seluruh Indonésia.* The examination requirements and regulations have been made the same for all of Indonesia. **2** to place on a par (with). *Ia diserupakan dengan pedagang yang bermodal dengkul.* He has been put on a par with traders without capital; → DENGKUL. **keserupaan** identity (of form), similarity. **penyerupaan** making similar, bringing into line with e.o. **perserupaan** similarity (of form), agreement, concurrence.

berupa I to have a distinct form/shape. *Roh itu dapat berpikir, berperasaan dan bergerak, tetapi tidak ~.* The soul can think, feel, and move, but it has no distinct shape. **2** to have/take the form of, be in the form of; to represent, resemble. *lambang yang ~ tangan memegang obor* a symbol in the form of a hand holding a torch. **3** good-looking, beautiful, attractive, handsome, pretty; → RUPAWAN.

berupa-rupa of various kinds, all kinds.

berupakan to take/be the form of. *Segala bantuan, baik ~ uang, maupun ~ barang, akan diterima dengan segala senang hati.* All aid, whether in the form of money or in kind, will be accepted wholeheartedly.

merupa I to materialize, appear. **2** to appear in a dream.

merupai to resemble, look like. *Penduduk aslinya ~ bangsa-bangsa kulit hitam di Afrika.* The aborigines look like the black races of Africa.

merupakan I to give/make into the form of. *Hulu keris itu dirupakan kepala orang.* The hilt of the kris was given the form of a human head. **2** to be in the form of. *cerita yang dirupakan dengan gambar* a story in (the form of) pictures. **3** (*adalah ~*) to represent, constitute, make up, be. *KOWARI yang terbentuk pada tanggal 6 Désémber 1979 adalah ~ salah satu anak organisasi LVRI.* The KOWARI formed on December 6, 1979, is one of the subsidiary organizations of the LVRI. *tidak lagi ~ halangan* it no longer poses an obstacle. *~ diri(nya)* a) to appear, show/turn up, take the form/shape of. *Kabarnya ia dapat ~ dirinya seperti harimau.* It is said that he can take the form of a tiger; → JADI-JADIAN. b) to pretend to be, represent o.s. as. *Dia selalu ~ dirinya seorang terpelajar.* He always pretended to be an intellectual.

terupa I imaginable. *~ di akal* reasonable. *tidak ~ di akal* unimaginable, impossible to imagine. **2** to appear in one's imagination. *~ di hadapannya wajah anaknya yang nakal itu.* He imagined that he saw the face of his naughty child in front of his face.

perupa artist; → ARTIS, SENI *rupa*.

perupaan forming, shaping.

rupawan (*Skr neo*) handsome, pretty, beautiful, good-looking. *gadis yang ~* a pretty girl. *Sukar juga mencari gadis yang berada, berbangsa lagi ~.* It's hard to find a girl who is well-to-do, of a good family, and good-looking.

kerupawanan being good-looking.

rupak and **rupek** (*Jv*) closed in, confined, restricted.

rupiah [Rp] (*Hind*) rupiah, the Indonesian monetary unit (= 100 *sén*). **2** (*coq*) (the Netherlands Indies) guilder.

serupiah I one rupiah. **2** one guilder.

merupiahkan to convert into rupiahs.

rupiahan a note worth ... rupiahs. *100 ~* a 100-rupiah note.

perupiahan converting into rupiahs. *~ valuta asing* converting foreign exchange into rupiahs.

RUPS [Rapat Umum Pemegang Saham] General Shareholders' Meeting.

ruralisasi (*E*) ruralization.

ruruh → LURUH I.

rurut I (*M*) to fall off (of leaves, etc.); → LURUT I. *- hati* affected, touched (by love). *- hati (kepada)* to fall in love (with).

rurut II **merurut** to slip off (of s.t. loose); to pull s.t. out (with the fingers).

rusa (*Skr*) (various species of) deer, *Cervus equinus*. *- di hutan, kancah sudah terjerang* to count one's chickens before they are hatched. *seperti - masuk kampung* like a fish out of water. *mati - karena tanduknya* pride comes before a fall. *- kena tambat* always restless. *- balar* albino deer. *- banyu/payau* sambar deer, *Cervus unicolor. - Bawéan* Bawean deer, spotted deer, *Cervus axis. - beruang* a large deer species. *- dandi* a short-haired deer. *- nibung* a black deer. *- sabun* albino deer. *- Timor* Timor deer, *Cervus timorensis. - totol (putih-cokelat)* a white-brown speckled deer species, spotted deer, *Cervus axis. - ubi* a deer with hairy antlers.

rusak I damaged. *Banyak rumah - karena gempa bumi.* Many houses were damaged due to the earthquake. **2** injured, bruised, lacerated. *Banyak pemain kita yang -.* Many of our players were injured. **3** old and broken-down, worn-out; rotten, rotting, bad (of fruit), decomposed. *Pondok-pondok yang lama dan - itu telah dirobohkan oléh pemerintah.* The old, broken-down cottages were demolished by the government. *Buah-buahan itu banyak yang -.* A lot of the fruit was rotten. *mayat yang sudah -* a decomposed/rotting corpse. **4** broken, not in working condition, out of order, inoperable (of a car/engine, etc.). *Kendaraan saya - lagi pagi ini.* My car was not working again this morning. **5** corrupt(ed), not following the norms, depraved. *bahasa yang sudah -* a corrupted language. **6** no longer intact, over, finished with (of a marriage). *Pernikahannya sudah lama -.* His marriage was finished a long time ago. **7** impaired. *- ingatannya karena gegar otak itu.* His memory was impaired due to a concussion. **8** destroyed, in ruins. *- negeri karena pengeboman yang dahsyat.* The country was destroyed due to the terrible bombing. **9** not good; tainted, in bad repute (of one's name/reputation). *cepat/mudah -* perishable. *- berat* heavily damaged. *- binasa* completely destroyed. **merusak-binasakan** to destroy s.t. completely. *- hatinya* a) to be sad/depressed. b) to have a bad character. *- ringan* slightly damaged. *- moralnya* morally depraved. *- namanya* to have a bad name/reputation. *- patah* broken into pieces. **merusak-patahkan** to break into pieces. *- susila* immoral.

berusak *~ diri* to torture o.s. by thinking/brooding about s.t. too much. *~ hati* a) to be sad/depressed. b) to have a bad character.

merusak I to destroy, damage, harm, ruin, spoil (s.t. that was good); to force, break open. *~ kesatuan dan persatuan bangsa* to destroy the nation's unity and integrity. *Hujan és ~ 175 ha tanaman sayuran di dataran tinggi Dieng.* The hail destroyed 175 hectares of vegetable cultivation in the Dieng plateau. *Senjata api jenis Colt Révolvér 38 itu dicuri dari lemari orangtuanya dengan ~ kuncinya.* The Colt 38 was stolen from his parents' cupboard by forcing the lock. **2** destructive, harmful, detrimental, negative (effects), crushing (defeat). *kritik ~* destructive criticism. *tenaga membangun dan tenaga ~* constructive and destructive forces. **3** to go bad, rot. *bahan makanan yang mudah ~* perishable foodstuffs. **4** → MERUSAKKAN.

merusaki [and **mengrusaki** (*infr*)] (*pl obj*) to destroy, spoil, make s.t. not work any longer, break (frequently or many things). *Sudah biasa anak kecil suka ~ tanam-tanaman.* It's not unusual for little children to destroy plants.

merusakkan [and **mengrusakkan** (*infr*) and **ngerusakin** (*J coq*)] **1** to destroy, devastate, ruin, spoil, damage, harm, hurt, make a mess of. *~ hati* a) to hurt s.o.'s feelings. b) to have a bad influence on s.o. **2** to ravage. **3** to render useless. *~ nama* to defame, destroy s.o.'s reputation, cast aspersions on, slander. *tidak dapat dirusakkan* indestructible.

terusak destroyed, damaged.

kerusakan I damage, harm, injury, devastation, decay, destruction, ravages, ruin. ~ *otak* brain damage. ~ *total* write-off. **2** downfall. **3** breakdown.

perusak [and **pengrusak** (*infr*)] **1** destroyer, damager. *faktor* ~ damage factor. *kapal* ~ destroyer. ~ *akhlak* offender against morality. **2** tool used for breaking. **3** disturber. ~ *keamanan* s.o. who disturbs public safety.

perusakan [and **pengrusakan** (*infr*)] destruction, damage, ruining, spoiling, harming, vandalism, desecration, mutilation. ~ *hutan alam, penyebab banjir Purbalingga* the destruction of natural forests is the cause of flooding in Purbalingga.

rusbang → RÉSBANG.

RUSI [Republic of the United States of Indonesia]; → RIS.

rusia I (*coq*) → RAHASIA.

Rusia II Russia, Russian.

merusiakan to Russianize.

Ruslan (*infr*) Russia, Russian.

rusléting → RITSLÉTING.

Ruspau → RUMAH *Sakit Pusat Angkatan Udara.*

rustig (*D infr*) /résteh/ calm, quiet.

rusuh I 1 disturbance(s) of the peace (such as riots/thefts/robberies, etc.); unsafe. **2** disorderly, chaotic, unsettled, troubled. *Di negara yang – itu sering timbul pemberontakan.* Uprisings frequently occur in that unsettled country. *biang* – trouble-maker. **3** indecent, improper (behavior/words, etc.). *perkataannya kasar dan –* his words were rude and improper. **4** rough, rude. *Kesebelasan kita tidak biasa bermain – seperti meréka.* Our soccer team isn't used to playing rough the way that they do. **5** indiscriminate. *Anak ini – benar makanannya.* This child eats anything. *– resah* all k.o. unrest, disturbances, riots, etc.; disturbed, perturbed.

merusuh 1 to create unrest, make a disturbance. *Masih banyak gerombolan bersenjata yang ~ di perkebunan-perkebunan.* There are still many armed gangs creating unrest on the plantations. **2** to become unsafe.

merusuhi to disturb, make trouble in, stir up trouble in/for, upset (s.o.'s plans), make unsafe. *Garong selalu ~ daérah itu.* Robbers always make trouble in that area.

merusuhkan to disturb, stir up.

kerusuhan 1 disturbances, riots, rioting, unrest, conflict. ~ *étnik* ethnic conflict. ~ *sosial* social conflict. **2** disorder, confusion, turbulence.

perusuh rioter, troublemaker; insurgent, dissident, rebel, terrorist.

perusuhan revolt, rebellion, insurrection, mutiny, disturbances.

rusuh II – *hati* anxious, restless; sad, sorrowful, upset. *berusuh hati* worried, upset; to mourn, grieve; nervous, on edge. *Banyak juga orang yang ~ hati dengan keberhentian pegawai tinggi itu.* There were very many people who were grieved by the discharge of the senior official. *– resah* completely nervous.

merusuh to become nervous/worried/grieved. *Ia sudah tenang sekarang, sudah dapat menguasai hatinya yang ~.* He has calmed down now and was able to control his nervousness.

memperusuh to disturb, perturb, make restless.

merusuhkan 1 to disturb, perturb, make restless/nervous. *Itulah yang ~ hatinya, tiada lain.* That's what made him nervous, nothing else. **2** to worry about, be sad about, grieve for. *Apa gunanya engkau ~ anakmu yang sudah meninggal?* What's the use of grieving for your child who died?

kerusuhan ~ *hati* anxiety, uneasiness, restlessness.

rusuk I 1 side, flank (of body/house, etc.). *tertémbak kena –nya* he was shot in the side. *dilihat dari –* seen from the side. *duduk di – to sit at the side.* **2** (road) side. *daérah –* fringe area. *pintu –* side door. **3** (*tulang –*) rib. *–nya patah akibat jatuh.* He broke his rib because of a fall. **4** rib, vane (part of a screw, etc.). *– antar* guide vane. *– badan* flank. *– bersayap* dovetail (carpentry). *– jalan* footpath (along a street/road), sidewalk; → TROTOAR. *– rangka* frame (of a ship, etc.). *– surat* margin (of a letter). *– tangan* side of the hand.

berusuk with a rib, ribbed.

merusuk 1 to stab from the side. *Orang itu dirusuknya dengan tombak.* He stabbed that person from the side with a spear. **2** to move/go along the side. *berjalan ~* to walk along the side. **3** on one's side/rib. *tidur ~* to sleep on one's side.

rusuk II temporary house or building.

rusun → RUMAH *susun.*

rusyd (*A*) age of discretion.

rut (*ob*) able, can hold out. (*tidak*) – (in)vulnerable; → LUT I.

rutan (*acr*) → RUMAH *tahanan.*

rute (*D*) route, the way to get from one place to another. *– gerak maju* (*mil*) approach route. *– penerbangan* route taken by a plane, airline route; → JALUR *penerbangan.*

rutin (*D*) routine.

merutinkan to routinize, make s.t. a routine/habit.

kerutinan routineness, habit. ~ *akan menghilangkan romantika perjuangan.* Habit will make the romance of the struggle disappear.

ruting (*M*) **1** (*baginda –*) k.o. snakehead fish, *Ophiocephalus striatus.* **2** a nickname for s.o. who behaves improperly towards women in his own or his wife's family.

rutinisasi (*E*) routinization.

rutinisme (*E*) routinism.

rutinitas routineness; → KERUTINAN.

rutuk merutuk to grumble, mutter, complain.

rutukan grumbling, muttering, complaining.

rutup noisy.

merutup to make a noise, be boisterous, tumultuous, vociferous.

RUU (*init*) → RENCANA *Undang-Undang.*

Ruwah the eighth month in the Muslim calendar, also called *Syaban,* the time for paying homage to one's ancestors.

ruwat I (*Jv*) **1** exorcised, driven out/away (of an evil spirit or spirits by prayers/incantations, etc.). **2** released from a spell, evil spirit, etc.

meruwat 1 to exorcise. **2** to protect s.o. from a spell, etc.

ruwatan a ceremony to protect the household, sometimes done with a *wayang* performance given as an act of exorcism, to protect a threatened household, *esp* an only child.

ruwat II → RUWET.

ruwet (*J/Jv*) **1** confused, perplexed; confusing, complicated, puzzling, bewildering. *Keadaan politik semakin –.* The political situation is becoming more and more confusing. **2** difficult, complicated, complex, tangled. *– bundet* very complicated. *– rénténg* worries, troubles, problems, complications.

beruwet complicated.

meruweti and **meruwetkan** to complicate, make difficult, confuse, tangle.

keruwet (*Jv*) to be complicated.

keruwetan 1 confusion. **2** complication, complexity, difficulty.

peruwetan complication.

ruyak meruyak to spread, extend, expand. ~*nya lagu pop* the spread of pop songs.

meruyaki to spread over/into.

ru'yat → RUKYAT.

ruyung I hardwood portion of a palm trunk which can be used for making hoe handles, poles, etc. *Pagar –* the capital city of the Minangkabau founded by Aditia Warman in 1347. *jika tidak pecah –, di mana boléh mendapat sagu* no pain, no gain; to achieve one's goal one must work hard. *awak yang payah membelah –, orang lain yang beroléh sagunya* to pull the chestnuts out of the fire for s.o. else.

ruyung II crooked, slanting (of a house/tree).

ruyung III (*J*) a sharp weapon.

ruyup 1 to droop with fatigue (of one's eyes), be drowsy, sleepy. **2** to go down, set, sink (of the sun).

meruyup to droop with fatigue, etc.

meruyupkan ~ *mata* to close one's eyes.

Rv (*D leg*) Rechtsvordering; → RÉGLEMÉN *Acara Perdata.*

RvJ Court of Justice; → RAAD *van Justitie.*

RW I [Rintek Wu'uk] (*Min*) dog meat (a Manadonese dish).

RW II (*init*) → RUKUN *warga.*

S

s and S I /és/ the 19th letter of the Latin alphabet used for writing Indonesian.

S II → STRATA *satu/dua/tiga.*

S III car license plate for Bojonegoro.

3S [Suka Sama Senang] lit. 'to want to be happy,' i.e., a kind of bribe.

sa- I prefix, the clipped form of **esa** (in Sundanese and Javanese words). *sajam* (*S*) one hour. *sadina* (*Jv*) one day.

sa II (in acronyms) → DÉSA.

saad (*A*) luck.

saadah (*A*) /sa'adat/ and **saadat** /sa'adat/ **1** majesty. *Baginda –* H.M. the King. **2** happiness, bliss.

saadiah (*A ob*) coat of mail.

saat (*A*) /sa'at/ **1** moment, instant, second, a very short period of time. *sudah sampai –nya* it's (high) time. *Diamatinya beberapa –.* He looked at it for a few seconds. *suatu – (nanti)* at some point/time (in the future). *Waktu itu tak pernah ia impikan bahwa suatu – akan menjadi pemain sépakbola terkenal.* At that time he never dreamed that he would at some point become a famous soccer player. *– ini* this very moment, right now. *dari – ini ke atas* from now on, in (the) future. *– itu* then, at that time. *pada tiap –* at any moment. *pada satu –* at one moment. *pada setiap –* at any moment. *– terakhir* the last moment/time. **2** the moment that (s.t. happened), when. *– diterimanya* the moment it was received. **3** (*cla*) a specific moment in time connected with good luck, etc. *– yang baik/naas/sempurna* an auspicious/unlucky/perfect moment. *– genting* crucial moment. *– lepas landas* (the moment of) takeoff. *– permulaan* start date. *– teduh* meditation hour. *– terakhir untuk memasukkan berita* deadline (of a newspaper). *– tutup* closing time. *– yang memutuskan/menentukan* decisive moment.

sesaat 1 (for) a moment. *Suara rintihnya hanya ~ terdengar.* The moaning was audible for only a moment. *~ kemudian* a moment later. *~ sebelum* just/right before. **2** instantaneous. **3** lasting only a brief time, momentary, ephemeral.

sesaat-sesaat at times, from time to time.

pensaatan timing.

saba I (*Skr*) to frequent, go to often (of restaurants/movie theaters, etc.).

bersaba to mix/associate with, go around with.

menyaba to visit regularly, frequent. *Dia ~ ke kota Jakarta.* He visited Jakarta often.

Saba II (*A*) **1** Sheba; Sabaea. **2** "Sabaens"; name of the 34th chapter of the Koran.

sabah (*A*) not distinctive, vaguely resembling.

sabak I (*M*) **1** dark; obscure; gloomy, cloudy, dull, somber. *hari –* a gloomy/cloudy/dull day; → KABUR I, MENDUNG. *Matanya –.* His eyes were dull. *Mukanya –.* His face was somber. *(meratap) berbiji –* to shed tears of sadness. **2** dejected, downcast, downhearted; sad, sorrowful, blue. **3** sulking, pouting.

menyabak to cry, weep.

sabak II baker's oven, vat for boiling palm sugar.

menyabak to boil palm sugar.

sabak III (*Jv*) slate; → BATU *tulis.*

sabak IV → SEBAK.

saban I (*J/Jv*) **1** each, every. **2** every time that.

saban-saban 1 each and every. **2** whenever. **3** frequently. **4** some time or other.

saban II and **sa'ban** → SYAKBAN.

sabana (*D*) savannah.

sabang I small jib used on small boats.

Sabang II island off the northern tip of Sumatra. *dari – ke Meraŭké* from Sabang to Merauke, an expression of the territorial unity of Indonesia.

sabar I (*A*) **1** patient, tolerant, able to endure/stand troubles/suf-

fering, etc. *harus belajar –* you have to learn to be patient/to put up with problems. *–lah dahulu!* be patient! *tahan –* to be patient. *tidak –* impatient. *Saya tidak – lagi.* I can't stand it any longer. **2** calm, relaxed. *tidak –* impatient, on edge. **ketidaksabaran** impatience.

bersabar (*~ hati*) to be patient/calm/tolerant, restrain o.s.

menyabari to calm s.o. down.

menyabarkan [and **nyabarin** (*J coq*)] and **mensabarkan** (*infr*) **1** to restrain, make s.o. patient. *~ hati* to control/restrain o.s., be patient. *Sabarkanlah hatimu!* Be patient! **2** to quiet/calm down, soothe, appease, pacify. *Aminah mencoba ~ ibunya yang sedang marah itu.* Aminah tried to calm down her angry mother.

tersabar the most patient.

sabaran (*J*) to be patient. *Ia sangat tidak ~.* He's very impatient.

kesabaran 1 patience, sociability, compatibility. **2** tolerance, toleration. **3** submissiveness, subservience, devotion.

penyabar a person who is patient/tolerant/sociable/easy to get along with.

penyabaran appeasement.

sabar II *penyakit –* → BÉRI-BÉRI.

sabas (*Pers*) **1** bravo, well done, good for you. **2** to like to.

sabasani (*Hind*) *pohon –* a legendary tree shaped like a snake.

sabat I → SABET.

Sabat II (*A*) Sabbath, Saturday.

sabat III → SOBAT.

sabatikal (*E*) sabbatical.

sabda (*Skr*) (polite term for) word (of God/the Prophet/a prince, etc.). *– Tuhan yang Mahaesa* the words of the One and Only God. *– pandita ratu* (*Jv*) a) words of a wise king. b) the king can do no wrong; an honest man's word is as good as his bond.

bersabda to say, speak.

mensabdakan and **menyabdakan** to say, order.

sabdapraja (*Skr neo*) dialect.

sabel (*D*) saber.

saben → SABAN I.

sabet (*J/Jv*) whip (with a long whip or cord), lash. *sekali –* at one blow, with one stroke.

menyabet [and **nyabet** (*coq*)] **1** to lash/whip (out at). *Ia ~ Mokhtar dengan telapak tangannya.* He lashed out at Mokhtar with the palm of his hand. **2** to strike, hit. *Sewaktu ia hendak menyeberang, ia disabet oléh sebuah mobil.* When he wanted to go across, he was struck by a car. **3** to grab, snatch; to steal, take s.t. or s.o. away from s.o. else. *Dompétnya disabet seorang pencopét.* His wallet was snatched by a pickpocket. *Pemuda itu ~ pacar temannya.* The young man stole his friend's girlfriend. **4** to cut, slash, hack. *Anggota Polri téwas disabet clurit oléh orang tak dikenal.* A member of the RI Police Force was slashed to death with a *clurit* by an unknown person. **5** to win, get, attain. *~ juara pertama* to get first prize.

menyabetkan to slash/whip s.t. against, hit hard with s.t. *Jopie ~ parang ke tubuh Rasyid.* Jopie slashed Rashid's body with his bolo knife.

tersabet [and **kesabet** (*coq*)] whipped, lashed, struck, snatched, etc.

sabetan 1 blow, stroke, lash(ing), slash. *mayat yang léhérnya nyaris putus akibat ~ senjata tajam* a corpse whose head was almost severed by a slash from a sharp weapon. **2** slamming shut (of a window, etc.). **3** s.t. snatched/stolen. **4** additional income (outside one's job).

penyabetan 1 lashing. **2** winning, getting (a medal/prize, etc.).

sabha (*Bal*) congress, conference.

sabhan (*A*) praising God.

Sabhara [Samapta Bhayangkara] Police Readiness (for Action) (Unit); it patrols, guards, maintains security, and is the first at the scene of a crime.

kesabharaan police readiness (*mod*).

sabhat (*A*) rosary bead.

sabi I (*Pers cla*) k.o. shirt.

Sabi II (*A cla*) **1** Sabaean. **2** unbeliever.

sabil (*A*) way, road, path, course. *mati* – to die a martyr's death, fall in battle in a Holy War. *perang* – crusade, Holy War (defending Islam against infidels); → JIHAD.

Sabilillah (*A*) **1** Allah's Road. **2** the name of the now defunct *Masyumi* militia organization during the 1945 independence movement.

sabit I 1 sickle. **2** crescent. *bintang* – star and sickle (as in the Turkish flag and as part of the Muslim emblem). *bulan* – crescent moon. *palu* – hammer and sickle (the Communist emblem); → PALU *arit*. – *Mérah* Red Crescent, an organization functioning like the Red Cross in Muslim countries.

menyabit to cut grass with a sickle, mow.

menyabiti (*pl obj*) to cut, mow.

menyabitkan to mow for s.o. else.

sabitan cut with a sickle, mowed.

penyabit mower. ~ *rumput* grass cutter (the person).

penyabitan cutting grass with a sickle, mowing.

sabit II (*A*) **1** fixed, certain, assured, definitive, inevitable. **2** of course.

menyabitkan to affirm, confirm, assert.

sabitah (*A*) fixed (of stars), i.e., not moving like the planets.

sableng (*J*) mentally unbalanced, crazy, not all there. *"Tak ada alasan untuk berdamai dengan si – Somad! Mengerti?"* "There's no reason to come to an agreement with that crazy guy Somad! Get it?"

nyableng to act crazy.

kesablengan craziness.

sablon (*D*) k.o. mold or template, a cut-out form which is used for making figures or letters, screening.

menyablon and **mensablon 1** to work with such a mold. **2** to plagiarize.

tersablon screened (onto a shirt, etc.).

penyablon and **pensablon 1** the person who works with such a mold. **2** plagiarist.

penyablonan 1 process or method of working with such a mold. **2** plagiarism.

sabluk (*Jv*) /-luk/ k.o. pot and steamer combined.

sabot (*D*) sabotage. *kaum* – saboteurs.

menyabot and **mensabot** to sabotage.

tersabot sabotaged.

penyabot saboteur.

penyabotan sabotage, sabotaging.

sabotase (*D*) sabotage. *Ledakan itu terjadi karena* –. The explosion was caused by sabotage.

menyabotase and **mensabotase** to sabotage.

penyabotasean sabotaging.

sabotir (*D*) **menyabotir** and **mensabotir** to sabotage.

sabrang (*Jv*) → SEBERANG.

Sabtu (*A*) *hari* – Saturday. *malam* – Friday evening. *petang – malam Minggu* Saturday night. – *malam* Saturday evening.

sabu (*sl*) methyl amphetamine.

sabuk I (*Jv*) **1** belt, sash; → ANGKIN. – *badai* chin strap. – *beranak* k.o. sash worn during pregnancy. – *dukung* sling. – *hijau* greenbelt. – *hitam* black belt (in judo). **bersabuk hitam** to have a black belt. – *kapas* cotton belt (in Central and East Java, NTB, NTT, or South and Southeast Sulawesi). – *keamanan/keselamatan* safety/seat belt. – *kulit* leather belt. – *peluru* cartridge belt. – *pengaman/penyelamat* safety/seat belt. – *pengangkut* conveyor belt. – *penolong* life belt. **2** loincloth.

bersabuk to wear a belt/sash/loincloth.

menyabuk to be shaped like a strap, strap-shaped.

sabuk II strip, narrow piece of land. *Sepanjang pantai terdapat sebuah – dataran rendah.* Along the coast is a strip of low land.

nyabuk ~ *gunung* contour planting.

sabun I (*A Port*) soap. *air* – soapsuds. *main* – to play in a game which has been fixed, pretend to fight (only for the sake of appearances). *pakaian yang belum pernah ketemu* – clothes which have never been washed.– *anjing* carbolic soap. – *batangan* bar

of soap. – *béko* (*J*) bar of soap. – *bubuk* soap powder. – *cair* liquid soap. – *colék* cream. – *cuci* laundry soap. – *cukur* lather (for shaving). – *karbol* carbolic soap. – *kecantikan* beauty soap. – *keringat buntet* soap for prickly heat. – *mandi* bath soap.

bersabun 1 to soap o.s. (before washing), apply lather to o.s. (before shaving). **2** soapy, with soap in it.

menyabun 1 to become soap-like. **2** to soap. **3** to deceive, cheat. **4.** (*coq*) to masturbate (using soap).

menyabuni [and **nyabunin** (*J coq*)] to put soap on, soap up, apply soap to, lather up. *Marina di kamar mandi* ~ *tubuhnya.* Marina soaped up her body in the bathroom.

menyabunkan to make s.t. into soap.

tersabun saponated.

penyabunan 1 soaping (up), washing with soap. **2** saponification.

sabun II off-white, light-colored. *anjing* – white dog. *mata* – light-colored, blue or gray eyes. *orang* – albino. *pinggan mangkuk* – white porcelain crockery/cups and saucers.

sabun III *penyakit/sakit* – gonorrhea.

sabung fight (usually between animals, and gambling is involved). *ayam* – fighting cock. *biar alah – asalkan menang sorak* happiness is more important than victory. – *selepas hari petang* to engage in a last-ditch effort.

bersabung 1 to fight, compete (of cocks, etc.). ~ *ayam* to pit fighting cocks against e.o. *ayam* ~ fighting cock. **2** to fight (against) s.t. ~ *dengan/melawan ketidakadilan* to fight against injustice. **3** to clash, flash (of lightning), collide, pound (of waves on the shore); clashed, collided, pounded. *kilat* ~ the lightning flashed. *ombak* ~ the waves pounded (on the shore); choppy seas. **4** to rage; to be fierce, furious. *topan* ~ a furious gale. ~ *mata/pandang* and *mata(nya)* ~ to strike/catch/meet one's eye. *kasih* ~ *dalam hati* to long for one's beloved. *angin berputar/bersiru ombak* ~ a very complicated matter/situation.

menyabung [and **nyabung** (*coq*)] **1** to pit (fighting cocks/kites, etc.) against e.o. **2** to put (one's life) in danger. ~ *jiwa/nyawa* to risk one's life in s.t. very dangerous. ~ *untung* a) if you're lucky, you'll win, if not you'll lose. b) to seek one's fortune/livelihood on the chance that one will find it.

sabung-menyabung 1 to lash out at e.o., rush at e.o. **2** to flash (of forked lightning). *Maka berbunyilah guruh petir, kilat* ~. And then the thunder roared and the lightning flashed.

menyabungkan 1 to make (fighting cocks, etc.) fight with e.o. **2** to hammer away at e.o. with.

tersabung competed, made to fight with e.o., unintentionally caused to fight with e.o. ~ *akan induk ayam* everyone thinks that his own geese are swans. ~ *di itik* to be friends with s.o. who is weak or powerless.

sabungan (animals, etc.) pitted against other (animals, etc.), fighting (*mod*). *Dia memelihara ayam* ~*nya dengan baik sekali.* He cared for his fighting cocks very well.

penyabung s.o. who holds cockfights. ~ *ayam* s.o. who pits fighting cocks against e.o.

penyabungan cockfighting; fighting, clashing, etc.

persabungan 1 arena for cockfighting. **2** fighting, clashing, competing. **3** fight, clash.

sabur 1 two or more elements mixed together in such a way that they are no longer distinguishable from e.o.; cacophony of sounds. **2** vague, hazy, dim, not bright, not clear. *Kaca jendéla ini – karena sudah lama tidak dibersihkan.* The windowpane isn't clear any longer because it hasn't been cleaned in a long time. – *limbur* a) all mixed together. b) dim, dark, dusky, not clear. *pada pagi buta waktu masih – limbur* very early in the morning when it is still dark.

menyabur 1 to disguise o.s. (so that one's true identity is hidden). *berhasil memasuki daérah lawan setelah* ~ *sebagai pengemis* to succeed in entering enemy territory after disguising o.s. as a beggar. **2** to join, disappear (into) (so that one becomes indistinguishable from others). *Ia* ~ *di antara kerumunan orang banyak itu.* He disappeared into the crowd.

menyaburkan 1 to mix (up together). ~ *bermacam-macam bahan pewarna untuk memperoléh warna yang diinginkan* to mix various coloring matters together to obtain the desired color. **2** to deaden (voices) (so that they become dim). *Pada* *dinding kamar kerjanya dipasang alat peredam untuk ~ suara bising.* A sound-absorbing coating was applied to the walls of his study to deaden noises.

tersabur mixed, blended together.

sabu-sabu → SHABU-SHABU.

sabut I coir, fibrous husk, mesocarp (of the coconut/areca-nut, etc.). *bungkuk* – hunched-over/round-shouldered (of old people). *tali* – coir rope. *untung – timbul, untung batu tenggelam* a) it's kill or cure, all or nothing. b) nobody can escape his fate. – *kelapa* coconut fiber.

bersabut fibrous.

sabut II *pohon* – a large tree whose timber is used for building materials, *Nauclea purpurascens*.

sacap → CAP IV.

sad- I (*Skr*) (a prefix) six. –.*Tunggal* the Six-in-One Unit consisting of the Regional/Provincial Head, Chief of Police, Army Commander, Public Prosecutor, Judge, and Chairman of the National Front (under President Soekarno).

sad II (*A*) **1** name of the 14th letter of the Arabic alphabet. **2** name of the 38th chapter of the Koran.

sada (*Jv*) main rib of a palm leaf.

pesada street sweeper.

sadab (*A*) rue, *Ruta graveolens*.

sadah (*M*) **1** lime (for betel chewing). **2** hard (of water). *air* – hard water. *termakan di* – looked blank/foolish; → KECELÉ.

kesadahan hardness (of water).

sadai bersadai 1 prone, lying stretched out. **2** beached, moved up to a higher level (of an unused boat), pulled up out of the water.

menyadaikan to ground (a boat on the beach).

tersadai 1 stranded, beached. *Apabila ribut sudah reda, tinggallah dua buah perahu itu ~ di batu.* When the storm abated, the two boats were left beached on the rocks. **2** stretched out. **3** remained on the shelf (of goods that didn't sell). *Karena mahal, banyak dagangannya ~.* Because they were expensive, his goods didn't move. **4** to remain unmarried, not asked for in marriage. *Karena angkuhnya, akhirnya gadis itu ~ sampai tua.* Due to her arrogance, in the end that girl remained unmarried into old age.

sadak I oblique, slanting, sloping; → CONDONG, MIRING.

sadak II 1 (*Jv*) betel roll (to be chewed). **2** bridal packet (a betel leaf rolled around the ingredients used for betel chewing) which is thrown down by bride and groom when they meet at the wedding ceremony (tradition has it that the first one to throw it down will be the dominant one in the marriage). **3** (*M*) betel-lime; → SADAH.

sadakah → SEDEKAH.

sadal → SADEL.

sadalinggam (*Skr?*) vermilion.

Sa'dan an ethnic group of southwest Sulawesi.

sadang-sading *pintu* – curtained entrance to bridal couch.

sadap I *pisau* – tapping knife (for tapping rubber trees). *tukang* – tapper (of rubber trees).

menyadap [and **nyadap** (*coq*)] to tap (rubber/palm-sap), draw (blood).

tersadap tapped.

sadapan 1 s.t. tapped, sap tapping. **2** container for holding what is tapped.

penyadap 1 tapper. **2** catheter.

penyadapan tapping. ~ *karét* rubber tapping.

sadap II menyadap [and **nyadap** (*coq*)] **1** to tap, intercept, bug (a telephone, etc.). ~ *pembicaraan* to tap/bug a conversation. **2** to poll. *Hampir 70% suara yang disadap pol Newsweek menyokong tindakan Présidén Bush.* Almost 70% of the voters polled by *Newsweek* support President Bush's measures.

penyadap tapper. *alat* ~ bug, bugging device.

penyadapan (wire)tapping, bugging, interception (of messages). *Agén-agén rahasia Sovyét pernah melakukan ~ suara terhadap Ratu Inggris dan suaminya.* Soviet secret agents once tapped the (telephone of the) Queen of England and her husband.

sadap III (*A*) mother-of-pearl.

sadaqah → SEDEKAH.

sadar I 1 conscious, aware. *bawah* – subconscious. **2** – *dari* to re-

cover from, get over (astonishment, etc.). **3** – *akan dirinya* a) to come to one's senses. b) and **sadarkan** *diri* and – *dari pingsan* to come to, regain consciousness. c) *tidak* **sadar(kan)** *diri(nya lagi)* unconscious. **4** – *dari tidur* to wake up, be awake; woken up. **5** to realize s.t., be aware of s.t. *Dia – akan kesalahannya.* He realized his mistake, he was aware of his mistake. *dalam keadaan* – being of sound mind. *dengan tak/tidak* – one is unaware (of s.t.), one (does s.t.) unconsciously/unawares. – *tak* – vaguely aware, not sure (about knowing s.t.). *tidak* – unconscious. *tidak* – *akan* to be out of touch with. *secara tidak* – unintentionally, inadvertently. *antara* – *dan tiada* semiconscious. *membuat* – *dari menungan* it startles s.o. out of his daydreams. *kurang* – only partly aware/conscious; *cp tidak* SADAR. *kekurangsadaran* lack of awareness. – *diri* self-conscious. – *status* status-conscious. – *tanggung-jawab* sense/feeling of responsibility. – *wisata* [darwis] tourist conscious.

menyadar ~ *arwah* (*M*) a *selamatan* in commemoration of the deceased (or, a *selamatan* in the month of *Syaban*).

menyadari [and **nyadarin** (*J coq*)] to realize, be aware of, understand, know, be conscious of. ~ *nasibnya/untungnya* to grieve over one's fate, complain about one's lot in life. *dengan tidak meréka sadari* without their being aware of it, without their realizing it, unbeknownst to them. *tidak* ~ to be out of touch with.

menyadarkan 1 to bring s.o. back to consciousness, bring s.o. around, awaken, arouse, revive. **2** to remind, make s.o. aware (of s.t.), convince s.o. (of s.t.). **3** to bring s.o. to his senses. ~ *daripada* to rid s.o. of (faults/stupidities), cure s.o. of.

tersadar 1 remembered/recalled suddenly, brought back to one's conscious awareness. **2** to become conscious/aware. **3** to regain/recover consciousness.

kesadaran 1 awareness, realization, consciousness, knowledge; minded(ness). *hilang* ~ to lose consciousness, become unconscious, pass out. ~ *diri* and ~ *akan diri sendiri* self-awareness. ~ *akan harga diri* sense of self-respect/one's own dignity. *menanam* ~ *berbangsa dan bernegara* to instill an awareness of nationhood and statehood. ~ *jiwa susila* moral/ethical awareness. ~ *keamanan* security-minded. ~ *kemasyarakatan* social awareness. ~ *menabung* savings-minded. ~ *pengamanan* security-minded. **2** repentance, regret, compunction. **3** true understanding, sense of reality. ~ *hukum* sense of justice.

penyadar reminder, s.t. that arouses/revives/awakens, reviver.

penyadaran awakening, waking up, reviving, arousing. *badan* ~ political awareness training center.

sadar II (*A*) **1** breast; chest; → DADA. **2** front; → DEPAN. **3** beginning; → PERMULAAN.

sadariah (*A*) *baju* – the *Haji*'s zouave-style waistcoat.

sadarulkalam (*A*) the beginning of a story, opening words; foreword, preface.

sadarusalam (*A*) paradise on earth.

sadau I menyadau to knock down a bee's nest.

sadau II menyadau (*ob*) to row a boat with long strokes of the oars (in a race).

sadaya (*Skr Jv cla*) all; → KALIAN, SEMUA.

sadd (*A cla*) wall; obstruction (in the way, etc.), barrier.

sadel (*D*) saddle, seat. – *sepéda* bicycle seat.

sadérék (*Jv*) sibling.

saderi → SADRI.

sadhumuk bathuk sanyari bumi (*Jv*) to defend every inch of the fatherland against the colonizer.

sadik I (*A*) sincere, honest, straight; loyal, faithful.

menyadikkan and **mensadikkan** to make the path straight (for a prophet or *nabi*).

sadik II (*A*) *fajar* – true dawn, daybreak; → SIDIK II.

sadin supernatural creature that has a dog's head, crocodile's legs and lives underwater.

sading I curtain; → SADANG-SADING.

sading II → SEDANG I.

sadir (*A*) sal-ammoniac, ammonium chloride.

sadis I (*D*) **1** sadist. **2** sadistic. **3** (*BG*) super, terrific, great. *Hébat, ya filmnya? –!* The film was great, wasn't it? super!

tersadis the most sadistic.

kesadisan sadism. ~ *penjahat harus ditanggulangi bersama.* As a group we must deal with criminal sadism.

sadis II (*A*) sixth.

sadisme (*D/E*) sadism.

sadistis (*D*) sadistic.

sadkona octagonal.

sadmatra hexameter.

sado (*D from Fr dos-à-dos*) a two-wheeled, horse-drawn carriage. *Nama – berasal dari bahasa Prancis "dos à dos."*

    bersado to ride in a *sado*.

sadrah (*S*) submissive, resigned; → PASRAH.

    kesadrahan submission.

sadran (*Jv*) to bring offerings to graves or to go to a holy place to take a vow for s.t. *musim* – the season to pay homage to one's deceased ancestors, i.e., during the month of *Sadran*, the eighth month of the Javanese/Muslim calendar.

    nyadran to participate in this ceremony.

    sadranan *tempat* ~ place where offerings are made.

sadri celery.

sad ripu (*Bal*) → MEMANGKAS *gigi*.

sadrulkalam → SADARULKALAM.

Sad Satya Sri Séna (the ethical code of *Puskowad*) the six promises of female soldiers, a reflection of actions and behavior based on the *Sapta Marga* and the *Sumpah Prajurit*, which have within them the values of the ancestors.

sadsudut hexagon.

Sadtunggal (*ob*) council of six highest government officials.

sadu I (*Skr ob*) preeminent, outstanding. – *perdana* most outstanding.

sadu II (*Skr*) k.o. Indian fakir who practices self-flagellation, sadhu.

sadur I (thin metal) layer/coating (on another metal, for protection/coating/plating); → SEPUH I. *sebagai – menimbulkan senam* "as a coat that lets its background appear," i.e., the veneer is wearing thin; to display one's true colors; murder will out; → *menunjukkan* BELANG*nya.* – *emas* gilt. – *listrik* electroplating.

    bersadur layered, coated, plated. *gelang pérak* ~ *emas* a gold-plated/gilt silver bracelet.

    menyadur to plate (metals), overlay/coat with. ~ *emas* to gild. ~ *pérak* to silver, coat with silver. ~ *séng* to galvanize, coat with tin.

    saduran plating, metal coating, veneer.

    penyadur plater (the person as well as the instrument used to plate s.t. else).

    penyaduran plating, coating.

sadur II menyadur [and **nyadur** (*coq*)] 1 to adapt. *Salah satu cerita sandiwara karangan Ibsen telah disadur oléh Armijn Pané.* One of Ibsen's plays has been adapted by Armijn Pane. 2 to edit, revise (and make ready) for publication. 3 to summarize (the results of an inspection, etc.).

    tersadur adapted.

    saduran 1 adaptation. ~ *cerita itu lebih hidup dari isi cerita aslinya.* The adaptation of the story was livelier than the original. 2 summary.

    penyadur 1 adaptor. 2 editor; → PENYUNTING.

    penyaduran 1 adaptation. 2 editing; → PENYUNTINGAN. 3 summarizing.

sadurungé (*Jv*) before, prior to. *ngerti/weruh – winarah* to be prophetic, foresee the future.

saé (*Jv*) good, virtuous.

saéran various species of drongos, *Dicrurus spp.*

saf I (*A*) 1 line, row, file. *Penumpang berhadap-hadapan dalam dua* –. The passengers were facing e.o. in two rows. 2 *as*– "The Formations"; name of the 61st chapter of the Koran.

    bersaf-saf(an) in line/rows (of troops/processions, etc.).

    saf-safan in rows.

saf II (*kertas* –) blotting paper; → SAP I.

safa (*A*) clear, pure.

safaat → SYAFAAT.

safakat → SEPAKAT.

safar I (*A*) trip, travel, journey.

Safar II (*A*) the second month of the Muslim calendar. Tradition has it that this month is full of dangers or is unlucky; therefore, on the last Monday of this month people take actions to ward off these dangers; → SYAFAR.

safari (*E*) 1 safari. *baju* – short-sleeved dress jacket for men (part of a suit), safari jacket, Nehru jacket. 2 itinerant group (of actors/singers, etc. – *Golkar* itinerant troops of actors, singers, musicians, etc. delegated to certain areas by *Golkar* as part of its election campaign.

    bersafari 1 to wear a safari jacket. 2 to go on a safari.

safarjal (*A*) quince, *Pyrus cydonia.*

safe (*E*) /séf/ → SIP I.

Saffat (*A*) *as*– "Those Who Stand in Rows"; name of the 37th chapter of the Koran.

safi (*A*) clean, pure, sincere. *sahabat yang* – a sincere friend.

safih (*A*) crazy, stupid, foolish; spendthrift.

safil → ASFAL I.

safinah and **safinat** (*A*) boat.

safir I (*D*) sapphire.

safir II (*A*) traveler; → MUSAFIR.

Safkar [Singapore Armed Forced Kartika] Joint Indonesian-Singapore Army Maneuvers.

safrah → SEPERAH.

safran (*D*) saffron, *Crocus sativus.*

safsaf (*A*) barren, uncultivated, underdeveloped, fallow (land).

sag (*Pers*) dog.

saga I 1 a tree whose fruit resembles *petai* (*Parkia speciosa*); it has fiery red seeds which are used as a standard weight for gold (*app* 1½ to 2 grams), either from a tree, – *pohon* red sandalwood, *Adenanthera pavonina/microsperma/bicolor,* or from a shrub, – *biji/betina* Chinese red bean, *Abrus pecatorius.* 2 red, bloodshot (of the eyes). *bak/seperti (biji)* – as red as a beet, fiery red, scarlet (blush/cheeks). *Wajah Fatimah mérah* –. Fatimah's face turned scarlet. *seperti – di atas talam* unstable behavior. *yang mérah* –, *yang kurik kundi* good manners, not appearance or face, are important. – *gajah* a larger *saga* variety with larger fruit, *Pithecellobium ellipticum.*

saga II (*D*) saga.

sagai (*ikan* –) horse-mackerel, long-finned trevally, jackfish, *Caranx armatus/gallus* and thread-fin jack, *Alectis indica.*

sagang I prop, support, (gun)rack, buttress.

    menyagang 1 to prop up, lean s.t. *Prajurit itu* ~ *senjatanya pada témbok.* The soldier propped his gun up against the wall. 2 to support s.t. with a piece of wood, etc. in a slanted position.

    tersagang propped up, supported, buttressed.

sagang II menyagang 1 to hold, take hold of. 2 to ward off, parry. *Ia* ~ *senjata lawannya dengan cekatan.* He parried his adversary's weapon skillfully. 3 to deflect.

sagar I palm leaf rib (from which writing pens/fish traps, etc. are made). – *jantan* a large round pen made from this rib.

    bersagar 1 with a palm leaf rib. 2 to use a palm leaf rib. *ijuk tidak* ~ a family which has no male children who are respected by others.

    menyagar 1 to fasten, pin, attach. *Karena tiada peniti,* ~ *dengan lidi pun jadi.* Because there's no safety pin, a palm leaf rib will also do to fasten it. 2 to become as hard as a palm leaf rib.

sagar II sugar; → SAKAR I.

sage → SAGA II.

sagir (*A*) small.

Sagitarius Sagittarius (*zod*).

sago → SAGU I.

sagon → SAGUN.

sagor → SAGUR.

sagotra (*Hind*) type of heirs according to Hinduism.

sagu I sago, pith of certain palm trees, *esp* of *rumbia* or sago palm, *Metroxylon spp., kabung* or sugar palm, *Arenga saccharifera. tepung* – sago flour. *pohon* – sago palm, *Metroxylon sagu.* – *belanda/betawi* arrowroot, *Maranta arundacea,* and the starch derived from it. – *moté* sago made into colored beads for use in porridge. – *pisang* starch made from the banana stem. – *rendang* the coarser ordinary sago. – *tampin* packet-sago (wrapped in *pandan* leaves), i.e., pearl sago (a commodity). – *tepung* tapioca.

    menyagu 1 to make sago. 2 (*coq*) to starch s.t. using sago.

    sagu-saguan plants of the sago family.

sagu II – *hati* a) money, etc. given as compensation. b) money, etc. given in appreciation for a service, bonus. *Para pengurus kapal ferry ini biasanya lebih senang memberikan – hati daripada harus terapung-apung diayun gelombang selama pemeriksaan hingga banyak penumpang yang mabuk.* The management of this ferryboat is usually happy to distribute money rather than float around tossed about by the waves during (customs) inspection so that many passengers become seasick. *hadiah – hati* consolation prize.

sagu III code name for narcotic powder.

saguér and **saguir** (*Min*) k.o. palm wine.

sagun(-sagun) a type of food made of rice flour fried with grated coconut and mixed with sugar (sometimes also with eggs).

sagur *perahu* – a river craft, dugout.

sah I (*A*) **1** valid, legal, lawful, rightful, done correctly (of a prayer, etc.). – *menurut hukumnya* judicially correct. *tidak* – a) illegal, unlawful. *transfer secara tidak* – illegal/unauthorized transfer. b) illegitimate (of a child), dishonestly (obtained goods, etc.). **2** genuine, authentic, authoritative, real, true. **3** reliable, trustworthy (news). **4** (officially) recognized/accepted. **5** to be realized/fulfilled/borne out, come to fulfillment (of a *bidal*). **6** convincing/persuasive (evidence, etc.). **7** original (document, such as a birth certificate, etc.). – *tanda* certification. **mensahtandakan** to certify.

sahnya properly; should be. *demi ~* on/under penalty of, under liability of.

mensahkan, meng(e)sahkan and (*infr*) **mengenyahkan 1** to confirm, sanction, approve. *disahkan (pen)corétan dua perkataan* (in the margin of notarial instruments) the deletion of two words is approved. **2** to recognize/acknowledge officially, grant official recognition to, authorize. **3** to legalize, certify, ratify, authenticate, validate, uphold (a decision); → MERESMIKAN. *~ menjadi undang-undang* to enact into law. **4** to affirm.

kesahan legality.

pengesah confirmatory, of confirmation.

pengesahan and **pensahan 1** confirmation, approval. **2** authorization, ratification, legalization, validation, authentication, endorsement.

sah II → SYAH I.

sahabat (*A*) **1** friend, comrade, companion; → KAWAN, TEMAN, SOBAT. – *Bumi* Friends of the Earth, an environmental protection organization. – *kandung/karib/kental* close friend. – *Nabi* the Prophet Muhammad's disciples. – *péna* pen pal. – *Satwa* Friends of the Zoo, an organization devoted to protecting wildlife. **2** disciple, those who were alive during Muhammad's lifetime. – *Nabi* disciples of Muhammad.

bersahabat 1 to be on friendly terms. **2** friendly, amiable. *tidak ~* unfriendly, hostile. *bersifat tidak ~* with an unfriendly nature. *tindak tidak ~* an unfriendly act. *~ dengan* to be friends with, associate with, go around with (people), rub shoulders with. *~ lagi* to make up (of friends who had been estranged).

mempersahabatkan to introduce s.o. (to).

sahabatan to be friends (with).

persahabatan friendship.

sahadat → SYAHADAT.

sahaja I → SAJA.

sahaja II intentionally, on purpose; → SENGAJA.

menyahajakan and **mempersahajakan** to do s.t. intentionally/on purpose.

sahaja III simple, natural, unaffected. *Makin – makin élok parasnya.* The simpler she is, the nicer she looks. – *basahan* to become one's second nature to do s.t. bad.

bersahaja simple, unaffected (dress, style), plain (food). **kebersahajaan** simplicity, simpleness, plainness, lack of affectation.

menyahaja to do s.t. deliberately.

menyahajakan, mempersahajakan, and **membersahajakan** (*infr*) to simplify, make plain/unaffected.

kesahajaan simplicity, simpleness, plainness.

persahajaan simplification.

saham (*A*) **1** part, role, share. *mempunyai* – to take part, play a role, have a share. *Pengaruh agama Hindu, Jawa, Sunda, Tiongkok dan agama Islam mempunyai – yang besar dalam prosés pem-* *bentukan budaya masyarakat Cirebon.* The influence of the Hindu, Javanese, Sundanese, and Chinese religions and of Islam has had a large share in the formation of the culture of Cirebon society. **2** contribution (of thoughts, etc.). **3** share, stock. *menjual – kepada masyarakat* to go public (of a corporation, etc.). *pemegang* – shareholder. – *atas nama* registered stock. – *atas penunjuk/tunjuk/unjuk* bearer stock. – *bagian* share. – *berhak suara/bersuara* voting stock. – *biasa* common stock. – *belum lunas* partly paid shares. – *bonus* bonus share. – *(dalam) blangko* bearer stock. – *dalam portepél* share in portfolio, unissued shares. – *diam* non-voting stock. – *ditempatkan* issued stock. – *élite* blue chip (stock). – *istiméwa* preferred stock. – *jempol* growth stock. – *kepada pembawa* bearer stock. – *lunas* fully paid stock. – *modal* capital stock. – *pendiri* founders stock. – *penggal* split share. – *perséroan* corporation stock. –.– *perséroan adalah* –.– *atas nama* corporation shares are registered shares. – *préférén* preferred stock. – *prioritas* preferred stock. – *tanpa nama* and – *tidak bernama* stock to bearer. – *terdaftar* registered stock. – *unggul(an)* blue chip stock. – *utama* preferred stock. – *utama timbun* cumulative preferred stock. – *yang dicap* assented shares. – *yang ditukarkan* assented stock. – *yang sudah ditempatkan* issued shares.

bersaham with shares.

pesaham shareholder; → PEMEGANG *saham.*

sahan (*A*) platter, plate, dish.

sahang (*K ob*) pepper, *Piper nigrum.*

sahap (*M*) **1** cover (of a cooking pot, etc.), lid (of a box, etc.), cap, door (in some compounds); → TUTUP. **2** (funeral) pall. *kaca* – cover glass.

bersahap covered, veiled, lidded.

menyahap to cover, put a lid on.

sahar (*A*) dawn.

sahara (*A*) **1** desert. **2** the Sahara, i.e., the vast desert region in North Africa.

saharah (*A*) large chest (for rice, etc.).

sahaya (*Skr cla*) **1** (household) slave, servant. *hamba* – serfs and slaves. **2** → SAYA.

sahayanda (*Skr cla*) your humble servant.

sahbandar → SYAHBANDAR.

sahda(h) and **sahdu** → SYAHDU.

sahdan → SYAHDAN.

sahi I (*A ob*) careless, thoughtless, negligent.

sahi II (*A J ob*) k.o. strong, aromatic tea.

sahi III (*ikan* –) skate.

sahib (*A*) (*esp* in compounds) possessor, owner, proprietor.

sahibulbait (*A*) host; → TUAN *rumah.*

sahibulhikayat (*A*) the (*usu* unknown) author (of the story; the author's "we"; historian. *Kata* – ... the story has it that ..., the story goes. *Namun, kata* –, *pada suatu hari, seorang PPP mengungkapkan sebuah cita-cita.* However, the story goes, one day a member of the PPP revealed one of their ideals.

sahid → SYAHID.

sahifah (*A*) written page; document.

sahih (*A*) **1** valid, authentic, genuine. **2** stainless, faultless, without fault. **3** perfect. **4** certain, proved, true (of a tradition).

tersahih the most authentic.

kesahihan 1 validity, authenticity. **2** accuracy.

penyahihan validation, authentification.

sahir → SIHIR.

sahkan clipped form of *usahkan* let alone that.

sahmura (*cla*) k.o. precious stone.

sahnio 120-gram package of morphine (sold clandestinely).

sahsiah (*A*) personality, individuality.

sahur (*A*) meal taken between midnight and dawn during the fasting month of *Ramadan*; → SAUR.

bersahur to eat this meal.

sahut /*usu* saut/ answer, reply (to a call or question). *"Betul," – si Amir.* "Right," answered Amir.

bersahut to answer, reply. *Sudah beberapa kali ia dipanggil, tetapi tidak juga ~.* He was called several times, but still no answer.

bersahut(-sahut)an to exchange words, respond to e.o. *bernyanyi*

~ to sing to e.o. ~ *cakap/kata/mulut* to hold an animated conversation.

menyahut [and **nyahut** (*coq*)] to answer, reply. *Saya ~, maka saya ada.* I answer therefore I am. *Tidak ada yang ~.* There's no answer (on the telephone).

sahut-menyahut to answer e.o., exchange words, etc. *Di kejauhan terdengar bunyi jangkerik ~.* In the distance the sound of crickets responding to e.o. could be heard.

menyahuti to respond to, answer.

sahutan answer, reply, response. *Kasno mengetuk pintu, tak ada ~.* Kasno knocked at the door, but there was no response.

penyahutan answering, responding, replying.

sahwat → SYAHWAT.

sai I (*A*) /sa'i/ the ritual walk back and forth seven times between Mt. Shafa and Mt. Marwah.

sai II (*coq*) → SAY.

said (*A*) **1** title given to male descendants of the Prophet. **2** an Arab descendant of the Prophet.

saidani (*A ob*) the two Lords, *Hasan* and *Hussain.*

Saidi (*A*) *ya ~!* O Lord!

saidina (*A*) master, title of the Prophet, his four companions, Muslim rulers and missionaries.

saif (*A*) sword. *-ullah* sword of God. *-uddin* sword of religion. *-ulislam* sword of Islam.

saikéiréi (*Jp*) to bow in honor of the Japanese Emperor; obligatory on all public occasions during the Japanese occupation in World War II.

saikosikikan (*Jp*) Supreme Commander.

Sailan (*A ob*) Sri Lanka, Ceylon.

saimah (*A*) livestock.

saing I equal, match, peer; rival. *perang –* competition. *perang – karét sintétik* the competition of synthetic rubber.

bersaing 1 to have an equal. *tak ~* matchless, unequaled, unparalleled. **2** to compete (with e.o.), be rivals, be competitive. *harga ~* competitive price(s). *~ melawan* to run against (s.o. in an election).

bersaingan 1 to compete (with e.o.), be rivals. *harga ~* competitive price(s). **2** unsecured (of a creditor or loan).

menyaingi [and **nyaingin** (*J coq*)] **1** to compete with, rival, emulate, match. **2** to beat, do better than, surpass. *Anda tidak bisa ~nya.* You can't beat him. *Ia ~ saya dalam ilmu pasti.* He beat me in math. *Tidak ada yang ~ makanan masakan sendiri.* Nothing beats home-cooked meals.

saing-menyaingi to compete with e.o.

mempersaingkan 1 to play ... off against e.o. **2** to compete for. *hal yang patut dipersaingkan* s.t. worth competing for.

tersaingi can be competed with/for. *tidak ~* a) unequaled, matchless, unparalleled. b) unchallenged (in an election). *Pemuda itu tidak ~ dalam mata pelajaran aljabar.* That young man excels in algebra.

saingan 1 competition, rivalry. **2** competitor, rival.

pesaing and **penyaing** competitor, rival.

persaingan competition, contest, rivalry, race. *~ bébas* laissez faire. *~ culas* unfair competition. *~ curang* unfair competition. *~ damai berkelanjutan* peaceful sustained competition. *~ séhat* healthy competition. *~ sempurna* pure competition. *~ tidak jujur/séhat/wajar* unfair competition.

saing II sesaing (*M*) the one beside/next to the other. *rumah ~* duplex consisting of two houses with a common wall.

bersaing to walk/sail side by side.

saing III (*M*) tusk (of an elephant/wild boar, etc.), fang (of a wolf, etc.).

saing-menyaing to bite e.o.

sains (*E*) (natural) science(s). *- fiksi* science fiction; → FIKSI *ilmiah.*

saintifik (*E*) scientific. *risét –* scientific research.

saintis (*E*) scientist.

saintisme (*D*) scientism.

sair I → SYAIR.

sair II (*A*) hellfire.

sais (*A Hind*) **1** coachman, cabby. **2** (disc) jockey. *- disko* disc jockey; → PERAMU *irama.*

persaisan jockey (*mod*). *bidang ~ disko* the field of disc jockeys.

sait → SAYAT I.

saja (*Skr*) **1** only, merely, solely; → CUMA, HANYA. *itu –* only that, nothing but that. **2** (following a number) only, just, no more than. *ambil dua –* take only two. *Berapa orang ada di situ? Seorang –.* How many people were there? Only one. *Sebutkan nama ikan sepuluh –.* Just name ten kinds of fish. **3** instead (of some alternative), just. *Saya takut, ayo pulang –!* I'm scared, come on, let's just go home (instead of going on). *Begini –!* (Just) like this! *Begitu –?* Is that all (there is to it)? *begitu-begitu –* in any old way. *Bila tidak, besar kemungkinannya kegiatan kepramukaan akan begitu-begitu –.* If not, there is a good possibility that scouting activities will just be carried out any old way. *Bilang –!* Just say it! *Saya pergi –.* I'll just go. *Tentu –!* Sure! Of course! **4** (indefinite) any ..., every ... *apa –* anything, everything. *Ia makan apa –.* He ate everything. *siapa –* whoever, everyone, anyone. *siapa – yang mau boléh datang* anyone who wants to can come. *bagaimana – in any way. *Itu bisa dipasang bagaimana –.* That can be installed in any way (you want). *Kapan-kapan – boléh datang ke rumah.* You can come to see me any time you like. *ada-ada –* he always has some new trick up his sleeve, he always has s.t. to say (when he shouldn't). *ada-ada – yang –* there's always s.o. who ... **5** (after question words, asks a question which expects a plural answer) (in some English dialects) ... all? *Siapa – yang datang?* Who (all) came? *Apa – yang dikerjakannya di situ?* What (all) did he do there? **6** (not) even. *Menjelaskan – tidak bisa.* He can't even explain (it). **7** anyway.

sajadah (*A*) prayer mat/rug.

sajak I (*A*) **1** rhyme. **2** meter. **3** poem, verse. **4** harmony. *- akhir* end rhyme. *- anak-anak* nursery rhyme. *- bébas* free verse. *- dalam* internal rhyme. *- percintaan* love poem. *- ratap* elegy. *- ...dalam seuntai* verse with ... lines in each stanza.

bersajak 1 to rhyme. **2** to be in rhyming form (of poetry). **3** to recite poetry. **4** to harmonize, be well-matched.

menyajak 1 to write poetry. **2** to rhyme.

menyajakkan to put into rhyme.

penyajak poet.

persajakan poetry.

sajak II (*Jv*) *-nya* as if, as it were, so to speak.

sajam [senjata tajam] blades, sharp weapons.

sajang (*ob*) spirits, arrack.

sajarah → SEJARAH.

Sajdah (*A*) *as-* "Prostration"; name of the 32nd chapter of the Koran.

sajén (*Jv*) an offering set out to appease the spirits.

sesajén to place an offering (of food, flowers, etc.) out.

saji I dish, food (presented/offered/served). *cepat –* fast food. *tudung –* dish cover (to prevent insects from getting into the food).

bersaji to make a sacrifice/offering.

menyajikan [and **nyajiin** (*J coq*)] **1** to serve (food). *Nyonya rumah ~ téh panas.* The hostess served hot tea. **2** to present, put on (a show, etc.). *Band itu ~ musik rok.* The band played rock music. *Mode terakhir akan disajikan kepada publik.* The latest fashions will be shown to the public. **3** to supply, provide, submit (articles for a magazine/newspaper, etc.). **4** to raise, bring up (problems, etc.), set forth.

tersaji served, presented, offered.

tersajikan served up. *méja makan yang telah ~ makanan di atasnya* a dining table on which the food was served up.

sajian 1 dish (offered). *Tamu mulai makan ~ itu.* The guests began to eat the food (that had been served). **2** presentation, performance. *~ tarian* dance performance.

penyaji 1 presenter, introducer (of exhibition, show, program, etc.). *~ makalah* presenter of a working paper. **2** server. **3** s.t. that serves up s.t. *~ informasi* source of information.

penyajian offer, offering, presentation.

persajian serving.

saji II *- balik* playback. *- ulang* replay.

sak I (*D*) **1** pocket. **2** bag (for cement, etc.); → ZAK.

sak II → SYAK.

sak- III (*Jv*) → SE-. *Saya -.keluarga.* My family and I. *-.a(m)breg-a(m)breg* **1** lots of. **2** in great numbers. *- bodo aja* who cares? It doesn't matter. *-.deksaknyet* instantly, all at once. *-.énak udelé déwé* at will, as one pleases; → *seénak* UDELNYA *sendiri. -. ini* now. *–.jagat* all over the world. *–.madya* (proper) moderation in living with what one has.

saka I 1 (clipped form of *pusaka*) heirloom, inheritance, estate (on the mother's side). **2** (*M*) family, relatives (on the mother's side). *Sang – (Mérah Putih)* Indonesia's Heirloom (and Venerated) Bicolor (Red and White Flag).

saka II (*Jv*) /soko/ pillar supporting a roof. *– guru* and **sakaguru 1** (originally) the four central pillars of a traditional Javanese house. **2** pillar (in general). **3** leader, leading figure.

saka III [satuan karya] Work Unit in the *Pramuka* Scout Movement. *– Bahari* Sea Work Unit. *– Bakti Husada* Health Care Work Unit. *– Bayangkara* Police Work Unit. *– Dirgantara* Air Work Unit. *– Wanabakti* Forestry Work Unit.

Saka IV (*Jv*) Javanese king whose reign began in A.D. 78 and the inventor of the Javanese calendar called *tahun –*, which begins in that year.

sakadang appellation for animals in folktales.

Sakai I an ethnic group of the Riau Archipelago and Malacca.

sakai II dependents, retainers, subjects.

sakal I contrary (of wind). *angin –* headwind.

sakal II blow, knock, slap, hit; mistreatment. *kena –* got hit.
　menyakal to hit, knock; to mistreat.

sakala concrete, material; *opp* NISKALA.

Sakalin Sakhalin, an island off the SE coast of the former Soviet Union.

sakalor (*S*) epidemic.

sakan big and sturdy. *akik/batu –* k.o. gemstone (from Bangka) which has magic power and which gives its owner courage.

sakang many, numerous.

sakap menyakap [and **nyakap** (*coq*)] to sharecrop.
　menyakapkan to lease out land on a sharecropping basis.
　sakapan sharecropped (land, crop).
　penyakap sharecropper.
　penyakapan sharecropping.

sakar I (*Pers*) sugar; → GULA. *– anggur* glucose. *– buah* fructose. *– darah* blood sugar. *– emping* maltose; → MALTOSA. *– nabati* sugar from plants. *– susu* lactose. *– susu muda* galactose.

sakar II (*M*) samun *– robbery with violence.
　menyakar to rob (with violence).
　penyakar robber.

sakar III (*A*) hell, hellfire.

sakarat → SEKARAT.

sakaratulmaut (*A*) → SAKRATULMAUT.

sakarida (*D*) saccharide.

sakarin (*D/E*) saccharine.

sakarosa (*D*) saccharose.

sakat I various species of epiphytes; → BENALU, PASILAN. *– batu* k.o. fern, *Cyclophorus adnascens*. *– bawang* k.o. epiphyte, *Acriopsis javanica*. *– belimbing* k.o. orchid, *Thecostele sp. – bunga* k.o. epiphyte, *Dendrobium glumaceum? – hitam* k.o. fern. *– lidah buaya* k.o. orchid, *Oberonia anceps*. *– ribu-ribu* k.o. tree fern, *Drymoglossum piloselloides*. *– sarang langsuir* k.o. epiphyte, *Cyclophorus spp. – tanduk rusa* stag horn fern, *Platycerium spp. – tulang ular* necklace orchid, *Coelogyne rochussenii*. *– ular* k.o. orchid, *Sarcanthus secundus*.

sakat II hindrance, obstruction, annoyance, difficulty.
　menyakat(kan) to tease, annoy, trouble, bother; → MENGGANGGU.
　tersakat bothered, troubled.
　penyakat bother, trouble.

sakat III menyakatkan (*naut*) to run (a boat) aground, beach.
　tersakat run aground, beached. *Perahu itu ~ di pulau karang.* The prau ran aground on a coral reef.

sakat IV → SUKU-SAKAT.

sakau(w) (*Pr from sakit?*) suffering from withdrawal symptoms (from lack of narcotics).

sakduk (*D*) handkerchief; → SAPUTANGAN.

saké (*Jp*) sake, a fermented rice drink.

sakelar (*D*) (electric) switch. *– tuas/ungkit* tumbler switch. *– untuk pemanfaat* appliance switch.

sakelat → SEKELAT.

sakelek → SAKLEK.

sakhalat → SEKELAT.

sakhariméter → SAKARIMÉTER.

sakharin → SAKARIN.

sakharosa → SAKAROSA.

sakhawat (*A*) generosity.

sakhi (*A*) generous.

sakhlat (*ob*) → SEKELAT.

sakhrat (*A*) rock, stone.

saki I → SAKÉ.

saki II (*Skr ob*) comrade, friend.

saki III *– baki* remainder, balance.

saki IV trash basket.

sakin (*coq*) → SEMAKIN.

sakinah and **sakinat** (*A*) **1** safe, peaceful. *keluarga –* (in planned parenthood) a small, happy, and prosperous family; → MAWADDAH. **2** a safe and peaceful place, haven.

saking (*J/Jv*) due to, because of, on account of. *Ia terdiam – bingungnya.* He fell silent because he felt confused. *– sembrononya* because of his carelessness.

sakit I 1 sick, ill, unwell. *– apa?* what are you sick with? what sickness do you have? *jangan pikir banyak, jangan sampai –* don't rack your brains about it. *jatuh –* to get sick, fall ill. *orang/si –* the patient, sick person. **2** pain, hurt, ache; it hurts. **3** to have the ... (disease), have a ... ache. *– flu* to have the flu. *Jangan bikin – orang lain.* Don't harm others. *– apa?* Where does it hurt? *Apa yang –?* Where does it hurt (you)? What hurts? *lain – lain diobat, lain luka lain dibebat* there's neither rhyme nor reason to it; it doesn't make any sense. *biar – dahulu senang kemudian* every cloud has a silver lining. *– menimpa, sesal terlambat* it's no use crying over spilt milk, what's done cannot be undone; → NASI *sudah menjadi bubur. tiada –, makan obat* to bring a hornet's nest down around one's ears. [THE FOLLOWING COMPOUNDS MEAN BOTH THE DISEASE AND TO SUFFER FROM THAT DISEASE] *– abuh* (*Jv*) dropsy; edema. *– akal* of unsound mind. *– angan-angan* not quite right in the head. *– asma* asthma. *penderita – asma* and *orang yang – asma* asthmatic. *– baka* mumps, struma. *– batuk kering* tuberculosis, TB. *– beranak* labor pains. *– bulanan* menstrual cramps. *– cahar* diarrhea; → DIARÉ. *– céléng* epilepsy; → PENYAKIT *ayan. – dada* tuberculosis. *– datang bulan* menstruation, period; → MÉNS. *– gajah-gajahan* elephantiasis. *– gembur-gembur* dropsy. *– gigi* toothache. *– gula* diabetes; → DIABÉTES. *– hati* a) annoyed, irritated. b) offended, hurt. c) sad, sorrowful. *melepaskan – hati kepada* to take revenge on. *– hosa* (*Pap*) asthma. *– hulu* (*ob*) headache. *– hulu hati* difficulty breathing. *– ingatan* insane, crazy. *– ingus* (horse) glanders. *– jantung* heart disease (of all kinds). *– jerih* short-winded. *– jiwa* insane, crazy. *– kantong* (*coq*) broke, out of money. *– karang* renal calculus, kidney stone. *– kepala* headache. *– kelintasan* a folk belief that if a young child dies, all other young children (up to 3, 5, or 7) will also die; if a parent dies, another parent will also die. *– keputihan* leucorrhea. *– kermi* to have intestinal worms. *– kuku dan mulut* (cattle) foot-and-mouth disease. *– kuning* hepatitis, jaundice. *– lambung* gastralgia. *– léver/liver* liver disease. *– malaria* malaria. *– mangga* swelling in the groin. *– menyebar* diffuse pain. *– napas* asthmatic. *– otak* crazy. *– panas* fever. *– paru(-paru)* tuberculosis, TB. *– pat(h)ék* yaws, framboesia. *– payah* seriously ill. *– perempuan* venereal disease. *– perut* upset stomach (indigestion/diarrhea, etc.). *– pikiran* insane, crazy. *– pinggang dan pegal* lumbago. *– punggung* to have a backache. *– radang* inflammation. *– raja* gonorrhea. *– rejan* stomachache accompanied by diarrhea. *– sabun* gonorrhea. *– sangat* seriously ill. *– senéwén/sinu* nervous disorder. *– tampak/tampek* to have the measles. *– telinga* to have an earache. *– tenggorokan* to have a sore throat. *– teruk* seriously ill. *– tua* illnesses relating to old age. *– tujuh keliling* (*J*) vertigo, dizziness.

sakit-sakit *dalam ~, ~ saja* and *sudah ~* sickly, ailing. **sesakit-sakit** no matter how ill/hurt.

bersakit *~ hati* to feel resentful (toward s.o.).

bersakit-sakit 1 to do one's best, toil away, work one's fingers to the bone, work hard at s.t. **2** to be ailing, sickly.

bersakit-sakitan to be ailing/sickly/in poor health. *Manusia yang*

~ tidak akan memiliki gairah hidup. A sickly person doesn't have the will to live.

menyakit to cause pain, make s.o. feel bad. *Segala caci maki tidak ~ padanya.* Insults don't make him feel bad.

menyakiti [and **nyakitin** (*J coq*)] 1 to torture, torment, plague, pester; to hurt, offend, injure. *Janganlah suka mengganggu dan ~ orang lain.* Don't enjoy teasing and torturing others. *~ hati* to hurt, offend. *Saya tidak sanggup ~ hati anda.* I can't hurt you. 2 (*ob*) to be in labor.

mempersakiti to torture, torment, plague, pester; to hurt, offend, injure.

menyakitkan 1 to pain, hurt, cause pain to. *Ucapannya yang pedas itu sangat ~ hati orang itu.* His sharp words hurt that person very much. 2 to feel hurt over s.t.

tersakit most painful, sickest.

sakitan (*coq*) more painful.

sakit-sakitan → BERSAKIT-SAKITAN.

kesakitan 1 (to be) in pain, suffer. *Ia menjerit ~.* He screamed in pain. 2 pain, trouble, torment.

pesakit (*BD*) patient (in hospital, etc.).

penyakit 1 disease, illness. *hama-hama ~* pathogenic germs/bacteria. *ilmu ~* pathology. *ilmu ~ kulit* dermatology. *ilmu ~ saraf* neurology. 2 physical disorder. *~ lelah* exhaustion, fatigue. 3 drawback, defect, problem, bad aspect of s.t. or s.o., bad habit. *Mobil itu banyak ~nya.* This car has a lot of problems. *Suka membual itulah yang menjadi ~nya.* His problem is his bragging. 4 bastard, louse, stinker, pain in the ass. *~, pergi kau!* beat it, you bastard! FOR OTHER ILLNESSES THAN THOSE LISTED BELOW, SEE THE WORD FOLLOWING *PENYA-KIT*. *~ anjing gila* rabies. *~ Apollo* a disease whose symptoms include bleeding from the cornea. *~ asam urat* gout. *~ ayan* epilepsy. *bang* brucellosis. *~ batu* (kidney) stones. *~ batuk kering* tuberculosis, TB. *~ beguk* struma, scrofula. *~ bengék* asthma. *~ bengok* goiter. *~ bercak daun* leaf spot disease. *~ biduren* (*Jv*) urticaria, hives. *~ buah pinggang* nephritis. *~ budug* (*Jv*) k.o. leprosy with swellings. *~ busuk akar* root rot disease. *~ busuk léhér* rice blast caused by a fungus, *Pyricularia oryzae*. *~ busung lapar* malnutrition. *~ cabuk putih* mildew (of apple trees). *~ cacar téh* blister blight, a disease of tea-shrubs. *~ cacar daun* fillustecta, a disease of clove plants. *~ cacing tambang* hookworm, ancylostomasis. *~ dalam* internal disease. *ahli ~ dalam* internist. *~ darah putih* leukemia. *~ demam kéong* schistosomiasis, disease caused by liver flukes. *~ dua bahasa* saying one thing but meaning another. *~ éltor* eltor, k.o. cholera. *embun tepung* powdery mildew disease. *- gajah* elephantiasis. *~ gatal-gatal "a go-go"* scabies. *~ gemuk* obesity. *~ gériatrik* geriatric disorder. *~ gila* lunacy. *~ GO* gonorrhea. *~ gondok* mumps. *~ gondongan* (*Jv*) goiter. *~ gudig* (*Jv*) torrhea. *~ hari senin* Monday-morning blues, i.e., reluctance to go back to work after a weekend. *~ inggris* rickets. *~ jamur karat* rust disease. *~ jembrana* cattle plague. *~ jirian* spermatorrhea. *~ kaki gajah* elephantiasis. *~ kanker batang* stem canker disease. *~ kanker darah* leukemia. *~ karang* (kidney) stones. *~ kegemukan* obesity. *~ kekurangan vitamin* avitaminosis, vitamin-deficiency disease. *~ kelamin* venereal disease. *~ kelingsir* scrotal hernia. *~ kencing manis* diabetes. *~ keputihan* discharge. *~ keluron* (*Jv*) disease related to miscarriage. *~ keturunan* hereditary disease. *~ koléra* cholera. *~ koro* stress-related temporary impotence. *~ kotor* venereal disease. *~ kronis* chronic illness. *~ krumut* smallpox. *~ kuku* hoof disease. *~ lanas* black-shank disease (of tobacco). *~ larat* syphilis. *~ layu* wilt. *~ léna* sleeping sickness. *~ lezat* (*ob*) venereal disease, VD. *~ lodoh* damping off (a disease of trees). *~ lumpuh separuh* hemiplegia. *~ lupa* amnesia; → AMNÉSI(A). *~ mati bujang* (*esp* in West Sumatra) "Sumatra disease" (of clove plants). *~ mati ranting* dieback (a fungal disease of clove plants). *~ menular* infectious disease. *~ menular séksual* [PMS] sexually transmitted disease, STD. *~ mérah* k.o. infantile rash. *~ mulut dan kuku* foot-and-mouth disease, FMD, *Aphtea epizootica*, AE. *~ mubeng* (*Jv*) surra. *~ mulut kuku* foot-and-mouth disease, FMD. *~ naik-naik* shortness of breath. *~ ngabeng* surra, a fatal infectious disease of cows, water buffaloes, and goats. *~ ngantuk* sleepiness,

wanting to sleep all the time. *~ ngorok* k.o. disease, hemorrhagic septicemia, *Septicemia epizootica*, SE. *~ nikmat* venereal disease. *~ orang kaya* (*coq*) hypertension, high blood pressure. *~ panggung* stage fright. *~ pangkal batang* foot rot, phytophtara. *~ paru(-paru)* pulmonary disease. *~ péktai* discharge, leucorrhoea. *~ pelupa* forgetfulness. *~ pengerasan pembuluh nadi* arteriosclerosis, hardening of the arteries. *~ perut membuncit* schistosomiasis, disease caused by a liver fluke. *~ pipi gemuk* goiter. *~ pitam* apoplexy, stroke. *~ psikosomatik* psychosomatic disease. *~ puru* psoriasis. *~ radang* inflammation. *~ radang kelenjar susu* mastitis. *~ radang limpa* anthrax (of cattle). *~ radang otak* encephalitis. *~ radang sinus* sinusitis. *~ radang paha* blackleg, *Gangrenosa temphysematosa*. *~ rama déwa* cattle plague. *~ saluran pencernaan* disease of the digestive tract, gastroenteritis. *~ sendi* arthritis. *~ sentrap-sentrup* cold, catarrh. *~ sikil gajah* (*Jv*) elephantiasis. *~ sindrom kehilangan kekebalan* AIDS. *~ sosial* social ill. *~ tampak* measles. *~ tekanan darah tinggi* hypertension, high blood pressure. *tétélo* Newcastle disease, N.D. *~ tidur* encephalitis. *~ tropis* tropical disease. *~ tua* infirmities of old age. *~ (dalam) tulang* arthritis. *~ tujuh keliling* (*Jv*) vertigo, dizziness. *~ usia lanjut* degenerative disease (of old age). *~ usus buntu* appendicitis. *~ waham kebesaran* megalomania. *~ yang ditimbulkan akibat pemakaian obat* drug-induced disease. **berpenyakit** to have the ... disease. *~ saraf* to suffer from a nervous disorder.

penyakitan and **berpenyakitan** to be sick all the time, be ailing, sickly. *Pegawai pénsiunan itu sudah gaék dan ~.* That retired employee is old and sickly.

persakitan 1 morbidity. 2 troubles, problems.

sakit II pesakitan 1 the accused. 2 prisoner, inmate.

saklar → SAKELAR.

saklek (*D*) business-like, pragmatic.

sakral (*D*) sacred, sacral. *tidak -* not sacred. **menidaksakralkan** to desanctify.

menyakralkan to sanctify, make sacred. *Pancasila perlu disakralkan. Pancasila* must be made sacred.

kesakralan sanctification, sacredness.

penyakralan sanctifying, making sacred.

sakramén (*D*) sacrament. *- Perminyakan* Extreme Unction. *memberkati - Minyak Suci* to administer Extreme Unction to. *menurut -* sacramental.

sakraméntal (*E*) sacramental.

sakrat → SEKARAT.

sakratulmaut (*A*) death agony/struggles. *puncak -* the peak of one's death agony.

sakristi (*D*) sacristy.

saksama (*Skr*) 1 accurate, meticulous, exact, precise. 2 patient, persevering, persistent. 3 thorough (investigation, etc.), close (observation, etc.).

kesaksamaan 1 exactness, precision, accuracy. 2 patience, perseverance, persistence.

saksang pork cooked with blood and spices.

saksi (*Skr*) 1 witness. *bukti -* evidence provided by a witness. *huruf -* vowels used in the Malayo-Arabic/Jawi script. *menjadi/naik -* to appear as a witness, give evidence, take the witness stand (in court). *uang -* conduct money. *satu - bukan -* "unus testis nullus testis," one witness is no witness, i.e., is insufficient evidence. 2 testimony. 3 second (at a duel). *- à charge* /a syars/ witness for the prosecution. *- à décharge* /a désyars/ witness for the defense. *- ahli* expert witness. *- alibi* witness who provides an alibi for the accused. *- baptisan* a) sponsor. b) godfather, godmother. *- bisu* silent witness. *- bohong/buatan/dengkul/dusta* false witness. *- hidup* living witness. *Saya adalah salah seorang - hidup yang melihat ...* I was one of the living witnesses who saw ... *- kenal* known witness. *- kunci* key witness. *- lelaki* best man (at a wedding). *- mahkota* witness for the prosecution. *- mata* eye witness. *- memberatkan* witness for the prosecution. *- palsu* false witness. *- pelemah* (*infr*) witness for the defense. *- pemberat* witness for the prosecution. *- pengenal* witness as to identity. *- penuduh* witness for the prosecution. *- perempuan* bridesmaid, maid of honor (at a wedding). *- peringan* witness for the defense. *- sah* legal witness. *- syak* questionable witness.

– yang memberatkan witness for the prosecution. *– yang meringankan* witness for the defense.

bersaksi 1 with a witness or witnesses, made with a witness, witnessed. **2** to appear as a witness, testify. **3** to appeal to s.o. or s.t. as witness/proof. **4** to have a best man or bridesmaid (at a wedding). *~ ke laut* to call a friend/one's relative as a witness. *~ ke lutut* to ask advice from a stupid person.

bersaksikan to call on … as one's witness.

menyaksikan and **mempersaksikan** [and **nyaksiin** (*J coq*)] **1** to witness. **2** to watch. *~ pertunjukan TV* to watch a TV show. **3** to ascertain, see for o.s. **4** to demonstrate, show.

tersaksikan (could be) witnessed/seen. *Yang ~ adalah semacam histéria massal.* A k.o. mass hysteria could be seen.

kesaksian 1 testimony, deposition. *memberikan ~* to testify (as to), give evidence/testimony (as to), make a deposition (as to). *~ yang diberikan Létkol Djudju itu bertentangan dengan keterangan empat orang – lainnya ketika dilaga.* The testimony given by Lieut. Col. Djudju was in contradiction to the statement made by the four witnesses when they were confronted. *~ dari pendengaran* hearsay evidence. *~ di bawah sumpah* affidavit, sworn testimony. **2** bearing witness, professing one's faith.

pesaksi (*geol*) outlier.

penyaksi witness. *~ mata* eyewitness.

penyaksian testimony, deposition, evidence.

persaksian testimony. *~ bumi dan langit* to swear by heaven and earth.

saksofon (*D/E*) saxophone.

saksofonis (*D*) saxophone player.

Sakson (*E*) Saxon.

saksrak (*S*) **menyaksrak** and **nyaksrak** to search for s.t. all over, look for a way to make a living.

sakti (*Skr*) **1** supernatural power (of Hindu deities, ascetics, weapons, etc.). **2** to have/possess magic power, magic. *Keris yang digunakan Hang Tuah dipercayai keris –.* It's believed that the kris used by Hang Tuah had magic powers. **3** sacred, holy, consecrated. *sumpah –* a solemn oath. *– mandraguna* (*Jv*) invulnerable, with supernatural powers.

menyaktikan to make s.t. sacred/invulnerable, sanctify. *Bulan Maulud dianggap waktu yang baik untuk ~ benda-benda pusaka kerajaan.* The month of Maulud is considered a good time to make the royal heirlooms sacred.

tersakti the most sacred.

kesaktian 1 (to have) supernatural powers. *Ia memperoléh ~ setelah bertapa.* He obtained supernatural powers after going into seclusion. **2** holiness, sanctity. *Hari ~ Pancasila* the Pancasila Sanctity Day (October 1).

saku I (*D*) pocket (of a coat/pants). *anak –* (waist)coat pocket. *kamus –* pocket dictionary. *uang –* pocket money. *– kempés* broke, penniless; → KANTONG *kempés*, TONGPÉS. *– pencernaan* digestive sac.

bersaku with/to have pockets.

menyakukan to pocket, put s.t. in one's pocket.

saku II (*cla*) **menyakukan** to separate.

tersaku separated, segregated.

sakulya (*Hind*) type of heirs under Hindu law.

sakura (*Jp*) (*bunga –*) cherry tree.

saku-saku stealthily, secretly, surreptitiously.

sakwasangka → SYAK *wasangka.*

sal I (*D? Pers*) **1** shawl. **2** scarf; → SYAL.

sal II (*D*) **1** (hospital) ward. **2** large hall for gatherings. **3** auditorium (of a theater). *– anak-anak* children's ward. *– bersalin* lying-in ward, maternity ward. *– rumah sakit jiwa* ward in lunatic asylum.

sala I an evergreen shrub, *Eurya japonica.*

Sala II an alternate spelling for Solo, another name for the city of Surakarta.

salad (*E*) salad.

salaf I (*A*) bragging, boasting.

salaf II (*A*) **1** ancestors, predecessors. **2** early Islamic times. *ulama –* clergymen in the early stages of Islam.

salafi (*A*) believer in a return to the practices of early Islamic times.

salafiyah (*A*) old-style *pesantren* which only teaches the *kitab kuning.*

salaga (*M*) an agricultural implement used to level the soil after plowing.

salah I 1 wrong, mistaken, incorrect, erroneous. **2** to fail, make a mistake, err. *tidak bisa –* infallible. **3** defect, fault, shortcoming. **4** imperfect, defective, faulty. **5** guilt, blame; guilty, at fault, to blame. **6** improper, indecent. **7** mis-, s.t. done the wrong way. *– arti* misunderstanding. *Apa –nya?* What does it matter? What's wrong with that? *berpendapat dengan –* to be mistaken in one's opinion. *dapat/kena –* to get the blame, get blamed. *tak – lagi* no doubt about it, certainly, surely, of course. *tidak ada –nya kalau …* there's nothing wrong in … it's all right to … *tidak akan –* unfailing, faultless, infallible, perfect. *secara –* done in the wrong way, mis-. *penggunaan sumber-sumber secara –* misuse of resources. *– sedikit* a) to differ slightly. b) it's a pity, it's too bad. *– sedikit ia tidak datang* it's too bad that he didn't come. *serba –* guilty. *Saya merasa serba –.* I have a guilty feeling. *terima –* to plead guilty, admit one's guilt. *bukan saya (hendak) – siasat (tapi)* (*M*) if I may ask; if it's not too indiscreet, may I ask; → NUMPANG *tanya. – adat* to run counter to society's unwritten rules of behavior; breach of customs; (*infr*) abuse, misuse. *– agak* a) mistakenly thought s.t. b) to be mistaken, wrong. *– air* badly educated; → SESAT *air. – alamat* a) wrong address; misdirected. b) (*leg*) error in persona. *– ambil* taken by mistake. *– ambilan* misunderstanding. *– anggapan* misconception, misunderstanding, misapprehension. *– anggaran* misestimated, miscalculated. *– angkuh* (*M*) indecent (e.g., for a woman to sit by herself without a female companion). *– arah* misdirection, wrong direction. **menyalaharahkan** to misdirect. *– arti* misunderstanding, misinterpretation. **menyalahartikan** to misunderstand, misinterpret, give a wrong interpretation of. *Orang sering ~ kebaikan saya.* People often misinterpret my good behavior. *– asuhan* poorly educated. *– bantal* to have a stiff neck (after sleeping). *– bebal* mistake due to one's stupidity, blunder. *– benang* (*M*) a) wrongly woven (of a fabric). b) not feeling well, ill. *– bentuk* deformed, misshapen. *– bentuk janin* fetal deformity. *– bercakap/ berkata* to misspeak. *– besar* blunder. *– buku* clerical error. *– bunuh* to kill, murder. *– cakap* to misspeak. *– cerna* indigestion. *– cétak* misprint, typographical error, typo. *– dengar* to mishear. *– dorong* to go too far. *– duga* to miscalculate; miscalculation. **kesalahdugaan** mistake, error, miscalculation. *– éjaan* to misspell; misspelling. *– faham* misunderstanding, to misunderstand. **kesalahfahaman** misunderstanding. *– gamak* (*M*) estimated incorrectly. *– gelogok* to work carelessly/hurriedly. *– guna* misused, abused. **menyalahgunakan** to misuse, abuse. **penyalah guna** abuser, misuser. *~ narkoba* drug user. **penyalahgunaan** misuse, abuse. *~ izin tinggal* (an immigration term) to overstay (one's visa). *~ kekuasaan* abuse of power/authority, wrongful action by the authorities. *– hati* displeased, irritated, annoyed; → JÉNGKÉL, KESAL, MENDONGKOL. *– hitung* to miscalculate; miscalculation, arithmetical error. *– intérpretasi* misinterpretation. **menyalahintérpretasikan** to misinterpret. *– jadi* monster; deformity. *– jalan* a) to get lost, lose one's way. b) to walk/drive on the wrong side of the road. *– jam* the wrong time. *– jamah* a) to touch by mistake. b) to touch a woman's body in an improper way. *– jawab* to answer incorrectly. *– kaprah* a) a mistake in the meaning of certain words or phrases generally accepted or sanctioned by members of the speech community. b) misnomer. *– kaprah dalam penggunaan kata-kata Indonésia asal Arab* the mistaken use of Indonesian words taken from Arabic. **menyalahkaprahkan** to misuse, mistakenly use (though generally accepted). *"Kodak" disalahkaprahkan untuk semua alat pemotrét.* The word "Kodak" is misused for all k.o. cameras. **kesalahkaprahan** (generally accepted) misuse, mistaken use. *– kata* to misspeak. *– kelola* mismanagement. *– kelola bisa ubah hutan menjadi gurun pasir.* Mismanagement can turn forests into deserts. *– kena* off-target. *– kira* a) misthought, mistaken thought. b) to be mistaken/wrong. *– kutip* to misquote; misquotation. *– langkah* a) to take a wrong step. b) to have bad luck en route (or, during a trip) (because of leaving on an inauspicious day). c) to embark on s.t. in the wrong way. d) bad behavior; to perform a forbidden act. *– lidah* to say s.t. inadvertently. *– lihat/ mata* a) (for a married person) to look at s.o. of the opposite sex in an improper way. b) to mistake s.t. or s.o. for (s.t. or s.o. else). *Soviét antara lain berdalih, pilot meréka – mata menémbak pesawat penumpang yang malang itu.* The Soviets, among other reasons, used the pretext that the pilot had mistakenly shot down the unfortunate passenger plane. *– manfaat* misused, abused. **menyalahmanfaatkan** to misuse, abuse. *– masa* anachronistic. *– melangkah* → **SALAH** *langkah*. *– menafsir* misinterpretation, miscalculation. *– mengatakan* to make a slip of the tongue. *– mengerti* a) to misunderstand, misinterpret. b) to take (s.o.'s remarks) amiss. **menyalahmengertikan** to misunderstand. *– mengutip* to misquote. *– (ng)omong* a) to misspeak; misspeaking. b) slip of the tongue. *– nguping* to mishear; mishearing. *– obat* giving/taking the wrong medicine. *téwas akibat – obat* died because given the wrong medicine. *– omong* to say the wrong thing. *– padanan* mismatch. *– paham* a) misunderstanding. b) to take (s.o.'s remarks) in the wrong way. **kesalahpahaman** misunderstanding. *– pakai* misused. **menyalahpakaikan** to misuse, abuse. *– pandang* a) (for a married person) to look at s.o. of the opposite sex in an improper way. b) to mistake s.t. or s.o. for (s.t. or s.o. else). *– penderitaan* half-truths and inaccuracies (in reporting). *– penerimaan* a) to misunderstand. b) angry, annoyed. *– pengamatan* observation error. *– pengertian* misunderstanding, misinterpretation, misconstruction. *untuk menghindarkan – pengertian yang berakibat – penggunaan* to avoid misunderstandings which can result in misuse. *– penggunaan* misuse, abuse. *– perasaan* a) to have an unpleasant feeling, have a bad presentiment. b) unhappy. c) misunderstanding. *– perhitungan* to miscalculate; miscalculation. *– periksa* a) examined wrongly. b) (*M*) (to do s.t.) in an improper way. *– pikiran* mistake in thinking. *– pilih* to choose wrongly, make the wrong choice. *– pukul* misdirected blow. *– raba* a) mistaken. b) to touch by mistake. c) to touch a woman's body in an improper way. *– rancang* misplanned, badly planned. *Pabrik yang kabarnya – rancang itu masih akan diselamatkan.* The factory which was said to have been badly planned can still be saved. *– rasa* a) to have an unpleasant feeling, have a bad presentiment. b) unhappy. c) misunderstanding. *– roman dipandang orang* (*M*) indecent, improper (e.g. for a woman to sit by herself without a female companion). *– rumah* to be at (or, go to) the wrong address. *– rupa dipandang orang* (*M*) indecent, improper (e.g. for a woman to sit by herself without a female companion). *– saji* misstatement. *– salih* various errors. *– sambung* wrong number (on the telephone). *– sangka* a) thought mistakenly, misthinking. b) to be mistaken. *mendatangkan – sangka* to give rise to/create mistrust. *– semat* misunderstanding. *– sendi* sprain. *– silih* various k.o. mistakes and errors. *– tafsir* misinterpretation. **menyalahtafsirkan** to misinterpret. **kesalahtafsiran** misinterpretation, misunderstanding. *– tampa* a) to be mistaken, make a mistake or an error. b) misconception, misunderstanding, misapprehension. c) to take s.t. amiss. *– tanggap* to misunderstand. *– tangkap* a) to misunderstand. b) seized/caught by mistake, wrongful arrest. *– tanya* (don't want) to ask an indiscreet question. *bukan aku – tanya* (*M*) if I may ask; if it's not too indiscreet, may I ask; → **NUMPANG** *tanya*. *– tebak!* (your guess is) wrong! *– telan* s.t. went down the wrong pipe, to choke on s.t. *– témbak* a miss (in shooting). *– tempat* out of place. *– terima* a) to misunderstand; misunderstanding. b) angry, annoyed. *– terjemahan* mistranslation. *– terka* to guess wrong. *– tertawa* to laugh in an improper way (said of a girl in the presence of a man). *– tingkah* [salting] not to know how to act (in the proper way in a situation). *Akh, saya jadi malu dan – tingkah.* Oh, I felt shy and didn't know what to do next. *– tulis* a) slip of the pen. b) misquoted. *– tutur* to talk in an improper way (said of a girl in the presence of a man). *– ucap* a) mispronunciation. b) to make a slip of the tongue. **menyalahucapkan** to mispronounce. *kalimat yang disalahucapkan* a mispronounced sentence. *– ukur* measuring error. *– urat* to sprain a muscle. *– urus* mismanagement. *– warna* discoloration. *– wésel* a) to miss the point, be off the mark. b) misaddressed. *– wewenang* abuse of power.

salah-salah 1 if you make the mistake of ...ing, you might (if you're unlucky). *~ bersikap takut akan tertuduh pula.* If you make the mistake of showing fear, you'll be accused too. *~ bisa*

konangan you might be discovered. *~ anda bisa dirampok di jalan.* You might be mugged (or, robbed) in the street. **2** even though (or, although) guilty. *~ dibébaskan juga.* Even though he was guilty, he was released anyway.

bersalah 1 to make a mistake, have an error. *Siapa yang ~ lebih dari lima tidak akan lulus.* Whoever has more than five errors won't pass. **2** to be guilty, be at fault, be in the wrong. *rasa ~* guilty feeling. *yang ~* the guilty party, offender. *Orang itu telah dibébaskan oléh hakim karena tidak ~.* That person was acquitted by the judge because he was innocent. *~ mencuri* guilty of theft. *tidak ~* innocent, not guilty. **kebersalahan** guilt.

bersalahan 1 to be different (from), be in conflict/contradiction/disagreement (with), conflict/contradict/disagree (with), be at variance/odds (with). *Raut mukanya ~ dengan raut muka ibunya.* Her features are different from her mother's. *~ paham/pendapat* to disagree with e.o., have different opinions from e.o. *Sépak terjangnya ~ dengan asas perkumpulan.* His actions conflict with the principles of the association. **2** (*M*) to be unhealthy.

bersalah-salahan to quarrel, have a dispute with e.o. *Apa sebabnya kedua orang itu selalu ~?* Why are those two always quarreling with e.o.?

menyalah 1 to deviate, digress. **2** to be contrary to (the rule). **3** to avoid (s.t.), ward off, dodge.

menyalahi 1 to contradict, run counter to, be contrary to, contra, versus, go against, break, violate. *~ hukum* to break the law. *~ peraturan-peraturan Pemerintah* to go against government regulations. **2** to blame, condemn, censure, put s.o. in the wrong. **3** to resist, oppose. **4** to break (a promise), not live up to (an obligation). *~ padan* to break one's word. **5** to abuse (alcohol, etc.).

menyalahkan [and **nyalahin** (*J coq*)] **1** to say that s.o. or s.t. is wrong. *Mengapa hitungan ini kausalahkan?* Why did you say that this calculation is wrong? **2** to blame, put the blame on, place the responsibility for (a fault/error, etc.) on s.o., find fault with. *harus disalahkan kepada A* the blame has to be put on A. *Kalau usaha saudara tidak berhasil, jangan ~ orang lain.* When your business is unsuccessful, don't blame s.o. else. **3** to deny, contradict, reject, oppose, repudiate, renounce. *Segala tuduhan disalahkannya.* He denied all the accusations.

salah-menyalahkan to accuse e.o.

mempersalahkan to blame, put the blame on, place the responsibility for (a fault/error, etc.) on s.o., find fault with.

tersalah 1 accidentally mistaken. **2** to be wrong, make a mistake. **3** blamed, accused.

tersalahkan considered wrong.

kesalahan 1 mistake, error. *~ besar* blunder. *melakukan ~ besar* to make a blunder. *~ dalam prakték kedokteran* malpractice. *~ manusia* human error. *~ pembulatan* error in rounding off. *~ pengadaan* misprocurement. *~ pengertian* misconception, misunderstanding, misapprehension. *~ penghukuman* wrongful conviction. *~ pilot* pilot error. **2** fault, guilt, defect. *di luar ~nya sendiri* through no fault of his own. *~ watak* defect of character. **3** accidentally make a mistake. **4** by mistake, in error, erroneously. **5** accusation, charge. **6** to be blamed for.

persalahan and **penyalahan 1** resistance, opposition; refutation. **2** blame.

salah II (premodifies the number *satu* or *se-* plus a counter word) one of (two or more), a (the indefinite article). *– satu daripada kepribadian Indonésia* one of the features of the Indonesian personality. *– seorang jago témbak* a sharpshooter. *– satu oléh-oléh* a gift. *– satu cara menangkal hal itu* one of the ways of preventing that. *– satu penyebab* one of the reasons. *– satu anaknya* one of her children. *– satu korban AIDS* a victim of AIDS. *– satu dari 17 anak-anak Bosnia* one of the 17 Bosnian children. *– sebuah perguruan tinggi di Manado* one of the institutions of higher learning in Manado. *– seorang pengusaha hutan* one of the forestry businessmen. *– seorang cucunya* one of his grandchildren. *– satu di/dari antaranya* and *– satunya* one of them.

salai dried by heat. *ikan –* fish dried over a fire, smoked/roasted fish. *pisang –* sun-dried banana strips.

bersalai to warm o.s. near a fire. *~ tidak berapi* to be an unmarried pregnant woman.

menyalai 1 to dry/smoke (fish/meat/bananas) over a fire. 2 to put a woman who has just given birth near a fire to warm her.

tersalai smoked, roasted, dried over a fire. *mati* ~ suffocated to death by smoke and heat.

salaian 1 roaster, grill. 2 kitchen rack/shelf; → PARA-PARA.

penyalaian 1 drying over a fire. 2 putting a woman who has just given birth near the fire.

salak I bark(ing) (of dogs, etc.).

menyalak 1 to bark, howl (of dogs, etc.). *Anjing* ~ *di buntut/pantat gajah.* His bark is worse than his bite. 2 to bark at. *Pada sangkanya anjingnya* ~ *pencuri.* He thought the dog had barked at a thief. *disalak anjing bertuah* (M) it can no longer be postponed/put off. 3 (M) to whine/nag, ask for s.t. again and again.

menyalaki to bark at.

menyalakkan to make s.t. bark. ~ *pistolnya* to shoot his pistol.

salakan barking.

salak II thorny palm, *Zalacca edulis*, almost stemless with edible fruit. *buah* – the *salak* fruit, a plum-sized, oval fruit with a brown, snake-skin exterior and an astringent taste, *Zalacca edulis. tinggal kelopak* – completely fleeced (left with only the clothes on one's back). – *Bali* k.o. thorny palm, *Zalacca amboinensis.* – *Condèt/Enrèkang* a variety of *salak* found in Jakarta and Sulawesi. – *hutan* k.o. palm, *Zalacca spp.* – *pasir* thorny palm, *Zalacca edulis.* – *pondoh/rimba/rimbo* a variety of *salak* found in Yogya, sweet and crisp instead of sour or astringent, *Zalacca blumeana.*

salam I (A) 1 peace (particularly used in compounds, such as *darussalam* abode of peace; → DAR II. 2 (*coq*) clipped form of either **asalamualaikum** peace be with you (a Muslim greeting) or the return greeting **waalaikum salam** and peace be with you too. 3 regards (through a handshake/greetings, etc.); phrase/form of etiquette. *Sampaikanlah* – *saya kepada seisi rumah* and *Kirimlah* – *saya kepada seisi rumah.* Please send my regards to the entire family. Remember me to your family. *berjabat* – to shake hands, greet e.o. *membalas* – to reciprocate/return s.o.'s greeting. *memberi* – to greet (by using the formula *asalamualaikum*, etc.). *menjawab* – to return a greeting (by using the formula *waalaikum salam*, etc.). *teriring/tertumpang* – with best/kind(est) regards. *hormat dan* – and *wa*– yours truly (at the end of a letter). – *dan takzim* yours truly. – *hangat* warmest regards. – *hormat* regards and respect. – *kompak* heartfelt greetings. – *métal* [*mérah total*] greeting by raising three fingers of the right hand, a greeting used by members of the Indonesian Democracy Party (PDI) (who wore red jackets during the general elections). – *mesra* → SALAM kompak. – *Natal* Christmas greetings. – *sayang* (to close a letter) affectionately, love. – *takzim* yours truly (at the end of a letter). – *témpél/témplék* k.o. bribe in the form of a banknote held in the palm of the hand and given by bus and truck drivers to officials when shaking hands.

bersalam to greet. *untuk* ~ in greeting.

bersalam(-salam)an to shake hands with e.o., greet e.o.

menyalam to greet, give a greeting. *Létnan itu tidak* ~ *kembali.* The lieutenant did not return the greeting.

menyalami [and **nyalamin** (J coq)] 1 to greet, shake hands with. *Tuan Wolcott* ~ *saya.* Mr. Wolcott greeted me. 2 to shake (s.o.'s hand). *Sambil menyerahkan kado, kusalami tangannya.* Handing over the present, I shook his hand.

salaman 1 (*coq*) to greet e.o. 2 greetings.

salam II *daun* – (*Jv*) bay leaf, *Eugenia cumini/polyantha.*

salam III (*ikan* -) salmon; → SALEM.

salam IV (A) k.o. Islamic futures or forward-purchase financing technique.

salamander (D) salamander.

salang I a long kris; → *keris* PENYALANG.

menyalang to execute s.o. by driving a kris through the shoulder to the heart. *mati disalang* executed in this manner.

penyalang → SALANG I.

salang II 1 a net or rattan receptacle for food that can be raised or lowered from the ceiling. 2 bags or baskets carried on a yoke.

salang III (M) → SEDANG II, SELANG I.

salang IV (M) borrowing.

menyalang to borrow.

menyalangi to lend to s.o.

menyalangkan to lend s.t.

salang-surup (*Jv*) a mix-up.

salap (D) salve, ointment; → SALEP.

salar → SELAR I.

salaris (D) salary, pay.

salasal (A) diabetes; → PENYAKIT *kencing manis.*

salasilah → SILSILAH.

salat I (A) the ritual prayer prescribed by Islam to be recited five times a day at stipulated times and in a stipulated way using Arabic phrases; the prayers are: MAGRIB, ISYA, SUBUH, LOHOR, ASAR (said through the day in that sequence); → SALAWAT, SEMBAHYANG, SHALAT, SHOLAT. – *asar/ashar* afternoon prayer. – *fardu* obligatory prayer. – *gaib* prayer for a dead person whose body is somewhere else. – *hajat* a special prayer for the fulfillment of a particular wish. – *id* prayer consisting of two *rakaat* performed on Idul Fitri (1 *Sawal*) and on Idul Adha (10 *Zulhijah*). – *istiska/istisqa/istisqo* prayer asking for rain. – *istikharah* prayer asking for guidance. – *isya* early evening prayer. – *jamaah* joint prayer with an *imam* in front of the group and a *makmum* behind the group. – *Jumat* Friday prayers. – *khusuf* prayer said in connection with an eclipse. – *lohor* noon prayer. – *mag(h)rib* sunset prayer. – *maktubah* the five daily prayers. – *nawafil* the five daily prayers. – *rawatib* optional prayers. – *subuh* dawn prayer. – *sunah/sunnat* recommended but not obligatory prayer. – *tahajud* night prayer (not obligatory). – *tarawih* recommended night prayers performed during the month of Ramadan. – *wajib* obligatory prayer. – *zuhur* noon prayer.

mensalati to say a prayer over.

salat II → SILATURAHIM.

salat III – *lidah buaya* an epiphytic orchid, *Oberonia anceps.*

salatin (A) sultans.

salawaku (*Pap*) shield.

salawat (A) prayer; → SALAT, SEMBAHYANG, SHALAT, SHOLAT. – *Badar* a song to praise the Prophet Muhammad after the victory at the Battle of Badar, the first war of the Muslims against the pagans of Mecca on the 17th or 19th of *Ramadan* in the second year of the Hegira.

salbiah (*Pers*) sage, *Salvia spp.*

saldo (D) balance (in a checkbook/account). – *akhir* closing balance. – *awal* opening/previous balance. – *bank* cash in bank. – *bersih tertimbang* weighted net balance. – *imbangan* compensating balance. – *krédit* credit balance. – *laba* credit balance, retained earnings. – *rugi* debit/adverse balance. – *terutang* unpaid balance.

bersaldo with a … balance. ~ *dibawah Rp 1 miliar* with a balance below one billion rupiah.

salé → SALAI.

saléh I (J) → SALAH I.

saléh II (A) 1 pious, devout. 2 virtuous.

kesaléhan 1 devotion, devoutness, piety. 2 virtuousness.

saléh III → SALIH II.

salem → SALAM III.

salep (D) salve, ointment. – *bibir* lip balm. – *kulit* skin salve. – *mata* eye ointment.

menyalep to apply salve to, rub with ointment.

sales (E) clipped form of **salesman/salesgirl**. *Dibutuhkan segera: tenaga* –. Needed immediately: salespeople. *Dicari segera: beberapa orang* –. Wanted immediately: several salespeople.

salesgirl (E) salesgirl; → PRAMUNIAGA(WATI).

salesman (E) salesman; → PRAMUNIAGA.

sali I strong, firm. *berhati* – stout-hearted, courageous. *sama* – equal in strength.

sali II (*Pap*) vagina cover.

sali III (A) warmed.

sali IV → SALAI.

salib I (A) 1 cross (for crucifixion). 2 cross (as a symbol). *benang* – cross wire. *perang* – crusade.

menyalib cruciate, cross-shaped.

menyalibkan to crucify.

tersalib crucified.

penyalib crucifier.

penyaliban crucifying, crucifixion. ~ *Yésus* the crucifixion of Jesus.

salib II (*Jv*) → SALIP I. **menyalib** [and **nyalib** (*coq*)] to pass/overtake (a car, etc.). *Bus yang berkecepatan tinggi itu berusaha ~ truk yang ada di depannya.* A bus riding at high speed tried to pass a truck in front of it.

tersalib passed, overtaken (of a car, etc.). *Pengemudi mempercepat agar dia tidak ~.* The driver sped up so as not to be passed.

salibi (*A*) *kaum* – the Crusaders.

salih I (*A ob*) to go; to come.

salih II → SALÉH I.

salik (*A*) a mystic; → SULUK I.

salim (*A*) healthy.

salin I bersalin to change. ~ *kulit* to slough off skin. ~ *warna* to change color. *Bunglon adalah binatang yang dapat ~ warna sesuai dengan alam sekitarnya.* The chameleon is an animal that can change color to accord with its surroundings. ~ *pakaian* to change one's clothes. ~ *rupa* to change appearance/shape.

bersalin-salin to keep on changing, changeable, erratic.

menyalin [and **nyalin** (*coq*)] **1** to change s.t. **2** to transpose. **3** to copy, transcribe, reproduce. **4** to translate; → MENTERJEMAHKAN.

menyalinkan to copy, etc. for s.o. else.

tersalin translated.

salinan 1 (signed) copy (of a letter), transcript; → KOPI II. ~ *sah* valid copy. **2** translation; → TERJEMAHAN.

penyalin 1 copier (the person), transcriber. **2** translator; → PEN(T)ERJEMAH.

penyalinan 1 copying. **2** translating; → PEN(T)ERJEMAHAN.

salin II bersalin to give birth. *klinik ~* maternity clinic. *ruang ~* delivery room.

persalinan childbirth, delivery, confinement.

salin III sesalin a suit of clothes.

menyalini and **mempersalin(i)** (*cla*) to give s.o. a suit of clothes as a present.

menyalinkan and **mempersalinkan** to give a suit of clothes (to s.o.).

pesalin a suit of clothes.

persalinan [and **pesalinan** (*cla*)] **1** change of clothes. **2** set of clothes. *persalinan selengkapnya* an outfit, suit.

saling (*J*) **1** e.o. **2** mutual, common. – *beli* cross purchase. – *berbaku hantam* to fight with e.o. – *berbatasan* with a common border. *negara yang – berbatasan* countries with a common border. – *bertélepon* to call e.o., talk to e.o. on the phone. *Seminggu kemudian kami – bertélepon lagi.* A week later we talked to e.o. again on the phone. – *imbang* evenly balanced, in equilibrium. **kesalingimbangan** equilibrium. – *bergantungan* interdependent. – *isi* to be complementary (to e.o.), complement e.o. – *kait* interconnect. **kesaling-kaitan** interconnection. – *kasih-mengasih* to love e.o. – *ketergantungan* interdependency. – *maafmemaafkan* to forgive/pardon e.o. – *melengkapi* to be complementary (to e.o.), complement e.o. *Filsafat dan sains – melengkapi.* Philosophy and science complement e.o. – *memerlukan* to need e.o. – *memukul* to hit e.o. – *mendahului* to overtake/pass e.o. – *menguntungkan* to benefit e.o., be mutually beneficial. – *menjauh* to stay away from e.o. – *pukul(-memukul)* to hit e.o. – *pengertian* mutual understanding. – *sikut* to elbow e.o. aside. – *silang* conflicting, to conflict with e.o. *koméntar yang – silang* conflicting commentaries. – *terhubung* interconnected. – *terikat* interdependent. – *tunjuk* finger-pointing, accusing e.o.

salinisasi (*E*) salinization.

salinitas (*D*) salinity, salt content.

salip I bersalip-salipan to keep on overtaking/passing e.o. (of a car/motorcycle, etc.).

menyalip to overtake/pass (of a car, etc.). *Sopir itu berusaha menghindari tabrakan dengan pengendara sepéda motor yang ~ dengan kecepatan tinggi dari sisi kanan.* The driver tried to avoid a collision with a motorcyclist who passed at a high speed on his right side.

tersalip overtaken, passed by.

penyalip s.o. who passes s.o. else on the road.

salip II → SALIB I.

salir drain(age).

menyalir(kan) to drain.

saliran drainage.

penyalir drain.

penyaliran draining, drainage.

salisilat (*D*) salicylate. *asam –* salicylic acid.

saliwah neutral gray.

salju (*A*) snow. *Manusia –* the Abominable Snowman. *– turun* it's snowing.

bersalju snowy, covered with snow, snow-covered. *gunung yang ~* a snow-covered mountain.

mensalju to turn as white as snow.

salla (*A*) blessing. *-llahualaihiwasalam(ma)* [saw] may God bless him and grant him salvation (*usu* uttered or written after mentioning the name of the Prophet Muhammad).

salmiak (*D*) **1** sal ammoniac. **2** k.o. licorice candy.

Salomé [Satu lobang untuk ramé-ramé] (*joc sl*) one hole for a lot of people, i.e., a prostitute.

salon I (*D*) **1** salon. *kursi –* armchair, easy chair. **2** amateur, not professional, armchair (*mod*). *sarjana –* armchair scholar. – *foto* photo studio. – *kecantikan* beauty salon. – *pijat uap* sauna. – *politikus* armchair politician. – *rambut* hairdresser's.

salon-salonan (*mod*) salon, drawing room.

salon II (*D*) console. – *radio* radio console.

salp → SALEP.

salting → SALAH *tingkah*.

salto (*D*) somersault; → JUNGKIR *balik*. – *mortal* somersault in the air.

bersalto to turn a somersault, turn around in the air. *Hondanya ~ setelah menabrak truk.* His Honda turned a somersault after colliding with a truck.

saluir (*D*) **bersaluir** to salute.

menyaluir to salute s.o.

saluk I (*M*) *destar –* headscarf (worn by the *penghulu adat* in the Minangkabau region).

bersaluk to wear such a headscarf.

saluk II → SELUK II.

salung (*M*) flageolet, (bamboo) fife. – *api* a) bamboo tube used as bellows. b) chimney (of a lamp).

bersalung to play the fife.

salur 1 channel, line. **2** stripe.

bersalur (*Mal*) corrugated.

bersalur-salur striped, lined.

menyaluri to pass (s.t.) through s.t., flow through. *tidak disaluri listrik dari PLN* PLN electricity does not flow through it.

menyalurkan [and **nyalurin** (*J coq*)] **1** to lead (in a certain direction/along/to), channel/funnel s.t. [(in)to], relay. **2** to grant/extend/channel (credit/money, etc.). ~ *uang (ke)pada* to channel funds to. **3** to distribute, transfer, send (to). *tidak dapat disalurkan ke jabatan lain* cannot be sent to another office. **4** to find an outlet for. ~ *aspirasi* to find an outlet for one's aspirations. ~ *hobinya di bidang tarik-menarik suara* found an outlet for his hobby of singing.

tersalur(kan) 1 channeled, found an outlet. *Dengan demikian kegemarannya mudah ~.* In that way his hobbies easily found an outlet. **2** distributed (of credit).

saluran 1 channel (in general and TV), (radio) station. **2** line (of a switchboard, etc.). *dalam ~* in line. ~ *induk* trunk line. ~ *tanah* land line. **3** (roof/street) gutter, conduit, pipe, sewer drain, duct, line, passage, flume. **4** tract/duct/canal (in the body). **5** pipeline (for information). ~ *air* waterworks; aqueduct, pipe(s), canal, tube. ~ *air kencing/seni* urethra. ~ *air yang tersumbat* clogged drain/sewer. ~ *alat kelamin* genital tract. ~ *angin* air duct. ~ *asap* flue. ~ *buang* exhaust pipe. ~ *Cakung* Cakung Drain (in Jakarta). ~ *diplomatik* diplomatic channels. *melalui ~ diplomatik* through diplomatic channels. ~ *empedu* bile duct. ~ *hawa* airshaft. ~ *hukum* legal channels. ~ *indung telur* fallopian tube. ~ *irigasi* irrigation canal. ~ *keluar* drain(age canal), outlet, outfall. ~ *kemih* urinary tract. ~ *kemih kelamin* urinogenital tract. ~ *komando* chain of command. ~ *kuras* drain. ~ *listrik* electric wiring. ~ *makanan* alimentary canal. ~ *mani* vas deferens. ~ *masuk* supply canal, inlet. ~ *napas* respiratory tract. ~ *panas* central heating. ~ *pembawa* feeder (line). ~ *pembuangan (limbah)* drainage, sewage system. ~ *pencernaan* digestive tract. ~ *pernapasan* respiratory tract. ~ *pernapasan atas* upper respiratory tract. *di luar* ~ *resmi* outside normal channels, without the knowledge of the official authorities. ~ *pimpinan* chain of command. ~ *pintas* by-pass. ~ *spérma* vas deferens. ~ *tataniaga* marketing channel. ~ *telur* fallopian tube, oviduct. ~ *tersumbat* clogged-up ditch. ~ *udara* a) windpipe. b) overhead line. ~ *urin* urinary tract.

penyalur 1 distributor, dealer. **2** *(elec)* conductor. ~ *aspirasi* outlet for aspirations. ~ *petir* lightning conductor. ~ *sandang pangan* food-and-clothing distributor. ~ *tenaga kerja* labor supplier. ~ *tunggal* sole distributor. ~ *utama* main/general distributor.

penyaluran 1 distribution, allocation, assignment, dispensing. ~ *bantuan bagi korban bencana alam Flores* distributing aid to the victims of the Flores natural disaster. **2** channeling, funneling. **3** conducting. *memerlukan* ~ *dari* the need to find an outlet for (one's frustration, etc.). ~ *pegawai-pegawai* reduction in force, rif, compulsory retirement. ~ *séksual* sexual release. *sistém* ~ *secara bersama* pooling (resources, etc.).

persaluran system of (blood, etc.) vessels.

salut I casing, coat, coating, lining, cover, wrapper, envelope; → **BALUT** I. - *biji (bot)* aril. - *gigi* dental crown. - *surat* envelope.

bersalut to be wrapped/covered/encased in. *gelang* ~ *emas* gold-plated bracelet. *gigi* ~ *emas* gold-plated tooth. *tinggal tulang* ~ *kulit* to be nothing but skin and bones, i.e., very emaciated; → **TULANG** I.

bersalutkan to have ... as an envelope/casing/covering, be enveloped in, be plated with. *Sarung pedangnya* ~ *kain sutera berwarna.* The case of his sword was covered with colored silk.

menyalut to cover, enwrap, encase, plate, envelop. ~ *sarung keris dengan pérak* to encase a kris in silver.

menyaluti to cover, encase, wrap.

tersalut covered, enwrapped, encased, enveloped. ~ *satu sisi* one-side coated.

salutan coating, covering, plating.

penyalut s.o. who covers/encases.

penyalutan coating.

salut II *(D)* **1** salute, honor, homage. **2** to pay homage (to). *memberi/menyatakan* ~ *kepada Indonésia* to pay homage to Indonesia.

salvarsan *(D/E)* salvarsan, a drug used in the treatment of syphilis and other spirochetal diseases.

salvo *(D)* salvo, volley.

salwat → **SALAWAT**.

Sam *(A)* Shem.

sama I *(Skr)* **1** same, alike, similar, equal(ly), identical, resembling. *Kedua soal itu* - *sulitnya.* The two questions are equally difficult. - *dengan* same as, equal to. *tidak* - *dengan* different/differs from. *Pendapat saya tidak* - *dengan pendapatnya.* My opinion differs from his. *dua kali dua* - *dengan empat* two times two is/equals four. *Lima tambah tiga* - *dengan delapan.* Five plus three is/equals eight. *Taraf kita tidak* - *dengan meréka.* Our social position is different from theirs. - *halnya dengan* as in the case of, the same holds/is true for, so is ... - *juga/saja* it doesn't matter, it's all the same. - *juga/halnya dengan* and - *seperti* the same as, similar to. *pada waktu yang* - simultaneously, at the same time. *Kedua mahasiswa itu datang pada waktu yang* -. The two students arrived at the same time. *yang* - *waktunya* simultaneous(ly). *Di mana-mana diadakan rapat samudra yang* - *waktunya.* Everywhere mass meetings were held simultaneously. *tidak* - not the same, different, unequal, not equal. **ketidak-samaan** difference, discrepancy. ~ *waktu* discrepancy in time. **pertidaksamaan** *(math)* inequality. **2** fellow-. - *manusia* fellow man. **3** (together) with, along with. *hidup* - *hidup, mati* - *mati* unanimous, in harmony; → **SEHIDUP** *semati*. *untung* - *untung, rugi* - *rugi* sharing the good and the bad. *Meréka itu pun berkelompok-kelompok, perempuan* - *perempuan, laki-laki* - *laki-laki.* They were in groups, the women with the women, the men with the men. *satu* - *lain* between them, to/with e.o. **4** *(coq)* a) with; → **DENGAN**. *Saya kawin* - *seorang gadis Jawa.* I married a Javanese girl. *aku sayang* - *kau* I'm in love with you. *satu* - *lain* s.t. or other, s.o. or other. b) against;

→ **TERHADAP**. *dia ikut berontak* - *pemerintah* he took part in the rebellion against the government. c) by; → **OLÉH**. *sudah dibeli* - *orang lain* bought by s.o. else. **5** (verb+*sama*+verb) mutual, reciprocal. *tahu* - *tahu* a) you scratch my back and I'll scratch yours. b) to connive through bribery or corruption. *Meréka nikah atas dasar suka* - *suka.* They married on the basis of love for e.o. **6** homo-, having the same, con-. - *bunyi* homophone. - *bunyinya* exact (copy). - *éja* homograph. - *pusat* concentric. - *rata* - *rasa* and - *rasa* - *rata* what's sauce for the goose is sauce for the gander, equal rights means equal burdens. - *arti* synonymous, having the same meaning. **menyama-artikan** to identify with, identify as equal (to). *Dia* ~ *"bangun" dengan "bentuk,"* padahal *"bentuk"* hanyalah salah satu arti dari *"bangun."* He identifies "structure" with "shape," but "shape" is only one of the meanings of "structure." - *dan sebangun (math)* congruent. - *duduk* put on a level/rank. **menyama-dudukkan** to put on the same level/rank, rank. - *jarak* equidistant. *Gerakan Nonblok bukanlah suatu kebijaksanaan nétral atau sebuah kebijaksanaan* - *jarak.* The Nonblock Movement is not a neutral policy nor is it an equidistant policy. - *kaki (math)* isosceles (triangle). - *kuat* a tie, the same score. - *kupuan* of the same/similar descent/origin. - *pusat* concentric. - *rata* a) equally, equitably. *membagi* - *rata* to divide equally. b) level(led) (with)/razed (to) (the ground). **menyama-ratakan 1** to equalize, make equal (to e.o.), generalize about, treat in the same way. *Kita tidak dapat* ~ *semua kemampuan.* We cannot generalize about all abilities. **2** to level (with)/raze (to the ground). *Jago mérah* ~ *kota itu dengan tanah.* The fire leveled the town to the ground. **kesama-rataan** equality, equity. *Tiada satu agama yang menghendaki* ~ *lebih daripada Islam.* No religion desires equality more than Islam does. **penyamarata** equalizer. **penyama-rataan** generalizing, generalization, making equal, equalizing. *tidak* - *rata* unequal. **ketidaksamarataan** inequality. *Semakin membesar tingkat atau kadar partisipasi khususnya rakyat kecil akan berkuranglah* ~ *atau kesenjangan sosial, ékonomi, politik dalam masyarakat.* As the level or degree of participation, especially of the masses, increases, the social, economic and political inequalities or gaps in society will decrease. - *rendah* equally low. **menyama-rendahkan** to belittle everyone. - *sebangun* equal. **menyama-sebangunkan** to equate. - *sekali* a) all (of them/it), completely. *Uang saya habis* - *sekali.* My money is all gone. b) (with negative) (not) at all, (not) in the least, by (no) means. *Meréka* - *sekali tidak mengharapkan apa-apa.* They didn't expect anything at all. - *sekali tidak!* absolutely not! - *sendirinya* between them, to himself. - *setentang* flush with e.o. - *sisi (math)* equilateral. - *taraf* same level. **menyama-tarafkan** to equate, put at the same level. - *tengah* a) (exactly) in the middle. b) neutral, impartial, unbiased. - *ucap (ling infr)* homonym.

sama-sama 1 *(coq)* both, all. *Sebagai keluarga yang* ~ *berasal dari Minangkabau, suami-istri ini saling menghargai.* As a couple who both come from the Minangkabau region, this couple respects e.o. *Kita* ~ *membutuhkan uang.* We both need money. ~ *tidak* neither. ~ *tidak tamat SMP* neither has finished Junior High School. *kita* ~ *manusia* we are all human beings. ~ *tahu* a) both/all know it. b) it mustn't go any further. **2** together, in concert/unison. **3** e.o., mutual. *meréka* ~ *suka* they love e.o. ~ *salah mengerti* to misunderstand e.o. *dengan dasar* ~ on an equal basis. **4** you're welcome, the same to you (reply to congratulations/thanks).

sesama 1 fellow-, -mate. *Suatu saat manusia itu mémang bisa jadi saudara yang akrab sekali antara ~nya.* At some point in time human beings can become very close brothers to their fellow men. *kita* ~ *anak Timur* we fellow Asians. ~ *anggota* fellow member. ~ *bangsa* fellow citizen, fellow countryman. ~ *blok* members of the same block. ~ *jenis* (of the) same sex. ~ *makhluk* fellow creature. ~ *main* playmate. ~ *manusia* fellow man. ~ *meréka* among themselves. ~ *Muslim* fellow Muslims. ~ *negara komunis* fellow communist countries. *kita* ~ *perempuan/wanita* we fellow women. ~ *serikat* ally. ~ *sukunya* fellow ethnic, member of the same ethnic group. **2** mutual(ly). ~ *menguntungkan* mutually beneficial.

bersama 1 joint, common, collective, together, in concert.

Meréka selalu ~. They are always together. *Dia mencari seorang untuk tinggal* ~. He looked for a housemate. *kegiatan* ~ *para kompétitor* concerted activities by competitors. *kepentingan* ~ common interest. *Pasar* ~ *Asia* Asian Common Market. *tindakan* ~ common action. 2 together (with). *kita* ~ all of us together. *pelajaran* ~ team-teaching. ~ *(surat) ini kami sampaikan* ... enclosed in this letter we are sending you ... **membersamakan** to do s.t. together/in common/simultaneously. *Sebaiknya kita* ~ *pengiriman tembakau dan pengiriman téh agar ongkos kirimnya lebih ringan.* The best thing would be for us to make a joint shipment of the tobacco and tea so that the shipping costs will be lower. **kebersamaan** sense of togetherness/community. *Saling percaya di antara kami itulah yang menjadi kunci suksés* ~ *kami.* It was mutual trust that was the key to the success of our sense of togetherness. *rasa* ~ *yang dekat* cohesiveness. ~ *kepentingan* mutuality of interest.

bersama-sama joint, common, collective, together, along with, in concert. *baik* ~, *maupun masing-masing* and *baik* ~, *maupun sendiri-sendiri* (in notarial instruments) both jointly and severally. *Apakah Linux dapat digunakan* ~ *Windows?* Can Linux be used along with Windows?

bersamaan 1 to coincide (with), occur/happen at the same time (as), coinciding, in real time. *HUTnya yang ke-25* ~ *dengan hari pernikahannya.* His 25th birthday coincided with the anniversary of his marriage. ~ *waktu* simultaneously. 2 of one/the same kind, similar, uniform. *Pakaian meréka* ~. Their dress is similar. 3 to agree/be in accordance (with). *Anggaran rumah tangga harus* ~ *dengan anggaran dasarnya.* The rules of association should be in accordance with the statutes. 4 to be equal, equivalent, be comparable. *Profésor madia di Amérika Serikat* ~ *dengan pensyarah kanan di Malaysia.* An Associate Professor in the United States is equivalent to a Senior Lecturer in Malaysia. ~ *kedudukannya di dalam hukum* to be equal under/in the eyes of the law.

menyama-nyama to act as/like. *Tak usahlah kita* ~ *orang kaya.* There's no need for us to act like rich people.

menyamai 1 to look like, resemble. *Wajahnya* ~ *wajah ayahnya.* His face resembles his father's face, he looks like his father. 2 to equal, match. *Kekayaannya tidak ada yang* ~*nya.* His wealth is unmatched. 3 to keep up (with doing the same thing). *Saya* ~ *kecepatan.* I kept up with the speed.

menyamakan and **mempersamakan** [and **nyamain** (*J coq*)] 1 to make equal, treat as equal/the same, make s.t. the same as s.t. else. *Semuanya disamakannya saja.* He treated everyone alike. *Meréka, kebanyakan orang Manado dan Ambon, minta dipersamakan haknya dengan bangsa Éropa.* They, mostly Manadonese and Ambonese, asked for the same rights as Europeans. *dapat disamakan dengan* is equal to, is tantamount to, is the same as. 2 *disamakan* to be entitled to the same rights (as); (with reference to privately owned universities) to be entitled to organize state examinations independently, without the supervision of *Kopertis*, the Coordinator of Private Higher Educational Institutions. 3 to liken, equate, compare.

menyama-nyamakan to compare s.t. with s.t. else. *Jangan* ~ *kehidupan di kota dengan kehidupan di désa.* Don't compare life in the city with life in the country.

mempersama-samakan 1 to treat equally/the same, put on a par (with). *Gadis Indonésia tidak boléh dipersama-samakan dengan gadis Barat.* Indonesian girls cannot be put on a par with Western girls. 2 to do s.t. jointly/in a group. *Tidak pernah kerja berat dilakukan oléh seorang saja, melainkan senantiasa dipersama-samakan.* A hard job is never done by only one person, but always in a group with others.

kesamaan alikeness, similarity, resemblance, equality, sameness. *Sangat sulit untuk memelihara* ~ *dan kesatuan dalam soal bahasa* it's very hard to maintain equality and unity in language problems. ~ *seimbang* proportional equality, equality of balance. ~ *senjata* arms equality.

penyama equalizer.

penyamaan making the same/similar/equivalent.

persamaan 1 resemblance, similarity, sameness, equality. *Ada* ~ *antara orang asli di Filipina dengan orang asli di Indonésia dan Malaysia.* There are similarities between the native peoples of the Philippines and those of Indonesia and Malaysia. ~ *dalam dunia pekerjaan* occupational equality. ~ *di hadapan hukum* equality before/in the eyes of the law. ~ *derajat/hak/kepentingan/kesempatan/pendapatan* equality of rank/rights/interests/opportunity/earnings. 2 community. ~ *barang-barang* community property. ~ *untung-rugi* community of profit and loss. 3 (*math*) equation.

sama II (*A*) heaven, sky, firmament; → SAMAWI.

sama III (*A*) transmission of a report concerning the words of the Prophet by the receiver hearing and memorizing it.

sama ada and **sama(a)da** (*Mal*) whether; → APA(KAH). *Saya tidak tahu – dia akan datang atau tidak.* I don't know whether he's coming or not.

samad (*A*) everlasting, eternal. *al-samad* and *assamad* the everlasting/eternal (one of the 99 names of God).

samadi → SEMADI.

samadya *makan* – to eat enough (but not overeat).

samai → SEMAI.

samak I 1 tanning. *pohon* – mangrove-like tree, *Eugenia spp.*, whose bark is used for tanning. 2 tannin. *asam* – tannic acid. *kulit* – tanned hide, leather. *tukang* – tanner.

menyamak to tan.

tersamak tanned.

samakan s.t. tanned.

penyamak tanner, tanning (*mod*). *bahan* ~ tanning agent.

penyamakan tanning.

samak II 1 cover, protection. 2 powdered glass (for coating kite strings).

bersamak covered/plated with.

menyamaki 1 to cover, cover with a protective coating. 2 to coat (a kite string) with powdered glass (used for fighting other kites); → *tali* BERGELAS.

penyamakan coating (a kite string) with powdered glass.

samak III (*J/Jv*) a mat made from pandanus leaves.

samak IV (*M*) → SEMAK I.

samama k.o. plant that grows in the Moluccas, *Anthocephalus macrophyllus.*

saman I (*E mostly Mal*) summons, writ, subpoena.

menyaman to issue a summons/subpoena to.

Saman II (*A*) Syeh Muhammad Saman (died A.D. 1720), founder of a mystical school. *ratib* – recital used in the *Samaniah* school. *tari* – a religious dance of North Sumatra.

samanéra (*Skr*) aspiring Buddhist monk.

Samaniah (*A*) the mystic's path to the Real as preached by Syeh Muhammad Saman, who claimed to be the receiver of the Prophet Muhammad's mandate, and which is able to grant peace to those at death's door and to bring good luck to its practitioners.

samapta (*Jv*) ready (for action), prepared, stand-by, (all) set. *tést* – *jasmani* squat jump test (in *ABRI*). – *Bhayangkara* tactical police unit.

kesamaptaan readiness, preparedness (for action). *memiliki* ~ *jasmani yang menggembirakan* to have a gratifying physical readiness.

samar and **samar-samar** 1 dim, vague, indistinct, unclear. *suara* – in a hushed voice. *warna* – subdued color. 2 obscure, hidden, secret, mysterious, inconspicuous, unknown, covert. *alam* – the invisible world. 3 disguised, masked. *tak* – *lagi* openly, candidly, plainly. *(hari)* – *muka* twilight, dusk.

menyamar [and **nyamar** (*coq*)] 1 to conceal o.s., disguise o.s. (as), pass o.s. off (as). *Larkin* ~ *sebagai seorang wartawan Swédia.* Larkin passed himself off as a Swedish reporter. 2 to be incognito. 3 (in wartime) to go into hiding.

menyamarkan 1 to hide/conceal s.t. 2 to camouflage, cloak, disguise. ~ *diri* to disguise o.s.

mempersamar to hide, conceal.

tersamar hidden, concealed, disguised, camouflaged, masked. *dalam bentuk kecil dan* ~ in a small and disguised form. *pengangguran* ~ disguised unemployment. *perusahaan* ~ mock company.

samaran 1 hiding, concealment, camouflage, mask, disguise,

guise. **2** hidden, concealed, disguised, pen-, pseudo-. *nama ~* pen name, pseudonym, cover name. *dengan nama ~* under/ using the alias of. *pakaian ~* camouflaged uniform, camouflage.

kesamaran 1 dusk, twilight. **2** obscurity. **3** confusion, indistinctness. **4** camouflage.

penyamar 1 s.o. in disguise. *~ musuh* spy. **2** camouflage.

penyamaran disguise, disguising, hiding, concealing, camouflaging.

samara winged seed.

samas (*PC*) deacon.

samatinggi accordant.

samawaktu synchronous.

samawi (*A*) celestial, heavenly, divine. *agama ~* revealed religion, such as Islam, Christianity, etc.

samba the samba (a Brazilian dance).

bersamba to dance the samba.

sambal hot spicy sauce/paste made from ground red chili peppers, salt, etc. and served along with cooked rice. *gertak ~* empty bluff (used just to intimidate). *ulam mencari ~* the woman courts the man. *~ bajak* fried hot pepper sauce. *~ déndéng* spicy shredded beef. *~ ébi* hot sauce containing dried shrimps. *~ goréng buncis* stir-fried green beans in coconut milk. *~ goréng printil* meatballs in hot sauce. *~ goréng telor* egg in red-pepper sauce. *~ goréng telor udang* shrimp in coconut cream. *~ jelantah* fried garlic hot sauce. *~ kacang* peanut sauce. *~ kécap* hot soy sauce. *~ pelecing* k.o. *sambal* using *belacan*, tomato, etc. *~ terasi* hot sauce with *terasi*. *~ tomat* hot sauce made with fresh tomatoes. *~ tumpang* hot sauce made with tempeh and other ingredients. *~ tutuk* hot sauce made with *ikan teri*. *~ ulak/ulek* ground chili paste.

menyambal to prepare *sambal*.

(sambal-)sambalan different k.o. *sambal*s.

sambalado (*M*) finely pounded chili mixed with onions and fish, a side dish served with rice.

sambaléwa nonchalant, uninterested, disinterested, indifferent, apathetic, lukewarm.

menyambaléwa (to work, etc.) not seriously, reluctantly, unwillingly.

menyambaléwakan to do s.t. reluctantly/lazily.

sambang I watch, guard, patrol; → RONDA.

bersambang to make their rounds (of the police/watchman), keep watch.

menyambangi to (keep) watch over, guard.

penyambangan making the rounds, keeping watch.

sambang II (*J*) visit. *~ kerja* working visit.

menyambangi to visit, pay a visit to, call on. *Hai Honolulu, kami tiba menyambangimu.* Hi, Honolulu, we've come to visit you.

sambang III (*Jv*) various diseases caused by evil spirits.

sambang IV abandoned/empty bees' nest.

sambang V (*M*) bamboo tube (used for storing spices). *~ api-api* match box. *~ tembakau* tobacco box.

sambang VI used as the first element of some plant names. *~ colok* amaranth, *Aerva sanguinolenta*. *~ darah* a) creeping, decorative plant, broad leaf flame ivy, *Hemigraphis colorata*. b) forb, Chinese croton, *Excoecaria cochinchinensis*. *~ getih* k.o. plant, *Strobilanthes crispus*.

sambangan I (*M*) k.o. bird.

sambangan II k.o. tree, *Vitis adnata, Spatholobus ferrugineus*.

sambar swoop, pounce, snatch. *~ gelédék!* (*coq*) damn, damn it, damn you, go to hell!

menyambar [and **nyambar** (*coq*)] **1** to swoop down on, pounce on, snatch and carry away, catch (prey) (of crocodiles/hawks/sharks/fish). *Burung elang itu ~ anak ayam.* The hawk swooped down on the baby chick. **2** to hit, tap, strike (suddenly/violently/unexpectedly); to reach/spread to (and touch). *disambar peluru* struck by a bullet. *cepat seperti kilat ~* as quick as lightning, with lightning speed. *Halilintar ~ batang nyiur.* Lightning hit the trunk of a coconut tree. *api ~ bénsin* the fire spread to the gasoline. *disambar gelédék* a) thunderstruck. b) bewildered, dazed. *disambar petir* struck by lightning. *Bau saté itu ~ hidung.* The smell of saté reached his nose. **3** to grab, snatch, steal. *Dompétnya disambar oléh seorang pen-*

copét di pasar. His purse was snatched by s.o. in the market. **4** to run over. *Empat pejalan kaki téwas disambar bus.* Four pedestrians were run over and killed by a bus.

sambar-menyambar 1 to pounce on e.o. **2** to take turns striking, strike one after the other.

menyambar-nyambar to keep pouncing on.

menyambari (*pl obj*) to pounce on, swoop down on.

menyambarkan to catch/snatch/grab with, put (one's claws) into. *laksana harimau mendekam dan ~ kuku kakinya pada mangsanya* like a tiger crouching and putting his back claws into his prey.

tersambar [and **kesambar** (*coq*)] swooped down on, snatched, struck, hit. *Bus itu ~ keréta api.* The bus was hit by a train. *Lima penduduk Jambi ~ petir.* Five residents of Jambi were struck by lightning.

sambaran 1 (bird, etc.) of prey. *yu ~* man-eating shark. **2** a pounce, swoop, snatching, quick grab. *Perahu itu oléng terkena ~ ombak besar.* The prau was rocked by the blow of a huge wave. *~ angin* gust of wind.

penyambar snatcher, thief who snatches s.t. from his victim. *~ sepéda* bicycle thief.

sambat I junction, splice.

bersambat *~ dengan* connected/joined/coupled/spliced with.

menyambat to connect, join, bind together, couple, splice. *~ dua batang bambu sehingga menjadi galah yang panjang* to join two bamboo stalks together into a long pole.

sambatan coupling.

penyambatan splicing.

sambat II (*Jv*) **sesambat** (to cry out) asking for help.

bersambat and **menyambat** [and **nyambat** (*coq*)] to ask s.o. for help (to carry out a task). *Tak ada seorang lain bisa disambat.* There's nobody else who we can ask for help.

sambatan help(ing hand).

sambat III (*Jv*) **menyambat** to complain, sigh (from misery/misfortune).

sambatan complaint.

sambat IV → SEBAT I.

sambat V menyambat to hit with s.t. flexible (like a rubber hose).

sambatan a blow with s.t. flexible.

sambau I *rumput ~* a hardy grass, goose grass, *Eleusina indica*, used for fodder, medicine, and a shaman's holy water sprinkler. *bagai ~ di tengah jalan* (a life of) ups and downs. *~ jangkang* a grass, *Trigonostemon longifolius*.

sambau II bloated (of one's stomach).

sambel → SAMBAL.

sambélakala (*Jv*) hindrance, trouble.

sambén (*Jv*) *pekerjaan ~* sideline, side job; → SAMBILAN, SAMPINGAN.

menyambén to work a side job.

samber → SAMBAR. *~ glédék!* may I be struck by lightning (if I am lying).

sambet → KESAMBET.

sambi (*Jv*) **menyambi** [and **nyambi** (*coq*)] **1** to do s.t. at the same time as s.t. else. *Usahanya bisa disambi.* He could do the (other) job as well as carry out his business at the same time. **2** to have a side job. *Bukan rahasia lagi bahwa artis kita banyak yang nyambi untuk menambah penghasilan.* It's no secret that many of our artists have a side job to increase their income.

sambil while, as (used to join two sentences which have the same subject). *Murid-murid sekolah melambai-lambai kepada kami ~ berteriak-teriak.* The schoolchildren kept waving at us as they shouted. *katanya ~ tertawa* he said (while) laughing. *~ menyelam minum air* and *~ berdiang nasi masak, ~ berdéndang biduk hilir* to kill two birds with one stone. *~ lalu* in passing, casual (glance, etc.). **menyambil-lalukan** to consider s.t. of secondary importance, do. s.t. in passing.

sambil-sambil in passing, incidentally, superficially.

menyambil to do s.t. as a sideline. *Anda dapat ~ pekerjaan yang lain.* You can get a second job.

menyambilkan to do s.t. at the same time (as s.t. else). *Dia pun ada kerja istiméwa agaknya yang boléh disambilkan apabila pergi ke pasar.* It seems that she has a special job which can be done when she goes to the market.

tersambil (to be) a matter of minor/secondary importance, accessory matter, side issue. *pekerjaan* ~ a side job.

sambilan 1 secondary, additional, part-time, side. *fungsi* ~ a secondary function, sideline. *pekerjaan* ~ sideline, second/side job. *Mémang salah satu usaha* ~ *penduduk Prapat ialah menangkap ikan.* In fact, one of the side jobs of the people in Prapat is fishing. *mahasiswa* ~ part-time student; → *mahasiswa* PENGGAL *waktu.* **2** pretext; → DALIH.

sambilata and **sambiloto** (*Jv*) green chiretta, a tree, *Andrographis paniculata,* whose stem can reach a length of 90 cm; it grows from 25 to 700 m above sea level; the leaves are used against malaria, fever, diabetes, flu, diarrhea, and snakebites.

sambit (*J/Jv*) **bersambit-sambit(an)** to throw at e.o. *Kedua pengantin* ~ *dengan daun sirih.* The bride and groom threw betel leaves at e.o. (part of the wedding ceremony).

menyambit [and **nyambit** (*coq*)] to throw at. *Anak itu* ~ *saya dengan/pakai sandal.* The child threw a sandal at me.

menyambiti [and **nyambitin** (*J coq*)] (*pl obj*) to throw repeatedly at, pelt. *Anak-anak* ~ *anjing geladak itu.* The children pelted the mongrel.

menyambitkan to throw/hurl s.t. *Kulit pisang itu disambitkannya kepada saya.* He threw the banana peel at me.

penyambit 1 thrower. **2** s.t. thrown, missile.

sambuk I → CAMBUK.

sambuk II (*A ob*) dinghy.

sambuk III (*J*) → SABUT I.

sambung 1 connection, continuation. *minta – dengan* please connect me with. *salah* ~ wrong number (in making a telephone call). **2** grafting. **3** continue, go on. *-nya* he continued. *- akar* root graft. *- cemeti* splice, graft. *- juang* continuous struggle. *- rasa* (to forge an) emotional link (with e.o.). *"Pada hari ini kita bersama untuk tatap muka, temu wicara, - rasa untuk dapat meninjau diri kita masing-masing,"* kata Kepala Negara. "We have gathered together today to face e.o., to speak to e.o., and to forge an emotional link with e.o. to examine ourselves," said the Head of State. *- sinambung* continuing, ongoing. *- singkat* short circuit. *- tangan* help, helping hand, assistance. **bersambung tangan** to give help, lend a hand.

bersambung 1 with an extension/piece that makes s.t. longer. *pita yang* ~ a ribbon with a piece added to it to make it longer. **2** continued, continuous; one after the other, relay. ~ *ke halaman IV* continued on page IV. *berenang* ~ relay swimming. *cerita* ~ [cerbér] serial, continuing story, feuilleton. *lari* ~ relay race. *nomor* ~ in sequence. *surat* ~ chain letter. *pertunjukan* ~ a continuous show. **3** to be connected/related/tied to e.o. *Rumahnya* ~ *dengan rumah saya.* His house is connected to my house. ~ *keluarga dengan* to be related to. **4** to follow (from), agree (with) *Jawabannya tidak* ~ *dengan pertanyaanku kepadanya.* His answer didn't follow from the question I asked him. **5** to come together. ~ *kembali* to knit (of a broken bone).

bersambung-sambung in a row, one after the other.

bersambungan connected to e.o. *rumah saling* ~ connected houses.

menyambung 1 to make longer, lengthen. *(akan) disambung* (to be) continued (of a story). *Jalan raya itu akan disambung lagi pada tahun depan.* The highway will be lengthened again next year. **2** to link up (the pieces of s.t.). ~ *rantai sepéda dengan dawai* to link up the bicycle chain with wire. **3** [and **nyambung** (*coq*)] (in telephone conversations) to connect, put s.o. (through to). *minta disambung dengan* please connect me with. **4** pursuant/further to, with reference to. ~ *Anda yang terakhir* pursuant to your last letter. **5** to make a go of, support (one's family, etc.). **6** to pick s.t. up (where one left off), continue. ~ *hidup* to survive, make ends meet, make a living. *berusaha* ~ *hidup di rantau* to try to make a go of one's life abroad. *berusaha* ~ *hidup sehari-hari* to make ends meet. ~ *hidupnya sekeluarga* to support one's family. ~ *keturunan* to multiply, propagate. ~ *lidah* to convey a message from s.o. to s.o. else. ~ *nyawa* to survive. ~ *pembicaraan/perkataan* continuing the conversation/discussions. ~ *rezeki* to survive. ~ *tali silaturrahmi/persahabatan* to strengthen the ties of friendship. ~ *tangan* to get help. ~ *umur* to survive.

sambung-menyambung and **sambung-bersambung** to follow e.o. in rapid succession, occur one after the other, nonstop. *Télepon itu berdering* ~. The telephone kept ringing nonstop. *Petir* ~ *tidak putus-putusnya.* The thunderclaps followed e.o. in rapid succession.

menyambungi to join in on. *Mendengar suara suaminya itu, disambunginya nyanyi suaminya.* Hearing her husband's voice, she joined in on his singing.

menyambungkan [and **nyambungin** (*J coq*)] **1** to connect, join (s.t. with s.t. else). *Léhér itu* ~ *kepala dengan badan.* The neck joins the head and body. **2** to connect, put through (on the telephone).

mempersambungkan to connect s.t. (to s.t. else).

tersambung 1 connected, in service (of telephones). *jumlah télepon yang* ~ the number of connected telephones. *télepon yang tidak* ~ *lagi* a disconnected telephone. *tidak* ~ disconnected (of conversation). **2** service (of electrical power).

sambungan 1 connecting (of flights, etc.). *penerbangan* ~ *dari Jakarta ke Singapura* a connecting flight from Jakarta to Singapore. **2** continuation, installment (of a continuing story). *Cerita ini ada ~nya lagi.* This story has a additional continuation. ~ *tangan* helper, helping hand; aid, assistance. ~ *terakhir* final installment. **3** telephone line, extension. ~ *induk* main line. ~ *khusus* hot line. **4** lengthening piece, extension. *Bambu ini dapat dijadikan* ~ *galah péndék ini.* The piece of bamboo can be made into an extension for this short pole. **5** connection, joint, coupler, coupling, bond, sleeve, scarf, patch, graft (in some compounds). (*pipa-pipa*) *tanpa* ~ seamless (pipes). ~ *bawah* root-stock. ~ *bergerigi* notched joint. ~ *celah* (*bot*) cleft graft (in grafting). ~ *flénsa* flange joint/sleeve. ~ *ganda* disk scarf. ~ *hidup* nest egg. ~ *jiwa* child; darling. ~ *langsung internasional* [SLI] international direct-dial call. ~ *langsung jarak jauh* [SLJJ] direct-dial long-distance call. ~ *lengkung* bend (in a pipe). ~ *lidah* spokesman, spokeswoman; → JURU *bicara,* JUBIR. ~ *menumpu* butt joint. ~ *nyawa* a) child; darling. b) nest egg. ~ *pemanfaat* appliance coupler/adaptor. ~ *pemuai* expansion joint. ~ *piranti lunak* software patch. ~ *rata* flat graft. ~ *silang* cross notching (of wood). ~ *sok* box coupling. ~ *tumpang* lap joint. ~ *tumpu* butt joint. **bersambungan** with an extension.

penyambung 1 connector. ~ *lidah* spokesman, mouthpiece. ~ *lidah rakyat* spokesman for the people, vox populi. ~ *télepon* telephone operator. **2** device used to connect two things to e.o. ~ *kata* ~ (*gram*) conjunction. *tanda* ~ (*gram*) hyphen; → SENGKANG. *Sebagai* ~ *hidup sehari-hari menjadi sukar.* It's getting hard to make ends meet.

penyambungan 1 connection. ~ *kabel télepon* telephone cable connection. *salah* ~ poor connection. **2** splicing.

persambungan 1 connection. **2** (*mostly Mal*) joint. ~ *tulang-tulang* bone joint.

sambur I and **sambur-limbur** twilight; → SABUR.

sambur II → SEMBUR I.

sambut 1 reply. **2** welcomed.

bersambut 1 to get a reply/answer/reaction/response, etc., be greeted, be accepted/approved. *Pidatonya* ~ *tepuk tangan para hadirin.* His speech was greeted by applause from the audience. *tidak* ~ to have no response. **2** to buy on credit. *Kami* ~ *ke warung itu.* We bought on credit from that stall. **3** ~ *pada* to meet the needs of, appeal to.

bersambutan 1 to answer e.o., exchange replies. *Muda-mudi berpantun* ~ *dengan riang.* The young people recited quatrains, exchanging replies cheerfully. **2** in response (to), with regard (to). ~ *dengan anjuran pemerintah* with regard to the government's recommendations. *Meréka* ~ *terus-menerus dalam diskusi itu.* They took turns in the discussion.

sambut-bersambut and **bersambut-sambutan** to answer/respond to e.o. in turn.

menyambut 1 to receive, accept. *Kami* ~ *penghargaan itu dengan rasa haru.* We accepted the reward with emotion. ~ *untung* to accept one's fate. **2** to react/respond to. *Penduduk* ~ *kebijaksanaan lurahnya dengan sikap positip.* The inhabitants reacted positively to the village head's policy. **3** to catch (an object). *Saya* ~ *bola yang dilémparkan kepada saya.* I caught the ball thrown to me. **4** to welcome, greet, look forward to. *Kami ~ hari depan yang lebih baik.* We look forward to a better future. **5** to approach (a problem), on the occasion of. **6** to avert, evade, dodge, parry. *Pasukan itu ~ serangan musuh dengan gigihnya.* The troops parried the enemy's attack with perseverance. **7** to buy on credit, buy on the installment plan. *Saya ~ sebungkus rokok ke warung.* I bought a pack of cigarettes on credit from the stall. *~ baik* to welcome, receive/accept positively. *Kongrés Kabilah Somalia ~ baik misi pasukan AS.* The Somali Clan Congress welcomed the mission of the U.S. troops. *~ untung* to accept one's fate.

sambut-menyambut to respond/answer e.o. in turn.

menyambuti (*pl obj*) to greet, respond to.

tersambut responded to, greeted. *cinta tidak ~* a love that is not accepted.

sambutan 1 reception, welcome. *~ positif terhadap misi pasukan AS ke Somalia* a positive reception to the mission of U.S. troops to Somalia. **2** answer, response, reaction, commentary (on a newspaper article, etc.). *Tulisannya mendapat ~ yang tajam.* His article got a sharp reaction. *~ tertulis* written response, response in writing. *Penegasan itu tertuang dalam ~ tertulis yang dibacakan Ketua DPP Golkar.* The explanation was couched in a written response read out by the chairman of *Golkar*'s Central Leadership Council. *~ tanpa téks* an impromptu response. **3** speech, address, remarks. *pidato ~* welcoming speech, opening remarks. **4** goods bought on credit. **5** consignment. *Pedagang itu memberikan ~ barang-barang kelontong di toko itu.* The merchant gave some small goods as a consignment to that store.

penyambut 1 receptionist, s.o. who receives guests, greeter. *Saya bertugas sebagai ~ tamu negara.* My duties were to greet state visitors. **2** goods or food to be presented to guests.

penyambutan reception, welcoming. *upacara ~* welcoming ceremony. *~ sederhana bagi tamu-tamu dari Pusat* a simple reception for visitors from the central government.

samédi → SEMADI.

samék (*M ob*) → SEMAT.

samenléven (*D*) to live together as husband and wife without being married; → KUMPUL *kebo*.

sami I (*Skr*) Buddhist monk.

sami II (*Jv*) alike, the same; → SAMA I. *- mawon* exactly the same, it's all the same. *Hasilnya - mawon.* The result is exactly the same.

Sami III (*A*) *as-Sami* the Hearkener, Listener (one of the names of God).

samijaga [sarana air minum dan jamban keluarga] facilities for drinking water and family toilets.

samin I (*A*) *minyak* - cooking oil extracted from goat's milk, k.o. ghee. *nasi* - rice cooked in this oil.

Samin II short for Kiayi Samin Surosentiko, exiled to Padang in 1907, died in 1914, founder of an anarchistic utopian community in Central Java.

Saminisme *ajaran* - the teachings of Samin *q.v.*

samir I 1 rough sheets of palm fronds stitched together to make a temporary roofing. **2** (*Jv*) a round banana leaf folded into a shallow inverted cone and used for covering foods.

samir II (*Jv*) a fringed yellow silk scarf worn by palace officials as an emblem of their office.

Samiri (*A*) *orang* - Samarian.

samodera → SAMUDRA.

samo-samo k.o. plant, sea grass, *Enhalus acoroides*.

sampa I → UBI *sampa.*

sampa II iron nail.

sampah garbage, waste (matter), trash, refuse. *bak/keranjang/tempat* - wastebasket, trash container/bin. *tempat pembuangan/penimbunan* - landfill. *tukang* - garbage collector/man. *- itu di tepi juga* people usually don't pay attention to worthless people. *teralang-alang bagaikan - dalam mata* an insult that always comes to one's mind and that is deeply felt. *- B2* [berbahaya] hazardous waste. *- B3* [berbahaya beracun] toxic waste. *- basah* kitchen and yard waste. *- bertoksik* toxic waste. *- dunia* a useless or worthless person. *- hijau* compost. *- masyarakat* social scum, scum of the earth. *- padat* solid waste. *- sarap* all k.o. trash.

menyampah 1 to rot, become polluted. *Tanggung jawab tidak jelas mengakibatkan waduk ~.* Unclear responsibility resulted in a polluted reservoir. **2** to pollute.

mempersampahkan to treat like rubbish, consider scum.

penyampah polluter.

penyampahan pollution, polluting.

persampahan rubbish/garbage heap, place to put garbage.

sampai I 1 to arrive (at), reach its destination; to finish (what one is doing). *Kami akan - di Singapura bésok.* We'll arrive in Singapore tomorrow. *Suratnya sudah - dengan selamat.* The letter arrived safely. *sudah -* arrived (of goods). *sudah - besarnya* has reached adulthood, has grown up. *Tidak - tamat pengajarannya.* (He) hasn't finished his studies. *Hendaklah - selesai baru berhenti.* Please finish the whole thing before you stop. **2** to expire (of a term/treaty, etc.). *Perjanjian sudah -.* The due date (to pay) has arrived. **3** to reach (out to and touch). *Tangannya tidak - buah mangga itu walaupun dia menjéngkét.* His hand couldn't reach the mango even though he stood on tiptoes. *Suaranya sayup-sayup -.* His voiced reached us vaguely. **4** to come true (of a dream), be realized/fulfilled (of a wish), achieved, reached, successful (of a plan). *Mudah-mudahan cita-citamu -.* I hope that your aspirations are fulfilled. *tak -* unrequited (of love). *marah yang tiada -* short-lived anger. **5** be as much as, enough (to), sufficient, reach as far as, go as far as. *Harganya tidak - seribu rupiah.* The price is less than a thousand rupiahs. *ada pula yang - lama* others (have stayed) longer. *cari - lama* to have looked for a long time (but in vain). *sekalipun tak usah - selama itu* even though it might not last that long. *Gaji ayah tidak - untuk hidup satu bulan.* Father's salary is not enough to live on for a month. *- dengan* [s/d] up to and including, through. *- dalam* sufficiently deep, deep enough. *- kuat* strong enough (to). *muka - baik* his face is pretty nice. *tak -* not quite (a certain amount of time). *jangan -* don't go so far as to, on no account should you. *Jangan - ketahuan Gubernur Supardjo.* Don't let Gov. Supardjo find out. *Golongan Karya jangan - menjadi organisasi yang sifatnya tertutup.* On no account should *Golkar* become a closed organization. **6** as a result of that. *Matanya silau -.* He become blind as a result of that. **7** to go so far as to, bring o.s. to the point of. *Saya tidak - membaca buku novél itu.* I can't bring myself to read that novel. **8** to (reach) such a point. *Mengapa peluhmu - begini?* Why are you sweating so much? *- ajal* to die, pass away. *- akal* logical, makes sense. *- akhir zaman* till the end of time, forever. *- bulannya* term (of a pregnancy). *- hari kiamat* till the end of time, forever. *- hati* to have the heart/nerve to, bring o.s. to (the point of). *Aku tidak - hati meninggalkan engkau.* I can't bring myself to leave you. *- jangka* to the exact amount. *- janji* to die, pass away. *- ke akar-akarnya* root and branch, to the very core. *- ke gunjainya* in every detail. *- ke liang kubur* unto death. *- ke sumsum* to the very marrow. *- kuping* to hear of s.t., come to one's attention. *- mati* to death, until ... died, fatal. *- rasa* to not hesitate, have the heart/nerve to, bring o.s. to. *- telinga* to hear of s.t., come to one's attention. *- tétés darah penghabisan* to the last drop of one's blood. *- tua* forever, for good. *- umur* a) adult, grown up. b) (*leg*) of age. c) advanced in years, old. *sudah - umurnya* to die, pass away.

sampai-sampai 1 so ... that *Ia asyik berjudi ~ ia lupa akan anaknya.* He was so absorbed in his gambling that he forget about his child. *Begitu kalemnya wanita langsing berkaca itu ~ ada yang menjulukinya biarawati.* The slender woman who wears glasses was so calm that some people nicknamed her the nun. **2** (immediately) upon arrival, as soon as ... arrived. *~ dia langsung merebahkan diri karena capéknya.* As soon as she arrived, she lay down right away because she was so tired. **3** to be forced (by circumstances) to, have to, even to the point of. *Bakal makan saja, ~ menjual pakaian.* Just in order to eat he had to sell his clothing.

sesampai 1 on arrival, upon reaching one's destination. *Barang-barang itu hilang ~ di tempat tujuan.* The goods disappeared when they reached their destination. **2** within reach of. *Aku lalu mencari tempat kos yang murah ~ gajiku.* Then I looked for a boardinghouse within reach of my salary.

nyampai (*J*) **1** to arrive. **2** to reach. **3** sufficient.

sampai-menyampai sufficient, enough. *Pendapatannya tidak ~. His income is not sufficient.*

menyampaikan 1 to deliver, convey, give, extend (an offer), offer (a suggestion), express (an opinion). *Saya akan ~ surat ini kepada S.* I'll deliver this letter to S. *~ pidato* to deliver a speech. *~ salam* to give one's greetings (to). *Sampaikan salam saya kepada Bu Sri.* Give my greetings to Bu Sri. **2** to send, forward, submit, pass s.t. on. *Kami sudah ~ surat permohonan melalui pos.* We've sent the petition by mail. **3** to make s.t. suffice, make last, stretch out. *Ia ~ gajinya untuk hidup satu bulan.* She made her salary last to live on for a month. **4** to fulfill (one's obligations, etc.). *Ia pergi merantau untuk ~ cita-citanya.* He went abroad to fulfill his dreams.

tersampaikan granted (of a wish), given. **ketersampaian** achievement.

kesampaian 1 arrival. *Orang ramai di situ tidak menghiraukan ~ meréka.* The crowd over there paid no attention to their arrival. **2** to reach, achieve, fulfill. *Ia ~ maksudnya.* He has achieved his goal. **3** to be reached, fulfilled, kept. *Janji-janjinya tidak pernah ~.* His promises are never kept. **4** sufficient, enough. *tak ~* not enough, insufficient. *Untuk membeli jagung sering tak ~.* It's often not even enough to buy corn. **5** accessibility. **berkesampaian** achieved; sufficient.

penyampai 1 messenger, deliverer, sender, conveyor. **2** transmitter. *~ berita* transmitter of news, media.

penyampaian presentation, conveyance, delivery, sending, submission, submitting, dissemination.

sampai II (preposition) to, until, till, as far as, up to. *- berapa besar untung-ruginya?* What are the chances? *- bertemu/ketemu (lagi)* so long, see you, 'bye. *- bésok* see you tomorrow. *- botak* forever. *- jauh malam* far into the night. *- kini* up to now. *dari Sabang – Merauké* from Sabang to Merauke, i.e., an expression of the territorial unity of the Republic of Indonesia, including Irian Jaya. *- mati* to death, until (s.o.) died, fatal. *- nanti* see you later. *- paha* up to one's thigh. *- saat ini* up to (or, until) this very moment. *- sekarang* up to now, to date, so far. *- sini* as far as here. *- tua* forever. *Tidak - di situ saja.* It didn't end there.

sampai III **menyampaikan 1** to hang out (clothing) to dry. **2** to place (a scarf, etc.) over one's shoulders.

tersampai hung out (of clothes) to dry.

sampaian clothesline or any line strung out for hanging clothes on; → SELAMPAI I.

sampak I metal collar to prevent tang or blade from splitting a wooden handle.

menyampak to provide s.t. with such a metal collar.

sampak II (*Jv*) *main -* (to toss a coin, etc. to see if it lands) heads or tails.

menyampak to toss.

menyampakkan to toss away.

sampak III (*Jv*) quick-paced *gamelan* music to accompany marching or a battle scene. *- sono* a tempo used in *gamelan* music near the denouement of a play.

sampakan war-like music.

sampak IV (*J*) tuft of hair; → JAMBAK II.

menyampak [and **nyampak** (*coq*)] **1** to pull/tear out one's hair. **2** to slap or beat with the hand in passing.

sampak V → SELUAR *sampak.*

sampan (*C*) sampan, flat-bottomed skiff *usu* propelled by oars, dugout. *- ada pengayuh tidak* not to have prepared o.s. well in advance. *ada – hendak berenang* to work o.s. to the bone for nothing. *- gandéng* double-hulled canoe. *- kolék* sampan without a sail. *- ludang* spathe-shaped boat. *- payang/pukat* fisherman's dinghy. *bagai – pukat* a stay-at-home, couch potato. *- tambang* (*BD*) gondola. *- tunda* towed sampan.

bersampan to travel/go by sampan.

bersampan-sampan to go around by sampan for pleasure.

sampang I a reddish-brown varnish.

menyampang to varnish s.t.

sampang II (*M*) a frame to hold the head of a buffalo/cow while its nose is pierced.

menyampang to hold the head of a buffalo while this is done.

tersampang 1 stuck, fastened. **2** remain fixed.

sampang III 1 to have enough time to; → SEMPAT. **2** in case, if.

sampang IV **menyampang** to paddle from the bow.

sampang V (*Jv*) k.o. tree, *Evodia latifolia.*

sampanye (*D*) champagne.

sampar epidemic, pest, plague. *- ayam* chicken pest. *- barah* bubonic plague. *- héwan* rinderpest. *- kaki* blackleg.

samparantu → SAPARANTU.

sampat *mandi -* ceremonial bathing of newlyweds on the third day after their marriage.

sampé → SAMPAI I. **nyampé** to arrive.

sampéan (*Jv*) **1** foot. **2** you; your (polite and respectful). *- andika* an honorific in archaic titles. *- Dalem* His Highness (title for a Javanese princess).

sampék (*Jv reg*) and (*coq pron of*) SAMPAI II.

sampel (*E*) sample; → CONTOH. *mengambil -* to take a sample.

samper (*J*) **menyamper(i)** and **nyamperin 1** to pick up s.o. (to go along). **2** to approach.

kesamper afflicted (by an illness due to an evil spirit or other mysterious power).

sampeu (*S*) k.o. cassava, *Manihot ultissima.*

sampéyan → SAMPÉAN.

sampi (*J*) → SAPI I. *- gamang* (in Lombok) wild buffalo.

sampil I (*Jv*) leg of meat (beef/lamb, etc.). *- babi* ham. *- kulit* husk at the lower end of a palm branch.

sampil II husk at the base of palm fronds.

samping I 1 side. *di -* a) beside, next to. *Ia berjalan di – ayahnya.* He was walking next to his father. *di – itu* besides that, moreover. *di – mana?* on which side? b) besides, in addition to, aside from; → LAIN I, SELAIN. *jalan -* feeder road, byway, shortcut. *léwat -* by the back door, in secret. *pintu -* side door. *ke -* to the side, lateral. **mengesampingkan** and **mengenyampingkan 1** to remove, set aside. *Amérika belum mengenyampingkan perundingan-perundingan dengan PLO.* America has not yet set aside negotiations with the PLO. **2** to ignore, disregard, not pay attention to. *Pejabat itu ~ pendapat yang baik dari bawahannya.* The official disregarded the good advice given by his subordinates. *Besar kemungkinan bahwa berita itu akan dikesampingkan.* It's quite possible that the news will be ignored. **terkesampingkan** put off/aside, shelved, postponed. *akibat dari ~nya ilmu-ilmu sosial itu* as a result of the social sciences being set aside. **pengenyampingan** setting aside, canceling. **2** lateral.

menyamping 1 to go along the side (of the road, etc.). *Ia berjalan ~ rumah.* He walked along the side of the house. **2** (*petro*) directional, lateral.

samping-menyamping 1 side by side. *Meréka ~ berlari-lari.* They were running side by side. **2** on either side of.

menyampingi 1 (to sit/lie, etc.) next to, at the side of. *Ia duduk ~ kepala kantornya.* He sat next to the head of his office. **2** to ignore, disregard. *Anak itu ~ nasihat ibunya.* The child ignored his mother's advice. **3** to aid, assist, support, second.

menyampingkan 1 to push s.t. to the side. **2** to set s.t. aside, ignore, pay no attention to.

tersamping(kan) pushed/put aside.

sampingan 1 side, not main. *akibat ~* side effect. *hasil ~* by-product. *kegiatan ~* side activity. *pekerjaan/usaha ~* side/part-time/second job. **2** sideline, secondary work. **bersampingan** side by side; on both sides, on either side. *Meréka duduk ~.* They were sitting side by side.

penyamping (*mod*) side. *dari jurusan ~* from the side.

penyampingan *~ perkara* setting aside, prosecutor's decision not to pursue a case.

samping II (*S*) **1** sarong. **2** *si -* a *sarong* which only hangs down to the knees.

bersamping 1 to wear a *sarong/kain.* **2** to wear a *sarong* which only hangs down to the knees.

samping III (*cla*) k.o. drum.

sampinur k.o. tree, *Dactylocladus stenostachys*; → JONGKONG III.

sampinyon (*D*) (canned) mushrooms; → JAMUR.

sampir I the upper part of a kris sheath, *usu* made from *kemuning* wood.

menyampir to make this part of the kris.

sampir II (*J/Jv*) **menyampir** to hang (over the shoulder). *Selembar seléndang ~ di pundaknya.* A shawl hung over her shoulder.

menyampiri to hang s.t. on. *Rumah disampiri spanduk.* The house was hung with banners.

menyampirkan 1 to hang s.t. up. **2** to place s.t. in the hands (of). *Hal itu disampirkan pada hakim.* Those matters are in the hands of judges.

sampiran 1 clothesline. **2** coatrack.

sampling (*E*) sampling. *- bertahap/bertingkat* multiphase/multistage sampling.

samplok bersamplokan 1 to run into e.o. **2** to meet (of glances).

samplong (in Klirong subdistrict, Kebumen) forest ghost which eats the rice and side dishes left after a *selamatan* and also runs after young widows on Thursday *Wagé* and Friday *Kliwon*.

sampo (*D*) shampoo.

sampu name of various diseases, such as anemia, jaundice, etc. *- pening* vertigo accompanied by a headache.

menyampu to ward off a disease caused by a charm.

sampuk bersampuk to collide (with e.o.).

menyampuk 1 to collide, crash/smash into, hit against. *Tangannya ~ tiang besi.* His hand hit against the iron pole. **2** to ward off (an attack), parry (a blow), push aside. *Polisi ~ tangan penodong yang bersenjata itu.* The policeman pushed aside the hand of the armed hold-up man. **3** to cut off, interrupt. *Kurang sopan kalau kita ~ pembicaraan orang lain.* It's impolite to interrupt s.o.'s conversation. **4** to meddle with, interfere in (s.o.'s business, etc.).

menyampukkan to crash/smash/ram s.t. into s.t.

tersampuk collided with, hit against. *kakinya ~ batu* his foot hit against a stone.

sampukan 1 clothesline, hanger. **2** (*leg*) assault.

kesampukan (*ob*) possessed (by the devil, etc.).

penyampuk assailant.

penyampukan (*leg*) assault.

sampul wrapper, envelope, cover. *gadis -* cover girl. *- bantal* pillowcase; → **SARUNG** *bantal. - buku* jacket (of book), book cover. *- gigi* filling (in a tooth). *- hari pertama* first-day cover. *- luar* outside cover. *- peringatan* commemorative cover. *- rokok* cigarette wrapper. *- surat* envelope; → **AMPLOP**.

bersampul covered, wrapped, placed in an envelope, with a cover/wrapper, etc.

menyampul to wrap, put into an envelope, cover.

menyampuli to put a wrapper/cover on, put (a letter) in an envelope.

menyampulkan to use s.t. as a wrapper for.

tersampul wrapped, covered.

penyampul cover, covering.

penyampulan wrapping, covering.

sampun (*Jv*) → **SUDAH**.

sampur I (*Jv*) a long sash worn as part of the classical costume of a female dancer; → **SELÉNDANG**. *ketiban -* to get one's chance (at s.t. good/lucky). *"Saya seperti ketiban -," kata Pak Haji.* "It's as if I've gotten my lucky break," said the Haji. *- gantung* garment that covers the breasts.

penyampur wrapper.

Sampur II (*col*) Zandvoort, a bathing resort in Jakarta.

sampurna → **SEMPURNA**.

sampyuh (*Jv*) to be killed (of two combatants simultaneously). *berakhir -* ended up with both of them killed.

samrah and **samroh** (*A*) (*- tonil*) k.o. Jakarta song and dance performance put on after Maulud Nabi. *lomba -* contest for singing religious poems; *cp* **KASIDAH**.

Sam Ratulangi 1 name of the airport in Manado. **2** name of a university in Manado.

samsam (*coq*) (to go) together.

sam sam sen [*sama-sama-senang*] (*Min*) to have fun together.

samsara → **SENGSARA**.

samseng (*C*) condolence call.

samséng (*C*) **1** gamecock. **2** hooligan, rowdy person.

samsir (*Pers cla*) scimitar.

samsiti (*C J*) a salad prepared from salted vegetables.

samsonit (*E*) samsonite (briefcase).

samsu I (*A*) the sun; → **SYAMSI, SYAMSU**.

samsu II (*C*) arrack (made from sugarcane).

samudana (*Jv*) having a pleasant, friendly expression hiding one's true feelings.

samudera → **SAMUDRA**.

samuderanisasi → **SAMUDRANISASI**.

samudra (*Skr*) ocean. *ketujuh -* the seven seas. *pemekaran lantai -* ocean-floor spreading. *punggungan tengah -* midocean ridge. *rapat -* mass meeting. *- Artika* Arctic Ocean. *- (H)india* Indian Ocean. *- Indonésia* (*ob*) the Indian Ocean. *- Pasifik* Pacific Ocean. *- raya* open sea.

samudranisasi making into s.t. oceanic. *- pelabuhan Semarang* making Semarang harbor into an oceanic port.

samudrawi oceanic.

samum (*A*) simoon, a hot dry dust storm in Central Asian and African deserts.

samun I *semak -* thick undergrowth, brush, shrubbery; → **SEMAK I**.

samun II *- sakal* highway robbery (with the threat of violence).

menyamun(i) to rob (on the highway).

samunan 1 loot. **2** robbery. **3** robbed, looted.

kesamunan to be/get robbed.

penyamun robber.

penyamunan robbery.

samur (*A*) marten, weasel.

samurai (*Jp*) samurai. *kaum -* the Japanese military caste. *pedang -* samurai sword.

samya *- suara* chorus, choir.

san (in acronyms) → **SÉRSAN**.

sana I 1 (over) there (not near either the speaker or the hearer); *cp* **SITU**. *di -* a) over there. b) (in correspondence) here, where the writer is (the sender is taking the point of view of the recipient, for whom the writer is "there"); *cp* **SINI I**. *dari -* from there. *(di) sebelah -* on the other side, over there. *(di) seberang -* across, on the other side of (the river, etc.). *suara di seberang -* the voice at the other end (of the telephone line). *ke -* there, to that place. *pergi ke -* to go there. *ke - ke mari* to and fro, back and forth, around and around. *ke - sedikit* (push/move) it over there a bit. *di AS -* over there in the United States. *dari -nya* (out) of that/which. *Kadang-kadang ganja kering itu saya jual Rp 1.500 per amplop, dr -nya Rp 1.000 ...* Sometimes I sell a bag of marijuana for Rp 1,500; Rp 1,000 of which ... **mengesanakan** to (move/take) s.t. over there. **2** other, opposing, different. *sudah ke -* has gone over (to the opposition). *tidak ke -* *tidak ke sini* impartial, neutral. *pihak -* the other side, the opposition. *menterjemahkan ke bahasa -* to translate into a foreign language. **3** (in compounds) place, position, site. *singgasana* throne.

sana-sini *di ~* here and there, everywhere.

sanaan (*J*) (somewhat) further (away), over in that direction. *duduk ~ sedikit* sit further over there.

sana II (*Jv*) he, she, they; *cp* **SITU II**. *- putranya présidén* he's the president's son.

sana III → **ANGSANA**. *- keling* k.o. plant, *Dalbergia latifolia*.

sanad (*A*) chain (of traditions about the Prophet); → **HADIS**.

sanak relative, (blood) relation, member of the family. *- famili/kadang* (*Jv*) family, relations, relatives. *- keluarga* family, relatives, relations. **kesanak-keluargaan** (family) relationship. *- saudara* family, relatives, relations. **sesanak saudara** (*dengan*) to be related (to). **bersanak saudara 1** to be related (to). **2** to have relatives. *tidak ~* to be all alone in the world, have no family; → **SEBATANG** *kara,* **SORANGAN**.

bersanak → **BERSANAK SAUDARA**.

menyanak to treat/consider s.o. a relative. *NU jangan disanak kalau ada perlunya saja!* Don't treat the NU as a close relative only when you need to!

kesanakan affinity; → **AFINITAS**.

sanan (*M*) over there; → **SANA I**.

sanat (*A*) **1** (Muslim) year. **2** year (in a certain calendar), date. *- Maséhi* A.D., Anno Domini, year of the Christian calendar. *- ul hijrah* A.H. year of the Hegira, year of the Muslim calendar.

bersanat with the date/year ...

sanatorium (*D*) sanatorium.

menyanatoriumkan to place in a sanatorium.

sanawiah → TSANAWIYAH.

sanca *(J) ular* – python; → PITON. – *bodo* Burmese python, *Python molurus*. – *hijau* green python, *Chondrophyton viridis*. – *timor* Timor python, *Python timorensis*.

sanda I clipped form of **sahaanda** your servant, I; → SAYA.

sanda II → SENDA I.

sanda III *(M)* pledge, pawn; → SANDAR II. *jual* – to pawn.
menyandakan to pledge, pawn.

sandal *(D)* sandal, open-toed slipper. – *Jepang/jepit* thongs, flip-flops. – *jinjit* high-heeled sandal.
bersandal to wear sandals, have sandals on. ~ *jepit* to wear thongs.
sandalan to wear sandals.

sandang I (leather/cloth, etc.) shoulder strap. *kata* – *(gram)* article.
bersandang to wear a ... strapped to one's shoulder.
menyandang 1 to sling s.t. over the shoulder, carry s.t. (slung) over the shoulder (of a satchel/bag). ~ *senapan* to carry a rifle over the shoulder, shoulder a rifle. ~ *seberkas kayu bakar* to carry a bundle of firewood on one's shoulder. 2 to bear, take on (a burden/task). *tugas pokok yang disandang R* the main task borne by R. ~ *derita* to suffer s.t. 3 to bear, have, hold (a title/degree/disease/name/position), have the position of. *Sebentar lagi ia akan ~ gelar MBA.* In a short time he'll have an MBA degree. ~ *gelar strata I* to have a bachelor's degree. ~ *jabatan guru besar* he has the position of professor.
menyandangi to give a certain title to.
menyandangkan and mempersandangkan 1 to put s.t. on s.o.'s shoulder (to be carried). *Dia ~ senapan mainan ke pundak anaknya.* He put a toy rifle over his son's shoulder. 2 to put/strap (s.t. over one's shoulder). *Wanita itu mempersandangkan seléndang pada pundaknya.* The woman put a shawl over her shoulder.
tersandang slung, strapped (over one's shoulder). ~ *di bahunya* strapped on one's shoulder. *Di punggungnya ~ ransel.* A backpack was slung over his back.
penyandang 1 for strapping over one's shoulder. *kain ~* (shoulder) strap. 2 carrier/bearer (of a disease or title), holder. ~ *cacat* a handicapped person. ~ *cacat fisik/tubuh* a physically handicapped person. ~ *dana* financier, provider of funds. ~ *gelar* bearer of a title. ~ *masalah kesejahteraan sosial* [PMKS] social undesirables (such as prostitutes/beggars, etc.). ~ *modal* financier. ~ *tunanétra* blind person.
penyandangan 1 strapping s.t. over the shoulder. 2 giving the name of.

sandang II *(Jv)* clothing. – *pangan* food and clothing (the basic necessities). – *pangan papan* food, clothing, and shelter (the basic necessities).
sandangan 1 clothing. 2 certain vowel symbols in the Javanese script.

sandang III *(Pal)* – *gawai* to pay s.o. else for performing required labor.

sandang IV – *lawé* woolly-necked stork, *Ciconia episcopus*.

sandar I prop, support. *kursi* – armchair.
bersandar 1 ~ *ke(pada)/atas/di* to lean (against/on) (a wall, etc.). ~ *di dinding* to sit or stand with one's back against the wall, leaning against the wall. 2 to rely/count/depend on, be based/founded (on), depend (on). *Jangan terlalu banyak ~ kepada bantuan pemerintah.* Don't depend too much on government aid. 3 *(naut)* to moor, tie up (a ship). ~ *di dermaga* to be moored at the quay.
bersandarkan 1 to lean on/up against. *Sepéda itu tidak akan roboh, karena ~ sebatang pohon.* The bike won't fall down it because it's leaning up against a tree. 2 to be based/founded on. 3 to depend/rely on. *Nasibnya ~ belas kasihan majikannya.* His fate depends on his employer's mercy.
menyandar to lean (up against s.t.). *Limah ~ ke dinding.* Limah was leaning against the wall.
sandar-menyandar 1 to lean on e.o. 2 to help/support e.o. 3 to be dependent on e.o.
menyandari 1 to support, provide support for. *Badannya masih lemah dan kalau mau duduk minta sandari kepada anak atau istrinya.* He's still weak, and when he wants to sit down he asks

his child or wife for support. 2 to lean on/against. *Jangan kau-sandari tiang bendéra itu, nanti roboh.* Don't lean against the flagpole, it might collapse. 3 to moor to/up against.
menyandarkan 1 put/lean s.t. (up against). *Saya ~ diri pada tiang télepon.* I leaned (up) against the telephone pole. 2 to entrust s.t. to s.o. ~ *nasib/untung kepada* to entrust one's fate to. 3a) to base/found/ground s.t. on. b) to set (one's hopes) on, entrust. *Ia ~ hidupnya pada hasil jualan rokok.* He entrusted his livelihood to what he made from selling cigarettes.
mempersandari to lean on/up against.
tersandar supported, leaning. ~ *di dinding* leaning against the wall.
sandaran 1 support, back (of a chair). ~ *buku* bookend. ~ *kaki* footrest. ~ *kepala* headrest (in a car). ~ *kepala yang dapat disetél* adjustable headrest. ~ *kursi* back of a chair. ~ *pendapat* accounting for one's vote (in Parliament). ~ *punggung* backrest. 2 base, foundation, source. ~ *hidup* source of one's livelihood. *30 ékor ayamnya merupakan ~ hidupnya.* Thirty chickens are the source of their livelihood. ~ *hukum* legal foundation. 3 rail, railing. bersandaran leaning (against s.t.). ~ *tiang bambu* leaning against a bamboo pole.
penyandar buttress, support. *Untuk ~ ténda itu digunakan pipa besi.* Iron pipes were used to support the tent. ~ *pipa* catwalk.
penyandaran 1 mooring place. 2 leaning (on).
pe(r)sandaran 1 point of support; place to lean on. 2 chair arm. 3 banisters.

sandar II pawn, pledge. *Arloji tangannya yang emas diberikan sebagai – utangnya.* His gold wristwatch was given as security for his loan.
menyandarkan to pawn, pledge.
sandaran ~ *utang* guarantee, collateral.

sandék [pesan péndék] short message.

sandékala *(Jv)* dusk, twilight.

sandel I *kayu* – sandalwood (found on Sumba).

sandel II *kuda* – horse from Sumba.

sandera *(Skr)* 1 hostage. 2 prisoner for debt.
menyandera 1 to take s.o. hostage. 2 to imprison for failure to follow a judicial order (*usu* to pay a debt).
menyanderakan to imprison for debt, throw into debtor's prison.
tersandera 1 taken hostage. *yang ~* hostage. 2 completely occupied/focused (of one's attention). *Kalau saja awal Novémber 1992 perhatian kita tidak ~ berita pemilihan Présidén AS.* If our attention at the beginning of November 1992 had not been completely focused on the US presidential election.
penyandera hostage-taker.
penyanderaan 1 hostage-taking. 2 imprisonment for debt.

sandhi → SANDI II.

sandi I *(Skr)* 1 (secret) code, in secret language, cipher. *nama* – code name. 2 concealed/hidden intention, ulterior motive. – *bangunan* building code. – *kata* code word. – *suara* password. – *télkom* telecommunications code; → TÉLKOM. – *Yudha* a) Special Mission (Forces). b) secret warfare.
bersandi code-named. *sebuah tim ~ "Operasi Purna Yudha"* a team code-named "Postwar Operation."
menyandi to (en)code, put into code. ~ *balik* to decode, put into plain text.
menyandikan to encode.
penyandi encoder.
penyandian encrypting, encoding.
persandian 1 cryptography, cryptographic; encryption, coding. 2 code service.

sandi II *(Skr gram)* sandhi, i.e., morphophonemic alternations, *esp* as determined by phonetic environment.

sandi III → SENDI I.

sandiasma cryptogram, concealment of the author's name, pen name.

sandibonéka puppet show.

sandikarsa *(Jv)* veiled intention.

sandiman *(Jv neo)* cryptographer.

sandinada *(Skr neo)* speed calling (a telephone service).

sandinama *(Skr neo)* initials.

sanding I close, near (by).

bersanding to be near e.o. *duduk* ~ to sit side by side (or, next to e.o.). ~ *bahu dengan* shoulder to shoulder with.
bersandingan to sit close to e.o.
menyandingi 1 to accompany, flank, be side by side with. *Kami ditugaskan ~ tamu itu.* We were assigned to accompany the guests. 2 to marry (a woman).
menyandingkan and **mempersandingkan** 1 to place side by side (or, next to e.o.), juxtapose. *Kami dipersandingkan di kursi yang dihias.* We were placed side by side on the decorated seat. 2 to bring/get together, unite (in marriage). *Ibu itu mau menyandingkan gadisnya dengan pemuda yang masih famili.* The mother wanted to get her daughter together with the young man who is related to them.
sandingan partner. *Gadis itu belum menemukan ~ yang diidamkannya.* The girl has not yet found the partner she has been yearning for.
penyandingan matching. ~ *pendapatan dengan biaya* matching revenues against costs.
sanding II 1 sharp angle, corner. 2 sharp, biting.
bersanding 1 with/to have a sharp angle/corner, angular. *Méja itu ~ empat.* The table has four corners. 2 sharp, biting.
sandirasa (*S gram*) interjection.
sandisastra cryptology, secret language.
sandisora (*S gram*) onomatopoeia.
sandisuara (*mil*) countersign.
sandiwara (*Skr*) 1 play, drama. 2 theatrical troupe. 3 comedy; comedian. 4 hypocrite. *main* – to act (in a play). *pengadilan* – mock court. – *keliling* traveling show. – *nyanyi* operetta, musical comedy. – *panggung* stage play. – *radio* radio play. – *sedih* tragedy, melodrama. – *terbuka* open-air theater.
bersandiwara 1 to act/be on the stage. 2 to put on a big show. *Jangan ~ di hadapan saya.* Don't put on a big show in front of me.
menyandiwarakan 1 to dramatize. 2 to adapt for the stage. *Pengarang itu sedang ~ cerita rakyat.* The author is adapting a folktale for the stage. 3 to poke fun at s.o.
kesandiwaraan theater (*mod*).
penyandiwaraan dramatization (of a novel, etc.), adaptation for the stage.
persandiwaraan theater (*mod*).
sandiwarawan (*Skr neo infr*) dramatist.
sando (*E*) tension bands (for physical exercise).
sandra → SANDERA.
sandro (in Sumatra) shaman; → DUKUN.
sandung I heddles of a loom, treadle of a weaving loom.
menyandung 1 to stumble, hit one's foot against s.t. 2 to trip s.o., make s.o. stumble. 3 to undermine, trip up.
tersandung [and **kesandung** (*coq*)] stumbled, tripped over, (one's foot) hit against s.t. *Kesandung buntut, ketiban sial.* Misfortune dogs his every step.
sandungan 1 heddles of a loom, treadle of a weaving loom. 2 s.t. stumbled over. *batu* ~ stumbling block. *Usul negara itu jadi batu ~ sidang OPÉC.* That country's proposal became a stumbling block at the OPEC meeting. 3 swing, rocking cradle, swinging cot (rocked by foot).
sandung II (in West Kalimantan) structure in which to preserve the ashes or bones of Dayak corpses.
sandyakala (*Skr*) 1 twilight. 2 twilight, the period of gradual decline after full development.
Sandya Kara Murti name of the women's association within the Department of Communication.
sanépa (*Jv*) k.o. metaphor in which s.t. is compared to the opposite of what is expected.
sanépan *cerita* ~ parable.
sanéring (*D*) currency reform, devaluation.
sang I (honorific article preceding a noun) 1 preceding the names of gods, monarchs, sovereigns, kings, etc.: – *Aji* the King. – *Buddha* Buddha. – *Hyang Tunggal* the One and Only God. – *Hyang Widi* Almighty God. – *Hyang Wenang* Almighty God. – *Hyang Widi* the Supreme Being of the Balinese. – *Khalik* the Creator (God). – *Nata* the Lord, Protector. – *Penebus* the Redeemer (Jesus Christ). – *Prabu* the King, His Majesty. – *Yang* God, the Divinity. – *Yang Guru* Siva the Teacher. 2 preced-

ingthe names of animals in fables: – *Belang* Mr. Tiger. – *Kancil* Mr. Mousedeer; → si KANCIL. – *Monyét* Mr. Monkey. 3 respectful title preceding personified nouns: – *Bumi Ruwa Jurai* the Province of Lampung, (*lit*) "the land of two layers (of people)," i.e., the indigenous population and the newcomers. – *Dwiwarna* the Bicolor, i.e., the Indonesian Red and White Flag. – *Kapal* the Ship. – *Mérah Putih* the Indonesian Red and White Flag. – *Saka Mérah Putih* the Indonesian Red and White Flag. – *Surya* the Sun. – *Waktu* Time. 4 shows humorous respect: – *Égo* me. – *istri/suami* one's better half, wife, husband.
persangan (*cla*) the set of courtiers who bear the title of *sang*.
sang II → ESANG.
sanga I dross (of metals).
sanga II (*J*) **tersanga-sanga** hurried, in a nervous rush.
sanga III (*Jv*) /sanga and songo/ nine. *wali* – the nine Muslim preachers who introduced Islam into Java.
sangadi (*Min*) village head.
sangai I lid/cover of rice steamer.
sangai II (*M*) **bersangai** to warm o.s.
menyangai to heat up, make s.t. warm. *Ibu ~ nasi sisa tadi malam.* Mother reheated last night's leftover rice.
tersangai 1 heated/warmed up. 2 not courted, not sought after (of a woman). *Gadis tua itu dianggap ~ oléh penduduk sekampungnya karena terlalu bertingkah.* That old maid was considered by her fellow villagers as s.o. not to be courted because she put on airs.
sangaji (in Bima) king.
sangan (*Jv*) earthen pot (for roasting).
menyangan to roast.
sangar I (*J/Jv*) 1 bringing misfortune, *esp* when one sets foot in a certain place, does s.t. on a certain day, etc. 2 enchanted, haunted, taboo. 3 terrifying, fearsome, frightening, aggressive. *Nada tanya satpamnya rada –.* The tone of the security guard's questions was rather frightening.
sangar II (*M*) strong-smelling (as of onions).
sangat very, extremely, highly. *amat* – very much, highly, greatly. *dengan* – urgently. *gemar* – very fond of, likes to very much. *Anaknya gemar – makan barang-barang yang manis.* His child is very fond of sweets. – *mudah terbakar* highly flammable. – *mungkin* probable. **kesangat-mungkinan** probability; → KEMENTAKAN.
sangat-sangat 1 very much. *meminta* ~ to ask very much for. 2 serious, important, burning (issue).
bersangatan extreme(ly), excessive, too much. *Dokter bilang, strés dan beban pikiran akibat ketakutan yang* ~. The doctor said that stress and the burden of too much thinking is the result of too much anxiety.
menyangatkan and **mempersangat** 1 to make more (intense), increase, intensify. 2 to make worse, change s.t. for the worse, exacerbate. *Bukan mengurangkan, bahkan ~ penderitaannya.* It did not diminish, but rather it exacerbated his sufferings.
tersangat very, extremely; excessive, extreme.
kesangatan 1 extreme, excessive. 2 vehemence, violence, intensity, severity. 3 excess.
sangau seaweed which is made into a k.o. jelly, *Gelidiopsis rigida.*
sangawali → WALI I.
sangé (*BG*) sexually excited, horny.
sangga I prop, support. – *bedil* rifle rack. – *buku* book rest. – *bunuh* charm against being killed in war. – *galah* place for putting punting pole. – *kejutan* shock absorber. – *kemudi* rudder beam. – *layar* forked supports for boom when boat is at anchor. – *mara* a) cross guard below spear blade. b) (*naut*) boat hook, gaff. – *payung* prop for keeping an umbrella open. – *pedang* cross guard on sword hilt.
menyangga to support, prop up. *Menjelang musim hujan dikhawatirkan bukit tanah yang ~ rél KA Jakarta-Depok tersebut akan longsor lagi.* It is feared that with the approach of the rainy season the earthworks which support the Jakarta-Depok railroad tracks will collapse again.
tersangga supported, buffered.
sanggaan support.
penyangga 1 support, prop, mainstay, girder. ~ *jembatan* pier. ~

pinggang lumbar support, backrest. ~ *senapan* gun rack. **2** buffer, support. *daérah* ~ buffer zone. *negara* ~ buffer state. *pasukan* ~ support troops, supports. *wilayah* ~ buffer zone. ~ *pembebanan* (*elec*) support loading. **3** cushion. ~ *pintu* automatic door closer. **4** pylon (aviation), stanchion. **5** (*botany*) receptacle.

penyanggaan support, buffering.

sangga II – *langit* a twining parasitic vine, *Cassytha filiformis, Quamoclit pennata*. – *lotong* k.o. fruit tree and its fruit, *Nephelium mutabile*; → PULASAN.

sangga III (*Jv*) unit of measurement for *padi*; one *sangga* = 5 *ikat* = 50 *kati*.

sangga IV the smallest unit in the *Pramuka* Boy Scout Movement consisting of *penegaks*; maximum membership is 10.

sanggah I menyanggah 1 to object to, protest against. ~ *perkataan yang tidak sepatutnya* to object to inappropriate words. **2** to oppose, go against, contradict. *raja adil raja disembah, raja lalim raja disanggah* a just king is respected, an unjust king is opposed. **3** to discuss/rebut (a thesis, etc.).

tersanggah objected to. *bukti tak* ~ an unimpeachable piece of evidence.

sanggahan 1 protest, opposition, resistance. *Segala macam* ~ *sepi saja*. All k.o. protests have just been ignored. **2** (*leg*) rebuttal, rejoinder.

penyanggah 1 adversary, opponent. **2** protester. **3** discussant. **4** (*leg*) complainant.

penyanggahan 1 opposition, opposing, protesting. **2** rebuttal (of a thesis).

sanggah II (*Bal*) **1** altar in Balinese houses. **2** bamboo place of worship for Balinese within a *subah*.

sanggam menyanggam to borrow for a single use/short time.

sanggama (*Skr*) sexual intercourse. – *terputus* coitus interruptus.

bersanggama to have sex(ual intercourse). *Diminum tak lama setelah* ~. It's drunk right after having sex.

menyanggamai to have sexual intercourse with.

persenggamaan sexual intercourse.

sanggamara (*Skr*) **1** crossbar (on a sword hilt). **2** boat hook.

sanggan I a low pedestal, saucer with feet.

sanggan II (*M*) basket.

sanggan III → HAK *sanggan*.

sanggang menyanggang to hold up s.t. heavy in two hands.

sanggar 1 (*Jv*) place of worship (in the home), family altar; chapel for prayer and meditation. **2** atelier, studio, workshop, gallery. – *foto* photographic studio. – *karya* collection of memorabilia of a historical hero. – *kerja/latihan* workshop; → LOKAKARYA. – *lukis/seni* art gallery. – *tari* dance studio (for Indonesian dancing). – *téh* tea house.

sanggarunggi (*Jv*) suspicious.

sanggat (*naut*) (run/go) aground; → KANDAS, SAKAT III.

tersanggat run aground; → TERKANDAS.

sanggep (*Jv? ob*) **menyanggep** to parry, ward off. *Pendékar itu* ~ *pukulan lawannya*. The champion parried his opponent's blows.

sanggerah I (*Port*) bloodletting.

menyanggerah to bleed s.o. (for medical purposes).

sanggerah II (*ob*) → SANGGRAH.

sanggit I bersanggit 1 to scrape/rub against s.t. **2** to quarrel, have a dispute.

menyanggit and **mempersanggit** to rub/scrape s.t. (against). ~ *gigi* to gnash one's teeth.

sanggit II version. *Pada dasarnya setiap dalang memiliki kebébasan membuat* – *terhadap setiap lakon*. Basically every puppeteer is free to make (his own) version of every *wayang* story.

sanggrah (*Jv*) **menyanggrah** to take a rest.

penyanggrahan sanatorium for *ABRI* personnel; → PASANGGRAHAN, PESANGGRAHAN.

sanggraloka resort.

sanggugu → SENGGUGU I.

sanggul 1 traditional women's hairdo consisting of a smooth bun at the nape of the neck; GELUNG II, KONDÉ. **2** modern hairdo for long hair; → KAPSEL. *terlindung oléh* – to be henpecked. – *bulat/kelong* low hair bun behind the head. – *gantung* bun

hanging down on the nape of the neck. – *lintang* big bow across the back of the head. – *lipat pandan* bun behind the head. – *miring* bun at the side of the head. – *nyonya* a quinquefoil knot. – *roda lambung* a hairdo covering the ears. – *siput* a shell-like roll of hair.

bersanggul to wear/twist one's hair in a bun.

menyanggul to twist/curl one's hair into a bun, do one's hair up.

menyangguli to twist s.o.'s hair into a bun.

menyanggulkan to twist/curl one's hair into a bun.

tersanggul twisted/put up into a bun.

sanggulan 1 bun **2** twisted into a bun.

sanggup 1 to declare/make o.s. available/ready, promise to do s.t. **2** ready/prepared to, willing to. *Saya* – *menunaikan tugas itu*. I'm ready to carry out that task. – *membuatkan kué anaknya* to be prepared to make a cake for one's child. **3** to be able to, capable of ...ing. – *membayar séwa rumahnya* to be able to pay the rent. – *belanja* (*euph*) to go shopping. *tidak* – unable, incapable. *ketidaksanggupan* inability.

sesanggup as (cap)able as. ~ *tenaga* to the best of one's ability.

menyanggupi [and **nyanggupin** (*J coq*)] **1** to be capable of, be prepared for. **2** to state one's willingness (to do s.t.), promise.

menyanggupkan 1 to promise (to do s.t.). **2** to enable.

kesanggupan 1 readiness, willingness, preparedness. **2** promise, commitment. **3** ability, capability, competence. *Itu di luar* ~ *saya*. That is beyond my capabilities. *surat* ~ promissory note, P/N. *menyatakan* ~*nya* to express one's readiness/willingness. ~ *berlayar* seaworthiness. **berkesanggupan** to be able, capable (of doing s.t.).

penyanggup acceptor.

sanggur (*Pers*) k.o. basket for drinks.

sanggurdi stirrup, stapes.

sangha (*Bal*) Buddhist priest.

sangih (*M*) to have a bloated stomach from overeating.

Sangihé Talaud (*kepulauan*) – the Sangihe and Talaud archipelago north of North Sulawesi.

Sangiin (*Jp*) /sangi'in/ Upper House.

Sangikai (*Jp*) (during the Japanese occupation) k.o. Parliament.

sangir I 1 tusk, fang. **2** canine tooth, eyetooth; → SIUNG I, TARUNG I.

Sangir II → SANGIHÉ.

sangit I (*Jv*) (it has a) burnt (smell), smells burnt/scorched; → ANGIT.

sangit II (*Jv*) *walang* – a noxious bug which attacks the rice plant, stink beetle.

sangitan Javanese elder, *Sambucus javanica*.

sangka I (*Skr*) **1** opinion, idea, supposition, presumption. **2** expectation, prognosis. **3** suspicion, mistrust. (*pada*) – *saya* in my opinion, I think. –*ku/-mu/-nya* in my/your/his opinion. *Kekuatannya tidak sekuat* –*nya*. He wasn't as strong as he thought. *kena* – to be under suspicion, be suspected. – *yang buruk/tak baik* and – *orang yang salah* scandal.

bersangka 1 to mean, think, be of the opinion (that). **2** to have doubts, entertain suspicions.

menyangka [and **nyangka** (*coq*)] to suppose, think, suspect, believe. *dengan tiada disangka* accidentally, without forethought. *tak disangka* and *tidak disangka-sangka* unexpectedly. *tidak kusangka* I never thought/suspected (that). *Dari perilakunya orang* ~ *dialah yang melakukan perbuatan itu*. They suspected from his behavior that he was the one who had done the deed.

menyangkakan and **mempersangkakan** [and **nyangkain** (*J coq*)] **1** to think, believe, consider, regard as, take ... for. *Saya* ~ *dia teman*. I considered him a friend. **2** to be doubtful/skeptical about, have doubts as to. *Kami* ~ *kebenaran ucapannya*. We were skeptical about the correctness of what he said. **3** to suspect (s.o.) in a case of. *perkara kejahatan yang dipersangkakan* the criminal case in which he is a suspect.

tersangka 1 suspected. *Ia* ~ *terlibat dalam kerusakan itu*. He was suspected of being implicated in the riot. **2** the suspect. *si* ~ the suspect. *Kedua* ~ *itu mengakui kesalahannya*. The two suspects admitted their guilt. **3** expected. *tidak* ~ unexpected(ly).

tersangka-sangka *tidak* ~ unexpected, unforeseen.

sangkaan 1 presumption, supposition, conjecture, allegation. **2** suspicion, mistrust. ~ *berfitnah* insinuation.

penyangka ~ *baik* inclined to think the best.

persangkaan → SANGKAAN.

sangka II (*Skr*) conch-shell (for making into a k.o. horn). *-kala* a) valveless trumpet used in military ceremonies. b) the Last Trumpet. *meniup -kala* to blow the trumpet. *suara tiupan - kala* the sound of the trumpet being blown.

sangkak I 1 (*M*) (*- kayu*) forked branch. **2** nest. *- ayam* hen's nest; → PETARANGAN. *menjunjung - ayam* (*M*) very confused/embarrassed.

bersangkak forked, bifurcated.

menyangkak 1 ~ *bulu* one's hair stands on end (from fright/the cold), one has goose flesh. ~ *bulu romanya mendengar berita yang buruk itu.* His hair stood on end when he heard the bad news. **2** ~ *hati* to be furious, in a rage. ~ *hatinya mendengar olok-olokan itu.* He was furious when he heard the joke.

sangkak II obstacle, obstruction.

menyangkak 1 to place an obstacle on/at. ~ *pohon* to place an obstacle under a tree so that nobody can climb it. **2** to thwart.

menyangkaki 1 to prevent. **2** to go counter (to), oppose, thwart.

penyangkak obstacle, obstruction.

sangkakala → SANGKA II.

sangkal I say in protest. *-nya* he protested.

bersangkal 1 to not comply with, not obey, not carry out an order, be unwilling to. ~ *terhadap perintah ortunya* not to obey one's parents orders. **2** to deny. *Walaupun bukti-buktinya sudah nyata, tetapi ia tetap ~ di hadapan hakim.* Even though the evidence was quite clear, he nevertheless persisted in his denial before the judge.

menyangkal [and **nyangkal** (*coq*)] **1** to deny s.t. **2** to act contrary to (or, against) (s.o.'s wishes/instruction). **3** to decline, refuse to obey (a request/order); → MENOLAK. **4** to dispute, challenge. **5** to resist, put up (or, offer) resistance to (the will of God). **6** to deny (God).

menyangkali to deny.

tersangkal denied, repudiated. *tidak* ~ undeniable, cannot be denied.

sangkalan denial, refusal, resistance. *mendapat* ~ *yang keras* to get a strong denial.

penyangkal s.o. who denies. ~ *Allah* atheist.

penyangkalan denial, refusal, noncompliance, resistance.

sangkal II (*Jv*) handle (of a hammer, etc.). *- putung* clamp for a broken arm or leg.

sangkala → SENGKALAN.

sangkan I (*Mal*) transvestite.

sangkan II (*Jv*) origin, source. *- paran* origin and destination. *- paraning dumadi* the origin and destination of mankind, life and death, rise and fall.

sangkan III (*M*) zeal, ardor.

bersangkan to do s.t. with enthusiasm.

sangkap name of a *ceki* card.

sangkar I (bird)cage, (chicken) coop. *sistém - terapung* pen culture system (in fishing for *udang windu* in the *Kepulauan Seribu* archipelago). *seperti burung di -* to live a happy life.

bersangkar to have a cage; to be caged.

menyangkarkan to cage, put in a cage.

sangkaran (bird)cage, (chicken) coop.

sangkar II diagonal. *bujur - a*) rectangle. b) square. *tiga méter bujur -* three square meters; → PERSEGI.

sangkayan → SENGKAYAN.

sangkeluk (*J*) stupid, idiotic.

sangkepan (*Bal*) meeting.

sangkét(an) various species of plants, musk basil.

sangkil I 1 (just) as far as, get to. **2** hits (the mark), effective, precise. **3** efficient; → ÉFISIÉN. **4** came true (what was predicted), arrived at the predicted time.

kesangkilan 1 efficacy. **2** efficiency.

sangkil II (*Jv*) **menyangkil** to carry on the hip.

sangkin (*coq*) more and more, increasingly, to an (ever) greater degree; → MAKIN, SEMANGKIN.

sangking → SAKING.

sangku glass or brass finger bowl.

sangkur bayonet. *mata -* bayonet blade. *ujung -* bayonet point.

bersangkur with/to have a bayonet. ~ *terhunus* with fixed bayonets.

menyangkur to bayonet, stab with a bayonet.

Sangkuriang (*S*) legendary hero who wants to marry his mother.

sangkut (*coq*) to hang, hook. *- paut* a) relation, connection, relationship. *Diduga bahwa penangkapan dua orang itu ada - pautnya dengan perkara penyelundupan senjata api.* It was believed that the arrest of the two persons was connected with arms smuggling. *Ia pun masih ada – pautnya dengan gubernur A.* He still has relations with governor A. b) detail, complications. *Amat banyak - pautnya.* That's a complicated business. c) financial obligations/commitments. *Pedagang itu masih ada - pautnya dengan mendiang ayah saudara.* That merchant still had financial obligations to your late father. **bersangkut-paut 1** to be connected (with), be linked/related (to). *soal-soal yang langsung* ~ *dengan peraturan itu* items directly related to that regulation. **2** to be relevant. *isu-isu yang tak* ~ irrelevant issues. **menyangkut-pautkan** to connect, link up, involve, bring in. *Sekarang anda sangkutpautkan soal pribadi.* Now you bring in personal matters. **tersangkut-paut** involved. **persangkut-pautan** implication, correlation, relation, connection. ~ *kausal* causal relationship.

bersangkut to be concerned/related/connected. ~ *dengan* to be related to, be connected with.

bersangkutan to be concerned, involved, interested; relevant, in question. *Beberapa orang yang* ~ *dengan perkara itu sudah diciduk.* Some of the people involved in that case have been arrested. *(pihak) yang* ~ those/the parties concerned/involved, the interested parties. *kepada yang* ~ to whom it may concern. *disertai surat-surat yang* ~ accompanied by the relevant documents. *rapat yang* ~ the meeting in question (or, referred to), the relevant meeting.

menyangkut [and **nyangkut** (*coq*)] **1** to be/get caught in (a tree, etc.), get stuck/held up somewhere, get hooked on/by. **2** to be related to, concern, be a matter of, come to; concerning, relating to, about, on. *Tabiat istrinya mémang selalu begitu, uring-uringan kalau sudah* ~ *soal uang.* His wife's really always like that, grumbling when it comes to money matters. *négosiasi* ~ *harga jual* negotiations on the sales price. *Ini tidak* ~ *kamu.* This doesn't concern you. **3** to hang s.t. (up). *Ia* ~ *lampu itu di tengah-tengah ruang duduk.* He hung the lamp up in the middle of the living room. **4** to implicate, involve, connect. *Beberapa surat kabar telah* ~ *namanya dengan kasus itu.* Several newspapers have connected his name with that case.

sangkut-menyangkut to have a connection/relationship with e.o.

menyangkuti to hang on to s.t.

menyangkutkan 1 to suspend, hang (over), hook. ~ *paruh* to ask for help. **2** to connect, relate, associate; to involve. **3** to connect s.t. with s.t. *dua hal yang tidak dapat disangkutkan begitu saja* two things that cannot be connected with e.o. just like that.

mempersangkutkan to connect with e.o.

tersangkut [and **kesangkut** (*coq*)] caught, stuck. *Ada duri* ~ *dalam kerongkongan.* A fishbone is stuck in my throat. *kesangkut batu* stumbled over a rock. **2** involved (in). *yang* ~ (*leg*) accomplice. **3** person concerned/involved. **4** (*fin*) drawee (of checks, etc.). **5** it depends on. *Pada engkau saja lagi ~nya.* It just depends on you. ~ *hati* in love (with). *Lama-kelamaan ~lah hatiku kepada anak itu.* Gradually I fell in love with that child. **ketersangkutan** involvement, connection.

tersangkut-sangkut jerked, yanked; jerky. *suara yang* ~ jerking sound. *tiada* ~ *keluarnya* uninterrupted flow of words.

sangkutan 1 hook, cradle (of a desk telephone). **2** hindrance, obstacle, impediment. **3** connection, relation(ship); involvement. *tidak ada ~nya dengan* to have no connection with, have nothing to do with.

penyangkut hook, cradle (of a desk telephone).

persangkutan connection, relation(ship); involvement.

sangling (*Jv*) **menyangling(kan)** to polish, burnish (metal).

sanglir (*Jv*) to have only one testicle or one large and one small testicle or one undescended testicle.

sangon <sangu> (*Jv*) **1** provisions, supplies (for a trip). **2** bonus, allowance, severance pay; → SANGU II.
    menyangoni and nyangoni **1** to supply, make provisions for. **2** to grant an allowance.
    pesangon bonus, allowance, severance pay.
sangrai (*J*) menyangrai to fry without oil; to roast (coffee).
sangsai → SENGSAI.
sangsaka → SANG *saka*.
sangsang (*J*) menyangsang to hang on s.t.
    tersangsang [and kesangsang (*coq*)] to be caught (in). *Layangan kesangsang di pohon.* The kite got caught in a tree.
    sangsangan necklace.
sangsara → SENGSARA.
Sangsekarta and Sangsekerta → SANSKERTA.
sangsi I (*Skr*) doubtful, suspicious. *dengan tidak usah – lagi* undoubtedly, without any doubt.
    bersangsi to be doubtful/dubious/uncertain/suspicious; → RAGU-RAGU, WASWAS I.
    menyangsikan **1** to be doubtful about, be suspicious of. *Mengapa kita harus ~ perhubungan meréka.* Why should we be suspicious of their relationship. **2** to doubt, question. *disangsikan* doubted, in doubt, in question, open to question, questionable. *masih (dapat) ~* it is still doubtful, it's still an open question. *Masih sangat ~ kebenarannya.* Its accuracy is still very much open to question. *tidak usah ~ lagi* it is no longer in doubt/ open to question. *dengan tidak usah ~ lagi* undoubtedly, without a doubt, certainly.
    kesangsian doubtfulness, dubiousness, suspicion.
    penyangsi doubter, skeptic.
    penyangsian doubt(fulness), uncertainty, skepticism.
sangsi II → SANKSI.
sangsing menyangsing to hold s.t. in one's hand.
sangsit k.o. insect that makes fowl sick.
sangsot (*J*) a blow (with a swung implement). *Sekali – dia jatuh menggelapar.* One blow and he fell sprawling.
    menyangsot to strike such a blow.
sangsrang (*J*) menyangsrang [and nyangsrang (*coq*)] to get caught (in a tree, etc.).
sangu I → SANGAU.
sangu II (*Jv*) provisions taken on a trip; → SANGON.
sangulun (*Jv*) your Majesty.
sangyang title of address for the gods; → SANG I, YANG II.
sani (*A*) exalted, most high.
sanik (*A*) the Creator.
sanitas (*D*) hygiene.
sanitasi (*E*) sanitation. *tenaga –* sanitation workers.
sanitér (*D*) sanitary.
sanjai I (*M*) tall and thin.
sanjai II (*M*) k.o. *krupuk* made from *ubi kayu* in the Bukittinggi area.
sanjak **1** rhyme. **2** poem; → SAJAK I.
sanjang a magic dance from Blambangan.
sanjung (*M*) menyanjung(-nyanjungkan) to flatter, coax, cajole; to praise, extol.
    tersanjung flattered, coaxed, cajoled.
    sanjungan **1** praise, adulation, flattery. **2** to like to be praised/ flattered.
    penyanjung flatterer, cajoler.
    penyanjungan praising, flattering.
sanksi (*D*) sanction, disciplinary action. *dikenakan –* to have sanctions imposed on one *mengenakan/menjatuhkan –* to impose sanctions on.
sanlat [pesantrén kilat] short course in Islamic studies.
sano (*M*) absent-minded, distracted.
sanok I green-billed malkoha, *Rhopodytes tristis*.
sanok II (*M*) pumpkin in coconut-milk syrup.
sans (*D*) (in bridge) no-trump.
sansai (*M*) → SANGSAI, SENGSAI.
sansak (*D*) (in boxing) punching ball, medicine ball, wall bag.
Sansibar Zanzibar.
Sanskerta Sanskrit.
Sanskrit → SANSKERTA.

Sans Souci (*col*) one of the names given to Bogor.
santa (*RC*) (female) saint. – *Maria* the Virgin Mary.
santai **1** to relax, take it easy, be relaxed/at ease, feel at home. *bersikap –* to relax/unwind. *pelayaran –* cruise, pleasure trip. *– saja* just take it easy. **2** informal. *bahasa –* informal style (of language). *Acaranya diatur lebih –.* The program will be more informal.
    sesantai as relaxed as.
    bersantai **1** (to do s.t.) at one's leisure, in a relaxed way. *santap ~* to eat informally. *sikap ~* a relaxed attitude. *tempat ~* recreation site. **2** to relax/take it easy. *Ia membaca koran atau ~.* He reads the paper or takes it easy.
    bersantai-santai to relax, take it easy. *Selama liburan kerjanya hanya ~ saja di rumah.* When he's on vacation, he just takes it easy at home.
    nyantai (*coq*) to relax
    menyantaikan to relax s.t. *~ diri dengan membaca* to take it easy reading.
    kesantaian **1** relaxation, taking it easy. *Jangan biarkan nyeri atau tegang otot mengganggu ~ sehabis berolah-raga.* Don't let pain or stiffness make it hard for you to relax after sports. **2** free time, leisure. *~, pengisi waktu yang univérsal* leisure, the universal pastime.
    pesantai vacationer, s.o. who is taking it easy.
    penyantaian relaxing, relaxation
santak → SENTAK I.
santam a shrub whose leaves produce indigo, *Marsdenia tinctoria*.
santan coconut milk (pressed from shredded coconut meat, sometimes also called coconut cream). *meramas – di kuku* to get blood from a stone. *seperti – dengan tengguli* to be hand and glove.
    bersantan (prepared) with coconut milk. *sayur gulai yang ~ kental* curry soup with thickened coconut milk.
    menyantani to put coconut milk into.
santana I (*Jv*) → SENTANA I.
santana II (*Bal*) child adoption.
santana III (*S*) title of lower nobility.
santap to eat. – *karya* working lunch. – *malam* dinner. **bersantap malam** to eat dinner. – *pagi* breakfast. – *sehidangan* to eat together. – *siaga* business lunch. – *siang* lunch. **bersantap siang** to lunch, eat lunch. – *siang karya* working lunch.
    bersantap to eat (now mostly used as an honorific word with reference to high government officials). *~ malam* to eat dinner, dine. *~ sirih* to chew betel.
    bersantap-santapan to feed e.o. (of bride and groom at the wedding ceremony).
    menyantap and nyantap (*coq*) **1** to eat. **2** to stuff (food down one's mouth/course notes into one's brain).
    santapan **1** food, meal. *~ laut* seafood. *~ rohani* spiritual nourishment; → HIDANGAN *rohani*. **2** s.t. pleasurable for. *~ mata* a delight to the eye. *~ telinga* a joy to hear.
    penyantap s.o. who eats, eater.
    penyantapan feeding.
    persantapan banquet, meal, feast; → ANDROWINO, PERJAMUAN.
santase (*D*) blackmail.
santau (*Mal*) a deadly mixture of poisons; poison used to stun fish.
santek (*Jv*) latch.
    santekan latch.
santél → CANTÉL I.
santen → SANTAN.
santeng (*Jv*) waist sash worn with traditional woman's dress.
    bersanteng to wear such a sash.
santer (*J/Jv*) **1** swift. **2** strong. *angin –* a strong wind. **3** severe (illness). **4** rife (of rumors), animated (of conversation). *Desas-desus tentang korupsi makin –.* Rumors about corruption have become rifer and rifer.
    menyanterkan to cause to be swift/strong/severe/loud.
santeri → SANTRI.
santét (*Jv*) k.o. black magic, hex. *tukang –* s.o. who practices black magic.
    menyantét to put a hex on, bewitch.
    tersantét hexed, bewitched.
    penyantét s.o. who practices black magic.

penyantétan and **persantétan** putting a hex on, hexing, bewitching.

Santiago the military resort command (*Korém* 131) in Manado.

santiaji (*Jv*) briefing; → BRI(E)FING, PENGARAHAN, TAKLIMAT.

menyantiaji to give a briefing.

penyantiaji s.o. who gives a briefing.

penyantiajian briefing.

santiajiwan → PENYANTIAJI.

santikrama (*mil*) practical spiritual education.

santing (*M*) beautiful, fine.

santio (*C Jv*) a silk fabric, shantung; → SANTUNG II.

santir (*M*) **santiran** 1 likeness, resemblance, comparison; → BANDING I, TARA I, TIMBANGAN. *tak ada ~nya* without comparison, unequaled, unique. 2 (reflected) image, reflection (in a mirror).

santo (*Port D RC*) Saint, St. – *Fransiskus Asisi* St. Francis of Assisi.

santri (*Jv*) 1 student of an Islamic seminary, Muslim seminarian. 2 steadfast Muslim of the Sunni Shafei school; a religious/pious person. – *kalong* a *santri* who visits the *pesantrén* and who participates in the recitation of Koranic verses but who doesn't live in the *pondok*. – *kelana* a *santri* who wanders from one *pesantrén* to another. – *kendil* a *santri* who doesn't study seriously. – *mukim* a live-in *santri*. – *pasaran* (in Garut) a *santri* who lives in the *pesantrén* for only a few months. – *sadar hukum* [tidurkum] a *santri* who is aware of the law.

nyantri to be a *santri*.

pesantrén [(*Jv*) from: *pe*+*santri*+*an*] Islamic seminary, a private educational institution run usually by one teacher-leader, usually a *haji* who is called *kiyai*.

santrinisasi making official conduct more in line with Islamic principles.

santriwan 1 male Muslim seminarian. 2 religious/pious man.

santriwati 1 female Muslim seminarian. 2 religious/pious woman.

santron (*J*) → SATRON. **menyantroni** to attack. *Empat pria bersenjata api ~ Kantor Pos.* Four armed men attacked the Post Office.

santuk → ANTUK I.

santun 1 politeness, civility, courteousness, courtesy, decency. *orang tak –* an ill-mannered person. 2 polite, benevolent, kind, sympathetic, helpful. 3 curator.

sesantun as polite as.

menyantun(i) 1 to sympathize/commiserate (with), feel sorry (for), be sympathetic (toward). *Membantu serta ~ fakir miskin adalah kewajiban kita semua.* To help and commiserate with the poor is the duty of all of us. 2 to help (support), aid, assist, support. *Tujuan mendirikan yayasan itu ialah untuk ~ anak yatim piatu.* The purpose of establishing that foundation is to help support orphans. 3 to treat s.o. politely.

santunan 1 benefit (paid by an insurance company), (insurance) payment. *~ pemutusan hubungan kerja* unemployment benefit payment. 2 compensation (for an accident, etc.), indemnity, indemnification. *~ kebijaksanaan* discretionary compensation, goodwill payment.

penyantun 1 civilized person. 2 sympathetic, willing to help, helpful. 3 curator. *Déwan ~* Board of Trustees (of a university/organization). *perkumpulan ~ mata tunanétra* eye donors for the blind.

penyantunan assistance, relief work, helping to support. *~ werdha* senior-citizen assistance.

santung I (*M*) tight, close. – *pelalai* magic spell to prevent a girl from marrying a rival.

santung II (*C*) Shantung. *cita/sutera –* shantung (textile).

sanubar (*Pers?*) fir, pine.

sanubari (*Pers*) feelings, emotions, heart as the seat of the emotions, mind, soul. *sudah berurat berakar dalam ~ kita* it is deeply rooted in our hearts. *hati –* a) innermost feelings. b) heart (the physical organ).

sanya → BAHWASANYA.

sanyo (*Jp*) (during the *Jp* occupation) informer.

saos I → SAUS.

saos II (*Jv*) to visit a social superior. – *bekti* to pay one's respects to (a superior). – *bekti ing Ngarso Dalem* to pay one's respects to His Majesty the Sultan of Yogyakarta.

sap I (*A?*) ink pad. *kertas –* blotting paper.

sap II → SAF I.

sapa I (*Skr*) 1 (say in) greeting. *"Selamat pagi, Pak," –nya.* "Good morning, Sir," he said. *Sopan tegur –nya.* He's very polite.

sesapanya (just) a brief greeting.

bersapa(-sapa)an and **sapa-menyapa** to greet e.o., say hello to e.o. *tidak bersapa-sapaan* not on speaking terms.

menyapa [and **nyapa** (*coq*)] to greet, speak to in a friendly fashion. *Seorang ibu tua di situ selalu ~ ramah.* An old lady over there always greets people in a friendly way. *disapa hantu* bothered/made sick by an evil spirit.

tersapa 1 greeted, addressed. 2 had a spell cast on one (making one ill).

sapaan 1 greeting, polite form of address. *~ salam* greeting, salutation. *Tiba-tiba terdengar ~ di dapur rumah.* All of a sudden a greeting was heard in the kitchen. 2 nickname.

penyapa address (*mod*). *sistém ~* address system.

penyapaan (extending a) greeting.

sapa II (*coq*) who; → SIAPA. *– nyang belon dateng?* Who hasn't arrived yet?

sapa III → SAFA.

sapa IV (*Skr Jv*) curse, imprecation.

nyapa to curse, put a curse on.

tersapa bewitched, had a spell cast on one (making one ill).

sapah → SEPAH I.

sapai-sapai (*M*) *angin si –* gentle breeze; → ANGIN *sepoi-sepoi basa*.

sapang → SEPANG.

sapapait samamanis (*S*) to go through thick and thin together, to share the good with the bad (used to describe the fighting spirit of the Siliwangi Division stationed in West Java); → ESA *hilang dua terbilang*.

sapar I (*Sg*) camp, improvised shelter for the night in the jungle.

bersapar to camp out.

Sapar II → SAFAR II.

saparantu k.o. tree and the medicine obtained from that tree, *Sindora sumatrana*.

saparila → SARSAPARILA.

sapat I (*S*) broken off all at once (of blades of grass).

sapat II → SEPAT II.

sapau → SAPAR I.

sapérsi (*D*) → ASPÉRSI.

sapfir (*A*) sapphire.

sapi I (*Jv*) cow, bull, ox; → LEMBU I. *(telor) mata –* fried egg, bull's eye egg. *minyak –* suet, beef drippings. *– anakan* calf. *– Banprés* cattle *usu* imported from Australia by the Indonesian government and distributed to farmers using special funds provided by the president; → BANPRÉS. *– bantai* slaughtered bull. *– Benggala* draft bull. *– betina/dara* heifer. *– Fries Holland* Holstein-Friesian. *– gadis* heifer. *– Grati* cross between Holstein-Friesian and Java cow. *– hutan* dwarf buffalo. *– jantan* bull. *– kebiri* steer. *– keréman* fattened cow. *– Madura* Madurese cow. *– mirit* a large species of cow, considered a cross between the Java cow and the (Indian) zebu. *– Onggolé* Brahman bull. *– paron* (in Timor) fattened cow. *– pedaging* beef cattle. *– pejantan* bull. *– pelacak/pemacak* stud bull. *– perah(an)* a) milch/dairy cow. b) cash cow (s.t. that produces a lot of income). *– Peranakan-Onggolé* (in Central and East Java) a white-gray cow with long legs, a large hump over the shoulders, and a large dewlap; used to pull plows or carts. *– potong* beef cow.

sapi II *pohon –* a tree-shrub, *Otophora spectabilis*.

sapi III (*zod*) Taurus.

sapi IV → SENJATA *api*.

sapih I (*Jv*) **menyapih** 1 to wean (a child/calf, etc.). 2 (*Jv*) (in South Sumatra) to part, separate (people fighting); → MELARAIKAN. 3 to plant (germinated seeds), put in beds. *~ diri* to separate, secede. *Tetapi ini gejala normal untuk ~ diri menjadi déwasa.* But this is a normal symptom of separating o.s. to become an adult.

tersapih weaned.

sapihan 1 weaned. *anak ~* child who has been weaned. *makanan ~* weaning food. 2 sapling.

penyapih *surat ~* letter for settling a quarrel.

penyapihan 1 weaning. *Jika anda mesti melakukan ~, sebaiknya lakukanlah secara bertahap.* If you must wean (a child), it's best to do it gradually. **2** lining out (in forestry).

sapih II partially paralyzed.

sapinda (*Hind*) type of heirs under Hindu law.

sapir I (*D mil*) sapper; → ZÉNI I.

sapir II (*D*) sapphire; → NILAM I.

sapir III (*A*) traveler; → MUSAFIR, SAFIR II.

sapir IV (*D*) jailer; → SIPIR.

sapit (*Jv*) tongs, pincers, chelae.

sapon <sapu> (*Jv*) sweepings. *Tanpa banyak mulut meréka bayar kewajibannya uang ~, walau hanya Rp 25,00,-.* Without much ado, they paid their obligations (in the form of) market sweeping money, even though it was only Rp 25.00.

saprodi → SARANA *produksi padi.*

saprofit (*D*) saprophyte.

saprolégnia fish mold.

saprotan [Sarana produksi pertanian] means of agricultural production.

sap sap sui (*Cantonese?*) to compete in wealth, extravagance, etc.

sapta (*Skr*) seven (only in compounds). – *Bhakti* Seven-Point Pledge of Allegiance (taken by government employees). – *Citra Diri Pemuda Indonésia* Seven Images of Indonesian Youth, i.e., nationalism, patriotism, no surrender, heroism, spirit of mutual help, devotion without expectation of recompense, and self-confidence. – *Krida (Kabinét Pembangunan)* the Seven Goals (of the Development Cabinet), i.e., political stability, security and law and order, economic stability, planning and implementation of *Pelita*, the well-being of the people, general elections, and the reorganization of the state apparatus. – *Marga* and –*marga* the "Seven Roads," i.e., the Seven-Point Military Code of Honor, i.e., we are citizens of the Unitary Republic of Indonesia, which is based on Pancasila; we are Indonesian patriots responsible for supporting and defending the State ideology and we are unconquerable; we are Indonesian warriors devoted to the One and Only God and we defend honesty, truth and justice; we are soldiers of the Republic of Indonesia Armed Forces and Guardians of the Indonesian State and People; we are soldiers of the Republic of Indonesia Armed Forces and are firmly disciplined, obedient and loyal to our leadership, and hold in high esteem the character and honor of the soldier; we are soldiers of the Republic of Indonesia Armed Forces and emphasize valor in carrying out our duties and we are always prepared to devote ourselves to the State and the People; we are soldiers of the Republic of Indonesia Armed Forces, loyal, keep our promises and fulfill the Soldier's Pledge, i.e., the *Sumpah Prajurit.* **Ber-Saptamarga** to adhere to the Seven-Point Military Code of Honor. – *Pesona* the Seven Charms to be used in attracting foreign tourists, i.e., security, public order, cleanliness, freshness, beauty, friendliness, and souvenirs. – *warsa* seven years.

saptadarma (*Skr neo*) the seven duties of Buddhists.

saptamarga (*Skr neo*) → SAPTA *marga.*

Saptamargais an adherent of the *Saptamarga.*

Saptu → SABTU.

sapu broom. *seperti – diikat dengan benang sutera* it's like a blacksmith with a white silk apron. – *bersih* clean sweep. **menyapubersihkan** to sweep clean, annihilate, wipe out. **penyapubersihan** wiping out, sweeping clean, annihilating. – *bulu ayam* feather duster. – *cat* (paint)brush. – *duk/ijuk* broom made of black sugar palm fibers. – *jagat* a) a large canon. b) a forest phantom. – *kaca mobil* windshield wiper. – *kapal* swab. – *kikis* skimmer. – *kuras* scrubber. – *lidi* broom or mosquito-swatter made of the veins of the (coconut) palm frond. *sistém – lidi* a sweep-clean system. – *listrik* (*coq*) vacuum cleaner. – *panjang* broom, *usu a sapu lidi* with a long broomstick. – *papan tulis* blackboard eraser. – *ragbol* dust mop, *esp* for dusting ceilings. – *rata* razed. **menyapu rata** to raze, demolish. – *sétan* witches' broom, a sickness of legumes. – *tangan* handkerchief. – *tangan penyegar* refreshing tissue. – *tangan pewangi* perfumed tissue.

menyapu [and **nyapu** (*coq*)] **1** to sweep (with a broom). *Halaman itu belum disapu.* The yard hasn't been swept yet. **2** to drag along,

sweep over. *Gaun panjangnya ~ lantai.* Her long gown dragged along the floor. *Matanya ~ ke arah saya.* Her eyes swept over toward me. **3** to wipe clean/dry, wipe (off), brush aside. *Ia ~ keringat di mukanya dengan lengannya.* He wiped the sweat off his face with his sleeve. **4** to wipe out, sweep/carry away and destroy. *Di Mauméré, dermaga pelabuan yang lama dilaporkan hilang disapu gelombang.* In Maumere it was reported that the old harbor quay was swept away by the waves. **5** to (apply) paint to, coat. *Ayah ~ dinding rumah dengan kapur.* Father coated the wall of the house with whitewash. **6** to clean up, clear (of hostile elements). **7** to rub. **8** to caress, fondle, pat. *Ibu ~ kepala anaknya dengan haru.* Mother caressed her child's head tenderly. **9** to buy up. *Lukisan Indonésia disapu pembeli.* Purchasers bought up Indonesian paintings. **10** (*Jv*) to lash, scourge.

nyapuin (*J coq*) to sweep.

menyapu-nyapu to rub (one's eyes). *Ia ~ matanya seperti orang yang baru bangun dari tidur.* He rubbed his eyes like s.o. who has just woken up.

menyapukan 1 to sweep/wipe for s.o. else. *~ sampahnya* to sweep up s.o. else's trash. **2** to sweep/wipe/rub with, apply/rub/smear/spread s.t. (on). *Ia ~ minyak macan pada punggung istrinya.* He rubbed Tiger Balm on his wife's back. **3** to pass over s.t. with.

tersapu swept, swept away, cleaned off, wiped, rubbed. *Naro dan kawan-kawannya ~ habis.* Naro and his buddies were swept away (out of office). *~ banjir* swept away by the flood.

sapuan 1 sweep, stroke, wipe, rub. *~ banjir* flood wash. *~ kuasnya* a stroke of his brush. **2** sweepings.

penyapu 1 sweeper. *~ jalan* street sweeper, scavenger. *~ permadani* carpet sweeper. *~ ranjau* mine sweeper. **2** wiper. *~ kaca* windshield wiper. *~ kakai* doormat.

penyapuan 1 sweeping, wiping, rubbing. *~ ranjau* mine sweeping. **2** elimination, deletion, obliteration.

sapuk (in Lombok) headband.

sapurwatin (in Lampung) a small hut where field agricultural officers give educational information on agricultural matters; → SAUNG I.

sapu-sapu *~ ringan* k.o. children's game in which the legs are extended and they are stroked with the hands.

saput thin film.

bersaput covered with a thin coat.

menyaput 1 to coat with a thin coat. **2** to cover with s.t. thin. **3** to disguise, hide.

menyaputi to cover/wrap up with s.t. thin. *Awan tipis ~ bulan sehingga tampak redup cahayanya.* Thin clouds covered the moon so that its rays seemed misty.

menyaputkan to apply a thin film with s.t.

tersaput 1 covered (up), coated. *~ awan* socked in by clouds. *~ polusi udara* covered in air pollution. **2** enveloped.

saputan thin cover, veil.

penyaput coat, coating.

penyaputan coating.

saputangan → SAPU *tangan.*

sar I (*onom*) sound of a tear.

sar II (in acronyms) → DASAR I, SARANA.

sara I (*A mostly Mal*) **1** maintenance, support, pension. **2** participation (in an enterprise); share. – *hidup* livelihood, sustenance.

bersara 1 retired, pensioned off. *Dia memilih ~ daripada tetap mengajar.* He chose to retire rather than continue to teach. **2** (*M*) to deliberate.

menyara(i) to give a pension to, pension off.

sara II – *bara* mixed up, pell-mell, in disorder, confused. *lari – bara* to run helter-skelter/head over heels).

sara III → SYARA'.

sara IV [Suku, Agama, Ras, Antargolongan] (pertaining to) ethnic, religious, racial, and intergroup relations. *masalah –* problems in these areas.

sara V (*Jv*) arrow.

sarad (*Jv*) **saradan** and **penyadaran** transporting teakwood logs by using oxen or tractors to pull them.

saradasi (suggested term for) subversion.

saraf I (*A*) *ilmu –* grammar; → TATA BAHASA.

saraf II (*A*) nerve. *ahli* – neurologist. *penyakit* – neurosis. *perang* – war of nerves. *urat* – nerve. – *kepala* cranial nerve. – *mata* optical nerve. – *otak* cranial nerve. – *paha* femoral nerve. – *parasimpatis* parasympathetic nerves. – *penciuman* olfactory nerve. – *périfér* peripheral nerves. – *pinggul* sciatic nerve. – *pusat* central nerves. – *séntral* central nervous system. – *simpati* sympathetic nerves. – *telinga* auditory nerve.
　kesarafan neurotic.
　persarafan (*mod*) nerve, nervous system.
saraf III (*A ob*) money-changer.
sarafi (*A*) neural.
sarak I separated, parted; → CERAI, PISAH, SAPIH I.
　bersarak legally separated. ~ *serasa hilang, bercerai serasa mati* absence makes the heart grow fonder.
　menyarak 1 to separate; to divorce. ~ *berkundang* (*Pal*) to leave one's parent's home and follow one's husband. **2** to wean.
sarak II → SYARAK, SYARIAT.
sarakah → SERAKAH.
saran suggestion, proposal, proposition, recommendation. *lekas kena* – suggestible. – *pribadi* autosuggestion.
　menyaran to be suggestive, suggest, hint at.
　menyarani to make a suggestion/proposal/recommendation to.
　menyarankan [and **nyaranin** (*J coq*)] to suggest, propose, offer/put forward a suggestion, etc. *Dokter* ~ *supaya si sakit dihospitalkan.* The doctor suggested that the patient be hospitalized. *Cita-cita kenegaraan yang disarankan kepada rakyat bertentangan dengan asas démokrasi.* The national aspirations proposed to the people contradicted democratic principles.
　tersaran *sudah* ~ suggestible.
　saranan 1 proposal, suggestion. **2** propaganda, announcement.
sarana (*Jv*) means, facilities, aid(s), media, services. *dengan* – by means of, through. – *angkutan* means of transportation. – *angkutan air* watercraft, craft for water transport. – *angkutan sungai* river-craft. – *antara* interface (computers). – *dan prasarana* equipment and infrastructure. – *fisik* physical aids. – *hukum* legal mechanism/means. – *ibadat* religious facilities (mosques/houses of worship, etc.). – *ikhtiar* ways and means. – *keamanan* safety/security provisions. – *kebijaksanaan* instrument of policy. – *komunikasi* means of communication (handy talkies, etc.). – *lapangan udara* airfield facilities. – *melawan hukum* ways of breaking the law. – *olahraga* sports facilities. – *parkir* parking facilities. – *pelayan masyarakat* public utilities. – *pemerintah* government apparatus. – *pendidikan* educational aids. – *pendukung darat* ground support equipment. – *pengangkutan* means of transportation. – *penggerak* drive, propulsion. – *penghidupan* facilities needed for living. – *penunjang* utilities. – *perhubungan* means of transportation. – *produksi* means of production. – *produksi padi* means of rice production. – *rékréasi* recreational facilities (swimming pools/tennis courts, etc.). – *umum* public utilities.
　bersarana with facilities.
sarang I 1 nest, web. **2** hotbed, breeding ground, den. **3** hideout, hideaway (*esp* for bandits/criminals, etc.). – *burung* bird's nest. – *burung walét* (edible) swallow's nest. – *Gestapu* hotbed of members of the *G30S/PKI*. – *judi* gambling den. – *laba-laba* cobweb, spider's web. – *lanun* pirates' den/nest. – *lebah* beehive. – *madu* honeycomb. – *meriam* emplacement for guns. – *misil* missile site. – *mitraliur* machine gun nest. – *nanah* pus in pimple. – *penjahat* criminal hideout. – *penyakit* breeding ground of disease, source of infection. – *penyakit malaria* breeding place for malaria. – *penyamun* robbers' den. – *perzinaan* den of adultery. – *pipit* a) sparrow's nest. b) dimple (in cheek). – *semut* ant hill. – *senapan mesin* (in aircraft) machine gun pod. – *siluman* "colony of ghosts," i.e., a reference to the corruption-ridden Indonesian Customs office. – *tikus* mousehole.
　bersarang 1 to nest, make a nest. *tempat* ~ breeding ground. **2** to hide out. **3** to lodge, enter and stay in. *Dua peluru* ~ *di perut.* Two bullets lodged in his stomach. *Sebuah cubitan kembali* ~ *di pinggang Burhan.* Burhan was pinched twice in the side. *Penjaga gawang itu gagal meraih bola yang akan* ~ *di jalanya.* The goalkeeper failed to catch the ball which was about to nest in his net.

bersarang-sarang 1 with many nests. **2** full of. ~ *di makan peluru* full of bullet holes.
　menyarang ~ *ke* to land in/on. *Banyak* ~ *di jaring lawan.* Many landed in the opponent's net.
　menyarangi to make its/their nest in/on.
　menyarangkan to put (a bullet/a ball, etc.) right in, hit right on. *Ia berhasil dilumpuhkan polisi yang* ~ *tiga peluru di kakinya.* He was paralyzed by the police who put three bullets in his legs. *Dua pukulan tangannya disarangkan ke muka S.* Two blows of his fist hit S's face.
　tersarang (*math*) nested.
　penyarangan nesting, hiding out.
sarang II porous.
　bersarang-sarang full of holes.
　sarangan s.t. porous. ~ *got* drain filter/trap.
　kesarangan porosity.
sarang III (– *tupai*) k.o. herb (eaten as uncooked food in Java), *Aneilema nudiflorum.*
sarangan (*Jv*) chestnut, *Castanea argentea*; → BERANGAN I.
sarangéngé (*S*) → SRENGÉNGÉ.
sarap I litter (dried leaves/paper, etc.), detritus, debris. – *sampah* and *sampah* – litter and rubbish. – *sehelai dituilkan, batu sebuah digulingkan* very accurate (in inspecting/investigating, etc.).
　menyarap 1 scattered around (of litter). **2** worthless, useless (like litter).
sarap II an infantile rash → PENYAKIT *mérah.*
sarap III menyarap to line. ~ *perut* to eat a light breakfast before going to work.
　menyarapi to line, put a substratum/under-layer on s.t., line (with leaves/cloth, etc.). *Tempat tidur bayi itu disarapi dengan kain tebal.* The baby's bed was lined with thick material.
　sarapan substratum, under-layer, lining.
sarap IV menyarap [and **nyarap** (*coq*)] to (eat/have) breakfast. *Kalau tidak* ~, *(me)ngantuk saja rasanya.* If you don't have breakfast, you just feel sleepy.
　menyarapi to serve breakfast to.
　sarapan 1 breakfast. *Mau* ~ *kesiangan, mau makan siang kepagian.* (*joc*) brunch. ~ *pagi* a) breakfast. *menyantap* ~ *pagi* to have breakfast. b) term used by some physicians to refer to an induced abortion. ~ *siang* brunch. **2** (*coq*) to eat breakfast. **bersarapan** to (eat/have) breakfast.
sarap V → SARAF II.
saraséhan (*Jv*) symposium, meeting to discuss s.t.
　bersaraséhan to hold discussions. *Pemulung akan* ~ *tentang lingkungan hidup.* Rag pickers are going to discuss the environment.
　menyaraséhankan to discuss in a symposium. *Makanan non-beras disaraséhankan.* Non-rice food will be discussed.
Saraswati Goddess of Wisdom; the patron of languages and literature, science and arts; spouse of the God Brahma.
sarat I 1 heavily laden (of a truck/ship/tree with fruit), full with/of. *pohon mangga yang* – *dengan buah* a mango tree full of fruit. *Perahu yang* – *tidak dapat laju.* A full prau cannot move fast. **2** to be full of, contain a lot of, be rich in. *mendung hitam* – *mengandung hujan* dark rain clouds. – *hati memikirkan anaknya itu* to be deeply affected by thinking about one's child. **3** pregnant; → HAMIL, MENGANDUNG, BUNTING. *sedang* – (of animals) with young. *Wanita itu dalam* –. That woman is pregnant. *bunting* – advanced pregnancy. **4** (*naut*) draft. – *air/kapal* draft (of ship). – *bertepas* fully laden. – *muatan* fully loaded. – *penumpang* full of passengers.
　menyarati to load/stuff with. *Kapal itu disarati beras berkarung-karung.* The ship was loaded with sacks of rice.
　menyaratkan to load s.t. (into), charge.
　kesaratan 1 overly laden, too full. **2** (*infr*) density; → KEPADATAN.
sarat II → SYARAT.
Sarathan and **Sarathon** (*A*) Cancer (*zod*).
sarau I 1 a large basket. **2** a hanging kitchen-rack.
sarau II (*M*) unlucky (of person).
　menyaraukan to make s.o. unlucky.
sardar (*Pers ob*) commander in chief.
sardén (*D*) sardine.
sardi (*Pers ob*) cold in the head.

saré (*Jv*) to sleep, go to bed.

(pa)saréan grave, tomb.

saréan (*Port*) 1 sergeant. 2 boatswain; → SERANG II. 3 (*J*) village head.

sarékat → SERIKAT. – *Islam* a Muslim mass organization founded in 1911.

sarén (*Jv*) black pudding of coagulated blood.

saréngat (*Jv*) → SYARAT.

saresmi (*K cla*) to have sexual intercourse.

sareukseuk (*S*) (in the Bandung area) unpleasant to look at, eyesore.

sargal (*J*) thick rope.

sargut menyargut to rip s.t. with one's teeth.

sarhad (*A cla*) limit, boundary.

sari I (*Skr*) essence, extract, quintessence, gist, nucleus. *benang* – stamen. *inti* – a) core, substance. b) digest. *serbuk/tepung* – pollen. *timah* – zinc. – *berita* news headlines. – *buah* fruit juice. – *buah-buahan* fruit juice. – *buah tomat* tomato juice. – *buah mangga* mango juice. – *buah sirsak* soursop juice. – *daging* meat stock, bouillon. – *delé* soybean powder. – *ganja* dried hemp, hashish. – *jeruk* orange juice. – *kedelé* soybean powder. – *kopi* instant coffee. – *madu* royal jelly. – *manis* sweetening. – *markisa* passion fruit juice. – *nanas* pineapple juice. – *pati* the essential, core, quintessence. **menyari-patikan** to take the essential of an article, etc., digest. – *pidato* the tenor of a speech. – *sagon* k.o. fried grated coconut. – *susu* cream. – *tebu* canesugar extract. – *téh* tea extract.

menyari 1 to extract. 2 to make juice.

menyarikan 1 to suck honey from; to pull juice out of. *kupu-kupu* ~ *bunga* butterflies suck the juice out of flowers. 2 to make an extract of, summarize, condense (a book).

tersarikan summarized, condensed.

penyari extractor.

penyarian extraction, extracting.

persarian digest, summary.

sari II (*Skr*) 1 flower. *cindai* – a fine flowered fabric, printed silk with flower pattern. *taman* – flower garden. 2 (it has lost its) bloom, freshness. – *naik ke wajahnya* blood came to s.o.'s face, i.e., he/she blushed.

persarian pollination.

sari III (*Skr*) a romantic name for women. *lambang* – (*Jv*) sexual intercourse. **nglambang** – to have sexual intercourse. – *rapat/rapet* (*Jv*) a *jamu* which helps tighten a woman's sexual organs (*nggeget-singset* in Javanese).

sari IV (*Skr*) a sari, saree, garment worn by Hindu women.

sari V (*J*) clipped form of **sehari**, a day. *saben* – and **sari-sari** every day, daily. *tidak seperti* –*nya* uncommon, out of the common, s.t. unusual.

sari-sarinya everyday, ordinary, usual.

sariat → SYARIAT.

sariawan aphtha, i.e., a small, white spot or pustule that is caused by a fungus and appears in the mouth, on the lips, or in the gastrointestinal tract in certain diseases, such as thrush; → SERIAWAN.

saridelé (*Jv*) soybean milk.

sarik I (*M*) bamboo variety with fine stems.

sarik II thief.

sarikan *akar* – a shrub from which rope is made, *Spatholobus ferrugineus.*

sarikat → SERIKAT, SARÉKAT. – *Buruh Muslim Indonésia* [SARBUMUSI] Indonesian Muslim Workers Association, founded in 1955.

saring I *kain/kertas* – filter cloth/paper. – *sinar lampu* light filter.

bersaring strained, filtered.

menyaring 1 to sift, strain, filter. *Kopi itu harus disaring dulu.* The coffee has to be filtered first. 2 to refine (a liquid), purify. 3 to screen. ~ *pelamar-pelamar yang akan diterima bekerja* to screen applicants who will be accepted/hired (for work); → MENYÉLÉKSI.

menyaringkan to filter/strain for s.o.

tersaring 1 sifted, sieved, strained, filtered. 2 screened.

saringan 1 filter, sieve, strainer. ~ *minyak/oli* oil filter (of car). ~ *udara* air filter. 2 filtered, sieved, strained. *air* ~ filtered water. 3 sifting, refining. 4 screening.

penyaring filter, strainer. *alat* ~ filter (the device), press.

penyaringan 1 filtering, straining. 2 screening.

saring II (*M*) slender.

saring III (*ob*) → SERING II.

sarip → SYARIF.

saripah → SYARIFAH.

saripati → SARI I.

sarira → SELÉRA II, SELIRA.

sarirah a shrub, *Acronychia laurifolia.*

sariri (*A*) k.o. chair, couch.

sari-sari → SARI V.

sarit (*M*) 1 difficult, laborious. 2 poor.

sarit-sarit seldom, rarely.

sarjan → SÉRSAN.

sarjana (*Skr*) 1 scholar, scientist. 2 academician. 3 (the academic degree of) master. 4 (university) graduate. – *Agama* [S.Ag] theologian. – *atom* atomic scientist. – *Ékonomi* [S.E.] Master of Economics. – *farmasi* pharmacist. – *géofisika* geophysicist. – *Hukum* [S.H./SH] a legal degree, Doctor of Jurisprudence, JD. – *ilmu agama* theologian. – *ilmu serangga* entomologist. – *Ilmu Politik* [S.IP] political scientist. – *Ilmu Sosial* [S.Sos] social scientist. – *Kedokteran* [S.Ked] physician. – *Kedokteran Gigi* [S.KG.] dentist. – *Kedokteran Héwan* [S.KH] veterinarian. – *Kehutanan* [S.Hut] sylvanologist. – *Keséhatan Masyarakat* [S.KM] public health official. – *kimia* chemist. – *lengkap* (*ob*) Ph.D. candidate. – *listrik* electrical engineer. – *Komputer* [S.Kom] computer expert. – *Muda* (*ob*) [S.M. and Sarmud] Bachelor (of Arts, etc.). – *Muda dalam Tarbiah* Bachelor of Education. – *Muda Ilmu Perawatan* [SMIP] Bachelor of Science in Nursing. – *nuklir* nuclear scientist. – *Pendidikan* [S.Pd] educationalist. – *peneliti* research scientist. – *Perikanan* [S.Pi.] piscatologist. – *Pertanian* [S.Pi] agriculturalist. – *Peternakan* [S.Pt.] expert in animal husbandry. – *Psikologi* [S.Psi] Master of Psychology. – *Sains* [S.Si] scientist. – *Sastra* [S.S.] Master of Arts. – *Seni* [S.Sn] artist. – *sujana* top scientist. – *Téknik* [S.T.] engineer. – *Téknik Kimia* chemical engineer. – *Téknik Listrik* electrical engineer. – *Téknik Mesin* mechanical engineer. – *Téknik Perminyakan* petroleum engineer. – *Téknologi Pertanian* [S.TP.] agricultural technologist. – *télékomunikasi* telecommunications expert. – *wisuda* degree candidate. – *Wiyata* name of the *Taman Siswa* University in Yogyakarta.

menyarjanakan to make senior high school teachers into *sarjana.*

kesarjanaan scholarship, i.e., the skills of a scholar.

sarjanisasi 1 turning out *sarjanas*/master's degree holders. 2 the replacement of nondegree senior high school teachers by *sarjanas.*

sarju (*Jv*) sympathy.

sarkasme (*D/E*) sarcasm.

sarkastik (*E*) and **sarkastis** (*D*) sarcastic.

sarkofagus (*E*) sarcophagus.

sarkom(a) (*D*) sarcoma.

sarkon [sarung-kontol] condom.

sarlir [sarung-pelir] condom.

sarmud [sarjana-muda] bachelor (academic degree).

saroja → SEROJA.

sarok → SARUK.

saron (*Jv*) xylophone-like *gamelan* instrument consisting of six or seven heavy bronze bars above a hollow wooden base. – *demung* larger such instrument; → KEDEMUNG. – *peking* smaller such instrument.

sarong → SARUNG I.

sarsaparila (*D*) drink made from the sarsaparilla root.

sarsar → SASAR I.

sarsaran to beat rapidly (of heart).

Sartan (*A zod*) Cancer. *garis balik* – tropic of Cancer.

saru I (*A*) *pohon* – cypress, *Casuarina equisetifolia.*

saru II (*J*) 1 dim, vague; unrecognizable. – *dengan* hard to distinguish from. 2 dummy (s.t. that looks like s.t. else and stands in for it).

menyaru [and **nyaru** (*coq*)] 1 disguised. 2 to disguise o.s. *Di antaranya ada yang* ~ *sebagai wanita.* Among them were also persons disguised as women.

menyarukan to cover up, disguise. *untuk ~ kegiatan gelap itu* to cover up that illegal activity.

tersaru disguised.

penyaru 1 s.o. who disguises himself. **2** (intelligence) secret agent; → AGÉN, MATA-MATA. ~ *asli* genuine/true agent. ~ *bantuan* support agent. ~ *keliling* roving agent. ~ *menetap* resident agent. ~ *palsu* bogus agent. ~ *penindak* action agent. ~ *penunggu* dormant agent. ~ *rangkap* dual agent. ~ *tunggangan* double agent. ~ *utama* principal agent.

penyaruan 1 disguise. **2** (intelligence) cover. **3** clandestine, covert. ~ *berlapis* cover within cover. ~ *mendalam* deep cover. ~ *perorangan* personal cover. ~ *pertemuan bersama* group cover.

saru III (*Jv*) ill-mannered, indecent, rude.

saru IV silver chain for a pet bird and nickname for the bird itself.

saruk saruk-saruk dragging (of feet).

menyaruk 1 to bump/run up against; to stumble, trip. **2** to be fortunate, be in luck (in gambling).

tersaruk(-saruk) (walked) stumbling, after falling and getting up.

sarun → SARON.

sarundéng → SERUNDÉNG.

sarung I 1 cover, case, envelope, wrapper. **2** sheath, scabbard, cover for the blade of a sword/kris/dagger, etc. – *angin* windsock (at airport). – *bantal* pillow cover. – *gigi* crown of tooth. – *jari* thimble. – *kaki* socks. – *kamasutra* Indian-made condom with the "Kamasutra" trademark. – *karét* condom. – *kelamin lelaki* condom. – *keris* kris sheath. – *kontol* [sarkon] condom. – *kursi* upholstery. – *pedang* sheath. – *pelekat* → KAIN *pelekat*. – *pelir* [sarlir] condom. – *pélor/peluru* cartridge case. – *pénis/penyelamat* condom. – *pistol* holster. – *rakét* racket cover. – *sepatu* overshoes. – *tangan* glove. – *tinju* boxing gloves. – *zakar* condom.

bersarung in a sheath; to provide with a sheath, wrapped in a sheath/scabbard; sheathed.

bersarungkan to use s.t. as a cover/sheath, etc.

menyarung(i) to put s.t. in a sheath/cover, wrap, encase.

menyarungkan 1 to put s.t. in a sheath/case, etc. **2** to use s.t. as a sheath.

tersarung sheathed, encased.

penyarung s.o. who makes sheaths/scabbards.

penyarungan sheath, sheathing.

sarung II *kain* – sarong, cloth worn round the middle of the body and tucked around the waist.

bersarung to wear a sarong.

sarungan *kaum/orang-orang* ~ the practicing/mosque-going Muslims.

sarung III menyarung to interrupt, intrude on.

sarungisasi the making available of sarongs with batik motifs in hotel rooms (in Yogyakarta).

saruni → SERUNAI III, SERUNI.

sarusun [saruan rumah susun] condo(minium).

sarut I (*M*) → CARUT *marut*.

sarut II menyarut **1** to scrape/rub against anything. **2** to gnaw.

sarut III (*M*) k.o. grass, goose grass, *Eleusine indica*.

sarwa (*Skr*) all. *Tuhan – sekalian alam* Lord of all creation. – *tunggal* everything merges into one.

bersarwa ~ *makna* meaningful.

sarwaboga (*Skr neo*) omnivore.

sarwal (*A*) → SELUAR.

sarwar (*Pers ob*) lord, master.

sasa (*cla*) sturdy, strong, robust.

sasah → SESAH.

sasak I 1 wattles, coarse wickerwork of bamboo strips (for fences/walls, etc.). *pagar* – a wattled fence. **2** bouffant (women's hairdo). *berambut* – with teased hair.

sasak-sasak bouffant.

bersasak *rambut* ~ backcombed hair.

menyasak to tease up one's hair in a bouffant backcomb.

sasakan bouffant. *memberéskan ~nya* to adjust one's teased hair.

Sasak II name of the main ethnic group on the island of Lombok.

sasakala (*Skr S*) at the time of. *dongéng* – legend.

sasan → SASA.

sasana (*Jv*) **1** lesson, advice. **2** place, location, venue, center; training site. **3** (*infr*) plaza. – *Bhakti Praja* "Place to devote to the State and Nation," i.e., the name given to the three-story auditorium building of the Department of the Interior in Jakarta. – *olahraga* sports venue. – *Réhabilitasi Wanita* Women's Rehabilitation Center. – *tinju* boxing arena. – *Triguna* Triguna Plaza. – *tresna wredha* senior citizens' home.

sasando a traditional musical instrument of Rote island.

sasap I (*M*) menyasap **1** to weed, clear of weeds, uproot; → MENCABUT, MENYIANG. **2** to clear away. **3** to rub/wipe out.

sasap II → SUSUP *sasap*.

sasap III → SESAP I.

sasar I (*Pers*) menyasar [and nyasar (*coq*)] **1** to lose one's way, go astray, end up in the wrong place. **2** to deviate from the expected course, stray. *peluru* ~ a stray bullet.

tersasar [and kesasar (*J*)] get lost, lose one's way.

menyasarkan to make s.t. go astray.

sasar II menyasar to aim at, target.

menyasarkan to aim with.

sasaran target, goal, objective. *menjadikan ... ~* to single s.o. out (for criticism), target s.t. ~ *akhir* final objective. ~ *antara* intermediate objective. ~ *bergerak* (*mil*) moving target. ~ *empuk* soft/easy target. ~ *ganti* alternate objective, supplementary target. ~ *keras* hard target. ~ *kesempatan* target of opportunity. ~ *lébar* target extending beyond the impact area. ~ *lelucon* butt of jokes, laughingstock. ~ *lunak* soft/easy target. ~ *permati* critical objective. ~ *pokok* main objective. ~ *semu aktif di luar kapal* (*mil*) off-board active decoy. ~ *semu aktif yang ditarik oléh kapal* (*mil*) towed-off-board active decoy. *menetapkan kembali ~* to retarget. *tidak kena ~* to miss the target. ~ *timbul hilang* fleeting target. **bersasaran** to have ... as a target/goal. ~ *ganda* to have a dual goal. *Usulan itu ~ ganda.* That proposal has two goals.

sasar III (*Pers*) **1** dazed, confused. **2** muddle-headed.

sasar IV sasaran drill/recreation ground.

sasaringan a batik pattern.

sasat (*J*) persasat to do as if.

sasaté (*S*) – *bandeng* k.o. milk-fish dish.

sasau I → SASAR I.

sasau II menyasau to eat large amounts.

sasdaya [sastra dan budaya] literature and culture.

sasi I (*Jv*) moon, month.

sasi II (*IBT*) prohibition against harvesting at certain periods. – *buaya* (*Pap*) prohibition against catching crocodiles.

sasi III a word ending in -sasi, such as *kulturisasi, problematisasi*, etc.

sasi IV (*M*) → SAKSI.

sasian (*M*) *anak* ~ student, pupil.

sasimi (*Jp*) sashimi.

sasirangan a traditional Kalimantan cloth formerly exclusively worn by the aristocracy to ward off disasters or diseases.

bersasirangan to wear a *sasirangan* cloth. *Saya ~ hanya untuk pertunjukan kedua saja.* I wore a *sasiranaan* cloth only for my second show.

sasis (*D*) chassis.

sasmita (*Skr Jv*) **1** sign, indication, omen. **2** symbolical. – *jelék* a bad omen.

sasmitaloka (*Skr neo*) former residence of a military hero.

sasono – *Langen Budoyo* Culture Building (in Jakarta); → SASANA.

sasrahan (*Jv*) gift (from person in love with a girl to her parents).

sas-sus clipped form of *desas-desus*.

mensas-suskan to spread rumors about.

sast(e)ra (*Skr*) **1** literature, belles lettres. *ahli* – literary scholar. *Fakultas* – Faculty of Letters. *karya* – literary work. *seni* – (art of) literature. **2** literary language. **3** (*cla*) (magical/holy) books. – *bandingan* comparative literature. – *Jawa kontémporér* contemporary Javanese literature. – *lisan* oral literature. – *wangi* chick-lit, literature for and by women.

bersastra to occupy o.s. with literature.

kesastraan literary.

sastrakanta (*Skr neo*) thesis.

sast(e)rawan (*Skr*) **1** man of letters, literary man; → PUJANGGA. **2** (*cla*) scribe.

kesast(e)rawanan (*mod*) literature, literary.

sast(e)rawati (*Skr neo*) 1 woman of letters, literary woman. 2 female author.

sasus rumor; → DESAS-DESUS.

menyasuskan to spread rumors about.

sat I (*ob*) a measure of capacity (for unhulled rice). – *besar* = 10 *gantang*. – *kecil* = 5 *gantang*.

sat II (in acronyms) → SATUAN.

sata (*Skr*) 100. *dwi-warsa* bicentennial.

satah (*A math*) plane; → SOTOH.

satai → SATÉ I.

Satal → SANGIHÉ *Talaud*.

satan (*D*) satan, devil; → SÉTAN.

satang I (*M*) punting pole.

satang II *udang* – crayfish, palaemon (prawn); → UDANG *galah*.

satanisme (*D/E*) Satanism.

satar (*A*) line (e.g., of writing/print).

satarat (*A*) silk and cotton fabric.

Satata Wiwéka Nirmala (the work slogan of the Army Fiscal Control Inspectorate) Eradicating Bureaucracy and Corruption within the Army.

saté I (*Tam*) pieces of meat roasted on a wooden skewer and customarily dipped in a special sauce before being eaten. *Gedung – "Saté Building,"* i.e., the epithet given by the population of Bandung to the Office of the Head of the First Level Area (the Governor's Office) due to its saté-like roofing. *setusuk* – a skewer of saté. *tukang* – saté vendor. – *ayam* chicken on skewers served with peanut sauce. – *babi manis* pork on skewers served with *kécap manis*. – *ganja* Buddha stick. – *(h)ati* liver served on skewers. – *kalong* flattened spiced beef served on skewers. – *kambing* lamb (or goat) on skewers served with (spicy hot) peanut sauce.

menyaté [and nyaté (*coq*)] 1 to make/grill *saté*. 2 to eat *saté*. 3 (*coq*) to dissent.

tersaté skewered.

persatéan (*coq*) dissension (divisions into small parts like saté).

saté II [Séhat, Aman, Tertib dan Élok] Healthy, Safe, Orderly and Beautiful.

saték various species of birds, tropic birds. – *putih* white-tailed tropic bird, *Phaethon lepturus*.

satelit (*D/E*) satellite. *kota/negara* – satellite town/state. – *antariksa* space satellite. – *buatan manusia* man-made satellite. – *bulan (tak berawak)* (unmanned) moon satellite. – *bumi (tak berawak)* (unmanned) earth satellite. – *cuaca* weather satellite. – *komunikasi* communications satellite. – *mata-mata* spy satellite. – *pengindra jarak jauh* remote-sensing satellite. – *siaran langsung* direct-broadcasting satellite. – *tarik* tethered satellite.

men(g)satelitkan to make (a certain town or country) a satellite of another town or country.

persatelitan satellite (*mod*) *bidang* ~ the satellite sector.

sateria → SATRIA.

satgas → SATUAN *tugas*.

satia → SATYA, SETIA.

satih (*M*) menyatih to fine s.o.

satin (*D*) satin.

satinét (*D*) sateen.

satir I (*D*) satyr; dirty old man, old goat.

satir II and satire (*D*) satire.

satir III (*M*) *sumpah* – oath of loyalty, irrevocable oath.

satirik (*E*) and satiris (*D*) satirical.

satirikus (*D*) satirist.

sato (*Jv*) → SATWA.

satori (in Buddhism) enlightenment.

satpam → SATUAN *pengaman(an)*.

satria and satrya (*Skr*) 1 nobleman; a man who devotes himself to the service of his country. 2 (*ob*) an aristocrat who helps rule the country and takes responsibility for dealing with dangers for the sake of his people.

kesatriaan and ksatrian 1 place where noblemen are quartered. 2 (*mil*) barracks.

Satriamandala (*Skr neo*) Armed Forces Museum.

satron <satru> (*J/Jv*) menyatroni 1 to consider s.o. as one's enemy; to be hostile toward. *Saya tidak merasa salah apa-apa kok disatroni*. I don't know what I've done that he's so hostile toward me. 2 to break into. *Désa itu akhir-akhir ini disatroni perampok*. Recently that village was broken into by bandits.

satru (*Skr Jv*) enemy.

satu I 1 one – *abad/rupiah* one century/rupiah. *halaman* – page one – *halaman* one page. – *demi/per* – one by one, one at a time. – *bangsa* – *bahasa* one nation, one language. – *dua* one or two, a few. – *dua hari* several days. – *dua, dua tiga!"* (yell of bus conductor to passengers already sitting in the bus) "Move up!" "Make place!" (to create more seating accommodation). *tak* – *yang betul* there is no one correct answer. *dihadapinya pada* – *antara dua* he was faced with a dilemma. – *di antaranya/antara meréka* one of them. *yang* – *ini berapa (harganya)?* what is the price of this one? *Yang* – *lagi berapa?* What does the other one cost? *Perancang mode yang* – *ini akhirnya menarik napas lega*. Finally, this fashion designer could breathe easy. *anaknya yang* – one of the two children. *yang* – *... yang lain ...* (the) one *...,* the other *... – dan lainnya* all this. – *dan lainnya asal saja tidak bertentangan atau melanggar ketertiban umum*. Provided that all this is not in conflict with or in violation of public order. – *lagi* one more. *yang* – *lagi* the other one – *sama lain* one another, mutual. *bertentangan* – *sama lain/yang* – *dengan yang lain* to be at odds/variance with one another (or, each other). *Mémang yang* – *itu kebangetan!* That one (i.e., she or he) is really too much! – *pun tidak* not even one, not (a single) one *Meréka* – *kata*. They were unanimous. 2 the same. *Meréka duduk* – *méja*. They sat at the same table. *memperoléh* –, *kepingin dua; dapat sedikit, kepingin banyak* give him an inch, and he will take a mile. – *arti* of the same meaning, synonymous. menyatuartikan to make s.t. synonymous with. *Kata "ambisi" itu kini sering disatuartikan dengan "ambisius.* The meaning of (the word) *"ambisi"* is nowadays often made synonymous with *"ambisius." – atap* under the same roof, one-stop (shopping, etc.). menyatu-atapkan to put under the same roof. penyatu-atapan putting under the same roof. – *bangsa* of the same nation. menyatubangsakan to make one nation, nationalize. *Sering sangat sulit upaya ~ para warga suatu negara*. Efforts to nationalize the citizens of a state are frequently very difficult. – *buyut* having the same great-grandparent. – *golong* one group. menyatugolongkan to place/put in a group, put in the same group. – *jalan* a) one way. b) of the same mind/orientation. bersatu jalan 1 to have the same orientation, be of the same mind, etc., be like-minded. 2 to go in the same direction. – *komando* one command. menyatukomandokan to place under a single command. – *nada* monotone. kesatunadaan monotony. – *padu* a whole, in harmony, unified. bersatu padu 1 to be unified, united, integrated. 2 unanimous, of one mind, at one, in harmony. *Sewajibnyalah meréka ~ dan bekerjasama untuk mencapai kemajuan*. They should be in harmony and cooperate to achieve progress. menyatu-padukan and mempersatu-padukan to unify, merge, unite, integrate, join (efforts). *Salah satu daripada tujuan ibadat haji ialah untuk ~ umat Islam*. One of the goals of the pilgrimage to Mecca is to unite Muslims. tersatu padu united, integrated. kesatu-paduan 1 union, harmony, unity, integration. 2 unanimity. – *pakét* one package. menyatupakétkan to make s.t. into a single package. *Obyék wisata Pulau Sumatera disatupakétkan*. Sumatra, an object of interest for tourists, has been made into a package deal. penyatupakétan package deal. – *ragam* one kind, uniform. penyaturagaman the process of making uniform, uniformizing. – *segi* one-sided. kesatusegian one-sidedness. – *sisi* one-sided. kesatusisian one-sidedness. – *tangan* of one hand. menyatutangankan to put/place in one/a single hand. *Perdagangan disatutangankan*. Trade was placed in one hand. – *taraf* one rank. menyatutarafkan to rank s.o. with. *satu waktu* of the same time, synchronous. menyatuwaktukan to synchronize. – *wangsa* kin. kesatu-wangsaan monodynasty. *tidak* – not united. ketidak-satuan lack of unity.

satu-satu 1 one by one, one at a time. *tamu berdatangan ~ the guests came one by one. 2 some, a few, one or two. *tak ~ a) not a little/few, (quite) a lot, very much. b) not only one, not alone, in a group, in great numbers. *tinggal ~ only that one remains.

satu-satunya only, sole, one and only. ~ *jalan ialah* ... the (one and) only way is ... ~ *kebon binating* the only zoo.

bersatu 1 to unite, ally, join; united, allied, joined. *Kaum tani ~ dengan kaum buruh.* The peasants united with the workers. *Kaum Buruh seluruh Dunia, ~!* Workers of the World, Unite! *Bangsa-Bangsa ~* (*Mal*) United Nations. ~ *kembali* to reunite. 2 to become one/united, coalesce, inseparably connected. *Zat makanan itu ~ dengan oksigén di dalam sél.* Nutrients coalesce with the oxygen in the cells. ~ *hati* to be of one mind, be in agreement, bring together in a common cause/interest, etc.; unanimous. ~ *kita teguh, bercerai kita runtuh/rubuh* united we stand, divided we fall; in union is strength. *tidak ~* not united. **ketidak-bersatuan** disunity. **membersatukan** to unify, unite. *"Saya puyeng," kata mantan profésor téologi di Univérsitas Kabul ini karena sulitnya para pejuang dibersatukan.* "I'm confused," said the professor of theology at the University of Kabul due to the difficulty of uniting the fighters. **kebersatuan** oneness, unity, integrity.

menyatu [and **nyatu** (*coq*)] to become one, converge, unite into one, be integrated into one *Genangan air di Kecamatan Penjaringan sampai Senén soré ~ dengan air yang merendam kompléks pemukiman méwah Pluit.* The floods in the Penjaringan District converged with the water that inundated the luxurious residential complex of Pluit as of Monday afternoon. ~ *diri* (*dengan*) to unite, join forces. *sistém yang ~* an integrated system.

menyatukan, mempersatukan, and **memersatukan** [and **nyatuin** (*J coq*)] 1 to unite, join, ally, bring together. *menyatukan hati* to work together for a common end. 2 to concentrate on. *Segenap minatnya dipersatukan pada masalah pengangguran.* All his attention was concentrated on the unemployment issue.

satuan unit, force, squad, squadron. ~ *bawahan* (*mil*) attached unit. ~ *berat/bobot* unit of weight. ~ *hitung uang* unit of currency. ~ *kontra* counterintelligence unit. ~ *korbankan diri* suicide squad. ~ *lahan* land unit. ~ *lintas udara* air-borne unit. ~ *Marinir Armada* Fleet Marine Force. ~ *(mata) uang* monetary unit. ~ *panjang* unit of length. ~ *pengaman(an)* [Satpam] a) security unit. b) security guard. ~ *setingkat kompi* [SSK] company-level unit. ~ *témbak* fire unit. ~ *tempur* [Satpur] combat unit. ~ *tentara* military unit. ~ *tugas* [Satgas] special unit. ~ *ukuran* unit of measure. ~ *usaha* business unit. ~ *waktu* unit of time. **bersatuan** to form a unit.

kesatu 1 first; → PERTAMA. *jilid ~* volume one. 2 firstly.

kesatuan 1 unit, lot (*fin*). ~ *bantuan* (*mil*) support unit. ~ *berdiri sendiri* separate unit. ~ *monétér* monetary unit. ~ *pemadam kebakaran* fire brigade. ~ *tempur* combat unit. ~ *tentara* army unit. 2 integrity, unity, oneness, entirety, totality. *satu ~ yang tidak terpisahkan* an inseparable unity, one integrated whole. *negara ~* unitary state. 3 union. ~ *Aksi Mahasiswa Indonésia* [KAMI] Indonesian University Students' Action Union. ~ *Aksi Mahasiswa Muslim Indonésia* [KAMMI] Indonesian Muslim University Students' Action Union. ~ *Aksi Pelajar Indonésia* [KAPPI] Indonesian Pupils' Action Union. ~ *Pabéan* Customs Union. **sekesatuan** of one (army) unit, in the same unit. *teman-teman ~nya* friends of his (army) unit.

pemersatu [and **penyatu** (*infr*)] unifier; unifying. *bahasa sebagai alat ~* language as a unifying tool. *suatu idéologi sebagai kekuatan ~* an ideology as a unifying force. *Jepang sendiri mengharapkan Indonésia sebagai pelopor ~ karaté di Asia.* Japan itself expects Indonesia to be the unifying vanguard of karate in Asia. **pemersatuan** unification.

penyatuan unification, union, joining. ~ *kembali* reunification. ~ *nada* unison. ~ *pemasaran minyak* the pooling of oil.

persatuan 1 association, club, union (*mod*). ~ *Advokat* Bar Association. ~ *Advokat Indonésia* [Peradin] Indonesian Lawyers Association. ~ *Bangsa-Bangsa* [PBB] United Nations, UN; *cp Bangsa-Bangsa* BERSATU. ~ *Émirat Arab* United Arab Emirates, U.A.E. ~ *Guru Républik Indonésia* [PGRI] Republic of Indonesia Teachers Association. ~ *istri Karyawan (Départemén) Pertanian* [Periskatani] Employees' Wives Association of the Department of Agriculture. ~ *Istri Tentara Kartika Chandra Kirana* [Persit KCK] Army Wives Association "Rays of the Stars and Moon." ~ *Mahasiswa Indonésia di Amérika*

Serikat [Permias] Association of Indonesian Students in the United States of America. ~ *Orang Tua Murid* [POTM] Parent-Students Association. ~ *Wanita Lembaga Administrasi Negara* [Perwalan] Women's Association of the National Institute of Administration. ~ *Wanita Républik Indonésia* [Perwari] Republic of Indonesia Women's Association (a social welfare organization). 2 unification. 3 community. ~ *barang-barang* community property.

satu II (*Jv*) cookie made from green-bean flour.

saturasi (*E*) saturation.

satwa (*Skr*) 1 (usually wild) animal, beast; → MARGASATWA. 2 (in police force) canine, K-9. ~ *buru* hunting animal. ~ *jinak* domesticated animal. ~ *langka* endangered animal. ~ *liar* game, wild animals. ~ *menyusui* mammal(s). ~ *pemangsa* predator.

satwaboga (*Skr neo*) carnivore.

satya (*ob*) → SETIA.

satyagraha (*Skr neo*) nonviolent resistance.

satyalencana reward or medal presented to military or government personnel. ~ *dwija sista* merit award for police academy teachers. ~ *pendidikan* merit award for education for teachers in isolated areas. ~ *penegak* medal for action against the G30S. ~ *seroja* medal for crushing local unrest (*esp* in East Timor). ~ *wira dharma* medal for action against Malaysia. ~ *wira karya* medal for civilians for exemplary deeds.

Satya Wacana (*Skr neo*) "Loyal to God's Commandment," i.e., the name of the Protestant university in Salatiga, Central Java.

Satya Wira Wicaksana (*Skr neo*) (motto of the Army Military Police) Act without Hesitation, Clearly and Wisely.

sau I (*onom*) rustling sound; → DESAU.

sau II → SAWO I.

saudagar (*Pers*) trader, merchant (*esp* Muslim); → BISNISMAN, PEDAGANG.

kesaudagaran merchandising.

saudara (*Skr*) 1 brother or sister of the same father and mother (or, only the father or the mother is the same), older or younger brother/sister, sibling; → ABANG I, ADIK, KAKAK I. ~ *perempuannya pergi ke pasar* his sister went to the market. ~ *seayah/sebapak* half-brother/-sister with the same father. ~ *seibu* half-brother/-sister with the same mother. *sanak* ~ relatives, family. 2 fellow (villager), person of the same (religion, etc.). *perang* ~ civil war. ~. ~ *kita di désa* our fellow villagers. 3 friend, comrade. ~ *sepermainan* playmate. 4 you a) (fairly formal, used to strangers of the same age or younger). ~, *boléh saya bertanya* may I ask you a question. ~ *(si) tertuduh* you, the accused. *"Melihat kejadian itu, apa yang ~ lakukan?" tanya hakim.* "When you saw what happened, what did you do?" asked the judge. b) used to audiences. ~ *pendengar* listeners (over the radio). c) Mr., Miss, Mrs. ~ *S* Mr. S. ~ *ketua* Mr. Chairman. 5 related to, the brother of. *menipu itu adalah ~ mencuri* deceiving is the brother of stealing. 6 placenta, afterbirth; → TEMBUNI, URI I. *anak* ~ nephew; niece. *bapak* ~ uncle. *mak* ~ aunt. *perang* ~ civil war. ~ *angkat* adopted sibling or s.o. raised by s.o.'s parents. ~ *anjing* half-brother/-sister with the same mother. ~ *baru* (*Mal*) a) a new convert to Islam. b) a Chinese Muslim. ~ *bau (em)bacang* distant relative. ~ *belahan* sibling from the same ancestors. ~ *daging* all distant and near relatives. ~ *dekat* close relatives. ~ *dua misan/pupu* second cousin. ~ *jauh/kandung renggang* distant relative. ~ *(se)kandung* one's own sibling (with the same father and mother). ~ *nénék* great aunt/uncle. ~ *pungut* adopted sibling. ~ *rapat* close relatives. ~ *saudari* ladies and gentlemen. ~ *sejalan/sejadi/sekandung* full sibling (with the same father and mother). ~ *senasib* companion in distress. ~ *sepengambilan* adopted sibling. ~ *seperjuangan* brother/comrade in arms. ~ *sepersusuan* → SAUDARA susu. ~ *sepupu* first cousin. ~ *susu(an)* foster brother/sister. ~ *tiri* stepbrother/-sister. ~ *tua* (during the Japanese occupation) the Japanese.

saudara-saudara gentlemen. ~ *yang terhormat!* Ladies and gentlemen!

bersaudara 1 to be siblings. *dua orang ~* two siblings. *Kami semuanya adalah ~.* We are all brothers. *Yvonne Agnés Sumlang merupakan anak bungsu dari 10 ~ dalam keluarga P.S. Sumlang alm.* Yvonne Agnes Sumlang is the youngest child of 10 siblings in the family of the late P.S. Sumlang. **2** to have a brother/sister or brothers/sisters. **3** to be related. **4** brothers (in the name of a firm). *Shaw ~* Shaw brothers.

mempersaudarakan to fraternize with; to treat s.o. as a brother/sister.

penyaudaraan fraternization.

persaudaraan 1 brotherhood, fraternity. **2** relationship, friendship. **3** fraternization. **berpersaudaraan** to have a sense of brotherhood/fraternity.

saudari (*Skr neo*) you (used toward women, *esp* in correspondence).

saudérék (*ob*) → SAUDARA.

sauh I (*naut*) anchor, drag; → JANGKAR I. *membongkar* – to weigh anchor. *membuang* – to cast anchor. – *buji* grappling anchor. – *cemat* kedge anchor. – *sekoci* boat anchor. – *larat* dragging anchor. – *terbang* mooring anchor, flying grapnel.

bersauh 1 with/to have an anchor. **2** to be/lie/ride at anchor.

sauh II → SAWO I.

saujana (*Skr*) *padang* – a plain stretching to the horizon; → YOJANA. – *mata memandang* as far as the eye can see.

sauk I 1 scoop, ladle, dipper. **2** long-handled net for catching fish/butterflies, etc. – *air mandikan diri* to pay one's way, be self-supporting, stand on one's own two feet. **3** scoopful.

sauk-sauk and **sesauk** butterfly/fishing net with a long handle.

menyauk 1 to scoop, dip up; to catch fish/butterflies, etc. with a long-handled net. **2** to acquire/gain knowledge; → MENGANGSU *~ ilmu/kawruh*. *~ uang di atas méja* to steal money from the table. **4** to hook s.t. onto (so as to trip up, preparatory to tying s.t. or s.o. up, etc.), lasso.

sauk-menyauk interlocked, interwoven.

menyaukkan to lasso (the legs of animals). *Disaukkannya jerat pada kaki gajah yang lepas itu.* He lassoed the leg of the elephant that had broken loose.

tersauk(kan) caught, scooped up.

sauk II sigh, sob. – *tangis* sobs and tears.

saum (*A*) **1** the Fast; → PUASA. **2** Lent.

sauna (*D/E*) sauna.

saung I (*S*) a small watchman's hut built in rice paddies. – *meeting* a meeting held in such a hut; this term is popular in West Java, *esp* among rice farmers. – *sawah* watcher's hut in rice paddy; → DANGAU.

saung II (*M*) cave, cavern.

saup (*J*) **nyaup** to pick up in a shovel, shovel.

saur I → SAHUR.

saur II (*M*) **bersaur** intertwined, interlocked.

menyaur 1 to entangle, wrap around. **2** to throw a rope/lasso (to capture animals by lassoing their legs).

menyauri to overgrow, twine around.

tersaur entangled, caught on, hooked on to. *Kakinya ~ pada akar.* His leg was caught on a root.

saur III (*Jv*) – *manuk* (to respond) in unison.

saur IV – *singkong* k.o. snack made of grated cassava, steamed and mixed with brown sugar.

saus (*D*) sauce, gravy. – *Inggris* Worcestershire sauce. – *kacang* peanut sauce. – *selada* mayonnaise. – *tomat* tomato catsup.

saut I *akar* – and **sautan** a climbing shrub, *Adenia singaporeana*.

saut II (*Jv*) **menyaut** to snatch. *Ia baru sadar setelah tasnya terjatuh dan segera disaut sang perampok.* She only realized it after her purse fell and immediately was snatched by the thief.

saut III → SAHUT. **bersaut-sautan** to respond to e.o. (of birds/crickets/talkers/saluting guns). *Dari kejauhan sesekali terdengar bunyi jengkerik – menyanyikan tembang malam.* From a distance from time to time there was heard the sound of crickets singing their evening song to e.o.

savana (*D*) savanna(h).

saw. [Salallahu Alaihi Wassalam] May the blessings of God and peace be upon him. (used after saying the name of the Prophet Muhammad.).

sawa python; → PITON, SAWO II, ULAR I.

sawab I (*A*) the truth. *wallahu alam bi–* only God knows what the real truth is.

sawab II (*A*) **1** compensation (after a death); → PAHALA, GANJARAN. **2** influence. – *dari pahlawan itu* the influence of that hero.

kesawaban to be influenced.

sawah irrigated rice field. – *air/(ber)bandar langit* rice field dependent on rainfall, rain-fed rice field. – *basah/bencah* artificially irrigated rice field. – *bengkok/lungguh* (*Jv*) a rice field given to s.o. in usufruct. – *bera/guluduk* (*S*)/*jajaran* rice paddy dependent on rainfall. – *kas* village treasury land. – *kitri* (*S*) rice field that can be inherited. – *klatakan* (*Jv*) unirrigated rice field. – *lebak* rice field in swampy area. – *liat* rice field that is too dry. – *pasang-surut* tidal rice field. – *rawang* rice field in a swampy area. – *rumput* grassland. – *tadah hujan* rain-fed rice field.

bersawah 1 to have/till rice fields. **2** to grow rice in *sawahs*.

menyawah to work a rice field.

menyawahkan to turn (a piece of land) into rice paddies.

pesawah and **penyawah** rice farmer.

pe(r)sawahan 1 cultivation of rice, rice growing. **2** plot of *sawah* land, rice-growing areas. *~ pasang-surut* tidal rice fields.

sawai various species of birds, large racket-tailed drongo, *Dissemurus paradiseus* and a k.o. drongo, *Surniculus malayanus*.

Sawal → SYAWAL.

sawala (*S*) discussion, debate.

bersawala to discuss, debate.

sawan 1 fits, convulsions. **2** epilepsy. *batuk* – whooping cough. *ibu* – boils on a child's head. – *agung* sudden dizziness. – *babi* epilepsy. – *bangkai* apoplexy. – *céléng* epilepsy. – *gila* recurrent mania. – *sesak* asthma. – *tangis* crying fits. – *ulu* chronic redness of the eyes, blepharitis.

sawanan to have convulsions. *jamu ~* k.o. herb for children with asthma or epilepsy.

sawang I – *langit* and (**pe**)**sawangan** the space between heaven and earth, the sky, atmosphere; → AWANG-AWANG(AN).

sawang II (*M*) *rimba* – uninhabited jungle, wilderness. – *pegunungan* vast and uninhabited mountain range.

bersawang forested, forest-covered.

pe(r)sawangan uninhabited region, desert, wasteland.

sawang III cobweb, dirt found in the corner of ceilings.

sawang IV dracaena, a plant used as medicine against ringworm and skin irritations, *Cordyline fruticosa*.

sawang V *punai* – cinnamon-headed green pigeon, *Treron fulvicollis*.

sawang VI (*Jv*) **nyawang** to stare at s.t. (from a distance).

sawangan (*Jv*) a very small bamboo whistle attached to the tail of a flying pigeon or kite.

sawar fence, barricade (to drive game or fish in a certain direction), barrier. – *darah otak* blood-brain barrier. – *jalan* barrier placed across a road. – *pohon* barrier placed around a tree trunk so that thieves cannot climb up and take the fruit. – *uri* placental barrier.

menyawar to place a barrier on, barricade.

penyawar barrier, barricade, block.

sawat I 1 cross belt, shoulder strap. **2** drive belt. – *sandang* shoulder belt, bandoleer (of sword).

sawat II → PESAWAT.

sawat-sawat vague (of hope).

sawér (*J*) the ceremony following the *sembah*. After the newlyweds have completed their rounds, they go outside the house to take their seats on a chair under a large umbrella which is held behind them by one of the relatives of the bride. An elderly woman then performs the *sawér*, i.e., throwing coins and rice grains at them from a bowl.

menyawér and **nyawér 1** to throw money, rice mixed with coins, etc. on the bridal couple or on a child just circumcised. **2** to ask money from the spectators or ask the spectators to give money to the performers (of a *kuda képang* show, etc.).

sawet → SAWAT I.

sawi I various species of vegetables, Indian mustard, spinach mustard, *Brassica spp.* – *granat* petchai, bok choy, *Brassica pekinensis*. – *bunga/hijau/ijo* choy sam, mustard greens, *Brassica rugosa*. – *jepun* dwarf white mustard, *Brassica sp.* – *lemah* (*Jv*) nasturtium, *Nasturtium indicum*. – *pahit* Indian mustard, *Brassica sp.* – *putih/slobor* bok choy, Chinese cabbage, *Brassica chinensis*; → PECAI. – *tanah* an edible weed, false pimpernel, *Ilysanthes antipoda, Nasturtium heterophyllum*.

sawi II *semut* – an ant species, red and black Indian ant, *Sima rufonigra*.

sawi III → SENAWI.

sawi-sawi → SAWI I.

sawit I kelapa – oil palm, *Elaeis guineensis. minyak* – palm oil.

sawit II (*Jv*) **sawitan** a matching *batik* outfit and headdress.

sawo I and **sawu 1** *buah* – chiku, sapodilla, sapote, zapote. – *durén* fruit and ornamental tree, star apple, *Chrysophyllum cainito*. – *kecik* name of a tree with very small fruits, wongai plum, *Manilkara kauki*. – *manila* sapodilla, *Achras zapota*. 2 *warna* – brown. *warna* – *matang/mateng/tua* dark brown (in color).

sawo II (*M*) → SAWA.

sawud and **sawut** (*Jv*) cookie made of steamed shredded cassava and palm sugar.

Sawunggalih name of a train running between Jakarta and Kutoarjo.

say clipped form of **tersayang**.

   tersay dearest. *Kak Léi –, saya sendiri tidak mengerti mengapa keanéhan ini ada pada diri saya*. Dearest sister Lei(la), I myself don't understand why I have this peculiarity. *bilang* – and

   bersay-say to say "dear" to e.o. *Saya berkenalan dengan seorang cowok léwat télepon. Sampai saat ini saya belum pernah melihat wajahnya, tetapi kami selalu ~*. I met a guy on the phone. I still haven't seen him in person, but we always call e.o. dear.

saya (*Skr*) **1** I, me, my. – *belum tahu*. I still don't know. *Dia melihat –*. He saw me. *rumah* – my house. – *tidak mengerti mengapa*. I don't know why. **2** yes (I have heard and I will obey). – *Ibu!* yes, Mother!

   saya-saya we. *~ saja yang disuruhnya, padahal orang lain yang lebih pandai pun banyak*. He just orders us around, but others know more than we do.

sayagi (*S*) ready, prepared, willing, equipped.

sayak I (*Port Jv*) a white pleated cloth worn under the front of a woman's jacket.

sayak II (*M*) a water vessel made from half a coconut. *dijual – dibeli tempurung* it's six of one and half a dozen of the other.

sayambara → SAYEMBARA.

sayang I 1 it's a pity/shame/too bad. – *kalau tidak kaulanjutkan studimu itu*. It's a pity if you don't continue your study. – *anda tidak bisa berenang*. It's too bad you can't swim. **2** I regret/am sorry. – *benar saudara tak dapat datang malam ini*. I'm really sorry that you can't make it tonight. **3** (it's) too bad. – *dia tidak tahu bahasa Jawa*. It's too bad he doesn't know Javanese.

   sayangnya 1 what a pity/shame! how sad! *~ perkara itu tidak langsung dilaporkan kepada polisi*. It's a shame that the matter wasn't immediately reported to the police. **2** the trouble/problem is that ... *~, nelayan di daérah ini kurang bisa memanfaatkan penghasilan yang diperoléhnya*. The problem is that fishermen in this area cannot make use of the catch they have obtained.

   menyayangi to regret, deplore, feel bad about s.t. *Karena sudah telanjur, tak perlu disayangi*. Since it's too late, you shouldn't regret it.

   menyayangkan [and **nyayangin** (*J coq*)] **1** to regret, deplore, feel sorry about. *Kejadian itu amat disayangkan*. That incident was most regrettable/deplorable. *Saya – apa yang terjadi padamu*. I feel sorry about what happened to you. **2** to take pity on.

   tersayang (*akan*) felt most regrettable.

   tersayang-sayang felt offended/annoyed with. *~ akan menteri kepercayaannya* he felt annoyed with his trusted minister.

   kesayangan pity, sorrow.

   penyayang merciful. *Tuhan yang Maha ~* the All-Merciful (God).

   penyayangan regret.

sayang II 1 *kasih* – affection. *dari mana datangnya –, dari mata turun ke hati* whence does affection come, from the eyes down to the heart. **2** – *akan/kepada* and *sayangkan* to be fond of, have a liking for, in love with. *Tiada ibu yang tak – kepada anaknya*. There is no mother who is not fond of her children. – *anak didatangi, kampung ditinggalkan* to love one's child is to visit him/her, to love one's *kampung* is to leave it. **3** honey, darling, etc. *"Duduk sini –," pintaku halus, sambil menarik lengan Éfra*. "Sit over here, honey," I asked gently, pulling Efra's arm.

   bersayang-sayangan to love e.o.

   menyayang (only in the passive: *disayang*) to be loved. *sebagai siswa yang disayang gurunya* as a pupil who is loved by the teacher.

   menyayangi to love, cherish, have affection for, be fond of. *~ segenap mahluk* love all creatures. *Istri yang tua engkau kasihi, tetapi yang muda engkau sayangi*. You care for the old wife, but you love the young one.

   menyayangkan to love. *sayangkan kain, buangkan baju* you can't have your cake and eat it too.

   tersayang to be a favorite. *Dia adalah anak saya yang ~*. She is my favorite child.

   kesayangan 1 love, affection. *~nya kepada menantunya lebih dari anaknya sendiri*. His love for his daughter-in-law is greater than for his own child. **2** favorite, darling, pet. *anak ~* favorite child. *anjing ~* pet dog. *nama ~* pet name. *Ia ~ orang tuanya*. She's her parents' favorite.

   penyayang lover, fan, aficionado. *~ binatang* animal lover.

sayap 1a) wing (of a bird, etc.). *Burung terbang dengan ~nya*. Birds fly with their wings. *Beberapa binatang seperti ayam mempunyai – tetapi tidak menggunakannya untuk terbang*. Some animals, such as chickens, have wings but they aren't used for flying. – *pesawat terbang itu patah*. A wing of that aircraft was broken. b) wing (part of the bodywork immediately above the wheel of an automobile/bike/motorcycle). – *roda* mudguard, fender; → SPATBOR. c) (either end of an army lined up for battle) – *pasukan* military wing. d) (either of the players in soccer/hockey, etc.) – *kanan/kiri* right/left wing. e) wing (an air-force unit of several squadrons). f) section of a political party or other group, with more extreme views than those of the majority. *membentang/menentang/merentang* – to spread one's wings and take off. **2** (*geol*) limb, flank. **3** main support. *patah – bertongkat paruh* unnecessarily trying to achieve one's goal. **4** outer chamber of a fish trap; → BELAT I. – *singkat, terbang hendak jauh* to bite off more than one can chew. – *belakang* a) rear guard (of a car/bike, etc.). b) defense (in sports). – *depan* front guard (of a car/bike, etc.). – *ikan* fin. – *kilang* sweep, vane. – *singkat* limited abilities. – *udara* wing, a unit of the air force.

   bersayap 1 winged; to have wings. *hendak terbang tiada ~* to bite off more than one can chew. **2** high-flown, high-sounding.

   menyayap to outflank.

sayarah and **sayarat** (*A*) *bintang* – planet.

sayat I (thin) slice. *dua –* two slices.

   sesayat a slice (of meat, etc.), a (little) bit (of). *~ senyum* a faint smile. *~ sebelanga juga* although it's only a little, it's considered sufficient, better s.t. than nothing. *kurang ~ sebelanga* a little shortcoming/defect.

   menyayat 1 to cut off bits of skin/flesh, carve. *~ daging* to carve (meat), cut into thin slices. **2** to wound, break (one's heart). *~ hati/jantung* to hurt/offend/wound deeply; heartbreaking, heartrending. *~ gitar* to play the guitar.

   menyayat-nyayat to cut to pieces.

   menyayati (*pl obj*) to slice, cut s.t. into thin slices.

   menyayatkan *~ hati* to hurt s.o.'s feelings.

   tersayat *~ hati* deeply hurt/offended.

   sayatan scratch, graze. *Terasa pedih juga ~ kecil itu*. Even though the scratch was small, it stung anyway. *~ pahat* cutting edge.

   penyayatan slicing.

sayat II → SAYÉT.

sayeg saékokapti (*Jv*) working together for a mutual purpose.

sayembara (*Skr*) competition, contest. – *roman* novel-writing contest.

   menyayembarakan to offer a prize (for the best ...). *~ siapa yang bisa membantu untuk memikul béaya itu* to offer a prize for whoever could help shoulder the expense.

sayét (*D*) sayette, knitting yarn. *benang –* worsted yarn.

sayib (*A*) non-virgin.

sayid → SAID.

sayidi (*A*) my Lord. *Ya –!* O (my) Lord!

sayidina (*A*) our Lord.

sayonara (*Jp*) good-bye! – *prints* multicolored tulle for ladies' blouses.

menyayonarakan to say good-bye to. *Tidak jarang meréka disa-yonarakan "sampai jumpa ésok malam."* Frequently they were greeted with a "till we meet again tomorrow evening."

sayu I sad, melancholy; dismal, depressing, gloomy; downcast, drooping; → KUYU, RAYU I, SEDIH. *Ia berangkat dengan –.* She left sadly. **2** somber, dull, pensive. *Mukanya pucat, matanya –.* He looked pale, his eyes were lusterless. *Gendang perang terlalulah – bunyinya.* The war drum sounded too somber. *sedih-pedih dan –, pilu dan –, suram lagi –,* and *– rawan/rayu* very deplorable/tragic.

   bersayu-sayu to be sad/unhappy/depressed, despondent/pitiful.

   menyayu to grieve, desolate, distress; to become downcast, droop. *perasaan yang* ~ a grievous/desolating/sad feeling.

   menyayukan 1 distressing, saddening, sad, pitiable. *keadaan yang* ~ a sad(dening) situation. **2** to touch, move, stir, rouse; touching. *Agaknya ada sesuatu yang* ~ *hatinya.* There is probably s.t. that touched his heart.

   kesayuan 1 sadness, melancholy, gloominess, lack of luster. **2** overcome by sadness.

sayung (*ob*) *– tirus* tapering unevenly.

   menyayung 1 to cut off/slice at an angle, cut at a sharp angle (of a pencil). **2** to sneer at, make sarcastic remarks about.

sayup indistinct, not clear, faint (of sounds), vague (of a noise/sound, due to distance), blurred. *Di kejauhan – terdengar gong-gongan anjing.* In the distance the barking of a dog could be heard faintly. *– bulan* a) the last few days of the lunar month. b) almost out of money (because it's the end of the month).

   sayup-sayup 1 ~ *mata memandang* as far as the eye can see. **2** ~ and ~ *sampai* "almost reaching the eye or ear," i.e., faintly, not clearly visible or audible because of the distance. ~ *terdengar gelegar meriam* the roaring/rumbling of guns was vaguely heard. *kedengaran azan* ~ *sampai* the muezzin's call to prayer was heard vaguely. **sesayup-sayup** ~ *mata memandang* as far as the eye can see.

   sesayup ~ *mata memandang* as far as the eye can see.

   bersayupan (*pl subj*) unclear, indistinct.

   sayup-menyayup and (**sayup-)semayup** almost, barely (audible/visible).

   menyayup to become unclear/indistinct/blurred.

   kesayupan faintness, blur, indistinctness, vagueness.

sayur I 1 vegetables. *pasar –* vegetable market. *tukang –* (roving) vegetable vendor. **2** a soup-like dish with vegetables. *seperti – dengan rumput* as different as night and day. *– asam/asem* a vegetable soup which uses tamarind as a main ingredient. *– asi-nan* spiced raw vegetables eaten as a salad. *– bening* spinach broth. *– brongkos* vegetables with *kluwak*. *– gudeg* vegetables prepared with *santan*. *– lelawar* vegetables prepared *lelawar* style. *– lodéh* eggplant stew that could be considered a soup since it does have enough liquid for both possibilities. *– mayur* all k.o. vegetables. *– menir* spinach and sweet corn. *– mentah* raw vegetables, a dish eaten with rice and red-pepper seasoning; → LALAP-LALAPAN. *– papasan* k.o. mixed vegetable soup. *– udang* k.o. plant, *Alternanthera sessilis*.

   menyayur to cook or prepare a vegetable dish.

   menyayurkan 1 to make *sayur* (of. *bisa disayur asam* can be used to prepare *sayur asam*. *Tetangganya itu membeli gabus tersebut bersama dua ékor lainnya yang telah disayur di Pasar Jatinegara seharga Rp 2.000.* His neighbor bought that *gabus* with two other ones already made into *sayur* at Jatinegara Market for Rp 2,000.00. **2** to smash to pieces.

   sayuran several k.o. vegetables. ~ *hijau* greens, i.e., green leafy vegetables, such as spinach, lettuce, turnip tops, etc.

   persayuran vegetable (*mod*).

   sayur-sayuran all k.o. vegetables.

sayur II *– babi* k.o. plant (its leaves are used to cure wounds), *Borreria ocimoides*.

sayuun ijtimayah (*A*) social/community matter.

sbb. (*abbr*) [sebagai berikut] as follows.

sbg. (*abbr*) [sebagai] as, like.

sbh (*abbr*) [sebuah] a, one.

SBPOA [Surat Bukti Pelaporan Orang Asing] Foreigners Report Document (k.o. passport issued internally to foreigners).

schakelschool (*D col*) /skhakelskhol/ k.o. middle school.

s/d (*abbr*) [sampai-dengan] up to and including, through.

SD (*init*) [Sekolah-Dasar] Elementary School.

sda. (*abbr*) [sama dengan di atas] as above.

SD Inprés [Sekolah Dasar Instruksi Présidén] an elementary school built with funds specially earmarked by the President and allocated by Presidential Instruction.

SDM (*init*) [Sumber Daya Manusia] human resources.

Sdn. Bhd. [Sendirian Berhad] (*Mal*) Private Limited, Pte. Ltd. (British).

sdr. (*abbr*) [Saudara] Mr. (as a title).

sdri. (*abbr*) [Saudari] Mrs., Miss, Ms. (as a title).

se- I (followed by some verbs) after having ... *seusai membaca Qur'an* after having finished reading the Koran. *sehilangnya ...* after the disappearance of.

se- II one, a (followed by a counter). *seékor kambing* a goat.

se III (in acronyms) → SEKOLAH.

SE IV [Septichomia Epizootica] *penyakit –* k.o. cattle disease; → PENYAKIT *ngorok*.

SE V [Surat-Édaran] Circular Letter.

S.E. VI [Sarjana-Ékonomi] economist.

sé (*C*) Chinese family or clan name.

seabreg-abreg (*S*) plenty, a lot of, many. *Sekolah ini berat sekali. Hafalannya –.* This school is very hard. There's a lot of memorization.

Sea Garuda the name of the Joint Naval Maneuvers between the Republic of Indonesia and Thailand.

seakan-akan → AKAN.

Sea Malindo Jaya the name of the Joint Naval Maneuvers between the Republic of Indonesia and Malaysia.

seantéro → ANTÉRO.

séba 1 (*Jv*) visit. **2** (*S*) (among the Baduis in the Lebak Regency, West Java) an *adat* ritual in the form of a "tribute" of various k.o. agricultural crops harvested and submitted to the Regent of Lebak.

   berséba to call upon, pay one's respect to (a social superior, *esp* at court).

   menyéba to present s.t. to an exalted person.

   peséban *q.v.*

sebab (*A*) **1** because, reason, cause; purpose, motive. *Itulah –nya!* That was the reason! That's why! *Apa –(nya)?* and *– apa?* Why? How did that happen/come about? **2** because of. *(oléh) – (itu)* and *dari – itu* for that reason. *dari/oléh –* because, on account of, through. *Oléh – itu ia tak berani datang.* That's the reason he's afraid to come. *– akibat* cause and effect, causality. *hubungan – akibat* causal connection. *– awal* reason behind. *Adapun raison d'être-nya, alias – awal semua itu, adalah karena Jo dan Ro pemalu, maka meréka sulit mendapatkan jodoh.* The reason behind all of that was that Jo and Ro are shy people and so it was hard for them to find mates. *– musabab* various/all k.o. reasons; the primary cause(s). *– utama* the main cause. *– yang halal* permissible cause.

   bersebab to have a reason/motive/purpose/cause, with a reason, etc. *mati* ~ dead from a certain cause (illness/drowning, etc.); to die an unnatural death. *tidak* ~ without reason. ~ *kepada* to depend on, be based/founded on, rest on.

   menyebabkan to cause, bring out, induce, produce, motivate, result in. *Dicarinya kata-kata tepat yang tak* ~ *salah paham.* He was looking for the precise words which wouldn't result in a misunderstanding. *Kelengahannya itulah yang* ~ *kerugian besar.* It was his negligence that caused a big loss. *disebabkan dari/karena* due to, to be caused by.

   tersebab caused, occasioned. ~ *oléh* as a result of, owing to, due to.

   kesebaban causal.

   penyebab 1 cause, originator, origin (of a fire, etc.). *itu* ~ *kematian* cause of death. ~ *utama* main/principal cause. **2** agent, s.t. that produces an effect or change. ~ *penyakit* pathogenic. ~ *perobahan* agent of change. *faktor-faktor* ~ *kecelakaan* accident-causing factors.

sebagai 1 like, resembling, as; → BAGAI I. **2** in the function of, acting as. *dituduh – mata-mata* to be accused of spying. *– berikut* [sbb.] as follows. *dan –nya* [dsb.] et cetera, etc., and the like.

sebagaimana as (wished/expected/planned, etc.), like, similar (conditions) to; → BAGAIMANA. ~ *direncanakan* as planned.

sebahat (*A*) league, pact, conspiracy.

sebai shawl worn over the shoulders, scarf.

sebak 1 to swell (of a river); freshet. **2** (tears) well up (in her eyes), to run, pour (of tears). – *air matanya* to shed tears. *bermata* – and – *matanya* one's eyes are swollen (from weeping).
menyebak 1 to swell (with water). **2** to fill (with tears).

sébak → SIBAK.

sebal I 1 resentful, disappointed, dissatisfied. **2** depressed, frustrated, sad, sullen; cranky; → KESAL *hati*, MENDONGKOL. – *hati* resentful.
menyebal to become resentful/frustrated.
menyebali to make s.o. resentful.
menyebalkan 1 to be sullen about, resent s.t. **2** to cause resentment, disappoint, frustrate; annoying, frustrating. ~ *hati* to annoy, displease.
sebal-sebalan to resent e.o.
kesebalan 1 resentment, dissatisfaction, frustration. **2** sulkiness, sullenness. *Sindiran dan éjékan kuli-kulinya itu menimbulkan ~ hatinya.* The insinuations and insults of his coolies made him resentful.
penyebal sullen person.

sebal II (*Jv*) unlucky, out of luck, down on one's luck; ill-omened, unfortunate, ominous, disadvantageous; → SIAL.

sebal III (*Jv*) **menyebal** [and **nyebal** (*coq*)] to deviate (from some religious or other principle).

sebam 1 blue-gray in color. **2** clouded, overcast; dull (of one's eyes); dim, dulled (of memory/affection).

seban-seban (*M*) to urinate in spurts.

sebar I (*J/Jv*) spread. – *luas* widespread. **menyebarluas** to spread widely. **menyebarluaskan** to spread s.t. widely, propagate, disseminate. **penyebarluasan** dissemination, spread, promulgation. – *rata* spread out equally. **menyebarratakan** to spread equally, announce/make known far and wide. – *pancar* radiate out. **menyebarpancarkan** to relay, receive and pass on news.
bersebaran (*pl subj*) to (be) spread/scattered all over. *ribuan kepulauan yang ~ di Laut China Selatan* thousands of islands scattered all over the South China Sea.
menyebar to spread out.
menyebar(kan) [and **nyebarin** (*J coq*)] **1** to scatter, strew, sow. ~ *benih* to scatter/sow seeds. **2** to spread, disseminate. ~ *kabar bohong* to spread false rumors. ~ *penyakit* to spread a disease. **3** to distribute. ~ *surat-surat sebaran* to distribute leaflets. **4** to deploy (forces).
menyebari to spread/fan out.
tersebar [and **kesebar** (*coq*)] **1** scattered. **2** spread, disseminated. **3** distributed. *Berita itu ~ cepat ke pelosok désa bagaikan api membakar ilalang di musim kering.* The news spread quickly to all corners of the village like wildfire in the dry season.
sebaran 1 s.t. spread/distributed. *buku ~* pamphlet, brochure. *surat ~* leaflet. **2** distribution. ~ *acak* random distribution.
penyebar 1 distributor, disseminator. ~ *penyakit* disease carrier. **2** propagator, spreader.
penyebaran 1 distribution, dissemination, range (of an animal), proliferation. **2** propagation, seeding. **3** deployment. ~ *biji* seeding. ~ *kekuatan* deployment of forces. ~ *seluas-luasnya* dispersion.
persebaran spread, dissemination.

sebar II (*ob*) numb (of one's limbs), asleep (of a leg/finger, etc.); → GERINGGING(EN), KESEMUTAN.

sebarang any, whatever, any old; → SEMBARANG. – *orang* anybody, who(so)ever.
sebarangan *sikap ~* an indifferent attitude.

sebarau a carp with a vertical bar on each side, silver and red barb, *Hampala macrolepidota*; → BARAU-BARAU II.

sebari → SEMBARI.

sebasa various species of tree shrubs, including *Aporosa frutescens*. – *hitam/minyak* k.o. tree, *Aporosa aurea*. – *jantan* k.o. shrub, *Aporosa sp.*

sebat I menyebat 1 to (beat with a) cane, whip, flog. **2** (*coq*) to steal, pinch. **3** to shake (one's hands) to dry them. **4** to brush s.t. aside with the hand.

sebatan caning, whipping, flogging.

sebat II breathing with difficulty due to a cold, etc.
tersebat stuffed (of one's nose).

sébat (*J*) quick, rapid, swift.
kesébatan quickness, rapidity, swiftness.

sebau to be in agreement, harmonize, be in accordance (with = *dengan*); → BAU I.

sebawahan → BAWAH.

sebaya of the same age; → BAYA I.

sebekah *ikan* – sea perch, *Apogon spp.* – *karang* blotch-eye/big-eye/crimson/pinecone soldier fish, *Myripristis murdjan*. – *laut* two-banded fish, *Diploprion bifasciatus*.

sebel → SEBAL I. **nyebelin** → MENYEBALKAN.

sebelah I → BELAH I.

sebelah II *ikan* – winter flounder, river sole, *Synaptura panoides*.

sebelas eleven; → BELAS II.
sebelasan around 11 (o'clock).
kesebelasan (soccer/hockey) eleven, i.e., eleven persons forming a team.

sebelum → BELUM.

sébéng *layar* – movable stage curtain.

sebentar a moment; → BENTAR I.

seberang 1 the opposite/other side, place across (the street, river, etc.), in front of. *daérah/tanah* – a) (viewed from Sumatra) Malaysia. b) (viewed from Java) all the Indonesian islands outside Java. *Menteri Daérah – Lautan* (the Dutch) Minister of Overseas Territories. *di – sana* on that side (further away), over there. *Tak berani aku memandang lelaki yang duduk di – ku itu.* I was afraid to look at the man sitting opposite me. **2** on the other end/side of (the telephone line). *"Ini siapa?" ditanya dari –.* "Whom am I speaking with?" was asked from the other end of the line. **3** foreign (place/person). *buatan –* manufactured abroad; imported goods. *negeri/tanah –* foreign land/country. *orang –* foreigner.
berseberangan and **seberang-menyeberang 1** to be on both sides (of a river/street, etc.), be on either side of; to be opposite/facing e.o., be face to face. *Ia duduk berseberangan dengan saya.* He sat facing me. *Penduduk seberang-menyeberang Selat Sunda menamakan gunung api itu Rakata.* The people on either side of the Sunda Straits call the volcano Rakata. **2** to be diametrically opposed (to). *Pandangannya berseberangan dengan pemerintah.* His views are diametrically opposed to those of the government.
menyeberang [and **nyeberang** (*coq*)] **1** to cross (over), go/move to the other side. *Soalnya, mobil-mobil yang léwat tidak mau memberikan kesempatan kita ~.* The problem is that passing cars do not want to give us the chance to cross (the street). *Susahnya ~ jalan.* The problem is in crossing the street. ~ *di sini* (traffic sign for pedestrians) Cross here. *Hampir semua wisatawan yang datang ke Parapat ~ ke Pulau Samosir.* Almost all tourists visiting Parapat cross over to Samosir Island. *Lebih énak naik perahu. Karena kalau siang hari kita tidak kepanasan seperti kalau ~ melalui jembatan.* It's more convenient to go by boat. That's because, in the daytime, we won't suffer from the heat as when we have to cross the bridge (since the boat has been provided with an awning). **2** to defect, go over to the other side. *Komponis Soviét menyeberang.* Soviet composer asks for (political) asylum.
menyeberangi [and **nyeberangin** (*J coq*)] **1** to go across/to the other side (of the street/river, etc.), cross (a street/river, etc.). *Perjalanan menyeberangi kali hanya memakan waktu satu menit, sebab itu tidak disediakan kursi dalam perahu.* The trip across the river only takes a minute, therefore no chairs have been provided in the boat. *Kenyataannya, di dalam hutan itu sendiri harus diseberangi beberapa sungai dan lembah curam.* The fact is that in the forest itself various rivers and steep valleys have to be crossed. **2** to go/pass through, experience, encounter, come across. *Seumur hidup saya, saya telah ~ seribu satu macam kesukaran.* My whole life, I have experienced one-thousand-and-one kinds of difficulties. **3** to defect (to the enemy), go over to the other side.

menyeberangkan to take s.o./s.t. to the other side (of the street/ river, etc.), take/transport across, ferry over. *Meréka menjual jasa ~ penduduk ke seberang dengan menggunakan perahu kayu sederhana.* They sell services to take residents across the river by using a simple wooden boat. *Ratusan pengemudi truk harus menunggu sampai empat hari sebelum mendapat giliran diseberangkan dengan féri dari Merak ke Bakauhéni.* Hundreds of truck drivers have to wait up to four days before they get their turn to be ferried from Merak to Bakauheni.

terseberang crossed (of a river/street, etc.).

terseberangi escaped from; averted, avoided. *Tiga kali kita menyeberang hidup, apabila ketiga kalinya telah kita ~ dengan selamat, bahagialah kita.* Three times we have to go through life; if at the third time we have crossed it safely, we are lucky.

terseberangkan (can) be carried across.

keseberangan 1 crossed (of a river, street, etc.). **2** known (its purpose, etc.). *dalam sudah keajukan, lébar sudah ~* it's already known what s.o. is up to.

penyeberang 1 (border-/river-/street-)crosser; → PELINTAS. *~ kanal* channel swimmer. **2** defector.

penyeberangan 1 the act of going across, crossing. **2** crossover, (place for) crossing (a street/river, etc.). *jembatan ~* skywalk, pedestrian overpass. *kapal ~* ferry(boat). **3** defection, going over to the other side.

perseberangan crossover point.

seberapa → BERAPA.

seberhana (*Skr*) *pakaian –* and *– pakaian* full dress.

sebermula → MULA.

seberot → SEBROT I.

sébet → SÉBAT.

sebih (*A ob*) *buah –* rosary beads, from the *bunga –, Canna orientalis*; → *buah* TASBIH.

sebik to pout (of infants about to cry); → CEBIK, MÉMÉK I.

sebisét (*J ob*) CBZ (the former name of RS Dr. Cipto Mangunkusumo).

sebit → SABIT 1.

sebodo (*J*) *– amatlah!* I don't care. I don't give a damn!; → *masa* BODOH. *Saya mah, – amatlah.* Me, I don't give a damn!

sébra (*D*) zebra. *– kros* (*J*) zebra crossing, i.e., the place to cross a (busy) road.

sebranan (*Jv*) (in Kediri, Central Java) ceremony asking for rain.

sebrang → SEBERANG.

sebrot I (*Jv*) **menyebrot** to snatch s.t., take by force, rob.

sebrot II (*J*) **menyebrot** to spray with large amounts of water.

kesebrot to get sprayed.

sebu 1 full (to the brim). **2** choked, stuffed (of nose/drain/pipe). *penyakit –* dyspepsia.

menyebu to fill to the brim; to fill in (a hole/grave/swamp).

menyebukan 1 to clog; to block. **2** to fill in (with soil, etc.); to close (a hole).

sebuk menyebuk 1 to intrude (on a group of people), worm one's way into (a crowd). **2** to butt into (a conversation).

penyebukan intrusion, butting in.

sébuk (*Mal*) → SIBUK I.

sebul (*Jv*) **menyebul** to blow on s.t. (with one's breath).

menyebulkan to blow s.t.

sebun 1 blind (of a boil). **2** unfinished (of clothes/mat work); → TERBENGKALAI.

sebura k.o. tree providing timber, *Adinandra dumosa*; → TIUP-TIUP.

seburas k.o. herbal plant, *Pollia aclisia/sorzogonensis*.

seburit → SEMBURIT.

seburu k.o. tree, *Ouratea sumatrana*.

seburus (*– hitam*) k.o. tree, *Gnetum funiculare*.

seburut a shrub with large purple flowers, *Thottea grandiflora*.

sebusuk 1 k.o. tree, *Cassia nodusa*. **2** k.o. shrub, *Clitoria laurifolia*.

sebut bersebut 1 → TERSEBUT. **2** → MENYEBUT.

menyebut [and **nyebut** (*coq*)] **1** to call, name, designate. *Jangan ~ saya Tuan.* Don't call me "Tuan." **2** to say, tell, quote (prices, etc.). *Wanita itu malu untuk ~ umurnya.* That woman is shy about telling her age. **3** to mention. *terlalu banyak untuk disebut* too numerous to mention. **4** to cite, evoke, recall. *Si*

sakit itu disuruhnya ~ nama Allah Taala. He let the patient evoke the name of God the Most High.

menyebut-nyebut to mention frequently/very often, bring s.t. up again and again. *Sejak mula tidak pernah ada disebut-sebut uang.* From the beginning money was never mentioned.

menyebuti to mention, say. *Tanggal 26 menjadi penting untuk disebuti.* It's important to mention the 26th of the month.

menyebutkan [and **nyebutin** (*J coq*)] **1** to call, name, designate. *Bisa disebutkan kampung, meskipun tidak ada rumah di sana.* We could call it a kampung, even though there are no houses there. **2** to disclose, reveal, indicate. *Ada seorang wartawan sénior yang tidak mau disebutkan namanya.* There was a senior news reporter who didn't want his name revealed.

tersebut [and **kesebut** (*coq*)] **1** mentioned, said, cited. *Buku ~ diterbitkan dua tahun yang lalu.* The book mentioned was published two years ago. **2** talked about, famous, well-known. *Ia seorang yang ~ di seluruh kotapraja.* He's a person known throughout the municipality.

tersebutkan mentioned. *Di samping beberapa nama yang telah ~ di atas, hanya beberapa nama lagi seperti Nurjanto yang bisa dibilang mempunyai poténsi sebagai kartunis.* Besides the various names already mentioned above, there are only a few other names, such as Nurjanto, of whom it can be said that they have potential as caricaturists.

sebutan 1 quotation, citation. *Buku itu berisikan banyak ~ dari berbagai majalah.* That book contains many quotations from various magazines. **2** title, term of address. *Di sana ia mendapat ~ "pak"* there he got the term of address "pak." *~ Radén dan Radén Mas* the titles Raden and Raden Mas. **3** designation, appellation, nickname. **4** pronunciation, the way s.t. is said. *– huruf k adalah ka* the pronunciation of the letter k is ka. **5** talk of the town. *Ia menjadi ~ sekota karena kejuaraan ténisnya.* He was the talk of the town because of his tennis championship. **6** (*gram*) predicate.

sebut-sebutan topic of conversation, much-talked-of, much-discussed, the talk of the town. *Ia menjadi ~ orang karena perbuatannya itu.* He is the talk of the town on account of his deeds.

penyebut 1 caller, mentioner, etc. **2** (*math*) denominator.

penyebutan mentioning, saying, etc.

Secaba [Sekolah Calon Bintara] Noncommissioned Officer Candidates School.

secang (*J*) a shrub which provides dark red dyewood, sapanwood, *Caesalpinia sappan*; → SEPANG.

Secapa [Sekolah-Calon-Perwira] Officer Candidate School.

secara → CARA.

secéng (*C*) one thousand (rupiahs).

séceng (*C*) syphilis.

secérék → SICÉRÉK.

secina k.o. bumblebee with long feelers.

seconlét manatee oil, i.e., oil of the *ikan duyung*, used in order to be loved by a girl or woman.

sedah (*ob*) → SADAH.

sedak tersedak and **kesedakan 1** to choke (from swallowing s.t. the wrong way). **2** stuffed. *kesedakan hidung* a stuffy nose.

sédak k.o. rattan band to make the parchment of a drum, etc. taut.

menyédak to insert such a band onto a drum, etc.

sedam(-sedam) (*onom*) sound of booming (of cannon).

bersedam(-sedam) to boom.

sedan sob. *– sedu* and *sedu –* sobbing, sobs.

tersedan-sedan to sob with a break in the voice and short, gasping breath. *meninggalkan kamar jenazah dengan ~* to leave the mortuary sobbing.

sédan (*D*) sedan, i.e., an enclosed two- or four-door car. *– atap terbuka* a convertible.

bersédan to ride in a sedan. *Penjahat ~ mencoba merampok toko di Jalan Jayakarta.* Criminals riding in a sedan tried to loot a store at Jayakarta Road.

sedang I 1 moderate, average. *Pendapatan saya – saja.* My income is just moderate. *tubuh –* of average height and size. **2** reasonable, acceptable. *– harganya* the price is reasonable. **3** sufficient. *Katanya, gajinya tidak – untuk hidup sebulan.* He said that his salary was insufficient to make ends meet for a month. **4** just right, fit just fine. *Pakaian ini – bagi saya.* These clothes fit me just fine. **5** simple. *Kehidupan meréka – saja.* They live simply.

sedang-sedangnya just enough, just what's needed.

menyedang to try on. ~ *pakaian* to try on clothes.

sedang-menyedang *tidak* ~ (*M*) insufficient, inadequate.

menyedang(-nyedang)kan (to try) to make ends meet.

sedangan medium, not too big or too small.

sedang II 1 (followed by an adjective) indicates a given condition or state. *Istrinya – hamil.* His wife is pregnant. **2** (followed by a verb) indicates an ongoing activity. *Ketika ia memanggil tadi, saya – mandi.* When he called a moment ago, I was still taking a bath; → TENGAH I. **3** → SEDANGKAN.

sedangkan 1 (when joining two sentences with different subjects) whereas, while, moreover; *cp* SAMBIL. *Istri saya menjahit, – saya melihat TV.* My wife was sewing, while I was watching TV. **2** even. *Jangankan membeli rumah, – membeli pakaian pun ia tidak sanggup.* He couldn't even buy clothes, let alone a house.

sedap I 1 delicious, nice, good (of taste). **2** pleased, amused. **3** refreshed, feeling well. **4** comfortable, snug, cozy. **5** agreeable, pleasant, pleasing. **6** spicy, pungent, well-seasoned. *sedaapp!* (*coq*) terrific! *badan kurang – and tidak – (rasa) badan* does not feel well, uncomfortable, (suffering from) malaise. *tidak – (di) hati, tak – hatinya,* and *hati sudah tak – lagi* a) hard to please, peevish, irritable, touchy, testy. b) uneasy (in mind). (*tentu) – tak – (Med)* can't tell whether it's pleasant. *tidak – di telinga* and *tak – didengar* unpleasant to hear, does not sound pleasant. *– dipandang (mata)* it's a pleasure to look at. *tidak – dipandang* unsightly. *– dahulu pahit kemudian* pleasant/good at first but unpleasant/bad afterwards. *tidak – tekak* off one's feed, not feel like eating.

menyedapkan 1 to refresh. **2** refreshing; pleasing (to the eye). *tidak ~ (bagi) hati* unpleasant, it puts one in a bad mood. **3** to content, satisfy, please. **4** to season, make s.t. taste good.

tersedap the most delicious.

(sedap-)sedapan delicacies, delicious food.

kesedapan 1 tastiness. **2** pleasantness, enjoyment, delight, refreshed feeling.

penyedap ~ *makanan* flavoring. ~ *rasa/masakan* seasoning.

sedap II (*bunga*) *– malam* a) tuberose, *Polianthes tuberosa.* b) prostitute.

sedar → SADAR I.

sedari → DARI.

sedaru → DARU.

sédasi (*D*) sedation.

sedat slow, tardy, indolent, sluggish, sloppy (in thought); → SENDAT.

sedati (*A*) k.o. Achehnese dance.

sédatif (*D*) sedative. *éfék –* sedative effect.

sedawa belch (in polite appreciation of a meal).

sedawai sarsaparilla, *Smilax calophylla.*

sedekah (*A*) **1** alms, charitable gift. **2** religious/ritual meal, **3** offerings (to spirits); → SELAMATAN, KENDURI. *– arwah* ritual meal for the dead. *– bumi* (*Jv*) village celebration held annually to honor the guardian spirits of the village. *– désa* the ceremony performed after the harvest in the form of a collective ritual meal. *– kubur* a) ritual meal after a burial. b) *sedekah* given to those present at the grave (reader of the *talkin,* gravediggers, etc.). *– laut* a traditional ceremony of the fishermen living in Tegal, Central Java, and other coastal towns in token of their gratitude to God; → KOMARAN.

bersedekah 1 to donate, contribute, give alms. ~ *ialah satu daripada amal kebaikan.* Giving alms is a good deed. **2** to hold a ritual feast.

menyedekahi 1 to give alms to. **2** to hold a ritual meal for. *Anak itupun disedekahi.* A religious meal was held for that child.

menyedekahkan to give s.t. as alms. *Dia ~ uangnya untuk si miskin.* He gave money to the poor man.

sedekala → SEDIAKALA.

sedekap (*ob*) with crossed arms; → DEKAP I.

sedelinggam (*Tam*) red lead.

sedemikian → DEMIKIAN.

sedeng (*J*) → SEDANG I.

sédeng (*D*) part (in hair); → SIBAK.

sedéng (*J*) crazy, silly, foolish.

sedep → SEDAP I.

séder (*D*) cedar (tree).

sederhana (*Skr*) **1** moderate, average. *Badan ayah saya –, tidak gemuk dan tidak kurus.* Father's body is average, not fat and not thin. **2** plain (of food/words), not fancy, modest. *Hidupnya sangat –.* He lives very modestly. **3** simple, easy, uncomplicated, not complex. *Gunakanlah kalimat-kalimat yang – supaya mudah dimengerti oléh pemeriksa.* Use simple sentences so that they are easily understood by the examiner. **4** (*leg*) summary. *terbukti secara –* proven summarily.

menyederhanakan 1 to simplify. **2** to economize, cut down (on expenses).

kesederhanaan simplicity, plainness. ~ *berpikir* intellectual simplicity.

penyederhanaan simplification, making simple, cutting down on.

sederiah → SADARIAH.

sedia (*Skr*) **1** prepared, ready, willing (to help, etc.), equipped (to act or to be used immediately); → SIAP I. *Rumah-rumah itu sudah – untuk didiami.* The houses are ready to be occupied. *Sewaktu-waktu ia – membantu kita.* He is willing to help us at any time. **2** available, at s.o.'s disposal, disposable, in stock. *ada – to* have in stock. *Makanan dan minuman sudah – di méja.* Food and drinks are already on the table. **3** (*cla*) in existence from the very beginning, of old, from ancient times, originally, (has) always (been like that). *Tuhan yang – God* who was from the beginning. *tidak – not* available, unavailable. **ketidak-sediaan** unavailability. *– maklum* it is admitted/already known. *Kita sudah – tahu akan kelakuannya yang sombong itu.* We already knew about his arrogant behavior. *– payung sebelum hujan* prevention is better than cure, better safe than sorry. *– muat* ready to load. *(dalam keadaan) – siaga* to be on the alert (or, at the ready) (of military force, etc.). *– tanam* ready to plant. *– (untuk) tempur* combat ready.

sedianya 1 willing. **2** in fact, actually. **3** should have (but didn't). *Ménlu Mochtar Kusumaatmadja sangat menyayangkan batalnya pertemuan antara Ménlu Muangthai dengan Ménlu Viétnam Nguyen Co Thach, yang ~ diadakan Kamis lalu.* Foreign Minister Mochtar Kusumaatmadja highly regretted the cancellation of the meeting between the foreign minister of Thailand and the foreign minister of Vietnam, Nguyen Co Thach, that in fact should have been held last Thursday.

bersedia 1 to be/get ready, be prepared/equipped, prepare o.s., make o.s. ready. *yang tidak ~ disebut namanya* who asked not to be quoted/identified, who insisted on anonymity. ~ *menghadapi* to come to terms with, be willing to face. **2** to get o.s. ready/prepared for. **3** to express/declare one's readiness/preparedness/willingness to. *tidak ~* unwilling, reluctant. **ketidak-bersediaan** unwillingness, reluctance.

bersedia-sedia to prepare o.s. to, make the necessary preparations to. *Penduduk kampung itu sudah ~ untuk menghadapi banjir.* The villagers have already made the necessary arrangements to cope with the flood.

menyediai (*Jv*) to make ready/available for s.o. *Tempat tidur sudah disediai untuk penumpang.* Beds were made ready for the passengers.

menyediakan and **mempersediakan** [and **nyediain** (*J coq*)] **1** to get s.t. ready, make things ready, prepare. *Ibu sedang ~ makanan untuk sarapan pagi.* Mother was getting food ready for breakfast. **2** to serve (food), set on the table. *Nasi goréng sudah disediakan.* The fried rice is already on the table. **3** to make available, provide, equip, supply, furnish, offer. *Beberapa hotél di Yogya ~ Qur'an dan Bibel.* Some hotels in Yogya provide Korans and Bibles. ~ *béasiswa* to provide scholarships. **4** to earmark, appropriate, set aside, reserve; → MEMPERUNTUKKAN. *disediakan untuk dibayar* to be made payable. ~ *waktu* to set aside time to.

tersedia available, in stock, on hand. *Pasanggrahan itu ~ bagi pegawai negeri.* The resthouse is available to government employees. ~ *untuk dijual* available for sale. **ketersediaan** availability. ~ *lahan* availability of land.

sediaan 1 preparation. ~ *darah* blood preparation. **2** spare. *ban ~*

spare tire. **3** materials for making s.t. ~ *sayur* materials for making soup. ~ *farmasi* pharmaceutical stock. **4** inventory, stock, stores; → PERSEDIAAN. ~ *dagangan* stock in trade. ~ *penyangga* buffer stock.

kesediaan readiness, preparedness, willingness. *menunjukkan ~nya* to show one's willingness (to *untuk*).

penyedia supplier. *Indonésia ~ minyak bumi terpercaya.* Indonesia is a reliable petroleum supplier. *perusahaan ~* supply company. ~ *berita* wire service. ~ *jasa* service provider. ~ *jasa jaringan* network service provider. ~ *kapal* carrier. *pusat pengendali dan ~ stok* stock control and supply center. *Sebagai adidaya yang sudah lama menjalin hubungan baik dengan India dan ~ senjata terbesar untuk negara ini, belum tentu bisa dipercaya.* As a superpower which for a long time has established good relations with India and which is the largest supplier of arms to this country, it is not sure whether it is reliable.

penyediaan 1 buffer stock. **2** stockpiling, creation of stocks. **3** supply, supplying, provision, appropriation; → PENYUPLAIAN. ~ *uang* monetary supply. ~ *lahan* land clearing.

persediaan 1 stock on hand, stock, supply. *dalam ~* ready stock. *dapat dijual dari ~* deliverable from stock. ~ *barang mati* dead stock. ~ *dagangan* stock in trade. *selama masih ada ~* while supplies last. ~ *habis/sedang kosong* we have run out of stock. ~ *uang* funds. **2** inventory. *~akhir/awal* closing/opening inventory. ~ *usang* obsolete inventory. *pengawasan ~ barang* inventory control. **3** preparation, provision. **4** reserve.

sediakala (*Skr neo*) **1** of old, former, long past. *adat –* ancient custom. **2** usual, habitual, customary, normal. *Selepas perayaan itu keadaan kampung itu kembali seperti –.* After the celebration, conditions in the kampung returned to normal again. **3** (*cla*) every. *– hari* every day.

sedih sad, sorrowful, unhappy, tragic, heartbreaking, distressed, grieved. *cerita –* a tragic story. *kabar –* sad news. *– hati* sad, distressed. **bersedih hati** to be sad/depressed/brokenhearted. *Janganlah terlalu lama ~ atas kematiannya.* Don't be depressed about his death for too long. *– pedih* grief, sorrow.

sedihnya the sad part of it. ~ *ialah bahwa ...* the sad part (of it) is that ...

bersedih-sedih sadly. *Dia menangis ~.* She cried sadly.

menyedihi to depress, make s.o. feel sad, sadden. *Satu hal yang ~ saya ialah melihat bocah membawa pelinteng.* What saddens me is to see a boy carrying a slingshot.

menyedihkan [and **nyedihin** (*J coq*)] **1** sad, saddening, make s.o. sad. **2** to grieve/be sad about. *Apa perlunya anda sedihkan semuanya itu?* What's the point of being sad about all of that?

mempersedih to make s.o. sadder/unhappier.

tersedih saddest.

kesedihan sadness, sorrow, unhappiness.

penyedih pessimistic/gloomy person.

sedikit → DIKIT. **1** a little, a bit, some. *Kasi(h) saya – gula.* Give me some sugar. *Dia minum – kopi.* He drinks a little coffee. *– demi –* little by little, by degrees; piecemeal; *– banyak* more or less, roughly, at a rough estimate. *bukan –* not few, a great many. *Dia ngomong –.* He said little. *tahu – bahasa Inggris* to know a little English. *–pun ada juga cacatnya* (nothing is perfect) there's still s.t. wrong. *–pun tidak* not at all, in the least, by no means. *tanpa kesulitan –pun* without the slightest difficulty. **2** a few, a small amount of. *– hari lagi pekerjaan itu akan selesai* in a few days that job will be finished. *tidak – jumlahnya* the quantity was not small. **3** somewhat, rather. *– tua* rather old. *– baik* slightly better. *dalam – waktu* soon, in a short time. *paling –* at least. *Umurnya paling – 15 tahun.* He's at least 15 years old. *– lagi!* a) a (little) bit more! b) a moment, please!

sedikitnya *banyak ~* more or less.

sedikit-sedikit 1 little by little, bit by bit, gradually. ~ *lama-lama jadi bukit* many a little makes a mickle (*BE*). **2** a little (bit), some but not too much.

sedikitnya, sedikit-(se)dikitnya at (the) least. ~ *ada dua tiga sampel.* At least there are two or three samples.

menyedikiti to reduce, diminish, curtail.

menyedikitkan and **mempersedikitkan** to lessen, abate, decrease. *Pemerintah mau ~ belanja supaya dapat menyimpan*

uang. The government wants to decrease expenses in order to save money.

sédimén (*D*) sediment. *gerakan – sejajar pantai* long-shore sand drift. *gerakan – tegak lurus pantai* offshore-onshore sand drift.

sédiméntasi (*D*) sedimentation.

sédiméntér (*D*) sedimentary.

sedingin k.o. plant used in magic and medicine; the leaves are used for fever, *Bryophyllum calycinum*.

sedit (*coq*) → SEDIKIT.

sedocong a freshwater fish.

sedot (*J/Jv*) **menyedot** [and **nyedot** (*coq*)] **1** to suck; sip; to siphon off. *Dia ~ sebotol Georgia Peach.* He sipped a bottle of Georgia Peach. ~ *bénsin* to siphon gasoline (from one tank to the tank of another car by first sucking it out through a rubber hose). ~ *dana masyarakat yang diduga masih tersimpan di bawah bantal atau terparkir di tempat yang kurang produktif* to siphon social funds which presumably are still stored under the pillow or parked in a less productive place. **2** to inhale, sniff; to take a puff (of a cigarette). *Kita hendaklah selalu ~ udara yang bersih.* We should always breathe clean air. ~ *hawa* to breathe in. **3** to swallow, gulp down; to consume, drain. *Ribuan ton beras berhasil disedot di daérah.* Thousands of tons of rice were consumed in the provinces. **4** to absorb, attract, draw, withdraw. ~ *pengunjung yang jumlahnya cukup banyak* to draw quite a lot of visitors. *Soal hak azasi manusia sempat ~ perhatiannya.* The human rights issue managed to get his attention.

menyedoti (*pl obj*) to suck up.

tersedot sucked, sipped, drawn, etc. *busuk ~* nasty-smelling.

kesedot (*coq*) **1** tapped (of electricity). **2** sucked.

sedotan 1 a straw (to sip a drink, etc. through). "*Dia selalu tanya kamu, lho,*" *potong Upit sambil melepaskan ~ plastik di mulut.* "He always asks you, you know," interrupted Upit taking the straw from his mouth. **2** draught, swallow, drink. *Dua ~ bir masuk kerongkongannya.* Two sips of beer went down his throat. **3** a puff (of a cigarette). ~ *pertamanya pada rokok itu panjang sekali.* He took a long first puff at the cigarette. **sesedotan** one puff (of a cigarette); ~ *rokok* a second (in time). *Tempat yang meréka tuju hanya tinggal satu ~ rokok.* It's only a second from their destination.

penyedot s.t./a device, etc. that sucks, swab (for wiping up spills). ~ *debu* vacuum cleaner. ~ *minyak di permukaan laut* oil skimmer. *mesin ~ kotoran* slime sizer. *mobil ~ kakus/tinja* septic tank pump truck.

penyedotan 1 sucking up; inhaling. **2** swallowing, gulping down; absorption; *tempat ~ air baku* water intake. ~ *lemak* liposuction. ~ *uang* the siphoning of money.

sedu I sob, hiccup. *– sedan* sobbing. **tersedu-sedan** to sob.

bersedu(-sedu) and **tersedu-sedu** to hiccup. *menangis ~* to cry and sob.

tersedu-sedu to sob; sobbing.

sedu II (*cla*) sad (and depressed), melancholy.

sedu III (*J*) → SEDUH II.

sedu IV excellent; sweet; charming; → SAHDA(H).

sedua (*M*) **menyeduai, menyeduakan** and **memperseduakan** to have a sharecropping agreement; → DUA.

seduayah a shrub whose flowers can be used for dyes, *Woodfordia floribunda/fruticosa*.

seduh I → SEDU I.

seduh II (*Jv*) **menyeduh** to pour boiling water over s.t. ~ *kopi* to make coffee. ~ *téh* to let make tea.

terseduh steeped.

seduhan prepared (of a hot drink), infused. *téh ~* prepared tea.

penyeduhan pouring boiling water on.

seduk (*ob*) → SEDU I.

sedulur (*Jv*) relative (of the same generation); → SAUDARA. *sanak – relatives.*

sedut → SEDOT.

seerrr (*BG*) great, fantastic!

sé és (*D*) with one's friends/companions/associates; → CUM SUIS, DKK. *–nya* et al, and others.

séf → SÉP II.

ség I (*D*) shag. *tembakau –* shag tobacco.

ség II (*D coq ob*) /sékh/ hey (you)!

sega I smooth and shiny, polished. *rotan –* → ROTAN *sega*.

sega II (*Jv*) cooked rice; → NASI I. – *aking* spoiled rice which has been dried and recooked.

segah – *perut* a stomach distended with gas.

segak menyegak to snarl/snap at.

ségak 1 smart, chic. **2** recuperated, recovered, regained one's strength (of a patient).

   menyégakkan to regain (one's strength). ~ *diri* to smarten o.s. up.

segala (*Tam Skr*) **1** all. – *keterangan* all information. **2** entire, whole. – *badannya berlumur darah*. His whole body was smeared with blood. **3** indicates a plural; → PARA I. – *menteri hulubalang sekalian* the highest government members and army commanders together. **4** entirely, totally; → SERBA. – *salah* caught in the middle, wrong whatever one says or does. **5** (*J*) (term of abuse) stinker, bastard. **6** and all that red tape, and all that nonsense/jazz/stuff/crap/sort of thing. *Saudara kira itu cukong-cukong apa mau répot-répot dengan kantor pajak dan surat fiskal –?* Do you think that those wheeler-dealers bother about the tax office, fiscal certificates, and all that other bullshit? *Duilah cakapnya, pakai tahi lalat - di pipi!* Gosh, what a beauty, she has beauty marks and all that kind of stuff on her cheek! – *apa/sesuatu* everything, anything. *Di jantung Jakarta ini – apa bisa terjadi*. Here in the heart of Jakarta anything can happen. – *macam* all k.o. things. *menyegala-macamkan* to try all k.o. things on s.o.

segalanya and **segala-galanya** everything. ~ *sedikit* a bit of everything.

   kesegalaan everything.

segalah (*infr*) → SEGALA.

segan I 1 averse, unwilling, reluctant. *Dia – memberi bantuan walaupun dia seorang yang kaya*. He's unwilling to help even though he's a rich person. **2** to be too shy to, have scruples about, hesitate to (do s.t. improper). *Gadis itu – untuk makan dan minum dengan orang-orang yang tidak dikenalnya*. That girl is too shy to eat and drink with people she doesn't know. – *kepada*, – *dan hormat akan*, – *dan gentar kepada* to feel socially awkward in front of. *tak* – even be willing to. *Zaman meléset ini ia tidak – menjadi tukang rumput*. During this depressed time he was even willing to become a grass cutter. *jangan* – don't hesitate to, feel free to. – *tak segan* to be willing. **3** to show proper respect (to a superior). *Para wasit terlalu – kepada présidén Persatuan Tinju Amatir Internasional*. The referees show too much respect to the president of the International Amateur Boxing Association. – *hormat* respect. *menyegan-hormati* to show respect to.

   segan-segan *Jangan ~!* don't be shy! (there's plenty more food, or do come in). *tidak ~* a) not hesitate. b) not scruple to. *(dengan) tidak ~ lagi* without hesitation, unhesitatingly.

   menyegani 1 to stand in awe of, respect. *Pilihlah orang yang jujur dan disegani*. Choose an honest and respected person. **2** to look up (to s.o.). *Ortu si Yakub disegani oléh isi kampung itu*. The villagers looked up to Yakub's parents.

   segan-menyegani to respect e.o.

   keseganan 1 reluctance, unwillingness; aversion, dislike. **2** shyness, scruple. **3** reserve, restraint. **4** respect.

   penyegan shy, timid, bashful (person).

segan II *burung* – and *si* – various species of birds, among others, the long-tailed nightjar, *Caprimulgus macrurus bimaculatus/indicus jotaka*. *bertabur* – k.o. weaving design. – *jawa* Javan frogmouth, *Batrachostomus javensis*.

seganda (*Skr*) **1** plant of the turmeric family. **2** odor, scent, fragrant (in flower names).

segandasuli → GANDASULI.

segani (*Pers ob*) helmsman.

segar 1 in good shape, fit, (feeling) refreshed. *Hasan merasa tubuhnya agak – setelah makan*. Hasan felt quite refreshed after eating. **2** fresh, refreshing. *angin yang* – a fresh wind. – *baunya*. It smells fresh. *minuman* – a refreshing drink. *susu* – fresh milk. **3** luxuriant, lush, not withered or faded. *Tumbuh-tumbuhan hidup – di taman ini*. The plants grow luxuriantly in this park. **4** fresh (in one's mind), vivid. *Segala apa yang terjadi antara dia dan teman-temannya masih – dalam ingatannya*. Everything

that occurred between him and his friends is still fresh in his mind. – *bugar/pugar* in perfect health, fit as a fiddle.

   menyegarkan [and **mempersegar** (*infr*)] **1** to refresh; refreshing. *menyegarkan ingatan seseorang* to refresh s.o.'s memory. **2** to revive; to charge (a battery). *menyegarkan aki* to charge a battery. *menyegarkan pengetahuannya* to brush up his knowledge.

   tersegar the most refreshing.

   kesegaran freshness, fitness, health, refreshment. ~ *jasmani* physical fitness.

   penyegar freshener. ~ *udara* air freshener.

   penyegaran 1 refreshment, refresher. *kursus ~* refresher course. **2** renewal, rejuvenation, change (for the better). ~ *pimpinan* change in management.

segara (*Skr*) sea, ocean. – *Anakan* the strait between Nusakambangan and Java. – *Kidul* the Indian Ocean.

segawé (*Jv*) k.o. plant, red sandalwood, *Adenanthera pavonina*.

segégér a medicinal herb, *Lycopodium cernuum*; → SEMUNIAN.

ségéh (*M*) (everything is) settled, fixed.

   berségéh in order, all prepared.

   menyégéh(i) to set things straight, settle everything.

ségel I (*D*) **1** seal (such as on documents/the packaging of medicine, etc.). *Jangan diterima apabila – telah terbuka*. Don't accept it if the seal is broken. **2** stamp (other than postal stamp). **3** (ration) coupon. *kertas –* stamped paper.

   berségel to be sealed/stamped. *surat ~* a letter stamped with a seal.

   menyégel 1 to seal, affix a seal on. **2** to seal off, close up. *Pémda ~ sebuah pabrik daur ulang timbal di Bekasi*. The provincial government closed up a lead recycling factory in Bekasi. **3** to attach.

   terségel sealed.

   penyégelan 1 sealing, closing up. ~ *pabrik itu dilakukan oléh sebuah tim di bawah pimpinan Asistén Sékwilda*. The closing up of that factory was carried out by a team under the supervision of the Assistant to the Provincial Territory Secretary. **2** attaching, sealing.

ségel II (*E naut*) shackle. – *tambat* mooring shackle.

segen → SEGAN I.

segenap all; → GENAP.

seger → SEGAR.

séger (*D*) piston.

segera (*Skr*) **1** swift, quick, fast, rapid, speedy. **2** immediately, directly, at once, right away, right now, soon. *Dapatkan –!* Get it now! **3** as soon as. *Datanglah – mungkin*. Come as soon as possible. **4** (for) urgent, immediate (delivery) (of letters/telegrams, etc.).

   sesegera ~ *mungkin* and **sesegeranya** as soon as possible.

   bersegera to hurry up, make haste; to do s.t. right away. ~ *datang* to come immediately.

   menyegerakan and **mempersegera(kan)** to speed up, quicken, accelerate, hasten, hurry up. *Ledakan bom atom di Hiroshima ~ berakhirnya perang dunia kedua*. The explosion of the atom bomb in Hiroshima accelerated the end of World War II. *Présidén: Segerakan pembangunan rumah di kawasan kumuh*. President: Speed up housing construction in slums.

   kesegeran being speedy, expeditiousness.

   penyegeraan and **persegeraan** speeding up, expedition, acceleration.

segi 1 side, one of the lines bordering a figure. **2** edge, line marking the outer limit/boundary of a surface. **3** facet, one of the many sides of a diamond, etc. **4** angle, aspect, facet. – *banyak* polygon(al). – *delapan* octagon(al). – *empat* quadrilateral. – *enam* hexagon(al). *dari – hukum* from a legal standpoint. – *pandangan* point of view, viewpoint. – *panjang* rectangle. – *ragam* modal aspects. – *tiga* a) triangle. b) tripartite. – *Tiga Emas* a) the Sudirman, Thamrin, and Kuningan area in Jakarta. b) the Golden Triangle (center of narcotics trade on the borders of Thailand, Burma, and Laos). – *tiga siku-siku* right triangle.

   bersegi with/to have ... angles/sides/edges/facets. ~ *empat/enam* four-/six-sided.

   persegi 1 ...-sided. ~ *delapan* octagonal. ~ *empat/enam* four-/six-sided. *empat* ~ *panjang* rectangular. ~ *enam* hexagonal. ~ *tiga* triangular. **2** square. *méter* ~ square meter.

segianya (*ob*) → SEYOGYANYA.

segini (*J coq*) as much as this/here, so and so much. – *aja déh!* just so much!; → BEGINI.

segitu (*J coq*) as much as that/there. ~ *kayanya dia sekarang?* Is he that rich now?; → BEGITU.

ségmén (*D*) segment.

ségméntasi (*D*) segmentation.

ségrégasi (*D*) segregation.

  terségrégasi segregated, segmented; → TERPISAH.

seguna – *sekaya* → GANA-GINI II.

seguni killer whale.

séh I → SYÉIKH, SYÉKH.

séh II → SÉG II.

séh III → SIH.

sehabis → HABIS.

sehaja → SAHAJA II.

seharah (*ob*) small covered chest for holding rice.

seharusnya → HARUS I.

séhat (*A*) **1** healthy, sound. *akal* – common sense. *alasan* – sound motive. *ékonomi* – sound economy. *pikiran* – sound mind. **2** recovered, recuperated (of a patient). *tidak* – unhealthy, unsound. **ketidak-séhatan** unhealthiness, unsoundness. – *otak* in one's right mind. – *sentosa/walafiat* safe and sound, fit and well, hale and hearty.

  séhat-séhat ~ *saja* (everyone is) fine.

  menyéhatkan 1 to make/keep s.o. healthy, restore to good health. **2** healthy, invigorating. **3** to reorganize (an unsound company, etc.).

  memperséhatkan to make healthier.

  terséhat healthiest, soundest.

  keséhatan health, physical and mental condition. *ilmu* ~ hygiene. *ilmu* ~ *anak* pediatrics. *perawatan* ~ health care. ~ *jiwa* mental health. ~ *masyarakat/rakyat/umum* public health.

  penyéhat s.t. which makes s.t. or s.o. healthy.

  penyéhatan 1 restoration to good health, soundness. **2** reorganization. ~ *aparatur negara* the reorganization of the state apparatus.

sehéding (*D*) part (in one's hair).

  bersehéding with a part. ~ *ke belakang* with a part at the back (of the head).

séher (*D*) piston.

séhér → SIHIR.

sehingga so (that), as a result of which, and (so) (as a result). *Ia terlambat bangun,* – *tidak sempat mandi lagi.* He woke up late, so he didn't have time for a bath. *Orang itu ditubruk mobil* – *mati.* The man was hit by a car, and he died. *begitu/demikian* – so … that. *Tulisannya begitu/demikian jelék,* – *saya tidak dapat membacanya.* Her writing was so bad that I couldn't read it; → HINGGA.

seia → IA II.

séikhul (*A*) chairman, president (of an organization/party, etc.).

seimbang → IMBANG I.

séin (*D*) → SÉN II.

Séinéndan (*Jp*) (during the occupation) Youth Corps.

Séinéndojo (*Jp*) (during the occupation) Youth Training Center.

séi-séi (*C*) (in Tanjung Pinang) a gambling game.

seismik (*E*) and **séismis** (*D*) seismic.

séismograf (*D*) seismograph.

séismogram (*D*) seismogram.

séismologi (*D*) seismology.

séismotéktonik (*D/E*) seismotechtonic.

sejadah (*A*) prayer mat; → SAJADAH, SUJADAH.

sejahtera (*Skr*) **1** prosperous. **2** safe, tranquil. *selamat* – safe and sound.

  menyejahterakan 1 to make prosperous. **2** to make safe.

  kesejahteraan 1 safety, security, tranquility. **2** prosperity, welfare, well-being. **3** (employee) benefits. ~ *karyawan* employee benefits. ~ *sosial* social security.

  penyejahteraan making prosperous/well-off.

sejajar → JAJAR I.

sejak 1 since, as of; from. *sudah* – as long ago as. – *awal* from the start. – *dahulu/dulu-dulu* for quite a while, for a long time (from the past to the present), from ancient times. – *kecil* since/from one's childhood. – *permulaan* from the beginning,

all along. – *sekarang* from this moment, henceforth. – *tadi* from a minute ago, just now.

sejak II (*coq*) → SAJAK I.

sejarah (*A*) **1** history. *ahli* – historian. *guru* – history teacher. – (*itu*) *berulang* history repeats itself. – *Indonésia* the history of Indonesia, Indonesian history. **2** story, account; annals. *Sekalian itu adalah* – *yang disangsikan lagi kebenarannya.* All that is a story whose truth has to be questioned again. **3** (*cla*) genealogy; → ASAL-USUL, SILSILAH. – *raja-raja Melayu* the genealogy of Malay sovereigns. – *kesenian* art history. – *kuno* ancient history. – *Pertumbuhan* Book of Genesis.

  sesejarah with the same history.

  bersejarah 1 historic, historical. *gedung/kejadian* ~ a historic building/event. *novél yang* ~ a historical novel. **2** to talk about one's family tree, trace back to see whether one is related.

  menyejarah to become history.

  menyejarahkan to relate/describe/tell the history/life story of.

  kesejarahan 1 historical. **2** historic character.

  sejara(h)wan male historian. *Soekarno bukan* – *melainkan pembikin sejarah.* Soekarno wasn't a historian but a maker of history.

  sejara(h)wati female historian.

sejat dried out (of a wet cloth), dehydrated, desiccated, evaporated, squeezed out.

  menyejatkan to (make) evaporate, make desiccated.

  kesejatan evaporation.

sejati true, real, genuine, authentic; → JATI II. *teman* – a real friend.

  sejatinya actually.

  kesejatian genuineness, authenticity.

sejeg (*J*) → SAJAK I.

sejeg-bujeg (*Jv*) from a long time ago. – *jadi manusia, baru sekarang nih gué masuk ke dalem gedong begini gedé.* Since I was a child, this is the first time that I've been in a building that's so big. – *'kan kita nggak pernah paké jas-ujan!* Isn't it true that we've never ever used a raincoat!

sejenak a moment; → JENAK I.

sejenis → JENIS.

seji → SAJI I.

sejingkat (*M*) **bersejingkat** to walk on tiptoes; → BERJÉNGKÉT.

sejoli → JOLI I.

sejuk I 1 cold, chilly. **2** cool, fresh.

  bersejuk(-sejuk) to refresh o.s.

  menyejuk to (become) cool. *udara* ~ *di gunung* the fresh air in the mountains.

  menyejuki and **menyejukkan** to cool off. *duduk-duduk* ~ *badan di téras* to sit around and cool off on the terrace.

  kesejukan 1 cold, coolness; cool. **2** freshness. **3** freezing, numb (from the cold).

  penyejuk s.t. that gives a cooling effect, cooler. *alat* ~ *ruangan* and *mesin* ~ air conditioner. *Gedung ini masih terasa remang-remang, sebab listrik PLN belum masuk, dan mesin* ~ *pun belum terpasang.* This building still seems dark because the PLN electricity hasn't gotten here yet and even the air conditioners haven't been installed. ~ *udara* air freshener.

  penyejukan cooling off.

sejuk II agreeable, pleasing. – *hati* satisfied, calm, composed; contented, relaxed, relieved. – *hatinya mendengar keterangan ayahnya itu.* He was relieved to hear his father's explanation.

  menyejuki to bring relief to.

  menyejukkan to comfort, solace, cheer up, ease pressure on, console. *Ia pandai* ~ *hati orang.* He knows how to cheer people up. ~ *mata* to be pleasing to the eye.

  kesejukan kindness, gentleness, pleasantness. *senyumnya yang penuh* ~ her smile which is full of kindness.

sejuk III *daun* – k.o. medicinal herb, Christmas tree plant, *Kalanchoe laciniata/pinnata.*

sejurus → JURUS I.

sek (*Jv*) *mak* – (killed) outright.

sék I (*D*) shag. *tembakau* – shag tobacco.

sék II (in acronyms) → SÉKRETARIAT, SÉKRETARIS, SÉKTOR.

sék III → SÉKS.

séka I (*Port*) **berséka** to rub (one's hands/eyes), wash o.s.

menyéka(i) to wipe off. *Sékai dulu keringatmu itu.* Wipe off your sweat first.

menyéka-nyéka to keep (on) wiping.

menyékakan to wipe away, rub out, wipe (off) with.

terséka wiped off.

penyéka wiper. ~ *kaca* windshield wiper. ~ *muka* towelette.

séka II → SIKA I.

Sékab and Sékkab [Sékretaris-kabinét] Cabinet Secretary.

sekadar just, only; → KADAR I.

sekah → SERKAH.

sékah (*ob*) → SÉGAK.

sekak I (*D*) chess. *main* – to play chess.

menyékak check! (called when threatening the opponent's king in chess).

Sekak II *orang* – nomads who live on boats between Bangka island and Belitung island.

sekakar and sekaker (*D?*) miserly, stingy, close-fisted.

sekakelar (*D*) (electric) switch.

sekaker → SEKAKAR.

sekakmat checkmate.

sekal I (*D*) scale (of a map,).

sekal II chubby, hefty.

sekala I → SEKAL I.

sekala II (*Bal*) tangible, can be perceived by the senses, the visible world; *opp* NISKALA.

sekalem link, joint, coupling.

sekali once; altogether, all; very, extremely; → KALI I. – *sekala* once in a while.

sekalian 1 all (of them). 2 together; → KALIAN, KALI I.

sekaligus all at once; all of a sudden.

sekalipun although, even though; → KALI I.

sekalor I epilepsy; epileptic (*mod*).

sekalor II (*Jv*) migraine.

sekam chaff, outer covering of grain, rice husk, glume; → DEDAK I. *bagai/seperti api dalam* – there is a snag somewhere; smoldering (of discontent/hatred). *tidak terbawa* – *segantang* a very weak person (due to old age, etc.). – *menjadi hampa berat* won't hurt a bit. – *kelopak* flowering glume, lemma. – *mahkota* palea, valvule.

menyekam 1 to imprison. 2 to suppress.

Sekanak *orang* – sea-nomads of the Riau archipelago.

sekanda torso.

sekang (*M*) plug, stopper. – *mata* nuisance, annoying person.

menyekang 1 to put a plug in s.t., plug up, stop. 2 to block. ~ *mata* unpleasant, disagreeable, annoying. ~ *perut* to stuff o.s. before leaving s.o.'s house.

tersekang plugged, stopped, blocked. ~ *nasi dalam rangkungan/ kerongkongan* rice plugged up the throat.

sekap I (*J*) menyekap to keep (fruits) (in a pile of *beras*, etc.) to ripen them artificially; → MEMERAM.

tersekap artificially ripened.

sekapan ripened (not on a tree). *matang* ~ artificially ripened (of fruits).

penyekapan the process of artificial ripening.

sekap II menyekap 1 to imprison, incarcerate, keep at home (of a marriageable girl). 2 to close, shut (up). ~ *mulut* to stop s.o.'s mouth, silence s.o. 3 to cover (up).

tersekap imprisoned, covered, trapped.

sekapan 1 prisoner, detainee. 2 prison.

penyekap s.o. who imprisons, confiner.

penyekapan imprisonment, locking up, blockade, confinement, confining.

sekapar k.o. marine fish.

sekar (*Jv*) flower; → BUNGA I, KEMBANG I. – *Kedaton* "Flower of the Kraton," i.e., the special designation for the firstborn daughter, descendant of a princess of the Kraton. – *mayang* blossoms of the coconut palm (also initiated ones) as decoration at wedding ceremonies. – *suhun* gold neck ornament.

menyekar [and nyekar (*coq*)] to put flowers on a grave.

sekarang now, at present, at this time, nowadays, today. *mulai* – from now on. *anak* – today's children/youth. *jaman* – the current period, nowadays. *lain dulu lain* – manners change with the times, that was then and this is now. – *ini* at this very moment, right now.

sekarang-sekarang at once, immediately, right away.

sekarat (*A*) (in) agony, at death's door. *sudah* – at death's door.

bersekarat to be at death's door. ~ *maut* to take one's life in one's hands.

sekat I 1 partition, screen. 2 obstacle, impediment. 3 bulkhead. 4 (*med*) septum. – *angin* windbreak. – *api* fire wall. – *bakar* firebreak. – *buritan bertekanan tinggi* aft high-pressure bulkhead (in aircraft). – *kisi-kisi* grating. – *pemisah génerasi* generation gap. – *rongga badan* midriff, diaphragm. – *rongga hidung* internasal septum. – *tembuni* section of the afterbirth.

bersekat 1 partitioned/sectioned off. 2 with partitions/bulkheads, etc.

bersekat-sekat divided up by partitions.

menyekat 1 to separate off (with a screen, etc.). *Kamarnya disekat dengan kain gordin.* Her room was separated off by a curtain. 2 to dam up, block. 3 to isolate, seclude. ~ *dirinya selama beberapa hari* to seclude o.s. for a couple of days. 4 to insulate.

menyekati 1 to separate by screens. 2 to dam up, block. ~ *diri* to control o.s.

tersekat 1 (s.t. got) stuck. *léhér/kerongkongan* ~ had a lump in the throat. 2 separated. 3 (*elec*) insulated.

sekatan 1 partition, screen. ~ *buku* flyleaf. 2 hindrance, obstacle, impediment, obstruction, partitioned-off space. 3 (*elec*) insulation. 4 cubicle.

penyekat 1 partition. 2 insulator, insulation. 3 obstacle, block(er). ~ *béta* beta blocker. 4 packer (a tool used in oil wells). berpenyekat insulated. *kotak pendingin* ~ insulated ice box.

penyekatan 1 enclosure, impediment, blockage. 2 segregating, separating. ~ *kalor* keeping s.t. warm.

sekat II (*D*) skate; to skate; skating.

sekata → KATA.

sekatén (*Jv*) a feast held in Yogyakarta, Surakarta, and Cirebon to commemorate the birth of the Prophet; → M(A)ULUD. *gamelan* – the *kraton gamelan* played on *sekatén*.

sekaténan 1 the celebration of *sekatén*. 2 to go to the *sekatén*.

sekater (*D ob*) evaluator, appraiser (of a pawnshop).

sekati (*Jv ob*) → SEKATÉN.

sekaut (*D col*) police inspector, bailiff.

Sékbergolkar → SÉKRÉTARIAT *Bersama Golongan Karya*.

Sékda [Sékretaris Daérah] Provincial Secretary; → SÉKWILDA I.

Sékdalopbang → SÉSDALOPBANG.

sékébér (*D ob*) district commissioner; → PÉTOR.

sekedar → KADAR I.

sekédéng (*D*) parting (of the hair).

sekedidi → KEDIDI.

sekeduduk → SENDUDUK.

sekedup (*A*) camel's packsaddle.

sekel (*J*) 1 to form a solid lump (of rice, etc.). 2 robust, strong (of person), firm (of breasts).

sekelar → SAKELAR.

sekelat (*Pers*) scarlet cloth.

sekelébatan → KELÉBAT.

sekelian → SEKALIAN.

sekeliling around; → KELILING.

seséma → SKÉMA.

sekén (*E*) secondhand, previously owned.

sekendal *pohon* – k.o. tree, Assyrian plum, *Cordia myxa/obliqua/ dichotoma.*

sekéndi *burung* – white ibis, *Threskiornis melanocephalus.*

séékéng (*Jv*) 1 weak, unable to resist. 2 poor, indigent.

sekengan dart (in clothes).

sekep → SEKAP I.

séker → SÉGER.

sékéram (*D*) curtain, screen, partition.

sekerba (*Skr*) full brother.

sekeri (*D*) hinge; → ÉNGSÉL.

sékering (*D*) fuse, circuit breaker.

sekerja → KERJA.

sékertaris → SÉKRETARIS.

sékertariat → SÉKRÉTARIAT.

sékertarés → SÉKRETARÉSE.

sekerup → SEKRUP.

sekésél (*D ob*) screen, partition.
sékéstrasi (*D*) sequestration.
sekét (*D*) sketch; → SKÉTSA.
  menyekét [and nyekét (*coq*)] to sketch.
sekéténg (*Jv*) *lawang* – (city) gate.
sékh → SYÉKH.
sekian → KIAN I.
sekilwak (*D*) 1 sentry. 2 to stand sentry.
sekin I (*A*) knife.
sekin II (*D*) bar, rule.
sekip (*D*) 1 target, mark; → BULAN-BULANAN. 2 rifle-range.
sekir (*D*) menyekir to sand down, grind.
sekira → KIRA.
sekiram (*D*) screen, shade.
sekis (*D*) schist.
  menyekis schistose.
sekitar → KITAR I.
Sékjén → SÉKRETARIS *jénderal*.
Sékkel → SÉKRETARIS *kelurahan*.
Sékko → SÉKRETARIS *kota*.
Sékmil → SÉKRETARIS *Militér*.
Séknég → SÉKRETARIS *negara*.
séko 1 scout. 2 spy; → AGÉN, MATA-MATA.
sekoci I (*D*) a small vessel, craft; sloop. – *kerja* work platform (for work on the side of a ship). – *pendarat* landing craft. – *penolong/penyelamat* lifeboat, life raft.
sekoci II (*D*) shuttle, bobbin case, container in a sewing machine which holds the bobbin or reel.
sekoi → SEKUI.
sekolah (*Port*) 1 school, place for teaching and learning. *Saya pergi ke – dengan berjalan kaki*. I go to school on foot. *Ia pernah duduk di bangku –*. He went/used to go to school. *anak* – schoolchild. *bis* – school bus. *guru* – schoolteacher. *kepala* – headmaster, school superintendent. *tidak makan* – uneducated. *masuk* – a) to enroll in school. b) to go into a school building. *meréka yang meninggalkan – sebelum waktunya* (school) dropouts. *pergi* – to go to school. *pulang* – to come home from school. *rumah* – school building. *uang* – school fee, tuition. 2 the period of instruction at any school, regular session of teaching. *Pukul berapa – mulai?* What time does school begin? *Selama bulan Puasa tidak ada –*. During the fasting month there's no school. 3 to attend school. *Saya ingin – di luar negeri*. I would like to go to school abroad. 4 study, schooling. *–nya tinggi* he has reached an advanced level of study. – *Aliyah* (*A*) Islamic senior high school. – *ambah* (*coq*) trade school. – *anak-anak nakal* reform school, reformatory. – *berasrama* boarding school. – *bina taat* reform school, reformatory. – *bruder* (*D*) Catholic seminary school; → BRUDERAN. – *bukan élit* nonelite school. – *Calon Bintara* [Secaba] Noncommissioned Officers Candidate School. – *Calon Bintara Tinggi* [Secabati] Senior Noncommissioned Officer Candidate School. – *calon Perwira* [Secapa] Officer Candidate School. – *Calon Tamtama* [Secatam] Recruitment Candidate School. – *dasar* [SD] elementary school. – *dagang* commercial school. – *désa* village school. – *Dokter Jawa* (*col coq*) → STOVIA. – *élit* elite school. – *Gajah Way Kambas* Way Kambas Elephant Training School (at Bandar Lampung, South Sumatra). – *(calon) guru* teacher training school (elementary and high school level). – *guru agama* theological seminar. – *ibtidaiyah* (*A*) Islamic elementary school. – *Jahat* (*Mal*) reform school, reformatory. – *kejuruan* vocational school. – *Kependidikan Ketrampilan Atas* [SKKA] Higher Skills Education School. – *kompréhénsif* comprehensive school. – *lanjutan* high school–level institution (after elementary school and before attending university). – *Lanjutan Tingkat Atas* [SLTA] Senior High School. – *Lanjutan Tingkat Pertama* [SLTP] Junior High School. – *Menengah Tingkat Atas* [SMTA] Senior High School. – *Menengah Tingkat Pertama* [SMTP] Junior High School, Middle School. – *Latihan Kejuruan* vocational training school. – *liar* illegal school. – *Menengah Atas* [SMA] Senior High School. – *Menengah Kejuruan* [SMK] Vocational High School. – *Menengah Pertama* [SMP] Junior High School, Middle School. – *Menengah Umum* [SMU] Senior High School. –

mengemudikan mobil driving school. – *menjahit* sewing school. – *main* play group; → KELOMPOK *bermain*. – *mode* fashion school. – *negeri* public school. – *nétral* nondenominational school. – *ongko loro* (*Jv col*) "number two school," the lowest type of school for Javanese village children. – *pagi* morning school (from 7 a.m. to 1 p.m.). – *partikelir* (*col*) private school. – *pelayaran* nautical (training) school. – *pembangunan* comprehensive school. – *penerbangan* flight school. – *pertukangan* trade school. – *Perwira Militér Sukaréla* [Sepamilsuk] Military Officers Volunteer School. – *prébel* (*col*) kindergarten; → PRASEKOLAH, TAMAN *kanak-kanak*. – *Raja* (*coq*) Teachers Training College (Yogyakarta). – *rakyat/rendah* grammar/elementary school; → SD. – *Républik Indonésia Tokyo* [SRTT] Republic of Indonesia School in Tokyo. – *siang* afternoon school. – *Staf Komando Angkatan Bersenjata Républik Indonésia* [Sésko ABRI, Séskoabri] Republic of Indonesia Armed Forces Staff and Command School. – *Staf Komando Angkatan Darat Téknologi Menengah Atas* [STMA] Senior Technological High School. – *swasta* private school. – *Téknologi Menengah Télékomunikasi* [STM Télkom] Telecommunications Technological High School. – *tinggi* college, academy. – *Tinggi Seni Rupa dan Désain* [STSRD] Academy of Plastic Arts and Design. – *Tinggi Téknologi Télékomunikasi* [STT Télkom] Telecommunications Technological College. – *Tsanawiyah* (*A*) (Islamic) Junior High School, Middle School. – *tukang* trade school. – *unggulan* elite school. – *vak* (*col*) vocational school.
bersekolah 1 to attend/go to school. 2 to be educated, have had an education. *kewajiban* ~ compulsory education. 3 to be a student (of).
menyekolahkan [and nyekolahin (*J coq*)] 1 to send to school. *Minat penduduk Irja untuk* ~ *anaknya meningkat*. The interest among Irian Jaya's population in sending their children to school is on the rise. 2 (*sl*) to pawn, hock.
mempersekolahkan to instruct/teach in school (a subject or art).
sekolahan 1 school (building). 2 educated, having been to school. *Saya bukan orang* ~. I'm not educated.
penyekolahan 1 schooling. 2 sending to school. 3 (*sl*) pawning, hocking.
persekolahan school system, school (*mod*). *masyarakat* ~ school community. *pendidikan* ~ *di masa depan* future education in school.
sekon (*D*) second (1/60 minute); → DETIK. *dalam se–* within a second.
sekonar (*D*) schooner.
sekondan (*D*) second (in a duel), strategic advisor.
sekonéng (*D*) beveling.
sekongkel and sekongkol (*D*) to plot, intrigue, conspire, scheme; plotting, intriguing, intrigues; engaged in underhanded dealings. *orang* – accomplice, accessory. *Penyelundup narkotika serta beberapa orang –nya sudah tertangkap*. The drug smugglers and their accomplices were apprehended.
bersekongkol to plot, intrigue, scheme, conspire, collude. *Ia dituduh* ~ *dengan kaum téroris*. He was accused of conspiring with terrorists.
(per)sekongkolan conspiracy, collusion, plot, scheme.
sekonyar (*ob*) → SEKONAR.
sekonyong-konyong suddenly, unexpectedly; → KONYONG.
sekop (*D*) shovel, spade.
  menyekop to shovel, spade.
sekopong (*D*) spades (card suit). *main* – to play European cards.
sekor(e)s → SKORS.
sekosol → SEKÉSÉL.
Sékot [Sékretaris-kotif] Administrative Town Secretary.
Sekota [sékretaris kota] municipal secretary.
sekotah (*cla*) total, all.
sekoténg (*CJ*) a hot ginger-flavored drink. *és* – the same drink iced.
sekout → SEKAUT.
sékpri [sékretaris-pribadi] private secretary.
sekréning → SEKRINING.
sékrési (*D*) secretion. – *asam* acid secretion.
  mensékrésikan to secrete s.t.
sékretarése (*D*) female secretary.

sékretariat (D) secretariat. – *Bersama Golongan Karya* [Sékbérgolkar] Joint Secretariat of Functional Groups. – *jénderal* [sétjén] secretariat general. – *Negara* [Séknég] State Secretariat, i.e., the Presidential Cabinet.

kesékretariatan secretarial. *di bidang* ~ in the secretarial sector.

persékretariatan secretarial. *Kursus Administrasi* ~ *TNI-AU ditutup*. The Secretarial Administration Course of the Armed Services-Air Force has been closed.

sékretaris (D) secretary. – *akaunting/akonting* accounting secretary. – *éksékutif* executive secretary. – *jénderal* [sékjén] secretary general. – *kabinét* [séskab] cabinet secretary. – *kelurahan* [sékkel] district secretary. – *kota* [sékko] municipal secretary. – *militér* [sékmil] military secretary. – *negara* [séknég] state secretary. – *perusahaan* business secretary. – *plus* a secretary who also works as a prostitute. – *satu* first secretary.

kesékretarisan secretarial sciences. *Akadémi* ~ Academy of Secretarial Sciences.

sekrétin (E) secretin.
sékring (D) fuse; → SÉKERING.
sekrining (D/E) screening.
sekrip (D) exercise book.
sékrit (E) secret.
sekrop (D) to scrub (the floor, etc.).
sekrup (D) screw, pin, bolt. – *jarum/penegang/tarik* turnbuckle.

menyekrup to screw s.t. *disekrup mati* (the screw) was tightened firmly.

menyekrupkan 1 to screw with (a tool). **2** to screw tight.

séks (D) sex. *ahli* – sexologist. *bom* – sex bomb. *film* – pornographic movie. *kelainan* – *dengan kekerasan* sadomasochism. *main* – to have sexual intercourse. – *anal* anal sex. – *bébas* free sex. – *oral* oral sex.

ngeséks (coq) to have sex.
seksama → SAKSAMA.
séksi I (D) **1** section. **2** (of a dead body) dissection, postmortem (examination). **3** (in army) platoon. **4** (police) precinct.
séksi II (E) sexy.
terséksi sexiest.
keséksian sexiness.
séksio section. – *sésaréa* caesarian section.
séksis (D) sexist.
séksisme (D/E) sexism.
séksmaniak (D/E) sexmaniac.
séksofon (D) saxophone.
séksofonis (D) saxophonist.
séksolog (D) sexologist.
séksologi (D/E) sexology.
Sékspir (coq) Shakespeare.
sékstan (D) sextant.
sékstét (D/E) sextet.
séksual (E) sexual. *rangsangan* – sexual stimulus.
séksualitas and **séksualitét** (D) sexuality.
séksuil (D) sexual.
séksuologi → SÉKSOLOGI.
séktarian (D) **1** a sect; → SÉKTARIS. **2** a member of a sect.
séktari(ani)sme (D) sectarianism.
séktaris (D) sectarian.
sékte (D) sect. – *keagamaan* religious sect.
séktor (D) sector. – *memimpin* leading sector. – *perhubungan* communications sector. – *riil* the real sector. – *swasta* private sector.
séktoral (E) sectoral.
sekuas (D) *limon* – lemon squash (a drink).
sekui k.o. millet, *Panicum viride*; → JAWAWUT.
sekuik *naga* – representation of a swimming dragon on batik designs.
sekul (Pers) a bowl made from three-quarters of a coconut shell with a rattan holder (for water/food, etc.).
sékular (E) secular.
mensékularkan to secularize.
sékularis secularistic.
sékularisasi (D) secularization.
sékularisme (D) secularism.
sékularitas (E) secularity.

sékulér (E) secular.
mensékulerkan to secularize.
sekunar → SEKONAR.
sékundér (D) secondary.
sekunyit a serving of yellow sweet glutinous rice.
sekuritas (E) pledge, security, pawn. – *dengan hasil tetap* fixed-income securities. – *tak terdaftar* unlisted securities.
sékuriti (E) security, security service. *polisi* – security police. – *bersandarkan asét* asset-backed securities, ABS.
sekut I 1 soporifics used by thieves to drug people they wish to rob, a Mickey Finn.
sekut II stingy, tight-fisted.
sekuténg → SEKOTÉNG.
sekuter → SKUTER.
sekutu (Tam) → KUTU II. **1** partner. **2** ally, associate; allied. *yg* – the Allied Powers. **3** accessory, accomplice. *Pemuda itu telah dihukum penjara juga sebab ia dianggap sebagai* – *dalam perampokan itu*. The young man was also convicted to imprisonment because he was considered an accomplice to the robbery. – *aktif/yang bekerja* active partner (in a corporation). – *kerja* working partner. – *komanditér* limited partner. – *pasif/yang beserta* silent partner (in a corporation). – *turutan* underpartner.
bersekutu 1 to join, combine, ally o.s., federate. *Portugal tetap nétral, tidak mau* ~ *dengan negara-negara tetangganya*. Portugal remained neutral, she didn't want to ally herself with her neighbors. **2** to be allied/united/federated. *Dua bank besar baru-baru ini* ~. Recently two large banks united. **3** to be an accomplice. *Di antara meréka itu ada yang* ~ *dengan penyelundup-penyelundup itu*. Among them there were some who became accomplices of the smugglers. *makhluk yang* ~ a social animal. *Tuhan tidak* ~ There is only one God.
menyekutui 1 to participate in, be a member of. **2** to be an accomplice with.
menyekutukan and **mempersekutukan** to make a member/partner. *perjanjian untuk mempersekutukan negara-negara itu* a treaty to unite those nations. **2** to consider as an ally/partner. ~ *Tuhan* to have other gods than the one God. *Jangan sekali-kali menyekutukan Allah dengan sesuatu yang lain*. On no account should you consider God a partner with s.o. else.
persekutuan 1 association, society, organization, club, partnership. ~ *dagang* trading company/partnership. ~ *komanditér* limited partnership. ~ *perdata* partnership. **2** federation. ~ *Tanah Melayu* (ob) Federation of Malaya. **3** league, alliance. – *segi-tiga* triple alliance.
penyekutuan polytheism.
sékwéstrasi (D) sequestration.
Sékwilda I [Sékretaris wilayah daérah] Provincial Territory Secretary.
sékwilda II (joc sl) [sekitar wilayah dada] petting, touching s.o.'s breasts.
Sékwilko [Sékretaris wilayah kota] City Territory Secretary.
Sékwilmat [Sékretaris wilayah kecamatan] Subdistrict Territory Secretary.
sel (in acronyms) → SELATAN.
sél (D) cell (biological/prison/battery, etc.). – *aki* battery cell. – *bicara* telephone booth. – *cagak* mast cell. – *darah* corpuscle. – *darah mérah* erythrocyte, red blood cell. – *darah putih* white blood cell. – *induk* mother cell. –.– *kelamin* spermatozoon, spermatozoa. – *kanker* cancerous cell. – *komunis* communist cell. – *limfosit* lymphocyte cell. – *macan* death row. – *pengasingan* solitary cell (for solitary confinement). – *penjara* prison cell. – *raba* taste bud. – *sikel* sickle cell. – *tandan* stem cell. – *télepon* telephone booth. – *tunas* stem cell.
bersél with/to have cells/a cell, cellular. ~ *tunggal* unicellular.
mengesél, mensél(kan) [and **ngesél** (coq)] to confine/lock up in a prison cell, imprison, incarcerate, put behind bars. *Tertuduh kagét karena disélkan*. The accused was shocked because he was put behind bars.
sela I 1 interval, break, time in between two events. *Hawa dingin menyelinap ke dalam dari* –.– *di bawah pintu*. The cold air slipped in through openings under the door. *Di* –.– *kesibukan tim Indonésia, Rudy menyempatkan diri main ténis*. At the

breaks during the Indonesian team's activities, Rudy made time to play tennis. *makanan* – between-meal snack. *tanaman* – catch crop. **2** cleft, crack, chink, crevice. *melihat dari* – *dinding* to look through the cracks in the wall. **3** interim, provisional. *putusan* – provisional decision. – *antara* clearance. **4** with an interval of. – *hari* with an interval of a day, every other day. **5** (*med*) symphysis.

sela-sela break (in a program). –.– *hukum* (*leg*) loopholes in the law.

bersela 1 with intervals/interstices. *tidak* ~ uninterrupted, continuous. **2** to have clefts/cracks/gaps, etc.

bersela-sela alternating. *Laki-laki dan perempuan duduk* ~. Men and women sat in alternating seats.

menyela [and **nyela** (*coq*)] **1** to interrupt, interfere, butt in. *Tiada seorang pun berani* ~ *perkataan Harmoko ini*. Nobody has the nerve to interrupt Harmoko's speech. **2** (*ob*) to intersperse, insert, put s.t. in between two other things. *Untuk menambah hasil, tanaman di pematang itu disela juga dengan kacang panjang*. To increase the yield, the plants on the dike were alternated with long beans. *Ia mau* ~ *saja, tidak mau antri*. He just wanted to break into the line because he didn't want to stand in line. **3** to streak. *Rambutnya sudah disela uban*. His hair is already streaked with gray.

sela-menyela alternate, intermittent.

menyelai → MENYELA 2.

menyelakan and **memperselakan** to insert, put s.t. into s.t. else.

selaan 1 interval. **2** interstice, interruption, intercalation.

penyela intervener, intervening third party.

penyelaan interruption, intervention.

sela II mixture.

séla I (*M*) cross-eyed, squinting; → JULING.

séla II (*Port ob*) saddle.

séla III (*Jv ob*) stone.
  menyélakan to cast a stone.

séla IV → SILA II.

selabar (*ob*) swab, mop.

selab(e)rak (*D ob*) saddle-cloth.

selada (*Port*) **1** lettuce, head (cabbage-)lettuce, *Lactuca sativa*. *daun* – lettuce leaves. **2** (*D?*) salad. *minyak* – salad oil. – *air* watercress, *Nasturtium officinale*. – *batang* k.o. asparagus, *Lactuca sativa*. – *buah* fruit salad. – *keriting* curly endive. – *tomat* tomato salad.

seladang I wild cattle, a type of wild ox which is dark brown or almost black in color, *Bos gaurus*.

seladang II on the same level.
  menyeladang to be spread out evenly.

selad(e)ri (*D*) celery; → SÉLEDERI.

selag and **selah** → SELAH II.

selagi → LAGI.

selah I → SELA II.

selah II (*D*) the hang of s.t. *Meréka belum mengetahui –nya*. They still don't have the hang of it.

selah III → SLAHRUM.

selai (*D*) jam, jelly. – *kacang* peanut butter. – *nenas* pineapple jam.

selain → LAIN I.

selaju I berselaju to skate. ~ *di atas és* ice-skating; → LAJU I.

selaju II → SALJU.

selak I bar (for a door/window), bolt.
  menyelak to bar (a door, etc.), lock a door, gate, etc. with a bolt. ~ *perisai* (*cla*) to carry a shield on one's arm (to parry blows).

selak II (*Jv*) on the point/verge of, just about to, can hardly (wait, etc., for s.t. one wishes or intends to do). *Cepat, – berangkat!* Hurry up! It's about to leave. *Meréka itu* – *kemudu-kudu melihat musuh besarnya mati*. They can hardly wait to see their archenemy die.
  menyelak [and **nyelak** (*coq*)] **1** to hurry s.o. up, urge s.o. (to do s.t.). **2** to jump (the line).
  penyelak s.o. who jumps (the line).

selak III (*Jv*) **terselak** [and **keselak** (*coq*)] choked, swallowed s.t. the wrong way.

selak IV (*D*) shellac.

selak V dazed, stunned.

sélak menyélak(kan) 1 to pull aside, lift up, raise. *Dia menyélak*

sarungnya untuk menunjukkan luka di lututnya. He lifted up his sarong to show the wound on his knee. *Kain selubung itu disélakkannya*. She raised the veil. **2** to turn, open (as of a book, etc.). *Album foto itu disélanya sehalaman demi sehalaman*. He opened the photo album page by page.
  tersélak raised (just a minute).

selaka I (*ob*) a rack for hanging clothes.

selaka II (*Jv*) silver.

selakangan (*J*) → SELANGKANG(AN).

sélakarang (*Jv*) mange (of cats/dogs/horses).

selak-seluk particulars, details; → SELUK II.

selaku as, as if, like.

selalap keselalapan ~ *duri* choked on a (fish-) bone.

selalu 1 always, frequently, incessantly, unceasingly. *Ia* – *mengingat ibunya*. He frequently thinks of his mother. **2** (*M*) entirely. *hitam* – entirely black. – *hari* the whole day.

selam I diving. *juru* – diver. *kapal* – submarine. – *skuba* scuba diving.

berselam 1 to go underwater. ~ *air* (*cla*) to take a test of going underwater as an oath (to prove one's innocence or guilt). **2** submersible.

menyelam [and **nyelam** (*coq*)] **1** to dive, submerge, plunge. *Orang itu membawa bekal oksigén yang cukup untuk* ~ *selama dua jam*. That man has taken enough oxygen to submerge for two hours. ~ *sambil minum air* to kill two birds with one stone. **2** to be immersed, stay under water, soak, disappear (into). *segera* ~ *di bawah lalang yang lebat* to vanish quickly under the dense coarse grass. **3** to enter, penetrate, thrust into. *Pisau* ~ *ke dalam perut*. The knife entered his stomach.

menyelami 1 to dive/plunge/dip into. ~ *air dalam tonggak* very difficult to observe s.o.'s character. **2** to dive to get/look for s.t. ~ *mutiara* to dive for pearls. **3** a) to fathom. *Pikirannya hendak* ~ *hati gadis itu*. He was thinking of fathoming that girl's mind. b) to examine, investigate, study. *Maksudnya hendak* ~ *sejarah filsafat Barat*. He intended to study the history of western philosophy. c) to understand. *Ia tidak sanggup dengan segera* ~ *kesedihan orang*. He wasn't able to understand people's sorrows easily.

menyelamkan to immerse, submerge, dip, stick into, duck. *Kepalanya diselamkan ke dalam air*. He stuck his head under the water.

terselam immersed, submerged.

terselami *tidak* ~ unfathomable, inscrutable.

penyelam and **peselam 1** diver. ~ *supit mutiara* pearl diver. **2** diving (goggles/suit, etc.).

penyelaman 1 diving. ~ *indah* fancy diving. **2** immersion, dipping. **3** probing, investigation.

Selam II (*coq*) Islam. *orang* – an Indonesian Muslim.
  menyelamkan 1 to Islamize, convert to Islam. **2** to circumcise.
  penyelaman 1 Islamization, conversion to Islam. **2** circumcision.

selama while, as long as, during; → LAMA.

selamat (*A*) **1** safe, unhurt, unscathed, uninjured, unharmed, safe and sound, secure. *Juru* – the Savior. – *dari bahaya maut* escaped from death. *biar lambat asal* – slow but sure, better late than never. *sampai di Surabaya dengan* – to arrive in Surabaya safely. *asal badan sendiri* – and *mau* – *sendiri* concerned with one's own safety. *Apakah saudara* –? (asked after s.o. has been in an accident, etc.) Are you O.K.? *memburu/mencari* – to save o.s., seek safety. *Penduduk nékad melarikan diri untuk mencari* –. Residents were determined to run away to seek safety. **2** (prayers/sayings/utterances/statements, etc.) hoping that s.o. will be safe/lucky, etc. *doa* – a) prayer to thank God (because one's relatives, etc. are doing well) *usu* expressed through a *selamatan*. b) prayer for the well-being of s.o. *Bila anak perempuan kita yang sulung itu lahir ke dunia, tidaklah kita menyambutnya dengan doa* – *besar-besaran*? When our firstborn daughter came into the world, shall we welcome her on a large scale with prayers for her well-being? *mendoa* – a) giving thanks to God or asking for one's well-being (*usu* linked to a *selamatan*). b) (= *membaca doa* –) to say a prayer of thanks. **3** expressions containing a hope that one will not lack (for) anything (or, will want for nothing). *Pada ketika ia kawin, banyak*

handai taulannya yang memberi – kepadanya. At his wedding, many friends wished him all the best. **4** congratulations, good wishes/luck. *–! Good luck! All the best! Saya memberi/mengucap(kan) – kepadanya.* I congratulated him. *– atas kelahiran anggota keluarga baru.* Congratulations on your new child. *– atas suksés anda.* Congratulations on your success. *– bekerja* Work hard. Success in your work. *– belajar.* Study hard. *– berbahagia* congratulations. *– berbahagia atas pernikahan anda.* Congratulations on your wedding. *– berharlah.* Happy anniversary; → HARLAH. *– berhut.* Many happy returns of the day; → HUT II. *– berjuang.* Victory! *– berjumpa.* How do you do. *– berkongrés.* Success with the congress. *– bermotor.* Happy motoring. *– berpuasa.* Have a successful fast (in the month of *Ramadan*). *– bertemu lagi.* See you soon. *– (ber)ulang tahun.* Many happy returns of the day. *– berusaha.* Success in your business! *– datang* welcome. **menyelamat-datangi** to welcome. *– diterima* duly received (of a letter, in commercial correspondence). *– erat* warm regards. *– hari lahir.* Happy birthday. *– jalan.* Good-bye (to the one leaving). Have a nice trip. Bon voyage. *– (Hari) Lebaran* Happy Lebaran. Congratulations (said at the end of the fasting month of *Ramadan*). *– Hari Natal.* Merry Christmas. *– hari raya* happy holidays. *– hari ulang tahun.* a) Many happy returns of the day. Happy birthday. b) Happy anniversary. *– jalan* have a good/safe trip, good-bye. *– lebaran.* Happy Lebaran. *– main.* Good luck (with your gambling). *– maju.* Continued success. *– makan.* Enjoy your meal. Bon appétit. *– malam.* a) Good evening. b) Good night (said on greeting as well as departing). *– minum.* To your health. Cheers. *– pagi.* Good morning. *– panjang umur* a) many happy returns of the day. b) speak of the devil (and he will appear). *– panjang umur, semoga sejahtera selalu.* Long life to you (and) may you always be prosperous. *– sampai* duly received (of a letter, in commercial correspondence). *– siang.* Good day (said around noontime). *– soré.* Good afternoon. *– tidur.* Good night. Sleep well, sleep well. *– tinggal.* Good-bye (said to one remaining behind). *memberi – tinggal kepada* to say good-bye to.
selamat-selamat *~ saja* take good care of yourself, be well.
menyelamati 1 to hold a *selamatan* on s.o. else's behalf. *Ibu ~ empat puluh hari bapaknya Siti.* Mother held a fortieth-day ceremony for Siti's father (commemorating the fortieth day after his death). **2** to congratulate. *Saya akan ~ George Bush, bila sudah pasti dia menang.* I will congratulate George Bush when it is certain that he has won.
menyelamatkan [and **nyelamatin** (*J coq*)] **1** to save, protect, rescue. *– muka* a) to save face. b) face saving. *kerugian yang tidak dapat diselamatkan* irretrievable losses. **2** to hold a *selamatan* on s.o. else's behalf. **3** to keep s.o. safe/well/secure. *Puluhan pengunjung "Jakarta Tower" terpaksa berlari ~ diri masing-masing.* Dozens of visitors to the "Jakarta Tower" had to run for their lives. **4** to relieve (a besieged city). **5** (*M*) the exchange of rings and the distribution of *nasi kunyit* after a wedding.
terselamatkan saved, salvageable. *tidak ~ could not be saved/rescued. Nyawanya tidak ~.* He could not be saved (i.e., he died).
selamatan ceremony which includes the custom of giving away sacred food which will provide security for the host and his family. *~ brokohan* ceremony held at childbirth and in connection with the naming ceremony. *~ hajat dalam malam selikuran* ceremony held to commemorate the end of the fasting month of Ramadan. *~ jenang abang* ceremony held after a circumcision. *~ kol* an annual ceremony in observance of the anniversary of s.o.'s death. *~ metik* village harvest ceremony. *~ mitoni* ceremony held on the seventh month of pregnancy. *~ nyepasari* ceremony held on the fifth day after birth. *~ puput puser* ceremony held on the occasion of the falling off of the umbilical cord. **berselamatan 1** to hold a *selamatan/kenduri.* **2** to congratulate e.o.
keselamatan 1 welfare, prosperity, security, salvation. *Bala (Tentara) ~.* Salvation Army. **2** safety. *~ kerja* job/occupational safety. *~ kesejahteraan rakyat yang tertinggi adalah hukum salus populi suprema lex esto,* the security of the people shall be the final law. **3** interest. *untuk ~ keluarga* in the interest of the family.

penyelamat 1 savior, redeemer; the Savior/Redeemer (in Christianity). *~ kehidupan* lifesaver (the person). **2** rescuer, rescue/safety (*mod*). *regu ~* rescue team.
penyelamatan salvation, rescue. *~ melalui kepercayaan* salvation by faith. *program ~* rescue program.
selamba (*ob*) **1** poker-faced, not showing any emotion. **2** not knowing how to behave properly, shameless, immodest, brazen-faced.
keselambaan shamelessness, improper behavior.
selampai I 1 (*cla*) piece of silk cloth about four centimeters wide worn around the neck or over the shoulder as a scarf or bandanna. **2** (*J*) handkerchief.
menyelampai (*cla*) to wear a *selampai* over the shoulder.
menyelampaikan to hang a *selampai* over the shoulder.
terselampai hanging down (like a *selampai*).
selampai II various species of marine fish such as bronze croaker, *Pseudosciaena diacanthus, Otolithoides biauritus.*
selampé → SELAMPAI I 2.
selampik (*J*) → SELAMPAI I 2.
selampit I flat braid or plait; thin and flat strands of thread/rope; skirt twisted between the thighs as a loincloth.
berselampit to wear a flat braid.
menyelampit to braid (hair). *~ ékor* to put one's tail between one's legs.
menyelampitkan *~ kain* to pass a skirt between one's thighs.
selampit II (*Mal*) storyteller.
selampuri *kain –* an Indian chintz.
Sélan → SAILAN.
selancak *burung –* a bird species, paddyfield pipit, *Anthus rufulus.*
selancang *burung –* pied triller, *Lalage nigra.*
selancar → LANCAR I.
berselancar 1 to windsurf. **2** to fling, pitch. **3** to surf (the web).
peselancar windsurfer.
Sélandia Baru New Zealand.
selang I 1 one after another/the other in regular order, by turns; turn about, alternate, occurring in turn; succeeding e.o.; one and then the other; at intervals. *buah –* fruits ripening in the interim. *pemilihan –* by-election. *Kainnya loréng, (–) mérah – putih.* The fabric was striped, alternately red and white. *– waktu* interval. *dengan – waktu* at intervals. *Meriam ditémbak –.– satu menit.* Guns were fired at intervals of one minute. *– sehari* a) every other/second day. b) one day later. *– sehari ia datang ke sini.* He comes here every other/second day. *– sehari Jumat* on alternate Fridays. *– seminggu* after a week, a week later. *– dua hari* a) every third day. b) after two days. c) two days ago. *– beberapa hari* after a couple of days. *– beberapa jam kemudian* some hours later. *– setengah jam* a) (the clock strikes) every half hour b) half an hour ago. *– setengah jam lamanya* every half hour. *belum – berapa lama ini* recently. *tidak – berapa lama* not long afterward. *– beberapa waktu yang lalu* some time ago. *– surap* (*Jv*) to misunderstand, misapprehend, misconstrue. **2** interval, throughout the entire time of; all through; → SEDANG I. *daftar ... yang dipegang – tahun 1949 di Morotai* the register of ... kept during the year of 1949 in Morotai. *Italia menjadi sekutu Jerman – perang dunia ke-2.* Italy was Germany's ally during World War II. **3** interval, gap. *Petani itu menanam pohon pisang dan pohon nenas sebagai tanaman –.* The farmers have planted banana and pineapple trees as an intercrop. *– seling* alternating. **(ber)selang-seling 1** in turn, alternatively, alternately; → SELAMENYELA. *Pelajaran berhitung diatur ~.* The mathematics lessons are arranged alternately (by turns). **2** uninterrupted, continuous, unbroken, unintermittent. *Dengan seketika itu juga ~ suara paluan gendang dan irama serunai memenuhi suasana.* At that very moment the uninterrupted sound of drumbeats and the rhythm of a bamboo flute filled the air. **menyelang-nyeling** to alternate s.t. (with s.t. else). **menyelang-nyelingi** to alternate with, vary with, punctuate by. *Tugas selaku anggota DPR hanyalah melakukan serangkaian rapat-rapat diselang-selingi dengan kunjungan kerja.* The work of DPR members is to hold a series of meetings alternating with work visits. **menyelang-nyeling(kan)** to alternate, vary.
berselang 1 with a break/interruption/interval. *hanya dua hari*

~ setelah ... only two days after ... *belum lama ~* not long ago. *tiada ~* always, ceaselessly. *Tiap-tiap hari dia mengantar(kan) susu kepada ibu-bapaknya dengan tidak pernah ~.* Every day he delivers milk to his parents without fail. *Ketiga peristiwa tersebut di atas terjadi ~ kira-kira tiap 10 menit.* The above-mentioned three events occurred at intervals of approximately 10 minutes. **2** every other (day, etc.); ... ago. *~ tiga hari* a) at three-day intervals. b) every fourth day; three days ago. **3** alternating. *Permata intan ~ dengan mirah.* A black jewel alternating with a ruby.

berselang-selang 1 in turns, changing, in succession. *~ hari* every other day. *duduk ~* to sit alternately a man between two women or a woman between two men. **2** with breaks/gaps/intervals/pauses. *tidak terus-menerus, melainkan ~* not uninterruptedly, but rather with pauses/breaks.

menyelang 1 to alternate, interpose, vary, do s.t. while still busy doing s.t. else. *Pekerjaannya tak lekas selesai, karena kerap kali diselang dengan pekerjaan lain.* His job was not finished quickly, because it is often alternated with another task. **2** to interrupt. *Sedang gurunya bercerita, ia ~, katanya ...* While his teacher was telling a story, he interrupted him, and said ... **3** to intervene, step in. *Ketika meréka bertengkar datanglah gurunya ~.* When they were quarrelling the teacher came and intervened. *~ kacang dengan jagung* to alternate peanuts with corn.

menyelangi to alternate/interrupt with. *Kawasan yang tipis pendudukan ini kadang-kadang diselangi oléh kampung-kampung nelayan.* This sparsely populated area sometimes alternates with fishing villages.

menyelang(-nyelang)kan to alternate, exchange, vary. *Wajib ia berpuasa enam puluh hari berturut-turut tidak boléh diselang-selangkan.* He is obliged to fast for sixty days in succession and is not allowed to do it at intervals.

selangan 1 interval. **2** s.t. that is/goes in between two other things, interim.

penyelang s.t. that alternates, alternative.

penyelangan interruption.

selang II (*M*) **(ber)selang-ténggang** to ask for help from e.o., help e.o., borrow from e.o.

menyelang to borrow (from). *~ uang* to borrow money (from).

menyelangi and **memperselangi** to loan (money) to.

menyelangkan and **memperselangkan** to lend, grant a loan of.

selang III (*Mal*) **berselang-pukang** (to run) helter-skelter.

selang IV place next to the staircase leading to the *serambi*, i.e., the place to wash one's feet and put on one's wooden clogs, shoes, etc. before entering the house.

selang V → SLANG I.

selangan – *batu* k.o. tree, *Shorea spp.*

selangat *ikan* – gizzard shad, *Anodontostoma/Dorosoma chacunda.* – *belau* k.o. fish, *D. nasus.*

selanggara → SELENGGARA.

selangit → LANGIT.

selangka *tulang* – collarbone.

selangkan → SEDANGKAN.

selangkang(an) (*J*) **1** groin, crotch (between the legs). *Bola meluncur masuk ke gawang léwat selangkangan kiper Jakarta itu.* The ball slid into the goal under the legs of Jakarta's goalie. **2** perineum. **3** basement (of a building).

selangkup menyelangkup to cover.

selantar-seluntur (*J*) to walk from one place to another like the proverbial cat on a hot tin roof.

selanting *burung* – long-billed partridge, *Rhizothera longirostris.*

selap unconscious, in a trance, possessed (by a spirit/sickness), hysterical (from being attacked by a spirit).

menyelap 1 to have fits (of fury). **2** to enter/penetrate into, take possession of (s.o. by an evil spirit). **3** to penetrate, infiltrate. *~ ke dalam organisasi geréja* to penetrate church organizations.

nyelap *~ nyelip* to slip in and out (of traffic, etc.).

menyelapi to enter into, take possession of.

menyelapkan to stir up, rouse. *~ marah* to arouse s.o.'s fury/rage.

terselap to be possessed (by an evil spirit).

keselapan possessed (by an evil spirit/fury/rage).

selapa a small container for keeping tobacco or betel-vine.

selapan I (*M*) eight; → DELAPAN.

selapan II (*Jv*) thirty-five. *– hari* thirty-five days.

selapanan *upacara ~* to celebrate a ceremony every 35 days. *~ désa* village meeting held every 35 days.

selapé (*mil acr*) [séléksi dan pelatihan pengemudi] selection and training of drivers.

selaput 1 film (over eye/cut/wound). **2** tarnish (on brass/silver). **3** membrane. **4** coat, coating. *– bening (mata)* cornea. *– biji* seed coat. *– dada* pleura. *– dara* hymen. *– gendang* tympanum. *– ikat* conjunctiva. *– jala* retina. *– jantung* pericardium. *– kegadisan* hymen. *– ketuban* amnion. *– lendir* mucus membrane. *– luka* thin skin that covers a wound when it begins to heal. *– mata* conjunctiva. *– mata keras* sclera. *– otak (keras)* dura mater (of the brain), cerebral membrane. *– otak lembut* pia mater (of the brain). *– otot* fascia. *– paru* pleurum. *– pelangi* iris (of the eye). *– pembuluh* (*med*) choroid. *– perut* peritoneum. *– putih* sclera. *– rahim* endometrium. *– renang* swimming web (of ducks). *– sawang* barrier membrane (in the brain). *– sega* membrane around the joints. *– tanduk* cornea. *– tulang* periosteum. *– urat* aponeurosis.

berselaput in/with a membrane, covered with a membrane.

menyelaputi to cover s.t. with a membrane, coat s.t.

selaputan 1 coating, casing. **2** lamination. *~ kartu mahasiswa* lamination of a university student's ID card.

selar I (*ikan* –) horse mackerel, *Caranx spp.* *– batang* k.o. fish, *Alepes kalla.* *– kuning* yellowstripe scad, *Selaroides leptolepis.* *– bentong* k.o. fish, big-eye scad, *Selar crumenophthalmus.*

selar II *tanda* – brand (on horses, etc.).

menyelar(kan) 1 to brand. **2** to cauterize, singe.

selar III menyelar to creep (of surface roots/some snakes). *– belar* → MEMBELAR.

selara I (*M*) thistledown, prickle, cilia, fine leaves on the leaves of some plants.

selara II *anak* – young of the *sembilang* fish.

selara III decayed leaves (of sugarcane: *daun – tebu*).

menyelara to decay.

selarak (*Jv*) wooden crossbar for fastening doors.

selaras → LARAS I.

selarung tracks made by large animals such as elephants, rhinos, etc.

Selasa (*A*) (*hari* –) Tuesday. *– Kelabu* Black Tuesday (May 12, 1998, when demonstrating Trisakti students were killed).

selasar 1 front verandah level with the floor of a house, gallery; → BERANDA, SERAMBI. **2** corridor.

selasih I (*Skr*) basil, *Ocimum spp. ayam* – chicken with black feathers, bones, and meat. *mabuk (bunga)* – drunk and weaving around. *– kemangi* holy basil, *O. sanctum.* *– putih* sweet basil, *O. basilicum.*

selasih II → TELUR *selasih.*

selat I 1 strait(s), narrows. **2** passage. *– Dardanélla* Dardanelles. *– Jabal-al-Tarik* Straits of Gibraltar. *– Hormuz* Strait of Hormuz. *– kantang* a strait which dries up at low tide. *– Sunda* Sunda Straits (between Java and Sumatra).

menyelat to sail through a strait(s).

selat II (*M*) interstice, crevice.

menyelat to squeeze (in).

menyelatkan to squeeze s.t. in, insert s.t., thrust s.t. in between.

terselat inserted, squeezed/jammed between.

penyelat s.t. inserted/squeezed in.

selatan south. *– barat daya* south-southwest, SSW. *– daya* south-southwest, SSW. *– menenggara/tenggara* south-southeast, SSE.

menyelatan to go south, southing.

menyelatani to cross going southward.

menyelatankan to move s.t. to the South, divert in a southerly direction.

terselatan most southerly, southernmost.

selaturahim → SILATURAHIM, SILATURAHMI.

selawat (*A pl* of *salat*) prayers to invoke God's blessing; → SALAWAT. *uang* – fee given to the prayer leader for his leading the prayers during a *selawatan. membaca* – to hold a prayer service. *– badar* a song to praise the Prophet Muhammad after the victory in the battle of Badar. *– jawi* this song in Javanese.

berselawat to hold a prayer service.

selawatan singing informally to the accompaniment of tambourines or tomtoms.

selawé (*Jv*) twenty-five. – *rénténg* (*coq*) reference to the freight train which consists of a long line of vans running between Jakarta and Surabaya.

selawéan the twenty-fifth. *malem* ~ the 25th of Ramadan.

selayak *burung* – k.o. bird, Raffles malkoha, *Phaenicophaeus chlorophaeus*.

selayang Japanese shad, *Decapterus maruadsi*.

selayang-seloyong (*J*) staggering; → SELOYONG.

selayun scarecrow, made from a taut piece of rope from which hang leaves/pieces of cloth, etc. to drive away birds, etc.

selayur *ikan* – hairtail or scabbard fish, *Trichiurus haumela/savala*.

selayut → SELAYUN.

Séldhi in Old Javanese annals the corruption of the Dutch name, van IJsseldijk. Wouter Hendrik van IJsseldijk was the director-general of Daendels's Council.

selé (*D*) jam, jelly; → SELAI. *kué(h)* – *gulung* jelly roll. – *nanas* pineapple jam.

selebaran *surat* – leaflet.

selébor → SLÉBOR I.

sélebran (*D*) celebrant.

sélébriti (*E*) celebrity.

sélébritis (*E*) *pl* celebrities.

selebu *laut* – open sea, high seas, distant hazy ocean.

selédér (*J/Jv*) **1** lazy-bones, sluggish person. **2** inattentive.

  berséléder to be lazy.

  keseléderan sluggishness.

selédri and **selédéri** (*D*) celery; *Apium graveolens*.

seledup → SELUDUP I.

seleguri a yellow-flowered mallow used in magic, *Clerodendron spp.*, *Sida rhombifolia*.

selek (*J*) → SELAK III.

selékéh stain, spot, dirt, mark, smudge, smear.

  berselékéh stained, dirty, smeary.

  menyelékéh to smear, stain.

  menyelékéhi to stain s.t.

séléknas [séléksi-nasional] national selection.

selékoh (*Mal*) **1** bend (in a road). **2** salient angle. – *kota* salient, bastion.

  berselékoh winding.

  menyelékoh to turn off.

selékor *ikan* – horse mackerel, silver pomfret, torpedo scad (?), *Caranx rottleri*.

séléksi (*D*) selection.

  menyéléksi to select. *Majelis hakim berwenang untuk* ~ *saksi yang akan didengar*. The judges council has authority to select the witnesses to be heard.

  terséléksi selected. *lagu-lagu yang* ~ selected songs.

  penyéléksi selecting, s.o. who selects.

  penyéléksian selecting.

séléktif (*D*) selective.

  keséléktifan selectiveness.

séléktir (*D*) **menyéléktir** to select.

séléktivitas (*D*) selectiveness.

seléler berseléléran **1** to trickle (of blood/sap/tears/water); → LÉLÉR I. **2** to drip all over. *makan* ~ to eat in a sloppy way so that the food drops all over.

seléma → SELESMA.

selembada → SELEMPADA.

selembana menyelembana to lie head to wind (of ships in a storm), ride out a storm.

selembubu *angin* – whirlwind; → HALIMBUBU.

selempada *semut* – a large biting ant (red- or black-colored).

selempang I (*J*) anxious, worried.

  menyelempangkan to worry about s.t.

selempang II (*ob*) **terselempang** fall down with legs spread apart.

selémpang 1 shoulder belt, bandoleer, sash. – *peluru di dada* bullet bandoleer. **2** crosswise.

  berselémpang with/to wear a sash.

  berselémpangkan to wear ... as a sash.

menyelémpang(kan) to wear s.t. over one shoulder and under the other.

selempit (*Jv*) **nyelempit** ~ *di antara* ... to be tucked in among. *Lokasinya kok* ~ *di dalam kompléks perumahan*. It's tucked in the housing complex.

  menyelempitkan to slip/tuck s.t. in.

  keselempit gotten mixed in with and hidden among other things.

selempukau *burung* – oriole, *Ariolus sp.*

selempuri → SELAMPURI.

selenat-selenét (*J*) to have a stinging pain.

seléndang a scarf-like batik women's garment worn over one shoulder for decoration, carrying infants, small baskets, dancing, etc. – *mayang* k.o. banana cake.

  berseléndang and **menyeléndang** to wear a *seléndang*.

  menyeléndangi to cover s.t. with a *seléndang*.

  menyeléndangkan and **memperseléndang(kan)** to use s.t. as a *seléndang*.

seléndér (*D*) → SILINDER.

seléndro (*Jv*) a five-tone scale system in Javanese *gamelan* music.

selengat k.o. scad, *Dorosoma chacunda*.

selénger (*D*) handle, crank.

selenggara menyelenggarakan [and **nyelenggarain** (*J coq*)] **1** to manage, organize, put on, hold, convene. *Beberapa perguruan tinggi di Australia Barat yaitu Univérsitas Murdoch dan Univérsitas Curtin telah* ~ *kursus Bahasa Indonésia untuk memenuhi keinginan masyarakat*. Some higher educational institutions in Western Australia, Murdoch and Curtin Universities, have organized Indonesian language courses in compliance with the desires of the community. *Tim itu akan dibentuk untuk* ~ *paméran itu*. The team will be set up to manage the exhibition. **2** to run. *Siapa yang sesungguhnya* ~ *pemerintahan di negara itu?* Who's really running things in that country? **3** to take care of, maintain (records, etc.). *Sawahnya diselenggarakannya dengan baik*. He takes good care of his rice fields. *Pembukuan perusahaan diselenggarakan dalam satuan Rupiah*. The company's accounting records are maintained in rupiahs. **4** to perform, undertake, conduct (an activity), fulfill (a function), exercise (control), provide (a service), institute (a program), say (mass in church), do s.t. ~ *kegiatan usaha* to do business.

terselenggara managed, run, taken care of, maintained, undertaken.

selenggaraan run, organized, managed.

penyelenggara 1 organizer, manager, producer (of a show). ~ *negara* administrator of the state, state official. ~ *perjalanan* tour operator. ~ *pembubaran* liquidator. ~ *perumahan* developer. **2** provider. ~ *jasa Internét* Internet Service Provider, ISP.

penyelenggaraan 1 organization, organizing, managing, holding, convening, running, exercising, setting up, implementing. ~ *kongrés bahasa Indonésia* organizing an Indonesian language congress. **2** providing (services).

seléngkang berseléngkangan (*pl subj*) crisscross.

  menyeléngkang to cross one's legs with one stuck out (a rude way to sit).

seléngkoh → SELÉKOH.

sélénium (*D*) selenium.

selentang → SELENTING. – *selenting* rumors.

selentik (*Jv*) **menyelentik 1** to snap s.t. with the finger by bending the fingernail against thumb and then releasing it suddenly. *Kalau nakal lalu diselentik kupingnya*. When he's bad, he gets a finger snap on the ear. **2** to snap one's fingers; to rap s.o. over the knuckles.

selenting (*Jv*) and **selentingan** (*J*) rumors, gossip, tittle-tattle.

  menyelentingkan to spread (rumors).

seléo → KESELÉO.

selép → SLÉP.

selepa(h) metallic box for tobacco or cigarettes, made in all shapes and designs.

selépang → SELÉMPANG.

selépar → SELIPAR.

selepat berselepat smeared.

selépé (*Jv*) a gold or silver waist buckle.

seléper (*D*) slipper.

selepét (*J*) **menyelepétkan** to shoot at with a slingshot.
 selepétan slingshot.
selepi a small *selepa*.
selepuh dust.
 berselepuh dusty.
seléra I 1 appetite. *membangkit* – to whet the appetite. *buruk* – greedy, covetous. *patah* – a) without appetite. b) anorexia. *patah* – *banyak makan* not having an appetite but eating out of habit. *titik air* – mouthwatering. **2** taste. *soal* – *mémang tidak dapat dipertengkarkan* there is no accounting for tastes. *masih pahit terasa* –*ku* I don't feel well. *sesuai dengan* – *saya* to my taste. **3** any strong desire or craving. *Acara TV tidak dapat memenuhi* – *para pirsawan*. TV programs cannot satisfy the entire TV audience. – *buruk* bad taste. – *tajam* great appetite.
 berseléra 1 with an appetite. *seorang yang* ~ *tinggi* a gourmet. **2** with … taste. ~ *tinggi* with a taste for luxury.
 terseléra 1 to desire, have a craving for (food, etc.). **2** zestful. **3** appetizing. **4** eager.
seléra II (*Skr cla*) → SELIRA.
selérak berselérak scattered all over (of clothes/rocks, etc.); → SÉRAK.
 menyelérakkan to scatter, strew.
selérang (*M*) **1** hard skin (on feet of man or animal). **2** outer skin. *kain* – a skirt woven in one broad piece.
selérét (*ob*) → LÉRÉT I. *rumah* – a long narrow house.
selésa (*Mal*) **1** space, opportunity. **2** spacious, wide; with a lot of space. **3** comfortable, pleasing, agreeable.
 berselésa to have the opportunity/time/chance. *tidak* ~ a) cramped, packed, crowded. b) not free, engaged (in work). c) to have no chance.
 keselésaan comfort, ease, pleasure.
selesai 1 finished, completed. *Cina ingin menonjolkan kepada dunia umum, bahwa proyék yang diberikan itu lebih cepat* –*nya*. China wanted to show the world at large that the projects handed over were completed more quickly. *belum* – unfinished. **2** settled, paid off (of debts). *Hutangnya sudah* –. His debts were paid off. **3** settled, come to an agreement/conclusion. *Sudah lama tawar-menawar belum* – *juga*. The bargaining went on for a long time and didn't reach a conclusion. **4** conclusion, end. *Dibacanya roman itu sampai* –. He read the novel to the end. **5** (*M*) neat, not tangled (of hair). *Rambutnya* – *diandam*. His hair was neat.
 seselesai upon completion, after finishing.
 menyelesaikan [and **nyelesaiin** (*J coq*)] **1** to complete, finish, conclude, bring to an end. *Selesaikan kalimat-kalimat di bawah ini*. Complete the sentences below. *Rapat ini sedapat-dapatnya akan diselesaikan sebelum tengah malam*. This meeting will conclude before midnight if possible. ~ *bertahap* to phase out. **2** to settle, pay off (debts). *Dia dipanggil ke kantor bank untuk* ~ *hutang piutang almarhum ayahnya*. He was summoned to the bank to pay off his late father's debts. ~ *segala rékening* to pay off all bills. ~ *tagihan* to settle one's bill. ~ *tunggakan* to pay off one's arrears. **3** to decide, resolve, settle. *Perkara itu tidak dapat diselesaikan sekarang*. That case cannot be decided now. **4** to arrange, put in order, make (the bed), comb (one's hair). ~ *tempat tidur* to make the bed. ~ *rambut yang kusut* to comb one's tangled hair. **5** to solve, resolve (a problem). *Ini pendekatan terbaik untuk* ~ *masalah itu*. This is the best approach to solving the problem.
 terselesaikan settled, finished, completed, resolved. *perkara-perkara yang belum* ~ unsettled/pending/outstanding lawsuits.
 keselesaian solution, decision.
 penyelesai settler, resolver; settling, liquidation. *juru* ~ liquidator. *tim* ~ settlement team. ~ *pertikaian* arbiter.
 penyelesaian settlement, resolution, solution, accomplishment, completion. *dalam* ~ in the process of completion, in progress. ~ *mata uang* currency readjustment. ~ *terakhir* finishing touch. ~ *tuntas* durable solution. ~ *perselisihan* resolution of disputes.
selesma and **selésma** (*Skr*) **1** head cold which causes a running nose. **2**a) nasal mucus, snot. b) to blow one's nose. *demam* – influenza.

seletuk (*J*) → CELETUK. **menyeletuk** [and **nyeletuk** (*coq*)] to interrupt.
seléwéng menyeléwéng [and **nyeléwéng** (*coq*)] **1** to deviate (from the right track). **2** to be on the wrong path, act deceitfully, be corrupt, practice fraud. **3** to carry on with another (wo)man, cheat (on one's spouse), be unfaithful (to one's spouse), commit adultery.
 menyeléwéngkan to make fraudulent use of, embezzle (money). *Ada indikasi kolusi untuk* ~ *fasilitas ékspor*. There are signs of collusion to make fraudulent use of export facilities.
 penyeléwéng s.o. who commits fraud, corrupt person.
 penyeléwéngan 1 deviation. **2** irregularity, fraud, corruption, deception. *kasus* ~ *dan penyimpangan* (*euph*) a case of corruption.
sélf-koréksi (*D*) self-correction.
seli selang-seli → SELANG I.
selia I menyelia (*mostly Mal*) **1** to supervise, manage. **2** to inspect, examine, investigate.
 penyelia 1 supervisor, manager. **2** inspector, examiner, investigator. ~ *penjualan* sales supervisor.
 penyeliaan 1 supervision, management. **2** inspection, examination, investigation.
selia II (*cla*) neatly, nicely.
seliak relating to the belly.
seliap *ikan* – marine horse mackerel, *Chorinemus spp*.
sélibat (*D*) celibate.
 bersélibat to be celibate.
selibu (*M*) rice stalks that grow after harvest. *padi* – late rice.
selibut (*ob*) **berselibut** to cause an uproar, make trouble.
selidik 1 exact, accurate, strict. **2** attentive. *kurang* – inattentive, careless.
 menyelidik and **menyelidiki** [and **nyelidikin** (*J coq*)] **1** to investigate, examine, look into. *Benar tidaknya kabar itu sedang diselidiki*. The truth of the news is being investigated. *sedang diselidiki* under investigation. **2** to reconnoiter, spy on. *Beberapa anasir asing* ~ *kekuatan dan kemampuan tentara kita*. Several foreign elements spied on the strength and capability of our army. **3** to search, frisk (a suspect). *Seluruh badannya diselidiki oléh pegawai pabéan*. His entire body was frisked by a customs officer. **4** to study, do (scientific) research on. *Bertahun-tahun lamanya ia menyelidik bahasa dan adat istiadat suku Toraja*. For years he studied the language and customs and traditions of the Toraja people.
 terselidiki investigated.
 selidikan investigation.
 penyelidik 1 investigator, researcher. *bagian* ~ intelligence service. *panitia* ~ inquiry committee. **2** examiner. **3** spy, scout.
 penyelidikan 1 research. ~ *ilmiah* scientific research. **2** inquiry, investigation, interrogation. *Perkara itu masih dalam* ~. The case is still under investigation. **3** surveillance.
seligi I wooden javelin, sharpened bamboo or *nibung* palm. – *tajam bertimbal tak ujung pangkat mengena* a) double-edged javelin. b) s.o. who wears two hats. c) to double dip, get income from both sides/parties.
 menyeligi to hurl/throw a javelin.
seligi II (*Jv*) k.o. plant, *Phyllanthus buxifolius*.
seligit and **seligut** confused mass movement (of bats/crowds).
 menyeligit to swarm.
selikur I twenty-one; → LIKUR.
selikur II → SELÉKOR.
selilit (*Jv*) toothpick.
selimang various species of freshwater fish. *ikan* – *batu* a small carp, *Crossocheilus oblongus*.
selimbu → SELIBU.
selimpang I menyelimpang to veer off, diverge from the right path.
selimpang II → SELÉMPANG.
selimpat I mat-making and wickerwork.
selimpat II *ular* – k.o. sea snake with a flat head.
selimpat III (*J*) – *selimput* to sneak around/away to avoid being seen or heard.
 berselimpatan (*pl subj*) to sneak around/away.
 menyelimpat 1 to avoid, shun (s.o.), stay away from. **2** to hide, conceal o.s.

selimpat IV arabesqued.
   berselimpat arabesqued.
selimpuh → SIMPUH I.
selimput → SELIMPAT III.
selimut 1 blanket. **2** cover, camouflage. *musuh dalam* - a wolf in sheep's clothing. - *hidup* a girl to sleep with, *usu* a prostitute.
   berselimut 1 with/to have a blanket. **2** to be covered in. *gunung ~ és abadi* eternally ice-capped mountains. **3** to hide (behind s.t.).
   berselimutkan wrapped/enveloped in. *Kapan kita berhenti bertugas adalah kalau kita sudah ~ tanah.* When we stop accomplishing our task is when we lie under the ground.
   menyelimut to cover.
   menyelimuti 1 to cover, envelope. *Puncak gunung itu diselimuti salju.* The mountain peak as enveloped with snow. **2** to cover up, hide. *Kata yang manis itu diselimuti maksudnya.* Sweet words hid his true purpose.
   menyelimutkan 1 to cover with, use s.t. as a blanket. **2** to shelter o.s. behind, conceal o.s.
   memperselimut to use s.t. as a cover.
   terselimuti blanketed. *Puncaknya ~ kabut.* The peak was blanketed with mist.
   penyelimut s.t. that covers. *kain ~ badan* a cloth for covering one's body.
   penyelimutan 1 covering. **2** camouflaging. *~ data* window-dressing.
selinap I - *sana* - *sini* sneak around in all directions.
   menyelinap [and **nyelinap** (*coq*)] **1** to sneak (into). *~ masuk/ke dalam* to slip/steal in(to). *Dia ~ di antara orang banyak.* He slipped away into the general public. **2** to come over one. *~ [ke (dalam) hati]* (a desire) came over him. **3** to penetrate (of cold, to the bone) *Hawa yang sejuk itu ~ ke dalam tubuh.* The chilly air penetrated to the bone. *~ ke dalam kalbunya/hati sanubarinya.* (My words) penetrated his brain. **4** to escape, sneak off, slip away. *Ular ~ ke dalam rumput* the snake escaped/slipped away into the grass. **5** to hide/conceal o.s., avoid. *Untung meréka itu dapat ~ dari mata polisi.* Fortunately they could avoid the watchful eye of the police.
   menyelinapi to slip/sneak into.
   menyelinapkan 1 to allow to slip in secretly. **2** to put/tuck away.
   terselinap penetrated secretly/surreptitiously.
   penyelinap infiltrator.
   penyelinapan infiltration.
selinap II menyelinap to gut, clean (fish/chicken).
selindit → SERINDIT.
selindung berselindung 1 to hide/conceal o.s. **2** to play hide-and-go-seek.
seling I interval, variety; → SELANG I.
   berseling to alternate, succeed e.o. in turn; to vary. *nyanyian yang ~ dengan tari-tarian* songs alternating with dances. *~ ganti* alternate, alternating.
   menyeling to alternate, vary. *Nyanyian itu diseling dengan tari-tarian* the songs alternated with dances.
   menyelingi to interrupt, alternate. *Mémang bukan Dr. Haryono Suyono, kalau bicaranya yang mengalir tanpa henti dan penuh semangat itu tidak diselingi tawa terbahak.* In fact, it wouldn't be Dr. Haryono Suyono, if his continuous and spirited speech did not alternate with roars of laughter.
   menyelingkan to put s.t. in between.
   terseling(i) varied, intermixed.
   selingan alternation, variation, variety. *kerja ~* alternate job. **2** intermezzo, entr'acte, interval, interlude. *lagu-lagu ~* musical interlude.
   penyeling s.t. that serves as a change, s.t. that alternates with s.t. else. *Sebagai ~, aku memutuskan untuk mencari banyak kesibukan.* For a change, I've made up my mind to look for a lot of activities.
seling II earthenware, crockery, pottery.
seling III (*D*) sling (to lift cargo into a ship).
seling IV → SALING.
selingar menyelingar dumbfounded.
selingkar → LINGKAR.
selingkit (*M*) **berselingkit** packed together (of crowds).

menyelingkit to make a place for o.s. (forcibly), force one's way into.
selingkuh (*Jv*) **1** dishonest, insidious, insincere, unreliable, surreptitious, secret. **2** embezzlement, defalcation, misappropriation. **3** converted fraudulently (to one's own use), misappropriated, embezzled. *berbuat* - to act dishonestly. *- dagang* insider trading. **4** cheating (on one's spouse), to have an affair (with s.o. not one's spouse).
   berselingkuh 1 to act dishonestly, act corruptly. **2** to cheat on one's spouse.
   menyelingkuhi to avoid (paying taxes).
   menyelingkuhkan to embezzle (money), misappropriate (funds), practice fraud.
   selingkuhan 1 (to have an) affair (with s.o. who is not one's spouse or boy/girlfriend). **2** person with whom one cheats on one's spouse or boy/girlfriend, the other man/woman.
   penyelingkuh dishonest person.
   perselingkuhan 1 fraud, deception. *~ politik* political deception. **2** cheating (on one's spouse).
selingkung → LINGKUNG.
selingkup → LINGKUP I. **menyelingkup(i)** to cover (up, in).
selinting → LINTING I.
selip I menyelip [and **nyelip** (*coq*)] **1** to insert, slide/slip in (of a knife into a slit/a page into a book/carbon paper under another paper, etc.). *~ surat ke dalam buku* to insert a letter into a book. *rasa ragu ~ ke dalam dadanya* hesitation slipped into him. *Tempat duduk pilih sendiri, ingin yang nyelip atau di tengah, terserah selera masing-masing.* You have to choose your own seat, whether you want to sit in a booth or at a table, according to your individual preference. *masih nyelip di ketiak ...* still under the jurisdiction of ... . **2** to slip (into). *Léo ~ di antara tower dan tiang bendéra di Lanud Adisutjipto.* Leo slipped in among the towers and flagpoles at Adisutjipto Airport.
   menyelipi to insert/attach with. *berita yang diselipi dengan koméntar* a news item with commentaries inserted into it.
   menyelipkan [and **nyelipin** (*J coq*)] to insert/slip s.t. between/into. *Dompétnya usu biasanya diselipkan di setagénnya tertinggal di rumah.* The purse which she *usu* slips into her sash she had forgotten (inadvertently) at home. *Ia baru meninggalkan kamar setelah lembaran lima rupee diselipkan ke tangannya.* He didn't leave the room until I had put a(n Indian) five-rupee bill into his hand.
   terselip [and **keselip** (*coq*)] slipped/squeezed (between), slipped (into). *Rumah meréka ~ di antara toko-toko.* Their house was squeezed between shops.
   selipan (*geol*) interbed.
   penyelipan slipping/inserting s.t. in, implanting.
selip II 1 to skid (of a car, etc.). *Bila hujan mobil mudah dapat -.* When it rains cars can easily skid. **2** (*coq*) to miss e.o.
   terselip 1 skidded (of a car, etc.). **2** let slip. *~ keluar dari mulut* said s.t. inadvertently.
selip III (*ob*) *mesin* - grinding machine.
   menyelip to grind.
selipar (*E*) slipper.
seliput I folder; → LIPUT.
seliput II berseliput full of.
   menyeliputi to fill, cover.
selir I (*Jv*) common-law wife, concubine, mistress. *- kinasih* favorite mistress. *- sampingan* secondary mistress.
   memperselirkan to take s.o. as a concubine.
   perseliran concubinage.
selir II (*onom*) rustling (of leaves).
   berselir and **menyelir** to rustle (of leaves).
selir III 1 veil. **2** covering. *- jendéla/pintu* window/door curtain.
selira (*Skr cla*) body; → SELÉRA II.
selirak berselirak scattered (everywhere); → SÉRAK.
selirang single/unpaired structure.
selirat berselirat tangled, confused, mixed up, reticulate (of nets/thread).
seliri (*A*) couch.
selisih 1 difference, disparity, differential. *dilaksanakan dengan jarak - 10 menit* to be done at 10-minute intervals. **2** difference

of opinion, quarrel, dispute. *silang* – a) to cross e.o. b) to differ in opinion. **3** space of (time). *dalam – waktu satu hari* in the space of one day. **4** variance. – *basah* to cruise (of ships). – *kata* quarrel. – *kurs* foreign exchange difference. – *lebih* excess. – *pendapat* difference of opinion. – *umur/usia* difference in age, age difference. – *paham* difference in understanding s.t. **berselisih paham** to have a different understanding of s.t. – *waktu* difference in time, space of time.

berselisih 1 to differ (in opinion), diverge, be different from e.o. ~ *pendapat* to disagree, differ in opinion. *Ada kalanya mémang kita ~ pendapat untuk suatu hal.* Naturally, we sometimes disagree about a case. ~ *setengah jam* with a half-hour difference. *si bungsu yang ~ umur/usia jauh dengan kakak-kakaknya* the youngest who differs very much in age from his older siblings. ~ *jalan/laku/lalu* to pass by e.o without meeting, cross (of letters). *Surat Tuan ~ jalan dengan surat saya.* Your letter crossed mine. ~ *semut* to have different opinions but not leading to a problem. **2** to quarrel, have a dispute. **3** to cross (by e.o. without meeting, of letters/people).

menyelisihi to quarrel with, take issue with.

menyelisihkan and **memperselisihkan** to disagree about/over. *Meréka memperselisihkan arti kata itu.* They disagreed about the meaning of that word.

perselisihan 1 difference. **2** dispute, quarrel, disagreement.

selisik I → SELIDIK.

selisik II menyelisik 1 delouse, debug (a computer program). *Dia ~ rambut anaknya.* She deloused her child's hair. **2** to investigate, look into. ~ *kitab-kitab klasik* to look into classic books.

penyelisikan delousing, debugging.

selisip → SELIP I. **menyelisip** to slip in.

menyelisipkan to insert s.t.

selisir I menyelisir to go along the side/edge of s.t., follow along. ~ *pantai* to sail along the coast.

selisir II k.o. quatrain set to music.

selit – *belit* complicated, difficult, hard. – *sepit* tight spot. **berselit-belit/-sepit** complicated; winding. *pandai ~ (ob)* good at wriggling out of difficulties.

berselit 1 inserted, slipped in. **2** enclosed.

berselit-selit complicated.

menyelit 1 to insert, slip in. *téknologi DNA untuk ~ ségmén gén virus dalam sél* the DNA technology for inserting a virus gene into a cell. **2** to be inserted (in). *Tangan kiriku terus menjalar ~ antara tilam dan bahagian depan tubuhnya.* My left hand crept between the mattress and the front part of his body.

menyelit-nyelit to push one's way (in), squeeze (through).

menyelitkan to stick/insert s.t. (between two things).

terselit(kan) jammed in between two surfaces, wedged in.

penyelitan interpolation, insertion.

seliu (*ob*) → KESELÉO.

seliwar → SELIWER.

seliwer berseliwer to crisscross.

(ber)seliweran 1 to lounge/loiter about, cruise around (of many cars, etc.), crisscross. **2** to come and go. *Orang berseliweran di jalan.* People are cruising around the streets. **3** to whistle about (of bullets). *Peluru-peluru seliweran sekeliling.* Bullets were whistling all around.

seliweran *pating* ~ and **seliwar-seliwer** cruising around (of many cars, etc.).

sélo (*D*) (violon)cello. *pemain* – (violon)cellist.

selobok collide with, meet, encounter; → SOBOK I.

selodang → SELUDANG.

selodok menyelodok to push one's way through using one's hands, crawl (into).

sélofan (*D*) cellophane.

selogan → SLOGAN.

seloka (*Skr*) **1** stanza, quatrain of four rhyming lines. **2** aphorism. **3** simile, metaphor.

berseloka 1 to recite a *seloka*. **2** to compose a *seloka*.

sélokan (*J*) **1** gutter, drain, ditch, chute, trench. **2** sewer; → PARIT I, SÉROKAN.

persélokan sewage system.

selokarang skin disease of horses and cattle, saccharomycosis.

seloki (*D*) **1** (small) draft, sip, swallow. **2** (small) glass; shot (of Dutch gin).

selom → SELUM.

selomor (*M*) slough (of a snake).

selomot (*J*) **menyelomot** to fool, trick, hoodwink.

menyelomoti 1 to hold a flame to s.t. *Orang itu dianiaya dengan diselomoti puntung rokok.* That man was tortured by holding a (burning) cigarette butt against him. **2** to pull one's leg, fool s.o., hoodwink.

terselomot [and **keselomot** (*coq*)] come into contact with a burning object unintentionally, get burned. *Tangannya ~ sampai hangus.* His hand came into contact with fire and was singed.

selomotan burn marks, burns. *Di sekujur tubuhnya ditemukan ~ rokok.* Cigarette burns were found all over his body.

selompong (in Ujungpandang) deck (on a traditional boat).

selomprét I (*D*) trumpet, horn.

menyelomprétkan to trumpet s.t., propagandize for s.t.

selomprét II (*J*) → SOMPRÉT.

selonang-selonong (*Jv*) moving precipitously; shooting forward. *Meréka terpaksa berlomba menggaruk penumpang, ngetém seénaknya, – di jalan raya.* They (the drivers and conductors of the buses) were forced to compete in scooping up passengers, waiting for passengers as they felt like, and moving precipitously on the highways.

Sélong I Ceylon; → LANGKAPURA, SRILANGKA.

sélong II menyélong to deport, expel from a country (read: Indonesia) to, formerly Ceylon, now any country. *Dr. Tjipto yang disélong ke Néderland* Dr. Tjipto, who was deported to the Netherlands.

selongkang bad (of a coin), debased (of metal).

selongkar → BONGKAR I. **menyelongkar 1** to rummage (in/about), ransack. **2** to turn over, put in disorder, throw/jumble together. **3** to examine s.t. carefully.

selongsong (*J*) **1** wrapper, case, casing, cover(ing), sleeve, sheath. **2** cartridge. **3** muzzle (for dogs); → BERONGSONG. – *kosong* blank cartridge. – *pancing* (*petro*) overshot. – *peluru* cartridge case.

menyelongsong(i) to envelop, wrap around, put in a (cartridge) case.

selonjor with one's legs stretched out before one.

berselonjor ~ *kaki* (to sit on the ground) with one's legs stretched out.

berselonjoran (*pl subj*) to sit around in a relaxed way.

selonong (*J/Jv*) to emerge/crop up suddenly. – *boy* offhand, extemporaneous, ad-lib. *Pengajuan calon Gubernur kali ini adalah Badah Musyawarah Betawi, maka harus dilakukan melalui musyawarah, tidak – boy begitu saja.* Submitting a candidate for the Governor this time is the Badah Musyawarah Betawi, so it has to be done by mutual agreement, not just offhandedly.

menyelonong 1 to emerge/turn up suddenly, enter (a room, etc.) without greeting or asking for permission. *Dia ~ dan duduk dekat Pak Camat.* Without any greeting, he came in and sat down next to the district head. **2** [and **nyelonong** (*coq*)] to enter (the wrong street, etc.) (all of a sudden); to go astray, lose one's way; to shoot forward, swerve, make a sudden movement. *Mobilnya ~ masuk kali.* All of a sudden his car rolled into the river.

menyelonongkan ~ *tangan* to interfere, stick one's hand (into).

selop I (*D*) slipper, mule; → SELIPAR. *sepatu* – pumps.

selop II → SLOF II.

sélopan → SÉLOFAN.

seloputu spotted wood owl, *Strix seloputo*.

seloroh 1 funny, amusing. **2** joke, jest, banter.

berseloroh to jest, joke, crack jokes.

memperselorohkan to make s.o. into a laughingstock.

selosoh → SELUSUH.

selot (*D*) lock. – *gantung* padlock; → GEMBOK.

menyelot to lock (a door, etc.).

sélotip (*E*) cellophane tape.

seloyak torn; → KOYAK, SOYAK II.

seloyong (*Jv*) **berseloyongan** to stagger, totter.

seloyongan staggering.

Sélsius Celsius.

sélter (E) shelter. – *bus* bus; → STOP.

seluang *ikan* – small carp, *esp Rasbora elegans. tak sungguh – me- laut* "small carp only pretend to go to sea," be it ever so humble there's no place like home.

seluar (*Pers*) trousers. – *Acéh* medium-length trousers. – *cina* long loose-fitting trousers. – *dalam/katok* underpants, panties. – *le- mang* tight trousers. – *pandak* short pants. – *sampak* short, tight Buginese trousers used for working in water.

berseluar 1 to wear trousers. **2** with trousers.

selubung 1 cover, veil, shawl. *membuka* – to unveil (a monument, etc.). **2** wrapper, envelopment, envelope. **3** case, casing. – *anak* caul, amnion.

berselubung 1 to veil o.s., cover o.s. up. *Dilihatnya seorang ~ kain putih.* He saw s.o. veil himself in a white cloth. **2** with a casing, cased, sheathed.

menyelubung 1 to envelop/wrap around with, cover up s.t., tuck in (a child in bed). **2** to cover with a veil, conceal. *Kedér- mawaannya itu tidak lain untuk ~ maksudnya yang buruk.* His charity was only to conceal his bad intentions.

menyelubungi to cover, encase. *Patung itu diselubungi dengan kain ungu.* The statue was covered in a purple cloth.

menyelubungkan to use as a cloak, cover over, hide, conceal.

terselubung disguised, hidden. *tempat-tempat ~ seperti kantor niaga* disguised facilities such as business offices. *membeli de- ngan cara ~* (a tactic to track narcotic traffickers) undercover buy. *~ kerahasiaan* shrouded in secrecy. *Penyebaran ranjau di Nikaragua adalah operasi ~ CIA.* The mining of Nicaragua was a CIA covert operation. **keterselubungan** dishonesty.

selubungan veil, covering, wrapping.

penyelubung s.t. that covers. *warna ~* protective coloration.

penyelubungan covering, hiding, camouflage.

seludang 1 sheath of the palm blossom, spathe. **2** covered racing skiff (shaped like a *seludang*). *seperti – menolak mayang* to re- veal the (hidden) truth/beauty behind s.t. – *pinang* k.o. plant, *Peliosanthes albida.*

seludu *ikan* – various species of catfish, *Arius macronotacanthu/ macronotacanthus, Silurus maculatus.*

seluduk menyeluduk to crawl crouching (under a house/forest trees). *~ sama bungkuk, melompat sama patah* friends through thick and thin.

seludup I menyeludup to crawl quietly (under/into).

seludup II → SELUNDUP.

selui *burung* – quail; → PUYUH.

seluk I menyeluk to feel/grope/fumble (for), put/stick (one's hand) in a hole or hollow, stick one's finger in (one's nose, etc.). *~ saku* to put one's hand into one's pocket to get s.t.

seluk II twist, coil, bend, turn, curve (in a line). – *beluk* a) particu- lars, details, the ins and outs. b) complications. c) (also – *jum- bai*) relations. **berseluk-beluk 1** complicated, intricate. *masalah yang ~ tidak keruan* an extremely complicated prob- lem. **2** to have relations with, still family of. *Meréka itu ~ karena sekampung.* They are still family because they are of the same village. *~ semeluk* winding, twisting.

berseluk winding, twisting; to be interlaced/intertwined.

menyelukkan to wind/twist s.t. (around s.t.).

memperselukkan to use s.t. which is wound/twisted).

selukat (*Jv*) a small *saron* in the *gamelan.*

menyelukat to play that instrument.

selukung a large shield to protect the whole body; → PERISAI.

sélulér (E) cellular. *télepon* – cellular phone.

séluloid (D/E) **1** celluloid. **2** film.

sélulosa (D) cellulose.

selulup (*Jv*) **berselulup** to plunge/dive into.

menyelulupi to plunge/dive into.

selulur terselulur slipped, slid; → LULUR I.

selum water parsley, *Oenanthe javanica*; → PIOPO.

selumar *pohon* – various species of trees, *Jackia ornata, Mussaen- dopsis beccariana.*

selumbar 1 splinter (of wood). **2** shard (of glass).

selumbari (*M*) day before yesterday.

selumbat (*J/Jv*) tool for husking coconuts.

selumput touchy, easily offended.

selumu (*M*) **berselumu 1** dirty. **2** frayed at the edge.

selumur slough, cast-off snakeskin.

menyelumur to slough.

selundap-selundup (various) acts of smuggling, contraband trades. – *dari Singapura léwat Halim* smuggling from Singapore via Halim.

selundat *ikan* – a marine fish.

selundup → SELUDUP. **menyelundup** [and **nyelundup** (*coq*)] **1** to dive/duck away, creep/hide away. *Anak itu ~ ke bawah kolong tempat tidur.* The child crept (into the space) under the bed. **2** to dive (of aircraft). *Pesawat pemburu itu ~ sambil memuntah- kan peluru.* The fighter plane dived while spewing bullets. **3** to infiltrate. *Satu kompi dapat ~ pertahanan musuh.* A company could infiltrate the enemy stronghold. **4** to smuggle. *Polisi di Kualalumpur telah berhasil menangkap dua orang wanita yang berniat ~ keluar héroin sebagai obat bius terlarang.* The police in Kuala Lumpur were successful in arresting two women who intended to smuggle heroin out of the country as a prohibited narcotic.

menyelundupi to enter s.o. (of a spirit).

menyelundupkan [and **nyelundupin** (*J coq*)] **1** to conceal, hide. *~ kepalanya ke dalam belukar* to hide his head in the under- brush. **2** to smuggle s.t. (into).

terselundupkan can be smuggled.

selundupan smuggled. *ban ~* smuggled tires. *barang ~* contra- band (goods).

penyelundup 1 smuggler. *kapal ~* smuggler ship. **2** infiltrator, intruder. *~ alkohol* bootlegger. *~ pajak* tax evader/dodger.

penyelundupan 1 smuggling, clandestine trade. **2** infiltration.

selungkang fake (of coins/metal). *iga* – the five lower ribs, costae spuriae.

selungkap menyelungkap to peel/scale off, be loose (of skin from abrasion); → JELUNGKAP.

selungkup menyelungkup(i) to cover, close.

selup (*D naut*) sloop.

selupan (*ob*) jasmine; → MELATI.

selupat 1 membrane. **2** caul (of newborns); → SELAPUT.

selurah (*ob*) → SELURUH.

selurai k.o. pasta.

seluru k.o. climber (leaves are used as medicine), *Pericampylus glaucus.*

seluruh 1 whole. – *kota* the whole town. **2** entire. – *dunia* the en- tire world. *di – dunia* global(ly). **3** all. *atas nama – yang hadir* on behalf of (or, in the name of) all those present. **4** total; → SEGENAP, SEMUA. *di – dunia* all over the world, everywhere, globally. *Kartu krédit itu diakui di – dunia.* That credit card is honored all over the world. **keseluruh** (noun +) ~ overall.

seluruhnya 1 in all, altogether, in total. *Ada sepuluh orang ~.* There were ten people in all. *Harga rumah dan tanah ~ sejuta dolar.* The total cost of the house and the land is one million dollars. **2** all the way through, from cover to cover. *Saya membaca buku itu ~.* I read that book from cover to cover.

menyeluruh 1 overall, comprehensive. *kebijakan keamanan ~* a comprehensive security policy. *kekuatan ~* overall strength. *persetujuan ~* an all-inclusive contract. **2** holistic. *kemampuan untuk berpikir secara ~ dan intégratif* the ability to think holis- tically and integratively. *secara ~* totally, wholly. *keterlibatan secara ~* totally involved.

menyeluruhi to do s.t. completely to.

keseluruhan entirety, whole, totality, entire amount. *Jembatan itu hancur ~nya.* The bridge was totally destroyed. *secara ~ all in all, as a whole, overall. Secara ~ keadaan kita baik.* All in all, we're in good shape.

selusar corridor.

selusuh (- *anak*) ecbolic, medicine to hasten or ease childbirth. – *tem- buni/uri* medicine used to hasten the expulsion of the afterbirth.

menyelusuh to slide, slip out.

menyelusuhi to spray this medicine on (the belly of a woman giving birth).

selusup menyelusup [and **nyelusup** (*coq*)] **1** to infiltrate, penetrate, enter (a place) stealthily. ~ *ke daérah yang dikuasai musuh* to penetrate into enemy-controlled territory. **2** to slip away, disappear. ~ *ke dalam belukar* to disappear into the bushes.

menyelusupi to slip (in), insert. *Ibu ~ jari-jarinya pada rambutnya.* Mother slipped her fingers in her hair.

menyelusupkan to infiltrate s.o. *Meréka ~ kadernya dalam parpol.* They infiltrated their cadres into political parties.

terselusup infiltrated, penetrated, entered.

penyelusup infiltrator.

penyelusupan infiltration, penetration.

selusur I menyelusur to slide/slip down.

menyelusurkan to make s.o. or s.t. slide/slip down.

terselusur slid/slipped down.

penyelusuran sliding s.t.

selusur II handrail (of a bridge).

menyelusuri to follow/go along, go through s.t. carefully.

selut mud, slime; muddy, slimy.

seluit lesser green broadbill, *Calyptomena viridis.*

séma [sénat mahasiswa] student senate.

semaan (*A? Jv?*) /sema'an/ collective recitation of the Koran.

semacam → MACAM.

semadi (*Skr*) concentration of thought, meditation.

bersemadi to meditate, commit concentration of thought.

menyemadikan to meditate upon, think over.

persemadian 1 meditation. **2** place for meditation.

penyemadian meditation.

semadya (*Jv*) → SAK *madya.*

sémafor (*D*) semaphore, signaling apparatus.

semagi a pall laid over a dead body in the house.

sémah I sacrifice, offering (to spirits).

menyémah 1 to make a sacrifice for. ~ *negeri* to make a sacrifice for the good of the nation. **2** to say a blessing over.

menyémah(kan) to sacrifice s.t., offer s.t. up as a sacrifice.

sémahan sacrifice, offering.

penyémahan sacrifice.

sémah II (*Jv*) **1** spouse. **2** household.

semai 1 seedling. **2** nursery. – *tumbuh* growing seedling. **menyemai-tumbuhkan** to grow, develop.

menyemai to sow, scatter or put seeds on or in (the ground). *Sawah ini baru kusemai.* I've just sown this rice field.

menyemaikan to plant/sow s.t., spread, scatter, propagate.

mempersemaikan to raise from a seedling.

tersemai sowed, sown, spread, scattered.

semaian 1 seedling. **2** nursery.

pe(r)semaian nursery.

penyemaian planting, sowing, spreading, propagation. ~ *awan* cloud seeding; → HUJAN *buatan.*

semaja (*Skr?*) in fact, actually, really; → MÉMANG, SEBENARNYA.

semak I undergrowth. *dari – ke belukar* a) it is six of one and half a dozen of the other. b) out of the frying pan into the fire. – *belukar* undergrowth, shrubs, bushes, etc. **menyemak-belukar** to turn into undergrowth. *Rumput dan ilalang di sana kelihatan telah ~.* It looks like the grasses there have turned into undergrowth. – *hati/pikiran* confused (thoughts). – *samun* undergrowth, shrubs, bushes, etc.

bersemak overgrown with undergrowth.

menyemak 1 to be overgrown. *Halaman rumahnya ~.* The yard of his house is overgrown. **2** thoroughly confused, all mixed/messed up. *Rambutnya ~(-nyemak).* His hair was all messed up. **3** confused (thoughts), disturbed.

menyemaki to be overgrown with ... seeds.

menyemakkan 1 to make into a wilderness. **2** ~ *hati* to alarm, disturb, perturb.

semak II (clipped from *seemak*) with the same mother (but different fathers).

sémak menyémak 1 to revise, proof. **2** to look at carefully; → SIMAK I.

semaka → SEMANGKA I.

semakin → MAKIN.

semalakama → SIMALAKAMA.

semalam 1 one night. **2** the night before, last night. **3** yesterday, the day before today; → MALAM I.

semalu sensitive plant, *Mimosa pudica;* → MALU II.

semama → SAMAMA.

semambu I (*rotan* –) k.o. large rattan, Malacca cane, *Calamus scipionum.*

semambu II *hantu* – k.o. evil spirit.

semambu III k.o. fish, tunny, *Germo sibi.*

semampai (*M*) slender, slim; → GEMULAI. *tinggi* – slender and lithe (of persons).

semampang (*ob*) suppose that.

semampat *pohon* – tree that provides timber, *Cratoxylon formosum/cochininensis;* → MERPITIS.

séman (*usu kesémanan*) **1** unsuccessful, abortive, didn't rise (of dough), didn't take (of an inoculation). **2** misshapen, not fully developed, rudimentary. **3** failed, went bankrupt. **4** lost (of one's memory).

semanak (*Jv*) jovial, friendly.

semanda → SEMENDA.

semandan (*ob*) *pesemandan* bridesmaid.

semandar (*Pers*) salamander.

semandarasa(h) (*Skr*) frangipani, *Plumeria acutifolia;* champac, *Michelia champaka;* → CEMPAKA, KEMBOJA. This flower *usu* suggests death, a girl lost, or love forlorn. – *wilis* the blue frangipani.

semandéra (*naut*) pennant attached to the bow of a boat.

semang *anak* – a) boarder. b) employed man; subordinate; personnel, staff, servants. c) debtor. *induk* – a) landlord. b) employer; supplier; bordello keeper.

semangat 1 soul, (vital) spirit, consciousness. *memanggil* – to raise/conjure up spirits. **2** gusto, zest, enthusiasm, lust, ardor, morale, energy. *tidak mempunyai* – *hidup* to have no zest for life. *kehilangan* – a) to have lost one's enthusiasm for work. b) unconscious, fainted. c) lost one's memory. *Berbunga* –*nya.* He was very happy. *dengan* – *yang tinggi* high-spirited. *dengan penuh* – enthusiastically. *sebagai ditinggalkan* – as if unaware; cowardly, fear-stricken. *keras* – powerful. *kurang/lemah* – a) sickly, ailing, ill. b) fearful, scared. *pulang* – come to o.s. again. *riang* – dizzy/nervous feeling. *terbang* –*nya* a) unconscious, fainted. b) memory loss. – *baja* resolve, determination. – *bekerja* enthusiasm/zest for work. – *bergelora* ardor. – *berjuang* combativeness. – *golongan* esprit de corps. – *kambing* cowardly. – *kampung* backwoods mentality. – *kedaérahan* provincialism. – *kelas* class spirit. – *kereguan* team spirit. – *menggebu(-gebu)* enthusiasm, energy. – *menyimpan* thrift. – *padi* the spirit causing the rice plant to grow and bear fruit. – *persamaan* egalitarianism. – *persatuan* esprit de corps. – *puputan* an undaunted spirit. – *témpé mlempem* dejection, discouragement. – *tinggi* resolve, determination, high spirits, willpower. – *zaman* Zeitgeist, the spirit of the age; trend of thought and feelings at a certain period of time.

bersemangat 1 to be conscious. *tidak ~* a) to be unconscious. b) to be fearful/scared. **2** enthusiastic, motivated, ardent, animated, active, -minded. ~ *pelaut* sea-minded. ~ *perang* bellicose, combative, militant. *kurang ~* in low spirits.

menyemangati and **mempersemangatkan** to animate, inspire, encourage.

penyemangat 1 stimulus, stimulator. **2** cheerleader. *Kita melihat perbédaan antara ~ di satu pihak dan pemimpin di pihak lain.* We can see the difference between the cheerleaders on the one side and the leaders on the other side. *menjadi ~* to incite, stimulate, fire up.

penyemangatan encouraging, encouragement.

semangga only, no one else but.

semanggi I (*Jv*) an herb that grows in moist places and is eaten as a vegetable, watercress, clover fern, *Hydrocotyle rotundifolia/sibthorpioides,* *Oxalis corniculata.* – *gunung* k.o. medicinal weed, Indian sorrel, yellow oxalis, *Oxalis corniculata.*

semanggi II clubs (in card games). *Jembatan* – The Cloverleaf Bridge in Jakarta. *setengah* – half clover leaf. *Tragédi* – → TRAGÉDI *Semanggi.*

semangka I watermelon, *Citrullus vulgaris;* → MENDIKAI. *papaya* – a red-colored and sweet papaya variety. – *belanda* cantaloupe, *Cucumis melo.* – *jingga* a variety of watermelon with red meat.

semangka II k.o. sea-perch, *Apogon spp.*

semangkin increasingly, the more; → MAKIN, SEMAKIN. – *lama* – *sakit* the more time passes the sicker (he is).

semangkok and **semangkuk** *kembang* – a tree, *Scaphium affinis*, whose seeds are used medicinally, such as for diarrhea; the seeds of this tree swell in water and fill a small *mangkok* or bowl.

semanja → SEMAJA.

semantan → SANTAN. *nyiur* – a ripe coconut whose milk or *santan* can be heard when it is shaken.

sémantik (*D/E*) 1 semantics. 2 semantic.

sémantis (*D*) semantic.

semantung thunder but no rain.

semaput (*Jv*) unconscious, fainted; → PINGSAN. *Dia – dan mati.* He lost consciousness and died.

Semar (in the *wayang* play) unmarried father of *Garéng, Pétruk,* and *Garong,* a divine being, the older brother of *Batara Guru* (Shiva), asexual. He is represented as a very short, thick-set figure with a flat nose, slit eyes, and a very large mouth with two teeth. A powerful weapon is his *kentut* or fart with which he blows away everything in the way. Former President Soekarno, after his fall, had to delegate broad security powers to (the then General) Soeharto, now President of the Republic of Indonesia, by *Surat Perintah Sebelas Maret* [March 11 Letter of Command (of 1966)]. Since then Soeharto is often referred to as *Super Semar,* the acronym for this letter of command. – *mendam/mendem* k.o. snack made from sticky-rice flour wrapped in a thin plain omelet instead of in banana leaves.

semar(a) (*ob*) passionate longing. – *mésem* (*Jv*) a charm that can make women fall in love.

kesemaran madly in love; → ASMARA.

semarai I (*M ob*) cracked, split.

semarai II *sorak* – (*ob*) applause, cheers.

semarak (*M*) 1 brilliant, glorious, excellent. *Namanya jadi –.* He became famous. 2 bright and brilliant, colorful. *Sepeninggal istrinya itu maka rumah dan halamannya tidak bersemarak seperti dulu.* After his wife's death his house and yard weren't as bright as they had been. 3 beauty; decoration. *Hilang –nya.* She lost her beauty.

bersemarak brilliant.

menyemarak to shine, brighten up.

menyemarakkan and **mempersemarakkan** to embellish, adorn, make more splendid/resplendent, brighten/liven up.

kesemarakan splendor, pomp, fame.

semaram I *pohon* – a large tree, *Payena obscura/leerii*, whose wood is used for making planks.

semaram II *ikan* – false scorpion fish, *Centrogenys vaigiensis*.

semaré (*Jv reg?*) to pass away. *Sowan pada yang – di Imogiri punya arti sendiri.* Visiting those who have passed away has a meaning all its own.

semasa during, throughout (the entire time); → MASA I.

sema-sema 1 cold (in the head). 2 catarrh; → SELESMA.

bersema-sema 1 to have a cold. 2 catarrhous.

séma-séma outrigger (of a prau).

semasih → MASIH I.

semat a sharpened coconut-leaf rib used for fastening leaf-wrapped packages. *salah* – (*M*) misunderstanding.

menyemat 1 to pin, fix, attach firmly. 2 (*sl*) to wear, put on (clothes).

menyemati to attach/pin s.t. firmly onto, give s.o. an award or medal by pinning it on them. *Dia disemati satu bintang mas.* He was awarded a gold star.

menyematkan 1 to attach/pin (a decoration) (to). *Présidén ~ bintang kehormatan kepada perwira itu.* The president pinned a badge of honor on the officer. 2 to append, attach. *Daftar kata-kata sulit yang terdapat dalam buku itu disematkan di belakang.* A glossary of difficult words found in that book is appended at the end.

tersemat fastened, pinned, affixed, stuck on. *Di dadanya ~ tidak kurang dari 10 buah medali.* No fewer than 10 medals are pinned on his chest. *~ dalam hati* remembered.

sematan s.t. that is pinned on, fastened or attached with a pin.

penyemat fastener. *lidi ~* a coconut-leaf rib used for fastening.

penyematan 1 fastening, pinning, attaching. 2 appending, including.

semata(-mata) (*Skr*) (simply and) solely, exclusively, merely. – *wayang* only, sole. *~ mobil wayang yang ada di kantornya* the only car found at his office.

semau – *gué* (*J*) as one thinks fit, just as one pleases, arbitrarily; → MAU. *Pengemudi jangan – gué di jalan raya.* Drivers should not act just as they please. *Kadang-kadang tarif penumpang atau barang lebih dari itu, ditentukan – gué oléh sang sopir.* Sometimes the fare for the passengers or goods is higher than that, since it is determined arbitrarily by the driver.

semau(-mau)nya 1 at will, as one likes/pleases, whatever one would like (to). 2 arbitrary. *Dia minta harga ~.* He asked whatever price he wanted.

semawang k.o. tree, *Kayea ferruginea*.

semawar a small oven fueled by oil.

semawat (*A*) heavens.

semawi → SAMAWI.

Semawis (*Jv*) Semarang, capital of the province of Central Java.

Semawisan of Semarang.

semaya (*Jv*) delay; to delay.

semayam bersemayam 1 (*cla*) to sit on a throne. *Baginda ~ di atas singgasana.* His Majesty was seated on his throne. 2 to reign, settle, establish o.s. (for royalty). *~ di Riau* residing in Riau. 3 to lie in rest (of honored people). *Di sinilah ~ para pahlawan nasional.* Here rest the national heroes.

menyemayamkan 1 to enthrone, place on a throne. 2 to place upon a bier, lie in state. *Dari bandara internasional Soekarno-Hatta, jenazah kemudian disemayamkan di rumah duka.* From Soekarno-Hatta international airport the mortal remains were then laid in state in the house of mourning.

persemayaman 1 (royal) residence. 2 last resting-place, grave.

semayi (*Jv?*) coconut pulp made into a food; the pulp which has putrefied for some days is then heated in banana-leaf package.

semayub → SAYUP.

sembab swollen (of one's eyes/face/feet), edema. *bermata* – with swollen eyes. *Wajah-wajah meréka – dan bengkak-bengkak akibat pukulan.* Their faces were swollen from blows. *– paru* oedema.

menyembab 1 to be swollen. 2 succulent.

sembabat (*J*) fitting, matching, exactly the same.

sembada (*Skr Jv*) 1 suitable, becoming, fitting, proper; → SWASEMBADA. 2 well-proportioned, well-built. *seorang pria yang berperawakan* – a well-built man.

sembah 1 respectful greeting made by raising the hands with the palms together, fingertips upward, to the height of the face, so that the thumbs touch the nose, as a token of homage to a superior, one's parents, etc. 2 (respectful) words, sayings, etc. *berdatang* – to speak respectfully/reverentially. *mengangkat* – to pay tribute by making the *sembah. uang* – (*M*) money given by the male to his prospective in-laws after his proposal has been accepted. *– berhala* a) idolatry. b) to worship idols. *– simpuh* respect, honoring. **menyembah menyimpuh** to show respect by kneeling. *– sujud/sungkem* expression of respect; the inferior kneels before the superior or parents, etc., holds the superiors' or parents' hands and puts his forehead against their knees. 3 say respectfully. *–nya* he spoke respectfully.

bersembah to say respectfully.

bersembah-sembahan to pay homage to e.o.

menyembah [and **nyembah** (*coq*)] 1 to pay homage to s.o. by making the *sembah*. 2 to worship, venerate (s.t. as a god or God). 3 (*cla*) to subject o.s. (to), submit to the rule of. *~ ke Majapahit* to submit to the rule of Majapahit. *~ panjang* to show respect standing up by bowing and lifting the hands to the face.

sembah-menyembah to pay homage to e.o.

menyembah-nyembah to do s.t. in a respectful way, treat in the respectful way described above.

menyembahkan and **mempersembahkan** 1 to offer, present, give respectfully, bestow. 2 to report (s.t. to a superior). 3 to dedicate (a book, etc.).

sembahan s.t. that is worshipped, God, idol.

penyembah worshipper, idolater, adorer. ~ *berhala* idol-worshipper, idolater.

penyembahan 1 worship, idolization, adoration, veneration. ~ *berhala* idolatry. **2** deep respect.

persembahan 1 tribute, present, gift, homage. **2** dedication. **3** offering (of s.t. respectfully given). **4** presentation.

sembahyang (from: *sembah* + *Hyang* or *Yang III*) to bring the *sembah* to *Hyang* or *Yang III*; → SALAT I. a canonical, ritual prayer; *cp* DOA; the second of the Five Pillars. It is composed of a series of movements repeated several times; → ISYA, SUBUH, LOHOR, ASAR I, MAGHRIB. *air* – water for washing the face, hands and feet before prayer. *tikar* – prayer mat. *meninggalkan* – to neglect one's obligations to pray. *– mencari akal, rukuk mencari kira-kira* hypocrite, externally good but internally wicked. – *asar* Islamic afternoon prayer. – *berjemaah* collective prayer under the guidance of an *imam* or leader of a congregation. – *doha* optional prayer performed before noon. – *fardu* the obligatory prayers. – *hajat* a special prayer at the request of s.o., such as for passing an examination, the speedy recovery of a sick person, etc. – *hari raya* recommended prayer, because it is performed only twice a year, on *Idul Fitri* and *Idul Adha* or, *Idul Kurban*. – *istiqa'/istiqo* collective religious service with prayers asking for rain. – *isya* Islamic evening prayers. – *jamaah* communal prayer. – *jari* the five daily prayers. – *jenazah* prayer for a dead person. – *Jumat* collective prayer on Friday in the mosque (at *Luhur*). – *kesyukuran* prayer of thanksgiving. – *k(h)usuf* commendable prayer because of an eclipse. – *loha* forenoon prayer. – *lima waktu* the obligatory five Islamic prayers. – *mayat/orang mati* prayer for a dead person. – *sun(n)at* recommended but optional prayer, intended for special purposes. – *sunnat rawatib* optional prayer after the obligatory prayer. – *tahajud* commendable (but not obligatory) night prayer. – *tarawih* prayer (in a *surau* or mosque with other people during the fasting month of Ramadan which begins before the *sembahyang/salat Isya*). – *wajib* the obligatory five Islamic prayers. – *witir* recommended prayer performed after the *sembahyang tarawih*.

bersembahyang to pray, worship. *orang-orang Islam ~ lima waktu sehari.* Muslims pray five times a day.

menyembahyangi to pray over. *Setelah dimandikan dan disembahyangi kedua mayat itu dikuburkan.* After having been bathed and prayed over, the two bodies were buried.

menyembahkan to pray for, say a prayer over.

sembahyangan worship, prayer. *kitab* ~ prayer book.

penyembahyangan praying, prayers.

persembahyangan 1 worship, veneration. **2** place of worship.

sémbai (*M*) **menyémbai** to catch (s.t. falling), grab (with a jerk); to snatch. **3** to interrupt.

sémbai-menyémbai to answer/respond to e.o.

penyémbai s.o. who interrupts.

sembak *ikan* – a) tunny, *Germo sibi.* b) bonito, *Euthynnus alletteratus.*

sembako [sembilan bahan pokok] the nine basic necessities/commodities: salt, granulated sugar, salted fish, cooking oil, kerosene, laundry soap, rough textiles, *batik* to wear, and soap.

sembam I (*M*) **menyembam** to roast s.t. in hot ashes.

sembam II → SEMBAB.

sembam III *sungkur* – to fall flat on one's face.

menyembamkan to throw s.t. face down.

tersembam to fall flat on one's face.

sembap → SEMBAB.

sembar → SABUR, SAMBAR.

sémbar k.o. parasitic plant.

sembarang no matter which/who, arbitrary, any (old), whatever, just any. *– orang* anybody at all. *bukan/tidak – orang* not just anyone. *– waktu* any time. *Bukan – jip.* Not just any old jeep. *Meréka bersalaman, ngobrol –. Masalah keséhatan nampaknya menjadi topik paling hangat bagi meréka.* They (i.e., the retirees) greeted e.o. and chatted about one thing and another. Health matters seemed to be the hottest topic for them. *dengan* – haphazard(ly).

menyembarangi to do impulsively/haphazardly/any old way.

sembarangan arbitrarily, any old (way/thing/person), at random, hit or miss; → BARANG II. *bertindak* ~ to act arbitrarily. *Ia bukan ~ orang* and *Ia bukan gadis –.* She is not just anybody. *Bagi saya ~ saja!* It's all the same to me! *Jangan omong ~!* Don't talk nonsense!

kesembarangan doing things any old way.

sembari (*J/Jv*) while. *Pria itu ngomong – makan.* The man talked with a full mouth; → SAMBIL.

sémbat menyémbat 1 to snatch, seize (a watch, etc.). **2** to draw in (a fishing rod, etc.) fast. **3** to pull out with a jerk (a weapon from its sheath, etc.). **4** to whip back to its original position, snap back, rebound.

sembawang → SEMAWANG.

sembayan (*M*) co-wife or mistress.

bersembayan to have a co-wife.

sembeb → SEMBAB.

sembelih menyembelih 1 to slaughter an animal by cutting its throat (as Islam ordains). **2** to kill, slaughter, assassinate, massacre, murder. *Ayah dan ibunya mati disembelih gerombolan.* His father and mother are dead, murdered by a gang.

tersembelih slaughtered.

sembelihan s.t. that is slaughtered. *sapi* ~ slaughtered cattle.

penyembelih 1 slaughterer, butcher, murderer. **2** *pisau* ~ knife used to slaughter cattle, etc.

penyembelihan slaughter, butchery, massacre. ~ *masal* mass murder, genocide.

sembelit I constipation.

menyembelitkan to constipate, constipating.

sembelit II (*ob*) small purse for holding money.

sembér (*J/Jv*) hoarse, cracked (of a voice/sound of a gong).

semberana → SEMBRONO.

semberani (*Tam Pers? cla*) *kuda* – flying/winged steed; → BORAK I.

semberap (*cla*) a full set of (clothes/betel appurtenances).

Sembérék (in Old Javanese annals the corruption of the Dutch proper name) Ossenberg.

semberip (*cla*) a small pedestal tray.

semberono → SEMBRONO.

semberut → CEMBERUT.

sembesi (*ob*) horse.

sembéta (*ob*) props to keep a boat steady on the beach.

sembiang small fish-spear.

sembilan nine. *– belas* nineteen. *– likur* twenty-nine. *– puluh* ninety.

bersembilan a total of nine, nine in all, nine together; to make nine (with eight others).

sembilanan ninth.

kesembilan 1 ninth (part). **2** (= **kesembilannya**) all nine (of them). **3** group of nine.

persembilan ninth. *se~* a ninth.

sembilang (*– betul*) catfish eel with a poisonous spine, *Plotosus canius.* – *karang* k.o. marine catfish, *Plotosus anguillaris.*

sembilat → SEMILAT.

sembilik and **sembilit** *puru* – hemorrhoids, piles.

sembilu 1 a bamboo splinter. **2** a razor-sharp) knife (made of bamboo) (used to cut the umbilical chord). *sebagai diiris dengan –* it cuts one to the heart/quick.

menyembilu to be sharp/harsh (as of words).

sembiluan very painful.

sembir 1 edge (of a tray/plate/paper). **2** ridge (of the *belimbing* fruit). **3** margin.

bersembir justified (lines of type).

menyembir 1 to deviate from the true reading (of a compass). **2** to justify (lines of type).

menyembirkan to justify (lines of type).

sembiran 1 border, edge (of a country). **2** deviation, error (of a compass). **3** justification (lines of type).

sembirat (*Jv*) **1** shine; blaze, glow. **2** to emit light.

sembodo → SEMBADA.

semboja → KEMBOJA.

semboyan (*Skr?*) **1** alarm (gun/gong), siren, signal (Morse, etc.). **2** slogan, catchword, motto, device. **3** shibboleth.

bersemboyan to have ... as a slogan; to use a siren/alarm/signal.

bersemboyankan to use ... as an alarm/siren/signal.

menyemboyankan to warn/announce by sounding an alarm/siren.

sembrani → SEMBERANI. name of a train running between Jakarta and Surabaya.

sembrono (*Jv*) **1** frivolous, thoughtless, imprudent, do things at random. **2** rash, hotheaded, reckless. *Kebanggaannya berubah jadi –.* His pride changed to recklessness. **3** arrogant, presumptuous.
menyembronokan to treat in an arrogant way.
kesembronoan 1 carelessness, imprudence, recklessness. **2** impoliteness, rudeness. **3** arrogance. *Bencana Bintaro merupakan pelajaran yang amat mahal untuk ~ anak manusia.* The Bintaro disaster is an expensive lesson of human arrogance.

sembuang I (*naut*) dolphin, a bundle of stakes tied together for mooring boats.

sembuang II offering to the spirits thrown into the jungle.

sembuh 1 cured, recovered, (got) well again. *Dia telah – sesudah dirawat di hospital.* He was cured after being hospitalized. *tak akan –.-nya* incurable (illness). **2** mended, corrected, all right again.
menyembuhkan [and **nyembuhin** (*J coq*)] **1** to cure s.o. or s.t. **2** to repair, mend.
tersembuhkan curable. *Pada usia senjanya ia mengidap penyakit Alzheimer yang tak ~.* At an advanced age he suffered from Alzheimer's disease, which is incurable.
kesembuhan 1 recovery (from an illness), getting well. *Keberangkatan kami bergantung pada ~ ibu.* Our departure depends on mother's recovery. **2** cure, healing. *mencari ~* to look for a cure.
penyembuh healer (the person). *secara ~* curative, curing.
penyembuhan recovery (from illness), healing.

sembul emerge, appear at the surface. (*geol*) horst. *– ibun* frost heave.
bersembul to emerge, come up (of a card/member, etc.), turn up, come to the surface, come into view, appear. *Saputangannya ~ dari sakunya.* The handkerchief stuck out of his pocket.
bersembulan (*pl subj*) to emerge, etc.
menyembul [and **nyembul** (*coq*)] **1** to appear, become visible, come into sight, emerge. *Ular ~ dari liang.* A snake appeared from a hole. *~ keluar* to peek/stick out. **2** to have (a kris hilt) sticking out. **3** to surface/come up. *Bila Anda menyelam, berhati-hatilah bila ingin ~ kembali ke permukaan.* If you dive, be careful when you want to come up again. **3** to turn up (a lamp wick). **4** to rise (of the sun). *pagi hari sebelum matahari ~* in the morning before sunrise. **5** to be prominent, bulge, protrude. *payudara yang ~* protruding breasts.
menyembulkan 1 to show s.t., make s.t. appear. *~ diri* to appear, crop up, turn up. *~ lidah* to stick out one's tongue. **2** to stick s.t. out. *~ kepala dari balik dinding.* She stuck her head out from behind the wall.
tersembul 1 to protrude, protruding, stick out (of eyes/bosom from a dress/a snake from a hole, etc.). *Tulang punggungnya agak ~.* His spinal column protruded somewhat. **2** to be outstanding (in contrast to others). **3** appeared, turned up, came out, emerged. **4** risen (of the sun from the sea). **5** gushed, spouted.
penyembulan 1 surfacing. **2** (*geol*) uplift.

sembung k.o. shrub, camphor plant, *Blumea balsamifera. daun –* leaves of this plant, used as a styptic.

sembuni → SEMBUNYI.

sembunyi secretly, on the sly, surreptitiously. *Meréka mengéjék secara –.* They ridiculed people surreptitiously. *– tuma/ékor kelihatan kepala tersuruk* ostrich policy; → POLITIK *burung unta.*
sembunyi-sembunyi 1 secretly, on the sly, stealthily. *~ puyuh* ostrich policy, i.e., purposely not wanting to know what is really happening around one. **2** sneaky. *main ~* and
bersembunyi to hide, conceal o.s.; hidden, concealed. *~ di balik alang-alang sehelai* to clear o.s. of blame. *Kaum téroris itu ~ di sebuah gua.* The terrorists were holed up in a cave.
bersembunyi-sembunyian to play hide-and-go-seek.
menyembunyikan [and **nyembunyiin** (*J coq*)] **1** to hide, conceal. *Céwék itu mencoba ~ rasa malunya.* That girl tried to conceal her embarrassment. **2** to hoard. *Dia ~ bahan makanan.* He

hoarded food supplies. **3** to hold inside of one, keep s.t. to o.s. *Jangan kau ~ kemarahanmu.* Don't hold your anger inside.
tersembunyi 1 concealed, hidden. *harapan yang ~* veiled hope. *Dia membawa senjata ~.* He carried a concealed weapon. **2** disguised. *pengangguran ~* disguised unemployment.
tersembunyi-bunyi hidden. *insinuasi ~* veiled insinuations.
sembunyi-sembunyian → BERSEMBUNYI-SEMBUNYIAN.
penyembunyi hider, s.o. who hides s.t.
penyembunyian secrecy, concealment, hiding.
persembunyian hiding place, hideout.

sembur I s.t. sprayed from the mouth (such as a cud of medications to treat a sick person or to chase away ghosts, etc.). *kena – a)* hit by such a spray. b) scolded. *seperti polong kena – a)* meek, docile, submissive. b) to run away head over heels. *– buatan* gas lift. *– gelak* (*M*) to burst into laughter.
sembur-sembur *~ galak* to burst out laughing.
bersemburan 1 to spout, gush (out). *Darah ~ keluar dari lukanya.* Blood gushed out of the wound. **2** (*plu subj*) to disperse, scatter. *Burung-burung ~ di udara.* Birds scattered in the sky.
bersembur-semburan to spray water at e.o.
menyembur [and **nyembur** (*coq*)] **1** to spout, gush. *Air ~ dari dalam tanah.* Water spouted from the ground. *Darah ~ ke mukanya.* His face became red (in anger). **2** to spray (on s.t.). *Besi yang akan disambung itu disembur dengan api sampai memijar.* Iron to be stretched is sprayed with fire until it glows. **3** to treat a sick person or chase away evil spirits by sprinkling exorcised water over them. *Sesudah disembur dukun, orang yang kemasukan itu siuman dan pulih sebagai semula.* After having been sprinkled by a shaman, the possessed person came to and returned to normal. **4** (*coq*) to reprimand, use abusive language to.
sembur-menyembur to spray water at e.o.
menyemburi → MENYEMBUR 2, 3.
menyemburkan to spray/spit s.t. out (of the mouth, etc.), gush, spew. *Daun-daunan itu dikunyah-kunyah lalu disemburkan dari tubuh orang yang sakit itu.* The leaves were chewed up in the mouth and then sprayed over the body of the patient. *Gunung Merapi ~ awan panas dan abu.* Mt. Merapi spat out hot clouds and ashes.
tersembur 1 sprayed, sprinkled, squirted. **2** scolded, jeered at. *~ gelak* (*M*) burst out laughing. *darah ~* startled, surprised.
semburan 1 spit, spittle. **2** spray, emission, flow, outpouring. *~ liar* (*petro*) blow out, i.e., an out-of-control eruption (of an oil well). *~ panas* hot flashes/flushes. **3** scolding.
penyembur 1 medications, etc. spewed out. **2** sprayer, thrower. *~ air otomatis* automatic sprinkler. *~ api* flame thrower. *~ gas* gas nozzle.
penyemburan (act of) spraying.

sembur II → SEMBUL.

semburat I (*Jv*) **1** tinge (of another color). *abu-abu dengan – mérah jambu* gray with tinges of pink. **2** ray (of light).
bersemburat to shine, gleam.
bersemburatkan to be tinged with.
menyemburat to shine, gleam.

semburat II bersemburat to burst forth, gush, pour out. *Darah amis pun ~ meléléh ke bawah.* The putrid blood gushed forth, dripping downward.
menyemburat to spout, pour, gush (forth), burst forth, spurt out. *api ~* fire poured forth. *Waktu itu ia hanya mendengar ledakan dan melihat ada api ~.* At that time he only heard explosions and saw that a fire had burst forth.
tersemburat to spurt (out).

semburit → BURIT. pederasty, homosexuality, sodomy. *main/ melakukan –* to commit sodomy.
bersemburit to commit sodomy.
menyeburit to sodomize.

Semdal [Studi Évaluasi Mengenai Dampak Lingkungan] Environmental Impact Evaluation Study.

semecah a children's game (played with candlenuts).

semedera (*cla*) → SAMUDERA, SAMUDRA.

semedi → SEMADI.

semejak → SEJAK I.

semek I (*Jv*) moist, damp, soggy, humid.

semek II → SEMAK I.

semek III → KESEMAK.

seméléh (*Jv*) to acquiesce to s.t., resign o.s. to s.t., resigned.

semémeh smeared, dirty (of the mouth with dried food particles).

semén (*D*) cement. – *asbés* asbestos cement. – *beton* reinforced concrete. – *biru* Portland cement.

  bersemén cemented.

  menyemén to cement.

  semén an cementing.

  penyeménan cementing.

sémén (*D*) semen.

semena-mena *(tidak)* – arbitrarily, without reason, just as one pleases; → MENA.

semenanjung peninsula. – *Ibéria* Iberian Peninsula. – *Krimia* Crimean Peninsula.

semenda 1 affinal/in-law relationship, for instance, a man who marries a sister or niece of one's wife. *adat* – matriarchate. *keluarga* – affinal relatives, kin related by marriage. *orang* – a man who has married into a tribe. *tanah* – reference to West Malaysia. *tempat* – his wife's relatives.

  bersemenda 1 related/be allied by marriage (to a matrilineal tribe). 2 to marry into. ~ *dengan* to have an affinal relationship (with).

  menyemenda to become related by marriage.

  semenda-menyemenda intermarriage between two families.

semendal mica.

semenderasa (*Skr*) frangipani, *Plumeria acutifolia*; → CEMPAKA. – *wilis* the blue frangipani, *Michelia spp.*

semenggah *tak* – improper, indecent. *Perempuan banyak yang tidak –.* Many women behaved improperly.

semenjak → SEJAK I.

semenjana (*Skr*) mediocre, average, medium.

sementang 1 = sementangpun although, even though. – *hendak pergi, nantilah makan dulu.* Even though you'd like to leave, stay to dinner. 2 as long as. – *lagi ada, élok dipakai* as long as there still is some (e.g., rice), use that first. 3 (= sementang-mentang and sementangkan) just/all because; → MENTANG. ~ *turunan priayi lantas akan diangkat jadi pembantu bupati* just because he is descended from *priayi*s he's going to be appointed as assistant *bupati*.

sementara I 1 while, as. – *saya membaca, suami saya menulis.* While I was reading, my husband was writing. 2 since. – *belum ada uang, jangan membeli-beli.* Since there is no money, don't go shopping. – *itu* meanwhile, in the meantime, at the same time.

sementara II temporary, provisional, interim, contingent. *aturan* – a temporary regulation. *laporan* – interim report. *penyidikan* – provisional investigation. *rencana* – contingency plans. *Undang-Undang Dasar* – Provisional Constitution. *untuk* – (*waktu*) a) for the time being. b) (e.g., that succeeds) only for a while.

  kesementaraan temporariness. *meyakini* ~ *masa kini* to convince of the temporariness of the present time.

sementara III (influence of Javanese *sawetara*) some. – *orang* some people.

seméntasi (act of) cementing.

sementelah after.

sementelahan moreover.

sementung I dull, stupid, clumsy.

sementung II → BIRAS II.

semér → SEMIR.

semerawut → SEMRAWUT.

semerbak fragrant, scented, pervasive (of scent).

semerdanta (*Skr*) snow-white (of teeth).

semesta (*Skr*) 1 whole, entire, total, universal. *dana pembangunan* – funds for universal development (in all sectors). 2 *alam* – universe. *Tuhan* – *alam* Lord of the universe. – *alam* the entire world, cosmos. – *kemaknaan* universe of meaning.

  kesemestaan 1 universal, worldwide. *Métodologi yang ada sudah sempurna dan mempunyai sifat* ~. The existing methodology is already perfect and has universal characteristics. 2 universalism.

seméster (*D*) semester. – *ganjil/gasal* odd-numbered semester (1, 3, 5, 7). – *genap* even-numbered semester (2, 4, 6, 8).

semésteran semestral, semi-annual. *ujian* ~ final exam.

semestinya → MESTI.

Sem Gim (*coq*) Asian Games.

semi (*Jv*) (young) shoot, sprout. *musim* – spring.

  bersemi and menyemi to sprout, bud.

sémi- (*D*) semi-, half-.

sémiacak partly at random. *Penyebaran angkét tersebut dilakukan secara* ~. Distribution of the inquiries was done partly at random.

semiang I (*M*) – *kalam* very little; → MIANG.

semiang II fish spear.

semidra *kayu* – a tree whose timber is made into charcoal, *Acronychia laurifolia.*

sémifinal semifinal.

sémifinalis (*D*) semifinalist (in contests).

sémikerajinan semi-handicrafted. *barang* – semi-handicrafted goods.

sémikonduktor (*E*) semiconductor.

semilat k.o. plant, *Rourea fulgens.*

semilih alternating.

  menyemilih to alternate.

semilir (*J*) a light/gentle breeze; → SILIR I.

sémiloka [s*éminar sekaligus lokakarya*] a seminar and workshop.

seminai k.o. tree providing very good timber, *Madhuca utilis.*

seminang k.o. small bamboo.

seminar radiating, shining; → SINAR I.

séminar (*D*) seminar.– *keliling* seminar held in different places.

  berséminar to hold a seminar.

  menyéminarkan to discuss in a seminar.

  séminar-séminaran all k.o. seminars. *Anda jangan kagét, karena di negara kita ini orang-orangnya paling senang dengan* ~. Don't be startled, because in our country the people are most happy with all k.o. seminars.

séminari (*D*) seminary.

séminaris (*D*) seminarian.

seminau shining, bright, flashing; → SINAU.

semingkin (*coq*) → SEMAKIN.

sémiologi (*D/E*) semiology.

sémiotik semiotic.

sémipemerintah semigovernment.

sémipérmanén (*D*) semipermanent.

semir (*D*) 1 (shoe) polish. 2 *minyak* – lubricant, engine oil. 3 *uang* – grease money, bribe. – *oli(e)* lubricating oil. – *rambut* hair oil. – *sepatu* shoe polish.

  menyemir [and nyemir (*coq*)] 1 to polish, spread with a greasing/polishing substance. "*Sepatunya mau disemir, ya?*" (said by a shoeshine to a passerby). "Need a shoeshine?" 2 to lubricate. 3 to grease s.o.'s palm, bribe.

  menyemirkan to smear s.t. (on), polish with s.t.

  tersemir polished, lubricated.

  penyemir s.t. or s.o. which polishes. ~ *sepatu* bootblack, shoeshine boy.

  penyemiran polishing, shining.

semisal like, resembling; → MISAL.

sémitik (*D/E*) Semitic.

semlohai and semlohay (*BG*) sexy.

semoga I hope (that), may it happen that; → MOGA-MOGA.

sémok (*Jv*) plump, chubby.

semokel (*D*) 1 smuggling. 2 to smuggle.

  menyemokel (*masuk*) to smuggle (in).

semokelar (*D*) smuggler.

semon (*Jv*) menyemoni to allude to, hint at; → SEMU.

semor → SEMUR.

sempada *ketam* – k.o. crab.

sempadan 1 frontier, boundary, border, limit (of a plot of land). 2 boundary post/mark, etc. *garis* – *jalan* street-building lines, street and building alignments.

  bersempadan ~ *dengan* limited/separated/bordered by, next to.

  bersempadankan bordered by.

  menyempadani to border, bound, define.

sempak bersempak-sempak to kick at e.o. (*usu* of fighting cocks).

sémpak splintered (of a wall, etc.), badly dented/chipped (of a dish, etc.).

sempal I shim, s.t. stuck between two things to strengthen the joint, s.t. stuffed into somewhere but part of it is sticking out. – *serat* stopper that is hard to remove.

menyempal 1 to stick out, appear partly, emerge; → MENYEMBUL. *Pucuk rebung itu telah ~.* The tip of the bamboo shoot is sticking out. **2** to stuff s.o.'s nose/mouth, gag; → MENYEMPAL. *Dokter ~ hidung pasiénnya dengan kapas karena berdarah.* The physician stuffed his patient's nose with cotton because it was bleeding.

tersempal 1 sticking out, appearing partly, emerged. **2** stuffed, stopped, got stuck, clogged up. *Tulang ayam ~ di tenggorokannya.* A chicken bone got stuck in his throat.

sempalan → SEMPAL I.

sempal II (*J/Jv*) broken off, hanging by a thread. *Cabangnya –.* The broken branch is held to the tree only by the bark. *tingkat – splintering* stage (of a political/religious party).

menyempal [and **nyempal** (*coq*)] **1** to break s.t. nearly off. **2** to separate, secede.

sempalan fragment, piece, part, splinter (group). *grup/kelompok ~* splinter group. *nasionalisme ~* breakaway nationalism. *~ goréng ayam* a piece of fried chicken.

sempalai tersempalai sprawled (on the ground), lying down unable to move.

sempana → SEMPENA I.

sémpang I hyphen.

bersémpang hyphenated.

menyémpang to hyphenate.

sémpang II → SIMPANG.

sempang-sempung to roll (of a boat).

sémpar (*Jv*) **menyémpar** to kick s.t. away.

sempat 1 to have/get the time/the chance/the opportunity (to do s.t. or act in some way), see one's way to, succeed in (escaping), get to, manage to, still be able to (do s.t.); to end up ...ing. *Saya tidak pernah – berkenalan dengan Amir.* I never got to meet Amir. *Tujuh orang – selamat.* Seven persons managed to save their skins. *Belum – dicari tahu sebabnya, tahu-tahu Go Yén sudah lari.* Not having had enough time to find out the cause, unexpectedly Go Yen took to his heels. *Meréka – merebut perhatian pérs.* They managed to attract the attention of the press. *Dia – gemetar.* She ended up quivering. *tidak –* to fail to. **2** to happen (to do s.t.), it (so) happens/happened that, what happened was [*usu* no translation]. *Masyarakat pedalaman Irian – melihat pasukan asing.* People in the interior of Irian happened to see foreign troops. *Minggu yang lalu Rupiah – menguat.* The rupiah appreciated last week. *Ma'af Daftar Alumni – Tidak Berfungsi.* Sorry, the Alumni List is Out of Order.

sempat-sempatnya seize the opportunity to. *Ketika Yati dioperasi, Syaf ~ mengintip dari balik jendéla.* When Yati was operated on, Syaf seized the opportunity to peep from behind the window.

menyempat to await/wait for an opportunity (to do s.t.).

menyempati to get a chance/an opportunity to, find the chance to let (s.o. do s.t.).

menyempatkan [and **nyempatin** (*J coq*)] **1** to give s.o. the chance/opportunity/time to. **2** to set aside (time) for, take time out to. *Ketika disempatkan bertanya kepada penduduk setempat, spontan tapi polos dan penuh cemas, menyahut: "Kami gelisah!"* When the opportunity was given to the local population to raise questions, spontaneously but in a simple way they answered apprehensively: "We're worried!" *~ diri* a) to take the trouble (to). b) to take the opportunity to, take time out (to), take the time (to).

kesempatan 1 opportunity, chance, possibility, break. **2** occasion. *Meréka diperintahkan meninggalkan Indonésia pada ~ pertama.* They were ordered to leave Indonesia at the first possible opportunity. *memberikan kepadanya ~ untuk membéla diri terhadap tuduhan-tuduhan terhadapnya* to offer him the opportunity to make a defense against the charges brought against him. *Saya pernah mendapat ~ (demikian).* I've had my day. *~ emas* golden opportunity. *~ kerja* employment opportunities. *~ untuk suksés* chance of success. **berkesempatan 1** to have a chance or an opportunity. **2** convenient, opportune, favorable.

sempayan k.o. tree, kadamba tree, *Anthocephalus spp.*; → JABON II.

sempelah 1 refuse, rubbish, reject. **2** dregs, lees, pulp, residue. **3** useless, worthless, scum (of society); → SAMPAH *masyarakat.* – *kelapa* squeezed-out coconut meat.

sempelat bersempelat dirty, smeared (with).

tersempelat 1 stuffed (with). **2** to get knocked down.

sempena I (*Skr mostly Mal*) blessing, bringing luck/safety, good luck, good fortune. *keris –* a kris with three, five, or seven curves.

menyempenakan to bless, bring happiness, keep safe/well/secure.

sempena II (*Skr*) dream. – *hati* inner feelings, conscience.

sémpér (*Jv*) paralyzed (of a hand/leg), lame.

semperah → SEMPELAH.

semperit → SEMPRIT I.

semperong → SEMPRONG.

semperot → SEMPROT.

sempidan Salvadori's pheasant, *Lophura inornata.*

sempil (*J*) (originally) dwelling built in between two houses so that a poor person who occupies it doesn't need sidewalls.

menyempil [and **nyempil** (*coq*)] to be squeezed (into), stuck in, slip (into/between). *Garuda Maintenance Facility yang ~ di salah satu sudut Hall C* the Garuda Maintenance Facility, which is squeezed into a corner of Hall C. *sisa-sisa makanan yang ~ di sela-sela giginya* bits of food stuck in the spaces between his teeth.

tersempil squeezed (in), sticking (into), slipped (into/between). *~ menonjol* sticking out.

sempilai k.o. fighting fish, *Betta spp.*

sempilur k.o. tree, satinwood, *Dacrydium elatum.*

sempit 1 narrow (of a passage/street/hole, etc.), tight, limited (also of time). *Keméja ini sudah –.* This shirt is tight. *Waktunya –.* a) Time is pressing. b) His time is limited. **2** narrow-minded, narrow (of vision/viewpoint). *Pandangannya –.* He has a narrow mind. **3** crowded (of a house, etc.). *Bandung semakin –.* Bandung is becoming increasingly crowded. – *akal* narrow-minded. – *alam* (*M*) quick-tempered. – *arti* narrow sense. – *dada* touchy, irritable. – *hati* touchy, quick to take offense. – *hidup* in distress/strained circumstances. – *kalang* quick to anger, irascible, bad-tempered. – *kening* touchy, quick to take offense. – *ketat* tight-fitting. – *mata* narrow-minded. – *pintu rezeki* in distress/strained circumstances. – *waktu* to have no time.

bersempit-sempit crushed (of people in crowds), packed in like sardines. *hidup ~ dalam sebuah rumah kecil* to live packed like sardines in a small house.

menyempit to narrow (down), crowd, be crammed.

menyempitkan and **mempersempit 1** to narrow, make narrower/smaller, take in. *Ia mempersempit roknya.* She took in her skirt. **2** to limit, reduce, diminish. *~ hak berbicara kebébasan bergerak* to limit freedom of movement. *Penyeléwéngan bisa dipersempit.* Fraud can be reduced.

tersempit narrowest.

sempitan narrows, narrow passage.

kesempitan 1 narrowness, limitation (of time). *~ akal* stupidity. **2** to be in a tight spot, with one's back to the wall. *Dia tidak dapat bergerak lagi karena ~* He could no longer move because he was with his back to the wall. **3** to be short of. *masa ~* depression, slump. *~ uang* to be hard-pressed. **4** (*coq*) too narrow. *Celana saya ~.* My pants are too tight.

penyempit s.t. that narrows (down) s.t.

penyempitan 1 narrowing, limiting; narrow passage. *~ pembuluh darah* arteriosclerosis. *~ arti* (*gram*) narrowing of meaning.

semplah (*Jv*) to hang off in pieces; hanging down useless, broken. – *hati* disheartened.

semplak (*Jv*) **menyemplak** [and **nyemplak** (*coq*)] to jump (on). *~ di belakang B.* to jump on the back of B.('s motorcycle/bicycle, etc.).

semplakan jump.

sempoa (*C*) abacus.

sempoyongan (*J*) to totter, stagger. *dalam keadaan –* groggy, staggering.

semprit I (*Jv*) **1** (small) whistle. **2** (small) syringe (used by physicians/drug addicts).

menyemprit 1 to whistle at (by a traffic policeman in order to stop traffic violators). **2** to inject with a syringe.

sempritan police whistle. *korban* ~ a traffic violator.

penyemprit whistle.

semprit II → KUÉ *semprit*.

semprong l glass, chimney. **2** tube. **3** (- *asap*) chimney (for smoke; also, of ships). **4** telescope, binoculars, spyglass. *kapal – Biru* a ship of the Blue Funnel Line. *kué –* rolled waffle, a crisp cylinder-shaped cookie. – *dompét* k.o. sweet roll; → KUÉ *semprong*. – *kacang* k.o. cookie.

semprot l spray gun, squirt gun, nozzle. **2** (physician's) syringe.

menyemprot l to spray. *Saya harus ~ kamar ini dengan DDT*. I have to spray this room with DDT. **2** [and **nyemprot** (*coq*)] to squirt. *Jangan ~ saya dengan pipa air itu*. Don't squirt me with that hose. **3** (*ob*) to inject (a liquid into s.o.'s body). *Juru rawat sudah ~ pasiennya*. A nurse injected s.t. into the patient. **4** to scold, reprimand. *Pejabat itu disemprot*. The official was scolded.

menyemproti to spray, squirt.

menyemprotkan to shoot, spray, squirt. *~ air itu ke api*. Squirt the water at the fire.

tersemprot [and **kesemprot** (*coq*)] sprayed.

semprotan l nozzle, spraying device. **2** spray. **3** scolding, criticism, reprimand. *dapat –* to get a scolding. *~ tinta* inkjet. *~ kabut* mist spray.

penyemprot l sprayer, spray, gun. *alat ~ mékanis* sprinkler. *~ air* water sprinkler. *~ asap* mistblower. *~ pasir* sandblaster. *~ tangan* hand sprayer. **2** nozzle.

penyemprotan l spraying, fogging. **2** injection.

semprul (*Jv*) l inferior quality (of tobacco). **2** worthless, insignificant, nonsense. *Itu hanya réka-rékaan pengacara –*. That was only a story made up by an insignificant lawyer. **3** nonsense.

sempudal dried food clinging to the mouth.

bersempudal dirty, smeared.

sempul (*ob*) tersempul emerged, turned up; → TERSEMBUL.

sempulur (*Jv*) l lucky. **2** to be prosperous; to grow prosperously. **3** prosperity, progress.

sempur (*S*) k.o. tree, *Dillenia spp*.

sempuras I (= **bersempuras**) untidy, dirty (of one's mouth/face).

sempuras II (*M*) refuse, rubbish, dregs; → SEMPELAH.

sempurna (*Skr*) l flawless, without fault, without any problems. *éksibisi yang –* a flawless exhibition. *dengan –* fully, in full, completely, perfectly. **2** perfect, complete, comprehensive. *kamus yang –* a complete/comprehensive dictionary. *Tidak ada orang yang –*. Nobody is perfect. **3** finished, completed, ended well. *Segala pekerjaannya –*. All his work was completed/finished. *kurang –* less than perfect. **kekurangsempurnaan** less than perfection, imperfection. *Ketua Mahkamah Agung mengungkapkan bahwa ~ kerja yang ia maksud itu terdapat baik di bidang administrasi maupun téknis yustisial*. The Chairman of the High Court disclosed that the work imperfections he was referring to are found in both judicial administration and technique. *tidak –* imperfect. **ketidaksempurnaan** imperfection. *~ pasar* market imperfection. *– akal* a) grown-up, adult. b) hale and hearty. *– umur* grown-up, adult. *– usia* passed away, died.

sesempurna as perfect/complete as.

sesempurna-sempurnanya as perfect/complete as possible, perfectly. *Répélita berjalan dengan ~*. The Five-Year Plan is proceeding perfectly.

menyempurnakan l to perfect, complete, make s.t. more perfect. **2** to improve, revamp (a cabinet/law), overhaul (an engine). *Sempurnakan keahlianmu*. Improve your skills. **3** to do s.t. with the proper ceremony. *~ mayat* to bury with the proper ceremonies.

tersempurnai *~ oléh* completed/perfected by.

kesempurnaan perfection, excellence, completeness. *ilmu –* mysticism.

penyempurna l s.t. for perfecting/revamping/overhauling. **2** perfectionist.

penyempurnaan perfecting, completion, improving, improvement, revamping, overhaul(ing). *~ menyeluruh* total revamping/overhaul.

semput short of breath.

semrawut (*Jv*) chaotic, disordered, disorganized, unruly. *keadaan yang paling –* a very chaotic situation.

kesemrawutan chaos, disorder, uproar, hubbub. *– dalam perjalanan lalu-lintas keréta api* the dislocation of railway traffic.

semringah → SUMRINGAH.

semsem → SENGSEM.

semu l quasi, mock (democracy, etc.), pseudo-, apparent. *Démokrasi yang hanya – saja lebih merugikan rakyat*. Only a quasi democracy places the people at a greater disadvantage. *dokter –* a fake physician. *mati –* apparently dead, in a state of suspended animation. *tinggi –* apparent altitude. **2** to bear some likeness to, somewhat, more or less, ...-ish. *– kuning* yellowish. *–.– lengkung* somewhat curved/arched. *– daya* deceit, ruse, pretence, trick, fraud. *– gerak* feint. *pujuk Melayu, – Jawa* Malay flattery/sweet words and Javanese deceit.

semu-semu somewhat, more or less, ...-ish.

bersemu l to be/look like. **2** to pretend to be s.t.

menyemui and **menyemu(kan)** to trick, cheat, deceive. *menyemukan diri* to disguise o.s. (as).

tersemui cheated, deceived.

kesemuan pseudo. *~ pendidikan* pseudo-education. *~ pséudo* fake, pseudo.

penyemu impostor, deceiver.

penyemuan imposition.

semua (*Skr*) l all (of), everything, in all, together. *– orang akan mati* all people will/must die. *– teman saya baik*. All of my friends are nice. *– meréka* they all, all of them. *Tidak – meréka dalang baru*. Not all of them were new puppeteers (in *wayang* performances). *– terjual habis*. Everything is sold out. *Jika – berjalan sesuai dengan rencana, kita akan kaya*. If things work out as planned, we'll be rich. *– serba ada* Everything is well-provided for. *– ini* all this. *– ini menjurus pada sikap tidak atau kurang rasional menghadapi berbagai perkembangan tertentu*. All this leads to an irrational or less rational attitude facing certain various developments. *– ... terkecuali* all ... but. *– teman saya terkecuali Achsan datang ke pésta saya*. All my friends came to my party but Achsan. **2** everyone, everybody. *Hidup di kota kecil, di mana – mengenal*. Life in a small village, where everybody knows everybody.

semuanya l all of it/them. **2** in all, altogether. *~ ada lima puluh orang*. There were 50 people in all. *Berapa ~?* How much does it cost altogether?

semua-semua everyone (without exception). *Tampangnya boléh juga. ~ pasti bilang ia céwék caem (khusus buat cowok yang rabun dilarang memberikan penilaian)*. Her figure isn't bad. Everyone will certainly say that she's a cute girl (nearsighted boys are forbidden from giving an evaluation).

semua-muanya everything; → SEGALA-GALANYA. *~ diangkut lintas udara* everything was airborne.

kesemua all. *~ tapol sudah dibébaskan*. All political detainees have been released.

kesemuanya all (of it), the whole (thing). *~ itu taklah berarti*. The whole thing was senseless.

kesemuaan totality.

semudera → SAMUDERA, SAMUDRA.

semuka alike (of the face). *Kedua-dua anak kembar itu agak –*. Those two twins are somewhat alike; → MUKA.

bersemuka in private, privately.

menyemukakan to confront, present s.o. face to face with s.o. else.

semula l from the beginning. **2** in the beginning, at first/the outset; → MULA.

semunian *daun –* k.o. medicinal plant, club moss, *Lycopodium cernuum*.

semunding (*ob*) k.o. monkey.

semuntu → SIMUNTU.

semur (*D*) meat boiled in spicy soy sauce. *– ati* braised liver. *– ayam* braised chicken in soy sauce. *– belut* braised eel. *– sapi* braised beef.

menyemur to braise s.t. in that sauce.

semurwat (*Jv*) → SEMADYA, SAK *madya*.

semut l ant. *dari – sampai gajah* from small to big; from high to low. **2** snow (on TV screen). *mati – karena gula* amenable to flattery. *di seberang lautan – kelihatan, gajah di pelupuk mata* *tidak kelihatan* to see the mote in one's brother's eye and not the beam in one's own. – *api* fire ant, *Solenopsis geminata*. – *asam* k.o. black ant. – *gajah* elephant ant, Bornean carpenter ant, *Camponotus gigas*. – *gatal* sugar ant, Pharaoh's ant, *Monomorium pharaonis*. – *geramang* long-legged ant, *Plagiolepis/Formica longipes*. – *gula* sugar ant, *Monomorium pharaonis*. – *hitam* black ant, *Dolichoderus sp*. – *kayu* carpenter ant, *Camponotus herculaneus*. – *kerangga/kerengga* weaver ant, *Oecophylla smaragdina*. – *keripik* a small brown or black ant, *Crematogaster difformis*. – *lada* dark red ant. – *manisan* sugar ant, Pharaoh's ant, *Monomorium pharaonis*. – *mérah* code word for PDI supporters. – *putih* termite. – *pudak* a small brown, red, or black ant, ghost ant, *Tapinoma melanocephalum*. – *rangrang* weaver ant, *Oecophylla smaragdina*. – *sabung/sabur* red and black stinging ant, *Sima rufonigra*. – *sentada* white ant, termite.

bersemut swarming with ants.

menyemut to swarm, teem. *Orang-orang ~ di jalan*. The street is teeming with people.

menyemuti to swarm all over s.t.

kesemutan, (ke)semut-semutan, and **semutan** pins and needles, prickling sensation in a part of the body, formication; to be "asleep" (of a numbed body part).

semuten → SEMUTAN.

sén I (*D*) *uang* – cent, 1/100 rupiah.

sénan 1 by/in cents. **2** cent (the coin), one-cent piece. *Saya sudah dari dulu jualan seperti ini. Mulanya ikut bapak saya, waktu zamannya uang ~*. I used to be a trader. It began when I joined my father at the time that the one-cent piece still had some value. *bilangan ~* (*J*) only some cents.

sén-sénan to live by/in cents, very poor.

sén II (*D*) sign, signal. *lampu* – a) flashing light. b) turn signal (of car).

ngesén to make a sign, give a signal.

sena (*Skr*) yellow-flowered shade tree, *Pterocarpus indicus*; → ANGSANA, ANGSÉNA.

séna (*Skr*) **1** army. **2** soldiers, troops. – *Jalasenastri* name of the Navy Wives' Association.

senak 1 clogged (of a ditch, so that it becomes full to overflowing). *Selokan-selokan – airnya, itulah yang menyebabkan banyak nyamuk*. The water in the ditches cannot flow, which is the reason why there are so many mosquitoes. **2** too full, feel uncomfortable due to overeating, etc., congested. *Perutnya – karena ia terlalu banyak makan dan minum di pésta itu*. He had a uncomfortable feeling in his stomach because he ate and drank too much at the party. *Sudah dua hari ini – rasa perutku*. These last two days I have had a full feeling in my stomach. **3** to have a tight feeling in the chest. **4** to be full (of thoughts, in one's head). **5** stagnant (water). – *napas* tight and spasmodic (of asthmatic breathing). – *perut* a swollen stomach (due to gas); → SENEP.

menyenak 1 to be clogged (up), congested. *Bendar air ~ The* ditch got clogged and overflowed. *air pasang ~* (of the tide) to flood and overflow. **2** to make s.t. too full/congested.

menyenak-nyenak to get all clogged up.

menyenakkan to make too full/congested, make s.o. feel uncomfortable. *Tingkah lakumu itu yang ~ hatiku*. It's your behavior that's makes me feel uncomfortable.

tersenak(-senak) 1 clogged (flow of water, etc.). **2** choked (up), suffocated, congested. *~ hati* have a depressed/dejected feeling. *~ kata* cannot utter a word, be tongue-tied.

kesenak(-senak)an suffer from indigestion/congestion/tightness/oppressiveness, suffocate.

senam I gymnastics; to do gymnastics. – *irama* calisthenics. – *kesegaran jasmani* [SKJ] physical fitness exercises. – *pagi* morning gymnastics. – *palang* gymnastics. – *séks* sexercise.

bersenam 1 to do physical exercises. **2** to stretch o.s. (after resting); → MENGGELIAT.

penyenam and **pesenam** gymnast.

senam II k.o. indigo plant, *Indigofera spp*. **2** dark blue, black, dark (of tigers). *bengkak* – (beaten) black and blue. **3** very pale. **4** the original color (of s.t. that has been varnished or gilded).

sénamaki (*A*) *pohon* – k.o. shrub, senna of Mecca, *Cassia angustifolia*, that can be used as a laxative.

senandung (*onom*) humming.

bersenandung to hum.

menyenandungkan to hum s.t. *~ nyanyian* to hum a tune.

senandungan humming.

penyenandung hummer.

senang 1 happy, to feel well, contented, satisfied, comfortable. – *lénang* (*Mal*) very comfortable. *orang yang – hidupnya* s.o. who takes pleasure/delight in his life. *merasa –* to be/feel at ease, feel comfortable/at home. *merasa kurang –* to be/feel ill at ease, feel uncomfortable, do not feel at home. *Ayah tidak/kurang – tinggal di sana*. Father didn't feel comfortable there. **2** in a good temper, good-humored, merry, cheerful. – *sekali* perfectly happy. **3** pleasant, agreeable, pleasing. **4** (*reg*) to like. – *dan tak –* likes and dislikes. – *dengan buah* to like fruit. – (*pada*) interested in. *Semasa hidupnya, almarhum – fotografi dan main ténis*. During his life, the deceased liked photography and tennis. *Rupanya kurang – kalau dikawinkan dengan dia*. It seems that she doesn't want to get married to him. – *bersaing* competitive. **5** well, in good health. *Sudah enam hari ini rasa badan tak –*. I haven't been feeling well for six days. *sudah agak – and berangsur –* getting better, recovering, improving in health. **6** (*Med Mal*) easy, simple. *Pulpén ini – memakainya*. This fountain pen is easy to use. *Gajinya besar, pekerjaannya –*. He has a high salary and his job is easy. **7** calm. **8** *ada –(.–) saja* be doing/getting on well. **9** (cannot sleep) quietly/peacefully. *tidak – dissatisfied*. **ketidak-senangan** dissatisfaction, resentment. *Syahrul menyatakan akan mengajukan ~nya kepada camat dan petugas keamanan supaya hal itu tidak terulang*. Syahrul stated his intention to express his dissatisfaction to the (administrative) district head and security officer so that the case won't recur. – *hati* pleased, delighted. **bersenang hati dengan/kepada** to be pleased/delighted with, get along (well) with s.o. **penyenang hati** s.t. pleasing, a pleasure.

senang-senang *~ susah* (*Med*) sometimes easy, sometimes hard. → GAMPANG-GAMPANG *angel/susah. Mengurus Surat Izin Bangunan di Médan ~ susah*. Applying for a Building Permit in Medan is unpredictable, sometimes it's easy and sometimes not.

bersenang to have a good time. *Taman hiburan itu berfungsi sebagai tempat bersantai dan ~*. That amusement park is a place for relaxation and having a good time.

bersenang-senang, bersenang(-senangkan) *diri*, and **menyenangkan** *diri* to take it easy, enjoy o.s., have a good time, have fun.

menyenangi to like. *Itu yang saya senangi*. That's what I like. **disenangi** to be popular.

menyenangkan [and **nyenangin** (*J coq*)] **1** [= mempersenang(kan)] to do s.o. a favor, please, amuse, let s.o. have his (own) way, satisfy, make s.o. content. *Senangkanlah hatimu*. a) Don't worry. b) Keep quiet. **2** attractive, inviting, pleasant, amusing, entertaining, kind, friendly, interesting, favorable, satisfying. *Pekerjaannya ~*. His work is satisfying. *orang yang ~* an agreeable person. *jawaban yang ~* a favorable answer. *tidak ~* offensive, unpleasant. **3** (*reg*) to like. *~ hati* to put one's mind at rest.

kesenangan 1 pleasure, happiness, enjoyment, entertainment, joy, gladness, delight, amusement, pastime. **2** comfort, ease, convenience. **3** fun. **4** what s.o. likes/wants most, one's favorite, hobby. *~nya teka-teki silang*. He is a crossword puzzle fan. *Anak-anak itu ~nya setengah mati*. Those children were delirious with joy.

penyenang s.t. pleasing, a pleasure. *~ mata* s.t. nice to look at.

penyenangan pleasing, making pleasant.

senangin *ikan* – thread fish, *Polynemus/Eleutheronema tetradactylus*.

senantan white (of fighting cocks); → KINANTAN.

senantiasa (*Skr*) always, incessantly, continuously, perpetually. – *hari* daily.

senapan [and **senapang** (*infr*)] (*D snaphaan*) gun, rifle. *–nya menyalak, granat ia lémparkan ke ténda-ténda lainnya*. His gun began to talk, he threw a grenade into the other tents. – *angin* air rifle. – *api* fire-arm. – *api lantak* muzzleloader. – *bambu/buluh* a) bamboo rifle (children's toy). b) it looks dangerous, but it isn't. – *berburu* sporting gun. – *cis* BB gun. – *bidik* sniper rifle. – *kembar* double-barreled shotgun. – *kopak* breech-loader. – *lantak/locok* muzzle-loader. – *mimis* BB gun. – *minimi* k.o. small machine gun. – *pengantin* double-barreled shotgun. – *serbu* assault rifle. – *submesin* submachine gun. – *sundut* flintlock gun. – *tumbuk* muzzleloader.

bersenapan to be armed with a gun/rifle.

sénapati → SÉNOPATI.

senar (*D*) 1 (violin/guitar, etc.) string. 2 string (on a tennis racket).

senarai (*Mal*) list; → DAFTAR. – *makalah* list of (newspaper) articles.

menyenaraikan to list.

sénario → SKÉNARIO.

senat and **sénat** (*D*) 1 senate, the upper branch of the U.S. legislature. *anggota* – (U.S.) senator. 2 senate, i.e., the governing/advisory council in a college/university. – *mahasiswa* [séma] student senate.

senator and **sénator** (*D*) senator; → anggota SÉNAT.

senawan k.o. venomous snake.

Senawangi [Sékretariat Nasional Pewayangan Indonésia] Indonesian Shadow Puppet National Secretariat.

senawar *pinang* – a palm variety, *Actinorhytis spp.*

senawat rattan buffalo-whip.

senawi a ship's passenger who works to pay his passage.

Senayan the area of Jakarta in which the DPR and a sports stadium are located.

senda I – *gurau* a) amusing, comic (of a person/conduct). b) joke, amusement, fun. ***bersenda gurau*** to joke around, banter.

bersenda-senda to joke around, banter, jest, flirt.

mempersendakan to tease, make fun of.

senda II (*ob*) → SANDA II, SENDA I.

sendal I (*J*) → SANDAL.

sendal II (*Jv*) **menyendal** 1 to jerk/pull at, tug on. 2 to snatch, pickpocket, pilfer.

menyendalkan to snatch, pickpocket.

tersendal 1 snatched, grabbed. 2 pickpocketed.

sendalan a pull, tug, jerk.

kesendalan to get pickpocketed.

sendal III wedge, shim.

menyendal to insert (a wedge to keep a door or window open).

sendalan s.t. inserted.

sendalu *angin* – (moderate) breeze.

sendam tersendam (*cla*) to plunge/dive down.

sendang (*Jv*) well, source, spring.

Sendangsono (*Jv*) the Indonesian "Lourdes" in Muntilan, Central Java.

sendar bersendar to snore (lightly).

penyendar snorer.

sendarat *ikan* – red snapper, mangrove jack, *Lutjanus argentimaculatus.*

sendat (*Jv*) 1 sluggish, slow(-moving), stagnant. *Arusnya air* –. The flow of water was sluggish. 2 tight (of a ring/clothes, etc.), narrow, closely fitting. *Celananya – sekali.* His pants are too tight. – *lubang kulup* (*med*) phymosis. 3 clogged (of a sewer/drain/nose, etc.). *perasaan – di kerongkongan* a choked-up feeling in one's throat. 4 chock-full, crammed.

menyendat-nyendat to come in fits and starts.

menyendat(kan) to stop/clog/choke/plug up, make s.t. jam. *Tumpukan sampah ~ selokan.* A pile of trash clogged up the ditch.

tersendat [and **kesendat** (*coq*)] 1 stagnant. 2 suspended, halted, held up. *Sidang pemilikan senjata genggam tanpa izin ini, dimulai selak bulan yang lalu dan agak ~ karena terhukum tidak menguasai bahasa Indonésia dengan baik.* The (court) session on owning hand-held weapons without a license which started last month was rather held up because the convicted person hadn't mastered Indonesian well enough. 3 stopped (in one's tracks), stood still. *Saya ~ oléh suaranya yang merdu.* I stopped in my tracks due to her sweet voice. **ketersendatan** stagnation, suspension, standstill. *Sekali-sekali terjadi – dalam gaya penulisannya dalam buku ini!* Time after time a standstill occurs in his style of writing this book.

tersendat-sendat [and **kesendat-sendat** (*coq*)] joltingly, jerk-

ingly, haltingly, in fits and starts. *dengan bahasa Inggris yang ~ in broken/halting English. menangis ~ to sob; sobbing. ucapan ~* a jerky speech.

sendatan clog.

kesendatan 1 clogged (up). 2 stagnation.

penyendatan clogging up, suspending, stopping (the flow).

sendawa I (*Skr*) saltpeter. *asam* – nitric acid. *obat* – gunpowder. *zat* – nitrogen.

bersendawa nitric.

menyendawakan to nitrify.

sendawa II (*M*) belch, burp; → SERDAWA.

tersendawa to belch, burp.

sendayan *rumput* – k.o. sedge, *Thorachostachyum bancanum.* – *masin* k.o. weed, *Pandanus oratus.* – *piah* k.o. sedge, sea grass, *Rhynchospora corymbosa.*

séndé I (*Jv*) *dijual* – to be sold with the right of repurchase.

menyéndékan to rent. *Sawahnya diséndékan kepada seorang bermodal di kota.* His irrigated rice fields were rented to a capitalist in the city.

nyéndé *sistém ~* rent system.

séndé II → SANTÉT.

séndél berséndél to lean (against). *~ bahu* shoulder to shoulder.

menyéndélkan to lean s.t. (against s.t.). *Punggungnya diséndélkan pada dinding.* He leaned his back on the wall.

séndéng I (*D*) Protestant mission. *sekolah* – missionary school.

séndéng II 1 slanting, sloping, tilting, listing. 2 squinty-eyed. 3 (*coq*) cracked, not in one's right mind. – *méndéng* staggering (around); → TERHUYUNG-HUYUNG.

berséndéng to lean, incline. *Ia ~ pada témbok itu* he leaned against that wall.

berséndéngan (*pl subj*) to slant/tilt. *Kalau angin kencang, layar perahu ~.* When there is a strong wind, the sails of the boat tilt.

menyéndéng to lean, slant, incline, bend over.

menyéndéngkan to put s.t. in a slightly slanting position, tilt, tip up slightly.

terséndéng-séndéng tottering, staggering.

sénder (*D*) transmitter, transmitting station.

séndér (*Jv*) **berséndér** to lean, incline.

menyéndér to lean.

menyéndérkan to lean s.t.

terséndér leaning.

séndéran 1 slope. 2 place where s.t. leans.

sendera → SANDERA.

senderik k.o. kris.

senderung *ikan* – a) coral trout, *Plectropoma maculatum.* b) black-tip grouper, *Epinephelus fasciatus.*

senderut (*ob*) surly, sour.

sendi I (*Skr*) 1 joint (of the bones), articulation. *berasa ngilu pada tulang –nya* to feel a pain in one's joints. *penyakit* – rheumatism; → SENGAL I. *salah* – sprained (one's ankle). 2 hinge (of a door/window, etc.), joint; → ÉNGSÉL. *Tangkai kacamataku patah –nya.* The hinge on the temple of my glasses is broken. 3 k.o. covering on s.t. *bagai tanduk – gading* s.t. that doesn't match up. – *éngsél* hinge-joint. – *kacamata* hinges on the temples of glasses. – *kejur* arthritis. – *lutut* knee-joint. – *pangkal paha* hip-joint. – *peluru* ball-and-socket joint. – *rahang* maxillary joint. – *rangka* spinal column. – *tercerai* disjointed, out of joint. – *tulang* joint, articulation.

bersendi 1 with a joint, hinged. 2 plated, covered.

bersendi-sendi with joints, articulated.

menyendi 1 (= **menyendikan**) to provide with hinges. 2 (= **menyendi-nyendi**) to chop/cut off (the legs or limbs of a slaughtered animal).

persendian 1 joints, articulation. *gerakan ~* movements of the joints. *peradangan ~* rheumatism. *~ tulangnya* the articulation of bones. 2 hinges.

sendi II (*Skr*) 1 base, foundation, substructure. *batu* – foundation stone. 2 foundation, principle, basis. *-.- kepercayaan* the foundations of faith.

bersendi to have a base/support/pillar. *rumah ~ batu* a house with a substructure of rocks.

bersendikan to be based on. *Républik Indonésia ~ Pancasila.* The Republic of Indonesia is based on Pancasila.

menyendi to lay down a base/foundation.

menyendikan and **mempersendikan** to base/found s.t. on.

persendian base, foundation.

sendiko (*Jv*) as you order or wish (answer of a subordinate to an instruction). – *dawuh* (a mental attitude) only waiting for orders from superiors.

sénding → SÉNDÉNG I.

sendiri I 1 (preceded by a personal pronoun) (self), myself, himself, herself, ourselves, themselves. *saya* – I myself. *dia* – he/she himself/herself. **2** own a) (preceded by a noun + possessive suffix, the possessive relationship is more precisely expressed) of one's own, (what one does at) home. *masakan* – home cooking. *rumahku* – my own house, *rumahnya* – his own house, etc. b) (depending on its position in a sentence). *Dia membawa kendaraan* –. He drove his own car; (*cp*) *Dia – membawa kendaraan*. He himself drove the car. **3** in person, personally. *Pelamar-pelamar harus datang* –. Applicants have to come in person. *Saya bertemu dengan dia* –. I met him personally. **4** (without external help) self-, by itself, independently. *alat perkakas yang dapat bergerak* – a self-propelled apparatus. *Dicari seorang pemegang buku yang dapat bekerja* –. Wanted: a bookkeeper able to work independently/on his own initiative, able to work without supervision, capable of taking responsibility for his own work. *berdiri tegak* – autonomous, independent. **5** single, unmarried. *Saya masih* –. I'm still single. **6** (entirely by o.s., not accompanied by others) all alone/by o.s. *Ia pergi ke Bandung – saja*. He went to Bandung all alone/by himself. *Sudah dingin, – lagi*. It was cold, and on top of that she was all by herself. *merasa – dan sepi*, → SORANGAN *waé*. **7** of one's own accord, without being asked (to). *Ia pergi* –. He left of his own accord. *Ada yang babat pohon cengkéh* –. There are persons who fell clove trees without being asked to. **8** to o.s. *Dia tertawa* –. She laughed to herself.

sendirinya *dengan* ~ by/of itself, of one's own free will, of its own accord, automatically, spontaneously. *bergerak dengan* ~ to move automatically. *(berkata) sama* ~ a) (to say) to o.s. b) (to say) to one's own friends or among themselves. *bertentangan sama* ~ in conflict with o.s.

sendiri-sendiri separately, one by one, individually. *Marilah, kita membayar* ~ *makanan kita*! Let's go Dutch! *Meréka masuk* ~. They entered one by one.

bersendiri 1 isolated, separated, severed. **2** to seclude o.s., be alone, retreat, recede, retire. *Éjaan bukanlah suatu pelajaran yang* ~ *atau tidak berkait dengan pelajaran-pelajaran yang lain*. Orthography isn't an isolated study or not linked to other studies.

bersendirian ~ *dengan* to be alone together with.

menyendiri 1 isolated, separated, severed. **2** to seclude o.s., isolate o.s., be alone, retreat, recede, retire. *suka* ~ likes to be by o.s. *mengakhiri masa* ~ *alias membujang* to give up one's bachelorhood.

menyendirikan to separate (out), set aside, isolate, segregate. *Mana-mana yang besar baik disendirikan, jangan dicampur dengan yang kecil-kecil*. Separate out the big ones; don't mix them with the small ones.

tersendiri 1 alone, separate. **2** special, particular. **3** isolated, individual, segregated. **4** all its own. *Bagi sebagian penduduk Padalarang, bukit kapur di sana mémang mendatangkan rezeki* ~. For part of the residents of Padalarang, the limestone mountains there indeed bring good luck all its own. **ketersendirian 1** aloneness. **2** isolation.

sendirian (*coq* form of *seorang diri*) **1** all alone, by o.s. *Saya berangkat tidak* ~, *tetapi bersama-sama dengan tim dari McDonald's*. I left not by myself, but together with a team from McDonald's. **2** lonely, solitary, isolated. *Kali Tanah Abang tidak* ~, *hampir semua kali dan kanal di Jakarta sama nasibnya*. The Tanah Abang River is not an isolated case, almost all rivers and canals in Jakarta have suffered a similar fate.

kesendirian solitariness, loneliness. *Tetapi masih lebih banyak yang melamun dalam* ~, *karena tak ada teman seperjalanan*. But there are still more who daydream in loneliness, because they don't have a travel companion. *dalam* ~ *di tempat yang jauh* all by o.s. at a faraway place.

penyendiri s.o. who likes to be alone, loner.

penyendirian isolation.

sendiri II (on the analogy of Javanese/Sundanese *déwé*) **1** -est, indicates a superlative. *Inilah yang terbesar/paling besar* –. This is the very biggest. **2** very, right (of position). *Dia duduk di muka* –. He sits right in the front (or, at the very front). *di atas* – right at the top (or, at the very top).

sendocong *ikan* – k.o. freshwater fish.

séndok I 1 spoon, ladle. **2** scoop, trowel. – *besar tak mengenyang* apt to promise, apt to forget. – *dan periuk lagi berantuk* and – *dengan belanga lagi berlaga* even the best friends (husband and wife) fall out once and again. – *air* scoop. – *bubur* pap spoon. – *ciduk* ladle. – *dapur* large spoons for cooking. – *isi* scoop. – *kapur* trowel. – *makan* dinner/table spoon. – *nasi* rice ladle. – *pengedang* (*M*) spoon used to scoop hot water out of a cooking pot. – *semén* trowel. – *sepatu* shoe horn. – *sop* soup spoon. – *téh* tea spoon. – *turap* trowel.

berséndok-séndok by the spoonful.

menyéndok [and **nyéndok** (*coq*)] **1** to ladle/spoon out. **2** to stuff/shovel s.t. (in). ~ *penumpang sebanyak-banyaknya* (city buses) stuff in as many passengers as possible.

menyéndoki 1 to ladle s.t. out to s.o., spoon feed. **2** (*pl obj*) to ladle/spoon out.

menyéndokkan to spoon out s.t.

terséndok ladled out. *nasi* ~ *tidak termakan* even though s.t. was gotten, it wasn't enjoyed.

penyéndok s.t. that spoons/ladles out.

penyéndokan ladling/spooning out.

séndok II séndok-séndok *daun* ~ name of a plant, *Endospermum sp.*

séndok III black cobra, *Naja bungarus*.

sendorong (*M*) **bersendorong** to slip forward; → DORONG.

tersendorong slipped forward.

sendratari [seni drama tari] ballet.

menyendratatarikan to dramatize in a ballet.

sendu sad, grieved, depressed, dejected, melancholy; → SEDU II.

menyendukan 1 to sadden. **2** saddening, distressing. *Kurangnya tenaga kerja begitu* ~. The shortage of manpower is so distressing.

kesenduan sadness, depression, dejection, melancholy.

senduduk Singapore/Straits rhododendron, *Melastoma malabathricum. akar* – k.o. shrub, *Marumia muscosa/nemorosa*.

sénduk → SÉNDOK I, II.

sendusin (*A*) brocade.

senél (*D*) *sepur* – fast train, express.

Senén (*A*) → SENIN. *(hari)* – Monday. *berpuasa* –.*Kemis* and *pasa* –.*Kemis* (*Jv*) to fast on Mondays and Thursdays (for a certain period of time; as an act of self-abnegation performed in the hope of having a wish fulfilled). *Napasnya sudah* –.*Kemis*. He's almost dead.

nyenén ~ *kemis* to live from hand to mouth. *Bank-bank perkréditan rakyat di Jawa Barat itu kebanyakan hidupnya masih* ~ *kemis*. The majority of people's credit banks in West Java still live from hand to mouth.

seneng → SENANG.

senentiasa → SENANTIASA.

senep (*Jv*) **1** to have a pain in one's stomach, stomachache. **2** desire to defecate (but unable to).

senéwan → SENÉWEN. **kesenéwanan** nervousness.

senéwen (*D*) I (to have a) nervous (fit). **2** neurotic, emotionally disturbed. **3** to lose one's head, be desperate. *membuat orang* – to get on one's nerves, set one's nerves on edge.

séng (*D*) zinc. *(Kepalanya) beratap* –. His hair has turned gray. – *atap/gelombang/kerdut* corrugated iron sheets (used for roofing).

sengaja *dengan* – on purpose, intentionally, deliberately, premeditated. *dengan tidak* – unintentionally. *tidak* – unintentional, unintended, inadvertent, not on purpose. **ketidaksengajaan** inadvertence.

menyengaja(kan) to do s.t. on purpose. *disengaja* (to be done) intentionally, intentional, on purpose, deliberately, premeditated. *Kejadian itu tidak disengaja*. That incident was not intentional. *disengajakan untuk* exclusively earmarked for.

tersengaja intended. *tidak* ~ unintended.

kesengajaan intent(ion), prepense, with forethought. ~ *bersyarat* recklessness. ~ *jahat* malice.

sengak I (*Jv*) → SENGAT.

sengak II → SENGUK *sengak*.

sengal I rheumatic, sciatic; gout. *(éncok) – pinggang* lumbago. – *puru* pains from yaws. – *tulang* rheumatism.

sengal II (*J*) **sengal-sengal** ~ *napas* panting, gasping, out of breath.

tersengal-sengal panting, gasping, out of breath. *Napas tuanya mulai ~, tatkala menikung di tanjakan jembatan.* He became out of breath at his old age, when he made a turn at the ascent near the bridge (on his bike). *Pendidikan kita ibarat pelari bernapas ~.* Our education is like a sprinter out of breath.

sengam menyengam to gorge on, eat up.

sengangar (*M*) flash of lightning. *panas* – sizzling hot.

sengangkang k.o. swallow.

sengap to be quiet/silent.

menyengap 1 to muffle, deaden (a sound); to keep s.t. silent. **2** to shut s.o. up.

menyengapkan 1 to silence s.o. **2** to keep s.t. a secret, conceal s.t., suppress s.t.

sengarat *ikan* – k.o. freshwater fish found in marshes.

sengaring *ikan* – k.o. freshwater fish, *Labeobarbus tambra*.

sengar-sengir to grimace, smirk; → SENGIR II.

menyengar-nyengirkan to twist, distort.

sengat 1 sting, sharp (often poisonous) pointed organ of some insects, etc.; → ANTUP. *kena* – stung. *Meréka kena – gas.* The smell of gas stung their nose. *seperti lebah, mulut membawa madu, pantat membawa* – a beautiful woman using sweet language, but with a dirty and treacherous character. – *matahari* sunstroke. – *panas* heatstroke. – *pari* poisonous stinger of a stingray. **2** pungent (odor).

bersengat 1 with/to have a sting. **2** feared (by other people).

menyengat [and **nyengat** (*coq*)] **1** to sting, prick with a sting; stinging (pain). *Kalajengking ~ tapak tangannya.* A scorpion stung the palm of his hand. **2** to sting/hurt (of words). *Katakatanya ~.* His words hurt.

menyengatkan to sting.

tersengat stung. ~ *(aliran) listrik* to get electrocuted; → KESETRUM. *Diduga almarhum ~ aliran listrik sewaktu menyambungkan arus untuk sebuah pabrik plastik di Teluk Gong.* It's believed that the deceased was electrocuted when hooking up electric current for a plastic factory at Teluk Gong. *Nyi Sayani téwas ~ listrik.* Nyi Sayani was electrocuted.

sengatan sting, prick, bite. ~*nya mampu menamatkan jiwa anda.* Its sting can kill you. ~ *dingin* frostbite. ~ *lebah* bee sting. ~ *panas* heat stroke. *terkena* ~ *panas* affected by heat stroke. ~ *surya* sunstroke.

penyengat 1 various species of wasps and gnats, *Vespa spp. Ropalidia spp.* **2** stinger. *memelihara ~ dalam baju* to nourish/cherish a viper in one's bosom.

penyengatan sting, stinging.

sengau to speak through one's nose; nasal. *bunyi* – (*gram*) nasal sound. *huruf* – (*gram*) the nasal letters/sounds (m/n/ng).

menyengau to speak through the nose, make nasal sounds. *Suaranya disengau oléh napas yang tidak teratur.* He talked through his nose because of his irregular breathing.

menyengaukan to pronounce s.t. through the nose, nasalize.

tersengaukan nasalized.

sengauan nasal sound.

sengau-sengauan to imitate s.o. who talks through the nose.

penyengauan nasalization, nasalizing.

persengauan nasalization.

sengélat rogue; → HÉLAT.

sénget slanting, sloping, tilted, listing. *Kopiah yang dipakainya itu – ke kanan.* The cap he wore tilted to the right. – *méngét* (to hang, etc.) totally slanting. *biar – méngét jangan tertiarap* it's better to sacrifice a bit than to lose a lot.

menyénget to slant, tilt, list, be at an angle.

menyéngétkan to put in a slanting position, tilt.

terséngét slanted, tilted.

séngétan (*geol*) dip-slope.

senggak I (*Jv*) calling out, shouts in time to the music, to accompany with shouts in time to the music.

menyenggaki to call out/shout during music.

senggakan repeat, refrain. *nyanyian dengan* ~ song with a refrain.

senggak II menyenggak to snarl at, scold, chide.

senggama → SANGGAMA.

senggan k.o. basket.

senggang I (*Jv*) **1** leisure, free (time). *waktu* – free time. **2** to be off duty, have a holiday, have time. **3** (to have/offer) space.

bersenggang(-senggang) to have free time, spend one's free time.

menyenggangkan to allow/make free time for s.t., free up time.

kesenggangan spare/leisure time.

senggang II (*M*) stubborn, obstinate.

sénggang – *itik* livid amaranth, wild blite, *Amaranthus lividus*.

senggani *bunga* – Indian/Straits rhododendron, a flower variety found in Indonesian graveyards, *Melastoma candidum/malabathricum*.

senggara → SELENGGARA.

senggat 1 graduation (marking with degrees for measuring). **2** up to, as far as.

bersenggat graduated.

senggau bersenggau-senggau to stand on tiptoe and reach for s.t.

menyenggau 1 to reach up for s.t. **2** to blaze up, spread to (of a fire).

senggayut bersenggayut hanging down, dangling, swing while hanging down; → GAYUT.

bersenggayutan (*pl subj*) hanging down, dangling.

senggerahan (*ob*) temporary residence; → PASANGG(E)RAHAN.

senggeruk (*Jv*) **1** snuff. **2** narcotic/drug that is sniffed.

sénggét I (*J/Jv*) a pole for picking fruit high up on a tree.

menyénggét to get (fruit) down with that pole.

sénggét II → SINGGIT.

senggiling → TENGGILING.

senggok menyenggok 1 to hit, punch. **2** to knock down.

sénggok bersénggok leaning.

menyénggok to hit, butt (with the head).

sénggol (*J/Jv*) touch, nudge. – *lari* hit-and-run.

bersénggol to touch/have contact with.

bersénggolan (*pl subj*) to touch. *Maka saya pesanlah segala macam makanan yang selama ini tak pernah ~ dengan lidah saya.* So I ordered all kinds of dishes I had never tasted before.

menyénggol [and **nyénggol** (*coq*)] **1** to touch, nudge. **2** to brush/bump against. **3** to collide with. *disénggol mobil* to be sideswiped. **4** to offend.

sénggol-menyénggol to touch e.o.

menyénggol-nyénggol to keep touching/nudging. *Tangan wanita-wanita itu kadang usil ~ lelaki yang léwat.* The hands of those women now and then annoyingly kept nudging passing men.

tersénggol [and **kesénggol** and **kesénggolan** (*coq*)] (to get) hit (in a collision), come into contact with.

sénggolan 1 touch, contact, impact. **2** collision, crash.

sénggol-sénggolan frequent clashes/contact/impacts/collisions. *Kerusuhan itu bermula dari ~ antara kelompok Solikin dengan sekelompok lain.* The riot started with a number of clashes between the Solikin group and the other group.

senggora *kucing* – k.o. Siamese cat.

sénggot (*J/Jv*) **1** equipment for dipping up water from a well: a bamboo lever weighted at one end and holding the bucket at the other. **2** crane (used in ports).

senggugu I a plant whose leaves and roots have curative properties, *Clerodendron serratum*.

senggugu II a very small shrimp, *Mysis spp.*; → UDANG *geragau*.

senggugut dysmenorrhea, painful menstruation. – *bangkai* painful menstruation from an abortion. – *bunga* a) discharge after confinement. b) leucorrhea. – *darah* dysmenorrhea with irregular menstruation. – *lintah* spasmodic dysmenorrhea with vomiting.

sengguk I menyengguk to nod (in assent).

tersengguk-sengguk keep nodding (from old age/fatigue/sleepiness, etc.).

sengguk II menyengguk to hit, knock (one's head).

tersengguk to get hit/knocked.

sengguk III to hiccup.
  tersengguk-sengguk and **sesunggukan** (*Jv*) to hiccup, have the hiccups.
  senggukan hiccups.
sengguk IV (*J*) **sengguk-sengguk** and **sesenggukan** to weep with choking sobs.
senggulung I large tropical millipede (it rolls up when touched), *Oniscomorpha spp., Chilognatha.*
senggulung II head-support (made of a rolled-up piece of cloth and the like) used when carrying a load on the head. *besar – dari beban* to live beyond one's means; → *besar* PASAK *dari tiang*.
  bersenggulung to use such a head-support.
senggur-senggur (*Jv*) 1 to snore. 2 to purr (of cats).
senggut → SENGGUK I.
sengih menyengih to grin/smile so as to show one's teeth; to draw back one's lips and show one's teeth.
  menyengihkan to open (the mouth) slightly showing the teeth.
  tersengih grinned (showing the teeth).
  sengihan grin (showing the teeth).
sengingih (*M*) → SENGIH.
sengir I (*J/Jv*) turpentine smell (of certain fruit).
sengir II menyengir [and **nyengir** (*coq*)] 1 to turn up one's nose at s.t., sneer at s.t. 2 to grin. *Mukanya ~.* He grinned. *~ kuda* to turn up one's nose like a horse.
sengit 1 sharp, pungent, powerful (of odors). *bau minyak wangi yang – sekali* the very pungent smell of perfume. 2 stinging, sharp, caustic (of words). *Tiap perkataan yang dilémparkan-nya kepada saya – sekali.* Every word that he hurled at me was very stinging. 3 violent, furious, intense (of a quarrel/conflict, etc.). *Pasukan kita terlibat dalam pertempuran –.* Our troops were involved in a violent battle. 4 cruel. *orang yang sangat – a* very cruel person.
  bersengit to feel bitter.
  bersengit-sengitan to have bitter feelings toward e.o.
  menyengit to become sharp/pungent/violent.
  menyengitkan *~ hati* to offend, hurt s.o.'s feelings.
  tersengit the bitterest, most violent.
  sengitan bite, sting.
  kesengitan 1 sharpness, pungency. 2 acrimony. 3 violence, virulence, intensity.
sengkak I menyengkak to massage the stomach (of midwives or to expel gas).
sengkak II → SANGKAK I.
sengkal (*cla*) thwart, crossbeam.
  sengkalan wooden board on which spices or curry-stuff are ground or crushed. *seperti – tak sudah* like an unfinished curry-board, ugly and unsightly.
sengkala (*Jv*) chronogram, i.e., a cryptic means of expressing the digits of calendar years (in reverse order) by the use of four ordinary words which mystically represent those digits: a practice used *esp* for dating structures.
sengkang 1 crossbar, crossbeam. 2 spoke (of a wheel). 3 bolt (of a door). 4 bar, rod. 5 diameter (of a circle). 6 yoke, clip, clamp, strap. *tanda* – hyphen. *– bor* drill yoke. *– émbér* crosspiece of a pail (for carrying). *– kaléng* crossbar on a can that is used for holding it. *– Mérah* (*ob*) Red Cross. *– mulut kuda* bit (of a bridle). *– orang hukuma/si terhukum* shackles, fetters. *– pintu* bar, rod (of a door).
  menyengkang 1 to support s.t. with a crossbar. *Kaki méja itu baik disengkang supaya kokoh.* There's no harm in that the table legs are supported by a crossbar for firmness. 2 to prop open (an animal's mouth with a bar so that it can't bite). *Mulut buaya itu disengkangnya dengan sekerat kayu.* He propped the crocodile's mouth open with a piece of wood.
  menyengkangkan 1 to use s.t. as a crossbar/bolt, etc. 2 to prop s.t. open. 3 to put s.t. across the grain.
  tersengkang 1 provided with a crossbar/bolt, etc. 2 kept open (of one's mouth, etc.). (with a splint/piece of wood, etc.). 3 got stuck in the throat (of a fish bone, etc.) *Tulang ayam ~ di mulutnya.* A chicken bone got stuck in his mouth.
  penyengkang s.t. used as a crossbar.
séngkang with (one's) legs apart. *– pedoman* gimbal.

menyéngkang (to walk) with (one's) legs apart. *duduk ~* to sit with one leg drawn up and the other stretched.
  terséngkang pulled up.
sengkar a crossbar or thwart in a boat (for the oarsmen).
sengkarut complication, entanglement. *Dangdut adalah gamba-ran kehidupan yang sesungguhnya, yang penuh –.* Dangdut is a picture of real life, which is full of complications.
  bersengkarut 1 in a tangle (of ropes/lianas); involved (of a story/debtors). *utang ~* monetary entanglements. 2 confused, chaotic.
sengkawang *pohon –* a tree which produces *minyak sengkawang, Isoptera sengkawang/sumatrana;* → TENGKAWANG. *– air* k.o. tree, *Shorea lepidota;* → MERANTI.
sengkawar → MALÉO.
sengkayan waterspout.
séngkéd (*S*) indentation, notch (in a tree for climbing).
  séngkédan terrace (flat platform of earth with sloping sides, rising one above the other).
sengkek (*J/Jv*) short-necked and so looks short.
séngkék (*C*) a recent immigrant from China.
sengkela (*Skr*) shackles, fetters, hobbles.
  bersengkela *~ kaki* with shackles on the leg.
  menyengkela to shackle, fetter.
sengkelang 1 crossed (of the arms or legs). 2 bar (across a road or roads into a port).
  bersengkelang crossed (of arms or legs).
  menyengkelangkan to cross (one's arms or legs).
sengkelat → SEKELAT.
séngkélat not to wash after defecating.
sengkeling bersengkeling to have the legs crossed or the hands behind the back. *duduk di kursi dengan ~ kaki* to sit in a chair with legs crossed.
  menyengkelingkan to cross (one's legs or one's hands behind the back).
sengkelit I 1 a band or loop into which the feet are placed when climbing a tree. 2 loop (in general).
  bersengkelit to use such a band.
sengkelit II (*Jv*) **menyengkelit** to slip/stick a *keris*/cleaver, etc. into the right side of a belt at the back of one's waist.
  menyengkelitkan to stick s.t. into one's belt.
sengkelit III bersengkelit crushed (of people in crowds), jostled.
  menyengkelit to force one's way (into).
sengkenit a small jungle tick, *Argasidae.*
sengker I (*Jv*) **menyengker** to confine (an unmarried girl) to her home until she's safely married (a once traditional practice), keep in seclusion.
  sengkeran 1 isolation, seclusion. 2 cage.
sengker II (*S*) **sengkeran** limit.
sengkéta (*Skr*) 1 dispute, quarrel, conflict. *dalam –* in dispute. *daérah –* disputed area. 2 lawsuit, action, case, proceedings. *tidak ada – yang tidak dapat diselesaikan* there's no conflict that cannot be settled. *– bersenjata* armed conflict. *masalah – tanah* problem of conflicts on landed property.
  bersengkéta 1 to quarrel, be in conflict, have a dispute (with). 2 to go to court.
  menyengkétakan and **mempersengkétakan** to dispute (a fact), quarrel about. *yang dipersengkétakan* in dispute/question.
  tersengkétakan disputed.
  persengkétaan 1 discord, disagreement, (matter in) dispute, conflict. *Agama sering merupakan pokok ~.* Religion is often the point/matter at issue. 2 bone of contention.
sengkil *duduk ~* **tersengkil** to sit in an open doorway (of a girl to be seen by passersby).
sengkilit (*J*) **menyengkilit** [and **nyengkilit** (*coq*)] 1 to trip s.o. up. 2 to cheat s.o.
sengkit k.o. tree, *Myristica elliptica.*
séngkléh (*J/Jv*) broken, hanging loose (of branches, etc.).
sengklek (*J*) stupid person, idiot.
séngkok (*J*) bent, twisted (of an arm after it's been broken).
séngkol → SÉNGKUL.
séngkong → SINGKONG I, II.
sengkuang yam-bean, used for food and starch, *Pachyrrhizus*

bulbosus/erosus; → BESUSU. *pohon* - walnut tree of Papua New Guinea, *Dracontomelum mangiferum.*

sengkuap canopy, awning.

sengkul painful when swallowing.

sengkulun (*J*) *kué* - k.o. cake made from sticky rice.

séngon and **songon** k.o. tree, yellow mimosa, *Albizia chinensis.* - *laut* white albizia, *Paraserianthes falcataria.*

séngonisasi encouraging the planting of *séngon* trees.

    menyéngonisasi to encourage the planting of *séngon* trees.

sengsai (*Skr*) **1** misery, suffering. **2** sad, distressed, miserable.

séngsai (*C*) → SINSÉ.

sengsam I (*M*) **tersengsam** and **kesengsaman** pricked (by a thorn).

sengsam II → SEMSEM.

sengsara (*Skr*) **1** miseries, sufferings, pain, agony. *menjalani/ menanggung* - to suffer difficulties in life. *azab/siksa* - various k.o. sufferings. **2** to suffer hardships, have difficulties. *sudah biasa hidup* - accustomed to a life of hardship.

    menyengsarakan 1 to torment, torture. **2** to give s.o. a hard time.

    kesengsaraan misery, suffering, torment.

    penyengsaraan torturing.

séngsé (*C*) → SINSÉ.

sengsem (*Jv*) **kesengsem 1** engrossed in; keen on s.t. **2** charmed, be taken with.

séngséong (*C?*) prostitute, whore.

séngsu [tongséng asu] delicacy made of dog meat made into saté.

sengsurit *burung* - ferruginous wood-partridge, *Caloperdrix oculea.*

senguk (*Jv*) snuffling (of a kiss with the nose). - *sengak* and **menyenguk 1** to snuffle, snivel. **2** to sob.

sengungut *ikan* - a freshwater fish.

sengut tersengut-sengut to sob.

seni I art. *ahli* - artist. *bakat* - artistic talent. *karya* - work of art. *rasa* - taste for art. - *balih-balihan* (*Bal*) secular (profane) art. - *bangunan* architecture. - *batik* art of batiking. - *bebali* (*Bal*) ceremonial art. - *berperan* art of acting. - *budaya* art and culture. - *cétak* typography. - *drama* dramatic art. - *drama tari* [sendratari] ballet. - *lukis* drawing. **keseni-lukisan** (art of) painting. *dunia* ~ the world of paintings. - *melipat kertas* origami, the traditional Japanese art of folding paper to form flowers, animals, etc. - *mendidik* art of teaching. - *murahan* kitch. - *murni* fine art. - *pahat* sculpture. - *panggung* theatrical arts. - *patung* sculpture. - *pencak* a traditional self-defense art. - *pentas* theatrical arts. - *peran* acting (in film). - *pewayangan* the art of the *wayang.* - *rakyat* folk/popular art. - *réklame* advertising. - *rupa* fine/plastic art. **kesenirupaan** fine arts (*mod*). - *sastra* (art of) word painting, literary arts, literature. - *suara* a) singing (an art form). b) singing (a school subject). - *sulap* prestidigitation, sleight of hand. - *sungging* art of enameling. - *taman* landscaping. - *tari* (art of) dancing. - *tarik suara* (art of) singing. - *tunggang* equitation. - *ukir* sculpture. - *wali* (*Bal*) sacred art. - *yudha* art of war.

    berseni to be artistic.

    nyeni (*coq*) arty.

    kesenian art. *ilmu* ~ the fine arts. *malam* ~ art evening. ~ *rakyat* folk/popular art. **berkesenian** to be artistic. *Meréka tidak* ~ *sebagai profési.* They are not artistic as a profession.

seni II 1 fine. *rambut yang* - fine hair. **2** shrill, treble (of voice). *Suaranya terlalu* -. His voice is too shrill.

seni III *air* - urine. *hajat/buang air* - to urinate.

seni IV *ular* - a small k.o. snake.

séni I (*D*) genius; genius (person).

séni II (*D*) (military) engineer; → ZÉNI I.

seniah artistic.

    keseniahan artistry.

senigai *tangga* - crossbeams (to climb a pole).

sénil (*D*) senile.

sénilitas (*D*) senility.

seniman artist. - *patung* sculptor.

    nyeniman (*coq*) to become an artist.

    kesenimanan artistry. *citra* ~ artistic image.

senin (*hari*) - Monday; → SENÉN. - *hitam/Kelabu Kelas* Black Monday (October 26, 1987).

sénior (*D*) **1** (one longer in service) senior. **2** (*university sl*) male sophomore and higher.

    kesénioran seniority.

sénioritas (*D*) seniority.

sénioriti (*university sl*) female sophomore and higher.

senirupawan artist of fine arts.

seniwan I → SENIMAN.

seniwan II → SENÉWEN.

seniwati female artist.

senja (*Skr*) sunset, dusk, twilight. *sebelum* - *tiba* before sunset. - *telah turun.* Night had fallen. *pada masa* - *jabatannya* near the end of his term of office. *pada masa* - *usianya* in his old age. - *buta/raya* late in the evening when it is dark. - *kala* nightfall. - *Utama* the express train between Jakarta and Yogyakarta-Surakarta. *berebut* - (*M*) darkness fell.

    menyenja to fall (of night).

    kesenjaan (*coq*) **1** too late in the afternoon. **2** to get caught (out) in the evening.

senjak → SEJAK I.

senjakala → SENJA.

senjang and **sénjang 1** asymmetrical. **2** not alike, different. - *terbang* jet lag. - *waktu* time lag.

    kesenjangan 1 asymmetry. **2** discrepancy, gap, imbalance. ~ *antardaérah* interregional gap. ~ *générasi* generation gap. ~ *hubungan* communications gap. ~ *internal* internal gap. ~ *jumlah tabungan dan invéstasi* savings-and-investment gap. ~ *kebudayaan* cultural lag. ~ *kekuatan* power gap. ~ *kepercayaan* credibility gap. ~ *organisasi* organizational gap. ~ *pendapatan* income gap. ~ *rasial* racial gap. ~ *sosial* social imbalance. ~ *sumber daya* resources gap. ~ *tabungan* savings gap. ~ *tenaga kerja* manpower/labor force gap. ~ *waktu* time lag.

    persenjangan difference, discrepancy.

senjata (*Skr*) **1** weapon, arm(s). *Pancasila merupakan* - *ampuh bangsa Indonésia.* Pancasila constitutes an effective weapon of the Indonesian nation. - *makan tuan* those who lay traps for others get caught themselves, to be a victim of one's own tricks, hoist by one's own petard. *alat* - arms, equipment. *gencatan* - armistice, ceasefire. *meletakkan* - to lay down one's arms. *mengacungkan* - *ke atas* (*mil*) to present arms. *mengangkat* - to take up arms. *perlombaan* - arms race. *meletuskan* - to fire a firearm. *kebudayaan merupakan* - *rakyat* culture is a weapon of the people. **2** (*euph*) penis. *Ada sejumlah penyebab mengapa* - *pria tidak mau siaga.* There are a number of reasons why the penis cannot become erect. - *ampuh* an effective weapon. - *antitank* antitank weapon(s). - *api* [sénpi] firearm. **bersenjata api** with firearms. - *api gelap* illegal firearms. - *api sémi-automatis* semi-automatic firearms. - *atom* atomic weapon(s). - *bahu* rifles. - *berat* heavy artillery. - *berburu* sporting gun, shotgun. - *défénsif* defensive weapon(s). - *dorgok* muzzleloader, zip gun. - *énténg* small arms, light arms. - *gelap* illegal weapon(s). - *genggam* handgun(s), side arm(s), such as pistols and revolvers. - *inti* nuclear weapon(s). - *konvénsional* conventional weapon(s). - *kuman* biological weapon. - *lantak* muzzleloader, zip gun. - *lawan tank* antitank weapon(s). - *locok* muzzleloader, zip gun. - *mainan* toy gun/rifles. - *membela diri* defensive weapon(s). - *nuklir* nuclear weapon(s). - *ofénsif* offensive weapon(s). - *organik* (*joc*) police dog. *Pistol Colt 38 adalah* - *organik Polri.* The Colt 38 is an organic weapon of the Republic of Indonesia Police. - *otomatik* automatic weapon(s). - *pamungkas* a) a lethal weapon. b) (*leg*) ultimate remedy. - *pantai* coastal guns/batteries. - *pemusnah massal* weapons of mass destruction. - *pengejut listrik* electric stun gun. - *penghancur massal* weapons of mass destruction. - *penusuk* pointed weapon(s). - *pukul* blunt object (used as a weapon). - *ringan* light arms. - *samping* door gun (of helicopter). - *serbu* assault weapon. - *stratégis* strategic weapon(s). - *super* supergun (of Iraq). - *tajam* (*sajam*) sharp weapon(s), blade(s). - *tanpa tolak balik* [STTE]. - *tidak berbalas/bertolak* recoilless gun. - *terkokang* a firearm cocked for firing. - *térmonuklir* thermonuclear weapon(s). - *untuk menyerang* offensive weapons.

    bersenjata to be armed. *Angkatan* ~ *Républik Indonésia* [ABRI] Armed Forces of the Republic of Indonesia. *gerombolan* ~ an armed band. ~ *lengkap* fully armed. ~ *sebelit pinggang* and ~ *serba lengkap* armed to the teeth. ~ *tajam* armed with sharp weapons.

bersenjatakan to be armed with. ~ *lengkap* fully armed.

mempersenjatai to arm, supply/equip with weapons. *Waktu perang beberapa kapal dagang dipersenjatai dengan meriam.* During the war some merchantmen were armed with guns.

kesenjataan 1 arm (i.e., any combatant branch of the military forces). ~ *infanteri/kavaleri* the infantry/cavalry arm. **2** arms, weapons (*mod*). *sistém* ~ weapons system.

penyenjataan arming, supplying with arms.

persenjataan and **pemersenjataan** (derived from a hypothetical form *memersenjatai*) armament, arms, weaponry. *Pemersenjataan Asia Tenggara* Southeast Asia's weaponry.

senjata II (*A*) a vowel sign in Arabic script.

senjolong → JOLONG-JOLONG.

senjong beam (of scales).

sénjong metal tray on a pedestal.

senjuang → LENJUANG.

senoh → SENUH.

senohong *ikan* – k.o. fish, threadfin, *Polynemus indicus*.

senoman (*J*) *maén* – to play *arisan*.

senonoh proper, decent, seemly, becoming. *tidak* – improper, indecent. ***ketidaksenonohan*** impropriety, indecency, unbecomingness, unseemliness.

sénopati (*Jv*) commander-in-chief. – *ing Ngalogo* respectful term for the Sultan of Yogyakarta.

senot – *ubi* k.o. dessert made from cassava.

senoyong tersenoyong to stagger, totter.

sénpal (*D*) signal post.

sénpi [*senjata api*] firearm. – *bahu* rifle. – *genggam* handgun. – *pinggang* sidearm.

sénsasi (*D*) sensation; sensational. *penuh* – sensational.

sénsasional (*E*) and **sénsasionsi** (*D*) sensational.

sénsasionalisme (*D/E*) sensationalism.

sénsitif and **sénsitip** (*D*) sensitive. *tidak* – insensitive. ***ketidaksénsitifan*** insensitivity.

sénsitivitas (*D*) sensitivity.

sénso (*E*) chainsaw.

sénsor (*D*) **1** censor. **2** censorship. *badan* – film board of film censors, viewing board. *kena* – censored. *tidak kena* – uncensored. *lolos* – passed the censor.

menyénsor to censor.

tersénsor censored.

sénsoran s.t. censored.

penyénsor censor.

penyénsoran censoring. – *Pémda Sumsél terhadap harian Sriwijaya Post bukan hal yang baru.* The censoring by the South Sumatra Provincial Government of the daily *Sriwijaya Post* is not s.t. new.

sénsual (*E*) and **sénsuil** (*D*) sensual.

sénsualisme (*D/E*) sensualism.

sénsualitas (*D*) sensuality.

sénsur → SÉNSOR.

sénsus (*D*) census; → CACAH *jiwa*.

mensénsus and **menyénsus** to take census.

senta (*naut*) longitudinal beam in a ship to support the deck.

sénta menyénta to reject, refuse (a request/demand, etc.).

sentada I various species of trees, brown pine, *Podocarpus neriifolius*; → KAYU *cina*.

sentada II *semut* – a white ant.

sentadu *belalang* – k.o. praying mantis, *Tenodera aridifolia*. *ulat* – → ULAT *sentadu*.

sentagi I → SETAGÉN.

sentagi II *akar* – k.o. medicinal herb.

sentak [and **séntak** (*M?*)] **I menyentak 1** to pull hard, jerk, tug. **2** to pull out quickly/suddenly, snatch. *Pencopét itu* ~ *jam tangannya.* The pickpocket suddenly snatched his wristwatch. ~ *keris* to draw one's kris. ~ *tumbuk* to punch very hard.

menyentak-nyentak to throb, pulsate.

menyentakkan → MENYENTAK.

tersentak 1 pulled, jerked. **2** woke up suddenly. *Oetojo* ~ *dari*

tidurnya. Oetojo suddenly woke up from sleep. **3** shocked. *membuat kita* ~ *kagét* made us shocked. **ketersentakan** shock.

tersentak-sentak jerky (of movements).

sentakan 1 (strong) pull, tug, jerk, surge. **2** puff. *satu* ~ *udara* a puff of air.

penyentakan twitching, jerking.

sentak II (*J/Jv*) → BENTAK, HARDIK. **sentaknya** he/she snarled/lashed out.

menyentak [and **nyentak** (*coq*)] to lash out angrily.

menyentak-nyentak to be angry and disagreeable accompanied by snarling or harsh words.

menyentaki snap at, lash out at.

penyentakan lashing out.

sentaka laurel-like trees with commercial timber used for furniture and planks, *Phoebe multiflora*, *Pygeum parviflorum*.

sental I → SINTAL, SINTAR I.

sental II menyental 1 to polish, rub, scrub. **2** to slap.

menyentalkan to rub (violently), scrub. ~ *punggung pada témbok* to rub one's back against a wall.

sentalan 1 rub, polish. **2** slap.

sentali *burung* – coppersmith barbet, *Megalaima haemacephala indica*.

sentana I (*Jv*) relatives, family (of noblemen).

sentana II (*M*) *kalau* – suppose/supposing/assuming (that), if possible, perhaps.

bersentana proper, appropriate, fitting, as it should be. *dengan tidak* ~ without further ado.

sentana III (*Jv*) cemetery.

Sentani name of the airport in Jayapura.

sentap and **séntap** → SENTAK I.

sentara → SEMENTARA II. **1** let alone that (...not even). **2** transient. **kesentaraan** transience.

sentausa → SENTOSA.

sénté k.o. giant wild taro, elephant ear, *Alocasia macrorrhiza*.

sénténg I (*M*) **1** too short (of a skirt, etc.). **2** shortage (of money/food, etc.), to live in straitened circumstances. **3** crazy; → SINTING I.

menyénténgi and **menyénténgkan 1** to shorten. **2** to cause a shortage.

kesénténgan shortage, scarcity, lack.

sénténg II (*Bal?*) breast cloth (wrapped around the upper part of a woman's body); → KEMBAN.

sénter I (*ob*) lantern slide. *lampu* – a) flashlight. b) searchlight.

menyénter(i) to illuminate, light up.

sénteran beam (of light).

sénter II (*E*) center; central.

senteri → SANTRI.

sénterpor (*D*) center forward (in soccer).

sénti (*D*) centimeter.

sentiabu (*cla*) → SETIABU.

séntiare (*D*) centiare, square meter.

sentiasa → SENANTIASA.

séntigram (*D*) centigram.

sentil I tersentil slightly protruding (as a quid from one's mouth/breast from a dress/kris out of a belt/head above water/roots above ground/snake from a hole, etc,); → TERSEMBUL.

sentil II (*J*) **menyentil** [and **nyentil** (*coq*)] **1** to flick/hit s.t. with one's finger(s). **2** to touch s.t., nudge. **3** to admonish, reprimand. **4** to criticize.

tersentil [and **kesentil** (*coq*)] **1** touched. **2** criticized.

sentilan 1 pinch, nip, flick. **2** touch, nudge, brush. **3** criticism, disapproval, discredit.

penyentilan touching.

séntiliter (*D*) centiliter.

séntimen 1 sentiment. **2** (*coq*) grudge, ill feelings (toward s.o.).

berséntimén 1 sentimental, compassionate. She's a compassionate lady. **2** to hold a grudge, have ill feelings.

menyéntiméni 1 to sentimentalize. **2** to hold a grudge against, have ill feelings toward.

séntimén tal (*E*) sentimental.

keséntiméntalan sentimentality.

séntiméntalis sentimentalist.

séntiméntalitas sentimentality.

sentiméntil (*D*) sentimental.
séntiméter centimeter.
senting I → GENTING I.
senting II (*Jv*) 1 plant, frequently used for hedges, *Cassia spp.* 2 bushes for green manure.
sentiong and **sentiung** (*C*) Chinese graveyard.
séntol squat, sturdy, strong (of stature/build).
sentolop 1 k.o. oil lamp in banging glass bell. 2 flashlight.
sentong (*Jv*) a small inner room in traditional Javanese homes, used for making offerings to the spirits, for wedding ceremonies, and for other special purposes.
sentono → SENTANA II.
sentosa (*Skr*) tranquil, serene, calm, live in peace and security.
  bersentosa peaceful, safe, secure.
  menyentosakan 1 to secure, protect, safeguard. 2 to give s.o. a rest.
  kesentosaan rest, tranquility, calm, peace.
séntra (*D*) 1 centers. 2 (sometimes used as singular) center.
séntral (*D*) 1 central. *Bank* – Central Bank. *komité* – central committee. *stasiun* – central station. 2 (of trade unions) federation. *– listrik* (electric) power station. *– télepon* telephone exchange.
séntralisasi (*D*) centralization.
  menyéntralisasikan to centralize.
  terséntralisasi centralized.
séntralisir (*D*) **menyéntralisir** to centralize.
  terséntralisir centralized, concentrated. *~nya perkembangan pariwisata di Jawa dan Bali saja akan menghasilkan berbagai dampak yang négatif.* The concentration of tourist development in Java and Bali will have a number of negative consequences.
séntralistik (*E*) and **séntralistis** (*D*) centralistic. *perencanaan* – centralistic planning.
sentrap-sentrup → PENYAKIT *sentrap-sentrup.*
séntrifugal (*D/E*) centrifugal.
séntrifuse (*D/E*) 1 centrifugal machine. 2 (of an automatic washing machine) spin-drier.
séntripetal (*D/E*) centripetal.
séntris (*D*) -centric. *agrari*– agraricentric. *ego*– egocentric. *étno*– ethnocentric. *Éuro*– Eurocentric. *industri*– industricentric. *Jawa*– Javacentric. *keluarga*– family-centric.
séntrum (*D*) center, business district.
sentuh bersentuh 1 to touch, brush slightly against. *Buku itu kotor karena ~ dengan tangannya yang penuh tinta.* That book is dirty because it touched his hands, which are full of ink. 2 to copulate.
  bersentuhan 1 to touch, nudge, brush against, come into contact with e.o. *Oléh karena bis sudah penuh sesak, penumpang ~.* Because the bus was chock-full, the passengers brushed up against e.o. 2 to have to do with, be concerned with. *tidak ~ dengan* to have nothing to do with, be unrelated to.
  bersentuh-sentuhan to keep on touching e.o.
  menyentuh [and **nyentuh** (*coq*)] 1 to touch s.t., come into contact with s.t. *Pesawat Garuda ~ landasan.* The Garuda plane touched down on the runway. *~ luka lama* to reopen old sores. *Jangan sentuh saya!* Hands off! Stay away from me! 2 to touch, hit, reach. *Wangi-wangian melati ~ hidung saya.* I noticed a jasmine fragrance. 3 to bump against. *Mobil itu rusak sedikit karena ~ témbok.* The car was somewhat damaged because it bumped against a wall. 4 (negative) to no longer touch, no longer have the desire to, refrain from. *Ia tidak ~ rokok lagi.* He refrained from smoking. *Ribut-ribut soal kapas belakangan ini sebenarnya belum ~ pokok persoalan.* The recent fuss made about cotton had actually not yet gotten to the very core of the matter.
  menyentuhkan to make s.t. touch (s.t. else).
  tersentuh [and **kesentuh** (*coq*)] 1 touched. *Tak ~ oléhnya makanan itu.* He didn't touch the food. 2 bumped, struck. *Kakinya ~ pada batu.* His foot struck a stone. 3 touched, moved, offended. *Hatinya mudah sekali ~.* He's easily offended.
  sentuhan touch, nudge. *tidak memiliki ~ pribadi* lack of the personal touch. *~ kecil* thoughtfulness, attention.
  kesentuhan to suffer from a disease from being touched by a spirit.
  penyentuh 1 s.t. that touches. *~ hati nurani* s.t. that touches one's inner feelings. 2 the person who touched.

penyentuhan process/way/act of touching.
persentuhan contact. *~ kultural* cultural contact.
sentuk tersentuk bumped, nudged.
sentul I *pohon* – tall (cultivated) tree with acid fruit, *Sandoricum koetjape.*
sentul II a lesbian who plays the male role, dyke.
sentulang k.o. tree, *Jackia ornata.*
sentulu k.o. tree, *Ixonanthes grandiflora.*
sentung I 1 wedge/shim/peg for tightening the parchment of a tambourine. 2 (*M*) tight, close. *– pelalai* k.o. magic which makes a woman not able to find a marriage partner or not want to marry. *– pintu* crossbar, bolt.
  menyentung to wedge/shim/peg.
sentung II circle, circular.
sénu (*D*) nerve(s).
senuh full (after meals).
  menyenuh to feel full.
senuhun (*ob*) → SINUHUN.
senuk I (*D*) *ikan* – pike, picklehandle barracuda, *Sphyraena jello.*
senuk II tapir, *Tapirus malayanus*; → TENUK.
senunggang I *ikan* – pinecone fish, *Monocentris japonicus.*
senunggang II upside down.
senungging → TUNGGING I.
senur (*D*) cord.
senut (*Jv*) sticking pain.
  senut-senut throbbing.
senyak → SENYAP.
senyampang → NYAMPANG.
senyam-senyum and **tersenyam-senyum** to keep on smiling; → SENYUM.
senyap 1 quiet; lonely, lone(some), desolate. *sunyi* – deserted, lonely (of places); there is not much doing in trade. 2 silent (of persons). 3 (sleep) soundly; → LENYAP.
  bersenyap-senyap to isolate o.s.
  menyenyapkan to silence, shut up.
  kesenyapan silence. *– yang mencekam* an oppressive silence.
senyar tingling (of the funny bone when hit).
senyawa → NYAWA.
senyum a smile. *mahal* – does not smile easily/readily. *murah* – smiles easily/readily. *– cerah* a bright and clear smile. *Seluruh Indonésia memperlihatkan wajah-wajah – cerah.* All of Indonesia shows bright and clear smiles. *– digumam* tongue in cheek. *– buaya* false smile. *– dikulum* weak smile. *– geli* smile of pleasure. *– getir* bitter smile. *– hampa* false smile. *– hambar* forced smile. *– kambing* put-on/fake smile. *– kanyur* affected smile (when ashamed). *– kecut* bitter smile. *– kemalu-maluan* smile of embarrassment. *– kemanja-manjaan* vacant smile. *– kucing* deceptive smile. *– manis* attractive smile. *– mekar* slight smile. *– menawan* captivating smile. *– meringis* smile through pain. *– mesra* friendly smile. *– monyét* toothy grin. *– nyinyir* grin. *– pahit* bitter smile. *– raja* hypocritical smile. *– selamba* pretending smile. *– simpul* simper. *– sinis* cynical smile. *– siput* simper. *– sumbing* sly smile, leer. *– tauké* (*Mal*) ingratiating (shopkeeper's) smile. *– tawar* smile meant to cover s.t. up. *– terkulum* weak smile. *– tipis* weak smile.
  senyum-senyum to keep on smiling.
  bersenyum to smile.
  bersenyum(-senyum)an to smile at e.o.
  menyenyumi to smile at.
  menyenyumkan to make s.o. smile.
  tersenyum to smile.
  senyuman smile. *kaya dengan ~* smiles easily.
senyur I and **senyor** (*Port ob*) senhor, sir, Mr.
senyur II (*coq*) → INSINYUR.
senyur III batfish, *Psettus/Monodactylus falsiformis.*
séok berséok-séok to look for s.t. with one's feet. *Kakinya ~ mencari kedua belah sandalnya.* He looked with his feet for his pair of slippers.
  terséok-séok stagger/stumble along, drag one's feet, move slowly along. *Ia berjalan ~.* He staggered along.
seolah(-olah) → OLAH I.
seorang → ORANG.

séot → SÉOK.

sep- also look under entries beginning with **sp-**.

sép I (*D*) chief.

  bersép *kepada* **1** to work for, serve, be at the service of. **2** subordinated to. *Lebih baik saya keluar daripada ~ kepada seorang pemarah.* I would rather resign than work for an angry person.

sép II → SIP I.

sepa (*Jv*) **1** tasteless, insipid. **2** not ingenious.

sepada → SPADA.

sepah I 1 residue, s.t. that has been chewed and the juice extracted, pulp, grounds; → AMPAS. **2** s.t. considered useless. *bertukar* – token of deep love between two lovers. *habis manis* – *dibuang* to take advantage of/make use of s.o./s.t. and then toss him/it away; the world's wages are ingratitude. – *kopi* coffee grounds. – *sirih* a masticated quid of betel. – *tebu* a piece of sugarcane that has been chewed and the juice extracted. – *tembakau* spit-out piece of chewed tobacco.

  bersepah to have residue/grounds.

  menyepah to extract the juice or essence from s.t. by chewing.

sepah II various species of birds, minivets, flower-peckers. *burung* – *gunung* Sunda minivet, fire-breasted flower-pecker, *Pericrocotus miniatus*, *Dicaeum sanguinolentum*. – *hutan* scarlet minivet, *Pericrocotus flammeus*. – *putri* a) scarlet-backed flower-pecker, *Dicaeum cruentatum*. b) orange-bellied flower-pecker, *Dicaeum trigonostigmum*. – *putri kecil/sulung* flower-pecker, *Dicaeum concolor*. – *raja* crimson sunbird, *Aethopyga siparaja*.

sepah III *pohon* – a tree with very hard wood; from its sap candles are made, dika tree, *Irvingia malayana*.

sepah IV – *bulan* rusty millipede, *Trigoniulus lumbricinus*.

sepah V k.o. precious stone (which looks like it contains an image of a root or tree).

sépah bersépah(-sépah) and **tersépah-sépah** scattered, strewn, littered; → BERSÉRAK-SÉRAK.

  bersépahan (*pl subj*) scattered, strewn, littered.

  menyépahkan to scatter, strew, litter.

  sépahan scattering.

sepai, bersepai(-sepai), and **tersepai-sepai** broken into small pieces and scattered everywhere, smashed to bits (of crockery).

  bersepaian (*pl subj*) scattered/strewn about.

sepak I (*D*) spoke (of a wheel).

sepak II (*onom*) slapping sound.

  menyepak to slap.

sépak a kick. – *ke atas* to kick upstairs. *kena* – *belakang* cheated by the behavior of s.o. who didn't want to be candid or who is dishonest. – *bola* soccer. **bersépak-bola** to play soccer. **pesépak-bola** soccer-player. **persépak-bolaan** (*mod*) soccer. *dunia* – world of soccer. – *raga* a game which is played by kicking a plaited rattan ball into the air and not allowing it to fall to the ground. – *sila* a kick with the inside of one's foot. – *singkur* a kick with the outside of one's foot. – *takraw* a game played by kicking a plaited rattan ball over a net and usually played between two teams. – *terjang* a) to kick and trample with the foot (out of anger, etc.). b) activity, behavior; → TINGKAH *laku*.

  bersépak-sépakan to kick e.o.

  menyépak [and **nyépak** (*coq*)] to kick, strike with the foot. *~ bola* to kick the ball. *Ia ~ punggung temannya.* He kicked his friend's back. *~ sila* to kick with the inside of the foot. *~ singkur* to kick with the outside of the foot.

  menyépak (*pl obj*) to keep kicking. *Ia ~ bangkai ular itu.* He kept kicking the carcass of the snake.

  menyépak-nyépak to keep on kicking.

  menyépakkan to kick with (one's foot).

  menyépak-nyépakkan to keep on kicking with (one's feet). *Bayi itu ~ kakinya di perut ibunya.* The baby kept kicking his mother's stomach with his feet.

  tersépak to be/get kicked.

  sépakan a kick, kicking.

  penyépak kicker.

  penyépakan kicking.

sepakat 1 unanimously. *Kami* – *mengangkatnya sebagai ketua.* We unanimously appointed him chairman. **2** agree(d). – *untuk tidak* – agree to disagree. **3** (*kata* –) permission, agreement,

consensus. *dengan/tanpa* – with/without the permission of. *Garuda Indonesian Airways dan Singapore Airlines akan melakukan perundingan untuk mencari kata – yang akan menguntungkan kedua belah pihak.* Garuda Indonesian Airways and Singapore Airlines are going to hold negotiations to seek an agreement that will be beneficial to both parties. *tidak* – to disagree. **ketidak-sepakatan** disagreement.

  bersepakat to agree (with e.o.). *Kedua negara ~ mengadakan pembicaraan mengenai lalulintas perbatasan.* The two countries agreed to hold discussions about border crossings.

  menyepakati to agree to. *Tiga menteri agama Indonésia, Malaysia, dan Brunéi Darussalam ~ menyelaraskan rukyat untuk menentukan hari ibadat dan hari raya Islam agar bisa dilakukan bersama di tiga negara.* The three ministers of religious affairs of Indonesia, Malaysia, and Brunei Darussalam have agreed to bring into line the sighting of the sickle moon to determine the Muslim days of worship and holidays so that they can be put into effect jointly in the three countries.

  sepakatan agreement, consensus. *mencapai ~* to reach an agreement. *~ penggabungan suara* ballot box accord. *~ sikap politik sipil* civil political consensus. *~ tak tertulis* gentlemen's agreement.

  kesepakatan agreement, covenant.

  penyepakatan agreeing on, reaching an agreement on.

  persepakatan agreement, concordance.

sépakbolawan soccer player.

sepakbor → SEPATBOR, SPATBOR(D).

sepala-pala → PALA II.

sepalek → SPALK.

sepam *pohon* – a wild mango tree, *Mangifera maingayi*.

sepan I (*D*) tight, narrow, skimpy; → SEMPIT. *rok* – a tight-fitting skirt.

  menyepan to tighten, draw in to tighten.

sepan II wart, verruca (sponge-like wart between the fingers or toes).

  bersepan to have this k.o. wart.

sepanar (*E ob*) spanner.

sepandri (*D col*) infantryman.

sepanduk → SPANDUK.

sepang (*Tam*) a thorny tree with yellow flowers whose wood is boiled to make dye for mats and batik cloths, sappan wood, *Caesalpinia sappan*. *mérah* – dark red.

sepanjang → PANJANG.

sepantasnya → PANTAS I.

sepantun → PANTUN I.

Sepanyol → SPANYOL.

séparasi (*E*) separation. – *warna* color separation.

séparatis (*D*) separatist. *gerakan* – separatist movement.

séparatisme (*D/E*) separatism.

separbang (*D ob*) Post Office Savings Bank.

separuh → PARO(H), PARUH II.

sepasan (*M*) → SEPESAN.

sepasi → SPASI.

sepasin (*M*) chrysalis of dragon-fly. – *dapat bersiang* to get a windfall unintentionally.

sepat I sour, acid, tart, harsh (of unripe fruits in the mouth).

sepat II *ikan* – various species of fish, *Trichogaster*. *bagai* – *ketohoran* to lie around and do nothing. *bagai anak* –, *tak makan pancing emas* though stupid, it's also able to choose what is good or bad for itself. – *jawa* → SEPAT *padi*. – *laut* a small climbing perch, common in rice fields, *Pempheris spp*. – *padi* blue/three-spot gourami, *Trichogaster trichopterus*. – *siam* a small climbing fish, snakeskin gourami, *Trichogaster pectoralis*.

sepat III *kayu* – a tree whose fruit and leaves are made into a remedy against diarrhea, *Macaranga triloba*. – *itu berada di kaki lain* the shoe is on the other foot.

sepatbor → SPATBOR(D).

sepatu I (*Port*) shoe, boots, footwear. *tukang* – a) shoemaker. b) cobbler. – *air* water ski. – *Ajaib* Puss in Boots. – *berduri/berpaku* spikes, spiked shoes. – *besi* horseshoe. – *bola* boots. – *Bruce Lee* kung fu slippers, cotton slip-ons. – *but* boots. – *duri* spikes, spiked shoes. – *és* ice skates. – *hak* high-heeled shoes. –

jéngki short boots. – *jinjit* high-heeled shoes. – *kanvas* sneakers. – *karét* sneakers. – *katak* scuba flippers. – *kayu* wooden shoes (of Holland). – *kéts* sneakers (from the trademark Keds). – *kuda* horseshoe. – *lapangan* (*mil*) boots. – *lars(a)* boots. – *luar* overshoe, galoshes. – *luncur* ski. – *olahraga* sports shoes. – *pantofel* slippers. – *perahu* platform shoes. – *rém* brake shoe/lining. – *roda* roller skates. **bersepatu roda** roller skating. – *sandal* a) sandals, open-toe slippers. b) laced shoes. – *spaik* spikes, spiked shoes. – *ténis* tennis shoes. – *tentara* army boots. – *tinggi* (woman's) boots. – *ulek-ulek* stubby shoes.

bersepatu 1 with/to have shoes. **2** to wear shoes, shod. *tidak ~* barefoot.

menyepatui to put shoes on s.o.

persepatuan pertaining to footwear, shoe (*mod*).

sepatu II *bunga/kembang* – hibiscus, *Hibiscus rosasinensis*.

sepatu III [separuh tua] (*coq*) middle-aged.

sepatung (*ob*) → CAPUNG.

sepéda (*D*) bicycle. *bél* – bicycle bell. *lampu* – cycle lamp. – *aérobik* exercise bicycle. – *air* peddle boat. – *balap* racing bicycle, racer. – *banci* sports cycle. – *berhenti* ergocycle, exercise bicycle. – *biasa* roadster. – *érobik* exercise bicycle. – *gembira* fun bike. – *gunung* mountain bike. – *jéngki* sports cycle. – *kayuh* an ordinary bike (not motorized but using pedals to propel it). – *kembar* tandem bicycle. – *kumbang* moped, motorized bicycle. – *mini* mini bike. – *motor* motorcycle. **bersepéda motor 1** to ride on a motorcycle. **2** (to go) by motorcycle. *Meréka ~ Kawasaki menuju sasaran*. They went on Kawasaki motorcycles to their target. – *motor bébék* the Suzuki Sprinter motorbike which looks like a duck, or any k.o. motorbike. – *motor bersetang tinggi* chopper. – *dengan keréta témpél* and *séspan* a motorcycle and sidecar. – *pancal* an ordinary bike (not motorized but using pedals by which it is propelled). – *santai* fun bike. – *stasionér* stationary bike, exercise bike. – *tandem* tandem bicycle. – *torpédo* bicycle with coaster/backpedaling brake. – *unta* (*Jv*) (*esp* in Yogya) a nonmotorized/pedal-operated bicycle.

bersepéda to (have a) bike, (go) by bike. *~ di gunung* mountain cycling.

pesepéda bicyclist. *Anda akan menjadi ~ sejati*. You'll become a real cyclist.

sepedas k.o. ginger, *Zingiber offininale*.

sepégoh k.o. oyster (provides poor-quality pearls).

sepekan one week. *warta* – a weekly; → PEKAN II.

sepéksi → INSPÉKSI

sepéktur → INSPÉKTUR.

sepékuk → SPÉKUK, SPÉK(K)OEK.

sepél I (*D ob*) **menyepél** to spell; → MENGÉJA.

sepélan spelling, orthography.

sepél II (*D*) game; exercise, practice match, training.

sepélé insignificant, trivial, futile. *barang* – trivia, trifles, unimportant matters. *menganggap* – to consider of no importance.

menyepélékan to consider insignificant, belittle; to underestimate, underrate, disregard, neglect.

kesepéléan triviality.

sepéling I (*D*) **1** loose. **2** play, tolerance, freedom of movement, wobbling (of wheel).

sepéling II (*J*) crazy; → GILA.

sepemeluk → PELUK.

sepén I → SPÉN.

sepén II (*D*) comforter, pacifier.

sepéng bald spot/patch.

sepenggalah → GALAH.

sepeninggal → TINGGAL.

sepenuh *daun* – k.o. bulbous plant, cardwell lily, *Eurycles amboinensis*.

seperah (*A*) white cloth, etc. which is spread over the floor and used under food served during a *selamatan*.

seperai, seperéi, and **sepréi** (*D*) **1** bed sheet. **2** bedspread, coverlet.

seperantu medicine made from the *Sindora sumatrana* tree.

seperitus → SPIRITUS.

sepérsi (*D*) asparagus.

seperti 1 like, as. *Badannya kurus – galah*. He's as lean as a rake. – *apa adanya* as is, in the condition that it's in. – *biasa* as usual. **2**

as if, like. *Ia berlagak – orang kaya*. He acted like a rich man. – *juga* a) just as (if). b) and (also). **3** as, in accordance with, according to. *buatlah – yang telah disuruhnya* do as he instructed. **4** such as. *Suratkabar-suratkabar Indonésia – Kompas, Suara Pembaruan, dll. banyak dibaca di kampung-kampung*. The Indonesian papers, such as Kompas, Suara Pembaruan, etc., are much read in villages.

sepertinya 1 it's as if, it seems that, it looks like. *~ tidak orang banyak yang mau menggunakannya*. It seems that few people want to use it. **2** for instance/example. *Sekalian binatang yang bertelur ~ ayam, burung, ikan, ular, dsb. tentu tidak berdaun telinga*. All egg-laying animals, for instance, fowls, birds, fishes, snakes, etc. have, for sure, no auricles. *kalau ~* supposed, supposing (that). *Kalau ~ kamu mendapat panggilan, bagaimana?* Supposing that you receive a summons, what would you do? *dengan ~* as it should be, it's as if. **3** properly, fittingly. *tidak ~* improper, indecent. *Rakyat tidak senang karena diperlakukan tidak ~*. The people weren't pleased because it was treated improperly.

sepertikan (*ob*) like. *Ia berjalan sangat perlahan ~ tidak berdaya lagi*. He walked very slowly like s.o. who has no more energy.

menyepertikan 1 (*cla*) to consider suitable. **2** to take as an example.

sepertimana (*Mal*) such as.

sepesan k.o. centipede, *Gryllacris spp. mengaki* – raveled.

sepésial → SPÉSIAL.

sepet I (*J/Jv*) **1** sour, acid, harsh (in the mouth). **2** (to have) burning eyes; → SEPAT I.

nyepet-nyepeti *~ mata* offensive (to the sight).

sepet II (*Jv*) outer fiber (of coconut).

sepét (*D*) syringe.

menyepét to inject, shoot up (a drug).

sépét → SIPIT I, II.

sepetir *pohon* – k.o. tree, *Sindora javanica*.

sepi (*Jv*) **1** calm, quiet, silent, tranquil. *Ia suka duduk-duduk di tempat yang* –. He likes to sit in a quiet place. **2** without (bustle/ulterior motive). – *ing pamrih* (*Jv*) a) without any ulterior motive. b) desireless. c) selfless. – *dari (bahaya/gangguan/malapetaka)* free from (dangers/disturbances/disasters), out of (danger). *tidak – dari (bahaya, dll)* one cannot get away from (dangers, etc.). – *duit* to not lack for money. **3** don't hear much more from. *cerita-cerita jadi* – you don't hear much more from those rumors. **4** (of market) dull, flat, inactive, slow, slack; without a lot of, with few. – *pembeli* with few buyers. *perdagangan telah* – there's little doing in trade, hardly any business is done, market is featureless/slack. *pekerjaan sedang* – there is no work at hand. **5** lonely; there's (almost) nobody. *sudah – orang berjalan* it's already perfectly silent in the street. *dianggap* – a) they ignore/negate s.o. or s.t. b) they don't talk about s.o. or s.t.

sepi-sepi *~ hangat* the calm/lull before the storm.

bersepi(-sepi) to be calm/quiet.

bersepi-sepi to go to a quiet place (for relaxation/to unwind).

menyepi [and **nyepi** (*coq*)] **1** to go into seclusion, isolate/seclude o.s. **2** to become quiet.

menyepikan 1 to isolate, seclude. *~ diri* to seclude o.s. **2** to ignore, pay no attention to. **3** to give the impression of being quiet.

mempersepi to quiet down, make quieter.

tersepi quietest.

kesepian 1 solitude, loneliness. **2** silence, quietness, tranquility. *memecahkan ~* to break the silence.

penyepian isolation.

sépia (*D*) sepia.

sepidol → SPIDOL.

sepih (*M*) → SERPIH.

sepiker (*E*) loudspeaker.

sepincang (*J*) one and a half cents.

sepintas – *lalu* in passing; → PINTAS.

sepion → SPION.

sepir (*D*) warden, jailer.

sepiritus → SPIRITUS.

sepit I 1 pincers, tweezers, tongs. **2** a clasping claw (as of a crab or lobster). **3** chopsticks; → SUMPIT IV. *kuat – karena kempa* strong because he has a powerful backer. *– angkup* tweezers. *– api* fire tongs. *– bara* blacksmith tongs. *– dasi* tie clasp. *– janggut* (beard) tweezers. *– rambut* hair clip. *– udang* loops (like the interspace of lobster's claws).

sepit-sepit pincers, tweezers.

bersepit to possess (such as a crab).

menyepit to nip, squeeze, or press between two surfaces. *Jarinya disepit ketam.* His finger was squeezed by a crab.

menyepitkan to squeeze with. *Anjing itu lari dengan ~ ékornya di sela pahanya.* The dog ran off with its tail between its legs.

tersepit 1 nipped, squeezed, clamped, cornered, with one's back to the wall. **2** fallen between two stools (having failed to satisfy either side).

penyepit pincers, tweezers.

sepit II (*D*) needle, hypodermic needle or substitute used for injection of a drug.

nyepit to take intravenous drugs, shoot up.

sepoa → SEMPOA.

sepoi-sepoi gentle (of breeze). *angin – basa* a soft zephyr.

sepokat code name for morphine.

sepon (*D*) sponge. *– bedak* powder sponge. *– cuci* kitchen sponge. *– mandi* bath sponge.

sepong menyepong to kiss.

nyepongin (*J*) to kiss.

sepong-sepongan kissing.

seponsor → SPONSOR.

sepor I (*D*) sport.

sepor II (*D*) → SEPUR.

sepora (*Jv*) excuse; → MAAF.

sepot (*D ob*) hodgepodge (a Dutch specialty: mashed potatoes, carrots, and onions with meat).

seprai and **sepréi** (*D*) bed sheet.

seprit → SEMPRIT I.

sépsis (*D/E*) sepsis.

Séptémber (*D*) September.

séptik (*E*) septic.

séptikténg (*D/E*) septic tank.

sepuh I 1 dark (color). **2** plating. *– emas* gilt, gold plating. *– pérak* silver plating; → SADUR I. hardening/tempering (of metals). *hilang – tampak senam* and then he showed the cloven hoof.

bersepuh gilded, plated. *barang yang ~ emas* gold-plated articles.

menyepuh 1 to gild, plate (with gold). *piala/gelang tembaga disepuh emas* a gold-plated cup/copper bracelet. **2** to temper (steel/iron). *~ sabit* to temper a sickle. **3** to cover s.t. with a metal. *disepuh pérak* silvered, silver-plated.

tersepuh gilded, plated; tempered.

sepuhan 1 plating, gilt. *~ rambut* hair dye. **2** fake, false.

penyepuh 1 liquid in which an object to be gilded is immersed. **2** s.o. who plates s.t.

penyepuhan tempering, hardening; plating (with a metal finish).

sepuh II (*Jv*) **1** old; parent (father or mother), parents; → SESEPUH. **2** an old relative. **3** old, mature, ripe. *dalam usia –* later in life.

sesepuh → SESEPUH.

sepuhan → SEPUH II.

kesepuhan 1 (old) age. **2** parental residence, i.e., parents' house. *kepala ~* the head of the parental residence. **3** senior citizens, old people.

sepui (*D*) → SEPIT II.

sepuit → SEPIT II.

sepuk I humus.

sepuk II menyepuk 1 to dump, slam down. **2** to snatch away.

tersepuk thrown away.

sepukal *keris –* kris with a straight blade.

sepukul (*Med*) video; television. *Meréka asyik nonton –.* They were busily engaged in watching TV.

sepul (*E*) spool.

sepulih *akar –* various species of plants and climbing shrubs that provide herbal remedies, *Ophioxylon serpentinum, Fragraea racemosa, Rauwolfia perakensis. daun – duduk* k.o. plant, *Plocoglottis sp.*

sepuluh → PULUH.

sepupu first cousin/niece; → PUPU.

sepur (*D*) **1** track, rails, railway. **2** (railway) train. *stasiun –* railroad station. *– balas* freight train. *– ejes-ejes* slow local train. *– genjreng* (*Jv*) the popular name given to the 1912 steam locomotive in Solo, now a tourist object. *– klutuk* slow local train. *– lempung* steam train. *– mati* siding with no egress. *– s(e)nél* express. *– simpang* siding. *– tumbuk* road roller.

nyepur (*coq*) to go by train.

sepuran (*Jv*) railway fare.

sepura → SPORA.

seput I (*D*) fast, quick. *kiriman –* express parcel.

seput II dull, discolored, faded.

seputar around; → PUTAR I.

ser- also see entries beginning with SR-.

sér (in acronyms) → SÉRSAN.

sera *tersera-sera* **1** hurried, hasty, **2** agitated.

serabai and **serabi** *kuéh –* a sort of pancake eaten with a sauce of sugar, flour, and coconut milk.

serabut I 1 fiber. **2** fibrous, filamentous; → SABUT. *akar –* secondary side-root. *– optik* optic fiber.

berserabut and **menyerabut** fibrous.

serabut II (*J/Jv*) **serabutan 1** chaotic, in disorder, disorganized. *buruh –* handyman. *Gerombolan tersebut pating mabur ~.* The gang run away in disorder. **2** all purpose, without a fixed job. *pelayan ~* factotum, jack-of-all trades, utility man. *Pemuda kelahiran Palémbang itu bekerja ~.* The young man from Palembang didn't have a fixed job.

berserabutan to have too many irons in the fire, bite off more than one can chew.

seradak-seruduk (*J*) **1** to swoop down (as a hawk on prey). **2** perfunctory, routine, hasty and superficial.

seraga *bantal –* a large round pillow or cushion with gold or silver end-plates, used at ceremonies.

seragam *pakaian –* uniform; → RAGAM I.

serah I turn over, surrender. *– kuasa* transfer of authority/power. *menyerah-kuasakan* to transfer authority/power. *Salah satu pihak tidak dapat ~ setiap dan semua hak dan kewajibannya di dalam perjanjian ini kepada siapapun, tanpa adanya ijin tertulis dari pihak yang lain.* One of the parties cannot transfer its power and all of its rights and obligations laid down in this agreement to whomsoever, without the written consent of the other party. *– nyata* physical delivery. *– pakai* surrender for use. *menyerah-pakaikan* to surrender s.t. for use. *– terima* transfer (of a function or command). *menyerah-terimakan* to transfer (a function or command). *penyerah-terimaan* transfer (of a function or command).

berserah to place s.t. in the hands of. *~ nasib pada dukun* to place o.s. completely in the hands of a dukun. *~ diri kepada* to surrender o.s. to, place o.s. completely in the hands of. *~ diri kepada Allah* to surrender to God. *~ diri kepada alam* fatalism.

menyerah [and **nyerah** (*coq*)] **1** to entrust one's fate to, submit (o.s.) to, reconcile o.s. to, surrender. *Jangan lekas ~ kepada takdir.* Don't submit to your fate so fast. **2** *~ kalah* a) to capitulate. b) to concede defeat. **3** *~ diri* to surrender o.s. to, place o.s. completely in the hands of. **4** to give in, not oppose or defy, just follow along. *Akhirnya saya ~ saja, disuruh apa pun, baiklah.* Finally, I just gave in; whatever I was told to do was OK.

menyerahi to entrust to, hand over to, charge (s.o. with a task or to do s.t.). *Dia telah diserahi tugas yang serupa.* He was entrusted with a similar task. *Ia diserahi mandat ... .* He was authorized to .... *Dia diserahi memberi bantuan.* He was charged with providing assistance.

menyerahkan [and **nyerahkan** (*J coq*)] **1** to turn over, give up, yield, surrender. *terpaksa ~ mobil kepada penodong* forced to turn over the car to a holdup artist. **2** to give, hand over, turn in, deliver, submit. *Ayahnya telah ~ uang yang diminta itu.* His father has handed over the money that was asked for. **3** to entrust s.t. to s.o., confide s.t. (a secret) to s.o. *Lebih baik uang ini diserahkan saja kepada istrinya.* It would be better to entrust this money to his wife. *~ jiwa raganya kepada nusa dan bangsa* to entrust one's body and soul to country and nation. *~*

nasibnya to entrust one's destiny (to). ~ *nyawanya* to entrust one's life (to). ~ *tanggung jawabnya* to entrust one's responsibility (to). ~ *diri* to submit o.s. to another's control, surrender.

terserah 1 it's up to (you), (I) leave it to (you). **2** surrendered, handed/turned over. *(itu)* ~ I leave it to you/to your discretion, it's up to you. ~ *kepada Anda* I leave it to you. ~ *mana yang akan dipilih* take your pick/choice. ~ *nanti* wait and see; *cp* TERGANTUNG *keadaan.*

serahan 1 s.t. that is surrendered. **2** *(geol)* yield. **seserahan** ceremony of surrendering s.t. as a bond for the bride and groom.

penyerah s.o. who surrenders/transfers.

penyerahan 1 surrender, capitulation, yielding, transfer. **2** delivery. ~ *hak* ceding (rights). ~ *kekuasaan* delegation of power/authority. ~ *kedaulatan* transfer of sovereignty. ~ *kembali* returns. ~ *kemudian* futures trading. ~ *nasib* fatalism. ~ *nyata* actual delivery. ~ *sampai gudang pembeli* cost, insurance, freight, cif. ~ *sampai ke kapal* free on board, fob. ~ *seadanya* as is. ~ *yang tidak bersyarat/tanpa syarat* unconditional surrender. ~ *yuridis* transfer of title.

serah II → SERA.

sérah *(M)* a vivid bright red.

serahi *(A)* **1** flagon. **2** flask, glass bottle.

serai I (– *betul/dapur/gulai/sayur/wangi*) citronella grass, lemon grass, *Andropogon nardus, Cymbopogon citratus/nardus. minyak* – citronella oil, used in cooking, also applied to the skin as a healing agent or insect repellent. – *kayu* k.o. plant, pink mempat, *Eugenia polyantha.*

serai II *(Pers)* palace.

serai III *(burung)* – *bakau* great tit, *Parus major.*

sérai tersérai scattered, dispersed.

serak I hoarse, husky (of one's voice).

serak-serak ~ *basah* husky and low (of one's voice).

serak II *burung* – barn owl (which makes a sound like a hoarse person), *Tyto alba.*

serak III – *serik/seruk* *(onom)* scrubbing noise.

sérak scatter, disperse.

bersérak(-sérak) scattered, dispersed, in disorder. *gudang senjata yang bersérak di seluruh negeri* arsenals scattered all over the country. *lari bersérak-sérak* to run in all directions.

bersérakan *(pl subj)* to be scattered/spread around, all over. *Puntung rokok dan kulit kacang* ~ *di méja.* Cigarette butts and peanut shells were scattered all over the table.

menyérak to disperse/spread out in all directions.

menyéraki to dilute, disperse, scatter, spread.

menyérakkan to sprinkle, scatter, pour.

tersérak(-sérak) scattered (all over), dispersed, in disorder. *Sekitar 300 pangkalan militér yang* ~ *di seluruh negara itu disiagakan.* About 300 military bases which are scattered all over the country were put on the alert.

sérakan s.t. scattered around.

penyérak dispersant.

serakah *(Jv)* greedy, voracious. *kaum berpunya yang* – the greedy rich.

menyerakahi to cast a covetous eye on.

keserakahan greed, gluttony, voracity, covetousness, avarice, stinginess.

serakahisme greedy mentality.

serak-serik *(onom)* the sound of scrubbing or cracking of joints or branches.

seram 1 (the hair at the base of one's neck) stands on end. *Mendengar cerita si A itu – bulu tengkukku.* When I heard A's story my hair stood on end. **2** (has a) creepy/eerie feeling. – *kudukku ketika lalu di bawah pohon waringin itu.* I had an eerie feeling in my neck when I passed under that banyan tree. **3** horrible, ghastly, gruesome. *Terdengar suara yang* –. A gruesome sound was heard. **4** cruel, ferocious. *Mukanya – kelihatan.* He looked ferocious. *Matanya* –. He looked ominous (and dangerous). – *kulit* goose flesh.

menyeramkan 1 to make one's hair stand on end. **2** terrifying. *"Tolong!" pekiknya dengan suara yang* ~. "Help!" he screamed in a terrifying voice.

keseraman creepiness, eeriness.

Séram Ceram, an island of Maluku/the Moluccas.

serama I → ASRAMA.

serama II *(Skr)* (from *se+irama*) in time/tune, rhythmical. *gendang* – → SERMANGIN.

berserama 1 to play such a *gendang.* **2** to play *silat* (with a sword).

serambi 1 lobby, vestibule. **2** ball. – *jantung* atrium. – *loténg* balcony. – *Mekah* a) Aceh. b) Banten. – *stasion* platform (of railroad).

séramik *(D)* ceramics.

serampak → REMPAK I, SEREMPAK.

serampang I a three-pronged fish spear, trident.

menyerampang to spear, stab with a trident.

terserampang speared/stabbed/pierced with a trident, etc.

serampang II *(M)* and **terserampang** stuck, caught (of a kite in a tree, etc.).

serampang III *(J/Jv)* **menyerampang 1** to hit (with a weapon), stab. *Kakinya diserampang dengan alu.* His leg was hit by a rice pestle. **2** to hit at random/haphazardly. *Pikir dulu, jangan asal* ~ *saja.* Look before you leap. **3** to steal, filch, pilfer.

menyerampangkan to hit wildly with, attack/assail with.

serampangan at random, wildly, hit or miss, arbitrarily.

keserampangan arbitrariness.

serampang IV – *dua belas* a traditional social dance.

serampangisme social attitude of doing exactly as one pleases.

serampin 1 a mat used for collecting sago. **2** sago leftovers.

serampu → SUMPAH *serampu.*

serampuk terserampuk bumped against.

séran stripe, hatching.

b* bersé ran striped (of fabrics).

serana I → SARANA.

serana II *(ob)* wasting away, languish(ing); → RANA I.

menyerana to waste away, languish.

seranah *(cla)* imprecation, curse; → SERAPAH. *sumpah* – various imprecations.

menyeranah to curse, revile.

serandang (bamboo) trestle, easel, sawhorse.

menyerandang to shore up, support, buttress.

serandau *burung* – purple heron, *Ardea purpurea manilensis.*

Serandib *(cla)* Ceylon, Sri Lanka.

serandung terserandung stumbled; → SANDUNG II. *kakinya* – *pada batu* his foot bumped against a rock.

serang I menyerang [and **nyerang** *(coq)*] **1** to attack, assault, charge. *Penjahat yang* ~ *polisi itu sudah tertangkap.* The criminal who assaulted the policeman was arrested. **2** to affect (s.o.'s health). *Orang-orang yang diserang penyakit pés, banyak yang meninggal.* Many who were affected by the plague died. **3** to accuse, indict, attack, criticize, oppose. *Ada yang membela dan ada yang* ~ *kebijaksanaan pemerintah.* Some defended and others criticized government policy. ~ *hari (M)* to ward off the rain.

serang-menyerang to attack e.o.

menyerangi *(pl obj)* to attack.

menyerangkan [and **nyerangin** *(J coq)*] **1** to attack. **2** to attack with s.t. – *bola* to put a ball (in the opponent's goal).

terserang [and **keserang** *(coq)*] attacked (by a disease). – *histéria* have an attack of hysteria. – *kantuk* overcome by sleep.

serangan attack, assault, charge, offensive. *mengadakan* ~ *terhadap beberapa hélikopter yang diduga dipakai oléh golongan yang setia kepada Marcos* to launch an attack on some helicopters which presumably were used by the Marcos loyalists. ~ *acak* random attack. ~ *amfibi* amphibious assault. ~ *balasan/balik* counterattack. ~ *dadakan awal* preemptive attack/strike ~ *gerilya* a) guerrilla attack. b) hit and run. ~ *jantung* heart attack. ~ *kilat* raid, sortie. ~ *komando* commando attack/strike. ~ *otak* stroke. ~ *panas* heatstroke. ~ *pembalasan* counterattack. ~ *pura-pura* feint. ~ *sambar* strafing (by aircraft). ~ *umum* general offensive.

serang-serangan attacks.

penyerang 1 attacker, assailant, aggressor. **2** (in sports) forward. ~ *tengah* center forward.

penyerangan offensive, attack, aggression. ~ *balasan* counterattack. ~ *dadakan/mendadak* surprise attack. ~ *secara frontal* frontal attack.

serang II (*Pers naut*) **1** boatswain. **2** quartermaster (aboard a ship).

serang III (*M*) **berserang** to increase, grow.

sérang I (*M*) dazzling, blinding; → SILAU.

    sérangan glare.

    kesérangan glare, blinding.

sérang II wide-meshed (of nets), coarse (of weaving), sparse (of fruit); → JARANG.

serangga I (*Skr?*) insect.

serangga II (*ob*) peak, summit.

seranggasida insecticide.

serangguh → SERANGGUNG.

seranggung berseranggung and **menyeranggung** (to sit) bent forward, squat (with one's head in one's hands/elbows on one's knees).

serangkai → RANGKAI.

serangkak I belt of thorns round a fruit tree to prevent thieves from stealing the fruit. – *payung* ribs of an umbrella or sunshade.

serangkak II (*M*) k.o. small crab. *bagai – tertimbakan* (*M*) to walk aslant/slantingly.

serangsang menyerangsang furious; → RANGSANG I.

Serani (*A*) → NASRANI. **1** Christian. **2** Roman Catholic. **3** (*ob*) an Indo-Portuguese (Catholic) Eurasian. **4** a Portuguese. *air* – baptismal water. *masuk* – to become a Christian.

    menyeranikan 1 to convert s.o. to Christianity. **2** to baptize. **3** (*col*) to marry legally (a European taking an Indonesian wife).

    keseranian Christianity.

seranta 1 proclamation. **2** pager.

    menyerantakan to proclaim, announce widely.

    penyeranta pager.

seranti → MERANTI.

serap penetrate, absorb. – *mesra* intimate.

    menyerap 1 to permeate, be absorbed. *Air dapat ~ ke dalam tanah pasir.* Water can permeate into sandy ground. **2** to absorb, soak/suck up. *Kertas yang ~ tinta disebut kertas lap.* Paper that absorbs ink is called blotting paper. **3** to penetrate, have a marked effect on the mind or emotions. *Kata-kata pemimpin itu telah ~ ke dalam jiwaku.* The words of that leader had a marked effect on my soul. **4** to possess (of an evil spirit). *diserap hantu* possessed by an evil spirit. **5** to employ (labor), take on (workers). *~ 800 tenaga kerja* to employ 800 workers. **6** to borrow (words from another language).

    menyerapi to penetrate, spread into. *Rasa dingin ~ tulangnya.* A cold sensation penetrated his bones.

    menyerapkan to make s.o. absorb s.t., implant.

    terserap(kan) absorbed, permeated (with). **keterserapan** absorption, absorbability.

    serapan 1 absorbed. **2** absorption. **3** borrowed (from another language). *kata ~* a borrowed word.

    keserapan absorbency.

    penyerap 1 absorbent. **2** absorber. *~ goncangan* shock absorber.

    penyerapan 1 absorption, permeation. **2** employment. *~ tenaga kerja* the employment of workers.

sérap (*D*) reserve, spare. *ban – a)* spare tire. *b)* (pitying reference to) the vice-president of the Republic of Indonesia.

    menyérapkan to set s.t. aside as a reserve.

serapa and **serapah** (*Skr*) **1** curse. *kena –* accursed. *sumpah –* all k.o. curses. **2** exorcism.

    menyerapah(i) 1 to curse, revile, swear at. **2** to exorcise, drive out an evil spirit, etc. by prayers or magic. *Pawang dan bomoh sibuk menjampi, ~ di kaki, di kepala si sakit.* The sorcerer and medicine man were busily engaged in casting a spell on the patient, driving out an evil spirit, at his feet and head.

    serapahan curse, cursing.

serapat k.o. tree which provides timber for ships' masts, *Cratoxylon ligustrinum, Salacia flavescens.* – *hitam* k.o. tree, *Urceola brachysepala.* *akar –* k.o. climbing plant, *Parameria polyneura.*

serasa I betel vine, *Piper betle;* → SIRIH.

serasa II → RASA I.

serasah I trash, rubbish, waste, fertilizer from decayed leaves, mulch.

serasah II (*Pers*) *kain –* printed cotton of Coromandel (India).

serasah III (*M*) rapids; waterfall, cataract.

serasi (*Skr*) **1** born under the same star; → RASI I. **2** harmonious,

matching, agreeing with, compatible, fitting. *hubungan –* a harmonious relationship. *kurang –* unharmonious. **kekurangserasian** lack of harmony. *tidak –* inharmonious. **ketidakserasian** lack of harmony, disharmony.

    menyerasikan to harmonize, reconcile, match, combine. *Kebutuhan rakyat harus diserasikan dengan kemampuan yang ada.* The needs of the people have to be matched with existing abilities.

    keserasian harmony, accord, compatibility.

    penyerasian harmonization, adaptation, restructuring.

serat I (*Jv*) **1** fiber. **2** strand. **3** grain (of wood). – *gelas* fiberglass. – *kaca* a) fiberglass. b) optical fiber. – *nanas* pineapple fiber. – *tambahan* fiber-trim.

    berserat with/to have fibers, fibrous. *makanan ~* fibrous food.

serat II (*Jv*) book; letter, document, certificate. – *kakaningan* certificate stating that the owner is of noble descent.

    seratan handmade (of *batik*); → TULIS.

serat III 1 blocked, tight, jammed. **2** (of money) blocked, frozen. *Keluarnya uang – sekali.* It was very difficult to unfreeze the money.

    menyerati to tighten up.

    menyeratkan to block, slow down. *~ jalannya usaha* to slow down the course of the business.

    terserat blocked, got stuck, slowed down.

serata the entire/whole; → RATA I.

seratah k.o. yam or taro, *Colocasia antiquorum.*

serati I (*Skr*) mahout.

serati II k.o. duck, *Anas moschata.*

seratung *pohon –* k.o. tree, *Tabernaemontana corymbosa.* – *padi* k.o. shrub, *Ixora pendula.*

seratus → RATUS I.

serau I loose (of weaving).

serau II *akar –* k.o. plant, *Parameria barbata;* → KAYU *rapat.*

seraut I k.o. paring knife; → RAUT I.

seraut II (*ob*) feature; → RAUT II.

serawak I *batu –* mineral containing sulfur and antimony.

serawak II banana fritter.

serawal (*A M*) → SELUAR.

seraya I (*Skr?*) (*cla*) while, and at the same time; → SAMBIL. *berkata – tersenyum* to speak while smiling.

seraya II (*M*) *uang –* money that has to be paid by villagers for village needs (such as the salary of the village head/his secretary, etc.).

    menyeraya to ask for help (in rice planting, etc.).

    seraya-menyeraya mutual aid (in performing s.t.).

seraya III k.o. timber tree, *Shorea curtisii;* → MERANTI. – *putih* k.o. tree, *Parashorea spp.*

serba (*Skr*) **1** completely, very, well- all-, purely, omni-, hetero-, super-, in every way. **2** -ism, istic, etc. – *ada* having everything. *toko – ada* [*toserba*] general store. – *akal* rationalism. – *aku* egoistic. – *anéka* various kinds. **keserba-anékaan** diversity. – *baru* brand new. – *béda* heterogeneous. – *bisa* all-purpose, well-rounded. – *boléh* permissive. **keserba-boléhan** permissiveness. – *cakup* comprehensive. – *cocok* compatible. – *dua* dualism. – *emas* pure gold. – *guna* versatile. **keserbagunaan** versatility. – *hitam* all black. – *kurang* completely lacking. – *malar* continuous. **keserbamalaran** continuum. – *salah* wrong in every way, wrong whatever one does. – *sama* homogeneous. **keserbasamaan** homogeneity. – *sedikit* a little bit. – *serbi* various, all sorts of, different kinds of. – *tunggal* only one, uniformity. *Pemerintah telah meninggalkan kebijakan "– tunggal" bagi organisasi-organisasi profési.* The government has abandoned the policy of "uniformization" for professional organizations. – *wah* totally fantastic.

    berserba with everything one needs.

serbah-serbih hanging down, slovenly (of a coat/shirt).

serbak → SEMERBAK. **menyerbak** to spread (of an odor, etc.), pervasive (of a smell); sweet-smelling, fragrant.

    menyerbakkan to spread (a smell).

    penyerbakan spread(ing).

serban (*Pers*) (Haji's) turban, a type of headdress made by winding a length of cloth around the head. *sudah memakai –* and **berserban** to wear a turban; to be a *haji.*

serbanéka various, different sorts, assorted.

serbasama → SERBA *sama*.

serbat (*A*) **1** sherbet. **2** k.o. ginger drink.

serbét (*D*) napkin.

   menyerbét(i) to wipe off with a napkin.

serbi → SERBA *serbi*.

serbih → SERBAH-SERBIH.

serbu menyerbu [and **nyerbu** (*coq*)] to invade, attack, assault, charge, rush. ~ *masuk ke* to break into, storm into.

   menyerbukan ~ *diri* to throw o.s. (into the fray/flames, etc.).

   serbuan charge, assault, attack, onslaught. ~ *kecil* incursion.

   penyerbu 1 attacker, assailant. **2** mechanized infantry rifleman.

   penyerbuan attack, rush, assault, invasion, onslaught.

serbuk 1 powder, dust. **2** pollen. – *ayam* powdered chicken broth. – *bakar* baking powder. – *batubara* coal dust. – *besi* iron filings. – *bor* (*petro*) cutting. – *bunga* pollen. – *gergaji* sawdust. – *gosok* scouring powder. – *henang* stamen. – *injéksi* injected powder. – *kelantang* bleaching powder. – *kikiran* filings. – *kopi* powdered coffee. – *mesiu* gunpowder. – *obat* a medicinal powder. – *sari* pollen. – *susu* powdered milk.

   berserbuk with powder.

   menyerbuk to be(come) (like) powder, pulverized.

   menyerbuki 1 to pollinate.

   menyerbukkan 1 to pulverize. **2** to pollinate.

   penyerbuk pollinator. *agén* ~ pollinating agent.

   penyerbukan 1 pulverizing. **2** pollination. ~ *bunga anggrék* the pollination of orchids. ~ *sendiri* autogamy. ~ *silang* cross-pollination.

sérda → SÉRSAN *dua*.

serdadu I (*Port*) **1** (neocolonialist/colonialist/imperialist) soldier; *cp* TENTARA. *masuk* – to become a soldier/military man. – *berkuda* cavalry. – *berpayung* paratrooper. – *jéngki* the American G.I. – *séwaan* mercenary. – *ubel-ubel* Gurkha soldier. – *Yankee* the American G.I. **2** (*joc*) penis.

serdadu II *ikan* – sharp-nosed catfish, *Arius macronotacanthus*.

serdadu III *kembang* – k.o. herbaceous plant, k.o. periwinkle, *Lochnera rosea*.

serdak dust, dirt.

serdam bamboo nose flute.

   beserdam to play (on) such a flute.

serdang *pohon* – k.o. tree, fan-palm, *Livistona cochinchinensis, Pholidocarpus sumatrana*, whose leaves are used for thatch, matting, and conical hats.

serdawa belch; → SEDAWA, SENDAWA II.

   beserdawa to belch.

serdi k.o. cold (of horses), strangles, glanders.

serdih (of one's chest/belly) prominent, sticking out, protruding.

seré → SERAI.

séréalia (*E*) cereals.

seréat and **seré'at** → SYARIAH.

seregang berseregang 1 to take a firm stand, brace o.s. → REGANG. **2** to fight.

sereh (*Jv?*) a pest of sugarcane.

seréh → SERAI I.

serek → SREG.

sérék → SIRIK I.

sérelak → SIRLAK.

serem → SERAM.

serembab terserembab to fall flat on one's face.

serembah-serembih to pour down (of tears).

seremban I (*cla*) a child's game played with shells or pebbles.

seremban II berseremban to wear a sarong high in front and low in back (e.g. when bathing).

sérémoni (*D/E*) ceremony.

sérémonial (*D/E*) ceremonial.

serempak → REMPAK I.

serempeng → SREMPENG.

serémpét (*J/Jv*) **berserémpétan** to brush against e.o. *Pesawat MIG-29 terbakar akibat* ~ *dengan MIG-29 yang lain.* A MIG-29 aircraft caught fire as a result of brushing against another MIG-29.

   menyerémpét [and **nyerémpét** (*coq*)] to sideswipe.

menyerémpét-nyerémpét [and **nyerémpét-nyerémpét** (*coq*)] to brush up against, be close to. ~ *bahaya* to live dangerously. *menggunakan bahasa Indonésia nyerémpét-nyerémpét logat Betawi* to use an Indonesian dialect which is close to Jakarta dialect.

   menyerémpétkan to make s.t. brush against s.t. else.

   terserémpét [and **keserémpét** (*coq*)] **1** to get grazed, sideswiped. ~ *mobil* sideswiped by a car. **2** to be touched on briefly. ~ *namanya dalam buku tersebut.* His name was mentioned in passing in that book.

   serémpétan grazing, brushing against.

   serémpét-serémpétan to sideswipe e.o.

   penyerémpét s.o. who grazes/sideswipes.

   penyerémpétan brushing against, grazing.

serempu (*cla*) **1** (*lunas* –) (*naut*) a long hollow keel (of praus). *biduk* – a prau with such a keel. **2** dugout.

sérénade (*D*) serenade.

serendah (*ob*) a short banana species, *Musa nana*.

serendéng 1 slanting, leaning, sloping (of a wall, etc.), keeling over, at an angle (like plates against a wall); → SÉNDÉNG II. **2** not quite right in one's head, a bit crazy.

   menyerendéng to lean, slant.

   menyerendéngkan to lean/slant s.t.

   terserendéng leaning, slanting, keeling over.

seréng (*J*) rocket (firecracker).

serengam excessive (of the hair in one's nose/one's appetite), very numerous.

seréngéh (*M*) → SERINGAI.

serengit (*ob*) → SERINGAI.

serenjak mousetrap.

serenjang (*ob*) erect (of a mast/person standing up).

   berserenjang to stand erect.

serenta (*J*) as soon as. – *ibu dengar anaknya jatuh, dia lari keluar rumah.* As soon as mother heard that her child had fallen, she ran out of the house; → SERTA I.

serentak jointly, together, as one, at the same time, collectively, simultaneously, concurrently. *serangan* – a simultaneous attack.

   keserentakan simultaneity.

serep (*J*) **menyerepi** and **nyerep-nyerepin** to dig thoroughly into, inquire into a thing thoroughly. ~ *kabar* to ferret out information.

sérep → SÉRAP.

serepet (*J*) between dark and light.

seresah mulch, (forest) litter.

seret (*J/Jv*) **1** stiff (of a lock/hinge/axle, etc.); jammed. *Pintu itu harus diminyaki supaya tidak* –. That door has to be oiled so that it doesn't jam. **2** turned a screw tight, screwed down. **3** hoarse (of voice). *Kalau* – *kau harus minum yang banyak.* When you have a hoarse voice you should drink a lot. **4** slow (to sell). *Sepéda motor* – *lakunya.* Motorcycles are not selling well. **5** blocked, sluggish, slowed down (of the flow of s.t.).

   menyeretkan and **memperseret** to block/slow down the flow of. *Iklim konfrontatif antara sumber peminjam dana dan yang berutang dikhawatirkan akan* ~ *arus dana dari negara pemberi pinjaman.* The confrontational climate between fund-granting sources and creditors will block the flow of funds from donor countries.

   keseretan blockage, sluggishness.

serét (*Jv*) **nyerét** to smoke opium.

sérét I dragging along, trailing.

   menyerét and **nyérét** (*coq*)] **1** to drag, trail along the ground. *Setelah S. tak berkutik, meréka* ~ *tubuh korban ke taman.* After S. didn't move, they dragged the victim's body to a park. **2** to take/drag by force. *Pencuri itu disérét ke séksi polisi.* The thief was taken to the police station. *Dia disérét ke muka persidangan Pengadilan Negeri.* He was summoned to appear before a session of the District Court. ~ (*ke pengadilan*) to prosecute. **3** to involve, implicate (in a case).

   menyerét-nyérét 1 to involve, implicate. *Dia disérét-sérét ke dalam perkara korupsi itu.* He was implicated in that incident of corruption. **2** to drag along.

   menyéréti (*pl obj*) to drag along, etc.

   tersérét [and **kesérét** (*coq*)] **1** dragged along. *Mahasiswa ITB téwas* ~ *arus Citarum.* A Bandung Institute of Technology student was dragged to his death by the current of the Citarum River. **2** involved, implicated.

terséret-séret 1 dragged. ~ *langkahnya* dragged one's feet. **2** dragged in, gotten involved.

séretan dragging, drag down, s.t. drawn down. ~ *ke bawah* draw-down.

penyéret s.o. who drags.

penyéretan dragging along, taking (to court, etc.), involving, implicating.

séret II (*Jv*) **1** stripe, band. **2** edge of cloth/umbrella, etc.

sergah snarl. *"Naik keréta perlu disiplin, karena terlambat semenit saja dari jadwal, kita akan tertinggal,"* *-nya.* "You have to be disciplined when you go by train because if you're late by even a minute you'll be left behind," he snarled.

menyergah 1 to speak sharply to, snarl/snap at. *Saya selalu ~ adik saya pabila dia bermain di tepi jalan raya.* I always snarled at my younger brother when he played at the side of the highway. **2** to startle (by a sudden noise/movement/remark).

sergahan snarl, snarling.

sergam tersergam 1 prominent, outstanding, conspicuous. *Bangunan hotél yang baru itu ~ indah di atas sebuah bukit.* The new hotel structure towers beautifully at the top of the hill. **2** to appear suddenly.

sergap I menyergap 1 to attack/assault suddenly, pounce on, ambush, intercept. **2** to catch and carry away.

tersergap attacked.

sergapan raid, ambush, attack, assault, interception.

penyergap attacker, interceptor.

penyergapan 1 attack, assault. **2** capture.

sergap II → SERGAH.

sergut badly done, rough (of workmanship).

seri I (*Skr*) shine, luster, glory, splendor, brilliancy, glamour. - *balai* (*cla*) the place of honor in the audience hall of the palace. - *gunung* beautiful from afar. - *muka* lit up countenance. - *panggung* star of the stage. - *pantai* beautiful from close up.

berseri(-seri) 1 to gleam, shine, be radiant, light up. *Mukanya berseri-seri.* His face lit up. **2** splendid, magnificent.

menyeri to gleam, glisten, shine.

menyerikan 1 to radiate, send off. *Semuanya ~ warna yang tak ada taranya di atas dunia.* Everything radiated a color unrivalled in this world. **2** to brighten up, enliven (a party, etc.).

keserian brilliance.

seri II (*Skr*) (honorable title for Majesty) His Royal Highness - *paduka* His Majesty (for kings/sultans, etc.). - *Maharaja* His Majesty. - *Paus* His Holiness the Pope.

perserian (*cla*) all courtiers with the title of *seri*.

Seri III (*Skr*) *Déwi* - the wife of Vishnu, goddess of the rice crop. - *panggung* leading lady.

seri IV substance; honey. *hilang* - to evaporate, vaporize.

menyeri to suck honey; → SARI I.

seri V 1 to tie, draw. *berakhir* - ended in a tie. **2** broke even (in a business venture).

seri VI first part of the names of some plants. - *gading* k.o. shrub, *Nyctanthes arbor-tristis*.

séri I (*D*) **1** series. *nomor* - serial number. *secara* - serially, in a series. - *perangko* a series of stamps. **2** serial. *film* - a serial.

berséri in a series.

séri II (*E*) *buah* - cherry (the fruit). *pohon* - cherry tree.

sérial (*E*) serial. *drama* - drama serial (on radio/TV). *kisah* - serial (story). - *drama* drama serial (radio, TV).

menyérialkan to serialize.

sériala → SÉRÉALIA.

seriap 1 dusky-gray heron, *Ardea sumatrana*. **2** gray heron, *Ardea cinerea rectirostris*.

seriat stop (of rain).

seriau shudder, feel queasy (at the sight of blood, etc.).

seriawan thrush (the disease), sprue, *Stomatitis aphthosa*, gingivitis, Indonesian sprue; also, scurvy. *daun* - leaves of a plant, *Elaeocarpus sp.*, used for the preparation of a medicine against sprue. - *usus/ucus* a stomachache which causes diarrhea (*usu* in children).

seribu one thousand; → RIBU.

seribulan *pohon* - a plant, *Phyllagathis rotundifolia*.

seribumi a plant, heliotrope, *Heliotropium indicum*.

seridanta → SERIGADING.

seriding I → SERÉNDÉNG.

seriding II → SERINDING.

serigading a shrub with scented leaves that yields a dye, *Nyctanthes arbor tristis*.

serigala (*Skr*) **1** jackal, *Cyon rutilans*. **2** wolf, *Canis lupus*.

serigunting various species of birds with scissors-like tails, drongo, *Dicrurus spp.* - *hitam* black drongo, *Dicrurus macrocercus*. - *kelabu* ashy drongo, *Dicrurus leucophaeus*. - *gunung* spangled drongo, *Dicrurus hottentottus*.

serik I learned one's lesson, had enough (of doing s.t.), cured; → JERA, KAPOK I. *Ia - untuk naik sepéda.* He's learned his lesson about riding a bike (after he had an accident).

serik II → SERAK II, SERAK-SERIK.

Serikandi → SRIKANDI.

serikat (*A*) → SARÉKAT, SYARÉKAT, SYARIKAT. **1** union, alliance, league. *Amérika* - [AS] United States of America, U.S.A. *negara-negara* - the Allied Powers (*esp* in WWII). *Negara/République Indonésia* - (*ob*) Republic of the United States of Indonesia. - *Bangsa-Bangsa* League of Nations. - *Yésus* Society of Jesus. **2** association, (commercial) society/company. - *dagang* commercial company. **3** syndicate, trade union. *orang* - syndicalist, trade unionist. - *buruh/(se)kerja* trade union. **keserikatkerjaan** trade unionism. **perserikat-buruhan** trade unionism. - *pekerja* trade union.

berserikat 1 to ally o.s. (with/to), join (with), make an alliance (with), associate (with). **2** to form or join a syndicate or association.

menyerikati to enter into an alliance with, participate in.

menyerikatkan and **memperserikatkan** to join together. ~ *Allah* to consider Allah as multiple (i.e., polytheism).

perserikatan alliance, association, union, league, confederacy, confederation; society; organization; trust. ~ *Bangsa-Bangsa* [PBB] United Nations. ~ *negara* Confederation. ~ *perdata* civil partnership. ~ *Sabda Allah* (Societas Verbi Divini) Society of the Word (Roman Catholic men's religious order).

serikaya I (*Skr?*) *ketan* - steamed banana pudding made of eggs, sugar, and coconut milk.

serikaya II (*Skr?*) *buah* - sugar apple, sweetsop, *Anona squamosa*. - *belanda* soursop.

serimala (*cla*) carpenter.

serimenganti (*Jv*) the true gate for entering the *kraton*.

serimpét → SERÉMPÉT.

serimpi (*Jv*) a classical female dance performed by a group of four principal dancers representing the heroines of the Menak romance.

menyerimpi [and **nyerimpi** (*coq*)] to perform this dance.

serimpung (*J*) a rope tied around the legs.

berserimpung-serimpung(an) to trip e.o. up.

menyerimpung 1 to fasten/tie the legs together. **2** to captivate. **3** to impede, block.

terserimpung entangled, entwined. *Kakinya ~ kain sarung yang dipakainya.* Their legs were entangled in the sarongs they were wearing.

penyerimpung s.o. or s.t. that ties such a rope.

penyerimpungan entangling, entwining.

serindai I a ghost which lives in the water and likes to bother women.

serindai II soft, pleasant, melodious (of the voice); → MERDU.

menyerindaikan to charm, enchant, fascinate.

serinding (*ikan* -) k.o marine fish, *Ambassis commersoni*.

serindit *burung* - and - *jawa* hanging parrot, Malay loriquet, *Loriculus pusillus/galgulus*.

sering I 1 (- *kali*) and **sering-sering** often, frequently, repeatedly. **2** sometimes, once in a while.

seringnya frequency.

sesering ~ *mungkin* as often as possible.

keseringan 1 too often. **2** frequency.

sering II twisted/woven tight, (closing) tight.

menyering 1 to twist tightly. **2** to twine.

sering III (*M*) slender.

sering IV (*M*) **menyering** to suck honey; → SERI IV.

seringai grin, grimace, smirk.

menyeringai 1 to grimace, grin, make faces. *Gadis itu cuma tersenyum* ~. The girl just grinned. **2** to move (one's lips, in anger), twist (one's mouth) into a grin.

seringaian grimace, smirk.

seringih → SERINGAI.

seringing menyeringing and **terseringing** to grimace.

sériosa (*D*) semiclassical (music). *lagu/musik* – semiclassical music.

serip fringe, edging, border.

seripah → SYARIFAH.

serit a fine comb for delousing.

menyerit to comb with such a comb.

sérius (*D*) **1** serious(ly). *Ia berbicara* –. He talked seriously. **2** critical, dangerous. *tidak* – not serious. **ketidak-sériusan** lack of seriousness.

mensériusi to become serious about, take s.t. seriously. *Tidak usah diseriusi*. It needn't be taken seriously.

kesériusan seriousness, gravity.

sériusitas seriousness.

Seriwijaya → SRIWIJAYA.

serkah torn (off), snapped, with a bite taken out of it.

menyerkah to break/smash to pieces, shatter, split apart.

serkai menyerkai to knead s.t. such as dough in a cloth to squeeze out the liquid, strain (rice-gruel) through a cloth, twist (wet cloth) to squeeze out the excess liquid.

serkap truncated conical scoop thrust down over fish in shallow waters or put over baby chicks for protection.

menyerkap 1 to catch with a scoop/in the hollow of one's hand. **2** to raid, arrest. **3** to cover with such a cover.

menyerkapi to put such a cover on.

penyerkapan 1 catching with such a scoop. **2** covering with such a cover. **3** raid, razzia, roundup (of suspects).

serkup menyerkup 1 to cover (with a hand/lid/basket/net/veil/plate); → SERGAP I. **2** (*geol*) to overthrust.

menyerkup to cover with s.t.

penyerkup s.o. or s.t. that covers.

serlah (*mostly Mal*) **te(r)serlah** distinct, clearly seen, gleaming against a dark background (of the face of the moon), glowing (of a beautiful countenance).

serling a pit for trapping large animals, pitfall.

te(r)serling fallen/walked into a trap.

sérma [*sérsan mayor*] sergeant-major.

sermangin a drum beaten on one side by a stick, on the other by hand; → GENDANG I.

sernak menyernak ~ *hati* to oppress; → SENAK.

séro I share (in a company). *untung* – dividend; → DIVIDÉN. *- pecahan* sub-share.

menyérokan and **mempersérokan 1** to issue shares for. **2** to convert (a state company) into a limited liability company.

pe(r)séro partner, associate, shareholder, s.o. who has an interest in (a business); → PEMEGANG *saham*. ~ *firma* partner. ~ *komanditér/pelepas uang* limited partner. ~ *(pen)diam* sleeping partner. ~ *pengurus* active/managing partner.

pe(r)séroan company, partnership. ~ *dagang* trading company. ~ *dengan/di bawah firma/nama* general partnership. ~ *induk* holding company. ~ *komanditér* limited partnership. ~ *patungan* joint corporation (owned partly by the government and partly by other companies). ~ *perdata* civil partnership. ~ *secara melepas uang* limited partnership. ~ *publik* publicly owned corporation. ~ *tanggung-jiwa* life insurance company. ~ *terbatas* [PT] corporation, limited company, incorporated. ~ *terbatas kosong* shell company. ~ *tunggal* single corporation (100 percent government owned).

séro II (*Jv*) large marine fish trap.

séro III (*S*) otter; → BERANG-BERANG.

serobéh unkempt and unbrushed (of hair), slovenly; → SERBAH-SERBIH.

serobok berserobok – *dengan* to run into, encounter by chance; → BERSUA/BERTEMU *dengan*.

serobot (*J/Jv*) *main* – arbitrary, high-handed. *tukang* – thief.

berserobotan to make a grab for e.o.'s things.

menyerobot [and **nyerobot** (*coq*)] **1** to take away (s.t. from), trick

out of (customers/passengers, etc.), pilfer, snatch, seize, take s.t. away (from s.o.). *Singapore Airlines selama dua tahun telah* ~ *penumpang Garuda Indonesian Airways*. Over the last two years Singapore Airlines has taken passengers away from Garuda Indonesian Airways. **2** to pickpocket. **3** to try to outdo s.o., try to get in front of s.o. in a line. **4** to act arbitrarily/high-handedly. **5** to sabotage (the instructions). **6** to usurp (s.o.'s position, etc.). **7** to kidnap, abduct; → MENCULIK. **8** to graze (a tree, etc., by a car). **9** to run over. ~ *masuk* to enter (a house) illegally. *bicara dengan* ~ to interrupt without further ado. **10** to jump (the line).

serobotan 1 arbitrary, high-handed. **2** s.t. stolen/snatched away. ~ *tanah* to squat (on s.o. else's land).

penyerobot thief, usurper. ~ *tanah* squatter.

penyerobotan theft, appropriation, taking possession, usurpation. ~ *tanah* squatting.

seroda → SERUDA.

serodok → SERUDUK.

seroja (*Skr*) **1** lotus, *Nelumbium speciosum* (*Willd*); → TERATAI. *- biru* blue lotus, *Nymphaea stella*. *- mérah* red lotus. *Nelumbium nelumbo*. **2** reference to military action against separatists in East Timor.

sérok I bay, inlet, bight; branch (of a river), creek.

sérok II → SÉRO II.

sérok III (*Jv*) scoop, ladle, spatula.

menyérok 1 to scoop s.t. (up). **2** to round up (suspects).

penyérok scoop (the tool).

sérokan canal, drain, sewer, conduit, pipe.

sérologi (*D/E*) serology.

sérologik (*E*) and **sérologis** (*D*) serologic.

serombong 1 pipe, tube. **2** hollow cylinder. *- asap* chimney.

serompok terserompok (*ob*) stuck.

serondéng → SERUNDÉNG.

serondok terserondok to stick/protrude up or out.

serondol → SUNDUL I.

serondong I menyerondong to bend/push forward.

terserondong pushed forward.

serondong II k.o. net for catching fish or shrimp.

menyerondong to fish using this net.

sérong 1 squinting, cross-eyed. **2** slanting, sloping (wall, etc.), skewed. **3** dishonest, unfaithful, cheating. *- hati* insincere, false, disloyal, crooked (of morals). *berbuat* – a) to deceive, cheat, take in. b) to be unfaithful to (one's husband/wife), commit adultery. *jalan/langkah* – cunning ways, fraudulent devices. *main* – a) to deceive, cheat, take in. b) to be unfaithful to (one's husband/wife). *main – dengan lelaki lain* to play around with other men. *pelampiasan dendam si ibu terhadap suaminya yang main – dengan wanita lain* a wife's revenge on her husband's infidelity.

menyérong 1 to go (off at a tangent). **2** slanting, oblique. *maju* ~ to go forward on the slant.

sérong-menyérong to go off at all angles.

menyérongi to commit an infidelity against.

menyérongkan 1 to slant, incline, tilt, angle. **2** to do s.t. in a dishonest way.

sérongan oblique angle, slant.

kesérongan 1 obscenity. **2** insincerity, disloyalty, unfaithfulness, falseness, falsity, treachery, meanness; corruption.

penyérongan skewing.

seronggong crib (in a mine shaft).

seronok 1 comfortable, pleasant. *Rumah ialah tempat yang paling –*. A house is the most pleasant place to be. *musik yang –* pleasant music. **2** (often with a negative and sarcastic connotation) improper. *tidak* – unpleasant. **ketidak-seronokan** unpleasantness. *- keluarga* broken home.

menyeronokkan to comfort, delight.

keseronokan delight, pleasure.

séropositif (*E*) seropositive.

seropot (*J*) **menyeropot** to suck up, lap. ~ *kopi* to lap up coffee.

serosoh (*M*) **menyerosoh** to slip/slide down; → MENYELIP.

serot (*J/Jv*) **menyerot 1** to suck up, sip. **2** to absorb.

terserot sucked up, sipped.

serotan straw (for drinking).
penyerot act/way of sucking/absorbing. *mesin ~ debu* vacuum cleaner.
serotonin (E) serotonin.
seroyong (J) seroyongan to stagger, totter, reel.
serpa (Skr) curse.
menyerpa to curse.
serpai → SERPIH.
serpih 1 chip, fragment, splinter. 2 chipped, broken at the edge. 3 flake, scale. *giginya –* his tooth was broken at the edge. 4 shale. *– jagung* corn flakes. *– kayu* woodchips. *– kudis/kulit* scar, peelings (of the skin). *– minyak* shale.
berserpih-serpih fragmented, splintered.
menyerpih to splinter, break up into splinters, crumble s.t.
menyerpihkan to splinter s.t., make s.t. crumble.
serpihan 1 splinter, crumb, piece. *~ kayu* and *kayu ~* wood-chips. *kelompok ~* splinter group. *~ kertas* scraps of paper. *penuh ~ kaca* full of glass fragments. 2 (sl) cocaine.
serpih-serpihan fragments, chips.
sérpis → SÉRVIS I, II.
serpuk terserpuk to fall down on one's face.
sérsan (D) sergeant. *– dua* [sérda] sergeant second class. *– kepala* [sérka] senior sergeant. *– mayor* [sérma] master sergeant. *– satu* [sértu] sergeant first class. *– taruna* [sértar] cadet sergeant.
ser-seran (BG) fantastic, great.
sérse and sérsi I (D) detective, plainclothesman.
sérsi II (D) serge.
serta I (Skr) 1 and (also), also, as well as. *Seorang yang baik hati – (dengan) murahnya.* A good-natured as well as generous person, a good-natured person and generous as well. 2 as soon as, while. *– menerima perintah, lalu menyerang.* As soon as he got the order, he attacked. *dengan – merta* a) at once, immediately, right away. *Perbaiki kesalahanmu dengan – merta.* Correct your mistake at once. b) on the spur of the moment. *Apa sebabnya maka dengan – merta ia berangkat ke Bali?* Why did he leave for Bali on the spur of the moment? *– merta* spontaneous. **keserta-mertaan** spontaneity. *– rata* to put o.s. in another's place, "do onto others as you would have them do onto you," be tolerant.
serta II (Skr) 1 to join, take part in, go along. *Beliau tidak – berunding.* He did not take part in the discussions. 2 together (with), along with. *wakil Présidén – (dengan) para wartawan* the Vice-President together with the reporters. *ikut –* accompany, go along. **keikut-sertaan** participation, taking part. *peran –* participation. *– bunyi* (ob) consonant. *– laku* (leg) to be an accomplice. **peserta-laku** accomplice.
beserta 1 together (with), along with, accompanied by. *Kirimkan kembali surat ini, ~ dengan uang langganan.* Return this letter together with the subscription fee. 2 to take part (in), join (in). *Meréka itu ~ juga mengerjakan tanah itu.* They also took part in tilling the soil. 3 to accompany, be with, be alongside. *Tuhan selalu ~mu.* God is always with you.
menyertai 1 to escort. *Beberapa pesawat pembom ~ pesawat B-29.* Several bombers escorted the B-29 plane. 2 to accompany, go along with. *Tari-menari disertai dengan nyanyian.* Dancing was accompanied by singing. 3 to assist. *Dalam perundingan itu wakil Indonésia disertai dua orang ahli keuangan.* At the meeting Indonesia's representatives were assisted by two financial experts. 4 to participate in, take part in. *Siapa yang hendak ~ kongrés itu dipersilakan mendaftarkan diri.* Those who want to take part in the congress are requested to register. 5 to join (another in doing s.t.).
menyertakan and mempersertakan 1 to include s.o. in the company, allow s.o. to join in, let s.o. participate. 2 to enclose s.t. *Céknya disertakan.* The check is enclosed.
sertaan accessory.
kesertaan participation. *fungsi ~* participatory function.
penyerta and peserta participant, partner. *untuk ~ beregu* for group participants. *~ didik* student. *~ komanditér* sleeping partner. *~ kongrés* congressee. *~ lélang* bidder. *~ pelatihan* trainee. *~ sederajat* equal partner. *~ pengurus* managing partner. *~ séminar* participant in a seminar. **kepesertaan** participation.
penyertaan 1 participation, co-. 2 equity participation, invest-

ment. *~ modal/pembiayaan* co-financing, equity participation. *~ saham* investment in shares of stock.
pesertaan → KESERTAAN.
sértifikasi (E) certification. *– kelaikan/kelayakan* certification of qualification.
sértifikat (D) certificate. *– déposito* certificate of deposit, C.D. *– dokter* physician's certificate; → SURAT *keterangan dokter. – kelahiran* birth certificate. *– kelaikan/kelayakan* certificate of qualification. *– kelaikan udara* certificate of airworthiness. *– kepemilikan* debenture. *– tanah* land certificate.
bersértifikat with a certificate.
menyértifikatkan to certify, legalize by a certificate. *~ tanah warisan* to certify land received as a bequest.
pensértifikatan and penyértifikatan certification. *HKTI (Himpunan Kerukunan Tani Indonésia) agar diikutsertakan dalam pendaftaran dan pensértifikatan tanah.* The Indonesian Peasant Solidarity Association should be included in the registration and certification of land.
sértipikat → SÉRTIFIKAT.
sertu ablutions after touching s.t. impure.
menyertu to clean o.s. after contact with s.t. filthy (such as the lick of a dog/touch of a pig, etc.).
sértu → SÉRSAN *satu.*
seru I call, shout, cry (to attract attention). *"Har!" – si Santoso.* "Har!" shouted Santoso. *kata – (gram)* interjection. *tanda – (gram)* exclamation mark (!).
berseru 1 to call out, shout. 2 to urge, appeal (to). *Dia ~ agar rakyat bekerja keras.* He urged the people to work hard. *~ kepada* to appeal to s.o.
menyeru 1 to shout/call out. *Teman saya ~ nama saya dari seberang jalan.* My friend called out my name from across the street. 2 to hail (a cab, etc.). *Ia ~ sebuah taksi untuk mengantarkannya ke stasiun.* He hailed a cab to take him to the station. 3 to urge, suggest strongly.
seru-menyeru to urge e.o.
menyerukan 1 to tout, cry out about. *Sebentar-sebentar kedengaran penjaja ~ barang dagangannya.* From time to time the peddlers could be heard touting their wares. 2 to announce. *~ azan* to announce the call to prayer. *Keputusannya akan diserukan kemudian dengan alat pengeras suara.* His decision will be announced by loudspeaker. 3 to suggest, propose, urge, call upon, call for, appeal (to). *Kami ~ agar semua penduduk diungsikan.* We called for the evacuation of all residents. *Meréka ~ kepada présidén supaya mengambil tindakan keras.* They urged/called on the president to take strong action.
menyeru-nyerukan to shout, shout about.
seruan 1 call, appeal. 2 (ling) exclamation.
penyeru 1 announcer. 2 calling (distance).
penyeruan 1 calling out, announcing. 2 appealing.
seru II violent, bloody, severe, sharp (of words). *pertempuran yang –* a violent fight. *pertandingan yang –* a tough match.
seru-serunya intense.
terseru the most exciting.
seru III all; → SARWA. *Tuhan – sekalian alam* Lord of the entire universe.
seru IV (A) *pohon –* cypress, *Schima bancana.*
seruak (M) menyeruak to make/force/push one's/its way through; to push aside; to penetrate, enter by force. *Ia ~ di antara hadirin.* He forced his way through the audience.
serual → SELUAR.
seruas k.o. shrub, *Fagraea racemosa.*
serubu menyerubu to hit. *Sepéda motor ~ témbok trotoar.* A motorcycle hit the wall of the sidewalk.
seruda a belt of thorns to stop pilferers from climbing fruit trees.
serudi grinding, polishing.
berserudi polished (of gems/precious stones).
menyerudi to polish (gems/precious stones).
seruduk to collide with, ram into. *Ambulans – penonton hiburan, 8 téwas, 10 cedera.* An ambulance rammed into entertainment spectators, 8 killed and 10 injured. *Truk - sepéda.* A truck collided with a bicycle.
berserudukan to collide with e.o.

menyeruduk 1 [and **nyeruduk**] (*J*) to ram into. *Kerbau ~ orang.* The water buffalo rammed into somebody. **2** (*M*) to crawl underneath. *~ ke dalam belukar* to crawl into the underbrush. **3** to do s.t. with the head lowered, butt.

menyeruduki to ram into again and again.

menyerudukkan to ram (s.t.) (into).

terseruduk [and **keseruduk** (*J*)] rammed into, hit, collided.

serudukan collision, ramming. *Akibat ~ mobil pembawa jenazah itu, 8 orang téwas dan 10 lainnya menderita luka berat dan ringan.* Due to the collision with the hearse, 8 people died and of the 10 others, some were seriously and some were slightly injured.

penyerudukan butting.

serugat k.o. orchid, *Tropidia curculigoides.*

seruh I (*ob*) → SERU II.

seruh II shrunken (of a boil).

seruh III (*onom*) sound of dragging feet along the ground.

seruit I one-barbed harpoon for spearing turtles.

menyeruit to harpoon.

seruit II (*J*) whistle.

menyeruit to blow a whistle.

seruitan whistle.

seruk a rice bin holding about 10 *gantang.*

serul loose, not sticking together.

seruling bamboo or wooden flute; → SULING I.

sérum (*D*) serum. *ilmu –* serology.

menyérum to inject with a serum.

serumat *akar –* k.o. plant, *Canthium aciculatum.*

serumpu *– telinga badak* k.o. tree, *Crypteronia griffithii.*

sérun hen-house.

serunai I (*Pers*) k.o. wind instrument like a clarinet. *– Sangkakala* the Last Trumpet.

serunai II *biawak –* k.o. iguana, roughneck(ed) monitor, *Varanus rudicollis.*

serunai III k.o. plant, *Wedelia montana. – laut* a yellow button-flower, *Wedelia biflora.*

serunci k.o. plant, *Hiptage sericea.*

serunda I menyerunda to drag (a boat) overland.

serunda II berserunda and **terserunda** dangling.

serundang menyerundang to grub around with the snout.

serundéng and **serunding** grated coconut pulp mixed with sugar (or spices and beans) and fried.

seruni → SERUNAI III.

serunjang (*cla*) k.o. wooden lance.

serunting k.o. climbing plant.

seruntul (*J/Jv*) **nyeruntul** to dash, sprint.

seruntun *akar –* k.o. climbing plant, *Tinospora tuberculata, Anamirta paniculata* which provides a diuretic and tonic; → PUTARWALI.

serupa → RUPA.

serupih → SERPIH.

seruput I (*Jv*) **menyeruput** to slurp, lap up. *~ kopi pagi hari* to slurp up one's early-morning coffee.

seruput II k.o. plant, *Justicia uber.*

seruru I → SELURU.

seruru II k.o. climber, *Pericampylus glaucus.*

serut (*J*) k.o. small plane (the carpentry tool).

berserut planed, smoothed.

menyerut to plane, smooth.

serutan shavings. *~ pénsil* pencil shavings.

penyerut s.t. used for planing.

penyerutan planing, smoothing.

serutu cigar.

serutup menyerutup to slurp. *~ kopi* to slurp one's coffee.

sérviks (*E*) cervix.

sérvis I (*E*) **1** service (in a restaurant/hotel, etc.). **2** maintenance (of a car, etc.). **3** service (in tennis, etc.). **4** (sexual) servicing. *–, tuan?* (prostitute's invitation) Want some sex? *– aki* battery-charging service.

menyérvis(kan) [and **nyérvis** (*coq*)] to service (car, etc.), service (s.o. sexually).

penyérvis one who services.

sérvis II (*D*) dinner/tea set.

serwa → SARWA.

sesah bersesah to beat e.o. *~ bertinju* to have a fistfight.

menyesah 1 to beat s.o. with a long cane. **2** to beat clothes on a stone.

penyesah *papan ~* beater for laundry.

penyesahan beating.

sesai *uang –* bridegroom's settlement on the bride, bride-price.

sesajén and **sesaji(an)** (*Jv*) offering (of flowers and victuals, for various spirits, at sacred sites).

sesak 1 narrow, tight, not spacious. *ruang itu –* that room is not spacious. **2** crowded, congested. *Bermacam-macam kendaraan – di jalan.* Various vehicles crowded the street. **3** clogged, obstructed (of breathing, due to asthma, etc.), out of breath. *Napasnya –.* It was hard for him to breathe. *Napasnya – setelah berlari-lari.* He was out of breath after he ran. **4** in straitened circumstances. **5** back-comb, rat (of hair). *– dada* a) pant, have difficulty breathing (from bronchitis/asthma). b) agitated (by emotion). *– hidup* living in difficult circumstances. *– kencing* a strong urge to urinate; → KEBELET. *– napas* short of breath. a) out of breath (due to walking). b) stuffy, lacking air (in too small a space). c) suppressed, suffocated; short of breath, asthmatic. *menyesak napas* to become short of breath, etc. *– padat* and *penuh –* chock-full. *bisnya – padat* the bus was chock-full. *– padat penduduknya* overpopulated (of a nation/land, etc.).

bersesak(-sesak) 1 to jostle, shove, push, crowd. *Para penonton ramai bersesak-sesak.* The spectators were busily jostling e.o. **2** (to live, etc.) cheek by jowl.

bersesak-sesakan to be crowded/jammed in tightly together.

menyesak(kan) 1 to urge, push, press. *Sekali lagi didesak(kan)nya supaya membayar utangnya.* Once again he was urged to pay his debts. *Ia didesak(kan) ke pagar.* He was pushed up to the fence. **2** to make s.t. crammed/congested/stuffy. *udara yang sangat menyesak(kan) napas* air which is causing congested breathing. **3** to tighten, narrow, constrict. *gerakan tentara yang bermaksud menyesakkan kedudukan musuh* the intended movement of the army to tighten enemy positions. **4** to hamper, hinder, thwart, make difficult. *Perusahaan asing itu menyesakkan penghidupan rakyat.* The foreign company made people's lives difficult. **5** to block. *menyesakkan jalan* to block a street (by double parking). *~ hati/sendiri* to make s.o. feel bad.

menyesak-nyesak to crowd around. *Polisi berusaha memisahkan orang yang ~ di depan rumah.* The police tried to separate the people crowding around in front of the house. *~ dada* breathtaking.

menyesaki 1 to tighten, make s.t. feel tight. **2** to cram, fill up.

tersesak 1 pressed, crowded. **2** to be short of money. **3** to be hard (of life). *~ padang ke rimba* not know what to do.

sesakan 1 to breathe with quick, shallow breaths. **2** excessively close, cramped. *Bajunya ~.* His shirt is too small on him.

kesesakan 1 crowdedness. *~ lalulintas* traffic jam. **2** difficulties, problems. **3** tightness (in the chest).

sesal regret. *penuh –* regretful. *– hati* repentance, contrition, compunction, remorse, regret. *– pikir dahulu pendapatan – kemudian tidak berguna* look before you leap.

bersesal (*~ hati*) → MENYESAL.

menyesal [and **nyesal** (*coq*)] be/feel sorry, regret, repent, feel bad, much to one's regret. *~ akan* to regret, be sorry for. *Ia tak ~ akan perbuatannya.* He isn't sorry for his action. **kemenyesalan** regret.

bersesal(-sesal)an and **sesal-menyesali** to blame/accuse e.o.

menyesali 1 to regret, be/feel sorry for, deplore. *Dia ~ perbuatannya.* He deplored his action. **2** to blame s.o. or s.t. for s.t. *Hampir semua orang ~ dia mengirimkan anaknya ke Éropa itu.* Almost everyone blamed him for sending his child to Europe. *~ diri* to reproach/blame o.s.

menyesalkan 1 to regret, repent, resent, feel sorry about. *Sebenarnya perkara itu tidak perlu kita sesalkan.* In fact, we needn't regret that matter. *~ diri* to reproach/blame o.s. for. **2** regrettable. *~ hati* to make s.o. regret, make s.o. feel bad. *Tindakanmu itu sangat ~ hatiku.* Your action made me feel bad.

sesalan and **penyesalan** repentance, remorse, regret. *penuh ~* regretful(ly). *bisa – seumur hidup* can regret all one's life.

sesama → SAMA 1. ~ *manusia* fellow man.
sesanti (*Jv*) 1 prayers. 2 blessings.
sesap I menyesap 1 to lap, lick up, feed (like birds or animals). *Burung ~ air.* Birds lap up water. 2 to suck (in or up), suckle on the breast. *disesap lembing* (*ob*) to be stabbed by a spear.
  sesapan 1 manger, crib, trough (for birds/fowls). *~ burung* bird bath. 2 suction; → PENGISAPAN.
sesap II (*M*) abandoned field.
sesapi – *laut* sea cow, manatee.
sesar I bersesar and **menyesar** to give way, shift, yield, move out of the way.
  menyesarkan to push aside, shift, move s.t.
  penyesaran yielding, giving way.
sesar II (*geol*) fault, a break in the continuity of a rock, etc., with dislocation along the plane of the fracture. *– jurus mendatar* transcurrent fault. *– miring* oblique fault. *– naik* upthrust. *– naik tersembunyi* hidden thrust fault. *– San Andréas* San Andreas Fault. *– sungkup* suture.
  persesaran fault system, faulting.
sesat 1 to lose one's way. 2 to be misled, go astray, deviate, be in error. *mengikuti pendapat yang –* to follow a different opinion. *mati –* to die an unnatural death (such as to commit suicide). *– surut, terlangkah kembali* to correct a mistake made. *malu bertanya – di jalan* if you're too shy to ask directions, you'll get lost. *– air* badly educated. *– akal* not quite right in one's head. *– barat* to be off course. *– berat* badly misled. *– fakta* error in fact. *– hukum* error in law. *– lalu* to go the wrong way. *– langkah* to take a false step. *– pikiran* to have a wrong opinion/position. *– pusat* confused.
  bersesat astray, lost.
  menyesatkan 1 to mislead, lead astray, misleading. *Ia sengaja ~ kita.* He purposely misled us. 2 to confuse. *~ pandangan/ pikiran* to confuse one's viewpoint/ideas.
  tersesat lost, gone astray, strayed from the right path.
  kesesatan 1 error, miscarriage. *~ peradilan* miscarriage of justice. 2 state of being lost. 3 digression.
  penyesat s.t. or s.o. that leads astray, misleading.
  penyesatan 1 misleading, leading astray, deluding, diversion, diversionary. *spésialis taktik ~* specialist in diversionary tactics. 2 deception, deceptive tactics.
sesawanan (*Jv*) ceremony in which the family in the Keraton and all the officials pay a visit to the Sultan (of Yogyakarta) to congratulate him on his birthday.
sesawi I mustard greens, *Brassica rugosa*; → SAWI(-SAWI). *– tanah* k.o. weed, *Nasturtium heterophyllum.*
sesawi II → SAWI II.
sesayuran – *mentah* uncooked vegetables functioning as a side dish to a rice menu; → LALAP(-LALAPAN).
sésdalopbang [Sékretaris pengendalian operasi pembangunan] Secretary for the Control of Development Operations.
sesek → SESAK.
sésék (*J/Jv*) k.o. rather coarse bamboo wickerwork (for ceilings, etc.).
sesel → SESAL. **nyesel** → MENYESAL. *~ tujuh rejeb/turunan* to regret forever.
sésél menyésél to retract, pull back.
sesembahan (*Jv*) s.o. who makes a *sembah.*
sesemutan pins and needles, pricking sensation in a body part; → SEMUT.
sesenap k.o. weed, cattle fodder, *Alysicarpus nummularifolius/ vaginalis.*
seséndok → SÉNDOK-SÉNDOK.
sesenggokan (*J*) and **sesenggukan** sobbing.
sesep (*Jv*) → SESAP I. **menyesep-nyesepkan** to suck (like an infant).
sesepuh (*Jv*) 1 elder, the older generation. 2 chairman. 3 ancestors, forbears. 4 éminence grise. 5 senior citizen. 6 godfather.
sésér (*Jv*) landing net.
  penyésér a fisherman who uses this k.o. net.
sését (*Jv*) to come/peel off.
  menyését to peel away.
sési I (*E*) session.
sési II (*D*) cession, assignment (of stock).
  mensésikan and **menyésikan** to cede, assign.

sesia → SIA I.
sesiak → SIAK II.
sesibar → SIBAR II.
sesira *pohon* – k.o. tree shrub, *Acronychia laurifolia.*
sesirik (*Jv*) prohibition (to eat). **menjalankan** – to begin fasting.
sesisihan (*bio*) phyllary.
sésium (*D*) cesium.
Sésko → SEKOLAH *Staf dan Komando.*
Séskowan (Army) Staff and Command School graduate.
sesoca (*Jv*) precious stone.
séspan (*D*) sidecar (of a motorcycle). *sepéda motor –nya* his motorcycle and sidecar.
sesuai 1 suitable, appropriate. 2 according (to), pursuant (to), in accordance (with), as per. *– dengan adat* traditional. *– dengan rencana* as planned/scheduled. *Segala sesuatu berjalan – dengan rencana.* Everything went according to plan. *sudah tidak – lagi* out of date, antiquated, archaic. *– dengan contoh* to come up to sample. *– dengan hatiku* after my own heart. *– dengan keadaan* in accordance with the situation. *– dengan jadwal* on schedule. *– dengan rencana* as planned, according to plan. *– seléra* what one likes to eat, one's taste in food. *– dengan sumpah jabatannya* mindful of one's oath of office. 3 in line (with). *Program ini – dengan politik pemerintah.* This program is in line with government policy. 4 in proportion (to), commensurate (with). *Saya akan menerima pekerjaan itu jika diberikan gaji yang – dengan keboléhan saya.* I'll accept that job if I'm given a salary that is commensurate with my skill. *Saudara harus memikul beban keuangan – dengan kekayaan saudara.* You have to bear a share of the financial burden commensurate with your wealth. 5 efficacious, effective (of remedies, etc.). *Obat ini – bagi kanak-kanak yang demam.* This remedy is effective for kids who have a fever. 6 in agreement. *Pendapat meréka – dengan pikiran saya.* Their opinion agrees with my ideas. 7 to cope. *Tidak mungkin – dengan tuntutan zaman.* It is impossible to cope with the requirements of the time. 8 under (a contract/law/regulation), pursuant to. *– artikel 18 perjanjian ini* under article 18 of this contract. *tidak –* unmatched, in contravention (of a law). **ketidak-sesuaian** mismatch, incompatibility, nonconformity.
  bersesuaian to be suitable/fitting, agree with. *tugas ini ~ benar untuk kaum wanita* this task is really fitting for women. **kebersesuaian** correspondence.
  menyesuaikan to adjust, adapt, set (a clock), coordinate, make fit/ suitable, harmonize. *~ diri* to adjust, adapt. *~ diri dengan iklim* to acclimatize o.s. *~ diri dengan kehendak zaman* to keep pace/ up with the times. *Bukanlah mudah ~ diri dengan orang-orang di tempat yang baru.* It isn't easy to adjust to people in new surroundings. *~ langkahnya dengan* to keep step/pace with. *~ arloji tangan anda dengan waktu setempat* to set your wristwatch to local time. *disesuaikan menurut* to be made compatible with.
  tersesuaikan adjusted.
  kesesuaian correspondence, agreement, similarity; suitability.
  berkesesuaian corresponding, matching, suitable, fit, qualified.
  penyesuai adjuster, adapter.
  penyesuaian 1 adjustment, adaptation. *~ diri* self-adaptation. 2 compatibility.
  persesuaian 1 agreement, harmony, concord, concurrence. *Kami telah mencapai ~ pendapat.* We've reached an agreement. *~ dalam* to fit in. *~ dan kesepadanan* link and match. 2 adjustment. *masa ~* adjustment period. *~ budaya* cultural adjustment. *~ kurs* currency realignment.
sesuatu → SUATU.
sesudah → SUDAH.
sesumbar (*Jv*) boasting, boast, bragging; defiant language; to brag, boast, bluster; → SUMBAR I.
sesunggukan to sob.
sesuru common milk hedge, fleshy spurge, *Euphorbia antiquorum.*
set- also see entries beginning with st-.
sét I (*E*) 1 set (of pans/cups/instruments, etc.). 2 (*D*) a move (in chess, etc.). 3 (*D/E*) a set (in tennis, etc.). *– langsung* straight set. 4 (in printing office) *tukang –* compositor.
  mengesét, mensét [and **ngesét** (*coq*)] 1 to compose/set up (a book in a printing office), typeset. 2 to set (one's hair).

sét II (in acronyms) → SÉKRÉTARIAT.

seta cubit, i.e., the length from elbow to the tip of the middle finger, 18 inches; → HASTA.

setabelan (D) artillery.

setabil → STABIL.

setadion → STADION.

setaf → STAF.

setagén and setagi (Jv) a strip of corded cotton measuring approximately 13 yards by 5 inches wound around the waist to secure the kain or sarung at one's waist.

setahu 1 (PC) conscience. 2 (J) I don't know. – jawabnya sambil meléngos. "I dunno," was his answer as he turned his head aside; → TAHU I.

setai bersetai-setai and tersetai-setai tattered, torn to shreds.

setaka I → ASTAKA.

setaka II k.o. shrub, Plumbago rosea.

setakona → ASTAKONA.

setal I (D) stable (for horses).

setal II (D) steel.

setala same tone, in tune/harmony; → TALA I.

setaman (Jv) kembang – water and flour mixture used ceremoniously.

setamat → TAMAT.

setambuk → STAMBUK.

setambul I (A) Istanbul. komidi/sandiwara – itinerant folk theater (in the first half of the 20th century).

setambul II (J) k.o. turban.

setambun k.o. tree, Baccaurea parviflora, with edible fruit.

sétan (A) 1 Satan, demon, devil, bad/evil spirit; → IBLIS. senja kala perulangan – twilight is the time for haunting. menonton gambar – berkejaran di layar tévé to watch an interfered-with picture on the TV screen; → SEMUT 2. – hantu wicked person. 2 (coq) a general term of abuse. – lu you devil! Mémang – engkau ini! The devil is really in you! You're really like one possessed! anak – imp, child of Satan. batu – lunar caustic, argentic (silver) nitrate. lingkaran – vicious circle. lombok – cayenne pepper; → CABÉ rawit. rumah – freemason's lodge. – alas tormentor. – belang gundul "bald devils," i.e., devils who have all their hair shaved off except for a topknot. 3 a member of the outlawed PKI or one of its mass organizations who must report to the Military District Command Headquarters. – jalan speed demon, speeder. – judi demon of gambling. – kerdil a very small devil. – laut purchaser in fish collecting centers. – léwat said when it all of a sudden becomes silent in a party/company, there is an angel passing, an angel passes through the room. – neraka hellish devil. – perempuan she-devil.

bersétan haunted by devils.

menyétan to perform a daredevil act.

mempersétan(kan) to ignore, take no notice of.

kesétanan possessed by the devil. orang ~ s.o. possessed by the devil.

persétan ~ sama the hell with. Boléh ~ saja! Drop dead! Go to hell!

setana → ISTANA.

setandar (D) 1 flag or banner used as a symbol of a military unit. 2 bicycle or motorcycle standard attached at the hub of the rear wheel or other place, for holding the bicycle or motorcycle upright when not in use. 3 standard (of quality). 4 a stand. Tarohlah TV-nya di –. Set the television on the stand.

menyetandar to put (a bike) on a stand.

setang (D) 1 handlebar (of a bicycle). 2 bar, rod. – putar kelly joint.

setangan handkerchief; → SAPU 1. – kepala headband.

setangga orang – neighbor; → TETANGGA.

setanggi (Skr) fragrant powder burnt as incense; → KEMENYAN I.

sétani (A) satanic, diabolical.

setanplas and setanplat (D) bus stop.

setap → STAF.

setapak → TAPAK I

setapsiun → SETASION.

setara – dengan equivalent to; → TARA 1.

kesetaraan equality, equivalency.

setasion (D) station. – bis bus terminal.

setat (D) list, roll, statement. – gaji payroll.

setater → STARTER.

setatis → STATIS.

setatistik → STATISTIK.

setatus → STATUS.

setatuten → STATUTEN.

setawar name for several plants thought to allay (= tawar) fever and keep away spirits which cause disease, Costus speciosus. menjadi – dan sedingin to be a consolation.

setebal k.o. tree, Alangium nobile.

setéger (D) scaffolding.

setéhéng (coq) insane.

seték (D) slip, cutting, i.e., a stem, root, twig, etc. cut or broken off a plant and used for planting or grafting; → STÉK.

menyeték to take cuttings, (take a) slip [from (a plant) for planting or grafting], propagate by cuttings.

penyetékan propagation by cuttings. Risét ~ pohon untuk réboisasi. Research regarding the propagation by cutting trees for reforestation.

setéker → STÉKER.

setél I (D) 1 a suite (of furniture); a suit (of clothes). – kartu deck of cards. dua – pakaian two suits. 2 (sl) stylish, in style.

menyetél to match (colors).

setélan 1 suit, dress, costume. Ia berpakaian ~ biru. She wore a blue dress. 2 dinner/tea set. satu ~ cangkir-piring a place setting. satu ~ kartu a deck of cards. 3 well-matched pair. bersetélan to have/wear a dress/costume.

setél II (D) menyetél [and nyetél (coq)] 1 to turn a knob/switch, wind (a clock/watch, etc.), adjust, tune, set. radio yang disetél keras-keras a radio tuned to a high volume. dapat disetél adjustable. tempat duduk yang dapat disetél an adjustable seat (in a car). ~ fokus kaméra berlénsa panjang to adjust focus of a telephoto lens. ~ jam to wind a watch. ~ radio/TV to change stations (on the radio/TV). 2 to fix (a game).

setélan 1 radio dial, tuning knob. 2 adjustment, tuning, setting.

penyetélan 1 adjusting, adjustment, fitting, tuning. 2 (car) tuneup.

setéla → KETÉLA.

setelah → TELAH I.

setéléng I (D) 1 exhibition, show; → PAMÉRAN. 2 show, performance; → PERTUNJUKAN.

menyetéléngkan to exhibit, show, perform.

setéléng II and setéling (D mil) position.

setém I (D) vote (in election), suffrage.

menyetém 1 to vote for. 2 to put s.t. to a vote.

setéman vote, election.

setém II (D) in harmony/tune (of the voice/sound). tidak – false, discordant, not in tune.

menyetém to tune (a violin/piano, etc.).

penyetém tuner. ~ piano piano tuner.

penyetéman tuning. ~ piano piano tuning.

setém III (E Mal) (postage) stamp.

setempat → TEMPAT.

setémpel → STÉMPEL I.

setén (Jv) clipped form of asistén (wedana), assistant to a district head, i.e., the present title for a former camat.

seténgan (E) sten-gun.

setengah → TENGAH I.

seténggar (ob) → ISTINGGAR.

seténsil → STÉNSIL.

setér (D coq ob) star, decoration.

séter → SÉT II.

seterap → SETRAP.

setérek (D) strong, full-flavored.

seteréng → STRÉNG.

seteria → SATRIA.

seterihat → ISTIRAHAT.

seterik (D) headband.

seterika → SETRIKA.

seteriman → SETIR.

seterimin → SETRIMIN.

seterip → SETRIP I.

seterongking → STOR(E)MKING, STROMKING.

seteru (*Skr*) (personal) enemy, foe. – *bebuyutan* archenemy.
 berseteru to be hostile. ~ *dengan* to be enemies with.
 menyeterui to dislike, be hostile toward s.o.
 menyeterukan 1 to dislike intensely. 2 to make an enemy of s.o.
 memperseterukan to be hostile toward s.o.
 perseteruan feud, enmity, hostility.

seterum → SETRUM.

seterup → SETRUP.

seti (*ob*) satin.

setia (*Skr*) 1 faithful, loyal. 2 frequent (flier, etc.), steady (customer). – *akan janji* to keep one's promise/word. *berubah* – to become unfaithful. *pengawal* – (*ob*) bodyguard. *tidak* – unfaithful, disloyal, infidel. **ketidak-setiaan** unfaithfulness, disloyalty, infidelity.
 bersetia to be loyal.
 menyetiai to be faithful to.
 kesetiaan faith(fulness), loyalty, allegiance, fidelity, dedication (to one's work). ~ *korps* esprit de corps.

setiabu (*cla*) 1 k.o. snake. 2 *pedang* – a) triangular foil. b) bayonet.

setiakawan solidarity.
 bersetiakawan feel solidarity (with).
 menyetiakawani to declare one's solidarity/sympathy with. ~ *kaum kumuh* sympathy for the poor.
 kesetia-kawanan solidarity.

setiap → TIAP I.

setiar (*J*) effort, endeavor; → IKHTIAR.

setiausaha (*Mal*) secretary. – *kerja* executive secretary.

setiawan 1 faithful, loyal. 2 loyal person.

setif → SETIP I.

setiga (*ob*) terza rima (of sonnet).

setik I (*D*) stitch (of needlework). – *balik* hem. – *hiasan* ornamental stitch. – *silang* cross-stitch.
 menyetik to stitch (a garment).

setik II (*D*) piece.

setik III (*J*) span (from thumb to middle finger; about nine inches); → JENGKAL.
 menyetik to measure in spans.

setikan (*J*) a children's game played with marbles.

setimbang → TIMBANG.

setimpal → TIMPAL.

séting (*E*) setting.
 sétingan setting.

setinggal (*ob*) setinggar → ISTINGGAR.

setinggan (*Mal*) 1 squatter, s.o. who settles on land without legal right. 2 illegal. *rumah* – an illegal house (built without the necessary permits); → LIAR.

setinggar → ISTINGGAR.

setinggi I (*naut*) clew on a sail.

setinggi II as high as; → TINGGI I.

setinggil → SITINGGIL.

setinja → ISTINJA.

setip I (*D*) India rubber, rubber eraser.
 menyitip [and nyetip (*coq*)] to erase (with an eraser).

setip II (*D*) convulsion, fit.

setir (*D*) driving/steering wheel (of car). *memegang* to drive, steer. – *kanan/kiri* right-/left-hand drive. – *kemudi* tiller. – *mobil* steering wheel of a car. – *stang* steering column.
 menyetir [and nyetir (*coq*)] 1 to drive, steer. 2 (*coq*) to have control over, run (s.o.'s life).
 menyetirkan 1 to drive (a vehicle) for s.o. else. 2 to drive (s.o.).
 penyetir driver, chauffeur.

setirman (*D naut*) steersman, mate (on ship); → JURUMUDI.

setiwal and setiwel (*D*) puttees, leggings.

sétjén → SÉKRETARIAT *jénderal*.

sétnég → SÉKRETARIAT *negara*.

setok (*D*) → STOK. menyetok to lay in a fresh supply of.

setoka *ikan pari* – a small sting-tailed ray, *Trygon spp.*

setoker (*D*) stoker, fireman (on steam-engine).

setokin (*E*) stocking.

setolop (*D*) 1 bell- ar. 2 *lampu* – k.o. hanging lamp.

setom → SETUM.

setomo → (*si*) JAGUR.

seton (*Jv*) water vessel; → GOMBANG I, GUCI.

setop I (*D ob*) fruit preserved in syrup.

setop II (*D coq*) to stop; stop! hold on!; → STOP.
 menyetop to stop, discontinue, cease.
 menyetopi (*pl obj*) to stop s.t. *Meréka secara bergiliran ~ bus-bus, truk-truk yang léwat.* They kept stopping passing buses and trucks.
 kesetop (*coq*) stopped, held up.
 setopan stopping place, (bus, etc.) stop, wayside station. *lampu* ~ and ~ *abang-ijo* (*coq*) traffic light(s). ~ *bis* bus stop.
 setop-setopan all k.o. stoppages.
 penyetop stopper; → STOPKERAN, STOPKONTAK, STOPLÉS.
 penyetopan 1 (act of) stopping, shutdown. 2 embargo.

setopelés → STOPLÉS.

setor (*D*) 1 deposit (money); deposited. 2 (*joc sl*) to move one's bowels.
 menyetor [and nyetor (*coq*)] to deposit (money), pay in, remit. *Uang itu harus disetor pada bank (dalam rékening).* The money must be paid into a bank (into an account). *disetor penuh* paid up fully/in full (of stock). *akan disetor dengan uang tunai* shall be paid up in cash. ~ (*uang*) to turn in one's receipts (to owner) (of cab drivers). ~ *muka sendiri* to report in person. *Anak-anak muda itu ~ muka sendiri kepada polisi.* The young kids reported in person to the police.
 menyetorkan 1 to deposit (money), make payment, remit (funds). 2 to deliver (rice, etc.) (at a fixed price). 3 to pay up (capital in a company).
 setoran 1 payment, deposit, contribution (of money), remittance. ~ *awal* initial deposit. ~ *jaminan* margin deposit. ~ *pajak* tax return. ~ *panjar* (*fin*) margin. ~ *penjinak* payola. 2 (rice, etc.) delivery. 3 rental fee.
 penyetor 1 depositor, person who makes a payment. 2 deliverer.
 penyetoran 1 storing. 2 depositing.

setori (*E*) 1 story, tale, account, narrative; → CERITA. – *yang menyedihkan* a sad story. 2 (*J coq*) quarrel, bickering; → PERCÉKCOKAN. *Dia mencari – dengan kelompok lainnya.* She looked for trouble with other groups. 3 gossip, rumor; → (DE)SAS-(DE)SUS.

setoromking → STOR(E)MKING.

setoter (*D*) k.o. card game.

sétra (*Skr Bal*) temporary burial place before cremation and burial.
 menyétrakan to isolate.

Sétra-Gand(h)amayu (*Skr*) legendary forest where the goddess Durga dwells with hosts of demons.

setrap (*D*) punishment, arrest, custody.
 menyetrap to punish, lock/shut up, confine.
 setrapan 1 punishment, sentence. 2 *orang* – (*ob*) prisoner, captive.
 penyetrapan punishment, conviction.

setrat (*D*) street.

setrén (*Jv*) foreland, forswore.

sétréng → STRÉNG.

setrik → SETERIK.

setrika (*D*) (flat)iron. – *arang* iron which is heated with the use of charcoal. – *buini* (*coq*) steam roller (for roads). – *listrik* electric iron.
 bersetrika to be ironed. *jas* ~ an ironed coat.
 menyetrika [and nyetrika (*coq*)] 1 to iron s.t. ~ *celana* to iron pants. 2 to ruin, flatten, shatter, smash.
 menyetrikakan 1 to iron for s.o. 2 to have s.t. ironed.
 tersetrika ironed. *celana hitam yang tak* ~ unironed black pants.
 setrikaan 1 (*J*) (flat)iron. 2 clothes, etc. which are (to be) ironed/pressed.

setrimin (*D*) gauze.

setrip I (*D*) 1 stripe; → JALUR I, SÉRAN. 2 line; → GARIS. 3 bar, slash. – *T* slant bar (in typography). 4 straight (hit in sports).
 bersetrip(-setrip) with/to have stripes; striped.
 menyetrip to mark (a passage in a book), put a stripe on.

setrip II (*J*) crazy, cracked.

setrop → SETRUP.

setru → SETERU.

setruk (*D*) strip, slip (of paper), voucher.

setrum (*D*) **1** electric current. *mencuri* – to tap electricity (clandestinely, without paying). **2** spiritual influence.

menyetrum [and **nyetrum** (*coq*)] **1** to electrify, charge, recharge, put (wires) in a circuit. **2** to induce. **3** to exercise spiritual influence on.

tersetrum [and **kestrum** (*coq*)] got an electric shock. *Empat pekerja téwas* ~. Four workers were killed by an electric shock.

penyetruman 1 charging (of a battery). **2** induction.

setrup (*D*) lemonade, sweet syrup of sugar and fruit juice; → SETROP. *és* – ditto with ice.

sétti (*ob*) merchant, moneylender.

setu I (*Jv*) favorable influence, blessing (of the gods); → RESTU.
menyetui to bless s.o., grant a favor to.

setu II (*Skr*) an aquatic plant with edible fruit, k.o. sea grass, *Enhalus acoroides*.

setua (*Skr*) wild animals, fauna; → (MARGA)SATWA.

setubuh sexual intercourse; → TUBUH.

setudén → STUDÉN.

setudio → STUDIO.

setuhuk *ikan* – various species of marlin and swordfish.

setui k.o. plant, *Derris uliginosa/trifoliata*.

setuju to agree, find acceptable, of one mind, at one, in agreement, in harmony. –*!* agreed! – *bahwa* to agree that. – *dengan syarat* agreed on condition, qualified opinion. – *untuk tidak* – agreed to disagree. *tidak* – disagree. **ketidak-setujuan** disagreement. *Dialah yang paling vokal menyatakan ~nya terhadap sistém cétak jarak jauh.* He was the most vocal in stating his disagreement with the long-distance printing system.

bersetuju to agree, to be in agreement/harmony, be reconciled. *tidak ~ tentang harganya* to disagree about the price.

bersetujuan ~ *dengan* to agree with, be in accordance/harmony with.

menyetujui to agree to (a resolution); to agree with (the last speaker).

mempersetujukan to bring into line (with).

penyetujuan approval.

persetujuan 1 approval. **2** agreement, concurrence. ~ *boreh* suretyship. ~ *Buruh Koléktif* Collective Labor Agreement. ~ *dengan persyaratan* conditional approval. ~ *Lintas Tapal Batas* Border Crossing Agreement. ~ *perdamaian* compromise, (out-of-court) settlement. ~ *prinsip* approval in principle. ~ *segi-tiga* tripartite agreement. *atas ~ kedua belah pihak* by joint consent. **sepersetujuan** with the consent/approval of.

setukin → SETOKIN.

setum (*D*) steam. *naik* – a) to get/put up steam, raise steam. b) to fly into a rage, lose one's temper.
menyetum to (clean by) steam.
penyetuman dry-cleaning with steam.

setumpu bersetumpu → TUMPU.

setung → RESTUNG.

setungging bersetungging to move with the rear end higher than the front; → TUNGGING I.

setup (*D*) **1** stewed (of fruit, etc.). **2** to stew (fruit, etc.).
menyetup to stew.
setupan fruit stew.

seturi I → SETORI.

seturi II → KESTURI I.

seturu (*J*) conspiracy, (own) clique. – *keluarga saja* within the family.

setyakawan → SETIAKAWAN.

seudati (*Ach*) an Achehnese dance.

séwa (*Skr*) **1** hire, rent, lease. – *dan kemudian beli tunai* lease with option to buy. **2** rented, rental. *uang* – rent, rental fee. – *beli* leasing, hire-purchase system. **menyéwa beli** to hire purchase. **menyéwa-belikan** to hire purchase out. **penyéwa beli** hire purchaser. – *guna (usaha)* leasing. **menyéwagunakan** to lease. – *kontrak* lease. **menyéwa-kontrakkan** to lease. – *modal* capital leasing. – *pakai* rent for use. – *rumah* house rent. – *tanah* land revenue.

menyéwa [and **nyéwa** (*coq*)] **1** to rent, lease, hire. ~ *mobil* to rent a car. ~ *sisip/ulang* to sublet. **2** to engage, employ. *seorang détéktip partikelir yang diséwa itu* a hired private detective.

séwa-menyéwa to let and sublet.

menyéwakan and **memperséwakan** [and **nyéwain** (*J coq*)] to rent, allow to be used in return for rent, lease. *apa yang diséwakan* (in notarial instruments) the rented property. ~ *kembali/ lagi* to sublet.

terséwa rented, leased.

séwaan rented, leased, hired. *sekolompok préman* ~ a bunch of hired hoodlums.

penyéwa 1 hirer; (of house) tenant, lessee. **2** charge (for admission), rental payment. ~ *awal* anchor tenant.

perséwaan rental, lease. ~ *ulang* subletting. ~ *vidéo* video rental.

penyéwaan renting, rental. ~ *ulang* subletting.

séwah I a curved knife.

séwah II *burung* – *tekukur* k.o. hawk-cuckoo, *Cuculus vagans*.

sewajarnya → WAJAR I.

séwaka (*Skr*) homage, tribute; service.
berséwaka to pay one's respects to (s.o.), wait upon.

séwal → SIAL.

sewang and **séwang** → WENANG.

séwar (*ob*) → SÉWAH I.

séwat menyéwat to grab, nab, nip. snatch; → MENYAMBAR, MENJAMBRÉT.

sewenang → WENANG.

sewelir (*D*) maiden-hair fern.

séwot (*J/Jv*) furious, angry.
menyéwoti to be angry at.
séwot-séwotan angry.

séwu (*Jv*) thousand.

séxava *hama* – pest which attacks coconut trees.

seyogya → **seyogyanya** (under YOGYA).

séyot → SÉOK.

sfinks (*D*) sphinx.

SH and **S.H.** (*init*) → SARJANA *Hukum*. – *gombal* shyster.

Shaad → SAD II.

shaan (*A*) open field.

shabara a special unit of the police.

shabas → SABAS.

shabu and **shabu-shabu** (*sl*) methamphetamine hydrochloride, amphetamine in crystal form.
nyabu to get high on such drugs.

shadakah (*A*) → SEDEKAH. **1** alms, charity gift, etc. (for the poor and needy). **2** offering for safety, etc. **3** food, flowers, etc. offered to the spirits. – *arwah* feast for the soul of the dead. – *bumi* offering after the general rice harvest as an expression of thanks (to *Déwi Sri*), village celebration held annually to honor the guardian spirits of the village; → BERSIH *désa*. – *kubur* a) *kenduri* after interment of s.o. b) offering presented to the dead (in the grave).

Shaf (*A*) *ash*– "Array"; name of the 61st chapter of the Koran.

shafalat → SYAFALAT.

Shaffat (*A*) *ash*– "Ranks"; name of the 37th chapter of the Koran.

shagar → SAKAR I.

shah → SYAH I.

shahada → SYAHADA, SYAHDA, SYAHDU.

shahadan → SYAHDAN.

shahadat → SYAHADAT.

shahbandar → SYAHBANDAR.

shahda → SYABDA.

shahdan → SYAHDAN.

shahdu → SHABDA, SYAHADA.

shahih → SAHIH.

shaikh → SYAIKH, SYÉKH.

shaitan → SÉTAN.

shak → SYAK I.

shakar → SAKAR III, SYAKAR.

shakduf → SYAKDUF.

shal → SYAL.

shalat (*A*) → SALAT I, SHOLAT. – *ied* prayer meeting held at *Hari Raya Idul Fitri* and (Hari Raya) Idul Adha; → ID. – *Istisqa* prayer for rain. – *Sunah* an extra prayer other than the five obligatory prayers.

shalér → SYAIR I.

shalawat (*A*) → SALAT I, SALAWAT. – *Badhar* → SALAWAT *Badar*. – *Badriyah* prayer to honor the Prophet.

shalir → SYAIR I.

Sham → SYAM I.

shamali → SYAMALI.

shamas → SAMAS, SYAMAS.

shamshir → SAMSIR.

shamsi → SYAMSI.

shamsiah → SYAMSIA.

shamsir → SAMSIR.

shapalat → SYAFAAT, SYAPAAT.

sharat → SYARAT.

sharab → SYARAB.

sharaf → SARAF II, SYARAF.

sharah → SYARAH I, II, III.

sharak → SYARAK, SYARAT, SYARIAT.

sharbat → SYARBAT, SERBAT.

sharékat → SYARÉKAT, SERIKAT, SYARIKAT.

shari'at → SYARIAH.

sharif → SYARIF.

sharifah → SYARIFAH.

sharik → SYARIK.

sharikat → SYARIKAT.

shaulam → SYAULAM.

shaum (A) fasting; → PUASA.

Shawal → SYAWAL.

shé (C) the first of three (Chinese) names, surname, clan name.

shéh and shékh → SYÉKH.

shg. (abbr) [sehingga] until.

shi (during the Japanese occupation) municipality; → KOTAMADYA.

Shia (A) Shia. Muslim – Shiite Muslim.

shidokan (during the Japanese occupation) leader, guide.

shin (A) name of the 13th letter of the Arabic alphabet.

shio (C) Chinese animal-name year, k.o. sign of the zodiac.
  bershio to be born in the year of the ... Ia percaya bahwa ~ kuda ditakdirkan bekerja keras. He believes that to be born in the year of the horse means that you will work hard.

shira(a)th (A) way, path, road.

shiréi (during the Japanese occupation) instruction, order, notice.

shirik → SYIRIK, SYIRK.

shiyar → SYIAR.

shodancho (during the Japanese occupation, in the PETA hierarchy) section commander.

shodaqoh → SHADAKAH.

shok → SYOK I, III.

sholat → SHALAT. – Jumat the Friday prayer.

sholatullail (A) late night prayer.

sholawat → SALAWAT.

Shonanto the Jp name given to Singapore during WWII.

shopping (E) shopping; → (BER)BELANJA, PERBELANJAAN.

SHP [Sampul-Hari-Pertama] First Day Cover.

SHU [sisa hasil usaha] surplus (of a cooperative).

Shuarna Bhumi an old Sanskrit name for Sumatra; → SUWARNAD-WIPA.

shubabat → SYUB(U)HAT.

shufalat → SYAFAAT, SYUFAAT.

shuhada → SYUHADA.

shuk → SYUK, SYOK I, II.

shukur → SYUKUR.

shulbi (A) testicles.

shur → SYUR I, II.

shurga → SURGA, SYURGA.

Shusangikat (during the Japanese occupation) Provincial Advisory Assembly.

si I k.o. definite article used: 1 before a proper name of a social equal to indicate a certain familiarity: – Amin Amin. – anu and – polan What's-his-/her-name. 2 to indicate the agent of a certain activity. – pengirim the sender (of a letter, parcel). – penipu the deceiver, impostor. – tersangka the suspect. – tertuduh the accused. 3 in front of nouns as a personification, call, mockery, darling/pet, etc. – ular besi itu terus saja melaju. The train continued to shoot forward. – palang kini bisa membuka-tutup sendiri. The railroad crossing can now open and close automatically. – bungsu the youngest one. – doyok the personification of

a village person living in Jakarta. – geulis (S) the beautiful (woman or girl). – hitam a) blacky (a black dog). b) asphalt. c) coal. – jelita code word for heroin and morphine. – kancil the clever/smart one; → TANCIL. – mamat the penis. 4 in front of adjectives as an appellation, in mockery, endearment, etc. – kecil the little one, the baby. – manis a) the sweetie. b) sugar. – sulung the oldest one. – tangan jail the bad guy.

si II (or se) is used with various names of plants and animals, usu as a prefix. – dingin life-plant, Bryophyllum calycinum, used in magic and medicine. – tawas a name for several plants thought to reduce fever. – gasir earth cricket. – kedidi sandpiper, plover.

si III seventh note in the musical scale.

si IV (C J) four. – ban forty thousand. – cap forty. – céng four thousand. – pék four hundred. – tiau four million.

si V → SIH.

si VI (in acronyms) → INSPÉKSI.

SI VII → SIDANG istiméwa.

sia I ikan – a small river cyprinid, Mystacoleucus marginatus.

sia II (C) interlocking food baskets; → RANTANG I.

sia III → SIA-SIA.

siaga I (Jv) 1 ready, alert, prepared, in readiness; → SIAP I. – Gatra Praja (motto of Golkar) Ready to Build Up the State. – penuh full alert. – satu first alert. – tempur combat ready. 2 standby. pembeli – standby buyer. 3 (euph) erect (of the penis).
  bersiaga to be ready/prepared, hold o.s. in readiness, stand by (to assist), be on the alert.
  menyiagakan to make/get ready, put in a state of alert. Marcos ~ kesiap-siagaan penuh Angkatan Perang Filipina menjelang peringatan setahun terbunuhnya pemimpin oposisi Benigno Aquino. Marcos put the Philippine Combat Forces in a state of alert prior to the anniversary of the killing of the opposition leader Benigno Aquino.
  kesiagaan readiness, alertness, preparedness.
  penyiagaan putting on the alert/standby.

siaga II member of the Pramuka Boy Scout Movement between 7 and 10 years old, cub.

siah – layah (J) to waver (like a drunken man or toddler).
  bersiah to give way, yield, move to one side.
  menyiah(kan) 1 to brush/push aside (one's hair/the opening of a curtain), avert (evil), winnow with a change of movement. 2 to eliminate, leave/rule out.
  tersiah brushed aside; eliminated.

siahwéé (C) society; → MASYARAKAT.

siak I (A) (a Muslim) caretaker of mosque (who lives on alms).

siak II (J) burung – owl; → SERAK II.

siak III rumput siak-siak a plant/herb, Dianella ensifolia, the root of which is used as a deworming medicine. ~ jantan k.o. weed, Mapanis humilis.

siakap ikan – giant sea-perch, Lates calcarifer; → KAKAP I.

sial 1 bad luck, unlucky, unfortunate. Hari ini ia – benar. He really has been unlucky today. gadis – a girl whom nobody wants to marry. Maryoto Hadisupono ketiban –. Maryoto Hadisupono was struck by bad luck. membawa – (kepada) to bring bad luck (to). membuang – to avert a calamity/disaster (such as by selling goods at a very low price in order to avert bad luck). 2 to be down on one's luck, have a run of bad luck. anak – a) an unlucky child. b) a child bringing bad luck. 3 unlucky, bringing bad luck. Keris yang dianggap – itu sudah dijualnya. He has sold the kris thought to bring bad luck. hari – an unlucky day. 4 cursed, damned. – kamu! to hell with you! damn you! Wah, – ini! Tough luck! – dangkalan extremely unlucky.
  menyialkan to bring bad luck.
  tersial the unluckiest.

sialan 1 an unlucky person, bird of ill omen. 2 ominous, damned. 3 damn it. ~, uang cuma sedikit dicuri orang. Damn it, the little bit of money I had on me was stolen. ~ dangkalan (J) damn it!

kesialan bad luck. Ia murung ditimpa ~. He was depressed, struck by bad luck.

sialang wild bees' nest. pokok – trees where wild bees like to nest. – bujang bees' nest that has not produced any wax yet.
  bersialang 1 to swarm (of wild bees). 2 (M) to gather honey from wild bees' nests.

menyialang to gather honey (in general).

penyialang honey gatherer.

sialit a plant providing medicine against gonorrhea, *Scleria sumatrensis/lithosperma.*

Siam I Siam(ese).

siam II (*A*) fast; → PUASA, SAUM.

siam III *burung* – k.o. bird, black-headed bulbul, *Pycnonotus atriceps.*

siamang I the long-armed black (tailless) gibbon, *Symphalangus continentis, Hylobates syndactylus. bagai – kurang kayu* sad because lacking one's daily necessities. *dirintang – berbual* wasting time watching s.t. useless. *– kerdil* the dwarf gibbon, *Hylobates klossii,* of the Mentawai Archipelago in West Sumatra.

siamang II wolfram, tungsten.

siamséng (*C*) gangster.

sian I (*coq*) like that.

sian II (*D*) cyan.

sianang a freshwater fish species.

siang I 1 (*– hari*) day, i.e., the period of light (of a 24-hour day) between sunrise and sunset. *buta* – day blindness, i.e., a defect in the eye in which the vision is reduced in the daylight or in bright light. **2** daytime, day; late morning, when the sun is practically at the zenith (from about 11 a.m. to 2 p.m.). *jam dua belas* – 12 noon. *Senin* – at noon on Monday. **3** early (in the afternoon), late (in the morning). *– menjadi angan-angan, malam menjadi buah mimpi* to live in a dream world, i.e., the world as seen by one full of illusions about life. *Tak – tak malam tamu-tamu berdatangan.* Guests were arriving all day long. *Hari pun –lah.* Day is breaking. *Hari sudah –.* It's daytime. *lebih* – earlier. *– tadi* earlier today/this morning. *makan* – lunch. *tidur –* to take a(n afternoon) nap/siesta. *– berpanas, malam berembun/berselimut embun, – bertudung awan* to be as poor as a church mouse. *ada – ada malam, ada sial ada mujur* after rain comes sunshine. *seperti/berbéda sebagai – dan malam* to be as different as day from night, differ as night from day. *kering di – (hari) bolong* in broad daylight. *– malam* day and night, around the clock. *Ia bekerja – malam.* He worked around the clock. *Pencurian itu terjadi di – bolong.* The theft occurred in broad daylight.

siangnya 1 in the afternoon (of that day). **2** later that day.

siang-siang early, before the expected time, in good time, at an early hour. *Datanglah ~ kalau mau mendapat tempat duduk yang baik.* Come early if you want to have a good seat. *Banyak orang yang ~ sudah mengungsi ke pedalaman.* Many people evacuated to the interior at an early hour.

sesiang a whole day. *~ suntuk* all day long. **sesiangan** all day long.

siangan (*coq*) later in the day. *Anda bisa datang agak ~.* You can come a bit later in the day.

kesiangan 1 to wake up after daylight, oversleep. **2** late (in the afternoon).

siang II cleaned, weeded (of a yard/garden), cleaned (of fish, etc.).

bersiang to clean, weed.

menyiang and **mempersiang** to trim dead branches off a tree; to clean, bone/gut (a fish); to pluck (a chicken/bird); to weed, remove the weeds from (a garden/lawn, etc.); to remove the skin from (a snake).

menyiangi to weed (a yard/garden).

mempesiang(i) 1 *~ diri* to dispose/get rid of, part with. **2** to weed (out). **3** to deprive (s.o. of).

penyiang weeder.

penyiangan weeding.

sianggit billy-goat weed, *Ageratum conyzoides.*

sianida (*E*) cyanide.

sianosis (*E*) cyanosis.

siantan *pohon* – k.o. tree, *Ixora concinna.*

sianu → *si ANU.*

siap I 1 ready, prepared, all set; → SEDIA. *makanan sudah* – the food is ready. *tetap* – stand by. **2** finished, completed. *Rumahya yang baru belum lagi –.* His new house is still not finished. **3** (*– sedia*) ready, fully prepared, equipped to act immediately. *ABRI – sedia menghadapi segala kemungkinan.* The Armed Forces of the Republic of Indonesia are fully prepared to face all possibilities. **4** (*mil*) (in commands) attention. *Maju ... jalan!* Attention!

Forward ... march! *jaman/bersiap/siap-siapan* the turbulent time immediately after the Japanese capitulation, i.e., the early days of the 1945 revolution for independence. **5** to be on one's guard. *Kedengaran bunyi kentungan dan teriak "–!"* The sound of beating on sounding-blocks and shouting of "be on your guard" were heard. **6** (in response to a command) sir. *"Kau punya rébewés?" –, tidak* (question asked by an army officer to a private and his answer). "Do you have a driver's license?" "Sir, no sir." *tidak* – unprepared. **ketidak-siapan** unpreparedness, unreadiness. *– bangun* ready to build. *– cétak* ready to print. **menyiap-cétak(kan)** to make s.t. ready for printing. *– dihuni* ready for occupancy. *rumah susun Kebon Kacang – dihuni.* The high-rises at Kebon Kacang are ready for occupancy. *– dimakan* ready to eat. *– diserahkan* ready for delivery. *– ditanam* ready to plant. **bersiap-lengkap** on the alert. *– édar* ready to distribute. *– muat* ready to load. *– pakai/untuk dipakai* a) ready to use/wear. *proyék – pakai* turnkey project. b) ready to shoot (a firearm). c) completely built up (of imported cars). *– potong* ready for slaughter (of cattle). *– saji* ready to serve. *– santap* ready to eat. *– sedia* a) fully prepared. b) standby, alert. **bersiap-sedia** to make preparations. **kesiap-sediaan** preparedness, on the alert. *– siaga* prepared and completely alert. **mempersiap-siagakan** to prepare and make s.t. completely alert. **kesiap-siagaan** preparedness and complete alertness. *– tanam* ready to plant. *– tempur* combat-ready. *– untuk dikapalkan* ready for shipment.

siap-siap to make preparations, get ready. *~ akan mati* to have a foot in the grave.

bersiap and **bersiap-siap** to be prepared/ready, get (o.s.) ready, stand at the ready, be on one's guard, be on the alert/watch.

menyiapi to provide/supply/furnish with, equip.

menyiapkan and **mempersiapkan** [and **nyiapin** (*J coq*)] **1** to get s.t. ready, prepare. *Suamiku sudah pulang lebih dulu untuk mempersiapkan segala keperluan dalam menyambut kembalinya Adinda ke tanah air.* My husband returned home earlier to get everything ready for welcoming Adinda back home. **2** to finish, complete. *diberi waktu seminggu untuk ~ laporan* one week's time was given to complete the report. **3** to make arrangements/preparations. *Ia ~ diri untuk melompat.* He made preparations to jump. **4** to establish, set up. *~ panitia untuk menyambut kedatangan Présidén* to set up a committee to welcome the President. **5** to make ready. *Apabila ada tanda bahaya segenap penduduk harus segera di(per)siapkan.* When there's a danger signal all the residents have to get ready immediately.

tersiap the most prepared.

siapan prearranged, preplanned.

siap-siapan (only) partly ready.

kesiapan preparedness, readiness, alertness. *~ di udara* air alert. *~ tempur* combat readiness.

penyiap preparer, s.o. who prepares.

penyiapan preparing, making ready.

persiapan preparations, arrangements. *pelajaran ~* lesson preparation.

siap II (*ob*) → KESIAP.

Siap III [Sisa Anggaran Pembangunan] Development Budgetary Surplus.

siapa who, whom, whose. *Ini rumah –?* Whose house is this? *Ada orang datang, saya tidak tahu –.* Somebody's coming, I don't know who. *– namanya?* What's his name? *– lagi?* (And) who else? *– orangnya yang tidak jéngkél?* Who wouldn't be annoyed? *– ngira/nyana ...?* Who would have thought/expected ...? *Ini –?* (over the telephone) Whom am I speaking with? *Ayo – lagi?* Come on, who's next (to buy s.t.)? *– itu?* a) Who is that? b) Who goes there? (Question posed by a watchman when addressing s.o.). c) (*– gerangan itu?*) Who could it be? *– gerangan menélepon malam-malam begini?* Who on earth could be calling this late at night? *– yang gatal, dialah yang menggaruk* as you sow, so will you reap. *– melejang, – patah (– melalah); – menyuruk, – bungkuk* more haste, less speed. *– pun/saja* a) who exactly, name the things, people, etc. *– saja yang datang?* Exactly who came? b) anyone, no matter whom. *– saja yang mengambil* no matter who took it. *– lu – gua* (*coq*) every man for himself.

siapa-siapa and **sesiapa** whoever, no matter who. *Sesiapa yang* *didapati bersalah akan dihukum.* Whoever is found guilty will be punished. *"– yang ada di rumah waktu itu?" "Tidak ada siapa-siapa."* Who was at home at that time?" "Nobody." *"Siapa-siapa yang tidak membawa KTP akan ditahan.* Anyone who doesn't have a Resident's Card with him will be detained.

Siapda [Sisa Anggaran Pembangunan Daérah] Provincial Development Budgetary Surplus.

siapuuuh 1 interjection of approval in *kroncong* songs. **2** would you ever! fancy that! (used as an exclamation of mild surprise).

siar I – *luas* dissemination. **menyiar-luaskan** to disseminate. – *pancar* broadcast. **menyiar-pancarkan** to broadcast.

menyiarkan [and **nyiarin** (*J coq*)] **1** to announce, make known, broadcast, show (on TV, etc.). *Ia minta agar soal ini jangan disiarkan.* He asked that the matter not be broadcast. *sedang disiarkan* on the air. *tidak untuk disiarkan* off the record. *Ia ~ pernikahannya* he announced his wedding. *Sebulan sekali RRI Yogya ~ wayang kulit semalam suntuk.* Once a month RRI broadcasts a shadow play with leather puppets the whole night through. *Setiap malam TV ~ kejahatan-kejahatan ngeri.* Every evening horrible crimes are shown on TV. **2** to spread, propagate. *~ agama Islam di Indonésia* to propagate Islam in Indonesia. **3** to publish. *Semua suratkabar akan ~ hasil pemilu.* Every newspaper will publish the election results. **4** to radiate, send forth. *Matahari mulai ~ cahayanya.* The sun began to send forth its rays.

tersiar broadcast, announced, spread, published, circulated. *ada kabar ~* there's a report abroad.

siaran 1 broadcast, telecast, show, program. **2** announcement, report. *~ cuaca* weather report. *~ gelap* illegal broadcast. *~ hidup* live report. *~ kilat* bulletin. *~ langsung* live broadcast. *~ luar negeri* foreign broadcast. *~ pedésaan* village program. *~ pemerintah* government announcement. *~ pendidikan* educational program. *~ pérs* press release. *~ radio* radio broadcast. *~ télévisi* television broadcast. *~ tunda* delayed broadcast. *~ ulang(an)* rebroadcast.

penyiar 1 spreader, propagator. **2** broadcaster, announcer. **3** transmitter. *~ radio* radio transmitter.

penyiaran 1 spreading, propagation, broadcast. *~ agama* spreading religion.

persiaran 1 announcement, notification. **2** proclamation.

siar II (*A*) **bersiar(-siar)** to stroll, walk around. *Sesudah makan, kami keluar ~ di tepi laut.* After dinner, we went outdoors to take a walk at the seashore.

pesiar 1 pedestrian. **2** tourist, sightseer.

siar III (*M*) – *bakar* arson. *– bakar berpuntung suluh* (*M*) a case can be decided after sufficient evidence and information.

menyiar 1 to set on fire, set fire to, burn. **2** to temper in the fire.

tersiar burnt.

siar IV 1 mortar, plaster, cement. **2** band, joint.

menyiar to joint, plaster.

siar V *daun* – k.o. fern, club moss, *Lycopodium cernuum.*

siarah (*A*) *bintang* – planet.

siasah → SIASAT II.

siasat I (*A*) **1** (close/searching) examination/investigation/inquiry, (investigative) question. *badan* – criminal investigation department, secret service. **2** tactic(s). **3** tact, discretion. **4** method, plan, operating system. **5** politics, strategy. *ahli – politik* politician; → AHLI *politik*. **6** criticism. *– bumi (h)angus* scorched-earth tactics. *– dan tegur* criticism. *– dunia* world policy. *– kura-kura* tactics undertaken according to the situation, improvised tactics. *– mengajar* teaching methods. *– negeri* state affairs. *– pemasaran* marketing strategy. *– perang* war strategy. *– perundingan* the line to be followed in negotiations. *– ulur waktu* a strategy of playing for time.

bersiasat 1 to use a policy/strategy (tactfully/diplomatically). **2** to interrogate, examine, question. **3** to ask. *bukan saya (hendak) salah ~* (*M*) if I may ask ... ? would it be indiscreet/impertinent for me to ask?

menyiasat(i) 1 to investigate, examine, inquire (look) into. *Ia ~ siapa yang salah.* He investigated the guilty ones. **2** to study, analyze, examine carefully. *Pakar-pakar pertanian itu sedang menyiasat untuk mengetahui jenis tumbuhan itu.* The agricul-

turists were analyzing it to find out what species the plant was. **3** to question, interrogate. *Tiap-tiap orang yang dicurigai sudah disiasat oléh seorang pegawai Béa Cukai.* Anybody who was suspicious was interrogated by a Customs official.

menyiasatkan to consider/take into consideration (a policy/plan).

penyiasat investigator.

penyiasatan investigation.

siasat II (*A*) punishment, penalty, chastisement.

menyiasat(kan) to punish, chastise.

sia-sia 1 of no use, useless, wasted, a waste of time, in vain, fruitless, doesn't help. *– juga saya mengeluarkan uang sebanyak itu.* It didn't help that I spent so much money. *Kalau begitu, – saja saya datang kemari ini.* In that case, it was pointless for me to come here. *Sudah minum obat ini tapi – belaka.* I've taken this medicine, but it was entirely fruitless. **2** nonsense, ridiculous. *Pada pendapatnya kepercayaan kita ini – belaka.* In his opinion our confidence is totally ridiculous. **3** unsuccessful, futile. *Harapanku – belaka.* My expectations were entirely futile. **4** not considered fully. *Kritik itu dilancarkan dengan – saja.* The criticism was made without giving it serious consideration.

bersia-sia useless. *anak yang –* a useless child.

menyia-nyiakan [and **nyia-nyiain**] (*J coq*) **1** to waste, squander. *Jangan ~ waktumu membantu orang yang tidak bertimbang rasa.* Don't waste your time helping people who don't show understanding. *~ tenaga, pikiran, dan uang untuk membuat bom waktu itu* to waste one's strength, ideas, and money to make nuclear bombs. **2** to miss out on (an opportunity), let s.t. slip by. *Kau sia-siakan peluang sebaik ini.* You're missing out on an opportunity as good as this. **3** to take no notice of, give the cold shoulder, cold-shoulder. *Gaji seorang ahli rokét atau seorang antariksawan sipil sama dengan penghasilan sopir taksi. Inikah yang menyebabkan para ilmuwan yang menganggap dirinya élite ini merasa disia-siakan?* The salary of a rocketeer or civilian cosmonaut is similar to the income of a cab driver. Is this why scientists who consider themselves the elite have the feeling of being ignored?

tersia-sia useless, wasted, fruitless. *Tak héran jika segala sesuatu di républik pulau itu seakan menunjukkan kepada warganya bahwa uang meréka tidak ~.* It is not surprising that everything in the island republic is as if it is showing their citizens that their money is not wasted.

kesia-siaan futility, frustration, triviality, waste.

penyia-nyiaan wasting (time, etc.).

siat I **menyiat** to slice s.t.; → SAYAT I. *Ibu ~ ubi kayu itu sebelum merebusnya.* Mother sliced the cassava before boiling it.

siat II (*C*) **siat-siat** to pretend; → PURA-PURA.

siau 1 cooled to a bearable temperature (of water/metal, etc.). **2** down (of a fever), back to normal (of temperature).

sibak (*M*) separated (to right and left), parted.

bersibak 1 to be separated/divided into two parts. *Jalan ~ dua.* The road was divided into two. *~ jalan* everyone went his own way. **2** to have a part (in one's hair). *Rambutnya ~.* He parted his hair.

menyibak-nyibak and **menyibak-nyibaki** (*pl obj*) to separate (the hair) (searching for lice).

menyibak(kan) 1 to separate, part. *rambutnya yg disibakkan* his parted hair. **2** to push aside (a curtain/veil). *Sekali-kali ia menyibak rambutnya yang sepanjang bahu.* From time to time he pushed aside his shoulder-length hair. **3** to cleave through (waves). *Kapal motor itu ~ gelombang.* The motorboat cleaved the waves. **4** to unveil, reveal. *~ mistéri* to unveil a mystery.

tersibak 1 separated, parted. **2** revealed, unveiled.

penyibakan unveiling.

sibar I and **sibar-sibar I 1** border or extra piece added (to a jacket, etc.). **2** annex (built on a house).

bersibar with such an extra piece.

sibar II bersibaran (*pl subj*) to splatter around.

sibar-sibar II various species of dragonfly, Chinese/scarlet skimmer, *Crocothemis servilia, Nannophya pygmaea.*

sibasol cibasol, i.e., a sulfa preparation.

sibayak (*Bat*) regional head.

sibérnétika (*D*) cybernetics.

sibi (*BG*) 1 [Sih Biasa] it's common/ordinary. 2 [Sikap Biasa] an ordinary attitude.

si-bi (from English: CB) a two-way radio service licensed by *Dirjén* Telkom to an Indonesian citizen.

sibilan (*D gram*) sibilant.

sibir (*M*) piece, slice.
　sesibir a shred.
　sibiran fragment, slice, section, piece. ~ *tulang* sweetheart, darling. ~ *tulangnya sendiri* his own beloved child.

SIBOR Singapore Interbank Offered Rate.

sibuk I busy, too busy (to do s.t.). *Dia* – *sekali*. He's very busy. *Dia* – *sekali dengan urusan sendiri*. He's very occupied with his personal affairs, He's wrapped up in himself. *tidak* – not busy. *ketidak-sibukan* slack season, period of unemployment. *Pekerjaan itu meréka lakukan di sela-sela ~nya sebagai petani.* They did the work during their slack period as farmers.
　sesibuk as busy as.
　bersibuk ~ *diri* to busy o.s. in.
　menyibuki to occupy, take up (in), keep busy (with). *Hari-hari disibuki dengan berbagai aktivitas.* The days were taken up in various activities.
　menyibukkan [and **nyibukin** (*J coq*)] 1 to occupy/busy o.s. (with). *RRC, Jepang, India juga sudah memiliki fasilitas peluncuran satelit, tetapi meréka bertiga ini masih disibukkan oléh kegiatan meréka sendiri.* The People's Republic of China, Japan, and India are also in possession of satellite launching pads, but the three of them are still busy with their own activities. 2 to be busily engaged in s.t. *Jangan kausibukkan benar perkara itu.* Don't get all wrapped up in that matter. ~ *diri* to occupy/busy o.s. (with), be occupied with (in ...-ing), be engaged in, devote o.s. to.
　mempersibukkan to busy s.o. (with some activity).
　kesibukan stir, bustle, liveliness, activity. *Ia selalu menyempatkan bermain catur dan bridge di tengah ~nya.* He always makes time to play chess and bridge in the midst of his activities. ~ *keseharian* daily activities.

sibuk II (*M*) **menyibuk** to spy on, peep at.
　penyibuk *si* ~ peeping Tom.

sibur ladle (of coconut shell) with handle.
　menyibur to ladle, draw (water).

sibur-sibur → SIBAR-SIBAR I.

sibusuk *pohon* – a tree species (supplies timber, and its roots are used as soap), *Cassia nodosa*.

sice (*D*) a five-piece sitting-room set consisting of a table and four chairs,

sicérék (*M*) k.o. shrub with officinal leaves, *Clausena excavata*.

sich → SIH.

sida I (*Skr ob*) (term of address for a) courtier.

sida II castrated.
　sida-sida eunuchs.
　menyidai to castrate.

sidaguri → SELEGURI.

sidai menyidai to air, dry out (clothes), dry on a clothesline. *tali* – clothesline.
　tersidai hung out to dry.
　penyidai clothesline.

sidak [inspéksi mendadak) spot check, unannounced inspection. *melakukan* – and **bersidak** to (carry out) a spot check.

sidamukti (*Jv*) bridal batik design.

sidang 1 session (of Parliament, etc.), meeting, assembly, sitting. 2 congregation, body (of men/members), board, council, etc. (to indicate a collectivity). 3 to be in session. *Meréka sedang* –. They are in session. *dalam* – *tertutup* in chamber. 4 (*leg*) hearing, court session. – *gabungan* joint session. – *geréja* church meeting, synod. – *hakim* tribunal. – *Istiméwa* [SI] Special Session. – *jemaah* a) [and – *Jum'at*] Friday prayers. b) (*PC*) congregation. – *kabinét* ministerial meeting. – *kilat* marathon trial. – *luar biasa* special session. – *paripurna* plenary session. – *pembaca* readership. – *pemeriksaan* examination hearing. – *pendengar* the listeners (of radio/television broadcasts, etc.). – *pengadilan* tribunal/court session. – *pengarang* editorial board. – *pengurus* board of directors, governing body, executive (board) (of a party). – *perang* war council. – *pléno* plenary session. – *puncak* summit meeting. – *ramai*. a) the public. b) the audience. – *terbuka* open session/court. – *tertutup* closed-door session. – *umum* general session.
　bersidang to convene, be in session.
　menyidang to be in session for s.t., hold a session on a certain subject.
　menyidangkan 1 to try/hear (a case), bring to trial. *Perkara pembunuhan disidangkan hari ini.* The murder case will be brought to trial today. 2 to convene for a meeting.
　penyidangan 1 reunion, gathering, assembly, meeting. 2 trial.
　persidangan 1 sitting, meeting, session, hearing. ~ *luar biasa* an extraordinary meeting. 2 (legal) procedure. 3 summoning to court.

Sidarta one of the names of Buddha.

sidat (*Jv*) (*ikan* –) an eel that lives in Lake Poso, Sulawesi, short-fin eel, *Anguilla spp.*

siddik → SIDIK I.

sidekah → SEDEKAH.

sidekap → DEKAP I.

sidi I (*Skr*) 1 full, complete. *bulan purnama* – full moon. 2 accepted as a full member of the Protestant church, confirmed. – *besar* confirmed. – *kecil* baptized.
　menyidi to confirm, accept as a full member of the church.

sidi II → SAIDI.

sidik I (*A*) *fajar* – daybreak; → *fajar* MENYINGSING.

sidik II – *jari* fingerprint. *ilmu* – *jari* dactyloscopy. – *midik* close investigation, scrutiny. – *Sakti* magic/supernatural investigator, i.e., the designation awarded the sleuth hounds of the Police Canine Brigade. *Unit* – *Sakti* [USS] Unit of Magic Investigators, popularly known as The Hunters. – *selidik* investigation, inquiry. – *suara* voice print.
　menyidik 1 to examine, investigate (*usu* by police), probe; → MENYELIDIK, MEMERIKSA. 2 to track, trace. *Disidik jarinya.* His fingerprints were taken.
　menyidiki (*pl obj*) to examine, investigate, look into.
　tersidik investigated.
　penyidik 1 investigator, investigating officer, researcher. ~ *samaran* agent provocateur. 2 probe, detector. ~ *kebohongan* lie detector.
　penyidikan 1 (police/criminal) investigation, probe. *dalam* ~ under investigation. 2 tracing and search.

sidik III (*A*) true, righteous, just; *opp* KIZIB.

siding 1 a long line of rattan nooses (= *aring*) to catch deer. 2 a sharp angle.
　menyiding at a slant. *tidur* ~ to sleep at an angle.

sidingin → SEDINGIN.

sido (*E coq*) eye shadow.

sidomukti (*Jv*) k.o. batik design.

sidrat al-muntaha and **sidratulmuntaha** (*A*) the Prophet Muhammad's final destination beyond the seventh heaven on his *mi'raj*, and the lote tree, the limit of human reach.

siduga (*M*) **bersiduga** to race, compete with e.o.

siduk (*S*) **menyiduk** to scoop (water).

Siéra Léoné Sierra Leone.

siésta (*D*) siesta.
　bersiésta to have a midday/afternoon nap.

sifar (*A*) zero.

sifat I (*A*) 1 appearance, look. 2 nature, innate character, disposition. –*nya gampang marah*. He's hot-tempered by nature. *kata* – (*gram*) adjective; → ADJÉKTIF. *pembawa* – gene. 3 attribute, characteristic, virtue. 4 (in letters) handling, priority, precedence (urgent, etc.). – *Allah* attributes of God; → SIFATULLAH. – *bawaan* inherited characteristic. – *bergado-gado* heterogeneous. – *dunia* that's life. – *jantan* male characteristics. – *khas* special characteristic. – *manis* kind appearance. – *pelupa* forgetfulness. – *pendiam* quiet disposition. – *perawakan* (*ob*) (human) description. – *tabiat/watak* (qualities of) character. – *tua* senility.
　bersifat to have the quality/character(istic) of, by nature. ~ *gado-gado* heterogeneous. ~ *keilmuan populer* popular science. ~ *khas* characteristic. ~ *maju* progressive, pushing. ~ *membangun* constructive. ~ *menyerang* aggressive, offensive.

~ *menerima* accepting. ~ *merusak* destructive. ~ *mobil* mobile, transportable. ~ *nasional* nationwide. ~ *penakut* cowardly. ~ *penjajagan* explorative, exploratory. ~ *seni* artistic. ~ *subvérsif* subversive in nature. ~ *tetap* permanent, constant. ~ *wajib* nondiscretionary, obligatory.

menyifati 1 to characterize s.t. *Sementara itu Hashimoto ~ peran Amerika tersebut sebagai pengkerdilan Asia.* Meanwhile Hashimoto characterized America's role as stunting Asia. **2** to be characteristic of, characterize. *sejumlah ciri yang ~ kondisi* a number of features which are characteristic of the situation.

menyifatkan 1 to describe. **2** to attach qualities/characteristics to. ~ *diri seperti* to conduct o.s. as.

tersifatkan describable, can be characterized (by). *tak ~ lagi* indescribable.

pensifatan and **penyifatan** description, characterization.

sifat II → SIPAT II.

sifatullah (*A*) attributes of God.

sifilis (*D/E*) syphilis.

sifir → SIFAR.

sifon I (*D*) chiffon.

sifon II (*D*) siphon.

sift (*E*) shift. - *pertama/kedua* the first/second shift.

sigai I 1 crossbeam, indentation, notch (in a pole/tree, used for climbing). **2** peg/rough ladder. *tangga -/senigai* a rough ladder. *kabung sebatang, dua -* "a sugar palm with two ladders," i.e., a woman with two lovers. - *dua segeragai* an affair connected with another affair.

bersigai with notches, notched.

menyigai to climb up (a tree) using these notches. ~ *sampai ke langit* and *tinggi -, besar ditebang* to investigate a case closely.

sigai II k.o. shellfish.

sigak scat! get away! (used to chase away dogs).

sigako (*Jp*) school inspector (during the Japanese occupation).

sigando (*M*) k.o. garlic, leek, *Allium odorum.*

sigap dexterous, skillful, adroit, proficient, energetic, smart, bright. **sesigap** as skillful, etc. as.

bersigap (to be) active, ready, in readiness, prepared.

kesigapan smartness, brightness, energy.

sigar I (*Jv*) split, cloven; folded. *terbelah - menjadi dua* split in two.

menyigar 1 to split, cleave, part. **2** to fold. ~ *rambut* to part the hair.

sigar II (*D*) cigar.

sigaran (*Jv*) - *nyowo* [garwo] spouse.

sigarét (*J*) cigarette, cigarillo; → ROKOK *putih*. - *kelembak kemenyan* [KLM] k.o. cigarette containing *kelembak* and *kemenyan.* - *putih* non-clove cigarette.

sigar-rotan (*Jv*) half-round.

sigasir I mole cricket, *Myrmeleon spp., Gryllotalpa spp.* **2** ant lion.

sigat (*A gram*) form.

sigéms (*E J*) SEA/Southeast Asian Games.

sigenting k.o. very small wasp, *Sceliphron madraspatanum.*

sigera (*ob*) → SEGERA.

sigi I 1 torch made of resin and bamboo. **2** investigation, survey.

menyigi 1 to light with such a torch. ~ *ikan* to fish using a torch light. **2** to go over, review, examine, inspect, investigate, survey. *Peserta Sipenmaru ~ pengumuman di Jakarta.* Participants in the *Sipenmaru* are examining (in the picture) the announcement in Jakarta.

sigian survey.

penyigian investigating, surveying.

sigi II metal band around a kris sheath.

sigi III menyigi to dig, excavate, gouge/hollow out, make a hole.

sigi IV *kayu* - k.o. pine tree, *Pinus mercusii.*

signifikan (*E*) significant.

signifikansi (*E*) significance.

sigung I → SINGGUNG I. **menyigung** to nudge with elbow, jostle, elbow.

sigung II polecat, badger, Javan stink badger, *Mydaus javanensis.*

sih (*J*) **1** (in questions, k.o. indirect question) I wonder ... *Dia kenapa -?* What's the matter with him? *Berapa - ini?* How much is this? How much would this be (if I were interested in buying it)? *Siapa - yang betah di tempat seperti ini?* Just tell me, who would feel at home in a place like this? **2** (after the subject)

as for. *Itu -, salah dirinya sendiri!* It's his own fault! *Saya - tidak percaya apa yang dikatakannya.* I, for one, don't believe what he said. **3** (at the end of a clause) because. *Habis, jauh -.* Well, because it's far. *Kamu yang nakal -!* You're the one who did wrong! **4** *X – X* it may be true that ... (but). *Dapat - dapat, cuma kagak semua!* (It's) true I've gotten s.t., but not all! *Bagus - bagus, tapi mahal!* Yes, it's nice, but it's expensive! *Jelék - jelék tapi saya punya.* She may be ugly but she's mine.

sihak (*A*) lesbianism.

sihir (*A*) sorcery, witchcraft, magic. *ilmu -* black magic. *kena -* bewitched, cast a spell on. *tukang -* sorcerer, magician. - *baz* sorcerer.

menyihir(i) and **menyihirkan** to cast a spell on, use magic on.

tersihir bewitched, with a spell cast on it.

penyihir charmer. - *ular* snake charmer.

siip (*coq*) → SIP I.

siji (*Jv*) one.

sijil (*A*) **1** list, register. **2** (*Mal*) certificate. - *anak buah* crew list.

menyijil to put on the manifest (of a ship).

sijingkat bersijingkat (*M*) to walk on tiptoe; → JINGKAT.

Sijori [Singapura-Johor-Riau] The Singapore-Johor-Riau Growth Triangle; in Malaysia known as *Nusa Tiga.*

sijundai → JUNDAI.

Sik Sikh, an Indian tribe from the state of Bengal.

sika I → SIKAP III.

sika II (*ob*) here.

sikah (*A*) k.o. currency.

sikai k.o. rattan whose leaf can be used for roofing.

sikak (*C*) an iron bar used as a weapon.

sikang (*ikan -*) k.o. fish, *Barilius guttatus.*

sikap I 1 bearing, carriage, posture, attitude. **2** figure, shape, stature, build. **3** standpoint, (point of) view, attitude, position. *membuang -* to pass o.s. off as dashing. - *berterima* a give-and-take attitude. - *berlebih-lebihan* overreacting. - *buatan* a pose. - *gagah-gagahan* bravado. - *hidup* one's attitude toward life, lifestyle. - *imbang* unsure of what to do. - *lunak* lenient. - *méntal* mental outlook. - *menunggu/tunggu dan lihat* a position of wait-and-see. **bersikap menunggu** (*saja*) to take a position of wait-and-see. *Pedagang emas di Jakarta masih ~.* The goldsmiths in Jakarta are still taking a position of wait-and-see. *berdiri dengan - sempurna* to stand at attention. - *yang lurus-lilin* straight as an arrow. - *yang mencla-menclé* constantly changing. **4** ready (to go/be used/for action, etc.). **5** traverse position (of a gun).

bersikap 1 to stand at attention. **2** to act (in a certain way), take a ... attitude, with an attitude of ... - *adil* to be/play fair. ~ *déwasa* to act adult. ~ *jantan* to act like a gentleman. ~ *masa bodoh* to be apathetic/indifferent. ~ *matang* to act like a mature person. ~ *menentang* to be aggressive. ~ *menerima* submissive, takes what comes along. ~ *menjauhkan diri* to hold s.o. aloof. ~ *sopan santun* to behave (properly). ~ *tegas* to get tough, act in a firm way. ~ *tenang* to stay calm. ~ *tuli* to pretend not to hear s.t., ignore.

menyikapi to take a position on/toward, respond to, deal with. *kebersamaan dalam ~ keprihatinan universal kemanusiaan* togetherness in responding to human universals.

penyikapan attitude, position.

sikap II → SIGAP.

sikap III *baju* - a close-fitting jacket.

sikap IV *burung (elang)* - (*malam*) a) crested goshawk, *Accipiter virgatus.* b) peregrine falcon, *Falco peregrinus.* - *madu* honey buzzard, *Pernis ptilorhyncus.*

sikap V (*Jv*) **menyikap 1** to embrace, hug. **2** to carry (a weapon).

sikat I 1 brush (for clothes, etc.). *potongan -* brush cut. *seorang bapak berambut potongan -* a gentleman with a crew cut. **2** bristle (stiff hair). **3** (in Sumatra) comb. **4** harrow, rake. - *arang* carbon brush. - *gigi* toothbrush. - *pakaian* clothes brush. - *pelentik bulu mata* eyelash curler. - *rambut* hairbrush. - *sepatu* shoe brush. - *sikut* to keep nudging with one's elbow.

menyikat [and **nyikat** (*coq*)] **1** to brush (the teeth, clothing, etc.). **2** to comb (the hair). **3** to harrow, rake (a rice paddy). **4** to mow down (with a machine gun, etc.), wipe out. **5** to eat up, devour, swallow. *Bubur sepiring itu disikatnya sendiri.* He himself ate up that plate of porridge. **6** to steal, rob, take away, embezzle (money), misappropriate (funds). *Empat puluh kasét mobil disikat maling.* Forty car cassettes were stolen by thieves. **7** to get (a decoration, etc.), score (a victory). **8** (*vulg*) to have sexual intercourse with. *Tahu-tahu suami saya nyikat adik nénék saya yang lagi mertamu di rumah.* My husband suddenly had sex with my grandmother's younger sister who was visiting us.

tersikat 1 brushed. **2** filched, pilfered. *Seorang dari buruh itu ~ uangnya.* Money was stolen from one of the workers.

penyikat 1 brush, rake. **2** thief.

penyikatan 1 brushing, combing, etc. **2** stealing, robbing, etc.

sikat II bunch (of bananas).

sesikat a bunch (of bananas). *pisang* – a bunch of bananas.

sikat III *pohon* – k.o. shrub, *Alchornea rugosa.*

sikatan various species of flycatcher birds, *Muscicapa/Ficedula spp.* – *belang* little pied flycatcher, *Ficedula sp.* – *bodoh* snowy-browed flycatcher, *Ficedula hyperthyra.* – *burik* gray-spotted/streaked flycatcher, *Muscicapa griseisticta.*

sikedempung k.o. fruit.

sikedidi → KEDIDI.

sikeduduk → SENDUDUK.

sikejut → SEMALU.

sikep I owner of communal land.

sikep II → SIGAP, SIKAP II.

sikep III – *madu* crested/Oriental honey buzzard, *Pernis ptilorhynchus.*

sikeras → KERAS. **bersikeras** to insist on; by all means, at any cost; (to act) firmly.

siketumbak → SIKUDOMBA.

sikik k.o. shrub with hard wood, hop bush, *Dodonaea viscosa.*

sikikih *burung* – a bird species.

sikil (*Jv*) foot.

sikin (*A*) **1** knife. **2** (in Sumatra) dagger.

sikit (*coq*) a bit/little; → DIKIT, SEDIKIT.

siklam (*D*) **1** cyclamen. **2** mauve.

siklamat (*D*) cyclamate.

siklis (*D*) cyclical.

sikloida (*D*) cycloid.

siklon (*D*) cyclone.

siklorana (*D*) cyclorama.

siklotron (*E*) cyclotron.

siklus (*D*) cycle (period of time); → DAUR. – *bisnis/usaha* business cycle. – *haid* menstrual cycle. – *produk* product cycle. – *waktu* time cycle.

sikon [situasi dan kondisi] situation and condition.

sikongkol → SEKONGKOL.

siksa (*Skr*) punishment, torment, torture. *kamar* – torture chamber.

menyiksa [and **nyiksa** (*coq*)] **1** to torture, torment, maltreat. ~ *hati* painful. ~ *tahanan* to torture detainees. **2** to be a torture, torturous, exasperating. *Bagi orang tua atau perempuan hamil, naik bis kota amat ~.* For senior citizens or pregnant women riding a city bus is a torture.

menyiksai (*pl obj*) to torture, torment, maltreat (again and again). *Kegemarannya ~ binatang.* He likes to torture animals.

menyiksakan to torment, torture, maltreat.

tersiksa tortured, tormented, maltreated.

siksaan 1 torture, mistreatment, punishment. **2** tortured. *Ian, yang tetap diborgol, tetap menerima ~.* Ian, who remained handcuffed, was continually tortured.

penyiksa tormentor, torturer.

penyiksaan torture, mistreatment, punishment. ~ *tingkat ke-3* third-degree torture.

siksak (*D*) zigzag.

siku 1 (– *tangan*) elbow. **2** turn (in a road/river). *jalan yang banyak liku dan –nya* a winding road. *p(em)atah* – benevolent, kind, willing. **3** carpenter's square. *sudut* – angle of 90 degrees, right angle. – *air* spirit level. – *bedil* rifle butt; → POPOR. – *jalan* hairpin turn. – *keluang* (*bio*) quincunx. – *kalong* zigzag. – *keluang* a) zigzag. b) zigzag design. *Untuk mengejar haluan ke timur pinisi berlayar – keluang.* To go in an easterly direction the pinisi sailed zigzag. – *seluang* zigzag, chevron.

siku-siku [and **sesiku** (*Mal*)] **1** right angle. **2** rifle butt. **3** ribs of a

boat. **4** L-shaped instrument for drawing or testing a right angle, carpenter's square. *tidak* ~ not straightforward. *makan* ~ to have a good character. *tidak makan* ~ that cannot be allowed.

bersiku with an elbow/right angle, etc.

bersiku-siku winding, tortuous, sinuous (of a road).

menyiku 1 to elbow, nudge. **2** right-angled, make a right angle.

siku-menyiku and **siku-sikuan** to elbow/nudge e.o.

menyikukan to nudge, elbow.

penyiku 1 blow given with elbow or rifle butt. **2** (*math*) complement(ary). *sudut* ~ complementary angle.

sikudidi a generic name for small sandpipers and plovers; → KEDIDI.

bersikudidi to hop, skip (*usu* because very happy).

sikudomba leviathan, sea monster.

sikukuh → KUKUH. **bersikukuh** to not back away from.

sikut (*Jv*) elbow. *main* –, **sikut-sikut** and **sikutan 1** to nudge with elbow, push aside. **2** to cheat, be dishonest. **3** to grab (a seat, etc.).

menyikut 1 to nudge with elbow, push aside. **2** to cheat, deceive.

sikut-menyikut to elbow e.o.

sikut-sikutan 1 to nudge with elbow. **2** to jostle e.o. **3** shoving match.

sil (*D*) warehouse/dock warrant.

sila I (*Skr*) – (mainly *Mal*) and **silakan(lah)** please, a polite form of request or command. – *masuk* please, come in. – *minum* please, have a drink. *Boléh saya masuk? –!* May I come in? Please do.

menyilakan and **mempersilakan** to invite, ask, request; to say go ahead (and do s.t.). *"Monggo sugeng dahar," katanya menyilakan sambil tersenyum.* "Enjoy your meal," he said, inviting us with a smile. *Ia telah menyilakan kalau AS mengémbargo.* She said go ahead if the US wants to embargo.

tersila 1 please yourself! **2** it's (now) up to you (you must make your choice); → TERSERAH. ~ *kepada anda, mau ikut atau tidak.* It's up to you whether you want to go along or not.

sila II cross-legged.

bersila to sit neatly/decently cross-legged, sit with one leg placed across the other. ~ *panggung* to sit with the knees pulled up.

menyilakan to cross one's legs, place one leg over the other.

sila III (*Skr*) (ethical/ideological/moral) principle, foundation; → PANCASILA. – *pertama dari Pancasila* the first principle of Pancasila.

bersila to have s.t. as a principle.

bersilakan to have s.t. as a principle. *UUD kita yang ~ Ketuhanan Yang Maha Esa* our Constitution, which is based on the principle of the One and Only God.

silabel (*D/E*) syllable.

silabi syllabus; → SILABUS.

silabik (*E*) and **silabis** (*D*) syllabic.

silabus (*D/E*) syllabus.

silaf (*A*) error, mistake; → KHILAF, SILAP.

tersilaf in error, erred, mistaken.

kesilafan error, mistake.

silah I → SILA I. **silahkan** → SILAKAN.

silah II (*A*) arms, weapons.

silah-silah → SILSILAH.

silalatu (*S*) spark.

silam I 1 past, ago, bygone, of a former time. *masa* – the past. *sebulan yang* – last month. **2** ago. *8 tahun* – eight years ago.

kesilaman the past.

silam II 1 overcast, gloomy, dark. **2** setting (of the sun), twilight, dusk.

menyilam to grow dark, obscure.

menyilamkan to obscure, darken, dim.

tersilam overtaken by night; → KEMALAMAN.

kesilaman darkness.

silam III → SELAM I.

silampukau oriole, *Oriolus maculatus;* → KEPUDANG.

silan (*gay sl*) male; → LANANG.

silang I cross. *garis* – small cross (+). *kayu* – cross(beam). *tanda* – a) sign of the cross. b) multiplication sign (x). *teka-teki* – crossword puzzle. – *balik* backcross. – *datar* (railroad) level crossing. – *dalam* inbreeding (of cattle). – *empat* crossroads, intersection. – *garis* linebreeding (of cattle). – *gunting* crisscross shape or figure. – *jalan* level crossing. – *melintang* messy, disorderly. – *pedang* crisscross shape or figure. – *pendapat* difference of opinion, disagreement. *Pengunduran diri ini mémang menimbulkan – pendapat.* This withdrawal has really caused conflicting opinions. – *selimpat* a) complications. *Tak pélak, suka atau tidak suka, menyerahnya Soekarno-Hatta inilah pangkal – selimpat hubungan sipil-militér di républik ini.* No doubt, whether one likes it or not, it was this surrender of Soekarno-Hatta that became the cause of complications in the civilian-military relationship. b) crisscross. – *selisih* a) quarrel, dispute, discord. b) to be at variance (or, at odds). *bersilang-selisih 1* to be at variance/at odds (with). *2* in the opposite direction; (to sail, etc.) to and fro, back and forth. – *sembur* (*petro*) Christmas tree. – *sengkéta* quarrel, dispute, discord. – *siur* a) to cross e.o. (of letters, etc.), (to go) back and forth; crisscrossing; → SIMPANG *siur*. b) covered with a dense network of roads. c) also said of (busily) incoming and outgoing orders, news items (via telephone connections). *bersilang siur* to cross back and forth, crisscross.

bersilang crossed, crisscrossed. *dengan tangan (yang) ~ di dada* with crossed arms over the chest. *tangan ~ pinggang* with arms akimbo. *~ jalan* to cross e.o. (pass without meeting). *~ kaki* to cross one's legs. *~ kata* to exchange harsh words. *~ mata dengan* to look in the eyes fixedly at. *~ pendapat* at odds with e.o.

bersilangan to crisscross, cross/pass e.o.

bersilang-silang *~ kayu dalam tungku, dengan begitu baru api hidup dan nasi masak* (*M*) the truth emerges from various opinions.

menyilang 1 to cut s.o. off. **2** to cross, intersect. *garis X ~ garis Y* line X intersects line Y. **3** to intersperse. **4** to cross (a check).

silang-menyilang to cross, meet and pass.

menyilangi to cut across, cross over.

menyilangkan and **mempersilangkan 1** to cross, put across/over. *menyilangkan kaki* to cross one's legs. *Kaki dipersilangkannya.* He crossed his legs. **2** to cross (animals/plants).

tersilang 1 crossed. **2** confused.

silangan 1 crossbreed, cross between ... and ... **2** crosspiece. **3** crossing (of one's legs).

penyilangan 1 crossing, crossbreeding. **2** crossing (of a check).

persilangan 1 grade/level crossing. *~ tidak dijaga* unguarded grade crossing. *~ yang dijaga* guarded grade crossing. *~ sebidang* grade/level crossing. *~ tidak sebidang* interchange. **2** (*bio*) cross, crossbreeding. **3** conflict, dispute.

silang II → SELANG I.

silap (*A*) **1** delusion, optical illusion; → KHILAF, SULAP I. *bermain –* to conjure, perform conjuring tricks. *tukang – (mata)* juggler, conjurer, illusionist. **2** wrong, mistaken, erroneous, amiss, misconstrued. *– mata pecah kepala* great accidents spring from small causes. *– hati* mad/frantic (due to disappointment in a love affair/losses at gambling, etc.). *– hitung* to make an arithmetical error. *– jalan* to get lost. *– mata* a) to look at s.o. of the opposite sex in an improper way (though one is already married). b) to mistake s.o. or s.t. for s.o. or s.t. else. c) dazzled, temporarily blinded by the glare. d) unconscious. e) imprudent.

bersilap to conjure, perform conjuring tricks. *awan ~* intricate decorative pattern/design.

menyilap to hoodwink, deceive, mislead, cheat s.o.

tersilap done in error, mistaken.

kesilapan 1 delusion. **2** fallacy, mistake, error. **3** deception.

penyilap 1 magician, conjuror. **2** cheat, trickster.

silara dry leaves.

silase (*E*) silage. *Téknologi – ini belum merakyat.* This silage technology is not yet popular.

silat martial art of self-defense, with or without pointed weapon. *cerita –* martial art stories (frequently illustrated). *pencak – a* system of self-defense. *kata/lidah* glib, talking cleverly. *Kampanye pemilu bukanlah aréna untuk mengadu kelihaian – dan débat kusir.* The election campaign isn't an arena for contesting the shrewdness of talking cleverly and senseless debates. *pandai – sharp talker, equivocator.

bersilat to engage in this martial art. *~ kata* to talk cleverly, quibble. *~ lidah* to debate, argue. *pandai ~ lidah* to have a way with words, be persuasive.

menyilat to dodge, ward off an attack or blow using a *silat* movement.

pesilat 1 a master of *silat*. **2** athlete.

persilatan *silat* (*mod*) *dunia ~* the world of *silat*. *~ kata* play upon words, pun.

silaturahim → SILATURAHMI.

silaturahmi (*A*) **1** friendship, good relationship. *mengikat ~* to enter into ties of friendship. *tali –* ties of friendship. **2** friendly get-together.

bersilaturahmi to maintain ties of friendship (with), become friendly (with). *Keluarga kami tidak pernah ~ dengan sanak-saudara.* Our family has never entered into ties of friendship with relatives.

silau dazzled, blinded (by a strong light). *membuat –* to dazzle. *Mérek impor membuat para konsumén ~.* Trademarks of imported goods dazzle consumers.

bersilau (*~ mata*) to be dazzled, temporarily blinded.

menyilau to be(come) glaring.

menyilaukan to dazzle, blind temporarily; blinding, glaring, dazzling.

tersilau become dazzled, blinded temporarily.

silauan glare.

kesilauan 1 dazzle, glare. **2** fascination.

penyilauan dazzling.

silempukau → SILAMPUKAU.

siléngah (*M*) **bersiléngah** to be indifferent; → LÉNGAH.

silés (*Pr*) lesbian.

silét (*E*) **1** (originally) a Gillette razor blade. **2** (now) any razor blade (sometimes used as a weapon in robberies, etc.).

menyilét to slash, slice/slit open. *Tas kulitnya disilét oléh pencopét.* Her leather handbag was slit open by a pickpocket.

menyilét-nyilét to slash up.

penyilétan attack with a razor blade. *~ muka* cutting up a person's face with a razor blade.

silhuét (*D*) silhouette.

silih I e.o., mutual(ly), reciprocal(ly). *– asah* to remind e.o., sharpen e.o.'s ideas. *– asih* to love e.o. *– asuh* to lead e.o., take care of e.o. *– (ber)ganti* a) to alternate, take turns, do s.t. in turn. b) one after the other, endless. *– mata* to wear s.t. just for show, for the sake of appearances. *– rugi* → GANTI *rugi.* *– sambung* continuous. *télepon yang berdering – sambung* a telephone which doesn't stop ringing. *– sambut* to alternate. *– semilih* by turns, in turn, alternately, one ... after another.

bersilih 1 to change (clothes). **2** to metamorphose, change into. *Dukun itu mampu ~ rupa jadi harimau.* That shaman is able to metamorphose his shape into a tiger. **3** to alternate, keep changing. *tahun ~ musim berganti* in the course of time. *– lapik* (*M*) to marry a sibling or relative of one's deceased spouse.

menyilih [and **nyilih** (*coq*)] **1** to change (one's clothes/opinion). **2** to pay restitution for (a financial loss). *~ tangan* to hire s.o. to do one's dirty work. **3** to cast off its skin (of a snake, etc.). **4** to change (into).

silihan replacement, substitution, reparation. *~ peran* role substitution. *~ perang* war reparations; → PAMPASAN *perang*.

persilihan and **penyilihan 1** metamorphosis. **2** alternating, alternation.

silih II *salah silih* → SALAH I.

silih III (*Jv M*) **menyilih** to borrow.

silik (*M*) **menyilik** to peep at, sneak a look at, glimpse.

silika (*E*) silica, silicon dioxide.

silikat (*D*) silicate.

silikon (*D*) silicon.

silikum silicon.

silinder (*D*) cylinder.

bersilinder with cylinders.

silinderkop (*D*) cylinder head.

silindris (*D*) cylindrical.

silindung (*bio*) sheathing stipule.

silir I cool and soothing (of breezes). *– semilir* and **(ber)silir-silir** to blow softly; to flutter (of a flag, etc.). *Anginnya – semilir.* There's a soft breeze blowing lightly.

silir-silir soft (of a breeze).

menyilir to turn windy.
siliran 1 *angin* ~ cool breeze. **2** flutter.
silir II – *bawang* the thin membrane of an onion.
silir III *keméja* – open-necked shirt.
silit (*Jv*) ass. –*!* you asshole!
Siliwangi 1 *Prabu* – the founder of the Pajajaran kingdom. **2** the white tiger, symbol of Pajajaran. **3** name of the army division stationed in West Java.
silo I (*D*) silo
silo II → SILAU.
silogisma and **silogisme** (*D*) syllogism.
silok (*M*) half-closed (of eyes). **2** dazzled, temporarily blinded by glare; → SILAU.
silom k.o. herb, water parsley, *Oenanthe javanica*.
silotip → SÉLOTIP.
silsilah (*A*) **1** genealogical/family tree, pedigree. **2** chronicle.
bersilsilah to have one's pedigree in. *Bonsai* ~ *ke negeri Cina.* The pedigree of the bonsai begins in China.
silu I 1 moved, touched, affected, hurt; → PILU I. **2** nerve-racking, unpleasant to the ears (such as the sound made by a saw, etc.); → NGILU.
menyilukan 1 horrible, ghastly; to set one's teeth on edge. **2** to move, affect, touch (of feelings).
silu II shy, bashful.
bersilu to be shy/bashful.
menyilukan to embarrass.
kesilu-siluan embarrassed.
siluét → SILHUÉT.
siluk I k.o. tree, *Gironniera nervosa/subaequalis.*
siluk II *ikan* – *mérah* Asian arowana, Asian bony tongue, dragon fish, *Sclerophages formosus.*
siluman 1 all k.o. ghosts, invisible (forest) elves. **2** an invisible mysterious (power that can appear suddenly). *golongan* – whisperers. *perusahaan* – a phantom enterprise producing items sold without permit; → *perusahaan* AKTENTAS. *uang* – bribes (payments under the table, invisible to the public). **3** (*ongkos/biaya* –) invisible costs, i.e., bribes, corruption.
silungkang k.o. material from Silungkang in West Sumatra.
silvikultur (*E*) silviculture.
SIM → SURAT *Izin Mengemudi.*
sima I (*Jv*) tiger; → HARIMAU I, MACAN I.
sima II → KESIMA.
simaharajaléla → (MAHA)RAJALÉLA.
simak I (*M*) **menyimak** to listen carefully to what is being said or read aloud by s.o., pay close attention to, monitor. *latihan* ~ a) listening exercise. b) memorization exercise (at school). ~ (*kembali*) to (re)consider, revise. *Gubernur tidak boléh* ~ *kembali keputusan kadi dalam masalah perkawinan.* The governor may not revise the decision of a judge (in Muslim matters) about marriage affairs.
menyimakkan to observe carefully.
tersimak observed.
penyimakan observing carefully, monitoring.
simak II bersimak to gather, get together.
menyimak to gather, collect.
simakan gathering.
simak III (*Jv*) mother.
simak IV (*A*) (– *al-azal*) Spica (the star). – *al-ramih* Arcturus.
simalakama a dilemma; → MALAKAMA.
simalu → MALU II.
simaung (*M*) k.o. tree and its fruit, football fruit, *Pangium edule*; → KEPAYANG.
simbah I bersimbah to be bathed/covered/drenched in. ~ *darah* to bathe in blood. *Di dekat tubuh Yuli* ~ *darah yang sudah mengering itu tergelétak pisau dapur.* Close to Yuli's body, which was bathed in clotted blood, lay a kitchen knife. *Parangnya yang* ~ *darah itu dicucinya di sumur.* He cleaned the knife that was covered in blood at the well. ~ *peluh* to be covered in sweat.
menyimbah 1 to stand in beads, break out. *Peluh* ~ *di dahinya.* The perspiration broke out on his forehead. **2** to splash with water, pour water over s.t. ~ *mobil yang berselisih dengan air banjir* to splash a passing car with flood water.

menyimbahi to splash, sprinkle.
tersimbah sprinkled, splattered, drenched.
simbah II (*M*) **bersimbah** tucked/rolled up. ~ *kain* with tucked-up cloth.
menyimbah(kan) to tuck/roll up, push aside, strip off (an article of dress).
tersimbah tucked/rolled up; to be open (a little bit).
simbah III (*Jv*) grandparents.
simbai 1 smart, making a good impression. **2** polite, discrete.
simbang I (*M*) k.o. children's game like jacks. *main* – to play jacks.
bersimbang to play jacks.
menyimbang to toss s.t. up and catch it.
simbang II *burung* – Christmas Island frigate-bird, *Fregata andrewsi.*
simbang III *musim* – season of uncertain weather between monsoons.
simbar I oak leaf fern, an epiphyte species with medicinal uses, *Drynaria sparsisora.* – *badak* a small tree species, *Tabernaemontana macrocarpa.* – *menjangan* staghorn fern, *Platycerium bifurcatum.*
simbar II – *dada* (*Jv*) hair on the chest.
simbat k.o. snare.
simbiosa, simbose and **simbosis** (*D*) symbiosis.
bersimbiose to be symbiotic.
menyimbiosekan to make symbiotic.
simbiotik (*D/E*) symbiotic.
simbok (*Jv*) mother; → EMBOK.
simbol (*D/E*) symbol.
bersimbol with symbols, symbolic.
bersimbolkan to be symbolic of, symbolize.
menyimbolkan to symbolize.
penyimbolan symbolizing.
simbolik (*E*) and **simbolis** (*D*) symbolic.
simbolisasi (*D*) symbolization.
simbolisme (*D/E*) symbolism.
simbukan a) a climbing plant (with bad-smelling leaves, *usu* used as a remedy against a bloated stomach), Indian ipecac, *Tylophora asthmatica.* b) k.o. shrub, *Saprosma ternatum. daun* – k.o. shrub, *Saprosma arboreum.*
simbul → SIMBOL.
simbur I bersimbur 1 to splash, gush/spurt out (of blood/water/a liquid); → BERPANCAR, MEMANCAR. *Darah* ~ *dari lukanya.* Blood spurted out of his wound. **2** covered, wrapped. *Hari pun* ~ *gelap.* The day was wrapped in darkness.
bersimburan (*pl subj*) to splash around, smash (of waves on the beach).
bersimbur-simburan to splash e.o., pour water with the hands over e.o. *mandi sambil* ~ *air di sungai* to take a bath in the river while pouring water over e.o. *Ombak* ~ *ke tepi.* The waves broke at the shore.
menyimbur to splash/gush/spurt out.
menyimburi to spray/sprinkle (a liquid) on.
menyimburkan to splash (water, etc.). *Di kamar mandi ia* ~ *air.* In the bathroom he got splashed with water.
tersimbur splashed/gushed/spurted out. *Air* ~ *dari tanah.* Water spurted out of the ground.
simburan splashing, gushing, spurting.
kesimburan → TERSIMBUR.
simbur II menyimbur to mount/rise to the head/face (of blood).
tersimbur to mount/rise to the head/face. *Darahnya* ~ *ke mukanya.* Blood rose to his face.
simduk [*sistém informasi kependudukan*] population information system.
Simelungun a subgroup of the Batak ethnic group.
simétri (*D*) symmetry.
simétris (*D*) symmetrical.
bersimétris ~ *dengan* to be symmetrical with.
simfoni (*D*) symphony. *orkés* – symphonic orchestra.
simia (*Pers cla*) necromancy.
simile (*E*) simile.
Simkim [*Sistém Manajemén Informasi Keimigrasian*] Immigration Information Management System.

simpai I 1 hoop, (flexible) band, loop. – *beduk* drum hoop. – *besi* iron band. – *pedoman* gimbals. – *senapan* sling of a rifle. – *tong* barrel hoop. **2** muzzle. **3** (*med*) capsule. – *sendi* joint capsule.
bersimpai 1 with a hoop/band/loop. **2** muzzled.
menyimpai(kan) 1 to hoop, bind, put a band around s.t. **2** to muzzle. ~ *mulut* to gag.
tersimpai 1 hooped, bound. **2** tightly fastened.
simpaian union, league, club, association. ~ *Seni Rupa Indonésia* Indonesian Plastic Arts Association.
simpai II k.o. leaf monkey, *Semnopithecus melalophos*; → CIPAI.
simpak → SÉMPAK.
simpan I storage, reserved. *hutan* – (*cla*) reserved forest. – *pinjam* savings and loan (cooperation).
menyimpan [and **nyimpan** (*coq*)] **1** to keep, store, preserve. *Ia ~ dokumén-dokumén penting itu ke dalam lemari besi.* He stored the important documents in a safe. **2** to save, keep, accumulate (money), lay away. *Ibu bapak patut menggalakkan anak-anak meréka ~ uang di bank.* Parents ought to encourage their children to save money in a bank. ~ *uang di bawah bantal* "to save money under the pillow," i.e., to save money at home (instead of depositing it in a bank). **3** to keep, retain. *Majikan pabrik itu telah menyingkirkan beberapa pekerja yang malas dan ~ meréka yang rajin bekerja.* The boss of that factory has gotten rid of some of the lazy workers and retained those who are hard-working. *Nasihat itu disimpan dalam hati.* The advice was taken to heart. **4** to secrete, put/keep in a secret place, hide s.t. inside somewhere. *Tidak siapa (pun juga) yang mengetahui bahwa ia ada ~ seorang madu.* Nobody knows that he kept a second wife in a secret place. **5** (*euph*) to imprison. *Pencuri itu disimpan di Bukit Duri.* The thief was imprisoned in Bukit Duri. ~ *dendam* to bear a grudge. ~ *di hati* to have feelings of resentment inside one. ~ *rahasia* to keep a secret. **6** (*math*) to carry (in adding).
menyimpankan 1 to have ... kept/saved/deposited, etc. *meminta tolong untuk ~ uangnya di bank itu* to ask for help to have his money deposited in the bank. **2** to save/deposit for s.o.
tersimpan 1 stored, kept, saved, deposited, laid away. *Bajunya ~ rapi di lemari.* His shirts were neatly stored in the wardrobe. **2** secreted. ~ *dalam hati* kept in one's heart. **3** contained in it, inserted, attached.
simpanan 1 place where s.t. is kept, storage place. **2** savings, deposits. *uang ~* savings. *dalam ~* in portfolio. **3** mistress, kept woman. *Sulit mempercayai bahwa suaminya punya ~.* It's hard to believe that her husband has a mistress. *"Kau pasti punya ~. Gendhak!" tuduhnya keji.* "You must have a mistress. A lover!" she accused him cruelly.
penyimpan 1 depositor, keeper. **2** depository. ~ *gas* gas depository/storehouse.
penyimpanan 1 savings (in bank). **2** depositing, storing, custody. *pendapatan ~* custody income. **3** place for storing s.t., storage. ~ *beton bawah tanah* (missile) underground silo. ~ *ikan* fish hold. *tempat ~ peluru* place for storing bullets.
persimpanan warehouse, storehouse.
simpan II (*cla*) **1** brief, short (history). *risalah yang* – a brief treatise; → RINGKAS, SINGKAT. **2** cleared away. *mengambil* – (*cla*) to summarize, sum up, recapitulate, condense, abridge.
bersimpan 1 to shorten, make brief. **2** to arrange/pack up clothes, etc. taken on a trip.
menyimpan(i) to put s.t. in order.
simpanan (*Mal*) reserved, only assigned in special cases. *Polisi ~* police force only called in to assist in special events, such as escorting VIPS, investigating complicated cases, etc.
simpan III bersimpan-simpan to tidy up.
menyimpani (*pl obj*) to neaten up.
menyimpan to arrange, tidy up. *Aminah sedang sibuk ~ pinggan mangkuk.* Aminah was busily engaged in arranging the crockery.
simpang crossing (of a road), branch, diversion. – *belahan* (*M*) family members who have moved to another place. – *dua* crossroads, crossing of two roads. – *empat* intersection of four roads. – *jalan ke* and *jalan* – *ke* side route to. – *pilih* dilemma; → DILÉMA. – *siur* a) swing(ing compass needle). b) dense (network of roads). c) crisscrossing (of telephone wires over a city, etc.). d) winding (of ribbons/aerial roots, etc.). e) conflicting (re-

ports). *segala* – *siur penghidupan* all the complications of life. *banyak* – *siurnya* a) complicated. b) not frank/candid, dishonest. **bersimpang siur 1** to move back and forth, fire bullets randomly. **2** to crisscross, zigzag. **3** to be complicated. *Ceritanya ~ tak keruan.* His story was terribly complicated. **kesimpangsiuran** confusion, complication, mess. **persimpang-siuran 1** crisscrossing. **2** confusion, mix-up. – *sungai* tributary. – *susun* interchange. – *Susun Cawang/ Jakarta* Cawang/Jakarta Interchange. – *tiga* three-way fork in the road.
bersimpang with crossings, forked (of a road). ~ *jalan* to cross (in the mail). ~ *kata* differing in opinion.
bersimpangan to cross e.o., meet and pass e.o. *jalan yang ~* intersecting roads.
menyimpang [and **nyimpang** (*coq*)] **1** to deviate (from), to be in contradistinction (to), violate. ~ *dari peraturan-peraturan* "to violate the regulations," i.e., to be corrupt. ~ *dari jalan besar* to take a detour from the main road. **2** deviant, odd. **3** to evade, sidestep, be evasive. *jawaban yang ~* an evasive answer. **4** to engage in misconduct. **5** to drift (away from the perpendicular).
menyimpangi to deviate from, violate. *tidak boléh ~ ketentuan Pasal 17 UU 4/1999* may not deviate from the provisions of article 17 of Law 4/1999.
menyimpangkan to cause to deviate/turn/swerve, etc.
tersimpang deviant. *perkataan ~* off the subject, non sequitur.
tersimpangkan deviated.
simpangan 1 branching off. ~ *jalan* byway, side route. **2** junction, crossroads. **3** (*math*) deviation. ~ *baku* standard deviation.
penyimpang s.o. who deviates (from).
penyimpangan 1 deviation (from the right path), digression, variance. ~ *dasar* standard deviation. **2** allowance. **3** impropriety, malfeasance, misconduct; violation (of the rules). **4** (*naut*) drift (off course).
persimpangan junction, crossroads, intersection. *industri otomotif di ~ jalan* the automotive industry at a crossroads.
simpansé (*D*) chimpanzee.
simpat (*J*) **kesimpatan** to choke (on s.t.), swallow s.t. the wrong way; → TERMENGKELAN, KESELAK.
simpati (*D*) sympathy.
bersimpati ~ *dengan/kepada* to sympathize with, be in sympathy with.
menyimpatii to have sympathy for.
simpatik (*D*) congenial (surroundings), likeable (fellow), nice (man), congenial.
kesimpatikan niceness.
simpatisan (*D*) sympathizer, supporter.
simpedés [simpanan-pedésaan] rural savings.
simpel (*D/E*) **1** simple (of a sentence/dress, etc.), plain; → SEDERHANA. *makanannya* – his food is plain. **2** limited, restricted, modest; → KECIL. *Modalnya sangat* –. His capital is very limited.
simpen → SIMPAN I.
simping I (*J/Jv*) a mollusk with a flat shell, common windowpen shell, *Placuna placenta*.
simping II (*J*) (*kué* -) a flattened cookie made out of wheat.
simpir 1 spread out its wings (of a peacock). *merak* – outboard gallery in a ship. **2** board (of a table saw).
menyimpirkan ~ *sayap* to spread out one's wings.
simplifikasi (*D*) simplification.
mensimplifikasikan ~ *secara berkelebihan* to oversimplify.
simplistis (*D*) simplistic.
simpoa → SEMPOA.
simponi → SIMFONI.
simposium (*D*) symposium.
men(g)simposiumkan to discuss s.t. at a symposium.
simptom (*D*) symptom.
simptomatik (*E*) and **simptomatis** (*D*) symptomatic.
simpuh I (*M*) *dengan sembah* – respectful, reverent, deferential.
bersimpuh to sit with the knees bent and folded back to one side. *duduk* – to sit with the feet backward (of a woman, on the floor).
tersimpuh (*jatuh ~*) to drop to one's knees (like a horse that has stumbled).
menyimpuhkan to fold (one's legs) back to the side.

simpuh II → SIMPUR.

simpuk menyimpuk 1 to touch s.o. passing by, bump into. 2 to accuse falsely.

    tersimpuk 1 touched, bumped into. 2 accused falsely.

simpul I 1 knot, hitch. 2 crux, node. 3 (police) checkpoint. *– anyam* a knot used to tie a large rope to a small one. *– balik* capstan knot. *– buku sila* small knot used for tying packages. *– bunga geti* knot used to tie string. *– daun* shamrock knot. *– delapan* figure of eight knot. *– erat* sheepshank knot. *– hidup* slipknot. *– ingatan* mnemonic device. *– jangkar* cat's-paw knot. *– mati* fast/reef knot. *– palsu* granny knot. *– pulih* slipknot. *– rawan* flashpoint, critical juncture. *– saraf* ganglion. *– sentak* slipknot that opens with one pull. *– syaraf* ganglion. *– tali* hitch, knot. *– tolong* fireman's knot. *– urat* ganglion.

    bersimpul knotted, with a knot in it.

    menyimpul 1 to knot, tie. *~ dasi* to knot one's tie. 2 to knot together, tie together. *Dia sedang ~ kedua ujung tali itu.* She is tying together the two ends of the rope. 3 to appear (of a smile).

    simpul-menyimpul to tie e.o. up.

    menyimpulkan [and **nyimpulin** (*J coq*)] 1 to knot, tie s.t. with a knot, fasten. *~ tali* to tie a rope. 2 to sum up, summarize, conclude. *Uraian tadi dapat disimpulkan sbb.* The aforementioned explanation can be summarized as follows.

    tersimpul 1 knotted, tied. 2 summarized. *sebagai ~ di bawah ini* as concluded hereunder. *~ dalam hati* in one's heart. *~ mati* tied tight. 3 implied.

    tersimpulkan summarized.

    simpulan 1 knotting, tying. 2 summary, conclusion, result.

    kesimpulan 1 summary, résumé, summing up, inference. 2 conclusion. *memberi ~* to conclude. *menarik ~ dari* to draw a conclusion from. *~ imbasan* inductive inference. *~ pungkasan* final conclusion. *~ rampat* general inference. **berkesimpulan** to conclude, come to the conclusion (that).

    penyimpul 1 tool used for making knots. 2 s.o. or s.t. that summarizes or brings s.t. to a conclusion.

    penyimpulan 1 knotting, tying. 2 drawing a conclusion, concluding.

simpul II → SENYUM. *senyum –* an embarrassed smile. *tersenyum –* to smile out of embarrassment.

    menyimpul (an embarrassed smile) formed. *Senyum ~ di bibir.* A smile was playing about her lips.

    menyimpulkan 1 to sketch (a smile). *~ senyum* to smile. 2 to keep s.t. hidden away inside.

    tersimpul hidden away inside.

simpur several k.o. small trees with hard wood and showy yellow flowers, *Dillenia spp., Wormia spp.,* such as *– air, Dillenia suffruticosa. – (h)utan, Dillenia sp. – paya* k.o. tree, *Dillenia pulchella.*

sim-salabin (*A*) [and **sim-sulap-salabim** (*infr*)] sleight of hand.

simtom → SIMPTOM.

simtomatis → SIMPTOMATIS.

simulasi (*D*) simulation.

    menyimulasi to stimulate.

simulator (*D/E*) simulator.

simultan (*D*) simultaneous. *penerjemah –* simultaneous interpreter.

    bersimultan to be simultaneous.

simuntu (*M*) masked children who take part in a Hassan-Husain procession.

sin (*A*) name of the 12th letter of the Arabic alphabet.

sinaga herpes, *Herpes zoster.*

sinagog(a) and **sinagogé** (*D*) synagogue.

sinambatan (*Jv*) to help e.o.

sinambung and **bersinambung** continuous; → SAMBUNG. *tidak sinambung* (*phys*) a) discrete. b) discontinuous. *ketidaksinambungan* discontinuity.

    menyinambungkan to continue, proceed.

    sinambungan continuity. **bersinambungan** continuous, sustainable. **kesinambungan** continuity. **berkesinambungan** continuous, uninterrupted, without interruption, sustainable. *pertumbuhan ékonomi yang ~* sustainable economic growth. *cerita yang ~* a serial.

sinandung → SENANDUNG.

sinangis k.o. fish.

Sinansari (*M*) Goddess of Rice; → DÉWI *Sri.*

sinar I 1 ray, beam (of light); light. 2 radiation. 3 gleam. *– api* light from a fire. *– bulan* moonlight. *– kosmik* (*E*) and *– kosmis* (*D*) cosmic ray. *– laser* laser beam. *– mata* glance, look. *– matahari* sunshine, sunray(s). *kena – matahari* to be sunburned. *– mengumpul* converging rays. *– menyinar/seminar/suminar* to glitter, glint, gleam. *– pantul* reflected light. *– ultraungu/ultraviolét* ultraviolet ray. *– X X* ray.

    bersinar and **menyinar** to shine, radiate light, beam, gleam. *disinar rontgen* to be X-rayed.

    bersinar-sinar shining, radiating, beaming, gleaming.

    menyinari 1 to illuminate, shine on, brighten up, light up. *Cahaya lampu itu ~ kamar yang gelap itu.* The light of the lamp illuminated the dark room. 2 to enlighten, make aware. *Qur'an telah berhasil ~ hatiku yang sedang gelap.* The Koran succeeded in enlightening my dark heart.

    menyinarkan 1 to illuminate, light up, brighten. 2 to radiate, shine. *~ cahaya* to shine a light (on s.t.).

    sinaran 1 radiation, ray. 2 glow, gleam.

    kesinaran radiance.

    penyinar radiator.

    penyinaran 1 illumination. *térapi ~* photo therapy. 2 radiation. *Dia akan menjalani ~ sinar X.* She will be X-rayed.

sinar II *daun –* k.o. herb, *Lycopodium cernuum.*

sinau sparkle. *– silau* glare. *– seminau* and **bersinau-sinau** shining, beaming, radiating, gleaming, give out brilliant light, shine brightly.

sinawar (*M*) *pohon –* k.o. large areca palm, calappa palm, *Actinorhytis calapparia.*

sincia (*C*) Chinese New Year.

sinda (*cla ob*) → SANDA II.

sindanglawé milky stork, *Mycteria cinerea.*

sindap (*Jv*) dandruff.

sindén (*Jv*) singing (by female singers) to the accompaniment of *gamelan* music.

    menyindén(i) to sing to the accompaniment of *gamelan* music (by a *pesindén*).

    sindénan dancing and singing to the above music.

    pesindén female vocalist with *gamelan* accompaniment.

sinder (*D col*) (plantation) supervisor; → OPSIN(D)ER.

sindik (*J*) **menyindik** to string (fish) together by the gills.

    sindikan bunch of fish strung together.

sindikalisme (*D/E*) syndicalism.

sindikasi (*D*) syndication. *pinjaman –* loan syndication.

    bersindikasi to syndicate.

sindikat (*D*) 1 syndicate. 2 gang (of criminals).

sindir teasing(ly), hint at, say indirectly. *– sampir* (*S*) to let s.o. know about his faults indirectly, *esp* by reprimanding s.o. else in his presence.

    menyindir [and **nyindir** (*coq*)] 1 to make slurring remarks to s.o. about s.t., tease, criticize. *pukul anak sindir menantu* "beat a daughter as a hint to a daughter-in-law," i.e., scold s.o. but that scolding is really aimed at s.o. else. 2 to make hints, be sarcastic.

    sindir-menyindir 1 to exchange banter, make allusions/insinuations at e.o., tease e.o. *Setiap hari kerjanya hanya ~ saja.* All they do is just tease e.o. 2 teasing. *~ dalam mengutarakan cinta adalah kuno.* Teasing in declaring love is old-fashioned.

    menyindirkan to allude to, hint at, quip.

    tersindir mocked, derided, ridiculed, teased.

    sindiran 1 allusion, hint. 2 satire. *gambar ~* caricature, cartoon. *nama ~* nickname, sobriquet.

    sindir-sindiran bantering, teasing.

    penyindir teaser.

sindrom (*D*) syndrome. *– kemiskinan désa* rural poverty syndrome. *– lawan bencana* counter-disaster syndrome.

sinduk → SÉNDOK I.

sindur (*Jv*) 1 white-bordered red sash tied at the rear, worn by the mother of the bride (Yogyakarta custom). 2 poppy red.

sinéas (*D*) filmmaker.

sinéma (*D*) cinema, movie/motion-picture theater. *– éléktronik* [sinétron] series (on TV).

sinématik (*E*) cinematic.
sinématika cinematics.
sinématis (*D*) cinematic.
sinématograf (*D*) cinematograph.
sinématografi (*D/E*) cinematography.
sinématografis (*D*) cinematographic.
sinérgi (*E*) synergy.
sinérgisme (*E*) synergism.
sinéstésia (*E*) synesthesia.
sinétron [sinéma éléktronik] series (on TV).
    menyinétronkan to turn into a series.
sing I (*onom*) sound of whizzing; → DESING.
sing II → SÉNG.
sing III (*Jv*) which, that, who; → YANG II.
singa (*Skr*) 1 lion, *Felis leo. raja* – syphilis. 2 Leo (*zod*). – *laut* sea lion.
singahak (*M*) **tersingahak** startled, surprised.
singaku (*Jp*) school inspector (during the occupation).
singangar → SENGANGAR.
Singapora and **Singapura** Singapore. *kayu* – k.o. strongly smelling shrub (used as a soil ameliorator), *Lantana camara. ubi* – a tuber variety, water yam, air potato, *Dioscorea bulbifera.*
singapuranisasi Singaporization. *Pemerintah Lee mempercepat prosés* –. The Lee administration accelerated the Singaporization process.
Singapurawan Singaporean.
Singasari name of the kingdom near Malang, East Java, preceding *Majapahit.*
singel (*E*) single.
singelar (*E*) (in sports) single player.
singga → SEHINGGA.
singgah 1a) to call (at s.o.'s house/a port, etc.). b) to stop (briefly) in/at/by. *Kapal itu akan* – *di Tanjung Priok.* The ship will call at Tanjung Priok. *tempat* – stop. 2 stopover.
    bersinggah (*infr*) → SINGGAH.
    singgah-menyinggah to stop frequently for a while; to make one call after another (as a mailman does).
    menyinggahi 1 to call at. *Pelabuhan itu tidak pernah disinggahi kapal berbendéra Panama.* No ship flying the Panamanian flag has ever called at that port. 2 to stop in/by. *Ia* ~ *pacarnya yang tinggal di ujung jalan itu.* He stopped in at his girlfriend's at the corner of the street. 3 to stop for a while at a place to pick up s.t. left for repair, deposit, etc. ~ *di/(ke)pada* a) to call, etc.). b) to stop (briefly at). *akan* ~ *di Tanjung Priok* will stop at Tanjung Priok.
    menyinggahkan 1 to hail/stop (a taxi/bus/car/ship, etc.) en route to a certain destination. *Wanita itu* ~ *taksi di jalan.* The woman hailed a cab on the street. 2 to drop off, drop s.t. on the way. *Kapal itu* ~ *surat-surat pos di Semarang.* The ship dropped off the mail in Semarang. 3 to invite s.o. while passing the house to come in (or, drop by). *Ia* ~ *temannya di rumah.* He invited his friend to drop in.
    mempersinggah (*M*) to invite s.o. while passing the house to drop in (to entertain him).
    singgahan stopping place, call. **bersinggahan** to make a stop.
    penyinggahan dropping off (on the way). *kampung* ~ *musafir* the village where the pilgrims were dropped off.
    persinggahan 1 stopover, transit, leg (of a journey). 2 port of call.
Singgala Singhalese.
singgan (*M ob*) → HINGGA.
singgang I *ikan* – fish boiled and preserved in salt.
singgang II (*M*) grilled; smoked. *ayam* – grilled chicken.
    bersinggang ~ *panas* to (have to) endure heat.
    menyinggang to prepare food that way. ~ *hati* to hurt s.o.'s feelings.
singgang III punishment in schools in which the pupil is made to squat then to get up while crossing his arms and pulling his ears several times.
    menyinggang to inflict this punishment on s.o.
singgasana (*Skr*) throne. – *Rini* royal throne.
    bersinggasana to be on the throne.
    menyinggasanakan to enthrone.

singgat → SINGGET.
singgel (*E*) single, unmarried. *Masih* –? Are you still single?
singget (*Jv*) **menyingget** to divide up with partitions.
    singgetan partition (*mod*). *dinding* ~ partition wall.
singgir menyinggir 1 to unfold (and make s.t. visible), disclose. 2 to show, display, exhibit.
singgit bersinggit to rub against e.o.
    menyinggit to rub.
    memperinggitkan to gnash (one's teeth).
    persinggitan gnashing.
singgul menyinggul to push aside; → SÉNGGOL.
singgung I touch, contact. *garis* – tangent. *titik* – point of contact.
    bersinggung to be in contact (with).
    bersinggungan and *saling* ~ 1 to touch/contact e.o. 2 to be related (to), overlap (with). *Kepentingan saya* ~ *dengan kepentingan anda.* My interests overlap with your interests.
    menyinggung [and **nyinggung** (*coq*)] 1 to push aside (with the elbow), nudge. *Ia kelihatan* ~ *teman-temannya dengan siku.* He was seen pushing his friends aside with his elbow. 2 to touch, brush against. *Tamu itu* ~ *gelas anggur itu hingga pecah.* The guest brushed against the wine glass and broke it. 3 to touch on (a subject); concerning, regarding. *Ia takut akan* ~ *soal yang pelik itu.* He was afraid to talk about that complicated matter. 4 to hurt, offend (s.o.'s feelings), violate (rights). *Kata-katanya* ~ *perasaan temannya.* His words hurt his friend's feelings.
    singgung-menyinggung touching e.o. *tidak ada* ~ *lagi* we no longer have anything to do with e.o.
    menyinggung-nyinggung *tidak* ~ not to touch on, leave out of account. *Rini maupun Boy tidak* ~ *peran meréka berdua dalam kehidupan Nétty setelah menjanda.* Neither Rini nor Boy touched on their role in Netty's life after she became a widow. *tidak* ~ *sedikitpun* a) to snub. b) does not mind at all.
    tersinggung [and **kesinggung** (*coq*)] 1 touched, brushed against. *Vasnya pecah karena* ~ *tanganku.* The vase broke because it touched my hand. 2 made mention of. 3 offended, hurt, insulted. *kesinggung pérnya* (*coq*) he felt offended. **ketersinggungan** sensitivity (to insult), touchiness.
    tersinggung-singgung *cepat/mudah* ~ touchy, apt to take offense on slight revocation, easily hurt emotionally. ~ *lebih dari kena* overly sensitive. ~ *puncak kudisnya* touched on s.t. very unpleasant for him.
    singgungan 1 touch, contact. 2 offense.
    penyinggungan touching (on).
    persinggungan contact. ~ *bébas* free sex.
singgung II badger, *Mydaus meliceps.*
singit I (*M*) **menyingit** 1 to open partly. ~ *selubung* to open a veil. 2 to become partly visible (of the sun or the moon on the horizon). *Cahaya fajar mulai* ~ *di timur.* The light of dawn began to become visible in the east.
    tersingit barely visible. *Rahasia itu baru sedikit* ~ *selimutnya.* Only a tip of the iceberg of the secret was visible.
singit II (*M*) slanting/sloping to one side, aslant (of a kite/ship, etc.); to list and capsize. *Ketika berada di perairan Masalémbo cuaca buruk dan ombak besar menyebabkan kapal* – 6 *derajat ke kanan.* When they were in Masalembo waters, the bad weather and high waves made the ship list 6 degrees to the right. *biar* – *jangan tertiarap* he who stops halfway is only half in error.
singit III (*J*) to grumble, complain, fret. *Anaknya* – *melulu, saya jadi kesal melihatnya.* Her child did nothing but cry; I got tired looking at him.
singit IV (*Jv*) **singitan** to hide, cover, conceal. *di tempat yang agak* ~ in a rather hidden spot.
singit V (*Jv*) holy, sacred.
singkak (*M*) → SINGKAP.
singkap open, exposed, revealed, cropping out. – *daun ambil isi (buah)* (to tell) in plain terms, bluntly, point-blank; not to mince words.
    menyingkapi to disclose, reveal.
    menyingkap(kan) 1 to push aside (a curtain, etc.), open (one's shirt/a book/door, etc.), lift (one's veil), unveil (a statue), turn back (of sheets). 2 to reveal (a secret), disclose.

tersingkap 1 opened, revealed, exposed. ~ *hati* (*M*) to want/feel moved (to do s.t.). 2 (*geol*) outcropped.

singkapan 1 disclosure, exposure. 2 (*geol*) outcrop. 3 s.t. drawn/folded back.

penyingkap 1 s.t. or s.o. that reveals/exposes/uncovers. 2 s.t. that draws back (curtains, etc.).

penyingkapan revealing, exposing, uncovering, disclosure, recovering (fingerprints).

singkat 1 short, brief. *dalam waktu yang* – in a short time. *paham/pikiran* – shortsighted. *"Saya sibuk, tidak ada waktu," katanya* –. "I'm busy, I've no time," he said in a curt way. 2 concise, brief, succinct. 3 shortened, abridged. – *tidak terluas, panjang tidak terkerat* everyone dies when his time is up. – *akal* a) narrow-minded, not very intelligent. b) s.o. who gives up easily. – *cerita* in short, to put it briefly, cut a long story short. – *ceritanya, begini.* The story goes like this. – *kata* in short/brief, the long and the short of it (is), all things considered. – *paham* narrow-minded, not sufficiently intelligent, easily losing hope. – *pengetahuan* inadequate knowledge. – *permintaan* died soon. – *pikiran* narrow-minded, not very intelligent, easily losing hope. – *pinta* to die young. – *sungu* (*M*) passionate, quick-tempered. – *tangan* a) avaricious, closefisted, stingy, ungenerous. b) unwilling to help. – *umur/usia* short-lived, die young.

singkatnya all things considered, in short/brief, in a word.

menyingkat 1 to shorten. *Untuk ~ waktu baiklah kita mulai saja rapat ini.* OK, let's start the meeting to shorten the time. 2 to summarize, condense. *Naskah itu disingkatnya.* He summarized the manuscript. *Buku ini perlu disingkat.* This book needs to be condensed. 3 to abbreviate, shorten. *Perkataan Républik Indonésia dapat disingkat menjadi RI.* Republic of Indonesia can be abbreviated as RI.

singkat-menyingkat abbreviating. *tradisi ~ kata* the tradition of abbreviating words.

menyingkatkan and **mempersingkat** to make shorter, shorten. *Oléh karena kekurangan uang, kami terpaksa ~ perjalanan kami.* Due to a shortage of money, we're forced to shorten our trip.

tersingkat briefest.

singkatan [and **kesingkatan** (*infr*)] abbreviation. *RI ~ perkataan Républik Indonésia.* RI stands for the Republic of Indonesia.

penyingkat s.t. that shortens.

penyingkatan abridgment, résumé, précis.

singkawang → TENGKAWANG.

singkéh and **singkék** (*C slur*) 1 an immigrant born in China; → TOTOK I. 2 an indentured coolie fresh from China.

singkil I on edge (of teeth).

singkil II → TALI *singkil.*

singkir menyingkir [and **nyingkir** (*coq*)] 1 to get out of the way, pull off to the side, step aside, move away. *Orang-orang ~ waktu truk lalu.* People got out of the way when a truck passed by. 2 to evacuate, move to a safer place, escape. *Ribuan orang pelarian Afganistan telah ~ ke Pakistan.* Thousands of Afghan evacuees had moved to a safer place in Pakistan. 3 to hop back and forth (of a rooster around a hen). *sebagai ayam jantan ~ betinanya* like a rooster hopping back and forth around the hen (before mating with her). 4 to quit, abandon, withdraw from. *Amérika ~ dari Viétnam.* The U.S. withdrew from Vietnam.

menyingkiri to shun, avoid, sidestep, evade. *Ia disingkiri oléh orang banyak.* He was shunned by the public.

menyingkirkan 1 to remove, smooth away (difficulties), clean up. *Rintangan-rintangan sudah disingkirkan.* The obstacles have been removed. 2 to put/set aside. *Segala perselisihan itu hendaklah disingkirkan dulu.* All disputes should be put aside first. 3 to evacuate, remove. *Anak-anak dan perempuan disingkirkan ke tempat yang lebih aman.* Children and women were evacuated to a safer place. 4 to eliminate, leave/rule out, get rid of s.o./s.t., purge. *Partai itu telah mengambil tindakan untuk ~ para anggota yang tersangkut dalam perkara korupsi.* The party has taken measures to get rid of the members who were involved in a corruption case. 5 to finish off, wipe out, kill. *Ia telah berhasil ~ penentang-penentangnya.* He succeeded in finishing off his opponents. ~ *diri* to withdraw, retire, go away.

tersingkir 1 avoided, prevented, safeguarded. ~ *dari* safeguarded against. 2 [and **kesingkir** (*coq*)] eliminated, gotten rid of, purged. *orang-orang ~* displaced persons.

tersingkirkan be shoved aside, eliminated. *tak ~* unavoidable, inevitable.

penyingkir evacuee, refugee. *kaum ~* evacuees.

penyingkiran removal, expulsion, exclusion, elimination, purge; evacuation.

singkong I (*Jv* from C?) 1 cassava, *Manihot utilissima.* – *bakar* k.o. hot cassava chips. – *gendruwo* bitter cassava, a species thought effective against cancer. – *goréng* fried cassava. – *Robunci* (fermented) cassava. – *SPP/Sao Pédro Prétol* a very poisonous cassava variety due to its high cyanic acid content.

singkong II of low descent. *anak/gadis* – a child/girl of low descent, from the poverty strata in capital cities as well as on the outskirts.

sinkron (*D*) synchronous.

mensinkronkan to synchronize.

singkup shovel, ladle.

singkur I **menyingkur** to kick aside.

menyingkuri to turn one's back on.

singkur II (*J*) leafy, shady.

single (*E*) 1 single (at tennis, etc.). 2 bachelor; → SINGGEL.

singlét (*E*) A-shirt, singlet, a sleeveless undershirt. (*kaos*) – a man's sleeveless undershirt.

singok the airspace between the top of the wall and the roof.

singsal (*Jv*) **kesingsal** left/remained behind.

singsat I 1 tight, taut (of clothing). 2 (*J*) (and **singset**) slender, thin. *galian/jamu/obat* – medicine to keep the body slender.

menyingsat to shrink, tighten.

menyingsatkan 1 to make tight(er). 2 to make slender, make s.o. stay youthful.

penyingsat slenderizer.

penyingsatan 1 making tighter. 2 making slender.

singsat II **penyingsat** a gift from the prospective bridegroom's family to the prospective bride's family as a sign of acceptance.

singsat III → SINGSING.

singsé → SINSÉ.

singset → SINGSAT I.

singsing menyingsing 1 to roll/pull up (one's sleeves/pants, etc.). 2 to lift, disappear (of fog, etc.). *Fajar ~.* Dawn is breaking.

menyingsing(kan) 1 to roll/tuck up. ~ *lengan baju* a) to roll up one's sleeves. b) to put one's shoulders to the wheel, get to work. 2 to push aside, remove.

tersingsing 1 tucked/rolled up (of sleeves, etc.). 2 pushed aside, removed.

penyingsingan rolling up.

singsring (*S*) **nyingsring** to blow one's nose.

singular (in sports) single player; → SINGELAR.

Sinhala Sin(h)hala. *orang* – Sin(g)halese.

sini I 1 *Aku orang* –. I'm from here. 2 –! come here! this way! → KEMARI. 3 *di* – a) here. *Saya tinggal di* –. I live here. b) there, at your place (only in letters). *dari* – *ke sana* from here to there. *ke* – a) to here. b) come here. *mengesinikan* to bring s.t. over here. *dikesinikan* (*coq*) to be brought here.

sinian (*ke ~*) a little bit over this way, come here. ~ *sedikit nanti saya bisiki.* Come over here, I'll whisper s.t. to you. *Ke ~ sedikit duduknya.* Sit a bit closer to me.

sini II (analogous to *Jv*) I, me; we, us. – *mau ke kampus.* I would like to go to the campus.

sinikal (*E*) cynical(ly).

sinis (*D*) 1 sarcastic. *ketawa* – to laugh sarcastically. 2 cynical.

kesinisan 1 sarcasm, scorn. 2 cynicism.

sinisme (*D*) 1 sarcasm, scorn. 2 cynicism; → KESINISAN.

siniwaka (*Jv*) to sit on the throne before the royal court.

sinkop(e) (*D*) syncope (i.e., *tak* for *tidak*).

sinkrétik (*E*) and **sinkrétis** (*D*) syncretic.

sinkrétisme (*E*) syncretization.

sinkron (*D*) synchronous. *tidak* – asynchronous. **ketidak-sinkronan** asynchronicity.

menyinkronkan to synchronize.

sinkronisasi (*D*) synchronization.
    men(g)sinkronisasikan and **menyinkronisasikan** to synchronize.
sinoda and **sinode** (*D*) synod. – *Godang* (*Bat*) Supreme Synod (of *HKBP*).
sinodistan (*Bat*) participant of *Sinode Godang*.
sinolog (*D*) sinologist.
sinologi (*D/E*) sinology. *ahli –* sinologist.
sinom (*Jv*) locks of hair on the temples of young women.
sinoman (*Jv*) youth who carry out services in the village community, k.o. *gotong-royong* by young people.
sinonim (*D/E*) synonym.
    bersinonim ~ *dengan* synonymous with.
    menyinonimkan to synonymize. *Kata "jihad" disinonimkan dengan pengertian "perang."* The word "jihad" has been made a synonym of the concept of "war."
    kesinoniman synonymy.
sinopsis (*D/E*) synopsis.
sinoptik (*E*) synoptic.
Sino-Soviét Sino-Soviet.
sinsé and **sinsyé** Chinese physician/healer.
sinso (*E*) chainsaw; → GERGAJI *mesin*.
sintagmatik (*E*) syntagmatic.
sintak → SÉNTAK.
sintaks (*D/E*) syntax; → ILMU *nah(w)u*.
sintaktis (*D*) syntactic.
sintal → SINTAR I.
sintar I (*M*) chubby, plump, fleshy, well-fed, bosomy.
sintar II various species of rails and crakes. *burung – (dada kelabu)* slaty-breasted rail, *Rallus striatus gularis*. – *api* red-legged crake, *Rallina fasciata*. – *kecil* Baillon's crake, band-bellied crake, *Porzana paykullii/pusilla*.
sinter (*D*) clinker, sinter.
    penyinteran sintering.
Sinterklas → SINYOKELAS. **Sinterklasan** Saint Nicholas celebration (December 5).
sintés, sintésa (*D*), and **sintésis** (*E*) synthesis.
    menyintésekan to synthesize.
    tersintése synthesized.
sintétik (*E*) and **sintétis** (*D*) synthetic.
sinting I a bit crazy.
    bersinting crazy.
    bersinting-sinting to act crazy.
    kesintingan foolishness, craziness.
sinting II (*Jv*) slanting. *Layangan saya –.* My kite is slanting to one side; → SÉNDÉNG II, SÉNTÉNG I.
sinting III short (of trousers).
sintir (*J*) dice, a gambling game. *main –* to play that game. *méja –* gambling table.
sintok → SINTUK.
sintrong (*S*) Brazilian fire weed, *Erechtites valerianifolia.*
sintua 1 elder (of a tribe, etc.). 2 (*Bat*) chairman, president (of a board, in the *HKBP* system).
sintuh → SENTUH.
sintuk *pohon –* a tree whose bark is used as hair wash, *Cinnamomum sintok.*
    bersintuk to wash o.s. (by rubbing o.s. with a liniment made from that tree, etc.).
    menyintuk to rub s.t. (on). *Badannya disintuk dengan sabun.* He rubbed his body with soap.
    menyintukkan to rub with. ~ *sabun ke badan* to rub the body with soap.
sintul short and stubby.
sintulang *pohon –* a tree whose timber is used for building houses, *Jackia ornata.*
sintung (*M*) **menyintung** to jostle, shove, nudge.
sinu (*D*) nerve, sinew. *perang –* war of nerves.
Sinuhun (*Jv*) exalted one. *Ingkang –* (title of the Sultan of Yogyakarta and of the Susuhunan of Surakarta) His Highness.
sinus (*E*) sinus.
sinuwen → SINU.
sinyal (*D*) signal (in general and at railway stations/road crossings,

etc.). – *digital pemrosés (pengolah)* digital signal processor. – *éléktromagnétik* electromagnetic signal.
    mensinyalkan to signal, indicate.
    pensinyalan signaling. *didukung oléh sistém* ~ supported by a signaling system.
sinyalemén (*D*) 1 description. 2 indication; suspicion; warning, admonition.
sinyalir (*D*) **mensinyalir** to warm/caution against, call attention to, point out, give a description of (s.o. wanted by the police, etc.). *Polda ~ masih ada senjata api gelap.* The Police Precinct warned that there still are illegal weapons.
sinyo (*Port*) 1 Caucasian or Eurasian young man. 2 (*ob*) young master of the house (term used by servants).
Sinyokelas and **Sinyokolas** Saint Nicholas, a white-bearded old man in a red suit with a white cross on the back, who makes toys for children and distributes gifts on December 5; he's always accompanied by one or more Black Peters. (Different from Santa Claus or Father Christmas who is associated with December 25.)
sio → SHIO.
sioca (*C*) girl; → NONI.
sioh → SHIO.
siomai and **siomay** (*C*) k.o. steamed dumplings filled with meat.
sional Naval Headquarters.
siong (*C*) *rokok –* an incense-flavored cigarette containing tobacco blended with *kelembak* root.
siongka (*C*) k.o. resin; → DAMAR I, II.
Sionisme (*D*) Zionism.
sip I (*E coq*) 1 safe, secure, certain. *untuk –nya, kami menggunakan semacam parasut* for security's sake, we used a k.o. parachute. 2 all set, certain to succeed; → BÉRÉS. – *déh!* It's all taken care of, no sweat! 3 okay.
sip II [*surat izin prakték*] license (to practice a profession).
sip III → SURAT *Izin Penghunian*.
sipa(h)i (*Pers Hind*) sepoy.
sipak I → SÉPAK.
sipak II [*siap-pakai*] ready to be used; → WANITA *sipak*.
sipat I → SIFAT I.
sipat II direction. *tali –* (carpenter's) plumb. – *datar* water level, i.e., a leveling instrument containing water in a glass tube. (*berlari*) – *kuping* (*Jv*) (to run) helter-skelter.
    menyipati to mark with a plumb line.
    menyipat(kan) 1 to measure with a plumb line. 2 to direct s.t. (in a certain direction).
    sipatan 1 (carpenter's) plumb. 2 plumb line. *garis* ~ building line, alignment.
sipat III – *alis* eyebrow pencil. – *mata* mascara; → CELAK.
sipat IV *daun –* a herb used medicinally, *Eclipta alba.*
sipatung → CAPUNG, SEPATUNG. *selama – mandi* a very short time.
sipedas (*M*) ginger, *Zingiber officinale.*
sipéng (*Bal*) → NYEPI.
Sipenmaru [*séléksi penerimaan mahasiswa baru*] university entrance selection.
sipesan millipede, *Gryllacris spp.*
sipi off center, go wild, grazing. *biar – jangan tepat/sesat* he who stops halfway is only half in error.
    menyipi to graze, not hit the mark in the center, be off center.
sipil (*D*) civil. *catatan –* vital statistics. *hukum –* private law. *perang – civil war.*
    mensipilkan and **menyipilkan** to convert to civilian administration.
sipir (*D*) warden, jailer.
sipit I (*J*) *mata –* (Mongolian) slanting eyes. *si mata –* the Chinese. *Banyak tanah dimiliki oléh orang-orang –.* A lot of land is owned by the Chinese.
    menyipit to close (of the eyes).
    menyipitkan to screw up (one's eyes).
    kesipitan slant (of the eyes).
sipit II → SEMPIT.
sipoa (*C*) abacus.
    nyipoin (*J*) to total on an abacus.
sipolan → POLAN.
sipon → SIFON I.

sipongang (*M*) echo.
  bersipongang to echo; echoing.
Siprus Cyprus.
sipu I *tersenyum* – to laugh shyly.
  kesipu(-sipu)an and **tersipu(-sipu)** *malu* very embarrassed/shy/ bashful. *Aku disérét oléh Liani, aku tersipu malu.* I was dragged along by Liani, I was very embarrassed.
sipu II (*J*) **tersipu-sipu** in a hurry.
sipulut glutinous/sticky rice; → PULUT II.
siput I generic names for shells and some k.o. shellfish. – *memuji buntut* "the snail praises its tail," i.e., self-praise. *berjalan lambat bak* – to go at a snail's pace, go as slowly as a snail. – *akik* k.o. mussel, *Helix sp.* – *babi* giant African snail, *Achatina fulica.* – *darat* snail. – *kena* clam. – *lintah* snail without a shell. – *mutiara* top shell.
siput II *burung* – blue whistling thrush, *Myophoneus caeruleus.*
SIPVA [*Surat Izin Pembelian Valuta Asing*] license to purchase foreign exchange.
sir I (*A*) mysterious, enigmatic, secret; → GAIB, RAHASIA.
sir II (*coq*) in love; to lust after, be after s.o. (sexually); → TAKSIR II. *Banyak lelaki pada* – *sama lu.* A lot of men are after you.
  mengesir to lust after.
  sir-siran 1 to be/fall in love; to flirt. **2** sweetheart, beloved; → PACAR.
sir III (*onom*) sound of hissing, sizzling, rushing (of wind through the leaves); → DESIR.
sir IV (*E*) sir.
sira (*ob*) **1** (respectful form of reference) he, she; → BELIAU. **2** you; → ANDA II.
sirah I (*M*) red; → MÉRAH.
  tersirah 1 reddest. **2** a most recent grave. *mendapat tanah* ~ a) dead. b) encountered a buried corpse.
sirah II (*A?*) – *Nabi* the story of the Prophet.
sirai combed, brushed (of the hair).
siram pour, flush, bathe, water. *toilét* – flush toilet.
  bersiram 1 to bathe/take a bath (of a *raja*). ~ *darah* to bathe in blood. ~ *tabal* (*cla*) to be anointed before being made king. **2** to bath with/in. *jalanan yang* ~ *cahaya terang* the road bathed in clear light.
  menyiram [and **nyiram** (*coq*)] **1** to pour water on/over, bathe, water. ~ *bunga dalam taman* to water the flowers in the garden. *Ibukota Révolusi disiram hujan.* It was raining cats and dogs over Yogyakarta. ~ *tersangka yang tengah diperiksa dengan air cabé* to sprinkle a suspect under investigation with water in which crushed chili pepper has been soaked (i.e., one of the practices applied by some police investigators to force a suspect to tell the truth). ~ *api* to make s.t. flare up. **2** to flush s.t. down (the toilet). ~ *kotorannya dengan air* to flush waste with water.
  siram-menyiram bathing.
  menyirami [and **nyiramin** (*J coq*)] to water, pour water on, sprinkle. ~ *tanaman* to water the plants.
  menyiramkan [and **nyiramin** (*J coq*)] **1** to water with, pour, sprinkle. *Ia* ~ *air karbol pada lantai yang akan dipél.* He poured diluted carbolic acid on the floor to be mopped. **2** to bathe s.o. ~ *putra baginda* to bathe the *raja*'s son.
  tersiram [and **kesiram** (*coq*)] watered, sprinkled. ~ *hujan* wet from the rain.
  siraman 1 splash, gush. *Tanah kering merindukan* ~ *hujan.* The dry soil yearns for a gush of rain. **2** bathing. *upacara* ~ a ritual bathing ceremony: a) following a circumcision. b) after the first menstruation. c) before the wedding (of a bride).
  penyiram sprinkler, s.o. or s.t. that waters.
  penyiraman watering, sprinkling.
  pe(r)siraman (*cla*) bathing place (of a *raja*).
sirap I slightly lifted. – *hati* angry.
  menyirapkan 1 to lift slightly. **2** to provoke/rouse/stir up anger/ rage. ~ *darah* to chill s.o.'s blood, terrifying. *serangan yang* ~ *darah* a terrifying attack.
  tersirap raised. *Darahnya* ~. and ~ *darahnya.* His heart throbbed (from fright/expectation, etc.), his blood mounted (to his head).

sirap II k.o. wooden roof shingle made from thin strips of *kayu ulin, Eusideroxylon wageri.*
  tersirap shingled.
sirap III → SIREP.
sirapa → JERAFAH, JERAPAH.
sirat I 1 mesh (of a net); network; → RAJUT. **2** spaces, interstices. –.– *gigi* spaces between the teeth.
  menyirat to weave. ~ *jala* to weave/make a net.
  menyiratkan to imply, state s.t. implicitly. *Pernyataan itu* ~ *bahwa Brigade Mérah telah memutuskan akan membunuh Jénderal Dozier.* The statement implied that the Red Brigade decided to kill General Dozier.
  tersirat 1 woven, intertwined, interlaced. **2** contained (within), hidden. *yang* ~ *di (dalam) hatinya* what is going on in one's mind. *yang* ~ *di muka* what shows on one's face. *ancaman yang* ~ a veiled threat. **3** implicit, implied. *ada yang tersurat dan ada yang* ~ one should read between the lines. *sesuai dengan apa yang tersurat dan* ~ in letter and in spirit.
  siratan 1 s.t. hidden, implication. **2** s.t. woven.
sirat II (*A*) bridge. *-ul-mustakim* the razor-edged bridge over which true believers pass into the Muslim heaven.
siraut (*M*) k.o. sharp knife.
sirawan k.o. plant.
  sirawan-sirawanan Menispermaceae.
siréibu (*Jp*) (army) headquarters (during the occupation).
siréne (*D*) siren.
sirep (*J/Jv*) **1** quiet, still, tranquil, calm, placed. **2** abated (of fever/ fire/war). **3** putting s.o. to sleep with a charm. **4** anesthetic (k.o. magic formula to put s.o. to sleep). *aji-aji/ilmu* – the art of learning how to put s.o. or an animal to sleep through sorcery.
  menyirep(kan) [and **nyirep** (*coq*)] **1** to hypnotize, put s.o. or an animal to sleep through magic formulas. **2** (*Jv*) to calm s.o. down.
  tersirep hypnotized, etc.
  penyirep hypnotist. *aji-aji/ilmu* ~ the art of learning how to put s.o. or an animal to sleep through sorcery.
  penyirepan hypnotizing.
siri (*A*) **1** spiritual, secret (places of the heart). **2** → SIRRI.
Siria → SURIAH.
sirih 1 betel vine, *Piper betle.* **2** betel leaves, used for chewing. *makan* – to chew betel. *uang* – a tip. *ada* – *hendak makan sepah* s.o. good wants s.t. bad. – *naik, junjungan patah* one is just about to get s.t. good when he suddenly has a disaster. – *pulang ke gagang* to get back to where one started. *seikat bagai* –, *serumpun bagai serai* unanimous; share for better and for worse. – *air* wild sirih, *Piper miniatum.* – *carang* young betel leaves. – *gading* pothos, *Rhaphidophora aurea.* – *kerakap* coarse lower leaves of the betel vine. – *kuning* (*Mal*) a beautiful girl. – *lezat* betel leaf given by the groom to the bride (during the ceremony of meeting the bride). – *masak* a prepared betel quid (with lime, areca nut, gambier, tobacco, etc.). – *pinang* articles taken to s.o. as a token of honor. – *sekapur/setampin* betel with appurtenances (for one quid). – *tanya* betel with accessories given to the parents of the girl asked in marriage.
  menyirih (*M*) to chew betel.
  menyirihi (*M*) to offer (*sirih*/tobacco/cigarettes) to a guest. *Saya disirihi rokok.* I was offered a cigarette.
  menyirihkan (*M*) to offer s.t. ~ *rokok/tembakau* to offer a cigarette/tobacco.
  penyirih confirmed betel chewer.
  penyirihan chewing sirih.
sirik I (*J*) envious, jealous; → DENGKI, IRI *hati.*
sirik II (*Jv*) to refrain from (do)ing. – *kalau ngemis* to refrain from begging.
  menyirik [and **nyirik** (*coq*)] to avoid. *Ali disirik teman-temannya.* Ali's friends avoided him. *Aku nyirik lombok sebab aku selalu sakit perut.* I don't eat chili peppers. They always give me a stomachache.
  sirikan 1 thing (to be) avoided. ~*ku udang.* I don't eat shrimp. **2** unpropitious by astrological reckoning. (*Hari*) *Jumat itu hari* ~*ku.* Friday is my unlucky day.
sirik III → SYIRIK.

sirine → SIRÉNE.

siring I rattan scoop for catching small fish, shrimp, etc.
  menyiring to catch fish, etc. with such a scoop.

siring II 1 gutter, drain, ditch. *ke* – to urinate. **2** (in *Sumsel*) irrigation.

siring III (*M*) border, edge (of a different color) of cloth.
  bersiring with such a border.

sirip 1 fin (of a fish). **2** crest (of a crocodile). *sop – ikan* shark fin soup. *– selam* "fin for diving," i.e., an award in the form of a wing for s.o. who has complied with applicable regulations. *– dada* pectoral fin. *– dubur* anal fin. *– ékor* tail fin. *– sayap* flap (on an airplane).
  bersirip overlapping (of wallboards, tiles, etc.). *papan dinding ~* overlapping wallboards.
  menyirip 1 to imbricate. **2** pinnate.

sirkah → SYIRKAH.

sirkam (*D*) ornamental comb (used in hair).

sirkaya → SERIKAYA II.

sirkel (*E*) circle.

sirkit circuit; → SIRKUIT. *– atlétik* athletic circuit. *– balap* race track. *– séwa* leased channel (of telephone line).

sirkol and **sirkul** (*D zuurkool*) sauerkraut.

sirkuit (*D*) circuit. *– listrik* electrical circuit. *– singkat* short circuit.
  bersirkuit with a ... circuit. *télévisi ~ tertutup* closed circuit television, CCTV.

sirkulasi (*D*) circulation. *bank –* circulation bank.
  bersirkulasi with a circulation of; → BERTIRAS. *koran ~ tinggi* a newspaper with a high circulation.

sirkulér (*D*) circular (letter).

sirkumsisi (*D*) circumcision; → SUNAT.
  menyirkumsisi to circumcise. *Hari itu R akan disirkumsisi.* That day R was to be circumcised.

sirkus (*D/E*) circus.
  pesirkus circus player.

sirkwit → SIRKUIT.

sirlak (*D*) shellac.

sirna (*Skr*) vanished, destroyed, disappeared, lost, exterminated. *Semua kenangan pahit – tak berbekas.* All bitter memories disappeared without leaving a trace.
  menyirnakan to destroy, wipe/root out, disappear, exterminate.

Sirnaning Jakso Katon Gapuraning Ratu motto of the Diponegoro army division stationed in Central Java, meaning "If the Demon has Disappeared the Gate to the King is visible."

sirobok (*M*) → SEROBOK.
  bersirobok to encounter, meet. *Aku ~ mata dengan Hamid.* My eyes encountered Hamid's by chance.

sirop (*D*) syrup. *– Betawi* purplish red. *– perambos* strawberry syrup.

sirosis (*E*) cirrhosis.

sirpé (*J*) a snack made of sugar and coconut.

sirri (*A*) *kawin/nikah/perkawinan –* a marriage performed before the religious authorities but not registered.

sirsak (*D zuurzak*) soursop, *Annona muricata. – gundul* a variety of soursop without thorns, pond apple, alligator apple, *Annona glabra.*

sirsekin (*D/E?*) sharkskin (a fabric).

sirtu → PASIR (*dan*) *batu.*

sirtukil [*pasir, batu, kerikil*] sand, stone, pebbles.

siru (*M*) **bersiru** to change (direction), shift/veer suddenly (of the wind), chop about.

sirup → STROP.

sis I (*onom*) sound of hissing; → DESIS.

sis II → ZUS.

sis III (*Pers cla*) k.o. head ornament.

sis IV (in acronyms) → SISTÉM.

sisa (*Skr*) **1** rest, remnant, remainder, balance, holdover, leftover, surplus, excess, residue. **2** residual. *bahan –* residual, refuse (by-)product. **3** waste, wreckage. *mangga – kamprét* a bat-eaten mango. *uang –* the amount of money left. *– hasil usaha* [SHU] surplus (of a cooperative). *– lebih* excess. *– makanan* leftovers (from a meal). *– purba* (*infr*) fossil. *– rasa* aftertaste. *– rimah* crumbs, leftovers. *– uang* balance (in one's checkbook, etc.).

bersisa to have a balance/surplus/remainder, remain, be left over. *tidak ~* without a remainder; complete; entirely. *Hidupnya tinggal ~ enam bulan.* He has only six months left to live.

menyisa to be left, remain. *satu-satunya kapal yang ~* the only remaining ship. *Kami tidak pernah ~ makanan di lemari és.* We never have any leftovers in the refrigerator.

menyisakan [and **nyisain** (*J coq*)] **1** to leave over, leave behind. **2** to set aside (for later use). *~ sebagian untuk ditabung* to set aside a part for savings. **3** to spare. *Api hanya ~ dua ruang kelas.* The fire spared only two classrooms.

tersisa left (aside/over). *Saté masih ~ dua tusuk.* Two skewers of satay are left. *Dunia ketiga ~ di luar garis.* The third world is left out of the community of nations. *tidak ~* nothing left over.

penyisaan the remaining. *~ 40%* the remaining 40%.

sisal (*D*) sisal (hemp).

sisalak (*M*) **bersisalak** to contend, dispute, quarrel.
  persisalakan quarrel, dispute.

sisi 1 (left/right) side, flank. *di – itu* besides. *di – jalan* at the side of the road, by the roadside. *Di – lain* on the other hand. *di – rumah* from the side of the house. *Semoga arwah almarhum diterima di – Tuhan.* May the soul of the deceased be received by God (in obituary notices). *Semoga arwah almarhum mendapat kebahagiaan kekal di – Tuhan Yang Maha Kasih.* May the soul of the deceased find eternal happiness at the side of God the All-Merciful. *ke –* aside, to the side. **mengesisikan** to set aside, ignore, keep at a distance. *Orang itu dikesisikan.* That person was kept at a distance. **2** (geometric) side. **3** side, view, aspect; → PIHAK. *pandangan satu –* unilateral consideration. *– kanan* right side. *– kapal* beam-side. *– kiri* left side. *– miring* (*math*) hypotenuse. *– penawaran* supply side. *sosialisme – penawaran* supply-side socialism. *– permintaan* demand side. *– perut* ventral. *– suplai* supply-side.

sesisi one-sided. *Téori sosial yang dikembangkan dalam Islam kebanyakan masih ~.* The social theories developed in Islam are for the greater part still one-sided.

bersisian to have ... on the side.

bersisi(-sisi)an side by side, abreast. *Meréka berjalan ~.* They walked side by side.

menyisi 1 to move aside/over/to the side. *~lah sedikit!* Move aside a bit! **2** to walk/go along the edge of, skirt. *~ pantai* to skirt/walk along the coast/shore.

menyisikan 1 to move s.t. to the side. **2** to set s.t. aside (for savings, etc.).

penyisian 1 moving s.t. aside. **2** setting s.t. aside.

sisih put/set aside, separated (from the rest). *– bagai antah* isolated, ignored, excluded.

bersisih to be separated (from *dari*). *~ antah dengan beras* the separation of the rich from the poor.

menyisih 1 to withdraw, seclude o.s., retire, be separate, secede, go away; → MENGHINDAR, MENYENDIRI. *hidup ~* to live secluded/sequestered. *Halim telah ~ dari perkumpulan itu setelah segala pendapatnya ditentang dengan hébat.* Halim withdrew from the party after all his opinions were vehemently opposed. **2** to step aside, make way/room, turn/move away, get out of the way. *Kalau ada mobil ~lah.* When there is a car, please step aside. **3** to blow over (of clouds). *Tak lama antaranya awan pun ~ dan bulan mulai tampak.* Not long thereafter the clouds blew over and the moon began to become visible.

menyisihkan [and **nyisihin** (*J coq*)] **1** to shun, avoid. **2** to exclude. *Dia disisihkan dari pergaulan sehari-hari.* He was excluded from daily intercourse. **3** to set apart/aside. *~ uang* to set money aside. **4** to make a distinction. **5** to eliminate (from the running in sports, etc.). *~ diri* to seclude o.s. (from society), retire (from the world).

tersisih 1 isolated (case), secluded, segregated, separated. *Hidupnya ~ dari kaum keluarga.* He lived separated from his family. **2** eliminated (from the game).

tersisihkan pushed aside/away. *Jangan kita sampai ~ oléh pendatang baru.* Don't let it get to the point that we are pushed aside by newcomers.

sisihan (*Jv*) spouse.

penyisih eliminating, elimination. *tahap ~* elimination stage.

penyisihan 1 (in sports) elimination (from the running). *babak* ~ elimination round. 2 (*fin*) exclusion, allowance (for), provision. ~ *kerugian aktiva* allowance for bad debts. ~ *persediaan usang* provision for inventory obsolescence. ~ *piutang ragu-ragu* allowance for doubtful accounts. ~ *rugi* provision for possible losses.

sisik I 1 fish scale(s), (hard) scale (of a tortoise, etc.). *minta - pada limbat* seek the impossible; → *seperti* CÉBOL *merindukan bulan*. 2 skin which scales off, squama. 3 name of certain species of turtle. *- karah* edible turtle, *Chelone mydas*. *- lilin* the shell turtle, *Chelone imbricata*. *- tempurung* inedible turtle, *Thalassochelys caretta*. 4 outer appearance.

bersisik to have scales, scaly, with a scale.

bersisikan with scales. *naga yang* ~ *emas* a dragon with gold scales.

menyisik 1 to scale, remove the scales from. ~ *ikan kakap mérah* the scrape the scales from a red snapper. ~ *limbat* to do the impossible. 2 to sharpen (bamboo/pencils, etc.). 3 to tell the qualities of a fighting cock from the scales on its legs. ~ *ayam sabungan* to judge the qualities of a fighting cock from the scales on its legs. 4 to be scaly, look like scales.

menyisiki 1 to scale, remove the scales/thorns from, strip (bamboo). 2 to see whether a fighting cock is good by examining the scales on its legs.

sisik II various species of creepers. *- naga/tenggiling* a creeper, k.o. beggar weed, *Desmodium heterophylla*. *- puyuh* k.o. tree, *Carallia suffruticosa*.

sisik III (*Jv*) (tobacco) quid. *tembakau* - chewing tobacco.

sisik IV (*Jv*) *- melik* clues, evidence for a crime. *memperoléh - melik* to obtain evidence.

Sisilia Sicily.

sisindiran (*S*) to make allusions to e.o., tease.

Si Singa Mangaradja name of the last Batak king defeated by the Dutch in 1906.

sisip insert, slip in.

bersisip to be inserted (into s.t.). *Sepucuk pistol* ~ *di pinggangnya*. A revolver was slipped into his waistband.

bersisipkan to have s.t. (e.g., a kris, etc.) inserted into it. *seorang bangsawan dengan pakaian yang indah*, ~ *keris* a nobleman in an attractive uniform with a kris slipped into his waistband.

menyisip 1 to insert, slip s.t. (into). *Ia* ~ *gambar itu ke dalam novél yang sedang dibacanya*. He inserted the picture into the novel he was reading. 2 to interleave (a book). *Tiap-tiap sepuluh halaman disisipi dengan sehelai kertas blangko*. A blank sheet was inserted every ten pages. 3 to replace (roof shingles/plants, etc. by inserting new ones). *Ia* ~ *bagian-bagian atap yang bocor dengan daun pisang*. He replaced the leaking portions of the roof with banana leaves. ~ *tanaman kopi* to replace good coffee plants with new ones in the gaps between the rows of plants. 4 to mend a torn piece of cloth, sock, net, etc.

menyisipi 1 to mend by inserting, fix up by inserting. 2 to insert (an infix) into a word. *Kata "kilau" disisipi "em" menjadi "kemilau."* The infix "em" has been inserted into the word *"kilau"* to form *"kemilau."* 3 to interleave.

menyisipkan and **mempersisipkan** [and **nyisipin** (*J coq*)] 1 to insert s.t. (into), slip s.t. (into). *Ia* ~ *kerisnya ke pinggang*. He inserted his kris at his waist. 2 to replace s.t. by replacing the old one. *Tukang itu* ~ *ubin di lantai*. The craftsman replaced the tiles in the floor. 3 (*gram*) to put an infix into a word. ~ *"er" dalam kata "gigi" menjadi "gerigi."* Infixing "er" into the word *"gigi"* makes it into *"gerigi."*

menyisip-nyisipkan to interlace.

tersisip 1 inserted, slipped in, intercalated. *Sebilah keris* ~ *di pinggangnya*. A kris was slipped into his waist. 2 included, implied, interpolated, contained. ~ *dalam pernyataan itu* included in that statement.

sisipan 1 insertion, intercalation. ~ *lepas* loose insert. 2 (*gram*) infix. **bersisipan** interlaced, infixed, with an insert.

sisip-sisipan interlacing.

kesisipan 1 to get s.t. (a splinter/needle, etc.) in the flesh accidentally. 2 to get s.t. accidentally inserted into it.

penyisip (in sports) reserve, stand-in.

penyisipan 1 insertion, interpolation, interleaving. 2 (*gram*) infixation.

sisir I 1 (hair-)comb. 2 harrow; → GARU. 3 bunch (of bananas); *cp* TANDAN. 4 shuttle comb (on a weaving loom).

sesisir a bunch (of bananas).

bersisir 1 to have/use a comb, comb one's hair. 2 combed. 3 to brush one's hair.

menyisir [and **nyisir** (*coq*)] 1 to comb. 2 to harrow (the ground). 3 to card.

menyisiri to comb out.

menyisirkan to comb/harrow for s.o. else.

tersisir combed, harrowed.

penyisir *mesin* ~ *serat* carder.

penyisiran 1 (*mil*) sweep. 2 sweeping, canvassing. 3 ~ *serat* carding.

sisir II menyisir 1 to skirt the edge of, walk along (the shore, etc.), go along the side of; → MENYUSUR. 2 to graze, brush against s.t. *Peluru itu hanya* ~ *lengangnya*. The bullet only grazed his arm.

pesisir the coast.

sisir III (*M*) **kesisiran** pricked by a thorn in the flesh, entered the flesh accidentally.

siskamling [Sistém Keamanan Lingkungan] neighborhood security system.

bersiskamling to patrol. ~ *semalam suntuk* to do an all-night patrol, night watch.

sisos → SISTÉM *sosial*.

sispan → SÉSPAN.

sista (*D*) cyst.

sisték → SISTÉM *téknik*.

sistém (*D*) system. *- angkum* [atasan yang berhak menghukum] system in which a *mil* superior has the right to punish a subordinate without going through civil law, military justice system. *- banyak partai* multi-party system. *- Bombardemén/Pemboman Orbit Fraksional* Fractional Orbital Bombardment System. *- démokrasi (parleménter)* (parliamentary) democratic system. *- dwipartai/dua partai* two-party system. *- famili* nepotism. *- gaduh* system whereby financial aid is reimbursed in kind. *- go-go* system in which a passenger has to pay a bribe to get a seat. *- hukum* legal system. *- kartu* card system (in computers). *- kawan* buddy system, spoils system. *- kecakapan* merit system. *- lingkungan ecosystem*. *- multi partai* multiparty system. *- Neraca Sosial Ékonomi* [SNSE] Social Accounting Matrix. *- partai tunggal* one-party system. *- pembuatan laporan* report-drafting system. *- pengendalian* control system. *- penggudangan* storage system. *- pilih bulu* favoritism. *- sosial* social system. *- surya untuk rumah tangga* solar system for the household. *- tanpalogam* ametallism. *- tekan tombol* push-button system. *- téknik* technical system. *- témbak* the system of activities that cannot bear the light of day, such as blackmailing, bribing, counterfeiting, etc. *- témbak di tempat* to obtain a birth certificate by bribing on the spot.

bersistém to be systematic; with a system. *Pembentukan akronim seharusnya* ~. The formation of acronyms should be systematic.

menyistémkan to systematize.

kesistéman systematically.

penyistéman systematization.

sistématik (*E*) systematic.

menyistématik(kan) to systematize.

sistématika (*D*) systematics.

tersistématitakan systematized.

sistématis (*D*) systematic.

sistématisasi (*D*) systematization.

menyistematisasikan to systematize.

tersistématisasi systematic.

sistématisir (*D*) **menyistématisir** to systematize.

sistémik (*E*) and **sistémis** (*D*) systemic.

sistén (*D*) clipped form of **asistén** (*wedana* or *camat*); → SETÉN.

sister (*D*) 1 female (hospital) nurse. 2 Catholic nun.

sistim → SISTÉM.

sistol (*D*) systole.

sistolik (*E*) systolic.

sisurut (*M*) **bersisurut** to withdraw, leave; → SURUT.

siswa (*Skr*) pupil, student (*esp* of elementary and secondary schools); *cp* PELAJAR, MAHASISWA. – *bidan* student midwife. – *pindahan* transfer student. – *siswi* male and female students. – *tamu* guest student. – *teladan* model student.

bersiswakan to have ... student(s). *sekolah itu ~ 60 anak* that school has 60 students.

siswi (*Skr neo*) female pupil/student (*esp* of elementary and secondary schools).

sit I (*onom*) sound of hissing, sizzling; → DESIR, DESIT.

sit II (*E*) sheet. – *sténsil* stencil sheet.

mengesit to make a master sheet.

SIT III (*init*) → SURAT *Izin Terbit*.

sita I (*leg*) seizure, foreclosure, confiscation. *juru* – bailiff, process server. *surat* – writ of execution. – *éksékutif/éksékutorial* attachment/seizure in execution/under foreclosure. – *jaminan/konsérvator* attachment/seizure before judgment, foreclosure. – *lélang* foreclosure sale. – *milik/révéndikasi/révéndikatur* revendicatory seizure.

menyita and **mensita** l (*leg*) to seize property/goods/possessions/(smuggled) items; to foreclose (on a mortgage); to confiscate. *Saya ~ barang-barang selundupan itu.* I seized the smuggled goods. 2 to take (up) one's time/attention. *~ perhatian* to draw one's attention. *~ (banyak) waktu* to take (a lot of) time, time-consuming. *~ seluruh waktunya* to take up all one's time. *suatu tawar-menawar yang ~ waktu* a time-consuming process of bargaining.

sita-menyita confiscation, seizure.

tersita (*leg*) l seized, confiscated. 2 taken over/up. *Hampir sebagian besar jalan yang ada ~ oléh pedagang kaki lima itu.* Almost the entire street was taken up by sidewalk vendors.

sitaan (*leg*) l seized, confiscated. 2 confiscated goods. 3 attachment. *dalam ~* in confiscation. *~ jaminan/pengekalan* attachment/seizure before judgment.

penyita and **pensita** (*leg*) l bailiff, process server. 2 confiscator.

penyitaan and **pensitaan** (*leg*) seizure, confiscation. *~ konsérvatoir/pengekalan* seizure/attachment before judgment.

sita II (*cla*) bright white (of color).

sitak valise.

sitampu → TETUPUK.

Sitarda [Integrasi taruna wreda] Senior Students Integration, i.e., the Program of the Armed Forces Academy with the People.

sitat (*D*) citation; → KUTIPAN.

sitawar → SETAWAR.

sitegang bersitegang (*urat léhér*) to take a firm stand, brace o.s.; → TEGANG.

sitekan bersitekan ~ to put one's hands on one's knees.

sitén → SETÉN.

siter (*D*) zither.

siteri (*ob*) → ISTERI, ISTRI.

siti (*A*) l lady. – *Hawa* Eve. – *Meriam* (the Virgin) Mary. 2 Miss (a title appearing before names) – *Nurbaya* Miss Nurbaya. 3 girl of a good family.

sitin (*E*) satin.

sitinggil (*Jv*) the main audience hall at the north end of the Yogyakarta palace, now used as a lecture hall for Gadjah Mada University.

sitir (*D*) **menyitir** and **mensitir** to cite, quote; → MENGUTIP.

sitiran citation.

Sitiung an area in West Sumatra.

mensitiungkan to relocate/transmigrate people to the Sitiung area.

sitokar → STOKER.

sitologi (*D*) cytology.

Si-Tosim (*E*) Cytozyme; → GUCI *wasiat*.

sitrat (*D*) citrate.

sitronélla (*D*) citronella (the grass), *Cymbopogon nardus*.

sitrun (*D*) citron.

sitti → SITI.

situ I there (a definite place nearer to the hearer than to the speaker). *dari* – from there. *ke* – (to) there. *Ke -nya pakai taksi.* I went there by taxi. *di* – a) over there. b) only then, only at that point. *Di – dia baru tahu penyakitnya berbahaya.* It was only then that he found out that his disease was dangerous.

situ-situ the very same place. *Menurut beberapa penjual barang-barang itu didapatkan di ~ juga.* Several vendors said that those goods could be obtained at the very same place.

situ II (*J*) you. – *mau ke mana?* Where are you going? *"Berapa ongkosnya untuk sekali pijat?" tanya SKM. "Ya, terserah – saja."* "How much for a massage?" asked SKM. "Well, that's up to you."

situ III (*S*) (man-made) lake.

situasi (*D*) l situation. 2 location.

mensituasikan and **menyituasikan** to situate s.t. somewhere.

situasional (*E*) and **situasionil** (*D*) situational. *faktor* – a situational factor.

situn black glazed earthenware pot.

situs (*L*) situs, site of an archeological find.

siu skimming push net.

siuh (*C coq*) go away, beat it!

siuk (*M*) **menyiuk** to sigh/groan in pain. *siapa sakit, siapa ~* s.o. who has made a mistake feels it when s.o. else ridicules him.

siul (*onom*) (sound of) whistling.

bersiul l to whistle (with the mouth). 2 to sing (of birds). 3 to blow air out of the mouth, make a hissing noise with the mouth.

menyiuli to whistle at, make a wolf-whistle at. *Anak-anak itu ~ gadis yang léwat itu.* The kids whistled at the girl passing by.

menyiulkan to whistle s.t.

siulan whistling, hissing. *~ angin* the whistling of the wind.

penyiul whistler.

siuman l – *daripada lupanya*, – *akan dirinya* and – *dari pingsannya* to come to (after fainting). 2 recovered (after fainting or passing out due to drinking too much). 3 – *dari khayalnya* to return to reality (after daydreaming or pondering over s.t.). 4 awakened (from a nightmare).

siung I (*Jv*) l canine tooth. 2 fang. 3 tusk.

bersiung tusked, fanged.

siung II (*Jv*) slice (of onion/garlic); → IRIS I. *dua – bawang* two slices of onion.

siung III (*onom*) buzzing sound (of bees), whizzing/whistling sound (of bullets passing overhead).

bersiung to buzz (of bees), whiz by (of bullets passing overhead).

SIUP (*init*) → SURAT *Izin Usaha Perdagangan*.

SIUPP (*init*) → SURAT *Izin Usaha Penerbitan Pérs*.

siur I → SIMPANG *siur*.

siur II (*onom*) rustling sound.

bersiuran and **berkesiuran** (*pl subj*) to make rustling/whistling/blowing sounds.

siut (*onom*) buzzing/sizzling/hissing sound.

siut-siut to make that sound.

bersiut and **menyiut(-nyiut)** l to make a buzzing/sizzling sound. 2 to blow (air out of the mouth to cool s.t.). 3 to whistle.

siutan buzz, sizzle, hiss.

sivik(s) (*E*) civics.

sivilisasi (*D*) civilization.

mensivilisasikan to civilize.

sivitas akadémika (*D*) civitas academica, community of scholars.

siwak (*A*) wooden toothbrush.

menyiwak to brush one's teeth.

siwalan I (*Jv*) *pohon* – Palmyra palm and its edible fruit, *Borassus flabellifer*.

siwalan II → SIALAN.

siwar → SÉWAH I,II, SÉWAR.

siwer (*Jv*) squinting, cross-eyed; → JULING.

siwilan (*Jv*) offshoot.

siwur (*Jv*) coconut ladle with a long handle.

siyaki (*A*) contextual.

siyasah (*A*) → SIASAT I. – *syariyyah* Islamic law policy.

sk- also see entries beginning with SEK-

SK (*init*) → SURAT *Keputusan*.

skadron (*E*) squadron. – *avionik* air squadron.

skak (*D*) l chess. 2 (in chess) check!

skakel (*D*) link.

skakelar (*D*) (electric) switch.

skala (*D*) scale. *dengan – 1:20.000* to a scale of 1 to 20,000. –

besar/kecil large/small scale. *dalam – besar ataupun kecil* on a large or small scale. *– nasional* national scale. *– Richter* Richter scale. *Gempa bumi itu berkekuatan sekitar 7 pada – Richter.* The earthquake measured about 7 on the Richter scale.

   berskala with a scale of, on a … scale. *pembangunan ~ besar* large-scale development. *usaha yang tidak lagi ~ kecil* a business which no longer runs on a small scale. *pembenihan udang ~ kecil* small-scale/backyard shrimp hatchery. *pemogokan ~ nasional* a national strike.

   penskalaan scaling.

skalanisasi scaling.

Skalu [Sekretariat Kerjasama Antar Lima Universitas] **1** Coordinating Secretariat among Five Universities: *Univérsitas Indonésia, Institut Téknologi Bandung, Institut Pertanian Bogor, Univérsitas Gadjah Mada,* and *Univérsitas Airlangga.* **2** admittance exam to any of these five universities.

skandal (*D*) scandal.

Skandinavia Scandinavia.

skap (*D*) (carpenter's) plane.

skarifikasi (*D*) scarification.

skarnir (*D*) hinge, joint.

skat (*D*) skate. *– indah* figure skating.

SKB (*init*) → SURAT *Keputusan Bersama.*

skédul (*E*) schedule; → JADWAL. *menurut –* on time.

   menskédulkan 1 to schedule. **2** to designate/set for a fixed time.

skélét (*D*) skeleton.

skéma (*D*) **1** scheme, sketch. **2** outline, diagram.

skématis (*D*) schematic.

skéna (*D*) scène (of theater).

skénario (*D*) scenario, screenplay.

skép I → SURAT *keputusan.*

skép II (*D auto*) sliding valve.

sképter (*D*) scepter.

sképtik (*E*) skeptic(al).

sképtikus (*D*) skeptic.

sképtis (*D*) skeptic(al).

sképtisi (*D*) skeptics.

sképtisisme (*D*) skepticism.

skét(s) and **skétsa** (*D*) sketch, draft, (sketchy) outline.

   menskéts(a) to sketch.

skétsel (*D*) wooden partition.

ski (*D*) ski. *(ber)main –* to ski, go skiing. *– air* water ski.

   berski to ski, go skiing.

skil (*E*) skill; → KETRAMPILAN.

skim I (*E*) *– milk* skim-milk; → SUSU *skim.*

skim II (*E*) scheme; → SKÉMA.

skip (*D*) target (in rifle shooting). *– bergerak* moving target.

skiping (*E*) skipping, jumping.

skisma (*D*) schism.

skismatis schismatic.

skizofrén (*D*) schizophrenic.

skizofréni (*D*) and **skizofrénia** (*E*) schizophrenia.

SKKA → SEKOLAH *Kependidikan Ketrampilan Atas.*

sklérosis (*E*) sclerosis.

SKM I (*init*) → SARJANA *Keséhatan Masyarakat.*

SKM II [Suara Karya Minggu] Sunday edition of the Golkar-oriented newspaper *Suara Karya.*

skolar (*E*) scholar.

skolastik (*D*) scholastic.

skolastis (*D*) scholastics.

skombroid *ikan –* scombroids (including mackerels, bonitos, tunas, etc.).

skontro (*D*) debit and credit side of a balance sheet.

skop I (*D*) shovel, spade.

skop II (*E*) scope; → RUANG *lingkup.*

skor (*D*) score (in sports).

   penskoran scoring.

skorbut (*D*) scurvy.

skors (*D*) suspended. *– tiga bulan tanpa gaji* suspended without pay for three months.

   menskors 1 to suspend. **2** to adjourn. *Hakim terpaksa ~ sidang.* The judge was forced to adjourn the session.

pen(g)skorsan 1 suspension. **2** adjournment.

skorsing (*D*) suspension; adjournment.

Skot (*D*) Scot, Scottish, Scotch. *orang bangsa –* Scotsman, Scotchman, Scot.

Skotlandia Scotland.

skrining (*E*) screening.

skrip I (*D*) exercise book; → BUKU *tulis.*

skrip II (*E*) script, scenario, screenplay.

skripsi (*D*) undergraduate thesis. *mempertahan –* to defend one's thesis.

skrotum (*D/E*) scrotum; → KANTUNG *buah pelir/zakar.*

sks [satuan krédit seméster] credit hours.

skuadron → SKADRON.

skul (in Bengkulu) school.

skuter (*E*) **1** (*motor –*) motor scooter. **2** scooter (a child's toy vehicle).

skwadron → SKADRON.

sl- also see entries beginning with **sel-**.

sla (*D*) salad.

slab (*E*) slab.

slada(h) SELADA.

slagorde (*D*) /slakh-/ order of battle, battle array.

slah (*D*) hang, knack. *belum tahu –nya* have not gotten the hang/knack of it.

slahrum (*D*) whipped cream.

slaid (*E*) slide.

slalom (*D*) slalom, i.e., a race in which automobiles, etc. have to show their ability to maneuver through a zigzag or winding course marked by obstacles or barriers.

slametan (*Jv*) → SELAMATAN.

slang I (*D*) tube, rubber hose, rubber pipe. *– kebakaran* fire hose.

slang II (*E*) /sléng/ slang.

sléb (*E*) slab (of crude rubber).

slebar (*Jv*) *pating –* scattered all over. *Gedung kantor ini dibangun dalam rangka menghapus kantor-kantor pemerintah yang pating – yang tidak menguntungkan.* This office building was built as part of the effort to eliminate government offices which were scattered all over (the city) and (thus) disadvantageous.

slébor I (*Jv*) fender, mudguard.

slébor II (*Pr*) **1** drunk, intoxicated. **2** stoned, high on drugs.

   sléboran *pakaian ~* inferior-quality clothes.

   kesléboran drunkenness, intoxication.

slék (*E*) slacks.

slém (*E*) (in bridge) slam. *– besar/kecil* grand/little slam.

sléndang (*Jv*) sling for carrying a child close to the body.

sléndér (*D*) **1** cylinder (of car engine). **2** steamroller.

sléndro (*Jv*) five-tone *gamelan* scale used in *wayang purwa,* etc. performances (the name may come from the *Sailendra* dynasty, which ruled Central Java in the eighth century).

sléngéan and **sléngékan** (*BG*) to do as one pleases/wants; messy, sloppy; to ad lib.

sléngér (*D*) crank (of a car), starting handle.

   mensléngér to crank, start a car with a crank.

slentik (*Jv*) **menylentik** [and **nylentik** (*coq*)] to snap s.t. with one's finger by placing the bent index finger against the back of the thumb and releasing it suddenly.

slép → BATU *slép.*

sléper (*D*) (pencil) sharpener.

slérétan zipper.

SLI [Sambungan Langsung Internasional] international long-distance direct dialing.

slilit (*Jv*) food particles stuck between the teeth. *mencukil-cukil –* to pick food particles from between the teeth.

slingkuh (*Jv*) secret, underhanded; → SELINGKUH. *berlaku –* to act in a secretive/underhanded way.

slintat-slintut (*Jv*) in secret, on the sly.

slintru (*Jv*) movable decorative screen used to partition a room, room divider.

slintutan (*Jv*) undercover, covertly, surreptitiously; → SLINTAT-SLINTUT.

slip I → SELIP II.

slip II (*E*) slip (of paper). *– krédit* credit voucher.

sliwar → SELIWAR, SELIWER.

SLJJ [Sambungan Langsung Jarak Jauh] direct-dial long-distance telephone service.

slof I (D) slipper(s), mule.

slof II (D) carton (of cigarettes).

  slof-slofan by the carton.

slogan (E) slogan.

  menslogankan to sloganize, turn s.t. into a slogan.

sloganisasi sloganization.

sloganistis (D) sloganistic.

sloka (Skr) stanza in Hindu/Buddhist texts.

sloki → SELOKI.

slomot → SELOMOT.

slomprét mild curse, damn it; → SELOMPRÉT II.

slonong (Jv) pushy, presumptuous, behaving arrogantly, too free in behavior or manners. *Masak, mentang-mentang kepala sekolah, sonder permisi main – boy aja masuk ke kelas.* Why does he think that just because he's the principal of the school that, boy, he can just push his way into the classroom.

slop → SLOF I, II.

slorok (Jv) crossbeam, crosspiece (for bolting a door).

SLTA (init) → SEKOLAH Lanjutan Tingkat Atas.

sluman, slumun, slamet (Jv) to go through thick and thin.

sm- also see entries beginning with sem-.

SM [Sebelum Maséhi] BC, Before Christ.

SMA (init) → SEKOLAH Menengah Atas.

smara (Jv) favorite, champion.

SMÉA (init) → SEKOLAH Menengah Ékonomi Atas.

smés (E) (in tennis) smash. – *setengah* half smash.

  mensmés to smash (the ball in tennis).

Sm.Hk. (init/abbr) → SARJANA Muda Hukum.

smok (E) smog.

smokel (D) smuggle.

  menyemokel to smuggle.

  persmokelan smuggling.

smoking (D) dinner jacket.

smoor → SEMUR.

SMP I (init) → SEKOLAH Menengah Pertama.

SMP II (init joc) [Sudah Makan Pulang] (coq) to eat and run.

SMU (init) → SEKOLAH Menengah Umum.

snék (E) snack.

snékbar (E) snack bar.

snélhéchter, snélhékter, and **snélhékhter** (D) k.o. binder with clips, clip binder.

snélvarband (D ob) long gauze bandage.

snob (D) snob.

snobisme (D) snobbishness.

snobismus (D) snobbery.

snobistis (D) snobbish.

snur (D) cable, cord, wire.

so (Min) → SU II.

soak (D J) /soak/ weak. *aki* – weak (car) battery; → SWAK.

soal (A) /so'al/ **1** question, problem, matter, point. *tidak menjadi –!* it's beside the point, it's not relevant; it's of no importance/consequence. *Itu bukan – saya.* That's no concern of mine, it's not my business. *bukan – baru* it's not news, it's nothing new. *itu – nanti* let's worry about that later. **2** problem, difficulty, trouble. *memecahkan suatu –* to solve a problem. *ada –* there's a problem. **3** problem, (exam) question, exercise, (set) paper. *– berhitung* arithmetic problem. *– ujian* examination question. **4** concerning, about, regarding. *– hidup-mati* and *– mati-hidup* a matter of life and death. *– jawab* a) debate. b) conversation, talk. c) question-and-answer (column in a newspaper). ***bersoal jawab*** to engage in a question-and-answer session, have a discussion. *– kecil-kecil* trivia. *– péséran buta* a trifle, s.t. unimportant.

soalnya the fact/thing/point is. *~ lama kita tak bicara léwat télepon.* The fact is that we haven't spoken on the telephone for a long time. *Apa ~?* What's up? What's the matter? *~ begini ...* the fact is that ... *itu bukan ~* that's not the point. *tentang ~* (in judgments) regarding the fact that.

  bersoal 1 to ask a question, discuss s.t. by means of questions and answers. **2** to have problems. **3** to raise a point.

  menyoal to ask s.o. a question. *Ketika disoal tentang ketatanega-*

raan, ia terdiam. When asked about the constitutional system, he remained silent.

  menyoalkan 1 to ask/inquire about. **2** to bring up for discussion. *Jangan ~ apa-apa yang belum pernah dipelajari oléh murid-murid.* Don't bring up s.t. that the students haven't learned yet.

  mempersoalkan to bring up a question about, question, find fault with, make a fuss about, bring s.t. up for discussion. *tidak usah ~ siapa yang bersalah* it's not necessary to ask who is at fault. *yang dipersoalkan* the issue is, what's at stake is.

  persoalan 1 problem, point (at issue). *Semakin hari ~ wanita semakin menjadi bertambah menarik.* From day to day the problems of women are becoming more and more interesting. **2** debate, discussion.

soang (J) goose.

soa-soa Malayan sail-finned lizard or water dragon, a lizard-like reptile (about half a meter long with hard fins extending the length of its back and tail; found only in Ambon), *Hydrosaurus amboinensis.*

SOB [Staat van Oorlog en Beleg] (D) State of War and Siege.

  men-SOB-kan to seize s.t. under this law.

soba (Jp) buckwheat.

sobat (A coq) friend, comrade, buddy; → KAWAN, SAHABAT, TEMAN. *– kental* close friend.

  bersobat to become friends, make friends (with). *~ dengan* to be on friendly terms with, be a friend of; to rub shoulders with.

  menyobati 1 to become friends with. **2** to strike up an acquaintance with.

  sobatan to make friends (with).

  persobatan friendship.

sobék torn, ripped.

  menyobék 1 to tear (a little bit/a small piece of). *Cepat-cepat sampul surat tadi disobéknya.* She quickly tore open the envelope of that letter. **2** to rip up, destroy. *~ ketenangan* to destroy tranquillity.

  menyobék-nyobék 1 to tear to shreds/pieces, tear up. *Anak kecil itu suka sekali ~ kertas.* That small child really likes to tear paper to shreds. **2** to tear repeatedly.

  menyobéki to tear s.t. up.

  menyobékkan 1 to tear s.t. away (from s.t. larger). **2** to tear s.t. for s.o. else.

  tersobék torn up, shredded, lacerated.

  sobékan 1 (a torn-off) piece, fragment. *~ buku* a torn-off piece of a book. *~ kertas* scraps of paper. **2** piece, part, portion. *Kota ini pun sebuah ~ dari neraka.* Even this town is a piece of hell. **sesobékan** a stub, a piece of s.t. torn off s.t. larger. *Dia menerima ~ tanda rétribusi parkir mobil.* He received a voucher stub as proof of having paid the parking fee. *~ kain* torn-off piece of cloth. *~ karcis* ticket stub.

  sobék-sobékan scraps, torn-up pieces.

  penyobék *~ karcis* ticket taker/collector; → PENCABIK karcis.

  penyobékan tearing (ripping) (up).

sobok I bersobok and **tersobok** *~ dengan* **1** to collide with. **2** to run into, meet. *~ langkah* to run/come across. *~ pandang* to glance at e.o.

sobok II (M) amalgam of two things in equal quantities.

  menyobokkan to mix two things in equal quantities.

societéit → SOSITÉT.

soda I (D) soda. *air –* soda water. *és – gembira* a cold drink made of soda water and red syrup.

soda II (D) sodium. *– abu* calcium hydroxide. *– api/kaustik* caustic soda. *– kué* natrium bicarbonate, baking soda.

sodét I (J) spatula.

sodét II menyodét 1 to carve up, cut through. **2** to make a waterway through.

  sodétan 1 cut, cutoff. **2** waterway, canal. **3** (geol) cut-off.

  penyodétan 1 carving up (of a territory, city). **2** broadening, widening. *proyék ~ Kali Grogol Jakarta Barat* the project of broadening the Grogol River in West Jakarta.

sodok I shovel, spade.

  menyodok to shovel, spade.

  menyodoki to shovel up. *Kuli-kuli perkuburan mulai ~ timbunan tanah.* The gravediggers began to shovel up the soil.

penyodok shovel, spade.

sodok II (*J*) *(main) bola* - (to play) billiards. *saling* - passing/overtaking s.o./another car. *Penumpang tidak suka bus saling* -. Passengers don't like it when buses pass e.o.

sodok-sodok to poke into. ~ *lubang itu, biar kodoknya keluar.* Poke into the hole so that the frogs come out.

bersodokan and **sodok-menyodok 1** to kick/push/shove e.o. **2** to push e.o. off the road.

menyodok [and **nyodok** (*coq*)] **1** to poke (into). **2** to thrust at. **3** to strike at (in *silat*). **4** (*vulg*) to have sexual intercourse with, screw. **5** (*coq*) to overtake, pass (a line of cars); → MENYALIP. **6** to arrest; → MENCIDUK. **7** to kick/throw (out). *Sodok keluar si A!* Kick A out! **8** to hit, smash. ~ *bola* to hit a ball (with a stick), i.e., play billiards.

menyodoki (*pl obj*) to poke at.

menyodokkan 1 to thrust s.t. forward, put forth (a proposal). **2** to thrust with s.t., thrust s.t. forward.

sodokan 1 shot (in billiards). **2** push, thrust, shove. ~ *siku* a push with the elbow. **3** punch.

sodok-sodokan to kick e.o., push e.o. away; to shove e.o. off the road.

penyodok s.o. who thrust s.t. forward, s.o. who puts forth s.t.

penyodokan thrusting s.t. forward.

sodok III sodokan (jargon used by pickpockets on Jakarta city buses) loot. *membawa turun ~nya di halte terdekat* to drop the loot at the nearest bus stop.

sodomi (*D/E*) sodomy; → SEMBURIT. *melakukan* - *dengan* to commit sodomy (with), sodomize. *Ia tertangkap basah melakukan* - *dengan seorang anak laki-laki.* He was caught red-handed sodomizing a boy.

bersodomi to commit sodomy.

mensodomi to sodomize.

penyodomi sodomist.

penyodomian sodomizing.

sodor I (*Jv*) **1** projecting, jutting out. **2** canopy. - *rapat* closed canopy.

menyodori [and **nyodorin** (*J coq*)] to offer, push (a chair, etc.) over to, present, hand to. ~ *kursi pada saya* to offer me a chair. *Ia disodori kertas kosong.* He was handed a blank piece of paper.

menyodorkan 1 to push forward, offer, give, hand over. **2** to stretch out (one's hand). **3** to project, propose.

tersodor presented, put forward.

penyodoran offer(ing), presenting, handing.

sodor II (*Jv*) (tournament) lance, spear with a round knob at the tip (instead of a point).

menyodor to prod with such a spear.

sodoran spear fight.

soé (*C coq*) **1** unlucky, unfortunate, ill-fated. **2** anything that brings bad luck, unlucky.

soék → SOBÉK.

Soekarno /su-/ name of the first president of the Republic of Indonesia (1901-1970).

Soekarnoisme /su-/ Soekarnoism.

soen (*D*) /sun/ a kiss; → SUN I.

mengesoen to kiss.

sofa (*D*) sofa.

sofbol (*E*) softball.

sofis (*D*) sophist.

sofisme (*D*) sophism.

sofistikasi (*E*) sophistication.

tersofistikasikan sophisticated.

soga 1 *pohon* - a tree whose bark supplies a reddish brown dyestuff, *Peltophorum pterocarpum.* **2** light brown.

menyoga to paint with *soga* (in making *batik*).

sogan a reddish-brown color.

sogang palisade of slanting posts joined by crossbeams.

sogili 1 (*ikan* -) an eel-like fish species found in Lake Poso, Central Celebes. **2** (*Min*) a Manadonese dish made from this fish.

sogok I (*uang* -) bribe, hush money. *kena* - to be bribed. *makan* - to take a bribe.

sogok-menyogok bribery. ~ *biasa di sini, bukan perkecualian.* Around here bribery is the rule, not the exception.

menyogok [and **nyogok** (*coq*)] to bribe. *Semua orang bisa disogok.* Everyone has his price.

sogokan bribe, hush money.

sogok-sogokan bribery.

penyogok bribe.

penyogokan bribery.

sogok II menyogok to prod at, poke into, stab into. ~ *saluran yang buntu* to poke into a clogged gutter.

sogok III (*Jv*) - *upil* a Javanese fancy dress consisting of a blouse and finery.

Sogo Shosa (*Jp*) Trading House.

sohib (*coq*) → friend, buddy.

sohiban to be friends.

sohibulbait (*A*) host; → SAHIBULBAIT.

sohih → SAHIH.

sohon → SOHUN.

sohor (*A*) famous, popular, noted, well-known; → BEKÉN, KONDANG I, MASYHUR. *Kota Bandung masih* - *dengan sebutan Parijs van Java.* Bandung is still well-known as the Paris of Java.

menyohorkan to make s.o./s.t. famous, put s.t. on the map.

tersohor [and **kesohor** (*coq*)] famous, popular, etc. **ketersohoran** fame, popularity.

sohun (*C*) transparent bean thread, k.o. vermicelli.

soja (*C*) bow low, kowtow (to show respect).

menyoja to bow low to, kowtow to.

tersoja-soja kowtowing, bowing low.

sok I to act as if, pretend to, not really/genuinely. *gadis cantik yang* - *jual mahal* an attractive girl pretending to be hard to get. - *aja/ aksi* to put on airs. - *iseng* to amuse o.s. by abusing/misusing one's authority. - *keminter/pinter* to be a pedant. - *tahu* to talk as if one knows about s.t. *kesok-tahuan* talking as if one knows about s.t.

kesokan pretension.

sok-sokan to give o.s. airs, brag, boast.

sok II (*D*) /sok/ sock, short stocking (reaching below the knee).

sok III (*E*) /sok/ socket, sleeve.

sok IV (*S*) often, frequently. - *kepanggih* to meet often. - *ke pasar* to go to the market often.

sok V → SYOK I.

soka → ANGSOKA.

sokah (*M*) wasteful, extravagant, spendthrift.

sokak k.o. tree, *Gnetum gnemon*; → MLINJO.

sokbréker (*D*) shock absorber; → PEREDAM *guncangan.*

sokét (*E*) socket, coupling, plug.

soklat 1 chocolate. **2** brown; → COK(E)LAT. - *pucat* pale brown.

sokoguru (*Jv*) pillar. *ASÉAN merupakan* - *politik luar negeri Indonésia.* ASEAN is the pillar of Indonesia's foreign policy.

sokom (*cla*) to smear o.s. (with charcoal).

bersokom smeared (with soot, etc.).

menyokomkan to smear (one's face), paint (with charcoal).

sokong prop, support. *tangga* - notched climbing pole. - *membawa rebah* to betray the trust placed on one.

menyokong 1 to prop (up), bear, support, back; to subsidize, sustain, maintain. *PPP yang disokong oléh Muslim* the Muslim-backed United Development Party. **2** to chip in. *Tiap orang ~.* Everybody chipped in.

sokongan 1 prop, support, backing. **2** maintenance, subsistence. **3** contribution. **4** gift, donation.

penyokong 1 supporter, backer. **2** contributor.

Soksi 1 [Séntral Organisasi Karyawan Sosialis Indonésia] Central Organization of Indonesian Socialist Workers. **2** [Swadiri Organisasi Karya Sosialis Indonésia] Independent Organization of Indonesian Socialist Work.

sok-sok (*Jv*) once in a while, every so often.

sol I (*D*) sole (of shoe). *Sepatu murah itu tak cepat habis -nya.* The soles of these cheap shoes don't wear out easily. *tukang* - shoemaker.

bersol with soles; soled. *sepatu yang ~ karét* rubber-soled shoes.

mengesol and **mensol** to sole, put a sole on (shoes).

mengesolkan and **mensolkan** to have a sole attached/repaired.

sol II (*D*) sol, the fifth note in the musical scale.

solah (*Jv*) way of acting, movements (of the body). *Dari cara berpakaian dan -nya sudah gampang ditebak. Meréka adalah* *penjual-penjual cinta "sesaat" alias tunasusila.* From their way of dressing and their actions it was easy to guess that they were sellers of "instant" love, in other words, prostitutes.

solak (*coq*) longing (for s.t.) (said of a pregnant woman who wants to eat a particular type of food); → NGIDAM.

solang (*M*) **menyolang** to contradict, go against, defy.
  solangan contradiction.

solar I (*D? E?*) *minyak –* automotive diesel oil.

solar II (*E*) solar. *sistém –* solar system.

solat → SALAT I.

solawat → SELAWAT.

soldadu → SERDADU I.

solder (*D*) attic.

soldér (*D*) solder; → PATRI.
  menyoldér to solder s.t.
  penyoldéran soldering.

soléh → SALÉH II.

solék I 1 well-dressed, dressy, elegant(ly dressed). **2** coquettish, flirtatious.
  bersolék 1 to make o.s. up, put on/apply makeup. *Rukmini sedang ~ di hadapan sebuah cermin muka yang besar.* Rukmini was putting on her makeup in front of a large mirror. **2** to dress up, be stylishly dressed, get all dressed up (usually of women).
  solék-menyolék dressing/making up.
  mempersolék to beautify, adorn. *Lampu-lampu néon ~ wajah kota.* Neon lights beautified the town.
  pemolék and **pesolék 1** coquette; dandy, fop. **2** s.o. who likes to make herself up.

solék II *buah pesolék* Japanese persimmon, *Diospyros kaki.*

Soléman Solomon. *– yang Bijak* King Solomon, the Wise.

solénoid (*D*) solenoid.

solfatar (*D*) solfatara.

solid (*E*) solid, solidary, united, cohesive.

solidaritas (*D*) solidarity, cohesiveness.

solidér (*D*) solidary, cohesive.
  kesolidéran solidarity, cohesiveness.

solilokui (*E*) soliloquy.

solis (*D*) soloist.

solo I (*D*) solo. *secara –* alone, by o.s.

solo II (*Port*) solitaire, k.o. card game.

Solo III also known as *Sala, Surakarta* and more formally as *Surakarta Hadiningrat,* a city in Central Java.

solok I penyolok and **pesolok** gift, contribution (in kind), such as food for a feast.

solok II (*ob*) **menyolok** *~ mata* striking; → COBLOS, COLOK III.

solok III (*M*) valley; → LEMBAH.
  solokan (*J*) gutter, ditch; → SELOKAN.

solot (*J*) very angry, furious, enraged. *Saya jadi – sama anak itu.* I became furious at that child.
  menyolotkan [and **nyolotin** (*J*)] to make s.o. angry, enrage.

solu (*Bat*) prau; → PERAHU, SAMPAN. *– bolon* a large prau paddled by many men. *– persadaan* a prau paddled by one man.

solusi (*E*) solution.
  menyolusi to solve (a problem).

solvabilitas (*D*) solvency.

solvén (*D*) solvent.

som I *perahu –* Siamese/Thai junk.

som II (*D*) hem.
  mengesom and **mensom** to hem.

som III (*D*) sum.

som IV *– jawa* panicled flame flower root, jewels of opar, *Talinum paniculatum.*

soma (*Skr*) **1** moon. **2** Monday.

somah (*Jv*) family, household. *– seperut* family related through the mother (irrespective of the father).

somai (*C*) Chinese snack resembling *bakso* but not using a sauce; consists of a mixture of bean curd, potatoes, and cabbage.

somasi (*D*) summons, call. *– atas tagihan* demand for payment.
  bersomasi to summon, call upon.
  menyomasi to summon.

somatik (*E*) and **somatis** (*D*) somatic, physical. *keluhan –* somatic complaints.

somay → SOMAI. *berdagang –* to deal in *somay. tukang –* seller of *somay.*

sombar (*Port IBT*) shadow.

sombé (*BG*) distant, forgetting one's friends; → SOMBONG.

sombéng (*J*) → SUMBING.

sombok (*J* from *E soundbox*) loudspeaker.

sombol menyombol to stuff, cram (food into a child's mouth).

sombong arrogant, conceited, proud, haughty, snobbish, stuck-up; → ANGKUH I, CONGKAK I, PONGAH I.
  bersombong and **menyombong** [and **nyombong** (*coq*)] to boast, brag, show off, act in a conceited/arrogant way. *Dia – di depan teman-temannya.* He boasted in front of his friends.
  menyombongi to be arrogant toward, brag to. *Tidak ada gunanya engkau ~ gurumu, engkau tidak akan lebih pandai daripadanya.* It's no use bragging to your teacher, you won't be smarter than he is.
  menyombongkan to be proud of, brag/boast about, vaunt. *~ diri* to boast about o.s. *Karena terlampau amat ~ dirinya, tidak ada lagi orang yang menaruh hormat kepadanya.* Because he brags about himself so much, nobody respects him any longer.
  kesombongan 1 conceit, arrogance, haughtiness, bragging, snobbishness, snobbery. *~ bangsa* a) racism. b) chauvinism. **2** arrogant, conceited.
  penyombong braggart, show-off.
  penyombongan boasting, bragging.

somél (*E*) sawmill.

soméng unpleasant (to see, hear); → SUMBANG I.

somoy → SOMAI.

sompak → SOMPLOK, SOMPOK.

sompal → SOMPEL I.

sompék chipped at the edge (of a table/car, etc.). *Piringnya –.* The plate is chipped.

sompel I (*Jv*) chipped at the edge.
  sompelan part (broken/chipped/bitten) off (of s.t. larger, such as a tree/arm, etc.). *Ia menyuruh anaknya Nur Asmah mencarikan ~ telinga Nurhayati Néhé, yang ditemukan di tempat kejadian.* He told his child Nur Asmah to look for the part bitten off of Nurhayati Nehe's ear which was found at the scene of the crime.

sompel II to laugh out of the wrong side of one's mouth.

sompéng (*M*) → SOMPÉK.

somp(e)lak (*J*) → SOMPÉK.

somplok (*J*) **bersomplokan** to meet/run into e.o.
  tersomplok [and **kesomplok** (*coq*)] **1** (*dengan*) run into, meet unexpectedly. *Ketika berbélok ke jalan kecil, ~ dengan polisi.* Turning into the small street, I ran into a policeman. **2** collided with, rammed into. *Sepédanya ringsek ~ mobil.* His bike was totally demolished (when it) rammed into a car.

sompoh menyompoh to carry (a child, etc.) (on the shoulders); → MENJULANG.

sompok → SOMPLOK.

sompong (*M*) full of holes.
  menyompong to put a hole in.

somprét (*J*) dammit! *–, lu!* Damn you! *– betul orang itu!* that son-of-a-gun!

somsom and **som-som** (*J*) arrogant, proud, haughty; → ANGKUH, SOMBONG.

sonar (*D/E*) sonar (detecting device).

sonata (*E*) sonata.

sonatina (*E*) sonatina.

sondai I (*M*) slanting, sloping, inclined; oblique, indirect.

sondai II → SONDÉK.

sondak → SUNDAK I.

sondang I (*M*) **menyondang** to carry on the shoulders.

sondang II menyondang to collide with, bang into.

sondéh and **sondék** *mayang –* a rubber-producing tree, *Payena leerii.*

sonder (*D*) without; → TANPA. *mét of –* with or without.

sondok (*M*) mane (of a horse).
  bersondok with a mane.

sondol I → SUNDUL I.

sondol II boost.

sondolan boost, boosting.
   penyondol booster.
sondong a shore net for catching shrimp.
   menyondong to catch shrimp with such a net.
   penyondong a shore net for catching shrimp.
sondor → SODOR I.
sonebril (*D*) sunglasses.
sonéta (*D*) sonnet.
songar (*J*/*Jv*) arrogant, haughty, affected; → SOMBONG.
   kesongaran arrogance, haughtiness, affectation.
songél tersongél (partly) protruding; → TERSEMBUL.
songér (*J*) joyful, in a good mood.
songgak (*M*) handsome, good-looking.
   menyonggakkan to improve, make s.t. better.
songgéng I → SUNGGING I.
songgéng II (*M*) to stick one's backside up (in leapfrog/cycling/
   prostrating o.s. in the Muslim prayer).
   tersonggéng with its bottom up in the air (of a sinking ship, etc.).
songgom (*Jv*) k.o. tree, *Barringtonia insignis*.
songkéh (*M*) loose, shaky, become detached.
songkét *kain* – fabric interwoven with gold or silver ornamentation
   (found in Palembang, Sumatra, and in Bali); → SUNGKIT I.
   bersongkét 1 embroidered with gold or silver threads. **2** to wear
   a *songket*.
   menyongkét to embroider with gold or silver threads.
songkok Malay fez-like cap usually made of velvet; → KOPIAH, PÉCI.
   bersongkok to wear such a cap.
songkong → SOKONG.
songkro (*Jv*) **1** pushcart; → GEROBAK *dorong*. **2** garbage cart.
songoh (*M*) **menyongoh-nyongohkan** ~ *auratnya* to keep on displaying one's genitals, be a flasher.
songong (*J*) impolite, impudent, ill-mannered, rude. *Anakmu –
   benar, orang lagi makan dia kentut.* Your child is very rude;
   while people were eating, he farted.
songsang → SUNGSANG I, II.
songsong I against, in a contrary direction to. *baju – barat* (*cla*) k.o.
   magic jacket (with which one can fly). *– arus* against the current/
   stream. *– runut* (*M*) k.o. witchcraft for predicting the future.
   bersongsong 1 to go to meet s.o. **2** oncoming. *dua mobil yang ~*
   two oncoming cars.
   menyongsong 1 to go against/into, go forward to meet. *Dengan
   susah payah kapal ~ setiap gelombang.* With great difficulty the
   ship moved forward into the waves. **2** to advance toward, meet.
   Musuh maju ~ lawan meréka. The enemy advanced to meet
   their opponents. **3** to greet, receive, welcome, extend hospitality to. *Ayah ~nya di pintu.* Father welcomed him at the door.
   ~ tamu to welcome a guest. **4** (to be) on the eve of, just before;
   on the occasion of. *~ hari kemerdékaan* on the occasion of independence day. *~ pemilihan umum* on the eve of the general
   elections.
   songsongan welcome, greeting.
   penyongsong 1 greeter. **2** welcome. *sepatah kata ~* a few words
   of welcome.
   penyongsongan greeting, welcoming.
songsong II menyongsong 1 to repay, reimburse, refund; →
   MENGGANTI. **2** to carry out, fulfill (an obligation), celebrate (a
   holiday); → MEMENUHI.
songsong III *ikan* – shell, *Murex tenuispinus*.
songsong IV (*Jv*) state umbrella.
   bersongsong to carry this state umbrella.
   penyongsong person who has the task of sheltering a dignitary
   from the sun or rain with a state umbrella.
sonji (*C*) bet, prediction of the winning lottery numbers.
sono I (*J*) over there; → SANA I. *seperti orang – bilang ...* as foreigners say ... *pemimpin sidang pun dari* – the leader of the
   session was also from over there (i.e., a Batak from Sumatra).
sono II (*Jv*) place, position, site (*esp* in names of buildings, etc.).
   senisono art gallery.
sono III (*Jv*) *dari –nya* from birth, by nature, from way back; in origin, originally. *Para Hoakiau ini suksés karena dari –nya
   sudah pandai dagang dan cukup modal.* The overseas Chinese
   are successful because from birth they are smart businessmen

with sufficient capital. *Pelaku bisnis juga bukan sétan yang dari
–nya mémang busuk.* Businessmen are also not devils who are
evil from birth.
sonokeling a tree which supplies hard wood, Indian rosewood,
   Dalbergia latifolia.
sonokembang *kayu* – sandalwood, *Pterocarpus indicus*; → ANGSANA.
sonor (*D*) sonorous; → NYARING.
sontak I (*J*/*Jv*) broken off, torn, dented, chipped.
   menyontakkan to cut/tear/rip (off), pull off, mutilate, deform,
   disfigure.
sontak II suddenly, abruptly. *Katarina – kagét dan menjerit keras.*
   Catherine was suddenly frightened and cried out loudly. *Setelah merenung, ia – mendapat ilham.* After thinking for a while,
   he suddenly got an inspiration.
   menyontakkan 1 to do s.t. suddenly, start all at once. **2** to tug at
   suddenly.
   tersontak all of a sudden, suddenly.
sonték I menyonték 1 to push/thrust aside. **2** to push/force s.t. forward. **3** to force/break open. *Pintunya sudah disonték maling.*
   The door was forced open by the thief. **4** to refuse, reject, set
   aside. **5** to violate, transgress.
   sontékan push/kick forward.
sonték II (*J*) **menyonték** [and **nyonték** (*coq*)] to cheat (on an exam
   by copying/using a crib, etc.). *Karena malas belajar, tiap kali
   ujian ia – kepada teman sebangkunya.* Because he is too lazy to
   study, every time there is an exam he copies from the person
   sitting next to him in school.
   sontékan 1 crib (sheet). **2** result of cheating/cribbing.
   penyonték cheater, cribber.
   penyontékan cheating, cribbing.
sontog (*S*) *celana* – k.o. knee-length peasant work trousers.
sontok I → SUNTUK I.
sontok II → SUNTUK II.
sontok III (*Jv*) **menyontok** to beat, strike, pound, crush to pieces/
   powder.
sontoloyo (*Jv*) **1** stupid, crazy, mad, idiotic. **2** worthless, contemptible, despicable. *Pada dasarnya ia tak menghendaki Islam –.*
   Basically he doesn't want a despicable Islam. **3** a mild curse.
sontong → SOTONG.
sontréng (*J*) talkative, garrulous, gossipy.
so'on → SOHUN.
soos → SOSITÉT.
sop (*D*) soup. *daun* – soup greens, such as celery, leeks, etc. *– ayam*
   chicken soup. *– buntut* oxtail soup. *– campur* soup with various
   k.o. cow meat in it. *– ikan* fish soup. *– kaki* soup made from goat
   legs. *– kaldu* broth. *– konro* k.o. ox-tail soup (a Makassarese specialty). *– kubis* cabbage soup. *– mokojong* soup made from dog
   meat. *– sayuran* vegetable soup. *– tito* tripe soup.
   mengesop [and **ngesop** (*coq*)] to make soup.
   mengesopkan to make a soup from (an ingredient).
sopak I a piebald skin disease, *Tinea albigena*, which appears on
   the hands and feet.
sopak II (*J*) **menyopak** to break down or force open (a door,
   etc.).
   sopak-sopak completely destroyed.
sopak III (*J*) **menyopak** to bind/wrap up, put a cast on (a broken
   limb).
sopan 1 polite, civil, courteous, correct (in behavior), well-mannered.
   Orangnya –. The person was polite. *menjawab dengan* – to answer politely. **2** decent, respectable, distinguished. **3** respectful,
   ladylike, gentlemanly. *Dengan – ia mempersilakan tamunya
   duduk.* He respectfully invited the visitor to have a seat. *bersikap
   –* to have a respectful attitude. *berlaku amat – kepada kedua orangtuanya* to behave respectfully toward both one's parents. *Sebagai gadis, kau lebih baik –.* As a girl, you should be ladylike. *–
   santun* ethical, correct, decorous, proper/refined (behavior).
   kesopan-santunan politeness, etiquette, manners, proper/cor-
   rect behavior.
   menyopani to be polite to, behave politely/courteously toward.
   menyopankan to cultivate (good manners), civilize, refine.
   menyopan-nyopankan to do s.t. with exaggerated politeness.
   kesopanan 1 politeness, decency, courteousness, courtesy, mo-

rality. *Itu dilakukannya untuk ~ saja.* He did it purely out of politeness. **2** civilization, norms of behavior; good behavior. *Bangsa-bangsa di dunia mempunyai ~ yang berbéda-béda.* The world's nations have different norms of behavior. *Perbuatannya sudah melanggar ~ timur.* His actions have gone against Asian norms of behavior.

sopi (*D zoopje*) alcoholic drink. *– manis* liqueur. *– pahit* gin, geneva, Dutch gin.

sopia (*C*) sweetened cake made from dried beans.

sopir (*D*) driver (of a car, etc.), chauffeur. *– batangan* the official licensed driver (of a bus or taxi). *– bécak* pedicab driver. *– maut* hearse driver. *– témbak* an unofficial unlicensed driver who drives a bus or taxi.

   menyopir to drive.

   menyopiri to drive s.t.

sopo (*Jv*) who; → SIAPA. *– siro – ingsung* every man for himself; → SIAPA *lu siapa gua.*

soporifik (*E*) soporific.

sopran (*D*) soprano. *penyanyi –* soprano.

soprano → SOPRAN.

sorah → SURAH.

sorai → SORAK *sorai.*

sorak 1 cry, shout, yell. **2** applause, cheering. *– gembira* shout of joy. *dulu – kemudian tohok* don't count your chickens before they're hatched. *– senang* jumping for joy. **bersorak senang** to jump for joy. *– sorai* cheers, shouts, applause; → TEMPIK II. *Dia disambut dengan ~ penonton.* She was welcomed by the applause of the spectators. **bersorak sorai** to shout with joy, applaud, greet with cheers. *Penduduk désa ~ mendengar suara letusan petasan.* The villagers shouted with joy on hearing the sound of the firecrackers exploding.

   menyoraki [and **nyorakin** (*J coq*)] **1** to acclaim, cheer. **2** to shout/hoot at, jeer, boo. *~ orang yang keplését* to hoot at the person who slipped. **3** to call out to.

   menyorakkan and **mempersorakkan 1** to cheer s.o. **2** to hoot at, jeer. **3** to shout out, cry out. *~ barang-barang yang akan dilélang* to shout out the goods up for auction.

   sorakan uproar, clamor, applause. *~ meréka masih berlanjut-lanjut.* Their applause went on and on.

   penyorak s.o. who cheers (a match, etc.), applauder.

sorang (*J*) clipped form of *seorang*, a (single) person.

   sorangan alone, by o.s.; → SENDIRIAN. *~ waé?* All alone? All by yourself? (said to a girl sitting in a pedicab, etc.). *Meréka masih ~.* They are still single/unmarried.

sorban → SERBAN.

sorbét (*D*) sorbet, sherbet.

sordam (*Bat*) a flute with five holes *usu* played by the Karo Batak to conjure up the spirits of the dead.

soré (*J/Jv*) (*hari –*) **1** afternoon. **2** early evening. *main –* to play vigorously (at the end of a soccer match). *. nanti – and – nanti* later (this afternoon) (said earlier in the same day). *-.- hari and – sekali* late in the afternoon. *– harinya* in the afternoon (of the same day).

   sorénya that (very) afternoon, in the afternoon (of that day). *Rombongan Présidén makan siang di hotél itu dan pada ~ Présidén menerima kunjungan kehormatan Menteri Luar Negeri Swiss Aubert.* The President's party had lunch at the hotel and that afternoon the President received a courtesy call from the Swiss Foreign Minister Aubert.

   soré-soré toward evening.

   kesoréan 1 (too) late, i.e., in the afternoon rather than in the *siang*, the next earlier time period. **2** (too) early, i.e., in the afternoon rather than in the *malam*, the next later time period.

soréh → SURIH.

sorék (*ob*) k.o. bamboo than can be used to make rope.

sorén I (*S*) **menyorén** to insert at the waist. *keris/pedang disorén* a kris/sword inserted at the waist.

   tersorén inserted at the waist.

sorén II (*J*) humus.

sorga → SURGA.

sorgawi → SURGAWI.

sorg(h)um (*E*) sorghum.

sori (*E*) sorry. *–, Man. Aku kemarin tak bisa datang.* Sorry, Man. I couldn't make it yesterday. *minta –* to apologize, ask forgiveness.

sorjan → SURJAN I.

sorog (*J*) **menyorog** to shake a tree until the fruits fall down; to prod at fruits with a pole so that they fall down.

   sorogan (fruit) fallen down as a result of shaking the tree or prodding the fruit with a pole (not because the fruit has ripened on the tree).

   sorogan (in a *pesantrén*) the study of the *kitab kuning* under the leadership of a *kiyai*; he dictates the translation, which the students, sitting cross-legged in front of him, write down under the Arabic original.

sorok I (*ob*) *pintu –* sliding door; → PINTU *sorong.*

sorok II → SURUK.

sorok III → SOGOK I.

sorolok a sifting device used to separate broken hulled rice from the grains.

sorong 1 pushed/slid forward; sliding. *kotak –* drawer (in a chest). *pintu –* sliding door. **2** push, shove. *air – buih* tide on the turn after the ebb tide. *angin – buritan* following/tailwind. *gerobak –* wheelbarrow. *keréta –* pushcart. **3** bribe; → UANG *suap. kena/makan –* bribed, taking bribes. **4** valve, damper, slide. *tahan jerat – kepala* those who lay traps for others get caught themselves.

   menyorong(kan) 1 to push/slide s.t. forward. *~ mobil mogok* to push a stalled car forward. **2** to bribe, grease s.o.'s palm. *Dia hendak ~ pegawai pabéan itu.* He was going to bribe the customs officer. **3** to extend, stretch forward, give, hand over, pass (over). *~ tepak sirih* to pass the betel box. *~ tangan* to hold out one's hand. **4** to propose, suggest. *~ damai* to ask for an armistice, offer terms. **5** to force s.t. (on). *Orang selalu ~ kegiatannya kepadanya.* People always forced their activities on him. **6** to urge (s.o. to do s.t.). **7** (*vulg*) to fuck, screw.

   menyorong-nyorongkan to force/intrude (o.s.) (on). *Ia selalu ~ dirinya kepada bakal menantunya.* He always intruded on his in-laws.

   tersorong 1 went too far. **2** pushed. (*M*) *~ kata-kata* to shoot off one's mouth; → KATA/MULUT *terdorong.*

   sorongan 1 s.t. pushed/shoved forward. **2** device used to push/shove s.t. forward. **3** gift, present. **4** bribe.

sorot ray, beam (of light), gleam, shine; → SINAR I. *di bawah – bulan* in the moonlight. *gambar –* a) slide projector. b) (*Mal*) movie theater. *– balik* flashback. *– mata* glance, look.

   menyorot 1 to shine, gleam, beam, glitter. **2** to draw attention to, focus on. *disorot* to be in the limelight. *saat kaméra télévisi ~ tersangka* when the television camera focused on the suspect. **3** to look/gaze (into).

   menyoroti [and **nyorotin** (*J coq*)] **1** to light (up), shine on, shine a light on, illuminate, spotlight. *Biliknya hanya disoroti dengan lampu minyak.* The room was only lit by an oil lamp. **2** to shed light on, look at critically. *kejadian yang ingin saya soroti* events I would like to shed some light on.

   menyorotkan [and **nyorotin** (*J coq*)] **1** to illuminate, throw light on, shine on, spotlight. **2** to radiate. **3** to shine s.t. (a flashlight, etc.) (onto s.t.). **4** to direct (one's eyes/a camera). *Ayah Yashiko ~ matanya ke muka adiknya.* Yashiko's father directed his gaze onto his sister's face.

   tersorot 1 shined, projected. *title yang ~ proyéktor ke layar bioskop* the titles projected by the projector on the movie screen. **2** focused on, illuminated. *personil yang jarang ~* personnel who are rarely focused on. **3** gazed at, looked at.

   tersoroti illuminated, spotlighted, focused on.

   sorotan 1 ray, beam; radiation. **2** illumination. **3** spotlight; focus of attention. *lepas dari ~* escaped one's attention, out of the spotlight. *Penyelundupan emas menjadi ~ masyarakat akhir-akhir ini.* Gold smuggling has become the focus of public attention recently. *dalam ~ masyarakat* in the public eye.

   penyorot reflector, projector. *lampu ~* a) searchlight. b) flashlight.

   penyorotan 1 illuminating, spotlighting. **2** elucidating.

sortasi sorting.

sortir (*D*) *tukang –* sorter, s.o. who sorts letters, etc.

   menyortir to sort (the mail, etc.).

   tersortir sorted.

penyortiran sorting (the mail, etc.).

sos I (D) 1 sauce. 2 gravy.

sos II clipped form of sositét.

sos III (in acronyms) → SOSIAL.

Sosba [(Ilmu Pengetahuan) Sosial dan Bahasa] (Department of) Social Sciences and Languages (in a Senior High School).

sosbud → SOSIAL budaya.

sosék → SOSIAL ékonomi.

sosékbud → SOSIAL, ékonomi, budaya.

sosi (C) key (to a lock).

sosial (D) 1 social. fungsi – social function. Départemén – [Dépsos] Department of Social Affairs. 2 sociable, gregarious, friendly. – Budaya [sosbud] sociocultural. – démokrasi social democracy. – démokrat social democrat. – ékonomi [sosék] socioeconomic. keadaan – ékonomi buruh the socioeconomic conditions of the workers. – kontrol social control. mensosialkontrolkan to exercise social control over. 3 charitable, generous.

mensosialkan to socialize.

kesosialan 1 social. 2 sociability.

pensosialan socialization.

sosialis (D) socialist. – kanan [soska] right-wing socialist. – kiri [soski] left-wing socialist.

mensosialiskan to make socialistic.

sosialisasi (D) 1 socialization. 2 putting s.t. out into the community to teach them about it or to get their reactions, publicizing.

mensosialisasikan and menyosialisasikan 1 to socialize. 2 to put s.t. out into the community for their reactions, publicize.

tersosialisasi socialized.

pensosialisasian socialization, putting out into the community, publicizing.

sosialisir (D) mensosialisir to socialize.

sosialisme (D/E) socialism.

sosialistis (D) socialistic.

sosialitas (D) sociality.

sosiatri sociology of deviant behavior.

sosiawan man who is concerned for his fellow human beings, social-minded man.

sosiawati woman who is concerned for her fellow human beings, social-minded woman.

sosiobudaya sociocultural.

sosiodrama (E) sociodrama.

sosiografi (E) sociography.

sosiokrat (E) sociocrat.

sosiokultural (E) sociocultural.

sosiolinguistik (E) sociolinguistics.

sosiolog (D) sociologist.

sosiologi (D/E) sociology; → WIDYAWARGA. – pedésaan rural sociology.

sosiologis (D) sociologist.

sosiométri (D) sociometrics.

sosiométris (D) sociometric.

sosiopat (E) sociopath.

sosiopolitik (E) sociopolitical.

sosiopsikologi (E) sociopsychological.

sosis (D) sausage.

sositét (D) social club; → KAMAR bola.

soska → SOSIALIS kanan.

soski → SOSIALIS kiri.

sosoh I (Jv) menyosoh to remove the husks from (rice) with a mortar and pestle, husk, hull; → MENCERUH.

sosohan husked, hulled. beras ~ husked rice.

penyosoh husker, huller. mesin ~ rice huller.

penyosohan husking, hulling. ~ beras rice-hulling mill.

sosoh II (M) bersosoh to do s.t. vigorously. perang ~ all-out war.

menyosoh 1 to do s.t. vigorously/in large amounts. ~ bekerja to work hard. ~ makan to eat a lot at one sitting. 2 to engage in combat, fight.

sosok I 1 hole through which s.t. is passed. – butang terdapat pada sebelah kiri keméja itu. The buttonholes are located on the left side of the shirt. 2 (naut) bend, hitch. – anyam (naut) sheet bend. – jaras hawser bend. – pikul carrick bend.

pesosok hole through which s.t. is passed.

sosok II 1 carcass, frame(work), skeleton (of a boat). 2 shape, appearance, (shape of the) body, figure, build, stature. – buku the outer appearance of the book. – tubuhnya sama seperti ayahnya. He has the same build as his father. 3 figure, person. – politik a political figure. 4 classifier for bodies/figures. sebuah/suatu – and se– tubuh a shape, form, figure. Se– mayat bayi ditemukan dalam tumpukan sampah. A baby's corpse was found in a garbage dump. Dua – mayat ditemukan mengambang di tengah laut. Two corpses were found floating on the high seas. Baru saja ia keluar, se– tubuh mengikutinya dari belakang. He had just gone out when a (shadowy) figure followed him from behind. 5 (M) a future (field/country, etc.); s.t. that is just taking shape. – cencang nénék moyang family heirlooms.

bersosok to have a form/shape, take shape, have the form/silhouette of.

menyosok 1 to set up the framework (of a house, etc.), frame. 2 to lay (a ship's keel). 3 to found (a town, state).

sosokan (J) /soso'an/ small box.

sosol I (J) menyosol to gobble up with its bill; → SOSOR I.

sosol II menyosol to appear suddenly/out of nowhere, emerge.

sosong I → SONGSONG I.

sosong II → SONGSONG II.

sosor I (Jv) beak, bill.

menyosor 1 to attack with the beak. 2 to peck.

sosor II (Jv) – bébék life plant, Kalanchoe pinnata.

sosot (BG) girlfriend, date.

nyosot to go on a date.

SosPol [(Ilmu Pengetahuan) Sosial dan Politik] Department of Sociopolitics (in a senior high school).

kesospolan sociopolitical.

sosro bahu pier (support for the ends of a bridge), a hydraulic nonfriction rotating device system.

SOTK [struktur organisasi dan tata kerja] organizational and methodological structure.

soto (C?) a soup-like dish, usu served with lontong. – ayam k.o. chicken soup with bean sprouts, scallions, cellophane noodles, lemon slices, hot chili, egg slices, fried onion bits, and sweet soy sauce. – babat tripe soup. – Betawi k.o. soto with meat and vegetable stock. – Madura similar to soto ayam, eaten with cooked rice and potato fritters cut into quarters. – tangkar k.o. meat soup.

menyoto to make soto out of s.t.

sotoh (A) flat roof.

bersotoh with such a roof.

sotok sotokan catch (of nenér fish).

penyotok s.o. who catches (nenér fish).

sotong various species of cuttlefish, squid, and octopus. – katak various species of cuttlefish, Sepia/Sepiella spp. – ketupat Indian squid, Loligo spp. – kurita various species of octopus, Octopus spp. and other species.

sotor → SOTOH.

sot tém (E coq) short time, one sex act with a prostitute. Saya tidak mau semalam. Saya maunya –. I don't want the whole night. I want a short time.

so'un → SOHUN, SUUN.

so(u)venir (D) souvenir.

Soviét (D) Soviet. – Rusia Soviet Russia. – Uni Soviet Union.

mensoviétkan to sovietize. Kuba ~ nonblok. Cuba sovietized the nonaligned nations.

Soviétisasi (E) sovietization.

sovinis (D) chauvinist.

sovinisme (D) chauvinism.

Sovyét → SOVIÉT.

sowan (Jv) and menyowani to visit (a social superior).

sowanan custom of visiting one's relatives of an older generation.

sowangan → KOANGAN.

sowék → SOBÉK.

soyak I blaze (on a tree).

soyak II – seloyak torn to shreds.

menyoyak-nyoyak to tear to shreds.

sp- also see entries beginning with SEP-

S.P. I [Sarjana Pendidikan] Master of Education, M.Ed.

S.P. II [Sri Paduka] His/Your Excellency.

spaakbor → SPATBOR(D).

spada (J) [siapa ada] anybody home? (said when entering s.o.'s house).

spagéti (E?) spaghetti.

spak (D coq) wheel spoke; → RUJI II.

spakbor(d) → SPATBOR(D).

spalk (D) splints.
menspalk to splint, insert splints into.

span (D) tight (of pants/skirt, etc.); → KETAT, METETET. celana – tights. rok – tight-fitting skirt; → SPANROK.

spanduk (D) banner attached at both ends to poles, trees, etc.

spaneng and **spaning** (D) **l** tension, voltage. turun – loss of tension. **2** pressure. **3** tension, strain, stress. naik – to become angry. **4** (sl) sexually excited, hot, horny. naik – to get sexually excited. – listrik electric tension. (arus listrik) – tinggi high tension (electric current). – udara atmospheric pressure.

spanrok (D) tight-fitting skirt.

Spanyol I (Port) **1** Spain. **2** Spanish.

spanyol II [separo nyolong] → KAYU spanyol.

sparepart (E) /spér-/ spare part; → ONDERDIL, SUKU cadang.

sparing (E) sparring (in boxing).

spasi (D) space (in typing/writing, etc.). – rangkap double space, double-spaced.

spat (D naut) spar.

spatbor(d) (D) (car) fender, mudguard (of a pedicab, etc.).
berspatbor(d) to have a fender.

SPAU [Sekolah Penerbangan Angkatan Udara] Air Force Flight School.

SPBU [Setasiun Pengisian Bahan Bakar (untuk) Umum] gas station.

special branch (E) (in Papua New Guinea) intelligence.

speedométer /spi-/ → SPIDOMÉTER.

speed terbang (in West Kalimantan) speedboat (at high speed it seems to fly over the water).

spék I (D) bacon.

spék II (E) specs, specifications.

spék(k)oek (D) (spiced) layer cake.

spéktakulér (D) spectacular.

spéktator (E) spectator.

spéktogram (D/E) spectrogram.

spéktrum (D/E) spectrum.

spékuk → SPÉK(K)OEK.

spékulaas (D) spiced windmill cookies.

spékulan (D) speculator. – beli bull (in the stock market).

spékulas → SPÉKULAAS.

spékulasi (D) **1** speculation. **2** conjecture, guess.
berspékulasi **1** to speculate. **2** to suppose, presume, conjecture. **3** to depend on (s.o.), count on (s.o. or s.t.).
menspékulasikan **l** to speculate with. **2** to suppose, take a guess at.

spékulatif (D) speculative.

spékulator (E) speculator.

spéleng and **spéling** (D) play, clearance.

spéléolog (D) speleologist, cave explorer.

spéléologi (D/E) speleology, cave exploring.

spén larder, small storeroom near the kitchen.

spérma (D) sperm; → PEJU(H).

spérmatogénésis (D) spermatogenesis.

spérmatologi (D/E) spermatology.

spérmatozoa (D/E) spermatozoa.

spérmiofag (E) spermatophage.

spési (D) mortar. – kapur lime mortar.

spésial (D) special, particular; with special ingredients; → ISTIMÉWA.
bakmi goréng – special fried noodles (with eggs).

spésialis (D) specialist. – penyakit kulit dermatologist.

spésialisasi 1 specialization. **2** to specialize.
berspésialisasi to specialize, specialized. ketrampilan yang ~ a specialized skill.
menspésialisasi ~ diri to specialize.
terspésialisasi(kan) specialized, to specialize (in). Dia ~ dalam bidang manajemén. He specializes in the field of management.

spésialitas (D) specialty.

spésiés (D) species.

spésifik (E) specific.
kespésifikan specificity.

spésifikasi (D) specification.
men(g)spésifikasi to specify.

spésimén (E) specimen, sample.

spét (D) syringe.

SPG [Sales Promotion Girl] girl who works at trade shows and exhibitions.

spidol (E?) k.o. felt pen, marker.

spidbot (E) speedboat.

spidométer (E) speedometer.

spiko → SPÉKULAAS.

spion (D) spy. – bermuka dua double agent. – Melayu amateurish spy. – top master spy.
menspioni and menyepioni to spy on.
spion-spionan (to play) spies.

spionase (D) espionage. – industri industrial espionage.

spir (D ob) muscle.

spiral (D) **1** spiral. **2** IUD (contraceptive device).
menspiralkan to insert an IUD.

spirit (E) spirit, enthusiasm. – konco-koncoan cronyism.

spiritis (D) spiritualist.

spiritisme (D) spiritualism.

spiritual (E) spiritual. material dan – material and spiritual.

spiritualisasi (D) spiritualization.

spiritualisme (D/E) spiritualism.

spiritualitas (D) spirituality.

spirituil (D) spiritual.

spiritus (D) spirit(s), alcohol. kompor – spirit stove. lampu – spirit lamp.

spirométer (D) spirometer.

SPJ (init) [Surat Perintah Jalan] Travel Order.
men-SPJ-kan to issue a travel order for. Uang makan bagi karyawan itu di-SPJ-kan. A travel order was issued for food money for the employees.

SPK → SURAT Perintah Kerja.

split (E) room (air conditioner).

SPLP (init) → SURAT perjalanan laksana paspor.

SPMB [séléksi penerimaan mahasiswa baru] new student acceptance selection.

spon(s) (D) (foam rubber) sponge; → SEPON.

sponéng (D) groove, rabbet.

sponsor (D/E) sponsor.
mensponsori to sponsor, act as a sponsor for.

sponsorisasi sponsoring, sponsorship.

spontan (D) spontaneous; → SWAKARYA.
kespontanan spontaneity.

spontanitas (D) spontaneity.

spor → SEPUR.

spora (D) spore.

sporadis (D) sporadic.

sport (D/E) sport(s).

sportif (D) sportsmanlike.
kesportifan sportsmanship.

sportivitas (D) sportsmanship.

spréi (D) (bed)sheet.

spréken (D infr) (jokingly) holand – to speak Dutch; → KARÉSÉH-PÉSÉH.

sprémpi (sl) a quarter of a gram (of drugs).

Spri [Staf pribadi] Personal Staff.

sprint (D) sprint.

sprinter (D) sprinter.

S.Psi. [Sarjana Psikologi] Master of Psychology, M.Ps.

spt I (abbr) [seperti] as, like.

SPT II → SURAT pemberitahuan.

spuit (D) /spét/ (hypodermic) needle, syringe; → SPÉT.

spur → SEPUR.

sputnik (D) sputnik.

sputum (D) sputum, saliva.

spy (abbr) [supaya] so that.

squash and – rakét /skwosy rakét/ racketball, a game played with rackets and a small ball in an enclosed court.

sr- also see entries beginning with **ser-**.

SR [Sekolah Rakyat/Rendah] Elementary/Grade School.

srabi (*Jv*) k.o. pancake.

srabutan → SERABUTAN.

srati (*Jv*) **1** mahout. **2** s.o. who takes care of people or who tends to animals. – *babi* swineherd.

sreet (*onom*) swish, sound of razor cutting into flesh.

sreg and **srek** (*Jv*) **1** adequate, fitting. *kurang* – not enough, insufficient. – *dengan* to match, suit, agree with. **2** to feel good/comfortable.

  mensregkan to make adequate.

sregep (*Jv*) industrious.

srempeng (*Jv*) enthusiastic, in earnest.

  menyrempeng *disrempeng* done with enthusiasm.

sréng (*Jv*) sizzling sound. *mercon* – skyrocket. – *dor* fireworks which explode in the air.

srengéngé (*Jv*) sun; → MATAHARI I, SURYA.

srepegan (*Jv*) k.o. Javanese musical form accompanying a fight scene.

sreset (*onom*) clip, clip, clip; sound made when cutting hair.

sri (*Jv*) **1** a personal name element. **2** title for royal persons. – *Baginda* His/Her Majesty. – *Paus* His Holiness the Pope (or, Pope ...). – *Ratu* Her Majesty the Queen. – *Sultan* His Majesty the Sultan (of Yogyakarta). **3** goddess of rice, and *Déwi* –.– *Sedana* a) the goddess of rice Sri and her spouse Sedana. b) symbol of prosperity.

sribombok (*Jv*) a long-necked, long-legged white-breasted water hen.

srigading coral jasmine, sorrowful tree, k.o. plant, *Nyctanthes arbortristis*.

srigunggu (*Jv*) → LAMPIN *budak*.

srigunting (*Jv*) various species of drongos, *Dicrurus spp.* – *hitam* black drongo, *Dicrurus macrocercus*. – *kelabu* ashy drongo, *Dicrurus leucophaeus*. – *lencana* spangled drongo, *Dicrurus bracteatus*.

Srikandi 1 one of *Arjuna*'s two main wives (the other is *Sumbadra*), a talkative, strong-willed, warm-hearted woman, fond of hunting and fighting other *satrya*, or members of the aristocratic warrior class. **2** brave female warrior, heroine. *kaum* – warlike women. – *Jamilah* Heroine Jamilah.

srikaya custard apple, *Annona squamosa*.

Srilangka and **Sri Langka** Sri Lanka, formerly Ceylon.

srimpét → SERÉMPÉT.

srimpi → SERIMPI.

srimpung (*Jv*) rope tied around the legs.

  menyrimpung to bind (around the legs). *Kakinya disrimpung tali rafia.* His feet were bound with a raffia rope.

srintil (*Jv*) very expensive first-quality tobacco.

sripah (*Jv*) dead person; death.

  kesripahan to lose (s.o. to death); → KEMATIAN. *Sri Sultan* ~. His Majesty the Sultan lost his ... (to death).

sripanggung prima donna.

srisip (*Jv*) tiller (on rice plant); → GERAGIH.

SRIT [Sekolah Républik Indonésia Tokyo] Republic of Indonesia School in Tokyo.

sriti (*Jv*) k.o. swallow, *Collacalia esculenta*.

sriwang (*Jv?*) *burung* – Asian paradise flycatcher, *Terpsiphone paradisi*.

Sriwijaya 1 the name of the South Sumatran maritime kingdom which existed from the seventh to the fourteenth centuries. *Bumi* – South Sumatra. *Gending* – a court dance of Sumatra. *kedatuan* – Principality of Sriwijaya. *Kota* – Palembang. **2** name of the army division stationed in South Sumatra.

srobot → SEROBOT.

sromo (*Jv*) k.o. sharecropping arrangement in Central Java in which the peasant *usu* takes care of the cultivation, and pays key money to the landowner for use of the land; 70 percent of the yield goes to the landowner and 30 percent to the cultivator.

srong (*Jv?*) *ikan* – whale; → IKAN *paus*.

sronggot (*Jv?*) snout (of a pig); tusk (of a boar).

  menyronggot to hit. *disronggot lokomotif* hit by a locomotive.

sroto k.o. chicken soup from Banyumas.

sruduk → SERUDUK.

sruput (*Jv*) gulp, draft. *secangkir kecil téh yang habis sekali* – a small cup of tea finished in one gulp.

SS → SHABU-SHABU.

SS-77 [Senjata Serbu-77] an attack weapon manufactured by *Pindad/Pusat Industri Angkatan Darat* in Bandung.

SSK → SATUAN *setingkat kompi*.

SSP → SURAT *setoran pajak*.

SSS (*init*) → SUKA *sama suka*.

ssst (*onom*) sh! shush! (exclamation calling for silence).

st- also see entries beginning with SET-.

ST [sarjana téknik] engineer.

Staatsblad (*D*) Statute Book, Official Gazette.

stabil (*D*) stable; → MANTAP I. – *terhadap* can withstand, will stand up to/against. *tidak* – unstable. *tidak* – unstable. **ketidak-stabilan** instability.

  meyetabil to stabilize, become stable.

  menyetabilkan and **menstabilkan** to stabilize s.t.

  kestabilan stability. ~ *harga* price stability.

  penstabil stabilizer. *faktor* ~ stabilizing factor.

  penstabilan stabilization.

stabilisasi (*D*) stabilization.

  menstabilisasikan to stabilize.

stabilisator (*D*) stabilizer.

stabilitas (*D*) stability.

stabilo (*a brand name*) **1** highlighter. **2** brightly colored.

stadia (*pl of stadium*) stages (of a disease).

stadion (*D*) stadium. – *balap anjing* dog track.

  perstadionan stadium (*mod*).

staf (*D*) **1** staff. *kepala* – chief of staff. *seorang* – staff member. **2** staff member. – *pengajar* a) teaching staff. b) member of the teaching staff. – *rédaksi* editorial board.

  berstaf staffed with; to have a staff consisting of. *sebuah grup yang* ~ 5 *mahasiswa FEUI* a group staffed with 5 students of the University of Indonesia School of Economics.

stafel (*D*) top to bottom of a balance sheet or budget page.

stagén → SETAGÉN.

stagflasi (*E*) [stagnasi dan inflasi] (an economic state of) stagnation and inflation.

stagnan (*E*) stagnant.

stagnasi (*D*) stagnation.

staking (*D coq*) strike, picketing; → PEMOGOKAN.

stal I (*D*) stable (for horses).

stal II (in acronyms) → INSTALASI.

stalagmit (*D*) /stalakmit/ stalagmite.

stalagtit (*D*) /stalaktit/ stalactite.

stales (*D*) stalls (in a theater), i.e., the set of seats in the part of a theater nearest to the stage.

Stalinisme (*D/E*) Stalinism.

stalpén (*Jv*) a pen (with a half-tubular metal point split into two nibs).

stambom (*D*) genealogy, pedigree, lineage, family tree.

stambuk (*D*) **1** (of persons) book of genealogy, family register. **2** (of horses/dogs, etc.) studbook. **3** (of cattle) herd book.

stambul I (*komidi* –) itinerant stage show.

Stambul II Istanbul/Constantinople (the former capital of Turkey).

stamina (*E*) stamina; → KETAHANAN.

  berstamina with stamina. ~ *tinggi* having a lot of endurance/stamina.

stamplas (*J*) → STANPLAT.

stampot (*D*) hotchpotch (of potatoes/cabbage/meat).

stan(d) I (*D*) score (in sports).

stan(d) II (*D*) stand, booth (in a trade fair, etc.). – *surat kabar* newsstand.

standar I (*D*) standard (of quality/living, etc.). – *ganda* double standard. – *hidup* standard of living, living standard.

  menstandarkan to standardize.

  penstandaran standardization.

standar II (*D*) standard, i.e., flag or banner used as a symbol of a military unit.

standar III (*D*) **1** (kick)stand, i.e., bicycle or motorcycle standard attached to the hub of the rear wheel or other spot, which holds the bike upright when not in use. 2 stand, rack, pedestal, etc. on which s.t. can be placed. *Tarohlah TVnya di –.* Put the TV set on the stand.

menstandarkan to put (a bike, etc.) on its stand.

standardisasi (*D*) standardization.

standpak (*D*) packaging.

stang (*D*) 1 bar (on a vehicle, etc.); → STIRSTANG. 2 handlebar(s) (of a bicycle). *– séger* piston rod.

staniol (*D*) tinfoil.

stanplat (*D*) 1 (bus) stop; → HALTE. 2 taxi stand.

stansa and **stanza** (*D*) stanza.

star (*D med*) cataract.

starko pager (from a Japanese brand name); → RADIO *panggil.*

start (*D/E*) 1 start. *uang – (coq)* initial capital. 2 to depart, leave; → BERANGKAT. *Kita harus – pagi-pagi benar.* We have to leave very early. *– pertama* flag fall (of taxicab).

menstart to start. *Mobil anda sukar distart?* Is your car hard to start?

starter (*D*) starter (of car, etc.).

menstarter and **menyetarter** to start (an engine). *Mobilnya distarter.* He turned on the ignition of his car.

Staséangraph (*infr*) a shorthand system developed for *ASEAN.*

stasi (*D*) station (of the Cross).

stasion → STASIUN.

stasionér (*D*) stationary.

stasiun (*D*) (railway/radio, etc.) station, terminal. *– bus* bus terminal. *– dirgantara* space station. *– hujan* rain gauge station. *– gangguan* jamming station (of radio broadcasts). *– induk* base station. *– kaméra* camera station. *– keberangkatan* departure terminal. *– keréta api* railway/road station. *– komunikasi* communication base. *– lintas tipis* light traffic station (for satellites). *– orbital* orbiting/space station. *– pancar-ulang* relay station. *– pemeriksaan* checking station. *– pelacak bertenaga nuklir* nuclear-powered tracking station. *– pengamatan* tracking/monitoring station. *– pengendali* (communications) tracking and command station (at Cibinong). *– pengisian bahan bakar umum* [SPBU] gas station. *– penguapan* evaporation station. *– pengukuran* gauging station. *– penyambung* (telecommunications) repeater station. *– peralihan* transfer station. *– pertanian* agricultural station. *– pertolongan pertama* first-aid station. *– radio* radio station. *– ruang angkasa* space station. *– satelit bumi* earth satellite station. *– tenaga listrik* power station. *– utama pengendali satelit* satellite master control station.

statemen(t) (*E*) /stét-/ statement; → PERNYATAAN.

stater → STARTER.

statif (*D*) stative.

statis (*D*) static. *listrik –* static electricity.

kestatisan staticness. *tetapi ~ itu jangan sampai mempengaruhi upaya menghadapi modernisasi* but that staticness should not affect efforts to face modernization.

statistik 1 (*D*) statistics. 2 (*E*) statistical.

perstatistikan statistics (*mod*). *kegiatan ~* statistics activities.

statistikawan (*infr*) and **statistikus** (*D*) statistician.

statistis (*D*) statistical.

statistisi (*kaum –*) statisticians.

status (*D*) status.

berstatus with/to have a status. *~ diplomat* with diplomatic status.

status quo (*L*) status quo, existing conditions.

statuta and **statuten** (*D*) statutes.

statutér (*D*) statutory.

stéarin (*D/E*) stearin.

stéger (*D*) pier, jetty, landing stage.

stégodon (*E*) stegodon.

sték cutting, slip (of a plant).

stéker (*D*) 1 (electric wall)plug; → TUSUK *kontak. – betina (elec)* jack. 2 cigarette lighter.

stél (*D*) a (matched) set; → SETÉL I.

stélan a) a (matched) set. b) a suit (jacket and matching trousers). c) uniform. *~ olahragawan* training suit. *~ Panglima AD Belanda* a Dutch army general's uniform. **berstélan** wearing a suit (of clothes). *~ abu-abu* wearing a gray suit.

stéling (*D mil*) position.

berstéling to take up a position. *Kawan-kawan bersenjata bambu runcing harus sudah ~ keliling rumah.* Friends armed with bamboo spears must have already taken up positions around the house.

menstéling and **menyetéling** 1 to place (soldiers) in position, position (troops). 2 to take up a position. 3 to surround, encircle (a house, etc.).

stélionat (*D leg*) swindle, fraud (*esp* in land or mortgage dealings).

stélsel (*D*) system; → SISTÉM.

stém (*D*) vote. *melakukan – untuk* to vote for.

menstém to vote (in favor of). *Perkara agama tidak bisa distém.* The religious issue cannot be voted for.

stémbusakkord (*D*) agreement between political parties.

stémpel I (*D*) 1 stamp (on a document); → CAP I. 2 punch, die, stamp. *– kering timbul* seal. *– pos* postmark.

berstémpel stamped.

berstémpelan with a ... stamp/seal (on it).

menstémpel and **menyetémpel** to stamp s.t. officially, put an official stamp on.

penstémpelan stamping.

stémpel II (in Kalimantan) a long, narrow river craft powered by an outboard motor.

sténding (*E*) standing; → GÉNGSI. *jagalah –* maintain your standing/position.

stén I (*D coq col*) clipped form of **asistén** (*wedana*) assistant to a district head.

stén II and **stén gun** (*E*) sten gun, i.e., a British light machine gun.

sténgkas (*D*) chain guard of a bicycle.

sténgky (*sl*) half a gram (of drugs).

sténo (*D*) clipped form of **sténografi** stenography, shorthand.

sténograf (*D*) stenographer.

sténografi (*D/E*) stenography.

sténografia stenography, shorthand. *– Karundéng* the Karundeng Stenographic System, i.e., the standard stenographic system used in Indonesia.

sténogram (*D/E*) stenographic report, shorthand notes.

sténotipis (*D*) stenotypist, shorthand typist, (*AE*) stenographer.

sténsil (*D/E*) stencil.

mensténsil to stencil.

sténsilan 1 a stencil. 2 stenciled, mimeographed. 3 a mimeographed pornographic book.

pensténsilan stenciling.

stép (*D*) convulsion(s); → KEJANG, STUIP.

stépa (*D*) steppe(s).

stépler (*E*) stapler (the device).

stérek (*D*) strong; *opp* SWAK.

mnstérek to recharge (a battery).

stéréo (*D*) clipped form of **stéréométri** stereometry.

stéréognosis (*E*) stereognosis.

stéréograf (*D/E*) stereometry.

stéréométri (*D/E*) stereometry.

stéréoskop (*D/E*) stereoscope.

stéréoskopis (*D*) stereoscopic.

stéréotip (*D/E*) stereotype.

menstéréotip(kan) to stereotype.

penstéréotipan stereotyping.

stéril (*D*) sterile. *perban –* sterile dressing.

menstérilkan to sterilize.

kestérilan sterility.

penstérilan sterilization.

stérilisasi (*D*) 1 sterilization. 2 security sweep.

menstérilisasi to sterilize.

stérilisator sterilizer. *– desakan tinggi* autoclave.

stérilitas (*D*) sterility.

stérling (*D/E*) (pound) sterling.

stéroid (*D*) steroid.

stérol (*D*) sterol.

stésen I (*E coq*) station wagon.

stésen II (*E*) station. *– minyak* gas station.

stétoskop (*D*) stethoscope.

stévia k.o. shrub originating in Uruguay and now cultivated in the village of Pekuncen (Banyumas); the plant contains a possible substitute for saccharine.

stéwal → STIWAL.

S.Th. (*abbr*) [Sarjana Théologi] Master of Theology.

stigma (*D*) stigma.

stigmatisasi (*D*) stigmatization.

stik (*D/E*) 1 stick, joint (a marijuana cigarette). 2 billiard cue. 3 club, bat (for golf/polo, etc.). – *bawang* k.o. snack food of fried dough.

stiker (*E*) sticker, decal.
  berstiker having/with a sticker.

stil (*E*) stylishly dressed.

stilir (*D*) menstilir to stylize (a dress, etc.).

stilisasi (*E*) stylization, stylizing.

stilistik (*E*) stylistic.

stilistika (*E*) stylistics.

stilistis (*D*) stylistics.

stimbat (*E*) steam bath.

stimulans (*D*) 1 stimulant. 2 stimulus.

stimulasi (*D*) stimulation.
  menstimulasikan to stimulate.

stimulatif (*E*) stimulative.

stip I (*D*) India rubber, eraser.

stip II (*D*) convulsion(s); → KEJANG, STUIP.

stir (*D*) 1 steering wheel (of a motor vehicle). – *kanan/kiri* right-/left-hand drive.
  menyetir to drive (a motor vehicle), steer.
  penyetir driver; → SUPIR.

'stirahat (*mil*) at ease!

stiréna (*E*) styrene.

stirstang (*D*) 1 (in general) steering column. 2 (of a bicycle) handlebar. 3 (of a car) drag link.

stiwal (*D*) gaiters.

STKI [Surat Tanda Kewarganegaraan Indonésia] Indonesian Citizenship Card.

stl (*abbr*) [setelah] after.

STM [Sekolah Téknik Menengah] Technical Middle School.

STMA [Sekolah Téknik Menengah Atas] Senior Technical Middle School.

STMD [Surat Tanda Melaporkan Diri] Registration Card for Non-diplomatic Foreign Nationals.

STMJ (*init*) → SUTEMAJA.

STNK [Surat Tanda Nomor Kendaraan] Vehicle Registration Card.

stofbril (*D*) sunglasses.

stofmap (*D*) file for keeping papers in order.

stok (*D/E*) stock. – *induk* brood stock. – *mati* iron stock. – *modal* capital stock. – *opname* stocktaking, inventory. – *timah* tin stock.
  menyetok to stock.
  penyetokan stocking.

stoker (*D*) stoker, fireman (of steam engine).

stoking (*E*) stocking.

stomatognatik (*E*) stomatognathic.

stomwals (*D*) steamroller.

stone (*E*) 1 code name for morphine. 2 to be high on drugs; → FLAAI, FLY.

stop (*D*) stop.
  menstop and menyetop to stop s.t.
  stopan (bus, etc.) stop. ~ *gantung* hanging traffic light.
  penyetopan stopping.

stopkeran (*D*) faucet, tap.

stopkontak (*D*) electric socket, wall plug, receptacle; → TUSUK *kontak*.

stopkran (*D*) stopcock.

stoplés (*D*) stoppered glass jar.

stopmap (*D*) folder (for holding papers).

stori (*E*) story; → CERITA, CERITERA.

storing (*D*) interference, static.

stor(e)mking → STROMKING.

STOVIA [School Tot Opleiding Van Indische Artsen] School for the Training of Indies Physicians (established in 1851; now the *FKUI* [Fakultas Kedokteran Univérsitas Indonésia].

strafoverplaatsing (*D*) punitive transfer, transfer to a remote station for punishment.

stranas [stratégi nasional] national strategy.

strap (*D*) punishment.
  menyetrap to punish.

strata (*pl* of *stratum* but often used for singular) (social, educational, etc.) levels. – *satu* [S 1] B.A. level. – *dua* [S 2] M.A. level. – *tiga* [S 3] Ph.D. level.

stratégi (*D*) strategy.

stratégis (*D*) and stratégik (*E*) strategic.

stratifikasi (*D*) stratification. – *sosial* social stratification.

stratigrafi (*D*) stratigraphy.

stratokumulus (*D/E*) stratocumulus.

stratosfér (*D*) and stratosfir (*E*) stratosphere.

stratum (*D*) stratum.

stratus (*D*) stratus, a continuous horizontal sheet of clouds.

stréng (*D*) severe, strict.

stréples (*E*) strapless, i.e., without shoulder straps.

stréptokokus (*E*) streptococcus.

stréptomisin (*D*) streptomycin.

strés (*E*) 1 stress. 2 emphasis.
  menstrés 1 to stress. 2 to emphasize.
  ngestrés to be stressed out.

strésor (*E*) stressor.

strika → SETRIKA.

striker (*E*) /strai-/ striker, s.o. or s.t. that strikes.

strimin (*D?*) fabric for lining.

stringbas (*E*) contrabass.

strip (*D*) line, stripe, streak. *bintara berpangkat – satu béngkok kuning* a noncommissioned officer, sergeant second class.

striptis (*E*) striptease.

strobila (*D*) strobila.

stroboskop (*D*) stroboscope.

Strodom k.o. LSD, a mind-altering drug.

strok → STRUK.

strom → STRO(O)M.

stromking a high-pressure kerosene lamp, Coleman lamp; from the brand name Stormking.

Strong-pa trademark of a medicinal capsule extracted from the *pasak bumi* root found in Central Kalimantan and used to increase male potency.

str(o)om (*D*) 1 electric current. *kena – (aliran listrik)* got an electric shock. 2 spiritual influence.
  menyetroom to wire up, put wires, etc. in a circuit.
  kestrom (*coq*) get an electric shock.

strowbéri (*E*) strawberry; → ARBÉI.

struk (*D*) strip (of paper), slip. – *(pembayaran atas) pembelian* proof of purchase, receipt.

struktur (*D*) structure.
  menstrukturkan to structure.
  terstruktur structured. *kegiatan* ~ structured activities.
  kestrukturan structure.
  penstrukturan structuring.

struktural (*E*) and strukturil (*D*) structural.

strukturalis (*D*) structuralist.

strukturalisasi (*E*) structuralization.

strukturalisme (*D*) structuralism.

strum → STROM.

struma (*D*) goiter; → GONDOK II.

strup (*D*) syrup.

STTB [Surat Tanda Tamat Belajar] Completion of Studies Certificate.

STTh [Sekolah Tinggi Théologi] Theological Academy.

STTS → SURAT *tanda terima setoran*.

studén (*D ob*) university student; → MAHASISWA.

studi (*D*) 1 study. *bahan* – study material. 2 study, den. 3 to study. *Ia* – *ékonomi di Berkeley.* She studied economics at Berkeley. – *grup* study group. – *kasus* case study. – *kawasan* area studies. – *kelayakan* feasibility study. – *sesudah-sarjana* postgraduate study. – *kawasan* area studies.

studio (*D*) studio. – *film* film studio.

stuip (*D*) /stép/ convulsion(s).

stupa (*Skr*) stupa.

stw (*abbr*) [setengah tuwa] middle aged.

su I → BUNGSU.

su II (*ITB*) → SUDAH.

Su- III (*Skr*) (also written as Soe- ; some Indonesians continue to use this spelling in their names) a personal name element meaning "beautiful, good," such as *Soeharto, Soekarno, Sumantri, Suhardiman*, etc.

SU IV [Sékretaris Umum] General Secretary.

SU V [Sidang Umum] General Assembly (of the MPR).

SU VI [Staf Umum] General Staff.

SU VII [Sumatera Utara] North Sumatra.

sua I meet (up with).
    bersua 1 to meet, run into/across. *Ia ~ dengan seorang sahabat lama.* He ran into an old friend. *~ kembali dengan* to see/meet again. **2** to come/get close to e.o. *Itulah pertama kalinya meréka ~.* That was the first time they had come close to e.o. **3** to find, meet up (with), come across (a lost item). *Ia tidak dapat ~ dengan apa yang dicarinya.* He couldn't find what he was looking for. **4** to be (found). *Di tempat itu ~ pula beberapa satwa langka.* Several endangered species are also found in that place. **5** to come true, be realized, fulfilled (of a prophecy). *~ alurnya* to come true.
    menyua to put/set (fighting cocks) up against e.o.
    menyuakan and **mempersuakan 1** to bring s.t. into contact with, confront. **2** to cause to meet, make meet.
    tersua met, encountered, come across.
    persuaan meeting, get-together.

sua II *bulu* – hackles, neck feathers (of cocks).

suah (*ob*) **1** once, ever; → PERNAH I. *belum* – never up to now; not yet ready. **2** finished, completed.

suai I – *tani* arable.
    bersuai well-fitting (of clothes/shoes/rings, etc.); for other derivatives → SESUAI.

suai II (*E?*) *tali* – stays (on a ship).

suak I 1 inlet, creek, small bay. **2** low-lying water-logged land. – *sungai* swamps between branches of a river (valueless land).
    menyuak to sail from creek to creek (along the coast).

suak II (*M*) **1** cancelled. *minta* – to ask that a (gambling) debt be cancelled. *belum pernah* – always. **2** failed. *Belum pernah M yang – menjelang pamannya.* M has never failed to visit her uncle.

suak III → SUA II.

suak IV part in the hair.
    menyuak *~ rambut* to part one's hair.

suak V (*D*) to have a weakness/failing. *Mémang biasanya orangtua – bertanya apakah ada guru yang ikut atau tidak.* Parents usually have the weakness of asking whether there's a teacher going along (with the children) or not.

suak VI (*M*) *minta* – to ask for a debt to be forgiven or reduced.

suaka I (*Skr*) **1** sanctuary (for birds), reserve (for wild animals). **2** asylum; → ASIL II. *minta* – to request/ask for asylum. *Peminta – Jerman Timur diperboléhkan ke Barat.* East German asylum seekers are allowed to go to the West. – *alam* nature reserve. – *alam laut* marine reserve. – *margasatwa* wildlife reserve. – *politik* political asylum. *menawarkan – politik* to offer political asylum.

suaka II → SÉWAKA.

sual → SOAL.

sualak → SOLAK.

suam warm. *dimandikan dengan air* – to be bathed with warm water.
    suam-suam *~ kuku* lukewarm, tepid. *badannya ~* he feels feverish.
    kesuaman warmth.

suami I (*Skr*) husband. *ikut* – (in Indonesian passports and visas) housewife. – *banyak* polyandry. *(sepasang) – istri* a) husband and wife, married couple. *kedua – istri* spouses, couple. b) marital. *hubungan – istri* marital relationship. **bersuami-istri** being married. *~ yang bertanggung-jawab* responsible parenthood. **persuami-istrian** matrimony. *mempelajari téori-téori ~* to study theories of matrimony.
    bersuami to have a husband, be married (said of a woman). *Ia belum ~.* She isn't married yet, She's still single.
    bersuamikan to be married to (said of a woman). *Wanita ini ~ Kolonél Polisi Mandagi.* This woman is married to Police Colonel Mandagi.

mempersuami to marry (a man), take s.o. as one's husband.
    mempersuamikan to marry off (a daughter), give (a daughter) in marriage. **2** to marry (a man), take s.o. as one's husband.
    persuamian husband (*mod*). *~ banyak* polyandry.

suami II (in Ambon) raw, compressed grated cassava which is steamed before being served.

suaminda husband (respectful term of address).

suang easy. – *marah* gets mad easily. *tidak* **suang(-suang)** a) not easy ... b) [*tidak suang(-suang)nya*] uninterruptedly, continuously, all the time. *~ mengunjungi pacarnya* to visit his girlfriend all the time. *tali tiga lembar tidak suang-suang putus* united we stand, divided we fall; in union there is strength; → BERSATU *kita teguh, bercerai kita runtuh* and BERSATU *kita kukuh, bercerai kita rubuh.*
    sesuang-suang as easy as possible.

suangat very, extremely → SANGAT.

suangi I evil spirit, nocturnal ghost. **2** (*IBT*) s.o. engaged in witchcraft/sorcery.

suangi II *ikan* – (*batu*) a sea fish, *Holocentrus rubrum.*

suangi III *burung* – a species of owl.

suap 1 mouthful, bite. **2** (*uang* –) bribe. *babi* – bribers. *makan* – to take bribes. *penerima* – the person bribed. – *balik* (*infr*) feedback; → UMPAN *balik.*
    sesuap a mouthful. *~ nasi* a mouthful of rice. *mencari ~ nasi* to seek one's livelihood. *~ pagi (dan) ~ petang* from hand to mouth.
    bersuap to eat with one's hands (not with a utensil), feed o.s.
    bersuap-suapan to feed e.o. using the hands (part of a marriage ritual). *Setelah sudah ~, maka ia pun memimpin tangan istrinya.* After feeding e.o., he led his wife by the hand.
    menyuap [and **nyuap** (*coq*)] **1** to eat with the hand (not with chopsticks, etc.). **2** to feed s.o. using the hand. **3** to bribe s.o.
    suap-menyuap 1 bribery. *~ antara calon dan pemilih dalam pemilihan pamong désa* bribery of a voter by a candidate in the election of village officials. **2** feeding e.o. by hand (of bride and groom).
    menyuapi [and **nyuapin** (*J coq*)] **1** to feed s.o. using the hand. **2** to support (one's family, etc.). *Di rumah ia harus ~ lima mulut manusia.* He has to support five people at home.
    menyuapkan to put (food, etc.) into s.o.'s mouth, feed.
    tersuap bribed. *Beberapa pemain bola ~.* Several soccer players were bribed. *si ~* the person bribed.
    suapan 1 bribe, bribery, corruption. **2** eating with the hand.
    penyuap briber.
    penyuapan 1 feeding (s.o. using the hand); supporting. **2** bribery, corruption, etc.
    persuapan (*mod*) bribery.

suar I 1 light signal, beam of light used as a signal. *memberi* – to signal (using a flare or beam of light). *mercu* – a) lighthouse. b) showcase. *proyék mercu* – a showcase project. **2** torch used to attract fish when fishing at night. – *anéka warna* alternating light. – *bakar* a) (*M*) to set (a house, etc.) on fire as an act of arson. b) (*petro*) flare. – *berantara* intermittent light. – *berputar* revolving light. – *cerlang* flashing light. – *pengarah* directional light. – *penuntun* leading light. – *putus/terputus-putus* occulting light. – *tetap* fixed light.
    bersuar to signal.
    menyuar to light a flare, light up; to fish with a torch at night. *~ lebah* to smoke out bees.
    menyuari to light up s.t.
    menyuarkan to lure by using a flare.
    tersuar lighted, lit. *Banyak ~ andang dan murang.* Many torches and fuses were lit.

suar II (*M*) sweat, perspiration. – *lelah* exertion, effort.

suara (*Skr*) **1** sound made by a human being when speaking, singing, laughing, etc., voice. – *itu nyatalah wanita.* It's clear that that sound is a woman's voice. **2** sound made by an animal, an apparatus, etc., sound, noise. – *harimau mengaum* the sound of a growling tiger. *Pesawat radio itu –nya sembér.* The radio makes a crackling sound. **3** words. *Hanya – saja, tidak ada buktinya.* It was only words, There was no proof. **4** pronunciation. *Huruf w dalam bahasa Belanda tidak sama –nya dengan huruf w dalam bahasa Indonésia.* The pronunciation of the letter *w* in Dutch differs from that of the letter *w* in Indonesian. **5** s.t. considered the equivalent of words, voice. *Majalah ini – para pekerja, bukan – suatu partai.* This magazine is the voice of the workers, not the voice of a particular party. **6** opinion. *Dalam rapat itu –nya tidak diindahkan sama sekali.* At that meeting his opinion was not heeded at all. **7** vote (in agreement or against). *dengan – bulat* (by) unanimous vote. *Usulnya diterima dengan – bulat.* His proposal was accepted unanimously/by acclamation. *apabila jumlah – yang setuju dan tidak setuju sama banyaknya, apabila –.– sama berat, dalam hal –.– sama banyaknya* in case of a tie vote. *dengan 20 – mufakat dan 5 – menyangkal* by twenty votes in favor and five against. *dengan – (yang) terbanyak* by majority vote. *– terbanyak biasa* simple majority. **8** support (in an election). *Banyak anggota yang memberi – memilih calon pemimpin baru itu.* Many members gave their support for the election of the new candidate. *ilmu –* acoustics; → AKUSTIK. *ilmu – kata* (*gram*) phonetics; → FONÉTIK. *kalah –* defeated (in an election), lost (the election). *kelebihan –* majority of votes. *melahirkan/ memberi(kan) –nya* to cast one's vote. *semua buruh yang berhak memberi –* all employees who have the right to vote. *tidak memberi –* to abstain (from voting). *menang –* to win (an election). *mengangkat –* to take the floor. *Lalu ketua érwé pun mengangkat –.* Then the chairman of the neighborhood association took the floor. *mengeluarkan –nya* to cast one's vote. *tiga – jatuh atas … –nya seperti perian pecah* he has a voice like a cracked violin. *– Amérika* Voice of America of the United States Information Agency, VOA. *– bising* noise. *– blangko* abstention, abstaining vote. *– bulat* acclamation, unanimity. *– burung* rumors. *– burung menyebutkan* rumors/unconfirmed reports have it that … *– genta* ringing voice. *– hati* conscience. *– Karya* the semi-official daily newspaper supported by *Golkar*. *– kumbang dijolok* angry sounds. *– menggelegar* rumbling (of a volcano). *– miring* criticism. *– pertama* (to sing) first part. *– pokok* key (in music), prevailing tone. *– rakyat* the voice of the people, vox populi (*L*). *– rakyat adalah – Tuhan* the voice of the people is the voice of God; vox populi, vox Dei (*L*). *– remang-remang* false voice. *– rendah (wanita)* alto. *– sumbang* opinion or view which differs from the majority. *– terbanyak biasa* majority vote.

sesuara with one voice, unanimously.

bersuara 1 to make (a) noise. *Jangan ~!* Don't make any noise! *tak ~* noiseless, quiet. **2** (*ling*) voiced. *tak ~* voiceless. **3** to express one's opinion. **4** to take a stand. *Anda harus ~, jangan hanya diam saja.* You have to take a stand; don't just remain silent. *ikut ~* to have a say (in the matter).

menyuarai to dub (a film).

menyuarakan 1 to voice (an opinion/demand, etc.), present, put s.t. forward. *Majalah itu ~ pendapat kaum buruh.* That magazine voices the opinions of the laborers. **2** to sing (a song). **3** to speak for. *~ rakyat* to speak for the people. **4** to cast a vote.

tersuara resonated.

penyuara drumbeater.

penyuaraan 1 dubbing (a film). **2** (*ling*) voicing.

suarang (*M*) **1** property jointly acquired by husband and wife, community property. **2** property belonging to a partnership. *– tagih, sekutu dibelah* (at a divorce) the community property is divided up.

bersuarang to work (of both husband and wife).

menyuarangkan to acquire (property) jointly.

suarawan (*Skr neo*) male singer.

suarawati (*Skr neo*) female singer.

suarga → SURGA.

suargaloka (*Skr cla*) heaven/abode of the gods.

suari I → KESUARI.

suari II → BANTAL *suari.*

suasa alloy of gold and copper; *cp* PANCALOGAM.

suasana (*Skr*) **1** atmosphere. **2** milieu. **3** situation. *– hati* mood. *– internasional* international milieu. *– jiwa* mood.

bersuasana with an atmosphere of.

menyuasanai 1 to give (a certain) atmosphere to. **2** to convey the atmosphere of.

suat a plaited bag made from the bark of a tree (by the *Badui* ethnic group in Banten).

suatu a certain (unknown or unidentified), a(n); → SATU. *mobil menjadi – kebutuhan dalam pengangkutan umum* a car has become a necessity in public transportation. *– apa juga* anything (at all). *– pagi/soré/malam* a certain morning/afternoon/evening. *–pun tidak ada* not even a single one *pada – ketika* at some point in time, once.

sesuatu 1 a certain (unspecified). *~ majalah* a certain magazine. **2** something. *barangkali ada ~ yang dibutuhkan* maybe there is s.t. required. *segala ~* everything. *segala ~ sudah selesai* everything was settled/fixed.

bersuatu (*ob*) united, joined. *kita berdua ini ~ perasaan* we are both united in our feelings.

mempersuatukan (*ob*) to unite, join.

sub- (prefix meaning) under, below, beneath; slightly, imperfectly, nearly; secondary, subordinate (for examples see below).

subagén (*D*) subagent.

subahat → SYUB(U)HAT.

subak (*Bal*) irrigation system organized and regulated by the people themselves.

subal 1 rough, coarse (of nets). **2** (*Jv*) (inferior) material mixed with s.t. else (to make the latter seem heavier or appear to be more than it really is; fraudulently). *daun-daun untuk – keranjang arang* leaves used to fill up a charcoal basket (fraudulently in place of charcoal).

menyubal to fill/stuff (with false material).

subalan → PAYUDARA *subalan.*

penyubal filling/stuffing (to increase the size or weight of s.t. fraudulently).

subam (*ob*) not shiny (of metal, etc.), dull, tarnished, faded.

suban splinter (of wood), shard (of glass).

menyuban splintery, full of splinters.

subang I earring.

bersubang to have/wear earrings.

subang II 1 slice (of sugarcane). **2** (*bio*) corm.

menyubang to cut into slices.

subang III *akar –* a creeping shrub species, *Sphenodesma pentandra.*

subatomik (*E*) subatomic.

subbab subchapter; under a chapter.

subbagian subdivision, subsection.

subbudaya subculture. *– Melayu* Malay subculture.

subbul khatimah (*A*) bad at the end.

subdiréktorat subdirectorate.

subéntri subentry (in dictionary).

Suberban → SUBURBAN.

subétnis subethnic. *kelompok –* a subethnic group.

subgéneralisasi subgeneralization.

subhah and **subhat** → SYUB(U)HAT.

subhana (*A*) *– (A)llah* God the Most Holy. *Allah –hu wa taala* [swt] God the Most Holy and Most High, i.e., a formula used after mentioning one of God's names.

subjék (*D*) subject. *– Hukum* Legal Subject, Person Holding Legal Rights.

subjéktif (*E*) subjective.

kesubjéktifan subjectivity.

subjéktivisme (*E*) subjectivism.

subjéktivitas and **subjéktivitét** (*D*) subjectivity.

subjudul subtitle.

subklas (*D*) subclass.

subkomité (*D*) subcommittee.

subkontrak (*E*) subcontract, sublease.

mensubkontrakkan to subcontract (out). *Proyék besar itu kini disubkontrakkan kepada Koréa Selatan.* That big project has now been subcontracted out to South Korea.

pen(g)subkontrakan subcontracting.

subkontraktor (*E*) subcontractor.

subkultur (*D*) subculture.

sublégaat (*D leg*) /sublégat/ devolved specific legacy.

sublégataris (*D leg*) devolved specific beneficiary.

subléma subentry.

sublim (*D/E*) sublime.

sublimasi (*D*) sublimation.

mensublimasikan to sublimate.
sublimat (*D*) sublimate.
sublimatif (*E*) sublimative.
sublimir (*D*) **mensublimir** to sublimate.
subordinasi (*D*) subordination.
　mensubordinasikan to subordinate.
subordinat (*E gram*) subordinate.
subpenyalur subdistributor.
subrayon (*D*) subarea, subdistrict.
subrogasi (*D*) subrogation.
subséktor (*E*) subsector.
subsidi (*D*) subsidy.
　bersubsidi subsidized. *sekolah* ~ subsidized school.
　menyubsidi and **mensubsidi** to subsidize.
　menyubsidikan to subsidize with s.t., give s.t. as a subsidy.
subsidi(é)r (*D*) 1 subsidiary, secondary. 2 (*leg*) or (before an alternative punishment for a crime).
subsisténsi (*D*) subsistence. *ékonomi* – subsistence economy.
substandar (*D*) substandard.
substansi (*D*) substance.
substansial (*E*) and **substansiil** (*D*) substantial.
substantif (*D gram*) substantive, noun.
　mensubstantifkan to make into a substantive, nominalize.
substitusi (*D*) substitution.
　mensubstitusi(kan) to substitute.
substitutif (*E*) substitutive.
substrat (*D*) substrate.
substratum (*E gram*) substratum.
subtil (*D*) subtle.
　kesubtilan subtlety.
subtilitas (*E*) and **subtilitét** (*D*) subtlety.
subtotal (*E*) subtotal.
subtropik (*E*) and **subtropis** (*D*) subtropic.
subuh (*A*) 1 (*waktu* –) dawn, daybreak (about 5 a.m.). *Ia mulai bekerja sejak* – *hingga larut malam.* He works from dawn to late at night. 2 (*salat/sembahyang* –) early morning prayer. *bakda* – period of time right after dawn, about 5 to 6 a.m. – *gajah* post-dawn period.
　subuh-subuh very early before dawn.
　subuhan *ikut* ~ to take part in early morning prayers.
Subulussalam (*A*) Area of Peace, i.e., the name of the capital of a *kecamatan* in North Sumatra.
subur 1 fruitful (of fields/minds/discussions, etc.). 2 fertile (soil/ground); productive. *masa* – productive age. 3 prolific (frequently reproducing or producing many descendants or fruit). *Pohon-pohon itu tumbuh* –. Those trees are growing luxuriantly. 4 healthy, sound (of the body), in good health (of a person). 5 flourishing, prosperous (of a business), booming; luxuriant, thriving (of plants, etc.), to thrive; → MURAH *rezeki. tidak* – infertile. *ketidaksuburan* infertility.
　menyubur to be(come) fertile.
　menyuburi (*pl obj*) to fertilize, make s.t. thrive.
　menyuburkan to fertilize, promote the growth of (plants).
　mempersubur to make s.t. thrive, make s.t. more fertile. ~ *korupsi* to make corruption thrive.
　tersubur the most fertile, etc.
　kesuburan 1 fertility. 2 prosperity.
　penyubur s.t. that fertilizes/enriches. ~ *rambut* hair conditioner. *pupuk* ~ *tanah* fertilizer to enrich the soil.
　penyuburan fertilizing.
Suburban k.o. station wagon or van used for interurban passenger transport.
suburu (*Pap*) sweet potato.
subvérsi (*D*) subversion, undermining (of authority), underground (illegal) action.
　mensubvérsi to subvert, overthrow.
subvérsif (*D*) subversive, undermining, insurgent, illegal.
subyék (*D*) → SUBJÉK.
subyéktif (*D*) → SUBJÉKTIF.
subyéktivisme (*D*) → SUBJÉKTIVISME.
sucad [*suku cadang*] spare parts.
sucéng (*J C?*) honest, fair (in soccer, etc.).

suci (*Skr*) 1 clean, untainted, impure (from a religious point of view). *Minuman keras adalah minuman yang dianggap tidak* – *bagi agama Islam.* Alcoholic drinks are beverages considered unclean for Islam. 2 clean, pure, sterilized, sterile, germfree; innocent, chaste, without sin. *Kanak-kanak yang baru lahir dikatakan masih* –. It's said that newborns are still innocent. 3 divine, holy, sacred. *orang* – holy person, saint. *Tanah* – the Holy Land (Mecca, etc.). *orang Islam menganggap Mekah sebagai Tanah* –. Muslims consider Mecca the Holy Land. – *dari* free of/from. – *dari sifat kecurangan* free from fraudulent characteristics. – *hama* sterile, aseptic, germfree. **menyucihamakan** to sterilize, purify. *Radiasi juga digunakan untuk* ~ *peralatan kedokteran, karena dianggap jauh lebih menguntungkan dari téknik* – *hama.* Radiation is also used to sterilize instruments, because it's considered far more beneficial than aseptic techniques. **penyucihama** sterilizer, purifier. – *hati* pure in heart, with pure motives. – *kuman* sterile, aseptic, germfree. **menyucikumankan** to sterilize, purify. **penyuci kuman** sterilizer, purifier. – *lamisan* hypocritical, sanctimonious.
　bersuci to clean/wash o.s. before praying; to cleanse o.s. (of sins), live a pure/chaste life.
　mensucikan and **menyucikan** 1 to cleanse (of sins). ~ *diri di bawah pohon* to meditate under a tree and therefore cleanse o.s. of sins. 2 to consecrate, purify, sanctify, regard as divine.
　mempersucikan to make s.t. pure, purify.
　tersuci most pure/holy. *Bunda Maria yang* ~ the most holy Mother Mary.
　kesucian 1 purity, cleanliness, chastity. 2 holiness, sanctity, sacredness. ~ *agama Islam* the sanctity of Islam.
　penyuci a purifying agent, purifier.
　persucian and **penyucian** purification, cleansing (of sins), sanctification, consecration. *api penyucian* purgatory.
suda (*cla*) pointed caltraps of bamboo planted around a fortress, stockade as a defense; → SUNGGA.
sudagar (*coq*) → SAUDAGAR.
sudah 1 completed, over, through, finished, done, accomplished, achieved, realized. *Rumah anda yang baru apa* – *rampung?* Is your new house finished yet? *Ia tidak akan* – *dengan pekerjaan itu.* He won't be through with that work. *barang* – finished product. 2 ceased, stopped, come to a stop/halt. *Hujan pagi ini belum* –. The morning rain hasn't stopped yet. 3 to have begun ...ing. *Kalau* – *belajar tidak ingat waktu.* When he's begun studying, he forgets the time. 4 (in prepredicate position) has occurred (and was expected to occur) [often no translation or translated by the English perfect] *Dia* – *datang.* He has arrived. *Meréka* – *kawin.* They are married. *Dia* – *hamil.* She's pregnant (now). *Dia* – *sembuh.* He's recovered (from his illness) (now). 5 (in postpredicate position) [same as 4 but more emphatic] *Hasil terakhir pemilu jelas* –. The final results of the general election are clear. *Bermacam-macam* – *obat yang saya coba.* I've tried a lot of medicines. 6 (before a time expression) [action started in the past and continues up to the present; often translated as English perfect]. – *lama* for a long time. – *lama dia dapat membaca jam.* He's been able to tell time for a long time (now). – *berapa lama* (for) how long (continuing into the present)? – *berapa lama anda di Indonésia?* How long have you been in Indonesia? – *lama saya menderita sakit éncok di kaki kiri.* I've been suffering from gout in my left leg for a long time. 7 *akan* – will (already) be, will have been. *Pasukan akan* – *ditarik pada akhir tahun.* The troops will have been withdrawn by the end of the year. 8 [before a time expression + *baru* + dependent clause] it didn't (won't) ... until/before. – *jam tiga baru keréta api berangkat.* The train didn't leave until three o'clock. 9 it's become, it's turned into, the expected result of a process/change of state has been reached, now; *opp* BELUM. *Sekarang* – *malam.* It's night now. *Dia* – *pénsiun.* He's retired (now). *Anak saya* – *besar.* My child is grown up now. – *akan* to be about to. *Meréka* – *akan berangkat.* They are about to leave. – *léwat* a) expired, run out; → KADULAWARSA, KEDALUARSA. b) too late. – *pernah* have done s.t. (at least once in the past). *Saya* – *pernah ke Pulau Bali.* I've been to Bali. – *tahu ia sakit* it's no news to me that he's sick. – *tentu* certain, sure, of course. – *tidak*

no longer, no ... more, not ... any longer. *Hanya sidangnya itu – tidak di sembarang tempat.* It's just that the court sessions are no longer held just anywhere. *– saatnya* and *– waktunya* it's (high) time. **10** OK, we're here (said to a *bécak* driver on arriving at one's destination). *– ya* OK, all right. *– ya, saya harus pergit.* OK, I've got to go (now). *–lah* a) all right! never mind, forget it! *"Yang –, –lah," kata Syamsidan kepada suaminya.* "Let bygones be bygones," said Syamsidan to her husband.

sudah-sudah past, gone by, last. *bulan yang ~* last month. *Jangan dibicarakan lagi soal yang ~.* Don't talk about the problems of the past.

sudah(-sudah)nya finally, eventually. *Semua yang hidup akan mati juga sudahnya.* All living creatures will die eventually. *tidak sudah-sudahnya* nonstop, continuously. *Istana bekas Kerajaan Siak bagai tak sudah-sudahnya dirundung pencuri.* The palace of the former Siak Principality is plagued by thieves so to speak nonstop.

sesudah after. *Dia makan ~ membasuh tangannya.* He ate after washing his hands. **menyesudahi** to close, end.

sesudahnya afterwards. *sebelum dan ~nya* (many thanks) in advance and afterwards (at the end of a letter).

sesudah-sudahnya afterwards. *Ia menyelesaikan tugasnya ~.* He finished his task afterwards.

bersudah with an ending.

bersudah-sudah severed, cut, ended (of friendship/ties/marriage, etc.). *~ berfamili* to break (off) with one's relatives.

menyudahi 1 to end, terminate, conclude. *Acara itu disudahi dengan doa.* The program was concluded with a prayer; → MENGAKHIRI. **2** to fulfill, realize, satisfy, meet. **3** to complete, finish. **4** to kill, put to death. *Ia disudahi sesama gali.* He was killed by his fellow criminals.

menyudahkan and **mempersudahkan** to complete, finish, conclude, terminate, end. *Saya akan makan setelah saya ~ pekerjaan saya.* I'll eat when I've finished my work.

kesudahan conclusion, end(ing), (final) result(s), completion, outcome, effect. *Bagaimana – cerita itu?* How did the story turn out? **berkesudahan** (*dengan*) to end/finish (with/in), result in. *tidak ~* to be endless, have no end. *Percintaannya akan ~ dengan kegagalan.* His love will end in failure.

tersudahi finished, settled. *kasus itu belum ~* the case hasn't been settled yet.

penyudah conclusion, end; last, final. *kata ~* last/final word.

penyudahan completion, termination, ending.

sudako k.o. public transportation vehicle.

sudamala → BARU II *cina.*

sudara (*coq*) → SAUDARA.

sudari (*coq*) → SAUDARI.

sudariah → SADARIAH.

sudat → SUDÉT. *– pandang* point of view.

sudayah → SUDUAYAH.

sudera → SUDRA.

sudét (*Jv*) diverted (of a stream).

menyudét 1 to divert (water). **2** to cut across an obstruction.

sudétan diversion.

penyudétan diversion (of a river).

sudi I (*Skr*) **1** ready, willing, prepared (to). *– tak –* a) whether one wants to or not. b) hesitant. **2** like, have a liking for, want. **3** please. *–lah anda duduk!* Please sit down! *– (apa)lah kiranya anda duduk!* Won't you please sit down!

bersudikan to like, approve of, willing (to do s.t. with pleasure).

menyudikan and **mempersudikan 1** to make s.o. like/want (to). *Itulah agaknya yang ~ PBB turun tangan mencampuri persengkétaan itu.* That might be what made the U.N. willing to interfere and get involved in the conflict. **2** to provoke, encourage. *Membuang témbakan ke atas untuk ~ pemuda kita bertempur.* To fire into the air to encourage them to fight. **3** to request, invite. *Tamu-tamu disudikannya masuk.* He invited the guests in.

kesudian readiness, willingness, acquiescence.

sudi II (*M*) *– siasat* to ask around (to find out s.t.).

menyudi to investigate, inquire into.

sudip 1 (wooden) spoon (to stir rice/turn over frying or boiling items, etc.). **2** spatula, trowel. *– cat* palette knife. *– lepa/lepo*

trowel (for mixing cement). *– lidah* (medial) tongue depressor. *– sepatu* shoehorn.

menyudip 1 to ladle out rice with a rice spoon. **2** spatulate.

sudipan chip, shaving.

Sudirman name of the first Commander-in-Chief of the Indonesian National Army, who led the fighting against the Dutch during the struggle for freedom in 1945. *lembaran – yang bernol empat* (*coq*) a 10,000-rupiah note (it has a picture of Sudirman on one side). *lembaran – dengan nol tiga* (*coq*) a 1,000-rupiah note.

Sudra (*Skr*) a member of the fourth and lowest Hindu caste, that of menial workers, the untouchables caste.

sudu I 1 goose-beak, duck-bill. **2** k.o. large ladle or spoon made from a coconut shell, from tinplate, etc., scoop, blade (of a stirring machine). *Hadiah – Kencana* Golden Spoon Award (for cooking). *–.– hati* and *tulang – hati* lower ribs, the xiphoid or ensiform cartilage of the sternum. *– turbin* turbine blade.

menyudu 1 to peck (with the beak/bill). **2** to ladle out (soup/tea, etc.). **3** to scoop s.t. up with the beak or bill.

tersudu pecked; could be scooped up/ladled out. *sudah tidak ~ oléh angsa, baharu diberikan kepada itik* the small fry only get what the big shots don't use.

penyudu ladle, large spoon.

sudu II rotor.

suduayah oleander, *Nerium oleander.*

suduk I (*Jv*) dagger. *– jiwa/selira* to commit suicide, kill o.s., stab o.s. to death.

menyuduk to stab, run through, pierce.

menyudukkan to stab with (a sharp weapon).

tersuduk pierced, stabbed. *Dadanya ~ tombak.* His chest was pierced by a spear.

suduk II → SODOK II.

sudung 1 shed, awning; → KAPA-KAPA, SENGKUAP. **2** small hut (on cropland). **3** hut, hovel (self-deprecatory for one's own house); → PONDOK.

sudung-sudung field hut.

sudur → SODOR I.

sudu-sudu a cactus-like shrub of the *lidah buaya* or aloe family, *Euphorbia neriifolia/antiquorum.*

sudut 1 angle. **2** corner (of a room/street, etc.). *di – halaman ruman* in the corner of the house yard. **3** direction, bearing. **4** point of view, viewpoint. **5** angle, angular. *jarak –* angular distance. *dari – penglihatan Indonésia* from an Indonesian point of view. *ditilik dari – ketatanegaraan* seen from a political angle. *– apit* included angle. *– arah* bearing. *– batas* critical angle. *– berhadapan* opposite angles. *– dalam* interior angle. *– damping* adjacent angle. *– dasar* basic angle. *– enam* hexagon. *– jarak* distance angle, parallax. *– kemudi* head/steering angle. *– kota* outskirts of the city. *– lancip* acute angle. *– lima* pentagon. *– lurus* straight angle. *– masuk* angle of incidence. *– mata* point of view, viewpoint, angle of vision. **menyudut-matakan** to look at s.o. out of the corner of one's eye. *– négatif* negative angle. *– pandangan/penglihatan* viewpoint, angle of vision. *– pelurus* (*math*) supplementary angle. *– penyiku* complementary angle. *– potong* angle of attack. *– ruang* solid angle. *– sérong* bevel edge. *– siku(-siku)* right angle. *– suplemén* supplementary angle. *– tajam* sharp angle. *– tegak* angle of convergence. *– tujuh* heptagon. *– tumpul* oblique angle.

bersudut 1 to have angles; angular. *~ enam* hexagonal. *~ lancip* to have an acute angle, be acute-angled. *bintang ~ lima* a five-pointed star. *~ sama* equiangular. **2** to have corners.

bersudut-sudut with many angles/corners.

menyudut 1 to form an angle; angular, acute. **2** to go into a corner, get elbowed out into an unimportant position.

sudut-menyudut at angles to e.o., diagonally, kitty-corner.

menyudutkan [and **nyudutin** (*J coq*)] to push aside/into an unimportant position, elbow out, oust; → MEMOJOKKAN. *Kemenangan Hongaria ~ Argéntina.* Hungary's victory elbowed out Argentina. *~ posisi* to put into an awkward position.

tersudut(kan) cornered.

penyudutan cornering.

suér (*E BG*) I swear. *– saya enggak tahu.* I swear I didn't know.

suf (*A*) woolen cloth.

sufal (*A cla*) notch (in arrow), indentation (in bow).

sufi (*A*) *ahli (al.)*– mystic. *ilmu* – Sufism.

sufiah (*A*) Sufism.

sufian (*A*) mysticism.

sufiks (*D gram*) suffix.

Sufisme (*D/E*) Sufism.

Sufistik (*E*) Sufistic.

sufrah and **sufran** (*A*) cloth spread on floor for meals; → SEPERAH.

sugar I **menyugar** to comb one's hair with one's fingers.

sugar II (*Pers ob*) sugar; → GULA.

sugeng (*Jv*) well, safe, secure. – *Natal dan Taon Anyar* (*Jv*) Merry Christmas and a Happy New Year. – *rawuh* (*Jv*) welcome. *menyugengrawuhi* to welcome. *akulturasi berbagai ragam budaya yang sejak dulu disugengrawuhi* the acculturation of various sorts of cultures that have been welcomed since past times.

sugésti (*D*) suggestion; → SARAN.

sugéstif (*D*) suggestive.

sugi 1 short pointed piece of wood (from a matchstick, etc.) used for removing food particles from between the teeth, k.o. toothpick. 2 (*M*) quid, lump of tobacco held in the mouth and chewed to clean the teeth.

bersugi 1 to pick one's teeth with a *sugi*. 2 to hold tobacco in the mouth while chewing betel leaf.

menyugi 1 to clean the teeth, clear food particles, etc. from between the teeth with a *sugi*. 2 to wipe off the lips, etc. with tobacco (while chewing betel leaf).

pesugi k.o. toothpick.

sugih (*Jv*) rich, wealthy, well-to-do. – *tanpa banda, digdaya tanpa aji, nglurug tanpa bala, menang tanpa ngasoraké* (*Jv*) rich without wealth, supernatural without mysticism, fighting without an army, gaining victory without defeat; i.e., a portion of an old (*Jv*) poem by R.M.P. Sosrokartono often cited by President Soeharto in his speeches. – *durung karuan, sombong didisikno* (*Jv*) to count one's chickens before they're hatched.

pesugihan riches, abundance.

sugi-sugi (*pohon* –) k.o. pine tree, *Mischocarpus sundaicus*, *Gandarusa vulgaris*.

Sugriwa (*Skr*) /-wo/ King of the Monkeys (in the *Ramayana* epic).

suguh (*Jv*) – *sumbangsih* contribution as proof of homage.

menyuguh 1 to treat s.o. (to s.t.), entertain, serve. ~ *tamu* to serve a guest. 2 to offer s.o. (something for entertainment).

menyuguhi to treat s.o. to, entertain s.o. with, serve s.o. (with s.t.), present s.o. (with s.t.). *Kami disuguhi téh*. We were served tea.

menyuguhkan [and **nyuguhin** (*J coq*)] 1 to serve (food, etc. to s.o.). ~ *sedap-sedapan kepada tamu* to serve the guests with delicacies. 2 to make available, offer, provide. *Majalah itu* ~ *cerita péndék*. The magazine offers short stories.

tersuguh offered (up). *Dalam homepage ini telah* ~ *3 buah ségmén menarik*. Three interesting segments were offered in this homepage.

suguhan 1 treat, food and drink offered to a guest. 2 contribution (in a newspaper, etc.).

penyuguh s.o. who treats, etc., host.

penyuguhan 1 treating. 2 presenting, offering, providing, presentation. ~ *seni tradisional kepada wisatawan* offering tourists traditional music.

sugul (*A coq*) → MASYGUL.

sugun disheveled, tousled (of hair after a fight, etc.). *(di)* – *hantu* tousled, tangled (of hair).

menyugun(kan) to seize s.o. by the hair.

suh I (*Jv*) bond, tie, band (of plaited rattan around a broom). *seperti lidi kehilangan –nya* without a leader (like a broom without a band around it).

suh II → SUHU II.

suhad (*A*) insomnia, sleeplessness; → SUKAR *tidur*.

suhartois Suharto supporter.

suhbat → SOBAT.

suhian (*C*) bordello, brothel.

suhu I (*A*) temperature (of one's body/a place/politics, etc.). *pengukur* – fever/clinical thermometer. *penurunan* – cooling down, tapering off. – *masih di bawah titik beku* the temperature is still below the freezing point. – *badan* body temperature. – *badan yang tinggi* a high fever. – *kamar* room temperature. – *lebur* melting point. – *politik* political tension. – *ruangan* room temperature. – *tubuh* body temperature. – *tubuh meninggi* hyperpyrexia. – *tubuh yang normal adalah 37 derajat* C normal body temperature is 37 degrees Centigrade. – *udara* outside temperature, temperature of the air.

bersuhu to have a temperature. ~ *kamar/ruangan* to be at room temperature.

suhu II (*C*) 1 (self-defense) instructor. 2 healer.

suhuf (*A*) 1 scriptures (written down through revelation from God). 2 → SAHIFAH.

suhun *sekar* – k.o. gold neck ornament; → SEKAR.

suipoa → SIPOA.

suir → LANGSUIR.

suit (*onom*) sound of whistling.

bersuit(-suit) 1 to whistle. 2 to whistle with one's fingers in one's mouth.

menyuit(i) to whistle at.

suitan 1 whistle, whistling (noise). 2 flute, whistle (the instrument).

suita (*D*) suite (music).

sujadah → SAJADAH.

sujana I (*Skr ob*) excellent, eminent (of person). – *alamiah* physicist.

sujana II (*ob*) → YOJANA.

sujén I (*Jv*) a wooden skewer used for roasting *saté*. – *saté* skewer for *saté*.

sujén II (*Med J*) dimple (in cheek).

suji I (*Skr*) embroidery. – *tenggelam* flat embroidery. – *timbul* embroidery in relief.

bersuji with embroidery on it, embroidered. *kain* ~ embroidered cloth.

menyuji to embroider.

tersuji embroidered.

sujian embroidery.

suji II (*Skr Hind? ob*) a flour-based gruel eaten with curry.

suji III → MERSUJI.

suji IV k.o. dracaena, *Pleomele angustifolia*.

sujud (*A*) prostration in prayer, the act of kneeling and bowing the head to the ground as part of praying. *sembah* – respectful homage. – *tawakal* to prostrate o.s. in resignation to God's will. *menyujud-tawakalkan* to resign to the will of God.

bersujud 1 to prostrate o.s. in prayer. *ketika aku* ~ *di hadapan Tuhan dalam sembahyang kesyukuranku* when I prostrated myself before God in my prayer of thanks. 2 to bow down, grovel.

tersujud prostrated, bowed-down.

persujudan prostration.

suka (*Skr*) 1 pleasure, delight, joy. *sahabat dalam* – *dan duka* a friend in joy and sorrow. – [*akan/dengan/(ke)pada*] to like, love, be fond of, care for. *saya* – *akan kamus ini* I like this dictionary. *Tanto* – *(ke)pada Tati*. Tanto likes Tati. *Saya kurang* – *ilmu pasti*. I'm not too fond of math. *ada yang* – *daging dan ada yang* – *ikan laut* some like meat and some like fish. *Tiada seorangpun* – *padanya*. Nobody likes him. 2 would like, to be willing, want. *Kalau tuan* – *datang, silakanlah*. If you'd like to come, please do. *Ia tidak* – *membayar sekian*. He isn't willing to pay so much. 3 (+ verb) to like to, like ...ing. – *makan/minum/tidur/membaca* like to eat/drink/sleep/read. 4 (*coq*) very, easily, frequently, often, prone to. *Mémang, dia* – *lupa*. Really, he's forgetful. – *menerima* receptive. *Pénsil semacam ini* – *patah*. Pencils like this break easily. *Ia* – *datang di rumah Ali*. He often visits Ali. 5 – *tidak* – favoritism. *(dengan perasaan yang)* – *tak* – a) indifferent; hesitant. b) willy-nilly, whether one wants to or not. *kurang* – to dislike. **kekurang-sukaan** dislike. *tidak* – to dislike. **ketidak-sukaan** dislike. ~ *pada yang serba asing* dislike of everything foreign. – *berkelahi* quarrelsome. – *berperang* warlike, belligerent. – *bertengkar* quarrelsome. – *berusaha* enterprising. – *bohong* deceitful. – *(dan) duka* joys and sorrows, ups and downs. – *gampang* easygoing. – *guyon* (*Jv*) always joking around, comical, amusing. *Pembawaannya sederhana, polos dan* –

guyon. His behavior is simple, unpretentious, and amusing. – *hati* happy, in high spirits, delighted. – *lupa* forgetful. – *melawan* disobedient, unruly. – *mengomél* nagging, complaining, grumbling. – *menyerang* aggressive. – *menyindir* to be sarcastic. – *mudah* easygoing. – *ria* → SUKARIA. – *sabar* accommodating, obliging. – *sama* – (*coq*) a) with mutual consent/agreement. b) between you and me. – *sok* to be a know-it-all, be a smart aleck. – *terima tamu* hospitable.

sesuka ~ *hati*, **sesukanya**, **sesuka-suka(nya)** at will, as one likes, to one's heart's content; with all one's heart, wholeheartedly. *Pedagang tidak boléh menaikkan harga sesuka-sukanya.* Merchants are not allowed to raise prices at will.

bersuka ~ *hati*, ~ *ria* to enjoy o.s.

bersuka-suka l to enjoy o.s., have a good time. *Tua muda, remaja putra dan putri, sekaliannya* ~. Old and young, teenage boys and girls, all had a good time. **2** to be cheerful, full of high spirits.

bersukaan (*J*) to go steady with e.o. *Ia* ~ *dengan gadis yang cantik itu.* He's going steady with that beautiful girl.

bersuka(-suka)an l to enjoy/amuse o.s. **2** to flirt with e.o., make love.

menyukai [and **nyukain** (*J coq*)] to like, love; to be fond of, favor, be attached to. *Keduanya* ~ *musik klasik.* They both love classical music. *lebih disukai yang belum berkeluarga* (in ads) unmarried (applicants) preferred. *Partai yang memerintah tidaklah boléh membuang pegawai pemerintah yang tidak disukainya.* The ruling party is not allowed to get rid of government employees it doesn't favor.

menyukakan to gladden, delight in, take pleasure in, rejoice in. *disukakan* to be accepted wholeheartedly.

menyuka-nyukakan ~ *hati* to make s.o. happy.

sukaan (*coq*) **l** sweetheart, darling. **2** favorite.

kesukaan l (~ *hati*) pleasure, enjoyment, amusement, what s.o. likes, ideal. **2** favor, kindness. **3** hobby. **4** inclination, willingness, readiness. **5** favorite. *~nya adalah makan sambel dan masakan Indonésia.* His favorite dishes are *sambel* and Indonesian food.

penyuka admirer, fan.

sukabumi (*lit*) "to like the earth."

mensukabumikan to shoot dead. (This term appeared in the press during the period of mysterious killings; → PÉTRUS).

sukacita (*Skr*) **l** joy, cheer, gladness. **2** glad, joyful, pleased, cheerful.

bersukacita to be cheerful, happy.

menyukacitakan to cheer up, delight, gladden.

sukamandi (*Jv*) unbleached cotton from Sukamandi.

sukan l k.o. herb with leaves used to heal wounds or eaten by women who have just given birth, *Coleus amboinicus*.

sukan II (*Mal*) sports; → OLAHRAGA.

sukar l difficult, hard, troublesome; → RUMIT, SULIT I, SUSAH. *Di kota ini – mencari pekerjaan.* It's hard to find work in this town. – *tidur* insomnia, difficulty in falling asleep. *Amat – menjalankannya* It's very hard to do it. **2** (of an illness) serious, severe, acute; → BERAT, SERIUS, PAYAH, TERUK. *penyakitnya terlalu –* his illness is very serious. **3** (*cla*) poor, needy, destitute. *hidupnya selalu –* he has always been poor.

sukarnya the difficulty (of doing s.t.), the hard thing about (doing s.t.).

menyukarkan and **mempersukar** to make difficult/hard, inconvenience, give s.o. a hard time. *Saya tidak mau ~ Saudara.* I don't want to inconvenience you.

tersukar the most difficult.

kesukaran l difficulty, trouble, hardship. *mendapat ~* to have problems, be having a hard time, get into hot water. **2** destitution. **3** to suffer hardships.

sukaréla (*Skr*) voluntary, of one's own free will. *pasukan –* volunteer troops. *tenaga –* volunteers.

kesukarélaan l voluntariness. **2** volunteership.

sukarélawan (*Skr neo*) (male) volunteer.

sukarélawati (*Skr neo*) (female) volunteer.

sukaria (*Skr*) **l** delight, pleasure. **2** happy, glad.

bersukaria to be happy, delighted; to gloat (over s.o.'s misfortune).

sukat I l cubic measure of 4 *gantang*s. *Ia membeli beras setengah –.* He bought 2 *gantang*s (about 6.25 kg) of rice. **3** gauge.

sesukat one *sukat* (about 3.125 kg). *yang ~ tak akan jadi segantang* one's fate cannot be changed.

bersukat measured by the *sukat*. ~ *darah* (*cla*) to kill s.o. ~ *darah, bertimbang daging* to wage war to the death; to launch a life-and-death struggle. *telah penuh sebagai ~* (*M*) lost one's patience, out of patience.

menyukat to measure s.t. by the *sukat*. ~ *penuh sudah* (*M*) lost one's patience, out of patience.

sukatan l (cubic) measure. *duduk dengan ~* to be rich/wealthy. *~nya sudah penuh* his hour has arrived. **2** gauge.

sukat II (*cla*) provided (that), on condition that; not earlier than. – *air menjadi batu* impossible.

sukduf (*A*) saddle on camel's back.

Sukernas [Survéi Kerja Nasional] National Workforce Survey.

sukerto (*Jv*) bringing bad luck. *orang yang –* s.o. who brings bad luck.

suket (*Jv*) **l** grass. – *gerinting* Bermuda grass, *Cynodon dactylon*. **2** (*sl*) marijuana-laced cigarette.

suki (*M*) (*ob*) enough, sufficient; abundant (of food).

sukma (*Skr*) **l** soul, spirit. **2** life. *keadaan rusak –* psychic trauma.

Sukrat (*A*) Socrates.

sukro clipped form of **sukrosa**.

sukrosa (*D*) sucrose.

suksara (*Jv*) village cash. *tanah –* land taken care of by a village head to finance the village organization.

suksés (*D*) **l** success. **2** successful. *tidak –* unsuccessful. – *ya!* good luck to you! – *médikal* medical success.

sesuksés as successful as.

me(ng)sukséskan and **menyukséskan** to make s.t. a success, make s.t. successful.

kesuksésan success.

penyuksés success, person or thing that is successful. *Ketenangan kerja, ~ pembangunan nasional.* Job security is the successful result of national development.

pe(ng)suksésan and **penyuksésan** success, successful result.

suksési (*D*) succession.

suku I (*Jv*) leg, foot; → KAKI I. – *lembu* cow's leg.

bersuku with/to have a leg/foot. *berdiri ~ tunggal* to stand on one foot.

suku II (*Jv*) **l** (*ob*) ¼ of a *réal*, i.e., a former Spanish monetary unit. **2** (*col*) half guilder. **3** half rupiah, fifty cents.

sesuku a/one half guilder; half a rupiah.

suku III l (*gram*) constituent part, clause, syllable. **2** part (of s.t. larger), section. – *cadang* spare parts. – *kalimat* constituent part of a sentence. – *buka/hidup* open syllable *bersuku hidup* containing an open syllable. – *kata* syllable. – *mati/tutup* closed syllable. *bersuku mati* containing closed syllables.

bersuku with ... syllable(s), word consisting of open syllables.

persukuan syllabification.

suku IV rate (of interest). – *bunga* interest rate. – *bunga jangka péndék* short-term interest. – *bunga perbankan* bank rate. – *bunga pinjaman* lending rate. – *bunga primér/utama* prime rate.

suku V l group. **2** family, genus. – *bangsa/sakat* ethnic group. *Negara kita terdiri dari beberapa ratus – bangsa.* Our nation is made up of several hundred ethnic groups. *rasa –* ethnic/tribal feelings. *pernikahan antar–* interethnic marriage. – *Déli* the Malay ethnic population of Eastern Sumatra; → MAYA-MAYA II, PENDUDUK *pesisir.– bangsa* ethnic group, tribe. – *Karo* Karo ethnic group. *kesukubangsaan* ethnic, tribal.

sesuku of the same ethnic background, belonging to the same ethnic group.

bersuku to belong to the ... ethnic group. *tidak ~* a) not belonging to any ethnic group. b) uneducated.

bersuku-suku in groups; grouped according to ethnic background.

kesukuan l ethnic, regional, tribal. *prasangka ~* ethnic prejudice. **2** tribalism, clannishness.

pensukuan syllabification.

persukuan ethnic relation(s). **sepe(r)sukuan** belonging to the same ethnic group.

suku VI l fourth part, quarter. **2** (– *emas*) k.o. gold coin also used as a measure for the weight of gold. *gelang tiga –* a bracelet that has the weight of three such gold coins. **3** (*math*) term in an equation, e.g., in *a:b*, both *a* and *b* are called *suku*. **4** a diacritical mark denoting the vowel *u* in Javanese. – *cadang* spare part. *penggantian* – *cadang* replacement of spare parts. – *jam* quarter (of an hour), fifteen minutes. – *tahun* quarter (of a year), three-month period.

sukuisme tribalism, ethnic chauvinism, feeling of ethnic solidarity.

sukun I (*buah* –) breadfruit, *Artocarpus communis*.

sukun II toothless.

sukun III (*A*) a diacritical mark that looks like a small zero over a consonant to indicate that the consonant ends the syllable, i.e., that no vowel follows the consonant.

sukur (*Jv*) → SYUKUR. – *kowé!* serves you right!

sukwan contraction of **sukarélawan**.

sukwati contraction of **sukarélawati**.

sula (*Skr*) **1** impaling stake. **2** device for husking coconuts.
   menyula 1 to open a coconut with a *sula*. **2** to impale with a *sula*.
   menyulakan to impale with a *sula*.
   sulaan 1 impaled. **2** impaling stake.
   penyula 1 tool used to impale s.o. **2** impaler.
   penyulaan impaling.

sulah bald (*esp* in the crown), hairless. *berkepala* – baldheaded. *lelaki agak beréwok dan berkepala* – a hairy but baldheaded man. *gunung* – bald/treeless mountain. *kepala* – *Bung Karno* Bung Karno's bald head; → BUNG *Karno*. *lada* – white pepper, *Piper retrofractum*. *si tua* – old baldy.

Sulaiman (*A*) (the biblical) Solomon.

sulaimani *batu* – onyx.

sulak (*Jv*) (chicken-)feather duster.
   menyulaki to dust with such a duster.

sulaksana (*Skr*) good omen/sign. *téja-téja* – a sign of good luck to come.

sulalah and **sulalat** (*A*) **1** ancestry, lineage, inheritance, descent. **2** derivate, derivative. – *karét* rubber derivatives.

sulam embroidery. *secara tambal* – in a makeshift way.
   bersulam embroidered. *bantal/seléndang* ~ an embroidered pillow/shawl.
   bersulamkan 1 embroidered with. *bantal beludru* ~ *emas* a velvet pillow embroidered with gold thread. **2** sprinkled with.
   menyulam 1 to embroider. **2** to replace dead plants with fresh ones, refill.
   sulam-menyulam 1 embroidery. **2** embroidering.
   menyulamkan to embroider s.t. (onto s.t.).
   tersulam embroidered.
   sulaman 1 embroidery. **2** embroidered.
   penyulaman 1 embroidering. **2** replacing dead plants with fresh ones, refilling.

sulang I (*ob*) **bersulang** to toast, drink a toast.
   bersulang-sulangan and **sulang-menyulang 1** to share drinks/food, drink/eat together. **2** to bill and coo, rub beaks together (of doves/pigeons). *berpantun* ~ to improvise quatrains and sing them to e.o. in turn.
   menyulang(i) to give drink/food to.
   menyulangkan to give drink/food.
   penyulang feeder.

sulang II (– *asap*) soot, lampblack.
   bersulang sooty.

sulap I juggling, sleight of hand, conjuring tricks. *bermain* – and
   bersulap to conjure, perform conjuring tricks/sleight of hand, juggle.
   menyulap [and **nyulap** (*coq*)] **1** to juggle, conjure up. *seperti disulap saja layaknya* as if by magic, magically. **2** to turn/change s.t. (into s.t. else). *Banyak komoditi bisa disulap menjadi dolar.* Many commodities can be turned into dollars. **3** (*coq*) to embezzle, misappropriate. *Ia* ~ *uang perkumpulan kita.* He misappropriated our club's money. **4** to falsify, forge. *Ia* ~ *surat jalan.* He forged a travel document.
   tersulap 1 fascinated, charmed. **2** as if by magic, magically.
   sulapan 1 deceit, deception, fraud. **2** magic show.
   penyulap 1 conjurer, juggler. **2** magician. ~ *faqir* conjurer who uses mysticism. ~ *ilusi* illusionist. ~ *manipulasi* conjurer who uses magic.

penyulapan 1 juggling, conjuring. **2** fooling. **3** deceit, deception.
   persulapan conjuring (*mod*).

sulap II (*J*) flaw in weaving due to raveling or a dropped thread.

sulat-salit I irregular (of teeth).

sulat-sulit II all k.o. difficulties.

Sulawesi Sulawesi, the Celebes. – *Selatan* [Sulsel] South Sulawesi. – *Selatan dan Tenggara* [Sulselra] South and Southeast Sulawesi. – *Tengah* [Sulteng] Central Sulawesi. – *Tenggara* [Sulra] Southeast Sulawesi. – *Utara* [Sulut] North Sulawesi. – *Utara dan Tengah* [Sulutteng]. North and Central Sulawesi.

sulbi (*A*) spinal column, loins, vertebrae. *tulang* – coccyx, tailbone.

sulfanilamida (*D*) sulfanilamide.

sulfat (*D*) sulfate.

sulfur (*D*) sulfur, brimstone.

sulfurisasi (*E*) sulfurization.

suli I (*S ob*) grandchild.

suli II → GANDASULI.

sulih (*Jv*) substitute, representative, stand-in, dummy. *guru* – substitute teacher. – *suara* dubbing. **menyulih-suarakan** to dub. **penyulih-suara** dubber.
   menyulih(i) to substitute, represent, act in place of or on behalf of.
   sulihan substitute.
   penyulih substitute, replacement.

suling I 1 flute, (bamboo) fife; → BANGSI, SERULING. **2** steam whistle (of a vessel/train, etc.). – *api* k.o. flute-shaped bellows. – *kapal* ship's horn.
   bersuling and **menyuling** to play the flute, blow on a whistle.
   penyuling flautist, flutist.

suling II distillate. *air* – distilled water.
   menyuling to distill. ~ *minyak wangi* to distill perfumes.
   sulingan 1 distillate. **2** distilled. *air* ~ distilled water. ~ *tengah* middle distillates.
   penyulingan 1 distilling, distillation. **2** distillery, refinery.

suling III (*M*) topsy-turvy, upside down; → SUNGSANG I. – *daling/paling* topsy-turvy.
   menyulingkan to turn upside down, invert.
   tersuling turned upside down, inverted.

sulinggih (*Bal*) Balinese priest.

sulit I 1 hard (to do), difficult, entangled, complicated, intricate. – *membelit* very complicated. **2** uncertain, precarious, critical. **3** (*mostly Mal*) hidden, concealed, secret, in secret; private, secluded, mysterious.
   sulitnya 1 the difficulty. ~ *menghapus pornografi* the difficulty of wiping out pornography. **2** the trouble/problem is. ~ *terkadang semua itu tidak konsistén*. The problem is that sometimes all of that is inconsistent. *apa* ~ why is it (so) hard (to do s.t.), what's so hard about (doing s.t.)?
   sulit-sulit ~ *gampang* not as hard as it looks.
   menyulitkan and **mempersulit** [and **nyulitin** (*J coq*)] to hamper, impede, complicate, make difficult; to trouble, inconvenience.
   kesulitan 1 complication, difficulty, hardship, entanglement, intricacy. *penyakit tampek dengan* ~ measles with complications. ~ *bahasa* language difficulties. ~ *yang sukar diatasi* deadlock; → JALAN *buntu*. **2** uncertainty, precariousness, criticalness. **3** concealment, privacy, seclusion, mystery. **4** shortage, scarcity. ~ *air* water shortage. *mengalami* ~ *air* suffering from a water shortage. ~ *uang* shortage of money, lack of funds. **5** to have a hard time ...*ing*, find it hard to. *Tapi ketika itu polisi* ~ *memperoléh bukti-bukti.* But then the police had a hard time finding evidence.
   penyulit complication(s).
   penyulitan complicating.

sulit II *ikan* – *batang* a fish species, brilliant rasbora, *Rasbora einthoveni*, found in swamps.

Suliwatang a high Buginese title.

Sulra → SULAWESI *Tenggara*.

Sulsel → SULAWESI *Selatan*.

Sulselra → SULAWESI *Selatan dan Tenggara*.

sultan (*A*) **1** sultan, monarch of Yogyakarta; → INGKANG. **2** (*Mal*) ruler.

bersultan → BERAJA *di hati, bersultan di mata.*

kesultanan 1 the territory over which a sultan rules. 2 sultan's palace, *kraton.* 3 Yogyakartanese court drama in which the performers sing and dance at the same time.

sultanah (*A Mal*) female sultan, sultan's consort; → PERMAISURI.

sultanat (*D*) 1 sultanate, the office or rule of a monarch. 2 the territory over which a monarch rules.

sultani monarchic. *nasab* – sultan's descent.

Sulteng → SULAWESI *Tengah.*

sulu (*ob*) → SULUH.

sulub → SULBI.

suluh 1 torch (*usu* made from dry coconut leaves or *damar*); → OBOR. 2 (*cla*) spy; scout.

bersuluh to use a torch, with a torch. *Ia ~ di jalan yang gelap.* He used a torch in the dark streets. *~ tengah hari* as clear as day.

bersuluhkan to have ... as one's torch. *~ bulan* to have the moon as one's torch, i.e., to sleep in the open, be homeless. *bagai ~ tengah hari* a) s.t. so obvious that it's known to everybody. b) to waste (money/energy, etc.).

menyuluh(i) 1 to light (up). *Meréka ~ lorong yang gelap itu dengan lampu sénter.* They lit up the dark alley with a flashlight. 2 to look for (fish or hunt) with a torch. 3 to investigate, look into, spy on. *~ keadaan musuh* to investigate the enemy situation. 4 to inform, give information to. *~ rakyat di pedésaan mengenai program keluarga berencana* to give the rural population information about birth control.

penyuluh 1 informer. 2 counselor. 3 investigator, spy.

penyuluhan 1 information (which educates). *~ pertanian* agricultural extension. 2 counseling. *bimbingan dan ~* guidance and counseling. 3 (*cla*) investigation, espionage.

pesuluh the person informed. *Terlebih dahulu penyuluh mencék kemampuan membaca dan menulis setiap ~.* First of all the informer has to check the reading and writing ability of each person informed.

suluk I (*A*) 1 mysticism. 2 (*RC*) retreat, seclusion; → KHALWAT. *ahli al.-* mystic. *ilmu –* mysticism.

bersuluk (*RC*) to go on retreat, go into seclusion.

suluk II (*Jv*) the *dalang*'s recitation.

sulung I oldest (child). *anak –* and *yang –* the oldest (child). *bahasa –* protolanguage. *buah –* first fruits. *gigi –* baby/deciduous teeth. *paling –* the oldest (child). *– tahun* beginning of the year.

sulung II *– akar* climbing plant on hedges, *Gynochthodes sublanceolata.*

sulup (*ob*) → SELUP.

sulur I 1 spiraling upward (of plants). 2 tendril. *akar –* aerial roots. 3 spiral, watch spring. 4 sprout from roots. 5 (*petro*) liner. *– batang* a) spiral, spiral-shaped. b) shoots on a tree trunk. *– bulur* incoherent, rambling, disjointed, confused (speech). *– gading* upward extensions of a boat's ribs. *– udara* aerial sucker.

bersulur 1 to climb upward, shoot up (of plants). 2 spiral-shaped.

menyulur to climb/creep upward, creep along (of plants).

sulur-suluran runners (from plants).

sulur II (*cla*) → SULUH.

sulut I (*J*) → SUNDUT III. menyulut 1 to light (a fire), kindle, ignite. *~ perang* to wage war. *disulut api* set on fire. 2 to light up (a cigarette, etc.) *~ rokok krték* to light up a clove cigarette. 3 to stimulate, instigate.

menyulutkan to light, kindle, ignite.

tersulut lit, set on fire.

penyulut igniter, instigator, trigger. *~ sumbu* provocation; trigger, s.t. which sets s.t. else off.

Sulut II → SULAWESI *Utara.*

Sulutteng → SULAWESI *Utara dan Tengah.*

sum I (*cla*) *perahu –* k.o. Siamese sailing vessel.

sum II (*D*) hem (of a dress, etc.).

mengesum to hem.

Sum III [Sumatera] Sumatra (in acronyms).

suma 1 *ikan –* k.o. marine fish. 2 (*Skr*) clipped form of kusuma, flower, used as an element in many Javanese and Sundanese personal names, such as *Sumadilaga*, etc.

sumah eager for praise, likes to be praised.

sumamburat (*Jv*) menyumamburat to glitter, sparkle, shimmer.

sumanda and sumando (*M*) s.o. related by marriage, affinal. *rang – a* relative by marriage.

sumangat → SEMANGAT.

sumaput → SEMAPUT.

sumarah (*Jv*) 1 obedient; to obey, comply with s.o.'s wishes. 2 to submit to God's will, put one's fate in God's hands; → PASRAH *pada "Yang di Atas."*

sumarak → SEMARAK.

sumasi giant perch (a fish species).

Sumatera Sumatra. *– bagian Selatan* [Sumbagsel] the southern part of Sumatra consisting of the provinces of Lampung, South Sumatra, Jambi, and Bengkulu. *– bagian Utara* [Sumbagut] the northern part of Sumatra consisting of the provinces of Aceh, North Sumatra, Riau, and West Sumatra. *– Barat* [Sumbar] West Sumatra. *– Selatan* [Sumsel] South Sumatra. *– Tengah* [Sumteng] Central Sumatra. *– Timur* [Sumtim] East Sumatra. *– Utara* [Sumut] North Sumatra.

sumatif (*E*) summative, additive.

Sumatra → SUMATERA.

sumba (*Skr*) 1 safflower, a thistle-like composite plant, *Carthamus tinctorius;* its dried florets are used as medicine or as a red dyestuff; → KESUMBA I. 2 name of an island in Nusa Tenggara Timur.

menyumba to dye/color with *sumba.*

Sumbadra and Sumbodro one of *Arjuna*'s two main wives (the other one is *Srikandi*), the epitome of the ladylike, obedient wife and the ideal aristocratic Javanese woman.

Sumbagsel → SUMATERA *bagian Selatan.*

Sumbagut → SUMATERA *bagian Utara.*

sumbang I 1 incest, incestuous. *perkawinan yang –* incest. 2 adultery, illicit sex. 3 treating s.o. in an improper way, e.g., looking at a woman in an impudent or licentious way or holding the hand of a woman who isn't one's wife, etc., indecent – *didengar* it sounds improper (e.g., of a proposal made by a girl, etc.). 4 (*M*) wrong, improper, false (move). *langkah –* a false/wrong step in *silat* or in fighting. *tegak –* a wrong posture in *silat*, e.g., to show one's armpit(s). *perjodohan yang –* misalliance, mésalliance. 5 not pleasing to hear or see (of musical instruments/behavior, etc.), out of tune, discordant, cracked (of the voice). 6 unbecoming, improper, indecent (of behavior), scurrilous. *– langkah* an improper act(ion). **menyumbangkan langkah** 1 to be improper, go against *adat.* 2 to feint, purposely make a false step in *silat*, etc. so as to fool one's opponent. *– pati* adultery with a full or half sibling. *– salah* adultery.

menyumbang to become false/wrong.

menyumbangkan 1 to make a mistake in. 2 to purposely make s.t. sound wrong.

menyumbang-nyumbangkan to insult, degrade.

kesumbangan 1 s.t. which goes against *adat*, indecent act(ion), impropriety. 2 outrage, offensiveness.

sumbang II (*Jv*) *– saran* suggestion. **menyumbang saran** to make a suggestion.

bersumbang to make a contribution, contribute s.t.

menyumbang 1 to give aid/assistance/help, assist, contribute, have a share. 2 to make a contribution to s.o. who is organizing a party.

menyumbangkan [and nyumbangin (*J coq*)] 1 to give s.t. (money/energy/one's voice in song, etc.) in support or assistance, contribute. *Dia ~ beras sebakul.* He contributed a basket of rice. 2 to devote one's energy to.

sumbangan 1 contribution, share (*esp* financial). *Dia minta ~ untuk mesjid.* He asked for a contribution for the mosque. 2 help, aid, assistance, support, relief, subsidies. *~ manasuka* voluntary support. 3 contribution (*esp* scientific). *~ seumur hidup* annuity.

sumbang-sumbangan contributions.

penyumbang 1 contributor, donor. *~ darah* blood donor. 2 helper, supporter.

penyumbangan contributing, supporting; contribution, support.

sumbangsaran → SUMBANG *saran.*

sumbangsih contribution, assistance, aid, support, backing.

sumbar I (*J/Jv*) ber(se)sumbar, menyumbar(-nyumbar) and sesumbar to boast, brag; → MENYOMBONG.

menyumbarkan to boast/brag about.

sumbar II → SUMBER.

Sumbar III → SUMATERA *Barat.*

sumbat 1 plug, stopper, cork, block, dowel. 2 plugged tight (of a hole). *penarik* – corkscrew. *– botol* cork, bottle stopper. *– cerat* drain plug. *– penutup* shutter. *– perintang* (*petro*) bridge plug.
  bersumbat plugged, stopped, blocked.
  menyumbat [and **nyumbat** (*coq*)] 1 to cork (up). ~ *mulut botol* to cork a bottle. 2 to plug (one's nostril/ear, etc.). ~ *telinganya dengan kapas* to plug one's ear with cotton. 3 to fill/plug/stop (up). ~ *lubang* to plug up a hole. 4 to stuff, cram full, clutter up. ~ *karung goni ke dalam gerbong* to stuff gunnysacks into a railway coach. 5 to gag. *Istrinya diikat dan disumbat mulutnya.* His wife was tied up and gagged. *Mulutnya disumbat dengan saputangan.* His mouth was gagged with a handkerchief.
  menyumbatkan 1 to fill a hole, etc. with. 2 to stuff s.t. with. 3 to seal s.t. up.
  tersumbat [and **kesumbat** (*coq*)] 1 corked, plugged (up), stopped/clogged (of a pipe, etc.); → MAMPET. *hidung* ~ a stuffed-up nose. *Pipa air itu* ~. The water pipe is clogged. 2 jammed/blocked (with traffic). *Bécak-bécak seringkali membuat jalan-jalan jadi* ~. Becaks often jam the streets. 3 gagged. 4 to have a lump (in one's throat). ~ *kerongkongan* a) to be off one's feed, have no desire to eat. b) unable to say anything, can't get out a single word.
  sumbatan plug, s.t. used to plug s.t., block, lock. ~ *uap* vapor lock.
  penyumbat cork, stopper. ~ *mulut* gag.
  penyumbatan 1 obstruction (in the urinary tract, etc.). ~ *pembuluh nadi* arteriosclerosis, hardening of the arteries, block. 2 obstructing, blocking.

sumbel in a hurry, head over heels, helter-skelter; → SUNGSANG I.

sumber (*Jv*) 1 well, spring. 2 source, origin, place from which s.t. comes (or, is obtained). *sang* – the source (of information); → NARASUMBER. 3 resource(s). *– air panas* hot spring. *– alam(i)* natural resources. *– api abadi* eternal flame. *– berita* news source. *– cahaya* luminary source. *– dana* capital resources. *– daya (alam)* (natural) resources. *– daya hutan* vegetation. *– daya insani* (*infr*) human resources. *– daya manusia* [SDM] human resources. *– daya laut* marine resources. *– daya yang langka* scarcity of resources. *– dévisa* foreign-exchange source. *– (di) tepi jalan* female tramp (who is also a prostitute). *– gempa* epicenter (of an earthquake). *– kekuasaan* source of power. *– kemarahan* subject/cause of discontent. *–.– keuangan* financial resources. *– minyak* oil well. *– nafkah* source of livelihood. *– pendapatan/penghasilan* source of income. *– rujukan* reference sources. *– sebabnya* cause, motive, grounds. *– sejarah* historical source. *– yang layak dipercaya* reliable source. *berita dari – yang layak dipercaya* news on good authority.
  bersumber (*dari*) 1 to originate (in), come (from), rest (upon), depend/rely (on). *Penyakit kejiwaan yang dideritanya itu* ~ *dari perasaan yang tertekan.* The mental disorder he was suffering from originated in suppressed feelings. 2 to be derived from.
  bersumberkan to have s.t. as its source, be based on. *Buku yang ditulis* ~ *falsafah Yunani.* The book he wrote is based on Greek philosophy.

sumbi I *gigi* – crowned/filled tooth; false tooth.
  menyumbi to fill (a tooth), put a crown on (a tooth), fix the damaged edge of s.t., repair a boat by replacing its damaged boards.

sumbi II rod used to hold the woven part of the cloth taut in a loom.

sumbi III → CELEMPUNG II.

sumbing jagged (of the edge of a blade, etc.), chipped, split (of a harelip). *bibir* – harelip. *gelak/senyum* – a forced laugh/smile.
  menyumbingkan to split s.t.

sumbu I 1 wick (for a candle/lamp). 2 fuse, fuze (for fireworks/cannon/explosives). 3 burner (on stove). *kompor 10* – a 10-burner stove. 4 (*infr*) percussion cap. *– kumpai/lampu* lamp wick. *– ledak* fuse, fuze. *– mercun* fuse of a firecracker. *– meriam* fuse of a cannon/gun. *– pengaman* safety fuse. *– waktu* time fuse.
  bersumbu to have a wick/fuse; provided with a wick/fuse. *roti* ~ cassava, *Manihot utilissima.*
  menyumbu to provide with a wick/fuse, put a wick on.

pesumbuan, persumbuan [and **penyumbuan** (*infr*)] 1 touchhole of a cannon/gun. 2 place for a wick/fuse.

sumbu II 1 axle (of a carriage). *berat* – axle load. 2 axis. 3 pivot. 4 coordinate (of a chart). *– baling-baling* propeller shaft. *– bumi* axis of the earth, earth's axis. *– datar* (*math*) abscissa. *– mata* optic axis. *– putar* propeller shaft. *– roda* wheel shaft. *– tegak* (*math*) ordinate.
  sesumbu with the same axle, coaxial.
  bersumbu with an axle. ~ *satu* with one axle (of vehicles).

sumbu III horn of a rhinoceros; → CULA, SUNGU I. *badak* – one horned rhinoceros, *Rhinoceros sondiacus. – badak* rhinoceros horn.

sumbuk (*Pers*) small boat, dinghy.

sumbul I (*Jv*) plaited-cane lidded hemispherical basket with a pedestal.

sumbul II (*M*) → SEMBUL, SUMBUR.

sumbung room for the head and members of the family in a Lodan Toraja house.

sumbur (*M*) **menyumbur** to project, protrude, stick out.
  menyumburkan ~ *diri* to appear, show o.s.
  tersumbur projecting/bulging/sticking out.

sumbut (*Jv*) worthwhile, worth the trouble.

suméh (*Jv*) friendly (smiling at customers, etc.).

sumek (*Jv*) not (smelling) fresh, stale, stuffy.

suméléh (*Jv*) 1 lying (down), put/placed down. *Kacamatamu – di méja.* Your glasses are on the table. 2 relieved of responsibilities (for one's children, etc.).

sumeng (in Semarang) k.o. cold, flu-like symptoms.

sumengit I k.o. herb, *Hyptis suaveolens.*

sumengit II easily offended; fierce, vicious.

sumerah (*Jv*) to surrender, give in, acquiesce; → SUMARAH.

sumilir (*Jv*) gentle (breeze); → SEPOI-SEPOI, SILIR I.

sumir (*D*) summary, brief, concise statement.
  menyumirkan to summarize, shorten, make brief.

sumirat (*Jv*) 1 radiant. 2 sparkling.

sumo (*Jp*) sumo (wrestling). *pemain* – and
  pesumo sumo wrestler.

sumonggo → MONGGO, SILAKAN.

sumpah I oath, vow. *atas/dengan* – on oath. *makan* – to break a vow. *mengambil* – to administer a vow. *mengangkat* – a) take an oath. b) to swear in. *mengikrarkan* – to take an oath. *mengkhianati* – to break a vow. *– bohong* perjury. *– celup* (*ob*) oath taken while immersing one's hand in boiling oil (no harm comes to one who is telling the truth). *– di bibir saja* oath taken under duress. *– dokter* Hippocratic oath. *– jabatan* oath of office. *– jilat besi* (*ob*) oath taken while licking hot iron (no harm comes to one who is telling the truth). *– kerak-keruk* solemn oath. *– keramat* oath taken at a shrine. *– mampus/mati* I swear. *– menyelam* oath taken on diving into water (the one telling the truth is the one who stays under the longest). *– mimbar* oath administered by a judge in a church. *– minum air keris* (*ob*) oath of fealty taken while drinking water into which a kris has been plunged. *– Palapa* the oath taken by Gadjah Mada. *– palsu* perjury. *melakukan – palsu* to commit perjury, perjure o.s. *– Pemuda* Youth Pledge taken in Jakarta on October 28, 1928, calling for the creation of an Indonesian nation and the use of Indonesian as the national language. *– pocong* an oath administered by a judge in a mosque in which the oath-taker is wrapped in a funeral shroud. *– potong ayam* oath taken over a cut-off chicken's head (administered by a judge in a Chinese temple). *– Prajurit* the Soldier's Pledge: I swear by God to be loyal to the government and submit to the laws and state ideology; a) to submit to military law; b) to carry out all duties and be fully responsible to the military and the Republic of Indonesia; c) to be well-disciplined, i.e., submissive, loyal, honorable, and obedient to superiors without questioning orders and decisions; d) to keep military secrets as firmly as possible regardless of any pressure. *– Qur'an* oath taken by swearing on the Koran. *– sakti* sacred oath. *– salah* perjury. *– serapah* all k.o. curses. *– setia* a) oath of allegiance. b) (*M*) solemn vow. *– tambahan* (*leg*) supplementary oath.
  bersumpah to swear on oath, take a vow. ~ *bohong* to commit

perjury. ~ *kerak-keruk* to swear a solemn oath. ~ *palsu* to perjure o.s. ~ *setia* to swear allegiance.

menyumpah 1 to swear in(to office). *disumpah menjadi Présidén* to be sworn in as president. *disumpah* sworn (translator, etc.). 2 to put under oath. *Anda harus disumpah.* You have to be put under oath.

menyumpahi to swear to s.o.

menyumpahkan and **mempersumpahkan** 1 to declare under oath. 2 to swear in(to office), administer the oath of office to.

tersumpah sworn. *penerjemah* ~ sworn translator.

penyumpah s.o. who swears an oath, s.o. who takes a vow.

penyumpahan swearing in, administering the oath of office.

persumpahan 1 swearing in. 2 taking an oath, oath-taking.

sumpah II curse, malediction, imprecation. *dimakan/kena* ~ be cursed, under a curse. ~ *serampu/seranah/serapah* imprecations and curses.

menyumpah 1 to use abusive language to. 2 to curse s.o.

menyumpahi [and **nyumpahin** (*J coq*)] to curse s.o. ~ *dan bahkan membunuh orang lain* to curse and even kill others.

tersumpah cursed.

penyumpah s.o. who curses, curser.

sumpah-sumpah poisonous green, long-tongued flying lizard, *Calotes cristatellus.*

sumpal cork, plug, stopper; → SUMBAT. ~ *kuping* earphones.

menyumpal 1 to plug (up), cork; to stuff, wad, cram, fill. *susur yang* ~ *mulut* (betel) quid that fills the mouth. ~ *bahu* to stuff the shoulders (of clothes). 2 to clot, lump up. *dahak* ~ *di tenggorokannya* phlegm clotted in his throat. 3 to be in groups, be crammed together. *murid-murid* ~ *di kelas* students crammed together in the classroom. *mobil yang* ~ *Jalan Massachusetts* cars riding in clumps on Massachusetts Avenue. ~ *mulut* a) to feed, give s.o. s.t. to eat; nourish, support. *Dia bekerja berat untuk* ~ *empat mulut.* He works hard to feed four mouths. b) to bribe (s.o. not to reveal a secret), pay blackmail to s.o.

menyumpalkan to plug up with, stuff s.t. (into).

tersumpal clogged (up), stopped (up).

sumpalan s.t. which obstructs a passageway.

penyumpal stuffing, s.t. used to stuff s.t.

penyumpalan stuffing, plugging up.

sumpek (*Jv*) 1 crowded, jammed. 2 choked, suffocated, stifled. – *berjubel* chock-full.

kesumpekan suffocation, choking, asphyxiation.

sumpel (*J/Jv*) → SUMPAL. **kesumpel** clogged (up), stopped (up).

sumpelan (*infr*) supplement.

sumpet (*J*) **kesumpet** tripped, stumbled.

sumpia (*C*) k.o. *lumpia* filled with *ébi* and fried.

sumping (*Jv*) leather ear ornament in the form of a wing, painted with gilt, worn as part of the costume for the classical (*Jv*) dance.

sumpit I blow-pipe. *lurus sebagai* – straightforward, honest.

menyumpit to shoot at (a bird, etc.) with a blowpipe.

menyumpitkan to use s.t. as a blowpipe.

tersumpit hit by a dart from a blowpipe.

sumpitan blowpipe.

penyumpit s.o. who shoots a blowpipe.

sumpit II *menegakkan* – *tak berisi* to labor in vain, perform a Sisyphean labor.

sumpit III (*C*) chopsticks.

sumpit IV (*ikan* –) and **sumpit-sumpit** blow-pipe fish, *Toxotes spp.*

sumpit-sumpit a small bag with string handles made from the screw pine, *Pandanus,* for carrying rice, salt, etc.

bersumpit-sumpit sackfuls.

SU MPR [Sidang Umum Majelis Permusyawaratan Rakyat] General Session of the People's Consultative Assembly.

sumprit (*BG*) I swear (it's true).

sumput (*S*) **menyumput** to hide, lie low.

sumribit (*Jv*) softly blowing (breeze); → SILIR I, SEPOI-SEPOI.

sumringah (*Jv*) cheerful, in good spirits.

bersumringah to look happy.

Sumsel → SUMATERA *Selatan.*

sumsum (*Jv?*) marrow. *bubur* – (*Jv*) porridge made of rice flour and coconut milk. *sampai ke tulang* – to the very marrow. *dinginnya*

terasa sampai ke tulang – the cold pierced you to the very marrow. – *belakang* spinal cord/marrow. – *lanjutan* medulla oblongata. – *tulang* bone marrow.

menyumsum(i) to penetrate to the very marrow (of). *menyumsum ke dada/tulang* (the cold) penetrated to one's very marrow. *Ketakutan itu merayap menyumsumi diriku.* Fear crept into my very marrow.

Sumteng → SUMATERA *Tengah.*

Sumtim → SUMATERA *Timur.*

sumuk (*Jv*) (the body feels) hot and clammy.

sumur I well, pit, shaft; → PERIGI, TELAGA. *gas* – well/free gas. – *digali air terbit* to get more than one asked for. – (*di*) *tepi jalan* prostitute. – *antara* infilling well. – *artésis/artétis* artesian well. – *bor* drilled well. – *buta* dry well. – *éksplorasi* test wells. – *éksplorasi taruhan* wildcat test well. – *gali* dug well. – *gas* natural gas well. – *imbuh* recharge well. – *injéksi* input well. – *jiran* offset well. – *kajian* appraisal well. – *kering/mati* dry well. – *lawas* stripper well. – *mati* dry well. – *minyak* oil well. – *panték* (*J*) drilled well. – *pelega* relief well. – *peluas* step-out well. – *pembantu* release well. – *pembuang* disposal well. – *penemuan* discovery well. – *pengembangan* development well. – *penunjang* service well. – *perintis* pioneer well. – *pompa* water well which uses a pump, beam well. – *resapan/serap* absorbing well. – *simak* monitor well. – *tambang* mine shaft. – *taruhan* wildcat well. – *témbak* foxhole. – *tinggal* abandoned well. – *uji* test pit.

sumuran pit. ~ *uji* test pit.

sumur II (*M*) → SEMUR.

sumurung to tower over others, exceptional. *kedudukan* – privilege.

Sumut 1 [Sumatera Utara] North Sumatra. 2 (*joc*) [Segala Urusan Mesti Uang Tunai] everything has to be settled in cash. 3 (*joc*) [Sopan, Ulet, Menarik, Unggul dan Takwa] Courteous, Persevering, Interesting, Excellent, and Devoted.

sun I (*D*) kiss; → SOEN. – *ceplok* a noisy kiss.

mengesun, mensun [and **ngesun** (*coq*)] to kiss.

sun-sunan kisses.

sun II (*C*) *tembakau* – high-quality tobacco.

sun III (*Jp*) term for the former *kewedanan.*

sunah (*A*) 1 commendable, though not obligatory, according to Islamic law. 2 proper conduct. 3 tradition. 4 the path or way of the Prophet; the body of traditions recording the deeds, pronouncements, examples, and things silently approved by the Prophet, cited by Muslims as a guide to personal and communal behavior. *ahli* – Sunni Muslims. *sembahyang* – recommended, additional but not obligatory, prayer.

menyunahkan to recommend; → SUNAT.

sunam menyunam 1 to dive (of aircraft). 2 to smuggle.

menyunamkan to put s.t. into a dive.

sunan (*Jv*) 1 the monarch of Surakarta (short for *susuhunan*), ruler. 2 Islamic title for the earliest preachers of Islam in Indonesia. – *Gunung Jati* the military resort command (*Korém* 063) in Cirebon.

kesunanan 1 the *kraton* in Surakarta. 2 the area ruled by the monarch of Surakarta.

sunat (*A*) commendable but not obligatory under Islamic law. *tukang* – circumciser. – *rasul* circumcision; → SUNAH. **menyunatrasulkan** 1 to circumcise. 2 to prescribe as s.t. meritorious in Islam.

bersunat circumcised. *orang yang tidak* ~ an uncircumcised person.

menyunat [and **nyunat** (*coq*)] 1 to circumcise. 2 to cut (currency/ allocation, etc.) (by cutting its value/amount, etc.). *Warga transmigrasi mengeluh karena jatahnya disunat.* The transmigrants complained that their (rice) allocation had been cut. 3 to steal, embezzle, skim (money off the top).

menyunati (*pl obj*) to circumcise.

menyunatkan 1 to have (a boy) circumcised. 2 to urge s.o. to do s.t. which is not obligatory.

tersunat circumcised.

sunatan 1 feast celebrating a circumcision. ~ *masal* mass circumcision. 2 circumcised. *anak* ~ a circumcised child.

penyunat circumciser.

penyunatan 1 circumcising. **2** cutting (the value of money, etc.), shortening (a *wayang* performance).

Sunbulah and **Sunbulat** (*A zod*) Virgo.

Sunda I *tanah* – and **Pasundan** the Sundalands of West Java, comprising the following regions: *Banten, DKI Jaya, (tanah) Priangan*, and *Cirebon. bahasa* – Sundanese (language). *orang* – Sundanese (person).

menyundakan to translate into Sundanese.

kesundaan Sundanese (*mod*). *unsur* ~ Sundanese elements (in music, etc.).

Sunda II – *Kelapa* the *Pasar Ikan* in Jakarta.

Sunda III – *wiwitan* the set of beliefs which the Badui people adhere to.

sundai (*M*) *limau* – k.o. lemon used for making curry.

sundak I (*M*) **menyundak 1** to bump (one's head against). **2** to rise (of tide).

tersundak bumped/hit (against).

sundak II sting(er) (of a bee, etc.), spine (of a fish).

sundal I 1 immoral, lewd. **2** whore, prostitute; → PELACUR, WATUNAS.

bersundal and **menyundal** to engage in prostitution, prostitute o.s.

sundalan prostitution.

persundalan 1 lewdness. **2** prostitution.

sundal II – *malam* Mexican tuberose, *Polianthes tuberosa*.

sundal III – *bolong* female devil who has a hole in her neck.

sundang a Buginese sword, often wavy in shape, with a metal-bound cockatoo-shaped hilt.

sundari I (*Skr cla*) a nymph in romances.

sundari II buzzer attached to a kite.

sundel → SUNDAL I.

sundep (*Jv*) (*hama* –) rice (stem) borer, *Tryporhyza spp.*

sundik → SONDÉK.

sunduk (*Jv*) skewer.

menyunduk 1 to stick, prick. **2** to skewer, put on a skewer.

menyunduki to skewer, put on a skewer.

sundukan things skewered (or, put on a skewer).

sundul I menyundul to hit with the head, head (a ball, in soccer).

tersundul hit with the head.

sundulan ~ *kepala* a header (in soccer), shot made by hitting the ball with the head.

penyundul s.o. who hits s.t. with the head.

penyundulan hitting with the head.

sundul II menyundul 1 to go up, rise, increase. *Harga roti bisa* ~ *ke Rp 2.000.* The price of bread may go up to Rp 2,000. ~ *angkasa/langit* (*coq*) sky-high; → SELANGIT. **2** to loom up.

sundus, sundusi, and **sundusin** (*A cla*) silk interwoven with gold.

sundut I (*M*) descendant; generation; heirloom, heritage.

bersundut with descendants.

sundut-bersundut by descent, from father to son, hereditary.

sundut II (*M*) **menyundut** to carry in a litter, etc.

sundut III (*J*) *meriam/senapan* – muzzleloader.

menyundut to set a match to, set fire to, light (a cigarette, etc. with a match).

menyunduti (*pl obj*) to light, set fire to.

tersundut [and **kesundut** (*coq*)] ~ *rokok* burnt by a cigarette.

sundutan burns ~ *rokok* cigarette burns.

penyundut 1 kindled, lit, ignited. **2** kindling (of fire), ignition.

penyunduran 1 burning, lighting with a cigarette, etc. ~ *dengan puntung rokok* burning with a lit cigarette. **2** firing up.

sungai 1 river. **2** (river) basin. *anak* – tributary, rivulet. *menganak* – to flow/stream continuously (of sweat, etc.). *ke* – (to go to the river) to defecate. *ke* – *sambil mandi* to do two or more things at the same time. – *bawah tanah* underground river. – *Gerong* an oil-rich satellite city of Palembang (South Sumatra). – *induk* main stream. – *lenyap* disappearing river. (*pergi*) *ke* – a) (to go) toward a river. b) (*coq*) to relieve o.s., answer a call of nature. – *mati* dry stream.

persungaian river system.

sungga (*cla*) **1** man-trap; → SUDA. **2** spur, spiked ball.

menyungga to spur.

sunggaran (*Jv*) k.o. bouffant hairstyle.

sunggi (*Jv*) **menyunggi** to carry s.t. on one's head. ~ *sebuah penampi di atas kepala* to carry a winnow on the head.

sungging I (*Jv*) **1** intricate painting on leather *wayang* puppets. **2** paint used for the intricate designs on leather *wayang* puppets. *seni* – enameling, painting on leather.

sesungging a wisp (of a smile). ~ *senyum cerah selalu tampak di wajahnya* a touch of a bright smile is always on her face.

menyungging to paint intricate and delicate designs (on leather *wayang* puppets).

menyunggingkan to sketch (a smile). *Para gadis* ~ *seulas senyum di bibir meréka yang mérah merekah, segenit mungkin.* The girls sketched a touch of a smile on their red lips, as flirtatious as possible.

tersungging 1 painted. **2** adorned (with a smile). *Bibirnya* ~ *senyum.* Her lips were adorned with a smile.

sunggingan painting (on leather *wayang* puppets).

penyungging painter (of leather *wayang* puppets).

penyunggingan painting, applying paint (to leather *wayang* puppets). ~ *wayang itu dilakukan oléh tangan-tangan seniman yang terampil.* Painting the *wayang* puppets was done by the hands of skillful artists.

sungging II (*M*) **menyungging** to bend down with the rear higher than the front.

sunggit → SUNGKIT I.

sungguh 1 true; truly, really. –? really? – *suatu yang ironis* really, s.t. ironic. **2** serious(ly); intense(ly). *berjanji dengan* – to swear solemnly. – *mati!* I swear to God! **3** really, very, extremely, excessively, too; → AMAT I, SANGAT, TERLALU. *bising* – *bunyi keduanya bertengkar* the noise made by the two of them quarreling was really deafening. *letih* – *rasa badan saya* I'm really very tired. **4** actually, in fact, as a matter of fact; → MÉMANG, SEBENARNYA. – *dia datang ke mari, tetapi tidak bertemu dengan saya.* He actually came here, but he didn't meet me. **5** – *hati* in earnest, seriously, for real. *dilaksanakan dengan* – *hati* carried out in earnest. *tidak* – insincere. **ketidak-sungguhan** insincerity.

sungguh-sungguh in earnest, seriously; (for) real. *Belajarlah* ~. Study hard/seriously. *Sinyokelah itu* ~, *bukan palsu.* That Santa Claus is real, not fake.

sesungguh ~ *hati* with all one's heart. *Aku berdoa* ~ *hati agar wanita malang itu segera sembuh.* I pray with all my heart that the unfortunate woman gets well soon.

sesungguhnya 1 *dengan* ~ in all seriousness. *menerangkan dengan* ~ to explain in all seriousness. **2** authentic, real, genuine, not fake.

bersungguh-sungguh to be sincere/truthful/honest/authentic. *Jika* ~, *pasti tercapai juga cita-citamu itu.* If you're sincere, your ideals will certainly be achieved anyway.

menyungguh(-nyungguh)i and **mempersungguhi** (*M*) to do s.t. in all earnestness (or, seriously), do one's very best, be zealous (in the cause of). *Meréka itu menyungguhi mempelajari soal-soal yang timbul pada akhir-akhir ini.* They did their very best to study recent problems.

menyungguhkan 1 to confirm; to admit that s.t. is real; to justify; to authorize. **2** to exert o.s.; to try seriously to. **3** (~ *diri*) to defend o.s.

sungguhan 1 authentic, real, genuine, not fake; → TULÉN. *emas* ~ pure gold. *motor* ~ a real engine (not a toy). ~ *atau sandiwara?* Real or a drama? **2** in all seriousness, truthfully.

kesungguhan seriousness, truthfulness, authenticity. *Aku merasa tak ada* ~ *dalam hidupku ini.* I've the feeling that there's nothing serious in my life. *dengan penuh* ~ in all seriousness, in earnest, joking aside, wholeheartedly, warmly (devoted). **berkesungguhan** in earnest, earnestly, seriously.

kesungguh-sungguhan to be serious. *Matanya hitam, besar,* ~. Her eyes were black, large, and serious.

penyungguhan confirmation, attestation, authentification.

sungguhpun although, even though, in spite of the fact that. – *bagus, tak mau saya membelinya.* Even though it's beautiful, I don't want to buy it. – *mahal, akan kubeli juga* Even though it's expensive, I'll buy it anyway. – *begitu/demikian* nevertheless, for all that.

sungil (*Jv*) impassible, difficult/hazardous to negotiate/pass through (of a mountain pass, etc.).

sungkah (*M*) → SENGAM. **menyungkah(kan)** to gorge o.s., eat greedily.

sungkai I a small tree used for hedges, *Peronema canescens*.

sungkai II *hantu* – a malignant forest spirit.

sungkal – *bajak* plowshare, coulter.

   menyungkal 1 to plow, dig/turn up the earth. 2 to pry s.t. out (of a hole, etc.).

sungkan (*Jv*) reluctant to approach a superior or take some action towards a superior; → ENGGAN I, SEGAN I.

   sungkan-sungkan to feel embarrassed before one's superiors.

   menyungkani to feel this k.o. reluctance toward s.o.

   sungkanan habitually unwilling.

   kesungkanan aversion, dislike, unwillingness, dislike (for).

sungkap tersungkap pulled loose (of a toe- or fingernail). *Kuku ~ kena batu.* His fingernail was pulled loose on a stone.

sungkawa (*Jv*) mourning.

   bersungkawa to express one's condolences; → BÉLASUNGKAWA.

sungkem (*Jv*) ways of showing esteem and humility toward s.o. (kneeling, making a *sembah*, pressing one's nose to the person's knee, making another *sembah*).

   menyungkem(i) to pay respect to (in that way).

   tersungkem with one's head bent down and touching the ground.

sungkit I bersungkit embroidered, interwoven; → SONGKÉT.

   menyungkit to embroider.

sungkit II menyungkit to extract, remove, pry out, take away. *~ tutup botol* to remove the lid of the bottle.

   penyungkit s.t. which extracts, etc. *~ tutup botol* bottle opener.

sungkuk tersungkuk-sungkuk nodding out (due to sleepiness).

sungkum menyungkum to lie prone (with the face touching the ground, etc.). *~ tanah* to lie with the face touching the ground.

   menyungkumkan to place s.t. face down on the ground.

   tersungkum fallen forward on one's face, prostrate.

sungkup concave cover/shelter, cap, bell. – *penggelembung* bell/bubble cap. – *penyelam* diving bell. – *udara* air chamber.

   bersungkup covered with such a cover/shelter.

   menyungkup(i) 1 to cover with such a cover/shelter. 2 to be/go around, surround, envelop.

   menyungkupkan to cover with (a hand/lid, etc.).

   tersungkup covered (with a hand/lid, etc.).

   sungkupan 1 lid, cover. 2 a basket used to cover drying clothes. 3 place covered by a concave cover/lid, etc., chamber.

   penyungkup bell jar.

sungkur I bersungkuran with lowered/bowed head. *jatuh ~* to fall flat on one's stomach.

   menyungkur 1 to lower one's head in order to butt. *Kerbau ~ hendak menyeruduk.* The buffalo lowered its head to attack. 2 to fall/pitch forward. 3 to dig/root up. *Babi ~ tanam-tanaman.* Pigs rooted up the plants.

   tersungkur 1 fallen/pitched forward; to fall flat on one's face. 2 (in sports) defeated.

sungkur II (*M*) spade, shovel; → SEKOP.

   menyungkur to spade, shovel.

   sungkuran (*nyiur –*) young coconut which is still soft.

sunglap to juggle, perform conjuring tricks; → SULAP I. *tukang –* conjurer, juggler.

   menyunglap(kan) to perform conjuring tricks with.

sunglir yellowtail (a fish species), rainbow runner, *Elagatis bipinnulatus.*

sungsang I 1 wrong side up, upside down, topsy-turvy, back to front. 2 against the grain. *letak –* breech (the position of a fetus in the womb). *letak bayinya –* it was a breech baby, i.e., the fetus was upside down in the womb. *– kalak* upside down. *– sumbal/sumbel* (*J*) a) somersault, head over heels, upside down. b) all topsy-turvy. *Buat apa – sumbel kerja?* Why such hasty and careless work? *hidup – sumbel* hand-to-mouth existence. *bagai/seperti air ditarik –* to work hard unnecessarily (due to a wrong approach, etc.).

   menyungsang to go against (the grain), sail against (the wind/current), be upside down/topsy-turvy.

   menyungsangkan to perform/do in a topsy-turvy way, do s.t. backwards, stand things on their head.

   tersungsang turned upside down.

sungsang II (*kembang –*) k.o. poisonous plant, flame/glory lily, *Gloriosa superba.*

sungsep (*J*) to fall headfirst.

menyungsep [and nyungsep (*coq*)] to fall forward/straight down, crash. *Kepala Tie ~ lembut di dada saya.* Tie's head fell forward tenderly on my chest. *Dua pesawat itu ~.* The two planes went straight down.

   menyungsepkan to make s.t. crash, bring down.

sungsum → SUMSUM.

sungsung (*Bal*) menyungsung to pray.

sungu I (*Jv*) horn (of animals). *singkat –* short-tempered. *– badak* rhinoceros horn.

sungu II (*M*) snout, beak.

sungu III filth, dirt, excrement.

sungut I *– létér* a) nagging, grumbling. b) glutton, greedy person.

   bersungut(-sungut) to grumble, grouse, complain.

   menyunguti to grumble about.

   sungutan complaint.

   penyungut constant complainer.

sungut II 1 antenna, palp, feeler, barbel (of a fish), whiskers (of a cat). 2 moustache.

suni I → SUNNI.

suni II (*M*) → SUNYI.

sunjam overturned.

   tersunjam fallen headfirst.

sunkist (*E*) *buah –* Sunkist orange.

sunnah → SUNAH. *– wal jama'ah* tradition and collective wisdom of theologians.

Sunni (*A*) Sunni, i.e., the tradition of most Muslims, who accept the historical experience of the early community as having been divinely guided and emphasize the importance of the community and communal tradition; *cp* SYIAH.

Sunnisasi Sunnization.

sunsum → SUMSUM.

sunti (*Skr*) 1 wart-like excrescence at the root of certain plants. 2 k.o. ginger used for folk medicine, *Zingiber gramineum*. *perawan/anak dara –* a very young girl, prepubertal girl. *– halia* ginger.

suntiabu → SETIABU.

suntih (*M*) menyuntih to cut pieces off, tear (prey) to pieces.

suntik I (*Jv*) inject, injection; → (IN)JÉKSI, VAKSIN. *jarum –* syringe, hypodermic needle. *obat –* vaccine. *– kebal* immunization.

   menyuntik [and nyuntik (*coq*)] 1 to vaccinate/inoculate against. *disuntik pés/cacar* to be vaccinated against the plague/smallpox. 2 to inject, infuse (ideas/money, etc.) into. *Meréka akan disuntik dengan pikiran-pikiran anti-Barat.* They would be injected with anti-Western ideas. *disuntik mati* to be killed by lethal injection. 3 to remove/pry out (a thorn from under the skin with a needle). 4 to engrave (metal, etc.) with a sharp object.

   menyuntikkan 1 to inject. *~ narkotik ke tubuhnya* to take drugs intravenously. *~ spérma ke dalam sél telur* to inject sperm into an ovum. 2 (*coq*) to inspire with. *Komandan mengumpulkan anak buahnya untuk ~ keberanian.* The commander convened his men to encourage them.

   tersuntik injected (with), stuck (with a needle).

   suntikan 1 inoculation, injection, vaccination, shot, infusion (of capital). *~ antitétanus* antitetanus shot. *~ di bawah kulit* subcutaneous injection. 2 injected, infused. *nilai modal ~* the value of infused capital. 3 (*coq*) inspiring (with courage, etc.).

   penyuntik device used to inject/vaccinate/inoculate. *jarum ~* hypodermic. *pihak ~ dana* the party infusing funds, financier.

   penyuntikan injecting, vaccinating, inoculating.

suntik II *getah –* → SONDÉK.

sunting 1 hair ornament (flower, etc.) put behind the ear. *– hati* darling, sweetheart. *– malai* hair ornament put behind the ear.

   bersunting with a hair ornament, to wear a hair ornament.

   bersuntingkan with ... as a hair ornament.

   menyuntingkan to put/stick (a flower, etc. behind the ear as an ornament). *~ belaian hatinya* to marry one's sweetheart.

   mempersunting 1 to put (a flower, etc.) behind the ear as an ornament. 2 to marry (a woman), take s.o. as one's wife. *~ ilmu* to acquire knowledge.

   tersunting ornamented (with a flower stuck in the hair, etc.).

   suntingan 1 flower, etc. put in the hair or behind the ear as an ornament. 2 (*bio*) corymb.

   penyuntingan putting (a flower, etc.) behind the ear.

sunting II menyunting 1 to edit (s.o. else's writing for publication); to edit (a movie by putting shots and scenes in a suitable sequence). **2** to supervise/direct the publication of (a newspaper/book/magazine, etc.).
 sunting-menyunting editing.
 tersunting edited, redacted.
 suntingan edited. ~ *manuskrip* edited manuscript.
 penyunting 1 editor. ~ *bahasa* language editor. ~ *bantu* assistant editor. ~ *berita* senior editor. ~ *kelola* managing editor. ~ *kepala* editor-in-chief. ~ *laksana* executive editor. ~ *matan/naskah* copy editor. ~ *pelaksana* executive editor. ~ *pengada* acquisitions editor. ~ *sejiran* associate editor.
 penyuntingan 1 editing. **2** editorial work.
suntrut (*Jv*) sad, depressed.
suntuk I 1 to have reached the limit, one cannot go further, one cannot continue; (time) is up, the time limit has passed, too late. *telah – waktunya* it's too late now, it's past the time limit. *takut – malam* afraid of being caught out after dark; → KEMALAMAN. *orang – tua* an old man who is trying to act young again. **2** the whole/entire (day/night, etc.), all ... long. *sehari –* all day long. *setahun –* all year long; → SEPANJANG. *sampai dua jam –* for two whole hours.
 tersuntuk 1 obstructed/thwarted/restrained (so that one cannot go ahead or up). **2** held up so that it is late.
 kesuntukan run out of, have no more left, be short of. ~ *akal* at one's wits end. ~ *masa* to run out of time. ~ *uang* out of money, broke.
suntuk II (*M*) **1** short, small; brief; narrow. **2** narrow-minded. *pikiran –* narrow-minded. *– akal* narrow-minded; not very smart, mentally limited; → SONTOK II.
suntuk III → ANTUK I.
suntung → SOTONG.
sunu (*M*) **menyunu** to light (a fire), ignite, kindle.
sunukung monkey.
sunyata (*Jv* from *Skr*) true.
 kesunyataan and **kesunyatan** (*Jv*) mystical truth. *ilmu –* mysticism.
sunyi (*Skr*) **1** quiet, silent. *Perpustakaan adalah tempat yang – dan sesuai untuk menelaah.* A library is a quiet place appropriate for studying. *Pasar malam itu sudah mulai –.* The fair began to quiet down. **2** lonely, deserted, empty, vacant. **3** free from, can escape. *Manusia di dunia ini tidak – dari melakukan kesalahan.* People in this world are not free from making mistakes. **4** (of business, etc.) quiet, slack. *Pasar uang hari ini –.* The money market was slack today. *tidak –.-nya* incessant. *– senyap* deathly quiet, silent as the grave.
 bersunyi(-sunyi) to seclude/isolate o.s.
 menyunyi to quiet down, become quiet.
 menyunyikan 1 to quiet s.o. down. **2** to free s.o. (from s.t.).
 kesunyian 1 stillness, quiet, silence. **2** calm(ness), tranquillity, composure. **3** (to feel) lonely, lonesome.
sup I (*D*) soup; → SOP. *– komputasi* computational soup.
sup II → SUF.
supa I (*Port IBT*) soup.
supa II (*S*) general name for mushrooms. *– lembar* Jew's ear fungus, *Auricularia auricula-judae.*
supai (*A Hind*) sepoy.
supas [*survéi penduduk antar sénsus*] inter-censal population survey.
supaya (*Skr*) in order to, so that, to, so as to; → AGAR I. *Kami harus selalu bersih, – tidak sakit.* We should always be clean so as not to get sick. *Saya mengusulkan – dia makan dulu.* I suggested that he eat first. *ingin – ...* to want (s.o.) to ... *– tidak/jangan* so as not to, so that ... doesn't ... *– kelapa jangan dimakan bajing* so that the squirrels wouldn't nibble away at the coconuts.
supel (*D*) **1** supple, flexible. **2** gets along with people easily, easygoing, sociable.
 kesupelan 1 flexibility. **2** sociability.
Supeltas [*Sukarélawan pengatur lalulintas*] Voluntary Traffic Regulators, who chase after *pengebut.*
super- 1 super-. **2** super (*mod*). *negara –* superstate.
supér (*J*) driver, chauffeur.
Super 98 1 supreme (gasoline) (used exclusively for luxury se-

dans). **2** bribes (code word in use at the Tanjung Priok port area in Jakarta).
superaktif (*E*) superactive.
Superban and **Superbén** the Suburban station wagon.
superberani supercourageous.
superburon superfugitive, reference to Philippine Colonel Gregorio Honasan.
supercanggih supersophisticated.
supercepat superfast.
superfisial (*E*) superficial.
superfosfat (*D*) superphosphate.
superinféksi (*D*) superinfection.
superior (*E*) **1** superior (*mod*). **2** superior, head of a religious community.
superioritas and **superioritét** (*D*) superiority.
superkaya superrich.
superkonduktivitas (*D*) superconductivity.
superkonduktor (*D*) superconductor.
superkuat superpower.
superlatif (*D*) superlative.
superlativisme (*E*) superlativism.
supermal hypermall.
superman (*E*) **1** superman. **2** an official or any backer who can be of help in quickly clearing incoming goods through customs at the port of Tanjung Priok.
supermarkét (*E*) supermarket; → PASAR *swalayan.*
supermi instant noodles.
supermodérn ultramodern.
 mensupermodérnkan to ultramodernize. *Pemerintah Lee Kuan Yew adalah suatu pemerintah modérn dengan tujuan untuk ~ Singapura.* The Lee Kuan Yew government is a modern administration whose goal is to supermodernize Singapore.
supernatural (*E*) supernatural.
superoksida (*E*) superoxide.
superorganik (*E*) superorganic.
superpower (*E*) superpower; → ADIKUASA.
superprioritas top priority.
 mengsuperprioritaskan to give top priority to. *Ya, Jambi mémang ~ olahraga perorangan.* Yes, Jambi is giving top priority to individual sports.
superramah extremely friendly/hospitable.
Supersemar [*Surat Perintah Sebelas Maret*] **1** the letter dated March 11, 1966, which handed power over to President Soeharto. **2** former President Soeharto's nickname; *cp* SEMAR. *béasiswa –* name of a presidential scholarship.
superskrip (*D*) superscript.
superskripsi (*D*) superscription.
supersonik (*D*) supersonic. *pesawat – (serbaguna)* (all-purpose) supersonic aircraft.
superstar (*E*) superstar.
supervisi (*D*) supervision.
 mensupervisi to supervise.
supervisor *D* supervisor.
supidol → SPIDOL.
supir driver, chauffeur.
 menyupir(i) to drive (a car).
supit I chopsticks (Chinese eating utensils); → SUMPIT III.
supit II (*Jv*) pincers, tongs.
 menyupit(i) to circumcise.
 supitan circumcision.
suplai (*E*) supply; → PASOK.
 mensuplai and **menyuplai** to supply.
 pensuplai and **penyuplai** supplier.
 pensuplaian and **penyuplaian** supply, supplying.
suplai(e)r and **suplayer** (*E*) supplier.
suplemén (*D*) supplement.
 menyupleménkan to supplement.
suplem<0x00E9>ntasi (*E*) supplementation.
suplési (*D*) suppletion.
supletoar (*D*) supplemental, supplementary. *anggaran –* supplementary budget.
suplir (*D*) maidenhair fern, *Adiantum cuneatum. – besi* silver-dollar

maidenhair fern, *Adiantum peruvianum*. - *gosong* delta maiden-hair fern, *Adiantum raddianum*. - *kipas* fan maidenhair fern, *Adiantum wrightii*. - *mawar* rough maidenhair fern, *Adiantum hispidulum*.

suplir-supliran maidenhair-fernlike.

supor(t) (*E*) support.

mensupor(t) to support.

suporter (*E*) supporter.

suportif (*E*) supportive.

supra- over-, super-, above, beyond the limits.

supra-alami supernatural.

Supradin and **Supradyn** brand name of a multivitamin preparation containing minerals and trace elements.

supranasional (*D/E*) supranational.

supranatural (*E*) supranatural; → SUPRA-ALAMI.

suprémasi (*E*) supremacy.

sur I → SYUR I, II.

sur II (in acronyms) → SURVÉI.

sura → SURAH.

surabi (*ob*) → SERABAI.

surah (*A*) a chapter of the Koran.

surahi (*A*) relating to a chapter in the Koran.

surai I 1 hair (of the head). **2** mane, long hair on the neck of a horse, lion, etc.

bersurai to have long hair on the neck.

surai II bersurai to disperse, scatter, break up.

menyurai(kan) to disperse, scatter, break s.t. up.

suralaya and **suraloka** (*Skr*) **1** Hindu heaven on Mount Meru. **2** abode of the gods.

suram → MURAM. **1** dim, not bright. **2** gloomy, overcast, cloudy. *Hari pun –.* The day was overcast. **3** tarnished, having lost its brightness. **4** gloomy, not cheerful, depressed. *– saja mukanya sehari ini.* He's been depressed all day. **5** not clear, dull. **6** bleak, uncertain (of the future), not having a good outcome. *Masa depannya –.* His future is bleak.

suram-suram slightly dim/dark, etc. *–.– gelap* dark.

menyuram to become dim/gloomy/dark, etc.

menyuramkan to blur, darken, dim, make gloomy, turn down (a light).

kesuraman 1 gloom, dreariness, cheerlessness, dimness. **2** dullness. **3** bleakness, uncertainty.

surat I 1 letter, mail. *Apa ada – buat saya?* Is there any mail for me? *– mengatakan ...* the letter stated ... *memberi kabar dengan –* to send a written message. *pelajaran dengan –* correspondence course. *sepucuk/secarik –* a letter. *juru –* secretary, writer. *tahu di mana –* literate. *tukang –* mailman. **2** certificate, (official) document. **3** writing. **4** ticket, note, notification. **5** receipt, check. *– aksép* promissory note. *– amanat Paus* Papal encyclical. *– andil* stock certificate. *– anggota* membership card. *– angkat(an)* letter of appointment. *– angkutan* bill of lading, B/L. *– asal usul* pedigree, family tree. *– bahari* (*ob*) receipt. *– bajak* letter of marques and reprisal. *– balik nama* certificate of transfer. *– banding* appeal. *– bantahan* defense, pleading. *– baptisan* baptismal certificate. *– bawa* bearer instrument. *– bébas fiskal* letter certifying that exit taxes have been paid. *– bébas ganti-rugi* letter of indemnity. *– bébas Gestapu* statement of noninvolvement in *Gestapu*. *– bébas narkoba* certificate of non-drug use. *– bébas pinjam* statement that all borrowed books have been returned. *– bébas tunggakan* statement that there are no arrears. *– berantai* chain letter. *–.– berharga* commercial paper, negotiable instrument, securities. *– berharga atas tunjuk* bearer documents. *– Berharga Bepergian* k.o. traveler's check issued by *Bank Bumi Daya*. *– Jangka Péndék* Treasury Bills. *– berharga pasar uang* [SBPU] money market instrument. *– berita peristiwa/perkara* protocol, record, minutes. *– berkala* periodical (publication). *– bersih Gestapu* statement of noninvolvement in *Gestapu*. *– bersumpah* (in Ambon) marriage notice. *– bom* letter bomb. *– budek* anonymous letter. *– bukti* a) voucher. b) certificate, written evidence. *–.– bukti (selayaknya)* (relevant) documentary evidence. *– bukti diri* proof of identity. *– bukti kewarganegaraan (Républik) Indonésia* [SBK(R)I] certificate of Indonesian citizenship, Indonesian citizenship papers. *– Bukti*

Pelaporan Orang Asing [SBPOA] Foreigners Registration Certificate. *– bukti pembayaran* receipt. *– bukti pengakuan utang* IOU. *– bukti penimbunan* warehouse receipt. *– buntu* undeliverable/dead letter. *– buta* anonymous letter. *– cacar* certificate of vaccination. *– cepat* special-delivery letter. *– cerai* certificate of divorce. *– cinta* love letter. *– dagang* a) business letter. b) commercial paper. *– dakwa* summons. *– dakwaan* indictment. *– denda* notification of a fine. *–.– di bawah No. ...* (in advertisements) write box ... *– di bawah tangan* private instrument. *– dinas* official letter. *– édaran* a) circular (letter). b) encyclical. *– éléktronik* [ratron] e-mail, electronic letter. *– fiskal* fiscal statement, i.e., document stating that one has paid all his taxes; the document is required if s.o. wants to leave the country. *– formulir* form. *– gadai/gadén* (*Jv*) a) pawn ticket. b) mortgage bond. *– ganti nama* name change certificate. *– garansi* guarantor's statement (in adoption verdicts). *– gelap* anonymous letter. *– Gembala* Pastoral letter. *– giro* (money) transfer card, giro form. *– gugat* (*leg*) verdict requested by the prosecutor. *– gugatan* (*leg*) complaint. *– hutang* debenture, debt instrument, IOU. *– ijazah/ijasah* diploma, certificate. *– ijin* → SURAT *izin*. *– ikrar* affidavit. *– Impor Valuta Asing* Foreign Exchange Import Permit. *– introduksi* letter of introduction. *– isian* form/blank (to be filled in). *– izin* permit, license. *– izin bangunan* building permit. *– izin jalan* travel permit. *– izin keluar* exit permit (an immigration document). *– izin mendirikan bangunan* building permit. *– izin mendarat* a) landing permit (for aircraft). b) disembarkation permit (for passengers arriving in Indonesia by plane or ship). *– izin mendirikan bangunan* building license. *– izin mengemudi* [SIM] driver's license. *– Izin Penduduk* Permission to Take up Residence. *– izin pengangkutan* transport permit. *– izin pengangkutan antarpulau* interisland transport permit. *– izin pengeluaran* export permit. *– izin penghunian* certificate of occupancy. *– izin pernikahan* marriage consent declaration (from the parents). *– Izin Perumahan* [SIP] Housing Permit. *– izin sakit* sick note. *– Izin Terbit* [SIT] Publication Permit. *– Izin Usaha Penerbitan Pers* [SIUPP] press publication permit. *– Izin Usaha Perdagangan* [SIUP] business license. *– jalan* a) travel documents (for shipped goods). b) pass allowing one to travel in certain parts of the outer islands. c) k.o. travel document for adopted babies. *– jaminan* a) guarantor's statement (in adoption verdicts). b) letter of indemnity. c) surety bond. *– jawatan* official letter. *– kabar* newspaper. *– kabar dinding* wall poster. *– kabar pagi* morning paper. **persurat-kabaran 1** the press. **2** journalism (*mod*). *– kaléng* anonymous letter. *– kapal* ship's papers. *– kawat* telegram, wire, cable. *– kawin* marriage certificate. *– keberatan* objection in writing, notice of objection. *– keluarga* family documents and papers. *– kematian* death certificate. *– kemilikan* title deed, deed of ownership. *– kenalan* letter of recommendation. *– kenal (ke)lahir(an)* certificate of recognition of birth (a document drawn up when a person has no birth certificate). *– kepada pembawa/pengganti* check payable to order. *–.– kepercayaan* credentials. *– keputusan* [SK] directive, decree. *– keputusan bersama* [SKB] joint decree/directive. *– keputusan Présidén* [Kepprés] executive order, presidential decree. *– kesanggupan* promissory note, P/N; → PROMÉS, SURAT *sanggup*. *– kesepakatan* letter of intent. *– keterangan* a) certificate, declaration. b) written reference. c) testimonial. d) identity card, identification papers, i.e., document explaining who the bearer is and what he/she does. *– keterangan adat-istiadat* certificate of good character. *– keterangan asal (barang)* and *– keterangan asal-usul* certificate of origin. *– keterangan atas sumpah* affidavit. *– keterangan bébas Gestapu/PKI* statement of noninvolvement in *Gestapu/PKI*. *– keterangan belum pernah menikah* certificate of unmarried status. *– keterangan berbadan séhat* certificate of good health. *– keterangan (ber)kelakuan baik* [SKBB] certificate of good character. *– keterangan cerai* divorce papers. *– keterangan dokter* physician's certificate, doctor's note. *– keterangan hidup* life certificate. *– keterangan keahlian* certificate stating that the holder has a certain skill, *esp* for medical specialists. *– keterangan kelahiran/lahir* certificate of clarification of birth (a different document than a birth certificate). *– keterangan kesaksian* dep-

osition, sworn statement of evidence. – *keterangan lahir* →
SURAT *keterangan kelahiran*. – *keterangan lolos butuh/keterangan tidak berkeberatan berhenti* certificate of dispensability. –
keterangan miskin proof of insolvency. – *Ketetapan Pajak*
[SKP] Tax Assessment Notice. – *Ketetapan Pajak Kurang
Bayar* [SKP-KB] Tax Deficiency Notice. – *Ketetapan Lebih Bayar*
Tax Overpayment Notice. – *muatan* manifest. – *keterangan sakit*
sick leave certificate. – *ketetapan pajak* tax notice. – *kewarganegaraan* citizenship papers. – *kilat* express letter. – *kilat khusus*
special-delivery letter. – *kir* inspection certificate. – *kiriman* letters to the editor. – *krédit* letter of credit, L/C. – *krédit perjalanan* traveler's check/letter of credit. – *kuasa* power of
attorney, authorization, warrant, proxy letter. – *kuasa di bawah
tangan* private authorization. – *kuasa khusus* special/limited
power of attorney. – *lahir* birth certificate. – *lamaran* application (form). – *lampiran* enclosure. – *laut* (*naut*) certificate of
registry. – *layang* (*Mal*) anonymous letter, poison-pen letter. –
légitimasi proof of identity. – *lélang* notice of auction. – *lepas* a)
discharge papers, pink slip. b) divorce certificate. – *mati* death
certificate. – *mentéga* letter of dismissal, pink slip. – *menyusul*
(in telegrams) letter follows. – *minat* letter of intent. – *muatan*
bill of lading, B/L. – *muatan cacat/kotor* foul bill of lading. –
muatan udara airway bill. – *mutasi* transfer notification. –
nadar/nazar letter promising s.t. – *ngablak* open letter. – *niaga*
commercial paper. – *nomor kendaraan* vehicle registration
certificate. – *obligasi* bond. – *order* check paid to order. – *pajak*
income tax form. – *paksa* warrant, writ, order. – *pancang tanah*
land survey document. – *panggilan* a) summons. b) notification
of arrival of a letter or package. – *panggilan sidang* notice to appear in court. – *pas* passport. – *patén* patent. – *pelepasan* release
order. – *Pembaca* Letters to the Editor. – *pembelaan politik*
apology, defense of a political position. – *pemberhentian* letter
of dismissal, pink slip. – *pemberitaan* notice, notification. – *pemberitahuan* declaration, notification, (tax) return. – *pemberitahuan pajak* tax return. – *pemberitahuan pajak terutang*
[SPPT] notification of tax liability. – *pemberitahuan pemasukan
barang* entry for home use (a customs term). – *Pemberitahuan
Tahunan Pajak Penghasilan* [SPTPPh] Annual Income Tax Return. – *pembukaan krédit* letter of credit, L/C. – *pemilihan* ballot (for voting). – *penagihan* dunning letter. – *penahanan* arrest
warrant. – *penawaran* letter of detention. – *penawaran* tender. – *penawaran harga* price quotation. – *penduduk* resident's
card. – *penetapan* letter of decision, decree. – *pengaduan* written complaint. – *pengakuan berutang/hutang* promissory note,
IOU. – *pengakuan lahir* certificate of clarification of birth (a different document than a birth certificate). – *pengangkatan* letter
of appointment. – *pengantar* a) delivery order. b) safe conduct
pass. c) letter/note of advice, advice notice. d) cover letter. e)
invoice. f) bill of lading, B/L. g) forwarding/shipping advice, advice of dispatch/shipment. – *pengantar dokumén* schedule of remittance. – *pengesahan* certification. – *penghargaan* letter of
appreciation. – *pengikat* bond. – *pengiriman* forwarding/shipping advice, advice of dispatch/shipment. – *pengunduran diri*
letter of resignation. – *penugasan* letter of appointment/assignment (to a position). – *penunjukan* a) award (for a tender). b)
letter of appointment. – *penutup* a) (insurance) covering/provisional/cover note, slip. b) (of broker) contract note. – *penyerahan* a) delivery advice. b) certificate of dedication (to God in the
Assemblies of God church). – *perbendaharaan* exchequer bill.
– *perceraian* divorce certificate. – *perdagangan* commercial paper. – *perdamaian* statement of amicable agreement (i.e., out-of-court settlement). – *peringatan* warning. – *perintah* a) warrant,
order. b) commission, mission. – *perintah jalan* [SPJ] travel order. – *perintah kerja* [SPK] work order. – *perintah penahanan*
arrest warrant. – *perintah penangkapan* arrest warrant. – *perintah penggeledahan* search warrant. – *perintah penyerahan* delivery order. – *perintah perjalanan* travel order. – *perjalanan* k.o.
travel document for adopted babies. – *perjalanan laksana
paspor* [SPLP] travel document in lieu of passport, pass. – *perjanjian* contract, pact, agreement. – *permandian* baptismal
certificate. – *permintaan/permohonan* request. – *permintaan
banding* appeal. – *permohonan* application, letter of request. –

perniagaan commercial paper. – *pernyataan* declaration. –
pernyataan ganti nama declaration of change of name. – *pernyataan hutang* acknowledgment of debt/indebtedness. – *pernyataan maksud* letter of intent. – *pernyataan pengunduran*
letter of resignation. – *pernyataan perdamaian* settlement
agreement. – *pernyataan persetujuan orangtua* marriage consent declaration from the parents. – *pernyataan terima kasih*
thank-you letter. – *persaksian hidup* life certificate. – *persetujuan* certification, certificate. – *pertanggungan jawab* statement
of accountability. – *petok* → GIRIK. – *pinjaman* certificate of
debt, IOU. – *piutang* debt instrument. – *polis* policy. – *promés*
promissory note. – *puji(an)* a) letter of recommendation, testimonial. b) attestation. – *putusan* verdict. – *rantai* chain letter. –
rékoméndasi letter of recommendation. – *saham* share/stock
certificate. – *sakti* a recommendation written by a superior or
high-ranking person asking that the holder be given a favor (a
certain job/immunity against legal measures, etc.); *cp*
KATABÉLECE. – *salinan* copy/duplicate. – *sanggup* (*bayar*)
promissory note, P/N. – *ségel* writ, letter on embossed stamped
paper. – *séro* share of stock. – *se(le)baran* circular (letter), pamphlet, leaflet. – *sembah* (*cla*) letter of subjection. – *setangan*
note, memo. – *setoran pajak* [SSP] tax payment form. – *sita*
writ of execution, summons. – *skorsing* suspension order. – *somasi* (*leg*) complaint. – *suara* ballot (for voting). – *sumpah*
official report of administering an oath or of confirmation on
oath. –.– official papers, documents (in court decisions, etc.). –
tagihan dunning letter. – *tagihan pajak* tax notice. – *tahniah* letter of congratulations. – *tahunan* annual reports and accounts.
– *takziah* letter of condolence, condolence note. – *talak* divorce
certificate of a repudiated wife. – *Tamat Belajar (Sekolah
Rakyat)* (Elementary School) Certificate of Graduation. –
tamu appointment-request form. – *tanda* a) (legal) instrument,
certificate. b) letter of identification. – *tanda anggota* membership card. – *tanda hutang* IOU, letter of debt. – *Tanda Kebangsaan* (*naut*) Certificate of Registry. – *tanda Nomor Kendaraan*
[STNK] Vehicle Registration Card. – *tanda pembayaran/pelunasan/penerimaan* receipt. – *tanda pengenal* identity card, ID. –
tanda setoran (in bookkeeping) deposit slip. – *tanda tamat (belajar)* [STTB] diploma, certificate. – *tanda terima setoran*
[STTS] (tax) payment receipt. – *tauliah* credentials. – *teguran*
a) dunning letter. b) warning. – *témpélan* poster, placard, bill. –
terbuka open letter. – *tercatat* registered letter. *dengan –.– tertutup* by secret ballot. – *tidak mampu* certificate of insolvency/
poverty. – *tuduhan* letter of accusation. – *tugas* a) mandatory
letter, instructions. b) mission, commission. – *tumpangan* letter
enclosed inside another letter. – *tunjuk* order document. – *ukur*
a) property title. b) map of premises, surveyor's certificate. c)
certificate of tonnage/measurement. – *uleman/undangan* invitation. – *undi(an)* lottery ticket. – *unjuk* bearer document. –
uraian explanatory letter. – *uraian banding* appellant's brief. –
usiran eviction notice. – *utang* debt instrument, debenture,
IOU. – *warisan/wasiat* (last) will (and testament). – *wésel* bill
of exchange, B/E. – *wésel pinjam nama* accommodation paper. –
yang bersambung-sambung chain letter.

bersurat 1 written. *tak ~* undocumented. **2** inscribed; → BATU
bersurat. **3** (*cla*) to write (a letter).

bersurat(-surat)an and **surat-suratan** to correspond, write to
e.o. *Saya ingin bersurat-suratan dengan dia.* I would like to
correspond with her.

menyurat to write. (*bagai*) *~ di atas air* it's like pouring water
into a sieve.

surat-menyurat 1 correspondence. **2** to correspond, write to
e.o. *Ia curiga setelah sekian lama anaknya tak ~.* He's suspicious that after such a long time his child hasn't corresponded.

menyurati 1 to write to. **2** to inscribe on.

menyuratkan 1 to write down. **2** to inscribe.

tersurat 1 written. **2** destined, ordained. *telah ~ sejak dahulu*
predestined, preordained. **3** explicit. *ada yang ~ ada yang tersirat* you have to read between the lines. *~ dalam hati* in one's
innermost thoughts.

suratan 1 writing. *ilmu ~* graphology. *~ nasib/takdir/tangan* fate,
destiny. *"Apa boléh buat. Sudah ~ nasib!" ujarnya lagi.* "What

can I do? It is my fate!" she went on to say. *Kematian mémang selalu menyedihkan walaupun itu mémang sudah ~ takdir.* Death is always sad even though it is fated. **2**a) *(~ tangan)* lines on the palm of the hand. b) one's fate. **3** manuscript.

penyurat (letter) writer.

penyuratan writing.

persuratan 1 library. **2** belles-lettres, literature. **3** bibliography.

surat II → SURAH. - *Makiyyah* the Meccan verses. - *Madaniyaah* the Medinah verses.

surati of Surat (the Indian port). *bébék/itik* - Manila duck.

suratron [surat éléktronik] e-mail.

surau a small Muslim chapel where there are too few worshipers for a mosque or a *musholla*; not used for the Friday prayers.

suraya *(A) bintang* - the Pleiades.

surban → SERBAN.

suréalis *(D)* surrealist.

suréalisme *(D/E)* surrealism.

suréalistik *(E)* and **suréalistis** *(D)* surrealistic.

surem → SURAM.

surén *(Jv)* Chinese toon, *Toona sinensis/sureni*, a tree whose wood is used for house frames.

surfaktan *(E)* surfactant.

surga *(Skr)* **1** *(esp* but not exclusively Muslim) heaven, paradise. **2** *Siva* or *Betara Guru*'s heaven. - *(berada/terletak) di bawah telepak kaki ibu* a mother's teachings will determine whether one goes to heaven or not. - *dunia* heaven/paradise on earth. - *jannah/jannat* Muslim heaven.

surgaloka → SURGA 2.

surgawi heavenly.

suri I comb (on a loom).

suri II - *teladan* model, example.

suri III *air* - *(M)* juice of the sugar palm, *Arenga pinnata*, before it becomes palm wine/*tuak*.

suri IV *mati* - apparently dead but not really.

suri V *(Skr) ibu* - Queen Mother; → PERMAISURI.

suri VI → SORÉ.

suria → SURYA.

Suriah *(A)* Syria.

suriakanta → SURYAKANTA.

Suriakencana the military resort command *(Korém* 061) in Bogor.

surian I → SURÉN.

surian II *(ob)* → SÉRSAN.

Suriani → SURYANI.

surih *(M)* line, scratch.

   bersurih lined, scratched, striped.

   menyurih to scratch, draw a line on.

   menyurihkan 1 to draw lines with, scratch with. **2** to strike, light. *~ api-api/gérétan* to strike a match. *~ jalan* to find a way to help s.o. *~ percakapan* to turn the conversation.

surili *(S)* banded/grizzled leaf monkey, a leaf monkey with black hair and a white spot on the chest, *Presbytis comata*.

surin → SURÉN.

Suriname Surinam.

surjan I *(Jv)* man's coat with a high collar and wide flaps in front.

   surjanan to wear/put on such a coat.

surjan II *(Jv)* raising the ground level to dry it.

   menyurjan to raise the level of the ground. *Lahan sawahnya disurjan.* The level of his rice field was raised (to dry it out).

suro *(Jv)* → ASYURA.

Suroboyo *(Jv)* Surabaya.

   suroboyoan Surabayan.

surogat *(D)* surrogate, substitute.

surplus *(D)* surplus. *daérah* - a region which produces surplus food.

   mensurpluskan to produce a surplus of. *Bukan mustahil ~ neraca perdagangan tanpa migas.* It's not impossible that it will produce a surplus in the balance of payments without oil and gas.

surprise *(E)* /-prais/ surprise.

sursak *(ob)* → SIRSAK.

surti *(Jv)* precaution, provision.

suru *(Jv)* spoon made from a banana leaf.

suruh I order, tell (s.o. to do s.t.). - *laku* have s.o. do s.t. *kepenyuruhlakuan* causing s.o. to perform a criminal act.

menyuruh [and **nyuruh** *(coq)*] **1** to order, command, instruct, direct. **2** to tell (s.o. to do s.t.), send (s.o. to do s.t.), have s.o. do s.t. *Dia disuruh gurunya ke kantor pos memasukkan surat.* He was told by his teacher to go the post office to mail a letter.

   menyuruh-nyuruh to order s.o. around.

   menyuruhkan to delegate, depute.

suruhan 1 message, order. **2** (s.o. who is) ordered. *budak ~* servant. **3** order, command, direction. **4** messenger, errand boy, emissary. *~ jaya (Mal)* → SURUHAN jaya.

suruh-suruhan *(orang ~)* errand boy, messenger.

pesuruh messenger, errand boy, gofer, agent. *~ Allah* God's apostle, prophet.

penyuruh 1 s.o. who gives orders, principal. **2** *(cla)* mission.

suruh II *(Jv)* betel-vine; → SIRIH.

suruhanjaya *(Mal)* **1** committee. **2** commission. - *Pilihanraya* Board of Elections.

suruk bersuruk(-suruk)an to play hide-and-go-seek.

   menyuruk 1 to crouch down, duck (down away from). **2** to hide, conceal o.s. *~ di bawah kursi* to hide under a chair. *~ di balik lumbung/lalang sehelai* to try in vain to hide. *~ hilang-hilang, memakan habis-habis* to conceal one's desire as perfectly as possible. **3** to creep into, infiltrate.

   menyuruk-nyuruk 1 to crawl crouching down (behind s.t.). **2** in hiding, not openly.

   menyuruki to creep under/behind. *Dia ~ pagar.* He crept under the fence.

   menyurukkan 1 to hide, conceal, put/stick s.t. away/under/inside/behind. *Ia ~ buku porno itu di bawah kasur.* He hid the pornographic book under the mattress. *Ia ~ mukanya di bawah bantal.* He buried his face in the pillow. **2** to bend s.t. down, lower (one's head, etc.).

   tersuruk 1 hidden. **2** ducked down (into). *~ dalam sofanya* ensconced in his couch.

   tersuruk-suruk (to do s.t.) secretly, on the sly, quietly. *Véspa tua itu ~ di jalan-jalan Jakarta mengantar penumpang.* These old Vespas are quietly taking passengers around the streets of Jakarta.

   surukan 1 hideout. **2** concealed/hidden item. *bermain ~* to play hide-and-go-seek.

   penyurukan hiding, concealment.

surung → SORONG.

surup I *(J)* proper, appropriate, suitable; → PATUT.

surup II *(Jv)* → RASUK I. **meyurup** to set (of heavenly bodies).

   kesurupan animated and dominated by an evil spirit; → KEMASUKAN. *mati ~* dead due to this condition.

surut 1 to retire, withdraw, draw back, retreat. *Ia - beberapa langkah.* She drew back several paces. - *langkah* to retreat, withdraw. **2** to ebb/recede (of the tide). *air/pasang* - ebb tide. **3** to diminish, lessen, decline, abate, decrease. *-nya kekuasaan Majapahit* the decline of Majapahit's power. **4** to become calm/quiet, quiet/calm down. *Semakin - rasa tidak senangku.* My dissatisfaction calmed down more and more. **5** to be retroactive, retrogressive. *berlaku -* to be retroactive. *diberlakukan -* to be made retroactive, be imposed retroactively. **6** to fade away. *soré mulai -* the day began to fade away. *Insidén ini kemudian - dari pemberitaan begitu saja.* Later this incident faded away by itself from news releases. *berjalan selangkah, melihat -* look before you leap; always think about tomorrow, not just about today. - *terendah* the lowest water level of the sea at ebb tide.

surut-surut *tidak juga ~nya* never diminishes/dies down.

bersurut and **bersisurut** *(M)* to withdraw, draw back. *Meréka ~ ke kampung.* They withdrew to the village.

menyurut to decrease, decline, diminish, lessen. *Sesudah saling mengusir diplomat hubungan Inggris-Nigéria ~.* After having expelled e.o.'s diplomats, the relationship between England and Nigeria declined. *Di wilayah Jakarta Timur, umumnya air mulai ~.* The water level in the area of East Jakarta in general began to decline.

menyuruti 1 to lessen, make less, decrease. **2** to return to, reunite with. *~ istri* to return to the wife one has previously divorced.

menyurutkan 1 to withdraw s.t. **2** to diminish, lessen, abate, decrease. **3** to put out, extinguish. *~ api* to put out a fire. *~ puntung* to extinguish/put out a cigarette. **4** to soothe, calm down.

~ *darah* to calm o.s. down. ~ *hati* to soothe, calm down, appease. ~ *napas* to cool down (after exercise).

tersurut 1 shrunk back. **2** returned, come back. ~ *pikiran* returned to one's original intention. **3** retired. **4** diminished, lessened. **5** calmed down. ~ *hatinya* calmed down.

surutan 1 withdrawal. **2** (*hydrology*) drawdown.

penyurutan diminishing.

survai and **survéi** (*E*) survey, investigation. – *udara* aerial survey.

mensurvei and **menyurvai** to survey, investigate.

pensurvei and **penyurvai** surveyor, investigator.

survéyor (*E*) surveyor.

surya (*Skr*) (*poet*) the sun. *sang* – the sun (personified). *tata* – solar system.

Suryahi (*ob*) Syrian.

suryakanta (*Skr*) **1** burning glass. **2** magnifying glass. **3** hand-microscope.

suryani (*A*) Syrian.

sus I (*D*) (*kué* –) cream puff.

sus II → ZUS.

sus III (in acronyms) → KHUSUS, KURSUS.

susah 1 trouble, inconvenience; pain, care, sorrow, anxiety, sadness; troubled, sad, sorrowful, anxious. *Ada yang senang, ada yang* –. Some were happy, and some were sad. – *hati* sorrowful. *dengan* – *payah* with great effort. **bersusah payah** to work hard, try one's hardest. **2** to be hard to find. – *dicari* hard to find/come by. **3** to shrink from, have a hard time (doing s.t.). **4** displeasure, annoyance, irritation, misery. **5** troublesome, burdensome, bothersome. **6** difficult/hard to find/get/come by. *Beras* –. Rice is hard to find. – *hilang* hard to get rid of. **7** poor, needy, destitute. *orang-orang* – the poor, paupers, homeless people.

susahnya the trouble/problem [is (that)], how hard it is to. *Ya, apa* ~ *sih mengucap kata 'tidak'*? What's so hard about saying "no"?

susah-susah 1 to go to a lot of trouble/bother to, go to the trouble of. *Meréka tidak usah* ~ *masak*. They don't have to go to the trouble of cooking. *tanpa* ~ without going to any trouble. **2** to work hard, put all one's efforts into. *Ketika ditanya mengapa ia masih* ~ *mengusahakan toko kué-kué ia menjawab ...* When asked why she was still putting all her efforts into running a pastry shop, she answered ... ~ *senang* it's not as bad as all that, it's not as bad as it seems; *cp* GAMPANG-GAMPANG *susah*.

bersusah ~ *hati* to be anxious/worried; to grieve.

bersusah-susah and to toil (away), exert o.s., work hard, try one's hardest. *jangan* ~ take it easy, relax! *tak usah* ~ don't make a big fuss, don't stand on ceremony.

menyusahi 1 to disturb, put s.o. out, cause worry for, cause s.o. a lot of trouble. **2** to be sad about s.t.

menyusahkan [and **nyusahin** (*J coq*)] **1** to impede, hamper, hinder, embarrass, interfere with; to obstruct; to make things difficult/hard for, get s.o. into trouble, inconvenience. *disusahkan oléh* to be inconvenienced by. **2** to busy o.s. (over), give o.s. a great deal of trouble (about); to worry/be worried (about).

mempersusah(kan) to make s.t. more difficult.

kesusahan 1 misery; trouble, bother, annoyance; anxiety, worry, uneasiness; hardships, pain, problems, difficulties. *mengalami* ~ to have problems/difficulties. **2** to have difficulties/problems, be in trouble.

susastra (*Skr*) **kesusastraan 1** literature, belles-lettres. **2** scientific literature. **3** poetry. **4** bibliography.

persusasteraan (*mod*) literary, literature.

susék (*C*) card game with four cards in four suites.

Susénas [Survéi Sosial Ékonomi Nasional] National Socio-Economic Survey.

susi 1 sister. **2** form of address to young, unmarried girls.

susila (*Skr*) **1** decorum, proper/good behavior; morals, ethics. **2** decency, morality. **3** civilized, cultured (person), ethical. *juru* – official in charge of dealing with prostitutes. *polisi* – vice squad. *tuna* – lacking morals, immoral. *wanita tuna* – [wts] prostitute. – *kedokteran* medical ethics.

bersusila moral, decent, ethical.

kesusilaan 1 morality, morals, ethics. **2** decency, propriety/ethical behavior, decorum, (good) manners. *norma* ~ norms of morality, norms of proper behavior.

susilat a boil on the neck.

susis → SOSIS.

suspénsi (*D*) **1** (*leg*) suspension, postponement. **2** (*chem*) suspension. **3** (*E*) suspense, tension. **4** the suspension (of a vehicle).

menyuspénsikan to suspend (s.t. in a liquid).

tersuspénsi suspended.

pensuspénsi (*chem*) suspensor.

Suspimpémdagri [kursus pimpinan pemerintahan dalam negeri] Civil Service Leadership Course.

suster (*D*) **1** nurse (in doctor's office or in hospital). **2** (*RC*) nun, sister. – *jaga* nurse on duty (in hospital).

susteran (*Jv*) **1** nurses' home. **2** (*RC*) convent, nunnery. *sekolah* ~ convent school.

susu I 1 (female) breast; → PAYUDARA. *mata/puntil/puting* – nipple (of the breast). **2** (*air* –) milk. *kepala* – cream. *kepala* – *kocok* whipped cream. **3** udder. *rusak* – *sebelanga karena tuba setitik* one rotten apple will decay a bushel. (*air*) – *dibalas dengan* (*air*) *tuba* the world's wages is ingratitude. – *asam* sour milk. – *awét* long-life milk. – *bawah* (*infr*) skim milk. – *beku* curdled milk. – *berlemak* whole/full-cream milk. – *bubuk* powered/dried milk, milk powder. – *bubuk bayi* powdered milk for babies. – *bubuk nonlemak/tanpa lemak* nonfat dried milk. – *bubuk rendah lemak* partly skim milk powder. – *cair pastéurisasi* pasteurized liquid milk. – *éncér* evaporated milk. – *és* (*infr*) ice cream. – *jolong* colostrum. – *kaléng(an)* canned milk. – *karét* latex. – *kental (manis)* (sweetened) condensed milk. – *kocok* buttermilk. – *kurus* nonfat/skim milk. – *lisut* dry breasts (of old women). – *macan* (in Sumatra) a beverage consisting of canned or powdered milk mixed with sweet syrup and water plus whiskey or brandy and possibly gin. – *murni* whole milk. – *pembersih* cleansing milk. – *segar* fresh milk. – *sisa* residual milk. – *skim* skim milk. – *stéril* sterilized milk. – *tak berlemak* skim milk. – *tante* → SUSU IV. – *tepung* powdered/dried milk. – *tepung tanpa lemak* nonfat dried milk. – *tin* canned milk. – *tumbukan* buttermilk. – *yang dipastéurisasi* pasteurized milk.

bersusu 1 to have (mother's) milk. **2** to have a (female) breast.

menyusu to suck, take milk at the breast.

menyusui [and **nyusuin** (*J coq*)] to suckle, nurse (a baby at the breast), breast-feed. *binatang* ~ mammal.

menyusukan to suckle, nurse (a baby at the breast), breast-feed.

susuan nursed. *anak* ~ a nursed child (not one's own). *ibu* ~ wet nurse. *saudara* ~ s.o. who has had the same wet nurse.

sesusuan nourished at the same breast. *saudara* ~ sibling with the same mother.

penyusu wet nurse.

penyusuan nursing (a baby at the breast).

persusuan milk (*mod*). *pengembangan* ~ *di dalam negeri* the growth of domestic milk (production). **sepersusuan** *saudara* ~ sibling with the same mother.

pesusu suckling.

susu II in various plant names and animal names. *getah* – rubber from the liana *Willughbeia firma*. *kembang* – an ornamental plant, crepe jasmine, *Tabernaemontana divaricata*. *pisang* – a short, fat banana species. – *bundar* k.o. topshell, *Trochus niloticus*. – *perada* k.o. wild herb, Himalayan cinquefoil, *Globba atrosanguinea*.

susu III kesusu in a hurry.

susu IV [sumbangan sukaréla] "Voluntary Contribution," i.e., a k.o. bribe. – *tante* [Sumbangan Sukaréla Tanpa Tekanan] "auntie's milk" ["Voluntary Contribution Without Pressure"], i.e., a k.o. bribe.

susuh I 1 large thorn. **2** spur (on a cock's leg or attached to the heel of a rider's boots). **3** peg, wooden pin, nail; hook.

susuh II (*Jv*) nest; breeding place. – *burung/manuk* bird's nest.

susuhunan title of the ruler of Surakarta.

susuk I – *tubuh* figure, shape; → SOSOK II.

menyusuk (*M*) to do work from the very beginning, pioneer.

susuk II 1 pin, peg, bolt; → SOSOK I. – *kondai/sanggul* hairpin. **2** (*J*) gold pin inserted into the lip or forehead (with the aid of magic formulas) to enhance one's beauty. **3** IUD, intrauterine (contraceptive) device, implant. **4** hole into which one inserts s.t. – *baju* buttonhole.

bersusuk 1 with a pin/peg/bolt. **2** to wear a hairpin or a *susuk* in the lip, etc.

bersusuk-susuk(an) to crowd/force one's way (into).

menyusuk 1 to stab; to stick a pin/peg/bolt into. **2** to implant a *susuk* in s.o.'s skin (as a beauty aid).

menyusukkan to stick/put s.t. [in(to)]. *Ia ~ kedua tangannya ke dalam saku celana.* He stuck his hands into his pockets.

susuk III (*J*) **susukan** canal; artificial channel joining two bodies of water.

susuk IV (*Jv*) change, small money.

susuk V (*Jv*) *– wangan* voluntary collective work to restore an irrigation system.

susul bersusul(-susul)an to follow e.o., succeed e.o.

menyusul [and **nyusul** (*coq*)] **1** to follow, catch up. *Pergilah sekarang saya akan ~.* Leave first; I'll catch up. **2** following, subsequent to, in the wake of. *~ naiknya suku bunga* in the wake of the rise in interest rates. **3** to follow and catch up to. *Ia dapat ~ lawan-lawannya melampaui garis finis.* He caught up to and passed his opponents crossing the finish line. *Ia dapat ~ pelajaran di sekolah.* He was able to catch up to the lessons in school. **4** to trace, follow (the track/trail/trace). *Sulit sekali ~ jejak kelahiran Gajah Mada.* It's very hard to trace Gajah Mada's birth. **5** in re, in reference to (a previous letter, etc.). *~ telegram yang kemarin* referring to yesterday's telegram. **6** to be next. *yang ~* the next person. *Siapa ~?* Who's next?

susul-menyusul to follow e.o., one after the other. *~ datang surat* letters came in one after the other.

menyusuli [and **nyusulin** (*J coq*)] **1** to follow (up) (with/by). *Ia mengangkat takbir yang disusuli dengan bacaan Fatihah.* He glorified God, which was followed by reciting the Muslim declaration of faith. **2** to follow, walk behind, tail. *Kata ku dan kau tidak ditulis terpisah dari kata dasar pasif yang ~nya.* The words *ku* and *kau* are not written separated from the passive base form that follows them. **3** to follow and add to s.t., add to s.t. previous. *Keterangan yang diberikan menteri itu ~ pernyataan Présidén.* The explanation given by the minister added to the President's statement.

menyusulkan 1 to allow to follow, let follow, send after. *Anak itu kami susulkan ke ibunya.* We let the child follow his mother. **2** to attach, annex, tack on, add (to s.t. written). *Sebaiknya Anda ~ keterangan kelakuan baik itu dalam surat lamaran Anda.* The best thing would be for you to attach the statement of good conduct to your letter of application.

tersusul [and **kesusul** (*coq*)] overtaken, passed, outstripped, be caught up to. *Kamu tidak usah kuatir ~.* Don't worry about being overtaken. *Akhir-akhir ini peristiwa-peristiwa politik ~ oléh peristiwa-peristiwa kenegaraan.* State events recently caught up to political events.

susulan s.t. that follows, follow-up; an addition, codicil; attachment, enclosure, s.t. added, after. *angin ~* tailwind. *berita ~* follow-up report. *gempa ~* aftershock. *pembakaran ~* afterburning. *surat ~* follow-up letter. *ujian ~* make-up test.

penyusul follower, s.o. or s.t. that follows.

penyusulan following up.

susun 1 heap, pile, stack, one on top of the other. *se– buku* a pile/stack of books. *rumah –* walk-up, apartment building. *sirih –* two betel leaves one on top of the other. **2** a (horizontal) layer. *se– batu bata* a layer of bricks. **3** nested set, set, series (of similar things, each fitting within the next larger one). *se– keranjang/kuali besar* a nested set of baskets/cooking pots. *rantang –* a set of food-baskets; → RANTANG I. **4** sequence, series, row. *se– kata itu* that sentence. *se– sajak* a poem. *se– genténg* a row of roof tiles. **5** double, dual. *bunga –* a double flower (with a dual crown). *– huruf* typography. *– paku* a large family, i.e., one in which the children are very close in age to e.o.

bersusun 1 piled/heaped (up), stacked. **2** stored (in layers), put one on top of the other; in rows/lines/files. *berdiri ~ lima-lima* standing in rows of fives, stacked five high/deep. *kué –* layer cake. *rumah ~* multistoried building, high-rise. *rumah ~ empat belas* a thirteen-story building [the 13th floor is omitted for superstitious reasons]. **3** placed/put together, (systematically) arranged, compiled, combined, put in order. *Nama-namanya*

dituliskan ~ menurut abjad. The names were written down arranged in alphabetical order. **4** in tiers, terraced, one after another, closely spaced. *Anaknya ~ paku.* His children were closely spaced one after the other in age. **5** shoulder to shoulder, one right next to the other. **6** (*gram*) *kalimat ~* compound sentence. *~ tindih* piled up (high), one on top of the other.

bersusun-susun (to stand/sit, etc.) in rows (of many people), in serried ranks.

menyusun [and **nyusun** (*coq*)] **1** to pile up, stack; to accumulate. **2** to compose, prepare, frame, draw up (a speech, etc.). **3** to hold (the palm of the hand against s.o. asking for help). **4** to arrange/sort in sequence, compile (a dictionary). **5** to order, regulate, put in order; to tidy up, put (away) (in the proper place or in proper order); to choose/select (one's words); to organize/put (one's words/thoughts, etc.) in order/so as to express o.s. fluently, express/couch/phrase/put in appropriate words/terms. **6** to concentrate, bring up (all one's resources); to be engaged in, devote o.s. to, occupy o.s. with. **7** to draft (a law), construct, erect, build. *~ acara* to draw up/prepare an agenda. *~ bahasa* to write, compose. *~ barisan* to close ranks. *~ batu* to lay stones. *~ buku* to write a book. *~ jari* to pay homage; to request, beg. *~ kabinét* to form a cabinet. *~ kalimat* to compose a sentence. *~ kamus* to compile a dictionary. *~ kembali* to reassemble. *~ laporan* to make/write a report. *~ panitia* to set up a committee. *~ pasukan* to close ranks. *~ pengurus* to appoint a manager. *~ piring* to stack plates (one on top of the other). *~ rencana pelajaran* to draw up a curriculum/syllabus. *~ undang-undang* to draft legislation. *~ wajah (suratkabar)* to lay out (a newspaper), do the layout work on (a newspaper).

menyusunkan 1 → MENYUSUN. **2** to arrange s.t. for s.o. else.

tersusun piled up, composed, compiled, stacked, arranged, ordered. *lis ~* an ordered list.

susunan 1 pile, heap, stack. **2** structure, system, organization. **3** s.t. erected, building, construction, structure. **4** composition. *~ kimia* chemical composition. **5** compilation. **6** form, formation, organization. **7** wording. *~ acara* the schedule. *~ bahasa* style. *~ berita* text of a report. *~ dalam* internal organization. *~ irama* rhythmic structure. *~ kalimat* sentence structure, syntax. *~ kata* wording (of a letter/story, etc.). *~ masyarakat* the fabric of society. *~ pegawai* table of organization (of the staff). *~ pemerintahan* polity. *~ pengairan* irrigation system. *~ permodalan* capital structure. *~ saraf pusat* [SSP] central nervous system. *~ tempur* battle array.

penyusun s.o. or s.t. that compiles, composes, etc., compiler, composer.

penyusunan 1 composition, composing. **2** compilation, compiling. **3** arrangement, arranging; construction, constructing. **4** organization, organizing; forming, formation; structure. *~ kekuasaan* power formation. *~ kembali* reconstruction, restructuring. *~ logis/masuk akal/secara mantik* logical construction. *~ peringkat* consolation round.

pesusun component.

susung → SONGSONG I, II, III.

susup *– sasap* to duck in and out, creep in and out of everything.

menyusup [and **nyusup** (*coq*)] **1** to duck (down), squeeze down (under), creep/crawl (under). *Dengan cepat ia ~ ke bawah untuk mengélak pukulan itu.* He quickly ducked down to dodge the blow. *Malingnya ~ di bawah pagar.* The thief squeezed under the fence. **2** to enter/go/run, etc. into. *Binatang yang ditémbak itu lari ~ ke dalam semak.* The animal which was shot ran into the undergrowth. **3** to intrude/penetrate (into) surreptitiously, infiltrate, encroach on. *Dia coba ~ ke dalam khémah musuh.* He tried to enter the enemy's tent surreptitiously.

menyusupi to infiltrate, enter surreptitiously. *disusupi komunis* communist-infiltrated.

menyusupkan 1 to push/shove/slip s.t. into/through/under. *~ dompétnya di bawah bantal* to slip one's wallet under the pillow. **2** to smuggle, infiltrate. *~ barang larangan melalui petugas béa dan cukai* to smuggle contraband past a customs officer.

tersusupi infiltrated.

susupan 1 infiltration. **2** s.t. that has been infiltrated. *orang ~* s.o. who has infiltrated (among the enemy).

kesusupan 1 stuck. ~ *duri* pricked by a thorn. 2 infiltrated, entered surreptitiously. ~ *komunis* communist-infiltrated.

penyusup 1 infiltrator, intruder. 2 s.t. which penetrates.

penyusupan 1 infiltration, infiltrating. 2 penetration, penetrating, encroachment.

susur I outer edge (of a cushion/pillow/beach, etc.), rim, fringe. – *bantal* edge of a pillow. – *daratan* coast. – *galur* genealogy. – *hutan* forest edge. – *kota* outskirts of a city. – *pantai* shoreline. – *tangga* handrails, banister.

menyusur to skirt (along the edge of the shore/a fence/the forest, etc.), along. *berjalan* ~ *pantai* to walk along the shore.

menyusuri [and **nyusurin** (*J coq*)] 1 to move/sail/walk along the edge/border/margin of. *Meréka berjalan lambat-lambat* ~ *pantai.* They walked slowly along the shoreline. 2 to follow, track, trace, trail; → MENELUSURI.

susuran s.t. to hold on to when walking along the edge. ~ *jembatan* guardrail (of a bridge). ~ *tangga* handrails, banister.

penyusur s.t. that skirts along. *kapal* ~ *pantai* coaster, ship that sails from port to port along the coast.

penyusuran 1 skirting (along). 2 tracking (down), tracing. ~ *gua* caving, spelunking. ~ *sumber-sumber tertulis itu* tracking down these written sources.

susur II (*Jv*) – *tembakau* plug/quid of tobacco held between the lips for cleaning the teeth after chewing betel; → SUGI.

susur III penyusur ~ *bayar* installment debt, hire-purchase.

susur IV *daging* – corned beef.

susut I 1 to decrease, be depleted, run low, reduce. 2 to fall, sink, subside (of water/flood/storm). 3 to (be on the) decline, become (physically) impaired. 4 loss, shrinkage, contraction. 5 to wane (of the moon). 6 to shrink (of wool, etc.). – *angkut* loss during shipping. – *berat* weight loss. – *isi* shrinkage. – *laut* sea regression. – *suling* distillation loss.

menyusut 1 to decrease, depreciate, decline, lessen. 2 to shrink, become smaller.

menyusuti to lessen, reduce, decrease.

menyusutkan 1 to decrease, lessen, reduce, diminish. ~ *diri* to make o.s. thinner. ~ *hutang* to decrease one's indebtedness. ~ *napas* to try to catch one's breath. 2 to write off, depreciate.

tersusut reduced, decreased.

tersusutkan depreciable.

susutan reduction, decrement.

penyusut 1 reductant. ~ *gas* gas reductant. 2 s.t. which decreases s.t. *gas-gas* ~ *lapisan ozon* gases which reduce the ozone layer.

penyusutan 1 reduction, decrease, decrement, shrinkage. 2 depreciation, writing off. ~ *arsip* file reduction, the destruction and transfer of dead files. ~ *dipercepat* accelerated depreciation. ~ *harga* depreciation.

susut II (*Jv*) **menyusut** to trace, track, scrutinize.

susut III (*Jv*) lost (weight), slimmed down, reduced (in weight).

menyusut to lose weight.

susut IV menyusut to wipe.

menyusuti (*pl obj*) to wipe.

sut I hush!

sut II (*Jv*) → SUTEN. **menyut** to play the game of *suten.* *Ayo mari disut!* Come on, let's play *suten.*

sut-sutan to play the game of *suten.*

sut III (*E coq*) **ngesut** to shoot up (drugs).

Sutan (*A M*) 1 an *adat* title, somewhat similar to Javanese *Radén* (the latter is a legally protected title on Java whereas *Sutan* is not). 2 (*M*) term of reference for children of the better classes. 3 (in the coastal areas of the Minangkabau, such as Padang) a hereditary title passed down from father to son; it usually precedes the personal name, i.e., *Sutan Mohammad Zain* and *Sutan Takdir Alisjahbana*, whereas in the interior areas of Sumatra, the title usually follows the personal name, i.e., *Rustam Sutan Palindih* and *Abbas Sutan Pamuntjak nan Sati.*

bersutan to address s.o. as *Sutan.* ~ *di mata, beraja di hati* to act arbitrarily/in a high-handed manner).

bersutan-sutan to boast of one's noble descent.

suté (*C*) fellow student of the same teacher.

sutemaja [*susu, telor, madu, dan jahé*] a hot drink made of condensed milk, raw eggs, honey, and ginger. *menyediakan* – to sell this drink (at a *warung*).

suten (*D from Jv*) **bersuten** to draw lots by throwing out a number of fingers to see who goes first.

sutera (*Skr*) silk. *baju* – silk coat. *ulat* – silkworm. – *gabus* crêpe. – *kembang* embroidered silk. – *tiruan* artificial silk, rayon.

menyutera silky.

persuteraan (*mod*) silk.

sutil (*Jv*) roasting spit.

sutradara director (of a film/play).

menyutradarai to direct (a film/play).

kesutradaraan stage management.

penyutradaraan directing (a film/play).

sutuh → SOTOH.

sutura (*E*) suture.

suud (*A*) luck.

suudh-dhon (*A*) bad prejudice.

bersuudh-dhon to have/feel prejudiced.

suul (*A*) – *adap* unethical. – *khatimah* evil ending.

suun → SOHUN, SO'UN.

suung (*S*) an umbrella-shaped species of mushroom.

su-uut (*onom*) whish, zipping or whistling sound made by s.t. passing by fast. – *naik lift* it zipped up in the elevator.

suuzan (*A*) → SUUDH-DHON.

suvelir (*D*) maidenhair fern, *Adiantum curatum.*

suvenir (*D*) souvenir. *kedai* – souvenir shop.

suwak → SWAK.

suwara → SUARA.

suwarnadwipa (*Skr*) gold island (an old name for Sumatra); → SUWARNABHUMI.

suwar-suwir (*D*) a dish containing pieces of duck, strongly seasoned with pepper and other spices.

suweg and **suwek** k.o. fruit, elephant's foot, *Amorphophallus campanulatus* and other species. – *raksasa* k.o. giant flower, *Amorphophallus titanum.*

suwing → SUMBING.

suwir (*Jv*) ripped up, torn to shreds.

menyuwir(i) to tear up, shred.

suwiran shreds. ~ *daging* shredded meat.

suwita (*Jv*) to live in the house of a prominent family in order to learn their manners, way of speaking, and style of living; in return for this one serves them; k.o Javanese system of patron-client relationship.

suwuk (*Jv*) **menyuwuk** medical treatment by a *dukun* consisting of incantations and blowing on the patient's head.

menyuwukkan to have s.o. treated in that way by a *dukun.*

suwukan treatment (of s.o. in that way).

penyuwukan action of healing s.o. in that way.

suwung (*Jv*) empty, vacant, unoccupied, uninhabited. *Rumahnya* –. The house is unoccupied. *Hatinya* –. Her heart felt empty. – *ing pamrih, tebih ajrih* because there is no selfishness, there is also no fear.

suyak (*M*) torn, ripped.

swa- (*Skr*) (prefix used in many of the following neologisms, see below) self-, auto-, own-.

swaaduk self-stirring. *panci* – self-stirring pan.

swa-atur self-regulating.

Swabhuwana Pakna (*Skr neo*) (motto of the Indonesian Air Force) With Wings We are the Masters in Our Own World. – *Pratama* medal awarded to those considered to have extraordinary merit beyond the call of duty and who, through their wisdom and ability, have contributed to the advancement and development of the Indonesian Air Force.

swabiaya (*Skr neo*) self-funded.

swacakap monologue.

berswacakap to hold a monologue.

swadana (*Skr*) own/private (financial) means, self-supporting, self-financing.

berswadana to be self-supporting.

swadanisasi self-sufficiency.

swad(h)arma (*Skr*) own right.

swadaya (*Skr*) own strength/means/expense; self-help. *(dengan)* *biaya –* (at) one's own expense.

berswadaya to do s.t. with one's own funds or with one's own powers (without external help).

menswadayakan to form/create s.t. with one's own funds or with one's own powers, without outside funding or help. ~ *koperasi adalah suatu tantangan.* Forming a cooperative with one's own funds is a challenge.

keswadayaan participatory, using one's own funding or powers. *Forum Pengembangan* ~ Participatory Development Forum.

penswadayaan self-helping, participation (using one's own funding, etc.).

swadayanisasi self-help, participation (using one's own funding, etc.). *invéstasi ~ masyarakat* investing in community self-help.

swadési (*Hind*) a national movement for the promotion and exclusive use of native manufactures and the boycott of foreign-made goods.

swadiri independent (organization, etc.), autonomous.

swadisiplin self-discipline.

swagaya (*Skr neo*) innate energy.

swaguna (*Skr neo*) self-use, for use by o.s. – *usaha* for its own account, on its own behalf.

swahara autotrophic.

swaharga (*Skr neo*) self-respect.

swaimbas self-induction.

swajana (*ling*) reflexive.

swajual right-to-sell.

swak (*D*) weak, not feeling good.

swakaji 1 self-study. **2** (*infr*) heuristic.

swakarsa (*Skr*) **1** spontaneous. *transmigrasi –* spontaneous transmigration (not sponsored by the government). **2** on one's own (initiative), vigilante. *atas –nya sendiri* on his own (initiative).

swakarya (*Skr*) auto-activity, self-motivation, doing s.t. on one's own (without outside initiative).

berswakarya to auto-activate, do s.t. on one's own, be self motivated.

swakelola self-management.

swakemudi self-steering. *mobil –* driverless car.

swakritik self-criticism.

swalayan self-service. *pasar –* supermarket. *toko –* self-service store.

swaloka in-house. *latihan –* in-house training.

swanama proper name.

swanggi (*Pap*) *daun –* a certain leaf used as a contraceptive.

swanyala autoignition.

swap (*E*) (currency) swap.

menswap to swap.

swapantau self-observation.

swapraja (*Skr*) self-government, autonomy. *daérah –* autonomous area.

Swa Prasidya Purna (*Skr*) Rehabilitation Center for the Handicapped.

swara → SUARA.

swarga → SURGA.

Swarnadwipa → SUWARNADWIPA.

swartepit (*D*) **1** (in card games) jack of spades. **2** k.o. card game like old maid.

swasadar self-conscious.

swasembada self-supporting. *– beras* self-supporting in rice.

berswasembada to be self-supporting in. ~ *pangan* to be self-supporting in food.

keswasembadaan self-support.

swasénsor self-censorship.

swasiswa (*Skr*) autodidact.

swasraya self-service.

swasta (*Skr*) private, nongovernmental. *pengusaha –* private entrepreneur.

men(g)swastakan to privatize, convert from government to private ownership.

pen(g)swastaan privatization, conversion from government to private ownership.

swastanisasi privatization.

menswastanisasikan to privatize.

swastawan private person.

swastika (*D*) swastika.

swasulut autoignition.

swatacana [swara, tari, dan wacana] singing, dancing, and speaking; *cp* SENDRATARI.

swatantra (*Skr*) autonomy; autonomous.

keswatantraan autonomy.

swausaha self-enterprise (independent of others).

swawédya self-cure.

swawinaya self-discipline.

swayasa self-made, made by an individual or group (not manufactured). *pesawat –* self-made aircraft.

berswayasa to make s.t. by o.s.

Swédia Sweden.

sweeping (*E*) /swiping/ sweep (by police/groups seeking to oust foreigners, etc.).

swémbak (*D*) swimming pool.

swémpak bathing/swim suit; → PAKAIAN *renang*.

swér (*D coq*) (to) swear.

swér-swéran swearing (by all that's holy). *Nggak usah ~.* You don't need all that swearing.

swéter (*E*) sweater.

berswéter to wear/have on a sweater.

swiké (*C*) (fried young) frog's legs.

swing (*E*) swing (music).

swipoa (*C*) abacus; → DEKAK-DEKAK.

Swis Switzerland, Swiss.

switer → SWÉTER.

swt. [Subhanahu Wa Taala] (*A*) praise be to God and He is sublime.

sya → INSYA ALLAH.

syabah (*A*) unclear; indistinguishable; almost similar.

Syaban → SYAKBAN.

syabas(h) and **syabi** (*A/Pers*) good! excellent!

syabi → SABI I.

syablon (*D*) stencil.

syafaat (*A*) intercession, mediation (of the Prophet on behalf of God).

syafakat (*A*) sympathy; pity.

syafar (*A*) **bersyafar** and **syafaran** to go in large numbers to a sacred place to pray to be spared danger.

Syafii (*A*) Imam Syafii or Mohammad bin Idris as-Syafii al-Shafi'i, born in Palestine in A.D. 767, the founder of one of the four schools of Islamic law. *mashab –* one of the four schools of Islamic law, founded by al-Shafi'i.

Syafiiah (*A*) **1** teachings of the al-Shafi'i school of Islamic law. **2** adherents to the al-Shafi'i school of Islamic law.

syafkah and **syafkat** → SYAFAKAT.

syagar → SAKAR I.

syah I (*Pers*) **1** king, ruler. **2** king (in chess). **3** (*Mal*) a name element suffixed to the personal names of Malaysian rulers, e.g., Sultan Muzaffar Shah. *– alam di rimba* king of the forest. *– peri* king of the fairies.

syah II → SAH I.

syahada → SYAHDA, SYAHDU.

syahadan → SYAHDAN.

syahadat (*A*) **1** testimony. **2** creed. **3** *kalimat (ul) –* the Muslim confession of faith; → KALIMAT *syahadat. – Rasul* the acknowledgment that Muhammad is God's messenger.

mensyahadatkan to convert s.o. to Islam.

pensyahadatan (ceremony) accepting Islam.

syahansyah (*A*) king of kings.

syahbandar (*Pers*) harbormaster.

kesyahbandaran 1 office of the harbormaster. **2** (*mod*) harbormaster's.

syahda → SYAHDU.

syahdan (*A*) further(more), then, moreover.

syahdu (*A*) **1** excellent. **2** lofty, solemn.

kesyahduan 1 excellence. **2** loftiness, solemnity.

syahi (*A J*) tea.

nyahi to drink tea.

syahid I (*A*) witness (to the Muslim faith), martyr. *mati –* martyred,

made a martyr (*esp* by being killed in the service of the faith). *alam* – the phenomenal world (which is illusory).
  kesyahidan martyrdom.
syahid II (*A*) behold!
syahid III (*A*) perceptible.
syahmat (*Pers*) checkmate (in chess).
syahmurah (*Pers*) magic stone.
syahriah (*A*) monthly.
syahriar (*A*) king.
syahru I (*A*) city.
syahru II (*A*) moon, month. *-n adzinum wa -n mubarokun* the most lofty month and the month of miracles (reference to *Ramadan*). *-sh shiyam* Ramadan.
syahrun → SYAHRU II.
syahwat (*A*) sexual desire, lust, libido. *lemah/mati* – impotent. *mencapai* – to have an orgasm, come. *puncak* – orgasm.
  kesyahwatan 1 sexual pleasure. *puncak ~* orgasm. 2 sex (*mod*).
syai (*A*) thing.
syaikh→ SYÉKH.
syair I (*A*) quatrain consisting of four rhyming lines, poem.
  bersyair 1 to write poetry. 2 to recite poetry.
  mensyairkan and **menyairkan** 1 to compose a poem about. 2 to chant (a poem).
  penyair poet. **kepenyairan** poetizing.
syair II (*A*) barley.
syairi (*A*) poetic.
syaitan → SÉTAN.
syaitani (*A*) Satanic.
syajar (*A*) tree. *- khuldi* the tree of life (in the Garden of Eden).
syajarat (*A*) → SEJARAH. 1 genealogy. 2 family tree.
syak I (*A*) suspicion, doubt, distrust. *menaruh* – (*wasangka*) to distrust, suspect, harbor suspicions about. *tidak* – *lagi* undoubtedly, without a doubt, no longer in doubt.
  mensyak to suspect, doubt.
  mensyaki 1 to distrust, mistrust. 2 to suspect, surmise.
syak II (*E*) to shuck (oysters or mollusks from their shells for sale or for eating).
Syaka (*Bal*) a calendrical year consisting of 210 days or 6 months.
syakar → SAKAR III.
Syakban the eighth month of the Muslim year; → RUWAH.
syakduf (*A*) saddle used on a camel; → SEKEDUP.
syakhsiah (*A*) personality.
syakir (*A*) a thankful/grateful person.
syal (*Pers D*) shawl.
syalat (*A*) prayer; → SALAT I, SYOLAT. *- Ied* prayer meeting held on (*Hari Raya*) Idul Fitri.
Syam I (*A*) Syria; → SIRIA, SURIAH.
Syam II (*A*) Shem (one of Noah's sons, the mythical forefather of the Semitic races).
Syamali (*A*) north. *kutub* – North Pole.
syaman shaman.
syamanisme shamanism.
syamas → SAMAS.
Syams (*A*) *ash*– "The Sun"; name of the 91st chapter of the Koran.
syamsi (*A*) sun.
syamsiah and **syamsiat** (*A*) solar. *tahun* – solar year.
syams(y)ir (*Pers*) scimitar.
syamsu → SYAMSI.
syanker (*D*) chancre.
Syantung Shantung.
syapaat → SYAFAAT.
syar (*A*) crime.
syara' → SYARIAH.
syarab (*A*) 1 alcoholic drink. 2 wine.
syaraf → SARAF II.
syarah I (*A*) 1 desire, longing. 2 fondness for eating sweets. 3 appetite for food.
syarah II (*A*) 1 explanation, exposition; commentary; information. 2 (*Mal*) lecture; sermon.
  bersyarah (*Mal*) and **mensyarah** to (give a) lecture.
  mensyarahkan 1 to explain. 2 to (give a) lecture about.
  syarahan (*Mal*) lecture; sermon.

pensyarah (*Mal*) lecturer; preacher.
syarah III and **syarahan** (*A ob*) publication (of newspaper, etc.); edition, issue. *- rakyat* cheap/popular edition.
syarak → SYARIAT.
syarat (*A*) 1 condition, proviso, term. *dengan* – *sebagai berikut* on/under the following conditions. *dengan tiada memakai* – unconditionally, without any conditions. *tanpa* – *apapun* without any conditions whatsoever. 2 requirement, (pre)requisite. *- yang paling mustahak untuk menyelesaikan perselisihan itu* the most important prerequisites for settling that dispute. 3 rule, stipulation/regulation, etc. that has to be met, provision. *Islamkah engkau kalau engkau tidak mengikut -.- dan undang-undang yang diwajibkan ke atas seorang Islam?* Are you a Muslim if you don't follow the rules and laws which are obligatory for a Muslim? 4 expenses, costs; fee, goods, etc. that have to be paid to a teacher (of *pencak*/Koranic reading, etc.). *- batal* (*leg*) condition subsequent, resolutory condition. *- damai* conditions can be discussed, we can come to an agreement, terms negotiable. *- hidup* living conditions. *- kawin* marriage contract. *- kepercayaan* requirement of credibility. *- kerja* working conditions, job description. *- mengadakan asuransi* insurance clauses. *- mutlak* absolute/indispensable conditions, *conditio sine qua non*. *- pembatalan* (*leg*) condition subsequent, resolutory condition. *- pembatasan séwa* stipulation in a mortgage contract forbidding rental without permission. *- pembayaran* terms of payment. *- penerimaan* entrance requirements. *-.- penjualan* terms of sale. *- perburuhan* working conditions, job description. *- pokok* essential conditions. *- tangguh/yang ditangguhkan* (*leg*) condition precedent, suspensory condition.
  syarat-syarat qualifications, prerequisites.
  bersyarat conditional, on condition (that), contingent, qualified. *dengan tidak ~* unconditionally. *tidak ~* unconditional. *penyerahan yang tak ~* unconditional surrender.
  bersyaratkan to have … as a condition.
  mensyaratkan to stipulate s.t. as a condition, make s.t. a condition.
  mempersyaratkan to stipulate/set as a condition.
  persyaratan (set of) requirements, conditions, rules and regulations, qualifications.
syarbat → SERBAT.
syarékat → SERIKAT.
syarh (*A*) *ash*– "Phlegmatic"; alternate name of the 94th chapter of the Koran.
syarhul (*A*) commentary. *- Qur'an* commentary on the Koran.
syariah and **syariat** (*A*) 1 (Islamic) canon law. 2 alternate name of the 45th chapter of the Koran; → JATSIAH.
  mensyariahkan to declare s.t. to be under Islamic law.
Syarif (*A*) designation for the male descendants of the Prophet Muhammad directly from Husain.
Syarifah (*A*) designation for the female descendants of the Prophet Muhammad directly from Husain.
syarik (*A*) partner; → MITRA.
syarikat (*A Mal*) company, enterprise, concern, undertaking; → SERIKAT.
syar'un man qablana (*A*) rules of law valid before Muhammad became the Prophet of God.
syatar (*A*) 1 page (of book, etc.). 2 board for ruling lines.
syatranj (*Pers*) chess.
syauk → SYOK I.
syaukaran (*Pers*) hemlock.
syaulam (*A cla*) magical formula (to make s.o. unconscious).
syawahid (*A*) evidence.
Syawal (*A*) the tenth month in the Muslim calendar, the month of hunting, the first day is Idul Fitri. *Grebeg/Lebaran* – (in Cirebon) festivities which consist of family members making devotional visits to the graves of ancestors of the Kanoman Palace in Cirebon.
syawalan (*Jv*) celebration of *Lebaran*.
syaz (*A*) exceptional (in *hadis*).
Syazilah (*A*) an order of mystics established by Abdul Hasan Ali asy-Syazili, who died in A.D. 1252.
syé (*C*) the first of a Chinese person's three names, surname, Chinese family name.

syéikh (*A*) **1** intimate term of address for the person one is speaking to, you. **2** professor; → SYÉKH.

syéikuha (*A*) our teacher.

syéir (*A*) wheat.

syékh (*A*) **1** designation for an Arab, *esp* a descendant of the Prophet Muhammad. **2** designation for an Arab who is a native of the Hadramaut. **3** designation for a theologian; *cp* KIAI. – *jemaah* guide for pilgrims to Mecca.

syérif (*E*) sheriff. – *dalam film koboi* a sheriff in a western.

syéti → CÉTI I.

syi (*Jp*) (during the Japanese occupation) municipality.

Syiah (*A*) Shiah, Shiite.

syiar (*A*) greatness; loftiness, sublimity.

Syidokan (*Jp*) (during the Japanese occupation) leader, guide.

syikak (*A*) conflict.

syin (*A*) the 13th letter of the Arabic alphabet.

syiréibu → SIRÉIBU.

syirik and **syirk** (*A*) **1** polytheism. **2** taboo (for religious reasons). **mensyirikkan 1** to deify s.t. (besides God). **2** to avoid doing s.t.

syirkah (*A*) partnership.

Syiwa Siva.

syodanco (*Jp*) (during the Japanese occupation) section commander (in PETA hierarchy).

syogun (*Jp*) shogun.

syohor → SOHOR.

syohrat (*A*) fame.

syok I (*A*) attractive, charming, delightful. **2** absorbed in.

syok II → SOK II.

syok III (*E*) shock, in a state of shock; → KEJUTAN.

syolat → SALAT I. – *Jumat* Friday services.

syolawat → SELAWAT.

Syonanto (*Jp*) the name which the Japanese occupiers gave to Singapore during World War II.

syor → SYUR I.

syorga → SURGA.

syuara(a) (*A*) *asy-* "The Poets"; name of the 26th chapter of the Koran.

syu'bah (*A*) position, post.

syubahat and **syub(u)hat** (*A*) **1** doubt. **2** uncertain, suspicious (as to whether s.t. is *haram* or not). *pemberitahuan agar konsumén hati-hati dengan makanan yang –* an announcement that consumers should be careful about food that is not clearly *haram* or *halal*. – *hati* doubtfulness. **bersyub(u)hat** to have one's doubts (about).

syuco (*Jp*) (during the Japanese occupation); → PEMBANTU *gubernur*.

syufaat → SYAFAAT.

syugul → SUGUL, MASYGUL.

syuhada (*A*) (plural of *syahid*) witnesses, martyrs.

syuk → SYOK I, II.

syukur (*A*) **1** thanks (to God). **2** thank God! luckily, fortunately (said in relief that s.t. bad didn't happen). *-lah anakku tidak mengalami cedera dalam kecelakaan itu.* Fortunately, my child was not injured in that accident. **bersyukur** to thank God, express one's thanks. *~ hati* thankful, grateful. **kebersyukuran** gratitude to God. **mensyukuri** and **menyukuri 1** to be thankful for. *Rakyat sudah mensyukuri pembangunan.* The people are thankful for development. **2** to congratulate. **syukuran** thanksgiving. *malam ~* thanksgiving evening. **kesyukuran** thankfulness, gratitude.

syur I (*A*) advice; proposal, suggestion. **mensyurkan** to advise, recommend, suggest.

syur II (*A*) **1** interesting. **2** appealing, exciting. *film-film yang paling –* the most interesting films. *merasa –* to be interested (in). **3** erotic.

syura (*A*) → SYUR I. **1** consultative. *maj(e)lis –* consultative body/council. **2** "The Council"; name of the 42nd chapter of the Koran.

syurah → SYARAH II.

syurga → SURGA.

syuriah and **syuriyah** (*A*) advisory.

syuruk (*A*) time of sunrise.

Syusangikai (*Jp*) (during the occupation) Provincial Advisory Assembly.

syuting (*E*) **1** shooting (a film). **2** to shoot (a film).

syuur → SYUR II.

T

t and **T** I /té/ the 20th letter of the Latin alphabet used for writing Indonesian.

T II car license plate for Karawang.

T-2 military rations.

ta I (*A*) **1** name of the third letter of the Arabic alphabet transliterated as the Latin letter t. – *marbuta* the Arabic letter *ha* with two dots above it indicating the pronunciation *t* rather than *h*. **2** name of the 16th letter of the Arabic alphabet.

ta II (in acronyms) → KOTA.

ta' → TAK I.

ta'addud (*A*) polytheism.

taajal (*A*) haste; hasty, hastily.

taajub (*A*) → TAKJUB.

taajul → TAAJAL.

taala (*A*) exalted, most high (mostly after Allah). *Allah* – God the Most High. *illahi* – due to God the Most High. *Sumbangan ini kuberikan kepada anak-anak yatim ini lillahi* –. I gave this contribution to these orphans thanks to God the Most High. *subhanabu wa* – [swt] praised be Almighty God!

ta'alik → TAKLIK.

taalim → TAKZIM.

taarof and **taaruf** (*A*) **1** acquaintance. **2** reception.

ta'arrub (*A*) to approach God and ask for His help.

taart (*D*) /tar/ tart.

ta'arud (*A*) clash.

taa(s)sub (*A*) **1** obstinacy. **2** obstinate, stubborn. **3** fanatical, overenthusiastic (and therefore easily taken in). **4** dogmatic, bigoted.

taat (*A*) **1** obedient. *hamba yang* – your obedient servant. – *kepada orang tua* obedient to one's parents. **2** pious, religious, devout. **3** faithful, loyal, dedicated. – *pada pemerintah* loyal to the government. **4** law-abiding. *warga yang* – a law-abiding citizen. – *asas* consistent. **bertaat-asas** to be consistent. *ketaatasasan* consistency. *kurang* – to fail to comply. *kekurang-taatan* disobedience, failure to comply. *tidak* – disobedient, disloyal. *ketidak-taatan* disobedience, disloyalty. *ketidak-taatasasan* inconsistency.

  bertaat to be faithful/obedient.

  men(t)aati 1 to obey, comply with, abide by, adhere to, stick to, go along with, play by (the rules). ~ *keputusan* to comply/go along with a ruling. ~ *undang-undang* to comply with the law. **2** to be faithful to. **3** to keep (one's promise).

  ketaatan 1 obedience, compliance. **2** piety, devotion. ~ *anak pada ortu* filial piety. **3** loyalty, allegiance, faithfulness.

  pen(t)aat obedient/faithful person.

  pentaatan obedience, respect, compliance, adherence.

taawud and **taawuz** (*A*) **1** prayer recited before reading the Koran. **2** an amulet carrying this prayer.

ta'awun (*A*) mutual help, cooperation; → TOLONG-MENOLONG.

taaziah (*A*) **bertaaziah 1** to feel sympathy. **2** to feel/express condolences, pay a condolence call.

taazur (*A*) hindrance; hindered; → UZUR I.

tabah I (*J/Jv*) – *hati* **1** bold, determined, unwavering, resolute, firm. **2** tough, able to endure (difficulties/hardship).

  menabahkan to make o.s. determined, strengthen, encourage. ~ *hati* to encourage, stiffen one's resolve. *Tabahkan hatimu.* Keep a stiff upper lip.

  mempertabah to reinforce, reaffirm, reassure, make firmer.

  ketabahan (~ *hati*) boldness, determination, resoluteness, firmness, resolution.

  penabah s.o. who is resolute.

tabah II (*M*) → TEBAH I.

tabak (*A*) a tray of food covered with a cloth; → TETAMPAN.

tabal (*A*) **1** (inauguration) drum. **2** inauguration.

  bertabal *naik* ~ to be inaugurated/installed.

  menabal(kan) to inaugurate, install, invest.

penabalan inauguration, installation, investing.

pertabalan inauguration, investiture.

taban name for various k.o. gutta-percha and rubber producing trees, *Palaquium spp.*

Tabanas [Tabungan pembangunan nasional] Savings for National Developments (which are not bound to a certain length of time, are exempt from property tax, and can be withdrawn any time)).

  mentabanaskan to put money into that k.o. savings account.

tabarak and **tabarakallah** (*A*) God bless.

tabar(r)uk (*A*) blessed.

tabar-tabar → SETAWAR.

tabarukan (*A*) to look for blessings/favors.

tabas (*M*) → TEBAS I.

tabat – *barito* k.o. epiphyte, mistletoe fig, *Ficus deltoidea*.

tabatul (*A*) ascetic.

tabay(y)un (*A*) confirmation, clarification.

tabé(k) → TABIK.

tabéat → TABIAT.

tabél (*D/E*) table, list. – *air-pasang* tide table.

  men(t)abélkan to register, put on a list.

tabela coffin.

tabélaris (*D*) tabular; in tabular form.

taberas menaberas to break through.

tabernakel (*D*) tabernacle.

tabi (*A*) follower, supporter, adherent.

tabia (*ob*) a small drum.

tabiat (*A*) **1** character, nature, disposition. **2** behavior, attitude, way of acting, style. *Bukan begitu* –*nya.* That's not his style.

  bertabiat to have a ... character/nature. ~ *kucing* untrustworthy.

tabib (*A*) **1** k.o. (Indian, Arab, or Pakistani) healer. **2** (*ob*) physician, medical doctor; → DOKTER.

  ketabiban medical, medicine (*mod*). *ilmu* ~ medical science. *sekolah* ~ school of medicine.

tabii (*A*) physical, (of the) natural (features), inborn. *ilmu* – physics, natural science. *mati* – dead from natural causes.

tabiin (*A*) **1** *pl* of **tabi**. **2** the second generation of Islam, who lived after Muhammad died.

tabiit – *tabiin* (*A*) the third generation of Islam, those who learned from the *tabiin*.

tabik (*A*?) **1** greetings. **2** hello. (*meng*)*angkat* – to greet. *kirim* – *kepada* remember me to, regards to. *memberi* – to greet, salute. *minta* – to say good-bye. **3** respect, esteem.

  tabik-tabik said when entering a holy place.

  bertabik [and **bersitabik** (*M*)] to greet.

  bertabikan to greet e.o.

  menabik(i) to greet.

tabir I curtain, partition, screen. *bekerja di belakang* – to work behind the scenes. – *asap* smoke screen. – *bambu* Bamboo Curtain, i.e., the barrier isolating the People's Republic of China from the free world. – *besi* Iron Curtain, i.e., the barrier isolating the Soviet Union and other countries in its orbit from the free world. – *kabut* air of secrecy. – *mabir* all k.o. curtains. – *surya* sunscreen.

  bertabir 1 to have/use a curtain. **2** to be in disguise.

  menabir to cover.

  menabiri 1 to put a screen/curtain on, screen off, cover with a screen/curtain. **2** to disguise.

  menabirkan to spread (a curtain, etc.).

  penabiran disguising, covering up.

tabir II (*A*) interpretation (of dreams).

  men(t)abirkan to interpret (a dream).

tablét (*D*) tablet. – *bergula/(ber)salut gula* sugar-coated tablet, dragée. – *(h)isap* lozenge, pastille. – *pelenyap batuk* cough-suppressant lozenge. – *pencegah mabuk perjalanan* anti-seasickness pill. – *salut/selaput* membrane-coated pill.

tablig and **tablih** (*A*) **1** sermon, preaching (*Isl*). **2** public assembly for religious purposes.

bertablig to preach.

men(t)abligkan to deliver a sermon on, preach about.

tablo (*D*) tableau vivant.

tabloid (*E*) **1** tabloid. **2** sensational newspaper.

tabo *bunga* – an ornamental herb, k.o. balsam, *Impatiens balsamina*, whose leaves can be used as nail polish.

tabok (*J/Jv*) **menabok** to slap, beat, strike, knock.

menaboki [and **nabokin** (*coq*)] **1** to beat/knock at. **2** (*pl obj*) to strike, hit, beat up.

tabokan slap.

tabrak collide; → TUBRUK. – *lari* hit and run. – *tubruk* (various) collisions.

bertabrak to collide (with).

bertabrakan to collide with e.o. *Empat kendaraan* ~. Four cars collided with e.o. *Kedua mobil itu* ~. The two cars collided.

menabrak [and **nabrak** (*coq*)] **1** to strike, hit, collide with, run into. *Kalau kendaraan kita* ~ *kucing hitam, ini pertanda akan datangnya malapetaka*. If our car hits a black cat, this is a sign that we'll have an accident. **2** to attack. **3** against, contrary to, in contravention/violation of. ~ *aturan* against regulations. *membongkar bangunan yang* ~ *aturan* to demolish buildings which (were built) contrary to the regulations.

menabraki (*pl obj*) to collide with.

menabrakkan [and **nabrakin** (*J coq*)] to run s.t. into s.t., ram, purposely smash s.t. (into s.t. else).

tertabrak [and **ketabrak** (*J*)] struck, hit, collided with (by a vehicle). *Sebuah bis* ~ *keréta api*. A bus was hit by a train. *Lampu belakangnya pecah* ~. The rear light of his car was smashed in a collision.

tabrakan collision. ~ *berantai/beruntun* a chain collision. ~ *frontal/dari depan* a head-on collision. ~ *kepentingan* conflict of interest; → BENTURAN *kepentingan*. ~ *maut* fatal collision.

penabrak hitter, s.o. or s.t. that hits. ~ *lari* hit-and-run driver.

penabrakan collision, colliding.

tabtiban *burung* – eared nightjar, *Eurostopodus temminckii*.

tabu I (*D*) taboo, not allowed, forbidden. *Wah saya* – *membicarakan itu*. Well, I can't discuss that matter.

men(t)abukan to taboo, consider s.t. taboo.

ketabuan sacredness.

tabu II – *kayu* k.o. plant used as a hedge-shrub, calabash tree, *Crescentia cujete*.

tabuan → TABUHAN.

tabuh 1 a long mosque-drum (smaller than a *beduk*). **2** drumstick. **3** drum beat. *jari* – drumstick fingers. *fitrah* drumming announcing the approach of Lebaran and reminding people to pay the *fitrah*. – *larangan* drumming announcing s.t. important.

menabuh [and **nabuh** (*coq*)] to beat (a drum), play (an instrument).

menabuhi (*pl obj*) to beat on.

tabuhan percussion instrument. ~ *rep-repan* k.o. *gamelan* instrument.

tabuh-tabuhan all k.o. percussion instruments.

penabuh drummer. ~ *drum* drummer (in a band); → PEMUKUL *drum*.

penabuhan sounding (a gong), beating (a drum).

tabuh II (*Bal*) – *rah* cockfighting.

tabuhan a large hornet or bee (*usu* builds its hive in trees), *Apis mellifera. sarang* – beehive. *menyolok sarang* – to stir up a hornet's nest. – *meminang anak labah-labah* "a bee asks for a young spider in marriage," i.e., not suited for each other (of a marriage). – *daun* sawfly. – *suruk* ichneumon fly, *Pimpla instigator*.

tabuk (*A M*) ceremony on the 10th of Muharram.

tabula rasa (*D*) **1** tabula rasa, sheet not written upon, blank paper. **2** newcomer, novice.

tabulasi (*D*) tabulation.

men(t)abulasikan to tabulate.

pen(t)abulasian tabulation.

tabulator (*D*) tabulator.

tabun menabun 1 to rise in clouds (of smoke/dust, etc.). **2** to make a bonfire of.

tabun-menabun rising in clouds.

tabunan bonfire; burning pile of garbage.

tabung 1 bamboo section between joints (used for storage). **2** money box. **3** tube; box, cylinder, canister, housing, sleeve, pipe, valve. *bayi* – test-tube baby. **4** bush, bushing. **5** fuse. – *air* a) bamboo container for carrying water. b) scuba. – *bantalan* bushing. – *cepat* instantaneous fuse. – *damak* container for darts. – *gambar télévisi* color-picture tube, CPT. – *gas* scuba. – *kaca* television, TV. – *kemudi* steering column. – *kimia* test tube, retort. – *lambat* delay fuse. – *logam* metal tubing. – *lucutan* discharge tube. – *luncur* launch tube. – *madat* opium pipe; → PENGUDUT. – *oksigén* oxygen cylinder. – *paking* packing gland, stuffing box. – *pekak* a piggy bank (originally made of bamboo). – *peledak* fuse. – *pemilihan* (*ob*) ballot box. – *pemasukan* inlet sleeve. – *pencernaan* digester. – *pengaduk beton* concrete mixer. – *pérak* piggy bank. – *pos* letter box. – *réaksi* test tube. – *seruas* can't keep a secret. – *surat* mailbox. – *tablét* a small glass pill box. – *takaran* measuring tube. – *tinta* ink holder (in a pen). – *waktu* time fuse.

bertabung with a tube, etc.

menabung [and **nabung** (*coq*)] to save (money). ~ *uang ke bank* to put/deposit money in a bank.

menabungkan 1 to save, put aside (money in savings) for s.o. else. **2** to save, put aside.

tabungan 1 money box; funds. **2** (*uang*) ~ savings. ~ *asuransi berjangka* [Taska] savings life insurance. ~ *haji* savings for the pilgrimage. ~ *hari tua* savings for old age, nest egg. ~ *langsung* direct saving(s). ~ *mesjid* funds for mosque requirements. ~ *Pembangunan Nasional* [Tabanas] National Development Savings Account. ~ *pemilihan* (*ob*) ballot box. ~ *pos* postal savings bank.

penabung saver; depositor.

penabungan saving, setting aside (money).

tabur strew, scatter. – *bunga* flower strewing. *melakukan* – *bunga* to strew flowers on a grave.

bertabur 1 speckled, spotted, spangled. ~ *bintang* star-spangled. *ayam* ~ a speckled chicken. **2** embroidered. *kain* ~ cloth shot with gold or silver thread. **3** to give alms. ~ *berderma* richly donated alms. ~ *bijan ke tasik* throwing away, wasting (money/time/energy). ~ *urai* generous.

bertabur(-tabur)an to be scattered all over, spread out, dispersed. *mulutnya* ~ with a flow/torrent of words. *Sak seménnya pecah dan isinya* ~ *di lantai gudang*. The sacks of cement cracked and the contents were scattered all over the warehouse floor.

bertabur-tabur → BERTABURAN.

bertaburkan 1 scattered/spread/spangled with. *duduk di karpét yang* ~ *bunga anéka warna* to sit on a carpet spangled with varicolored flowers. *langit* ~ *bintang* a star-spangled sky. **2** all covered with. *Di dadanya tersemat bros yang* ~ *intan berlian*. A brooch covered with jewelry was fastened to her breast.

menabur 1 to scatter, strew (flowers, etc.). ~ *bunga di pekuburan* to strew flowers on a grave. ~ *biji di atas batu* to carry coals to Newcastle, do s.t. useless. ~ *tenaga/uang* to waste/squander energy/money. **2** to sow (seeds).

menaburi to scatter s.t. (with), spread/sprinkle on/all over. ~ *peti jenasah dengan bunga mawar dan melati* to scatter roses and jasmine on the coffin.

menaburkan 1 to scatter, strew, throw. ~ *benih di atas batu* to do s.t. useless. **2** to broadcast, spread (knowledge/understanding, etc.).

tertabur scattered, strewn. *Dia mengumpulkan remah-remah roti yang* ~ *di atas méja makan*. She picked up the bread crumbs scattered all over the dinner table.

taburan 1 s.t. that is scattered/strewn. **2** dispersion. ~ *bunga di Pusara* the dispersion of flowers on the cemetery.

penabur 1 sower, spreader. **2** seeder. ~ *benih* an automatic tractor-towed seeder. **3** small pellets/bullets.

penaburan scattering, spreading, strewing, dispersion, sowing. ~ *benih padi* sowing of paddy seeds.

taburik horned helmet shell, k.o. sea snail, *Cassis cornuta*.

tabut (*A*) **1** a chest made of plaited bamboo or an imitation wooden *bouraq* bird with the head of a smiling girl and the body of a horse carried around in a procession on the day commemorating Hasan-Husain (Muharram 10). **2** the procession to commemorate Hasan-Husain by carrying it around the *tabut*. *bulan* – Muharram 1-10 (Hasan-Husain festival). **3** ark. – *perjanjian* Ark of the Covenant containing the two stone tablets inscribed with the Ten Commandments proclaimed to Moses in the Sinai Desert.

taci(k) (*C coq*) **1** elder sister. **2** term of address for Chinese woman.

tada (*ob*) → TIADA.

tadabur (*A*) – *alam* k.o. outdoor religious retreat.

  mentadaburkan to ponder, contemplate.

tadad (*A*) contradiction.

tadah I 1 receptacle, container (used to catch s.t. which is falling or dripping). **2** s.t. used to provide a base for another object (such as a saucer for a cup, etc.). **3** fencing, receiving stolen goods. *tukang* – receiver of stolen goods, fence. *ilmu* – *gaman* the knowledge of how to be invulnerable to weapons. **4** dependent on rain for irrigation. – *angin* wind break. – *cangkir* saucer. – *embun* the topmost bunch of bananas on a tree. – *gelas* coaster. – *hujan* cistern, reservoir. *sawah* – *hujan* rice field dependent on rainwater for irrigation. – *keringat/peluh* a) cloth attached to the inside of a shirt back, back lining. b) (*coq*) T-shirt. – *liur* bib. – *mangkok* saucer.

  bertadah to use a *tadah*.

  menadah [and **nadah** (*coq*)] **1** to catch or store s.t. (rainwater/ fruits, etc.) in a receptacle. *Kamu yang nyénggét, aku yang nadah*. You knock the fruits from the tree and I'll catch them. *Disediakan bak untuk ~ air hujan*. A receptacle was provided to catch rainwater. ~ *matahari* to oppose a man in power. **2** to receive stolen goods, fence.

  menadahi (*pl obj*) to catch.

  menadahkan [and **nadahin** (*J coq*)] to use s.t. as a receptacle for catching or storing s.t. *Émbérnya ditadahkannya air hujan*. He used a bucket to catch rainwater.

  tadahan 1 s.t. caught or stored in a receptacle. **2** act/way of catching s.t. from above. *air* – water caught in a receptacle. *sawah* ~ *hujan* rice field dependent on rain for irrigation. **3** s.t. fenced. *barang* ~ stolen goods received by a fence.

  penadah 1 container, receptacle. **2** receiver of stolen goods, fence. **3** (in sports) catcher, fielder. ~ *derita* butt, laughingstock, victim. ~ *barang-barang loak* dealer in secondhand goods.

  penadahan and **pertadahan 1** receptacle for storing clothes or finery. **2** receiving or storing s.t. in a receptacle. **3** fencing, receiving stolen goods.

tadah II bertadah ~ *amin* to say "amen" with the hands placed before the face in Muslim praying style.

  menadahkan ~ *tangan* to lift up and stretch out both hands as if asking for s.t. ~ *amin* to say "amen" while praying.

  tertadah (hands) lifted and stretched out.

tadah III long-tailed broadbill, *Psarisomus dalhousiae*.

tadaruk (*A*) humility.

tadarus (*A*) alternate Koran reading during Ramadan and on other occasions (in mosques/*surau*, etc.) by various persons; → DARAS.

  bertadarus and **tadarusan** to recite the Koran in alternate singing.

tadbir (*A mainly Mal*) administration, management.

  men(t)adbirkan to administer, manage.

  pen(t)adbir administrator, manager.

  pen(t)adbiran and **pertadbiran** administration, management, government.

tadi 1 just now. *Siapa yang datang –?* Who just came? – *ia duduk di sini*. He was sitting here not long ago. **2** some time ago. *dari/ sejak* – for some time. **3** in the earlier part of the day. – *pagi* and *pagi* – this morning. – *malam* last night. – *siang* today, during the day. – *soré* and *soré* – this afternoon (when speaking in the evening of that day). **4** mentioned earlier/before/previously, just mentioned. *sebagai yang tersebut di atas* – as mentioned above earlier. *orang* – the person referred to (earlier), the person mentioned previously.

  tadinya at first, in the beginning, at the outset, formerly, origi-

nally. *Pengakuan Bahasa Indonésia pada tahun 1945 kelak akan membuka peluang-peluang yang ~ tertutup bagi meréka*. The recognition of the Indonesian language in 1945 will in the future open job opportunities which originally were closed to them. ~ *rumah ini hanya dua jendélanya*. Originally, this house had only two windows. ~ *akan* was (supposed) to have (taken place, etc.). *Rapat itu ~ akan diadakan kemarin*. The meeting was to have taken place yesterday.

  tadi-tadinya originally, from the start.

tadir (*M*) wall of rice barn (made of plaited bamboo).

tadkik (*A*) scrutinizing.

tadlis (*A*) fraud.

tadmin (*A*) guarantee.

tadris (*A*) secular sciences. *jurusan* – the department of secular studies.

tadrus → TADARUS.

taduh → TEDUH.

Tadulako 1 the military resort command (*Korém* 132) in Palu. **2** name of a university in Palu.

tadulaku (*Sulteng*) **1** a respected social leader. **2** patriotism.

tadung I to trip. *Kakinya –*. He tripped.

  bertadung and **tertadung** to trip.

tadung II *ayam* – fowl with black feathers on the legs.

tadwin (*A*) registration, recording; codification of the Koran.

  mentadwinkan to register, record, codify.

taéfah (*A*) company, tribe.

taék (*Jv*) bullshit! – *sama meréka!* To hell with them! → TAHI I.

Taékwondo Korean art of self-defense.

Taékwondoin (*Jp*) taekwondo athlete.

taél → TAHIL.

taf (*D*) *kain* – taffeta.

tafa (*IBT*) k.o. long machete.

tafad(h)al (*A*) please.

tafahus (*A*) **1** meticulous inquiry, thorough investigation. **2** examination.

  men(t)afahusi and **men(t)afahus(kan) 1** to search (a person for concealed weapons, etc.), frisk. **2** to examine.

tafakur, tafakkur, and **tafkur** (*A*) meditation, contemplation.

  bertafakur 1 to meditate. **2** to be reflective.

  men(t)afakurkan to meditate on, reflect upon.

  tafakuran 1 meditation. **2** to meditate.

tafdis (*A*) **menafdiskan** to validate.

taf(e)ril (*D*) picture, scene.

tafrit (*A*) excess.

tafsil (*A*) detailed.

tafsir (*A*) commentary, elucidation, interpretation, exegesis (of parts of the Koran), explanation. *juru* – commentator. *salah* – to misinterpret, get s.t. wrong. *Jangan salah –*. Don't get the wrong idea. – *harfiah* literal interpretation. – *mimpi* dream interpretation.

  menafsiri to interpret s.t.

  men(t)afsir(kan) 1 to interpret s.t., construe. (*esp* the Koran), elucidate, explain. *Ia diminta ~ ayat-ayat Qur'an yang baru saja disebutkannya itu*. They asked him to interpret the Koranic verses he had just recited. **2** to figure s.t. out, understand.

  tertafsirkan interpreted, explained.

  tafsiran 1 interpretation, explanation. ~ *harfiah/hurufiah* literal interpretation. **2** commentary.

  pen(t)afsir 1 commentator, explainer. **2** exegete.

  pen(t)afsiran 1 explanation, interpretation. **2** commentary, exegesis.

taftah (*Pers*) → *kain* TAF.

tafwid (*A*) authorization.

tagak I menagak 1 to postpone/delay/put off (work). **2** to avert (danger), overcome (an obstacle).

  menagak-nagak to put off (work) repeatedly.

  tertagak-tagak put off (of work), neglected.

tagak II (*geol*) monadnock.

tagal I (*ob*) → TEGAL I.

tagal II large stones thrown up by the waves onto the beach.

tagan I stake(s) (in gambling).

  bertagan to bet.

penaganan betting.

tagan II separated, divorced.

  bertagan to be separated, divorced.

tagar (onom) thunder(clap).

  bertagar to thunder.

Tagaroa name of the God of the Sea controlling the Indo-Pacific Ocean.

tagéh I k.o. river catfish, *Macrones nigriceps*.

tagéh II (M) with lots of stamina.

Taghaabun (A) at– "Mutual Deceit"; name of the 64th chapter of the Koran.

tagih I menagih [and nagih (*coq*)] 1 to dun (a debtor for payment), request payment of a debt, bill. *dapat ditagih* (of a debt) due and payable. 2 to demand fulfillment of a promise.

  menagihkan to dun, collect a debt (for s.o. else).

  tertagih 1 dunned, billed, collected (of a debt). *tidak ~* uncollectible. 2 billable.

  tagihan 1 claim, claim for payment. *surat ~* dunning letter, bill. *~ listrik* electric bill. *~ muatan* bill of lading. *~ susulan* supplementary claim for payment (of a tax, etc.). *~ yang diistiméwakan* preferred claim. 2 receivable.

  penagih creditor. *~ bersaing* unsecured creditor. *~ (h)utang* creditor, dunner. *~ peserta* joint creditor. *~ rékening* bill collector. *~ utama* preferred creditor.

  penagihan request/reminder to pay a debt, billing, dunning, collection (of money owed). *~ berdaur* cycle billing. *~ pajak* tax collection.

tagih II addiction to s.t., obsession with s.t. *– tidur* lethargy.

  menagih(i) addictive, habit-forming. *Candu itu ~.* Opium is addictive.

  ketagih (*coq*) addicted to, habitually accustomed to. *Orang itu ~ rokok dan dapat menghisapnya tanpa berkeputusan.* That man is addicted to smoking and can smoke without stopping.

  ketagihan [and ketagian (*J*)] 1 addiction. 2 to be addicted to, obsessed by. *~ candu/narkotik* addicted to opium/drugs. *Kalau sudah ~ rokok, susah untuk menghentikannya.* Once one is addicted to smoking, it's hard to stop. *Ia ~ membaca buku.* He's a bookworm. 3 to crave. *Istrinya yang sedang hamil ~ rujak.* His pregnant wife craved *rujak*; → NGIDAM.

  penagih addict. *~ alkohol* alcoholic. *~ dadah* drug addict.

  penagihan addiction. *~ dadah* drug addiction.

tagir (M) → TAGIH I, II.

tagorub (A) to approach God.

tagut idol (worshiped by pagans).

-tah interrogative suffix expressing doubt or wonder. *Apatah faédahnya?* What use is it, I wonder? *Initah gambarannya?* Is this his portrait, I wonder?

tah → ENTAH.

tahabus (M) menahabus(kan) to imprison, detain.

tahadi → TADI.

tahajud (A) *salat –* optional midnight prayer.

  bertahajud to make that prayer.

tahak (*J*) belch.

  bertahak to belch, burp.

tahakik → TAHKIK.

tahala k.o. tree, *Santiria griffithii*; → BERAS-BERAS II.

tahalil → TAHLIL II.

tahaluf (A leg) the swearing in of both parties to a suit.

tahalul and tahallul (A) cutting the hair, an action performed after completing the *hajj* rituals.

  bertahalul to perform this act.

tahan I 1 durable, (long-)lasting, strong, hold up (well). *Cat seperti ini tak akan – kena panas matahari.* Paint like this won't hold up if exposed to the sun. 2 (can) bear/stand/suffer/endure, tolerate. *Benar-benar ia – sakit.* He really can endure pain. 3 to stand/take (-ing s.t.). *Ia tidak – tinggal lama-lama di sini.* He can't stand staying here too long. *Jarang yang – bekerja di tambang batu bara.* Rarely can one stand working in a coal mine. *Saya héran, ia – melihat orang yang tergilas mobil itu.* I'm amazed that he could stand to look at s.o. run over by a car. *– menghadapi* to put up with s.o. 4 to last, be enough/sufficient for. *Persediaan makanan hanya – (untuk) dua minggu.* A food supply lasts only for two

weeks. 5 sensitive, susceptible. *tidak – terhadap* allergic to, sensitive to a specific substance (such as a food/pollen/dust, etc.). *putih – sesah, hitam – terpa* unchangeable, able to resist everything. *– air* watertight, waterproof. *– api* fireproof, flame-resistant. *– asam* acid-resistant. *– bakar* fireproof. *– banting* to be able to take it, hold out (in hard times). *– basah* moisture-resistant. *– besi* invulnerable; → KEBAL. *– bocor* leak-proof. *– busuk* spoil resistant. *– cuaca* weatherproof. *– cuci* (of colors) fast, washable. *– debu* dustproof. *– érosi* erosion-resistant. *– gelombang* seaworthy (of a boat/ship, etc.). *– getaran/goncangan* shockproof. *– gorésan* scratchproof. *– harga* a) self-respect. b) to stick to a price. *– hati* steadfast, firm, consistent, constant, persistent; *cp* MENAHAN hati. *– hidup* to survive. *– hina* thin-skinned, not quick to anger when insulted. *– jenis* specific resistivity. *– karat* rustproof, rust resistant. *– kemarau* drought-resistant. *– kena api* fireproof. *– kias* doesn't get mad when an insinuation is made. *– kota* city detainee, s.o. under city arrest. *– lama* a) durable, lasting, firm, tough, resistant. b) strong and energetic. *tidak – lama* perishable. *– lapar* hardened against hunger. *– larat* have a nest egg. *– lasak* long-lasting. *– lembab* moistureproof/-resistant. *– lipat* resistant to bending. *– luntur* colorfast. *– magnit* antimagnetic. *– mengalami* to go through with. *– menghadap* to put up with. *– nafsu* self-controlled. *– nyala* flame resistant. *– ombak* seaworthy (of a boat/ship, etc.). *– palu* to be able to take a beating. *– panas* heat-resistant. *– peluru* bulletproof. *– pukul* feel no pain when beaten. *– retak* crack-resistant. *– sabar* with endless patience. *– selama hidup* will last a lifetime. *– selip* nonskid. *– sesah* fast (of color). *– sobék* tear-resistant. *– sopi* can hold one's liquor. *– susut* non-shrink. *– tangan* doesn't cry out when beaten. *– témbak* bulletproof. *– tuak* can hold one's liquor. *– turut* (naut) backstay. *– udara* airtight. *– uji* a) tested, tried (and true). b) to persevere, be tough. *– warna* colorfast.

bertahan 1 to adhere (to), keep (to), stick (to), abide (by). *Ia ~ pada pendiriannya.* He sticks to his opinions. 2 to last, hold out, stand one's ground, stand firm, hold on, keep going, hold up (of prices/improvements, etc.), maintain its position (of prices/rate (of exchange)], be maintained, be upheld, stay firm. *~ hidup* to survive. *tidak ~ lama* nondurable (of commodities) perishable. *bahan makanan yang sifatnya tidak ~ lama* food that spoils quickly, perishables. *~ mati-matian* to fight to the finish. 3 to be a holdover (from the past). *Ada 19 menteri yang ~.* There are 19 holdover ministers. *~ diri* to defend o.s. *~ harga* doesn't say yes to the first suitor, is choosy. *~ menghadapi* to put up with s.t.

bertahan-tahan to hold out over a long time. *~ larat* to put s.t. aside for a rainy day.

menahan [and nahan (*coq*)] 1 to hold (back), contain, restrain, control, check, curb, keep down, keep back. *~ diri* to restrain/contain/control o.s., resist. *tanggul untuk ~ banjir* flood-control dam. *peraturan untuk ~ meningkatnya harga barang-barang* regulations to keep down increases in the price of goods. *~ airmata* to hold/choke back one's tears. *~ gelak* to refrain from laughing, bite one's tongue. *~ kantuk* to hold back feelings of sleepiness. *~ lidah* to hold one's tongue. *~ lapar* to hold back one's hunger. *tidak dapat ~ ketawa* couldn't help but laugh. *~ rasa marah* to keep one's anger bottled up inside one. *~ rasa sakit* to endure pain. *~ kemarahan* to hold in one's anger. *~ sabar* to be patient. *tidak dapat lagi ~ sabarnya* to lose one's patience. *~ tertawanya* to suppress one's laughter. 2 to detain, arrest. *~ luar* to put under house arrest. 3 to keep, hold on to, withhold. *Paspornya ditahan.* They held on to his passport.

menahan-nahan to keep s.t. inside o.s., not let s.t. out. *Jangan ditahan-tahan.* Out with it!

menahani 1 to control, restrain. 2 (*pl obj*) to detain, etc.

menahankan to stand, endure, put up with.

mempertahankan 1 to defend, protect, safeguard. *Tentara ~ negara.* The army protects the nation. *~ kemerdékaan* to defend independence. *~ disertasi* to defend one's dissertation. *~ diri* to defend o.s., be defensive. 2 to maintain, preserve, retain, keep (alive), stand behind, keep (the same thing). *Tidak perlu ~ adat yang telah usang.* It's not necessary to keep outdated customs alive. *~ pendirian* to stick to one's opinion.

tertahan checked, impeded, hindered, hampered, held back/ up; stuck, backed up (of traffic). *tidak ~* a) unbearable. b) irresistible.

tertahan-tahan 1 delayed. 2 to fail, break down, falter. 3 there was a catch (in one's throat). *tidak ~* insuppressible, could not be held back. 4 limited, restricted.

tertahankan resistible. *tidak ~* unbearable.

tahanan 1 resistance, s.t. for resisting. 2 detention, custody, arrest. *~ kota* restricted to a city, (under) city arrest. *~ luar* house arrest. *~ muka* pretrial arrest. *~ (di) rumah* (under) house arrest. 3 s.t. held back, reserves. *~ buat hidup* nest egg. 4 detainee, prisoner. *~ politik* political prisoner. 5 resistivity.

ketahanan 1 resistance, tenacity, endurance, immunity (to disease), stamina, resilience, staying power, tolerance. 2 survival. *~ di hutan* jungle survival. *~ diri* self-endurance. *~ hidup* survival. *~ gosok* scuff resistance. *~ lipat* bend resistance. *~ méntal* mental stability. *~ nasional* [tannas] national resistance. *~ retak* crack resistance. *~ sobék* tear resistance. *~ tumbuk* impact resistance.

penahan 1 s.t. which holds back/protects against/resists/restrains s.t., retainer, guard. *~ angin* windbreak. *~ api* flame arrester, fireproofing. *~ arus air laut* jetty. *~ baju/celana* suspenders, braces. *~ buku* bookend. *~ gelombang* breakwater. *~ kejut* shock absorber. *~ kerusuhan* antiriot (police). *(simpanan) ~ larat* nest egg. *~ listrik* lightning arrester. *~ longsor* retaining wall. *~ lumpur* mudguard. *~ pintu* door check. *~ sinar matahari* sunblock. *~ terik* awning. 2 support, prop, mainstay. *~ kaus kaki* garters. 3 resistor.

penahanan 1 arrest, detention. *~ kota* restriction to a city. *~ lanjutan* detention in custody. *~ rumah* house arrest. 2 captivity. 3 retention, withholding.

pertahanan 1 resistance, endurance, stamina, strength, durability. 2 defense. *perjanjian ~* defense treaty. *~ diri* self-defense. *~ keamanan nasional* [Hankamnas] national defense and security. *~ ke dalam* in-depth defense. *~ sipil* [Hansip] civil defense.

tahan II menahan(kan) 1 to set (a trap). 2 to put up a sign prohibiting s.o. from doing s.t. (such as an *unduh*).

tertahan set (of a trap).

tahan III (*naut*) *– turut* backstay, stay or rope extending from a masthead to the side or stern of the ship.

tahana (*Skr*) 1 dignity, loftiness. 2 (*geol*) state.

bertahana to sit in state (of chiefs/high-ranking officials, etc.).

tahang I (*C*) tub, barrel, drum, cask; (wooden) pot, bowl. *– minyak* oil barrel. *– penggerak* hoist drum. *– penggulung* winding drum.

tahang II (*ob*) ravine.

tahap I stage, phase, leg (of a journey). *dalam – penyelesaian* in the final stages, nearing completion. *– akhir* final stage. *– awal* initial stage. *– lanjut* advanced stage. *– pembangunan* development phase. *– pendahuluan* preliminary stage. *– percobaan* testing stage.

setahap at the same stage/level. *~ demi ~* step by step.

bertahap(-tahap) 1 in stages/phases. *secara ~* step by step, gradual(ly). 2 fractional.

mentahapkan to do ... in stages. *Waktu harus ditahapkan secara terencana.* Time must be planned out in stages.

tahapan stage, phase.

pen(t)ahapan phasing. *~ kembali* rephasing.

tahap II (*S*) **tahapan** rank, class; → TINGKATAN.

tahar bertahar (*naut*) to maintain one's course (in a gale, etc.), sail on (of a ship in bad weather).

menaharkan to keep (a ship) on course, make s.t. sail on; make s.o. carry s.t. out/through.

taharah (*A*) 1 purification. 2 circumcision and its ceremonies.

bertaharah to purify o.s.

tahayul → TAKHYUL.

tahbis (*A*) consecrated, ordained.

men(t)ahbiskan to consecrate, ordain.

tahbisan consecration, ordination.

pen(t)ahbisan consecration, ordination.

Tahdiriyah (*A*) kindergarten.

tahfidz (*A*) knowing by heart, memorization.

tahi I 1 excrement, feces, shit. 2 dung, manure. 3 dirt, filth, grounds. 4 sludge. *sebesar – kuku pun* (not) even a little bit, (not) at all. *– air* scum on water. *– angin* a) light, fleecy clouds. b) nonsense, empty talk. c) beard moss. *– ayam* a) chicken droppings. b) bullshit! *– arak* drunkard. *– besi* iron rust. *– bintang* shooting star, meteorite. *– burung* a) guano. b) parasite. *– candu* a) opium dross. b) opium addict. *– gagak* meconium. *– gergaji* sawdust. *– gigi* tartar (on teeth). *– hidung* nasal mucus, snot. *– kerbau* bullshit! *– kelelawar* guano. *– ketam* shavings. *– kikir* iron filings. *– kopi* coffee grounds. *– kotok* chicken droppings. *– kucing* bullshit! *– kuda* manure. *– kuku* dirt under the nails. *– kuping* earwax. *– lalat* a) birthmark. b) freckles, mole. **bertahi lalat** with a birthmark. *– mata* mucus at corners of eyes. *– minyak* a) sludge. b) scum. *banyak – minyaknya* a lot of excuses. *– panas* heat rash. *– penyakit* fever rash. *– serutan* shavings. *– tangki* tank sludge. *– telinga* earwax, cerumen. *– tembaga* verdigris. *– tuwak* a k.o. yeast derived from *tuak*.

tahi II in plant and animal names: *– angin* plant used for medicinal purposes, *Usnea spp. – anjing/asu* k.o. herbaceous plant, billy-goat weed, *Ageratum conyzoides. – ayam* k.o. shrub, *Lantana camara. – babi* k.o. plant, *Adenostemma viscosum. – gigi* k.o. tree, *Elaeocarpus sp. – kerbau* a) k.o. sedge, fimbry, *Fimbristylis miliacea.* b) k.o. snake, *Coluber radiatus?*

tahiat → TAHIYAT.

tahil unit of measurement for gold: 1 *tahil* = 16 *mayam*; for opium: 1 *tahil* = 10 *ci(e)* = 100 *mata* = 1,500 *cekak*.

menahil to measure by this unit.

tahir (*A*) pure, untainted, innocent.

menahirkan to purify.

ketahiran purity.

pen(t)ahiran purification.

tahiyat (*A*) *duduk –* sitting at the second *rakaat* and at the end of the *salat* (in prayer).

tahkik (*A*) verification; valid. *ahli –* philosopher.

men(t)ahkikkan to verify, validate.

tahkim (*A*) appointment of a judge; judgment

bertahkim to use a judge (to adjudicate a disagreement).

tahlik → TAKLIK.

tahlil I (*A*) praise to God by repeating *la ilaha ilallah*.

bertahlil to repeat that phrase.

menahlilkan to repeat that phrase over s.t.

tahlilan gathering at which that confession is chanted.

tahlil II (*A*) to legalize remarriage to one's original husband (said of a woman who has divorced three times) by marriage to an intermediary; → CINABUTA, MUHALLIL.

tahmid (*A*) the repetition of *alhamdulillah(i)*.

tahniah (*A*) congratulations.

tahrif (*A*) falsification (of the religious message of Islam).

tahrim (*A*) *at-* "Prohibition"; name of the 66th chapter of the Koran.

tahsil (*A*) obtaining, acquiring, acquisition, collecting (rent, etc.).

tahta → TAKHTA.

tahu I /*usu* tau/ 1 to know, understand; to know how to. *Kamu –? You know what? Guess what? Saya tidak – pasti.* I'm not sure. *Mau – saja.* Just curious. *siapa –* who knows, possible. *– benar dalam* to be thoroughly familiar with. *– nggak* you know. *– membaca dan menulis* to know how to read and write. *ambil –* a) to find out. b) to care about (*akan*). *beri – →* BERITAHU. *cari – to make inquiries, inquire. *dapat –* to get information, find out. *tak –nya* unbeknownst (to him, etc.). *yang saya –* as far as I know, to the best of my knowledge. 2 to tell, figure out. *Bagaimana kau –?* How can you tell? 3 to recognize. 4 to be well informed of, be acquainted with. 5 to care about, pay attention to. *Saya tidak mau – tentang/dengan hal itu.* I don't want to think about it. 6 competent, skilled, able. 7 to be aware (of). *– akan* to be aware of. *udang tak – akan bungkuknya* nobody sees the mote in his own eye. *– and –, ya* (*coq*) (I) don't know. 8 (in some regions in negative and interrogative sentences) ever; → PERNAH. *Ia belum – minum vodka.* He's never drunk vodka. *Apa kau sudah – melihat gambar itu?* Have you ever seen that picture? *– makan – simpan* to know how to keep a secret. *– senang saja* and *tak – apa-apa yang kurang* impudent, not to know one's proper place, to act as if one is unaware that one is in an inferior position. *mau – sedia saja* not to bother about a thing. *tidak –* ignorant. **ketidak-tahuan** ignorance. *– ada saja* leave it to me! *– adanya* to be sure of o.s. *– adat* civilized, well-bred, polite. *tidak – adat* not nice (of behavior), unethical. *– akal* to have/get an idea. *– bahasa* decent, respectable. *– balas* grateful. *– benar* to know for sure. *– bérés* a) no problem. b) to leave it to others to do s.t., I leave it to you. *– bérés saja* and *– bérés déh* leave it to me. *– di alif* literate. *– di mata huruf* literate. *– diri* a) conscious. b) to be aware. c) to know one's place. *tidak – (di) diri* and *tidak – diuntung diri* a) not know how to do things properly. b) insolent, impertinent. c) unconscious. *sudah – akan dirinya* to regain consciousness, come to o.s. *Biar dia – diri sedikit.* He needs a good lesson. *– madu* to know which side one's bread is buttered on. *– mahu* all k.o. skills. *tak – malu* without shame. *– sama tahu* [TST] you scratch my back and I'll scratch yours, you take care of me and I'll take care of you.

tahunya 1 knowledge. *Banyak ~.* He has a lot of experience. *bawa ~ sendiri* to follow one's own ideas. *di luar ~* unbeknownst to him. **2** (*coq*) what one knows/finds out. *~ dari mana?* How did you find out? How do you know (that)? **3** it turned out. *tak ~* unexpectedly.

tahu-tahu all of a sudden, suddenly, before you know it.

setahu as far as ... knows. *~ saya* as far as I know. *dengan ~ saya* with my knowledge.

bertahu 1 informed. *unjuk ~* (*Jv*) to inform, announce, report. **2** conceited. **bertahuan** to know e.o.

bertahu-tahu 1 to pretend to know. **2** (*M*) with the knowledge (of).

bertahukan 1 (*ob*) to be acquainted (with). **2** to inform, announce, report, advise.

nauin (*J coq*) to know, understand. *yang ~ dan bukan yang mauin* those who know, not those who want.

tahu-menahu *tidak ~* a) not to know anything (about). b) not to care (about).

mengetahui 1 to know, find out about. *agar setiap orang ~nya* to ensure that all persons are informed, so that it may be known to all persons. *diketahui* known, understood. *Belum diketahui idéntitasnya.* His identity is still unknown. *supaya ~ saja* for your information. *untuk diketahui* for your attention. *untuk diketahui dan dijalankan* for your attention and action. *dengan tidak diketahuinya* unbeknownst to him. *dengan ~ dan menghendaki* knowingly and willfully. *tidak ~ daratan lagi → LUPA daratan.* **2** to figure out. **3** to recognize. *Serdadu Inggris dapat diketahui dari topi bajanya.* British soldiers can be recognized by their steel helmets. **4** to hear, understand. *Saya ~ bahwa dia baru pindah.* I've heard he's just moved. **5** informed. *kalangan yang sangat ~* well-informed circles. **6** acknowledged/seen by (above a signature verifying that a document has been seen by a superior or by one's parents).

mempertahukan (*ob*) to announce, notify, report; → MEMBERITAHUKAN.

tahuan (*infr*) information.

ketahuan 1 found out, discovered; perceived, noticed. *Akhirnya ~ juga perbuatannya.* Finally, his actions were discovered. **2** caught (in the act of). *Dia ~ mencuri.* He was caught stealing. *~ budi* his true nature has been discovered. **3** to be known, recognized. *Belum ~ lulus tidaknya.* It's not known whether he passed or not. **berketahuan 1** to get acquainted (with), get to know. **2** to be informed, be knowledgeable about. *tak ~* irregular, disorderly.

pengetahuan knowledge, science. *~ éskakta* exact sciences. *~ kejuruan* professional skill, specialized knowledge. *~ terapan* applied sciences. **sepengetahuan 1** as far as ... knows. **2** knowledge gained from experience, skills. **3** of similar knowledge. *tanpa ~* unbeknownst. **berpengetahuan 1** to have knowledge, be knowledgeable, informed. **2** intelligent, clever, able, skillful.

tahu II (*C*) /tahu/ bean curd, tofu. *– andir* k.o. soybean cake that can be fried without oil. *– campur* mixture of soybean cake and vegetables. *– gejrot* k.o. bean curd cooked with garlic and chilies. *– gimbal* k.o. vegetable dish with *bakwan udang*. *– goréng* fried tofu. *– gunting* spicy bean curd with potatoes, etc. *– isi* stuffed soybean cake. *– kering* soybean cake fry. *– perkedél* soy-

bean cake fritters. *– pong* soybean cake cut into small pieces and baked. *– sumpel* stuffed bean cake. *– telor* soybean cake omelet. *– témpé* combination dish of tofu and tempeh.

tahu-témpéwan s.o. who makes *tahu témpé.*

tahun I (*coq*) /taun/ year. *tiga – sekali* triennial. *dari – ke –* year after year, from year to year. *– berselisih musim berganti* over the course of time. *– ajaran* academic year. *– akadémik* academic year. *– alif* first year in the *windu* cycle. *– anggaran* fiscal year. *– baru* New Year's. *– baru Hijrah* Muslim New Year's. *– berjalan* current year. *– buku* fiscal/accounting/bookkeeping year. *– cahaya* light-year. *– depan* next year. *– fiskal* fiscal/financial year. *– hadapan* next year. *– hijrah/hijriah* date according to the Muslim calendar. *– Islam* lunar year. *– jagung* about three months. *– Jawa* a year in the Javanese calender. *– kabisah/kabisat* leap year. *– kamariah* lunar year. *– kering* a year with a long dry season. *– kuliah* academic year. *– lalu* previous year. *– Maséhi* date in the Christian calendar. *– pajak* tax year. *– panjang* leap year. *– pelajar* school year. *– pelajaran/pengajaran* academic year. *– pembukuan* fiscal/accounting/bookkeeping/ financial year. *– saka* the Javanese calendar. *– syamsiah* solar year. *– takwim* calendar year. *– ukuran bintang* sidereal year.

setahun one year. *~ dua* fly-by night, short-lived. *~ jagung* about three or four months. *umur baru ~ jagung* very young and inexperienced. *~ padi* about five or six months.

setahun-(tahun)nya every year, annual.

setahun-tahunan throughout the year.

bertahun for years.

bertahun-tahun for years (and years).

menahun to last for years, be chronic. *Penyakit ini bisa menjadi ~.* This disease can become chronic.

tahunan 1 annual, yearly. *secara ~* year on year. **2** for years. **3** about ... years. *20 ~* about 20 years. **bertahunan** perennial.

tahun II **bertahun** to plant rice.

tahuwa (*C*) by-product of tofu.

tahuwan tofu maker.

tahwé walking over live coals.

tahyat → TAHIYAT.

tahyul → TAKHYUL.

tahzibi (*A*) didactic.

tai I → TAHI I. *– tuwak* k.o. yeast made from *tuwak.*

tai II (in acronyms) → (PENG)INTAI(AN).

taib (*A*) good.

taici (*C*) tai chi.

taifun (*C*) typhoon.

taik I → TAÉK.

taik II → NAIK.

taikéng bayonet.

taiko (*C*) leprosy.

taikong (*C*) shipmaster, skipper.

taipak (*C*) **1** an idol which is supposed to help a gambler. **2** gambling. **3** banker (in gambling).

taipan (*C*) head or owner of a business, magnate.

taipun → TAIFUN.

tairu (*Tam?*) milk curd; → DADIH.

tais dirty, unwashed.

taiso (*Jp*) drill, exercise.

bertaiso to exercise.

taitut red-wattled lapwing, *Lobivanellus indicus.*

ta'iyah (*coq*) yes or no; right?

taja (*Mal*) sponsor.

menaja to sponsor.

menajai to sponsor.

penajaan sponsoring, sponsorship.

tajak hoe used for weeding, trowel. *– kebat* collateral.

menajak(i) to use such a hoe (on).

tajakan (*petrol*) spudding in.

penajak (*petrol*) spudder.

penajakan (*petro*) spudding in.

tajali (*A*) **1** open. **2** proven, attested. **3** revelation.

tajam 1 sharp, acute. **2** keen. **3** tough, unbeatable (competition). **4** caustic, corrosive. **5** incisive. *– akal* quick-witted, sharp-witted. *– hidung* good at sniffing out crime. *– lidah* sharp-tongued, sarcastic. – *mata* careful. – *mulut* sharp-tongued. – *otak* smart, intelligent. – *penciuman* good at sniffing out crime. – *pendengaran* with sharp hearing. – *penglihatan* with good vision. – *perasaan* sensitive. – *pikiran* smart, intelligent. – *seléra* not finicky about food. – *siasat* careful, not easily tricked.

menajam to come to a head, reach a critical point, intensify. ~ *kupingnya* to strain one's ears.

menajamkan 1 to sharpen, whet. **2** to aggravate, make worse.

mempertajam(kan) 1 to sharpen, make s.t. sharper. **2** to exacerbate, worsen. ~ *sanding* to make the situation worse.

tertajam the sharpest.

ketajaman 1 sharpness, acuity, acuteness. **2** too sharp.

penajam sharpener.

penajaman 1 sharpening. **2** exacerbation, exacerbating.

tajang menajang to carry in the hands.

tajau large porcelain jar.

tajdid (*A*) renovation, reform(ation).

tajén (*Bal*) cockfighting.

taji I spur. *laksana – dibentuk* with a beautiful curve. – *bentuk* spur with bent blade. – *golok* dagger-like spur. – *tiruan* artificial spur used in cockfighting.

bertaji with a spur on it. *belum ~ sudah berkokok* arrogant without being in a position to be so. *tidak ~ lagi* powerless, defenseless.

taji II k.o. tree used for house frames, *Podocarpus imbricata/neriifolia*.

tajil → TAKJIL.

tajin 1 starch; → KANJI I. – *susu* whey. **2** rice water.

menajin 1 to feed a child rice water. **2** to starch s.t.

menajini to starch s.t.

menajinkan to starch s.t.

tajir [harta banjir] very rich.

tajiran k.o. fine imposed on Muslim students.

tajribah (*A*) experiment.

taju (*A*) **1** crown; → TAJUK I. **2** (*anat*) process.

tajub → TAKJUB.

tajuk I (*Pers*) **1** crown. **2** title, heading, entry (in a catalog); subject, topic (of book, etc.). **3** outward projection on small vessel. **4** canopy (of forest). **5** (*bio*) perianth. – *gigi* crown on tooth. – *perahu* oarlocks. – *rencana* editorial. – *surat* letterhead.

bertajuk 1 wearing a crown, crowned. **2** titled, with a title/heading, etc. *sajak tak ~* an untitled poem.

menajuk 1 to protrude. **2** prominent, well-known.

menajukkan to editorialize about.

tajuk II tier, story.

tajung *kain –* k.o. silk *sarong*.

tajur I (*J*) pagoda flower, *Clerodendrum buchanani*.

tajur II fixed fishing pole.

penajur line of fixed fishing poles.

tajwid (*A*) rules for reciting the Koran correctly.

bertajwid to recite the Koran correctly.

tak I → TIDAK.

tak II (*D*) stroke, cycle, phase. *kendaraan 2-tak* two-stroke vehicle.

takabur → TAKBUR.

takaful (*A*) (the principle acceptable to Islam of) joint guarantee in a business undertaking.

takah I (*M*) **1** dashing, handsome. **2** appearance. – *takuh* various k.o. of showing off.

takah-takahnya it seems.

menakah to act dashing.

takah II → TAKUH-TAKAH.

takajub → TAKJUB.

takak bertakak (of two pieces of cloth) sewn together to make a garment.

menakak to sew two pieces of cloth together in this way.

takal (*D*) tackle, pulley. – *kait* hook block. – *luar* yard tackle. – *susun* block.

takang – *takik* various notches.

takar I measure, measuring. *mangkok –* measuring cup. **2** glass jar. – *coba* test batch. – *lajak* overdose. – *lebih* overdose.

setakar 1 to match, measure up to. **2** appropriate.

menakar(i) 1 to measure (out). **2** to set a limit to.

takaran 1 measure (the tool). ~ *pemberian* dosage measure. **2** a

measured amount, dose, dosage. ~ *obat* dosage. ~ *penghidupan* standard of living. ~ *sudah hampir penuh* to be near the end of one's life.

ketakaran standard.

penakar s.o. or s.t. that measures out.

penakaran measuring out.

takarir (*A*) marginal note.

Takasur (*A*) *at–* "Multiplying"; name of the 102nd chapter of the Koran.

takat I 1 limit, level. **2** until, up to, as far as.

setakat as far as, up to. ~ *ini* up to now, thus far.

takat II able to put up with illness, etc.

takau various species of birds: coppersmith barbet, *Megalaima haemacephala indica*; green broadbill, *Calyptomena viridis*.

takbil (*A*) the practice of a Muslim not descended from the Prophet Muhammad kneeling and kissing the hand of those descended from the Prophet.

takbir I (*A*) repetition of *Allahu akbar*. *–ul-ihram* that phrase used at the beginning of the liturgy. – *di pangkal lidah* to be on the point of death.

bertakbir to recite that phrase.

takbiran 1 religious gathering at which that phrase is recited. **2** (*malam ~*) the night of the last day of Ramadhan. **bertakbiran** to recite that phrase in a group.

takbir II (*A*) interpretation (of dreams).

mentakbirkan to interpret (dreams).

takbur (*A*) arrogant, conceited.

takdim (*A*) **1** introduction. **2** performing one required prayer before another because the first could not be done at the proper time.

takdir I (*A*) fate, destiny.

men(t)akdirkan to destine, predestine, preordain, fate, doom.

takdir II supposing that. *–pun* even if.

takdis (*A*) sanctification, hallowing.

mentakdiskan to sanctify, hallow, consecrate.

ketakdisan holiness, sanctity.

takel → TAKAL.

taker → TAKAR.

takhayul → TAHAYUL, TAKHYUL.

takhlik (*A*) **men(t)akhlikkan** to create, form.

takhsis (*A*) limitation.

mentakhsiskan to limit.

takhta (*Pers*) throne, crown. *naik –* to ascend the throne. *turun –* to abdicate.

bertakhta to sit on the throne, reign, be crowned.

men(t)akhtakan to crown, enthrone.

ketakhtaan (*mod*) royal.

takhyul (*A*) superstition.

ketakhyulan belief in superstition.

taki I bertaki 1 to deny. **2** to debate.

menaki 1 to deny, oppose. **2** to debate s.t.

taki II (*ob*) **bertaki** to promise.

takiah (*A*) fear.

takik notch, groove, incision. – *telinga* earmark.

bertakik(-takik) to have a notch/notches/grooves; notched, grooved.

menakik 1 to notch, groove. ~ *darah di batu* to get blood from a turnip. ~ *rezeki* to seek profits. **2** to tap (a rubber tree).

menakikkan to set a time for (a feast, etc.).

takikan 1 notch, groove. **2** tapping.

penakik 1 (*petrol*) tap. **2** tapper.

takir (*J/Jv*) **1** food container made of a banana leaf folded into a cone. **2** portion of rice wrapped in such a container.

takjil (*A*) k.o. sweet eaten to break the fast.

takjim → TAKZIM.

takjiran (*A*) special services for those unable to fast during Ramadhan.

takjub (*A*) **1** astonished, dazed, surprised. **2** wondering, marveling.

men(t)akjubi to admire. *yang patut ditakjubi* admirable.

men(t)akjubkan 1 to amaze, astonish. **2** amazing, astounding. **3** to admire.

ketakjuban 1 amazement, astonishment, surprise. **2** admiration.

takkan and *ta'kan* won't; → *tak* AKAN.

taklid (*A*) 1 unquestioning acceptance of a particular interpretation of religious doctrine. 2 gullible, easily fooled. – *buta* blind faith.

   bertaklid to have unquestioning acceptance of a particular interpretation of religious doctrine.

taklif (*A*) giving s.o. a difficult task or duty.

taklik (*A*) 1 (– *talak*) part of the marriage ceremony in which the bridegroom agrees to certain conditions under which the bride can ask for a divorce. 2 (*leg*) conditional (sentence).

   bertaklik to make the above promise.

   menaklik to read s.t. carefully.

   penaklikan collation.

taklikat and ta'likat (*A*) marginal notes.

taklim (*A*) 1 information, instructions. 2 teachings. 3 training, schooling, education. 4 advisory. *majelis* – Islamic study group (usually of women).

taklimat (*A*) briefing.

taklit → TAKLID.

takluk (*A*) to surrender, yield, give in. – *kepada* subject to.

   men(t)aklukkan to defeat, make ... surrender, subjugate, subdue, conquer.

   taklukan subject, s.t. subjected.

   penakluk conqueror.

   pen(t)aklukan conquering, subjecting.

takma splice, twining, braiding.

   menakma to splice, braid.

tako snack made of bamboo shoots topped with *santan* and rice flour served in a banana leaf.

takoa(h) (*C*) a soybean dish.

takokak → TEKOKAK.

takol (*J*) menakol to hit, beat.

takor various species of birds, *Megalaima spp.* – *akar* blue-eared barbet, *Megalaima australis*.

takowah → TEKUA.

takrau and takraw (*Thai*) rattan ball; → SÉPAK *takraw*.

takrif (*A*) 1 definition. 2 statement, informing. 3 determination.

   men(t)akrifkan 1 to define. 2 to state, inform. 3 to determine, set.

   ketakrifan definition.

takrim (*A*) honor, respect.

takrir (*A*) argumentation.

takro → TAKRAU.

taksa ambiguous.

   ketaksaan ambiguity.

taksah → *tidak* SAH.

Taksaka the executive-class train running between Jakarta and Yogyakarta.

taksasi (*D*) estimate; → TAKSIRAN.

taksi (*D*) taxi.

   bertaksi to ride in a taxi, go by taxi.

   menaksi to drive a taxi.

   menaksikan to turn (a private vehicle) into a taxi.

   pertaksian taxi (*mod*).

taksiméter taximeter.

taksir I (*D*) appraisal, evaluation, estimate. *kurang* –, *hilang laba* look before you leap.

   menaksir(kan) to estimate, appraise, value, evaluate. *Dia akan* ~ *rumah saya.* He's going to appraise my house.

   taksiran 1 estimate, appraisal, evaluation, valuation, calculations. 2 assessed, appraised. *harga* ~ assessed value. 3 provision for. ~ *pajak penghasilan* provision for income tax. ~ *tagihan pajak* estimated claims for tax refunds.

   penaksir adjuster, appraiser. ~ *kerugian* claims adjuster.

   penaksiran assessment, evaluation, estimation.

taksir II (*sl*) menaksir [and naksir (*coq*)] to chase after (a girl). *Émang, banyak lelaki pada* ~ *samé lu.* Really, a lot of men are running after you.

taksir III (*A*) neglect, negligence, defect.

taksis → TAKHSIS.

taksiun → STASIUN.

taksonomi (*D*) taxonomy.

taksub → TA'AS(S)UB.

takt → TAK II.

tak-tak (*onom*) crackling.

taktik (*D/E*) tactics.

taktis (*D*) tactical.

tak-tok (*onom*) clicking, ticking.

takua → TEKUA.

takuh-takah all k.o. notches/grooves.

takuk 1 groove, large notch (e.g., used for climbing up a tree). 2 curved part on head of penis (the uncircumcised part). 3 chevron, herringbone. – *takak* various k.o. notches.

   bertakuk grooved, notched.

   menakuk(kan) 1 to groove, notch (a tree). 2 to set, fix (a date to do s.t.). *Ia* ~ *hari untuk mengunjungi anaknya.* He set a date to visit his son.

tak-umpet peek-a-boo.

takung bertakung to settle (of a liquid).

   menakung 1 to let (a liquid) settle. *Ia* ~ *air sungai untuk minum.* He let the river water settle so he could drink it. 2 to let (a liquid) accumulate, puddle.

   tertakung (of liquids) settled, accumulated, puddled.

   takungan puddle, water that has settled in a spot.

takup menakup to close up (of two symmetrical things). *Bibirnya* ~. His lips closed.

   menakupkan to close (two symmetrical things). *Aku menggerakkan kedua tanganku turun dan* ~ *telapak tanganku di pantatnya dan meremasnya.* I moved my hands down and closed the palms over her behind and massaged it.

   tertakup closed (of two symmetrical things).

takur → TAKOR, TEKUR.

takut 1 to be afraid, scared, frightened. –*nya saya* ... (*coq*) what I'm afraid of is ... 2 to be cowardly. 3 to worry, be concerned. – *mayat, terpeluk bangkai* penny wise and pound foolish. – *tujuh keliling* to be scared to death.

   takut-takut 1 afraid, fearfully. 2 hesitantly. ~ *berani* hesitatingly.

   bertakutan (*pl subj*) to be afraid, scared.

   menakuti 1 to be afraid of, fear. *Tak ada yang saya takuti.* I'm not afraid of anything. 2 to frighten, intimidate.

   menakut-nakuti [and nakut-nakutin (*J coq*)] to frighten, intimidate, scare off.

   mempertakut(-takut)i to intimidate.

   menakutkan 1 to frighten. 2 frightening, scary, terrifying, spooky. *penerbangan yang* ~ a terrifying flight. 3 to be afraid of, concerned about.

   takutan easily frightened. ~ *segan* somewhat reluctant.

   takut-takutan bashful, nervous.

   ketakutan 1 fear, scare, fright. 2 concern, worry. 3 out of fright, with fright, in fear. *lari* ~ to flee in fear. *menjerit* ~ to scream with fright. 4 (*coq*) afraid, scared. berketakutan to be (too) scared (to).

   penakut coward.

   penakutan frightening, scaring.

takuwéh and takuwih k.o. bird, banded bay cuckoo, *Penthoceryx sonneratii malayanus*.

takwa I (*A*) piety, religious devotion.

   bertakwa to be pious.

   ketakwaan piety, religious devotion.

takwa II → TEKUA.

takwil (*A*) Koranic interpretation.

   menakwilkan to interpret.

   pen(t)akwilan interpretation.

takwim (*A*) calendar. *hari* – calendar day. *tahun* – calendar year.

takwinul alam (*A*) cosmogony.

Takwir (*A*) *at-* "Folding Up"; name of the 81st chapter of the Koran.

takwo (*Jv*) *baju* – dark blue Yogya jacket closed with a broad lapel and button on the shoulder.

takziah (*A*) condolence, mourning, consolation; → TAAZIAH.

   bertakziah to grieve with, send condolences to, sympathize with.

takzim (*A*) honor, respect, esteem. *salam* – → SALAM *takzim*.

   mentakzimkan to respect, honor.

   ketakziman respect, esteem.

takzir and takziz (*A*) punishment less than that prescribed by Islamic law.

takzirah (*A*) warning, admonition.

tal Palmyra palm, *Borassus fiabellifera*.

tala I (*Skr*) modulation (of pitch), tuning. *garpu* – tuning fork.
　setala in tune. **menyetalakan** to tune. **kesetalaan** resonance; → RÉSONANSI. **penyetala** resonator.
　bertala-tala to resound, respond to e.o.
　menala to tune (an instrument).
　menalakan to adjust (the sound).
　talaan tuning.
　penala tuner, tuning fork.
　penalaan tuning.

tala II (*Skr*) base. – *loka* the underworld.
　penala and **petala** layer.

talaah → TELAAH.

talabiah → TALBIYAH.

talah (*M*) hastily.
　(ber)talah-talah hastily.
　tertalah-talah in haste.

talai → LALAI I.

talak I (*A*) 1 divorce. – *bain kubra/kubro* irrevocable divorce. – *bain sughro/syughra* revocable divorce. – *bid'i* forbidden divorce. – *dua* second divorce. – *khul* divorce initiated by the wife; → KHULAK. – *raji/raj'i* first and second divorces (reunion is still allowed). – *rujuk* repudiation of divorce. – *satu* first divorce. – *tiga* third (and final) divorce (after two reconciliations). 2 *at*– "Divorce"; name of the 65th chapter of the Koran.
　men(t)alak to divorce s.o.
　menalaki to repudiate.
　tertalak divorced, repudiated.

talak II → TALEK.

talam I (*Tam*) tray made of wood or metal with feet for carrying food. *seperti* – *dua muka* said of s.o. who gets s.t. from both sides that are having a dispute. – *dua muka* tray that can be used on either side. – *gelembung* bubble tray.

talam II rice-flour cake.

talang I *ikan* – a) horse mackerel, *Chorinemus, spp*. b) (double-spotted) queen fish, *Scomberoides lysan*.
　talang-talang various k.o. marine fish, *Chorinemus spp*.

talang II (*Jv*) agent, broker, buyer of options. – *kuda* horse trader. – *uang* moneylender.
　menalangi [and **nalangin** (*J coq*)] to advance money to.
　menalangkan to lend/advance money at interest.
　talangan *krédit* ~ bridge loan. ~ *utang* bail-out.
　penalang ~ *uang* moneylender.
　penalangan advancing (money), advance financing.

talang III 1 (*Jv*) (roof) gutter. 2 a bamboo that holds a lot of water. *bujang* – a) bachelor. b) childless widower. *tak air* – *dipancung* to take emergency measures. – *air* aqueduct. – *daun* driptip (of a leaf). – *pencuci* sluice box. – *perindu* Aeolian harp. – *tegak* downspout. – *udara* air duct.
　bertalang with/to have a gutter.
　talangan launder (an instrument used in mining).

talang IV (= petalangan) hamlet, small village.

talaqqi (*A*) system of learning to read the Koran face to face with a teacher.

talar I frank, open.
　bertalar, bertalar-talar, and **bertalaran** open, frank, outspoken.
　penalaran outspokenness.

talar II *menalar* to allow, let.

talas taro, *Colocasia esculenta*. – *pérak* k.o. decorative plant, *Xanthosa sp*.
　talas-talasan Araceae, taro-like plants.

talbiah (*A*) to surrender o.s. to God. – *bilhaj* to form the intention of making the pilgrimage to Mecca.

talédék → TLÉDÉK.

talek (*D*) talc, talcum powder.

talem → TALAM II.

talémpong (*M*) a small gong.

talén (*col*) 25-cent piece.
　setalén 25 cents.
　talénan 25-cent piece.

talenan (*J/Jv*) cutting board.

tales → TALAS.

talfik and **talfiq** (*A*) following a legalist school other than the one usually followed.

tali I 1 rope, cord, string, line. 2 belt, strap. – *jangan putus, kaitan jangan serkah* settle a matter so that both parties are satisfied. – *agas* (*ob*) rope hung over the bed of a woman who has just given birth to help her get up and down. – *air* a) stream. b) perineum. – *ali-ali* slingshot. – *alir* a baited line for catching crocodiles. – *alit* string for a top. – *ambin* strap for carrying a load. – *anak* small line. – *anduh* a) sling. b) (*naut*) gun-lashing. – *angkat* tackle rope. – *antar* guide cord. – *api* fuse. – *ari-ari* umbilical cord. – *arus* main channel (of a river). – *bahu* shoulder strap. – *bandar* drainage. – *barut* abdominal strap. – *batong/batung* sash. – *bawat* brace. – *belakang* tail rope. – *belati* hemp rope. – *besi* cable. – *BH* bra strap. – *buangan* mooring line. – *bulan* cat line. – *busur* a) bowstring. b) chord (in geometry). – *cabang* branch line. – *cemat* tow rope. – *dagu* bit. – *dahi* horse's brow band. – *dasi* necktie. – *datar* flat rope. – *duga* sounding line. – *dugang* a) (*naut*) support line. b) rope tied to a tree being felled. – *gasing* string for a top. – *getah* rubber tie. – *giring-giring* bell rope. – *hidung* nose band. – *ikat* twine. – *jangkar* anchor chain. – *jantung* sweetheart. – *jemuran* clothesline. – *jentera* thread being spun. – *jiwa* the heart as the source of life. – *kail* fishing line. – *kang/kekang* bridle, reins. – *kasi* the bonds of love. – *kelat* (*naut*) boat's sheet. – *kemudi* tiller rope, steering line. – *kendali* reins; guidelines. – *kendit* belt. – *kepala* strap for carrying s.t. on the head. – *kepil* mooring rope. – *keselamatan* safety belt. – *kincir* thread being spun. – *kipas* fan belt. – *kolor* purse line. – *komando* (gold) aiguilletee (of army commanders). – *kursi* seat belt. – *laberang* ship's stays. – *lalai* (*naut*) mast rope. – *lari* escape line. – *léhér* horse collar. – *lés* reins. – *liang* k.o. belt. – *lidah* tissue connecting tongue with mouth. – *liung-liung* cord for tying a kris to one's waist. – *malang* (*naut*) breast line. – *manik-manik* (*naut*) lifeline (for lifeboat). – *menali* (ship's) rigging. – *nyawa* a) the heart as the source of life. b) sweetheart. – *pancing* fishing line. – *pangkal* mast rope. – *paranti* tradition. – *payung* suspension line. – *peduga* sounding line. – *pegangan* grip line. – *penahan* rope line. – *penarik* towline. – *pencemat* tow rope. – *pendarat* hawser. – *péndék* poor. – *pending* k.o. belt. – *pengaman* safety rope. – *pengangguk* (*naut*) forestay. ~ *penggantung* suspension line. – *penggulung* winding rope. – *penyandang* shoulder strap. – *peranti* tradition. – *pergantungan* a) s.o. who is always asked for help. b) sweetheart. – *persahabatan* ties of friendship. – *perum* lead line. – *perut* a) bellyband. b) intestines. – *pusar* a) funiculus, filament. b) umbilical cord. – *pusat* umbilical cord. – *putri* k.o. plant, *Cassytha filiformis*. – *rafia* raffia cord. – *ruai* twine. – *sabut* fiber rope. – *sandang* laces for clothing. – *sauh* anchor chain. – *sawar* rope for leading cattle. – *sepatu* shoelace. – *sidai* clothesline. – *singkil* rope used by women in labor. – *singkur* (*naut*) brace. – *sipat* plumb line. – *suai* (*naut*) stays. – *suci* the bonds of matrimony. – *statik* ripcord. – *tandur* cord for blinds. – *tarik* ripcord (on parachute). – *temali* all k.o. ropes, rigging. **bertali-temali** to be connected to. *Kematiannya masih* ~ *dengan berbagai mistéri korupsi*. His death is connected to various mysteries of corruption. – *tambat* mooring line. – *tiang* stay (on ship). – *tipis* twine. – *tom* reins. – *tudung* chin strap. – *tunda* tow rope, dragline. – *ukur* measuring rope. – *umban* sling rope. – *utama* main line.

tali-tali ropelike object.

setali connected.

bertali 1 to use/have a rope. 2 to be tied, bound. *sudah* ~ to be spoken for, already having a fiancé(e). 3 to refer to, bear on. 4 to be related (by blood or marriage). ~ *darah/keluarga* related.

tali-bertali connected/related to e.o., continuous.

bertali-tali 1 various ropes. 2 interconnected, involved with e.o. 3 continuously, ceaselessly.

bertalian 1 to be related to e.o. *Meréka masih* ~ *darah*. They are related to e.o. by blood. ~ *nasab* to be related to e.o. 2 relevant, germane. ~ *dengan* in connection with.

menali to tie (with a rope).

menalikan to tie up, to tie s.t. (to).

mempertalikan to tie/connect two things together, link, join (in marriage).

talian (*Mal*) (telephone) line.

penali 1 tie, bind. *cinta* ~ *dua hati* the love binding two hearts together. **2** tying up, conclusion.

pertalian relationship, connection. ~ *darah* blood relationship. ~ *jiwa* congeniality. ~ *keluarga* family relationship. ~ *kerabat semenda* relationship by marriage. ~ *sesusuan* relationship because suckled by the same wet nurse.

tali II (*col*) coin worth 25 cents.

setali ~ *tiga uang* six of one and half a dozen of the other.

tali III *pring* – k.o. bamboo, *Gigantochloa apus*.

talib (*A*) student (of a religion).

talibun (*A? cla*) k.o. poetry with more than four lines and several different possible rhyming patterns, ode.

taligram → TELEGRAM.

taligrap → TÉLEGRAP.

talik – *talak* the conditions under which a marriage can be dissolved.

ta'lik → TAKLIK.

ta'lim → TAKLIM.

talimarga communication. *alat* – means of communication.

bertalimarga to communicate.

taling (*ling*) acute accent used to distinguish é from e. *é* – e acute.

talipon and **talipun** → TÉLEPON.

talisai various species of trees, *Terminalia spp.*

tali-tali cypress vine, *Quamoclit pennata*.

talk and **talkum** (*D*) **1** powder, talc. **2** tallow.

talkin and **talqin** (*A*) prayer for the dead which takes the form of instructions given to the deceased on how to answer questions posed to them by the angels Nakir and Munkar. *membaca* – to recite this prayer for the dead.

men(t)alkinkan to recite this prayer over.

talon (*D*) stub (a form attached to a stock certificate which can be used to obtain new dividend coupons), counterfoil.

talu I bertalu-talu repeatedly, incessantly.

menalu to beat on.

talu II (*Jv*) **1** *gamelan* overture. **2** prelude.

bertalu to play this overture.

ta'luk → TAKLUK.

taluki → TELUKI II.

talun I (*onom*) resounding sound. – *temalun* various resounding sounds.

bertalun to resound/resonate.

bertalun-talun and **talun-temalun** keep on resounding.

talunan resonance.

penalun resonator.

talun II *pisang* – k.o. banana.

Talut (*A*) (the biblical) Saul.

tam (*onom*) → DENTAM.

tama → PERTAMA.

tama(d)dun (*A*) culture, civilization.

bertama(d)dun 1 cultured, refined. **2** with a ... civilization.

tamah → RAMAH *tamah*.

tamak (*A*) **1** greedy. **2** greed. – *kedekut* greed and avarice.

menamak to be greedy for, covet.

ketamakan greed.

tamam (*A*) **1** finished. **2** perfect.

taman I park, garden, reserve. – *atap* roof garden. – *bacaan* a) reading room. b) library. – *bahagia* cemetery. – *bunga* flower garden. – *buru* game preserve. – *burung* aviary. – *dalam* inner court. – *déwasa* junior high school. – *guru* teachers' college. – *hiburan* amusement park. – *hiburan rakyat* [THR] amusement park. – *hutan* arboretum. – *indria/kanak-kanak* kindergarten. – *karang* rock garden. – *madya* senior high school. – *makam pahlawan* heroes'/military cemetery. – *margaswatwa* a) zoo. b) game preserve. – *Mini Indonésia Indah* [TMII] Beautiful Indonesia in Miniature. – *muda* elementary school. – *pahlawan* (military) cemetery. – *parkir* parking lot. – *pendidikan Alquran* [TPA] Koran Education School. – *pustaka* library. – *remaja* playground. – *ria* amusement park. – *sari* park. – *Siswa* an educational association of the first quarter of the 20th century. – *tangki* tank farm. – *tani* peasants school. – *wisata alam* national recreation park.

pertamanan 1 (*mod*) park, garden. **2** landscaping.

taman II (*M*) hard-working.

tamanisasi laying out of parks.

tamar (*A*) date (the fruit). – *hindi* tamarind.

tamasya (*Pers*) **1** tour, excursion. **2** view, scenery. **3** performance, spectacle.

bertamasya to go on an excursion, go sightseeing, take a trip (for pleasure).

tamasyawan tourist, sightseer.

tamat (*A*) finished, done, over. – *belajar* to graduate. – *riwayat* (*euph*) demise, death.

setamat 1 upon ending, when it ended. **2** after graduating from. *Bahkan saya nyaris dinikahkan* ~ *SD.* In fact, I almost got married after graduating from elementary school.

menamatkan to finish, end, conclude. ~ *riwayatnya* to kill o.s.

tamatan 1 finish, ending. **2** graduate. ~ *SMA* a high-school graduate. **3** graduation.

penamatan termination.

tamatulkalam (*A ob*) the end of the story.

tambah 1 more, additional. **2** plus. *2 – 2 sama dengan 4.* 2 plus 2 is 4. **3** what one adds. *-nya* he added. **4** increasingly, to get ...er. – *x – y* the x-er ... the y-er. – *malam – gelap* the later it got the darker it got. *yang kaya – kaya* the rich get richer. – *kurang* added and omitted. – *pula* moreover.

bertambah 1 to increase, grow, mount, get greater/bigger, accrue. **2** increasingly. ~ *baik* to feel/get better, improve, recover (from an illness). ~ *berat badan* to gain/put on weight. ~ *cepat* to speed up. ~ *kuat* to recover, regain one's strength. ~ *kurang* to get less and less. ~ *lama* ... ~ ... the more ... the more ... .

bertambah-tambah 1 to keep on increasing. **2** and besides, in addition.

menambah [and **nambah** (*coq*)] **1** to add to, supplement, make more, increase, boost. *Tambah!* Take some more, have another helping! **2** to add. *Dua ditambah tiga jadi lima.* Two plus three is five. *ditambah dengan* to be eked out by. *belum ditambah* not counting, exclusive of.

menambahi to add to, increase the amount of, put more of s.t. (in, etc.).

menambahkan [and **nambahin** (*J coq*)] **1** to add s.t., supplement, increase the amount of. *Kami juga* ~ *situs baru.* We're also adding a new site. **2** to make s.t. more.

mempertambah to increase.

tertambah added, increased.

tambahan 1 additional, extra, more. ~ *data* additional data. ~ *jalur* out of one's way. ~ *pembayaran* surcharge. ~ *tumbuh* accretion. **2** supplementary, ancillary, secondary, supplement. ~ *Berita Lembaran Negara* Supplement to the State Gazette. ~ *pula* in addition. **3** lagniappe.

ketambahan to be increased/augmented.

penambah 1 addition, increment, additive, extra, replenisher. **2** (*math*) enumerator.

penambahan adding, increasing, supplementing; addition, increment, supplement. ~ *isi* replenishment.

pertambahan increase in, growth of. ~ *jiwa* increase in population. ~ *nilai* added value.

tambak I (*Jv*) **1** fish/aquaculture pond. **2** dike, levee. **3** brackish water. **4** banking, leveling.

menambak 1 to dam up. **2** to control (the flow or supply of) s.t. **3** to apply a poultice to.

penambak and **petambak** fish-pond fisherman.

pertambakan rearing pond.

tambak II k.o. snapper, *Lutjanus vaiquiensis? – dapur* k.o fish, black pomfret, *Parastromateus niger.*

tambak III – *bukit* and **tambak-tambak** little iron weed, *Vernonia cinerea.*

tambakan → TEBAKANG.

tambal (*Jv*) patch. – *ban* tire repairs. – *gigi* filling. – *sulam* patch. *secara – sulam* in a makeshift way. **menambal-sulam(kan)** to patch (up). *pak* – appellation for a man who has to marry a woman because she is pregnant.

bertambal patched.

bertambal-tambal patched up. *pakaian yang* ~ patched clothes.

bertambalkan patched with.

menambal [and nambal (*J coq*)] to patch (up), fill (a hole/cavity in a tooth, etc.); to mend, repair, fix.
menambali to patch up (a road/wall, etc.).
menambalkan 1 to patch for s.o. else. 2 to use s.t. as a patch.
tambalan 1 patch, filling (in a tooth). 2 patched up. bertambalan with patches, patched.
penambal 1 s.o. who patches. 2 s.t. used to patch with.
penambalan patching up, mending.
tamban various species of sardines, herrings, sprats, *Clupea spp.* – *bulat/buluh* rainbow sardine, *Dussumieria acuta.* – *jebur* round herring, *Dussumieria hasseltii.* – *nipis* k.o. sprat, *Clupea perforata.* – *sisik* k.o. sprat, fringetail sardine, *Clupea jussieu/fimbriata.*
tambang I 1 mine. – *basah* hydraulic mine. – *batu* quarry. – *emas* a) gold mine. b) source of profit. – *hanyutan* placer mine. – *milik* captive mine. – *semprot* hydraulic mine. – *terbuka* surface mine, open pit, strip mine. – *uang* source of profit.
menambang [and nambang (*J coq*)] to mine, excavate, dig.
tertambang mined.
penambang and petambang miner.
penambangan mining, excavating, digging. ~ *dalam tanah* underground mining. ~ *terbuka* open-pit mining.
pertambangan mining. *Départemén* ~ *dan Énérgi* Department of Mining and Energy.
tambang II 1 ferry. 2 crossing, passage, transportation. *ongkos* – transportation costs. 3 (*ob*) fare.
menambang 1 to ferry (passengers). 2 to cross using a ferry.
menambangkan 1 to carry across, ferry. 2 to use s.t. as a ferry.
tambangan 1 ferry, rented (vehicle). 2 passenger. 3 fare. 4 crossing point.
penambang 1 ferryman. 2 ferry.
penambangan ferrying, carrying across.
tambang III (*J/Jv*) 1 tether, thick rope. 2 tethering post.
menambang 1 to tether. 2 to refuse to grant a divorce to one's wife but also refuse to support her.
menambangkan to tether, tie up.
penambangan tethering, tying up.
tambar I medicine, cure.
menambari to treat (an illness).
tambar II not completely white (of rice).
tambat tether, moor. – *tarik* (*naut*) towing bollard.
bertambat 1 to be tethered, tied. 2 to moor.
bertambatkan to be tethered/tied with.
menambat 1 to tether, tie. 2 to moor. ~ *hati* to be attractive to, enthrall. ~ *tidak bertali* to live together without being married; → KUMPUL *kebo*. 3 (*geol*) to retain.
menambatkan to tether/tie (up) (a boat/animal, etc.). ~ *simpati* to gain one's sympathy.
tertambat 1 tied, moored. 2 attracted. *hatinya* ~ to be attracted, in love. ~ *budaya* culture bound. ketertambatan attachment.
tambatan 1 tie, mooring post. 2 lashing. ~ *batin* shelter. ~ *hati* beloved, sweetheart, lover. ~ *kabel* tie down. bertambatan 1 with a tie. 2 tied, connected, related. 3 (*geol*) retention.
penambat s.t. used to tie with, tether.
penambatan 1 tethering, mooring. 2 tie, alliance, relationship. 3 (*bio*) fixation.
pertambatan 1 moorings. 2 tie, connection, relationship.
tambel → TAMBAL.
tambeng (*Jv*) disobedient. – *macam gedék* opinionated and annoying.
tambera I k.o. freshwater fish, *Labeobarbus tambra.*
tambera II 1 bronze. 2 inscription on bronze.
tambi (*Tam reg*) 1 term of address for s.o. of Indian origin. 2 errand boy.
tambo (*M*) annals, chronicles; history, legend. *membuka (si)* – *lama* to dig up the past, rake up old stories.
tambra → TAMBERA I.
tambuh (*M*) more, additional; seconds (of rice); → TAMBAH.
bertambuh to have seconds (of rice).
menambuhkan to offer seconds (of rice).
tambuhan seconds (of rice).
tambul I snack, dessert, s.t. eaten with drinks, refreshments; drinks as refreshments.

bertambul 1 with a snack/refreshments. 2 to have a snack/refreshments.
menambul serve s.t. as a snack.
tambul II acrobatics and other theatrical stunts.
bertambul and menambul to do these stunts.
penambul acrobat or performer of theatrical stunts.
tambun I chubby.
menambunkan to make chubby.
tambun II (*M*) pile, heap; → TIMBUN.
bertambun 1 to pile up. 2 to be crowded.
bertambun-tambun to keep on piling up. *Hutang* ~. Debts keep piling up.
menambun to pile up.
tertambun piled up.
tambunan pile, heap. ~ *budi* a wise person.
pertambunan pile, heap.
Tambun Bungai (*ob*) name of the Army division stationed in Central Kalimantan.
tambung rude, impertinent, impudent.
menambungi to be rude to.
tambur I drum.
bertambur and menambur to beat a drum.
menamburi to beat on.
penambur drummer.
tambur II one of the Chinese playing cards.
tamburin (*D*) tambourine.
tambus I → TEMBUS.
tambus II menambus to bake in hot ashes.
taméng (*Jv*) 1 shield, guard. 2 disguise.
bertaméng 1 to use a shield. 2 to hide behind a shield, shielded by.
tertaméngi shielded.
menaméngi to shield.
penaméngan shielding.
tamimah (*A*) amulet.
tammat → TAMAT.
tammatulkalam → TAMATULKALAM.
tampa I → TANPA.
tampa II *salah* – to make a mistake, be wrong.
menampa to think, suppose, understand.
tampah (*Jv*) winnow; → NYIRU.
tampak I 1 to appear, seem, look. 2 to appear, be(come) visible, come into sight, show up; → NAMPAK. *-nya* apparently, it seems. – *oléhku* I saw. – *oléhnya* he saw. *tak* – invisible. – *sekali* obvious, conspicuous. *Tidak* – *batang hidungnya.* He didn't show up. *tidak begitu* – not so obvious, subtle. 3 view, way of looking at s.t. – *depan/muka* front view. – *samping* side view.
tampaknya 1 obviously, apparently. 2 by the look of it, it seems (that), it looks like. ~ *akan hujan.* It looks like rain.
tampak-tampak and nampak-nampak 1 vaguely visible. ~ *apung* vaguely visible. 2 to appear in one's imagination. *tak* ~ *lagi* didn't show up.
menampak [and nampak (*coq*)] to (be able to) see.
menampakkan 1 to display, exhibit, show. 2 to perceive, see. ~ *diri/hidung/muka* to show up, appear.
tertampak visible, can be seen.
penampak displayer, s.t. which makes s.t. visible.
penampakan appearance.
tampak II measles; → CAMPAK II.
tampal patch, mend; → TAMBAL. – *roti* jelly, etc. smeared on bread.
menampal 1 to patch (up), mend. 2 to patch with.
menampalkan 1 to attach a patch, mend (*usu* with plaster). 2 to affix, put up. ~ *kersik ke buluh* to give s.o. unheeded advice.
tampalan 1 patch. 2 s.t. affixed/attached. 3 appendix (to a book).
penampal sticker.
penampalan affixing, putting up.
tampan I 1 to look smart/stylish/great, good-looking. 2 look, appearance. 3 fitting, appropriate. – *di badan* (the clothes) look good on s.o. – *muka* features. – *rupa* appearance, the way one looks.
tampannya at first sight.
tampan-tampannya apparently, it looks like.
menampan to make s.o. look smart/stylish, spruce up.
ketampanan smart looks/appearance.

tampan II block.
  menampan to block, stanch (the flow of blood).
  tertampan blocked.
  penampan block(ade).
tampang I 1 appearance, look, view, profile. **2** (flat) section, slice. *- Afrika* Afro (haircut). *- atas* top view. *- bawah* bottom view. *- lintang* cross section. *- muka* front view. *- samping/sisi* side view, profile.
  bertampang to have a ... look. *Polisi tak boléh ~ militér.* The police may not have a military look.
  menampang 1 to look at o.s. in the mirror. **2** to show off, put on airs. **3** to slice, cut into sections, section.
  penampang section. *~ bagan* schematic section. *~ datar* horizontal section. *~ gabungan* composite section. *~ kerucut* conic section. *~ melintang* cross section. *~ memanjang* longitudinal section. *~ pipa* size of a wire. *~ tegak* vertical section. *~ tumpuk* columnar section. **berpenampang** with a cross section of.
  penampangan profiling.
tampang II (*M*) **1** seed, cutting. **2** source, origin.
tampang III (*J/Jv*) wad (of tobacco), roll, slice, ingot (of tin), tin coin.
tampang IV k.o. tree, Indian valerian, *Vernonia wallichii.*
tampang V (*ob*) a tin coin.
tampar I 1 blow (with the palm), slap, smack. **2** beater (for rugs, etc.).
  bertampar *~ tangan* to applaud.
  menampar [and **nampar** (*coq*)] to slap. *~ angin* to miss the mark. *~ dada* to beat one's chest (with pride).
  tampar-menampar to slap e.o.
  menampari (*pl obj*) to slap/hit.
  menamparkan 1 to slap/hit/smack with s.t. **2** to slap, etc. on s.o. else's orders.
  tertampar slapped, hit, smacked.
  tamparan 1 slap, blow, smack. *~ nyamuk* shoulder blade. **2** clapping.
  penampar s.o. or s.t. that slaps.
  penamparan slapping, smacking.
tampar II and **tamparan** *hantu* k.o. tree, *Sindora wallichii/sumatrana.*
tampas (*ob*) lopped off, trimmed.
  menampas to lop off.
  tertampas lopped off.
tampek → CAMPAK II, TAMPAK II.
tampel → TAMPAL.
tampél (*J?*) **menampél 1** to slap (not on the face), bump, knock into, hit. **2** to parry.
tampi winnow.
  menampi 1 to winnow. *tumpah padinya kalau ~* to go too far, overdo s.t. **2** to throb. *dada ~* to be out of breath.
  tertampi winnowed.
  tampian 1 winnow. **2** (s.t.) winnowed.
  penampi winnowing basket, thresher.
  penampian winnowing (out).
tampias → TEMPIAS.
tampik I (*Jv*) **menampik 1** to reject, deny, decline (an offer), repulse (an attack). **2** to shun, not have anything to do with.
  tampikan 1 refusal, rejection. **2** s.t. refused/rejected.
  penampikan refusal, rejection.
tampik II → TEMPIK I.
tampil and **menampil** (*ob*) **1** to appear, become visible, come into sight, emerge, come into being. *- béda* to (try to) look different. **2** to come/step (forward), come (before), advance. *Jabatannya telah memberikan banyak kesempatan -.* His position has given him a lot of opportunities to come forward.
  menampilkan [and **nampilin** (*J coq*)] show, display, perform, feature; to present, bring up, come up with. *Upacara ~ parade kekuatan ABRI.* The ceremony displayed an ABRI show of force. *acara yang ~ Marzuki* the program at which Marzuki appeared.
  tampilan 1 display. **2** appearance (on TV, etc.).
  ketampilan appearance, presence.
  penampil s.o. who appears. *~ mula* debutante.
  penampilan 1 profile, appearance, debut. *~ luar* putting on a front. *~ perusahaan* company profile. **2** performance, presen-

tation, display. **berpenampilan** with the appearance of. *Dia ~ sangat meyakinkan.* He appeared to be very convincing.
tampin I 1 quid. **2** k.o. container. *- rumbia* leaves used to wrap food, etc.
  setampin a quid.
tampin II (*M*) stake, bet.
  bertampin to have a stake, bet for a stake. *~ taruh* to match s.o.'s bet.
  menampin to stake.
tamping (*Jv*) **1** edge, verge, border. **2** shore, beach. **3** screen, protection (against the wind, etc.). **4** (prison) trustee, guard; foreman.
tampoi k.o. tree, *Xerospermum intermedium.*
tampon (*D*) plug, tampon; → SUMBAT.
tamprak (*J*) **namprakin** to spread s.t. out.
tampu 1 k.o. tree, *Macaranga hullettii* and other species. **2** k.o. shrub, sword fern, *Melochia umbellata.*
tampui → TEMPUI.
tampuk I 1 calyx, end of stem to which the fruit is attached. **2** socket, fitting. **3** power, position of authority, reins (of power). **4** decorative or ornamental cover similar in design or form to a calyx. **5** butt (of gun). *- bertangkai* with strong evidence or reason. *- kekuasaan* reins of power. *- labu* clitoris. *- lampu* lamp socket. *- mata* eyelid. *- negeri* reins of power. *- pemerintahan* supreme power. *- pimpinan* central authority, supreme power, top leadership. **bertampuk pimpinan** to have supreme power. *- pistol* butt of a pistol. *- subang* part of earring that goes through the ear. *- susu* aureola (around the nipple).
  setampuk *darah ~ pinang* too young and inexperienced.
  bertampuk 1 to have a calyx/socket. **2** to be centered (of power).
tampuk II k.o. bird, green broadbill, *Calyptomena viridis.*
tampuk III tampuk-tampuk k.o. fish, slender silver biddy, *Gerres oblongus.*
tampunai → TEMPUNAI.
tampung I menampung [and **nampung** (*coq*)] **1** to catch s.t. which is falling, collect s.t. falling from above. *~ air hujan* to catch rainwater (in a bucket, etc.). *~ doa* to say one's prayers (with upraised hands). **2** to accommodate, handle, receive and take in, provide s.o. with a job, put s.o. up (at one's house), provide a haven for, collect. *hotél yang dapat ~ tamu-tamu dari luar kota* a hotel which can accommodate out-of-town guests. **3** to intercept, seize in transit. *rémbés dipalit, titik ditampung* though small it was accepted anyway.
  menampungi (*pl obj*) to catch, etc.
  menampungkan to catch s.t. with, intercept with, use s.t. to collect s.t. *~ tabung di bawah* to put a tube below s.t. to catch it with. *~ tangan* to raise one's hands (to collect s.t.)
  tertampung [and **ketampung** (*coq*)] **1** received and taken in, collected. *Beras di beberapa daérah Krawang melimpah dan tidak ~ pemerintah.* Rice in a number of areas of Krawang was overflowing and the government couldn't take in all of it. **2** accommodated. *Banyak lulusan tidak ~.* Many graduates could not be accommodated.
  tampungan 1 catcher, scraper (in mining). *~ tikusan* scraper tap. **2** place for collecting s.t. *~ air* cistern.
  penampung 1 container, place for collecting s.t. *bak ~* reservoir. *~ debu* dust collector. **2** s.o. who intercepts/collects, etc., collector.
  penampungan receiving and taking in, collecting, reception. *pusat ~* reception center. *tempat ~* shelter (for battered women, etc.). *tempat ~ kembali* resettlement site. **sepenampungan** fellow receivers. *teman-teman ~* fellow receivers (of this message).
tampung II patch.
  bertampung patched (of clothes/a floor with new planks, etc.).
  menampung to patch (up), sew a patch on, mend, fix. *~ lantai* to fix a floor.
  penampung patch, replacement.
tampung III menampung to slap (on the face).
tampung IV (*- besi*) k.o. plant, *Callicarpa longifolia.*
tampung V (*- bajau*) Chinese pond heron, *Ardeola bacchus.*
tampur → TEMPUR.
tampus (*M*) reddish yellow.

tamsil (*A*) parable, analogy, allegory. – *ibarat* example.
  bertamsil allegorical, analogical.
  men(t)amsilkan 1 to analogize, compare. 2 to tell (a story) as an allegory.
  tertamsilkan can be understood by analogy.
  tamsilan analogy, comparison.
  pen(t)amsil allegorist.
tamtam I (*D*) k.o. drum.
tamtam II (*M*) indigo plant, *Marsdenia tinctoria.*
tamtama (*mil*) enlisted man.
tamu guest, visitor, caller, company. – *negara/negeri* state visitor. – *tidak diundang* uninvited visitor, i.e., a burglar.
  bertamu to be a guest/visitor, visit, socialize. *Dia terlalu sibuk untuk* ~. He's too busy to socialize.
  menamu 1 to be a guest of. 2 to entertain.
  mertamu to be a guest of.
  menamui to visit, go to see.
  ketamuan to be visited, receive visitors.
tamuk k.o. mullet, *Mugil sp.*
tamyiz (*A*) the ability to discriminate (right from wrong).
  mentamyizkan to distinguish (right from wrong).
tamzil → TAMSIL.
Tan I → SUTAN, TUN I.
tan- II without, not having; → TANPA.
tana land (in some place names). – *Toraja* the Toraja highlands in Sulawesi.
tanah 1 land. 2 earth, soil. *di mana – dipijak, di situ langit dijunjung* when in Rome do as the Romans. *ke –* to the land. **mengetanahkan** 1 to bury, inter. 2 to raze to the ground. ~ *bendéra* to lower the flag. – *adat* land whose use is regulated by *adat*. – *air* fatherland, native land. **bertanah air** to have a fatherland. – *bagian atas* topsoil. – *bagian bawah* subsoil. – *bangunan* building site. – *basah* wetlands. – *bata* sod. – *bawahan* subsoil. – *bencah* muddy soil. – *bendang* wet rice land. – *bengkok* land received in lieu of wages. – *berkapur* calcareous soil. – *bero* fallow land. – *berumput* turf. – *dara* virgin soil. – *darat* land not used for wet rice fields. – *dasar* subsoil. – *datar* flatlands. – *daun* humus. – *dawas* badlands. – *dingin* reference to Europe (*esp* the Netherlands). – *érpah* leasehold land. – *gambut* fenland. – *garapan* crop/arable land. – *geluh* loamy ground. – *gembur* fertilized land. – *gemuk* peat. – *genting* isthmus. – *girik* → TANAH *adat.* – *gogolan* (*Jv*) community-held land. – *goyang* earthquake. – *gundul* bare land. – *guntai* a) land situated outside the area where the government employee owner resides. b) land owned by an absentee owner. – *hak* individually owned land. – *hidup* cultivated land. – *Hijau* Greenland. – *Hijaz* Mecca and the surrounding area. – *hitam* humus. – *HO* (*D ob*) tenancy agreement land. – *isi* landfill. – *jabatan* land received in lieu of wages. – *kampung* communal land. – *kelam* muck soil. – *kerajaan* uncultivated land outside a village. – *kering* unirrigated land. – *kosong* uncultivated land. – *kuripan* privately owned land. – *kurus* poor soil. – *labu* humus. – *lapang* a) field, heath. b) village square. – *lapisan teratas* topsoil. – *lapukan* topsoil. – *lempung* loam. – *liat* clay, loam. – *longsor* earth slide. – *lus* loess. – *mati* uncultivated land. – *menanjung* spit (of land). – *mérah* lateritic soil. – *Mérah* colonial time site in Boven Digul. – *milik* privately owned land. – *milik-bersama* communally held land. – *napal* marl. – *negara* state land. – *pangonan* pasture. – *papas* marginal land. – *partikelir* privately owned land. – *pekarangan* land and property. – *pekat* loam. – *pelungguh* appanage. – *penggembalaan* pasture. – *penutup* overburden. – *perawan* virgin soil. – *Perjanjian* the Promised Land. – *perkebunan* plantation. – *persil* long-lease land. – *pertapalan* land that has been demarcated into lots. – *pertanian* agricultural land. – *perumahan* land to be used for housing. – *pucuk* topsoil. – *pusaka* (*cla*) ancestral lands. – *rata* level ground. – *rawang* bog. – *raya* continent. – *remah* granulated soil. – *rembang* open land. – *Réncong* Aceh. – *ringan* light soil. – *seberang* a) Sumatra, etc. (as seen from Java). b) Malacca (as seen from Sumatra). – *Sepi* West Sumatra. – *suci* the Holy Land, *esp* Mecca and Medina. – *suku* communally held land. – *tambak* polder. – *terbis* eroded land. – *tersirah/tersirat* recent grave site. – *tidur* fallow land, land not being used for agriculture. – *timbul* sand bank. –

timbun landfill. – *tinggi* highland. – *titisara* land owned by a village. – *tuang* groin (a structure built out from the shore). – *tumpah darah* one's native land. – *ulayat* (*M*) village *adat* land. – *uruk* landfill. – *usaha* a) land used for a business enterprise. b) landed property. – *wakaf* land for public purposes.
  bertanah to take root, to put down roots.
  menanahkan (*elec*) to ground.
  pentanahan (*elec*) grounding.
  pertanahan land (*mod*).
tanahair → TANAH *air.*
tanai (*M*) **menanai** to lift or carry s.t. on the palms of the hand.
tanak bertanak 1 to cook rice. 2 (rice/potatoes) boiled in water.
  menanak and **mempertanak** [and **nanak** (*coq*)] to cook (rice, etc.) in boiling water, boil. *ditanaknya semua berasnya* he has shot his wad.
  tanak-tanakan playing at cooking.
  penanak person who or instrument which cooks rice. ~ *nasi* rice cooker. **sepenanak** and **sepertanak** the time it takes rice to cook, about 20 minutes.
  petanak *kayu* ~ firewood.
tanakud (*A*) incompatibility.
tanam plant. – *akar* root crop. **menanam-akarkan** to instill, inculcate. – *paksa* forced planting; → CULTUURSTÉLSEL. – *sela* interplanting.
  bertanam to plant/raise (a crop for a living), be a ... planter. *Dia* ~ *jagung.* He raises corn. *musim* ~ the planting season. ~ *tebu di bibir* to cajole. ~ *biji hampa* to do s.t. useless. ~ *budi* to do a good deed.
  bertanam-tanaman to be a planter.
  menanam [and **nanam** (*coq*)] 1 to plant, sow. 2 to invest (money). 3 to implant, instill, inculcate, place. 4 to bury (a body, etc.). *Pencuri* ~ *hasil rampokannya.* The robber buried his loot. ~ *kebaikan* to do good deeds, do favors for others. ~ *mumbang* to do s.t. hopeless.
  tanam-menanam planting, cultivating.
  menanami to plant (a field, etc.). *dapat ditanami* cultivable. *tanah ditanami* land under cultivation.
  menanamkan 1 to invest. 2 to instill, implant, inculcate, sow. *Kebiasaan membaca buku masih harus ditanamkan.* The habit of reading books still must be instilled (among the people). ~ *kesadaran* to make s.o. realize. ~ *mumbang* to hope for the impossible, do s.t. useless. 3 to cultivate, foster, promote. ~ *kerjasama* to foster cooperation.
  tertanam 1 planted. 2 invested. 3 embedded. 4 instilled, implanted. 5 buried.
  tanaman 1 plant, crop. ~ *bermusim* seasonal crop. ~ *bidan* k.o. decorative plant, *Quisqualis indica.* ~ *biji-bijian* cereals. ~ *campuran* mixed cropping. – *dua musim* biennial. ~ *ékspor* export crop. ~ *gantung* hanging plant. ~ *genjah* short crop. ~ *hari panjang* long-day plant. ~ *hari péndék* short-day plant. ~ *hias* ornamental plant. ~ *hias ruangan* indoor plant. ~ *hijauan* forage plant. ~ *industri* industrial crop. ~ *keras* tree crop. ~ *lurik* seersucker plant, *Geogenanthus undatus.* ~ *makanan* food crops. ~ *memanjat* climber. ~ *menahun* perennial plant. ~ *menjalar* creeper. ~ *merambah* vine. ~ *muda* annuals. ~ *musiman* annuals. ~ *obat* medicinal plant. ~ *paksa* forced cultivation; → CULTUURSTÉLSEL. ~ *pangan* food crop. ~ *pembatas* border plant. ~ *pengganggu* weeds. ~ *penyangga* buffer crop. ~ *perdagangan* commercial crops. ~ *perkebunan* estate crop. ~ *polongan* root crops. ~ *sela* intercrop, catch crop. ~ *semusim* field crop. ~ *setahun* annual. ~ *sisipan* interculture. ~ *tahunan* perennial plant. ~ *tumpang gilir* multiple cropping. ~ *tumpang sari* intercrop. ~ *umbi-umbian* root crops. 2 growth, vegetation.
  tanam-tanaman various k.o. plants, crops.
  penanam 1 planter, grower. 2 investor. ~ *modal* investor.
  penanaman 1 planting, cropping. ~ *berurutan* sequential cropping. ~ *ikan* aquaculture. ~ *kepala kerbau* burying a buffalo head on a building lot (to bring good luck). 2 investing. ~ *modal* investing, investment. ~ *modal dalam negeri* [PMDN] Domestic Investment. 3 instilling, placing. 4 planting area. 5 burying.
  pertanaman cropping. ~ *tumpang sari* intercropping.
  petanaman field.

Tanamur [Tanah Abang Timur] a well-known nightclub and discotheque.

tanang → TANAI.

tanas [ketahanan nasional] National Defense.

tanat (*D*) tannic.

tanau various species of birds, *Psittinus spp.* – *ru* lineated dull barbet, *Megalaima zeylanicus hodgsoni*.

tanbiat (*A*) prophecy, forecast.

tanbih (*A*) note the following, n.b.

tancang I mangrove, *Bruguiera spp.*

tancang II menancang to tether, tie, fasten.

tancap (*J*) 1 to step on (the gas). 2 to stay (at a hotel).
 menancap [and **nancap** (*coq*)] 1 to be stuck in, embedded, implanted. 2 to step on (the gas).
 menancapkan to stick s.t. (in), (im)plant s.t., stick s.t. (into). ~ *kukunya* to stick one's claws in(to).
 tertancap 1 stuck, embedded, (im)planted. ~ *dan terpaku* permanently fixed/attached. 2 impaled. *Dadanya* ~ *sebatang kayu.* Her breast was impaled on a stick of wood. 3 vested (interests).
 tancapan sticking in, stepping (on the pedal).
 penancap 1 place to stick s.t. 2 machine for implanting s.t.
 penancapan implanting, implant. ~ *silikon* silicon implant.

tancep → TANCAP. – *kayon* the curtain falls.

tanda sign, mark, signal, token, cue, badge, omen. – *air* watermark. – *akad* sign of approval. – *akar* root sign. – *alangan* dash. – *aman* all-clear signal. – *anggota* membership card. – *apkir* reject mark. – *baca(an)* punctuation mark. – *badan* inherited mark on the body. – *bagi* division sign. – *bahaya* alarm. – *bakti* testimonial. – *batas* boundary marker. – *bekas réman* skid marks. – *beti* incriminating evidence. – *bintang* asterisk. – *buka-kata* open quotes. – *bukti* a) affidavit, testimonial. b) proof. – *bukti diri* identification. – *bukti hak* proof of title. – *bukti pencatatan* proof of registry. – *bulatan* circle (written as a symbol). – *cerai* hyphen. – *daftar perusahaan* certificate of company registration. – *dividén* dividend coupon. – *dua garis miring* slash marks, //. – *dua jari* V for victory sign. – *ésrar* holy sacrament. – *gambar* party symbol. – *garis* dash. – *garis miring* slash, /. – *hajat* memento. – *hayat* souvenir. – *hidup* a) signs of life. b) souvenir. – *hormat* a) sign of respect. b) salute. – *hubung* hyphen. – *isyarat* cue. – *jadi* (*sl*) deposit. – *jalan* traffic signal. – *jasa* (*mil*) order of merit, decoration, distinction. – *kali* multiplication sign. – *kebesaran* insignia of rank/title. – *kehormatan* decoration. – *kenaldiri* identification card, ID. – *kendaraan bermotor* motorized vehicle license plate. – *kepangkatan* insignia of office. – *keselamatan* safety label/mark. – *kurang* minus sign. – *kurawal* brace(s). – *kurung* parentheses, brackets. – *kurung besar/siku* square brackets. – *kutip* quotation mark. – *kutip pembuka* opening quotes. – *kutip penutup* closing quotes. – *laba* (*fin*) profit dividend. – *masuk* admission stub. – *mata* memento, souvenir. – *mati* symbol in Arabic writing showing that the accompanying letter is not pronounced. – *naik* lucky. – *pagar* number/pound sign, hash mark, #. – *panah* directional arrow. – *panggilan* call sign. – *pangkat* insignia, chevrons. – *pembayaran* receipt. – *penerimaan* receipt, return receipt (for letters). – *pengenal* a) identifying/distinguishing mark, symbol. b) badge. – *penghubung/penyambung* hyphen. – *penyeru* exclamation point. – *penyingkat* apostrophe. – *peringatan* monument, memorial. – *petik* (double) quotation mark, quotes. – *petik tunggal* single quotation mark. – *pisah* dash. – *pundak* attribute placed on epaulet. – *putus* deposit. – *rasa* token. – *sah (diri)* validation, verification. **menanda-sahkan** to validate, verify. – *salib* sign of the cross. – *sama* equal sign. – *selar* a) brand, stigma. b) registration mark. – *sémpang/sengkang* dash, hyphen. – *serah* legal expenses. – *seru* exclamation point. – *setoran* deposit slip. – *setuju* sign of approval, go ahead, green light. – *siaran* synchronizing signal. – *silang* check mark, tick. – *simpanan gudang* warehouse receipt. – *strip* dash. – *takik* blaze (on a tree). – *tambah* plus sign. – *tangan* a) signature. b) (*coq*) to sign. – *tangan pendamping* countersignature. – *tangan pengesahan* countersignature. **bertandatangan** signed. *yang* ~ *di bawah ini* the undersigned. **menandatangani** to sign. **penandatangan** signatory, signer. **penandatanganan** signing.

– *tanya* question mark. – *tekanan* stress mark. – *tera* calibration, gauge mark. – *terima* receipt. – *terima gudang* warehouse receipt. – *terimakasih* (*sl*) bribe. – *titik* period, full stop. – *titik dua* colon. – *titik koma* semicolon. – *tudung* circumflex. – *turun* unlucky. – *tulis* diacritic. – *tutup-kata* close quotes. – *ujar* quotation mark. – *uji* inspection sticker (on a vehicle). – *ulang* a superscript 2 to indicate reduplication. – *usaha* (*infr*) trade mark; → MÉREK.
 bertanda 1 marked, labeled. 2 to mean, signify.
 bertanda-tandaan to exchange rings as a sign of an engagement.
 menandai 1 to mark, designate, brand (cattle, etc.), label, (put a) check (mark on), tick. 2 to note, perceive.
 menandakan to mean, signify, indicate, show, prove. ~ *irama* to keep time, beat out the rhythm.
 tertanda marked, labeled. **ketertandaan** markedness.
 ketandaan symbols. *ilmu* ~ semiotics.
 penanda 1 marker, sign. 2 (*ling*) marker.
 penandaan 1 labeling, marking, branding. ~ *tanggal* dating. 2 signaling, indicating. 3 (*ling*) markedness.
 pe(r)tanda 1 omen, indication, sign. ~ *minyak* (*petrol*) show. 2 landmark.
 pertandaan indication, sign.

tandak (*Jv*) **bertandak** and **menandak** to dance.
 penandak (female) dancer.

tandan (*Jv*) raceme, hand (of fruit), bunch. – *ékor* (*coq*) behind, ass.
 setandan a hand (of bananas, etc.).
 bertandan with a hand (of bananas, etc.).

tandang – *duduk* to visit.
 bertandang (*ke*) to go (to), visit. ~ *ke surau* to go to s.o.'s house and not be offered anything (to eat or drink). ~ *membawa lapik* to visit s.o. and bring one's own food and drink. ~ *diam* to visit and stay one or two nights.
 tandang-bertandang to visit back and forth.
 menandangi to visit.
 pe(r)tandang visitor.

tandarasa → TANDA *rasa.*

tandas I what s.o. asserts/states firmly. *–nya* he asserted/stated. – *ulang* restate. **menandas-ulangkan** to reassert.
 menandaskan 1 to assert, state firmly. 2 to stress, emphasize, underscore. 3 to intensify.
 tandasan intensity.
 ketandasan intensity.
 penandas intensifier, intensifying.
 penandasan asserting, assertion, emphasizing, intensifying.

tandas II completely finished, wiped out, all used up, with nothing left. *Sebotol besar bir – diminumnya.* He drank up a big bottle of beer.
 tandas-tandas all up, completely. *Kopi itu kuminum* ~. I drank the coffee all up.
 menandaskan to wipe out completely, finish/use up completely.

tandas III (*Mal*) latrine, toilet.

tanda-tanda brown-stripe red snapper, *Lutjanus vitta.*

tandatangan → TANDA *tangan.*

tandem (*D*) tandem, two-seater bicycle.

tandes → TANDAS I, II.

tandik (insect) sting.

tandikat k.o. tree in which bees make their nest, *Canarium pseudodecumanum.*

tandil (*Tam*) foreman, overseer.

tanding I match, equal.
 setanding be equal/comparable to.
 bertanding 1 to compete (with), play (against). ~ *panco* to armwrestle. 2 to match, compare. *tidak* ~ unmatched, unequaled. 3 competitive.
 menanding to compare.
 mempertandingkan 1 to compare. 2 to put into combat, enter into competition.
 menandingi [and **nandingin** (*J coq*)] 1 to match, equal, compare with. 2 to stand up to.
 menandingkan to compare, set (two things) side by side and compare them.
 tertanding comparable. *tidak* ~ incomparable.

tertandingi to be matched. *tidak* ~ unmatched, incomparable.

tandingan 1 (one's) match, equal. *bertemu ~nya* he met his match. *tak ada ~nya* and *tidak akan bersua ~nya* incomparable. **2** rival. *partai* ~ rival party. **3** counterpart. **4** counter. *propaganda* ~ counterpropaganda.

petanding opponent (in sports such as boxing).

penandingan match, contest.

pertandingan 1 one's match. **2** match, game, meet, contest. ~ *pemanasan* tryouts. **3** comparison. ~ *kembar campuran* mixed doubles. ~ *persahabatan* friendly game.

tanding II pile, heap.

menanding to pile up, heap, stockpile.

tandingan in bulk. *cabé* ~ hot peppers in bulk.

tandiri impersonal.

tando → KOLAM *tando*. **menando** to keep in reserve.

tandon I (*Jv*) reservoir, cistern.

tandon II 1 (*Jv*) security, collateral. **2** stock, provisions, supplies.

tandu litter, sedan chair.

bertandu carried on a litter.

menandu to carry in a litter/on a stretcher.

penandu litter bearer.

tanduk I 1 horn (the part of an animal and the material of which it consists). **2** s.t. shaped like a horn. **3** (*coq*) front bumper. *bagai* – *bersendi gading* a mismatch. *macam* – *dengan gading* very close to e.o. *di ujung* – hanging in the balance. *keluar –nya* he got angry. *minta/menghendaki* – *[(ke)pada] kuda* to ask for the impossible. *seperti telur di ujung* – precarious. – *Afrika* the Horn of Africa. – *diberkas* an impossible task. – *cakah* straight horns. – *capah* widely separated horns. – *kemudi* rudder horn. – *lok* head of a locomotive. – *ragum* horns which curve inward. – *rusa* antler. – *semboyan* hooter. – *tegak* vertical horns with the tips near e.o. – *télepon* telephone receiver.

bertanduk 1 with horns, horned. *menantikan kucing* ~ a futile hope. **2** powerful.

menanduk 1 to butt, hit with the head, gore (with a horn). **2** to shoot (billiards).

tandukan butting. ~ *kepala* headshot (in soccer).

tanduk II → TINDAK *tanduk*.

tandun remote past, long ago.

tandur (*Jv*) – *alih* transplant(ing). – *jajar* to plant rice in rows.

menandur to plant rice.

menanduri to plant in/on.

tandus 1 infertile, not arable. **2** to lie fallow. **3** wiped/cleaned out.

menanduskan 1 to render infertile. **2** to wipe out, render powerless.

ketandusan barrenness, infertility.

penandusan wiping out.

tanem → TANAM.

tanfidziah and **tanfiziah** (*A*) executive.

tang I (*D*) tongs, pliers, pincers. – *cawan* crucible shank. – *cucut* long-nose pliers. – *kacip* nippers. – *kunci* locking pliers. – *las* crucible tongs. – *paku* nail clippers. – *pegas* pincers. – *pelipat* pliers. – *picak* flat pliers.

tang II (*mil*) tank.

tang III (*onom*) clanking sound.

tangan 1 hand, arm. **2** lever. – *kanan jangan percaya akan* – *kiri* don't trust anybody. – *mencencang bahu memikul* you have to be responsible for your actions. – *baju* sleeve. – *di bawah* the recipient. – *berulas* with a good assistant. – *besi* strict, firm. ***bertangan besi*** to act firmly and harshly. – *berulas* s.o. who helps. – *di atas* the giver. – *dingin* successful, lucky. – *gaib* invisible hand. – *gatal* to have to touch everything. – *hampa* empty handed. – *jahat* the bad guy(s). – *jahil* delinquent, mischievous. – *kanan* helper, assistant. *dari* – *kedua* (heard) secondhand. – *kemudi* helm, rudder. – *kosong* a) empty-handed. b) the bare hand, (with) bare hands. ***bertangan-kosong*** empty-handed. – *kotor* crime. – *lébar* generous. – *manis* right hand (as opposed to the left). – *naik* successful, lucky. – *panas* unsuccessful, unlucky. – *panjang* a) long sleeves. b) thievish, kleptomaniacal. – *pasak* wedge grip. – *péndék* short sleeves. *dari* – *pertama* firsthand, from the horse's mouth. – *tangga* handrail. – *terbuka* generous. – *terkokot* hands curved from disease. *dengan* – *ter-*

buka warmly, with open arms. – *turun* always failing, unsuccessful. – *usil* paw, caress (improperly). – *yang manis* the right (as opposed to the left) hand.

tangan-tangan 1 handholds/rests (on a ladder/bike/chair). **2** interference. ~ *siluman* unknown elements.

bertangan with hands, handed.

tangan-menangan through many hands, not directly from the source.

menangani 1 to handle, deal with, address (a problem/issue), tackle (a job). **2** to strike, hit, beat.

tertangani can be handled. *tak* ~ unmanageable, out of control.

tanganan 1 handhold. **2** handiwork, handmade.

penanganan handling, dealing with, addressing, administration.

Tanganyika Tanganyika.

tangap (*M*) **menangap** to hold back, stop, restrain; → MENANGKAP.

tangar (*J*) careful, circumspect.

tangas bertangas to take a steam bath.

menangas to steam, cook in steam.

penangas steamer.

penangasan steaming.

tangéh (*Jv*) a long time/way off.

tangén(s) (*D math*) tangent.

tangénsial (*D math*) tangential.

tangga 1 stairs, steps, ramp (of airplane). **2** s.t. that has levels/steps. – *balon darurat* escape ladder. – *bangku* step stool. – *berjalan* escalator. – *bunyi* musical scale. – *gaji* pay scale. – *gantung* hanging ladder. – *gésér* extendible ladder. – *Jakob* Jacob's ladder. – *jenjang* stepladder. – *kapal* ship's/accommodation ladder. – *kimbul* (*naut*) poop ladder. – *kubu-kubu* (*naut*) bulwark ladder. – *lagu* chart (of most popular recordings). – *lambung* (*naut*) accommodation ladder. – *lipat* folding ladder. – *mobil* running board. – *nada* musical scale. – *naik* the way up (in one's job). – *pengait* flexible portable ladder. – *pesawat* ramp (of plane). – *pilin* circular staircase. – *pusing* spiral staircase. – *putar* ramp. – *sigai* portable ladder. – *sokong* notched climbing pole. – *suara* musical scale. – *tapak* stairway. – *tegak* vertical ladder.

setangga → TETANGGA.

bertangga 1 with stairs. **2** stepped.

bertangga-tangga 1 stepped, terraced, graduated. **2** by degrees, gradually.

tanggah I penanggah and **penanggahan** kitchen.

tanggah II (*Pers cla*) k.o. currency.

tanggak → TAGAK I.

tanggal I (*J/Jv*) date. – *berapa*? What's the date? – *akhir-ténggang* expiration date. – *alih hak* date of assignment. – *berlaku* effective date. – *dikirim* shipping date. – *diterima* date received. – *habis waktu* expiration date. – *jatuh témpo/waktu* due date, maturity date. – *kadaluwarsa* expiration date. – *kelahiran/lahir* date of birth. – *main* performance date. – *maju* antedated. – *mérah* red-letter day, official holiday. – *muda* a) early in the month. b) first quarter of the moon. – *mundur* postdated. ***bertanggal mundur*** postdated. – *niaga* trade date. – *pembayaran* payment date. – *pembelian* date of acquisition. – *pembukuan* posting date. – *pencatatan* recording date. – *penetapan* cutoff date. – *pengeluaran* date of issue. – *pengembalian* return due date. – *penyerahan* a) date of issue (from the warehouse). b) settlement date. – *pilahan* cutoff date. – *penutupan* closing date. – *terakhir* deadline. – *tua* a) late in the month. b) last quarter of the moon.

bertanggal dated. *tidak* ~ undated.

menanggali to date, assign a date to.

menanggalkan to date. ~ *surut* to predate.

tertanggal dated. ~ *25 Oktober 1999* dated October 25, 1999.

tanggalan calendar. **bertanggalan** with a date on it.

penanggalan 1 calendar, almanac. **2** dating.

tanggal II 1 fall out/off, get loose, slip off. **2** stripped, removed.

bertanggalan (*pl subj*) to come/drop off. *Satu per satu kedok itu mulai* ~. One by one the masks began to drop off.

menanggali to strip off, take off, remove. **2** to dismantle.

menanggalkan to take off, remove, pull out. ~ *kewarganegaraan* to renounce/give up one's citizenship.

penanggal repudiator.

penanggalan 1 stripping, taking off, removing, renouncing/giving up (one's citizenship). **2** dismantling. **3** (*ob*) k.o. ghost.

tanggam dovetail, joint. – *budaya* culture-bound. – *temu* butt joint. – *tindih* clinker joint.

bertanggam dovetailed.

menanggam 1 to dovetail. **2** to bring close together.

tertanggam dovetailed.

tanggang (*M*) – *berjaga* to stay up all night.

bertanggang to refrain/abstain from (doing s.t.). ~ *malam* to stay up all night. ~ *istri/suami* to refuse to have sex with one's wife/husband.

menanggang to abstain from, not to do s.t. that one usually does. ~ *anak* (*bayi*) to deny one's child the breast. ~ *mata* to stay up all night. ~ *perut* to fast.

tanggap I (*Jv*) **1** responsive, perceptive. *secara* – responsively. **2** (*gram*) passive (voice). *kata kerja* – passive verb. – *segera* immediately responsive. **ketanggap-segeraan** immediate responsiveness. –, *tanggon dan trengginas* (*Jv*) responsive, trustworthy and quick-acting.

bertanggap to respond, be responsive.

menanggap 1 to listen carefully to. **2** to understand/grasp quickly, perceive, be responsive to. ~ *cinta* to respond to love.

menanggapi [and **nanggapin** (*J coq*)] to respond/react to, take (the news), handle (a situation), comment on. ~ *usul-usul* to welcome/be open to suggestions.

menanggapkan to imagine, picture.

tanggapan 1 response, reaction. **2** concept, idea, viewpoint, approach (to a problem). **3** image.

ketanggapan response.

penanggap respondent, s.o. who responds.

penanggapan perception, way of looking at s.t., way of responding to s.t.

tanggap II (*Jv*) **menanggap** and **nanggap** to hire s.o. to perform, put on (a performance).

tanggapan performance.

tanggar 1 answerable for. **2** feasible.

menanggar to be responsible for (a job, etc.).

ketanggaran feasibility.

tanggep → TANGGAP I.

tanggok → TANGGUK.

tanggon (*Jv*) dependable, reliable, trustworthy.

ketanggonan reliability, trustworthiness.

tanggor (*Jv*) **ketanggor** run into, encounter by chance.

tangguh I 1 not easily defeated, unbeatable, strong, solid. **2** steady, steadfast, not easily discouraged. **3** of integrity.

ketangguhan 1 strength, firmness, tenacity. **2** integrity, honesty.

tangguh II postponement, delay, stay.

bertangguh 1 to postpone, delay; to hold back, hesitate to, be reluctant to, be hesitant/reluctant. **2** postponed, put off, deferred.

menangguhkan and **mempertangguhkan** to postpone, put off, defer, stay, adjourn.

tertangguh postponed, deferred, put off, stayed.

tertangguh-tangguh kept on being postponed/delayed/deferred/adjourned.

tangguhan deferred.

penangguhan s.t. which postpones/puts off/delays/adjourns.

penangguhan and **pertangguhan** postponement, delay, deferral, moratorium, stay, adjournment.

tangguk 1 basket or net used for catching fish. **2** trap, ruse, trick. – *lerak dengan bingkainya* a happily married couple.

menangguk 1 to scoop up, net. ~ *di air keruh* a) to fish in troubled waters. b) to profit from a bad situation. **2** to take in, collect. *Diréktorat itu harus bisa* ~ *pajak sekitar Rp 79 triliun.* That directorate has to be able to take in about Rp 79 trillion.

tertangguk netted, trapped.

penangguk 1 s.o. who or s.t. which nets. **2** s.o. who gets s.t. by trickery.

tanggul I (*Jv*) **1** dam, dike, bund, levee, weir, embankment, causeway. **2** (*elec*) baffle. – *alam* natural dam. – *api* fire wall. – *jalan* berm. – *pengaman* speed bump; → POLISI *tidur*. – *penyangga* coffer dam.

menanggul to dam up, build a dike.

menangguli to put a dike on.

penanggulan 1 embankment. **2** tackling (a problem). **3** prevention (of crime, etc.).

tanggul II bobbing up and down.

menanggul to shake up and down.

tanggulang (*Jv*) sluice gate.

menanggulangi to deal/cope with, cope with, handle, fight, combat, face up to. ~ *inflasi* to fight inflation.

tertanggulangi coped with, handled.

penanggulangan handling, dealing/coping with, combating. ~ *banjir* flood control.

tangguli → TENGGULI I.

tanggung I 1 guaranteed. **2** → MENANGGUNG. – *baik* guaranteed to be good. *berani* – (I) guarantee (it), (I) assure you. – *béres* a) to take care of s.t. b) Leave it to me! – *derita* suffering. **menanggung-deritakan** to suffer, endure. – *gugat* accountability. **bertanggung-gugat** to be liable/accountable. **menanggung-gugat** to be accountable for. **pertanggung-gugatan** liability, accountability. – *jamin* guarantee. – *jawab* a) responsible, liable. b) responsibility, liability. *mempunyai* – *jawab* fully qualified. – *jawab bersama* joint liability. – *jawab hukum* legal liability. – *jawab mutlak* strict liability. **bertanggung-jawab** to be responsible (for), be in charge (of), be liable (for), (be) accountable (for), report to. *dapat* ~ accountable. **menanggung-jawab** to be responsible for. **mempertanggung-jawabkan 1** to account for, justify. *yang tidak dapat dipertanggung-jawabkan* unaccounted for. *alasan yang dapat dipertanggungjawabkan* justifiable reasons. **2** to hold s.o. accountable/liable for. **3** to take up (a question), address. *Pemberitaan itu harus dipertanggungjawabkan.* That report must be addressed. **terpertanggung-jawabkan** accounted for. **ketertanggung-jawaban** responsibility. *kurang* ~ diminished responsibility. **penanggung-jawab** responsible party, manager. **pertanggung-jawaban** and **pertanggungan-jawab 1** accounting, an account. **2** accountability, responsibility. **3** liability. – *rénténg* joint and several. *secara* –*rénténg* jointly and severally (responsible). – *wajib* responsibility.

menanggung and **nanggung** (*coq*)] **1** to bear (a burden/loss). ~ *akibatnya* to suffer the consequences. ~ *kasih* to feel grateful for. ~ *malu* to feel shameful. ~ *ragam* to put up with trials and tribulations. ~ *rindu* to long for. ~ *rugi* to suffer a loss. ~ *sakit* to put up with an illness. ~ *sabar* to be patient. **2** to assume (a risk). **3** to guarantee, be responsible for. *ditanggung halal* guaranteed to follow Islamic dietary restrictions, strictly *halal*. ~ *pinjaman* to guarantee a loan. ~ *rahasia* to keep a secret.

tanggung-menanggung jointly and severally.

menanggung to bear, be responsible for.

menanggungkan 1 to bear, put up with. **2** to take responsibility for, be accountable for. **3** to give s.t. as a guarantee.

mempertangguhkan 1 to hold s.o. responsible for. **2** to vouch for, guarantee. **3** to suffer, endure, put up with.

tertanggung 1 the insured, insuree. **2** endured, put up with. *tidak* ~ unbearable.

tertanggungkan bearable. *tak* ~ unbearable, insufferable.

tanggungan 1 a dependent, s.o. for whom one is responsible. **2** burden, load. **3** guarantee, security, collateral, bond. **4** responsibility. **5** liability. ~ *keuangan* financial liability. *atas* ~ *sendiri* at one's own risk. *atas* ~ *si berpiutang* at the risk of the creditor. *di luar* ~ not chargeable to, not payable by. **6** insurance. ~ *jiwa* life insurance.

penanggung 1 guarantor. ~ *utang* guarantor. (~ *émisi*) underwriter. **2** person responsible. ~ *pajak* taxpayer.

penanggungan 1 assuming responsibility for. **2** burden. **3** guarantee, suretyship.

pertanggungan 1 responsibility. **2** guarantee, security. **3** insurance, insuring. ~ *asuransi* coverage. ~ *jiwa* life insurance. ~ *kebakaran* fire insurance. ~ *kecelakaan* accident insurance. ~ *kembali* reinsurance. ~ *kerugian* property and casualty insurance. ~ *laut* marine insurance. ~ *pencurian* theft insurance. ~ *sosial* social security. ~ *ulangan* reinsurance.

tanggung II 1 not quite adequate/enough (in quantity/size, etc.), neither too ... or too ... **2** not quite on time (just too late). *lagi* – I'm almost done! *tidak* – not by half, not halfhearted. –

bulan at the end of the month (just before payday). **3** difficult (choice/moment, etc.).

tanggung-tanggung in a halfhearted way, without enthusiasm. *pekerjaan yang* ~ halfhearted work.

tan-gir [tante-girang] older woman who likes young men.

tangis cry, weep. - *berhiba-hiba* to weep bitterly. - *kejan* holding the breath (of a child having a tantrum, etc.).

bertangisan (*pl subj*) to weep.

bertangis-tangisan to keep on weeping.

menangis [and **nangis** (*coq*)] to weep, cry, be in tears. ~ *bombay* to cry one's eyes out. ~ *pijar* to wail. ~ *sepuas-puasnya* to cry one's eyes out. ~ *tersedu-sedu* to sob and moan.

menangis-nangis to keep on weeping.

menangisi 1 to weep/cry over, bemoan, lament. **2** to regret. **3** to make s.o. weep.

menangiskan to weep over.

mempertangis to make s.o. weep.

tertangis to burst into tears.

tangisan 1 weeping, crying. **2** s.t. wept over.

penangis crybaby.

penangisan lamentation, weeping over.

tangkahan (*Med*) broker, middleman.

tangkai 1 stem, shaft, shank, handle, stem, butt. **2** classifier for flowers. - *baut* shank. - *bedil* gun butt. - *besi* rod. - *buah* (*bot*) stalk. - *bunga* (*bot*) pedicel. - *daun* petiolus. - *dayung* paddle. - *gagang* shaft, handle. - *hati* a) sweetheart. b) aorta. - *jangkar* anchor shank. - *kacamata* eyeglass temples. - *katup* valve stem. - *kering* miser. - *palu* shaft, handle. - *pengayun* rocker arm (in engine). - *péna* penholder. - *putik* stylus, style (of a plant). - *sapu* broom handle. - *sari* filament (of a plant). - *sudu* stirrer.

tangkaian 1 granary, storehouse for rice. **2** by the individual flower, by the stem.

tangkal 1 fending off, interception, repulsion, refusal (of entry). **2** charm, talisman, amulet. - *bisa* antidote.

menangkal 1 to deter. *ditangkal* (in immigration law) entrance prohibited. **2** to ward s.t. off.

tertangkal deterred, prevented.

tangkalan deterrence.

penangkal 1 barrier, anti-, fending off, repulsion, prevention, arrester, deterrent. ~ *petir* lightning rod. ~ *racun* antidote. **2** amulet, charm.

penangkalan 1 deterrence, preventive measure. **2** (an immigration term) ban on entrance into the country. **3** warding s.t. off.

tangkap catch, seize.

bertangkap to do battle with e.o.

menangkap [and **nangkap** (*coq*)] **1** to catch, seize. **2** to arrest, hold, detain, apprehend. **3** to grasp, get, manage to understand (what s.o. said, etc.). **4** to pick up (a signal), overhear (a conversation). ~ *angin* to work hard with no results, fail. ~ *basah* to catch red-handed. ~ *bayang-bayang* to work in vain. ~ *tangan* to catch red-handed.

tangkap-menangkap to seize e.o.

menangkapi [and **nangkapin** (*J coq*)] (*pl obj*) to catch, arrest, detain.

menangkapkan to catch, etc. for s.o. else.

tertangkap [and **ketangkap** (*coq*)] caught, arrested, seized, detained. ~ *basah/tangan* caught red-handed/in the act. ~ *muka* to meet s.o. unexpectedly. *tidak* ~ inaudible.

tertangkap-tangkap *tiada* ~ faint, disappearing in the distance.

tangkapan 1 s.t. caught, prey, catch, haul. ~ *pancing* angling catch. ~ *sampingan* bycatch. ~ *terkumpul* accumulated catch. **2** prisoner, detainee.

ketangkapan suddenly attacked by an illness.

penangkap s.o. who or s.t. that catches, etc., catcher, captor, capturer. ~ *ikan* fisherman. ~ *suara* recorder.

penangkapan 1 catching. **2** arrest, seizure, detention.

tangkar I (*Jv*) **menangkar** to breed, cultivate; → MEMBIAKKAN.

penangkar breeder, raiser. ~ *benih* nursery.

penangkaran 1 breeding, raising, cultivating; → PEMBIAKAN. **2** stockyard.

tangkar II (*J/Jv*) **1** animal's breastbone. **2** k.o. stew.

tangkas skillful, adroit, agile.

bertangkas-tangkas to compete.

ketangkasan skill, agility, adroitness, dexterity, skillfulness. ~ *lidah* being quick-witted/mentally agile. ~ *jasmani* physically agile.

tangkep I → TANGKAP.

tangkep II (*Jv*) a pair which fits together.

setangkep a pair which fits together. *roti* ~ a sandwich.

tangker (*E*) tanker.

tangki (*D*) tank. - *bénsin* gas tank. - *pemberat* ballast tank. - *penampung* reservoir. - *penimbun/penyimpanan* storage tank. - *séptik* septic tank. - *tampung* rundown tank. - *timbun* storage tank.

setangki a tankful.

tangkil I **bertangkil-tangkil** lined up.

menangkil to file.

tangkil II (*Jv*) **menangkil** to pay one's respects to.

tangkil III 1 various species of climbing plants. **2** k.o. *mlinjo, Gnetum spp.*

tangkin k.o. basket.

tangkis levee. - *alam* natural levee. - *balik* (*leg*) counterplea.

menangkis(kan) 1 to ward off, parry, fend off. **2** to repulse, repel. **3** (*leg*) to object to.

tertangkis warded off, repulsed, objected to.

tangkisan 1 defense. **2** resistance. **3** (*leg*) objection. **4** denial. **5** parry.

penangkis defense, antidote. ~ *petir* lightning rod.

penangkisan 1 warding off, parrying. **2** repelling, repulsing. **3** resisting. **4** objecting to.

tangkol k.o. fig tree, *Ficus racemosa.*

tangkring menangkring [and **nangkring** (*coq*)] to perch, sit/be located in a high spot.

menangkringkan to perch s.t. (up on s.t.).

tangkué → TANGKUWÉH.

tangkuk (*M*) → TANGKUP.

tangkul k.o. net.

menangkul to catch in that k.o. net.

tangkup 1 a hollow space. **2** stopper. **3** symmetry. - *telentang* over and over, back and forth, turning over and over. **menangkup-telentangkan** to turn s.t. over in one's mind, consider.

setangkup 1 symmetrical. *tidak* ~ asymmetrical. **2** a cupped hand forming a hollow. ~ *tangan* a cupped handful. **kesetangkupan** symmetry.

bertangkup and **menangkup 1** to close up (of two things that come together). **2** to catch in cupped hands. **3** to fall face downward.

menangkupkan 1 to lay s.t. face down. **2** to fall down and hit. ~ *tanah* to fall down on the ground, hit the ground. **3** to enclose in a hollow space. ~ *tangan* to cup one's hands.

tertangkup 1 cupped (of the hand). **2** to be caught (of s.o. in a children's game). **3** closed up. **4** laid facedown. ~ *makan tanah* to bite the dust.

tangkupan embrace.

ketangkupan symmetry.

penangkupan embrace (in a hollow space).

tangkur (*J/Jv*) **1** - (*kuda*) sea horse, *Hippocampus spp.* **2** (*anat*) hippocampus. - *buaya* a) alligator/double-ended pipefish, *Syngnathoides biaculeatus.* b) k.o. aphrodisiac.

tangkut → TANGKUP.

tangkuwéh candied (citrus fruit peel).

tanglung (*C*) paper lantern.

tangpu (*C*) pawnshop.

tangsa k.o. drum.

tangsel (*J/Jv*) wedge.

menangsel to insert a wedge into. *ditangsel* (*J*) stuffed to the gills.

penangsel s.t. used to fill/stuff s.t. ~ *perut* (*coq*) s.t. filling, s.t. which fills the stomach.

tangsi I (*C*) barracks. - *militér* military barracks.

menangsikan to confine to barracks.

tangsi II (*Jv*) rice field given as payment to the village head.

tangsin (*C*) spiritualist, medium.

tangtang II - *angin* k.o. food made from rice.

tangtang II → TANTANG.

tani I (*J/Jv*) **1** farmer. - *penggarap* tiller of the soil. **2** peasant.

bertani to farm (for a living). ~ *tradisionil* to engage in traditional farming.

petani 1 farmer. 2 peasant. ~ *berdasi* gentleman farmer. ~ *gurem* dirt-farmer, small farmer, subsistence farmer.

pertanian agriculture, farming. ~ *(yang) berpindah-pindah* shifting agriculture. ~ *menetap* sedentary agriculture. ~ *rakyat* small-scale farming.

tani II rigging (on ship).

tani III (*ob*) *pintu* – outer main gate entrance to a palace.

tanih (*mostly Mal*) soil; *cp* TANAH.

tanin (*D/E*) tannin.

taniwan farmer.

pertaniwanan farm(ing).

taniwati farmer wife.

tanjak to rise, slope upwards, slant(ing), tilt(ing) upward. – *tunjuk* to show up here and there.

bertanjak to slope upward. ~ *kaki* to rise up on one's tiptoes. ~ *harus bertinjau* look before you leap.

menanjak [and nanjak (*coq*)] 1 to slope upward, rise, ascend, go up(hill), rising. *Jalannya* ~ The road is rising. 2 to ascend, climb. 3 to move upward, move ahead, become well known. 4 to be (a certain age). ~ *déwasa* to enter adulthood.

menanjaki to climb (a ladder).

menanjakkan 1 to move s.t. upwards, make s.t. go upwards, hoist. 2 to bring s.t. up. ~ *ilmu* to go abroad to study. ~ *kaki* to stand on one's tiptoes.

tanjakan 1 grade, rise, gradient, slope. 2 ascent, climb. 3 riser (of steps).

penanjak (*petro*) spudder.

penanjakan 1 going upward, ascending, climbing, bringing s.t. up. 2 (*petro*) spudding in.

tanjang k.o. mangrove, *Bruguiera spp.*

tanjek → TANJAK.

tanji k.o. large drum.

tanjidor and tanjidur (*Port?*) k.o. Jakartan form of music using trumpets and drums.

tanjis (*A*) contamination.

tanju k.o. wall lamp.

tanjul snare in the form of a noose used to trap small animals, noose.

menanjul to snare (such animals).

tertanjul snared, trapped.

tanjung I cape, promontory. – *C*ina the southern tip of Sumatra. – *Harapan* Cape of Good Hope. – *Hijau* Cape Verde. – *Jabung* the eastern edge of Jambi province. – *Pérak* the port of Surabaya. – *Priok* the port of Jakarta.

menanjung 1 to protrude out into the sea (like a cape). 2 to follow along the cape. *berlayar* ~ to sail along the cape.

tanjung-menanjung (to sail) from cape to cape.

tanjung II (*bunga* –) k.o. shade tree, tanjung tree, Spanish cherry, *Mimusops elengi*.

tanjung III (*paku* –) vegetable fern, *Diplazium esculentum*.

tanjung IV medal, decoration.

Tanjungpura 1 name of the Army division stationed in West Kalimantan. 2 name of a university in West Kalimantan.

tanjur (*M*) scoop made from coconut shell.

menanjur 1 to scoop up water using such a scoop. 2 to try to get s.o. to talk.

tank (*E*) /téng/ tank. – *kanon* casemate tank.

tanker /téngker/ tanker (ship). – *raksasa* supertanker.

tanki → TANGKI.

tanorganik inorganic.

tanpa (*Jv*) without (sometimes also spelled together with following word). – *bayaran* free, gratis. – *bentuk* amorphous. – *bersyarat* without conditions, unconditional. – *bobot* weightless. – *bunga és* frost-free (refrigerator). – *busana* naked, nude. – *daksa* deformed, crippled. – *dipikir panjang* on the spur of the moment, on impulse. – *dipungut bayaran* free, gratis. – *dosa* innocent. – *ganggu* without a hassle, hassle-free. – *hasil* in vain, to no avail. – *kecuali* without exception. – *krana* without reason. – *nama* anonymous. – *negara* stateless. – *pamrih* without ulterior motives. – *pandang* regardless of. – *persiapan* impromptu. – *pikir panjang* on the spur of the moment, impromptu. – *prasangka* unprejudiced. **ketanpa-prasangkaan** lack of prejudice. – *ragu-ragu* unhesitatingly. – *sepatu* shoeless. – *sepenge-*

tahuan unbeknownst. – *syarat* unconditional. – *tanding* unmatched. – *tujuan* aimless. – *wujud* abstract.

tanpasta toothpaste.

tansi → TANGSI.

tansiém → TANTIÉME.

tansuara voiceless.

tansuku nonsyllabic.

tanta → TANTE.

tantal (*D*) tantalum.

tantama → TAMTAMA.

tantang (*Jv M*) challenge.

menantang(i) [and nantang (*coq*)] 1 to challenge (to a fight). 2 to be challenging (of s.t. difficult).

tertantang challenged.

tantangan 1 challenge, defiance. 2 opposition, resistance. 3 a challenge, s.t. that must be overcome.

penantang 1 challenger, opponent. 2 s.o. who likes to challenge/fight.

penantangan challenging.

tante (*D*) 1 aunt. 2 term of address and reference for older European, Chinese, or Westernized women. – *girang* older woman who runs after younger men.

ketante-tantean acting like s.o. who would be called *tante*.

tanti I → NANTI.

tanti II (*M*) gold-threaded edges for trousers or a woman's garment.

bertanti to wear such an edge.

tanting (*Jv*) menanting to carry s.t. in the palm of one's hand.

tantiéme (*D*) bonus, percentage of profits, director's fee, (author's) royalty.

tantra (*Skr*) tantra, tantric.

tanur (*A*) furnace. – *busur api* arc furnace. – *kapur* lime kiln. – *putar* kiln. – *tiup/tinggi* blast furnace.

tanwin (*A*) diacritic used in Arabic writing to show a following nasal, nunation.

menawinkan to use such a diacritic on.

tanwir (*A*) advice.

tanwujud

tanya 1 question. *Apa –nya?* What did he ask? 2 to ask a question; → BERTANYA. – *jawab* question and answer. **bertanya-jawab** to discuss. – *sidik* inquiry.

bertanya to ask (a question). ~ *dalam hati* to wonder. ~ *pada diri sendiri* to ask o.s. ~ *jalan* to ask directions. ~ *tentang sesuatu* to ask about s.t.

bertanya-tanya 1 to keep on asking questions, ask around. ~ *dalam hatinya* to wonder. 2 to be uncertain.

bertanya-tanyaan to ask e.o. questions.

bertanyakan to ask a question about.

menanya [and nanya (*coq*)] 1 to ask s.o. a question. 2 to ask for a girl's hand in marriage.

menanyai 1 to ask s.o. a question. 2 to question/interrogate (a suspect, etc.). *Dia ditanyai polisi.* He was questioned by the police.

menanyakan [and nanyain (*J coq*)] to ask/inquire about/for. *Ada yang mau saya tanyakan.* There's s.t. I want to ask you about.

mempertanyakan 1 to question, raise questions about. ~ *masalah* to raise questions about a problem. 2 to wonder (about). *Ribuan orang lainnya* ~ *siapa sebenarnya di balik pembunuhan ini.* Thousands of other people wonder who is actually behind those murders.

tertanya(-tanya) to ask o.s. questions.

penanya 1 questioner. 2 interrogator.

penanyaan 1 questioning. 2 interrogating.

pertanyaan question. ~ *keliling* questions from the floor.

tanzil (*A*) liturgy, revelation; the Koran.

tao → TAHU I.

taocang (*C*) pigtail.

taoci (*C*) k.o. fish jelly.

taoco (*C*) fermented soybean paste.

taodék (*C*) to steal.

taogé (*C*) bean sprouts.

taoké and taokéh (*C*) boss, foreman.

taon → TAHUN I.

taosi (C) soybeans soaked in saltwater.
tap I (D) 1 gudgeon, journal; tenon, pin. 2 tap (rubber, etc.). 3 tap, faucet. – *bulat* ball journal. – *léhér/putar* journal. – *tuang* runner stick. – *ulir* screw tap. – *ungkit* tipping spindle.
  mengetap to tap.
  pengetap tapping. *sekrup* ~ tapping screw.
tap II [ketetapan] ruling, resolution.
Tap III (in acronyms) Tapanuli.
tapa I (Skr) 1 hermit. 2 asceticism. – *brata* (Jv) a) asceticism. b) initiation period (in university). – *sungsang* asceticism involving standing on one's head.
  bertapa 1 to live as a hermit, seclude o.s. 2 (coq) to be in prison.
  mempertapakan to achieve s.t. through asceticism.
  pertapa hermit, ascetic.
  pertapaan 1 retreat, hermitage. 2 asceticism.
tapa II strips of salted and dried fish.
tapa(h) III various k.o. freshwater fish, *Wallago spp.*
tapa IV (M) *tahan* – immune to pain.
tapa V (M) **menapa** to strike, hit.
tapai I food or drink made from fermented rice or cassava. *rusak – karena ragi* a small slip can have serious consequences. – *keladi* this food made from taro. – *ketan* this food made from glutinous rice. – *ketéla/ubi kayu* this food made from cassava. – *laos* remedy for s.o. who has difficulty getting pregnant. – *uli* (J) a mixture of *tapai* and *uli*.
  menapai 1 to ferment, become fermented. 2 to make this food from s.t. by fermentation.
  penapaian making this food by fermentation.
  pertapaian and **petapaian** 1 (mod) making this food by fermentation. 2 pot in which this food is made.
tapai II **tapaian** water barrel; → TEMPAYAN.
tapak I 1 sole (of the foot/shoe); palm (of one's hand). 2 trace, track, footprint. 3 pace, step, stride. *Kami berjalan beberapa* –. We took a few steps. *putih –nya lari* (M) to run helter-skelter (from fear). 4 a measure of length (palm of the hand or sole of the foot). 5 base. 6 in certain expressions refers to the time of day. *delapan – bayang-bayang* about 8 a.m. *tengah – bayang-bayang* exactly midday when the sun is at the zenith. *tiga – bayang-bayang* (phrase indicating) the time of the day when a shadow has the length of three palms of the hand. *cium – tangan, berbaukah atau tidak* to search one's own soul. *kecil – tangan, nyiru ditadalkan* wanting to have as much as possible. – *ani* two parallel beams connected by a sliding laze-rod (part of a loom). – *batu jalak* k.o. magic stone. – *besi* horseshoe. – *canai* completed, finished. – *cangkir* saucer. – *catur* a square (on a chessboard). – *itik* gusset at the heel of trousers. – *jalak* cross, mark, an X used as a signature. – *jempol* thumbprint (used as a signature). – *kaki* a) sole of foot. b) footprint. – *kasut* sole of shoe. – *kuku* horseshoe. – *lawang* the underside/bottom of the mangosteen fruit showing how many segments are inside the fruit. – *léper* flat-footed. – *rata* flat-footed. – *sepatu* sole (of a shoe). – *Sulaiman* the five-pointed seal of Solomon, the pentacle. – *tangan* a) palm of hand. b) signature; → TANDA *tangan*. – *tatu* (Jv) scar. – *tilas* a) footprint, track. b) following in the footsteps of. *menapak-tilas* (*jejak*) to follow in s.o.'s footsteps; to repeat s.o. else's experience. *menapak-tilasi* to follow in s.o.'s footsteps. – *tukul* s.t. barely begun.
tapak-tapak slippers, sandals.
setapak 1 a step. ~ *demi* ~ step by step. 2 a palm's/sole's breadth. ~ *pun tak* not (even) an inch. *jalan* – a footpath.
  bertapak 1 having a sole, with a sole made of. 2 to step, tread. 3 to have a firm footing, take root. (*dapat*) ~ able to have a firm hold/footing. ~ *catur* tessellated.
  menapak 1 to step/tread on, touch (with the feet). *Kakinya* ~ *tanah.* His feet touched the ground. ~ *jejak* to follow the trail, stalk. 2 to measure with the palm of the hand or sole of the foot. *Sebelum digali, tanah itu ditapaknya dulu, berapa panjangnya dan lébarnya.* Before digging, he first measured the length and width of the land (with the sole of his foot). 3 to stride. 4 to follow in the footsteps of.
  menapaki 1 to set foot on, enter into. *Dia* ~ *usia remaja.* He entered his adolescent years. *Seorang pelajar ibukota mendapat-*

kan kesempatan untuk ~ *karirnya dan suatu keteguhan hati.* A high-school student of the capital city had the opportunity to get into his career through determination. 2 to track down, investigate, look into.
  menapakkan to put (one's foot down on), step (on). *Ia ingin* ~ *kakinya sendiri ke tangga anéh.* He wanted to put his own foot down on the strange step.
tapak II site, location, place, base. – *bangunan* building site. – *rumah* house site. – *warna* color base.
  bertapak to have a site/place.
  bertapakan to rest on.
  bertapakkan to be based/founded on, rest on (solid grounds).
  (ke)tapakan *balai* ~ place of honor in a reception hall. *batu tapakan* a) stepping-stone. b) base.
tapak III (in compounds) names of various types of plants and animals. – *burung* k.o. plant, *Mollugo pentaphylla/stricta, Aneilema nudiflorum.* – *dara* periwinkle, *Catharanthus roseus, Vinca rosea.* – *gajah* a) k.o. tree, *Phyllagathis rotundifolia.* b) k.o. snail, helmet shell, *Cassis cornuta.* – *harimau* k.o. shrub, *Trevesia cheirantha.* – *kasut* k.o. sea fish, remora, *Echineis naucrates.* – *kerbau* k.o. climbing plant, *Bauhinia*, spp., *Cleroden-dron villosum.* – *kuda* a) k.o. shrub, beach morning glory, *Ipomoea pes-caprae.* b) k.o. mollusk, *Navicella*, spp. – *léman/ liman* (Jv) k.o. medicinal shrub and herb, prickly-leaved elephant's foot, *Elephantopus scaber, Nothopanax scutellarium.* – *Sulaiman* a) common starfish, *Asterias rubens.* b) k.o. tree, *Phyllagathis rotundifolia;* → TAPAK *gajah.* – *tangan* → TAPAK *liman.*
tapakdara periwinkle, a decorative plant, *Lochnera rosea, Vinca rosea, Catharanthus roseus.*
tapak-tapak → TAPAK *Sulaiman.*
tapakur → TEPEKUR.
tapal I paste. – *gigi* toothpaste.
tapal II (Jv) limit. – *batas* boundary line. – *batas kota* city limits.
  pertapalan boundary.
tapal III – *kuda* a) horseshoe. b) the north and east coast of East Java.
  penapal ~ *kuda* blacksmith who makes horseshoes.
ta'pang and **tapang** (C? J) k.o. sofa.
tapas (Jv) large leaf sheath of the coconut (used for wrapping food).
tapa-tapa slice of dried salted fish.
tapaut apart, difference, gap; → TERPAUT. – *tiga tahun* three years apart.
tape (E) /tép/ tape.
tapé → TAPAI I.
tapék-o (coq) *ndak* – not so much.
tapékong → TOA-PÉKONG.
tapel → TAPAL I.
tapelak → TAPLAK.
tapi → TETAPI.
tapian (M) → TEPIAN.
tapih (Jv) long batik skirt.
taping prison trustee.
tapioka (D) tapioca.
tapir (D) tapir, *Tapirus indicus.*
tapis filter, sieve, screen.
  menapis 1 to filter, sift. 2 to censor. 3 to select.
  menapisi (pl obj) to filter.
  tertapis filtered, screened.
  tapisan 1 screen, sieve, strainer. 2 filtrate. 3 what has been censored. 4 what has been selected.
  penapis 1 strainer, sieve. 2 censor.
  penapisan 1 straining, sifting, filtering. 2 censoring.
taplak (D) (– *méja*) tablecloth.
  bertaplak covered with a tablecloth.
  menaplaki to put a tablecloth on.
tapol [tahanan politik] political prisoner.
  pertapolan (mod) political prisoner.
Tapos I the place where former president Suharto's farm was located. *peristiwa* – a meeting that took place between President Suharto and top businessmen in Tapos on March 4, 1990, in which conglomerates were asked to make contributions to small businesses.

tapos II → TAPUS II.

tapos III a tree whose wood is used for making furniture, *Elateriospermum tapos*.

tapsir → TAFSIR.

tapsiun → STASIUN.

taptap (*onom*) 1 sound of trickling water. 2 clicking sound.

Tapténg [Tapanuli Tengah] Central Tapanuli.

taptibau great eared nightjar, *Eurostopodus temminckii*.

taptu (*D mil*) taps.

tapuk I pockmarked; → CAPUK.
  bertapuk-tapuk 1 heavily pockmarked. 2 with a bad reputation.

tapuk II → TAMPUK I.

tapuk III (*Jv*) menapuk to slap.

tapung I long narrow skirt.

tapung II (*Jv*) steamer.
  menapung to steam.

tapung III (*M*) blow, hit.
  menapung to hit.

tapus I (*J*) squeeze.
  menapus to squeeze, milk.

tapus II → TAPOS III.

taqarrub → TA'ARRUB.

taqwa → TAKWA I.

tar I (*onom*) 1 bang, sound made by gun or pistol. 2 whipping sound.

tar II (*D*) tart.

tar III → TÉR I.

tar IV → ENTAR.

tar V (in acronyms) → PENATARAN.

tara I same, equivalent, match, counterpart. *tidak ada –nya* a) unequaled, unmatched. b) unbeatable. *belum ada –nya* unprecedented.
  setara 1 equivalent. ~ *kas* cash equivalent. 2 a match for e.o.
  menyetarakan to make equivalent. kesetaraan equivalency, equivalence. penyetaraan making equivalent.
  bertara matched, matching, equaled. *tidak* ~ unequaled, unmatched.
  menarakan 1 to compare. 2 match.
  tertara compared. *tidak* ~ incomparable.

tara II (*A/D*) tare, difference between gross and net weight to account for the weight of the container, wrapping, etc.

tara III → KENTARA.

tara IV (*M*) a tool for scratching lines on wood.

taraf (*A*) 1 boundary, border. 2 level, degree, phase, stage, standard, grade, status, class, position. 3 layer. *- dan umur* position and age. *- dua* two-stage. bertaraf dua two-stage. *- hidup* standard of living. *- nyata* level of significance. *- penyelesaian* final stage. *- rendah* lower class. *- warna* shade of color.
  setaraf at the same level/degree/grade, on a par, equal. ~ *dengan* at the same level as, equivalent to, on a par with, equal to.
  menyetarafkan to set s.t. at the same level as, make s.t. equivalent to s.t., place s.o. on a par with, consider equal to.
  bertaraf 1 to have a level/degree. ~ *internasional* at an international level. 2 prestigious.
  menarafkan to evaluate by grading, rank.
  penarafan ranking, grading.

tarah planed (of a piece of wood). *- kasau* filed down so they are even (of teeth).
  bertarah planed (of a piece of wood). *sudah* ~ *berdongkol pula* it's just one problem after another.
  menarah 1 to plane (wood). 2 to level off (a rice field).
  tarahan s.t. that has been planed or leveled off.
  penarah a plane, s.t. or s.o. that planes.
  penarahan planing, leveling.

tarak (*A*) 1 abstinence (to achieve an objective). 2 to abstain from. *- garam* to be on a salt-free diet.
  bertarak to go to an isolated or holy place.
  penarak s.o. who abstains from s.t. ~ *alkohol* teetotaler.
  penarakan abstinence, abstaining (to achieve an objective).
  pertarakan retreat.

taram (*ob*) dark, dim. *- temaram* dark, dim.

tarang (*Jv*) menarang to hang s.t. up high; → PETARANGAN.

tarap I (*Jv*) row, line.

bertarap in rows/lines.

tarap II → TARAF.

tarasul (*A*) 1 manuscript. 2 correspondence.

taratai and taraté → TERATAI.

tarawangsa (*S*) a two-stringed musical instrument.

tarawéh and tarawih (*A*) *salat* – evening prayer during Ramadan.
  bertarawéh to recite that prayer.

tarbantin (*A*) (*minyak –*) turpentine.

tarbil catapult, pellet bow.

tarbi(y)ah (*A*) 1 training, education. 2 upbringing.
  mentarbiahkan to train, educate.

tarbus (*A*) Turkish fez.

tarcis (*D*) tartlets.

tarékah and tarékat (*A*) 1 path, way. 2 mystic path to the Truth. 3 regimen, way of life. 4 spiritual fraternity.

targét (*E*) target.
  targét-targétan (*coq*) to do s.t. just to fulfill a quota.
  men(t)argétkan to target.
  pen(t)argétan targeting.

tari dance. *- balét* ballet. *- barat* Western-style dancing. *- barong* a Balinese dance. *- bedaya* a classical dance. *- bondan* a Javanese dance. *- cakalélé* a war dance of Minahasa. *- gambus* a dance accompanied by the *gambus* and Arabic-style music. *- gebyar* a Balinese dance. *- inai* candle dance. *- kécak* the Balinese "monkey" dance. *- kejang* break dance. *- keléwang* sword dance. *- keris* sword dance. *- kipas* fan dance. *- kupu-kupu* the Balinese "butterfly" dance. *- lénso* handkerchief dance. *- lilin* candle dance. *- payung* the "umbrella" dance. *- pedang* sword dance. *- pencak silat* martial arts dance. *- perang* war dance. *- piring* candle dance. *- saputangan* handkerchief dance. *- seléndang* scarf dance. *- sikin/séwar* sword dance. *- topéng* masked dance.
  bertari to dance. ~ *kejang* break dancing.
  menari to dance. ~ *di ladang orang* to strut in borrowed plumes. *tak tahu* ~, *dikatakan lantai terjungkit* a bad workman blames his tools.
  tari-menari 1 dancing. 2 dance party.
  menari-nari dancing with joy, dance up and down.
  menarikan to dance (a dance). ~ *tari-tarian daérah* to dance regional dances.
  tarian dance. ~ *kejang* break dance. ~ *jumpalitan* break dance.
  tari-tarian various k.o. dances.
  penari dancer. ~ *perut* belly dancer. ~ *strip* striptease dancer.

tarif (*D*) tariff, fee, rate. *- angkutan* fare. *- béa masuk* import duty tariff. *- biaya tambangan* freight rate. *- bongkar* unloading costs. *- dasar listrik* [TDL] basic electricity rates. *- makan(an)* menu. *- muat* loading costs. *- pajak* tax rate. *- penyusutan* depreciation rate. *- rata* flat rate.
  pen(t)arifan 1 tariff (*mod*). *kebajikan* ~ tariff policy. 2 pricing, rating. ~ *télepon lokal* pricing local telephone calls.

ta'rif (*A*) → TAKRIF.

tarih → TARIKH.

tarik I 1 pull, draw, attract. 2 (bus conductor's command to driver) OK, go ahead! *- layar* to hoist sail. *- langkah* a) to step back (in *silat*). b) to run away. *- léhér* to shout out one's wares. *- muka* to make a face. *- muka duabelas* to grimace. *- suara* to sing. *- tali/tambang* tug of war. *- tunai* cash withdrawal. *- ulur* to drag one's feet. *setelah – ulur selama lebih dari 2 tahun* after dragging their feet for more than 2 years. *- urat (léhér)* to stand firm, hold one's ground, make a stand, stubbornly resist giving in, hold out.
  bertarik-tarikan to pull at e.o.
  menarik [and narik (*coq*)] 1 to pull, drag. ~ *keréta* to pull a wagon. ~ *pelatuk* to cock the hammer. 2 to drive. ~ *bécak* to drive a pedicab. 3 to pull out, draw, extract, unsheathe, withdraw, recall. ~ *akar* (math) to extract the root. ~ *garis* to draw a line. ~ *pedang* to pull out one's sword. ~ *pengalaman* to draw a lesson (from an experience). *tidak dapat ditarik kembali* cannot be withdrawn. ~ *mundur* to withdraw, retreat. ~ *pulang* to countermand. ~ *tuduhan* to drop charges. 4 to attract; attractive, charming, interesting. ~*nya* the interesting thing is, what's interesting about it is. ~ *anggota baru* to attract new members (of a political party). ~ *hati* to attract, interest, be appealing. 5

to collect. ~ *bayaran* to collect payment. ~ *bunga* to charge interest. *ditarik harganya* it'll cost you (money). ~ *diri* to withdraw, back out. ~ *iuran* to collect dues. ~ *jiwa* at death's door. ~ *kembali* to withdraw, recall. ~ *ke pengadilan* to take s.o. to court. ~ *kesimpulan* to draw a conclusion. ~ *keuntungan* to take advantage of, reap a profit from, cash in on, sponge off s.o. ~ *lagu* to sing. ~ *langkah* to take a step. ~ *langkah seribu* to run away. ~ *langkah surut* to withdraw. ~ *layar* to unfurl a sail. ~ *loteré* to hit the jackpot. ~ *muka duabelas* to show one's disappointment. ~ *mundur* to withdraw. ~ *napas panjang* to breathe a sigh of relief. ~ *napas penghabisan* to breathe one's last. ~ *nyawa* to die. ~ *nyawa sekarat* to be at death's door. ~ *ongkos* a) to cost money. b) to ask for payment. ~ *otot* stubborn, obstinate. ~ *pajak* to collect taxes. ~ *panjang* to stretch out, prolong. ~ *pembayaran* to ask for payment. ~ *perhatian* to attract attention, be interesting, appeal to. ~ *piutang* to ask for repayment. ~ *senyum* to smile. ~ *suara* to sing. ~ *surat wésel* to draw up a draft. ~ *tuduhan* (*leg*) to drop charges. ~ *undian* to win a drawing. ~ *usul* to withdraw one's suggestion. **kemenarikan** attractiveness, charm. *tidak* ~ uninteresting, unattractive. *ketidak-menarikan* lack of attractiveness/charm.

tarik-menarik tug-of-war.

menarik-narik 1 to keep on pulling/dragging. **2** to involve, implicate, pull s.o. into s.t.

menariki (*pl subj*) to pull, drag, draw.

menarikkan 1 to pull, drag, draw (for s.o. else).

mempertarikkan 1 to drag s.t. **2** to pull, stretch.

tertarik [and **ketarik** (*coq*)] **1** interested, attracted. *tertarik perhatian* to become interested. **2** sympathetic, captivated. **3** drawn, pulled, dragged. ~ *hati* moved, touched. **4** pulled out, extracted. **5** drawee. **ketertarikan** interest, attraction.

tarikan 1 pull, traction, draught. ~ *napas* respiration. ~ *udara* air current. **2** attraction. **3** drive (in a vehicle). ~ *roda belakang* rear-wheel drive.

tarik-tarikan 1 tug-of-war. **2** (*sl*) to try to pass e.o. (of drivers).

penarik 1 puller, attracter, extractor. *kuda* ~ draft horse. ~ *hati* attraction. ~ *perhatian* eye-catcher, s.t. that makes you sit up and notice. ~ (*se*)*persepuluhan* s.o. who has the right to 10 percent of a receivable. **2** drawer (of a draft). **3** driver. ~ *bécak* pedicab driver. **4** collector. ~ *pajak* tax collector.

penarikan 1 withdrawal, disbursement. ~ *diri* withdrawal. **2** recall. ~ *kembali* withdrawal, recall; revocation, retraction, repeal. **3** drawing, pulling, dragging. **4** stretching. **5** collecting, collection. ~ *contoh* sampling. ~ *keluar* pull-out. ~ *kembali* cancellation. ~ *pajak* tax collection. ~ *tunai* cash withdrawal.

tarik II → TARIKH.

tarikah and **tarikat** → TARÉKAT.

tarikh (*A*) **1** date. **2** era, calendar. **3** history, chronicle, annals, chronology. **4** in the year ... – *Hijriah* Muslim calendar, A.H. – *Maséhi* Christian calendar, A.D.

men(t)arikhkan 1 to date. **2** to chronicle.

taring 1 fang, tusk. – *Padi* name of a populist art movement in Yogyakarta. **2** canine (tooth).

bertaring fanged, tusked.

tarip → TARIF.

Tariq (*A*) *al*– "The Night Star"; name of the 86th chapter of the Koran.

taris I floor.

taris II menaris to wrap/tie/bind up.

tarjamah and **tarjemah** → TERJEMAH.

tarjih (*A*) *Majelis* – organ of Muhammadiyah that studies problems of religious law.

tarkas (*A*) quiver (for arrows).

tarling [*gitar dan suling*] guitars and flutes.

tarmak (*E*) tarmac.

taro tart, cake.

Taroada Tarogaru the military resort command (*Korém* 142) in Pare Pare.

taro(h) → TARUH.

tarok → TARO, TARUH.

tarombo (*Bat*) patrilineal family tree.

tarompét → TROMPÉT.

tarpentin (*D*) turpentine.

tart (*D*) tart, cake.

Tartar (*D/E*) Tartar.

tar-tar-tar and **tar-tor** (*onom*) sound of gun shots.

tartil (*A*) slow rhythmic recitation of the Koran.

tarub → TARUP.

taruf (*A*) reception.

taruh 1 place, put, lay. **2** stake, bet. **3** security deposit. – *beras dalam padi* to keep a secret. – *kata* let's say, supposing that. – *mata* to watch, see. – *muka* to meet face to face.

bertaruh 1 to (place a) bet. **2** to bet (that).

bertaruhkan 1 to bet s.t. **2** to entrust, give s.t. (to s.o.) for safekeeping.

menaruh [and **naruh** (*coq*)] **1** to place, put, lay, put down. **2** to take care of, raise, keep. ~ *aib* to feel ashamed. ~ *barang* to give s.t. to s.o. for safekeeping. ~ *dahsyat* to be afraid. ~ *dendam* to bear a grudge. ~ *di bawah paha* to ignore. ~ *harga* to set a price on, ask for a certain price. ~ *hati pada* to be interested in s.o. romantically. ~ *hormat* to esteem, respect, show respect (for). ~ *insaf* to be compassionate. ~ *kasihan kepada* to feel pity/sorry for. ~ *kepercayaan* (*kepada*) to put trust (in). ~ *malu* to feel ashamed. ~ *mata* to watch, pay attention to. ~ *minat* to take interest (in s.t.). ~ *modal* to draw on one's capital. ~ *perhatian* (*terhadap*) to show interest (in). ~ *pikiran* to show interest in. ~ *rindu* to long for. ~ *télepon* to hang up. ~ *uang* to deposit money. *taruhlah* let's say, supposing we say. *Taruhlah empatpuluh.* Let's say forty.

menaruhi 1 to put (s.t.) on s.t. **2** to lay a bet on.

menaruhkan 1 to place, put (for s.o. else). **2** to bet (for s.o. else).

mempertaruhkan 1 to pawn. **2** to bet (money) (on), risk, put s.t. at risk/stake, jeopardize. ~ *jiwa/nyawa* to risk one's life. ~ *kehormatan* to stake one's reputation. *dipertaruhkan* at stake. **3** to entrust s.t. to s.o. for safekeeping.

taruhan 1 s.t. bet, stake, a gamble. *Nyawa* ~*nya*. He's risking his life. ~ *nyawa* putting one's life at stake. *jadi* ~ to be at stake. ~*nya menyangkut nasib bangsa ini.* The stakes involve the fate of this nation. *Citra ABRI jadi* ~. ABRI's image is at stake. **2** favorite, best-loved. **bertaruhan 1** to stake. **2** to entrust s.t. for safekeeping.

penaruh s.o. who places bets, etc. ~ *perhatian* s.o. who is interested.

petaruh 1 better. **2** last will and testament. **3** security deposit. **4** backer. **berpetaruh** to advise. **mempetaruhkan** to risk (one's life, etc.).

penaruhan 1 placement, placing, putting, laying, storing. **2** place s.t. is put. **3** money box, storage box. **berpenaruhan** well off, rich.

pertaruhan 1 bet. **2** savings. **3** s.t. entrusted to s.o. for safekeeping. ~ *senjata* cease-fire.

taruk I → TARUH.

taruk II sprout, bud, shoot.

bertaruk to sprout, bud.

tarum I indigo, *Indigofera tinctoria*. – *akar* a climbing plant, *Marsdenia tinctoria*. – *hutan* a shrub, *Indigofera sp.*, *Didissandra frutescens*. – *kembang* a shrub, *Indigofera suffruticosa*.

tarum II blue rock thrush, *Monticola solitaria*.

Tarumanegara the military resort command (*Korém* 062) in Garut.

taruna → TERUNA.

tarung I (*onom*) sound of clashing swords.

bertarung to fight, argue, dispute, debate. ~ *melawan* to play against.

bertarungan to fight with e.o.

menarung to fight/dispute/debate/argue against.

menarungkan to have animals fight e.o. ~ *jiwa/nyawa* a) to risk one's life. b) to fight to the death.

mempertarungkan 1 to have animals fight e.o. **2** to risk (one's life, etc.).

petarung combatant.

pertarungan 1 combat, fight, battle, match, struggle. **2** dispute.

tarung II (*M*) stumble, trip.

tertarung to stumble. ~ *batu* to trip on a stone.

penarung obstacle, s.t. stumbled over. *batu* ~ stumbling block.

taruni female cadet.

tarup (*Jv*) temporary building erected for wedding guests, etc. – *agung* grandstand.

  bertarup to use such a building.

  menarupi to build such a building on/over.

tarwiah (*A*) the eighth of *Zulhijjah*.

tarwih → TARAWÉH.

tas I (*onom*) **1** boom (of gun); → DAS I. **2** crackling (as of fireworks); → DETAS.

tas II (*D*) bag, briefcase, attaché case, pouch. – *belanja* shopping bag. – *bepergian* travel bag. – *cangkingan/jinjing* handbag. – *krések* plastic bag without handle. – *mahasiswa* shoulder bag. – *pesiar* travel bag. – *punggung* backpack. – *samsonite* Samsonite attaché case. – *sekolah* school bag.

tas III (*ob*) forthwith, (and) immediately; → LANTAS.

tas IV *kayu* – a small tree, *Kurrimia paniculata* whose wood is believed to frighten away tigers.

tas V (in acronyms) → ATAS, PEMBERANTASAN.

tasa (*M*) k.o. drum.

tasai k.o. tree, *Mischocarpus lessertianus*.

tasak *obat* – styptic.

  menasak to stop bleeding with a styptic.

  penasak styptic pencil.

tasalsul (*A*) genealogy.

tasamuh (*A*) free from bigotry/prejudice, tolerant.

tasar [kata dasar] root word.

tasauf → TASAWUF, TASAW(W)UF.

tasawuf and **tasawwuf** (*A*) mysticism. *ilmu* – Islamic mysticism. *mengaji* – to study mysticism. *orang* – mystic.

tasbéh → TASBIH.

tasbih (*A*) **1** extolling God. **2** (*buah* –) rosary beads. *menghitung* (*buah*) – and *mengucap* – to count/say one's beads. *bunga* – seeds of the wild canna, *Canna orientalis*.

  bertasbih to tell one's beads, extol God.

  men(t)asbihkan to extol God.

  pen(t)asbihan extolling God.

tasdid → TASYDID.

tasdik (*A*) confirmation, verification, attestation.

  mentasdikkan to confirm, verify, attest.

tasik I lake.

Tasik II clipped form of **Tasikmalaya**.

tasiun (*coq*) → STASIUN.

Taska → TABUNGAN *Asuransi Berjangka*.

Taskin [pengentasan kemiskinan] eradication of poverty.

taslim I (*A ob*) obedience (to God), loyalty.

  men(t)aslimkan to entrust, hand over (a letter).

taslim II (*A*) salutation.

tasmak → TESMAK.

taspén [tabungan asuransi pegawai negeri] Government Employees' Insurance Savings.

tasrif (*A*) declension (of nouns); conjugation (of verbs).

  mentasrifkan to decline; to conjugate.

tasrih (*A*) anatomy.

taswir (*A*) **1** sketch; portrait. **2** speech, address.

tasyahud → TASYHID.

tasyakur (*A*) thanking God.

tasyakuran (*A*) to prostrate o.s. in prayer.

tasybih (*A*) characterizing God as having human attributes.

tasydid and **tasjid** (*A*) duplication mark, diacritical mark in Arabic script to indicate the doubling of the sound of a letter.

tasyhid (*A*) – confession of faith/creed.

  bertasyhid to pronounce the confession of faith.

  mentasyhidkan to confess the faith.

Tasykén Tashkent.

tasyrif (*A*) honoring.

tasyrih (*A*) *ilmu* – anatomy.

  mentasyrihkan to analyze.

tasyrik (*A*) legal practice.

tata (*Jv*) [also see **tata** written together with the following root] arrangement, order, system, grouping, organization, pattern, regulation, classification, *esp* in compounds. *negara mawa* –, *désa mawa cara* (*Jv*) "the cities have their own customs and the villages their own traditions," i.e., the principle of observing ethical codes. – *bahasa* grammar. – *bangunan* architecture. – *cahaya* lighting, illumination. – *cara* procedures. – *guna* use. – *guna lahan* land use. – *hidup* way of life. – *hutan* forest management. – *kelola* management. – *kelola risiko* risk management. – *kelola wiraswasta* entrepreneurial management. – *kerajaan* monarchy. – *kerja* (working) method, methodology. – *kota* city planning, townscape. – *krama* methods. – *laku* conduct, behavior. – *laksana* systems and procedures, ways of doing s.t. **ketatalaksanaan** matters of systems and procedures, administrative procedures. – *letak* layout. – *naskah* documentation. – *niaga* commerce. – *pemerintahan* governance. – *persuratan* record-keeping. – *rambut* hairdo. – *ruang* a) layout (of structure/land, etc.). b) interior design. c) zoning. – *susun* layout. – *susunan* structure. *tanam* landscaping. – *tertib* regulations. – *usaha* administration. **ketatausahaan** administrative affairs.

  menata to put in order, organize, manage. ~ *ulang* to reorganize.

  pemenataan justifying (lines of text).

  menatakan to organize, put into order.

  tertata put in order, ordered, arranged, organized. ~ *apik/rapi* neatened up.

  tataan 1 arrangement, organization. **2** staging.

  penata 1 s.o. or s.t. that puts s.t. in order, arranger, organizer. ~ *rontgén* radiologist. ~ *rambut* hairdresser. **2** a civil-service rank. ~ *muda/tingkat 1* various civil-service ranks. ~ *musik* musical arranger. ~ *tari* choreographer.

  penataan structuring; system, order, arrangement, alignment. ~ *kembali* restructuring, adjustment. ~ *masyarakat* governance.

tataacara 1 agenda, program. **2** procedures, proceedings.

tataacuan frame of reference.

tataadab good manners/breeding, politeness, civility.

tataadegan grouping (in theatrical life).

tataair water regulation, irrigation. – *pegunungan* mountain hydrology.

tataajaran curriculum.

tatabahasa grammar.

  bertatabahasa to be grammatical. ~ *yang benar* grammatically correct.

  ketatabahasaan grammatical.

tatabahasawan grammarian.

tatabahasawi grammatical, pertaining to grammar.

tatabentuk 1 (*ling*) morphology. **2** design.

tataboga food management.

  penataboga food manager.

tatabuku bookkeeping, accounting. – *berpasangan* double-entry bookkeeping. – *tunggal* single-entry bookkeeping.

  penatabuku bookkeeper, accountant.

tatabumi land use.

tatabunyi (*ling*) phonology.

tatabusana 1 costume, dress. **2** fashion designing.

  penatabusana fashion designer.

tatacahaya lightning, illumination.

tatacara 1 etiquette, protocol, customs and manners. **2** procedure. – *ibadat* liturgy. – *mistik* mystic rites. – *pelélangan* tender procedure. – *peradilan* proceedings.

tatacipta fashion designing.

tatadaérah regional planning.

tatadunia world/global order. – *baru* the new world order.

tataédar distribution.

tataéjaan (*ling*) orthography.

tataékonomi economic order.

tatafoném (*ling*) phonemics.

tatag → TATAK.

tatagaul (social) manners.

tatageréja (*PC*) church rituals.

tatagraha housekeeping.

  ketatagrahaan housekeeping. *masalah-masalah* ~ housekeeping problems.

  penatagraha housekeeper.

tataguna use. – *biologi/hayati* bio-management. – *lahan/tanah* land use.

penatagunaan use.
tatah I (*Jv*) chisel.
  bertatah carved, chiseled.
  menatah 1 to carve, chisel, sculpt. **2** to carve out (leather puppets).
  tatahan 1 carving, sculpture. **2** form and composition. ~ *negara* form and structure of the state.
  penatah carver, sculptor.
  penatahan carving out, sculpting.
tatah II inlay, inlaid work.
  bertatah(kan) inlaid, studded. *bertatahkan mutu manikan* studded with jewels.
  menatah (*cla*) to inlay, set (jewels) into a surface.
tatah III (*M*) tottering, unsteady on one's feet, shaky, wobbly. – *tatih* to wobble, totter, toddle.
  menatah to lead a child who is learning to walk.
tatah IV tatah-tatah (*ob*) rumors, gossip.
  tatahan ~ *kata* small talk, gossip.
tatahalaman landscape gardening.
tatahukum (*leg*) legal structure.
tatai (*ob*) **bertatai-tatai** in rows.
tatainformasi information order.
tataistilah terminology.
tatak (*Jv*) /tatak/ intrepid, fearless, determined, resolute.
tatakalimat (*gram*) syntax.
tatakamar housekeeping.
tatakan (*Jv*) /tata'an/ **1** underlayer, base, pedestal. **2** coaster, saucer. – *kertas* doily. **3** tray.
tatakantor office management.
tatakarya (working) method.
tatakata (*ling*) morphology.
tatakelola management. – *risiko* risk management.
tatakerajaan monarchy.
tatakerja work procedures.
tatakota city planning.
tatakrama code of conduct, etiquette, good manners.
tatal I wood chips/shavings. – *halus* wood wool. – *kayu* wood chips. – *ketam* shavings.
tatal II tertatal 1 to get squashed. **2** to be in trouble.
tatalaksana management, implementation.
  menatalaksanakan to manage.
  ketatalaksanaan management.
  penatalaksana manager. ~ *penjualan* sales manager.
  penatalaksanaan managing.
tatalampu lighting.
tatalayan stewardship.
  penatalayanan stewardship.
tataletak 1 layout. **2** pilot/site plan.
  penataletak layout man.
tatalingkungan environment. – *hidup* ecosystem.
tataloka layout, site plan.
tatamasyarakat social order.
tataméja table setting.
tataminuman drinks, beverages.
  penataminuman bartender.
tatamode clothing design.
  penatamode clothing designer.
tatamonétér monetary system.
tatamuka 1 cover layout. **2** makeup.
tatamusik (music) arrangement.
  penatamusik (music) arranger.
tatanada (musical) arrangement.
  penatanada (musical) arranger.
tatanama nomenclature.
tatanan (*Jv*) **1** order, arrangement. – *rambut* hairdo. **2** (system of) regulations, rules, order. – *dalam* inner setting. *Dalam – démokrasi Pancasila Parpol bukan pelengkap.* In the Pancasila democratic order the political parties are not complements. – *ékonomi baru* the new economic order. – *luar* outer setting. – *politik* political order.
tatanegara 1 constitution/organization of the State, form of government, political science. **2** State regulation. **3** State institution.

bertatanegara having a constitutional system, constitutional.
ketatanegaraan 1 of/pertaining to the State. **2** political. **3** of/pertaining to constitutional law.
tatang menatang to lift or carry s.t. (carefully) in the palm of the hand; to treat very carefully; → **MENATING**. *ditatang bagai minyak yang penuh* and *seperti – minyak penuh* to treat with tender loving care. – *di anak lidah* to love one's wife and children.
tatangkalan (*S*) trees.
tataniaga marketing, commerce; → **PEMASARAN**.
  ketataniagaan business administration.
tatanilai set of values. *pergéséran* ~ *dalam NU* shift of values in the NU organization.
tatap – *muka* face-to-face. *pertemuan* – *muka* a face-to-face meeting. *bertatap muka* to have a face-to-face meeting (with). *Panglima ABRI* ~ *dengan karyawan ABRI.* The Armed Forces Commander of the Republic of Indonesia had a face-to-face meeting with the Armed Forces staff.
  bertatapan, bertatap-tatapan, and **bersitatap** to stare/look closely at e.o., look into e.o.'s eyes, be face to face. *Lantas kedua orang itu* ~ *sebentar.* Then the two persons stared at e.o.
  menatap to look closely at, stare at, observe closely.
  menatapi 1 to look closely at s.t. or s.o., look over carefully, scrutinize, scan, observe carefully. **2** to stare at. *Jangan* ~ *matahari.* Don't keep staring at the sun. *dengan saling* ~ *mata* with locked eyes.
  menatapkan to fix (one's eyes on), stare (at).
  tertatap stared at, looked at closely.
  tatapan 1 scrutinizing, inspection, observation, looking carefully at. ~ *ke masa depan* looking ahead to the future. *menjadi* ~ *mata* stared at (or, paid attention to) by the public; to become the focus of attention/center of interest of the public. **2** look, stare. *dengan* ~ *bengis* with a cruel stare.
  penatapan fixing one's eyes on, staring, scrutinizing, observing.
tatapan (*ob*) a piece of yellow silk that is placed on the shoulder when in the audience of a king or used to cover gifts for a king.
tatapanggung staging.
  penatapanggung stage manager.
tatapelajaran curriculum.
tatapemerintahan governmental system.
tatapentas setting (in film).
tatapenulisan graphology.
tataperabotan ~ *rumah* household furniture.
tatapergaulan ~ *hidup* way of life, lifestyle.
tatapérsonalia personnel management.
tataperusahaan business administration.
tatapimpinan management; → **MANAJEMÉN**.
tatapola regulation.
  menatapola to regulate.
tatapraja state administration.
tatapuspa flower arrangement.
tatar (*Jv*) (and **tataran**) foothold/stepping place cut into a steep place (e.g., a cliff/coconut palm trunk) to enable s.o. to climb it.
  menatar to upgrade.
  tataran 1 step (toward a goal). **2** stage, level.
  penatar upgrader, trainer.
  petatar upgradee.
  penataran 1 upgrading. ~ *P4* P4 upgrading; → *P4*. **2** (*euph*) indoctrination.
tatarambut hairdressing. *ahli* – hairdresser. *seni* – the art of hairdressing.
  penatarambut hairdresser.
  penataan ~ *rambut* hairdressing.
tatarias makeup. – *fantasi* fancy makeup. – *surat kabar* makeup of newspaper.
tatarompétan k.o. decorative plant, *Ipomoea tripida.*
tatarontgén radiology.
  penatarontgén radiologist.
tataruang → **TATA** *ruang.*
tatarupa cover design (of magazine).
tatasopan courtesies.
tatasuara sound system.
  penatasuara (sound) engineer.

tatasurya solar system.
tatataman landscaping.
tatatanam agriculture.
tatatari choreography.
    menatatari to choreograph.
    penatatari choreographer.
tatatéhnik engineering.
    penatatéhnik engineer, mechanic.
tatatempat layout; → TATALOKA.
tatatentrem – *kertaraharja* (*Jv*) the golden age of peace and prosperity.
tatatertib 1 discipline, order. 2 regulations, rules. – *lalulintas* traffic regulations. ~ *sidang* rules of order.
tatatingkat hierarchy; rank, scale.
tatatiti bureaucratic red tape.
tatatulis writing.
tataudara ventilation, air-conditioning.
tataupacara protocol.
tataurut(an) position in a sequence, hierarchy.
tatausaha administration.
    menatausahakan to administer.
    ketatausahaan administrative. *dari sudut* ~ from the administrative point of view.
    penatausahaan administration.
tatawarna Technicolor. *dalam* – in color.
tatawiraswasta business science.
tatayur (*A*) evil omen.
tatera crested fire-back pheasant, *Lophura ignita rufa*.
tatib → TATATERTIB.
tatih unsteady (of steps, walking).
    bertatih(-tatih) to toddle, walk unsteadily.
    menatih to help s.o., such as a child, walk by holding his hand, etc.
    tertatih-tatih shaky, wobbly, wobbling.
tating menating to carry in one's hands; lift with both hands; → TATANG, TAYANG II. *Piala Citra itu diarak, dipayungi, ditating oléh wanita cantik.* The Image Trophy was carried along in procession, protected by an umbrella, and lifted up with both hands by a beautiful woman.
tatkala (*Skr*) when (in the past).
tato (*E*) tattoo.
    bertato tattooed.
    mentato to tattoo.
    pentatoan tattooing.
taton → KETATON.
tatorruf (*A*) extreme.
Tat Twam Asi (*Skr*) 1 You are Me and I am You, i.e., to be considerate; → TEPO SELIRO. 2 name of the women's association of the Department of Social Affairs.
tatu (*Jv*) wound, wounded.
    menatui to wound.
    tertatu wounded.
tau I → TAHU I. *-lah* (*coq*) I don't know.
tau II (*daun* –) k.o. palm, *Livistona tahanensis*.
Taubah (*A*) *at-* "Repentance"; name of the ninth chapter of the Koran.
taubat → TOBAT.
taucang (*C*) pigtail.
tauci and **tauc(y)o** (*C*) fermented bean paste.
taufah (*A*) careless, negligent.
taufan (*C*) typhoon. – *pasir* sandstorm.
taufik (*A*) piety.
taugé → TAOGÉ.
tauhid → TAWHID.
tauk I → (*coq*) TAHU I. –, *ya* I don't know.
tauk II (*A*) vault of the heavens.
tauké → TAOKÉH.
taukid (*A*) confirmation.
taukua (*C*) dried soybean cake.
taul menaul to make fast (an oar/anchor).
taula (*E?*) towel; → HANDUK.
tauladan → TELADAN.
taulan (*Tam*) friend, buddy.

tauliah (*A*) 1 permit, permission. 2 license, warrant. 3 credential, commission.
    bertauliah commissioned, authorized.
    men(t)auliahkan to commission, authorize.
taun I → TAHUN I.
taun II k.o. plant, *Pometia tomentosa/pinnata*; → LENGSAR.
ta'un (*A*) pestilence, *esp* cholera.
taung dust eddy, sand devil.
    menaungi to cover, dust (with clouds or with a dusting of). *Kepalanya mulai ditaungi uban.* His head has begun to be covered with a dusting of gray.
taup → TAUT. **bertaupan** interlocking.
taur (*M*) **menaur** to redeem, recover, buy back.
    menauri to redeem.
    tauran redemption, buying back.
Taurat, Taurét, and **Taurit** (*A*) the Old Testament, *esp* the Pentateuch, Torah.
tausi → TAUCI.
tausiah (*A*) advice; → NASIHAT.
taut I fusion.
    bertaut 1 to fit close together, close up (of a wound), fuse/join into one, join up, grow together, link up, (one's eyes are) fixed on. ~ *matanya* to close one's eyes. ~ *menjadi satu* to fuse into one ~ *tangan* to shake hands. 2 to dock, moor. 3 related, connected, linked.
    bertautan to be linked/related to e.o., related, interrelated.
    men(t)autkan and **mempertautkan** 1 to combine/unite into one, tie together. ~ *tangan* to join hands. 2 to close up, sew up. 3 to dock, moor, hook up. 4 to bring into, involve.
    tautan link, connection. ~ *hati* sweetheart.
    pen(t)autan linking up, connecting.
    pertautan 1 coherence. 2 contact. 3 docking, mooring. 4 joining together, uniting into one. 5 (*chem*) linkage.
taut II fishing line.
tau-tau (in Tanatoraja) wooden effigies of the dead.
Tauwab (*A*) a name of God, the forgiver.
tauziah (*A*) recommendation.
Tavip [Tahun Viveré Pericoloso] the Year of Living Dangerously (Soekarno speech of August 17, 1964).
tawa I laugh, laughter. – *gemuruh* roaring laughter. – *kecil* smile. – *sumbang* laughing on the outside but crying on the inside. – *ria* pleasant laughter. – *terkékéh* giggle.
    tertawa [and **ketawa** (*coq*)] to laugh. ~ *besar* to laugh heartily. ~ *cekikikan* to giggle. ~ *dekah-dekah* to roar with laughter. ~ *gelak-gelak* to roar with laughter. ~ *gemuruh* to roar with laughter. ~ *kecil* to smile. ~ *kecut* to laugh out of the wrong side of one's mouth. ~ *ketiwi* to laugh uproariously. ~ *lébar/lepas* to laugh heartily. ~ *pahit* to laugh bitterly. ~ *ria* to laugh with pleasure. ~ *sendiri* to laugh to o.s. ~ *sumbang* to laugh on the outside but cry on the inside. ~ *terkékéh* to giggle. ~ *terpingkal-pingkal* to shake with laughter. **tertawai** laughed at, ridiculed, mocked. **men(t)ertawai, mengetawai, men(t)ertawai,** and **men(t)ertawakan** [and **ngetawain** (*J coq*)] 1 to laugh at, ridicule. 2 to make s.o. laugh. **tertawaan** and **ketawaan** 1 object of ridicule, laughingstock. 2 mocking, mockery.
tawa II → TAHUWA.
tawadhu and **tawadzu** → TAWADU II.
tawadu(k) I and **tawadhu** (*A*) humility; humble, modest, docile.
tawadu II, tawad(l)u, and **tawadlu'** (*A*) ablutions before prayer.
    bertawadu to do one's ablutions.
tawaf and **towaf** (*A*) (to) walk around the Kaabah seven times reciting the appropriate prayers.
    bertawaf to perform that action.
tawajuh and **tawajuk** (*A*) (*hati*) religious devotion, turning one's face to God.
    bertawajuh devoted.
tawak I (*cla*) **men(t)awaki** to throw stones at.
tawak II mentawakkan to move (one's lips, etc.).
tawak(k)al (*A*) trust in God, rely on God, surrender to God.
    bertawak(k)al to place one's trust in God, surrender to God.
    ketawak(k)alan resignation to God's will.
tawak-tawak small signal gong.

tawan I menawan 1 to capture, imprison, detain, intern. ~ *hati* charming, captivating, appealing, fascinating. **2** to seize (property, etc. belonging to the enemy, etc.).

tertawan 1 captured, imprisoned, detained, interned. **2** seized.

tawanan 1 prisoner, detainee, internee. ~ *jaminan* hostage. ~ *karang* booty looted from grounded ship. ~ *perang* prisoner of war. **2** detention, internment, captivity. **3** seized. *harta* ~ seized property.

penawan captor. ~ *hati* s.o. who captivates.

penawanan capturing, captivity, detaining, imprisoning, interning.

tawan II → AKAR *tawan hutan.*

tawang I k.o. gold or silver necklace.

tawang II (*Jv*) → AWANG-AWANG.

Tawang Jaya name of a train running between Jakarta and Semarang.

Tawang Mas name of a train running between Jakarta and Semarang.

tawang-tawang k.o. insect.

tawar I 1 offer. - *tunai* cash offer. **2** bargain.

bertawar-tawaran to bargain with e.o.

menawar [and **nawar** (*coq*)] **1** to make an offer. **2** to bargain (for). *tidak dapat ditawar* nonnegotiable, no bargaining.

menawar-nawar to negotiate about. *tidak bisa ditawar-tawar lagi* nonnegotiable.

tawar-menawar bargaining, negotiating. *tidak bisa* ~ *lagi* it's final.

menawari [and **nawarin** (*J coq*)] to (make an) offer to. *Meréka* ~ *saya untuk jadi anggota.* They made me an offer to become a member.

menawarkan to offer s.t. *Dia* ~ *pertolongan kepada saya.* He offered me some help.

tertawar offered.

tawaran 1 offer. **2** bid.

penawar s.o. who offers, bidder.

penawaran 1 offering, bid, bidding. ~ *harga* price quotation. ~ *perdana saham* initial public offering, IPO. ~ *saham terbatas* right issue. ~ *terbatas* limited offering. ~ *umum* tender, public (invitation to) tender, public offering. **2** supply. ~ *dan permintaan* supply and demand.

tawar II 1 fresh (water). **2** tasteless, bland. **3** dull, uninteresting. **4** become powerless (of a mantra), ineffective (of a medicine). *Apa kabar?* - *saja.* How are you? Not too good. **5** unaffected, indifferent. - *bisa* antidote. - *hambar* tasteless, insipid. - *hati* a) dejected, discouraged, down. b) indifferent. - *mawar* tasteless, insipid. - *tular* neutralized. **menawartularkan** (*mil*) to neutralize.

setawar ~ *sedingin* consolation. *disetawar-sedingini* to be consoled.

menawar to neutralize, make weaker (poison, etc.).

menawari 1 to imbue (*air obat*) with magic power. **2** to treat s.o. (with *air obat*). **3** to calm s.o. down. ~ *hati* to calm s.o. down, console. **4** to try to seduce.

menawarkan 1 to neutralize, make ineffective. ~ *hati* to discourage.

penawar 1 incantation, charm, spell (to neutralize the effects of black magic). **2** remedy, antidote, neutralizer. ~ *bisa* antidote. ~ *hati* consolation, s.t. to cheer one up. ~ *jambi* k.o. tree fern used to stop the flow of blood from a wound, *Cibotium sp.* ~ *nyeri* analgesic. ~ *pahit* k.o. medicinal plant, *Eurycoma*; → BIDARA *laut.* ~ *perut* s.t. to fill one's stomach. ~ *racun* antidote.

penawaran neutralizing, exorcism (of black magic).

pentawaran (*petrol*) sweetening. ~ *air asin* desalinization.

Tawarikh Chronicles (in the Bible); → TARIKH.

tawar(r)uk (*A*) (*duduk* -) posture at the end of a prayer (left leg under the right and the sole of the right foot raised vertically).

tawar-tawar → SETAWAR.

tawas I alum.

tawas II → TAWES.

tawas(s)ul (*A*) intercession (of Muhammad on behalf of Muslims).

bertawas(s)ul to pray asking for Mohammad's intercession.

tawa-tawa gong-type instruments in the *gamelan.*

tawes (*Jv*) *ikan* - k.o. fish, white bream, *Puntius javanicus.* - *loréng* k.o. fish, tiger barb, *Barbus/Capoeta tetrazona.*

tawfik → TAUFIK.

tawhid (*A*) **1** oneness (of God), monotheism. **2** acknowledgment of the oneness of God. **3** "Unity"; name of the 112th chapter of the Koran.

bertawhid to acknowledge the oneness of God.

mentawhidkan to unite, unify.

ketawhidan the unity of God.

ta'wil → TAKWIL.

tawon (*Jv*) wasp; → TABUHAN.

Tawrah → TAURAT.

tawur I (*Jv*) brawl.

menawuri to brawl with.

tawuran brawl, fight.

tawur II → TABUR.

Tawwab → TAUWAB.

tayam(m)am and **tayam(m)um** (*A*) *wudhu* with sand when water is not available.

bertayam(m)um to do that action.

tayang I present, show (film, etc.). - *ulang* rerun (of TV show). *menayang ulang* to show reruns. - *panjang* extension (of a show). *menayang-panjangkan* to extend (a show).

menayang 1 to show. **2** to appear in a show.

men(t)ayangkan [and **nayangin** (*J coq*)] to present, show, display.

tertayang displayed, presented, shown.

tertayangkan presented, shown, displayed.

tayangan presentation, show. ~ *langsung* real-time, direct. ~ *tunda* delayed broadcast.

pen(t)ayangan presentation, performance, display. ~ *ulang* rerun.

tayang II menayang (*ob*) **1** to carry in the hands. **2** to carry (on the wind, etc.).

tertayang carried in the hands.

tayangan s.t. carried in the hands.

tayang III → MAIN *tayang.*

taypak (*C*) banker, croupier.

tayub (*Jv*) k.o. dance performed by young women in which men in the audience are invited to join in (Central and East Java).

menayub to dance that dance.

tayuban that k.o. dance.

penayub dancer of that dance.

tayum-temayum evening, sunset.

ta'ziah → TAKZIAH.

ta'zim → TAKZIM.

ta'zir → TAKZIR.

tazkirah (*A*) Islamic teachings.

tbc tuberculosis.

Tbk (*abbr*) [Terbuka] publicly listed/traded.

tc [training center] /tésé/ training center.

men-tc-kan to send to a training center.

pen-tc-an sending to a training center.

tcd (*init*) [typhus, cholera, dysentery] /tésédé/ vaccine against these diseases.

TDL [tarif dasar listrik] basic electricity rate.

té I street vendor's call; → SATÉ

té II name of the letter t.

team → TIM.

téater (*D*) theater. - *kendaraan* drive-in theater. - *mobil* drive-in theater. - *réstoran* dinner theater.

bertéater to engage in theatrical performances.

mentéaterakan to stage, perform in the theater.

pertéateran theatrical.

téater(a)wan actor, player.

téatrikal (*E*) theatrical.

tebah I menebah(kan) 1 to beat. ~ *dada* to beat one's breast. **2** to thresh.

tebahan beating.

penebah 1 beater. *mesin* ~ thresher. **2** bat (in sports).

penebahan beating, threshing.

tebah II menebah to catch in the palm of the hand.

tebak I (*J?*) guess, conjecture.

tebak-tebak(an) to keep on guessing. *main* ~ to play riddles.

menebak [and **nebak** (*coq*)] to (take a) guess, guess at.

tertebak 1 guessed, surmised. **2** can be guessed.

tebakan 1 guess, conjecture. **2** riddle; → TEKA-TEKI.

penebak guesser.

penebakan guessing, surmising.

tebak II crowbar.

menebak to use a crowbar to (break up stones/dig up the soil).

tébak menébak 1 to chop/cut/hew away at. **2** to till/turn over (the soil).

tebakang k.o. catfish, kissing gurami, java combtail, *Helostoma teminckii, Belontia hasselti*.

tebal I 1 thick, viscous, dense; thickness. **2** strong (of coffee/beliefs). **3** bold(face) (print). *– bibir* not talkative, taciturn. *– hati* cruel, pitiless. *– iman* strong of faith. *– jangat* insensitive. *– kantong* rich. *– kocék* rich. *– kulit* cruel, pitiless. *– lidah* with a thick accent. *– muka* a) insensitive. b) without shame. **bertebal muka 1** to be insensitive/shameless. **2** to be impudent, insolent. *– semangat* enthusiastic, spirited. *– telinga* a) stubborn, obstinate. b) thick-skinned.

setebal as thick as, with a thickness of. *buku ~ 82 halaman* an 82-page thick book. *~ bandul* very thick. *~ kulit bawang* weak, not firm.

menebal to become thick(er)/denser/stronger/firmer.

menebali to add thickness to, thicken.

menebalkan 1 to thicken, make denser. **2** to strengthen, reinforce, boost. *untuk ~ kepercayaan meréka* to strengthen their confidence. *~ nyali* to desensitize (s.o. to problems). *~ telinga* to strengthen o.s. against insults, etc.

mempertebal(kan) 1 to thicken. **2** to strengthen. *~ semangat* to strengthen one's resolve.

tertebal thickest.

ketebalan thickness, density.

penebal s.t. that thickens/strengthens.

penebalan 1 thickening. *~ pembuluh darah* arteriosclerosis. **2** strengthening, reinforcing, boosting. **3** overlay.

pertebalan thickening.

tebal II first part of some names of fishes. *– bibir* grunter, painted sweet lip, *Plectorhynchidae spp. – pipi* k.o. sea fish, *Pamadasys spp. – sisik* k.o. freshwater fish, two-spot barb, *Puntius binotatus spp.*

téban bet, stake. *– tiga* pays three to one.

menébankan to bet.

tébanan bet, stake.

tebang I fell, chop/cut down, cut. *– bakar* slash and burn. *– habis* clear cutting. *– penyelamatan* salvage cutting. *– perawatan/pemeliharaan* salvage felling/cutting. *– sungkuran* grub felling (removing the roots). *– ulang* relogging.

menebang [and **nebang** (*coq*)] **1** to cut/chop down, fell, clear away (forest). **2** (*coq*) to knock down.

menebangi (*pl obj*) to cut down, etc.

tertebang felled.

tebangan 1 s.t. that has been felled. *~ pohon* felled tree. **2** cut.

penebang 1 logger. **2** tool for felling.

penebangan felling, cutting/chopping down, clearing, lumbering. *~ habis* clear cutting. *~ liar* illegal cutting.

tebang II (*burung*) *– mentua* helmeted hornbill, *Rhinoplax vigil*.

tebar (*Pers ob*) axe; → KAPAK I.

tébar I spread, scatter, disperse.

bertébar spread, scattered, dispersed. **kebertébaran** (*phys*) dispersion.

bertébaran (*pl subj*) **1** spread out, spread all over, lie scattered, lying about. *Majalah ~ di atas méja.* Magazines were scattered all over the table. **2** to look around (of one's glance).

menébar 1 to spread. **2** to spread s.t. **3** to cast (a net). *~ pandang* to look around.

menébari to spread/scatter on/in s.t. *Halaman ditebari kursi.* Chairs were scattered all over the yard.

menébarkan 1 to spread, distribute. **2** to exude, release. **3** to cast (a net). **4** to stock (fish in a pond). *~ pandang* to cast a glance around.

mempertébarkan to spread, disperse. *~ kécék* to spread lies.

tertébar 1 spread, scattered. **2** broadcast. *Matanya ~.* His eyes glanced around.

tébaran 1 s.t. spread. **2** spread. **3** seed. **4** circular, bulletin. *~ pandang* looking around.

ketébaran 1 spread. **2** (*phys*) dispersion.

penébar s.o. who or s.t. that spreads, disperser, dispersant, broadcaster. *~ isyu* rumormonger.

penébaran 1 spreading, dispersion, broadcasting. **2** restocking (fish in ponds).

pertébaran dispersion.

tébar II *– layar* triangular section covering the space between two crossing rafters.

tebas I (*Jv*) *– mentah* to ask s.o. for money equal in value to a gift in place of the gift itself.

menebas 1 to buy up before the harvest. **2** to buy up the entire crop. **3** to buy s.t. wholesale.

menebaskan to sell one's crop before it is harvested.

tebasan crop bought before it is harvested.

penebas 1 s.o. who buys crop before it is harvested. **2** wholesale purchaser.

tebas II menebas 1 to cut, clear away. *~ hutan* to clear the forest. *~ jalan* to cut a road. *~ menebang* to cut down and fell. **2** to cut out, cancel. *Pemerintah ~ delapan kerja sama bisnis.* The government cancelled eight joint business ventures.

menebasi 1 (*pl obj*) to cut, clear away. **2** to open (a road) by clearing.

menebaskan 1 to cut/clear away with/using. **2** to cut/clear away for s.o. else.

tertebas cut off.

tebasan s.t. cut/cleared away.

penebas cutter, clearer.

penebasan cutting, clearing (away).

tebat I 1 fish pond. **2** dam.

menebat 1 to dam up. **2** to make a pond by damming a stream.

penebatan 1 damming a stream. **2** making a pond by damming a stream.

tebat II insulator.

tebel → TEBAL I.

tébésé → TBC.

tébéng I protective screen (against the sun, etc.). *– jendéla* window screen. *– topi* sun brim.

menébéngi to screen, put up a screen on.

menébéng(kan) to put up (a screen) (against the sun).

tébéng II (*J*) **menébéng** [and **nébéng** (*coq*)] **1** to hitchhike. **2** to freeload, eat or drink, etc. with s.o. but not pay, mooch (cigarettes), get a free ride on; *~ ngetop* to become well known through s.o. else's actions. *Soal séminar, silakan Saudara Judi yang bicara, paling-paling saya nanti ~ ngetop di forum itu.* As for the seminars, you please speak, at the most I'll also become known in the forum (he said).

menébéngi to ride on s.t. for free, hitch a ride on.

menébéngkan to let s.o. get s.t. for nothing or live with you for free.

tébéng III menébéng to get a haircut.

tebengau k.o. shrub, *Ehretia timorensis*.

teberau a tall river reed, hardy sugarcane, *Erianthus/Saccharum arundinaceum*.

tebersih → TERBERSIH.

tebing 1 steep bank (of a river/the side of a mountain), escarpment. **2** slope. *– kawah* crater rim. *– laut* marine escarpment.

bertebing banked, sloped.

menebing to be abrupt, like a bank/slope.

menebingi to run along the bank (of a river, etc.).

tebir → TABIR I.

tébok I small tool for threshing rice.

menébok to hit hard.

tébok II menébok to strike, hit s.t. hard.

tebu sugarcane, *Saccharum officinarum. dapat – rebah* to get lucky. *– masuk di mulut gajah* completely destroyed, cannot be saved. *– betung* large sugarcane variety. *– biasa* milling cane. *– bibit* seed cane. *– gading* yellowing sugarcane. *– gajah* k.o. climbing plant, *Albizzia myriophylla*. – *hitam* black sugarcane. – *kapur* greenish sugarcane. – *keprasan* sucker growing from cut-down sugarcane. – *kera* k.o. herbaceous plant, *Forestia sp.* – *madu* a very sweet sugarcane variety. – *salah* hardy sugarcane, *Saccharum arundinaceum*. – *telur* sugarcane with green stalks. – *tunas* ratoons.

tebu-tebu k.o. design on hilt of kris, etc. which looks like sugarcane joints/bands.

bertebu jointed (similar to sugarcane joints).

bertebu-tebu jointed, banded.

menebu-nebu to make a design which looks like sugarcane joints.

tebuan → TABUHAN.

tebuk 1 small hole, perforation, eyelet. 2 perforated.

menebuk to pierce, perforate, bore into.

menebuki to perforate, pierce, drill a hole in.

tebukan drilled (hole).

penebuk drill, punch.

penebukan drilling, perforating, boring.

tebus I redeem.

menebus [and **nebus** (*coq*)] 1 to redeem, buy back, cash in. 2 to catch up on, make up for, compensate for. ~ *kekurangan tidur* to make up for one's sleep deficit. 3 to expiate, wipe out (one's sins). ~ *dosa* to expiate a sin. 4 to ransom. 5 to pay (s.o.) back for. 6 to get s.t. through sacrifice. ~ *darah* to seek revenge. ~ *janji* to fulfill a promise. ~ *kehormatan* to defend one's name. ~ *jiwa* to save s.o.'s life. ~ *kata* to keep one's word. ~ *kebaikan* to pay (s.o.) back for their kindness. ~ *kekalahan* to avenge o.s. ~ *nyawa* to save s.o.'s life. ~ *talak* to seek divorce by giving back the dowry. ~ *wésel* to cash in a money order.

menebusi to redeem, pay back. ~ *talak* to seek divorce by giving back the dowry.

menebuskan to expiate (one's sins, etc.).

tertebus 1 bought back, redeemed. 2 ransomed.

tebusan 1 s.t. used for buying back/redeeming/redemption. ~ *darah* revenge, vengeance, vendetta. 2 indemnification, compensation. 3 lump sum (payment).

ketebusan redemption.

penebus 1 redemptor, redeemer. *Sang* ~ the Redeemer, Christ. ~ *dosa* s.t. that makes up for past bad actions. 2 s.o. who pays a ransom or indemnification.

penebusan 1 redeeming, buying back, redemption. 2 making up for, catching up on. 3 expiation. 4 ransoming. 5 indemnification, compensation.

tebus II → TEMBUS.

tedak (*Jv*) – *siti* ceremony at which a child first touches the ground.

tedarus (*A*) recitation of the Koran.

bertedarus to recite the Koran.

tedas I clear, distinct, sharp, vivid.

tedas II rings or circles around a column.

tédéng (*Jv*) 1 screen. 2 sun hat. – *aling-aling* to cover up, hide a secret. *tanpa* – *aling-aling* frank, straightforward.

bertédéng(an) 1 screened, hidden, disguised, covered up. 2 on the sly.

teduh 1 sheltered, in the shade, shaded. 2 quiet, calm, died down (of the wind), stop (of heavy rain). 3 to drop (of a fever).

berteduh to take shelter. ~ *di bawah pohon* to take shelter under a tree. ~ *di bawah betung* to get insufficient help.

berteduhkan to make a shelter of, use s.t. as shelter, take shelter under. ~ *diri* to shelter o.s.

meneduh 1 to take shelter. 2 to calm down. 3 to be shady.

meneduhi 1 to shelter, provide shelter for, protect from the sun, etc. 2 to calm down.

meneduhkan 1 to shade, protect from the sun, etc. 2 to take shelter under. 3 to quiet, calm down.

teduhan shade, shelter.

keteduhan 1 shelter, shade. 2 quiet, calmness.

peneduh shelter, s.t. that provides shelter.

peneduhan 1 sheltering, shading. 2 quieting, calming down.

perteduhan shelter, place of shelter.

tedun (*Jv*) hernia.

tedung I → ULAR *tedung*.

tedung II → AYAM *tedung*.

téécu (*C ob*) (said to a superior) I, me.

tefakur and **tefekur** → TAFAKUR.

tég (*E*) tag.

téga (*Jv*) 1 to have the heart to, be able to bring o.s. to, bear to. 2 to do s.t. without thinking about the consequences. – *larané ora patiné* (*Jv*) to have the heart to see s.o.'s sufferings but not his death, the attempted blending of irreconcilable principles.

tegah prohibition, s.t. prohibited. – *larang* interdiction. – *suruh* interdictions and orders.

bertegah forbidden. *tempat* ~ forbidden places.

menegah(kan) to forbid, interdict, prevent.

tertegah forbidden, interdicted, prevented.

tegahan s.t. forbidden/interdicted/prevented.

penegah s.o. who forbids.

penegahan prohibition, interdiction, prevention.

tegak 1 erect, (standing) upright, vertical. *berdiri* – standing erect. 2 a stand (for holding s.t. upright). – *pada* to stick/hold firm to (one's position). -*nya kebenaran* upholding the truth. – *bulu kuduk/roma/tengkuk* one's hair stands on end. – *sama tinggi, duduk sama rendah* at the same level/rank. – *pada yang datang* firm (in beliefs, etc.). – *berdiri* to stand up straight. – *cancang* pointing upward. – *damar* torch stand. – *duduk* to get up and sit down again. – *kaku* rigid (of corpse). – *lurus* perpendicular, vertical, at right angles. – *lurus dengan kepala* straight overhead. – *sebagai alif* as straight as an arrow. – *sendiri* autonomous.

tegak-tegak 1 upright, erect. *berdiri* ~ to stand upright. 2 without much ado, just like that. *membunuh orang* ~ to kill s.o. just like that. *dijual* ~ and *tertipu* ~ to be tricked.

setegak as tall as s.o. standing up.

bertegak 1 to erect, put up. 2 to inaugurate, hold a ceremony putting s.o. into office. ~ *lutut* to sit with the knee up. ~ *nama* to hold a name-giving ceremony.

bersitegak to hold on to one's opinions.

menegak 1 upright. 2 to uphold, enforce.

menegakkan 1 to uphold/enforce (the law), maintain. 2 to raise (one's head, etc.), prick up (one's ears), turn/lift up, put in an upright position. 3 to erect, build. 4 to spread, propagandize for. 5 to straighten s.t. up, pick up s.t. that has fallen down. *ibarat* ~ *benang basah* to try to do s.t. that can't succeed, do s.t. that's a waste of time. ~ *bulu kuduk* to make one's hair stand on end. ~ *kebenaran* to uphold the truth. ~ *semangat* to inspire.

tertegak stood/standing bolt upright. *Dia* ~ *menunggu perintahnya.* He stood bolt upright waiting for orders.

tegakan 1 stand (of trees or for holding s.t.). ~ *mati* snag. ~ *sisa* residual stand. 2 standing upright.

ketegakan 1 upright position, being upright. 2 enforcement. 3 high position.

penegak 1 s.o. who erects, runs, enforces, upholds, maintains. ~ *hukum* law enforcement (agency/official). 2 founder. 3 member of the Pramuka Boy Scouts between 16 and 20 years of age.

penegakan 1 enforcement, enforcing, maintaining, upholding. ~ *hukum* law enforcement. 2 erecting, putting up.

pertegak sepertegak 1 as tall as s.o. standing up. 2 (*ob*) a set of clothes.

tegal I (*Jv cla*) because. – *sebab* for the reason that.

tegal II dry (not irrigated) field; (*opp*) *sawah*; → LADANG.

tegalan dry field.

penegalan cultivation in unirrigated fields.

tegal III k.o. sea fish, finny scad, *Megalaspis cordyla*.

Tegal Arum name of a train running between Tegal and Jakarta.

tegang 1 taut, tight. 2 stiff (of hair, muscles, neck), firm (of flesh), tough (of meat). 3 tense, strained, in suspense. – *syaraf* nervous, worried. 4 stubborn. 5 suspenseful. 6 erect (of one's penis).

ber(si)tegang 1 to refuse (to surrender), persevere, hold out to the end. 2 to be stubborn, obstinate. ~ *urat léhér* obstinate, stubborn.

menegang 1 to stiffen, become stiff/tense/tight/taut. 2 to have an erection. 3 to stretch.

menegangi to pull s.t. tight, tighten, make taut.

menegangkan 1 to tighten, stretch (tight), make taut. 2 to strain, make s.t. tense. 3 thrilling, exciting, suspenseful.

mempertegang(kan) to stiffen, make s.t. tight/tense.

tegangan 1 tension, stress, pressure. *dalam* ~ under tension. ~ *tarik* tensile strength. ~ *tekan* compressive strength. ~ *tinggi* high tension. 2 voltage; → VOLTASE. 3 (*biol*) potential. **bertegangan** with ... tension. ~ *tinggi* high-tension.

ketegangan 1 tightness, tenseness. 2 tension, voltage. 3 strain, stress, tense situation, suspense. ~ *jiwa* mental strain. ~ *mata* eyestrain. 4 erection (of one's penis).

persitegangan stubbornness.

pertegangan tension.

tegap I 1 sturdy, well-built. 2 firm, unshakable, determined. – *hati* firm, unshakable, determined. – *sasa/tegun* sturdy, strong.

menegapkan and **mempertegap** 1 to make sturdy. 2 to strengthen, firm up. ~ *badan* to stand at attention.

ketegapan 1 sturdiness. 2 firmness, determination.

penegap s.t. that strengthens, strengthener.

tegap II k.o. marine fish, wolf herring, *Chirocentrus dorab*.

tegar I 1 stiff (and dry), rigid, inflexible, unyielding. 2 obstinate, stubborn. 3 determined. – *hati* obstinate, stubborn. **bertegar hati** to be strong and resolved (in facing problems). **menegarkan hati** to stiffen one's resolve. ~ *kemudi* to stick to one's course. – *pelupuk mata* brave, courageous. – *tengkuk* obstinate, stubborn.

menegarkan to harden, stiffen.

ketegaran 1 stiffness, rigidity, inflexibility. 2 obstinacy, stubbornness. 3 determination.

tegar II menegarkan ~ *kemudi* to stick to one's course.

tegar III → TAGAR.

tegari (*J*) k.o. herbaceous plant with fragrant roots, *Dianella ensifolia*.

tegarun *kain* – k.o. silk fabric with gold threads.

tegas (*Jv*) 1 certain, sure, clear, obvious. 2 explicit, s.t. stated explicitly, s.t. stressed/asserted. 3 distinct (difference). –*nya* a) he asserted. b) in other words, to state it more clearly/explicitly. **bersikap** – to take a strong position, be assertive. *dengan* – clearly, firmly, flatly (refuse/deny), emphatically. *secara* – expressly, explicitly. 4 firm, resolute, tough. *langkah yang* – a firm step. *tidak* – indistinct, uncertain, not explicit. **ketidaktegasan** indistinctness, lack of certainty, lack of explicitness. – *bergas* (right) to the point, state explicitly, assert. – *ringkas* brief but explicit.

tegasnya in short/brief.

bertegas 1 to be clear. 2 to confirm.

menegas to firm up.

menegasi to confirm, stress.

menegaskan 1 to clarify, explain. 2 to insist, assert, state explicitly, articulate. 3 to confirm, affirm. 4 to stress, emphasize, underscore.

mempertegas(kan) 1 to stress. 2 to confirm.

ketegasan 1 assertion, explicit statement. 2 firmness, resoluteness. 3 emphasis, stress.

penegasan 1 explicit assertion. 2 clarifying, clarification. 3 determination. 4 confirmation, affirmation.

pertegasan 1 definition. 2 confirmation, affirmation. 3 emphasis.

tegel (*Jv*) to be able to do s.t. that is disgusting/despicable. – *hati* resolute.

tégel (*D*) floor tile. – *marmer* marble tile. – *porselin* wall tile.

bertégel lined with tiles.

menégel to tile.

tégelté (*D*) tea in bricks.

tégenpréstasi (*D*) consideration, quid pro quo, s.t. given in exchange.

tegep → TEGAP I.

teges → TEGAS.

tegil (*J*) cock's spur.

bertegil to have such a spur.

tegor → TEGUR.

teguh 1 firm, strong. *keyakinan yang* – a firm conviction. 2 unwavering, tenacious. 3 dependable. 4 close (of relations). *yang – disokong, yang rebah ditindih* the strong get helped and the weak get crushed. *tidak* – unstable. **ketidak-teguhan** instability. – *hati* firm, resolute. – *(dalam) iman* firm in one's faith. – *setianya* always loyal.

seteguh-teguhnya 1 with all one's might. 2 as firm/dependable as possible.

ber(si)teguh to stick to one's guns, stand firm, hold to ...ing s.t.

berteguh-teguhan to strengthen e.o. ~ *janji* to reaffirm their promises to e.o.

meneguhkan and **memperteguh(kan)** 1 to strengthen, make firmer. *Teguhkan iman*. Don't be discouraged. 2 to confirm, reaffirm. **meneguhkan kembali** to reconfirm.

terteguh the firmest.

keteguhan 1 firmness, strength, resistance. ~ *belah* split resistance. ~ *gésér* slip resistance. ~ *hati* resolution, perseverance. ~ *iman* unwavering faith. ~ *lentur* warp resistance. ~ *pukul* resistance to blows. ~ *tekan* pressure resistance. 2 stability. 3 dependability.

peneguh s.o. who supports, stands behind.

peneguhan confirming, strengthening, making more resolute, stabilizing.

teguk I gulp, swallow.

seteguk one gulp, a mouthful.

meneguk to gulp (down).

meneguki (*pl obj*) to gulp down repeatedly.

tegukan gulp, swallow.

ketegukan to swallow s.t. the wrong way.

teguk II stubborn.

teguk III → TETAGUK.

tegun static.

setegun for a moment.

bertegun and **menegun** to stop for a moment.

menegunkan to stop s.t., stop s.o. in his tracks.

tertegun to stop suddenly, stupefied, (struck) speechless. **ketertegunan** being startled/struck speechless.

tertegun-tegun to start and stop, keep stopping, falter, stall.

tegunan stupefaction, amazement.

tegur way of opening a conversation, greeting. – *ajar* admonition, warning. – *sapa* way of greeting s.o. or of starting a conversation. **bertegur sapa** to have conversations (with), talk (to). **menegur sapa** to talk to.

bertegur(an) to talk to e.o., converse. ~ *dahulu maka berkenalan* you don't get to know s.t. until you experience it.

menegur [and **negur** (*coq*)] 1 to start a conversation (with), greet. *pandai* – *orang* to be affable. 2 to issue a warning to, admonish, remind. 3 to criticize. *ditegur hantu* bothered by an evil spirit.

meneguri 1 to talk to. 2 to admonish, remind.

menegur-neguri to examine s.o. to discover whether he/she is ill because of an evil spirit.

teguran 1 greeting. 2 warning, notice, notification. ~ *lisan* oral warning. ~ *tertulis* written notice/warning. 3 criticism.

keteguran bothered by/become ill due to an evil spirit.

penegur 1 s.o. who speaks. 2 s.o. who admonishes.

peneguran warning, admonition.

téh I (*C*) tea, *Camellia sinensis*. – *bohéa* broken tea. – *botol* bottled tea. – *bungkus* teabag. – *celup* teabag. – *daun* whole-leaf tea. – *és* iced tea. – *hijau* green tea. – *hitam* black tea. – *hutan/kampung* k.o. shrub, *Acalypha siamensis*. – *kosong* (*Mal*) unsweetened tea. – *kotak* tea in a carton. – *makau* k.o. herbaceous plant, broom weed, sweet broom, *Scorparia dulcis*. – *manis* sweetened tea, tea with sugar. – *pahit* a) (*J*) beverage made from certain roots and used as an aphrodisiac. b) unsweetened tea. – *pucuk* pekoe tea. – *susu* tea with cream or milk. – *tawar* unsweetened tea. – *tubruk* tea made by pouring boiling water over tea leaves. – *uncang* tea made using teabags.

téh II (*S*) particle showing the previous old information is stressed. *Siapa wanita yang cantik tadi* – Who was that beautiful woman?

téhel → TÉGEL.

téhnik and **téhnis** (*D*) → TÉKNIK.

téhnikus → TÉKNIKUS.

téhnisi (*D*) → TÉKNISI.

téhnokrasi technocracy.

téhnokrat technocrat.

téhnokratis technocratic.

téhnologi → TÉKNOLOGI.

téja (*Skr*) 1 red, yellow, or orange sunset clouds. 2 rainbow. 3 first part of some plant names. – *badak* k.o. plant, wild cinnamon, roots used as medicine, *Cinnamomum iners*. – *betina* k.o. tree, its wood is used for furniture, *Neolitsea zeylanica*. – *keluang* glow in the sky after a storm. – *lawang* → TÉJA *badak*. – *membangun* vertical rainbow. – *pasir* → TÉJA *betina*.

téji (*Pers*) swift (of horses).

ték I → KETÉK I.

ték II → (KE)TIK I.

teka → TERKA.

Tékab [Team Khusus Anti-Banditisme] Special Anti-bandit Team.

tékad (*A*) determination, resolution, will. – *bulat* firm determination.

setékad in agreement.

bertékad to be determined, with a firm purpose, resolute, committed to. ~ *baja* to be totally determined. ~ *bulat* resolute. ~ *hati* determined, resolved. ~ *mantap* to make a determined effort to.

menékadkan to determine, be determined that (s.o. do s.t.). ~ *diri* to determine, resolve.

ketékadan determination, resolution.

penékadan being committed to.

tekah k.o. gibbon, *Hylobates leuciscus*.

tekak I 1 soft palate, velum, pharynx. *anak* – uvula. 2 (after)taste (in the mouth). *tak sedap –nya* unpalatable, unpleasant to the taste. *kering –nya* thirsty. *umpan* – appetizer. *payau/langu –nya* unpleasant tasting. – *haus/kering* a dry throat.

bertekak 1 to have a pharynx, etc. 2 to quarrel, argue.

menekak (a taste that) stays in the mouth. *manis* ~ a sweet aftertaste.

tekak II (*cla*) fanatical, stubborn, obstinate.

tekam k.o. tree, *Shorea collina*.

tekan press, pressure.

bertekan and **bersitekan** to lean (on). ~ *lutut* to lean on one's knees. ~ *pinggang* with arms akimbo.

menekan [and **nekan** (*coq*)] 1 to press (down on). ~ *gas* to step on the gas. 2 to reduce, drive/hold down, cut down on, exert downward pressure on. ~ *harga produksi* to drive down production costs. 3 to suppress, oppress, repress. 4 to pressure, force. 5 to emphasize, stress. ~ *perasaan/perut* to keep one's feelings under control. 6 to compress into a shorter amount of time.

menekan-nekan to keep on pressing on.

menekankan [and **nekanin** (*J coq*)] 1 to stress, emphasize. 2 to push down with/using, press.

tertekan 1 pressed/pushed down, depressed. 2 driven down, reduced, lowered. 3 depressed (psychologically). 4 suppressed, oppressed.

tertekan-tekan to start and stop.

tekanan 1 pressure. ~ *darah* blood pressure. ~ *dasar (lubang)* bottom hole pressure (in mining). ~ *inflasi* inflationary pressure. ~ *jiwa* (psychological) stress. ~ *julang* uplift pressure. ~ *ke atas* uplift. ~ *kempa* pressure. ~ *knop* a press of the button. ~ *lawan* back pressure. ~ *méntal* psychological pressure. ~ *nadi* pulse. ~ *sosial* social pressure. ~ *sukat* gauge pressure. ~ *tegun* static pressure. ~ *tinggi* high-pressure. ~ *tumpu* abutment pressure. ~ *udara* air/atmospheric pressure. 2 strain, stress, pressure. 3 thrust (of an argument). 4 (*ling*) stress, accent. ~ *bunyi* stress, accent. 5 domination, oppression. **bertekanan** with ... pressure. 2 stressed, accented.

penekan 1 pressure (*mod*). *kelompok* ~ pressure group. 2 leverage. ~ *paking* packing gland.

penekanan 1 pressure, pressuring, pressurization. 2 driving down, cutting down (on), reducing, lowering. 3 emphasis, stress, thrust. 4 accenting, stressing.

tékan → TÉKEN.

tekang crossbeam.

menekang to put a crossbeam on.

tekap closed, plugged. – *kepala* head covering. – *mulut* gag. *bertekap* and *menekap mulut* to cover one's mouth. – *sampan* cover for a boat.

bertekap to cover.

menekap to close, plug (up). ~ *telinga* to close one's ears.

menekapi to cover, close up, plug up.

menekapkan to cover s.t. with, use s.t. as a cover.

tertekap sealed off.

tekapan 1 s.t. used as a cover(ing), covering. 2 dome, cupola.

tekar-takih obstacle, obstruction.

tekat embroidery. – *berakam* embroidery using gold thread. – *berawan* embroidery with cloud-like motif. – *bersuji* embroidery using silk thread. – *bertekat* flower motif at edge of embroidery. – *timbul* raised embroidery.

bertekat embroidered. ~ *emas* with gold embroidery.

bertekatkan embroidered with.

menekat to embroider.

tekatan 1 s.t. that has been embroidered. 2 embroidery.

tékat → TÉKAD.

teka-teki riddle, puzzle. – *jenaka* tricky puzzle. – *silang* crossword puzzle.

berteka-teki to play/ask riddles.

tékdung (*coq*) 1 homemade rifle. 2 (*J*) pregnant out of wedlock.

téké (*sl*) Special Anti-bandit Team.

tekebur → TAKBUR.

tekek (*J*) stupid.

tékék → TOKÉK I.

tékék (*M*) **menékék** to hit with the knuckles.

tékel menékel to handle, deal with, work on.

penékelan and **pertékelan** handling, dealing with, working on.

tekelék (*Jv*) wooden clog.

tékelok → TÉKLOK.

teken → TEKAN. **neken** to take ecstasy orally.

téken (*D*) 1 signature; to sign. – *kontrak* to execute/sign a contract. – *mati* ready to risk one's life. 2 drawing, sketch.

menéken [and **néken** (*coq*)] to sign. ~ *serdadu* to sign on (for *mil* service).

tékenan 1 signature. 2 signing on (for *mil* service). 3 signed (by s.o.). *surat* ~ *X* a letter signed by X. 4 drawing, sketch, picture.

penéken signer, signatory.

penékenan signing.

tekep → TEKAP.

téker (*batu* –) flint.

menéker to light with a flint.

tékeran flint.

tékhnik and **tékhnis** → TÉKNIK.

teki I k.o. grass with edible tubers, purple nut sedge, *Cyperus rotundus*. – *bodoh/rawa* k.o. herbaceous plant, *Killinga sp.*

teki II → TEKA-TEKI.

tekik I cigarette butt; → PUNTUNG *rokok*.

tekik II **menekik** to split; → TAKIK.

tekik III (*Jv*) k.o. plant, *Albizia lebbekoides*.

tekis 1 very close, almost but not quite. – *tertabrak* almost hit. 2 too near the edge (in sewing).

teklak-teklik (*onom*) clicking sounds.

teklak-tekluk (*Jv*) bobbing/nodding up and down.

teklék → TEKELÉK.

téklok (*J*) exhausted.

téknik 1 (*D*) engineering. 2 (*E*) technique. 3 technical. – *arsitéktur* architectural engineering. – *bangunan* structural engineering. – *éléktro* electrical engineering. – *industri* industrial engineering. – *kelautan* marine engineering. – *keséhatan* sanitary engineering. – *kimia* chemical engineering. – *listrik* electrical engineering. – *penerbangan* aeronautical engineering. – *perkapalan* marine engineering. – *sipil* civil engineering. – *terbang* aerial techniques.

ketéknikan engineering.

téknikus (*D*) technician.

téknis (*D*) technical; engineered.

téknisi (*D*) technician. – *minyak bor* mud engineers (in mining).

téknokrat (*E*) technocrat.

téknokratis (*D*) technocratic.

téknologi (*D/E*) technology, engineering. – *madya* mid-level technology. – *maju* advanced technology. – *tepat-guna* appropriate technology. – *tinggi* high-tech.

bertéknologi with ... technology. ~ *canggih* with sophisticated technology, high technology.

téknologis (*D*) technological.
téknologiwan techie.
téko(an) (*C*) tea pot.
tékoh (*C?*) warehouse.
    tékohan warehouse keeper.
tekokak (*S*) k.o. shrub, *Solanum tarvum*; → **TERUNG** *pipit*.
tekong internode; → **RUAS**.
tékong I (*C*) **1** ship's captain under the orders of the owner. **2** (*Mal*) "coyote," hustler who assists Indonesians entering Malaysia illegally.
    menékongi to run such an operation. *Meréka bergerak dengan boat yang ditékongi Adam.* They moved in a boat run by Adam.
tékong II → **TIKUNG**.
tekor (*D*) shortfall, deficit.
    ketekoran 1 shortage, deficit. ~ *neraca perdagangan* trade deficit. **2** to be short of. *Saya* ~ *uang.* I'm short of money.
tekoran (*J*) dipper made of banana leaves or palm spathe; → **TAKIR**.
tékpai (*C*) dowry.
tékpi (*C?*) trident.
téks (*E*) text. – *bawah* subtitle. **menéks-bawahi** to subtitle.
tékstil (*D/E*) textile.
    pertékstilan textile (*mod*). *Asosiasi* ~ *Indonésia* Indonesian Textile Association [API].
tékstur (*E*) texture.
tékté (*C*) key money.
ték-ték I (*onom*) tapping sound.
tékték II → **TÉTÉK**.
téktonik(a) (*E*) and **téktonis** (*D*) (*geol*) tectonic.
    ketéktonikan tectonics.
tekua (*Jv*) *baju* – k.o. long sleeveless vest.
tekuk I (*J/Jv*) **1** bent over, folded. **2** (*geol*) knick point. – *lutut* bend the knee. **bertekuk lutut 1** to bend at the knee. **2** to submit, surrender. **3** to do whatever s.o. wishes. **menekuk-lututkan** to force (s.o.) to his knees, subdue. – *simpuh* kneeling. **bertekuk simpuh** to kneel down. ~ *tangan* a) to fold one's arms across one's chest. b) to sit around and do nothing.
    menekuk 1 to bend over, fold (s.t. stiff). **2** to arrest, collar.
    menekukkan to bend s.t. ~ *lutut* to do knee bends. ~ *pinggang* to do waist bends.
    tertekuk bent over, folded over.
    tekukan 1 bend, fold. **2** tool for bending/folding.
tekuk II k.o. marine fish, croaker, *Halieutia stellata*.
tekukur (– *api*) little cuckoo dove, *Macropygia ruficeps malayana*. – *api besar/gunung* bar-tailed cuckoo dove, *Macropygia unchall*. – *jawa* colored turtledove, *Turtur risorius/bitorquatus*. – *jerum* Malay spotted dove, *Streptopelia chinensis tigrina*. – *merbuk* barred ground dove, *Geopelia striata*.
tekun persevering, zealous, hardworking, diligent, dedicated.
    bertekun 1 to be diligent/hardworking. **2** to adhere strongly to (one's *adat*, etc.).
    menekuni and **menekunkan** to go deeply into, study seriously, work hard at, put one's mind to, be devoted to.
    tertekun to persevere (at), hardworking.
    tekunan application, zeal.
    ketekunan persistence, zeal, perseverance, diligence, application, intensity.
    penekun devotee.
    penekunan diligence, working hard at.
tekung joint (of sugarcane/bamboo, etc.).
tekup → **TEKAP**. **tertekup** (*geol*) superimposed.
tekur bent down/over, bowed (of the head).
    menekur 1 to bow one's head. **2** to meditate.
    menekuri to look down at, bend one's head over (in working on s.t.). ~ *masalah* to bend one's head over a problem.
    menekurkan to bow (one's head).
    tertekur bowed (of the head).
tékwan (*C*) k.o. soup containing *pémpék*, noodles, etc.
tékyan (*sl*) street child; → **ANAK** *jalanan*.
tél I (*D ob*) number (in counting).
tél II (*abbr*) → **TÉLEPON**.
tela (*ob*) woman's pavilion in a palace compound.
téla I → **KETÉLA**.

téla II fact, specification.
    pertélaan list, register, proceedings, description.
téla III pan of an old-fashioned gun.
telaah (*A*) study, research. – *kelayakan/keterlaksanaan* feasibility study. – *perbandingan* comparative study. – *ulang* review.
    men(t)elaah 1 to study, do research on, scrutinize. **2** to predict, forecast.
    telahaan 1 study, research. **2** review.
    penelaah researcher.
    penelaahan 1 study, research. ~ *terbatas akuntan* accountant's partial audit. **2** review.
telabang k.o. long shield; → **TAMÉNG**.
telabat (*ob*) walking in a respectful way when approaching the king.
    bertelabat to walk in that way.
telacak footprint.
teladan model, s.t. or s.o. to be emulated.
    meneladan to follow the example of, emulate.
    meneladani to set an example for.
    meneladankan to make s.t. an example, provide a model for.
    keteladanan being exemplary. *hal* ~ *berbahasa Indonésia* being exemplary in speaking Indonesia.
teladas low rapids.
telaga (*Skr*) **1** lake, pond. **2** pit, well. – *di bawah gunung* a woman who brings good fortune to her husband. – *mencari timba* a woman looking for a man. – *tahi* cesspool.
telah I marker of past time. *Dia* – *meninggal dunia.* He has passed away.
    setelah after.
telah II (*J?*) **menelah(kan)** to predict, forecast.
    penelah forecaster, predictor.
    penelahan forecast, prophesy, prediction.
telak (*J*) **1** sharp-sighted. **2** clear, distinct, exact. **3** right on target, right, exactly, accurate, precise. *kena tebak* – to guess right. *kalah* – to be roundly defeated. *menang* – *atas* to score a definite victory over.
    tertelak hit right on the spot.
telakan → **TELEKAN**.
telampung → **PELAMPUNG**. **1** k.o. raft, float, buoy. **2** flotsam.
telan swallow.
    menelan [and **nelan** (*coq*)] **1** to swallow, take (a pill). **2** to cost. ~ *biaya sebanyak Rp 10.000,00* to cost Rp 10,000.00. ~ *korban* to claim victims. ~ *korban luka-luka* to injure. ~ *korban téwas* to kill. **3** to destroy, gut; to defeat. *Rumah itu ludes ditelan jago mérah.* The house was gutted by fire. *ditelan usia* out of date, antiquated. ~ *ludah* to gulp down one's saliva from fear or anxiety. ~ *mentah-mentah* to defeat, beat. **4** to take (insults, time, etc.). *ditelan mentah-mentah* tricked, taken in. ~ *pil pahit* to have to swallow a bitter pill (because of defeat/criticism). ~ *waktu* to take time.
    menelani (*pl obj*) to swallow.
    tertelan [and **ketelan** (*coq*)] **1** swallowed (by accident). **2** taken, used up, consumed. **3** caught up (in the current of events).
    penelan s.o. who swallows (up).
    penelanan swallowing.
télan small worm or worm-like fish.
Telanaipura appellation for Jambi.
telancang k.o. bird, mangrove brown babbler, *Aethostoma rostratum*.
telang I 1 (*buluh* –) k.o. bamboo, *Gigantochlea spp.* **2** (*bunga* –) k.o. climbing plant with blue flowers, butterfly pea, *Clitoria ternatea*.
telang II striped, streaked.
    bertelang-telang striped.
telangkai I marriage broker, intermediary for marriage, go-between.
    menelangkai to ask for a girl's hand in marriage on behalf of s.o.
    penelangkaian asking for a girl's hand in marriage on behalf of s.o.
telangkai II menelangkai to attack.
telangkup → **TELUNGKUP**.
telanjang 1 naked. **2** bare, uninsulated. *kabel* – a bare wire. *dijual* – sold without a tax stamp (of cigarettes). – *bogél/bugil/bulat/loncos* stark naked. – *kaki* barefoot. **bertelanjang kaki** to go barefoot.

bertelanjang 1 to be naked. ~ *dada* to bare one's chest, go topless. 2 unsheathed (of a kris).

menelanjangi [and **nelanjangin** (*J coq*)] 1 to strip naked, undress. 2 to expose, uncover, unmask. 3 to reveal (a secret). 4 to strip s.o. of all his possessions.

ketelanjangan nudity, being naked.

penelanjangan baring, stripping (naked), denuding, undressing.

telanjur (*Jv*) 1 to have gone too far, cannot be undone. *Itu sudah –.* It's all over now. 2 premature, overhasty.

ketelanjuran 1 extremely. *Ia ~ nakalnya.* He's extremely naughty. 2 having gone too far, extreme behavior.

telantar 1 abandoned, neglected. 2 miserable, suffering.

menelantarkan to abandon, neglect.

ketelantaran neglect.

penelantaran neglecting, abandonment.

telap I 1 permeable. 2 vulnerable (usually with a negative). *tidak – * invulnerable. 3 sharp enough (to cut s.t.).

menelap 1 to permeate, soak into. 2 to penetrate (of a weapon).

tertelapkan permeable.

telapan permeation.

ketelapan permeability.

telap II → HARIMAU *telap*.

telap III and **telapa** small box, casket (for tobacco, etc.).

telapak palm, sole. *sebagai – tangannya sendiri* at one's fingertips. *tidak semudah membalik – tangan* not as easy as that, it's not so easy. *– ban* tire tread. *– kaki* a) sole. b) lowest step on stairs. *– kembar* dual tread, two-ply. *– kuda* horseshoe. *– tangan* palm.

menelapak to measure s.t. with the span of the hand.

telapakan palm, sole.

telas petelasan base.

telasak menelasak to make one's way (into/across, etc.). ~ *masuk ke* to make one's way into.

telasih (*Jv*) → SELASIH I.

telat (*D*) too late, overdue, tardy, late (of menstruation). *– dua minggu* two weeks late (and so might be pregnant). *– datang* to arrive late. *– membayar* delinquent.

ketelatan lateness, tardiness.

telatah I (*Jv*) district, region, territory.

telatah II 1 mannerisms, ways, idiosyncrasies, behavior. 2 evidence.

telatap hut for spending the night in the woods.

telatén (*J/Jv*) 1 patient, persevering. 2 painstakingly, carefully.

menelaténi 1 to be painstaking/persevering in ...ing. 2 (*sl*) to have sex with.

ketelaténan patience, perseverance.

telau patchy (of light, coloring), with spots or stains (of color).

bertelau(-telau) 1 spotted, spotty, with lighter stains of color, patchy. 2 uneven, not all the same stage.

télé I (*M?*) **bertélé(-télé)** long-winded, long and trivial.

télé II (*D*) tulle.

télé III (*M*) stupid.

teledék → TLÉDÉK.

teledor (*Port*) careless, neglectful.

men(t)eledorkan to be careless about, neglect.

keteledoran 1 carelessness, negligence. 2 default, failure to pay.

teledu badger, *Mydaus meliceps*.

telefon → TÉLEPON.

teléfoni telephony.

teléfonis (*D*) 1 telephonically. 2 telephone operator.

teléfoto telephoto.

télégraf → TÉLÉGRAP.

télégrafi (*D*) telegraphy.

télégrafis (*D*) 1 telegraphist. 2 telegraphically.

telegram and **télégram** (*D*) telegram.

menélegram to telegram.

telegrap and **télégrap** (*D*) telegraph.

télégrapis → TÉLÉGRAFIS.

téléjénik (*E*) telegenic.

telek → TELAK.

telék (*Jv*) chicken droppings. *– lencung* watery chicken droppings.

telekan *– lutut* to lean with one's hands on one's knees. *– pinggang* arms akimbo.

bertelekan 1 to lean forward with both hands, 2 to lean on s.t.

---

bersitelekan to hold onto (with the hands).

menelekankan to place part of the body (on).

telekap → TEKAP.

télékomunikasi (*D*) telecommunications.

pertélékomunikasian (*mod*) telecommunications.

téléks (*D*) telex.

teleku berteleku to lean on one's elbows.

telekung a short white veil worn by Muslim women during prayers.

telekup → TEKUP.

telempap handbreadth.

setelempap a handbreadth.

bertelempap to measure, assess.

menelempap to measure (with the hand).

menelempapkan to put (one's hands on).

telémpong (*M*) a percussion instrument.

bertelémpong to play such an instrument.

telen → TELAN.

telenan → TALENAN.

teleng I (*Jv*) pupil (of the eye). *jadi –nya* to become the center of one's attention.

teleng II → TELANG I.

téléng turned at an angle, cocked, crossed (of the eyes). *– telinga* to prick up one's ears.

menélengi to be at an angle to.

menélengkan to turn s.t. so that it is at an angle.

tertéléng(-téléng) at an angle.

telengkup → TELUNGKUP.

telentang face/front part facing upward, on one's back.

menelentang to lie, etc. with the face/front part upward, lie, etc. on one's back.

menelentangkan to place s.t. face/front part upward, place on its back.

tertelentang lying face upwards, on one's back.

telep (*sl*) pilfer.

telepa → SELEPA(H).

télépati (*D*) telepathy.

télépisi → TÉLÉVISI.

télépok and **télépok** water lily, *Nymphaea stellata. – mérah/putih* lotus, *Nymphaea lotus.*

télepon and **télépon** (*D*) 1 telephone. 2 (tele)phone call. *Ada – untuk anda.* There's a phone call for you. *Sejumlah – datang ke kantornya.* A number of phone calls came in to his office. *Masih –?* Are you still on the phone? *meletakkan pesawat –nya* to hang up the phone. *mengambil/mengangkat gagang –* to pick up the phone. *buku (petunjuk) –* telephone book, directory. *kantor –* telephone office. *kawat –* telephone wire. *kios –* telephone booth. *mesin penjawab –* telephone answering machine. *pembicaraan (léwat) –* telephone conversation. *penyambung –* telephone operator. *percakapan (léwat) –* telephone conversation. *pesawat –* telephone instrument. *sél –* telephone booth. *– bébas pulsa* toll-free call. *– bergerak* mobile phone. *– digital* digital phone. *– éngkol* old-fashioned, crank-operated telephone. *Hubungan dengan – éngkol, seperti yang sudah-sudah, mémang tidak memadai.* Communications with old-fashioned, crank-operated telephones, as in the past, are really unsatisfactory. *– genggam* hand/cell phone. *– interlokal* long-distance call. *– intérn* intercom. *– jinjing* portable phone. *– kepala* headphone. *– kepala awal* the first three digits of a seven-digit telephone number, excluding the area code. *– koboi* old-fashioned, crank-operated telephone. *– langsung* hotline. *– mobil* car phone. *– mobil sélular* cellular car phone. *– ontélan* old-fashioned, crank-operated telephone. *– pencét putar* pushbutton dial-system telephone. *– radio* radiophone. *– saku* handset. *– sélular* [ponsél] cellular phone, cell phone. *– tangan* cellular phone. *– tanpa kabel* cordless/wireless telephone. *– tetap* fixed line. *– tidur* a) a telephone left behind by the occupant in a vacated house. b) a telephone as a show piece and status symbol. c) suspended service due to lack of payment. *– udara* sky-phone. *– umum* public telephone. *– vidéo* videophone.

bertélepon 1 to have a telephone. 2 to talk over the telephone; → BERHALO-HALO. *Soeharto-Mahathir akan ~ jarak jauh.* Soeharto-Mahathir will make a long-distance call.

bertélepon-téleponan to telephone e.o., make phone calls.

menélepon [and **nélepon** (*coq*)] to telephone, call s.o. (on the telephone).

menéleponkan to call on s.o.'s behalf.

penélepon (telephone) caller.

pertéléponan 1 telephone system. 2 telephone (*mod*).

téléprinter (*D*) teleprinter.

telepuk *kain* – glazed linen stamped with a gilt pattern from wooden blocks; → TELÉPOK. – *serasah* k.o. fabric made in India.

bertelepuk to have that k.o. fabric.

bertelepukkan to be stamped with ... in that k.o. pattern.

télepun → TÉLEPON.

télér I foul discharge from an infected ear.

télér II (*J/Jv*) 1 drunk, high (on drugs) *Penyalahgunaan obat-obatan keras bisa membuat pemakainya menjadi* –. Drug abuse can intoxicate the user. 2 to use drugs, be a drug addict. 3 dizzy with exhaustion.

télér-téléran to be dead drunk.

télér III *és* – k.o. soft ice (with bits of jackfruit and other fruits).

télerama a TV program involving rhythmic music and dance.

telesan (*Jv*) clothing worn while bathing in public.

téléskop (*D*) telescope.

teléték menelétékan to drop, let fall.

telétong (*Jv*) dung, manure.

télevisi and **télévisi** (*D*) television. – *12 inci* a 12-inch television. – *berwarna* a color TV set. – *hitam-putih* black-and-white television. – *jaringan* network television. – *kabel* cable television. – *komérsial* commercial television. – *komunitas* community television. – *layar lébar* wide-screen television. – *lingkup dekat* closed-circuit TV – *lokal* local television. – *pendidikan* educational television. – *publik* public television. – *warna* color television.

bertélévisi to have a TV set.

men(t)élévisikan to televise.

penélévisian televising.

pertélévisian television business, television (*mod*).

télgram → TÉLEGRAM.

telik (*S*) sharp (of vision). – *sandi* secret intelligence, spies.

menelik to observe, check on.

penelik spy, observer.

telikung (*Jv*) **menelikung(kan)** to fasten, tie up (hands and feet).

telimpuh (*ob*) **bertelimpuh** to sit with the legs bent backward.

telimpung → TELÉMPONG.

telinak k.o. climbing plant, *Gnetum tenuifolium*.

telinga I 1 ear. 2 handle (of a jar, etc.). 3 loop (of curtains). 4 one's attention. *mampir di – saya* that's come to my attention. *Itu sampai ke -ku.* That's come to my attention. *melébarkan –* to prick up one's ears, listen attentively. *memasang/memberi –* to listen attentively. *masuk – kiri, keluar – kanan* to go in one ear and out the other. *– rabit dipasang subung* out of place. *– bedil* (*ob*) pan of a gun. *– berok* ears that are close to the head. *– biola* tuning pegs. *– dalam* inner ear. *– gajah* big ears. *– jebang* ears that stick out. *– kambing* ears that stick up. *– kuali* a) handles of a pan. b) s.o. who is thick skinned. **bertelinga kuali** to have ears but not hear (what one is told). *– kucing* ears that stick up. *– luar* external ear. *– panas* one's ears are burning (hearing s.t.). *– panci* panhandle. *– putus* detached ear. *(ber) – rawah* (be) s.o. who won't listen to advice. *– rusa* ears that stick up. *– telepok layu* beautiful ears. *– tempayan* said of s.o. who doesn't want to listen. *– tengah* middle ear. *– tipis* touchy, overly sensitive. **bertelinga tipis** to be touchy, overly sensitive.

bertelinga to have ears, with ears. *~ lembut* stupid. *~ mérah* thick-skinned.

penelinga auditory.

telinga II first part of the names of some plants and animals. *– anjing* mother-of-pearl oyster. *– badak*, k.o. plant, *Cryptocoryne griffithii*. *– gajah*, coral-reef fish, *Platax teira*. *– ke(le)lawar* k.o. plant, *Thottea grandiflora*. *– kerbau* balsam plant, *Blumea balsamifera*; → SEMBUNG. *– tikus* black mushroom, Judas ear, *Auricularia auricula judae*.

telingkah 1 (*ob*) conduct, behavior. 2 incompatible.

bertelingkah to disagree, dispute, argue, quarrel.

ketelingkahan incompatibility.

pertelingkahan disagreement, dispute, quarrel.

telingkung – *daun* k.o. rattan, *Calamus javensis*.

telingkup → TELUNGKUP.

telisik → SELISIK I.

teliti careful, thorough. *– sebelum membeli* caveat emptor. *kurang* – careless. **kekurang-telitian** carelessness. *– penuh* check and recheck.

meneliti to examine, investigate, look into, study. *diteliti* under study. *~ kembali/ulang* to reexamine.

memperteliti to look carefully at, scrutinize.

terteliti most carefully examined.

ketelitian 1 investigation. 2 carefulness.

peneliti investigator, researcher, surveyor.

penelitian research, investigation, survey, checking, assay. *~ dasar* basic research. *~ guna* applied research. *~ lapangan* fieldwork. *~ mula* preliminary survey. *~ pembukuan* auditing. *~ permulaan* pilot study. *~ pustaka* library research. *~ silang* cross-checking. *~ tanah* soil survey. *~ terapan* applied research.

Télkom [Télékomunikasi] telecommunications.

télmi (*BG*) [telat mikir] slow thinking, stupid.

telon → MINYAK *telon*.

telor → TELUR I.

télor having an accent (in speech) or a speech defect.

ketéloran speech defect.

télp (*abbr*) [télepon] telephone.

télpon → TÉLEPON.

telu (*Jv*) three.

telu(h) (*Jv*) 1 black magic. 2 killing by black magic. *– braja* a) magic power. b) shooting star, meteorite.

meneluh 1 to hex, put a spell on. 2 to kill by black magic.

peneluhan 1 hexing, putting a spell on. 2 killing by black magic.

teluk I gulf, bay. *jadi – ulakan air* to go round and round in circles. *– Bayur* port of Padang. *– Benggala* Bay of Bengal. *– Cenderawasih* Bird of Paradise Bay. *– Iran* Persian Gulf. *– Parsi* Persian Gulf. *– rantau* a) region, district. b) bends and reaches (of a river), bends in a river. *– Yos Sudarso* the former Humboldt Baai.

berteluk-teluk with many bays.

meneluk to curve around like a bay.

teluk II (*M*) – *belanga* a collarless Malay shirt.

teluk III berteluk to kneel.

teluki I k.o. silk.

teluki II 1 k.o. herbaceous plant, beach sunflower, *Wedelia biflora*. 2 pinkish white.

telukup → TELUNGKUP.

telumpang menelumpang to overlap.

telungkup lying facedown.

menelungkup to lie facedown.

menelungkupi to lie facedown on.

menelungkupkan to place s.t. facedown, turn s.t. over.

tertelungkup (suddenly fall, etc.) facedown, flat on one's face. *Dia jatuh ~.* He fell facedown.

penelungkupan laying (one's body) facedown.

telunjuk index finger. *– lurus kelingking berkait* to have a catch to it; to be hypocritical. *– merosok mata sendiri* to be hoist on one's own petard.

telur I 1 egg, ovum. 2 head (of cabbage). 3 manure, feces. 4 kindergarten. *bagai – di ujung tanduk* hanging in the balance, in a precarious situation. *– aduk* scrambled eggs. *– asin* salted egg. *– belangkas* k.o. cake. *– berlada* eggs in chili sauce. *– besar* second level of kindergarten. *– bumbu bali* eggs in a tomato and chili sauce. *– bungkus* mincemeat-coated eggs. *– busuk* rotten egg. *– ceplok* fried egg. *– dadar* omelet. *– gabus* a snack made from rice flour or wheat flour. *– godog* boiled egg. *– ikan* fish roe. *– isi* stuffed eggs. *– kecil* first level of kindergarten. *– kemungkus* an egg that becomes addled after the chick is formed. *– kocokan* scrambled egg. *– kutu* nit. *– mandi* poached egg. *– masak setengah* soft-boiled egg. *– mata sapi* fried egg sunny-side up. *– mata sapi matang* egg over well. *– penyu* turtle egg (believed to be an aphrodisiac). *– pindang* egg boiled in tamarind water and other seasonings. *– puyuh* quail egg. *– rebus* hard-boiled egg. *– selasih* rotten egg. *– setengah matang* soft-boiled egg. *– tembelang* egg that addles after the chick is formed. *– terubuk* herring roe.

bertelur 1 to lay eggs, spawn. 2 to grow (of an investment).

menelur ~ *burung* said of beautiful heels.

menelurkan [and **nelurin** (*J*)] 1 to lay (eggs). 2 to produce, come up with, drop (bombs).

petelur (*ayam* ~) layer.

peneluran egg laying/production.

perteluran place where eggs are laid.

telur II first word in compounds for various k.o. grasses. – *ayam* k.o. plant, *Psychotria rostrata*. – *belalang* k.o. tree, *Sporobolus diandrus*. – *buaya* k.o. tree, *Homalium longifolium*. – *cecak/cicak* k.o. tree, *Myrica farquhariana*. – *ikan* torpedo grass, *Cyrtococcum patens, Panicum repens/radicans*. – *kodok*, k.o. herbaceous plant, *Hygrophila sp.* – *sentadu* k.o. weed, ditch millet, *Paspalum scrobiculatum*.

telus 1 permeable. 2 (*Mal*) transparent. – *air* permeable to water.

menelus to penetrate, pierce, percolate.

penelusan 1 leaching, percolation. 2 penetration, piercing. 3 permeability.

telusup menelusup 1 to go into hiding, hide out. 2 to infiltrate. ~ *masuk* to infiltrate into.

telusur trace, scan(ning), search (on website).

menelusur to investigate, examine, unravel.

menelusuri 1 to follow/go along. 2 to trace. 3 to research, investigate. 4 to scan. 5 to scroll through.

telusuran scanning, searching.

penelusur investigator. ~ *gua* caver, speleologist.

penelusuran 1 investigation, tracing, searching. ~ *kembali* retracing. ~ *minat dan kemampuan* [PMDK] talent scouting. 2 scrutiny, research into.

telut I bertelut 1 to kneel. 2 to submit.

telut II → LUT I, TELAP I. invulnerable. *tak – oléh senjata* invulnerable.

telutuh spot/stain on fabric.

telutut → TELUT I.

tém (*E*) time.

ngetém (*J*) to wait for enough passengers to fill a public vehicle.

téma (*D*) theme, topic, subject of a dissertation.

bertémakan to have the theme of. ~ *drama rumah tangga* to have the theme of a family drama.

temaah (*M*) greedy.

temabur scattered all over.

temadun → TAMAD(D)UN.

temaha I wrong, mistaken.

temaha II intentionally, on purpose.

temaha(k) → TEMAAH.

temak k.o. tree, *Shorea cochinchinensis*.

temakul → TEMBAKUL.

temalang k.o. conical basket used in bees' nest hunting.

temali → TALI I. **bertemali** to be tied/connected.

temambah (*math*) additive.

teman 1 friend, companion. 2 companion, s.o. with whom one does s.t., -mate, partner, associate. *Cari –?* Looking for company? (invitation by prostitute or pimp). 3 accompaniment, trimming, dressing, topping. – *duka sukar dicari* a friend in need is a friend indeed. – *akrab* close friend. – *bercakap* person one is talking to, interlocutor. – *bermain* playmate. – *bertanding* sparring partner. – *dekat* close friend. – *hidup* life companion, mate. – *karib* close friend. – *kencan* boy/girlfriend, date; sex partner. – *main* boy-/girlfriend. – *nasi* a dish served along with the rice. – *ngobrol* person one is talking to. – *seasrama* dorm-mate. – *sejawat* colleague. – *sekamar* roommate. – *sekapal* shipmate. – *sekelas* classmate. – *sekerja* colleague. – *selapik seketiduran* bosom friend. – *senegeri* fellow countryman. – *sepantar* peer. – *sepekerjaan* colleague. – *sepembuangan* fellow exile. – *sepemondokan* housemate. – *sependeritaan* fellow sufferer. – *seperjalanan* traveling companion. – *seperjuangan* comrade-in-arms. – *sepermainan* playmate. – *serumah* housemate. – *setanahair* fellow countryman. – *temin* (*coq*) friends. – *tidur* s.o. to go to bed with, bedmate.

berteman 1 with friends. 2 to have a friend. 3 to go around (with), keep company (with), be friends (with). 4 to be(come) friends (with e.o.).

bertemankan to have ... as a friend.

menemani [and **nemanin** (*J coq*)] to accompany, keep s.o. company, go along with, keep s.o. company. *ditemani semangkok téh* over a cup of tea. ~ *orang tiada takut* to help s.o. who doesn't need help.

peneman s.o. that accompanies. ~ *nasi* a dish served with the rice.

penemanan accompanying, going along.

pe(r)temanan friendship, companionship.

temangau k.o. tree, *Vernonia javanica*.

temantén (*Jv*) bride, bridegroom. – *baru* newlyweds.

temara (*ob*) lance, spear.

temaram 1 dark, unlit. 2 darkness.

temarang → TERANG.

temas temas-temas 1 to cure an illness due to sorcery. 2 a way to predict the future using two pieces of saffron.

temas(y)a → TAMASYA.

tématik (*E*) and **tématis** (*D*) thematic.

tématisasi thematization.

tematu → TEMBATU I.

temayun → AYUN-TEMAYUN.

tembadau k.o. wild ox, *Bos sondaicus*.

tembaga (*Skr*) copper. – *batangan* copper rod. – *kuning* brass. – *lantak* copper bar. – *mérah* copper. – *perunggu* bronze. – *putih* pewter. – *suasa* alloy of gold and copper.

menembaga to turn copper-colored.

témbak I 1 shot, fire, firing (of a gun). *menghukum –* to execute by firing squad. *kena –* to get shot. 2 (*M*) direction, course. *Tak berketentuan – katanya*. It's not clear to whom his words were directed. – *beralamat, tujuan bermaksud* the end justifies the means. – *cepat* rapid fire. – *ganggu* harassing fire. – *gawar* (*Mal*) warning shot. – *gusar* interdiction fire. – *jitu* direct hit. – *lambung* flanking fire. – *langsung* a) shoot on sight. b) to go right to the point, do s.t. without any preliminaries. – *lindung* covering fire. – *memusat* converging fire. – *mengaur* random shots. – *pinta* fire on call. – *sasaran* target shooting.

bertémbak-témbakan to shoot at e.o. 2 shoot-out.

menémbak [and **némbak** (*coq*)] 1 to shoot, fire. ~ *jatuh* to shoot down (a plane). ~ *mati* to shoot to death. *ditémbak tustél* to be photographed. ~ *di tempat* to shoot on sight. 2 to aim at; to kick (a soccer ball towards the goal). 3 to direct to; to intend, mean. *Siapa yang ditémbaknya?* Whom did he mean? 4 to strike. *ditémbak petir* struck by lightning. 5 to blackmail. 6 to bribe. ~ *di tempat* bribing on the spot. 7 (*BG*) to ask a girl to be your girlfriend. ~ *tanah di gunung* to carry coals to Newcastle.

témbak-menémbak 1 to shoot at e.o., exchange fire. 2 shoot-out.

menémbaki [and **némbakin** (*J coq*)] (*pl obj*) to shoot at, shell. *Kami ditémbaki.* We were under fire.

menémbakkan 1 to fire (a gun), shoot with (a gun/camera). 2 to kick (a ball towards the goal). 3 to project (a film), use (a projector) for showing (a film).

tertémbak [and **ketémbak** (*coq*)] 1 shot. 2 struck (by s.t. hurled or moving).

témbakan 1 a shot, shooting, gunfire. ~ *cepat* rapid fire. ~ *kehormatan* salvo. ~ *pengampunan* coup de grace. ~ *peringatan* warning shot. 2 a bribe.

témbak-témbakan shooting, rifle drill.

penémbak 1 shooter, gunner. ~ *bersembunyi/gelap* sniper. ~ *jitu* sharpshooter. ~ *mahir* marksman. ~ *mistérius* vigilante. ~ *runduk* sniper. ~ *tepat* sharpshooter. ~ *tersembunyi* sniper. ~ *titis* sharpshooter. ~ *ulung* marksman. 2 weapon used for shooting at s.t. *meriam* ~ *pesawat terbang* A.A.-gun, Anti-Aircraft gun.

petémbak (*sport*) target shooter.

penémbakan 1 shooting, firing, bombardment. ~ *jatuh* shooting down. 2 shot. *melepaskan –* to fire a shot. ~ *meriam* cannonade. ~ *pantul* ricochet shot. ~ *peringatan* warning shot. ~ *sunyi* a single shot now and then.

témbak II (*coq*) counterfeit, fraudulent; → PALSU. *sopir –* unofficial driver.

témbakan replacement. *sopir* ~ an unlicensed replacement driver.

tembakang k.o. freshwater fish, kissing gourami, *Helostoma temmincki, Polycanthus spp.*

tembakau (*Port*) tobacco, *Nicotina tabacum*. – *asli* native tobacco. – *belati* imported tobacco. – *garang* dried tobacco. – *hutan* wild tobacco which has medical uses, *Solanum verbascifolium*. – *iris* fine-cut tobacco. – *kepala* high-quality tobacco. – *kerosok* dried tobacco leaves. – *lémpéng(an)* thin flat pieces of tobacco. – *pengisi* filler. – *pépéan* dried (in the sun) tobacco. – *rajangan* cut tobacco. – *molé* k.o. tobacco product. – *sék* shag tobacco. – *sisik* tobacco used with betel nut chewing. – *tengkuk* mid-quality tobacco. – *warning* shag tobacco.
  pertembakauan tobacco (*mod*).
tembako → TEMBAKAU.
tembakul k.o. marine fish, goby, *Periophthalmus koelreuteri* and other species.
tembam (*Jv*) plump, puffy, chubby, fleshy (*esp* of cheeks).
  ketembaman plumpness, puffiness.
tembang (*Jv*) sung or recited Javanese, Madurese or Sundanese poetry.
  menembang and **nembang** to sing or recite this poetry.
  menembangi to sing or recite this poetry to.
  menembangkan to sing or recite (this poetry).
  penembang singer of this poetry.
témbang k.o. sardine, *Clupea (Harengula) fimbriata*. – *moncong* k.o. fish, *Clupea longiceps*. – *perempuan*, k.o. fish, *Clupea sp*.
tembatar k.o. pile worm or shipworm.
tembarau k.o. grass, *Saccharum arundinaceum*; → TEBERAU.
tembatu I k.o. tree, *Neoscortechinia kingii, Angelesia splendens*.
tembatu II (*M*) k.o. banana with hard seeds.
témbék near miss.
tembékar → TEMBIKAR.
témbél I sty (in the eye).
témbél II → TAMBAL.
tembelang rotten (of an egg).
tembélékan prickly lantana, *Lantana camara*.
tembelian k.o. freshwater fish, golden-price barb, *Probarbus jullieni*.
tembeliung whirlwind.
tembélok toredo, pile worm, shipworm, *Toredo navalis*. – *masam* k.o. parasite of chickens caused by a virus.
tembem → TEMBAM.
tembera → TAMBRA.
temberam k.o. fish trap used in rivers.
tembérang I boasting, bragging. – *keling* boasting, bragging.
  menembérang to boast, brag.
tembérang II ship's stays, shroud. – *belakang* backstays. – *buritan* backstays. – *haluan* forestays. – *lénggang* side stays. – *turut* backstays.
temberas k.o. carp, cyprinid, *Cyclocheilichthys apogon*.
tembérék glazed earthenware.
tembéréng 1 ceramics, glazed earthenware. **2** potsherd, fragment. **3** (*math*) segment. **4** outer edge, border.
temberih k.o. fish, *Pseudosciaena diacanthus*.
tembesu various species of hardwood trees, *Fagraea, spp*. – *bukit/hutan/tembaga* k.o. tree, *Fagraea gigantea*. – *kapur/talang* k.o. tree, *Fagraea sororia*. – *padang* k.o. tree, *Fagraea fragrans*. – *paya* k.o. tree, *Fagraea racemosa*.
tembikai watermelon, *Citrullus edulis*.
tembikar pottery; → TEMBÉRÉNG. – *lingkaran* segment of a circle.
tembilang spade.
tembilar fish trap.
tembilu → SEMBILU.
tembiring → TEMBÉRÉNG.
tembis (*ob*) **menembis** to scold.
témbok I (exterior masonry) wall. – *Bérlin* the Berlin Wall. – *Cina* the Great Wall of China. – *kering* miser. – *laut* breakwater. – *penahan tanah* retaining wall. – *pertahanan* rampart. – *Ratapan* Western/Wailing Wall.
  menémbok to put a wall on. *Rumah bambunya sudah ditémbok.* They've put a wall on their bamboo house.
  menémboki to wall in, immure.
  témbokan brickwork.
  penémbokan 1 masonry. **2** bricking in.
témbok II (*Jv*) **menémbok** to cover batik with wax to keep the dye off the parts that are to be kept white.

témbok III menémbok to cool a hot liquid by stirring it.
tembola → TOMBOLA.
tembolok 1 crop, craw. **2** (*coq*) paunch. – *masam* candidiasis.
témbong (*Jv*) mark on the face.
tembosa (*Pers/Hind*) curry puff, sambosa.
tembra → TAMBERA I.
tembuk I → TEMBUS.
tembuk II – *tebing* k.o. freshwater fish, pike head, *Luciocephalus pulcher*.
tembuku k.o. knob on the mast of a ship.
tembung I 1 k.o. stick used to ward off blows in *silat*. **2** k.o. whip.
  menembung to ward off blow using that stick.
tembung II bertembung and **menembung** to meet, run into.
  pertembungan meeting.
tembuni placenta.
tembus 1 pierced, penetrated. – *panser* armor-piercing. – *kena peluru* pierced by a bullet. *tidak* – *peluru* bulletproof. – *terkaannya* he guessed it right away. **2** transparent, see-through. **3** to go through, come out, lead to. *jalan ini* – *ke ...* this street comes out on ... – *cahaya* translucent. – *mata/pandang/penglihatan* see-through, transparent.
  menembus [and **nembus** (*coq*)] **1** to go through, penetrate and come out the other side, cross, go/break through. *Jalan ini ~ jalan raya.* This road crosses the highway. **2** to make one's way through. **3** to exceed, surpass. *Ékspor nonmigas ~ 1 miliar dolar.* Nonoil and gas exports exceeded 1 billion dollars.
  menembusi [and **nembusin** (*J coq*)] to go through, pierce, break through.
  menembuskan 1 to send a copy of. *Laporannya juga ditembuskan ke Polri.* A copy of the report was also sent to the police. **2** to pierce/penetrate with.
  tertembus riddled, perforated, pierced.
  tembusan 1 copy (formerly carbon copy but no longer necessarily so). **2** way through, passage. **3** tunnel. **4** (*anat*) hiatus. **bertembusan** riddled.
  penembus punch.
  penembusan 1 breaking through, crossing, penetrating, penetration. **2** exceeding, surpassing.
tembusu → TEMBESU.
téméh → RÉMÉH *téméh*.
temen → TEMAN.
temenan (*Jv*) really, truly.
temengalan → TENGALAN.
temenggang k.o. bird, white-winged black jay, *Platyurus leucopterus*.
Temenggung I → TUMENGGUNG.
temenggung II k.o. marine fish, *Priacanthus tayenus*.
temenggung III Bornean carpenter ant, *Camponotus gigas*.
temenggung IV k.o. shrub, *Gendarussa vulgaris*.
temenong and **temenung** k.o. freshwater fish, Indian mackerel, *Rastrelliger kanagurta*.
temesar k.o. tree, *Croton argyratum*.
temiang k.o bamboo used for making blowpipes, *Bambusa wrayi*.
temilang k.o. tree, *Aglaia odoratissima*.
temin I (*joc*) female friend.
temin II metal band or ring used for binding or mounting.
  bertemin having such a ring.
  menemin to provide s.t. with such a ring.
temoléh → TEMBELIAN.
temon pengantén (*Jv*) the ceremony in which the bride and groom meet e.o.
tempa metalwork. – *selagi besi masih panas* strike while the iron is hot.
  menempa 1 to forge, shape by tempering, make metal objects. **2** to work s.t. into a desired shape, give special training to. *sudah ditempa* have been through the mill. ~ *diri* to undergo severe training.
  tertempa forged, tempered.
  tertempakan malleable.
  tempaan 1 tempered. **2** wrought (iron). **3** made in. ~ *Bali* made in Bali.
  penempa smith.

penempaan forging, tempering.

tempah in advance, ahead of time, pre-. *uang* - down payment, deposit.

menempah(kan) 1 to order/book s.t. in advance/ahead of time, buy futures. ~ *padi* to buy rice while it is still in the field by paying for it in advance. 2 to order, have s.t. made to order.

mempertempahkan to sell s.t. in advance by taking a down payment on it.

tempahan 1 order, booking. 2 deposit (of money).

penempah s.o. who buys s.t. in advance, futures buyer.

penempahan ordering in advance, booking.

tempala the hop of an animal about to pounce.

tempalak → TEMPELAK.

témpang → TIMPANG.

tempap → TELEMPAP.

tempat 1 place, locality, site; facility, point. *di* - a) of this (city, etc.), at this address. *Firma Natuna & Co. di* - Natuna, Inc. of this city. b) (stay) in a place. *Harap di* -. Please stay put. *pada suatu* - somewhere. *latihan di* - on-the-job training. c) on the spot, on sight. *di* - *terpisah* separately. 2 place to put s.t., place where s.t. is kept. *Pedagang-pedagang kali-lima selalu mengambil* - *hampir setengah jalan.* 3 place where one lives or is domiciled. - *kedudukan* residence. 4 spot, proper or natural position, seat, holder. *-nya* its place. *sudah pada -nya* a) right. b) with good reason, fitting, proper. *tidak pada -nya* improper, out of place, not in place. *tidak pada -nya lagi* a) no longer fitting/proper. b) out of place. *di* - *istirahat* at ease, at rest. 5 position (in a race, etc.). 6 in which, where (adverbial relative) *rumah* - *dia tinggal* the house in which he lives. 7 (business) center. - *abu* ashtray. - *air* water container. - *asal* place of origin. - *bekerja* workplace. - *berdiri* standing room (in bus, etc.). - *ber(h)utang* creditor. - *beribadat* place of worship. - *berkata* a) interlocutor. b) (*gram*) second person. - *berlabuh* anchoring berth, anchorage. - *berlindung* shelter. - *bertanya* oracle. - *bertaut* rendezvous, meeting place. - *biaya* cost center. - *buang air/hajat* toilet, bathroom. - *cuci muka* washbasin. - *curahan hati* a shoulder to cry on. - *dawat* inkstand. - *duduk* seat. - *gadai* pawnshop. - *garam* saltshaker. - *gula* sugar bowl. - *hajat* toilet. - *hati* sweetheart. - *hiburan* amusement park. - *hiburan malam* nightclub. - *ibadah* house of worship. - *indekos(t)* boardinghouse. - *jalan kaki* footpath. - *kediaman* residence, abode. - *kedudukan hukum* legal domicile/residence. - *kejadian perkara* [TKP] the scene of the crime, crime scene. - *kelahiran* place of birth. - *kencing* urinal. - *kontrol* checkpoint. - *kos(t)* boardinghouse. - *kotoran* trash. - *labuh* berth. - *lada* pepper mill. - *lahir* place of birth. - *lain* somewhere else. - *lapang* square, plaza. - *lilin* candlestick. - *ludah* spittoon. - *makan* manger, trough. - *mandi* bathhouse. - *mayat* morgue. - *menyeberang* crossing. - *minum* bar. - *minyak* oilcan. - *nasi* rice bowl. - *nongkrong* hangout. - *pacuan kuda* racetrack. - *parkir* parking lot. - *parkir pesawat* apron. - *parkir susun* parking structure. - *pelarian* asylum. - *pelepas dahaga* refreshment stand. - *peluncuran* launch site. - *peluru* (bullet) clip. - *pembakaran mayat* crematorium. - *pembenihan udang* shrimp hatchery. - *pemberian* place of issue. - *pemberian suara* voting booth. - *pembuangan akhir/sampah* [TPA] garbage dump. - *pemesanan tempat* booking office. - *pemungutan suara* [TPS] polling station. - *penampungan* a) relocation center. b) rehabilitation center, shelter. - *pendaratan* landing site. - *pengantar* departure lounge. - *pengasingan* a) internment camp. b) isolation ward. - *pengobatan* medical facility. - *pengumpulan* depot. - *penimbunan berikat* entrepot. - *penitipan anak* [TPA] day-care center. - *penitipan harta* custodian. - *penitipan pakaian* cloakroom. - *penjudian* gambling den. - *penjualan karcis* ticket counter. - *penyeberangan* crossing point. - *penyimpanan dingin* cold storage. - *penyimpanan mesiu* ammunition dump. - *peranginan* vacation spot. - *percontohan* demonstration plot. - *perhentian (bus)* (bus) stop. - *peribadatan* place of worship. - *peristirahatan* and *persemayaman* rest area. - *persembunyian* hideout. - *persinggahan* stopover (on airplane trip). - *pondokan* accommodations. - *rapat* berth. - *rawan* hardship post. - *rékréasi* resort. - *rokok* cigarette case. - *sabun* soap dish. - *sam-*

pah trashcan. - *sandar* berth (of a ship). - *senjata* armory. - *sepéda* bicycle stand. - *simpan* container. - *singgah* a stop. - *sirih* betel holder. - *surat* letter case. - *susu* milk pitcher. - *tambatan* berth. - *tawanan* interment camp. - *teduh* the shade, lee, shelter. - *temu* meeting place. - *terluang* vacancy. - *tidur* bed. - *tidur dorong* stretcher. - *tidur lipat* folding cot. - *tidur susun* bunk bed. - *tinggal* residence, home. **bertempat tinggal** to reside, stay in a place. - *tinta* inkwell. - *tujuan* destination. - *tumpah darah* a) native country, father/motherland. b) birthplace.

setempat 1 (of) the same place. 2 local. *secara ~.~* from place to place, in places. **menyetempatkan** 1 to bring together into a certain place. 2 to localize.

setempat-setempat local, localized, not everywhere.

bertempat 1 to take place, happen, occur (in a certain place). 2 to have a place, stay/reside in a place. ~ *kedudukan* to be domiciled, reside.

bertempat-tempat local.

menempati 1 to reside in, stay in, occupy. 2 to fill (an office/vacancy). *langsung tinggal ditempati* turnkey (project).

menempatkan 1 to place, deploy, plant (spies), assign (to a place), set s.t. down. 2 to pay-in (capital). *modal yang ditempatkan* paid-in capital.

tertempati to be occupied.

tempatan (*Mal*) local. ~ *hati* sweetheart.

ketempatan to be occupied.

penempatan 1 placing, placement, deployment, investment. ~ *dana* call money. ~ *jangka péndék* short-term investment. ~ *kembali ke masyarakat* rehabilitation. ~ *secara berlapis* layering. 2 stand, place (where s.t. is kept). ~ *sepéda* bicycle stand. 3 occupying, occupation. 4 arrangement.

tempaus a fragrance used in making cigarettes.

tempawak k.o. tree, *Elaeocarpus floribundus.*

tempawan hammered, beaten, wrought. *emas* - native gold. *gadis* - golden girl.

tempayak larva, grub.

tempayan large earthenware jar for storing water, etc. - *tertiarap di air* said about s.o. who doesn't listen to advice.

tempayang jar. - *gubang* narrow-necked jar. - *taban* wide-bodied jar. - *tapak gajah* narrow-necked jar.

tempayung k.o. weed, Lyon's grass, *Themeda villosa.*

témpé (*Jv*) 1 tempeh, soybean cake. 2 good-for-nothing, small and insignificant. *bangsa* - small and insignificant nation. - *ajojing* tempeh made by treading on it (not made by machine). - *bongkrék* tempeh made from peanut residue. - *bungkil* tempeh made from peanut cakes. - *gembos/gembus/gerubus* tempeh made from soybean residue. - *jagung* tempeh made from corn. - *koro* tempeh made from *koro* residue. - *mendoan* partly cooked tempeh prepared with various spices. - *turi* tempeh made from the seeds of the *turi* shrub. - *wurung* soybean cake whose fermentation process is defective.

menémpékan 1 to make s.t. into tempeh. 2 to consider s.t. small and insignificant.

témpél affix, adhere, patch. - *ban* service for patching inner tubes.

bertémpél 1 to be affixed with. ~ *prangko* affixed with a stamp.

bertémpélan to stick to e.o.

bertémpelkan to have s.t. affixed to it. ~ *tanda gambar Ka'abah* to have a picture of the Ka'abah affixed to it.

menémpél [and **némpél** (*coq*)] 1 to stick (onto), adhere/cling (to), hang on (to). *Dia* ~ *di mobil-mobil di lampu mérah.* She hangs on to cars at red lights. 2 to lodge (in), be implanted (in). *Pelurunya* ~ *di témbok.* The bullet was lodged in the wall. 3 to patch. 4 (*coq*) to be right next (to), stick (to), hang out (with).

menémpéli 1 to stick/adhere to. 2 to freeload off of. 3 to stick s.t. on to s.t.

menémpélkan [and **némpélin** (*J coq*)] to stick s.t. (onto s.t.), affix. ~ *poster pada dinding* to stick a poster on the wall.

tertémpél stuck, adhered.

témpélan 1 a sticker, poster. 2 s.t. attached. 3 revenue stamp. 4 place where s.t. is affixed, billboard. 5 person who is sponged off.

penémpél s.o. or s.t. that sticks s.t. up/on.

penémpélan attachment, sticking, adhering.
tempelak blame, reproach.
　bertempelak-tempelakan to reproach e.o.
　menempelak(kan) to blame, reproach.
　tempelakan reproach.
tempelas *akar* – k.o. climbing plant, *Tetracera indica*.
tempéléng and tempéling a slap on the face, a box on the ear.
　menémpéling(i) to slap on the face or box the ears.
　témpéléng a slap or a box.
　penempéléngan slapping, boxing.
témperamén (*D*) temperament.
　bertémperamén temperamental.
temperas I k.o. fish, barb, *Cyclocheilichthys apogon*.
temperas II (*ob*) in disorder.
　bertemparasan 1 in complete disarray. 2 (*pl subj*) to spread.
témperatur (*D*) temperature.
témperau bertémperau to criticize e.o. in public.
tempiar bertempiar(an) scattered all over.
tempias 1 splash, splatter. 2 (*petrol*) drift.
　bertempias and menempias to splash, splatter (on).
　menempiaskan to splash s.t. (onto s.t.).
tempik I (*Jv*) vagina.
tempik II shout, yell. – *sorak* shouting and yelling. ***bertempik sorak*** to shout and yell.
　bertempik to shout, yell.
　menempikkan to shout s.t.
　tempikan shout, yell.
tempil → TAMPIL.
tempilan increased credit ceiling.
tempinah k.o. herbaceous plant, *Hydrocera triflora*.
tempinis k.o. hardwood tree, *Sloetia elongata*, *Streblus elongatus*.
témplék (*J/Jv*) attached, affixed, stuck; → TÉMPÉL.
　menémplék to be attached, affixed, stuck.
　témplék-témplékan (*Jv coq*) to be close to e.o.
témplok (*J/Jv*) némplok 1 to stick, be attached (to), stuck on (to). *Cecak itu ~ di loténg.* The house lizard was attached to the ceiling. 2 to perch, alight. *Burung ~ di jendéla.* A bird perched on the window. 3 to depend on. 4 to be in a certain position.
　némplokin to be stuck to, attached to.
témpo I (*Port*) 1 time. *sudah –nya* it's time to … . *sudah sampai – nya* expired, out of date. 2 when (*coq*) → KETIKA, WAKTU. 3 period of time. – *tiga hari* three days. 4 tempo, rhythm, pace. *ada –nya* sometimes, now and then. – *doeloe* /dulu/ the good old days (the colonial period). – *hari* a) the other day. b) formerly, in the past, former.
　témpo-témpo from time to time, sometimes.
témpo II (*Port*) 1 delay. 2 (*coq*) to take a break/vacation. *tidak tahu* – never takes a break.
　bertémpo to take a break/vacation.
　menémpokan to have s.o. take a break.
témpoh → TÉMPO I.
témpohari → TÉMPO *hari*.
tempolong (*J/Jv*) spittoon, cuspidor.
temponék → TEMPUNAI.
témpong I (*ob*) menémpong to throw s.t. at a target.
témpong II menémpong to push off (a boat from the shore).
témporér (*D*) temporary.
temporong → TEMPURUNG I.
tempoyak pickled durian.
tempoyan k.o. tree, brown malletwood, *Rhodamnia trinervia*.
tempua weaverbird, *Ploceus philippinus*.
tempuh I setempuh ~ *lalu sebondong turut* with concerted efforts.
　bertempuh-tempuh and tempuh-menempuh (*ob*) to attack, assault.
　menempuh and menempuhi 1 to undergo, undertake, experience, take (an exam/a course of study/trip/step, etc.), endure. ~ *hidup baru* to start a new life, marry. ~ *jalan tengah* to take the middle course. *réstrukturisasi yang telah ditempuh* restructuring already undertaken. ~ *ujian* to take an exam. 2 to attack, assault, hit hard at, beat (of the waves against the shore, etc.). ~ *musuh* to attack the enemy. 3 to go/get through s.t. difficult. ~ *hutan* to go through the forest. ~

jalan to make one's way through. ~ *jarak* to cover a distance. *kawasan yang sulit ditempuh* an inaccessible region.
　tertempuh undergone, experienced, taken.
　penempuh s.o. who undergoes, experiences, takes, etc.
　penempuhan 1 undergoing, taking. 2 attacking, assaulting. 3 getting through.
tempuh II (*Jv*) compensation for s.t. broken, etc., replacement.
　menempuhkan to blame and demand compensation for s.t. broken, etc., hold s.o. responsible for s.t.
　ketempuhan 1 to be responsible (for s.t. broken, etc.). 2 to be liable for damages and forced to pay compensation.
tempui k.o. tree, wood can be used for timber and fruit can be made into *arak*, *Baccaurea macrophylla/malayana*.
tempuling harpoon.
　menempuling(i) to harpoon.
tempunai k.o. tree with fruit like small *nangka*, *Artocarpus rigida*.
tempur battle, combat, action. – *dekat* close combat. – *sergap* interceptor (type of aircraft).
　bertempur to fight, do battle, be in combat, in action, clash. *Dia téwas ~.* He was killed in action. *siap ~* ready for battle. *téwas ~* to die in action.
　ber(si)tempuran (*ob*) to fight e.o.
　menempur to attack, assault.
　menempurkan 1 to make s.o. fight. 2 to fight for.
　mempertempurkan to fight/battle/struggle for/over. ~ *kemerdékaan* to fight for freedom.
　tempuran confluence (of two rivers).
　penempur battler, assailant.
　pertempuran battle, fight, clash, engagement, combat. ~ *udara* air battle.
tempuras → TEMPERAS II.
tempurung I part of a coconut shell. *dari luar* – from outsiders. – *betina* bottom half of a coconut shell. – *jantan* top half of a coconut shell. – *kepala* skull. – *lutut* kneecap, patella. – *rebab* body of a *rebab*.
tempurung II (*buah* –) avocado, *Persea gratissima*.
tempuyung (*Jv*) a perennial herb used as medicine, corn sow thistle, gut weed, *Sonchus arvensis*, *Nasturtium indicum*.
temtu (*Jv*) → TENTU.
temu I meet, get together, run into. – *akal* rational. – *alumni* reunion. – *batunya* found his match. – *darat* to meet face to face. – *duga* (job) interview. **bertemu duga** to hold an interview. **menemuduga(i)** to interview. – *ilmiah* academic meeting. – *karya* working meeting. – *kangenan* reunion. – *kenal* familiarization. **menemu-kenali** and **menemu-kenalkan** 1 to identify, recognize. 2 to become familiar with, familiarize o.s. with. **penemu-kenalan** familiarization. – *muka* reunion, face-to-face meeting. **bertemu muka** to have a face-to-face meeting. – *rindu/ulang* reunion. – *usaha* business meeting. – *wicara* a) colloquium. b) briefing, interview, dialogue. **bertemu wicara** 1 to hold a colloquium. 2 to hold an interview.
　bertemu 1 to meet, encounter, run into. *Baru-baru ini saya ~ dengan dia.* I ran into him recently. ~ *dengan bahaya* to meet up with dangers. 2 to visit, see, have an interview with. *Ia hendak ~ dengan tuan rumah.* He wanted to see the landlord. *Sampai ~ lagi.* Good-bye, see you again. 3 to find, come across, discover. *Meréka berjalan kaki sebentar sebelum ~ bécak kosong.* They walked along for a while before they found an empty becak. *Kalau ~ arloji itu, akan kuserahkan kepada polisi.* If I come across the watch, I'll turn it over to the police. ~ *balik* to come across again (of s.t. that was lost). ~ *hati* to fall in love. ~ *jodoh* to meet one's mate, find a life partner. ~ *roma* to have a dispute. ~ *ruas dengan buku* to have found one's mate in life. 4 to be found, come across. *Batu permata seélok ini tak akan ~ di negeri ini.* Such a beautiful precious stone cannot be found in this country. 5 to merge, converge, join up. *Kuala Lumpur di-bina di tempat Sungai Kelang ~ dengan Sungai Gombak.* K.L. was founded at the spot where the Kelang River converged with the Gombak River. 6 to prove true. *Téori yang tak ~ dalam prakték.* A theory that doesn't prove true in practice. 7 to match, agree. ~ *ruyung dengan beliung* to meet one's match.
　menemu to find, come across, meet up with.

menemui [and **nemuin** (*J coq*)] 1 to go and visit s.o., go to see. *Ia tidak mau ~ para démonstran.* He didn't want to go and meet with the demonstrators. 2 to meet (with), reach, encounter, experience, run into (*usu s.t.* unpleasant), come up against. *~ ajal* to meet one's death. *~ jalan buntu* to reach a deadlock. *~ kegagalan* to meet up with failure. 3 to comply with, obey. *Semalam saya tak sempat datang ~ panggilanmu.* Last night I couldn't comply with your call.

menemukan 1 to find, locate, detect. *~ kebocoran* to detect a leak. *~ kembali* to recover. 2 to come up with. *Kami ~ pikiran.* We came up with an idea. 3 to discover, come/run across. 4 to invent.

mempertemukan 1 to bring together, match up, (re)unite. *~ jodoh* to marry off. 2 to connect with, contact. 3 to make two parties confront e.o.

ketemu (*coq*) 1 to meet, see. *Sampai ~ (lagi).* Good-bye. *~ batunya* a) to get into trouble. b) to get caught; → KENA *batunya.* 2 to find, come across. 3 after. *X ~ X X* after X. *minggu ~ minggu* week after week. 4 to be found, come across. **mengetemui** 1 to meet. 2 to find. **mengetemukan** 1 to find, discover. 2 to unite, bring together.

tertemui can be found, findable. *tidak ~* unfindable.

tertemukan found, discovered.

temuan 1 finding, s.t. found, find. *~ kepurbakalan* archeological find. 2 found. *barang ~* found item.

penemu 1 inventor, discoverer. 2 innovator.

penemuan 1 discovery, invention, find, finding. *salah satu ~ dalam survai* one of the findings in the survey. 2 innovation. 3 finding, locating, detecting. *~ kembali* recovery.

pertemuan 1 meeting, coming together, gathering, talks. *~ empat mata* tête-à-tête. *~ kekeluargaan* family reunion. *~ langit dan air* horizon. *~ pejabat tinggi* senior officials' meeting. *~ perpisahan* farewell meeting. *~ ramah-tamah* social get-together. *~ tatap muka* face-to-face meeting. *~ tingkat atas/tinggi* high-level meeting. *~ udara* air combat. *~ untuk penglepasan* farewell meeting. 2 meeting place, confluence. *~ sungai* confluence of two rivers.

temu II first element in the names of various k.o. plants of the *Curcuma* family. *- giring* a yellow tuber, *Curcuma viridiflora/heyneana.* *- hitam/ireng* a plant similar to turmeric, *Curcuma aeruginosa.* *- kunci* Chinese ginger, *Kaempferia pandurata.* *- kuning/kunyit* turmeric, *Curcuma domestica, Gastrochilus panduratum.* *- lalab/mangga/pauh* k.o. herb, *Curcuma mangga.* *- lawak/lawas* white turmeric, *Curcuma xanthorrhiza.* *- putih* k.o. wild ginger, zedoary. *Curcuma zedoaria.* *- putri* a medicinal plant, round-rooted galangal, *Curcuma petiolata/Kaempferia rotunda.*

temu-temuan Zingiberaceae.

temucut love-grass, *Chrysopogon aciculatus.*

temukus → KEMUKUS.

temukut broken grains of rice.

temulawak → RIMPANG *kuning.*

temuni → TEMBUNI.

temuras k.o. shrub, *Ardisia oxyphylla.*

temurun → TURUN.

temus [*tenaga musiman*] seasonal manpower/worker.

temut-temut 1 to bob up and down, twitch. 2 to mumble (the lips move up and down).

Tenabang (*coq*) Tanah Abang (a section of Jakarta).

tenaga 1 power, energy. 2 capacity, output, thrust (of engines). 3 zip, pep. 4 personnel, labor. *- atom* atomic power. *- ahli* expert. *- air* hydraulic power. *- bantuan* support forces. *- baru* new employee. *- batin* spiritual power. *- beli* purchasing power. *- berguna* efficiency. *- dalam* inner/spiritual force. *- gerak* kinetic energy. *- hayati* vitality, life force. *- hidup* vitality. *- hidrolik* hydraulic power. *- ikat inti* nuclear binding energy. *- kasar* manual labor. *- kerja* [NAKER] manpower, work force, labor, staff. *- kerja (warga negara) asing* expatriate. *- kerja Indonésia* [TKI] Indonesian worker in a foreign country. *- kerja lepas* day/seasonal laborer, freelance, subcontractor. *- kerja rumah tangga* [TKRT] household help, servant. *- kerja terlatih* skilled manpower. *- kerja tetap* regular employee. *-*

kerja trampil skilled manpower. **ketenagakerjaan** manpower (*mod*). *- kerja wanita* [TKW] (Indonesian) female worker (abroad). *- kinétis* kinetic power. *- kuda* horse power [TK]. *- lama* an old hand. *- lepas* casual/day labor. *- listrik* electric power. **bertenaga listrik** electrified. **ketenaga-listrikan** a) electric power (*mod*). *séktor ~* electric power sector. b) electric power system. *- luar* external/visible power. *- manusia* manpower, personnel. *- matahari* solar energy. *- médis* medical advisor. *- mékanik* rig mechanic. *- musiman* [temus] seasonal manpower/worker. *- nuklir* nuclear power. **ketenaganukliran** nuclear power (*mod*). *- panas bumi* geothermal power. *- pejuang* fighter. *- pekerja* labor force. *- pembeli* purchasing power. *- pendorong* momentum. *- penentang* resistance. *- pengajar* teaching staff. *- penguat/penggiat* exciter capacity. *- pengukur* scaler. *- pimpinan* executive. *- prima* energy peak. *- rélawan* volunteer. *- semu* apparent output. *- tempat* (*phys*) potential energy. *- teralan* (*phys*) excitation energy. *- terdidik* trained staff. *- térmis* caloric energy.

bertenaga energized, energetic, with energy, full of energy/pep, vigorous, active.

men(t)enagai to energize, power.

ketenagaan (*mod*) power, energy.

tenahak (*ob*) disappointed.

tenak k.o. marine fish, *Sphyraena spp.*

tenam k.o. tree, mascal wood, *Anisoptera costata.*

tenan (*Jv*) real(ly), true, very.

tenang quiet, peaceful, calm. *tidak -* not quiet. **ketidak-tenangan** disquiet.

bertenang *~ diri* to calm down.

(ber)tenang-tenang to calm/quiet down.

menenang to become quiet, calm down.

menenangkan [and **nenangin** (*J coq*)] 1 to quiet/calm down, silence. 2 to soothe, comfort, relax. *~ keadaan* to let things quiet down. *~ pikiran* to set s.o.'s mind at ease.

tertenang the quietest.

ketenangan calm, peace, peace of mind, quiet.

penenang 1 s.o. or s.t. that calms/quiets down. 2 s.t. that soothes/relaxes. *~ saraf* sedative. 3 tranquillizer.

penenangan *masa ~* cooling-off period.

ténang menénang to (take) aim at.

ténar and **tenar** 1 well-known, famous, popular. 2 noisy.

menénarkan to make s.o. well-known.

keténaran 1 fame, renown, popularity. 2 noise.

tenat exhausted, very tired; → PENAT.

ténda (*Port*) 1 tent. 2 awning, blind. 3 top of a pedicab or vehicle. *- buka* convertible (of a vehicle). *- rumah* awning.

berténda with a tent, tented.

tendang kick. *- gol* (*coq*) to have sex (homosexual term). *- tumit* to stamp one's feet. *- terajang* kicking and stamping one's feet.

menendang [and **nendang** (*coq*)] 1 to kick. *~ lidah* to stimulate the appetite. 2 to kick out, expel.

menendangkan to kick.

menendangi (*pl obj*) to kick.

tertendang 1 kicked. 2 kicked out, expelled.

tendangan 1 kick. *~ penjuru* corner kick. *~ pertama* kickoff. *~ pisang* banana kick. *~ sudut* corner kick.

penendang s.o. or s.t. that kicks, kicker.

penendangan kicking.

téndanisasi pitching tents.

tendas (*ob*) **menendas** to decapitate.

téndéns(i) tendency.

berténdéns(i) to have a tendency (to).

téndénsius (*D*) tendentious.

ténder (*E*) tender, bid; → PENAWARAN.

menénderkan to offer a tender.

téner (*E*) paint thinner.

teng exactly, precisely. *- jam 12 siang* exactly at 12 noon.

téng I (*onom*) ding (of a clock).

téng II (*D*) 1 armored car, tank. 2 tank (a container).

téng III (*C*) Chinese lantern. *- loléng* paper lantern.

tengadah look upward.

menengadah to look upward. ~ *ke langit hijau* hopeless. ~ *matahari* to oppose the authorities.

menengadahi to look upward at.

menengadahkan to point/lift s.t. upward.

tengah I 1 middle, center, central. *Jawa* – Central Java. *di* – a) in the middle of. b) while, during. c) among. *di* – *meréka* among them. *di* – *ramainya antréan rakyat kecil untuk membeli sembako* while the common people are lining up to buy the nine basic commodities. **2** median. **3** in the process of, in the middle of, be ...ing; → LAGI, SEDANG. *Dia* – *makan*. He's eating. **4** halfway (to the next point). – *200* 150. – *40* 35. – *empat* three and a half. **5** twice every. – *bulanan* semimonthly. – *harga* half price. – *hari* noon. – *hari bolong* around noon. – *hari rembang* high noon. – *hati* halfhearted(ly), grudgingly. – *jalan* on the way, right in the middle of things. – *kapal* amidships. – *kiri* left of center (politically). – *malam* midnight. – *masa* midterm. – *naik* a) about 9 a.m. b) about 14–15 years old. – *tahunan* semiannual. – *tanggal* mean date. – *tapak bayang-bayang* noon. – *turun* about 3 p.m. *ke* – to the middle. **mengetengahi 1** to interfere in, intercede in, mediate between, get between (two people fighting). **2** to interrupt. **mengetengahkan 1** to present, set forth, cite. **2** to subpoena, summon.

tengah-tengah center, very middle. *di* ~ in the midst of.

setengah 1 half, semi, middle, central. ~ *baya* middle-aged. ~ *hari* part-time. ~ *hati* halfhearted. ~ *jadi* half/semifinished. ~ *jalan* halfway. ~ *jam* half an hour. ~ *lingkaran* semicircular. ~ *masak* not finished, unfinished. ~ *matang* a) partly ripe. b) partly cooked. c) soft-boiled. d) partly developed. ~ *mati* a) desperate, in bad shape. b) extreme, (work o.s.) to death. *Panasnya* ~ *mati*. It's extremely hot. ~ *mengerti* to understand partly. ~ *miring otak* somewhat crazy. ~ *resmi* semiofficial. ~ *sadar* semiconscious. ~ *tiang* half mast. ~ *tua/umur* middle-aged. **2** halfway to the next hour. *jam* ~ *tiga* two-thirty. **3** some. ~ *orang* some people. **4** stupid. *orang* ~ half-wit.

setengah-setengah to do things halfway. *Menteri Kehakiman tak mau* ~. The Minister of Justice didn't want to do things halfway.

menengah 1 to be in the middle. **2** to move to the middle. **3** middle. *sekolah* ~ middle school. ~ *atas* upper middle (class). **4** moderate (not radical). **5** neutral. **6** to intervene, intercede, mediate.

menengahi 1 to interfere/intervene/intercede in, mediate between, get between (two people fighting). **2** to interrupt.

menengahkan to come between.

tengahan 1 mid-level. **2** coin worth 50 cents. **3** (*coq*) more to the middle.

penengah 1 mediator, intermediary, arbiter, arbitrator, middleman. **2** neutral party.

penengahan mediation, intercession.

pertengahan middle, center. *Abad* ~ the Middle Ages. ~ *kedua* the second half (of a month). ~*nya* the average.

tengah II → TENGAR.

tengahari noon.

tengak confused, desperate.

téngak-téngok to keep looking around; → TÉNGOK.

tengal (*J*) **1** not yet ripe, tough (of cooked food). **2** rude.

tengalan k.o. marine fish, *Puntius bulu*.

tengar k.o. mangrove tree, *Ceriops tagal/candolleana*. – *hutan* k.o. tree, *Ternstroemia bancana*.

tengara (*Jv*) signal, sign.

menengarai to point out, allege. *ditengarai oléh* allegedly due to.

tengari → TENGAHARI.

tengas I k.o. freshwater fish, mahseer, *Acrossocheilus hexagonolepis*. – *daun* k.o. freshwater fish, *Acrossocheilus deauratus*.

tengas II earmark on cattle.

menengas to earmark.

tengel → TENGAL.

téngél-téngél shaky, on the point of falling down.

tengeran (*Jv*) landmark.

tenggadai k.o. swamp tree, *Bruguiera parvifolia*.

tenggak (*Jv*) throat.

menenggak [and **nenggak** (*coq*)] to swallow, gulp down.

menenggakkan to force s.t. down s.o.'s throat.

tenggala (*Skr*) plow.

menenggala to plow.

penenggala plowman.

tenggalung k.o. civet cat, Malay civet, *Viverra tangalunga*.

ténggang I fixed period of time. – *batas* time limit. *tanpa* – *batas* ad infinitum. – (*ka*)*daluwarsa* period of time before s.t. expires. – *daya* time limit. – *penyerahan* delivery date. – *tangguh* postponement period. – *waktu* time frame, lead time, grace period.

berténggang with a time limit.

ténggang II 1 consideration. **2** ways and means, methods, efforts. – *hati/rasa* a) tolerant, considerate. b) keeping one's feelings to o.s.

berténggang 1 to find the way to carry on. **2** to negotiate, reach an agreement.

berténggang-ténggang(an) and **ténggang-menénggang** to be considerate of e.o.

menénggang(kan) 1 to be considerate of. **2** to tolerate. **3** to find the ways and means. *tidak* ~ *lagi* at one's wits' end.

memperténggangkan 1 to take into consideration. **2** to economize, save (money).

terténggang taken into consideration.

keténggangan consideration, tolerance.

tenggar (*J/Jv*) spacious, roomy, broad, wide.

tenggara southeast.

menenggara to head southeast.

tenggarang stove, oven.

tenggat time limit, deadline.

menenggat to interrupt, disturb.

tenggayun(g) k.o. tree whose wood is used for making furniture, *Parartocarpus triandra*.

ténggék berténggék and **menénggék 1** to perch. **2** to sit at an angle, sit in an insecure position.

menénggékkan to perch s.t., put s.t. up high (or, at an angle).

terténggék perched, set at an angle.

ténggékan perch.

penénggék perch.

tenggelam 1 go under water, sink, submerge. **2** to drop below the surface (of the setting sun). **3** to be absorbed (in). **4** to fail, go under.

menenggelamkan 1 to push under water, sink s.t., scuttle. **2** to make s.t. drop out of sight. **3** to involve (o.s.) deeply (in), get caught up (in).

tertenggelamkan sinkable.

penenggelaman making s.t. sink under (the water), sinking, scuttling.

tenggen(g) (*sl*) to be high on drugs, get drunk.

ténggér I perch.

berténggér 1 to perch, sit on. **2** to stay put (and not move).

menénggér(kan) to perch, put on. *Hélmnya diténggérkan di kaca spion sepéda motor*. He perched a helmet on the rearview mirror of the motorcycle.

ténggéran perch.

penénggéran 1 perch. **2** perching.

Ténggér II an ethnic group which lives on the slopes of Mt. Bromo in East Java.

tenggérét → TONGGÉRÉT.

tenggiling anteater, pangolin, *Manis javanica/pentadactyla*.

tenggiri Spanish mackerel, *Scomberomorus, spp.*; → LUDING. – *batang* k.o. Spanish mackerel, *Scomberomorus commersonii*. – *bunga/papan* stick mackerel, *Scomberomorus guttatus*. – *musang/tikus* civet/streaked mackerel, *Scomberomorus lineolatus*.

ténggok (*J/Jv*) basket; → BAKUL I, KERANJANG.

tenggorok(an) throat, trachea.

tengguli I 1 k.o. bush, golden shower tree, *Cassia fistula*. **2** reddish brown, brown madder.

tengguli II (*M*) molasses.

tenggulung → SENGGULUNG I.

tengik I 1 rancid, stinking. **2** snide, nasty, sharp (of words).

bertengik-tengik to be nasty to e.o.

ketengikan 1 rancidness. **2** snideness, nastiness, spitefulness.

tengik II k.o. tree, bark cloth tree, *Antiaris toxicaria*; → UPAS I.

tengil I snide, nasty, sarcastic.

tengil II (*Jv*) swelling.

  menengil to swell up.

tengkalak long fish trap.

tengkalang rice granary on stilts.

tengkaluk immature edible mango seed.

tengkam (*ob*) gold measure = 6 *kupang* or 14.18 grams.

tengkang the space between the eyes.

tengkar I quarrel, squabble, get into an argument. - *mulut* quarrel.
  bertengkar mulut to quarrel.

  bertengkar(an) to quarrel (with e.o.)

  menengkari to dispute.

  menengkarkan and mempertengkarkan to quarrel/argue over,
  dispute. *dipertengkarkan* at issue/stake, in question.

  tengkar-tengkaran to keep on quarreling.

  pertengkaran quarrel, argument, dispute.

tengkar II stubborn, obstinate.

  menengkar to refuse to obey.

  penengkar stubborn/obstinate person.

tengkarah dispute, altercation.

tengkarap (*A*) destroyed.

  menengkarapkan 1 to destroy. 2 to denigrate s.o.

tengkaras k.o. tree, *Aquilaria malaccensis*.

tengkawang k.o. tree, *Shorea spp.*, and its fruit, illipe nuts.

téngkék (*J/Jv*) k.o. bird with blue feathers, *Halcyon chloris*.

téngkél granule in form, such as sheep, etc. droppings.

  menéngkél to form such granules.

tengkélék wooden clogs.

téngkér → TÉNGGÉR.

tengkérong k.o. fish, tiger-toothed croaker, *Otolithes ruber*.

téngkés (*ob*) underdeveloped, small for its age.

téngki (*E?*) 1 tank car. 2 tank (container).

téngkik → TÉNGKÉK I.

tengking snarling.

  bertengking to snarl, scold.

  menengking to snarl at, scold.

  tengkingan snarling, scolding.

téngkoh (*C*) prepared opium.

tengkok → TENGKUK.

tengkolak → TENGKULAK.

tengkolok headdress for women.

  bertengkolok to wear a headdress.

  bertengkolokkan to wear a headdress made of.

tengkorak skull, cranium.

tengku a royal Malay title. - *mahkota* (*Mal*) Crown Prince.

tengkujuh (*ob*) rainy season.

tengkuk 1 nape (of the neck); → KUDUK I. *bulu* - a) hair at the back
  of the neck. *bulu -nya merinding* it gave him the creeps, his hair
  stood on end. b) horse's mane; → SURAI I. *pusar* - upper part of
  the nape. 2 s.t. resembling the nape, bunch, stalk. - *padi* stalk
  of rice.

  setengkuk as high/tall as the nape of s.o.'s neck.

  bertengkuk humped.

tengkulak (*J/Jv*) broker, middleman.

tengkulak → TENGKOLOK.

tengkurap lying prostrate, on one's stomach; to fall flat on the ground.

  bertengkurap and menengkurap to lie prostrate, flat on one's
  stomach.

  menengkurapkan to lay s.t. down flat.

tengkurup → TENGKURAP.

tengkuyung cowrie, *Murex sp.*

ténglang (*C*) Chinese person.

téngloléng → TÉNG III.

téngnéng (*onom*) ding, ding, ding.

téngok menéngok [and néngok (*coq*)] 1 to look at, see. - *kanan!*
  eyes right! 2 to visit. 3 to predict, forecast.

  menéngoki (*pl obj*) to look at.

  menéngokkan to turn (one's head) to look at.

  terténgok seen.

  penéngok 1 observer. 2 visitor.

téngsin (*Pr*) embarrassed (because caught doing or saying s.t. embarrassing).

téngténg I (*J*) k.o. chewy candy; → ENTING-ENTING, TINGTING II. -
  gepuk k.o. sweet made with peanuts and sugar. - *jahé* k.o.
  sweet made with ginger. - *kacang* sweet peanut brittle.

téngténg II → TÉNTÉNG I.

tengu → TUNGAU I.

tenguh → LENGUH I.

tenguk-tenguk (*Jv*) to sit around with nothing to do.

ténis (*D*) tennis. - *dinding* squash. - *lapangan* outdoor tennis. -
  méja Ping-Pong, table tennis.

  peténis tennis player.

  perténisan (*mod*) tennis.

ténja → TINJA.

ténjét berténjét to stand or walk on tiptoes.

ténok (*M ob*) menénok to aim at.

ténon (*D*) tenon.

ténong (*J/Jv*) container made of woven bamboo for carrying food.

ténor (*D*) tenor.

ténsi (*E*) 1 tension. 2 high blood pressure.

ténsimétér instrument for measuring blood pressure.

ténsor (*D/E*) tensor.

téntakel (*D*) tentacle.

téntamén (*D*) preliminary examination.

téntamina (*D*) preliminary examinations.

tentang 1 concerning, on, about, regarding. *Dia menayangkan laporan - skandal dioksin.* She presented a report on the dioxin
  scandal. 2 facing, opposite, directly above. *di - stasion* opposite
  the station. *di - kepala* directly overhead.

  setentang right on top of, right/exactly opposite. *sama* ~ right
  up against. bersetentang(an) (*dengan*) right in front of.

  bertentang 1 ~ *dengan* facing, right in front of, opposite. ~ *mata*
  face to face. 2 facing e.o. *berdiri* ~ to stand facing e.o.

  bertentangan 1 to be in conflict (with), contrary (to), contrast
  (with). ~ *paham/pandangan/pendapat* to have conflicting opinions. ~ *dengan kemauan* to go against one's will. ~ *dengan kebiasaan* to be contrary to customs. 2 conflicting, opposing, counter,
  opposite. *pernyataan yang* ~ conflicting statements. *arah yang*
  ~ the opposite direction. 3 in violation (of), in defiance (of), go
  (against). ~ *dengan hukum* against the law. 4 to face, be opposite, be face to face (with). *Rumahnya* ~ *dengan mesjid.* His
  house is opposite the mosque. ~ *musuh* face to face with the
  enemy. ~ *pandang* looking right at e.o.

  menentang 1 to oppose, resist, go/be against, con. ~ *kekuasaan*
  antiestablishment. *suara* ~ opposing votes. *tidak dapat ditentang lawan* irresistible. 2 to violate, defy, be in defiance of. ~
  hukum to violate the law. 3 to face, facing toward. ~ *angin*
  against the wind. 4 to look directly at, confront. ~ *matahari* to
  gaze at the sun. ~ *bahaya* to face danger.

  menentangi 1 to oppose. 2 to face, be facing, be directly opposite. 3 to go against, violate.

  menentangkan to bring/put s.t. up in front of, make s.o. or s.t.
  face.

  mempertentangkan 1 to have a conflict over, make an issue of.
  *Perbédaan latar belakang suku, agama dan pendidikan tidak
  perlu dipertentangkan.* There should be no conflict over differences of ethnic, religious, and educational backgrounds. 2
  to oppose. 3 to contrast, be in contrast (with).

  tertentang 1 opposed. *tidak* ~ cannot be contradicted. 2 seen,
  viewed. *tidak* ~ *mata* out of sight.

  tentangan 1 opposition, resistance. 2 (s.t. is) at stake. *Jiwanya
  menjadi* ~. His life is at stake. 3 concerning, regarding. *di* ~
  in front of, before.

  penentang opponent, opposition.

  penentangan 1 resistance, opposition. 2 conflict.

  pertentangan 1 conflict, dispute, controversy, contradiction. ~
  kepentingan conflict of interest. ~ *pendapat* difference of
  opinion. 2 opposition, resistance.

tentara (*Skr*) 1 army, military. 2 soldier. 3 unit (in the military),
  troops. - *darat* infantryman. - *Darat Diraja Malaysia* Royal
  Malaysian Army. - *Nasional Indonésia* [TNI] Indonesian National Army (has now replaced ABRI as the preferred term). -
  payung parachute unit. - *pembébasan* liberation army. - *Pembébasan Nasional Papua* [TPNP] Papua National Liberation

Army. – *pendudukan* army of occupation. – *pilihan* elite troops. – *rakyat* people's army. – *sekutu* allied forces. – *séwaan* mercenary army. – *tetap* regular army. – *upahan* mercenary army.

ketentaraan (*mod*) military, army.

pertentaraan (*mod*) **1** military, army. **2** barracks, garrison.

téntatif (*E*) tentative.

tentawan 1 k.o. creeping plant, *Conocephalus naucleiflorus*. **2** k.o. parasitic plant, *Concephalus suaveoleus*.

ténténg I menénténg to carry s.t. dangling from the hand.

terténténg dangling, carried in the hand.

téntëngan 1 hanging down. **2** portable, hand. *barang* ~ hand baggage. *lampu* ~ portable lamp.

ténténg II → PETANTAN(G)-PETÉN(G)TÉNG.

ténténg III → TINGTING II.

tentera → TENTARA.

tenteram (*Jv*) quiet, peaceful, calm, not nervous.

meneteramkan to quiet/calm s.o. down, reassure. ~ *hati* to comfort, give s.o. peace of mind to, assure. ~ *keadaan* to return the situation to normal, restore law and order.

ketenteraman peace and quiet, calm, tranquillity.

penenteram s.o. who quiets down or reassures.

peneteraman 1 quieting down. ~ *hati kembali* reassurance. **2** reassurance.

téntir (*D*) preliminary exam.

menéntir to give s.o. a preliminary exam.

tentram → TENTERAM.

tentu 1 certain, sure. *belum* – not necessarily. *masih belum* – still uncertain, still up in the air. *sudah* – certain, for sure. *sudah barang* – a) as a matter of course. b) very likely, in all probability. **2** fixed, definite, permanent. *tidak* – a) odd (jobs), not fixed (of employment). b) varying, not fixed (in type), irregular (intervals). c) uncertain. *ketidak-tentuan* uncertainty. *tidak* – *arahnya* changeable, in no fixed direction. *tidak* – *rimbanya* without a trace. *tidak* – *sebabnya* for no definite reason. **3** of course, certainly. – *saja* of course. *tidak* – *ujung pangkalnya* rambling (about a speech).

tentunya certainly, of course.

bertentu certain, sure. *Ia belum* ~ *datangnya*. It's not sure that he's coming.

bertentu-tentu certain(ly), definite(ly), positive(ly).

menentu certain, definite, stabilized. *tidak* ~ a) not fixed, variable, unstable. b) indefinite, indefinable. *ketidak-menentuan* uncertainty.

menentui 1 to examine, investigate. **2** to visit (a sick person), pay a call on. **3** to settle/pay off (debts).

menentukan [and **nentuin** (*J coq*)] **1** to decide, determine, settle on, set, establish, specify. *batas waktu yang ditentukan* deadline. *persyaratan yang ditentukan dalam undang-undang No. …* conditions established in law No. … *tanggal yang ditentukan* specified date. ~ *letak* to determine the position. *diundurkan sampai waktu yang belum ditentukan* postponed indefinitely. ~ *tempat* to set up a place (for a meeting, etc.). **2** to foreordain, destine. *Dia ditentukan akan menjadi pemimpin besar.* He was destined to become a great leader. **3** decisive, crucial, critical. *Kedua hal ini sangat* ~. These two matters are crucial. **4** to find out definitely about s.t., diagnose.

tertentu certain, specified, specific, special, particular, some. *pada hari-hari* ~ on some days.

ketentuan 1 provision (of a contract, etc.). ~ *hukum* legal provision. *dengan* ~ *bahwa* with the provision that. ~ *larangan* prohibiting order. ~ *pelaksanaan* executory provisions. ~ *pembatas* restrictive provision. ~ *penutup* closing provisions. ~ *peralihan* transitional provisions. ~ *pidana* provisions of the penal code. ~ *yang mengikat* binding provisions. **2** definiteness, certainty. **berketentuan** sure, certain. *tidak* ~ uncertain, unsure.

penentu 1 s.o. who determines, setter. ~ *kualitas* grader. ~ *trénd* trendsetter. **2** determiner, determinant, determining, key. *faktor* ~ determining/key factor.

penentuan decision, determination, setting, fixing. ~ *biaya* costing. ~ *diri sendiri* self-determination. ~ *harga* pricing. ~ *nasib sendiri* self-determination. ~ *nilai* assessment. ~ *séks* sexing (animals). ~ *tempat* localization. ~ *tingkat* rating.

tenuk tapir, *Tapirus indicus/malayanus*.

tenun weaving, textile. *barang* – woven goods.

bertenun to weave. ~ *sampai ke bunjainya* when you do s.t., do it until you're finished.

menenun to weave s.t.

tenun-menenun weaving.

tenunan woven fabric, cloth, tissue. ~ *kelarai* twill.

penenun weaver.

penenunan weaving.

pertenunan 1 mill, place where weaving is done. **2** weaving, spinning.

tenung (*Jv*) **1** black magic. **2** sorcerer. **3** fortune-telling. **4** horoscope.

bertenung to tell fortunes.

menenung 1 to prophesy. **2** to bring misfortune to s.o. through black magic, cast a curse/spell on. *Saya ditenung.* Someone has cast a spell on me.

menenungkan to prophesy.

tenungan prophesy.

penenung and **petenung** fortune-teller, seer.

penenungan fortune-telling, prophesying.

pertenungan fortune-telling.

tenusu (*mostly Mal*) dairy.

téodolit (*D*) theodolite.

téokrasi (*D*) theocracy.

téokratis (*E*) theocratic.

téolog (*D*) theologian.

téologi(a) (*D*) theology.

téologis (*D*) theological.

téorém(a) (*D*) theorem.

téorétik (*E*) theoretical.

téorétikus (*D*) theoretician.

téorétis (*D*) theoretical.

téori (*D*) theory. – *himpunan* (*math*) set theory.

bertéori to theorize.

men(t)éorikan to theorize about.

téoris theorist.

téorisasi theorizing.

téoritikus → TÉORÉTIKUS.

téoritis (*D*) theoretical.

téoritisi (*D*) theoretician(s).

téoriwan theoretician.

téosof (*D*) theosophist.

téosofi (*D*) theosophy.

tép I → TIP III.

tép II → TIK I.

tepa → TEPO.

tepak I light tap/slap. – *tepuk* tapping.

menepak to tap/slap lightly.

tepakan tap, light slap.

tepak II a climber, *Melodorum cylindricum*.

tépak small box for holding s.t. – *rokok* cigarette case. – *sirih* betel nut case. – *tembakau* tobacco pouch.

tepam menepam 1 to touch/feel with the palm of the hand. **2** to hit with the hand.

tepang k.o. climbing plant, *Desmodium chinensis*. – *asu* k.o. fodder, *Desmodium capitatum*.

tepas I (*Jv*) front veranda, office. – *pariwisata* tourist office.

tepas II bamboo wickerwork.

bertepas using this k.o. wickerwork.

menepas(i) to wall/screen in an area with this k.o. wickerwork.

tepas III direction, point of the compass. *empat* – *dunia* the four points of the compass.

tepas IV completely full.

tepaselira → TEPOSELIRO.

tepat 1 accurate, exact, correct. *diagnosa yang* – the right diagnosis. *paling* – the best. **2** right, precisely, exactly, direct (hit). – *di atas* right above. – *di hadapan* right opposite. – *di muka* right in front. – *jam enam* exactly six o'clock. **3** perfectly right (for some situation), suited. *tidak* – imprecise, inaccurate, out of adjustment, ill-advised (decision). *ketidak-tepatan* imprecision, inaccuracy. – *guna* effective, appropriate (technology).

ketepatgunaan appropriateness, effectiveness. – *jadwal* on schedule. – *janji* keep a promise. – *kena* direct hit. – *sasaran* on target. – *waktu/pada waktunya* timely, on time.

tepatnya to be precise, precisely, exactly.

tepat-tepat right, straight, directly.

bertepatan to coincide (with), coinciding (with), in conjunction (with).

menepat to go directly (to). *jalan ini* ~ *ke* this road goes directly to.

menepati [and **nepatin** (*J coq*)] 1 to keep (a promise), fulfill (a commitment), live up to (an agreement), meet (an obligation), follow through with (a plan). *tidak* ~ to go back on (a promise). 2 to head straight for.

menepatkan 1 to adjust, adapt. 2 to direct, send s.t.

tertepat the best, perfectly right.

tepatan 1 destination. 2 aim, purpose. *menjadi* ~ *pandangan orang* to become the center of attention. 3 s.o. who is asked for help, etc.

ketepatan 1 precision, accuracy. 2 correctness. **berketepatan** to coincide (with).

penepatan adjustment, adaptation.

pertepatan coincidence.

tepaus → TAFAHUS.

tepaut → TERPAUT.

tépdék (*E*) tape deck.

tépéh (*ob*) k.o. edible mollusk, intertidal clam, *Gafrarium divaricatum.*

tépék I 1 counter word for lump-like objects. **2** plaque.

setépék a lump (of sugar), plug (of tobacco).

bertépék-tépék in lumps/plugs.

tépék II stick, adhere.

bertépék to be spattered/smeared (with s.t. that sticks like mud).

menépék(kan) to stick, make s.t. adhere.

tepékong I → TOA-PÉKONG.

tepékong II – *kumis* mustached tree-swift, *Hemiprocne mystacea.*

tepekur (*A*) 1 absorbed in thought. 2 meditation.

bertepekur 1 to be absorbed in thought. 2 to meditate.

men(t)epekurkan to think deeply about, reflect upon.

teperam (*ob*) k.o. bride's head ornament.

tepes (*Jv*) coconut fiber.

tépét → TÉPÉK I.

tepi edge, border, rim, side, periphery. – *baju* hem of a garment. – *Barat* West Bank. – *cekung* concave bank. – *hutan* edge of the forest. – *jalan* side of the road. – *jurang* edge of the abyss. – *kota* outskirts of town. – *langit* horizon. – *laut/pantai* seashore. – *Pasifik* Pacific Rim. – *sungai* river bank/edge. *ke* – to the edge.

mengetepikan 1 to move s.t. to the edge/side, pull s.t. over. 2 to ignore, neglect.

bertepi 1 to have an edge/border/rim. *tidak* ~ without end, infinite. 2 bordered, edged, trimmed.

bertepikan 1 to border on. 2 to have ... along the edge, trimmed with.

menepi 1 to move to the edge, pull over (of vehicles), move out of the way. 2 to go along the edge/rim.

menepi-nepi to keep following along the edge.

tepi-menepi on either side of.

menepikan 1 to push to the side, order (a car) to pull over. 2 to ignore, neglect.

tepian 1 margin (of sea and land), shallows, edge. ~ *benua* continental margin. ~ *ilmu* s.o. who knows a lot, learned person, scholar. ~ *laut* seashore. ~ *mata* sweetheart. 2 marginal. *manusia* ~ marginal human beings (homeless people, etc.).

tepik menepik to slap, smack. ~ *mata pedang* to oppose s.o. powerful.

tepinis → TEMPINIS.

tepis I counter, ward off, parry.

menepis(kan) to counter, parry, ward off. *Présidén* ~ *dua hal sekaligus.* The president will counter two things at the same time.

tertepis countered, parried, warded off, pushed away.

penepisan countering, parrying, warding off.

tepis II menepis to skim (off), skim (over the top of).

menepisi to skim over (the top of).

téplék (*J*) thin and flat.

téplok (*J/Jv*) attached to. *lampu* – oil lamp hanging on wall.

tépo (*C*) k.o. gambling.

tepok I → TEPUK. – *bulu* badminton.

tepok II (*J*) rotten, dilapidated.

tépok I lame, paralyzed.

tépok II → TIPU *tépok.*

tépos (*J/Jv*) flat (of buttocks).

teposeliro (*Jv*) empathy.

teptibau → TAPTIBAU.

tepu (*penuh* –) 1 full, brimming. 2 with sails unfurled.

tepuk clap, tap. – *berbalas alang berjawat* to return good for good, evil for evil. – *dada tanya seléra* fight or flight. – *berbalas* tit for tat. – *kuduk* praise. – *sétan* a child's game involving clapping. – *sorak* applause and shouting. **bertepuk sorak** to clap and shout. – *tangan* applause, clapping. **bertepuk tangan** to applaud, clap. – *tari* k.o. dance accompanied by clapping. – *tepak* all k.o. clapping.

bertepuk 1 to beat. ~ *dada* to boast, brag. ~ *paha* to beat one's thighs as a sign of pleasure. ~ *sebelah tangan tak akan berbunyi* it takes two to tango. ~ *sebelah tangan* to have an unrequited love. 2 to applaud.

bertepuk-tepuk to keep on clapping, splash (of waves).

menepuk to beat, pound on. ~ *dada* to beat one's chest (from happiness/unhappiness/pride).

menepuk-nepuk to keep on clapping/beating.

menepukkan to beat with s.t.

tepukan 1 clapping, applause. 2 beater (the instrument). – *bedak* powder puff.

penepukan beating (one's chest, etc.).

tepung I 1 flour. 2 powder. – *beras* rice flour. – *cat* paint powder. – *gula* confectioners' sugar. – *hun(g)kué/hungkwé/hunkwé* green bean flour, powdered bean. – *gandum* wheat flour. – *ikan* fish meal. – *jagung* cornstarch. – *kanji* tapioca flour. – *kerang* grit. – *ketan* glutinous rice flour. – *limpa* flour made from dried spleen. – *masina* cornstarch. – *mesiu* gunpowder. – *panir* breadcrumbs. – *pati* starch. – *pulut* glutinous rice flour. – *ragi* baking powder. – *sagu* sago flour. – *sari* pollen. – *singkong* manioc flour. – *susu* powdered milk. – *tawar* rice flour mixed with water and leaves of the *setawar.* **menepung-tawari** to smear this flour on s.o. – *telur* powdered egg. – *terigu* wheat flour. – *tulang* bone meal. – *ubi jalar* sweet potato powder.

menepung 1 to pound into flour. ~ *beras* to pulverize rice. 2 (*M*) to pummel.

menepungkan to pound into flour.

penepungan pulverization.

tepus I various k.o. herbaceous plants, gingerwort, *Zingiber aromaticum,* and others. – *belalah* k.o. plant, *Languas spp.* – *halia/tanah* k.o. plant, black gingerwort, *Zingiber spectabilis.* – *hinggap/lada* k.o. epiphyte, *Hedychium longecornutum.* – *mérah* k.o. plant, *Amomum uliginosum/aculeatum.* – *wangi* k.o. plant, *Elettariopsis spp.*

tepus II various species of tree babblers, *Stachyris spp.*

ter superlative. – *apa saja* the best in every way.

tér I (*D*) tar. – *minyak* petroleum tar.

mentér to tar.

tér II → TIR I.

tér III (*D leg*) third section under the same article number (after *bis*).

tera I official seal, stamp.

bertera with an official seal.

menera 1 to stamp, apply a seal to. 2 to calibrate. 3 to print.

menerakan 1 to stamp, apply a seal to. 2 to imprint.

tertera 1 printed, inscribed. 2 embodied (in an agreement), included, appear (on a list).

teraan 1 imprint, print. 2 stamp, seal.

penera inspector of weights and measures.

peneraan 1 stamping, sealing. 2 calibration.

perteraan printing office.

tera II – *tangki* tank strapping.

peneraan strapping.

terabas shortcut.

menerabas to take a shortcut.

terabasan shortcut.

penerabasan cutting short.

teracak 1 hoof, hoofprint (of cattle).

terada I various species of trees, *Sloetia elongata*.

terada II → TRADA.

terai k.o. tree with edible fruit.

terajam → MERTAJAM.

terajang → TERJANG.

teraju (*Pers*) 1 scales, balance (for weighing). 2 kite strings attached to the frame. – *dua* kite strings only attached in two places. 3 guy lines (for a tent) 4 chain from which a lamp hangs. – *kepemimpinan* top leadership.

menerajui (*mostly Mal*) to head, lead.

terak I cinder, slag, clinker; waste. – *api* cinders. – *asam* acid slag. – *baja* iron slag. – *dapur* kitchen trash. – *las* weld slag. – *logam* cinder, slag. – *nasi* rice crust which clings to the bottom of the pot. – *semén* clinker.

menerak to toss aside (like waste).

terak II hen's nest.

terak III (*ob*) very (only in certain fixed expressions).

térakota (*D*) terracotta.

teraktir → TRAKTIR.

terakup greater coucal, *Centropus sinensis*.

teral activation.

meneral to excite, instigate, incite, activate, encourage.

terteral excited, instigated, incited, activated, encouraged.

teralan (*phys*) excitation.

terala (*A*) exalted, noble.

terali (*D*) railings, trellis, window bars. – *besi* iron railing. – *kapal* ship's railing. – *roda* spokes.

berterali with a railing.

berteralikan using ... as a railing.

teraling I k.o. tree, *Tarrietia simplicifolia, Engelhardtia nudiflora*.

teraling II blue rumped parrot, *Psittinus cyanurus*.

teralis → TRALI(S).

teram I → TERAM-TEMARAM.

teram II → TRÉM.

terambo and **terambu** → TAMBO.

terampa (*J*) bamboo bars holding the posts of a fence together.

terampil (*Jv*) skill, skillful.

keterampilan skill. **berketerampilan** skilled.

teram-temaram overcast.

teran (*M*) **meneran** to strain in childbirth or while defecating; → MEREJAN.

teranas (*ob*) layer of hard soil under the sea.

terang 1 clear, bright. 2 evident, obvious. *sudah –lah* it goes without saying. – *akal* smart, intelligent, quick-witted. – *benderang* bright, clear. – *bintangnya* lucky. – *bulan* a) moonlight. b) k.o. pancake made with peanuts, etc. – *cuaca* nice weather. – *gemblang* bright and clear. – *hari* a nice day. – *hati* a) bright, smart. b) clearsighted. – *jelas* absolutely clear. **menerang-jelaskan** to make s.t. absolutely clear, clarify. – *kain* not so clear yet. – *lampu* lamplight. – *lengkap* the full particulars. – *mata* a) clairvoyant. b) with good vision. – *matahari* sunlight, sunshine. – *otak/pikiran* intelligent. – *tanah* predawn. – *temarang/temerang* brilliant, shining brightly, radiant. – *terbang lalat* dawn. – *terus* transparent.

terangnya in other words. *untuk* ~ to be clear about it, for the sake of clarity.

terang-terang 1 frankly, openly. 2 bright, clear. ~ *gelap* dusk, twilight. ~ *kain* not too clear. ~ *larat* vague.

seterang as bright as.

seterang-terangnya as bright as possible.

berterang-terang(an) bluntly, frankly, candidly.

menerang to become light, dawn.

menerangi 1 to light (up), 2 to cast light on, elucidate, explain.

menerangkan [and **nerangin** (*J coq*)] 1 to explain, clarify. 2 to declare, state, certify (in official documents), testify (in court). 3 to illuminate. 4 to indicate, point to, show. 5 to describe, set forth.

terang-terangan 1 frank, open, candid, blunt. 2 out in the open, not concealed. *dengan* ~ openly.

keterangan 1 explanation, (official) statement, declaration, version/accounting (of events). *atas* ~ *tersebut di atas akte ini diperbuat oléh saya* in witness whereof this instrument has been drawn up by me. *memberi* ~ *di depan pengadilan* to appear as a witness before the court. ~ *ahli* expert testimony. ~ *asas/azas* statement of policy. ~ *gambar* caption. ~ *kelakuan baik* statement of good conduct. ~ *kerja* (*gram*) grammatical object. ~ *lahir* birth declaration (a different document from a birth certificate). ~ *lebih lanjut* further information. ~ *lisan* oral declaration. ~ *pabéan* custom's declaration. ~ *palsu* false testimony, perjury. ~ *saksi* a) deposition. b) testimony. ~ *sumpah* sworn statement. ~ *waktu* (*gram*) adjunct of time. 2 (~ *tanda-tanda*) legend (on a map). ~ *pakai* directions for use. 3 particulars, details, description (as the heading of a chart). *memberi* ~ *lebih jauh* to provide further particulars. 4 testimony. 5 subject (in an e-mail message).

penerang explainer.

penerangan 1 informing, clarifying. 2 information, clarification. 3 illumination, lighting.

terantai k.o. tree, *Santiria laevigata*.

terap I 1 arranging, applying. 2 cookie mold.

menerap to apply, arrange.

menerapkan 1 to apply, put (a law) into effect, enforce (a law). *salah* ~ *hukum* misapplication of the law. 2 to adopt (a policy), put into practice. *dapat diterapkan* can be applied, applicable.

terapan applied. *ilmu* ~ applied science.

penerap applier.

penerapan 1 application, practice, putting into effect. 2 adoption (of a policy), putting into practice. 3 calibration. 4 assembly.

terap II (– *nasi*) k.o. tree, the bark of which is used for making rope, etc., *Artocarpus elasticus*.

menerap to catch birds using sap from that tree.

terap III a groove in the blade of a kris.

berterap inlaid.

menerap to do inlay work on.

terapan 1 inlaid. 2 part of the kris which has an inlay.

terap IV → TIARAP.

térapéutik and **térapétik** (*E*) therapeutic.

térapéutis and **térapétis** (*D*) therapeutic.

terapi k.o. shrub, Jamaica mandarin orange, *Glycosmis pentaphylla*.

térapi (*D*) therapy. – *bahasa* speech therapy. – *kejiwaan* psychotherapy. – *kejutan* shock therapy. – *kerja* occupational therapy.

térapis (*E*) therapist.

teras I 1 core, body (of fasteners). 2 pith, kernel, essence. 3 key (figure), senior, elite (troops). *pejabat* – key official.

berteras to have a core/pith, etc. – *ke dalam* to know s.t. without seeming to, said about s.o. who is knowledgeable but quiet. ~ *ke luar* said about s.o. who brags but doesn't know what he's talking about. ~ *ke ujung dahan* a henpecked husband.

berteraskan to be based on, have as its essence.

meneras to get to the essence/core.

penerasan coring.

teras II and **téras** (*D*) porch, terrace.

berteras to have a terrace.

teras III (*D*) trass.

terasi → TRASI.

térasing (*E*) terracing.

téraso (*D*) terrazzo.

terasul (*A ob*) correspondence.

teratai lotus, *Nelumbium nelumbo*. – *besar* → PADMA. – *kecil* blue water lily, *Nymphaea lotus/stellata*. – *kerikil* Indian lotus, *Nelumbium nelumbo*. – *kerdil* dwarf water lily, *Nymphaea tetragona*. – *raksasa* Victoria water lily, *Victoria amazonica*. – *utan* → TERATAI *kecil*.

teratak 1 hut, temporary structure. 2 hamlet. 3 house (self-deprecating).

meneratak to erect a hut.

teratu (*Port ob*) torture.

terau menerau to transfer thread from a spool to a weaver's spool on the loom.

terawang lace, openwork, fretwork.

berterawang full of holes, with fretwork.

menerawang 1 to make lace/fretwork. 2 to daydream. ~ *di angkasa angan-angan* and ~ *khayal/langit/udara* and ~ *mengukir jagat* to daydream, build castles in Spain.

terawangan porous, full of holes.

penerawang daydreamer.

terawéh → TARAWIH.

terban 1 collapsed, fallen down, totally destroyed. 2 (*geol*) graben.

terbang I 1 to fly. *Pesawat udara – rendah di atas kota.* A plane flew low above the town. *tidak boléh –* grounded (of aircraft). 2 flight. *dalam keadaan –* in flight. *kapal –* airplane, aircraft. *kelas –* fly-weight class (in boxing). *lapangan –* [lapter] airfield. *mesin –* (*ob*) and *pesawat –* (air)plane. *pakaian –* G-suit. 3 to fly, travel in an aircraft. *Ia terpaksa – ke Jakarta hari ini juga.* She had to fly to Jakarta this very day. 4 to evaporate, volatilize (of liquids, salt, etc.). *minyak –* volatile oil. 5 (= **beterbangan**) to fly (of many things), fly everywhere. *Debu – ke mana-mana.* The dust flew in all directions. 6 to run away, make/run off, disappear (without a trace); → HILANG *lenyap,* KABUR II. *Mobil yang menubruk orang itu terus –.* The car which hit s.o. disappeared immediately. *Sepédanya – entah ke mana.* His bike disappeared God knows where. 7 rapidly escalating. *inflasi yang – ini* this rapidly escalating inflation. 8 to wander (referring to thoughts, etc.). *Pikirannya selalu – pada perkara yang lain semasa di dalam kelas.* His thoughts always wander to other matters when in class. 9 by air. *Jarak antara A dan P adalah lebih kurang satu jam –.* The distance between A and B is about one hour by air. *– bertumpu, hinggap mencekam* when visiting places beyond your ethnic homeland, please look for friends and family where you could stay. 10 to evaporate (of liquids). *– arwah* to lose consciousness, faint. *– bébas rokok* smoke-free flight. *– bergembira* joy flight. *– berhenti* to hover (of a helicopter). *– darahnya* very frightened. *– diam* to hover (of helicopter). *– instrumén* to fly by instrument. *– lalat* a) very early in the morning. b) to jump around without stopping anywhere, in fits and starts. *membaca –.– lalat* to read in fits and starts. *– layang* glider flying. *– lintas médan* cross-country flight. *– lintas rendah* fly by. *– mengapung di tempat* to hover (of helicopter). *– merahap* to fly down and alight. *– nyawa* to give up the ghost. *– pikiran* to lose one's head, lose one's mind, take leave of one's senses. *– rendah* low-level flight. *– sendirian/solo* solo flight. *– tukik* diving. *– uji* test flight.

terbang-terbang ~ *hinggap* with no permanent home. ~ *lalat* in fits and starts.

be(r)terbangan (*pl subj*) 1 to fly around/everywhere/in large numbers, be scattered in the air. *Banyak burung layang-layang kelihatan ~ di udara.* Many swallows can be seen flying in the sky. 2 floating in the air. *Apabila kipas angin dipasang, debu ~ di udara.* When the fan is turned on, dust floats in the air.

menerbangi to fly through/to/over, travel by air over. ~ *rute Jakarta-Singapura* to fly the Jakarta-Singapore route.

menerbangkan 1 to release into the air, allow/cause s.t. to fly. *Dalam upacara itu diterbangkan burung merpati perdamaian.* In that ceremony peace doves were released. 2 to fly (an aircraft/passengers). *Ia ~ pesawat MNA.* He flew an MNA plane. 3 to run away/off with, abscond with. ~ *uang kas perkumpulan* to abscond with the association's cash.

penerbang [Pnb] pilot, flyer, aviator, flight (*mod*). ~ *angkasa* astronaut. ~ *layang* glider pilot. ~ *layang gantung* hang-glider. ~ *pembantu* copilot. ~ *pencoba* test pilot. ~ (*pesawat*) *tempur* fighter (plane). ~ *pencoba(an)/uji* test pilot.

penerbangan flight; aviation, aeronautics. *alat perekam ~* black box (in an airplane); → KOTAK *hitam. maskapai/perusahaan ~* airline. *pelayanan selama ~* in-flight service. *rute ~* flight route. ~ *amal* charity flight. ~ *angkasa* (*bermanusia*) (manned) space flight. ~ *angkasa bolak-balik/ulang-alik/pulang-pergi* shuttle flight. ~ *berjadwal* scheduled flight. ~ *borongan/carteran* charter flight. ~ *dalam negeri* domestic flight. ~ *dirgantara* aerospace flight. ~ *domésik* domestic flight. ~ *intai* reconnaissance flight. ~ *internasional* international flight. ~ *keliling* sightseeing flight. ~ *kembali* home flight. ~ *komérsial* commercial flight. ~ *lanjutan* connecting flight; → PENERBANGAN *sambungan.* ~ *lintas médan* (*jarak jauh*) (long-distance) cross-country flight. ~

luar-negeri international flight. ~ *melintas* overhead flight. ~ *militér* military aviation. ~ *niaga* commercial flight. ~ *percobaan* test flight. ~ *perdana* maiden/inaugural flight. ~ *perintis* maiden flight. ~ *pesiar* joy flight. ~ *regional* regional flight. ~ *sambungan* connecting flight; *cp* PENERBANGAN *lanjutan.* ~ *sipil* civil aviation. ~ *tamasya udara* joy flight. ~ *tanpa asap rokok* nonsmoking flight. ~ *ujian* test flight. **sepenerbangan** of/on the same flight. *teman ~ saya* my fellow passenger (on a plane).

terbang II (*Pers*) tambourine.

terbangan to play music on the *terbang.*

terbang III *ikan –* flying fish, *Exocoetidae spp.*

terbangun → BANGUN-BANGUN.

terbil → TARBIL.

terbis 1 collapse, slide (of a mountain slope/side of a ravine, etc.). 2 mountain slope.

terbit 1 appear, be published, come out, be made public. *– lagi* to resume publication. 2 to rise (of the sun). 3 arise, come about, appear, emerge. *– soré* evening edition (of a newspaper).

menerbitkan [and **nerbitin** (*J coq*)] 1 to publish. ~ *kembali* to republish. 2 to issue. 3 to produce, provoke, cause. ~ *air liur* it makes one's mouth water. ~ *ingat kepada* it reminds one of.

terbitan 1 publication, edition, issue. 2 published, issued.

penerbit publisher. ~ *éfék* issuer.

penerbitan 1 publishing, making public, issuing. 2 publishing house. 3 edition, issue.

terbosan → TEROBOSAN.

terbul k.o. freshwater fish, hard-lipped barb, *Osteochilus hasseltii.*

terbus → TARBUS.

terbut (*D*) large nail or peg.

teréak → TERIAK.

terém → TRÉM.

terenang (*ob*) earthenware jar with a lid.

teréndak sun hat.

terentang k.o. tree, *Campnosperma spp.* and *Buchanania spp. – ayam/burung/manuk* k.o. tree, *Buchanania arborescens/sessilifolia. – malung* k.o. tree, *Campnosperma macrophyllum. – putih* k.o. tree, *Campnosperma auriculatum.*

terenyuh → TRENYUH.

terépés → TRÉPÉS.

térés → TERAS II.

terét (*D*) to go back, in reverse (of a car).

terét → DÉRÉT.

terétét (*onom*) ra-ta-tat-tat.

teri 1 various k.o. small fish, such as Japanese anchovy, white bait, *Stolephorus spp., Engraulis japonicus.* 2 small fry, insignificant (criminal, etc.). *– asin* dried salted *teri.*

teriak shout, yell, scream.

berteriak to shout, yell, scream. ~ *minta tolong* to shout for help. ~ *semampu urat léhérnya* to scream at the top of one's lungs. ~ *seperti cina kebakaran jénggot* to scream bloody murder.

berteriak-teriak to keep screaming/shouting.

meneriaki to shout at. *anak yang diteriaki* the child who was shouted at.

meneriakkan to shout s.t. (out). ~ *yél-yél Hidup Bung Joko* to shout out Long Live Joko.

teriakan shouting, yelling, screaming.

peneriak screamer.

teriba k.o. shrub, the root of which is used against worms, *Rhinacanthus nasuta.*

terigu (*Port*) wheat. *tepung –* wheat flour.

terik I 1 tight, taut. 2 blazing hot (of sun). *panas –* blazing hot. 3 difficult, hard. *pekerjaan yang –* a hard job.

menerik(kan) 1 to tighten. 2 to intensify.

keterikan blazing heat. *Meréka berjalan cepat menuju rumah masing-masing, ingin istirahat, menghindar dari ~ siang hari.* They walked quickly to their respective homes, wanting a rest, to avoid the blazing midday heat.

terik II *burung –* k.o. bird, black-naped oriole, *Oriolus chinensis.*

terik III a way of preparing beef, chicken, etc.

terika → SETRIKA.

teriko (*D*) tricot.

terima acceptance; taking, receiving. *salah* – a) misunderstanding, misapprehension. b) taking s.t. ill/amiss. *serah/timbang* – transfer. *(secara)* – *jadi* turnkey *(mod)*. *perumahan secara* – *jadi* turnkey housing. – *bérés* it's taken care of, don't worry; → TAHU *bérés*. – *kasih* a) expression of thanks/gratitude. *menyatakan* – *kasih kepada* to express one's thanks to. b) thank you. *kurang* – *kasih* and *tidak punya rasa* – *kasih* ungrateful. *meminta/menerima* – *kasih* to thank, express one's thanks, be grateful. **berterima kasih** *(atas)* to thank (for). *Ia* ~ *kepada Garuda atas bantuannya yang diberikan kepada Kedutaan Besar Australia.* He expressed his thanks to Garuda for the aid rendered to the Australian Embassy. *menerima-kasihi* to thank s.o. *Siapa yang harus kami terimakasihi untuk jamuan ini?* Whom do we have to thank for this treat? *menerima kasihkan* to be grateful for. – *kosong* (the house) is handed over vacated. – *kost* we take in boarders. – *nasib* resigned, submissive, nonresistant. – *salah* to admit one's guilt.

 berterima acceptable. **keberterimaan** acceptability, acceptance.

 menerima [and **nerima** and **nrima** *(coq)*] 1 to accept; to get, fetch, receive, accommodate (s.t. given/forwarded, etc.); *(leg)* to admit (evidence, etc.). *dapat diterima* a) acceptable. b) *(leg)* admissible. *tidak bisa/dapat diterima* a) can't be accepted, unacceptable. b) *(leg)* inadmissible. *diterima seperti adanya* taken for granted. ~ *apa adanya* to take things as they come. ~ *gadai* to take as security. ~ *kenyataan* to be realistic. ~ *nasib* to resign o.s.; → TERIMA *nasib*, NRIMO. *yang* ~ recipient. ~ *pénsiun* to collect a pension. ~ *tamu* to receive guests. ~ *pesanan* to receive an order to be accepted or that has been accepted. 2 ~ *baik* to legalize, approve; to agree to s.t. *Laporan panitia itu diterima baik oléh rapat.* The report of the committee was approved by the meeting. 3 *(Jv)* to accept or suffer s.t. (with resignation). ~ *salah* → TERIMA *salah*. 4 to consider (as). *Nasihatku diterimanya sebagai éjékan.* He considered my advice an insult. 5 to admit (as a member/student/employee, etc.). *Ia diterima jadi anggota PDI.* He was admitted to the PDI. *diterima bekerja* to be hired. 6 to take up one's duties. ~ *jabatan baru yang lebih berat tanggungjawabnya* to take up a new function with greater responsibility. 7 *(mil)* to review (a parade). ~ *parade militér dari seluruh jajaran taruna Akabri Militér di Magelang* to review the military parade of all the ranks and files of the cadets of the Military Academy at Magelang.

 menerimakan to convey, hand over, transfer, assign, delegate (power). *Bantuan uang itu diterimakan kepada rakyat.* The assistance was handed directly over to the people.

 terterima [and **keterima** *(coq)*] accepted. *Aku tahun depan harus* ~ *di UI.* Next year I have to be accepted as a student of the University of Indonesia. **keterterimaan** acceptability.

 penerima 1 receiver. *pesawat* ~ (radio) receiver. ~ *amanat* agent. ~ *aval* guaranteed party. ~ *darah* blood donee. ~ *fidusia* fiduciary. ~ *gadai* pledgee. ~ *hibah* donee. ~ *konsinyasi* consignee. ~ *krédit* borrower. ~ *kuasa* *(leg)* agent (for a principal), proxy. ~ *mandat* mandatee, receiver. ~ *muatan* consignee. ~ *pantulan gelombang* radio receiver. ~ *perintah* agent. ~ *tamu* receptionist. ~ *télévisi satelit* satellite TV receiver. ~ *titipan* depository. ~ *tugas* agent. ~ *uang* cashier. ~ *waralaba* franchisee. 2 recipient, beneficiary (in a bank transfer). 3 *(coq)* s.o. who is resigned.

 penerimaan 1 hiring, employment (of new personnel), acceptance (of new members). 2 acceptance. 3 receipts, revenue, income. ~ *dan pengeluaran* income and expenditures. 4 reception, ~ *tamu* reception of guests. 5 front desk (in hotel). 6 opinion, view. *berdasarkan* ~ *yang salah* based on a wrong opinion/view. 7 response.

terindil *(J)* → TRINDIL.

téring *(D coq)* tuberculosis, t.b., T.B.

teripang 1 dried sea slugs or Holothurians, beche-de-mer, *Holothuria edulis.* 2 *ikan* – Queensland smelt, *Saurus indicus.*

teripel *(E) main* – play a card game for three persons.

teriska *(coq)* → SETRIKA.

terisula *(cla)* → TRISULA.

teriti meneriti to stand on, perch on.

teritik I *(S ob) pohon* – k.o. large tree, *Parinarium corymbosum.*

teritik II → TITIK I, TRITIK I.

teritip barnacle (that attacks ships' bottoms). – *karang* k.o. bivalve, *Spondylus sp.*

teritis(an) porch, space under eaves (around a house).

téritor *(D)* territory.

téritorial *(D)* territorial. *perairan* – territorial waters.

téritorialisasi territorialization.

téritorium *(D)* territory (a military administrative division).

teriwulan → TRIWULAN.

terjal steep, sheer; → CURAM.

 keterjalan steepness.

terjali → TAJALI.

terjang 1 kick, lunge. *sépak* – action; → SÉPAK. – *ke* be surprised by, taken by surprise by. 2 attack. – *tumit* digging the heel into the ground.

 menerjang 1 to kick. 2 to attack, assault, assail, lunge at. *diterjang wabah influénsa* attacked by a flu epidemic. 3 to go/run into, run through. *diterjang peluru* to be hit by bullets. *Dua butir peluru* ~ *tubuhnya.* Two bullets hit his body. ~ *sebuah ranjau darat* to run into a land mine.

 menerjang-nerjang 1 to keep on kicking/assaulting. 2 to convulse.

 menerjangi to step/trample on.

 menerjangkan to kick against, give a kick with, butt with.

 terterjang hit, overwhelmed (by). *Trenggalék dan Tulungagung* ~ *banjir lagi.* Trenggalek and Tulungagung were hit again by floods.

 terjangan attack, lunge, rain (of bullets).

 penerjangan 1 kicking. 2 attack, assaulting, piercing, lunging.

terjemah *(A)* translate, interpret.

 men(t)erjemahkan to translate, interpret. ~ *ke dalam bahasa Prancis* to translate into French.

 terjemahan translation. ~ *dari bahasa Indonésia ke dalam bahasa Inggris* a translation from Indonesian into English. ~ *bébas* free translation. ~ *harfiah* literal translation. ~ *ilmiah* scientific translation. ~ *katawi/lurus/menurut huruf* literal/word-by-word translation. ~ *sastra* literary translation.

 terjemah-men(t)erjemahan translating, interpreting.

 pen(t)erjemah translator, interpreter. ~ *bersumpah/di bawah sumpah/tersumpah* authorized and sworn translator.

 pen(t)erjemahan translating, translation, interpreting. *melakukan* ~ to translate, interpret. ~ *mesin* machine translation, MT.

terjun 1 to jump (from a higher to a lower place). 2 to get/go into (a field of study/employment, etc.), go out (into), be involved (in). – *bébas* free fall. **menerjunbébaskan** to send s.t. or s.o. into free fall. **penerjun bébas** skydiver. **penerjunan bébas** free fall. – *berduaan* tandem jumping. – *bersusun* canopy teamwork (in parachuting). – *kuyup* to jump right (in). – *payung* parachute jumping. – *(payung) tandem* tandem parachute jumping.

 be(r)terjunan *(pl subj)* to jump down.

 menerjuni to get/go into (a field of study, etc.).

 menerjunkan to parachute, throw s.o. (into), throw s.t. down, drop. *Pihaknya diterjunkan ke SD-SD.* His group was thrown into the elementary schools. ~ *diri ke* to take part in, join.

 keterjunan to be hit/affected by (a sickness).

 penerjun (parachute) diver. ~ *payung* parachutist.

 penerjunan (parachute) diving, jumping. ~ *biasa* static fall.

terka *(Skr)* guess, supposition, conjecture.

 menerka to guess, conjecture, suppose. *dapat diterka* predictable.

 menerka-terka to keep on guessing.

 terkaan guess, conjecture, supposition.

 terka-terkaan guessing game.

 penerka guesser, s.o. who suspects.

 penerkaan guessing, conjecturing.

terkam menerkam to attack, pounce on.

 menerkami to attack, invade.

 terkaman 1 pounce, attack. 2 grasp, grip.

 penerkam s.o. or s.t. that pounces/attacks.

 penerkaman pouncing, attacks.

terkap menerkap to cover.

terkul *(ob)* carbine.

terkup berterkup to fight by butting horns.

menerkup 1 to grasp, seize. 2 to infiltrate.
menerkupkan to put on a fight between animals that butt horns.
terlak (*ob*) k.o. martial art.
terlalu → LALU I.
terlat → TELAT.
térmal (*D*) thermal.
termasa → TAMASYA.
térmik thermal.
términ (*D*) 1 installment. 2 (*E*) term (of office).
términal (*E*) terminal.
términologi (*D*) terminology.
térmis (*D*) thermal.
térmisida termicide.
térmit (*D/E*) termite.
térmodinamika thermodynamics
térmométer (*D*) thermometer.
térmonuklir thermonuclear.
térmos (*E*) thermos bottle.
térmostat (*D*) thermostat.
ternah (*ob*) unusual.
ternak 1 native of. *Dia – Jakarta.* He's a native of Jakarta. *orang –* native, son of the soil. 2 cattle, livestock. *– besar* livestock. *– bibit* parent stock. *– kecil* small ruminants, goats, lambs, sheep. *– potong* butcher stock. *– susu perah* dairy cattle. *– unggas* fowl, poultry.
be(r)ternak 1 to raise/breed cattle. 2 to lend. (*coq*) ~ *uang* to lend out money.
mempeternakkan to raise/breed (cattle).
men(t)ernakkan 1 to raise/breed (cattle). 2 (*coq*) to lend (money).
peternak and **penernak** rancher, cattle raiser. ~ *sapi perah* dairy farmer.
peternakan 1 raising, breeding. 2 place where animals are raised. ~ *ayam* poultry raising. ~ *kuda* stud farm. ~ *lebah* apiary. ~ *pembibitan* breeding farm, ranch. ~ *sapi perah* dairy farm.
ternang (*ob*) carafe, jug.
terobong → CEROBONG.
terobos (*Jv*) break through/into.
menerobos 1 to break through. 2 to run (a traffic light). ~ *masuk (ke)* to force one's way (into), break into. 3 to invade, penetrate. 4 (*geol*) to intrude.
menerobosi 1 to run through, penetrate, invade. 2 to cut into (line).
terteroboskan penetrable. *tidak* ~ impenetrable.
terobosan 1 breakthrough, penetration. 2 intrusion. 3 shortcut. 4 (*geol*) emplacement.
penerobos s.o. who breaks through/into, burglar.
penerobosan 1 tunneling. 2 breakthrough. 3 break-in, burglary. 4 (*geol*) intrusion, emplacement.
térok menérok to poke into a bag to see what's inside.
penérok s.o. or s.t. that pokes into a bag.
penérokan poking into a bag.
teroka (*Mal*) **meneroka** 1 to open up new land. 2 to do research.
peneroka 1 well-known figure. 2 pioneer. 3 smallholder. 4 researcher.
penerokaan research.
terokmok (*J*) big but not well shaped.
teromel → TROMOL.
teromok plump.
teromol (*D*) 1 drum. 2 box, canister.
teromolpos → TROMOLPOS.
terompa(h) sandal, shoe. *– kayu* clog. *– kuda* horseshoe.
terompét (*D*) trumpet, horn.
menerompétkan to proclaim.
penerompét trumpeter.
térong → TERUNG.
terongko → TERUNGKU.
térop (*J?*) temporary building.
teropong telescope, glass.
meneropong 1 to look at through a telescope. 2 to scrutinize.
meneropongi to scrutinize, examine.
peneropongan observation, examination. ~ *bintang* stargazing.

téror (*D*) terror.
men(t)éror to terrorize.
tertéror terrorized.
pen(t)éror terrorist.
pen(t)éroran terrorism.
téroris (*D*) terrorist.
térorisme (*D/E*) terrorism.
terowong (*Jv*) tunnel, trench. *– angin* wind tunnel. *– sejajar* drift (in mining).
menerowong to tunnel (into).
terowongan 1 tunnel. ~ *air* aqueduct. ~ *layang* air bridge. ~ *pengélak* diversion tunnel. ~ *pengering* culvert. ~ *silang* crosscut. 2 (mine) shaft.
penerowongan tunneling.
terpa attack.
menerpa 1 to jump at, pounce/jump on. 2 to attack.
terpa-menerpa to attack e.o.
terpaan 1 pounce, jump, leap. 2 attack.
terpal (*D*) canvas, tarpaulin, sail. *– dék* awning.
terpaut → TAPAUT, TEPAUT.
terpédo → TORPÉDO.
terpekur → TAFAKUR.
térpéntin → TARPENTIN.
térsiér (*D*) tertiary.
tertawa → TAWA I.
tertib and **tertip** (*A*) 1 orderly, in order. 2 rules, regulations. *– acara* rules of order. *– hukum* legal system. *– lalu lintas* traffic regulations. *tidak –* in disorder, disorganized. **ketidak-tertiban** disorder, disorganization.
bertertib well-mannered, well-behaved, polite, courteous.
menertibkan 1 to control, curb, bring under control. 2 to put into order. 3 to chase away (of street vendors from their stalls).
ketertiban order. ~ *umum* public order.
penertib s.o. who restores order.
penertiban sweeping up, putting in order, clearance. ~ *kembali* rearranging. *terkena* ~ (*euph*) fired (from a job).
terubuk Toli shad, *Alosa macrura, Hilsa toli*. *– padi* k.o. fish, *Clupea sinensis/toli*.
terucuk (*Jv*) stakes set in the sea.
terucuk(an) (*J/Jv*) yellow-vented bulbul, *Pycnonotus goiavier*.
teruf (*D*) 1 trump (in cards). 2 k.o. card game like poker.
terugval basis (*D*) redoubt.
teruk 1 acute, severe, serious (of illness). 2 aggravating. 3 hard. *bekerja –* to work hard.
terulak k.o. twining plant, moon flower, *Calonyction bona/aculeatum*.
terum I to kneel down (of an animal on two or four feet).
menerumkan to make s.t. kneel down.
terum II → DERUM I.
terumba saga.
terumbu reef (visible at low tide). *– anjungan* platform reef. *– belakang* back-reef. *– birih* fringing reef. *– buatan* artificial reef. *– depan* fore-reef. *– jumbai* fringing reef. *– karang/koral* coral reef. *– penghalang/sawar/sampir* barrier reef. *– tepi(an)* fringing reef.
terumbuk clods of earth.
teruna (*Skr*) 1 (*mil*) cadet. 2 freshman. 3 young people. *– wisata* youth hostel. *– Wreda* senior (at the Armed Forces Academy).
terung and **térung** eggplant, aubergine, *Solanum melongena*. *– asam* Thai eggplant, *Solanum ferox*. *– balado* k.o. fried eggplant. *– bali* wild tomato, *Solanum lycopersicum*. *– belanda* tree tomato, *Cyphomandra betacea*. *– hitam* black nightshade, *Solanum nigrum*. *– kuning* naranjilla, *Solanum quitoense*. *– meranti* → TERUNG *hitam*. *– pait* k.o. shrub that produces edible fruits, *Solanum undatum*. *– pipit* k.o. medicinal shrub, *Solanum tarvum*. *– susu* k.o. shrub, apple of Sodom, *Solanum mammosum*.
terungku (*Port ob*) prison.
menerungkukan to imprison.
keterungkuan imprisonment.
teruni → TARUNI.
teruntum various species of mangrove trees. *– bunga putih*, k.o. tree, sandy mangrove, *Lumnitzera racemosa*. *– mérah* k.o. small tree, *Lumnitzera littorea*.

terup → TERUF.

terus 1 continue, go on, keep on. *Rupiah bakal – menguat.* The rupiah will continue to appreciate. *Sidang Umum ditunda –.* The Special Session kept on being postponed. *– bisa hidup* to survive. 2 keep going (command to taxi driver, etc. to go on, continue), straight ahead. 3 and then. 4 straight, directly, immediately, right away. *Dia – makan.* He ate right away. *Saya – pulang.* I went straight home. *– mata/penglihatan* clear-sighted. *– terang* frank, candid, blunt, honest. **berterus-terang** to be frank, candid, honest. **keterus-terangan** frankness, candor, honesty. **ketidak-terusterangan** dishonesty, lack of candidness.

  seterusnya from now on, as of now, from here on in. *dan begitulah ~* and so forth and so on.

  berterus-terus continually, constantly, keep on ...ing.

  berterusan continually, without interruption.

  menerus continuous.

  terus-menerus 1 sustained, continued; continuous, nonstop, in a row; to keep ...ing. *dua hari ~* two days in a row. *Dia ~ mengganggu saya.* He keeps bothering me. 2 permanent.

  menerusi 1 to continue. 2 to pass/break through.

  meneruskan [and **nerusin** (*J coq*)] 1 to continue, pursue, resume. 2 to convey, send, pass along, forward. 3 to follow/go through with (a plan, etc.).

  terterus transmittable. **keterterusan** transmittability.

  terusan 1 passage, canal, channel, gully, aqueduct. *~ laut* seaway. 2 continuation, sequel. 3 extension. 4 sheath (k.o. skirt).

  terus-terusan continuously, on and on, constantly.

  keterusan 1 to go on, continue. *Ia ~ membasuh mukanya.* He went on and washed his face. 2 continuity. 3 to go straight ahead inadvertently. 4 transmissivity. **berketerusan** continuous.

  penerus 1 s.o. who continues what s.o. else has started. *générasi ~* the next generation. *~ ajaran Soekarno* [PAS] the continuer of Soekarno's teachings. *~ hak* (*leg*) assigns. 2 relay, repeater. *stasion ~* relay station.

  penerusan 1 continuation, sequel, succession. 2 continuing. *~ pinjaman* two-step loan. *~ suara* projection of the voice. 3 continuity. *~ pemijaran* afterglow.

terusi (*Tam*) verdigris, copper sulfate, hydrated sulfate of copper.

terwélu (*Port Jv*) rabbit; → KELINCI.

tés (*E*) test; → UJIAN. *– bakat* aptitude test. *– isian* fill-in test. *– kebohongan* lie-detector test. *– lisan* oral exam. *– penempatan* placement test. *– pilihan ganda* multiple-choice test. *– préstasi* achievement test. *– tertulis* written exam. *– tidak tersangkut organisasi terlarang* clearance test.

  men(ge)tés to test.

  pen(ge)tés tester.

  pengetésan testing.

tésala → MINYAK *tesala*.

tésaurus (*D*) thesaurus.

tesbih → TASBIH.

tésédé [Typhus Cholera Dysentery] TCD.

tésis (*D*) 1 thesis. 2 paper (for a course).

tesmak (*Pers*) eyeglasses.

  bertesmak wearing glasses.

tést → TÉS.

téstamén (*D*) testament.

tésting (*E*) test, exam.

téstis (*D*) testes.

tét (*Jv*) exactly, on the dot; → TEPAT.

tetabuhan musical instruments, orchestra.

tetaguk brown hawk owl, *Ninox scutulata malaccensis.*

tetak I 1 gash, slash, cut. *luka –* slash wound. 2 circumcised.

  bertetakan to slash e.o.

  menetak to gash, slash, cut.

  tetak-menetak to slash e.o.

  menetaki to slash/hack at.

  menetakkan 1 to slash/hack with. 2 to slash/hack at.

  tetakan 1 slash, gash, cut. 2 notch. 3 (*Jv*) circumcise.

  penetak s.o. who hacks, slasher.

  penetakan gashing, slashing, cutting, hacking.

tetak II **menetak** (*ob*) to decide, fix, set.

tetal closely woven, compressed, compact, packing.

menetal(kan) to compress, compact.

  penetalan compressing, compacting.

tetampah (*J*) winnow, sieve; → TAMPAH.

tetampan piece of yellow silk placed on one's shoulders when in the presence of the king or used to cover gifts for the king.

tetamu guest; → TAMU.

tetanaman plants, crops.

tetangga neighbor. *– duduk* the person sitting next to s.o.

  bertetangga (*dengan*) to be a neighbor (of).

  bertetanggakan to be neighbors of.

  menenangga to visit the neighbors.

  tetanggaan to be neighbors of e.o.

  ketetanggaan (*mod*) neighborly.

  pertetanggaan neighborliness, neighborhood (*mod*).

tétanus (*D*) tetanus.

tetap I 1 to remain, stay, continue, still. *– pada* to stick to, stay with, hold to. *Mahasiswa – pada tuntutannya.* The students stuck to their demands. *Dia – menolak.* He still refuses. *sekali ... – ...* once ... always ... 2 to keep (on) ...ing, still. *Dia ingin – menjadi présidén.* He wants to keep on being president. *– hidup* to survive. 3 steady, fixed, permanent, constant, unchanging, regular. *guru –* permanent teacher. *pegawai –* permanent employee. *pekerjaan –* steady employment. *penghasilan –* steady income. *secara –* permanent. 4 certain, sure, final (of a court's decision), (already) decided, settled. *belum –* not certain, unsure, not necessarily the case. *– hati* determined, resolute. *– ingin* to insist on. *Meréka – ingin tinggal.* They insisted on staying.

  menetap 1 to live, settle down (in a place). *Saya ~ di Surabaya.* I'm living in Surabaya. 2 to remain, settle, stay (in a certain place or position and not move), stabilize. 3 to be permanent, unchanging.

  menetapi 1 to keep (a promise). 2 to implement, carry out. 3 to comply with.

  menetapkan [and **netapin** (*J coq*)] 1 to determine, reach a determination about, set, establish. *~ biaya* to set fees. 2 to decree, enact, promulgate, pass (a law). *ditetapkan di Jakarta* enacted/promulgated in Jakarta. *pada tanggal ditetapkan* on the date it is enacted/promulgated. 3 to stipulate (s.t. in an agreement). 4 to maintain, make sure that s.t. continues.

  mempertetap(kan) to make more permanent/settled, etc.

  tetapan (*phys math*) constant.

  ketetapan 1 [TAP] resolution, decision, (court) ruling. 2 determination. *~ hati* determination, resolve. *~ pajak* tax assessment. **berketetapan** to be resolved/determined, reach a decision; to be ruled on.

  penetap 1 s.o. who stays behind. 2 permanent resident.

  penetapan 1 determining, determination, deciding, decreeing, fixing. *~ biaya* costing. *~ harga* pricing. *~ peringkat* ranking. *~ waktu* scheduling, timing. 2 [TAP] decree, finding, ruling, resolution. 3 appointing. 4 fulfilling, meeting, keeping. *~ janji* fulfillment of a promise/agreement. 5 stipulating, enacting, promulgating, passing (a law). 6 confirmation (of an order).

tetap II **menetap** to blot up, dry.

  penetap s.t. that blots up, blotter, dishtowel.

tetapi (*Skr*) but.

  tetapi-tetapian ifs, ands, and buts.

tetar **menetar** 1 to aim (a weapon). 2 to arrange the warp in a loom.

  menetarkan to brandish.

tetarub (*J*) temporary construction for a festivity.

tetas lay eggs.

  menetas 1 to hatch (of eggs). 2 to crack open (from the inside). *~ jahitan* to pull open stitches.

  menetaskan 1 to hatch s.t. 2 to cause s.t. to break out from the inside.

  tetasan hatched. *~ ayam* newly hatched chicks.

  penetas *alat ~ telur* incubator.

  penetasan 1 hatching. 2 hatchery.

tetawak → TAWAK-TAWAK.

teteguk → TETAGUK.

téték teat. *babu –* wet nurse.

  setéték *saudara ~* foster sibling.

  menéték to suckle.

menétéki to suckle, breast-feed. *Dia ~ anaknya.* She breast-fed her child.

menétékkan to have s.o. else suckle/breast-feed.

teték-bengék trivia, unimportant details, odds and ends.

tetel (*Jv*) glutinous rice steamed in coconut milk.

tétél (*J*) **nétélin** to cut off meat adhering to bones.

tételan (*Jv*) meat adhering to bones.

tételo Newcastle disease.

teteluk bight.

téténg → TÉNTÉNG I.

teténgék hard tail/finny scad, *Megalaspis cordyla;* → CENCARU, CINCARU.

tetenger (*Jv*) inscription on gravestone.

tetep → TETAP I.

teter (*Jv*) k.o. shrub, wild tobacco, *Solanum verbascifolium.*

tétér (*Jv*) **menétér** to hit, beat.

ketetéran 1 to get hit, beaten. 2 to fail, failed (to reach a target).

tétés (*J/Jv*) 1 drop, drip. - *hidung* nosedrops. - *hujan* raindrop. - *mata* eyedrops. - *riak* droplet. - *tebu* molasses. - *telinga* eardrops. 2 fluent, smooth.

setétés a drop. **setétés-setétés** drop by drop, a little at a time.

bertétés(-tétés)an (*pl subj*) dripping, dropping.

bertétéskan to drip with, with ... dripping off it.

menétés to drip, trickle down.

menétés-nétés to keep (on) dripping.

menétési to drip on, sprinkle, put drops into.

menéteskan 1 to drip, dribble; to dispense (medicine in drops). 2 to shed (tears). *~ air mata* to shed tears.

tétésan drip, trickle. *~ darah* a) descendants. b) drop of blood. *~ ke bawah* trickle down.

ketétésan of ... descent, with ... blood. *~ darah ningrat* of noble descent.

penétés drip (an instrument), dropper.

penétésan dripping, sprinkling, dispensing, sweating.

tetibar and **tetibau** → TAPTIBAU.

tetimun → TIMUN.

tetirah (*Jv*) to go somewhere to recover from a disease or for a rest.

bertitirah to go on such a vacation.

menetirahkan to send on such a vacation.

petetirahan sanatorium.

tetiron imitation, fake; → TIRU.

tetiruk k.o. bird, fantail/pintail snipe, *Capella stenura.*

tétoron a synthetic fiber.

tétralogi (*D*) tetralogy.

tétra-(siklin) (*D/E*) tetracycline.

tetua I parent (plant or animal). - *induk* female parent. - *pejantan* male parent.

tetua II blackhead, pimple, mole, age spots.

tetuang (*ob*) 1 bamboo horn; → TUANG-TUANG. 2 (*Mal*) - *udara* radio transmitter.

tetuban → KETUBAN, TUBAN-TUBAN.

tetuhu → TUHU.

tetulung (*Jv*) → PERTOLONGAN.

Tétum an ethnic group in Timor.

tetumbuhan plants, flora; → TUMBUHAN.

tetupuk k.o. shrub, *Claoxylon polot.*

Teuku (*Ac*) Achehnese *adat* title.

Teungku (*Ac*) Achehnese religious title.

tévé → TV I.

téwas (*A*) 1 to die, dead, killed in action or in an accident. - *terbunuh* murdered. - *tertémbak* shot to death. 2 lose (a battle, etc.), defeated, lost.

menéwas *~ menjadi* to degenerate into.

menéwaskan 1 to kill, murder. 2 to defeat, beat.

tertéwaskan killed, murdered.

ketéwasan 1 death. 2 defeat. 3 mishap, disaster.

téwél (*Jv*) unripe jackfruit.

téyan (*C*) collection of money for a specific purpose.

téyol(an) (*Jv*) exhausted.

tézi → TÉJI.

tezrau (*Pers*) pheasant.

Tgk (*abbr*) → TEUNGKU.

tgl. (*abbr*) [tanggal] date.

tha (*A*) name of the fourth letter of the Arabic alphabet.

Thaamah (*A*) → NAZI'AT.

Thaariq (*A*) ath- "Morning Star"; name of the 86th chapter of the Koran.

thabaqaatur (*A*) ranking.

Thadarta Samiti name of a hall in the MPR building.

thafizil (*A*) recitation from memory.

Thaha (*A*) "The letter Ta Ha"; name of the 20th chapter of the Koran.

thaharah → TAHARAH.

Thailand Thailand.

Thalaq (*A*) ath- "Divorce"; name of the 65th chapter of the Koran; → TALAK I.

thali (*Pap*) single girl's skirt.

thaodék → TAODÉK.

tharékat and **thariqah** → TARÉKAT.

thasauf → TASAWWUF.

Thaul ath- → MUKMIN.

thawaf → TAWAF.

thaypak (*C*) caretaker of a *klenténg.*

theklak-thekluk - *ngantuk* to nod out from drowsiness.

théologia (*D*) theology.

théologiawan theologian.

théologiawati female theologian.

thésaurir (*D*) - *Jénderal* chief treasurer.

thibburrahany (*A*) faith healing.

thiwul → TIWUL.

thoifah → JEMAAH.

thok → TOK I.

thoriqat → TARÉKAT.

THR I (*init*) → TAMAN *Hiburan Rakyat.*

THR II (*init*) → TUNJANGAN *Hari Raya.*

THT I (*init*) [Telinga, Hidung, Tenggorokan] ear, nose, and throat; ENT.

THT II (*init*) [Tunjangan Hari Tua] old-age pension.

Thuur (*A*) ath- "Mountain"; name of the 52nd chapter of the Koran.

ti (in acronyms) → TINGGI I.

tiada 1 not; → TIDAK. 2 there aren't any; → *tidak* ADA.

tiadanya lack of, absence, nonexistence.

meniada 1 to become nothing. 2 to say "no."

meniadakan and **mempertiadakan** 1 to get rid of, scrap, do away with, cancel, revoke, repeal, quash, lift (an embargo), withdraw. 2 to abolish. 3 to deny the existence of. 4 to undo, unfasten.

ketiadaan 1 nothingness. 2 lack, shortage. *~ berat* weightlessness. *~ jalan kembali* no return.

peniadaan 1 canceling, abolishing, discontinuance, getting rid of, lifting (an embargo). 2 negating. *~ beban* discharging.

tiaga (*M*) → NIAGA I.

tiah (*A*) wilderness. *padang* - desert.

tian 1 uterus, womb. 2 belly of a pregnant woman. *dalam* - pregnant.

bertian pregnant.

meniani to make pregnant.

tiang 1 mast, pole, tower, pile, pier, staff, pillar, peg, column. 2 main source, backbone. - *agung* mainmast. - *anténa* antenna mast. - *api* flare stand. - *bendéra* flagstaff. - *bergantung* main source of hope. - *buritan* sternpost. - *cabang* gaff. - *cerocok* piling. - *depan* foremast. - *gantungan* gallows. - *hidup* main source of income. - *ibu rumah* main pillars of a house. - *induk* main pillars. - *kampung* village elders. - *kapal* mast. - *keluarga* backbone of the family. - *kepil* bollard. - *kili-kili* capstan. - *kisi* latticed boom. - *layar depan* foremast. - *menyusur* luffing boom. - *muat* derrick. - *negara* backbone of the nation, pillars of the state. - *pagar* fence post. - *pancang* piling, pile, pier. **meniang-pancangi** to support. - *penambat* bollard. - *penggantungan* gallows. - *penghidupan* main source of income. - *penyangga* cantilever. - *pikét* peg. - *pintu* doorpost. - *salib* upright of a cross. - *sandaran* baluster. - *seri* main pillar of a house. - *silang* mizzenmast. - *tambat* mooring post. - *tanam* house pillars planted in the ground. - *topang* foremast. - *turus* a) post holding up a fence, etc. b) important figure in the history of a nation.

setiang ~ *penuh* full mast.
bertiang with a post, pillar, pole, etc.
meniang columnar.
meniangi to provide with posts, etc.
tiap I each, every. – *miap* (*ob*) each and every. – *sebentar* from time to time.
tiap-tiap each and every.
setiap 1 every, each. **2** every time that. ~ *dia minta uang* every time he asks for money. ~ *kali* every time. ~ *kita* each of us. ~ *waktu* whenever, every time.
tiap II (*C J*) **1** dosage. **2** key money.
meniap to give key money.
meniapkan to rent out and ask for key money.
tiara (*D*) tiara.
tiarap and **bertiarap 1** lying prone. **2** to lie low, try to avoid being noticed.
meniarap to lie facedown, lie prone.
meniarapi to lie facedown on.
meniarapkan to lay s.t. down on its front or s.o. on his/her stomach.
tertiarap lying/falling/facing front down.
tiau (*C*) name of one of the cards in *ceki*.
tib I (*A*) *ilmu* – knowledge of magic spells or medical prescriptions. *kitab* – book of magic spells or medical prescriptions, charm book.
tib II (in acronyms) → TERTIB.
tiba I to arrive, come. (*sudah*) – *saatnya* the time has come.
tiba-tiba suddenly, unexpectedly. **ketiba-tibaan** suddenness.
setiba upon arrival. ~*nya* after his/her arrival, when he/she arrived.
ketibaan arrival.
tiba II (*Jv*) **1** to fall, drop.
menibani and **nibani** to strike, fall on. *Lagi nongkrong ia ditibani beton.* While he was squatting a piece of concrete fell on him.
ketiban to be hit/struck by. *Meréka belum* ~ *rezeki.* Luck has not befallen them. ~ *bulan* to hit the jackpot. ~ *pulung* to get lucky, luck out.
tiban → TIBA II.
tibang – *cukup/pas* just enough.
tibér k.o. rubber mixed with calfskin-like material.
Tibum [ketertiban umum] public order.
tidak [for words containing *tidak* see the root] **1** no, not. **2** (negative prefix) in-, un-, dis-, non-. – *adil* unjust. For negated nouns in the form *ketidak...an* see the root.
tidaknya or not, or (opposite of previous word). *suksés* ~ the success or failure.
tidak-tidak 1 keep on saying "no." *Kok* ~ *melulu sih.* Why do you keep on saying "no"? **2** nonsensical, inane. *yang* ~ stupid things, nonsense.
setidak-tidaknya at the very least.
bersitidak (*M*) to keep on saying "no," keep on refusing.
menidakkan 1 to deny. **2** to abolish, wipe out.
tidur I 1 to sleep, be asleep. – *seranjang dengan* to sleep in the same bed as. **2** to have sex. – *masih sendiri* still unmarried. – *seperti mami dan papi* (*euph*) to go to bed together. – *tak lelap makan tak kenyang* very anxious. – *ayam* to nap, doze. – *awal* to go to bed early. – *bergelung* to sleep in a fetal position. – *léna/lelap/ nyenyak/senyap* to be sound asleep. – *membungkuk* to sleep huddled up (due to the cold/cramped space, etc.). – *menyidik/ miring* to sleep on one's side. – *terbungkung* to sleep in a stretched out position. – *terkedah* to sleep on one's back with legs spread apart.
tidur-tidur to laze about. ~ *ayam* to doze, sleep with one eye open.
bertiduran 1 (*pl subj*) to sleep. **2** to lie around.
bertidur-tiduran to lie around, stretch out (on a bed, etc.).
meniduri [and **nidurin** (*J coq*)] **1** to sleep on. **2** to sleep with, have sex with.
menidurkan 1 to put s.o. to bed. **2** to bed, take to bed. **3** to lay s.t. down in a horizontal position.
tertidur to fall asleep, doze off.
tiduran to lie down, recumbent.
tidur-tiduran to lie down.

ketiduran 1 to be overcome by sleepiness. **2** to oversleep, sleep late. **3** slumber, sleepiness. **4** bed.
seketiduran ~ *dengan* a) to sleep together. b) to have sex with. *selapik* ~ to be bosom friends. **berseketiduran** (*ob*) to have sex with e.o.
penidur sleeper (agent).
peniduran 1 putting to bed. **2** place for sleeping.
petiduran place for sleeping, bed.
tidur II beating on the *beduk* during *Ramadhan.*
tiem (*Pr*) black, dark-skinned; → HITAM.
tifa (*IBT*) small drum.
tifoid (*D/E*) typhoid.
tifus (*D*) typhus.
tiga three. – *Buta* the three Blindnesses: *Buta Askara* "illiteracy." *Buta Bahasa Indonesia* "ignorance of Indonesian," and *Buta Pendidikan Dasar* "without primary education." – *belas* thirteen. – *Daérah* the area of Brebes, Tegal, and Pemalang where a separate government was briefly formed in 1945. – *hari* a) three days. b) third day after s.o.'s death. *meniga hari* to celebrate this day. – *lai* a Chinese card game in which a hand consists of three cards. – *persegi* triangle, triangular. – *puluh* thirty. – *ratus* three hundred. – *roda* pedicab. – *sejoli* troika. – *sekawan* a group of three friends. – *serangkai* triad. – *tragédi nasional* the three national tragedies: a) Gestapu/PKI. b) the economic collapse. c) moral decay. – *warna* the tricolor, the Dutch flag.
bertiga to be a group of three, the three of ... *kami* ~ the three of us.
(ber)tiga-tiga to do s.t. in threes (or, three at a time).
meniga 1 to become three. **2** to do s.t. for the third time.
mempertiga(kan) to divide into three.
ketiga 1 group of three, all three ~ *orang itu* all three of those people. **2** third. *yang* ~ the third one. **3** tertiary. *kerugian* ~ tertiary damages.
ketiganya and **(ke)tiga-tiganya** all three of them.
tigaan around three.
ketigaan trinity.
pertiga third. **sepertiga** one-third. *dua* ~ two-thirds. ~ *malam* after midnight.
pertigaan T-intersection.
tigabelas thirteen.
tigapuluh thirty.
tigari [tiga hari] three days.
menigari to celebrate on the third day after s.o.'s death.
tigas menigas to decapitate.
tihang → TIANG.
tiin (*A*) *at*– "The Fig"; name of the 95th chapter of the Koran.
tijak (*M*) → PIJAK.
tik I → KETIK I. **mentik** and **mengetik** to type.
tik-tikan typing, something typed.
ketikan typescript.
pengetik typist.
tik II (*onom*) ticking sound.
tik III (*D/E?*) *kain* – bedspread.
tik IV (*sl*) strip (of illegal pills).
tika counter for reel or spool.
tika-tika reel/spool (of yarn).
menika-nika to wind thread on a spool.
tikai (*M*) difference.
bertikai to quarrel, disagree with e.o., dispute. *dua partai yang* ~ two disputing parties. ~ *paham* to have different opinions. ~ *pangai* to have a dispute.
menikai to contradict, have a dispute (with).
mempertikaikan to argue over, debate about, have a dispute over.
menikai to oppose, go against, disagree with.
pertikaian 1 disagreement, quarrel, dispute, conflict, controversy. **2** difference, discrepancy. ~ *agama* religious conflict. ~ *bathin* pangs of conscience. ~ *pendapat* conflict.
tikal (*Jv*) **menikal** to snap in two.
tikalan pieces (of s.t. cut).
tikam I stab, thrust (with a sharp weapon).
bertikam(-tikam)an and **tikam-menikam** to stab e.o.

menikam 1 to strike/stab (with a blade). **2** biting, cutting (words). *~ hati* to hurt one's feelings.

menikami 1 to strike/stab/cut into. **2** (*pl obj*) to strike, stab, cut.

menikamkan to strike/stab with s.t.

tertikam stabbed, hit, struck.

tikaman stab, thrust, blow, jab.

penikam 1 s.o. or s.t. which stabs/strikes a blow. **2** killer.

penikaman stab, stabbing, jabbing, striking a blow.

pertikaman knife fight.

tikam II menikam to place a bet.

tikaman bet, stake.

tikar plaited mat. *– gulung* – to go out of business. *– (ber)ganti/meng-gantikan* – to marry the younger sister of one's deceased wife. *– bangkar* thick coarse mat. *– bantal* bedding. *– gantung* hammock. *– kelarai* k.o. woven mat. *– kumbuh* coarse mat. *– ladang* a rough mat. *– pacar* colorful mat. *– putih* plain undecorated mat. *– sajadah/salat/sembahyang* prayer mat. *– tidur* sleeping mat.

setikar on the same mat. *teman ~ sebantal* a close friend.

bertikarkan to use s.t. as a mat, sleep on.

tikas I 1 trace, mark (of place where pressure was applied or after the tide recedes), impression, imprint. **2** mold, cast. *– garit* (*geol*) flute cast. *– pokok* main course (of a ship).

tikas II menikas to roar.

tiké I (C?) opium (prepared for smoking).

tiké II (*J*) k.o. plant with edible tubers, Chinese water chestnut, *Heleocharis plantaginoidea/dulcis*.

tiker (*D*) typist.

tikét (*E*) ticket. *– pulang pergi* round-trip ticket. *– sekali jalan* one-way ticket. *– terusan* through ticket.

tikim (*J*) k.o. herbaceous plant, k.o. pennywort, *Hydrocotyle sibthorpioides*.

tiko (C? *J*) (a slur term for) native Indonesian.

tikpi (C) trident.

tiktak and **tiktok** (*onom*) tick-tock.

bertiktak and **bertiktok** to make that sound.

tiku → TIKUNG.

tikung bend, curve, turn.

menikung to take a bend/curve, turn.

menikungkan to turn, change the direction of.

tikungan curve, bend.

tikus I 1 mouse, rat. **2** (*coq*) thief. *dimakan* – to be stolen. *ditebuk/dikerebok* – to be deflowered (of a virgin). *macam – basah* with tail between its legs. *marahkan –, rengkiang terbakar* to neglect the important for the trivial. *rumah terbakar, – habis keluar* the rats leave the sinking ship. *seperti – jatuh di beras* to get a stroke of good luck. *– babi* lesser moon rat, *Hylomys suillus*. *– belanda* a) rabbit. b) guinea pig, *Cavia cobaya*. *– berkantung* various species of marsupial carnivores. *– bulan* moon rat, *Echinosorex gymnurus*. *– ce(n)curut* musk-shrew, *Crocidura spp*. *– gunung* marmot. *– haji bulan* moon rat, *Echinosorex gymnurus*. *– hitam* Norwegian rat, *Rattus norvegicus*. *– kesturi* lesser white-toothed shrew, *Crocidura suaveolens*. *– ladang* field mouse, *Rattus rattus*. *– mondok* Norway rat, *Rattus norvegicus*. *– nyingnying* small house mouse. *– padi* field mouse, *Rattus rattus*. *– raksasa* giant rat, *Papagomys armandvillei*. *– riul* Norwegian rat, *Rattus norvegicus*. *– rumah* house mouse, *Mus musculus*. *– sawah* rice-field mouse, *Rattus argentiventer*. *– tanah* → TIKUS padi. *– wistar* → TIKUS hitam. *– tanah* field mouse, *Rattus rattus*.

menikus to be silent.

tikusan 1 (*petrol*) pig, go-devil. **2** squib.

tikus-tikusan toy mouse.

tikus II → AKAR *tikus*, KUPING *tikus*, ROTAN.

tikusan 1 k.o. bush, *Clausena excavata*. **2** various species of crakes. *– alih putih* white-browed crake, *Porzana cinerea*. *– kaki kelabu* slaty-legged crake, *Rallina eurizoenoides*.

tikusisai being overrun by rats.

ti kwéé (C) → KUWÉ *cina*.

tilam mattress; → KASUR.

bertilam with/having a mattress. *~ pasir* homeless.

menilami to put a mattress on.

tilan spiny eel, *Mastacembelus spp*.

tilang I → KUTILANG.

tilang II [bukti pelanggaran] ticket, summons (for a traffic offense). *– kena* – to get a (traffic) summons/ticket.

men(t)ilang(kan) to issue a summons/ticket.

tertilang ticketed, given a summons.

tilap → TILEP.

tilas (*Jv*) ruins.

petilasan tomb, burial place, grave.

tilawah and **tilawat** (*A*) reciting the Koran.

tilawatil and **tilawatul** (*A*) reciting the Koran.

men(t)ilawatil and **men(t)ilawatul** to recite the Koran.

tilé (*D*) tulle.

tilem-timbul bobbing up and down.

tilep menilep [and **nilep** (*coq*)] **1** to relieve s.o. of his/her office. **2** to steal, embezzle.

tilgram → TÉLEGRAM.

tilgrap → TÉLEGRAP.

tilik I 1 glance at. **2** check, observation. **3** sharp look. *titik* – checkpoint. *baik –nya* sharp-eyed. *jahat –nya* to be evil-looking. *kurang –nya* unobservant. *pada –nya* from his point of view. *– jahat* evil eye.

tilik-tilik to stare.

menilik 1 to stare at. **2** to check, supervise, control, inspect. **3** to observe/examine carefully. **4** to consider. **5** to distinguish (between). **6** to visit.

tilik-menilik to glance at e.o.

menilik-nilik to peer at.

tilikan 1 examination, observation. **2** check, checking, supervision, control. **3** point of view.

penilik checker, inspector, supervisor. *~ keséhatan* health inspector. *~ sekolah* school supervisor.

penilikan 1 supervision, control. **2** observation. **3** point of view. *pada ~ saya* from my point of view.

tilik II menilik to foretell the future. *~ nujum* to tell the future based on astrology.

tilikan prediction.

penilik fortune-teller, clairvoyant.

tilisim (*A*) talisman.

tilpon and **tilpun** → TÉLEPON.

tim I (*E*) team. *– jihandak* bomb squad. *– pencari fakta* [TPF] fact-finding team. *– pendahuluan* advance team.

tim II (C) very soft (of cooked rice). *nasi* – steamed rice.

mengetim to cook rice until it is very soft.

pengetim rice cooker (person or implement).

pengetiman cooking rice until it is very soft.

petiman rice cooker, steamer.

tim III (in acronyms) → TIMUR.

TIM IV [Taman Ismail Marzuki] cultural center in Jakarta.

timah 1 tin. **2** (*sl*) bullet. *dahulu – sekarang besi* s.o. who has gone down in social position. *– batang* tin ingot. *– campuran* pewter. *– daun* tin foil. *– hitam* lead. *– lémpéng* tin plate. *– mérah* red lead. *– panas* (*sl*) bullet. *– putih* tin. *– sari* zinc. *– wurung* bismuth.

timah-timah I k.o. tree, *Ilex cymosa*.

timah-timah II k.o. freshwater fish, *Trichirus savala*.

timang I menimang(-nimang) 1 to hold s.o. in the hand and move it up and down, dandle, rock (a baby in one's arms), pet (an animal). **2** to weigh/consider s.t. carefully.

menimangkan to weigh, consider.

timangan darling, sweetheart. *anak ~* favorite child. *nama ~* affectionate name for s.o.

timang-timangan repeated rocking motion.

timang II (*Jv*) belt buckle.

timarah tin foil; → TIMAH.

timba bailer, dipper, bucket, pail. *– ruang* bailer.

bertimba to bail/scoop with a bucket, etc. *~ karang* to start a fight. *~ uang* to live in luxury.

bertimbakan *~ darah* to shed blood in war.

menimba 1 to bail out (water), scoop; to draw (water) from a well. **2** to acquire knowledge. *~ ilmu* to study, learn.

tertimba bailed out.

tertimbakan accidentally scooped up, etc.

penimba 1 bailer, scoop. 2 person who bails/scoops.

penimbaan bailing.

timbal I balance, equilibrium. – *balik* reciprocal, two-way, mutual, on both sides. *perdagangan* – *balik* countertrade. *bertimbal-balik* mutual, reciprocal, on both sides/parts. *menimbal-balikkan* to make reciprocal/mutual. *ketimbal-balikan* and *ketertimbalbalikan* reciprocity.

setimbal 1 in balance, in proportion. 2 just, equitable. **kesetimbalan** balance, proportion.

bertimbal 1 equivalent, just the same (as). 2 on both sides. 3 ambivalent.

bertimbalan 1 ~ *(dengan)* commensurate (with). 2 to exchange s.t. ~ *surat* to exchange letters. *duduk* ~ to sit at the same height.

bertimbal-timbalan to balance e.o., alternate.

menimbali to counterbalance, match.

tertimbal balanced, in balance. ~ *balik* reciprocal, mutual.

timbalan 1 balance. 2 *(Mal)* vice-, deputy. ~ *Perdana Menteri* Deputy Prime Minister.

timbal II → TIMBEL I.

timbang 1 fair, unbiased. 2 weigh, weight. 3 rather than; → KETIMBANG. – *pas* no more, no less. – *rasa* consideration (of other people's feelings), sympathy. – *taruh* an equal bet. *bertimbang taruh* to match a bet. *bertimbang rasa* to be considerate (of other people's feelings), sympathetic. – *terima* transfer of power/office. *bertimbang terima* to make a transfer. *menimbang-terimakan* to transfer, hand over (power, etc.). – *tunai* C.O.D.

setimbang 1 balanced, in balance. 2 in proportion. **menyetimbangkan** to balance, set in proportion, harmonize. **mempersetimbangkan** to counterbalance, compensate. **kesetimbangan** equilibrium, balance, harmony, stability.

bertimbang 1 commensurate, of equal (weight, etc.). 2 to exchange, trade. ~ *kata* to exchange words. ~ *pandang* to exchange glances. ~ *rasa* to make decisions based on one's feelings. ~ *tanda* to exchange engagement rings. 3 to weigh, have a weight of.

bertimbangan commensurate, of equal (weight, etc.).

menimbang [and **nimbang** *(J coq)*] 1 to weigh. 2 to consider, (in notarial instruments) considers, considering. *dapat ditimbang dari* it can be derived from. *dapat/tahu* ~ *rasa* a) sensitive. b) ready to help. *tahu* ~ *buruk-baiknya* to know how to balance the pros and cons.

timbang-menimbang 1 to consider e.o.'s feelings. 2 to weigh carefully.

menimbang-nimbang to weigh, consider.

mempertimbangkan 1 to take into consideration/account. *kurang cukup dipertimbangkan (leg)* insufficiently motivated. 2 to think about, considering whether (to). 2 to ask for s.o.'s opinion on.

menimbangi 1 to repay (with s.t. equivalent). 2 to be in proportion to. 3 to match, equal.

menimbangkan 1 to consider, take into consideration/account, deliberate over. 2 to weigh for s.o. else. 3 to give s.t. to s.o. for weighing.

ketimbang *(Jv)* rather than, compared to. ~ *menunggu empat jam, lebih baik ke Yogya naik bis.* Rather than wait four hours, it would be better to go to Yogya by bus.

tertimbang weighted. *rata-rata* ~ weighted average.

timbangan 1 match, equal, comparison. ~ *badan/nyawa* sweetheart, spouse. 2 scale, balance. ~ *daging* meat scales. ~ *duduk* scale, balance. 3 weight. 4 opinion, consideration. 5 rather than; → KETIMBANG.

penimbang 1 s.o. who weighs. 2 advisor, counselor. 3 scale for weighing.

penimbangan 1 weighing. 2 considering, taking into consideration. 3 assessment, appraisal.

pertimbangan 1 weighing. 2 scales. 3 consideration, judgment, thinking, the reason given for doing s.t., ground, view. – *bisnis yang baik* commercial considerations. *dalam* ~ under consideration. *menurut* ~ in the view of, at the discretion of. *penuh* ~

deliberate. 4 advisory. *Déwan* ~ *Agung* Supreme Advisory Council. 5 review.

timbau menimbau to add a piece, piece out.

timbel I lead (the metal).

timbel II *(S)* cooked rice rolled up in a banana leaf (taken on a trip). **menimbel** to give s.o. such food for taking on a trip.

timber *(E)* timber.

timbil sty (in the eye).

timbris tamper (tool used in road construction). **menimbris** to tamp down.

timbrung *(J/Jv)* **menimbrung** [and **nimbrung**] 1 to interfere, intervene, interrupt, butt in. 2 to jam (signals). 3 to play (in a film, band).

timbrungan interference.

penimbrung jammer (of signals).

timbuk menimbuk to hit (with a downward motion).

timbul I 1 emerge, (float to the) surface, come/spring up, appear, rise, arise, occur, break out, go through (one's mind). – *karena* to stem/result from. 2 (in) relief. 3 to be in debt. *baru* – up-and-coming. – *marah* become angry. – *tenggelam* to bob up and down.

bertimbulan *(pl subj)* to appear, etc.

menimbul to be raised above the surface.

menimbulkan 1 to bring to the surface, bring up. 2 to bring about, arouse, produce, provoke, lead to, give rise to, cause, bring back (memories). ~ *kecurigaan* to arouse suspicion. ~ *kekhawatiran* to evoke concern. ~ *kesan* to give the impression. ~ *kortsléting* to cause a short circuit. ~ *perhatian* interesting. ~ *protés* to lead to protests. ~ *tawa* to provoke laughter. ~ *tenaga* to energize, pep up.

tertimbul to arise.

timbulan relief.

timbul II, penimbul, and ~ *raksa* mercury that is rubbed into the body to give invulnerability.

timbul III k.o. tree, breadfruit, *Artocarpus communis/altilis.*

timbun pile, heap.

setimbun a pile/heap.

bertimbun in piles/heaps.

bertimbun-timbun (to be) piled/heaped up/high.

menimbun 1 to pile up, collect. 2 to accumulate, hoard. 2 to dump.

menimbuni 1 to pile/heap on. 2 to bury in piles of s.t. *ditimbuni utang* drowning in debt.

menimbunkan to pile/heap up, accumulate, amass, stock up on.

tertimbun 1 piled up, accumulated. 2 [and **ketimbun** *(J coq)*] buried under a pile of.

timbunan 1 pile, heap. 2 build up (of fat, etc.). 3 (~ *persediaan*) stockpile. 4 (land)fill, dump. ~ *limbah* waste (disposal) dump. ~ *puing* a heap of rubble.

penimbun hoarder.

penimbunan 1 piling up, accumulating, stockpiling, hoarding. 2 dumping. *tempat* ~ dump. 3 reclaiming (land).

timburu → CEMBURU.

timbus fill in, bury. – *pantai* beach accretion.

menimbus(i) to fill in, cover up with earth, etc.

tertimbus buried, covered up.

timi *(D)* thyme, *Thymus vulgaris.*

timlo *(Jv)* k.o. chicken soup.

timnas [tim nasional] national team.

Timor Timor. – *Dili* East Timor. – *Lésté* East Timor. – *Loro Sa'e* the official name of the independent nation of East Timor. – *Portugés* [Timport] East Timor (before the Indonesian takeover in 1975). – *Timur* [Timtim] East Timor.

timpa I blow, hit.

timpa-bertimpa to come one after the other.

bertimpa-timpa to come in large amounts/stacks one after another.

bertimpaan overlapping, coming one after another.

menimpa to strike, hit, fall on, sweep over, crush. *ditimpa kemalangan* struck by bad luck.

timpa-menimpa 1 to throw s.t. at e.o., hit e.o. with. 2 to hit one after the other.

menimpai to fall on, strike.

menimpakan 1 to strike. **2** to drop. **3** to hit with s.t. **4** to lay/place (blame) (on s.o. else).

tertimpa [and **ketimpa** (*coq*)] struck, hit. ~ *bahaya kelaparan* struck by famine. *Dia téwas ~ pohon.* He died when he was struck by a tree.

timpaan blow, collapse.

timpa II menimpa to steal.

timpaan stolen.

timpah (*sl*) **menimpah** to have sex with.

timpal (*J*) **setimpal 1** balanced, equivalent. **2** fair, equitable. **3** appropriate, in harmony.

menimpali 1 to back s.o. up, take s.o.'s side. **2** [and **nimpalin** (*J coq*)] to equal, balance, match, answer, echo. *Ledakan ini ditimpali réntétan suara témbakan.* The explosions were answered by a series of explosions.

nimpali (*coq*) to agree with, consent to.

timpalan match.

timpang 1 unstable, unbalanced. **2** lame. **3** biased. **4** defective.

menimpang 1 to be unstable/unbalanced. **2** to limp.

menimpang-nimpang to keep limping.

menimpangkan to make s.t. unbalanced, make (one's leg) limp.

ketimpangan 1 inequality, imbalance. **2** lameness. **3** defect. **4** one-sidedness.

timpas I 1 dried up, run out (of energy/money). **2** low tide. – *perbani* low tide with very little fall. – *purnama* neap tide.

timpas II (*M*) **bertimpas-timpas** one after the other, again and again.

timpé (*J*) **menimpé** to steal, pilfer.

Timport [Timor Portugés] Portuguese Timor.

timpuh → DUDUK *bertimpuh.*

timpuk (*J*) **menimpuk** [and **nimpuk** (*coq*)] **1** to throw/toss at. **2** to hit, smash into.

timpuk-menimpuk to throw things at e.o.

menimpukkan [and **nimpukin** (*coq*)] to throw, hurl, toss.

menimpuki (*pl obj*) to throw at, pelt. *Anak itu suka ~ anjing saya.* That child likes to throw things at my dog.

timpukan projectile, s.t. thrown.

timpus tapering, pointed.

timsuis [intim suami isteri] husband-wife intimate (relations), i.e., a euphemism for (having) sex.

Timténg [Timur Tengah] Central Timor.

Timtim [Timor Timur] East Timor.

timun → MENTIMUN.

timung (in Surabaya) massage parlor.

timur I east. – *Dekat* Near East. – *Jauh* Far East. – *laut* northeast, NE. – *menenggara* east-southeast, ESE. – *Tengah* Middle East. – *tenggara* east-southeast, ESE. – *timur laut* east-northeast, ENE.

timur-timur ~ *laut* east-northeast.

menimur to move to the east, easterly, easting.

tertimur easternmost, most easterly.

ketimuran eastern, Asian, oriental.

timur II *kayu* – bark from the *Peltophorum pterocarpum*, yellow poinciana.

timus I (*D/E med*) thymus.

timus II [tipu muslihat] dirty tricks.

timus III – *panggang* k.o. potato cake.

timu-timu (*ob*) appropriate, proper.

tin I (*E*) tin can.

tin II (*A*) fig.

tinambah (*math*) addend.

tindak (*Jv*) **1** step, stride. **2** measure, act(ion), step. *saling* – interact. – *balas* reaction. *bertindak balas* to react. – *laku* behavior, conduct, demeanor. – *lanjut* continuation, follow-up. **menindaklanjuti** to follow up on, take the next step on. – *kejahatan* a criminal act. – *pidana* criminal/punishable act, crime. – *pidana aduan* offense prosecutable only in case of complaint. – *pidana berat* felony. – *pidana jabatan* official misconduct. – *pidana khusus* special criminal acts (abuse of authority and corruption). – *pidana pérs* press offense. – *pidana ringan* misdemeanor. – *pidana ulang* recidivism. – *pidana umum* general criminal act. – *tanduk* behavior, manners, conduct, demeanor.

setindak one step. ~ *demi* ~ step by step.

bertindak 1 to step, pace, stride. **2** to act, behave, take action/measures/steps, proceed. ~ *atas nama* to act on behalf of. ~ *berlebihan* to overreact. ~ *keras* a) to get tough, to take drastic action. b) to resort to violence. ~ *untuk dan atas nama* to act for and on behalf of. ~ *sendiri* to act in a high-handed way. **3** to commit (a crime, etc.).

menindak 1 to take (legal) action against, crack down on, deal with. **2** to prosecute. *Penimbum beras akan ditindak tegas.* Rice hoarders will be prosecuted.

menindakkan to put into practice, practice, exercise, carry out, initiate.

tertindak taken action against.

tindakan 1 action, act, step, measures (taken). ~ *balasan* countermeasure. ~ *balikan* reprisal. ~ *darurat* emergency measure. ~ *hukuman* punitive action. ~ *keamanan* precautions. ~ *kekerasan* violence, force. ~ *kendali* control measures. ~ *keras* stern measure. ~ *lanjut(an)* follow-up. ~ *paksaan* compulsory measure. ~ *pelambatan* delaying action. ~ *pembalasan* retaliatory measures. ~ *pembetulan* corrective action. ~ *pencegah* preventive action/measure. ~ *penyesuai* adaptive action/measure. ~ *perbaikan* corrective action. ~ *perdata* civil action. ~ *sita jaminan* (*leg*) seizure of property before judgment. **2** (medical) procedure. **3** behavior.

penindak and **petindak** person who does s.t. *petindak pidana ulang* recidivist, career criminal.

penindakan 1 taking action/measures (against). ~ *huru-hara* riot control. **2** upholding, enforcement. ~ *hukum* law enforcement. **3** (*mil*) operations.

tindan overlapping.

bertindan piled up (in a disorderly way), stacked.

bertindan-tindan piled up on top of e.o.

menindankan to pile up, stack.

tindas crush, oppress.

menindas 1 to crush between the fingers (like an insect), crush using s.t. hard. **2** to suppress, oppress, crush, repress, wipe out. ~ *pemberontakan* to crush a revolt. **3** to exploit.

menindaskan to make (a copy of). *Surat itu ditindaskan Muis.* Muis made a copy of that letter.

tertindas 1 coerced. **2** oppressed, repressed, crushed, repressed.

ketertindasan 1 coercion. **2** suppression.

tindasan 1 oppression, suppression. **2** copy, duplicate.

penindas oppressor, suppressor.

penindasan oppression, oppressing, suppression, suppressing, persecution, crushing.

tindawan (*M*) → CENDAWAN.

tindes → TINDAS.

tindih I overlapping. – *suara* dubbing.

bertindih 1 to be squeezed (between), lie (in the middle of). **2** piled up. ~ *bangkai* piled high with corpses.

tindih-bertindih to squeeze together.

bertindih-tindih one on top of the other, on top of e.o., crowded closely together.

bertindihan 1 to be squeezed together. **2** to lie one on top of the other, superimposed, overlap.

menindih [and **nindih** (*J coq*)] **1** to put s.t. on top of, press down on s.t., hold s.t. down. **2** to squeeze together. **3** to overlap. **4** to oppress, suppress. **5** to restrain. **6** (*sl*) to have sex with.

tindih-menindih overlapping, one on top of the other.

menindihi to press/squeeze down on, lie on top of.

menindihkan to press down on s.t.

tertindih [and **ketindih** (*coq*)] overlapped, overlaid, pinned down.

tindihan 1 squeezing, pressing down, pressure. **2** copy, duplicate. **3** overlap.

ketindihan 1 squeezed, pressed, caught (between two things pressing on it). **2** to have a cramp in … . *Tangannya ~.* He has a cramp in his arm.

penindih 1 oppressor, suppressor. **2** s.t. pressing down on s.t. ~ *kertas* paperweight.

penindihan 1 pressure, pressing down on. **2** overlapping. **3** suppressing, oppressing.

pertindihan overlap.

tindih II (*Jv*) **ketindihan** to have a nightmare.
tindik pierced (of ears). – *telinga* pierced ears.
  bertindik pierced (of ears). ~ *telinga* ear-piercing.
  menindik to pierce.
  tertindik pierced.
  penindikan piercing.
tindis menindis to oppress, suppress.
  tertindis oppressed.
  tindisan pressure, oppression.
  penindis bully.
  penindisan oppressing, oppression.
tinébar (*phys*) dispersoid; → TÉBAR I.
ting I (*Jv*) lantern. – *pal* streetlight.
ting II (*onom*) metallic sound.
tingak-tinguk to look around in a puzzled way.
tingau hook needle used to repair nets.
tinggal 1 to stay, rest. – *di hotél* to stay in a hotel. **2** to live. *–nya di mana?* Where do you live? **3** to remain, remaining, left (behind/over), stay around (after everyone else has left). – *tiga orang* three people are left. **4** nothing left to do but, all you have to do is, all that's left to do is. *(Hanya)* – *memilih saja.* All you have to do is choose. **5** (*coq*) it's up to... – *bagaimana lu!* It's up to you! – *kita lihat saja* it remains to be seen. **6** pending. – *menunggu pembongkarannya saja* pending clearance. **7** to stop, finish. *tak* – *berpuasa* to keep on fasting. **8** (in certain expressions) ready to ... **9** except. **10** left back (of a student who wasn't promoted). **11** neglected, ignored. – *bersiul-siul* sit around happily after work is finished. – *diam* to remain silent and do nothing. – *gelanggang colong playu* (of a leader) to run away from one's responsibilities. – *kelopak salak* bankrupt, all assets gone. – *tulang terbalut kulit* and – *tulang membalut kulit* and – *tulang dengan kulit* and *hanya* – *kulit dan tulang saja* nothing but skin and bones. – *kelas* to be left back, not be promoted (in school). – *ke popak salak* flat broke. – *kenangan* all that's left is the memory. – *landas(an)* a) to take off (of planes, ventures). b) to lose one's bearings. – *muat* ready to load. – *nadi* very sick, near death. – *nama* deceased. – *pakai* ready to wear. – *pilih saja* take your pick. – *tulang* very thin. – *tunggu waktu saja* it's just a matter of time. – *waktu* did not say one's prayers.
  bertinggal ~ *kata* to take one's leave.
  meninggal 1 (~ *dunia*) (*euph*) to pass away, die. ~ *tak wajar* to die an unnatural death. ~ *lebih dahulu* to predecease. **2** *ditinggal* left, abandoned, lost (s.o. to death). *Saya ditinggal pergi.* Everybody left me behind. *Saya ditinggal tidur.* Everybody went to sleep on me. *Ia ditinggal (mati) ayahnya.* He lost his father. *Dia ditinggal ke Amérika.* She was left behind (by s.o. who went) to America.
  ninggal (*coq*) **1** to desert. **2** to leave s.t. ~ *surat* to leave a note.
  meninggali 1 to live in, stay at. **2** to leave to, bequeath.
  meninggalkan [and **ninggalin** (*J coq*)] **1** to leave (behind), abandon, walk out on, turn one's back on, desert. ~ *jabatan/tugas* to resign (one's position). ~ *kapal* to abandon ship. ~ *landasan* to take off (of a plane). ~ *rél* to jump the rails, go off the track. *Usiaku sudah* ~ 8 *tahun.* I've passed my 8th birthday. *meréka yang ditinggalkan* the survivor(s) (referring to s.o., e.g., whose spouse, etc. has died in an accident, etc.). ~ *zaman* passed away. **2** to leave out, omit. ~ *huruf* to leave out a letter. **3** to neglect. ~ *waktu* to neglect to say one's prayers.
  tertinggal [and **ketinggal** (*coq*)] **1** left behind, abandoned. **2** behind. *Saya* ~ *dalam pekerjaan.* I'm behind on my work. **3** backward, behind the times, passé. *tak* ~ not precluded/omitted. **2** remainder, left-over. **3** underdeveloped. **4** arrears. **5** missed. ~ *bis* missed the bus. *jauh* ~ *dari* cannot be compared to, far surpassed by. *tidak* ~ to leave nothing undone (in order to do s.t.).
  petinggal evader.
  peninggal death. **sepeninggal 1** after ... died. ~ *ayahnya* after his father died. **2** after ... left.

peninggal(an) 1 estate, inheritance. **2** remains, remainder, rest. **sepeninggal(an) 1** after the death of. **2** after ... left.
peninggalan 1 relic. **2** inheritance, estate.
pertinggal 1 counterfoil (of a bank check). **2** file copy. **3** ledger.
tinggam (*M*) k.o. black magic which kills s.o. by piercing his/her likeness.
  meninggam to use black magic on, hex.
tinggi I 1 high, tall. **2** height, level, altitude. **3** old. *umur* – old age. **4** expensive (of prices). **5** near the zenith (of the sun). **6** advanced, higher (of civilization, education, age, etc.), high-ranking (of one's position). – *terbawa oléh ruas* big but stupid. *hendak* – *terlalu jatuh* pride goeth before a fall. – *diseluduki, rendah dilangkahi* do everything as best as possible. – *duduk dari rendah* s.t. improper. – *awan* sky-high. – *bébas* clearance. – *cakapnya* to brag. – *hari* late in the morning. – *hati* haughty, conceited, boasting, snobbish. – *himmah* ambitious. – *kaji/kecerdasan/kepintaran* advanced (in one's studies, learning). – *lawak* to spend more than one earns. – *rasi* to have a lucky star. – *rendahnya* standards, height. – *sejati* true altitude. – *semu* apparent altitude. – *tegap* tall and strong. – *usia* old.
  setinggi-tinggi no matter how high/tall, etc. ~ *terbang bangau, surutnya ke kekubangan jua* a) east, west, home is best. b) no matter how high one's position, one comes down to earth after retirement or the job is finished.
  setinggi-tingginya the highest possible.
  meninggi 1 to become higher, go higher. *Kecepatan kian* ~. The speed kept on going up and up. **2** to advance (in one's position). **3** to boast, brag.
  meninggikan to raise, heighten, elevate, increase. ~ *diri* to boast.
  mempertinggi(kan) to heighten, increase, boost. ~ *diri* to boast, brag about o.s.
  tertinggi the highest.
  ketinggian 1 height, elevation, altitude. **2** (*coq*) too/very high. **3** elevated place. **4** boasting. ~ *hati* boasting. **berketinggian** with/at an altitude/height of.
  peninggi 1 (in forestry) height, the average height of the 100 tallest trees per hectare of forest land. **2** heightener.
  peninggian heightening, raising, increasing, boosting.
  petinggi high-ranking official.
tinggi II (*Jv*) bedbug; → KUTU *busuk.*
tinggir → TÉNGGÉR I.
tinggung bertinggung and **meninggung** to squat.
tingi (*Jv*) a bark used for making dyes.
tingkah I 1 behavior. **2** whim, caprice. *banyak –nya* with a lot of fuss. *dengan tidak banyak* – without much ado. – *laku/langkah/perangai* behavior, demeanor, manners. *bertingkah laku* to behave. – *polah* way of behaving.
  bertingkah to behave (*usu* badly), act up, put on airs.
  meningkahi to put on airs toward s.o.
tingkah II k.o. drum.
  bertingkah(-tingkah) and **tingkah-bertingkah** to alternate, respond to e.o. (of musical instruments).
  meningkah to respond, answer.
  tingkah-meningkah to alternate/respond.
  meningkahi 1 to accompany (one musical instrument by another). **2** to respond to.
  tingkahan 1 drumbeat. **2** musical accompaniment.
  peningkah accompaniment.
tingkah III meningkah to interrupt.
  meningkahi to object to, contradict.
  peningkahan interruption, contradiction.
tingkal (*Skr*) borax, solder.
tingkalak (*M*) k.o. fish trap. – *menghadap mudik, lukah menghadap hilir* you can tell a leopard by his spots.
tingkap 1 louver frame, light, small window. – *atas* skylight. **2** flap.
  bertingkap with such a window.
  meningkap observe, spy on.
  tingkapan porthole.
tingkar (*S*) **meningkar** to surround, encircle, lay siege to.
  tertingkar surrounded, besieged.
  tingkaran siege, encirclement.

peningkaran encirclement.

tingkarah → TENGKARAH.

tingkarang (*M*) shard, fragment (of porcelain).

tingkas → NASI *tingkas*.

tingkat 1 level. *hingga ke – yang merata* to reach a level. **2** rung (of a ladder). **3** rate. **4** floor, story (of a building). **5** social stratum/class. **6** phase, stage. *– akhir* final stage. *– banjir* flood stage. *– batas* a) (*fin*) hurdle rate, i.e., the minimum amount of return required before s.o. will make an investment in something. b) entry level (position). *– bawah tanah* basement level. *– bunga* interest rate. *– bunga utama* prime rate. *– diskonto* discount rate. *– harga* price level. *– hasil* rate of return. *– hidup* standard of living. *– hunian* occupancy rate. *– isian (kursi)* load factor (for airplanes). *– kebisingan* noise level. *– kecerdasan otak* IQ. *– kecermatan* accuracy level. *– kedua/ketiga* to the second/third degree (of family relationships). *– kegempaan* seismicity. *– kejahatan* crime rate. *– kelahiran* birth rate. *– kematian* mortality rate. *– kewaspadaan* state of alert. *– mekar* development. **meningkat-mekarkan** to develop. *– kematian* death rate. *– kepercayaan* level of reliability. *– ketajaman otak* IQ. *– mutu* grade. *– pemulihan* (*fin*) recovery rate. *– pendapatan* rate of return. *– pengangguran* rate of unemployment, unemployment figures. *– pengembalian* recovery rate. *– penghidupan layak* subsistence level. *– penghunian/pengisian kamar* occupancy rate. *– penyusutan* depreciation rate. *– perputaran* turnover rate. *di – pertama* (*leg*) (court) of the first instance. *– piutang* rank of a debt. *– potongan* discount rate. *– pulang pokok* break-even point. *– sarjana* post-graduate. *– sempurna* upgrade. **meningkat-sempurnakan** to upgrade. *– tarif* rate. *– tinggi* high-level. **meningkat-tinggikan** to step up, increase.

setingkat 1 a step/level. *~ demi ~* step by step, gradually. **2** at the same level.

setingkat-setingkat step by step, gradually.

bertingkat 1 with more than one story (of a building), multistory. *~ tiga* three-story. **2** graduated.

bertingkat-tingkat 1 gradually, in stages/phases, by degrees. **2** stratified, terraced, multistoried.

meningkat 1 to improve, get better. **2** to reach (a stage of life). *Kini ia sudah ~ déwasa.* She's all grown up now. **3** to increase, escalate, heighten, mount. *~ melebihi* to reach and surpass. *~ menjadi* to develop into. **4** to climb, ascend, go up. **5** to get promoted. **6** to terrace.

meningkat-ningkat 1 to keep increasing. **2** to terrace.

meningkatkan 1 to increase, raise, heighten, beef/step/build up. *~ hukuman menjadi* to increase a sentence to. **2** to improve, develop. *~ mutu* to upgrade.

tingkatan 1 level, stage, phase. **2** class, level, standard. *~ hidup* standard of living. **3** floor, story. **4** gradient.

peningkat 1 improver. **2** s.t. that augments. *~ tegangan* booster.

peningkatan 1 increasing, increase, escalation, raising, boosting, augmenting. *~ kebutuhan* rising demands. **2** improving, improvement, upgrading. *~ arti* (*ling*) amelioration.

tingkep (*Jv*) ceremony to celebrate s.o.'s seventh month of pregnancy.

meningkepi to hold a ceremony in s.o.'s seventh month of pregnancy.

tingkepan this ceremony.

tingker → TINGKAR.

tingkis k.o. marine fish.

tingkrang (*ob*) **bertingkrang** and **meningkrang** to sit in an improper manner.

tingkuh (*M?*) **bertingkuh** to quarrel.

tingting I (*J*) net for catching shrimp.

tingting II sugared beets. *– jahé* ginger candy. *– wijén* k.o. sesame-seed brittle.

tingting III (*J*) genuine, pure, unused. *gadis –* a virgin. *jaka –* a confirmed bachelor.

tingting IV and **tingtong** (*onom*) ding-a-ling, sound of a bell ringing.

meningting 1 to strike a coin to make sure it is genuine. **2** to shake rice, etc. with a winnow to clean it. **3** to separate the good from the bad.

ting-tong (*onom*) ding-dong.

berting-tong to make such sounds.

tingtur (*D/E*) tincture.

tingwé (*Jv*) [nglinting déwé] roll your own (cigarette).

tinimbang (*Jv*) compared to, rather than; → KATIMBANG. *Mode pakaian bahkan sebaiknya lebih konsérvatif ~ yang mutakhir.* The way of dressing in fact should be more conservative than up-to-date.

tinja (*Jv*) **1** feces. **2** waste, sewage.

tinjak → INJAK. **bersitinjak** (*ob*) to do s.t. step by step.

tinjau I observe. *– karang* lookout (on a boat for coral reefs).

bertinjau-tinjau(an) to be observant, on one's guard, look around.

meninjau 1 to observe, watch. **2** to consider, view. *~ kembali* a) to reconsider, review. b) (*euph*) to wipe out, eliminate. *sedang ditinjau* under consideration. **3** to reconnoiter, look around. **4** to figure out, fathom, guess. *Siapa yang bisa ~ perasaan orang?* Who can fathom people's feelings?

meninjau-ninjau to look around.

tinjau-meninjau 1 to look around, survey. **2** to watch e.o.

tinjauan 1 observation. **2** consideration, review. *~ buku* book review. *~ gaji* salary review. *~ umum* overview. **3** reconnaissance.

peninjau observer. *~ depan* (*mil*) forward observer.

peninjauan 1 observation, review. *~ kembali* review. *~ depan* forward observation post. **2** reconnoitering, reconnaissance. **3** consideration.

tinjau II 1 various species of plants and trees.

tinju 1 fist. **2** boxing match.

bertinju to box.

bertinju-tinjuan to punch e.o.

meninju to punch, hit.

tinju-meninju to punch e.o., engage in fisticuffs.

meninjui to punch at, strike out at.

meninjukan *~ tangan* to make a fist.

tertinju punched, hit.

petinju boxer.

pertinjuan boxing match.

tinta (*Port*) ink. *– cétak* printing ink. *– Cina* India ink. *– emas* gold ink. *– koran* news ink.

bertinta inked, with ink in it.

menintai to ink, put ink on.

penintaan inking.

tinting → TINGTING III.

tintir kerosene lamp.

tintong → TING-TONG.

tiong → TIUNG.

tiongcupia (*C*) moon cake.

tionghoa and **tionghwa** (*C*) Chinese; → CINA. *– peranakan* Chinese born in Indonesia. *– totok* Chinese born in China.

ketionghwaan Chinese (*mod*).

pertionghwaan Chinese (*mod*).

Tiongkok (*C*) China. *– Daratan* Mainland China. *– Mérah* Red China.

tip I (*E*) **1** tip, gratuity. **2** piece of information.

men(t)ip to tip.

men(t)ipkan to give ... as a tip.

tip II → TIK I.

tip III (*E*) **1** recording tape. **2** tape recorder. **3** (Scotch) tape.

men(t)ip and **mengetip** to tape, tape-record.

tipa and **tipe** (*D*) type, kind.

tipak (*M*) share, allotment, quota.

bertipak shared out, allotted.

tipar (*J/Jv*) dry rice field.

menipar to work such a field.

tip-éks k.o. correction fluid, white-out.

mentip-éks to white-out, remove with correction fluid.

tip-éksan whited out.

tipes (*D*) typhus.

tipi → TIVI I.

tipikal (*E*) typical.

tipis 1 thin. **2** thinning (of head hair). **3** slight, remote (of hope), low (of profit). **4** sheer (of fabric), fine (of thread). *– bibir* always complaining. *– telinga* overly sensitive, touchy.

setipis as thin as. *~ kulit ari* very narrow/remote/short (distance).

menipis 1 to become thin(ner), thin out. **2** to decrease, decline, become fewer and fewer, deplete, taper down, run low (of supplies), fade away (of memories). *Jumlah muridnya makin ~.* He is getting fewer and fewer students. *Hujan sudah agak ~.* The rain has slowed down.

menipiskan 1 to thin s.t. out, make s.t. thin, dilute. **2** to cut down on, reduce.

mempertipis to make s.t. thinner.

tertipis the thinnest.

penipis *bahan ~* thinner.

penipisan thinning, making thinner.

tipografi (*D/E*) typography.

tipologi (*D/E*) typology.

tipologis (*D*) typological.

tipp-éx → TIP-ÉKS.

tipu 1 trick, ruse, cunning. **2** deceit, deception. *- Acéh gurindam barus* watch out for tricks. *- Acéh* cunning tricks. *- daya* cunning tricks, gimmicks. *- helat* tricks. *- mata* optical illusion. *- muslihat* cunning tricks. *- tepok* ruse, trick.

menipu [and **nipu** (*coq*)] **1** to trick, fool, swindle, deceive. *ditipu bulat-bulat* swindled. **2** to make a fool of s.o.

tertipu [and **ketipu** (*coq*)] tricked, cheated, deceived. *mudah ~* gullible.

tipuan 1 fraud, trickery. **2** ruse. **3** sham, fake, dummy.

ketipuan to be disappointed, let down.

penipu deceiver, imposter. *~ ulung* con man.

penipuan deceit, deception, fraud.

tipulogi trickery, deceit.

tir I (*Pers*) castle (the chess piece).

tir II → TÉR I.

tirah → TETIRAH.

tirai (*Tam*) **1** blinds, curtains. **2** partition, screen, (protective) sheath. *- api* fire screen. *- bambu* bamboo blinds. *negara - bambu* China. *- bantal* pillow fringe. *- belakang* background. *- kelambu* mosquito curtain. *- mirai* all k.o. blinds. *- radar* radar screen.

bertirai with a screen, etc., screened, etc.

bertiraikan *~ banir* to have tree-buttresses for one's bed curtains, i.e., to have no house.

tirakat (*A*) austerity through fasting and meditation.

bertirakat to meditate.

tirakatan 1 night vigil. **2** k.o. feast.

tiram I oyster, *Ostrea spp. - bakau* plicate oyster, *Ostrea parasitica. - batu* rock oyster, *Ostrea cuculata.*

petiraman oyster bed.

tiram II k.o. marine fish, *Clupea kanagurta.*

tiran (*D*) tyrant.

tirani (*E*) tyranny.

tiras I circulation (of a magazine, etc.); → OPLA(A)H.

bertiras with a circulation of.

tiras II (*Port*) **1** cloth remnants. **2** fringe, raveled edge.

bertiras(-tiras) fringed.

tirau (*M*) goblin, gnome.

tiri (of family relationships) step, half. *adik -* half brother/sister. *ibu -* stepmother.

tirik *tirik-tirik* in detail.

tiris 1 permeable. **2** to spring a (slow) leak, leak through. *- miris* leaking badly.

meniris to drain, ooze.

meniriskan 1 to make permeable. **2** to cause a leak. **3** to drain (the water out of s.t.).

tirisan leak, place where s.t. is leaking.

ketirisan 1 permeated. **2** wet from being leaked on.

penirisan place where s.t. is drained.

tirjup k.o. bird, shrike, *Lanius tigrinus.*

tirkah (*A*) heirlooms.

tiroid (*D/E*) thyroid.

tirtakencana golden water.

tirtamarta nectar.

tirta yatra (*Bal*) pilgrimage to a holy place to seek holy water.

Tirtonadi name of a train running between Jakarta and Solo.

tiru imitate. *- teladan* example to follow.

meniru [and **niru** (*coq*)] **1** to imitate, ape, do an impression of. **2** to simulate. **3** to copy.

tiru-meniru to ape e.o.

meniru-niru to imitate, do an imitation of.

menirukan to imitate, do the same as, make a copy of, repeat after.

tertiru imitated.

tiruan 1 imitation, dummy. **2** synthetic, artificial, man-made, ersatz. **3** counterfeit, forgery. **4** a copy of s.t. in miniature.

tiru-tiruan to do an imitation of.

peniru imitator, imposter.

peniruan imitation, imitating, copying.

tirus tapering, conical, becoming narrower toward one end, telescoping.

menirus to taper, telescope.

penirusan attenuation.

tis (*Jv*) → PANAS *tis.*

tisik (*J/Jv*) **1** mend, darn. **2** stitch.

menisik(i) to darn, mend, stitch up.

menisikkan 1 to darn, mend (for s.o.). **2** to give s.t. to s.o. for mending.

tisikan 1 s.t. darned/mended. **2** darn, mend. **3** stitch.

tisor (*D*) k.o. silk.

tisu (*D/E*) tissue (paper).

tit I (*onom*) beep (sound of a car horn).

tit II (*sl*) **1** to die, dead. **2** marijuana.

titah (royal) order, command.

bertitah to pronounce an order, issue a command.

menitahkan to order, command s.o.

titar, bertitar-titar, and **tertitar-titar** to move back and forth quickly.

menitar-nitarkan to move s.t. back and forth quickly.

titel (*D*) **1** degree. **2** title. *- yang memberatkan* onerous title.

bertitel with a title/degree.

bertitelkan with the title/degree of.

titi I small wooden footbridge. *- gantung* suspension bridge. *- laras* notation.

bertitian *diberi ~* bridged.

meniti to pass over, walk on (a plank, etc.). *~ air (polongan asap)* middle-man, broker. *~ batang kayu* and *~ buih/kawat* to do s.t. very difficult. *~ kariér* to pursue one's career. *~ kehidupan* to try one's luck.

titian 1 footbridge. *~ batu* stepping-stones. *~ gantung* suspension bridge. *~ peraga* catwalk. *~ siratulmustakim* narrow path for believers on Judgment Day. *~ biasa lapuk, janji biasa mungkir* don't trust people's promises. *membuat ~ berakuk* to trick people. **bertitian** with a footbridge. **2** jumper (in computer).

titi II (*Jv*) attentive. *~, Tatag, Tuntas* Boy Scout motto (attentive, undaunted, thorough).

titiang (*Jv*) (self denigrating) I, me.

titih → PETITIH.

titihan (*- telaga*) little grebe, *Tachybaptus ruficollis.*

titik I 1 a drop. **2** dot, spot, point, period. *- air mata* teardrop. *- alir (petro)* yield point. *- antara* intermediate point. *- api* focus, focal point. *- apung* flotation point. *- asap (petro)* smoke point. *- awal* initial point. *- bakar* fire point. *- balik* turning point. *- beku* freezing point. *- benam* center of buoyancy. *- berat* a) center of gravity. b) center/heart of s.t. **menitik-beratkan** to emphasize, place emphasis (on), stress, consider important. **penitik-beratan** stressing, emphasizing. *- bertindih* colon (the punctuation mark). *- biaya kembali* break-even point. *- buhul* where the roof joists meet. *- buta* blind spot. *- cair* melting point, liquefaction point. *- cekik* choke point. *- dasar* a) (*fin*) basic points. b) the low point, nadir. *- didih* boiling point. *- dua* colon (the punctuation point). *- emas* gold point. *- embun* dew point. *- ikat* reference point (in surveying). *- impas* break-even point. *- jenuh* a) saturation point. b) high point. *- kaki* nadir, low point. *- kata* decision. *- kenal* checkpoint. *- keramaian* public place. *- kering* dry point. *- keruh* cloud point. *- keseimbangan* break-even point. *- koma* semicolon. *tidak karuan/ tentu - komanya* hard to figure out. *- kumpul* accumulation point. *- layu* wilting point. *- lebur/léléh* melting point. *- lepas* outfall (in mining). *- lidah* a saying. *- luluh* a) melting point. b) yield point. *- masuk* entry point. *- mata* point of view. *- mati* dead center. – *menengah* center. – *minat* points of interest. – *mula* starting point. – *nadir* low point. – *nol* zero. – *nyala* flash point. – *padu* fusion point. – *panas* hot spot. – *pandang* viewpoint. – *pangkal* basic starting point for a discussion. – *pecah* breaking point. – *pembagi* distribution point. – *pemeriksaan* checkpoint. – *penggabungan* assembly point. – *penggal batas* cut-off point. – *penyatuan* rallying point. – *permati* critical point. – *permulaan* starting point. – *pertalian/pertautan* point of contact, connection point. – *pertemuan* point of contact, pickup point. – *perubahan pokok* turning point. – *pijak* starting point, stepping-off point. – *pisah* (*petro*) cut point. – *pulang pokok* break-even point. – *puncak* climax, high point. – *pusat* center, focus. – *putar* pivot. – *rawan* critical/vulnerable point, flash point. – *rendah* low point. – *seimbang* break-even point. – *sela* break point. – *seléra* one's mouth waters. – *simpang* point of divergence. – *simpul* node. – *singgung* point of contact. – *tak dapat balik* point of no return. – *taut* connection point. – *temu* meeting point. – *terang* bright spot. – *terendah* low point. – *tetap* benchmark. – *tétés* (*petro*) dropping point. – *tilik* checkpoint. – *tolak* departure point. **bertitik tolak** to depart/start off. – *tumpu* starting mark.

setitik ~ *lidah* a word or two, a few words. ~ *demi* ~ drop by drop.

bertitik 1 to drip, drop. ~ *tolak dari* starting from. 2 to have a period (of a sentence).

bertitikan (*pl subj*) to drip, drop.

bertitik-titik dotted.

menitik(-nitik) 1 to drip. 2 to place a period on.

menitiki to sprinkle/drip on.

menitikkan to make drip, sprinkle, shed (tears).

titikan drop, drip.

penitikan dotting.

titik II menitik to hammer, forge. *laksana emas baru dititik* like newly hammered gold.

titilaras musical scale.

titimangsa (*Jv*) 1 chronicle. 2 date.

titinada musical note, pitch level.

titip (*Jv*) **menitip** [and **nitip** (*coq*)] 1 to ask s.o. to do a favor, run an errand, etc. *Boléh saya titip?* Can you do me a favor. – *salam* send one's regards (to s.o.). 2 to entrust s.t. to s.o. temporarily. 3 to give s.t. to s.o. for safekeeping.

menitipi to give s.o. s.t. for safekeeping.

menitipkan [and **nitipin** (*J coq*)] to put/leave s.t. somewhere or with s.o. for safekeeping, entrust. *dititipkan tidur* to be put to sleep (at). *dititipkan menjualkan* to be taken on commission. *tempat* ~ *barang* place for checking items (in a store, etc.). ~ *pesan* ask s.o. to do an errand.

titipan 1 deposit, custody. ~ *sepéda* bicycle parking. 2 deposited, entrusted, left for safekeeping. *orang* ~ s.o. put in a certain position because he knows a VIP or an insider, not because he is qualified for the job.

ketitipan to receive s.t. for safekeeping.

penitip 1 person who puts s.t. somewhere for safekeeping. 2 (in espionage) live drop.

penitipan 1 depositing, putting s.t. somewhere for safekeeping, safekeeping, bailment, custody. ~ *koléktif* (*fin*) collective custody. 2 storage place. 3 (in espionage) dead drop.

titir I (*Jv*) alarm signal (beaten out on a drum/gong).

menitir (~ *lesung*) to beat the alarm signal.

titir II and **ketitiran** k.o. bird, barred ground dove, *Geopelia striata*.

titiran (*Jv*) 1 propeller. 2 windmill.

titis I (*Jv*) **menitis** and **nitis** 1 to reincarnate. 2 (*coq*) to be passed down (by heredity), be inherited.

titis-menitis to reincarnate.

titisan (*Jv*) reincarnation. ~ *darah* descendants. ~ *péna* composition, essay.

penitisan (*Jv*) reincarnation.

titis II → TÉTÉS.

titisara (*Jv*) village land (whose produce is used to finance village needs).

titit I (*J*) young boy's penis. *bulu* – incipient pubic hair.

titit II (*onom*) honking sound (of vehicle horn).

titulér (*D*) titulary.

tiung various species of birds that imitate human words. – *batu kecil* broad-billed roller, pied bush chat, whistling thrush, *Myophonus glaucinus, Eurystomus orientalis, Saxicola caprata*. – *belacan* blue whistling thrush, *Myophonus caeruleus/flavirostris*. – *(e)mas* grackle, hill myna, *Gracula religiosa*. – *lampu* dollar bird, *Eurystomus orientalis*. – *mungkal* Javan cochoa, *Cochoa azurea*.

tiup blow (of wind), wind (instrument). – *besar* blown up, exaggerated. **meniup-besarkan** to blow s.t. up out of all proportion.

bertiup 1 to blow. *Angin* ~. The wind is blowing. 2 to spread (of rumors).

meniup to blow (of the wind), blow (a whistle, etc.), blow out (a candle), blow up (a balloon), play (a wind instrument). ~ *api dalam air* to perform a difficult task. ~ *mati* to blow out (a candle). ~ *semangat* to encourage.

meniup-niup to blow s.t. up out of all proportion.

meniupi 1 to blow on s.t. 2 to blow onto s.o. (part of a healing ceremony).

meniupkan 1 to fan. 2 to spread, make s.t. fan out. 3 to spread (rumors). *Dia sempat ditiupkan bakal jadi pesaing Pak S.* It is rumored that he is going to be Mr. S's rival. 4 to blow (for s.o. else). 5 to blow (one's breath on s.o. for curing an illness).

tertiup blown.

tiupan 1 blowing, blast (of wind), gust. 2 blowing on (to cure illness).

peniup s.o. who blows, player (of a wind instrument). ~ *gelas* glassblower. ~ *selomprét* bugler. ~ *suling* flautist. ~ *trombom* trombonist.

peniupan blowing. ~ *pasir* sandblasting.

tiup-tiup k.o. tree, *Adinandra dumosa*.

tivi → TV.

tiwas → TÉWAS.

tiwikrama (*Skr*) 1 change of form, transformation. 2 (in *wayang*) Kresna changing into Wisnu.

bertiwikrama to transform o.s., change form.

tiwul (*Jv*) snack made from dried cassava.

tk I *rev*) [tingkat] level, floor.

TK II (*init*) [taman kanak-kanak] kindergarten.

TKI (*init*) [Tenaga Kerja Indonésia] Indonesian worker abroad.

TKP (*init*) [Tempat Kejadian Perkara] crime scene.

TKW (*init*) [tenaga kerja wanita] (Indonesian) female worker (abroad).

tl- also see entries beginning with *tel-*.

tlédék (*Jv*) female dancer and singer.

tlembuk (*Jv*) whore.

tlh (*init*) → TELAH I.

tlundak (*Jv*) steps, stairs.

tlusub (*Jv*) infiltrated.

Tn (*abbr*) → TUAN.

TNI (*init*) → TENTARA *Nasional Indonésia*.

to I (*Jv*) right? Isn't that so?; → KAN III. *Musti gitu, –?* That's the way it is, right? *ya* – right?

to II → DATUK.

to III (*C*) close, fail (of a business).

to IV → ATAU.

toa (*C*) indent, order form used in certain illegal deals between Singapore and Tanjung Pinang.

toako (*C*) k.o. ship, lighter.

toalét (*D*) /twalét/ toilet.

toa-pékong (*C*) 1 Chinese deity. 2 Chinese temple.

tobak bertobak to cut one's nails (for the first time).

menobak to cut s.o.'s nails (for the first time).

tobang (*mil*) s.o. ordered around to do minor errands, gofer.

tobat (*A*) 1 repentance, remorse. 2 reclamation. 3 to mend one's ways. 4 mild exclamation, good gracious. 5 to learn one's lesson from a bad experience. *Baru engkau –!* That taught you a good lesson!

bertobat 1 to repent, feel remorse. 2 to regret, feel sorry. 3 to have learned a good lesson. 4 to return (to one's religion/the right path, etc.).

men(t)obatkan 1 to teach s.o. a good lesson. 2 to feel remorse about. 3 ~ *orang* to lead s.o. to Islam.

pertobatan remorse, regret.

tobel → TOBIL.

toberos → TOBROS.

tobil mild exclamation, good gracious, heavens.

toblos → COBLOS.

toboh (*M*) group, team.

   bertoboh-toboh in groups.

tobong I → TOMBONG I.

tobong II (*Jv*) theater (for *ketoprak/wayang* performances).

tobralko k.o. fabric.

tobros (*J*) break through; → TEMBUS.

   menobros to break through, penetrate. ~ *pertahanan musuh* to break through enemy defenses.

   tobrosan breakthrough.

   penebrosan breakthrough, breaking through, penetrating.

toco → TAUCO.

todak → IKAN *todak*.

todat [tokoh adat] traditional-law leaders.

Toddopuli the military resort command (*Korém* 141) in Watambone.

todong (*J/Jv*) threaten with a weapon.

   menodong [and **nodong** (*coq*)] **1** to threaten with a weapon, pull ... on s.o. *kalau sudah ditodong pistol di kepala* if a pistol were put to my head. **2** to commit armed robbery, stage a holdup. **3** to put pressure on s.o. to do s.t.

   menodongkan [and **nodongin** (*J coq*)] to aim (a weapon), threaten with (a weapon).

   tertodong threatened (with a weapon).

   todongan threat with a weapon, stickup, holdup.

   penodong holdup man.

   penodongan threatening with a weapon, stickup, holdup, armed robbery.

tofan → TOPAN.

toga I (*L*) toga, academic robe, robe of office, judge's gown.

toga II [tokoh agama] religious leaders.

togan (*ob*) **menogan** to throw s.t. at a target.

togé → TAOUGÉ.

togél I tailless.

   menogél(kan) to cut off the tail.

togél II [toto gelap] k.o. illegal lottery.

Togog **1** character in the *wayang* who is not loyal. **2** opportunistic person.

togok I **1** stump, trunk (without branches). **2** trunk (of the body). **3** (*J*) stupid.

   bertogok and **menogok** to sit around and do nothing.

togok II (*M*) k.o. lamp. – *damar* lamp stand.

togok III k.o. marine fish, Indian spiny turbot, *Psettodes erumei*.

toh I (*D*) and yet, still, nevertheless.

toh II large birthmark.

tohok I harpoon. – *lembing ke semak* to do s.t. useless.

   menohok **1** to harpoon/stab. **2** to betray. ~ *kawan seiring* to betray one's comrades. ~ *sepeninggal ciling* to remember s.t. too late.

   menohokkan to harpoon/stab with.

tohok II *bintang* – Southern Cross.

tohok III k.o. fish, *Scombero morus*.

tohor I **1** dried up (in low tide), shallow (of rivers). **2** superficial. **3** all gone (of money).

   bertohor to be dry. ~ *air liur* to give too much advice so that it's not listened to. *tidak* ~ *kaki* to work and work without a break.

   menohorkan to dry up.

   ketohoran **1** too dry. **2** dryness. **3** out of (money).

tohor II → KAPUR *tohor*.

toilét (*D*) /twalét/ toilet.

tojang prop, support, underpinning.

toji (*Jv*) [moto siji] one-eyed person.

tojin (*C*) Buddhist or Taoist monk.

tojok *bola* – billiards.

   menojok to prod, poke.

tojor (*J*) **menojor** to punch.

tojos (*J*) **menojos** [and **nojos** (*coq*)] **1** to pierce, perforate. **2** to vote (by perforating a ballot); → COBLOS.

penojosan punch, perforate. ~ *tanda gambar* voting by punching an illustrated ballot (used by illiterates).

tok I **1** just, only. **2** pure, without anything added. *kopi* – black unsweetened coffee.

tok II (*onom*) knocking sound.

tokai (*Pr*) shit; → TAHI I.

tokak I k.o. marine fish, Diana's hogfish, *Bodianus diana*.

tokak II **menokak** to bite (of animals).

tokak III k.o. sore on leg, etc. *bagai* – *lekat di kening* shame which cannot be hidden.

tokak-takik cut unevenly.

tokcér (*J?*) **1** instant, to start instantly. *penerbit* – publisher who pays right away. **2** effective. *obat yang* – effective medicine. **3** fertile.

toké(h) → TAOKÉH, TAUKÉ.

tokék I **1** gecko. **2** (mild curse) fool!

tokék II scabies on head.

tokét (*Pr vulg*) (female) breast, tits; → TÉTÉK.

tokh → TOH I.

Tokio Tokyo.

toko (*C*) store, shop. – *bébas béa* duty-free shop. – *berangkai* chain store. – *besi* hardware store. – *buku* bookstore. **pertoko-bukuan** (*mod*) bookstore. – *cabang* branch store. – *emas* jewelry store. – *grosir* wholesaler. – *jaring* chain store. – *kelontong* variety store. – *kerinting rambut* beauty shop. – *khusus* specialty shop. – *loak* secondhand shop. – *makanan* grocery store. – *M dan M* food and beverage shop. – *mandiri* independent store. – *me(u)bel* furniture store. – *palén* store selling household utensils. – *P dan D* food and beverage shop. – *pangan serbada* supermarket. – *pengécér* retail shop. – *penuntun* distributor. – *sandang pangan* clothing and food store. – *serba ada* [toserba] department store. – *swadaya* independent store. – *swalayan* self-service store. – *tempat jual* outlet. – *tukang jahit* tailor shop.

   bertoko to have a shop, be a shopkeeper.

   tokoan secondary gate (in fishpond).

   pertokoan shopping (center).

tokoh I **1** leading figure, important person, big shot (in a certain field), celebrity. **2** shape, form. **3** leading character (in a story), hero. – *badan* body shape. – *bulat* leading character (in a story). – *datar* secondary character (in a story). – *kunci* key figure. – *masyarakat* informal leader. – *panutan* leading figure. – *penopang* key supporter. – *penting* important figure. – *pipih* secondary character (in a story). – *sastra* literary figure. – *tahun ini* the man of the year. – *utama* main character.

   bertokoh to have the shape of.

   menokohi **1** to be the leader of, run, organize. **2** to play the lead (in a film, etc.).

   menokohkan **1** to make s.o. the leading figure in. **2** to play (a character).

   ketokohan being an important figure, fame.

   penokohan characterizing, making s.o. the leading figure in, playing the lead.

   pertokohan (*mod*) leading figure/character.

tokoh II **menokoh** to cheat, deceive.

   penokoh cheat, deceiver.

tokok I s.t. extra added.

   bertokok with s.o. extra added. ~ *lagi/pula* and furthermore.

   menokok to give or say s.t. extra, add s.t.

   tokokan increase, increment.

tokok II (*M*) hammer.

   menokok to tap (at/on), hit. ~ *kawat* to send a wire. ~ *pintu* to knock at the door.

   tokok-menokok to hit e.o.

   penokok knocker.

tokolan (*Jv*) **1** very young shrimp (3–5 cm in size). **2** young bean sprouts.

tokong I (*M?*) lump, bump, mass.

tokong II → TOA-PÉKONG.

tokong III rocky waterless islet. – *pulau* chain of rocky islets.

tokong IV **1** with short hair, without a tail (of rooster). **2** with shaven hair (a punishment).

menokong to shave s.o.'s hair.

tokong V – *bulu* k.o. weed, *Hedyotis vestita*.

tokowan shopkeeper.

toksik (*E*) toxic.

toksikolog (*D*) toxicologist.

toksikologi (*D/E*) toxicology.

toksin (*D/E*) toxin.

toksis (*D*) toxic.

toksisitas toxicity.

toktok piece of wood beaten as a signal.

tol (*E*) toll.

tolak push, push away, reject. *barang* – rejected items. – *angsur* give and take, bargaining. – *bahar* ballast. – *bala* talisman for driving away evil spirits or warding off misfortune. – *ba(ha)ra* ballast. – *balik* back and forth. – *bayar* (*fin*) charge back. – *belakang* to take one's leave. – *landas* to take off (of a plane). – *peluru* (in sports) shot put. – *pinggang* with arms akimbo. – *raih* give and take, bargaining. – *senjata* k.o. tribute paid so as not to be attacked, protection money. – *sumpah* k.o. necklace; → DOKOH I. – *ukur* yardstick.

bertolak 1 to go, leave. ~ *belakang* a) conflicting, be the complete opposite of, to go in the opposite direction, turn away (from). b) to differ, be different from e.o. ~ *pinggang* with arms akimbo. ~ *punggung* to leave. **2** to start from, take s.t. as a starting point. ~ *angsur* to compromise. ~ *dari* on grounds of.

bertolak-tolak to accuse/blame e.o.

bertolak-tolakan to jostle e.o.

menolak [and **nolak** (*coq*)] **1** to reject, deny (a request), turn down, decline, dismiss (a lawsuit), refuse, vote down. *Permohonannya ditolak*. His request was denied. **2** to push away/aside. **3** to ward off, repel. ~ *bara* to ward off disaster. **4** to subtract. ~ *salah* to put the blame (on s.o. else).

tolak-menolak to push e.o.

menolakkan 1 to push back/away. **2** to push s.t. off onto s.o. else. ~ *kesalahan kepada orang lain* to put the blame on s.o. else.

tertolak 1 pushed. **2** turned down, rejected, denied, declined.

tolakan 1 push, shove. **2** rejection, denial, dismissal; s.t. rejected. **3** subtraction. **4** reduction (in price).

penolak 1 s.o. or s.t. that rejects/refuses/wards off. ~ *bisa* antidote. **2** repellent. ~ *serangga* insect repellent. ~ *nasi* sidedishes (that go along with rice); → LAUK-PAUK.

penolakan 1 rejection, denial, declining, dismissal, refusal. ~ *kerja* refusal to perform (military) service. **2** warding off. **3** disclaimer. **4** subtracting.

tolan → TAULAN.

tolap bertolap embroidered.

tolé (*Jv*) boy.

toléh I menoléh [and **noléh** (*coq*)] **1** to look around (toward). *Dia ~ ke arah datangnya bunyi itu*. He looked around in the direction that the sound came from. *Dia ~ ke orang yang memanggilnya*. He looked toward the person who had called him. ~ *belakang* to look back/behind. ~ *ke dalam* a) to look inward. b) inward-looking. ~ *ke kanan/kiri* look to the right/left. **2** to turn around.

menoléh-noléh to keep on looking around.

menoléhkan to turn (one's face to look at s.t.). ~ *muka* to turn one's head.

toléhan movement of the head to(ward)/in the direction of.

toléh II pertoléhan ~ *hari* (*ob*) when the sun seems to halt at 9 a.m. or hesitates before descending (3 p.m.). ~ *tenggala muda* about 8–9 a.m. ~ *tenggala tua* about 9–11 a.m. (when plows are turned around because the buffaloes can no longer bear the heat).

toleran (*E*) tolerant.

toleransi (*E*) tolerance, play (in a brake).

bertoleransi to be tolerant.

men(t)oleransi(kan) to tolerate.

tolerir (*D*) tolerate.

mentolerir to tolerate; → BERTOLERANSI. *Pemerintah tidak akan ~ setiap kapal ompréngan beroperasi di wilayah perairan Indonésia*. The government will not tolerate any tramp steamers operating in Indonesian waters. *suatu perbuatan yang tidak bisa ditolérir* an intolerable act.

tolk (*D ob*) /tolek/ interpreter.

tolo I (*ob*) → TOLOL.

tolo II → KACANG *tolo*. – *lembut* Sarawak bean, *Vigna hosei*.

tolok I 1 equal, identical, match, peer. **2** partner. **3** gauge. **4** standard. *waktu* – standard time. *tiada –nya* unparalleled, peerless, matchless, unequaled. – *banding* equal, match. – *ukur* landmark; benchmark, criterion, yardstick.

setolok equal, similar, tantamount. *tiada* ~ unequaled. *kunci* ~ a key similar to other keys.

bertolok matched, equaled. *tiada ~nya* unparalleled, peerless, matchless, unequaled.

menolok 1 to compare, liken, contrast. **2** to make equal to. **3** to gauge.

penolok 1 an equal. **2** standard (measure), norm.

tolok II → TOLK.

tolok III k.o. plant, tree, Tahitian chestnut, *Inocarpus edulis*.

tolol stupid, foolish, silly. *si* – a stupid, foolish person.

nolol-nololin (*J*) to keep calling s.o. stupid.

men(t)ololkan and **mempertololkan** to consider s.o. a fool, make a fool of s.o.

ketololan stupidity, foolishness.

tolong 1 help; → BANTU. –! help! *minta* – a) to ask for a favor. *Boléhkah saya minta – saudara* May I ask you for a favor? b) to cry for help. (*suara*) *jeritan minta* – a cry for help. **2** please (used for politeness in requests or commands); → COBA. – *bawakan saya buku itu*. Please, bring me that book.

bertolong-tolongan, tolong-menolong, and **tolong-bertolongan** to help/support e.o. (voluntarily, based on *adat*), render mutual assistance.

menolong [and **nolong** (*coq*)] **1** to aid, help, assist, provide relief for, support, come to the aid of. *obatnya dapat ~* the medicine can provide relief. ~ *nyawa* to save, rescue, retrieve. ~ *daripada pingsan* to restore to consciousness. **2** to solace/comfort.

menolongi [and **nolongin** (*J coq*)] **1** to come to s.o.'s assistance. **2** to help (*pl obj*).

tertolong [and **ketolong** (*coq*)] helped, aided, assisted. *tidak ~* cannot be saved, past recovery, irretrievable. ~ *daripada* helped against.

tolongan → PERTOLONGAN.

ketolongan 1 received help, helped. **2** (could be) rescued. *tidak ~* irretrievable, (one's life) could not be saved.

penolong 1 aide, assistant, deputy. **2** obliging, helpful, willing to help/aid. **3** auxiliary (in compounds), support, prop. **4** manual, guide. **5** rescuer, rescuing, rescue. *regu ~* rescue team.

penolongan helping, aiding, etc.

pertolongan help, aid, assistance. *atas ~* a) with the help/assistance (of). b) with the aid of (crutches, etc.). *tanpa ~* without anyone's help/assistance, unaided, unassisted. ~ *pertama pada kecelakaan* [PPPK] first aid.

tolor (*ob*) → TOLOL.

tom I (*D col*) bridle, rein(s).

tom II (*Jv*) indigo; → TARUM I.

tomah → TUHMAH.

toman (*ikan*) – murrel, snakehead fish, *Ophiocephalus striatus*. *seperti – makan anak* s.o. who acts or speaks improperly. – *barong/bunga* giant snakehead, *Ophiocephalus micropeltes*, a fish species which eats its young. – *jela/ékor kuang*, *Channa melanoptera*.

tomas [*tokoh masyarakat*] community leaders.

tomat (*E*) tomato, *Solanum lycopersicum*. *sari* – tomato juice. *saus* – tomato sauce. – *gondol* the Rome tomato.

tombak I 1 spear, lance. – *pancing* spear.

bertombak (armed) with a spear/lance.

tombak-menombak to spear e.o.

bertombak-tombakan to spear e.o.

menombak to attack/stab/pierce with a lance or spear.

menombaki (*pl obj*) to stab, etc.

tertombak speared.

tombak II a linear measure of 12 feet.

tomboi (*E*) tomboy.

tombok I (*J/Jv*) **1** compelled to pay the difference, obliged to pay in addition. **2** additional payment (due to a shortfall). **3** money given to a dancer by her partner (in the *jogét* or *tayuban* dance).

menombok [and **nombok** (*coq*)] **1** to have to add money to.

Harganya seratus lima puluh, saudara kasi uang hanya seratus, jadi saya harus ~ lima puluh. The price is 150, you gave me only 100, so I have to add 50. **2** to bet on.

menomboki [and **nombokin** (*J coq*)] **1** to add money to. **2** (*pl obj*) to add money. **3** to bet on.

penombok 1 additional source (of funds). **2** person who has to pay s.t. additional.

penombokan increase.

tombok II (*J*) to knock, bang (against s.t.); → TUMBUK I. *main* – to play marbles (in which one marble has to hit another).

nombok to bet on.

tombol 1 bump, lump (on a person/animal/wood). **2** knob, switch, button, pushbutton. – *bintang* the star key (*) (on a telephone keypad). – *lampu* (light) switch. – *lift* elevator button. – *pagar* the pound/number key (#) (on a telephone keypad). – *pintu* doorknob. – *putaran* winder (of a watch). – *spasi* space bar. – *tekan* push button.

menombol to stick out (like a bump).

tombola (*E*) tombola.

tombong I (*Jv*) kiln for processing earthenware/bricks/lime.

tombong II → TUMBUNG I.

tombong III → TOMONG.

tombong IV (*J*) seed in a coconut.

tomong 1 (*meriam* –) mortar **2** cannon.

tompang → TUMPANG.

tompék k.o. small cake made from sago meal.

tompél (*J*) **1** black scar (from a wound/injury, etc.) on the face, etc. **2** birthmark, mole.

tompélan to have a birthmark.

tomplok I (*J*) **nomplok** to stick (to), stay (in). *Banyak dokter ~ di Jakarta.* Many physicians stick to Jakarta.

tomplok II (*J*) **1** a leap forward to rush at prey. **2** to knock/strike together.

menomplok [and **nomplok** (*coq*) and **nomplokin** (*J coq*)] to run into s.o, crash into. *rezeki ~* to get a windfall or an unexpected piece of good luck.

ketomplok (*coq*) run into, crashed into s.o. head-on. *mati ~* to die in a crash.

ketomplokan collision.

tompok 1 small heap/pile/stack. **2** small group. **3** spot (on animals, clothes, etc.).

bertompok-tompok 1 in heaps/piles/stacks. **2** in small groups. **3** spotted.

menompok(kan) 1 to arrange in small heaps/piles/stacks. **2** to pile up.

tertompok arranged in heaps, etc.

tompokan 1 group. **2** heap, pile, stack.

tomprok (*J*) **nomprok** to pounce on.

ton I (*D*) **1** metric ton (= 2,200 lbs). **2** unit of area (1 square meter = about 0.84 square yards). **3** monetary unit (1,000 rupiahs). – *bobot mati* dead weight ton (DWT).

berton-ton in tons, by the ton.

ton II (in acronyms) → PELETON. – *tindak* (*mil*) action company.

tonaas (*Min*) **1** ancestors. **2** s.o. who uses magic incantations in fishing. **3** s.o. who has great influence, plays an important role in society and, for that reason, is honored.

tonang k.o sea-eel, conger, *Muraenesox talabon.*

tonarigumi (during the Japanese occupation) neighborhood association.

tonase (*E*) tonnage.

tonda → TUNDA I.

tonéél (*D*) → TONIL.

tong I (*C? D*) pail, bucket, barrel, cask, keg. – *kosong nyaring bunyinya* empty barrels make more noise. – *penuh tak bergoncang,* – *setengah bergoncang* those who know don't say and those who don't know talk too much. – *sampah* trash/garbage can. – *Sétan* Hell Hole, i.e., a barrel in which a daredevil rides his motorcycle against the wall.

bertong-tong by the bucket.

tongan by the bucketful/barrelful, etc.

tong II (*J*) the clipped form of *entong*; vocative for boys. –, *babé lu udé di rumé apé nggak?* Is your father at home or not?

tong III (*onom*) sound of a gong, etc.

tongak (*J*) **nongak** to look upward/up to.

tongcay (*C*) dried cabbage.

tonggak I 1 post, pole, pillar. **2** log, billet (of wood). **3** milestone, landmark. **4** basic foundation. **5** tree stump. **6** milestones placed about 1,500 meters apart. – *bermata kucing* delineator. – *gantungan* gallows. – *guntung* a house post that only reaches to the floor and doesn't go into the ground. – *jembatan* bridge pillar. – *karang* stack (in the ocean). – *penghalang* obstacle, impediment, obstruction, hindrance. – *perjalanan* boundary-stone, milestone, landmark (along roads). – *pintu* doorjamb. – *rumah* house pillar. – *sejarah* a historic landmark/milestone. – *tambat* mooring post. – *tua* main house post. – *ukur* measuring pole (for measuring the depth of water, etc.).

menonggak to erect s.t.

tonggak II menonggak to pour water into one's mouth from a *kendi*, etc.

tonggék protruding buttocks; → TUNGGIK.

menonggék to walk wriggling the posterior.

menonggékkan to turn s.t. bottom upward.

tertonggék turned a somersault, fell with the buttocks upward.

tonggéng → TUNGGING I.

tonggérét (*J*) a black tree-cricket.

tonggok I (*ob*) heap, pile, stack; → ONGGOK I.

setonggok a pile.

bertonggok heaped/piled up.

menonggok to heap/pile up.

tonggok II (*M*) **bertonggok 1** to perch, roost. **2** to stick up (of an object).

menonggokkan to put s.t. in a high place, perch.

tertonggok perched, roosted.

tonggong I (*ob*) → TONGGOK II.

tonggong II (*M*) oversized (of persons or animals).

tonggong III (*M*) bump, hump, lump.

bertonggong with a hump, humped.

bertonggong-tonggong bumpy.

tonggos (*J*) **1** prominent, protruding. *gigi* – protruding upper front teeth. **2** overbite.

bertonggos bucktoothed.

tongkah I *papan* – planks, etc. used to span a muddy area.

bertongkah to glide along.

menongkah 1 to place planks, etc. (over the mud, etc.). **2** to cross (s.t. difficult). **3** to oppose. ~ *arus* to go against the current. ~ *perintah* to disobey an order.

tongkah II piece of cloth used to lengthen a sarong.

bertongkah lengthened with a piece of cloth.

menongkah to lengthen (a sarong in this way).

tongkang (*C*) sea-going barge, lighter. – *minyak* oil barge. – *pelabuhan* harbor lighter.

tongkat cane, stick, rod, wand. *tidak dua kali orang tua kehilangan* – and *jangan dua kali hilang* – once bitten twice shy. – *Ali* k.o. plant used as an aphrodisiac, *Eurycoma longifolia*; → BABI *kurus*, PASAK *bumi.* – *ampai* divining rod. – *bilyar* billiard cue. – *duga* sounding rod. – *éstafét* relay stick. – *giok* (*euph*) penis. – *kebesaran* mace of authority. – *kejut listrik* electric shock wand. – *kerajaan* royal mace. – *ketiak* crutch. – *komando* swagger stick. – *kuning* cane (used by the blind). – *pemindah* gear shift. – *pengais* stick used by ragpickers to pick up useful pieces of garbage. – *penongkat/penopang/penyangga* crutch. – *peramal* divining rod. – *perontok* threshing stick with V-shaped end. – *polri* police nightstick. – *putih* cane (used by the blind). – *silang* crossbar. – *ukur* ruler.

bertongkat to use a cane, etc. ~ *senduk* very old. ~ *tebu* to go walking with one's wife or sweetheart. ~ *tempurung* very old.

bertongkatkan resting on.

menongkat(kan) to hold s.t. up, raise (by putting a support under it), assist.

penongkat 1 s.t. used as a cane, etc. **2** assistant to village head.

tongkéng I rump, lower back. *tulang* – coccyx.

tongkéng II k.o. ivy; → KETONGKÉNG.

tongkol I tuna, *Thynnus tunnina.*

tongkol II 1 ear, cob (of corn), spadix. **2** nugget, lump. *se–* an ear (of corn).

bertongkol like a lump.

tongkong (*ob*) piece of cut wood.

tongkos → TONGGOS.

tongkrong (*J/Jv*) **menongkrong** [and **nongkrong** (*coq*)] 1 to squat. 2 to sit around and do nothing, hang out. 3 to be out of commission, on the blink, not work. 4 (*sl*) to sit (in jail). 5 (*coq*) to lie in wait.

menongkrongi [and **nongkrongin** (*J coq*)] to squat on, sit in, occupy (a post), hang around at, sit in front of. *Dia sudah ~ posnya dua periode.* He's been in his post for two terms.

menongkrongkan to put s.t. in mothballs, retire, let s.t. sit idle.

tongkrongan 1 hangout, (place) where one sits around or hangs out. *kedai ~* roadside eating stall. 2 peer group. 3 (*J*) talent, aptitude. 4 physical appearance. 5 performance.

tongol (*J/Jv*) to stick out, protrude.

menongol [and **nongol** (*coq*)] to appear, rise, show up.

nongolin (*J*) to show, make s.t. visible.

menongolkan to stick s.t. out (of the window, etc.).

tongong (*Jv*) stupid.

tongpau (*C*) comrade, pal.

tongpés [*kantong kempés*] broke, penniless.

tongsan (*C*) ancestral land, China. *pulang –* to go back to China.

tongséng (*Jv*) a dish prepared with sautéed ingredients, usually includes lamb, beef, or goat.

tongsit (*C? ob*) hair bun.

tongtong k.o. signal drum.

tonikum (*D*) tonic.

tonil (*D*) 1 the theater, stage. 2 show, performance.

men(t)onilkan 1 to perform, put on. 2 to dramatize.

toning (*E*) highlighting (of hair).

mentoning to highlight. *Rambutnya ditoning.* Her hair was given highlights.

tonjok (*J*) 1 fist. 2 punch. 3 boxing match.

menonjok [and **nonjok** (*coq*)] 1 to punch, hit with the fist. 2 to move onto (s.t. else). *Apa yang terjadi Senin itu langsung ~ ke soal besar dan pokok 'réformasi'.* What occurred on that Monday moved onto to a major and basic matter "reform."

tonjokan blow (with the fist), punch.

tonjol 1 prominent. 2 protrusion, bump.

bertonjol(-tonjol) bumpy.

bertonjolan 1 (*pl subj*) to bulge out. 2 rugged (of the landscape).

menonjol [and **nonjol** (*coq*)] 1 to be prominent, stand out, dominate, dominant. 2 to bulge/stick (out), protrude. *gigi ~* bucktoothed. **kemenonjolan** prominence, conspicuousness.

menonjolkan [and **nonjolin** (*J coq*)] 1 to stick s.t. out, thrust s.t. forward, show off. *~ diri* to show off. 2 to show, manifest, bring out.

menonjol-nonjolkan to show off, brag about.

tertonjol 1 pushed forward. 2 conspicuous.

tonjolan 1 bulge, protrusion, protuberance; (*med*) condyle, process. *~ tanah* knoll. 2 outstanding. *tokoh ~* outstanding figure.

penonjolan 1 sticking out, protruding. 2 making s.t. stand out, showing off. 3 conspicuousness. 4 appearance.

tonsil (*D/E*) tonsils.

tonsus [*peleton khusus*] special platoon.

tonton (*J/Jv*) **menonton** [and **nonton** (*coq*)] to watch a performance (of a movie/TV/show, etc.). *nonton bareng* to watch TV or a video in a group (in a café, etc.).

menontoni 1 to look at. 2 (*Jv*) to visit the family of one's future in-laws (in an arranged marriage).

menontonkan and **mempertontonkan** 1 to put on (a performance), exhibit, perform. 2 to show off.

tontonan performance, presentation, show, exhibit, exhibition, spectacle, s.t. that people look at (in a negative sense).

penonton viewer, spectator, audience. *para ~* the audience. *~ filem* movie-goer. *~ télévisi* televiewer, TV audience.

tonus (*D*) (muscle) tone.

tonyoh menonyoh to touch with the fingers.

to'ol (*sl*) penis.

toos (*D*) /tos/ to toast (by lifting glasses).

top I *perahu –* Thai or Indochinese cargo boat.

top II (*C?*) *main –* to play dice, gamble.

petopan gambling den.

top III *baju –* k.o. loose dress.

top IV (*E*) top, most prominent, the most. *pendidik –* top educators.

ngetop 1 to be at the top, be popular. 2 (*BG*) far out!

topan (*A*) typhoon, hurricane, tornado. *– badai* storm. *– dalam segelas air* a tempest in a teapot.

topang I support, prop, abutment. *– sudut* angle bracket.

bertopang 1 to lean on, be supported by. *~ dagu* to twiddle one's thumbs. 2 to be split, branch.

menopang 1 to prop up. *~ diri* to lean (against). 2 to support (by providing money, etc.).

menopangi (*infr*) to support.

menopangkan to support, prop up, hold up.

topangan support, prop; supporting.

penopang support, prop. *~ kehidupan* life support.

penopangan support, supporting.

topang II bertopang *tidak ~* a) to quarrel, have a dispute. b) to be in conflict (with), contradict.

menopang to contradict, dispute.

pertopangan conflict, contradiction, dispute.

topas (*D*) topaz.

topdal (*E*) ship's log.

topék menopék to slice (meat) thin for drying.

topékong → TOA-PÉKONG.

topéng 1 mask. 2 disguise (of one's true nature). *– debu* respirator. *– gas* gas mask. *– monyét* k.o. theater; → KOMEDI kéték. *– pelindung muka* visor.

bertopéng 1 with a mask, to wear a mask. 2 disguised, pretend to be s.t. *~ alim/dua* hypocritical. 3 covered up.

bertopéngkan to hide behind s.t.

mempertopéng 1 to mask, disguise, hide. 2 to masquerade as.

menopéngi 1 to put a mask on. 2 to hide one's true intentions.

topéngan hidden, disguised, masked, fictional.

topés overhanging (of cliffs).

topi (*Hind*) 1 hat, helmet. 2 (*sl*) condom. *– baja* helmet; → HÉLM. *– bangunan* hard hat. *– caping* k.o. hat made of plaited bamboo. *– cetok* (*J*) European hat. *– gabus* pith hat. *– helm* helmet. *– jaksi* Panama/straw hat. *– keselamatan* safety helmet. *– lapangan* field cap (in the army). *si – Mérah* Little Red Riding Hood. *– pandan* Panama/straw hat. *– pelindung* hard hat. *– pengaman (kepala)* crash helmet. *– pét* cap. *– prop* pith helmet. *– proyék* hard hat. *– rumput/tikar* Panama/straw hat.

bertopi to wear a hat, with a hat. *~ baja* with a steel helmet.

topik (*D*) topic.

men(t)opikkan to talk about, make one's topic.

penopikan making s.t. into a topic.

toplés (*D*) a glass jar with an airtight cover used for storing cookies, tobacco, etc.; → SETOPELÉS, STOPLÉS.

topo (*J C*) rag.

topobroto (*Jv*) to go into seclusion to meditate.

topografi (*D/E*) topography, topographic. *– bumbunan* accretion topography.

topong I 1 k.o. small basket. 2 conical in shape.

topong II → KETOPONG.

Torah → TAURAT.

Toraja an area and ethnic group in Sulawesi.

torak I 1 piston. 2 bobbin-holder.

torak-torak (automobile) cylinder.

torak II k.o. bird, *Rhinoplax vigil*.

toraks (*D/E*) thorax.

torang (*Min*) (inclusive) we, us, our; → KITORANG.

torani flying fish, *Cypselurus oligolepis*.

torap (*Jv*) **menorap** 1 to inundate, flood. 2 to irrigate.

penorapan 1 inundation, flooding. 2 irrigation.

Torat → TAURAT.

torbus → TARBUS.

toréh incision, slit.

menoréh 1 to incise, cut into, slit open. 2 to tap (rubber).

tertoréh incised, cut into.

toréhan 1 incision, notch, slit. 2 blaze (on a tree). 3 tapped.

penoréh 1 s.o. or s.t. that slits. 2 rubber tapper.

penoréhan 1 incising, slitting. 2 rubber tapping.
torék an ear disease which leads to being hard of hearing.
torés I → TORÉH.
torés II → TURIS II.
Torét → TAURAT.
torium (D/E) thorium.
torka (D/E) torque.
torné → TURNÉ.
toro I (J) baju – k.o. long pullover dress.
toro II – busi-busi k.o. cookie.
torop k.o. breadfruit.
toros → TURUS I.
torpédo 1 (D/E) torpedo. – kendali homing torpedo. 2 goat penis (used in a k.o. soup). 3 (sl) penis. 4 (pickpocket sl) wallet, purse.
 men(t)orpédo to torpedo.
torsar [motor besar] large motor.
torsi (D) torsion, torque.
torti hide-and-go-seek.
tortor a Batak dance.
tos (E) toss of a coin.
 mengetos to toss a coin.
 tos-tosan tossing a coin.
Toserba [Toko Serba ada] department store.
tosan (Jv) iron. – aji precious weapon, such as a kris.
total (D) total. – jénderal grand total. – keseluruhan grand total. – purna grand total. – suku subtotal.
 men(t)otal(kan) to total (up).
 totalan in total.
 ketotalan totality.
totalisator 1 sweepstakes. 2 soccer pool.
totalitas totality.
totalitér (D) 1 total. 2 totalitarian.
totalitérisme (D) totalitarianism.
totalitét (D) totality.
totemisme (D/E) totemism.
toto k.o. lottery. – Koni/Raga k.o. lotteries.
totok I (J/Jv) 1 full-blooded, pure-blooded. Belanda – a full-blooded Dutchman. 2 (coq) newcomer, inexperienced. 3 an immigrant born in China; → SINGKÉH.
totok II → TUTUK.
totokromo → TATAKRAMA.
totol (J) freckles, spots.
 totol-totol speckles, spots. **menotol-notol** to put spots on s.t.
 menotolkan to make s.t. spatter, splash, splatter.
 penotolan splattering.
tour of duty (E) tour of duty.
 mentour-of-dutykan to transfer to a different post.
towél (J) a light touch with one's fingers. J(ohn) – a racketeer who extorts money from winners at a casino.
 men(t)owél [and **nowél** (coq)] to touch lightly with one's fingers.
 towélan a light touch with one's fingers.
toya, toyah and **toyak** (C) k.o. staff or cudgel used in silat.
toyoko a three-wheeled vehicle with a small gas-powered engine.
toyor (J) **menoyor** to hit, punch.
TPA I (init) → TEMPAT Pembuangan Akhir.
TPA II (init) → TEMPAT Penitipan Anak.
TPA III (init) → TAMAN Pendidikan Alquran.
TPNP (init) → TENTARA Pembébasan Nasional Papua.
TPS (init) → TEMPAT Pemungutan Suara.
TPT [Tékstil dan Produk Tékstil] Textiles and Textile Products.
tr- → ter- (except in many foreign and international words).
tra (ob) → TAK I, TIDAK. – usah not necessary, no need.
trabas → TERABAS.
trada (IBT) (is) not, not (exist); → TIADA.
tradang-tréding (J) **bertradang-tréding** to speculate (in business).
tradisi (D) tradition. – lisan oral tradition.
 mentradisi to become a tradition.
 mentradisikan to make into a tradition.
tradisional (E) traditional, time-honored.
 ketradisionalan traditionalism.
tradisionalis (E) traditionalist.
tradisionalisme (D/E) traditionalism.

tradisionil (D) traditional, time-honored.
trafo (D) (elec) 1 transformer. 2 voltage regulator. – penstabil tegangan tension stabilizing transformer.
tragédi (D) tragedy. – Semanggi the events of Friday, 13 November 1998 when protesting students were shot outside Atmajaya University in Jakarta.
tragik (E) and **tragis** (D) tragic.
 mempertragis to make a show of, dramatize.
 ketragisan tragedy.
tragikomis (D) tragicomic.
trah (Jv) pedigree, lineage. anjing – pedigree dog.
trail (E) trial.
trainingspak → TRÉNINGSPAK.
trak (onom) clicking noise.
trakéa (E) trachea, windpipe.
trak(h)om(a) (D) trachoma.
traksi (D) traction.
traktasi (D) treat(ing).
traktat (D) treaty. – Persahabatan dan Kerjasama di Asia Tenggara. Treaty of Amity and Cooperation in Southeast Asia.
traktir (D) – Arab (coq) Dutch treat.
 mentrakir to treat (to a meal, etc.).
 traktiran treating.
traktor (D) tractor. – tangan rototiller.
 mentraktor(i) to till with a tractor.
 pentraktoran bulldozing; → PEMBULDOSERAN.
traktornisasi tractorization.
trak-trok (onom) clickety-clack.
trakum trachoma.
tra-la-la (D) tralala. – trilili high-spirited, cheerful.
trali(s) (D) door/window bars; → TERALI.
tram → TRÉM.
trampil skilled, competent.
 mentrampilkan to train.
 trampilan skill, competence, know-how.
 ketrampilan skill, know-how. **berketrampilan** skilled. tenaga (yang) ~ skilled workers.
trancam (Jv) k.o. salted salad with hot sauce.
trandal relevant.
 ketrandalan relevance.
trans I (D) trance.
trans II (coq) → TRANSMIGRASI.
trans III prefix meaning 'across, beyond'. – Kalimantan Trans-Kalimantan.
Transad → TRANSMIGRASI Angkatan Darat.
transaksi (D) transaction, deal. – batal (fin) bust the trade. – berjalan current account. – langsung off-board transaction. – lugas arm's-length transaction. – nyata/riil on balance-sheet transaction. – sedang berjalan current account. – setaraf arm's-length transaction.
transatlantik (E) transatlantic.
Transau → TRANSMIGRASI Angkatan Udara.
transéndén (D) transcendent.
transéndénsi (D) transcendence.
transéndéntal (D) transcendental.
transfer (E) transfer.
 mentransfer(kan) to transfer.
 tertransfer transferred.
 pentransfer transferrer.
 pentransferan transference.
transfigurasi (D) transfiguration.
transformasi (D) transformation.
 mentransformasikan to transform.
 tertransformasikan transformed.
transformator (D elec) transformer.
transfusi (D) transfusion. – darah blood transfusion.
 mentransfusikan to transfuse (blood), apply a transfusion.
transisi (D) transition.
transistor (D/E) transistor.
transit (E) transit; (goods, passengers) are in transit.
transitif (D gram) transitive.
transito (D) → TRANSIT. perdagangan – transit trade.

mentransitokan to transit.

transkaryawan 1 settler. 2 migrant.

Transkaukasia Transcaucasia.

Transkopemada [(Départemén) Transmigrasi, Koperasi dan Pembangunan Masyarakat Désa] (Department of) Transmigration, Cooperatives, and Village Community Development.

transkrip (E) transcript. - akadémik academic transcript.

transkripsi (D) transcription; → ALIH aksara.
  mentranskripsikan to transcribe.
  pentranskripsian transcribing.

translasi (E) translation; → TERJEMAHAN.

translator (E) translator; → PEN(T)ERJEMAH.

transliterasi (D) transliteration.
  mentransliterasikan to transliterate.

translok [transmigrasi lokal] local transformation.
  mentranslokkan to transmigrate locally.

transmigran (D) transmigrant.

transmigrasi (D) transmigration. - angkatan darat [transad] transmigration of army personnel. - angkatan udara [transau] transmigration of air force personnel. - bedol désa Interisland Village Resettlement. - lokal [translok] local transmigration. mentransmigrasi-lokalkan to transmigrate locally. - musim seasonal transmigration. - nelayan [transnél] transmigration of fishermen. - pemukiman [transkim] transmigration of residency. - Polisi Républik Indonésia [transpolri] transmigration of police personnel. - pramuka [transpram] transmigration of Boy Scouts. - sisipan interspersed transmigration. - spontan transmigration not financed by the government. - swakarsa [transwakarsa] voluntary transmigration. - swakarsa murni pure self-supported transmigration. - swakarsa mandiri [TSM] independent spontaneous transmigration. - swakarsa berbantuan [TSB] aided self-supported transmigration. - udara airborne transmigration. - véteran lokal [transvétlok] transmigration of local veterans. - (yang terdiri dari para) perwira menengah [transpamén] transmigration of field-grade officers.
  bertransmigrasi to transmigrate.
  mentransmigrasikan to transmigrate s.o.
  ketransmigrasian transmigration.
  pentransmigrasian transmigrating.
  pertransmigrasian transmigration (mod). berpartisipasi di bidang ~ to take part in the transmigration field.

transmisi (D) transmission.
  pentransmisi ~ penyakit disease carrier.

transmiter (E) transmitter; → PEMANCAR.

transmutasi (D) transmutation.
  mentransmutasikan to transmute.

transnasional (E) transnational.

transnél (acr) → TRANSMIGRASI nelayan.

transparan (D) transparent, open. tidak - not transparent.
  ketidak-transparanan lack of transparency.
  ketransparanan transparency.

transparansi (E) transparency.

transpirasi (D) transpiration.

transplantasi (D) transplantation. - jantung heart transplant.
  mentransplantasikan to transplant (of a human heart, etc.).

transpolri → TRANSMIGRASI Polisi Républik Indonésia.

transponder (D/E) transponder.

transpor(t) (D) transport.
  mentranspor(t) to transport.

transportabel (E) transportable.

transportasi (E) transportation. - udara air transportation.

transpram → TRANSMIGRASI pramuka.

transvétlok → TRANSMIGRASI véteran lokal.

transwakarsa → TRANSMIGRASI swakarsa.

Trantib [ketenteraman dan ketertiban] (aparat/petugas) - peace and order (officers), municipal guards.

trap I (Jv) → TERAP I. mengetrapan and mentrapkan to apply.
  pengetrapan and pentrapan 1 application. 2 enforcement (of law).

trap II (D) stairs (of a building).

trapel cék (E coq) traveler's check.

trapésium (D) trapezium.

trapéze (D) trapeze.

trapis(t) (D) Trappist.

trapo → TRAFO.

trapsila and trapsilo (Jv) well-mannered; → SANTUN.

tras (D) trass, tarras, k.o. cement. batu - a brick made from trass.

trasé (D) (ground)plan.
  mentrasé to trace.
  pentraséan tracing.

trasi (Jv) shrimp paste.

trasir (D) mentrasir to trace.

traso → TÉRASO.

tratak (Jv) temporary bamboo or iron platform with thatched roof of palm leaves or canvas roofing added to a building to function as a seating structure for spectators.

trauma (D) trauma.

traumétik (E) and traumatis (D) traumatic.

travel (E) travel. - biro travel bureau/agency. - cék traveler's check.

travésti (D) travesty.

travo (ob) → TRANSFORMATOR.

trawang (Jv) nrawang transparent.

trawl (D) (shrimp) trawl.
  ngetrawl to catch shrimp by using a trawl.

trayék (D) 1 transportation line, designated route. 2 range. - didih boiling range. - pokok trunk line. - samping(an) feeder/branch line. - utama main/trunk line.
  bertrayék to run on a certain route.

trayéktori (D) trajectory.

TRC [Truth and Reconciliation Commission] → KOMISI Kebenaran dan Rékonsiliasi.

tréak → TERIAK.

trék 1 (D) (in sports) center, twister. 2 (E) track, trail, trace; trek. 3 designated route; → TRAYÉK. 4 track (on a music CD).
  ngetrék (coq) 1 to run on a designated route. 2 to drive fast.
  trék-trékan 1 operating a vehicle on a designated route. 2 wild reckless speeding; → KEBUT-KEBUTAN.

trékbal (D) twister.

trékbom (D) land mine.

trék(k)er (D) trigger; → PICU.

trékkers (D col) Dutch who returned to the Netherlands after their period of service in the Indies was completed; cp BLIJVERS.

trékpén (D) drawing pen.

tréktor → TRAKTOR.

trék-trok (onom) creaking noise.

trém (D) tram, streetcar.

tréma (D) dieresis.

trembesi (Jv) pohon – designation for trees, belonging to the Pithecolobium family, from which sometimes a rain of dampness comes down, rain tree, Piptorus incanus, Samanea saman.

trémor (E) tremor.

trémos → TÉRMOS.

trén and trénd (E) trend. - menurun a decreasing trend.
  bertrénd ~ naik to show an upward trend.
  ngetrén(d) (coq) 1 to have a general and continued tendency. 2 to be trendy/stylish.

tréndi (E) trendy.

trenggiling → TENGGILING.

trengginas (Jv) swift, quick.
  ketrengginasan swiftness.

tréningspak (D) tracksuit.

trenyuh (Jv) 1 brokenhearted. 2 touched, moved, affected. Amat – bila mendengar keluh kesah meréka. Amat was touched when he heard their groans.
  mentrenyuhkan to touch, move, affect, moving.
  ketrenyuhan feelings of being touched.

trépés (Jv) flat (of the breasts/buttocks).

trés (D) braid.

tresna and tresno (Jv) (full of) love, loving.
  mentresnani to love s.o. or s.t.
  ketresnoan love.

trét (onom) rattling noise. - tét tét rat-a-tat-tat.

tri- I (Skr) three, tri- (used in many of the neologisms listed below).

TRI II [Tebu Rakyat Inténsifikasi] Smallholders' Sugarcane Intensification (Program).

    men-TRI-kan to subject to the Smallholders' Sugarcane Intensification (Program).

TRI III [Tentara Rakyat Indonesia] Indonesia People's Army (replaced ABRI); → TNI.

triangulasi (D) triangulation.

triadik (E) triadic.

Tri Arga the three mountains surrounding Bukittinggi: Mount Sago, Mount Singgalang, and Mount Marapi.

trias I ~ *politika* (D) trias politica, i.e., the three powers of the state: legislative, judicial, and executive powers.

Trias II (geol) Triassic.

Tribrata (Kepolisian) (Skr neo) the three duties of the police: a) Rastrasewakottama (Prime Servant of the Country and Nation); b) Nagarayanottama (Prime Citizen of the Country and Nation); c) Yana Anucasandharma (Duty to Guard the People's Personal Security).

Tribuana district military command in Hamadi, Irian Jaya.

tribulan quarter.

tribun(e) (D) 1 tribune. 2 reviewing stand.

tribunal (D) tribunal.

tribus (D) tribe.

tribut → ATRIBUT.

tributa the three blindnesses/shortcomings in national development: a) lack of knowledge; b) lack of the Indonesian language, and c) lack of health matters; → TIGA *buta*.

trica(k) (ob) k.o. tricycle.

Trid(h)arma (Skr neo) 1 the three devotions: a) to have the feeling of co-owning the country and nation; b) to have the obligation to defend the fatherland; c) to have the courage to carry out introspection for collective progress. 2 the three religions: a) Confucianism; b) Taoism; c) Buddhism. – *Perburuhan* the three principles of labor relations: a) *Rumongso Handarbéni* partnership; b) *Melu Hangrukebi* responsibility for the organization; c) *Mulatsariro Hangrosowani* introspection. – *Perguruan Tinggi* the three principles of education: a) education in the framework of pursuing science; b) research to develop science; c) devotion to the people in the framework of applying science.

tridasawarsa (Skr neo) three decades, 30 years.

Tri Daya Sakti (Skr neo) the three capabilities of the cavalry.

trifraksi the three factions in the MPR: → F-KP, F-ABRI, F-UD.

triftong (gram) triphthong.

Trifungsi Ditjén Imigrasi the three functions of the Directorate General of Immigration: law enforcement, security apparatus, and server of the community.

Tri Gatra (Skr neo) the three geopolitical fields (location, resources, population).

trigonométri (D/E) trigonometry.

trigu → TERIGU.

trik (E) 1 trick, ruse. 2 (cards) a point or scoring unit.

trikarya (Skr neo) the Triumvirate: SOKSI, Kosgoro, and MKGR.

trikembar triplet.

Trikendala Risténas [Trikendala Risét dan Téknologi Nasional] The three constraints of National Research and Technology: funds, technology, and high-quality men.

triko (D) tricot, a knitted fabric.

Trikora 1 [Tri komando rakyat] People's Threefold Command announced by President Soekarno on December 19, 1961: (1) Raise the Indonesian flag in West Irian; (2) Defeat the establishment of a "State of Papua" by the Dutch; (3) Prepare for a General Mobilization. 2 the military district command for Irian Jaya and Maluku.

Tri Krama Adhaksa (Skr neo) The three duties of the public prosecutor's office: honesty, responsibility, and wisdom.

trik-trak (D onom) creaking sound.

trilateral (E) trilateral.

trilili → TRA-LA-LA.

    bertrilili to sing without words.

trilingga (Jv) reduplication of the original morpheme twice with vowel variation, for instance dag-dig-dug, nang-ning-nong, etc.

trilipat (in) threefold.

triliun trillion; → TRILYUN.

    triliunan trillions.

trilogi (D/E) trilogy (applied by the Department of Education and Culture): discipline, dedication, and loyalty. – *pembangunan* development trilogy, i.e., the three basic principles for the strategy of Indonesian development programs: equality, growth, and national stability.

trilomba triathlon: swimming, bicycle racing, and sprinting.

trilyun 1 (AE) trillion (1 million with 12 zeros). 2 (BE) trillion (1 million with 18 zeros).

trima → TERIMA.

trimatra (Skr neo) three-dimensional.

triméster (D) term, three months.

trimitra three-party call (a telephone service).

trimo → NRIMA, NRIMO.

trim(s) (coq) → TERIMAKASIH.

trimurti (Skr) trinity, the oneness of Brahma, Siva, and Vishnu.

trindil (J) robbed, fleeced.

    mentrindil to rob/fleece.

    mentrindili to rob/fleece s.o.

trinil (Jv) various species of sandpipers and greenshanks, *Tringa spp.* – *betis mérah* common redshank, *Tringa totanus*. – *hijau* green sandpiper, *Tringa ochropus*. – *karang* ruddy turnstone, *Arenaria interpres*. – *pantai* common sandpiper, *Tringa hypoleucus*. – *rawa* marsh sandpiper, *Tringa stagnatilis*. – *semak* wood sandpiper, *Tringa glareola*.

trinitas (D) trinity; → TRIMURTI, TRITUNGGAL.

trio (D) trio.

trip I (E) trip, a short voyage; → PERJALANAN, TRAVEL.

TRIP II [Tentara Républik Indonésia Pelajar] Republic of Indonesia Army of Students.

Tripandita [(daérah) industri, pertanian, pendidikan, dan pariwisata] an industrial, agricultural, educational, and tourist area.

tripang a variety of edible sea cucumber (shellfish).

tripartit (D) tripartite.

Tripida [Tri pimpinan daérah] Regional Leadership Trio, consisting of the subdistrict head, *Kodim* commander, and Sector Police Head; → MUSPIKA.

Tripitaka (Skr) "Three Baskets of the Law," the scripture or holy writings of the Buddhists.

triplék(s) (D) plywood.

tripod (E) tripod.

triprogram three-part program.

trirangkap triple, triplicate.

Trisakti 1 (Skr Bal) Sang Hyang Widi's three principal manifestations: Brahma, the Creator (symbolized by red), Vishnu, the Preserver (symbolized by black), and Shiva, the Destroyer (symbolized by white). 2 (RC) the Trinity.

trisila threefold. *sumpah* – threefold oath.

trisilabik (E) and **trisilabis** (D) trisyllabic.

trisna → TRESNA.

trisudut triangle.

trisula (Skr) trident, a three-pronged spear.

tritia → TÉRSIÉR.

tritik (Jv) resist process for dying.

tritis → TERITIS(AN).

Tritugas the threefold task (announced by President Soekarno on August 17, 1964): a) Freedom; b) Socialism; c) A New World.

trituna the three "withouts," i.e., a collective term for *tunakarya* (jobless persons), *tunawisma* (homeless persons), and *tunasusila* (prostitutes).

Tritunggal 1 The Regional Triumvirate consisting of a) the Head of the Civil Service; b) the Chief of Police; c) the Chief of the Regional Army Detachment. 2 (after September 30, 1965) a) the Great Leader of the Revolution/President/Supreme Commander of the Armed Forces (Soekarno); b) the Armed Forces; c) the People.

    ketritunggalan trinity.

Tritura [Tri tuntutan ampera] Ampera's Three Demands: a) Banning the Communist Party of Indonesia; b) Purging Gestapu/PKI elements from the Dwikora Cabinet; c) Lowering the Price of Basic Necessities.

Tri Ubaya Cakti/Sakti The Three Sacred Vows; an army doctrine evolved around 1964/5, consisting of: a) the Army's work doctrine; b) the Revolutionary Doctrine; c) developing the Revolutionary Doctrine.

triumvirat (*D*) triumvirate.

triunsur triadic.

triwangsa (*Bal*) the three castes: Brahman, Kshatriya, and Vaisya.

triwarna the (Dutch) tricolor.

triwarsa three years.

triwarsan triennial.

triwikrama assume a demonic form.

triwindu three *windu*s, 24 years.

triwulan quarter (of a year).

  triwulanan quarter(ly). *secara* ~ quarterly.

trobos → TEROBOS.

trofi (*D*) trophy.

trofoblas (*D*) trophoblast.

trol → PATROLI.

trombolisis (*E*) thrombolysis.

trombon (*D*) trombone.

trombose (*D*) and **trombosis** (*E*) thrombosis.

trombus (*D*) thrombus.

tromel (*D*) → TROMOL.

tromol box, case, tin, drum, canister.

tromolpos post office box, PO Box. – *5000* complaint box.

tromolrém (*D*) brake drum.

trompét (*D*) trumpet.

  mentrompétkan to trumpet out.

trompétis (*D*) trumpet player.

trompong a *gamelan* instrument.

trondol (*Jv*) **1** plucked, bare of feathers. *ayam* – a featherless chicken. **2** leafless.

  mentrondoli to squeeze s.o. dry of his money.

trondolo (*Jv*) and **troondooloo** dummy, stupid person.

tronton *truk* – a large flatbed truck.

trop → TRUF.

trope (*D gram*) figure of speech.

tropik(a) (*D*) **1** the tropics. **2** tropical.

tropikalisasi making s.t. suitable for use in the tropics.

tropis (*D*) tropical.

tropong → TEROPONG.

tropongan k.o. perennial grass, *Sacciolepis interrupta*.

troposfér troposphere.

tros (*D*) hawser, mooring line.

trotoar sidewalk; footpath, pavement.

  bertrotoar with/to have a pavement.

trotoir (*Fr D*) /trotoar/ → TROTOAR.

trotok *burung* – k.o. thrush.

trotol (*J*) k.o. skin disease or white spots on leaves.

  trotolan affected by that disease.

trotskis (*D*) Trotskyite.

trowongan → TEROWONGAN.

trubuk (*Jv*) *ikan* – long-tail shad, Chinese herring, *Clupea macrura, Alosa macrura. telor* – salted trubuk spawn, Indonesian caviar.

truck (*D*) → TRUK.

trucuk → TERUCUK.

trucut (*Jv*) *ketrucut* slip of the tongue.

truf (*D*) trump.

truk I (*E*) truck. – *balak* truck for transporting beams (of wood). – *beban* articulated truck, tractor-trailer truck. – *gandéngan* trailer truck. – *jungkit* dump truck. – *keran* crane truck. – *lossing* a truck used for unloading/discharging good directly from the ship's hold to a private warehouse. – (*pengangkat*) *sampah* garbage truck. – *tanki (bénsin)* tank truck. – *telanjang* flatbed truck. – *tertutup* compactor. – *yang diperlengkapi pengeras suara* sound truck.

  bertruk-truk by the truckload, in truckloads.

  trukan trucking.

  pertrukan trucking (*mod*).

Truk II [Tim Rélawan untuk Kemanusiaan] Volunteer Team for Humanity.

trukbyangmu (*vulg*) motherfucker!

trulek (*Jv*) – *Jawa* Javan wattled lapwing, *Vanellus macropterus/tricolor*. – *kli'it* golden plover, *Pluvialis dominica*. – *lidi* black-winged stilt, *Himantopus himantopus*.

trundul → TRONDOL.

truntum a *batik* pattern.

trusa(h) (*ob*) → *tidak* USAH.

trusi → PRUSI.

trutuk *kapal* – an old ship.

t.s. (*init*) → TEMAN *sejawat*.

tsamrah (*A leg*) the purpose of doing s.t.

Tsanawi(y)ah → SEKOLAH *tsanawiyah*.

tsani (*A*) second (chairman, etc.).

tsar (*D*) czar, tsar.

Tsaur (*A*) Taurus (*zod*).

tsb. (*abbr*) [tersebut] above-mentioned.

TSP (*init*) → TOKO *Sandang Pangan*.

tst. I (*init*) [Tahu Sama Tahu] **1** you scratch my back and I'll scratch yours. **2** to collude by bribery or kickbacks.

TST II (*init*) [Transplantasi Sumsum Tulang] Bone-Marrow Transplant.

tsunami (*Jp*) tsunami; → GELOMBANG *pasang*.

t.t. (*abbr*) [tukar tambah] (in advertisements) trade-in.

ttd. (*abbr*) [tertanda] signed.

ttg. (*abbr*) [tertanggal] dated.

tu I (*J*) → ITU. – *orang* that person.

tu II one; → SATU I.

tu III (in acronyms) → SATU I, TUGAS, TUA.

tua 1 old, aged; *opp* MUDA. *si* – the old guy. *bini* – one's first/oldest wife, co-spouse (about men who have two or three wives). *budak lampau* – *tidak* a young fellow. *bulan* – that part of the month after the 20th (when one is hard up, since salaries are paid on the last day of the month); *cp* BULAN *muda. hamil* – advanced stage of pregnancy. *hari/masa* – one's old age. *kakak* – a) the oldest sibling, b) → KAKAK I. *mak* – father's/mother's older sister. *Nénék sudah* –. Grandmother is already old. *orang* – an old person, a senior citizen. *orangtua* → ORANG I. *pak* – father's/mother's older brother. *saudara* – a) elder sibling. b) (during the Japanese occupation) reference to the Japanese. *sudah terlampau* – obsolete. **2** older in age. *Saya – dua bulan daripada istri saya*. I'm two months older than my wife. **3** old, not new; *opp* BARU I. *barang-barang* – junk. *besi* – scrap. *harta* – inherited wealth, legacy; → HARTA *pusaka. paham* – an old concept. **4** head, chief, → TUA-TUA. – *kampung* village head; → LURAH I. – *rumah* head of the family; → KEPALA *keluarga.* **5** late, far advanced (of night). *Malam sudah – dan keadaan di bandara makin sunyi*. It's already late at night and the airport is more and more deserted. **6** to have magic powers (of weapons, etc., because they were made in olden days). *keris* – a kris with magic powers. **7** already boiled (of water/oil, etc.); cooked, done. *Bubur ini belum sampai –nya*. The porridge is not yet done. **8** ripe, can be plucked (referring to fruits). *Mangga ini sudah* –. This mango is ripe. **9** dark, deep (referring to colors). *mérah* – dark/deep red. **10** pure, of a high quality (metal). *emas* – pure gold. **11** old-fashioned. *sudah terlampau* – obsolete. *Rumahnya sudah* –, *lagi jauh dari jalan besar*. His house is old fashioned and is far from the main road. **12** classic. *makin – makin banyak santannya* the older you get, the wiser you become. – *bangka* very old, senile, decrepit, worn out with age. – *bangkot* (*J*) old but behaving like a young person. – *catuk* senile. – *datuk* old and dignified. – *ganyut* old and tough. – *gayut* trying to look younger than one really is. – *kejemur* (*J*) very old, senile, decrepit. – *kutuk* an old fart. – *lara* an old man with a bad character. – *lélér* a) very old. b) dilapidated. – *lengkuas* old but full of beans. – *lontok* old and senile. – *muda* both old and young. – *péot* decrepit, dilapidated. – *rénta* very old, senile, decrepit. – *rumah* head of the household. – *sulah* old and bald. – *suntuk* old but behaving like a young person. – *uzur* very old, decrepit.

tua-tua 1 the elders, leaders. *Siapa nama* ~ *meréka?* What are the names of their leaders? ~ *désa* village elders. **2** although old, still ... ~ *masih séhat* though old but still healthy. ~ *keladi/kelapa, tambah/makin* – *tambah/makin jadi* there is no fool like an old fool, i.e., an old rake. ~ *terung asam* the older he gets the sourer he gets. **3** foster father. **ketua-tuaan** acting like an old person.

setua 1 of the same age. **2** as old as.

bertua-tua(an) (*M*) **1** by seniority. **2** married till old in years.

mentua parents-in-law, in-laws; → MERTUA.

menua 1 to grow old, mature; senescent. **2** to get later. *Malam kian ~.* It became later and later at night.

mempertua to designate as leader.

menuakan 1 to consider s.o. senior/the head. **2** to make old(er), age, make s.t. mature. **3** to let s.t. ripen. **4** to make s.t. purer. **5** to let s.t. get darker (in color).

menua-nuakan to make (o.s.) older.

tertua 1 oldest. **2** chairman. *~ kelas* class president; → KETUA.

ketua chairman, head. *~ kelas* class president. **mengetuai** to chair, head, preside over. **pengetua** head, leader.

tuaan 1 elderly, old. **2** age spots.

ketuaan 1 old age. **2** too old.

ketua-tuaan senile, act like an old person.

pengetua chairman, head, dean (of the diplomatic corps).

penuaan aging, senescence.

tetua → KETUA.

tuagama R.C. sacristan.

tuah 1 fortunate, lucky; happiness, luck. **2** supernatural power. **3** respect, prestige, honor. *- ada, untung tiada* he has luck but doesn't profit from it. *- anjing, celaka kuda* one man's meat is another man's poison. *- ayam boléh dilihat, - manusia siapa tahu* only God knows whether s.o. is fortunate. *- melambung tinggi* a well-off person will also get a high position.

bertuah 1 to be fortunate, lucky; to bring good luck. **2** to have supernatural power.

menuahi to bring s.o. good luck.

menuahkan to glorify, extol.

ketuahan 1 luck, fortune. **2** magical power.

tuai small crescent-shaped harvesting knife. *mesin -* harvester.

bertuai 1 harvested, plucked. **2** to harvest (for a living). *~ padi* to harvest rice for a living.

menuai to harvest (using such a knife), reap, make (a profit).

tertuai harvested, plucked.

tuaian what has been harvested. *padi ~* harvested rice.

penuai harvester, reaper, s.o. or s.t. that harvests.

penuaian 1 harvesting, harvest. **2** reaping.

tuak 1 toddy, fermented coconut milk. **2** palm wine. **3** fermented milk. *- terbeli, tunjang hilang* to have bad luck. *- anggur* palm wine. *- keras* hard toddy. *- manis* sweet toddy.

tual piece of wood, block.

bertual-tual cut up into pieces.

menual to saw wood into blocks.

tuala (*Port*) towel.

tualang I vagabond.

bertualang 1 to go from place to place, wander about, have no permanent home. **2** to like to travel, etc. for the adventure of it. **3** to swarm (of bees, etc.).

petualang 1 adventurer. **2** tramp, homeless person. **kepetualangan** adventurous.

petualangan 1 wandering about. **2** adventure, escapade.

tualang II a very tall species of tree, *Koompassia excelsa.*

tuam anything used to warm the body, such as a hot compress, hot ashes.

bertuam and **menuam** to treat s.o. with a hot compress, etc.

menuami to apply a hot compress, etc. to.

tuan 1 sir, Mr. (*usu* for Europeans/foreign Asians/Arabs/Hajis, etc.). **2** you, your. **3** boss, master. *- besar* a) the big boss. b) VIP. *- guru* religious teacher (in the NU). *- hamba* you (respectful). *-ku* (*M*) title for leader of a religious school. *- pabrik* factory owner. *- putri* a) princess. b) consort. *- rumah* host. **menuan-rumahi** and **menuan-rumahkan** to host (an event). *- tamu* host. *- tanah* landlord. *- toko* shop owner.

bertuan 1 with a master, serve s.o. *daérah tak ~* no-man's land. **2** to address s.o. as *tuan.* **3** to act as boss/master.

bertuankan 1 to have ... as boss/master. **2** to call s.o. *tuan.*

menuani and **mempertuani** to domineer, dominate, have control over.

menuankan 1 to make s.o. master. **2** to call s.o. master.

mempertuan(kan) 1 to regard s.o. as lord/master. **2** to accept as sovereign. *yang dipertuan* (mainly *Mal*) His Majesty, the ruler. *hak yang dipertuan* sovereignty. **3** to respect.

ketuan-tuanan to act as if one were boss/master.

pertuanan 1 sovereignty. *hak ~* sovereign rights. **2** rule, government, dominion. **3** ruling, rule, government. **4** ruling class.

tuang I pour, cast.

bertuang cast. *besi ~* cast iron.

menuang 1 to pour (a liquid). **2** to cast. **3** to smelt.

menuangi to pour into. *Produk tersebut dapat dikonsumsi setelah dituangi air panas ke dalam wadahnya dan dibiarkan selama kurang lebih 5 menit.* The product can be eaten after hot water is poured into the container and it is allowed to sit for at least 5 minutes.

menuangkan 1 to pour out. **2** to embody (in a document/constitution, etc.). *Prinsip itu dituangkan ke dalam peraturan perundang-undangan.* Those principles have been embodied in statutes. **3** to mold, cast.

tertuang 1 poured out. **2** cast. **3** embodied (in a document).

tuangan 1 pouring, casting. **2** mold, shape. **3** cast.

ketuangan pouring out. *Hari ~ Rohulkudus* Pentecost.

penuang s.o. or s.t. that molds/casts, founder.

penuangan 1 molding, shaping, casting. **2** foundry.

tuang II → TUANG-TUANG.

tuanku a title used in parts of Sumatra for religious teachers.

tuangku → TENGKU.

tuang-tuang bamboo horn.

tuap splint for wrapping broken limb.

tuar (*M?*) sticks or branches set up in a rice field as a scarecrow.

tuarang dry season, dry spell.

tuas I lever, arm. *- balik* link lever. *- gas* accelerator. *- gigi* gearshift lever. *- kaki pemutar motor* kick starter. *- kendali* control stick. *- kotrék* ratchet lever. *- kulis* rocker arm. *- penahan* dolly bar. *- pengénténg* relief lever. *- sékundér* idler lever.

menuas to lever, raise with a lever.

penuas lever.

tuas II tuasan k.o. fish trap made of branches.

tuat → KETUAT.

tuba 1 k.o. medicinal plant, derris, *Derris elliptica.* **2** fish poison derived from this plant. *- tikus* rat poison. *- dibalas dengan susu* to return good for evil. *- habis ikan tak dapat* to make unnecessary work for o.s.

bertuba poisoned.

menuba to spread this poison in (to catch fish).

menubai to poison (fish) with this poison.

penuba 1 fish poison. **2** poisoner.

penubaan poisoning.

Tubagus title of nobility for descendants of the former Sultans of Banten; → *Tu* BAGUS II.

tuban-tuban fetal membranes and placenta.

tube (*E*) tube.

tuberkulosa (*D*) tuberculosis.

tubi I bertubi-tubi repeatedly, continuously, again and again.

menubi to persevere at, keep on ...ing.

menubi(-nubi)kan to keep on ...ing.

mempertubi-tubi(kan) to intensify, make stronger (by repetition).

pentubian drilling, exercising.

tubi II (*A*) *pohon -* k.o. tree found in Muslim paradise.

tubin the fourth day from now.

tubir ravine, gully, chasm, abyss. *- bibir* edge of the lips. *- jurang* edge of the abyss.

bertubir with a ravine, etc.

bertubir-tubir with many ravines, etc.

menubir steep, precipitous.

menubiri to walk/follow along a precipitous edge.

tubles (*J*) **menubles** to stick, prick.

tubruk (*J/Jv*) **1** collide; → TABRAK. **2** lunge.

bertubrukan to collide with e.o.

menubruk [and **nubruk** (*coq*)] **1** to collide with, run into. **2** to lunge at. **3** to finish off (food), gobble down.

menubrukkan to crash s.t. (into s.t.). ~ *truknya ke sebuah kendaraan* to crash one's truck into a vehicle.

tertubruk [and **ketubruk** (*coq*)] collided, hit.

tubrukan 1 collision, crash. ~ *beruntun* chain collision. **2** impact. **ketubrukan** collision.

penubrukan colliding, crashing, hitting, running into.

tubuh 1 body, figure. *dalam* – in vivo. *di luar* – in vitro. **2** person. *menghadap* – to appear in person. **3** the body (of an organization). – *badan* one's entire body. – *berita* body (of a news story). – *bumi* the land (under the soil). – *cebakan* (mineral) deposit. – *halus* a) small in build. b) spirit, ghost. **bertubuh halus** possessed by a spirit. – *kapal* hull. – *kasar* the physical body. **bertubuh kasar** having a physical body. – *oléh tutup* said about s.t. that's really right. – *pesawat* fuselage.

setubuh 1 sexual intercourse. **bersetubuh** to have sexual intercourse. **menyetubuhi** to have sexual intercourse with. **menyetubuhkan** to realize, bring about. **persetubuhan** sexual intercourse. **2** (*ob*) in harmony.

bertubuh 1 with a ... body/figure. ~ *kekar* well-built. *tidak* ~ intangible (rights). **2** to have the body of a woman (said of girls).

menubuhkan 1 to bring about, realize, make come true. **2** to set up (an organization, etc.).

pertubuhan organization.

tudak → TODAK.

tuding I (*Jv*) **1** index finger. **2** hand of a clock. **3** guidance.

menuding [and **nuding** (*coq*)] **1** to point. **2** to point at (with the finger). **3** to accuse, blame. *Hampir semua pengusaha bis kota* ~ *tarif Rp 50.* Almost all city bus entrepreneurs blame the Rp 50 rate.

menuding-nuding to keep on pointing at, keep on accusing.

menudingi (*pl obj*) to keep pointing at, keep on accusing.

menudingkan 1 to point with. ~ *senapan* to point a gun. **2** to accuse of. *bukti yang ditudingkan* the evidence for what they were accused of.

tertuding accused.

tudingan 1 accusation. **2** s.t. indicated. *arah* ~ indicated direction.

penuding accuser.

penudingan accusation, accusing.

tuding II 1 at an angle, sloping, aslant. **2** to form a blunt angle.

menudingkan to slant s.t., make s.t. slant.

tuduh accuse, charge.

menuduh [and **nuduh** (*coq*)] to accuse, charge (with a crime) claim. *karena dituduh* on a charge of.

tuduh-menuduh to accuse e.o.

menuduhkan 1 to charge with, accuse of, blame. *Apa yang meréka tuduhkan kepada saya?* What did they charge me with? *Semua dituduhkan ke saya.* Everything is blamed on me. **2** to base one's accusations on.

tertuduh accused. *si* ~ (*leg*) the accused.

tuduhan charge, accusation, complaint, allegation. *atas* ~ on the charge of. *dengan* ~ charged with (the crime of).

penuduh 1 accuser, plaintiff. **2** prosecutor.

penuduhan charging, accusing, accusation.

tudung 1 cap, cover, shade. **2** veil. – *akar* root cap. – *belanga* pot cover. – *cetus* fuse. – *hidang* → TUDUNG *saji.* – *kepala* a) head cover. b) veil. – *lampu* lamp shade. – *lingkup* k.o. veil. – *lutut* kneecap. – *muka* veil. – *saji/tepak* movable protective cover for food or drink so that insects don't fall in. – *wajah* veil.

bertudung wear/have a cover/cap/veil.

bertudungkan to cover s.t. with.

menudung(i) to cover, put a protective cover on.

menudungkan to cover with, put s.t. over as a cover.

tertudung covered.

penudung cover.

penudungan covering, veiling.

tuf(a) (*D*) tuff.

tuf(f)ah (*A*) *buah* – apple.

tufangka (*Pers ob*) firearm.

tug (in acronyms) → TUGAS I.

tugal dibble stick.

menugal to plant using a dibble stick.

menugali to dibble (in land).

menugalkan to plant s.t. using a dibble stick.

tugalan s.t. dibbled.

penugal person who dibbles.

penugalan dibbling.

tugar (*ob*) → TUGAL.

tugas I 1 task, duty, job, chore, mission. **2** assignment, function. – *akhir* final tasks (to obtain an academic diploma). – *belajar* study assignment. **menugas-belajarkan** to send s.o. on a study assignment. – *berat* heavy-duty. – *intai* reconnaissance mission. – *karya* civilian job for a military man. **penugaskaryaan** placing a military man in a civilian position. – *kata* (*ling*) arguments. – *kewajiban* duty. – *negara* official duties. – *penguatan* annealing task. – *pokok/utama* primary mission, key task.

bertugas 1 to be on duty, one's duty is, have an assignment, be on assignment, be stationed (in or at), serve. **2** to work. *selesai* ~ finished work. *tidak* ~ off duty.

menugasi to assign (a job) to. *Bulog ditugasi memonitor masalah minyak goréng.* Bulog was assigned the job of monitoring the cooking oil problem.

menugaskan 1 to engage, hire. ~ *penasihat yang berpengalaman* to engage experienced advisors. **2** to assign, send out on assignment. *Urusan ini ditugaskan kepada pemerintah daérah.* These matters are assigned to the provincial government.

tertugas assigned.

petugas official, functionary, officer. ~ *angkut* shipping clerk. ~ *bali* s.o. who works in the front office of a company. ~ *Béa Cukai* Custom's Official. ~ *bimbingan* counselor. ~ *darat* ground crew. ~ *imigrasi* immigration official. ~ *keamanan* security guard. ~ *lapangan* field worker. ~ *pabéan* customs official. ~ *parkir* parking attendant. ~ *pimpinan* manager. ~ *ukur* surveyor.

penugasan assignment (of a job), engagement. ~ *kembali* reassignment.

tugas II (*ob*) **menugas** to accuse without evidence, allege.

tugel → TUGAL.

tugu (*Jv*) **1** pillar, post, column. **2** boundary marker. **3** monument, statue. – *Kemenangan* Victory Arch. – *lembur* neighborhood association. – *Monas* [Monumén Nasional] the National Monument (in Jakarta). – *perbatasan* boundary marker. – *peringatan* cenotaph, commemorative column. – *Tani* Farmer's Statue (in Jakarta).

menugu monumental. *karyanya yang* ~ his monumental opus.

tugunisasi the erection of monuments.

tugur (*Jv*) to stand watch.

menuguri to stand watch over.

tuguran standing watch all night long.

tu(h) → ITU.

tuha → TUA.

Tuhan God. – *Allah* God. – *yang Kaya* Almighty God. – *yang Kudrati* Almighty God. – *yang maha esa* God the only one, God Almighty.

bertuhan 1 having a God, believing in God. *perasaan* ~ belief in God. *tidak* ~ atheistic. **2** to worship as a god.

bertuhankan to have ... as a god, worship. ~ *harta benda* to worship material goods.

menuhankan to consider a god.

mempertuhankan to deify, worship as divine.

tuhan-tuhanan false god.

ketuhanan deity, divinity. **berketuhanan** believing in the deity, devout.

tuhfah and **tuhfat** (*A ob*) **1** present, gift. **2** jewels.

tuhfatulajnas (*A ob*) valuable gifts sent with letters.

tuhmah (*A*) suspicion, distrust.

tuhu (*J*) k.o. night bird, cuckoo, *Eudynamis orientalis.*

tuhur → TOHOR I.

tui I (*C?*) private bet (not betting against the house in gambling).

tui II to soak one's feet in hot water.

tui III k.o. tree, *Dolichandrone spathacea.*

tuidi (*J ob*) assistant village head.

tuil jack, lever.

menuil to jack/lever up.

menuilkan to jack s.t. up.

tuit (*D/E?*) tweed.

tujah (*Pal*) **menujah** to stab with a spear.

menujahkan to stab (a spear into).

tuji repeatedly.

tuju I 1 direction. 2 intention. 3 bewitching s.o. by pointing a finger at him/her.

setuju 1 to agree, approve. *tidak* ~ to disagree, disapprove. **ketidaksetujuan** disagreement, disapproval. 2 (*coq*) to like s.t., approve of the way s.t. is. **bersetuju** to agree. ~ *dengan* in accordance with. **menyetujui** to approve. **menyetujukan** and **mempersetujukan** to bring together in agreement, coordinate, bring into line.

menuju 1 to head for, heading toward, set out (for). ~ *ke arah* to move in the direction of. 2 to practice witchcraft on.

menujui to go toward.

menujukan 1 to aim, direct, point s.t. (at). 2 to concentrate (one's attention, etc.).

ketuju agreed.

tertuju ~ *kepada* addressed (to), meant (for), directed (toward).

tertujukan addressed (to).

tujuan 1 goal, objective, aim, purpose. 2 destination. ~ *akhir* final destination, ultimate goal. ~ *menghalalkan semua cara* the end justifies the means. 3 (*gram*) object. ~ *penderita* direct object. **setujuan** having the same goal, going in the same direction. **bersetujuan** simultaneous(ly), at the same time.

bertujuan 1 to have the goal/purpose of, be aimed at; to head for. 2 (*gram*) transitive. 3 purposeful. *tiada* ~ aimless. **persetujuan** 1 approval, consent, permission. 2 agreement, settlement, treaty; → PERJANJIAN. *dengan* ~ with the approval of. ~ *boreh* suretyship. ~ *prinsip* agreement in principle. **sepersetujuan** 1 with the permission of. 2 agreement, pact. 3 approval.

penuju indicator of direction. ~ *hati* one's favorite (dish, etc.).

penujuan directing, aiming, direction, orientation.

tuju II spell, hex; → JAMPI.

menujukan to put a spell on, hex.

tujuh seven. – *belas* seventeen. **tujuhbelasan** on August 17th, Indonesian independence day. *pidato upacara* ~ speech given on that day. – *Agustus* (*ob*) name of the Army division stationed in West Sumatra. – *bulan/hari* seven months/days. **menujuh bulan/hari** and **menujuh-bulani** to celebrate the seventh month/day of pregnancy/death. – *keliling* a) the seven rounds of the *Kabah* (part of the *hajj* ceremonies). b) *puluh* seventy.

bertujuh to be a group of seven.

bertujuh-tujuh in groups of seven, seven at a time.

ketujuh 1 (after the noun) seventh. 2 (before the noun) all seven, a group of seven.

tujuhan around seven.

pertujuh seventh. *se*~ one seventh.

tujul straight to the target.

tuk I → DATUK.

tuk II (*onom*) shortened form of many onomatopoetic words ending in *tuk*.

TUK III [Téater Utan Kayu] a theater and cultural center in Jakarta.

tukai I (*vulg*) cunt, pussy.

tukai II → TUGAL.

tukak ulcer, sore. – *lambung* ulcer.

menukak to ulcerate, fester.

tukal (classifier for) skein of yarn.

setukal a measure of cloth = 16 *rian*.

tukam menukam to pay a condolence call.

tukang I 1 skilled laborer, mechanic, (handi)craftsman, artisan; *cp* AHLI, JURU I. 2 street vendor, door-to-door salesman, peddler, hawker, repairman. 3 person who carries out a certain job. 4 person who usually does or likes to do s.t. 5 (pejorative term) person who has a certain bad habit. – *air* water carrier. – *amin* yes man. – *angkat barang* porter. – *angkut* porter, bellboy. – *angkut barang* porter, red-cap (at airports). – *angkut sampah* garbage collector. – *angon* shepherd. – *antar surat* letter carrier. – *api* stoker. – *arloji* watchmaker. – *asut* agitator. – *aur* peddler. – *azan* muezzin. – *bakul* basket maker. – *bantai* butcher. –

banyol clown, jokester. – *batu* bricklayer; mason. – *béca(k)* pedicab driver. – *belék/belik* tinman. – *bénde* (*Jv*) public auctioneer. – *béngkong* circumciser. – *besi* blacksmith. – *botol* dealer in used bottles, bottle collector. – *bénder* bookbinder. – *berkelahi* fighter. – *besi* blacksmith. – *besi kuda* farrier. – *besi bersih jalan* street sweeper. – *bikin duit* moneylender. – *bikin kacau* troublemaker. – *bikin sajak* composer of poetry. – *binatu* laundryman. – *blék* tinman, tinsmith. – *bodor* clown, comedian. – *bohong* liar. – *bola* (*Pr*) pickpocket. – *boncéng* sponger, freeloader. – *bubut* fitter. – *cakap perut* ventriloquist. – *canai* knife and scissors grinder. – *cap* printer. – *cap batu* lithographer. – *cari adperténsi* advertising salesman. – *cat* painter. – *catut* black-marketeer, (ticket) scalper, swindler. – *cekék* thug. – *celup* dyer. – *ceritera* storyteller. – *cét* → TUKANG cat. – *cétak* printer. – *cincang* film censor. – *copét* pickpocket. – *cor* (metal) founder. – *cukur* barber. – *cungo* pickpocket. – *cuplik* plagiarizer. – *dagel* clown, comedian. – *daging* meat vendor, – *dansa* (*ob*) acrobat, entertainer. – *dérék* winch driver. – *diesel* diesel engine operator. – *diko* car spray painter. – *doa* (pejorative term for) pious person. – *dobi* laundryman. – *dongkél* burglar. – *enggih* (*Jv*) yes man. – *fitnah* slanderer. – *gangsir rumah* burglar. – *ganyang lampu mobil* automobile lamp thief. – *gedor* burglar. – *gelap mata* conjurer, magician. – *gencét* bully. – *gendem* hypnotist. – *genténg/genting* (roof-) tile maker. – *gergaji mesin* chainsaw operator. – *gerobak* cart driver. – *gerogoti uang* corruptor. – *gigi* unlicensed Chinese dentist and dental technician. – *godot* corrupt government employee. – *gosok* intriguer, provocateur. – *gunting rambut* barber, hairdresser. – *guyon* joker, comedian. – *hambur uang negara* corruptor of state funds. – *hasut* agitator. – *ijon* purchaser of paddy while still in the field. – *ikan* fishmonger. – *intip* a) peeping Tom. b) knothole watcher (at sports events). c) spy. – *itung-itungan* astrologer. – *jam* watch repairer. – *jamas* person who cleans *pusaka* with arsenic. – *jahit* seamstress, tailor. – *jambrét* (purse) snatcher. – *jentera* helmsman. – *jarah* rustler. – *jilat* ass kisser. – *jilid* bookbinder. – *jiplak* plagiarist, plagiarizer. – *jotos* bodyguard. – *jual obat* medicine man, quack (doctor). – *kacau* troublemaker. – *kacip* sniper. – *kaplok* person in the claque. – *kasut* shoemaker. – *kawin* s.o. who marries many times. – *kayu* carpenter. – *kebun* gardener. – *kebut* irresponsible and reckless driver. – *kelontong* peddler. – *kemasan* goldsmith. – *keplok* → TUKANG kaplok. – *kepruk* member of a pressure group, member of a strong-arm squad, bouncer (in a night club). – *keréta* cart driver. – *ketok* auto body repairman. – *kipas* (in volleyball) person who is known for his smashes. – *kisar* miller. – *kompas* blackmailer. – *kompor* instigator, inciter. – *koran* newspaper boy. – *krédit* lender. – *kuda* stableboy, groom. – *kué* a) baker. b) bread seller. – *kunci* locksmith. – *ladén* (*S*) cement mixer helper. – *langsir* yardman, shunter. – *lapor* informant. – *las* welder. – *las pipa* pipe welder. – *lawak* joker, clown. – *lédéng/léding* a) bill collector for the water company. b) plumber. – *lélang* auctioneer. – *lémpar duit* spendthrift. – *lepas uang* moneylender. – *listrik* electrician. – *loténg* roofer. – *lo(w)ak/luak* a) secondhand dealer. b) rag dealer. – *lumas* lube man. – *mabok/mabuk* drunkard. – *madat* opium smoker. – *madon* womanizer. – *main biola* violinist. – *main piano* pianist. – *makan* s.o. who likes to eat, glutton. – *masak* cook. – *mas* goldsmith; → TUKANG kemasan. – *mbolos* a habitual truant, work dodger. – *melucu* clown, comedian. – *mencabut nyawa* hired assassin, killer. – *mengiakan* yes man. – *mengocok* masturbator. – *métsel* bricklayer. – *menyuka* jack-of-all-trades. – *mindering* a) moneylender. b) supplier on the installment plan. – *nébéng* freeloader. – *ngadu* informant. – *ngamén* troubadour. – *ngarang buku* author, writer. – *ngarit* grass cutter. – *ngéntot* cocksman. – *ngesét* typesetter. – *ngobrol* chatterbox. – *ngompol* bed-wetter. – *ngorok* snorer. – *nrimo* easygoing person who accepts whatever comes along. – *nunut* freeloader. – *nyepom* shoplifter. – *obat* quack (doctor). – *pacak* dummy, puppet. – *palak* mugger. – *pamér* showoff. – *pancing* angler. – *panggil tamu* page (in hotel). – *pangkas* barber. – *parkir* parking lot attendant. – *pasang sihir* s.o. who practices black magic. – *pat(e)ri* solderer. – *pedati* cart driver. – *pél* janitor. – *pelat* plate worker. – *pengkorankan* (*ob*) rumormonger. – *perah* s.o. who milks cows.

– *perahu* boatman. – *peras* blackmailer, extortionist. – *perkosa* rapist. – *pidato* big talker. – *pijat/pijit* masseur, masseuse. – *pipa* pipe fitter, plumber. – *plakat* person who puts up posters. – *pola* pattern-maker (in making *batik* and in tailoring). – *pos* mailman, postman. – *potong* a) cutter (in general). b) butcher. – *potong rambut* barber. – *potrét* photographer. – *pukul* a) hatchet man, strong-arm man. b) bodyguard. c) pressure group. – *pungut puntung rokok* collector of cigarette butts. – *ramal* fortuneteller. – *rém* a) (railroad) brakeman. b) person whose task it is to corner a victim (in pickpocket jargon on Jakarta city buses). – *rénte* moneylender. – *résénsi* reviewer, critic. – *rias* makeup artist. – *riba* usurer. – *ribut* troublemaker. – *rogo* (*J*) pickpocket. – *rombéng(an)* a) secondhand dealer. b) rag dealer, junkman. – *roti* a) baker. b) bread man. – *royal* man about town. – *réwél* fuss-budget. – *rumah* mason. – (*sabit*) *rumput* grass cutter. – *samak* tanner. – *sambrah* dancing girl. – *sampah* garbage collector/man. – *sapu* trash man, garbage collector. – *sapu jalan* street sweeper. – *sayur* door-to-door greengrocer. – *semir sepatu* bootblack, shoeshine boy. – *sepatu* a) shoemaker. b) shoe repairman. – *sepatu kuda* blacksmith. – *sepéda* bicycle repairman. – *serobot* pickpocket. – *sihir* hypnotist. – *sikari* hunter. – *sikut* deceiver, cheater, con man. – *silap mata* conjurer, magician. – *sol sepatu* cobbler. – *sosot* a man who has one girlfriend after another. – *spanduk* banner fastener. – *suap* briber. – *sulap* a) juggler, conjurer. b) magician. – *sunat* circumciser. – *sundut* arsonist. – *suntik* vaccinator. – *sunglap* → TUKANG *sulap*. – *susu* milkman. – *tadah* fence, receiver of stolen property. – *tambal ban sepéda* (roadside) bicycle tire repairman. – *tambur* drummer (*mil* music). – *tangkap anjing* dogcatcher. – *tanji* (*ob*) musician. – *tarohan/taruhan* bettor, gambler. – *tawar* s.o. who likes to drive a hard bargain. – *télepon* telephone installer. – *teluh* s.o. who practices black magic. – *tembaga* coppersmith. – *tembang* male singer with gamelan orchestra. – *tembérang* big talker. – *tempa* forger (of metal). – *tempah* futures buyer. – *tenung* fortune-teller. – *tepok* claque. – *tera* inspector of weights and measures. – *teriak* auctioneer. – *ternak uang* moneylender. – *tidur* sleepyhead, sleep hound. – *tilik* fortune-teller. – *tin* tinsmith. – *tinju* boxer. – *todong* gangster, holdup man. – *tunjuk* stoolpigeon. – *uang* a) cashier. b) purser. – *ukur* surveyor. – *ukur jalan* vagabond, bum. – *ular* snake charmer. – *urut* masseur, masseuse. – *warang* person who cleans *pusaka* with arsenic.

bertukang and **menukang** to be an artisan, be a skilled workman.

tukang-menukang 1 ply (all k.o.) trades, be a jack-of-all-trades. **2** handicraft, handiwork, craftsmanship.

menukangi 1 to work at making/constructing. **2** to repair, mend.

ketukangan skill, craftsmanship.

pertukangan 1 trade. *sekolah* ~ (*coq*) trade school. **2** handicraft. **3** craftsmanship. **4** craft, guild of craftsmen.

tukang II 1 – *besi* coppersmith barbet, *Megalaima haemacephala Indica*. **2** long-tailed nightjar, *Caprimulgus macrurus bimaculatus*; → BURUNG *malas/segan*.

tukar (*coq*) to change, exchange; → BERTUKAR. – *barang* barter. – *cincin* a) to exchange rings, i.e., to be engaged to marry; → BERTUNANG(AN). *Meréka akan* ~ *cincin bulan depan*. They are going to be engaged next month. b) engagement. – *cincin itu akan diadakan di Médan*. The engagement will take place in Medan. – *ganti* substitution, replacement. – *guling* land swap; → RUILSLAG. – *haluan* tack (of a ship). – *jaga* to change the guard, changing of the guard. – *pesawat* to change planes. – *pikir* exchange of views. **menukar-pikirkan** to exchange views about. – *tambah* trade-in. *terima* – *tambah* trade-ins accepted.

bertukar 1 to exchange (cables/words/glances/smiles, etc); → BERGANTI, BERSILIH. ~ *rupa* to change one's appearance/shape; → BERSALIN *rupa*. **2** to change. ~ *dari* to change from (what it was originally). ~ *dari yang sudah-sudah* to be different from before. **3** ~ *dengan* to turn/change (into). *siang* ~ *dengan malam* daytime has changed to evening. ~ *adat* a) to abandon/give up old habits. b) to change one's habits. ~ *akal* (to go) crazy, not all there, not in one's right mind. ~ *bulu* a) to molt/shed one's feathers/plumage. b) to change one's mind c) to change fundamentally/profoundly/radically. ~ *baju/pakaian* to change one's clothes. ~ *haluan* a) to change direction. b) to change policy. ~ *iman* to change religions. ~ *jalan* a) to pass e.o. b) to take another road/course. ~ *kain* to change the topic. ~ *kapal* to change ships, transship. ~ *kécék* to change the topic. ~ *keréta* to change trains. ~ *kulit* a) to slough (of snakes). b) to change one's opinion. ~ *lagu* → BERTUKAR *suara*. ~ *pandang* a) to discuss. b) to exchange views. ~ *pesawat* to change planes. ~ *pikiran* a) to change one's mind. b) to exchange views. c) to go crazy. ~ *omong* to converse. ~ *ranjang* to change wives. ~ *sebut* to argue back and forth. ~ *sepah* token of deep love between two lovers. ~ *suara* to sing a different tune; to shift one's grounds. ~ *tambah* trade in (a car). ~ *tangan* to change hands. ~ *tempat* to change places.

bertukar-tukar 1 to take turns, alternate. **2** alternating. **3** to keep on changing.

bertukar-tukaran to exchange, interchange.

menukar [and **nukar** (*coq*)] **1** to exchange, barter, trade. *ditukar tambah dengan* to be traded in for. **2** to change, cash, convert. ~ *ban* to change a tire. ~ *lagu* to change one's tune. ~ *seléra* to change what one eats.

tukar-menukar 1 to exchange with e.o., interchange. **2** an exchange, exchanging. ~ *pendapat* an exchange of ideas.

menukari 1 to exchange s.t. for. **2** (*pl obj*) to change.

menukarkan 1 to change (s.t. into s.t. else), convert, trade. ~ *cék* to cash a check. ~ *rupiah dengan dolar* to convert rupiahs into dollars. **2** to trade, exchange. *Inggeris* ~ *Bengkulu dengan Pulau Singapura*. The English traded Bengkulu for Singapore. **3** to fill (a prescription). ~ *résép* to fill a prescription.

mempertukarkan 1 to change, convert. **2** to exchange, trade (one thing for another). ~ *barang* to exchange goods. ~ *bentuk* to change its form. *uang yang dapat dipertukarkan* convertible currency. *dapat dipertukarkan* exchangeable, convertible.

tertukar accidentally exchanged.

tukaran exchange.

penukar exchange, changer, s.o. who exchanges. *alat* ~ medium of exchange. ~ *uang* money changer.

penukaran 1 change, exchange, swap, the act/process of substitution, change. *tempat* ~ *uang* money changer. ~ *hawa* ventilation. ~ *zat* metabolism. **2** filling (a prescription).

pertukaran change, alteration, replacement, swap, exchange. *alat* ~ medium of exchange. ~ *agama* religious conversion. ~ *barang* exchange of goods. ~ *bentuk* change of form, transformation. ~ *iklim* change of climate. ~ *pelajar* student exchange. ~ *pikiran* exchange of ideas. ~ *udara* ventilation. ~ *zat* metabolism.

tukas I 1 false accusation, slander. **2** to say in an accusatory way. –*nya* he said accusingly.

menukas(i) to accuse without evidence, slander.

tukasan slander, aspersions, false accusation.

penukas false accuser.

tukas II (*M*) repeat, the same thing all over again.

bertukas-tukas repeatedly.

menukas to repeat, do/say again.

tukas III 1 (*ling*) interpolated clause, parenthetical phrase. **2** retort, respond. –*nya* he retorted/countered. *Jangan cepat-cepat percaya," -nya*. "Don't believe it so quickly," he countered.

tukas IV k.o. rattan palm (usually used to snare wild animals), *Caryota mitis*.

tuker → TUKAR.

tukik I (*M*) dive, plunge down.

menukik to plunge/dive/dash/swoop down, aim/look, etc. downward. *Pesawat pembom itu* ~ *sambil menjatuhkan bom*. The bomber swooped down and dropped bombs. ~ *api* to ignite a fire with a flint.

menukiki to dive/swoop down on.

menukikkan 1 to make s.t. plunge/dip/come down/descend/swoop down. ~ *layang-layang* to make a kite dive down. ~ *pandang/pemandangan* to look downward. ~ *tombak* to jab a spear downward. **2** to direct, concentrate (one's attention).

tertukik (of airplane) to make a dive.

tukikan incline, inclination.

penukikan dive (of an airplane).

tukik II (M) notch, nick, indentation; → TAKIK. *keras ditukik, lunak disudu* giving orders should be done wisely.

menukik to nick, indent, notch, carve a notch in.

tukik III baby green turtle, *Chelonia mydas.*

tukil I a bamboo cylinder for juice obtained from the blossom of the coconut palm or sugar palm.

tukil II → NUKIL.

tukmis [batuk klimis] (*Jv*) philanderer, womanizer; → MATA *keranjang. Ia dikenal* –. He is known as a womanizer.

tukon (*Jv*) bought.

tuk-tuk motorboat.

tuku → TENGKU.

tukuk → TOKOK I, II.

tukul hammer, mallet. – *besi* hammer made of steel. – *kayu* wooden hammer, mallet.

menukul to hammer.

penukul 1 hammer. **2** hammerer.

tukun underwater rock.

tukung (*Jv*) a tailless variety of chicken.

tukup (M) lid, shutter.

tukus *angin* – first breeze (after the rainy season).

tuku-takal (*Jv*) a plant the leaves of which are used to keep away malicious spirits, usually hung above a door, *Baccaurea wallichii.*

tul I clipped form of **betul.**

tul II main – a child's game.

Tula Libra (*zod*).

tulad (*Jv*) **menulad** [and **nulad** (*coq*)] to imitate.

tulah I (*D*) allowance, bonus (above one's salary); → TUNJANGAN, TUSLAH. – *anak* child allowance.

tulah II (*A*) calamity, bad luck, misfortune (brought on by a curse or due to misbehavior toward one's parents, etc.). – *papa* miserable luck.

menulahi to curse, damn.

ketulahan curse, malediction.

tulalit (*BG*) stupid, out of it.

tulang 1 bone. **2** s.t. resembling a bone or skeleton. *tinggal – dan/dengan kulit* and *tinggal – terbalut kulit* and *tinggal kulit membalut/pembalut –* and – *dan kulit saja lagi* and *hanya tinggal kulit dan – saja* nothing but skin and bones. *minta – kepada lintah* to demand the impossible. – *air mata* lachrymal bone. – *alah mak* ankle bone. – *babi* spareribs. – *baji* sphenoid bone. – *belakang* backbone, spine. – *belikat* shoulder blade, scapula. – *belulang* a) skin and bones. b) carcass, bones. – *bercagak* cheekbone. – *betis* tibia. – *biji* raphe. – *biduk* navicular bone. – *buku lali* ankle bone. – *bulan* lunate bone. – *bundar* fetlock join (of a horse). – *cabang* lateral nerve (of a plant). – *cenak* clavicle. – *cenonot* coccyx. – *ceruk* alveolar bone. – *dada* breastbone, sternum. – *dahi* frontal bone. – *daun* veins of a leaf. – *dayung* a) blade of an oar. b) shoulder blade. – *delapan kerat* a) the whole body. b) (M) the extremities. – *duduk* ischium. – *ékor* coccyx. – *empat kerat* the limbs. – *halus* cartilage. – *hasta* ulna. – *hidung* nasal bone. – *hitam* marrow. – *iga* rib. – *jari* fetlock, pastern. – *jorong* foramen ovule. – *kelangkang* sacrum. – *kélék buyung* the crest of the ileum. – *kemaluan* pubis, pubic bone. – *kéng* the condyle at the end of the lower jaw. – *kepala belakang* occipital. – *kering* tibia, shinbone. – *ketuk jari* knuckles. – *ketul* cartilage. – *kucing* humerus. – *ketul* cartilage. – *kipas* scapula. – *kongkéng* coccyx. – *landasan* incus. – *langit-langit* hard palate. – *layanglayang* skeleton of a kite. – *léhér* collar bone. – *lembusir* shoulder blade. – *lengan atas* humerus. – *lidah* hyoid bone. – *lunas* wishbone. – *mata duli* ankle bone. – *mata kaki* ankle bone. – *mérah* hyoid bone. – *muda* cartilage. – *paha* femur. – *panggul* hip bone. – *pangkal lengan* humerus. – *pangkal paha* femur. – *pantat* ischium. – *papan bahu* shoulder blade. – *papan breastbone. – *pelipis(an)* temporal bone. – *pengumpil* radius (bone in wrist). – *pengancing* cheekbone. – *pemutar* axis. – *pergelangan* carpus. – *pergelangan kaki* tarsus. – *pinggul* pelvic bone. – *pinggul atas* ileum. – *pipi* cheekbone. – *pukang* ileum. – *punggung* a) spine, spinal column, ischium. b) backbone, main support. *Perdagangan merupakan – punggung meréka.* Trade is their bread-

and-butter. **menulang-punggungi** to support fully, be the main support of. *Hanoi akan tetap ~ Kamboja.* Hanoi will remain Cambodia's main supporter. – *punggung negara* a) teenagers. b) the nation's youth, hope of the future. *Mahasiswa sering dianggap sebagai putra-putri terbaik, – punggung negara.* Students are often considered the best sons and daughters, the nation's hope for the future. – *pungkur* a) lumbar vertebrae b) pubic bone. – *rahang* jawbone, mandible. – *rawan* cartilage. – *rawan cincin* cricoid cartilage. – *rawan gondok* thyroid cartilage. – *rimau menangis* breastbone. – *rusuk* rib. – *sanggurdi* stapes. – *sayap* wing spar (of aircraft). – *selangka* clavicle, collarbone. – *selangka katak* femur. – *sendi* joint. – *sendi siku* condyles of the humerus. – *som* pubic bone. – *sulbi* coccyx. – *sumsum* bone and marrow. *sampai di – sumsum* through and through. **menulang sumsum** to penetrate to the bone. **menulang-sumsumi** to form the very backbone/core of s.t. – *tangan* ulna. – *tempurung* patella. – *tengah* midrib (of a plant). – *tongkéh* lower part of backbone. – *tongkéng* coccyx. – *tudung* temporal bone. – *tumit* heel bone, calcaneus, pastern (of a horse). – *tungging* coccyx. – *tunjang* astralagus, leg bone of fowl. – *tutup dahi* supraorbital ridge of the frontal bone. – *ubun-ubun* parietal bone. – *ujung belikat* acromonium. – *usus* ileum.

tulang-tulang ossicles.

bertulang 1 bony, full of bones. **2** with bones. *binatang ~ belakang* vertebrates. *tidak ~* a) boneless. b) spineless, weak. *lidah tak ~* makes empty promises. *binatang tidak ~* invertebrates. **3** reinforced (concrete).

menulang 1 to be(come)bony, osseous. **2** to harden, become adamant. – *sumsum* very painful.

menulangi to bone, remove the bones from, fillet.

tertulang 1 to be felt to the very marrow. **2** as lean as a rake, as skinny as a rail. **3** as poor as a church mouse.

tulangan armature, reinforcement.

tulang-tulangan 1 various bones. **2** framework of a house. **3** skeleton.

ketulangan to have a bone stuck in one's throat.

penulangan 1 steelwork for reinforced concrete. **2** reinforcing.

pertulangan (*Bal*) cremation site.

tulang II – *daing* k.o. tree, purple milletia, *Milletia atropurpurea. kayu –* → KAYU *tulang.*

tulang-tulang various k.o. trees, *Euphorbia tirucalli, Prismatomeris malayana.*

tular infect, contaminate.

menular [and **nular** (*coq*)] **1** to infect, contaminate. **2** to spread (of a disease/s.t. bad). *Perbuatan buruk itu mudah sekali ~.* That bad behavior spreads very easily. **3** infectious, contagious.

menulari to infect, spread to/over. *program yang ditulari virus* a program infected by a virus.

menularkan to transmit/spread a disease/skill/feeling, carry (a disease). *Kecintaan terhadap laut ditularkannya kepada para anaknya.* He transmitted his love of the sea to his children.

tertular infected. *wilayah ~* infected zone.

tertulari to get infected.

tularan 1 contagion, infection. **2** s.t. infected, affected by a disease.

ketularan to be contaminated/infected, catch (a disease).

penular (disease) vector.

penularan infection, spread, contagion. *~ penyakit* spread of a disease.

tulat (*ob*) three days from now.

tulban (*D*) raisin cake.

tulé (*D*) tulle.

tulén (*Jv*) genuine, authentic, pure, unadulterated.

ketulénan purity, authenticity, genuineness.

tuli deaf. – *bisu* deaf and dumb.

menuli to become deaf.

menulikan *~ (telinga)* a) deafening. b) to turn a deaf ear.

ketulian 1 deafness. **2** to suffer from deafness.

tulip (*D*) tulip.

tulis 1 write, writing. – *baca* reading and writing. *Ia sama sekali tidak tahu – baca.* He didn't know at all how to write and read. **2** handmade (batik). *batik –* handmade batik; *opp batik cap/*

cétak printed batik. *batu* – slate (for writing). *buku* – exercise book. *méja* – desk. *mesin* – *(éléktronik)* (electronic) typewriter. *papan* – blackboard, chalkboard. – *halus* handmade (batik). – *tangan* handwriting. **bertulis-tangan** handwritten. – *ulang* rewrite. **menulis-ulang** to rewrite.

bertulis written on, inscribed. *batu* ~ stone tablet; → PRASASTI. ~ *tangan* handwritten. *surat yang* ~ *tangan* a handwritten letter.

bertuliskan to have s.t. written on, inscribed with. *Spanduk itu* ~ "*mohon diperhatikan nasib kami penghuni proyék pemukiman Lhok Pineung.*" The banner has written on it the words "please, pay attention to our plight, dwellers of the Lhok Pineung resettlement project." *Tak jauh dari tempat Musa menjajakan sepatu bekas ada papan dari séng: "Daérah terlarang untuk pedagang kakilima dan penempatan barang.*" Not far from the place where Musa was hawking used shoes was a zinc signboard inscribed with the words: "Prohibited area for sidewalk vendors and placement of goods."

menulis [and **nulis** (*coq*)] 1 to write, make letters or other symbols with a pen/pencil, etc. on paper, draw. ~ *gambar* to draw a picture, illustrate. ~ *roman* to write a novel. ~ *ulang* to rewrite. *ditulis serangkai* written as a single word. 2 to form (letters/words/a message, etc.) in this way. *dengan ditulis tangan* handwritten. ~ *cék* to write a check. 3 to compose in written form for publication, to be an author, write (for). *Ia* ~ *dalam majalah "Témpo."* He wrote for the magazine "Tempo." 4 to write and send a letter. *Tulislah saya sering-sering.* Write me often. 5 to batik. 6 (*coq*) to fill out (a form).

tulis-menulis 1 writing (of articles, stories, etc.). 2 correspondence. *Maju-mundurnya perniagaan, banyak bergantung pada* ~. The progress of commerce depends, to a large extent, on correspondence. *alat* ~ writing implement.

menulisi [and **nulisin** (*J coq*)] to write on s.t. or to s.o. ~ *kertas ini* to write on this paper. ~ *kain* to batik cloth.

menuliskan [and **nulisin** (*J coq*)] 1 to write s.t. down/out. ~ *nama dalam buku tamu* to write one's name in a guest book. 2 to write with s.t., use s.t. to write with. *Bagaimana hendak* ~ *pénsil tumpul ini?* How do you write with a blunt pencil? 3 to write s.t. for s.o. else. *Saya yang* ~ *surat untuknya.* It's I who wrote the letter for him.

tertulis written, in writing. *memberikan jaminan* ~ to issue a guarantee in writing. *keterangan/ujian* written statement/examination

tulisan 1 s.t. written; manner/style of writing. *masyarakat yang belum mengenal* ~ an illiterate society. 2 writings, article (in a magazine/newspaper, etc.); books. *Saya ingin membaca* ~ *Mochtar Lubis.* I would like to read Mochtar Lubis's books. 3 writing, written language, script. *belum mengenal* ~ illiterate. 4 picture of s.t., drawing. 5 *batik* ~ handmade batik. 6 fate, destiny. *dengan* ~ in writing (not orally). ~ *cepat* shorthand, stenography. ~ *nasib* fate, destiny. ~ *penghinaan* (*leg*) libel. ~ *rahasia* cryptogram. ~ *tangan* handwriting. **bertulisan** with/to have a notice. *Papan itu* ~ "*Awas anjing galak.*" The signboard reads: "Beware of the vicious dog."

penulis 1 writer (of a letter/books, etc.), author. 2 secretary (of a club/association, etc.). 3 the author (of this book, etc.). ~ *cerita panggung* playwright. ~ *kepariwisataan* travel writer. ~ *naskah* copywriter. ~ *pariwisata* travel writer. ~ *rahasia* cryptographer. ~ *siluman* ghost writer. ~ *tajuk* editorialist. **kepenulisan** writing, authoring.

penulisan process/way of writing. ~ *kembali* rewriting. ~ *kréatif* creative writing. ~ *sejarah* historiography.

pertulisan inscription.

tuli-tuli (*ob*) a silver cord to tie a kris to one's belt.

tultul polka-dot(s).

tulu stupid, foolish.

tulung I → TOLONG.

tulung II – *tumpuk* black-banded barbet, *Megalaima javensis*.

tulup (*Jv*) blowpipe.

menulup to blow with a pipe.

tulus honest, sincere. – *hati* sincere. – *ikhlas* honest, sincere, straightforward. **ketulus-ikhlasan** sincerity.

setulus-tulus *dengan* ~ *hatinya* in good faith.

ketulusan and ~ *hati* honesty, sincerity, integrity, candor.

tum I (*onom*) thumping sound.

tum II bridle, reins.

tum III (*Jv*) banana-leaf wrapping.

mengetum to cook in a banana leaf.

tuma k.o. louse. *takutkan* – *dibuangkan kain* to throw out the baby with the bathwater.

bertuma having lice.

tuman I → TOMAN.

tuman II (*J/Jv*) to be used to, accustomed to.

tumang I 1 (tent) peg, stake. 2 support (for a cooking pan).

tumang II a measurement of about 10 kg of sago.

tumang III bertumang refused, rejected.

menumang(kan) to refuse, reject.

tumbak I a measurement of area = 14 square meters.

tumbak II → TOMBAK I.

tumbakan (*Jv*) marriage between parallel cousins.

tumbal (*J/Jv*) 1 antidote, charm or offering (against sickness). 2 s.o. who protects s.o. else from getting hurt, protection.

bertumbal 1 antidotal. 2 to use ... as protection. *asal jangan* ~ *rakyat kecil saja* as long as you don't just use the common people as protection.

menumbalkan to use s.t. or s.o. as protection (against misfortune, etc.), sacrifice for one's own benefit.

tumbang I fall down (with a crash), collapse and fall down, crash, topple. *jika bank-bank itu dibiarkan* – if those banks are allowed to crash.

bertumbangan (*pl subj*) to collapse, crash.

menumbangkan 1 to topple, overturn, overthrow. 2 to knock down, uproot. 3 to break (a record), beat s.o. in a game. 4 to slaughter (animals).

tertumbangkan beaten, beatable (of a record).

tumbangan topping (of trees).

penumbang s.o. who topples. ~ *rékor* record breaker.

penumbangan 1 toppling, knocking down. 2 breaking (a record).

pertumbangan overthrow, collapse.

tumbang II (*M*) – *pisang* k.o. snack made from bananas.

menumbang to cook ... in that way.

tumbar (*Jv*) → KETUMBAR.

tumbas → TUMPAS I.

tumbén (*J*) 1 what a surprise! how odd! 2 I'm surprised! – *nih*...? How come...? *Wah, kok – ke sini!* I'm surprised that you're here! *baru* – for the first time, just starting out to ...

tumbén-tumbénan it's really odd (that).

tumbila bedbug.

tumbrak (*J*) to kick, knock, bang; → TABRAK.

tumbu (*Jv*) k.o. lidded coarse basket for carrying rice. *seperti* – *oléh tutup* well-matched.

tumbuh 1 to grow, develop. 2 to sprout, come out (of teeth). 3 to accrue. 4 to grow/do well. 5 to appear, come out (of feelings). 6 to occur, happen. – *kembang* grow and develop. **menumbuh-kembangkan** to make s.t. grow and develop. – *luas* fostering, stimulating. **menumbuh-luaskan** to foster/stimulate the growth of. – *mekar* to make s.t. grow. **menumbuh-mekarkan** to cultivate. – *subur* prosper. **menumbuh-suburkan** to make s.t. prosper.

bertumbuh to grow.

bertumbuh-tumbuhan overgrown, full of plants.

bertumbuhan (*pl subj*) to grow.

bertumbuhkan overgrown with.

menumbuh (*coq*) to grow.

menumbuhi to grow over, let s.t. overgrow.

menumbuhkan 1 to make s.t. grow. 2 to cultivate, foster, promote, develop. ~ *cinta tanah air* to foster love toward one's country. 3 to lead to. *Ini* ~ *cerita lain.* That's another story. 4 to cause s.t. to arise, bring about.

mempertumbuhkan to make s.t. grow, develop, raise.

tumbuhan 1 vegetation, plant. 2 offshoot. 3 s.t. that grows. 4 a growth. ~ *inang* host (to parasites). ~ *memanjat* climbers. ~ *(men)jalar* creeper. ~ *pengganggu* weed. ~ *polong* legumes. ~ *semusim* annual. ~ *tahunan* perennial.

tumbuh-tumbuhan plants, vegetation, flora.

ketumbuhan 1 growth, development. 2 to be overgrown with. 3 a growth on the skin, skin eruption.

penumbuhan 1 growing. 2 emergence. 3 bringing about.

pertumbuhan growth, increase, development.

tumbuk I I celebration of one's *windu* birthday (every eight years). *- yuswo* 72nd birthday (= nine *windu*). 2 pounding, striking. 3 crushed, pounded.

bertumbuk 1 to collide with, crash into, slam against. *saling ~* to clash. 2 to fight. 3 to coincide (with), occur at the same time (as).

bertumbukan to collide with e.o.

menumbuk 1 to strike. *~ mata* to be striking (of a view, etc.). 2 to collide with, crash into. 3 to pound, crush by pounding. 4 to let (one's eyes) light (on).

menumbukkan 1 to smash s.t. (against s.t.). 2 to smash with s.t., use s.t. to smash with.

tertumbuk 1 collided. *~ di/ke/pada jalan* emerge on the street. *~ dengan/ke/pada* (your eyes) will fall on. *~ pada batasnya* reached its limit. *~ pada diri sendiri* to fall back on one's own resources. *~ akal/pikiran* to be at one's wits' end. *~ kata* in difficulties. 2 hit by accident. 3 depressed, down. 4 to light on s.t. (of the eyes).

tumbukan 1 blow. 2 impact, shock. 3 crash, collision. *~ balik* recoil. 4 clash. 5 s.t. struck, crashed into.

penumbuk crusher, pounder, rammer.

penumbukan 1 collision, crash. 2 blow, strike, stroke. 3 pounding, crush by pounding.

pertumbukan meeting, coming across.

tumbuk II *(burung)* *- ketampi* k.o. owl, *Ketupa zeylonensis.*

tumbuk III → TUMPAK I.

tumbung I protrusion, prolapse. *- dubur* prolapsed anus. *- kelapa* coconut seed bud. *- rahim* prolapsed uterus.

penumbungan bulging out.

tumbung II → TOMBONG I.

tumbur bertumburan to collide with e.o.

ketumbur *(coq)* got hit.

tumenggung 1 *(Mal)* Minister. 2 high-ranking official (under the *bendahara*). 3 *(Jv col)* title conferred on a Bupati. 4 authority in charge of internal security.

tumimbal *- lahir* reincarnation, to reincarnate.

tumis sauté, stir-fry. *- arcis* stir-fried snow peas. *- telur* poached eggs in stock.

bertumis sautéed, stir-fried.

menumis(i) to cook s.t. that way.

tumisan stir-fried.

tumit heel. *- bedil* butt of a rifle.

bertumit with ... heels.

tumon *(Jv)* to notice. *Apa –?* Did you ever see/hear of such a thing?

tumor *(D)* tumor. *- ganas* malignant tumor. *- jinak/tenang* benign tumor.

bertumor with a tumor.

tumpah spill/pour (out), overflow. *- darah* one's birthplace. **bertumpah darah** to shed blood. *- ruah* overflowing. **bertumpah-ruah** abundant, copious, plentiful. *- tindih* one on top of the other.

menumpahi to spill/pour out on/over. *~ méja* it spilled out over the table.

menumpahkan 1 to pour s.t. out, spill. *~ isi hati* to confide (in s.o.), pour one's heart out (to s.o.). 2 to shed. *~ darah* to shed blood. 3 to concentrate, pour.

tertumpah 1 spilled. *negara tempat darahnya ~* his native land. 2 shed. 3 ascribed/attributed to. *Kesalahan ~ pada séktor perhubungan saja.* Mistakes are only attributed to the transportation sector. 4 concentrated.

tumpahan 1 flow, spill. 2 s.t. spilled, shed. *~ hati* sweetheart.

ketumpahan 1 spill. 2 wet with s.t. that spilled.

penumpahan 1 spilling, shedding. *~ darah* bloodshed. 2 concentrating, concentration.

pertumpahan spilling, shedding. *~ darah* bloodshed.

tumpak I *(M)* 1 group, collection, mass. 2 batch. 3 place, spot. 3 plot (of land). *se- tanah* a plot of land. *- tampak* field of vision.

bertumpak(-tumpak) in groups/batches.

tumpak II *(Jv J)* **numpak** to ride on. *~ bécak* to ride in a pedicab.

menumpaki to ride on.

tumpal *(Jv)* border design on the edge of a sarong.

tumpang do s.t. with s.o. else or use s.t. belonging to s.o. else. *- gilir* multiple cropping. *- kaki* one leg on top of the other. *- sari* intercrop. **menumpang-sarikan** to intercrop. *- sisip* intercropping. *- suh* overlapping. **bertumpang-suh** to overlap. *- susun* overlay. *- tindih* overlapping. **bertumpang-tindih** a) to overlap. b) to be piled up, one on top of the other. **ketumpang-tindihan** overlap.

bertumpang *duduk ~ dagu* to sit with one's chin in one's hands, i.e., to do nothing.

menumpang [and **numpang** *(coq)*] 1 to pile up. *Gumpalan awan hitam ~ di atas puncak gunung.* Masses of clouds piled up on top of the mountain. 2 to travel by, catch a ride on. *dengan ~ pesawat* by plane. 3 (most commonly **numpang**) to use s.t. that belongs to s.o. else. *~ alamat* to have an address at, be housed at (s.o. else's place). *~ dengar* to listen, eavesdrop. *~ hidup* to live at s.o. else's expense. *~ makan* to eat at s.o. else's expense. *~ ke kamar mandi* to take a bath in s.o. else's house. *~ nama* to use s.o. else's good name. *~ nonton* to watch (TV) in s.o. else's house. *~ télepon* to borrow s.o.'s telephone. *~ tidur* to sleep over (at s.o.'s house). *~ (tinggal)* to board, be a paying guest, stay. 4 to do s.t. together with others. 5 to do s.t. with others. *~ ketawa* to join in the laughter. *~ mati* to die at the same time (as s.o. else). 6 ask permission. *~ jalan/léwat* excuse me (when passing in front of s.o.), just passing by. *~ tanya?* May I ask you a question?

tumpang-menumpang to overlap. *~ taruh* to bet on the same number (as s.o. else).

menumpangi 1 to ride in (a vehicle). 2 to stay in/at (a place). 3 to overlay. 4 to make use of s.t. belonging to s.o. else. 5 to pin (one's hopes on). *dara-dara Bali yang ditumpangi harapan sepenuhnya* Balinese girls on whom all hopes are pinned.

menumpangkan 1 to lay s.t. on. *Tangannya ditumpangkannya di atas kepalaku.* He laid his hands on my head. 2 to put s.o. on a vehicle, let s.o. ride on a vehicle. *Anaknya ditumpangkannya di kapal.* He put his son on the boat. 3 to put s.o. up (in a hotel, etc.). *Peserta kongrés itu ditumpangkan di Hotél Borobodur.* The participants at the congress were put up at the Borobudur Hotel. 4 to entrust, give s.t. to s.o. (for safekeeping or to take along with them). *Saya hendak ~ surat.* I'd like to give you a letter to take (to s.o.). *Kita ~ sépeda kita di warung itu.* We put our bike in the shop for safekeeping.

tertumpang 1 included, sent along. *Dalam surat ini ~ surat pak guru.* The teacher's letter is included in this one. 2 accompanied. *~ salam kepada* my greetings to.

tumpangan 1 a lift, ride on a vehicle. *memberi ~* to give s.o. a lift. *mencari ~* to look for passengers. 2 s.t. or s.o. given a ride, cargo, load, passenger. 3 lodgings. *belanja ~* board, money paid to stay in lodgings. *rumah ~* boarding house, inn. *uang ~* board.

penumpang 1 passenger. *~ yang berdiri* standing passenger, strap hanger. *~ gelap* stowaway. *~ singgah* transit passengers. *~ setia* frequent flier. **berpenumpang** to have ... passengers. 2 boarder, lodger.

penumpangan 1 the act of entrusting s.t. to s.o. 2 housing, lodging. 3 riding, transportation. *~ umum* public transportation. 4 overlaying (s.t. on top of s.t. else).

tumpas I destroyed, wiped out, exterminated, annihilated.

menumpas 1 to crush, wipe out, destroy, quash. *~ habis* to wipe out completely. 2 to put out, extinguish.

menumpaskan 1 to destroy, wipe out, exterminate. 2 to destroy for s.o.

tertumpas crushed, destroyed.

penumpas destroyer, exterminator.

penumpasan destroying, exterminating, wiping out, extermination, annihilation.

tumpas II and **tumpasan** stain, spot.

tumpat 1 clogged, stuffed up. 2 chock-full, crammed, solid. 3 to be at the end of one's rope. *Pikirannya sudah –.* He's at his wits' end. *- mampat/pedat/padat/tumpul* chock-full, crammed, crowded, packed.

menumpat to fill in (a hole), plug up.

menumpatkan to cram, stuff full.
tertumpat crammed, stuffed full.
tumpatan filling (in a tooth).
penumpatan plotting. ~ *berbantuan komputer* computer-aided plotting.
tumpeng(an) (*Jv*) *nasi* – a cone of steamed rice with turmeric and meat, eaten at ceremonies.
tumper (*J*) stump, cigarette butt.
tumpes → TUMPAS I.
tumpil (*J*) support, prop, strut.
menumpil to support, prop up.
tumplak [and **tumplek** (*Jv*)] 1 spilled, poured out. 2 to pour (into), inundate. – *ponjén* (*Jv*) a Javanese ceremony relating to the marriage of the youngest child. – *bleg/bleg* spilled all over. *menumplek-blekkan* to concentrate s.t. (on). – *ruek* piled up.
menumplek-ruek to pile up.
menumplak [and **numplak** (*coq*)] to spill out, pour out.
menumplaki to inundate. *ditumpleki* to be crawling (with), overrun (with).
menumplakkan 1 to turn over, overturn. 2 to pour out. 3 to make s.t. inundate.
tertumplek piled up.
ketumplakan inundation, place where s.t. pours out.
tumpu 1 footing. 2 foothold. 3 sping board. 4 abutment, butt (in some compounds).
setumpu stepping-stone. **bersetumpu** → BERSITUMPU.
bertumpu ~ (*pada*) 1 to be based (on), rest (on), based/resting (on). 2 to rest (lean) (on). 3 to focus (on), be centered (on). 4 to adjoin.
bertumpukan to use s.t. as a base, base o.s. on.
bersitumpu to lean (on). ~ *kaki* to gain a foothold.
menumpu 1 to concentrate. 2 to support, hold up. 3 butt (in some compounds).
menumpukan 1 to lean (s.t. on s.t.). 2 to support, hold up. 3 to rest (s.t. on s.t.). *Dia ~ kakinya di tangga.* He rested his foot on the step. 4 to base, ground. 5 to concentrate (one's attention, efforts, etc.). ~ *orang* to kick s.o. out of the way.
tertumpu 1 leaned. 2 concentrated, focused.
tumpuan 1 support, bracket, brace, carrier, pedestal, pillar, fulcrum. 2 base, basis. 3 stepping-stone. 4 center, focus, focal point. ~ *arus* scapegoat. ~ *busur* abutment. ~ *gelombang* breakwater. ~ *harapan* s.t. on which one's hopes are based, a hope for the future. ~ *hidup* life support. ~ *injakan* pedal stop. ~ *kaki* footrest. ~ *kasih sayang* sweetheart. ~ *keluarga* means of support for one's family. ~ *kepercayaan* s.o. whom one trusts. ~ *kesalahan* scapegoat. ~ *pantai* beachhead. ~ *udara* airhead.
penumpu 1 support. ~ *kaki* a) footstool. b) kneeler (in church pew). 2 (*bot*) stipule.
penumpuan abutting, convergence.
pertumpuan overlapping.
tumpuk pile, stack, heap. – *sesak* piled up. **bertumpuk sesak** to pile up.
setumpuk a pile/stack. ~ *roti* a sandwich.
bertumpuk 1 to pile up. 2 a lot, many.
bertumpuk-tumpuk 1 in piles/stacks/groups, piled up, in large groups, in clusters. 2 in various forms.
menumpuk to pile up, amass.
menumpuki to pile up on top of s.t.
menumpukkan [and **numpukin** (*J coq*)] 1 to pile s.t. up, accumulate, amass. ~ *lapisan* to sandwich. 2 to hoard.
tertumpuk 1 stacked/piled (up). 2 hoarded. 3 accumulated.
tumpukan pile, stack, heap, mound. ~ *kendaraan* car dump. ~ *pekerjaan* workload. ~ *perkataan* in the limelight, the talk of the town. ~ *sampah* pile of garbage, garbage dump.
ketumpukan 1 group. 2 piled up on, get covered with.
penumpuk s.t. used to pile up or accumulate.
penumpukan 1 piling up, loading. *tempat ~ peti kemas* container yard. ~ *utang* (*fin*) pyramid debt. 2 hoarding. 3 concentration.
tumpul 1 dull, blunt. 2 not pointed. 3 slow-witted. 4 obtuse (angle).
menumpul to dull, become dull, obtuse
menumpulkan 1 to blunt, dull. *Upaya pengetatan monétér*

dapat ~ inisiatif. Efforts at monetary tightening can blunt initiatives. 2 to make s.o. slow-witted.
tertumpul dulled, blunted.
tumpulan stub, s.t. blunt or dull.
ketumpulan 1 bluntness, dullness. 2 slow-wittedness.
penumpulan blunting, dulling.
tumpur (*Jv*) 1 ruined, destroyed. 2 broke, bankrupt. *jatuh* – to go bankrupt.
menumpur(kan) to destroy, ruin.
tertumpur to be crushed.
penumpur man about town, playboy.
tumtam (*onom*) sound of a drum roll.
tumu k.o. mangrove tree, *Bruguiera spp.*
tumus tertumus (dived or fell) face forward.
tun I 1 the clipped form of *Tuan*; usually inherited title for prominent people. 2 title given to the holders of the *Seri Segara* or Grand Knight of the Most Distinguished Order of the Defense of the Realm yg DiPertuan Agung, e.g., to Tun Abdul Razak. 3 as *Tan*, an honorific surviving in a few titles; → SUTAN.
pertunan all those with the title Tun.
tun II (*C J*) rupiah, rup. *cap* – ten rups.
tun III (in acronyms) → TUNJANGAN.
TUN IV [Tata Usaha Negara] State Administration.
tuna I (*Skr*) a wound, injury. – *diri* self-inflicted wound.
tertuna wounded, injured. *Hatinya ~.* Her feelings were hurt.
tuna II *ikan* – tuna(fish), *Thunus spp.*; → CAKALANG I, TONGKOL I. – *bersirip biru* bluefin tuna, *Thunnus thynnus.* – *sirip kuning* yellowfin tuna.
tuna- III (*Skr*) privative affix indicating negation, absence, or loss, i.e., a-, il-, un-, non-. (used in many of the neologisms given below). – *risiko* risk-free.
ketunaan deprivation (of some basic need), disadvantage.
tunaakal witless.
tunaaksara (*Skr neo*) analphabetic, illiterate; → BUTA *huruf*.
ketunaaksaraan illiteracy
tunaanggota lacking a limb.
Tuna Bina Warga correctional institution.
tunabudi (*Skr neo*) characterless.
tunabusana (*Skr neo*) nude.
tunacacat a mentally and/or physically handicapped person who is unable or unwilling to work and who has no permanent housing.
ketunacatatan unemployment.
tunadaksa physically handicapped; → CACAT. *penyandang* – physically handicapped person.
tunadiri without personality.
tunagana underprivileged.
tunaganda mentally as well as physically handicapped.
tunagizi undernourished, malnutrition.
tunagra(h)ita retarded, mentally handicapped.
tunaharga-diri disrespect, lack of respect, discourtesy.
tunahasta (*Skr neo*) one-armed.
tunai 1 cash. *melakukan penjualan secara* – to make a cash sale. *membayar* – to pay cash. 2 spot (sale). – *bawa* cash and carry. – *kirim* cash in advance.
menunaikan 1 to pay cash for. 2 to cash. ~ *cék* to cash a check. 3 to carry out, fulfill, do, perform. ~ *hajat* to fulfill a vow (by holding a *selamatan*). ~ *kewajiban* to do one's duty. ~ *perintah* to carry out orders. ~ *perjanjian* to keep a promise. ~ *tugas* to do one's duty. ~ *wamilnya* to fulfill one's military service.
penunaian 1 cash payment. 2 accomplishment, completion, fulfillment, keeping (a promise). ~ *tugas* performance of one's duty. 3 settlement.
pertunaian fulfillment, completion. ~ *tidak sempurna* non-fulfillment.
tunak 1 steady, steady-state. *aliran* (*tak*) – (un)steady flow. *tidak* – transient. 2 persistent.
(ke)tunakan persistence.
tunakarna (*Skr neo*) deaf, hearing impaired.
tunakarya (*Skr neo*) unemployed, jobless. – *biasa* an able-bodied person who has neither work nor permanent housing. – *cacat* handicapped person who is unable or unwilling to work.
ketunakaryaan unemployment.

tunakawaca → TUNABUSANA.
tunakawat wireless.
tunakembang underdeveloped.
tuna-ketegangan nonstress.
tunakisma landless.
  ketunakismaan landlessness.
tunalaras unsociable person, misfit.
tunalistrik without electricity.
tunam I fuse (made from coconut fiber, etc. for firing cannons). *bagai membakar – basah* trying to teach s.o. who is slow-witted.
tunam II tertunam stuck, implanted.
tunaméntal mentally deficient.
tunan tool for leveling out drying rice.
tunanétra (*Skr neo*) blind, visually impaired.
  ketunanétraan blindness.
tunang I bertunang(an) (*dengan*) to be/get engaged (to). *Meréka sudah ~ sejak tahun yang lalu.* They have been engaged since last year.
  menunang to get engaged to, propose marriage to.
  menunangi to get engaged to.
  menunangkan and mempertunangkan to engage (as parents). *Ia sudah ditunangkan dengan pemuda pilihan orangtuanya sendiri.* She was already engaged to the young man chosen by her own parents.
  tunangan fiancé(e).
  penunang fiancé(e).
  penunangan betrothal, engagement.
  pertunangan engagement, the act of getting engaged.
tunang II penunang and petunang magic formula directed to musical instruments, such as a flute, etc. so that the sounds of the flute, etc. will affect the listener. *juru – (penunang)* a bullet on which a spell has been cast to make it hit the target.
tunapidana convict.
tunaraga (*Skr neo*) physically handicapped.
tunarasa (*Skr neo*) apathetic, not interested.
tunaredam underdamped.
tunarisiko risk-free.
tunarungu hard of hearing, deaf.
tunas bud, shoot, sucker. *– bangsa* the future generation. *– harapan* a ray of hope. *– kecambah* shoot, budding. *– ketiak* axillary bud. *– muda/mudi* children. *– pengisap* sucker. *– tanduk* place on an animal's head where the horn begins to sprout. *– tunggul* stool shoot. *– ujung* leader (of a plant).
  bertunas to bud, sprout.
  menunas 1 to bud, sprout. 2 to prune.
  menunasi 1 to have s.t. bud/sprout. 2 to prune.
  menunaskan to give rise to, produce.
  penunasan pruning.
tunasemangat apathetic.
tunasosial unsociable, misfit, social undesirable.
tunasusila (*Skr neo*) amoral. *lelaki –* gigolo; → PELACUR *pria. wanita –* [wantunas, WTS] a woman of loose morals, prostitute.
tunasusilawan (*Skr neo*) male prostitute.
tunasusilawati (*Skr neo*) female prostitute.
tunatangkar underbred.
tunatertib a disturber of the peace.
tunawan indigent.
tunawangun (*geol*) anhedral.
tunawarga (*Skr neo*) 1 prisoner, captive. 2 stateless person.
tunawarganegara (*Skr neo*) stateless.
tunawicara (*Skr neo*) dumb, unable to speak.
tunawisma (*Skr neo*) homeless. *– biasa* a person who has a job but no permanent home.
tuncep (*J*) → TANCAP.
tunda I s. t. towed by a rope behind a boat. *kail –* a fishing line towed behind a boat. *kapal –* tugboat, towboat, towing vessel. *pukat –* a seine/dragnet towed by a boat.
  bertunda to have/take in tow.
  bertunda-tunda to move one behind the other, one after another. *Orang datang di jalan raya itu ~.* People came in waves along the road.
  menunda to tow, pull along by a rope or chain.

tunda-menunda to shove e.o. aside trying to get ahead.
  penunda s.t. used for towing. *kapal ~* tug(boat); → KAPAL *tunda.*
  penundaan towing. *~ kewajiban pembayaran utang* debt moratorium.
tunda II delay, postpone, defer, put off.
  bertunda to take a long time. *mandi ~* to bathe for a long time.
  menunda(kan) to put off, procrastinate, adjourn, bring to a stop temporarily, defer, suspend, delay, postpone. *Karena sesuatu hal rapat ditunda.* For one reason or another the meeting was postponed. *Keberangkatannya ditunda.* He put off his departure. *sedang ditunda* in abeyance.
  menunda-nunda to postpone again and again. *Penangkatan itu selalu ditunda-tunda.* The appointment was postponed again and again.
  tertunda postponed, delayed, adjourned.
  tertunda-tunda repeatedly postponed/called off.
  tundaan delay.
  penundaan adjournment, postponement, suspension, delay, deferral. *~ hak* vested remainder.
tunda III (*M*) bertunda to leave, depart; → BERTOLAK. *kapal hendak ~* the ship is about to leave.
  menundakan to shove, push forward.
tundak (*BD*) crest, tuft (of hair).
tundan (*Jv*) place where post horses were replaced by fresh ones.
tundang (*J*) → TUNANG I.
tundra (*D*) tundra.
tunduk 1 to bow, bend (one's head); to bend over (of plants), bow their ears (of rice plants). 2 to bow down to, surrender, give up. *– tanpa syarat* unconditional surrender. 3 to obey, carry out instructions, be obedient, biddable. *– kepada istri* henpecked; → KERBAU *dicocok hidungnya.* 4 subject (to). *– pada syarat-syarat tertera di belakang* subject to the conditions on the back. *– tengadah* a) to go up and down, bowing and then looking up. b) to think, ponder.
  bertunduk to bow down, submit.
  menunduk [and nunduk (*coq*)] 1 to bow, bend, incline (one's head). 2 to defeat, subjugate, conquer.
  menunduk-nunduk to keep on bowing, humble o.s. (before s.o. else.
  menunduki 1 to bow toward. 2 to bend one's head over.
  menundukkan 1 to lower/bow (one's head). 2 to defeat, beat, subjugate, conquer, vanquish, overcome.
  tertunduk 1 bowed, bent over; to bow one's head. 2 submissive, obedient.
  ketundukan 1 bowing of the head. 2 submission. 3 defeat, subjugation. 4 loyalty.
  penunduk and petunduk (*M*) magic spell for making an enemy submit.
  penundukan 1 bowing (of the head). 2 defeat, submission, subjection. *~ dianggap (leg col)* implied subjection.
tundun I (*Jv*) banana stalk with bunches of fruit growing on either side.
  setundun a stalk (of bananas).
tundun II (*M*) 1 nape of the neck (of horses). 2 female pubic area, mons veneris.
tundung menundung 1 to chase/drive away, evict. 2 to exile, expel.
  tundungan exile, exiled, evicted person.
tunét → TUNANÉTRA.
tung (*onom*) shortening for various *onom* words ending in *tung.*
tungau I dust mite, acarid, Sarcoptidae. *– bulu* northern fowl mite, Ornithonyssus sylviarum. *– mérah* a) two-spotted mite, Tetranychus telarius. b) chicken mite, Dermanyssus gallineae. *– tepung* flour mite.
tungau II menungau (*ob*) to look down by bowing the head.
tunggak I (*J/Jv*) bertunggak in arrears.
  menunggak [and nunggak (*coq*)] 1 to be in arrears, behind (in payments), skip payment. 2 to put off (work).
  tunggakan 1 overdue payment, arrears, delinquent. 2 pending. *~ aplikasi* backlog. *~ mérah* bad debt. *~ pajak* delinquent taxes. *~ perkara* pending cases.
  penunggak debtor, s.o. in arrears. *~ pajak* tax delinquent.
  penunggakan delinquency (in payment).

tunggak II 1 stump of tree. **2** base, foundation; → TONGGAK I.

tunggal 1 one and only, only, just one, single. *anak* – only child. *berkaki* – on one foot. *rumah* – one-family house. **2** exclusive, sole. *agén* – sole agent. **3** (*gram*) a) singular (number). b) simple (sentence). **4** whole, full, complete. *dengan hati* – and *dengan – hati* wholeheartedly. – (*ber*)*béléng* all alone. – *ika* being a single entity. *ketunggal-ikaan* unity. – *nada* monotonous. *ketunggal-nadaan* and *penunggal-nadaan* monotony. – *putra* men's singles (in tennis and badminton). – *putri* women's singles (in tennis and badminton).

setunggal of one kind, the same kind. *bapak dan anaknya ~* like father like son. *~ derajat/serajat* of the same rank. *~ darah* related by blood.

menunggal 1 to be single, alone. **2** to be one and the same; → MANUNGGAL.

menunggalkan to unite into one single entity, concentrate. *~ pikiran* to concentrate one's thoughts.

tertunggal sole, only.

ketunggalan 1 solitude, being all alone. **2** oneness, singleness, unity. **3** concentration.

penunggalan uniting into one single entity, concentration.

tungganai (*M*) head (of a family/clan).

tunggang I – *air* range of tide. – *gunung* around sunset. – *harawan* straight (of the chest-bone of a horse). – *indah* dressage. – *serasi* dressage.

menunggang [and **nunggang** (*coq*)] to ride, mount.

menunggangi [and **nunggangin** (*J coq*)] **1** to ride on. **2** to ride on s.o. else's coattails, to (mis)use s.o. else's actions or reputation for one's own purposes, exploit. *Aksi-aksi di sana ditunggangi pihak ketiga.* The demonstrations were being used for their own purposes by a third party.

menunggangkan to have s.o. ride.

tunggangan 1 mount, animal ridden on. **2** carriage, vehicle.

penunggang rider. *~ kuda* equestrian. *~ sepéda* cyclist.

penunggangan 1 riding. **2** riding on s.o. else's coattails, (mis)using s.o. else's actions for one's own purposes; misuse, abuse.

tunggang II upside down, head over heels. – *balik* topsy-turvy, head over heels. **menunggang-balikkan** to turn s.t. upside down. – *hati* a) keen (about s.t.). b) steadfast. – *langgang* a) head over heels. b) helter-skelter. **bertunggang langgang** to run helter-skelter. **menunggang-langgangkan** to make s.o. run helter-skelter. – *pukang* head over heels. – *tunggik/tunggit* to bob up and down, pitch (of ships).

bersetunggang to turn somersaults. *~ balik* to turn upside down.

tunggang-menunggang head over heels, upside down.

menunggangkan to turn/hold s.t. over, invert. *~ air ke laut* to help s.o. who doesn't need help.

mempertunggangkan to hold upside down.

tertunggang upside down. *~ balik* to turn upside down.

penunggangan turning upside down, inverting.

tunggang III steep. – *hilang berani mati* very brave. – *hati* zealous, determined.

tunggang IV – *hati* steadfast.

tunggik 1 → TUNGGANG II. **2** with the spine bent forward.

menunggik bent forward.

menunggikkan to overturn with the head down and the tail up.

tertunggik bent downward.

tungging I 1 with tail/rear end up in the air. **2** turned over, upside down. **3** caudal, tail. *tulang* – tail bone, coccyx. **4** to sink bow first (of a ship). **5** to dive down. **6** downward.

menungging [and **nungging** (*coq*)] **1** to bend over (with the behind up). *gaya nungging* doggy style (in sexual intercourse). **2** to be upside down, topsy-turvy. **3** to dive down with one's bottom up. **4** to protrude, stick out.

menunggingkan 1 to place s.t. upside down. **2** to overthrow, topple. **3** to lift s.t. so that the bottom is up.

tertungging with the rear end up.

tungging II the fourth day after today, four days from now.

tunggir (*J*) tail bone.

tunggit → TUNGGANG II, TUNGGING I.

tunggu I wait. – *dulu* wait a minute. – *dawuh* to wait for instructions. – (*tanggal*) *mainnya* wait and see.

bertunggu to watch, keep guard.

menunggu [and **nunggu** (*coq*)] **1** to wait (for), await. **2** to look forward to, expect. **3** to be in store, lie ahead. **4** (*Jv*) to stay somewhere and watch over it, take care of. *~ angin lalu* to wait for s.t. in vain. *~ laut kering* to do s.t. pointless. *diminta ~ di luar sekolah* (*euph*) to be fired (of teachers).

menunggu-nunggu to look forward to.

menunggui [and **nungguin** (*J coq*)] **1** to watch over, guard. **2** to take care of, nurse (a sick person).

menunggukan [and **nungguin** (*J coq*)] **1** to wait for s.t. for s.o. **2** to expect.

tertunggu 1 waited. **2** watched over.

penunggu 1 s.o. who waits, watches; watchman, guard, attendant, caretaker. *~ bayi* baby-sitter. *~ dunia* human beings. *~ lift* elevator operator. *~ malam* night watchman. *~ rumah sakit* orderly (in a hospital). *~ toko* store clerk. **2** inhabitant, spirit (that lives in a tree, etc.). **berpenunggu** haunted.

penungguan 1 waiting, expecting. **2** watching over.

tunggu II – *taman* k.o. paradise fly-catcher, *Terpsiphone sp.*

tunggu III (*M*) menunggu to ask for s.t. back.

tunggul I 1 tree trunk/stump. **2** bump. – *jerawat* bumps left on the skin after pimples have cleared up. – *mati baharu ia berkata* as silent as the grave. – *padi* stem of rice plant. – *punggur* dead stump.

bertunggul-tunggul bumpy.

ketunggulan *~ silsilah* dynasty, lineage.

tunggul II pennant, streamer, banner. – *angin* clouds that pile up around a mountain. – *pelangi* rainbow that is beginning to form.

tunggul III → TUNGKUL I.

tungkahan (*M*) **1** wooden seat. **2** bridge support. **3** piece of wood for holding s.t. being sawed.

tungkai (*M*) **1** foot, leg. *yang panjang* – rain. *penderita cacat* – paraplegic. – *hitam* k.o. disease of cattle. **2** (*geol*) limb.

menungkai 1 to turn a cow on its side after tying its legs (for slaughter). **2** to kick.

tungkak (*Jv*) heel.

tungkap tongue-tied.

tungkat → TONGKAT.

tungket → PERSNÉLING, TUNGKAT.

tungku I 1 brazier. **2** hearth, brick fireplace with a grill. **3** oven, stove, furnace. **4** kiln, forge. – *api* fire box. – *arang* charcoal stove. – *bakar* incinerator. – *listrik* electric stove. – *pembakar* incinerator, furnace. – *sambang* beehive oven (for making coke). – *sampah* incinerator. – *tahanan* resistance furnace. – *tempa* forge, smithy.

tungku II → TENGKU, TUNGKU.

tungkul I menungkul to lower (the head).

menungkuli 1 to lower the head toward. **2** to submit.

menungkulkan to lower s.t.

penungkul tribute, homage.

tungkul II → TONGKOL I.

tungkulan (*J*) for a long time, unhurried.

tungkup (*M*) **1** face down, prostrate. **2** overlay (on chart). – *telentang* up and down. **menungkup-telentangkan** to turn s.t. over and over to examine it, consider s.t. from every angle.

menungkup to lie prostrate/face down. *Aku balikkan dia ~.* I turned him over face down.

menungkupkan to place s.o. or s.t. face down.

tertungkup 1 prostrate. **2** face down. *daripada ~ baik tertéléng* half a loaf is better than none.

tungkus I package, bundle; → BUNGKUS.

menungkus to wrap, bundle.

tungkusan package, bundle.

tungkus II submerged.

(ter)tungkus *~ lumus* overwhelmed (with debts/problems, etc.).

tungro a virus that attacks rice plants.

tungstén (*D*) tungsten.

tunik (*D*) tunic.

tunil → TONIL.

Tunisia Tunisia.

tunjal bertunjal to brace o.s. (with a foot on the ground) getting ready for a jump.

menunjal(kan) to find support (for a jump). *Kakinya ditunjal.* He found his footing.

tunjam menunjam to plunge; → HUNJAM.
menunjam (*geol*) to subduct.
tunjaman (*geol*) subduction.
penunjaman (*geol*) subducting, subduction.
tunjang 1 support. *akar* – aerial support (root). – *terima* acceptance. 2 (*M*) leg (of certain animals). 3 jellied meat from trotters.
menunjang 1 to support (financially or otherwise), promote. 2 to kick.
tertunjang supported, aided.
tunjangan 1 allowance, (fringe) benefit, subsidy. 2 alimony. ~ *anak* child support. ~ *belajar* scholarship. ~ *berdiri* hardship allowance. ~ *biaya hidup* cost-of-living allowance. ~ *cacad/ cacat* disability benefit. ~ *duka* condolence benefit. ~ *gaji* benefit. ~ *hari raya* [THR] *keagamaan* religious holiday allowance. ~ *hari tua* [THT] old-age pension. ~ *jabatan* extra allowance for being at a certain rank or position, k.o. expense account. ~ *kecelakaan* disability allowance. ~ *keluarga* family allowance. ~ *kemahalan* cost-of-living allowance. ~ *kematian* death benefit. ~ *kerja* bonus. ~ *konjungktur* cost-of-living allowance. ~ *nafkah* allowance. ~ *pengangguran* unemployment compensation. ~ *perceraian* alimony. ~ *préstasi* bonus. ~ *sosial* fringe benefit. ~ *tahunan* annual allowance. 3 kick. **bertunjangan** to have/with an allowance, receive support.
penunjang 1 auxiliary, service, accessory. *sumur* ~ (*petro*) service well. 2 supporting, support. ~ *harga* price support. 3 bracket, girder. ~ *lintang* cross-girder. ~ *tegak* guide post, upright. 4 supporter, fan.
penunjangan support, supporting.
tunjuk 1 (*M*) index finger. 2 show; → MENUNJUK. 3 point out. *-nya* he pointed out. *atas* – bearer (security, etc.). – *hidung* finger pointing, naming names. – *muka* to appear, make an appearance. – *silang* cross-reference. **menunjuk-silangkan** to cross-reference. **penunjuk-silangan** cross-referencing. – *tangan* to claim to be.
bertunjuk-tunjukan 1 to point at e.o. 2 to accuse e.o.
menunjuk [and nunjuk (*coq*)] 1 to indicate, point at/toward, show. 2 to appoint, designate. *ditunjuk dengan jalan undi* chosen by lot. 3 with reference to. ~ *surat saudara* with reference to your letter. 4 to raise one's hand (in class, etc.).
tunjuk-menunjuk 1 to point at e.o. 2 to accuse e.o.
menunjuki 1 to show to. *sebagai ditunjuki Tuhan* as if inspired by God. 2 to advise, give s.o. advice.
menunjukkan [and nunjukin (*J coq*)] 1 to point out. 2 to display, express, indicate, show. ~ *belangnya/bulu* to show s.o.'s true colors, call a spade a spade. ~ *gigi* a) to show one's teeth (in smiling). b) to make a show of one's bravery. ~ *pendirian* to take a stand. ~ *perasaan* to show one's feeling; to demonstrate. ~ *kesediaannya* to express one's willingness. 3 to place (an order). 4 to give notice of. 5 to designate.
mempertunjukkan to demonstrate, show, exhibit, put on, perform. *dipertunjukkan lagi* being shown again, in rerun.
tertunjuk 1 pointed to. *kepada* ~ to order/bearer. 2 designate. *Perdana Menteri* ~ Prime Minister designate.
tunjukan indication.
penunjuk 1 indicator, pointer, signal. 2 guide. ~ *angin* weather vane. ~ *arah* directional signal. ~ *halaman* bookmark. ~ *jalan* signpost, road sign. ~ *jarak tempuh* odometer. ~ *kecepatan* speedometer. ~ *putaran mesin* tachometer. ~ *télepon* telephone directory.
petunjuk 1 indication, hint, clue, omen. 2 guidance, advice, instructions, guidelines. ~ *Tuhan* divine guidance. 3 sign, signal, omen. ~ *jalan* directions. ~ *memakai* directions for use. ~ *navigasi* navigational aids. ~ *pelaksanaan* [juklak] operational manual. ~ *perjalanan keréta api* railroad timetable. ~ *téknis* [juknis] technical manual. ~ *Tuhan* revelation.
penunjukan 1 indicating, pointing to, showing, displaying. ~ *kembali* referral. 2 appointing, appointment, nomination. 3 placing, placement (of) (an order). 4 notice, notification (of default, etc.). 4 designating, designation.
pertunjukan show, display, exhibition, performance, act, engagement. ~ *amal* benefit (performance). ~ *bioskop* movie show. ~ *bugil* burlesque show. ~ *keliling* itinerant/touring performance. ~ *perasaan* demonstration. ~ *perdana/pertama* premiere, opening performance.
petunjukan appointment, designation.
tunjul → TONJOL.
tunjung – *biru* lotus, *Nymphaea lotus*. – *(e)mas* white or rose-colored water-lilies, *Nymphet stellata*.
Tunku → TENGKU.
tuntas (*Jv*) 1 completed, finished. 2 thorough, conclusive, exhaustive, once and for all. *sampai* – thoroughly. *secara* – thoroughly, completely. 3 secure and stable. 4 drained, emptied. – *atau gagal* all or nothing. *kurang* – incomplete. **kekurangtuntasan** incompleteness.
setuntas-tuntasnya as thorough(ly) as possible.
men(t)untaskan to do s.t. thoroughly/exhaustively, completely finish; to settle a matter conclusively, solve (a crime). ~ *wajib belajar* to complete one's educational requirements.
tertuntaskan able to be completed.
ketuntasan completeness, conclusiveness, thoroughness.
penuntas s.t. which concludes or completes s.t.
penuntasan 1 completing. 2 draining completely. ~ *air* drainage.
tuntun I (*Jv*) guide, lead.
bertuntun (*pada*) to be guided/led (by). ~ *tangan* to be led by the hand. *terbeli kerbau* ~ tricked, deceived.
menuntun 1 to guide, lead (by the hand, etc.); → MEMBIMBING. 2 to push by hand. ~ *sepéda* to push a bike by hand. 3 to guide by teaching, teach. ~ (*supaya*) to teach s.o. (to).
tertuntun led, guided.
tuntunan guidance, guide, leadership.
penuntun 1 s.t. or s.o. that guides, guide, leader. 2 manual, guide book.
penuntunan 1 guidance, leadership. 2 leading (with a line, etc.).
tuntun II (*M*) bertuntun (face, eyes) covered, veiled. *membeli kerbau* ~ to buy a pig in a poke.
menuntun to cover up, veil, close (one's eyes).
tuntung I point, sharp end, tip.
setuntung a small piece/slice (of rattan/sugarcane, etc.).
menuntung to cut up into small pieces.
tuntung II (*M*) menuntung(kan) 1 to overturn, turn upside down (so that the contents fall out). 2 to pout out (one's feelings).
tertuntung captivated.
tuntung III freshwater tortoise, river terrapin, *Batagur baska*.
tuntung IV (*M*) small box/case.
tuntung V slender, tall and thin.
tuntut – *malu* to take revenge. **penuntut malu** s.o. who takes revenge. – *pulang* request for extradition. **menuntut-pulangkan** to request that ... be extradited.
menuntut [and nuntut (*coq*)] 1 to insist (on/that). ~ *agar/supaya* to insist that, to demand that. *Meréka* ~ *agar tabloid itu meminta maaf*. They demanded that the tabloid apologize. 2 to demand, claim, have a claim on; be demanding. ~ *hak* to claim one's rights. 3 to prosecute. ~ *berbareng* to prosecute simultaneously (on several charges). ~ *dakwa* to prosecute, bring charges. 4 to sue, take to court. ~ *balik* to countersue. ~ *di muka hakim/pengadilan* to summon to appear in court. ~ *ganti rugi/kerugian* to sue for compensation, claim damages. 5 to petition (the court). 6 to strive/fight for. 7 to pursue, take action against. ~ *balas* to seek revenge. ~ *béla* an eye for an eye, a tooth for a tooth. ~ *hak sendiri* to stand up for one's rights. ~ *ilmu* to pursue knowledge. ~ *janji* to demand that s.o. fulfill his promise. ~ *kembali* to revendicate, call in. ~ *malu* to seek revenge for having been shamed. ~ *pelajaran* to pursue one's studies.
menuntutkan 1 to demand. 2 demanding.
tertuntut 1 demanded. 2 prosecuted.
tuntutan 1 demand, claim, petition. 2 prosecution, indictment. 3 striving, pursuit, insistence. ~ *akan kedudukan* claim for recognition (as one's lawful child). ~ *asal* original claim. ~ *balasan/ balik* counterclaim, cross-petition. ~ *dahulu* provisional claim. ~ *darah* vendetta. ~ *ganti rugi* claim. ~ *hak* legal action, claim. ~ *hukum* prosecution. ~ *jaksa* prosecutor's demand. ~ *kebendaan* action in rem. ~ *kembali* revendication, claim for refund. ~ *perdata* civil suit. ~ *pidana* a) prosecution, criminal proceedings. b) prosecutor's closing statement. ~ *pokok* basic

claim/demand. ~ *semula* original complaint. ~ *tambahan* alternative claim.

penuntut 1 prosecutor. ~ *umum* public prosecutor. **2** petitioner, claimant; → PEMOHON.

penuntutan 1 prosecuting, prosecution. ~ *hukum* prosecution, criminal proceedings. ~ *kembali* revendication, calling in. ~ *pidana* criminal prosecution. ~ *rangkap* double jeopardy. **2** claiming. **3** demand(ing). **4** pursuit, study.

tunu combustion. *bahan* – combustibles.

menunu 1 to burn, be on fire. **2** to burn s.t., burn down. ~ *hati* a) to offend, hurt s.o.'s feelings. b) to annoy.

menunukan 1 to burn up/down. **2** to burn for s.o. ~ *hati* to annoy, irritate. **3** to light, ignite.

tertunu burned, on fire, roasted.

tertunukan combustible.

penunu 1 arsonist. **2** burner.

penunuan arson, burning, roasting.

tup (*onom*) sound of explosion.

tupai I squirrel, tree shrew. *sependai-pandai* – *melompat sekali akan gawal/terjatuh (juga)* everyone makes mistakes. – *akar* k.o. squirrel, *Tupaia ferruginea*. – *akar malam* pen-tailed tree shrew, *Ptilocercus lowii*. – *belang* striped ground squirrel, *Lariscus spp.* – *cerlih* k.o. small squirrel. – *jenjang/kerawak (hitam)* giant squirrel, *Ratufa bicolor*. – *kampung/kelapa/ nyiur* coconut/plantain squirrel, *Sciurus notatus*. – *kericik* pygmy squirrel, *Nannosciurus exilis*. – *layang/terbang* Japanese giant flying squirrel, *Petaurista leucogenys*.

tupai II 1 k.o. herbaceous plant, white shrimp plant, *Justicia betonica*. **2** k.o. weed, *Aneilema nudiflorum*.

tupai-tupai clamp, wedge, peg, cleat. – *pintu* place where door bar is attached.

tupang brace, strut, stay, prop, bracket; → TOPANG I.

tur I (*D/E*) tour.

Tur II (*A*) *at–* "The Mount"; name of the 52nd chapter of the Koran.

tura (*M*) **bertura-tura 1** to get angry. **2** to talk in one's sleep.

turah excess.

turah-turah to have more than enough.

turang (*M*) s.t. added. – *atap* horn-shaped additions to a roof. – *jala* additional mesh added to a fishing net.

menurang to add s.t.

turangga 1 horse. **2** *dun* (in color).

turap I erosion-retaining dam, sea wall, bulkhead, crib.

menurap to dam.

turapan wall of a dam.

penurapan damming, putting up a retaining wall.

turap II plaster.

berturap plastered, coated, layered.

menurap to plaster, coat, line.

turapan 1 plastering, coating. **2** (*Mal*) pavement.

penurapan plastering.

turas I to urinate.

peturasan urinal.

turas II sieve, filter.

menuras to sift, filter.

penuras sieve, filter.

penurasan sifting, filtering.

turba [*turun ke bawah*] *q.v.* **berturba** to be in close contact with the people (of politicians/students working in villages, etc.).

menurbakan to send into close contact with the people.

turban (*D?*) turban.

tubiditas turbidity.

turbin (*D*) turbine. – *bantu* auxiliary turbine.

turbulénsi turbulence.

turi an ornamental shrub, West Indian pea tree, *Sesbania grandiflora*.

turiang 1 ratoon, rice shoot which grows after rice has been harvested. **2** (*agric*) ratooning.

turih → TORÉH.

turinisasi planting *turi* shrubs.

turis I (*D*) tourist. – *asing* foreign tourist. – *dari utara* reference to Chinese. – *lokal* domestic tourist.

turis II notch, scratch; → TORÉS II.

menuris to notch, scratch.

turisme (*D*) tourism.

turistik (*E*) tourist (*mod*).

Turki Turkey, Turkish.

turkis (*D*) turquoise.

turnamén (*D*) tournament.

turné tour, go on tour.

berturné to make a tour.

turnoi (*D*) tournament.

tursa [*turun ke désa*] going into the villages (to check on public opinion, etc.).

tursi → TERUSI.

Tursina Sinai.

turta → TURUN *tangan*.

turu (*J*) **turu-turu** and **seturu** just (us), nobody but (us).

turuk (*Jv vulg*) cunt, pussy.

turun 1 to go down, descend, step down (from an office), set (of the sun). *tengah* – (the sun) is beginning to go down (about 3 p.m.). – *dari Mekah* to return from Mecca. – *dari ranjang* to get out of bed. – *(dari kursinya)* to resign/step down. – *(dari) takhta* to abdicate. **2** to come down (from higher up), be issued. *Dana pemugaran belum* –. Funds for restoration have not come down yet. **3** to get off (a vehicle). – *kapal* and – *ke darat* a) to go ashore. b) to disembark. – *ke tanah* the ceremony accompanying stepping on the ground for the first time. – *mobil* to get out of a car. **4** to be handed down, passed on (to the next generation). **5** to fade (of colors). **6** to become lower, decrease, decline. **7** to befall, affect. **8** to take to the dance floor. **9** to settle (of liquids). – *berat badan* to lose weight. – *berok* hernia. – *coloknya* to come down in life. – *darah* to calm down. – *derajat* a) to be demoted. b) degeneracy. – *gunung* a) to come down from the mountains. b) to show/turn up again (after having been away or out of touch for a while). – *haji* to return from the *hajj*. – *ke air* to go to the river to take a bath. – *harga* to be reduced (of prices), go down in price. – *ke bawah* [*turba*] a) to go down to the people, grass-roots movement. b) reconnoitering. – *ke jalan* to take to the streets. *ilmu ayahnya* – *kepadanya* his father's knowledge passed on to him. – *main* to have a recess (at school), take a break. – *makan* to take a lunch break. – *mandi* a) to go and take a bath (in the river). b) to hold a ceremony for a child's first bath. – *menjadi* to drop (down) to (to s.t. lower). – *menogan* (*ob*) to jump ship. – *mér(e)k* to decline (of a brand name), lose its prestige. – *mesin* overhaul. – *minum* to take a break, half time (in soccer). – *naik* to go up and down, fluctuate. ***menurun-naikkan*** to make s.t. fluctuate, make s.t. go up and down, lower and raise, unload and load. – *pangkat* to get demoted. – *peringkat* to go down in rank(ing). – *perut* prolapse (of uterus). – *pesawat* to deplane. – *ranjang* to marry one's deceased wife's younger sister. – *takhta* to abdicate. – *tangan* a) to intervene, interfere. b) to take action. *Sudah selayaknya BI* – *tangan melindungi nasabah*. It's time BI intervened to protect depositors. – *tangga* a) to descend the steps, get off a ladder. b) stepped, stepwise. c) to go down a step, go down the scale. ***menurun-tangga*** and ***menurun-tanggai*** to go down the steps. – *tanpa konsép* to turn up without any ideas. – *temurun* a) from generation to generation. b) handed down from generation to generation, traditional. ***menurun-temurunkan*** to pass s.t. on from generation to generation, hand down. ***keturun-temurunan*** descent, lineage.

berturun to diminish, become lower/less.

berturunan (*pl subj*) to get off a vehicle.

menurun [and **nurun** (*coq*)] **1** (of stationary objects) to go down, slope down, descend. **2** to go (from generation to generation), be hereditary, run in the family. *bersifat* ~ hereditary. ~ *kepada* to be inherited by. *Sifat baik ayahnya* ~ *kepadanya*. He's inherited his father's good traits. **3** to decrease, decline, become lower, sink. **4** to decline, become worse. **5** to make a copy of. **6** down (in a crossword puzzle). **7** (*ling*) falling (tone).

turun-menurun traditional, handed down from generation to generation.

menuruni to go down s.t., go down along s.t., go down into, descend (into). ~ *tangga* to go down the steps.

menurunkan [and **nurunin** (*J coq*)] 1 to make lower, reduce, demote. ~ *dari jabatan* to demote. ~ *harga* to lower prices. ~ *pangkat* to demote. *Diturunkan pangkatnya.* He was demoted. 2 to lower, take down. ~ *bendéra* to lower the flag. 3 to send s.t. down. 4 to publish (a news report). 5 to disburse (funds from the government). 6 to issue, send down (a directive/warning/ order). 7 to turn down (the volume). 8 to disembark, discharge, let off (passengers), unload (cargo). 9 to introduce, put (actors on stage). 10 to transmit (from generation to generation). 11 to produce/have (descendants). 12 to drop (anchor, etc.).

memperturunkan ~ *hujan* to produce rain by prayers.

terturun derived.

temurun descent. **ketemurunan** heredity.

turunan 1 copy. ~ *yang ditandai* certified copy. *yang mengambil* ~ copyist. 2 (*fin*) derivative. 3 descendant. *Ia masih ada* ~ *ningrat.* She is of aristocratic stock. 4 descent. 5 hereditary. *penyakit* ~ hereditary disease. 6 slope, descent. 7 (*ling*) derived. *kata* ~ derived word. 8 (*coq*) of Chinese descent. *WNI* ~ an Indonesian citizen of Chinese descent. **seturunan** cognate. **berturunan** (*coq*) to have descendants.

keturunan 1 of ... descent, of ... heredity. ~ *Arab* of Arab descent. *habis* ~*nya* extinct. 2 descendant, offspring, issue. ~ *menyambung* adopted child of a childless person. 3 (an indirect way of saying) of Chinese descent. 4 reduction, decline, lowering. 5 copy, duplicate. 6 to inherit (a trait). ~ *sétan* possessed by the devil. **berketurunan** 1 for generations and generations. 2 of ... descent.

penurun s.t. that lowers/reduces. ~ *panas* antipyretic.

penurunan 1 lowering, reducing, reduction, decline, decrement, loss. ~ *berat badan* weight loss. ~ *harga* lowering prices. ~ *nilai* decrement. ~ *pangkat* demotion. ~ *tingkat* phasing out. 2 taking down, lowering (of a flag, etc.). 3 discharging (passengers), unloading (cargo). ~ *penumpang* disembarkation. 4 slope, descent. 5 downgrading. ~ *arti* (*ling*) pejoration. 6 subsidence, settlement (of land). ~ *dataran* subsidence. 7 derivation, deriving.

turus I 1 post, pillar, column, stake (for holding up climbing plants). 2 classifier for long narrow objects, bars. - *belat/empang* posts holding up the sides of a fishpond. - *negara* s.o. who has made a lasting contribution to a nation and people.

menurus straight as an arrow.

menuruskan (*ob*) to tie s.t. to a post for punishment.

turus II shoot, sucker, runner.

turut 1 to join in, take part in (doing s.t. with others), ... along, follow along in, share in, play a role/part in, help. *Berbagai hambatan - mempengaruhi lambatnya pertumbuhan.* Several other obstacles played a role in influencing slow growth. *pak* - s.o. who goes along with what others say. - *pergi* to go along. 2 to obey. - *perintah* to obey/follow orders. 3 (*leg*) co-. - *penggugat* third-party plaintiff. - *tergugat* co-defendant, co-respondent. - *berdukacita* to offer one's condolences. - *campur* to meddle, intervene, interfere. - *munding* to follow blindly. - *nafsu/ renyut hati* impulsive(ly). - *serta* to participate, take part (in), go along with. - *serta melakukan tindak pidana* to be a co-perpetrator. *menurut-sertakan* to have ... participate, make ... take part, involve s.o. in ...ing. *peturut-sertaan* making s.o. take part, involving s.o. in ...ing.

turut-turut to join in.

seturut ~ *dengan* in accordance/line with, as a follow-up to.

berturutan successive.

berturut-turut 1 in succession, in a row, continually, one after another, at a stretch, unending. *Kami sakit* ~. We got sick one after another. *masalah* ~ unending problems. *sepuluh hari* ~ ten days in a row. 2 continued (from s.t. preceding).

menurut [and **nurut** (*coq*)] 1 to follow. 2 to obey, go along with. 3 to imitate. 4 according to. 5 under, pursuant to (a certain law/regulation). ~ *abjad* alphabetically, in alphabetical order. ~ *akal* reasonable. ~ *angka* numerical. ~ *banyaknya* quantitatively. ~ *dugaan* in one's estimation. ~ *imbangan* proportionally. ~ *jadwal* on schedule. ~ *hukum* by law. ~ *keadaan* according to the situation. ~ *kias* on the analogy of. ~ *nilai* ad valorem. ~ *pendapat* in one's opinion. ~ *pengalaman* from ex-

perience. ~ *peraturan* to follow the rules. ~ *permintaan* on demand/request. ~ *rencana* according to plan, as planned, as scheduled. ~ *tingkat* gradually. ~ *urutan* in order. ~ *usik hati* intuitively. ~ *waktu* chronological.

turut-menurut 1 to follow along. 2 to agree with e.o.

menuruti [and **nurutin** (*J coq*)] 1 to follow, obey, listen to. ~ *nasihat* to follow s.o.'s advice. ~ *perintah* to obey a command. 2 to grant, allow, permit. *Jangan* ~ *dia.* Don't let her get her way. 3 to comply with. ~ *keinginan* to comply with s.o.'s wishes. ~ *nafsu* to indulge o.s. in ..., give in to one's wishes.

menurutkan 1 to follow, obey. 2 to copy, imitate. 3 to have s.o. follow/obey.

memperturuti to follow, obey.

memperturutkan 1 to follow, obey. ~ *hati* to follow one's heart. 2 to let ... take part.

memperturut-turutkan 1 to get s.o. involved. 2 to repeat, do s.t. one after another.

keturut (*coq*) along with.

terturut-turut in a row, consecutive.

turutan 1 guidance, example set for s.o. else to follow; exemplar. 2 succession, sequence. 3 outbuilding. 4 ancillary (services). 5 appurtenances, fixtures.

turut-turutan accommodating, always goes along with others.

penurut 1 s.o. who follows along, docile person. 2 follower.

penurutan following, obedient, accommodating.

perturutan 1 succession. 2 continuation.

tus (*onom*) whistling sound (of bullets flying by, etc.); → DETUS.

tusam (*kayu* -) tropical pine, *Pinus mercusii*.

tusam-tusaman pines, *Pinaceae*.

tuslag and **tuslah** (*D*) 1 surcharge, extra charge. 2 supplementary payment.

tustél (*D*) camera.

tusuk 1 pin. 2 skewer (and counter for skewered food). *sepuluh* - 10 sticks (of saté). 3 mandril, awl. - *biku* embroidery stitch. - *gigi* toothpick. - *jarum* a) stitch. b) acupuncture. - *kondé* hairpin. - *kontak* (electric) plug. - *kundai/sanggul* hairpin. - *pipa* mandril. - *rantai* chain stitch. - *saté* a) saté stick/skewer. b) at a T-intersection (a house location that brings bad luck); → RUMAH *tusuk saté.*

bertusuk stuck, jabbed, skewered.

bertusukan to jab e.o.

menusuk 1 to stick, stab. ~ *dari belakang* to stab s.o. in the back. ~ *hati* to hurt s.o.'s feelings. 2 to penetrate. ~ *hidung* penetrating (odor). ~ *tulang* bone-chilling (cold). 2 to stab, jab. 3 to skewer. 4 to vote (in an election).

tusuk-menusuk to jab/stab e.o.

menusuk-nusuk to instigate. ~ *hati* to offend, hurt.

menusuki 1 to pierce, stick s.t. through. 2 (*pl obj*) to stick, jab.

menusukkan 1 to stick/jab s.t. (into). 2 to vote for.

tertusuk [and **ketusuk** (*coq*)] stuck, jabbed, pricked. ~ *duri* pricked by a thorn. ~ *hati* offended, hurt (feelings)

tusukan 1 stick, jab. 2 s.t. that is stuck/jabbed. - *gigi* toothpick. 3 puncture. 4 sticking pain, twinge.

penusuk 1 s.o. or s.t. that stabs/sticks, etc. 2 plug. 3 acupuncturist.

penusukan 1 sticking, jabbing. 2 plugging. 3 perforation.

tut I (*D onom*) sound of a car horn.

tut II (*A*) mulberry.

tut III graft (of a plant).

mengetutkan to graft (one plant onto another).

tut-buri → TUTWURI.

tuter (*D*) car horn.

men(t)uter to blow the horn.

tutor (*E*) tutor.

tutorial (*E*) tutorial.

tuts (*D*) 1 key (of a piano/typewriter, etc.). 2 valve (of a musical instrument).

tutu (*onom*) cooing sound.

bertutu cooing.

tutug (*J/Jv*) entire, until the end. *puasa sebulan* - to fast for an entire month.

ketutugan to get large amounts of s.t.

tutuh clip, clipping, clipper, prune.

menutuh 1 to clip, prune, trim. 2 to break up a ship to reuse the wood.

tutuhan clipping.

penutuh clipper, trimmer.

tutuk (*Jv*) **menutuk** 1 to tap/knock on. 2 to strike (in *pencak*). 3 to scold.

menutukkan to tap/knock with s.t.

tertutuk tapped, knocked.

tutukan 1 tap, knock. 2 striking. 3 scolding.

penutuk s.o. or s.t. that taps/knocks.

tutul I (*Jv*) 1 pockmarked. 2 spotted, stained (of the surface); → MACAN *tutul*.

menutuli to put spots on, spot.

menutul(-nutul)kan to smear/dab s.t. on.

tutul II k.o. children's game.

tutup I 1 cover, covering, cap, lid. 2 closed, shut. 3 whole, complete, full. *setahun* – a full year. – *buku* balanced (of the books in accounting). – *got* drain cover. – *ikat* blindfold. **menutup-ikat** to blindfold. – *jendéla* curtain. – *kantor* closing time. – *kejepit* flat broke. – *kepala* headwear, headgear. – *léhér* scarf. – *malu* a way of hiding s.t. shameful. – *muka* k.o. face covering. – *mulut* to remain silent. – *panci* pot cover. – *rantai* chain guard. – *sumur* (*petro*) shut/closed in. – *tahun* year-end balancing of books. – *usia* (*euph*) to pass away.

bertutup 1 with a cover, etc., covered. 2 closed.

bertutupkan to be covered with. ~ *dengan kain bandana biru* covered with a blue bandana.

menutup [and **nutup** (*coq*)] 1 to cover, put a cover on, plug/fill in (a hole/ditch, etc.). *asuransi yang telah ditutup* insurance (already) in effect. 2 to close, shut; to close down, close off, bar, stop, get in the way of. *Kita tidak* ~ *mata.* We didn't close our eyes. ~ *diri dari kenyataan* to shut one's eyes to the facts. ~ *kegiatan perbankan nasional* to close down domestic banking activities. ~ *mulut* to keep one's mouth shut. 3 to hide, conceal. 4 to preclude (a possibility). 5 to conclude (a contract, speech, etc.). 6 to lock up (a prisoner, etc.). 7 to pay off a debt (by borrowing from someone else); → MENGGALI *lubang*. ~ *buku* to close the books. ~ *diri* to isolate o.s., refuse to listen to advice. ~ *gigi* to clench one's teeth. ~ *hati* to refuse to listen to advice. ~ *mata* a) to cover one's eyes. b) to refuse to see what is happening, shut one's eyes to the fact that. ~ *méja* to set the table. ~ *mulut* to shut up. ~ *ongkos* to cover expenses. ~ *riwayat* to kill. ~ *tangan* to be tight-fisted. ~ *telinga* to close one's ears (either on purpose or not). ~ *télepon* to hang up the telephone.

menutup(-nutup)i [and **nutupin** (*J coq*)] 1 to cover up (a crime, etc.), conceal, hide. *Skandal itu ditutup-tutupi oléh pejabat yang berwenang.* The scandal was covered up by the officials in charge. 2 to put a cover on.

menutupkan 1 to use s.t. as a cover, cover with. 2 to close for s.o.

tertutup [and **ketutup** (*coq*)] 1 covered, eclipsed. *Minggu lalu, berita ékonomi agak* ~ *oléh peristiwa penting.* Last week the economic news was rather eclipsed by important events. 2 closed off, shut. *Jakarta sudah* ~ *bagi ...* Jakarta is closed to... *wilayah* ~ bonded area. 3 locked up. 4 precluded, closed off. ~ *untuk umum* closed to the public. ~ *kemungkinan* the possibility has been excluded. *tidak.* ~ *kemungkinan* the possibility is not precluded, it's possible. 5 reclusive, introverted. 6 clandestine, covert. 7 healed (of a wound). 8 closely/privately held. **ketertutupan** 1 closedness. 2 reticence.

tertutupi 1 to be covered/concealed. 2 can be covered.

tutupan 1 covering, cover, lid. ~ *awan* cloud cover. ~ *langit* overcast. 2 lock-up. 3 detained, imprisoned.

ketutupan (*coq*) to be covered.

penutup 1 covering, cover, s.o. which covers (up)/conceals, lid, casing, top, cap. ~ *botol* bottle cap. ~ *dinding* wall covering. ~ *lénsa* shutter (of a camera). ~ *muka* face shield. ~ *rambut* hair cap. ~ *tahun* end of year. ~ *tempat tidur* bedspread. 2 hood (of an engine). 3 closing (remarks). *sebagai* ~ in closing.

penutupan 1 coverage, covering. ~ *atap* roofing. 2 closing (off), shutting (down). 3 lockout. 4 end, closing. ~ *sidang* the end of the session.

tutup II – *bumi* k.o. herbaceous plant, prickly-leaved elephant's foot, *Elephantopus scaber*; → TAPAK LIMAN.

tutur I what one says. –*nya* he/she said. – *bayi* baby talk. – *bicara* topic of conversation. – *kata* spoken word. – *sapa* form of address for s.o. **bertutur sapa** to address s.o. with the proper form of address.

bertutur to talk, speak. ~ *kata* to talk, converse.

bertutur-tutur to talk, converse, have a conversation. ~ *seorang* to talk to o.s.

menuturkan and **mempertuturkan** 1 to say, express, pronounce. 2 to narrate, tell about, relate, tell about.

tertutur said, spoken, expressed.

tuturan 1 s.t. said, utterance. *berita* ~ feature article. 2 story, narrative, narration.

penutur speaker, narrator. ~ *asing* non-native speaker. ~ *asli* native speaker. ~ *bahasa* a speaker of a language. ~ *cerita* narrator.

penuturan 1 talk, saying, speaking, expressing. 2 conversing, conversation.

pertuturan 1 pronunciation. 2 conversation. 3 what one says.

tutur II **tuturan** and **penuturan** lowest part of roof.

penuturan and **petuturan** (*ob*) descendant.

tuturuga Manadonese dish made with meat cooked in a spice mixture.

tutus (*J/Jv*) thin strips, etc. of bamboo used as bindings.

tutwuri (*Jv*) to follow. – *handayani* influencing from behind. *ing madya mangun karsa, ing ngarsa sung tuladha*, – *handayani* motivating from within, providing an example from in front, influencing from behind.

tu-wa-ga yo-heave-ho.

tuwék (*joc*) old.

tuwuhan (*Jv*) ceremonial decorations for wedding symbolizing fertility.

tuwur various species of koel (birds), *Eudynamis spp.* – *Asia* Asian koel, *Eudyamis scolopacea*.

tuyu (*J*) drooping (of the eyes of s.o. tired).

tuyul 1 a spirit that can help one. 2 an individual who has been successful overnight; short-lived, fly-by-night. – *jalanan* illegal fee; → PUNGLI.

TV I /tévé/ or /tivi/ television. – *hitam-putih* black-and-white TV. – *kabel* cable TV. – *mata-mata* closed-circuit TV.

ber-TV with a TV.

men-TV-kan to televise.

TV II (*joc D*) [Twééde Vrouw] second wife, i.e., mistress.

TVRI [Télévisi Républik Indonésia] /té-vé-ér-i/ Republic of Indonesia Television.

twédehan (*D coq*) secondhand, used.

U

u and U /u/ the 21st letter of the Latin alphabet used for writing Indonesian.

ua 1 (*abbrev of tua*); → WA I. **2** (= *uak, wak*) *abbrev of pak/mak* – uncle/aunt older than father.

uaah → WAH I.

uai (*ob*) mother.

UAJ (*init*) [Univérsitas Atma Jaya] (Jakarta).

uak I polite form of address to elders; *cp* TUA, WAK I. *pak* – uncle older than father. *mak* – aunt older than mother; sister or brother of father and mother.
  beruak to call s.o. using that form of address.

uak II 1 moo (sound made by a cow). **2** croak (sound made by a frog or raven). **3** roar (sound made by a lion). **4** bellow (sound made by a bull). **5** quack (sound made by a duck). **6** hoot (sound made by an owl). **7** whoop (sound made by a gibbon).
  menguak 1 to produce one of these sounds. **2** to shout loudly.

uan I (*ob*) → TUAN (as a form of address). **menguani** and **menguankan** to have authority over, govern; to have power over.

uan II (*ob*) gray (of hair); → UBAN I.

uanda (*ob*) polite form of address to one's elders.

uang 1 money. **2** wages, salary. **3** wealth. **4** (*ob*) an obsolete copper coin valued at less than one cent or 1/3 *tali*. *tiga* – 25 cents; → SETALI. *Ada berapa – anda sekarang?* How much money do you have with you now? *Sangat sulit mencari –*. It's very hard to make money. *anak/bunga* – interest (on money). *kaum* – the rich, rich people. *mata* – currency. *melepas/memperbuangkan/menganakkan/menjalankan* – to lend money (and to get paid back with interest). *menanam(kan)/melekatkan* – to invest money (in an enterprise, etc.). *pasar* – money market. *pelepas/tukang lepas* – money lender. *tukang* – cashier. *(pandai) memutar(kan)* – to be able to handle/manage money (well), able to deal with money (well). *mencari* – to seek a living. *setali tiga* – six of one and half a dozen of the other; (it's) all the same to me. *– itu pangkal segala kejahatan* love of money is the root of all evil. *ada – ada sayang, tak ada – abang melayang* he's a fair-weather friend; fair-weather friendship. *– acaram* earnest money. *– adat* bail. *– adem arem-arem* consolation money. *– administrasi* administrative fee. *– alas* bribe. *– angkutan* freight. *– angus* a) bridegroom's share of wedding expenses. b) unspent part of budget (because the period for spending the funds has passed) which must be reimbursed to the government. *– antaran* (from *antaran kawin*) wedding present given by the bridegroom to the bride's parents to defray wedding expenses. *– awal* seed money. *– baik/bajik* merit pay. *– bakti masuk* → UANG bangku. *– bandar* a bet, money bet on s.t., stake. *– bangku* a contribution made to gain admission to a school. *– bantuan* grant-in-aid. *– béa pendaratan* aircraft landing fee. *– bedol(an)* restitution for transportation costs. *– belanja* a) money for daily necessities. b) (*ob*) salary. *– berédar* money supply. *– berobat* medical expenses. *– besar* large bills. *– bolong* (*ob*) a nickel coin with a hole in the middle. *– buta* a) salary paid to s.o. for doing nothing, pay for a no-show job. b) unemployment compensation pending one's retirement or resignation. c) reduced/half salary. *makan – buta* to be put on reduced salary. *– cadangan* reserve fund(s). *– capé* honorarium. *– cegatan* bribe paid to be admitted somewhere. *– céndol* spending money. *– cengkeram* advance/down payment, deposit (partial payment in advance). *– cicilan* installment payment. *– cincai-cincai* k.o. bribe. *– confirm* /konfirem/ (in the port of Belawan, Medan) a bribe collected by dockworkers for putting goods into or taking goods out of a warehouse. *– cuké* money tipped to the banker by a winner. *– curai* loose cash, pocket money. *– dalam perédaran* currency in circulation. *– damai* damages paid in an out-of-court settlement. *– dengar* money given to s.o. because of what he knows about a certain transaction, k.o. hush money. *– diam* (in

Tanjung Pinang) hush money paid when a ship from Singapore is unloaded without the proper documents. *– duduk* attendance fee (paid to members of Parliament when in session). *– duka* compensation paid for the suffering caused by the death of a spouse, etc. *– éntré* admission/entrance fee. *– erakan* statute-labor tax money. *– ganda* duplicate money (because it has the same serial number as legal money). *– ganéfo* (in the port of Belawan, Medan) a bribe that truck drivers had to pay to dockworkers for loading and unloading their trucks. *– ganti rugi/kerugian* amends, compensation, recompense. *– gantung* advance/down payment. *– gedung* contribution a prospective student pays toward the cost of erecting a school building. *– giral* demand deposits. *– hadiah* dispatch money. *– hangat* hot money. *– hangus* a) (*fin*) points. b) forced contribution (so as to get s.t.). c) → UANG angus. *– hantaran* → UANG antaran. *– haram* money from illegal sources. *– hasil* money earned. *– hilang* key money (in order to rent housing). *– idah* money paid to wife until she can marry again after divorce. *– ikhlas* k.o. bribe. *– imbalan* fee, consideration. *– inséntif* financial incentive. *– iuran* contribution, dues. *– iuran usaha* rent. *– jadi* money paid up front as a token that a transaction has been conducted. *– jaga* a) money paid to a guard. b) protection money. *– jaga-jaga* reserve fund(s). *– jago* a) protection money, an illegal contribution made to street thugs. b) k.o. bribe paid in the West Kalimantan citrus-fruit trade. *– jajan* pocket money, allowance. *– jalan* travel expenses. *– jaminan* a) security/guarantee deposit. b) bail. *– jasa* bonus, honorarium, royalty. *– jempling* bribe paid to railroad employees by s.o. who is trying to evade paying the full fare. *– jemputan* (*M*) money given to a prospective son-in-law as part of a marriage proposal. *– jerih* a tip. *– jujur(an)* money given by the groom to his prospective parents-in-law. *– kagét* money given to s.o. who has experienced a shock (e.g., in a car accident or plane crash, etc.) as partial compensation for the bad experience. *– kancing* security deposit. *– kartal* currency, cash, money in circulation. *– karun* a) money obtained illegally. b) part of a hidden treasure. *– kas* cash (on hand). *– keamanan* protection money. *– kecil* small change. *– kehidupan* alimony. *– kelebihan berlabuh* demurrage. *– kelip* (*col*) nickel coin with a hole in the middle. *– keluar* [u/k] debits. *– kematian* donation given to the family of a deceased person. *– kembali(an)* change, money returned as the difference between the price and the payment offered. *– kemeng* (*Jv*) money paid in extra recompense for a painful strained feeling in the legs caused by standing too long in front of a class. *– kepercayaan* fiduciary money. *– keping* coins. *– keras* hard currency. *– kerja lembur* overtime pay. *– kertas* paper money; bank notes (issued by banks or the government). *– kertas pemerintah* Federal note. *– ketat* tight money. *– khartal* → UANG kartal. *– kol* call money. *– komisi* commission fee. *– kontan* cash, ready money. *– konvérsi* funded debt. *– kopi* → UANG jerih. *– kuliah* tuition (at a university). *– kunci* a) key money, down payment on the rental or purchase price of a home, *esp* money given to the former tenants to persuade them to leave. b) deposit. *– kupatan* the very small 1971 Lebaran bonus. *– lambat* demurrage. *– lancung* counterfeit money. *– langganan* subscription fee. *– lauk-pauk* extra money given to members of the army who do not receive a food ration. *– lelah* honorarium; tip. *– lembur* a) overtime pay. b) bribe given to government official to stay overtime so as to obtain a needed document. *– lendir* bribe given by prostitutes to local officials to allow them to work in sealed or closed buildings. *– lepas* severance pay. *– logam* coin. *– logam peringatan* commemorative coin. *– lusuh* base coins. *– mahal* tight money. *– mainan* play money. *– makan* official per diem. *– masa kerja* length-of-service payment. *– masak* money given by dancers to musicians. *– masuk* [u/m] credits. *– mas ukon* a gold coin used as an ornament. – *mati* uninvested money. – *méja* a) (*J*) cost of a lawsuit. b) an unofficial tax levied by officials of the Road Traffic Service on newspaper boys who sell papers at Jakarta bus terminals. – *menderingan* → UANG *minderingan*. – *mengenggur* idle funds. – *minderingan* loan repaid in installments at a high interest rate. – *miskin* alms, charity. – *muka* down payment, deposit, advance. – *murah* cheap money. – *mutah* one-time monetary payment to one's wife after divorce. – *nafkah* alimony. – *oto-bon* (at the port of Belawan, Medan) an illegal fee levied by port guards on truckers entering or leaving the port area. – *pakaian* clothing allowance. – *paksa* default fine, penalty. – *palsu* counterfeit money. – *pamit* (in Kupang) a bribe paid to the head of the junior high school to obtain one's certificate. – *panas* a) loan at a high rate of interest. b) surplus money in circulation. c) money earned through gambling or corruption, illegal money. – *pancang* bribe. – *pandu* pilotage. – *pangjeujeuh* (*S*) recompense. – *pangkal* a) admission/entrance fee. b) capital. c) registration fee. – *panjar* down payment. – *parkir* a) parking fee. b) aircraft ramp fee. – *pas* exact change. – *pecah(an)* → UANG *kecil*. – *pelancar* a) → USIL II. b) bribe to make s.t. move along faster. – *pelécét* hush money. – *pelicin/pelincir/pelumas* bribe, grease money. – *pemasukan pajak* tax revenues. – *pembeli jarum* pin money. – *pencil keluarga* family separation allowance. – *pendaftaran* registration fee. – *pendaratan* landing fee. – *penegur* → UANG *tegur*. – *pengertian* bribe so that "you scratch my back and I'll scratch yours" → TST I. – *pengusiran/pengusutan* money given to s.o. to vacate the house he is occupying. – *peningset* (*Jv*) engagement present. – *penjaga* nest egg, money put aside for future needs. – *penyambung hidup* a) money needed to make ends meet. b) k.o. bribe. – *perkenalan* k.o. protection money paid to a thug in Medan by s.o. who has moved into a new house, opened a new store, etc. – *persekot* advance. – *persén* a tip. – *pesangon* a) severance pay. b) money given to renter or leaser who is being asked to move out. – *pintu* bribe, illicit commission. – *pisah* → UANG *pesangon*. – *pitingan* a) bribe paid by a college student to pass an exam. b) illegal road tariff. – *plastik* credit card. – *plécét* hush money. – *pokok* a) cost, what one pays for s.t. b) principal. – *prémi* premium. – *primér* base money. – *pulasi* (in Yogya) money paid the village administration by a buyer for the sale and purchase of land. – *rapat* honorarium paid for attending a meeting. – *récéh/réncéh* → UANG *kecil*. – *ringgit* a) (*ob*) a two-and-a-half-guilder/rupiah coin. b) the ringgit, the Malaysian currency. – *rokok* → UANG *jerih*. – *sabun* a bribe to make s.t. go smoothly. – *sagu hati* a) compensation. b) money given to the heirs of members of the police, army, etc. who died in the line of duty. – *saksi* witness's fee. – *saku* pocket money. – *sangu* traveling money. – *sara* a) relief, assistance, maintenance. b) pension. – *sekolah* school fees, tuition. – *selawat* money paid to person who reads prayers at a *selamatan*. – *sembah* (*J*) money given by the prospective bridegroom to the bride's parents after the acceptance of the proposal. – *semir/senin* bribe, grease money. – *seraya* money paid by resident for community services. – *sérvis* bribe. – *sesai* → UANG *jujur*. – *séwa* rent. – *sidang* pay to council members while in session. – *siluman* [usil] bribes. – *simpanan* nest egg, money put aside for later use. – *sirih* a) a tip. b) bribe. – *sogok(an)/sorok/suap* bribe. – *sokongan* allowance. – *srono* (*Jv*) dowry; → (E)MAS *kawin*. – *sumbangan* contribution, e.g., money to a charity. – *susuk* → UANG *kecil*. – *syukuran* bribe given to a member of IAIN's examining board. – *tabungan* savings. – *tagihan* a claim. – *tali* 25-cent coin. – *tambang(an)* passage, fare, ferriage. – *tanda (jadi)* binder, token money. – *tandu* (in Semarang) demurrage. – *tanggung botol* deposit for empty bottles. – *tanggungan* bail. – *taruhan* stake (in gambling). – *tebusan* a) ransom (money). b) lump sum payment. – *tegur* (*J*) money paid to a newlywed wife to have intercourse. – *téh* a) a tip. b) bribe. – *tembaga* copper coin. – *tempah* advance money, earnest money. – *témpél* bribe. – *tengahan* a half-rupiah coin. – *terima kasih* bribe. – *terjun* paratrooper's extra pay for jumping. – *tiap/thiap* → UANG *kunci*. – *tikaman* stake (in gambling). – *tinta* pay to s.o. who has drafted a letter, signed a letter, etc. for one. – *titipan* escrow account. – *tolak* bribe to hasten an action. – *tolong* rescue charges. – *tulis* clerical

fee (in official documents). – *tumpangan* board, money for board. – *tunai* cash. – *tunggu* a) retainer. b) (*mil*) early-retirement payment. – *tunjangan* a) unemployment pay. b) allowance, subsidy, grant. – *tutup mulut* hush money. – *upeti* rental fee. – *utangan* borrowed money. – *vakasi* money paid to s.o. to administer or grade an exam. – *wajib* fee. – *yang ngangguur* idle money. – *yang terbatas* limited funds.

beruang 1 to have money. **2** to be well off, rich. *kalau tidak* ~, *ke mana pergi terbuang* no money no honey.

menguangi to finance, fund, subsidize. *Persatuan Orang Tua Murid* ~ *pendirian gedung sekolah itu.* The Parents' Association financed the erection of the school building.

menguangkan 1 to cash (a check, etc.). **2** to sell s.t. for cash.

uang-uangan 1 counterfeit money. **2** tokens, play money.

keuangan finance; financial. *berada dalam kesulitan* ~ to be in financial difficulties. *harta-harta* ~ financial assets. *Kementerian* ~ Ministry of Finance.

penguangan cashing (a check, etc.).

peruangan monetary system.

uap I vapor, steam, smoke, fume. *daya* – steam power. *mandi* – steam bath. *mesin* – steam engine. – *air* water vapor. – *atas* (*petro*) top steam. – *bakda* after damp. – *jenuh* saturated. – *puncak* (*petro*) overhead. – *tak jenuh* unsaturated vapor.

beruap 1 to steam. **2** carbonated. *minuman* ~ carbonated beverage(s). **3** steamy.

menguap 1 to evaporate, vaporize, turn to vapor, boil away. *Airnya* ~. The water boiled away. **2** to disappear. **3** volatile.

menguapi 1 to steam. **2** to dry-clean. **3** to let s.t. evaporate.

menguapkan 1 to cause to evaporate, boil away. ~ *air* to let water evaporate, boil (water) away. **2** to steam.

meruap → BERUAP.

terupa evaporated.

teruapkan *tidak* ~ unevaporated.

uapan 1 vapor. ~ *air* water vapor. **2** s.t. steamed.

penguap vaporizer, evaporator. *alat* ~ evaporator.

penguapan evaporation, vaporization, distillation.

uap II → KUAP.

uar I (*Jv*) **uar-uar** public announcement (by loudspeaker or by crying it out).

beruar announced, publicized.

menguar(-uar)kan 1 to announce to the public, make public. **2** to spread (the news).

penguaran announcing to the public, making public.

uar II → KELUAR. **menguar** to emit (steam/an odor, etc.).

menguarkan to expel, emit (an odor, etc.).

uas → UWAS.

u.b. and **u/b** (*abbr*) [untuk beliau] for, on his behalf (used when signing a letter on s.o. else's behalf).

uba a vat for sago porridge.

ubah different, unlike, not the same (as). *tak* – *dari/sebagai/seperti* and *tak* ~ *nya dengan/sebagai/seperti* no different from, the same as, just like, identical to. *Merazia ladang ganja tak-nya dengan memencét balon.* Raiding a marijuana field is just like squeezing a balloon. *jauh* –*nya* entirely different (from s.t. else). – *bentuk* transformation, change of form. **mengubah-bentukkan** to transform, change the form of. – *suai* modification. **mengubah-suaikan** to modify. ~ *bangunan lama* to modify old buildings. **pengubah-suaian** processing, modifying, modification.

berubah 1 to be different, differ. ~ *dari yang sudah-sudah* different from the past/the earlier ones. **2** not steadfast/firm/constant. *tidak* ~ invariant. ~ *setia* to become disloyal. **3** to change (color/form/character/appearance, etc.), alter. ~ *air mukanya.* His facial expression changed. ~ *arah* to change direction. ~ *jadi* and ~ *kepada* to change for/into. ~ *kepada yang baik/buruk* and ~ *(men)jadi baik/buruk* to change for the better/worse. *angin* ~ shifting wind. ~ *akal/ingatan* to go/become crazy. ~ *hatinya/niatnya/pendapatnya* to change one's mind/plans/opinion. ~ *kelakuan* to change character. ~ *menjadi* to change/turn into. ~ *mulut* to break one's promise. ~ *pikiran* to change one's mind.

berubah-ubah to keep on changing; (to be) capricious/fickle, changeable, fluctuating. *Kemauannya ~ dari waktu ke waktu.* His wishes kept changing. *tidak ~* invariable.

mengubah [and **ngubah** (*coq*)] to change, transform, modify, alter, amend, convert, turn (one thing into another). *~ buku* to revise a book. *~ hukuman* to commute a sentence. *Hukuman matinya diubah menjadi hukuman penjara seumur hidup.* His death sentence was commuted to life imprisonment. *~ kata* to break a promise. *~ monyét jadi bekantan* to change into the same thing; plus ça change, plus c'est la même chose. *~ menjadi* to transform/change into, commute. *selalu boléh/dapat diubah* and *sewaktu-waktu boléh/dapat diubah* to be subject to change at any time. *tak dapat diubah* irreversible.

mengubah-ubah to twist around, alter.

mengubahi 1 to cause/bring about a change/alteration in; to break (a contract). **2** (*pl obj*) to change, etc.

mengubahkan 1 to change/alter for s.o. else's benefit. *Ibu ~ celana anaknya.* Mother altered her child's pants. **2** to cause to change.

memperubahkan (*dengan*) to differentiate/discriminate/distinguish (from); to treat differently. *~ anak ini dengan anak-anak lainnya* to treat this child differently from the other children.

terubah changed, can be changed.

ubahan 1 change, alteration. **2** variation. *~ berterusan* continuous variation. *~ persekitaran* environmental variation. **3** (*math*) variable. *~ antara* intermediate variable. *~ bébas* independent variable. *~ bergantung* dependent variable.

keubahan transformation.

peubah (*math*) variable.

pengubah 1 reformer, remodeler. **2** (*elec*) converter. *~ arus listrik* rectifier, converter (for changing AC into DC).

pengubahan 1 alteration, change. **2** conversion.

perubahan change, alteration, modification, changeover, transition. *usul ~* amendment. *zaman ~* transitional era. *~ alamat* change of address. *~ Anggaran Dasar* a) constitutional amendment. b) alteration of the Articles of Association. *~ bentuk* a) metamorphosis. b) conversion, changeover. *~ cuaca* change in the weather. *~ haluan* a) change of course. b) change in policy, new orientation. *~ kecil* minor adjustment. *~ kurs antarmata* currency realignment. *~ mendasar* fundamental change. *~ méntal* change in attitude. *~ nama* name change. *~ téknologi* technological change. *~ yang terus-menerus* flux, constant change.

ubak-ubak (*Jv*) **mengubak-ubak 1** to stir up. **2** to search/rummage through. *Setiap pojok Pasar Malam Sekatén di Alun-alun Utara diubak-ubak polisi.* The police searched through every corner of the Sekaten Fair on North Alun-alun.

ubal-ubal → UBEL-UBEL.

uban I gray/white hair, hair that is turning or has turned white. *menjunjung ~ (di dalam kebesarannya)* grown gray (in the service); no longer serviceable.

beruban 1 to have gray/white hair; (have) become gray, turned gray. **2** elderly. **3** to have lots of experience in life, seasoned; → GARAM. *sudah ~ baru berguam* to behave childishly (of an elderly person).

menguban 1 to turn/grow gray. *Rambutnya sudah ~ semua.* His hair has turned completely gray. **2** to be grayish, look gray, be hoary. **3** worn out (of clothes).

mengubani 1 to pull out gray hairs. **2** to give s.o. gray hair (through worry), make s.o.'s hair turn gray.

ubanan (*J*) **1** to be gray (of a person), grown gray. **2** to be/find o.s. in an awkward position.

uban II (*burung*) *pipit ~* sharp-tailed munia, *Munia striata.*

ubang mengubang to fell/cut down a tree by cutting notches on opposite sides, one higher than the other.

ubar I 1 *pohon ~* and *~ serai* a tree species whose bark produces a dark red coloring matter for tanning casting nets, Java lemon, river jambu, and whose leaves are used for cooking, *Eugenia cymosa/densiflora.* **2** the coloring matter produced from that tree. **3** paint. **4** dark ruby (color).

mengubar 1 to dip (nets, etc.) in that coloring matter. **2** to paint.

ubar II berubar *~ hati* to unbosom o.s.

mengubar to unroll s.t. and spread it out.

ubar III → UBER.

Ubara [Univérsitas Bhayangkara] (Surabaya).

ubarampé, uba-rampé and **uba rampé** (*Jv*) accessories, things needed for a special purpose. *dengan segala - ritual baru* with all new ritual accessories. *mengembalikan - tali pertunangan yang pernah kami terima dulu* to return the engagement gifts we have received.

ubas (*sl from shabu*) methyl amphetamine, meth; → SHABU-SHABU. **ngubas** to use this drug.

ubat I (*Mal*) → OBAT.

ubat III → HOBAT.

ubaya → HUBAYA-HUBAYA.

Ubaya [Univérsitas Surabaya] University of Surabaya.

ubek I (*J/Jv*) **ngubek(-ubek) 1** to mess up; to mix up. **2** to look for s.t. by rummaging through (wardrobes, etc.); to keep looking for s.t. **3** to clean, wash out (a tank/reservoir, etc.); to drain. *Siapa yang mau ~ empang yang penuh dengan tahi?* Who is willing to drain a fishpond full of feces?

ubekan s.t. mixed/stirred up.

ubek-ubekan to be in disorder.

ubek II (*Jv*) **ngubek** to hang out/about. *Mula-mula ia hanya ~ di sekitar kampungnya.* At first he just hung out around the village.

ubek-ubekan to mill about. *mencari ~* to look all over for, hunt about for.

ubel-ubel (*J*) turban, head scarf. *serdadu ~* Indian soldier (Sikh) (serving with British army in Indonesia right after the Japanese occupation).

ubeng ngubeng (*J*) **1** to walk around without any specific goal. **2** to swarm (of bees).

uber (*J/Jv*) chase (after), pursue. *tukang - céwék* womanizer, woman-chaser.

menguber(-uber) [and **nguber(-nguber)** (*coq*)] to pursue, chase (after), hunt down, go after. *~ duit* to chase after money. *diuber waktu* to be rushed for time.

uber-uberan to chase (after) e.o.

penguber pursuer, one who chases after s.t.

penguberan pursuit, chasing after.

ubet persevering in seeking additional sources of income.

Ubhitka [Univérsitas Bhinneka Tunggal] (Jakarta).

ubi edible tubers/roots. *gedé-gedé - (J)* brawny but brainless. *ada - ada talas, ada budi ada balas* a) tit for tat. b) nothing for nothing. *- aung* birch-rind yam, *Dioscorea aculeata. - benggala/inggris/jénderal/kayu/kaspé/pohon/prancis/singkong* manioc, cassava, *Manihot ultissima. - buton* a bluish white ubi. *- gandola* k.o. red sweet potato. *- garut* arrowroot, *Maranta arudinacea. - gembili* (*Jv*) birch-rind yam, *Dioscorea aculeata. - halia* artichoke. *- jalar/jawa/kelapa/keledék/kenduduk/kipas/manis/menjangan* (*J*)/*mengari* (*J*)/*rambat/senggani* yam, *Dioscorea alata, Ipomoea batatas. - keladi éddo* wild taro, *Colocasia esculentum. - kemayung/teropong* low-grade species of *ubi, Dioscorea aculeata. - kembili/kemili*, **GEMBILI, KEMBILI.** *- nasi* buck yam, greater yam, *Dioscorea alata. - pasir/sunda* half-wild variety of the *ubi,* buck yam, *Dioscorea pentaphylla. - sampa* cassava. *- Singapura* air potato, *Dioscorea bulbifera. - tiyang* → UBI *nasi.*

ubi-ubian various kinds of edible tubers/roots.

ubin 1 (*batu -*) (floor)tile, flag; → JUBIN, TÉGEL. *- porselin* wall tile. **2** diamond (in deck of cards). **3** tile (in mah-jongg).

mengubini to tile, line with tiles.

pengubinan tessellation.

ubinan unit of land measurement of about 0.56 square rods = 14.19 square meters.

ubing → OBÉNG I.

ubit mengubit-ubit to flicker (of a burning lamp wick, etc.).

UBK (*init*) Univérsitas Bung Karno (Jakarta).

ublak-ublek (*Jv*) → UBRAK-ABRIK.

ubleg (*Jv*) **ngubleg-ngubleg** to meddle in. *~ keamanan dalam negeri* to meddle in internal security.

ubo rampé → UBARAMPÉ.

ubrak-abrik (*Jv*) → OBRAK-ABRIK. **mengubrark-abrik** to turn upside down, mess s.t. up completely.

ubrat-abrit → UBRAK-ABRIK.

ubrug (*J*) **1** large statue of a human being. **2** epithet for a large woman. **3** k.o. Betawi theater.

ubub(an) (*Jv*) a (pair of) bellows; → EMBUSAN, PUPUTAN.

ubudi(y)ah and **ubudiyyah** (*A*) (prayer) ritual.

ubun berubun to loom (before one's eyes).

ubun-ubun I 1 crown (of head). **2** fontanel. *sudah napas di* – to be afraid. *di/ke* – the highest point. *Dendamnya telah memuncak hingga ke ujung* –. His resentment has mounted to the highest point. **3** coronet.

ubun-ubun II (*ob*) Hindu nun.

ubung I stable.
  mengubungi to stable, put in a stable.

ubung II → HUBUNG. **ngubungin** → MENGHUBUNGI.

ubur-ubur I jellyfish, *Scyphozoa spp.* – *api* k.o. jellyfish.

ubur-ubur II (*payung* –) a fringed umbrella (used as part of royal regalia).

ubur-ubur III (*M ob*) k.o. excise tax levied on marine products, such as fish, salt, etc.

ubuwah (*A*) paternity.

ubyang-ubyang and **ubyang-ubyung** (*Jv*) to loaf around.

ucap 1 what s.o. says/expresses; word, utterance, phrase, expression. **2** said. *"Sekedar menyambung hidup," – Suryana.* "Just to make ends meet," said Suryana. *"Naik bécak,"-ku asal berucap.* "I took a pedicab," I said for the sake of saying s.t. – *habis, niat sampai* so let it be written, so let it be done. **3** counter for words; → PATAH II. *se- kata* a word.

  berucap 1 to speak, say s.t. **2** (*ob*) ~ *kata* to say, talk, speak. *Saya terdengar dia ~ dengan Sumarni.* I overheard him speaking to Sumarni. **3** to give/make a speech. ~ *dalam rapat raksasa* to deliver a speech at a mass meeting; → MENGUCAPKAN *pidato.*

  mengucap to worship God by pronouncing His names and attributes.

  mengucapi to call (out) s.o.'s name. *Dia menyuruh ~ Pak Sumarno.* He had s.o. call Mr. Sumarno.

  mengucap(kan) [and **ngucapin** (*J coq*)] **1** to express, say (a conventional phrase). *Ucapkanlah dengan bunga!* Say it with flowers! ~ *selamat datang* to welcome s.o. ~ *selamat kepada* to wish s.o. good luck, congratulate. ~ *selamat Lebaran* to wish s.o. a happy *Lebaran.* ~ *selamat Tahun Baru* to wish s.o. a happy New Year. ~ *banyak terima kasih atas* to express thanks for. ~ *sepatah dua patah kata* to say a few words. ~ *suksés* to wish s.o. good luck. ~ *syukur* to thank God. **2** to say, deliver (s.t. verbal), articulate. ~ *keputusan* (*leg*) to hand down a verdict/ruling. ~ *pidato* to deliver a speech. **3** to worship God by pronouncing His names and attributes. **4** to express/utter certain tenets of the Muslim faith. ~ *Allahu Akbar tiga kali* to utter "God is Great" three times. ~ *dua kalimah/kalimat syahadat* to utter the Muslim profession of faith; → KALIMAH. ~ *Minal Aidin Walfaidzin* to express joy in having successfully completed the fast.

  terucap said, pronounced. *Tak ada kata yang* ~. Not a word was said.

  terucapkan (can be) pronounced/said. *Banyak kata yang tidak jelas* ~. Many words were not clearly pronounced. *tak* ~ unutterable, indescribable.

  ucapan utterance, statement, expression, remark, what one says. *Saya seakan-akan terpesona dengan segala ~nya itu.* It was as though I was spellbound by everything he said. ~ *keras* ranting. ~ *lantang* topping cue. ~ *terakhir* tag. ~ *bahasa* saying, proverb. **2** spoken word, pronunciation, way of saying s.t., expression. *dalam* ~ *dan perbuatan* in word and deed. *pola* ~ pronunciation pattern. ~ *tepat* correct pronunciation. **3** speech, talk, lecture. *memberi* ~ *péndék* to give a short lecture/speech. ~ *penutup* closing address. **4** expression (of a conventional statement). *memberikan* ~ *selamat kepada* to congratulate. ~ *dukacita* expression of condolence/sympathy. ~ *syukur* thanks to God. ~ *terima kasih atas* expression of thanks for.

  pengucap 1 speaker, user of a language; → PENUTUR. ~ *asli* native speaker. **2** (*alat* ~) the speech organs.

  pengucapan expression, utterance; expressing, uttering, pronunciation.

ucek (*Jv*) **mengucek(-ucek)** [and **ngucek-ngucek** (*coq*)] and **mengucekkan** to rub (one's eyes, etc.).

ucel (*Jv*) **mengucel** [and **ngucel** (*coq*)] to crumple.

uci-uci (*Jv*) (hard, flesh-like fatty) tumor.

ucis detonator, fuse; → PENGGALAK.

ucok I (*M ob*) **1** to negotiate peacefully. **2** to make peace, come to an agreement. *hendak* – *dilawan damai, hendak perang giling peluru* you have to choose between war and peace.

ucok II (*Bat*) boy, lad.

ucu (*ob*) youngest, last-born (child); *cp* CUCU.

ucul (*Jv*) freed, released.

ucus (*J*) → USUS.

UD → UTUSAN *daérah.*

ud (in acronyms) → UDARA.

uda I (clipped form of *muda*) younger. *mak/pak* – aunt/uncle younger than one's father or mother.

uda II (*M*) elder brother/male cousin.

UDA [Univérsitas Darma Agung] (Medan).

uda(h) (*J*) → SUDAH.

udag → UDAK I.

udah (*J/Jv*) → SUDAH. – *déh* come on!
  udahan 1 well OK, come on! **2** → SUDAH. ~ *dulu* that's all for now.

udak I (*J*) **udak-udak** to chase e.o.
  mengudak to chase, pursue, follow; → MENGUBER.

udak(-udak) II (*Jv*) **mengudak** to stir with a round-and-round movement (rather than up and down); → MENGADUK.
  mengudak-udak to stir up, upset.

udal-adul (*Jv*) **mengudal-adul** to rumple one's hair.

udal-udal (*Jv*) **mengudal-udal 1** to open up and spread around the contents of s.t. **2** to break up into pieces. *Mayat petugas itu diudal-udal.* The body of the official was totally destroyed. **3** to reveal and spread (a secret).

udam dull, dim, faded.

udan-iris (*Jv*) k.o. batik design.

udang I shrimp, prawn. *ada (ber)* – *di balik batu* a) there's a snake in the grass, there's s.t. going on here. b) there's a catch to this. *(seperti)* – *(di) dalam tangguk* uneasy, worried, anxious. *seperti* – *dipanggang* a very stupid person. *bungkuk* – slouch, drooping position. *kepala/otak* – very stupid. *benih* – shrimp fry; → BENUR. *pusat pembenihan* – shrimp hatchery. *tepung* – shrimp meal. *banyak* – *banyak garam* people's wishes vary. – *hendak mengatai ikan* to be unaware of one's own mistakes. – *tak tahu dibungkuknya* not to recognize one's own faults. – *api-api* brown shrimp. *Metapenaeus sp.* – *bago/pancét/windu* tiger prawn, *Penaeus monodon.* – *barong* spiny lobster. – *basah* fresh shrimp (sold in markets). – *batu* rock shrimp, *Sicyonia brevirostris.* – *beku* slipper lobster, *Thenus orientalis.* – *belado* slipper lobster, *Thenus orientalis.* – *belang* rock tiger shrimp, cat tiger shrimp, *Parapenaeopsis sculptilis.* – *bubuk* → UDANG *geragau.* – *cendana* yellow-white shrimp, *Metapenaeus brevicornis.* – *darat* flowerbud of the *durian* fruit. – *dogol* brown shrimp, *Metapenaeus monoceros.* – *galah* a) freshwater prawn, *Macrobrachium rosenbergii.* b) lobster; → LOBSTER. – *geragau/gerangau/kepai/pepai/senggugu/rebon* shrimp species, *Mysis spp.* used for *belacan/terasi.* – *goréng tepung* batter-fried shrimp. – *harimau* various species of prawns, *Penaeus spp.* – *jerbung/jrebung/menjangan/pengantin/putih* white/banana prawn, *Penaeus merguiensis.* – *kali* river prawn. – *kara* spiny lobster, *Palinurus polyphagous.* – *karang* spiny lobster, *Panuliris.* – *kecapi* small dried shrimp. – *kembang* green tiger prawn, *Panaeus semisulcatus.* – *kering* dried shrimp; → ÉBI. – *kipas* Spanish/slipper lobster, *Thenus orientalis.* – *krosok* small white shrimp, *Metapenaeus lysianassa.* – *kupas-rebus-beku* peeled, boiled, and then frozen shrimp. – *kupas-segar-beku* uncooked, peeled, and then frozen shrimp. – *laut* lobster, *Palinurus homarus.* – *lubuk* shrimp which lives in a pool in a stream, slipper lobster, *Thenus orientalis.* – *mutiara* pearl shrimp, *Panulirus versicolor.* – *papai* → ÉBI. – *pasir* sand prawn, *Metapenaeopsis spp.* – *raja* Western king prawn, *Penaeus latisulcatus.* – *rebon* mysid shrimp, *Mysidopsis bahia* – *ronggéng* matis shrimp. – *satang* → UDANG *galah.* – *sétan* k.o. shrimp. – *werus* k.o. shrimp used to make *krupuk udang.*

  berudang with shrimp in it.

  udang-udangan 1 various species of shrimp. **2** imitation shrimp.

udang II *burung* – various species of kingfishers, *Alcedo/Totanus spp. burung raja* – kingfisher, *Alcedo atthis bengalis.*

udang III *rotan* – k.o. rattan used for baskets, shrimp rattan.

udani k.o. climbing plant, woody vine, Chinese honeysuckle, *Quisqualis indica*; → WEDANI.

udap **mengudap** to eat the following k.o. salad.
  udap-udapan salad made of a mixture of vegetables or fruits with a hot spicy sauce; → KUDAP.

udar (*Jv*) loose(ned).
  mengudar(i) 1 to loosen, untangle (one's hair/a knot, etc.). **2** to solve, figure out.

udara (*Skr*) **1** air. *di* – on the air (of a radio program). *di* – *terbuka* in the open air. *menghirup* – *segar* to breathe fresh air. *hampa* – vacuum. *kedap* – airtight. – *balik* return air. – *lengas* damp air. – *segar* intake air. – *mampat* compressed air. **2** sky, aerospace, atmosphere, firmament. *ilmu* – meteorology. **3** weather, climate; → IKLIM. – *dalam musim hujan* the weather in the rainy season. **4** atmosphere, climate, ambience, milieu. – *désa* village ambience. – *politik* political climate. **5** relating to aviation, flight, air transportation, air (*mod*). *Angkatan* – [AU] Air Force. *bandar* – [bandara] airport. *hubungan* – air communications/travel. *kapal/pesawat* – airplane, aircraft. *pos* – airmail. – *luar* atmosphere.
  berudara to have a certain k.o. climate/weather/atmosphere. *Bandung ~ sejuk.* Bandung has a cool climate.
  mengudara 1 to take off (of a plane). **2** to be aired (on the radio/TV), be on (the air). *TVRI belum ~ pagi begini.* Republic of Indonesia TV is not on this early.
  mengudarakan 1 to broadcast (over the airwaves), televise. *~ pidato kenegaraan* to broadcast the state-of-the-nation address. **2** to release s.t. into the air, let s.t. fly, send into space. *~ pesawat antariksa ulang-alik* to send a space shuttle into space.
  keudaraan (*mod*) air. *perjanjian* – air treaty.
  pengudaraan 1 broadcasting, putting s.t. on the airwaves. *~ wawancara* broadcasting an interview. **2** releasing/sending s.t. (up) into the air. **3** aeration.

udarasa (*Jv*) (in one's) opinion.
  pengudarasa opinion. *Tulisan ini hanyalah sebuah ~.* This article only states an opinion.

Udayana 1 name of the Army division stationed in Nusatenggara. **2** name of a university in Bali.

udé(h) (*J*) → SUDAH.

udek (*J/Jv*) **mengudek 1** to stir. **2** to go/search through.

udel (*Jv*) navel. *seénak* – *nya (sendiri)* (to act) as one pleases (without concern for others or the proprieties); to one's heart's content.

udeng (*Jv*) a square piece of cloth (about 1.1 x 1.1 meters) for making one *blangkon*.

udet (*Jv*) (female's) sash, waistband.

udhu → WUDUK.

udhu guyub → UDU *guyub*.

udi (*M*) unlucky, unfortunate; misfortune, adversity; disastrous.

udik I 1 upper reaches (of river); → HULU. – *sungai* upper reaches of a river. **2** village, country, hamlet; *opp* KOTA. *di* – *sekali* deep in the country, far from town. **3** unsophisticated, hickish. *orang* – a) country person. b) bumpkin, hick, yokel.
  mudik (*Jv*) to move upstream against the current; → MUDIK. *pulang ~ ke kampung* to go back to one's rural home (or, birthplace).
  mengudik 1 to go upstream. **2** to return to one's ancestral village.
  ngudik (*J*) → MUDIK.
  udikan country person.

udik II (*J*) south; → SELATAN.
  beludik be in the south. *Ruményé di ~.* His house is to the south.
  ngudikin to go south.
  udikan southerly.

udik-udik (*Jv*) ceremony involving throwing money to the poor held on the afternoon before the two *Sekaten gamelan* are taken back to the *Kraton* in Yogyakarta,

udim (*D*) edema.

udo (*J*) → UDA II.

UDT (*init*) [Uniao Démocratica Timorénsé] Timorese Democratic Union (a conservative party in East Timor).

udu I (*A*) enemy, adversary.
  berudu to be hostile, enemies.

udu II → WUDUK II.

udu III (*J*) in trouble because it's hard to obtain s.t.

udu guyub (*Jv*) friendly contribution in the form of money.

udud (*Jv*) straw cigarette, tobacco rolled in *kawung* leaf; → TINGWÉ, UDUT.

uduh I foolish, silly, stupid; → ODOH.

uduh II (*M*) talisman used to prevent thieves from entering a compound, etc.

uduk I (*J/Jv*) *nasi* – rice cooked in coconut milk; → WUDUK I.

uduk II → WUDUK II.

udur → UZUR II.

udut (*Jv*) **mengudut 1** to smoke (usually opium). **2** to take it easy, relax.
  udutan (opium) pipe.
  pengudut 1 (opium) smoker. **2** opium pipe.

udzur → UZUR II.

ué I (*C*) small covered pan with handles.

ué II → OWÉ(H).

uék → UIK.

uénak very delicious; → ÉNAK.

ufti → UPETI.

ufuk (*A*) horizon; → HORISON, KAKI *langit. di* – *barat* in the west.
  berufuk with a horizon. *tidak ~* boundless.
  mengufuk horizontal.

ugahari (*Skr*) moderate, average, temperate.

ugal-ugalan (*J/Jv*) **1** mischievous, boyish, naughty; (to act) improperly/inconsiderately. **2** (to be driven) recklessly. *bis kota yang* – *di jalan umum* city buses which are driven recklessly on public roads.
  keugal-ugalan 1 naughtiness. **2** recklessness.

ugama → AGAMA.

ugel-ugelan I (*Jv*) **1** ankle-joint. **2** wrist-joint.

ugel-ugelan II (*J*) kneecap, patella.

ugem (*Jv*) property.
  mengugem claim as one's own.
  mengugemi to believe in, be faithful/loyal to, hold (fast) to, stick to.

uger (*Jv*) rules, regulations.
  mengugeri to play by the rules of the game.
  ugeran rule, norm.
  paugeran procedure(s).

uget-uget (*Jv*) mosquito larvae; → CUK II, JENTIK-JENTIK.

UGM (*init*) [Univérsitas Gadjah Mada] Gadjah Mada University (Yogyakarta).

ugut (*mostly Mal*) intimidation, threat; → GERTAK. – *keling* empty threat; → GERTAK *sambal.*
  mengugut to intimidate, threaten.
  ugutan threat, intimidation.
  pengugut intimidator, bully.
  pengugutan intimidation.

uh (exclamation of distaste/disgust) ugh, yuck! –, *pahitnya obat ini!* Yuck, this medicine is bitter!

uhau loyal to one's parents.

UHT (*init*) [Univérsitas Hang Tuah] Hang Tuah University (Surabaya).

uhu 1 (*onom*) sound made by an owl. **2** owl.

Uhud → PERANG *Uhud.*

uhuk (*onom*) sound of coughing/crying.

UI (*init*) [Univérsitas Indonésia] University of Indonesia.

UIA (*init*) [Univérsitas Islam As-syafi'iyah] (Jakarta).

UIB (*init*) [Univérsitas Indonesia Baru].

uih (exclamation drawing s.o.'s attention to s.t.) hey! hey!

UII (*init*) [Univérsitas Islam Indonésia] Islamic University of Indonesia.

uik (*onom*) **menguik** to make a sound (of a young animal); to quack (of ducks), to squeal (of pigs); to cry (of babies).

UIK [Univérsitas Ibnu Khaldun] (Bogor).

UIM [Univérsitas Indonésia Muda] (Jakarta).

UIR [Univérsitas Islam Riau].

uir-uir (*M?*) cicada, *Dundubia mannifera.* – *minta getah* a) to dig one's own grave. b) to be a seductress.

uis menguis-uis to rake, scratch at; → KUIT.

UISU [Univérsitas Islam Sumatra Utara] (Medan).

uit menguit to lift, raise; to shift s.t. a little bit.

teruit *tidak ~ (hatinya)* unshakable (viewpoint).

UIT [Univérsitas Islam Tribakti] (Kediri).

uitkéring (*D ob*) /ét-/ payment.

uitklaring (*D ob*) /ét-/ clearance (from Customs).

uitvoerbaar bij voorraad (*D leg*) provisionally enforceable, to take effect immediately.

uja menguja to excite/force animals to fight; → OJA(H).

teruja excited.

ujaan excitation.

penguja exciter.

pengujaan excitation.

ujan → HUJAN I. **ujan-ujanan 1** to go out in the rain on purpose. **2** even though it's raining.

ujana I → YOJANA.

ujana II playground, garden, park; → TAMAN I.

ujang I (*J*) polite pronoun used to boys; → BUJANG I.

ujang II (*S vulg*) *si* – penis.

ujar 1 remark, words, saying, turn of speech, what one says. *-nya* he said. **2** (*Ling*) utterance.

berujar to say, speak. *Soedarmadji ~ kepada para protokol istana* ... Soedarmadji spoke to all the masters of ceremony in the palace ...

mengujarkan to say, speak, state, express.

ujaran statement, announcement.

ujar-ujaran sayings, proverbs; proper behavior.

pengujaran announcing.

ujat calumny, slander, defamation; → HUJAH I.

uji test, trial. *batu* – touchstone. *tabung* – test tube. *tahan* – a) to stand the test (of time), pass muster. b) guaranteed (value). *- asal* provenance test. *- bakat* aptitude test. *- bubuk bata* brick dust test. *- cincin coklat* browning test. *- coba* a) a random test, spot-check. *melakukan – coba* to spot-check, test at random. *pelayaran – coba di laut* sea trial (for ships.) b) a tryout. *- coba terbang* ground test. **menguji-coba(kan)** to try out, test in operation. *pesawat yang diuji-coba itu* the plane being tried out. **penguji-cobaan** trying out, testing in operation. *- dengar* listening test. *- endap-apung* sink and float testing. *- ganda* double test. *- getaran* vibration test (for aircraft). *- hantam* crash test. *- imbuh* recharge test. *- jalan* a test drive. *- kadar* assaying. *- kandung lapisan* (*petro*) drill stem test, DST. *- kelayakan dan kepatutan* fit and proper test. *- keletihan* fatigue test (for aircraft). *- kepatutan dan kepantasan* fit and proper test. *- ketercucian* washability test. *- keturunan* progeny test (for plants). *- klinis* clinical trial. *- laik operasi* [ULO] operational acceptance test. *- luncur* test launch. **menguji-luncurkan** to test launch. *- matériil* judicial review. *- média bata* red brick test. *- pentas* try out. **menguji-pentaskan** to try out (a play, etc.). *- petik* a) multiple-choice exam. b) sampling. *- pompa* pumping test. *- pulih* recovery test. *- resap* infiltration test. *- silang* cross-check. *- terbang* test flight. *mengadakan – terbang* to test-fly. **menguji-terbang** to test-fly (an aircraft). *- tuntas* due diligence.

beruji 1 to give a test/examination; to compete. **2** to take/sit for an examination.

menguji 1 to verify, inspect, check. **2** to give an exam to, test, give an examination to. *Semua mahasiswa diuji.* All university students are subject to examinations. **3** to test, put s.t. to the test. *~ kejujurannya* to test his honesty. **4** to assay. *~ emas* to assay gold. *diuji sama mérah, di hati (diteliti) sama berat* a husband and wife who get along very well.

mengujikan 1 to test (s.t. on an exam). *pelajaran yang diujikan* the lesson tested. **2** to have s.t. tested.

teruji to be tested/examined. *Belum ~ validitasnya.* Its validity has not yet been tested. *~ waktu* has withstood the test of time. *diteruji* (*infr*) tested.

ujian 1 exam(ination), test. *calon peserta ~ gadungan* ringer, s.o. who takes a test for s.o. else; → JOKI II. *sekali lancung ke ~, seumur hidup orang tak percaya* do one bad thing and people will never trust you again. *maju ~* to take/stand for an exam. *~ akhir* posttest. *~ awal* pretest. *~ bakat* aptitude test. *~ dinas*

trial period (for civil servants). *~ hér* re-examination. *~ kandidat B.A.* exam (in the older system). *~ kedinasan* service test. *~ kenaikan kelas* promotion exam (in schools). *~ kesetiaan* loyalty test. *~ ketangkasan* proficiency test. *~ lisan* oral exam. *~ masuk* admission/entrance exam. *~ negara* state exam. *~ pendadaran* oral exam of one's thesis (and may also cover course content), orals. *~ penghabisan* final exam. *~ persiapan* preparatory exam. *~ pilihan ganda* multiple-choice test. *~ prakték* practical exam, practicum. *~ saringan* screening exam. *~ sarjana muda* B.A. exam. *~ SIM* driver's test. *~ susulan* make-up exam. *~ tulis* [utul] and *~ tertulis* written (part of an) exam. *~ ulangan* re-examination. **2** what is used to test. *bahan ~* examination paper. **3** test, trial, experiment. **4** assay. **5** (*coq*) to take an exam. *Dalam bulan Oktober dia akan ~.* He'll take his exam in October.

keujian 1 (*M*) found out, detected, discovered. *sekali lancung ~ seumur hidup orang tak percaya* if you are shown to be false/ unfaithful once, nobody will trust you ever again. **2** to suffer/ sustain/incur a loss (in a contest). **3** (*cla*) to fail.

penguji 1 examiner, examining. *panitia ~* examining board. *~ kayu lapis* plywood grader. **2** tester, assayer.

pengujian 1 examination, trial, testing. *~ secara terbatas* limited review. **2** assay. **3** audit.

ujmah (*A*) barbarism.

ujrah and **ujrat** (*A*) **1** wages. **2** rent (in an *ijarah* transaction).

uju and **ujub** (*A*) arrogant, pride.

ujud I → WUJUD I.

ujud II intention, aim.

berujud to intend, aim at.

mengujud(kan) to intend, want.

ujug-ujug (*Jv*) suddenly, all of a sudden, unexpectedly, without saying a word. *Istrinya – minta cerai.* His wife suddenly asked for a divorce.

ujuk hand s.o. over without being asked.

ujul k.o. plant, *Willughbeia coriacea* whose sap is used to trap birds. *getah* – sap of that plant.

ujung I 1 (sharp) end, point, tip; *opp* PANGKAL. *dari – kaki hingga/ sampai – pangkal* from stem to stern. **2** nose, head (of a weapon). **3** end, conclusion (of discussions, etc.), where s.t. is leading to. *- pembicaraan* conclusion of the discussions. *- perkataan* intention of what s.o. is saying. **4** end (of a period of time); → AKHIR. *- minggu* weekend; → AKHIR *minggu*. **5** the most remote from the center, outskirts, suburbs. *tinggal di – kota Jakarta* to live in the suburbs (or, far from the center) of Jakarta. *dari – dunia ke – dunia yang lain* from one end to the other. *yang paling –* a) (to) the utmost. b) in the background (of a picture). c) the furthest (in a certain direction). *yang paling – sebelah barat* the westernmost. *berada dalam posisi di – tanduk* to be in an awkward/difficult position. **6** promontory, headland, isthmus, peninsula. **7** meaning, purport, bearing (on a topic). *lalu/lulus –, lalu/lulus kelindan* if you achieve your highest goal, your other goals will also be achieved. *makin ke – makin manis* a) an extraordinary situation. b) her children get prettier and prettier (as you go from one to the next). *mengadu – penjahit* a) to meet s.o. b) to show e.o. one's expertise, etc. *- balok* beam end. *- buritan* cant end. *- gigi* crown. *- hidung* tip of the nose. *- jari* finger tip. *- jari sambungan lidah* spokesman, representative in negotiations. *- jarum* tip of a needle. *- jarum halus kelindan sutera* a very subtle trick. *mengadakan – jarum* to carry out a very difficult task. *- jalan* the end of the street. *- kota* the outskirts of town. *- kuku* a little bit. *- Kulon* a wildlife preserve at the southwestern tip of Java. *- laras* muzzle. *- lidah* a) tip of the tongue. *kata-kata yang sudah di – lidahnya* words on the tip of his tongue. b) (*M*) spokesman; → JUBIR, JURU *bicara*. *jadi – lidah* to be(come) a spokesman/mouthpiece. *selalu di – lidah* get talked about, be the talk of the town. *mengadu – lidah* to quarrel, squabble. *berniaga di – lidah* to be smart but dishonest. *- mata* a) corner of the eye. b) tip (of a knife). *di – mulut* to be the talk of the town; → SELALU *di ujung lidah*. *- panah* arrowhead. *- pangkal* a) both lower and upper ends (of s.t.). b) the gist/essentials of a matter, its essence. *tak jelas pangkalnya* Heaven knows why, it is unclear why. *Tak jelas –*

pangkalnya tiba-tiba Pak Camat mengeluarkan kata-kata pe-das. Heaven knows why all of a sudden the Subdistrict Head uttered some sharp words. *tanpa – pangkal* indiscriminate(ly), without rhyme or reason. *tak tentu – pangkalnya* a) does not make any sense, incoherent; doubtful, questionable. b) to be completely off center, lose one's bearings completely. *tidak berujung berpangkal* incoherent. *– pengabut* nozzle head. *– perkataan* intention. *tidak dapat menangkap – percakapan itu* cannot understand the meaning of that conversation. *– péna* nib of a pen. *– pijak (mil)* beachhead. *– pipa pompa* nozzle (at end of gasoline hose). *– rambut* from head to toe. *– rembang* terminal; apex. *– susu* nipple. *– tanah* a) the southernmost tip of the Malaysian peninsula. b) cape. *di – tanduk* on the horns of a dilemma. *– tap* stud bolt. *– tombak* spearhead.

ujungnya at long last, finally, in the end; it finally turned out that. *~ Susanto diserahkan kepada familinya.* Sunanto was finally turned over to his relatives.

ujung-ujungnya in the long run, finally, eventually. *Sebagian dari keuntungan itu dibagikan kepada para pemegang saham, yang ~ juga terkena PPh.* Part of the profits were distributed to the shareholders, who in the long run are subject to the income tax.

seujung *~ kuku* a little/tiny bit.

berujung 1 to have a head; → BERKEPALA. *peluru kendali ~ nuklir* missile with a nuclear warhead. 2 with an end/point. *yang ~ tajam* with a sharp point. 3 to have an end, be finite. *jalan yang tak ~* an endless road. *perdébatan tak ~* an endless debate. *memainkan pisau ~ dua* to be an unreliable/fickle person. 4 to end (in), culminate (in). *Rapat itu ~ pada pemungutan suara.* The meeting ended in a vote.

mengujung 1 to taper to a point. 2 to draw to a close, come to an end, be over. *Musim rambutan sudah ~.* The *rambutan* season has come to an end. 3 to reach a high point, culminate, intensify. *Perselisihannya sudah ~.* Their conflict has reached the culmination point.

terujung the furthest end/tip. *di bagian ~ perkampungan itu* in the furthest reaches of the settlement.

pengujung end, conclusion (of a period of time). *~ bulan* the end of the month.

ujung II *– atap* k.o. shrub, *Baeckea frutescens.*

Ujung Pandang and **Ujungpandang** Ujung Pandang, the name used for a number of years for Makassar; the name has now been changed back to Makassar.

ujungan *(J/Jv)* k.o. fencing with rattan sticks.

ujur → UZUR II.

ujut → WUJUD I.

u/k [uang keluar] (banking) debit.

UKA [Univérsitas Karo] (Kabanjahe).

ukab *(A)* the Prophet's banner.

ukas k.o. shellfish, *Lammellibranch sp.*

UKAW [Univérsitas Kristen Artha Wacana] (Kupang).

UKDW [Univérsitas Kristen Duta Wacana] (Yogya).

ukel k.o. snack made from sticky-rice flour.

ukh-ukh-ukh *(onom)* sounds produced by deaf-mutes.

  berukh-ukh-ukh to produce such sounds.

ukhdud *(A)* trench, moat.

ukhrawi(yah) *(A)* eschatological.

ukhrowi → UKHRAWI(YAH).

ukhuwah *(A)* brotherhood, fraternity. *– Basariyah* human brotherhood. *– Islami(y)ah* Islamic/Muslim brotherhood. *– Wathaniah/Wathoniah* National Brotherhood.

UKI [Univérsitas Kristen Indonésia] (Jakarta).

ukik child's game using hard fruit or coins.

UKIM [Univérsitas Kristen Indonésia Maluku] (Ambon).

ukir carve, engrave. *juru/pandai/tukang –* carver, engraver, sculptor. *seni –* art of carving/engraving/sculpting. *– kencana* carvings on gold.

  berukir 1 carved, engraved. 2 with carvings/engravings. *kursi ~* a chair with carvings on it.

  berukir-ukir 1 embellished with carvings. 2 pockmarked; → BOPÉNG, BURIK. *Mukanya ~.* His face is pockmarked.

  mengukir 1 to carve, engrave, chisel. *~ dalam hati* to imprint on one's heart. *~ langit* to build castles in the air. 2 to show, dis-

play (a smile). *Mulutnya ~ senyuman.* Her mouth showed a smile. *~ senyum di kedua ujung bibirnya* to smile a full smile.

ukir-mengukir (the art of) carving. *~ kayu* wood carving.

mengukirkan 1 to have engraved. *~ nama kekasihnya pada cincin* to have his sweetheart's name engraved on the ring. 2 to engrave s.t. *~ dalam hati* to engrave s.t. in one's heart.

  terukir 1 carved, engraved. *Cerita Rama ~ pada dinding Candi Prambanan.* The Ramayana story is carved on the walls of the Prambanan Temple. 2 became/was visible, show, appear (of a smile). *Di mukanya ~ senyum lébar.* A broad smile appeared on her face. *~ di lauhilmahfud* fated.

  ukiran 1 carved work, carving, sculpture; statue. *~ kayu* woodcut. *~ terawang* lacy carving. 2 embossing, engraving. *~ timbul* bas-relief. 3 design (on cloth). **berukiran** with carvings on it, having carvings.

  pengukir 1 carver, engraver, sculptor. 2 carving knife.

  pengukiran the act/way of carving/engraving.

Ukit [Univérsitas Kristen Indonésia Tomohon].

UKM I [Univérsitas Kristen "Maranatha"] (Bandung).

UKM II → USAHA *kecil (dan) menengah.*

UKM III → UNIT *kegiatan mahasiswa.*

uknum → OKNUM.

ukon *(Jv col)* a silver 50-cent coin. *– mas* a gold 10-guilder coin (used as an ornament).

UKP [Univérsitas Kristen Pétra] (Surabaya).

Ukrida [Univérsitas Kristen Djaya] (Jakarta).

UKSW [Univérsitas Kristen Satya Wacana] (Salatiga).

uktab *(A)* (*burung –*) eagle; → RAJAWALI.

ukuf *(A)* "Remaining Behind," i.e., used to describe the life of prayer of one who was constantly in the mosque.

ukulélé ukulele.

ukup 1 perfume. 2 incense, i.e., all types of perfumes, scents, or fragrances (such as incense) burned to fumigate clothes and to give them an aromatic smell. 3 flowers, such as jasmine, used to impart aroma to tea. *air –* perfumed water.

  berukup 1 to fumigate o.s. by burning incense, etc. 2 perfumed, scented. *kain ~* a perfumed piece of cloth.

  mengukup(i) 1 to fumigate clothes with incense. 2 to burn incense.

  ngukup *(J)* 1 to burn various k.o. incense. 2 to fumigate a room to drive out mosquitoes.

  ukupan 1 perfume. 2 incense. 3 censer.

  pengukup censer.

  perukupan 1 censer. 2 place where clothes are fumigated.

ukur 1 measure, gauge. 2 rating. *– baju (di) badan sendiri* judge others as you would yourself. *Jika belum – berpantang mati.* Nobody dies before his allotted time. *– alit (M cla)* regulations. *– jangka (M)* fixed period of time. *– tanah* land-surveying. *alat – air* water meter. *ilmu –* geometry. *mantri –* surveyor, cadastral official. *pita –* measuring tape. *surat –* surveyor's certificate. *tukang – jalan (coq)* idler, loafer. *nggak –.–* beyond measure.

  seukur 1 of the same size. 2 *(M)* matching, harmonizing, agreeing. *telah ~* a) to be well matched. b) identical. c) appropriately, properly. d) to agree in every respect. *~ mata dan/dengan telinga* according to what one sees and hears.

  seukuran the size of. *dipotong kecil-kecil ~ kertas untuk résép dokter* cut into small pieces the size of a doctor's prescription form.

  mengukur [and **ngukur** *(coq)*] 1 to measure, survey (length/area, etc.); to weigh (by means of a scale), take (s.o.'s temperature). *sibuk ~ tubuh-tubuh orang* (a tailor) was busily engaged in measuring people. *~ berat badan anda setiap pagi.* Weigh yourself every morning. *~ jalan (coq)* to loaf about, hang out and do nothing. *~ tempat tidur (coq)* to go to bed. 2 to weigh, compare. *Jangan ~ kekayaan orang dengan kekayaan ortumu.* Don't compare other people's wealth with that of your parents. *~ keberanian* sizing e.o. up. *~ bayang-bayang sepanjang badan* to cut your coat according to your cloth. 3 to measure s.o. or s.t. against s.t.

  ukur-mengukur calibration. *~ térmométer* thermometer calibration.

  mengukurkan to measure s.t. against s.t. else.

  terukur 1 measured. 2 rated.

ukuran 1 measure(ment). *kayu* ~ ruler, measuring stick. ~ *induk* standard measure. ~ *isi* cubic measure. ~ *kapal* admeasurement (of ship). ~ *luas* square measure. ~ *panas* temperature. ~ *panjang* linear measure. ~ *sejari* fingerling. ~ *vital* vital statistics. ~ *yang berlaku* accepted measures. **2** criterion, norm, standard, principle. *mempergunakan* ~ *ganda* to use a double standard. ~ *zaman* according to the times. **3** scale, size, dimension, gauge, value, caliber (of bullets). ~ *jangka* pair of compasses. ~ *lebih* oversize. ~ *masyarakat* social values. ~ *mini* in a small way, on a small scale, in miniature. ~ *tonggak* tide gauge. *dalam* ~ in the sense of. **3** grounds. *menurut* ~ *derajat saja* on the grounds of prestige alone. **berukuran** to measure. *kertas yang* ~ *8x10 inci* paper measuring 8x10 inches. *16 meriam yang* ~ *100 mm* 16 100-mm guns.

pengukur 1 surveyor, measurer. **2** meter, -meter, measuring device/instrument, surveyor's chain, counter, checker, gauge. ~ *ampére/arus* ammeter. ~ *api* pyrometer. ~ *ban* tire gauge. ~ *bunyi* audiometer. ~ *cepat* speedometer. ~ *demam* fever thermometer. ~ *gigi perangko* perforation gauge (for stamps). ~ *harga* measure of value. ~ *hujan* rain gauge. ~ *jam ampére* ampere-hour meter. ~ *jarak* odometer. ~ *kalori* calorimeter. ~ *kawat* wire gauge. ~ *kecepatan* speedometer. ~ *kedalaman* depth finder. ~ *ketinggian* altimeter. ~ *lembab* hygroscope. ~ *lengas* hygrometer. ~ *putaran poros* tachometer. ~ *suara* soundfinder (artillery). ~ *suhu* clinical thermometer. ~ *tanah* surveyor. ~ *tarikan* draft gauge. ~ *tekanan darah* blood-pressure measuring device, sphygmomanometer. ~ *tinggi* altimeter. ~ *waktu* timer. **sepengukur** as far as (the eye and ear) can tell.

pengukuran measurement, measuring, mensuration, survey(ing), -metry. ~ *sudut arah* bearing. ~ *suhu* temperature measurement. ~ *tanah* surveying. ~ *tinggi* altimetry.

perukuran measurement.

ul (*BG*) [*ulangan*] test, quiz.

ulah comportment, behavior, manners, ways, caprice, whim; → OLAH I. *- alam* whim of nature. *- asmara* behavior in a love affair, such as flirtation, sexual intercourse, etc. *- gombal* a cheap trick.

berulah to behave, comport o.s.

ulaiti the original Arab community in Jakarta from the Hadramaut and South Yemen.

ulak I eddy, whirlpool, swirl. *- air* whirlpool; → PUSARAN.

berulak to swirl, eddy; to move in an eddy.

ulakan vortex, turbulence. ~ *air* whirlpool.

ulak II (*J*) **mengulak** to crush, pound, grind spices in a *cobék* or mortar; → ULEG, ULEK I.

mengulakkan ~ *janji* to break a promise.

ulak-ulak *- pinggang* small of the back.

ulam raw, young leafy vegetables eaten as a side dish with rice; → LALAP. *hendak - pucuk menjulai* and *pucuk dicinta - datang/tiba* "you wanted a shoot and out came a salad"; to get an unexpected piece of luck, to hit the jackpot. *- mencari sambal* a woman looking for a man. *- raja* a plant, *Cosmos caudatus* whose leaves are made into *lalap*; → KENIKIR.

berulam with ... as a side dish. *sakit hati ~ jantung* feel depressed because emotionally wounded. ~ *airmata* to feel sad.

ulama (*A* plural of *alim* but often used as a singular) ulema, learned man, Islamic scholar, theologian in Islamic matters. *alim -* Islamic scholars.

keulamaan 1 Islamic scholarhood, an ulema's reputation. **2** (*mod*) ulama.

ulam-ulam and **ulaman** concubine; → GUNDIK.

ulamawan → ULAMA.

ulan various species of climbing plants. *- putih* whitejacket, *Aniseia martinicensis*.

ulang I 1 return, go/come back (to a former place). **2** *verb +* *-* to do again, re-. *(men)cétak -* to reprint. *- alik* to commute, go back and forth. *- aling* a) often, frequently, repeatedly. b) to come and go, back and forth. *- bicara* recession (as of a court). *- gelar* redeployment (of missiles). *- pola* pattern practice. *- sebar* (*mil*) redeployment. *- séwa* sublet. **mengulang-séwakan** to sublet. (*hari*) *- tahun* [HUT] a) birthday. b) anniversary, celebration of an event on the date that the event occurred. **beru-**

lang tahun 1 to celebrate one's birthday. *Selamat ~ tahun!* Happy birthday! **2** to celebrate an anniversary.

seulang repeated once.

berulang 1 to return again, go back (to a place). **2** to recur, happen again, be repeated. *Kita tidak mau tuduhan itu ~ lagi.* We don't want that accusation to be repeated. ~ *kali* repeatedly, again and again, over and over again. ~ *kata* to repeat a remark, keep saying the same thing again and again. ~ *kembali* to happen again, recur, repeat itself. *sejarah ~ kembali* history repeats itself. **3** iterative, repeated.

ulang-berulang recurring. *soal yang ~* a recurring problem.

berulang-ulang 1 to move back and forth constantly. **2** (= **berulang-ulangan**) to do s.t. repeatedly/often/again and again, over and over again. *Saya ~ ke rumahnya.* I visited him again and again. *Dia menyebut nama anaknya ~.* He said his child's name over and over again.

mengulang to do over again, repeat, review, go (back) over. *Yang salah dihukum supaya ia tidak akan ~ kesalahannya.* The wrongdoer was punished so that he wouldn't repeat his wrongdoing. *Anak-anak harus ~ pelajarannya di rumah.* The children have to study their lessons again at home. ~ *jejak* a) to do s.t. again, repeat. b) to reconcile with one's estranged wife; → RUJUK *kembali*.

mengulangi [and **ngulangin** (*J coq*)] **1** (= **mengulang-ulang** and **mengulang-ulangi**) to repeat once, to do s.t. once again. *diulangi (lagi)* repeat it, say it again. *mengulang-ulang kaji lama* to rake up old stories. **2** (= **mengulang-ulangi**) to do over and over again. **3** to redo/study, etc. (what has already been done/studied, etc.).

mengulangkan to repeat for s.o.

terulang repeated, happened again, recurred. *Saya harap kejadian itu tidak ~ lagi.* I hope that that event won't happen again. **keterulangan** repetition.

ulangan 1 test, quiz. ~ *umum* general test (of all subjects studied). **2** repetition, re-. *pertunjukan ~* rerun. *siaran ~* rebroadcast, rerun. *ujian ~* re-examination. **3** refrain, chorus.

pengulang 1 reviser, coach, (private) tutor, instructor. **2** repeater. *stasiun ~* repeater station.

pengulangan 1 repetition, revision, repeating. ~ *kejahatan/tindak pidana* recidivism. **2** (*ling*) reduplication.

perulangan repetition, recurrence, return, reduplication. ~ *kata* (*ling*) word reduplication.

ulang II *- uli* a freshwater fish, clown loach fish, *Botia macracantha*.

ulang-alik 1 to come and go, move/go back and forth rapidly/frequently; to ply, shuttle, commute. *- dengan kereta api* to commute by train. **2** (*mod*) shuttle, commuter. *pelayanan -* commuter service. *penduduk yang bersifat -* commuters. *pesawat antariksa -* space shuttle.

berulang-alik 1 to go and return, go back and forth, commute. *Dia ~ mendatangi sebuah klinik bersalin.* She's been going back and forth to a maternity clinic. **2** to shuttle (of aircraft).

pengulang-alik commuter.

ulang-aling again and again.

ulang-balik → ULANG-ALIK.

ulap *ulap-ulap* (*J*) waving, beckoning (to call s.o. over), gesture.

mengulap [and **ngulapin** (*J*)] **1** to wave, beckon with the hand. **2** (*Jv*) gesture made with the hand in front of the eyes as though looking into the distance (used as a choreographic movement).

ngulap to look into the distance.

mengulap-ngulapkan to beckon to, wave at.

ulap-ulap k.o. porridge made of bananas or yams boiled with sugar and coconut milk.

ular I snake, serpent. *ahli -* herpetologist. *sop -* snake soup. *bagai - dengan legundi* a young person very attached to his beloved. *bagai - orang* two brothers who don't want to know e.o. *naga didengarkan siul -* to always be careful. *kerosok - di rumpun bambu* don't be afraid of people's threats. *seperti ketiak - dan berketiak -* wordy, tedious, talking interminably. *seperti - ular, panjang lanjut tidak putus-putusnya* not sure whether s.t. is good or bad. *- bukan, ikan pun bukan* neither fish nor fowl. *- kena bedal/palu/pukul* restless (due to anger, etc.). *seperti - dicubit ékor* to face one's enemy with anger. *sekerat -, sekerat belut* a hypocrite. *sudah tampak kaku -* s.o.'s bad behavior has become known. *-*

menyusur akar to keep a low profile without losing prestige. – *palu biar mati* strike while the iron is hot. *melangkahi* – to perform a dangerous task. FOR OTHER NAMES OF SNAKES BEGINNING WITH ULAR SEE THE SPECIFIC TERM. – *air* puff-faced water snake, *Tropidonotus spp.*, *Homalopsis buccata*. – *anang/babi* king cobra, *Ophiophagus hannah*. – *ari* k.o. venomous snake, *Doliophis*. – *babi* → ULAR *séndok*. – *bakau* crab-eating water snake, *Fordonia leucobalia*. – *bandotan* → ULAR *tanah*. – *bandotan puspa* Russel's viper, *Vipera russeli*. – *belang* banded krait, *Bungarus fasciatus*. – *belérang* yellow-bellied sea snake, *Pelamis platurus*. – *beludak/biludak* → ULAR *tanah*. – *berbisa* poisonous/venomous snake. – *bula/bura* a poisonous snake, Asian spitter, *Naja sputatrix*. – *bungka* pope's pit viper, *Trimeresurus sp.* – *cabai* banded Malayan coral snake, *Maticora intestinalis*. – *cabai besar* red-bellied long-glanded snake, *Maticora bivirgata*. – *cincin emas* gold/yellow-ringed cat snake, banded mangrove snake, *Boiga dendrophila*. – *cindai* (*cla*) reticulated python, *Python reticulatus*. – *cintamani* Wagler's pit viper, a golden snake which is believed to give success in love, *Trimeresurus* and other species. – *danau* a) python, *Python reticulatus*. b) rainbow; → PELANGI. – *danau mengiang* (*M*)/*minum* rainbow; → PELANGI. – *derik* rattlesnake. – *emas* → ULAR *jelutung*. – *gadung* white-lipped pit viper, *Trimesurus albolabris*. – *gebuk* → ULAR *tanah*. – *hanjaliwan* (in East Kalimantan) k.o. flying cobra. – *hijau* → ULAR *gadung*. – *hijau Sumatra* Sumatran pit viper, *Trimeresurus sumatranus*. – *hitam* → ULAR *séndok*. – *jelmaan* a ghost that takes the form of a snake. – *jelutung* spotted greenish snake, Celebes flying snake, *Chrysopelea paradisi*. – *kadut* little file snake, *Acrochordus granulatus*. – *kapak* viper, *Trimeresurus wagleri*. – *karung* Javan wart snake, *Acrochordus javanicus*. – *katam tebu* banded krait, *Bungarus fasciatus*. – *kembang* irresponsible person, person who seems good but is bad at heart. – *kepala dua* a) red-tailed pipe snake, *Cylindrophis rufus*. b) two faced. – *kisi* striped keelback, k.o. snake, *Coluber melanzostus/vittatus*. – *lanang* large *ular séndok*. – *laut* yellow-bellied sea snake, *Pelamis platurus*. – *lidi* long poisonous snake, *Ahaetulla sp.* – *matahari* coral snake, *Maticora intestinalis*. – *mengiang* rainbow. – *minum* rainbow. – *naga* dragon. – *patola* (*Min*) Menadonese dish made from the green python, *Chondrophyton viridis*. – *picung* red-necked keel back, a nonpoisonous snake, *Natrix subminiata*, *Tropidonotus trianguligerus*. – *pucuk* green whip snake, short-nosed vine snake, *Dryophis prasinus*. – *puspokajang* python, *Python reticulatus*. – *putih* white snake found in Irian Jaya. – *sanca/sawa* python, *Python reticulatus*. – *séndok* Asian spitter, common black cobra, *Naja sputatrix*. – *siput* snail-eating snake, keeled slug snake, *Pareas carinatus*. – *tanah* ground pit viper, *Agkistrodon/Trigonocephalus rhodostoma*. – *tebu* → ULAR *belang*. – *tedung cobra, Naja naja*. – *tedung abu/séndok* hamadryad, king cobra, *Naja/Ophiophagus hannah/bungarus*. – *tedung séndok/sénduk* black snake, *Naja tripudians*. – *tiong/tiung* Sumatran pit viper, *Trimesurus sumatranus*. – *welang* banded krait, *Bungarus fasciatus*. – *welang kepala mérah* red-headed krait, *Bungarus flaviceps*. – *weling* Malayan krait, *Bungarus candidus*.

mengular to be long and snake-like in shape. *Antréan masih ~ panjang hingga ke pintu masuk*. The line still snaked around to the entrance.

ular-ular and **ularan** rubber hose/tube.

ular II *akar* – a climbing plant, *Freycinetia angustifolia*. *kayu* – k.o. climbing shrub, *Strychnos ligustrina* (used as a remedy against snake bites). *paku* – a species of fern, *Pleopeltis phymatodes*.

ular-ularan k.o. climbing plant, *Tinospora coriacea*.

ular-ular I pennon, pennant.

ular-ular II (*Jv*) welcoming speech, words of wisdom.

ular-ularan (*M*) cramp in the calf of the leg.

ulas I **1** piece of cloth or material used for a covering or wrapper; cover, slip, case, envelope, wrapper. – *bantal* pillowcase. **mengulas bantal** to put a case on a pillow. – *buku* book cover. – *kasur* bed sheet. – *méja* tablecloth. – *surat* envelope. – *tangan* assistant. **2** bark, rind, husk, peel.

berulas covered (with), wrapped (in), with a cover/case. *Bantalnya ~ kain bersulam*. The pillow was wrapped in an embroidered case.

mengulas 1 to cover, envelope, wrap. **2** to put a coat of paint on.

mengulasi 1 to cover, envelope, wrap. **2** (*pl obj*) to put coats of paint on.

mengulaskan to use s.t. as a cover.

ulasan 1 cover, case (of pillow). **2** putting a coat of paint on.

ulas II **1** slice, section, small piece, segment (of an orange), clove (of garlic). **2** classifier used to count segments, pips/pits of the *durian* fruit, jackfruit, etc.

seulas 1 a slice, a pip, etc. *durian* ~ a pip/pit of the *durian* with its flesh. *jeruk* ~ a slice of an orange. *limau masak* ~ smarter than his/her other siblings. **2** a little bit, barely. ~ *senyum* a faint smile.

mengulas ~ *senyum* to smile faintly/out of politeness.

mengulaskan to divide into sections. ~ *senyum* to have a faint smile on one's face.

ulasan ~ *Pap* Pap smear.

ulas III (*Jv*) *juru* – commentator.

mengulas 1 to comment (on), review (a book, etc.). **2** to interpret, explain. **3** to analyze.

ulasan exegesis, explanation, interpretation, commentary, criticism, analysis, review. ~ *buku* book review. ~ *keuangan* financial commentary/review. ~ *pérs* press roundup.

pengulas commentator, reviewer.

pengulasan commenting on, reviewing.

ulas IV (*M*) sequel, extension, continuation. – *tangan* a) helper, assistant. b) accomplice, stooge. **berulas tangan** to have an assistant/helper. **berulas tangan dan lidah** to be helped materially and with advice. **mengulas tangan** to help, assist, support, lend a helping hand to. *Tanganku diulas oléhnya*. He lent me a helping hand.

berulas with a sequel/extension/continuation.

mengulas 1 to appoint (a helper/assistant). **2** to lengthen, continue, prolong. ~ *bicara* to continue to talk (or, keep on talking). ~ *kayu* to lengthen a piece of wood. ~ *nyawa* to save, rescue; to cure, restore to health.

ulasan sequel, extension, continuation. ~ *lidah* spokesman; → JURU *bicara*.

perulasan place where s.t. is connected/joined on.

ulas V mengulas-ulas to caress, stroke, fondle; → ELUS.

ulat I worm, maggot, caterpillar. *macam* – crowded (with people), packed in like sardines. *mengorék lubang* – to look for a reason to quarrel with s.o. FOR OTHER NAMES OF WORMS, ETC. BEGINNING WITH ULAT SEE THE SPECIFIC TERM. – *air* athlete's foot. – *api* a pest of oil-palm leaves, *Sentora nitten*. – *apung* → ULAT *layar*. – *bulu* hairy caterpillar, *Aloa sanguinolenta*. – *bulu laut* a marine worm. – *bungkus* bagworm, *Thyridopteryx ephemeraeformis*. – *cawai* → ULAT *ratus*. – *daun* gypsy moth, *Lymantria dispar*. – *gading* caseworm, a rice pest, *Nymphula depunctalis*. – *grayak* a caterpillar which attacks rice plants, k.o. cutworm, *Spodoptera littoralis*. – *gulung* roll worm, rice case worm, *Nymphula depunctalis*. – *jengkal* inchworm, *Hyposidra talaca*. – *kantung* bagworm, *Thyridopteryx ephemeraeformis*. – *kapas* cotton boll worm, *Helicoverpa armigera*. – *kelolong pisang* banana leaf roller, *Erionata thrax*. – *kilau* inchworm. – *kipat* golden cocoon, *Cricula trifenestrata* that attacks cashew-nut trees. – *kubis* cabbage worm, diamond-back moth, *Plutella xylostella*. – *layar* rice case worm, *Nymphula depunctalis*. – *pangkas* black cut-worm, *Agrotis ipsilon*. – *pelombong daun* leaf-miner. – *pelombong lepuh* blister miner. – *penambang daun* leaf borer. – *pemakan/penggulung daun* leaf roller, *Homona coffearia*. – *perangka daun* skeletonizer. – *rangkak* tent caterpillar. – *ratus* lawn armyworm, *Spodoptera mauritia*. – *sarung* faggot worm. – *sentadu* green caterpillar or leaf-insect. – *serangga* insects, bugs. – *sutera* a) silkworm, *Bombyx mori*. b) *si* – *Sutera* the Silkworm, an antiship missile made in the PRC. – *tentara* armyworm, *Psodoptera exempta* and other species.

berulat worm-eaten, wormy; maggoty. ~ *mata melihat* unable to stand the sight of s.o.

ulat II → ULET I.

ulat III (*J*) **ngulat 1** to plait. **2** to make *ketupat* skins.

ulati → ULU *hati*.

ula-ula pennon, pennant.

ulayah and **ulayat** (*A*) region, territory; → WILAYAH. *hak* – collective rights of a group of residents to a piece of land. *harto* – (*M*) a form of property, mainly uncultivated forest land, under the authority of the village as a whole. *tanah* – communal reserved land.

uled (*J/Jv*) no longer crisp (of *krupuk*, etc.).

uleg → ULEK I.

ulek I (*Jv*) ulek-ulek pestle, crusher, slightly bent piece of wood or stone used to pound or grind spices, etc. in a *cobék* or mortar; → ULAK II.

   mengulek to grind, pound, pulverize (spices, etc.).

   ulekan 1 pestle. **2** what has been ground up/pounded.

ulek II → ULAK I.

ulek III (*gay sl*) anal sex.

ulem (*Jv*) ulem-ulem(an) invitation (to a social event).

   mengulem [and **ngulem** (*coq*)] and **mengulemi** to invite s.o. to a social event.

   uleman 1 (invited) guest. **2** invitation.

ulén → ULI I.

uler (*J/Jv*) caterpillar; → ULAT I. – *kepalé dué* (*J*) a hypocrite. *paspasan* – castoff slough. – *bulu/jengkal* caterpillar. – *kambang* leech.

   nguler ~ *kambang* to float along with the current, take it easy. ~ *kambang yén trimo alon-alon* (*Jv*) slow but sure.

   uleran worm-eaten, wormy.

uler-uler k.o. *kué basah* made with grated coconut.

ules I (*J*) mengules to pulverize.

ules II → ULAS I.

ulet I (*Jv*) **1** solid, strong, substantial, strong, tough (of s.t.); → KUAT. *Tali ini kurang* –. This rope isn't strong enough. **2** tenacious, obstinate, stubborn, persistent, hard-nosed, to strike a hard bargain; → TANGGUH I. *Meréka* – *sekali dalam berbisnis*. They're very hard-nosed in business. **3** ductile.

   mengulet [and **ngulet** (*coq*)] to stretch (after sleeping).

   memperulet to make s.t. tough, toughen, make s.t. persevere.

   keuletan 1 solidity, strength, durability. **2** perseverance, steadiness, stamina, tenacity. ~ *bekerja* perseverance in work.

ulet II → ULAT I.

uleti (*J*) → WALAITI.

uleuebalang (*Ac*) officials who determine and rule on customary law in Aceh.

uli I sticky rice cooked with coconut. *tapé* – (*J*) a mixture of *tapai* and *uli*.

   menguli [and **menguléni** and **nguléni** (*Jv*)] to knead/mix into a paste.

   ulian batter.

   penguli s.o. or s.t. that kneads.

   pengulian kneading.

uli II (*cla*) beautiful, pretty, pet name for a pampered child.

ulia → AULIA.

ulik I (*S*) mengulik to investigate, examine thoroughly.

   pengulikan investigation, examination.

ulik II → ULIT I.

ulil (*A*) – *albab* intellectuals. – *amri/amr* government administrative order.

ulin (*kayu* -) Borneo ironwood, a tall hardwood tree from Kalimantan, *Eusiderodoxylon zwageri*.

uling (*J/Jv*) – *anjing* a large marine eel, Murray/shortfin eel, *Anguilla bicolor*.

ulir (*Jv*) screw thread, spiral, worm. – *dalam* female thread. – *rumah siput* modiolus.

   ulir-ulir (*J?*) screwdriver.

   berulir threaded, with threads.

   mengulir to put in a screw. ~ *kembali* to retread (a tire).

   uliran 1 thread. ~ *mur* female thread. **2** threaded. **3** (*bio*) bostryx, helicoid cyme.

   penguliran ~ *kembali* retreading (a tire).

ulit I berulit to lull a child to sleep. ~ *dengan* to sleep together with. *Dia* – *dengan anaknya*. He slept in the same bed as his child.

   mengulit, mengulit-ulit, menguliti and **mengulitkan 1** to sing to sleep. **2** (*M*) to hug, embrace.

   pengulit 1 lullaby. **2** singer of lullabies.

ulit II stingy, cheap.

uli-uli k.o. marine fish, Bombay duck, *Harpodon nehereus*.

ulkus (*D*) ulcer.

ulo (*S*) snake. – *marani gebuk* (*S lit*) "a snake is nearing a stick," i.e., to look for trouble.

ulos (*Bat*) a handmade piece of cloth, 85 cm wide by 1 to 2 meters long, worn like a shawl or stole over one shoulder; → UWIS GARA.

   mengulos to wear this cloth around one's shoulders.

   mengulosi to offer an ulos.

   pengulosan offering an ulos.

ultah [ulang tahun] **1** anniversary. **2** birthday.

   berultah to celebrate an anniversary/one's birthday.

ultimatum (*D*) ultimatum.

   mengultimatum to deliver an ultimatum, deliver an ultimatum to.

ultra- (*D/E*) ultra-, prefix meaning extremely, excessively.

ultrabunyi ultrasonic.

ultracanggih ultrasophisticated.

ultradogmatis ultradogmatic.

ultrakanan ultrarightist.

ultrakiri ultraleftist.

ultralembayung ultraviolet.

ultramarin (*D*) ultramarine.

ultramodern ultramodern.

ultrasonik (*D*) ultrasonic.

ultrasonografi ultrasonography.

ultraungu ultraviolet.

ultraviolét (*E*) ultraviolet.

ulu → HULU. – *hati, uluati* (*J*) and *ulati* epigastrium, the upper middle portion of the abdomen.

uluamah uncontrollable desire to eat and drink.

uluati → ULU hati.

ulubalang → HULUBALANG.

uluhiyah Godhead, divinity.

uluk (*Jv*) uluk-uluk to send a message, let know. ~ *salam* Islamic greeting. **beruluk salam** *dengan* and **(me)nguluki** ~ *salam* to greet.

   mengulukkan [and **ngulukkan**] ~ *layangan* to fly a kite.

   ulukan greeting.

ululazam and **ululazmi** (*A*) "the possessors of constancy," i.e., a title given to certain prophets in the Koran.

ulumuddiniyah (*A*) Islamic religious science.

ulun (*cla*) servant, slave, I (the pronoun); → HAMBA I.

ulung I 1 experienced, skilled, capable. **2** having worked in a particular occupation for a long time, veteran (*mod*). *sudah* – *bekerja* to have worked for a long time. *diplomat* ~ a veteran diplomat. *pencoléng/pencuri* – a professional thief. *penjahat* – an archvillain. **3** superior, predominant (in a particular field), unbeatable. *pemain* – *dunia* a world-class player.

   mengulungi to predominate (in a field).

   keulungan 1 superiority, excellence. **2** craftiness, cunning, deceit.

ulung II oldest, firstborn → SULUNG I.

ulung-ulung (*J/Jv*) k.o. hawk, *Haliastur indus* which attacks chickens and other small animals.

ulup (*naut*) haws pipe.

ulur I mengulur **1** to pay out (line). ~ *tali layang-layang* to pay out the line of a kite. **2** to let s.o. down along a rope. **3** to prolong. ~ *umur* to prolong (one's life); to put off, postpone. ~ *waktu* to play for time. **4** to stick out (of the tongue), protrude. *Lidah anjing itu* ~. The dog's tongue stuck out. **5** to reach, hand over, pass. *Sambil* ~ *minuman ia meminta uangnya*. He asked for the money while handing over the drink. ~ *tarik* to twist. *Maksud itu diulur tariknya*. He twisted its meaning.

   ulur-mengulur obliging, accommodating, compliant.

   mengulur-ulur [and **mengulur-ngulur** and **ngulur-ngulur** (*coq*)] **1** to play for time, stall, put off (doing s.t.). *Jangan* ~ *waktu*. Don't put it off until later. **2** (*coq*) to interpret s.t. to one's liking (by twisting the meaning around). **3** to stretch s.t. out. ~ *uang belanja* to make ends meet.

   menguluri to give/hand over to.

   mengulurkan [and **ngulurin** (*J coq*)] **1** to pay out (rope, etc.). **2** to extend, stretch out, crane, hold/stick out, reach out. ~

bendéra to raise the flag. ~ *lidah* to stick out one's tongue. ~ *kepala* to crane one's neck. **3** to put off, postpone, stall on (doing s.t.). *Waktu perundingan itu dapat diulurkan sampai minggu muka.* The discussions can be put off until next week. **4** to hand (over), give (with outstretched hand). *Ia* ~ *segelas air kepada suaminya.* She handed her husband a glass of water. **5** (*M*) to deliver, take. ~ *makanan ayah ke kebun* to deliver father's food to the plantation. **6** to comply with (a wish), fulfill (a wish). *Jangan diulurkan kehendak orang itu.* Don't do what that person wants. *Tidak baik selalu* ~ *kemauan anakmu.* It's not right to do what your child wants all the time. ~ *tangan* a) to hold out the hand (in greeting, etc.). b) to lend a helping hand. c) to settle differences. d) to poke one's nose into s.o. else's business.

terulur 1 extended, outstretched. **2** protruding, sticking out, projecting. ~ *lidah* exhausted.

uluran 1 s.t. handed over; aid, assistance. ~ *tangan* a) a helping hand. b) a gesture, offer. **2** paying out (rope, etc.), handing over. **3** the part of s.t. that has been paid out.

penguluran 1 paying out, extending. **2** postponing. **3** handing over.

pengulur-uluran constant postponement.

ulur II (*cla*) serf, bond(s)man, villain, (feudal) praedial slave. *masuk* – to become a serf, etc.

ulur III *rotan* – rattan, *Calamus ulur*.

ulu-ulu (*Jv*) (– *banyu*) village official in charge of irrigation.

ulwi (*A*) high, sublime.

u/m [uang masuk] (banking) credit.

um (*A*) mother; → UMM, UMMI I. – *al-khabith* mother of impurity, i.e., alcoholic drinks.

uma I → HUMA.

uma II (Mentawai island) longhouse.

UMA III [Univérsitas Médan Aréa].

umah (*ob*) → RUMAH.

Umaiyah (*A*) Omayyad, a member of the dynasty that ruled in Damascus (661-750 A.D.), which claimed descent from Omayya, Muhammad's grandfather's cousin.

umak (*ob*) → EMAK.

umak-umik (*Jv*) to mutter, mumble (inaudibly), speak indistinctly. *Bibirnya* –. His lips mouthed words.

mengumak-umak [and **ngumak-umak** (*coq*)] to move the lips inaudibly.

uman I (*Jv ob*) **menguman(-uman)** to use abusive language; to inveigh against, assault with words.

uman II (*J*) **1** useless, in vain, unproductive. **2** but in the end. *Segalényé disediain,* – *dié nyolong jugé.* Everything was made available (to him), but in the end he stole (s.t.) anyway.

umanah and **umanat** → AMANAH.

umang → UMANG-UMANG.

umang-umang 1 hermit crab, *Coenobita clypeatus; cp* KEPITING *kelapa. bagai* – to deck o.s. out in borrowed plumes. *si* – *menumpang sahaja kulit orang* a sponger, s.o. who lives off others. **2** a dandy who struts around in borrowed clothes.

umara(k) and **umaro(k)** (*A*) (Muslim) government official/functionary.

umat (*A*) **1** followers of a religion, members of a religious group. – *Islam* Muslims. – *Kristen* Christians. – *Muhammad* Muslims. – *Nabi* followers of the Prophet. **2** the people, folk. **3** community, group, race. – *baru* novices, neophytes. – *manusia* mankind, the human race, humanity.

umbai I → RUMBAI I.

umbai II – *cacing* (*anat*) appendix.

umbai III → UMBUK I.

umbalan (*J/Jv*) fare, freight, fee, charge (for using a ferry or other means of transportation).

umbalang → HEMBALANG.

umban (– *tali*) sling (for hurling a stone); catapult, slingshot.

mengumban(kan) 1 to hurl a stone. **2** to throw away.

mengumbani to sling at s.o.

umbanan projectile.

pengumban sling. **sepengumban** as far as a catapult can throw a stone.

umbang I mengumbang (*ob*) → AMBANG II.

umbang II (*ob*) appear big and terrifying. *naga* – sea serpent.

umbang-ambing mengumbang-ambingkan to make s.t. drift to and fro, toss about.

terumbang-ambing tossed about; → OMBANG-AMBING.

umbar (*Jv*) *jangan* –.– *uang dulu* a) don't squander your money in advance. b) don't count your chickens before they hatch.

mengumbar [and **ngumbar** (*coq*)] **1** to let loose, free, let s.t. wander around free. **2** to give free rein to one's passions, etc. ~ *ancaman* to make a threat. ~ *hawa nafsu* to vent one's feelings, give free rein to one's strong feelings; emotional. *terlalu* ~ *janji* to make too many promises. ~ *kata-kata* to talk a lot. ~ *kemarahannya* to vent one's rage. ~ *tubuh* a) to display the parts of one's body that should be hidden. b) to let o.s. gain weight.

mengumbar(kan) ~ *kesedihannya* to show one's sorrow.

pengumbaran release, letting free, giving free rein to.

umbara mengumbara → MENGEMBARA.

umbi I 1 tuber, storage stem (of a yam/potato/ginger, etc.). **2** bulb, storage leaves (onion/tulip/lily, etc.). **3** storage root (of a carrot/tapioca/turnip, etc.). – *akar* root which becomes an *umbi*. – *dan akar* completely, drastically, root and branch. **4** (*akar* –) a) bulbous root. b) taproot. **5** that part of a stake/pole/pile in the ground. **6** source, the place from which s.t. originates/is gotten. *tercabut dengan urat-nya* rooted out, cut out root and branch.

berurat umbi deep rooted (feelings, etc.). – *batang* stem tuber. – *bunga* bulb. – *gula* sugar beet. – *iles-iles* → ILES-ILES. – *lapis* (*bio*) bulb. – *semu* pseudo bulb.

seumbi of the same plant.

berumbi to have a root, be rooted.

umbi-umbian 1 all k.o. tubers/roots, etc. **2** tuberoses.

umbi II umbuk-umbi (*ob*) → UMBUK-UMBAI.

umbilikus (*E*) umbilicus.

umbin woven mat made of pandanus.

umbing (*J*) a large landing net made from a network of threads.

ngumbing to catch fish in such a net.

umbisi corm.

umbo protruding part of the navel.

umbra (*D*) umbra, total darkness due to an eclipse of the sun. *11 buah pelabuhan akan mengalami* – *akibat gerhana matahari total.* Eleven ports will experience total darkness due to a total eclipse of the sun.

umbrang-ambing (*J*) panicky, in a panic. – *lari-larian anak itu.* The children ran back and forth in a panic.

mengumbrang-ambringin (*J*) to waste, squander. *Duitnya diumbrang-ambringin.* He wasted his money.

umbruk (*J/Jv*) **ngumbruk** to pile up.

ngumbrukin to pile s.t. up.

umbrukan heap, pile.

umbu ancestors.

umbuk I (*J/Jv*) heap, pile; → UMBRUK, TUMPUK. *Duitnya ada se-.* He has a pile of money.

umbuk II persuasion, deception (with words or promises). – *.umbai* and – *.umbi* (*ob*) persuasive and wheedling talk.

mengumbuk 1 to flatter, wheedle, persuade by words and promises. **2** to cheat, swindle.

pengumbuk 1 flatterer. **2** deceiver, swindler.

umbul I (*M*) grown rapidly, grown up quickly (of children); hypertrophic.

mengumbul to rise rapidly.

umbul II → UMBUT-UMBUT.

umbul III – *air* source of drinking water.

umbul-umbul I (*J/Jv*) long pennon, pennant, banner, tassel.

umbul-umbul II (*J/Jv*) **umbulan** to jump up, bounce up, bump (on a bumpy road), jounce around.

umbul-umbulan (*Jv*) k.o. children's game.

umbul-umbul III – *mérah* k.o. folk art resembling Jakartan *dogér*.

umbun-umbun → UBUN-UBUN I.

umbur → UMBUL I.

umbur-umbur (*M*) scarecrow.

umbut I palm cabbage, edible soft shoot of palm-tree stems. *mencari* – *dalam batu* a hopeless quest. *cari* – *kena buku* to look for the good but get the bad.

mengumbut 1 to remove the shoot of a palm tree. 2 to dig s.t. out, get to the heart of the matter.

terumbut gone/cut, etc. into too deeply.

umbut II mengumbut to pull in (a rope that has been let out, etc.); to withdraw. ~ *hati* to attract, captivate. ~ *nyawa* to kill s.o.

umbut-umbut (*ikan* –) carp, *Dangila cuvieri/lineata.*

umbut-umbutan (*J*) a *rambutan* whose hairy outer skin has been removed, leaving the inner skin.

umega [usaha menambah gaji] *lit* "efforts to increase one's salary," i.e., corruption.

UMGM [Univérsitas Mahapatih Gajah Mada] (Jakarta).

umi I → UMMI I.

umi II → UMMI II.

UMI [Univérsitas Muslim Indonésia] (Ujungpandang).

umiah (*A*) illiteracy.

umik-umik (*Jv*) to recite magic formulas.

UMJ [Univérsitas Muhammadiyah Jakarta] (Jakarta).

UMK [Univérsitas Muria Kudus] (in Kudus).

umm (*A*) mother (in compounds). *umm-al-qura* mother of all cities, i.e., Mecca. *umm-ul-buldan* capital city; *cp* IBU *kota.*

ummat → UMAT.

ummi I (*A*) term of address for one's mother.

ummi II (*A*) illiterate (person); → AMI I, AMMI.

Ummul Mu'minin (*A*) Mother of the Faithful, the title applied to each of Muhammad's wives.

ummulkitab the mother of the Book, i.e., the name given in the Hadis to the first Surah of the Koran.

ummulqura mother of cities, i.e., a title given to Mecca.

umpag-ampig (*J*) **ngumpag-ampigin** to make s.o. unhappy by ordering them around.

umpak I (*J/Jv*) 1 base, foundation, support, pedestal. 2 stone block used as the base of construction.

berumpak with a base/foundation.

mengumpak 1 to provide (pillars with) stone bases. 2 to praise insincerely, flatter.

umpak-umpakan praise, flattery.

pengumpak flatterer.

umpak II (*ob*) **mengumpak-umpak** 1 to run after, chase. 2 to hasten, accelerate, urge that s.t. be done quickly.

umpama (*Skr*) 1 example, model. – *yang dikemukakan kurang tepat.* The example put forth was not to point. *sebagai* – as an example. 2 supposition, assumption, hypothesis. 3 let's say that, supposing that. – *kata* supposing that.

(se)umpamanya for example. *jika* ~*nya* and **umpamakan** suppose, supposing that; for example. *dan yang* ~*nya* and the like, etc.

berumpama to use a simile/example/model; to hypothesize.

mengumpama (*ob*) to respect.

mengumpamai (*ob*) 1 same as, like; to resemble. 2 → MENGU-PAMA(KAN).

mengumpamakan and **memperumpamakan** 1 to compare with. *Batu karang diumpamakan dengan keteguhan hati kita.* Our firmness has been compared to a coral reef. 2 to give/present s.t. as an example. *Ia telah* ~ *bagaimana ia dapat mengélakkan diri dari tikaman pencuri.* He has given us an example of how he could avoid being stabbed by a thief. 3 to suppose, assume, imagine. *Dalam latihan perang itu ada pasukan yang diumpamakan musuh yang hendak menyerang.* In the war games there were troops who were supposed to be the attacking enemy. 4 to use as an example (and so to respect/honor/esteem). *Ia tak betah tinggal di sini, karena merasa dirinya tidak diumpamakan orang.* He isn't comfortable living here because he feels people don't respect him.

perumpamaan 1 parable, metaphor. ~ *kepada* allusion to, a hint at. 2 resemblance, likeness. 3 proverb, maxim, adage. 4 (*infr*) example.

umpan 1 bait, lure. 2 decoy, enticement. 3 prey, victim (of passions). 4 (*coq*) chow, food, fodder (for domestic animals). 5 (soccer) set up, pass. – *lambung* long pass. – *silang* cross/diagonal crosses. – *tarik* cut-in-cross/back pass. 6 material such as seeds put into a machine to be processed. – *habis, ikan tak kena* to carry coals to Newcastle. – *seumpan, kail sebentuk* to be not

fully prepared (for). – *alir* floating bait, trap with live bait for catching crocodiles. – *api* shavings used to create a flame. – *balik* feedback. – *balik biologis* biofeedback. – *golok/harimau/keris* doomed to die a violent death (by a chopper/tiger/dagger). – *meriam* cannon fodder. – *pancing* fish bait. – *peluru* cannon fodder. – *pengolahan* mill head. – *pisau* doomed to die a violent death (by the knife). – *tank* (*mil*) tank mock-up. – *tekak* appetizer, hors d'oeuvres.

berumpan to have bait in it, be baited.

mengumpan to bait, lure, trap, tempt. ~ *ikan dengan cacing* to bait fish with worms. ~ *bola* (soccer) to pass the ball to another player.

mengumpani 1 to feed bait to, feed. 2 to seduce, entice, lure into a trap.

mengumpankan to use as bait, bait with. *Apa yang kauumpankan dalam jebak itu?* What did you bait that trap with?

pengumpan 1 one who uses bait. 2 the passer (in soccer). 3 feeder. ~ *kertas* paper feeder.

pengumpanan feeding.

umpat I 1 false accusation, slander, defamation, backbiting, criticism; curse, cursing, swear word. 2 mockery, ridicule, sneering, derision. 3 anger, irritation. – *tidak membunuh, puji tidak mengéyang* (*M*) pay no attention to criticism or praise.

mengumpat 1 to speak ill of, slander. 2 to abuse, insult, criticize, blame. 3 to swear at, curse.

umpat-mengumpat to insult e.o.

mengumpati to curse at.

umpatan slander, calumny; curse, cursing, verbal abuse.

pengumpat slanderer, backbiter, scandalmonger.

pengumpatan slander, calumny, speaking ill of s.o.

umpat II → UMPET.

umpel-umpelan (*Jv*) jam-packed, chock-full, filled to capacity, bulging out from being overfilled; *cp* SUMPAL, SUMPEL.

umpet (*J/Jv*) *petak* – to play hide-and-(go-)seek.

mengumpet [and **ngumpet** (*coq*)] to hide, lie low, go into hiding. ~ *rahasia* to keep a secret.

mengumpetkan [and **ngumpetin** (*J*)] to hide s.t. ~ *muka* to hide one's face in shame.

umpet-umpetan 1 hide-and-(go-)seek. 2 hidden, concealed, covert. 3 in secret, on the sly.

umpi (*Bat*) family head.

umpiak (*J*) → ÉMPÉR.

umpiang (*J*) *diumpiang* (his wishes) are just carried out.

umpil mengumpil 1 to lever up (with a crowbar, etc.), lift. 2 to paddle without lifting the blade; to row, scull.

pengumpil lever, crowbar.

pengumpilan levering, lifting.

umplek (*J*) → UPLEK.

umpuk (*M*) heap, pile, stack, mass. *se-cabai* a pile of chili peppers.

berumpuk piled up, heaped, stacked; in heaps/piles/stacks.

mengumpukkan to heap up, pile up, stack.

umpun (*ob*) → RUMPUN I.

umput → UMPUK.

umrah (*A*) and **umroh** the so-called lesser pilgrimage to Mecca, which can be performed at any time of year and only includes worship at the *Kaaba* and other shrines adjacent to the Great Mosque; → HAJI *kecil. visa* – visa valid for a two-week trip to Mecca to perform the *umrah.* – *mufradhah* out-of-season *umrah.*

berumrah to perform the "lesser pilgrimage" to Mecca.

umran – *badawi* (*A*) subtribal group.

umrat → UMRAH.

umroh → UMRAH.

UMS [Univérsitas Muhammadiyah Surakarta] (Solo).

umu → UMMI.

umuk (*Jv*) arrogant; to brag, boast, show off.

umum I (*A*) 1 general, common, universal, public, communal. *di depan/muka* – in public, in open court. *anggapan* – public opinion. *bentuk kalimat* – (*ling*) general sentence structure. *dapur* – public/soup kitchen. *gedung-gedung* – public buildings. *ilmu penyakit* – general pathology. *jalan* – public road. *kendaraan* – public transport. *kepentingan* – public interest. – *pemilihan* – general election. *pendapat* – public opinion. *penuntut* – public prosecutor. *rapat* – general/public meeting. *rumah sakit* – general hospital. *télepon* – public telephone. **2** commonly, publicly. *sudah – diketahui* it's public knowledge. **3** common practice, widespread. **4** the public, people (in general). *– telah mengetahui bahwa ...* people know that ... *memberitahukan kepada –* to notify the public.

umumnya in general, generally, on the whole, usually. *diambil ~* generally/broadly speaking. *pada ~* generally, by and large, in general, in a general sense. *... pada khususnya ... pada ~ ...* in particular ... in general. *umat Islam pada khususnya dan manusia lain pada ~* Muslims in particular and other people in general.

seumumnya 1 all of it/them; everything. **2** on the whole, in general, generally.

mengumumkan [and **ngumumin** (*J coq*)] **1** to announce, notify. **2** to declare, proclaim. *~ perang* to declare war. *perang tak diumumkan* an undeclared war. **3** to publish, issue, bring s.t. out into the public, make public.

keumuman generality.

pengumuman 1 announcement, notification. *~ resmi* official notification. **2** declaration, proclamation. *~ perang* declaration of war. **3** publication.

umum II → UMUN.

umumiyah (*A*) maternity.

umun (*M*) not clear yet, still vague, still kept secret.
   berumun to discuss s.t. which is still unclear (or, kept secret).
   mengumun(kan) to keep s.t. a secret.

umur (*A*) **1** age, years old. *–nya berapa?* a) How old is he? b) How old are you? *–nya 20 tahun.* He's 20 years old. *– berapa ia meninggal?* How old was he when he died? *Dia 30 tahun di atas –ku.* He's 30 years older than I am. *Kalau masih ada –, mudah-mudahan kita dapat berjumpa lagi.* If (I'm) still alive, let's hope we can meet again. *Rupanya sesuai dengan –nya.* He looks his age. *kelihatan lebih muda daripada –nya* to look younger than one's age. *–nya sudah tinggi.* He's very old. *dalam – tuanya* in his old age. *(di) bawah –* and *belum cukup/sampai –* underage. *anak di bawah –* a minor. *cukup –* a) adult, grown-up; → AKIL balig, DÉWASA I. b) mature. *sudah lanjut/tinggi –nya* to be of an advanced age. *dimakan –* antiquated, out of date. *panjang/péndék –* long (short-)lived. *Saudara akan panjang –!* Speak of the devil (and he will appear). *sudah sampai –* of age. *untuk segala/sekalian/semua –* for all ages, i.e., for children as well as for adults. *separoh/separuh/setengah –* middle aged. *singkat –* short-lived. *– setahun jagung* still very young (and inexperienced). *– asosiasi kami ini baru setahun jagung.* Our association was established only recently. **2** at the age of. *Ia menikah – delapan belas.* He married at 18. **3** life span. *Panjang –nya.* He had a long life. *ada – ada rejeki* with time comes counsel. *– bermanfaat* useful life. *– harapan hidup* life expectancy. *– pakai* useful life. *– paro/paruh* half life. *– piutang* days receivable. *– rerata* average life. *– tahan* shelf life.

seumur 1 of the same age as; → SEPANTARAN. *teman ~* peer. **2** of the life span of; during (one's lifetime), while still alive. *~ dunia* as old as the world. *~ hidup* lifelong. *~ hidupnya* during his lifetime, as long as he lived. *hukuman ~ hidup* life imprisonment. *dihukum ~ hidup* sentenced to life imprisonment. *Présidén ~ Hidup* [Présmurhi] President for Life (of President Soekarno). *~ jagung* a) a period of 3 to 4 months. b) the 3½-year Japanese occupation of Indonesia. c) a very short period of time. *Pernikahannya dengan A baru ~ jagung.* She married A very recently. *~ jaman* for many years to come. *~ manusia* a lifetime.

seumur-umur lifelong. *profésor bukan gelar ~* professor is not a lifelong title.

seumuran to be the same age as.

berumur 1 to be ... years old. *~ lima puluh tahun* to be 50 years old. **2** to be old/aged; to be an adult. *~ separuh jalan* at the awkward age. *gadis yang belum ~* a young girl. *wanita yang ~* an old woman.

umyeg (*Jv*) /umyek/ and **umyek 1** to be engaged in arguing about/discussing. **2** animated (discussion). *– sekali tanya-jawab* an animated question and answer period.

Unair [Univérsitas Airlangga] (Surabaya).

unak → ONAK.

unam I k.o. sea mollusk, Venus comb, *Murex ternispina*.

unam II beautiful jewel.

Unamét [United Nations Mission in East Timor].

Unand [Univérsitas Andalas] (Padang).

unanim (*D*) unanimous(ly).

Unanti [Univérsitas Tridinanti] (Palembang).

unap mengunap to travel unaccompanied.

Unas [Univérsitas Nasional] (Jakarta).

Unbhara [Univérsitas Bhayangkara] (Surabaya).

Unbo [Univérsitas Bogor] Bogor.

uncal barred cuckoo dove, *Macropygia unchall. – Ambon* slender-billed cuckoo dove, *Macropygia amboinensis*.

uncang cloth slipknot bag used for carrying one's belongings on a trip, travel kit. *– beras* a small bag used to contain rice collected by panhandlers. *– téh* teabag. *– uang* money bag.

uncang-uncang (*J*) to dangle down. *duduk –* to sit with feet dangling. *– kaki* a) to dandle a child on one's feet. b) lazy.

uncang-uncit I to move from one place to another, not stay in one place, be restless.

uncang-uncit II to pay in installments.

Uncén I [Univérsitas Cendrawasih] (Jayapura).

uncén II watchman; → KUNCÉN.

uncit → UNCANG UNCIT II.

uncluk (*J*) **uncluk-uncluk** forthwith, directly (without pause).
   menguncluk and **nguncluk** (*Jv*) to walk without looking to either side.

Uncok [Univérsitas Cokroaminoto] (Yogya).

uncu (*M coq*) youngest, last (of children). *mak –* youngest aunt. *pak –* (shortened to *pak 'cu*) youngest uncle.

uncué and **uncui → HUNCUÉ.**

uncuing (*burung –*) brush cuckoo, rusty-breasted/barred cuckoo, *Cuculus sepulchralis*.

unda clipped form of **bunda**.

undagi (*Jv*) carpenter.
   keundagian and **perundagian** carpentry. *ahli perundagian* builder of traditional houses.

undak I (*Jv*) **1** to climb, ascend, mount; to increase, rise, go up. **2** step, level. *fungsi – héréng* (*math*) slanting step function. **3** to progress, advance, make headway. **4** higher, of a higher order. **5** step, rung (of ladder). *dua –* two steps. **6** (*geol*) terrace. *– kikisan* erosion terrace.
   undak-undak step (of stairs/ladder). **berundak-undak 1** to have stairs/steps. **2** to have stories. **3** wavy.
   berundak(-undak) stepped, terraced.
   mengundakkan (*Jv*) **1** to raise, increase (prices). **2** to increase, grow (of capital through investment, etc.).
   undakan 1 story, floor (of a building); podium, dais, raised platform. **2** stair, step, riser. **3** staircase, stairway, flight of stairs (leading up to a house). *naik –* to go upstairs. **4** terracing (of rice fields). **5** (*Jv*) shoulder (of a road).
   undak-undakan 1 stairs, steps. **2** s.t. one step higher.

undak II mengundak to fail to make headway (of a boat).
   pengundak s.t. that causes a boat to make no headway.

undak-usuk (*S*) language levels.

undaki architecture.

undan I various species of pelicans. *– kacamata* Australian pelican, *Pelecanus conspicillatus. – paruh totol* spot(ted)-billed pelican, *Pelecanus roseus. – putih* great white pelican, *Pelecanus onocrotalus*.

undan II berundan(-undan) to dawdle, dally, take one's time (doing s.t.), linger, loiter; to hang out, sit around.

Undana [Univérsitas Nusa Cendana] (Kupang).

undang I (*Jv*) invite, summon.
   mengundang [and **ngundang** (*coq*)] **1** to invite (s.o. to attend a party, etc.). *~ makan malam* to invite s.o. to dinner. *~ rapat* to call/hold a meeting. **2** to call (to mind). *Pertanyaan itu ~ bayangan tentang satu perkawinan yang diatur orang tua.* That question calls to mind a marriage arranged by one's parents. **3** to summon, send for. *~ dokter* to send for a doctor. **4** to provoke, cause, lead to. *~ kesulitan* to ask/look for trouble. *~ protés* to lead to protests. *~ réaksi* to provoke a reaction. *~ tawa* to provoke laughter.

mengundangi (*pl obj*) to invite, etc.

terundang invited.

undangan 1 invitation. *surat* ~ letter of invitation. ~ *penawaran* invitation to submit a bid. **2** person invited, (invited) guest.

pengundang host (who invites s.o.).

undang II undang-undang law, act, regulation. *rancangan* ~ [RUU] draft law, bill. *melanggar* ~ to break/violate the law. ~ *bagi hasil* production-sharing law. ~ *darurat* emergency regulations. ~ *Dasar* [UUD] Constitution. ~ *féderal* federal law. ~ *gangguan* nuisance law. ~ *hak cipta* copyright act. ~ *hukum pidana* criminal law. ~ *Kerajaan* Kingdom Act. ~ *organik* organic law. ~ *pekaryaan* employment act. ~ *pemilu* election laws. ~ *perburuhan* labor act. ~ *perkawinan* [UUP] marriage act/law. ~ *perniagaan* commercial law. ~ *pokok* outline law (on). ~ *Pokok Agraria* [UUPA] Land Act/Law. **berundang-undang** to have laws. **pengundang-undang** legislator. **perundang-undangan 1** legislation. *penyusun peraturan perundangan* drafter of legislation. **2** legislative, legally constituted. *dalam* ~ statutory. *aturan pidana dalam* ~ statutory penal provisions.

berundang(an) (*M*) *pandai* ~ a) to be thoroughly acquainted with *adat* law. b) eloquent.

mengundangkan to legislate, enact, promulgate.

undangan legislature, legislative. *majelis* ~ legislative council.

pengundangan enactment (of a law), promulgation.

perundangan legislation.

undang III district chief in Malaysia.

UNDAP (*joc*) [Univérsitas Dapur] joking reference to becoming a housewife, an Mrs. degree.

Undapa [Univérsitas Sunda Kelapa] (Jakarta).

Undar I [Univérsitas Darul(-Ulama)] (Jombang).

Undar II [Univérsitas Iskandar] (Ciputat, Jakarta).

undat (*Jv*) **mengundat-undat** to reproach s.o. (about s.t. that happened in the past), dig up old grievances.

unda-unda berunda-unda towed one behind the other; → TUNDA I.

mengunda-unda to tow one behind the other.

unda-usuk (*Jv*) to address and treat s.o. in accordance with his standing in society.

keunda-usukan addressing and treating s.o. in accordance with his standing in society.

undat (*Jv*) **ngundat** to engage in recriminations.

undi lot (in a drawing). *buang* – to cast a lot. *kena* – to win the lottery. *main* – to play the lottery. *membuang* – to cast lots.

berundi to determine by lot, draw lots.

mengundi to draw lots, toss a coin. ~ *suara* to vote.

memperundikan to raffle off.

terundi drawn (of lots).

undian 1 lottery, raffle. ~ *berhadiah* lottery with prizes. ~ *Nalo* national lottery; → NALO. *menarik* ~ a) to win the lottery. b) to draw lots. *nasib di dalam* ~ the fate of s.t. is at stake. ~ *suara* voting. ~ *uang* money lottery. **2** lottery prize.

pengundi s.o. who draws a lot/lottery ticket, winner in a lottery.

pengundian lottery, raffle, drawing by lot.

Undip [Univérsitas Diponegoro] (Semarang).

unduh I (*M*) prohibition sign put up in yards to deter thieves.

unduh II (*Jv infr*) download.

mengunduh and **ngunduh 1** to gather, pick (fruit, etc.). **2** to hunt for (bird's nests). **3** to reap (the results). ~ *mantu* to acquire a son-/daughter-in-law. ~ *pengantin/temantén* to receive the newlyweds (said of the bridegroom's family).

unduk-unduk sea horse, *Hippocampus histrix/guttulatus*.

undung-undung I (*M*) veil (which a woman wears over her head).

berundung-undung to wear such a veil.

mengundung-undungkan to use s.t. as such a veil.

memperundung-undungkan to put (such a veil) over s.o.'s head.

undung-undung II berundung-undung to sob.

undur (*J/Jv*) **1** to go back, retreat, back off, move backward; → MUNDUR. *tidak mau – selangkah* do not want to move back (or, retreat) a single step. **2** to withdraw. **3** to be withdrawn (from circulation).

berundur (*mostly Mal*) to step down, resign.

mengundur to postpone, put off, adjourn, delay, defer. *Dialog ASÉAN-Australia diundur lagi.* Talks between ASEAN and Australia have been postponed again.

mengundurkan [and **ngundurin** (*J coq*)] **1** to set back, put back, back up, move back. *Ia* ~ *mobilnya.* He backed up his car. *Jamnya diundurkan.* He set his watch back. ~ *pembayaran* to delay payment. ~ *rapat itu* to adjourn the meeting. ~ *tanggal* to antedate. **2** to pull back (troops), withdraw (candidacy/ remark, etc.). ~ *pasukan* to pull back troops. ~ *suara* to withdraw one's vote. ~ *diri* a) to resign (one's position), step down. ~ *diri dari jabatannya sebagai ketua* to resign the chairmanship. b) to retire. ~ *diri dari dunia bisnis* to retire from the business world. c) to withdraw. ~ *diri karena alasan keséhatan* to withdraw for health reasons. d) to back out.

mengundur-undurkan to keep on putting back, etc.

pengunduran retreat, withdrawal, resignation, postponement, adjournment, delay, putting off, procrastinating. ~ *diri* a) resignation. ~ *diri Gubernur Maluku disetujui Présidén.* The president has approved the resignation of the governor of the Moluccas. b) withdrawal. ~ *dirinya dari pencalonan* his withdrawal from candidacy. ~ *diri dari gelanggang* withdrawal from the fray. ~ *pembayaran* debt moratorium.

undur-undur (*Jv*) ant-lion, *Emerita spp.*

uneg-uneg /unek-unek/ and **unek-unek** (*Jv*) **1** embitterment, grudge, pent-up anger. **2** to be vindictive/bitter. *Meréka lebih senang membuka –nya kepada wartawan.* They preferred to vent their spleen on the reporters. *mengeluarkan –* and *menyampaikan* **panguneg-uneg** to say what is on one's mind.

Unéj [Univérsitas Negeri Jember] (Jember).

ungah-angih and **ungah-ungah** shaky, wobbly.

ungam mengungam to be delirious.

ungap ungap-ungap panting, gasping for breath.

mengungap-ungap to pant, gasp for breath.

ungar *ikan* – sea perch, *Lutianus argentimaculatus/johnii*.

UNGAT [Univérsitas Gatot] (Mangkoepradja) (Jakarta).

unggah (*infr*) upload.

unggah-ungguh (*Jv*) etiquette.

unggal (*ob*) → TUNGGAL.

unggang-anggit and **unggang-unggit** to bob/go up and down, play on a seesaw.

unggap → UNGGANG-ANGGIT.

unggas fowl. – *angkasa* birds that fly high in the sky.

mengunggas ~ *puding* (*M*) to run away in fear.

perunggasan poultry husbandry.

unggat-unggit → UNGGANG-UNGGIT.

unggis mengunggis to nibble/gnaw at (*esp* mice/rabbits, etc.).

unggit → UNGGAT-ANGGIT.

ungguh-ungguh (*Jv*) manners, etiquette; → BASA-BASI.

ungguk → ONGGOK I.

unggul (*Jv*) **1** excellent, outstanding, superior, choice, the best. *olahragawan yang* – a great athlete. **2** first-class, first-rate, prime. *bibit* – prime seed. *rasa* – feeling of superiority. **3** to be ahead/winning (in an election), win, come out ahead, lead.

mengungguli 1 to surpass, exceed, go beyond, best, do better than. *Ia berhasil* ~ *para penentangnya.* He succeeded in surpassing his opponents. **2** to defeat, beat. *Tim kesebelasan nasional Malaysia diungguli PSSI.* The PSSSI defeated the Malaysian national soccer team. *Tiada siapa yang dapat ~nya.* Nobody can beat him.

unggul-mengungguli to surpass/outdo e.o.

mengunggulkan 1 to raise, elevate. **2** to consider superior, rank high. *Cina diunggulkan di posisi pertama.* China was considered to be in the first position. **3** to seed (of tennis players). *diunggulkan* to be seeded (of tennis players).

mengunggul-unggulkan to show off.

terunggul most superior, the best.

unggulan high-ranking, favored, thought likely to win. *menempatkan peserta* ~ *sesuai dengan préstasinya* to place high-ranking participants according to their achievements. *daftar* ~ *pemain* seeding, placing in rank order of achievement.

unggul-unggulan to compete with e.o. for supremacy.

keunggulan supremacy, eminence, excellence, superiority, advantage, merit. ~ *regu Indonésia atas Cina* the Indonesian team's superiority to the Chinese. ~ *ketrampilan/pengetahuan* superior skill/knowledge. ~ *komparatif* comparative advantage. ~ *kompétitif* competitive advantage. ~ *udara* air superiority.

pengunggulan making s.t. superior, favoring.

unggun 1 pile of wood/logs, etc., stack. *membakar* – to set a pile of wood on fire. **2** campfire, bonfire.

berunggun(-unggun) 1 to pile up, in piles/stacks. **2** to make a campfire.

mengunggun(kan) to pile/stack up (wood).

unggunan pile, heap, stack (of wood, etc.). ~ *api* campfire, bonfire.

unggut → RENGGUT. **berunggut-unggutan** to play tug-of-war.

mengunggut to pull/tug at.

unggutan a tug; tugging.

ungka various species of gibbon, *Hylobates lar/agilis*.

ungkah (*M*) **mengungkah** to loosen, disentangle (one's hair, a fastening, etc.).

ungkai come undone, come off.

mengungkai 1 to untie, loosen. **2** to demolish, wreck (a building). *Rumahnya diungkai polisi*. The police demolished his house. **3** to undo, strip, take off (clothes). **4** to disclose, reveal, uncover (secret/plot, etc.). *Adiknya ~ kekhilafannya*. His brother revealed his mistakes.

terungkai untied, undone, loosened.

ungkaian loosening, release.

pengungkai ~ *rantai* magic charm to loosen chains/handcuffs.

ungkak (*naut*) the space or opening between the two posts where the anchor chain is raised and lowered, hawse pipe. – *dék* chain hole. – *tarik* towing hole.

ungkal stubborn, unwilling to listen to advice.

ungkang-ungkang → ONGKANG-ONGKANG.

ungkang-ungkit → UNGGANG-UNGGIT.

ungkap I mengungkap 1 to pant/gasp for breath.

terungkap-ungkap panting/gasping for breath.

ungkap II (*Jv*) express.

berungkap to express (o.s./one's words).

mengungkap 1 to show/express/vent (one's feelings, etc.). **2** to uncover, unmask, disclose, expose, bring to light, shed light on.

mengungkapi to do research on, check out, scrutinize. ~ *kembali jalan hidupku selama ini* to rethink my life up to now.

mengungkapkan 1 to disclose, reveal, uncover, expose, unveil. **2** to pronounce, utter, relate, state, express.

terungkap 1 expressed, pronounced. **2** unmasked, revealed, disclosed (of a secret). *Kedok rahasianya ~*. His secret was revealed.

ungkapan 1 expression; way of saying s.t. **2** idiom(atic expression). **3** phrase. **4** cliché. **5** disclosure. ~ *data lengkap* full disclosure. ~ *lembut* euphemism. ~ *muka* facial expression. ~ *pelembut* euphemism. ~ *pengeras* emphasizing phrase. ~ *surat-menyurat* epistolary formula.

pengungkap s.o. who uncovers, etc.

pengungkapan 1 disclosure. **2** expressing s.t.

perungkapan expression.

ungkat (*J*) **mengungkat-ungkat** to drag/bring up the past; → MEMBANGKIT-BANGKIT.

ungkat-ungkit repeated oscillating motion.

ungkau night-eagle.

ungkil → UNGKIT.

ungkir → MUNGKIR.

ungkit ungkit-ungkit to go/bob up and down; → UNGGANG-UNG-GIT, UNGKANG-UNGKIT.

mengungkit 1 to lever up, raise, lift, hoist, pry (up/open), jimmy (up/open). ~ *penutup lubang got itu dengan tongkat besi* to pry open the manhole cover with an iron bar. *tidak dapat diungkit dengan besi hangat* inseparably connected to e.o. *hanya selintas diungkit* only touched on in passing, only referred to briefly. **2** to bring s.t. up for discussion, raise (questions); to dig up old grievances or past help in hope of reward. *Jangan ~ perkara lama*. Don't rake up old stories, let bygones be bygones. *Jangan ~ soal itu*. Don't bring that matter up. *Anda tidak perlu ~nya*. Don't rub it in! **3** to raise (a matter for discussion). *Harno tidak pernah ~ uang saku kepada majikannya*. Harno never raised the matter of pocket money with his boss.

mengungkit-ungkit and **mengungkit-ngungkit 1** to bring s.t. up for discussion, raise (questions), rake up (the past). **2** to bob up and down.

terungkit 1 levered up, raised, pried up. **2** raised for discussion.

pengungkit lever. ~ *daun jendéla* window-opener. ~ *katup* valve rocker arm.

pengungkitan leverage, lifting, raising.

ungkluk I (*J*) calf.

ungkluk II (*J*) pile, heap.

ungko → UNGKA.

ungkrak-ungkrak (*J*) **1** to jump up and down (with joy). **2** to mess up, make a mess of.

ungkret (*Jv*) **mengungkret** to shorten, curtail; → MUNGKRET.

ungku → ENGKU.

ungkulan 1 funds. **2** power, ability.

ungkur (*Jv*) **(ber)ungkur-ungkuran 1** back to back. *Kedua rumah itu ~*. The two houses are back to back. **2** to miss e.o., pass e.o. (one leaves before the other arrives, etc.).

mengungkuri to turn one's back on. *Ia selalu ~ anaknya*. He always turned his back on his son; → PUNGKUR.

ungkut-ungkut I (*J*) all bent over.

ungkut-ungkut II coppersmith barbet, *Megalaima haemacephala*.

ungsep (*Jv*) **ngungsep 1** to fall face down. **2** to crash (of airplane). *Pesawat terbang ~ di gunung*. The plane crashed in the mountains.

ungsi (*Jv*) **mengungsi** [and **ngungsi** (*coq*)] to flee (for safety), retreat (from danger), evacuate. *Karena banjir datang penduduk berlarian ~*. Because the flood was rising, the population ran away.

mengungsikan to remove/evacuate s.o. or s.t. from (danger/a threatened area). ~ *anak-istrinya ke Yogya* to evacuate his wife and children to Yogya.

pengungsi refugee, evacuee.

pengungsian 1 evacuation. **2** (place of) refuge, asylum, haven, sanctuary.

ungti (*C*) a giant puppet (a person operates it from the inside); → ONDEL-ONDEL.

ungu purple, violet. *léwat* – ultraviolet. – *muda* violet. – *terung* bluish violet.

mengungu to become/turn purple/violet.

keungu-unguan purplish.

Unhair [Univérsitas "Hairun"] (Ternate).

Unhalu [Univérsitas Halu Oléo] (Kendari).

Unhas [Univérsitas Hasanuddin] (Ujungpandang).

Unhasy [Univérsitas Hasyim Asy'ari] (Jombang).

Unhul [Univérsitas Hulu] (Kendari).

uni I (*M*) older sister.

uni II (*D*) union. – *Afrika Selatan* Union of South Africa. – *Soviét/Sovyét* [US] Soviet Union.

uni III → HUNI.

Uniat [Univérsitas Islam Attahiriyah] (Jakarta Selatan).

Unib [Univérsitas Bengkulu] (Bengkulu).

Unibang [Univérsitas Bangkalan] (Bangkalan).

Unibraw [Univérsitas Brawijaya] (Malang).

Unida [Univérsitas Djuanda] (Bogor).

Unidayan [Univérsitas Dayanu (Ikhsanuddin)] (Buton).

uniférsum (*D*) universe.

unifikasi (*D*) unification.

terunifikasi unified.

uniform (*D*) **1** (*pakaian* –) uniform (of clothes); → SERAGAM. **2** uniform (in appearance, etc.).

beruniform to wear a uniform; uniformed.

menguniformkan to make uniform, standardize.

penguniforman uniformizing, uniformization, standardization.

uniformisasi (*E*) and **penguniformisasian** uniformization.

uniformitas uniformity.

Unigha [Univérsitas (Jabal) Ghafur] (Pidie, Aceh).

Unija [Univérsitas Indonésia Jakarta] (Jakarta).

unik I (*D*) unique, sole.

keunikan 1 uniqueness. **2** s.t. which is unique.

Unik II [Univérsitas Kediri] (Kediri).

Unika Atma Jaya (*acr*) [Univérsitas Katolik Atma Jaya] (Jakarta).

Unika Soegijapranata (*acr*) [Univérsitas Katolik Soegijapranata] (Semarang).

Unikal [Univérsitas Pekalongan] (Pekalongan).

unikameral (*D*) unicameral.

Unikapar [Univérsitas Katolik Parahiyangan] (Bandung).

Unikass [Univérsitas Kiansantang Siliwangi] (Bandung).

unikum (*D*) s.t. or an action which is unique.

Unila [Univérsitas Lampung] (Lampung).

Unilak [Univérsitas Lancang Kuning] (Pekanbaru).

unilateral (*D*) unilateral.

Unima [Univérsitas Mahadjaja] (Jakarta).

Uninus [Univérsitas Islam Nusantara] (Bandung).

Unipa [Univérsitas Paderi] (Jakarta).

uniporem → UNIFORM.

Uni Raya [Univérsitas Palangka Raya] (Palangka Raya).

Unis [Univérsitas Islam Sjéch (Jusuf)] (Jakarta).

Unisba [Univérsitas Islam Bandung] (Bandung).

uniséks (*D/E*) unisex.

Unisemar [Univérsitas Sebelas Maret] (Jakarta).

Uniskar [Univérsitas Islam Kalimantan] (Banjarmasin).

Unisma [Univérsitas Islam Malang] (Malang).

Unismu [Univérsitas Mu(h)ammadiyah].

Unisula [Univérsitas Islam Sultan Agung] (Semarang).

unit (*E*) /yunit or unit/. 1 unit, constituent, member, part, section. 2 unit (of measure), quantity. - *Gawat Darurat* Intensive Care Unit, ICU (in a hospital). - *kegiatan mahasiswa* [UKM] student club, student extracurricular activity. - *kesatuan* unit. - *kesediaan* stock-keeping unit. - *Pelaksana Téknis Dinas* [UPTD] Technical Implementing Service Unit (of the government). - *pembidikan* aiming/sighting device. - *pencatatan* event logger.

unitarisme (*D*) unitarism.

univérsal (*E*) universal.

   menguniversalkan to make universal.

   keuniversalan universality.

univérsalisme (*D*) universalism.

univérsalitas universality.

univérse (*E*) universe.

universil (*D*) universal.

univérsitas (*D*) university. - *di kampung* (*coq*) small regional university. - *Terbuka* [UT] Open University.

   beruniversitas to attend a university.

   keuniversitasan university (*mod*). *kalangan* ~ university circles.

universitér (*D*) university (*mod*).

universitit (*ob*) → UNIVÉRSITAS.

Unizar [Univérsitas Islam al-Azhar] (Jakarta).

Unja [Univérsitas Jambi] (Jambi).

unjai → UNYAI.

Unjam I [Univérsitas Jambi] (Jambi).

unjam II → HUNJAM.

unjam III palm fronds anchored at sea to attract fish.

Unjaya [Univérsitas Jayakarta] (Jakarta).

unjuk I - *ber(i)tahu/periksa* (*coq*) to inform, notify, announce, let know. - *yang tidak diberikan* to go back on one's word, break a promise.

   mengunjuk 1 to extend, stretch/hold out one's hand, stick out (the tongue, etc.), put out (the flag, etc.). 2 to hand over, hand-deliver. *"Ini surat dari pacarmu," Santo* ~. "This is a letter from your girlfriend," said Santo, handing it over.

   mengunjukkan 1 to extend, hold/put out (one's hand). *Ketika ditanya hanya dua orang yang* ~ *tangannya*. When asked, only two persons held out their hands. 2 to deliver (with outstretched hand), hand over, hand-deliver. ~ *surat permohonan* to hand-deliver a petition.

   pengunjuk sepengunjuk ~ *tangan* as far as the hand can reach.

   pengunjukan presentation, handing over, extending (the hand, etc.).

unjuk II → TUNJUK. - *gigi* (*coq*) to show one's fangs, treat angrily, show hostility. - *kekuatan* show of force. - *kerja* working method, performance. - *muka* to appear (before a high-ranking person/official, etc.). - *otot* to flex one's muscles. - *rasa/*

perasaan demonstration. *melakukan/melancarkan/mengadakan - rasa/perasaan* to demonstrate, hold a demonstration. *aksi - perasaan* activities during a demonstration. - *upaya* showdown.

   berunjuk ~ *(pe)rasa(an)* to demonstrate.

   mengunjuk 1 to point toward, indicate. ~ *rumah yang kosong dengan telunjuknya* to point toward a vacant house with one's index finger. 2 to show, indicate. 3 to appoint (to a position), designate (to a function). 4 to raise one's hand/one's index finger asking to be called on, etc. *Siapa yang tahu jawabnya hendaklah* ~. Those who know the answer please raise their hand. 5 to show one's feelings. ~ *perasaan* to demonstrate (against s.t.). 6 ~ *kepada* to refer to; → MERUJUK/MENGACU *kepada*. 7 to point to, put forward as proof. *Ia* ~ *pasal 10 sebagai dasar tindakannya itu*. He pointed to article 10 as the basis of his action.

   mengunjukkan to show, point out, display, exhibit.

   unjukan indication.

   pengunjuk s.o. who shows/displays, bearer (of a bond). ~ *rasa* demonstrator.

   pengunjukan sign, indication, clue. *Ada* ~ *bahwa dia terlibat dalam pembunuhan itu*. There are signs that he was implicated in the murder.

unjuk III (*Jv*) **munjuk** to inform/tell s.o. respectfully about s.t.

   mengunjukkan to offer/address/give notice of (in the address of a letter to a high-ranking person).

unjuk IV (*Jv*) **mengunjuk** to have (a respected person) drink s.t. **(unjuk-)unjukan** /unju'an/ beverage, drink (of a respected person).

unjul (*A*) badger.

unjun mengunjun to thrust out/pay out (hand/line, etc.) and then pull back firmly.

unjung I → KUNJUNG I.

unjung II → UNJUK I.

unjur belunjur stretched out, outstretched, extended (of legs). *duduk* ~ to sit with outstretched legs. *belum duduk* ~ *dahulu* to count one's chickens before they are hatched.

   mengunjur 1 to stretch out (in the grass, etc.). 2 (to lie) stretched out, at one's ease. 3 with outstretched legs.

   mengunjurkan 1 to stretch out (one's legs). 2 to have s.o. lie with outstretched legs.

   terunjur stretched out.

   unjuran foot (of a bed, table, etc.).

unjut (*M*) bundle made with a square piece of cloth the four ends of which are tied together in a knot.

   mengunjutkan to wrap up in such a bundle.

Unklab [Univérsitas Klabat] (Air-Madidi, Sulut).

Unkris [Univérsitas Krisnadwipayana] (Jakarta).

unku → UNGKA.

Unlam [Univérsitas Lambung Mangkurat] (Banjarmasin).

Unmad [Univérsitas Madura] (Pamekasan).

Unmer [Univérsitas Merdéka] (Malang).

Unmirham [Univérsitas Amir Hamzah] (Medan).

Unmu [Univérsitas Muhammadiyah].

Unmul [Univérsitas Mulawarman] (Samarinda).

Unpad [Univérsitas Padjadjaran] (Bandung).

Unpadip [Univérsitas Pangéran Diponegoro](Jakarta).

Unpak [Univérsitas Pakuan] (Bogor).

Unpal [Univérsitas Palémbang] (Palembang).

Unpar I [Univérsitas (Katolik) Parahiyangan] (Bandung).

Unpar II [Univérsitas Palangka Raya] (Palangka Raya).

Unpas [Univérsitas Pasundan] (Bandung).

Unpatti [Univérsitas Pattimura] (Ambon).

Unram [Univérsitas Mataram] (Ampenan).

Unri [Univérsitas Riau] (Pekan Baru).

UNS Semar [Univérsitas Negeri Surakarta Sebelas Maret] (Surakarta).

UNS (*init*) [Univérsitas Negeri Sebelas (Maret)] (Surakarta).

Unsa [Univérsitas Sawerigading] (Makassar).

Unseb [Univérsitas Semarak Bengkulu] (Bengkulu).

Unsil [Univérsitas Siliwangi] (Bandung).

Unsila [Univérsitas Pancasila] (Jakarta).

Unsoed [Univérsitas Negeri (Jénderal) Soedirman] (Purwokerto).

Unsrat [Univérsitas Sam Ratulangi] (Manado).

Unsri [Univérsitas Sriwijaya] (Palembang).

unsur (*A* singular of *anasir*) **1** element, substance (of which s.t. is made), component. **2** element, member (of a group). –.– *pemerintah* members of the government. **3** item, particulars. – *gramatikal* (*ling*) grammatical item. **4** (*leg*) count (in a prosecutor's charge). –.– *bantuan tempur* (*mil*) combat support elements. – *abus* trace element. – *budaya* cultural element. – *hara* nutritive element. – *kebudayaan* → UNSUR budaya. – *kimia* chemical element. – *léksikal* (*ling*) lexical item. – *pembangun* constituent element. – *pengaman* security feature. – *perasaan* emotional element. – *perdagangan* commercial element. – *perselisihan* controversial point, point at issue, question in dispute. – *perunut* trace element. – *polusi* pollutant. – *radioaktif* radioactive element. – *runut(an)* trace element.

 berunsur with/to have a(n) ... element, with ... as component. *Pencurian paku rél KA tak* ~ *subvérsi.* The theft of railroad rivets had no elements of subversive activity in it.

 berunsurkan to have ... as an element/component/member. ~ *agama Hindu* to have elements of the Hindu religion in it.

 mengunsuri to be the constituents of.

Unsuri [Univérsitas Sunan Giri] (Malang).

unsuri(ah) (*A*) elementary, elemental.

Unswagati [Univérsitas Swadaya Gunung Jati] (Cirebon).

Unsyiah [Univérsitas Syiah (Kuala)] (Banda Aceh).

unta I (*Hind Skr*) camel, *Camelus spp. – Arab* dromedary, one-humped camel. – *Asia Tengah* Bactrian camel, two-humped camel. – *berpunuk satu* one-humped camel, *Camelus dromedarius.*

unta II *burung –* ostrich, cassowary, *Struthio camelus.*

Untad [Univérsitas Tadulako] (Palu).

Untaét [United Nations Transitional Authority for East Timor].

Untag [Univérsitas Tujuhbelas Agustus] (Semarang).

untai 1 thread, string, lace, strand (*esp* of beads, etc.). **2** numeral classifier for objects occurring in a string or strands, such as necklaces, rosaries, etc. *tiga – kalung mutiara* three pearl necklaces.

 beruntai → MENGUNTAI. *pélor* ~ ammunition belt.

 beruntaian 1 to dangle, hang down loosely. **2** (to hang) on strings/skeins/hanks.

 beruntaikan with ... dangling/hanging down loosely. *sebuah peti jenazah* ~ *kembang-kembang anggrék* a coffin with garlands of orchids hanging loosely over it.

 menguntai 1 to string (beads, etc.) on string. **2** to dangle, hang down (loosely).

 menguntaikan to string out (a long story).

 teruntai hung, suspended.

 untaian 1 string, chain, garland. **2** series. **3** couplet, stanza. **4** (*ling*) string. **5** (*elec infr*) circuitry.

 penguntai s.t. that strings together s.t.

untal I 1 pellet. **2** pill, tablet.

 menguntal to roll/make pills.

 menguntal-untal to wad up into a ball.

untal II (*Jv*) **menguntal 1** to swallow whole. *Ular* ~ *ayam.* A snake swallowed a chicken whole. ~ *pil* to take a pill. **2** to stuff o.s., eat voraciously. **3** to annex, take over, swallow up. *Vésted interests* ~ *pabrik.* Vested interests swallow up factories.

untal III teruntal-untal dangling and swaying (of female breasts, etc.).

Untan [Univérsitas Tanjungpura] (Pontianak).

untang-anting dangling and swaying.

Untar [Univérsitas Tarumanagara] (Jakarta).

Untid [Univérsitas Tidar] (Magelang).

until I menguntil to dangle, hang down.

 teruntil-until to dangle, sway.

until II → UNTAL I.

Untim [Univérsitas Timtim] (Dili).

unting I 1 classifier for things that are tied together at one end, such as fringes, skeins, hanks, etc. *tiga – benang emas* three hanks of gold thread. **2** strand. – *rambut* strand of hair.

 unting-unting fringes on a kite.

 berunting stranded, with strands.

 untingan bunch of things tied together at one end, strand.

unting II mengunting to plumb, sound (depths).

 unting-unting 1 (plumb line with) plumb (bob). **2** (*naut*) fairlead. **3** sight (on a gun).

untir (*Jv*) → PUNTIR. *gelang –* a plaited bracelet.

 menguntir 1 to plait. **2** to hold s.t. firmly and twist it.

 teruntir sprained, twisted.

Untirta [Univérsitas Tirtayasa] (Banten).

untit (*J/Jv*) **nguntit** to hide or take s.t. little by little.

untu (*Jv*) tooth.

untuk 1 (*ob*) allotted share. **2** set aside/intended/meant for. *Tanah sawah ini – adikmu.* This rice field is for your brother. **3** (to be used) for, to (be used for). *ruang – bekerja* a room for working in, study. *uang – membeli makan* money to buy food with, money for buying food. – *anak-anak/ibu* (*euph*) a bribe. **4** (to be used) as, in order to, for the purpose of. *Peti ini dipakai – méja.* This box was used as a table. *Ditumbuknya kulit kayu itu halus-halus – obat.* He pulverized the bark for medicine. – *diketahui* for announcement. **5** (with the intention) of, to. *Saya terlalu takut – lari.* I'm too afraid to run away. **6** to (be given/sent). *Ayahnya telah mengirim uang kuliah – anaknya yang pria.* The father has sent college tuition to his son. **7** in order (to be able) to (do s.t.). – *memahami keadaan sekarang* in order to understand the current situation. **8** for (a span of time). – *beberapa bulan* for several months; → SELAMA.

 beruntuk 1 to have one's share. **2** to be determined (of respective shares). *harta peninggalannya telah* ~ the respective shares of the estate have been determined.

 menguntukkan and **memperuntukkan** to allot, assign, apportion, dole/parcel out, allocate to, set aside (for), zone (land). *Pemerintah telah* ~ *tanah itu bagi para transmigran.* The government has allotted the land to the transmigrants. *Panitia* ~ *seluruh hasil malam dana kepada sebuah yayasan.* The committee has allocated the entire proceeds of the charity evening to a foundation.

 teruntuk intended/destined/used for.

 peruntukan 1 allocation. **2** allotment. *pemantapan* ~ *tanah* land consolidation.

untuk-untuk (*J*) **1** to go or come in secret. **2** and then, right away. *Dié dateng – makan.* He came and then ate.

untun → RUNTUN I, II.

untung 1 fate, destiny, lot. *mengadu –* to try one's luck, chance one's fate. – *jahat/malang* bad luck. **2** to be fortunate/in luck, lucky. – *akan celaka* as ill luck would have it. **3** profit, gain. *mendapat banyak –* to make a lot of money. – *bersih/kotor* net/gross profit. **4** use, benefit, profit, advantage. *Kita tidak akan mendapat – apa-apa dengan menganiaya orang lain.* We won't get the slightest advantage by mistreating others. *paling –* under the best of circumstances. – *ada tuah tiada* easy come, easy go. *ada yang –, ada yang buntung* one man's meat is another man's poison. *mau – jadi buntung* for wanting too much all was lost. – *sabut timbul, – batu tenggelam* nobody can escape his fate. – *sepanjang jalan, malang sekejap mata* great accidents spring from small causes. – *baik* good fate. – *batu* the fate of stones (is to sink in the water), i.e., to have bad luck. – *besar* big profit, to do well financially. – *buntungnya* the way it turns/turned out. – *malang* a) fate, destiny, lot. b) adversity, bad luck. – *nasib* adventures. – *rugi* a) profit and loss. b) advantages and disadvantages. c) pros and cons. – *sabut* the fate of husks (is to float on water), i.e., to have good luck, always prospering. – *séro* dividend. – *terselubung* patronage dividend.

 untungnya fortunately, luckily. *sudah* ~ *begitu* it is foreordained for him, it is his fate.

 untung-untung 1 perhaps, maybe, possibly, who knows?, one might be lucky (speaker hopes and believes that the result will be positive); *cp* JANGAN-JANGAN. *Pergilah cepat-cepat,* ~ *masih ada tempat yang kosong.* Go right away, maybe, if you're lucky, there is still a vacant seat. *Tak apalah saya tertipu,* ~ *memberi sedekah.* It doesn't matter if I'm cheated; if I'm lucky, I'll give s.t. to charity.

 seuntung to have the same fate as, be in the same boat as.

 seuntung-untungnya under the best of circumstances, no matter how profitable; not exceeding, no more than.

beruntung 1 lucky, fortunate. *Siapa ~, dialah menang.* The lucky person will win. *kalau ~* with luck. 2 to profit by, to make a profit on. 3 successful, prosperous, helpful, advantageous. *tidak ~* unlucky. **ketidak-beruntungan** bad luck, misfortune. **seberuntung** as lucky as. **keberuntungan** chance, (good) fortune/luck.

beruntung-untung to try one's luck.

menguntungi *~ uang orang* to use s.o. else's money to make a profit.

menguntungkan [and **nguntungin** (*J coq*)] 1 to produce benefits; to benefit, be beneficial for, favorable to; favorable, beneficial. *keadaan yang ~* a favorable situation. *~ diri sendiri* to serve one's own purposes, forward one's own ends. *tidak ~* unfavorable. 2 to yield profits, (be) profitable/advantageous, makes money. *usaha yang sangat ~* a highly profitable business.

untung-untungan 1 to take a chance, risk one's luck. *Meskipun belum siap, dengan sikap ~, dia menempuh ujian itu.* Even though he wasn't ready yet, he took a chance and took the exam. 2 at random, on the off chance, aleatory.

keuntungan 1 profit, gain, yield, revenue; fee. *mencari ~* to seek a profit/gain. *pembagian ~* revenue sharing. *~ cepat* short-term gain. *~ modal* capital gain. *~ sesaat* (*fin*) hit-and-run profit taking. *~ yang ditahan* retained profits. *~ yang melimpah* a bonanza. 2 benefit, gain, advantage. *memberi ~ kepada dirimu* beneficial for you. 3 fortune, chance, luck. *~ besar bagimu kalau dapat diangkat menjadi karyawan bank.* It would be a piece of good luck if you could be appointed to a position in the bank. *mengambil ~ kepada* to profit by. 4 to make a profit on.

peruntungan destiny, fate, lot. *melihat ~* to have one's fortune told through astrology, consult the stars.

untut elephantiasis, beriberi in the form of swelling of the lower limbs. *kaki ~* a leg swollen from elephantiasis. *kaki ~ dipakaikan gelang* it suits you as a saddle suits a sow, i.e., it's completely wrong for you.

Unud [Univérsitas Udayana] (Denpasar).

unun (*S*) **mengunun** to smoke (over a fire).

unus → HUNUS.

Unwar [Univérsitas Warmadéwa] (Denpasar).

Unwiku [Univérsitas Wijaya Kusuma] (Purwokerto).

Unwira [Univérsitas Widya Mandira] (Kupang).

unyai (*M*) soft, tender (of meat).

berunyai(-unyai) 1 (to do a job) very slowly. 2 little by little, gradually.

mengunyi to slacken, slow down (one's work).

unyeng (*Jv*) k.o. roulette game consisting of a black disk with numbers running from 1 to 24 along its perimeter. A needle is attached to the outside edge and the disk is spun around. The winning player is paid 12 times his bet.

unyeng-unyeng (*J*) → UNYENG. 2 (*Jv*) → PUSAR *rambut*.

ngunyeng-nguyeng 1 to pull and twist. 2 to go round and round looking for s.t.

unyi → HUNI.

unyil 1 boy. 2 (*si ~*) name of a popular puppet on TV. 3 small and cute.

unying-unyingan (*J*) to feel restless (in mind or body).

Unzah [Univérsitas Zainul Hasan] (Probolinggo).

uok a form of address to young children.

u.p. (*abbr*) [untuk perhatian] for the attention of (in correspondence), att.

upa- I and **upa** (*Skr*) a prefix or word meaning: below, lower than, assistant, deputy, under-, sub-. *~ guru besar* associate professor.

upa II gift.

mengupa-upa to give a gift.

upaboga (*Skr*) (*ob*) food, meal, daily bread. *seni ~* gastronomy, culinary art.

upacara (*Skr*) 1 ceremony, ritual. *dengan ~* ceremoniously. *memberikan hadiah tanpa/tidak dengan ~* to present an award unceremoniously. *pakaian ~* full dress (uniform). 2 regalia. 3 state equipment for s.o.'s personal use assigned to him as a token of his high rank; includes umbrella, betel nut box, mat, spittoon, box with smoking utensils, etc. 4 honor, homage. *~ adat* traditional ceremony, ceremony which follows traditional law. *~*

bendéra flag ceremony. *~ bersih désa* (*Jv*) cleaning up a village from evil spirits, powers and misfortunes. *~ ngruwet* (*Jv*) ritual to ward off evil. *~ pelantikan* inaugural ceremony. *~ pelepasan* farewell ceremony. *~ pembukaan* opening ceremony. *~ perkawinan/pernikahan* wedding ceremony. *~ Wis(h)uda Para* (in the Air Force) Wing Day.

mengupacarai 1 to pay homage to. 2 to make s.t. official with a ceremony, officialize.

mengupacarakan to hold a ceremony for, celebrate s.t.

upaduta (*Skr*) envoy extraordinary (ranking below an ambassador).

upah 1 wages, salary, fee, compensation for services rendered, pay(ment for services), labor (costs). *asal diberi ~* for a fee. 2 commission. 3 gratuity, tip. 4 reward, premium. *Itulah ~ nya!* Serves you right! *daftar ~* payroll. *kenaikan ~* wage increase, raise. *makan/mengambil ~* a) to be paid. b) to be a wage earner. c) to take bribes. *pajak ~* (*Jv*) income tax. *~ angkutan* freight. *~ basi kerja* overtime pay. *~ bersih* net pay. *~ borongan* piece wages. *~ bulanan* monthly wages. *~ dasar* base pay. *~ harian* daily wages. *~ hati* s.o. that comforts o., comforter. *~ jahit* seamstress's wages. *~ jam-jaman* hourly wage. *~ (kerja) lembur* overtime pay. *~ mingguan* weekly wages. *~ minimum* minimum wage. *~ minimum régional* [UMR] regional minimum pay. *~ natura* payment in kind. *~ nyata* real wages. *~ pelaksanaan* handling fee. *~ pengangkutan* freight. *~ penolongan/pertolongan* rescue charges. *~ perangsang* incentive award. *~ pokok* base pay. *~ prémi* bonus. *~ tahunan* annual salary. *~ tahunan terjamin* guaranteed annual salary. *~ tempa-uang* mintage. *~ terutang* back pay, accrued wages. *~ tulis* administrative fee/charge. *~ yang dibawa pulang* take-home pay.

berupah 1 to receive payment/wages, be paid. 2 to have a salary, get paid for doing s.t. *belum ~* not yet paid/rewarded (for doing s.t.).

mengupah to hire, employ, engage. *Perusahaan itu ~ beberapa pekerja untuk mengecat gedungnya.* The company hired several workers to paint the building.

mengupahi to pay a fee (wages/commission, etc.) to.

mengupahkan to hire, have s.o. perform a task/carry out s.t. for pay/a fee; to pay s.o. to make s.t. *Ayah ~ orang itu untuk memotong rumput.* Father hired that man to cut the grass.

upahan 1 (= *orang ~*) wage earner, hired man. 2 wage, fee, payment. *pajak ~* (*Jv*) income tax. 3 paid. *kerja ~* paid work.

pengupah employer.

pengupahan payment, fee, remuneration.

perupahan (*mod*) pay, wage.

upajiwa (*Jv*) livelihood, means of support.

mengupajiwa to earn one's living.

upak mengupak 1 to stir smoldering ashes. 2 to stir up old quarrels; → OPAK II.

upakarti (*Skr*) (*penghargaan ~*) a government award for helping, guiding, promoting, and developing small-scale industries and handicrafts.

upal [uang palsu] counterfeit money.

upam (*Tam*) **mengupam** to polish, shine, burnish, make smooth and shiny by rubbing. *~ piala-piala pérak* to polish silver trophies.

terupam polished, shined (up) (of metal), burnished.

upaman 1 polished, shined (up). 2 s.t. polished. 3 polishing.

pengupam 1 polish (substance used for polishing). 2 polisher, person who polishes.

pengupaman polishing.

upama → UMPAMA.

upan k.o. bird, sultan tit, *Melanochlora sultanea*.

Upancas [Univérsitas Pancasila] (Jakarta).

upanisada (*Skr*) sermon, preaching.

upanisat (*Skr*) (Buddhist) religious lecture.

upar mengupar(kan) to make a ball out of leaves, dough, etc. by rolling it between the palms.

upas I (*Jv*) 1 (*pohon ~*) a tree, bark cloth tree, *Antiaris toxicaria*. 2 poison made from this tree. *makan ~ berulam racun* misfortunes do not come singly.

upas-upasan *~ uler* a) caterpillar toxin. b) place where the caterpillar sheds its skin.

mengupasi (ob) to poison by using this toxin.

upas II → OPAS.

upat I → UMPAT I.

upat II torpedo grass, *Panicum repens*.

upau (C) bead purse worn on the belt.

upaya I (*Skr*) 1 means/efforts to achieve a goal. *tiada* – cannot find the means to do it. 2 contrivance, expedient, remedy; → DAYA-UPAYA. *– administratif* administrative remedy. *– bantahan* (*leg*) defense. *– hukum* legal remedy. *– paksa* forcible means. *– pengamanan* seizure before judgment. *– tangkisan* legal defense.

seupaya-upayanya and *seberapa* upayanya as much as one is able to; to the best of one's ability, do one's best.

berupaya to make an effort (to do s.t.), do one's best/utmost to, try to; to exert o.s., take pains.

mengupayakan to make an effort to (do s.t.), seek to, strive for, take steps to, attempt (to achieve s.t.).

terupaya enabled. *tidak* ~ disabled.

Upaya II [Univérsitas Pangéran Jayakarta] (Jakarta).

UPB (*init*) [Univérsitas Patriot] (Bekasi).

upet (*J/Jv*) wick/fuse made of a coconut-blossom sheath; used for lighting cigarettes, as a torch, etc.;→ TALI *api*.

upeti (*Skr*) 1 tribute (paid by a subject to those in authority or by a subject people to their conquerors). 2 (*coq*) bribe paid to a higher-up; → UANG *pelicin*.

upeti(i)sme the practice of a subordinate giving a tip or bribe to his superior in order to please him and buy his favor.

upgrade (*E*) /apgrét/ upgrade; → TATAR.

mengupgrade to upgrade.

pengupgradean upgrading.

upgrading (*E*) /apgréding/ upgrading.

UPI [Univérsitas Pembangunan Indonésia] (Jakarta).

upi(a)h *burung* – a) milky stork, *Ibis cinereus*. b) painted stork, *Ibis leucocephalus*.

upih spathe, sheath of the spadix of the unexpanded fruit of certain palms. *– cabang* rameal sheath. *– jatuh* the old die first.

mengupih faded (of colors).

upih-upih → UPI(A)H.

upik (*M*) *si* – affectionate term of address for a young girl; *cp* SI *buyung*. *si* – *jantan* tomboy. *belum tentu* – *si buyungnya* the outcome is still up in the air.

upil I (*J/Jv*) 1 dried nasal mucus/snot. 2 scab.

mengupil [and ngupil (*coq*)] 1 to pick one's nose. 2 to form a scab.

upil II (*J*) seupil an insignificant amount (of money, etc.). *bantuan* ~ a ridiculously small amount of aid.

upleg → UPLEK.

uplek 1 (*J*) very busy, overburdened with work. 2 (*S*) noisy, boisterous.

uplek-uplekan completely tied up in s.t., very occupied with some activity.

uplik (*J*) tool for making holes in shoes, belts, etc.

UPN (*init*) [Univérsitas Pembangunan Nasional] (Yogya).

upruk (in East Java) prostitute; → PELACUR.

UPTD [Unit Pelaksana Téknis Dinas] Technical Implementing Service Unit (of the government).

upuk → UFUK.

uqba (*A*) end reward or punishment; the life to come.

uqubah (*A*) punishment.

urab → URAP II.

urah I (*M*) mengurah to pull down, destroy, demolish.

urah II mengurah to narrate, recount, tell.

urai 1 not solid, not compact. *emas* – gold dust. 2 loose, not tied together, apart, asunder, decompose(d). *ilmu* – anatomy. *– sendi* dislocation. 3 to scatter, disperse.

urai-uraian strands, pieces.

berurai to be open/detached/unfastened/separated, fall apart; to be liberated/freed/released/spread apart; to let s.t. flow, disperse. ~ *air mata* a) to weep. b) to express one's sorrow.

berurai *keringat* ~ the sweat was pouring off him.

mengurai 1 to get/come loose, loosen, become untangled, get detached/unfastened, etc., relax. *Gadis itu* ~ *rambutnya*. The girl let down her hair. ~ *ketegangan otot* to relax one's muscles. 2 to let s.t. (hang) down. 3 to expand, open up. *mayang* ~ an

unfolding spadix/palm blossom. 4 → MENGURAIKAN. ~ *sila* to get up and go.

menguraikan 1 to let (one's hair) hang down. 2 to untie, undo (a knot, etc.); to unravel. ~ *benang* to untangle thread. ~ *borgol* to break the fetters. ~ *simpul* to untie/undo a knot. 3 to break (a contract/promise, etc.). ~ *janji* to break a promise. ~ *nikah* (*M*) to divorce one's spouse. 4 to break/split (s.t. into its constituent parts). *Air dapat diuraikan menjadi hidrogén dan oksigén.* Water can be split into hydrogen and oxygen. 5 to explain, expound on, elucidate, set forth. ~ *pendirian partainya* to explain his party's position. 6 to analyze, examine closely. 7 to let flow; → BERURAI.

terurai 1 hanging down loosely. *Rambutnya* ~. Her hair was hanging loosely. 2 knocked down into component parts, completely knocked down, CKD. *setrika listrik dalam keadaan* ~ knocked-down electric irons. 3 can be decomposed/unraveled. 4 loose, scattered. 5 to break down (into component parts). keteruraian decomposability.

uraian 1 explanation, account, clarification. 2 description. ~ *pekerjaan* job description. 3 (*anat*) dissection. 4 analysis, breakdown, details. ~ *lebih jauh* further details. ~ *tugas* job breakdown. 5 (*Ling*) parsing. ~ *kalimat* sentence parsing.

urai-uraian loose pieces.

pengurai 1 analyzer. 2 dissector. 3 chemical used for decomposing, decomposer.

penguraian 1 analyzing. 2 dissecting. 3 decomposition.

peruraian dissociation, disentanglement.

urak → ORAK.

urakan (*Jv*) 1 boorish, ill-mannered. 2 eccentric. *orang* – a) rabble, hoi polloi, populace. b) boorish person. *kaum* – literary group of the 1970s.

urakanisme anti-elitist movement.

urang I (*M S*) → ORANG I. *– awak* the Minangkabau people (term they use for themselves). *– rantau* people from Padang, West Sumatra. *– sumando* a non-Minangkabau man married to a Minangkabau woman; *cp* ANAK *pisang*.

urang II *kayu* – a tree species with hard timber, *Erythroxylon cuneatum*.

urang-aring 1 (*S*) k.o. herb, *Pouzolzia zeylanica*. 2 (*Jv*) an herbaceous plant, *Ecliptica alba/prostata*, source of a black stain used to color the hair; the plant's juice is used as a hair tonic and as medicine for worms, dental ailments, and respiratory problems.

uran-uran → URO-URO.

uranium (*D*) uranium.

uranologi (*E*) uranology.

Uranus (*D*) 1 the god Uranus. 2 the planet Uranus.

urap I 1 ointment, unguent, liniment, salve, cream; a perfumed cosmetic. 2 (*med*) smegma.

berurap-urap(an) to rub ointment on o.s., scent o.s. with perfume.

mengurap(i) to rub ointment, etc. on.

mengurapkan 1 to apply (an ointment, etc.) to the body. 2 to use s.t. to rub with. *Saputangan itu diurapkannya ke muka wanita itu.* He rubbed the woman's face with a handkerchief.

urapan 1 (*rel*) ordination, consecration. ~ *imamat suci* ordination to the priesthood. 2 ointment, liniment, unguent, cream.

urap-urapan ointment, liniment, salve, unguent, cream.

pengurapan anointing.

urap II (*Jv*) 1 a miscellaneous mixture. 2 grated coconut mixed with spices and vegetables. *ketan* – cooked glutinous rice mixed with grated coconut and spices. *– sari* a) a mixture of various kinds of flowers. b) miscellany.

urap-urap → URAPAN.

mengurap 1 to mix a variety of things. 2 to mix s.t. with grated coconut and spices.

urapan 1 medley, hodgepodge, jumble. 2 salad of mixed vegetables, vegetables used to make this salad.

uras (*M*) 1 curative/healing ointment, liquid embrocation. 2 (*ob*) healthy, sane, sound; recovered, cured, healed.

beruras 1 to be rubbed with this ointment. 2 cured, healed. ~ *hati* to be happy. ~ *katang-katang* to be furious.

menguras(i) 1 to rub this ointment on o.s. 2 to cure, heal.

menguraskan to rub s.t. on o.s.

urat I 1 – *daging* tendon, sinew. **2** nerve, muscle. **3** fiber, filament (of plant or root). *daun* – k.o. plantain with leaves used for medicine, *Plantago major*. **4** vein, vena, vessel, artery. *menghendaki* – *lesung* to get blood from a stone. – *belikat* shoulder-blade muscle. – *bumi* train. – *daging* sinew. – *darah* blood vessel. – *darah halus* vein. – *daun* vein (rib) in a leaf. – *daun lintang* transverse rib. – *kayu* grain in wood. – *keting* Achilles tendon. – *léhér* cervical muscle. *menarik/bersitegang/tertegang* – *léhér* stubborn. – *lembar* aponeurosis. – *magel (J)* a) tendon. b) *(sl)* penis. – *merih* jugular (vein). – *nadi* a) pulse, radial artery. b) arterial road, thoroughfare. c) very important, the main. – *pembuluh* carotid artery. – *pengetul* adductor muscle. – *penyokong* brace vein. – *saraf* nerve(s), nervous system. *dokter ahli* – *saraf* neurologist. – *sesar* fault line. – *tengah* midvein. – *tunggang* tap root.
  berurat 1 with/having nerves/veins/muscles/tendons, etc. **2** muscular, sinewy, tough. ~ *keras* a) sinewy, muscular. b) tough (of wood). **3** to take root, become rooted. ~ *selirat* net-veined. ~ *umbi/berakar* a) to be firmly/deeply rooted (in), ingrained. b) to have lived in a place for a long time. *berhati baja*, ~ *kawat* determined and persevering.
  mengurat 1 to take root. **2** to toughen, become tough.
  uratan veinlet.

urat II *daun* – plantain, *Plantago major*.

urat III numeral classifier for bangles or small, fine, long things, such as rattan, thread, etc. *tiga* – *gelang* three bangles. *dua* – *rotan* two pieces of rattan.

urat IV → AURAT. *gila* – woman-crazy.

ura-ura I meeting, discussion.
  berura-ura to hold a meeting, have a discussion.
  mengura-urakan and **memperurakan** to discuss, talk over.

ura-ura II proposal, suggestion, intention.
  berura-ura to intend, propose, suggest.
  mengura-urakan to plan, propose, suggest.

urban *(E)* urban, city *(mod)*, citified. *wilayah* – urban zone.

urbanis urbanite, city dweller. *kaum* – urbanites, city dwellers.

urbanisasi *(E)* urbanization, migration to the city.
  berurbanisasi 1 to become urbanized. *Penduduk pedésaan* ~. Villagers are becoming urbanized. **2** to move to the city. **3** urbanized, citified.

urbanisme *(E)* urbanism.

urdi → ORDI I.

Urdu Urdu.

uréa *(E)* urea (based fertilizer).

urén *(Jv) jalak* – black mynah bird.

urét *(Jv)* grub, larva; → HAMA *tebu*.

uréter *(E)* urethra.

urf *(A)* customary law.

urgén *(D)* urgent.

urgénsi *(D)* urgency.

uri I placenta, afterbirth; → ARI-ARI. *tali* – umbilical cord.

uri II menguri *(cla)* to spin around very fast.

urian *(A)* naked; naked gymnast.

uriani *(A)* naked.

uribang *(J)* hibiscus, *Hibiscus rosa-sinensis*.

urik I *(J)* **mengurik(-urik)** and **ngurik-ngurik 1** to pick, pluck. **2** to bore (with a small tool). **3** to go deeply into.

urik II *(Jv)* falsely, by cheating, behind one's back.

uril [*urusan moril*] *pegawai* – official for moral matters.

urine *(D)* urine.
  berurine to urinate.

uring *(M)* philtrum, i.e., the curved groove above the upper lip.

uring-uringan *(J/Jv)* cranky, in a bad mood.

urip I *(Jv)* **1** life. **2** to live; → HIDUP. – *manungsa pinasti ing Pangéran* however well a human being plans his life, in the end it is God who determines it.

urip II *pohon* – tirucalli, *Euphorbia Tirucalli*.

uris *(M)* line, stripe, streak, dash; → GARIS, GORÉS. – *datar* dash. – *miring* slanted line, virgule.
  beruris-uris and **teruris-uris** striped, streaked.

urita → BERITA.

uritan *(Jv)* ovary, roe.

urna I → WARNA.

urna II crown.

urolog *(D)* urologist.

urologi *(D/E)* urology.

uro-uro *(Jv)* to sing/chant solo without musical accompaniment.

URSS *(init)* [Uni Républik Sovyét Sosialis] USSR.

uruf *(A)* local custom.

urug and **uruk** *(J geol)* rock fall.
  menguruk 1 to heap up (with soil, etc.), fill up (land with soil). **2** to bury.
  menguruki to put land or soil on.
  mengurukkan to heap up (soil).
  teruruk buried under. ~ *salju* buried under the snow.
  urukan *(Jv)* **1** earth used for filling, fill. **2** mound (of earth). ~ *tanah* landfill.
  keuruk(an) overloaded, overburdened.
  pengurukan filling (up land with soil). ~ *lahan* landfill. ~ *laut* reclamation.

urun *(Jv)* to make a contribution. *hanya* – *awak* to contribute only one's body (and nothing else). – *biaya* cost-sharing. – *pemikiran/pikir(an)* to contribute one's thinking. – *rembug* a) to contribute to a discussion. b) discussions leading to a decision; caucusing, parlaying. – *rembug antarpimpinan itu berlangsung Selasa pagi dan malam*. Caucusing among the leaders took place Tuesday morning and night. – *suara* to speak up. – *sumbang* negotiations, discussions.
  berurun to make a contribution.
  mengurun to contribute.
  urunan contribution (financial/to a feast, etc.).

urung I 1 failed, unsuccessful. **2** not to come off, not happen, not take place. **3** to be canceled, declared null and void. *tak* –, *tidak(kan)* – and *kagak* – *(coq)* have to, must be; for certain, can't be avoided. *tak* – *dari* not exempt from. *tetapi tak* – and yet, still.
  mengurungkan 1 to defer, delay, put off, postpone. **2** to cancel, drop, abandon, cross/strike out. **3** to frustrate, make/cause to fail; to give up (on). ~ *niatnya* to give up (on) a plan.

urung II *(M)* **berurung** to swarm; in masses/swarms.
  mengurung to swarm (around).

urung-urung *(Jv)* culvert, drain, sewer, underground watercourse.

urup *(Jv)* **urup-urupan** money changing.
  mengurup *(cla)* **1** to change (money into smaller denominations, etc.). **2** to exchange, barter.
  urupan 1 the thing exchanged. **2** change (money).
  pengurup 1 money-changer. **2** barterer.

urus arrange, organize (in an orderly way). *tidak* – *(coq)* in disorder. – *niaga* business deal. – *niaga pepak* blanket deal.
  mengurus [and **ngurus** *(coq)*] **1** to arrange for, make arrangements for, regulate, organize. *Siapa yang* ~ *pembagian beras?* Who is arranging for the rice distribution? *bisa diurus* it can be arranged/taken care of (through bribery, etc.); → BISA *diatur*. **2** to make (the bed), pick up (the room, etc.). ~ *tempat tidur* to make the bed. **3** to take care of s.t. (so that it runs smoothly), care for. ~ *rumah tangga* to keep house. **4** to manage, supervise, run, look after (a store/factory/child, etc.), be in charge of. ~ *hotél dan rumah makan* to manage a hotel and restaurant. **5** to investigate, look into, examine (a matter in order to clear it up), tackle (a problem). *Penggedoran gudang itu sedang diurus polisi*. The warehouse break-in is being looked into by the police. *tidak* ~ *panjang* to do nothing about a matter, let the matter rest. *tuntutan campur* ~ *(leg)* to demand a say (in a matter).
  mengurusi 1 to look after, take care of, watch, baby-sit. ~ *anak* to look after the children. **2** to be in charge of, be responsible for. *Seorang kelasi* ~ *jangkar*. A sailor was responsible for the anchor.
  menguruskan [and **ngurusin** *(J coq)*] to manage, supervise, run, organize (s.t. for s.o. else). *Tidak ada siapa-siapa yang dapat* ~ *kebun kelapanya*. There's nobody to run the coconut plantation for him.
  terurus managed, run, organized, taken care of, looked after. *tidak* ~ to be a mess, be in disorder, neglected. *harta peninggalan yang tak* ~ *(leg)* vacant succession, *bona vacantia*.

teruruskan *tiada* ~ to be a hopeless task, be a vain quest.
urusan 1 affair, matter, business. ~ *belakang* a matter for future consideration. *Itu 'kan* ~ *belakang!* That's s.t. for the future (or, for future consideration)! *Itu* ~*nya.* That's his business. *(Itu) bukan* ~ *saya.* I have nothing to do with it. It's none of my business. *bukan* ~ *menang atau kalah* not to be a question of winning or losing. *kecuali dalam* ~ *yang perlu* except as necessary. *Saya banyak* ~. I'm very busy. *Ada* ~ *apa?* What's up? *mau tahu* ~ *orang* to like to stick one's nose into other people's business. 2 duties; affairs, division (of the government, etc.) administration. ~ *agama* religious matters. ~ *dinas* official duties. ~ *keuangan* financial division. ~ *perburuhan* labor affairs. ~ *sajian* catering department. ~ *tagihan* billing department. ~ *hukum* legal affairs. ~ *véteran* veteran affairs. 3 arrangement(s).
berurusan l to do business (with), have dealings (with). *Saya* ~ *banyak.* I am busy. *Dia* ~ *dengan orang asing itu.* He has dealings with that foreigner. *tidak mau* ~ *dengan* not to want to bother with, not to have any dealings with. *Ia tidak mau* ~ *dengan perkara yang kecil-kecil.* He doesn't want to bother with small cases. *Saya tidak mau* ~ *dengan kamu.* I don't want to have anything to do with you. 4a) to make contact (with), contact, get in touch (with). *Negara itu akan* ~ *lagi dengan badan-badan PBB.* That country will no longer contact UN agencies. b) to be in contact with, communicate with. 5 to be connected (to), refer (to), relate (to), have some bearing (on). 6 to have to do (with), be concerned (with), bother/deal with. *Dia pernah* ~ *dengan polisi.* He has had trouble with the police. *Dia* ~ *dengan pengadilan.* He was indicted by the court.
keurus(an) *(J)* managed, organized; → TERURUS. *tidak* ~ not well-managed, poorly managed.
pengurus l (managing) board, management. ~ *besar* board of directors. ~ *darurat* caretaker (in an emergency). ~ *harian* day-to-day executive board/committee. ~ *penjara* warden (of a prison). ~ *pusat* general executive board, board of directors. 2 manager, director, administrator. ~ *tata-usaha* administrator, manager.
pengurusan l handling, management, administration, treatment. *masih dalam prosés* ~ currently being finalized. ~ *keuangan* financial management. ~ *rumah tangga* housekeeping. ~ *uang* money management. 2 arrangement(s). **kepengurusan** management, leadership (of a council/assembly, etc.). *Dia duduk dalam* ~ *Déwan Nasional Indonésia untuk Kesejahteraan Sosial.* She is on the leadership of the Indonesian National Council for Social Welfare.
urus-urus *(Jv)* 1 laxative, purgative. 2 to take a laxative/purgative.
urut I massage. *minyak* – liniment. *rumah* – massage parlor. *tukang* – masseur, masseuse.
berurut to get a massage.
mengurut l to massage, rub. ~ *dada* to feel disappointed. *tinggal* ~ *dada* to look blank/foolish/sheepish. ~ *hati* to cajole, seduce (into doing s.t.). ~ *muka* to give s.o. a facial (massage). ~ *rambut* to give s.o. a cream rinse. 2 to caress, stroke. *Ibu* ~ *kepala saya.* Mother stroked my hair. ~ *janggut* to stroke one's beard (a sign of courage).
menguruti to rub.
mengurutkan to rub with, rub s.t. (on).
pengurut masseur, masseuse.
pengurutan massage, massaging.
urut II l one in a series. –*nya* follow-up. –*nya surat kami tanggal 2 Méi* following our letter of May 2. 2 serial, successive. *angka/nomor* – serial number. *(dalam)* – *kacang* to be in a series, be ranked in a series, by seniority. *Tidak ada istilah* – *kacang dalam pimpinan suatu kesatuan.* There's no such thing as seniority in the leadership of a (police) unit. – *tanggal/témpo/waktu* chronology.
berurut in sequence/succession, consecutively.
berurutan in a row/series, one after the other, sequential. *dua buah mobil* ~ two cars one after the other.
berurut-urut l one after the other. *masuk* ~ to enter (a room) one after the other. 2 consecutively, chronologically.
mengurut l to put in the right order. 2 trace (according to a certain order).

mengurutkan to put in the right order, straighten up. *dan diurutkan* and working down (the list) from there. *mulai dari A dan diurutkan* starting with A and working down.
urutan l order, succession, sequence, chronology. ~ *besarnya* order of magnitude. ~ *cerita* continuity, plot. ~ *kata (ling)* word order. 2 rank. *menduduki* ~ *kedua* to rank second, be the runner-up. ~ *kedudukan* ranking, position (in a sequence). ~ *pertama* first place, ranked first. ~ *terakhir* final (in a ranking), last (place). **berurutan** sequential.
urut-urutan l consecutively, in sequence. 2 (in sports) seeded, ranking. *pemain* ~ a seeded player. 3 sequence, succession.
pengurutan ranking, sorting.
US *(init)* [*Uni Sovyét*] Soviet Union.
usada *(Jv)* 1 remedy, medicine. 2 medical science; → HUSADA.
usadawan *(Bal)* → DUKUN.
usah I *tidak* – not needed; it is not necessary to, not need to, not have to. *tidak* – *membayar* no need to pay. *tak* – *akan sesuatu* not to need s.t. *tak* – *dikata* not to say. *tak* – *dikata menolong, malahan mengéjék* you can't say he helped; on the contrary, he ridiculed (me).
usah II *(M)* don't; → JANGAN. *Sebab itu pulanglah engkau,* – *merintang aku berangkat.* Please go home; don't prevent me from leaving.
usahkan l far from being. ~ *cerdik, ia bodoh* far from being smart, he's stupid. 2 let alone, not to speak of. ~ *makan, minumpun tak dihidangkannya.* He didn't even serve a drink, let alone food. 2 instead of. ~ *belajar, pergilah ia menonton bioskop.* Instead of studying, he went to see a movie.
usaha *(Skr)* l effort, attempt, venture, endeavor, undertaking. – *untuk meningkatkan mutu pendidikan* efforts to increase the quality of education. *melakukan segala* – *untuk mensukséskan acara ini* to make every effort to make the program a success. *kuasa* – chargé d'affaires. *kuasa* – *sementara* chargé d'affaires ad interim. *kuasa* – *tetap* chargé d'affaires en pied. *setia* – secretary. 2 business, work, labor, industry, enterprise, activity, service, trade. *badan* – a business. *daftar* – work program. *ijin* – business license. 3 initiative(s), instigation, auspices, aegis. *Dia bermaksud melakukan* – *itu.* He plans to take the initiative. *atas* – under the auspices/aegis of, on the initiative of, sponsored by. *bertindak atas* – *sendiri* to act on one's own initiative, of one's own accord. – *pemerintah* government initiatives/efforts. 4 measures, steps. *mengambil* –.– *préventif* to take preventive measures. 5 business operations, operating. *laba* – operating profit. – *asuransi* insurance firm. – *bagus* a nice try. – *bersama* joint venture, partnership. – *campuran* mixed enterprise. – *gelap* illegal/clandestine operation. – *gabungan* joint venture. – *kecil (dan) menengah* [UKM] small and medium businesses. – *kecil menengah dan koperasi* [UKMK] small and medium businesses and cooperatives. – *kemasyarakatan* community service. – *kemauan* effort of will. – *kerajinan tangan* handicrafts. – *kongsi* joint venture. – *melawan/menentang* reaction. – *negara* state-owned company. – *paksa* means of coercion. – *patungan* joint venture/enterprise. – *pemulihan* rehabilitation. – *pencegahan* prevention. – *penyembuhan* curing, healing. – *(peternakan) sapi perah* dairy farm. – *sejenis* congeneric enterprise. – *sendiri* a) self-employment. b) one's own efforts. – *spionase* espionage. – *sungguh-sungguh* exertion. – *tamasya* excursion service. – *tanah dan bangunan* real estate. – *tani* farm, agricultural enterprise. – *témpél-menémpél* patchwork.
berusaha l to work/try (hard) to, endeavor to, strive to, make every effort to, make it a point to. *Dia* ~ *mendapatkan dokumén itu.* He made every effort to obtain that document. 2 to have/run/operate a business, manage an enterprise; to be in the ... business. *Dia* ~ *dalam bidang perdagangan.* He runs a commercial enterprise. ~ *sendiri* to be self-employed. *kebébasan* ~ free enterprise. *surat izin* ~ business license. 3 to see to it (that). *Dia* ~ *supaya ...* He saw to it that.
mengusahakan [and **ngusahain** *(J coq)*] l to do everything in one's power to, make an effort to, use every means in one's power to, work on ...ing, make sure that. *Pemerintah* ~ *sejumlah penambahan modal.* The government has been working on increasing its capital. 2 to effect, bring about, achieve, accom-

plish, manage, ensure that, get to. **3** to till, work, cultivate, prepare (the land), undertake (a task). **4**a) to grow, cultivate (a crop). b) to compile (a book). c) to manufacture (a product). **5**a) to organize (a congress). b) to supervise, finance (a school). c) to run (an enterprise). ~ *dirinya* to exert o.s., make the effort (to). *boléh diusahakan* it can be handled/taken care of.

memperusahakan 1 to till, cultivate (the land). **2** to raise (crops). **3** to engage in, run (a business).

usahaan 1 entrepreneurship. **2** entrepreneurial.

pengusaha 1 businessman, businesswoman, entrepreneur, industrialist. ~ *bunga* florist. ~ *pembuat kunci duplikat/tiruan* locksmith. ~ *kapal/perkapalan* ship owner. ~ *kecil* small businessman. ~ *plat mérah* government employee whose name also appears in the memorandum of association of a corporation. ~ *rumah gelap* madam (in charge of a brothel). ~ *tanaman* nurseryman, gardener. ~ *toko* storekeeper, shopkeeper. **2** a business.

pengusahaan working, exploiting; work, exploitation. ~ *hutan* forest exploitation. **kepengusahaan** exploitation.

perusahaan company, business, corporation, firm, concern, enterprise, undertaking; (particular k.o. business, such as) farm, store. *anak* ~ branch (office). *di dalam* ~ in-house. ~ *air (minum)* water company, waterworks. ~ *angkutan* transportation business. ~ *asosiasi* associated companies. ~ *benah tubuh* figure salon. ~ *bongkar-muat* stevedoring company. ~ *campuran* joint enterprise. ~ *daérah* [perusda] provinical corporation. ~ *Dagang Negara* [PDN] State Trading Company. ~ *film* movie industry. ~ *gabungan* joint enterprise. ~ *guna umum* public utility. ~ *induk* holding/parent company. ~ *jamu* traditional medicine firm. ~ *jasa pengurusan transportasi laut* freight forwarder. ~ *jasa umum* public utility. ~ *jawatan* [perjan] departmental company. ~ *Jawatan Keréta Api* [PJKA] Railroad Company. ~ *kapal* shipping company. ~ *kartu-krédit* credit card company. ~ *kosong* a paper company, i.e., one that exists on paper but has no assets. ~ *Listrik Negara* [PLN] State Electric Power Company. ~ *manfaat umum* public utility. ~ *mentéga-kéju/kiju* dairy. ~ *nasional WNI* nonnative (usually Chinese) national corporation. ~ *Negara* [PN] State Enterprise. ~ *Negara Jawatan* State Enterprise (fully controlled by the government). ~ *Negara Umum* State Public Corporation (partly controlled by the government). ~ *Negara Perséroan* State Public Utility (not controlled by the government). ~ *niaga* trading company. ~ *obat tradisional* traditional medicine firm. ~ *patungan* joint venture/enterprise. ~ *pelaksana amanat* trust company. ~ *pelayaran* shipping company. ~ *pemasakan karét* remilling factory. ~ *pemasok makanan* catering business. ~ *pembangunan rumah* developer (the company). ~ *pembangunan perumahan* realty, real estate. ~ *pembawa bendéra* flag carrier. ~ *pembenihan udang* shrimp hatchery. ~ *pembiayaan* finance company. ~ *pembibitan ayam* chicken ranch. ~ *pemborong dan bangunan* building contractors. ~ *penaksir/penilai* appraisal company. ~ *pencuci mobil* car wash. ~ *penerbangan* airline. ~ *pengangkutan* transportation company. ~ *penjamin* (insurance) underwriter. ~ *penukar uang* money-changing firm. ~ *penyéwaan kasét vidéo* video (rental) store. ~ *penyosohan beras* rice-hulling works. ~ *perékayasaan* engineering firm. ~ *perkapalan* shipping company. ~ *perkebunan* agricultural enterprise. ~ *perséroan* [PERSÉRO] corporation. ~ *Pertambangan Minyak dan Gas Bumi Negara* [Pertamina] State Oil and Natural Gas Mining Company. ~ *pertanian* agribusiness. ~ *pesanan persurat* mail-order company. ~ *peternakan ayam* chicken ranch. ~ *plat mérah* government-owned company. ~ *réasuransi* reinsurance company. ~ *samping* subsidiary business, branch. ~ *sapi perah* dairy farm. ~ *sepatu* shoe factory. ~ *siluman* paper company (one that exists in name only). ~ *swasta* private/nongovernmental company. ~ *tanah* plantation, estate. ~ *tanah dan bangunan* real estate company realtor. ~ *terbatas* limited liability company. ~ *terbuka* open shop. ~ *ternak* livestock company. ~ *tertutup* closed shop. ~ *trans-nasional* cross-frontier company. ~ *umum* [Perum] public corporation. ~ *(Negara) Umum Asuransi Sosial ABRI* [Perum Asabri] ABRI Social Insurance Public Corporation. ~ *(Negara) Umum Asuransi Sosial Tenaga Kerja*

[Perum Asték] Workforce Social Insurance Public Company. ~ *(Negara) Umum Husada Bakti* [Perum Husada Bakti] Husada Bakti Public Corporation. ~ *(Negara) Umum Keréta Api* [Perumka] Railroad Public Corporation. ~ *(Negara) Umum Pegadaian* [Perum Pegadaian] Pawnbroking Public Corporation. ~ *(Negara) Umum Pelabuhan* [Perumpél] Harbor Public Corporation. ~ *(Negara) Umum Perumahan Nasional* [Perum Perumnas] National Housing Public Corporation. ~ *(Negara) Umum Percétakan Uang Républik Indonésia* [Perum Peruri] Republic of Indonesian Mint Public Corporation. ~ *(Negara) Umum Perusahaan Film Negara* [Perum PFN] National Film Public Corporation. ~ *(Negara) Tabungan Asuransi Pegawai Negeri* [Perum Taspén] Civil Servants' Insurance Savings Public Corporation. ~ *(Negara) Umum Télékomunikasi* [Perumtél] Telecommunication Public Corporation; (now replaced by *PT Télkom Indonésia*). ~ *yang bergerak dalam séwa kendaraan* car-rental company. ~ *yang cepat/lambat menghasilkan* quick-/slow-yielding enterprise.

usahatani → USAHA *tani*.

usahawan (*Skr neo*) **1** businessman, entrepreneur. **2** industrialist. **keusahawanan** business (*mod*), entrepreneurial. *latihan* ~ entrepreneurial training.

usahawati (*Skr neo*) **1** businesswoman, female entrepreneur. **2** female industrialist.

usai 1 over, finished, ended, out, concluded. *Hari sudah siang, sekolah - sudah.* It's late in the morning and school is already over. *tak -.-* unending. *perang yang tak -.-* a protracted war. **2** over, out (of a period of time); → *sudah* LAMPAU. *Minggu sudah -.* The week is over. **3** to disperse, scatter, break up. *Pertunjukan itu telah tamat dan para penonton pun telah -.* The show ended and the spectators dispersed. **4** disorderly, unruly, untidy. *Dia membetulkan pakaiannya yang -.* She fixed her untidy clothes. **5** spent, all gone; → HABIS. *Uangnya -.* His money is all gone.

seusai after, after ... has finished, after ... is/was over. ~ *bioskop meréka pergi ke réstoran.* After the movie (was over), they went to a restaurant.

mengusai 1 to separate, disperse. *Pelajar-pelajar yang baku hantam itu akhirnya ~.* The students who were fighting finally dispersed. **2** to overturn, make a mess of. **3** to unravel, undo, let down (one's hair, etc.). ~ *rambutnya setelah mandi* to let down one's hair after taking a bath.

mengusaikan to break up, loosen.

usak (*M*) **1** lessened, diminished, decreased. **2** fallen (of water level).

berusak (*geol*) retrograde.

mengusak to decrease, ebb.

mengusaki to reduce, diminish, abate, curtail, decrease, lessen.

keusakan deficiency.

Usakti [Univérsitas Trisakti] (Jakarta).

usal(l)i (*A*) intention to pray.

berusali and *membaca* - to utter the prayer indicating the intention to pray.

usam I (*J*) **1** waste, dregs. **2** refuse left after the oil has been pressed out of coconuts.

usam II dull, faded (of color); → KUSAM.

usang 1 dried up and empty, withered, shriveled up. **2** obsolete, archaic, outdated, out of date. *adat lama pusaka* - inherited traditions. **3** worn-out, no longer useful; broken, out of order. *mesin bekas yang telah* - a secondhand worn-out engine. **4** no longer busy, quiet.

mengusang to become dry/withered/worn-out/outdated/obsolete.

keusangan 1 dryness. **2** obsolescence.

pengusangan obsolescence.

usap wipe (off), stroke.

seusap a small amount, a touch/breath of. ~ *angin* a breath of wind.

mengusap(i) 1 to wipe off (tears/sweat, etc.). *Dia ~ keringat yang meléléh di dahinya dengan handuk.* He wiped the dripping sweat off his forehead with a towel. **2** to caress, stroke. *Orang tua itu ~ rambut cucunya.* The old man caressed his grandchild's hair. ~ *dada* to stroke one's chest (as a sign of disappointment).

mengusap-usap to stroke, caress.

mengusapkan to rub/stroke/caress with s.t., smear (s.t. on). ~ *saputangannya ke dahinya* to wipe one's handkerchief on one's forehead. *Meréka ~ sambal ke muka korban.* They smeared sambal on the victim's face.

usapan 1 rubbing. **2** stroke, pat, light touch, caress. ~ *angin* a breath of wind. **3** swab.

pengusapan rubbing, stroking.

usar vetiver or khus-khus, i.e., a grass whose roots yield a fragrant oil used in perfumes, cosmetics, etc., *Andropogon/Vetiveria zizanioides*.

usar-usar → USER-USERAN.

usat k.o. marine catfish, *Plotosus anguillaris*.

usawan → USAHAWAN.

Usdék and **USDÉK 1** [U(ndang-undang Dasar 1945); S(osialisme ala Indonésia); É(konomi Terpimpin); K(epribadian Indonésia)] The guiding principles President Soekarno promulgated in 1959: The 1945 Constitution; Indonesian-style Socialism; Guided Democracy; Indonesian Identity. **2** (*Jv joc*) [U(dané) S(aya) D(eres), É(naké) K(emulan)/K(elonan)] It's getting rainier; it would be nice to bundle up with e.o. **3** (*joc*) [U(ang) S(udah) D(ipotong), É(konomi) K(acau)] The money's been cut and the economy's a mess.

Usdékis a supporter of *Usdék*.

Usdékisme the political movement for the establishment of *Usdék*.

usek ngusek (*J/Jv*) to erase, wipe off.

user-useran (*J*) crown of the head; → PUSAR-PUSAR, PUSAR *kepala*.

ushalli → USAL(L)I.

ushuludin → USULUDDIN.

ushulul fiqhi (*A*) legal principle.

USI [Univérsitas Simalungun] (Pematang Siantar).

usia (*Skr*) **1** one's age; → UMUR. *umur* – age. *Berapa tahun –mu?* How old are you? *seorang anak laki-laki yang sama –nya* a boy of the same age; → SEPANTARAN *dengan.* *dalam – yang begitu muda* at such a young age. *lanjut* – advanced in age, elderly. *yang –nya di atasnya* those who are older than she is. *– belajar* school age. *– formatif* formative years. *– harapan hidup* life expectancy. *– kawin* marriageable age. *– kerja* working age. *– lanjut* advanced age. *penyakit – lanjut* degenerative disease. *– muda* youth. *– pakai* duration of use. *– pénsiun* retirement age. *– rawan* a difficult age. *– sekolah* school age. *– senja* the twilight years. *– sepatu* middle-aged. *dalam* **2** the right age for, ready for/to. *– jati yang sudah – tebang* teak trees ready to cut down.

usia-usia –.– *ini* at this old age.

seusia as old as. *mesin jahit yang mungkin ~ dengannya* a sewing machine which might be as old as she is.

berusia to be ... years old; at the age of ... ~ *40 tahun* 40 years old. ~ *madya* middle-aged. ~ *lanjut/tinggi* advanced in years, elderly.

usiat (*J*) → WASIAT I.

usiawan (*Skr neo*) an elderly person.

usik – *hati* intuition. – *rumah* trespass.

mengusik 1 to annoy, tease, bother, disturb, be a nuisance (to). **2a)** to touch. **b)** to exploit. *belum pernah diusik* untouched, virgin (forest). **c)** to touch on (a matter). **3** to criticize, find fault with. **4** to meddle in (other people's business), interfere in (other people's affairs). **5** (*phys*) to perturb.

mengusik-usik to dig up (the past).

terusik 1 troubled, annoyed, disturbed, hurt. *Égonya akan ~.* Their egos will be hurt. **2** obstructed. *Sinar matahari ~ oléh kabut.* The rays of the sun were obstructed by haze.

usikan 1 annoyance, criticism. **2** disturbance, meddling in, interference. **3** (*phys*) perturbation, perturbation.

pengusik 1 teaser, disturber. **2** meddler, busybody.

pengusikan teasing, bothering.

usil I (*J/Jv*) **1** troublesome, bothersome, annoying, (fond of) teasing. *Jangan –!* Hands off! *mulut –* meddlesome. *tidak mau – a)* do not want to be an annoyance. **b)** do not care about. *– ajé amé orang* (*J*) constantly teasing people. **2** to meddle with, interfere in. *suka – mengurusi persoalan orang lain* to like to meddle in other people's affairs. **3** talkative, gabby. *mulut –* to be a bigmouth, have a sharp tongue.

ngusil to stick one's nose into other people's business.

ngusilin (*J coq*) to stick one's nose into (s.o. else's business).

mengusil-usilkan to get involved in, meddle in.

usilan (fond of) teasing.

keusilan meddling, interference; annoyance, teasing.

pengusil s.o. who interferes/bothers.

usil II [uang siluman] bribe paid to customs officials to speed up the importation procedures.

usir chase away.

berusir-usiran and **usir-mengusir** to chase after e.o.

mengusir [and **ngusir** (*coq*)] **1** to expel, banish, eject, evict, chase away, throw out, get rid of, exile. *Kubaca sebuah buku atau majalah untuk ~ kebosanan.* I read a book or magazine to chase away boredom. ~ *rasa kantuk* to get rid of a sleepy feeling. **2** to chase after, pursue, run after, hunt. ~ *asap, meninggalkan api* to throw away old shoes before getting new ones.

terusir 1 to be expelled, ejected, evicted, driven out, thrown out. **2** to be pursued, chased after.

usiran 1 *orang* ~ fugitive, exile. **2** *surat* ~ eviction notice.

pengusir ejector, evictor, s.o. or s.t. that chases away s.t. ~ *burung* scarecrow.

pengusiran ejection, eviction, expulsion, banishment, ouster. ~ *dari aparteménnya yang méwah* her eviction from her luxury apartment.

usis → UCIS.

uskup (*D*) bishop. – *agung* archbishop.

keuskupan bishopric, diocese. ~ *agung* archbishopric, archdiocese.

uslub (*A*) manner, way, style.

Usmani(yah) Ottoman.

usolli → USAL(L)I.

usrah → USROH.

usreg (*Jv*) nervous, restless, fidgety; → RESAH.

keusregan restlessness, nervousness.

usroh (*A*) Islamic study group.

ustad(z) (*A Pers*) **1** male Muslim religious teacher. **2** (*cla*) lord, master. **3** → GURU *mengaji.* **4** professor in a *madrassah*.

mengustad(z)kan to ordain as an *ustad*.

ustada, ustaja and **ustadzah** (*A*) female Muslim religious teacher.

ustana tomb (of the rulers of Pagarruyung in Sumatra).

ustat and **ustaz** → USTAD(Z).

ustazah → USTADAH.

Ustrali (*coq*) Australia.

Ustria (*coq*) Austria.

USU [Univérsitas Sumatra Utara] University of North Sumatra.

usuk (*Jv*) rafter; → KASAU.

usul I (*A*) **1** origin, source, beginning. *bangsawan –* inherited nobility. **2** original. **3** character, disposition, behavior, nature. – *asal* a) genealogy, pedigree, descent. b) details, ins and outs of s.t. – *menunjukkan asal* by their fruit ye shall know them. – *bangsawan/budiman* noble. – *pikiran* leading thought, basic idea.

usul II (*A*) **1** proposal, suggestion. *menerima segala – yang dikemukakan* to accept all the proposals made. **2** motion (in court/ at a meeting). – *balasan* counterproposal. – *damai/perdamaian* peace proposal. – *perubahan* amendment.

mengusulkan [and **ngusulin** (*J coq*)] **1** to suggest/propose s.t. to s.o. *Dia ~ supaya diadakannya sayembara.* He suggested holding a contest. **2** to move (a motion at a meeting).

usulan 1 hint, proposal, suggestion. **2** motion (at a meeting).

pengusul 1 proposer, person who proposes s.t. **2** mover (of a motion at a meeting). ~ *intérpelasi* interrogator.

pengusulan suggestion, suggesting, proposal, proposing.

usul III (*A*) – *periksa* thorough investigation. *dengan tiada – periksa* a) peremptorily, summarily. b) rashly, thoughtlessly, inconsiderately. c) (to believe s.t.) without thinking about it.

mengusul(i) to investigate, look into.

pengusulan investigation, inquiry.

usul IV (*A*) *ilmu* – and *–uddin* knowledge of the basic tenets of Islam as found in the Koran and Islamic religious texts.

usuluddin → USUL IV.

usung berusung carried on the shoulders.

mengusung 1 to carry s.t. on the shoulders along with other people. *Orang-orang ~ lemari.* They carried the armoire together. **2** (*BG*) to play (a particular k.o. music). **3** to support, back.

usungan 1 equipment for carrying s.t. 2 litter, stretcher; → TANDU. ~ *mayat/jenazah* bier.

pengusung 1 s.o. who carries s.t. on his shoulders, carrier, porter, bearer. ~ *peti jenazah* pallbearer. 2 (*BG*) s.o. who plays (a kind of music).

pengusungan carrying s.t. on the shoulders, transporting, porterage, conveying.

usur I (*A*) one tenth, tithe.

usur II → UZUR I.

usur III – *patol* confiscation; taking away by force.

usurpasi (*D*) usurpation.

usus (*Jv*) intestine(s). *ujung* – rectum. – *besar* large intestine, colon. *pemeriksaan* – *besar* colonoscopy. – *buntu* appendix, caecum. *radang* – *buntu* appendicitis. – *dua belas jari* duodenum. – *halus/kecil* small intestine, ileum. – *kucing* catgut. – *mulas* colic.

usut I (*J/Jv*) **usut-usut**, and **mengusut** to grope around, feel about; to fondle, caress.

usut II (*J/Jv*) investigate. – *punya* – after a lot of investigation.

mengusut to investigate, examine, check s.t. out, look into s.t. for evidence/proof, etc. ~ *jejak* to trace s.t. *sedang diusut* under investigation.

terusut to be investigated, examined, looked into. *Pembunuhan itu sudah* ~. The murder has been investigated.

pengusut investigator, researcher.

pengusutan investigating, examining; investigation, examination, inquiry. ~ *fiskal* (*ob*) tax investigation.

uswah (*A*) example.

usyah (*coq*) → USAH I.

usyur → USUR I.

UT I (*init*) → UNIVÉRSITAS *Terbuka*.

ut II (in acronyms) → UTAMA, UTARA II.

utak-atik and **utak-utik** (*Jv*) **mengutak-ngatik** [and **ngutak-ngatik/ngutik** (*coq*)] to put one's fingers on; to tinker with, fiddle around with, tweak. *cp* KUTAK-KATIK.

utama (*Skr*) 1 superior, excellent, outstanding, eminent, top, distinguished, first, leading. *abdi* – *daripada bangsa* the first servant of the nation. *pemain* – *nasional* the top national player. 2 basic, essential, vital, fundamental, primary, principal, prime. *beras makanan* – rice is the basic food. *kewajiban yang* – primary obligation. *nada* – key note, prevailing tone. *pengerjaan* – (*math*) elementary operation. 3 main, chief, principal, most important, key(note). *hasil* – chief product. *makanan* – staple diet. *pembicara* – keynote speaker. *peran* – main role. *saksi* – main witness.

mengutamakan to prioritize, give top priority to, stress, emphasize, consider most important, make the first consideration. *Pangan harus diutamakan.* Food must come first. *Utamakan keselamatan!* Safety first!

terutama 1 especially, particularly, in particular, mainly, specifically. 2 best, top, superior. *pelajar yang* ~ *di kelasnya* the star of his class. 3 most important. ~*nya* especially. **men(t)erutamakan** to consider of utmost importance, give the highest priority to.

keutamaan 1 importance, significance, excellence, superiority. 2 virtue, decency, moral superiority.

pengutamaan prioritizing.

utan → HUTAN.

utang → HUTANG. 1 debt, loan, money or things borrowed from s.o., accounts payable, liabilities. *kaya* – to be heavily in debt. *kesanggupan lunasi* – solvency. *membayar* – to pay off a debt. *memberi* – to sell s.t. on credit. *mendapat* – to obtain a loan. *penghapusan* – write-off (of debts). *perbandingan* – *luar negeri dengan nilai ékspor* debt service ratio. *surat* – certificate of indebtedness. 2 (nonmonetary) obligation, debt, duty (as payback for s.t. received). 3 (*infr*) fault. – *emas dapat dibayar; - budi dibawa mati* a monetary debt can be repaid; a debt of gratitude is carried to the grave, i.e., can never be fully repaid. – *nyawa dibayar nyawa* an eye for an eye and a tooth for a tooth. – *bank* bank loan, bank liability. – *budel* claim against an estate. – *budi* moral obligation, debt of gratitude. **berutang budi** to have a moral obligation, have a debt of gratitude, be beholden. – *dagang* accounts payable. – *ditangguhkan* deferred liability. –

hipoték mortgage payable. – *jangka panjang* long-term debt/liability. – *jangka péndék* short-term debt/liability. – *kayu ara* a debt that will probably never be paid off. – *lancar* current/short-term liabilities. – *macet* bad debt, nonperforming loan. – *nyawa* saving s.o.'s life. **berutang nyawa** to owe one's life (to s.o.). – *pajak* taxes payable. – *pemerintah* public/sovereign debt. – *piutang* debt and credit, debts and receivables. – *pokok* principal. – *sebelit/selilit pinggang* to be up to one's ears in debt. – *semahaméru* mountainous debts. – *tetap* fixed liabilities. – *tiap helai bulu* to be up to one's ears in debt. – *usaha* operating liabilities, trade payables. – *yang belum lunas* outstanding debts. – *yang mungkin tak dapat ditagih* bad debts. – *yang sudah dipakai* disbursed debts.

berutang 1 to owe money, be in debt. 2 to borrow money, go into debt. ~ *nyawa* to owe one's life (to s.o.). *si* ~ debtor. *orang tempat* ~ creditor. *orang yang turut* ~ co-debtor, joint debtor.

mengutang [and **ngutang** (*coq*)] to be in debt, get into debt. ~ *kanan-kiri/sana-sini* to be deeply in debt.

mengutangi, memperutangi [and **ngutangin** (*J coq*)] 1 to lend money to. *Saya diutangi 10.000 rupiah.* He lent me 10,000 rupiahs. 2 put s.o. into one's debt. *Dia* ~ *saya.* He put me in his debt.

mengutangkan to lend s.t. *tidak mau* ~ *kalau tidak ada jaminan* not to want to lend (money) without collateral. *yang* ~ creditor.

memperutangkan to borrow from, buy on credit from. *Saya* ~ *kain.* I bought cloth on credit.

terutang owed, payable.

utangan indebted, having a debt.

pengutang debtor.

pengutangan putting into debt.

perutangan 1 (*mod*) debt. 2 creditor.

utara I (*Skr*) north. *angin* – north wind. *bintang* – North Star, polar star. *musim* – northwest monsoon. *Sumatra* – North Sumatra. – *barat laut* north-northwest, NNW – *magnétik* magnetic north. – *sebenarnya/sejati* true north. – *semata timur* and – *timur laut* north-northeast, NNE – *tepat* due north.

mengutara to head north, northing.

terutara northernmost.

utara II (*Skr*) state, express.

mengutarakan 1 to state, explain, clarify, point/spell out, get across (an idea), make (a point). 2 to suggest, put forward, propose. 3 to tell, narrate, relate, recount, deliver (a speech). 4 to show, indicate. 5 to exhibit, display, publicize, air. ~ *keluh-kesah meréka di depan umum* to air their grievances in public.

pengutara spokesman, mouthpiece.

pengutaraan explanation, clarification, airing, etc.

Utarid (*A*) *bintang* – (the planet) Mercury.

utar-utar small round shield.

utas I 1 string for stringing beads, pearls, etc. 2 numeral classifier for strings, ropes, cords, threads, etc.

seutas one strand/length (of rope, etc.).

berutas with a string, stringed. ~ *permata* with a string of gems.

utas II 1 clever, skillful, competent, capable, expert. *orang* – a) craftsman. b) lumberjack.

utasan *orang* ~ craftsman.

pengutas craftsman.

utek (*Jv*) brains. *pikir* **utek-utek** turn s.t. over in one's mind.

Uthmaniyyah → USMANI(YAH).

uterus *D* uterus.

uter-uter (*J*) k.o. caterpillar which is a pest of the *durian* tree, *Xystrocera festiva pascoe*.

UTI [Univérsitas Terbuka Indonésia] (Jakarta).

utih clipped form of *putih* used as a polite address for the fourth or sixth child in a family, a younger member of a family.

utik spotted catfish, *Arius maculatus*; → OTÉK I.

utik-utik I (*Jv*) **mengutik-utik** 1 to tinker with, fiddle around with. ~ *radio* to tinker with a radio. 2 to touch (with the finger). *Saya tidak berani* ~ *uang amanat itu.* I'm afraid to touch the money entrusted to me. 3 to meddle with, interfere with (s.t. that is not one's business).

utik-utikan tinkering, fiddling around with.

utik-utik II (*J/Jv*) **ngutik-ngutik 1** to rake up old stories. **2** to vex, tease. **3** to tackle a difficult job.

util (*Jv*) **mengutil** [and **ngutil** (*coq*)] to shoplift.

utilitas (*D*) utility, usefulness.

utk (*abbr*) [untuk] for, in order to.

utomo (*Jv*) → UTAMA. *Budi* – → BUDI *Utomo*.

utopi (*D*) and **utopia** (*E*) **1** utopia. **2** dream.

utopiawan → UTOPIS.

utopis (*D*) **1** utopian. **2** dreamer.

utopisme (*D*) utopism.

UTP (*init*) [Univérsitas Tunas Pembangunan] (Surakarta).

utri (*Jv*) k.o. dessert made from steamed cassava and sugar.

UTT (*init*) [Univérsitas Timor Timur] (Dili).

utuh (*Jv*) **1** intact, undamaged, uninjured, unscathed, sound, unimpaired, unmarred, in good condition. *dengan –nya* unimpaired. **2** whole, integral, complete, perfect.

  seutuh(nya) whole, intact, complete, as perfect as it was before, in its entirety.

  mengutuhkan to make intact/whole/complete (again), leave unimpaired. ~ *wilayah* to make a territory intact (again).

  utuhan (*math*) integer.

  keutuhan wholeness, unity, oneness, totality, integrity. ~ *wilayah* territorial integrity. *menjaga* ~ *negara* to protect the integrity of the nation.

  pengutuhan overhauling, restoration (to its former state); integrating, unifying, making whole/one (again).

utul [ujian tertulis] written exam.

utun (*Jv*) **1** simple. **2** industrious, diligent, assiduous. *petani* – the industrious farmer.

utus mengutus(kan) to send an envoy/representative, delegate (as an envoy).

  mengutusi (*pl obj*) to send off, delegate.

  utusan delegate, envoy, representative, messenger, emissary, delegation. ~ *Allah* God's messenger. ~ *Daérah* [UD] Provincial Delegates. - *Golongan* Group Delegates. ~ *Injil* missionary. *para* ~ *Injil* messengers of the Gospel. ~ *negara* ambassador. ~ *Yésus* disciple(s).

  pengutus s.o. or s.t. that sends off/delegates.

  pengutusan mission, (diplomatic) legation.

  perutusan delegation, deputation.

UU [Undang-Undang] law, act.

UUD [Undang-Undang Dasar] Constitution. ~ *45* the 1945 Constitution.

UUDS [Undang-Undang Dasar Sementara] Provisional Constitution.

UUPA → UNDANG-UNDANG *Pokok Agraria*.

uuuh (exclamation) oops!

Uvaya [Univérsitas Achmad Yani] (Banjarmasin).

uwak (*Jv*) aunt or uncle older than father or mother; → UA, UAK I.

uwak-uwak burrowing marine worm.

uwar-uwar → UAR I.

uwas (*J*) a bit crazy.

uwa-uwa (*Jv*) gibbon; → WAWA,WAKWAK.

uwé → OWÉ(H).

uwi I → HUWI I.

UWI II (*acr*) [Univérsitas Wiraswasta Indonésia] (Jakarta).

uwis gara a k.o. red-gold *ulos* made in the Karo area.

UWMY [Univérsitas Widya Mataram] (Yogyakarta).

uwong → ORANG.

uwungan (*J*) → BUBUNGAN.

uwur → KRÉTÉK I.

uyah-uyah k.o. plant used as fodder, *Struchium sparganophorum*.

  uyah-uyahan various species of plants, including *Procris laevigata/penduculata*.

uyak (*J*) **nguyak-nguyak** to mix up, stir.

uyang (*J/Jv*) to feel unwell, restless.

uyeg-uyeg (*J/Jv*) **nguyeg-nguyeg** to massage the knee with circular motions of the hand.

uyel-uyel (*Jv*) **(ber)uyel-uyel** to elbow one's way through, jostle.

  beruyelan and **uyel-uyelan** to jostle e.o.

  menguyelkan to push aside (by using the elbows).

uyon-uyon (*Jv*) playing the *gamelan* for the pleasure of it and not connected to any ceremony.

uyung → HUYUNG.

uyungan → BUBUNGAN, UWUNGAN.

Uzair (*A*) (the Biblical) Ezra.

uzlah and **uzlat** (*A*) isolation.

  beruzlah to isolate o.s., become a hermit (for mystical purposes).

uzur I (*A*) hindrance, obstacle, obstruction, s.t. that prevents one from doing s.t. *Kalau tidak ada* –, *saya akan datang*. If all goes well, I'll come.

uzur II (*A*) **1** weak, feeble (*esp* due to old age); senile; ill, sick, indisposed. *nénék saya yang* – *itu* my feeble old grandmother.

  keuzuran 1 weakness, feebleness, debility. **2** sickness, illness. **3** to suffer from feebleness (too old, weak, etc.). **4** to be old and worn out, no longer usable. *Rumah ini sudah sangat* ~. This house is beyond repair. *usia* ~ old/advanced age.

uzur III (*A*) **1** menstruation. *datang –nya* she has her period. **2** pregnant.

V

/v/ is usually pronounced /f or p/. Words beginning with a V not found under this letter should be looked for under F or P.

v and V I /fé/ the 22nd letter of the Latin alphabet used for writing Indonesian.
v II (*L*) versus.
V III Roman numeral for 5.
V IV (*chem*) symbol for vanadium.
vacum → VAKUM.
vadémécum (*L*) /vadémékum/ vademecum, a handbook or other small useful reference work.
vagina (*D*) vagina.
vaginal (*D*) vaginal.
vak (*D*) 1 subject of study. 2 discipline, branch of knowledge. 3 vocational. *sekolah* – vocational school; → SEKOLAH *kejuruan*. 4 profession, line of work.
vakansi (*D*) vacation, holiday; → PAKANSI.
   bervakansi to take a vacation, be away on vacation.
vakasi (*D*) attendance fee.
vakature (*D*) /fakatur/ vacancy.
vakbon (*D*) trade union; → SERIKAT *buruh/sekerja.*
vaksin (*D*) vaccine; → VAKSINA. – *influénsa* influenza vaccine, flu shot. – *polio* polio vaccine.
   memvaksin(kan) to vaccinate, inoculate.
vaksina (*D*) vaccine; → VAKSIN. – *DAPAT* [Diptéri, Pertussis, Tetanus] a vaccine against diphtheria, pertussis, and tetanus, DPT shot.
vaksinasi (*D*) vaccination, shot. – *penyakit gila anjing* rabies shot.
   memvaksinasi(kan) to vaccinate, inoculate.
vaksinator (*D*) vaccinator.
vakum (*D*) 1 vacuum.
   memvakumkan to put in a vaccum.
   kevakuman 1 vacuum. ~ *politik* political vacuum. 2 suction device to abort a fetus.
   pemvakuman vacuuming.
valas [valuta asing] foreign currency. *pinjaman* – foreign currency loan.
valénsi (*D*) valency.
Valéntine Saint Valentine. *Hari* – Valentine's Day.
valid (*E*) valid.
validasi (*D*) validation.
validitas (*D*) validity.
valis (*D*) valise.
valium (*E*) valium.
valuta (*D*) currency. – *asing* [valas] foreign currency/exchange.
vam (in Ambon) clan; → FAM.
vampir (*D*) vampire.
vandal (*D*) vandal.
vandalis (*D*) vandal.
vandalisme (*D*) vandalism.
vandalistis (*D*) vandalistic.
vandel (*D*) banner, ensign.
vanili (*D*) 1 vanilla. 2 vanilla tree; → KERNÉLI, PANILI, PANÉLI.
varan (*D*) varan, monitor lizard. – *Komodo* Komodo dragon, *Varanus komodoensis.*
varia (*D*) miscellanea.
variabel (*D*) variable; → PEUBAH.
variabilitas (*D*) variability.
varian (*D*) variant.
variasi (*D*) variation.
   bervariasi to vary, various. *suku bunga yang* ~ varied interest rates.
   memvariasikan to vary s.t.
variétas (*D*) variety. – *unggul* superior variety; → VUTW.
varises (*D*) varicose veins.
varitas → VARIÉTAS.
Varuna → BARUNA.
vas I (*D*) vase; → JAMBANG(AN). – *bunga* (flower) vase.

vas II (*L*) a vessel or duct. – *déferén* vas deferens.
vasal (*D*) vassal.
vaséktomi (*D/E*) vasectomy.
   memvaséktomi to perform a vasectomy on.
vaselin (*D*) vaseline.
   memvaselinkan to grease with vaseline.
vaskular (*E*) vascular.
vasodilatasi (*D*) vasodilatation.
Vatikan (*D*) Vatican. *Duta Besar* – Apostolic Nuncio. *Kedubés/ Kedutaan Besar* – Apostolic Nunciature.
VB [Véstigings Bewijs] (*D*) /féstihingsbewés/ 1 certificate of right to take up one's residence. 2 (*col*) company house.
VBS [Visa Berdiam Sementara] Temporary Resident Visa (an immigration document).
vé /fé/ name of the letter *v.*
Véda (*Skr*) the Vedas (ancient Hindu scriptures).
Védda Vedda, a member of the aboriginal people of Srilangka/ Ceylon.
véém (*D*) /fém/ goods warehouse (in port areas).
   memvéémkan to store in a warehouse (in port areas).
   pervééman wharfage business.
végetariér and **végetarir** (*D*) vegetarian.
végetaris (*D*) vegetarian. *seorang* – a vegetarian.
végetarisme (*D*) vegetarianism.
végetasi (*D*) vegetation.
végetatif (*D*) vegetative.
véktor (*D biol* and *math*) vector. – *malaria* malaria vector.
vélar (*D ling*) velar.
vélbak → PÉLBAK.
vél(d)béd (*D*) camp/folding bed; → PÉLBÉD.
vél(d)flés (*D*) canteen, water bottle; → PÉLPLÉS.
vél(e)g (*D*) rim, the outer edge of a wheel on which a tire is fitted; → PÉLEK.
vélodrom (*D*) velodrome.
vélositas (*D*) velocity, speed.
vélplés (*D mil*) water bottle, canteen.
véna (*L*) vena, vein.
vénéréologi (*E*) venereology. *ahli* – venereologist.
Vénésia Venice.
Vénésuéla Venezuela.
vénotip(e) (*D*) phenotype; → FÉNOTIP(E).
ventil (*D*) valve; → PENTIL I.
véntilasi (*D*) ventilation.
véntilator (*D*) ventilator.
véntrikel (*D*) ventricle.
véntura (*E*) venture.
Vénus 1 (Roman mythology) the goddess Venus. 2 the morning star Venus.
ver- I also see entries beginning with **per-**.
vér II clipped form of **visum et repertum.**
vérba (*L ling*) verb; → KATA *kerja.* – *bantu* auxiliary verb. – *déféktif* defective verb (missing some of its parts). – *ékuatif* equational verb, copula. – *finit* finite verb. – *impérsonal* impersonal verb. – *intransitif* intransitive verb. – *kausatif* causative verb. – *pérsonal* personal verb. – *réfléksif* reflexive verb. – *résiprokal* reciprocal verb. – *statif* stative verb. – *tak teratur* irregular/strong verb. – *teratur* regular/weak verb. – *utama* main/nonauxiliary verb.
vérbal (*D/E*) 1 oral (rather than written). *ujian* – oral examination. 2 verbatim, word for word. *terjemahan* – verbatim translation. 3 (*ling*) verbal.
   memvérbalkan to verbalize, put into words.
vérbalisan (*D*) summoner.
vérbalisasi (*D*) verbalization.
vérbalisme (*D*) verbalism.
vérbalistis (*D*) verbalistic.

vérbatim (D) verbatim, word for word.

verdah (D) suspected (of having a certain disease). – *tifus* suspected of having typhus.

   memverdah to suspect.

vergén (D) vergence, a turning movement of the eyeballs. *Ia menyandang cacat –.* He has a vergency deficiency.

verhang (D) the slope of a water surface, the ratio between the difference in the levels of a river and the distance across which the fall has been measured.

vérifikasi (D) verification.

   memvérifikasi(kan) to verify.

vérifikator (D) checker, verifier.

verjaring (D) /feryaring/ expire; → DALUWARSA.

verkéneng and **verkéning** (D mil) reconnaissance, reconnoitering.

Verklaring van Ingezétenschap (D ob) Certificate of Occupation.

verkoper (D) salesman.

vermaak (D) → PERMAK.

vernikel (D) (plate with) nickel, nickel-plate.

vernis (D) varnish; → PERNIS.

verpléher (D) male nurse.

verpléhster (D) nurse.

vérsi (D) version.

versnéling (D) gear; → PERSNÉLING. *bak* – gearbox. *ganti* – to change gears.

versték (D) 1 (leg) default, nonappearance. *menghukum secara – (tanpa kehadiran tersangka)* to sentence in default (in the absence of the accused). 2 (mil) hiding place.

vérsus (L) versus, against.

vértebrata (L) vertebrates.

vértikal (D) vertical.

verzét (D leg) /fersét/ objection.

Véspa 1 (originally) a "Vespa" motor scooter. 2 (now) any motor scooter.

vésted interés (E) *kaum* – those with vested interests.

Vésuvius the volcano Vesuvius.

vét (D) 1 (animal) fat. 2 grease, lubricant. 3 boldface. *dicétak dengan huruf* – printed in boldface.

   mengevét(i) to grease, lubricate.

véter (D) shoe lace.

véteran (D) veteran.

   memvéterankan to retire s.o. from service. *divéterankan* s.o. of long experience in some position, for example, an ex-criminal, a student who has been left back and has to repeat a class.

véto (D) veto.

   memvéto to veto.

vétor (in the East Lesser Sundas) local area head.

vétsin monosodium glutamate, MSG.

via (L) via.

viabel (E) viable.

viaduk(t) (D) 1 viaduct. 2 overpass, fly-over.

vibrafon (D) vibraphone.

vibrasi (D) vibration.

   bervibrasi to vibrate.

vidé (L) see; refer to: used to direct attention to a particular page, book, document, etc.

vidéo (D/E) video. *pita* – videotape. *– kasét* videocassette. *– porno* X-rated videotape.

   bervidéo 1 to watch video. 2 to be equipped with video.

   memvidéokan to record on a videocassette.

vidéotek (D/E) videotheque.

vidio → VIDÉO.

Viétkong and **Viét Kong** Vietcong, Viet Cong, V.C.

Viétnam Vietnam. *– Selatan/Utara* South/North Vietnam.

viétnamisasi Vietnamization.

Viétsel [Viétnam Selatan] South Vietnam.

Viétut [Viétnam Utara] North Vietnam.

vihara (Skr) Buddhist monastery; → WIHARA.

vikariat (D) vicariate.

vikaris (D) vicar. *– apostolik* apostolic vicar. *– jénderal* vicar general.

vikép [vikaris épiskopal] episcopal vicar.

viksi (D) fiction; → FIKSI.

viktimologi (E) victimology.

vil(l)a (D) villa, country house for weekend use.

vilt (D) felt (the material).

vinil (D) vinyl.

vinyét (D) vignette.

violét (D) violet in color.

violis (D) violinist.

vip, VIP and **V.I.P.** /fip/ abbreviation for Very Important Person.

   memvipkan 1 to reserve s.t. for VIPs. 2 to give s.o. VIP status.

vipiawan and **VIPiawan** male VIP.

vipiawati and **VIPiawati** female VIP.

VIPwan → VIPIAWAN.

Virgi-Tab trademark of medicinal capsule to increase women's sexual potency (extract from a root found along the Barito river in Central Kalimantan).

Virgo (zod) Virgo.

virologi (D) virology. *ahli* – virologist.

virtuos (D) virtuoso.

virtuositas (D) virtuosity.

virulén (D) virulent; → GANAS.

virulénsi (D) virulence; → KEGANASAN.

virus (D) virus. *pembawa* – vector.

visa (D) visa. *– berdiam sementara* temporary visa. *– biasa* ordinary visa. *– dinas* service visa. *– diplomatik* diplomatic visa. *– kehormatan* courtesy visa. *– kunjungan* visitor's visa. *– kunjungan berkali-kali* multiple entry visa. *– kunjungan usaha* business visit visa. *– kunjungan usaha beberapa kali perjalanan* [VKUBP] multiple-trip business visit visa. *– saat kedatangan* visa on arrival/entry. *– transit* transit visa. *– turis* tourist visa.

visi (D) 1 point of view, perspective, view. 2 a vision. 3 sight, observation.

visionér (D) visionary, s.o. who sees visions; prophet, seer.

visitador(es) (D?) detailman/-men

viskosa (D) viscose. *rayon* – viscose rayon.

visual (E) visual.

   memvisualkan 1 to visualize. 2 to put into visual form, represent visually.

visualisasi (D) visualization.

   memvisualisasikan to visualize, put into visual form.

visuil (D) → VISUAL.

visum 1 (in passport) → VISA. 2 written document from authorities stating that a matter has been considered (and approved). *– (ét) répértum* autopsy/postmortem report.

   memvisum to perform an autopsy on.

visus (D) vision, eyesight.

vit-A vitamin A.

vital (D) vital.

   memvitalkan to vitalize.

   kevitalan vitality.

vitalitas and **vitalitét** (D) vitality.

vitamin (D) vitamin. *– D/Duit* (coq) money, dough.

vitrase (D) /fitrasye/ lace.

vivéré péricoloso (Italian) living dangerously.

   bervivéré péricoloso to pursue brinksmanship (under President Soekarno).

VJ (E init) video jockey.

vla (D) /fla/ custard (used as topping for cakes and puddings); → FLA.

vlék (D) blot, stain.

V.O.C. [Verénigde Oostindische Compagnie] /fé o sé/ Dutch East India Company (1602–1800).

voering → VURING.

voile (D) /foal/ veil.

vokabulér (D) vocabulary.

vokal (D) 1 (ling) vowel. *– bundar* rounded vowel. *– disengaukan* nasalized vowel. *– hampar/tak bundar* unrounded vowel. *– kardinal* cardinal vowel. *– kendur* lax vowel. *– nasal* nasal vowel. *– tengah* central vowel. *– ternasal* nasalized vowel. 2 vocal, i.e., a sung musical piece, usually with instrumental accompaniment. 3 (E?) outspoken.

vokalia (D) vocal music.

vokalis (D) vocalist.

vokasional (E) vocational. *ahli térapi* – vocational therapist.

vokatif (*D*) vocative. *kasus* – vocative case.
vol (*D*) volume control; → POL I.
vol. [volume] volume.
volentér (*D*) unsalaried clerk, volunteer; → POLONTÉR, VOLONTÉR.
voli (*D*) (to play) volleyball.
volkan → VULKAN.
volkanik (*E*) and **volkanis** (*D*) volcanic.
Volksraad (*D col*) /-rat/ People's Council, k.o. parliament.
volontér (*D ob*) volunteer, unsalaried clerk.
volt (*D*) volt; → POL II.
Volta-Hulu Upper Volta.
volt(a)méter (*D*) voltmeter.
voltase (*D*) voltage.
volume (*D*) volume.
Volvo trademark of a Swedish car.
  bervolvo to drive a Volvo.
vonis (*D*) verdict. *menjatuhkan* – to pass verdict.
  memvonis to sentence to. *divonis bébas* to be acquitted (of a prisoner of a charge). *divonis mati* to be sentenced to death.
voorfinanciering (*D*) /forfinansiring/ pre-financing.
voorganger (*D*) minister, pastor.
voorman (*D*) foreman, overseer, head of a block (in a prison).
voorrijder (*D*) /vorayder/ advance motorcycle escort/outrider; → PEMBUKA *jalan*, PENGENDARA *pendahulu*.
  memvoorrijderi to precede by an advance escort.
vooruitslag (*D*) /forétslakh/ (customs term) release of goods from a warehouse anticipating the settlement of the related documents.

voorverkoop (*D*) /forferkop/ advance sale.
voorzitter (*D Bat*) chairperson; → ÉPHORUS.
Vorstenlanden (*D col*) the Sultanates of Yogyakarta and Surakarta, the Princely States.
votum (*L*) vote. – *kepercayaan* vote of confidence.
vrij (*D*) /fré, pré, préi, frai/ 1 free (time). 2 neutral gear.
Vrisaba (*Skr zod*) Taurus.
vs I /fé-és/ [vérsus] versus.
VS II /fé-és/ –*nya* her vital statistics (chest, waist, hips).
vulgair (*D*) → VULGAR, VULGÉR.
vulgar (*E*) vulgar.
vulgarisasi (*D*) vulgarization.
vulgér (*D*) vulgar, common.
vulkan (*D*) volcano.
vulkanis → VOLKANIS.
vulkanisasi (*D*) vulcanization.
  memvulkanisasikan to vulcanize.
vulkanisir (*D*) (to) vulcanize.
vulkanit (*D*) vulcanite.
vulkanolog (*D*) vulcanologist.
vulkanologi (*D*) vulcanology. *ahli* – volcanologist.
vulpén (*D*) fountain pen; → PULPÉN.
vuring (*D*) lining (of clothing).
VUTW (*init*) [Vari(é)tas Unggul Tahan Wereng] *wereng*-proof Superior Variety, i.e. a rice variety from the *Balai Penelitian Pertanian Bogor* (Bogor Agricultural Research Institute).
vuurcontact (*D*) firefight.

W

w and W /wé/ the 23rd letter of the Latin alphabet used for writing Indonesian.

wa I (*Jv*) term of address for parent's older sibling or person in the parents' age group.

wa II (*A*) 1 and (in various Arabic expressions). –*llahu alam* and God knows best. 2 by (in taking an oath). –*llahi!* by God!

wa III 1 (particle of mild emotion on receiving some information) my! 2 (particle of disappointment or complaint) oh! 3 (particle showing discomfort at not being able to fulfill a request) gee!

wa IV (in acronyms) → WAJIB, WAKIL, SISWA, WANITA.

waad, waadah, waadat, and waat (*A*) treaty, contract.

berwaad to conclude a treaty/contract, contract, pledge o.s.

wa'aung (*J*) gorilla, orangutan.

wabadahu → WABAKDAHU.

wabah (*A*) epidemic. – *raya* pandemic.

mewabah 1 to be epidemic (of a disease). 2 to be all the rage. *Break dance ~ di masyarakat.* Break dancing is all the rage.

mewabahi to spread to (of a disease). *Narkoba juga telah ~ dunia atlét.* Narcotics have also spread to the athletics world.

mewabahkan 1 to spread (a disease). 2 to spread s.t. widely.

pewabahan spreading (of a disease).

wabakdahu and wabakdu (*A*) and then, after that. –*lkalam* and after that speech.

wabarakatuh (*A*) and with His blessings.

wabihi nastainu billahi (*A*) and to call upon Him for help.

wacana (*Skr*) 1 speech; discourse. 2 lecture.

mewacanakan to express, say.

pewacanaan discussion, discussing.

Wacanasabha *MPR* Meeting Hall.

wad → WAAD.

wada' (*A*) farewell, leave-taking, adieu, valediction.

wadag (*Jv*) 1 corporeal, physical, body, bodily. 2 businesslike.

wadah (*Jv*) 1 receptacle, container. – *gula* sugar bowl. 2 coalition (of political parties), union, umbrella organization, association, coordinating association. *nama – tunggal* the name of the sole organization. 3 forum (for expressing ideas).

berwadah to have a container.

berwadahkan to have ... as its umbrella organization.

mewadahi to organize, put into an organization. *menjadi wahana untuk ~ kegiatan tersebut* to become the means for organizing those activities.

mewadahkan to use s.t. as a container.

terwadahi organized under.

pewadahan providing a place/container/umbrella organization.

wadak → WADAG.

wadal (*Jv*) sacrifice to wipe out sins; expiatory sacrifice to make s.t. evil committed good again. [According to folk belief, in the month of Maulud one monkey from each pack of monkeys is sacrificed to the tigers].

mewadalkan *diwadalkan* to be at the mercy of the devil.

wadam [wanita adam] homosexual; transvestite; → WARAS.

kewadaman transvestitism.

wadan [wakil komandan] deputy commander.

wadana → WEDANA.

wadar → BADER I.

wadas (*J/Jv*) sandstone-like ground, rocky ground/soil; → CADAS.

wadat (*Jv*) 1 bachelor. 2 celibate.

berwadat to be unmarried.

wadau (*J*) → WADUH.

wadduh → ADUH, WADUH.

wader (*Jv*) a river fish. – *bang* goldfish. *Teri itu dimakan ikan –, kemudian –nya dimakan yang lebih besar dan seterusnya.* Big fish gobble up little fish, and big fish are gobbled up by bigger fish, etc. *ikan – mérah* brill-like fish, *Puntius bramoides.*

waderan k.o. grass, swamp millet, *Isachne globosa.* – *beludru* a perennial grass, *Isachne pangerangensis.*

wadi I (*Jv*) 1 secret that may not be disclosed. 2 mysterious.

wadi II (*A*) wadi, dry (except after a heavy rainfall) river basin in the desert.

wadi III (*A*) semen or urine.

wadiah and wadi'ah (*A*) (bank) deposit, savings, giving s.t. of value to s.o. else for safekeeping; a k.o. Islamic banking in which the customer deposits money in a bank for safekeeping and the bank pays the customer by a bonus or gift.

wadian female sorcerer.

wadir [wakil diréktur] deputy director.

waditra (*S*) k.o. musical instrument.

wadon I (*Jv*) 1 female. 2 woman.

wadon II *ikan – gunung* k.o. fish, *Labeo erythropterus.*

wadud (*A*) the Loving One (one of Allah's 99 names).

waduh (*Jv*) 1 (exclamation of astonishment/surprise) wow! – *cantiknya!* Wow, she's cute! – *lega rasa hatiku!* What a relief! 2 (expression of pain) ouch! – *sakit perutku!* Ouch, my stomach hurts! 3 (particle on noticing s.t.) my!

waduk (*Jv*) 1 rumen. 2 stomach, belly, paunch. 3 reservoir, basin, pond, sump. – *air* a) water reservoir. b) water tower. c) dam. – *listrik* condenser. – *penampung limbah* aeration lagoon.

wadul (*Jv*) a tattletale; to tattle (to).

wadung I (*Jv*) axe, hatchet.

wadung II (*Jv*) jack (in the set of playing cards).

wadyabala (*K*) soldier, troops.

waé (*J/Jv*) just, only. *Sorangan –?* All by yourself? Want some company? (said when approaching a girl who is alone).

waéhé (*J*) → BERÉNGSÉK.

Wafa (*A*) 1 faithful. 2 name of the Palestinian news agency.

wafak I (*A*) a written amulet. *cincin –* a ring with an amulet engraved on it.

wafak II (*A*) 1 definite time (regarding a certain event). 2 in accord/agreement.

wafat (*A*) 1 to pass away, die. 2 deceased.

mewafatkan to cause s.o.'s death.

kewafatan death, demise.

pewafatan causing death.

wagal k.o. fish, *Wallago miostoma* and k.o. catfish, *Pangasius micronema.*

Wagé (*Jv*) the fourth day of the five-day market week.

wagen (*D*) typewriter carriage.

wagon (*D*) → WAHON. – *réstorasi* dining car.

wagu (*Jv*) awkward, rude, clumsy, poorly executed.

wagub [wakil gubernur] vice-governor.

wah I 1 (exclamation of surprise/wonder/pleasure/pain, etc.) heavens! my! wow! – *énaknya!* How delicious (they were)! 2 enormous, exorbitant, magnificent, fantastic. *Bisnis mainan anak yang kian –!* The fantastic children's toy business! *dengan tarifnya yang cukup –* at exorbitant rates. *kapal yang –* a luxurious boat.

wah II (in acronyms) → BAWAH.

waha(h) (*A*) oasis.

wahab (*A*) Giver (= God). *Abdul–* a man's name; → ABDU.

wah(h)abi (*A*) Wahhabi, a strict Muslim sect.

wahadah and wahadat (*A*) oneness, unity (of God).

wahadaniyah and wahadiah → WAHADAH.

wahah (*A*) fertile area (with water and vegetation) in a desert, oasis.

wahai (exclamation to get s.o.'s attention) hey! hello!

waham (*A*) 1 suspicion, expectation, opinion. *menaruh syak (dan) –* to entertain suspicion and mistrust. 2 imagination, fantasy, delusion, -mania. – *kebesaran* megalomania. 3 syndrome.

mewaham to surmise, suspect.

mewahamkan to surmise, suspect s.t.

wahana I (*Jv*) vehicle, conveyance, means, device. – *antariksa (tak berawak)* (unmanned) space vehicle. – *Lingkungan Hidup Indonésia* [Walhi] Indonesian Environmental Society. – *sandi* cipher device.

wahana II (*Jv*) sign, interpretation of a dream.

wahdani(y)ah (*A*) **1** unity. **2** unanimity.

wahdat (*A*) individuality.

wahdatul – *Islamiah* (*A*) Islamic association.

wahéng → WAHING.

wahi (*A*) → WAHYU.

wahib (*A*) the Giver (i.e., God).

wahid (*A*) **1** one, single, unique (*esp* of God). **2** alone, without peer. *nomor* – first class.

wahidiat (*A*) unity.

wahing (*Jv*) **1** a sneeze. **2** to sneeze.

wahon (*D*) railway car.

wahyu (*A*) **1** divine source of power. **2** (divine) revelation, Revelation (in the Bible); fortunate/victorious power. – *cakraningrat* a) godlike powers bestowed on mortals. b) the charisma of President Soekarno. – *kepada Yahya* the Revelation of St. John the Divine.

mewahyui 1 to inspire. **2** to make a revelation to.

mewahyukan to reveal (in a vision).

pewahyu revealer.

pewahyuan revelation.

wai I (exclamation indicating shock) dear me! dear God! o dear! – *apa bicara kita!* What are we talking about!

wai II (in names of rivers in southern Sumatra) river; → KALI III, SUNGAI.

Waicak Buddhist Holy Day commemorating the three important events in Buddha's life: his birth, enlightenment, and death.

waid → WAAD.

waiduri → BAIDURI.

waima (*ob*) although.

wain(g) → WAHING.

Waisak(a) → WAICAK.

waisakan the month of May (when *Waicak* is held).

Waisya (*Skr ob*) Vaisya, a member of the third Hindu (trading) caste.

waitangkung (*C*) (to do) a certain k.o. gymnastics.

berwaitangkung to do that k.o. gymnastics.

waja (*Jv*) steel; → BAJA I.

wajad (*A*) spiritual ecstasy.

wajah (*A*) **1** looks, face, facial appearance, countenance; facade. – *lama dalam kémasan baru* old wine in new bottles. – *baru* newcomer. – *tirus* oval face. **2** view, aspect. **3** cover. *dengan – baru* (a magazine) with a new cover.

berwajah ... with a facade of ...

perwajahan layout, design.

wajan → BAJAN.

wajar I (*A*) **1** plain, (self-)evident, proper, unadorned, unembellished, without embellishment/artifice. *nasi* – just plain rice (without coconut cream, etc.). **2** authentic, natural, genuine, real; logical; normal, ordinary. *Semuanya berjalan dengan –.* Everything takes its natural course, everything's going along normally. **3** fair; → ADIL. *secara* – fairly. *tidak* – a) anomalous, abnormal. b) unreasonable, unfair. **ketidak-wajaran 1** anomaly, abnormality. **2** unreasonableness, unfairness.

sewajar ~ *dengan* in concord/harmony/line with. *Hasil usahanya* ~ *dengan tenaga yang dipergunakannya.* The results of his efforts were in line with the energy he expended. **kesewajaran 1** concord, harmony, agreement. **2** genuineness, naturalness.

sewajarnya 1 it is only fair/just/right that. *~lah kalau dia mendapat penghargaan sebesar itu.* It is only right that he gets such great appreciation. **2** naturally, as was to be expected. *sudah* – it's only right/natural that. *mati* – to die of natural causes. **3a)** automatically. b) it is assumed/taken for granted. **4** of one's own accord/free will. *Biarkan pikiran meréka tumbuh dengan* ~. Let their thoughts develop of their own free will. **5** exactly as it should be. *Kalimat-kalimat dalam undang-undang itu harus ditafsirkan* ~, *jangan diputarbalikkan.* The sentences in that law should be interpreted exactly as they should be; don't twist them around.

mewajarkan and **memperwajar(kan) 1** to bring s.t. in harmony/accordance/line with. *Tingkat suku bunga untuk para peminjam masih perlu diperwajarkan dengan cara menurunkan tingkat suku bunga.* The interest rate for lenders still needs to be brought into line with the way of lowering it. **2** to make s.t. what it should be. **3** to take for granted, consider natural.

kewajaran 1 plainness, lack of embellishment, simplicity. **2** naturalness, genuineness, spontaneity. **3** fairness.

wajar II [wajib belajar] compulsory education.

wajé (*J*) → BAJA I. *tudung* – (*mil*) helmet.

wajib (*A*) **1** obligatory, required, necessary, essential, compulsory, unavoidable, inevitable. *Orangtua* – *memberi asuhan yang cukup.* Parents must provide (their children with) an adequate education. *Tiap-tiap pengemudi mobil* – *menggunakan sabuk pengaman.* Every driver is required to wear a safety belt. **2** to be obligated/compelled/obliged/forced, have no choice/alternative. **3** must, should, ought to; to have to. – *ain* Islamic obligation on individuals. – *béla umum* [WBU] general defense obligation. – *belajar* [wajar] compulsory education. **mewajib-belajarkan** to require compulsory education for. – *daftar* compulsory registration. – *dinas militér* [WDM] conscription. – *hadir* compulsary attendance. – *hélm* the obligation to wear a safety helmet (on motorcycles). – *kerja* [waker] compulsory labor. – *kifayah* Islamic obligation on a community. – *lapor* [WALOP] s.o. who is liable to reporting (i.e., presenting o.s. or making one's presence known to the police or military authorities, etc.). – *latih* [WALA] compulsory military training. – *latih mahasiswa* [WALAWA] k.o. university military training. – *militér* [WAMIL] conscription. – *muat* obligation of transport companies to provide services for the government. – *pajak* [WP, wapa] a) taxable, assessable. b) taxpayer, s.o. liable for taxation. – *pajak siluman* tax evader. – *puasa* obligation to fast. – *putar* (in the film industry) the obligatory showing of Indonesian films in certain first-class movie theaters. – *sumbang* compulsory contribution. – *tentara* a) compulsory military service, conscription. b) s.o. who is liable to military service, conscript.

sewajibnya should, ought to. ~ *meréka bersatu-padu.* They should form a strong unity.

berwajib competent, proper (of authorities), the one(s) concerned/responsible for. *yang* ~ the competent/proper authorities, the authorities concerned.

mewajibkan to oblige, compel, make compulsory/obligatory, force, require. *Pemerintah* ~ *setiap penduduk* ... The government requires every resident to ... *diwajibkan* a) to be required. b) to be entrusted to. *yang diwajibkan* compulsory (subjects). *vak/mata pelajaran yang tidak diwajibkan* optional/elective subjects. *orang yang diwajibkan masuk tentara* s.o. liable to military service, conscript.

kewajiban obligation, responsibility, duty, task, liability. *menjalankan/melakukan* ~*nya* to perform/discharge one's duties. *melalaikan* ~*nya* to neglect one's duties. *tahu/mempunyai rasa* ~ to have a sense of (one's) duty. *terkena* ~ to be (legally) obliged (to). *tugas* ~ duties. ~ *belajar/bersekolah* (*ob*) compulsory education. ~ *bersyarat* contingencies. ~ *gantung* contingent obligation. ~ *lancar* current liabilities. ~ *membayar* obligation/liability to pay. ~ *pajak* tax liability. **berkewajiban** to have the obligation/responsibility/duty/task/liability.

pewajib s.o. who is subject to certain things. ~ *daftar* s.o. who is liable to registration. ~ *militér* conscript.

pewajiban requiring, obligating.

wajid (*A*) the Finder or Maker (= God).

wajik (*Jv*) **1** a diamond-shaped pastry made of glutinous rice grains, coconut milk, and sugar. **2** rhomboid shape. **3** (cards) diamonds.

wajip → WAJIB.

wajir → WAZIR.

wajit (*S*) → WAJIK.

wajur (*A*) medicine.

wak I (*Jv*) uncle or aunt, i.e., an elder brother or sister of father or mother and their spouses; → UA, UAK I.

wak II sound made by ducks, frogs, etc., quack.

wak III term of address, title for older and/or higher-ranking male, corresponding to *bapak*. – *haji* = *pak haji*.

wak IV (*S*) (*onom*) splitting or breaking sound: crack, snap.

waka [wakil kepala] deputy head.

wakaf I (*A*) **1** legacy, bequest, benefaction, endowment. **2** property donated for religious/community purposes, mortmain. **3** religious institution. *sumur* – a well donated in the public interest. *tanah* – land left to a mosque or for other purposes such as a school, a *pesantren*, etc.
    berwakaf to donate; donated.
    mewakafkan to donate/bequeath land, etc. for religious purposes or in the public interest.
    pewakaf benefactor.
    pewakafan and **perwakafan** donating for religious purposes or in the public interest.

wakaf II (*A*) pause, temporary stop (in reading).

wakalah (*A*) embassy; agency; subdistrict.

wakap → WAKAF I.

Wakapri [Wakil kepala Perwakilan Républik Indonésia] Deputy Chief of the Delegation of the Republic of Indonesia.

wakas [wakil kepala staf] deputy head of staff.

wakhen → WAGEN.

waki'ah (*A*) an accident or unavoidable circumstance. *al-* "The Inevitable"; name of the 56th chapter of the Koran.

wakif (*A*) founder, donor.

wakil (*A*) **1** representative, deputy, vice-. *sebagai* – on behalf of (s.o. else). **2** ambassador, emissary, envoy, diplomat. **3** agent, messenger, operative. – G.M. G.M.'s agent. **4** the Guardian (= God). – *Duta Besar* Deputy Chief of Mission, DCM. – *gubernur* [wagub] deputy governor. – *Kepala Perwakilan Républik Indonésia* [Wakapri] Deputy Chief of the Delegation of the Republic of Indonesia. – *ketua* deputy chairman. – *komandan* second in command. – *mahkota* viceroy. – *mutlak* plenipotentiary. – *muwakal* representative, deputy. – *nikah* proxy for the groom at a wedding. – *présidén* [waprés] vice-president. – *rakyat* people's representative (Member of Parliament). – *tetap* permanent representative. – *tunggal* sole representative
    berwakil with/to have a representative, etc.
    mewakili to represent (a country/enterprise/party, etc.), act for/in place of; to be an agent, proxy, substitute, etc. *bersifat* ~ representative (*mod*); speaking in the place or on behalf of another or others.
    mewakilkan [and **ngewakilin** (*J coq*)] **1** to hand over, transfer. ~ *kepada* to delegate/authorize (work/activities, etc.) to s.o. *Pak Kasim* ~ *pengurusan tokonya kepada anaknya.* Mr. Kasim delegated the management of his store to his son. **2** to delegate, empower, authorize. *Setiap pemohon tidak boléh* ~ *orang lain untuk menggantikannya.* No delegate is allowed to authorize s.o. else to replace him. **3** to do s.t. by proxy.
    terwakil(i) to be represented. *Semua provinsi* ~. All provinces are represented. **keterwakilan 1** representativeness. ~ *politik* political representativeness. **2** representation. ~ *berlebih* overrepresentation. ~ *rendah* underrepresentation.
    wakilan representation. **berwakilan** to be represented.
    pewakil representative.
    perwakilan [and **pewakilan** (*mostly Mal*)] **1** delegation; liaison unit. **2a**) representation. ~ *berimbang/diplomatik* proportional/diplomatic representation. b) representative. *Déwan Rakyat* [DPR] House of Representatives, Parliament. **3** agency. ~ *mutlak/tunggal* sole agency.

waktu (*A*) **1** time (past, present, or future). *jangka* – period of time. ~ *yang telah lampau* the past. ~ *yang akan datang* the future. **2** certain amount of time. – *tiga jam* three hours. *Tidak ada – untuk belajar.* There is no time to study. **3** a definite time to do s.t., the stipulated/scheduled/proper time to say prayers. – *belajar membaca* reading time; lesson hour for reading. *sudah sampai –nya untuk* ... the time has come to ... *sembahyang lima* – the five obligatory prayers (for Muslims) → ISYA, SUBUH, LOHOR, ASAR I, MAGRIB. – *sudah habis* time is up. *Ia kehabisan –.* He ran out of time. **4** a point in time; moment; instant; occasion. *pada tiap-tiap* – every moment, at any moment; without previous notice. *pada* – a) by the time that. b) when, as, while. *pada* – *ini* at present, now, nowadays. *pada* – *itulah* at that moment/point in time. *pada –nya* on time. **5**

chance, opportunity. *menantikan* – *yang baik* to wait for a favorable opportunity. **6** a period of the day. – *pagi/siang/soré/malam* in the morning/daytime/afternoon/evening. **7** system of measuring duration. – *tolok* standard time. **8** when (in the past). – *dia datang* when he arrived. **9** while. **10** time zone. *beberapa* – *yang lalu* some time ago. *untuk beberapa* – *lamanya* for some time. *dalam* – ... *tahun mendatang* ... years from now. *dalam* – *dekat/singkat* (*ini*) shortly, before (very) long, in the near future. *dalam* – *rélatif singkat* in a relatively short time. *dalam* – *yang bersamaan* simultaneously. *dalam* – *yang sesingkat-singkatnya/sependék-pendéknya* in the shortest time possible. *dari* – *ke* – from time to time. (*me*)*makan/menelan* – time-consuming. *membuang* – to waste time. *mempunyai/punya/ada* – to have the time, can afford the time. *menurut* – chronological. *tidak menurut* – a) unpunctual. b) irregular. *banyak menyita* – to take a lot of time. *pada* – *ini juga* right now, at this very moment. *pada* – *itu juga* at the same time. *pada suatu* – a) (in the past) once, one day. b) (in the future) one day. *pengisi* – pastime. *sampai* – *ini* up till now. *sang* – time (personified). *sang* – *berjalan dengan cepatnya* time flies. *sebarang* – a) at any time. b) always. *sebelum* – premature. *sedikit* – *lagi* in the near future. *setiap* – any time. *untuk* – *yang tidak ditentukan* (*lamanya*) indefinitely, for an indefinite (period of) time. *untuk* –*. selanjutnya* henceforth, from now on. – *berarti duit* time is money. – *itu* in those days, then. *Hanya* – *yang dapat memberikan jawabnya.* Only time will tell. *kerja/pekerjaan sebagian* – part-time work/job/employment; → PENGGALWAKTU. – *yang akan menjawab* time will tell. – *antara* pass time (between two military vehicles). – *belajar* apprenticeship, period of study. – *berdiri* term of incorporation. – *berkunjung* visiting hours (in hospital). – *berlaku* period of validity. – *bertelur* laying season. – *dinas* length of service. – *duga berangkat* estimated time of departure. – *duga tiba* estimated time of arrival, ETA. – *garapan* time it takes to produce a product. – *gencat* idle/down time. – *hamil* pregnancy period, time of being pregnant. – *henti-sela* shut-down time. – *hilang* down time. – *Indonésia Barat* [WIB] West Indonesian Time (Zone). – *Indonésia Tengah* [WITA] Central Indonesian Time (Zone). – *Indonésia Timur* [WIT] East Indonesian Time (Zone). – *istirahat* rest, pause. – *jeda* break, pause, recess. – *kosong* unoccupied time. – *lampau* past tense. – *lintas* pass time (between two military vehicles). – *luang* spare time. – *matahari* solar time. – *mati* down time. – *melapor* date of report. – *menjenguk* visiting hours (in hospital). – *nganggur* down time. – *operasi* on-stream time. – *paro/paruh* (*phys*) half-life. – *pelunasan* term/period of repayment. – *pembayaran* due date (for payment). – *pencapaian* target date. – *penyerahan* delivery date. – *pergantian* turnover time. – *pesan* lead time. – *putar* a) screen/running time (of film). b) turnaround time. – *réhat* break (from work). – *samar muka* late dusk or dawn. – *seketika* real-time. – *senggang* a) leisure time. b) slack season, off-time. – *setempat* local time. – *tanggap* response time. – *telu/tiga* "three prayers a day," i.e., a modified form of Islam found in Lombok; → WEKTU *telu*. – *tempuh* a) the time that it takes to do s.t. b) travel time. – *terluang* spare time. – *termakan* elapsed time. – *tolok* standard time. – *tunda* delay time. – *tunggu* waiting period. – *tuntas* draining time. – *turun* down time. – *turun ke sawah* period of rice-field tilling. – *yang paling sibuk* peak hours.
    waktunya *pada* ~ in (good) time; (according to a timetable or schedule) on time, punctual. *sampai pada* ~ ultimately. *tepat pada* ~ timely. *sebelum* ~ a) before the time specified. b) interim. *sudah* ~ it is time for. *Sudah* ~ *kita pulang.* It's time for us to go home. *sudah léwat* ~ expired, lapsed. ~ *telah sangat mendesak* it is high time, time is pressing.
    sewaktu when → WAKTU 8; at the same time. **sesewaktu** and
    sewaktu-waktu 1 at any time, at all times, any moment. ~ *téroris itu dapat dibekuk.* The terrorist could be caught at any moment. **2** always. **3** from time to time, now and then, every now and then/again, at times, occasionally.
    berwaktu with fixed/definite time. *sembahyang diberi* ~, *janji diberi berketika* there is a time for everything.

pewaktu timer.

wakun veil made of strings of beads for covering the bride's face.

wakuncar (*BG joc*) [wajib kunjungi pacar] the obligation to visit one's girlfriend.

berwakuncar to visit one's girlfriend.

wakwak (white-handed) gibbon, *Hylobates spp*.

wakwakkung and **wakwak gong** (*J*) a child's game.

wala [wajib latih] compulsory military training.

walaah (*A*) /wala:h/ **1** (exclamation of disbelief) Come on! – *gimana nih, mau nonton kagak punya duit!* Come on, you want to go to the movies but you don't have any money! **2** (exclamation of disapproval or of surprise) Oh, no! Oh, my God! – *saya lupa.* Oh, my God, I forgot.

walabi (*E*) wallaby.

walad (*A*) son/child of.

walafiat → SÉHAT.

walah I (*A J*) by God!

walah II → KEWALAHAN, KU(W)ALAHAN

walahu'alam (*A*) → WALLAHUALAM.

walaikum salam (*A*) the response to *assalam alaikum*.

walaiti (*J*) reference to a native-born Arab (not the Indonesian-born Arab).

walak (*A*) right of succession.

walak (*M ob*) **mewalakkan** to place, put.

terwalak placed, put.

walakhir (*A*) in the end, finally.

walakin (*A*) **1** (al)though. **2** however, but.

walama [wajib latih mahasiswa] student military training obligation.

walang (*Jv*) grasshopper, locust. – *sangit* noxious pest of the rice plant, green padi bug, *Leptocorisa acuta*.

berwalang ~ *hati* anxious, concerned.

walangan culantro, long coriander, *Eryngium foetidum*.

walap [wajib lapor] required to report.

walat (*J/Jv*) punishment from a higher power (for insulting treatment of one's elders); → KUALAT.

walau (*A*) **1** (*cla*) and (even) if, though. **2** (= **walaupun**) although, even if, though. – *... sekalipun* even ... – *di toko buku besar seperti Harpers ini sekalipun* even in a large bookstore such as Harpers. – *begitu/demikian* despite this, nevertheless, in spite of that.

walaupun → WALAU 2.

walawa [wajib latihan mahasiswa] obligatory training period for students.

waledan (*Jv*) arrears; back pay.

waléh (*J/Jv*) **1** to tell the truth. **2** plain-spoken, straightforward.

waléhan straightforward, honest.

walét (*J*) various species of swifts, swiftlets; name of a swallow species, the salangane, *Collocalia fuciphaga*. – *Maluku* Moluccan swiftlet, *Aerodramus infuscatus*. – *sapi* glossy/white-bellied swiftlet, *Collocalia esculenta*.

waletan → WALEDAN.

walhal (*A*) whereas, while, (al)though, even though, in actual fact, notwithstanding. – *itu* a) in spite of (the fact) that. b) even if/though, (al)though.

walhasil (*A*) **1** in the end, with the result that. **2** actually, in actual fact, whereas.

Walhi → WAHANA Lingkungan Hidup Indonésia.

wali I (*A*) **1** the one near(-by), to be near/close to (God), (a trusted) friend, benefactor, nearest relative. **2** appellation for the first preachers of Islam in Java who, as governors, were in command of the areas converted to Islam; they used the title of *sunan* and are venerated as saints. **3** male next of kin and guardian whose consent is required for the marriage of a girl or woman; he represents her, in person or in writing, before the clergyman (*penghulu*). *surat* – the written consent of the *wali* for the marriage of his ward. **4** guardian, i.e., s.o. (in Islam) who is given the right to look after an orphan and his/her property until he/she is of age. **5** (– *Allah, waliullah*) Muslim saint. **6** head of an area, *nagari* or village (in West Sumatra), etc. *Pak* – intimate title of address for a mayor. – *amanat* trustee. **perwali-amanatan** trust (*mod*). – *faqih* religious leader. – *geréja*

bishop. – *hakim* person (appointed by the court) who is not related to the bride (for instance, the *penghulu*) who acts as *wali*, in the absence of an appropriate male nearest relative. – *jorong* (in Payakumbuh) hamlet head. – *kelas* homeroom teacher (in a school). – *kota* mayor; → WALIKOTA. – *mujbir* the enforcing *wali*. – *murid* (in school) guardian, i.e., the person to whose care a student is committed. – *nagari* (in West Sumatra, Padang) village head. – *nasab* male next of kin. – *negara* head of a (partition) state, i.e., during the formation of the federal *Républik Indonésia Serikat*. – *negeri* a) head of state. b) (*ob*) Governor General. – *nikah* → WALI I **3**. – *pemilih* elector. – *pengawas* co-guardian. – *rumah* → TUNGGANAI *rumah*. – *Sanga/Songo* the first nine (= *songo* in Javanese) *walis* who spread Islam throughout Java, the Great Proselytizers. *Tim/Team – songo* the team established in 1971 to combat corruption in the Tanjung Priok port area; official name: Tanjung Priok Port Control Team. –*yul Amri Daruri Bisysyaukah* "The President of the Country though not Perfect should be Strong," i.e., the designation conferred on Pres. Soekarno in the 1950s by the NU party.

berwalikan to have ... as a *wali*.

me(mper)walikan 1 to appoint s.o. as a *wali*. **2** to act as a *wali* for, become the *wali* for.

kewalian guardian status.

perwalian 1 trusteeship. **2** guardianship, conservatorship, custody. ~ *pengawas* co-guardianship. **3** protectorate.

wali II (*cla*) *kain* – a long yellow stole worn on the shoulder or around the neck by the court pages who carry the regalia.

wali III *pisau* – a small knife.

wali IV → RAJAWALI.

wali V walian (in the northern Celebes) s.o. who has great influence, plays an important role in society and is honored; → TONAAS.

walik the green wild pigeon or black-naped fruit dove, *Ptilinopus melanospila*. – *kembang* black-naped fruit dove, *Ptilinopus melanospila*. – *raja* superb fruit dove, *Ptilinopus superbus*.

walikorong (in West Sumatra) a functionary one level lower in rank than the village head.

walikota mayor.

kewalikotaan mayoral.

walikotamadya mayor, i.e., the chief administrator of a *kota-madya*.

walikukun (*J/Jv*) name of a tree, *Schoutenia obovata*, with very hard and tough wood, used for making axle trees, spinning wheels, wheel rims, etc.

walimah and **walimat** (*A*) festive meal presented to the *wali* at the bridegroom's house; wedding party.

walimana (*Skr ob*) harpy, legendary bird used as a mount.

walimé (*J*) → WALIMAH.

walisongo umbrella tree, *Schefflera grandifolia*, *Brassaia actinophylla*.

waliullah (*A*) glorifying title for a *wali*; → WALI I.

walkie-talkie (*E*) /woki-toki/ walkie-talkie.

walkot [wali kota] mayor.

wallah(i) and **wallohi** (*A*) **1** God! **2** by God; → WALAH I. – *wabillahi* I swear to God.

wallahualam (*A*) **1** and God knows (the truth). **2** I don't know. – *bissawab* God alone knows the truth; → SAWAB I.

walmana → WALIMANA.

walo I (in Irian Jaya) a penis sheath, larger and longer than the *kotéka* used in Jayawijaya and Nabire.

walo II → WALAU.

waloh → WALUH.

wals(a) and **waltz** (*D/E*) waltz.

waluh (*Jv*) → LABU. **1** pumpkin. **2** calabash. **3** gourd, designating a family (Cucurbitaceae) of plants that includes the squash, melon, pumpkin, etc, *Cucurbita moschata*. – *Jepang* chayote, *Sechium edule*.

waluku (*J*) plow.

berwaluku to plow.

waluya (*Jv*) to be healthy, in good health.

wambrau (in Irian Jaya) hot dry wind, Föhn.

wamil [wajib militér] 1 compulsory military service, conscription. 2 s.o. who is liable to military service, conscript.

mewamilkan to make s.o. liable to conscription.

wampa [wakil menteri pertama] deputy prime minister.

-wan I suffix for the formation of male persons, such as *wartawan*, etc.

wan II (in acronyms) → DÉWAN.

Wan III title for s.o. of Malay noble family or for male Arab; clipped form of *tu(w)an*: – *Empu* and – *Malini*, two women of noble blood who received Sang Sipurba in *Pelémbang* (now *Palémbang*).

wana I (*Jv*) forest; uncultivated land.

wana II → WANNA.

wanadri (*Jv*) 1 wilderness, terrain. *pendidikan* – terrain familiarization (for mountaineers). 2 name of a mountaineering club.

Wanapati (*Jv*) Minister of Forestry.

wanara (*Skr*) monkey.

wanatani agroforestry.

wanda I (*Jv*) physiognomy, facial features and expression; the face.

wanda II (*Jv gram*) syllable.

sewanda monosyllabic. *kata* ~ a monosyllabic word.

wandu (*Jv*) homosexual, hermaphrodite, transvestite.

wanéh kawanéhan by chance, accidentally.

wang I → UANG.

wang II clipped form of awang.

wanga (*IBT*) k.o. tree, wanga palm, *Pigafetta filaris*.

wangi 1 fragrant. *air/minyak* – scent, perfume. 2 fragrance, scent. 3 scented. *tissue* – scented tissue.

mewangi 1 sweet-smelling, smelling fragrant. 2 to scent, perfume.

mewangikan to scent, perfume, make fragrant/sweet-smelling/smell fragrant.

wangian fragrance, perfume.

wangi-wangian all types of perfumes/scents/fragrances.

kewangian fragrance, perfume, scent.

kewangi-wangian sweet-smelling, perfumed.

pewangi s.t. which perfumes. ~ *ruangan* air freshener. ~ *WC/Toilét* bathroom deodorizer.

pewangian perfuming.

wangkang (*C*) outrigger canoe; Chinese oceangoing junk.

wangkawa rainbow.

wangsa (*Skr*) 1 relatives, kinsmen, family. 2 descendant. – *Kartarajasa* family or descendant of Kartarajasa. 3 people, race, nation. 4 dynasty.

kewangsaan kinship.

wangsat (*Jv*) you bastard!; → BANGSAT I.

wangsit (*Jv*) inspiration from a supernatural power, spiritual guidance.

wangwung → KUMBANG *badak/kelapa/nyiur*.

wani I (*Jv*) to dare. – *ngalah luhur wekasané* one who has the courage to give in, will, in the end, be victorious and glorious.

Wani II *Séhat* – [acronym for (Senam keséhatan) waitangkung-néitangkung [= (*Jv*) courageous health] the Indonesian substitute name for waitangkung and néitankung.

wanita (*Skr*) 1 woman (more refined term than *perempuan*). *Tujuh* – *Bersaudara* the Seven Sisters, i.e., the seven major oil producers: Exxon, Royal Dutch Shell, Texaco, Standard Oil Co. of California, Mobil, Gulf, British Petroleum. 2 female, feminine. 3 wife. 4 lady. – *adam* [wadam] transvestite. – *gituan* prostitute. – *kudus* female saint. – *metakil* shrew, scolding woman. – *P* prostitute (the P is from *pelacur*). – *panggilan* call girl. – *penghibur/penjaja cinta* (*euph*) prostitute. – *plesiran/sipak/T/TS/tunasusila* prostitute.

kewanitaan 1 womanhood; womanliness, femininity. 2 female sex organ.

kewanita-wanitaan effeminate.

Wanjakti [Déwan Pertimbangan Jabatan dan Kepangkatan AD Tingkat Tinggi] High-Ranking Army Council for Assignments and Ranks.

wanna (*C*) term used by Chinese for Indonesians, *lit* "Southern Barbarian." *sama – boléh kasih makan, tapi jangan kasih tahu. cara cari makan* (Indonesian-Chinese saying) you can give food to Indonesians, but don't tell them how to (make the money to) get it.

wanoja (*Jv*) young girl.

wanpréstasi (*D*) breach of contract, default.

wanra [perlawanan rakyat] People's Militia.

wantah (*Jv*) 1 in one's own, true character/shape. 2 simple, without s.t. particular to it. *besi* – pig iron.

wanték (*Jv*) dye.

mewanték to dye.

pewantékan dyeing.

wantilan I 1 one-man sawmill operation. 2 sawmill for ironwood.

wantilan II (*Jv*) stake to which an elephant is tethered.

wanti-wanti (*Jv*) time after time, again and again, repeatedly. *dengan* – repeatedly, again and again.

mewanti-wanti to say s.t. repeatedly/again and again.

wantunas → WATUNAS.

wanua (in the southern Celebes) village.

wap → UAP I, II.

wapa → WAJIB *pajak*.

Wapangab [Wakil Panglima Angkatan Bersenjata] Deputy Commander of the Armed Forces.

wapat → WAFAT.

waperdam [Wakil Perdana Menteri] Deputy Prime Minister.

Waprés [Wakil Présidén] Vice-President.

waqaf → WAKAF.

war → UAR.

wara I (*Jv*) to announce, make known/public, give notice of.

wara-wara announcement.

pewara announcer. ~ *télévisi* TV announcer.

WARA II [Wanita Angkatan Udara] Women's Air Force.

warak I (*A*) deep devotion to God (by not violating prohibitions, etc.), abstinence, abstemiousness.

berwarak to be abstinent/abstemious.

warak II (*Jv*) rhinoceros; → BADAK I.

warakat → WARKAT.

warakawuri (*Jv*) widow of an Armed Forces member.

waralaba franchise.

mewaralabakan to franchise.

pewaralaba franchisee.

pengwaralaba franchisor.

waran (*D/E*) warrant, option.

warana I (*Jv*) screen.

warana II → WAKIL.

warangan (*Jv*) 1 arsenic. 2 rat poison made of arsenic; → BARANGAN, BERANGAN II. 3 mixture used to clean krises.

mewarangkan to rub (a *keris*) with arsenic to clean it.

waranggana (*Jv*) 1 nymph. 2 female singer with the *gamelan*, chanteuse.

warangka (*Jv*) sheath (of kris).

waras (*Jv*) healthy, well, sound, sane. *kurang/tidak – akalnya/ingatannya/otaknya/pikirannya* (*coq*) slightly insane, a bit crazy. *tidak* – crazy. **ketidak-warasan** madness, insanity.

sewaras as sane as.

kewarasan sanity, soundness, health, well-being.

warasa(h) (*A*) (plural of *waris*) heirs (to property or title).

Warastratama the military resort command (*Korém* 074) in Solo.

warawiri I (*Jv*) *kembang* – hibiscus, shoe-flower, *Hibiscus rosa-sinensis*; → KEMBANG *sepatu*.

warawiri II (*J*) → WIRAWIRI.

wardi (*ob*) → ORDI II.

warek (*Jv J*) satiated, full.

warembol (*D*) bun, (hamburger) roll.

warga (*Skr*) 1 member (of a family/company, etc.). 2 citizen (of a country), resident (of a certain address). 3 (*Jv*) family, relatives. 4 (reference to) Chinese. 5 (*ob*) caste (such as *Brahmana, Satria, Waisya*, and *Sudra*). – *ABRI* a member of the Armed Forces (of the Republic of Indonesia). – *dalam* member of Sultan's family. – *dunia* cosmopolite, citizen of the world. – *Éropa* European. – *kota* townsman, city resident. – *masyarakat* community members. – *Nahdiyin/Nah(l)ijén/Nah(l)ijin* members of the Islamic organization NU. – *negara* citizen; → WARGANEGARA. – *sekolah* pupil, student.

sewarga allied, related; co-member (of an organization). ~ *Aséan* co-member(s) of ASEAN.

kewargaan 1 membership. 2 citizenry. ~ *negara* a) civic consciousness. b) civics.

pewargaan naturalizing.

wargadunia cosmopolite.

kewargaduniaan cosmopolitan(ism).

wargajagat (*Skr neo*) cosmopolite.

wargakota (*Skr neo*) city dweller.

warganegara (*Skr neo*) citizen; national (of a country). – *asing* [WNA] foreign citizen. – *asli* citizen by birth. – *bunglon* a) bipatride. b) Chinese who has obtained dual citizenship. – *Indonésia* [WNI] Indonesian citizen (often a code word for an ethnic Chinese Indonesian). – *Indonésia keturunan Tionghoa* Indonesian citizen of Chinese descent. – *kambing/kelas dua* second-class citizen. – *keturunan* citizen by descent. – *peroléhan* naturalized citizen. – *tiri* second-class citizen.

berwarganegara to be a citizen of.

mewarganegarakan to naturalize, to make a citizen (of a country).

kewarganegaraan 1 citizenship. 2 civics. *surat-surat* ~ citizenship papers. ~ *rangkap* dual citizenship. **berkewarganegaraan** to have citizenship, be a citizen of. *orang yang tidak* ~ a stateless person.

pewarganegaraan naturalization.

wari (*M ob*) **berwari** (*cla*) well then! (at the beginning of a story).

waria [wanita pria] homosexual, transvestite; intersex.

warid I (*A*) 1 traditional. 2 (*membaca -*) to recite prayers in the traditional way.

warid II (*A*) jugular vein.

warik (*A*) abstain from the unlawful; abstemious, pious; → WARAK I.

waringin (*Jv*) banyan tree; → BERINGIN.

waris I (*A*) 1 inheritor, heir (to property or title). *ahli* – the joint heirs. *hukum* – law of succession, hereditary law. 2 heritage, inheritance, legacy, estate. – *asli* lineal heir, e.g., one's wife's child. – *(yang) karib* nearest heirs (children/grandchildren, etc.). – *sah* legal heir.

mewarisi to inherit.

mewariskan 1 to leave (behind). 2 to bequeath, will, pass down. 3 to make s.o. one's heir. 4 (*ob*) to inherit.

warisan inheritance, bequest, legacy, heritage. *memperoléh* ~ to receive a bequest, inherit. *surat* ~ (last) will (and testament). ~ *kebudayaan* cultural heritage. ~ *terbuka* devolved estate.

kewarisan 1 get an inheritance, inherit. 2 inheritance (*mod*).

pewaris testator.

pewarisan 1 inheriting. 2 inheritance, heritage.

perwarisan inheritance (*mod*).

waris II (*J*) (= warisan) always fortunate/lucky in undertaking s.t.

warita (*ob*) news, report; story; → BERITA.

warkaf (*A*) document.

warkah and **warkat** (*A*) 1 letter, epistle, note. 2 draft, bill. 3 contents of letters. 4 item, document. *tanpa* – scripless. – *ambangan* float. – *bank* bank draft. – *berharga* paper money. – *inkaso* collection item. – *invéstasi* investment bill. – *kliring* paper-based clearing, clearing document. – *krédit* credit item (in account). – *lancar* negotiable instrument. – *niaga* commercial paper, such as checks, promissory notes, bills of exchange and other negotiable papers used in business. – *pos* aerogram, letter paper which folds to form envelope (similar to an air letter). – *pos udara* aerogram. – *tagihan* bill. – *témpélan* poster. – *warta* newsletter.

warkatulikhlas (*A*) a letter written/sent sincerely and frankly (usually used for old-style correspondence).

warkop [warung kopi] coffee shop.

warmbol → WAREMBOL.

warna (*Skr*) 1 color, tint, hue. *Mérah –nya.* It's red. 2 shade (of color). 3 (in some compounds) diversified, varied, assorted, different. 4 (*ob*) caste, any of the distinct, hereditary Hindu social classes; → WARGA 4. 5 character (of a political movement, etc.). – *asli* natural color. – *bahasa* speech level. – *bunga terung* purple. – *bunyi* vowel color. – *cempaka* yellow like the frangipani flower. – *cok(e)lat* reddish brown. – *darah* blood red. – *delima* red like the pomegranate. – *hijau lapangan* field green (of army uniform). – *keramat* the Indonesian national colors (red and white). – *muda* a light color. – *riang* bright color(s). – *sari* anthology. – *sawo* a) various shades of brown.

b) flesh-colored; yellowish-pink. – *sawo matang/tua* dark brown. – *suara* timbre. – *tua* a dark color. – *warni* various k.o. colors. **berwarna-warni** varicolored. **mewarna-warnikan** to make s.t. multicolored.

sewarna of the same color.

berwarna colored. *bangsa* ~ people of color. *tidak* ~ achromatic. ~ *gading* cream-colored. ~ *menyolok* flashy.

berwarna-warna 1 various. 2 multicolored, colorful.

mewarna to become colored, to gain color.

mewarnai to color, give color to, tinge; to slant (a story); to influence.

mewarnakan to color.

terwarnai colored, tinged.

pewarna dye, coloring matter, pigment, stain. ~ *alami* natural dye. ~ *kayu* wood dyes. ~ *kulit* tan. ~ *tambahan* color additive.

pewarnaan dying, coloring, pigmentation; color (*mod*).

warnabunyi phoneme; sound.

warnada (*Skr neo*) timbre.

warnasari (*Skr neo*) 1 various/all types of flowers. 2 a collection of poems and prose or essays, chosen by the compiler; anthology; → BUNGA *rampai.*

warnawarta (*Skr neo*) various/all k.o. news.

warnét [warung internét] cyber café.

waro' (*J*) pious, faithful to God's commandments.

warok I (*Jv*) 1 master (in the arts of fighting), expert. 2 leader. 3 village chief.

warok II (*Jv*) pederast, man who has sex with young boys; → GEMBLAKAN.

warsa (*Skr poet*) year.

Warsawa (*D*) Warsaw.

warta (*Skr*) news, report. *juru* – journalist. – *dibawa pikat dan langau* (*ob*) rumor. – *berita* (miscellaneous) news. – *harian* daily newspaper. – *sepekan* weekly magazine. – *yudha* war news.

mewartakan to report, announce, give the news about.

pewarta journalist, reporter. – *Rahayu* the Gospel.

pewartaan reporting, informing, announcing.

wartah (*A*) dilemma.

wartawan reporter, journalist, person who collects news for newspapers or magazines. – *amplop* "envelope news reporter," i.e., a news reporter who receives bribes for writing nicely about certain events. – *Bodréx* a hack reporter; → BODRÉX. – *gadungan* [wargad] fake/self-styled journalist. – *foto* newspaper photographer. – *lepas* freelance reporter, stringer. – *Muntabér/ Muncul tanpa Berita* a reporter who doesn't write articles. – *potrét* photo journalist. – *tulis* newsman, reporter. – *yang tidak terikat kepada suatu suratkabar* and – *bébas* (*Mal*) freelancer, freelance journalist. – *WTS/Wartawan Tanpa Suratkabar* "news reporter without a newspaper;" *cp* WTS.

kewartawanan journalism.

wartawati female journalist.

wartég → WARUNG *tegal.*

Warték [Warta Ékonomi] Economic News (name of a magazine).

wartél [warung télékomunikasi] telecommunications shop.

wartén [warung ténda] outdoor restaurant under a tent.

waru I (*J/Jv*) k.o. hibiscus tree whose bark fibers (*agel*) are used for making rope and sacking material, *Hibiscus tiliaceus.* – *gading* nyssa, *Nyssa javanica.* – *geli/geni* k.o. hibiscus, *Hibiscus grewiifolius.* – *gunung* k.o. hibiscus, *Hibiscus similis.* – *jembut/ lanang/payung/songsong* k.o. tree, *Hibiscus macrophyllus.* – *laut* k.o. tree, *Hibiscus tiliaceus.* – *lilin* k.o. hibiscus, *Litsea sebifera.*

waru II spade (in pack of cards).

waruga (from wa+ruga meaning "become soft and pulverized") sarcophagus, a stone coffin, found in parts of the Minahasa area in northern Celebes.

Waruna (*Skr*) Varuna, the Hindu God of the sea.

warung (*J/Jv*) (roadside) food booth, usually consisting of a small wood and straw hut with a central table. The customers sit on one side, usually on a long bench; the persons who prepare the food stand on the other side. – *angkringan/(ber)jalan* mobile food cart. – *berbunga* food stall with charming waitresses to attract truck drivers on the Trans-Sumatran Highway. – *hidup* a yard planted with vegetables for daily consumption. – *kelap-kelip* k.o. disguised brothel which offers food and prostitutes. – *keliling* k.o. chuck wagon (pushed by a man) or (recently) a van equipped with a kitchen. – *kopi* coffee shop. – *lamsam* (*J*) store selling kitchen necessities (salt, etc.). – *léséhan* (in Yogyakarta) stall where the customers sit on a mat spread on the ground. – *nasi* a) roadside eating stall. b) (in Cianjur, West Java, also) a term used by restaurants to evade taxes. – *pengécér* retail stall. – *pinggir jalan* roadside stall. – *pojok* "corner roadside food stall," located outside Tangerang, West Java; it offers prostitutes as well as food. – *remeng-remeng* → WARUNG *kelap-kelip*. – *sénggol* a small food stand. – *Tegal* [*wartég*] Jakarta food stalls open 24 hours a day to serve inexpensive food to *becak* drivers, etc.

    berwarung to own/run a *warung*.

warwar (*ob*) → UAR(-UAR).

was I clipped form of **waswas**.

was II clipped form of **wassalam**.

was III (in acronyms) → PENGAWASAN, WASIT, WAWASAN.

wasahlan (*A*) welcome.

wasak (*A*) rice, wheat, etc. in the amount that can be loaded on a camel's back (in Java corresponds to about 180 *kati*s).

wasal → WASLAH.

wasalam → WASSALAM.

wasana (*Jv*) end, close, final. – *kata* and finally, to sum it all up.

wasanakata peroration (of a speech), closing/final remarks.

wasangka (*A + Skr*) *syak* – [from: *syak + wa + sangka* = suspicion and doubt/mistrust] suspicion, distrust, doubt, uncertainty. – *yang jelék* fallacy, fallacious ideas. *menaruh syak* – *kepada* to suspect (s.o.).

    berwasangka to be suspicious.

wasantara [*wawasan nusantara*] national outlook.

wasbang [*pengawasan pembangunan*] development oversight.

waserai → WASSERIJ.

wasfah (*A*) description.

washup (*E mil*) exercise evaluation meeting.

wasi I (*A*) *Al*– the omnipresence (of God).

wasi II (*A*) executor of a will.

wasiat (*A*) **1** last will and testament (usually verbal). *surat* – last will and testament, a document containing the legal statement of s.o.'s wishes concerning the disposal of his property after his death. – *di bawah tangan* will not drawn up before a notary public. – *hukum* will drawn up before notary public. – *rahasia* sealed will. **2** heirloom. *keris* – hereditary kris having *sakti*, i.e., supernatural powers. **3** Testament. *Kitab* – *Baru* New Testament. *Kitab* – *Lama* Old Testament.

    berwasiat to make a (verbal or written) will/testament.

    mewasiatkan to bequeath, leave by will.

wasikah (*A*) document.

wasil (*A*) united (with God), of mystics.

wasilah and **wasilat** (*A*) close/intimate relationship explained as the site where the close allies (Muhammad and his companions) are found in heaven; bond, association, union (of persons).

wasilkan (*A*) to convey (a letter) to a recipient.

wasir (*Jv*) hemorrhoids; → BAWASIR.

wasis (*Jv*) able, clever, skillful, experienced, expert.

wasit (*A*) **1** referee, umpire. – *kehormatan* honorary referee. **2** mediator, arbiter. **3** medium. **4** procuress.

    mewasiti to umpire, act as an umpire of, referee.

    pe(r)wasitan 1 arbitration. **2** arbitration (*mod*).

wasitah (*A*) **1** arbitress, mediatress. **2** matchmaker, go-between. **3** medium, spirit. *ilmu* – spiritualism.

wasi-wasiyat (*A*) executor of an estate.

waskat [*pengawasan melekat* and *kewaspadaan melekat*] self-control, built-in controls.

waskita (*Jv*) to foresee the future, be prophetic. *orang* – clairvoyant.

    kewaskitaan ability to see the future, clairvoyance.

    pewaskitaan clairvoyance.

waskom (*D*) washbasin; → BASKOM.

waslah (*A*) **1** mark in the written language which indicates that the *alif* over which it is placed has lost its vowel sound in favor of the preceding vowel (similar to an apostrophe to mark a con-

traction): *fi 'l-bait*, in the house (instead of *fi al-bait*). **2** chaining, connecting.

waslap (*D*) washcloth, bath brush.

wasmat [*pengawas dan pengamat*] supervising and controlling.

wasnas [*kewaspadaan nasional*] national alertness.

waspada (*Jv*) cautious, watchful, on the alert, wary. *-lah!* be vigilant! – *éling* self-knowledge and self-control. – *purpa wisésa* (*mil*) always being alert to correct the mistakes of one's crew.

    berwaspada to beware, be cautious/on guard/alert/careful.

    mewaspadai to guard against, watch out for, be on the alert for.

    mewaspadakan to put on the alert.

    kewaspadaan and **pewaspadaan** caution, care(fulness), watchfulness, vigilance, alertness.

Wasrik [*pengawasan dan pemeriksaan*] supervision and inspection.

    ke-Wasrik-an relating to supervision and inspection. *ceramah* ~ a lecture on supervision and inspection.

wass clipped form of **wassalam**.

wassalam (*A*) **1** and peace be with you! **2** (as a closing phrase of a letter) yours truly, sincerely, respectfully; → SALAM I.

wassalumualaikum → WASSALAM.

wasserij (*D*) /waseray/ laundry or dry-cleaning establishment.

    mewasserijkan to send to the dry cleaners.

    wasserijan dry-cleaned (clothes).

wastafel (*D*) washstand.

wastra (*Jv*) **1** clothing. **2** batik wraparound skirt. – *Préma* "Batik Wraparound Skirt Business Company," i.e., the name of the association of Indonesian batik and textile lovers.

wastu (*Skr*) architecture.

wastuwidyawan master builder, architect.

waswas (*A*) **1** suspicion, distrust. **2** (– *hati*) anxious, worried. **3** apprehensive, nervous, restless. **4** evil thoughts; torment.

    kewaswasan anxiety, uneasiness.

waswisu (*J*) → WASWAS I. **1** anxious (person). **2** slightly crazy person.

wat I (*D*) watt.

wat II (Thai) Buddhist temple.

watak (*Jv*) **1** character. *pendidikan* – formation of character. **2** attitude, nature, disposition. – *berulang* stock character. – *pribadi* character, nature. – *wantu* behavior.

    berwatak to have character; characteristic. *tak* ~ characterless.

    mewataki to form one's character, permeate one's character.

    pewatak character (in a play).

    pewatakan role, character.

    perwatakan characterization.

watan → WAT(H)AN.

watang (*Jv*) bamboo spear, long pole.

watas (*Jv*) border, boundary, frontier, limit; → BATAS. – *kesabarannya* the limits of his patience.

    berwatas(an) to be bordered.

    mewatasi 1 to border, enclose. **2** to limit, restrict, confine, modify.

    terwatas bounded. *tak* ~ unbounded.

    pewatas (*ling*) modifier.

    perwatasan 1 border, frontier. **2** restriction, confinement, limitation. **3** (*ling*) modification.

watase → WATTASE.

watek → WATAK.

watermantel (*D*) water-cooled machine gun.

watermér(e)k (*D*) watermark.

waterpas (*D*) **1** leveling instrument. **2** level (*mod*).

waterpoken (*D*) chicken pox.

waterpruf (*E*) waterproof.

wates → WATAS.

wat(h)an (*A*) fatherland, native country.

wat(h)ania(h) (*A*) concerning/relating to the fatherland, native country (*mod*).

-wati (*Skr*) suffix for the formation of female persons; *cp* -WAN, such as *wartawati*.

wati I 1 (*ob*) (in several compounds) firmament, heaven, universe, sky.

wati II *pohon* – (in the eastern part of Indonesia) name of a tree, *Piper sp.*, which produces a k.o. liquor that can be highly intoxicating.

watik (A) sexual intercourse.

waton I → WAT(H)AN.

waton II – *garang, sanajan garing* (Jv) all is not gold that glitters.

Watt (E) Watt(s).

wattase (E) wattage.

watu (Jv) rock, (natural) stone. – *pengilon* yoni, representation of the female genitalia.

watunas [wanita tunasusila] prostitute.

wau I (D) paper kite (in various shapes). *main* – to fly a kite. – *melawan angin* a useless act.

wau II (A) name of the 27th letter of the Arabic alphabet.

wauw wow!

wauwau → WAKWAK.

wawa → WAKWAK.

wawaderan a perennial grass, *Isachne albens*.

wawancara (Jv) interview. – *ajuk* interview in depth. – *bébas* open-ended interview. – *sambil lalu* casual interview. – *télepon* telephone interview. – *tivi/tipi* TV-interview.

berwawancara to hold an interview. ~ *dengan* and

mewawancarai [and ngewawancarain (J coq)] to interview s.o. *orang yang diwawancarai* the interviewee.

mewawancarakan to hold an interview about.

terwawancara interviewee.

pewawancara interviewer.

pewawancaraan interviewing.

wawancarawan male interviewer.

wawancarawati female interviewer.

wawankata dialogue.

berwawankata to hold a dialogue.

wawanmuka face-to-face.

berwawanmuka to hold face-to-face talk, personally.

wawanrembug dialogue.

wawansabda → WAWANCARA.

wawansantap friendly, informal dinner.

wawanwuruk (Jv) to teach/instruct e.o.

wawar k.o. sandwich board; → RÉKLAME *berjalan*.

wawas (Jv) insight, perception, view(point), outlook, vision.

berwawaskan which takes ... as its viewpoint/point of view.

wawasan l insight, outlook. 2 geopolitical concept. ~ *hari kiamat* doomsday model. ~ *bahari* the sea as a geostrategic concept. ~ *buwana* the land as a geostrategic concept. ~ *dirgantara* airspace as a geostrategic concept. ~ *kebangsaan* nationalistic viewpoint. ~ *kebudayaan* cultural viewpoint. ~ *kejuangan* (armed) struggle viewpoint. ~ *Nusantara* archipelagic principle, which gives Indonesia control over what are now considered international waters. berwawasan with a ... viewpoint. ~ *luas* with a broad outlook, broad-minded. ~ *péndék* short-sighted.

wawasdiri introspection.

mewawasdiri to introspect.

wawuh (Jv) l agreement, accord, harmony; → RUKUN II. 2 reconciliation.

way → WAI II.

wayah (J/Jv) l o'clock. – *kapan* at what time? 2 when; → WAKTU. – *titét* early in the morning. – *dur* afternoon. – *soré* evening.

Wayan (in Bali) a noncaste name element placed before personal names to indicate the firstborn child, such as *Wayan Diya*.

wayang I (Jv) l shadow play performance with puppets (made of buffalo hide or carved wood) manipulated by the puppeteer (*dalang*) and which cast their shadows against a cloth screen (*kelir*), illuminated by an oil lamp. The *dalang* is accompanied by a *gamelan* and by a female singer or singers [= *pesind(h)én*]. *menanggap* – a) to have players perform a *wayang* play for money. b) (= *menonton* –) to watch a *wayang* performance. 2 the shadow puppets themselves. *dunia* – the world of the *wayang*. – *bébér* a shadow play in which the *dalang* is aided by a scroll on which the scenes of the story are painted. – *gambar/gelap* (Mal) movie(s). – *gedog* shadow play with leather puppets; stories are from the Panji cycle; → PANJI. – *golék* performance using three-dimensional wooden puppets; stories are from the Amir Hamza cycle in Central Java and from the Ramayana and Mahabharata in West Java. – *k(e)litik/kercil/*

k(e)rucil show using flat wooden puppets with leather arms; stories are about Damar Wulan. – *kulit* shadow play with leather puppets. **mewayang-kulitkan** to perform as a shadow play. – *madia/madya* shadow play based on 19th-century stories about Djojobojo. – *Makao* Chinese shadow play. – *mbeling* k.o. *wayang* similar to – *purwo*; the language is popular, relaxed, often slightly pornographic; first introduced in Semarang in 1981. – *orang* dance-drama using real people instead of puppets; → WAYANG *wong*. – *Pancasila* shadow play in which the five Pandawas are symbolically represented as the Pancasila. – *planét* a k.o. *wayang* with modern themes and characters. – *pompa* show with inflated rubber puppets. – *potéhi* Chinese puppet show. – *purwa/purwo* performance in which leather puppets project their shadows on a canvas; stories are based on the Ramayana and the Mahabharata. – *sadat* k.o. Islamic shadow play. – *suluh* a 20th-century shadow play used by the Ministry of Information for the purpose of telling recent Indonesian history and for disseminating information. The leather puppets are human figures in profile. – *tahunengul* shadow play peculiar to Blora, East Java. – *timplong* → WAYANG *klitik*. – *titi* Chinese hand-puppet show. – *topéng* → TOPÉNG. – *wahyu* shadow puppet show of biblical stories. – *wong* show with actors who speak the lines themselves and do not use a *dalang*.

mewayangkan to perform a shadow play.

wayangan (*euph*) not sleeping (for four days and four nights); during this period college students usually start to read the prescribed books for the exam.

pewayang *wayang* play performer.

pewayangan 1 place where a shadow play is performed. 2 the *wayang* plays. *cantrik dalam* ~ a) student in the art of shadow plays. b) reference to a *santri* or student of an Islamic seminary.

perwayangan (*mod*) shadow play. *cerita/tokoh* ~ a shadow play story/character.

wayang II *semata* – → MATA III.

wayer (D) electric fan.

wayu → BAYU I, II, III.

wayuh (Jv) 1 to have/take an additional wife. 2 polygamy. – *arti* (*joc*) ambiguous.

berwayuh to commit bigamy.

wazifah (A) a daily lesson or portion of the Koran read.

wazir (A *cla*) l vizier; premier. 2 bishop (in chess).

wb. → WB.

W.C. /wésé/ toilet, restrooms. – *cemplung/gantung* toilet located above a stream.

per-W.C.-an toilet/restroom system.

W.C.-nisasi encouraging the installation of restrooms.

WDP [Wajib Daftar Perusahaan] obligation to register as a business.

me-WDP-kan to register s.t. as a business.

wé I (K) water; *cp* WEDANG.

wé II (Jv) and wéh interjection of astonishment: ah, oh.

wéda (Skr) l the Veda. 2 the wisdom contained in the Vedas.

wédam → WÉDA.

wedana (Jv) head of a (government administrative) district; this function has been replaced by the *Pembantu Bupati*. *asistén* – assistant district head; → CAMAT, STÉN.

kewedanaan office/residence of the *wedana*; district under the *wedana*; → KAWEDANAN.

wedang pest of the tobacco plant which causes brown rot, *Pseudomonas solanacearum*.

wédang (Jv) hot cooked/boiled water (for making hot drinks). – *jahé* a hot ginger drink. – *kopi* hot coffee. – *ronda* a soupy ginger dessert. – *téh* hot tea.

wedani (Jv) k.o. climbing ornamental plant, Rangoon creeper, *Quisqualis indica*.

wedar (Jv) mewedarkan to disclose, let down, explain.

terwedar 1 disclosed (of a secret). 2 let down (of hair).

wedaran explanation, clarification.

Wédatama (Book of) Javanese ethics.

wédé (D *col* w.d. *waarnemend*) acting (chief, etc.).

wedel (Jv) mewedel to dye blue.

wedelan dyeing blue, s.t. dyed blue.

wedi-wedi (*Jv*) pink-headed imperial pigeon, *Ducula rosaceae*.

weduk (*J*) invulnerable.

   kewedukan invulnerability.

wedung (*Jv*) cleaver.

wedusan (*Jv*) k.o. weed, goat weed, *Ageratum conyzoides*.

wegah (*Jv*) not willing/inclined; reluctant; opposed/averse (to); → OGAH I.

   kewegahan reluctance, unwillingness.

wéger (*D*) to misfire.

weharima (*cla*) (in Sumbawa) mutual cooperation; → GOTONG-ROYONG.

Wéhrkreis (*German*) komando – (in the early days of the struggle for independence) similar to the present Military Area Command; → KORÉM.

wejang (*Jv*) mewejang(i) to advise/instruct, etc.

   mewejangi to use s.t. to instruct.

   mewejangkan to use s.t. to instruct with.

   wejangan 1 instruction; advice; guide(lines). **2** speech containing advice/guidance, etc.

   pewejangan instructing.

wekel (*Jv*) serious, diligent.

wéker (*D*) alarm clock.

wektu (*Jv*) – *telu* religion peculiar to Lombok; combines elements of Islam and other faiths.

welahar (*Jv*) soggy marsh land; land inundated now and then, such as land at the edge of the sea.

welang → BELANG.

welas (*Jv*) compassion, pity, commiseration; → BELAS I. – *asih* pity, compassion, affection. – *tanpo alis* to get no thanks for earlier favors.

   memelas pitiful, pitiable.

   kewelasan pity, affection.

welasan (in Palembang; *ob*) extra, a small addition (one for every 10) given to please the customer, lagniappe.

weling (*Jv*) **1** message. **2** (*leg*) last will and testament, document containing s.o.'s wishes concerning the disposal of his property after death.

welirang (*Jv*) sulfur; → BELÉRANG.

welit (*Jv*) k.o. *nipah* used for roofing.

wélter (*E*) welter(weight).

wenang (*Jv*) (to have) authority, power; authorized, rightful. *tanpa* – without authorization. *tidak* – unauthorized. – *garis* direct command authority.

   sewenang-wenang 1 arbitrarily, at will, as one wishes. **2** tyrannical, cruel, despotic. **3** (to do s.t.) haphazardly, in a slapdash manner. **kesewenang-wenangan 1** arbitrariness. **2** despotism, tyranny. **bersewenang-wenang** and **bersiwenang-wenang** → SEWENANG-WENANG. **menyewenang-wenangi** to treat arbitrarily. **persewenang-wenangan** reign of terror.

   berwenang 1 with/to have the authority, competent (court, etc.), have jurisdiction, authorized. *pihak yang* ~ the competent authorities. *sumber-sumber yang* ~ *mengatakan…* authoritative sources stated that… **2** in charge.

   berwenang-wenang ~ *penuh* fully competent.

   mewenangkan to authorize.

   kewenangan 1 right and power/authority (to do s.t.). ~ *mengadili* jurisdiction. ~ *pimpinan* authority. ~ *otorisasi* financial authority. **2** jurisdiction (of a court), competence (of a court/judge).

   kewenang-wenangan 1 arbitrariness. **2** despotism, tyranny.

   pewenang person with the authority (in that matter).

wénéh *diwénéhi ati ngrogoh rempelo* (*Jv*) → MEMPEROLÉH *satu, kepingin dua; dapat sedikit, kepingin banyak*.

wérak and **wérek** (*D coq*) s.o. who looks for laborers, recruiter of laborers.

   mewérak to recruit as a laborer.

werangka → WARANGKA.

werda (*Jv*) old, senior. *golongan* – senior citizens.

wérda (*D? ob*) Who goes there?

werdatama → WREDATAMA.

werdawan senior citizen.

werdha → WERDA.

Werdi Budaya Art Center.

wérék → WÉRAK.

wereng I (*Jv*) black insect which attacks rice and other plants. (*hama*) – *cokelat* brown (rice) plant-hopper, *Nilaparvata lugens*.

wereng II (in Banyuwangi, East Java) prostitute.

werit (*Jv*) **1** holy, awe-inspiring. **2** unsafe (due to the presence of tigers or bandits). **3** weird. **4** ominous, sinister, spooky.

weru (*Jv*) k.o. tall albizzia, *Albizzia procera*.

werus (*Jv?*) – *kuning* yellow-white shrimp; → UDANG *cendana*.

Wésak → WAICAK.

wésé → W.C.

wésel I (*D*) **1** (demand) draft, bill (of exchange); → SURAT *wésel*. **2** (– *pos*) postal money order. – *atas unjuk* sight draft. – *bayar* promissory note (to be paid at a fixed time). – *berjangka* usance draft. – *ékspor* export bill. – *lihat* sight draft. – *tagih* a) promissory note (time to be determined). b) reimbursement draft, bill for collection. – *tunai* payment bill. – *unjuk* sight draft. – *utang* notes payable. – *waktu* time draft. – *yang diaval* protected bill of exchange.

   mewéselkan to transmit (money) by postal money order.

wésel II (*D*) railway switch. *salah* – misunderstand, make a mistake.

wéselbor (*D*) switchboard.

wéselpos → POSWÉSEL, POS *wésel*. – *inkaso* collection draft.

   mewéselposkan to transmit by postal money order.

wesi (*Jv*) iron; → BESI. – *aji* "precious weapon," such as the kris; → TOSAN *aji*.

wésio Buddhist monk; → WAISYA.

wéskét (*E*) waistcoat.

wésminster (*E*) → JAM *wésminster*.

wésternis (*D*) Western(-oriented).

wésternisasi (*D*) westernization.

wét (*D*) law.

wétan (*J/Jv*) east.

wé-té-és → WTS, WANITA *tunasusila*.

weton (*Jv*) birthday determined by combining the five-day week and the seven-day week, e.g., *Selasa Kliwon*.

wewangian (*ob*) perfumes; → WANGI-WANGIAN.

wewarah (*Jv*) instruction, teaching.

wewaton (*Jv*) **1** rule, regulation. **2** yardstick.

wéwé – (*gombél*) (*Jv*) (female) forest ghost.

weweg (*Jv*) **1** large, compact, and muscular; *opp* flabby. **2** stacked (of a woman).

weweja (*Jv*) → ÉCÉNG.

wéwéka → WIWÉKA.

wewenang (*Jv*) **1** power, ability, competence, authority. ~ *resmi* formal authority. **2** jurisdiction; → WENANG.

   berwewenang to have the authority/right to. ~ *mengadakan pemeriksaan* to have the authority to investigate.

wewengkon (*Jv*) supremacy, control; area under one's authority.

wewohan (*Jv*) → ÉCÉNG.

white (*E sl*) morphine.

wiara → WIHARA.

WIB [Waktu Indonésia Barat] West Indonesia Time.

wibawa (*Jv*) authority. *tata* – system of power.

   berwibawa authoritative, influential.

   mewibarakan to authorize, give authority to.

   kewibawaan power/authority to give orders (that have to be obeyed). ~ *Seroja Nugraha* an award given to *Lémhannas* students for high achievement. **berkewibawaan** with the authority. ~ *untuk* to have the authority (to).

   wibawa-wibawaan authority.

wicaksana (*Jv*) **1** endowed with wisdom. **2** to foresee. **3** with clear insight.

   kewicaksanaan statesmanship; wisdom.

wicara (*Jv*) **1** speech. **2** (*infr*) conversation; dialogue. *ahli térapi* – speech pathologist/therapist.

wicitra (*Skr*) motion-picture theater, cinema.

widak (*A*) good-bye.

widara → BIDARA.

widaran (*Jv*) k.o. *kué*.

widarén (in Tuban, Central Java) ceremony asking for rain.

widia- → WIDYA-.

widoro (*Jv*) name of various trees with edible fruit; → BIDARA.

Widura (Mahabharata) brother of Dasaratha and Pandu.

widuren (*Jv*) nettle rash, hives, urticaria; → KALIGATA.

widuri (*Jv*) giant milkweed, *Calotropis gigantea*.

widya (*Skr*) [also see words beginning with **widya** below] 1 knowledge, skill, ability. – *Graha* "House of Knowledge," i.e., the *Gedung Lembaga Ilmu Pengetahuan Indonésia* or Indonesian Sciences Institute Building. – *prasara* science advocate/pioneer. – *Yudha* "War Skills," i.e., a training exercise for advanced cadets in the Armed Forces Academy. 2 (used as a prefix in neologisms) -ology.

widyabasa (*Skr neo*) linguistics; → ILMU *bahasa*.

widyabasawan (*Skr neo*) linguist.

widyaiswara (*Skr neo*) (university) lecturer.

widyajanma (*Skr neo*) anthropology.

widyajanmawan (*Skr neo*) anthropologist.

widyakalawan (*Skr neo*) historian.

widyakarya (*Skr neo*) workshop, experts' meeting.

widyaléka (*Skr neo*) epigraphy.

widyalékawan (*Skr neo*) epigraphist, epigrapher.

widyapurba (*Skr neo*) arch(a)eology.

widyapurbawan (*Skr neo*) arch(a)eologist.

widyaswara (*Skr neo*) spokesman, spokeswoman.

widyawarga (*Skr neo*) sociology.

widyawargawan (*Skr neo*) sociologist.

widyawisata (*Skr neo*) study tour. – *pérs* press tour.
  berwidyawisata to go on a study tour.

widyayudha (*Skr neo*) field tactics.

Wiéna Vienna.

wig (*E*) wig.

wigah-wigih (*Jv*) timid, diffident. *tidak* – undaunted, fearless.

wigati (*Jv*) urgent, important, serious.

wigih (*Jv*) to fear, dread, hesitate.

wih exclamation to draw attention.

wihara (*Skr*) Buddhist place of worship.

Wihdatul Wujud (*A*) Pantheism.

wijadah (*A*) transmission of the words of the Prophet by inadvertent discovery.

wijan (*Jv*) → BIJAN.

wijawiyata training. – *manajemén* management training.

wijaya I (*Skr*) winning, victorious.
  kewijayaan victory.

wijaya II (*Skr*) first part of some plant names. – *kusuma* a) night-blooming cereus, Queen of the Night, an ornamental plant, *Epiphyllum oxypetalum*. b) the military resort command (*Korém* 071) in Purwokerto. – *mala/mulia/kesuma* a legendary flower (of the *sentolong* plant, k.o. pisonia) which brought all it touched to life. It is found on the island of *Nusakembangan* off Java's south coast.

Wijayakarta the military resort command (*Korém* 051) in Jakarta Timur.

Wijayakrama the military resort command (*Korém* 052) in Jakarta Barat.

wijén (*Jv*) sesame, *Sesamum indicum/orientale*; → BIJAN.

wiji → BIJI I.

wijik (*Jv*) to wash one's hands/feet.
  wijikan water vessel for washing.

wijil (*Jv cla*) door; exit.

wikalat (*A*) representative, proxy.

wiku (*Kawi cla*) an ascetic sage.

Wiku Yudha Wirottama (motto of the Infantry Training Center) Master of Military Science.

wil I [*wanita idaman lain*] girlfriend, mistress (of a married man).

wil II (in acronyms) → WILAYAH.

wila I bel-fruit tree, *Aegle marmelos*.

Wila II Negritos of Kedah (Malaysia).

wiladah (*A*) childbirth; pregnancy. *mandi* – ceremonial washing of a pregnant woman or after confinement; → MANDI *tian/lénggang perut*.

wiladé (*J*) → WILADAH.

wilahar (*ob*) → WELAHAR.

wilangon and **wilangun** (*Jv cla*) frantic, frenzied; lust.

wilayah (*A*) domain, territory, district, province, zone, area, sphere. – *daérah* province. – *hukum* jurisdiction. – *industri* industrial estate. – *kecamatan* subdistrict. – *kepentingan* sphere of interest. – *kota* city/town territory. – *kumuh* slum. – *Pabéan* Customs Zone. – *Pembantu Gubernur* → KERÉSIDÉNAN. – *pencacahan* enumeration area. – *pendudukan* occupied territory. – *perairan* territorial waters. – *peralihan* border area. – *perdagangan bébas* free-trade zone. – *perdésaan* rural area. – *perkotaan* urban area. – *Persekutuan* (*Mal*) Federal Territory. – *pertambangan* mining area. – *sénsitif* erogenous zone. – *udara* air space.

sewilayah 1 in the same area. 2 all-... *lomba tarik tambang untuk tingkat SD ~ Bandung* a tug-of-war contest for all elementary schools in the Bandung area.

kewilayahan area (*mod*) specialist. *studi ~* area studies.

berwilayah to comprise a zone of.

mewilayahi to have ... within its area/territory, etc.

pewilayahan 1 zoning. 2 territorial.

perwilayahan regional, district (*mod*).

wildop (*D*) hubcap.

wilem (*Jv*) [*dijawil gelem*] *wanita* – an easy lay.

wilis (*Jv*) bluish green, myrtle green, emerald. *ratna* – a green diamond.

wili-wili thick-knee, *Esacus neglectus*. – *besar* beach thick-knee, *Esacus magnirostris*.

wilmana → WAL(I)MANA.

Wil-Wo (*Jv*) the system of "to be touched" (to get attention = *dijaWIL*) and then "to be dragged along" (= *digoWO*); a system introduced into East Java as part of the campaign for family planning.

wimana (*Skr cla*) carriage, vehicle.

Wina Vienna.

winanajaka hostess on a train.

winaya (*Skr*) guidance; education; teaching; discipline. – *diri* self-discipline.

winayadati *Ibu* – *Kanyaséna* Air Force Women Governess.

windu I (*Jv*) a period of eight years (in Javanese calendrical reckoning).
  berwindu-windu for some periods of eight years.

windu II → UDANG *windu*.

winéka (*Skr*) attentive.

wing I (*E*) air force unit of several squadrons, wing.

wing II (*E*) (football) winger.

wingit (*Jv*) 1 impressive, imposing, awe-inspiring, demanding respect when approaching. 2 magically.

wingking (*Jv*) rear, back. *konco* – "the friend in the back of the house," i.e., the woman of the house, one's wife.

wingko (*Jv*) k.o. cookie made from sticky-rice flour.

wings (*E*) a pilot's badge.

wiper (*E*) /waiper/ windshield wiper.

wira (*Skr*) 1 man, male. 2 manly, courageous; hero. – *amur* army aviator. – *cipta busana* fashion designer. – *penjualan* salesman.
  kewiraan manly (*mod*). *kursus ~* course in citizenship.

Wirabhakti the military resort command (*Korém* 162) in Mataram.

Wirabima military resort command (*Korém* 031) in Pekanbaru.

Wirabraja military resort command (*Korém* 032) in Padang.

Wirabuana name of the Army division stationed in Sulawesi.

wiracarita and **wiracerita** (*Jv*) epic.

Wiradharma the military resort command (*Korém* 164) in Dili.

wiraga (*Jv*) swift and graceful (in posture/movements/manners).

wirakarya (*Skr neo*) jamboree.

wirama I → IRAMA.

wirama II → KEKAWIN.

wirang (*Jv cla*) 1 shy, ashamed; to feel shame. *membalas lara* – to take revenge on being made to feel ashamed. 2 shame, humiliation, loss of self-respect/face, mortification.

wiraniaga salesman, salesperson.
  kewiraniagaan salesmanship.

wirapraja (*Skr neo*) statesman.
  kewiraprajaan statesmanship.

wirapuspaniaga (*Skr neo*) sales promoter, canvasser.

wirapuspawisata (*Skr neo*) tour promoter.

wirasa (*Jv*) meaning.

Wirasakti the military resort command (*Korém* 161) in Kupang.

wirasat (*Jv*) 1 facial expression. 2 physiognomy; → FIRASAT, PIRASAT.

Wirasatya the military resort command (*Korém* 163) in Den Pasar.

wirasuara and wiraswara (*Jv*) female singer with a *gamelan* orchestra.

wiraswasta (*Skr neo*) entrepreneur, businessman.

  berwiraswasta to be an entrepreneur, trade/do business.

  kewiraswastaan entrepreneurship.

wiraswastawati and wiraswasti businesswoman.

wira(ta)tama (*Skr neo*) special-forces soldier.

wirausaha (*Skr neo*) entrepreneur, businessman.

  kewirausahaan entrepreneurship, entrepreneurial.

wirausahawan (*Skr neo*) businessman.

wirawan (*cla*) hero(ic).

wirawati female soldier. *(Yayasan)* – *Catur Panca* 1945 Female Soldiers (Foundation).

wirawicara (*Skr neo*) speaker (in election campaign).

wira-wiri and wirawiri (*J*) (to go/move) back and forth. *bus* – shuttle bus; *cp* ULANG-ALIK.

wirid (*A*) 1 division of the Koran (to be read, studied, etc.). 2 extra, personal prayers said after the ritual prayers.

  berwirid to recite passages from the Koran.

  mewiridkan to read the wirid.

  wiridan reading of passages from the Koran.

wiro → WIRA.

wiron (*Jv*) pleats in batik skirt.

  berwiron pleated.

Wiropati name of a group of political guards.

wiro(t)ama (*Jv*) bold and reckless; daredevil.

wiru and wiron (*Jv*) pleat, fold (in a batik wraparound skirt) made at the time the wearer puts on the garment.

  berwiru-wiru (a wraparound skirt) with pleats.

  mewiru to pleat, fold.

wiruk (*Jv*) – *hitam* great bandicoot rat, *Bandicota indica*.

wirwir → UIR-UIR.

wirya (*Skr*) male.

  wiryaan heroism.

wisa → BISA II.

wisata (*Skr*) 1 excursion, trip, tour; → DARMAWISATA, PARIWISATA. *bis* – tour bus. – *borongan* package tour. – *budaya* cultural tour. – *karya* work-tour. – *konvénsi* convention tour. – *satu hari penuh* one-day tour. 2 recreation. – *bahari* marine recreation.

  berwisata 1 tourist (*mod*). 2 to be a tourist, sightsee.

wisatawan (male) tourist. – *domestik* domestic/internal tourist.

wisaya 1 animal trap. 2 black magic, witchcraft.

wisel (*D*) → WÉSEL II.

wisésa (*Jv*) 1 powerful, mighty. 2 supreme power, supremacy. 3 dominant.

wisik (*Jv*) 1 whispering. 2 communication/warning/admonition in secrecy or in a dream. 3 prompting, inspiration, revelation, oracle; → BISIKAN *gaib*.

wisit (*J*) → WASIT.

wiski (*E*) whiskey. – *soda* whiskey and soda.

wisma (*K*) 1 house, dwelling; building where a group of employees of a corporation or organization live together; place of business, business firm, commercial establishment. 2 used in the name of such structures: ... House. – *budaya* art gallery. – *dagang* trading house, firm. – *Kusnul Qatimah* Drug Dependency Home. – *Mulya Jaya* rehabilitation center for prostitutes at Pasar Rebo, Jakarta. – *Nusantara* a 30-story high-rise in Jakarta containing offices and a restaurant. – *pangkas* barbershop. – *perawatan orang-orang lanjut usia* home for the aged. – *pijat keséhatan* massage parlor. – *ramah tamah* (*infr*) open house. -*rini* the University of Indonesia's dormitory for girls. – *tamu* guest house. – *Warta* Press House. – *Werd(h)a* Retirement Home, Old Person's Home. – *Yaso* the Jakarta house in which President Soekarno died; now used for the Armed Forces Struggle Museum.

  mewismakan to billet, put up (in housing).

  perwismaan housing.

wisman [wisatawan mancanegara] foreign tourist.

Wisnu I Vishnu, one of the principal gods of Javanese mythology.

wisnu II [wisatawan nusantara] domestic tourist.

wisuda I (*Skr*) graduation, inauguration, installation (in a college/university, etc.). *Acara* – Wing Day (in Air Force). *Hari* – graduation day. – *jurit* the promotion from candidate cadet to cadet at the Armed Forces Academy. – *purnabhakti* retired from service. **mewisma-purnabhakti** to retire (from the police force). – *purnoyudha* retired from the army. **mewisuda-purnoyudha** to retire from the army.

  me(ng)wisuda to inaugurate, install.

  pewisudaan (~ *sarjana*) commencement, graduation.

wisuda II clean, pure, genuine.

wisudapurnawira (*Skr neo*) ceremony at one's retirement from the army.

  mewisudaprunawira to retire from the army.

wisudawan (*Skr neo*) male graduate (from a university, etc.).

wisudawati (*Skr neo*) female graduate (from a university, etc.).

wisudha → WISUDA.

wit I (*D*) blank space (between words or pages in printing).

WIT II [Waktu Indonésia Timur] East Indonesia Time.

WITA [Waktu Indonésia Tengah] Central Indonesia Time.

witing (*Jv*) – *bosen amarga saka kulino* hate arises from too frequent meeting; familiarity breeds contempt. – *tresno jalaran (saka/soko) kulina/kulino* love rises from frequently meeting e.o.

witir (*A*) odd (not even). *salat/sembahyang* – a) a voluntary prayer at least three prayers following the *salat tarawih*. b) prayer done between *isya* and *subuh*.

wiwaha (*Skr*) marriage, wedding; wedding feast/party. *Arjuna* – the wedding of Arjuna.

  berwiwaha marriageable.

  mewiwaha to marry (of s.o. performing the ceremony), perform the marriage ceremony for s.o.).

wiwéka (*Jv*) 1 precaution. 2 to take precautions. 3 cautious.

wiwik (*Jv*) various species of cuckoo. – *kelabu* plaintive cuckoo, *Cacomantis merulinus*. – *lurik* banded bay cuckoo, *Cacomantis sonneratii*. – *rimba* brush cuckoo, *Cacomantis variolosus*. – *uncuing* rusty-breasted cuckoo, *Cacomantis sepulcralis*.

wiwit (*Jv*) a ritual performed before the rice harvest.

  wiwitan beginning, origin.

wiyaga (*Jv*) *gamelan* player.

wiyata (*Jv*) education, instruction, teaching. – *bakti* a) volunteer teaching. b) (*infr*) temporary employee. – *Bhayangkara* Police Education. – *mandala* teacher training.

wiyatamandala 1 educational surroundings. 2 alma mater.

wiyatapraja (*Jv*) (in Yogya) (Office of) Education and Culture.

wiyatawan educationalist.

wiyatawisata study tour.

wiyosan (*Jv*) birthday. – *Dalem* Birthday of the Sultan (of Yogyakarta).

wizurai (*Port*) viceroy.

wlijo (*Jv*) middleman in the fishing industry; he sells the fish from another middleman to the wholesaler.

WNA [Warga Negara Asing] Foreign Citizen (usually a code word for an ethnic Chinese).

WNI → WARGANEGARA *Indonésia*. **ke-WNI-an** Indonesian citizenship (*mod*).

  me-WNI-kan to naturalize as an Indonesian citizen.

wodka (*D*) vodka.

woki-toki (*E*) (*alat* –) walkie-talkie.

woku (C?) a way of cooking fish.

wokwok ketekur (*onom*) cooing, the sound made by pigeons or doves.

  berwokwok ketekur to bill and coo, be in love.

wol (*D*) wool. – *kayu* woodwool. – *lacakan* uneven wool mixed with hair and pieces of rough wool.

Wolanda (*ob*) → BELANDA.

wolfram (*D*) wolfram.

wong I (*Jv*) man, person. – *agung* important person. – *angon bébék* boy who tends ducks; → PENGGEMBALA *bébék*. – *cilik* the man in the street. – *londo* Dutchman. – *Majapahit* (in Bali) most Balinese; they consider themselves descendants of 15th-century Javanese migrants; *cp* BALI *aga*. – *Palémbang/Pelémbang* a native of the town of Palembang, South Sumatra. – *Solo* Solonese, a native of Surakarta.

wong II (*Jv*) **1** (word of explanation) you know. – *persoalannya belum selesai orang sudah ribut di luar.* You know, the problem hasn't been settled and people are already excited outside. **2** (exclamation of disagreement) what do you mean? ...

wongké (*Jv*) **mewongké** to appreciate.

wonti *ikan* – k.o. mullet, *Mugil troscheli.*

Worasatya the military resort command (*Korém* 163) in Denpasar.

worawari → WARAWIRI I.

wortel (*D*) carrot, *Daucus carota.*

wot (*Jv*) bridge.

wow (*E*) wow!

WP → WAJIB *pajak.*

wr. [wb.] [warakhmatullahi (wabarakatuh)] may God be merciful (and bless you), formal opening or ending to a letter.

wreda (*Jv*) **1** old; → WERDA. **2** ex-, former; → MANTAN.

wredatama a retired government employee.

Wrekudara Bima, among the most admired and feared of the *wayang* figures; he has a terrible club and long fingernails.

wts and **WTS** (*init*) [Wanita Tuna Susila] prostitute.

   per-wts-an prostitute (*mod*).

wuah → WAH I.

wudani → WEDANI.

wudel (*Jv*) navel; → UDEL. – *bodong* swelling of the navel. ***berwudel bodong*** to have a swollen navel. *orang yang tidak punya* – a tireless person.

wudlu → WUDU. **berwudlu** to make a ritual ablution. *tempat ~ Mesjid Istiqlal* place for the ritual ablution before prayers in the Istiqlal Mosque (in Jakarta).

wudo (*Jv*) nude, naked.

wudu (*A*) ritual washing of the face, hands, and feet before praying.

   berwudu to wash the face, hands, and feet ritually before praying.

wuduk I (*Jv*) *nasi* – rice boiled in coconut milk.

wuduk II → WUDU.

wuih and **wuihh** (*exclam*) wow!

wujud (*A*) **1** being, existence. **2** s.t. of substance. **3** (a real) thing, object. **4** (a visible) shape, form, appearance. *dengan* – to be in a ... form, take the shape of. – *mutlak* absolute (as opposed to phenomenal) being. **5** intention, aim.

   berwujud 1 to really exist. **2** concrete, existing. **3** to be in a ... form, take the shape of.

   mewujud to appear.

mewujudkan 1 to shape, create, translate into reality, realize, bring about, make ... come true. *~ ... menjadi ...* to turn ... into *... ~ cita-cita* to realize one's ambitions. *~ keadilan yang merata* to bring about equal justice for all. **2** to explain/show by presenting objective evidence.

terwujud realized, come true, become a reality, come about. **keterwujudan** realization, materialization.

kewujudan existence, material.

perwujudan 1 form, shape (that can be seen, etc.). **2** a real thing (as visible in a dream, etc.). **3** a concrete object. **4** realization, materialization, actualization. *~ diri* self-actualization.

wujudiah existential.

wujut → WUJUD.

wuku (*Jv*) a period of seven days (each with its own name, such as Kuningan, Marakih, Madangkungan, etc.; in total there are 30 seven-day periods or 210 days constituting the Javanese *tahun Jawa* or Javanese calendar).

wukuf (*A*) a stop at Arafah (while performing the *hajj*).

   berwukuf to stop, stay (at Arafah).

wul (*E*) wool; → WOL.

wulan → BULAN I.

wulang (*Jv*) **wulangan** teachings.

wulangréh (*Jv*) a literary work on Javanese philosophy by Mangkunegoro IV.

wulu I (*Jv*) – *cumbu* hanger-on, follower. – *wetu* agricultural products.

wulu II name of a *ceki* card.

wuluh the Pleiades.

wulung (*Jv*) blue-black, bluish black, slate blue.

wungkul (*Jv*) in full, in its entirety, as a whole (not divided).

wungon (*Jv*) to stay up all night (as part of an ascetic regime).

wungu (*Jv*) purple, violet; → UNGU.

wuquf (*A*) → WUKUF.

wuring → PURING I.

wurung → URUNG I.

wushu (*C*) a Chinese martial art form.

wusssh (*onom*) word for sound of s.t. bursting into flame.

wutuh → UTUH.

wuwu (*Jv*) bow-net, fish trap.

wuwungan I (*J*) rooftop, house peak, roof beam.

wuwungan II (in Cirebon) landless farmer, not a fully entitled member of the village community.

wuyungan (*J*) → UBUBUNGAN, UWUNGAN, UYUNGAN.

WvK (*D leg*) [Wetboek van Koophandel] Commercial Code.

WvS (*D leg*) [Wetboek van Strafrecht] Penal Code.

X

x and X /éks/ the 24th letter of the Latin alphabet used for writing Indonesian (used only in spelling some foreign words and slang).

XTC [ékstasi] Ecstasy, an illegal drug.

Y

y and Y I /yé/ the 25th letter of the Latin alphabet used for writing Indonesian.

y II (*math*) a symbol for the second of a set of unknown quantities.

Y III (*chem*) yatrium.

ya I 1 (answer to a question) yes, OK. *Mau pergi?* – Do you want to go out? Yes. *Rasanya énak. Apa* –? It tastes good. Really? *Barangkali* –. Probably so. – *halo* hello (said by person called to the phone). 2 do you hear me; get this straight. *Jangan main-main sama saya,* –! Don't make a fool of me, do you hear? 3 also, too; both ... and ... *Waktu masih kecil saya* – *gitu.* When I was young, I was like that too. *Héwan – bisa membalas kebaikan.* Animals, too, can return kindness. 4 (at the end of the sentence) makes a statement, command or question less blunt or more polite. *Bagaimana* –? What should we do? *Berapa* –? How much is this? *entah* – I don't know. *Permisi* –? Excuse me, please. *Sebentar,* –? one minute, OK? *Terima kasih* –. Thank you. *Jangan nakal* –. Don't be naughty, OK? 5 (at the end of the subject or a subordinate clause and before the predicate or main clause) well, as for. *Lauknya – masih perlu tambahan dari rumah.* As for the side dishes, well, they had to be supplemented from home (said by a prisoner). *Kalau tidak di Hongkong,* – *di Singapura.* If he's not in Hong Kong, well, he must be in Singapore. *Kalau mau kawin,* – *kawin.* If you want to get married, well (go ahead and) get married. 6 – ... – ... either ... or ..., (both) ... and ..., ... and ... – *pemandangan alamnya,* – *kesenian rakyatnya* its natural beauties and its folk arts. – *bawang,* – *kentang,* – *jeruk* onions, potatoes, and oranges. *Dia – gembira – sedih.* She was both happy and sad.

ya II (*A*) – *Allah!* a) O God! b) My God! – *Rabbi/Robbi* O Lord!

ya III (*A*) name of the 28th letter of the Arabic alphabet.

ya IV (in acronyms) → RAYA.

yaani (*A*) that is, i.e.; → YAKNI.

yach → YAH I.

yad I (*A*) 1 (human) hand. 2 front paw (of a quadruped). 3 wing (of a bird).

yad II (*abbr*) [yang akan datang] next, (up)coming; → MENDATANG. *(Hari) Natal* – next Christmas.

Yafit (*A*) (the Biblical) Japheth.

yah I /yaaa/ long-drawn-out pronunciation of *ya I.* weeell ... – *kami ingin lihat-lihat dulu.* Weeell, we want to look around first.

yah II (*coq*) clipped form of *ayah.*

yahud (*D sl*) very good, fantastic.
  beryahud-yahud to have a great time. *tempat* ~ lovers' lane.

Yahudah (*A*) Judea.

Yahudi (*A*) Jew(ish). *agama* – Judaism. *orang* – Jew. – *asal Eropah* Ashkenazi (Jew). – *asal Timur* Sephardic (Jew).
  memperyahudikan to revile, abuse; make fun of, pull s.o.'s leg.
  keyahudian Judaism.
  pengyahudian judaization.

Yahudiah (*A*) Judaism; Jewish.

yahut → YAHUD.

Yahwé Yahweh, God.

Yahya (*A*) (the biblical) John.

yaini → IA *ini,* YAANI, YAKNI.

yais (*A*) menopause.

yaitu → IA *itu.*

yajnu (*A?*) sacrifice.

Yajuj (*A*) (the biblical) Gog. – *wa Majuj* Gog and Magog, the nations that, under Satan, are to wage war against the kingdom of God.

yak (*coq*) yes, OK; → YA I. *Terus! Mundur!* –, *stop!* Forward! Back! OK, stop!

yakarim (in Semarang) beggar who comes to Semarang to beg just before *Lebaran.*

yakin (*A*) confident, sure, certain, positive, convinced. – *akan kejujurannya* confident of his sincerity. – *diri* to persuade o.s. *pada -ku* I'm convinced (that). *tidak* – unsure, undecided.
  seyakin-yakinnya absolutely convinced, beyond any doubt.
  meyakini to believe (in), be convinced/persuaded (that). *setelah* ~ *bahwa tidak ada orang yang mengintip* ... after being convinced that nobody was watching secretly ... ~ *Tuhan* to believe in God. *diyakini* to be believed (to). *Meréka diyakini memiliki dana Rp 80 juta.* They are believed to have Rp 80 million.
  meyakin-yakini to investigate s.t. so as to be convinced, make sure; to determine, ascertain. ~ *suatu hal yang buruk* to convince o.s. that s.t. is bad.
  meyakinkan [and ngeyakinin (*J coq*)] 1 to convince, persuade, assure. ~ *diri* to convince o.s. (that), be persuaded (of). 2 convincing. *Keterangannya tidak* ~. His testimony was not convincing. 3 high, excessive (of price). *harga yang cukup* ~ a stiff price.
  keyakinan 1 faith, belief, conviction. ~ *politik* political conviction. 2 confidence, trust, reliance. *Kita harus menaruh* ~ *kepada Tuhan.* We should place our confidence in God. 3 determination, assurance. ~ *memadai* reasonable assurance.
  berkeyakinan to be convinced (that), have confidence/faith (in). ~ *bahwa ia akan lulus ujiannya* to be convinced that he will pass the exam.
  peyakinan act of convincing, assurance.

yakis (*ob*) baboon.

yakjuj → YAJUJ.

yakni (*A*) that is, namely, i.e.

Yakobus (the biblical) James.

yaksa (*Skr*) demigod.

Yakub (*A*) (the biblical) Jacob.

yakun (*A*) *kun fa* – be and it was (the words by which God created the world).

yakut (*A*) 1 hyacinth, *Hyacinthus spp.* 2 green or blue precious stone, jacinth (also applied to rubies and sometimes to garnet).

yala *détasemén – Mengkara* an antihijacking unit in the Armed Forces.

yalah → IALAH.

yalamlam (*A*) the stage in the pilgrimage where the pilgrims from Yemen assume the pilgrim's garb.

Yalasénastri name of the Navy wives' association.

yalavéva jayamahé marines' slogan ("on sea we are victorious").

Yamaha brand name of a Japanese motorbike. – *bébék* the 79-cc V80 Yamaha motorbike.

Yaman (*A*) Yemen.

yamin and **yami'en** (*C*) k.o. cooked noodles with sweet soy sauce.

yamtuan who is Lord; → YANG dipertuan.

Yana Badra (*Skr*) "Salutary Path," i.e., the initiation undergone by students at the Basic School for Supply Officers in Surabaya.

yang I 1 deity. **2** God.

   beryang-yang to worship the deities.

   beryang-yangkan (*déwa-déwa*) to worship (the gods).

   keyangan (in *pantuns*) where the gods reside.

yang II (nominalizing particle which picks out a specific one or group from a number of possibilities). **1**a) (before verb phrases) the (one or ones) who/which/that. *banyak* – ... there are many who ... – *berkepentingan* those concerned, those who have business here. – *bertandatangan di bawah ini* the undersigned. – *buta* the blind. – *hadir* the audience/attendees. – *kuasa* the authorities. – *(me)nonton* the viewers/audience. – *(em)punya* the owner. – *lumpuh* the paralyzed. – *punya rumah* a) the host(ess). b) the landlord/lady. – *satu ini* this (particular) one. – *tidak berkepentingan tidak boléh masuk* (signpost) employees/customers, etc.) only. – *sakit boléh pulang* the sick (person) may go home/be discharged from the hospital. b) (in some modern Malay titles) – *Dipertuan* title for the chairman of the *Déwan Negara* and *Déwan Negeri*. – *Dipertuan Agung* title for the Head of State. – *Dipertuan Negara* title for the Head of Brunei Darussalam. – *Dipertuan Negeri* title for Head of a Negeri/ Province in Malaysia. c) (before *adj* phrases) the (one or ones) which is/are (forms a specific adjective clause as opposed to a descriptive adjective clause). *rumah* – *kecil* the small house (as opposed to any other type of house; *cp rumah kecil* the small house (merely descriptive). **2** the specific one/ones in a set. – *mana?* which one? – *satu/dua*, etc. ... *dan satunya/duanya*, etc. *lagi* ... and – *satu lagi* one (of a pair or set) and the other(s) (of a pair or set). *ada* – ... *ada* – ... some ... some ... *ada* – *mérah*, *ada* – *biru* some are red and some are blue. **3** (+ noun + *-nya*) whose, which has the/a, with the/a. *orang* – *istrinya meninggal* the man whose wife died. *rumah* – *pintunya mérah itu* the house with a red door. **4** (*Jv* influence; *coq*) forms adverbs. – *baik, ya!* Do it right! *Duduk* – *baik!* Sit right! *Hidup* – *tenang dan santai!* Live quietly and relaxed. **5** (before noun phrases) a) (in Old Malay *cla*) the. – *Bhumi Jawa* the isle of Java. – *kadatuan* the kingdom. – *mitranya* their friends. b) (in contemporary Indonesian) the (introducing a phrase in apposition) *A. H. Nasution.* – *jénderal* A. H. Nasution, the general. *Ayam mutiara, kalau musim kawin* – *jantan lebih perlénté.* In the mating season, the male of the guinea fowl is more elegant.

yang III the clipped form of **sayang**.

yang-yang *akar* – a climbing plant, *Vitis hastata*.

yanhué (*C*) fireworks.

Yankee Délta (CB-ers' slang) a CB-er who has a call-sign.

yan-oh (*C?*) edible bird's nest.

yapon (*D*) dress, gown.

yar(d) (*E*) yard.

yareh and **yarig** (*D*) /yarikh/ **1** a year old. **2** birthday. *merayakan* – *nya* to celebrate one's birthday. **3** to celebrate one's birthday. *dua hari setelah Tuty* – two days after Tuty celebrated her birthday.

yargon (*D*) jargon, lingo.

yarhamukallah (*A*) (when s.o. sneezes) God bless you.

yarkan (*A*) jaundice.

yas → HIAS.

yasa (*Jv*) **1** building. **2** structure, foundation.

yasan (*Jv*) *sawah* – rice field cultivated by individual labor.

yashém (*D ob*) k.o. jacket.

yasin (*A*) *surah/surat* – the 36th chapter of the Koran, which is read to the dying.

yasmén (*D*) and **yasmin** (*A*) jasmine.

yaspis (*D*) jasper. – *mérah* sardius.

yassin → YASIN.

yasyib (*A*) jasper.

yatim (*A*) **1** a motherless or fatherless child, orphan. **2**a) a motherless and fatherless child. b) a neglected orphan. – *piatu* a motherless and fatherless child. *rumah* – *piatu* orphanage.

yaum (*A*) day. – *alkiamat* Day of Judgment. – *uddin* the Day of Judgment, doomsday. – *ul-akhir* the hereafter, afterworld. *–ul-mukiamah* and *–ul-kiamah* Day of Judgment. – *ul-mahsyar* the day of reckoning. *–ulmizan* Day of Judgment.

yayang → YAYI.

yayasan (*Jv*) **1** foundation (a corporate body). – *Ford* Ford Foundation. **2** a building specially earmarked for a certain purpose (such as a hospital).

yayi (*Jv cla*) younger sibling.

yayu (*Jv*) older sister; → YU II.

yb (*abbr*) [yang berikut] next, following.

ybl (*abbr*) [yang baru lalu] last, past.

ybs (*abbr*) [yang bersangkutan] the person concerned/in question.

yé I (*J*) → YA I.

yé II name of the letter *y*.

Yéhézkiel (*A*) (the biblical) Ezekiel.

Yéhova (*A*) Jehovah; → YAHWÉ.

yék (in acronyms) → PROYÉK.

yéksi (*D*) a clipped form of *injéksi*.

yél (*D/E*) yell.

Yellow Baby (*E*) /yélo bébi/ a variety of Taiwan watermelon grown in Indonesia.

yellow paper (*E*) /yélo péper/ or **yellow press** /yélo prés/ the yellow press, a tabloid.

yem name of a *ceki* card.

yén (*Jp*) yen, the Japanese monetary unit.

yéndaka (*Jp*) the yen shock.

Yéremiah (*A*) (the biblical) Jeremiah.

yérikén → JÉRIKÉN.

Yérusalem Jerusalem.

Yésaya (*A*) (the biblical) Isaiah.

Yésuit (*D*) Jesuit.

Yésus Jesus.

yét (*E*) → JÉT.

yeyunum (*D*) jejunum, the middle part of the small intestine.

yg (*abbr*) [yang] who, which, etc.

yi (*abbr*) [yaitu] that is, i.e.

yl I (*abbr*) [yang lain] the other.

y.l. II (*abbr*) [yang lalu] past, last.

YME (*abbr*) [yang maha esa] the Almighty.

ymj (*abbr*) [yang menjalankan jabatan] acting, temporary.

yo → AYO.

yodisasi (*D*) iodizing.

yodium (*D*) iodine. – *tingtur* tincture of iodine.

   beryodium iodized.

yodiumisasi treating with iodine.

yodur (*D*) iodide.

Yoél (the biblical) Joel.

yoga (*Skr*) yoga. *ahli* – yogi.

   beryoga to practice yoga.

yoghurt (*E*) yoghurt.

yogi (*Skr*) yogi.

yogia and **yogya** (*Skr*) proper, fitting, suitable, appropriate, adequate.

   seyogia → YOGIA.

   seyogianya 1 it is/would be proper/right/good/advisable/a good idea (to). *Jika hendak membawa mobil jauh-jauh, ~ dipenuhi dulu tangki bénsinnya.* If you want to take a long trip in your car, it is advisable to fill up the gas tank first. **2** really, as a matter of fact. *~ dokter adalah tumpuan harapan pasién.* In fact, a patient puts his hopes in a doctor.

   menseyogianyakan to make s.t. proper, fitting.

Yohan(n)es (*D*) John.

yo'i (*sl*) come on, let's go; → AYO(H).

yojana (*Skr ob*) a measure of length; (great) distance; field of vision.

   seyojana ~ *mata* as far as the eye can see.

yok → AYO.

yokal (in Irian Jaya) woman's native dress.

yoker (*E*) joker (in card games).
yokwan (*C*) k.o. Chinese *jamu* for increasing stamina.
yon (in acronyms) → BATALYON.
yonang [batalyon angkutan] transport battalion.
yonangmor [batalyon angkutan bermotor] motor transport battalion.
yonarhanudri [batalyon artileri pertahanan udara ringan] light air defense artillery battalion.
yonarhanudse [batalyon artileri pertahanan udara sedang] medium air defense artillery battalion.
yonbekal [batalyon perbekalan peralatan] supply and maintenance battalion.
yongab [batalyon gabungan] joint battalion.
yongenskop (*D*) a boy's-style haircut for girls, pageboy.
yongker (*D*) young nobleman.
yong tahu (*C*) tofu filled with meat.
yonhub [batalyon perhubungan] communications battalion.
yoni (*Skr*) 1 vulva, womb. 2 symbol of the female sexual organs.
yonif [batalyon infanteri] infantry battalion.
yonint [batalyon inténdans] quartermaster battalion.
yonkav [batalyon kavaleri] cavalry battalion.
yonkavtai [batalyon kavaleri intai] reconnaissance cavalry battalion.
yonkavtank [batalyon kavaleri tank] tank cavalry battalion.
yonkés [batalyon keséhatan] health battalion.
yonkomlék [batalyon komunikasi éléktronika] electronics and communications battalion.
yonlinud [batalyon lintas udara] airborne infantry battalion.
yonmar [batalyon marinir] marine battalion.
yonpal [batalyon peralatan] equipment battalion.
yonparafib [batalyon parasut amfibi] amphibious parachute battalion.
yonpasrat [batalyon pasukan pendarat] landing force battalion.
yonpur [batalyon tempur] combat battalion.
yonranratfib [batalyon kendaraan pendarat amfibi] amphibious landing vehicle battalion.
yontaifibmar [batalyon intai amfibi marinir] marine amphibious reconnaissance battalion.
yontankfib [batalyon tank amfibi] amphibious tank battalion.
yonzi [batalyon zéni] engineer battalion.
yonzikon [batalyon zéni konstruksi] construction engineer battalion.
yonzipi [batalyon zéni pionir] pioneer engineer battalion.
yonzipur [batalyon zéni tempur] combat engineer battalion.
Yordani(a) Jordan.
Yosua (the biblical) Joshua.
you (*E*) /yu/ you (to equals or inferiors only). *Kalau – gagal sekali ini, – tidak bisa motrét saya lagi.* If you fail this time (to take my picture), you can't take my picture again.
yowana → YUWANA.
yoyo (*E*) yo-yo (the toy).
yth (*abbr*) [yang terhormat] the honorable, dear (in correspondence).
yts (*abbr*) [yang tersebut] the aforementioned, the above.
yu I 1 (*ikan –*) shark, *Carcharinidae*; → HIU. 2 dogfish. 3 sawfish, beaked ray. – *belangkas/gila/minyak* bamboo shark, *Chiloscyllium indicum*. – *beléngkong/laras* dogfish, *Scyllium spp.* – *béngkong/mata jauh/sanggul/tukul* hammerhead shark, *Pristis cuspidatus* and other species. – *bodoh/cecak/cicak/rimau/tenggiri/tokék* tiger/zebra shark, *Stegostoma fasciatum, Galeocerdo spp.* – *cemangi/jerong/pandak/péndék/sambaran* ground shark, marbled cat shark. – *gergaji/palang/parang/tanduk/todak* sawfish, *Pristis spp.* – *kemenyan/kia-kia* beaked ray?, guitar fish, *Rhynchobatus djiddensis/thonii.* – *punai/toléh* brown-banded bamboo shark, *Chiloscyllium punctatum*.
yu II (*Jv coq*) (form of address to) older sister; → MBAK *yu*.
yu III → YOU.
yu IV → AYO(H).
yu V *pohon* – k.o. tree, *Ryparosa sp.*

yu VI k.o. card game; → CEKI.
yubilaris (*D*) one who celebrates his jubilee.
yubiléum (*D*) and **yubilium** anniversary, jubilee.
yuda → YUDHA. – *kelana* straggler (in combat zone).
Yudas (the biblical) Jude.
yudasmara (*Skr*) lovers' tiff.
yudha (*Skr*) 1 fight, combat, battle, war. 2 soldier. – *Pratid(h)ina (Marhaénis)* (Marhaenist) Struggle without End, i.e., the slogan of the *Partai Nasional Indonésia*.
yudhagama (*Skr neo*) art of war.
Yudha-loka (*Skr neo*) (in the *Bina Graha*) War Room.
yudhawarta (*Skr neo*) war news.
yudhya → YUDHA.
yudikatif (*E leg*) judicative, judicial. *di bidang –* in the judicial sector.
yudisium (*L D*) judicium, judgment (on diploma). *Ia lulus dengan – magna cum laude.* He graduated magna cum laude.
Yudistira the oldest of the five *Pandawa* brothers, the gentle, wise, introspective and just king but with a weakness for gambling. *Prabu –* the *wayang* character King Yudistira (also known as Puntadewa).
yudo (*D*) judo; → JUDO.
yudoka (*Jp*) yudoka, a judo expert.
yu-és dolar (*E*) U.S. dollar.
yugékitai (*Jp*) guerrilla section of the *Péta/Pembéla Tanah Air* during the Japanese occupation.
Yugo Yugoslav(ia).
Yugoslavia Yugoslavia.
yuh and **yuk** → AYO(H).
yujitsu (*Jp*) jujitsu.
yuk → AYO.
Yuli I → JULI.
yuli II (*D*) you (*pl*).
yumén [kayu semén] k.o. wallboard used in low-income housing.
Yunani (*A*) 1 Greek. *Geréja – Ortodoks* Greek Orthodox Church. 2 Greece. – *Kuno* Ancient Greece.
yuncto → JUNCTO.
yunda → AYUNDA.
yungyun (*Jv*) **keyungyun** attracted (by), charmed, enchanted; madly in love (with).
yunior (*D*) junior; → JUNIOR.
yuniorat (*D col*) college preparatory school emphasizing the classics.
yunta → JUNTA.
Yunus (*A*) 1 (the biblical) Jonah. 2 "Jonas"; name of the 10th chapter of the Koran.
yura science of law.
yuran → IURAN.
yuri → JURI I.
yuridis (*D leg*) 1 jurist, lawyer. 2 law-school graduate. 3 legal, judicial.
yuris (*D leg*) jurist.
yurisdiksi (*D leg*) jurisdiction.
yurisprudénsi (*D leg*) jurisprudence.
yurk (*D*) /yurek/ dress, frock. – *maksi/landung* long dress.
Yusak (*A*) (the biblical) Joshua.
Yustika Rini the woman's organization under the jurisdiction of the Department of Justice and the Supreme Court.
yustisi (*D leg*) administration of justice; → JUSTISI.
yustisial (*D leg*) judicial.
Yusuf (*A*) 1 (the biblical) Joseph. 2 "Joseph"; name of the 12th chapter of the Koran.
yuta I and **yute** (*D*) jute.
yuta II (*ob*) → JUTA.
yuwana (*Skr*) youth, juvenile. *Yayasan Pro –* Pro Juventute Foundation.
yuwelir (*D*) jeweler.
yuyu (*J/Jv*) rice-paddy crab, *Gecarcinidae spp., Sesarma spp.* – *kangkung* k.o. river crab.
YW an uncovered goods car (in train formation).

Z

/z/ is usually pronounced /s/. Words beginning with a Z not found under this letter should be looked for under D, DZ, J and L.

z and Z /sét/ the 26th letter of the Latin alphabet used for writing Indonesian.

za (*A*) 1 → ZAI. 2 name of the 17th letter of the Arabic alphabet.

zabad → JEBAT.

zabah (*A*) to chop, slaughter, butcher.

Zabaniah (*A*) the angels who push the damned into hellfire, keepers of the gates of Hell.

zabarjad (*A*) chrysolite, topaz.

zabat → JEBAT I.

zabib (*A*) raisin; → KISMIS.

Zabur (*A*) *Al* – and *Kitab* – the Psalms.

zadah (*Pers*) *anak* – illegitimate child, bastard; → JADAH I.

zadat [zat padat] (*phys*) solid.

zadir sal ammoniac.

zafaran (*A*) saffron.

zafin (*A*) k.o. dance.

zahid (*A*) pious, ascetic, hermit, not greedy.

zahir → LAHIR I.

zai (*A*) name of the 11th letter of the Arabic alphabet.

zaim (*A*) leader.

zain (*A*) adornment, grace, beauty.

zair [zat cair] fluid.

zaitun (*A*) 1 olive tree, *Olea europea*. 2 olive (the small, oval-shaped fruit of this tree). *minyak* – olive oil.

zak (*D*) /sak/ sack, bag. *pembongkaran 12.500 – atau 500 ton semén* unloading 12,500 sacks or 500 tons of cement.

zakar (*A*) penis. *batang* – shaft of the penis. *buah* – testicle(s), testis, testes. *lemah* – impotent.

Zakariya (*A*) Zacharias.

zakat (*A*) obligation to contribute to those in need or to religious activities. – *an'am* charity in the form of cattle. – *badan/fitrah* the *zakat* which has to be paid once a year after Ramadhan. – *ma'din* charity in the form of minerals. – *mal* charity given because one has more than enough. – *rikaz* charity on *harta terpendam*. – *zuru'* charity in the form of food.

berzakat to pay the *zakat*.

menzakati and menzakatkan to give s.t. as *zakat. harta yang dizakati* wealth on which a tithe is levied.

zakelijk (*D*) /sakelek/ 1 businesslike; → LUGAS. 2 practical; → PRAKTIS.

zaken (*D*) – *kabinét* cabinet made up of experts.

zakiah (*A*) pure, sincere; → FUAD al-zakiah.

zakum (*A*) a tree that grows in Hell and provides food for the damned.

zal (*D*) /sal/ ward (in hospital). *Ia dirawat dalam – B.* He was treated in ward B.

zalf (*D*) /salep/ → SALEP.

zalim (*A*) → LALIM.

zalir [zat alir] fluid.

zalm → SALAM III.

Zalzalah (*A*) *al-* "The Earthquake"; name of the 99th chapter of the Koran.

zaman (*A*) 1 (stretch of) time, period, epoch. *manusia/wartawan tiga* – s.o. who has lived through the Dutch colonial period, the Japanese occupation and independence. *tanda* – sign of the times. – *pemerintahan Belanda* the period of Dutch rule. 2 (at the time) when, during. – *pendudukan Jepang* during the Japanese occupation. *umur* – (*ob*) (a certain) age. *akhir* – the end of time. *sampai akhir* – till the end of time, forever; eternal, everlasting, perpetual. *tidak cocok dengan kemauan* – (that is) not in accordance with the present situation. – *sudah tua* the world is coming to an end. *ketinggalan* – and *sudah tidak sesuai dengan* – and *sudah lalu* and *sudah dimakan* – behind the times, archaic, out of date, old fashioned. *meninggalkan* – (*ob*) to die, pass away. – *beralih musim bertukar* the times are changed and we are changed with them. – *airbatu* the ice age. – *atom* the atomic age. – *bahari* olden/ancient days, former ages, long ago, time immemorial. – *baheula* the dim past. – *batu* the stone age. – *batu madya* Mesolithic era. – *batu muda* Neolithic era. – *Buda* the pre-Islamic period in Indonesia. – *dahulu* → ZAMAN bahari. – *depan* the future. – *édan, nék ora édan ora oman* (*Jv*) crazy times (when public order/security/norms, etc. are upset or suspended), if one does not also become crazy, one will not get one's piece of the cake. – *és* → ZAMAN airbatu. – *jahiliah* the time prior to the birth of Islam (in Arabia). – *keemasan* the golden age. – *Kegelapan* Dark Ages. – *kuda gigit besi* the distant past. – *madya* the Middle Ages. – *melését* depression, recession, slump, bad/hard times. – *normal* the period when prices were normal or stable, i.e., the postwar Dutch period up to the transfer of sovereignty in December 1949. – *Pencerahan* the Enlightenment. – *penjajahan* the colonial period. – *pertengahan* → ZAMAN madya. – *perunggu* the Bronze Age. – *purbakala* ancient times. – *révolusi* the time of the Indonesian revolution. – *sekarang* nowadays, the present (time). – *tandun* ancient times, long ago.

sezaman contemporary, contemporaneous.

menzaman *sudah tidak ~ lagi* out-of-date.

zamin (*Pers ob*) land, country.

zamindar (*Pers cla*) landowner.

zamrud (*A*) emerald. *Nusantara "serangkaian – di katulistiwa"* the Indonesian archipelago is "a girdle of emeralds around the equator."

zamzam (*A*) 1 copious, abundant (*esp* water). 2 name of a well in Mecca. *air* – the water from this well, which has a bitter taste, is considered sacred by Muslims and a cure-all for various diseases; therefore, if possible, some of it is taken home from the pilgrimage to Mecca. – *durja* facial expression; → AIR muka.

zan (*A*) doubt, suspicion, lack of confidence/trust.

zanggi (*Pers*) *orang* – Abyssinian, Ethiopian, (African) Negro/black; → JANGGI I.

zani (*A*) adulterer, fornicator.

zaniah and zaniat adulteress.

zanjabil (*A*) water or springs in Paradise.

zann → ZAN.

zantara [zat antara] (*phys*) medium.

zapin (*A*) (Arabic) beat/rhythm.

zarafah → ZIRAFAH.

za(r)rah (*A*) 1 crumb; (a small) bit; grain; mite. 2 atom, particle. sezarah a bit.

menzarah *pecah ~* pulverized.

zarbaf (*A*) brocade.

zariah and zariat (*A*) 1 seed, semen. 2 descendants.

zarkar (*Pers*) golden.

zat (*A*) 1 being, existing. 2 (in compounds) substance, matter, agent, essence. 3 essence (of God). – *Allah* Allah's being/existence. *pertukaran* – *makanan* metabolism. – *adiktif* addictive substance. – *air* hydrogen. – *air belérang* hydrogen sulphide. – *alir* fluid. – *antara* medium (through which s.t. flows). – *anti* antimatter, antibody. – *arang* carbon. – *asam* oxygen. – *asam arang* carbon dioxide. – *berkhasiat* active ingredient. – *cair* liquid, fluid. – *celup* dyestuff. – *dalam suspénsi* suspended solid. – *dasar* matrix. – *garam* salts. – *gizi* nutrient. – *hara* nutrient. – *hijau (daun)* chlorophyll. – *hirup* volatile substance. – *kapur* calcium. – *kayu* lignin. – *kedap* sealant. – *kekebalan* immune body; → ANTIBODI. – *kimia* chemical substance. – *lemas* nitrogen. – *makanan* a) vitamin. b) nutrient. – *menghawa* volatile substance. – *padat* (*phys*) solid matter, solids. – *pati* amylum. – *peledak* blasting agent. – *pelemas* → ZAT lemas. – *pembakar* oxygen. – *pembersih* detergent. – *pemurni* refining agent. – *pemutih* bleach. – *penangkal* antidote. – *pencahar* gastric lavage.

– *pendingin* refrigerant. – *pengasap* fumigant. – *pengawét* preservative. – *pengenal* reagents. – *penggumpal* flocculant. – *penularan* germ of infection. – *penyédar* dispersing agent. – *penyerap* desiccant. – *perangsang* antigen, such as pollen, dust, etc. – *perangsang tubuh* growth hormone. – *peréduksi* reducing agent. – *pewarna* coloring matter. – *psikoaktif* psychoactive substance. – *putih telur* albumen. – *racun* toxin. – *sakar* glucose. – *sendawa* nitrogen. – *tambahan* supplementary ingredient, additive. – *tanduk* keratin. – *telur* protein, albumen. – *terbang* volatile matter. – *terlarut* dissolved solid. – *tumbuh* auxin. – *warna* dye(stuff). – *yang mahatinggi* the supreme essence (God).

zati (*A*) innate.
zauhal → ZUHAL.
zauj (*A*) counterpart.
zaujiah (*A*) matrimony.
zawal (*A naut*) declination.
zawiat (*A*) a small Muslim chapel, not used for Friday prayers, in an area where there are too few people for a mosque; → LANGGAR I, SURAU.
zébra (*D*)/sébra/ zebra. ikan – zebra fish, any of a number of unrelated fishes with barred, zebralike markings, such as the *zebra danio, Brachydanio rerio*, often kept in aquariums. *penyeberangan* – zebra crossing.
zébu (*D*) zebu, *Bos taurus indicus*.
Zelfbesturen (*D col*) self-governing (territories), native states.
zém (*D*) /jém/ jam, preserves.
Zén Zen.
zénding (*D*) /sénding/ Protestant mission.
zenggi → ZANGGI I.
zéni I (*mil D*) army engineers. – *alat-alat besar* [ZIALBER] heavy equipment engineers. – *amfibi* [ZIBI] amphibious engineers. – *bangunan* [ZIBANG] construction engineers. – *daérah militér* [ZIDAM] regional engineers. – *gerak cepat* [ZIPAT] rapid-deployment engineers. – *jembatan* [ZIBAT] bridge engineers. – *konstruksi* [ZIKON] construction engineers. – *pionir* [ZIPI] pioneer engineers. – *pontonir* [ZIPON] pontoon engineers. – *tempur* [ZIPUR] combat engineers.
zéni II *D*) genius.
zénit (*D*) zenith.
zéolit (*D*) zeolite.
zéro (*E*) zero.
zét I (*D*) /sét/ composition, setting-up of type.
 menzét and **mengezét** to set type.
zét II the name of the letter *z*.
zétter (*D*) /séter/ (type)setter, compositor; → LÉTERSÉTER.
zh- also see roots beginning with z-.
zi (in acronyms) → ZÉNI I.
ziadah (*A*) addition, excess.
ZIALBER → ZÉNI *alat-alat besar*.
ziarah and **ziarat** (*A*) visit (to a shrine/grave/holy place), pilgrimage.
 berziarah ~ *ke* and **menziarahi** to visit (a shrine, etc.), go on a pilgrimage to.
 ziarahan pilgrimage.
 pe(n)ziarah 1 visitor (to a shrine, etc.). 2 pilgrim.
 penziarahan and **perziarahan** act of going to somewhere sacred.
zib I (*naut*) (*A*) triangular-shaped sail, jib (sail).
zib II (*A*) k.o. jackal → SERIGALA.
ZIBANG → ZÉNI *bangunan*.
ZIBAT → ZÉNI *jembatan*.
ZIBI → ZÉNI *amfibi*.
ZIDAM → ZÉNI *daérah militér*.
zigot (*D*) zygote.
zigzag (*D*) /siksak/ zigzag; → SIKU *keluang*.
 berzigzag to zigzag.
zihar (*A*) continence.
zikir I (*A*) to chant in praise of Allah.
ZIKON → ZÉNI *konstruksi*.
zill (*A*) shadow. *–ullah* and *– ullah* the shadow of Allah, i.e., a ruler. *– filalam* (a sovereign is) the shadow of Allah on the world.
Zilzaal → ZALZALAH.
Zimbabwé Zimbabwe (formerly Rhodesia).
zimmi → DIMI.

zina (*A*) fornication, adultery, illicit sexual intercourse. – *sedarah* incest. – *tangan* masturbation.
 berzina to commit adultery, fornicate, go whoring.
 menzinai to commit adultery/fornicate with. *Ia berulang kali ~ gadis semarganya.* He had often had illicit sex with a girl of the same *marga*.
 pezina [and **penzina** (*Mal*)] adulterer, fornicator.
 perzinaan → ZINA.
zinah → ZINA.
zindik and **zindiq** (*A*) 1 heresy. 2 heretic; atheist; fire worshiper.
zinkwit (*D*) /singkwit/ zinc-white.
Zionis (*D*) Zionist.
Zionisma and **Zionisme** (*D*) Zionism.
ZIPAT → ZÉNI *gerak cepat*.
ZIPI → ZÉNI *pionir*.
ZIPON → ZÉNI *pontonir*
ZIPUR → ZÉNI *tempur*.
zir → *zir* BAD.
zirafah (*A*) giraffe.
zirah (*Pers*) *baju* – coat of mail, armor.
zirbad (*Pers*) leeward.
zirnikh (*A*) arsenic, *Acidum arsenicosum*.
ziter (*D*) zither.
zitje → SICE.
zodiak (*D*) zodiac.
 berzodiak to be born under the sign of. *Ia ~ Libra.* She was born under the sign of Libra.
Zohal → ZUHAL.
zohor → LOHOR.
Zohrah and **Zohrat** → ZUHARA.
zolim → LALIM.
zona → ZONE.
zonasi (*E*) zonation, dividing s.t. up into zones.
zonder (*D*) /sonder/ without; → SONDER, TANPA. *Dia mengendarai mobilnya – rébewés.* He drove his car without a driver's license.
zone (*D*) 1 any of the five great latitudinal divisions of the earth's surface named according to the prevailing climate, such as – *dingin* frigid zone. – *panas* the tropics. – *penyangga* buffer zone. – *sederhana* temperate zone. 2 any area/region considered as separate/distinct from others because of its particular use, crops, plant or animal life, status in time of war, etc. – *bébas, damai dan nétral* Zone of Peace, Freedom and Neutrality (in Southeast Asia). – *bébas pajak* duty-free zone. – *Bébas Senjata Nuklir Pasifik Selatan* [ZBNPS] South Pacific Nuclear Free Zone. – *Bébas Senjata Nuklir di Asia Tenggara* Southeast Asia Nuclear Weapons Free Zone [SEANWFZ]. – *ékonomi* economic zone. – *Ékonomi Éksklusif* [ZEE] Exclusive Economic Zone. – *Ékonomi Éksklusif Indonésia* [ZEEI] Indonesian Exclusive Economic Zone. – *industri* industrial zone. – *Industri Lhok Seumawé* [ZILS] Lhok Seumawe Industrial Zone (in Aceh). – *industri penghasil dévisa* foreign-exchange producing industrial zone. – *inti* core zone. – *keamanan* safety/security zone. – *kebisingan* noise zone (of landing aircraft). – *kematian* death zone. – *Kerjasama* Zone of Cooperation (to enable cooperation between Indonesians and Australians in exploiting oil fields in the Timor gap). – *pemanfaatan* utilization zone. – *Penangkapan Ikan Australia* [ZPIA] Australian Fishery Zone (guaranteeing Indonesian traditional fisherman the right to fish within this zone). – *penyangga* buffer zone. – *perang* war zone. – *perikanan* fishing zone. – *perlindungan* protected zone. – *pertanian* agricultural zone. – *peruntukan* allotment zone, zoning. – *peruntukan tanah* land allotment zone. – *terhalang* zone of avoidance. – *téror* terroristic zone.
 menzonekan to zone, divide up into zones.
 penzonean zoning.
zoning (*E*) zoning; → PENZONEAN.
zoofit (*D*) zoophyte.
zoolog (*D*) /so'olok/ zoologist.
zoologi (*D/E*) /so'ologi/ zoology. *ahli* – zoologist. *muséum* – zoological museum.
zoologis (*D*) /so'ologis/ zoological.
zooplankton (*D*) /so'oplangton/ zooplankton.

zu (*A*) 1 possessed of. *Iskandar -lkarnain* Alexander with two horns, i.e., Alexander the Great. 2 endowed with.

zuadah (*A*) sweetmeats; → JUADAH.

zuama (*A pl* of *zaim*) leaders.

zubur *pl* of **zabur** *q.v.*

zufa (*A*) hyssop, *Hyssopus officinalis.*

zuhal (*A*) (*bintang* -) the planet Saturn.

zuhara, zuharah, zuhrah and **zuhrat** (*A*) (*bintang* -) the planet Venus.

zuhud (*A*) → ZAHID.

zuhur (*A*) → LOHOR. *sembahyang* - the noon/midday prayer. *waktu* - noon (about 1:15 p.m.).

zukhruf (*A*) 1 decorative art. 2 *az*- "Ornaments of Gold"; name of the 43rd chapter of the Koran.

Zulhijjah (*A*) the 12th month of the Muslim calendar, the month of the pilgrimage, often referred to as *bulan Haji.*

Zulkaédah (*A*) 1 the 11th month of the Muslim calendar. 2 the month of the Truce (in which Arab feuds should cease).

zulkarnain → ZU.

zulmah and **zulmat** (*A*) darkness, ignorance.

Zulu 1 a member of the Zulu tribe of South Africa. 2 the Zulu language.

Zumar (*A*) *az*- "The Troops"; name of the 39th chapter of the Koran.

zumurruh (*Pers*) emerald; → ZAMRUD.

zunub → JUNUB.

zurafah and **zurapah** → ZARAFAH.

zuriah and **zuriat** → ZARIAH.

zus (*D*) /ses, sis, sus/ Miss, respectful and friendly term of address for a) a girl or woman about the same age as the male speaker. b) telephone operators, etc.

zuster (*D*) /sester, sister, suster/ nurse; → SUSTER.

zuurzak (*D*) /sirsak/ → SIRSAK.